# CONCISE  Y

## ENGLISH
## GERMAN
—
## GERMAN
## ENGLISH

LAROUSSE
DICTIONNAIRES

# KOMPAKTWÖRTERBUCH

## ENGLISCH
## DEUTSCH
—
## DEUTSCH
## ENGLISCH

© Larousse, 2010
21, rue du Montparnasse
75283 Paris Cedex 06
France

Published in the United States of America and Canada by:
Für die Ausgabe in den USA und Kanada:
Éditions LAROUSSE
21, rue du Montparnasse
75283 Paris Cedex 06
France
www.larousse.fr

ISBN 978 203 541052 8

Sales/Vertrieb: Houghton Mifflin Harcourt, Boston
Library of Congress CIP Data has been applied for

Typeset by/Satz: Ingénierie Graphisme Services, France

# CONTENTS
## *INHALTSVERZEICHNIS*

# PREFACE

This dictionary has been designed as a reliable and user-friendly tool for use in all language situations. It provides accurate and up-to-date information on written and spoken German and English as they are used today.

Its 90,000 words and phrases and 120,000 translations give you access to German texts of all types. The dictionary aims to be as comprehensive as possible in a book of this size, and includes many proper names and abbreviations, as well as a selection of the most common terms from computing, business and current affairs.

The new German spelling system has been used throughout, with both old and new forms shown on the German–English side of the dictionary

Carefully constructed entries and a clear page design help you to find the translation that you are looking for fast. Examples (from basic constructions and common phrases to idioms) have been included to help put a word in context and give a clear picture of how it is used.

The dictionary provides extra help for students of German with the inclusion of boxes on German life and culture that appear within the dictionary text itself, and a 16-page central section which gives fuller background details on political and cultural life in Germany, Austria and Switzerland.

# VORBEMERKUNG

Dieses Wörterbuch wurde als zuverlässiger und benutzerfreundlicher Begleiter für Schule, Beruf und Freizeit entwickelt. Es gibt schnell und präzise Auskunft über den aktuellen Wortschatz des Englischen und des Deutschen in seiner geschriebenen und gesprochenen Form.

90000 Wörter und Ausdrücke mit 120000 Übersetzungen eröffnen den Zugang zu englischen Texten aller Art. Um dieses Nachschlagewerk innerhalb des vorgegebenen Umfangs so umfassend wie möglich zu gestalten, wurden zudem viele Eigennamen und Abkürzungen sowie eine Auswahl der gebräuchlichsten Begriffe aus den Bereichen EDV/Internet, Wirtschaft und Tagespolitik aufgenommen.

Die Schreibung des Deutschen folgt konsequent den neuen amtlichen Rechtschreibregeln, im deutsch–englischen Teil werden zur besseren Auffindbarkeit alte und neue Formen nebeneinander angegeben.

Mit großer Sorgfalt gestaltete Einträge und eine übersichtliche Seitengestaltung helfen dem Benutzer, die gesuchte Übersetzung schnell zu finden. Zusätzlich veranschaulichen zahlreiche Beispiele (von grammatischen Basiskonstruktionen und gebräuchlichen Kollokationen bis zu idiomatischen Wendungen) die Benutzung des betreffenden Wortes im Kontext. Das Wörterbuch bietet dem deutschsprachigen Benutzer besondere Hilfestellung in Form von landeskundlichen Erläuterungen, die in den Text integriert sind und wertvolle Hintergrundinformationen zum jeweils gesuchten englischen Begriff liefern.

Editor-in-Chief
*Gesamtleitung*
Patrick White

Project Manager
*Koordinierung*
Helen Bleck

Editorial Team
*Redaktion*

Joaquín Blasco
Stuart Fortey
Helen Galloway
Elaine O'Donoghue

Christina Reinicke
Stefan Rosenland
Veronika Schilling
Anna Stevenson

with
*mit*

Alexander Behrens
Anna Canning
Lynda Carey
Steffen Krug
Elisabeth Lauer
Dörthe und Günter Lügenbuhl

Friedemann Lux
Úna ní Chiosáin
Ruth Noble
Ingrid Schumacher
Liliane Seifert
Katerina Stein

Supplement on German language and culture
*Deutsche Landeskunde*
Helen Galloway
Veronika Schnorr

Data Management
*Datenverwaltung*
Abdul Aziz Ndao

| ABKÜRZUNGEN | | ABBREVIATIONS |
|---|---|---|
| Akkusativ | *A* | accusative |
| Abkürzung | *abk/abbr* | abbreviation |
| abwertend<br>bezeichnet die subjektive negative<br>Wertung des Sprechers, z. B. **Banause** | *abw* | pejorative<br>implies disapproval, e.g. **Banause** |
| Adjektiv | *adj* | adjective |
| Adverb | *adv* | adverb |
| amerikanisches Englisch | *Am* | American English |
| amtssprachlich, formell | *amt* | official language |
| australisches Englisch | *Austr* | Australian English |
| Hilfsverb | *aux* | auxiliary |
| britisches Englisch | *Br* | British English |
| kanadisches Englisch | *Can* | Canadian English |
| ein zusammengesetztes<br>Substantiv bildend<br>ein Substantiv, das zur näheren<br>Bestimmung eines anderen dient,<br>z. B. **gardening** in **gardening book**<br>oder **airforce** in **airforce base** | *comp* | compound-forming element<br>a noun used to modify another noun,<br>e.g. **gardening** in **gardening book** or<br>**airforce** in **airforce base** |
| Komparativ | *compar* | comparative |
| Konjunktion | *conj* | conjunction |
| Verlaufsform | *cont* | continuous |
| Dativ | *D* | dative |
| demonstrativ, hinweisend | *dem* | demonstrative |
| Determinant<br>bezeichnet Artikelwörter und andere<br>artikelähnliche Substantivbegleiter | *det* | determinant<br>indicates article words and similar |
| eigentliche Bedeutung | *eigtl* | literal |
| etwas | *etw* | something |
| Femininum | *f* | feminine noun |
| umgangssprachlich | *fam* | informal |
| übertragene Bedeutung | *fig* | figurative |
| gehoben | *fml* | formal |
| Femininum im Plural | *fpl* | plural feminine noun |
| nicht trennbar | *fus* | inseparable |
| Genitiv | *G* | genitive |
| gehoben | *geh* | formal |
| generell, allgemein | *gen* | generally |
| humorvoll | *hum* | humorous |
| unbestimmt | *indef* | indefinite |
| umgangssprachlich | *inf* | informal |
| Interjektion | *interj* | interjection |
| unveränderlich<br>kennzeichnet bei Substantiven die<br>Übereinstimmung der Plural- und<br>Singularform, wie z. B. bei sheep<br>*pl inv*: **four sheep** | *inv* | invariable<br>applied to a noun to indicate that<br>plural form same as singular, e.g.<br>**sheep** *pl inv*: **four sheep** |
| ironisch | *iron* | ironic |
| jemand | *jd* | someone (nominative) |
| jemandem | *jm* | someone (dative) |
| jemanden | *jn* | someone (accusative) |
| jemandes | *js* | someone (genitive) |
| Komparativ | *kompar* | comparative |
| Konjunktion | *konj* | conjunction |

## ABKÜRZUNGEN

## ABBREVIATIONS

| | | |
|---|---|---|
| eigentliche Bedeutung | *lit* | literal |
| | | in conjunction with *fig*, shows that both a literal and figurative sense is being covered by the same translation |
| Maskulinum | *m* | masculine noun |
| Maskulinum und Femininum | *mf* | feminine and masculine noun |
| Maskulinum im Plural | *mpl* | plural masculine noun |
| Norddeutsch | *Norddt* | northern German |
| Neutrum bei Städte- und Ländernamen | *nt* | neuter noun (used with place names) |
| Städte und Ländernamen gehören zu den Neutra. Sie werden in den meisten Fällen ohne Artikel benutzt: **ich fahre nach Deutschland/nach Berlin**. Es gibt jedoch Ausnahmen: **das Deutschland/das Berlin der 90er Jahre** | | The names of countries and cities are generally neutral, and used without an article: **ich fahre nach Deutschland/ nach Berlin**. There are some exceptions, however: **das Deutschland/ das Berlin der 90er Jahre** |
| Zahlwort | *num* | numeral |
| ohne Plural | *ohne pl* | uncountable noun |
| sich | *o.s.* | oneself |
| Ostdeutsch | *Ostdt* | East German |
| Österreichisch | *Österr* | Austrian |
| abwertend | *pej* | pejorative |
| bezeichnet die subjektive negative Wertung des Sprechers, z. B. **bimbo, catty** | | implies disapproval, e.g. **bimbo, catty** |
| Perfekt | *perf* | perfect |
| persönlich | *pers* | personal |
| Redewendung(en) | *phr* | phrase(s) |
| Plural | *pl* | plural |
| besitzanzeigend | *poss* | possessive |
| Partizip Perfekt | *pp* | past participle |
| Präposition | *präp* | preposition |
| Präsens | *präs* | present |
| Präteritum | *prät* | preterite |
| Vorsilbe | *pref* | prefix |
| Präposition | *prep* | preposition |
| Pronomen | *pron* | pronoun |
| reflexives Verb | *ref* | reflexive verb |
| regelmäßig | *reg* | regular |
| Redewendung(en) | *RW* | phrase(s) |
| salopp | *salopp* | very informal |
| jemand | *sb* | someone |
| Schweizerdeutsch | *Schweiz* | Swiss German |
| schottisches Englisch | *Scot* | Scottish English |
| trennbar | *sep* | separable |
| singular | *sg* | singular |
| Slang | *sl* | slang |
| etwas | *sthg* | something |
| Subjekt | *Subj/subj* | subject |
| Süddeutsch | *Süddt* | southern German |
| Superlativ | *superl* | superlative |
| ohne Plural | *U* | uncountable noun |
| unregelmäßig | *unreg* | irregular |

## ABKÜRZUNGEN

## ABBREVIATIONS

| | | |
|---|---|---|
| unveränderlich | *unver* | invariable |
| Verb | *vb* | verb |
| intransitives verb | *vi* | intransitive verb |
| unpersönliches Verb | *v impers* | impersonal verb |
| salopp | *vinf* | very informal |
| vor dem Substantiv | *vor Subst* | before noun |

vor dem Substantiv
zeigt an, dass die Übersetzung grundsätzlich attributiv verwendet wird, d. h. unmittelbar vor dem Substantiv steht, welches es näher bezeichnet

before noun
indicates that the translation is always used attributively, i.e. directly before the noun which it modifies

| | | |
|---|---|---|
| transitives Verb | *vt* | transitive verb |
| vulgär | *vulg* | vulgar |
| ohne Plural | *U* | uncountable noun |
| kulturelle Entsprechung | ≃ | cultural equivalent |
| | \| | |

a) Im Verb: Trennbarkeit des deutschen Verbs
b) Im zusammengesetzten Substantiv: Angaben zum Plural unter dem Wort nach dem Balken (z. B. steht der Plural von **Ab|bild** under dem Stichwort **Bild**)

a) In a German verb: indicates that verb is separable
b) In a compound noun: shows the root of the word, where the plural will be found (e.g. the plural of **Ab|bild** is under the headword **Bild**)

## SACHBEREICHSANGABEN

## FIELD LABELS

| | | |
|---|---|---|
| Verwaltung | ADMIN | administration |
| Flugwesen, Luftfahrt | AERON | aeronautics, aviation |
| Landwirtschaft | AGRIC | agriculture |
| Anatomie | ANAT | anatomy |
| Archäologie | ARCHAEOL | archaeology |
| Architektur | ARCHIT | architecture |
| Astrologie | ASTROL | astrology |
| Astronomie | ASTRON | astronomy |
| Kfz-Technik | AUT(O) | automobile, cars |
| Biologie | BIOL | biology |
| Botanik | BOT | botany |
| Chemie | CHEM | chemistry |
| Handel | COMM | business |
| Datenverarbeitung | COMPUT | computers, computer science |
| Bauwesen | CONSTR | construction, building trade |
| Kochkunst | CULIN | culinary, cooking |
| Wirtschaft | ECON | economics |
| Datenverarbeitung | EDV | computers, computer science |
| Elektrotechnik | ELEKTR/ELEC | electricity, electronics |
| Finanzen | FIN | finance, financial   Flugwesen, |
| Luftfahrt | FLUG | aeronautics, aviation |
| Fotografie | FOTO | photography |
| Fußball | FTBL | football |
| Geografie | GEOGR | geography, geographical |
| Geologie | GEOL | geology, geological |
| Geometrie | GEOM | geometry |
| Grammatik | GRAM(M) | grammar |
| Geschichte | HIST | history |
| Industrie | IND | industry |
| Rechtswesen | LAW | legal |
| Kochkunst | KÜCHE | culinary, cooking |
| Linguistik | LING | linguistics |
| Mathematik | MATH | mathematics |
| Medizin | MED | medicine |
| Meteorologie | METEOR | weather, meteorology |
| Militärwesen | MIL | military |
| Musik | MUS | music |
| Mythologie | MYTH | mythology |
| Schifffahrt | NAUT | navigation |
| Fotografie | PHOT | photography |
| Physik | PHYS | physics |
| Politik | POL | politics |
| Psychologie | PSYCH | psychology, psychiatry |
| Eisenbahn | RAIL | railways |
| Rechtswesen | RECHT | law |
| Religion | REL(IG) | religion |
| Schifffahrt | SCHIFF | navigation |
| Schule | SCH(ULE) | school |
| Sport | SPORT | sport |
| Börse | ST EX | stock exchange |
| Technik, Technologie | TECH | technology, technical |
| Telekommunikation, Fernmeldewesen | TELEKOM/TELEC | telecommunications |
| Fernsehen | TV | television |
| Druckwesen | TYPO | printing |
| Universität | UNI(V) | university |
| Wirtschaft | WIRTSCH | economics |
| Zoologie | ZOOL | zoology |

## LAUTSCHRIFT

### Deutsche Vokale

| | |
|---|---|
| [ a ] | Affe, Banane |
| [ a: ] | Arzt, Antrag |
| [ ɐ ] | Gallier |
| [ ɐ̯ ] | Dessert |
| [ e ] | Beton |
| [ e: ] | edel |
| [ ɛ ] | echt, Händler |
| [ ɛ: ] | Rätsel |
| [ ə ] | Aktie |
| [ i: ] | vier |
| [ i ] | Radio |
| [ i̯ ] | Kalzium |
| [ ɪ ] | Winter |
| [ o ] | Melodie |
| [ o: ] | apropos |
| [ o̯ ] | loyal |
| [ ɔ ] | sollen |
| [ ø ] | ökologisch |
| [ ø: ] | Öl |
| [ œ ] | Köchin, Pumps |
| [ u ] | Kuvert, aktuell |
| [ u: ] | Kuh |
| [ u̯ ] | Silhouette |
| [ ʊ ] | Kunst |
| [ y ] | Büchse, System |
| [ y: ] | Tür |
| [ y̆ ] | Nuance |

### Deutsche Diphthonge

| | |
|---|---|
| [ ai ] | Deichsel |
| [ au̯ ] | Auge |
| [ ɔy̯ ] | EuroCity |

### Deutsche Nasale

| | |
|---|---|
| [ ã ] | Chanson |
| [ ã: ] | Abonnement |
| [ ɛ̃: ] | Pointe |
| [ ɔ̃ ] | Chanson |

### Halbvokale

| | |
|---|---|
| Jubiläum | [j] |
| Hardware | [w] |

### Konsonanten

| | |
|---|---|
| Baby | [b] |
| Chemie | [ç] |

## PHONETICS

### English vowels

| | |
|---|---|
| [ɑ:] | barn, car, laugh |
| [æ] | pat, bag, mad |
| [ɒ] | pot, log |
| [e] | pet, tend |
| [ɜ:] | burn, learn, bird |
| [ə] | mother, suppose |
| [i:] | bean, weed |
| [ɪ] | pit, big, rid |
| [ɔ:] | born, lawn |
| [u:] | loop, loose |
| [ʌ] | run, cut |
| [ʊ] | put, full |

### English diphthongs

| | |
|---|---|
| [aɪ] | buy, light, aisle |
| [aʊ] | now, shout, town |
| [eɪ] | bay, late, great |
| [ɔɪ] | boy, foil |
| [əʊ] | no, road, blow |
| [ɪə] | peer, fierce, idea |
| [eə] | pair, bear, share |
| [ʊə] | poor, sure, tour |

### Semi-vowels

you, spaniel
wet, why, twin

### Consonants

bottle, bib

## LAUTSCHRIFT

| | | PHONETICS |
|---|---|---|
| Achse, Kaviar | [ k ] | come, kitchen |
| Duett, Medien | [ d ] | dog, did |
| Gin | [dʒ] | jet, fridge |
| Fantasie, vier | [ f ] | fib, physical |
| Algerien, gut | [ g ] | gag, great |
| Hobby | [ h ] | how, perhaps |
| alphabetisch, Laser | [ l ] | little, help |
| Alphabet, Laser | [ l̩ ] | |
| Material, Alarm | [m] | metal, comb |
| großem | [m̩] | |
| November, Angabe | [n] | night, dinner |
| lieben | [n̩] | |
| singen | [ŋ] | sung, parking |
| Pony, Pappe | [p] | pop, people |
| Apfel | [pf] | |
| Revue, rot | [ r ] | right, carry |
| Slalom, Sauce | [ s ] | seal, peace |
| Stadion, Schule | [ ʃ ] | sheep, machine |
| Toast, Volt | [ t ] | train, tip |
| Konversation | [ts] | |
| Chili | [tʃ] | chain, wretched |
| | [θ] | think, fifth |
| | [ð] | this, with |
| Vase, Wagen | [ v ] | vine, livid |
| Macht, lachen | [ x ] | loch |
| Sauce, Sonne | [ z ] | zip, his |
| Etage | [ ʒ ] | usual, measure |

Die Betonung der deutschen Stichwörter wird mit einem Punkt für einen kurzen betonten Vokal (z. B. Berg) und mit einem Strich für einen langen betonten Vokal (z. B. Magen) angegeben.

German headwords have the stress marked either by a dot for a short stressed vowel (e.g. Berg) or by an underscore for a long stressed vowel (e.g. Magen). A phonetic transcription is only given when the pronunciation is problematic.

Der Hauptton eines englischen Wortes ist durch ein vorangestelltes ['] markiert, der Nebenton durch ein vorangestelltes [ˌ].

The symbol ['] indicates that the following syllable carries primary stress and the symbol [ˌ] that the following syllable carries secondary stress.

Das Zeichen [r] zeigt in der englischen Phonetik an, dass der Endkonsonant "r" ausgesprochen wird, wenn das folgende Wort mit einem Vokal beginnt. Im amerikanischen Englisch wird dieses "r" so gut wie immer mitgesprochen.

The symbol [r] in English phonetics indicates that the final "r" is pronounced only when followed by a word beginning with a vowel. Note that it is nearly always pronounced in American English.

## HOW TO USE THE DICTIONARY

### How to find the word or expression you are looking for:

First ask yourself some basic questions:

Is it a single word, a hyphenated word or an abbreviation?
Is it a compound noun?
Is it a German separable verb?
Is it a German feminine form?
Is it a phrase?
Is it a reflexive verb?
Is it a German irregular verb form?

### Single words, hyphenated words and abbreviations

As a rule, you can find the word you are looking for in its alphabetical order. If you want to translate an English word into German, you should look on the English–German side of the dictionary, and if you want to know what a German term means, you should look on the German–English side. The word in **bold** at the start of each entry is called the 'headword'.

Entries beginning with a *capital* appear after those spelled the same way but with a small letter.

> **kosten** vi [probieren] to have a taste ...
> **Kosten** pl costs ...

Words with a *hyphen*, a *full stop* or an *apostrophe* come after those spelled the same way but without any of these punctuation marks.

> **ob** konj whether; ich weiß nicht, ~ er kommt I don't know whether ODER if he'll come ...
> **o. B.** abk für ohne Befund ▷ Befund.

In some cases, the entry is followed by a number in *superscript*. This means that just before or just after there is another entry, also followed by a number, which is written the same way but which has a completely different meaning or pronunciation. You must take care not to choose the wrong entry.

> **modern**[1] (perf hat/ist gemodert) vi to moulder.
> **modern**[2] adj modern; [modisch] fashionable ◇ adv - **1.** [zeitgemäß] in a modern way; ~ denken to have modern ideas - **2.** [zeitgenössisch] in a modern style.

You will sometimes see words followed by a grey lozenge, called sub-entries. English phrasal verbs fall into this category.

> **afternoon** [ˌɑːftəˈnuːn] n Nachmittag der; in the ~ am Nachmittag; good ~ guten Tag.
> ➤ **afternoons** adv esp Am nachmittags.
>
> **amount** [əˈmaʊnt] ...
> ➤ **amount to** vt fus - **1.** [total] sich belaufen auf (+ A) - **2.** [be equivalent to] hinauslaufen auf (+ A).

If you are looking up a noun which has a form with an initial capital which has a different meaning from the form without a capital, you should look at the form without a capital.

> **ascension** [əˈsenʃn] *n* [to throne] Thronbestei-gung *die.*
> ◆ **Ascension** *n* RELIG Christi Himmelfahrt *die.*

If you are looking up a noun which, in the plural, has a different meaning from the noun in its singular form (like **glass/glasses** in English), you will find it under the singular form; the plural form will be there as a sub-entry, indicated by the symbol ◆.

> **glass** [glɑːs] *n* - **1.** [gen] Glas *das;* **a ~ of wine** ein Glas Wein - **2.** *(U)* [glassware] Glaswaren *pl* ◇ *comp* Glas-.
> ◆ **glasses** *npl* [spectacles] Brille *die;* [binoculars] Fernglas *das;* **a pair of ~es** eine Brille.

Some plural nouns appear as headwords in their own right when they are never or rarely used in the singular (e.g. **Teigwaren** in German, **scissors** in English).

## Compound nouns

A compound is a word or expression which has a single meaning but is made up of more than one word, e.g. **point of order, kiss of life, virtual reality, International Monetary Fund**. It is a feature of this dictionary that English compounds appear in the A–Z list in strict alphabetical order. The compound blood donor will therefore come after bloodcurdling which itself follows blood count.

> **blood count** *n* Blutbild *das.*
>
> **bloodcurdling** [ˈblʌdˌkɜːdlɪŋ] *adj* marker-schütternd.
>
> **blood donor** *n* Blutspender *der.*

Most compounds in German have their two elements joined together to form a single word. A vertical line is used to separate the constituent elements of a compound.

> **Schul|jahr** *das* - **1.** [Jahr] school year - **2.** [Klas-se] year.

In order to check the plural of this noun, you should refer to the entry **Jahr**.

> **Jahr** (*pl* -e) *das* year; **im ~(e) 1992** in 1992; **die 90er ~e** the nineties; **seit ~en** for years ...

Other German compound nouns made up of two separate words are entered in the same way as English compounds, e.g. **Schwarze Markt** *der,* **Rote Kreuz** *das.*

## German separable verbs

Verbs of the type **an sein** which used to be written in one word (**an|sein**) are now written in two words following the German spelling reform but are still entered in the same place alphabetically.

> **an|seilen** vt to rope up.
> ➡ **sich anseilen** ref to rope o.s. up.
>
> **an sein** (perf **ist an gewesen**) vi (unreg) to be on.
>
> **an|setzen** vt - **1.** [in Stellung bringen - Werkzeug] to place in position ...

## German feminine forms

The feminine form of a German noun is entered alongside the masculine form when the two forms are identical or alphabetically adjacent. **Lehrerin** is thus entered at **Lehrer**.

> **Lehrer, in** (mpl -; fpl -**nen**) der, die [in Schule] teacher; [in Sportverein] instructor.

Otherwise the feminine appears as a separate headword.

> **Ärztin** ['ɛːɐ̯tstɪn] (pl -**nen**) die doctor.

## Phrases

If looking for a phrase, you should look first under the noun that is used in the phrase. If there is no noun, then you should look under the adjective, and if there is no adjective, under the verb. Phrases appear in entries in bold, the symbol ~ standing for the headword.

> **Zeit** (pl -**en**) die - **1.** [gen] time; **in letzter ~** lately; **im Laufe der ~** in the course of time; **von ~ zu ~** from time to time; **die ~ stoppen** to stop the clock; **~ raubend** time-consuming; **~ sparend** time-saving; **sich** (D) **für jn/etw ~ nehmen** to spend time on sb/sthg; **die ~ drängt** fig time is short; **wir dürfen keine ~ verlieren** we have no time to lose; **sich** (D) **die ~ (mit Kartenspielen) vertreiben** to pass the time (playing cards); **sich** (D) **~ lassen** to take one's time ...

Some very fixed phrases like **in spite of** in English or **auf jeden Fall** in German are entered under the first important element and preceded by ➡ .

> **spite** [spaɪt] n (U) Bosheit die; **to do sthg out of** ODER **from ~** etw aus reiner Bosheit tun ⬦ vt ärgern.
> ➡ **in spite of** prep trotz (+ G) ...

> **Fall** (pl **Fälle**) der [gen] case ...
> ➡ **auf alle Fälle** adv - **1.** [unbedingt] definitely - **2.** [vorsichtshalber] in any case.
> ➡ **auf jeden Fall** adv in any case ...

## Reflexive verbs

German reflexive verbs are entered under the main form, after the symbol ➡ .

> **an|schnallen** vt [Skier, Rollschuhe] to put on; [Sicherheitsgurt] to fasten.
> ➡ **sich anschnallen** ref to fasten one's seat belt.

## German irregular verb forms

If you are unsure what the infinitive of a certain verb form is, and so where to look for it, then it may be an irregular form. These irregular forms are entered in the A–Z list.

**aß** *prät* ⊳ **essen.**

## How to find the right translation

Once you have found the word or phrase that you are looking for, there may be several different translations given from which to choose. However, all the necessary information to help you find the right translation is given.

**Step 1** Imagine that you want to translate 'he accepted the blame' into German.

Go first to the entry **accept** on the English-German side of the dictionary. At sense 3 you will find the verb used in this context: ein|gestehen.

**accept** [ək'sept] *vt* - **1.** [gift, advice, apology, invitation, offer] an|nehmen - **2.** [change, situation] akzeptieren, hin|nehmen - **3.** [defeat, blame] ein|gestehen; [responsibility] übernehmen - **4.** [person - as part of group] akzeptieren; [ - for job] nehmen; [ - as member of club] auf|nehmen ...

**Step 2** Go now to the entry for the second word that needs to be translated, **blame**.

**NB** It is important first to find the correct grammatical category (each new category is introduced by ◇). **Blame** is a noun in this example and so you should look under the noun category (labelled *n*).

**blame** [bleɪm] *n* Schuld *die;* **to take the ~ for sthg** die Schuld für etw auf sich *(A)* nehmen ◇ *vt* beschuldigen; **to ~ sthg on sb/sthg** jm/ etw die Schuld an etw *(D)* geben ...

**Step 3** On examining the noun category, you will find that the translation used is **Schuld**.

**Step 4** The words selected can now be put together in the phrase to be translated, to give: **er hat die Schuld eingestanden.**

## Extra information given in this dictionary

### Labelling the gender of German nouns

The gender of German nouns is indicated on both sides of the dictionary by the definite article placed after the noun (*der* for masculine, *die* for feminine and *das* for neuter).

The label pl was chosen to mark plural forms in order to avoid the confusion with *die*.

When a German noun accompanied by an adjective is given as a translation on the English–German side, the adjective ending (**-er, -e** or **-es**) tells you what gender the noun is and no *der, die* or *das* label is given. At the entry **adjustable spanner**, for example, the gender of **Schraubenschlüssel** is indicated by the **-er** ending of the adjective **verstellbarer.**

**Baum** (*pl* **Bäume**) *der* tree ...

**Hand** (*pl* **Hände**) *die* - **1.** [Körperteil] hand ...

**Kind** (*pl* **-er**) *das* child ...

**kosten** *vi* [probieren] to have a taste ...

**adjustable spanner** *n* Engländer *der*, verstellbarer Schraubenschlüssel.

## German adjectives only used attributively

With German adjectives of this type, the feminine form is shown first, followed by the masculine and neuter endings.

> **letztere, r, s** *adj* the latter; **in ~m Fall** in the latter case ◇ *pron* the latter.

## German adjectives used as nouns

Nominalized German adjectives are, like all other nouns, labelled with the definite article. When used with an indefinite article, the ending of this type of noun changes according to the gender. Hence **Blinde** *der*, *die* becomes **ein Blinder** and **eine Blinde**.

> **Blinde** (*pl* -n) *der, die* blind man (*f* blind woman).

## Labelling case information

Some German prepositions can take either the accusative or dative case and these are always labelled accordingly, e.g. at the entry **adept: to be ~ (at sthg) (in etw (D)) geschickt sein.**
Case is also indicated when it is not predictable, e.g. **to be able to afford sthg** sich (D) etw leisten können. Here the reflexive pronoun is dative, rather than the usual accusative.

## Indicating the auxiliary

We indicate when a verb can be conjugated with both the auxiliary verb **haben** and the auxiliary verb **sein**, as at the entry **fahren**.

> **fahren** (*präs* fährt; *prät* fuhr; *perf* hat/ist gefahren) *vi*

## Separability of German verbs

A vertical line is used in the dictionary after the prefix of a verb to indicate that it is separable.

> **ab|fahren** (*perf* hat/ist abgefahren) (*unreg*) *vi* (*ist*) [losfahren] to leave; [Zug] to depart, to leave; **auf jn/etw ~** *fam fig* to be into sb/sthg ◇ *vt* (*hat*) **- 1.** [Ladung] to take away ...

## German prefixes as translations for English adjectives

Some English adjectives are translated by a noun prefix that is joined to the noun to form a compound noun.

Thus, when translating **aggregate amount** into German, the prefix **Gesamt-** should be joined to **Summe** to give **Gesamtsumme**.

> **aggregate** ['ægrɪgət] *adj* Gesamt-; **~ earnings** Gesamtverdienst *der* ◇ *n* [total] Gesamtsumme *die*, Gesamtheit *die*; **on ~** ingesamt.

## Alphabetical order and new German spelling

The German spelling reform sometimes means changes in alphabetical order on the German–English side of the dictionary. In order to help the reader to find what they are looking for, we have decided to show both the old and the new spellings in cases like these.

When the new spelling of a word means that its alphabetical order must be changed, the old spelling is always given but with a cross-reference to the new spelling where the full entry appears.

> **Stengel** *der* = Stängel.
> **Stängel** (*pl* -) *der* stalk.

In many cases, however, the new spelling is alphabetically very close to the old one. In these cases, a cross-reference is not necessary.

> **potenziell, potentiell** [poten'tsiɛl] *adj* potential ⬦ *adv* potentially.

Sometimes cross-references are used when both the old spelling and new spelling are allowed. In these cases, the entry appears at the new spelling.

> **selbständig** = selbstständig.
> **selbstständig** *adj* - **1.** [unabhängig] independent - **2.** [im Beruf] self-employed ...

Compound words which used to be written in one word but which are now written in two have been left in their 'usual' place.

**Kennen lernen** thus appears where **kennenlernen** did before.

> **kennen** (*prät* kannte; *perf* hat gekannt) *vt* to know ...
> **kennen lernen** *vt* - **1.** [Person] to get to know, to meet ...
> **Kenner** (*pl* -) *der* expert; [von Wein] connoisseur.

In some cases, however, we have left the old spelling and given a cross-reference to the new spelling.

> **rad|fahren** *vi* (*unreg*) ⬥ Rad.
> **Rad** (*pl* Räder) *das* - **1.** [von Fahrzeug] wheel; **unter die Räder kommen** *fam* [überfahren werden] to be knocked over; *fam fig* [scheitern] to go to the dogs - **2.** [Fahrrad] bike; **~ fahren** to cycle ...

On the English–German side, only the new spelling is used without any labelling.

> **river** ['rɪvəʳ] *n* Fluss *der* ...

When both the old and new spellings are allowable, just the new spelling is shown in translations.

> **fantastically** [fæn'tæstɪklɪ] *adv* - **1.** [extremely] unwahrscheinlich - **2.** [bizarrely] fantastisch.

## Cultural information

An appreciation of the culture of a foreign country is key to being able to understand and speak its language well. Cultural information on Germany is provided in this dictionary in boxes on the German–English side of the dictionary.

As a **Volkshochschule** is part of an education system unique to Germany, there is no real equivalent in English and a box is required to explain it.

> **Volkshoch|schule** *die* ≃ college of adult education.
>
> **VOLKSHOCHSCHULE**
>
> Colleges of adult education in Germany offer academic as well as practical courses, usually in the form of evening classes and lectures. These courses are offered in a variety of subjects and can in some cases lead to a certificate or other recognized qualification.

### WARENZEICHEN

Als Warenzeichen geschützte Wörter sind in diesem Wörterbuch durch das Zeichen ® gekennzeichnet. Die Markierung mit diesem Symbol, oder sein Fehlen, hat keinen Einfluss auf die Rechtskräftigkeit eines Warenzeichens.

### TRADEMARKS

Words considered to be trademarks have been designated in this dictionary by the symbol ®. However, neither the presence nor the absence of such designation should be regarded as affecting the legal status of any trademark.

## LIST OF ENGLISH CULTURAL BOXES
### *LISTE DER ENGLISCHEN LANDESKUNDLICHEN ERLÄUTERUNGEN*

ALBERT HALL
A LEVEL
APRIL FOOLS' DAY
BANK HOLIDAY
BED AND BREAKFAST
BILL OF RIGHTS
BRITISH COUNCIL
BUILDING SOCIETY
BURNS' NIGHT
CAPITOL HILL
CAUCUS
CEILIDH
CHURCH OF ENGLAND
THE CITY
CIVIL SERVICE
CIVIL WARS
COCKNEY
COMMONWEALTH
COMPREHENSIVE SCHOOL
CONGRESS

CONSTITUTION
COVENT GARDEN
DEVOLUTION
DOWNING STREET
FISH AND CHIPS
-GATE
GCSE
GOOD FRIDAY AGREEMENT
GRAMMAR SCHOOL
GREAT BRITAIN
GUY FAWKES NIGHT
HALLOWEEN
HOUSE OF COMMONS
HOUSE OF LORDS
HOUSE OF
  REPRESENTATIVES
MS
OPEN UNIVERSITY
PENTAGON
PILGRIM FATHERS

POLITICALLY CORRECT
PRIMARIES
PRIVY COUNCIL
PROMS
PUB
PUBLIC SCHOOL
PUNCH-AND-JUDY SHOW
RHYMING SLANG
SAT
SENATE
SOAP OPERA
STATE SCHOOL
TEA
THANKSGIVING
WALL STREET
WEST END
WESTMINSTER
WHITEHALL
YELLOW LINES

## LIST OF GERMAN CULTURAL BOXES
### *LISTE DER DEUTSCHEN LANDESKUNDLICHEN ERLÄUTERUNGEN*

ABITUR
ADVENT
AUTOBAHN
BAUSPARKASSE
BEAMTE
BERLINER MAUER
BIER
BIERGARTEN
BILDZEITUNG
BROT
BUNDESLAND
BUNDESRAT
BUNDESVERFASSUNGS-
  GERICHT
DEUTSCHE BUNDESBANK
DEUTSCHER BUNDESTAG
DEUTSCHER
  GEWERKSCHAFTSBUND
DIALEKT
FÜNFPROZENTKLAUSEL
GRUNDGESETZ
HANSESTÄDTE
20. JULI 1944

KANZLER
KARNEVAL
KIRCHENSTEUER
KIRCHENTAG
KNEIPE
KRANKENKASSE
LOVEPARADE
NUMERUS CLAUSUS
NUMMERNSCHILD
ODER-NEISSE-LINIE
PARAGRAF 218
GRÜNER PFEIL
PREUSSEN
REFORMHAUS
REICHSTAG
SCHÜTZENFEST
SILVESTER
DER SPIEGEL
STAATSEXAMEN
STAMMTISCH
STASI
STIFTUNG WARENTEST
STUDENTENVERBINDUNG

TAG DER DEUTSCHEN
  EINHEIT
TÜV
UMWELTBEWUSSTSEIN
VEREIN
VOLKSHOCHSCHULE
WALDORFSCHULE
WEIHNACHTEN
WEIHNACHTSMARKT
WEIMARER REPUBLIK
WIEDERVEREINIGUNG
WIRTSCHAFTSWUNDER
WURST
DIE ZEIT
ZIVILDIENST

# ENGLISH – GERMAN
# ENGLISCH – DEUTSCH

**a¹** (*pl* as *OR* **a's**), **A** (*pl* **As** *OR* **A's**) [eɪ] *n* [letter] a *das,* A *das;* **to get from A to B** von A nach B kommen; **from A to Z** von A bis Z, von Anfang bis Ende.

➡ **A** *n* - **1.** MUS [note] A *das* - **2.** SCH [mark] ≈ eins.

**a²** [stressed eɪ, unstressed ə] (before vowel or silent "h" **an** [stressed æn, unstressed ən]) indef art - **1.** [gen] ein, -e; **~ woman** eine Frau; **~ restaurant** ein Restaurant; **~ friend** ein Freund, eine Freundin; **an apple** ein Apfel - **2.** [referring to occupation]: **I'm ~ doctor** ich bin Arzt - **3.** [instead of the number one] ein, -e; **~ hundred** hundert; **~ hundred and twenty** hundertzwanzig; **for ~ week** eine Woche lang - **4.** [in prices, ratios] pro; **£2 ~ kilo** £2 pro Kilo; **£10 ~ head** £10 pro Kopf; **twice ~ week/year** zweimal in der Woche/im *OR* pro Jahr; **50 km an hour** 50 km pro Stunde, 50 Stundenkilometer - **5.** [preceding person's name]: **~ Mr Jones** ein Herr Jones - **6.:** **not ~** kein, -e; **not ~ soul** kein Mensch; **I haven't understood ~ (single) word** ich habe kein (einziges) Wort verstanden.

**a.** *abbr of* **acre.**

**A-1** *adj inf* 1a.

**A4** *n Br* A4.

**AA** *adj abbr of* **antiaircraft** ◇ *n* - **1.** (abbr of Automobile Association) ≈ ADAC *der* - **2.** (abbr of Associate in Arts) Hochschulabschluss in einem geisteswissenschaftlichen Fach nach zweijährigem Studium - **3.** (abbr of Alcoholics Anonymous) AA *pl.*

**AAA** *n* - **1.** (abbr of Amateur Athletics Association) ≈ DLV *der* - **2.** (abbr of American Automobile Association) ≈ ADAC *der.*

**AB** *n Am* (abbr of Bachelor of Arts) Hochschulabschluss in einem geisteswissenschaftlichen Fach nach drei- oder vierjährigem Studium ◇ abk für Alberta, in Postanschrift verwendet.

**aback** [ə'bæk] *adv:* **to be taken ~ (by sthg)** schockiert sein (über etw (A)).

**abacus** ['æbəkəs] (*pl* **-cuses** *OR* **-ci** [-saɪ]) *n* Abakus *der,* Rechenbrett *das.*

**abandon** [ə'bændən] *vt* - **1.** [leave, desert] verlassen - **2.** [give up] aufgeben ◇ *n* (U): **with ~** ausgelassen.

**abandoned** [ə'bændənd] *adj* [deserted] verlassen.

**abashed** [ə'bæʃt] *adj* verlegen, beschämt.

**abate** [ə'beɪt] *vi fml* nachlassen.

**abattoir** ['æbətwɑːr] *n* Schlachthaus *das.*

**abbess** ['æbes] *n* Äbtissin *die.*

**abbey** ['æbɪ] *n* Abtei *die.*

**abbot** ['æbət] *n* Abt *der.*

**abbreviate** [ə'briːvɪeɪt] *vt* abkürzen.

**abbreviation** [ə,briːvɪ'eɪʃn] *n* Abkürzung *die.*

**ABC** *n* - **1.** [alphabet] ABC *das* - **2.** *fig* [basics]: **the ~ of** das ABC von - **3.** (abbr of American Broadcasting Company) eine der vier überregionalen Fernsehanstalten in den USA.

**abdicate** ['æbdɪkeɪt] *vi* abdanken ◇ *vt* [responsibility] von sich schieben.

**abdication** [,æbdɪ'keɪʃn] *n* Abdankung *die.*

**abdomen** ['æbdəmən] *n* [of person] Unterleib *der;* [of animal, insect] Hinterleib *der.*

**abdominal** [æb'dɒmɪnl] *adj* Unterleibs-.

**abduct** [əb'dʌkt] *vt* entführen.

**abduction** [æb'dʌkʃn] *n* Entführung *die.*

**aberration** [,æbə'reɪʃn] *n* Abweichung *die;* **a mental ~** eine geistige Verwirrung.

**abet** [ə'bet] (*pt* & *pp* **-ted;** *cont* **-ting**) *vt* ▷ aid.

**abeyance** [ə'beɪəns] *n fml*: **to be in ~** [law] außer Kraft sein.

**abhor** [əb'hɔːr] (*pt* & *pp* **-red;** *cont* **-ring**) *vt* verabscheuen.

**abhorrent** [əb'hɒrənt] *adj* abscheulich, abstoßend.

**abide** [ə'baɪd] *vt* auslstehen.
➤ **abide by** *vt fus* sich halten an (+ *A*).

**abiding** [ə'baɪdɪŋ] *adj* bleibend.

**ability** [ə'bɪlətɪ] (*pl* **-ies**) *n* - **1.** (U) [capability] Fähigkeit *die;* **a manager of great ~** ein Manager von großen Fähigkeiten; **to do sthg to the best of one's ~** etw nach besten Kräften OR bestem Vermögen tun - **2.** [capability] Fähigkeit *die*, Gabe *die;* [talent] Begabung *die;* **linguistic abilities** Sprachbegabung *die*.

**abject** ['æbdʒekt] *adj* - **1.** [poverty] bitter; **~ misery** tiefes Elend - **2.** [person] unterwürfig, demütig; **to offer an ~ apology** unterwürfig um Entschuldigung bitten.

**ablaze** [ə'bleɪz] *adj* - **1.** [on fire] in Flammen - **2.** *fig* [bright]: **to be ~ with light** hell erleuchtet sein.

**able** ['eɪbl] *adj* - **1.** [capable] fähig; **to be ~ to do sthg** etw tun können; [due to circumstances] imstande OR in der Lage sein, etw zu tun - **2.** [competent] tüchtig; [gifted] begabt; **an ~ teacher** ein tüchtiger Lehrer.

**able-bodied** [-ˌbɒdɪd] *adj* kräftig und gesund; MIL tauglich.

**ablutions** [ə'bluːʃnz] *npl fml* Toilette *die*.

**ably** ['eɪblɪ] *adv* geschickt, gekonnt.

**ABM** *n abbr of* **antiballistic missile.**

**abnormal** [æb'nɔːml] *adj* [behaviour] abnorm; [interest] krankhaft; [workload] übermäßig.

**abnormality** [ˌæbnɔː'mælətɪ] (*pl* **-ies**) *n* [of behaviour] Abnormität *die;* [physical defect] Missbildung *die*.

**abnormally** [æb'nɔːməlɪ] *adv* ungewöhnlich.

**aboard** [ə'bɔːd] *adv* [on ship, plane] an Bord ◇ *prep*: **to go ~** an Bord gehen; **~ the ship/plane** an Bord des Schiffes/Flugzeugs; **~ the bus/train** im Bus/Zug.

**abode** [ə'bəʊd] *n fml*: **of no fixed ~** ohne festen Wohnsitz.

**abolish** [ə'bɒlɪʃ] *vt* ablschaffen.

**abolition** [ˌæbə'lɪʃn] *n* Abschaffung *die*.

**A-bomb** *n abbr of* **atom bomb.**

**abominable** [ə'bɒmɪnəbl] *adj* [behaviour, treatment] abscheulich; [performance] furchtbar.

**abominable snowman** *n*: **the ~** der Yeti, der Schneemensch.

**abominably** [ə'bɒmɪnəblɪ] *adv* [behave, treat] abscheulich; [perform] furchtbar.

**aborigine** [ˌæbə'rɪdʒənɪ] *n* Ureinwohner *der*, -in *die* Australiens, Aborigine *der*.

**abort** [ə'bɔːt] *vt* - **1.** [pregnancy] ablbrechen; [baby] abltreiben - **2.** *fig* [plan, mission] ablbrechen - **3.** COMPUT ablbrechen ◇ *vi* COMPUT ablbrechen.

**abortion** [ə'bɔːʃn] *n* [of pregnancy] Abtreibung *die*, Schwangerschaftsabbruch *der;* **she's going to have an ~** sie wird eine Abtreibung vornehmen lassen.

**abortive** [ə'bɔːtɪv] *adj* misslungen, fehlgeschlagen.

**abound** [ə'baʊnd] *vi* - **1.** [be plentiful] in großer Fülle vorhanden sein - **2.** [be full]: **to ~ with** OR **in sthg** reich an etw (*D*) sein.

**about** [ə'baʊt] *adv* - **1.** [approximately] ungefähr, etwa; **~ 50** ungefähr 50; **at ~ six o'clock** gegen sechs Uhr - **2.** [referring to place] herum; **to walk ~** herumllaufen; **is Mr Smith ~?** ist Herr Smith da?; **there's a lot of flu ~** die Grippe geht um - **3.** [on the point of]: **to be ~ to do sthg** im Begriff sein, etw zu tun ◇ *prep* - **1.** [concerning] um, über (+ *A*); **a book ~ Scotland** ein Buch über Schottland; **what's it ~?** worum gehts?; **to talk ~ sthg** über etw sprechen; **to quarrel ~ sthg** sich wegen etw streiten; **what ~ a drink?** wie wärs mit etwas zu trinken? - **2.** [referring to place] herum; **there are lots of hotels ~ the town** es gibt viele Hotels in der Stadt; **to wander ~ the streets** in den Straßen umherschlendern.

**about-turn** *esp Br*, **about-face** *esp Am n* - **1.** MIL Kehrtwendung *die* - **2.** *fig* [change of attitude] Wendung *die* um hundertachtzig Grad.

**above** [ə'bʌv] *prep* - **1.** [higher than] über (+ *A, D*); **to fly ~ the clouds** über den Wolken fliegen; **no trees grow ~ the snowline** oberhalb der Schneegrenze wachsen keine Bäume - **2.** [more than] über (+ *A*); **children ~ the age of twelve** Kinder über zwölf Jahren - **3.** [in rank, status] über (+ *D*); **a colonel is ~ a major** ein Oberst steht über einem Major - **4.** [too good for]: **she is ~ suspicion** sie ist über jeden Verdacht erhaben; **to be ~ doing sthg** sich (*D*) zu gut für etw sein; **she's not ~ lying** sie schreckt vor einer Lüge nicht zurück ◇ *adv* - **1.** [on top, higher up] oben; **the flat ~** die Wohnung oben; **see ~** [in text] siehe oben - **2.** [more]: **children aged ten and ~** Kinder ab zehn Jahren.
➤ **above all** *adv* vor allem.

**aboveboard** [əˌbʌv'bɔːd] *adj* ehrlich, einwandfrei.

**abracadabra** [ˌæbrəkə'dæbrə] *excl* Abrakadabra!

**abrasion** [ə'breɪʒn] *n fml* [graze] Abschürfung *die*, Schürfwunde *die*.

**abrasive** [ə'breɪsɪv] *adj* - **1.** [for cleaning] Scheu-

er- - **2.** *fig* [person] ungehobelt; [manner] grob
◇ *n* Schleifmittel *das*, Scheuermittel *das*.

**abreast** [ə'brest] *adv* nebeneinander, Seite
an Seite; **to walk three ~** zu dritt nebeneinander gehen.
➤ **abreast of** *prep:* **to keep ~ of sthg** auf dem
Laufenden in Bezug auf etw *(A)* bleiben.

**abridged** [ə'brɪdʒd] *adj* gekürzt.

**abroad** [ə'brɔːd] *adv* [live] im Ausland; [travel,
go] ins Ausland.

**abrupt** [ə'brʌpt] *adj* - **1.** [sudden] abrupt
- **2.** [person] kurz angebunden; [manner]
brüsk.

**abruptly** [ə'brʌptlɪ] *adv* - **1.** [suddenly] abrupt
- **2.** [brusquely, rudely] barsch.

**ABS** (*abbr of* **antilock braking system**) *n* ABS
*das*.

**abscess** ['æbsɪs] *n* Abszess *der*.

**abscond** [əb'skɒnd] *vi* [from detention centre] ent-
fliehen; [from boarding school] wegl|laufen; **to**
**~ with sthg** sich mit etw davon|stehlen.

**abseil** ['æbseɪl] *vi* sich abseilen; **to ~ down**
**sthg** sich an etw *(D)* abseilen.

**absence** ['æbsəns] *n* - **1.** [of person] Abwesenheit *die*; **in his ~** in seiner Abwesenheit
- **2.** [lack] Mangel *der*; **in the ~ of sthg** aus Mangel an etw *(D)*, mangels etw *(G)*.

**absent** ['æbsənt] *adj* - **1.** [not present]: **~ (from)**
abwesend (von); **to be ~ without leave** MIL oh-
ne Beurlaubung abwesend sein - **2.** [absent-
minded - person] zerstreut, geistesabwesend;
[ - expression] geistesabwesend.

**absentee** [ˌæbsən'tiː] *n* Abwesende *der, die*.

**absent-minded** [-'maɪndɪd] *adj* zerstreut,
geistesabwesend.

**absolute** ['æbsəluːt] *adj* - **1.** [complete, utter] absolut, vollkommen; **it's an ~ disgrace** es ist
eine ausgesprochene Schande - **2.** [ruler,
power] absolut.

**absolutely** [ˌæbsə'luːtlɪ] *adv* [completely, utterly]
vollkommen, ausgesprochen; **I'm ~ starving**
ich bin ausgesprochen hungrig ◇ *excl* [ex-
pressing agreement] auf jeden Fall!

**absolute majority** *n* absolute Mehrheit
*die*.

**absolution** [ˌæbsə'luːʃn] *n* Absolution *die*.

**absolve** [əb'zɒlv] *vt:* **to ~ sb (from sthg)** [from
crime] jn (von etw) frei|sprechen; [from sin] jn
(von etw) los|sprechen; [from responsibility] jn
(von etw) entbinden.

**absorb** [əb'zɔːb] *vt* - **1.** [liquid] auf|saugen; [gas,
heat] absorbieren - **2.** *fig* [learn] auf|nehmen
- **3.** [interest] fesseln; **to be ~ed in sthg** in etw *(A)*
vertieft OR versunken sein - **4.** [take over]
übernehmen.

**absorbent** [əb'zɔːbənt] *adj* absorbierend,
saugfähig.

**absorbing** [əb'zɔːbɪŋ] *adj* fesselnd.

**absorption** [əb'zɔːpʃn] *n* - **1.** [soaking up] Absorption *die* - **2.** [interest] Versunkenheit *die*
- **3.** [taking over] Übernahme *die*.

**abstain** [əb'steɪn] *vi* - **1.**: **to ~ from sthg** [from
drinking, smoking] sich etw *(G)* enthalten; [from
sex, food] auf etw *(A)* verzichten - **2.** [in vote]
sich der Stimme enthalten.

**abstemious** [æb'stiːmjəs] *adj fml* enthaltsam.

**abstention** [əb'stenʃn] *n* [in vote] Enthaltung
*die*.

**abstinence** ['æbstɪnəns] *n:* **~ (from sthg)** Abstinenz *die* (von etw), Enthaltsamkeit *die* (in
Bezug auf etw *(A)*).

**abstract** ['æbstrækt] *adj* abstrakt ◇ *n* [summa-
ry] Abstract *der*.

**abstraction** [æb'strækʃn] *n* - **1.** [distractedness]
Geistesabwesenheit *die* - **2.** [abstract idea]
Abstraktion *die*.

**abstruse** [æb'struːs] *adj* schwer verständlich.

**absurd** [əb'sɜːd] *adj* absurd.

**absurdity** [əb'sɜːdətɪ] (*pl* **-ies**) *n* Absurdität
*die*.

**absurdly** [əb'sɜːdlɪ] *adv* [large, rich] unsinnig;
[low] lächerlich.

**ABTA** ['æbtə] (*abbr of* **Association of British**
**Travel Agents**) *n Verband britischer Reiseveranstalter.*

**abundance** [ə'bʌndəns] *n* Fülle *die;* **in ~** in
Hülle und Fülle.

**abundant** [ə'bʌndənt] *adj* reichlich.

**abundantly** [ə'bʌndəntlɪ] *adv* - **1.** [extremely]:
**it's ~ clear** es ist mehr als klar - **2.** [in large
amounts] in Hülle und Fülle.

**abuse** [*n* ə'bjuːs, *vb* ə'bjuːz] *n* - **1.** (U) [offensive re-
marks] Beschimpfungen *pl*, Schimpfworte *pl*
- **2.** [maltreatment] Missbrauch *der* - **3.** [mis-
use - of alcohol, drugs, power] Missbrauch *der*
◇ *vt* - **1.** [insult] beschimpfen - **2.** [maltreat, mis-
use] missbrauchen.

**abusive** [ə'bjuːsɪv] *adj* ausfallend.

**abut** [ə'bʌt] (*pt* & *pp* **-ted;** *cont* **-ting**) *vi:* **to ~**
**onto sthg** grenzen an (+ *A*).

**abysmal** [ə'bɪzml] *adj* [behaviour, performance,
weather] miserabel; [failure, performance] erbärmlich.

**abysmally** [ə'bɪzməlɪ] *adv* [behave, perform] miserabel.

**abyss** [ə'bɪs] *n* Abgrund *der; fig* [between people,
groups] Kluft *die*, Abgründe *pl*.

**Abyssinia** [ˌæbɪ'sɪnjə] *n* Abessinien *nt*.

**Abyssinian** [ˌæbɪ'sɪnɪən] *adj* abessinisch ◇ *n*
Abessinier *der*, -in *die*.

**a/c** (*abbr of* **account (current)**) Kto.

**AC** *n* - **1.** *Br* (*abbr of* **athletics club**) *Leichtathletik Club* - **2.** *abbr of* **alternating current.**

**acacia** [əˈkeɪʃə] *n* Akazie *die.*

**academic** [ˌækəˈdemɪk] *adj* - **1.** [of college, university] wissenschaftlich, akademisch - **2.** [studious] intellektuell - **3.** [hypothetical] theoretisch ⬦ *n* Akademiker *der,* -in *die.*

**academic year** *n* akademisches Jahr.

**academy** [əˈkædəmɪ] (*pl* -ies) *n* Akademie *die.*

**ACAS** [ˈeɪkæs] (*abbr of* **Advisory Conciliation and Arbitration Service**) *n unabhängige britische Organisation, die bei Konflikten zwischen Arbeitgebern und Gewerkschaften vermittelt.*

**accede** [ækˈsiːd] *vi* - **1.** *fml* [agree]: **to ~ to sthg** in etw (A) einlwilligen - **2.** [monarch]: **to ~ to the throne** den Thron besteigen.

**accelerate** [əkˈseləreɪt] *vt* [pace, rhythm, decline, event] beschleunigen ⬦ *vi* - **1.** [car, driver] beschleunigen - **2.** [inflation, growth] sich beschleunigen, zulnehmen.

**acceleration** [əkˌseləˈreɪʃn] *n* Beschleunigung *die.*

**accelerator** [əkˈseləreɪtər] *n* Gaspedal *das.*

**accelerator board, accelerator card** *n* COMPUT Beschleunigerkarte *die.*

**accent** [ˈæksent] *n* - **1.** [gen] Akzent *der* - **2.** *fig* [emphasis] Betonung *die,* Akzent *der.*

**accentuate** [ækˈsentjʊeɪt] *vt* hervorlheben, betonen.

**accept** [əkˈsept] *vt* - **1.** [gift, advice, apology, invitation, offer] anlnehmen - **2.** [change, situation] akzeptieren, hinlnehmen - **3.** [defeat, blame] einlgestehen; [responsibility] übernehmen - **4.** [person - as part of group] akzeptieren; [ - for job] nehmen; [ - as member of club] auf lnehmen - **5.** [admit]: **to ~ that** zugeben, dass; **it is generally ~ed that** es ist allgemein anerkannt, dass - **6.** [subj: shop, bank] akzeptieren; [subj: machine] nehmen.

**acceptable** [əkˈseptəbl] *adj* akzeptabel.

**acceptably** [əkˈseptəblɪ] *adv* passend.

**acceptance** [əkˈseptəns] *n* - **1.** [of gift, advice, apology, piece of work] Annahme *die* - **2.** [of change, situation] Hinnahme *die* - **3.** [of defeat, blame] Eingeständnis *das;* [of responsibility] Übernahme *das* - **4.** [of person - as part of group] Akzeptierung *die;* [ - for job] Anstellung *die;* [ - as member of club] Aufnahme *die.*

**accepted** [əkˈseptɪd] *adj* [wisdom, fact] anerkannt.

**access** [ˈækses] *n (U)* - **1.** [entry, way in] Zutritt *der,* Zugang *der;* **to gain ~ to** [place, building] sich (D) Zutritt verschaffen zu - **2.** [opportunity to use, see]: **to have ~ to sthg** zu etw Zugang haben ⬦ *vt* COMPUT zulgreifen auf (+ A).

**accessibility** [əkˌsesəˈbɪlətɪ] *n* - **1.** [of place] Zu-

gänglichkeit *die,* Erreichbarkeit *die* - **2.** [availability] Verfügbarkeit *die.*

**accessible** [əkˈsesəbl] *adj* - **1.** [place] zugänglich, (leicht) erreichbar - **2.** [available] verfügbar - **3.** [understandable] zugänglich.

**accession** [ækˈseʃn] *n (U):* **~ (to the throne)** Thronbesteigung *die.*

**accessory** [əkˈsesərɪ] (*pl* -ies) *n* - **1.** [extra part, device] Extra *das;* **accessories** Zubehör *das,* Zubehörteile *pl* - **2.** LAW Helfershelfer *der,* -in *die.*
⬦ **accessories** *npl* [to outfit] Accessoires *pl.*

**access road** *n* - **1.** [to building site, housing estate] Zufahrt *die,* Zufahrtsstraße *die* - **2.** *Br* [to motorway] Auffahrt *die.*

**access time** *n* COMPUT Zugriffszeit *die.*

**accident** [ˈæksɪdənt] *n* - **1.** [unpleasant event] Unfall *der;* [more serious] Unglück *das;* [mishap] Missgeschick *das;* **to have an ~** [in car] einen Autounfall haben; **I had an ~ in the garden** mir ist im Garten ein Missgeschick passiert - **2.** [unintentional act] Versehen *das,* Missgeschick *das* - **3.** *(U)* [chance]: **we met by ~** wir haben uns zufällig getroffen.

**accidental** [ˌæksɪˈdentl] *adj* - **1.** [meeting, discovery] zufällig - **2.** [mistake] versehentlich.

**accidentally** [ˌæksɪˈdentəlɪ] *adv* - **1.** [drop, break] versehentlich - **2.** [meet, find, discover] zufällig.

**accident-prone** *adj:* **he is ~** er ist vom Pech verfolgt.

**acclaim** [əˈkleɪm] *n* Anerkennung *die,* Beifall *der* ⬦ *vt* feiern.

**acclamation** [ˌækləˈmeɪʃn] *n* Beifall *der,* Beifallsbekundung *die.*

**acclimatize, -ise** [əˈklaɪmətaɪz], **acclimate** *Am* [ˈækləmeɪt] *vi:* **to ~ (to sthg)** sich (in etw (D)) akklimatisieren.

**accolade** [ˈækəleɪd] *n* Anerkennung *die,* Auszeichnung *die.*

**accommodate** [əˈkɒmədeɪt] *vt* - **1.** [subj: building, car] Platz bieten für; [subj: person] unterlbringen - **2.** [oblige] entgegenlkommen (+ D), berücksichtigen.

**accommodating** [əˈkɒmədeɪtɪŋ] *adj* entgegenkommend.

**accommodation** *Br* [əˌkɒməˈdeɪʃn] *n,* **accommodations** *Am* [əˌkɒməˈdeɪʃnz] *npl* - **1.** [lodging] Unterkunft *die* - **2.** [work space] Raum *der.*

**accompaniment** [əˈkʌmpənɪmənt] *n* MUS Begleitung *die.*

**accompanist** [əˈkʌmpənɪst] *n* MUS Begleiter *der,* -in *die.*

**accompany** [əˈkʌmpənɪ] (*pt* & *pp* -ied) *vt* - **1.** [gen] begleiten - **2.** MUS: **to ~ sb (on sthg)** jn (auf etw (D)) begleiten.

**accomplice** [əˈkʌmplɪs] *n* Komplize *der.*

**accomplish** [əˈkʌmplɪʃ] *vt* [achieve] erreichen, leisten; [complete] vollbringen.

**accomplished** [əˈkʌmplɪʃt] *adj* fähig; [performance] vollendet.

**accomplishment** [əˈkʌmplɪʃmənt] *n* - **1.** [feat, deed] Leistung *die* - **2.** [action] Vollendung *die*.
➡ **accomplishments** *npl* Fähigkeiten *pl*.

**accord** [əˈkɔːd] *n* - **1.** [settlement] Einigung *die* - **2.** [agreement, harmony]: **to be in ~ (with sb)** (mit jm) übereinlstimmen; **to be in ~ (with sthg)** (mit etw) im Einklang sein; **with one ~** geschlossen; **to do sthg of one's own ~** etw aus eigenem Antrieb tun, etw aus freien Stücken tun.

**accordance** [əˈkɔːdəns] *n*: **in ~ with** entsprechend (+ D), gemäß (+ D); **in ~ with your wishes** Ihren Wünschen entsprechend.

**according to** [əˈkɔːdɪŋ-] *prep* - **1.** [as stated or shown by] zufolge (+ D), laut (+ D); **to go ~ plan** nach Plan gehen - **2.** [with regard to, depending on] entsprechend (+ D).

**accordingly** [əˈkɔːdɪŋlɪ] *adv* - **1.** [appropriately] (dem)entsprechend - **2.** [consequently] folglich, demgemäß.

**accordion** [əˈkɔːdjən] *n* Akkordeon *das*, Ziehharmonika *die*.

**accordionist** [əˈkɔːdjənɪst] *n* Akkordeonspieler *der*, -in *die*.

**accost** [əˈkɒst] *vt* belästigen.

**account** [əˈkaʊnt] *n* - **1.** [with bank, building society] Konto *das* - **2.** [with shop, company] Kundenkonto *das* - **3.** [report] Bericht *der*, Darstellung *die* - **4.** *phr:* **to call sb to ~** jn zur Rechenschaft ziehen; **to give a good ~ of o.s.** sich gut schlagen; **to take ~ of sthg, to take sthg into ~** etw berücksichtigen, etw in Betracht ziehen; **to be of no ~** ohne Bedeutung sein; **on no ~** auf keinen Fall, keinesfalls.
➡ **accounts** *npl* [of business] Buchführung *die*.
➡ **by all accounts** *adv* nach allem, was man hört.
➡ **on account of** *prep* aufgrund (+ G), wegen (+ G).
➡ **account for** *vt fus* - **1.** [explain] erklären, Rechenschaft abllegen über; **all the missing people have been ~ed for** der Verbleib aller vermissten Personen ist geklärt worden - **2.** [represent] auslmachen.

**accountability** [ə,kaʊntəˈbɪlətɪ] *n* Verantwortlichkeit *die*.

**accountable** [əˈkaʊntəbl] *adj:* **~ (for sb/sthg)** [responsible] verantwortlich (für etw/jn); **~ to sb** [answerable] jm (gegenüber) verantwortlich.

**accountancy** [əˈkaʊntənsɪ] *n* Buchhaltung *die*, Buchführung *die*.

**accountant** [əˈkaʊntənt] *n* Buchhalter *der*, -in *die*.

**accounting** [əˈkaʊntɪŋ] *n* Buchhaltung *die*, Buchführung *die*.

**accounts department** *n* Buchhaltungsabteilung *die*, Buchführungsabteilung *die*.

**accoutrements** *Br* [əˈkuːtrəmənts], **accouterments** *Am* [əˈkuːtərmənts] *npl fml* [baggage] Ausrüstung *die*.

**accredited** [əˈkredɪtɪd] *adj* [authorized] bevollmächtigt; [recognized] (offiziell) anerkannt.

**accrue** [əˈkruː] *vi* FIN sich anlsammeln.

**accumulate** [əˈkjuːmjʊleɪt] *vt* [money, belongings] anlhäufen; [evidence] sammeln ⬦ *vi* [money, belongings] sich anlhäufen, sich anlsammeln.

**accumulation** [ə,kjuːmjʊˈleɪʃn] *n* - **1.** (U) [action - of money, belongings] Anhäufen *das;* [ - of evidence] Sammeln *das* - **2.** [collection - of money, belongings] Anhäufung *die;* [ - of people] Menge *die*.

**accuracy** [ˈækjʊrəsɪ] *n* - **1.** [truth, correctness] Korrektheit *die*, Richtigkeit *die* - **2.** [precision - of weapon, marksman] Präzision *die;* [ - of typing, typist] Fehlerlosigkeit *die;* [ - of figures, estimate] Genauigkeit *die*.

**accurate** [ˈækjʊrət] *adj* - **1.** [true] korrekt, richtig - **2.** [precise - weapon, marksman] präzis(e); [ - typing, typist] fehlerlos; [ - figures, estimate] genau.

**accurately** [ˈækjʊrətlɪ] *adv* - **1.** [truthfully] korrekt, richtig - **2.** [precisely - aim, estimate] genau; [ - type] fehlerlos.

**accusation** [,ækjuːˈzeɪʃn] *n* - **1.** [charge, criticism] Vorwurf *der*, Beschuldigung *die* - **2.** LAW [formal charge] Anklage *die*.

**accuse** [əˈkjuːz] *vt* - **1.** [charge, criticize]: **to ~ sb of sthg** jn etw (G) beschuldigen; **to ~ sb of doing sthg** jn beschuldigen, etw getan zu haben - **2.** LAW: **to be ~d of murder/fraud** des Mordes/Betrugs angeklagt sein OR werden, wegen Mord(es)/Betrug(s) angeklagt sein OR werden; **to be ~d of doing sthg** beschuldigt werden, etw getan zu haben.

**accused** [əˈkjuːzd] *n* LAW: **the ~** der/die Angeklagte.

**accusing** [əˈkjuːzɪŋ] *adj* vorwurfsvoll.

**accusingly** [əˈkjuːzɪŋlɪ] *adv* vorwurfsvoll.

**accustomed** [əˈkʌstəmd] *adj:* **to be ~ to sthg** etw gewohnt sein, an etw (A) gewöhnt sein; **to be ~ to doing sthg** gewohnt sein, etw zu tun.

**ace** [eɪs] *n* - **1.** [gen] As *das* - **2.** *phr:* **he came within an ~ of being run over** er wäre um ein Haar OR beinahe überfahren worden ⬦ *adj* [topclass] erstklassig.

**acerbic** [əˈsɜːbɪk] *adj* bissig.

**acetate** [ˈæsɪteɪt] *n* Acetat *das*.

**ache** [eɪk] *n* [dull pain] (dumpfer) Schmerz ⬦ *vi* - **1.** [be painful] weh tun, schmerzen;

my head ~s mein Kopf tut mir weh - **2.** *fig* [want]: **to be aching for sthg** sich nach etw sehnen; **to be aching to do sthg** sich danach sehnen, etw zu tun.

**achieve** [ə'tʃiːv] *vt* [success] erzielen; [goal] erreichen; [ambition] verwirklichen; [victory] erringen; [fame] erlangen.

**achievement** [ə'tʃiːvmənt] *n* - **1.** [feat, deed] Leistung *die* - **2.** (U) [process of achieving] Erreichen *das*.

**Achilles' heel** [ə'kɪliːz-] *n* Achillesferse *die*.

**Achilles' tendon** *n* Achillessehne *die*.

**acid** ['æsɪd] *adj* - **1.** [substance, food, drink] sauer - **2.** *fig* [remark, person] bissig <> *n* - **1.** CHEM Säure *die* - **2.** *inf* [LSD] Acid *das*.

**acidic** [ə'sɪdɪk] *adj* sauer.

**acidity** [ə'sɪdətɪ] *n* (U) - **1.** [of substance, food, drink] Säure *die* - **2.** *fig* [of remark, person] Bissigkeit *die*.

**acid rain** *n* saurer Regen.

**acid test** *n* *fig* Feuerprobe *die*.

**acknowledge** [ək'nɒlɪdʒ] *vt* - **1.** [accept, admit] einlgestehen, zulgeben - **2.** [recognize]: **to ~ sb as sthg** jn als etw anlerkennen; **to ~ sb's presence** js Anwesenheit zur Kenntnis nehmen - **3.** [letter]: **to ~ (receipt of) sthg** den Eingang OR Empfang von etw bestätigen - **4.** [greet] grüßen.

**acknowledg(e)ment** [ək'nɒlɪdʒmənt] *n* - **1.** [thanks, gratitude] Anerkennung *die* - **2.** [acceptance] Eingeständnis *das* - **3.** [letter] Empfangsbestätigung *die*.

➤ **acknowledg(e)ments** *npl* [in book] Danksagungen *pl*.

**ACLU** (*abbr of* **American Civil Liberties Union**) *n* US-amerikanische Organisation, die Rechtsfälle daraufhin untersucht, ob die Freiheitsrechte der betroffenen Personen verletzt wurden.

**acme** ['ækmɪ] *n* Gipfel *der*, Höhepunkt *der*.

**acne** ['æknɪ] *n* Akne *die*.

**acorn** ['eɪkɔːn] *n* Eichel *die*.

**acoustic** [ə'kuːstɪk] *adj* akustisch.
➤ **acoustics** *npl* [of room] Akustik *die*.

**acoustic guitar** *n* Akustikgitarre *die*.

**ACPO** (*abbr of* **Association of Chief Police Officers**) *n* Verband britischer Polizeipräsidenten.

**acquaint** [ə'kweɪnt] *vt*: **to ~ sb with sthg** [information] jn über etw (A) informieren; [method, technique] jn mit etw vertraut machen; **to be ~ed with sb** mit jm bekannt sein, jn kennen.

**acquaintance** [ə'kweɪntəns] *n* - **1.** [personal associate] Bekannte *der*, *die* - **2.** (U) *fml*: **to make sb's ~** [meet] js Bekanntschaft machen.

**acquiesce** [ˌækwɪ'es] *vi*: **to ~ (to** OR **in sthg)** (in etw (A)) einlwilligen.

**acquiescence** [ˌækwɪ'esns] *n* (U) Einwilligung *die*.

**acquire** [ə'kwaɪəʳ] *vt* - **1.** [house, company, book] erwerben; [information, document] erhalten - **2.** [habit] anlnehmen; [skill, knowledge] erwerben; **to ~ a taste for sthg** Gefallen an etw (D) finden.

**acquired taste** [ə'kwaɪəd-] *n*: **whisky/modern jazz is an ~** Whisky/Modern Jazz ist ein Genuss, wenn man sich erst daran gewöhnt hat.

**acquisition** [ˌækwɪ'zɪʃn] *n* - **1.** [purchase, find] Anschaffung *die* - **2.** (U) [act of purchasing, obtaining] Erwerb *der*.

**acquisitive** [ə'kwɪzɪtɪv] *adj* habgierig.

**acquit** [ə'kwɪt] (*pt* & *pp* **-ted**; *cont* **-ting**) *vt* - **1.** LAW: **to ~ sb (of sthg)** jn (von etw) freilsprechen - **2.** [conduct]: **to ~ o.s. well/badly** seine Sache gut/schlecht machen.

**acquittal** [ə'kwɪtl] *n* LAW Freispruch *der*.

**acre** ['eɪkəʳ] *n* ≃ Morgen *der*, = 4047,9 m².

**acreage** ['eɪkərɪdʒ] *n* Größe eines Gebietes in „acres".

**acrid** ['ækrɪd] *adj* - **1.** [smoke, smell] beißend; [taste] bitter - **2.** *fig* [words] verletzend; [remarks] beißend.

**acrimonious** [ˌækrɪ'məʊnjəs] *adj* erbittert.

**acrobat** ['ækrəbæt] *n* Akrobat *der*, -in *die*.

**acrobatic** [ˌækrə'bætɪk] *adj* - **1.** [display] akrobatisch - **2.** [person] (körperlich) geschickt.
➤ **acrobatics** *npl* akrobatische Kunststücke *pl*.

**acronym** ['ækrənɪm] *n* Akronym *das*.

**across** [ə'krɒs] *adv* - **1.** [from one side to the other - to the other side] hinüber; [- from the other side] herüber - **2.** [in measurements] breit; [of circle] im Durchmesser - **3.** [in crossword] waag(e)recht - **4.** *phr*: **to get sthg ~ to sb** jm etw verständlich machen <> *prep* - **1.** [from one side to the other] über (+ A); **he drew a line ~ the page** er machte einen Strich quer über die Seite - **2.** [on the other side of] auf der anderen Seite (+ G).
➤ **across from** *prep* gegenüber von.

**acrylic** [ə'krɪlɪk] *adj* Acryl-, aus Acryl <> *n* Acryl *das*.

**act** [ækt] *n* - **1.** [action, deed] Tat *die*, Akt *der*; **an ~ of mercy** ein Gnadenakt; **to catch sb in the ~** jn auf frischer Tat ertappen - **2.** LAW Gesetz *das* - **3.** [of play, opera] Akt *der*; [in cabaret etc] Nummer *die* - **4.** *fig* [pretence] Komödie *die*, Schau *die*; **to put on an ~** Komödie spielen - **5.** *phr*: **to get in on the ~** mit von der Partie sein; **get your ~ together!** reiß dich mal am Riemen <> *vi* - **1.** [take action] handeln - **2.** [behave] sich benehmen OR verhalten; **to ~ as if/like** sich benehmen OR verhalten als ob/wie - **3.** [in play, film] spielen - **4.** *fig* [pretend] Komödie spielen, schauspielen; **to ~ innocent** unschuldig tun - **5.** [take effect] wirken - **6.** [fulfil function]: **to ~ as sthg** als etw fungieren; **to ~ for** OR **on behalf of sb** jn vertreten <> vt [role] spielen; **to ~ the fool/innocent** den Dummen/Unschuldigen spielen.

◆ **act out** vt sep - **1.** [thoughts, feelings] zum Ausdruck bringen; [fantasy] ausleben - **2.** [event, story] nachlspielen.

◆ **act up** vi inf - **1.** [not work] verrückt spielen - **2.** [misbehave] Theater machen.

**acting** [ˈæktɪŋ] adj [interim] stellvertretend <> n (U) [performance] Spiel das; [profession] Schauspielerei die; **Olivier's ~ was always marvellous** Olivier hat immer fantastisch gespielt; **I enjoy ~** ich spiele gerne Theater/ in Filmen.

**action** [ˈækʃn] n - **1.** (U) [fact of doing sthg] Handeln das; **to take ~** etwas unternehmen, handeln; **to put sthg into ~** etw in die Tat umlsetzen; **in ~** [person] in Aktion; [machine] in Betrieb; **out of ~** [person] nicht in Aktion; [machine] außer Betrieb - **2.** [deed] Tat die - **3.** (U) [in battle, war] Gefecht das, Kampf der; **killed in ~** gefallen - **4.** LAW [trial] Prozess der; [charge] Klage die; **to bring an ~ against sb** eine Klage gegen jn anlstrengen - **5.** [in play, book, film] Handlung die - **6.** [effect] Wirkung die.

**action group** n [lobby] (Bürger)initiative die.

**action replay** n Wiederholung die.

**activate** [ˈæktɪveɪt] vt [device, machine] in Gang setzen; [alarm] ausllösen.

**active** [ˈæktɪv] adj aktiv; [mind, interest] rege.

**actively** [ˈæktɪvlɪ] adv aktiv.

**active service** n MIL: **on ~** im Einsatz.

**activist** [ˈæktɪvɪst] n Aktivist der, -in die.

**activity** [ækˈtɪvətɪ] (pl -ies) n - **1.** (U) [movement, action] Geschäftigkeit die, geschäftiges Treiben - **2.** [pastime, hobby] Betätigung die, Aktivität die.

◆ **activities** npl Aktivitäten pl.

**act of God** n höhere Gewalt.

**actor** [ˈæktər] n Schauspieler der.

**actress** [ˈæktrɪs] n Schauspielerin die.

**actual** [ˈæktʃʊəl] adj eigentlich; [cost, amount, cause] tatsächlich, wirklich; **in ~ fact** eigentlich.

**actuality** [ˌæktʃʊˈælətɪ] n (U): **in ~** in Wirklichkeit.

**actually** [ˈæktʃʊəlɪ] adv - **1.** [really, in truth] wirklich, tatsächlich - **2.** [by the way] übrigens - **3.** [with contradictory statement] eigentlich.

**actuary** [ˈæktjʊərɪ] (pl -ies) n Aktuar der.

**actuate** [ˈæktjʊeɪt] vt [device, mechanism] in Gang setzen; [alarm] ausllösen.

**acuity** [əˈkjuːətɪ] n fml [of thought, judgement] Scharfsinn der; [of sight] Schärfe die.

**acumen** [ˈækjʊmen] n: **business ~** Geschäftssinn der.

**acupuncture** [ˈækjʊpʌŋktʃər] n Akupunktur die.

**acute** [əˈkjuːt] adj - **1.** [pain, shortage] akut; [embarrassment, anxiety] groß - **2.** [observer, mind] scharf; [analysis, judgement, person] scharfsinnig - **3.** [sight] scharf; [hearing, sense of smell] fein - **4.** MATH spitz.

**acutely** [əˈkjuːtlɪ] adv [extremely] äußerst; **to be ~ aware/conscious of sthg** sich (D) einer Sache (G) genau OR sehr bewusst sein.

**ad** [æd] (abbr of **advertisement**) n inf [in newspaper] Inserat das, Annonce die; [on TV] Werbung die; [in shop window] Angebot das.

**AD** (abbr of **Anno Domini**) A. D.

**adage** [ˈædɪdʒ] n Sprichwort das.

**adamant** [ˈædəmənt] adj: **to be ~ (about sthg)** (in Bezug auf etw (A)) unnachgiebig sein; **to be ~ that** darauf bestehen, dass.

**Adam's apple** [ˈædəmz-] n Adamsapfel der.

**adapt** [əˈdæpt] vt - **1.** [adjust, modify] anlpassen; [machine, system] umlstellen; [text, materials] umlarbeiten - **2.** [book, play] adaptieren, bearbeiten <> vi: **to ~ to sthg** sich etw (D) anlpassen; [idea] sich mit etw anlfreunden.

**adaptability** [əˌdæptəˈbɪlətɪ] n Anpassungsfähigkeit die.

**adaptable** [əˈdæptəbl] adj anpassungsfähig.

**adaptation** [ˌædæpˈteɪʃn] n [of book, play] Adaptation die, Bearbeitung die.

**adapter, adaptor** [əˈdæptər] n [for foreign plug] Adapter der; [for several plugs] Mehrfachstecker der.

**ADC** n abbr of **aide-de-camp**.

**add** [æd] vt - **1.** [gen]: **to ~ sthg (to)** etw hinzulfügen (zu) - **2.** [total] addieren, zusammenlzählen.

◆ **add in** vt sep [include] hinzulfügen, einlbeziehen.

◆ **add on** vt sep - **1.** [build on, attach]: **to ~ sthg on (to sthg)** etw (an etw (A)) anlbauen - **2.** [include]: **to ~ sthg on (to sthg)** etw (zu etw) hinzulfügen; [number, amount] etw (zu etw) dazulrechnen.

◆ **add to** vt fus [increase] vergrößern, vermehren.

◆ **add up** vt sep [total up] zusammenlrechnen, zusammenlzählen <> vi inf [make sense] einen Sinn ergeben, zusammenlpassen.

◆ **add up to** vt fus [represent] ergeben.

**addendum** [əˈdendəm] (pl -da [- də]) n [of speech] Nachtrag der; [of book] Anhang der.

**adder** [ˈædər] n [snake] Viper die.

**addict** [ˈædɪkt] n - **1.** [taking drugs] Süchtige der, die, Abhängige der, die - **2.** fig [fan]: **to be a**

chocolate ~ süchtig nach Schokolade sein; **to be an exercise ~** ein Sportfanatiker sein.

**addicted** [ə'dıktıd] *adj lit* & *fig:* **~ (to)** süchtig (nach).

**addiction** [ə'dık∫n] *n lit* & *fig:* **~ (to)** Sucht *die* (nach).

**addictive** [ə'dıktıv] *adj:* **to be ~** [drug] süchtig machen; *fig* [exercise, food, TV] zu einer Sucht werden können.

**addition** [ə'dı∫n] *n* - **1.** MATH Addition *die* - **2.** [extra thing] Zusatz *der*, Ergänzung *die* - **3.** [act of adding] Hinzufügen *das;* **in ~** außerdem; **in ~ to** zusätzlich zu.

**additional** [ə'dı∫ənl] *adj* zusätzlich.

**additive** ['ædıtıv] *n* Zusatz *der*.

**addled** ['ædld] *adj* - **1.** [egg] verdorben, faul - **2.** *inf* [brain] verwirrt.

**add-on** COMPUT *adj* Zusatz- <> *n* Zusatzgerät *das*.

**address** [ə'dres] *n* - **1.** [location] Adresse *die*, Anschrift *die* - **2.** [speech] Ansprache *die* <> *vt* - **1.** [letter, parcel] adressieren - **2.** [meeting, conference] eine Ansprache halten bei, sprechen zu - **3.** [person] ansprechen; **to ~ sb as sthg** jn etw nennen, jn mit etw anlreden - **4.** [problem, issue]: **to ~ (o.s. to) sthg** sich etw (D) widmen, sich mit etw befassen.

**address book** *n* Adressbuch *das*.

**addressee** [ædre'si:] *n* [of letter, parcel] Empfänger *der*, -in *die*, Adressat *der*, -in *die*.

**adenoids** ['ædınɔıdz] *npl* Polypen *pl*.

**adept** ['ædept] *adj:* **to be ~ (at sthg)** (in etw (D)) geschickt sein; **he is ~ at cooking** er kann gut kochen.

**adequacy** ['ædıkwəsı] *n* - **1.** [of amount, supply] ausreichender Umfang, Zulänglichkeit *die* - **2.** [quality of being good enough] Adäquatheit *die*, Angemessenheit *die;* [of person, material] Eignung *die*.

**adequate** ['ædıkwət] *adj* - **1.** [sufficient] ausreichend - **2.** [good enough] adäquat, angemessen.

**adequately** ['ædıkwətlı] *adv* - **1.** [sufficiently] ausreichend, hinlänglich - **2.** [well enough] adäquat, angemessen.

**adhere** [əd'hıər] *vi* - **1.** [stick]: **to ~ (to)** kleben (an (+ D)) - **2.** [observe]: **to ~ to sthg** sich an etw (A) halten, etw befolgen - **3.** [uphold]: **to ~ to sthg** an etw (D) festlhalten.

**adherence** [əd'hıərəns] *n:* **~ to sthg** [rule] Befolgung *die* einer Sache (G); [decision, law] Festhalten *das* an etw (D) *.*

**adhesive** [əd'hi:sıv] *adj* klebend; **~ label** Haftetikett *das* <> *n* Klebstoff *der*.

**adhesive tape** *n* Klebestreifen *der*.

**ad hoc** [ˌæd'hɒk] *adj* ad hoc.

**ad infinitum** [ˌædınfı'naıtəm] *adv* ad infinitum.

**adjacent** [ə'dʒeısənt] *adj* angrenzend, Neben-; **to be ~ to sthg** an etw (A) anlgrenzen, neben etw (D) liegen OR sein.

**adjective** ['ædʒıktıv] *n* Adjektiv *das*.

**adjoin** [ə'dʒɔın] *vt* grenzen an (+ A).

**adjoining** [ə'dʒɔınıŋ] *adj* angrenzend, Neben-.

**adjourn** [ə'dʒɜːn] *vt* [postpone] **to ~ sthg (until)** etw vertagen (auf (+ A)) <> *vi* - **1.** [stop temporarily] sich vertagen; **to ~ for lunch** zur Mittagspause unterbrechen - **2.** *inf* [go]: **they ~ed to the pub** sie begaben sich in die Kneipe.

**adjournment** [ə'dʒɜːnmənt] *n* Vertagung *die*.

**adjudge** [ə'dʒʌdʒ] *vt* [declare]: **to be ~d the winner** zum Sieger erklärt werden; **the court ~d him (to be) guilty** das Gericht befand OR erklärte ihn für schuldig.

**adjudicate** [ə'dʒuːdıkeıt] *vt* [contest] Preisrichter sein bei; [claim] entscheiden über (+ A) <> *vi* als Preisrichter fungieren; **to ~ on** OR **upon sthg** entscheiden OR urteilen bei etw.

**adjudication** [əˌdʒuːdı'keı∫n] *n* [act] Entscheidung *die*, Beurteilung *die;* [result] Urteil *das*

**adjust** [ə'dʒʌst] *vt* regulieren; [settings] einlstellen; [clothing] zurechtlrücken <> *vi:* **to ~ (to sthg)** sich (auf etw (A)) einlstellen, sich (etw (D)) anlpassen.

**adjustable** [ə'dʒʌstəbl] *adj* [machine] regulierbar; [chair] verstellbar.

**adjustable spanner** *n* Engländer *der*, verstellbarer Schraubenschlüssel.

**adjusted** [ə'dʒʌstıd] *adj* [person]: **to be well ~** ausgeglichen sein.

**adjustment** [ə'dʒʌstmənt] *n* - **1.** [gen] Regulierung *die;* [of settings] Einstellung *die;* **to make an ~ to sthg** eine Änderung an etw (D) vorlnehmen - **2.** [to situation]: **~ (to)** Anpassung *die* (an (+ A)).

**adjutant** ['ædʒutənt] *n* Adjutant *der*.

**ad lib** [ˌæd'lıb] (*pt* & *pp* **ad-libbed;** *cont* **ad-libbing**) *adj* [improvised] Stegreif- <> *adv* [freely] aus dem Stegreif <> *n* [improvised joke] Stegreifwitz *der*.
➤ **ad-lib** *vi* improvisieren.

**adman** ['ædmæn] (*pl* **-men** [-mən]) *n* Werbefachmann *der*.

**admin** ['ædmın] *n Br inf* Verwaltung *die*.

**administer** [əd'mınıstər] *vt* - **1.** [company] verwalten - **2.** [punishment] verhängen; **to ~ justice** Recht sprechen - **3.** [drug, medication] verabreichen.

**administration** [ədˌmını'streı∫n] *n* - **1.** [gen] Verwaltung *die* - **2.** [of punishment] Verhängung *die;* **the ~ of justice** die Rechtsspre-chung.

**~ Administration** *n Am* [government]: **the Admin-istration** die Regierung.

**administrative** [əd'mɪnɪstrətɪv] *adj* Verwal-tungs-, administrativ.

**administrator** [əd'mɪnɪstreɪtəʳ] *n* Adminis-trator *der,* -in *die.*

**admirable** ['ædmərəbl] *adj* [worthy of admiration] bewundernswert; [excellent] großartig.

**admirably** ['ædmərəblɪ] *adv* bewunderns-wert.

**admiral** ['ædmərəl] *n* Admiral *der.*

**Admiralty** ['ædmərəltɪ] *n Br:* **the ~** die Admi-ralität.

**admiration** [ˌædmə'reɪʃn] *n* Bewunderung *die.*

**admire** [əd'maɪəʳ] *vt* bewundern; **to ~ sb for sthg** jn wegen etw *(G)* bewundern.

**admirer** [əd'maɪərəʳ] *n* - **1.** [suitor] Verehrer *der,* -in *die* - **2.** [enthusiast, fan] Bewunderer *der,* -in *die.*

**admiring** [əd'maɪərɪŋ] *adj* [look] bewundernd.

**admiringly** [əd'maɪərɪŋlɪ] *adv* bewundernd.

**admissible** [əd'mɪsəbl] *adj LAW* zulässig.

**admission** [əd'mɪʃn] *n* - **1.** [permission to enter] Zulassung *die;* [to museum etc] Eintritt *der* - **2.** [cost of entrance] Eintrittspreis *der* - **3.** [con-fession - of crime] Geständnis *das;* [ - of guilt, mis-take] Eingeständnis *das;* **by his/her own ~** nach eigenem Eingeständnis.

**admit** [əd'mɪt] (*pt* & *pp* **-ted;** *cont* **-ting)** *vt* - **1.** [crime] gestehen; [mistake] ein|gestehen; **to ~ that** zugeben, dass; **to ~ doing sthg** zul-geben, etw getan zu haben; **to ~ defeat** *fig* auf|geben - **2.** [allow to enter] herein|lassen, hinein|lassen, Zutritt gewähren; **to be ~ted to hospital** *Br OR* **to the hospital** *Am* ins Kran-kenhaus eingeliefert werden - **3.** [allow to join]: **to ~ sb (to sthg)** jn (in etw *(A)*) auf|-nehmen ◇ *vi:* **to ~ to sthg** etw zugeben.

**admittance** [əd'mɪtəns] *n:* **to gain ~ to sthg** Zutritt erhalten zu etw; **'no ~'** 'kein Zutritt'.

**admittedly** [əd'mɪtɪdlɪ] *adv* zugegebener-maßen.

**admixture** [æd'mɪkstʃəʳ] *n* Beimischung *die.*

**admonish** [əd'mɒnɪʃ] *vt fml* ermahnen.

**ad nauseam** [ˌæd'nɔːzɪæm] *adv* bis zum Überdruss.

**ado** [ə'duː] *n: without further OR more ~* ohne weitere Umstände.

**adolescence** [ˌædə'lesns] *n* Jugend *die.*

**adolescent** [ˌædə'lesnt] *adj* - **1.** [teenage] ju-gendlich, halbwüchsig - **2.** *pej* [immature] un-reif, pubertär ◇ *n* [teenager] Jugendliche *der, die,* Halbwüchsige *der, die.*

**adopt** [ə'dɒpt] *vt* - **1.** [child] adoptieren - **2.** [plan, method] übernehmen; [attitude, man-nerism, recommendation] an|nehmen.

**adoption** [ə'dɒpʃn] *n* - **1.** [of child] Adoption *die* - **2.** *(U)* [of plan, method] Übernahme *die;* [of atti-tude, mannerism, recommendation] Annahme *die.*

**adoptive** [ə'dɒptɪv] *adj* Adoptiv-.

**adorable** [ə'dɔːrəbl] *adj* entzückend.

**adoration** [ˌædə'reɪʃn] *n* innige Liebe *die.*

**adore** [ə'dɔːʳ] *vt* über alles lieben; **I ~ these chocolate biscuits** ich esse diese Schokola-denkekse für mein Leben gern.

**adoring** [ə'dɔːrɪŋ] *adj* [look, smile] anbetend.

**adorn** [ə'dɔːn] *vt* schmücken.

**adornment** [ə'dɔːnmənt] *n* Schmuck *der.*

**ADP** (*abbr of* **automatic data processing)** *n* EDV *die.*

**adrenalin** [ə'drenəlɪn] *n* Adrenalin *das.*

**Adriatic** [ˌeɪdrɪ'ætɪk] *n:* **the ~ (Sea)** die Adria.

**adrift** [ə'drɪft] *adj* [boat, ship] treibend ◇ *adv:* **to go ~** *fig* [go wrong] schief gehen, schief laufen.

**adroit** [ə'drɔɪt] *adj* geschickt.

**ADT** (*abbr of* **Atlantic Daylight Time)** *n Sommerzeit in den Staaten an der Ostküste der USA.*

**adulation** [ˌædjʊ'leɪʃn] *n* Anbetung *die.*

**adult** ['ædʌlt] *adj* erwachsen; [animal] ausge-wachsen; [book, film] für Erwachsene ◇ *n* [person] Erwachsene *der, die.*

**adult education** *n* Erwachsenenbildung *die.*

**adulterate** [ə'dʌltəreɪt] *vt* [wine, whisky] pan-schen; [food] *die Qualität eines Produkts durch die Beigabe von etwas anderem ver-schlechtern.*

**adulterer** [ə'dʌltərəʳ] *n* Ehebrecher *der,* -in *die.*

**adultery** [ə'dʌltərɪ] *n (U)* Ehebruch *der.*

**adulthood** ['ædʌlthʊd] *n* Erwachsenenalter *das.*

**advance** [əd'vɑːns] *n* - **1.** [of army] Vorrücken *das* - **2.** [improvement, progress] Fortschritt *der* - **3.** [money] Vorschuss *der* ◇ *comp:* **~ booking** Vorbestellung *die;* **~ payment** Vorauszah-lung *die;* **~ warning** Vorwarnung *die* ◇ *vt* - **1.** [improve - cause] voran|bringen, fördern; [ - interest] fördern - **2.** [bring forward in time] vor|-verlegen - **3.:** **to ~ sb sthg** [money] jm etw vor|-schießen ◇ *vi* - **1.** [go forward - army] vor|-rücken - **2.** [improve] Fortschritte machen.

**~ advances** *npl:* **to make ~s to sb** [sexual] bei jm Annäherungsversuche machen.

**~ in advance** *adv* im Voraus.

**~ in advance of** *prep* - **1.** [ahead of]: **to be in ~ of sb/sthg** jm/etw voraus|sein - **2.** [prior to] vor *(+ D).*

**advanced** [əd'vɑːnst] *adj* - **1.** [developed - plan] weit entwickelt; [ - stage] vorgerückt; **~ in years** *euphemism* [elderly] in fortgeschrittenem Alter - **2.** [student, pupil] fortgeschritten.

**advancement** [əd'vɑːnsmənt] *n* - **1.** *(U)* [promotion in job] Aufstieg *der* - **2.** [improvement] Förderung *die*.

**advantage** [əd'vɑːntɪdʒ] *n* Vorteil *der;* **to be to one's ~** für jn von Vorteil sein; **to have** *OR* **hold the ~ (over sb)** (jm gegenüber) im Vorteil sein; **to take ~ of sb/sthg** jn/etw auslnutzen.

**advantageous** [ˌædvən'teɪdʒəs] *adj* vorteilhaft.

**advent** ['ædvənt] *n* [of invention] Aufkommen *das;* [of period] Beginn *der*.
◆ **Advent** *n* RELIG Advent *der*.

**Advent calendar** *n* Adventskalender *der*.

**adventure** [əd'ventʃəʳ] *n* Abenteuer *das;* **to have no sense of ~** keinen Sinn für Abenteuer haben.

**adventure holiday** *n* Abenteuerurlaub *der*.

**adventure playground** *n* Abenteuerspielplatz *der*.

**adventurer** [əd'ventʃərəʳ] *n* - **1.** [adventurous person] Abenteurer *der*, -in *die* - **2.** [unscrupulous person] Schlitzohr *das*.

**adventurous** [əd'ventʃərəs] *adj* - **1.** [person] abenteuerlustig - **2.** [life, project] abenteuerlich.

**adverb** ['ædvɜːb] *n* Adverb *das*.

**adversary** ['ædvəsərɪ] (*pl* **-ies**) *n* Gegner *der*, -in *die*.

**adverse** ['ædvɜːs] *adj* [weather] schlecht; [conditions] ungünstig; [criticism] negativ, nachteilig; [effect] nachteilig.

**adversely** ['ædvɜːslɪ] *adv* negativ.

**adversity** [əd'vɜːsətɪ] *n* Unglück *das*.

**advert** ['ædvɜːt] *n Br* = **advertisement**.

**advertise** ['ædvətaɪz] *vt* [job, product] Reklame *OR* Werbung machen für; **to ~ for sb/sthg** jn/etw per Anzeige suchen.

**advertisement** [əd'vɜːtɪsmənt] *n* - **1.** [in newspaper] Inserat *das*, Annonce *die;* [on TV] Werbung *die;* [in shop window] Angebot *das* - **2.** *fig* [recommendation] Aushängeschild *das*.

**advertising** ['ædvətaɪzɪŋ] *n (U)* - **1.** [advertisements] Werbung *die*, Reklame *die* - **2.** [industry] Werbebranche *die*.

**advertising agency** *n* Werbeagentur *die*.

**advertising campaign** *n* Werbekampagne *die*.

**advice** [əd'vaɪs] *n (U)* Rat *der;* **to give sb ~** jm einen Rat geben; **to take sb's ~** js Rat befolgen; **a piece of ~** ein Ratschlag *der*.

**advice note** *n* Benachrichtigung *die*, Avis *der*.

**advisability** [əd,vaɪzə'bɪlətɪ] *n* Ratsamkeit *die*.

**advisable** [əd'vaɪzəbl] *adj* ratsam.

**advise** [əd'vaɪz] *vt* - **1.** [give advice to]: **to ~ sb to do sthg** jm raten, etw zu tun; **to ~ sb against sthg** jm von etw ablraten; **to ~ sb against doing sthg** jm davon ablraten, etw zu tun - **2.** [professionally]: **to ~ sb on sthg** jn in etw *(D)* beraten - **3.** *fml* [inform]: **to ~ sb of sthg** jn über etw *(+ A) OR* von etw unterrichten, jn von etw in Kenntnis setzen ◇ *vi:* **to ~ against sthg** von etw ablraten; **to ~ against doing sthg** davon ablraten, etw zu tun.

**advisedly** [əd'vaɪzɪdlɪ] *adv* mit Bedacht, bewusst.

**adviser** *Br*, **advisor** *Am* [əd'vaɪzəʳ] *n* Berater *der*, -in *die*.

**advisory** [əd'vaɪzərɪ] *adj* [group, organization] beratend; **in an ~ capacity** *OR* **role** in einer beratenden Funktion *OR* Rolle.

**advocacy** ['ædvəkəsɪ] *n (U)* [support] Befürwortung *die*.

**advocate** [*n* 'ædvəkət, *vb* 'ædvəkeɪt] *n* - **1.** *Scot* LAW (Rechts)anwalt *der*, -wältin *die* - **2.** [supporter] Befürworter *der*, -in *die*, Verfechter *der*, -in *die* ◇ *vt* befürworten, einltreten für.

**advt.** (*abbr of* **advertisement**) Anz.

**AEA** (*abbr of* **Atomic Energy Authority**) *n* britische Organisation, die für die Entwicklung und Überwachung von Atomenergie verantwortlich ist.

**AEC** (*abbr of* **Atomic Energy Commission**) *n* US-amerikanische Organisation, die für die Entwicklung und Überwachung von Atomenergie verantwortlich ist.

**Aegean** [iː'dʒiːən] *n:* **the ~ (Sea)** die Ägäis.

**aegis** ['iːdʒɪs] *n:* **under the ~ of** unter der Schirmherrschaft von.

**Aeolian Islands** *npl:* **the ~** die Äolischen Inseln.

**aeon** *Br*, **eon** *Am* ['iːən] *n* Äon *der; fig* [very long time] Ewigkeit *die*.

**aerial** ['eərɪəl] *adj* Luft-; **~ photograph** Luftaufnahme *die* ◇ *n Br* [antenna] Antenne *die*.

**aerobatics** [ˌeərəʊ'bætɪks] *n (U)* Kunstfliegen *das*.

**aerobics** [eə'rəʊbɪks] *n (U)* Aerobic *das*.

**aerodrome** ['eərədrəʊm] *esp Br* *n* Flugplatz *der*.

**aerodynamic** [ˌeərəʊdaɪ'næmɪk] *adj* aerodynamisch.
◆ **aerodynamics** *n (U)* [science] Aerodynamik *die* ◇ *npl* [aerodynamic qualities] Aerodynamik *die*.

**aerogramme** [ˈeərəgræm] n Aerogramm das, Luftpostleichtbrief der.

**aeronautics** [ˌeərəˈnɔːtɪks] n (U) Luftfahrt die, Aeronautik die.

**aeroplane** Br [ˈeərəpleɪn], **airplane** Am n Flugzeug das.

**aerosol** [ˈeərəsɒl] n Spraydose die.

**aerospace** [ˈeərəuspeɪs] n: **the ~ industry** die Raumfahrtindustrie.

**aesthete, esthete** Am [ˈiːsθiːt] n Ästhet der, -in die.

**aesthetic, esthetic** Am [iːsˈθetɪk] adj ästhetisch.

**aesthetically, esthetically** Am [iːsˈθetɪklɪ] adv ästhetisch.

**aesthetics, esthetics** Am [iːsˈθetɪks] n (U) Ästhetik die.

**afar** [əˈfɑːr] adv: **from ~** aus der Ferne.

**affable** [ˈæfəbl] adj umgänglich.

**affair** [əˈfeər] n - **1.** [event, concern] Angelegenheit die, Sache die - **2.** [extramarital relationship] Verhältnis das.
→ **affairs** npl [matters, interests] Angelegenheiten pl.

**affect** [əˈfekt] vt - **1.** [influence] beeinflussen, sich auslwirken auf (+ A); [health] beeinträchtigen - **2.** [move emotionally] berühren, bewegen - **3.** [pretend, feign] vorltäuschen.

**affectation** [ˌæfekˈteɪʃn] n - **1.** [mannerism] Affektiertheit die; [habit] affektierte Angewohnheit - **2.** [pretence] Vortäuschung die.

**affected** [əˈfektɪd] adj [mannered] affektiert.

**affection** [əˈfekʃn] n Zuneigung die.

**affectionate** [əˈfekʃnət] adj liebevoll, zärtlich.

**affectionately** [əˈfekʃnətlɪ] adv liebevoll, zärtlich.

**affidavit** [ˌæfɪˈdeɪvɪt] n eidesstattliche Erklärung.

**affiliate** [n əˈfɪlɪət, vb əˈfɪlɪeɪt] n Tochtergesellschaft die <> vt: **to be ~d to** OR **with sthg** an etw (A) angegliedert sein.

**affiliation** [əˌfɪlɪˈeɪʃn] n Angliederung die; **what are her political ~s?** in welche politische Richtung tendiert sie?

**affinity** [əˈfɪnətɪ] (pl -ies) n - **1.** (U) [attraction] Verbundenheit die; **to have an ~ with sb/sthg** sich mit jm/etw verbunden fühlen - **2.** [connection, similarity] Verwandtschaft die, Affinität die; **to have an ~ with sb/sthg** eine Ähnlichkeit mit jm/etw haben.

**affirm** [əˈfɜːm] vt - **1.** [declare] versichern - **2.** [confirm] bestätigen.

**affirmation** [ˌæfəˈmeɪʃn] n - **1.** [declaration] Versicherung die - **2.** [confirmation] Bestätigung die.

**affirmative** [əˈfɜːmətɪv] adj positiv <> n: **to answer in the ~** mit „ja" antworten.

**affix** [əˈfɪks] vt [stamp] kleben.

**afflict** [əˈflɪkt] vt plagen; **to be ~ed with sthg** von etw geplagt sein.

**affliction** [əˈflɪkʃn] n Plage die; **the ~s of old age** die Beschwerden des Alters.

**affluence** [ˈæfluəns] n Wohlstand der.

**affluent** [ˈæfluənt] adj wohlhabend.

**affluent society** n Wohlstandsgesellschaft die.

**afford** [əˈfɔːd] vt - **1.** [gen]: **to be able to ~ sthg** sich (D) etw leisten können; **to be able to ~ the time (to do sthg)** die Zeit haben (, etw zu tun); **I can't ~ two weeks off work** ich kann mir zwei Wochen Urlaub nicht leisten; **we can't ~ to let this happen** wir können es uns nicht leisten, dies geschehen zu lassen - **2.** fml [provide - protection, shelter] gewähren; [- assistance] leisten.

**affordable** [əˈfɔːdəbl] adj erschwinglich.

**afforestation** [æˌfɒrɪˈsteɪʃn] n Aufforstung die.

**affray** [əˈfreɪ] n Br fml [disturbance] Schlägerei die.

**affront** [əˈfrʌnt] n Beleidigung die, Affront der <> vt beleidigen.

**Afghan** [ˈæfgæn], **Afghani** [æfˈgænɪ] adj afghanisch <> n Afghane der, -nin die.

**Afghan hound** n Afghane der, afghanischer Windhund.

**Afghani** adj & n = **Afghan**.

**Afghanistan** [æfˈgænɪstæn] n Afghanistan nt.

**afield** [əˈfiːld] adv: **far ~** weit weg OR entfernt.

**AFL-CIO** (abbr of **American Federation of Labor and Congress of Industrial Organizations**) n ≃ DGB, Dachverband US-amerikanischer Gewerkschaften.

**afloat** [əˈfləʊt] adj - **1.** [above water] schwimmend - **2.** fig [out of debt]: **to stay ~** sich über Wasser halten.

**afoot** [əˈfʊt] adj: **there's something ~** da ist irgendetwas im Gange; **there are plans ~** es sind Pläne in Vorbereitung.

**aforementioned** [əˌfɔːˈmenʃənd], **aforesaid** [əˈfɔːsed] adj fml oben erwähnt, oben genannt.

**afraid** [əˈfreɪd] adj - **1.** [frightened, reluctant]: **to be ~ (of sb/sthg)** (vor jm/etw) Angst haben, sich (vor jm/etw) fürchten; **to be ~ of doing** OR **to do sthg** Angst (davor) haben, etw zu tun; **to be ~ that** Angst (davor) haben; **don't be ~ to call** scheuen Sie sich nicht (davor,) anzurufen - **2.** [in apologies]: **I'm ~ we can't**

**come** wir können leider nicht kommen; **I'm ~ so/not** leider ja/nicht.

**afresh** [ə'freʃ] adv: **to start ~** noch einmal von vorn anfangen; **to look at sthg ~** etw erneut betrachten.

**Africa** ['æfrɪkə] n Afrika nt.

**African** ['æfrɪkən] adj afrikanisch ◇ n Afrikaner der, -in die.

**African American** adj afro-amerikanisch ◇ n Afro-Amerikaner der, -in die.

**Afrikaans** [ˌæfrɪ'kɑːns] n Afrikaans das.

**Afrikaner** [ˌæfrɪ'kɑːnəʳ] n Afrikaner der, -in die.

**aft** [ɑːft] adv achtern; **to go ~** nach achtern gehen.

**after** ['ɑːftəʳ] prep - **1.** [in time] nach; **day ~ day** Tag für Tag; **time ~ time** immer wieder; **the day ~ tomorrow** übermorgen; **the week ~ next** übernächste Woche - **2.** [in order] nach; **~ you!** nach Ihnen!; **shut the door ~ you** schließe die Tür hinter dir - **3.** [in search of]: **to be ~ sb/sthg** jn/etw suchen - **4.** [with the name of] nach; **he is named ~ his father** er ist nach seinem Vater benannt - **5.** [directed at sb moving away]: **to call (sb) ~ sb** jm (etw) nachrufen - **6.** [enquiring]: **to ask ~ sb/sthg** sich nach jm/etw erkundigen - **7.** ART [in imitation of] nach; **~ Titian** nach Tizian - **8.** [telling the time] nach; **a quarter ~ ten** Am Viertel nach zehn ◇ adv danach; **the rest followed ~** die Übrigen folgten nach; **I heard about it ~** ich habe erst nachher or später davon erfahren ◇ conj nachdem; **I came ~ he had gone** ich kam, nachdem er gegangen war.
● **afters** npl Br inf Nachtisch der.
● **after all** adv - **1.** [in spite of everything] doch - **2.** [it should be remembered] schließlich.

**afterbirth** ['ɑːftəbɜːθ] n Nachgeburt die.

**aftercare** ['ɑːftəkeəʳ] n (U) [for recovering patient] Nachbehandlung die; [for ex-prisoner] Resozialisierungshilfe die.

**aftereffects** ['ɑːftərɪˌfekts] npl [of war, storm] Folgen pl; [of heavy drinking] Nachwirkungen pl.

**afterlife** ['ɑːftəlaɪf] (pl -lives [-laɪvz]) n Leben das nach dem Tode.

**aftermath** ['ɑːftəmæθ] n Nachwirkungen pl; **in the ~ of sthg** nach etw.

**afternoon** [ˌɑːftə'nuːn] n Nachmittag der; **in the ~** am Nachmittag; **good ~** guten Tag.
● **afternoons** adv esp Am nachmittags.

**after-sales service** n Kundendienst der.

**aftershave** ['ɑːftəʃeɪv] n Rasierwasser das, Aftershave das.

**aftershock** ['ɑːftəʃɒk] n Nachbeben das.

**aftersun (lotion)** ['ɑːftəsʌn-] n Aftersunlotion die.

**aftertaste** ['ɑːftəteɪst] n lit & fig Nachgeschmack der.

**afterthought** ['ɑːftəθɔːt] n nachträgliche Idee.

**afterwards** ['ɑːftəwədz], **afterward** esp Am ['ɑːftəwəd] adv danach; **three weeks ~** drei Wochen später; **she died soon ~** sie starb bald danach.

**again** [ə'gen] adv - **1.** [one more time] wieder; **~ and ~** immer wieder; **time and ~** immer wieder; **never ~** nie wieder; **all over ~** noch einmal von vorn; **please don't do that ~!** tu das bitte nicht wieder! - **2.** [once more as before] wieder; **he was ill, but he's well ~ now** er ist krank gewesen, aber jetzt ist er wieder gesund; **she promised to come back ~ one day** sie versprach, eines Tages wiederzukommen - **3.** [asking for repetition] wieder, noch einmal; **what is his name ~?** wie heißt er noch gleich? - **4.** [besides] außerdem; **~, we must remember his age** außerdem müssen wir sein Alter berücksichtigen - **5.** phr: **half as much ~** noch mal halb so viel; **(twice) as much ~** doppelt or noch einmal so viel; **come ~?** inf wie bitte?; **then** or **there ~** andererseits; **he may come, but then ~ he may not** vielleicht kommt er, aber vielleicht auch nicht.

**against** [ə'genst] prep - **1.** [gen] gegen; **he was leaning ~ the wall** er stand an die Wand gelehnt; **~ the law** rechtswidrig - **2.** [in contrast to]: **as ~** verglichen mit, im Gegensatz zu ◇ adv: **are you for or ~?** bist du dafür oder dagegen?

**age** [eɪdʒ] (cont ageing or aging) n - **1.** [gen] Alter das; **she's 20 years of ~** sie ist 20 Jahre alt; **he's about my ~** er ist ungefähr mein Alter; **he was still writing at the ~ of 80** mit 80 schrieb er immer noch; **what ~ are you?** wie alt sind Sie?; **to be of ~** Am volljährig or mündig sein; **to come of ~** volljährig or mündig werden; **to be under ~** minderjährig or unmündig sein; **act your ~!** sei nicht kindisch! - **2.** [of history] Zeitalter das ◇ vt altern lassen, alt werden lassen ◇ vi [person] altern, alt werden; [wine] reifen.
● **ages** npl [a long time]: **~s ago** schon ewig or Urzeiten her; **I haven't seen her for ~s** ich habe sie eine Ewigkeit or ewig lang nicht gesehen.

**aged** [adj sense 1 eɪdʒd, adj sense 2 & npl 'eɪdʒɪd] adj - **1.** [of the stated age]: **a girl ~ 5** ein fünfjähriges Mädchen - **2.** [very old] betagt ◇ npl: **the ~** [the elderly] die alten Menschen.

**age group** n Altersgruppe die.

**ageing** ['eɪdʒɪŋ] adj [person, thing] alternd ◇ n [process of getting old] Altern das ◇ comp: **the ~ process** der Alterungsprozess.

**ageless** ['eɪdʒlɪs] adj [thing] zeitlos; **he seems to be ~** er scheint überhaupt nicht zu altern.

**A**

**agency** ['eɪdʒənsɪ] (*pl* **-ies**) *n* - **1.** [business] Agentur *die* - **2.** [organization] Organisation *die*.

**agenda** [ə'dʒendə] (*pl* **-s**) *n* Tagesordnung *die;* **what's on the ~ for today?** was steht heute auf dem Programm?

**agent** ['eɪdʒənt] *n* - **1.** COMM [representative] Agent *der*, -in *die* - **2.** [substance] Mittel *das;* [chemical] Wirkstoff *der* - **3.** [spy] Agent *der*, -in *die*.

**age-old** *adj* uralt.

**aggravate** ['ægrəveɪt] *vt* - **1.** [make worse] verschlimmern - **2.** [annoy] ärgern.

**aggravating** ['ægrəveɪtɪŋ] *adj* [person, behaviour] unangenehm; [problem] ärgerlich.

**aggravation** [ˌægrə'veɪʃn] *n* [irritation] Ärger *der*.

**aggregate** ['ægrɪgət] *adj* Gesamt-; **~ earnings** Gesamtverdienst *der* <> *n* [total] Gesamtsumme *die*, Gesamtheit *die;* **on ~** ingesamt.

**aggression** [ə'greʃn] *n* (*U*) [behaviour] Aggressionen *pl;* [feeling] Aggressivität *die;* **an act of ~** eine aggressive Handlung.

**aggressive** [ə'gresɪv] *adj* - **1.** [belligerent - person] aggressiv - **2.** [forceful - person] energisch; [ - campaign] aggressiv.

**aggressively** [ə'gresɪvlɪ] *adv* aggressiv.

**aggressor** [ə'gresəʳ] *n* [country] Aggressor *der;* [person] Angreifer *der*, -in *die*.

**aggrieved** [ə'griːvd] *adj* [upset, hurt] gekränkt.

**aggro** ['ægrəʊ] *n Br inf* - **1.** [violent behaviour] Rauferei *die* - **2.** [hassle] Theater *das*.

**aghast** [ə'gɑːst] *adj:* **~ (at)** entsetzt (über (*+ A*)).

**agile** [*Br* 'ædʒaɪl, *Am* 'ædʒəl] *adj* - **1.** [person] beweglich, agil; [body] gelenkig - **2.** [mind]: **to have an ~ mind** geistig sehr beweglich sein.

**agility** [ə'dʒɪlətɪ] *n* - **1.** [physical] Beweglichkeit *die*, Agilität *die* - **2.**: **mental ~** geistige Beweglichkeit.

**aging** *adj* & *n* = **ageing**.

**agitate** ['ædʒɪteɪt] *vt* - **1.** [disturb, worry] auf l- regen, aus der Fassung bringen - **2.** [shake] schütteln <> *vi* [campaign actively]: **to ~ for/ against sthg** für/gegen etw Propaganda machen.

**agitated** ['ædʒɪteɪtɪd] *adj* [disturbed, anxious] auf l- geregt.

**agitation** [ˌædʒɪ'teɪʃn] *n* [anxiety] Aufregung *die*.

**AGM** (*abbr of* **annual general meeting**) *n Br* JHV *die*.

**agnostic** [æg'nɒstɪk] *adj* agnostisch <> *n* Agnostiker *der*, -in *die*.

**ago** [ə'gəʊ] *adv* vor; **that was a long time ~** das ist schon lange her; **three days/years ~** vor drei Tagen/Jahren.

**agog** [ə'gɒg] *adj* gespannt; **the children were all ~ (with excitement)** die Kinder waren ganz gespannt (und aufgeregt).

**agonize, -ise** ['ægənaɪz] *vi:* **to ~ (over** OR **about sthg)** sich (*D*) den Kopf (über etw (*A*)) zerbrechen.

**agonized** ['ægənaɪzd] *adj* gequält.

**agonizing** ['ægənaɪzɪŋ] *adj* qualvoll.

**agony** ['ægənɪ] (*pl* **-ies**) *n* Qual *die;* **to be in ~** Qualen erleiden.

**agony aunt** *n Br inf* Kummerkastentante *die*.

**agony column** *n Br inf der Teil einer Zeitung oder Zeitschrift, in dem Leserbriefe mit persönlicher Problematik abgedruckt und beantwortet werden.*

**agoraphobia** [ˌægərə'fəʊbjə] *n* Platzangst *die*.

**agree** [ə'griː] *vi* - **1.** [concur - two or more people] einer Meinung sein, sich einig sein; [ - one person] der gleichen Meinung sein; **to ~ with sb/ sthg** jm/etw zulstimmen; **to ~ on sthg** sich auf etw (*A*) einigen - **2.** [consent] einlwilligen, zulstimmen; **to ~ to sthg** sich mit etw einverstanden erklären - **3.** [statements] übereinlstimmen - **4.** [food]: **curries don't ~ with me** Currygerichte bekommen mir nicht, ich vertrage keine Currygerichte - **5.** GRAMM: **to ~ (with)** übereinlstimmen (mit) <> *vt* - **1.** [price, terms] vereinbaren - **2.** [concur]: **I ~ that ...** ich bin auch der Meinung, dass ...; **it was ~d that ...** man einigte sich darauf, dass ... - **3.** [consent]: **to ~ to do sthg** sich bereit OR einverstanden erklären, etw zu tun - **4.** [concede]: **to ~ that ...** zugeben, dass ...

**agreeable** [ə'grɪəbl] *adj* - **1.** [weather, experience] angenehm; [person] nett, angenehm - **2.** [willing]: **to be ~ to sthg** mit etw einverstanden sein.

**agreeably** [ə'grɪəblɪ] *adv* angenehm.

**agreed** [ə'griːd] *adj:* **to be ~ on sthg** sich über etw (*A*) einig sein <> *adv* - **1.** [decided] einverstanden - **2.** [admittedly]: **~ (that) it's not the most attractive of cars, but ...** es ist zugegebenermaßen nicht das ansprechendste Auto, aber ...

**agreement** [ə'griːmənt] *n* - **1.** [accord] Einigkeit *die*, Übereinstimmung *die;* **to be in ~ with sb/sthg** mit jm/etw übereinlstimmen - **2.** [settlement] Vereinbarung *die*, Übereinkunft *die;* [contract] Vertrag *der*, Abkommen *das;* **to reach an ~** eine Einigung erzielen - **3.** [consent] Einwilligung *die*, Zustimmung *die* - **4.** GRAMM Übereinstimmung *die*.

**agricultural** [ˌægrɪ'kʌltʃərəl] *adj* landwirtschaftlich; **~ land** Agrarland *das;* **~ worker** Landarbeiter *der*, -in *die*.

**agriculture** ['ægrɪkʌltʃəʳ] n Landwirtschaft die.

**aground** [ə'graʊnd] adv: **to run ~** auf Grund laufen, stranden.

**ah** [ɑː] excl [expressing surprise, pleasure] ah!, ach!; [expressing pity] ach!; [expressing pain] au!, aua!

**aha** [ɑː'hɑː] excl aha!

**ahead** [ə'hed] adv - **1.** [in front]: **the road ~** die Straße vor uns/ihnen/etc; **straight ~** geradeaus; **to go on ~** vor(aus)gehen/vor(aus)fahren; **to be sent on ~** vorgeschickt werden - **2.** [in competition, game]: **to be ~** führen - **3.** [indicating success]: **to get ~** vorwärts kommen - **4.** [in time]: **to plan ~** voraus|planen, im Voraus planen; **the weeks ~ are going to be difficult** die nächsten Wochen werden schwierig sein.
➡ **ahead of** prep - **1.** [in front of] vor (+ D); **the road ~ of them** die Straße vor ihnen - **2.** [in competition, game]: **they are 10 points ~ of the other teams** sie sind den anderen Mannschaften um 10 Punkte voraus - **3.** [in time] vor; **~ of schedule** früher als geplant.

**ahoy** [ə'hɔɪ] excl NAUT ahoi!; **ship ~!** Schiff ahoi!

**AI** n - **1.** abbr of **Amnesty International** - **2.** abbr of **artificial intelligence** - **3.** abbr of **artificial insemination**.

**aid** [eɪd] n - **1.** [help] Hilfe die; **to go to the ~ of sb** OR **to sb's ~** jm zu Hilfe kommen; **in ~ of** zugunsten (+ G); **with the ~ of** mithilfe (+ G) - **2.** [device] Hilfsmittel das; **teaching ~** Lehrmittel das ⬦ vt - **1.** [help] unterstützen, helfen (+ D) - **2.** LAW: **to ~ and abet** Beihilfe leisten (+ D).

**aide** [eɪd] n POL persönlicher Berater, persönliche Beraterin.

**aide-de-camp** [eɪddə'kɑː] (pl **aides-de-camp**) n Adjutant der.

**AIDS, Aids** [eɪdz] (abbr of **acquired immune deficiency syndrome**) n Aids das ⬦ comp: **~ specialist** Aids-Spezialist der, -in die; **~ patient** Aids-Patient der, -in die.

**aid worker** n humanitärer Helfer, humanitäre Helferin.

**ailing** ['eɪlɪŋ] adj - **1.** [ill] kränkelnd, kränklich - **2.** fig [economy] kränkelnd.

**ailment** ['eɪlmənt] n Leiden das; [not serious] Wehwehchen das.

**aim** [eɪm] n - **1.** [objective] Ziel das, Zweck der - **2.** [in firing gun, arrow] Zielen das; **to take ~ at sthg** auf etw (A) zielen ⬦ vt - **1.**: **to ~ a gun at sb/sthg** ein Gewehr auf jn/etw zielen, ein Gewehr auf jn/etw richten; **to ~ a camera at sb/sthg** eine Kamera auf jn/etw richten - **2.** [plan, programme]: **to be ~ed at doing sthg** darauf ausgerichtet sein, etw zu tun; **the campaign is ~ed at influencing public opinion** die Kampagne zielt darauf ab, die öf-

fentliche Meinung zu beeinflussen - **3.** [remark, criticism]: **to be ~ed at sb** gegen jn gerichtet sein ⬦ vi - **1.** [point weapon]: **to ~ (at)** zielen (auf (+ A)) - **2.** [intend]: **to ~ at** OR **for sthg** etw an|streben, auf etw (A) ab|zielen; **to ~ to do sthg** vor|haben OR beabsichtigen, etw zu tun.

**aimless** ['eɪmlɪs] adj [person, life] ziellos; [task, activity] planlos.

**aimlessly** ['eɪmlɪslɪ] adv [wander, look] ziellos.

**ain't** [eɪnt] inf = **am not, are not, is not, have not, has not**.

**air** [eəʳ] n - **1.** [gen] Luft die; **to throw sthg into the ~** etw in die Luft werfen; **by ~** [travel] mit dem Flugzeug; **to be (up) in the ~** fig ungewiss OR unentschieden sein - **2.** [look] Aussehen das; [facial expression] Miene die; **he had a certain ~ of mystery about him** er hatte etwas Geheimnisvolles an sich - **3.** literary [tune] Weise die - **4.** RADIO & TV: **to be on the ~** [programme] gesendet werden; **we're on the ~ in five minutes** wir werden in fünf Minuten auf Sendung sein - **5.** phr: **to clear the ~** fig Klarheit schaffen ⬦ comp Luft- ⬦ vt - **1.** [washing] nachtrocknen lassen - **2.** [room, bed] lüften - **3.** [feelings, opinions] äußern - **4.** [broadcast] senden ⬦ vi [washing] nachtrocknen.
➡ **airs** npl: **~s and graces** Allüren pl; **to give o.s. ~s, to put on ~s** wichtig tun.

**air bag** n AUT Airbag der.

**airbase** ['eəbeɪs] n Luftstützpunkt der.

**airbed** ['eəbed] n Br Luftmatratze die.

**airborne** ['eəbɔːn] adj - **1.** [troops, regiment] Luftlande- - **2.** [plane] in der Luft.

**airbrake** ['eəbreɪk] n [of bus, train] Druckluftbremse die.

**airbus** ['eəbʌs] n Airbus der.

**air-conditioned** [-kən'dɪʃnd] adj klimatisiert.

**air-conditioning** [-kən'dɪʃnɪŋ] n [device] Klimaanlage die; [process] Klimatisierung die.

**aircraft** ['eəkrɑːft] (pl inv) n Flugzeug das.

**aircraft carrier** n Flugzeugträger der.

**airfield** ['eəfiːld] n Flugplatz der.

**airforce** ['eəfɔːs] n Luftwaffe die.

**air freight** n Luftfracht die.

**air freshener** [-ˌfreʃnəʳ] n Raumspray das.

**airgun** ['eəgʌn] n Luftgewehr das.

**airhostess** ['eəˌhəʊstɪs] n Stewardess die.

**airing** ['eərɪŋ] n: **to give sthg an ~** [clothes] etw nachtrocknen lassen; [room] etw lüften.

**airing cupboard** n Br Schrank, der durch den Heizkessel der Zentralheizung erwärmt wird und in dem man Wäsche trocknen lassen kann.

**airlane** ['eəleɪn] n Flugroute die.

**airless** ['eəlɪs] *adj* [room] stickig; [weather] windstill.

**airletter** ['eəletəʳ] *n* Luftpostbrief *der.*

**airlift** ['eəlɪft] *n* Luftbrücke *die* ◇ *vt* über eine Luftbrücke befördern.

**airline** ['eəlaɪn] *n* Fluglinie *die,* Fluggesellschaft *die.*

**airliner** ['eəlaɪnəʳ] *n* Verkehrsflugzeug *das.*

**airlock** ['eəlɒk] *n* - 1. [in tube, pipe] Lufteinschluss *der* - 2. [airtight chamber] Luftschleuse *die.*

**airmail** ['eəmeɪl] *n* Luftpost *die;* **by ~** mit OR per Luftpost.

**airman** ['eəmən] (*pl* -men [- mən]) *n* [aviator] Flieger *der.*

**air mattress** *n* Luftmatratze *die.*

**air miles** *npl* Flugmeilen *pl.*

**airplane** ['eəpleɪn] *n Am* = aeroplane.

**airplay** ['eəpleɪ] *n:* **to get a lot of ~** oft im Radio gespielt werden.

**airpocket** ['eə,pɒkɪt] *n* Luftloch *das.*

**airport** ['eəpɔːt] *n* Flughafen *der.*

**air raid** *n* Luftangriff *der.*

**air-raid shelter** *n* Luftschutzkeller *der.*

**air rifle** *n* Luftgewehr *das.*

**airship** ['eəʃɪp] *n* Luftschiff *das.*

**airsick** ['eəsɪk] *adj:* **I often get ~** im Flugzeug wird mir leicht übel.

**airspace** ['eəspeɪs] *n* Luftraum *der.*

**airspeed** ['eəspiːd] *n* Fluggeschwindigkeit *die.*

**air steward** *n* Steward *der.*

**air stewardess** *n* Stewardess *die.*

**air strike** *n* MIL Luftangriff *der.*

**airstrip** ['eəstrɪp] *n* Start- und Landebahn *die.*

**air terminal** *n* Terminal *das* OR *der.*

**airtight** ['eətaɪt] *adj* luftdicht.

**airtime** ['eətaɪm] *n* [on radio] Sendezeit *die.*

**air-to-air** *adj* [missile] Luft-Luft-.

**air-traffic control** *n* Flugsicherung *die;* [people] Fluglotsen *pl.*

**air-traffic controller** *n* Fluglotse *der,* -sin *die.*

**air travel** *n* Flugverkehr *der.*

**airwaves** ['eəweɪvz] *npl:* **on the ~** im Radio.

**airy** ['eərɪ] (*compar* -**ier**; *superl* -**iest**) *adj* - 1. [room] luftig - 2. [notions] abstrus; [promises] vage - 3. [nonchalant] lässig, nonchalant.

**aisle** [aɪl] *n* - 1. [in church - central] Mittelgang *der;* [ - at side] Seitenschiff *das* - 2. [in plane, theatre, shop] Gang *der.*

**ajar** [ə'dʒɑːʳ] *adj* angelehnt.

**AK** *abk für Alaska, in Postanschrift verwendet.*

**aka** (*abbr of* **also known as**) alias.

**akin** [ə'kɪn] *adj:* **~ to** vergleichbar mit.

**AL** *abk für Alabama, in Postanschrift verwendet.*

**alacrity** [ə'lækrətɪ] *n fml* [eagerness] Eifer *der;* **she accepted our offer with ~** sie nahm unser Angebot ohne zu zögern an.

**alarm** [ə'lɑːm] *n* - 1. [fear] Beunruhigung *die,* Besorgnis *die* - 2. [device] Alarmanlage *die;* **to raise** OR **sound the ~** [by activating device] Alarm geben; [by shouting] Alarm schlagen ◇ *vt* [scare] beunruhigen, alarmieren.

**alarm clock** *n* Wecker *der.*

**alarming** [ə'lɑːmɪŋ] *adj* beunruhigend.

**alarmingly** [ə'lɑːmɪŋlɪ] *adv* beunruhigend.

**alarmist** [ə'lɑːmɪst] *adj* schwarzseherisch.

**alas** [ə'læs] *excl literary* leider.

**Albania** [æl'beɪnjə] *n* Albanien *nt.*

**Albanian** [æl'beɪnjən] *adj* albanisch ◇ *n* - 1. [person] Albaner *der,* -in *die* - 2. [language] Albanisch(e) *das.*

**albatross** ['ælbətrɒs] (*pl inv* OR -**es**) *n* Albatros *der.*

**albeit** [ɔːl'biːɪt] *conj fml* wenn auch.

**Albert Hall** ['ælbət-] *n:* **the ~** große Konzerthalle in London.

**albino** [æl'biːnəʊ] (*pl* -**s**) *n* Albino *der* ◇ *comp* Albino-.

**album** ['ælbəm] *n* Album *das.*

**albumen** ['ælbjʊmɪn] *n* Albumin *das.*

**alcohol** ['ælkəhɒl] *n* Alkohol *der.*

**alcoholic** [,ælkə'hɒlɪk] *adj* [drink] alkoholisch ◇ *n* [person] Alkoholiker *der,* -in *die.*

**alcoholism** ['ælkəhɒlɪzml] *n* Alkoholismus *der.*

**alcove** ['ælkəʊv] *n* [in room] Alkoven *der;* [in wall] Nische *die.*

**alder** ['ɔːldəʳ] *n* Erle *die*

**alderman** ['ɔːldəmən] (*pl* -men [-mən]) *n* Ratsherr *der.*

**ale** [eɪl] *n* Ale *das.*

**alert** [ə'lɜːt] *adj* - 1. [vigilant] wachsam - 2. [perceptive] aufmerksam; [as character trait] aufgeweckt - 3. [aware]: **to be ~ to sthg** sich (D) einer Sache (G) bewusst sein ◇ *n* Alarm *der;* **on the ~** [watchful] auf der Hut; MIL in Gefechtsbereitschaft ⟨⟩ vt **- 1.** [police, fire brigade] alarmieren; [to imminent danger] warnen **- 2.** [make aware]: **to ~ sb to sthg** jm etw bewusst machen.

**A level** (abbr of **Advanced level**) n einzelne Prüfung des Schulabschlusses weiterführender Schulen in England, Wales und Nordirland.

**A LEVEL**

Die „A level"-Prüfungen entsprechen in etwa dem deutschen Abitur bzw. der schweizerischen Matura und werden von Schülern im Alter von 18 Jahren abgelegt. Ihr Bestehen ist Voraussetzung für ein Hochschulstudium in Großbritannien. Im britischen Schulsystem wählen die Schüler bis zu vier Fächer, und in jedem Fach wird eine „A level"-Prüfung abgelegt. Die „A level"-Endnoten sind sehr wichtig, da sie mit entscheiden, ob ein Schüler an der Universität der eigenen Wahl angenommen wird.

**alfalfa** [æl'fælfə] n Alfalfa die, Luzerne die.

**alfresco** [æl'freskəʊ] adj & adv im Freien.

**algae** [ˈældʒiː] npl Algen pl.

**Algarve** [æl'gɑːv] n: **the ~** die Algarve.

**algebra** [ˈældʒɪbrə] n Algebra die.

**Algeria** [æl'dʒɪərɪə] n Algerien nt.

**Algerian** [æl'dʒɪərɪən] adj algerisch ⟨⟩ n Algerier der, -in die.

**Algiers** [æl'dʒɪəz] n Algier nt.

**algorithm** [ˈælgərɪðm] n Algorithmus der.

**alias** [ˈeɪlɪəs] (pl **-es**) adv alias ⟨⟩ n Deckname der.

**alibi** [ˈælɪbaɪ] n Alibi das.

**alien** [ˈeɪlɪən] adj **- 1.** [foreign] ausländisch **- 2.** [from outer space] außerirdisch **- 3.** [unfamiliar] fremd ⟨⟩ n **- 1.** [from outer space] Außerirdische der, die **- 2.** LAW [foreigner] Ausländer der, -in die.

**alienate** [ˈeɪljəneɪt] vt [voters, supporters] verärgern, entfremden; **his time in prison has ~d him from his family** seine Haftzeit hat ihn seiner Familie entfremdet.

**alienation** [ˌeɪljəˈneɪʃn] n Entfremdung die; **to have a sense of ~** ein Gefühl des Nicht-Dazugehörens haben.

**alight** [əˈlaɪt] (pt & pp **-ed** OR alit) adj: **to be ~** brennen; **to set sthg ~** etw anlzünden ⟨⟩ vi fml **- 1.** [bird, insect] sich niederllassen **- 2.** [from train, bus] auslsteigen.

**align** [əˈlaɪn] vt **- 1.** [line up] auslrichten **- 2.** [ally]: **to ~ o.s.** with sb sich mit jm verbünden.

**alignment** [əˈlaɪnmənt] n **- 1.** [of car wheels, brakes] Ausrichtung die **- 2.** [with an ally] Zusammenschluss der.

**alike** [əˈlaɪk] adj & adv [similar] ähnlich; [identical]

gleich; **to look ~** [similar] ähnlich auslsehen; [identical] gleich auslsehen.

**alimentary canal** [ˌælɪmentərɪ-] n Verdauungskanal der.

**alimony** [ˈælɪmənɪ] n Unterhaltszahlung die.

**alive** [əˈlaɪv] adj **- 1.** [living, lively] lebendig; **is he still ~?** lebt er noch?, ist er noch am Leben?; **to keep a tradition ~** eine Tradition aufrechtlerhalten **- 2.** [aware]: **to be ~ to sthg** sich (D) etw (G) bewusst sein **- 3.** [full]: **to be ~ with sthg** wimmeln von etw; **the house was ~ with rats** in dem Haus wimmelte es von Ratten.

**alkali** [ˈælkəlaɪ] (pl **-s** OR **-es**) n Alkali das.

**alkaline** [ˈælkəlaɪn] adj alkalisch.

**all** [ɔːl] adj **- 1.** [the whole of – with sg noun] ganze; **~ the money** das ganze Geld; **~ the food** das ganze Essen; **~ the time** immer, die ganze Zeit; **~ day/evening** den ganzen Tag/Abend; **~ his life** sein ganzes Leben lang; **we condemn ~ violence** wir verurteilen jegliche Art von Gewalt; **~ Paris** ganz Paris **- 2.** [every one of – with pl noun] alle, -r, -s; **~ the people** alle Menschen, alle Leute; **~ trains stop at Tonbridge** alle Züge halten in Tonbridge; **~ three died** alle drei starben; **at ~ hours** zu jeder Tages- und Nachtzeit ⟨⟩ pron **- 1.** [everything]: **~ of the cake** der ganze Kuchen; **is that ~?** [in shop] ist das alles?; **she ate it ~, she ate ~ of it** sie aß alles auf; **it's ~ gone** es ist nichts mehr da **- 2.** [everybody] alle; **~ of us went, we ~ went** wir sind alle gegangen **- 3.** (with superl): **the best of ~** der/die/das Allerbeste; **the biggest of ~** der/die/das Allergrößte; **he is the cleverest of ~** er ist der klügste von allen; **and, best of ~, ...** und (was) das Beste ist, ... ⟨⟩ adv **- 1.** [completely] ganz; **~ alone** ganz allein; **dressed ~ in red** ganz in rot gekleidet; **the water spilled ~ over the carpet** das Wasser ergoss sich über den Teppichboden; **I'd forgotten ~ about that** das hatte ich völlig vergessen; **~ told** [in total] insgesamt; **that's ~ very well, but ...** das ist (ja) alles schön und gut, aber ... **- 2.** [in scores] beide; **it's two ~** es steht zwei beide **- 3.** (with compar): **you'll feel ~ the better for it** du wirst dich danach umso besser fühlen; **to run ~ the faster** noch schneller laufen **- 4.** phr: **~ over** [finished] alles vorbei.

➤ **above all** adv ▷ **above**.

➤ **after all** adv ▷ **after**.

➤ **all but** adv fast; **~ but empty** fast leer.

➤ **all in all** adv alles in allem.

➤ **all that** adv: **she's not ~ that pretty** so hübsch ist sie nun auch wieder nicht.

➤ **at all** adv ▷ **at**.

➤ **for all** prep trotz (+ G); **for ~ his money** trotz seines (ganzen) Geldes ⟨⟩ conj: **for ~ I know** so viel ich weiß; **for ~ I care** meinetwegen.

➤ **in all** adv [in total] zusammen; [in summary] alles in allem.

**Allah** [ˈælə] n Allah.

**all-around** adj Am = all-round.

**allay** [əˈleɪ] vt fml [fears, doubts] weitgehend zerstreuen; [anger] vermindern.

**all clear** n - **1.** [signal] Entwarnung die - **2.** fig [go-ahead] Bewilligung die.

**allegation** [ˌælɪˈgeɪʃn] n Behauptung die; to make ~s (against sb) Beschuldigungen erheben (gegen jn).

**allege** [əˈledʒ] vt behaupten; they ~d misconduct on the part of the police sie beschuldigten die Polizei eines Fehlverhaltens; he is ~d to have passed on the information er soll die Informationen weitergegeben haben.

**alleged** [əˈledʒd] adj angeblich.

**allegedly** [əˈledʒɪdlɪ] adv angeblich.

**allegiance** [əˈliːdʒəns] n: ~ (to) Treue die (gegenüber).

**allegorical** [ˌælɪˈgɒrɪkl] adj allegorisch.

**allegory** [ˈælɪgərɪ] (pl -ies) n Allegorie die.

**alleluia** [ˌælɪˈluːjə] excl alleluia!, halleluja!

**allergic** [əˈlɜːdʒɪk] adj: ~ (to) allergisch (gegen).

**allergy** [ˈælədʒɪ] (pl -ies) n Allergie die; to have an ~ to sthg eine Allergie gegen etw haben.

**alleviate** [əˈliːvɪeɪt] vt mildern.

**alley(way)** [ˈælɪ(weɪ)] n [street] (enge) Gasse die; [in garden] Weg der.

**alliance** [əˈlaɪəns] n Bündnis das.

**allied** [ˈælaɪd] adj - **1.** MIL verbündet, alliiert - **2.** [related] verwandt.

**alligator** [ˈælɪgeɪtəʳ] (pl inv OR -s) n Alligator der.

**all-important** adj [crucial] entscheidend.

**all-in** adj Br [price] Pauschal-.
➤ **all in** adj [tired] völlig OR total erledigt ◇ adv Br [inclusive] alles inklusive.

**all-in wrestling** n Freistilringen das.

**alliteration** [əˌlɪtəˈreɪʃn] n Alliteration die.

**all-night** adj [party, session] die ganze Nacht dauernd; [shop] nachts durchgehend geöffnet.

**allocate** [ˈæləkeɪt] vt: to ~ sthg to sb [money, resources] jm etw zur Verfügung stellen; [task, seats] jm etw zuweisen; [tickets] etw an jn verteilen.

**allocation** [ˌæləˈkeɪʃn] n - **1.** [sharing out - of money, resources, tickets] Verteilung die; [ - of task, responsibility, seats] Zuweisung die - **2.** [share - of money, resources] Anteil der; [ - of tickets, seats] Quote die.

**allot** [əˈlɒt] (pt & pp -ted; cont -ting) vt [task] zuweisen; [money, resources] zur Verfügung stellen; [time] vorsehen.

**allotment** [əˈlɒtmənt] n - **1.** Br [garden] Schre-

bergarten der - **2.** [sharing out - of task] Zuweisung die; [ - of money, resources] Verteilung die; [ - of time] Vorsehen das - **3.** [share - of money, resources] Anteil der; [ - of time] Zeitrahmen der.

**all-out** adj [effort] äußerst; [war] total; [attack] massiv.

**allow** [əˈlaʊ] vt - **1.** [permit] erlauben, gestatten; they don't ~ smoking in the office sie gestatten das Rauchen im Büro nicht; to ~ sb to do sthg jm erlauben OR gestatten, etw zu tun; to be ~ed to do sthg etw tun dürfen; you're not ~ed to park here Sie dürfen hier nicht parken; ~ me! gestatten (Sie)! - **2.** [allocate - money] einrechnen; [ - time] einplanen - **3.** [admit]: to ~ that ... einräumen, dass ...
➤ **allow for** vt fus einkalkulieren.

**allowable** [əˈlaʊəbl] adj zulässig.

**allowance** [əˈlaʊəns] n - **1.** [grant] finanzielle Unterstützung die; **travel ~** Reisekostenzuschuss der; **clothing ~** Kleidungsgeld das - **2.** Am [pocket money] Taschengeld das - **3.** FIN [for tax] Freibetrag der - **4.** [excuse]: to make ~s for sb mit jm Nachsicht haben; to make ~s for sthg etw berücksichtigen.

**alloy** [ˈælɔɪ] n Legierung die.

**all-powerful** adj allmächtig.

**all right** adv - **1.** [healthy, unharmed]: to feel ~ sich ganz gut fühlen; did you get home ~? bist du gut nach Hause gekommen? - **2.** inf [acceptably] ganz gut - **3.** inf [indicating agreement] okay, in Ordnung - **4.** inf [certainly] it's pneumonia ~ es ist sicher Lungenentzündung - **5.** [do you understand?]: all right? okay?, in Ordnung? - **6.** [now then]: ~, let's go okay, auf gehts ◇ adj - **1.** [healthy, unharmed]: are you ~? bist du in Ordnung? - **2.** inf [acceptable]: it was ~ es war ganz ordentlich; that's ~ [never mind] das ist schon in Ordnung - **3.** [permitted]: is it ~ if I make a phone call? haben Sie etwas dagegen, wenn ich (kurz) telefoniere?

**all-round** Br, **all-around** Am adj - **1.** [athlete] Allround-; [worker] vielseitig begabt - **2.** [improvement] allgemein.

**all-rounder** [-ˈraʊndəʳ] n - **1.** [versatile person] vielseitig begabter Mensch - **2.** SPORT Allroundsportler der, -in die.

**all-time** adj [record, best] absolut.

**allude** [əˈluːd] vi: to ~ to sthg auf etw (A) anlspielen.

**allure** [əˈljʊəʳ] n Reiz der, Anziehungskraft die.

**alluring** [əˈljʊərɪŋ] adj verführerisch.

**allusion** [əˈluːʒn] n Anspielung die.

**ally** [n ˈælaɪ, vb əˈlaɪ] (pl -ies; pt & pp -ied) n Verbündete der, die ◇ vt: to ~ o.s. with sb sich mit jm verbünden.

**almighty** [ɔːlˈmaɪtɪ] adj inf [noise, fuss] Riesen-.
➤ **Almighty** n: the Almighty der Allmächtige.

**almond** [ˈɑːmənd] n Mandel die; ~ **(tree)** Mandelbaum der.

**almond paste** n Marzipan der or das.

**almost** [ˈɔːlməʊst] adv fast, beinahe; I ~ **missed the bus** ich hätte beinahe den Bus verpasst.

**alms** [ɑːmz] npl dated Almosen pl.

**aloft** [əˈlɒft] adv - **1.** [in the air]: **to hold sthg ~** etw in die Höhe halten - **2.** NAUT (oben) in der Takelung.

**alone** [əˈləʊn] adj allein, -e ◇ adv - **1.** [without others] allein, -e; **to go it ~** [in career] sich selbstständig machen - **2.** [only] nur, allein; **you ~ can help me** nur du or du allein kannst mir helfen - **3.** [untouched, unchanged]: **to leave sthg ~** etw in Ruhe lassen; **leave me ~!** lass mich in Ruhe!
➥ **let alone** conj geschweige denn.

**along** [əˈlɒŋ] adv - **1.** [indicating movement]: **to stroll ~** dahinlschlendern; **they went ~ to the demonstration** sie gingen zu der Vorführung - **2.** [with others]: **to take sb/sthg ~** jn/etw mitlnehmen; **to come ~** mitlkommen ◇ prep entlang (+ A); **they walked ~ the river** sie liefen den Fluss entlang; **they walked ~ the forest path** sie folgten dem Waldweg; **the trees ~ the path** die Bäume neben dem Weg.
➥ **all along** adv die ganze Zeit.
➥ **along with** prep zusammen mit.

**alongside** [əˌlɒŋˈsaɪd] prep neben (+ D); [with verbs of motion] neben (+ A) ◇ adv daneben.

**aloof** [əˈluːf] adj unnahbar ◇ adv: **to remain ~ (from)** sich fernlhalten (von).

**aloud** [əˈlaʊd] adv laut.

**alpaca** [ælˈpækə] n Alpaka das.

**alphabet** [ˈælfəbet] n Alphabet das.

**alphabetical** [ˌælfəˈbetɪkl] adj alphabetisch; **in ~ order** in alphabetischer Reihenfolge.

**alphabetically** [ˌælfəˈbetɪklɪ] adv alphabetisch.

**alphabetize, -ise** [ˈælfəbətaɪz] vt alphabetisieren.

**alphanumeric key** [ˌælfənjuːˈmerɪk-] n COMPUT alphanumerische Taste.

**alpine** [ˈælpaɪn] adj alpin.

**Alps** [ælps] npl: **the ~** die Alpen pl.

**already** [ɔːlˈredɪ] adv schon.

**alright** [ˌɔːlˈraɪt] adv & adj = **all right**.

**Alsace** [ælˈsæs] n Elsass nt.

**Alsatian** [ælˈseɪʃn] adj elsässisch ◇ n - **1.** [person] Elsässer der, -in die - **2.** [dog] (deutscher) Schäferhund.

**also** [ˈɔːlsəʊ] adv auch.

**also-ran** n: **to be an ~** unter „ferner liefen" sein.

**Alta.** abk für Alberta, in Postanschrift verwendet.

**altar** [ˈɔːltəʳ] n Altar der.

**alter** [ˈɔːltəʳ] vt ändern; [appearance] verändern; [text] abländern ◇ vi sich ändern; [appearance] sich verändern.

**alteration** [ˌɔːltəˈreɪʃn] n Änderung die; [of appearance] Veränderung die; [of text] Abänderung die; **to make ~s to sthg** Änderungen an etw (D) vorlnehmen.

**altercation** [ˌɔːltəˈkeɪʃn] n fml Auseinandersetzung die.

**alter ego** [ˈɔːltəʳ-] (pl -s) n Alter Ego das.

**alternate** [adj Br ɔːlˈtɜːnət, Am ˈɔːltərnət, vb ˈɔːltərneɪt] adj - **1.** [by turns] abwechselnd - **2.** [every other]: **on ~ days** jeden zweiten Tag ◇ vt ablwechseln ◇ vi: **to ~ (with)** sich ablwechseln (mit); **to ~ between sthg and sthg** zwischen etw (D) und etw (D) (ablwechseln.

**alternately** [ɔːlˈtɜːnətlɪ] adv abwechselnd.

**alternating current** [ˈɔːltəneɪtɪŋ-] n ELEC Wechselstrom der.

**alternation** [ˌɔːltəˈneɪʃn] n (U) Wechsel der.

**alternative** [ɔːlˈtɜːnətɪv] adj - **1.** [different, other] andere, -r, -s - **2.** [nontraditional] alternativ ◇ n Alternative die; **an ~ to sb/sthg** eine Alternative zu jm/etw; **to have no ~ (but to do sthg)** keine (andere) Wahl haben(, als etw zu tun).

**alternatively** [ɔːlˈtɜːnətɪvlɪ] adv oder aber, aber auch; **~, you could just stay at home** Sie könnten aber auch einfach zu Hause bleiben.

**alternative medicine** n (U) alternative Heilmethoden pl.

**alternator** [ˈɔːltəneɪtəʳ] n ELEC Wechselstromgenerator der; [in car] Lichtmaschine die.

**although** [ɔːlˈðəʊ] conj obwohl.

**altitude** [ˈæltɪtjuːd] n Höhe die.

**alto** [ˈæltəʊ] (pl -s) n [female voice] Alt der ◇ comp [flute, saxophone] Alt-.

**altogether** [ˌɔːltəˈgeðəʳ] adv - **1.** [completely] vollkommen - **2.** [in general, in total] insgesamt.

**altruism** [ˈæltruɪzm] n Altruismus der.

**altruistic** [ˌæltruˈɪstɪk] adj altruistisch.

**aluminium** Br [ˌæljʊˈmɪnɪəm], **aluminum** Am [əˈluːmɪnəm] n Aluminium das ◇ comp Aluminium-; **~ foil** Aluminiumfolie die.

**alumnus** [əˈlʌmnəs] (pl -ni [-naɪ]) n ehemaliger Schüler, ehemalige Schülerin.

**always** [ˈɔːlweɪz] adv immer; **you can ~ stay at my place** du kannst auch bei mir übernachten.

**am** [æm] vb ⊳ **be**.

**a.m.** (abbr of ante meridiem) vormittags; **at 3 ~** um 3 Uhr morgens or früh; **12 ~** 12 Uhr.

**AM** (*abbr of* **amplitude modulation**) *n* AM.

**AMA** (*abbr of* **American Medical Association**) *n US-amerikanische Bundesärztekammer.*

**amalgam** [ə'mælgəm] *n* - **1.** *fml* [combination] Mischung *die* - **2.** TECH [of metals] Amalgam *das*.

**amalgamate** [ə'mælgəmeɪt] *vt* mischen <> *vi* sich verbinden.

**amalgamation** [ə‚mælgə'meɪʃn] *n* - **1.** (U) [process] Verbindung *die* - **2.** [merger] Fusion *die*.

**amass** [ə'mæs] *vt* [fortune, power, information] anhäufen.

**amateur** ['æmətəʳ] *adj* - **1.** [nonprofessional] Amateur- - **2.** *pej* [unprofessional] dilettantisch <> *n* - **1.** [nonprofessional] Amateur *der*, -in *die* - **2.** *pej* [unskilled person] Dilettant *der*, -in *die*.

**amateurish** ['æmətəːrɪʃ] *adj pej* [unprofessional] dilettantisch.

**amaze** [ə'meɪz] *vt* erstaunen, verblüffen.

**amazed** [ə'meɪzd] *adj* erstaunt, verblüfft.

**amazement** [ə'meɪzmənt] *n* Erstaunen *das*.

**amazing** [ə'meɪzɪŋ] *adj* [incredible] erstaunlich.

**amazingly** [ə'meɪzɪŋlɪ] *adv* [very] erstaunlich.

**Amazon** ['æməzn] *n* - **1.** [river]: **the ~** der Amazonas - **2.** [region]: **in the ~** am Amazonas; **the ~ (Basin)** das Amazonasbecken; **the ~ rainforest** der Regenwald am Amazonas - **3.** [woman] Amazone *die*.

**Amazonian** [‚æmə'zəʊnjən] *adj* [woman] amazonisch; [region] Amazonas-.

**ambassador** [æm'bæsədəʳ] *n* Botschafter *der*, -in *die*.

**amber** ['æmbəʳ] *adj* - **1.** [amber-coloured] bernsteinfarben - **2.** *Br* [traffic light] gelb <> *n* - **1.** [substance] Bernstein *das* - **2.** *Br* [colour of traffic light] Gelb *das* <> *comp* [made of amber] aus Bernstein, Bernstein-.

**ambiance** *n* = ambience.

**ambidextrous** [‚æmbɪ'dekstrəs] *adj* beidhändig.

**ambience** ['æmbɪəns] *n* Ambiente *das*.

**ambiguity** [‚æmbɪ'gjuːətɪ] (*pl* **-ies**) *n* [two possible meanings] Zweideutigkeit *die*; [many possible meanings] Mehrdeutigkeit *die*.

**ambiguous** [æm'bɪgjuəs] *adj* [two possible meanings] zweideutig; [many possible meanings] mehrdeutig.

**ambiguously** [æm'bɪgjuəslɪ] *adv* [two possible meanings] zweideutig; [many possible meanings] mehrdeutig.

**ambition** [æm'bɪʃn] *n* - **1.** Ehrgeiz *der* - **2.** [objective, goal] Ambition *die*.

**ambitious** [æm'bɪʃəs] *adj* ehrgeizig.

**ambivalence** [æm'bɪvələns] *n* Ambivalenz *die*.

**ambivalent** [æm'bɪvələnt] *adj* ambivalent.

**amble** ['æmbl] *vi* schlendern.

**ambulance** ['æmbjuləns] *n* Krankenwagen *der*, Ambulanz *die* <> *comp:* **~ service** Rettungsdienst *der*; **~ man** Sanitäter *der*; **~ woman** Sanitäterin *die*.

**ambush** ['æmbuʃ] *n* Hinterhalt *der* <> *vt* [attack] aus dem Hinterhalt überfallen.

**ameba** [ə'miːbə] *n Am* = amoeba.

**ameliorate** *fml* [ə'miːljəreɪt] *vt* verbessern <> *vi* sich verbessern.

**amen** [‚ɑː'men] *excl* [at end of prayer] Amen.

**amenable** [ə'miːnəbl] *adj:* **~ (to sthg)** (einer Sache (D)) zugänglich.

**amend** [ə'mend] *vt* [change] abländern.
➣ **amends** *npl*: **to make ~s (for sthg)** Entschädigungen (für etw) bieten.

**amendment** [ə'mendmənt] *n* Änderung *die*.

**amenities** [ə'miːnətɪz] *npl* Einrichtungen *pl*.

**America** [ə'merɪkə] *n* Amerika *nt*.
➣ **Americas** *npl*: **the ~s** das Amerika, Nord- und Südamerika.

**American** [ə'merɪkn] *adj* amerikanisch <> *n* Amerikaner *der*, -in *die*.

**American football** *n Br* American Football *der*.

**American Indian** *n* Indianer *der*, -in *die*.

**Americanism** [ə'merɪkənɪzm] *n* Amerikanismus *der*.

**americanize, -ise** [ə'merɪkənaɪz] *vt* amerikanisieren.

**amethyst** ['æmɪθɪst] *n* Amethyst *der*.

**Amex** ['æmeks] *n* - **1.** (*abbr of* **American Stock Exchange**) *zweitwichtigste US-amerikanische Börse* - **2.** (*abbr of* **American Express**) *American Express, US-amerikanisches Kreditkartenunternehmen.*

**amiable** ['eɪmjəbl] *adj* freundlich.

**amiably** ['eɪmjəblɪ] *adv* freundlich.

**amicable** ['æmɪkəbl] *adj* freundschaftlich; [agreement] gütlich.

**amicably** ['æmɪkəblɪ] *adv* in aller Freundschaft.

**amid(st)** [ə'mɪd(st)] *prep fml* inmitten (+ G).

**amino acid** [ə'miːnəʊ-] *n* Aminosäure *die*.

**amiss** [ə'mɪs] *adj*: **is there anything ~?** stimmt etwas nicht? <> *adv*: **to take sthg ~** etw übel nehmen.

**ammo** ['æməʊ] *n inf* MIL Munition *die*.

**ammonia** [ə'məʊnjə] *n* Ammoniak *der*.

**ammunition** [‚æmjʊ'nɪʃn] *n* Munition *die*.

**ammunition dump** *n* Munitionslager *das*.

**amnesia** [æm'niːzjə] *n* Amnesie *die*.

**amnesty** ['æmnəstɪ] (*pl* **-ies**) *n* Amnestie *die*.

**Amnesty International** *n* Amnesty International.

**amniocentesis** [ˌæmnɪəʊsen'tiːsɪs] *n* Fruchtwasseruntersuchung *die*.

**amoeba, ameba** *Am* [ə'miːbəl] *n* Amöbe *die*.

**amok** [ə'mɒk] *adv:* **to run ~** Amok laufen.

**among(st)** [ə'mʌŋ(st)] *prep* unter (+ D); **~ other things** unter anderem; **I count him ~ my friends** ich zähle ihn zu meinen Freunden; **they were talking ~ themselves** sie unterhielten sich.

**amoral** [ˌeɪ'mɒrəl] *adj* amoralisch.

**amorous** ['æmərəs] *adj* amourös.

**amorphous** [ə'mɔːfəs] *adj* amorph; [body, ideas] ungestaltet.

**amortize** [ə'mɔːtaɪz] *vt* FIN tilgen.

**amount** [ə'maʊnt] *n* - **1.** [quantity] Menge *die* - **2.** [sum of money] Betrag *der*.

◆ **amount to** *vt fus* - **1.** [total] sich belaufen auf (+ A) - **2.** [be equivalent to] hinausllaufen auf (+ A).

**amp** [æmp] *n* - **1.** *abbr of* **ampere** - **2.** *inf abbr of* **amplifier**.

**amperage** ['æmpərɪdʒ] *n* ELEC Amperezahl *die*.

**ampere** ['æmpeəʳ] *n* Ampere *das*.

**ampersand** ['æmpəsænd] *n* Und-Zeichen *das*.

**amphetamine** [æm'fetəmiːn] *n* Amphetamin *das*.

**amphibian** [æm'fɪbɪən] *n* Amphibie *die*.

**amphibious** [æm'fɪbɪəs] *adj* amphibisch.

**amphitheatre** *Br,* **amphitheater** *Am* ['æmfɪˌθɪətəʳ] *n* Amphitheater *das*.

**ample** ['æmpl] *adj* - **1.** [enough] reichlich - **2.** [large] großzügig.

**amplification** [ˌæmplɪfɪ'keɪʃn] *n (U)* - **1.** [of sound] Verstärkung *die* - **2.** [of idea, statement] Ausführung *die*.

**amplifier** ['æmplɪfaɪəʳ] *n* Verstärker *der*.

**amplify** ['æmplɪfaɪ] (*pt* & *pp* **-ied**) *vt* - **1.** [sound] verstärken - **2.** [idea, statement] ausllführen.

**amply** ['æmplɪ] *adv* - **1.** [sufficiently] reichlich - **2.** [considerably] großzügig.

**ampoule** *Br,* **ampule** *Am* ['æmpuːl] *n* Ampulle *die*.

**amputate** ['æmpjʊteɪt] *vt* & *vi* amputieren.

**amputation** [ˌæmpjʊ'teɪʃn] *n* Amputation *die*.

**Amsterdam** [ˌæmstə'dæm] *n* Amsterdam *nt*.

**amt** *abbr of* **amount**.

**Amtrak** ['æmtræk] *n* Nordamerikanische Eisenbahngesellschaft.

**amuck** [ə'mʌk] *adv* = **amok**.

**amulet** ['æmjʊlɪt] *n* Amulett *das*.

**amuse** [ə'mjuːz] *vt* - **1.** [make laugh] amüsieren - **2.** [entertain] unterhalten; **to ~ o.s. (with sthg)** sich (D) (mit etw) die Zeit vertreiben.

**amused** [ə'mjuːzd] *adj* amüsiert; **to be ~ at** OR **by sthg** von etw erheitert sein; **to keep o.s. ~** sich die Zeit vertreiben.

**amusement** [ə'mjuːzmənt] *n* - **1.** [enjoyment] Vergnügen *das* - **2.** [diversion, game] Unterhaltungsmöglichkeit *die*.

**amusement arcade** *n* Spielhalle *die*.

**amusement park** *n* Vergnügungspark *der*.

**amusing** [ə'mjuːzɪŋ] *adj* [funny] amüsant.

**an** [*stressed* æn, *unstressed* ən] *indef art* ➞ **a²**.

**anabolic steroid** [ˌænə'bɒlɪk-] *n* Anabolikum *das*.

**anachronism** [ə'nækrənɪzm] *n* Anachronismus *der*.

**anachronistic** [əˌnækrə'nɪstɪk] *adj* anachronistisch.

**anaemia** *Br,* **anemia** *Am* [ə'niːmjə] *n* Anämie *die*.

**anaemic** *Br,* **anemic** *Am* [ə'niːmɪk] *adj* [suffering from anaemia] anämisch.

**anaesthesia** *Br,* **anesthesia** *Am* [ˌænɪs-'θiːzjə] *n (U)* Anästhesie *die*, Narkose *die*.

**anaesthetic** *Br,* **anesthetic** *Am* [ˌænɪs'θetɪk] *n* Anästhetikum *das*, Narkosemittel *das;* **under ~** unter Narkose, in der Narkose.

**anaesthetist** *Br,* **anesthetist** *Am* [æ'niːsθətɪst] *n* Anästhesist *der*, -in *die*.

**anaesthetize, -ise** *Br,* **anesthetize** *Am* [æ'niːsθətaɪz] *vt* betäuben, narkotisieren.

**anagram** ['ænəgræm] *n* Anagramm *das*.

**anal** ['eɪnl] *adj* anal.

**analgesic** [ˌænæl'dʒiːsɪk] *adj* schmerzstillend ➪ *n* Analgetikum *das*.

**analog** *adj* & *n Am* = **analogue**.

**analogous** [ə'næləgəs] *adj fml* [comparable]: **~ (to)** vergleichbar (mit).

**analogue** *Br,* **analog** *Am* ['ænəlɒg] *adj* analog ➪ *n fml* [similar object, device] Gegenstück *das*.

**analogy** [ə'nælədʒɪ] (*pl* **-ies**) *n* Analogie *die;* **to draw an ~ between** eine Analogie herstellen zwischen (+ D); **by ~** analog dazu.

**analyse** *Br,* **-lyze** *Am* ['ænəlaɪz] *vt* analysieren.

**analysis** [ə'næləsɪs] (*pl* **-ses** [ə'næləsiːz]) *n* - **1.** [gen] Analyse *die* - **2.** *phr:* **in the final** OR **last ~** letzten Endes.

**analyst** ['ænəlɪst] *n* - **1.** [political, computer, statistics] Analytiker *der*, -in *die* - **2.** [psychoanalyst] Psychoanalytiker *der*, -in *die*.

**analytic(al)** [ˌænə'lɪtɪk(l)] *adj* analytisch.

**analyze** *vt Am* = **analyse**.

**anarchic** [æ'nɑːkɪk] adj anarchisch.

**anarchist** ['ænəkɪst] n POL Anarchist der, -in die.

**anarchy** ['ænəkɪ] n Anarchie die.

**anathema** [ə'næθəmə] n Anathema das.

**anatomical** [ˌænə'tɒmɪkl] adj anatomisch.

**anatomy** [ə'nætəmɪ] (pl -ies) n Anatomie die.

**ANC** (abbr of African National Congress) n ANC der.

**ancestor** ['ænsestə'] n - 1. [person] Vorfahr der, Ahn der - 2. fig [of machine, vehicle] Vorläufer der.

**ancestral home** [æn'sestrəl-] n Stammsitz der.

**ancestry** ['ænsestrɪ] (pl -ies) n Abstammung die.

**anchor** ['æŋkə'] n - 1. NAUT Anker der; to drop/weigh ~ Anker werfen/lichten - 2. TV Moderator der, -in die <> vt - 1. [secure] sichern - 2. TV [present] moderieren <> vi NAUT ankern.

**anchorage** ['æŋkərɪdʒ] n - 1. NAUT Ankerplatz der - 2. [means of securing] Verankerung die.

**anchorman** ['æŋkəmæn] (pl -men [-menl) n TV Moderator der (eines Nachrichtenmagazins).

**anchorwoman** ['æŋkəˌwumən] (pl -women [-ˌwɪmɪn]) n TV Moderatorin die (eines Nachrichtenmagazins).

**anchovy** ['æntʃəvɪ] (pl inv OR -ies) n Sardelle die.

**ancient** ['eɪnʃənt] adj - 1. [dating from distant past] alt - 2. hum [very old] alt, uralt.

**ancillary** [æn'sɪlərɪ] adj [staff, device] Hilfs-, Neben-.

**and** [stressed ænd, unstressed ənd, ənl conj - 1. [gen] und; ~ you? und du/Sie?; my wife ~ I meine Frau und ich; nice ~ warm schön warm - 2. [in numbers]: a hundred ~ one hunderteins; an hour ~ a quarter eineinviertel Stunden - 3. [with repetition]: more ~ more immer mehr; for days ~ days tagelang - 4. (with infinitive) [in order to]: to try ~ do sthg versuchen, etw zu tun; wait ~ see! warte es ab!, warten Sie es ab!

➤ **and all that** adv und dergleichen.

➤ **and so on, and so forth** adv und so weiter, und so fort.

**Andes** ['ændiːz] npl: the ~ die Anden pl.

**androgynous** [æn'drɒdʒɪnəs] adj androgyn.

**android** ['ændrɔɪd] n Androide der.

**anecdote** ['ænɪkdəut] n Anekdote die.

**anemia** n Am = anaemia.

**anemic** adj Am = anaemic.

**anemone** [ə'nemənɪ] n Anemone die.

**anesthetic** etc n Am = anaesthetic etc.

**anew** [ə'njuː] adv von neuem.

**angel** ['eɪndʒəl] n lit & fig Engel der.

**Angeleno** [ˌændʒə'liːnəul n Bürger von Los Angeles.

**angelic** [æn'dʒelɪk] adj engelsgleich.

**anger** ['æŋgə'] n Zorn der, Wut die <> vt ärgern.

**angina** [æn'dʒaɪnə] n Angina pectoris die.

**angle** ['æŋgl] n - 1. MATH [corner] Winkel der - 2. [point of view] Standpunkt der - 3. [slope] Schräge die; at an ~ im schrägen Winkel <> vt [remarks, report] ausrichten <> vi - 1. [fish] angeln - 2. [manoeuvre]: to ~ for sthg nach etw angeln.

**Anglepoise (lamp)**® ['æŋgəlpɔɪs-] n verstellbare Klemmleuchte.

**angler** ['æŋglə'] n Angler der, -in die.

**Anglican** ['æŋglɪkən] adj anglikanisch <> n Anglikaner der, -in die.

**anglicism** ['æŋglɪsɪzm] n Anglizismus der.

**angling** ['æŋglɪŋ] n Angeln das.

**Anglo-** ['æŋgləul prefix Anglo-.

**Anglo-Saxon** adj Angelsächsisch <> n - 1. [person] Angelsachse der, -sächsin die - 2. [language] Angelsächsisch(e) das.

**Angola** [æŋ'gəulə] n Angola nt.

**Angolan** [æŋ'gəulən] adj Angolanisch <> n Angolaner der, -in die.

**angora** [æŋ'gɔːrə] n - 1. [goat] Angoraziege die; [rabbit] Angorakaninchen das - 2. [material] Angora das.

**angrily** ['æŋgrəlɪ] adv wütend.

**angry** ['æŋgrɪ] (compar -ier; superl -iest) adj böse, wütend; to be ~ (with sb) (jm) böse sein, wütend sein (auf jn); to get ~ (with sb) böse OR wütend werden (auf jn).

**angst** [æŋst] n Existenzangst die.

**anguish** ['æŋgwɪʃ] n Qual die.

**anguished** ['æŋgwɪʃt] adj qualvoll; [look, expression] gequält.

**angular** ['æŋgjulə'] adj [face, jaw, body] kantig; [furniture, car] eckig.

**animal** ['ænɪml] adj - 1. [gen] Tier- - 2. [physical] animalisch <> n - 1. [living creature] Tier das - 2. inf pej [brutal person] Bestie die.

**animate** ['ænɪmət] adj [alive] lebend.

**animated** ['ænɪmeɪtɪd] adj [lively] lebhaft.

**animated cartoon** n Zeichentrickfilm der.

**animation** [ˌænɪ'meɪʃn] n - 1. [excitement] Lebhaftigkeit die - 2. [of cartoons] Animation die.

**animosity** [ˌænɪ'mɒsətɪ] (pl -ies) n Feindseligkeit die.

**aniseed** ['ænɪsiːd] n Anis der.

**ankle** ['æŋkl] n Knöchel der <> comp Knöchel-; ~ socks Söckchen pl.

**annals** ['ænlz] *npl fml* Annalen *pl.*

**annex** ['æneks] *vt* annektieren.

**annexation** [ˌænek'seɪʃn] *n* Annektion *die.*

**annexe** ['æneks] *n* [building] Anbau *der.*

**annihilate** [ə'naɪəleɪt] *vt* vernichten, auslöschen.

**annihilation** [əˌnaɪə'leɪʃn] *n* Vernichtung *die,* Auslöschung *die.*

**anniversary** [ˌænɪ'vɜːsərɪ] (*pl* **-ies**) *n* Jahrestag *der.*

**annotate** ['ænəteɪt] *vt fml* mit Anmerkungen versehen.

**announce** [ə'naʊns] *vt* **- 1.** [make public] ankündigen, bekannt geben **- 2.** [state, declare] verkünden.

**announcement** [ə'naʊnsmənt] *n* [public statement] Bekanntmachung *die;* **government ~** Regierungserklärung *die.*

**announcer** [ə'naʊnsəʳ] *n* Ansager *der,* -in *die;* **television ~** Fernsehansager *der,* -in *die;* **radio ~** Radioansager *der,* -in *die.*

**annoy** [ə'nɔɪ] *vt* ärgern.

**annoyance** [ə'nɔɪəns] *n* Ärgernis *das.*

**annoyed** [ə'nɔɪd] *adj* verärgert; **to be ~ at sthg** über etw (A) verärgert sein; **to be ~ with sb** über jn verärgert sein; **to get ~** sich ärgern.

**annoying** [ə'nɔɪɪŋ] *adj* ärgerlich.

**annual** ['ænjʊəl] *adj* jährlich, Jahres- ◇ *n* **- 1.** [plant] einjährige Pflanze **- 2.** [book] Jahrbuch *das.*

**annual general meeting** *n* Jahreshauptversammlung *die.*

**annually** ['ænjʊəlɪ] *adv* jährlich.

**annuity** [ə'njuːtɪ] (*pl* **-ies**) *n* FIN Jahresrente *die.*

**annul** [ə'nʌl] (*pt* & *pp* **-led;** *cont* **-ling**) *vt* annullieren.

**annulment** [ə'nʌlmənt] *n* Annullierung *die.*

**annum** ['ænəm] *n:* **per ~** pro Jahr.

**Annunciation** [əˌnʌnsɪ'eɪʃn] *n:* **the ~** Mariä Verkündigung.

**anode** ['ænəʊd] *n* TECH Anode *die.*

**anoint** [ə'nɔɪnt] *vt* RELIG salben.

**anomalous** [ə'nɒmələs] *adj fml* anomal.

**anomaly** [ə'nɒməlɪ] (*pl* **-ies**) *n* Anomalie *die.*

**anon.** [ə'nɒn] *abbr of* **anonymous.**

**anonymity** [ˌænə'nɪmətɪ] *n* Anonymität *die.*

**anonymous** [ə'nɒnɪməs] *adj* anonym.

**anonymously** [ə'nɒnɪməslɪ] *adv* anonym.

**anorak** ['ænəræk] *n esp Br* Anorak *der.*

**anorexia (nervosa)** [ˌænə'reksɪə(nɜː'vəʊsə)] *n* Anorexie *die,* Magersucht *die.*

**anorexic** [ˌænə'reksɪk] *adj* magersüchtig ◇ *n* Magersüchtige *der, die.*

**another** [ə'nʌðəʳ] *adj* **- 1.** [additional] noch eine, -r, -s; **in ~ few minutes** in einigen Minuten **- 2.** [different] ein anderer, eine andere, ein anderes ◇ *pron* **- 1.** [an additional one] noch eine, -r, -s; **one after ~** einer/eine/eines nach dem/der anderen **- 2.** [a different one] etwas anderes; **they love one ~** sie lieben einander, sie lieben sich; **they are always arguing with one ~** sie streiten immer miteinander, sie streiten (sich) immer.

**ANSI** (*abbr of* **American National Standards Institute**) *n* ≃ DIN.

**answer** ['ɑːnsəʳ] *n* **- 1.** [reply] Antwort *die;* **in ~ to** als Antwort auf (+ A) **- 2.** [solution] Lösung *die* ◇ *vt* **- 1.** [reply to - question, letter, advertisement] beantworten **- 2.** [respond to]: **to ~ the door** die Tür öffnen; **to ~ the phone** den Hörer abnehmen ◇ *vi* [reply] antworten.

➡ **answer back** *vt sep* & *vi* widersprechen (+ D).

➡ **answer for** *vt fus* verantworten.

**answerable** ['ɑːnsərəbl] *adj* [accountable] verantwortlich; **~ to sb** jm gegenüber verantwortlich; **~ for sthg** für etw verantwortlich.

**answering machine** ['ɑːnsərɪŋ-] *n* Anrufbeantworter *der*

**ant** [ænt] *n* Ameise *die.*

**antacid** [ˌænt'æsɪd] *n* Säure bindendes Mittel.

**antagonism** [æn'tægənɪzm] *n* Feindlichkeit *die,* Feindseligkeit *die.*

**antagonist** [æn'tægənɪst] *n* Kontrahent *der,* -in *die.*

**antagonistic** [ænˌtægə'nɪstɪk] *adj* feindlich, feindselig.

**antagonize, -ise** [æn'tægənaɪz] *vt:* **to ~ sb** jn gegen sich aufbringen.

**Antarctic** [æn'tɑːktɪk] *n:* **the ~** die Antarktis ◇ *adj* antarktisch.

**Antarctica** [æn'tɑːktɪkə] *n* Antarktis *die.*

**Antarctic Circle** *n:* **the ~** der südliche Polarkreis.

**Antarctic Ocean** *n:* **the ~** das Südpolarmeer.

**ante** ['æntɪ] *n inf fig:* **to up** OR **raise the ~** den Einsatz erhöhen.

**anteater** ['æntˌiːtəʳ] *n* Ameisenbär *der.*

**antecedent** [ˌæntɪ'siːdənt] *n fml* [earlier event] Vorgeschichte *die.*

**antediluvian** [ˌæntɪdɪ'luːvjən] *adj hum* [outdated] vorsintflutlich.

**antelope** ['æntɪləʊp] (*pl inv* OR **-s**) *n* Antilope *die.*

**antenatal** [ˌæntɪ'neɪtl] *adj* Schwangerschafts-.

**antenatal clinic** *n* Sprechstunde *die* für Schwangere.

**antenna** [æn'tenə] (*pl sense 1* **-nae** [-niː], *pl sense 2* **-s**) *n* - **1.** [of insect, lobster] Fühler *der* - **2.** *Am* [aerial] Antenne *die*.

**anteroom** ['æntɪrum] *n* - **1.** [antechamber] Vorsaal *der* - **2.** [waiting room] Vorzimmer *das*.

**anthem** ['ænθəm] *n* Hymne *die*.

**anthill** ['ænthɪl] *n* Ameisenhügel *der*.

**anthology** [æn'θɒlədʒɪ] (*pl* **-ies**) *n* Anthologie *die*.

**anthrax** ['ænθræks] *n* Milzbrand *der*.

**anthropologist** [ˌænθrə'pɒlədʒɪst] *n* Anthropologe *der*, -in *die*.

**anthropology** [ˌænθrə'pɒlədʒɪ] *n* Anthropologie *die*.

**anti-** ['æntɪ] *prefix* - **1.** [opposed to] Anti- - **2.** [preventive] -abwehr.

**antiaircraft** [ˌæntɪ'eəkrɑːft] *adj* Flugabwehr-.

**antiapartheid** [ˌæntɪə'pɑːtheɪt] *adj* gegen Apartheid.

**antiballistic missile** [ˌæntɪbə'lɪstɪk-] *n* Raketenabwehr-Rakete *die*.

**antibiotic** [ˌæntɪbaɪ'ɒtɪk] *n* Antibiotikum *das*.

**antibody** ['æntɪˌbɒdɪ] (*pl* **-ies**) *n* BIOL Antikörper *der*.

**anticipate** [æn'tɪsɪpeɪt] *vt* - **1.** [expect] erwarten, vorauslsehen - **2.** [preempt]: **to ~ sb** jm zuvorlkommen.

**anticipation** [ænˌtɪsɪ'peɪʃn] *n* Erwartung *die;* **thanking you in ~** vielen Dank im Voraus; **in ~ of** in Erwartung von.

**anticlimax** [ˌæntɪ'klaɪmæks] *n* Enttäuschung *die*.

**anticlockwise** *Br* [ˌæntɪ'klɒkwaɪz] *adj* [direction] Links- ⟨⟩ *adv* gegen den Uhrzeigersinn, nach links.

**antics** ['æntɪks] *npl* - **1.** [of children, animals] Possen *pl* - **2.** *pej* [of politician *etc*] Eskapaden *pl*.

**anticyclone** [ˌæntɪ'saɪkləʊn] *n* Hoch *das*, Hochdruckgebiet *das*.

**antidepressant** [ˌæntɪdɪ'presnt] *n* Antidepressivum *das*.

**antidote** ['æntɪdəʊt] *n lit &* **fig: ~ (to)** Gegenmittel *das* (gegen).

**antifreeze** ['æntɪfriːz] *n* Frostschutzmittel *das*.

**antihero** ['æntɪˌhɪərəʊ] (*pl* **-es**) *n* Antiheld *der*, -in *die*.

**antihistamine** [ˌæntɪ'hɪstəmɪn] *n* Antihistamin *das*.

**antinuclear** [ˌæntɪ'njuːklɪəʳ] *adj* gegen Atomkraft OR Kernkraft.

**antipathy** [æn'tɪpəθɪ] *n:* **~ (to** OR **towards)** Abneigung *die* (gegen).

**antipersonnel** ['æntɪˌpɜːsə'nel] *adj* MIL gegen Menschen gerichtet.

**antiperspirant** [ˌæntɪ'pɜːspərənt] *n* Deodorant *das*.

**Antipodes** [æn'tɪpədiːz] *npl:* **the ~** die Antipoden *pl*.

**antiquarian** [ˌæntɪ'kweərɪən] *adj* antiquarisch ⟨⟩ *n* Antiquar *der*, -in *die*.

**antiquated** ['æntɪkweɪtɪd] *adj* antiquiert, veraltet.

**antique** [æn'tiːk] *adj* antik ⟨⟩ *n* Antiquität *die*.

**antique dealer** *n* Antiquitätenhändler *der*, -in *die*.

**antique shop** *n* Antiquitätenhandlung *die*.

**antiquity** [æn'tɪkwətɪ] (*pl* **-ies**) *n* - **1.** [ancient times] Antike *die*, Altertum *das* - **2.** [antique object] Gegenstand *der* aus der Antike.

**anti-Semitic** [ˌæntɪsɪ'mɪtɪk] *adj* antisemitisch.

**anti-Semitism** [ˌæntɪ'semɪtɪzəm] *n* Antisemitismus *der*.

**antiseptic** [ˌæntɪ'septɪk] *adj* steril, desinfiziert ⟨⟩ *n* Antiseptikum *das*, Desinfektionsmittel *das*.

**antisocial** [ˌæntɪ'səʊʃl] *adj* - **1.** [damaging to society] unsozial - **2.** [unsociable] ungesellig; [working hours] unsozial.

**antistatic** [ˌæntɪ'stætɪk] *adj* antistatisch.

**antitank** [ˌæntɪ'tæŋk] *adj* MIL Panzerabwehr-.

**antithesis** [æn'tɪθɪsɪs] (*pl* **-theses**) [θɪsiːz] *n fml* Antithese *die*.

**antlers** ['æntləz] *npl* Geweih *das*.

**antonym** ['æntənɪm] *n* Antonym *das*.

**Antwerp** ['æntwɜːp] *n* Antwerpen *nt*.

**anus** ['eɪnəs] *n* After *der*.

**anvil** ['ænvɪl] *n* Amboss *der*.

**anxiety** [æŋ'zaɪətɪ] (*pl* **-ies**) *n* - **1.** [worry, cause of worry] Sorge *die* - **2.** [keenness] Ungeduld *die*.

**anxious** ['æŋkʃəs] *adj* - **1.** [worried] besorgt; **to be ~ about sb/sthg** sich um jn/etw sorgen, sich über jn/etw Sorgen machen - **2.** [keen]: **to be ~ to do sthg** darauf brennen, etw zu tun; **I'm ~ that he doesn't find out** ich möchte auf keinen Fall, dass er es erfährt.

**anxiously** ['æŋkʃəslɪ] *adv* - **1.** [nervously] besorgt - **2.** [eagerly] gespannt.

**any** ['enɪ] *adj* - **1.** *(in questions):* **have you got ~ money?** hast du Geld?; **have you got ~ postcards?** haben Sie Postkarten?; **can I be of ~ help?** kann ich Ihnen irgendwie behilflich sein? - **2.** *(with negatives):* **I haven't got ~ money** ich habe kein Geld; **we don't have ~ rooms**

wir haben keine Zimmer frei; **he never does ~ housework** er tut nie etwas im Haushalt; **it isn't ~ good** [pointless] es nützt nichts; [poor quality] es taugt nichts - **3.** [no matter which] irgendein, -e; **take ~ one you like** nimm, welches du willst; **~ beer will do** jedes Bier ist recht; **at ~ time** jederzeit; ▷ **case, day, moment, rate** ◇ pron - **1.** (in questions) welche; **I'm looking for a hotel – are there ~ nearby?** ich suche ein Hotel – gibts hier welche in der Nähe?; **can ~ of you change a tyre?** kann jemand von euch/Ihnen einen Reifen wechseln? - **2.** (with if): **if ~** wenn überhaupt; **few foreign films, if ~, are successful here** nur wenige ausländische Filme haben hier Erfolg - **3.** (with negatives): **I don't want ~ (of them)** ich möchte keinen/keines/keine (von denen) - **4.** [no matter which one] jede, -r, -s; **take ~ you like** nimm, welches du willst; **you can sit at ~ of the tables** Sie können sich an jeden beliebigen Tisch setzen ◇ adv - **1.** (in questions): **is there ~ more ice cream?** ist noch Eis da?; **is that ~ better?** ist das besser? - **2.** (with negatives): **we can't wait ~ longer** wir können nicht mehr länger warten; **I can't see it ~ more** ich kann es nicht mehr sehen.

**anybody** ['enɪˌbɒdɪ] pron = anyone.

**anyhow** ['enɪhaʊ] adv - **1.** [in spite of that] trotzdem - **2.** [carelessly] durcheinander, wahllos - **3.** [returning to topic in conversation] jedenfalls.

**anyone** ['enɪwʌn] pron - **1.** [any person] jeder; **~ can tell you that** (ein) jeder kann dir das sagen; **~ else would have given up** jeder andere hätte es aufgegeben; **if ~ asks, you haven't seen me** wenn jemand fragt, du hast mich nicht gesehen - **2.** (in questions) irgendjemand; **has ~ seen my book?** hat irgendjemand mein Buch gesehen?; **do you know ~ else?** kennst du sonst noch jemanden? - **3.** (in negative statements): **there wasn't ~ in** niemand war zu Hause; **I didn't see ~ else** ich habe sonst niemanden gesehen; **there was hardly ~ there** es war kaum jemand dort.

**anyplace** ['enɪpleɪs] adv Am = anywhere.

**anything** ['enɪθɪŋ] pron - **1.** [no matter what] alles; **he eats ~** er isst alles; **if ~ should happen to him** falls ihm irgendetwas zustoßen sollte; **please can I have something to write with, ~ will do** gib mir bitte etwas zu schreiben, egal was - **2.** (in questions) irgendetwas; **would you like ~ else?** darf es noch etwas sein?; **is there ~ more pleasant than ...?** gibt es denn etwas Angenehmeres als ...? - **3.** (in negative statements): **I don't want ~ at all** ich möchte überhaupt nichts (haben); **he didn't tell me ~** er hat mir nichts gesagt; **hardly ~** kaum etwas; **not for ~** um keinen Preis.

➡ **anything but** adv: **he is ~ but mad** er ist alles andere als verrückt.

**anyway** ['enɪweɪ] adv - **1.** [in any case] sowieso

- **2.** [in spite of that] trotzdem; **but we went along ~** aber wir sind trotzdem hingegangen - **3.** [in conversation] jedenfalls; **~, there we were, ... nun ja, jedenfalls standen wir da ...

**anywhere** ['enɪweəʳ] adv - **1.** [any place] überall; **sit ~ you like** setz dich einfach irgendwohin; **~ else** woanders, anderswo - **2.** (in questions) irgendwo; **have you seen my jacket ~?** hast du meine Jacke irgendwo gesehen?; **did you go ~ else?** bist du/seid Ihr noch irgendwo anders hingegangen? - **3.** (in negative statements): **I can't find it ~** ich kann es nirgends finden; **we didn't see ~ interesting** wir haben nichts Interessantes gesehen - **4.** [unspecified amount, number]: **we're expecting ~ between 50 and 100 people** wir erwarten mindestens 50, vielleicht sogar 100 Leute.

**Anzac** ['ænzæk] (abbr of **Australia New Zealand Army Corps**) n australisch-neuseeländisches Korps.

**AOB, a.o.b.** (abbr of **any other business**) Verschiedenes.

**Apache** [ə'pætʃɪ] n Apache der, -in die.

**apart** [ə'pɑːt] adv - **1.** [separated in space] getrennt; **she stood ~ from the group** sie hielt sich abseits der Gruppe - **2.** [in several pieces] auseinander; **to fall ~** auseinander fallen; **to take sthg ~** etw auseinander nehmen - **3.** [aside, excepted] beiseite; **joking ~** Spaß beiseite.

➡ **apart from** prep [except for] mit Ausnahme von ◇ conj [in addition to] abgesehen von.

**apartheid** [ə'pɑːtheɪt] n Apartheid die.

**apartment** [ə'pɑːtmənt] n esp Am Wohnung die.

**apartment building** n Am Wohnblock der.

**apathetic** [ˌæpə'θetɪk] adj teilnahmslos, apathisch.

**apathy** ['æpəθɪ] n Teilnahmslosigkeit die, Apathie die.

**APB** (abbr of **all points bulletin**) n Fahndungsaufruf der.

**ape** [eɪp] n [animal] Menschenaffe der ◇ vt pej [imitate] nachläffen.

**Apennines** ['æpɪnaɪnz] npl: **the ~** der Apennin.

**aperitif** [əperə'tiːf] n Aperitif der.

**aperture** ['æpəˌtjʊəʳ] n - **1.** [hole, opening] Öffnung die - **2.** PHOT Blende die.

**apex** ['eɪpeks] (pl -es OR apices) n [top] lit Spitze der; fig Gipfel der.

**APEX** ['eɪpeks] (abbr of **advance purchase excursion**) n Br zeitlich reglementierter Vorverkauf verbilligter Flugtickets und Bahnfahrkarten.

**aphid** ['eɪfɪd] n Blattlaus die.

**aphorism** [ˈæfərɪzm] *n* Aphorismus *der.*

**aphrodisiac** [ˌæfrəˈdɪzɪæk] *n* Aphrodisiakum *das.*

**apices** [ˈeɪpɪsiːz] *pl* ➪ **apex.**

**apiece** [əˈpiːs] *adv* [object] pro Stück.

**aplomb** [əˈplɒm] *n* Selbstsicherheit *die.*

**apocalypse** [əˈpɒkəlɪps] *n* Apokalypse *die.*

**apocalyptic** [əˌpɒkəˈlɪptɪk] *adj* apokalyptisch.

**apogee** [ˈæpədʒiː] *n fig* & *fml* Höhepunkt *der.*

**apolitical** [ˌeɪpəˈlɪtɪkəl] *adj* unpolitisch.

**apologetic** [əˌpɒləˈdʒetɪk] *adj* entschuldigend; **to be ~ (about sthg)** sich (für etw *OR* wegen etw *(G))* entschuldigen.

**apologetically** [əˌpɒləˈdʒetɪklɪ] *adv* entschuldigend.

**apologize, -ise** [əˈpɒlədʒaɪz] *vi* sich entschuldigen; **to ~ to sb for sthg** sich bei jm für etw entschuldigen.

**apology** [əˈpɒlədʒɪ] (*pl* **-ies**) *n* Entschuldigung *die.*

**apoplectic** [ˌæpəˈplektɪk] *adj* **- 1.** MED apoplektisch **- 2.** *inf* [very angry]: **to be ~ (with rage)** außer sich sein (vor Wut).

**apoplexy** [ˈæpəpleksɪ] *n* MED Apoplexie *die.*

**apostle** [əˈpɒsl] *n* RELIG Apostel *der.*

**apostrophe** [əˈpɒstrəfɪ] *n* GRAMM Apostroph *der.*

**appal** *Br* (*pt* & *pp* **-led**; *cont* **-ling**), **appall** *Am* [əˈpɔːl] *vt* entsetzen.

**Appalachian** [ˌæpəˈleɪtʃjən] *n:* **the ~s, the ~ Mountains** die Appalachen *pl.*

**appall** *vt Am* = **appal.**

**appalled** [əˈpɔːld] *adj* entsetzt.

**appalling** [əˈpɔːlɪŋ] *adj* entsetzlich, furchtbar.

**appallingly** [əˈpɔːlɪŋlɪ] *adv* entsetzlich, furchtbar.

**apparatus** [ˌæpəˈreɪtəs] (*pl inv OR* **-es**) *n* Apparat *der;* [device] Gerät *das;* [in gym] Geräte *pl.*

**apparel** [əˈpærəl] *n Am* Kleidung *die.*

**apparent** [əˈpærənt] *adj* **- 1.** [evident] offensichtlich; **for no ~ reason** aus keinem ersichtlichen Grund **- 2.** [seeming] scheinbar.

**apparently** [əˈpærəntlɪ] *adv* **- 1.** [according to rumour] anscheinend; **~ they're quite good** anscheinend sind sie ganz gut **- 2.** [seemingly] scheinbar.

**apparition** [ˌæpəˈrɪʃn] *n fml* [ghost] Erscheinung *die.*

**appeal** [əˈpiːl] *vi* **- 1.** [request] (dringend) bitten; **to ~ to sb for sthg** jn (dringend) um etw bitten; **to ~ to the public to do sthg** die Öffentlichkeit dazu aufrufen, etw zu tun **- 2.** [to sb's honour, common sense]: **to ~ to** appellieren an (+ *A*) **- 3.** LAW: **to ~ (against)** Berufung einlegen (gegen) **- 4.** [attract, interest]: **to ~ to sb** jm gefallen, jm zusagen ◇ *n* **- 1.** [for help, money] Aufruf *der,* Appell *der;* [for mercy] Gesuch *das* **- 2.** LAW Berufung *die* **- 3.** [charm, interest] Reiz *der,* Anziehungskraft *die.*

**appealing** [əˈpiːlɪŋ] *adj* [person] ansprechend; [baby] süß; [idea] reizvoll.

**appear** [əˈpɪəʳ] *vi* **- 1.** [gen] erscheinen **- 2.** [in play] auftreten ◇ *vt* [seem] scheinen; **it would ~ that ...** es hat den Anschein *OR* es scheint, als ob ...

**appearance** [əˈpɪərəns] *n* **- 1.** [gen] Erscheinen *das;* [of symptoms] Auftreten *das;* **to put in** *OR* **make an ~** sich sehen lassen **- 2.** [outward aspect] äußere Erscheinung; [facial features] Aussehen *das;* **to keep up ~s** den Schein wahren; **by** *OR* **to all ~s** allem Anschein nach **- 3.** [in play, film, on TV] Auftritt *der.*

**appease** [əˈpiːz] *vt* [person, anger] (durch Zugeständnisse) beschwichtigen; [hunger, curiosity] stillen.

**appeasement** [əˈpiːzmənt] *n* **- 1.** [of person, anger] Beschwichtigung *die* (durch Zugeständnisse); [of hunger, curiosity] Stillen *das* **- 2.** POL Beschwichtigung *die* (durch Zugeständnisse).

**append** [əˈpend] *vt fml:* **to ~ sthg (to)** [add] etw hinzufügen (zu); [enclose] etw beifügen (+ *D*).

**appendage** [əˈpendɪdʒ] *n* Anhängsel *das.*

**appendices** [əˈpendɪsiːz] *pl* ➪ **appendix.**

**appendicitis** [əˌpendɪˈsaɪtɪs] *n* (*U*) Blinddarmentzündung *die.*

**appendix** [əˈpendɪks] (*pl* **-dixes** *OR* **-dices**) *n* **- 1.** MED Blinddarm *der;* **to have one's ~ out** *OR* **removed** sich (*D*) den Blinddarm herausnehmen lassen **- 2.** [in book] Anhang *der.*

**appertain** [ˌæpəˈteɪn] *vi fml:* **to ~ to** verbunden sein mit.

**appetite** [ˈæpɪtaɪt] *n:* **~ (for)** Appetit *der* (auf (+ *A*)); **he's lost his ~ for politics** er hat die Lust an der Politik verloren.

**appetizer, -iser** [ˈæpɪtaɪzəʳ] *n* (appetitanregendes) Häppchen; [starter] Vorspeise *die.*

**appetizing, -ising** [ˈæpɪtaɪzɪŋ] *adj* appetitlich.

**applaud** [əˈplɔːd] *vt* **- 1.** [person] applaudieren (+ *D*), Beifall klatschen (+ *D*) **- 2.** *fig* [effort] loben; [decision] begrüßen ◇ *vi* applaudieren, (Beifall) klatschen.

**applause** [əˈplɔːz] *n* Applaus *der,* Beifall *der.*

**apple** [ˈæpl] *n* Apfel *der;* **to be the ~ of sb's eye** js Liebling sein.

**apple pie** *n* eine Art gedeckter Apfelkuchen mit dünnen Teigwänden.

**apple tree** *n* Apfelbaum *der.*

**appliance** [əˈplaɪəns] *n* Gerät *das.*

**applicable** [ə'plɪkəbl] *adj* zutreffend; **delete where not** ~ Nichtzutreffendes streichen; **to be** ~ **to sb/sthg** auf jn/etw zutreffen.

**applicant** ['æplɪkənt] *n:* ~ **(for)** [for job] Bewerber *der*, -in *die* (um *OR* für); [for state benefit] Antragsteller *der*, -in *die* (für).

**application** [,æplɪ'keɪʃn] *n* - **1.** [for job, college]: ~ **(for)** Bewerbung *die* (um *OR* für) - **2.** [for club]: ~ **(for)** Antrag *der* (auf (+ A)) - **3.** [of knowledge, rule] Anwendung *die;* [of invention] Einsatz *der* - **4.** [use] Verwendung *die* - **5.** [diligence] Fleiß *der* - **6.** COMPUT: ~ **(program)** Anwendungsprogramm *das.*

**application form** *n* [for job] Bewerbungsformular *das;* [for state benefit, club] Antragsformular *das.*

**applied** [ə'plaɪd] *adj* [science] angewandt.

**apply** [ə'plaɪ] (*pt* & *pp* **-ied**) *vt* - **1.** [rule, skill] anlwenden; **to** ~ **o.s. (to)** sich anlstrengen (bei); **to** ~ **one's mind to sthg** intensiv über etw (A) nachldenken - **2.** [paint, ointment] auf ltragen; **to** ~ **the brakes** bremsen *⋄ vi* - **1.** [for work, grant]: **to** ~ **(for)** sich bewerben (um *OR* für); **to** ~ **to sb for sthg** sich bei jm um *OR* für etw bewerben - **2.** [be relevant]: **to** ~ **(to)** zultreffen (auf (+ A)).

**appoint** [ə'pɔɪnt] *vt* - **1.** [to job, position] einlstellen; [to office] ernennen - **2.** *fml* [time, place] vereinbaren, festllegen.

**appointment** [ə'pɔɪntmənt] *n* - **1.** (U) [to job, position] Einstellung *die;* [to office] Ernennung *die;* '**by** ~ **to Her Majesty the Queen**' 'Hoflieferant Ihrer Majestät der Königin' - **2.** [job, position] Stelle *die* - **3.** [with doctor, hairdresser, in business] Termin *der;* **to have an** ~ einen Termin haben; **to make an** ~ einen Termin vereinbaren; **by** ~ nach Vereinbarung.

**apportion** [ə'pɔːʃn] *vt* [money] auf lteilen; [blame] zulweisen.

**apposite** ['æpəzɪt] *adj fml* treffend.

**appraisal** [ə'preɪzl] *n* Beurteilung *die.*

**appraise** [ə'preɪz] *vt fml* beurteilen.

**appreciable** [ə'priːʃəbl] *adj* [difference] merklich; [amount] beträchtlich.

**appreciably** [ə'priːʃəblɪ] *adv* [different] merklich; [larger, smaller] beträchtlich, merklich.

**appreciate** [ə'priːʃɪeɪt] *vt* - **1.** [value] schätzen; **her books were not** ~**d at the time** ihre Bücher wurden damals nicht gewürdigt - **2.** [recognize, understand] sich (D) bewusst sein (+ G) - **3.** [help, advice] dankbar sein für; **thanks, I really** ~ **it!** danke schön, sehr nett von dir/ Ihnen! *⋄ vi* FIN im Wert steigen.

**appreciation** [ə,priːʃɪ'eɪʃn] *n* - **1.** [liking] Anerkennung *die*, Würdigung *die* - **2.** [understanding] Verständnis *das* - **3.** [gratitude] Dankbarkeit *die* - **4.** FIN Wertsteigerung *die* - **5.** [assessment] Kritik *die*, Rezension *die.*

**appreciative** [ə'priːʃjətɪv] *adj* [person, audience] dankbar; **to be** ~ **of sthg** etw zu schätzen wissen.

**apprehend** [,æprɪ'hend] *vt fml* [arrest] festlnehmen.

**apprehension** [,æprɪ'henʃn] *n* [worry] Besorgnis *die.*

**apprehensive** [,æprɪ'hensɪv] *adj:* ~ **(about)** besorgt (wegen (+ G)).

**apprehensively** [,æprɪ'hensɪvlɪ] *adv* besorgt, ängstlich.

**apprentice** [ə'prentɪs] *n* Lehrling *der*, Auszubildende *der*, *die;* **an** ~ **mechanic** ein Mechanikerlehrling *⋄ vt:* **to be** ~**d to sb** bei jm in der Lehre sein.

**apprenticeship** [ə'prentɪsʃɪp] *n* Lehre *die.*

**appro.** ['æprəʊ] (*abbr of* **approval**) *n inf:* **on** ~ zur Probe.

**approach** [ə'prəʊtʃ] *n* - **1.** [arrival] (Heran)nahen *das* - **2.** [access] Zugang *der;* [road] Zufahrt *die* - **3.** [method] Ansatz *der* - **4.** [proposal]: **to make an** ~ **to sb** an jn heranltreten *⋄ vt* - **1.** [come near to] sich nähern (+ D); **temperatures** ~**ing 35°C** Temperaturen von bis zu 35°C - **2.** [speak to]: **to** ~ **sb about sthg** wegen etw (G) an jn heranltreten - **3.** [problem, task] anlgehen *⋄ vi* sich nähern.

**approachable** [ə'prəʊtʃəbl] *adj* - **1.** [person] umgänglich - **2.** [place] erreichbar.

**approaching** [ə'prəʊtʃɪŋ] *adj* sich nähernd.

**approbation** [,æprə'beɪʃn] *n fml* Zustimmung *die.*

**appropriate** [*adj* ə'prəʊprɪət, *vb* ə'prəʊprɪeɪt] *adj* angemessen; [clothing, moment] passend *⋄ vt* - **1.** LAW [steal] sich anleignen - **2.** [allocate] bestimmen.

**appropriately** [ə'prəʊprɪətlɪ] *adv* angemessen.

**appropriation** [ə,prəʊprɪ'eɪʃn] *n* - **1.** [stealing] Aneignung *die* - **2.** [allocation] Bestimmung *die.*

**approval** [ə'pruːvl] *n* - **1.** [liking, admiration] Anerkennung *die* - **2.** [official agreement] Genehmigung *die* - **3.** COMM: **on** ~ zur Probe.

**approve** [ə'pruːv] *vi:* **to** ~ **of sb** etwas von jm halten; **to** ~ **of sthg** mit etw einverstanden sein, etw gutlheißen; **I don't** ~ **of him** ich halte nichts von ihm *⋄ vt* genehmigen.

**approved** [ə'pruːvd] *adj* - **1.** [accepted] anerkannt - **2.** [authorized] staatlich anerkannt.

**approving** [ə'pruːvɪŋ] *adj* [showing satisfaction] anerkennend; [showing consent] zustimmend.

**approx.** [ə'prɒks] *abbr of* **approximately.**

**approximate** [*adj* ə'prɒksɪmət, *vb* ə'prɒksɪmeɪt] *adj* ungefähr *⋄ vi:* **to** ~ **to sthg** etw (D) in etwa entsprechen.

**approximately** [ə'prɒksɪmətlɪ] *adv* ungefähr, circa.

**approximation** [ə‚prɒksɪ'meɪʃn] *n* Annäherung *die;* **to be an ~ to the truth** in etwa der Wahrheit entsprechen.

**Apr.** *abbr of* **April.**

**APR** *n* - **1.** (*abbr of* **annualized percentage rate**) jährlicher Gebührenzinssatz - **2.** (*abbr of* **annual purchase rate**) jährlicher Gebührenzinssatz.

**après-ski** [ˈæpreɪ-ln] Après-Ski *das.*

**apricot** [ˈeɪprɪkɒt] *n* - **1.** [fruit] Aprikose *die* - **2.** [colour] Apricot *das* <> *comp* Aprikosen-.

**apricot tree** *n* Aprikosenbaum *der.*

**April** [ˈeɪprəl] *n* April *der; see also* **September.**

**April Fools' Day** *n* der erste April.

**APRIL FOOLS' DAY**

> Der 1. April wird wie im deutschsprachigen Raum auch mit Aprilscherzen begangen: an diesem Tag spielt man anderen gerne Streiche oder treibt sonst allerlei Schabernack. Aprilscherze sind allerdings nur bis zur Mittagszeit erlaubt.

**apron** [ˈeɪprən] *n* - **1.** [clothing] Schürze *die;* **to be tied to sb's ~ strings** *inf* jm am Schürzenzipfel hängen - **2.** AERON Vorfeld *das.*

**apropos** [ˈæprəpəʊ] *fml adj* [pertinent] treffend <> *prep:* **~ (of)** hinsichtlich (+ *G*).

**apt** [æpt] *adj* - **1.** [pertinent] treffend - **2.** [likely]: **to be ~ to do sthg** dazu neigen, etw zu tun.

**Apt.** (*abbr of* **apartment**) Whg.

**aptitude** [ˈæptɪtjuːd] *n* Begabung *die;* **to have an ~ for sthg** eine Begabung für etw haben.

**aptitude test** *n* Eignungstest *der.*

**aptly** [ˈæptlɪ] *adv* treffend.

**aqualung** [ˈækwəlʌŋ] *n* Presslufttauchgerät *das.*

**aquaplane** [ˈækwəpleɪn] *vi Br* AUT durch Aquaplaning ins Rutschen geraten.

**aquarium** [əˈkweərɪəm] (*pl* **-riums** OR **-ria** [-rɪə]) *n* Aquarium *das.*

**Aquarius** [əˈkweərɪəs] *n* Wassermann *der.*

**aquatic** [əˈkwætɪk] *adj* Wasser-.

**aqueduct** [ˈækwɪdʌkt] *n* Aquädukt *der* OR *das.*

**AR** *abk für Arkansas, in Postanschrift verwendet.*

**Arab** [ˈærəb] *adj* arabisch <> *n* - **1.** [person] Araber *der,* -in *die* - **2.** [horse] Araber *der.*

**Arabia** [əˈreɪbjə] *n* Arabien *nt.*

**Arabian** [əˈreɪbjən] *adj* arabisch.

**Arabic** [ˈærəbɪk] *adj* arabisch <> *n* [language] Arabisch(e) *das.*

**Arabic numeral** *n* arabische Ziffer.

**arable** [ˈærəbl] *adj:* **~ land** Ackerland *das.*

**Arab League** *n:* **the ~** die Arabische Liga.

**arbitrary** [ˈɑːbɪtrərɪ] *adj* willkürlich.

**arbitrate** [ˈɑːbɪtreɪt] *vi* als Schiedsrichter fungieren.

**arbitration** [ˌɑːbɪ'treɪʃn] *n* Schlichtungsverfahren *das;* **to go to ~** vor eine Schlichtungskommission gehen.

**arc** [ɑːk] *n* Bogen *der.*

**ARC** (*abbr of* **AIDS-related complex**) *n* ARC.

**arcade** [ɑːˈkeɪd] *n* - **1.** [for shopping] Passage *die* - **2.** ARCHIT [covered passage] Arkade *die.*

**arch** [ɑːtʃ] *adj* [knowing] schelmisch <> *n* - **1.** ARCHIT Bogen *der;* [arched entrance] Torbogen *der* - **2.** [of foot] Wölbung *die* <> *vt* [back] krümmen <> *vi* sich wölben.

**arch-** [ɑːtʃ] *prefix* [chief] Erz-; **~rival** Erzrivale *der.*

**archaeological** [ˌɑːkɪə'lɒdʒɪkl] *adj* archäologisch.

**archaeologist** [ˌɑːkɪ'ɒlədʒɪst] *n* Archäologe *der,* -in *die.*

**archaeology** [ˌɑːkɪ'ɒlədʒɪ] *n* Archäologie *die.*

**archaic** [ɑːˈkeɪɪk] *adj* [language] veraltet.

**archangel** [ˈɑːkˌeɪndʒəl] *n* Erzengel *der.*

**archbishop** [ˌɑːtʃ'bɪʃəp] *n* Erzbischof *der.*

**archduchess** [ˌɑːtʃ'dʌtʃɪs] *n* Erzherzogin *die.*

**archduke** [ˌɑːtʃ'djuːk] *n* Erzherzog *der.*

**arched** [ɑːtʃt] *adj* - **1.** [roof] gewölbt; [window] (Rund)bogen- - **2.** [eyebrows] hochgezogen; [back] gekrümmt.

**archenemy** [ˌɑːtʃ'enɪmɪ] (*pl* **-ies**) *n* Erzfeind *der,* -in *die.*

**archeology** *etc* [ˌɑːkɪ'ɒlədʒɪ] = **archaeology** *etc.*

**archer** [ˈɑːtʃər] *n* Bogenschütze *der.*

**archery** [ˈɑːtʃərɪ] *n* Bogenschießen *das.*

**archetypal** [ˌɑːkɪ'taɪpl] *adj* typisch.

**archetype** [ˈɑːkɪtaɪp] *n* [typical specimen] Prototyp *der.*

**archipelago** [ˌɑːkɪ'pelɪgəʊ] (*pl* **-es** OR **-s**) *n* Archipel *der.*

**architect** [ˈɑːkɪtekt] *n* - **1.** [of buildings] Architekt *der,* -in *die* - **2.** *fig* [of plan, event] Urheber *der,* -in *die.*

**architectural** [ˌɑːkɪ'tektʃərəl] *adj* architektonisch.

**architecture** [ˈɑːkɪtektʃər] *n* - **1.** [gen & COMPUT] Architektur *die* - **2.** [style of building] Baustil *der.*

**archive file** [ˈɑːkaɪv-] *n* COMPUT Archivdatei *die.*

**archives** [ˈɑːkaɪvz] *npl* [of documents] Archiv *das.*

**archivist** [ˈɑːkɪvɪst] *n* Archivar *der,* -in *die.*

**archway** ['ɑːtʃweɪ] *n* Torbogen *der*.

**Arctic** ['ɑːktɪk] *adj* - **1.** GEOGR arktisch - **2.** *inf* [very cold] eiskalt ⬦ *n:* **the ~** die Arktis; **in the ~** in der Arktis.

**Arctic Circle** *n:* **the ~** der nördliche Polarkreis.

**Arctic Ocean** *n:* **the ~** das Nordpolarmeer.

**ardent** ['ɑːdənt] *adj* leidenschaftlich; [desire] brennend.

**ardour** *Br*, **ardor** *Am* ['ɑːdəʳ] *n* [patriotic, revolutionary] Eifer *der;* [romantic] Leidenschaft *die*.

**arduous** ['ɑːdjʊəs] *adj* [task] mühselig; [climb, journey] anstrengend.

**are** [weak form əʳ, strong form ɑːʳ] *vb* ⬥ **be**.

**area** ['eərɪə] *n* - **1.** [region] Gegend *die;* [in town] Viertel *das;* **do you live in the ~?** wohnen Sie/ wohnst du hier in der Gegend?; **in the Bristol ~** im Raum Bristol - **2.** *fig* [approximate size, number]: **in the ~ of** im Bereich von - **3.** [surface size] Fläche *die* - **4.** [space] Bereich *der;* **a parking ~** ein Parkplatz - **5.** [of knowledge, interest, subject] Gebiet *das*.

**area code** *n Am* Vorwahl *die*.

**arena** [əˈriːnə] *n lit* & *fig* Arena *die*.

**aren't** [ɑːnt] = **are not**.

**Argentina** [ˌɑːdʒənˈtiːnə] *n* Argentinien *nt*.

**Argentine** ['ɑːdʒəntaɪn], **Argentinian** [ˌɑːdʒənˈtɪnɪən] *adj* argentinisch ⬦ *n* Argentinier *der*, -in *die*.

**arguable** ['ɑːgjʊəbl] *adj* [points, ideas, comments] fragwürdig; **it is ~ whether he will ever succeed** es ist (noch) die Frage, ob er es jemals schafft.

**arguably** ['ɑːgjʊəblɪ] *adv* möglicherweise.

**argue** ['ɑːgjuː] *vi* - **1.** [quarrel]: **to ~ (with sb about sthg)** sich (mit jm über etw *(A)*) streiten - **2.** [reason] argumentieren; **to ~ for/against sthg** für/gegen etw ein|treten ⬦ *vt:* **to ~ the case for sthg** für etw ein|treten; **to ~ that** die Meinung vertreten, dass.

**argument** ['ɑːgjʊmənt] *n* - **1.** [quarrel] Streit *der*, Auseinandersetzung *die;* **to have an ~ (with sb)** sich (mit jm) streiten - **2.** [reason] Argument *das* - **3.** (U) [reasoning] Diskussion *die*.

**argumentative** [ˌɑːgjʊˈmentətɪv] *adj* streitsüchtig.

**aria** ['ɑːrɪə] *n* Arie *die*.

**arid** ['ærɪd] *adj* trocken.

**Aries** ['eəriːz] *n* Widder *der*.

**arise** [əˈraɪz] (*pt* **arose**; *pp* **arisen** [əˈrɪzn]) *vi* [problems, difficulties] auf|treten; [opportunities] sich ergeben; **to ~ from sthg** sich aus etw ergeben; **if the need ~s** falls sich die Notwendigkeit ergibt.

**aristocracy** [ˌærɪˈstɒkrəsɪ] (*pl* **-ies**) *n* Aristokratie *die*.

**aristocrat** [*Br* 'ærɪstəkræt, *Am* əˈrɪstəkræt] *n* Aristokrat *der*, -in *die*, Adlige *der*, *die*.

**aristocratic** [*Br* ˌærɪstəˈkrætɪk, *Am* əˌrɪstəˈkrætɪk] *adj* [person, family] adlig; [manners, bearing] vornehm, kultiviert.

**arithmetic** [əˈrɪθmətɪk] *n* Arithmetik *die*, Rechnen *das;* [calculation] Rechnung *die*.

**ark** [ɑːk] *n* [ship] Arche *die*.

**arm** [ɑːm] *n* - **1.** [of person] Arm *der;* **~ in ~** Arm in Arm; **to chance one's ~** sein Glück versuchen; **to keep sb at ~'s length** *fig* jn auf Distanz halten; **do you want a drink? - oh, go on, twist my ~** möchtest du was trinken? - bevor ich mich schlagen lasse - **2.** [of garment] Ärmel *der* - **3.** [of chair] Armlehne *die* - **4.** [of organization] Zweig *der* ⬦ *vt* [with weapons] bewaffnen.

➣ **arms** *npl* [weapons] Waffen *pl;* **to take up ~s** zu den Waffen greifen; **to be up in ~s (about sthg)** (wegen etw *(G)*) aufgebracht sein.

**armadillo** [ˌɑːməˈdɪləʊ] (*pl* **-s**) *n* Gürteltier *das*.

**armaments** ['ɑːməmənts] *npl* Waffen *pl*.

**armband** ['ɑːmbænd] *n* Armbinde *die;* [for swimming] Schwimmflügel *der*.

**armchair** ['ɑːmtʃeəʳ] *n* Sessel *der*, Lehnstuhl *der*.

**armed** [ɑːmd] *adj* - **1.** [police, thieves] bewaffnet - **2.** *fig* [with information]: **~ with sthg** mit etw ausgestattet.

**armed forces** *npl* Streitkräfte *pl*.

**armed robbery** *n* bewaffneter Raubüberfall.

**Armenia** [ɑːˈmiːnjə] *n* Armenien *nt*.

**Armenian** [ɑːˈmiːnjən] *adj* armenisch ⬦ *n* - **1.** [person] Armenier *der*, -in *die* - **2.** [language] Armenisch(e) *das*.

**armhole** ['ɑːmhəʊl] *n* Armloch *das*.

**armistice** ['ɑːmɪstɪs] *n* Waffenstillstand *der*.

**armour** *Br*, **armor** *Am* ['ɑːməʳ] *n* - **1.** [for person] Rüstung *die* - **2.** [for military vehicle] Panzerung *die*.

**armoured** *Br*, **armored** *Am* ['ɑːməd] *adj* MIL gepanzert.

**armoured car** *n* MIL Panzerwagen *der*.

**armour-plated** [-pleɪtɪd] *adj* MIL gepanzert.

**armoury** *Br*, **armory** *Am* ['ɑːmərɪ] (*pl* **-ies**) *n* Arsenal *das*.

**armpit** ['ɑːmpɪt] *n* Achselhöhle *die*.

**armrest** ['ɑːmrest] *n* Armlehne *die*.

**arms control** ['ɑːmz-] *n* Rüstungskontrolle *die*.

**army** ['ɑːmɪ] (*pl* **-ies**) *n* - **1.** MIL Heer *das*, Armee *die;* **to be in the** ~ beim Militär sein - **2.** *fig* [large group] Heer *das.*

**A road** *n Br* ≃ Bundesstraße *die.*

**aroma** [əˈrəʊmə] *n* Duft *der.*

**aromatherapy** [əˌrəʊməˈθerəpɪ] *n* Aromatherapie *die.*

**aromatic** [ˌærəˈmætɪk] *adj* aromatisch.

**arose** [əˈrəʊz] *pt* ▷ arise.

**around** [əˈraʊnd] *adv* - **1.** [here and there] herum; **to travel** ~ herumlreisen; **to sit** ~ **doing nothing** untätig herumlsitzen - **2.** [on all sides] herum; **all** ~ auf allen Seiten, rundherum - **3.** [present, nearby]: **is she** ~? ist sie da?; ~ **here** [in the area] hier in der Gegend; **cars have been** ~ **for over a century** Autos gibt es schon seit über hundert Jahren - **4.** [in a circle]: **to go** ~ sich drehen; **to spin** ~ **(and** ~**)** sich im Kreis drehen - **5.** [to the other side]: **to go** ~ herumlgehen; **to turn** ~ sich umldrehen; **to look** ~ sich umlsehen - **6.** *phr:* **to have been** ~ *inf* [travelled a lot] (viel) herumgekommen sein ▷ *prep* - **1.** [surrounding] um … herum; **the country** ~ **the town** das Land rund um die Stadt *OR* um die Stadt herum - **2.** [near]: ~ **here/there** hier/dort in der Nähe; **is there a bank anywhere** ~ **here?** gibt es hier irgendwo eine Bank? - **3.** [all over]: **150 offices** ~ **the world** 150 Büros in der ganzen Welt; **all** ~ **the country** im ganzen Land; **we walked** ~ **the town** wir spazierten durch die Stadt - **4.** [in a circle]: **we walked** ~ **the lake** wir gingen um den See herum; **to go/drive** ~ **sthg** um etw herumlgehen/herumlfahren; ~ **the clock** *fig* rund um die Uhr - **5.** [approximately] ungefähr - **6.** [in circumference]: **she measures 30 inches** ~ **the waist** um die Taille misst sie 75 cm - **7.** [so as to avoid] um … herum; **to get** ~ **an obstacle** um ein Hindernis herumlgehen; **to find a way** ~ **a problem** einen Ausweg für ein Problem finden.

**arousal** [əˈraʊzl] *n* [of feelings] Erregung *die;* [of interest, suspicion] Erweckung *die.*

**arouse** [əˈraʊz] *vt* - **1.** [excite] erregen; [interest, suspicion] erwecken - **2.** [wake] (auf)wecken.

**arrange** [əˈreɪndʒ] *vt* - **1.** [flowers] arrangieren; [books, objects] (an)ordnen; [furniture] (um)l-stellen - **2.** [event] planen; [meeting] vereinbaren; [party] arrangieren; **to** ~ **to do sthg** vereinbaren, etw zu tun; **to** ~ **for sb to do sthg** dafür sorgen *OR* veranlassen, dass jd etw tut; **to** ~ **a hotel for sb** für jn ein Hotel buchen; **to** ~ **a taxi for sb** für jn ein Taxi bestellen - **3.** *MUS* bearbeiten, arrangieren.

**arranged marriage** [əˈreɪndʒd-] *n* arrangierte Heirat.

**arrangement** [əˈreɪndʒmənt] *n* - **1.** [agreement] Vereinbarung *die;* **to come to an** ~ eine Einigung erzielen - **2.** [of objects] Anordnung *die;*

**flower** ~ Blumenarrangement *das* - **3.** *MUS* Bearbeitung *die,* Arrangement *das.*

⬥ **arrangements** *npl* [preparations] Vorbereitungen *pl;* **to make** ~**s** Vorbereitungen treffen; **please make your own** ~**s for accommodation** bitte arrangieren Sie Ihre Unterkunft selbst.

**array** [əˈreɪ] *n* - **1.** [of objects, people, ornaments] Aufgebot *das* - **2.** *COMPUT* (Daten)feld *das,* Array *das* ▷ *vt* [ornaments] auf lstellen.

**arrears** [əˈrɪəz] *npl* [money owed] Rückstände *pl;* **to be paid in** ~ rückwirkend bezahlt werden; **to be in** ~ im Rückstand sein.

**arrest** [əˈrest] *n* [by police] Verhaftung *die,* Festnahme *die;* **to be under** ~ verhaftet *OR* festgenommen sein ▷ *vt* - **1.** [subj: police] verhaften, festlnehmen - **2.** *fml* [sb's attention] erregen - **3.** *fml* [stop - development] hemmen; [ - spread of disease] auf lhalten.

**arresting** [əˈrestɪŋ] *adj* [striking] faszinierend.

**arrival** [əˈraɪvl] *n* - **1.** [at place] Ankunft *die;* **on** ~ bei der Ankunft; **late** ~ [of train, bus, mail] verspätete Ankunft - **2.** [of new system, technology] Aufkommen *das* - **3.** [person] Ankömmling *der;* **new** ~ [person] Neuankömmling *der;* **we're expecting a new** ~ [baby] wir erwarten Familienzuwachs.

**arrive** [əˈraɪv] *vi* - **1.** [gen] anlkommen; **to** ~ **at a conclusion/decision** zu einem Schluss/einer Entscheidung kommen - **2.** [moment, event] kommen.

**arrogance** [ˈærəgəns] *n* Arroganz *die,* Überheblichkeit *die.*

**arrogant** [ˈærəgənt] *adj* arrogant, überheblich.

**arrogantly** [ˈærəgəntlɪ] *adv* arrogant, überheblich.

**arrow** [ˈærəʊ] *n* Pfeil *der.*

**arse** *Br* [ɑːs], **ass** *Am* [æs] *n vulg* [buttocks] Arsch *der.*

**arsenal** [ˈɑːsənl] *n* Arsenal *das.*

**arsenic** [ˈɑːsnɪk] *n* Arsen *das.*

**arson** [ˈɑːsn] *n* Brandstiftung *die.*

**arsonist** [ˈɑːsənɪst] *n* Brandstifter *der,* -in *die.*

**art** [ɑːt] *n* Kunst *die* ▷ *comp* Kunst-.

⬥ **arts** *npl* - **1.** *SCH & UNIV* [humanities] Geisteswissenschaften *pl* - **2.** [fine arts]: **the** ~**s** die schönen Künste *pl* ▷ *comp SCH & UNIV* [subject] geisteswissenschaftlich; ~**s graduates** (Hochschul)absolventen *pl* der Geisteswissenschaften.

⬥ **arts and crafts** *n* Kunsthandwerk *das.*

**art deco** [-ˈdekəʊ] *n* Art deco *die.*

**artefact** [ˈɑːtɪfækt] *n* = artifact.

**arterial** [ɑːˈtɪərɪəl] *adj* - **1.** [blood] arteriell - **2.** [road]: ~ **road** Hauptverkehrsstraße *die.*

**arteriosclerosis** [ɑːˌtɪərɪəʊskliə'rəʊsɪs] n Arteriosklerose die.

**artery** ['ɑːtərɪ] (pl -ies) n Arterie die.

**artful** ['ɑːtfʊl] adj raffiniert.

**art gallery** n Kunstgalerie die.

**arthritic** [ɑː'θrɪtɪk] adj arthritisch.

**arthritis** [ɑː'θraɪtɪs] n Arthritis die.

**artic** [ɑː'tɪk] n Br inf Sattelschlepper der.

**artichoke** ['ɑːtɪtʃəʊk] n Artischocke die.

**article** ['ɑːtɪkl] n - 1. [item] Gegenstand der; comm Ware die, Artikel der; ~ of clothing Kleidungsstück das - 2. [in newspaper, magazine] Artikel der - 3. [in agreement, contract] Paragraph der; [in constitution] Artikel der - 4. gramm Artikel der.

**articled clerk** ['ɑːtɪkld-] n Br Rechtsreferendar der, -in die.

**articles of association** ['ɑːtɪklz-] npl Gesellschaftsvertrag der.

**articulate** [adj ɑː'tɪkjʊlət, vb ɑː'tɪkjʊleɪt] adj [speech] leichtverständlich; to be ~ [person] sich gut ausdrücken können <> vt [thought, wish] zum Ausdruck bringen, artikulieren.

**articulated lorry** [ɑː'tɪkjʊleɪtɪd-] n Br Sattelschlepper der

**articulation** [ɑːˌtɪkjʊ'leɪʃn] n - 1. [of sound] Artikulation die - 2. [of thought, wish] Ausdruck der, Artikulation die.

**artifact** ['ɑːtɪfækt] n Artefakt das.

**artifice** ['ɑːtɪfɪs] n List die.

**artificial** [ˌɑːtɪ'fɪʃl] adj - 1. [non-natural] künstlich - 2. [insincere] gekünstelt.

**artificial insemination** n künstliche Befruchtung.

**artificial intelligence** n künstliche Intelligenz.

**artificially** [ˌɑːtɪ'fɪʃəlɪ] adv - 1. [non-naturally] künstlich - 2. [insincerely] gekünstelt.

**artificial respiration** n künstliche Beatmung.

**artillery** [ɑː'tɪlərɪ] n Artillerie die.

**artisan** [ˌɑːtɪ'zæn] n Handwerker der, -in die.

**artist** ['ɑːtɪst] n Künstler der, -in die.

**artistic** [ɑː'tɪstɪk] adj - 1. [gen] künstlerisch; [person] künstlerisch begabt - 2. [attractive] kunstvoll.

**artistically** [ɑː'tɪstɪklɪ] adv - 1. [inclined, gifted] künstlerisch - 2. [arranged] kunstvoll.

**artistry** ['ɑːtɪstrɪ] n Kunstwertigkeit die.

**artless** ['ɑːtlɪs] adj unschuldig, arglos.

**art nouveau** [ˌɑːnuː'vəʊ] n Jugendstil der.

**as** [unstressed əz, stressed æz] conj - 1. [referring to time] als; ~ the plane was coming in to land als das Flugzeug beim Landeanflug war; he became more patient ~ he grew older mit zunehmendem Alter wurde er geduldiger - 2. [referring to manner] wie; ~ expected ... wie erwartet ...; do ~ I say tu, was ich dir sage; ~ it is ohnehin, sowieso; it's hard enough ~ it is es ist ohnehin schon schwierig genug; ~ it turns out wie sich herausstellt; ~ things stand so, wie die Dinge liegen; be that ~ it may wie dem auch sei - 3. [introducing a statement] wie; ~ I told you ... wie ich dir bereits gesagt habe ...; ~ you know, ... wie du weißt, ... - 4. [because] weil, da <> adv (in comparisons): ~ ... ~ so ... wie; he's ~ tall ~ I am er ist so groß wie ich; ~ many ~ so viele wie; ~ much ~ so viel wie <> prep als; she works ~ a nurse sie arbeitet als Krankenschwester; to consider sb ~ a friend jn als Freund betrachten; she treats it ~ a game sie betrachtet das Ganze als (ein) Spiel.

➤ **as it were** adv sozusagen.

➤ **as for** prep: ~ for me was mich betrifft.

➤ **as from, as of** prep ab; ~ from OR of Monday ab Montag.

➤ **as if, as though** conj als ob, als wenn; he looked at me ~ if I were mad er sah mich an, als ob ich verrückt wäre; ~ if by chance wie durch Zufall.

➤ **as to** prep Br: she questioned him ~ to his motives sie fragte ihn nach seinen Beweggründen.

**AS** n (abbr of Associate in Science) von einer US-Universität verliehener naturwissenschaftlicher Grad oder dessen Inhaber <> abk für American Samoa, in Postanschrift verwendet.

**ASA** (abbr of American Standards Association) n ASA.

**a.s.a.p.** (abbr of as soon as possible) baldmöglichst.

**asbestos** [æs'bestəs] n Asbest der.

**asbestosis** [ˌæsbes'təʊsɪs] n Asbestose die.

**ascend** [ə'send] vt [hill] besteigen; [staircase] hinauf lgehen; [ladder] hinauf lsteigen; to ~ the throne den Thron besteigen <> vi [climb] auf lsteigen; [subj: path, road etc] anlsteigen.

**ascendancy** [ə'sendənsɪ] n Vorherrschaft die.

**ascendant** [ə'sendənt] n: to be in the ~ im Aufstieg begriffen sein.

**ascendency** [ə'sendənsɪ] n = ascendancy.

**ascending** [ə'sendɪŋ] adj [increasing] zunehmend; in ~ order in aufsteigender Reihenfolge.

**ascension** [ə'senʃn] n [to throne] Thronbesteigung die.

➤ **Ascension** n relig Christi Himmelfahrt die.

**ascent** [ə'sent] n - 1. [gen] Aufstieg der - 2. [upward slope] Steigung die.

**ascertain** [ˌæsə'teɪn] *vt* ermitteln.

**ascetic** [ə'setɪk] *adj* asketisch.

**ASCII** ['æskɪ] (*abbr of* **American Standard Code for Information Interchange**) *n* ASCII *das*.

**ascorbic acid** [ə'skɔːbɪk-] *n* Askorbinsäure *die*.

**ascribe** [ə'skraɪb] *vt:* **to ~ sthg to sthg** einer Sache *(D)* etw zuschreiben; **to ~ sthg to sb** jm etw zuschreiben.

**ASE** (*abbr of* **American Stock Exchange**) *n* Börse *in New York*.

**aseptic** [ˌeɪ'septɪk] *adj* aseptisch, keimfrei.

**asexual** [ˌeɪ'sekʃʊəl] *adj* BIOL ungeschlechtlich.

**ash** [æʃ] *n* **- 1.** [from cigarette, fire] Asche *die* **- 2.** [tree] Esche *die*.

➤ **ashes** *npl* [from cremation] Asche *die*.

**ASH** [æʃ] (*abbr of* **Action on Smoking and Health**) *n britische Anti-Raucherbewegung*.

**ashamed** [ə'ʃeɪmd] *adj* beschämt; **to be ~ of sb/sthg** sich js/einer Sache *(G)* schämen, sich für jn/etw schämen; **to be ~ to do sthg** sich schämen, etw zu tun.

**ash can** *n Am* Mülleimer *der*.

**ashen-faced** ['æʃn̩ˌfeɪst] *adj* kreidebleich.

**ashore** [ə'ʃɔːʳ] *adv* [go, swim] an Land.

**ashtray** ['æʃtreɪ] *n* Aschenbecher *der*.

**Ash Wednesday** *n* Aschermittwoch *der*.

**Asia** [*Br* 'eɪʃə, *Am* 'eɪʒəl *n* Asien *nt*.

**Asia Minor** *n* Kleinasien *nt*.

**Asian** [*Br* 'eɪʃn, *Am* 'eɪʒn] *adj* asiatisch; **the ~ community** *Br aus Indien, Pakistan und Bangladesh stammende Bevölkerungsgruppe* <> *n* [from Far East] Asiat *der*, -in *die*.

**Asiatic** [ˌeɪʒɪ'ætɪk] *adj* asiatisch.

**aside** [ə'saɪd] *adv* **- 1.** [to one side] beiseite, zur Seite; **step ~!** treten Sie zur Seite!; **to take sb ~** jn beiseite nehmen; **to brush** OR **sweep sthg ~** etw vom Tisch wischen **- 2.** [apart]: **joking ~,** ... Spaß beiseite, ...; **~ from** abgesehen von <> *n* **- 1.** [in play] Apart *das*, Beiseitesprechen *das* **- 2.** [remark] beiläufige Bemerkung.

**ask** [ɑːsk] *vt* **- 1.** [gen] fragen; **to ~ a question** eine Frage stellen; **to ~ sb sthg** jn etw fragen; **if you ~ me** ... wenn du mich fragst, ... **- 2.** [request - permission, forgiveness] bitten um; **to ~ sb for sthg** jn um etw bitten; **to ~ sb for advice** jn um Rat fragen; **to ~ sb to do sthg** jn (darum) bitten, etw zu tun **- 3.** [invite] einladen; **to ~ sb (round) to dinner** jn zum Abendessen einladen **- 4.** [price] verlangen <> *vi* **- 1.** [enquire] fragen **- 2.** [request] bitten.

➤ **ask after** *vt fus* sich erkundigen nach.

➤ **ask for** *vt fus* **- 1.** [ask to talk to] verlangen; **he's ~ing for you** er will Sie sprechen **- 2.** [request] bitten um.

**askance** [ə'skæns] *adv:* **to look ~ at sb** jn mißbilligend an|schauen; **to look ~ at sthg** einer Sache *(D)* ablehnend gegenüber|stehen.

**askew** [ə'skjuː] *adj* schief.

**asking price** ['ɑːskɪŋ-] *n* Verkaufspreis *der*.

**asleep** [ə'sliːp] *adj* schlafend; **to fall ~** ein|schlafen; **to be fast** OR **sound ~** fest schlafen.

**ASM** (*abbr of* **air-to-surface missile**) *n* Luft/Boden-Rakete *die*.

**asparagus** [ə'spærəgəs] *n* Spargel *der*.

**aspect** ['æspekt] *n* **- 1.** [facet] Aspekt *der* **- 2.** [appearance] Aussehen *das* **- 3.** [of building] Lage *die*.

**aspen** ['æspən] *n* Espe *die*.

**aspersions** [ə'spɜːʃnz] *npl:* **to cast ~ (on sthg)** abfällige Bemerkungen (über etw *(A)*) machen.

**asphalt** ['æsfælt] *n (U)* Asphalt *der*.

**asphyxiate** [əs'fɪksɪeɪt] *vt* ersticken.

**aspic** ['æspɪk] *n* Aspik *der* OR *das*.

**aspidistra** [ˌæspɪ'dɪstrə] *n* Aspidistra *die*.

**aspirate** ['æspərət] *adj* LING aspiriert.

**aspiration** [ˌæspə'reɪʃn] *n* **- 1.** [desire, ambition] Bestrebung *die* **- 2.** LING Aspiration *die*, Behauchung *die*.

**aspire** [ə'spaɪəʳ] *vi:* **to ~ to sthg** nach etw streben; **to ~ to do sthg** danach streben, etw zu tun.

**aspirin** ['æsprɪn] *n* Aspirin® *das*.

**aspiring** [ə'spaɪərɪŋ] *adj* aufstrebend.

**ass** [æs] *n* **- 1.** Esel *der* **- 2.** *Am vulg* = **arse**.

**assail** [ə'seɪl] *vt* **- 1.** [attack physically] an|greifen **- 2.** *fig* [beset]: **to ~ sb with questions/insults** jn mit Fragen/Beleidigungen überschütten; **to be ~ed by worries/doubts** von Sorgen/Zweifeln geplagt werden.

**assailant** [ə'seɪlənt] *n* Angreifer *der*, -in *die*.

**assassin** [ə'sæsɪn] *n* Attentäter *der*, -in *die* (*dessen Mordanschlag glückt*).

**assassinate** [ə'sæsɪneɪt] *vt* ermorden; **to be ~d** einem Attentat OR Mordanschlag zum Opfer fallen.

**assassination** [əˌsæsɪ'neɪʃn] *n* (geglücktes) Attentat, (politischer) Mord.

**assault** [ə'sɔːlt] *n* **- 1.** MIL: **~ (on sthg)** Sturmangriff *der* (auf etw *(A)*) **- 2.** [physical attack]: **~ (on sb)** (tätlicher) Angriff (auf jn); **~ and battery** LAW Körperverletzung *die* <> *vt* [attack - physically] (tätlich) an|greifen; [- sexually] belästigen.

**assault course** *n* Übungsgelände *das*.

**assemble** [ə'sembl] *vt* **- 1.** [gather - people] zusammen|rufen; [ - evidence, material] zusammen|tragen; [ - Parliament] einberufen **- 2.** [fit together] zusammenlbauen ◇ vi [people] sich versammeln; [Parliament] zusammenltreten.

**assembler language** n = assembly language.

**assembly** [ə'semblɪ] (pl -ies) n - **1.** [gen] Versammlung die; [at school] Morgenandacht die - **2.** (U) [fitting together] Zusammenbau der; [of device, machine] Montage die.

**assembly language** n COMPUT Assemblersprache die.

**assembly line** n Fließband das.

**assent** [ə'sent] n Zustimmung die ◇ vi zustimmen; **to ~ to sthg** etw (D) zustimmen.

**assert** [ə'sɜːt] vt - **1.** [conviction, belief] behaupten; [innocence] beteuern - **2.** [authority] geltend machen; **to ~ o.s.** sich behaupten.

**assertion** [ə'sɜːʃn] n Behauptung die.

**assertive** [ə'sɜːtɪv] adj [person, tone] energisch; [attitude] selbstbewusst.

**assess** [ə'ses] vt - **1.** [judge] einlschätzen, beurteilen - **2.** [estimate - value] schätzen; [ - damages] festlsetzen.

**assessment** [ə'sesmənt] n - **1.** [judgement] Einschätzung die, Beurteilung die - **2.** [estimate - of value] Schätzung die; [ - of damages] Festsetzung die.

**assessor** [ə'sesə'] n FIN Sachverständiger (meist Finanzbeamter), der z. B. Vermögenswerte, Einkommen oder Steuern berechnet.

**asset** ['æset] n - **1.** [valuable quality] Vorteil der - **2.** [valuable person] Stütze die; **the new secretary is an ~ to the company** die neue Sekretärin ist ein Gewinn für die Firma.
➤ **assets** npl COMM Vermögen das.

**asset-stripping** [-ˌstrɪpɪŋ] n Aufkauf einer Firma zu einem niedrigen Preis, um die einzelnen Vermögenswerte gewinnbringend zu verkaufen und die Firma dann zu schließen.

**assiduous** [ə'sɪdjʊəs] adj gewissenhaft.

**assiduously** [ə'sɪdjʊəslɪ] adv gewissenhaft.

**assign** [ə'saɪn] vt - **1.** [allot]: **to ~ sthg (to sb/sthg)** (jm/etw) etw zulteilen OR zulweisen - **2.** [appoint]: **to ~ sb (to sthg)** jn (einer Sache (D)) zulteilen OR zulweisen; **to ~ sb to do sthg** jn damit beauftragen, etw zu tun.

**assignation** [ˌæsɪg'neɪʃn] n fml geheimes Treffen; [between lovers] Stelldichein das.

**assignment** [ə'saɪnmənt] n - **1.** [task] Aufgabe die; [at school] Projekt das; [job] Auftrag der - **2.** [act of appointing] Zuteilung die; [to task] Betrauung die; [to post] Berufung die.

**assimilate** [ə'sɪmɪleɪt] vt - **1.** [gen] auflnehmen - **2.** [people]: **to ~ sb (into sthg)** jn (in etw (A)) integrieren.

**assimilation** [əˌsɪmɪ'leɪʃn] n - **1.** [gen] Aufnahme die - **2.** [of people] Integration die.

**assist** [ə'sɪst] vt helfen (+ D); **to ~ sb with sthg** jm bei etw helfen; **to ~ sb in doing sthg** jm helfen, etw zu tun.

**assistance** [ə'sɪstəns] n (U) Hilfe die; **to be of ~ (to sb)** (jm) helfen OR behilflich sein.

**assistant** [ə'sɪstənt] n - **1.** [helper] Assistent der, -in die - **2.** [in shop] Verkäufer der, -in die ◇ comp stellvertretend; **~ editor** Redaktionsassistent der, -in die.

**associate** [adj & n ə'səʊʃɪət, vb ə'səʊʃɪeɪt] adj [member] außerordentlich ◇ n [business partner] Partner der, -in die ◇ vt [connect] in Verbindung bringen, assoziieren; **to ~ sb with sb/sthg** jn mit jm/etw in Verbindung bringen; **to ~ sthg with sb/sthg** etw mit jm/etw in Verbindung bringen OR assoziieren; **to be ~d with sb/sthg** mit jm/etw in Verbindung gebracht werden ◇ vi: **to ~ with sb** mit jm verkehren.

**association** [əˌsəʊsɪ'eɪʃn] n - **1.** [organization] Verband der, Vereinigung die - **2.** (U) [relationship] Verkehr der, Umgang der; **in ~ with sb/sthg** in Zusammenarbeit mit jm/etw - **3.** [of ideas] Assoziation die.

**assonance** ['æsənəns] n Assonanz die.

**assorted** [ə'sɔːtɪd] adj [colours, sizes] verschieden; [sweets] gemischt.

**assortment** [ə'sɔːtmənt] n [mixture - of people] Mischung die; [ - of goods] Auswahl die, Sortiment das.

**Asst.** abbr of **assistant.**

**assuage** [ə'sweɪdʒ] vt fml [grief] lindern; [thirst, hunger] stillen.

**assume** [ə'sjuːm] vt - **1.** [suppose, adopt] anlnehmen - **2.** [undertake] übernehmen.

**assumed name** [ə'sjuːmd-] n falscher Name.

**assuming** [ə'sjuːmɪŋ] conj: **~ (that)** vorausgesetzt(, dass).

**assumption** [ə'sʌmpʃn] n - **1.** [supposition] Annahme die - **2.** (U) [of power] Übernahme die.
➤ **Assumption** n RELIG: **the Assumption** Mariä Himmelfahrt die.

**assurance** [ə'ʃʊərəns] n - **1.** [promise] Zusicherung die, Versicherung die - **2.** [confidence] Selbstsicherheit die - **3.** (U) FIN [insurance] Versicherung die.

**assure** [ə'ʃʊə'] vt [reassure] versichern (+ D); **to ~ sb of sthg** jn einer Sache (G) versichern; **to be ~d of sthg** [be certain] sich (D) einer Sache (G) sicher sein; **I ~ you that it will be ready tomorrow** ich versichere Ihnen, dass es morgen fertig ist.

**assured** [ə'ʃʊəd] adj selbstsicher.

**AST** (abbr of **Atlantic Standard Time**) n Standardzeit in der östlichen Zeitzone der USA.

**asterisk** ['æstərɪsk] n Sternchen das.

**astern** [ə'stɜːn] adv NAUT achtern; [towards the rear] achteraus.

**asteroid** ['æstərɔɪd] n Asteroid der.

**asthma** ['æsmə] n Asthma das.

**asthmatic** [æs'mætɪk] adj asthmatisch ◇ n Asthmatiker der, -in die.

**astigmatism** [eɪ'stɪgmətɪzm] n Astigmatismus der.

**astonish** [ə'stɒnɪʃ] vt erstaunen.

**astonished** [ə'stɒnɪʃd] adj erstaunt.

**astonishing** [ə'stɒnɪʃɪŋ] adj erstaunlich.

**astonishment** [ə'stɒnɪʃmənt] n Erstaunen das.

**astound** [ə'staʊnd] vt verblüffen.

**astounded** [ə'staʊndɪd] adj verblüfft.

**astounding** [ə'staʊndɪŋ] adj verblüffend.

**astrakhan** ['æstrəkɑːn] n Astrachan der.

**astray** [ə'streɪ] adv: **to go ~** [object] verloren gehen; [animal] sich verirren; **to lead sb ~** fig jn vom rechten Weg abbringen.

**astride** [ə'straɪd] adv rittlings ◇ prep rittlings auf (+ D).

**astringent** [ə'strɪndʒənt] adj - **1.** [lotion] adstringierend - **2.** [criticism] beißend ◇ n Adstringens das.

**astrologer** [ə'strɒlədʒəʳ] n Astrologe der, -gin die.

**astrological** [ˌæstrə'lɒdʒɪkl] adj astrologisch.

**astrologist** [ə'strɒlədʒɪst] n = **astrologer.**

**astrology** [ə'strɒlədʒɪ] n Astrologie die.

**astronaut** ['æstrənɔːt] n Astronaut der, -in die.

**astronomer** [ə'strɒnəməʳ] n Astronom der, -in die.

**astronomical** [ˌæstrə'nɒmɪkl] adj lit & fig astronomisch.

**astronomy** [ə'strɒnəmɪ] n Astronomie die.

**astrophysics** [ˌæstrəʊ'fɪzɪks] n Astrophysik die.

**astute** [ə'stjuːt] adj clever.

**asunder** [ə'sʌndəʳ] adv literary: **to tear ~** auseinander reißen.

**asylum** [ə'saɪləm] n - **1.** dated [mental hospital] psychiatrische Anstalt - **2.** (U) [protection] Asyl das.

**asymmetrical** [ˌeɪsɪ'metrɪkl] adj asymmetrisch.

**at** [unstressed ət, stressed æt] prep - **1.** [indicating place, position]: **there was a knock ~ the door** es klopfte an der Tür; **he studies ~ Cambridge** er studiert in Cambridge; **~ the bottom of the hill** am Fuß(e) des Hügels; **~ my father's** bei meinem Vater; **~ home** zu Hause; **~ school** in der Schule; **~ work** bei der Arbeit - **2.** [in-

dicating direction]: **to aim ~ sb/sthg** auf jn/etw zielen; **to smile ~ sb** jn anllächeln; **to look ~ sb/sthg** jn/etw anlsehen - **3.** [indicating a particular time]: **~ midnight/noon/eleven o'clock** um Mitternacht/zwölf Uhr mittags/elf Uhr; **~ Christmas/Easter** zu OR an Weihnachten/ Ostern; **~ night** bei Nacht, nachts - **4.** [indicating age, speed, rate]: **~ your age** in deinem Alter; **~ 52 (years of age)** mit 52 (Jahren); **~ 100 miles per hour** mit 100 Meilen pro Stunde; **~ high speed** mit hoher Geschwindigkeit - **5.** [indicating price]: **~ £50 (a pair)** für 50 Pfund (das Paar) - **6.** [indicating particular state, condition]: **~ peace/war** im Frieden/Krieg; **~ lunch** beim Mittagessen - **7.** [indicating tentativeness, noncompletion]: **to pull ~ sthg** an etw (D) ziehen; **to snatch ~ sthg** nach etw greifen; **to nibble ~ sthg** an etw (D) knabbern - **8.** (after adjectives): **amused/appalled/puzzled ~ sthg** über etw (A) belustigt/entsetzt/verblüfft; **to be bad/good ~ sthg** in etw (D) schlecht/gut sein.

➝ **at all** adv - **1.** (with negative): **not ~ all** [when thanked] keine Ursache; [when answering a question] überhaupt nicht; **she's not ~ all happy** sie ist überhaupt nicht glücklich - **2.** [in the slightest]: **have you done anything ~ all today?** hast du heute überhaupt irgendetwas gemacht?; **do you know her ~ all?** kennst du sie überhaupt?

**ATC** (abbr of **Air Training Corps**) n Trainingseinheit der britischen Luftwaffe.

**ate** [Br et, Am eɪt] pt ➣ **eat.**

**atheism** ['eɪθɪɪzm] n Atheismus der.

**atheist** ['eɪθɪɪst] n Atheist der, -in die.

**Athenian** [ə'θiːnjən] adj athenisch ◇ n Athener der, -in die.

**Athens** ['æθɪnz] n Athen nt.

**athlete** ['æθliːt] n Leichtathlet der, -in die; **to be a good ~** [sporty] (sehr) sportlich sein.

**athlete's foot** n Fußpilz der.

**athletic** [æθ'letɪk] adj - **1.** [relating to athletics] athletisch - **2.** [sporty] sportlich.

➝ **athletics** npl Leichtathletik die.

**Atlantic** [ət'læntɪk] adj atlantisch ◇ n: **the ~ (Ocean)** der Atlantik, der Atlantische Ozean.

**Atlantis** [ət'læntɪs] n Atlantis nt.

**atlas** ['ætləs] n Atlas der.

**Atlas** ['ætləs] n: **the ~ Mountains** das Atlas-Gebirge, der Atlas.

**ATM** (abbr of **automatic teller machine**) n Geldautomat der.

**atmosphere** ['ætməˌsfɪəʳ] n - **1.** [gen] Atmosphäre die - **2.** [in room] Luft die.

**atmospheric** [ˌætməs'ferɪk] adj - **1.** [pressure, pollution] atmosphärisch - **2.** [music, place, film] stimmungsvoll.

**atoll** ['ætɒl] n Atoll das.

**atom** ['ætəm] n - **1.** TECH Atom das - **2.** *fig* [tiny amount]: **an ~ of truth** ein Körnchen Wahrheit; **he hasn't an ~ of sense** er hat keinen Funken Verstand.

**atom bomb** n Atombombe die.

**atomic** [ə'tɒmɪk] adj Atom-.

**atomic bomb** n = atom bomb.

**atomic energy** n Atomenergie die, Kernenergie die.

**atomic number** n PHYS Ordnungszahl die.

**atomizer, -iser** ['ætəmaɪzəʳ] n Zerstäuber der.

**atone** [ə'təʊn] vi: **to ~ for sthg** [crime, sin] (für) etw büßen; [mistake, behaviour] etw wieder gutlmachen.

**atonement** [ə'təʊnmənt] n [for crime, sin] Buße die; [for mistake, behaviour] Wiedergutmachung die.

**A to Z** n Stadtplan der (im Buchformat).

**ATP** (abbr of Association of Tennis Professionals) n internationaler Tennisverband.

**atrocious** [ə'trəʊʃəs] adj grauenhaft.

**atrocity** [ə'trɒsətɪ] (pl **-ies**) n Greueltat die.

**attach** [ə'tætʃ] vt - **1.** [fasten] befestigen; [document] beilheften; **to ~ sthg to sthg** etw an einer Sache (D) befestigen; [document] etw (D) etw beilheften - **2.** [attribute]: **to ~ sthg to sthg** [importance] einer Sache (D) etw beimessen; [blame] einer Sache (D) etw zulschreiben - **3.** COMPUT anlheften, anlhängen.

**attaché** [ə'tæʃeɪ] n Attaché der.

**attaché case** n Aktenkoffer der.

**attached** [ə'tætʃt] adj - **1.** [fastened]: **~ (to sthg)** (an etw (D)) befestigt; [document] (etw (D)) beigeheftet - **2.** [assigned]: **to be ~ to sthg** etw (D) zugeteilt sein - **3.** [fond]: **to be ~ to sb/sthg** an jm/etw hängen.

**attachment** [ə'tætʃmənt] n - **1.** [device] Zusatzgerät das - **2.** [fondness]: **~ (to sb/sthg)** Anhänglichkeit die (an jn/etw) - **3.** COMPUT Attachment das, Anhang der.

**attack** [ə'tæk] n - **1.** [physical]: **~ (on sb)** [on person] Überfall der (auf jn); [on enemy] Angriff der (auf jn) - **2.** [verbal]: **~ (on sthg)** Angriff der (auf etw (A)) - **3.** [of illness] Anfall der ◇ vt - **1.** [physically - person] überfallen; [ - enemy] anlgreifen - **2.** [verbally] anlgreifen - **3.** [affect] befallen - **4.** [deal with] in Angriff nehmen ◇ vi anlgreifen.

**attacker** [ə'tækəʳ] n Angreifer der, -in die.

**attain** [ə'teɪn] vt [rank, objectives] erreichen; [success, happiness] erlangen.

**attainment** [ə'teɪnmənt] n - **1.** [of rank, objectives] Erreichen das; [of success, happiness] Erlangen das - **2.** [skill] Fertigkeit die.

**attempt** [ə'tempt] n Versuch der; **an ~ at a smile** ein Versuch zu lächeln; **to make an ~ on sb's life** einen Mordanschlag auf jn verüben ◇ vt [try] versuchen; **to ~ to do sthg** versuchen, etw zu tun.

**attend** [ə'tend] vt - **1.** [meeting] teillnehmen an; [party] gehen zu - **2.** [school, church] besuchen ◇ vi - **1.** [be present] anwesend sein - **2.** [pay attention]: **to ~ (to sthg)** auf lpassen (bei etw).
◆ **attend to** vt fus - **1.** [deal with] sich kümmern um - **2.** [look after - customer] bedienen; [ - patient] behandeln.

**attendance** [ə'tendəns] n - **1.** [number present - at meeting] Teilnehmerzahl die; [ - at concert, cinema] Besucherzahl die - **2.** [presence] Anwesenheit die, Teilnahme die; **to have a poor ~ record** oft fehlen.

**attendant** [ə'tendənt] adj [accompanying] damit verbunden; **~ on sthg** mit etw verbunden ◇ n [at museum] Aufseher der, -in die; [at petrol station] Tankwart der; **car park ~** Parkplatzwächter der, -in die.

**attention** [ə'tenʃn] n (U) - **1.** [awareness, interest] Aufmerksamkeit die; **to attract sb's ~** jn auf sich (A) aufmerksam machen; **js Aufmerksamkeit erregen**; **to bring sthg to sb's ~**, **to draw sb's ~ to sthg** jn auf etw (A) aufmerksam machen; **to pay ~ to sb/sthg** jm/einer Sache Aufmerksamkeit schenken; **to pay ~ auf**lpassen - **2.** [care] Fürsorge die - **3.** COMM: **for the ~ of** zu Händen (von) - **4.** MIL: **to stand to ~** stilllstehen ◇ excl MIL stillgestanden!

**attentive** [ə'tentɪv] adj aufmerksam.

**attentively** [ə'tentɪvlɪ] adv aufmerksam.

**attenuate** [ə'tenjʊeɪt] fml vt [make thin] dünn machen; [risk] reduzieren; [weaken] ablschwächen; **attenuating circumstances** LAW mildernde Umstände ◇ vi schwächer werden.

**attest** [ə'test] vt [affirm] bestätigen; [signature, will] beglaubigen ◇ vi: **to ~ to sthg** etw beweisen.

**attic** ['ætɪk] n Dachboden der.

**attire** [ə'taɪəʳ] n (U) fml Kleidung die.

**attitude** ['ætɪtjuːd] n - **1.** [way of thinking]: **~ (to OR towards sb/sthg)** Einstellung die (gegenüber jm/zu etw) - **2.** [behaviour, posture] Haltung die.

**attn** (abbr of for the attention of) z. Hd.

**attorney** [ə'tɜːnɪ] n Am [lawyer] (Rechts)anwalt der, -wältin die.

**attorney general** (pl attorneys general) n ≈ Generalbundesanwalt der, -wältin die.

**attract** [ə'trækt] vt - **1.** [draw, cause to come near] anlziehen, anllocken - **2.** [be attractive to] anziehend wirken auf (+ A); **to be ~ed to sb** jn anziehend finden; **to be ~ed to sthg** etw mögen - **3.** [support] gewinnen; [criticism] auf sich (A) ziehen - **4.** [magnetically] anlziehen.

**attraction** [ə'trækʃn] n - **1.** [liking] Anziehungskraft die; **to feel an ~ to sb** sich zu jm hingezogen fühlen - **2.** (U) [appeal, charm] Reiz der - **3.** [attractive feature, event] Attraktion die.

**attractive** [ə'træktɪv] adj - **1.** [person] anziehend - **2.** [thing, idea] attraktiv, ansprechend.

**attractively** [ə'træktɪvlɪ] adv ansprechend.

**attributable** [ə'trɪbjʊtəbl] adj: **to be ~ to sb/ sthg** jm/etw zuzuschreiben sein.

**attribute** [vb ə'trɪbju:t, n 'ætrɪbju:t] vt - **1.** [ascribe]: **to ~ sthg to sb/sthg** etw jm/etw zulschreiben - **2.** [work of art, remark]: **to ~ sthg to sb** jm etw zulschreiben <> n [quality] Eigenschaft die.

**attribution** [ˌætrɪ'bju:ʃn] n (U) Zuschreibung die.

**attrition** [ə'trɪʃn] n (U) Zermürbung die; **war of ~** Zermürbungskrieg der.

**attuned** [ə'tju:nd] adj: **~ (to sthg)** vertraut (mit etw).

**Atty. Gen.** abbr of **Attorney General.**

**ATV** n (abbr of **all terrain vehicle**) Geländewagen der.

**atypical** [ˌeɪ'tɪpɪkl] adj atypisch.

**atypically** [ˌeɪ'tɪpɪklɪ] adv atypisch.

**aubergine** ['əʊbəʒi:n] n Br Aubergine die.

**auburn** ['ɔ:bən] adj [hair] rotbraun.

**auction** ['ɔ:kʃn] n Auktion die, Versteigerung die; **at** OR **by ~** bei einer Auktion OR Versteigerung; **to put sthg up for ~** etw zur Versteigerung anlbieten <> vt versteigern.

➤ **auction off** vt sep versteigern.

**auctioneer** [ˌɔ:kʃə'nɪəʳ] n Auktionator der.

**audacious** [ɔ:'deɪʃəs] adj [daring] kühn; [impudent] dreist.

**audacity** [ɔ:'dæsətɪ] n [daring] Kühnheit die; [impudence] Dreistigkeit die.

**audible** ['ɔ:dəbl] adj hörbar.

**audience** ['ɔ:djəns] n - **1.** [gen] Publikum das; [of TV programme] Zuschauer pl; [of radio programme] Zuhörer pl; [of books] Leserschaft die - **2.** [formal meeting] Audienz die.

**audio** ['ɔ:dɪəʊ] adj Ton-; **~ tape** Audiokassette die.

**audio frequency** n Tonfrequenz die.

**audiotyping** ['ɔ:dɪəʊˌtaɪpɪŋ] n das Schreiben eines auf Band gesprochenen Textes.

**audiotypist** ['ɔ:dɪəʊˌtaɪpɪst] n Fonotypist der, -in die.

**audio-visual** adj audiovisuell.

**audit** ['ɔ:dɪt] n Buchprüfung die <> vt prüfen.

**audition** [ɔ:'dɪʃn] n [of actor] Vorsprechen das; [of singer] Probesingen das; [of musician] Probe-

spiel das <> vi: **to ~ for sthg** [actor] für etw vorlsprechen; [singer] für etw vorlsingen; [musician] für etw vorlspielen.

**auditor** ['ɔ:dɪtəʳ] n Buchprüfer der, -in die.

**auditorium** [ˌɔ:dɪ'tɔ:rɪəm] (pl **-riums** OR **-ria** [-rɪə]) n Zuschauerraum der.

**au fait** [ˌəʊ'feɪ] adj: **~ with sthg** vertraut mit etw.

**Aug.** (abbr of **August**) Aug.

**augment** [ɔ:g'ment] vt vergrößern.

**augur** ['ɔ:gəʳ] vi: **to ~ well/badly** etwas Gutes/ nichts Gutes verheißen.

**august** [ɔ:'gʌst] adj literary [person, institution] ehrwürdig; [gathering, guest] illuster.

**August** ['ɔ:gəst] n August der; see also **September.**

**Auld Lang Syne** [ˌɔ:ldlæŋ'saɪn] n Lied, das nach alter Tradition in Großbritannien am Silvesterabend um Mitternacht angestimmt wird.

**aunt** [ɑ:nt] n Tante die.

**auntie, aunty** ['ɑ:ntɪ] (pl **-ies**) n inf Tantchen das.

**au pair** [ˌəʊ'peəʳ] n Aupairmädchen das.

**aura** ['ɔ:rə] n Aura die.

**aural** ['ɔ:rəl] adj SCH: **~ comprehension** Hörverständnis das.

**aurally** ['ɔ:rəlɪ] adv: **~ handicapped** hörbehindert.

**auspices** ['ɔ:spɪsɪz] npl: **under the ~ of** unter der Schirmherrschaft (+ G).

**auspicious** [ɔ:'spɪʃəs] adj [start] vielversprechend; [day, occasion] günstig.

**Aussie** ['ɒzɪ] inf adj australisch <> n Australier der, -in die.

**austere** [ɒ'stɪəʳ] adj - **1.** [person] streng; [life] asketisch - **2.** [room, building] karg.

**austerity** [ɒ'sterətɪ] n - **1.** [of person] Strenge die; [of life - for religious reasons] Entsagung die; [ - for economic reasons] Entbehrung die - **2.** [of room, building] Kargheit die.

**austerity measures** npl Sparmaßnahmen pl.

**Australasia** [ˌɒstrə'leɪʒə] n Australien und Ozeanien nt.

**Australia** [ɒ'streɪljə] n Australien nt.

**Australian** [ɒ'streɪljən] adj australisch <> n Australier der, -in die.

**Austria** ['ɒstrɪə] n Österreich nt.

**Austrian** ['ɒstrɪən] adj österreichisch <> n Österreicher der, -in die.

**authentic** [ɔ:'θentɪk] adj authentisch.

**authenticate** [ɔ:'θentɪkeɪt] vt authentifizieren, die Echtheit bestätigen von.

**authentication** [ɔːˌθentɪˈkeɪʃn] n (U) Authentifizierung die, Echtheitserklärung die.

**authenticity** [ˌɔːθenˈtɪsətɪ] n Authentizität die.

**author** [ˈɔːθəʳ] n Autor der, -in die; [by profession] Schriftsteller der, -in die.

**authoritarian** [ɔːˌθɒrɪˈteərɪən] adj autoritär.

**authoritative** [ɔːˈθɒrɪtətɪv] adj - 1. [person, voice] Respekt einflößend - 2. [report] verlässlich.

**authority** [ɔːˈθɒrətɪ] (pl -ies) n - 1. [official organization] Behörde die, Amt das - 2. (U) [power] Autorität die; to have ~ over sb Weisungsbefugnis gegenüber jm haben; in ~ verantwortlich - 3. [permission] Erlaubnis die - 4. [expert] Autorität die - 5. phr: to have it on good ~ aus zuverlässiger Quelle wissen.
➤ **authorities** npl: the authorities die Behörden.

**authorize, -ise** [ˈɔːθəraɪz] vt genehmigen; [biography] autorisieren; [money] bewilligen; to ~ sb to do sthg jn ermächtigen, etw zu tun.

**Authorized Version** n: the ~ englische Bibelübersetzung von 1611.

**authorship** [ˈɔːθəʃɪp] n Autorschaft die.

**autistic** [ɔːˈtɪstɪk] adj autistisch.

**auto** [ˈɔːtəʊ] (pl -s) n Am Auto das.

**autobiographical** [ˈɔːtəˌbaɪəˈɡræfɪkl] adj autobiografisch.

**autobiography** [ˌɔːtəbaɪˈɒɡrəfɪ] (pl -ies) n Autobiografie die.

**autocrat** [ˈɔːtəkræt] n Autokrat der, -in die.

**autocratic** [ˌɔːtəˈkrætɪk] adj autokratisch.

**autocross** [ˈɔːtəʊkrɒs] n Br Autocross das.

**Autocue**® [ˈɔːtəʊkjuː] n Br Teleprompter der.

**autofocus** [ɔːtəʊˌfəʊkəs] n Autofokus der.

**autograph** [ˈɔːtəɡrɑːf] n Autogramm das ◇ vt signieren.

**Automat**® [ˈɔːtəmæt] n Am Automatenrestaurant das.

**automata** [ɔːˈtɒmətə] pl ➢ automaton.

**automate** [ˈɔːtəmeɪt] vt automatisieren.

**automatic** [ˌɔːtəˈmætɪk] adj automatisch ◇ n - 1. [car] Wagen der mit Automatikgetriebe - 2. [gun] automatische Waffe, Maschinenwaffe die - 3. [washing machine] Waschautomat der.

**automatically** [ˌɔːtəˈmætɪklɪ] adv automatisch.

**automatic pilot** n AERON & NAUT Autopilot der; I was working on ~ fig ich habe völlig mechanisch meine Arbeit getan.

**automation** [ˌɔːtəˈmeɪʃn] n Automatisierung die.

**automaton** [ɔːˈtɒmətən] (pl -tons OR -ta) n Roboter der.

**automobile** [ˈɔːtəməbiːl] n Am Auto(mobil) das.

**automotive** [ˌɔːtəˈməʊtɪv] adj Kraftfahrzeug-; ~ industry Auto(mobil)industrie die.

**autonomous** [ɔːˈtɒnəməs] adj autonom.

**autonomy** [ɔːˈtɒnəmɪ] n (U) Autonomie die.

**autopilot** [ˌɔːtəʊˈpaɪlət] n = automatic pilot.

**autopsy** [ˈɔːtɒpsɪ] (pl -ies) n Autopsie die.

**autumn** [ˈɔːtəm] n Herbst der; in ~ im Herbst ◇ comp [leaves, weather] Herbst-; [colours, weather] herbstlich.

**autumnal** [ɔːˈtʌmnəl] adj herbstlich.

**auxiliary** [ɔːɡˈzɪljərɪ] (pl -ies) adj - 1. [providing assistance] Hilfs-; ~ nurse Schwesternhelferin die - 2. GRAMM [verb] Hilfs- ◇ n [in hospital] Hilfskraft die.

**Av.** abbr of avenue.

**AV** n abbr of Authorized Version ◇ (abbr of audiovisual) AV.

**avail** [əˈveɪl] n: to no ~ vergeblich, ohne Erfolg ◇ vt: to ~ o.s. of sthg von etw Gebrauch machen.

**availability** [əˌveɪləˈbɪlətɪ] n Verfügbarkeit die; [of product] Lieferbarkeit die.

**available** [əˈveɪləbl] adj verfügbar; [product] lieferbar; to be ~ [person] zur Verfügung stehen.

**avalanche** [ˈævəlɑːnʃ] n lit & fig Lawine die.

**avant-garde** [ˌævɒŋˈɡɑːd] adj avantgardistisch.

**avarice** [ˈævərɪs] n Habgier die, Habsucht die.

**avaricious** [ˌævəˈrɪʃəs] adj habgierig, habsüchtig.

**Ave.** abbr of avenue.

**avenge** [əˈvendʒ] vt rächen.

**avenue** [ˈævənjuː] n Allee die (in der Stadt).

**average** [ˈævərɪdʒ] adj - 1. [mean] durchschnittlich - 2. [typical]: the ~ Englishman der Durchschnittsengländer - 3. pej [mediocre] durchschnittlich, mittelmäßig ◇ n Durchschnitt der; on ~ im Durchschnitt ◇ vt: we ~d 80 miles per hour wir sind durchschnittlich 80 Meilen pro Stunde gefahren.
➤ **average out** vt sep den Durchschnitt ermitteln von ◇ vi: to ~ out at durchschnittlich betragen.

**averse** [əˈvɜːs] adj: to be ~ to sthg etw (D) abgeneigt sein; to be ~ to doing sthg abgeneigt sein, etw zu tun.

**aversion** [əˈvɜːʃn] n - 1. [dislike]: ~ (to) Abneigung die (gegen) - 2. [object of dislike] Gräuel der.

**avert** [əˈvɜːt] vt - 1. [problem] vermeiden; [acci-

A

dent, disaster] verhindern **- 2.** [eyes, glance] ablwenden.

**aviary** ['eɪvjərɪ] (pl **-ies**) n Vogelhaus das.

**aviation** [ˌeɪvɪ'eɪʃn] n (U) Luftfahrt die.

**aviator** ['eɪvɪeɪtəʳ] n dated Flieger der, -in die.

**avid** ['ævɪd] adj begeistert, passioniert; ~ **for** sthg begierig auf etw (A).

**avocado** [ˌævə'kɑːdəʊ] (pl **-s** OR **-es**) n: ~ **(pear)** Avocado die.

**avoid** [ə'vɔɪd] vt **- 1.** [problem, accident, mistake] vermeiden; **to ~ doing sthg** vermeiden, etw zu tun **- 2.** [keep away from] meiden.

**avoidable** [ə'vɔɪdəbl] adj vermeidbar.

**avoidance** [ə'vɔɪdəns] n ⊳ **tax avoidance**.

**avowed** [ə'vaʊd] adj erklärt.

**AWACS** ['eɪwæks] (abbr of **airborne warning and control system**) n AWACS das.

**await** [ə'weɪt] vt erwarten.

**awake** [ə'weɪk] (pt **awoke** OR **awaked**; pp **awoken**) adj [not sleeping] wach; **to be wide ~** hellwach sein ⇔ vt **- 1.** [person] wecken **- 2.** fig [memories, feelings] erwecken ⇔ vi aufl-wachen, erwachen.

**awakening** [ə'weɪknɪŋ] n Erwachen das.

**award** [ə'wɔːd] n **- 1.** [prize] Preis der; [for bravery] Auszeichnung die **- 2.** [compensation] Entschädigungszahlung die ⇔ vt: **to ~ sb sthg, to ~ sthg to sb** [prize] jm etw verleihen; [free kick, penalty] jm etw geben; [damages, compensation] jm etw zulsprechen.

**aware** [ə'weəʳ] adj **- 1.** [conscious]: **to be ~ of sthg** sich (D) einer Sache (G) bewusst sein; **to be ~ that** sich (D) bewusst sein, dass **- 2.** [informed, sensitive] (gut) informiert; **to be ~ of sthg** über etw (A) informiert sein.

**awareness** [ə'weənɪs] n Bewusstsein das

**away** [ə'weɪ] adv **- 1.** [indicating movement] weg; **to walk ~ (from)** weglgehen (von); **to run ~ (from)** weglaufen (von); **to look ~ (from)** weglsehen (von); **to turn ~ (from)** sich ablwenden (von) **- 2.** [at a distance]: **far ~** weit entfernt; **10 miles ~ (from here)** 10 Meilen (von hier) entfernt; **it's still two weeks ~** bis dahin sind es noch zwei Wochen **- 3.** [absent] weg; [not at home or in the office] nicht da; **Mr Stone is ~ on a business trip** Herr Stone ist auf Geschäftsreise **- 4.** [in a safe place]: **to put sthg ~** etw weglräumen **- 5.** [indicating removal or disappearance]: **to fade ~** verblassen; **to take sthg ~ (from sb)** (jm) etw weglnehmen; **to give sthg ~** [as a present] etw verschenken **- 6.** [continuously]: **to work ~** in einem fort arbeiten **- 7.** phr: **straight** OR **right ~** sofort ⇔ adj SPORT: **~ game** Auswärtsspiel das.

**awe** [ɔː] n Ehrfurcht die; **to be in ~ of sb** Ehrfurcht vor jm haben.

**awesome** ['ɔːsəm] adj [impressive] ehrfurchtgebietend.

**awestruck** ['ɔːstrʌk] adj von Ehrfurcht ergriffen; [expression, voice] ehrfurchtsvoll.

**awful** ['ɔːfʊl] adj **- 1.** [terrible] furchtbar, schrecklich **- 2.** inf [very great]: **an ~ lot** sehr viel; **an ~ lot of time/money/books** eine Menge Zeit/Geld/Bücher.

**awfully** ['ɔːflɪ] adv inf [very] furchtbar.

**awhile** [ə'waɪl] adv literary eine Weile.

**awkward** ['ɔːkwəd] adj **- 1.** [clumsy - movement] ungeschickt, unbeholfen; [ - position] ungünstig; [ - person] unbeholfen **- 2.** [embarrassed - person] verlegen; [ - silence] betreten; [ - situation, questions] peinlich **- 3.** [uncooperative] unkooperativ **- 4.** [inconvenient] ungünstig **- 5.** [difficult, delicate] schwierig.

**awkwardly** ['ɔːkwədlɪ] adv **- 1.** [clumsily - move] ungeschickt, unbeholfen; [ - dance] unbeholfen **- 2.** [in an embarrassed way] verlegen **- 3.** [inconveniently] ungünstig.

**awkwardness** ['ɔːkwədnɪs] n **- 1.** [clumsiness - of movement] Ungeschicktheit die, Unbeholfenheit die; [ - of person] Unbeholfenheit die **- 2.** [unease - of person] Verlegenheit die; [ - of situation] Peinlichkeit die **- 3.** [inconvenience] Ungünstigkeit die.

**awning** ['ɔːnɪŋ] n **- 1.** [of tent] Vordach das **- 2.** [of shop] Markise die.

**awoke** [ə'wəʊk] pt ⊳ **awake**.

**awoken** [ə'wəʊkn] pp ⊳ **awake**.

**AWOL** ['eɪwɒl] (abbr of **absent without leave**) ⊳ **absent**.

**awry** [ə'raɪ] adj schief ⇔ adv: **to go ~** schief gehen.

**axe** Br, **ax** Am [æks] n Axt die; **to have an ~ to grind** ein persönliches Interesse haben ⇔ vt [project] auflgeben; [jobs] streichen, kürzen.

**axes** ['æksiːz] pl ⊳ **axis**.

**axiom** ['æksɪəm] n Axiom das.

**axis** ['æksɪs] (pl **axes**) n Achse die.

**axle** ['æksl] n Achse die.

**aye** [aɪ] adv **- 1.** Scot [yes] ja **- 2.** NAUT [yes] zu Befehl, jawohl ⇔ n [vote] Jastimme die.

**AZ** abk für Arizona, in Postanschrift verwendet.

**azalea** [ə'zeɪljə] n Azalee die.

**Azerbaijan** [ˌæzəbaɪ'dʒɑːn] n Aserbaidschan nt.

**Azeri** [ə'zerɪ] adj aserbaidschanisch.

**Azores** [ə'zɔːz] npl: **the ~** die Azoren pl; **in the ~** auf den Azoren.

**AZT** (abbr of **azidothymidine**) n AZT das.

**Aztec** ['æztek] *adj* aztekisch ◇ *n* Azteke *der*, -kin *die*.

**azure** ['æʒəʳ] *adj* azurblau, tiefblau.

# B

**b** (*pl* **b's** OR **bs**), **B** (*pl* **B's** OR **Bs**) [biː] *n* [letter] b *das*, B *das*.
➤ B *n* - **1.** MUS H *das* - **2.** SCH [mark] ≃ zwei.

**b.** *abbr of* **born**.

**BA** *n* - **1.** *abbr of* **Bachelor of Arts** - **2.** (*abbr of* **British Airways**) BA *die*.

**BAA** (*abbr of* **British Airports' Authority**) *n* unabhängige Organisation, die viele der britischen Flughäfen betreibt.

**babble** ['bæbl] *n* [noise] Gemurmel *das* ◇ *vi* plappern.

**babe** [beɪb] *n* - **1.** *literary* [baby] Kindlein *das* - **2.** *Am inf* [term of address] Babe *das* - **3.** *inf* [beautiful woman]: **she's a ~** sie ist 'ne tolle Braut.

**baboon** [bə'buːn] *n* Pavian *der*.

**baby** ['beɪbɪ] (*pl* **-ies**) *n* Baby *das*; **don't be such a ~!** benimm dich nicht wie ein Baby!

**baby boomer** [-,buːməʳ] *n* Am Angehöriger der ersten Generation nach dem Zweiten Weltkrieg, geboren zwischen 1945 und 1950.

**baby buggy** *n* - **1.** Br [pushchair] Sportwagen *der* - **2.** Am = **baby carriage**.

**baby carriage** *n* Am Kinderwagen *der*.

**baby food** *n* Babynahrung *die*.

**Baby-gro**® ['beɪbɪɡrəʊ] *n* Strampelanzug *der*.

**babyish** ['beɪbɪʃ] *adj pej* kindisch, Baby-.

**baby-minder** *n* Br Tagesmutter *die*.

**baby-sit** *vi* babysitten.

**baby-sitter** [-,sɪtəʳ] *n* Babysitter *der*, -in *die*.

**bachelor** ['bætʃələʳ] *n* Junggeselle *der*.

**Bachelor of Arts** *n* [degree] erster akademischer Grad der Geisteswissenschaften an Universitäten in englischsprachigen Ländern.

**Bachelor of Science** *n* [degree] erster akademischer Grad der Naturwissenschaften an Universitäten in englischsprachigen Ländern.

**bachelor's degree** *n* erster akademischer Grad an Universitäten in englischsprachigen Ländern.

**back** [bæk] *adv* - **1.** [backwards] zurück; **stand ~ (please)!** (bitte) zurückltreten!; **to tie ~** zurücklbinden; **to push ~** [shove] zurücklschieben - **2.** [to former position or state] zurück; **when will you be ~?** wann bist du wieder da?; **~ and forth** hin und her; **to give sthg ~** etw zurücklgeben; **we went ~ to sleep** wir sind wieder eingeschlafen; **~ home** bei uns zu Hause - **3.** [earlier]: **two weeks ~** vor zwei Wochen; **it dates ~ to 1960** es stammt aus dem Jahr(e) 1960; **I found out ~ in January** ich habe es schon im Januar erfahren; **to think ~ to sthg** an etw (A) zurückldenken - **4.** [in reply, in return]: **to write/phone/pay ~** zurücklschreiben/-rufen/-zahlen - **5.** [in fashion again]: **to be ~ (in fashion)** wieder modern sein ◇ *n* - **1.** [of person, animal, hand] Rücken *der*; [of chair] Lehne *die*; **to break the ~ of the work** *fig* den größten Teil der Arbeit erledigen; **to do sthg behind sb's ~** etw hinter js Rücken tun; **he knows London like the ~ of his hand** er kennt London wie seine Westentasche; **to put sb's ~ up** jn irritieren; **to stab sb in the ~** jm in den Rücken fallen; **to turn one's ~ on sb/sthg** [abandon] jn/etw im Stich lassen; **to put one's ~ into sthg** sich bei etw anlstrengen; **get off my ~!** lass mich in Ruhe! - **2.** [opposite or reverse side - of bank note, page] Rückseite *die*; **~ of the head** Hinterkopf *der* - **3.** [not front - inside car] Rücksitz *der*; [ - of room] hinterer Teil *der*; **at the ~ of, in ~ of** Am hinter (+ D); **at the ~ of the cupboard** hinten im Schrank; **the ~ of beyond** Br das Ende der Welt - **4.** SPORT [player] Verteidiger *der*; [in rugby] Spieler *der* der Hintermannschaft ◇ *adj* (in compounds) - **1.** [at the back - wheels, legs, door] Hinter-; **~ seat** Rücksitz *der*; **~ street** kleine Seitenstraße - **2.** [overdue - rent] überfällig; **~ pay** Nachzahlung *die* ◇ *vt* - **1.** [reverse] zurücklsetzen - **2.** [support] unterstützen - **3.** [bet on]: **to ~ a horse** (Geld) auf ein Pferd setzen - **4.** [provide lining for] füttern ◇ *vi* [car, driver] rückwärts fahren.
➤ **back to back** *adv* [stand] Rücken an Rücken.
➤ **back to front** *adv* [the wrong way round] verkehrt herum, auf links.
➤ **back away** *vi* zurücklweichen.
➤ **back down** *vi* nachlgeben.
➤ **back off** *vi* zurücklweichen; **~ off!** weg da!
➤ **back onto** *vt fus Br*: **our garden ~s onto a river** unser Garten grenzt an einen Fluss.
➤ **back out** *vi* [of arrangement] auslsteigen.
➤ **back up** *vt sep* - **1.** [support] unterstützen - **2.** [confirm] bestätigen - **3.** [reverse] zurücklsetzen - **4.** COMPUT ein Backup machen von ◇ *vi* [car, driver] zurücklsetzen.

**backache** ['bækeɪk] *n* (U) Rückenschmerzen *pl*.

**backbencher** [ˌbæk'bentʃəʳ] n Br POL parlamentarischer Hinterbänkler.

**backbiting** ['bækbaɪtɪŋ] n Lästern das.

**backbone** ['bækbəʊn] n lit & fig Rückgrat das.

**backbreaking** ['bækˌbreɪkɪŋ] adj erschöpfend.

**back burner** n: to put sthg on the ~ etw zurücklstellen.

**backchat** Br ['bæktʃæt], **backtalk** Am ['bæktɔːk] n (U) inf Widerrede die.

**backcloth** ['bækklɒθ] n Br = backdrop.

**backcomb** ['bækkəʊm] vt Br toupieren.

**back copy** n = back number.

**backdate** [ˌbæk'deɪt] vt zurückldatieren.

**back door** n Hintertür die; to get in through OR by the ~ fig durch ein Hintertürchen hereinlschlüpfen.

**backdrop** ['bækdrɒp] n lit & fig Hintergrund der.

**backer** ['bækəʳ] n FIN Geldgeber der.

**backfire** [ˌbæk'faɪəʳ] vi - 1. [motor vehicle] Fehlzündungen haben - 2. [plan] fehllschlagen; to ~ on sb auf jn zurücklfallen.

**backgammon** ['bækˌgæmən] n Backgammon das.

**background** ['bækgraʊnd] n - 1. [gen] Hintergrund der; in the ~ lit & fig im Hintergrund - 2. [upbringing] Herkunft die, Verhältnisse pl ⟷ comp Hintergrund-.

**backhand** ['bækhænd] n Rückhand die.

**backhanded** ['bækhændɪd] adj fig [compliment] zweifelhaft.

**backhander** ['bækhændəʳ] n Br inf [bribe] Schmiergeld das.

**backing** ['bækɪŋ] n - 1. (U) [support] Unterstützung die - 2. [lining] Verstärkung die - 3. MUS Begleitung die.

**backing group** n MUS Begleitband die.

**back issue** n = back number.

**backlash** ['bæklæʃ] n [adverse reaction] Gegenschlag der, Gegenreaktion die.

**backless** ['bæklɪs] adj rückenfrei.

**backlog** ['bæklɒg] n Rückstände pl; to have a ~ of work mit der Arbeit im Rückstand sein.

**back number** n alte Ausgabe.

**backpack** ['bækpæk] n esp Am Rucksack der.

**backpacker** ['bækpækəʳ] n esp Am Rucksacktourist der, Tramper der.

**backpacking** ['bækpækɪŋ] n esp Am: to go ~ trampen, wandern.

**back passage** n euphemism After der.

**back pay** n ausstehender Lohn.

**backpedal** [ˌbæk'pedl] (Br pt & pp -led; cont -ling, Am pt & pp -ed; cont -ing) vi fig: to ~ (on sthg) einen Rückzieher (bei etw) machen.

**back seat** n [in car] Rücksitz der; to take a ~ fig sich im Hintergrund halten.

**back-seat driver** n Beifahrer, der dem Fahrer ständig ungefragt Ratschläge gibt.

**backside** [ˌbæk'saɪd] n inf Hintern der.

**backslapping** ['bækˌslæpɪŋ] n (U) inf Schulterklopfen das.

**backslash** ['bækslæʃ] n COMPUT Backslash der, umgekehrter Schrägstrich.

**backslide** [ˌbæk'slaɪd] (pt & pp -slid) vi rückfällig werden.

**backspace** ['bækspeɪs] n [key] Backspacetaste die, Rücktaste die ⟷ vi zurücklsetzen.

**backstage** [ˌbæk'steɪdʒ] adv hinter den Kulissen.

**back street** n Br kleine Seitenstraße.

**back-street abortion** n Br illegale Abtreibung.

**backstroke** ['bækstrəʊk] n Rückenschwimmen das.

**backtalk** n Am = backchat.

**backtrack** ['bæktræk] vi = backpedal.

**backup** ['bækʌp] adj - 1. [reserve] Hilfs-, Reserve- - 2. COMPUT Sicherungs-, Backup- ⟷ n - 1. (U) [support] Unterstützung die - 2. COMPUT Sicherungskopie die.

**backward** ['bækwəd] adj - 1. [gen] rückwärts gerichtet; a ~ glance ein Blick über die Schulter - 2. pej [child, country] zurückgeblieben ⟷ adv Am = backwards.

**backward-looking** [-ˌlʊkɪŋ] adj pej rückwärtsgewandt, rückwärtsgerichtet.

**backwards** ['bækwədz], **backward** Am ['bækwəd] adv - 1. [towards the rear] rückwärts; to fall ~ nach hinten fallen; ~ and forwards hin und her; to look ~ zurücklblicken - 2. [back to front] verkehrt herum.

**backwater** ['bækˌwɔːtəʳ] n fig [place] Kaff das.

**backwoods** ['bækwʊdz] npl [remote place] abgelegene Gegend.

**backyard** [ˌbæk'jɑːd] n - 1. Br [yard] Hinterhof der - 2. Am [garden] Garten der hinter dem Haus.

**bacon** ['beɪkən] n (U) Schinkenspeck der, durchwachsener Speck.

**bacteria** [bæk'tɪərɪə] npl Bakterien pl.

**bacteriology** [bækˌtɪərɪ'ɒlədʒɪ] n Bakteriologie die.

**bad** [bæd] (compar **worse**; superl **worst**) adj - 1. [unpleasant, unfavourable - gen] schlecht; [- smell] übel; ~ **breath** Mundgeruch der; things are going from ~ to worse es wird immer schlimmer; he is in a ~ way es geht ihm gar nicht gut; smoking is ~ for you Rauchen ist schädlich; **too** ~! Pech! - **2.** [serious] schwer; **to have a** ~ **cold** einen starken Schnupfen haben - **3.** [inadequate - eyesight, excuse] schwach; **to be** ~ **at sthg** etw schlecht können; **he's** ~ **at English** er ist schlecht in Englisch; **not** ~ nicht schlecht - **4.** [injured, unhealthy] schlimm; **my** ~ **leg** mein schlimmes Bein; **he has a** ~ **heart** er hat ein schwaches Herz - **5.** [naughty] ungezogen; [wicked] böse, übel; **he's a** ~ **lot** er ist ein übler Bursche - **6.** [food - rotten, off] verdorben; **to go** ~ verderben - **7.** [guilty]: **he really feels** ~ **about it** es tut ihm wirklich leid ⬦ adv Am = **badly.**

**bad blood** n [anger] böses Blut.

**bad cheque** n ungedeckter Scheck.

**bad debt** n unbegleichbare Schuld.

**baddy** ['bædɪ] (pl -ies) n inf Böse der, Schurke der.

**bade** [bæd] pt ▷ **bid.**

**bad feeling** n (U) [resentment] ungutes Gefühl.

**badge** [bædʒ] n - **1.** [for fun] Button der - **2.** [for employee, visitor] Schild(chen) das - **3.** [sewn-on] Abzeichen das - **4.** [on car] Emblem das.

**badger** ['bædʒə'] n Dachs der ⬦ vt [pester]: **to** ~ **sb** jm keine Ruhe lassen.

**badly** ['bædlɪ] (compar **worse;** superl **worst**) adv - **1.** [poorly] schlecht; **to treat sb** ~ jn schlecht behandeln; **to think** ~ **of sb** von jm schlecht denken - **2.** [wounded, beaten, affected] schwer - **3.** [very much]: **to be** ~ **in need of sthg** etw dringend benötigen.

**badly-off** adj - **1.** [poor] nicht gut gestellt - **2.** [lacking]: **to be** ~ **for sthg** ein Mangel an etw (D) haben.

**bad-mannered** [-'mænəd] adj unhöflich.

**badminton** ['bædmɪntən] n (U) Federball das; SPORT Badminton das.

**bad-mouth** vt esp Am inf herziehen über (+ A).

**badness** ['bædnɪs] n Schlechtigkeit die.

**bad-tempered** [-'tempəd] adj - **1.** [by nature] übellaunig - **2.** [in a bad mood] schlecht gelaunt.

**baffled** ['bæfld] adj ratlos.

**baffling** ['bæflɪŋ] adj verwirrend.

**bag** [bæg] (pt & pp **-ged;** cont **-ging**) n - **1.** [container] Tasche die; [for shopping] Tüte die; [large, for coal, cement] Sack der; [of tea, rice] Beutel der; **to be a** ~ **of bones** nur Haut und Knochen sein; **to be in the** ~ inf [contract] unter Dach und Fach sein; [game] gelaufen sein; **to pack one's** ~**s** fig [leave] seine Sachen packen - **2.** [handbag] Handtasche die; [when travelling] Reisetasche die - **3.** [bagful]: **a** ~ **of crisps** Br eine Tüte Chips; **a** ~ **of potatoes** ein Sack Kartoffeln ⬦ vt - **1.** [put into bags] einpacken - **2.** Br inf [get] sich (D) schnappen - **3.** Br [reserve] belegen, besetzen.

**bags** npl - **1.** [under eyes] Tränensäcke pl - **2.** [lots]: ~**s of time/room** inf eine Menge OR jede Menge Zeit/Platz.

**bagel** ['beɪgl] n kleines ringförmiges Brötchen.

**baggage** ['bægɪdʒ] n Gepäck das.

**baggage car** n Am Gepäckwagen der.

**baggage reclaim** n Gepäckausgabe die.

**baggage room** n Am Gepäckaufbewahrung die.

**baggy** ['bægɪ] (compar **-ier;** superl **-iest**) adj weit (geschnitten), ausgebeult.

**Baghdad** [bæg'dæd] n Bagdad nt.

**bag lady** n inf Stadtstreicherin die.

**bagpipes** ['bægpaɪps] npl Dudelsack der.

**bagsnatcher** ['bægsnætʃə'] n Handtaschendieb der.

**bah** [bɑ:] excl bah!

**Bahamas** [bə'hɑ:məz] npl: **the** ~ die Bahamas; **in the** ~ auf den Bahamas.

**Bahrain** [bɑ:'reɪn] n Bahrain nt.

**bail** [beɪl] n (U) LAW Kaution die; **on** ~ gegen Kaution.

**bail out** vt sep - **1.** LAW [pay bail for] (die) Kaution stellen für - **2.** [rescue] aus der Klemme helfen (+ D) - **3.** [boat] ausschöpfen ⬦ vi [from plane] abspringen.

**bailiff** ['beɪlɪf] n [in charge of repossession] Gerichtsvollzieher der; [in court] Gerichtsdiener der.

**bait** [beɪt] n (U) Köder der; **to rise to** OR **take the** ~ fig anlbeißen, sich ködern lassen ⬦ vt - **1.** [hook, trap] mit einem Köder versehen - **2.** [torment - person] piesacken; [ - bear, badger] quälen.

**baize** [beɪz] n Bezugsstoff für Billiard- und Kartentische.

**bake** [beɪk] vt - **1.** [bread, cake etc] backen - **2.** [ground] ausldörren; [clay, brick] brennen ⬦ vi backen.

**baked beans** [beɪkt-] npl weiße Bohnen pl in Tomatensoße.

**baked potato** n in der Schale gebackene Kartoffel.

**baker** ['beɪkə'] n Bäcker der, -in die; ~**'s (shop)** Bäckerei die, Bäckerladen der.

**bakery** ['beɪkərɪ] (pl -ies) n Bäckerei die.

**baking** ['beɪkɪŋ] adj inf [hot] brütend heiß ⬦ n [cooking] Backen das.

**baking powder** n Backpulver das.

**baking tin** n Backform die.

**baking tray** n Backblech das.

**balaclava** [ˌbælə'klɑːvə] n Br eng anliegende Kopfbedeckung, die nur das Gesicht freilässt.

**balance** ['bæləns] n - **1.** [equilibrium] Gleichgewicht das; **to keep/lose one's** ~ das Gleichge-

wicht halten/verlieren; **off ~** aus dem Gleichgewicht **- 2.** *fig* [counterweight] Ausgleich *der* **- 3.** *fig* [weight, force]: **~ of power** Gleichgewicht *das* der Kräfte **- 4.** [scales] Waage *die;* **to be** OR **hang in the ~** in der Schwebe sein **- 5.** [remainder] Rest *der* **- 6.** [of bank account] Kontostand *der* ⬦ *vt* **- 1.** [keep in balance] im Gleichgewicht halten **- 2.** [compare]: **to ~ sthg against sthg** etw gegen etw ablwägen **- 3.** [in accounting]: **to ~ the books/the budget** die Bilanz machen ⬦ *vi* **- 1.** [maintain equilibrium] das Gleichgewicht halten **- 2.** [in accounting] sich auslgleichen.
➤ **on balance** *adv* alles in allem.

**balanced** ['bælənst] *adj* **- 1.** [view, report] ausgewogen **- 2.** [person] ausgeglichen.

**balanced diet** [ˌbælənst-] *n* ausgewogene Ernährung.

**balance of payments** *n* Zahlungsbilanz *die.*

**balance of trade** *n* Handelsbilanz *die.*

**balance sheet** *n* Bilanz *die.*

**balancing act** ['bælənsɪŋ-] *n* *fig* Balanceakt *der.*

**balcony** ['bælkənɪ] (*pl* **-ies**) *n* **- 1.** [on building] Balkon *der* **- 2.** [in theatre] oberster Rang.

**bald** [bɔːld] *adj* **- 1.** [head, man] glatzköpfig, kahl(köpfig) **- 2.** [tyre] völlig abgenutzt **- 3.** *fig* [unadorned] nüchtern, unverblümt.

**bald eagle** *n* Weißkopfseeadler *der.*

**balding** ['bɔːldɪŋ] *adj:* **to be ~** eine Glatze bekommen.

**baldness** ['bɔːldnɪs] *n* Kahlköpfigkeit *die.*

**bale** [beɪl] *n* Ballen *der.*
➤ **bale out** *Br* *vt sep* [boat] auslschöpfen ⬦ *vi* [from plane] ablspringen.

**Balearic Islands** [ˌbælɪˈærɪk-], **Balearics** [ˌbælɪˈærɪks] *npl:* **the ~** die Balearen; **in the ~** auf den Balearen.

**Bali** ['bɑːlɪ] *n* Bali *nt;* **in ~** auf Bali.

**balk** [bɔːk] *vi:* **to ~ (at)** zurücklschrecken (vor (+ D)).

**Balkan** ['bɔːlkən] *adj* Balkan-.

**Balkans** ['bɔːlkənz], **Balkan States** *npl:* **the ~** der Balkan; **in the ~** auf dem Balkan.

**ball** [bɔːl] *n* **- 1.** [in game] Ball *der;* [in snooker, bowling] Kugel *die;* **to start the ~ rolling** den Anfang machen; **to keep the ~ rolling** die Sache in Gang halten; **to be on the ~** auf Draht sein; **to play ~** *fig* mitlmachen **- 2.** [of wool] Knäuel *das* **- 3.** [of foot] Ballen *der* **- 4.** [dance] Ball *der;* **to have a ~** *fig* sich prima amüsieren.
➤ **balls** *vinf* *n* (U) [nonsense] Schwachsinn *der* ⬦ *npl* [testicles] Eier *pl* ⬦ *excl* Scheiße!

**ballad** ['bæləd] *n* Ballade *die.*

**ball-and-socket joint** *n* Kugelgelenk *das.*

**ballast** ['bæləst] *n* Ballast *der.*

**ball bearing** *n* Kugellager *das.*

**ball boy** *n* Balljunge *der.*

**ballcock** ['bɔːlkɒk] *n* Schwimmerhahn *der.*

**ballerina** [ˌbæləˈriːnə] *n* Ballerina *die.*

**ballet** ['bæleɪ] *n* Ballett *das.*

**ballet dancer** *n* Balletttänzer *der,* -in *die.*

**ball game** *n* **- 1.** *Am* [baseball match] Baseballspiel *das* **- 2.** *fig* [situation]: **it's a whole new ~** *inf* das ist eine ganz neue Lage.

**ball girl** *n* Ballmädchen *das.*

**ballistic missile** [bəˈlɪstɪk-] *n* ballistische Rakete.

**ballistics** [bəˈlɪstɪks] *n* Ballistik *die.*

**balloon** [bəˈluːn] *n* **- 1.** [toy] Luftballon *der* **- 2.** [hot-air balloon] Heißluftballon *der* **- 3.** [in comic strip] Sprechblase *die* ⬦ *vi* [swell] sich blähen.

**ballooning** [bəˈluːnɪŋ] *n* Ballonfahren *das.*

**ballot** ['bælət] *n* **- 1.** [voting paper] Stimmzettel *der* **- 2.** [voting process] Abstimmung *die,* Wahl *die* ⬦ *vt* [members] abstimmen lassen ⬦ *vi:* **to ~ for sthg** über etw (A) ablstimmen.

**ballot box** *n* Wahlurne *die.*

**ballot paper** *n* Stimmzettel *der.*

**ball park** *n* *Am* Baseballstadion *das.*

**ball-park figure** *n* *inf* [estimate] Richtzahl *die.*

**ballpoint (pen)** ['bɔːlpɔɪnt-] *n* Kugelschreiber *der.*

**ballroom** ['bɔːlrʊm] *n* Ballsaal *der,* Tanzsaal *der.*

**ballroom dancing** *n* (U) Gesellschaftstanz *der.*

**balls-up** *Br,* **ball-up** *Am* *n* *vinf* Durcheinander *das.*

**balm** [bɑːm] *n* Balsam *der.*

**balmy** ['bɑːmɪ] (*compar* **-ier;** *superl* **-iest**) *adj* [evening] mild.

**baloney** [bəˈləʊnɪ] *n* **- 1.** *inf* [rubbish] Quatsch *der,* Blödsinn *der* **- 2.** *Am* [sausage] Fleischwurst *die,* Mortadella *die.*

**balsa** ['bɒlsə] *n* = **balsawood.**

**balsawood** ['bɒlsəwʊd] *n* Balsaholz *das.*

**Baltic** ['bɔːltɪk] *adj* [port, coast] Ostsee-, baltisch ⬦ *n:* **the ~ (Sea)** die Ostsee.

**Baltic Republic** *n:* **the ~s** die Baltischen Republiken *pl.*

**Baltic State** *n:* **the ~s** die Baltischen Staaten.

**balustrade** [ˌbæləsˈtreɪd] *n* Balustrade *die.*

**bamboo** [bæmˈbuː] *n* Bambus *der.*

**bamboozle** [bæmˈbuːzl] *vt* *inf* verwirren.

**ban** [bæn] (*pt* & *pp* **-ned;** *cont* **-ning**) *n* Verbot *das;* **~ on smoking** Rauchverbot *das* ⬦ *vt* verbieten; **to ~ sb from doing sthg** jm etw verbieten; **to be ~ned from driving** Fahrverbot erteilt bekommen.

**banal** [bə'nɑːl] adj pej banal.

**banana** [bə'nɑːnə] n Banane die.

**banana republic** n Bananenrepublik die.

**banana split** n Bananensplit das.

**band** [bænd] n - 1. [musical - pop] Gruppe die; [ - traditional, classical] Kapelle die; [ - jazz] Band die - 2. [gang] Bande die - 3. [of colour, metal] Streifen der - 4. [range] Klasse die.

➤ **band together** vi sich zusammenlschließen.

**bandage** ['bændɪdʒ] n Verband der ⬦ vt verbinden.

**Band-Aid**® n Heftpflaster das.

**bandan(n)a** [bæn'dænə] n farbiges Baumwolltuch, als Halstuch oder (gefaltet) als Stirnband getragen.

**b and b, B and B** n abbr of bed and breakfast.

**bandit** ['bændɪt] n Bandit der.

**bandmaster** ['bænd,mɑːstəʳ] n Kapellmeister der.

**band saw** n Bandsäge die.

**bandsman** ['bændzmən] (pl -men [-mən]) n Musiker der.

**bandstand** ['bændstænd] n Musikpavillon der.

**bandwagon** ['bændwægən] n: **to jump on the ~** auf den fahrenden Zug auf lspringen.

**bandy** ['bændɪ] (compar -ier; superl -iest; pt & pp -ied) adj [bandy-legged] krummbeinig.

➤ **bandy about, bandy around** vt sep [words] um sich werfen mit.

**bandy-legged** [-ˌlegd] adj = bandy.

**bane** [beɪn] n: **the ~ of my life** der Nagel zu meinem Sarg.

**bang** [bæŋ] adv - 1. [right]: **~ in the middle** genau in der Mitte; **his description was ~ on** seine Beschreibung passte aufs Haar; **~ on time** auf die Minute pünktlich - 2. phr: **~ goes our holiday!** inf unser Urlaub ist geplatzt! ⬦ n - 1. [blow] Schlag der - 2. [loud noise] Knall der; **to go with a ~** inf fig sein Bombenerfolg sein ⬦ vt - 1. [hit] anlschlagen, (anl)stoßen - 2. [door] zulschlagen ⬦ vi - 1. [knock]: **to ~ on the door/wall** [once] gegen die Tür/die Wand schlagen; [more than once] gegen die Tür/die Wand hämmern - 2. [make a loud noise] (herum)poltern, Krach machen - 3. [crash]: **to ~ into sb/sthg** gegen jn/etw stoßen ⬦ excl peng!

➤ **bangs** npl Am Pony der.

➤ **bang down** vt sep hinlknallen.

**banger** ['bæŋəʳ] n Br - 1. inf [sausage] Würstchen das - 2. inf [old car] alte Kiste - 3. [firework] Knallkörper der.

**Bangkok** [ˌbæŋ'kɒk] n Bangkok nt.

**Bangladesh** [ˌbæŋglə'deʃ] n Bangladesh nt.

**Bangladeshi** [ˌbæŋglə'deʃɪ] adj aus Bangladesh ⬦ n Bangladeshi der, die.

**bangle** ['bæŋgl] n Armreif der.

**banish** ['bænɪʃ] vt lit & fig verbannen, vertreiben.

**banister** ['bænɪstəʳ] n, **banisters** ['bænɪstəz] npl Geländer das.

**banjo** ['bændʒəʊ] (pl -s OR -es) n Banjo das.

**bank** [bæŋk] n - 1. FIN Bank die - 2. [of data, blood etc] Bank die - 3. [of river, lake] Ufer das - 4. [slope] Böschung die, Abhang der - 5. [of fog, cloud] Bank die; **a ~ of snow** eine Schneeverwehung ⬦ vt FIN einlzahlen ⬦ vi - 1. FIN: **who do you ~ with?** bei welcher Bank sind Sie/bist du? - 2. [plane] sich in die Kurve legen.

➤ **bank on** vt fus sich verlassen auf (+ A).

**bank account** n Bankkonto das.

**bank balance** n Kontostand der.

**bankbook** ['bæŋkbʊk] n Sparbuch das.

**bank card** n = banker's card.

**bank charges** npl Bankgebühren pl.

**bank draft** n Banküberweisung die.

**banker** ['bæŋkəʳ] n FIN Bankier der.

**banker's card** n Br Scheckkarte die.

**banker's order** n Br Dauerauftrag der.

**bank holiday** n Br Feiertag der.

**BANK HOLIDAY**

> Bank holidays sind gesetzliche Feiertage (pro Jahr etwa vier), die stets auf einen Montag fallen, so dass sich ein verlängertes Wochenende ergibt. Die Banken haben an diesen Tagen geschlossen; fällige Rechnungen werden erst am folgenden Tag bezahlt.

**banking** ['bæŋkɪŋ] n Bankwesen das.

**banking house** n Bankhaus das.

**bank loan** n Bankkredit der.

**bank manager** n Filialleiter der, -in die.

**bank note** n Banknote die, Geldschein der.

**bank rate** n Diskontsatz der.

**bankrupt** ['bæŋkrʌpt] adj bankrott; **to go ~** bankrott machen, in Konkurs gehen ⬦ n Bankrotteur der ⬦ vt ruinieren.

**bankruptcy** ['bæŋkrəptsɪ] (pl -ies) n Bankrott der.

**bank statement** n Kontoauszug der.

**banner** ['bænəʳ] n Transparent das, Spruchband das.

**bannister** n, **bannisters** npl = banister.

**banns** [bænz] npl: **to publish the ~** das Aufgebot ausl hängen.

**banquet** ['bæŋkwɪt] n Festessen das, Bankett das.

**bantam** ['bæntəm] n Bantamhuhn das.

**bantamweight** ['bæntəmweɪt] n Bantamge-
wicht das.

**banter** ['bæntəʳ] n (U) Frotzeleien pl.

**bap** [bæp] n Br weiches Brötchen, Milchbrötchen das.

**baptism** ['bæptɪzm] n Taufe die; ~ of fire Feu-
ertaufe die.

**Baptist** ['bæptɪst] n Baptist der, -in die.

**baptize, -ise** [Br bæp'taɪz, Am 'bæptaɪz] vt taufen.

**bar** [baːʳ] (pt & pp **-red**; cont **-ring**) n - **1.** [of wood,
metal] Stange die; [of gold] Barren der; [of soap]
Stück das; [of chocolate - slab] Tafel die; [ - long and
thin] Riegel der; **to be behind ~s** hinter Gittern
sitzen; **the ~** [in gymnastics] der Balken - **2.** fig
[obstacle] Hindernis das - **3.** [in hotel] Bar die;
[pub] Kneipe die - **4.** [counter] Theke die, Tresen der - **5.** mus Takt der <> vt - **1.** [door, window]
verriegeln - **2.** [block] (ver)sperren; **to ~ sb's
way** jm den Weg versperren - **3.** [ban]: **to ~ sb
(from doing sthg)** jn (von etw) ausschließen;
**to ~ sb (from somewhere)** jm den Zutritt (zu
einem Ort) verweigern <> prep [except] ausgenommen, außer (+ D); **~ none** ohne Ausnahme, ausnahmslos.

➤ **Bar** n: **during his time at the Bar** während seiner Zeit als Anwalt; **to be called to the Bar** Br
als Anwalt zugelassen werden.

**Barbados** [baː'beɪdɒs] n Barbados nt; **in ~** auf
Barbados.

**barbarian** [baː'beərɪən] n lit & fig Barbar der,
-in die.

**barbaric** [baː'bærɪk] adj barbarisch.

**barbarous** ['baːbərəs] adj pej - **1.** [uncivilized]
barbarisch - **2.** [cruel] roh, grausam.

**barbecue** ['baːbɪkjuː] n - **1.** [grill] Grill der
- **2.** [party] Barbecue das, Grillparty die <> vt
grillen.

**barbed** ['baːbd] adj - **1.** [hook, spear] mit Wider-
haken (versehen) - **2.** [comment] bissig, spitz.

**barbed wire** [baːbd-] n Stacheldraht der.

**barber** ['baːbəʳ] n (Herren)friseur der; **~'s
(shop)** (Herren)friseursalon der.

**barbiturate** [baː'bɪtjʊrət] n Barbiturat das.

**bar chart, bar graph** Am n Balkendia-
gramm das.

**bar code** n Strichkodierung die, Strichcode
der.

**bare** [beəʳ] adj - **1.** [feet, legs, body] nackt, bloß;
[rock, branches, landscape] kahl - **2.** [basic]: **the
~ facts** die reinen Tatsachen; **the ~ minimum**
das strikte Minimum; **the ~ essentials** das
Allernotwendigste - **3.** [room, cupboard] leer
- **4.** [mere]: **a ~ 15%** gerade mal 15% <> vt entblößen; **to ~ one's teeth** die Zähne fletschen.

**bareback** ['beəbæk] adj & adv ohne Sattel.

**barefaced** ['beəfeɪst] adj schamlos, frech.

**barefoot(ed)** [,beə'fʊt(ɪd)] adj barfüßig
<> adv barfuß.

**bareheaded** [,beə'hedɪd] adj & adv ohne
Kopfbedeckung.

**barelegged** [,beə'legd] adj & adv mit nack-
ten Beinen.

**barely** ['beəlɪ] adv [scarcely] kaum, knapp.

**bargain** ['baːgɪn] n - **1.** [agreement] Geschäft
das; **into the ~** obendrein, noch dazu
- **2.** [good buy] Schnäppchen das, günstiges
Angebot <> vi (ver)handeln; **to ~ with sb for
sthg** mit jm um etw handeln oʀ feilschen.

➤ **bargain for, bargain on** vt fus erwarten,
rechnen mit.

**bargaining** ['baːgɪnɪŋ] n (Ver)handeln das.

**bargaining power** n Verhandlungsspiel-
raum der.

**barge** [baːdʒ] n Schleppkahn der, Lastkahn
der <> vi inf: **to ~ into sb** jn anrempeln; **to ~
into a room** in ein Zimmer hereinplatzen;
**to ~ past sb/sthg** an jm/etw vorbeistürmen.

➤ **barge in** vi: **to ~ in (on sb)** hereinplatzen
(bei jm).

**barge pole** n inf: **I wouldn't touch it with a ~**
das würde ich nicht mal mit der Kneifzan-
ge anfassen.

**bar graph** n Am = bar chart.

**baritone** ['bærɪtəʊn] n Bariton der.

**bark** [baːk] n - **1.** [of dog] Bellen das; **his ~ is
worse than his bite** inf Hunde, die bellen,
beißen nicht - **2.** [on tree] Rinde die, Borke die
<> vt [order] bellen <> vi [dog] bellen; **to ~ at sb/
sthg** jn/etw anbellen.

**barking** ['baːkɪŋ] n Bellen das.

**barley** ['baːlɪ] n Gerste die.

**barley sugar** n Br Malzbonbon der oʀ das.

**barmaid** ['baːmeɪd] n Bardame die.

**barman** ['baːmən] (pl **-men** [-mən]) n Barkeeper der.

**barmy** ['baːmɪ] (compar **-ier**; superl **-iest**) adj Br
inf idiotisch, bescheuert.

**barn** [baːn] n Scheune die.

**barnacle** ['baːnəkl] n Rankenfüßer der.

**barn dance** n Bauerntanz der.

**barn owl** n Schleiereule die.

**barometer** [bə'rɒmɪtəʳ] n lit & fig Barometer
das

**baron** ['bærən] n Baron der; **oil ~** Ölmagnat
der; **press ~** Pressezar der.

**baroness** ['bærənɪs] n Baronin die; [not married]
Baronesse die.

**baronet** ['bærənɪt] n Baronet der.

**baroque** [bə'rɒk] adj Barock-.

**barrack** ['bærək] vt Br auspfeifen, ausbuhen.

➤ **barracks** npl Kaserne die.

**barracking** ['bærəkɪŋ] *n Br* Auspfeifen *das*, Ausbuhen *das*.

**barracuda** [ˌbærə'kuːdə] *n* Barracuda *der*.

**barrage** ['bærɑːʒ] *n* **- 1.** [of firing] Sperrfeuer *das*; **a ~ of complaints/questions** eine Flut von Beschwerden/Fragen **- 2.** *Br* [dam] Staudamm *der*.

**barred** [bɑːd] *adj* [window, door] vergittert.

**barrel** ['bærəl] *n* **- 1.** [for beer, wine] Fass *das* **- 2.** [for oil] Tonne *die*; [as measure] Barrel *das* **- 3.** [of gun] Lauf *der*.

**barrel organ** *n* Drehorgel *die*.

**barren** ['bærən] *adj* **- 1.** [woman, land, soil] unfruchtbar **- 2.** [subject] trocken; [time] unproduktiv.

**barrette** [bə'ret] *n Am* Haarspange *die*.

**barricade** [ˌbærɪ'keɪd] *n* Barrikade *die* ◇ *vt* verbarrikadieren; **to ~ o.s. in** sich verbarrikadieren.

**barrier** ['bærɪəʳ] *n* Barriere *die*; [at car park, level crossing] Schranke *die*.

**barring** ['bɑːrɪŋ] *prep*: **~ accidents** falls nichts passiert.

**barrister** ['bærɪstəʳ] *n Br* Rechtsanwalt *der*, -wältin *die*.

**barroom** ['bɑːruːm] *n Am* Bar *die*.

**barrow** ['bærəʊ] *n* [market stall] Karren *der*, Karre *die*.

**bar stool** *n* Barhocker *der*.

**Bart.** *abbr of* **baronet**.

**bartender** ['bɑːtendəʳ] *n Am* Barkeeper *der*.

**barter** ['bɑːtəʳ] *n* Tauschhandel *der* ◇ *vt & vi* tauschen.

**base** [beɪs] *n* **- 1.** [of post, lamp, mountain] Fuß *der*; [of triangle] Basis *die*; [of box] Boden *der*, Grundfläche *die* **- 2.** [of food, paint] Basis *die* **- 3.** [centre of activities - gen] Standort *der*; [ - military, in mountaineering] Stützpunkt *der* **- 4.** [in baseball] Mal *das* ◇ *vt* **- 1.** [locate] MIL stationieren; **he's ~d in Paris** er arbeitet in Paris **- 2.** [use as stating point]: **to ~ sthg (up)on sthg** etw auf etw *(A)* gründen *OR* basieren; **~d on a novel** nach einem Roman ◇ *adj pej* [dishonourable] niederträchtig.

**baseball** ['beɪsbɔːl] *n (U)* Baseball *der*.

**baseball cap** *n* Baseballkappe *die*.

**Basel** [bɑːl] *n* Basle *nt*.

**baseless** ['beɪslɪs] *adj* unbegründet, grundlos.

**baseline** ['beɪslaɪn] *n* SPORT Grundlinie *die*.

**basement** ['beɪsmənt] *n* [of house] Keller *der*; [of department store] Untergeschoss *das*.

**base rate** *n* Leitzins *der*.

**bases** ['beɪsiːz] *pl* ⊳ **basis**.

**bash** [bæʃ] *inf n* **- 1.** [blow] (heftiger) Schlag **- 2.** [attempt]: **to have a ~ (at sthg)** (etw) mal

probieren **- 3.** [party] Party *die* ◇ *vt* **- 1.** [hit] schlagen, hauen; **to ~ one's head** sich *(D)* den Kopf anlhauen **- 2.** [criticize] attackieren.

**bashful** ['bæʃfʊl] *adj* schüchtern.

**basic** ['beɪsɪk] *adj* grundlegend, wesentlich; [vocabulary, principle] Grund-; [meal, accommodation] einfach.
➤ **basics** *npl*: **the ~s** die Grundlagen *pl*.

**BASIC** ['beɪsɪk] (*abbr of* **Beginner's All-purpose Symbolic Instruction Code**) *n* BASIC *nt*.

**basically** ['beɪsɪklɪ] *adv* grundsätzlich, im Grunde.

**basic rate** *n Br* [of taxation] Eingangssteuersatz *der*; [of interest] Grundzinssatz *der*.

**basic wage** *n* Grundlohn *der*, Grundgehalt *das*.

**basil** ['bæzɪl] *n* Basilikum *das*.

**basin** ['beɪsn] *n* **- 1.** [sink] Waschbecken *das* **- 2.** *Br* [bowl] Schüssel *die* **- 3.** GEOGR Becken *das*.

**basis** ['beɪsɪs] (*pl* **-ses**) *n* **- 1.** [reason] Grundlage *die*, Basis *die*; **on the ~ that** in der Annahme, dass **- 2.** [foundation, arrangement] Basis *die*; **she works for us on a regular ~** sie arbeitet regelmäßig für uns; **on a weekly ~** wöchentlich; **on the ~ of** auf der Grundlage (+ *G*), aufgrund (+ *G*).

**bask** [bɑːsk] *vi* sich aalen; **to ~ in sb's praise/approval** *fig* sich in js Lob/Anerkennung sonnen.

**basket** ['bɑːskɪt] *n* Korb *der*.

**basketball** ['bɑːskɪtbɔːl] *n* Basketball *der*.

**basket case** *n inf* Verrückte *der*, *die*.

**basking shark** ['bɑːskɪŋ-] *n* Riesenhai *der*.

**Basque** [bɑːsk] *adj* baskisch ◇ *n* **- 1.** [person] Baske *der*, -kin *die* **- 2.** [language] Baskisch(e) *das*.

**bass¹** [beɪs] *adj* [part, singer] Bass- ◇ *n* **- 1.** [singer] Bass *der* **- 2.** [double bass] Kontrabass *der* **- 3.** = **bass guitar**.

**bass²** [bæs] (*pl inv OR* **-es**) *n* [fish] (See)barsch *der*.

**bass clef** [beɪs-] *n* Bassschlüssel *der*.

**bass drum** [beɪs-] *n* große Trommel.

**basset (hound)** ['bæsɪt-] *n* Basset *der*.

**bass guitar** [beɪs-] *n* Bassgitarre *die*, Bass *der*.

**bassoon** [bə'suːn] *n* Fagott *das*.

**bastard** ['bɑːstəd] *n* **- 1.** [illegitimate child] Bastard *der* **- 2.** *vinf pej* [unpleasant person] Scheißkerl *der*; **the poor ~** die arme Sau.

**baste** [beɪst] *vt* begießen *(Braten)*.

**bastion** ['bæstɪən] *n fig* Bastion *die*.

**bat** [bæt] (*pt & pp* **-ted**; *cont* **-ting**) *n* **- 1.** [animal] Fledermaus *die* **- 2.** [for cricket, baseball] Schlagholz *das*; [for table tennis] Schläger *der* **- 3.** *phr*: **to do sthg off one's own ~** etw auf eigene Faust tun ⬦ *vt* [hit] schlagen ⬦ *vi* [in cricket, baseball] schlagen.

**batch** [bætʃ] *n* **- 1.** [of papers, letters, work] Stapel *der* **- 2.** [of products] Ladung *die* **- 3.** [of people] Schwung *der*.

**batch file** *n* COMPUT Stapeldatei *die*.

**batch processing** *n* COMPUT Stapelverarbeitung *die*.

**bated** ['beɪtɪd] *adj*: with ~ breath mit angehaltenem Atem.

**bath** [bɑːθ] *n* Bad *das*; [bathtub] (Bade)wanne *die*; to have OR take a ~ ein Bad nehmen, baden ⬦ *vt* baden.

➤ **baths** *npl Br* Bad *das*.

**bathe** [beɪð] *vt* **- 1.** [wound] auslwaschen, baden **- 2.** [in light, sweat] baden; to be ~d in sweat in Schweiß gebadet sein ⬦ *vi* baden.

**bather** ['beɪðə'] *n* Badende *der*, *die*.

**bathing** ['beɪðɪŋ] *n* Baden *das*.

**bathing cap** *n* Badekappe *die*.

**bathing costume, bathing suit** *n* Badeanzug *der*.

**bathing trunks** *npl* Badehose *die*.

**bath mat** *n* Bademate *die*, Badvorleger *der*.

**bath oil** *n* Badeöl *das*.

**bathrobe** ['bɑːθrəʊb] *n* Bademantel *der*.

**bathroom** ['bɑːθrʊm] *n* **- 1.** *Br* [room with bath] Badezimmer *das* **- 2.** *Am* [toilet] Toilette *die*.

**bath salts** *npl* Badesalz *das*.

**bath towel** *n* Badetuch *das*.

**bathtub** ['bɑːθtʌb] *n* Badewanne *die*.

**batik** [bə'tiːk] *n* Batik *der* OR *die*.

**baton** ['bætən] *n* **- 1.** [of conductor] Taktstock *der* **- 2.** [in relay race] Staffelstab *der* **- 3.** *Br* [of policeman] Schlagstock *der*.

**baton charge** *n Br* [by police] Schlagstockeinsatz *der*.

**batsman** ['bætsmən] (*pl* **-men** [-mən]) *n* Schlagmann *der*.

**battalion** [bə'tæljən] *n* Bataillon *das*.

**batten** ['bætn] *n* Latte *die*.

➤ **batten down** *vt fus*: to ~ down the hatches *fig* sich warm anlziehen.

**batter** ['bætə'] *n* CULIN Teig *der* ⬦ *vt* [person] schlagen, verprügeln ⬦ *vi* [on door, wall] hämmern, trommeln.

➤ **batter down** *vt sep* einlschlagen, zertrümmern.

**battered** ['bætəd] *adj* **- 1.** [person] verprügelt **- 2.** [car, hat, suitcase] verbeult **- 3.** CULIN im Teigmantel.

**battering** ['bætərɪŋ] *n*: to take a ~ Prügel bekommen OR beziehen.

**battering ram** *n* Rammbock *der*.

**battery** ['bætəri] (*pl* **-ies**) *n* Batterie *die*.

**battery charger** *n* Batterieladegerät *das*.

**battery hen** *n* Batteriehuhn *das*.

**battle** ['bætl] *n* **- 1.** [in war] Schlacht *die* **- 2.** [struggle]: ~ (for/against) Kampf *der* (für/gegen); ~ of wits geistiger Wettkampf; to be fighting a losing ~ auf verlorenem Posten kämpfen; that's half the ~ damit ist schon eine Menge gewonnen ⬦ *vi*: to ~ (for/against) kämpfen (für/gegen).

**battledress** ['bætldres] *n Br* Kampfanzug *der*.

**battlefield** ['bætfiːld], **battleground** [-graʊnd] *n lit* & *fig* Schlachtfeld *das*.

**battlements** ['bætlmənts] *npl* Zinnen *pl*.

**battleship** ['bætlʃɪp] *n* Schlachtschiff *das*.

**bauble** ['bɔːbl] *n* Christbaumkugel *die*.

**baud** [bɔːd] *n* COMPUT Baud *das*.

**baud rate** *n* COMPUT Baudrate *die*.

**baulk** [bɔːk] *vi* = **balk**.

**Bavaria** [bə'veərɪə] *n* Bayern *nt*.

**Bavarian** [bə'veərɪən] *adj* bay(e)risch ⬦ *n* Bayer *der*, -in *die*.

**bawdy** ['bɔːdɪ] (*compar* **-ier**; *superl* **-iest**) *adj* derb.

**bawl** [bɔːl] *vt* [shout] brüllen ⬦ *vi* **- 1.** [shout] brüllen **- 2.** [weep] heulen.

**bay** [beɪ] *n* **- 1.** GEOGR Bucht *die* **- 2.** [for loading] Ladeplatz *der* **- 3.** [for parking] Parkbucht *die* **- 4.** [horse] Braune *der* **- 5.** *phr*: to keep sb at ~ jn auf Abstand halten ⬦ *vi* [dog, wolf] bellen.

**bay leaf** *n* Lorbeerblatt *das*.

**bayonet** ['beɪənɪt] *n* Bajonett *das*.

**bay tree** *n* Lorbeerbaum *der*.

**bay window** *n* Erkerfenster *das*.

**bazaar** [bə'zɑː'] *n* **- 1.** [market] Basar *der* **- 2.** *Br* [charity sale] Wohltätigkeitsbasar *der*.

**bazooka** [bə'zuːkə] *n* Panzerfaust *die*.

**B & B** *n abbr of* **bed and breakfast**.

**BBC** (*abbr of* **British Broadcasting Corporation**) *n* BBC *die*.

**BC - 1.** (*abbr of* **before Christ**) v. Chr. **- 2.** *abbr of* **British Columbia**.

**BCG** (*abbr of* **Bacillus Calmette-Guérin**) *n* BCG *nt*.

**B/D** *n abbr of* **bank draft**.

**BDS** (*abbr of* **Bachelor of Dental Science**) *n akademischer Grad in der Zahnheilkunde oder dessen Inhaber*.

**be** [biː] (*pt* **was** OR **were**; *pp* **been**) *vi* **- 1.** [exist] sein; there is/are es ist/sind ... da, es gibt; are there any shops near here? gibt es hier in der Nähe irgendwelche Geschäfte?; there is someone in the room es ist jemand im Zimmer; ~ that as it may wie dem auch sei **- 2.** [referring to location] sein; the hotel is near the airport das Hotel ist in der Nähe des Flughafens; he will ~ here tomorrow er kommt morgen - **3.** [referring to movement] sein; **have you ever been to California?** warst du schon mal in Kalifornien?; **I'll ~ there in ten minutes** ich komme in zehn Minuten; **where have you been?** wo bist du gewesen? - **4.** [occur] sein; **my birthday is in June** mein Geburtstag ist im Juni - **5.** [identifying, describing] sein; **he's a doctor** er ist Arzt; **I'm British** ich bin Brite/Britin; **I'm hot/cold** mir ist heiß/kalt; **you are right** du hast Recht; **~ quiet!** sei still!, seid still!; **one and one are two** eins und eins ist zwei - **6.** [referring to health]: **how are you?** wie geht es Ihnen?; **I'm fine** mir geht es gut; **she is ill** sie ist krank - **7.** [referring to age]: **how old are you?** wie alt bist du?; **I am 14 (years old)** ich bin 14 (Jahre alt) - **8.** [referring to cost] kosten; **how much is it?** wie viel kostet es?; **it's £10** es kostet 10 Pfund - **9.** [referring to time, dates] sein; **what time is it?** wie viel Uhr ist es?, wie spät ist es?; **it's ten o'clock** es ist zehn Uhr; **today is February 17th** heute haben wir den 17. Februar - **10.** [referring to measurement] sein; **it's ten metres long/high** es ist zehn Meter lang/hoch; **I'm 8 stone** ich wiege 50 Kilo - **11.** [referring to the weather] sein; **it's hot/cold** es ist heiß/kalt - **12.** [for emphasis] sein; **is that you?** bist du das?; **yes, it's me** ja, ich bins ⟨⟩ aux vb - **1.** (in combination with present participle to form continuous tense): **I'm learning German** ich lerne Deutsch; **what is he doing?** was macht er?; **it's snowing** es schneit; **we've been visiting the museum** wir waren im Museum; **I've been living in London for 10 years** ich wohne seit 10 Jahren in London; **he is going on holiday next week** nächste Woche fährt er in Urlaub - **2.** (forming passive) werden; **they were defeated** sie wurden geschlagen; **the flight was delayed** das Flugzeug hatte Verspätung; **to ~ loved** geliebt werden; **it is said** man sagt - **3.** (with infinitive to express an order): **all rooms are to ~ vacated by 10.00 a.m.** alle Zimmer müssen bis 10 Uhr geräumt sein; **you are not to tell anyone** das darfst du niemandem erzählen - **4.** (with infinitive to express future tense): **the race is to start at noon** das Rennen ist für 12 Uhr angesetzt - **5.** (in tag questions): **it's cold, isn't it?** es ist kalt, nicht wahr?; **you're not going now, are you?** willst du schon gehen?

**B/E** abbr of **bill of exchange.**

**beach** [biːtʃ] n Strand der ⟨⟩ vt auf (den) Strand setzen.

**beach ball** n Wasserball der.

**beach buggy** n Strandbuggy der.

**beachcomber** [ˈbiːtʃˌkəʊmər] n Strandgutsammler der.

**beachhead** [ˈbiːtʃhed] n MIL Brückenkopf der.

**beachwear** [ˈbiːtʃweər] n (U) Strandkleidung die.

**beacon** [ˈbiːkən] n - **1.** [fire, lighthouse] Leuchtfeuer das - **2.** [radio beacon] Funkfeuer das.

**bead** [biːd] n [of glass, wood, sweat] Perle die.

**beaded** [ˈbiːdɪd] adj [dress, bag] mit Perlen besetzt.

**beady** [ˈbiːdɪ] (compar -ier; superl -iest) adj [eyes] wach.

**beagle** [ˈbiːgl] n Beagle der.

**beak** [biːk] n [of bird] Schnabel der.

**beaker** [ˈbiːkər] n Becher der.

**be-all** n: **money/winning is not the ~ and end-all** das Gewinnen/Geld ist nicht alles.

**beam** [biːm] n - **1.** [of wood] Balken der; [of steel] Träger der - **2.** [of light] Strahl der - **3.** Am AUT: **high/low ~s** Fern-/Abblendlicht das ⟨⟩ vt [signal, news] auslstrahlen ⟨⟩ vi strahlen.

**beaming** [ˈbiːmɪŋ] adj strahlend.

**bean** [biːn] n Bohne die; **to be full of ~s** inf voller Tatendrang sein; **to spill the ~s** inf [confess] singen.

**beanbag** [ˈbiːnbæg] n [seat] Sitzsack der.

**beanshoot** [ˈbiːnʃuːt], **beansprout** [-spraʊt] n (Soja)bohnensprosse die.

**bear** [beər] (pt bore; pp borne) n - **1.** [animal] Bär der - **2.** ST EX Baissespekulant der ⟨⟩ vt - **1.** [gen] tragen - **2.** [tolerate] ertragen, auslhalten - **3.** [fruit] tragen; [interest] einlbringen - **4.** [child] gebären - **5.** [ill will, hatred] hegen ⟨⟩ vi - **1.** [turn]: **to ~ left/right** sich links/rechts halten - **2.** [have effect]: **to bring pressure/influence to ~ on sb** bei jm Druck/Einfluss geltend machen.

◆ **bear down** vi: **to ~ down on sb/sthg** auf jn/etw zulsteuern.

◆ **bear out** vt sep bestätigen.

◆ **bear up** vi: **to ~ up well** sich tapfer halten.

◆ **bear with** vt fus: **~ with me for a minute, will you?** einen Moment Geduld, bitte.

**bearable** [ˈbeərəbl] adj erträglich.

**beard** [bɪəd] n Bart der.

**bearded** [ˈbɪədɪd] adj bärtig.

**bearer** [ˈbeərər] n - **1.** [of stretcher, coffin] Träger der - **2.** [of news, letter] Überbringer der, -in die - **3.** [of cheque, passport] Inhaber der, -in die - **4.** [of name, title] Träger der, -in die.

**bear hug** n inf kräftige OR warmherzige Umarmung.

**bearing** [ˈbeərɪŋ] n - **1.** [relevance] Bedeutung die; **to have a ~ on sthg** bei etw eine Rolle spielen - **2.** [deportment] (Körper)haltung die - **3.** TECH Lager das - **4.** [on compass]: **to take a ~** die Richtung bestimmen; **to get one's ~s** sich orientieren; **to lose one's ~s** fig die Orientierung verlieren.

**bear market** n ST EX Baissemarkt der.

**bearskin** [ˈbeəskɪn] n - **1.** [fur] Bärenfell das - **2.** [hat] Bärenfellmütze die.

**beast** [biːst] *n* - **1.** [animal] Tier *das* - **2.** *inf pej* [person - unpleasant] Ekel *das;* [ - evil] Bestie *die.*

**beastly** ['biːstlɪ] (*compar* -**ier;** *superl* -**iest**) *adj dated* scheußlich.

**beat** [biːt] (*pt* beat; *pp* beaten) *n* - **1.** [of drum, heart, pulse] Schlag *der;* **the ~ of wings** das Flügelschlagen - **2.** [mus - rhythm] Rhythmus *der;* [ - measure] Takt *der* - **3.** [of policeman] Runde *die* ◇ *adj inf* [exhausted] todmüde, geschafft ◇ *vt* - **1.** [gen] schlagen; **to ~ a record** einen Rekord brechen; **it ~s me** *inf* ich habe keine Ahnung - **2.** [arrive ahead of] zuvorkommen (+ D); **you've ~en me to it!** du bist mir zuvorgekommen! - **3.** mus: **to ~ time** (den) Takt schlagen *or* anlgeben - **4.** *phr:* **~ it!** *inf* [go away] verschwinde!, hau ab! ◇ *vi* - **1.** [rain - on roof] trommeln - **2.** [heart, pulse] schlagen.

**beat down** *vi* - **1.** [sun] niederlbrennen - **2.** [rain] niederlprasseln ◇ *vt sep* [seller] herunterlhandeln.

**beat off** *vt sep* [resist] ablwehren.

**beat up** *vt sep* *inf* [person] zusammenlschlagen.

**beaten** ['biːtn] *adj* - **1.** [metal] gehämmert - **2.** [path] ausgetreten.

**beater** ['biːtəʳ] *n* - **1.** [for eggs] Schneebesen *der* - **2.** [for carpet] Teppichklopfer *der.*

**beating** ['biːtɪŋ] *n* - **1.** [punishment] Prügel *pl;* **to give sb a ~** jm eine Tracht Prügel verabreichen - **2.** [defeat] Niederlage *die;* **to take some ~** *inf* nicht leicht zu schlagen sein.

**beat-up** *adj inf* [shabby] heruntergekommen.

**beautician** [bjuːˈtɪʃn] *n* Kosmetikerin *die.*

**beautiful** ['bjuːtɪfʊl] *adj* - **1.** [person] schön - **2.** [picture, music, weather] wundervoll, herrlich - **3.** *inf* [goal, player] herrlich, toll.

**beautifully** ['bjuːtəflɪ] *adv* - **1.** [dressed, decorated] bezaubernd - **2.** *inf* [cook, sing, play] wunderbar.

**beauty** ['bjuːtɪ] (*pl* -**ies**) *n* Schönheit *die;* **the goal was a ~** das war ein Traumtor ◇ *comp* [product] Schönheits-.

**beauty contest** *n* Schönheitswettbewerb *der.*

**beauty parlour** *n* Schönheitssalon *der.*

**beauty queen** *n* Schönheitskönigin *die.*

**beauty salon** *n* = beauty parlour.

**beauty spot** *n* - **1.** [place] schönes Fleckchen - **2.** [on skin] Schönheitsfleck *der.*

**beaver** ['biːvəʳ] *n* Biber *der;* [fur] Biberpelz *der.*

**beaver away** *vi:* **to ~ away at sthg** an etw (D) schuften.

**becalmed** [bɪˈkɑːmd] *adj* in einer Flaute liegend.

**became** [bɪˈkeɪm] *pt* ▷ become.

**because** [bɪˈkɒz] *conj* weil.

**because of** *prep* wegen (+ G, D).

**beck** [bek] *n:* **to be at sb's ~ and call** nach js Pfeife tanzen.

**beckon** ['bekən] *vt* - **1.** [make a signal to] zulwinken (+ D) - **2.** *fig* [call] rufen ◇ *vi:* **to ~ to sb** jm zulwinken.

**become** [bɪˈkʌm] (*pt* became; *pp* become) *vt* werden; **to ~ old/rich/famous** alt/reich/berühmt werden; **to ~ accustomed to sthg** sich an etw (A) gewöhnen; **what became of him?** was ist aus ihm geworden?; **to ~ a priest** Priester werden.

**becoming** [bɪˈkʌmɪŋ] *adj* - **1.** [attractive] **it's very ~** es steht ihr/dir/*etc* gut - **2.** [appropriate] schicklich.

**BECTU** ['bektuːl] (*abbr of* Broadcasting, Entertainment, Cinematograph and Theatre Union) *n* britische Gewerkschaft der Techniker aus den Bereichen Rundfunk, Unterhaltung, Film und Theater.

**bed** [bed] (*pt* & *pp* -**ded;** *cont* -**ding**) *n* - **1.** [to sleep on] Bett *das;* **to go to ~** zu *or* ins Bett gehen; **to get out of ~** auf lstehen; **to make the ~** das Bett machen; **to go to ~ with sb** *euphemism* mit jm ins Bett gehen - **2.** [flowerbed] Beet *das;* **it's no ~ of roses** *fig* das ist kein Zuckerschlecken - **3.** [of sea] Meeresgrund *der;* [of river] Flussbett *das.*

**bed down** *vi* kampieren.

**BEd** [ˌbiːˈed] (*abbr of* Bachelor of Education) *n* erziehungswissenschaftlicher Grad mit Lehrbefähigung oder dessen Inhaber.

**bed and breakfast** *n* Zimmer *das* mit Frühstück.

**BED AND BREAKFAST**

Bei „Bed and Breakfast", meist einfach „B & B" oder auch „guest house" genannt, handelt es sich um eine in Großbritannien sehr verbreitete Unterkunftsmöglichkeit bei Privatleuten, die ein oder mehrere Zimmer für zahlende Gäste bereitstellen. Das Frühstück, ein „English breakfast", besteht aus Würstchen, Eiern, gebratenem Speck, Toast und Tee oder Kaffee und ist im Zimmerpreis inbegriffen.

**bedbug** ['bedbʌg] *n* Wanze *die.*

**bedclothes** ['bedkləʊðz] *npl* Bettzeug *das.*

**bedcover** ['bedˌkʌvəʳ] *n* Tagesdecke *die.*

**bedding** ['bedɪŋ] *n* (U) = bedclothes.

**bedding plant** *n* Setzling *der.*

**bedeck** [bɪˈdek] *vt:* **to ~ sthg with sthg** etw mit etw dekorieren *or* verzieren.

**bedevil** [bɪˈdevl] (*Br pt* & *pp* -**led;** *cont* -**ling,** *Am pt* & *pp* -**ed;** *cont* -**ing**) *vt:* **to be ~led with sthg** von etw geplagt werden.

**bedfellow** ['bedˌfeləʊ] *n* *fig* [colleague] Bettgenosse *der.*

**bedlam** ['bedləm] *n* Chaos *das.*

**bed linen** n Bettwäsche die.

**Bedouin** ['beduɪn] adj Beduinen- ⟨> n Beduine der, -nin die.

**bedpan** ['bedpæn] n Bettpfanne die.

**bedraggled** [bɪ'drægld] adj schmutzig und nass.

**bedridden** ['bed,rɪdn] adj bettlägerig.

**bedrock** ['bedrɒk] n - **1.** GEOL Felsenuntergrund der - **2.** fig [solid foundation] stabile Grundlage.

**bedroom** ['bedrʊm] n Schlafzimmer das.

**Beds** [bedz] abk für Bedfordshire, in Postanschrift verwendet.

**bedside** ['bedsaɪd] n: at sb's ~ an js Bett.

**bedside manner** n das Verhalten eines Doktors gegenüber seinem Patienten.

**bedside table** n Nachttisch der.

**bed-sit(ter)** n Br Wohnschlafzimmer das.

**bedsore** ['bedsɔːr] n wundgelegene Stelle.

**bedspread** ['bedspred] n Tagesdecke die.

**bedtime** ['bedtaɪm] n Schlafenszeit die.

**Beduin** ['beduɪn] adj & n = **Bedouin.**

**bed-wetting** [-,wetɪŋ] n Bettnässen das.

**bee** [biː] n Biene die; to have a ~ in one's bonnet eine fixe Idee haben.

**Beeb** [biːb] n Br inf: the ~ die BBC.

**beech** [biːtʃ] n - **1.** [tree] Buche die - **2.** [wood] Buchenholz das.

**beef** [biːf] n Rindfleisch das.
➡ **beef up** vt sep inf [report, story] auf|polieren; [flavour] verstärken.

**beefburger** ['biːf,bɜːgər] n Hamburger der, Rinderhacksteak das.

**Beefeater** ['biːf,iːtər] n Beefeater der.

**beefsteak** ['biːf,steɪk] n Beefsteak das.

**beehive** ['biːhaɪv] n [for bees] Bienenstock der.

**beekeeper** ['biː,kiːpər] n Imker der, -in die.

**beeline** ['biːlaɪn] n: to make a ~ for sb/sthg inf geradewegs auf jn/etw zu|steuern.

**been** [biːn] pp ⊳ be.

**beep** [biːp] inf n Pieps(ton) der ⟨> vi piepen.

**beeper** ['biːpər] n [device] Piepser der.

**beer** [bɪər] n Bier das.

**beer garden** n Biergarten der.

**beermat** ['bɪə,mæt] n Bierdeckel der.

**beeswax** ['biːzwæks] n Bienenwachs das.

**beet** [biːt] n - **1.** [sugar beet] Zuckerrübe die - **2.** Am [beetroot] rote Rübe, rote Bete.

**beetle** ['biːtl] n Käfer der.

**beetroot** ['biːtruːt] n rote Rübe, rote Bete.

**befall** [bɪ'fɔːl] (pt befell [-'fel], pp befallen [-'fɔːlən]) vt literary [subj: misfortune] zu|stoßen (+ D); [subj: fate, harm] treffen.

**befit** [bɪ'fɪt] (pt & pp **-ted**; cont **-ting**) vt fml sich gehören für.

**before** [bɪ'fɔːr] prep - **1.** [in time] vor (+ D); they arrived ~ us sie sind vor uns angekommen; the week ~ last vorletzte Woche; the day ~ yesterday vorgestern; the day ~ der Tag zuvor; she had arrived the day ~ sie war am Tag(e) zuvor angekommen; ~ long bald - **2.** [in front of, facing] vor (+ D); ~ my (very) eyes vor meinen Augen; we have a difficult task ~ us wir haben eine schwierige Aufgabe vor uns ⟨> adv [previously] schon einmal; never ~ noch nie ⟨> conj bevor; ~ you go bevor du gehst.

**beforehand** [bɪ'fɔːhænd] adv vorher, im Voraus.

**befriend** [bɪ'frend] vt sich an|freunden mit.

**befuddled** [bɪ'fʌdld] adj benebelt.

**beg** [beg] (pt & pp **-ged**; cont **-ging**) vt - **1.** [money, food] betteln um - **2.** [favour, forgiveness] bitten um; to ~ sb for sthg jn um etw bitten; to ~ sb to do sthg jn bitten, etw zu tun ⟨> vi - **1.** [for money, food]: to ~ (for) betteln (um) - **2.** [for favour, forgiveness]: to ~ (for) bitten (um).

**began** [bɪ'gæn] pt ⊳ begin.

**beggar** ['begər] n Bettler der, -in die.

**begin** [bɪ'gɪn] (pt began; pp begun; cont **-ning**) vt beginnen, an|fangen; to ~ doing OR to do sthg beginnen OR an|fangen, etw zu tun ⟨> vi beginnen, an|fangen; to ~ with zunächst, zu Anfang.

**beginner** [bɪ'gɪnər] n Anfänger der, -in die.

**beginning** [bɪ'gɪnɪŋ] n Anfang der; in OR at the ~ am Anfang; from the ~ von Anfang an.

**begonia** [bɪ'gəʊnjə] n Begonie die.

**begrudge** [bɪ'grʌdʒ] vt - **1.** [envy]: to ~ sb sthg jm etw missgönnen - **2.** [do unwillingly]: to ~ doing sthg etw widerwillig tun.

**beguile** [bɪ'gaɪl] vt [charm] bezaubern.

**beguiling** [bɪ'gaɪlɪŋ] adj [charming] bezaubernd.

**begun** [bɪ'gʌn] pp ⊳ begin.

**behalf** [bɪ'hɑːf] n: on Br OR in Am ~ of im Namen (+ G), im Auftrag (+ G).

**behave** [bɪ'heɪv] vt: to ~ o.s. sich benehmen ⟨> vi sich verhalten; [with good manners] sich benehmen.

**behaviour** Br, **behavior** Am [bɪ'heɪvjər] n Benehmen das.

**behead** [bɪ'hed] vt enthaupten, köpfen.

**beheld** [bɪ'held] pt & pp ⊳ behold.

**behind** [bɪ'haɪnd] prep - **1.** [at the back of] hinter (+ D); [with verbs of motion] hinter (+ A) - **2.** [causing, responsible for] hinter (+ D); what's ~ this campaign? was hat es mit dieser Kampagne auf sich?; what's ~ it? was steckt dahinter?

- **3.** [supporting]: **to be ~ sb** *fig* jn unterstützen - **4.** [indicating deficiency, delay]: **~ schedule** im Rückstand; **the train is 15 minutes ~ time** der Zug hat 15 Minuten Verspätung ⬦ *adv* - **1.** [at, in the back] hinten; **the others followed ~** die anderen kamen hinterher; **to leave sthg ~** etw zurücklassen; **to stay ~** (noch) (da)bleiben - **2.** [late]: **to be ~ (with sthg)** (mit etw) im Verzug sein ⬦ *n inf* [buttocks] Hintern *der*.

**behold** [bɪ'həʊld] (*pt* & *pp* **beheld**) *vt literary* erblicken.

**beige** [beɪʒ] *adj* beige ⬦ *n* Beige *das*.

**Beijing** [ˌbeɪ'dʒɪŋ] *n* Peking *nt*.

**being** ['biːɪŋ] *n* - **1.** [creature] Wesen *das*, Geschöpf *das* - **2.** [existence]: **in ~** existierend, vorhanden; **to come into ~** entstehen.

**Beirut** [ˌbeɪ'ruːt] *n* Beirut *nt*.

**belated** [bɪ'leɪtɪd] *adj* verspätet.

**belatedly** [bɪ'leɪtɪdlɪ] *adv* verspätet.

**belch** [beltʃ] *n* Rülpser *der* ⬦ *vt* [smoke, fire] (aus)speien ⬦ *vi* - **1.** [person] rülpsen - **2.** [smoke, fire] (aus)speien.

**beleaguered** [bɪ'liːgəd] *adj lit* & *fig* belagert.

**belfry** ['belfrɪ] (*pl* -ies) *n* Glockenturm *der*.

**Belgian** ['beldʒən] *adj* belgisch ⬦ *n* Belgier *der*, -in *die*.

**Belgium** ['beldʒəm] *n* Belgien *nt*.

**Belgrade** [ˌbel'greɪd] *n* Belgrad *nt*.

**belie** [bɪ'laɪ] (*cont* **belying**) *vt* [claim, statement] nicht entsprechen *(+ D)*; **his looks ~ his age** er sieht jünger/älter aus, als er ist.

**belief** [bɪ'liːf] *n* - **1.** [gen]: **~ (in)** Glaube *der (+ A)*; **beyond ~** unglaublich - **2.** [opinion] Meinung *die*; **it's my ~ that ...** ich bin davon überzeugt, dass ...; **in the ~ that** im Glauben, dass.

**believable** [bɪ'liːvəbl] *adj* glaubwürdig, glaubhaft.

**believe** [bɪ'liːv] *vt* glauben; **to ~ sb** jm glauben; **I ~ so** ich glaube ja; **I don't ~ it!** das darf (ja wohl) nicht wahr sein!; **~ it or not** ob du/Sie es glaubst/glauben oder nicht ⬦ *vi* glauben; **to ~ in sb/sthg** an jn/etw glauben; **I ~ in getting up early** ich halte viel davon, früh aufzustehen.

**believer** [bɪ'liːvəʳ] *n* RELIG Gläubige *der*, *die*; **I'm a great ~ in corporal punishment** ich halte viel von der Prügelstrafe.

**belittle** [bɪ'lɪtl] *vt* schmälern, herabwürdigen.

**Belize** [be'liːz] *n* Belize *nt*.

**bell** [bel] *n* Glocke *die*; [of phone, door, bike] Klingel *die*; **that rings a ~** *fig* das kommt mir bekannt vor.

**bell-bottoms** *npl* Schlaghose *die*.

**bellhop** ['belhɒp] *n Am* Page *der*, Hotelboy *der*.

**belligerence** [bɪ'lɪdʒərəns] *n* Aggressivität *die*.

**belligerent** [bɪ'lɪdʒərənt] *adj* - **1.** [at war] kriegführend - **2.** [aggressive] angriffslustig.

**bellow** ['beləʊ] *vt* & *vi* brüllen.

**bellows** ['beləʊz] *npl* Blasebalg *der*.

**bell push** *n Br* Klingelknopf *der*.

**bell-ringer** *n* Glöckner *der*.

**belly** ['belɪ] (*pl* -ies) *n* Bauch *der*.

**bellyache** ['belɪeɪk] *n* Bauchschmerzen *pl* ⬦ *vi inf* [complain] jammern.

**belly button** *n inf* Bauchnabel *der*.

**belly dancer** *n* Bauchtänzerin *die*.

**belong** [bɪ'lɒŋ] *vi* gehören; **to ~ to sb** jm gehören; **to ~ to a party/club** einer Partei/einem Verein anlgehören.

**belongings** [bɪ'lɒŋɪŋz] *npl* Sachen *pl*, Habseligkeiten *pl*.

**beloved** [bɪ'lʌvd] *adj* geliebt ⬦ *n* Geliebte *der*, *die*.

**below** [bɪ'ləʊ] *adv* - **1.** [in a lower position] unten; **they live on the floor ~** sie wohnen ein Stockwerk tiefer; **see** ~ [in text] siehe unten - **2.** [with numbers, quantities]: **children of 5 and ~** Kinder bis zu 5 Jahre - **3.** NAUT: **to go ~** unter Deck gehen ⬦ *prep* - **1.** [lower than] unter *(+ D)*; [with verbs of motion] unter *(+ A)*; **~ the tree line** unterhalb der Baumgrenze - **2.** [in rank, status] unter *(+ D)*; **a sergeant is ~ a captain** ein Feldwebel steht unter einem Hauptmann - **3.** [less than] unter *(+ D)*; **10 degrees ~ (zero)** 10 Grad unter Null; **~ average** unter dem Durchschnitt, unterdurchschnittlich.

**belt** [belt] *n* - **1.** [for clothing] Gürtel *der*; **that was below the ~** das war ein Schlag unter die Gürtellinie; **to have sthg under one's ~** [qualification] etw in der Tasche haben; [experience] etw gesammelt haben; **to tighten one's ~** den Gürtel enger schnallen - **2.** TECH Riemen *der* - **3.** [of land, sea] Zone *die*, Gürtel *der* ⬦ *vt inf* [hit] verprügeln ⬦ *vi Br inf* [move at speed] rasen, brausen.

➡ **belt out** *vt sep inf*: **to ~ out a song** ein Lied aus voller Kehle singen.

➡ **belt up** *vi Br inf* [be quiet] die Klappe halten.

**beltway** ['belt,weɪ] *n Am* Umgehungsstraße *die*.

**bemused** [bɪ'mjuːzd] *adj* verwirrt.

**bench** [bentʃ] *n* - **1.** POL [seat] Bank *die* - **2.** [in workshop] Werkbank *die*; [in laboratory] Labortisch *der*.

**benchmark** ['bentʃmɑːk] *n* [standard] Standard *der*; COMPUT Benchmark *der*.

**bend** [bend] (*pt* & *pp* **bent**) *n* - **1.** [in river, pipe] Biegung *die*; [in road] Kurve *die* - **2.** *phr*: **round the ~** *inf* verrückt, bekloppt ⬦ *vt* [arm, leg, knee] beugen; [back] krümmen; [head] neigen; [wire, fork, tube] (ver)biegen ◇ *vi* - **1.** [arm, leg] beugen; [branch, tree] biegen - **2.** [person] sich bücken, sich beugen - **3.** [road] eine Kurve machen; [river] eine Biegung machen.

◆ **bends** *npl* MED: **the ~s** die Caissonkrankheit.

◆ **bend down** *vi* sich bücken, sich herunterlbeugen.

◆ **bend over** *vi* sich bücken, sich nach vorn beugen; **to ~ over backwards for sb** alles für jn tun.

**beneath** [bɪˈniːθ] *adv* [below] unten ◇ *prep* - **1.** [under] unter (+ *D*); [with verbs of motion] unter (+ *A*); **it's ~ the bridge** es ist unter der Brücke; **she shoved it ~ the bed** sie schob es unter das Bett - **2.** [unworthy of]: **that is ~ him** das ist unter seiner Würde.

**benefactor** [ˈbenɪfæktəʳ] *n* Wohltäter *der*, -in *die*.

**beneficial** [ˌbenɪˈfɪʃl] *adj* nützlich, nutzbringend; **to be ~ to sb/sthg** jm/etw zugute kommen.

**beneficiary** [ˌbenɪˈfɪʃərɪ] (*pl* -**ies**) *n* - **1.** LAW [of will] Begünstigte *der*, *die* - **2.** [of change in law, new rule] Nutznießer *der*, -in *die*.

**benefit** [ˈbenɪfɪt] *n* - **1.** (*U*) [advantage] Nutzen *der*; **to be to sb's ~**, **to be of ~ to sb** zu js Nutzen sein, für jn von Nutzen sein; **for the ~ of** zum Nutzen von (+ *G*); **to give sb the ~ of the doubt** jm trotz Zweifels Glauben schenken - **2.** [good point] Vorteil *der* - **3.** [allowance of money] Unterstützung *die* ◇ *comp* [concert, match, performance] Benefiz- ◇ *vt* nützen (+ *D*) ◇ *vi:* **to ~ from sthg** von etw profitieren.

**Benelux** [ˈbenɪlʌks] *n:* **the ~ countries** die Beneluxstaaten, die Beneluxländer.

**benevolent** [bɪˈnevələnt] *adj* wohlwollend.

**BEng** [ˌbiːˈeŋ] (*abbr of* **Bachelor of Engineering**) *n* akademischer Abschluß in den Ingenieurwissenschaften oder dessen Inhaber.

**benign** [bɪˈnaɪn] *adj* - **1.** [influence] gut; [climate] mild - **2.** MED gutartig.

**Benin** [beˈniːn] *n* Benin *nt*.

**bent** [bent] *pt* & *pp* ⊳ **bend** ◇ *adj* - **1.** [wire, bar] gebogen, verbogen - **2.** [person, body] gebeugt - **3.** *Br inf* [dishonest] korrupt - **4.** [determined]: **to be ~ on sthg** etw unbedingt wollen/ haben wollen; **to be ~ on doing sthg** etw unbedingt tun wollen ◇ *n* [natural aptitude]: **~ (for)** Neigung *die* (zu).

**bequeath** [bɪˈkwiːð] *vt lit* & *fig* hinterlassen; **to ~ sb sthg**, **to ~ sthg to sb** jm etw hinterlassen.

**bequest** [bɪˈkwest] *n* Nachlass *der*.

**berate** [bɪˈreɪt] *vt* schelten.

**Berber** [ˈbɜːbəʳ] *adj* berberisch ◇ *n* - **1.** [per-

son] Berber *der*, -frau *die* - **2.** [language] Berbersprache *die*.

**bereaved** [bɪˈriːvd] (*pl inv*) *adj:* **to be ~** trauern ◇ *npl:* **the ~** die Hinterbliebenen *pl*.

**bereavement** [bɪˈriːvmənt] *n* Trauerfall *der*.

**bereft** [bɪˈreft] *adj literary* mangelnd; **~ of sthg** einer Sache (*G*) beraubt.

**beret** [ˈbereɪ] *n* Baskenmütze *die*.

**Bering Strait** [ˈberɪŋ-] *n:* **the ~** die Beringstraße.

**berk** [bɜːk] *n Br inf* Dussel *der*.

**Berks** [bɑːks] *abk für* **Berkshire**, *in Postanschrift verwendet*.

**Berlin** [bɜːˈlɪn] *n* Berlin *nt*; **East ~** Ostberlin *nt*; **West ~** Westberlin *nt*; **the ~ Wall** die Mauer.

**Berliner** [bɜːˈlɪnəʳ] *n* Berliner *der*, -in *die*.

**berm** [bɜːm] *n Am* Grünstreifen *der*.

**Bermuda** [bəˈmjuːdə] *n* Bermudainseln *pl*, Bermudas *pl*.

**Bermuda shorts** *npl* Bermudashorts *pl*.

**Bern** [bɜːn] *n* Bern *nt*.

**berry** [ˈberɪ] (*pl* -**ies**) *n* Beere *die*.

**berserk** [bəˈzɜːk] *adj:* **to go ~** wild werden.

**berth** [bɜːθ] *n* - **1.** [in harbour] Liegeplatz *der*, Ankerplatz *der* - **2.** [on ship] Koje *die*; [on train] Schlafwagenplatz *der* - **3.** *phr:* **to give sb a wide ~** einen großen Bogen um jn machen ◇ *vt* [ship]: **to ~ a ship** mit einem Schiff (am Kai) anlegen ◇ *vi* [ship] anllegen.

**beseech** [bɪˈsiːtʃ] (*pt* & *pp* **besought** OR **beseeched**) *vt literary* [implore]: **to ~ sb (to do sthg)** jn anlflehen(, etw zu tun).

**beset** [bɪˈset] (*pt* & *pp* **beset**; *cont* -**ting**) *adj:* **~ with** OR **by sthg** von etw heimgesucht ◇ *vt* heimlsuchen.

**beside** [bɪˈsaɪd] *prep* - **1.** [next to] neben (+ *A*, *D*) - **2.** [compared with] verglichen mit - **3.** *phr:* **to be ~ o.s. with joy/anger** vor Freude/Wut außer sich sein.

**besides** [bɪˈsaɪdz] *adv* außerdem; **~ being expensive, it's also ugly** es ist nicht nur teuer, sondern auch hässlich ◇ *prep* [in addition to] außer (+ *D*).

**besiege** [bɪˈsiːdʒ] *vt lit* & *fig* belagern; **to be ~d with sthg** *fig* mit etw überschüttet werden.

**besotted** [bɪˈsɒtɪd] *adj:* **~ (with sb)** vernarrt (in jn).

**besought** [bɪˈsɔːt] *pt* & *pp* ⊳ **beseech**.

**bespectacled** [bɪˈspektəkld] *adj* bebrillt.

**bespoke** [bɪˈspəʊk] *adj Br* [clothes] maßgeschneidert, nach Maß.

**best** [best] *adj* beste, -r, -s; **my ~ friend** mein bester Freund/meine beste Freundin ◇ *adv* am besten; **which car do you like ~?**

welches Auto gefällt dir am besten?; **what type of beer do you like ~?** welches Bier magst du am liebsten? $\diamondsuit$ *n* - **1.** Beste *der, die, das;* **to do one's ~** sein Bestes tun - **2.** *phr:* **to make the ~ of sthg** das Beste aus etw machen; **for the ~** nur zum Guten; **all the ~!** alles Gute!; **he wants the ~ of both worlds** er will weder auf das eine noch auf das andere verzichten.

➡ **at best** *adv* bestenfalls.

**bestial** ['bestjəl] *adj* bestialisch.

**best man** *n* Trauzeuge *der.*

**bestow** [bɪ'stəʊ] *vt fml:* **to ~ sthg on sb** jm etw gewähren.

**best-seller** *n* [book] Bestseller *der,* Kassenschlager *der.*

**best-selling** *adj* meistverkauft.

**bet** [bet] (*pt & pp* bet *OR* -ted; *cont* -ting) *n* - **1.** [wager] Wette *die;* **to hedge one's ~s** sich absichern - **2.** *fig* [prediction]: **it's a safe ~ that ...** man kann sicher sein, dass ... $\diamondsuit$ *vt* wetten $\diamondsuit$ *vi* - **1.** [gamble]: **to ~ (on sthg)** (auf etw *(A)*) wetten - **2.** *fig* [predict]: **to ~ on sthg** sich auf etw *(A)* verlassen - **3.** *phr:* **you ~!** *inf* darauf kannst du wetten!, und ob!

**Bethlehem** ['beθlɪhem] *n* Bethlehem *nt.*

**betray** [bɪ'treɪ] *vt* verraten; [trust] missbrauchen.

**betrayal** [bɪ'treɪəl] *n* Verrat *der;* **~ of trust** Vertrauensmissbrauch *der.*

**betrothed** [bɪ'trəʊðd] *adj dated:* **~ (to sb)** (jm) versprochen.

**better** ['betər] *adj (compar of good, well)* besser; **to get ~** besser werden; **I hope you get ~ soon** ich hoffe, es geht dir bald besser; **to get ~ and ~** immer besser werden $\diamondsuit$ *adv* besser; [like] lieber $\diamondsuit$ *n* [best one] Bessere *der, die, das;* **to get the ~ of sb** die Oberhand über jn gewinnen; **my curiosity got the ~ of me** meine Neugier war stärker $\diamondsuit$ *vt* [improve] verbessern; **to ~ o.s.** sich verbessern.

**better half** *n inf* bessere Hälfte.

**better off** *adj* besser dran.

**betting** ['betɪŋ] *n (U)* - **1.** [bets] Wetten *das* - **2.** [odds] Wetten *pl.*

**betting shop** *n Br* Wettannahmestelle *die.*

**between** [bɪ'twiːn] *prep* zwischen (+ *D*); [with verbs of motion] zwischen (+ *A*); **~ now and next month** bis nächsten Monat; **we had only twenty pounds ~ us** wir hatten (zusammen) nur zwanzig Pfund $\diamondsuit$ *adv:* **(in) ~** zwischen.

**bevelled** *Br,* **beveled** *Am* ['bevld] *adj* abgeschrägt.

**beverage** ['bevərɪdʒ] *n fml* Getränk *das.*

**bevy** ['bevɪ] (*pl* -ies) *n* [group] Schar *die.*

**beware** [bɪ'weər] *vi* sich in Acht nehmen; **to**

**~ of sthg** sich vor etw in Acht nehmen; '**~ of the dog**' 'Vorsicht bissiger Hund'.

**bewildered** [bɪ'wɪldəd] *adj* verwirrt.

**bewildering** [bɪ'wɪldərɪŋ] *adj* verwirrend.

**bewitched** [bɪ'wɪtʃt] *adj* verzaubert.

**bewitching** [bɪ'wɪtʃɪŋ] *adj* bezaubernd.

**beyond** [bɪ'jɒnd] *prep* - **1.** [in space] jenseits (+ *G*), über (+ *A*) ... hinaus; **it's just ~ the park** es ist direkt auf der anderen Seite des Parks - **2.** [in time]: **~ the year 2010** über das Jahr 2010 hinaus; **~ midnight** bis nach Mitternacht; **~ the age of five** ab dem fünften Lebensjahr - **3.** [outside the range of] über (+ *D, A*); **the matter is now ~ my control** die Angelegenheit liegt nicht mehr in meiner Hand; **the town has changed ~ all recognition** die Stadt hat sich bis zur Unkenntlichkeit verändert $\diamondsuit$ *adv* - **1.** [in space] jenseits (davon) - **2.** [in time] darüber hinaus, danach.

**b/f** (*abbr of* brought forward) $\triangleright$ bring.

**bhp** *abbr of* brake horsepower.

**biannual** [baɪ'ænjʊəl] *adj* halbjährlich.

**bias** ['baɪəs] *n* - **1.** [prejudice] Voreingenommenheit *die* - **2.** [tendency] Tendenz *die.*

**biased** ['baɪəst] *adj* - **1.** [person]: **to be ~ (against)** voreingenommen sein (gegenüber) - **2.** [system]: **to be ~ against/towards sb** jn benachteiligen/bevorteilen.

**bib** [bɪb] *n* [for baby] Latz *der,* Lätzchen *das.*

**Bible** ['baɪbl] *n* Bibel *die.*

**biblical** ['bɪblɪkl] *adj* biblisch.

**bibliography** [ˌbɪblɪ'ɒɡrəfɪ] (*pl* -ies) *n* Bibliografie *die.*

**bicarbonate of soda** [baɪ'kɑːbənət-] *n* Natron *das.*

**bicentenary** *Br* [ˌbaɪsen'tiːnərɪ] (*pl* -ies), **bicentennial** *Am* [ˌbaɪsen'tenjəl] *n* Zweihundertjahrfeier *die.*

**biceps** ['baɪseps] (*pl inv*) *n* Bizeps *der.*

**bicker** ['bɪkər] *vi* sich zanken.

**bickering** ['bɪkərɪŋ] *n* Gezänk *das.*

**bicycle** ['baɪsɪkl] *n* Fahrrad *das* $\diamondsuit$ *vi* radeln, Rad fahren.

**bicycle path** *n* Fahrradweg *der.*

**bicycle pump** *n* Luftpumpe *die.*

**bid** [bɪd] (*pt & pp vt sense 1 & vi* bid; *pt vt senses 2 & 3* bid *OR* bade; *pp vt senses 2 & 3* bid *OR* bidden; *cont* -ding) *n* - **1.** [attempt] Versuch *der;* **his ~ for power** sein Griff nach der Macht - **2.** [at auction] Gebot *das* - **3.** *COMM* Angebot *das* $\diamondsuit$ *vt* - **1.** [at auction] bieten - **2.** *literary* [request]: **to ~ sb do sthg** jn bitten, etw zu tun - **3.** *fml* [say]: **to ~ sb good morning** jm einen guten Morgen wünschen; **to ~ sb farewell** von jm Abschied nehmen $\diamondsuit$ *vi* [at auction]: **to ~ (for)** bieten (für).

**bidder** ['bɪdəʳ] n Bietende der, die.

**bidding** ['bɪdɪŋ] n [at auction] Bieten das.

**bide** [baɪd] vt: **to ~ one's time** (eine Gelegenheit) ablwarten.

**bidet** ['biːdeɪ] n Bidet das.

**biennial** [baɪ'enɪəl] adj zweijährlich ◇ n [plant] zweijährige Pflanze.

**bier** [bɪəʳ] n Bahre die.

**bifocals** [baɪ'fəʊklz] npl Brille die mit Bifokalgläsern.

**BIFU** ['bɪfuː] (abbr of **The Banking, Insurance and Finance Union**) n ≃ HBV die, britische Gewerkschaft der Arbeitnehmer in den Bereichen Finanzwesen, Banken und Versicherungen.

**big** [bɪg] (compar **-ger**; superl **-gest**) adj - **1.** [gen] groß; **how ~ is it?** wie groß ist es?; **my ~ brother** mein großer Bruder; **~ ideas** hochfliegende Ideen - **2.** [important] bedeutend; **the ~ day** der große Tag - **3.** [conceited]: **to have a ~ head** eingebildet sein - **4.** [phr] inf: **he's into motorbikes in a ~ way** er ist vernarrt in Motorräder.

**bigamist** ['bɪgəmɪst] n Bigamist der.

**bigamy** ['bɪgəmɪ] n Bigamie die.

**Big Apple** n umgangssprachliche Bezeichnung für New York (City).

**Big Ben** [-'ben] n Big Ben der.

**big business** n (U) [large companies] Hochfinanz die.

**big cat** n Großkatze die.

**big deal** inf n: **it's no ~** das ist kein Problem; **what's the ~?** was ist schon dabei? ◇ excl und wenn schon!

**Big Dipper** [-'dɪpəʳ] n - **1.** Br [rollercoaster] Achterbahn die - **2.** Am ASTRON: **the ~** der Große Bär.

**big end** n AUT Pleuelfuß der.

**big fish** n inf [person] hohes Tier.

**big game** n Großwild das.

**big hand** n - **1.** [on clock] großer Zeiger - **2.** inf [applause] großer Beifall.

**bighead** ['bɪghed] n inf Angeber der.

**bigheaded** [bɪg'hedɪd] adj inf eingebildet.

**big-hearted** [-'hɑːtɪd] adj großherzig, großzügig.

**big money** n inf: **he earns ~** er verdient einen Haufen Geld.

**big mouth** n inf [person] Großmaul das; **he's got a ~** er hat eine große Klappe.

**big name** n inf Größe die.

**bigot** ['bɪgət] n bigotter Mensch.

**bigoted** ['bɪgətɪd] adj bigott.

**bigotry** ['bɪgətrɪ] n Bigotterie die.

**big shot** n inf hohes Tier.

**big time** n inf: **to make** OR **hit the ~** ganz groß rauslkommen.

**big toe** n großer Zeh.

**big top** n Zirkuszelt das.

**big wheel** n - **1.** Br [at fairground] Riesenrad das - **2.** inf [big shot] hohes Tier.

**bigwig** ['bɪgwɪg] n inf pej hohes Tier.

**bike** [baɪk] n inf - **1.** [cycle] Rad das - **2.** [motorcycle] Motorrad das.

**bikeway** ['baɪkweɪ] n Am Radweg der.

**bikini** [bɪ'kiːnɪ] n Bikini der.

**bilateral** [baɪ'lætərəl] adj bilateral.

**bilberry** ['bɪlbərɪ] (pl -ies) n Heidelbeere die.

**bile** [baɪl] n Galle die.

**bilingual** [baɪ'lɪŋgwəl] adj zweisprachig.

**bilious** ['bɪljəs] adj - **1.** [colour] widerlich - **2.** [nauseous] übel.

**bill** [bɪl] n - **1.** [statement of cost] Rechnung die - **2.** [in parliament] Gesetzentwurf der - **3.** [of show, concert] Programm das - **4.** Am [bank note] Geldschein der, Banknote die - **5.** [poster]: **'post** OR **stick no ~s'** 'Plakate ankleben verboten' - **6.** [of bird] Schnabel der - **7.** phr: **to be given a clean ~ of health** MED eine gute Gesundheit bescheinigt bekommen ◇ vt: **to ~ sb (for sthg)** jm eine Rechnung (für etw) schicken.

**billboard** ['bɪlbɔːd] n Plakatwand die.

**billet** ['bɪlɪt] n Quartier das ◇ vt einlquartieren.

**billfold** ['bɪlfəʊld] n Am Brieftasche die.

**billiards** ['bɪljədz] n (U) Billard das.

**billion** ['bɪljən] num - **1.** [thousand million] Milliarde die - **2.** Br dated [million million] Billion die.

**billionaire** [bɪljə'neəʳ] n Milliardär der, -in die.

**bill of exchange** n Wechsel der.

**bill of lading** [-'leɪdɪŋ] n Konnossement der.

**Bill of Rights** n: **the ~** die ersten zehn Zusätze zu den Grundrechten der Vereinigten Staaten.

**BILL OF RIGHTS**

Bezeichnung für die ersten zehn Amendments (Ergänzungen) der Verfassung der USA, die 1791, zwei Jahre nach Inkrafttreten der Verfassung, ratifiziert wurden. Sie schützen die Rechte des Bürgers in Bezug auf Rede-, Religions-, Versammlungsfreiheit usw.

**bill of sale** n Kaufvertrag der.

**billow** ['bɪləʊ] n [of smoke] Schwaden der ◇ vi - **1.** [smoke, steam] in Schwaden ziehen - **2.** [skirt, sail] sich blähen.

**billposter** ['bɪl‚pəʊstəʳ] *n* Plakatankleber *der.*

**billycan** ['bɪlɪkæn] *n* Kochgeschirr *das.*

**billy goat** ['bɪlɪ-] *n* Ziegenbock *der.*

**bimbo** ['bɪmbəʊ] (*pl* -s *OR* -es) *n inf pej* Tussi *die.*

**bimonthly** [‚baɪ'mʌnθlɪ] *adj* - **1.** [every two months] zweimonatlich - **2.** [twice a month] vierzehntäglich ⇔ *adv* - **1.** [every two months] jeden zweiten Monat - **2.** [twice a month] zweimal monatlich.

**bin** [bɪn] (*pt* & *pp* -ned; *cont* -ning) *n* - **1.** *Br* [for rubbish] Abfalleimer *der* - **2.** [for coal] Eimer *der;* [for grain] Tonne *die* - **3.** [for bread] Brotkasten *der;* [for flour] Dose *die* ⇔ *vt inf* [discard] wegschmeißen.

**binary** ['baɪnərɪ] *adj* binär.

**bind** [baɪnd] (*pt* & *pp* **bound**) *vt* - **1.** [gen] binden - **2.** [bandage] verbinden - **3.** [constrain] verpflichten ⇔ *n inf* - **1.** *Br* [nuisance]: it's a real ~ es ist sehr lästig - **2.** [difficult situation] Klemme *die.*

  ➤ **bind over** *vt sep* verwarnen.

**binder** ['baɪndəʳ] *n* - **1.** [machine] Bindemaschine *die* - **2.** [person] Buchbinder *der,* -in *die* - **3.** [cover] Ordner *der,* Hefter *der.*

**binding** ['baɪndɪŋ] *adj* verbindlich, bindend ⇔ *n* [of book] Einband *der.*

**binge** [bɪndʒ] *inf n:* to go on a ~ [on drink] auf Sauftour gehen; [on food] eine Fresstour machen ⇔ *vi:* to ~ on sthg [drink] etw saufen; [food] etw fressen.

**bingo** ['bɪŋgəʊ] *n* Bingo *das.*

**bin-liner** *n Br* Müllsack *der.*

**binoculars** [bɪ'nɒkjʊləz] *npl* Fernglas *das.*

**biochemistry** [‚baɪəʊ'kemɪstrɪ] *n* Biochemie *die.*

**biodegradable** [‚baɪəʊdɪ'greɪdəbl] *adj* biologisch abbaubar.

**biodiversity** [‚baɪəʊdaɪ'vɜːsətɪ] *n* Artenvielfalt *die.*

**biographer** [baɪ'ɒgrəfəʳ] *n* Biograph *der,* -in *die.*

**biographic(al)** [‚baɪə'græfɪk(l)] *adj* biographisch.

**biography** [baɪ'ɒgrəfɪ] (*pl* -ies) *n* Biografie *die.*

**biological** [‚baɪə'lɒdʒɪkl] *adj* biologisch.

**biological weapon** *n* biologische Waffe.

**biologist** [baɪ'ɒlədʒɪst] *n* Biologe *der,* -gin *die.*

**biology** [baɪ'ɒlədʒɪ] *n* Biologie *die.*

**biopic** ['baɪəʊpɪk] *n inf* biografischer Film.

**biopsy** ['baɪɒpsɪ] (*pl* -ies) *n* Biopsie *die.*

**biotechnology** [‚baɪəʊtek'nɒlədʒɪ]*n* Biotechnik *die.*

**bipartite** [‚baɪ'pɑːtaɪt] *adj* [treaty] zweiseitig.

**biplane** ['baɪpleɪn] *n* Doppeldecker *der.*

**birch** [bɜːtʃ] *n* - **1.** [tree] Birke *die* - **2.** [stick]: **the ~** die Rute.

**bird** [bɜːd] *n* - **1.** [creature] Vogel *der;* to kill two ~s with one stone zwei Fliegen mit einer Klappe schlagen - **2.** *inf* [woman] Braut *die.*

**birdcage** ['bɜːdkeɪdʒ] *n* Vogelkäfig *der.*

**birdie** ['bɜːdɪ] *n* - **1.** [bird] Vögelchen *das* - **2.** [in golf] Birdie *das.*

**bird of paradise** *n* Paradiesvogel *der.*

**bird of prey** *n* Raubvogel *der.*

**birdseed** ['bɜːdsiːd] *n* (*U*) Vogelfutter *das,* Körner *pl.*

**bird's-eye view** *n* Vogelperspektive *die.*

**bird-watcher** [-‚wɒtʃəʳ] *n* Vogelbeobachter *der,* -in *die.*

**Biro**® ['baɪərəʊ] *n* Kugelschreiber *der.*

**birth** [bɜːθ] *n* - **1.** [of baby] Geburt *die;* to give ~ (to) gebären - **2.** *fig* [of idea, system, country] Geburtsstunde *die.*

**birth certificate** *n* Geburtsurkunde *die.*

**birth control** *n* (*U*) Geburtenregelung *die;* to use ~ verhüten.

**birthday** ['bɜːθdeɪ] *n* Geburtstag *der* ⇔ *comp* Geburtstags-.

**birthmark** ['bɜːθmɑːk] *n* Muttermal *das.*

**birthplace** ['bɜːθpleɪs] *n* Geburtsort *der.*

**birthrate** ['bɜːθreɪt] *n* Geburtenrate *die.*

**birthright** ['bɜːθraɪt] *n* Geburtsrecht *das.*

**Biscay** ['bɪskeɪ] *n:* the Bay of ~ der Golf von Biskaya.

**biscuit** ['bɪskɪt] *n* - **1.** *Br* [thin dry cake] Keks *der* - **2.** *Am* [bread-like cake] Hefebrötchen, *das* üblicherweise mit Bratensaft gegessen wird.

**bisect** [baɪ'sekt] *vt* - **1.** GEOM halbieren - **2.** [cut in two] durchschneiden.

**bisexual** [‚baɪ'sekʃjʊəl] *adj* bisexuell ⇔ *n* Bisexuelle *der, die.*

**bishop** ['bɪʃəp] *n* - **1.** [in church] Bischof *der* - **2.** [in chess] Läufer *der.*

**bison** ['baɪsn] (*pl inv OR* -s) *n* Bison *der.*

**bistro** ['biːstrəʊ] (*pl* -s) *n* Bistro *das.*

**bit** [bɪt] *pt* ▷ **bite** ⇔ *n* - **1.** [small piece] Stück *das,* Stückchen *das;* ~s and pieces *Br* [objects] Krimskrams *der;* to fall to ~s kaputtgehen, auseinander fallen - **2.** [unspecified amount]: **a ~ of** ein bisschen; **quite a ~ of** eine ganze Menge - **3.** [short time]: **for a ~** für ein Weilchen - **4.** [of drill] Bohrer *der,* Bohreinsatz *der* - **5.** [of bridle] Trensengebiss *das* - **6.** COMPUT Bit *das* - **7.** *phr:* to do one's ~ *Br* sein(en) Teil (dazu) beitragen; **every ~ as ... as** genauso ... wie; **it's a ~ much** [overwhelming] es ist ein bisschen zuviel; [unreasonable] es ist ein starkes Stück; **not a ~** kein bisschen.

  ➤ **a bit** *adv* [tired, late, confused] ein bisschen.

➤ **bit by bit** *adv* Stück für Stück.

**bitch** [bɪtʃ] *n* - **1.** [female dog] Hündin *die* - **2.** *vinf pej* [unpleasant woman] Miststück *das*, Schnepfe *die* ◇ *vi inf* - **1.** [complain] meckern - **2.** [talk unpleasantly]: **to ~ about sb** über jn herziehen.

**bitchy** [bɪtʃɪ] (*compar* -**ier**; *superl* -**iest**) *adj inf* gehässig, gemein.

**bite** [baɪt] (*pt* **bit**; *pp* **bitten**) *n* Biss *der*; **to have a ~ (to eat)** einen Happen essen ◇ *vt* beißen ◇ *vi* - **1.** [animal, person, insect] beißen; **to ~ into sthg** in etw (hineinl)beißen; **to ~ off more than one can chew** den Mund zu voll nehmen, sich übernehmen - **2.** [tyres, clutch] greifen - **3.** *fig* [sanction, law] greifen.

**biting** [baɪtɪŋ] *adj* - **1.** [wind, cold] schneidend, beißend - **2.** [caustic - comment] bissig.

**bitmap** [bɪtmæp] *n* COMPUT Bitmap *das*.

**bit part** *n* kleine Rolle, Nebenrolle *die*.

**bitten** [bɪtn] *pp* ➤ **bite.**

**bitter** [bɪtə'] *adj* - **1.** [gen] bitter; **it's ~ (weather) today** es ist heute bitterkalt; **to the ~ end** bis zum bitteren Ende - **2.** [argument, war] erbittert - **3.** [resentful] verbittert ◇ *n Br* [beer] *dem Altbier ähnliches Bier.*

**bitter lemon** *n* Bitter Lemon *das*.

**bitterly** [bɪtəlɪ] *adv* [disappointed] bitter; [weep, regret] bitterlich; **~ cold** bitterkalt.

**bitterness** [bɪtənɪs] *n* Bitterkeit *die.*

**bittersweet** [bɪtəswiːt] *adj* [taste] bittersüß; **~ memories** schmerzlich-schöne Erinnerungen.

**bitty** [bɪtɪ] (*compar* -**ier**; *superl* -**iest**) *adj Br inf* [story, film] zusammengestückelt.

**bitumen** [bɪtjumɪn] *n* Bitumen *das.*

**bivouac** [bɪvʊæk] (*pt* & *pp* -**ked**; *cont* -**king**) *n* Biwak *das* ◇ *vi* biwakieren.

**biweekly** [ˌbaɪwiːklɪ] *adj* & *adv* - **1.** [every two weeks] vierzehntäglich - **2.** [twice a week] zweimal wöchentlich.

**bizarre** [bɪzɑːʳ] *adj* exzentrisch; [house, landscape] bizarr.

**bk** - **1.** *abbr of* **bank** - **2.** *abbr of* **book.**

**bl** *abbr of* **bill of lading.**

**blab** [blæb] (*pt* & *pp* -**bed**; *cont* -**bing**) *vi inf* quatschen.

**black** [blæk] *adj* - **1.** [gen] schwarz; **he beat her ~ and blue** er hat sie grün und blau geschlagen; **~ and white** [films, photos] schwarz-weiß - **2.** [future] finster, düster - **3.** [look] finster; **to be in a ~ mood** deprimiert sein ◇ *n* - **1.** [colour] Schwarz *das*; **in ~ and white** [in writing] schwarz auf weiß; **in the ~** [solvent] in den schwarzen Zahlen - **2.** [person] Schwarze *der, die* ◇ *vt Br* [boycott] boykottieren.

➤ **black out** *vt sep* [city] verdunkeln ◇ *vi* [faint] ohnmächtig werden.

**blackball** [blækbɔːl] *vt* stimmen gegen.

**black belt** *n* schwarzer Gürtel.

**blackberry** [blækbərɪ] (*pl* -**ies**) *n* Brombeere *die.*

**blackbird** [blækbɜːd] *n* Amsel *die.*

**blackboard** [blækbɔːd] *n* Tafel *die.*

**black box** *n* [flight recorder] Flugschreiber *der.*

**black comedy** *n* schwarze Komödie.

**blackcurrant** [ˌblækˈkʌrənt] *n* schwarze Johannisbeere.

**black economy** *n* Schattenwirtschaft *die.*

**blacken** [blækn] *vt* - **1.** [in colour] schwärzen - **2.** *fig* [reputation, name] anlschwärzen ◇ *vi* [sky] sich verdunkeln.

**black eye** *n* schwarzes Auge.

**Black Forest** *n* Schwarzwald *der*; **in the ~** im Schwarzwald.

**blackhead** [blækhed] *n* Mitesser *der.*

**black hole** *n* ASTRON schwarzes Loch.

**black ice** *n (U)* Glatteis *das.*

**blackjack** [blækdʒæk] *n* - **1.** [card game] Siebzehnundvier *das* - **2.** *Am* [weapon] Totschläger *der.*

**blackleg** [blækleg] *n pej* Streikbrecher *der*, -in *die.*

**blacklist** [blæklɪst] *n* schwarze Liste ◇ *vt* auf die schwarze Liste setzen.

**black magic** *n* schwarze Kunst, schwarze Magie.

**blackmail** [blækmeɪl] *n* Erpressung *die* ◇ *vt* erpressen.

**blackmailer** [blækmeɪlə'] *n* Erpresser *der*, -in *die.*

**Black Maria** [-məraɪə] *n inf* Grüne Minna.

**black mark** *n* Minuspunkt *der.*

**black market** *n* Schwarzmarkt *der.*

**blackout** [blækaʊt] *n* - **1.** [in wartime] Verdunkelung *die* - **2.** [power cut] Stromausfall *der* - **3.** [suppression of news] Nachrichtensperre *die* - **4.** [fainting fit] Ohnmachtsanfall *der.*

**black pudding** *n Br* Blutwurst *die.*

**Black Sea** *n*: **the ~** das Schwarze Meer.

**black sheep** *n* schwarzes Schaf.

**blacksmith** [blæksmɪθ] *n* Schmied *der*, -in *die.*

**black spot** *n* [for road accidents] Gefahrenstelle *die.*

**black-tie** *adj* in Abendkleidung.

**bladder** [blædə'] *n* ANAT Blase *die.*

**blade** [bleɪd] *n* - **1.** [of knife, razor] Klinge *die* - **2.** [of propeller, saw, oar] Blatt *das* - **3.** [of grass] Halm *der.*

**blame** [bleɪm] *n* Schuld *die*; **to take the ~ for**

sth**g** die Schuld für etw auf sich (A) nehmen ◇ vt beschuldigen; **to ~ sthg on sb/sthg** jm/ etw die Schuld an etw (D) geben; **they ~d her for the defeat** sie gaben ihr die Schuld an der Niederlage; **to be to ~ for sthg** an etw (D) schuld sein.

**blameless** ['bleɪmlɪs] adj schuldlos, unbescholten.

**blanch** [blɑːntʃ] vt cuLIN blanchieren ◇ vi [go white] erbleichen.

**blancmange** [bləˈmɒndʒ] n Pudding der.

**bland** [blænd] adj - **1.** [person] farblos - **2.** [food] fad - **3.** [music, style] nichtssagend.

**blank** [blæŋk] adj leer ◇ n - **1.** [empty space] Leere die, leere Stelle - **2.** MIL [cartridge] Platzpatrone die - **3.** phr: **to draw a ~** keinen Erfolg haben.

**blank cheque** n Blankoscheck der; **to give sb a ~ to do sthg** fig jm freie Hand lassen, etw zu tun.

**blanket** ['blæŋkɪt] adj [ban, coverage] allgemein ◇ n - **1.** [bed cover] Decke die - **2.** [layer] Schicht die ◇ vt [subj: snow, fog] zudecken.

**blanket bath** n Br MED: **to give sb a ~** jn im Bett waschen.

**blankly** ['blæŋklɪ] adv [stare] ausdruckslos.

**blare** [bleəʳ] vi plärren.
➡ **blare out** vi plärren.

**blasé** [blɑːˈzeɪ] adj blasiert.

**blasphemous** ['blæsfəməs] adj blasphemisch, lästerlich.

**blasphemy** ['blæsfəmɪ] (pl -ies) n Blasphemie die.

**blast** [blɑːst] n - **1.** [of bomb] Explosion die - **2.** [of air] Windstoß der - **3.** Am inf : **John's party was a ~** John's Party war total geil; **we had a real ~** wir haben einen Riesenspaß gehabt ◇ vt [hole, tunnel] sprengen ◇ excl Br inf verdammt!
➡ **(at) full blast** adv - **1.** [maximum volume] auf höchster Lautstärke - **2.** [maximum effort, speed] auf Hochtouren.
➡ **blast off** vi SPACE starten.

**blasted** ['blɑːstɪd] adj inf [for emphasis] verdammt.

**blast furnace** n Hochofen der.

**blast-off** n SPACE Start der.

**blatant** ['bleɪtənt] adj [shameless] unverhohlen.

**blatantly** ['bleɪtəntlɪ] adv offensichtlich.

**blaze** [bleɪz] n - **1.** [fire] Brand der, Feuer das - **2.** fig [of colour, light] Pracht die; **in a ~ of publicity** mit großem Werbeaufwand ◇ vi - **1.** [fire] lodern - **2.** fig [with colour, emotion] brennen.

**blazer** ['bleɪzəʳ] n Blazer der.

**blazing** ['bleɪzɪŋ] adj - **1.** [sun, heat] brennend;

**~ hot** brennend heiß - **2.** [argument, row] hitzig.

**bleach** [bliːtʃ] n (U) [for clothes] Bleichmittel das; [for cleaning] Reinigungsmittel das ◇ vt [hair, clothes] bleichen.

**bleached** [bliːtʃt] adj [hair, jeans] gebleicht.

**bleachers** ['bliːtʃəz] npl Am sport nicht überdachte Zuschauertribüne.

**bleak** [bliːk] adj - **1.** [weather] trüb, trostlos; [place] trostlos - **2.** [future, face, person] trüb.

**bleary** ['blɪərɪ] (compar -ier; superl -iest) adj [eyes] trüb, verschlafen.

**bleary-eyed** [ˌblɪərɪˈaɪd] adj verschlafen.

**bleat** [bliːt] n [of sheep] Blöken das; [of goat] Meckern das ◇ vi - **1.** [sheep] blöken; [goat] meckern - **2.** fig [person] meckern.

**bleed** [bliːd] (pt & pp bled [bled]) vt [drain] entlüften ◇ vi bluten.

**bleep** [bliːp] n Piepton der, Signalton der ◇ vt [call] rufen ◇ vi piepen.

**bleeper** ['bliːpəʳ] n Piepser der, Funkrufempfänger der.

**blemish** ['blemɪʃ] n lit & fig Makel der ◇ vt [reputation] beflecken.

**blend** [blend] n lit & fig Mischung die ◇ vt (ver)mischen ◇ vi [colours, sounds] sich (ver)mischen; **to ~ with sthg** mit etw mischen.
➡ **blend in** vi - **1.** [person] sich einlfügen - **2.** [colours, sounds] verschmelzen.
➡ **blend into** vt fus [background] sich einlfügen in (+ A).

**blender** ['blendəʳ] n [food mixer] Mixer der.

**bless** [bles] (pt & pp -ed OR blest) vt - **1.** RELIG segnen - **2.** [endow]: **to be ~ed with sthg** mit etw gesegnet sein - **3.** phr: **~ you!** [after sneezing] Gesundheit!; [thank you] du bist ein Engel!

**blessed** ['blesɪd] adj - **1.** [wonderful & RELIG] gesegnet - **2.** inf [for emphasis] verdammt.

**blessing** ['blesɪŋ] n lit & fig Segen der; **to count one's ~s** seinem Schöpfer danken können; **it's a ~ in disguise** das ist Glück im Unglück; **a mixed ~** kein ungetrübtes Vergnügen.

**blest** [blest] pt & pp ⊏▶ **bless**.

**blew** [bluː] pt⊏▶ **blow**.

**blight** [blaɪt] n - **1.** (U) [plant disease] Brand der - **2.** fig [curse] dunkler Schatten - **3.** (U) fig [of city] Verfall der ◇ vt beeinträchtigen.

**blimey** ['blaɪmɪ] excl Br inf herrje!

**blind** [blaɪnd] adj - **1.** [gen] blind; **to be ~ to sthg** fig gegenüber einer Sache (+ D) OR für etw blind sein - **2.** Br inf [for emphasis]: **it doesn't make a ~ bit of difference** das ist doch völlig egal! ◇ adv: **~ drunk** sinnlos betrunken ◇ n [for window] Jalousie die ◇ npl: **the ~** die

Blinden pl ◇ vt blenden; **to ~ sb to sthg** fig jn für etw blind machen.

**blind alley** n lit & fig Sackgasse die.

**blind corner** n unübersichtliche Kurve.

**blind date** n Rendezvous mit einem oder einer Unbekannten.

**blinders** ['blaɪndəz] npl Am Scheuklappen pl.

**blindfold** ['blaɪndfəʊld] adv mit verbundenen Augen ◇ n Augenbinde die ◇ vt: **to ~ sb** jm die Augen verbinden.

**blinding** ['blaɪndɪŋ] adj [light] grell.

**blindingly** ['blaɪndɪŋlɪ] adv [obvious] völlig

**blindly** ['blaɪndlɪ] adv lit & fig blindlings.

**blindness** ['blaɪndnɪs] n Blindheit die.

**blind spot** n - **1.** [when driving] toter Winkel - **2.** fig [inability to understand]: **to have a ~ about sthg** (überhaupt) keine Begabung für etw haben.

**blink** [blɪŋk] n - **1.** [of eyes, light] Blinzeln das - **2.** phr: **to be on the ~** inf [machine] eine Macke haben ◇ vt - **1.** [eyes] anlblinzeln, zulzwinkern - **2.** Am AUT: **to ~ one's lights** die Scheinwerfer aufleuchten lassen ◇ vi - **1.** [eyes] blinzeln, zwinkern - **2.** [light] auflscheinen, aufleuchten.

**blinkered** ['blɪŋkəd] adj - **1.** [horse] mit Scheuklappen - **2.** fig [view, attitude] engstirnig.

**blinkers** ['blɪŋkəz] npl Br [for horse] Scheuklappen pl.

**blinking** ['blɪŋkɪŋ] adj Br inf [for emphasis] verflixt.

**blip** [blɪp] n - **1.** [sound] Piepton der, Piepen das - **2.** [on radar] leuchtendes Pünktchen.

**bliss** [blɪs] n Glück das, (Glück)seligkeit die; **it was sheer ~** es war die reinste Wonne.

**blissful** ['blɪsfʊl] adj herrlich; **in ~ ignorance** in völliger Ahnungslosigkeit.

**blissfully** ['blɪsfʊlɪ] adv [happy, unaware] vollkommen.

**blister** ['blɪstər] n Blase die ◇ vi - **1.** [skin] Blasen bekommen - **2.** [paint] Blasen werfen.

**blistering** ['blɪstərɪŋ] adj - **1.** [heat, sun] glühend - **2.** [attack] scharf.

**blister pack** n Verpackung für Tabletten mit einer hubbeligen Oberseite aus Plastik.

**blithe** [blaɪð] adj - **1.** [unworried] unbekümmert, sorglos - **2.** dated [cheerful] heiter.

**blithely** ['blaɪðlɪ] adv unbekümmert.

**blitz** [blɪts] n MIL Luftangriff der; **I had a ~ on my bedroom** Br fig ich habe in meinem Zimmer einmal schnell gründlich aufgeräumt.

**blizzard** ['blɪzəd] n Schneesturm der.

**bloated** ['bləʊtɪd] adj - **1.** [body, face] aufgedunsen - **2.** [with food] übersatt.

**blob** [blɒb] n - **1.** [of paint] Klecks der; [of cream] Klacks der - **2.** [indistinct form] Fleck der.

**bloc** [blɒk] n POL Block der.

**block** [blɒk] n - **1.** [building]: **~ (of flats)** Wohnhaus das; **office ~** Bürohaus das - **2.** [of ice, wood, stone] Klotz der - **3.** Am [of buildings] Block der; **it's three ~s away** es ist drei Blocks OR Straßen weiter - **4.** [mental] geistige Sperre - **5.** TECH: **~ and tackle** Flaschenzug der ◇ vt - **1.** [road, path, law] blockieren; [pipe] verstopfen - **2.** [view] versperren.

➤ **block off** vt sep [road, channel, entrance] ablsperren; [pipe] blockieren.

➤ **block out** vt sep - **1.** [from mind] verdrängen - **2.** [light] nicht durchllassen.

➤ **block up** vt sep verstopfen; **my nose is all ~ed up** meine Nase ist völlig verstopft.

**blockade** [blɒ'keɪd] n Blockade die ◇ vt blockieren, sperren.

**blockage** ['blɒkɪdʒ] n Verstopfung die.

**block booking** n Gruppenreservierung die.

**blockbuster** ['blɒkbʌstər] n inf Kassenschlager der.

**block capitals** npl Blockschrift die.

**blockhead** ['blɒkhed] n inf Dummkopf der, Esel der.

**block letters** npl Blockschrift die.

**block vote** n Br Stimmenblock der.

**bloke** [bləʊk] n Br inf Typ der.

**blond** [blɒnd] adj blond.

**blonde** [blɒnd] adj blond ◇ n [woman] Blondine die.

**blood** [blʌd] n Blut das; **new** OR **fresh ~** fig frisches Blut; **in cold ~** kaltblütig; **it's in his ~** es liegt ihm im Blut; **to make sb's ~ boil** jn rasend machen; **to make sb's ~ run cold** jm das Blut in den Adern erstarren lassen.

**blood bank** n Blutbank die.

**bloodbath** ['blʌdbɑːθ] n Blutbad das.

**blood brother** n Blutsbruder der.

**blood cell** n Blutzelle die.

**blood count** n Blutbild das.

**bloodcurdling** ['blʌdkɜːdlɪŋ] adj markerschütternd.

**blood donor** n Blutspender der.

**blood group** n Blutgruppe die.

**bloodhound** ['blʌdhaʊnd] n Bluthund der.

**bloodless** ['blʌdlɪs] adj - **1.** [face, lips] blutleer - **2.** [coup, victory] unblutig.

**bloodletting** ['blʌdˌletɪŋ] n Blutvergießen das.

**blood money** n Blutgeld das.

**blood orange** n Blutorange die.

**blood poisoning** n Blutvergiftung die.

**blood pressure** n Blutdruck der.

**blood relation, blood relative** n Blutsverwandte der, die.

**bloodshed** ['blʌdʃedl] n Blutvergießen das.

**bloodshot** ['blʌdʃɒt] adj [eyes] blutunterlaufen.

**blood sports** npl Sportarten, die das Töten von Tieren zum Ziel haben.

**bloodstained** ['blʌdsteɪndl] adj blutbefleckt.

**bloodstream** ['blʌdstriːml] n Blutstrom der.

**blood test** n Blutprobe die.

**bloodthirsty** ['blʌd,θɜːstɪl] adj blutrünstig.

**blood transfusion** n Transfusion die.

**blood type** n Blutgruppe die.

**blood vessel** n Blutgefäß das.

**bloody** ['blʌdɪ] (compar **-ier**; superl **-iest**) adj - 1. [gen] blutig - 2. Br vinf [for emphasis] verdammt; ~ hell! verdammt noch mal! <> adv Br vinf verdammt.

**bloody-minded** [-'maɪndɪdl] adj Br inf stur.

**bloom** [bluːml] n Blüte die <> vi blühen.

**blooming** ['bluːmɪŋl] adj - 1. Br inf [for emphasis] verflixt; ~ heck! verflixt noch mal! - 2. [healthy]: to be ~ with health sich blühender Gesundheit erfreuen <> adv Br inf verflixt.

**blossom** ['blɒsəml] n Blüte die; in ~ in Blüte <> vi - 1. [tree] blühen - 2. fig [person] aufl- blühen.

**blot** [blɒtl] (pt & pp **-ted**; cont **-ting**) n - 1. [of ink etc] (Tinten)klecks der - 2. fig [blemish] Makel der; a ~ on the landscape ein Schandfleck in der Landschaft <> vt - 1. [dry] abllöschen - 2. [spot with ink] beklecksen.

➤ **blot out** vt sep - 1. [sun, light] verdecken - 2. [memory] ausllöschen.

**blotch** [blɒtʃl] n Fleck der.

**blotchy** ['blɒtʃɪl] (compar **-ier**; superl **-iest**) adj fleckig.

**blotter** ['blɒtəʳl] n Löscher der.

**blotting paper** ['blɒtɪŋ-] n (U) Löschpapier das.

**blouse** [blaʊzl] n Bluse die.

**blouson** ['bluːzɒnl] n Br Blouson das OR der.

**blow** [bləʊl] (pt **blew**; pp **blown**) vi - 1. [wind] wehen; [stronger] blasen - 2. [move in the wind] wehen; **the door blew open/shut** die Tür flog auf/zu - 3. [person] blasen; **to ~ on one's coffee to cool it down** in den Kaffee pusten um ihn abzukühlen - 4. [fuse] durchlbrennen - 5. [whistle] ertönen <> vt - 1. [subj: wind] wehen; [stronger] blasen - 2. [clear]: **to ~ one's nose** sich (D) die Nase putzen - 3. [whistle, horn, trumpet] blasen - 4. [bubbles] machen - 5. inf [money] verpulvern <> n Schlag der; **to come to ~s** handgreiflich werden; **to strike a ~ for sthg** fig etw (D) einen großen Dienst erwei-

sen; **to soften the ~** [of bad news] die Härte der Nachricht abImildern.

➤ **blow away** vi [in wind] weglfliegen.

➤ **blow out** vt sep auslblasen <> vi - 1. [candle] auslgehen - 2. [tyre] platzen.

➤ **blow over** vi - 1. [storm] sich legen - 2. [argument] in Vergessenheit geraten.

➤ **blow up** vt sep - 1. [inflate] aufllblasen; [with pump] auflpumpen - 2. [with bomb] in die Luft jagen - 3. [photograph] vergrößern <> vi [explode] explodieren.

**blow-by-blow** adj detailliert.

**blow-dry** n Fönen das; **a cut and ~** Schneiden und Fönen <> vt fönen.

**blowfly** ['bləʊflaɪl] (pl **-flies**) n Schmeißfliege die.

**blowgun** n Am = blowpipe.

**blowlamp** Br ['bləʊlæmp], **blowtorch** esp Am ['bləʊtɔːtʃl] n Lötlampe die.

**blown** [bləʊnl] pp ⊳ blow.

**blowout** ['bləʊaʊtl] n - 1. [of tyre]: **he had a ~** ihm platzte ein Reifen - 2. inf [big meal] Gelage das.

**blowpipe** Br ['bləʊpaɪpl], **blowgun** Am [bləʊgʌnl] n Blasrohr das.

**blowtorch** n esp Am = blowlamp.

**blowzy** ['blaʊzɪl] (compar **-ier**; superl **-iest**) adj Br schlampig.

**blubber** ['blʌbəʳl] n Walfischspeck der <> vi pej flennen, heulen.

**bludgeon** ['blʌdʒənl] vt prügeln.

**blue** [bluːl] adj - 1. [in colour] blau - 2. inf [sad] trübsinnig, melancholisch - 3. [film] Porno-; [joke] unanständig <> n Blau das; in ~ (ganz) in Blau; **out of the ~** aus heiterem Himmel.

➤ **blues** npl - 1. MUS: **the ~s** der Blues - 2. inf [sad feeling]: **the ~s** ein Anfall von Melancholie.

**blue baby** n Baby mit angeborenem Herzfehler.

**bluebell** ['bluːbell] n Glockenblume die.

**blueberry** ['bluːbərɪl] (pl **-ies**) n Blaubeere die, Heidelbeere die.

**blue-black** adj blauschwarz.

**blue-blooded** [-'blʌdɪdl] adj blaublütig.

**bluebottle** ['bluː,bɒtll] n Schmeißfliege die.

**blue cheese** n Blauschimmelkäse der.

**blue chip** n ST EX [share] Blue chip der; [company] erstklassige Firma.

**blue-collar** adj: ~ **worker** Arbeiter der, -in die; ~ **job** Stelle die für einen Arbeiter/eine Arbeiterin.

**blue-eyed boy** [-aɪd-] n inf Liebling der.

**blue jeans** npl Am (Blue) Jeans die.

**blue moon** n inf: **once in a ~** alle Jubeljahre einmal.

**blueprint** ['blu:prɪnt] *n* - **1.** CONSTR Blaupause *die* - **2.** *fig* [plan, programme] Entwurf *der*.

**bluestocking** ['blu:ˌstɒkɪŋ] *n* *pej* Blaustrumpf *der*.

**blue tit** *n Br* Blaumeise *die*.

**blue whale** *n* Blauwal *der*.

**bluff** [blʌf] *adj* [person, manner] raubeinig ◇ *n* - **1.** [deception] Bluff *der;* **to call sb's ~** jn dazu auf lfordern, seine Drohung wahr zu machen - **2.** [cliff] Steilhang *der* ◇ *vt* bluffen; **he ~ed his way through** er hat sich durchgemogelt ◇ *vi* bluffen.

**blunder** ['blʌndə'] *n* Schnitzer *der;* **to make a social ~** einen Fauxpas begehen ◇ *vi* - **1.** [make mistake] einen Schnitzer machen; [socially] sich blamieren - **2.** [move clumsily] tappen.

**blundering** ['blʌndərɪŋ] *adj* stümperhaft.

**blunt** [blʌnt] *adj* - **1.** [knife, pencil, instrument] stumpf - **2.** [person] geradeheraus; [manner, question] unverblümt ◇ *vt* - **1.** [knife] stumpf machen - **2.** *fig* [enthusiasm] dämpfen; [impact] ablschwächen.

**bluntly** ['blʌntlɪ] *adv* unverblümt, geradeheraus.

**bluntness** ['blʌntnɪs] *n* Unverblümtheit *die*.

**blur** [blɜ:'] (*pt* & *pp* **-red;** *cont* **-ring**) *n* verschwommener Fleck; **he couldn't remember anything about the accident, it was all a ~** er konnte sich an nichts bezüglich des Unfalls erinnern, alles war verschwommen ◇ *vt* - **1.** [outline, photograph] unscharf machen - **2.** [distinction] undeutlich machen; **his eyes were ~red with tears** seine Augen schwammen in Tränen.

**blurb** [blɜ:b] *n inf* [on book] Klappentext *der*.

**blurred** [blɜ:d] *adj* - **1.** [outline, photograph] unscharf - **2.** [distinction] undeutlich.

**blurt** [blɜ:t] ◆ **blurt out** *vt sep* herauslplatzen mit.

**blush** [blʌʃ] *n* Röte *die;* **to spare sb's ~es** jn nicht in Verlegenheit bringen ◇ *vi* rot werden, erröten.

**blusher** ['blʌʃə'] *n* Rouge *das*.

**bluster** ['blʌstə'] *n* großes Geschrei, Toben *das* ◇ *vi* toben.

**blustery** ['blʌstərɪ] *adj* stürmisch.

**Blvd** *abbr of* boulevard.

**BMA** (*abbr of* **British Medical Association**) *n* britischer Ärzteverband.

**BMJ** (*abbr of* **British Medical Journal**) *n* Zeitschrift des britischen Ärzteverbandes.

**BMX** (*abbr of* **bicycle motorcross**) *n:* **~ bike** BMX -Rad *das*.

**BNP** (*abbr of* **British National Party**) *n* rechtsextreme britische Partei.

**BO** *n abbr of* body odour.

**boa constrictor** ['bəʊəkən'strɪktə'] *n* Boa *die*.

**boar** [bɔ:'] *n* - **1.** [male pig] Eber *der* - **2.** [wild pig] Keiler *der*.

**board** [bɔ:d] *n* - **1.** [plank] Brett *das* - **2.** [for notices - large] schwarzes Brett; [ - small] Pinnwand *die* - **3.** [for games] Spielbrett *das* - **4.** [blackboard] Tafel *die* - **5.** ADMIN: **~ (of directors)** Vorstand *der;* **~ of examiners** Prüfungskommission *die;* **~ of enquiry** Untersuchungsausschuss *der* - **6.** *Br* [at hotel, guesthouse] Verpflegung *die;* **~ and lodging** Unterkunft und Verpflegung; **full/half ~** Voll-/Halbpension *die* - **7.** *phr:* **above ~** offen, einsichtig; **to go by the ~** *fig* ins Wasser fallen; **to sweep the ~** auf der ganzen Linie siegen ◇ *vt* [train, bus] einlsteigen in (+ A); **to ~ a ship/aircraft** an Bord eines Schiffes/Flugzeugs gehen.

◆ **across the board** *adj* [increase] generell ◇ *adv* [apply] überall.

◆ **on board** *prep* [ship, plane] an Bord (+ G); [bus, train] in (+ D) ◇ *adv:* **to be on ~** [on ship, plane] an Bord sein; [on train] im Zug sein; **to take sthg on ~** [knowledge] etw berücksichtigen; [advice] etw anlnehmen.

◆ **board up** *vt sep* mit Brettern vernageln.

**boarder** ['bɔ:də'] *n* - **1.** [lodger] Pensionsgast *der* - **2.** [at school] Internatsschüler *der,* -in *die*.

**board game** *n* Brettspiel *das*.

**boarding card** ['bɔ:dɪŋ-] *n* Bordkarte *die*.

**boardinghouse** ['bɔ:dɪŋhaʊs, *pl* -haʊzɪz] *n* Pension *die*.

**boarding school** ['bɔ:dɪŋ-] *n* Internat *das*.

**board meeting** *n* Vorstandssitzung *die*.

**Board of Trade** *n Br:* **the ~** das Handelsministerium.

**boardroom** ['bɔ:drʊm] *n* Sitzungssaal *der*.

**boardwalk** ['bɔ:dwɔ:k] *n Am* Bohlenweg *der*.

**boast** [bəʊst] *n* Prahlerei *die;* **her proudest ~ is that she can windsurf** es ist ihr ganzer Stolz, windsurfen zu können ◇ *vt* [special feature] sich rühmen (+ G) ◇ *vi* prahlen; **to ~ about sthg** mit etw prahlen OR anlgeben.

**boastful** ['bəʊstfʊl] *adj* prahlerisch, angeberisch.

**boasting** ['bəʊstɪŋ] *n (U)* Prahlerei *die*.

**boat** [bəʊt] *n* Boot *das;* [large] Schiff *das;* [for rowing] Ruderboot *das;* [for sailing] Segelboot *das;* **by ~** mit dem Boot; [large] mit dem Schiff; **to be in the same ~** im selben Boot OR in einem Boot sitzen; **to rock the ~** für Aufregung sorgen.

**boater** ['bəʊtə'] *n* [hat] steifer Strohhut.

**boating** ['bəʊtɪŋ] *n* Bootfahren *das*.

**boat people** *npl* Bootsflüchtlinge *pl*.

**boatswain** ['bəʊsn] *n* NAUT Bootsmann *der*.

**bob** [bɒbl] (*pt* & *pp* **-bed;** *cont* **-bing**) *n* - **1.** [hair-style] Bubikopf *der* - **2.** *Br inf dated* [shilling] Schilling *der* - **3.** [bobsleigh] Bob *der* <> *vi* [boat, ship] auf und ab schaukeln.

**bobbin** [ˈbɒbɪn] *n* Spule *die.*

**bobble** [ˈbɒbl] *n* Pompom *der*, Bommel *der.*

**bobby** [ˈbɒbɪ] (*pl* **-ies**) *n Br inf* [policeman] Polizist *der.*

**bobby pin** *n Am* Haarklammer *die.*

**bobby socks, bobby sox** *npl Am* kurze Söckchen *pl.*

**bobsleigh** [ˈbɒbsleɪ] *n* Bob *der.*

**bode** [bəʊd] *vi literary:* **to ~ well/ill (for sb/sthg)** ein gutes/schlechtes Zeichen (für jn/etw) sein; **to ~ well (for sb/sthg)** ein gutes Zeichen (für jn/etw) sein.

**bodice** [ˈbɒdɪs] *n* Oberteil *das.*

**bodily** [ˈbɒdɪlɪ] *adj* körperlich; **~ functions** Körperfunktionen *pl* <> *adv* [carry, lift] mit dem ganzen Körper.

**body** [ˈbɒdɪ] (*pl* **-ies**) *n* - **1.** [of human, animal] Körper *der;* **to keep ~ and soul together** Leib und Seele zusammenhalten - **2.** [corpse] Leiche *die;* **over my dead ~!** nur über meine Leiche! - **3.** [organization] Organisation *die* - **4.** [of car] Karosserie *die;* [of plane] Rumpf *der* - **5.** [group] Gruppe *die* - **6.** [of wine] Körper *der* - **7.** [of hair] Volumen *das* - **8.** [garment] Body *der.*

**body bag** *n* Leichentransporthülle *die.*

**body building** *n* Bodybuilding *das.*

**bodyguard** [ˈbɒdɪgɑːd] *n* [one person] Leibwächter *der;* [group of people] Leibwache *die.*

**body odour** *n* Körpergeruch *der.*

**body search** *n* Leibesvisitation *die.*

**body shop** *n* - **1.** [garage] Karosseriewerkstatt *die* - **2.** *Am inf* [gym] Fitnesscenter *das.*

**body stocking** *n* Bodystocking *der.*

**bodywork** [ˈbɒdɪwɜːk] *n* Karosserie *die.*

**boffin** [ˈbɒfɪn] *n Br inf* [scientist] Eierkopf *der.*

**bog** [bɒg] *n* - **1.** [marsh] Sumpf *der* - **2.** *Br inf* [toilet] Klo *das.*

**bogey** [ˈbəʊgɪ] *n* [in golf] Bogey *das.*

**bogeyman** [ˈbəʊgɪmæn] *n* schwarzer Mann.

**bogged down** [ˌbɒgd-] *adj:* **~ (in sthg)** *lit* & *fig* (in etw (*D*)) festgefahren; **to get ~ in details** sich in Details verzetteln.

**boggle** [ˈbɒgl] *vi:* **the mind ~s!** es übersteigt den Verstand!

**boggy** [ˈbɒgɪ] (*compar* **-ier;** *superl* **-iest**) *adj* sumpfig, morastig.

**bogie** [ˈbəʊgɪ] *n RAIL* Drehgestell *das.*

**Bogotá** [bɒgəˈtɑː] *n* Bogota *nt.*

**bog-standard** *adj inf* stinknormal.

**bogus** [ˈbəʊgəs] *adj* [identity] falsch; [emotion] geheuchelt.

**Bohemia** [bəʊˈhiːmjə] *n* Böhmen *nt.*

**bohemian** [bəʊˈhiːmjən] *adj* [lifestyle] unkonventionell <> *n* Bohemien *der.*

→ **Bohemian** *adj* böhmisch <> *n* Böhme *der*, -min *die.*

**boil** [bɔɪl] *n* - **1.** [on skin] Furunkel *der* - **2.** [boiling point]: **to bring sthg to the ~** etw zum Kochen bringen; **to come to the ~** zu kochen beginnen <> *vt* kochen; **to ~ the kettle** Wasser aufsetzen <> *vi* kochen; **the kettle is ~ing** das Wasser im Kessel kocht.

→ **boil away** *vi* [evaporate] verkochen.

→ **boil down to** *vt fus fig* hinauslaufen auf (+ *A*).

→ **boil over** *vi* - **1.** [liquid] überlkochen - **2.** *fig* [feelings] ihren Höhepunkt erreichen.

**boiled** [ˈbɔɪld] *adj* gekocht; **~ potatoes** Salzkartoffeln *pl;* **~ sweets** Bonbons *pl;* **~ egg** gekochtes Ei.

**boiler** [ˈbɔɪləʳ] *n* Boiler *der.*

**boiler suit** *n Br* Overall *der*, Blaumann *der.*

**boiling** [ˈbɔɪlɪŋ] *adj* [hot liquid] kochend heiß; [weather] wahnsinnig heiß; **I'm ~ (hot)!** mir ist fürchterlich heiß!; **to be ~ with rage** vor Wut kochen.

**boiling point** *n* Siedepunkt *der.*

**boisterous** [ˈbɔɪstərəs] *adj* ungestüm, wild.

**bold** [bəʊld] *adj* - **1.** [person, plan] kühn, mutig - **2.** ART [lines, colour] kräftig; [design] kühn - **3.** TYPO: **~ type** OR **print** Fettdruck *der.*

**boldly** [ˈbəʊldlɪ] *adv* [confidently] kühn, mutig.

**Bolivia** [bəˈlɪvɪə] *n* Bolivien *nt.*

**Bolivian** [bəˈlɪvɪən] *adj* bolivianisch <> *n* Bolivier *der*, -in *die.*

**bollard** [ˈbɒlɑːd] *n* Poller *der.*

**bollocks** [ˈbɒləks] *Br vinf npl* Eier *pl* <> *excl* Scheiße!

**Bolshevik** [ˈbɒlʃɪvɪk] *adj* bolschewistisch <> *n* Bolschewik *der*, -in *die.*

**bolster** [ˈbəʊlstəʳ] *n* Nackenrolle *die* <> *vt* [confidence] stärken.

→ **bolster up** *vt fus:* **to ~ up the economy** die Wirtschaft stärken.

**bolt** [bəʊlt] *n* - **1.** [on door, window] Riegel *der* - **2.** [type of screw] Bolzen *der* <> *adv:* **~ upright** kerzengerade <> *vt* - **1.** [fasten together] verschrauben - **2.** [close] verriegeln - **3.** [food] hinunterlschlingen <> *vi* [run - horse] durchlgehen; [ - person] flüchten.

**bomb** [bɒm] *n* Bombe *die* <> *vt* [from the air] bombardieren; [on the ground] einen Bombenanschlag verüben auf (+ *A*).

**bombard** [bɒmˈbɑːd] *vt* [from the air] bombardieren; [from gun] beschießen; **to ~ sb with sthg** *fig* jn mit etw bombardieren.

**bombardment** [bɒm'bɑːdmənt] n [from the air] Bombardement das; [by big guns] Beschuss der.

**bomb disposal squad** n Bombenräumkommando das.

**bomber** ['bɒmə'] n - **1.** [plane] Bomberflugzeug das - **2.** [person] Bombenleger der, -in die.

**bomber jacket** n Fliegerjacke die.

**bombing** ['bɒmɪŋ] n [from the air] Bombardierung die; [on the ground] Bombenanschlag der.

**bombproof** ['bɒmpruːf] adj bombensicher.

**bombshell** ['bɒmʃel] n fig schwerer Schlag.

**bombsite** ['bɒmsaɪt] n Trümmerfeld das.

**bona fide** [ˌbəʊnə'faɪdɪ] adj [genuine] echt.

**bonanza** [bə'nænzə] n Goldgrube die.

**bond** [bɒnd] n - **1.** [emotional link] enge Beziehung, Bindung die; **~s of friendship** freundschaftliche Bande pl - **2.** [binding promise]: **my word is my ~** was ich verspreche, halte ich auch - **3.** FIN Obligation die ◇ vt - **1.** [glue]: **to ~ sthg to sthg** etw an etw (A) kleben - **2.** fig [people]: **the experience ~ed them together** die Erfahrung band sie aneinander ◇ vi - **1.** [stick together]: **to ~ (together)** zusammenkleben - **2.** fig [people] Bande knüpfen.

**bondage** ['bɒndɪdʒ] n literary Sklaverei die.

**bonded warehouse** ['bɒndɪd-] n Zolldepot das.

**bone** [bəʊn] n Knochen der; [of fish] Gräte die; **~s** [of skeleton] Gebeine pl; **~ of contention** Zankapfel der; **to feel** OR **know sthg in one's ~s** etw im Gefühl haben; **to make no ~s about sthg** keinen Hehl aus etw machen ◇ vt [meat] von den Knochen lösen; [fish] entgräten.

**bone china** n feines Porzellan.

**bone-dry** adj knochentrocken.

**bone-idle** adj inf stinkfaul.

**boneless** ['bəʊnlɪs] adj [meat] ohne Knochen; [fish] ohne Gräten.

**bone marrow** n Knochenmark das.

**bonfire** ['bɒnˌfaɪə'] n großes Feuer (im Freien).

**bonfire night** n Br 5. November, Jahrestag der Pulververschwörung; ▷ **Guy Fawkes' Night**.

**bongo** ['bɒŋgəʊ] (pl **-s** OR **-es**) n: **~ (drum)** Bongo das OR die.

**bonk** vt & vi Br vinf bumsen.

**Bonn** [bɒn] n Bonn nt.

**bonnet** ['bɒnɪt] n - **1.** Br [of car] Kühlerhaube die, Motorhaube die - **2.** [hat - for woman] Haube die; [ - for baby] Häubchen das; .

**bonny** ['bɒnɪ] (compar **-ier;** superl **-iest**) adj Scot [baby] prächtig; [girl] hübsch.

**bonus** ['bəʊnəs] (pl **-es**) n - **1.** [extra money] Prämie die; **Christmas ~** Weihnachtsgratifikation die - **2.** fig [added advantage] Pluspunkt der.

**bonus issue** n Br FIN Extradividende die.

**bony** ['bəʊnɪ] (compar **-ier;** superl **-iest**) adj - **1.** [person, hand, face] knochig - **2.** [meat] voller Knochen; [fish] voller Gräten.

**boo** [buː] (pl **-s**) excl buh! ◇ n Buhruf der ◇ vt ausbuhen, auspfeifen ◇ vi buhen.

**boob** [buːb] n inf [mistake] Schnitzer der.
➤ **boobs** npl Br vinf [woman's breasts] Möpse pl.

**boob tube** n - **1.** Br [garment] Bustier das - **2.** Am inf [TV] Röhre die.

**booby prize** ['buːbɪ-] n Preis für den schlechtesten Teilnehmer.

**booby trap** ['buːbɪ-] n - **1.** [bomb] getarnte Bombe - **2.** [prank] Falle die (mit deren Hilfe ein Streich gespielt wird).
➤ **booby-trap** vt eine Bombe verstecken in (+ D).

**boogie** ['buːgɪ] inf n: **to have a ~** rocken ◇ vi rocken.

**book** [bʊk] n - **1.** [for reading] Buch das; **to do sthg by the ~** etw genau nach Vorschrift tun; **to throw the ~ at sb** jn nach allen Regeln der Kunst fertigmachen - **2.** [of stamps, matches, tickets] Heftchen das; [of cheques] Heft das ◇ vt - **1.** [table, room] reservieren lassen; [ticket] bestellen; [performer] engagieren; [plane seat] buchen; **to be fully ~ed** [restaurant, hotel] ausgebucht sein; [performance] ausverkauft sein - **2.** inf [subj: police] auf|schreiben - **3.** Br FTBL verwarnen ◇ vi [book table, room] reservieren lassen; [book ticket] vor|bestellen; [book plane seat] buchen.
➤ **books** npl COMM Bücher die; **to do the ~s** die Bücher führen; **to be in sb's good/bad ~s** bei jm gut/schlecht angeschrieben sein.
➤ **book in** vt sep [register] an|melden; [make reservation for] ein Zimmer/Zimmer reservieren lassen für ◇ vi sich an|melden.
➤ **book up** vt sep buchen; **to be ~ed up** [restaurant, hotel] ausgebucht sein; [performance] ausverkauft sein.

**book bag** n Am = **booksack**.

**bookbinding** ['bʊkˌbaɪndɪŋ] n Buchbinderei die.

**bookcase** ['bʊkkeɪs] n Bücherregal das.

**book club** n Buchklub der.

**bookends** ['bʊkendz] npl Buchstützen pl.

**bookie** ['bʊkɪ] n inf Buchmacher der.

**booking** ['bʊkɪŋ] n - **1.** esp Br [of seat, room] Reservierung die; [of ticket] Bestellung die - **2.** FTBL Verwarnung die.

**booking clerk** n esp Br Schalterbeamte der, -tin die.

**booking office** *n esp Br* [in station] Fahrkartenschalter *der;* [in theatre] Theaterkasse *die.*

**bookish** ['bʊkɪʃ] *adj:* **to be ~** ein Bücherwurm sein.

**bookkeeper** ['bʊkˌkiːpə'] *n* COMM Buchhalter *der, -in die.*

**bookkeeping** ['bʊkˌkiːpɪŋ] *n* COMM Buchhaltung *die.*

**booklet** ['bʊklɪt] *n* Broschüre *die.*

**bookmaker** ['bʊkˌmeɪkə'] *n* Buchmacher *der.*

**bookmark** ['bʊkmɑːk] *n* Lesezeichen *das.*

**booksack** ['bʊksæk] *n Am* Schultasche *die.*

**bookseller** ['bʊkˌselə'] *n* Buchhändler *der, -in die.*

**bookshelf** ['bʊkʃelf] (*pl* **-shelves** [-ʃelvz]) *n* Bücherbord *das.*

**bookshop** *Br* ['bʊkʃɒp], **bookstore** *Am* ['bʊkstɔː'] *n* Buchhandlung *die.*

**bookstall** ['bʊkstɔːl] *n Br* Bücherstand *der.*

**bookstore** ['bʊkstɔː'] *n Am* = **bookshop.**

**book token** *n esp Br* Büchergutschein *der.*

**bookworm** ['bʊkwɜːm] *n* Bücherwurm *der.*

**boom** [buːm] *n* - **1.** [of cannons, guns] Donnern *das;* [of voice] Dröhnen *das* - **2.** [in business, economy] Boom *der,* Aufschwung *der* - **3.** NAUT Baum *der* - **4.** [for TV camera, microphone] Galgen *der* ◇ *vi* - **1.** [cannons, guns] donnern; [voice] dröhnen - **2.** [business, economy] einen Aufschwung nehmen.

**boomerang** ['buːməræŋ] *n* Bumerang *der.*

**boon** [buːn] *n* Segen *der.*

**boor** [bʊə'] *n* Flegel *der,* Rüpel *der.*

**boorish** ['bʊərɪʃ] *adj* flegelhaft, rüpelhaft.

**boost** [buːst] *n* - **1.** [in profits, production] Zunahme *die;* **to give a ~ to sthg** etw ankurbeln - **2.** [in popularity] Steigerung *die;* [in spirits, morale] Verbesserung *die;* **to give a ~ to sthg** [popularity] etw steigern; [spirits, morale] etw heben; **to give sb a ~** [encourage] jm Auftrieb geben ◇ *vt* - **1.** [profits, production] ankurbeln - **2.** [popularity] steigern; [morale, spirits] heben - **3.** *Am inf* [steal] klauen.

**booster** ['buːstə'] *n* [vaccine] Auffrischimpfung *die.*

**booster seat** *n* Kindersitz *der.*

**boot** [buːt] *n* - **1.** [footwear] Stiefel *der;* [for football, rugby] Schuh *der* - **2.** *Br* [of car] Kofferraum *der* ◇ *vt* - **1.** *inf* [kick] einen Tritt geben (+ *D*); [ball] kicken - **2.** COMPUT booten, hochfahren.

→ **to boot** *adv* noch dazu.

→ **boot out** *vt sep inf* rausschmeißen.

→ **boot up** *vi* COMPUT booten.

**booth** [buːð] *n* - **1.** [at fair] (Markt)bude *die* - **2.** [for telephone] Telefonzelle *die* - **3.** [for voting] Kabine *die.*

**bootleg** ['buːtleg] *adj inf* [recording] schwarz hergestellt; [alcohol] schwarz gebrannt.

**bootlegger** ['buːtˌlegə'] *n inf* Schwarzhändler *der.*

**booty** ['buːtɪ] *n literary* Beute *die.*

**booze** [buːz] *inf n* [alcohol] Alkohol *der* ◇ *vi* saufen.

**boozer** ['buːzə'] *n inf* - **1.** [person] Säufer *der, -in die* - **2.** *Br* [pub] Kneipe *die.*

**bop** [bɒp] (*pt & pp* **-ped;** *cont* **-ping**) *inf n* - **1.** [on head] Kopfnuss *die* - **2.** [dance] **to have a ~** rocken ◇ *vt* [hit]: **to ~ sb on the head** jm eins auf den Kopf geben ◇ *vi* [dance] rocken.

**border** ['bɔːdə'] *n* - **1.** [between countries] Grenze *die* - **2.** [of dress, handkerchief] Bordüre *die;* [of plate] Rand *der* - **3.** [outer limit] Rand *der* - **4.** [in garden] Rabatte *die* ◇ *vt* - **1.** [country] grenzen an (+ *A*) - **2.** [field, garden] umschließen; [path] säumen.

→ **border on** *vt fus* [verge on] grenzen an (+ *A*).

**borderline** ['bɔːdəlaɪn] *adj:* **~ case** Grenzfall *der* ◇ *n fig* Grenze *die.*

**Borders** ['bɔːdəz] *n* **the ~** *an England grenzender südlicher Teil Schottlands.*

**bore** [bɔː'] *pt* ⟾ **bear** ◇ *n* - **1.** [person] Langweiler *der;* [situation, event] Plage *die;* **it's a ~ being sick** es ist ärgerlich, krank zu sein - **2.** [of gun] Kaliber *das;* **a 12-~ shotgun** eine Flinte vom Kaliber 12 ◇ *vt* - **1.** [not interest] langweilen; **to ~ sb stiff** OR **to tears** OR **to death** jn zu Tode langweilen - **2.** [drill] bohren.

**bored** [bɔːd] *adj* gelangweilt; **he was ~ with his toys** seine Spielsachen langweilten ihn; **she is ~ with always staying in** es langweilt sie, immer zu Hause zu bleiben.

**boredom** ['bɔːdəm] *n* Langeweile *die.*

**boring** ['bɔːrɪŋ] *adj* langweilig.

**born** [bɔːn] *adj:* **to be ~** geboren werden; **I was ~ in London/1968** ich bin OR wurde in London/1968 geboren; **~ and bred** in geboren und aufgewachsen in (+ *D*); **a ~ entertainer** ein geborener Entertainer.

**born-again** *adj* [Christian] wiedergeboren.

**borne** [bɔːn] *pp* ⟾ **bear.**

**Borneo** ['bɔːnɪəʊ] *n* Borneo *nt.*

**borough** ['bʌrə] *n* Regierungsbezirk, *der entweder eine Stadt oder einen Stadtteil umfasst.*

**borrow** ['bɒrəʊ] *vt* sich (*D*) leihen; [book from library] ausleihen; **to ~ sthg from sb** sich (*D*) etw von jm leihen OR borgen.

**borrower** ['bɒrəʊə'] *n* [from bank] Kreditnehmer *der, -in die.*

**borrowing** ['bɒrəʊɪŋ] *n* [from bank] Kreditaufnahme *die.*

**Bosnia** ['bɒznɪə] n Bosnien nt.

**Bosnia-Herzegovina** [-ˌhɜːtsəgəˈviːnə] n Bosnien-Herzegowina nt.

**Bosnian** ['bɒznɪən] adj bosnisch ◇ n Bosnier der, -in die.

**bosom** ['buzəm] n - **1.** [woman's breasts] Busen der; [of dress] Brustteil der - **2.** fig [of family] Schoß der; ~ friend Busenfreund der, -in die.

**Bosporus** ['bɒspərəs], **Bosphorus** ['bɒsfərəs] n: the ~ der Bosporus.

**boss** [bɒs] n - **1.** [gen] Chef der, -in die; to be one's own ~ sein eigener Chef sein - **2.** fig [of gang] Boss der.
➤ **boss about, boss around** vt sep pej herumlkommandieren.

**bossy** ['bɒsɪ] (compar -ier; superl -iest) adj herrisch.

**bosun** ['bəʊsn] n = boatswain.

**botanic(al)** [bəˈtænɪk(l)] adj [drawing] Pflanzen-; [studies, books] botanisch.

**botanical garden** n botanischer Garten.

**botanist** ['bɒtənɪst] n Botaniker der, -in die.

**botany** ['bɒtənɪ] n Botanik die.

**botch** [bɒtʃ] ➤ **botch up** vt sep inf mehr schlecht als recht machen.

**both** [bəʊθ] pron beide; ~ of us wir beide; ~ of them speak German sie sprechen beide Deutsch; do you prefer music or painting? – I like them ~ bevorzugst du die Musik oder Malerei? – ich mag beides ◇ adj beide ◇ adv: ~ my sister and I sowohl meine Schwester als auch ich.

**bother** ['bɒðəʳ] vt - **1.** [worry, hurt] stören; what you told me yesterday has been ~ing me was du mir gestern gesagt hast, hat mich beschäftigt; she/can't be ~ed to do it sie hat keine Lust, das zu tun - **2.** [annoy] ärgern; [pester] belästigen; I'm sorry to ~ you entschuldigen Sie die Störung ◇ vi sich bemühen; no, don't ~! nein, das ist nicht nötig!; to ~ about sthg sich um etw kümmern; don't ~ to phone me Sie brauchen mich nicht anzurufen; I didn't ~ to lock up ich habe mir nicht die Mühe gemacht abzuschließen; don't ~ getting up bleiben Sie doch sitzen ◇ n Mühe die; it's no ~ at all überhaupt kein Problem; if it isn't too much of a ~ wenn es Ihnen nichts ausmacht ◇ excl verflixt!

**bothered** ['bɒðəd] adj [annoyed] verärgert.

**Botswana** [bɒtˈswɑːnə] n Botswana nt.

**bottle** ['bɒtl] n - **1.** [container, quantity] Flasche die - **2.** [for baby] Fläschchen das, Flasche die - **3.** (U) Br inf [courage] Mumm der ◇ vt - **1.** [wine] in Flaschen ablfüllen - **2.** [fruit] einlmachen.
➤ **bottle out** vi Br inf einen Rückzieher machen.

➤ **bottle up** vt sep [feelings] in sich (D) auflstauen.

**bottle bank** n Altglascontainer der.

**bottled** ['bɒtld] adj [water, gas] in Flaschen; ~ beer Flaschenbier das.

**bottle-feed** vt mit der Flasche auf lziehen OR ernähren.

**bottleneck** ['bɒtlnek] n Engpass der.

**bottle-opener** n Flaschenöffner der.

**bottom** ['bɒtəm] adj - **1.** [lowest] unterste, -r, -s - **2.** [least successful] schlechteste, -r, -s; to be ~ in sthg [subject] der Schlechteste in etw (D) sein ◇ n - **1.** [of glass, bottle, bag] Boden der; [of page, list, ladder] unteres Ende; [of sea, lake] Grund der; [of hill, mountain] Fuß der; at the ~ unten - **2.** [of street, garden]: at the ~ of am Ende (+ G) - **3.** [of organization] unteres Ende; he worked his way up from the ~ er hat sich hoch gearbeitet - **4.** [buttocks] Hintern der - **5.** [cause]: what's at the ~ of it? was steckt dahinter?; to get to the ~ of sthg etw auf den Grund gehen.
➤ **bottom out** vi den Tiefstand erreichen.

**bottomless** ['bɒtəmlɪs] adj - **1.** [pit, chasm] bodenlos - **2.** [supply] unerschöpflich.

**bottom line** n fig [result]: the ~ das Endergebnis.

**botulism** ['bɒtjʊlɪzm] n Nahrungsmittelvergiftung die

**bough** [baʊ] n Ast der.

**bought** [bɔːt] pt & pp ⊳ buy.

**boulder** ['bəʊldəʳ] n (gerundeter) Felsbrocken.

**boulevard** ['buːləvɑːd] n Boulevard der.

**bounce** [baʊns] vi - **1.** [ball] springen; the ball ~d onto the car der Ball prallte auf das Auto - **2.** [light, sound] reflektiert werden - **3.** [person - with energy, enthusiasm] hüpfen; to ~ on sthg [jump up and down] auf etw (D) springen - **4.** inf [cheque] platzen ◇ vt [ball] aufprallen lassen ◇ n - **1.** [of ball] Sprungkraft die; [rebound] Aufprall der - **2.** (U) [vigour] Schwung der.
➤ **bounce back** vi [after illness, setback] wieder auf die Beine kommen.

**bouncer** ['baʊnsəʳ] n inf Rausschmeißer der.

**bouncy** ['baʊnsɪ] (compar -ier; superl -iest) adj - **1.** [lively] munter - **2.** [springy] federnd.

**bound** [baʊnd] pt & pp ⊳ bind ◇ adj - **1.** [certain]: to be ~ to do sthg etw bestimmt tun; it was ~ to happen das musste so kommen; he's ~ to win er gewinnt hundertprozentig - **2.** [forced, morally obliged]: ~ by sthg durch etw gebunden; ~ to do sthg gezwungen, etw zu tun; he's morally ~ to tell the truth er ist moralisch verpflichtet, die Wahrheit zu sagen; I'm ~ to say OR admit ich muss sagen OR zugeben - **3.** [en route]: to be ~ for unterwegs sein nach ◇ *n* [leap] Sprung *der* ◇ *vt* [border]: **to be ~ed by** begrenzt sein von ◇ *vi* [leap] springen, hüpfen.

➤ **bound up with** *prep*: **to be ~ up with** zusammenlhängen mit.

➤ **bounds** *npl* Grenzen *pl*; **out of ~s** verboten.

**boundary** ['baʊndrɪ] (*pl* -ies) *n* Grenze *die*.

**boundless** ['baʊndlɪs] *adj* grenzenlos.

**bountiful** ['baʊntɪfʊl] *adj literary* reich, üppig.

**bounty** ['baʊntɪ] *n (U) literary* Freigebigkeit *die*.

**bouquet** [bʊ'keɪ] *n* **- 1.** [bunch] Strauß *der* **- 2.** [smell] Bukett *das*, Blume *die*.

**bouquet garni** [-'gɑːnɪ] *n* Kräutermischung *die*.

**bourbon** ['bɜːbən] *n* Bourbon *der*.

**bourgeois** ['bɔːʒwɑː] *adj pej* spießbürgerlich.

**bourgeoisie** [ˌbɔːʒwɑː'zɪ] *n pej*: **the ~** die Spießbürger *pl*.

**bout** [baʊt] *n* **- 1.** [attack, session] Anfall *der* **- 2.** [boxing match] Kampf *der*.

**boutique** [buː'tiːk] *n* Boutique *die*.

**bow¹** [baʊ] *n* **- 1.** [act of bowing] Verbeugung *die* **- 2.** [of ship] Bug *der* ◇ *vt* [lower] beugen ◇ *vi* **- 1.** [make a bow] sich verbeugen **- 2.** [defer]: **to ~ to sthg** sich einer Sache (*D*) beugen.

➤ **bow down** *vi* [give in]: **to ~ down (to sb)** sich (jm) fügen.

➤ **bow out** *vi* sich verabschieden.

**bow²** [baʊ] *n* **- 1.** [weapon, for musical instrument] Bogen *der* **- 2.** [knot] Schleife *die*.

**bowels** ['baʊəlz] *npl lit* & *fig* Eingeweide *pl*.

**bowl** [baʊl] *n* Schüssel *die*; [of pipe] Kopf *der* ◇ *vt* [in cricket] werfen ◇ *vi* [in cricket] den Ball werfen.

➤ **bowls** *n* britische Variante des französischen Boulespiels, bei der die Spielkugeln gerollt werden.

➤ **bowl over** *vt sep* umlwerfen.

**bow-legged** [ˌbaʊ'legɪd] *adj* O-beinig.

**bowler** ['baʊləʳ] *n* **- 1.** [in cricket] Werfer *der*, -in *die* **- 2.** [headgear]: **~ (hat)** Melone *die*.

**bowling** ['baʊlɪŋ] *n*: **(tenpin) ~** Bowling *das*.

**bowling alley** *n* Bowlingbahn *die*.

**bowling green** *n* Rasen- oder Kunstrasenfläche, auf der „bowls" gespielt wird.

**bow tie** [baʊ-] *n* Fliege *die*.

**bow window** [baʊ-] *n* Erkerfenster *das*.

**box** [bɒks] *n* **- 1.** [made of wood or metal] Kiste *die*; [smaller] Kasten *der*; [made of cardboard] Karton *der*; [smaller] Schachtel *die*; **a ~ of chocolates** eine Schachtel Pralinen **- 2.** [in theatre] Loge *die* **- 3.** [on form] Kästchen *das* **- 4.** *Br inf* [television]: **the ~** die Glotze **- 5.** (*U*) [shrub, tree]

Buchsbaum *der* ◇ *vt* **- 1.** BOXING boxen **- 2.** [put in boxes] einlpacken ◇ *vi* [fight] boxen.

➤ **box in** *vt sep* **- 1.** [hem in] einlklemmen **- 2.** [build a box around] verkleiden, verschalen.

**boxer** ['bɒksəʳ] *n* **- 1.** [fighter] Boxer *der* **- 2.** [dog] Boxer *der*, -hündin *die*.

**boxer shorts** *npl* Boxershorts *pl*.

**boxing** ['bɒksɪŋ] *n* Boxen *das*.

**Boxing Day** *n* Zweiter Weihnachtsfeiertag.

**boxing glove** *n* Boxhandschuh *der*.

**boxing ring** *n* Boxring *der*.

**box junction** *n Br* Kreuzung mit gelber Schraffierung, die im Falle eines Staus freizuhalten ist.

**box number** *n* Postfach *das*.

**box office** *n* Kasse *die (von Kino, Theater, bei Konzert)*.

**boxroom** ['bɒksrʊm] *n Br* sehr kleiner Raum in einer Wohnung oder einem Haus, oft als Abstellkammer genutzt.

**boy** [bɔɪ] *n* **- 1.** [young male, son] Junge *der* **- 2.** [male friend]: **the ~s** die Jungs ◇ *excl*: **(oh) ~!** *inf* oh Mann!

**boycott** ['bɔɪkɒt] *n* Boykott *der* ◇ *vt* boykottieren.

**boyfriend** ['bɔɪfrend] *n* Freund *der*.

**boyish** ['bɔɪɪʃ] *adj* jungenhaft.

**boy scout** *n* Pfadfinder *der*.

**Br** *abbr* of **brother**.

**BR** *n abbr* of **British Rail**.

**bra** [brɑː] *n* Büstenhalter *der*, BH *der*.

**brace** [breɪs] (*pl sense 3 inv*) *n* **- 1.** [on teeth] Klammer *die*, Zahnspange *die* **- 2.** [on leg] Stützapparat *der* **- 3.** [pair] Paar *das* ◇ *vt* **- 1.** [steady, support]: **to ~ o.s.** sich festlhalten **- 2.** *fig* [mentally prepare]: **to ~ o.s. (for sthg)** sich (auf etw (*A*)) gefasst machen.

➤ **braces** *npl Br* [for trousers] Hosenträger *pl*.

**bracelet** ['breɪslɪt] *n* Armband *das*.

**bracing** ['breɪsɪŋ] *adj* belebend.

**bracken** ['brækn] *n (U)* Farnkraut *das*.

**bracket** ['brækɪt] *n* **- 1.** [support] Halterung *die*; (angle) **~** Winkelträger *der* **- 2.** [parenthesis] Klammer *die*; **in ~s** in Klammern **- 3.** [group] Klasse *die*; **income ~** Einkommensklasse *die* ◇ *vt* **- 1.** [enclose in brackets] einlklammern, in Klammern setzen **- 2.** [group]: **to ~ sb/sthg (together) with sb/sthg** jn/etw in dieselbe Gruppe wie jn/etw einlordnen; **he ~s all criminals together** er wirft alle Kriminellen in einen Topf.

**brackish** ['brækɪʃ] *adj* brackig.

**brag** [bræg] (*pt* & *pp* **-ged;** *cont* **-ging**) *vi* prahlen.

**braid** [breɪd] *n* - **1.** *(U)* [on uniform] Tresse *die* - **2.** *esp Am* [hairstyle] Zopf *der* ⟨⟩ *vt esp Am* flechten.

**braille** [breɪl] *n (U)* Blindenschrift *die*.

**brain** [breɪn] *n* - **1.** [organ] Gehirn *das* - **2.** [mind, person] Kopf *der;* **to have sthg on the ~** etw im Kopf haben.

➣ **brains** *npl* [intelligence] Grips *der*, Intelligenz *die;* **to pick sb's ~s** jn um Hilfe OR Rat bitten; **to rack** Br OR **cudgel** Am **one's ~s** sich *(D)* den Kopf zerbrechen.

**brainchild** ['breɪntʃaɪld] *n* Geistesprodukt *das*.

**brain death** *n (U)* Gehirntod *der*.

**brain drain** *n* Abwanderung *die* von Wissenschaftlern.

**brainless** ['breɪnlɪs] *adj* hirnlos.

**brainstorm** ['breɪnstɔːm] *n* - **1.** Br [moment of aberration]: **to have a ~** (geistig) weggetreten sein - **2.** Am [brilliant idea] Geistesblitz *der*.

**brainstorming** ['breɪnˌstɔːmɪŋ] *n (U)* Brainstorming *das*.

**brainteaser** ['breɪnˌtiːzəʳ] *n* Denksportaufgabe *die*.

**brainwash** ['breɪnwɒʃ] *vt:* **to ~ sb** jn einer Gehirnwäsche unterziehen.

**brainwave** ['breɪnweɪv] *n* Geistesblitz *der*.

**brainy** ['breɪnɪ] (*compar* **-ier;** *superl* **-iest**) *adj inf* gescheit.

**braise** [breɪz] *vt* schmoren.

**brake** [breɪk] *n* - **1.** [on vehicle] Bremse *die* - **2.** *fig* [restraint] Zurückhaltung *die* ⟨⟩ *vi* bremsen.

**brake horsepower** *n (U)* Bremsleistung *die*.

**brake light** *n* Bremslicht *das*.

**brake lining** *n* Bremsbelag *der*.

**brake pedal** *n* Bremspedal *das*.

**brake shoe** *n* Bremsbacke *die*.

**bramble** ['bræmbl] *n* [bush] Brombeerbusch *der;* [fruit] Brombeere *die*.

**bran** [bræn] *n (U)* Kleie *die*.

**branch** [brɑːntʃ] *n* - **1.** [of tree] Zweig *der*, Ast *der* - **2.** [of river] Arm *der;* [of railway] Nebenstrecke *die* - **3.** [of company, bank, organization] Zweigstelle *die* - **4.** [of subject] Zweig *der* ⟨⟩ *vi* [road] sich teilen, sich gabeln.

➣ **branch off** *vi* [road, track] ablzweigen, ablbiegen.

➣ **branch out** *vi* sein Tätigkeitsfeld erweitern OR ausldehnen.

**branch line** *n* Nebenlinie *die*.

**brand** [brænd] *n* - **1.** COMM [make] Marke *die* - **2.** *fig* [type, style] Sorte *die*, Art *die* - **3.** [on cattle] Brandzeichen *das* ⟨⟩ *vt* - **1.** [cattle] mit einem Brandzeichen versehen - **2.** *fig* [classify]: **to ~ sb (as) sthg** jn als etw brandmarken.

**brandish** ['brændɪʃ] *vt* schwingen.

**brand leader** *n* führende Marke.

**brand name** *n* Markenname *der*.

**brand-new** *adj* nagelneu, brandneu.

**brandy** ['brændɪ] (*pl* **-ies**) *n* Brandy *der*, Weinbrand *der*.

**brash** [bræʃ] *adj pej* [person, manner] laut.

**brass** [brɑːs] *n* - **1.** [metal] Messing *das* - **2.** MUS: **the ~** die Blechbläser *pl*.

**brass band** *n* Blaskapelle *die*.

**brasserie** ['bræsərɪ] *n* Bierstube *die*.

**brassiere** [Br 'bræsɪəʳ, Am brə'zɪr] *n* Büstenhalter *der*.

**brass knuckles** *npl* Am Schlagring *der*.

**brass tacks** *npl inf:* **to get down to ~** zur Sache kommen.

**brat** [bræt] *n inf pej* Balg *das*.

**bravado** [brə'vɑːdəʊ] *n* Wagemut *der*.

**brave** [breɪv] *adj* mutig, tapfer ⟨⟩ *n* [warrior] Krieger *der* ⟨⟩ *vt* [weather] trotzen *(+ D);* [anger, displeasure, punishment] über sich *(A)* ergehen lassen.

**bravely** ['breɪvlɪ] *adv* mutig, tapfer.

**bravery** ['breɪvərɪ] *n* Mut *der*, Tapferkeit *die*.

**bravo** [ˌbrɑː'vəʊ] *excl* bravo!

**brawl** [brɔːl] *n* Handgemenge *das*, Rauferei *die*.

**brawn** [brɔːn] *n (U)* - **1.** [muscle] Muskelkraft *die* - **2.** Br [meat] Schweinskopfsülze *die*.

**brawny** ['brɔːnɪ] (*compar* **-ier;** *superl* **-iest**) *adj* muskulös.

**bray** [breɪ] *vi* [donkey] schreien.

**brazen** ['breɪzn] *adj* unverschämt, frech.

➣ **brazen out** *vt sep:* **to ~ it out** sich *(D)* nichts anmerken lassen.

**brazier** ['breɪzjəʳ] *n* Kohlenbecken *das*.

**Brazil** [brə'zɪl] *n* Brasilien *nt*.

**Brazilian** [brə'zɪljən] *adj* brasilianisch ⟨⟩ *n* Brasilianer *der*, -in *die*.

**brazil nut** *n* Paranuss *die*.

**breach** [briːtʃ] *n* - **1.** [of law, agreement] Bruch *der;* **to be in ~ of sthg** gegen etw verstoßen; **~ of contract** Vertragsbruch *der* - **2.** [opening, gap] Bresche *die;* **to step into the ~** *fig* in die Bresche springen - **3.** *fig* [in friendship, marriage] Bruch *der* ⟨⟩ *vt* - **1.** [disobey] verletzen - **2.** [make hole in] durchbrechen.

**breach of the peace** *n* öffentliche Ruhestörung *die*.

**bread** [bred] *n (U)* - **1.** [food] Brot *das;* **~ and but-**

ter [food] Butterbrot *das; fig* [main income] Lebensunterhalt *der* - **2.** *inf* [money] Kies *der*.

**bread bin** *Br*, **bread box** *Am n* Brotkasten *der*.

**breadboard** ['bredbɔːd] *n* Brettchen *das*.

**bread box** *n Am* = **bread bin**.

**breadcrumbs** ['bredkrʌmz] *npl* Brotkrümel *pl;* [for coating food] Paniermehl *das*.

**breaded** ['bredɪd] *adj* paniert.

**breadline** ['bredlaɪn] *n:* **to be on the ~** am Existenzminimum leben.

**breadth** [bretθ] *n* - **1.** [in measurements] Breite *die* - **2.** *fig* [scope] Spektrum *das*.

**breadwinner** ['bred,wɪnəʳ] *n* Ernährer *der*, -in *die*.

**break** [breɪk] (*pt* **broke;** *pp* **broken**) *n* - **1.** [gap, interruption] Unterbrechung *die; ~* **in sthg** Unterbrechung in etw *(D)* - **2.** [fracture, rupture, change] Bruch *der; ~* **with sthg** Bruch *der* mit etw - **3.** [pause, rest] Unterbrechung *die*, Pause *die;* sch Pause *die;* **coffee ~** Kaffeepause *die;* **weekend ~** Urlaubswochenende *das;* **to take** *or* **have a ~** eine (kurze) Pause machen; **to have a ~ from sthg** mit etw pausieren; **without a ~** ohne Unterbrechung - **4.** *inf* [luck, chance] Chance *die* - **5.** *literary* [of day]: **at ~ of day** bei Tagesanbruch ⬦ *vt* - **1.** [gen] brechen; [smash] zerbrechen; [windows] einlschlagen; **the river broke its banks** der Fluss stieg über die Ufer; **to ~ sb's hold** js Fesseln sprengen - **2.** [cause to stop working] kaputtlmachen - **3.** [interrupt - journey, silence] unterbrechen; **to ~ sb's fall** js Fall bremsen - **4.** [tell]: **to ~ the news of sthg to sb** jm etw mitlteilen *or* beilbringen - **5.** tennis: **to ~ sb's serve** jm den Aufschlag *or* das Aufschlagspiel ablnehmen ⬦ *vi* - **1.** [gen] brechen, zerbrechen - **2.** [stop working] kaputtlgehen - **3.** [pause] eine Pause machen, unterbrechen - **4.** [day] anlbrechen - **5.** [weather] umlschlagen - **6.** [wave] sich brechen - **7.** [escape]: **to ~ loose** *or* **free** loslbrechen, sich loslreißen - **8.** [voice] brechen - **9.** [news] bekannt werden - **10.** *phr:* **to ~ even** seine Kosten decken.

➤ **break away** *vi* - **1.** [escape] weglaufen, sich loslreißen - **2.** [end relationship]: **to ~ away (from sb)** sich (von jm) loslreißen.

➤ **break down** *vt sep* - **1.** [destroy] einlschlagen, einlbrechen - **2.** [analyse] auflschlüsseln - **3.** [cause to decompose] zersetzen ⬦ *vi* - **1.** [gen] zusammenlbrechen; **the car has broken down** das Auto hat eine Panne - **2.** [decompose] sich zersetzen.

➤ **break in** *vi* - **1.** [enter by force] einlbrechen - **2.** [interrupt]: **to ~ in (on sb/sthg)** (jn/etw) unterbrechen ⬦ *vt sep* - **1.** [horse] zulreiten - **2.** [person] einlarbeiten - **3.** [shoes] einllaufen.

➤ **break into** *vt fus* - **1.** [enter by force] einl-

brechen in *(+ A)* - **2.** [begin suddenly] auslbrechen in *(+ A)* - **3.** [become involved in] Fuß fassen in *(+ D)*.

➤ **break off** *vt sep* & *vi* ablbrechen.

➤ **break out** *vi* - **1.** [begin suddenly] auslbrechen - **2.** [become covered]: **to ~ out in spots/a rash** Pickel/Ausschlag bekommen; **he broke out in a sweat** ihm brach der Schweiß aus - **3.** [escape]: **to ~ out (of)** auslbrechen (aus).

➤ **break through** *vt fus* & *vi* durchbrechen.

➤ **break up** *vt sep* - **1.** [object] zerbrechen; [ice, soil] auflbrechen - **2.** [bring to an end]: **he broke up their relationship** er beendete ihre Beziehung; **the police broke up the party** die Polizei sprengte die Party; **she broke up the fight** sie trennte die Kämpfenden ⬦ *vi* - **1.** [object] auseinander brechen, zerbrechen - **2.** [relationship] in die Brüche gehen; [fight, party] enden; **to ~ up with sb** sich von jm trennen - **3.** [crowd] auseinander laufen - **4.** [school] enden; [pupils, teachers] in die Ferien gehen.

➤ **break with** *vt fus* brechen mit.

**breakable** ['breɪkəbl] *adj* zerbrechlich.

**breakage** ['breɪkɪdʒ] *n* Bruchschaden *der*.

**breakaway** ['breɪkəweɪ] *adj* Splitter-.

**breakdown** ['breɪkdaʊn] *n* - **1.** [of system] Zusammenbruch *der;* [of car] Panne *die;* [of machine] Störung *die;* [in talks] Scheitern *das* - **2.** [analysis] Aufschlüsselung *die*.

**breaker** ['breɪkəʳ] *n* [wave] Brecher *der*.

**breakeven** [,breɪk'iːvn] *n (U)* Gewinnschwelle *die*.

**breakfast** ['brekfəst] *n* Frühstück *das;* **to have ~** frühstücken ⬦ *vi:* **to ~ (on sthg)** frühstücken (etw).

**breakfast cereal** *n* Frühstücksflocken *pl*.

**breakfast television** *n Br* Frühstücksfernsehen *das*.

**break-in** *n* Einbruch *der*.

**breaking** ['breɪkɪŋ] *n (U):* **~ and entering** Einbruch *der*.

**breaking point** *n* Grenze *die* der Belastbarkeit.

**breakneck** ['breɪknek] *adj:* **at ~ speed** in halsbrecherischem Tempo.

**breakthrough** ['breɪkθruː] *n* Durchbruch *der*.

**breakup** ['breɪkʌp] *n* - **1.** [of system, group] Zusammenbruch *der* - **2.** [of relationship] Scheitern *das*.

**breakup value** *n* comm Liquidationswert *der*.

**bream** [briːm] (*pl inv or* -s) *n* Brasse *die*.

**breast** [brest] *n* - **1.** Brust *die* - **2.** *phr:* **to make a clean ~ of it** alles gestehen.

**breast-feed** *vt* & *vi* stillen.

**breast pocket** *n* Brusttasche *die*.

B

**breaststroke** ['brestsrəʊk] n Brustschwimmen das.

**breath** [breθ] n Atem der; **bad ~** Mundgeruch der; **to go out for a ~ of (fresh) air** frische Luft schnappen gehen; **he took a deep ~** er holte tief Atem; **out of ~** außer Atem; **to get one's ~ back** Luft holen; **to hold one's ~** lit & fig den Atem anlhalten; **to save one's ~** sich seine Worte sparen; **to say sthg under one's ~** etw vor sich (A) hin murmeln; **to take sb's ~ away** jm den Atem verschlagen; **to waste one's ~** in den Wind reden, seine Worte verschwenden.

**breathalyse** Br, **-yze** Am ['breθəlaɪz] vt (ins Röhrchen) blasen lassen.

**Breathalyser**® Br, **-yzer**® Am ['breθəlaɪzəʳ] n Promillemesser der.

**breathe** [briːð] vi atmen; **to ~ more easily** fig auflatmen ◇ vt - **1.** [inhale] einlatmen - **2.** [whisper] flüstern.
◆ **breathe in** vt sep & vi einlatmen.
◆ **breathe out** vi [exhale] auslatmen.

**breather** ['briːðəʳ] n inf Atempause die.

**breathing** ['briːðɪŋ] n Atmen das.

**breathing space** n fig Atempause die.

**breathless** ['breθlɪs] adj atemlos.

**breathtaking** ['breθ.teɪkɪŋ] adj atemberaubend.

**breath test** n Atemkontrolle die, Alkoholtest der.

**breed** [briːd] (pt & pp bred [bred]) n - **1.** [of animal] Rasse die - **2.** fig [sort, style] Art die ◇ vt - **1.** [animals, plants] züchten - **2.** fig [suspicion] säen ◇ vi züchten.

**breeder** ['briːdəʳ] n Züchter der, -in die.

**breeder reactor** n Brutreaktor der.

**breeding** ['briːdɪŋ] n (U) - **1.** [of animals] Aufzucht die; [of plants] Züchtung die - **2.** [manners] Erziehung die.

**breeding-ground** n fig Nährboden der.

**breeze** [briːz] n Brise die ◇ vi: **to ~ in** hereinlschneien; **to ~ out** verschwinden.

**breezeblock** ['briːzblɒk] n Br Schlackebetonstein der.

**breezy** ['briːzɪ] (compar **-ier**; superl **-iest**) adj - **1.** [windy] windig - **2.** [cheerful] leichtherzig, fröhlich.

**brevity** ['brevɪtɪ] n Kürze die.

**brew** [bruː] vt [beer] brauen; [tea, coffee] auflgießen, auflbrühen ◇ vi - **1.** [tea, coffee] ziehen - **2.** fig [trouble, storm] sich zusammenlbrauen.

**brewer** ['bruːəʳ] n Brauer der, -in die.

**brewery** ['bruːərɪ] (pl **-ies**) n Brauerei die.

**briar** ['braɪəʳ] n BOT Baumheide die.

**bribe** [braɪb] n Bestechung die ◇ vt: **to ~ sb (to do sthg)** jn bestechen(, etw zu tun).

**bribery** ['braɪbərɪ] n (U) Bestechung die.

**bric-a-brac** ['brɪkəbræk] n Nippes der.

**brick** [brɪk] n Ziegelstein der, Backstein der.
◆ **brick up** vt sep zumauern.

**bricklayer** ['brɪk.leɪəʳ] n Maurer der.

**brickwork** ['brɪkwɜːk] n (U) Backsteinmauerwerk das.

**bridal** ['braɪdl] adj Braut-.

**bride** [braɪd] n Braut die.

**bridegroom** ['braɪdgrʊm] n Bräutigam der.

**bridesmaid** ['braɪdzmeɪd] n Brautjungfer die.

**bridge** [brɪdʒ] n - **1.** [gen] Brücke die; **I'll cross that ~ when I come to it** alles zu seiner Zeit - **2.** [card game] Bridge das ◇ vt fig [gap] überbrücken.

**bridging loan** ['brɪdʒɪŋ-] n Br Überbrückungskredit der.

**bridle** ['braɪdl] n Zaum der ◇ vt auflzäumen ◇ vi: **to ~ (at sthg)** sich (gegen etw) sträuben.

**bridle path** n Reitweg der.

**brief** [briːf] adj - **1.** [short] kurz - **2.** [skimpy, concise] knapp; **please be ~** fassen Sie sich kurz; **in ~** kurz (gesagt) ◇ n - **1.** LAW [statement] Unterlagen pl - **2.** Br [instructions] Auftrag der ◇ vt: **to ~ sb (on sthg)** jn (über etw (A)) unterrichten.
◆ **briefs** npl [underwear] Slip der; **a pair of ~s** ein Slip.

**briefcase** ['briːfkeɪs] n Aktentasche die.

**briefing** ['briːfɪŋ] n Einsatzbesprechung die.

**briefly** ['briːflɪ] adv kurz.

**Brig.** abbr of brigadier.

**brigade** [brɪ'geɪd] n - **1.** MIL Brigade die - **2.** [organization] Truppe die.

**brigadier** [.brɪgə'dɪəʳ] n Br Brigadegeneral der.

**bright** [braɪt] adj - **1.** [room, light] hell - **2.** [colour] leuchtend - **3.** [lively, cheerful] strahlend - **4.** [intelligent] klug, gescheit; **a ~ girl** ein aufgewecktes Mädchen - **5.** [future, prospects] glänzend.
◆ **brights** npl Am inf AUT Fernlicht das.
◆ **bright and early** adv in aller Frühe.

**brighten** ['braɪtn] vi sich auflhellen.
◆ **brighten up** vt sep - **1.** [room, house] auflhellen - **2.** [situation, prospects] auflheitern ◇ vi - **1.** [become more cheerful] fröhlicher werden; [face] sich auflhellen - **2.** [weather] sich auflhellen, sich auflheitern.

**brightly** ['braɪtlɪ] adv - **1.** [shine] hell - **2.** [coloured] leuchtend - **3.** [cheerfully] heiter.

**brightness** ['braɪtnɪs] n (U) - **1.** [of light] Helligkeit die, Helle die - **2.** [of colour] Leuchtkraft die.

**brilliance** ['brɪljəns] n - **1.** [cleverness] Großartigkeit die - **2.** [of colour, light] Strahlen das.

**brilliant** ['brɪljənt] adj - **1.** [gen] glänzend, brilliant - **2.** [colour, light] strahlend - **3.** inf [wonderful, enjoyable] toll; iron oh ~! na toll!

**brilliantly** ['brɪljəntlɪ] adv - **1.** [cleverly] großartig, brilliant - **2.** [coloured] leuchtend - **3.** [shine] glänzend.

**Brillo pad**® ['brɪləʊ-] n Scheuerschwämmchen aus Stahlwolle, mit Reinigungsmittel getränkt.

**brim** [brɪm] (pt & pp -med; cont -ming) n - **1.** [edge] Rand der - **2.** [of hat] Krempe die <> vi - **1.** [with liquid]: to ~ with sthg randvoll mit etw sein - **2.** [with feeling]: to ~ with ideas vor Ideen überIsprudeln; to ~ with self-confidence vor Selbstbewußtsein strotzen.
➡ **brim over** vi - **1.** [with liquid] überIlaufen - **2.** [with feeling]: to ~ over with sthg vor etw (D) überIlaufen, mit etw übervoll sein.

**brine** [braɪn] n (U) Sole die, Lake die.

**bring** [brɪŋ] (pt & pp **brought**) vt - **1.** [take along] mitbringen; [move] bringen; to ~ sb good luck jm Glück bringen - **2.** [cause] führen zu; to ~ sthg to an end etw zu Ende bringen; to ~ sthg into being etw ins Leben rufen - **3.** LAW: to ~ charges against sb jn anIklagen; to ~ sb to trial in vor Gericht stellen - **4.** phr: I couldn't ~ myself to do it ich konnte es nicht über mich bringen.
➡ **bring about** vt sep verursachen.
➡ **bring along** vt sep mitbringen.
➡ **bring around** vt sep [make conscious] zu Bewusstsein bringen.
➡ **bring back** vt sep - **1.** [return] zurückIbringen - **2.** [shopping, gift] mitIbringen - **3.** [reinstate - custom] wieder einIführen; [ - government] wieder an die Macht bringen - **4.** [cause to remember]: to ~ back memories Erinnerungen wachrufen.
➡ **bring down** vt sep - **1.** [shoot down - plane] abIschießen - **2.** [government, tyrant] stürzen - **3.** [prices] senken - **4.** THEATRE: to ~ the house down stürmischen Beifall ernten.
➡ **bring forward** vt sep - **1.** [meeting, election] vorIverlegen - **2.** [in bookkeeping] übertragen.
➡ **bring in** vt sep - **1.** [introduce] einIführen - **2.** [earn] einIbringen - **3.** [involve] einIschalten - **4.** [verdict] fällen.
➡ **bring off** vt sep [plan] in die Tat umIsetzen; [deal] zustande bringen; you'll never ~ it off das schaffst du nie.
➡ **bring on** vt sep [cause] hervorIrufen; you brought it on yourself das hast du dir selber zuzuschreiben.
➡ **bring out** vt sep - **1.** [new product, book] herausIbringen - **2.** [reveal - flavour] betonen;

to ~ sthg out in sb [characteristic] etw in jm wachIrufen.
➡ **bring round, bring to** vt sep = bring around.
➡ **bring up** vt sep - **1.** [child] erziehen; I was brought up in Liverpool ich bin in Liverpool aufgewachsen - **2.** [subject] anIsprechen; did you have to ~ that up again? komm mir doch nicht schon wieder damit! - **3.** [food] erbrechen.

**brink** [brɪŋk] n: on the ~ of am Rand(e) (+ G).

**brisk** [brɪsk] adj - **1.** [walk, swim] flott - **2.** [business, trading] rege - **3.** [manner, tone] forsch - **4.** [wind, weather] frisch.

**brisket** ['brɪskɪt] n (U) Bruststück das.

**briskly** ['brɪsklɪ] adv - **1.** [walk] zügig - **2.** [speak, act] schnell.

**bristle** ['brɪsl] n Borste die <> vi - **1.** [hair] sich sträuben - **2.** [person]: to ~ (at sthg) zornig reagieren (auf etw (A)).
➡ **bristle with** vt fus strotzen vor (+ D), voll sein von.

**bristly** ['brɪslɪ] (compar -ier; superl -iest) adj stoppelig.

**Brit** [brɪt] n inf (abbr of Briton) Brite der, -tin die.

**Britain** ['brɪtn] n Großbritannien nt.

**British** ['brɪtɪʃ] adj britisch <> npl: the ~ die Briten pl.

**British Columbia** [- kə'lʌmbɪə] n Britisch-Kolumbien nt.

**British Council** n: the ~ das British Council, Organisation für die Förderung und Verbreitung englischer Sprache und Kultur im Ausland.

**BRITISH COUNCIL**

Eine Art britisches Gegenstück zum deutschen Goethe-Institut, dient das „British Council" der Förderung der britischen Kultur und englischen Sprache und der Pflege der kulturellen Beziehungen zum Ausland.

**Britisher** ['brɪtɪʃəʳ] n Am Brite der, -tin die.

**British Isles** npl: the ~ die Britischen Inseln.

**British Rail** n British Rail die, ehemals staatliche britische Eisenbahn-gesellschaft.

**British Summer Time** n britische Sommerzeit die.

**British Telecom** [-'telɪkɒm] n British Telecom die.

**Briton** ['brɪtn] n Brite der, -tin die.

**brittle** ['brɪtl] adj [china] zerbrechlich; [material] spröde; [bones] schwach.

**Bro** [brəʊ] = Br.

**broach** [brəʊtʃ] vt [subject] anIschneiden.

**broad** [brɔːd] adj - **1.** [wide] breit - **2.** [wide-ranging, extensive] weit - **3.** [introduction, description] umfassend **- 4.** [hint] deutlich **- 5.** [accent] stark ⇔ *n Am inf* [woman] Braut *die.*

➤ **in broad daylight** *adv* am helllichten Tag.

**B road** *n Br* ≃ Landstraße *die.*

**broad bean** *n* dicke Bohne, Saubohne *die.*

**broadcast** ['brɔːdkɑːst] (*pt* & *pp* **broadcast**) RADIO & TV *n* Sendung *die,* Übertragung *die* ⇔ *vt* senden, übertragen.

**broadcaster** ['brɔːdkɑːstəʳ] RADIO & TV *n* jemand, der kulturell anspruchsvolle Sendungen präsentiert.

**broadcasting** ['brɔːdkɑːstɪŋ] *n (U)* Sendung *die,* Übertragung *die.*

**broaden** ['brɔːdn] *vt* **- 1.** [make wider] verbreitern, erweitern **- 2.** [make more wide-ranging] vergrößern; **to ~ one's mind** seinen Horizont erweitern ⇔ *vi* [become wider] sich verbreitern.

➤ **broaden out** *vi* sich weiten.

**broadly** ['brɔːdlɪ] *adv* **- 1.** [generally] allgemein; **~ speaking** allgemein gesprochen **- 2.** [smile] breit.

**broadminded** [‚brɔːd'maɪndɪd] *adj* tolerant.

**Broads** [brɔːdz] *npl* ➣ **Norfolk Broads.**

**broadsheet** ['brɔːdʃiːt] *n* großformatige Tageszeitung.

**brocade** [brə'keɪd] *n (U)* Brokat *der.*

**broccoli** ['brɒkəlɪ] *n* Broccoli *der.*

**brochure** ['brəʊʃəʳ] *n* Prospekt *der.*

**brogues** [brəʊgz] *npl* feste Halbschuhe *pl.*

**broil** [brɔɪl] *vt Am* grillen.

**broiler** ['brɔɪləʳ] *n* **- 1.** [young chicken] Brathähnchen *das* **- 2.** *Am* [pan] Rost *der.*

**broke** [brəʊk] *pt* ➣ **break** ⇔ *adj inf* [penniless] pleite; **to go ~** pleite gehen; **to go for ~** alles aufs Spiel setzen.

**broken** ['brəʊkn] *pp* ➣ **break** ⇔ *adj* **- 1.** [damaged, in pieces] zerbrochen **- 2.** [fractured] gebrochen **- 3.** [not working] kaputt **- 4.** [interrupted] unterbrochen **- 5.** [promise, contract] gebrochen **- 6.** [marriage, home] kaputt, zerrüttet **- 7.** [hesitant, inaccurate] gebrochen.

**broken-down** *adj* **- 1.** [car, machine] kaputt **- 2.** [building] verfallen, heruntergekommen.

**broker** ['brəʊkəʳ] *n* [of shares, commodities] Broker *der,* -in *die;* (insurance) ~ Versicherungsmakler *der,* -in *die.*

**brokerage** ['brəʊkərɪdʒ] *n (U)* **- 1.** [business] Maklergeschäft *das* **- 2.** [fee] Maklergebühr *die.*

**brolly** ['brɒlɪ] (*pl* **-ies**) *n Br inf* (Regen)schirm *der.*

**bronchitis** [brɒŋ'kaɪtɪs] *n (U)* Bronchitis *die.*

**bronze** [brɒnz] *n* Bronze *die* ⇔ *comp* [made of

bronze] aus Bronze ⇔ *adj* [bronze-coloured] bronzefarben.

**bronzed** [brɒnzd] *adj* braun, gebräunt.

**bronze medal** *n* Bronze *die,* Bronzmedaille *die.*

**brooch** [brəʊtʃ] *n* Brosche *die.*

**brood** [bruːd] *n* Brut *die* ⇔ *vi:* **to ~ (over** OR **about sthg)** (über etw *(D)*) brüten.

**broody** ['bruːdɪ] (*compar* **-ier;** *superl* **-iest**) *adj* **- 1.** [person] schwermütig **- 2.** [bird] brütig.

**brook** [brʊk] *n* Bach *der* ⇔ *vt fml* dulden.

**broom** [bruːm] *n* **- 1.** [brush] Besen *der* **- 2.** *(U)* [shrub] Ginster *der.*

**broomstick** ['bruːmstɪk] *n* Besenstiel *der.*

**Bros, bros** (*abbr of* **brothers**) Gebr.

**broth** [brɒθ] *n* Brühe *die.*

**brothel** ['brɒθl] *n* Bordell *das.*

**brother** ['brʌðəʳ] *n* Bruder *der* ⇔ *excl Am inf:* (oh) ~! Junge, Junge!

**brotherhood** ['brʌðəhʊd] *n* **- 1.** *(U)* [companionship] Brüderschaft *die* **- 2.** [organization] Gemeinschaft *die;* [religious] Bruderschaft *die.*

**brother-in-law** (*pl* **brothers-in-law**) *n* Schwager *der.*

**brotherly** ['brʌðəlɪ] *adj* brüderlich.

**brought** [brɔːt] *pt* & *pp* ➣ **bring.**

**brow** [braʊ] *n* **- 1.** [forehead] Stirn *die* **- 2.** [eyebrow] Braue *die;* **to knit one's ~s** die Stirn runzeln **- 3.** [of hill] Bergkuppe *die.*

**browbeat** ['braʊbiːt] (*pt* **browbeat;** *pp* **-en**) *vt* unter Druck setzen.

**brown** [braʊn] *adj* **- 1.** [colour] braun; **~ bread** Graubrot *das,* Mischbrot *das* **- 2.** [tanned] braun, gebräunt ⇔ *n* [colour] Braun *das;* **in ~** in Braun ⇔ *vt* [food] bräunen, anlbraten.

**Brownie (Guide)** ['braʊnɪ-] *n* Pfadfinderin *die.*

**Brownie point** *n fig* Pluspunkt *der.*

**brown paper** *n (U)* Packpapier *das.*

**brown rice** *n* brauner Reis.

**brown sugar** *n* brauner Zucker.

**browse** [braʊz] *vt* COMPUT: **to ~ the Web** im Web surfen ⇔ *vi* **- 1.** [in shop] sich umlsehen **- 2.** [read]: **to ~ through sthg** in etw *(D)* blättern **- 3.** [graze] weiden.

**browser** ['braʊzəʳ] *n* COMPUT Browser *der.*

**bruise** [bruːz] *n* Bluterguss *der,* blauer Fleck ⇔ *vt* **- 1.** [part of body] sich prellen; [fruit] beschädigen; **she ~d her arm** sie holte sich einen blauen Fleck am Arm **- 2.** *fig* [pride, feelings] verletzen ⇔ *vi* [person] blaue Flecken bekommen; [fruit] Druckstellen bekommen.

**bruised** [bruːzd] *adj* **- 1.** [skin, part of body] mit

blauen Flecken; [fruit] mit Druckstellen
- **2.** *fig* [pride, feelings] verletzt.

**Brum** [brʌm] *n* *Br inf* Birmingham.

**Brummie, Brummy** ['brʌmɪ] *Br inf* *adj* Birminghamer, aus Birmingham ⬦ *n* Bürger von Birmingham.

**brunch** [brʌntʃ] *n* Brunch *der.*

**brunette** [bru:'net] *n* Brünette *die*

**brunt** [brʌnt] *n:* **to bear** OR **take the ~ of sthg** die Hauptlast von etw tragen OR auf sich (A) nehmen.

**brush** [brʌʃ] *n* - **1.** [with bristles] Bürste *die;* [for painting] Pinsel *der* - **2.** [encounter] (flüchtige) Begegnung; **to have a ~ with the law** mit dem Gesetz in Konflikt kommen ⬦ *vt* - **1.** [clean with brush - hair] bürsten; [ - teeth] putzen - **2.** [move with hand] wischen - **3.** [touch lightly] berühren, streifen.
- ➤ **brush aside** *vt sep* [disregard] vom Tisch wischen.
- ➤ **brush off** *vt sep* [dismiss] zurücklweisen; **to ~ sb off** jn ablblitzen lassen.
- ➤ **brush up** *vt sep* *fig* [revise] auflfrischen ⬦ *vi:* **to ~ up (on sthg)** (etw) auflfrischen.

**brushed** [brʌʃt] *adj* [fabric] aufgeraut.

**brush-off** *n inf:* **to give sb the ~** jm eine Abfuhr erteilen.

**brush-up** *n inf:* **to have a wash and ~** sich frisch machen.

**brushwood** ['brʌʃwʊd] *n (U)* Unterholz *das,* Gestrüpp *das.*

**brushwork** ['brʌʃwɜ:k] *n (U)* Pinselführung *die.*

**brusque** [bru:sk] *adj* brüsk.

**Brussels** ['brʌslz] *n* Brüssel *nt.*

**brussels sprouts** *n pl* Rosenkohl *der.*

**brutal** ['bru:tl] *adj* brutal.

**brutality** [bru:'tælətɪ] *(pl* -**ies**) *n* Brutalität *die.*

**brutalize, -ise** ['bru:təlaɪz] *vt* - **1.** [make brutal] verrohen lassen - **2.** [treat brutally] brutal behandeln.

**brute** [bru:t] *adj:* **~ force** rohe Gewalt ⬦ *n* Tier *das,* Vieh *das.*

**bs** *abbr of* bill of sale.

**BS** (*abbr of* **Bachelor of Science**) *n Am* an US-Universitäten verliehener naturwissenschaftlicher Grad oder dessen Inhaber.

**BSc** *abbr of* Bachelor of Science.

**BSE** (*abbr of* **bovine spongiform encephalopathy**) *n* BSE *das.*

**BSI** (*abbr of* **British Standards Institution**) *n* ≈ DIN, *britisches Normungsinstitut.*

**B-side** *n* Rückseite *die.*

**BST** *abbr of* British Summer Time.

**BT** *abbr of* British Telecom.

**B**

**BTA** (*abbr of* **British Tourist Authority**) *n* britisches Amt für Tourismus.

**btu** (*abbr of* **British thermal unit**) *n* Btu.

**bubble** ['bʌbl] *n* (Luft)bläschen *das,* (Luft)blase *die* ⬦ *vi* - **1.** [produce bubbles] Bläschen bilden - **2.** [make a bubbling sound] blubbern - **3.** *fig* [person]: **to ~ with sthg** vor etw (D) sprühen.

**bubble bath** *n (U)* Schaumbad *das.*

**bubble gum** *n (U)* Kaugummi *das* OR *der.*

**bubblejet printer** ['bʌbldʒet-] *n* Tintenstrahldrucker *der.*

**bubbly** ['bʌblɪ] (*compar* -**ier;** *superl* -**iest**) *adj* - **1.** [water, wine] spritzig - **2.** [person, personality] sprühend ⬦ *n inf* Schampus *der.*

**Bucharest** [ˌbju:kə'rest] *n* Bukarest *nt.*

**buck** [bʌk] (*pl sense 1 inv* OR -**s**) *n* - **1.** [male animal - rabbit, hare] Rammler *der;* [ - deer] Bock *der* - **2.** *esp Am inf* [dollar] Dollar *der;* **to make a fast ~** eine schnelle Mark machen - **3.** *inf* [responsibility]: **the ~ stops here** ich bin letztlich verantwortlich; **to pass the ~** die Verantwortung weiterlreichen OR ablschieben ⬦ *vt* - **1.** [subj: horse] ablwerfen - **2.** *inf* [trend] sich sträuben gegen; **to ~ the system** sich dem System widersetzen ⬦ *vi* [horse] bocken.
- ➤ **buck up** *inf* ⬦ *vt sep* - **1.** [improve]: **~ your ideas up** gib dir mehr Mühe - **2.** [cheer up] auflmuntern ⬦ *vi* - **1.** [hurry up] sich beeilen - **2.** [cheer up] auflleben.

**bucket** ['bʌkɪt] *n* Eimer *der.*
- ➤ **buckets** *npl inf fig:* **~s of money** ein Haufen Geld.

**Buckingham Palace** ['bʌkɪŋəm-] *n* Buckingham Palace *der.*

**buckle** ['bʌkl] *n* Schnalle *die,* Spange *die* ⬦ *vt* - **1.** [fasten] zulschnallen - **2.** [bend] einldellen, verbeulen ⬦ *vi* [wheel] sich verbiegen; [knees, legs] nachlgeben.
- ➤ **buckle down** *vi* [work harder] sich dahinter klemmen; **to ~ down to sthg** sich hinter etw (A) klemmen; **to ~ down to work** sich an die Arbeit machen.

**Bucks** [bʌks] *abk für* Buckinghamshire, *in Postanschrift verwendet.*

**buckshot** ['bʌkʃɒt] *n* Schrot *der* OR *das.*

**buckskin** ['bʌkskɪn] *n* Wildleder *das.*

**buckteeth** [ˌbʌk'ti:θ] *npl* vorstehende Zähne *pl.*

**buckwheat** ['bʌkwi:t] *n* Buchweizen *der.*

**bud** [bʌd] (*pt* & *pp* -**ded;** *cont* -**ding**) *n* Knospe *die;* **to nip sthg in the ~** etw im Keim ersticken ⬦ *vi* Knospen treiben, auslschlagen.

**Budapest** [ˌbju:də'pest] *n* Budapest *nt.*

**Buddha** ['bʊdə] *n* Buddha *der.*

**Buddhism** ['bʊdɪzm] *n* Buddhismus *der.*

**Buddhist** [ˈbʊdɪst] *adj* buddhistisch ◇ *n* Buddhist *der*, -in *die*.

**budding** [ˈbʌdɪŋ] *adj* [aspiring] angehend.

**buddy** [ˈbʌdɪ] (*pl* -ies) *n esp Am inf* [friend] Kumpel *der*.

**budge** [bʌdʒ] *vt* - **1.** [move] bewegen - **2.** [change mind of] beeinflussen ◇ *vi* - **1.** [move] sich rühren - **2.** [change mind] nachlgeben.

**budgerigar** [ˈbʌdʒərɪɡɑːˌ] *n* Wellensittich *der*.

**budget** [ˈbʌdʒɪt] *adj* [cheap - travel, holiday] kostengünstig; [- prices] niedrig ◇ *n* Budget *das;* **the Budget** *Br* POL der Haushaltsplan ◇ *vt* planen ◇ *vi* wirtschaften.

◆ **budget for** *vt fus* einlplanen.

**budgetary** [ˈbʌdʒɪtrɪ] *adj* Budget-.

**budgie** [ˈbʌdʒɪ] *n inf* Wellensittich *der*.

**Buenos Aires** [ˌbwenəsˈaɪrɪz] *n* Buenos Aires *nt*.

**buff** [bʌf] *adj* [brown] braun ◇ *n inf* [expert] Kenner *der*, -in *die*.

**buffalo** [ˈbʌfələʊ] (*pl inv* OR -es OR -s) *n* Büffel *der*, Buffalo *der*.

**buffer** [ˈbʌfəˌ] *n* - **1.** [gen] Puffer *der* - **2.** [for trains] Prellbock *der*.

**buffer state** *n* Pufferstaat *der*.

**buffet¹** [ˈbʊfeɪ] *n* - **1.** [meal] Buffet *das* - **2.** [cafeteria] Stehimbiss *der*.

**buffet²** [ˈbʌfɪt] *vt* [physically] rütteln.

**buffet car** [ˈbʊfeɪ-] *n* Speisewagen *der*.

**buffoon** [bəˈfuːn] *n* Clown *der*.

**bug** [bʌɡ] (*pt & pp* -ged; *cont* -ging) *n* - **1.** *esp Am* [small insect] Insekt *das;* [beetle] Käfer *der* - **2.** *inf* [germ] Bazillus *der* - **3.** *inf* [listening device] Wanze *die* - **4.** COMPUT Programmfehler *der* - **5.** [enthusiasm]: **the travel ~** die Reiselust ◇ *vt inf* - **1.** [room, phone] verwanzen - **2.** [annoy] nerven.

**bugbear** [ˈbʌɡbeəˌ] *n* Schreckgespenst *das*.

**bugger** [ˈbʌɡəˌ] *Br vinf n* - **1.** [unpleasant person] Scheißkerl *der*; **he's a lazy ~!** er ist ein fauler Sack!; **the poor ~!** der arme Kerl! - **2.** [difficult, annoying task]: **a ~ of a job** eine Scheißarbeit ◇ *excl* Scheiße! ◇ *vt:* **~ it!** Scheiße!

◆ **bugger off** *vi:* **~ off!** hau ab!

**buggy** [ˈbʌɡɪ] (*pl* -ies) *n* Kinderwagen *der*.

**bugle** [ˈbjuːɡl] *n* Signalhorn *das*.

**build** [bɪld] (*pt & pp* built) *vt* - **1.** [construct] bauen - **2.** *fig* [form, create] auf lbauen ◇ *n (U)* Statur *die*, Körperbau *der*.

◆ **build in** *vt sep* - **1.** CONSTR ein lbauen - **2.** [include] ein lschließen.

◆ **build on** *vt fus* [further] auf lbauen) ◇ *vt sep* [base on] **to ~ sthg on sthg** etw auf etw (D) auf lbauen).

**build up** *vt sep* [strengthen] auf lbauen ◇ *vi* [increase] zu lnehmen.

◆ **build upon** *vt fus & vt sep* = **build on.**

**builder** [ˈbɪldəˌ] *n* Bauarbeiter *der*, -in *die*.

**building** [ˈbɪldɪŋ] *n* - **1.** [structure] Gebäude *das*, Bau *der* - **2.** *(U)* [profession] Bau *der*, Bauwesen *das*.

**building and loan association** *n Am* Bausparkasse *die*.

**building block** *n* - **1.** [toy] Bauklotz *der*, Bauklötzchen *das* - **2.** *fig* [element] Baustein *der*.

**building contractor** *n* Bauunternehmer *der*, -in *die*.

**building site** *n* Baustelle *die*.

**building society** *n Br* Bausparkasse *die*.

**BUILDING SOCIETY**

Die den deutschen Bausparkassen vergleichbaren „Building Societies" entstanden als Genossenschaften, die ihren Mitgliedern Bauhypotheken vermittelten. Sie sind heute einer der Grundpfeiler der privaten Vermögensbildung und finanziellen Vorsorge. Ende der 1990er Jahre sind mehrere von ihnen von „mutual" (d. h. im Besitz der Sparer befindlichen) Building Societies zu konventionellen Girobanken umstrukturiert worden.

**buildup** [ˈbɪldʌp] *n* [increase] Steigerung *die*, Zunahme *die*.

**built** [bɪlt] *pt & pp* ▷ **build** ◇ *adj* [person] gebaut; **~ for sthg** für etw gemacht.

**built-in** *adj* - **1.** CONSTR eingebaut - **2.** [inherent] automatisch.

**built-up** *adj:* **~ area** bebautes Gebiet.

**bulb** [bʌlb] *n* - **1.** [for lamp] (Glüh)birne *die* - **2.** [of plant] Zwiebel *die* - **3.** [of thermometer, vessel] Kolben *der*.

**bulbous** [ˈbʌlbəs] *adj* [fruit] bauchig; **~ nose** Knollennase.

**Bulgaria** [bʌlˈɡeərɪə] *n* Bulgarien *nt*.

**Bulgarian** [bʌlˈɡeərɪən] *adj* bulgarisch ◇ *n* - **1.** [person] Bulgare *der*, -rin *die* - **2.** [language] Bulgarisch(e) *das*.

**bulge** [bʌldʒ] *n* - **1.** [lump] Beule *die* - **2.** [sudden increase] Anschwellen *das* ◇ *vi:* **to ~ (with sthg)** (mit etw) voll gestopft sein.

**bulging** [ˈbʌldʒɪŋ] *adj* [muscles] sich wölbend; [pocket, bag] voll gestopft.

**bulimia (nervosa)** [bʊˈlɪmɪə-] *n* Bulimie *die*.

**bulk** [bʌlk] *n* - **1.** [mass] Ausmaß *das* - **2.** [of person] Masse *die* - **3.** COMM: **in ~** en gros - **4.** [majority]: **the ~ of** der Großteil (+ G) ◇ *adj* en gros, Groß-.

**bulk buying** [-ˈbaɪɪŋ] *n (U)* Einkauf en gros *der*, Großeinkauf *der*.

**bulky** ['bʌlkɪ] (compar **-ier;** superl **-iest**) adj sperrig, unhandlich; [garment] unhandlich.

**bull** [bʊl] n **- 1.** [male cow] Stier der, Bulle der **- 2.** [male elephant, seal] Bulle der **- 3.** ST EX Hausse-Spekulant der, -in die **- 4.** (U) vinf esp Am [nonsense] Geschwafel das.

**bulldog** ['bʊldɒg] n Bulldogge die.

**bulldog clip** n Klemme die.

**bulldoze** ['bʊldəʊz] vt **- 1.** [with bulldozer] planieren **- 2.** fig [force]: **to ~ one's way** seinen Weg erzwingen; **to ~ sb into sthg** jn zu etw zwingen; **to ~ sb into doing sthg** jn zwingen, etw zu tun.

**bulldozer** ['bʊldəʊzər] n Bulldozer der, Planierraupe die.

**bullet** ['bʊlɪt] n [for gun] Kugel die, Patrone die.

**bulletin** ['bʊlətɪn] n **- 1.** [brief report] Bericht der **- 2.** [regular publication] Bulletin das.

**bulletin board** n esp Am schwarzes Brett.

**bullet-proof** adj kugelsicher.

**bullfight** ['bʊlfaɪt] n Stierkampf der.

**bullfighter** ['bʊl͵faɪtər] n Torero der, Stierkämpfer der.

**bullfighting** ['bʊl͵faɪtɪŋ] n (U) Stierkampf der.

**bullion** ['bʊljən] n (U) Barren der.

**bullish** ['bʊlɪʃ] adj ST EX zuversichtlich.

**bull market** n Haussemarkt der.

**bullock** ['bʊlək] n Ochse der.

**bullring** ['bʊlrɪŋ] n Stierkampfarena die.

**bullrush** ['bʊlrʌʃ] n = **bulrush.**

**bull's-eye** n Schwarze das, Zentrum das.

**bullshit** ['bʊlʃɪt] (pt & pp **-ted;** cont **-ting**) vulg n Unfug der, Bockmist der ◇ vi Scheiß erzählen OR reden.

**bull terrier** n Bullterrier der.

**bully** ['bʊlɪ] (pl **-ies;** pt & pp **-ied**) n Tyrann der ◇ vt drangsalieren, tyrannisieren; **to ~ sb into doing sthg** jn so drangsalieren, dass er/sie etw tut.

**bullying** ['bʊlɪɪŋ] n Drangsalieren das, Tyrannisieren das.

**bulrush** ['bʊlrʌʃ] n Rohrkolben der.

**bum** [bʌm] (pt & pp **-med;** cont **-ming**) n **- 1.** esp Br inf [bottom] Hintern der **- 2.** Am inf pej [tramp] Gammler der, -in die **- 3.** Am inf pej [idler] Faulpelz der.
➡ **bum around** esp Am vi inf **- 1.** [waste time] gammeln **- 2.** [travel aimlessly] herumlziehen.

**bum bag** n inf Gürteltasche die.

**bumblebee** ['bʌmblbiː] n Hummel die.

**bumbling** ['bʌmblɪŋ] adj inf trottelig.

**bumf** [bʌmf] n (U) Br inf Reklamewisch der.

**bump** [bʌmp] n **- 1.** [lump] Beule die; [in road] Unebenheit die, Hubbel der **- 2.** [knock, blow] Delle die **- 3.** [noise] Bums der ◇ vt [knock, damage] anlschlagen ◇ vi **- 1.** [move unevenly] holpern **- 2.** [knock, hit]: **to ~ into sthg** gegen etw stoßen.
➡ **bump into** vt fus [meet by chance] treffen.
➡ **bump off** vt sep inf ablmurksen, kaltlmachen.
➡ **bump up** vt sep inf erhöhen.

**bumper** ['bʌmpər] adj Riesen-; **~ harvest** Rekordernte die ◇ n **- 1.** [on car] Stoßstange die **- 2.** Am RAIL Rammbohle die.

**bumper-to-bumper** adj dicht an dicht.

**bumph** [bʌmf] n = **bumf.**

**bumptious** ['bʌmpʃəs] adj pej wichtigtuerisch.

**bumpy** ['bʌmpɪ] (compar **-ier;** superl **-iest**) adj holp(e)rig.

**bun** [bʌn] n **- 1.** [cake] Rosinenbrötchen das **- 2.** [bread roll] Milchbrötchen das **- 3.** [hairstyle] Knoten der.

**bunch** [bʌntʃ] n [group - of people] Traube die, Haufen der; [ - of flowers] Strauß der; [ - of grapes] Traube die; [ - of parsley, asparagus, keys] Bund der ◇ vt (zusammenl)bündeln ◇ vi sich bauschen.
➡ **bunches** npl [hairstyle] Zöpfe pl.

**bundle** ['bʌndl] n Bündel das ◇ vt stopfen.
➡ **bundle off** vt sep verfrachten.
➡ **bundle up** vt sep [put into bundles] bündeln.

**bundled software** n COMPUT Software-Paket das.

**bung** [bʌŋ] n Stöpsel der, Zapfen der ◇ vt Br inf [put] schmeißen.

**bungalow** ['bʌŋgələʊ] n Bungalow der.

**bunged up** [bʌŋd-] adj verstopft.

**bungee jump** ['bʌndʒɪ-] n Bungeesprung der.

**bungee-jumping** n (U) Bungeespringen das.

**bungle** ['bʌŋgl] vt verpfuschen.

**bunion** ['bʌnjən] n Ballen der.

**bunk** [bʌŋk] n **- 1.** [bed] Koje die; [in dorm] Bett das **- 2.** = **bunk bed - 3.** (U) inf [nonsense] Quatsch der **- 4.** phr: **to do a ~** inf ablhauen.

**bunk bed** n Etagenbett das.

**bunker** ['bʌŋkər] n Bunker der.

**bunkhouse** ['bʌŋkhaʊs, pl -haʊzɪz] n Schlafbaracke die.

**bunny** ['bʌnɪ] (pl **-ies**) n: **~ (rabbit)** Häschen das.

**Bunsen burner** ['bʌnsn-] n Bunsenbrenner der.

**bunting** ['bʌntɪŋ] n (U) Wimpel pl.

**buoy** [Br bɔɪ, Am 'buːɪ] n Boje die.
➡ **buoy up** vt sep [encourage] beleben, stärken.

B

**buoyancy** ['bɔɪənsɪ] *n (U)* - **1.** [ability to float] Auftrieb *der* - **2.** [optimism] Schwung *der*.

**buoyant** ['bɔɪənt] *adj* - **1.** [able to float] schwimmfähig - **2.** [optimistic] beschwingt.

**BUPA** ['bjuːpə] (*abbr of* **British United Provident Association**) *n private Krankenversicherung.*

**burden** ['bɜːdn] *n* Bürde *die*, Last *die;* **to be a ~ on sb** eine Last für jn sein ⟨> *vt:* **to ~ sb with sthg** jn mit etw belasten.

**bureau** ['bjʊərəʊ] (*pl* -**x**) *n* - **1.** *Am* [government department] Amt *das* - **2.** [office, branch] Büro *das* - **3.** *Br* [desk] Sekretär *der* - **4.** *Am* [chest of drawers] Kommode *die*.

**bureaucracy** [bjʊə'rɒkrəsɪ] (*pl* -**ies**) *n* Bürokratie *die*.

**bureaucrat** ['bjʊərəkræt] *n pej* Bürokrat *der*, -in *die*.

**bureaucratic** [ˌbjʊərə'krætɪk] *adj pej* bürokratisch.

**bureau de change** (*pl* **bureaux de change**) *n* Wechselstube *die*.

**bureaux** ['bjʊərəʊz] *pl* ⟼ **bureau**.

**burger** ['bɜːɡəʳ] *n* Hamburger *der*.

**burglar** ['bɜːɡləʳ] *n* Einbrecher *der*, -in *die*.

**burglar alarm** *n* Alarmanlage *die*.

**burglarize** *vt Am* = **burgle**.

**burglary** ['bɜːɡlərɪ] (*pl* -**ies**) *n* Einbruch *der*.

**burgle** ['bɜːɡl], **burglarize** *Am* ['bɜːɡləraɪz] *vt* einlbrechen in (+ *A*).

**burial** ['berɪəl] *n* Begräbnis *das*.

**burial ground** *n* Begräbnisstätte *die*.

**Burkina Faso** [bɜːˌkiːnə'fæsəʊ] *n* Burkino Faso *nt*.

**burly** ['bɜːlɪ] (*compar* -**ier**; *superl* -**iest**) *adj* stämmig, kräftig.

**Burma** ['bɜːmə] *n* Birma *nt*.

**Burmese** [ˌbɜː'miːz] *adj* birmanisch ⟨> *n* - **1.** [person] Birmane *der*, -nin *die* - **2.** [language] Birmanisch(e) *das*.

**burn** [bɜːn] (*pt* & *pp* **burnt** *OR* -**ed**) *vt* - **1.** [gen] verbrennen; [house] ablbrennen ; **to ~ o.s.** sich verbrennen - **2.** [overcook] anbrennen lassen - **3.** [use as fuel] verbrauchen - **4.** [with chemical] verätzen ⟨> *vi* - **1.** [gen] brennen - **2.** [food] anlbrennen - **3.** [face, cheeks] glühen - **4.** [get sunburned] einen Sonnenbrand bekommen - **5.** [feel strong emotion]: **to ~ with anger** vor Wut kochen; **to ~ with shame** vor Scham rot anllaufen ⟨> *n* - **1.** [wound, injury] Brandwunde *die* - **2.** [mark - on carpet, sofa] Brandfleck *der*.

➤ **burn down** *vt sep* niederlbrennen ⟨> *vi* - **1.** [building, town] ablbrennen, niederlbrennen - **2.** [fire, candle] herunterlbrennen.

➤ **burn out** *vt sep* [exhaust]: **to ~ o.s. out** sich total verausgaben ⟨> *vi* [fire] auslgehen.

➤ **burn up** *vt sep* [use up] verbrauchen ⟨> *vi* [be destroyed] verglühen.

**burner** ['bɜːnəʳ] *n* [on cooker] Brenner *der*.

**burning** ['bɜːnɪŋ] *adj* - **1.** [on fire] brennend - **2.** [very hot] sengend - **3.** [face, passion, desire] glühend.

**burnish** ['bɜːnɪʃ] *vt* polieren.

**burnout** *n* - **1.** TECH [of rocket] Burnout *das* - **2.** *fig* [of person] totale Erschöpfung.

**Burns' Night** [bɜːnz-] *n der Abend des 25. Januar, an dem mit Feiern der Geburtstag des schottischen Dichters Robert Burns begangen wird.*

**BURNS' NIGHT**

Am 25. Januar jedes Jahres feiern die Schotten den Geburtstag ihres Nationaldichters Robert Burns (1759–96). Dazu trifft man sich der Tradition gemäß zum Abendessen, den sogenannten „Burns' suppers", bei denen die Anwesenden reihum Gedichte von Burns rezitieren. Es werden typische schottische Spezialitäten wie „Haggis" (mit Innereien gefüllter Schafsmagen) serviert. Dazu trinkt man Whisky.

**burnt** [bɜːnt] *pt* & *pp* ⟼ **burn**.

**burnt-out** *adj lit* & *fig* ausgebrannt.

**burp** [bɜːp] *inf n* Rülpser *der* ⟨> *vi* auf lstoßen.

**burrow** ['bʌrəʊ] *n* Bau *der* ⟨> *vi* - **1.** [dig] graben - **2.** *fig* [search] wühlen.

**bursar** ['bɜːsəʳ] *n* Schatzmeister *der*.

**bursary** ['bɜːsərɪ] (*pl* -**ies**) *n Br* Stipendium *das*.

**burst** [bɜːst] (*pt* & *pp* **burst**) *vi* - **1.** [break open] platzen, auf lplatzen - **2.** [explode] explodieren - **3.** [door, lid]: **to ~ open** auf lspringen - **4.** [go suddenly]: **to ~ in** hineinlplatzen, hineinlstürmen ⟨> *vt* [tyre, balloon, bubble] platzen lassen; [dam, river bank] durchlbrechen ⟨> *n* [bout] Explosion *die*.

➤ **burst into** *vt fus* auslbrechen in (+ *A*); **the house ~ into flames** im Haus brach Feuer aus.

➤ **burst out** *vt fus* - **1.** [say suddenly] loslplatzen - **2.** [begin suddenly]: **to ~ out laughing/crying** in Gelächter/Tränen auslbrechen.

**bursting** ['bɜːstɪŋ] *adj* - **1.** [with emotion]: **to be ~ with laughter** vor Lachen platzen - **2.** [eager]: **to be ~ to do sthg** darauf brennen, etw zu tun.

**Burundi** [bʊ'rʊndɪ] *n* Burundi *nt*.

**bury** ['berɪ] (*pt* & *pp* -**ied**) *vt* - **1.** [in ground - person] begraben; [ - thing] vergraben - **2.** [hide] vergraben - **3.** *fig* [immerse]: **to ~ o.s. in sthg** sich in etw (*A*) vergraben.

**bus** [bʌs] *n* Bus *der;* **by ~** mit dem Bus.

**bus conductor** *n* Busschaffner *der*, -in *die*.

**bus driver** n Busfahrer der, -in die.

**bush** [buʃ] n - **1.** [gen] Busch der - **2.** phr: **to beat about the ~** um den heißen Brei herumlreden.

**bushel** ['buʃl] n Scheffel der.

**bushy** ['buʃɪ] (compar **-ier;** superl **-iest**) adj buschig.

**business** ['bɪznɪs] n - **1.** (U) [commerce] Geschäft das; **on ~** geschäftlich; **to mean ~** inf es ernst meinen; **to go out of ~** zulmachen, schließen - **2.** [company] Firma die - **3.** (U) [concern] Angelegenheit die; **to have no ~ doing** OR **to do sthg** kein Recht haben, etw zu tun; **mind your own ~!** inf kümmere dich um deine eigenen Sachen OR deinen eigenen Kram! - **4.** [affair, matter] Sache die ⬦ comp Geschäfts-.

**business address** n Geschäftsadresse die.

**business card** n Visitenkarte die.

**business class** n Businessclass die.

**businesslike** ['bɪznɪslaɪk] adj sachlich.

**businessman** ['bɪznɪsmæn] (pl **-men** [-men]) n Geschäftsmann der.

**business school** n Wirtschaftshochschule die.

**business trip** n Geschäftsreise die.

**businesswoman** ['bɪznɪsˌwʊmən] (pl **-women** [-ˌwɪmɪn]) n Geschäftsfrau die.

**busker** ['bʌskəʳ] n Br Straßenmusikant der, -in die.

**bus lane** n Busspur die.

**bus shelter** n Wartehäuschen das.

**bus station** n Busbahnhof der.

**bus stop** n Bushaltestelle die.

**bust** [bʌst] (pt & pp **bust** OR **-ed**) adj inf - **1.** [broken] kaputt - **2.** [bankrupt]: **to go ~** pleite gehen ⬦ n - **1.** [bosom] Busen der - **2.** [statue] Büste die - **3.** police sl [raid] Razzia die ⬦ vt inf - **1.** [break] kaputt machen - **2.** inf [arrest] festlnehmen - **3.** police sl [raid]: **this club has been ~ed twice** in diesem Klub sind zwei Razzien durchgeführt worden ⬦ vi inf kaputt gehen.

**bustle** ['bʌsl] n [activity] reges Treiben ⬦ vi: **to ~ about** OR **around** hin und her eilen.

**bustling** ['bʌslɪŋ] adj geschäftig, rege.

**bust-up** n inf - **1.** [quarrel, fight] Streit der - **2.** [of marriage, relationship] Ende das.

**busy** ['bɪzɪ] (compar **-ier;** superl **-iest**) adj - **1.** [active] (viel) beschäftigt - **2.** [hectic - life] bewegt; [ - week] hektisch; [ - place] belebt; [ - office] geschäftig; **to be ~ doing sthg** damit beschäftigt sein, etw zu tun - **3.** esp Am TELEC [engaged] besetzt ⬦ vt: **to ~ o.s. doing sthg** sich damit beschäftigen, etw zu tun.

**busybody** ['bɪzɪˌbɒdɪ] (pl **-ies**) n pej Wichtigtuer der, -in die.

**busy lizzie** n fleißiges Lieschen.

**busy signal** n Am TELEC Besetztzeichen das.

**but** [bʌt] conj aber; [with negatives] sondern; **we were poor ~ happy** wir waren arm, aber glücklich; **she owns not one ~ two houses** sie hat nicht nur eins, sondern zwei Häuser; **~ now let's talk about you** jetzt aber zu dir ⬦ prep [except] außer; **he has no one ~ himself to blame** das hat er sich (D) selbst zuzuschreiben; **the last ~ one** der/die/das Vorletzte; **anyone ~ him would have helped** jeder andere hätte geholfen; **anything ~ that** alles, nur nicht das ⬦ adv fml [only] nur; **had I ~ known** hätte ich das nur gewusst; **we can ~ try** wir müssen es wenigstens versuchen; **she has ~ recently joined the firm** sie hat erst vor kurzem bei der Firma angefangen.
➤ **but for** prep ohne; **~ for her I would have died** ohne sie wäre ich gestorben.
➤ **but then** adv: **he's very good at it, ~ then he's been doing it for years** er kann es sehr gut, aber er hat natürlich auch jahrelange Erfahrung.

**butane** ['bjuːteɪn] n Butan das.

**butch** [bʊtʃ] adj Br inf [woman] maskulin.

**butcher** ['bʊtʃəʳ] n - **1.** [shopkeeper] Fleischer der, Metzger der; **~'s (shop)** Fleischerei die, Metzgerei die - **2.** fig [killer] Schlächter der ⬦ vt - **1.** [kill for meat] schlachten - **2.** fig [massacre] ablschlachten.

**butchery** ['bʊtʃərɪ] n fig Abschlachten das.

**butler** ['bʌtləʳ] n Butler der.

**butt** [bʌt] n - **1.** [of cigarette] Kippe die; [of cigar] Stummel der - **2.** [of rifle] Kolben der - **3.** [for water] Fass das - **4.** [target] Zielscheibe die - **5.** esp Am inf [bottom] Hintern der ⬦ vt [hit with head] mit dem Kopf stoßen.
➤ **butt in** vi [interrupt] sich einlmischen, dazwischenlplatzen; **to ~ in on sb/sthg** sich bei jm/etw einlmischen.

**butter** ['bʌtəʳ] n Butter die; **~ wouldn't melt in her mouth** inf sie könnte kein Wässerchen trüben ⬦ vt buttern, mit Butter bestreichen.
➤ **butter up** vt sep inf: **to ~ sb up** jm schönltun, jm um den Bart gehen.

**butter bean** n Wachsbohne die.

**buttercup** ['bʌtəkʌp] n Butterblume die.

**butter dish** n Butterdose die.

**buttered** ['bʌtəd] adj gebuttert, mit Butter.

**butterfingers** ['bʌtəˌfɪŋgəz] (pl inv) n inf Tolpatsch der.

**butterfly** ['bʌtəflaɪ] (pl **-ies**) n - **1.** [insect] Schmetterling der; **to have butterflies in one's stomach** inf ein flaues Gefühl im Magen haben - **2.** (U) [swimming style] Schmetterlingsstil der.

**buttermilk** ['bʌtəmɪlk] n Buttermilch die.

**butterscotch** [ˈbʌtəskɒtʃ] n (U) Karamelle die.

**buttocks** [ˈbʌtəks] npl Hintern der.

**button** [ˈbʌtn] n - **1.** [on clothes, machine] Knopf der - **2.** Am [badge] Anstecker der ◇ vt = button up.
➤ **button up** vt sep zulknöpfen.

**button-down** adj mit angeknöpften Kragenenden.

**buttonhole** [ˈbʌtnhəʊl] n - **1.** [hole] Knopfloch das - **2.** Br [flower] Blume die für das Knopfloch ◇ vt inf zum Zuhören zwingen.

**button mushroom** n junger Champignon.

**buttress** [ˈbʌtrɪs] n Stützpfeiler der ◇ vt [wall] stützen.

**buxom** [ˈbʌksəm] adj vollbusig.

**buy** [baɪ] (pt & pp bought) vt - **1.** [purchase] kaufen; [company] auflkaufen; **to ~ sthg from sb** etw von jm kaufen - **2.** fig [bribe] kaufen, bestechen ◇ n Kauf der.
➤ **buy in** vt sep Br einlkaufen.
➤ **buy into** vt fus sich einlkaufen in (+ A).
➤ **buy off** vt sep kaufen.
➤ **buy out** vt sep - **1.** [in business] auslzahlen - **2.** [from army]: **to ~ o.s. out** sich freilkaufen.
➤ **buy up** vt sep auf lkaufen.

**buyer** n - **1.** [purchaser] Käufer der, -in die - **2.** [profession] Einkäufer der, -in die.

**buyer's market** n Käufermarkt der.

**buyout** [ˈbaɪaʊt] n Aufkauf der.

**buzz** [bʌz] n [noise - of insect, machinery] Summen das, Brummen das; [ - of conversation] Gemurmel das, Stimmengewirr das; **to give sb a ~** inf TELEC jn anlrufen ◇ vi - **1.** [insect, machinery] summen, brummen - **2.** fig [place]: **the office was ~ing** with excitement im Büro herrschte große Aufregung - **3.** fig [head] schwimmen; [thoughts] schwirren; **my head was ~ing** mir schwirrte der Kopf ◇ vt [on intercom] rufen.
➤ **buzz off** vi Br inf: ~ **off!** zisch ab!

**buzzard** [ˈbʌzəd] n - **1.** Br [hawk] Bussard der - **2.** Am [vulture] Geier der.

**buzzer** [ˈbʌzəʳ] n Summer der.

**buzzing** [ˈbʌzɪŋ] n (U) Summen das; Brummen das.

**buzzword** [ˈbʌzwɜːd] n inf Modewort das.

**by** [baɪ] prep - **1.** [expressing cause, agent] von; **he was hit ~ a car** er ist von einem Auto angefahren worden; **~ Mozart** von Mozart - **2.** [indicating method, means, manner] mit; **~ car/train** mit dem Auto/Zug; **to pay ~ credit card** mit Kreditkarte bezahlen; **to dine ~ candlelight** bei Kerzenlicht speisen; **to take sb ~ the hand** jn an der Hand nehmen; **made ~ hand** handgemacht; **he got rich ~ buying land** er wurde durch Grundstückskäufe reich

- **3.** [near to, beside] an (+ D); **~ the sea** am Meer; **~ my side** an meiner Seite, neben mir - **4.** [past] an (+ D) ... vorbei; **a car went ~ the house** ein Auto fuhr am Haus vorbei - **5.** [via] durch; **exit ~ the door on the left** Ausgang durch die Tür auf der linken Seite; **we came ~ way of Paris** wir kamen über Paris - **6.** [with time]: **it will be ready ~ tomorrow** bis morgen wird es fertig sein; **be there ~ nine** sei spätestens um neun da; **she should be there ~ now** sie müsste inzwischen da sein; **I'll be ready ~ then** bis dahin bin ich fertig; **~ then it was too late** zu diesem Zeitpunkt war es bereits zu spät; **~ day** tagsüber; **~ night** nachts - **7.** [expressing quantity]: **sold ~ the dozen** im Dutzend verkauft; **prices fell ~ 20%** die Preise fielen um 20%; **~ the day/week/month/hour** pro Tag/Woche/Monat/Stunde - **8.** [expressing meaning]: **what do you mean ~ that?** was meinst du damit? - **9.** [in division] durch; **to divide 20 ~ 2** 20 durch 2 dividieren; [in multiplication] mit; **to multiply 20 ~ 2** 20 mit 2 multiplizieren; **two metres ~ five** zwei mal fünf Meter - **10.** [according to] nach; **~ law** nach dem Gesetz; **it's fine ~ me** ich bin damit einverstanden; **to judge ~ appearances** nach dem Äußeren urteilen; **~ nature** von Natur aus; **~ profession** von Beruf - **11.** [expressing gradual process]: **day ~ day** Tag für Tag; **they came out one ~ one** sie kamen einer nach dem anderen heraus; **little ~ little** nach und nach - **12.** phr: **~ mistake** versehentlich; **~ chance** durch Zufall; **~ the way** übrigens ◇ adv ⊳ **go, pass** etc.
➤ **by and large** adv im Großen und Ganzen.
➤ **(all) by oneself** adv allein; **did you do it all ~ yourself?** hast du das ganz allein gemacht? ◇ adj allein; **I'm all ~ myself today** ich bin heute ganz allein.

**bye(-bye)** [baɪ(baɪ)] excl inf tschüs!, tschüss!

**bye-election** n = by-election.

**byelaw** [ˈbaɪlɔː] n = bylaw.

**by-election** n Nachwahl die.

**bygone** [ˈbaɪɡɒn] adj vergangen.
➤ **bygones** npl: **to let ~s be ~s** die Vergangenheit ruhen lassen.

**bylaw** [ˈbaɪlɔː] n Verordnung die.

**by-line** n Seitenlinie die.

**BYOB** (abbr of bring your own bottle) Getränke bitte selbst mitbringen.

**bypass** [ˈbaɪpɑːs] n - **1.** [road] Umgehungsstraße die - **2.** MED: **~ (operation)** Bypassoperation die ◇ vt - **1.** [place] umlfahren, umgehen - **2.** [issue, person] umgehen.

**by-product** n lit & fig Nebenprodukt das.

**bystanders** [ˈbaɪˌstændəz] npl : **the ~** die Umstehenden pl.

**byte** [baɪt] n COMPUT Byte das.

**byword** ['baɪwɜːd] *n* [symbol]: **to be a ~ for sthg** ein Synonym für etw sein.

**c¹** (*pl* **c's** *OR* **cs**), **C** (*pl* **C's** *OR* **Cs**) [siː] *n* [letter] c *das*, C *das*.
➡ **C** *n* - **1.** MUS C *das;* **C major** C-Dur - **2.** SCH [mark] ≈ drei - **3.** (*abbr of* **celsius, centigrade**) C.

**c²** [siː] - **1.** *abbr of* **century** - **2.** *abbr of* **cents.**

**c., ca.** (*abbr of* **circa**) ca.

**c/a** - **1.** *abbr of* **credit account** - **2.** *abbr of* **current account.**

**CA** *n* - **1.** *abbr of* **chartered accountant** - **2.** (*abbr of* **Consumers' Association**) *Verbraucherschutzorganisation in Großbritannien* ⬦ - **1.** *abbr of* **Central America** - **2.** *abk für* „California", *in Postanschrift verwendet.*

**CAA** *n* - **1.** (*abbr of* **Civil Aviation Authority**) *britische Zivilluftfahrtsbehörde* - **2.** (*abbr of* **Civil Aeronautics Authority**) *amerikanische Zivilluftfahrtsbehörde.*

**cab** [kæb] *n* - **1.** [taxi] Taxi *das* - **2.** [of lorry] Führerhaus *das*.

**CAB** *n abbr of* **Citizens' Advice Bureau.**

**cabaret** ['kæbəreɪ] *n* Varieté *das*, Kabarett *das*.

**cabbage** ['kæbɪdʒ] *n* [vegetable] Kohl *der*.

**cabbie, cabby** ['kæbɪ] *n inf* Taxifahrer *der*, -in *die*.

**caber** ['keɪbəʳ] *n:* **tossing the ~** Pfahlwerfen *das*, *das Werfen eines grob behauenen Baumstamms, schottische Sportart.*

**cabin** ['kæbɪn] *n* - **1.** [on ship, in aircraft] Kabine *die* - **2.** [house] Hütte *die*.

**cabin class** *n* zweite Klasse.

**cabin crew** *n* Begleitpersonal *das*.

**cabin cruiser** *n* Kajütboot *das*.

**cabinet** ['kæbɪnɪt] *n* - **1.** [cupboard] Vitrine *die* - **2.** POL Kabinett *das*.

**cabinet-maker** *n* Tischler *der*, -in *die*, Möbelschreiner *der*, -in *die*.

**cabinet minister** *n* Minister *der*, -in *die*, Mitglied *das* des Kabinetts.

**cable** ['keɪbl] *n* - **1.** [rope] Seil *das* - **2.** [telegram] Telegramm *das* - **3.** ELEC Kabel *das* - **4.** TV = **cable television** ⬦ *vt* [telegraph] telegrafieren.

**cable car** *n* Drahtseilbahn *die*.

**cablegram** ['keɪblgræm] *n* Telegramm *das*.

**cable railway** *n* Bergbahn *die*, Drahtseilbahn *die*.

**cable television, cable TV** *n* Kabelfernsehen *das*.

**caboodle** [kə'buːdl] *n inf:* **the whole (kit and) ~** der ganze Klumpatsch.

**cabriolet** ['kæbrɪəleɪ] *n* Kabriolett *das*.

**cache** [kæʃ] *n* - **1.** [store] geheimes Lager, Versteck *das* - **2.** COMPUT Zwischenspeicher *der* ⬦ *vt* COMPUT zwischenspeichern.

**cachet** ['kæʃeɪ] *n fml* Ansehen *das*, Prestige *das*.

**cackle** ['kækl] *n* - **1.** [of hen] Gackern *das* - **2.** [of person] Kichern *das* ⬦ *vi* - **1.** [hen] gackern - **2.** [person] kichern.

**cacophony** [kæ'kɒfənɪ] *n* Kakophonie *die*.

**cactus** ['kæktəs] (*pl* -**tuses** *OR* -**ti** [-taɪ]) *n* Kaktus *der*.

**CAD** (*abbr of* **computer-aided design**) *n* CAD.

**caddie** ['kædɪ] *n* Golfjunge *der*, Caddie *der* ⬦ *vi:* **to ~ for sb** für jn Caddie sein.

**caddy** ['kædɪ] (*pl* -**ies**) *n* Teedose *die*.

**cadence** ['keɪdəns] *n* Kadenz *die*.

**cadet** [kə'det] *n* [in police] Kadett *der*, -in *die*.

**cadge** [kædʒ] *Br inf* *vt:* **to ~ sthg (off** *OR* **from sb)** etw (von jm) schnorren ⬦ *vi:* **to ~ off** *OR* **from sb** von jm schnorren.

**Caesar** ['siːzəʳ] *n* Cäsar *der*.

**caesarean (section)** [sə'zeərɪən] *n Br* Kaiserschnitt *der*.

**CAF** (*abbr of* **cost and freight**) *Kosten und Fracht.*

**cafe, café** ['kæfeɪ] *n* Café *das*.

**cafeteria** [ˌkæfɪ'tɪərɪə] *n* Cafeteria *die*.

**caffeine** ['kæfiːn] *n* Koffein *das*.

**cage** [keɪdʒ] *n* Käfig *der*.

**caged** [keɪdʒd] *adj* eingesperrt, im Käfig.

**cagey** ['keɪdʒɪ] (*compar* -**ier**; *superl* -**iest**) *adj inf* zugeknöpft, verschlossen.

**cagoule** [kə'guːl] *n Br* Regenjacke *die*.

**cahoots** [kə'huːts] *n inf:* **to be in ~ (with sb)** (mit jm) unter einer Decke stecken.

**CAI** (*abbr of* **computer-aided instruction**) *n* CUU, RGU.

**cairn** [keən] *n* [heap of stones] Steinhügel *der*.

**Cairo** ['kaɪərəʊ] *n* Kairo *nt*.

**cajole** [kə'dʒəʊl] *vt* zulreden; **to ~ sb into doing sthg** jn überreden, etw zu tun.

**cake** [keɪk] n - **1.** [sweet food] Kuchen der; **to sell like hot ~s** inf wie warme Semmeln weglgehen; **you can't have your ~ and eat it** inf beides auf einmal geht nicht; **a piece of ~** inf fig ein Kinderspiel - **2.** [of soap] Stück das.

**caked** [keɪkt] adj: **~ with sthg** verkrustet mit etw.

**cake pan** n Am Kuchenform die, Backform die.

**cake tin** n Br [for baking] Kuchenform die, Backform die; [for storing] Keksdose die, Plätzchendose die.

**cal** [kæl] n abbr of **calorie.**

**calamine lotion** [ˌkæləmaɪn-] n Galmeilotion die.

**calamitous** [kə'læmɪtəs] adj fml verhängnisvoll.

**calamity** [kə'læmətɪ] (pl -**ies**) n fml Unheil das, Katastrophe die.

**calcium** ['kælsɪəm] n Kalzium das.

**calculate** ['kælkjoleɪt] vt - **1.** [work out] auslrechnen - **2.** [plan, intend]: **to be ~d to do sthg** darauf ausgelegt sein, etw zu tun.

➤ **calculate on** vi: **to ~ on sthg** mit etw rechnen; **to ~ on doing sthg** damit rechnen, etw zu tun.

**calculated** ['kælkjoleɪtɪd] adj [planned] berechnet; [insult] beabsichtigt; [lie] bewusst.

**calculating** ['kælkjoleɪtɪŋ] adj pej berechnend.

**calculation** [ˌkælkjo'leɪʃn] n [sum] Berechnung die.

**calculator** ['kælkjoleɪtə'] n Taschenrechner der, Rechenmaschine die.

**calculus** ['kælkjoləs] n MATH [differential] Differentialrechnung die; [integral] Integralrechnung die.

**calendar** ['kælɪndə'] n - **1.** [gen] Kalender der - **2.** [list of events] Veranstaltungskalender der.

**calendar month** n Kalendermonat der.

**calendar year** n Kalenderjahr das.

**calf** [kɑːf] (pl **calves**) n - **1.** [young animal] Kalb das - **2.** [leather] Kalbsleder das - **3.** [of leg] Wade die.

**calfskin** n Kalbsleder das.

**caliber** n Am = **calibre.**

**calibrate** ['kælɪbreɪt] vt kalibrieren.

**calibre, caliber** Am ['kælɪbə'] n Kaliber das.

**calico** ['kælɪkəʊ] n Kaliko der.

**California** [ˌkælɪ'fɔːnjə] n Kalifornien nt.

**Californian** [ˌkælɪ'fɔːnjən] adj kalifornisch ◇ n Kalifornier der, -in die.

**calipers** npl Am = **callipers.**

**call** [kɔːl] n - **1.** [shout - of person, animal] Ruf der; **a ~ for help** Hilferuf der - **2.** [visit] Besuch der; **to pay sb a ~** bei jm vorbeilgehen - **3.** [demand]: **she has a lot of ~s on her time** ihre Zeit ist stark beansprucht; **there are ~s for a referendum** verschiedentlich wird nach einem Referendum verlangt; **there's no ~ for that sort of behaviour!** das gehört sich nicht! - **4.** [telephone call] Anruf der; **to give sb a ~** jn anlrufen - **5.** [for flight] Aufruf der - **6.** [lure, fascination] Ruf der ◇ vt - **1.** [name, describe] nennen; **to be ~ed** heißen; **what's he ~ed?** wie heißt er?; **to ~ sb names** jn beschimpfen; **let's ~ it £10** sagen wir 10 Pfund - **2.** [shout] rufen - **3.** [telephone] anlrufen; [doctor] rufen - **4.** [meeting] einlberufen; [election] anlsetzen; [flight] auflrufen; [strike] auslrufen ◇ vi - **1.** [shout] rufen - **2.** [telephone] anlrufen; **who's ~ing?** wie war der Name? - **3.** [visit] vorbeilkommen; **this train ~s at ...** dieser Zug hält in ...

➤ **on call** adj: **to be on ~** [doctor, nurse] Bereitschaftsdienst haben.

➤ **call back** vt sep zurücklrufen ◇ vi - **1.** [phone again] zurücklrufen - **2.** [visit again] wiederlkommen.

➤ **call by** vi inf vorbeilschauen.

➤ **call for** vt fus - **1.** [come to fetch] ablholen - **2.** [demand] verlangen; [require] erfordern; **that ~s for an explanation** das verlangt eine Erklärung; **this ~s for a drink** darauf müssen wir anstoßen.

➤ **call in** vt sep - **1.** [send for - army, riot police] einlsetzen - **2.** COMM [goods] aus dem Verkehr ziehen; FIN [loan] einlfordern ◇ vi: **to ~ in (on sb)** (bei jm) vorbeilschauen.

➤ **call off** vt sep - **1.** [cancel] ablsagen - **2.** [dog, attacker] zurücklrufen.

➤ **call on** vt fus - **1.** [visit] besuchen - **2.** [ask]: **to ~ on sb to do sthg** jn auf lfordern, etw zu tun.

➤ **call out** vt sep - **1.** [shout out] auslrufen - **2.** [doctor, fire brigade] rufen - **3.** [workers] zum Streik auf lrufen ◇ vi [shout out] rufen.

➤ **call round** vi vorbeilkommen.

➤ **call up** vt sep - **1.** MIL einlberufen - **2.** [on telephone] anlrufen - **3.** COMPUT auf lrufen.

**call box** n Br Telefonzelle die.

**caller** ['kɔːlə'] n - **1.** [visitor] Besucher der, -in die - **2.** [on telephone] Anrufer der, -in die.

**call girl** n Prostituierte die.

**calligraphy** [kə'lɪgrəfɪ] n Schönschreibkunst die.

**call-in** n Am RADIO & TV Fernseh- oder Radioshow, in der Zuschauer bzw. Zuhörer anrufen und ihre Meinung zu einem Thema äußern können.

**calling** ['kɔːlɪŋ] n - **1.** [profession, trade] Beruf der - **2.** [vocation] Berufung die.

**calling card** n Am Visitenkarte die.

**callipers** Br, **calipers** Am ['kælɪpəz] npl

- **1.** MATH Taster der, Zirkel der - **2.** MED Beinschienen die.

**callous** [ˈkæləs] adj gefühllos, herzlos.

**callously** [ˈkæləslɪ] adv gefühllos, herzlos.

**callousness** [ˈkæləsnɪs] n Grausamkeit die.

**call-up** n Br Einberufung die.

**callus** [ˈkæləs] (pl **-es**) n Schwiele die.

**calm** [kɑːm] adj - **1.** [person, voice] ruhig - **2.** [weather, day] windstill - **3.** [water] still ◇ n Ruhe die ◇ vt beruhigen.
◆ **calm down** vt sep beruhigen ◇ vi sich beruhigen.

**calmly** [ˈkɑːmlɪ] adv ruhig.

**calmness** [ˈkɑːmnɪs] n Ruhe die.

**Calor gas**® [ˈkælə-] n Br britische Handelsmarke für Butangas.

**calorie** [ˈkælərɪ] n Kalorie die.

**calorific** [ˌkæləˈrɪfɪk] adj kalorienreich.

**calve** [kɑːv] vi kalben.

**calves** [kɑːvz] pl ⊏ **calf.**

**cam** [kæm] n Nocken der.

**CAM** (abbr of **computer-aided manufacturing**) n CAM.

**camaraderie** [ˌkæməˈrɑːdərɪ] n Kameradschaft die.

**camber** [ˈkæmbəʳ] n Wölbung die.

**Cambodia** [kæmˈbəʊdjə] n Kambodscha nt.

**Cambodian** [kæmˈbəʊdjən] adj kambodschanisch ◇ n Kambodschaner der, -in die.

**Cambs** abk für Cambridgeshire, in Postanschrift verwendet.

**camcorder** [ˈkæmˌkɔːdəʳ] n Camcorder der.

**came** [keɪm] pt ⊏ **come.**

**camel** [ˈkæml] adj [coat] Kamelhaar- ◇ n [animal] Kamel das.

**camellia** [kəˈmiːljə] n Kamelie die.

**cameo** [ˈkæmɪəʊ] (pl **-s**) n - **1.** [piece of jewellery] Kamee die - **2.** [in film] kleine Nebenrolle, in der ein berühmter Schauspieler zu sehen ist.

**camera** [ˈkæmərə] n Kamera die.
◆ **in camera** adv LAW unter Ausschluss der Öffentlichkeit.

**cameraman** [ˈkæmərəmæn] (pl **-men** [-men]) n Kameramann der.

**camomile** [ˈkæməmaɪl] n Kamille die ◇ comp: ~ **tea** Kamillentee der.

**camouflage** [ˈkæməflɑːʒ] n - **1.** MIL Tarnung die - **2.** [of bird] Tarngefieder das; [of animal] Tarnkleid das ◇ vt MIL tarnen.

**camp** [kæmp] n - **1.** [for tents] Lagerplatz der - **2.** MIL Feldlager das, Militärlager das - **3.** [for refugees, faction] Lager das ◇ vi MIL lagern; [holiday] campen, zelten.
◆ **camp out** vi campen, zelten.

**campaign** [kæmˈpeɪn] n - **1.** [project, crusade] Kampagne die - **2.** [in war] Feldzug der ◇ vi: **to ~ for sthg** sich für etw einlsetzen; **to ~ against sthg** gegen etw anlgehen.

**campaigner** [kæmˈpeɪnəʳ] n Kämpfer der, -in die, Aktivist der, -in die.

**camp bed** n Feldbett das.

**camper** [ˈkæmpəʳ] n - **1.** [person] Camper der, -in die - **2.** [vehicle]: ~ **(van)** Wohnmobil das.

**campground** [ˈkæmpgraʊnd] n Am Campingplatz der, Zeltplatz der.

**camphor** [ˈkæmfəʳ] n Kampfer der.

**camping** [ˈkæmpɪŋ] n Camping das; **to go ~** zelten gehen.

**camping site, campsite** [ˈkæmpsaɪt] n Campingplatz der, Zeltplatz der.

**campus** [ˈkæmpəs] (pl **-es**) n Universitätsgelände das, Campus der.

**camshaft** [ˈkæmʃɑːft] n Nockenwelle die.

**can**[1] [weak form kən, strong form kæn] (pt & pp **-ned**; cont **-ning**) n [container] Dose die ◇ vt konservieren, einldosen.

**can**[2] [weak form kən, strong form kæn] (pt & conditional **could**; negative **cannot** OR **can't**) aux vb - **1.** [be able to] können; **~ you help me?** können Sie mir helfen?; **I ~ see you** ich kann dich sehen, ich sehe dich; **~ you see/hear anything?** sehen/hören Sie etwas?, können Sie etwas sehen/hören?; **as soon/fast as I ~** so bald/schnell ich kann - **2.** [know how to] können; **~ you drive?** kannst du Auto fahren?; **I ~ speak German/play the piano** ich spreche Deutsch/spiele Klavier - **3.** [be allowed to] können, dürfen; **you ~'t smoke here** Sie können OR dürfen hier nicht rauchen; **you ~ use my car if you like** du kannst mein Auto nehmen - **4.** [in polite requests] können; **~ you tell me the time?** können Sie mir sagen, wie viel Uhr es ist?; **~ I speak to John, please?** kann ich bitte John sprechen? - **5.** [indicating disbelief, puzzlement] können; **what ~ she have done with it?** was hat sie bloß damit gemacht?; **we ~'t just leave him here** wir können ihn nicht einfach hier lassen; **you ~'t be serious!** das ist doch wohl nicht dein Ernst! - **6.** [indicating possibility] können; **they could be lost** sie könnten sich verlaufen haben - **7.** [indicating occasional occurrence] können; **it ~ get cold at night** es kann nachts kalt werden; **she ~ be a bit difficult sometimes** sie ist manchmal etwas schwierig.

**Canada** [ˈkænədə] n Kanada nt.

**Canadian** [kəˈneɪdjən] adj kanadisch ◇ n Kanadier der, -in die.

**canal** [kəˈnæl] n Kanal der.

**Canaries** [kəˈneərɪz] npl: **the ~** die Kanaren pl.

**canary** [kə'neərı] (pl -ies) n Kanarienvogel der.

**Canary Islands** npl: the ~ die Kanarische Inseln pl; in the ~ auf den Kanarischen Inseln.

**Canberra** ['kænbərə] n Canberra nt.

**cancel** ['kænsl] (Br pt & pp -led; cont -ling, Am pt & pp -ed; cont -ing) vt - 1. [call off - event, party] ausfallen lassen, absagen; [ - appointment, meeting] ablsagen; [ - order, booking] stornieren; **the concert has been ~led** das Konzert fällt aus; **the train has been ~led** der Zug fährt heute nicht; **the flight has been ~led** der Flug ist gestrichen worden - 2. [invalidate - stamp] entwerten; [ - cheque] stornieren; [ - debt] streichen; [- subscription] ablbestellen <> vi: **we had to ~** wir mussten absagen.

➤ **cancel out** vt sep: **to ~ each other out** einander auslgleichen, sich gegenseitig auf l-heben.

**cancellation** [ˌkænsə'leıʃn] n Stornierung die; [of meeting, visit] Absage die; [of subscription] Abbestellung die.

**cancer** ['kænsə'] n Krebs der <> comp Krebs-.
➤ **Cancer** n Krebs der.

**cancerous** ['kænsərəs] adj Krebs-, krebsartig.

**candelabra** [ˌkændɪ'lɑːbrə] n Leuchter der, Kandelaber der.

**C and F, C & F** (abbr of cost and freight) Kosten und Fracht.

**candid** ['kændɪd] adj offen, ehrlich.

**candidacy** ['kændɪdəsɪ] n Kandidatur die.

**candidate** ['kændɪdət] n - 1. [for job] Kandidat der, -in die, Bewerber der, -in die - 2. [for exam] Prüfling der.

**candidature** ['kændɪdətʃə'] n Kandidatur die.

**candidly** ['kændɪdlɪ] adv offen, ehrlich.

**candidness** ['kændɪdnɪs] n = candour.

**candied** ['kændɪd] adj kandiert.

**candle** ['kændl] n Kerze die; **to burn the ~ at both ends** inf sich zu viel zulmuten OR auf l-halsen.

**candlelight** ['kændllaɪt] n Kerzenlicht das.

**candlelit** ['kændllɪt] adj im Kerzenschein, bei Kerzenlicht.

**candlestick** ['kændlstɪk] n Kerzenständer der.

**candour** Br, **candor** Am ['kændə'] n Offenheit die.

**candy** ['kændɪ] (pl -ies) n esp Am - 1. (U) [confectionery] Süßigkeiten pl - 2. [sweet] Bonbon das.

**candy bar** n Am Schokoriegel der.

**candyfloss** Br ['kændɪflɒs], **cotton candy** Am n (U) Zuckerwatte die.

**candy store** n Am Süßwarenladen der.

**cane** [keɪn] n - 1. (U) [for making furniture] Rohr das - 2. [walking stick] Spazierstock der - 3. [for punishment]: **the ~** der Rohrstock - 4. [for supporting plant] Stock der <> comp Rohr- <> vt mit dem Rohrstock züchtigen.

**cane sugar** n Rohrzucker der.

**canine** ['keɪnaɪn] adj Hunde- <> n: ~ (tooth) Eckzahn der.

**canister** ['kænɪstə'] n Kanister der, Behälter der; [for tea, film] Dose die.

**cannabis** ['kænəbɪs] n Cannabis der.

**canned** [kænd] adj - 1. [food] Konserven-; [drink] Dosen- - 2. inf fig [prerecorded] Tonband-.

**cannelloni** [ˌkænɪ'ləʊnɪ] n italienische Nudelspezialität.

**cannery** ['kænərɪ] (pl -ies) n Konservenfabrik die.

**cannibal** ['kænɪbl] n Kannibale der, -in die, Menschenfresser der, -in die.

**cannibalize, -ise** ['kænɪbəlaɪz] vt auslschlachten.

**cannon** ['kænən] (pl inv OR -s) n - 1. [on ground] Kanone die - 2. [on aircraft] Bordkanone die.
➤ **cannon into** vt fus Br zusammenlprallen mit.

**cannonball** ['kænənbɔːl] n Kanonenkugel die.

**cannot** ['kænɒt] vb fml ⊳ can².

**canny** ['kænɪ] (compar -ier; superl -iest) adj umsichtig, sparsam.

**canoe** [kə'nuː] (cont canoeing) n Paddelboot das, Kanu das <> vi Kanu fahren.

**canoeing** [kə'nuːɪŋ] n Kanufahren das.

**canon** ['kænən] n - 1. [clergyman] Domherr der - 2. [general principle] Grundregel der.
➤ **Canon** n [of Mass]: **the Canon** der Kanon.

**canonize, -ise** ['kænənaɪz] vt heilig sprechen.

**canoodle** [kə'nuːdl] vi Br inf schmusen.

**can opener** n Dosenöffner der.

**canopy** ['kænəpɪ] (pl -ies) n - 1. [over bed, seat] Baldachin der - 2. [of trees, branches] Blätterdach das.

**cant** [kænt] n (U) pej Heuchelei die.

**can't** [kɑːnt] = cannot.

**Cantab.** (abbr of Cantabrigiensis) von der Universität Cambridge.

**Cantabrian Mountains** [kæn'teɪbrɪən-] npl: **the ~** das Kantabrische Gebirge.

**cantankerous** [kæn'tæŋkərəs] adj streitsüchtig.

**canteen** [kæn'tiːn] n - 1. [restaurant - in workplace] Kantine die; [ - in university] Mensa die - 2. [box of cutlery] Besteckkasten der.

**canter** ['kæntə'] *n* Kanter *der* <> *vi* im Handgalopp reiten.

**cantilever** ['kæntılı:və'] *n* Ausleger *der*.

**Cantonese** [ˌkæntə'ni:z] *adj* kantonesisch <> *n* [language] Kantonesisch(e) *das* <> *npl*: **the** ~ die Kantonesen.

**canvas** ['kænvəs] *n* - **1.** (*U*) [cloth] Segeltuch *das;* **under** ~ [in a tent] im Zelt - **2.** [art - for painting] Leinwand *die;* [ - finished painting] Gemälde *das*.

**canvass** ['kænvəs] *vt* - **1.** POL: **to** ~ **an area** in einer Gegend Wahlwerbung betreiben; **to** ~ **voters** um Wählerstimmen werben - **2.** COMM: **to** ~ **opinion** eine Meinungsumfrage durchlführen <> *vi* POL [campaign] um Stimmen werben.

**canvasser** ['kænvəsə'] *n* - **1.** POL [campaigner] Wahlhelfer *der*, -in *die* - **2.** [for opinion poll] Interviewer *der*, -in *die*.

**canvassing** ['kænvəsıŋ] *n* (*U*) - **1.** POL [campaigning] Stimmenwerbung *die* - **2.** [for opinion poll] Befragung *die*, Umfrage *die*.

**canyon** ['kænjən] *n* Cañon *der*.

**cap** [kæp] (*pt* & *pp* -**ped**; *cont* -**ping**) *n* - **1.** [hat] Mütze *die*, Kappe *die;* **to go** ~ **in hand to sb** *fig* jm demütig gegenüberltreten - **2.** [lid, top] Deckel *der;* [on pen, lipstick] Kappe *die* - **3.** *Br* [contraceptive device] Diaphragma *das* <> *vt* - **1.** [cover top of] bedecken - **2.** [outdo] **to** ~ **it all** als Krönung des Ganzen.

**CAP** (*abbr of* **Common Agricultural Policy**) *n* GAP *die*.

**capability** [ˌkeɪpə'bɪlətɪ] (*pl* -**ies**) *n* - **1.** [ability] Fähigkeit *die* - **2.** MIL Potenzial *das*.

**capable** ['keɪpəbl] *adj* - **1.** [able, having capacity]: **to be** ~ **of sthg** zu etw fähig sein; **to be** ~ **of doing sthg** fähig sein, etw zu tun - **2.** [competent, skilful] kompetent.

**capably** ['keɪpəblɪ] *adv* gekonnt.

**capacious** [kə'peɪʃəs] *adj fml* geräumig.

**capacitor** [kə'pæsɪtə'] *n* Kondensator *der*.

**capacity** [kə'pæsɪtɪ] (*pl* -**ies**) *n* - **1.** (*U*) [limit] Fassungsvermögen *das;* [of room, hall] Sitzplätze *pl;* **the theatre has a** ~ **of 200** das Theater fasst 200 Personen; **to work at full** ~ voll ausgelastet sein; **full to** ~ vollbesetzt - **2.** [ability] Fähigkeit *die;* ~ **for sthg** die Fähigkeit zu etw; ~ **for doing** *OR* **to do sthg** die Fähigkeit, etw zu tun - **3.** [position] Stellung *die;* **in my** ~ **as ...** in meiner Eigenschaft als ...; **in a ...** ~ in der Funktion (+ *G*) ... <> *comp* Fassungs-.

**cape** [keɪp] *n* - **1.** GEOGR Kap *das* - **2.** [cloak] Cape *das*, Umhang *der*.

**Cape Canaveral** [-kə'nævərəl] *n* Cape Canaveral *nt*.

**Cape Horn** *n* Kap Horn *nt*.

**Cape of Good Hope** *n*: **the** ~ das Kap der guten Hoffnung.

**caper** ['keɪpə'] *n* - **1.** [food] Kaper *die* - **2.** *inf* [escapade] Eskapade *die* <> *vi* herumltollen.

**Cape Town** *n* Kapstadt *nt*.

**capillary** [kə'pɪlərɪ] (*pl* -**ies**) *n* Kapillare *die*.

**capita** [⊃ per capita.

**capital** ['kæpɪtl] *adj* - **1.**: ~ **letter** Großbuchstabe *der* - **2.** [offence] Kapital- <> *n* - **1.** [of country]: ~ **(city)** Hauptstadt *die* - **2.** [letter] Großbuchstabe *der;* **in** ~**s** in Großbuchstaben - **3.** (*U*) [money] Kapital *das;* **to make** ~ **out of sthg** *fig* aus etw Kapital schlagen.

**capital allowance** *n* steuerpflichtige Abschreibung.

**capital assets** *npl* Kapitalanlagen *pl*, Kapitalvermögen *das*.

**capital expenditure** *n* Kapitalaufwand *der*.

**capital gains tax** *n* Kapitalertragssteuer *die*.

**capital goods** *npl* Investitionsgüter *pl*.

**capital-intensive** *adj* kapitalintensiv.

**capitalism** ['kæpɪtəlɪzm] *n* Kapitalismus *der*.

**capitalist** ['kæpɪtəlɪst] *adj* kapitalistisch <> *n* Kapitalist *der*, -in *die*.

**capitalize, -ise** ['kæpɪtəlaɪz] *vi*: **to** ~ **on sthg** aus etw Nutzen ziehen.

**capital punishment** *n* (*U*) Todesstrafe *die*.

**capital stock** *n* Grundkapital *das*.

**capital transfer tax** *n* Schenkungs- und Erbschaftssteuer *die*.

**Capitol** ['kæpɪtl] *n*: **the** ~ das Kapitol.

**Capitol Hill** ['kæpɪtl-] *n* Capitol Hill.

**CAPITOL HILL**

> Das Areal in Washington, D.C., auf dem die Hauptinstitutionen der US-Regierung liegen, wie der Kongress (im Kapitol), die Kongressbibliothek („Library of Congress") und der Oberste Gerichtshof („Supreme Court"). Oft bezeichnet der Ausdruck „Capitol Hill" oder kurz „the Hill" auch den Kongress oder die US-Regierung allgemein.

**capitulate** [kə'pɪtjʊleɪt] *vi*: **to** ~ **(to sthg)** kapitulieren (vor etw (*D*)).

**capitulation** [kəˌpɪtjʊ'leɪʃn] *n* Kapitulation *die*.

**cappuccino** [ˌkæpʊ'tʃi:nəʊ] (*pl* -**s**) *n* Cappuccino *der*.

**capricious** [kə'prɪʃəs] *adj* launisch, unberechenbar.

**Capricorn** ['kæprɪkɔːn] *n* Steinbock *der*.

**caps** [kæps] (*abbr of* **capital letters**) *npl* Großbuchstaben *pl*.

**capsicum** ['kæpsɪkəm] *n* Pfefferschote *die*.

**capsize** [kæp'saɪz] vt zum Kentern bringen ⟨⟩ vi kentern.

**capsule** ['kæpsju:l] n - **1.** [gen] Kapsel die - **2.** [on spacecraft] Raumkapsel die.

**Capt.** abbr of captain.

**captain** ['kæptɪn] n Kapitän der; [in army] Hauptmann der ⟨⟩ vt - **1.** [ship] kommandieren - **2.** [sports team] führen.

**caption** ['kæpʃn] n Bildunterschrift die.

**captivate** ['kæptɪveɪt] vt bezaubern, fesseln.

**captivating** ['kæptɪveɪtɪŋ] adj bezaubernd.

**captive** ['kæptɪv] adj - **1.** [imprisoned] gefangen - **2.** fig [unable to leave] gebannt; ~ audience unfreiwilliges Publikum; ~ market monopolistischer Markt ⟨⟩ n Gefangene der, die.

**captivity** [kæp'tɪvətɪ] n: in ~ in Gefangenschaft.

**captor** ['kæptəʳ] n Person, die jemanden gefangen nimmt.

**capture** ['kæptʃəʳ] vt - **1.** [take prisoner - person] gefangen nehmen; [ - animal] einlfangen - **2.** [city, market, audience] erobern; [interest, imagination, votes] gewinnen - **3.** [in words, pictures, music] einlfangen - **4.** COMPUT erfassen ⟨⟩ n Gefangennahme die; [of city] Eroberung die.

**car** [kɑːʳ] n - **1.** [motor car] Auto das, Wagen der - **2.** [on train] Wagen der ⟨⟩ comp Automobil-, Auto-.

**carafe** [kə'ræf] n Karaffe die.

**caramel** ['kærəməl] n - **1.** [burnt sugar] Karamell der - **2.** [sweet] Karamellbonbon das.

**carat** ['kærət] n Br Karat das.

**caravan** ['kærəvæn] n - **1.** Br [vehicle - towed by car] Wohnwagen der, Caravan der; [ - towed by horse] Pferdewagen der - **2.** [travelling group] Karawane die ⟨⟩ comp Wohnwagen-.

**caravanning** ['kærəvænɪŋ] n (U) Br Ferien pl im Wohnwagen.

**caravan site** n Br Wohnwagenplatz der.

**caraway seed** ['kærəweɪ-] n Kümmelkorn der.

**carbohydrate** [,kɑːbəʊ'haɪdreɪt] n (U) Kohle(n)hydrat das.
➤ **carbohydrates** npl [food] Kohle(n)hydrate pl.

**carbon** ['kɑːbən] n - **1.** [element] Kohlenstoff der - **2.** = carbon copy - **3.** = carbon paper.

**carbonated** ['kɑːbəneɪtɪd] adj mit Kohlensäure versetzt.

**carbon copy** n - **1.** [document] Durchschlag der - **2.** fig [exact copy]: **she's a ~ of her mother** sie ist ihrer Mutter wie aus dem Gesicht geschnitten.

**carbon dating** [-'deɪtɪŋ] n (U) Radiokarbonmethode die.

**carbon dioxide** [-daɪ'ɒksaɪd] n Kohlendioxyd das.

**carbon fibre** n (U) Kohlenstofffaser die.

**carbon monoxide** n Kohlenmonoxid das.

**carbon paper** n (U) Kohlepapier das.

**car-boot sale** n Br auf einem (Park)platz oder in einem Parkhaus stattfindender Trödelmarkt.

**carburettor** Br, **carburetor** Am [,kɑːbə'retəʳ] n Vergaser der.

**carcass** ['kɑːkəs] n [of animal] Kadaver der.

**carcinogenic** [,kɑːsɪnə'dʒenɪk] adj krebserregend.

**card** [kɑːd] n - **1.** [playing card] Spielkarte die; **to play one's ~s right** fig seine Karten richtig auslspielen; **to put OR lay one's ~s on the table** die Karten auf den Tisch legen - **2.** [for identification] Karte die - **3.** [greetings card] Grußkarte die - **4.** [postcard] Postkarte die - **5.** (U) [cardboard] Pappe die.
➤ **cards** npl [game] Kartenspiel das; **to play ~s** Karten spielen.
➤ **on the cards** Br, **in the cards** Am adv inf durchaus möglich.

**cardamom** ['kɑːdəməm] n Kardamom der OR das.

**cardboard** ['kɑːdbɔːd] n (U) Pappe die ⟨⟩ comp Papp-.

**cardboard box** n Pappkarton der.

**card-carrying** adj eingetragen.

**card catalog** n Am Kartei die.

**cardiac** ['kɑːdiæk] adj Herz-.

**cardiac arrest** n Herzstillstand der.

**cardigan** ['kɑːdɪgən] n Strickjacke die.

**cardinal** ['kɑːdɪnl] adj äußerste, -r, -s; ~ **sin** Todsünde die ⟨⟩ n RELIG Kardinal der.

**cardinal number, cardinal numeral** n Kardinalzahl die.

**card index** n Br Kartei die.

**cardiograph** ['kɑːdɪəgrɑːf] n Kardiograf der.

**cardiology** [,kɑːdɪ'ɒlədʒɪ] n Kardiologie die.

**cardiovascular** [,kɑːdɪəʊ'væskjʊləʳ] adj kardiovaskular.

**cardsharp** ['kɑːdʃɑːp] n Falschspieler der, -in die.

**card table** n Kartentisch der.

**card vote** n Br Abstimmung durch Wahlmänner bei Gewerkschaftswahlen in Großbritannien.

**care** [keəʳ] n - **1.** [protection, looking after] Pflege die; **to be in ~** Br in Pflege sein; **to be taken into ~** in Pflege genommen werden; **to take ~ of sb** [look after] für jn sorgen; **to take ~ of sth** etw erledigen; **take ~!** inf [when saying goodbye] pass auf dich auf!, gib auf dich

Acht! - 2. [caution] Sorgfalt die; to take ~ to do sthg darauf achten, etw zu tun; take ~! [be careful] pass auf!, sei vorsichtig! - 3. [cause of worry] Sorge die <> vi - 1. [be concerned]: you really don't ~, do you? dir ist das wohl ganz egal, wie?; to ~ about sb/sthg an jn/etw denken - 2. [mind] sich kümmern; I don't ~ if/that/how ... es ist mir egal, ob/dass/wie ...; who ~s? wen interessiert das schon?; I don't honestly ~ what I look like es kümmert OR interessiert mich ehrlich gesagt nicht, wie ich aussehe; I couldn't ~ less! inf das ist mir völlig egal!

➤ care of prep bei.

➤ care for vt fus [like] Interesse haben für; I don't much ~ for opera ich mache mir nichts aus Oper; does she still ~ for him? bedeutet er ihr noch immer viel?; would you ~ for a drink? möchtest du etwas trinken?

**CARE** [keə'] (abbr of **Cooperative for American Relief Everywhere**) n CARE.

**career** [kə'rɪə'] n - 1. [job] Beruf der; ~s such as acting, writing ... Berufe wie Schauspieler, Autor ...; he's hoping for a ~ in the sciences er möchte eine wissenschaftliche Laufbahn einschlagen; to make a ~ out of sthg etw zum Beruf machen - 2. [working life] Laufbahn die; [in retrospect] Werdegang der - 3. [very successful] Karriere die; to make a ~ for o.s. Karriere machen; she had a very successful ~ as a businesswoman sie hat als Geschäftsfrau Karriere gemacht <> vi rasen.

**careerist** [kə'rɪərɪst] n pej Karrieremacher der, -in die.

**careers** [kə'rɪəz] comp Berufs-.

**careers adviser** n Berufsberater der, -in die.

**career woman** n Karrierefrau die.

**carefree** ['keəfriː] adj sorglos, sorgenfrei.

**careful** ['keəful] adj - 1. [cautious] vorsichtig; to be ~ with sthg vorsichtig mit etw umliegehen; to be ~ to do sthg darauf achten, etw zu tun - 2. [thorough] gründlich, sorgfältig.

**carefully** ['keəflɪ] adv - 1. [cautiously] vorsichtig - 2. [thoroughly] gründlich, sorgfältig.

**careless** ['keəlɪs] adj - 1. [inattentive] unaufmerksam - 2. [unconcerned] nachlässig.

**carelessly** ['keəlɪslɪ] adv - 1. [inattentively] unaufmerksam - 2. [unconcernedly] nachlässig.

**carelessness** ['keəlɪsnɪs] n - 1. [inattention] Unaufmerksamkeit die - 2. [lack of concern] Nachlässigkeit die.

**carer** ['keərə'] n Pfleger der, -in die.

**caress** [kə'res] n Liebkosung die <> vt liebkosen.

**caretaker** ['keə,teɪkə'] n Br Hausmeister der, -in die.

**caretaker government** n Übergangsregierung die.

**car ferry** n Autofähre die.

**cargo** ['kɑːgəʊ] (pl -es OR -s) n Ladung die, Fracht die <> comp Fracht-.

**car hire** n (U) Br Autovermietung die.

**Caribbean** [Br kærɪ'biːən, Am kə'rɪbɪən] adj karibisch <> n - 1. [sea]: the ~ (Sea) das Karibische Meer, die Karibische See - 2. [region]: the ~ die Karibik.

**caribou** ['kærɪbuː] (pl inv OR -s) n Karibu das OR der.

**caricature** ['kærɪkə,tjʊə'] n lit & fig Karikatur die <> vt karikieren.

**caries** ['keəriːz] n Karies die.

**caring** ['keərɪŋ] adj mitfühlend.

**caring professions** npl: the ~ die Pflegeberufe.

**carnage** ['kɑːnɪdʒ] n (U) Gemetzel das.

**carnal** ['kɑːnl] adj literary fleischlich.

**carnation** [kɑː'neɪʃn] n Nelke die.

**carnival** ['kɑːnɪvl] n - 1. [festive occasion] Karneval der - 2. [fair] Volksfest das, Jahrmarkt der.

**carnivore** ['kɑːnɪvɔː'] n Fleischfresser der.

**carnivorous** [kɑː'nɪvərəs] adj Fleisch fressend.

**carol** ['kærəl] n: (Christmas) ~ Weihnachtslied das.

**carouse** [kə'raʊz] vi zechen.

**carousel** [,kærə'sel] n - 1. esp Am [at fair] Karussell das - 2. [at airport] Gepäckband das.

**carp** [kɑːp] (pl inv OR -s) n Karpfen der <> vi nörgeln; to ~ about sb über jn meckern.

**car park** n Br Parkplatz der.

**carpenter** ['kɑːpəntə'] n [working on buildings] Zimmermann der; [making furniture] Tischler der, Schreiner der.

**carpentry** ['kɑːpəntrɪ] n [working on buildings] Zimmerhandwerk das; [making furniture] Tischlerhandwerk das, Schreinerhandwerk das.

**carpet** ['kɑːpɪt] n - 1. [floor covering] Teppich(boden) der; to sweep sthg under the ~ fig etw unter den Teppich kehren - 2. fig [of flowers, snow] Teppich der <> vt - 1. [floor] mit Teppich(boden) auslegen - 2. fig: ~ed with snow schneebedeckt.

**carpet slipper** n Pantoffel der.

**carpet sweeper** [-,swiːpə'] n Teppichkehrmaschine die.

**car phone** n Autotelefon das.

**car pool** n Br [fleet of cars] Wagenpark der.

**carport** ['kɑː,pɔːt] n Unterstellplatz der.

**car radio** n Autoradio das.

**car rental** n (U) Am Autovermietung die.

**carriage** ['kærɪdʒ] n - **1.** [horsedrawn vehicle] Kutsche die - **2.** Br [railway coach] Wagen der - **3.** [transport of goods] Transport der; ~ **paid** OR **free** Br frachtfrei, frei Haus; ~ **forward** Br Fracht zahlt Empfänger - **4.** [on typewriter] Wagen der - **5.** (U) literary [deportment] Karosse die.

**carriage return** n Wagenrücklauf der.

**carriageway** ['kærɪdʒweɪ] n Br Fahrbahn die.

**carrier** ['kærɪə'] n - **1.** COMM Spediteur der - **2.** [of disease] Überträger der, -in die - **3.** MIL: (aircraft) ~ Flugzeugträger der - **4.** [on bicycle] Gepäckträger der - **5.** = **carrier bag**.

**carrier bag** n Tragetasche die.

**carrier pigeon** n Brieftaube die.

**carrion** ['kærɪən] n (U) Aas das.

**carrot** ['kærət] n - **1.** [vegetable] Möhre die, Karotte die - **2.** inf [incentive] Köder der.

**carry** ['kærɪ] (pt & pp -ied) vt - **1.** [transport] tragen - **2.** [be equipped with] dabeilhaben, mit sich führen - **3.** [disease] übertragen - **4.** [involve] mit sich bringen - **5.** [motion, proposal] anlnehmen - **6.** [be pregnant with] tragen - **7.** MATH: **5 ~ 1** 5 Rest 1 <> vi [sound] tragen.

→ **carry away** vt fus: **to get carried away** sich hinreißen lassen.

→ **carry forward** vt sep übertragen.

→ **carry off** vt sep - **1.** [plan, performance] schaffen - **2.** [prize] gewinnen.

→ **carry on** vt fus [continue] fortlführen; **to ~ on doing sthg** etw weiterhin tun <> vi - **1.** [continue] weiterlmachen; **to ~ on with sthg** mit etw weiterlmachen - **2.** inf [make a fuss] sich auf lführen - **3.** inf [have affair]: **to ~ on with sb** ein Verhältnis mit jm haben.

→ **carry out** vt fus [task, plan, order] auslführen; [experiment, investigation] durchlführen; [promise, threat] wahr machen.

→ **carry through** vt sep [accomplish] durchlführen.

**carryall** ['kærɪɔːl] n Am Reisetasche die.

**carrycot** ['kærɪkɒt] n esp Br Babytragetasche die.

**carry-on** n Br inf Durcheinander das.

**carry-out** n Am & Scot Essen oder Getränke zum Mitnehmen.

**carsick** ['kɑːˌsɪk] adj reisekrank.

**cart** [kɑːt] n - **1.** [vehicle] Wagen der - **2.** COMPUT abbr of **cartridge** - **3.** Am [for shopping]: **(shopping** OR **grocery) ~** Einkaufswagen der <> vt inf schleppen.

**carte blanche** n uneingeschränkte Vollmacht.

**cartel** [kɑːˈtel] n Kartell das.

**cartilage** ['kɑːtɪlɪdʒ] n (U) Knorpel der.

**carton** ['kɑːtn] n Karton der; [of cream, yoghurt] Becher der; [of milk] Tüte die.

**cartoon** [kɑːˈtuːn] n - **1.** [satirical drawing] Karikatur die - **2.** [comic strip] Comic(strip) der - **3.** [film] Zeichentrickfilm der.

**cartoonist** [kɑːˈtuːnɪst] n - **1.** [of satirical drawings] Karikaturist der, -in die - **2.** [of comic strips] Comiczeichner der, -in die.

**cartridge** ['kɑːtrɪdʒ] n - **1.** [for gun, pen] Patrone die - **2.** [for camera] Film der - **3.** [for record player] Tonabnehmer der.

**cartridge paper** n Zeichenpapier das.

**cartwheel** ['kɑːtwiːl] n Rad das; **to do ~s** Rad schlagen.

**carve** [kɑːv] vt - **1.** [wood] schnitzen; [stone] hauen, meißeln - **2.** [meat] auf lschneiden, in Scheiben schneiden - **3.** [cut] ritzen <> vi den Braten/das Fleisch auf lschneiden.

→ **carve out** vt sep: **to ~ out a career** sich eine Karriere auf lbauen.

→ **carve up** vt sep [divide] auf lteilen.

**carving** ['kɑːvɪŋ] n - **1.** (U) [art, work] Schnitzerei die - **2.** [object] Skulptur die.

**carving knife** n Tranchiermesser das.

**car wash** n - **1.** [process] Autowaschen das - **2.** [place] Autowaschanlage die.

**Casanova** [kæsəˈnəʊvə] n Casanova der.

**cascade** [kæˈskeɪd] n Wasserfall der <> vi herablstürzen.

**case** [keɪs] n - **1.** [gen] Fall der; **a ~ in point** ein typischer Fall; **that's not the ~** das ist nicht der Fall; **in that ~** in dem Fall; **unless it's a draw, in which ~ I'll make the decision** außer bei einem Unentschieden, dann treffe ich die Entscheidung; **as** OR **whatever the ~ may be** je nachdem; **in ~ of emergency/doubt** im Notfall/Zweifelsfall - **2.** [argument] Angelegenheit die, Sache die; **the ~ for the defence** die Verteidigung - **3.** [packing case] Kiste die; [small box] Kästchen das; [for glasses, cigarettes] Etui das; [for musical instrument] Kasten der - **4.** Br [suitcase] Koffer der.

→ **in any case** adv wie dem auch sei, wie auch immer.

→ **in case** conj falls <> adv: **(just) in ~** für alle Fälle.

**case history** n Vorgeschichte die.

**casement window** ['keɪsmənt-] n Flügelfenster das.

**case study** n Fallstudie die.

**cash** [kæʃ] n (U) - **1.** [notes and coins] Bargeld das; **to pay (in) ~** bar bezahlen - **2.** inf [money] Geld das; **I'm a bit short of ~** ich bin etwas knapp bei Kasse - **3.** [payment]: **~ in advance** Vorkasse die; **~ on delivery** zahlbar bei Empfang <> vt einlösen.

→ **cash in** vi: **to ~ in on sthg** inf von etw profitieren.

**cash and carry** n [for retailers] Großhandelsmarkt der; [for public] Verbrauchermarkt der.

**cashbook** ['kæʃbʊk] n Kassenbuch das.

**cash box** n Geldkassette die.

**cash card** n Kontokarte die.

**cash crop** n für den Verkauf bestimmte Feldfrucht.

**cash desk** n Br Kasse die.

**cash discount** n Skonto das.

**cash dispenser** [-dɪˌspensə'] n Geldautomat der.

**cashew (nut)** ['kæʃuː-] n Cashewnuss die.

**cash flow** n Cash-flow der.

**cashier** [kæ'ʃɪə'] n Kassierer der, -in die.

**cash machine** n = cash dispenser.

**cashmere** [kæʃ'mɪə'] n Kaschmir der <> comp Kaschmir-.

**cash payment** n Barzahlung die.

**cashpoint (machine)** ['kæʃpɔɪnt-] n Geldautomat der.

**cash price** n Barpreis der.

**cash register** n Registrierkasse die.

**cash sale** n Barverkauf der.

**casing** ['keɪsɪŋ] n Gehäuse das; [of cable] Hülle die; [of tyre] Mantel der.

**casino** [kə'siːnəʊl] (pl -s) n Kasino das.

**cask** [kɑːsk] n Fass das.

**casket** ['kɑːskɪt] n - 1. [for jewels] (Schmuck)kästchen das - 2. Am [coffin] Sarg der.

**Caspian Sea** ['kæspɪən-] n: the ~ das Kaspische Meer.

**casserole** ['kæsərəʊl] n - 1. [stew] Fleischeintopf der - 2. [pan] Schmortopf der, Kasserolle die.

**cassette** [kæ'set] n Kassette die.

**cassette deck** n Kassettendeck das.

**cassette player** n Kassettenspieler der.

**cassette recorder** n Kassettenrekorder der.

**cassock** ['kæsək] n [Catholic] Soutane die; [Protestant] Talar der.

**cast** [kɑːst] (pt & pp cast) n - 1. [of play, film] Besetzung die - 2. MED Gipsverband der <> vt - 1. [gen] werfen; to ~ one's eye over sthg einen Blick auf etw (A) werfen; to ~ doubt on sthg etw in Zweifel ziehen; to ~ a spell on sb jn verhexen - 2. [choose for play, film]: she ~ him in the role of Hamlet sie gab ihm die Rolle des Hamlet - 3. POL: to ~ one's vote seine Stimme abⅼgeben - 4. [metal, statue] gießen - 5. [skin]: to ~ its skin sich häuten <> vi [in fishing] die Angel ausⅼwerfen.

◆ **cast about, cast around** vi: to ~ about for sthg nach etw suchen.

◆ **cast aside** vt sep fallen lassen.

◆ **cast off** vt sep fml [get rid of] abⅼlegen <> vi - 1. NAUT abⅼlegen - 2. [in knitting] Maschen abⅼnehmen.

◆ **cast on** vi [in knitting] Maschen anⅼschlagen.

**castanets** [ˌkæstə'nets] npl Kastagnetten pl.

**castaway** ['kɑːstəweɪ] n Schiffbrüchige der, die.

**caste** [kɑːst] n [class] Kaste die.

**caster** ['kɑːstə'] n Rolle die.

**caster sugar** n Br Feinkristallzucker der.

**castigate** ['kæstɪgeɪt] vt fml [criticize] tadeln.

**casting** ['kɑːstɪŋ] n (U) [for film, play] Rollenverteilung die.

**casting vote** n entscheidende Stimme.

**cast iron** n (U) Gusseisen das.

◆ **cast-iron** adj - 1. [made of cast iron] gusseisern - 2. fig [will] eisern; [alibi, guarantee] hieb- und stichfest.

**castle** ['kɑːsl] n - 1. [fortress] Burg die; [mansion] Schloss das - 2. [in chess] Turm der.

**castoff** ['kɑːstɒf] n abgelegtes Kleidungsstück.

**castor** ['kɑːstə'] n = caster.

**castor oil** n Rizinusöl das.

**castor sugar** n = caster sugar.

**castrate** [kæ'streɪt] vt kastrieren.

**castration** [kæ'streɪʃn] n Kastration die.

**casual** ['kæʒʊəl] adj - 1. [relaxed] gleichgültig - 2. pej [offhand] nachlässig - 3. [chance] zufällig - 4. [clothes]: ~ clothes zwanglose Kleidung; ~ wear Freizeitkleidung - 5. [work, worker] Gelegenheits-.

**casually** ['kæʒʊəlɪ] adv - 1. [in a relaxed manner] gleichgültig - 2. [dress] leger, zwanglos.

**casualty** ['kæʒʊəltɪ] (pl -ies) n - 1. [dead person] Todesopfer das; [injured person] Unfallopfer das - 2. = casualty department - 3. fig [of change, policy, system] Opfer das.

**casualty department** n Ambulanz die.

**cat** [kæt] n - 1. [domestic] Katze die; to let the ~ out of the bag die Katze aus dem Sack lassen; to be like a ~ on hot bricks Br OR on a hot tin roof Am wie auf glühenden Kohlen sitzen; that's put the ~ among the pigeons Br das hast du ja toll hingekriegt; it's raining ~s and dogs es regnet in Strömen; she thinks she's the ~'s whiskers Br sie hält sich für was Besonderes - 2. [wild] Raubkatze die - 3. (abbr of catalytic converter) AUT Kat der.

**cataclysmic** [ˌkætə'klɪzmɪk] adj [change] umwälzend; [disaster] katastrophal.

**catacombs** ['kætəkuːmz] npl Katakomben pl.

**Catalan** ['kætəˌlæn] adj katalanisch <> n

**- 1.** [person] Katalane *der*, -nin *die* **- 2.** [language] Katalanisch(e) *das*.

**catalogue** *Br*, **catalog** *Am* ['kætəlɒg] *n* **- 1.** [of items] Katalog *der* **- 2.** *fig* [of accidents, disasters] Serie *die*, Reihe *die* ⋄ *vt* katalogisieren.

**Catalonia** [ˌkætə'ləʊnɪə] *n* Katalonien *nt*.

**Catalonian** [ˌkætə'ləʊnɪən] *adj* katalonisch ⋄ *n* [person] Katalonier *der*, -in *die*.

**catalyst** ['kætəlɪst] *n* **- 1.** CHEM Katalysator *der* **- 2.** *fig* [cause] Auslöser *der*.

**catalytic converter** [ˌkætə'lɪtɪk-] *n* Katalysator *der*.

**catamaran** [ˌkætəmə'ræn] *n* Katamaran *der*.

**catapult** *Br* ['kætəpʊlt] *n* **- 1.** [hand-held] Katapult *das* OR *der*, (Stein)schleuder *die* **- 2.** HIST [machine] Katapult *das* ODER *der* ⋄ *vt* schleudern; **she was ~ed to fame** *fig* sie wurde über Nacht berühmt.

**cataract** ['kætərækt] *n* **- 1.** MED grauer Star **- 2.** *literary* [waterfall] Wasserfall *der*.

**catarrh** [kə'tɑːr] *n* Katarrh *der*.

**catastrophe** [kə'tæstrəfɪ] *n* Katastrophe *die*.

**catastrophic** [ˌkætə'strɒfɪk] *adj* katastrophal.

**cat burglar** *n Br* Fassadenkletterer *der*.

**catcall** ['kætkɔːl] *n* Buhruf *der*.

**catch** [kætʃ] (*pt* & *pp* **caught**) *vt* **- 1.** [ball, fish, animal] fangen **- 2.** [criminal] fassen **- 3.** [discover] überraschen; **to ~ sb doing sthg** jn bei etw ertappen **- 4.** [train, plane] erreichen **- 5.** [hear clearly] hören, verstehen **- 6.** [interest] wecken; [imagination] anregen; **I tried to ~ his attention** ich versuchte, ihn auf mich aufmerksam zu machen; **to ~ sight of sb/sthg, to ~ a glimpse of sb/sthg** jn/etw flüchtig zu Gesicht bekommen **- 8.** [illness, disease]: **to ~ malaria/measles** an Malaria/Masern erkranken; **to ~ a cold** sich erkälten **- 9.** [trap]: **to ~ one's finger in the door** sich den Finger in der Tür einklemmen **- 10.** [light]: **the watch face glinted when it caught the light** das Zifferblatt schimmerte, als das Licht darauf fiel **- 11.** [strike] treffen ⋄ *vi* **- 1.** [clothing] hängen bleiben; [foot, limb] stecken bleiben **- 2.** [fire] angehen ⋄ *n* **- 1.** [of ball etc]: **good ~!** sehr gut gefangen! **- 2.** [of fish] Fang *der* **- 3.** [fastener] Verschluss *der* **- 4.** [snag] Haken *der*.

⬥ **catch at** *vt fus* greifen nach.

⬥ **catch on** *vi* **- 1.** [become popular] Anklang finden, sich durchsetzen **- 2.** *inf* [understand] begreifen; **to ~ on to sthg** hinter etw (A) kommen, etw herausfinden.

⬥ **catch out** *vt sep* [trick] hereinlegen.

⬥ **catch up** *vt sep* **- 1.** [come level with] einlholen **- 2.** [involve]: **to get caught up in sthg** in etw (A) verwickelt werden ⋄ *vi* auflholen; **to ~ up on sthg** etw nachlholen.

⬥ **catch up with** *vt fus* **- 1.** [in race, work] einlholen **- 2.** [criminal] ausfindig machen.

**catch-22** [-twentɪ'tuː] *n*: **we're in a ~ situation** wir sind in einer Zwickmühle.

**catch-all** *adj*: **~ term** universeller Begriff.

**catching** ['kætʃɪŋ] *adj* ansteckend.

**catchment area** ['kætʃmənt-] *n* Einzugsgebiet *das*.

**catchphrase** ['kætʃfreɪz] *n* [of performer] Lieblingsspruch *der*.

**catchword** ['kætʃwɜːd] *n* [slogan] Schlagwort *das*.

**catchy** ['kætʃɪ] (*compar* **-ier**; *superl* **-iest**) *adj*: **a ~ tune** ein Ohrwurm.

**catechism** ['kætɪkɪzm] *n* Katechismus *der*.

**categorical** [ˌkætɪ'gɒrɪkl] *adj* kategorisch.

**categorically** [ˌkætɪ'gɒrɪklɪ] *adv* kategorisch.

**categorize, -ise** ['kætəgəraɪz] *vt* kategorisieren.

**category** ['kætəgərɪ] (*pl* **-ies**) *n* Kategorie *die*.

**cater** ['keɪtər] *vi* [provide food]: **to ~ for sb** jn mit Lebensmitteln versorgen.

⬥ **cater for** *vt fus Br* **- 1.** [tastes, needs] befriedigen **- 2.** [anticipate]: **I hadn't ~ed for that** darauf war ich nicht vorbereitet.

**caterer** ['keɪtərər] *n* Lebensmittellieferant *der*, -in *die*.

**catering** ['keɪtərɪŋ] *n (U)* [industry] Gaststättengewerbe *das;* [at wedding, party] Essen *das*.

**caterpillar** ['kætəpɪlər] *n* Raupe *die*.

**caterpillar tracks** *npl* Gleisketten *pl*, Ketten *pl*.

**cat flap** *n Br* Katzenklappe *die*.

**catharsis** [kə'θɑːsɪs] *n fml* Katharsis *die*, Läuterung *die*.

**cathedral** [kə'θiːdrəl] *n* Kathedrale *die*.

**catheter** ['kæθɪtər] *n* Katheter *der*.

**cathode ray tube** ['kæθəʊd-] *n* Kathodenstrahlröhre *die*.

**Catholic** ['kæθlɪk] *adj* katholisch ⋄ *n* Katholik *der*, -in *die*.

⬥ **catholic** *adj*: **to have very ~ tastes** vielseitig interessiert sein.

**Catholicism** [kə'θɒlɪsɪzm] *n* Katholizismus *der*.

**catkin** ['kætkɪn] *n* Kätzchen *das*.

**cat litter** *n* Katzenstreu *das*.

**Catseyes®** ['kætsaɪz] *npl Br* Katzenaugen *pl*.

**catsuit** ['kætsuːt] *n Br* einteiliger, enganliegender Hosenanzug für Frauen.

**catsup** ['kætsəp] *n Am* Ketschup *der*.

**cattle** ['kætl] *npl* Vieh *das*.

**cattle grid** n Br Gitter auf Landstraßen, um Vieh am Überqueren zu hindern.

**catty** ['kætɪ] (compar -ier; superl -iest) adj inf pej [spiteful] gehässig.

**catwalk** ['kætwɔːk] n Laufsteg der.

**Caucasian** [kɔː'keɪzjən] adj kaukasisch ◇ n - **1.** GEOGR Kaukasier der, -in die - **2.** [white person] Weiße der, die.

**caucus** ['kɔːkəs] n - **1.** Am POL Sitzung die, Versammlung die - **2.** Br POL Gremium das.

**CAUCUS**

> Die amerikanischen „caucuses" sind riesige politische Versammlungen der beiden großen politischen Parteien (Republikaner und Demokraten), auf denen diese ihre Kandidaten auswählen und ihre Programme formulieren.

**caught** [kɔːt] pt & pp ⊳ catch.

**cauldron** ['kɔːldrən] n Kessel der.

**cauliflower** ['kɒlɪˌflaʊəʳ] n Blumenkohl der.

**causal** ['kɔːzl] adj kausal.

**cause** [kɔːz] n - **1.** [reason why sthg happens] Ursache die - **2.** [grounds]: ~ (for) Grund der (zu); **to have no ~ to do sthg** keinen Grund haben, etw zu tun; **I have no ~ for complaint** ich habe keinen Grund zur Klage - **3.** [movement, aim] Sache die; **for a good ~** für eine gute Sache ◇ vt verursachen; **to ~ sb to do sthg** jn veranlassen, etw zu tun; **heavy rain ~d the match to be postponed** aufgrund starken Regens musste das Spiel verschoben werden.

**causeway** ['kɔːzweɪ] n Damm der.

**caustic** ['kɔːstɪk] adj - **1.** CHEM ätzend - **2.** fig [comment] bissig; ~ **wit** beißender Humor.

**caustic soda** n Ätznatron das.

**cauterize, -ise** ['kɔːtəraɪz] vt ausⱵbrennen.

**caution** ['kɔːʃn] n - **1.** [care] Vorsicht die; [prudence] Umsicht die; **'proceed with ~'** 'vorsichtig vorgehen' - **2.** [warning] Warnung die - **3.** Br LAW Verwarnung die ◇ vt - **1.** [warn]: **to ~ sb against doing sthg** jn davor warnen, etw zu tun - **2.** Br LAW verwarnen.

**cautionary** ['kɔːʃənrɪ] adj belehrend.

**cautious** ['kɔːʃəs] adj [careful] vorsichtig; [prudent] umsichtig.

**cautiously** ['kɔːʃəslɪ] adv [carefully] vorsichtig; [prudently] umsichtig.

**cautiousness** ['kɔːʃəsnɪs] n Vorsicht die.

**cavalier** [ˌkævə'lɪəʳ] adj unbekümmert, gleichgültig.

**cavalry** ['kævlrɪ] n (U) - **1.** [on horseback] Kavallerie die - **2.** [in armoured vehicles] motorisierte Truppen pl.

**cave** [keɪv] n Höhle die.

**cave in** vi - **1.** [physically collapse] einⱵstürzen - **2.** [give up] nachⱵgeben.

**caveman** ['keɪvmæn] (pl -men [-men]) n Höhlenmensch der.

**cavern** ['kævən] n Höhle die.

**cavernous** ['kævənəs] adj [room, building] höhlenartig.

**caviar(e)** ['kævɪɑːʳ] n Kaviar der.

**caving** ['keɪvɪŋ] n Br Höhlenklettern das.

**cavity** ['kævətɪ] (pl -ies) n - **1.** [in object, structure] Hohlraum der; [in body] Höhle die - **2.** [in tooth] Loch das.

**cavity wall insulation** n (U) Br Schaumisolierung die.

**cavort** [kə'vɔːt] vi herumⱵtollen.

**cayenne (pepper)** [keɪ'en-] n Cayennepfeffer der.

**CB** n - **1.** (abbr of **Citizens' Band**) CB - **2.** (abbr of **Companion of (the Order of) the Bath**) Auszeichnung des britischen Königreichs oder deren Inhaber.

**CBC** (abbr of **Canadian Broadcasting Corporation**) n nationale kanadische Rundfunkanstalt.

**CBE** (abbr of **Companion of (the Order of) the British Empire**) n Auszeichnung des britischen Königreichs oder deren Inhaber.

**CBI** (abbr of **Confederation of British Industry**) n britischer Unternehmerverband.

**CBS** (abbr of **Columbia Broadcasting System**) n CBS.

**cc** n (abbr of **cubic centimetre**) cm³ ◇ abbr of **carbon copy.**

**CCTV** (abbr of **closed circuit television**) n betriebs- oder schulinternes Fernsehen.

**CD** n (abbr of **compact disc**) CD die.

**CDI** (abbr of **compact disc interactive**) n CDI die.

**CD player** n CD-Player der, CD-Spieler der.

**Cdr.** (abbr of **commander**) n Kdt.

**CD-R** n (abbr of **compact disc recordable**) CD-R die.

**CD-ROM** [ˌsiːdiː'rɒm] (abbr of **compact disc read-only memory**) n CD-ROM die.

**CDT** (abbr of **Central Daylight Time**) n Sommerzeit in der zentralen Zeitzone der USA.

**CDW** (abbr of **collision damage waiver**) Versicherungspolice für Mietfahrzeuge.

**CE** abbr of **Church of England.**

**cease** [siːs] fml vt beenden, einⱵstellen; **to ~ doing** OR **to do sthg** auf ⱵÞhören, etw zu tun ◇ vi auf ⱵÞhören, enden.

**cease-fire** n Waffenruhe die.

**ceaseless** ['siːslɪs] adj fml unaufhörlich.

**ceaselessly** [ˈsiːslɪslɪ] *adv* unaufhörlich.

**cedar (tree)** [ˈsiːdəˀ-] *n* Zeder *die*.

**cede** [siːd] *vt* abltreten; **to ~ sthg to sb** etw an jn abltreten.

**cedilla** [sɪˈdɪlə] *n* Cedille *die*.

**Ceefax®** [ˈsiːfæks] *n Br* Videotext *der* BBC.

**ceilidh** [ˈkeɪlɪ] *n besondere Tanzveranstaltung in Schottland und Irland mit traditioneller Musik*.

**CEILIDH**

In Schottland und Irland sind die „ceilidhs" traditionelle gesellige Abende mit Volksmusik, Tanz und Gesang. Ursprünglich traf man sich dazu im Kreise der Familie und Freunde, heute versteht man darunter meist öffentliche Tanzveranstaltungen.

**ceiling** [ˈsiːlɪŋ] *n* - **1.** [of room] Decke *die* - **2.** [limit] oberste Grenze.

**celebrate** [ˈselɪbreɪt] *vt* - **1.** [victory, anniversary] feiern - **2.** [praise] preisen - **3.** RELIG zelebrieren ⟨⟩ *vi* feiern.

**celebrated** [ˈselɪbreɪtɪd] *adj* berühmt.

**celebration** [ˌselɪˈbreɪʃn] *n* - **1.** (U) [activity] Feiern *das* - **2.** [event] Feier *die*.

**celebrity** [sɪˈlebrətɪ] (*pl* -**ies**) *n* [star] Star *der*, Berühmtheit *die*.

**celeriac** [sɪˈlerɪæk] *n* Knollensellerie *der or die*.

**celery** [ˈselərɪ] *n* Stangensellerie *der or die*.

**celestial** [sɪˈlestjəl] *adj* Himmels-.

**celibacy** [ˈselɪbəsɪ] *n* RELIG Zölibat *der or das*; *fig* Enthaltsamkeit *die*.

**celibate** [ˈselɪbət] *adj* RELIG zölibatär; *fig* enthaltsam.

**cell** [sel] *n* - **1.** [gen] Zelle *die* - **2.** COMPUT Feld *das*.

**cellar** [ˈseləˀ] *n* - **1.** [basement] Keller *der* - **2.** [stock of wine] Weinkeller *der*.

**cellist** [ˈtʃelɪst] *n* Cellist *der*, -in *die*.

**cello** [ˈtʃeləʊ] (*pl* -**s**) *n* Cello *das*.

**Cellophane®** [ˈseləfeɪn] *n* Zellophan *das*.

**cellphone** [ˈselfəʊn], **cellular phone** [ˈseljʊləˀ-] *n* Mobiltelefon *das*, Handy *das*.

**cellulite** [ˈseljʊlaɪt] *n* Zellulitis *die*.

**Celluloid®** [ˈseljʊlɔɪd] *n* Zelluloid *das*.

**cellulose** [ˈseljʊləʊs] *n* Zellulose *die*.

**Celsius** [ˈselsɪəs] *adj* Celsius-, Celsius; **20 degrees ~** 20 Grad Celsius.

**Celt** [kelt] *n* Kelte *der*, -tin *die*.

**Celtic** [ˈkeltɪk] *adj* keltisch ⟨⟩ *n* [language] Keltisch(e) *das*.

**cement** [sɪˈment] *n* (U) - **1.** [for concrete] Zement *der* - **2.** [glue] Klebstoff *der* ⟨⟩ *vt* - **1.** [cover with

cement] betonieren - **2.** [glue] kleben - **3.** *fig* [friendship] festigen.

**cement mixer** *n* Betonmischmaschine *die*.

**cemetery** [ˈsemɪtrɪ] (*pl* -**ies**) *n* Friedhof *der*.

**cenotaph** [ˈsenətɑːf] *n* Mahnmal *das*.

**censor** [ˈsensəˀ] *n* Zensor *der* ⟨⟩ *vt* zensieren.

**censorship** [ˈsensəʃɪp] *n* Zensur *die*.

**censure** [ˈsenʃəˀ] *n* Tadel *der* ⟨⟩ *vt* tadeln.

**census** [ˈsensəs] (*pl* **censuses**) *n* Volkszählung *die*.

**cent** [sent] *n* Cent *der*.

**centenary** *Br* [senˈtiːnərɪ] (*pl* -**ies**), **centennial** *Am* [senˈtenjəl] *n* Hundertjahrfeier *die*, hundertster Jahrestag.

**center** *n*, *adj* & *vt Am* = **centre**.

**centigrade** [ˈsentɪgreɪd] *adj* Celsius-; **16 degrees ~** 16 Grad Celsius.

**centigram(me)** [ˈsentɪgræm] *n* Zentigramm *das*.

**centilitre** *Br*, **centiliter** *Am* [ˈsentɪˌliːtəˀ] *n* Zentiliter *der*.

**centimetre** *Br*, **centimeter** *Am* [ˈsentɪˌmiːtəˀ] *n* Zentimeter *der*.

**centipede** [ˈsentɪpiːd] *n* Tausendfüßler *der*.

**central** [ˈsentrəl] *adj* zentral; **to be ~ to sthg** [crucial] das Wesentliche an etw (D) sein.

**Central African Republic** *n*: **the ~** die Zentralafrikanische Republik.

**Central America** *n* Mittelamerika *nt*.

**Central Asia** *n* Zentralasien *nt*.

**Central Europe** *n* Mitteleuropa *nt*.

**central government** *n* Zentralregierung *die*.

**central heating** *n* Zentralheizung *die*.

**centralization** [ˌsentrəlaɪˈzeɪʃn] *n* Zentralisierung *die*.

**centralize, -ise** [ˈsentrəlaɪz] *vt* zentralisieren.

**centralized** [ˈsentrəlaɪzd] *adj* zentralisiert.

**central locking** [-ˈlɒkɪŋ] *n* Zentralverriegelung *die*.

**centrally** [ˈsentrəlɪ] *adv* zentral.

**centrally heated** *adj* zentralbeheizt.

**central nervous system** *n* Zentralnervensystem *das*.

**central processing unit** *n* COMPUT [component] Hauptprozessor *der*; [box] Computer *der*, PC *der*.

**central reservation** *n Br* Mittelstreifen *der*.

**centre** *Br*, **center** *Am* [ˈsentəˀ] *n* - **1.** [gen] Mitte *die*, Zentrum *das*; [of circle] Mittelpunkt *der* - **2.** [building, place] Zentrum *das* - **3.** [of event, activity] Zentrum das, Mittelpunkt der; **she always wants to be the ~ of attention** sie will immer im Mittelpunkt stehen; **~ of gravity** Schwerpunkt der - **4.** POL Mitte die - **5.** [in basketball, netball] Center der ⬦ adj - **1.** [middle] Mittel-, mittlere, -r, -s - **2.** POL: **~ party** Partei der Mitte ⬦ vt [text, image] zentrieren; **the party's support is ~d in the capital** die Unterstützung der Partei konzentriert sich auf die Hauptstadt.

➤ **centre around, centre on** vt fus (sich) konzentrieren auf (+ A).

**centre back** n Mittelläufer der, -in die.

**centre-fold** n doppelseitige Abbildung in der Mitte einer Zeitung oder Zeitschrift.

**centre forward** n Mittelstürmer der, -in die.

**centre half** n = centre back.

**centrepiece** Br, **centerpiece** Am ['sentəpiːs] n Hauptelement das.

**centre-spread** n = centre-fold.

**centrifugal force** [sentrɪ'fjuːgl-] n Fliehkraft die.

**century** ['sentʃərɪ] (pl -ies) n Jahrhundert das.

**CEO** (abbr of **chief executive officer**) n Am geschäftsführender Direktor.

**ceramic** [sɪ'ræmɪk] adj keramisch.

➤ **ceramics** npl [objects] Keramik die.

**cereal** ['sɪərɪəl] n - **1.** [crop] Getreide das - **2.** (U) [breakfast food] Frühstücksflocken pl.

**cerebral** ['serɪbrəl] adj - **1.** [intellectual] geistig; [person] durchgeistigt - **2.** ANAT zerebral.

**cerebral palsy** n (U) MED zerebrale Lähmung.

**ceremonial** [serɪ'məʊnjəl] adj feierlich ⬦ n - **1.** [event] Zeremoniell das - **2.** [formality] Förmlichkeit die.

**ceremonious** [serɪ'məʊnjəs] adj förmlich, zeremoniell.

**ceremony** ['serɪmənɪ] (pl -ies) n - **1.** [event] Zeremonie die - **2.** [formality] Förmlichkeit die; **without ~** ohne Umstände; **to stand on ~** sehr förmlich sein.

**cert** [sɜːt] n Br inf: **it's a ~** es ist eine todsichere Sache.

**cert.** abbr of **certificate**.

**certain** ['sɜːtn] adj - **1.** [gen] sicher; **he is ~ to be late** er kommt bestimmt zu spät; **she is ~ of a bronze medal** sie hat eine Bronzemedaille sicher; **to make ~** nachı̈prüfen, sich vergewissern; **I always make ~ of being on time** ich achte immer darauf, pünktlich zu sein; **for ~** sicher - **2.** [particular, individual] gewiss; **she has a ~ charm** sie hat einen gewissen OR ganz eigenen Charme; **to a ~ extent** bis zu einem gewissen Grad - **3.** [named person]: **a ~ Mr Davis** ein gewisser Herr Davis.

**certainly** ['sɜːtnlɪ] adv sicher(lich); **can I bring a friend along? - ~!** kann ich einen Bekannten/eine Bekannte mitbringen? – na klar!; **do you dye your hair? - ~ not!** färbst du dir die Haare? – natürlich nicht!

**certainty** ['sɜːtntɪ] (pl -ies) n Sicherheit die, Gewissheit die; **it's a ~ that he will win the race** es steht fest, dass er das Rennen gewinnen wird.

**CertEd** [sɜːt'ed] (abbr of **Certificate in Education**) n britische Qualifikation für das Lehramt.

**certifiable** [sɜːtɪ'faɪəbl] adj [insane] unzurechnungsfähig.

**certificate** [sə'tɪfɪkət] n Bescheinigung die; [from school, college] Zeugnis das; [of birth] Urkunde die.

**certified** ['sɜːtɪfaɪd] adj - **1.** [teacher, accountant] geprüft - **2.** [document] beglaubigt.

**certified mail** n Am Einschreiben das.

**certified public accountant** n Am Buchhalter der, -in die.

**certify** ['sɜːtɪfaɪ] (pt & pp -ied) vt - **1.** [declare true] bescheinigen; **this is to ~ that ...** hiermit wird bescheinigt, dass ... - **2.** [declare insane] für unzurechnungsfähig erklären.

**cervical** [sə'vaɪkl] adj Gebärmutter-.

**cervical smear** n Abstrich der.

**cervix** ['sɜːvɪks] (pl -ices [-ɪsiːz]) n Gebärmutterhals der.

**cesarean (section)** n Am = caesarean section.

**cessation** [se'seɪʃn] n fml Einstellung die, Ende das; **~ of hostilities** Waffenstillstand der.

**cesspit** ['sespɪt], **cesspool** ['sespuːl] n Senkgrube die.

**CET** (abbr of **Central European Time**) n MEZ.

**cf.** (abbr of **confer**) vgl.

**c/f** (abbr of **carried forward**) ⟹ **carry**.

**CFC** (abbr of **chlorofluorocarbon**) n FCKW das.

**ch.** (abbr of **chapter**) Kap.

**Chad** [tʃæd] n Tschad der.

**chafe** [tʃeɪf] vt [rub] scheuern ⬦ vi - **1.** [be sore] sich wund scheuern - **2.** [be annoyed]: **to ~ at** sthg sich über etw (A) ärgern.

**chaff** [tʃæːf] n [husks] Spreu die.

**chaffinch** ['tʃæfɪntʃ] n Buchfink der.

**chain** [tʃeɪn] n Kette die; **a ~ of events** eine Kette OR Folge von Ereignissen ⬦ vt anketten, mit einer Kette befestigen.

**chain letter** n Kettenbrief der.

**chain reaction** n Kettenreaktion die.

**chain saw** n Kettensäge die.

**chain smoker** n Kettenraucher der, -in die.

**chain store** n Filiale die einer Ladenkette.

**chair** [tʃeəʳ] n - **1.** [gen] Stuhl der - **2.** [university post] Lehrstuhl der - **3.** [of meeting - position] Vorsitz der; [ - person] Vorsitzende der, die; **to take the ~** den Vorsitz führen <> vt [meeting, discussion] den Vorsitz führen bei, leiten.

**chair lift** n Sessellift der.

**chairman** ['tʃeəmən] (pl -men [-mən]) n Vorsitzende der.

**chairmanship** ['tʃeəmənʃɪp] n Vorsitz der.

**chairperson** ['tʃeə,pɜːsnl] (pl -s) n Vorsitzende der, die.

**chairwoman** ['tʃeə,wumən] (pl -women [-,wɪmɪn]) n Vorsitzende die.

**chaise longue** [ʃeɪz'lɒŋ] (pl chaises longues) n Chaiselongue die.

**chalet** ['ʃæleɪ] n [in mountains] Chalet das.

**chalice** ['tʃælɪs] n Kelch der.

**chalk** [tʃɔːk] n - **1.** [for drawing] Kreide die - **2.** (U) [type of rock] Kalkstein der.
➤ **by a long chalk** adv mit Abstand.
➤ **not by a long chalk** adv bei weitem nicht.
➤ **chalk up** vt sep [attain] verzeichnen.

**chalkboard** ['tʃɔːkbɔːd] n Am Tafel die.

**challenge** ['tʃælɪndʒ] n - **1.** [gen] Herausforderung die - **2.** [to authority] Infragestellung die <> vt - **1.** [to fight, competition]: **to ~ sb (to sthg)** jn (zu etw) herausⱡfordern; **I ~ you to beat that!** wetten, dass du das nicht schaffst! - **2.** [question] in Frage stellen.

**challenger** ['tʃælɪndʒəʳ] n Herausforderer der, -derin die.

**challenging** ['tʃælɪndʒɪŋ] adj herausfordernd.

**chamber** ['tʃeɪmbəʳ] n - **1.** [room] Kammer die, Zimmer das - **2.** TECH Kammer die.
➤ **chambers** npl [of barrister] Amtszimmer das.

**chambermaid** ['tʃeɪmbəmeɪd] n Zimmermädchen das.

**chamber music** n Kammermusik die.

**chamber of commerce** n Handelskammer die.

**chamber orchestra** n Kammerorchester das.

**chameleon** [kə'miːljən] n Chamäleon das.

**chamois**[1] ['ʃæmwɑː] (pl inv) n [animal] Gämse die.

**chamois**[2] ['ʃæmɪ] n: **~ (leather)** Waschleder das.

**champ** [tʃæmp] n inf Meister der -in die, Champion der <> vi [horse] geräuschvoll kauen.

**champagne** [,ʃæm'peɪn] n Champagner der.

**champion** ['tʃæmpjən] n - **1.** [of competition] Meister der, -in die, Champion der - **2.** [of cause] Verfechter der, -in die,.

**championship** ['tʃæmpjənʃɪp] n Meisterschaft die.

**chance** [tʃɑːns] n - **1.** (U) [luck] Glück das; **by ~** zufällig, durch Zufall; **by any ~** vielleicht - **2.** [likelihood] Chance die, Möglichkeit die; **she doesn't stand a ~ of winning the match** sie hat keine Chance, das Spiel zu gewinnen; **on the off ~** auf gut Glück - **3.** [opportunity] Gelegenheit die, Chance die - **4.** [risk]: **to take a ~** es riskieren <> adj [meeting] zufällig <> vt - **1.** [risk] riskieren; **he's chancing his luck a bit** er fordert sein Glück heraus - **2.** [happen]: **to ~ to do sthg** zufällig etw tun.

**chancellor** ['tʃɑːnsələʳ] n Kanzler der.

**Chancellor of the Exchequer** n Br Schatzkanzler der.

**chancy** ['tʃɑːnsɪ] (compar -ier; superl -iest) adj inf riskant.

**chandelier** [,ʃændə'lɪəʳ] n Kronleuchter der.

**change** [tʃeɪndʒ] n - **1.** [alteration] Änderung die; [difference] Veränderung die; **~ in sb/sthg** Veränderung in jm/etw; **a ~ for the better** eine Verbesserung; **for the worse** eine Verschlechterung - **2.** [contrast, for variety] Abwechslung die; **that makes a ~!** das ist mal was anderes!; **for a ~** zur Abwechslung - **3.** [switch, replacement] Wechsel der; **a ~ of clothes** Kleidung zum Wechseln - **4.** (U) [money returned after payment] Wechselgeld das - **5.** (U) [coins] Kleingeld das; **have you got ~ for a £5 note?** können Sie mir einen Fünfpfundschein wechseln? <> vt - **1.** [alter, make different] ändern; **to ~ sthg into sthg** etw in etw (A) umⱡwandeln; **to ~ one's mind** seine Meinung ändern - **2.** [replace] ausⱡwechseln; [product purchased] umⱡtauschen - **3.** [switch] wechseln; **to ~ clothes, to get ~d** sich umⱡziehen; **to ~ trains/planes** umⱡsteigen; **to ~ hands** COMM den Besitzer wechseln - **4.** [money] wechseln - **5.** [bed] wechseln; [baby] trockenlegen <> vi - **1.** [alter, become different] sich ändern, sich verändern; **to ~ into sthg** sich in etw (A) verwandeln - **2.** [put on different clothes] sich umⱡziehen; **to ~ into a suit** sich einen Anzug anⱡziehen - **3.** [on train, bus] umⱡsteigen; **all ~!** alles ausⱡsteigen!
➤ **change over** vi: **to ~ over to sthg** auf etw (A) umⱡstellen.

**changeable** ['tʃeɪndʒəbl] adj - **1.** [mood] wechselnd - **2.** [weather] wechselhaft.

**changed** [tʃeɪndʒd] adj [person] verändert.

**change machine** n Geldwechselautomat der.

**change of life** n: **the ~** die Wechseljahre.

**changeover** ['tʃeɪndʒ,əuvəʳ] n: **~ (to sthg)** Umstellung die (auf etw (A)).

**change purse** n Am Portmonee das.

**changing** ['tʃeɪndʒɪŋ] adj sich (ver)ändernd, wechselnd.

**changing room** n [in sports] Umkleideraum der; [in shop] Umkleidekabine die.

**channel** ['tʃænl] (*Br pt* & *pp* **-led;** *cont* **-ling,** *Am pt* & *pp* **-ed;** *cont* **-ing**) *n* **- 1.** [gen] Kanal *der* **- 2.** [route] Fahrrinne *die* ⬦ *vt* [water] leiten.

➤ **Channel** *n:* **the (English) Channel** der Ärmelkanal.

➤ **channels** *npl:* **to go through the proper ~s** sich an die richtigen Stellen wenden.

**channel-hopping** *n* TV *ständiges Umschalten von einem Fernsehkanal zum anderen.*

**Channel Islands** *npl:* **the ~** die Kanalinseln *pl.*

**Channel Tunnel** *n:* **the ~** der Kanaltunnel.

**chant** [tʃɑ:nt] *n* **- 1.** RELIG [song] Gesang *der* **- 2.** [repeated words] Sprechchor *der* ⬦ *vt* **- 1.** RELIG singen **- 2.** [words] im Sprechchor rufen ⬦ *vi* **- 1.** RELIG [sing] singen **- 2.** [repeat words] Sprechchöre anlstimmen.

**chaos** ['keɪɒs] *n* Chaos *das.*

**chaotic** [keɪ'ɒtɪk] *adj* chaotisch.

**chap** [tʃæp] *n Br inf* [man] Kerl *der.*

**chapat(t)i** [tʃə'pætɪ] *n indische Spezialität, ein aus Weizenmehl hergestelltes Fladenbrot.*

**chapel** ['tʃæpl] *n* **- 1.** [part of church] Kapelle *die* **- 2.** [in prison, hospital, school - small church] Kapelle *die;* [ - room] *Raum, in dem Gottesdienste stattfinden.*

**chaperon(e)** ['ʃæpərəʊn] *n* Anstandsdame *die* ⬦ *vt* als Anstandsdame begleiten.

**chaplain** ['tʃæplɪn] *n* Hausgeistliche *der.*

**chapped** [tʃæpt] *adj* aufgesprungen.

**chapter** ['tʃæptə'] *n* Kapitel *das.*

**char** [tʃɑ:'] (*pt* & *pp* **-red;** *cont* **-ring**) *n Br* [cleaner] Putzfrau *die* ⬦ *vt* [burn] verkohlen ⬦ *vi* [work as cleaner] als Putzfrau arbeiten.

**character** ['kærəktə'] *n* **- 1.** [nature - of place] Charakter *der;* [ - of person] Wesen *das;* **out of ~** untypisch; **in ~** typisch **- 2.** [unusual quality, style] Originalität *die* **- 3.** [in film, book, play] Gestalt *die* **- 4.** *inf* [unusual person] Original *das* **- 5.** [letter, symbol] Schriftzeichen *das.*

**character code** *n* COMPUT Zeichenkode *der.*

**characteristic** [ˌkærəktə'rɪstɪk] *adj* charakteristisch ⬦ *n* Kennzeichen *das.*

**characteristically** [ˌkærəktə'rɪstɪklɪ] *adv* charakteristischerweise.

**characterization** [ˌkærəktəraɪ'zeɪʃn] *n* Charakterisierung *die.*

**characterize, -ise** ['kærəktəraɪz] *vt* **- 1.** [typify] kennzeichnen **- 2.** [portray] **to ~ sthg as sthg** etw als etw beschreiben.

**charade** [ʃə'rɑ:d] *n* Farce *die.*

➤ **charades** *n* (U) Scharade *die.*

**charcoal** ['tʃɑ:kəʊl] *n* (U) [for drawing] Kohle *die;* [for barbecue] Holzkohle *die.*

**charge** [tʃɑ:dʒ] *n* **- 1.** [cost] Gebühr *die;* **free of ~** gebührenfrei **- 2.** LAW Anklage *die* **- 3.** [com-

mand, control] Verantwortung *die;* **to take ~ (of sthg)** [of organization, group of people] die Leitung (einer Sache (G)) übernehmen; **in ~** zuständig, verantwortlich; **in ~ of** verantwortlich für **- 4.** ELEC Ladung *die* **- 5.** MIL Sturmangriff *der* ⬦ *vt* **- 1.** [customer] berechnen (+ *D*); **to ~ £ 10 for sthg** für etw 10 Pfund verlangen; **to ~ sthg to sb** jm etw in Rechnung stellen **- 2.** [suspect, criminal] anlklagen; **to ~ sb with sthg** jn wegen etw anlklagen **- 3.** [attack] anlgreifen **- 4.** ELEC auf lladen ⬦ *vi* **- 1.** [ask for payment]: **to ~ sthg (for sthg)** etw berechnen (für etw) **- 2.** [rush] stürmen **- 3.** [attack] anlgreifen.

**chargeable** ['tʃɑ:dʒəbl] *adj* **- 1.** [costs]: **to be ~ to sb** auf js Kosten gehen **- 2.** [offence]: **a ~ offence** ein Vergehen, für das man belangt werden kann.

**charge account** *n* Kundenkonto *das.*

**charge card** *n* Kundenkreditkarte *die.*

**charged** [tʃɑ:dʒd] *adj* [tense] angespannt.

**chargé d'affaires** ['ʃɑ:zeɪdæ'feə'] (*pl* **chargés d'affaires**) *n* Diplomat, *der anstelle eines Botschafters ein Land vertritt.*

**charge hand** *n Br* Vorarbeiter *der,* -in *die.*

**charge nurse** *n Br* Stationsschwester *die.*

**charger** ['tʃɑ:dʒə'] *n* **- 1.** [for batteries] Ladegerät *das* **- 2.** *literary* [soldier's horse] Schlachtross *das.*

**charge sheet** *n Br* Anklageprotokoll *das.*

**chariot** ['tʃærɪət] *n* Streitwagen *der.*

**charisma** [kə'rɪzmə] *n* Charisma *das.*

**charismatic** [ˌkærɪz'mætɪk] *adj* charismatisch.

**charitable** ['tʃærətəbl] *adj* **- 1.** [person] gütig; [remark] mitfühlend **- 2.** [organization] Wohltätigkeits-, karitativ.

**charity** ['tʃærətɪ] (*pl* **-ies**) *n* **- 1.** (U) [gifts, money] Spenden *pl* **- 2.** [organization] Wohltätigkeitsorganisation *die,* karitative Einrichtung **- 3.** [kindness] Nächstenliebe *die.*

**charlatan** ['ʃɑ:lətən] *n* Scharlatan *der.*

**charm** [tʃɑ:m] *n* **- 1.** (U) [appeal, attractiveness] Charme *der* **- 2.** [spell] Bann *der* **- 3.** [on bracelet] Anhänger *der;* **lucky ~** Glücksbringer *der* ⬦ *vt* bezaubern.

**charm bracelet** *n* Armband *das* mit Anhängern.

**charmer** ['tʃɑ:mə'] *n:* **to be a real ~** wirklich charmant sein.

**charming** ['tʃɑ:mɪŋ] *adj* bezaubernd; [person] charmant.

**charmingly** ['tʃɑ:mɪŋlɪ] *adv* bezaubernd, entzückend.

**charred** [tʃɑ:d] *adj* verkohlt.

**chart** [tʃɑ:t] *n* **- 1.** [diagram] Diagramm *das;* [for weather forecast] Wetterkarte *die* **- 2.** [map] Karte *die* <> *vt* - **1.** [map - seas, skies] kartieren; [ - movements] auf einer Karte erfassen - **2.** *fig* [record] auf lzeichnen.

➤ **charts** *npl:* **the ~s** die Hitparade.

**charter** [ˈtʃɑːtəʳ] *n* [document - of organization] Charta *die;* [ - of town] Gründungsurkunde *die* <> *vt* [plane, boat] chartern.

**chartered accountant** [ˌtʃɑːtəd-] *n Br* Wirtschaftsprüfer *der*, -in *die*.

**charter flight** *n* Charterflug *der*.

**charter plane** *n* Charterflugzeug *das*.

**chary** [ˈtʃeərɪ] (*compar* -**ier**; *superl* -**iest**) *adj:* **to be ~ of doing sthg** zögern, etw zu tun.

**chase** [tʃeɪs] *n* Verfolgungsjagd *die;* [hunt] Jagd *die;* **a car ~** eine Verfolgungsjagd im Auto; **to give ~** [chasing animals] jagen; [chasing people] die Verfolgungsjagd auf lnehmen <> *vt* - **1.** [pursue] jagen; [criminal] verfolgen - **2.** [drive away] fortljagen - **3.** [money, jobs] nachjagen <> *vi:* **to ~ after sb/sthg** jm/etw nachjagen.

➤ **chase up** *vt sep Br* [person, information]: **to ~ sb up to do sthg** jn daran erinnern, etw zu tun.

**chaser** [ˈtʃeɪsəʳ] *n* [drink] *ein schwächeres alkoholisches Getränk, das nach einem starken getrunken wird, oder umgekehrt.*

**chasm** [ˈkæzm] *n* - **1.** [deep crack] tiefe Felsspalte - **2.** *fig* [divide] Kluft *die*.

**chassis** [ˈʃæsɪ] (*pl inv*) *n* [of vehicle] Fahrgestell *das*.

**chaste** [tʃeɪst] *adj* keusch.

**chasten** [ˈtʃeɪsnl] *vt* zur Einsicht bringen.

**chastise** [tʃæˈstaɪz] *vt fml* schelten.

**chastity** [ˈtʃæstətɪ] *n* Keuschheit *die*.

**chat** [tʃæt] (*pt* & *pp* **-ted**; *cont* **-ting**) *n* Plauderei *die*, Plausch *der;* **to have a ~** plaudern <> *vi* plaudern.

➤ **chat up** *vt sep Br inf* sich heranlmachen an (+ *A*).

**chat room** *n* COMPUT Diskussionsforum *das*, Chatroom *der*.

**chat show** *n Br* Talkshow *die*.

**chatter** [ˈtʃætəʳ] *n* - **1.** [of person] Geplapper *das* - **2.** [of animal, bird] Gezwitscher *das* <> *vi* - **1.** [person] plappern - **2.** [animal, bird] zwitschern - **3.** [teeth] klappern.

**chatterbox** [ˈtʃætəbɒks] *n inf* [child] Plappermäulchen *das*.

**chattering classes** *npl pej:* **the ~** Klatschkreise *pl, Intellektuelle, die selbstherrlich über das aktuelle Tagesgeschehen diskutieren.*

**chatty** [ˈtʃætɪ] (*compar* -**ier**; *superl* -**iest**) *adj* - **1.** [person] gesprächig - **2.** [letter] im Plauderton geschrieben.

**chauffeur** [ˈʃəʊfəʳ] *n* Chauffeur *der* <> *vt* chauffieren.

**chauvinist** [ˈʃəʊvɪnɪst] *n* Chauvinist *der*.

**chauvinistic** [ˌʃəʊvɪˈnɪstɪk] *adj* chauvinistisch.

**cheap** [tʃiːp] *adj* - **1.** [inexpensive] billig - **2.** [reduced in price] preiswert - **3.** [poor - quality] billig, minderwertig - **4.** [vulgar] billig; **to feel ~** sich schäbig fühlen <> *adv* billig <> *n:* **on the ~** auf die billige Tour.

**cheapen** [ˈtʃiːpn] *vt* [degrade - thing, place] herablsetzen; [ - person] erniedrigen.

**cheaply** [ˈtʃiːplɪ] *adv* billig.

**cheapness** [ˈtʃiːpnɪs] *n* - **1.** [low cost] billiger Preis - **2.** [poor quality] Billigkeit *die*, Minderwertigkeit *die*.

**cheap rate** *n* TELEC Billigtarif *der*.

**cheapskate** [ˈtʃiːpskeɪt] *n inf pej* Knauser *der*, -in *die*.

**cheat** [tʃiːt] *n* - **1.** [person] Betrüger *der*, -in *die;* [in exam, game] Mogler *der*, -in *die* - **2.** [act] Betrug *der* <> *vt* betrügen; **to ~ sb out of sthg** jn um etw betrügen; **to feel ~ed** sich betrogen fühlen <> *vi* [in exam, game] mogeln.

➤ **cheat on** *vt fus inf* [be unfaithful to] betrügen.

**cheating** [ˈtʃiːtɪŋ] *n* [at cards, in exam] Mogeln *das*.

**check** [tʃek] *n* - **1.** [inspection, test]: **~ (on sthg)** Überprüfung *die* (von etw); **to keep a ~ on sthg** etw regelmäßig überprüfen - **2.** [restraint]: **to put a ~ on sthg** etw unter Kontrolle halten; **in ~** unter Kontrolle - **3.** *Am* [bill] Rechnung *die* - **4.** [pattern] Karomuster *das;* **a ~ tablecloth** ein Tischtuch mit Karomuster - **5.** *Am* = **cheque** <> *vt* - **1.** [test, verify] kontrollieren - **2.** [restrain] unter Kontrolle halten; [advance] auf lhalten; **to ~ o.s.** innelhalten <> *vi* [have a look] nachlsehen; [ask sb] nachlfragen; **to ~ on sthg** etw überprüfen.

➤ **check in** *vt sep* [luggage] abfertigen lassen; [coat] ablgeben <> *vi* - **1.** [at hotel] sich anlmelden - **2.** [at airport] einlchecken.

➤ **check off** *vt sep* ablhaken.

➤ **check out** *vt sep* [investigate] überprüfen <> *vi* [from hotel] sich ablmelden.

➤ **check up** *vi:* **to ~ up on sb** [supervise] jn kontrollieren; [investigate] über jn Nachforschungen anlstellen; **to ~ up on sthg** etw überprüfen.

**checkbook** *n Am* = **chequebook**.

**checked** [tʃekt] *adj* [patterned] kariert.

**checkered** *adj Am* = **chequered**.

**checkers** [ˈtʃekəz] *n* (U) *Am* Damespiel *das*.

**check guarantee card** *n Am* Scheckkarte *die*.

**check-in** *n* Abfertigung *die;* [check-in desk] Abfertigungsschalter *der*.

**checking account** [ˈtʃekɪŋ-] *n Am* Girokonto *das*.

**checklist** ['tʃeklɪst] n Checkliste die.

**checkmate** ['tʃekmeɪt] n Schachmatt das.

**checkout** ['tʃekaut] n - **1.** [in supermarket] Kasse die - **2.** [in hotel]: ~ **(time) is 11 a.m** das Zimmer ist bis 11:00 zu räumen.

**checkpoint** ['tʃekpɔɪnt] n Kontrollpunkt der.

**checkup** ['tʃekʌp] n Kontrolluntersuchung die, Vorsorgeuntersuchung die.

**Cheddar (cheese)** ['tʃedə'-] n Cheddar (käse) der.

**cheek** [tʃiːk] n - **1.** [of face] Backe die, Wange die - **2.** [buttock] Pobacke die - **3.** inf [impudence] Frechheit die <> vt inf frech sein zu.

**cheekbone** ['tʃiːkbəʊn] n Wangenknochen der, Backenknochen der.

**cheekily** ['tʃiːkɪlɪ] adv frech.

**cheekiness** ['tʃiːkɪnɪs] n Frechheit die, Unverschämtheit die.

**cheeky** ['tʃiːkɪ] (compar -ier; superl -iest) adj frech.

**cheep** [tʃiːp] vi piepsen.

**cheer** [tʃɪə'] n [shout] Hurraruf der; [cheering] Jubelgeschrei das; **three ~s for Linda!** ein dreifaches Hurra für Linda! <> vt - **1.** [shout approval, encouragement at] zujubeln (+ D) - **2.** [gladden] auf!muntern, auf!heitern <> vi jubeln.

⬥ **cheers** excl - **1.** [said before drinking] prost! - **2.** Br inf [goodbye] tschüs! - **3.** Br inf [thank you] danke!

⬥ **cheer on** vt sep an!feuern.

⬥ **cheer up** vt sep auf!muntern, auf!heitern <> vi vergnügter werden; ~ **up!** Kopfhoch!

**cheerful** ['tʃɪəfʊl] adj heiter; [music, colour] fröhlich.

**cheerfully** ['tʃɪəfʊlɪ] adv - **1.** [happily] fröhlich - **2.** [willingly] gern.

**cheerfulness** ['tʃɪəfʊlnɪs] n Heiterkeit die.

**cheering** ['tʃɪərɪŋ] adj [news, story] erfreulich <> n (U) Jubelgeschrei das; [of encouragement] Anfeuerungsrufe pl.

**cheerio** [ˌtʃɪərɪˈəʊ] excl Br inf tschüs!

**cheerleaders** ['tʃɪəˌliːdəz] npl Cheerleader pl.

**cheerless** ['tʃɪəlɪs] adj trostlos.

**cheery** ['tʃɪərɪ] (compar -ier; superl -iest) adj heiter, fröhlich.

**cheese** [tʃiːz] n Käse der.

**cheeseboard** ['tʃiːzbɔːd] n - **1.** [board] Käsebrett das - **2.** [on menu] Käseplatte die.

**cheeseburger** ['tʃiːzˌbɜːgə'] n Cheeseburger der.

**cheesecake** ['tʃiːzkeɪk] n Käsekuchen der.

**cheesed off** [ˌtʃiːzd-] adj inf angeödet, verärgert.

**cheesy** ['tʃiːzɪ] (compar -ier; superl -iest) adj

- **1.** [tasting of cheese] Käse- - **2.** [grin] breit - **3.** inf [of poor quality] mies.

**cheetah** ['tʃiːtə] n Gepard der.

**chef** [ʃef] n [cook] Koch der, Köchin die; [head cook] Chefkoch der, -köchin die.

**chemical** ['kemɪkl] adj chemisch <> n Chemikalie die.

**chemically** ['kemɪklɪ] adv chemisch.

**chemical weapons** npl chemische Waffen pl.

**chemist** ['kemɪst] n - **1.** Br [pharmacist] Apotheker der, -in die; ~'**s (shop)** [dispensing] Apotheke die; [non-dispensing] Drogerie die - **2.** [scientist] Chemiker der, -in die.

**chemistry** ['kemɪstrɪ] n - **1.** [science] Chemie die - **2.** [composition, characteristics] chemische Zusammensetzung.

**chemotherapy** [ˌkiːməʊˈθerəpɪ] n Chemotherapie die.

**cheque** Br, **check** Am [tʃek] n Scheck der; **to pay by ~** mit Scheck bezahlen.

**cheque account** n Girokonto das.

**chequebook** Br, **checkbook** Am ['tʃekbʊk] n Scheckheft das.

**cheque (guarantee) card** n Br Scheckkarte die.

**chequered** Br ['tʃekəd], **checkered** Am ['tʃekərd] adj - **1.** [patterned] kariert - **2.** [varied] bewegt.

**Chequers** ['tʃekəz] n der offizielle Landsitz des britischen Premierministers.

**cherish** ['tʃerɪʃ] vt [person] liebevoll sorgen für; [thing] hegen und pflegen; [hope] hegen; **a memory I'll ~ all my life** eine Erinnerung, die mir immer teuer sein wird.

**cherished** ['tʃerɪʃt] adj [dear] kostbar.

**cherry** ['tʃerɪ] (pl -ies) n - **1.** [fruit] Kirsche die - **2.**: ~ **(tree)** Kirschbaum der.

**cherry-picking** n der Erwerb nur der gewinnbringendsten Firmen bei der Privatisierung eines Industriezweigs.

**cherub** ['tʃerəb] (pl -s OR -im) n - **1.** [angel] Cherub der - **2.** [child] Engelchen das.

**chervil** ['tʃɜːvɪl] n Kerbel der.

**chess** [tʃes] n Schach das.

**chessboard** ['tʃesbɔːd] n Schachbrett das.

**chessman** ['tʃesmæn] (pl -men [-men]) n Schachfigur die.

**chest** [tʃest] n - **1.** ANAT Brust die; **to get sthg off one's ~** fig inf sich (D) etw von der Seele reden - **2.** [trunk] Truhe die.

**chestnut** ['tʃesnʌt] adj [colour] kastanienbraun <> n - **1.** [nut] Kastanie die - **2.**: ~ **(tree)** Kastanienbaum der.

**chest of drawers** (pl **chests of drawers**) n Kommode die.

**chesty** ['tʃestɪ] (compar **-ier;** superl **-iest**) adj [cough] schnarrend.

**chevron** ['ʃevrən] n **- 1.** [on roadsign] Winkel der **- 2.** [on uniform] Abzeichen das.

**chew** [tʃuː] n [sweet] Kaubonbon der OR das <> vt **- 1.** [food] kauen **- 2.** [nails, pencil] kauen an (+ D).

➤ **chew over** vt sep fig [think over]: **to ~ sthg over** sich (D) etw durch den Kopf gehen lassen.

➤ **chew up** vt sep zerkauen; [by dog] zerbeißen.

**chewing gum** ['tʃuːɪŋ-] n (U) Kaugummi der.

**chewy** [tʃuːɪ] (compar **-ier;** superl **-iest**) adj [meat] zäh; **to be nice and ~** angenehm zu kauen sein.

**chic** [ʃiːk] adj schick <> n Schick der.

**chicanery** [ʃɪˈkeɪnərɪ] n Machenschaften pl.

**chick** [tʃɪk] n **- 1.** [baby bird] Junge das, Küken das **- 2.** inf [girl] Braut die.

**chicken** ['tʃɪkɪn] adj inf [cowardly] feige <> n **- 1.** [bird] Huhn das; **it's a ~ and egg situation** man kann nicht sagen, was Ursache und was Wirkung ist **- 2.** (U) [food] Hähnchen das **- 3.** inf [coward] Feigling der.

➤ **chicken out** vi inf: **to ~ out of sthg** vor etw (D) kneifen; **to ~ out of doing sthg** sich (aus Angst) davor drücken, etw zu tun.

**chickenfeed** ['tʃɪkɪnfiːd] n (U) fig [small sum of money] ein paar Pfennige pl.

**chickenpox** ['tʃɪkɪnpɒks] n Windpocken pl.

**chicken wire** n Maschendraht der.

**chickpea** ['tʃɪkpiː] n Kichererbse die.

**chicory** ['tʃɪkərɪ] n [vegetable] Chicorée die.

**chide** [tʃaɪd] vt literary schelten; **to ~ sb for sthg** jn für etw schelten.

**chief** [tʃiːf] adj **- 1.** [most important] Haupt- **- 2.** [head] leitend <> n **- 1.** [of organization] Leiter der, -in die, Chef der, -in die; **~ of police** Polizeipräsident der, -in die **- 2.** [of tribe] Häuptling der.

**chief constable** n Br Polizeipräsident der.

**chief executive** n [of company] Direktor der, -in die.

➤ **Chief Executive** n Am [US president]: **the Chief Executive** der Präsident der USA.

**chief justice** n Am oberster Bundesrichter, oberste Bundesrichterin.

**chiefly** ['tʃiːflɪ] adv hauptsächlich.

**chief of staff** n Stabschef der, -in die.

**chieftain** ['tʃiːftən] n [of tribe] Häuptling der; [of Scottish clan] Oberhaupt das.

**chiffon** ['ʃɪfɒn] n Chiffon der.

**chihuahua** [tʃɪˈwɑːwə] n Chihuahua der.

**chilblain** ['tʃɪlbleɪn] n Frostbeule die.

**child** [tʃaɪld] (pl **children**) n Kind das.

**childbearing** ['tʃaɪld,beərɪŋ] n Gebären das; **a woman of ~ age** eine Frau im gebärfähigen Alter.

**child benefit** n Br Kindergeld das.

**childbirth** ['tʃaɪldbɜːθ] n Geburt die.

**childcare** n (U) Kinderbetreuung die.

**childhood** ['tʃaɪldhʊd] n Kindheit die.

**childish** ['tʃaɪldɪʃ] adj pej kindisch.

**childishly** ['tʃaɪldɪʃlɪ] adv pej kindisch.

**childless** ['tʃaɪldlɪs] adj kinderlos.

**childlike** ['tʃaɪldlaɪk] adj kindlich.

**childminder** ['tʃaɪld,maɪndəʳ] n Br Tagesmutter die.

**child prodigy** n Wunderkind das.

**childproof** ['tʃaɪldpruːf] adj kindersicher.

**children** ['tʃɪldrən] pl ⊏➤ child.

**children's home** n Kinderheim das.

**Chile** ['tʃɪlɪ] n Chile nt.

**Chilean** ['tʃɪlɪən] adj chilenisch <> n Chilene der, -nin die.

**chili** ['tʃɪlɪ] n = **chilli**.

**chill** [tʃɪl] adj kühl <> n **- 1.** [illness] Erkältung die mit leichtem Fieber **- 2.** [in temperature]: **there's a ~ in the air** es ist kühl draußen **- 3.** [feeling of fear] Schauder der <> vt **- 1.** [drink] kühlen; [food] kalt stellen **- 2.** [person - with cold]: **I'm ~ed to the bone** ich bin bis auf die Knochen durchgefroren <> vi [drink, food] kühl werden.

**chilli** ['tʃɪlɪ] (pl **-ies**) n [vegetable] Chili der; **~ (con carne)** Chili con carne.

**chilling** ['tʃɪlɪŋ] adj **- 1.** [very cold] eisig **- 2.** [frightening] schaudererregend.

**chilli powder** n Chillipulver das.

**chilly** ['tʃɪlɪ] (compar **-ier;** superl **-iest**) adj kühl.

**chime** [tʃaɪm] n [of bells] Geläut das; [of clock] Schlagen das; [of door bell] Läuten das <> vt [time] schlagen <> vi [bell] läuten; [clock] schlagen.

➤ **chime in** vi sich einlschalten.

**chimney** ['tʃɪmnɪ] n Schornstein der.

**chimneypot** ['tʃɪmnɪpɒt] n Schornsteinaufsatz der.

**chimneysweep** ['tʃɪmnɪswiːp] n Schornsteinfeger der.

**chimp** [tʃɪmp] n inf Schimpanse der.

**chimpanzee** [tʃɪmpənˈziː] n Schimpanse der.

**chin** [tʃɪn] n Kinn das.

**china** ['tʃaɪnə] n Porzellan das <> comp Porzellan-.

**China** ['tʃaɪnə] n China nt; **the People's Republic of ~** die Volksrepublik China.

**china clay** n Porzellanerde die, Kaolin das.

**Chinatown** ['tʃaɪnətaʊn] *n* von Chinesen bewohntes Viertel in manchen Großstädten der USA und Großbritanniens.

**chinchilla** [tʃɪn'tʃɪlə] *n* - **1.** [animal] Chinchilla die - **2.** (U) [fur] Chinchillapelz der.

**Chinese** [ˌtʃaɪ'niːz] *adj* chinesisch <> *n* [language] Chinesisch(e) das <> *npl:* the ~ die Chinesen *pl.*

**Chinese cabbage** *n* Chinakohl der.

**Chinese lantern** *n* Lampion der.

**Chinese leaves** *npl Br* Chinakohl der.

**chink** [tʃɪŋk] *n* - **1.** [narrow opening] Ritze die; a ~ of light ein dünner Lichtstrahl - **2.** [sound] Klimpern das <> *vi* klimpern.

**chinos** ['tʃiːnəʊz] *npl* Hose aus Baumwollköper.

**chintz** [tʃɪnts] *n* Chintz der <> *comp* Chintz-.

**chinwag** ['tʃɪnwæg] *n inf:* to have a ~ einen Plausch halten.

**chip** [tʃɪp] (*pt* & *pp* -**ped**; *cont* -**ping**) *n* - **1.** *Br* [fried potato] *pl* Pommes frites: ~s - **2.** *Am* [potato crisp] Chip der - **3.** [fragment - of wood] Span der; [ - of stone, metal] Splitter der - **4.** [flaw] angeschlagene Stelle - **5.** [microchip, token] Chip der; when the ~s are down wenn es hart auf hart kommt - **6.** *phr:* to have a ~ on one's shoulder Komplexe haben <> *vt* [damage] anl schlagen.
➤ **chip in** *inf vt fus* [contribute] beilsteuern <> *vi* - **1.** [contribute] etwas beilsteuern - **2.** [interrupt] sich einlschalten.
➤ **chip off** *vt sep* ablkratzen.

**chip-based** [-beɪst] *adj* COMPUT chip-gestützt.

**chipboard** ['tʃɪpbɔːd] *n* (U) Spanplatte die.

**chipmunk** ['tʃɪpmʌŋk] *n* Streifenhörnchen das.

**chipolata** [ˌtʃɪpə'lɑːtə] *n* Cocktailwürstchen das.

**chipped** [tʃɪpt] *adj* [flawed] angeschlagen.

**chippings** ['tʃɪpɪŋz] *npl* [of wood] Späne *pl;* 'loose ~' 'Rollsplit'.

**chip shop** *n Br* Imbissbude die.

**chiropodist** [kɪ'rɒpədɪst] *n* Fußpfleger der, -in die.

**chiropody** [kɪ'rɒpədɪ] *n* Fußpflege die.

**chiropractor** ['kaɪrəʊˌpræktəˈ] *n* Chiropraktiker der, -in die.

**chirp** [tʃɜːp] *vi* [bird] zwitschern; [cricket] zirpen.

**chirpy** ['tʃɜːpɪ] (*compar* -**ier**; *superl* -**iest**) *adj esp Br inf* [cheerful] munter.

**chisel** ['tʃɪzl] (*Br pt* & *pp* -**led**; *cont* -**ling**, *Am pt* & *pp* -**ed**; *cont* -**ing**) *n* [for metal] Meißel der; [for wood] Beitel der <> *vt* [in metal] meißeln; [in wood] stemmen.

**chit** [tʃɪt] *n* Zettel der.

**chitchat** ['tʃɪttʃæt] *n inf* Geplauder das.

**chivalrous** ['ʃɪvlrəs] *adj* ritterlich.

**chivalry** ['ʃɪvlrɪ] *n* - **1.** *literary* [of knights] Rittertum das - **2.** [courtesy] Ritterlichkeit die.

**chives** [tʃaɪvz] *npl* Schnittlauch der.

**chivy, chivvy** ['tʃɪvɪ] (*pt* & *pp* -**ied**) *vt inf:* to ~ sb along jn anltreiben.

**chloride** ['klɔːraɪd] *n* Chlorid das.

**chlorinated** ['klɔːrɪneɪtɪd] *adj* gechlort.

**chlorine** ['klɔːriːn] *n* Chlor das.

**chlorofluorocarbon** ['klɔːrəʊˌflɔːrəʊ'kɑːbən] *n* Chlorfluorkohlenwasserstoff der.

**chloroform** ['klɒrəfɔːm] *n* Chloroform das.

**chlorophyll** ['klɒrəfɪl] *n* Chlorophyll das.

**choc-ice** ['tʃɒkaɪs] *n Br* Eis mit Schokoladenüberzug.

**chock** [tʃɒk] *n* Keil der.

**chock-a-block, chock-full** *adj inf* überfüllt.

**chocolate** ['tʃɒkələt] *n* - **1.** (U) [food] Schokolade die - **2.** [sweet] Praline die - **3.** [drink]: **(hot) ~** heiße Schokolade <> *comp* [made of chocolate] Schokoladen-.

**choice** [tʃɔɪs] *n* - **1.** [gen] Wahl die; by/from ~ freiwillig; to have no ~ but to do sthg keine andere Wahl haben, als etw zu tun - **2.** [variety, selection] Auswahl die <> *adj* auserlesen, ausgesucht.

**choir** ['kwaɪəˈ] *n* Chor der.

**choirboy** ['kwaɪəbɔɪ] *n* Chorknabe der.

**choke** [tʃəʊk] *n* AUT Choke der <> *vt* - **1.** [strangle] würgen; to ~ sb to death jn erwürgen; the fumes ~d her durch den Rauch bekam sie keine Luft mehr - **2.** [block] verstopfen <> *vi* keine Luft mehr kriegen; [on fishbone] sich verschlucken; to ~ to death ersticken.
➤ **choke back** *vt fus* unterdrücken.

**choker** *n* [necklace] enge Halskette; [collar] Vatermörder der.

**cholera** ['kɒlərə] *n* Cholera die.

**cholesterol** [kə'lestərɒl] *n* Cholesterin das.

**choose** [tʃuːz] (*pt* chose; *pp* chosen) *vt* - **1.** [select - career] wählen; [ - cake, dress] auslwählen; there's little OR not much to ~ between them sie sind gleich gut - **2.** [opt]: to ~ to do sthg beschließen, etw zu tun <> *vi* [select]: to ~ (from sthg) eine Wahl treffen (zwischen etw (D)).

**choos(e)y** ['tʃuːzɪ] (*compar* -**ier**; *superl* -**iest**) *adj* wählerisch.

**chop** [tʃɒp] (*pt* & *pp* -**ped**; *cont* -**ping**) *n* - **1.** [meat] Kotelett das - **2.** [blow] Hieb der; to be for the ~ vor dem Aus stehen <> *vt* - **1.** [wood] hacken; [food] schneiden - **2.** *inf* [funding, budget] kürzen - **3.** *phr:* to ~ and change es sich (D) dauernd anders überlegen.
➤ **chops** *npl inf* [mouth] Maul das.

← **chop down** *vt sep* fällen.

← **chop up** *vt sep* [wood] klein hacken; [food] klein schneiden.

**chopper** ['tʃɒpəʳ] *n* - **1.** [axe] Hackbeil *das* - **2.** *inf* [helicopter] Hubschrauber *der*.

**chopping board** ['tʃɒpɪŋ-] *n* Hackbrett *das*.

**choppy** ['tʃɒpɪ] (*compar* -ier; *superl* -iest) *adj* kabbelig.

**chopsticks** ['tʃɒpstɪks] *npl* Stäbchen *pl*.

**choral** ['kɔːrəl] *adj* Chor-.

**chord** [kɔːd] *n* MUS Akkord *der*; **to strike a ~ (with sb)** auf Zustimmung (bei jm) treffen.

**chore** [tʃɔːʳ] *n* lästige Pflicht; **household ~s** Hausarbeit *die*.

**choreographer** [ˌkɒrɪ'ɒɡrəfəʳ] *n* Choreograf *der*, -in *die*.

**choreography** [ˌkɒrɪ'ɒɡrəfɪ] *n* Choreografie *die*.

**chortle** ['tʃɔːtl] *vi* glucksen.

**chorus** ['kɔːrəs] *n* - **1.** [part of song] Refrain *der* - **2.** [singers] Chor *der* - **3.** *fig* [of approval, complaints] Chor *der*.

**chose** [tʃəʊz] *pt* ⊳ **choose**.

**chosen** ['tʃəʊzn] *pp* ⊳ **choose**.

**choux pastry** [ʃuː-] *n* Brandteig *der*.

**chow** [tʃaʊ] *n* [dog] Chow-Chow *der*.

**chowder** ['tʃaʊdəʳ] *n* Suppe *mit Fisch oder Meeresfrüchten*.

**Christ** [kraɪst] *n* Christus *der* ⊳ *excl* oh Gott!

**christen** ['krɪsn] *vt* taufen.

**christening** ['krɪsnɪŋ] *n* Taufe *die* ⊳ *comp* Tauf-.

**Christian** ['krɪstʃən] *adj* christlich ⊳ *n* Christ *der*, -in *die*.

**Christian Democrat** *n* POL Christdemokrat *der*, -in *die*.

**Christianity** [ˌkrɪstɪ'ænətɪ] *n* Christentum *das*.

**Christian name** *n* Vorname *der*.

**Christmas** ['krɪsməs] *n* Weihnachten *das*; **Happy OR Merry ~!** Frohe OR Fröhliche Weihnachten! ⊳ *comp* Weihnachts-.

**Christmas cake** *n* Br *Früchtekuchen mit Zuckerguss, der an Weihnachten gegessen wird*.

**Christmas card** *n* Weihnachtskarte *die*.

**Christmas cracker** *n* Br Weihnachtsknallbonbon *das*.

**Christmas Day** *n* erster Weihnachtstag.

**Christmas Eve** *n* Heiligabend *der*.

**Christmas pudding** *n* Br *schwere Süßspeise aus Trockenfrüchten, die an Weihnachten gegessen wird*.

**Christmas stocking** *n* Strumpf, der mit kleinen Weihnachtsgeschenken gefüllt wird.

**Christmastime** ['krɪsməstaɪm] *n* Weihnachtszeit *die*.

**Christmas tree** *n* Weihnachtsbaum *der*.

**chrome** [krəʊm], **chromium** ['krəʊmɪəm] *n* Chrom *das* ⊳ *comp* Chrom-.

**chrome-plated** *adj* verchromt.

**chromosome** ['krəʊməsəʊm] *n* Chromosom *das*.

**chronic** ['krɒnɪk] *adj* - **1.** [illness, unemployment] chronisch - **2.** [alcoholic] Gewohnheits-; [liar] chronisch.

**chronically** ['krɒnɪklɪ] *adv* chronisch.

**chronicle** ['krɒnɪkl] *n* Chronik *die* ⇔ *vt* (chronologisch) auflzeichnen.

**chronological** [ˌkrɒnə'lɒdʒɪkl] *adj* chronologisch.

**chronologically** [ˌkrɒnə'lɒdʒɪklɪ] *adv* chronologisch.

**chronology** [krə'nɒlədʒɪ] *n* Chronologie *die*.

**chrysalis** ['krɪsəlɪs] (*pl* -lises [-lɪsiːz]) *n* Puppe *die (eines Schmetterlings/eines Nachtfalters)*.

**chrysanthemum** [krɪ'sænθəməm] (*pl* -s) *n* Chrysantheme *die*.

**chubby** ['tʃʌbɪ] (*compar* -ier; *superl* -iest) *adj* mollig.

**chuck** [tʃʌk] *vt inf* - **1.** [throw] schmeißen - **2.** [job] hinlschmeißen; [girlfriend, boyfriend] Schluss machen mit.

← **chuck away, chuck out** *vt sep inf* weglschmeißen.

**chuckle** ['tʃʌkl] *n* leises Lachen ⇔ *vi* in sich (A) hineinllachen.

**chuffed** [tʃʌft] *adj* Br *inf*: **to be ~ with sthg** sich sehr über etw (A) freuen; **to be ~ to do sthg** sich sehr darüber freuen, etw zu tun.

**chug** [tʃʌɡ] (*pt* & *pp* -ged; *cont* -ging) *vi* tuckern.

**chum** [tʃʌm] *n inf* [friend] Kumpel *der*.

**chummy** ['tʃʌmɪ] (*compar* -ier; *superl* -iest) *adj inf*: **to be ~ with sb** auf freundlichem Fuß mit jm stehen.

**chump** [tʃʌmp] *n inf* Dummkopf *der*.

**chunk** [tʃʌŋk] *n* - **1.** [of bread, cheese] Stück *das* - **2.** *inf* [large amount] großer Teil.

**chunky** ['tʃʌŋkɪ] (*compar* -ier; *superl* -iest) *adj* - **1.** [person] untersetzt - **2.** [jewellery, furniture] klobig; [jumper] grob gestrickt.

**church** [tʃɜːtʃ] *n* Kirche *die*; **to go to ~** in die Kirche gehen.

**churchgoer** ['tʃɜːtʃˌɡəʊəʳ] *n* Kirchgänger *der*, -in *die*.

**churchman** ['tʃɜːtʃmən] (*pl* -men [-mən]) *n* Geistliche *der*.

**Church of England** *n:* **the ~** die Anglikanische Kirche.

**CHURCH OF ENGLAND**

Die „Church of England" oder Anglikanische Kirche ist die traditionelle englische Staatskirche. Sie hat eine episkopalische (bischöfliche) Struktur; ihr weltliches Oberhaupt ist der/die jeweils amtierende König/Königin, ihr geistlicher Leiter der Erzbischof von Canterbury. Dagegen ist die schottische Staatskirche, die Church of Scotland, synodal-presbyterianisch und wird von einer General Assembly (Generalsynode) geleitet; theologisch gehört sie zu den Reformierten Kirchen.

**Church of Scotland** *n:* **the ~** die Kirche von Schottland.

**churchyard** ['tʃɜːtʃjɑːd] *n* Friedhof *der*.

**churlish** ['tʃɜːlɪʃ] *adj* [impolite] unhöflich; [loutish] ungehobelt.

**churn** [tʃɜːn] *n* **- 1.** [for making butter] Butterfass *das* **- 2.** [for milk] Milchkanne *die* ◇ *vt* [stir up] auf|wühlen ◇ *vi:* **my stomach ~ed** mein Magen drehte sich um.

➡ **churn out** *vt sep inf* am laufenden Band produzieren.

➡ **churn up** *vt sep* auf|wühlen.

**chute** [ʃuːt] *n* Rutsche *die*; [for rubbish] Müllschlucker *der*.

**chutney** ['tʃʌtnɪ] *n* Chutney *das*.

**CI** *abbr of* **Channel Islands.**

**CIA** (*abbr of* **Central Intelligence Agency**) *n* CIA *der or die*.

**cicada** [sɪ'kɑːdə] *n* Zikade *die*.

**CID** (*abbr of* **Criminal Investigation Department**) *n* ≈ Kripo *die*.

**cider** ['saɪdə'] *n* Cidre, Apfelwein *der*.

**CIF** (*abbr of* **cost, insurance and freight**) CIF.

**cigar** [sɪ'gɑː'] *n* Zigarre *die*.

**cigarette** [ˌsɪgə'ret] *n* Zigarette *die*.

**cigarette butt, cigarette end** *Br n* Zigarettenstummel *der*.

**cigarette holder** *n* Zigarettenspitze *die*.

**cigarette lighter** *n* Feuerzeug *das*.

**cigarette paper** *n* Zigarettenpapier *das*.

**C-in-C** *n abbr of* **commander in chief.**

**cinch** [sɪntʃ] *n inf:* **it's a ~** es ist ein Kinderspiel.

**cinder** ['sɪndə'] *n* Asche *die*.

**Cinderella** [ˌsɪndə'relə] *n* Aschenputtel *das*.

**cinecamera** ['sɪnɪˌkæmərə] *n* Filmkamera *die*.

**cinefilm** ['sɪnɪˌfɪlm] *n* Film für eine Filmkamera.

**cinema** ['sɪnəmə] *n* Kino *das*; **the ~ industry** die Filmindustrie.

**cinematic** [ˌsɪnɪ'mætɪk] *adj* filmisch; [arts, effect] Film-.

**cinnamon** ['sɪnəmən] *n* Zimt *der*.

**cipher** ['saɪfə'] *n* [secret writing system] Chiffre *die*, Kode *der*.

**circa** ['sɜːkə] *prep* etwa, zirka.

**circle** ['sɜːkl] *n* **- 1.** [gen] Kreis *der*; **to come full ~** an den Ausgangspunkt zurück|kehren; **to go round in ~s** sich im Kreis bewegen **- 2.** [in theatre, cinema] Balkon *der* ◇ *vt* **- 1.** [draw a circle round] ein|kreisen **- 2.** [move round] umkreisen ◇ *vi* kreisen.

**circuit** ['sɜːkɪt] *n* **- 1.** ELEC Stromkreis *der* **- 2.** [lap] Runde *die* **- 3.** [motor racing track] Rennstrecke *die* **- 4.** [series of venues] Tour *die*.

**circuit board** *n* Platine *die*, Leiterplatte *die*.

**circuit breaker** *n* Stromkreisunterbrecher *der*.

**circuitous** [sɜː'kjuːɪtəs] *adj* umständlich.

**circular** ['sɜːkjʊlə'] *adj* **- 1.** [in shape] rund, kreisförmig **- 2.** [route] Rund- **- 3.** [argument] sich im Kreis bewegend ◇ *n* **- 1.** [letter, memo] Rundschreiben *das* **- 2.** [advertisement] Wurfsendung *die*.

**circulate** ['sɜːkjʊleɪt] *vi* **- 1.** [gen] zirkulieren **- 2.** [rumour, story] um|gehen, kursieren **- 3.** [socialize] sich unter die Leute mischen ◇ *vt* **- 1.** [document] zirkulieren lassen **- 2.** [rumour, story] in Umlauf setzen.

**circulation** [ˌsɜːkjʊ'leɪʃn] *n* **- 1.** [of blood] Zirkulation *die*, Kreislauf *der* **- 2.** [of money, document] Umlauf *der*; **in ~** im Umlauf **- 3.** [of magazine, newspaper] Auflage *die* **- 4.** [of heat, air] Zirkulation *die*.

**circumcise** ['sɜːkəmsaɪz] *vt* beschneiden.

**circumcision** [ˌsɜːkəm'sɪʒn] *n* Beschneidung *die*.

**circumference** [sə'kʌmfərəns] *n* Umfang *der*.

**circumflex** ['sɜːkəmfleks] *n:* **~ (accent)** Zirkumflex *der*.

**circumnavigate** [ˌsɜːkəm'nævɪgeɪt] *vt* umfahren; [by sailing boat] umsegeln.

**circumscribe** ['sɜːkəmskraɪb] *vt fml* [restrict] beschränken.

**circumspect** ['sɜːkəmspekt] *adj* umsichtig.

**circumstances** ['sɜːkəmstənsɪz] *npl* Umstände *pl*; **under** or **in no ~** unter keinen Umständen, auf keinen Fall; **under** or **in the ~** unter diesen Umständen.

**circumstantial** [ˌsɜːkəm'stænʃl] *adj fml* [account, description] ausführlich; **~ evidence** Indizienbeweis *der*.

**circumvent** [ˌsɜːkəm'vent] *vt fml* um|gehen.

**circus** ['sɜːkəs] n Zirkus der; [in place names] Platz der.

**cirrhosis** [sɪ'rəʊsɪs] n Zirrhose die.

**cissy** ['sɪsɪ] (pl -ies) n Br inf Weichling der.

**cistern** ['sɪstən] n - 1. Br [in roof] Wassertank der - 2. [in toilet] Spülkasten der.

**citation** [saɪ'teɪʃn] n - 1. [official praise]: ~ (for sthg) Belobigung die (für etw) - 2. [quotation] Zitat das.

**cite** [saɪt] vt - 1. [mention, quote] zitieren - 2. LAW vorlladen.

**citizen** ['sɪtɪzn] n - 1. [of country] Staatsbürger der, -in die - 2. [of town] Bürger der, -in die.

**Citizens' Advice Bureau** n Bürgerberatungsstelle die.

**Citizens' Band** n CB-Funk der.

**citizenship** ['sɪtɪznʃɪp] n [nationality] Staatsangehörigkeit die.

**citric acid** ['sɪtrɪk-] n Zitronensäure die.

**citrus fruit** ['sɪtrəs-] n Zitrusfrucht die.

**city** ['sɪtɪ] (pl -ies) n Stadt die; [large] Großstadt die.
➤ **City** n Br: **the City** Londoner Finanzviertel.

**city centre** n Innenstadt die, Stadtzentrum das.

**city hall** n Am Rathaus das.

**civic** ['sɪvɪk] adj - 1. [leader, event] Stadt- - 2. [duty, pride] bürgerlich, Bürger-.

**civic centre** n Br Verwaltungszentrum das einer Stadt.

**civil** ['sɪvl] adj - 1. [disorder, marriage] zivil - 2. [polite] höflich.

**civil defence** n Bürgerwehr die.

**civil disobedience** n ziviler Ungehorsam.

**civil engineer** n Hoch- und Tiefbauingenieur der.

**civil engineering** n Hoch- und Tiefbau der.

**civilian** [sɪ'vɪljən] n Zivilist der, -in die ◇ comp [government] Zivil-; [organization] zivil; **in ~ clothes** in Zivil.

**civility** [sɪ'vɪlətɪ] n Höflichkeit die.

**civilization** [ˌsɪvəlaɪ'zeɪʃn] n - 1. [advanced world] Zivilisation die - 2. [society, culture] Kultur die.

**civilize, -ise** ['sɪvɪlaɪz] vt zivilisieren.

**civilized** ['sɪvəlaɪzd] adj - 1. [advanced] zivilisiert - 2. [polite] zivilisiert.

**civil law** n bürgerliches Recht.

**civil liberties** npl Freiheitsrechte pl.

**civil list** n Br Geldsumme, die das britische Parlament jedes Jahr an den König bzw. die Königin von England und an einige andere Leute gibt.

**civil rights** npl Bürgerrechte pl.

**civil servant** n Beamte der, -in die (im Staatsdienst).

**civil service** n Staatsdienst der.

**civil war** n Bürgerkrieg der.

**CJD** (abbr of **Creutzfeldt-Jakob disease**) n CJK die.

**cl** (abbr of **centilitre**) n cl.

**clad** [klæd] adj literary [dressed]: ~ **in sthg** in etw (D) gekleidet.

**cladding** ['klædɪŋ] n Br Verkleidung die.

**claim** [kleɪm] n - 1. [for territory, expenses, refund] Anspruch der; [demand] Forderung die; **to lay ~ to sthg** etw für sich beanspruchen - 2. [assertion] Behauptung die ◇ vt - 1. [money] beantragen; [lost property] beanspruchen; [expenses] einreichen; [credit] für sich in Anspruch nehmen; **he ~ed responsibility for it** er bekannte, dafür verantwortlich zu sein; **the earthquake ~ed 50 lives** das Erdbeben forderte 50 Menschenleben - 2. [assert]

behaupten ◇ *vi:* **to ~ on one's insurance** Ansprüche an die Versicherung geltend machen; **to ~ for sthg** Ansprüche auf etw *(A)* geltend machen.

**claimant** ['kleɪmənt] *n* Antragsteller *der,* -in *die;* LAW Kläger *der,* -in *die.*

**claim form** *n* Antragsformular *das.*

**clairvoyant** [kleə'vɔɪənt] *adj* hellseherisch ◇ *n* Hellseher *der,* -in *die.*

**clam** [klæm] (*pt & pp* -med; *cont* -ming) *n* Klaffmuschel *die.*

◆ **clam up** *vi inf* keinen Pieps mehr sagen.

**clamber** ['klæmbəʳ] *vi* klettern.

**clammy** ['klæmɪ] (*compar* -ier; *superl* -iest) *adj inf* [skin] feucht und klamm; [weather] schwül.

**clamor** ['klæməʳ] *n & vi Am* = clamour.

**clamorous** ['klæmərəs] *adj* [applause] tosend.

**clamour** *Br,* **clamor** *Am* ['klæməʳ] *n* - **1.** [noise] [of voices] Geschrei *das* - **2.** [demand] **~ (for sthg)** lautstark erhobene Forderung (nach etw) ◇ *vi:* **to ~ for sthg** etw lautstark fordern.

**clamp** [klæmp] *n* - **1.** [fastener] Schraubzwinge *die* - **2.** MED & TECH Klemme *die* ◇ *vt* - **1.** [with fastener] fest|klemmen - **2.** [parked car] Parkkralle anlegen *(+ D).*

◆ **clamp down** *vi:* **to ~ down (on)** durch|greifen (gegen).

**clampdown** ['klæmpdaʊn] *n:* **~ (on)** Durch|greifen *das* (gegen).

**clan** [klæn] *n* Clan *der.*

**clandestine** [klæn'destɪn] *adj* geheim.

**clang** [klæŋ] *n* [of bell] lautes Tönen ◇ *vi* [bell, gong] laut ertönen.

**clanger** ['klæŋəʳ] *n Br inf* Fauxpas *der;* **to drop a ~** ins Fettnäpfchen treten.

**clank** [klæŋk] *n* [of chains] Gerassel *das;* [of metallic objects] Scheppern *das* ◇ *vi* [chain] rasseln; [iron gate] scheppern.

**clap** [klæp] (*pt & pp* -ped; *cont* -ping) *n* - **1.** [of hands] Klatschen *das* - **2.** [of thunder] Donnerschlag *der* ◇ *vt* Beifall klatschen *(+ D);* **to ~ one's hands** in die Hände klatschen; **to ~ eyes on sb/sthg** jn/etw zu Gesicht bekommen ◇ *vi* Beifall klatschen.

**clapboard** ['klæpbɔːd] *n Am* Schindel *die.*

**clapped-out** [klæpt-] *adj Br inf* [machine] klapprig.

**clapperboard** ['klæpəbɔːd] *n* Klappe *die.*

**clapping** ['klæpɪŋ] *n* Beifall *der.*

**claptrap** ['klæptræp] *n inf* Gewäsch *das.*

**claret** ['klærət] *n* - **1.** [wine] roter Bordeaux - **2.** [colour] Bordeauxrot *das.*

**clarification** [klærɪfɪ'keɪʃn] *n* (nähere) Erläuterung.

**clarify** ['klærɪfaɪ] (*pt & pp* -ied) *vt* (näher) erläutern.

**clarinet** [klærə'net] *n* Klarinette *die.*

**clarity** ['klærətɪ] *n* Klarheit *die.*

**clash** [klæʃ] *n* - **1.** [incompatibility]: **a ~ of interests** ein Interessenkonflikt; **a ~ of personalities** ein Zusammenprall verschiedener Persönlichkeiten - **2.** [fight] Zusammenstoß *der* - **3.** [disagreement] Meinungsverschiedenheit *die* - **4.** [of cymbals] lautes Tönen ◇ *vi* - **1.** [ideas, beliefs] aufeinander prallen; [colours] sich beißen - **2.** [fight]: **to ~ (with sb)** (mit jm) zusammen|stoßen - **3.** [disagree]: **to ~ (with sb)** (mit jm) aneinander geraten - **4.** [coincide]: **to ~ (with sthg)** sich (mit etw) überschneiden - **5.** [cymbals] laut ertönen.

**clasp** [klɑːsp] *n* [on necklace, bracelet] Verschluss *der;* [on belt] Schnalle *die* ◇ *vt* ergreifen; **to ~ one's hands together** die Hände falten.

**class** [klɑːs] *n* - **1.** [gen] Klasse *die;* **to be in a ~ of one's own** eine Klasse für sich sein - **2.** [lesson] Stunde *die;* **an evening ~** ein Abendkurs - **3.** [social group] Schicht *die;* **upper ~** Oberschicht *die;* **the working ~** die Arbeiterklasse ◇ *comp* [system, war] Klassen- ◇ *vt* ein|stufen; **to ~ sb as sthg** jn als etw ein|stufen.

**class-conscious** *adj pej* standesbewusst.

**classic** ['klæsɪk] *adj* klassisch ◇ *n* Klassiker *der.*

◆ **classics** *npl* Altphilologie *die.*

**classical** ['klæsɪkl] *adj* - **1.** [gen] klassisch - **2.** [sculpture, architecture] klassizistisch.

**classical music** *n* klassische Musik.

**classification** [klæsɪfɪ'keɪʃn] *n* - **1.** [gen] Klassifizierung *die* - **2.** [category] Klassifikation *die.*

**classified** ['klæsɪfaɪd] *adj* [secret]: **~ information** Verschlusssache *die.*

**classified ad** *n* Annonce *die.*

**classify** ['klæsɪfaɪ] (*pt & pp* -ied) *vt* klassifizieren.

**classless** ['klɑːslɪs] *adj* klassenlos.

**classmate** ['klɑːsmeɪt] *n* Klassenkamerad *der,* -in *die.*

**classroom** ['klɑːsrʊm] *n* Klassenzimmer *das.*

**classy** ['klɑːsɪ] (*compar* -ier; *superl* -iest) *adj inf* [clothes, restaurant] nobel; [car] edel; [person] vornehm.

**clatter** ['klætəʳ] *n* Geklapper *das* ◇ *vi* klappern.

**clause** [klɔːz] *n* - **1.** [in legal document] Klausel *die* - **2.** GRAMM Satz *der.*

**claustrophobia** [klɔːstrə'fəʊbjə] *n* Klaustrophobie *die.*

**claustrophobic** [klɔːstrə'fəʊbɪk] *adj* klaustrophobisch; **it's very ~ in here** hier bekommt man wirklich Platzangst.

**claw** [klɔː] *n* - **1.** [of animal, bird] Kralle *die* - **2.** [of insect, sea creature] Schere *die* <> *vt* kratzen <> *vi:* **to ~ at sthg** sich an etw *(A)* krallen.

➤ **claw back** *vt sep Br* sich *(D)* zurück|holen.

**clay** [kleɪ] *n* [soil] Lehm *der*; [for pottery] Ton *der*.

**clay pigeon shooting** *n* Tontauben-schießen *das*.

**clean** [kliːn] *adj* - **1.** [gen] sauber - **2.** [reputation, driving licence] tadellos; **to come ~ about sthg** *inf* etw zulgeben - **3.** [joke] harmlos - **4.** [line, movement] klar - **5.** [break] glatt <> *adv* [completely] ganz, völlig <> *vt* sauber machen; **to ~ one's teeth** *Br* sich *(D)* die Zähne putzen <> *vi* putzen <> *n:* **to give sthg a ~** etw sauber machen.

➤ **clean out** *vt sep* - **1.** [room, cupboard] gründlich auf|räumen - **2.** *inf fig* [leave penniless] aus|nehmen; **the burglars ~ed us out** die Einbrecher haben unser Haus vollkommen ausgeräumt.

➤ **clean up** *vt sep* [mess] auf|räumen; [with cloth] sauber machen; **to ~ o.s. up** sich waschen <> *vi inf* [win] ab|kassieren.

**cleaner** [ˈkliːnər] *n* - **1.** [person] Putzfrau *die* - **2.** [substance] Reiniger *der* - **3.** [shop]: **~'s** Reinigung *die*.

**cleaning** [ˈkliːnɪŋ] *n:* **to do the ~** sauber machen.

**cleaning lady** *n* Putzfrau *die*.

**cleanliness** [ˈklenlɪnɪs] *n* Reinlichkeit *die*.

**clean-living** *adj* anständig.

**cleanly** [ˈkliːnlɪ] *adv* sauber.

**cleanness** [ˈkliːnnɪs] *n* [of room] Sauberkeit *die*; [of air] Reinheit *die*.

**cleanse** [klenz] *vt* - **1.** [skin, wound] säubern, reinigen - **2.** [society, soul] läutern.

**cleanser** [ˈklenzər] *n* - **1.** [for skin] Reinigungsmilch *die* - **2.** [detergent] Reinigungsmittel *das*.

**clean-shaven** [-ˈʃeɪvn] *adj* glatt rasiert.

**cleanup** [ˈkliːnʌp] *n:* **to have a ~** auf|räumen; [with cloth] sauber machen.

**clear** [klɪər] *adj* - **1.** [gen] klar; **to make sthg ~ (to sb)** (jm) etw klar machen; **to make it ~ that** deutlich machen, dass; **to make o.s. ~** sich klar aus|drücken - **2.** [obvious] eindeutig - **3.** [sound] deutlich; [speaker] deutlich hörbar - **4.** [skin, complexion, conscience] rein - **5.** [road, view] frei; **try and keep Friday ~** versuch dir Freitag freizuhalten - **6.** [profit] Netto- <> *adv:* **stand ~!** zurücktreten!; **to be ~ of sthg** etw nicht berühren; **to stay ~ of sb, to steer ~ of sb** jm aus dem Wege gehen; **to stay ~ of sthg, to steer ~ of sthg** etw meiden <> *n:* **in the ~** [out of danger] außer Gefahr; [free from suspicion] außer Verdacht <> *vt* - **1.** [path, road] räumen; [pipe] reinigen; **to ~ the table** den Tisch ab|räumen; **to ~ one's throat** sich räuspern

- **2.** [take out of the way] aus dem Weg räumen - **3.** [jump over] überspringen - **4.** [debt] begleichen - **5.** [authorize] genehmigen - **6.** [prove not guilty] freisprechen; **to ~ one's name** seinen Namen rein|waschen; **to be ~ed of sthg** von etw freigesprochen werden - **7.** [cheque] verrechnen <> *vi* [fog, smoke] sich verziehen; [weather] sich auf|klären.

➤ **clear away** *vt sep* weg|räumen.

➤ **clear off** *vi Br inf* ab|hauen.

➤ **clear out** *vt sep* [room, cupboard] gründlich auf|räumen <> *vi inf* [leave] verschwinden.

➤ **clear up** *vt sep* - **1.** [tidy] auf|räumen; [toys, litter] weg|räumen - **2.** [mystery] auf|klären; [problem, confusion] klären <> *vi* - **1.** [weather] sich auf|klären - **2.** [illness] zurück|gehen - **3.** [tidy up] auf|räumen.

**clearance** [ˈklɪərəns] *n (U)* - **1.** [removal] Entfernen *das*, Beseitigung *die* - **2.** [permission] Genehmigung *die*; [for takeoff] Starterlaubnis *die* - **3.** [free space] Spielraum *der*.

**clearance sale** *n* Ausverkauf *der*.

**clear-cut** *adj* klar umrissen.

**clear-headed** [-ˈhedɪd] *adj* scharfsinnig.

**clearing** [ˈklɪərɪŋ] *n* [in forest] Lichtung *die*.

**clearing house** *n* [bank] Clearingstelle *die*.

**clearing up** *n:* **to do the ~** auf|räumen.

**clearly** [ˈklɪəlɪ] *adv* - **1.** [speak, write] deutlich - **2.** [think, explain] klar - **3.** [obviously] eindeutig.

**clearout** [ˈklɪəraʊt] *n esp Br inf* Großreinemachen *das*; **to have a ~** gründlich auf|räumen.

**cleavage** [ˈkliːvɪdʒ] *n* - **1.** [between breasts] Dekolletee *das* - **2.** [division] Kluft *die*.

**cleaver** [ˈkliːvər] *n* Hackbeil *das*.

**clef** [klef] *n* Notenschlüssel *der*.

**cleft** [kleft] *n* [in rock] Spalt *der*.

**cleft palate** *n* Gaumenspalte *die*.

**clematis** [ˈklemətɪs] *n* Klematis *die*.

**clemency** [ˈklemənsɪ] *n fml* Milde *die*.

**clementine** [ˈkleməntaɪn] *n* Klementine *die*.

**clench** [klentʃ] *vt* [fist] ballen; [teeth] zusammen|beißen.

**clergy** [ˈklɜːdʒɪ] *npl:* **the ~** die Geistlichkeit.

**clergyman** [ˈklɜːdʒɪmən] *(pl* **-men** [-mən]*) n* Geistliche *der*.

**cleric** [ˈklerɪk] *n* Geistlicher *der*.

**clerical** [ˈklerɪkl] *adj* - **1.** [in office] Büro- - **2.** [in church] geistlich.

**clerk** [*Br* klɑːk, *Am* klɜːrk] *n* - **1.** [in office] Büroangestellte *der, die* - **2.** [in court] Gerichtsschreiber *der*, -in *die* - **3.** *Am* [shop assistant] Verkäufer *der*, -in *die*.

**clever** [ˈklevər] *adj* - **1.** [person] klug; **to be ~ with one's hands** geschickte Hände haben - **2.** [idea, device] raffiniert; **he had the ~ idea to ... iron** er war so schlau, ...

**cleverly** ['klevəlı] adv - **1.** [intelligently] klug - **2.** [ingeniously] raffiniert - **3.** [skilfully] geschickt.

**cleverness** ['klevənıs] n - **1.** [intelligence] Klugheit die - **2.** [ingenuity] Raffiniertheit die - **3.** [skill] Geschicklichkeit die.

**cliché** ['kliːʃeɪ] n Klischee das.

**click** [klık] n Klicken das; [of tongue] Schnalzen das <> vt [fingers] schnippen mit; [tongue] schnalzen mit <> vi [gen & COMPUT] klicken; **to ~ on sthg** COMPUT etw anlklicken; **the door ~ed shut** die Tür schnappte ins Schloss; **suddenly it all ~ed** plötzlich wurde alles klar.

**client** ['klaıənt] n Kunde der, -din die; [of lawyer] Klient der, -in die.

**clientele** [ˌkliːənˈtel] n Kundschaft die, Klientel die.

**cliff** [klıf] n [by sea] Klippe die; [of mountain] Felsen der.

**cliffhanger** ['klıfˌhæŋəʳ] n inf Thriller der.

**climactic** [klaıˈmæktık] adj: **~ point** Höhepunkt der.

**climate** ['klaımıt] n lit & fig Klima das.

**climatic** [klaıˈmætık] adj klimatisch.

**climax** ['klaımæks] n - **1.** [culmination] Höhepunkt der - **2.** [orgasm] Orgasmus der.

**climb** [klaım] n [of mountain] Aufstieg der <> vt [tree, wall] hochlklettern; [rope] hochlklettern an (+ D); [ladder, stairs] hinauflsteigen; [hill] steigen auf (+ A); [mountain] besteigen <> vi - **1.** [person, plant] klettern - **2.** [road, prices, costs] anlsteigen; [plane] (auf l)steigen.
◆ **climb down** vi [admit mistake] klein beilgeben.

**climber** ['klaıməʳ] n - **1.** [person] Kletterer der, -in die; [mountaineer] Bergsteiger der, -in die - **2.** [plant] Kletterpflanze die.

**climbing** ['klaımıŋ] n Klettern das; [mountaineering] Bergsteigen das; **to go ~** bergsteigen gehen.

**climbing frame** n Br Klettergerüst das.

**climes** [klaımz] npl literary Breiten pl.

**clinch** [klıntʃ] vt [deal] ablschließen.

**cling** [klıŋ] (pt & pp clung) vi - **1.** [hold tightly]: **to ~ to** sich klammern an (+ A) - **2.** [clothes]: **to ~ (to sb)** sich (an jn) anlschmiegen.

**clingfilm** ['klıŋfılm] n (U) Br Frischhaltefolie die.

**clinging** ['klıŋıŋ] adj - **1.** [person, child] anschmiegsam - **2.** [clothes] sich anschmiegend.

**clinic** ['klınık] n Klinik die.

**clinical** ['klınıkl] adj - **1.** MED klinisch - **2.** [coldly rational] nüchtern.

**clinically** ['klınıklı] adv - **1.** MED klinisch - **2.** [coldly] nüchtern.

**clink** [klıŋk] n Geklirr das <> vi klirren.

**clip** [klıp] (pt & pp -ped; cont -ping) n - **1.** [fastener] Klammer die; [on earring] Klipp der - **2.** [of film, video] Ausschnitt der, Clip der <> vt - **1.** [fasten]: **to ~ sthg onto sthg** [papers] etw an etw (A) heften - **2.** [cut] schneiden - **3.** inf [hit] streifen; **to ~ sb round the ear** jm eins über die Ohren geben.
◆ **clip on** vi [fasten] anlklemmen.

**clipboard** ['klıpbɔːd] n Klemmbrett das.

**clip-on** adj: **~ earrings** Klipps pl.

**clipped** [klıpt] adj [speech] abgehackt.

**clippers** ['klıpəz] npl - **1.** [for hair] Haarschneidemaschine die - **2.** [for nails] Nagelknipser der, Nagelzange die - **3.** [for plants, hedges] Heckenschere die.

**clipping** ['klıpıŋ] n [newspaper cutting] Zeitungsausschnitt der.

**clique** [kliːk] n pej Clique die.

**clitoris** ['klıtərıs] n Klitoris die.

**cloak** [kləuk] n - **1.** [garment] Umhang der - **2.** fig [for secret] Deckmantel der <> vt: **~ed in mystery** geheimnisumwittert.

**cloak-and-dagger** adj [story] geheimnisvoll.

**cloakroom** ['kləukrum] n - **1.** [for clothes] Garderobe die - **2.** Br [toilets] Waschraum der.

**clobber** ['klɒbəʳ] inf n [things] Kram der <> vt - **1.** [hit - person] hauen; [ - ball] schlagen - **2.** [defeat] fertiglmachen.

**clock** [klɒk] n - **1.** [gen] Uhr die; **round the ~** rund um die Uhr; **to put the ~ back** lit die Uhr zurücklstellen; fig die Zeit zurückldrehen; **to put the ~ forward** die Uhr vorlstellen - **2.** [mileometer] Tachometer der.
◆ **clock in** vi Br [at work] (den Arbeitsbeginn) stechen ODER stempeln.
◆ **clock off** vi Br [at work] (das Arbeitsende) stechen ODER stempeln.
◆ **clock up** vt fus [miles] fahren; [victories] erreichen.

**clock radio** n Radiowecker der.

**clockwise** ['klɒkwaız] adj & adv im Uhrzeigersinn.

**clockwork** ['klɒkwɜːk] n: **like ~** wie am Schnürchen <> comp [toy, train] zum Aufziehen.

**clod** [klɒd] n [of earth] Klumpen der.

**clog** [klɒg] (pt & pp -ged; cont -ging) vt verstopfen.
◆ **clogs** npl Clogs pl.
◆ **clog up** vt sep & vi verstopfen.

**clogged** [klɒgd] adj verstopft.

**cloister** ['klɔıstəʳ] n ARCHIT Kreuzgang der.

**cloistered** ['klɔıstəd] adj literary [sheltered] behütet.

**clone** [kləun] n Klon der <> vt klonen.

**close¹** [kləus] *adj* - **1.** [near] nahe; **~ to** nahe an (+ *D*), dicht bei; [with verbs of motion] nahe an (+ *A*); **the house is ~ to the river** das Haus steht nahe *OR* dicht am Fluss; **she sat down ~ to me** sie setzte sich in meine Nähe; **don't get too ~ to the edge** geh nicht zu nahe an den Abgrund; **~ to tears** den Tränen nahe; **that was a ~ shave** *OR* **thing** *OR* **call** das war knapp; **when seen from ~ up** *OR* **to** aus der Nähe betrachtet - **2.** [friend, contact, link] eng; **to be ~ to sb** jm nahe stehen - **3.** [resemblance] stark - **4.** [examination, inspection] genau; **on ~r examination** bei näherer Betrachtung - **5.** [weather] schwül - **6.** [race, contest] knapp ⬦ *adv* nah; **~ by, ~ at hand** in der Nähe; **~ behind** dicht dahinter; **to stand ~ together** nahe *OR* dicht beieinander stehen ⬦ *n* [street] Sackgasse *die.*

◆ **close on, close to** *prep* [almost] beinahe.

**close²** [kləuz] *vt* - **1.** [gen] schließen - **2.** [road] sperren - **3.** [meeting, event] beenden - **4.** [speech, novel] beschließen - **5.** [bank account] auflösen - **5.** [deal] abschließen ⬦ *vi* - **1.** [door, eyes, wound] sich schließen - **2.** [shop, office, book, share price] schließen - **3.** [factory - permanently] stillgelegt werden - **4.** [deadline, offer] enden ⬦ *n* [end] Schluss *der;* **to draw to a ~** zu Ende gehen.

◆ **close down** *vt sep* [shut] schließen ⬦ *vi* [shut down] stillgelegt werden.

◆ **close in** *vi* - **1.** [fog] fallen; **night was closing in** die Dunkelheit brach herein - **2.** [person]: **to ~ in on sb/sthg** sich jm/etw nähern.

◆ **close off** *vt sep* sperren.

**close-cropped** [ˌkləus-] *adj* [hair] kurzgeschnitten.

**closed** [kləuzd] *adj* - **1.** [gen] geschlossen - **2.** [society] abgeschottet.

**closed circuit television** *n* (U) Fernsehüberwachungsanlage *die.*

**closed shop** *n* Gewerkschaftszwang *der.*

**close-fitting** [ˌkləus-] *adj* eng anliegend.

**close-knit** [ˌkləus-] *adj* eng verbunden.

**closely** [ˈkləuslɪ] *adv* - **1.** [gen] eng; [resemble] stark - **2.** [watch, guard, listen] genau; [follow] dicht.

**closeness** [ˈkləusnɪs] *n* - **1.** [proximity] Nähe *die* - **2.** [of relationship] Innigkeit *die.*

**close quarters** [ˌkləus-] *npl*: **at ~** aus nächster Nähe.

**close season** [ˌkləus-] *n Br* [for hunting, fishing] Schonzeit *die.*

**closet** [ˈklɒzɪt] *adj inf* heimlich; **he's a ~ socialist** er ist ein verkappter Sozialist ⬦ *n Am* Schrank *der* ⬦ *vt*: **to be ~ed with sb** mit jm hinter verschlossenen Türen sitzen.

**close-up** [ˈkləus-] *n* Nahaufnahme *die.*

**closing** [ˈkləuzɪŋ] *adj* [final] abschließend.

**closing price** *n* Schlusskurs *der.*

**closing time** *n* [for pubs] Sperrstunde *die;* [for shops] Ladenschlusszeit *die.*

**closure** [ˈkləuʒə] *n* - **1.** [of business, company] Schließung *die* - **2.** [of road, railway line] Sperrung *die.*

**clot** [klɒt] (*pt* & *pp* -**ted;** *cont* -**ting**) *n* - **1.** [lump] Klumpen *der;* [of blood] Blutgerinnsel *das* - **2.** *Br inf* [fool] Hornochse *der* ⬦ *vi* [blood] gerinnen.

**cloth** [klɒθ] *n* - **1.** (U) [material] Stoff *der* - **2.** [for cleaning] Lappen *der;* [floor cloth] (Boden)wischlappen *der* - **3.** [tablecloth] Tischtuch *das.*

**clothe** [kləuð] *vt fml* [dress] kleiden; **~d in white** in Weiß gekleidet.

**clothes** [kləuðz] *npl* Kleider *pl;* **to put one's ~ on** sich anziehen; **to take one's ~ off** sich ausziehen.

**clothes basket** *n* Wäschekorb *der.*

**clothes brush** *n* Kleiderbürste *die.*

**clotheshorse** [ˈkləuðzhɔːs] *n* Wäscheständer *der.*

**clothesline** [ˈkləuðzlaɪn] *n* Wäscheleine *die.*

**clothes peg** *Br,* **clothespin** *Am* [ˈkləuðzpɪn] *n* Wäscheklammer *die.*

**clothing** [ˈkləuðɪŋ] *n* Kleidung *die;* **a piece of ~** ein Kleidungsstück.

**clotted cream** [ˈklɒtɪd-] *n* sehr dicke Sahne, *Spezialität Südwestenglands.*

**cloud** [klaud] *n* Wolke *die;* [of insects] Schwarm *der;* **to leave under a ~** *fig* unter zweifelhaften Umständen aus dem Dienst scheiden ⬦ *vt* - **1.** [mirror, window] beschlagen - **2.** [memory] trüben; **to ~ the issue** die Angelegenheit kompliziert machen.

◆ **cloud over** *vi* - **1.** [sky] sich bewölken - **2.** [face] sich verdüstern.

**cloudburst** [ˈklaudbɜːst] *n* Wolkenbruch *der.*

**cloudless** [ˈklaudlɪs] *adj* wolkenlos.

**cloudy** [ˈklaudɪ] (*compar* -**ier;** *superl* -**iest**) *adj* - **1.** [day, sky] bedeckt - **2.** [beer, water] trüb.

**clout** [klaut] *inf n* - **1.** [blow] Schlag *der* - **2.** (U) [influence] Schlagkraft *die* ⬦ *vt* [hit] schlagen.

**clove** [kləuv] *n*: **a ~ of garlic** eine Knoblauchzehe.

◆ **cloves** *npl* [spice] Gewürznelken *pl.*

**clover** [ˈkləuvə] *n* Klee *der.*

**clown** [klaun] *n* - **1.** [performer] Clown *der* - **2.** [fool] Idiot *der* ⬦ *vi* herumalbern.

**cloying** [ˈklɔɪɪŋ] *adj* - **1.** [scent] süßlich - **2.** [sentimentality] kitschig.

**club** [klʌb] (*pt* & *pp* -**bed;** *cont* -**bing**) *n* - **1.** [association] Klub *der* - **2.** [nightclub] Nachtklub *der* - **3.** [weapon] Knüppel *der,* Prügel *der* - **4.** SPORT [equipment]: **(golf) ~** (Golf)schläger *der* ⬦ *comp* Klub- ⬦ *vt* [hit] prügeln.

➤ **clubs** npl [playing cards] Kreuz das; **the six of ~s** die Kreuz Sechs.

➤ **club together** vi Br zusammenllegen.

**club car** n Am RAIL Speisewagen der.

**clubhouse** ['klʌbhaus, pl -hauzɪz] n Klubhaus das.

**cluck** [klʌk] vi - **1.** [hen] gackern - **2.** [person] schnalzen.

**clue** [kluː] n - **1.** [hint] Hinweis der, Tipp der; [in crime] Spur die; [in crossword] Frage die; **I haven't (got) a ~ (about)** ich habe keine Ahnung (von) - **2.** [key to problem]: **~ (to sthg)** Schlüssel der (zu etw).

**clued-up** [kluːd-] adj Br inf gut informiert.

**clueless** ['kluːlɪs] adj Br inf ahnungslos.

**clump** [klʌmp] n - **1.** [of trees, flowers] Gruppe die; **~ of bushes** Gebüsch das - **2.** [sound] dumpfer Laut ◇ vi [move heavily] trampeln.

**clumsily** ['klʌmzɪlɪ] adv ungeschickt.

**clumsy** ['klʌmzɪ] (compar **-ier;** superl **-iest)** adj - **1.** [person] tollpatschig; [movement, remark] ungeschickt - **2.** [unwieldy] klobig; [tool] unhandlich.

**clung** [klʌŋ] pt & pp ⊳ cling.

**cluster** ['klʌstəʳ] n Gruppe die; [of grapes] Traube die ◇ vi - **1.** [people] sich scharen - **2.** [things] sich drängen.

**clutch** [klʌtʃ] n AUT Kupplung die ◇ vt festlhalten ◇ vi: **to ~ at sb/sthg** nach jm/etw greifen.

➤ **clutches** npl: **in the ~es of** in der Gewalt (+ G).

**clutch bag** n Unterarmtasche die.

**clutter** ['klʌtəʳ] n Unordnung die.

**cm** (abbr of **centimetre)** n cm.

**CNAA** (abbr of **Council for National Academic Awards)** n von den Universitäten unabhängiger Ausschluss für die Vergabe von akademischen Auszeichnungen.

**CND** (abbr of **Campaign for Nuclear Disarmament)** n Kampagne für nukleare Abrüstung.

**c/o** (abbr of **care of)** ⊳ care.

**Co. - 1.** abbr of **Company - 2.** abbr of **County.**

**CO** n abbr of **commanding officer** ◇ - **1.** abbr of **Company - 2.** abbr of **County - 3.** abk für Colorado, in Postanschrift verwendet.

**coach** [kəutʃ] n - **1.** [bus] (Reise)bus der - **2.** RAIL Wagen der - **3.** [horsedrawn] Kutsche die - **4.** SPORT Trainer der, -in die - **5.** [tutor] Nachhilfelehrer der, -in die ◇ vt - **1.** SPORT trainieren - **2.** [tutor]: **to ~ sb (in sthg)** jm Nachhilfestunden (in etw (D)) geben.

**coaching** ['kəutʃɪŋ] n - **1.** SPORT Training das - **2.** [tutoring] Nachhilfe die.

**coach station** n Busbahnhof der.

**coach trip** n Br Ausflug der mit dem Bus.

**coagulate** [kəu'ægjuleɪt] vi [blood] gerinnen; [sauce] einlldicken.

**coal** [kəul] n - **1.** (U) [mineral] Kohle die - **2.** [piece of coal] Stück das Kohle.

**coalface** ['kəulfeɪs] n Streb der.

**coalfield** ['kəulfiːld] n Kohlenrevier das.

**coalition** [ˌkəuə'lɪʃn] n POL Koalition die; **~ government** Koalitionsregierung die.

**coalman** ['kəulmæn] (pl **-men** [-men]) n Br Kohlenmann der.

**coal merchant** n Kohlenhändler der, -in die.

**coalmine** ['kəulmaɪn] n Kohlenbergwerk das.

**coalminer** ['kəulˌmaɪnəʳ] n Bergmann der.

**coalmining** ['kəulˌmaɪnɪŋ] n Kohlenbergbau der.

**coarse** [kɔːs] adj - **1.** [rough - hair] dick; [ - skin] derb; [ - sandpaper, fabric] grob - **2.** [vulgar - remark, laugh] ordinär; [ - joke] derb; [ - person] ordinär.

**coarse fishing** n Br das Angeln von Süßwasserfischen (mit Ausnahme aller Lachs- und Forellenarten) in Flüssen und Seen.

**coarsen** ['kɔːsn] vt - **1.** [manners] ungehobelter machen - **2.** [skin] derber machen ◇ vi - **1.** [manners] ungehobelter werden - **2.** [skin] derber werden.

**coast** [kəust] n Küste die ◇ vi - **1.** [car] im Leerlauf fahren - **2.** fig: **you can't just ~ through life** du kannst nicht so ziellos durchs Leben gehen; **to ~ through an exam** eine Prüfung mit links schaffen.

**coastal** ['kəustl] adj Küsten-.

**coaster** ['kəustəʳ] n Untersetzer der.

**coastguard** ['kəustgɑːd] n - **1.** [person] Mitglied das der Küstenwache - **2.** [organization]: **the ~** die Küstenwache.

**coastline** ['kəustlaɪn] n Küste die.

**coat** [kəut] n - **1.** [garment] Mantel der - **2.** [of animal] Fell das - **3.** [of paint, varnish] Schicht die ◇ vt: **to ~ sthg (with sthg)** etw (mit etw) überziehen.

**coat hanger** n Kleiderbügel der.

**coating** ['kəutɪŋ] n [of chocolate] Überzug der; [of dust] Schicht die; [of metal] Beschichtung die.

**coat of arms** (pl **coats of arms)** n Wappen das.

**coat stand** n Garderobenständer der.

**coauthor** [kəu'ɔːθəʳ] n Mitverfasser der, -in die.

**coax** [kəuks] vt: **to ~ sb (to do OR into doing sthg)** jn überreden(, etw zu tun).

**coaxial cable** [ˌkəu'æksɪəl-] n COMPUT Koaxialkabel das.

**cob** [kɒb] n ⊳ corn on the cob.

**cobalt** ['kəʊbɔːlt] n - **1.** [colour] Kobaltblau das - **2.** CHEM Kobalt das.

**cobbled** ['kɒbld] adj: ~ **street** Straße die mit Kopfsteinpflaster.

**cobbler** ['kɒbləʳ] n Schuster der, -in die.

**cobbles** ['kɒblz], **cobblestones** ['kɒbls-təʊnz] npl Kopfsteinpflaster das.

**cobble ⇌ cobble together** vt sep zusammenbasteln; [book, article] zusammenstoppeln.

**Cobol** ['kəʊbɒl] (abbr of **Common Business Oriented Language**) n COMPUT COBOL.

**cobra** ['kəʊbrə] n Kobra die.

**cobweb** ['kɒbweb] n Spinnennetz das; **the room is full of ~s** der Raum ist voller Spinnweben.

**Coca-Cola®** [ˌkəʊkə'kəʊlə] n Coca-Cola® die OR das.

**cocaine** [kəʊ'keɪn] n Kokain das.

**cocaine addict** n Kokainsüchtiger der, -süchtige die.

**cock** [kɒk] n - **1.** [male chicken] Hahn der - **2.** [male bird] Männchen das - **3.** vulg [penis] Schwanz der ⟨⟩ vt - **1.**: **to ~ a gun** den Hahn einer Schusswaffe spannen - **2.** [head]: **to ~ one's head (to one side)** den Kopf auf die Seite legen.

**⇌ cock up** vt sep Br vinf versauen.

**cock-a-hoop** adj inf [delighted] außer sich vor Freude; [boastful] triumphierend.

**cockatoo** [ˌkɒkə'tuː] (pl -s) n Kakadu der.

**cockerel** ['kɒkrəl] n junger Hahn.

**cocker spaniel** [ˌkɒkə-] n Cockerspaniel der.

**cockeyed** ['kɒkaɪd] adj inf - **1.** [lopsided] schief - **2.** [foolish] verrückt.

**cockfight** ['kɒkaɪt] n Hahnenkampf der.

**cockle** ['kɒkl] n Herzmuschel die.

**Cockney** ['kɒknɪ] (pl -s) n - **1.** [person] Cockney der - **2.** [dialect, accent] Cockney das ⟨⟩ comp Cockney-.

**COCKNEY**

Traditionelle Bezeichnung für die Bewohner des Londoner East End. Ihr ebenfalls „Cockney" genannter Akzent ist fast ein eigener Dialekt und hat einen unverkennbaren „rhyming slang".

**cockpit** ['kɒkpɪt] n Cockpit das.

**cockroach** ['kɒkrəʊtʃ] n Küchenschabe die, Kakerlak der.

**cocksure** [ˌkɒk'ʃɔːʳ] adj von sich eingenommen.

**cocktail** ['kɒkteɪl] n Cocktail der ⟨⟩ comp Cocktail-.

**cocktail dress** n Cocktailkleid das.

**cocktail party** n Cocktailparty die.

**cocktail shaker** [-ˌʃeɪkəʳ] n Cocktailshaker der.

**cocktail stick** n Cocktailpicker der.

**cock-up** n vinf: **to make a ~** Scheiße bauen; **to make a ~ of sthg** etw versauen.

**cocky** ['kɒkɪ] (compar -ier; superl -iest) adj inf überheblich.

**cocoa** ['kəʊkəʊ] n Kakao der.

**coconut** ['kəʊkənʌt] n Kokosnuss die.

**cocoon** [kə'kuːn] n - **1.** ZOOL Kokon der - **2.** fig [protective environment] Hülle die ⟨⟩ vt behüten.

**cod** [kɒd] (pl inv OR -s) n Kabeljau der.

**COD** (abbr of **cash/collect on delivery**) ▷ **cash/collect.**

**code** [kəʊd] n - **1.** [cipher] Kode der - **2.** [set of rules] Kodex der; **~ of behaviour** Verhaltenskodex der - **3.** TELEC Vorwahl die ⟨⟩ vt - **1.** [encode] verschlüsseln, chiffrieren - **2.** [give identifier to] kennzeichnen.

**coded** ['kəʊdɪd] adj verschlüsselt, chiffriert.

**codeine** ['kəʊdiːn] n Kodein das.

**code name** n Deckname der.

**code of practice** n Verfahrensregeln pl.

**cod-liver oil** n Lebertran der.

**codswallop** ['kɒdzˌwɒləp] n Br inf Blödsinn der.

**coed** adj abbr of **coeducational** ⟨⟩ n - **1.** (abbr of **coeducational student**) Am Studentin (manchmal auch Student) an einer gemischten Universität - **2.** (abbr of **coeducational school**) Br gemischte Schule.

**coeducational** [ˌkəʊedjuː'keɪʃənl] adj koedukativ; [school] gemischt.

**coefficient** [ˌkəʊɪ'fɪʃnt] n Koeffizient der.

**coerce** [kəʊ'ɜːs] vt zwingen; **to ~ sb into doing sthg** jn dazu zwingen, etw zu tun.

**coercion** [kəʊ'ɜːʃn] n Zwang der.

**coexist** [ˌkəʊɪg'zɪst] vi nebeneinander existieren, koexistieren.

**coexistence** [ˌkəʊɪg'zɪstəns] n Koexistenz die.

**C. of C.** n abbr of **chamber of commerce.**

**C of E** n abbr of **Church of England.**

**coffee** ['kɒfɪ] n Kaffee der.

**coffee bar** n Br Café das.

**coffee beans** npl Kaffeebohnen pl.

**coffee break** n Kaffeepause die.

**coffee cup** n Kaffeetasse die.

**coffee-maker** n Kaffeemaschine die.

**coffee mill** n Kaffeemühle die.

**coffee morning** n Br morgendliches Kaffeetrinken, das zu Wohltätigkeitszwecken organisiert wird.

**coffeepot** ['kɒfɪpɒt] n Kaffeekanne die.

**coffee shop** n - **1.** Br [café] Café das - **2.** Am [restaurant] Café das - **3.** [shop selling coffee] Kaffeegeschäft das.

**coffee table** n Couchtisch der.

**coffee-table book** n Bildband der.

**coffers** ['kɒfəz] npl Kasse die.

**coffin** ['kɒfɪn] n Sarg der.

**cog** [kɒg] n [tooth on wheel] Zahn der; [wheel] Zahnrad das; **he's just a ~ in the machine** er ist nur ein Rädchen im Getriebe.

**cogent** ['kəʊdʒənt] adj [argument] stichhaltig; [reason] zwingend.

**cogitate** ['kɒdʒɪteɪt] vi fml nachldenken.

**cognac** ['kɒnjæk] n Cognac der.

**cognitive** ['kɒgnɪtɪv] adj kognitiv.

**cogwheel** ['kɒgwiːl] n Zahnrad das.

**cohabit** [ˌkəʊˈhæbɪt] vi: **to ~ (with sb)** (mit jm) in nichtehelicher Gemeinschaft zusammenlleben.

**coherent** [kəʊˈhɪərənt] adj [answer] folgerichtig; [theory, ideas, story, speech] schlüssig; [account] zusammenhängend.

**coherently** [kəʊˈhɪərəntlɪ] adv [speak, write] zusammenhängend; [argue] folgerichtig.

**cohesion** [kəʊˈhiːʒn] n [of society] Zusammenhalt der; [of ideas] Zusammenhang der.

**cohesive** [kəʊˈhiːsɪv] adj [united - group] einheitlich; [ - image] stimmig.

**COI** (abbr of Central Office of Information) n zentrales Informationsamt der britischen Regierung.

**coil** [kɔɪl] n - **1.** [of rope, wire] Rolle die; [of hair] Locke die; [of smoke] Kringel der - **2.** ELEC Spule die - **3.** Br [contraceptive device] Spirale die ⬦ vt auf lrollen; **to ~ sthg around sb/sthg** etw um jn/etw wickeln ⬦ vi sich ringeln.
➤ **coil up** vt sep auf lrollen.

**coiled** [kɔɪld] adj aufgerollt.

**coin** [kɔɪn] n Münze die ⬦ vt [invent] prägen; **to ~ a phrase** um es mal ganz originell zu sagen.

**coinage** ['kɔɪnɪdʒ] n - **1.** (U) [currency] Währung die - **2.** [invented word, phrase] Neuprägung die, Neuschöpfung die.

**coin-box** n Br Münztelefon das.

**coincide** [ˌkəʊɪnˈsaɪd] vi - **1.** [occur simultaneously]: **to ~ (with sthg)** (mit etw) zusammenlfallen - **2.** [be in agreement] übereinlstimmen.

**coincidence** [kəʊˈɪnsɪdəns] n Zufall der.

**coincidental** [kəʊˌɪnsɪˈdentl] adj zufällig.

**coincidentally** [kəʊˌɪnsɪˈdentəlɪ] adv zufällig.

**coin-operated** [-ˈɒpəˌreɪtɪd] adj Münz-.

**coitus** ['kəʊɪtəs] n fml Koitus der.

**coke** [kəʊk] n - **1.** [fuel] Koks der - **2.** drugs sl [cocaine] Koks der.

**Coke**® [kəʊk] n [Coca-Cola] Coke® das.

**Col.** abbr of colonel.

**cola** ['kəʊlə] n Cola die OR das.

**colander** ['kʌləndəʳ] n Sieb das.

**cold** [kəʊld] adj - **1.** [gen] kalt; **I'm ~** mir ist kalt - **2.** [unfriendly - eyes, smile, voice] kalt; [ - person] gefühlskalt ⬦ n - **1.** [illness] Erkältung die; **to catch (a) ~** sich erkälten - **2.** [low temperature] Kälte die.

**cold-blooded** [-ˈblʌdɪd] adj - **1.** BIOL wechselwarm, kaltblütig - **2.** [unfeeling - person] gefühllos; [ - attitude] herzlos - **3.** [ruthless] kaltblütig.

**cold cream** n Coldcream die.

**cold cuts** npl esp Am Aufschnitt der.

**cold feet** npl: **to get ~** inf kalte Füße kriegen.

**cold-hearted** [-ˈhɑːtɪd] adj [person] kaltherzig; [action] herzlos.

**coldly** ['kəʊldlɪ] adv kalt.

**coldness** ['kəʊldnɪs] n Kälte die.

**cold shoulder** n: **to give sb the ~** inf jm die kalte Schulter zeigen.

**cold sore** n Bläschenausschlag der.

**cold storage** n Kühllagerung die.

**cold sweat** n kalter Schweiß der; **he was in a ~** ihm brach der kalte Schweiß aus.

**cold war** n: **the ~** der Kalte Krieg.

**coleslaw** ['kəʊlslɔː] n Krautsalat der.

**colic** ['kɒlɪk] n Kolik die.

**collaborate** [kəˈlæbəreɪt] vi - **1.** [work together]: **to ~ (with sb)** (mit jm) zusammenlarbeiten - **2.** pej [with enemy]: **to ~ (with sb)** (mit jm) kollaborieren.

**collaboration** [kəˌlæbəˈreɪʃn] n - **1.** (U) [teamwork - of two parties] Zusammenarbeit die; [ - of one party] Mitarbeit die - **2.** pej [with enemy]: **~ (with)** Kollaboration die (mit).

**collaborative** [kəˈlæbərətɪv] adj gemeinschaftlich.

**collaborator** [kəˈlæbəreɪtəʳ] n - **1.** [colleague] Mitarbeiter der, -in die - **2.** pej [traitor] Kollaborateur der, -in die.

**collage** ['kɒlɑːʒ] n Collage die.

**collagen** ['kɒlədʒən] n Kollagen das.

**collapse** [kəˈlæps] n - **1.** [destruction] Einsturz der - **2.** [failure - of marriage, government] Scheitern das; [ - of empire] Untergang der; [ - of system, business, company] Zusammenbruch der - **3.** MED Kollaps der ⬦ vi - **1.** [fall down, fall in - house, building, roof] einlstürzen; [ - stage, bridge] zusammenlbrechen; [ - lung] zusammenlfallen; **I ~d into bed** ich ließ mich aufs Bett fallen - **2.** [fail - marriage, government] scheitern; [ - system, business, company] zusammenlbrechen - **3.** MED kollabieren - **4.** [folding table, chair] sich zusammenklappen lassen.

**collapsible** [kə'læpsəbl] *adj* zusammenklappbar.

**collar** ['kɒlə'] *n* - **1.** [on clothes] Kragen *der* - **2.** [for dog] Halsband *das* - **3.** TECH Bund *der* ◇ *vt inf* [detain] fassen.

**collarbone** ['kɒləbəʊn] *n* Schlüsselbein *das*.

**collate** [kə'leɪt] *vt* - **1.** [information, evidence] sammeln - **2.** [pages, photocopies] sortieren.

**collateral** [kə'lætərəl] *n* Sicherheit *die*.

**collation** [kə'leɪʃn] *n* - **1.** [of information, evidence] Sammeln und Vergleichen *das* - **2.** [of pages, photocopies] Sortierung *die*.

**colleague** ['kɒliːg] *n* Kollege *der*, -gin *die*.

**collect** [kə'lekt] *vt* - **1.** [gen] sammeln; [empty glasses, bottles] einlsammeln; [dust] anlziehen; [one's belongings] zusammenlsuchen; [taxes] einlziehen; **~ on delivery** Am bei Lieferung bezahlen; **~ o.s.** sich sammeln - **2.** [go to get, fetch] ablholen ◇ *vi* - **1.** [crowd, people] sich versammeln - **2.** [dust, dirt] sich anlsammeln - **3.** [for charity, gift] sammeln ◇ *adv* Am TELEC: **to call (sb) ~** ein R-Gespräch (mit jm) führen.

➤ **collect up** *vt sep* zusammenlsammeln.

**collectable** [kə'lektəbl] *adj* sammelwürdig ◇ *n* Sammlerstück *das*.

**collected** [kə'lektɪd] *adj* - **1.** [person] gelassen - **2.** [works, poems] gesammelt.

**collecting** [kə'lektɪŋ] *n* Sammeln *das*.

**collecting tin** *n* Sammelbüchse *die*.

**collection** [kə'lekʃn] *n* - **1.** [gen] Sammlung *die* - **2.** (U) [of taxes] Einziehen *das;* [of rubbish] Abfuhr *die;* [of mail] Leerung *die*.

**collective** [kə'lektɪv] *adj* kollektiv ◇ *n* Produktionsgenossenschaft *die*.

**collective bargaining** *n* (U) Tarifverhandlungen *pl*.

**collectively** [kə'lektɪvlɪ] *adv* gemeinsam.

**collective ownership** *n* Kollektiveigentum *das*.

**collector** [kə'lektə'] *n* - **1.** [as a hobby] Sammler *der*, -in *die* - **2.** [of taxes] Einnehmer *der*, -in *die* - **3.** [of debts] Eintreiber *der*, -in *die;* [of rent] Kassierer *der*, -in *die*.

**collector's item** *n* Sammlerstück *das*.

**college** ['kɒlɪdʒ] *n* - **1.** [for further education] ≃ Fachhochschule *die;* **~ of technology** technische Hochschule - **2.** [of university] College *das* - **3.** [organized body] Kammer *die*, Bund *der*.

**college of education** *n* pädagogische Hochschule.

**collide** [kə'laɪd] *vi*: **to ~ (with sb/sthg)** (mit jm/etw) zusammenlstoßen, (mit jm/etw) kollidieren.

**collie** ['kɒlɪ] *n* Collie *der*.

**colliery** ['kɒljərɪ] *(pl* -**ies)** *n* Kohlengrube *die*.

**collision** [kə'lɪʒn] *n* - **1.** [crash]: **~ (with sb/sthg)** Zusammenstoß *der* (mit jm/etw), Kollision *die* (mit jm/etw); **to be on a ~ course with sb/ sthg** *fig* mit jm/etw auf Kollisionskurs sein - **2.** *fig* [conflict] Kollision *die*, Konflikt *der*.

**colloquial** [kə'ləʊkwɪəl] *adj* umgangssprachlich.

**collude** [kə'luːd] *vi*: **to ~ with sb** mit jm gemeinsame Sache machen.

**collusion** [kə'luːʒn] *n*: **in ~ with** in geheimer Absprache mit.

**cologne** [kə'ləʊn] *n* Kölnischwasser *das*.

**Colombia** [kə'lɒmbɪə] *n* Kolumbien *nt*.

**Colombian** [kə'lɒmbɪən] *adj* kolumbianisch ◇ *n* Kolumbianer *der*, -in *die*.

**colon** ['kəʊlən] *n* - **1.** ANAT Dickdarm *der* - **2.** [punctuation mark] Doppelpunkt *der*.

**colonel** ['kɜːnl] *n* Oberst *der*.

**colonial** [kə'ləʊnjəl] *adj* kolonial-.

**colonialism** [kə'ləʊnjəlɪzm] *n* Kolonialismus *der*.

**colonist** ['kɒlənɪst] *n* Siedler *der*, -in *die*, Kolonist *der*, -in *die*.

**colonize, -ise** ['kɒlənaɪz] *vt* kolonisieren.

**colonnade** [ˌkɒlə'neɪd] *n* Säulengang *der*, Kolonnade *die*.

**colony** ['kɒlənɪ] *(pl* -**ies)** *n* Kolonie *die*.

**color** *etc n, adj, vt & vi* Am **= colour** *etc*.

**colorado beetle** [ˌkɒlə'rɑːdəʊ-] *n* Kartoffelkäfer *der*.

**colossal** [kə'lɒsl] *adj* gewaltig.

**colostomy** [kə'lɒstəmɪ] *(pl* -**ies)** *n* Kolostomie *die*.

**colour** Br, **color** Am ['kʌlə'] *n* Farbe *die;* **in ~** in Farbe ◇ *adj* [not black and white] Farb- ◇ *vt* - **1.** [give colour to] färben; [with pen, crayon] kolorieren - **2.** *fig* [affect] beeinflussen ◇ *vi* [blush] erröten.

➤ **colours** *npl* - **1.** [of school, team] Farben *pl* - **2.** [flag] Fahne *die*.

➤ **colour in** *vt sep* auslmalen.

**colour bar** *n* Rassenschranke *die*.

**colour-blind** *adj* farbenblind.

**colour-coded** *adj* farbig gekennzeichnet.

**coloured** Br, **colored** Am ['kʌləd] *adj* farbig.

**colourfast** Br, **colorfast** Am ['kʌləfɑːst] *adj* farbecht.

**colourful** Br, **colorful** Am ['kʌləfʊl] *adj* - **1.** [brightly coloured] farbenfroh - **2.** [story] ereignisreich; [description] farbig - **3.** [person] schillernd.

**colouring** Br, **coloring** Am ['kʌlərɪŋ] *n* - **1.** [dye] Farbstoff *der* - **2.** [complexion] Gesichtsfarbe *die;* [of hair] Farbe *die* - **3.** [colours] Farben *pl.*

**colourless** *Br,* **colorless** *Am* ['kʌlǝlɪs] *adj lit & fig* farblos.

**colour scheme** *n* Farbzusammenstellung *die.*

**colour supplement** *n Br* Farbbeilage *die.*

**colt** [kǝʊlt] *n* Hengstfohlen *das.*

**column** ['kɒlǝm] *n* - **1.** [structure, of smoke] Säule *die* - **2.** [of people, vehicles, numbers] Kolonne *die* - **3.** [of text] Spalte *die* - **4.** [article] Kolumne *die.*

**columnist** ['kɒlǝmnɪst] *n* Kolumnist *der,* -in *die.*

**coma** ['kǝʊmǝ] *n* Koma *das.*

**comatose** ['kǝʊmǝtǝʊs] *adj* komatös, im Koma.

**comb** [kǝʊm] *n* Kamm *der* ⬦ *vt* - **1.** [hair] kämmen - **2.** [search] durchkämmen.

**combat** ['kɒmbæt] *n* Kampf *der* ⬦ *vt* bekämpfen.

**combative** ['kɒmbǝtɪv] *adj* aggressiv.

**combination** [ˌkɒmbɪ'neɪʃn] *n* - **1.** (U) [act of combining] Verbindung *die* - **2.** [mixture, for safe] Kombination *die.*

**combination lock** *n* Kombinationsschloss *das.*

**combine** [*vb* kǝm'baɪn, *n* 'kɒmbaɪn] *vt* vereinigen, verbinden; **to ~ sthg with sthg** [two substances, activities] etw mit etw verbinden; [two qualities] etw mit etw vereinigen ⬦ *vi* [businesses, political parties]: **to ~ (with sb/sthg)** sich (mit jm/etw) zusammenlschließen ⬦ *n* - **1.** [group] Firmengruppe *die,* Konzern *der* - **2.** = **combine harvester.**

**combined** [kǝm'baɪnd] *adj:* **~ with sb/sthg** zusammen mit jm/etw; **~ efforts** vereinte Anstrengungen *pl;* **~ attack** gemeinsamer Angriff.

**combine harvester** [-'hɑ:vɪstǝʳ] *n* Mähdrescher *der.*

**combustible** [kǝm'bʌstǝbl] *adj* brennbar.

**combustion** [kǝm'bʌstʃn] *n* Verbrennung *die;* **~ engine** Verbrennungsmotor *der.*

**come** [kʌm] (*pt* came; *pp* come) *vi* - **1.** [move] kommen; **we came by taxi** wir sind mit dem Taxi gekommen; **~ here!** komm her!; **coming!** ich komme schon! - **2.** [arrive] kommen; **to ~ home** nach Hause kommen; 'coming soon' 'demnächst'; **the time has ~** es ist an der Zeit; **the news came as a shock (to him)** die Nachricht war ein Schock (für ihn); **he doesn't know whether he's coming or going** *fig* er weiß nicht, wie er dran ist; **to ~ to one's senses** *inf* Vernunft anlnehmen - **3.** [in competition, in order]: **to ~ first/last** Erster/Letzter werden; **P ~s before Q** P kommt vor Q - **4.** [become] werden; **to ~ true** wahr werden; **to ~ undone** auf lgehen - **5.** [be sold]: **they ~ in packs**

of six es gibt sie im Sechserpack - **6.** [happen]: **how did you ~ to fail your exam?** wieso hast du eigentlich die Prüfung nicht geschafft?; **~ what may** was auch geschieht - **7.** [begin gradually]: **we have ~ to think that ...** wir sind zu der Ansicht gekommen, dass ...; **he has ~ to like Baltimore** inzwischen gefällt ihm Baltimore recht gut - **8.** *inf* [have orgasm] kommen - **9.** *phr:* **~ to think of it** wenn ich es mir recht überlege.

⬥ **to come** *adv:* **for generations to ~** auf Generationen hin; **in years to ~ we will look back on today with pride** wir werden später mit Stolz auf diesen Tag zurückblicken.

⬥ **come about** *vi* [happen] geschehen; [come into being] entstehen; **how did it ~ about?** wie ist es dazu gekommen?

⬥ **come across** *vt fus* [find] stoßen auf (+ A) ⬦ *vi* [speaker, message]: **how did I ~ across?** wie bin ich beim Publikum angekommen?; **to ~ across as friendly** freundlich wirken; **she came across as being very knowledgeable** sie schien viel zu wissen.

⬥ **come along** *vi* - **1.** [arrive] kommen - **2.** [progress] voranlkommen - **3.** *phr:* **~ along!** komm!

⬥ **come apart** *vi* auseinander fallen.

⬥ **come at** *vt fus* [attack] loslgehen auf (+ A).

⬥ **come back** *vi* - **1.** [gen] zurücklkommen; **to ~ back to sthg** auf etw (A) zurücklkommen - **2.** [memory]: **it will ~ back to me in a minute** es wird mir gleich einfallen - **3.** [become fashionable again] wieder in Mode kommen.

⬥ **come by** *vt fus* - **1.** [get, obtain]: **to ~ by sthg** an etw (A) kommen; **they are hard to ~ by** sie sind schwer zu finden - **2.** [visit]: **he came by my place yesterday** er ist gestern bei mir vorbeigekommen.

⬥ **come down** *vi* - **1.** [price, rain] fallen - **2.** [descend] herunterlkommen.

⬥ **come down to** *vt fus:* **it ~s down to a choice between money and happiness** es läuft auf eine Entscheidung zwischen Geld und Glückhinaus; **it all ~s down to profitability** letztlich ist die Rentabilität entscheidend.

⬥ **come down with** *vt fus* [illness] bekommen.

⬥ **come forward** *vi* sich melden.

⬥ **come from** *vt fus* - **1.** [person]: **I ~ from Ireland** ich komme aus Irland; **my family ~s from Belgium** meine Familie stammt aus Belgien - **2.** [originate from]: **caviar ~s from sturgeon** Kaviar stammt vom Stör; **where is that noise coming from?** woher kommt dieses Geräusch?

⬥ **come in** *vi* - **1.** [enter] hereinlkommen; **~ in!** herein! - **2.** [arrive - train] einlfahren - **3.** [finish race] anlkommen, einllaufen; **to ~ in first** Erste/Erster werden - **4.** [be involved]: **where do I ~ in?** was ist mit mir?; **that's where you ~ in** hier kommst du ins Spiel.

⬥ **come in for** *vt fus* [criticism] einstecken OR hinnehmen müssen.

⬥ **come into** *vt fus* - **1.** [inherit] erben - **2.** [begin to be]: **to ~ into being** entstehen; **to ~ into sight** in Sicht kommen.

🔹 **come of** *vt fus* [result from]: **what will ~ of it?** was wird daraus?; **did anything ~ of your plans?** ist etwas aus deinen Plänen geworden?; **that's what ~s** of telling lies das kommt davon, wenn man lügt.

🔹 **come off** *vi* - **1.** [button, top] ablgehen - **2.** [succeed] klappen - **3.** [finish]: **to ~ off well/badly** [person] gut/schlecht ablschneiden - **4.** [dirt, mud] ablgehen - **5.** *phr:* **~ off it!** *inf* hör doch auf!

🔹 **come on** *vi* - **1.** [start] anlfangen; **I have a cold coming on** ich kriege eine Erkältung; **the rain came on** es fing an zu regnen - **2.** [start working - light, machine] anlgehen - **3.** [progress] voranlkommen - **4.** *phr:* **~ on!** [as encouragement, hurry up] komm!; [in disbelief] hör doch auf!

🔹 **come out** *vi* - **1.** [become known] herauslkommen - **2.** [appear - book, record] erscheinen, herauslkommen; [ - stars] zu sehen sein; **the sun came out from behind a cloud** die Sonne kam von hinter einer Wolke hervor - **3.** [turn out]: **my cake/painting came out well** der Kuchen/das Bild ist mir gut gelungen; **to ~ out well/badly** gut/schlecht ablschneiden - **4.** [go on strike] streiken - **5.** [declare publicly]: **to ~ out for/against sthg** sich für/gegen etw auslsprechen - **6.** [photograph]: **only two photos came out** nur zwei Bilder sind etwas geworden - **7.** [stain] herauslgehen.

🔹 **come out in** *vt fus*: **to ~ out in spots** [acne] Pickel bekommen.

🔹 **come out with** *vt fus* [idea] anlkommen mit; [remark] machen; **to ~ out with the truth** mit der Wahrheit herauslrücken.

🔹 **come over** *vt fus* [subj: sensation, emotion] überkommen; **I don't know what has ~ over her** ich weiß nicht, was in sie gefahren ist ◇ *vi* [visit] vorbeilkommen.

🔹 **come round** *vi* - **1.** [visit] vorbeilkommen - **2.** [change opinion] seine Meinung ändern; **he eventually came round to my way of thinking** letzendlich schloss er sich meiner Ansicht an - **3.** [regain consciousness] zu sich kommen.

🔹 **come through** *vt fus* - **1.** [war, illness, difficult situation] überstehen - **2.** [survive] durchlkommen ◇ *vi* [cheque] einltreffen; **have your results ~ through yet?** hast du deine Ergebnisse schon?

🔹 **come to** *vt fus* - **1.** [reach]: **to ~ to an end** zu Ende gehen; **to ~ to power** an die Macht kommen; **to ~ to a decision** zu einer Entscheidung kommen - **2.** [amount to]: **the bill ~s to £20** das macht 20 Pfund ◇ *vi* [regain consciousness] zu sich kommen.

🔹 **come under** *vt fus* - **1.** [be governed by - jurisdiction, rules] fallen unter (+ A); **this matter ~s under local government authority** für diese Angelegenheit ist die Lokalregierung zuständig; **to ~ under sb's influence** unter js

Einfluss geraten - **2.** [heading] kommen OR stehen unter (+ D) - **3.** [suffer]: **to ~ under attack (from)** angegriffen werden (von).

🔹 **come up** *vi* - **1.** [go upstairs] herauf lkommen - **2.** [be mentioned] erwähnt werden; **to ~ up for discussion** zur Diskussion kommen - **3.** [happen] passieren - **4.** [job] frei werden - **5.** [sun, moon] auf lgehen - **6.** [be imminent] bevorlstehen; **my birthday is coming up** ich habe bald Geburtstag.

🔹 **come up against** *vt fus* [difficulties, obstacles] stoßen auf (+ A); [opponent] treffen auf (+ A).

🔹 **come upon** *vt fus* [thing, place] stoßen auf (+ A); [person] treffen.

🔹 **come up to** *vt fus* - **1.** [approach - person, object] kommen zu; **it's coming up to Christmas/six o'clock** es ist bald Weihnachten/gleich sechs Uhr - **2.** [reach]: **the water ~s up to my waist** das Wasser reicht mir bis zur Taille - **3.** [equal - standard] erreichen; **to ~ up to sb's expectations** js Erwartungen erfüllen.

🔹 **come up with** *vt fus* [answer, idea, solution] sich (D) ausldenken.

**comeback** ['kʌmbæk] *n* [of person] Comeback *das*; **to make a ~** [person] ein Comeback schaffen; [activity, style] wieder in Mode kommen.

**Comecon** ['kɒmɪkɒn] (*abbr of* **Council for Mutual Economic Aid**) *n* Comecon *das*.

**comedian** [kə'miːdjən] *n* Komiker *der*, -in *die*.

**comedienne** [kə,miːdɪ'en] *n* Komikerin *die*.

**comedown** ['kʌmdaʊn] *n inf* Abstieg *der*.

**comedy** ['kɒmədɪ] (*pl* **-ies**) *n* - **1.** [play, film] Komödie *die* - **2.** [humour] Komik *die*.

**comely** ['kʌmlɪ] *adj literary* ansehnlich.

**come-on** *n inf*: **to give sb the ~** jn anlmachen.

**comet** ['kɒmɪt] *n* Komet *der*.

**come-uppance** [,kʌm'ʌpəns] *n inf*: **to get one's ~** die Quittung kriegen.

**comfort** ['kʌmfət] *n* - **1.** [ease] Behaglichkeit *die* - **2.** [luxury] Komfort *der* - **3.** [solace] Trost *der*; **to take ~ from sthg** Trost in etw (D) finden ◇ *vt* trösten.

**comfortable** ['kʌmftəbl] *adj* - **1.** [chair, shoes, sofa, life] bequem; [house, hotel, coach] komfortabel - **2.** [at ease]: **to be ~** sich wohl fühlen; **make yourself ~** machen Sie es sich bequem - **3.** [financially secure - income] ausreichend; **to be ~** keine finanziellen Sorgen haben - **4.** [after operation, accident]: **his condition is ~** ihm geht es (den Umständen entsprechend) gut - **5.** [lead] sicher; [victory] leicht.

**comfortably** ['kʌmftəblɪ] *adv* - **1.** [sit] bequem; [sleep] gut - **2.** [without financial difficulty] bequem, ohne Probleme; **he's ~ off** es geht ihm finanziell gut - **3.** [win] mühelos.

**comforter** ['kʌmfətə*r*] *n* - **1.** [person] Tröster *der*, -in *die* - **2.** *Am* [quilt] Deckbett *das*.

**comforting** ['kʌmfətɪŋ] *adj* tröstlich.

**comfort station** *n Am euphemism* Bedürfnis-anstalt *die.*

**comfy** ['kʌmfɪ] (*compar* -ier; *superl* -iest) *adj inf* - **1.** [chair, shoes, sofa, life] bequem; [house, hotel, coach] komfortabel - **2.** [person]: **to be ~** sich wohl fühlen; **make yourself ~** machs dir ge-mütlich.

**comic** ['kɒmɪk] *adj* komisch ⬦ *n* - **1.** [comedian] Komiker *der*, -in *die* - **2.** [magazine] Comicheft *das.*
➤ **comics** *npl Am* [in newspaper] Comics *pl.*

**comical** ['kɒmɪkl] *adj* ulkig, komisch.

**comic strip** *n* Comicstrip *der.*

**coming** ['kʌmɪŋ] *adj* [future] kommend ⬦ *n:* **~s and goings** Kommen und Gehen *das.*

**comma** ['kɒmə] *n* Komma *das.*

**command** [kə'mɑːnd] *n* - **1.** [order] Befehl *der;* MIL Kommando *das* - **2.** (*U*) [control] Komman-do *das*, Befehlsgewalt *die;* **to be in ~ of sthg** [in charge of] für etw verantwortlich sein - **3.** [mastery] Beherrschung *die;* **to have sthg at one's ~** etw zur Verfügung haben; **she has four languages at her ~** sie beherrscht vier Sprachen - **4.** COMPUT Befehl *der* ⬦ *vt* - **1.** [or-der]: **to ~ sb (to do sthg)** jm befehlen(, etw zu tun) - **2.** MIL [control] befehligen, kommandie-ren - **3.** [deserve - respect, attention, admiration] ver-dienen; **to ~ a high price** einen hohen Preis verlangen können.

**commandant** [ˌkɒmən'dænt] *n* Komman-dant *der.*

**commandeer** [ˌkɒmən'dɪəʳ] *vt* MIL beschlag-nahmen.

**commander** [kə'mɑːndəʳ] *n* - **1.** [in army] Kom-mandant *der*, Befehlshaber *der* - **2.** [in navy] Fregattenkapitän *der.*

**commander in chief** (*pl* **commanders in chief**) *n* Oberbefehlshaber *der.*

**commanding** [kə'mɑːndɪŋ] *adj* - **1.** [position, view] beherrschend; [lead] groß - **2.** [voice, man-ner] gebieterisch.

**commanding officer** *n* befehlshabender Offizier.

**commandment** [kə'mɑːndmənt] *n* RELIG Gebot *das.*

**command module** *n* Kommandokapsel *die.*

**commando** [kə'mɑːndəʊ] (*pl* **-s** OR **-es**) *n* - **1.** [unit] Kommandotrupp *der* - **2.** [soldier] Angehörige *der*, *die* eines Kommando-trupps.

**command performance** *n* königliche Galavorstellung.

**commemorate** [kə'meməreɪt] *vt* - **1.** [honour] gedenken (+ *G*) - **2.** [subj: statue, plaque] erin-nern an (+ *A*).

**commemoration** [kəˌmemə'reɪʃn] *n:* **in ~ of** zum Gedenken an (+ *A*).

**commemorative** [kə'memərətɪv] *adj* Ge-denk-.

**commence** [kə'mens] *fml vt* beginnen; **to ~ doing sthg** (damit) beginnen, etw zu tun ⬦ *vi* beginnen.

**commencement** [kə'mensmənt] *n fml* Be-ginn *der.*

**commend** [kə'mend] *vt* - **1.** [praise]: **to ~ sb (on** OR **for sthg)** jn (wegen etw) loben - **2.** [recom-mend]: **to ~ sthg (to sb)** (jm) etw empfehlen.

**commendable** [kə'mendəbl] *adj* lobenswert.

**commendation** [ˌkɒmen'deɪʃn] *n* Auszeich-nung *die.*

**commensurate** [kə'menʃərət] *adj fml:* **to be ~ with sthg** etw (*D*) entsprechen.

**comment** ['kɒment] *n* Bemerkung *die;* **no ~** kein Kommentar ⬦ *vt:* **to ~ that** bemerken OR äußern, dass ⬦ *vi:* **to ~ (on sthg)** sich (über etw (*A*)) äußern.

**commentary** ['kɒməntrɪ] (*pl* -ies) *n* - **1.** RADIO & TV Livereportage *die* - **2.** [written] Kommentar *der.*

**commentate** ['kɒmənteɪt] *vi* RADIO & TV: **to ~ (on sthg)** (über etw (*A*)) live berichten.

**commentator** ['kɒmənteɪtəʳ] *n* - **1.** RADIO & TV Reporter *der*, -in *die* - **2.** [expert] Kommenta-tor *der*, -in *die.*

**commerce** ['kɒmɜːs] *n* Handel *der.*

**commercial** [kə'mɜːʃl] *adj* - **1.** [regarding busi-ness - law, organization] Handels-; [- premises] Ge-schäfts- - **2.** [profit-making] kommerziell ⬦ *n* [advertisement] Werbespot *der.*

**commercial bank** *n* Geschäftsbank *die.*

**commercial break** *n* Werbepause *die.*

**commercial college** *n* kaufmännische Schule, Handelsschule *die.*

**commercialism** [kə'mɜːʃəlɪzm] *n pej* Kom-merz *der.*

**commercialize, -ise** [kə'mɜːʃəlaɪz] *vt* kom-merzialisieren.

**commercialized** [kə'mɜːʃəlaɪzd] *adj pej* kom-merzialisiert.

**commercially** [kə'mɜːʃəlɪ] *adv* kommerziell.

**commercial traveller** *n Br dated* Handels-vertreter *der*, -in *die.*

**commercial vehicle** *n Br* Nutzfahrzeug *das.*

**commie** ['kɒmɪ] *inf pej adj* rot ⬦ *n* Rote *der*, *die.*

**commiserate** [kə'mɪzəreɪt] *vi:* **to ~ (with sb)** (jm) sein Mitgefühl auslsprechen.

**commiseration** [kəˌmɪzə'reɪʃn] *n* Mitgefühl *das.*

**commission** [kə'mɪʃn] n - **1.** (U) [money] Provision die - **2.** [piece of work] Auftrag der - **3.** [investigative body] Kommission die <> vt [work] in Auftrag geben; **to ~ sb to do sthg** jn damit beauftragen, etw zu tun.

**commissionaire** [kə‚mɪʃə'neəʳ] n Br Portier der.

**commissioned officer** [kə'mɪʃənd-] n Offizier der.

**commissioner** [kə'mɪʃnəʳ] n - **1.** [of police] Präsident der, -in die - **2.** [member of commission] Kommissionsmitglied das.

**Commission for Racial Equality** n Br: the ~ britische Regierungsorganisation mit dem Auftrag, die Gleichstellung aller ethnischen Gruppen im Arbeitsleben, in Schulen etc sicherzustellen.

**commit** [kə'mɪt] (pt & pp **-ted**; cont **-ting**) vt - **1.** [crime, sin] begehen - **2.** [money, resources] bestimmen für; **to ~ o.s. (to sthg)** sich (auf etw (A)) festlegen; **to ~ o.s. to doing sthg** sich verpflichten, etw zu tun - **3.** [consign] einlweisen; **to ~ sthg to memory** sich (D) etw merken, sich (D) etw einlprägen.

**commitment** [kə'mɪtmənt] n - **1.** [dedication] Engagement das - **2.** [responsibility] Verpflichtung die.

**committed** [kə'mɪtɪd] adj [writer, Christian] engagiert; **to be ~ to sb/sthg** sich für jn/etw einlsetzen.

**committee** [kə'mɪtɪ] n Ausschuss der, Komitee das.

**commode** [kə'məʊd] n - **1.** [chamber pot] Nachtstuhl der - **2.** [chest of drawers] Kommode die.

**commodity** [kə'mɒdətɪ] (pl **-ies**) n [product] Produkt das.

**commodity exchange** n Warenbörse die.

**common** [‘kɒmən] adj - **1.** [ordinary, widespread] häufig; [practice] weit verbreitet; **the ~ cold** die Erkältung; **the ~ man** der Normalbürger - **2.** [shared] gemeinsam; **it's ~ to us all** es ist uns allen gemein - **3.** Br pej [vulgar] gewöhnlich <> n [land] Gemeinde die.

➤ **in common** adv gemein; **we've got a lot in ~** wir haben viel gemein.

**commoner** [‘kɒmənəʳ] n Bürgerliche der, die.

**common good** n: **for the ~** im allgemeinen Interesse, für das Gemeinwohl.

**common ground** n: **there's no ~** es gibt keine gemeinsame Basis.

**common knowledge** n: **it's ~ that ...** es ist allgemein bekannt, dass ...

**common land** n (U) Gemeindeland das.

**common law** n Gewohnheitsrecht das.

➤ **common-law** adj: **she is his common-law wife**

sie lebt mit ihm in eheähnlicher Gemeinschaft.

**commonly** [‘kɒmənlɪ] adv [generally] allgemein.

**Common Market** n: **the ~** der Gemeinsame Markt.

**commonplace** [‘kɒmənpleɪs] adj alltäglich.

**common room** n Aufenthaltsraum der.

**Commons** [‘kɒmənz] npl Br: **the ~** das (britische) Unterhaus.

**common sense** n gesunder Menschenverstand.

**Commonwealth** [‘kɒmənwelθ] n: **the ~** das Commonwealth.

Als freiwilliger Zusammenschluss von 54 unabhängigen Staaten, die früher zum Britischen Weltreich gehörten, tritt der Commonwealth für Entwicklung, Gleichheit zwischen den Rassen und wirtschaftliches Wachstum ein und bietet seinen Mitgliedern Hilfen dabei an. Sein derzeitiges Oberhaupt ist Queen Elizabeth II, obwohl die meisten der Gliedstaaten mittlerweile gänzlich unabhängig von der britischen Krone sind. Daneben dient das Wort Commonwealth„ auch zur Bezeichnung gewisser Länder, wie z. B. Australien („Commonwealth of Australia"), die aus mehreren Gliedstaaten bestehen.

**commotion** [kə'məʊʃn] n [activity] Aufregung die; [noise] Lärm der; **to cause a ~** für Aufregung sorgen.

**communal** [‘kɒmjʊnl] adj [kitchen] Gemeinschafts-; [garden, ownership] gemeinsam.

**commune** [n ‘kɒmjuːn vb kə'mjuːn] n Kommune die <> vi: **to ~ with** Zwiesprache halten mit.

**communicate** [kə'mjuːnɪkeɪt] vt mitlteilen <> vi sich verständigen; **to ~ with** kommunizieren mit.

**communicating door** [kə'mjuːnɪkeɪtɪŋ-] n Verbindungstür die.

**communication** [kə‚mjuːnɪ'keɪʃn] n - **1.** (U) [contact] Kommunikation die, Verständigung die; **to be in ~ with sb** Kontakt mit jm haben - **2.** [letter, phone call] Mitteilung die.

➤ **communications** npl [traffic] Verkehrsverbindungen pl; [telephone etc] Kommunikationsmittel pl.

**communication cord** n Br Notbremse die.

**communications satellite** n Nachrichtensatellit der.

**communicative** [kə'mjuːnɪkətɪv] adj gesprächig, mitteilsam.

**communicator** [kə'mjuːnɪkeɪtəʳ] n: **to be a**

**good/bad ~** sich gut/schlecht verständigen können.

**communion** [kə'mju:njən] *n* Zwiesprache *die.*

➤ **Communion** *n* [RELIG - Protestant] Abendmahl *das;* [ - Catholic] Kommunion *die.*

**communiqué** [kə'mju:nɪkeɪ] *n* (offizielle) Bekanntmachung.

**Communism** ['kɒmjʊnɪzm] *n* Kommunismus *der.*

**Communist** ['kɒmjʊnɪst] *adj* kommunistisch ◇ *n* Kommunist *der,* -in *die.*

**community** [kə'mju:nətɪ] *(pl* -ies) *n* - **1.** [group] Gemeinschaft *die;* [local] Gemeinde *die;* [ethnic] Bevölkerungsgruppe *die* - **2.** [people in general]: **the ~** die Gesellschaft.

**community centre** *n* Gemeindezentrum *das.*

**community home** *n* Br Fürsorgeanstalt *die.*

**community service** *n* [charitable work] ehrenamtliche Arbeit; [for criminal] gemeinnütziger Dienst.

**community spirit** *n* Gemeinschaftsgeist *der.*

**commutable** [kə'mju:təbl] *adj* LAW umwandelbar.

**commutation ticket** [ˌkɒmju:'teɪʃn] *n* Am Zeitnetzkarte *die.*

**commute** [kə'mju:t] *vt* LAW umlwandeln ◇ *vi* [to work] pendeln.

**commuter** [kə'mju:tə'] *n* Pendler *der,* -in *die.*

**commy** ['kɒmɪ] *(pl* -ies) *adj* & *n* = **commie.**

**compact** [*adj* & *vb* kəm'pækt, *n* 'kɒmpækt] *adj* kompakt; [style, text] gedrängt ◇ *n* - **1.** [for face powder] Puderdose *die* - **2.** Am AUT: **~ (car)** Kompaktauto *das* ◇ *vt* [with foot] festltreten; [with vehicle] festlfahren.

**compact disc** *n* Compactdisc *die.*

**compact disc player** *n* CD-Player *der.*

**companion** [kəm'pænjən] *n* - **1.** [person] Gefährte *der,* -tin *die* - **2.** [one of pair] Pendant *das* - **3.** [book] Ratgeber *der.*

**companionable** [kəm'pænjənəbl] *adj* freundlich.

**companionship** [kəm'pænjənʃɪp] *n (U)* Gesellschaft *die.*

**company** ['kʌmpənɪ] *(pl* -ies) *n* - **1.** [business] Firma *die;* **insurance ~** Versicherung *die* - **2.** [of actors] Schauspieltruppe *die* - **3.** *(U)* [companionship] Gesellschaft *die;* **she's good ~** es ist schön, mit ihr zusammen zu sein; **to keep sb ~** jm Gesellschaft leisten; **to part ~ (with sb)** sich *(D)* (von jm) trennen - **4.** [guests] Besuch *der* - **5.** MIL Kompanie *die* - **6.** NAUT Besatzung *die.*

**company car** *n* Firmenwagen *der.*

**company director** *n* Firmenchef *der,* -in *die.*

**company secretary** *n* Prokurist *der,* -in *die.*

**comparable** ['kɒmprəbl] *adj:* **~ (to** OR **with)** vergleichbar (mit).

**comparative** [kəm'pærətɪv] *adj* - **1.** [relative] relativ - **2.** [study, literature] vergleichend - **3.** GRAMM: **~ form** Komparativ *der.*

**comparatively** [kəm'pærətɪvlɪ] *adv* [relatively] relativ, verhältnismäßig.

**compare** [kəm'peə'] *vt* vergleichen; **to ~ sb/sthg with** OR **to** jn/etw vergleichen mit; **~d with** OR **to** verglichen mit, im Vergleich zu ◇ *vi* - **(with sb/sthg)** sich (mit jm/etw); vergleichen lassen **to ~ favourably/unfavourably with sthg** im Vergleich mit etw gut/schlecht ablschneiden.

**comparison** [kəm'pærɪsn] *n* Vergleich *der;* **in ~ (with** OR **to)** im Vergleich (zu).

**compartment** [kəm'pɑ:tmənt] *n* - **1.** [in fridge, desk, drawer] Fach *das* - **2.** RAIL Abteil *das.*

**compass** ['kʌmpəs] *n* - **1.** [for finding direction] Kompass *der* - **2.** *fml* [scope] Rahmen *der;* **within the ~ of** im Bereich von.

➤ **compasses** *npl:* **(a pair of) ~es** ein Zirkel.

**compassion** [kəm'pæʃn] *n* Mitgefühl *das.*

**compassionate** [kəm'pæʃənət] *adj* mitfühlend.

**compatibility** [kəmˌpætə'bɪlətɪ] *n* - **1.** [of people]: **there's no ~ between them** sie passen nicht zueinander - **2.** COMPUT Kompatibilität *die.*

**compatible** [kəm'pætəbl] *adj* - **1.** [people]: **to be ~** zueinander passen - **2.** COMPUT kompatibel.

**compatriot** [kəm'pætrɪət] *n* Landsmann *der,* -männin *die.*

**compel** [kəm'pel] *(pt* & *pp* -led; *cont* -ling) *vt* - **1.** [force] zwingen; **to ~ sb to do sthg** jn (dazu) zwingen, etw zu tun - **2.** [sympathy] ablnötigen; [interest, attention] ablverlangen.

**compelling** [kəm'pelɪŋ] *adj* zwingend.

**compendium** [kəm'pendɪəm] *(pl* -diums OR -dia [-dɪə]) *n* Handbuch *das.*

**compensate** ['kɒmpenseɪt] *vt:* **to ~ sb for sthg** [financially] jn für etw entschädigen ◇ *vi:* **to ~ for sthg** etw gutlmachen.

**compensation** [ˌkɒmpen'seɪʃn] *n:* **~ (for sthg)** Entschädigung *die* (für etw).

**compere** ['kɒmpeə'] Br *n* Showmaster *der* ◇ *vt:* **to ~ a show** bei einer Show (der) Showmaster sein.

**compete** [kəm'pi:t] *vi* - **1.** [vie]: **to ~ (for sthg)** (um etw) kämpfen - **2.** COMM: **to ~ (with sb/sthg)** (mit jm/etw) konkurrieren; **to ~ for sthg** [contract, business] um etw kämpfen

**- 3.** [take part] teil|nehmen; **to ~ in sthg** an etw (D) teil|nehmen.

**competence** ['kɒmpɪtəns] n Fähigkeit die, Tüchtigkeit die.

**competent** ['kɒmpɪtənt] adj fähig, kompetent.

**competently** ['kɒmpɪtəntlɪ] adv sachkundig, kompetent.

**competing** [kəm'pi:tɪŋ] adj [theories, views] (miteinander) konkurrierend.

**competition** [ˌkɒmpɪ'tɪʃn] n **- 1.** [rivalry & COMM] Konkurrenz die **- 2.** [race, contest] Wettbewerb der.

**competitive** [kəm'petətɪv] adj **- 1.** [person] vom Konkurrenzdenken geprägt **- 2.** [exam] Auswahl-; [sport] Wettkampf- **- 3.** COMM [goods, prices, company] konkurrenzfähig.

**competitively** [kəm'petətɪvlɪ] adv **- 1.** [play] um die Wette **- 2.** COMM [priced] konkurrenzfähig.

**competitor** [kəm'petɪtəʳ] n **- 1.** COMM Konkurrent der, -in die **- 2.** [in race, contest] Teilnehmer der, -in die.

**compilation** [ˌkɒmpɪ'leɪʃn] n **- 1.** [of book, report] Abfassung die **- 2.** [collection] Zusammenstellung die.

**compile** [kəm'paɪl] vt [programme, album] zusammen|stellen; [book, report] ab|fassen.

**complacency** [kəm'pleɪsnsɪ] n Selbstzufriedenheit die.

**complacent** [kəm'pleɪsnt] adj selbstzufrieden.

**complacently** [kəm'pleɪsntlɪ] adv selbstzufrieden.

**complain** [kəm'pleɪn] vi **- 1.** [moan]: **to ~ (about)** sich beschweren (über (+ A)) **- 2.** MED: **to ~ of sthg** über etw (A) klagen.

**complaint** [kəm'pleɪnt] n **- 1.** [gen] Beschwerde die; **to have no ~s** [be satisfied] sich nicht beklagen können **- 2.** MED Leiden das.

**complement** [n 'kɒmplɪmənt, vb 'kɒmplɪˌment] vt gut ergänzen; [food] vervollkommnen ⬦ n **- 1.** [accompaniment & GRAMM] Ergänzung die **- 2.** NAUT Besatzung die; **full ~** volle Anzahl.

**complementary** [ˌkɒmplɪ'mentərɪ] adj [colour] (einander) ergänzend; **~ medicine** alternative Medizin.

**complete** [kəm'pli:t] adj **- 1.** [entire] vollständig; **~ with** komplett mit **- 2.** [finished] abgeschlossen, fertig **- 3.** [total - disaster, surprise] völlig; **she was a ~ stranger to me** sie war mir völlig fremd ⬦ vt **- 1.** [make whole] vervollständigen **- 2.** [finish] beenden, fertig|stellen **- 3.** [questionnaire, form] aus|füllen.

**completely** [kəm'pli:tlɪ] adv vollkommen, völlig.

**completion** [kəm'pli:ʃn] n [finishing] Beendigung die, Fertigstellung die.

**complex** ['kɒmpleks] adj [complicated] kompliziert ⬦ n **- 1.** [of buildings] (Gebäude)komplex der **- 2.** PSYCH Komplex der.

**complexion** [kəm'plekʃn] n **- 1.** [of face] Teint der **- 2.** [aspect] Aspekt der; **that puts a different ~ on things** das lässt die Dinge in einem neuen OR anderen Licht erscheinen.

**complexity** [kəm'pleksətɪ] (pl -ies) n **- 1.** [complex nature] Kompliziertheit die **- 2.** [complex thing] Schwierigkeit die.

**compliance** [kəm'plaɪəns] n Einverständnis das; **~ with sthg** [with rules] Einhalten das einer Sache (G).

**compliant** [kəm'plaɪənt] adj fügsam.

**complicate** ['kɒmplɪkeɪt] vt komplizieren.

**complicated** ['kɒmplɪkeɪtɪd] adj kompliziert.

**complication** [ˌkɒmplɪ'keɪʃn] n **- 1.** [complexity] Kompliziertheit die **- 2.** MED Komplikation die.

**complicity** [kəm'plɪsətɪ] n: **~ (in sthg)** Mittäterschaft die (bei etw).

**compliment** [n 'kɒmplɪmənt, vb 'kɒmplɪˌment] n Kompliment das ⬦ vt: **to ~ sb (on sthg)** jm ein Kompliment/Komplimente (wegen etw (G)) machen.

➤ **compliments** npl fml: **with ~s** mit den besten Empfehlungen; **my ~s to the chef!** mein Kompliment an den Küchenchef!

**complimentary** [ˌkɒmplɪ'mentərɪ] adj **- 1.** [admiring] schmeichelhaft; **to be ~** [person] sich bewundernd äußern **- 2.** [drink] Frei-.

**complimentary ticket** n Freikarte die.

**compliments slip** n Empfehlungszettel der.

**comply** [kəm'plaɪ] (pt & pp -ied) vi: **to ~ with sthg** [contract] etw erfüllen; [request] etw (D) nachkommen; [law, standards] etw ein|halten.

**component** [kəm'pəʊnənt] n Teil das, Bestandteil der.

**compose** [kəm'pəʊz] vt **- 1.** [constitute] bilden; **to be ~d of sthg** sich aus etw zusammensetzen **- 2.** [poem] verfassen; [music] komponieren; [letter] ab|fassen **- 3.** [make calm]: **to ~ o.s.** sich fassen.

**composed** [kəm'pəʊzd] adj [calm] beherrscht, gelassen.

**composer** [kəm'pəʊzəʳ] n Komponist der, -in die.

**composition** [ˌkɒmpə'zɪʃn] n **- 1.** (U) [of music] Komponieren das; [of poetry] Verfassen das **- 2.** [piece of music] Komposition die **- 3.** [contents] Zusammensetzung die **- 4.** [essay] Aufsatz der.

**compost** [Br 'kɒmpɒst, Am 'kɒmpəust] n Kompost der.

**composure** [kəm'pəuʒə'] n Beherrschung die, Fassung die.

**compound** [adj & n 'kɒmpaund, vb kəm'paund] adj GRAMM zusammengesetzt <> n - **1.** CHEM Verbindung die - **2.** [mixture] Mischung die - **3.** [enclosed area] umzäuntes Gelände - **4.** GRAMM zusammengesetztes Wort, Kompositum das <> vt - **1.** [mixture, substance]: to be ~ed of sthg sich aus etw zusammenlsetzen - **2.** [mistake, problem] vergrößern.

**compound fracture** n offener Bruch.

**compound interest** n Zinseszins der.

**comprehend** [ˌkɒmprɪ'hend] vt [understand] begreifen, verstehen.

**comprehension** [ˌkɒmprɪ'henʃn] n Verständnis das; it's beyond my ~ es ist mir unbegreiflich.

**comprehensive** [ˌkɒmprɪ'hensɪv] adj - **1.** [wide-ranging] umfassend - **2.** [insurance] Vollkasko- <> n Br [school] = comprehensive school.

**comprehensively** [ˌkɒmprɪ'hensɪvlɪ] adv umfassend.

**comprehensive school** n Gesamtschule die.

**compress** [n 'kɒmpres, vb kəm'pres] n MED Kompresse die <> vt - **1.** [squeeze] zusammenlpressen; ~ed air Pressluft die - **2.** [text] kürzen.

**compression** [kəm'preʃn] n - **1.** [of air] Kompression die - **2.** [of text] Kürzung die.

**comprise** [kəm'praɪz] vt - **1.** [consist of]: to be ~d of bestehen aus, umlfassen - **2.** [constitute] bilden.

**compromise** ['kɒmprəmaɪz] n Kompromiss der <> vt kompromittieren; to ~ o.s. sich kompromittieren <> vi einen Kompromiss schließen.

**compromising** ['kɒmprəmaɪzɪŋ] adj kompromittierend.

**compulsion** [kəm'pʌlʃn] n Zwang der.

**compulsive** [kəm'pʌlsɪv] adj - **1.** [behaviour, gambler, liar] zwanghaft - **2.** [compelling]: this programme is ~ viewing dieses Programm muss man sehen.

**compulsory** [kəm'pʌlsərɪ] adj [retirement] Zwangs-; it is ~ to do sthg es ist Pflicht, etw zu tun; attendance is ~ die Teilnahme ist verpflichtend.

**compunction** [kəm'pʌŋkʃn] n (U) Gewissensbisse pl; [stronger] Schuldgefühle pl.

**computation** [ˌkɒmpjuː'teɪʃn] n Berechnung die.

**compute** [kəm'pjuːt] vt berechnen.

**computer** [kəm'pjuːtə'] n Computer der <> comp Computer-.

**computer dating** n Partnervermittlung die per Computer.

**computer game** n Computerspiel das.

**computerization** [kəmˌpjuːtəraɪ'zeɪʃn] n Computerisierung die; [of system, office] Umstellung die auf Computer.

**computerize, -ise** [kəm'pjuːtəraɪz] vt computerisieren; [system, office] auf Computer umlstellen.

**computerized** [kəm'pjuːtəraɪzd] adj computerisiert.

**computer language** n Computersprache die.

**computer-literate** adj: to be ~ mit Computern vertraut sein.

**computer science** n Informatik die.

**computing** [kəm'pjuːtɪŋ] n elektronische Datenverarbeitung; [subject] Informatik die.

**comrade** ['kɒmreɪd] n - **1.** POL Genosse der, -sin die - **2.** [companion] Kamerad der, -in die.

**comradeship** ['kɒmreɪdʃɪp] n Kameradschaft die.

**comsat** ['kɒmsæt] n abbr of communications satellite.

**con** [kɒn] (pt & pp -ned; cont -ning) inf n - **1.** [trick] Schwindel der - **2.** (abbr of convict) prison sl Knacki der <> vt [trick] reinlegen; to ~ sb out of sthg jn um etw bringen; to ~ sb into doing sthg jn durch einen Trick dazu bringen, etw zu tun.

**concave** [ˌkɒn'keɪv] adj konkav.

**conceal** [kən'siːl] vt [object] verstecken; [feelings, information] verbergen; to ~ sthg from sb etw vor jm verstecken; [feelings, information] etw vor jm verbergen.

**concede** [kən'siːd] vt [a point] zulgeben; [defeat] einlgestehen <> vi seine Niederlage einlgestehen.

**conceit** [kən'siːt] n Arroganz die.

**conceited** [kən'siːtɪd] adj eingebildet.

**conceivable** [kən'siːvəbl] adj denkbar, vorstellbar.

**conceivably** [kən'siːvəblɪ] adv: he could ~ win er könnte möglicherweise gewinnen; I can't ~ agree to that ich kann dem unmöglich zustimmen.

**conceive** [kən'si:v] *vt* - **1.** [plan, idea] sich *(D)* ausldenken - **2.** MED [child] empfangen ◇ *vi* - **1.** MED empfangen - **2.** [imagine]: to ~ of sthg sich *(D)* etw vorlstellen.

**concentrate** ['kɒnsəntreɪt] *vt* konzentrieren ◇ *vi:* to ~ (on) sich konzentrieren (auf (+ A)).

**concentrated** ['kɒnsəntreɪtɪd] *adj* - **1.** [substance]: ~ orange juice Orangensaftkonzentrat *das* - **2.** [activity] verstärkt.

**concentration** [,kɒnsən'treɪʃn] *n* Konzentration *die.*

**concentration camp** *n* Konzentrationslager *das,* KZ *das.*

**concentric** [kən'sentrɪk] *adj* konzentrisch.

**concept** ['kɒnsept] *n* [idea] Vorstellung *die;* [principle] Konzept *das;* he has no ~ of what's involved er hat keine Ahnung, was damit zusammenhängt.

**conception** [kən'sepʃn] *n* - **1.** [idea] Vorstellung *die* - **2.** [formation of idea] Konzeption *die* - **3.** MED Empfängnis *die.*

**conceptualize, -ise** [kən'septʃʊəlaɪz] *vt* begrifflich fassen.

**concern** [kən'sɜːn] *n* - **1.** [worry] Besorgnis *die;* [cause of worry] Sorge *die;* to show ~ for sb/sthg sich Gedanken um jn/etw machen - **2.** [matter of interest] Angelegenheit *die;* it's no ~ of mine das geht mich nichts an - **3.** COMM [company] Unternehmen *das* ◇ *vt* - **1.** [worry] beunruhigen; to be ~ed (about) besorgt sein (um) - **2.** [involve] anlgehen, betreffen; to be ~ed with sthg [subj: person] mit etw zu tun haben; to ~ o.s. with sthg sich mit etw befassen; as far as I'm ~ed was mich betrifft - **3.** [subj: book, film] handeln von.

**concerning** [kən'sɜːnɪŋ] *prep* bezüglich (+ G).

**concert** ['kɒnsət] *n* Konzert *das.*
➥ in concert *adv* - **1.** [group, singer] live - **2.** *fml* [acting as one] gemeinsam.

**concerted** [kən'sɜːtɪd] *adj* [effort] vereint, gemeinsam.

**concertgoer** ['kɒnsət,gəʊə'] *n* Konzertbesucher *der,* -in *die.*

**concert hall** *n* Konzerthalle *die.*

**concertina** [,kɒnsə'ti:nə] *n* Konzertina *die.*

**concerto** [kən'tʃɜːtəʊ] (*pl* -s) *n* Konzert *das.*

**concession** [kən'seʃn] *n* - **1.** [allowance] Zugeständnis *das* - **2.** COMM [franchise] Konzession *die* - **3.** [special price] Preisermäßigung *die.*

**concessionaire** [kən,seʃə'neə'] *n* Konzessionär *der,* -in *die.*

**concessionary** [kən'seʃnərɪ] *adj* [fare, price] ermäßigt.

**conciliation** [kən,sɪlɪ'eɪʃn] *n* [between people]

Versöhnung *die;* to go to ~ [industrial dispute] ein Schlichtungsverfahren durchllaufen.

**concise** [kən'saɪs] *adj* präzis(e), exakt.

**concisely** [kən'saɪslɪ] *adv* präzis(e), exakt.

**conclave** ['kɒŋkleɪv] *n:* to be in ~ in Klausur tagen.

**conclude** [kən'kluːd] *vt* - **1.** [end] beenden - **2.** [deduce]: to ~ (that) schließen(, dass), folgern(, dass) - **3.** [agreement, deal] ablschließen ◇ *vi* [finish] enden, schließen.

**conclusion** [kən'kluːʒn] *n* - **1.** [opinion] Schlussfolgerung *die;* to jump to ~s voreilige Schlüsse ziehen - **2.** [ending] Abschluss *der,* Schluss *der;* it was a foregone ~ (that ...) es war von vornherein klar(, dass ...) - **3.** [of agreement, deal] Abschluss *der.*

**conclusive** [kən'kluːsɪv] *adj* eindeutig.

**concoct** [kən'kɒkt] *vt* - **1.** [story, excuse, alibi] sich *(D)* ausldenken - **2.** [meal] kreieren; [drink] zusammenlbrauen.

**concoction** [kən'kɒkʃn] *n* [meal] selbst kreiertes Gericht; [drink] Gebräu *das.*

**concourse** ['kɒŋkɔːs] *n* [hall] Eingangshalle *die.*

**concrete** ['kɒŋkriːt] *adj lit* & *fig* konkret ◇ *n* Beton *der* ◇ *comp* [made of concrete] Beton- ◇ *vt* betonieren.

**concrete mixer** *n* Betonmischmaschine *die.*

**concur** [kən'kɜː'] (*pt* & *pp* -red; *cont* -ring) *vi* [agree]: to ~ (with sthg) (etw *(D)*) zulstimmen.

**concurrently** [kən'kʌrəntlɪ] *adv* gleichzeitig.

**concussed** [kən'kʌst] *adj:* to be ~ eine Gehirnerschütterung haben.

**concussion** [kən'kʌʃn] *n* Gehirnerschütterung *die.*

**condemn** [kən'dem] *vt* - **1.** [disapprove of]: to ~ sb (for sthg) jn (wegen etw *(G)*) verurteilen - **2.** [force] verdammen - **3.** LAW [sentence]: to ~ sb to sthg jn zu etw verurteilen - **4.** [building] für unbewohnbar erklären.

**condemnation** [,kɒndem'neɪʃn] *n* Verurteilung *die.*

**condemned** [kən'demd] *adj* - **1.** LAW [man, criminal] zum Tode verurteilt - **2.** [building] für unbewohnbar erklärt.

**condensation** [,kɒnden'seɪʃn] *n* [on windows etc] Kondenswasser *das.*

**condense** [kən'dens] *vt* - **1.** PHYS [gas, steam] kondensieren - **2.** [text] zusammenlfassen ◇ *vi* [gas] kondensieren.

**condensed milk** [kən'denst-] *n* Kondensmilch *die.*

**condescend** [,kɒndɪ'send] *vi* - **1.** [behave patronizingly]: to ~ to sb jn von oben herab behandeln - **2.** [lower o.s.]: **to ~ to do sthg** sich dazu herabllassen, etw zu tun.

**condescending** [ˌkɒndɪ'sendɪŋ] *adj* herablassend.

**condiments** *npl fml* Salz, Pfeffer, Tomatenketschup und anderes, was zum Würzen von Speisen am Tisch dient.

**condition** [kən'dɪʃn] *n* - **1.** [of object, building] Zustand *der;* [of person, patient] Verfassung *die;* **out of ~** schlecht in Form - **2.** MED [illness] Leiden *das* - **3.** [requirement] Bedingung *die,* Voraussetzung *die;* **on ~ that ...** unter der Bedingung, dass ... ◇ *vt* - **1.** PSYCH konditionieren - **2.** [determine] bestimmen - **3.** [hair] pflegen.

➧ **conditions** *npl* [circumstances] Verhältnisse *pl.*

**conditional** [kən'dɪʃənl] *adj* [provisional] vorbehaltlich; **to be ~ (up)on sthg** von etw abhängen ◇ *n* GRAMM Konditional *der.*

**conditionally** [kən'dɪʃnəlɪ] *adv* mit OR unter Vorbehalt.

**conditioner** [kən'dɪʃnəʳ] *n* - **1.** [for hair] Pflegespülung *die* - **2.** [for clothes] Weichspüler *der.*

**conditioning** [kən'dɪʃnɪŋ] *n* PSYCH Konditionierung *die.*

**condo** ['kɒndəʊ] *n Am inf abbr of* **condominium.**

**condolences** [kən'dəʊlənsɪz] *npl* Beileid *das.*

**condom** ['kɒndəm] *n* Kondom *das* OR *der,* Präservativ *das.*

**condominium** [ˌkɒndə'mɪnɪəm] *n Am* - **1.** [apartment] Eigentumswohnung *die* - **2.** [building] Apartmenthaus *das.*

**condone** [kən'dəʊn] *vt* hinweglsehen über (+ A).

**condor** ['kɒndɔːʳ] *n* Kondor *der.*

**conducive** [kən'djuːsɪv] *adj:* **to be ~ to sthg** einer Sache (D) förderlich sein.

**conduct** [*n* 'kɒndʌkt *vb* kən'dʌkt] *n* - **1.** [behaviour] Verhalten *das,* Benehmen *das* - **2.** [of business, talks] Durchführung *die* ◇ *vt* - **1.** [carry out] durchlführen - **2.** [behave]: **to ~ o.s. well/badly** sich gut/schlecht benehmen - **3.** MUS dirigieren - **4.** PHYS [heat, electricity] leiten ◇ *vi* MUS dirigieren.

**conducted tour** [kən'dʌktɪd-] *n* Führung *die.*

**conductor** [kən'dʌktəʳ] *n* - **1.** MUS Dirigent *der,* -in *die* - **2.** [on bus] Schaffner *der* - **3.** *Am* [on train] Zugführer *der.*

**conductress** [kən'dʌktrɪs] *n* [on bus] Schaffnerin *die.*

**conduit** ['kɒndjuːt] *n* [for gas] Leitungsrohr *das;* [for water] Kanal *der.*

**cone** [kəʊn] *n* - **1.** [shape] Kegel *der* - **2.** [for ice cream] Eistüte *die* - **3.** [from tree] Zapfen *der* - **4.** [on roads] Pylon *der,* Pylone *die.*

**confectioner's** *n* [shop] Süßwarenladen *der.*

**confectionery** [kən'fekʃnərɪ] *n (U)* Süßwaren *pl.*

**confederation** [kənˌfedə'reɪʃn] *n* Bund *der.*

**Confederation of British Industry** *n:* **the ~** ≃ der Bundesverband der deutschen Industrie.

**confer** [kən'fɜːʳ] (*pt* & *pp* **-red;** *cont* **-ring**) *vt fml:* **to ~ sthg (on sb)** [title, degree] (jm) etw verleihen ◇ *vi:* **to ~ (with sb on** OR **about sthg)** sich (mit jm über etw *A*) beraten.

**conference** ['kɒnfərəns] *n* Konferenz *die,* Tagung *die;* **in ~** in einer Besprechung.

**conference call** *n* Konferenzschaltung *die.*

**conference centre** *n* Konferenzzentrum *das.*

**conference hall** *n* Konferenzhalle *die.*

**confess** [kən'fes] *vt* - **1.** RELIG beichten - **2.** [admit] gestehen ◇ *vi* - **1.** [admit]: **to ~ (to sthg)** (etw) gestehen - **2.** RELIG beichten.

**confession** [kən'feʃn] *n* - **1.** [of guilt] Geständnis *das* - **2.** *(U)* RELIG Beichte *die.*

**confessional** [kən'feʃənl] *n* Beichtstuhl *der.*

**confetti** [kən'fetɪ] *n (U)* Konfetti *pl.*

**confidant** [ˌkɒnfɪ'dænt] *n* Vertraute *der,* die.

**confidante** [ˌkɒnfɪ'dænt] *n* Vertraute *die.*

**confide** [kən'faɪd] *vt* anlvertrauen ◇ *vi:* **to ~ in sb** sich jm anlvertrauen.

**confidence** ['kɒnfɪdəns] *n* - **1.** *(U)* [self-assurance] Selbstvertrauen *das* - **2.** *(U)* [trust] Vertrauen *das;* **to have ~ that ...** zuversichtlich sein, dass ...; **to have ~ in sb** Vertrauen zu jm haben - **3.** [secrecy]: **in ~** im Vertrauen - **4.** [secret] vertrauliche Information.

**confidence trick** *n* Schwindel *die.*

**confident** ['kɒnfɪdənt] *adj* - **1.** [self-assured] selbstsicher, selbstbewusst - **2.** [sure] überzeugt; **to be ~ of sthg** von etw überzeugt sein.

**confidential** [ˌkɒnfɪ'denʃl] *adj* vertraulich.

**confidentiality** ['kɒnfɪˌdenʃɪ'ælətɪ] *n* Vertraulichkeit *die.*

**confidently** ['kɒnfɪdəntlɪ] *adv* - **1.** [with self-assurance] selbstsicher - **2.** [with certainty] sicher.

**configuration** [kənˌfɪgə'reɪʃn] *n* - **1.** [arrangement] Anordnung *die* - **2.** COMPUT Konfiguration *die.*

**confine** [*vb* kən'faɪn, *npl* 'kɒnfaɪnz] *vt* beschränken; **to be ~d to** beschränkt sein auf (+ *A*); **to ~ o.s. to sthg** sich auf etw (*A*) beschränken; **to ~ o.s. to doing sthg** sich darauf beschränken, etw zu tun; **she was ~d to the house** sie war ans Haus gefesselt.

➧ **confines** *npl* Grenzen *pl.*

**confined** [kən'faɪnd] *adj* [space, area] beschränkt.

**confinement** [kən'faɪnmənt] *n* - **1.** *(U)* [act of imprisoning] Einsperren *das;* [state of imprisonment] Haft *die* - **2.** *dated* & MED Niederkunft *die.*

**confirm** [kən'fɜːm] *vt* - **1.** [gen] bestätigen - **2.** RELIG konfirmieren; [Roman Catholic] firmen.

**confirmation** [ˌkɒnfəˈmeɪʃn] *n (U)* - **1.** [ratification] Bestätigung *die* - **2.** RELIG Konfirmation *die;* [of Roman Catholic] Firmung *die.*

**confirmed** [kən'fɜːmd] *adj* [bachelor, spinster] überzeugt.

**confiscate** ['kɒnfɪskeɪt] *vt* beschlagnahmen, konfiszieren.

**confiscation** [ˌkɒnfɪ'skeɪʃn] *n* Beschlagnahme *die,* Konfiszierung *die.*

**conflagration** [ˌkɒnfləˈgreɪʃn] *n fml* Feuersbrunst *die.*

**conflict** [*n* 'kɒnflɪkt, *vb* kən'flɪkt] *n* Konflikt *der;* ~ **of interest** Interessenkonflikt *der* <> *vi* [clash] sich *(D)* widersprechen; **to ~ with sb/sthg** im Widerspruch zu jm/etw stehen.

**conflicting** [kən'flɪktɪŋ] *adj* widersprüchlich.

**conform** [kən'fɔːm] *vi* - **1.** [behave as expected] sich anlpassen - **2.** [be in accordance]: **to ~ (to** OR **with sthg)** sich (nach etw *(D)*) richten.

**conformist** [kən'fɔːmɪst] *pej adj* konformistisch <> *n* Konformist *der,* -in *die.*

**conformity** [kən'fɔːmətɪ] *n:* ~ **(to** OR **with)** Übereinstimmung *die* (mit).

**confound** [kən'faʊnd] *vt* [confuse] verblüffen.

**confounded** [kən'faʊndɪd] *adj inf* [for emphasis] verflixt.

**confront** [kən'frʌnt] *vt* - **1.** [opponent, enemy, problem] sich stellen (+ *D*); **to be ~ed with a problem** mit einem Problem konfrontiert werden; **the problem that ~s us** das Problem, das sich uns stellt - **2.** [present]: **to ~ sb (with sthg)** jn (mit etw) konfrontieren.

**confrontation** [ˌkɒnfrʌn'teɪʃn] *n* Konfrontation *die,* Auseinandersetzung *die.*

**confuse** [kən'fjuːz] *vt* - **1.** [bewilder] verwirren - **2.** [mix up]: **to ~ sb/sthg (with)** jn/etw verwechseln (mit) - **3.** [complicate - situation] verworren machen.

**confused** [kən'fjuːzd] *adj* [person] verwirrt, konfus; [ideas, thoughts, situation] verworren, durcheinander; **to get ~** konfus werden.

**confusing** [kən'fjuːzɪŋ] *adj* verwirrend.

**confusion** [kən'fjuːʒn] *n* - **1.** [perplexity] Verwirrung *die* - **2.** [mixing up] Verwechslung *die* - **3.** [bewilderment] Verlegenheit *die* - **4.** [disorder] Durcheinander *das.*

**congeal** [kən'dʒiːl] *vi* [blood] gerinnen; [food] fest werden.

**congenial** [kən'dʒiːnjəl] *adj* angenehm.

**congenital** [kən'dʒenɪtl] *adj* MED angeboren.

**conger eel** ['kɒŋgə-] *n* Seeaal *der.*

**congested** [kən'dʒestɪd] *adj* [roads, nose] verstopft.

**congestion** [kən'dʒestʃn] *n (U)* - **1.** [overcrowding] Stau *der* - **2.** MED Blutandrang *der.*

**conglomerate** [ˌkən'glɒmərət] *n* COMM Großkonzern *der (aus mehreren Firmen bestehend).*

**conglomeration** [kənˌglɒmə'reɪʃn] *n fml* Konglomerat *das.*

**Congo** ['kɒŋgəʊ] *n:* **the ~** [country, river] der Kongo.

**congratulate** [kən'grætʃʊleɪt] *vt:* **to ~ sb (on sthg)** jm (zu etw) gratulieren; **they ~d her on passing her exams** sie gratulierten ihr zum Bestehen ihrer Prüfungen; **to ~ o.s. (on sthg)** sich (zu etw) beglückwünschen.

**congratulations** [kənˌgrætʃʊ'leɪʃənz] *npl* Glückwunsch *der,* Glückwünsche *pl* <> *excl* herzlichen Glückwunsch!

**congratulatory** [kən'grætʃʊlətrɪ] *adj* Glückwunsch-.

**congregate** ['kɒŋgrɪgeɪt] *vi* [people] sich versammeln; [animals] sich sammeln.

**congregation** [ˌkɒŋgrɪ'geɪʃn] *n* RELIG Gemeinde *die.*

**congress** ['kɒŋgres] *n* [meeting] Kongress *der,* Tagung *die.*
➤ **Congress** *n* Am POL der Kongress.

**CONGRESS**

Der Kongress, das Gesetzgebungsorgan der USA, besteht aus zwei „Häusern": dem „Senate" (Senat) und dem House of Representatives (Repräsentantenhaus). Gesetzesvorlagen müssen separat von beiden Häusern verabschiedet werden, um Gesetzeskraft zu erlangen. Ein Amtsenthebungsverfahren („Impeachment") gegen einen US-Präsidenten kann nur durch den Kongress betrieben werden (die Anklage muss durch das Repräsentantenhaus erhoben werden, das eigentliche Verfahren obliegt dem Senat). Der Kongress hat auch die Befugnis, die amerikanische Verfassung zu ändern.

**congressional** [kəŋ'greʃənl] *adj* Am POL Kongress-.

**congressman** ['kɒŋgresmən] (*pl* -men [-mən]) *n* Am POL Kongressabgeordnete *der.*

**congresswoman** ['kɒŋgresˌwʊmən] (*pl* -women [-ˌwɪmɪn]) *n* Am POL Kongressabgeordnete *die.*

**conical** ['kɒnɪkl] *adj* konisch, kegelförmig.

**conifer** ['kɒnɪfə-] *n* Nadelbaum *der,* Konifere *die.*

**coniferous** [kə'nɪfərəs] *adj* Nadel-.

**conjecture** [kən'dʒektʃəʳ] n Vermutung die, Mutmaßung die <> vt: **to ~ (that)** vermuten(, dass), mutmaßen(, dass) <> vi Vermutungen an|stellen.

**conjugal** ['kɒndʒʊgl] adj fml Ehe-.

**conjugate** vt GRAMM konjugieren.

**conjugation** [ˌkɒndʒʊ'geɪʃn] n GRAMM Konjugation die.

**conjunction** [kən'dʒʌŋkʃn] n - **1.** GRAMM Konjunktion die - **2.** [combination] Verbindung die; [of events] Zusammentreffen das; **in ~ with** in Verbindung mit.

**conjunctivitis** [kənˌdʒʌŋktɪ'vaɪtɪs] n (U) Bindehautentzündung die.

**conjure** ['kʌndʒəʳ] vt & vi zaubern.
➤ **conjure up** vt sep [evoke] herauf|beschwören.

**conjurer** ['kʌndʒərəʳ] n Zauberer der, -in die.

**conjuring trick** ['kʌndʒərɪŋ-] n Zaubertrick der.

**conjuror** ['kʌndʒərəʳ] n = conjurer.

**conk** [kɒŋk] n inf [nose] Zinken der.
➤ **conk out** vi inf - **1.** [person] zusammen|klappen - **2.** [car, machine] den Geist auf|geben.

**conker** ['kɒŋkəʳ] n Br (Ross)kastanie die.

**conman** ['kɒnmæn] (pl **-men** [-men]) n Betrüger der.

**connect** [kə'nekt] vt - **1.** [join]: **to ~ sthg (to sthg)** etw (mit etw) verbinden - **2.** [on telephone] verbinden - **3.** [associate] in Verbindung OR Zusammenhang bringen; **to ~ sb/sthg to, to ~ sb/sthg with** jn/etw in Verbindung bringen mit; **to be ~ed** [two things] miteinander zu tun haben - **4.** ELEC [to power supply]: **to ~ sthg (to sthg)** etw (an etw (A)) an|schließen <> vi [train, plane, bus]: **to ~ with** Anschluss haben an (+ A).

**connected** [kə'nektɪd] adj [related]: **to be ~ with** sthg mit etw in Zusammenhang stehen.

**connecting** [kə'nektɪŋ] adj [flight, train] Anschluss-.

**connecting rod** n AUT Pleuelstange die.

**connection** [kə'nekʃn] n - **1.** [relationship]: **to have a ~ with** in Zusammenhang stehen mit; **~ between** Zusammenhang zwischen; **in ~ with** im Zusammenhang mit; **to be in ~ with** in Zusammenhang stehen mit - **2.** ELEC [between wires] Schaltung die - **3.** [on telephone] Verbindung die - **4.** [plane, train, bus] Anschluss der - **5.** [professional acquaintance]: **~s** Beziehungen pl.

**connective tissue** [kə'nektɪv-] n Bindegewebe das.

**connexion** [kə'nekʃn] n Br = connection.

**connive** [kə'naɪv] vi - **1.** [plot]: **to ~ (with sb)** sich (mit jm) verschwören - **2.** [allow to happen]: **to ~ at sthg** etw dulden.

**conniving** [kə'naɪvɪŋ] adj pej hinterhältig.

**connoisseur** [ˌkɒnə'sɜːʳ] n Kenner der, -in die; **a ~ of wine** ein Weinkenner.

**connotation** [ˌkɒnə'teɪʃn] n Konnotation die.

**conquer** ['kɒŋkəʳ] vt - **1.** [take by force - land, city] erobern; [- people] besiegen - **2.** fig [overcome] besiegen.

**conqueror** ['kɒŋkərəʳ] n [of land, city] Eroberer der, -in die; [of people] Sieger der, -in die.

**conquest** ['kɒŋkwest] n - **1.** [act - of land, city] Eroberung die; [- of people] Sieg der - **2.** [thing conquered] Eroberung die.

**cons** [kɒnz] npl - **1.** Br inf (abbr of **conveniences**): **all mod ~** mit allem modernen Komfort - **2.** ⊳ **pro.**

**Cons.** abbr of **Conservative.**

**conscience** ['kɒnʃəns] n Gewissen das; **to have a clear/guilty ~** ein reines/schlechtes Gewissen haben; **in all ~** mit gutem Gewissen.

**conscientious** [ˌkɒnʃɪ'enʃəs] adj gewissenhaft.

**conscientiously** [ˌkɒnʃɪ'enʃəslɪ] adv gewissenhaft.

**conscientiousness** [ˌkɒnʃɪ'enʃəsnɪs] n Gewissenhaftigkeit die.

**conscientious objector** n Kriegsdienstverweigerer der (aus Gewissensgründen).

**conscious** ['kɒnʃəs] adj - **1.** [awake] bei Bewusstsein - **2.** [aware]: **to be ~ of sthg** sich einer Sache (G) bewusst sein; **fashion-~** modebewusst; **to be money-~** sehr auf Geld achten - **3.** [intentional - effort, decision] bewusst; [- insult] absichtlich.

**consciously** ['kɒnʃəslɪ] adv absichtlich

**consciousness** ['kɒnʃəsnɪs] n Bewusstsein das.

**conscript** [n 'kɒnskrɪpt, vb kən'skrɪpt] MIL n Wehrpflichtige der <> vt ein|ziehen.

**conscription** [kən'skrɪpʃn] n Wehrpflicht die.

**consecrate** ['kɒnsɪkreɪt] vt weihen.

**consecration** [ˌkɒnsɪ'kreɪʃn] n Weihe die.

**consecutive** [kən'sekjʊtɪv] adj aufeinanderfolgend; [numbers] fortlaufend; **for four ~ days** vier Tage hintereinander.

**consecutively** [kən'sekjʊtɪvlɪ] adv hintereinander; [numbered] fortlaufend.

**consensus** [kən'sensəs] n Übereinstimmung die.

**consent** [kən'sent] n (U) - **1.** [permission] Zustimmung die - **2.** [agreement]: **he is, by common ~, a good minister** man hält ihn allgemein für einen guten Minister <> vi: **to ~ (to sthg)** (einer Sache (D)) zu|stimmen.

**consequence** ['kɒnsɪkwəns] n - **1.** [result] Folge die; **to take the ~s** die Konsequenzen tragen; **in ~** folglich - **2.** (U) [importance] Bedeutung die; **a person of ~** eine bedeutende Person.

**consequent** ['kɒnsɪkwənt] adj daraus folgend.

**consequently** ['kɒnsɪkwəntlɪ] adv folglich.

**conservation** [ˌkɒnsə'veɪʃn] n [of buildings] Schutz der, Erhaltung die; **nature ~** Naturschutz der; **~ of energy/water** sorgsamer Umgang mit Energie/Wasser.

**conservation area** n [natural] Naturschutzgebiet das; [historical, architectural] unter Denkmalschutz stehendes Gebiet.

**conservationist** [ˌkɒnsə'veɪʃənɪst] n [of nature] Umweltschützer der, -in die; [of buildings] Denkmalpfleger der, -in die.

**conservatism** [kən'sɜːvətɪzm] n Konservatismus der.
➤ **Conservatism** n POL Konservatismus der.

**conservative** [kən'sɜːvətɪv] adj - **1.** [traditional] konservativ - **2.** [cautious] vorsichtig ◇ n Konservative der, die.
➤ **Conservative** POL adj konservativ ◇ n Konservative der, die.

**Conservative Party** n: **the ~** die Konservative Partei.

**conservatory** [kən'sɜːvətrɪ] (pl -ies) n Wintergarten der.

**conserve** [n 'kɒnsɜːv, vb kən'sɜːv] n Marmelade die ◇ vt [energy, supplies, electricity] sorgsam umlgehen mit; [nature, wildlife] schützen.

**consider** [kən'sɪdər] vt - **1.** [think about] erwägen - **2.** [take into account] berücksichtigen; **all things ~ed** alles in allem - **3.** [believe]: **I ~ him (to be) an expert** ich halte ihn für einen Experten.

**considerable** [kən'sɪdrəbl] adj beträchtlich.

**considerably** [kən'sɪdrəblɪ] adv beträchtlich.

**considerate** [kən'sɪdərət] adj rücksichtsvoll.

**consideration** [kənˌsɪdə'reɪʃn] n - **1.** [thought] Überlegung die; **to take sthg into ~** etw berücksichtigen - **2.** [thoughtfulness] Rücksichtnahme die - **3.** [factor] Gesichtspunkt der - **4.** [discussion]: **the matter is under ~** die Angelegenheit wird zur Zeit geprüft.

**considered** [kən'sɪdəd] adj: **~ opinion** wohlüberlegte Meinung.

**considering** [kən'sɪdərɪŋ] prep in Anbetracht (+ G) ◇ conj wenn man bedenkt, dass ◇ adv eigentlich; **the play was quite good, ~** das Stück war eigentlich ganz gut.

**consign** [kən'saɪn] vt: **to ~ sthg to the attic/shed/etc** etw auf den Dachboden/in den Schuppen/etc verbannen; **to ~ sthg to the scrapheap** fig etw rauslwerfen.

**consignee** [ˌkɒnsaɪ'niː] n Empfänger der, -in die.

**consignment** [kən'saɪnmənt] n Sendung die; [bigger] Ladung die.

**consignment note** n Frachtbrief der.

**consist** [kən'sɪst] ➤ **consist in** vt fus: **to ~ in sthg** in etw (D) bestehen; **to ~ in doing sthg** darin bestehen, etw zu tun.
➤ **consist of** vt fus bestehen aus.

**consistency** [kən'sɪstənsɪ] (pl -ies) n - **1.** [coherence] Beständigkeit die; [of several things] Einheitlichkeit die - **2.** [texture] Konsistenz die.

**consistent** [kən'sɪstənt] adj - **1.** [constant] beständig - **2.** [steady] stetig - **3.** [coherent]: **to be ~ (with)** im Einklang stehen (mit).

**consistently** [kən'sɪstəntlɪ] adv - **1.** [constantly] ständig - **2.** [coherently] konsequent.

**consolation** [ˌkɒnsə'leɪʃn] n Trost der.

**consolation prize** n Trostpreis der.

**console** [n 'kɒnsəʊl, vt kən'səʊl] n [control panel] Bedienungsfeld das; [of computer game] Spielkonsole die ◇ vt trösten; **to ~ o.s. with sthg** sich mit etw trösten.

**consolidate** [kən'sɒlɪdeɪt] vt - **1.** [strengthen] festigen - **2.** COMM [merge] vereinigen ◇ vi COMM fusionieren, sich zusammenlschließen.

**consolidation** [kənˌsɒlɪ'deɪʃn] n (U) - **1.** [strengthening] Festigung die - **2.** COMM [merging] Fusion die, Zusammenschluss der.

**consols** ['kɒnsɒlz] npl Br ST EX Konsols pl.

**consommé** [kɒn'sɒmeɪ] n Brühe die.

**consonant** ['kɒnsənənt] n Konsonant der.

**consort** [vb kən'sɔːt, n 'kɒnsɔːt] vi fml: **to ~ with sb** mit jm verkehren ◇ n [spouse] Gemahl der, -in die.

**consortium** [kən'sɔːtjəm] (pl -tiums OR -tia [-tjə]) n Konsortium das.

**conspicuous** [kən'spɪkjʊəs] adj auffällig.

**conspicuously** [kən'spɪkjʊəslɪ] adv auffällig.

**conspiracy** [kən'spɪrəsɪ] (pl -ies) n Verschwörung die.

**conspirator** [kən'spɪrətər] n Verschwörer der, -in die.

**conspiratorial** [kənˌspɪrə'tɔːrɪəl] adj verschwörerisch.

**conspire** [kən'spaɪər] vt: **to ~ to do sthg** heimlich planen, etw zu tun ◇ vi - **1.** [plan secretly]: **to ~ against/with sb** sich gegen jn/mit jm verschwören - **2.** [combine]: **events ~d to ruin our holiday** eine Verkettung unglücklicher Umstände hat unseren Urlaub ruiniert.

**constable** ['kʌnstəbl] n Br Wachtmeister der, -in die.

**constabulary** [kən'stæbjʊlərɪ] (pl -ies) n Polizei die.

**constancy** ['kɒnstənsɪ] n (U) - **1.** [continuity - of

temperature] Beständigkeit *die*; [ - of purpose] Unwandelbarkeit *die* - **2.** *literary* [faithfulness] Treue *die*.

**constant** ['kɒnstənt] *adj* - **1.** [unvarying] konstant, beständig - **2.** [recurring] ständig - **3.** *literary* [faithful] treu.

**constantly** ['kɒnstəntlɪ] *adv* [always] dauernd, ständig.

**constellation** [ˌkɒnstə'leɪʃn] *n* Sternbild *das*.

**consternation** [ˌkɒnstə'neɪʃn] *n* Bestürzung *die*.

**constipated** ['kɒnstɪpeɪtɪd] *adj* verstopft.

**constipation** [ˌkɒnstɪ'peɪʃn] *n (U)* Verstopfung *die*.

**constituency** [kən'stɪtjʊənsɪ] *(pl* -ies) *n* Wahlkreis *der*.

**constituency party** *n Br Ortsgruppe einer politischen Partei.*

**constituent** [kən'stɪtjʊənt] *adj* Bestandteil *der* <> *n* - **1.** [voter] Wähler *der*, -in *die* - **2.** [element] Bestandteil *der*.

**constitute** ['kɒnstɪtjuːt] *vt* - **1.** [represent] darlstellen - **2.** [form] bilden - **3.** [set up] einlrichten.

**constitution** [ˌkɒnstɪ'tjuːʃn] *n* - **1.** [health] Konstitution *die* - **2.** [composition] Zusammensetzung *die*.

➤ **Constitution** *n:* the (United States) Constitution die Verfassung (der Vereinigten Staaten).

**CONSTITUTION**

> Die USA haben eine Verfassung in Form eines verbindlichen schriftlichen Dokuments; sie ist durch mehrere „Amendments" ergänzt worden, darunter die Bill of Rights von 1791. Dagegen ist die Verfassung von Großbritannien nie schriftlich niedergelegt worden; sie basiert im Wesentlichen auf dem Präzedenzprinzip, also auf der Gesetzeslage, wie sie sich im Laufe der Geschichte entwickelt hat.

**constitutional** [ˌkɒnstɪ'tjuːʃənl] *adj* - **1.** [regarding the constitution] Verfassungs- - **2.** [allowed by the constitution] konsitutionell; [government, rights] verfassungsmäßig.

**constrain** [kən'streɪn] *vt* - **1.** [coerce] **to ~ sb** js Freihein einlschränken; **to ~ sb to do sthg** jn zwingen, etw zu tun - **2.** [restrict] hemmen.

**constrained** [kən'streɪnd] *adj* [inhibited] gezwungen.

**constraint** [kən'streɪnt] *n* - **1.** [restriction] Beschränkung *die*; **to place ~s on sthg** etw *(D)* Beschränkungen auf lerlegen - **2.** [coercion]: **under ~** unter Zwang.

**constrict** [kən'strɪkt] *vt* - **1.** [compress] einzwängen - **2.** [limit] einlschränken.

**constricting** [kən'strɪktɪŋ] *adj* - **1.** [clothes] beengend - **2.** [circumstances, lifestyle] einschränkend.

**construct** [*vb* kən'strʌkt, *n* 'kɒnstrʌkt] *vt* - **1.** [build] bauen - **2.** [sentence] konstruieren; [argument] entwickeln <> *n fml* [concept] Konstrukt *das*.

**construction** [kən'strʌkʃn] *n* - **1.** [act of building] Bau *der*; **under ~** im Bau - **2.** [building industry] Bauindustrie *die* - **3.** [structure] Konstruktion *die* <> *comp* Bau-.

**construction industry** *n* Bauindustrie *die*.

**constructive** [kən'strʌktɪv] *adj* konstruktiv.

**constructively** [kən'strʌktɪvlɪ] *adv* konstruktiv.

**construe** [kən'struː] *vt fml* [interpret]: **to ~ sthg as** etw auf lfassen als.

**consul** ['kɒnsəl] *n* Konsul *der*.

**consular** ['kɒnsjʊləʳ] *adj* konsularisch.

**consulate** ['kɒnsjʊlət] *n* Konsulat *das*.

**consult** [kən'sʌlt] *vt* - **1.** [ask advice of - doctor, lawyer] konsultieren; [ - friend] um Rat fragen - **2.** [refer to - dictionary] nachlschlagen in *(+ D)*; [ - map] nachlsehen auf *(+ D)* <> *vi:* **to ~ with sb** sich mit jm beraten.

**consultancy** [kən'sʌltənsɪ] *(pl* -ies) *n* [company] Beratungsbüro *das*.

**consultancy fee** *n* Beratungsgebühr *die*.

**consultant** [kən'sʌltənt] *n* - **1.** [expert] Berater *der*, -in *die* - **2.** *Br* [hospital doctor] Facharzt *der*, -ärztin *die*.

**consultation** [ˌkɒnsəl'teɪʃn] *n* [meeting, discussion] Beratung *die*.

**consulting room** [kən'sʌltɪŋ-] *n* Sprechzimmer *das*.

**consume** [kən'sjuːm] *vt* - **1.** [food, drink] zu sich nehmen - **2.** [fuel, energy] verbrauchen; [time] in Anspruch nehmen - **3.** *literary* [burn up] verzehren.

**consumer** [kən'sjuːməʳ] *n* Verbraucher *der*, -in *die* <> *comp* Verbraucher-; **~ rights** Rechter *pl* der Verbraucher.

**consumer credit** *n (U)* Verbraucherkredit *der*.

**consumer durables** *npl* (langlebige) Gebrauchsgüter *pl*.

**consumer goods** *npl* Konsumgüter *pl*.

**consumerism** [kən'sjuːmərɪzm] *n (U) pej* [excessive consumption] Konsumdenken *das*.

**consumer society** *n* Konsumgesellschaft *die*.

**consumer spending** *n* Ausgaben *pl* für Konsumgüter.

**consuming** *adj* [passion] verzehrend; [interest] brennend.

**consummate** [adj kən'sʌmət, vb 'kɒnsəmeɪt] adj - **1.** [skill] vollendet; with ~ ease mit spielender Leichtigkeit - **2.** [liar, actor] unübertrefflich ◇ vt - **1.** [marriage] vollziehen - **2.** [deal, achievement] vollenden.

**consummation** [ˌkɒnsə'meɪʃn] n - **1.** [of marriage] Vollzug der - **2.** [culmination] Vollendung die.

**consumption** [kən'sʌmpʃn] n (U) - **1.** [of food, drink] Konsum der - **2.** [of fuel, energy] Verbrauch der - **3.** dated [tuberculosis] Schwindsucht die.

**cont.** (abbr of continued) Forts.

**contact** ['kɒntækt] n Kontakt der; to be in ~ with sthg [touching] etw berühren; to lose ~ with sb den Kontakt zu jm verlieren; to make ~ with sb mit jm Kontakt auf lnehmen, sich mit jm in Verbindung setzen; in ~ (with sb) in Kontakt (mit jm) ◇ vt sich in Verbindung setzen mit, kontaktieren.

**contact lens** n Kontaktlinse die.

**contact number** n Telefonnummer, unter der man erreicht werden kann.

**contagious** [kən'teɪdʒəs] adj lit & fig ansteckend.

**contain** [kən'teɪn] vt - **1.** [hold, include] enthalten - **2.** fml [control - enthusiasm, anger, excitement] unter Kontrolle halten; [ - epidemic, riot] unter Kontrolle bringen; [ - enemy troops] in Schach halten; [ - population growth] in Grenzen halten; to ~ o.s. sich beherrschen.

**contained** [kən'teɪnd] adj [person] beherrscht.

**container** [kən'teɪnəʳ] n - **1.** [box, bottle etc] Behälter der - **2.** COMM [for transporting goods] Container der.

**containerize, -ise** [kən'teɪnəraɪz] vt COMM - **1.** [transport] in Container verpacken - **2.** [adapt for containers] auf Container umlstellen.

**container ship** n Frachtschiff das.

**containment** [kən'teɪnmənt] n (U) [limitation] Eindämmung die.

**contaminate** [kən'tæmɪneɪt] vt [make impure] verunreinigen; [make poisonous] verseuchen.

**contamination** [kənˌtæmɪ'neɪʃn] n [making impure] Verunreinigung die.

**cont'd** (abbr of continued) Forts.

**contemplate** ['kɒntempleɪt] vt - **1.** [consider] erwägen; to ~ doing sthg erwägen, etw zu tun - **2.** literary [look at] betrachten ◇ vi [meditate] Betrachtungen anlstellen.

**contemplation** [ˌkɒntem'pleɪʃn] n (U) - **1.** [thought] Kontemplation die, Betrachtung die; she was lost in ~ sie war in Gedanken versunken - **2.** literary [looking at] Betrachtung die.

**contemplative** [kən'templətɪv] adj kontemplativ.

**contemporary** [kən'tempərərɪ] (pl -ies) adj [life] zeitgenössisch ◇ n Zeitgenosse der, -sin die.

**contempt** [kən'tempt] n (U) - **1.** [scorn] ~ (for) Verachtung die (für); to hold sb in ~ jn verachten - **2.** LAW: ~ (of court) Missachtung die des Gerichts.

**contemptible** [kən'temptəbl] adj verachtenswert.

**contemptuous** [kən'temptʃʊəs] adj verächtlich; to be ~ of sthg etw verachten.

**contend** [kən'tend] vi - **1.** [deal]: to ~ with sthg mit etw zu kämpfen haben; I've got enough to ~ with ich habe genug, womit ich fertig werden muss - **2.** [compete]: to ~ for sthg um etw kämpfen ◇ vt fml [claim]: to ~ that behaupten, dass.

**contender** [kən'tendəʳ] n - **1.** [in fight, race] Konkurrent der, -in die - **2.** [in election] Kandidat der, -in die.

**content** [n 'kɒntent, adj & vb kən'tent] adj: ~ (with) zufrieden (mit); to be ~ to do sthg etw gerne tun ◇ n - **1.** [amount contained] Gehalt der - **2.** [subject matter] Inhalt der ◇ vt: to ~ o.s. with sthg sich mit etw zufrieden geben.

➡ **contents** npl - **1.** [of container, document] Inhalt der - **2.** [at front of book] Inhaltsverzeichnis das.

**contented** [kən'tentɪd] adj zufrieden.

**contentedly** [kən'tentɪdlɪ] adv zufrieden.

**contention** [kən'tenʃn] n - **1.** [assertion] Behauptung die - **2.** (U) [disagreement]: to be a source of ~ ein Streitpunkt sein - **3.** (U) [competition]: to be in ~ wetteifern.

**contentious** [kən'tenʃəs] adj fml [statement, issue, view] strittig; [decision] umstritten.

**contentment** [kən'tentmənt] n Zufriedenheit die.

**contest** [n 'kɒntest, vb kən'test] n - **1.** [competition] Wettkampf der; a beauty ~ ein Schönheitswettbewerb - **2.** [for power, control] Kampf der ◇ vt - **1.** [compete for] kämpfen um - **2.** [dispute - statement] bestreiten; [ - decision] Einspruch erheben gegen; [ - will] anlfechten.

**contestant** [kən'testənt] n [in sports] Wettkampfteilnehmer der, -in die; [in quiz, election] Kandidat der, -in die.

**context** ['kɒntekst] n - **1.** [of word, phrase] Kontext der; to take sthg out of ~ etw aus dem Kontext reißen - **2.** [of event, idea] Zusammenhang der.

**continent** ['kɒntɪnənt] n Kontinent der.
➡ **Continent** n Br: the Continent Kontinentaleuropa das.

**continental** [ˌkɒntɪ'nentl] adj - **1.** GEOGR kontinental - **2.** *Br* [European] kontinentaleuropäisch; **~ holidays** Ferien auf dem europäischen Festland ◇ *n Br inf* Festlandseuropäer *der*, -in *die*.

**continental breakfast** *n* Frühstück mit Kaffee oder Tee, Brötchen und Marmelade.

**continental climate** *n* kontinentales Klima.

**continental quilt** *n Br* Steppdecke *die*.

**contingency** [kən'tındʒənsɪ] (*pl* -ies) *n* Eventualität *die*.

**contingency plan** *n* Ausweichplan *der*.

**contingent** [kən'tındʒənt] *adj fml*: **~ (up)on sthg** von etw abhängig ◇ *n* - **1.** MIL Kontingent *das* - **2.** [group] Gruppe *die*.

**continual** [kən'tınjuəl] *adj* - **1.** [without interruption - noise] pausenlos; [ - growth] ununterbrochen; [ - jealousy] dauernd - **2.** [frequently repeated] ständig, dauernd.

**continually** [kən'tınjuəlɪ] *adv* - **1.** [without interruption] ununterbrochen - **2.** [frequently] ständig.

**continuation** [kən,tınju'eɪʃn] *n* Fortsetzung *die*.

**continue** [kən'tınjuː] *vt* [carry on] fortlsetzen; **to ~ singing/working/***etc* OR **to sing/work/***etc* weiterlsingen/arbeiten/*etc*; **"And now ...," he said ~d** „Und nun ...", fuhr er fort ◇ *vi* - **1.** [carry on] anldauern; **to ~ as director** weiterhin Direktor/Direktorin bleiben; **to ~ with sthg** etw fortlsetzen - **2.** [begin again] weiterlgehen; [- people] - weiterlmachen - **3.** [resume speaking] fortlfahren - **4.** [resume travelling] weiterlfahren; [on foot] weiterlgehen.

**continuity** [,kɒntɪ'njuːətɪ] *n* (*U*) - **1.** [coherence] Kontinuität *die* - **2.** TV & CINEMA Anschluss *der*; **~ girl** Scriptgirl *das*.

**continuous** [kən'tınjuəs] *adj* ununterbrochen.

**continuous assessment** *n* fortlaufende Beurteilung.

**continuously** [kən'tınjuəslɪ] *adv* ununterbrochen.

**contort** [kən'tɔːt] *vt* [face, image] verzerren; [one's body] verrenken.

**contortion** [kən'tɔːʃn] *n* - **1.** (*U*) [twisting - of face, image] Verzerrung *die*; [ - of body] Verkrümmung *die* - **2.** [position] Verrenkung *die*.

**contour** ['kɒn,tuəʳ] *n* - **1.** [outline] Kontur *die* - **2.** [on map] Höhenlinie *die* ◇ *comp* [map] mit Höhenlinien; [line] Höhen-.

**contraband** ['kɒntrəbænd] *adj* geschmuggelt ◇ *n* (*U*) Schmuggelware *die*.

**contraception** [,kɒntrə'sepʃn] *n* Empfängnisverhütung *die*.

**contraceptive** [,kɒntrə'septɪv] *adj* Verhü-

tungs-; [advice] zur Empfängnisverhütung ◇ *n* Verhütungsmittel *das*.

**contraceptive pill** *n* Antibabypille *die*.

**contract** [*n* 'kɒntrækt, *vb* kən'trækt] *n* Vertrag *der*; **a ~ of employment** ein Arbeitsvertrag ◇ *vt* - **1.** [through legal agreement]: **to ~ (to do sthg)** sich vertraglich verpflichten(, etw zu tun) - **2.** COMM: **to ~ sb** jn unter Vertrag nehmen - **3.** *fml* [disease] sich (*D*) zulziehen - **4.** [reduce in size, length] zusammenlziehen ◇ *vi* [decrease in size, length] sich zusammenlziehen.

◆ **contract in** *vi esp Br* beiltreten.

◆ **contract out** *vt sep* vergeben ◇ *vi esp Br*: **to ~ out (of sthg)** (aus etw) ausltreten.

**contraction** [kən'trækʃn] *n* - **1.** [reduction in size, length] Zusammenziehen *das* - **2.** [short form] Kontraktion *die*.

**contractor** [kən'træktəʳ] *n* [person] Auftragnehmer *der*, -in *die*; [company] beauftragte Firma.

**contractual** [kən'træktʃuəl] *adj* vertraglich.

**contradict** [,kɒntrə'dıkt] *vt* widersprechen (+ *D*).

**contradiction** [,kɒntrə'dıkʃn] *n* Widerspruch *der*; **~ in terms** Widerspruch in sich.

**contradictory** [,kɒntrə'dıktərɪ] *adj* widersprüchlich.

**contraflow** ['kɒntrəfləu] *n* Umleitung auf die Gegenfahrbahn (bei Baustellen auf der Fahrbahn).

**contralto** [kən'træltəu] (*pl* -s) *n* [voice] Alt *der*; [singer] Altistin *die*.

**contraption** [kən'træpʃn] *n* Apparat *der*.

**contrary** ['kɒntrərɪ, *adj sense 2* kən'treərɪ] *adj* - **1.** [opposing] gegensätzlich; **to be ~ to sthg** im Gegensatz zu etw stehen - **2.** [stubborn] widerspenstig ◇ *n* Gegenteil *das*; **on the ~** im Gegenteil; **evidence to the ~** gegenteilige Beweise.

◆ **contrary to** *prep* im Gegensatz zu.

**contrast** [*n* 'kɒntrɑːst, *vb* kən'trɑːst] *n*: **~ (with** OR **to)** Gegensatz *der* (zu); **the ~ between** der Unterschied zwischen; **by** OR **in ~** im Gegensatz dazu; **in ~ with** OR **to sthg** im Gegensatz zu etw ◇ *vt*: **to ~ sthg with sthg** etw einer Sache (*D*) gegenüberlstellen ◇ *vi*: **to ~ (with sthg)** im Gegensatz (zu etw) stehen; [colours] sich (gegen etw) ablheben.

**contrasting** [kən'trɑːstıŋ] *adj* [personalities, views] gegensätzlich; [colours] kontrastierend.

**contravene** [,kɒntrə'viːn] *vt* verstoßen gegen.

**contravention** [,kɒntrə'venʃn] *n*: **~ (of sthg)** Verstoß *der* (gegen etw).

**contribute** [kən'trıbjuːt] *vt* - **1.** [ideas] beiltragen; [money] beilsteuern; [help, advice] zur Verfügung stellen - **2.** [to magazine, newspaper] beiltragen ◇ *vi* - **1.** [donate]: **to ~ (to sthg)** (für etw) spenden - **2.** [be part of cause]: **to ~ to sthg** zu etw beiltragen - **3.** [write material]: **to ~ to sthg** für etw einen Beitrag/Beiträge schreiben.

**contributing** [kən'trɪbjuːtɪŋ] *adj*: **it's a ~ factor** es ist ein Faktor, der mit eine Rolle spielt.

**contribution** [ˌkɒntrɪ'bjuːʃn] *n*: **~ (to sthg)** Beitrag *der* (zu etw).

**contributor** [kən'trɪbjʊtəʳ] *n* - **1.** [of money] Spender *der*, -in *die* - **2.** [to magazine, newspaper] freier Mitarbeiter, freie Mitarbeiterin; [regular] Mitarbeiter *der*, -in *die*.

**contributory** [kən'trɪbjʊtərɪ] *adj*: **it's a ~ factor** es ist ein Faktor, der mit eine Rolle spielt.

**contributory pension scheme** *n* beitragspflichtige Rentenversicherung.

**contrite** ['kɒntraɪt] *adj literary* reuig.

**contrition** [kən'trɪʃn] *n literary* Reue *die*.

**contrivance** [kən'traɪvns] *n* - **1.** [contraption, device] Vorrichtung *die*; [machine] Maschine *die* - **2.** [ploy] List *die*.

**contrive** [kən'traɪv] *vt fml* - **1.** [engineer] entwickeln; [meeting] arrangieren - **2.** [manage]: **to ~ to do sthg** es zuwege bringen, etw zu tun.

**contrived** [kən'traɪvd] *adj* gewollt.

**control** [kən'trəʊl] (*pt* & *pp* -**led**; *cont* -**ling**) *n* - **1.** (U) [power to manage - of situation, language] Beherrschung *die*; [ - of traffic] Regelung *die*; [ - of disease, crowd, fire] Kontrolle *die*; [ - of budget] Aufsicht *die*; **to gain ~ of sthg** [of area, country] die Gewalt über etw *(A)* gewinnen; [of government, company, radio station] die Kontrolle über etw *(A)* gewinnen; **to take ~ of sthg** [one's life] etw in die (eigene) Hand nehmen, etw in seine Gewalt bringen; **due to circumstances beyond our ~** durch nicht in unserer Hand liegende Umstände; **to be in ~ of** [situation, place] unter Kontrolle haben; **out of ~** außer Kontrolle; **his car went out of ~** er verlor die Gewalt über seinen Wagen; **under ~** unter Kontrolle; **to get a situation under ~** eine Situation in den Griff bekommen - **2.** [of emotions] Beherrschung *die*; **to lose ~** [become angry] die Beherrschung verlieren - **3.** [limit] Beschränkung *die* - **4.** [in experiment - group] Kontrollgruppe *die*; [ - person] Kontrollperson *die* - **5.** COMPUT Control, Steuerung *die* ◇ *vt* - **1.** [have power to manage - company] leiten; [ - government] unter sich *(D)* haben; [ - country] beherrschen; [ - traffic] regulieren; [ - crowds, rioters] unter Kontrolle haben - **2.** [operate - car, plane] steuern; [ - machine] bedienen - **3.** [curb] unter Kontrolle bringen - **4.** [emotions] beherrschen; **to ~ o.s.** sich beherrschen ◇ *comp* Kontroll-.
➡ **controls** *npl* [of machine, plane] Bedienungsfeld *das*.

**control group** *n* Kontrollgruppe *die*.

**control key** *n* COMPUT Control- OR Steuerung-Taste *die*.

**controlled** [kən'trəʊld] *adj* - **1.** [person] beherrscht - **2.** ECON [prices] gebunden.

**controller** [kən'trəʊləʳ] *n* [of finances] Leiter *der*, -in *die* des Finanzwesens; RADIO & TV Programmdirektor *der*, -in *die*.

**controlling** [kən'trəʊlɪŋ] *adj* [factor] beherrschend.

**controlling interest** *n* Mehrheitsanteil *der*.

**control panel** *n* [of car] Armaturenbrett *das*; [of plane, machine] Bedienungsfeld *das*.

**control room** *n* Kontrollraum *der*.

**control tower** *n* Kontrollturm *der*.

**controversial** [ˌkɒntrə'vɜːʃl] *adj* umstritten.

**controversy** ['kɒntrəvɜːsɪ, *Br* kən'trɒvəsɪ] (*pl* -**ies**) *n* Streit *der*.

**conundrum** [kə'nʌndrəm] (*pl* -**s**) *n fml* Rätsel *das*.

**conurbation** [ˌkɒnɜː'beɪʃn] *n* Ballungsgebiet *das*.

**convalesce** [ˌkɒnvə'les] *vi* genesen.

**convalescence** [ˌkɒnvə'lesns] *n* Genesungszeit *die*.

**convalescent** [ˌkɒnvə'lesnt] *adj* Genesungs- ◇ *n* Genesende *der*, *die*.

**convection** [kən'vekʃn] *n* Konvektion *die*.

**convector** [kən'vektəʳ] *n*: **~ heater** Heizlüfter *der*.

**convene** [kən'viːn] *vt* [meeting, conference] einlberufen; [people] versammeln ◇ *vi* sich versammeln; [court, parliament] zusammenltreten.

**convener** [kən'viːnəʳ] *n Br* Organisator *der*, -in *die* einer Versammlung.

**convenience** [kən'viːnjəns] *n* - **1.** [ease of use]: **I like the ~ of it** ich finde es so praktisch; **for ~** aus praktischen Gründen - **2.** [benefit]: **please reply at your earliest ~** *fml* wir bitten um baldmöglichste Antwort; **a telephone is provided for your ~** ein Telefon wird Ihnen zur Verfügung gestellt - **3.** [facility] Annehmlichkeit *die*; **the house has every modern ~** das Haus hat allen modernen Komfort.

**convenience food** *n* Fertiggericht *das*, Fertigmahlzeit *die*.

**convenience store** *n Am kleiner* Supermarkt.

**convenient** [kən'viːnjənt] *adj* - **1.** [suitable] günstig; **to be ~ for sb** jm passen - **2.** [handy] praktisch; **to be ~ for the shops** günstig in der Nähe von Geschäften gelegen sein.

**conveniently** [kən'viːnjəntlɪ] *adv* günstig.

**convent** ['kɒnvənt] *n* Kloster *das* (für Frauen).

**convention** [kən'venʃn] *n* - **1.** [practice] Brauch *der;* [social rule] Konvention *die* - **2.** [agreement] Abkommen *das* - **3.** [assembly] Tagung *die.*

**conventional** [kən'venʃənl] *adj* - **1.** *pej* [dull] konventionell; [person] konventionsgebunden - **2.** [traditional] üblich - **3.** [weapon, war] konventionell.

**conventionally** [kən'venʃnəlɪ] *adv* - **1.** *pej* [in a dull way] konventionell - **2.** [traditionally] auf herkömmliche Weise.

**convent school** *n* Klosterschule *die.*

**converge** [kən'vɜːdʒ] *vi* - **1.** [come together] zusammenlaufen; **to ~ on sb/sthg** von überall her zu jm/etw strömen; **to ~ on Denver** von überall her nach Denver strömen - **2.** [become similar] sich einander annähern.

**conversant** [kən'vɜːsənt] *adj fml:* **~ with sthg** mit etw vertraut.

**conversation** [ˌkɒnvə'seɪʃn] *n* Gespräch *das;* **to have a ~** sich unterhalten; **to make ~** Konversation machen.

**conversational** [ˌkɒnvə'seɪʃənl] *adj* leger.

**conversationalist** [ˌkɒnvə'seɪʃnəlɪst] *n:* **a good ~** ein guter Unterhalter, eine gute Unterhalterin.

**converse** [*n* & *adj* 'kɒnvɜːs, *vb* kən'vɜːs] *adj fml* [opposing] gegenteilig <> *n* [opposite]: **the ~** das Gegenteil <> *vi fml* [talk]: **to ~ (with sb)** sich (mit jm) unterhalten.

**conversely** [kən'vɜːslɪ] *adv fml* umgekehrt.

**conversion** [kən'vɜːʃn] *n* - **1.** [process] Umwandlung *die* - **2.** [converted building, room] Umbau *der* - **3.** RELIG [change in belief] Bekehrung *die* - **4.** [in rugby] Verwandlung *die.*

**conversion table** *n* Umrechnungstabelle *die.*

**convert** [*vb* kən'vɜːt, *n* 'kɒnvɜːt] *vt* - **1.** [change]: **to ~ sthg (in)to sthg** [miles, pounds] etw in etw (A) umlrechnen; [energy] etw in etw (A) umlwandeln; **we're ~ing the system to a computerized one** wir rüsten (das System) auf Computer um - **2.** RELIG & *fig:* **to ~ sb (to sthg)** jn (zu etw) bekehren - **3.** [building, room, ship]: **to ~ sthg (in)to sthg** etw zu etw umlbauen - **4.** RUGBY verwandeln <> *vi:* **to ~ from sthg to sthg** [gas, electricity] sich von etw auf etw (A) umlstellen; [religion] von etw zu etw konvertieren <> *n* Bekehrte *der, die.*

**converted** [kən'vɜːtɪd] *adj* - **1.** [building, room, ship] umgebaut - **2.** RELIG [person] bekehrt.

**convertible** [kən'vɜːtəbl] *adj* - **1.** [bed, sofa] ausziehbar - **2.** [currency] konvertibel - **3.** [car] mit aufklappbarem Verdeck <> *n* [car] Kabrio *das.*

**convex** [kɒn'veks] *adj* konvex; **~ lens** Konvexlinse *die.*

**convey** [kən'veɪ] *vt* - **1.** *fml* [people, cargo] befördern - **2.** [feelings, thoughts] vermitteln; **to ~ sthg to sb** jm etw vermitteln.

**conveyancing** [kən'veɪənsɪŋ] *n* Eigentumsübertragung *die.*

**conveyer belt** [kən'veɪəʳ-], **conveyor belt** *n* [in factory] Fließband *das;* [at airport] Förderband *das.*

**convict** [*n* 'kɒnvɪkt, *vb* kən'vɪkt] *n* Strafgefangene *der, die* <> *vt:* **to ~ sb of sthg** jn wegen etw verurteilen.

**convicted** [kən'vɪktɪd] *adj* verurteilt, schuldig gesprochen.

**conviction** [kən'vɪkʃn] *n* - **1.** [gen] Überzeugung *die* - **2.** LAW [of criminal] Verurteilung *die;* **previous ~s** Vorstrafen *pl.*

**convince** [kən'vɪns] *vt* [persuade] überzeugen; **to ~ sb of sthg** jn von etw überzeugen; **to ~ sb to do sthg** jn überreden, etw zu tun.

**convinced** [kən'vɪnst] *adj:* **~ (of sthg)** (von etw) überzeugt.

**convincing** [kən'vɪnsɪŋ] *adj* - **1.** [person, argument, speech] überzeugend - **2.** [win, victory] klar.

**convivial** [kən'vɪvɪəl] *adj* gesellig.

**convoluted** ['kɒnvəluːtɪd] *adj* [plot, reasoning] verwickelt; [sentence] gewunden.

**convoy** ['kɒnvɔɪ] *n* Konvoi *der;* **in ~** im Konvoi.

**convulse** [kən'vʌls] *vt:* **to be ~d with laughter** sich vor Lachen schütteln; **to be ~ d with pain** sich vor Schmerzen krümmen.

**convulsion** [kən'vʌlʃn] *n* MED Konvulsion *die.*

**convulsive** [kən'vʌlsɪv] *adj* [shiver, movement] konvulsiv; **~ laughter** Lachkrämpfe *pl.*

**coo** [kuː] *vi* gurren.

**cook** [kʊk] *n* Koch *der*, Köchin *die* <> *vt* - **1.** [food, meal] machen, zulbereiten; [boil] kochen; [roast, fry] braten; **to ~ sthg (in the oven)** etw im Ofen garen lassen - **2.** *inf* [falsify] frisieren <> *vi* [boil] kochen; [roast, fry] braten.
➤ **cook up** *vt sep* [invent] sich zusammenlbasteln.

**cookbook** ['kʊkˌbʊk] *n* = **cookery book.**

**cooked** [kʊkt] *adj* [food] gekocht; **a ~ meal** ein warmes Essen.

**cooker** ['kʊkəʳ] *n esp Br* [stove] Herd *der.*

**cookery** ['kʊkərɪ] *n* Kochen *das.*

**cookery book** *n* Kochbuch *das.*

**cookie** ['kʊkɪ] *n* Keks *der*, Plätzchen *das.*

**cooking** ['kʊkɪŋ] *n* (U) - **1.** [activity] Kochen *das* - **2.** [food] Küche *die;* **her ~'s awful** ihre Kochkünste sind grauenvoll <> *comp* Koch-; **~ oil** Öl *das* (zum Kochen und Braten); **~ choco-**

**late** Blockschokolade *die;* ~ **sherry** Sherry *der* (zum Kochen).

**cooking apple** *n* Kochapfel *der.*

**cookout** ['kukaut] *n Am Kochen/Grillen am Lagerfeuer oder Kastengrill.*

**cool** [ku:l] *adj* - **1.** [gen] kühl; [dress] leicht - **2.** [person] ruhig, gelassen; **to keep a ~ head** einen kühlen Kopf behalten - **3.** *inf* [excellent, fashionable] cool <> *vt* kühlen <> *vi* ablkühlen <> *n inf* [calm]: **to keep one's ~** die Ruhe bewahren, einen kühlen Kopf bewahren; **to lose one's ~** die Nerven verlieren.

▸ **cool down** *vt sep* - **1.** [make less warm] ablkühlen - **2.** [make less angry] beruhigen <> *vi* - **1.** [become less warm] ablkühlen; [person] kühler werden - **2.** [become less angry] sich beruhigen.

▸ **cool off** *vi* - **1.** [become less warm] ablkühlen; [person] kühler werden - **2.** [become less angry] sich beruhigen.

**coolant** ['ku:lənt] *n* Kühlmittel *das.*

**cool bag** *n* Kühltasche *die.*

**cool box** *Br*, **cooler** ['ku:lə'] *Am n* Kühlbox *die.*

**cool-headed** [-'hedɪd] *adj* kühl und besonnen.

**cooling-off period** ['ku:lɪŋ-] *n Zeitraum, in dem die Betroffenen nach einem Disput ihre Besonnenheit wiedergewinnen können.*

**cooling tower** ['ku:lɪŋ-] *n* Kühlturm *der.*

**coolly** ['ku:lɪ] *adv* - **1.** [calmly] ruhig, gelassen - **2.** [coldly] kühl.

**coolness** ['ku:lnɪs] *n (U)* Kühle *die.*

**coop** [ku:p] *n* Käfig *der.*

▸ **coop up** *vt sep inf* einlpferchen.

**co-op** ['kəu,ɒp] *n abbr of* **cooperative.**

**cooperate** [kəu'ɒpəreɪt] *vi* zusammenlarbeiten, kooperieren; **to ~ with sb** mit jm zusammenlarbeiten.

**cooperation** [kəu,ɒpə'reɪʃn] *n (U)* - **1.** [collaboration] Zusammenarbeit *die* - **2.** [assistance] Mitarbeit *die,* Kooperation *die.*

**cooperative** [kəu'ɒpərətɪv] *adj* - **1.** [helpful] kooperativ - **2.** [collective] auf Genossenschaftsbasis <> *n* [enterprise] Genossenschaft *die,* Kooperative *die.*

**co-opt** *vt:* **to ~ sb** jn hinzulwählen; **to ~ sb into/onto sthg** jn in etw *(A)* hineinlwählen.

**coordinate** [*n* kəu'ɔ:dɪnət, *vt* kəu'ɔ:dɪneɪt] *n* [on map, graph] Koordinate *die* <> *vt* koordinieren.

▸ **coordinates** *npl* [clothes] Kleidung *die* zum Kombinieren.

**coordination** [kəu,ɔ:dɪ'neɪʃn] *n* Koordination *die.*

**coot** [ku:t] *n* Blässhuhn *das.*

**co-ownership** *n (U)* Mitbesitz *der.*

**cop** [kɒp] (*pt & pp* **-ped;** *cont* **-ping**) *n inf* [policeman] Polizist *der,* -in *die.*

▸ **cop out** *vi inf:* **to ~ out (of sthg)** kneifen (vor etw *(D)*).

**cope** [kəup] *vi* zurechtlkommen; **to ~ with sthg** etw schaffen.

**Copenhagen** [,kəupən'heɪgən] *n* Kopenhagen *nt.*

**copier** ['kɒpɪə'] *n* [photocopier] Kopierer *der.*

**copilot** ['kəu,paɪlət] *n* Kopilot *der,* -in *die.*

**copious** ['kəupjəs] *adj* reichlich.

**cop-out** *n inf* Rückzieher *der.*

**copper** ['kɒpə'] *n* - **1.** [metal] Kupfer *das* - **2.** *Br inf* [policeman] Polizist *der,* -in *die.*

**coppice** ['kɒpɪs], **copse** [kɒps] *n* Wäldchen *das.*

**copulate** ['kɒpjuleɪt] *vi fml:* **to ~ (with)** kopulieren (mit).

**copulation** [,kɒpju'leɪʃn] *n* Kopulation *die.*

**copy** ['kɒpɪ] (*pt & pp* **-ied**) *n* - **1.** [gen] Kopie *die* - **2.** [of book, magazine] Exemplar *das* <> *vt* - **1.** [imitate] nachlahmen - **2.** [photocopy] kopieren <> *vi* [cheat - at school] ablschreiben.

▸ **copy down** *vt sep* auflschreiben.

▸ **copy out** *vt sep* ablschreiben.

**copycat** ['kɒpɪkæt] *n inf* Nachahmer *der,* -in *die* <> *comp* Nachahmungs-.

**copy protected** *adj* comput kopiergeschützt.

**copyright** ['kɒpɪraɪt] *n* Copyright *das,* Urheberrecht *das.*

**copy typist** *n Br* Schreibkraft *die.*

**copywriter** ['kɒpɪ,raɪtə'] *n* Texter *der,* -in *die.*

**coral** ['kɒrəl] *n (U)* Koralle *die* <> *comp* Korallen-.

**coral reef** *n* Korallenriff *das.*

**cord** [kɔ:d] *n* - **1.** [string] Schnur *die* - **2.** [wire] Kabel *das* - **3.** *(U)* [fabric] Kord *der* <> *comp* Kord-.

▸ **cords** *npl inf* Kordhose *die.*

**cordial** ['kɔ:djəl] *adj* freundlich <> *n* Fruchtsirup *der.*

**cordially** ['kɔ:dɪəlɪ] *adv* freundlich.

**cordless** ['kɔ:dlɪs] *adj* kabellos.

**cordon** ['kɔ:dn] *n* Kette *die.*

▸ **cordon off** *vt sep* ablsperren.

**cordon bleu** [-blɜ:] *adj* [cook] Meister-; **~ cookery** feine Küche.

**corduroy** ['kɔ:dərɔɪ] *n (U)* Kord *der* <> *comp* Kord-.

**core** [kɔ:'] *n* - **1.** [of apple, pear] Kerngehäuse *das* - **2.** [of Earth, nuclear reactor] Kern *der* - **3.** [of cable] Seele *die* - **4.** *fig* [of group of people] Zentrum *das;* [of argument, policy] Kern *der* <> *vt* entkernen.

**corer** ['kɔ:rə'] *n* Apfelstecher *der.*

**corespondent** [ˌkəʊrɪ'spɒndənt] n LAW Dritte der, die.

**core time** n Br Kernzeit die

**corgi** ['kɔːgɪ] (pl -s) n Corgi der.

**coriander** [ˌkɒrɪ'ændəʳ] n Koriander der.

**cork** [kɔːk] n - **1.** [material] Kork der - **2.** [stopper] Korken der.

**corkage** ['kɔːkɪdʒ] n (U) Korkengeld das.

**corked** [kɔːkt] adj korkig.

**corkscrew** ['kɔːkskruː] n Korkenzieher der.

**cormorant** ['kɔːmərənt] n Kormoran der.

**corn** [kɔːn] n - **1.** (U) Br [cereal] Korn das, Getreide das - **2.** (U) esp Am [maize] Mais der - **3.** [callus] Hühnerauge das.

**Corn** abk für Cornwall, in Postanschrift verwendet.

**corn bread** n Maisbrot das.

**cornea** ['kɔːnɪə] (pl -s) n Hornhaut die.

**corned beef** [kɔːnd-] n Corned beef das.

**corner** ['kɔːnəʳ] n Ecke die; fig from all ~s of the earth aus aller Welt; to cut ~s oberflächlich arbeiten ⬦ vt - **1.** fig [person, animal] in die Enge treiben - **2.** [market] monopolisieren.

**corner flag** n Eckfahne die.

**corner kick** n FTBL Eckstoß der.

**corner shop** n Laden der an der Ecke.

**cornerstone** ['kɔːnəstəʊn] n fig Grundstein der.

**cornet** ['kɔːnɪt] n - **1.** [instrument] Kornett das - **2.** Br [ice-cream cone] Hörnchen das.

**cornfield** ['kɔːnfiːld] n - **1.** Br [of wheat] Kornfeld das - **2.** esp Am [of maize] Maisfeld das.

**cornflakes** ['kɔːnfleɪks] npl Cornflakes pl.

**cornflour** Br ['kɔːnflaʊəʳ], **cornstarch** Am [-staːtʃ] n (U) Stärkemehl das.

**cornice** ['kɔːnɪs] n Zierleiste die.

**Cornish** ['kɔːnɪʃ] adj aus Cornwall ⬦ npl: the ~ die Einwohner von Cornwall.

**Cornishman** ['kɔːnɪʃmən] (pl -men [-mən]) n Einwohner der von Cornwall.

**Cornishwoman** ['kɔːnɪʃˌwʊmən] (pl -women [-ˌwɪmɪn]) n Einwohnerin die von Cornwall.

**corn oil** n (U) Maiskeimöl das.

**corn on the cob** n Maiskolben der.

**cornstarch** ['kɔːnstaːtʃ] n Am = cornflour.

**cornucopia** [ˌkɔːnjʊ'kəʊpjə] n literary Füllhorn das.

**corny** ['kɔːnɪ] (compar -ier; superl -iest) adj inf abgedroschen.

**corollary** [kə'rɒlərɪ] (pl -ies) n Folgeerscheinung die.

**coronary** ['kɒrənrɪ] (pl -ies), **coronary thrombosis** [-θrɒm'bəʊsɪs] (pl coronary thromboses [-siːz]) n Herzinfarkt der.

**coronation** [ˌkɒrə'neɪʃn] n Krönung die.

**coroner** ['kɒrənəʳ] n für die Untersuchung ungeklärter Todesfälle zuständiger Beamter.

**Corp.** abbr of corporation.

**corpora** ['kɔːpərə] pl ⬅ corpus.

**corporal** ['kɔːpərəl] n Hauptgefreite der.

**corporal punishment** n (U) körperliche Züchtigung die, Prügelstrafe die.

**corporate** ['kɔːpərət] adj - **1.** [business] körperschaftlich - **2.** [collective] gemeinsam.

**corporate hospitality** n (U) PR-Veranstaltung die.

**corporate identity, corporate image** n Firmenidentität die.

**corporation** [ˌkɔːpə'reɪʃn] n - **1.** [council] Gemeindeverwaltung die, Stadtverwaltung die - **2.** [large company] Handelsgesellschaft die.

**corporation tax** n Br Körperschaftssteuer die.

**corps** [kɔːʳ] (pl inv) n Korps das.

**corpse** [kɔːps] n Leiche die.

**corpulent** ['kɔːpjʊlənt] adj fml korpulent.

**corpus** ['kɔːpəs] (pl -pora OR -puses) n Korpus der.

**corpuscle** ['kɔːpʌsl] n Blutkörperchen das.

**corral** [kɒ'raːl] n esp Am Korral der.

**correct** [kə'rekt] adj - **1.** [right, accurate] korrekt, richtig; you're quite ~ du hast ganz Recht - **2.** [appropriate, suitable] angemessen ⬦ vt korrigieren.

**correction** [kə'rekʃn] n - **1.** (U) [act of correcting] Korrigieren das - **2.** [change] Korrektur die, Berichtigung die.

**correctly** [kə'rektlɪ] adv - **1.** [accurately] richtig - **2.** [appropriately, suitably] korrekt, angemessen.

**correlate** ['kɒrəleɪt] vt einen Zusammenhang herstellen zwischen ⬦ vi: to ~ (with sthg) in Wechselbeziehung stehen (zu etw).

**correlation** [ˌkɒrə'leɪʃn] n (U): ~ (between) Wechselbeziehung die (zwischen).

**correspond** [ˌkɒrɪ'spɒnd] vi - **1.** [be equivalent]: to ~ (with OR to sthg) (etw (D)) entsprechen - **2.** [tally]: to ~ (with OR to sthg) (mit etw) übereinstimmen - **3.** [write letters]: to ~ (with sb) (mit jm) korrespondieren.

**correspondence** [ˌkɒrɪ'spɒndəns] n - **1.** [letters] Briefe pl - **2.** (U) [letter-writing]: ~ with/between Briefwechsel der mit/zwischen (D) - **3.** [relationship]: ~ with sthg Übereinstimmung die mit jm.

**correspondence course** n Fernkurs der.

**correspondent** [ˌkɒrɪ'spɒndənt] n Korrespondent der, -in die.

**C**

**corresponding** [ˌkɒrɪ'spɒndɪŋ] adj entsprechend.

**corridor** ['kɒrɪdɔːr] n Gang der, Korridor der.

**corroborate** [kə'rɒbəreɪt] vt bestätigen.

**corroboration** [kəˌrɒbə'reɪʃən] n (U) Bestätigung die.

**corrode** [kə'rəʊd] vt zerfressen ◇ vi korrodieren.

**corrosion** [kə'rəʊʒn] n Korrosion die.

**corrosive** [kə'rəʊsɪv] adj korrosiv.

**corrugated** ['kɒrəgeɪtɪd] adj gewellt.

**corrugated iron** n Wellblech das.

**corrupt** [kə'rʌpt] adj - 1. [gen] korrupt - 2. [depraved] verdorben ◇ vt - 1. [deprave] verderben - 2. COMPUT [damage] beschädigen.

**corruption** [kə'rʌpʃn] n (U) - 1. [dishonesty] Korruption die - 2. [depravity] Verdorbenheit die - 3. [debasement] Verführung die.

**corsage** [kɔː'sɑːʒ] n Ansteckblume die.

**corset** ['kɔːsɪt] n Korsett das.

**cortege, cortège** [kɔː'teɪʒ] n Prozession die.

**cortisone** ['kɔːtɪzəʊn] n Kortison das.

**cos¹** [kɒz] Br inf = because.

**cos²** [kɒz] n = cos lettuce.

**cosh** [kɒʃ] n Knüppel der ◇ vt niederlknüppeln.

**cosignatory** [ˌkəʊ'sɪgnətrɪ] (pl -ies) n Mitunterzeichner der, -in die.

**cosine** ['kəʊsaɪn] n Kosinus der.

**cos lettuce** n Br römischer Salat.

**cosmetic** [kɒz'metɪk] adj fig [superficial] kosmetisch ◇ n Kosmetikum das, Schönheitsmittel das.
⭢ **cosmetics** n Kosmetik die, Kosmetika pl.

**cosmetic surgery** n (U) Schönheitschirurgie die.

**cosmic** ['kɒzmɪk] adj kosmisch.

**cosmonaut** ['kɒzmənɔːt] n Kosmonaut der, -in die.

**cosmopolitan** [kɒzmə'pɒlɪtn] adj [city, place] kosmopolitisch, international; [person] welterfahren.

**cosmos** ['kɒzmɒs] n: the ~ der Kosmos.

**Cossack** ['kɒsæk] n Kosake der, -kin die.

**cosset** ['kɒsɪt] vt verhätscheln.

**cost** [kɒst] (pt & pp sense 1 cost; pt & pp sense 2 -ed) n - 1. [price] Kosten pl - 2. fig [loss, damage] Preis der; at the ~ of his health auf Kosten seiner Gesundheit; at all ~s um jeden Preis ◇ vt - 1. [gen] kosten - 2. COMM: to ~ sthg die Kosten einer Sache (G) kalkulieren.
⭢ **costs** npl LAW Kosten pl.

**cost accountant** n Kostenbuchhalter der, -in die.

**co-star** n: to be the ~ in a film eine der Hauptrollen in einem Film spielen ◇ vt [subj: film] in einer der Hauptrollen zeigen ◇ vi: to ~ (with) in einer der Hauptrollen auftreten (neben (+ D)).

**Costa Rica** [ˌkɒstə'riːkə] n Costa Rica nt.

**cost-benefit analysis** n Kosten-Nutzen-Rechnung die.

**cost-effective** adj kosteneffektiv.

**cost-effectiveness** n Kosteneffizienz die.

**costing** ['kɒstɪŋ] n Kalkulation die.

**costly** ['kɒstlɪ] (compar -ier; superl -iest) adj kostspielig, teuer.

**cost of living** n: the ~ die Lebenshaltungskosten pl.

**cost-of-living index** n Lebenshaltungsindex der.

**cost price** n Selbstkostenpreis der.

**costume** ['kɒstjuːm] n - 1. THEATRE Kostüm das - 2. (U) [dress] Tracht die - 3. [swimming costume] Badeanzug der.

**costume jewellery** n Modeschmuck der.

**cosy** Br, **cozy** Am (compar -ier; superl -iest; pl -ies) ['kəʊzɪ] adj - 1. [warm and comfortable] gemütlich - 2. [intimate] behaglich ◇ n [for teapot] Wärmer der.

**cot** [kɒt] n - 1. Br [for child] Kinderbett das - 2. Am [folding bed] Feldbett das.

**cot death** n plötzlicher Kindstod.

**cottage** ['kɒtɪdʒ] n Häuschen das, Cottage das.

**cottage cheese** n (U) Hüttenkäse der.

**cottage hospital** n Br Krankenhaus für unkomplizierte Fälle.

**cottage industry** n Heimindustrie die.

**cottage pie** n Br Hackfleisch mit einer Lage Kartoffelbrei, im Ofen überbacken.

**cotton** ['kɒtn] n (U) - 1. [fabric] Baumwolle die - 2. [plant] Baumwollstrauch der - 3. [thread] Faden der ◇ comp [fabric] Baumwoll-.
⭢ **cotton on** vi inf: to ~ on (to sthg) (etw) kapieren.

**cotton bud** Br, **cotton swab** Am n Wattebausch der.

**cotton candy** n Am = candyfloss.

**cotton swab** n Am = cotton bud.

**cotton wool** n Watte die.

**couch** [kaʊtʃ] n - 1. [sofa] Sofa das, Couch die - 2. [in doctor's surgery] Liege die ◇ vt: the letter was ~ed in polite terms der Brief war in höflichen Worten abgefasst.

**couchette** [kuː'ʃet] n Br Liegewagen der.

**couch potato** *n inf Person, die ständig vor dem Fernseher sitzt.*

**cougar** ['ku:gər] (*pl inv* OR **-s**) *n* Puma *der.*

**cough** [kɒf] *n* Husten *der* <> *vt* & *vi* husten.

➤ **cough up** *vt sep* - **1.** [blood, phlegm] aus|husten - **2.** *inf* [money] raus|rücken, aus|spucken.

**coughing** ['kɒfɪŋ] *n* (*U*) Husten *das.*

**cough mixture** *n Br* Hustensaft *der.*

**cough sweet** *n Br* Hustenpastille *die.*

**cough syrup** *n* = cough mixture.

**could** [kʊd] *pt* ⊳ can².

**couldn't** ['kʊdnt] = could not.

**could've** ['kʊdəv] = could have.

**council** ['kaʊnsl] *n* - **1.** [local authority] Stadtverwaltung *die* - **2.** [group, organization] Rat *der* - **3.** [meeting] Beratung *die* <> *comp* [of local authority] Stadtverwaltungs-.

**council estate** *n* Sozialsiedlung *die.*

**council house** *n Br* ≃ Sozialwohnung *die, mit öffentlichen Mitteln gebautes Einfamilienhaus für eine Familie mit niedrigem Einkommen.*

**councillor** ['kaʊnsələr] *n* Stadtrat *der,* -rätin *die.*

**Council of Europe** *n* Europarat *der.*

**council of war** *n* Kriegsrat *der.*

**council tax** *n Br* Gemeindesteuer *die.*

**counsel** ['kaʊnsl] (*Br pt* & *pp* **-led;** *cont* **-ling,** *Am pt* & *pp* **-ed;** *cont* **-ing**) *n* - **1.** *fml* [advice] Rat *der* - **2.** [lawyer] Rechtsanwalt *der,* -wältin *die; ~* **for the defence** Verteidiger *der,* -in *die; ~* **for the prosecution** Anklagevertreter *der,* -in *die* <> *vt* beraten; **to ~ sb to do sthg** *fml* jm raten, etw zu tun.

**counselling** *Br,* **counseling** *Am* ['kaʊnsəlɪŋ] *n* (*U*) Beratung *die.*

**counsellor** *Br,* **counselor** *Am* ['kaʊnsələʳ] - **1.** [adviser] Berater *der,* -in *die* - **2.** *Am* [lawyer] Rechtsanwalt *der,* -wältin *die.*

**count** [kaʊnt] *n* - **1.** [total] Zählung *die;* **to keep ~ of sthg** etw mit|zählen; **to lose ~ of sthg** den Überblick über etw (*A*) verlieren - **2.** [point] Punkt *der* - **3.** LAW [charge] Anklagepunkt *der* - **4.** [aristocrat] Graf *der* <> *vt* - **1.** [add up] zählen - **2.** [consider, include]: **to ~ sb/sthg as sthg** jn/etw als etw an|sehen; **there are six, not ~ing the broken ones** es sind sechs, die zerbrochenen nicht mitgezählt <> *vi* zählen; **to ~ (up) to** zählen bis; **to ~ for something** etwas wert sein, etwas bedeuten; **to ~ for nothing** umsonst gewesen sein; **to ~ as sthg** als etw zählen.

➤ **count against** *vt fus* sprechen gegen.

➤ **count in** *vt sep inf* rechnen mit.

➤ **count on** *vt fus* - **1.** [rely on] zählen auf (+ *A*) - **2.** [expect] rechnen mit.

➤ **count out** *vt sep* - **1.** [money] ab|zählen - **2.** *inf* [leave out]: **~ me out!** ohne mich!

➤ **count up** *vt fus* zusammen|zählen.

➤ **count upon** *vt fus* = count on.

**countdown** ['kaʊntdaʊn] *n* Countdown *der.*

**countenance** ['kaʊntənəns] *n literary* [face] Angesicht *das;* [expression] Gesichtsausdruck *der* <> *vt* [approve of] unterstützen.

**counter** ['kaʊntəʳ] *n* - **1.** [in shop] Ladentisch *der* - **2.** [in board game] Spielmarke *die* - **3.** *Am* [in kitchen] Theke *die* <> *vt:* **to ~ sthg with sthg** etw (*D*) mit etw begegnen <> *vi:* **to ~ with sthg** mit etw reagieren.

➤ **counter to** *adv* entgegen (+ *D*); **to run ~ to sthg** etw (*D*) zuwider|laufen.

**counteract** [ˌkaʊntəˈrækt] *vt* entgegen|wirken (+ *D*).

**counterattack** ['kaʊntərəˌtæk] *n* Gegenangriff *der* <> *vt* einen Gegenangriff führen gegen <> *vi* einen Gegenangriff führen.

**counterbalance** [ˌkaʊntəˈbæləns] *vt fig* aus|gleichen.

**counterclaim** ['kaʊntəkleɪm] *n* Gegenanspruch *der.*

**counterclockwise** *Am* [ˌkaʊntəˈklɒkwaɪz] *adj* & *adv* gegen den Uhrzeigersinn.

**counterespionage** [ˌkaʊntərˈespɪənɑːʒ] *n* Gegenspionage *die.*

**counterfeit** ['kaʊntəfɪt] *adj* gefälscht <> *vt* fälschen.

**counterfoil** ['kaʊntəfɔɪl] *n* Kontrollabschnitt *der.*

**counterintelligence** [ˌkaʊntərɪnˈtelɪdʒəns] *n* Spionageabwehr *die.*

**countermand** [ˌkaʊntəˈmɑːnd] *vt* widerrufen.

**countermeasure** [ˌkaʊntəˈmeʒəʳ] *n* Gegenmaßnahme *die.*

**counteroffensive** [ˌkaʊntərəˈfensɪv] *n* Gegenoffensive *der.*

**counterpane** ['kaʊntəpeɪn] *n* Tagesdecke *die.*

**counterpart** ['kaʊntəpɑːt] *n* Gegenstück *das.*

**counterpoint** ['kaʊntəpɔɪnt] *n* (*U*) MUS Kontrapunkt *der.*

**counterproductive** [ˌkaʊntəprəˈdʌktɪv] *adj* die entgegengesetzte Wirkung habend.

**counter-revolution** *n* Konterrevolution *die.*

**countersank** ['kaʊntəsæŋk] *pt* ⊳ countersink.

**countersign** ['kaʊntəsaɪn] *vt* gegen|zeichnen.

**countersink** ['kaʊntəsɪŋk] (*pt* **-sank;** *pp* **-sunk**) *vt* versenken.

**countess** ['kaʊntɪs] *n* Gräfin *die.*

**countless** [ˈkaʊntlɪs] *adj* unzählig.

**countrified** [ˈkʌntrɪfaɪd] *adj pej* ländlich.

**country** [ˈkʌntrɪ] (*pl* -ies) *n* - 1. [nation] Land *das;* the ~ [countryside] das Land; they live in the ~ sie leben auf dem Land - 2. [area of land, region] Gebiet *das* ◇ *comp* Land-.

**country and western** *n* Country- und Westernmusik *die* ◇ *comp* Country- und Western-.

**country club** *n exklusiver Klub auf dem Land.*

**country dancing** *n (U)* Volkstanz *der.*

**country house** *n* Landhaus *das.*

**countryman** [ˈkʌntrɪmən] (*pl* -men [-mən]) *n* Landsmann *der.*

**country music** *n* & *comp* = **country and western.**

**country park** *n Br* Freizeitpark *der.*

**countryside** [ˈkʌntrɪsaɪd] *n (U)* Landschaft *die.*

**countrywoman** [ˈkʌntrɪˌwʊmən] (*pl* -women [-ˌwɪmɪn]) *n* Landsmännin *die.*

**county** [ˈkaʊntɪ] (*pl* -ies) *n* Grafschaft *die.*

**county council** *n Br* Grafschaftsrat *der.*

**county court** *n Br* Grafschaftsgericht *das.*

**county town** *Br,* **county seat** *Am n Verwaltungszentrum einer Grafschaft.*

**coup** [kuː] *n* - 1. [rebellion] ~ (d'état) Staatsstreich *der,* Coup d'Etat *der* - 2. [masterstroke] Coup *der.*

**coupé** *n* AUT Coupé *das.*

**couple** [ˈkʌpl] *n* - 1. [in relationship] Paar *das* - 2. [small number]: a ~ (of) [two] zwei; [a few] ein paar ◇ *vt* - 1. [join]: to ~ sthg (to sthg) etw (an etw (A)) koppeln - 2. *fig* [associate]: to ~ sthg with sthg etw mit etw verbinden; ~d with verbunden mit.

**couplet** [ˈkʌplɪt] *n* Verspaar *das.*

**coupling** [ˈkʌplɪŋ] *n* RAIL Kupplung *die.*

**coupon** [ˈkuːpɒn] *n* Gutschein *der.*

**courage** [ˈkʌrɪdʒ] *n* Mut *der,* Courage *die;* to take ~ (from sthg) sich (durch etw) ermutigt fühlen; to have the ~ of one's convictions Zivilcourage haben.

**courageous** [kəˈreɪdʒəs] *adj* mutig.

**courageously** [kəˈreɪdʒəslɪ] *adv* mutig.

**courgette** [kɔːˈʒet] *n Br* Zucchini *die.*

**courier** [ˈkʊrɪəʳ] *n* - 1. [on holiday tour] Reiseleiter *der,* -in *die* - 2. [to deliver letters, packages] Kurier *der.*

**course** [kɔːs] *n* - 1. [of study - for student] Kurs(us) *der;* [ - for employee] Lehrgang *der;* a ~ of lectures eine Vorlesungsreihe - 2. MED [of treatment] Reihe *die* - 3. [path, route] Kurs *der;* in the ~ of time im Laufe der Zeit; during the ~ of the ne-gotiations im Verlauf der Verhandlungen; to run *OR* take its ~ seinen Verlauf nehmen; on ~ *lit* & *fig* auf Kurs; off ~ vom Kurs abgewichen - 4. [plan]: ~ (of action) Vorgehensweise *die* - 5. [of time]: in due ~ zu gegebener Zeit; in the ~ of im Laufe (+ G) - 6. [in meal] Gang *der* - 7. SPORT [for horseracing] Bahn *die,* Strecke *die;* [for golf] Platz *der* ◇ *vi literary* [flow] fließen, strömen.

➡ **of course** *adv* natürlich; **of ~ not** natürlich nicht.

**coursebook** [ˈkɔːsbʊk] *n* Lehrbuch *das.*

**coursework** [ˈkɔːswɜːk] *n (U)* Mitarbeit *die* im Unterricht.

**court** [kɔːt] *n* - 1. [for trial] Gericht *das;* to appear in ~ vor Gericht erscheinen; to settle out of ~ sich außergerichtlich einigen; to go to ~ vor Gericht gehen; to take sb to ~ jn verklagen *OR* vor Gericht bringen - 2. SPORT Platz *der;* on ~ auf dem Platz - 3. [courtyard, of monarch] Hof *der* ◇ *vt* [danger, disaster] herausfordern; [favour, popularity] werben um ◇ *vi dated:* ~ing couples Liebespärchen; is he ~ing? hat er ein Mädchen?

**courteous** [ˈkɜːtjəs] *adj* höflich.

**courtesan** [ˌkɔːtɪˈzæn] *n* Kurtisane *die.*

**courtesy** [ˈkɜːtɪsɪ] *n* Höflichkeit *die.*

➡ **courtesy of** *prep* [thanks to] dank (+ G); [reproduced ~ of mit freundlicher Genehmigung (+ G).

**courtesy car** *n Fahrzeug, das kostenlos zur Verfügung gestellt wird.*

**courthouse** [ˈkɔːthaʊs, *pl* -haʊzɪz] *n Am* Gerichtsgebäude *das.*

**courtier** [ˈkɔːtjəʳ] *n* Höfling *der.*

**court-martial** (*pl* -s *OR* courts-martial, *Br pt* & *pp* -led; *cont* -ling, *Am pt* & *pp* -ed; *cont* -ing) *n* - 1. [court] Kriegsgericht *das* - 2. [trial] Kriegsgerichtsverhandlung *die* ◇ *vt* vor ein Kriegsgericht stellen.

**court of appeal** *Br,* **court of appeals** *Am n* Berufungsgericht *das.*

**court of inquiry** *n* - 1. [investigation] Untersuchung *die* - 2. [group] Untersuchungskommission *die.*

**court of law** *n* Gericht *das.*

**courtroom** [ˈkɔːtrʊm] *n* Gerichtssaal *der.*

**courtship** [ˈkɔːtʃɪp] *n (U)* - 1. [of people] Werbung *die* - 2. [of animals] Paarung *die;* [of birds] Balz *die.*

**court shoe** *n* Pumps *der.*

**courtyard** [ˈkɔːtjɑːd] *n* Hof *der.*

**cousin** [ˈkʌzn] *n* Cousin *der,* Cousine *die,* Kusine *die.*

**couture** [kuːˈtʊəʳ] *n:* haute ~ die Haute Couture.

**cove** [kəʊv] *n* Bucht *die.*

**coven** ['kʌvən] n Hexenzirkel der.

**covenant** ['kʌvənənt] n - **1.** [of money] Zahlungsverpflichtung die - **2.** [pact] Vertrag der.

**Covent Garden** [ˌkɒvənt-] n Covent Garden der, exklusive Londoner Einkaufsmeile.

**COVENT GARDEN**

Covent Garden, der frühere Obst-, Gemüse- und Blumenmarkt der Londoner Innenstadt, ist heute ein großes überdachtes Areal mit Geschäften und Kunstgewerbemärkten. Künstler unterhalten die Besucher mit Straßentheater, Konzerten, Pantomimen usw. Der Name „Covent Garden" bezeichnet auch das gleich neben dem Markt gelegene Royal Opera House.

**Coventry** ['kɒvəntrɪ] n: **to send sb to ~** jn schneiden.

**cover** ['kʌvəʳ] n - **1.** [of machine, typewriter] Abdeckung die; [of seat, cushion] Überzug der - **2.** [lid] Deckel der - **3.** [of book, magazine] Einband der - **4.** [blanket] Decke die - **5.** (U) [protection, shelter, insurance] Schutz der; **to take ~** [from weather] sich unterIstellen; [from gunfire] in Deckung gehen; **under ~** [from weather] geschützt; **under ~ of darkness** im Schutz der Dunkelheit; **to break ~** aus der Deckung kommen - **6.** [disguise] Tarnung die ◇ vt - **1.** [gen] bedecken; **to be ~ed in blood** blutüberströmt sein - **2.** [traverse] zurücklegen - **3.** [insure]: **to ~ sb (against sthg)** [subj: policy] jn (gegen etw) versichern - **4.** [report on] berichten über (+ A) - **5.** [deal with] behandeln - **6.** [pay for - damage] decken.
◆ **cover up** vt sep - **1.** [to keep warm] einIwickeln - **2.** fig [to conceal] vertuschen.

**coverage** ['kʌvərɪdʒ] n (U) [of news] Berichterstattung die.

**coveralls** ['kʌvərɔːlz] npl Am Overall der.

**cover charge** n Gedeckgebühr die.

**cover girl** n Covergirl das, Titelmädchen das.

**covering** ['kʌvərɪŋ] n Belag der; **a ~ of snow/dust** eine Schneedecke/Staubdecke.

**covering letter** Br, **cover letter** Am n Begleitbrief der.

**cover note** n Br vorläufiger Versicherungsschein.

**covert** ['kʌvət] adj verdeckt, versteckt; [look, glance] verstohlen.

**cover-up** n Vertuschung die.

**cover version** n Coverversion die.

**covet** ['kʌvɪt] vt fml begehren.

**cow** [kaʊ] n Kuh die ◇ vt einIschüchtern.

**coward** ['kaʊəd] n Feigling der.

**cowardice** ['kaʊədɪs] n Feigheit die.

**cowardly** ['kaʊədlɪ] adj feige.

**cowboy** ['kaʊbɔɪ] n - **1.** [cattlehand] Cowboy der - **2.** Br inf [dishonest workman] Gauner der ◇ comp [western] Cowboy-.

**cower** ['kaʊəʳ] vi sich ducken; [squat] kauern.

**cowhide** ['kaʊhaɪd] n (U) Rindsleder das.

**cowl neck** [kaʊl-] n Schalkragen der.

**cowpat** ['kaʊpæt] n Kuhfladen der.

**cowshed** ['kaʊʃed] n Kuhstall der.

**cox** [kɒks], **coxswain** ['kɒksən] n Steuermann der.

**coy** [kɔɪ] adj kokett, neckisch.

**coyly** ['kɔɪlɪ] adv kokett, neckisch.

**coyote** [kɔɪ'əʊtɪ] n Kojote der.

**cozy** adj & n Am = cosy.

**CP** (abbr of Communist Party) n KP die.

**CPA** n abbr of certified public accountant.

**CPI** (abbr of Consumer Price Index) n Verbraucherpreisindex der.

**Cpl.** abbr of corporal.

**c.p.s.** (abbr of characters per second) Zeichen pro Sekunde ◇ (abbr of cycles per second) Hz.

**CPS** (abbr of Crown Prosecution Service) n Staatsanwaltschaft in England und Wales.

**CPSA** (abbr of Civil and Public Services Association) n britische Gewerkschaft der Angestellten des öffentlichen Dienstes und des Dienstleistungssektors.

**CPU** n COMPUT abbr of central processing unit.

**cr. - 1.** abbr of credit - **2.** abbr of creditor.

**crab** [kræb] n Krabbe die, Krebs der.

**crab apple** n - **1.** [fruit] Holzapfel der - **2.** [tree] Holzapfelbaum der.

**crabby** (compar -ier; superl -iest) adj mürrisch.

**crack** [kræk] n - **1.** [fault] Riss der; [in cup, glass, mirror] Sprung der - **2.** [in curtains, door] Spalt der; [in wall] Ritze die; **at the ~ of dawn** bei Tagesanbruch - **3.** [sharp noise] Knall der - **4.** [joke] Witz der - **5.** inf [attempt]: **to have a ~ at sthg** sich an etw (D) versuchen - **6.** [cocaine] Crack das ◇ adj toll, erstklassig ◇ vt - **1.** [damage] einen Riss machen in (+ D); [cup, glass, mirror] anIschlagen; [skin] rissig machen - **2.** [open - nut, safe] knacken; [ - bottle] öffnen; [ - egg] aufIschlagen - **3.** [whip] knallen mit - **4.** [bang, hit] anIschlagen; **I ~ed my head on the doorpost** ich habe mir den Kopf am Türrahmen gestoßen - **5.** [solve] lösen; [code] knacken - **6.** inf [make]: **to ~ a joke** einen Witz reißen ◇ vi - **1.** [be damaged] einen Riss bekommen; [cup, glass, mirror] springen; [skin] aufIspringen - **2.** [whip] knallen - **3.** [person] zusammenIbrechen; [marriage] auseinanderIbrechen - **4.** Br inf [act quickly]: **to get ~ing** losIlegen.
◆ **crack down** vi: **to ~ down (on sb/sthg)** (bei jm/etw) hart durchIgreifen.

➤ **crack up** *vi* durchldrehen.

**crackdown** ['krækdaʊn] *n:* ~ **(on sthg)** hartes Durchgreifen(bei etw).

**cracked** ['krækt] *adj* - **1.** [damaged] rissig; [cup, glass, mirror] gesprungen, angebrochen - **2.** *inf* [mad] verrückt.

**cracker** ['krækə'] *n* - **1.** [biscuit] Keks *der* - **2.** *Br* [for Christmas] Knallbonbon *das.*

**crackers** ['krækəz] *adj Br inf* [mad] verrückt.

**cracking** ['krækɪŋ] *adj inf:* **to walk at a ~ pace** in scharfem Tempo laufen.

**crackle** ['krækl] *n* Knacken *das;* [of leaves, paper] Rascheln *das;* [of cooking] Brutzeln *das* <> *vi* knacken.

**crackling** ['kræklɪŋ] *n (U)* - **1.** [noise] Knacken *das* - **2.** [pork skin] Kruste *die.*

**crackpot** ['krækpɒt] *inf adj* verrückt <> *n* Spinner *der,* -in *die.*

**cradle** ['kreɪdl] *n* - **1.** [bed, birthplace] Wiege *die* - **2.** [hoist] Hängebühne *die* <> *vt* an sich (A) drücken.

**craft** [krɑːft] (*pl sense 2 inv*) *n* - **1.** [trade, skill] Handwerk *das* - **2.** [boat] Boot *das.*

**craftsman** ['krɑːftsmən] (*pl* -**men** [-mən]) *n* Handwerker *der.*

**craftsmanship** ['krɑːftsmənʃɪp] *n (U)* Handwerkskunst *die.*

**craftsmen** *pl* ➤ craftsman.

**crafty** ['krɑːftɪ] (*compar* -**ier**; *superl* -**iest**) *adj* schlau.

**crag** [kræg] *n* Felszacken *der.*

**craggy** ['krægɪ] (*compar* -**ier**; *superl* -**iest**) *adj* - **1.** [cliff, mountain] zerklüftet - **2.** [face] kantig.

**cram** [kræm] (*pt* & *pp* -**med**; *cont* -**ming**) *vt* - **1.** [stuff]: **to ~ sthg into sthg** etw in etw (A) stopfen - **2.** [overfill]: **to be ~med (with sthg)** (mit etw) vollgestopft sein <> *vi* [study] pauken, büffeln.

**cramming** ['kræmɪŋ] *n* [studying] Pauken *das,* Büffeln *das.*

**cramp** [kræmp] *n* Krampf *der;* **I've got ~** ich habe einen Krampf; **stomach ~s** Magenkrämpfe <> *vt* [hinder] hemmen, behindern.

**cramped** [kræmpt] *adj* [flat] eng; [conditions] beengt; **it's a bit ~ in here** es ist etwas eng hier.

**crampon** ['kræmpɒn] *n* Steigeisen *das.*

**cranberry** ['krænbərɪ] (*pl* -**ies**) *n* Preiselbeere *die.*

**crane** [kreɪn] *n* - **1.** [machine] Kran *der* - **2.** [bird] Kranich *der* <> *vt:* **to ~ one's neck** den Hals recken.

**crane fly** *n* Schnake *die.*

**cranium** ['kreɪnjəm] (*pl* -**niums** OR -**nia** [-njə]) *n* Kranium *das.*

**crank** [kræŋk] *n* - **1.** TECH Kurbel *die* - **2.** *inf* [eccen-

tric] Spinner *der,* -in *die* <> *vt* - **1.** [handle, mechanism] kurbeln - **2.** AUT anlkurbeln.

**crankshaft** ['kræŋkʃɑːft] *n* Kurbelwelle *die.*

**cranky** ['kræŋkɪ] (*compar* -**ier**; *superl* -**iest**) *adj inf* - **1.** [odd] wunderlich, verschroben - **2.** *Am* [bad-tempered] griesgrämig.

**cranny** ['krænɪ] (*pl* -**ies**) *n* ➤ nook.

**crap** [kræp] *n vinf* Scheiße *die.*

**crappy** ['kræpɪ] (*compar* -**ier**; *superl* -**iest**) *adj vinf* beschissen.

**crash** [kræʃ] *n* - **1.** [of car] Unfall *der;* [of plane] Absturz *der;* [of train] Unglück *das;* [collision] Zusammenstoß *der;* **to have a ~** verunglücken; [collide] zusammenlstoßen - **2.** [loud noise] Krachen *das* - **3.** FIN Zusammenbruch *der* <> *vt* [car] einen Unfall haben mit; **she ~ed her car into a tree** sie krachte mit dem Auto gegen einen Baum <> *vi* - **1.** [car driver] verunglücken; [plane] ablstürzen; [collide] zusammenlstoßen; **to ~ into sthg** [in car] mit dem Auto gegen etw krachen - **2.** [make loud noise] krachen - **3.** FIN [business, company] bankrott gehen; [stock market] zusammenlbrechen - **4.** COMPUT ablstürzen.

**crash barrier** *n* Leitplanke *die.*

**crash course** *n* Intensivkurs *der.*

**crash diet** *n* Radikaldiät *die.*

**crash helmet** *n* Sturzhelm *der.*

**crash-land** *vt* eine Bruchlandung machen mit <> *vi* eine Bruchlandung machen.

**crash landing** *n* Bruchlandung *die.*

**crass** [kræs] *adj* dumm und geschmacklos.

**crate** [kreɪt] *n* Kiste *die;* [of milk bottles, beer] Kasten *der.*

**crater** ['kreɪtə'] *n* Krater *der.*

**cravat** [krə'væt] *n* Halstuch *das.*

**crave** [kreɪv] *vt* sich sehnen nach; [subj: pregnant woman] Gelüste haben auf (+ A) <> *vi:* **to ~ for sthg** sich nach etw sehnen; [subj: pregnant woman] Gelüste auf etw (A) haben.

**craving** ['kreɪvɪŋ] *n:* ~ **(for)** Verlangen *das* (nach); [of pregnant woman] Gelüste *pl* (auf (+ A)).

**crawl** [krɔːl] *vi* - **1.** [gen] kriechen; [baby, insect] krabbeln; **to ~ along** [traffic] im Schneckentempo vorwärtslkommen - **2.** *inf* [be covered]: **to be ~ing with** wimmeln von - **3.** *inf* [grovel]: **to ~ (to sb)** (vor jm) kriechen <> *n* - **1.** [slow pace]: **to move at a ~** sich im Schneckentempo bewegen - **2.** [swimming stroke]: **the ~** das Kraulen; **to do the ~** kraulen.

**crawler lane** [ˌkrɔːlə-] *n Br* Kriechspur *die.*

**crayfish** ['kreɪfɪʃ] (*pl inv* OR -**es**) *n* [saltwater] Languste *die.*

**crayon** ['kreɪɒn] *n* [pencil] Buntstift *der;* [of wax] Wachsmalstift *der.*

**craze** [kreɪz] n Mode die (die gerade „in" ist); **the latest ~** der letzte Schrei.

**crazed** [kreɪzd] adj verrückt.

**crazy** ['kreɪzɪ] (compar **-ier;** superl **-iest**) adj inf - **1.** [mad] verrückt - **2.** [enthusiastic]: **to be ~ about sthg** auf etw (A) verrückt sein; **to be ~ about sb** nach jm verrückt sein.

**crazy paving** n Br Mosaikpflaster das.

**CRE** n abbr of **Commission for Racial Equality.**

**creak** [kri:k] n [of door, floorboard] Knarren das; [of bed, hinge, handle] Quietschen das <> vi [door, floorboard] knarren; [bed, hinge, handle] quietschen.

**creaky** ['kri:kɪ] (compar **-ier;** superl **-iest**) adj [door, floorboard] knarrend; [bed, hinge, gate] quietschend.

**cream** [kri:m] adj [in colour] creme(farben) <> n - **1.** [food] Sahne die; [filling for chocolates, biscuits] Creme die - **2.** (U) [cosmetic] Creme die - **3.** [colour] Creme das - **4.** [elite]: **the ~** die Besten pl <> vt [potatoes, parsnips] pürieren; [butter, cake mix] (schaumig) rühren.

◆ **cream off** vt sep sich (D) das Beste sichern.

**cream cake** n Br Sahnetorte die; [bun] Sahnetörtchen das.

**cream cheese** n Frischkäse der.

**cream cracker** n Br Kräcker der

**cream tea** n Br Nachmittagstee mit Gebäck, Marmelade und Sahne.

**creamy** ['kri:mɪ] (compar **-ier;** superl **-iest**) adj - **1.** [taste] sahnig - **2.** [texture] cremig - **3.** [colour] creme(farben).

**crease** [kri:s] n [in fabric - deliberate] Bügelfalte die; [ - accidental] Falte die <> vt [deliberately] falten; [accidentally] zerknittern <> vi - **1.** [fabric] knittern - **2.** [face, forehead] sich runzeln.

**creased** [kri:st] adj - **1.** [fabric] zerknittert - **2.** [face] gerunzelt.

**crease-resistant** adj knitterfrei.

**create** [kri:'eɪt] vt - **1.** [gen] schaffen; [the world] erschaffen - **2.** [noise, fuss] verursachen; [impression] machen; [difficulties] bereiten.

**creation** [kri:'eɪʃn] n - **1.** [gen] Schaffung die; [of the world] Erschaffung die - **2.** (U) literary [universe] Schöpfung die - **3.** [work of art] Werk das; [dress, hat, hairstyle] Kreation die.

**creative** [kri:'eɪtɪv] adj kreativ; [energy] schöpferisch.

**creativity** [ˌkri:eɪ'tɪvətɪ] n Kreativität die.

**creator** [kri:'eɪtəʳ] n Schöpfer der, -in die.

**creature** ['kri:tʃəʳ] n - **1.** [animal] Lebewesen das, Geschöpf das - **2.** literary [person] Geschöpf das.

**crèche** [kreʃ] n Br (Kinder)hort der.

**credence** ['kri:dns] n: **to give** OR **lend ~ to sthg** etw glaubwürdig machen.

**credentials** [krɪ'denʃlz] npl - **1.** [papers] (Ausweis)papiere pl - **2.** fig [qualifications] Qualifikationen pl - **3.** [references] Referenzen pl, Zeugnisse pl.

**credibility** [ˌkredə'bɪlətɪ] n Glaubwürdigkeit die.

**credible** ['kredəbl] adj glaubwürdig; [excuse, story] glaubhaft.

**credit** ['kredɪt] n - **1.** [financial aid] Kredit der; **to be in ~** im Plus sein; **on ~** auf Kredit - **2.** (U) [honour] Ehre die; [approval] Anerkennung die; **it is to your ~ that you admitted your crime** es ehrt dich, dass du dein Verbrechen zugibst; **to do sb ~** jm Ehre machen; **he was never given any ~ for it** man hat ihm nie Anerkennung dafür gezollt - **3.** SCH & UNIV [mark] Auszeichnung die; [unit of work] Schein der - **4.** FIN [money credited] Guthaben das <> vt - **1.** FIN gutschreiben - **2.** inf [believe] glauben - **3.** [attribute]: **to ~ sb with sthg** jm etw zuschreiben; **~ me with** SOME **intelligence!** ein bisschen Intelligenz kannst du mir schon zutrauen!; **he's ~ed with having discovered her** er soll sie entdeckt haben.

◆ **credits** npl CINEMA Nachspann der.

**creditable** ['kredɪtəbl] adj fml [effort, attempt] anerkennenswert; [behaviour] lobenswert.

**credit account** n Br Kundenkonto das.

**credit card** n Kreditkarte die.

**credit facilities** npl Kreditmöglichkeiten pl.

**credit limit** Br, **credit line** Am n Kreditgrenze die.

**credit note** n COMM & FIN Gutschrift die.

**creditor** ['kredɪtəʳ] n Gläubiger der, -in die.

**credit rating** n Kreditwürdigkeit die.

**creditworthy** ['kredɪtˌwɜːðɪ] adj kreditwürdig.

**credulity** [krɪ'dju:lətɪ] n fml Leichtgläubigkeit die.

**credulous** ['kredjʊləs] adj leichtgläubig.

**creed** [kri:d] n - **1.** [political] Kredo das - **2.** RELIG Konfession die.

**creek** [kri:k] n - **1.** [of sea] Meeresarm der - **2.** Am [stream] Bach der.

**creep** [kri:p] (pt & pp **crept**) vi - **1.** [gen] kriechen; [person] schleichen - **2.** inf [grovel]: **to ~ (to sb)** (vor jm) kriechen <> n inf [loathsome person] widerlicher Typ; [groveller] Schleimer der.

◆ **creeps** npl: **to give sb the ~s** inf jm nicht geheuer sein.

◆ **creep in** vi [mistakes, doubts] sich einschleichen.

◆ **creep up on** vt fus - **1.** [subj: person, animal] sich anschleichen an (+ A) - **2.** [subj: deadline] langsam zukommen auf (+ A).

**creeper** ['kri:pə'] *n* [plant - growing along ground] Kriechpflanze *die;* [ - growing upwards] Kletterpflanze *die.*

**creeping** ['kri:pɪŋ] *adj* [gradual] schleichend.

**creepy** ['kri:pɪ] (*compar* **-ier;** *superl* **-iest**) *adj inf* unheimlich.

**creepy-crawly** [-'krɔ:lɪ] (*pl* **creepy-crawlies**) *n inf* Krabbeltier *das.*

**cremate** [krɪ'meɪt] *vt* einläschern.

**cremation** [krɪ'meɪʃn] *n* Einäscherung *die.*

**crematorium** *Br* [ˌkremə'tɔ:rɪəm] (*pl* **-riums** *OR* **-ria** [-rɪə]), **crematory** *Am* ['kremətrɪ] (*pl* **-ies**) *n* Krematorium *das.*

**creosote** ['krɪəsəʊt] *n* Kreosot *das* ◇ *vt* mit Kreosot streichen.

**crepe** [kreɪp] *n* - **1.** [cloth] Krepp *der* - **2.** [rubber] Kreppgummi *der* - **3.** [thin pancake] Crêpe *die.*

**crepe bandage** *n Br* elastische Binde.

**crepe paper** *n* Krepppapier *das.*

**crepe-soled shoes** *npl Br* Schuhe *pl* mit Kreppsohlen.

**crept** [krept] *pt & pp* ⊳ **creep.**

**Cres.** *abbr of* **crescent.**

**crescendo** [krɪ'ʃendəʊ] (*pl* **-s**) *n MUS* Crescendo *das.*

**crescent** ['kresnt] *adj:* **~ moon** Mondsichel *die* ◇ *n* - **1.** [shape] Halbmond *der* - **2.** [street] *halbkreisförmig verlaufende Straße.*

**cress** [kres] *n* Kresse *die.*

**crest** [krest] *n* - **1.** [of bird] Haube *die;* [of cock, hill, wave] Kamm *der* - **2.** [of school, noble family] Wappen *das.*

**crestfallen** ['krestˌfɔ:ln] *adj* geknickt, niedergeschlagen.

**Crete** [kri:t] *n* Kreta *nt;* **in ~** auf Kreta.

**cretin** ['kretɪn] *n inf pej* [idiot] Idiot *der,* -in *die,* Schwachkopf *der.*

**crevasse** [krɪ'væs] *n* Gletscherspalte *die.*

**crevice** ['krevɪs] *n* Spalte *die.*

**crew** [kru:] *n* - **1.** [of ship, plane] Besatzung *die,* Crew *die* - **2.** CINEMA & TV Crew *die* - **3.** *inf* [gang] Bande *die.*

**crew cut** *n* Bürstenschnitt *der.*

**crewman** ['kru:mæn] (*pl* **-men** [-men]) *n* Mitglied *das* der Besatzung.

**crew-neck** *n* runder Halsausschnitt.

**crib** [krɪb] (*pt & pp* **-bed;** *cont* **-bing**) *n* - **1.** [cradle] Krippe *die* - **2.** *Am* [cot] Kinderbett *das* ◇ *vt inf* [copy]: **to ~ sthg off** *OR* **from sb** etw von jm abschreiben.

**cribbage** ['krɪbɪdʒ] *n Kartenspiel, bei dem der Punktestand dadurch angezeigt wird, dass kleine Holzstücke in die Löcher eines Holzbrettes gelegt werden.*

**crick** [krɪk] *n:* **I've got a ~ in my neck** ich habe einen steifen Hals ◇ *vt:* **to ~ one's neck/back** sich (D) den Hals/Rücken verrenken.

**cricket** ['krɪkɪt] *n* - **1.** [game] Kricket *das* - **2.** [insect] Grille *die* ◇ *comp* Kricket-.

**cricketer** ['krɪkɪtə'] *n* Kricketspieler *der,* -in *die.*

**crikey** ['kraɪkɪ] *excl Br inf dated* verflixt!

**crime** [kraɪm] *n* - **1.** [gen] Verbrechen *das;* **~ is on the decrease** die Zahl der Verbrechen nimmt ab - **2.** *fig* [shameful act] Schande *die,* Sünde *die* ◇ *comp:* **~ prevention** Verbrechensverhütung *die;* **~ novel** Kriminalroman *der,* Krimi *der.*

**Crimea** [kraɪ'mɪə] *n:* **the ~** die Krim; **in the ~** auf der Krim.

**crime wave** *n* Verbrechenswelle *die.*

**criminal** ['krɪmɪnl] *adj* kriminell; [act, offence] strafbar; **~ lawyer** Anwalt *der,* -wältin *die* für Strafsachen; [in court] Strafverteidiger *der* ◇ *n* Kriminelle *der, die.*

**criminalize, -ise** ['krɪmɪnəlaɪz] *vt* kriminalisieren.

**criminal law** *n* Strafrecht *das.*

**criminology** [ˌkrɪmɪ'nɒlədʒɪ] *n* Kriminologie *die.*

**crimson** ['krɪmzn] *adj* - **1.** [in colour] purpurrot - **2.** [with embarrassment] knallrot ◇ *n* Purpur *der.*

**cringe** [krɪndʒ] *vi* - **1.** [out of fear] zurücklweichen - **2.** *inf* [with embarrassment] schaudern; **to ~ at sthg** vor etw (D) zurücklschrecken.

**crinkle** ['krɪŋkl] *n* [wrinkle] Knitterfalte *die;* [in skin] Fältchen *das* ◇ *vt* [paper, clothes] zerknittern ◇ *vi* [clothes] knittern; [face] sich in Fältchen legen.

**cripple** ['krɪpl] *n offensive* Krüppel *der* ◇ *vt* - **1.** MED [disable] zum Krüppel machen - **2.** [ship, plane] aktionsunfähig machen - **3.** *fig* [country, industry] lähmen.

**crippling** ['krɪplɪŋ] *adj* [taxes, prices, debts] erdrückend; **a ~ disease** eine Krankheit, die zu Lähmungen führt.

**crisis** ['kraɪsɪs] (*pl* **crises** ['kraɪsi:z]) *n* Krise *die.*

**crisp** [krɪsp] *adj* - **1.** [pastry, bacon] knusprig; [apple, vegetables] frisch und knackig; [bank note] frisch gedruckt - **2.** [weather] frisch - **3.** [manner, tone] forsch.
  ◆ **crisps** *npl Br* Chips *pl.*

**crispbread** ['krɪspbred] *n* Knäckebrot *das.*

**crispy** ['krɪspɪ] (*compar* **-ier;** *superl* **-iest**) *adj* [pastry, bacon] knusprig; [apple, vegetables] frisch und knackig.

**crisscross** ['krɪskrɒs] *adj* [pattern] gitterartig ◇ *vt* [subj: roads] kreuz und quer führen durch ◇ *vi* [lines] sich kreuzen.

**criterion** [kraɪ'tɪərɪən] (*pl* **-rions** *OR* **-ria** [-rɪə]) *n* Kriterium *das.*

**critic** ['krɪtɪk] n Kritiker der, -in die.

**critical** ['krɪtɪkl] adj kritisch; [illness] schwer; [crucial] entscheidend; **to be ~ of sb/sthg** jn/ etw kritisieren.

**critically** ['krɪtɪklɪ] adv kritisch; [ill] schwer; **to be ~ important** von entscheidender Bedeutung sein.

**criticism** ['krɪtɪsɪzm] n - **1.** [gen] Kritik die - **2.** [unfavourable comment] Kritikpunkt der; **I have a few small ~s** ich habe nur einige kleinere Kritikpunkte.

**criticize, -ise** ['krɪtɪsaɪz] vt & vi kritisieren.

**critique** [krɪ'tiːk] n Kritik die.

**croak** [krəʊk] n [of frog] Quaken das; [of raven, person] Krächzen das <> vi [frog] quaken; [raven, person] krächzen.

**Croat** ['krəʊæt] adj kroatisch <> n - **1.** [person] Kroate der, -tin die - **2.** [language] Kroatisch(e) das.

**Croatia** [krəʊ'eɪʃə] n Kroatien nt.

**Croatian** [krəʊ'eɪʃn] adj & n = **Croat.**

**crochet** ['krəʊʃeɪ] n Häkeln das <> vt häkeln.

**crockery** ['krɒkərɪ] n Geschirr das.

**crocodile** ['krɒkədaɪl] (pl inv OR -s) n Krokodil das.

**crocus** ['krəʊkəs] (pl -cuses) n Krokus der.

**croft** [krɒft] n Br vor allem in Schottland Bezeichnung für einen kleinen Bauernhof.

**croissant** ['kwæsɒn] n Croissant das.

**crony** ['krəʊnɪ] (pl -ies) n inf [friend] Kumpel der.

**crook** [krʊk] n - **1.** [criminal] Gauner der - **2.** [of road, river] Biegung die; [of arm, elbow] Beuge die - **3.** [of shepherd] Hirtenstab der <> vt [finger] krümmen; [arm] beugen.

**crooked** ['krʊkɪd] adj - **1.** [picture, tie, teeth] schief; [path] gewunden - **2.** inf [dishonest - person] unehrlich; [- deal] krumm.

**croon** [kruːn] vt & vi [softly] sanft singen; [sentimentally] schmalzig singen.

**crop** [krɒp] (pt & pp -ped; cont -ping) n - **1.** [kind of plant] Feldfrucht die - **2.** [harvest] Ernte die - **3.** fig [group] Schwung der - **4.** [whip] Reitpeitsche die - **5.** [of bird] Kropf der - **6.** [haircut] Kurzhaarschnitt der <> vt - **1.** [hedge] stutzen; [hair] kurz schneiden - **2.** [subj: cows, sheep] abfressen.

⬥ **crop up** vi [problem] auf tauchen.

**cropper** ['krɒpər] n inf: **to come a ~** [fall] auf die Nase fallen; [fail - person] auf die Nase fallen; [- scheme] ein Reinfall sein.

**crop spraying** n Schädlingsbekämpfung die (durch Besprühen).

**croquet** ['krəʊkeɪ] n Krocket das.

**croquette** [krɒ'ket] n Krokette die.

**cross** [krɒs] adj [angry] böse; **to be ~ with sb** böse auf jn sein <> n - **1.** [gen] Kreuz das - **2.** [hybrid]

Kreuzung die <> vt - **1.** [street, road, river] überqueren; [room, desert] durchqueren; **it ~ed my mind that ...** der Gedanke ging mir durch den Kopf, dass ... - **2.** [place one across the other] (über)kreuzen; [arms] verschränken; [legs] übereinander schlagen - **3.** RELIG: **to ~ o.s.** sich bekreuzigen - **4.** Br [cheque] als Verrechnungsscheck kennzeichnen - **5.** [thwart] verärgern - **6.** [animals, plants] kreuzen <> vi - **1.** [intersect] sich kreuzen - **2.** [cross road] die Straße überqueren; [cross river] den Fluß überqueren; **we ~ed into Hungary** wir überquerten die Grenze nach Ungarn.

⬥ **cross off** vt sep streichen.

⬥ **cross out** vt sep aus streichen.

**crossbar** ['krɒsbɑːr] n - **1.** [of goal] Querlatte die - **2.** [of bicycle] Stange die.

**crossbow** ['krɒsbəʊ] n Armbrust die.

**crossbreed** ['krɒsbriːd] n Kreuzung die.

**cross-Channel ferry** n Fähre die über den Ärmelkanal.

**cross-check** n Gegenprobe die.

**cross-country** adj [run] Querfeldein-, Gelände-; [skiing] Langlauf- <> adv querfeldein; [travel] über Land <> n Querfeldeinlauf der, Geländelauf der.

**cross-cultural** adj interkulturell.

**cross-dressing** n Transvestismus der.

**cross-examination** n lit & fig Kreuzverhör das.

**cross-examine** vt lit & fig ins Kreuzverhör nehmen.

**cross-eyed** [-aɪd] adj schielend; **to be ~** schielen.

**cross-fertilize** vt kreuzbefruchten.

**crossfire** ['krɒs,faɪər] n Kreuzfeuer das.

**crossing** ['krɒsɪŋ] n - **1.** [place] Übergang der - **2.** [sea journey] Überfahrt die.

**cross-legged** [-legd] adv im Schneidersitz.

**crossly** ['krɒslɪ] adv böse.

**cross-purposes** npl: **to talk at ~** aneinander vorbeireden.

**cross-question** vt ins Kreuzverhör nehmen.

**cross-refer** vt verweisen.

**cross-reference** n Querverweis der.

**crossroads** ['krɒsrəʊdz] (pl inv) n Kreuzung die; **to be at a ~** fig am Scheideweg stehen.

**cross-section** n Querschnitt der.

**crosswalk** ['krɒswɔːk] n Am Fußgängerüberweg der.

**crosswind** ['krɒswɪnd] n Seitenwind der.

**crossword (puzzle)** ['krɒswɜːd-] n Kreuzworträtsel das.

**crotch** [krɒtʃ] n - **1.** [of man] Hodengegend die;

[of woman] Schamgegend *die* - **2.** [of clothes] Schritt *der.*

**crotchet** ['krɒtʃɪt] *n* Viertelnote *die.*

**crotchety** ['krɒtʃɪtɪ] *adj Br inf* griesgrämig; [child] quengelig.

**crouch** [krautʃ] *vi* kauern.

**croup** [kru:p] *n* - **1.** (U) [illness] Krupp *der* - **2.** [of horse] Kruppe *die.*

**croupier** ['kru:pɪə] *n* Croupier *der.*

**crouton** ['kru:tɒn] *n* Crouton *der.*

**crow** [krəʊ] *n* Krähe *die;* **10 miles as the ~ flies** 10 Meilen Luftlinie ◇ *vi* - **1.** [cock] krähen - **2.** *inf* [gloat]: **to ~ over sthg** sich mit etw brüsten.

**crowbar** ['krəʊbɑː'] *n* Brecheisen *das.*

**crowd** [kraʊd] *n* - **1.** [mass of people] Menschenmenge *die;* **~s of people** große Menschenmengen - **2.** [social group]: **the usual ~** der übliche Haufen ◇ *vi* sich drängen ◇ *vt* [streets, town] bevölkern; **we were ~ed into a small room** wir wurden in ein kleines Zimmer gedrängt.

**crowded** ['kraʊdɪd] *adj* voll; [train, shop, bar] überfüllt; [timetable, flat] eng; **to be ~ with people** voller Menschen sein.

**crown** [kraʊn] *n* - **1.** [of monarch, tooth] Krone *die* - **2.** [top - of hat] oberes Ende; [ - of head] Scheitel *der;* [ - of hill] Kuppe *die* ◇ *vt* - **1.** [king, queen] krönen - **2.** [tooth] überkronen - **3.** [top] bedecken.

➡ **Crown** *n:* **the Crown** [monarchy] die Krone.

**crown court** *n* Strafgericht *das* (*in England und Wales*).

**crowning** ['kraʊnɪŋ] *adj:* **his ~ achievement** die Krönung seiner Leistung.

**crown jewels** *npl* Kronjuwelen *pl.*

**crown prince** *n* Kronprinz *der.*

**crow's feet** *npl* Krähenfüße *pl.*

**crow's nest** *n* Mastkorb *der.*

**crucial** ['kru:ʃl] *adj* entscheidend.

**crucially** ['kru:ʃlɪ] *adv:* **~ important** von entscheidender Bedeutung.

**crucifix** ['kru:sɪfɪks] *n* Kruzifix *das.*

**Crucifixion** [ˌkru:sɪ'fɪkʃn] *n:* **the ~** die Kreuzigung.

**crucify** ['kru:sɪfaɪ] (*pt & pp* -ied) *vt* - **1.** [kill] kreuzigen - **2.** *fig* [treat cruelly] fertig machen.

**crude** [kru:d] *adj* - **1.** [raw] Roh-, roh - **2.** [vulgar] derb, ordinär - **3.** [drawing] grob; [method, shelter] primitiv ◇ *n* = **crude oil.**

**crudely** ['kru:dlɪ] *adv* - **1.** [vulgarly] ordinär - **2.** [drawn] grob; [built] primitiv.

**crude oil** *n* Rohöl *das.*

**cruel** [kruəl] (*compar* -ler; *superl* -lest) *adj* grausam; **to be ~ to animals** Tiere quälen.

**cruelly** ['kruəlɪ] *adv* grausam.

**cruelty** ['kruəltɪ] *n* Grausamkeit *die;* **~ to children** Kindesmisshandlung *die;* **~ to animals** Tierquälerei *die.*

**cruet** ['kru:ɪt] *n* Menage *die.*

**cruise** [kru:z] *n* Kreuzfahrt *die* ◇ *vi* [ship] kreuzen; [plane] fliegen.

**cruiser** ['kru:zə'] *n* - **1.** [warship] Kreuzer *der* - **2.** [cabin cruiser] Vergnügungsjacht *die.*

**crumb** [krʌm] *n* - **1.** [of food] Krümel *der*, Krume *die* - **2.** [of information] Brocken *der.*

**crumble** ['krʌmbl] *n* mit Streuseln bedeckte überbackene Obstnachspeise ◇ *vt* zerkrümeln; [into larger pieces] zerbröckeln ◇ *vi* - **1.** [plaster] bröckeln; [bread] krümeln; [building, wall] zerbröckeln, verfallen - **2.** *fig* [society, empire] verfallen; [hopes] dahinschwinden.

**crumbly** ['krʌmblɪ] (*compar* -ier; *superl* -iest) *adj* [plaster] bröckelig; [bread, cake] krümelig.

**crummy** ['krʌmɪ] (*compar* -ier; *superl* -iest) *adj inf* mies.

**crumpet** ['krʌmpɪt] *n kleines rundes Brot aus Hefeteig zum Toasten.*

**crumple** ['krʌmpl] *vt* [clothes] zerknittern; [paper] zerknüllen ◇ *vi* - **1.** [clothes] knittern; [face] sich (beim Weinen) verziehen - **2.** [metal object] eingedrückt werden - **3.** [legs, body] nachgeben.

➡ **crumple up** *vt sep* [clothes] zerknittern; [paper] zerknüllen.

**crunch** [krʌntʃ] *n* [sound] Krachen *das;* [of gravel, snow] Knirschen *das;* **if OR when it comes to the ~** *inf* wenn es darauf an|kommt ◇ *vt* [with teeth] (krachend) kauen ◇ *vi* [snow, gravel] knirschen.

**crunchy** ['krʌntʃɪ] (*compar* -ier; *superl* -iest) *adj* - **1.** [apple, vegetables] frisch und knackig; [chocolate bar] knusprig - **2.** [snow, gravel] verharscht.

**crusade** [kru:'seɪd] *n lit & fig* Kreuzzug *der* ◇ *vi:* **to ~ for/against sthg** für/gegen etw zu Felde ziehen.

**crusader** [kru:'seɪdə'] *n* - **1.** HIST Kreuzritter *der* - **2.** *fig* [campaigner] Verfechter *der*, -in *die.*

**crush** [krʌʃ] *n* - **1.** [crowd] Gedränge *das* - **2.** *inf* [infatuation] Schwärmerei *die;* **to have a ~ on sb** für jn schwärmen - **3.** *Br* [drink]: **lemon ~** Zitronensaftgetränk *das* ◇ *vt* - **1.** [squeeze - limb] quetschen; [ - clothes, garlic] zerdrücken - **2.** [ice, tablet] zerstoßen - **3.** [destroy] zerquetschen; **to be ~ed to death** zu Tode gequetscht werden - **4.** *fig* [army, hopes] vernichten; [opposition] niederschlagen.

**crush barrier** *n Br* Absperrung *die.*

**crushing** ['krʌʃɪŋ] *adj* [defeat, remark] vernichtend.

**crust** [krʌst] *n* Kruste *die.*

**crustacean** [krʌ'steɪʃn] n Schalentier das.

**crusty** ['krʌstɪ] (compar -ier; superl -iest) adj - **1.** [bread] knusprig - **2.** [person] barsch.

**crutch** [krʌtʃ] n - **1.** [stick] Krücke die; **she uses him as an emotional ~ fig** sie klammert sich an ihn - **2.** [crotch - of man] Hodengegend die; [ - of woman] Schamgegend die.

**crux** [krʌks] n Kern der; **the ~ of the matter** der springende Punkt.

**cry** [kraɪ] (pl **cries**; pt & pp **cried**) n - **1.** [weep]: **to have a ~** weinen - **2.** [shout] Ruf der; [louder] Schrei der; **a ~ of pain** ein Schmerzensschrei; **a ~ for help** ein Hilferuf; **to be a far ~ from** ... vollkommen anders sein als ... - **3.** [of bird] Schrei der ⬦ vt & vi - **1.** [weep] weinen - **2.** [shout] rufen; [louder] schreien.

⬦ **cry off** vi einen Rückzieher machen.

⬦ **cry out** vt sep & vi schreien.

⬦ **cry out for** vt fus [demand] dringend brauchen.

**crybaby** ['kraɪ‚beɪbɪ] (pl **-ies**) n inf pej Heulsuse die.

**crying** ['kraɪɪŋ] adj inf: **it's a ~ shame** es ist jammerschade; **there is a ~ need for sthg** etw ist dringend notwendig ⬦ n Weinen das.

**crypt** [krɪpt] n Krypta die.

**cryptic** ['krɪptɪk] adj rätselhaft.

**crypto-** [krɪptəʊ] prefix: **~-communist** verkappter Kommunist, verkappte Kommunistin.

**crystal** ['krɪstl] n Kristall der ⬦ comp [glass] Kristall-.

**crystal ball** n Glaskugel die (einer Hellseherin).

**crystal clear** adj glasklar.

**crystallize, -ise** ['krɪstəlaɪz] vi - **1.** [form crystals] kristallisieren - **2.** [ideas, plans] Form anl nehmen ⬦ vt [fruit] kandieren.

**CSE** (abbr of **Certificate of Secondary Education**) n ≃ Hauptschulabschluss der, früherer britischer Schulabschluss.

**CS gas** n CS-Gas das.

**CST** (abbr of **Central Standard Time**) n Standardzeit in der zentralen Zeitzone der USA.

**ct** abbr of **carat**.

**CT** abk für Connecticut, in Postanschrift verwendet.

**cu.** abbr of **cubic**.

**cub** [kʌb] n - **1.** [young animal] Junge das - **2.** [boy scout] Wölfling der.

**Cuba** ['kju:bə] n Kuba nt; **in ~** auf Kuba.

**Cuban** ['kju:bən] adj kubanisch ⬦ n Kubaner der, -in die.

**cubbyhole** ['kʌbɪhəʊl] n [room] Kabäuschen das; [compartment] Fach das.

**cube** [kju:b] n - **1.** [object, shape] Würfel der

- **2.** MATH dritte Potenz ⬦ vt MATH in die dritte Potenz erheben; **3 ~d** 3 hoch 3.

**cube root** n Kubikwurzel die.

**cubic** ['kju:bɪk] adj Kubik-.

**cubicle** ['kju:bɪkl] n Kabine die.

**cubism** ['kju:bɪzm] n Kubismus der.

**cub reporter** n junger Reporter, junge Reporterin.

**Cub Scout** n Wölfling der.

**cuckoo** ['kʊku:] n Kuckuck der.

**cuckoo clock** n Kuckucksuhr die.

**cucumber** ['kju:kʌmbə'] n Gurke die.

**cud** [kʌd] n: **to chew the ~** [cow] wiederlkäuen; inf [person] vor sich hin grübeln.

**cuddle** ['kʌdl] n: **to give sb a ~** jn in den Arm nehmen; **I need a ~** ich brauche jemand zum Schmusen ⬦ vt an sich (A) drücken, in den Arm nehmen; [doll, dog] knuddeln ⬦ vi schmusen.

⬦ **cuddle up** vi sich zusammenlkuscheln; **to ~ up to sb** sich an jn kuscheln.

**cuddly** ['kʌdlɪ] (compar -ier; superl -iest) adj knuddelig.

**cuddly toy** n Knuddeltier das.

**cudgel** ['kʌdʒəl] (Br pt & pp -led; cont -ling, Am pt & pp -ed; cont -ing) n Knüppel der; **to take up the ~s for sb/sthg** für jn/etw auf die Barrikaden gehen ⬦ vt prügeln.

**cue** [kju:] n - **1.** RADIO, THEATRE & TV Stichwort das; **on ~** wie gerufen; **to take one's ~ from sb** sich nach jm richten - **2.** fig [signal] Signal das - **3.** [in snooker, pool] Queue das.

**cuff** [kʌf] n - **1.** [of sleeve] Manschette die - **2.** Am [of trouser] Aufschlag der ⬦ vt: **to ~ sb round the ear** jm eine aufs Ohr geben.

**cuff link** n Manschettenknopf der.

**cu. in.** (abbr of cubic inch) = 16,3871 cm³.

**cuisine** [kwɪ'zi:n] n Küche die.

**cul-de-sac** ['kʌldəsæk] n Sackgasse die.

**culinary** ['kʌlɪnərɪ] adj kulinarisch; [art, expertise, skills] Koch-.

**cull** [kʌl] n Kontrolle der Größe eines Viehbestands durch das Töten der schwächsten Tiere ⬦ vt - **1.** [kill]: **to ~ seals** Robbenschlag betreiben - **2.** fml [gather] sammeln.

**culminate** ['kʌlmɪneɪt] vi: **to ~ in sthg** in etw (D) gipfeln.

**culmination** [‚kʌlmɪ'neɪʃn] n Höhepunkt der.

**culottes** [kju:'lɒts] npl Hosenrock der.

**culpable** ['kʌlpəbl] adj fml strafbar; [person] schuldig; **~ homicide** fahrlässige Tötung.

**culprit** ['kʌlprɪt] n Schuldige der, die; [guilty of a crime] Täter der, -in die.

**cult** [kʌlt] n - **1.** RELIG Kult der - **2.** [book, film] Kultsymbol das ⬦ comp [book, film] Kult-.

**cultivate** ['kʌltɪveɪt] vt - **1.** [farm - land] bebauen; [ - crops] anlbauen, kultivieren - **2.** [develop - interest, taste] entwickeln; [ - friendship] pflegen; [ - trust] stärken; [ - image] kultivieren.

**cultivated** ['kʌltɪveɪtɪd] adj kultiviert.

**cultivation** [ˌkʌltɪ'veɪʃn] n [farming] Kultivieren das.

**cultural** ['kʌltʃərəl] adj kulturell.

**culture** ['kʌltʃə'] n Kultur die.

**cultured** ['kʌltʃəd] adj kultiviert.

**cultured pearl** n Zuchtperle die.

**culture shock** n Kulturschock der.

**culture vulture** n inf Kulturfanatiker der, -in die.

**cumbersome** ['kʌmbəsəm] adj - **1.** [object] unhandlich; [parcel] sperrig - **2.** [system] mühselig, beschwerlich.

**cumin** ['kjuːmɪn] n Kümmel der.

**cumulative** ['kjuːmjʊlətɪv] adj kumulativ; ~ interest Zins und Zinseszins.

**cunning** ['kʌnɪŋ] adj [plan] schlau; [person] gerissen; [device] schlau ausgedacht <> n [of plan] Schlauheit die; [of person] Gerissenheit die.

**cup** [kʌp] (pt & pp -ped; cont -ping) n - **1.** [gen] Tasse die; a ~ of tea eine Tasse Tee; it's not my ~ of tea fig das ist nicht mein Fall - **2.** [trophy, competition] Pokal der - **3.** [of bra] Körbchen das <> vt: to ~ one's hands die Hände hohl machen.

**cupboard** ['kʌbəd] n Schrank der.

**cupcake** ['kʌpkeɪk] n in Papier oder Folie gewickelter kleiner runder Kuchen mit Zuckerguss.

**Cup Final** n: the ~ das Pokalendspiel.

**cupid** ['kjuːpɪd] n MYTH Amor der.

**cupola** ['kjuːpələ] (pl -s) n ARCHIT Kuppel die.

**curable** ['kjʊərəbl] adj heilbar.

**curate** ['kjʊərət] n Vikar der.

**curator** [ˌkjʊə'reɪtə'] n [of museum] Kustos der.

**curb** [kɜːb] n - **1.** [control]: to put a ~ on sthg etw im Zaum halten - **2.** Am [of road] Bordstein der <> vt zügeln.

**curd cheese** n Br Quark der.

**curdle** ['kɜːdl] vi gerinnen.

**cure** [kjʊə'] n - **1.** MED: ~ (for) Heilmittel das (für) - **2.** [solution]: ~ (for sthg) Mittel das (gegen etw), Lösung die (für etw) <> vt - **1.** MED [illness, person] heilen, kurieren - **2.** [solve] beheben - **3.** [rid]: to ~ sb of sthg fig jn von etw heilen OR befreien; [preserve - smoke] räuchern; [ - salt] pökeln; [ - dry] trocknen.

**cure-all** n Allheilmittel das.

**curfew** ['kɜːfjuː] n Ausgangssperre die.

**curio** ['kjʊərɪəʊ] (pl -s) n Kuriosität die.

**curiosity** [ˌkjʊərɪ'ɒsətɪ] n - **1.** [inquisitiveness] Neugier die - **2.** [rarity] Kuriosität die.

**curious** ['kjʊərɪəs] adj - **1.** [inquisitive]: ~ (about) neugierig (auf (+ A)); I'm ~ to see what happens next ich bin gespannt, was als Nächstes passiert - **2.** [strange] merkwürdig, seltsam.

**curiously** ['kjʊərɪəslɪ] adv - **1.** [inquisitively] neugierig - **2.** [strangely] merkwürdig, seltsam.

**curl** [kɜːl] n - **1.** [of hair] Locke die - **2.** [of smoke] Kringel der <> vt - **1.** [hair] in Locken legen - **2.** [tail, ribbon] (ein)rollen <> vi - **1.** [hair] sich locken - **2.** [paper, leaf] sich zusammenlrollen; to ~ into a ball sich einlrollen OR zusammenlrollen - **3.** [road, smoke, snake] sich schlängeln.

➤ **curl up** vi [person, animal] sich zusammenlrollen; to ~ up in bed sich ins Bett kuscheln.

**curler** ['kɜːlə'] n Lockenwickler der.

**curling** ['kɜːlɪŋ] n SPORT Curling das.

**curling tongs** npl Lockenstab der.

**curly** ['kɜːlɪ] (compar -ier; superl -iest) adj [hair] lockig.

**currant** ['kʌrənt] n Korinthe die.

**currency** ['kʌrənsɪ] (pl -ies) n - **1.** [money] Währung die - **2.** fml [acceptability]: to gain ~ sich verbreiten, Verbreitung finden.

**current** ['kʌrənt] adj gegenwärtig, aktuell <> n - **1.** [flow - of water] Strömung die; [ - of air] Luftströmung die; [ - of electricity] Strom der - **2.** fig [of opinion] Tendenz die.

**current account** n Br Girokonto das.

**current affairs** npl aktuelle Fragen pl.

**current assets** npl Umlaufvermögen das.

**current liabilities** npl kurzfristige Verbindlichkeiten pl.

**currently** ['kʌrəntlɪ] adv gegenwärtig, momentan.

**curricular** [kə'rɪkjələ'] adj lehrplanmäßig.

**curriculum** [kə'rɪkjələm] (pl -lums OR -la [-lə]) n Lehrplan der.

**curriculum vitae** [-'viːtaɪ] (pl curricula vitae) n Lebenslauf der.

**curried** ['kʌrɪd] adj mit Curry(sauce).

**curry** ['kʌrɪ] (pl -ies) n Currygericht das; chicken ~ Huhn mit Curry(sauce).

**curry powder** n (U) Curry das OR der.

**curse** [kɜːs] n - **1.** [evil spell, swearword] Fluch der - **2.** [source of problems] Plage die <> vt verfluchen <> vi [swear] fluchen.

**cursor** ['kɜːsə'] n COMPUT Cursor der.

**cursory** ['kɜːsərɪ] adj flüchtig.

**curt** [kɜːt] adj barsch.

**curtail** [kɜː'teɪl] vt - **1.** [visit] ablkürzen

**- 2.** [rights, expenditure] einlschränken, beschneiden.

**curtailment** [kɜː'teɪlmənt] n [of rights, expenditure] Einschränkung die, Beschneidung die.

**curtain** ['kɜːtn] n **- 1.** [gen] Vorhang der **- 2.** fig [of smoke] Wand die.

◆ **curtain off** vt sep durch einen Vorhang abltrennen.

**curtain call** n [encore] Vorhang der.

**curtain raiser** n fig kurzes Vorspiel.

**curts(e)y** ['kɜːtsɪ] (pt & pp curtsied) n Knicks der ◇ vi knicksen.

**curvaceous** [kɜː'veɪʃəs] adj kurvenreich.

**curvature** ['kɜːvətʃə‘] n (U) **- 1.** [of Earth] Krümmung die **- 2.** MED [of spine] Verkrümmung die.

**curve** [kɜːv] n Kurve die ◇ vi [road, river] einen Bogen machen; [surface] sich wölben.

**curved** [kɜːvd] adj [surface] gewölbt; [shape] gebogen, gekrümmt

**curvy** ['kɜːvɪ] (compar -ier; superl -iest) adj kurvenreich.

**cushion** ['kʊʃn] n **- 1.** [for sitting on] Kissen das **- 2.** [protective layer] Polster das ◇ vt dämpfen, ablfangen; **to be ~ed against sthg** gegen etw geschützt sein.

**cushy** ['kʊʃɪ] (compar -ier; superl -iest) adj inf bequem, lässig.

**custard** ['kʌstəd] n ≃ Vanillesoße die.

**custard powder** n ≃ Vanillesoßenpulver das.

**custodian** [kʌ'stəʊdjən] n Wächter der, -in die.

**custody** ['kʌstədɪ] n **- 1.** [of child] Sorgerecht das **- 2.** [of suspect]: **in ~ in** Untersuchungshaft.

**custom** ['kʌstəm] n **- 1.** [tradition] Brauch der; [habit] Gepflogenheit die **- 2.** COMM [trade] Einkauf der.

◆ **customs** n (U) [place] Zoll der.

**customary** ['kʌstəmrɪ] adj üblich, gewöhnlich.

**custom-built** adj in Sonderausführung.

**customer** ['kʌstəmə‘] n Kunde der, -din die.

**customer services** npl Kundendienst der.

**customize, -ise** ['kʌstəmaɪz] vt **- 1.** [make] individuell herlrichten **- 2.** [modify] anlpassen, modifizieren.

**custom-made** adj [clothes] maßgeschneidert; [furniture] einzeln angefertigt.

**Customs and Excise** n (U) Br britische Finanzbehörde, die indirekte Steuern (Ex- und Importsteuer, Mehrwertsteuer und Verbrauchssteuer) einzieht und verwaltet.

**customs duty** n (U) Zoll der.

**customs officer** n Zollbeamte der, -tin die.

**cut** [kʌt] (pt & pp cut; cont -ting) n **- 1.** [slit]

Schnitt der **- 2.** [wound] Schnittwunde die **- 3.** [of meat] Fleischstück das **- 4.** [in salary, film, article] Kürzung die **- 5.** inf [share] Anteil der **- 6.** [style - of clothes, hair] Schnitt der **- 7.** phr: **to be a ~ above the rest** dem Rest überlegen sein ◇ vt **- 1.** [gen] schneiden; **to ~ one's finger** sich (D) in den Finger schneiden **- 2.** [salary, costs, expenditure] reduzieren, senken **- 3.** [grass] mähen **- 4.** [tooth]: **to ~ a tooth** einen Zahn bekommen **- 5.** [cards] ablheben **- 6.** inf [lecture, class] schwänzen ◇ vi **- 1.** [gen] schneiden **- 2.** [intersect] sich kreuzen.

◆ **cut across** vt fus [as short cut]: **to ~ across a field** querfeldein gehen.

◆ **cut back** vt sep **- 1.** [prune] zurücklschneiden **- 2.** [reduce] reduzieren, senken ◇ vi: **to ~ back on sthg** etw einlschränken.

◆ **cut down** vt sep **- 1.** [chop down] fällen **- 2.** [reduce] reduzieren, einlschränken ◇ vi: **to ~ down on sthg** etw einlschränken.

◆ **cut in** vi **- 1.** [interrupt]: **to ~ in (on sb)** (jn) unterbrechen **- 2.** [in car]: **to ~ in on** OR **in front of sb** jn schneiden.

◆ **cut off** vt sep **- 1.** [sever] ablschneiden **- 2.** [disconnect - electricity, gas, telephone] ablstellen; **I got ~ off** [on telephone] das Gespräch wurde unterbrochen **- 3.** [isolate]: **to be ~ off (from sb/sthg)** (von jm/etw) abgeschnitten sein **- 4.** [discontinue] stoppen, unterbrechen.

◆ **cut out** vt sep **- 1.** [article, photo] auslschneiden; [tumour] herauslschneiden **- 2.** [sewing] zulschneiden; **to be ~ out for sthg** fig zu etw (D) geeignet sein **- 3.** [stop] auflhören mit; **~ it out!** lass das sein! **- 4.** [exclude] auslschließen ◇ vi [engine] auslsetzen.

◆ **cut up** vt sep [vegetables] schneiden; [wood] hacken; [meat] auf lschneiden.

**cut-and-dried** adj abgesprochen.

**cut and paste** COMPUT vt & vi ausschneiden und einlfügen.

**cutback** ['kʌtbæk] n: **~ (in)** Kürzung die (von).

**cute** [kjuːt] adj süß.

**cut glass** n geschliffenes Glas ◇ comp: **a ~ bowl** eine geschliffene Glasschale.

**cuticle** ['kjuːtɪkl] n Nagelhaut die.

**cutlery** ['kʌtlərɪ] n (U) Besteck das.

**cutlet** ['kʌtlɪt] n Kotelett das.

**cutoff (point)** ['kʌtɒf-] n Grenzlinie die.

**cutout** ['kʌtaʊt] n **- 1.** [on machine] Stopschalter der **- 2.** [shape] Ausschneidemodell das.

**cut-price, cut-rate** Am adj Billig-.

**cutter** ['kʌtə‘] n [tool] Schneidwerkzeug das.

**cut-throat** adj [ruthless] gnadenlos, unbarmherzig.

**cutting** ['kʌtɪŋ] adj [wit] scharf; [remark] spitz, verletzend; [person] sarkastisch ◇ n **- 1.** [of plant] Ableger *der* - **2.** [from newspaper] Ausschnitt *der* - **3.** *Br* [for road, railway] Durchstich *der*.

**cuttlefish** ['kʌtlfɪʃ] (*pl inv*) *n* Tintenfisch *der*.

**cut up** *adj Br inf* [upset] aufgewühlt; **he was very ~ about the divorce** die Scheidung hat ihn schwer mitgenommen.

**CV** *n abbr of* **curriculum vitae.**

**C & W** (*abbr of* **country and western (music)**) *n* Country- und Westernmusik *die*.

**cwo** (*abbr of* **cash with order**) zahlbar bei Bestellung.

**cwt.** *abbr of* **hundredweight.**

**cyanide** ['saɪənaɪd] *n* Cyanid *das*.

**cybernetics** [saɪbə'netɪks] *n* Kybernetik *die*.

**cyclamen** ['sɪkləmən] (*pl inv*) *n* Alpenveilchen *das*.

**cycle** ['saɪkl] *n* - **1.** [series of events] Kreislauf *der*, Zyklus *der* - **2.** [of machine] Durchlauf *der*, Durchgang *der* - **3.** [bicycle] Fahrrad *das* - **4.** [of poems, songs] Zyklus *der* ◇ *comp* Fahrrad- ◇ *vi* Fahrrad fahren.

**cyclic(al)** ['saɪklɪk(l)] *adj* zyklisch.

**cycling** ['saɪklɪŋ] *n* Fahrradfahren *das*.

**cycling helmet** *n* Fahrradhelm *der*.

**cyclist** ['saɪklɪst] *n* Fahrradfahrer *der*, -in *die*.

**cyclone** ['saɪkləʊn] *n* Zyklone *die*, Tiefdruckgebiet *das*.

**cygnet** ['sɪgnɪt] *n* junger Schwan.

**cylinder** ['sɪlɪndə'] *n* - **1.** [gen] Zylinder *der* - **2.** [for gas, oxygen] Flasche *die*.

**cylinder block** *n* Zylinderblock *der*.

**cylinder head** *n* Zylinderkopf *der*.

**cylinder-head gasket** *n* Zylinderkopfdichtung *die*.

**cylindrical** [sɪ'lɪndrɪkl] *adj* zylindrisch.

**cymbals** ['sɪmblz] *npl* Becken *das*.

**cynic** ['sɪnɪk] *n* Zyniker *der*, -in *die*.

**cynical** ['sɪnɪkl] *adj* zynisch.

**cynically** ['sɪnɪklɪ] *adv* zynisch.

**cynicism** ['sɪnɪsɪzml] *n* Zynismus *der*.

**cypher** ['saɪfə'] *n* = **cipher.**

**cypress** ['saɪprəs] *n* Zypresse *die*.

**Cypriot** ['sɪprɪət] *n* Zypriot *der*, -in *die*.

**Cyprus** ['saɪprəs] *n* Zypern *nt;* **in ~** auf Zypern.

**cyst** [sɪst] *n* Zyste *die*.

**cystic fibrosis** [sɪstɪkfaɪ'brəʊsɪs] *n (U)* Mukoviszidose *die*.

**cystitis** [sɪs'taɪtɪs] *n (U)* Blasenentzündung *die*.

**cytology** [saɪ'tɒlədʒɪ] *n* Zytologie *die*.

**CZ** (*abbr of* **canal zone**) *den Panamalkanal umgebende Zone*.

**czar** [zɑ:'] *n* Zar *der*.

**Czech** [tʃek] *adj* tschechisch ◇ *n* - **1.** [person] Tscheche *der*, -hin *die* - **2.** [language] Tschechisch(e) *das*.

**Czechoslovak** [tʃekə'sləʊvæk] *adj* & *n* = **Czechoslovakian.**

**Czechoslovakia** [tʃekəslə'vækɪə] *n* Tschechoslowakei *die*.

**Czechoslovakian** [tʃekəslə'vækɪən] *adj* tschechoslowakisch ◇ *n* Tschechoslowake *der*, -kin *die*.

**Czech Republic** *n:* **the ~** die Tschechische Republik.

**D**

**d¹** (*pl* **d's** *or* **ds**), **D** (*pl* **D's** *or* **Ds**) [di:] *n* [letter] d *das*, D *das*.

➡ **D** *n* - **1.** mus D *das;* [D flat] Des *das* - **2.** sch [mark] ≈ vier ◇ *abbr of* **Democratic.**

**d²** (*pl* **d's** *or* **ds**), **D** (*pl* **D's** *or* **Ds**) [di:] *Symbol für den alten britischen Penny*.

**d.** (*abbr of* **died**) *abbr of* **died.**

**DA** *n abbr of* **district attorney.**

**dab** [dæb] (*pt* & *pp* **-bed;** *cont* **-bing**) *n* [small amount] Klecks *der* ◇ *vt* - **1.** [skin, wound] abtupfen - **2.** [cream, ointment]: **to ~ sthg on(to) sthg** etw auf etw (A) tupfen ◇ *vi:* **to ~ at sthg** etw betupfen.

**dabble** ['dæbl] *vt* planschen, plantschen ◇ *vi:* **to ~ (in sthg)** (in etw (D)) planschen *or* plantschen.

**dab hand** *n Br inf:* **to be a ~ (at sthg)** (in etw (D)) sehr geschickt sein.

**dachshund** ['dækshʊnd] *n* Dackel *der*.

**dad** [dæd], **daddy** ['dædɪ] (*pl* **-ies**) *n inf* Vati *der*.

**daddy longlegs** [-'lɒŋlegz] (*pl inv*) *n* Schnake *die*.

**daffodil** ['dæfədɪl] *n* Osterglocke *die*, Narzisse *die*.

**daft** [dɑ:ft] *adj Br inf* doof, blöd.

**dagger** ['dægə'] *n* Dolch *der*.

**dahlia** ['deɪljə] *n* Dahlie *die*.

**Dáil (Eireann)** [dɔːl'eərən] *n:* the ~ *Unterhaus der Republik Irland.*

**daily** ['deɪlɪ] (*pl* **-ies**) *adj* täglich ◇ *adv* täglich ◇ *n* **- 1.** [newspaper] Tageszeitung *die* **- 2.** *esp Br* [cleaning woman] Putzfrau *die.*

**daintily** ['deɪntɪlɪ] *adv* [walk, move] anmutig; [made, dressed] fein, zierlich.

**dainty** ['deɪntɪ] (*compar* **-ier;** *superl* **-iest**) *adj* zierlich.

**dairy** ['deərɪ] (*pl* **-ies**) *n* **- 1.** [on farm] Molkerei *die* **- 2.** [shop] Milchgeschäft *das.*

**dairy cattle** *npl* Milchvieh *das.*

**dairy farm** *n* *auf Milchwirtschaft spezialisierter Bauernhof.*

**dairy products** *npl* Molkereiprodukte *pl,* Milchprodukte *pl.*

**dais** ['deɪɪs] *n* Podium *das.*

**daisy** ['deɪzɪ] (*pl* **-ies**) *n* Gänseblümchen *das.*

**daisy wheel** *n* Typenrad *das.*

**daisy-wheel printer** *n* Typenraddrucker *der.*

**dale** [deɪl] *n literary* Tal *das.*

**dalmatian** [dæl'meɪʃn] *n* [dog] Dalmatiner *der.*

**dam** [dæm] (*pt & pp* **-med;** *cont* **-ming**) *n* (Stau)damm *der* ◇ *vt* (auf)stauen.
◆ **dam up** *vt sep* auf|stauen.

**damage** ['dæmɪdʒ] *n:* ~ (to sthg) Schaden *der* (an etw *(D)*) ◇ *vt* **- 1.** [physically] beschädigen **- 2.** *fig* [chances, reputation] schaden *(+ D).*
◆ **damages** *npl* ʟᴀᴡ Schaden(s)ersatz *der.*

**damaging** ['dæmɪdʒɪŋ] *adj:* ~ (to) schädlich (für).

**Damascus** [də'mæskəs] *n* Damaskus *nt.*

**Dame** [deɪm] *n Br* Dame *die.*

**damn** [dæm] *adj & adv inf* verdammt ◇ *n inf:* not to give *OR* care a ~ (about sthg) sich einen Dreck scheren (um etw) ◇ *vt* **- 1.** ʀᴇʟɪɢ [condemn] verdammen **- 2.** [curse] verfluchen; ~ it! *inf* verdammt! ◇ *excl inf* verdammt!, Mist!

**damnable** ['dæmnəbl] *adj dated* [appalling] abscheulich.

**damnation** [dæm'neɪʃn] *n* ʀᴇʟɪɢ Verdammung *die.*

**damned** [dæmd] *inf adj* verdammt; I'm ~ if ... mich soll der Teufel holen, wenn ...; well I'll be *OR* I'm ~! Donnerwetter! ◇ *adv* verdammt.

**damning** ['dæmɪŋ] *adj* vernichtend.

**damp** [dæmp] *adj* feucht ◇ *n* Feuchtigkeit *die* ◇ *vt* an|feuchten, befeuchten.
◆ **damp down** *vt sep* [unrest, violence] ein|dämmen.

**damp course** *n Br* Feuchtigkeitsisolierung *die.*

**dampen** ['dæmpən] *vt* **- 1.** [make wet] an|feuchten, befeuchten **- 2.** *fig* [emotion] dämpfen.

**damper** ['dæmpə*ʳ*] *n* [for fire] Luftklappe *die;* to put a ~ on sthg etw *(D)* einen Dämpfer verpassen.

**dampness** ['dæmpnɪs] *n* Feuchtigkeit *die.*

**damp-proof course** *n* = damp course.

**damson** ['dæmzn] *n* Damaszenerpflaume *die.*

**dance** [dɑːns] *n* **- 1.** [gen] Tanz *der* **- 2.** [social event] Tanzabend *der* **- 3.** [art form] Tanzen *das* ◇ *vi* tanzen.

**dance floor** *n* Tanzfläche *die.*

**dance hall** *n* Tanzlokal *das.*

**dancer** ['dɑːnsə*ʳ*] *n* Tänzer *der,* -in *die.*

**dancing** ['dɑːnsɪŋ] *n* Tanzen *das.*

**D and C** (*abbr of* dilation and curettage) *n* ᴍᴇᴅ Dilatation und Kürettage.

**dandelion** ['dændɪlaɪən] *n* Löwenzahn *der.*

**dandruff** ['dændrʌf] *n* Schuppen *pl.*

**dandy** ['dændɪ] (*pl* **-ies**) *n* Dandy *der.*

**Dane** [deɪn] *n* Däne *der,* -nin *die.*

**danger** ['deɪndʒə*ʳ*] *n* Gefahr *die;* in ~ in Gefahr; out of ~ außer Gefahr; ~ to sb/sthg Gefahr für jn/etw; to be in ~ of doing sthg Gefahr laufen, etw zu tun.

**danger list** *n Br:* to be on/off the ~ in/außer Lebensgefahr sein.

**danger money** *n (U) Br* Gefahrenzulage *die.*

**dangerous** ['deɪndʒərəs] *adj* gefährlich.

**dangerous driving** *n (U)* ʟᴀᴡ Verkehrsgefährdung *die.*

**dangerously** ['deɪndʒərəslɪ] *adv* [riskily] gefährlich, riskant; ~ ill lebensbedrohlich erkrankt.

**danger zone** *n* Gefahrenzone *die.*

**dangle** ['dæŋgl] *vt* baumeln lassen; to ~ sthg in front of sb *fig* jn mit etw locken ◇ *vi* baumeln.

**Danish** ['deɪnɪʃ] *adj* dänisch ◇ *n* **- 1.** [language] Dänisch(e) *das* **- 2.** = Danish pastry ◇ *npl:* the ~ die Dänen *pl.*

**Danish blue** *n (U)* Blauschimmelkäse *der.*

**Danish (pastry)** *n* Hefeteilchen *das.*

**dank** [dæŋk] *adj* naßkalt.

**Danube** ['dænjuːb] *n:* the ~ die Donau.

**dapper** ['dæpə*ʳ*] *adj* adrett.

**dappled** ['dæpld] *adj* scheckig.

**Dardanelles** [ˌdɑːdə'nelz] *npl:* the ~ die Dardanelle *pl.*

**D**

**dare** [deəʳ] *vt* - **1.** [be brave enough]: **to ~ to do sthg** sich trauen, etw zu tun - **2.** [challenge]: **to ~ sb to do sthg** jn herauslfordern, etw zu tun - **3.** *phr*: **I ~ say** ich glaube schon ⬦ *vi* es wagen, sich trauen; **how ~ you!** was fällt dir ein! ⬦ *n* Mutprobe *die*.

**daredevil** ['deə‚devl] *n* Draufgänger *der*, -in *die*.

**daren't** [deənt] = **dare not.**

**daring** ['deərɪŋ] *adj* [person, action] kühn, verwegen; [comment, clothes] gewagt ⬦ *n* Wagemut *der*, Kühnheit *die*.

**dark** [dɑːk] *adj* - **1.** [gen] dunkel - **2.** [gloomy] düster - **3.** [sinister] finster ⬦ *n* - **1.** [darkness]: **the ~** die Dunkelheit; **to be in the ~ about sthg** *fig* keine Ahnung von etw haben - **2.** [night]: **before/after ~** vor/nach Einbruch der Dunkelheit.

**Dark Ages** *npl*: **the ~** das frühe Mittelalter.

**darken** ['dɑːkn] *vt* verdunkeln ⬦ *vi* - **1.** [gen] sich verdunkeln - **2.** *fig* [face] sich verfinstern.

**dark glasses** *npl* Sonnenbrille *die*.

**dark horse** *n fig* [person] stilles Wasser.

**darkness** ['dɑːknɪs] *n* Dunkelheit *die*.

**darkroom** ['dɑːkrʊm] *n* Dunkelkammer *die*.

**darling** ['dɑːlɪŋ] *adj* - **1.** [dear] lieb - **2.** *inf* [cute] süß, goldig ⬦ *n* - **1.** [loved person, term of address] Schatz *der* - **2.** [favourite] Liebling *der*.

**darn** [dɑːn] *adj* & *adv inf* verdammt, verflixt ⬦ *n* gestopfte Loch ⬦ *vt* [repair] stopfen ⬦ *excl inf* [damn] verdammt!, verflixt!

**darning** ['dɑːnɪŋ] *n* Stopfen *das*.

**darning needle** *n* Stopfnadel *die*.

**dart** [dɑːt] *n* - **1.** [arrow] (Wurflpfeil *der* - **2.** [in sewing] Abnäher *der* ⬦ *vt*: **to ~ a look/glance at sb** jm einen Blick zulwerfen ⬦ *vi* [move quickly] flitzen; **to ~ at sb/sthg** sich auf jn/etw stürzen.

➠ **darts** *n* (U) [game] Darts *pl*.

**dartboard** ['dɑːtbɔːd] *n* Dartscheibe *die*.

**dash** [dæʃ] *n* - **1.** [of liquid] Schuß *der* - **2.** [in punctuation] Gedankenstrich *der* - **3.** AUT Armaturenbrett *das* - **4.** [rush]: **to make a ~ for sthg** sich auf etw (A) stürzen ⬦ *vt* - **1.** *literary* [throw] schleudern - **2.** [hopes] zerstören ⬦ *vi* stürzen, sausen; **I must ~!** ich muß los!

➠ **dash off** *vt sep* [write quickly] hinlhauen.

**dashboard** ['dæʃbɔːd] *n* Armaturenbrett *das*.

**dashing** ['dæʃɪŋ] *adj* [man] schneidig, flott.

**dastardly** ['dæstədlɪ] *adj dated* niederträchtig, gemein.

**DAT** [dæt] (*abbr of* **digital audio tape**) *n* DAT.

**data** ['deɪtə] *n* Daten *pl*.

**databank** ['deɪtəbæŋk] *n* Datenbank *die*.

**database** ['deɪtəbeɪs] *n* Datenbank *die*.

**data capture** *n* Datenerfassung *die*.

**data processing** *n* Datenverarbeitung *die*.

**data transmission** *n* (U) Datenübertragung *die*.

**date** [deɪt] *n* - **1.** [in time] Datum *das*; **to bring sb up to ~** jn über den Stand der Dinge informieren; **to bring sthg up to ~** etw auf den neuesten Stand bringen; **out of ~** [fashion, dictionary] veraltet; [passport] abgelaufen; **to keep sb/sthg up to ~** jn/etw auf dem Laufenden halten; **to ~** bis heute - **2.** [appointment, person] Verabredung *die* - **3.** [fruit] Dattel *die* ⬦ *vt* - **1.** [gen] datieren - **2.** [go out with] auslgehen mit ⬦ *vi* [go out of fashion] altmodisch werden.

➠ **date back to, date from** *vt fus* stammen aus.

**dated** ['deɪtɪd] *adj* altmodisch.

**date of birth** *n* Geburtsdatum *das*.

**date rape** *n Vergewaltigung im Verlauf eines Rendezvous*.

**date stamp** *n* Datumsstempel *der*.

**daub** [dɔːb] *vt*: **to ~ sthg with sthg** etw mit etw beschmieren; **to ~ sthg on sthg** etw auf etw (A) schmieren.

**daughter** ['dɔːtəʳ] *n* Tochter *die*.

**daughter-in-law** (*pl* **daughters-in-law**) *n* Schwiegertochter *die*.

**daunt** [dɔːnt] *vt*: **to be ~ed by sthg** durch etw entmutigt werden.

**daunting** ['dɔːntɪŋ] *adj* überwältigend, gewaltig.

**dawdle** ['dɔːdl] *vi* trödeln.

**dawn** [dɔːn] *n* - **1.** [of day] Morgengrauen *das*, Tagesanbruch *der*; **at ~** im Morgengrauen, bei Tagesanbruch; **from ~ to dusk** von morgens bis abends - **2.** *fig* [of era, period] Beginn *der* ⬦ *vi lit* & *fig* anlbrechen; **the day is ~ing** es dämmert.

➠ **dawn (up)on** *vt fus*: **it finally ~ed on me that ...** mir dämmerte schließlich, dass ...

**dawn chorus** *n* morgendliches Konzert der Vögel.

**day** [deɪ] *n* - **1.** [gen] Tag *der*; **the ~ before/after** am Tag zuvor/danach; **the ~ before yesterday** vorgestern; **the ~ after tomorrow** übermorgen; **any ~ now** jeden Tag (*in Kürze*); **one ~, some ~, one of these ~s** irgendwann, eines Tages; **to call it a ~** Schluss machen; **to make sb's ~** jn sehr erfreuen; **~ and night** Tag und Nacht; **to save sthg for a rainy ~** etw für später auflheben; **it's early ~s yet** es ist noch zu früh; **his ~s are numbered** seine Tage sind gezählt - **2.** [period]: **in those ~s** damals; **in my ~** zu meiner Zeit; **in this ~ and age** heutzutage.

**days** *adv* [work] tagsüber.

**dayboy** ['deɪbɔɪ] *n Br* sch Externe *der.*

**daybreak** ['deɪbreɪk] *n* Tagesanbruch *der;* at ~ bei Tagesanbruch.

**daycare centre** ['deɪkeə-] *n* Tagesstätte *die.*

**daycentre** ['deɪsentəʳ] *n Br* [for old people] Altentagesstätte *die;* [for children] Kindertagesstätte *die.*

**daydream** ['deɪdriːm] *n* Tagtraum *der* <> *vi* [not concentrate] vor sich hin träumen; [be idealistic] Luftschlösser bauen.

**daygirl** ['deɪgɜːl] *n Br* sch Externe *die.*

**Day-Glo**® ['deɪgləʊ] *adj* Day-Glo®.

**daylight** ['deɪlaɪt] *n* - **1.** [light] Tageslicht *das* - **2.** [dawn] Tagesanbruch *der* - **3.** *phr inf:* to scare the (living) ~s out of sb jn furchtbar erschrecken.

**daylight robbery** *n inf* Halsabschneiderei *die.*

**daylight saving time** *n* Sommerzeit *die.*

**day nursery** *n* Kindertagesstätte *die.*

**day off** (*pl* days off) *n* arbeitsfreier Tag.

**day pupil** *n Br* Externe *der, die.*

**day release** *n (U) Br* britisches System, das Arbeitnehmern einen freien Tag zur Weiterbildung einräumt.

**day return** *n Br* Tagesrückfahrkarte *die.*

**dayroom** ['deɪruːm] *n* Aufenthaltsraum *der (im Krankenhaus).*

**day school** *n* Tagesschule *die.*

**day shift** *n* Tagschicht *die.*

**daytime** ['deɪtaɪm] *n* Tag *der* <> *comp:* ~ job Arbeit am Tage or über Tag; ~ television tagsüber ausgestrahlte Fernsehprogramme.

**day-to-day** *adj* [routine, life] (all)täglich; on a ~ basis tageweise.

**day trip** *n* Tagesausflug *der.*

**day-tripper** *n Br* Tagesausflügler *der,* -in *die.*

**daze** [deɪz] *n:* in a ~ benommen, betäubt <> *vt* benommen machen.

**dazed** [deɪzd] *adj* benommen.

**dazzle** ['dæzl] *vt* blenden.

**dazzling** ['dæzlɪŋ] *adj* blendend.

**DC** *n abbr of* **direct current** <> *abk für „District of Columbia", in Postanschrift verwendet.*

**D/D** *abbr of* **direct debit.**

**DDS** (*abbr of* **Doctor of Dental Science**) *n* Doktorgrad der Zahnmedizin oder dessen Inhaber.

**DDT** (*abbr of* **dichlorodiphenyltrichloroethane**) *n* DDT *das.*

**DE** *abk für Delaware, in Postanschrift verwendet.*

**DEA** (*abbr of* **Drug Enforcement Administration**) *n amerikanische Drogenfahndung.*

**deacon** ['diːkn] *n* Diakon *der.*

**deaconess** [ˌdiːkəˈnes] *n* Diakonisse *die.*

**deactivate** [ˌdiːˈæktɪveɪt] *vt* entschärfen.

**dead** [ded] *adj* - **1.** [person, animal, flower] tot; the ~ man/woman der/die Tote; to shoot sb ~ jn erschießen; I wouldn't be seen ~ wearing that *inf* darin möchte ich nicht einmal tot gesehen werden - **2.** [battery] leer; [telephone line, radio] tot - **3.** [numb - arm, fingers] wie abgestorben, taub - **4.** [lifeless - town] wie ausgestorben; [ - party] öde <> *adv* - **1.** [precisely] genau; it's ~ ahead es ist genau geradeaus; ~ on time auf die Minute pünktlich - **2.** *inf* [very] total; '~ slow' 'Schrittgeschwindigkeit'; ~ tired todmüde; to be ~ against sthg völlig gegen etw sein; to be ~ set on sthg zu etw fest entschlossen sein - **3.** [suddenly]: to stop ~ [in car] plötzlich stehen bleiben <> *n:* at ~ of night mitten in der Nacht; in the ~ of winter im tiefsten Winter <> *npl:* the ~ die Toten *pl.*

**deadbeat** ['dedbiːt] *n Am inf* Gammler *der,* -in *die.*

**dead centre** *n* exakter Mittelpunkt.

**dead duck** *n inf* [plan] aussichtsloser Fall.

**deaden** ['dedn] *vt* - **1.** [noise] dämpfen - **2.** [feeling] betäuben.

**dead end** *n lit &* fig Sackgasse *die.*

**dead-end job** *n* Job *der* ohne Aufstiegsmöglichkeiten.

**dead heat** *n* totes Rennen.

**deadline** ['dedlaɪn] *n* letztmöglicher Termin.

**deadlock** ['dedlɒk] *n* Stillstand *der,* toter Punkt.

**deadlocked** ['dedlɒkt] *adj* festgefahren.

**dead loss** *n inf* Reinfall *der;* ~ at sthg Niete *die* in etw (*D*).

**deadly** ['dedlɪ] (*compar* -**ier**; *superl* -**iest**) *adj* tödlich; [enemy, sin] Tod- <> *adv* tödlich.

**deadly nightshade** *n (U)* Tollkirsche *die.*

**deadpan** ['dedpæn] *adj* [delivery, manner] ausdruckslos; [humour] trocken <> *adv* ausdruckslos, mit unbewegter Miene.

**Dead Sea** *n:* the ~ das Tote Meer.

**dead wood** *Br,* **deadwood** *Am* ['dedwʊd] *n* fig Ballast *der.*

**deaf** [def] *adj* taub; to be ~ to sthg fig sich in Bezug auf etw (*A*) taub stellen <> *npl:* the ~ die Gehörlosen *pl.*

**deaf-aid** *n Br* Hörgerät *das.*

**deaf-and-dumb** *adj* taubstumm.

**deafen** ['defn] *vt* taub machen.

**deafening** ['defnɪŋ] *adj* ohrenbetäubend.

**deaf-mute** adj taubstumm ◇ n Taubstumme der, die.

**deafness** ['defnɪs] n Taubheit die.

**deal** [diːl] (pt & pp dealt) n - **1.** [quantity]: **a good** OR **great** ~ (sehr) viel; **a good** OR **great** ~ **of** eine Menge - **2.** [business agreement] Geschäft das; **to do** OR **strike a** ~ **with sb** ein Geschäft mit jm abschließen - **3.** inf [treatment]: **to give sb a fair/rough** ~ jn fair/unfair behandeln; **big** ~! iron wie wichtig! ◇ vt - **1.** [strike]: **to** ~ **sb/sthg a blow, to** ~ **a blow to sb/sthg** jm/etw einen Schlag versetzen - **2.** [cards] austeilen, geben ◇ vi - **1.** [in cards] geben - **2.** [in drugs, arms] handeln.

◆ **deal in** vt fus COMM handeln mit.

◆ **deal out** vt sep - **1.** [cards] austeilen, geben - **2.** [share out] verteilen.

◆ **deal with** vt fus - **1.** [handle, cope with] sich kümmern um, erledigen - **2.** [be concerned with] handeln von - **3.** [be faced with] es zu tun haben mit.

**dealer** ['diːləʳ] n - **1.** [trader] Händler der, -in die - **2.** [in cards] Kartengeber der, -in die.

**dealership** ['diːləʃɪp] n Vertretung die.

**dealing** ['diːlɪŋ] n [trading] Handel der.

◆ **dealings** npl [relations] Umgang der; **to have** ~**s with sb** mit jm (geschäftlich) zu tun haben.

**dealt** [delt] pt & pp ⊳ **deal.**

**dean** [diːn] n UNIV & RELIG Dekan der.

**dear** [dɪəʳ] adj - **1.** [loved] lieb; **to be** ~ **to sb** jm lieb und teuer sein - **2.** esp Br [expensive] teuer - **3.** [in letter]: **Dear Tony** Lieber Tony; **Dear Mr Blair** Sehr geehrter Herr Blair; **Dear Sir** OR **Madam** Sehr geehrte Damen und Herren ◇ n: **my** ~ mein Lieber, meine Liebe ◇ excl: **oh** ~! ach je!; ~ **me!** du meine Güte!

**dearly** ['dɪəlɪ] adv [love] von ganzem Herzen; [hope, wish] sehr.

**dearth** [dɜːθ] n: ~ **(of)** Mangel der (an (+ D)).

**death** [deθ] n Tod der; **to frighten/worry sb to** ~ jn zu Tode erschrecken; **to be bored to** ~ zu Tode gelangweilt sein; **to be sick to** ~ **of sthg** etw gründlich satt haben; **to be put to** ~ hingerichtet werden; **to be at** ~'**s door** an der Schwelle zum Tod stehen.

**deathbed** ['deθbed] n Sterbebett das.

**death certificate** n Totenschein der.

**death duty** Br, **death tax** Am n Erbschaftssteuer die.

**death knell** n fig Todesstoß der.

**deathly** ['deθlɪ] (compar **-ier**; superl **-iest**) adj [silence] tödlich ◇ adv: ~ **white** totenbleich.

**death penalty** n Todesstrafe die.

**death rate** n Sterblichkeitsrate die.

**death row** n Am Todestrakt der.

**death sentence** n Todesurteil das.

**death squad** n Todesschwadron die.

**death tax** n Am = death duty.

**death toll** n Zahl die der Todesopfer.

**death trap** n inf Todesfalle die.

**deathwatch beetle** ['deθwɒtʃ-]n Klopfkäfer der.

**death wish** n Todeswunsch der.

**deb** [deb] n Br inf Debütantin die.

**débâcle** [deɪ'bɑːkl] n Debakel das.

**debar** [diː'bɑːʳ] (pt & pp **-red**; cont **-ring**) vt ausschließen.

**debase** [dɪ'beɪs] vt [quality, value, concept] entwerten; **to** ~ **o.s.** sich erniedrigen.

**debasement** [dɪ'beɪsmənt] n [of person] Entwürdigung die.

**debatable** [dɪ'beɪtəbl] adj fraglich.

**debate** [dɪ'beɪt] n Debatte die, Diskussion die; **to be open to** ~ zur Debatte stehen ◇ vt debattieren, diskutieren; **to** ~ **whether to do sthg** darüber diskutieren, ob etw getan werden soll ◇ vi debattieren, diskutieren.

**debating society** [dɪ'beɪtɪŋ-] n Debattierklub der.

**debauched** [dɪ'bɔːtʃt] adj verdorben, liederlich.

**debauchery** [dɪ'bɔːtʃərɪ] n Ausschweifung die.

**debenture** [dɪ'bentʃəʳ] n Schuldschein der.

**debilitate** [dɪ'bɪlɪteɪt] vt schwächen.

**debilitating** [dɪ'bɪlɪteɪtɪŋ] adj [illness] schwächend; [heat] lähmend.

**debit** ['debɪt] n Soll das, Debet das ◇ vt debitieren, belasten.

**debit card** n Bankkarte die (kann zum Bezahlen verwendet werden, wobei der jeweilige Betrag vom Konto abgebucht wird).

**debonair** [debə'neəʳ] adj flott.

**debrief** [diː'briːf] vt befragen, Bericht erstatten lassen.

**debriefing** [diː'briːfɪŋ] n Einsatzbesprechung die.

**debris** ['deɪbriː] n (U) Trümmer pl; GEOL Geröll das.

**debt** [det] n Schuld die; **to be in** ~ Schulden haben; **to be in sb's** ~ in js Schuld stehen.

**debt collector** n Schuldeneintreiber der.

**debtor** ['detəʳ] n Schuldner der, -in die.

**debug** [diː'bʌg] (pt & pp **-ged**; cont **-ging**) vt - **1.** [remove microphones from] entwanzen - **2.** COMPUT [program] Fehler beseitigen in.

**debunk** [diː'bʌŋk] vt entlarven.

**debut** ['deɪbjuː] n Debüt das.

**debutante** ['debjutɒnt] n Debütantin die.

**Dec.** (*abbr of* **December**) Dez.

**decade** ['dekeɪd] n Jahrzehnt *das*, Dekade *die*.

**decadence** ['dekədəns] n Dekadenz *die*.

**decadent** ['dekədənt] *adj* dekadent.

**decaff** ['dɪːkæf] n *inf* entkoffeinierter Kaffee.

**decaffeinated** [dɪ'kæfɪneɪtɪd] *adj* entkoffeiniert.

**decal** ['diːkæl] n *Am* Aufkleber *der*.

**decamp** [dɪ'kæmp] vi *inf* sich davonlmachen.

**decant** [dɪ'kænt] vt umlfüllen, dekantieren.

**decanter** [dɪ'kæntə'] n Karaffe *die*.

**decapitate** [dɪ'kæpɪteɪt] vt enthaupten.

**decathlete** [dɪ'kæθliːt] n Zehnkämpfer *der*, -in *die*.

**decathlon** [dɪ'kæθlɒn] n Zehnkampf *der*.

**decay** [dɪ'keɪ] n - **1.** [of body] Verwesung *die;* [of plant, wood] Verrotten *das;* **(tooth)** ~ Karies *die* - **2.** *fig* [of building] Zerfall *der;* [of society] Untergang *der* <> vi - **1.** [tooth] faulen; [body] verwesen; [plant, wood] verrotten - **2.** *fig* [building] zerfallen; [society] unterlgehen.

**deceased** [dɪ'siːst] (*pl inv*) *fml adj* verstorben <> n: **the ~** der/die Verstorbene.

**deceit** [dɪ'siːt] n Betrug *der*.

**deceitful** [dɪ'siːtful] *adj* betrügerisch, hinterlistig.

**deceive** [dɪ'siːv] vt [trick] betrügen; [subj: memory, eyes] täuschen; **to deceive o.s.** sich (*D*) selbst etwas vorlmachen.

**decelerate** [ˌdiː'seləreɪt] vi die Geschwindigkeit verringern.

**December** [dɪ'sembə'] n Dezember *der; see also* **September.**

**decency** ['diːsnsɪ] n [respectability] Anstand *der;* **he didn't have the ~ to thank me** er hat es nicht für nötig gehalten, sich bei mir zu bedanken.

**decent** ['diːsnt] *adj* anständig; **are you ~?** [dressed] hast du was an?

**decently** ['diːsntlɪ] *adv* anständig.

**decentralization** [diːˌsentrəlaɪ'zeɪʃn] n Dezentralisierung *die*.

**decentralize, -ise** [ˌdiː'sentrəlaɪz] vt dezentralisieren.

**deception** [dɪ'sepʃn] n Täuschung *die*.

**deceptive** [dɪ'septɪv] *adj* irreführend, trügerisch.

**deceptively** [dɪ'septɪvlɪ] *adv* täuschend

**decibel** ['desɪbel] n Dezibel *das*.

**decide** [dɪ'saɪd] vt - **1.** [resolve] (sich) entscheiden, beschließen; **to ~ to do sthg** (sich) entscheiden, etw zu tun, beschließen etw zu tun; **to ~ that ...** entscheiden, ... dass ...

beschließen, ... dass ... - **2.** [issue, case, match] entscheiden; **what finally ~d you?** was hat dich schließlich dazu gebracht? <> vi [make up one's mind] (sich) entscheiden, (sich) entschließen.

➡ **decide (up)on** vt *fus* sich entscheiden für.

**decided** [dɪ'saɪdɪd] *adj* - **1.** [distinct] entschieden - **2.** [resolute] bestimmt, entschlossen.

**decidedly** [dɪ'saɪdɪdlɪ] *adv* - **1.** [distinctly] entschieden - **2.** [resolutely] bestimmt.

**deciding** [dɪ'saɪdɪŋ] *adj:* ~ **vote** entscheidende Stimme.

**deciduous** [dɪ'sɪdjuəs] *adj* Laub-.

**decimal** ['desɪml] *adj* dezimal <> n Dezimalzahl *die*.

**decimal currency** n Dezimalwährung *die*.

**decimalize, -ise** ['desɪməlaɪz] vt dezimalisieren.

**decimal place** n Dezimalstelle *die*.

**decimal point** n Dezimalpunkt *der*.

**decimate** ['desɪmeɪt] vt dezimieren.

**decipher** [dɪ'saɪfə'] vt entziffern.

**decision** [dɪ'sɪʒn] n - **1.** [choice, judgement] Entscheidung *die;* **to make a ~** eine Entscheidung treffen - **2.** [decisiveness] Entschlossenheit *die*.

**decision-making** n Entscheidungsfindung *die*.

**decisive** [dɪ'saɪsɪv] *adj* - **1.** [person] entschlossen - **2.** [factor, event] entscheidend.

**decisively** [dɪ'saɪsɪvlɪ] *adv* - **1.** [confidently] entschieden - **2.** [conclusively] entscheidend.

**decisiveness** [dɪ'saɪsɪvnɪs] n Entschlossenheit *die*.

**deck** [dek] n - **1.** [of ship, bus, plane] Deck *das* - **2.** [of cards] Spiel *das* - **3.** *Am* [of house] Terrasse *die* <> vt [decorate]: **to ~ sthg (with)** etw schmücken (mit).

➡ **deck out** vt *sep* schmücken.

**deckchair** ['dektʃeə'] n Liegestuhl *der*.

**declaration** [ˌdeklə'reɪʃn] n - **1.** [statement, proclamation] Erklärung *die* - **2.** [to customs] Zollerklärung *die;* [to tax office] Steuererklärung *die*.

**Declaration of Independence** n: **the ~** die (amerikanische) Unabhängigkeitserklärung.

**declare** [dɪ'kleə'] vt - **1.** [state, proclaim] erklären - **2.** [goods at customs, taxes] deklarieren.

**declassify** [ˌdiː'klæsɪfaɪ] (*pt & pp* -**ied**) vt freigeben.

**decline** [dɪ'klaɪn] n Niedergang *der;* **to be in** ~ sich verschlechtern; **to be on the ~** (ab)sinken <> vt [offer, request] abllehnen; **to ~ to do sthg** es abllehnen, etw zu tun <> vi

**- 1.** [deteriorate] sich verschlechtern **- 2.** [refuse] abllehnen.

**declutch** [dɪ'klʌtʃ] *vi* AUT auslkuppeln.

**decode** [ˌdiː'kəʊd] *vt* entschlüsseln.

**decoder** [ˌdiː'kəʊdə'] *n* TV Decoder *der*.

**decommission** [ˌdiːkə'mɪʃn] *vt* stilllegen.

**decompose** [ˌdiːkəm'pəʊz] *vi* [vegetable matter] verfaulen; [flesh] verwesen.

**decomposition** [ˌdiːkɒmpə'zɪʃn] *n* [of vegetable matter] Fäulnis *die;* [of body] Verwesung *die.*

**decompression sickness** [ˌdiːkəm'preʃn-] *n* Taucherkrankheit *die.*

**decongestant** [ˌdiːkən'dʒestənt] *n* schleimlösendes Mittel.

**decontaminate** [ˌdiːkən'tæmɪneɪt] *vt* dekontaminieren, entgiften.

**décor** ['deɪkɔːʳ] *n* Dekor *der.*

**decorate** ['dekəreɪt] *vt* **- 1.** [make pretty - cake, dessert] verzieren; [ - with balloons, streamers, flags] dekorieren, schmücken **- 2.** [with paint] streichen; [with wallpaper] tapezieren **- 3.** [with medal] auslzeichnen.

**decoration** [ˌdekə'reɪʃn] *n* **- 1.** [ornament] Dekoration *die;* [on cake] Verzierung *die;* **Christmas tree ~s** Christbaumschmuck *der* **- 2.** (U) [act of making pretty] Dekorieren *das;* [of cake] Verzieren *das* **- 3.** [appearance of room, building] Dekor *das* **- 4.** [medal] Auszeichnung *die.*

**decorative** ['dekərətɪv] *adj* dekorativ.

**decorator** ['dekəreɪtəʳ] *n* Maler *der*, -in *die.*

**decorous** ['dekərəs] *adj fml* schicklich.

**decorum** [dɪ'kɔːrəm] *n* Anstand *der.*

**decoy** [*n* 'diːkɔɪ, *vt* dɪ'kɔɪ] *n* **- 1.** [for hunting] Köder *der* **- 2.** [person] Lockvogel *der* ◇ *vt* anllocken.

**decrease** [*n* 'diːkriːs, *vb* dɪ'kriːs] *n:* **~ (in sthg)** [crime, unemployment] Rückgang *der* **(an etw (D))**; [size, spending] Abnahme *die* **(einer Sache (G))** ◇ *vt* verringern; [price] herablsetzen, reduzieren ◇ *vi* [in size] abllnehmen; [of numbers] zurücklgehen, sinken.

**decreasing** [diː'kriːsɪŋ] *adj* sinkend.

**decree** [dɪ'kriː] *n* **- 1.** [order, decision] Erlass *der* **- 2.** *Am* [judgment] Urteil *das* ◇ *vt* verordnen.

**decree absolute** (*pl* **decrees absolute**) *n Br* LAW endgültiges Scheidungsurteil.

**decree nisi** [-'naɪsaɪ] (*pl* **decrees nisi**) *n Br* LAW vorläufiges Scheidungsurteil.

**decrepit** [dɪ'krepɪt] *adj* [person] altersschwach; [house, car] heruntergekommen.

**decry** [dɪ'kraɪ] (*pt & pp* **-ied**) *vt fml* bemängeln.

**dedicate** ['dedɪkeɪt] *vt* **- 1.** [book, song, poem]: **to ~ sthg to sb** jm etw widmen **- 2.** [devote]: **to ~ one's life to sthg** sein Leben einer Sache (D) widmen; **to ~ o.s. to sthg** sich etw (D) widmen.

**dedicated** ['dedɪkeɪtɪd] *adj* **- 1.** [person] engagiert **- 2.** COMPUT dediziert.

**dedication** [ˌdedɪ'keɪʃn] *n* **- 1.** [commitment] Hingabe *die* **- 2.** [in book] Widmung *die.*

**deduce** [dɪ'djuːs] *vt* schließen; **to ~ sthg from sthg** etw aus etw schließen.

**deduct** [dɪ'dʌkt] *vt:* **to ~ sthg (from)** etw ablziehen (von).

**deduction** [dɪ'dʌkʃn] *n* **- 1.** [conclusion] Folgerung *die* **- 2.** [of money, number] Abzug *der.*

**deed** [diːd] *n* **- 1.** [action] Tat *die* **- 2.** LAW Urkunde *die;* **~ of sale** Kaufvertrag *der.*

**deed poll** (*pl* **-s**) *n Br:* **to change one's name by ~** seinen Namen durch eine einseitige Rechtserklärung ändern.

**deem** [diːm] *vt fml* erachten; **to ~ it wise to do sthg** es für sinnvoll erachten, etw zu tun.

**deep** [diːp] *adj* **- 1.** [gen] tief; **to be thrown in at the ~ end** *fig* ins kalte Wasser geworfen werden **- 2.** [colour] dunkel **- 3.** [thoughts, feelings] stark **- 4.** [sigh, breath] schwer ◇ *adv* tief; **to be ~ in thought** tief in Gedanken versunken sein; **~ down** *fig* innerlich.

**deepen** ['diːpn] *vt* [hole, channel] vertiefen ◇ *vi* **- 1.** [river, sea] tiefer werden **- 2.** [crisis, recession, feeling] sich verstärken.

**deepening** ['diːpnɪŋ] *adj* [crisis, recession] sich verschlimmernd.

**deep-fat fryer** *n* Fritteuse *die.*

**deep freeze** *n* Tiefkühltruhe *die.*
➣ **deep-freeze** *vt* tiefkühlen.

**deep-fry** *vt* frittieren.

**deeply** ['diːplɪ] *adv* **- 1.** [gen] tief **- 2.** [grateful, sorry, regret, moving] zutiefst **- 3.** [sigh] tief; **~ religious** tief religiös.

**deep-rooted** *adj* tief verwurzelt.

**deep-sea** *adj* Tiefsee-.

**deep-seated** [-'siːtɪd] *adj* [belief, fear] tief sitzend.

**deep-set** *adj* [eyes] tief liegend.

**deer** [dɪəʳ] (*pl inv*) *n* [male] Hirsch *der;* [female] Reh *das.*

**deerstalker** ['dɪəˌstɔːkəʳ] *n* [hat] *Mütze mit Ohrenklappen.*

**de-escalate** [ˌdiː'eskəleɪt] *vt* deeskalieren.

**deface** [dɪ'feɪs] *vt* [poster] verunstalten.

**defamation** [ˌdefə'meɪʃn] *n fml* Verleumdung *die.*

**defamatory** [dɪ'fæmətrɪ] *adj fml* verleumderisch.

**default** [dɪ'fɔːlt] *n* **- 1.** [failure] Versäumnis *das;* **to win by ~** durch Nichtantreten des Gegners gewinnen **- 2.** COMPUT Voreinstellung *die* ◇ *adj* COMPUT voreingestellt ◇ *vi* nicht erscheinen; [in sports] nicht anltreten; **to ~ on**

**sthg** seinen Verpflichtungen hinsichtlich einer Sache (G) nicht nachlkommen.

**defaulter** [dɪ'fɔːltəʳ] n [on payment] säumiger Zahler, säumige Zahlerin.

**default value** n COMPUT Voreinstellung die.

**defeat** [dɪ'fiːt] n Niederlage die; [of motion] Ablehnung die; **to admit ~** sich geschlagen geben <> vt **- 1.** [team, opponent] schlagen **- 2.** [motion, proposal] abllehnen **- 3.** [plans] zunichte machen.

**defeatism** [dɪ'fiːtɪzm] n Defätismus der.

**defeatist** [dɪ'fiːtɪst] adj defätistisch <> n Defätist der.

**defecate** ['defəkeɪt] vi fml defäkieren.

**defect** [n 'diːfekt, vi dɪ'fekt] n Mangel der, Fehler der <> vi POL überllaufen.

**defection** [dɪ'fekʃn] n Überlaufen das.

**defective** [dɪ'fektɪv] adj defekt.

**defector** [dɪ'fektəʳ] n Überläufer der, -in die.

**defence** Br, **defense** Am [dɪ'fens] n **- 1.** [gen] Verteidigung die; **in my ~** zu meiner Verteidigung **- 2.** [protective device, system] Abwehr die.

➡ **defences** npl [of country] Verteidigungsanlagen pl.

**defenceless** Br, **defenseless** Am [dɪ'fenslɪs] adj schutzlos.

**defend** [dɪ'fend] vt verteidigen; **to ~ sb against sb/sthg** jn gegen jn/etw verteidigen; **to ~ o.s.** sich verteidigen <> vi SPORT verteidigen.

**defendant** [dɪ'fendənt] n Angeklagte der, die, Beklagte der, die.

**defender** [dɪ'fendəʳ] n Verteidiger der, -in die.

**defense** n Am = defence.

**defenseless** adj Am = defenceless.

**defensive** [dɪ'fensɪv] adj **- 1.** [weapons, tactics] Verteidigungs- **- 2.** [person] defensiv <> n: **on the ~** in der Defensive.

**defer** [dɪ'fɜːʳ] (pt & pp **-red**; cont **-ring**) vt verschieben <> vi: **to ~ to sb** sich jm beugen, sich jm fügen.

**deference** ['defərəns] n Achtung die, Respekt der.

**deferential** [defə'renʃl] adj respektvoll, ehrerbietig.

**defiance** [dɪ'faɪəns] n Trotz der; **in ~ of sb/sthg** jm/etw zum Trotz.

**defiant** [dɪ'faɪənt] adj trotzig.

**defiantly** [dɪ'faɪəntlɪ] adv trotzig.

**deficiency** [dɪ'fɪʃnsɪ] (pl **-ies**) n **- 1.** [lack] Mangel der **- 2.** [inadequacy] Mangelhaftigkeit die.

**deficient** [dɪ'fɪʃnt] adj **- 1.** [lacking]: **~ in sthg** es

mangelt ihm an etw (D) **- 2.** [inadequate] ungenügend.

**deficit** ['defɪsɪt] n Defizit das.

**defile** [dɪ'faɪl] vt besudeln.

**define** [dɪ'faɪn] vt **- 1.** [give meaning of] definieren **- 2.** [describe] bestimmen, festllegen.

**definite** ['defɪnɪt] adj **- 1.** [plan, date] bestimmt, definitiv **- 2.** [answer] eindeutig; [improvement, difference] deutlich **- 3.** [confident - person] bestimmt.

**definitely** ['defɪnɪtlɪ] adv definitiv, auf jeden Fall.

**definition** [defɪ'nɪʃn] n **- 1.** [of word, expression, concept] Definition die; **by ~** per Definition **- 2.** [of problem, function] Bestimmung die **- 3.** [of image] Bildschärfe die.

**definitive** [dɪ'fɪnɪtɪv] adj **- 1.** [answer] entschieden **- 2.** [book, version] maßgeblich.

**deflate** [dɪ'fleɪt] vt **- 1.** [balloon, tyre] die Luft ablassen aus **- 2.** fig [person] zurechtstutzen **- 3.** ECON: **to ~ the economy** eine Deflation herbeilführen <> vi [balloon, tyre] Luft verlieren.

**deflation** [dɪ'fleɪʃn] n ECON Deflation die.

**deflationary** [dɪ'fleɪʃnərɪ] adj ECON deflationär.

**deflect** [dɪ'flekt] vt abllenken.

**deflection** [dɪ'flekʃn] n Ablenkung die.

**defog** [diː'fɒg] vt Am AUT belüften.

**defogger** [diː'fɒgəʳ] n Am AUT Scheibenbelüftung die.

**deforest** [diː'fɒrɪst] vt ablholzen.

**deforestation** [diːˌfɒrɪ'steɪʃn] n Abholzung die.

**deform** [dɪ'fɔːm] vt deformieren.

**deformed** [dɪ'fɔːmd] adj deformiert.

**deformity** [dɪ'fɔːmətɪ] (pl **-ies**) n Deformität die.

**defraud** [dɪ'frɔːd] vt betrügen.

**defray** [dɪ'freɪ] vt tragen.

**defrost** [diː'frɒst] vt **- 1.** [fridge] abltauen; [frozen food] auf ltauen **- 2.** Am [- DE-ICE] enteisen; [ - demist] belüften <> vi **- 1.** [fridge] abltauen **- 2.** [frozen food] auf ltauen.

**deft** [deft] adj geschickt.

**deftly** ['deftlɪ] adv geschickt.

**defunct** [dɪ'fʌŋkt] adj [organization] nicht mehr bestehend.

**defuse** [diː'fjuːz] vt Br lit & fig entschärfen.

**defy** [dɪ'faɪ] (pt & pp **-ied**) vt **- 1.** [disobey] trotzen (+ D) **- 2.** [challenge]: **to ~ sb to do sthg** jn herauslfordern, etw zu tun **- 3.** fig: **that defies description** das spottet jeder Beschreibung; **that defies belief** das ist nicht zu glauben.

**degenerate** [adj & n dɪ'dʒenərət, vb dɪ'dʒe-nəreɪt] adj degeneriert, entartet <> n Degenerierung die, Entartung die <> vi: **to ~ (into)** auslarten (zu).

**degradation** [ˌdegrə'deɪʃn] n Entwürdigung die, Degradierung die.

**degrade** [dɪ'greɪd] vt entwürdigen, degradieren.

**degrading** [dɪ'greɪdɪŋ] adj entwürdigend, degradierend.

**degree** [dɪ'griː] n - **1.** [unit of measurement] Grad der - **2.** [qualification] akademischer Grad; **to have/take a ~ (in sthg)** einen akademischen Abschluss (in etw (D)) haben/machen - **3.** [amount - of risk, truth] Maß das; **to a (certain) ~** bis zu einem gewissen Grad; **by ~s** allmählich, nach und nach.

**dehumanizeg -ise** [diː'hjuːmənaɪz] vt entmenschlichen.

**dehydrated** [ˌdiːhaɪ'dreɪtɪd] adj - **1.** [food]: **~ milk** Milchpulver - **2.** [person] ausgetrocknet.

**dehydration** [ˌdiːhaɪ'dreɪʃn] n [of person] Austrocknung die.

**de-ice** [diː'aɪs] vt enteisen.

**de-icer** [diː'aɪsəʳ] n Enteiser der, Enteisungsmittel das.

**deign** [deɪn] vi: **to ~ to do sthg** sich herablassen, etw zu tun.

**deity** ['diːɪtɪ] (pl -ies) n Gottheit die.

**déjà vu** n: **a feeling of ~** ein Déjà-vu-Erlebnis.

**dejected** [dɪ'dʒektɪd] adj niedergeschlagen.

**dejection** [dɪ'dʒekʃn] n Niedergeschlagenheit die.

**del.** (abbr of delete) [on keyboard] Entf.

**delay** [dɪ'leɪ] n Verspätung die; **without ~** unverzüglich <> vt - **1.** [plane, train, traveller] aufl-halten; [start, operation, recovery] verzögern - **2.** [postpone - meeting, journey, decision] verschieben; **to ~ doing sthg** es auf lschieben, etw zu tun <> vi zögern; **to ~ in doing sthg** es verschieben, etw zu tun.

**delayed** [dɪ'leɪd] adj verspätet.

**delayed-action** [dɪ'leɪd-] adj mit Zeitverzögerung; **~ shutter** PHOT Selbstauslöser der.

**delectable** [dɪ'lektəbl] adj - **1.** [food] köstlich - **2.** [person] reizend.

**delegate** [n 'delɪgət, vb 'delɪgeɪt] n Delegierte der, die <> vt delegieren; **to ~ sb to do sthg** jn beauftragen, etw zu tun; **to ~ sthg to sb** jn mit etw beauftragen <> vi delegieren.

**delegation** [ˌdelɪ'geɪʃn] n - **1.** [group of people] Delegation die - **2.** (U) [act of delegating] Delegieren das.

**delete** [dɪ'liːt] vt [word, line, name] streichen; COMPUT löschen, entfernen.

**deletion** [dɪ'liːʃn] n Streichung die; COMPUT Löschen das.

**deli** ['delɪ] n abbr of delicatessen.

**deliberate** [adj dɪ'lɪbərət, vb dɪ'lɪbəreɪt] adj - **1.** [intentional] absichtlich - **2.** [slow] bedächtig <> vi fml beraten.

**deliberately** [dɪ'lɪbərətlɪ] adv - **1.** [on purpose] absichtlich - **2.** [slowly] bedächtig.

**deliberation** [dɪˌlɪbə'reɪʃn] n - **1.** [careful consideration] Überlegung die - **2.** [slowness] Bedächtigkeit die.

◆ **deliberations** npl Beratungen.

**delicacy** ['delɪkəsɪ] (pl -ies) n - **1.** [of lace, china] Feinheit die; [of health, instrument] Empfindlichkeit die; **because of the ~ of the situation** weil die Situation so heikel ist - **2.** (U) [tact] Feingefühl das - **3.** [food] Delikatesse die.

**delicate** ['delɪkət] adj - **1.** [lace, china, flavour] fein; [fingers, colour] zart - **2.** [child, person, health, instrument] empfindlich - **3.** [situation, subject] heikel.

**delicately** ['delɪkətlɪ] adv [made, drawn] fein; [flavoured, coloured] zart.

**delicatessen** [ˌdelɪkə'tesn] n Delikatessengeschäft das.

**delicious** [dɪ'lɪʃəs] adj - **1.** [tasty] köstlich - **2.** fig [delightful] entzückend.

**delight** [dɪ'laɪt] n Freude die; **to take ~ in doing sthg** Freude daran haben, etw zu tun <> vt erfreuen <> vi: **to ~ in doing sthg** sich damit vergnügen, etw zu tun.

**delighted** [dɪ'laɪtɪd] adj sehr erfreut; **can you come? - I'd be ~** können Sie kommen? – mit Vergnügen; **~ by** OR **with sthg** hocherfreut über etw (A); **to be ~ to do sthg** etw mit Vergnügen tun; **to be ~ that ...** sich freuen, dass ...

**delightful** [dɪ'laɪtfʊl] adj reizend; [meal] köstlich.

**delightfully** [dɪ'laɪtfʊlɪ] adv erfrischend.

**delimit** [diː'lɪmɪt] vt fml ablgrenzen.

**delineate** [dɪ'lɪnɪeɪt] vt fml umreißen.

**delinquency** [dɪ'lɪŋkwənsɪ] n Kriminalität die.

**delinquent** [dɪ'lɪŋkwənt] adj straffällig <> n Straftäter der, -in die.

**delirious** [dɪ'lɪrɪəs] adj - **1.** MED im Delirium - **2.** [ecstatic] ekstatisch.

**delirium** [dɪ'lɪrɪəm] n - **1.** MED Delirium das - **2.** [state of excitement] Ekstase die.

**deliver** [dɪ'lɪvəʳ] vt - **1.** [distribute]: **to ~ sthg (to sb)** [mail, newspaper] (jm) etw zustellen; COMM (jm) etw liefern - **2.** [give - speech, lecture] halten; [ - message, warning] überbringen - **3.** [a blow, kick] versetzen - **4.**: to ~ a woman's baby eine Frau von ihrem Baby entbinden - **5.** *fml* [liberate]: **to** ~ **sb (from sthg)** jn (von etw) erlösen - **6.** *Am* POL [votes] stellen ⟨⟩ *vi* - **1.** COMM liefern - **2.** [fulfil promise] erfüllen.

**deliverance** [dɪ'lɪvərəns] *n fml* Erlösung *die.*

**delivery** [dɪ'lɪvərɪ] (*pl* -**ies**) *n* - **1.** [of goods] Lieferung *die;* [of letters] Zustellung *die* - **2.** (*U*) [way of speaking] Vortragsweise *die* - **3.** [birth] Entbindung *die.*

**delivery note** *n* Lieferschein *der.*

**delivery van** *Br*, **delivery truck** *Am n* Lieferwagen *der.*

**delphinium** [del'fɪnɪəm] (*pl* -**s**) *n* Rittersporn *der.*

**delta** ['deltə] (*pl* -**s**) *n* GEOGR Delta *das.*

**delude** [dɪ'luːd] *vt* täuschen; **to** ~ **o.s.** sich etwas vor|machen.

**deluge** ['deljuːdʒ] *n* - **1.** [flood] Sintflut *die* - **2.** *fig* [of questions, letters] Flut *die* ⟨⟩ *vt*: **to be** ~**d with** überschwemmt werden mit.

**delusion** [dɪ'luːʒn] *n* Täuschung *die;* ~**s of grandeur** Größenwahnsinn *der.*

**de luxe** [də'lʌks] *adj* Luxus-.

**delve** [delv] *vi* - **1.** [into mystery]: **to** ~ **into sthg** sich in etw (*A*) vertiefen - **2.** [in bag, cupboard] greifen.

**Dem.** - **1.** *abbr of* Democrat - **2.** *abbr of* Democratic.

**demagogue** *Br*, **demagog** *Am* ['deməgɒg] *n* Demagoge *der*, -gin *die.*

**demand** [dɪ'mɑːnd] *n* - **1.** [claim, firm request] Forderung *die;* **it makes great** ~**s on my time** es nimmt viel von meiner Zeit in Anspruch; **wage** ~ Gehaltsforderung *die;* **on** ~ bei Bedarf - **2.** (*U*) COMM: ~ **(for)** Nachfrage *die* (nach); **in** ~ [product, person] gefragt ⟨⟩ *vt* - **1.** [request forcefully] fordern, verlangen; **to** ~ **to do sthg** verlangen, etw zu tun - **2.** [enquire forcefully] zu wissen verlangen - **3.** [require] erfordern.

**demanding** [dɪ'mɑːndɪŋ] *adj* - **1.** [job] anstrengend - **2.** [person, public] anspruchsvoll.

**demarcation dispute** [diːmɑː'keɪʃn-] *n* Kompetenzstreit *der.*

**dematerialize, -ise** [diːmə'tɪərɪəlaɪz] *vi* sich entmaterialisieren.

**demean** [dɪ'miːn] *vt* erniedrigen; **to** ~ **o.s.** sich erniedrigen.

**demeaning** [dɪ'miːnɪŋ] *adj* erniedrigend.

**demeanour** *Br*, **demeanor** *Am* [də'miːnəʳ] *n* (*U*) *fml* Verhalten *das.*

**demented** [dɪ'mentɪd] *adj* wahnsinnig.

**dementia** [dɪ'menʃə] *n* Schwachsinn *der.*

**demerara sugar** [ˌdeməˈreərə-] *n Br* brauner Zucker.

**demigod** ['demɪgɒd] *n* Halbgott *der.*

**demilitarized zone, demilitarised zone** [ˌdiːˈmɪlɪtəraɪzd-] *n* entmilitarisierte Zone.

**demise** [dɪ'maɪz] *n* (*U*) *fml* - **1.** [death] Ableben *das* - **2.** *fig* [of company, custom] Ende *das.*

**demist** [ˌdiːˈmɪst] *vt Br* AUT belüften.

**demister** [ˌdiːˈmɪstəʳ] *n Br* AUT Scheibenbelüftung *die.*

**demo** ['deməʊ] (*pl* -**s**) *n inf abbr of* demonstration.

**demobilize, -ise** [ˌdiːˈməʊbɪlaɪz] *vt fml* entlassen.

**democracy** [dɪ'mɒkrəsɪ] (*pl* -**ies**) *n* Demokratie *die.*

**democrat** ['deməkræt] *n* Demokrat *der*, -in *die.*

➤ **Democrat** *n Am Wähler bzw. Angehöriger der Demokratischen Partei der USA.*

**democratic** [ˌdeməˈkrætɪk] *adj* demokratisch.

➤ **Democratic** *adj Am die Demokratische Partei der USA betreffend.*

**democratically** [ˌdeməˈkrætɪklɪ] *adv* demokratisch.

**Democratic Party** *n Am*: **the** ~ die Demokraten.

**democratize, -ise** [dɪ'mɒkrətaɪz] *vt* demokratisieren.

**demographic** [ˌdeməˈgræfɪk] *adj* demografisch.

**demolish** [dɪ'mɒlɪʃ] *vt* - **1.** [building] ab|reißen - **2.** [idea, argument] zunichte machen - **3.** *inf* [food] vertilgen.

**demolition** [ˌdeməˈlɪʃn] *n* [of building] Abbruch *der.*

**demon** ['diːmən] *n* Dämon *der* ⟨⟩ *comp inf* [skilled] verdammt gut.

**demonstrable** [dɪ'mɒnstrəbl] *adj* beweisbar.

**demonstrably** [dɪ'mɒnstrəblɪ] *adv* nachweislich.

**demonstrate** ['demənstreɪt] *vt* - **1.** [prove] beweisen - **2.** [appliance, machine] vorführen - **3.** [ability, talent] zeigen ⟨⟩ *vi*: **to** ~ **(for/against)** demonstrieren (für/gegen).

**demonstration** [ˌdemən'streɪʃn] *n* - **1.** [public meeting] Demonstration *die* - **2.** [proof] Beweis *der* - **3.** [of new appliance, machine] Vorführung *die* - **4.** *fml* [of feelings] Ausdruck *der.*

**demonstrative** [dɪ'mɒnstrətɪv] *adj* demonstrativ.

**demonstrator** ['demənstreɪtəʳ] *n* - **1.** [protester] Demonstrant *der*, -in *die* - **2.** [of machine, product] Vorführer *der*, -in *die.*

**demoralize, -ise** [dɪ'mɒrəlaɪz] *vt* demoralisieren.

**demoralized** [dɪ'mɒrəlaɪzd] *adj* demoralisiert, entmutigt.

**demote** [ˌdiː'məʊt] *vt* degradieren.

**demotion** [ˌdiː'məʊʃn] *n* Degradierung *die*.

**demotivate** [ˌdiː'məʊtɪveɪt] *vt* demotivieren.

**demure** [dɪ'mjʊəˈ] *adj* sittsam.

**demystify** [ˌdiː'mɪstɪfaɪ] (*pt* & *pp* **-ied**) *vt* entmystifizieren.

**den** [den] *n* [of animal] Höhle *die*.

**denationalization** [ˈdiːˌnæʃnəlaɪˈzeɪʃn] *n* Entnationalisierung *die*.

**denationalize, -ise** [ˌdiː'næʃnəlaɪz] *vt* entnationalisieren.

**denial** [dɪ'naɪəl] *n* - **1.** [refutation] Leugnung *die* - **2.** (U) [refusal] Verweigerung *die*.

**denier** ['denɪəˈ] *n* Denier *das*.

**denigrate** ['denɪɡreɪt] *vt fml* verunglimpfen.

**denim** ['denɪm] *n* (U) Jeansstoff *der*.
→ **denims** *npl* Jeans *pl*.

**denim jacket** *n* Jeansjacke *die*.

**denizen** ['denɪzn] *n* *literary* OR *hum* Bewohner *der*.

**Denmark** ['denmɑːk] *n* Dänemark *nt*.

**denomination** [dɪˌnɒmɪ'neɪʃn] *n* - **1.** RELIG Konfession *die* - **2.** FIN Nennwert *der*.

**denominator** [dɪ'nɒmɪneɪtəˈ] *n* Nenner *der*.

**denote** [dɪ'nəʊt] *vt fml* anizeigen.

**denouement** [deɪ'nuːmɒnn] *n* (Auf)lösung *die*.

**denounce** [dɪ'naʊns] *vt* [person] anigreifen; [actions] aniprangern.

**dense** [dens] *adj* - **1.** [thick] dicht - **2.** *inf* [stupid] schwer von Begriff.

**densely** ['densli] *adv* [thickly] dicht; ~ **packed** dicht gedrängt.

**density** ['densətɪ] (*pl* -ies) *n* Dichte *die*.

**dent** [dent] *n* Beule *die* ◇ *vt* einibeulen.

**dental** ['dentl] *adj* Zahn-; ~ **appointment** Termin *der* beim Zahnarzt.

**dental floss** *n* Zahnseide *die*.

**dental plate** *n* Gaumenplatte *die*.

**dental surgeon** *n* Zahnarzt *der*, -ärztin *die*.

**dental surgery** *n* Zahnarztpraxis *die*.

**dental treatment** *n* (U) zahnärztliche Behandlung.

**dented** ['dentɪd] *adj* verbeult.

**dentist** ['dentɪst] *n* Zahnarzt *der*, -ärztin *die*; **to go to the dentist('s)** zum Zahnarzt gehen.

**dentistry** ['dentɪstrɪ] *n* Zahnmedizin *die*.

**dentures** ['dentʃəz] *npl* Gebiss *das*.

**denunciation** [dɪˌnʌnsɪ'eɪʃn] *n* [of person] Angriff *der*; [of action] Anprangern *das*.

**deny** [dɪ'naɪ] (*pt* & *pp* **-ied**) *vt* - **1.** [refute] bestreiten; [publicly] dementieren - **2.** *fml* [refuse] verweigern; **to** ~ **sb sthg** jm etw verweigern.

**deodorant** [diː'əʊdərənt] *n* Deodorant *das*.

**depart** [dɪ'pɑːt] *vi fml* - **1.** [leave] weglgehen; [by car, bus *etc*] weglfahren; [on journey] ablreisen; **to** ~ **from** [train] ablfahren von; [plane] ablfliegen von - **2.** [differ]: **to** ~ **from sthg** von etw ablweichen.

**department** [dɪ'pɑːtmənt] *n* - **1.** [in organization, shop] Abteilung *die* - **2.** SCH & UNIV Fachbereich *der* - **3.** [in government] Ministerium *das*.

**departmental** [ˌdiːpɑːt'mentl] *adj* [of organization, shop] Abteilungs-; SCH & UNIV Fachbereichs-; [in government] Ministeriums-.

**department store** *n* Kaufhaus *das*.

**departure** [dɪ'pɑːtʃəˈ] *n* - **1.** [leaving - on journey] Abreise *die*; [ - of train] Abfahrt *die*; [ - of plane] Abflug *der*; **there are several ~s for Los Angeles every day** es gehen täglich mehrere Busse/Züge/Flüge nach Los Angeles; **'departures'** [in airport] 'Abflug' - **2.** [variation]: ~ **(from sthg)** Abweichung *die* (von etw) - **3.** [orientation]: **a new** ~ ein Neubeginn.

**departure lounge** *n* Abflughalle *die*.

**depend** [dɪ'pend] *vi* - **1.**: **to** ~ **on sb/sthg** [financially] von jm/etw ablhängen; [rely on] auf jn/etw angewiesen sein; **I can** ~ **on you** ich kann mich auf dich verlassen - **2.** [be determined]: **to** ~ **on sb/sthg** von jm/etw ablhängen; **it ~s on what happens/who is there** das hängt davon ab, was passiert/wer da ist; **it all ~s on you** das hängt alles von dir ab; **~ing on the weather** je nachdem, wie das Wetter wird.

**dependable** [dɪ'pendəbl] *adj* verlässlich, zuverlässig.

**dependant** [dɪ'pendənt] *n* versorgungsabhängige Angehörige *der, die*.

**dependence** [dɪ'pendəns] *n* - **1.**: ~ **(on sb/sthg)** [financially] Abhängigkeit *die* (von jm/etw); [reliance] Angewiesenheit *die* (auf jn/etw) - **2.** [addiction]: ~ **(on sthg)** Abhängigkeit *die* (von etw).

**dependent** [dɪ'pendənt] *adj* - **1.** [reliant]: **to be** ~ **(on sb/sthg)** [financially] abhängig sein (von jm/etw); [rely on] angewiesen sein (auf jn/etw); **do you have any** ~ **children?** haben Sie unterhaltsberechtigte Kinder? - **2.** [addicted] abhängig - **3.** [determined by]: **to be** ~ **on sb/sthg** von jm/etw abhängig sein .

**depict** [dɪ'pɪkt] *vt* - **1.** [show in picture] darstellen - **2.** [describe]: **to** ~ **sb/sthg as sthg** jn/etw als etw beschreiben.

**depilatory** [dɪ'pɪlətrɪ] *adj* Enthaarungs-.

**deplete** [dɪ'pliːt] *vt* vermindern.

**depletion** [dɪ'pliːʃn] *n* Verminderung *die*.

**deplorable** [dɪ'plɔːrəbl] *adj* beklagenswert.

**deplore** [dɪ'plɔː'] *vt* verurteilen.

**deploy** [dɪ'plɔɪ] *vt* einsetzen.

**deployment** [dɪ'plɔɪmənt] *n* (U) Einsatz *der*.

**depopulated** [ˌdiː'pɒpjʊleɪtɪd] *adj* entvölkert.

**depopulation** [diːˌpɒpjʊ'leɪʃn] *n* Entvölkerung *die*.

**deport** [dɪ'pɔːt] *vt* ausIweisen.

**deportation** [ˌdiːpɔː'teɪʃn] *n* Ausweisung *die*.

**deportation order** *n* Ausweisungsanordnung *die*.

**depose** [dɪ'pəʊz] *vt* [king, ruler] ablsetzen.

**deposit** [dɪ'pɒzɪt] *n* - **1.** GEOL [of gold, oil] Ablagerung *die* - **2.** [in wine] Bodensatz *der* - **3.** [payment into bank] Einzahlung *die;* **to make a ~** eine Einzahlung machen - **4.** [down payment] Anzahlung *die* - **5.** [returnable payment - on bottle] Pfand *das;* [ - on hired goods] Kaution *die* <> *vt* - **1.** [subj: river] ablagern - **2.** [in bank] deponieren - **3.** [bag, case, shopping] ablegen.

**deposit account** *n Br* Sparkonto *das*.

**depositor** [də'pɒzɪtə'] *n* [of money] Einzahler *der*, -in *die*.

**depot** ['depəʊ] *n* - **1.** [storage area - for buses] Depot *das;* [ - for goods] Lagerhaus *das* - **2.** *Am* [terminus - for trains] Bahnhof *der;* [ - for buses] Busbahnhof *der*.

**depraved** [dɪ'preɪvd] *adj* verderbt.

**depravity** [dɪ'prævətɪ] *n* Verderbtheit *die*.

**deprecate** ['deprɪkeɪt] *vt fml* missbilligen.

**deprecating** ['deprɪkeɪtɪŋ] *adj* missbilligend.

**depreciate** [dɪ'priːʃɪeɪt] *vi* an Wert verlieren.

**depreciation** [dɪˌpriːʃɪ'eɪʃn] *n* Wertverlust *der*.

**depress** [dɪ'pres] *vt* - **1.** [sadden] deprimieren - **2.** ECON [economy, market] sich hemmend auswirken auf *(+ A);* [prices/share values] verringern - **3.** [slow down] verlangsamen; [reduce] reduzieren.

**depressant** [dɪ'presənt] *n* MED Beruhigungsmittel *das*.

**depressed** [dɪ'prest] *adj* - **1.** [person] deprimiert, niedergeschlagen - **2.** ECON flau - **3.** [area] unterentwickelt *(in wirtschaftlicher Hinsicht)*.

**depressing** [dɪ'presɪŋ] *adj* deprimierend.

**depression** [dɪ'preʃn] *n* - **1.** [sadness] Niedergeschlagenheit *die;* MED Depression *die* - **2.** ECON Depression *die* - **3.** *fml* [hollow] Vertiefung *die*.

➤ **Depression** *n:* **the (Great) Depression** die Weltwirtschaftskrise *(in den 30er Jahren)*.

**depressive** [dɪ'presɪv] *adj* depressiv; [effect] depressiv machend.

**deprivation** [ˌdeprɪ'veɪʃn] *n* Entbehrung *die;* **sleep ~** Schlafentzug *der;* **~ of freedom** Freiheitsberaubung *die*.

**deprive** [dɪ'praɪv] *vt:* **to ~ sb of sthg** [to take sthg away] jn einer Sache *(G)* berauben; [to prevent sb from having sthg] jm etw vorlenthalten.

**deprived** [dɪ'praɪvd] *adj* [person] unterprivilegiert; **a ~ background** soziale Verhältnisse, in denen der Person fundamentale Rechte wie das auf eine angemessene Ausbildung verweigert werden.

**dept.** *abbr of* **department.**

**depth** [depθ] *n* Tiefe *die;* **to be out of one's ~** [in water] nicht mehr stehen können; *fig* [unable to cope] überfordert sein; **the ~ of her knowledge** die Breite ihres Wissens; **to show great ~ of feeling/understanding** sehr viel Gefühl/ Verständnis zeigen; **in ~** eingehend.

➤ **depths** *npl:* **the ~s of the sea** die Tiefen des Meeres; **in the ~s of winter** im tiefsten Winter; **to be in the ~s of despair** in tiefster Verzweiflung sein.

**depth charge** *n* Wasserbombe *die*.

**deputation** [ˌdepjʊ'teɪʃn] *n* Abordnung *die*.

**deputize, -ise** ['depjʊtaɪz] *vi:* **to ~ for sb** jn vertreten *(eine Person höheren Rangs)*.

**deputy** ['depjʊtɪ] *(pl* -ies) *adj* stellvertretend <> *n* - **1.** [second-in-command] Stellvertreter *der*, -in *die* - **2.** *Am* [deputy sheriff] Hilfssheriff *der*.

**derail** [dɪ'reɪl] *vt* [train] entgleisen lassen.

**derailment** [dɪ'reɪlmənt] *n* Entgleisung *die*.

**deranged** [dɪ'reɪndʒd] *adj* geistesgestört.

**derby** [*Br* 'dɑːbɪ, *Am* 'dɜːbɪ] *(pl* -ies) *n* - **1.** [sports event] Derby *das* - **2.** *Am* [hat] Melone *die*.

**deregulate** [ˌdiː'regjʊleɪt] *vt* dem freien Wettbewerb überlassen.

**deregulation** [ˌdiːregjʊ'leɪʃn] *n* (U) Wettbewerbsfreiheit *die*.

**derelict** ['derəlɪkt] *adj* verfallen.

**deride** [dɪ'raɪd] *vt* verhöhnen.

**derision** [dɪ'rɪʒn] *n* Hohn *der*.

**derisive** [dɪ'raɪsɪv] *adj* höhnisch.

**derisory** [də'raɪzərɪ] *adj* - **1.** [ridiculous] lächerlich - **2.** [scornful] höhnisch.

**derivation** [ˌderɪ'veɪʃn] *n* [of word] Ursprung *der*.

**derivative** [dɪ'rɪvətɪv] *adj pej* nachgeahmt <> *n* Derivat *das*.

**derive** [dɪ'raɪv] *vt* - **1.:** **to ~ pleasure from sthg** Freude an etw *(D)* haben; **to ~ satisfaction from sthg** Befriedigung aus etw ziehen - **2.:** **to be ~d from sthg** [from language] aus etw stammen; [from word] von etw abgeleitet sein

◇ vi: **to ~ from sthg** [from language] aus etw stammen; [from word] von etw abgeleitet sein.

**dermatitis** [ˌdɜːmə'taɪtɪs] n (U) Hautentzündung die.

**dermatologist** [ˌdɜːmə'tɒlədʒɪst] n Dermatologe der, -gin die.

**dermatology** [ˌdɜːmə'tɒlədʒɪ] n Dermatologie die.

**derogatory** [dɪ'rɒgətrɪ] adj abfällig.

**derrick** ['derɪk] n - 1. [crane] Derrickkran der - 2. [over oil well] Bohrturm der.

**derv** [dɜːv] n Br Diesel der.

**desalination** [diːˌsælɪ'neɪʃn] n Entsalzung die; ~ **plant** Meerwasserentsalzungsanlage die.

**descant** ['deskænt] n Diskant der.

**descend** [dɪ'send] vi - 1. fml [go down - person] herunter|gehen/hinunter|gehen; [ - in vehicle] herunter|fahren/hinunter|fahren; [ - from carriage, ladder etc] herunter|steigen/hinunter|steigen; [ - plane] die Flughöhe verringern - 2. [fall]: **to ~ on sb/sthg** [silence] sich über jn/etw legen; [gloom] jn/etw befallen - 3. [invade]: **to ~ on** herfallen über (A) - 4. [stoop]: **to ~ to sthg** sich zu etw herablassen ◇ vt fml [go down] hinunter|gehen.

**descendant** [dɪ'sendənt] n Nachkomme der.

**descended** [dɪ'sendɪd] adj: **to be ~ from sb** von jm ablstammen.

**descending** [dɪ'sendɪŋ] adj: **in ~ order** in absteigender Reihenfolge.

**descent** [dɪ'sent] n - 1. [downwards movement]: **a steep ~** ein steiler Abstieg; **the ~ will take us an hour** [walking] wir brauchen eine Stunde für den Abstieg - 2. (U) [origin] Abstammung die.

**describe** [dɪ'skraɪb] vt beschreiben

**description** [dɪ'skrɪpʃn] n - 1. [account] Beschreibung die - 2. [type] Art die.

**descriptive** [dɪ'skrɪptɪv] adj [passage] beschreibend, anschaulich; ~ **writing** Beschreibung die.

**desecrate** ['desɪkreɪt] vt entweihen.

**desecration** [ˌdesɪ'kreɪʃn] n Entweihung die.

**desegregate** [ˌdiː'segrɪgeɪt] vt Rassentrennung auf|heben in (+ D).

**deselect** [ˌdiːsɪ'lekt] vt Br nicht mehr als Kandidat auf|stellen (ein Parlamentsmitglied).

**desert** [n 'dezət, vb & npl dɪ'zɜːt] n - 1. GEOGR Wüste die - 2. fig [boring place] Einöde die ◇ vt [abandon - place] verlassen; [ - person] im Stich lassen ◇ vi MIL desertieren.

◆ **deserts** npl: **to get one's just ~s** bekommen, was man verdient hat.

**deserted** [dɪ'zɜːtɪd] adj verlassen, öde.

**deserter** [dɪ'zɜːtəʳ] n Deserteur der.

**desertion** [dɪ'zɜːʃn] n - 1. MIL Fahnenflucht die - 2. [of person] Verlassen das.

**desert island** ['dezət-] n einsame Insel.

**deserve** [dɪ'zɜːv] vt verdienen; **to ~ to do sthg** verdienen, etw zu tun.

**deserved** [dɪ'zɜːvd] adj verdient.

**deservedly** [dɪ'zɜːvɪdlɪ] adv verdientermaßen, zu Recht.

**deserving** [dɪ'zɜːvɪŋ] adj verdienstvoll; **to be ~ of sthg** fml etw verdienen.

**desiccated** ['desɪkeɪtɪd] adj getrocknet.

**design** [dɪ'zaɪn] n - 1. [plan, drawing] Entwurf der - 2. [art] Design das - 3. [pattern] Muster das - 4. [shape] Konstruktion die; [of dress] Schnitt der - 5. [intention] Absicht die; **by ~** absichtlich; **to have ~s on sb/sthg** es auf jn/etw abgesehen haben ◇ vt entwerfen; **to be ~ed for sthg** vorgesehen sein für etw; **to be ~ed to do sthg** dafür vorgesehen sein, etw zu tun.

**designate** [adj 'dezɪgnət, vb 'dezɪgneɪt] adj designiert; **minister ~** der designierte Minister ◇ vt [appoint - area] bestimmen; [ - person] ernennen; **to ~ sb as sthg** jn zu etw ernennen; **to ~ sb to do sthg** bestimmen, dass jd etw tut.

**designation** [ˌdezɪg'neɪʃn] n fml [name] Bezeichnung die.

**designer** [dɪ'zaɪnəʳ] adj [jeans, glasses, stubble] Designer- ◇ n [in industry] Konstrukteur der; [in theatre] Bühnenbildner der, -in die; [of clothes] Modedesigner der, -in die.

**desirable** [dɪ'zaɪərəbl] adj - 1. fml [appropriate] wünschenswert - 2. [attractive] reizvoll - 3. [sexually attractive] begehrenswert.

**desire** [dɪ'zaɪəʳ] n - 1. [wish]: ~ **(for sthg/to do sthg)** der Wunsch (nach etw/etw zu tun) - 2. (U) [sexual longing] Begierde die ◇ vt - 1. [want] wünschen; **it leaves a lot to be ~d** es lässt viel zu wünschen übrig - 2. [feel sexual longing for] begehren.

**desirous** [dɪ'zaɪərəs] adj fml: **to be ~ of sthg** den Wunsch nach etw haben.

**desist** [dɪ'zɪst] vi fml: **to ~ (from doing sthg)** davon ablsehen (etw zu tun).

**desk** [desk] n - 1. [piece of furniture] Schreibtisch der; [in school] Pult das - 2. [service point] Schalter der; [in hotel] Empfang der.

**desk clerk** n Am Empfangschef der, -in die.

**desk diary** n Tischkalender der.

**desk lamp** n Schreibtischlampe die.

**desktop** ['desktɒp] adj [computer] Desktop-.

**desktop publishing** n Desktop-Publishing das.

**desolate** ['desələt] *adj* **- 1.** [place] trostlos **- 2.** [person] tieftraurig.

**desolation** [ˌdesə'leɪʃn] *n* **- 1.** [barrenness, emptiness] Trostlosigkeit *die* **- 2.** [devastation] Verwüstung *die* **- 3.** [despair] tiefe Traurigkeit.

**despair** [dɪ'speəʳ] *n* Verzweiflung *die;* in ~ verzweifelt <> *vi* verzweifeln; **to ~ of sb/sthg** an jm/etw verzweifeln; **to ~ of doing sthg** die Hoffnung auf lgeben, etw zu tun.

**despairing** [dɪ'speərɪŋ] *adj* verzweifelt.

**despairingly** [dɪ'speərɪŋlɪ] *adv* verzweifelt.

**despatch** [dɪ'spætʃ] *n* & *vt* = **dispatch**.

**desperate** ['despərət] *adj* **- 1.** [reckless - criminal, person] zum Äußersten entschlossen; [ - attempt, measures] verzweifelt **- 2.** [serious, hopeless] hoffnungslos **- 3.** [despairing] verzweifelt **- 4.** [in great need]: **to be ~ for sthg** etw dringend benötigen.

**desperately** ['despərətlɪ] *adv* **- 1.** [seriously, hopelessly] hoffnungslos **- 2.** [very - busy, sorry] äußerst; **to be ~ in love** über beide Ohren verliebt sein; **she ~ wants to travel** sie wünscht sich nichts mehr als zu reisen.

**desperation** [ˌdespə'reɪʃn] *n* Verzweiflung *die;* in ~ aus Verzweiflung.

**despicable** [dɪ'spɪkəbl] *adj* [person] verachtenswert; [behaviour, act] verabscheuungswürdig.

**despise** [dɪ'spaɪz] *vt* [person] verachten; [racism] verabscheuen.

**despite** [dɪ'spaɪt] *prep* trotz (+ G), ungeachtet (+ G).

**despondent** [dɪ'spɒndənt] *adj* verzagt, mutlos.

**despot** ['despɒt] *n* Despot *der*.

**despotic** [de'spɒtɪk] *adj* despotisch.

**dessert** [dɪ'zɜːt] *n* Dessert *das*, Nachtisch *der*.

**dessertspoon** [dɪ'zɜːtspuːn] *n* Dessertlöffel *der*.

**dessert wine** *n* Dessertwein *der*.

**destabilize, -ise** [ˌdiː'steɪbɪlaɪz] *vt* destabilisieren.

**destination** [ˌdestɪ'neɪʃn] *n* [of means of transport] Bestimmungsort *der;* [of traveller] Reiseziel *das*.

**destined** ['destɪnd] *adj* **- 1.** [intended]: **to be ~ for sthg** zu etw bestimmt sein; **to be ~ to do sthg** dazu bestimmt sein, etw zu tun; **we were ~ never to meet again** das Schicksal wollte es, dass wir uns nie wieder begegneten **- 2.** [bound]: ~ **for** unterwegs nach.

**destiny** ['destɪnɪ] *(pl* **-ies)** *n* Schicksal *das*.

**destitute** ['destɪtjuːt] *adj* notleidend; **to be ~** Not leiden.

**destroy** [dɪ'strɔɪ] *vt* **- 1.** [ruin] zerstören **- 2.** [kill] töten.

**destroyer** [dɪ'strɔɪəʳ] *n* Zerstörer *der*.

**destruction** [dɪ'strʌkʃn] *n (U)* Zerstörung *die*, Vernichtung *die*.

**destructive** [dɪ'strʌktɪv] *adj* [power] zerstörerisch; [feeling, behaviour] destruktiv.

**destructively** [dɪ'strʌktɪvlɪ] *adv* destruktiv.

**desultory** ['desəltrɪ] *adj fml* [attempt] planlos; [conversation] nicht zielgerichtet.

**detach** [dɪ'tætʃ] *vt* **- 1.** [remove] ablnehmen; [tear off] abltrennen; **to ~ sthg from sthg** etw von etw ablnehmen *OR* abltrennen **- 2.** [dissociate]: **to ~ o.s. from sthg** sich von etw distanzieren.

**detachable** [dɪ'tætʃəbl] *adj* abnehmbar; [by tearing off] abtrennbar.

**detached** [dɪ'tætʃt] *adj* [unemotional] distanziert, unbeteiligt.

**detached house** *n* Einfamilienhaus *das*.

**detachment** [dɪ'tætʃmənt] *n* **- 1.** [aloofness] Distanziertheit *die* **- 2.** MIL Sonderkommando *das*.

**detail** ['diːteɪl] *n* **- 1.** [small point] Detail *das;* [specific] Einzelheit *die* **- 2.** *(U)* [collection of facts, points] Details *pl;* **to go into ~** ins Detail gehen; in ~ im Detail **- 3.** MIL Sondertrupp *der* <> *vt* [list] auf llisten.

↪ **details** *npl* [information] Informationen *pl;* [personal information] Personalien *pl*.

**detailed** ['diːteɪld] *adj* detailliert.

**detain** [dɪ'teɪn] *vt* **- 1.** [in police station] in polizeilichem Gewahrsam behalten; [in hospital] zur stationären Behandlung behalten **- 2.** [delay] auf lhalten.

**detainee** [ˌdiːteɪ'niː] *n:* **political ~** politischer Häftling.

**detect** [dɪ'tekt] *vt* **- 1.** [subj: person] bemerken, entdecken **- 2.** [subj: machine] ausfindig machen.

**detection** [dɪ'tekʃn] *n* **- 1.** *(U)* [discovery] Entdeckung *die* **- 2.** [investigation] Ermittlungsarbeit *die*.

**detective** [dɪ'tektɪv] *n* [private] Detektiv *der*, -in *die;* [police officer] Kriminalbeamte *der*, -tin *die*.

**detective novel** *n* Kriminalroman *der*.

**detector** [dɪ'tektəʳ] *n* Detektor *der*.

**détente** [deɪ'tɒnt] *n* POL Détente *die*.

**detention** [dɪ'tenʃn] *n* **- 1.** [of suspect] Untersuchungshaft *die;* in ~ in Untersuchungshaft **- 2.** [at school] Nachsitzen *das;* **to be in ~** nachlsitzen.

**detention centre** *n Br* Jugendstrafanstalt *die*.

**deter** [dɪ'tɜːʳ] *(pt* & *pp* **-red;** *cont* **-ring)** *vt* ablhalten; **to ~ sb from doing sthg** jn davon ablhalten, etw zu tun.

**detergent** [dɪ'tɜːdʒənt] n [for clothes] Wasch-
mittel das; [for dishes] Spülmittel das.

**deteriorate** [dɪ'tɪərɪəreɪt] vi sich verschlechtern.

**deterioration** [dɪ,tɪərɪə'reɪʃn] n Verschlechterung die.

**determination** [dɪ,tɜːmɪ'neɪʃn] n - 1. [resolve]
Entschlossenheit die - 2. [fixing, establishment]
Festlegung die.

**determine** [dɪ'tɜːmɪn] vt - 1. [establish, find out]
bestimmen, ermitteln - 2. [control] entscheiden - 3. fml [resolve]: to ~ to do sthg sich dazu
entschließen, etw zu tun - 4. [fix, establish]
festlegen.

**determined** [dɪ'tɜːmɪnd] adj - 1. [person] resolut; to be ~ to do sthg fest entschlossen sein,
etw zu tun - 2. [effort] angestrengt.

**deterrent** [dɪ'terənt] adj abschreckend <> n
Abschreckungsmittel das.

**detest** [dɪ'test] vt verabscheuen.

**detestable** [dɪ'testəbl] adj verabscheuungswürdig.

**dethrone** [dɪ'θrəʊn] vt entthronen.

**detonate** ['detəneɪt] vt zur Detonation bringen <> vi detonieren.

**detonator** ['detəneɪtəʳ] n Sprengkapsel die.

**detour** ['diː,tʊəʳ] n Umweg der.

**detox** ['diːtɒks] n (U) inf Entziehungskur die
(im Krankenhaus).

**detoxification** [,diːtɒksɪfɪ'keɪʃn] n Entgif-
tung die.

**detract** [dɪ'trækt] vi: to ~ from [quality] beeinträchtigen; [enjoyment, achievement] schmälern.

**detractor** [dɪ'træktəʳ] n Kritiker der, -in die.

**detrain** [,diː'treɪn] vi aus dem Zug aus|
steigen.

**detriment** ['detrɪmənt] n: to the ~ of sb/sthg
zum Schaden von jm/etw.

**detrimental** [,detrɪ'mentl] adj [effect] schädlich; [consequences] nachteilig.

**detritus** [dɪ'traɪtəs] n (U) Abfälle pl.

**deuce** [djuːs] n TENNIS Einstand der.

**Deutschmark** ['dɔɪtʃ,mɑːk] n deutsche
Mark.

**devaluation** [,diːvæljʊ'eɪʃn] n FIN Abwertung
die.

**devalue** [,diː'væljuː] vt ab|werten.

**devastate** ['devəsteɪt] vt - 1. [destroy] verwüs-
ten - 2. fig [person] sehr mit|nehmen.

**devastated** ['devəsteɪtɪd] adj - 1. [area, city]
verwüstet - 2. fig [person] am Boden zerstört.

**devastating** ['devəsteɪtɪŋ] adj - 1. [disas-
trous - hurricane, storm] verheerend; [- news, expe-
rience] niederschmetternd - 2. [very effec-

tive - charm, wit] umwerfend; [- remark, argument]
vernichtend; [- player, speaker] überragend.

**devastation** [,devə'steɪʃn] n (U) [destruction]
Verwüstung die.

**develop** [dɪ'veləp] vt - 1. [land, area, resources]
erschließen - 2. [illness] bekommen; [habit]
an|nehmen; to ~ one's mind seine geistigen
Fähigkeiten weiter|entwickeln; the ma-
chine ~ed a fault an der Maschine ist ein
Fehler aufgetreten - 3. [industry, sector] för-
dern - 4. [machine, weapon, product] weiter|
entwickeln - 5. [business, company] aus|bauen;
[idea, argument, plot] entfalten - 6. PHOT entwickeln <> vi - 1. [gen] sich entwickeln; [plot]
sich entfalten - 2. [fault, problem] auf|tau-
chen; [illness] sich entwickeln.

**developer** [dɪ'veləpəʳ] n - 1. [of land] Geschäftsmann, der Land kauft, erschließt und
danach gewinnbringend wiederverkauft
- 2. [person]: to be an early ~ frühreif sein; to be
a late ~ ein Spätentwickler sein - 3. PHOT
[chemical] Entwickler der.

**developing country** [dɪ'veləpɪŋ-] n Ent-
wicklungsland das.

**development** [dɪ'veləpmənt] n - 1. [gen] Entwicklung die; [of business, company] Ausbau der;
[of idea, argument, plot] Entfaltung die - 2. (U) [of
land, area, resources] Erschließung die - 3. [devel-
oped land] Neubausiedlung die.

**development area** n Br Gebiet mit hoher
Arbeitslosigkeit, in dem durch Investitionen
neue Arbeitsplätze geschaffen werden sollen.

**deviant** ['diːvjənt] adj abweichend; [sexually]
sexuell abnormal <> n Person, die in ihrem
Sexualverhalten von der Norm abweicht.

**deviate** ['diːvɪeɪt] vi: to ~ (from sthg) (von etw)
ab|weichen.

**deviation** [,diːvɪ'eɪʃn] n - 1. (U) [abnormality] De-
vianz die - 2. [departure] Abweichung die.

**device** [dɪ'vaɪs] n - 1. [apparatus] Gerät das
- 2. [plan, method] Mittel das; to leave sb to his/
her own ~s jn sich selbst überlassen
- 3. [bomb] Sprengkörper der; incendiary ~
Brandbombe die.

**devil** ['devl] n - 1. [evil spirit] Teufel der - 2. inf
[person] Teufel der; poor ~! armer Teufel!; you
silly ~! du Trottel!; you lucky ~! du Glücks-
pilz! - 3. [for emphasis]: who/where/why the
~ ...? wer/wo/warum zum Teufel ...?
➤ **Devil** n [Satan]: the Devil der Teufel.

**devilish** ['devlɪʃ] adj teuflisch.

**devil-may-care** adj Nach-mir-die-
Sintflut-.

**devil's advocate** n Advocatus Diaboli der.

**devious** ['diːvjəs] adj [plan, means] fragwürdig;
[person] verschlagen.

**deviousness** ['diːvjəsnɪs] n [of person] Ver-

schlagenheit *die;* [of plan, means] Fragwürdig-
keit *die.*

**devise** [dɪ'vaɪz] *vt* entwerfen.

**devoid** [dɪ'vɔɪd] *adj fml:* ~ of bar *(+ G).*

**devolution** [ˌdiːvə'luːʃn] *n* POL Dezentralisierung *die.*

**DEVOLUTION**

Im Jahre 1998 gab die Zentralregierung in
Westminster bestimmte Befugnisse und
Pflichten an kleinere Parlamente in Schottland und Wales ab. Für Wales war dies die
erste praktische Erfahrung mit dem Dezent-
ralisierungsprozess der Devolution. Schottland hatte schon immer sein eigenes
Rechts- und Schulsystem; jetzt hat es auch
die Eigenzuständigkeit für Gesundheitswesen, Verkehr u. a. Die Zuständigkeit für die
Bereiche, die das gesamte Vereinigte Königreich angehen (etwa Verteidigung), liegt
nach wie vor beim Parlament in Westminster. In Zukunft könnten auch einige der
größeren Regionen in England in den Genuss der Dezentralisierung kommen.

**devolve** [dɪ'vɒlv] *vi fml:* to ~ (up)on sb jm übertragen werden.

**devote** [dɪ'vəʊt] *vt:* to ~ sthg to sthg etw für
etw verwenden; to ~ o.s. to sthg sich etw *(D)*
widmen.

**devoted** [dɪ'vəʊtɪd] *adj* [mother] hingebungs-
voll; [husband, wife] liebevoll und treu; to be
~ to sb/sthg jn/etw innig lieben.

**devotee** [ˌdevə'tiː] *n* [fan] Fan *der.*

**devotion** [dɪ'vəʊʃn] *n:* ~ (to sb/sthg) Hingabe
*die* (an jn/etw).

**devour** [dɪ'vaʊəʳ] *vt lit* & *fig* verschlingen.

**devout** [dɪ'vaʊt] *adj* RELIG fromm.

**dew** [djuː] *n* Tau *der.*

**dexterity** [dek'sterətɪ] *n* Geschicklichkeit
*die.*

**dexterous** ['dekstrəs] *adj* geschickt.

**dextrose** ['dekstrəʊs] *n* Traubenzucker *der.*

**dextrous** ['dekstrəs] *adj* = **dexterous**.

**DFEE** *(abbr of* **Department for Education and
Employment)** *n britisches Bildungs- und Ar-
beitsministerium.*

**diabetes** [ˌdaɪə'biːtiːz] *n* Diabetes *der.*

**diabetic** [ˌdaɪə'betɪk] *adj* - **1.** [person] zuckerkrank - **2.** [foods] Diabetiker- ⬦ *n* Diabetiker *der,* -in *die.*

**diabolic(al)** [ˌdaɪə'bɒlɪk(l)] *adj* - **1.** [evil] teuflisch - **2.** *inf* [very bad] sauschlecht.

**diaeresis** *Br,* **dieresis** *Am* [daɪ'erɪsɪs] *(pl -eses
[-ɪsiːz]) n* Trema *das.*

**diagnose** ['daɪəgnəʊz] *vt* - **1.** [illness] diagnostizieren - **2.** *fig* [problem] erkennen.

**diagnosis** [ˌdaɪəg'nəʊsɪs] *(pl -oses* [-əʊsiːz]) *n*
- **1.** [of illness] Diagnose *die* - **2.** *fig* [of problem]
Erkennen *das.*

**diagnostic** [ˌdaɪəg'nɒstɪk] *adj* MED diagnos-
tisch.

**diagonal** [daɪ'ægənl] *adj* diagonal ⬦ *n* Diagonale *die.*

**diagonally** [daɪ'ægənəlɪ] *adv* diagonal.

**diagram** ['daɪəgræm] *n* Schaubild *das.*

**diagrammatic** [ˌdaɪəgrə'mætɪk] *adj:* in ~ form
in einem Schaubild dargestellt.

**dial** ['daɪəl] *(Br pt* & *pp* -**led;** *cont* -**ling,** *Am pt* &
*pp* -**ed;** *cont* -**ing)** *n* - **1.** [of watch, clock] Zifferblatt *das;* [of meter] Skala *die* - **2.** [of radio] Skala
*die* - **3.** [of telephone] Wählscheibe *die* ⬦ *vt*
[number] wählen.

**dialect** ['daɪəlekt] *n* Dialekt *der.*

**dialling code** ['daɪəlɪŋ-] *n Br* Vorwahl *die.*

**dialling tone** *Br* ['daɪəlɪŋ-], **dial tone** *Am n*
Amtszeichen *das.*

**dialogue** *Br,* **dialog** *Am* ['daɪəlɒg] *n* Dialog
*der.*

**dial tone** *n Am* = **dialling tone.**

**dialysis** [daɪ'ælɪsɪs] *n* Dialyse *die.*

**diamanté** [daɪə'mɒnteɪ] *adj* Strass-.

**diameter** [daɪ'æmɪtəʳ] *n* Durchmesser *der.*

**diametrically** [ˌdaɪə'metrɪklɪ] *adv:* ~ opposed
diametral entgegengesetzt.

**diamond** ['daɪəmənd] *n* - **1.** [gem] Diamant *der*
- **2.** [shape] Raute *die.*
➤ **diamonds** *npl* Karo *das;* the six of ~s die Karo sechs.

**diamond wedding** *n* diamantene Hochzeit.

**diaper** ['daɪəpəʳ] *n Am* Windel *die.*

**diaphanous** [daɪ'æfənəs] *adj* durchscheinend.

**diaphragm** ['daɪəfræm] *n* - **1.** ANAT Zwerchfell
*das* - **2.** [contraceptive] Diaphragma *das.*

**diarrh(o)ea** [ˌdaɪə'rɪə] *n* Durchfall *der.*

**diary** ['daɪərɪ] *(pl -ies) n* - **1.** [appointment book]
(Termin)kalender *der* - **2.** [personal record] Tagebuch *das.*

**diatribe** ['daɪətraɪb] *n* [spoken] Schmährede
*die;* [written] Schmähschrift *die.*

**dice** [daɪs] *(pl inv) n* [for games] Würfel *der;* no
~! *Am inf* keine Chance! ⬦ *vt* würfeln.

**dicey** ['daɪsɪ] *(compar -ier; superl -iest) adj esp Br
inf* riskant.

**dichotomy** [daɪ'kɒtəmɪ] *(pl -ies) n fml* Dicho-
tomie *die.*

**dickens** ['dɪkɪnz] *n Br inf dated:* who/what/
where the ~ ...? wer/was/wo zum Teufel ...?

**Dictaphone®** ['dɪktəfəʊn] *n* Diktiergerät *das.*

**D**

**dictate** [*vb* dɪk'teɪt, *n* 'dɪkteɪt] *vt* - **1.** [read out] diktieren; **to ~ sthg to sb** jm etw diktieren - **2.** [impose] vorlschreiben ⇔ *vi* - **1.** [read aloud]: **to ~ to sb** jm diktieren - **2.** [give orders]: **to ~ to sb** jm Vorschriften machen.

◆ **dictates** *npl* [of fashion] Diktat *das;* **the ~s of his conscience** die Stimme seines Gewissens.

**dictation** [dɪk'teɪʃn] *n* Diktat *das;* **to take** OR **do ~** ein Diktat auf lnehmen.

**dictator** [dɪk'teɪtəʳ] *n* POL Diktator *der*, -in *die*.

**dictatorship** [dɪk'teɪtəʃɪp] *n* Diktatur *die*.

**diction** ['dɪkʃn] *n (U)* Aussprache *die*.

**dictionary** ['dɪkʃənrɪ] (*pl* -**ies**) *n* Wörterbuch *das;* [for a particular subject] Lexikon *das*.

**did** [dɪd] *pt* ⊳ **do.**

**didactic** [dɪ'dæktɪk] *adj* didaktisch.

**diddle** ['dɪdll *vt inf* übers Ohr hauen.

**didn't** ['dɪdnt] = **did not.**

**die** [daɪ] (*pt* & *pp* **died;** *cont* **dying;** *npl sense 2 only* **dice**) *vi* - **1.** [person] sterben; [animal, plant] einlgehen; **to be dying** im Sterben liegen; **to be dying for sthg** *inf* sich nach etw sehnen; **to be dying to do sthg** *inf* darauf brennen, etw zu tun - **2.** *fig* [love, anger] vergehen; [memory] schwinden ⇔ *n* - **1.** [for shaping metal] Gussform *die* - **2.** *esp Am* [dice] Würfel *der*.

◆ **die away** *vi* [sound] leiser werden; [wind] nachllassen.

◆ **die down** *vi* [wind] sich legen, ablflauen; [sound] leiser werden; [fire] herunterlbrennen.

◆ **die out** *vi* auslsterben.

**diehard** ['daɪhɑːdl *n* Ewiggestrige *der*, *die*.

**dieresis** [daɪ'erɪsɪs] *n Am* = **diaeresis.**

**diesel** ['diːzl] *n* - **1.** [vehicle] Diesel *der* - **2.** [fuel] Dieselöl *das*.

**diesel engine** *n* - **1.** [of car] Dieselmotor *der* - **2.** LOCOMOTIVE Diessellokomotive *die*.

**diesel fuel, diesel oil** *n* Dieselkraftstoff *der*, Dieselöl *das*.

**diet** ['daɪət] *n* - **1.** [eating pattern] Ernährung *die;* **they have a poor ~** ihre Ernährung ist schlecht; **to exist on a ~ of sthg** sich (ausschließlich) von etw ernähren - **2.** [to lose weight, for medical reasons] Diät *die;* **to be/go on a ~** eine Diät machen ⇔ *comp* [low-calorie] Diät- ⇔ *vi* [to lose weight] eine Diät machen.

**dietary** ['daɪətrɪ] *adj* diätisch, Ernährungs-.

**dietary fibre** *n* Ballaststoff *der*.

**dieter** ['daɪətəʳ] *n* Person, *die eine Diät macht*.

**dietician** [ˌdaɪə'tɪʃn] *n* Ernährungswissenschaftler *der*, -in *die*.

**differ** ['dɪfəʳ] *vi* - **1.** [be different] verschieden sein; **to ~ from sb/sthg** sich von jm/etw unterscheiden - **2.** [disagree]: **to ~ with sb (about sthg)** mit jm (über etw *(A)*) verschiedener

Meinung sein; **to agree to ~** sich *(D)* verschiedene Meinungen zugestehen.

**difference** ['dɪfrəns] *n* Unterschied *der;* **it doesn't make any ~** es ist egal; **to make all the ~** einen gewaltigen Unterschied machen; **~ of opinion** Meinungsverschiedenheit *die*.

**different** ['dɪfrənt] *adj* - **1.** [not like before] anders; [not identical] verschieden, unterschiedlich; [various] verschieden; **to be ~ from** Br OR **than** Am **sb/sthg** anders sein als jd/etw - **2.** [unusual] außergewöhnlich.

**differential** [ˌdɪfə'renʃl] *adj* unterschiedlich, verschieden ⇔ *n* - **1.** [between pay scales] Gehaltsunterschied *der* - **2.** TECH Differential *das*.

**differentiate** [ˌdɪfə'renʃɪeɪt] *vt*: **to ~ sthg from sthg** etw von etw unterscheiden ⇔ *vi*: **to ~ (between)** unterscheiden (zwischen (+ *D*)).

**differently** ['dɪfrəntlɪ] *adv* anders.

**difficult** ['dɪfɪkəlt] *adj* - **1.** [hard] schwierig; **to make life ~ for sb** jm das Leben schwer lmachen - **2.** [awkward] schwierig.

**difficulty** ['dɪfɪkəltɪ] (*pl* -**ies**) *n* Schwierigkeit *die;* **to have ~ (in) doing sthg** Schwierigkeiten haben, etw zu tun; **with ~** mit Mühe.

**diffidence** ['dɪfɪdəns] *n* Schüchternheit *die*.

**diffident** ['dɪfɪdənt] *adj* schüchtern; [approach] zaghaft.

**diffuse** [*adj* dɪ'fjuːs, *vb* dɪ'fjuːz] *adj* - **1.** [light] diffus - **2.** [speech] weitschweifig ⇔ *vt* - **1.** [light] auslstrahlen - **2.** [information] verbreiten ⇔ *vi* - **1.** [light] auslstrahlen - **2.** [information] sich verbreiten.

**diffusion** [dɪ'fjuːʒn] *n (U)* - **1.** [of light] Ausbreitung *die* - **2.** [of information] Verbreitung *die*.

**dig** [dɪg] (*pt* & *pp* **dug;** *cont* -**ging**) *n* - **1.** *fig* [unkind remark] Seitenhieb *der* - **2.** ARCHAEOL Ausgrabung *die* ⇔ *vt* - **1.** [hole] graben; [garden] umlgraben - **2.** [press, jab]: **to ~ sthg into sb/sthg** etw in jn/etw bohren; **to ~ sb in the ribs with one's elbow** jm den Ellbogen in die Rippen stoßen ⇔ *vi* - **1.** [in ground] graben - **2.** [press]: **my belt's ~ging into me** mein Gürtel schneidet ein; **her nails were ~ging into his skin** ihre Fingernägel gruben sich in seine Haut.

◆ **dig out** *vt sep lit* & *fig* auslgraben.

◆ **dig up** *vt sep lit* & *fig* auslgraben.

**digest** [*n* 'daɪdʒest, *vb* dɪ'dʒest] *n* [book] Sammlung zusammengefasster Texte ⇔ *vt lit* & *fig* verdauen.

**digestible** [dɪ'dʒestəbl] *adj* verdaulich.

**digestion** [dɪ'dʒestʃn] *n* Verdauung *die*.

**digestive** [daɪ'dʒestɪv] *adj* Verdauungs-.

**digestive biscuit** *n* Br mürber Keks aus Vollkornmehl.

**digestive system** *n* Verdauungsapparat *der*.

**digger** ['dɪgər] n [machine] Bagger der.

**digit** ['dɪdʒɪt] n - 1. [figure] Ziffer die - 2. [finger] Finger der; [toe] Zehe die.

**digital** ['dɪdʒɪtl] adj digital.

**digital camera** n digitale Kamera.

**digital recording** n Digitalaufnahme die.

**digital television** n digitales Fernsehen.

**digital watch** n Digitaluhr die.

**digitize, -ise** ['dɪdʒɪtaɪz] vt digitalisieren.

**dignified** ['dɪgnɪfaɪd] adj würdevoll.

**dignify** ['dɪgnɪfaɪ] (pt & pp -ied) vt würdigen.

**dignitary** ['dɪgnɪtrɪ] (pl -ies) n Würdenträger der, -in die.

**dignity** ['dɪgnətɪ] n Würde die.

**digress** [daɪ'gres] vi: to ~ (from sthg) (von etw) abschweifen.

**digression** [daɪ'greʃn] n Abschweifung die.

**digs** [dɪgz] npl Br inf Bude die.

**dike** [daɪk] n - 1. [wall, bank] Damm der - 2. inf pej [lesbian] Lesbe die.

**dilapidated** [dɪ'læpɪdeɪtɪd] adj baufällig.

**dilate** [daɪ'leɪt] vt erweitern <> vi sich erweitern.

**dilated** [daɪ'leɪtɪd] adj erweitert.

**dilemma** [dɪ'lemə] n Dilemma das.

**dilettante** [ˌdɪlɪ'tæntɪ] (pl -tes OR -ti) n pej Dilettant der, -in die.

**diligence** ['dɪlɪdʒəns] n Sorgfalt die.

**diligent** ['dɪlɪdʒənt] adj sorgfältig.

**dill** [dɪl] n Dill der.

**dillydally** ['dɪlɪdælɪ] (pt & pp -ied) vi inf trödeln.

**dilute** [daɪ'luːt] adj verdünnt <> vt: to ~ sthg (with sthg) etw (mit etw) verdünnen.

**dilution** [daɪ'luːʃn] n: ~ (with sthg) Verdünnung die (mit etw).

**dim** [dɪm] (compar -mer; superl -mest; pt & pp -med; cont -ming) adj - 1. [room] halbdunkel; [light] trüb, schwach - 2. [indistinct - shape, sight] undeutlich; [ - sound, memory] schwach - 3. [eyes] schwach - 4. [gloomy]: to take a ~ view of sthg wenig von etw halten - 5. inf [stupid] beschränkt, begriffsstutzig <> vt dämpfen <> vi [memory, beauty] verblassen; [light, hope] schwinden.

**dime** [daɪm] n Am Zehncentstück das; they're a ~ a dozen sie sind reine Dutzendware.

**dimension** [dɪ'menʃn] n Dimension die.
 → **dimensions** pl [of room, object] Abmessungen pl; in three ~s dreidimensional.

**-dimensional** [dɪ'menʃənl] suffix -dimensional.

**diminish** [dɪ'mɪnɪʃ] vt [subj: person] herabsetzen; [subj: thing] verringern <> vi [responsibil-ity] sich vermindern; [importance, popularity] abnehmen.

**diminished** [dɪ'mɪnɪʃt] adj - 1. [profits, budget] reduziert - 2. [reputation] verschlechtert.

**diminished responsibility** n LAW verminderte Zurechnungsfähigkeit.

**diminishing returns** npl fig: it's a case of ~ obwohl man immer mehr hineinsteckt, kriegt man immer weniger heraus.

**diminutive** [dɪ'mɪnjutɪv] adj fml winzig <> n GRAMM Verkleinerungsform die.

**dimly** ['dɪmlɪ] adv - 1. [shine] schwach - 2. [see] verschwommen; [remember] schwach.

**dimmer** ['dɪmər] n Dimmer der.
 → **dimmers** npl Am - 1. [dipped headlights] Abblendlicht das - 2. [parking lights] Begrenzungsleuchten pl.

**dimmer switch** n = dimmer.

**dimple** ['dɪmpl] n Grübchen das.

**dimwit** ['dɪmwɪt] n inf Schwachkopf der.

**dim-witted** [-'wɪtɪd] adj inf beschränkt.

**din** [dɪn] n inf Getöse das.

**dine** [daɪn] vi fml speisen.
 → **dine out** vi auswärts speisen.

**diner** ['daɪnər] n - 1. [person] Gast der (in einem Restaurant) - 2. Am [restaurant] Lokal das.

**dingdong** [ˌdɪŋ'dɒŋ] adj inf [battle, argument] hin- und herwogend <> n [of bell] Bimbam das.

**dinghy** ['dɪŋgɪ] (pl -ies) n [for sailing] kleines Segelboot; (rubber) ~ Schlauchboot das.

**dingo** ['dɪŋgəʊ] (pl -es) n Dingo der.

**dingy** ['dɪndʒɪ] (compar -ier; superl -iest) adj schmuddelig.

**dining car** ['daɪnɪŋ-] n Speisewagen der.

**dining room** ['daɪnɪŋ-] n - 1. [in house] Esszimmer das - 2. [in hotel] Speisesaal der.

**dining table** ['daɪnɪŋ-] n Esstisch der.

**dinner** ['dɪnər] n - 1. [meal - in the evening] (warmes) Abendessen; [ - at noon] Mittagessen das - 2. [formal event] (Abend)essen das.

**dinner dance** n Abendgesellschaft die mit Tanz.

**dinner jacket** n [jacket] Smokingjacke die; [suit] Smoking der.

**dinner party** n Abendgesellschaft die (mit Essen).

**dinner service** n Tafelservice das.

**dinner table** n: the ~ die Tafel.

**dinnertime** ['dɪnətaɪm] n Essenszeit die.

**dinosaur** ['daɪnəsɔːr] n Dinosaurier der.

**dint** [dɪnt] n fml: by ~ of mittels (+ G).

**diocese** ['daɪəsɪs] n Diözese die.

**diode** ['daɪəʊd] n Diode die.

**dip** [dɪp] (*pt & pp* **-ped;** *cont* **-ping**) *n* - **1.** [in road, ground] Senke *die* - **2.** [sauce] Dip *der* - **3.** [swim]: **to go for a ~** (kurz) schwimmen gehen, ins Wasser gehen ◇ *vt* - **1.** [into liquid]: **to ~ sthg in (to) sthg** etw in etw (A) (ein)tauchen - **2.** *Br* [headlights] ab|blenden ◇ *vi* - **1.** [wing, road, ground] sich senken - **2.** [sun, temperature, price] sinken.

**Dip.** *Br abbr of* diploma.

**diphtheria** [dɪf'θɪərɪə] *n* Diphterie *die.*

**diphthong** ['dɪfθɒŋ] *n* LING Diphthong *der.*

**diploma** [dɪ'pləʊmə] (*pl* **-s**) *n* Diplom *das.*

**diplomacy** [dɪ'pləʊməsɪ] *n* Diplomatie *die.*

**diplomat** ['dɪpləmæt] *n* - **1.** [official] Diplomat *der*, -in *die* - **2.** [tactful person] diplomatischer Mensch.

**diplomatic** [ˌdɪplə'mætɪk] *adj* diplomatisch.

**diplomatic corps** *n* diplomatisches Korps.

**diplomatic immunity** *n* Immunität *die (für Mitglieder des diplomatischen Korps).*

**diplomatic relations** *npl* diplomatische Beziehungen *pl.*

**dipsomaniac** [ˌdɪpsə'meɪnɪæk] *n* Trunksüchtige *der, die.*

**dipstick** ['dɪpstɪk] *n* AUT Ölmessstab *der.*

**dipswitch** ['dɪpswɪtʃ] *n Br* AUT Abblendschalter *der.*

**dire** ['daɪəʳ] *adj* [serious - warning] dringend; [ - consequences] schwerwiegend; **to be in ~ need of sthg** etw dringend brauchen.

**direct** [dɪ'rekt] *adj* - **1.** [gen] direkt - **2.** [exact] genau ◇ *vt* - **1.** [aim]: **to ~ sthg at sb** [question, remark] etw an jn richten; **to ~ sb's attention to sthg** js Aufmerksamkeit auf etw (A) lenken; **the campaign is ~ed at teenagers** die Kampagne zielt auf Teenager ab - **2.** [person to place] den Weg erklären (+ D) - **3.** [manage, be in charge of] leiten - **4.** [TV programme] leiten; [film, play] Regie führen bei - **5.** [order]: **to ~ sb to do sthg** jn anweisen, etw zu tun ◇ *adv* direkt.

**direct action** *n* (U) Protestaktionen *pl.*

**direct current** *n* Gleichstrom *der.*

**direct debit** *n Br* Dauerauftrag *der.*

**direct dialling** *n* Durchwählen *das.*

**direct hit** *n* Volltreffer *der.*

**direction** [dɪ'rekʃn] *n* - **1.** [orientation] Richtung *die* - **2.** [of play, film] Regie *die*; [of TV programme] Leitung *die* - **3.** [control]: **under the ~ of** unter (+ D) der Leitung von.

➥ **directions** *npl* - **1.** [to place] Wegbeschreibung *die*; **to ask (sb) for ~** (jn) nach dem Weg fragen - **2.** [for use] Gebrauchsanweisung *die.*

**directive** [dɪ'rektɪv] *n* Direktive *die.*

**directly** [dɪ'rektlɪ] *adv* - **1.** [gen] direkt - **2.** [exactly] genau - **3.** [very soon] sofort.

**direct mail** *n* Postwurfsendung *die.*

**director** [dɪ'rektəʳ] *n* - **1.** [of company] Direktor *der*, -in *die* - **2.** [of film, play] Regisseur *der*, -in *die*; [of TV programme] Leiter *der*, -in *die.*

**directorate** [dɪ'rektərət] *n* Aufsichtsrat *der.*

**director-general** (*pl* **directors-general** OR **director-generals**) *n* Generaldirektor *der*, -in *die.*

**Director of Public Prosecutions** *n Br* Leiter der Anklagebehörde für schwere Straffälle.

**directorship** [dɪ'rektəʃɪp] *n* - **1.** [position] Direktorenposten *der* - **2.** [period] Amtszeit *die (eines Direktors).*

**directory** [dɪ'rektərɪ] (*pl* **-ies**) *n* - **1.** [book, list] Verzeichnis *das*; **(telephone) ~** Telefonbuch *das* - **2.** COMPUT Directory *das*, Inhaltsverzeichnis *das.*

**directory enquiries** *n Br* Fernsprechauskunft *die.*

**direct rule** *n* das Regieren einer Provinz durch eine Zentralregierung.

**direct selling** *n* Direktverkauf *der.*

**direct speech** *n* direkte Rede.

**direct taxation** *n* direkte Besteuerung.

**dire straits** *npl*: **in ~** in großen Nöten.

**dirge** [dɜːdʒ] *n* Klagegesang *der.*

**dirt** [dɜːt] *n* - **1.** [mud, dust] Schmutz *der* - **2.** [earth] Erde *die.*

**dirt cheap** *inf adj* spottbillig.

**dirt track** *n* Feldweg *der.*

**dirty** ['dɜːtɪ] (*compar* **-ier;** *superl* **-iest;** *pt & pp* **-ied**) *adj* - **1.** [not clean] schmutzig - **2.** [unfair] gemein; **~ trick** Gemeinheit *die*; **to play a ~ trick on sb** jm übel mitspielen - **3.** [smutty] schmutzig, unanständig; **~ joke** schmutziger Witz ◇ *vt* beschmutzen.

**disability** [ˌdɪsə'bɪlətɪ] (*pl* **-ies**) *n* Behinderung *die.*

**disable** [dɪs'eɪbl] *vt* [subj: illness, accident] eine Behinderung zur Folge haben bei.

**disabled** [dɪs'eɪbld] *adj* behindert ◇ *npl*: **the ~** die Behinderten *pl.*

**disabuse** [ˌdɪsə'bjuːz] *vt fml*: **to ~ sb (of sthg)** jn (von etw) befreien.

**disadvantage** [ˌdɪsəd'vɑːntɪdʒ] *n* Nachteil *der*; **to be at a ~** im Nachteil sein; **to be to one's ~** zu js Nachteil sein.

**disadvantaged** [ˌdɪsəd'vɑːntɪdʒd] *adj* benachteiligt.

**disadvantageous** [ˌdɪsædvɑːn'teɪdʒəs] *adj* nachteilig.

**disaffected** [ˌdɪsə'fektɪd] *adj* [party voters] illoyal; [voters in general] am politischen Geschehen desinteressiert.

**disagree** [ˌdɪsəˈɡriː] vi - **1.** [with another person] nicht übereinstimmen; [two people] sich nicht einig sein; **to ~ with sb** mit jm nicht übereinstimmen; **to ~ with sthg** mit etw nicht einverstanden sein - **2.** [statements, accounts] nicht übereinstimmen - **3.** [subj: food, drink]: **to ~ with sb** jm nicht bekommen.

**disagreeable** [ˌdɪsəˈɡriːəbl] adj - **1.** [smell, job] unangenehm - **2.** [person] unfreundlich.

**disagreement** [ˌdɪsəˈɡriːmənt] n - **1.** [of opinions] Uneinigkeit die; [of records] Diskrepanz die - **2.** [argument] Meinungsverschiedenheit die; **to be in ~ about sthg** [people] verschiedener Ansicht in Bezug auf etw (A) sein.

**disallow** [ˌdɪsəˈlaʊ] vt - **1.** fml [appeal, claim] zurücklweisen - **2.** [goal] nicht anlerkennen.

**disappear** [ˌdɪsəˈpɪəʳ] vi verschwinden.

**disappearance** [ˌdɪsəˈpɪərəns] n Verschwinden das.

**disappoint** [ˌdɪsəˈpɔɪnt] vt enttäuschen.

**disappointed** [ˌdɪsəˈpɔɪntɪd] adj: **~ (in OR with sthg)** (von etw) enttäuscht.

**disappointing** [ˌdɪsəˈpɔɪntɪŋ] adj enttäuschend.

**disappointment** [ˌdɪsəˈpɔɪntmənt] n Enttäuschung die.

**disapproval** [ˌdɪsəˈpruːvl] n Missfallen das.

**disapprove** [ˌdɪsəˈpruːv] vi: **to ~ of sthg** etw missbilligen; **to ~ of sb** etwas gegen jn haben.

**disapproving** [ˌdɪsəˈpruːvɪŋ] adj missbilligend.

**disarm** [dɪsˈɑːm] vt lit & fig entwaffnen <> vi ablrüsten.

**disarmament** [dɪsˈɑːməmənt] n Abrüstung die.

**disarming** [dɪsˈɑːmɪŋ] adj entwaffnend.

**disarray** [ˌdɪsəˈreɪ] n: **to be in ~** fml [clothes, hair, room] in Unordnung sein; [group] schlecht organisiert sein.

**disassociate** [ˌdɪsəˈsəʊʃieɪt] vt: **to ~ o.s. from sb/sthg** sich von jm/etw distanzieren

**disaster** [dɪˈzɑːstəʳ] n Katastrophe die; **to court ~** eine Katastrophe herauflbeschwören.

**disaster area** n [after natural disaster] Katastrophengebiet das.

**disastrous** [dɪˈzɑːstrəs] adj katastrophal.

**disastrously** [dɪˈzɑːstrəslɪ] adv katastrophal; **to fail ~** vollkommen versagen.

**disband** [dɪsˈbænd] vt aufllösen <> vi sich aufllösen.

**disbelief** [ˌdɪsbɪˈliːf] n: **in OR with ~** ungläubig.

**disbelieve** [ˌdɪsbɪˈliːv] vt [person] nicht glauben (+ D).

**disc** Br, **disk** Am [dɪsk] n - **1.** [shape] Scheibe die - **2.** MED Bandscheibe die - **3.** [record] Platte die.

**discard** [dɪˈskɑːd] vt weglwerfen.

**disc brake** n Scheibenbremse die.

**discern** [dɪˈsɜːn] vt - **1.** [see] wahrlnehmen - **2.** [detect] erkennen.

**discernible** [dɪˈsɜːnəbl] adj - **1.** [visible] wahrnehmbar - **2.** [detectable] erkennbar.

**discerning** [dɪˈsɜːnɪŋ] adj kritisch.

**discharge** [n ˈdɪstʃɑːdʒ, vt dɪsˈtʃɑːdʒ] n - **1.** [of patient, prisoner, soldier] Entlassung die - **2.** fml [fulfilment] Erfüllung die - **3.** [toxic emission] Ausstoß der - **4.** MED [from wound] Ausfluss der - **5.** [payment] Begleichung die <> vt - **1.** [patient, prisoner, soldier] entlassen - **2.** fml [fulfil] erfüllen - **3.** [emit] auslstoßen - **4.** [pay] begleichen.

**discharged bankrupt** [dɪsˈtʃɑːdzd-] n entlasteter Konkursschuldner.

**disciple** [dɪˈsaɪpl] n - **1.** RELIG Jünger der - **2.** fig [follower] Anhänger der, -in die.

**disciplinarian** [ˌdɪsɪplɪˈneərɪən] n Zuchtmeister der, -in die.

**disciplinary** [ˈdɪsɪplɪnərɪ] adj Disziplinar-, disziplinarisch; **to take ~ action against sb** disziplinarisch gegen jn vorlgehen.

**discipline** [ˈdɪsɪplɪn] n Disziplin die <> vt - **1.** [train] disziplinieren - **2.** [punish] bestrafen.

**disciplined** [ˈdɪsɪplɪnd] adj [person] diszipliniert.

**disc jockey** n Discjockey der.

**disclaim** [dɪsˈkleɪm] vt fml ablstreiten.

**disclaimer** [dɪsˈkleɪməʳ] n Dementi das.

**disclose** [dɪsˈkləʊz] vt enthüllen.

**disclosure** [dɪsˈkləʊʒəʳ] n Enthüllung die.

**disco** [ˈdɪskəʊ] (pl -s) n abbr of discotheque.

**discoloration** [dɪsˌkʌləˈreɪʃn] n Verfärbung die.

**discolour** Br, **discolor** Am [dɪsˈkʌləʳ] vt verfärben <> vi sich verfärben.

**discoloured** Br, **discolored** Am [dɪsˈkʌləd] adj verfärbt.

**discomfort** [dɪsˈkʌmfət] n - **1.** (U) [physical pain] Beschwerden pl; **to be in ~** Beschwerden haben - **2.** [anxiety, embarrassment] Unbehagen das - **3.** [uncomfortable condition] Beschwerlichkeit die.

**disconcert** [ˌdɪskənˈsɜːt] vt verunsichern.

**disconcerting** [ˌdɪskənˈsɜːtɪŋ] adj verunsichernd.

**disconnect** [ˌdɪskəˈnekt] vt - **1.** [detach] trennen - **2.** [remove plug of] den Stecker herauslziehen von; [from water/gas supply] von der

**D**

Wasserzufuhr/Gaszufuhr trennen; **to ~ sb's telephone** jm das Telefon ablstellen; **we've been ~ed** man hat uns das Telefon/das Gas/das Wasser/den Strom abgestellt **- 3.** [when talking]: **we've been ~ed** die Verbindung wurde unterbrochen.

**disconnected** [ˌdɪskə'nektɪd] *adj* **- 1.** [remarks, thoughts] zusammenhanglos **- 2.** [telephone, wire] nicht angeschlossen.

**disconsolate** [dɪs'kɒnsələt] *adj* untröstlich.

**discontent** [ˌdɪskən'tent] *n:* **~ (with sthg)** Unzufriedenheit *die* (mit etw).

**discontented** [ˌdɪskən'tentɪd] *adj:* **to be ~ (with sthg)** (mit etw) unzufrieden sein.

**discontentment** [ˌdɪskən'tentmənt] *n:* **~ (with sthg)** Unzufriedenheit *die* (mit etw).

**discontinue** [ˌdɪskən'tɪnjuː] *vt* [service, supply] einlstellen; [visits] beenden; [production] auslaufen lassen.

**discontinued line** [ˌdɪskən'tɪnjuːd-] *n* COMM ausgelaufene Serie.

**discord** ['dɪskɔːd] *n* **- 1.** *fml* [conflict] Uneinigkeit *die* **- 2.** MUS Disharmonie *die*.

**discordant** [dɪ'skɔːdənt] *adj* **- 1.** [conflicting] nicht miteinander harmonierend **- 2.** MUS disharmonisch.

**discotheque** ['dɪskəʊtek] *n* Diskothek *die*.

**discount** [*n* 'dɪskaʊnt, *vb, Br* dɪs'kaʊnt, *Am* 'dɪskaʊnt] *n* Rabatt *der* ◇ *vt* **- 1.** [disregard] verwerfen **- 2.** COMM [product] zu einem geringeren Preis anlbieten; [price] senken.

**discount house** *n* **- 1.** FIN Diskontbank *die* **- 2.** COMM [store] Discountgeschäft *das*.

**discount rate** *n* Rabattrate *die*.

**discount store** *n* COMM Discountgeschäft *das*.

**discourage** [dɪs'kʌrɪdʒ] *vt* **- 1.** [dishearten] entmutigen **- 2.** [dissuade]: **to ~ sb from doing sthg** jn davon ablbringen, etw zu tun.

**discouraging** [dɪ'skʌrɪdʒɪŋ] *adj* entmutigend.

**discourse** ['dɪskɔːs] *n:* **~ (on sthg)** Diskurs *der* (über etw (A)).

**discourteous** [dɪs'kɜːtjəs] *adj fml* unhöflich.

**discourtesy** [dɪs'kɜːtɪsɪ] *n* Unhöflichkeit *die*.

**discover** [dɪ'skʌvəʳ] *vt* **- 1.** [find] entdecken; [cause of sthg] herauslfinden **- 2.** [realize] festlstellen.

**discoverer** [dɪ'skʌvərəʳ] *n* Entdecker *der*, -in *die*.

**discovery** [dɪ'skʌvərɪ] (*pl* -ies) *n* Entdeckung *die*.

**discredit** [dɪs'kredɪt] *n* [shame] Misskredit *der* ◇ *vt* diskreditieren.

**discredited** [dɪs'kredɪtɪd] *adj* diskreditiert.

**discreet** [dɪ'skriːt] *adj* diskret.

**discreetly** [dɪ'skriːtlɪ] *adv* diskret; [coloured, dressed] dezent.

**discrepancy** [dɪ'skrepənsɪ] (*pl* -ies) *n:* **~ (in/between)** Diskrepanz *die* (zwischen (+ D)).

**discrete** [dɪs'kriːt] *adj fml* verschieden.

**discretion** [dɪ'skreʃn] *n* **- 1.** [tact] Diskretion *die* **- 2.** [judgment]: **use your own ~** handeln Sie nach eigenem Ermessen; **at the ~ of** nach Ermessen (+ G).

**discretionary** [dɪ'skreʃənrɪ] *adj* Ermessens-; **to be ~** Ermessenssache sein; **~ powers** Ermessensspielraum *der*.

**discriminate** [dɪ'skrɪmɪneɪt] *vi* **- 1.** [distinguish]: **to ~ (between)** unterscheiden (zwischen (+ D)) **- 2.** [treat unfairly]: **to ~ against sb** jn diskriminieren.

**discriminating** [dɪ'skrɪmɪneɪtɪŋ] *adj* [person, eye, audience] kritisch; [taste] fein.

**discrimination** [dɪˌskrɪmɪ'neɪʃn] *n* **- 1.** [prejudice] Diskriminierung *die* **- 2.** [good judgment] Urteilsvermögen *das*.

**discus** ['dɪskəs] (*pl* -es) *n* Diskus *der*.

**discuss** [dɪ'skʌs] *vt* besprechen; [in political, academic context] diskutieren; **to ~ sthg with sb** etw mit jm besprechen.

**discussion** [dɪ'skʌʃn] *n* **- 1.** (U) [act of discussing] Besprechen *das;* [in political, academic context] Diskussion *die;* **to be under ~** zur Diskussion stehen **- 2.** [talk] Gespräch *das;* [in political, academic context] Diskussion *die*.

**disdain** [dɪs'deɪn] *fml n:* **~ (for sb/sthg)** Verachtung *die* (für jn/etw) ◇ *vt* verachten ◇ *vi:* **to ~ to do sthg** es für unter seiner Würde halten, etw zu tun.

**disdainful** [dɪs'deɪnfʊl] *adj* verächtlich.

**disease** [dɪ'ziːz] *n lit* & *fig* Krankheit *die*.

**diseased** [dɪ'ziːzd] *adj* **- 1.** [plant] befallen; [body] krank **- 2.** *fig* [mind] krank.

**disembark** [ˌdɪsɪm'bɑːk] *vi* von Bord gehen.

**disembarkation** [ˌdɪsembɑː'keɪʃn] *n* (U) Landung *die*.

**disembodied** [ˌdɪsɪm'bɒdɪd] *adj* körperlos; [voice] geisterhaft.

**disembowel** [ˌdɪsɪm'baʊəl] (*Br* pt & pp **-led;** cont **-ling,** *Am* pt & pp **-ed;** cont **-ing**) *vt* auslweiden; [person] die Eingeweide herauslnehmen (+ D).

**disenchanted** [ˌdɪsɪn'tʃɑːntɪd] *adj:* **~ (with sthg)** (von etw) ernüchtert.

**disenchantment** [ˌdɪsɪn'tʃɑːntmənt] *n* Ernüchterung *die*.

**disenfranchise** [ˌdɪsɪn'fræntʃaɪz] *vt* POL: **to ~ sb** jm das Wahlrecht verwehren.

**disengage** [ˌdɪsɪn'geɪdʒ] *vt* **- 1.** [release]: **to ~ o.s./sthg (from sthg)** sich/etw (von etw) loslmachen **- 2.** TECH [gears, mechanism] auslrücken.

**disentangle** [ˌdɪsɪn'tæŋɡl] *vt* entwirren; **to ~ sthg from sthg** etw von etw lösen; **to ~ o.s. from sthg** sich aus etw befreien.

**disfavour** *Br*, **disfavor** *Am* [dɪs'feɪvə'] *n (U)*: **to look on sthg with ~** etw mit Missfallen betrachten; **to fall into ~ with sb** bei jm in Ungnade fallen.

**disfigure** [dɪs'fɪɡə'] *vt* verunstalten.

**disgorge** [dɪs'ɡɔːdʒ] *vt* auslspeien.

**disgrace** [dɪs'ɡreɪs] *n* Schande *die;* **to be in ~** in Ungnade gefallen sein ◇ *vt:* **to ~ sb** jm Schande machen; **to ~ o.s.** sich blamieren.

**disgraceful** [dɪs'ɡreɪsfʊl] *adj* skandalös.

**disgruntled** [dɪs'ɡrʌntld] *adj* verstimmt.

**disguise** [dɪs'ɡaɪz] *n* Verkleidung *die;* **in ~** verkleidet ◇ *vt* - **1.** [dress up] verkleiden; **to ~ o.s. as sb/sthg** sich als jd/etw verkleiden - **2.** [voice, handwriting] verstellen - **3.** [disappointment, surprise] verbergen; [fact] verschleiern; [taste of sthg] überdecken.

**disgust** [dɪs'ɡʌst] *n:* **~ (at sthg)** Abscheu *der* (vor etw *(D)*); **in ~** empört ◇ *vt* anlekeln.

**disgusting** [dɪs'ɡʌstɪŋ] *adj* ekelhaft.

**dish** [dɪʃ] *n* - **1.** [bowl] Schüssel *die;* [shallow] Schale *die* - **2.** *Am* [plate] Teller *der* - **3.** [food] Gericht *das.*
- **dishes** *npl* Geschirr *das;* **to do** OR **wash the ~es** Geschirr spülen OR ablwaschen.
- **dish out** *vt sep inf* aus[teilen.
- **dish up** *vt sep inf* [food] auf [tun.

**dish aerial** *Br*, **dish antenna** *Am n* Parabolantenne *die*, Satellitenschüssel *die.*

**disharmony** [ˌdɪs'hɑːmənɪ] *n* Disharmonie *die.*

**dishcloth** ['dɪʃklɒθ] *n* Spültuch *das.*

**disheartened** [dɪs'hɑːtnd] *adj* entmutigt.

**disheartening** [dɪs'hɑːtnɪŋ] *adj* entmutigend.

**dishevelled** *Br*, **disheveled** *Am* [dɪ'ʃevəld] *adj* [hair] zerzaust; [person] unordentlich.

**dishonest** [dɪs'ɒnɪst] *adj* - **1.** [person] unehrlich; [trader] unredlich - **2.** [action] unredlich, unlauter.

**dishonesty** [dɪs'ɒnɪstɪ] *n* [of person] Unehrlichkeit *die;* [of trader, action] Unredlichkeit *die.*

**dishonor** *n* & *vt Am* = dishonour.

**dishonorable** *adj Am* = dishonourable.

**dishonour** *Br*, **dishonor** *Am* [dɪs'ɒnə'] *n* Unehre *die* ◇ *vt* entehren.

**dishonourable** *Br*, **dishonorable** *Am* [dɪs'ɒnərəbl] *adj* unehrenhaft.

**dish soap** *n Am* Spülmittel *das.*

**dish towel** *n Am* Geschirrtuch *das.*

**dishwasher** ['dɪʃˌwɒʃə'] *n* [machine] Geschirrspülmaschine *die.*

**dishy** ['dɪʃɪ] (*compar* -ier; *superl* -iest) *adj Br inf* [attractive] aufregend.

**disillusioned** [ˌdɪsɪ'luːʒnd] *adj* desillusioniert; **~ with sb/sthg** von jm/etw enttäuscht.

**disillusionment** [ˌdɪsɪ'luːʒnmənt] *n (U):* **~ (with sb/sthg)** Desillusionierung *die* (in Bezug auf jn/etw).

**disincentive** [ˌdɪsɪn'sentɪv] *n* Abschreckungsmittel *das.*

**disinclined** [ˌdɪsɪn'klaɪnd] *adj:* **to be ~ to do sthg** abgeneigt sein, etw zu tun.

**disinfect** [ˌdɪsɪn'fekt] *vt* desinfizieren.

**disinfectant** [ˌdɪsɪn'fektənt] *n* Desinfektionsmittel *das.*

**disinformation** [ˌdɪsɪnfə'meɪʃn] *n (U)* Desinformation *die.*

**disingenuous** [ˌdɪsɪn'dʒenjʊəs] *adj* unaufrichtig.

**disinherit** [ˌdɪsɪn'herɪt] *vt* enterben.

**disintegrate** [dɪs'ɪntɪɡreɪt] *vi* - **1.** [object] zerfallen - **2.** *fig* [project] sich auf[lösen; [marriage] auseinander gehen.

**disintegration** [dɪsˌɪntɪ'ɡreɪʃn] *n* [of object] Zerfall *der;* [of project] Auflösung *die;* [of marriage] Auseinandergehen *das.*

**disinterested** [ˌdɪs'ɪntrəstɪd] *adj* - **1.** [objective] unparteiisch - **2.** *inf* [uninterested]: **~ (in sb/sthg)** nicht interessiert (an jm/etw).

**disjointed** [dɪs'dʒɔɪntɪd] *adj* zusammenhanglos.

**disk** [dɪsk] *n* - **1.** COMPUT: (floppy) **~** Diskette *die;* (hard) **~** Festplatte *die* - **2.** *Am* = disc.

**disk drive** *Br*, **diskette drive** *Am n* COMPUT [for floppy disk] Diskettenlaufwerk *das.*

**diskette** [dɪs'ket] *n* COMPUT Diskette *die.*

**diskette drive** *n Am* = disk drive.

**disk operating system** *n* COMPUT Betriebssystem *das.*

**dislike** [dɪs'laɪk] *n:* **~ (of)** Abneigung *die* (gegen); **to take a ~ to sb/sthg** eine Abneigung gegen jn/etw empfinden ◇ *vt* nicht mögen.

**dislocate** ['dɪsləkeɪt] *vt* - **1.** MED auslrenken - **2.** [disrupt] durcheinander bringen.

**dislodge** [dɪs'lɒdʒ] *vt:* **to ~ sb/sthg (from)** jn/etw entfernen (von OR aus).

**disloyal** [ˌdɪs'lɔɪəl] *adj:* **~ (to sb)** illoyal (gegenüber jm).

**dismal** ['dɪzml] *adj* - **1.** [gloomy, depressing] trist - **2.** [attempt, failure] kläglich.

**dismantle** [dɪs'mæntl] *vt* auseinander nehmen; [power plant, nuclear weapons] demontieren.

**dismay** [dɪs'meɪ] *n* Bestürzung *die;* **to sb's ~** zu js Bestürzung ◇ *vt* bestürzen.

**dismember** [dɪs'membə'] *vt* zerstückeln.

**dismiss** [dɪs'mɪs] *vt* - **1.** [employee, class, troops]: **to ~ sb (from sthg)** jn (aus etw) entlassen - **2.** [refuse to take seriously] abltun - **3.** LAW [case] ablweisen.

**dismissal** [dɪs'mɪsl] *n* - **1.** [from job] Entlassung *die* - **2.** [refusal to take seriously] Abtun *das* - **3.** LAW Abweisung *die*.

**dismissive** [dɪs'mɪsɪv] *adj* geringschätzig; **to be ~ of sb/sthg** jn/etw gering achten.

**dismount** [ˌdɪs'maʊnt] *vi*: **to ~ (from sthg)** ablsteigen (von etw).

**disobedience** [ˌdɪsə'biːdjəns] *n* Ungehorsam *der*.

**disobedient** [ˌdɪsə'biːdjənt] *adj* ungehorsam.

**disobey** [ˌdɪsə'beɪ] *vt* [rule] übertreten; [person] nicht gehorchen (+ D) <> *vi* [by disobeying rule] eine Regel/Regeln übertreten; [by disobeying person] nicht gehorchen.

**disorder** [dɪs'ɔːdə'] *n* - **1.** [disarray]: **in ~** in Unordnung - **2.** [rioting] Unruhen *pl* - **3.** MED Funktionsstörung *die*.

**disordered** [dɪs'ɔːdəd] *adj* - **1.** [in disarray] unordentlich - **2.** MED: **mentally ~** geistig gestört.

**disorderly** [dɪs'ɔːdəlɪ] *adj* - **1.** [untidy] unordentlich - **2.** [unruly - behaviour] ungehörig.

**disorderly conduct** *n* LAW ungebührliches Verhalten.

**disorganized, -ised** [dɪs'ɔːgənaɪzd] *adj* [person] unorganisiert; [system] unstrukturiert.

**disorientated** *Br* [dɪs'ɔːrɪənteɪtɪd], **disoriented** *Am* [dɪs'ɔːrɪəntɪd] *adj* desorientiert.

**disown** [dɪs'əʊn] *vt* [son, daughter] verstoßen; [friend] verleugnen; **the screenwriter ~ed the film** der Drehbuchautor distanzierte sich von dem Film.

**disparage** [dɪ'spærɪdʒ] *vt* herabsetzen.

**disparaging** [dɪ'spærɪdʒɪŋ] *adj* geringschätzig.

**disparate** ['dɪspərət] *adj fml* disparat.

**disparity** [dɪ'spærətɪ] (*pl* **-ies**) *n:* **~ (between/in)** Ungleichheit *die* (zwischen (+ D)).

**dispassionate** [dɪ'spæʃnət] *adj* objektiv.

**dispatch** [dɪ'spætʃ] *n* Bericht *der* <> *vt* [person, troops, submarine] entsenden; [message, letter, parcel] senden.

**dispatch box** *n Br* POL: **to be at the ~** als Vertreter des Kabinetts/Schattenkabinetts im Unterhaus eine Rede halten.

**dispatch rider** *n* Kurier *der;* MIL Meldefahrer *der*.

**dispel** [dɪ'spel] (*pt* & *pp* **-led;** *cont* **-ling**) *vt* [doubts, fears] zerstreuen; [illusions] nehmen.

**dispensable** [dɪ'spensəbl] *adj* entbehrlich.

**dispensary** [dɪ'spensərɪ] (*pl* **-ies**) *n* Stelle in einem Krankenhaus, wo Medizin zubereitet und ausgehändigt wird.

**dispensation** [ˌdɪspen'seɪʃn] *n* Dispens *der*.

**dispense** [dɪ'spens] *vt* - **1.** [advice] erteilen; **to ~ justice** Recht sprechen - **2.** [drugs, medicine] ablgeben.

◆ **dispense with** *vt fus* - **1.** [do without] verzichten auf (+ A) - **2.** [make unnecessary] unnötig machen.

**dispenser** [dɪ'spensə'] *n* [for drinks, cash] Automat *der;* [for soap] Spender *der*.

**dispensing chemist** *Br,* **dispensing pharmacist** *Am* [dɪ'spensɪŋ-] *n* Apotheker *der,* -in *die*.

**dispersal** [dɪ'spɜːsl] *n* - **1.** [of crowd] Zerstreuung *die* - **2.** [of substance, oil slick] Auflösung *die;* [of gas] Verbreitung *die*.

**disperse** [dɪ'spɜːs] *vt* - **1.** [crowd] zerstreuen - **2.** [knowledge, news] verbreiten <> *vi* [crowd] sich zerstreuen.

**dispirited** [dɪ'spɪrɪtɪd] *adj* entmutigt, niedergeschlagen.

**dispiriting** [dɪ'spɪrɪtɪŋ] *adj* entmutigend.

**displace** [dɪs'pleɪs] *vt* - **1.** [supplant] abllösen - **2.** CHEM & PHYS verdrängen.

**displaced person** [dɪs'pleɪst-] *n* [expelled] (Zwangs)vertriebene *der,* (Zwangs)vertriebene *die;* [fleeing] Flüchtling *der*.

**displacement** [dɪs'pleɪsmənt] *n (U)* - **1.** [of people - expulsion] Vertreibung *die;* [ - flight] Flucht *die* - **2.** CHEM & PHYS Verdrängung *die*.

**display** [dɪ'spleɪ] *n* - **1.** [of goods, merchandise] Auslage *die;* [in museum] Ausstellung *die;* **to be on ~** ausgestellt werden - **2.**: **it was a fine ~ of courage/skill from him** er zeigte viel Mut/Geschick - **3.** [performance] Vorführung *die* - **4.** COMPUT Display *das* <> *vt* - **1.** [goods, merchandise] auslstellen - **2.** [courage, skill, self-control] zeigen.

**displease** [dɪs'pliːz] *vt* verärgern; **to be ~d with sthg** mit etw unzufrieden sein.

**displeasure** [dɪs'pleʒə'] *n* Missfallen *das*.

**disposable** [dɪ'spəʊzəbl] *adj* - **1.** [to be thrown away after use] Wegwerf-; **~ nappy** *Br,* **~ diaper** *Am* Wegwerfwindel *die* - **2.** [available] verfügbar.

**disposal** [dɪ'spəʊzl] *n (U)* - **1.** [removal] Beseitigung *die* - **2.** [availability]: **to be at sb's ~** jm zur Verfügung stehen; **to put sthg at sb's ~** jm etw zur Verfügung stellen.

**disposed** [dɪ'spəʊzd] *adj* - **1.** [willing]: **to be ~ to do sthg** geneigt sein, etw zu tun - **2.** [friendly]: **to be well ~ to** OR **towards sb** jm wohlwollend gegenüberstehen.

**dispose** [dɪ'spəʊz] ◆ **dispose of** *vt fus* [rubbish, problem] beseitigen.

**disposition** [ˌdɪspə'zɪʃn] *n* - **1.** [temperament]

Naturell *das;* **he has a cheerful ~** er ist ein fröhlicher Mensch **- 2.** [willingness]: **~ to do sth** Bereitschaft *die,* etw zu tun.

**dispossess** [ˌdɪspə'zes] *vt fml:* **to ~ sb** jn enteignen; **she was ~ed of her land** ihr Land wurde enteignet.

**disproportion** [ˌdɪsprə'pɔːʃn] *n* Missverhältnis *das.*

**disproportionate** [ˌdɪsprə'pɔːʃnət] *adj:* **to be ~ to sthg** in keinem Verhältnis zu etw stehen.

**disprove** [ˌdɪs'pruːv] *vt* widerlegen.

**dispute** [dɪ'spjuːt] *n* **- 1.** [quarrel] Streit *der* **- 2.** *(U)* [disagreement] Meinungsverschiedenheit *die;* **to be in ~** [matter] umstritten sein; **they are in ~** zwischen ihnen herrschen Unstimmigkeiten **- 3.** IND Auseinandersetzung *die* <> *vt* **- 1.** [question, challenge] bestreiten **- 2.** [fight for - championship] jm streitig machen; [- territory] beanspruchen; **to ~ ownership of sthg** sich über den Besitz von etw streiten.

**disqualification** [dɪsˌkwɒlɪfɪ'keɪʃn] *n:* [from sporting event] Disqualifizierung *die;* [from standing for election] Ausschluss *der;* **~ from driving** Führerscheinentzug *der.*

**disqualify** [ˌdɪs'kwɒlɪfaɪ] (*pt* & *pp* **-ied**) *vt* **- 1.** [subj: illness, criminal record]: **to ~ sb from doing sthg** jn dafür ungeeignet machen, etw zu tun **- 2.** SPORT disqualifizieren **- 3.** Br: **to ~ sb from driving** jm den Führerschein entziehen.

**disquiet** [dɪs'kwaɪət] *n* Unruhe *die.*

**disregard** [ˌdɪsrɪ'gɑːd] *n:* **~ (for sthg)** Geringschätzung *die* (für etw) <> *vt* ignorieren.

**disrepair** [ˌdɪsrɪ'peəʳ] *n* Baufälligkeit *die;* **to fall into ~** verfallen.

**disreputable** [dɪs'repjʊtəbl] *adj* in einem schlechten Ruf stehend.

**disrepute** [ˌdɪsrɪ'pjuːt] *n:* **to bring sthg into ~** etw in Verruf bringen; **to fall into ~** in Verruf geraten.

**disrespectful** [ˌdɪsrɪ'spektfʊl] *adj* respektlos.

**disrupt** [dɪs'rʌpt] *vt* [meeting, lesson] stören; [transport system] behindern.

**disruption** [dɪs'rʌpʃn] *n* Störung *die.*

**disruptive** [dɪs'rʌptɪv] *adj* störend.

**dissatisfaction** ['dɪsˌsætɪs'fækʃn] *n* Unzufriedenheit *die.*

**dissatisfied** [ˌdɪs'sætɪsfaɪd] *adj:* **~ (with sthg)** unzufrieden (mit etw).

**dissect** [dɪ'sekt] *vt* **- 1.** MED [animal] sezieren; [plant] präparieren **- 2.** *fig* [poem, novel, idea, argument] analysieren.

**dissection** [dɪ'sekʃn] *n* **- 1.** MED [of animal] Sektion *die;* [of plant] Präparation *die* **- 2.** *fig* [of poem, novel, idea, argument] Analyse *die.*

**disseminate** [dɪ'semɪneɪt] *vt* verbreiten.

**dissemination** [dɪˌsemɪ'neɪʃn] *n (U)* Verbreitung *die.*

**dissension** [dɪ'senʃn] *n (U)* Differenz *die.*

**dissent** [dɪ'sent] *n (U)* Nichtübereinstimmung *die* <> *vi:* **to ~ from sthg** in Bezug auf etw anderer Meinung sein.

**dissenter** [dɪ'sentəʳ] *n* Abweichler *der,* -in *die.*

**dissenting** [dɪ'sentɪŋ] *adj:* **hers was the only ~ voice** sie war die Einzige, die Kritik übte.

**dissertation** [ˌdɪsə'teɪʃn] *n* [for degree] schriftliche Abschlussarbeit; [for PhD] Dissertation *die.*

**disservice** [ˌdɪs'sɜːvɪs] *n:* **to do sb a ~** jm einen schlechten Dienst erweisen.

**dissident** ['dɪsɪdənt] *n* Regimekritiker *der,* -in *die.*

**dissimilar** [ˌdɪ'sɪmɪləʳ] *adj:* **~ (to)** verschieden (von); **to be not ~ to sthg** etw *(D)* nicht unähnlich sein.

**dissipate** ['dɪsɪpeɪt] *vt* **- 1.** [heat, oil spill] beseitigen **- 2.** [efforts, money] verschwenden, vergeuden <> *vi* [crowd] sich zerstreuen; [heat] verschwinden.

**dissipated** ['dɪsɪpeɪtɪd] *adj* [life] ausschweifend; [person] verlebt.

**dissociate** [dɪ'səʊʃɪeɪt] *vt:* **to ~ sb/sthg from sthg** jn/etw von etw unabhängig betrachten; **to ~ o.s. from sthg** sich von etw distanzieren.

**dissolute** ['dɪsəluːt] *adj* [way of life] ausschweifend; [person, behaviour] zügellos.

**dissolution** [ˌdɪsə'luːʃn] *n (U)* [of organization, relationship] Auflösung *die.*

**dissolve** [dɪ'zɒlv] *vt* auflösen <> *vi* **- 1.** [substance] sich auflösen **- 2.** *fig* [disappear] schwinden.

➤ **dissolve in(to)** *vt fus:* **to ~ in(to) tears/laughter** in Weinen/Gelächter ausbrechen.

**dissuade** [dɪ'sweɪd] *vt:* **to ~ sb from doing sthg** jn davon abbringen, etw zu tun.

**distance** ['dɪstəns] *n* **- 1.** [between two places] Entfernung *die;* [distance covered] Strecke *die* **- 2.** [distant point]: **at a ~ of five metres** in 5 Metern Entfernung; **to follow sb at a ~** jm in einiger Entfernung folgen; **from a ~** aus der Entfernung; **in the ~** in der Ferne <> *vt:* **to ~ o.s. from sb/sthg** sich von jm/etw distanzieren.

**distant** ['dɪstənt] *adj* **- 1.** [place] weit entfernt; **~ from** weit entfernt von **- 2.** [future] fern; **in the not too ~ future** in nicht allzu ferner Zukunft; **it's all in the ~ past** das ist alles schon lange her - **3.** [relative] entfernt - **4.** [manner] kühl, distanziert.

**distaste** [dɪsˈteɪst] n (U): ~ **(for sthg)** Widerwille der (gegen etw).

**distasteful** [dɪsˈteɪstfʊl] adj sehr unangenehm.

**Dist. Atty** abbr of district attorney.

**distemper** [dɪˈstempəʳ] n - **1.** [paint] Temperafarbe die - **2.** [disease] Staupe die.

**distended** [dɪˈstendɪd] adj aufgebläht.

**distil** Br (pt & pp -**led**; cont -**ling**), **distill** Am [dɪˈstɪl] vt - **1.** [water] destillieren; [whisky] brennen - **2.** fig [information] herausldestillieren.

**distiller** [dɪˈstɪləʳ] n Brenner der, -in die.

**distillery** [dɪˈstɪlərɪ] (pl -**ies**) n Brennerei die.

**distinct** [dɪˈstɪŋkt] adj - **1.** [different]: ~ **(from)** verschieden (von); **as ~ from** im Unterschied zu - **2.** [clear] deutlich, klar.

**distinction** [dɪˈstɪŋkʃn] n - **1.** [difference] Unterschied der; **to draw** OR **make a ~ between** einen Unterschied machen zwischen (+ D) - **2.** (U) [excellence] Rang der - **3.** [in exam result] Auszeichnung die; **she got a ~ in French** sie hat das Examen in Französisch mit Auszeichnung bestanden.

**distinctive** [dɪˈstɪŋktɪv] adj unverkennbar.

**distinctly** [dɪˈstɪŋktlɪ] adv - **1.** [see, speak] deutlich; [remember] genau - **2.** [very - rude, drunk] ausgesprochen; [ - improve] entscheidend.

**distinguish** [dɪˈstɪŋgwɪʃ] vt - **1.** [tell apart]: **to ~ sthg from sthg** etw von etw unterscheiden - **2.** [discern, perceive] erkennen - **3.** [make different] unterscheiden; **to ~ o.s.** sich auslzeichnen ◇ vi: **to ~ between** unterscheiden zwischen (+ D).

**distinguished** [dɪˈstɪŋgwɪʃt] adj [visitor, politician] bedeutend; [career] glänzend.

**distinguishing** [dɪˈstɪŋgwɪʃɪŋ] adj charakteristisch.

**distort** [dɪˈstɔːt] vt - **1.** [shape, face, sound] verzerren - **2.** [truth, facts] verzerrt darlstellen.

**distorted** [dɪˈstɔːtɪd] adj verzerrt.

**distortion** [dɪˈstɔːʃn] n - **1.** [of shape, face, sound] Verzerrung die - **2.** [of truth, facts] verzerrte Darstellung.

**distract** [dɪˈstrækt] vt: **to ~ sb (from sthg)** jn (von etw) ablenken.

**distracted** [dɪˈstræktɪd] adj geistesabwesend.

**distraction** [dɪˈstrækʃn] n - **1.** [interruption, diversion] Ablenkung die - **2.** [madness]: **to drive sb to ~** jn zum Wahnsinn treiben - **3.** [absentmindedness] Geistesabwesenheit die.

**distraught** [dɪˈstrɔːt] adj verzweifelt.

**distress** [dɪˈstres] n (U) - **1.** [suffering - mental]

Kummer der; [ - physical] Leiden das; **to be in ~** leiden - **2.** [danger]: **in ~** in Not ◇ vt [upset] Kummer machen (+ D).

**distressed** [dɪˈstrest] adj bestürzt.

**distressing** [dɪˈstresɪŋ] adj bestürzend.

**distress signal** n Notsignal das.

**distribute** [dɪˈstrɪbjuːt] vt - **1.** [gen] verteilen; [prizes] verleihen - **2.** COMM [goods] vertreiben.

**distribution** [ˌdɪstrɪˈbjuːʃn] n - **1.** [gen] Verteilung die; [of prizes] Verleihung die - **2.** COMM [of goods] Vertrieb der.

**distributor** [dɪˈstrɪbjʊtəʳ] n COMM & AUT Verteiler der.

**district** [ˈdɪstrɪkt] n - **1.** [of country] Gebiet das; [of city] Stadtteil der - **2.** [administrative area] Bezirk der.

**district attorney** n Am LAW Bezirksstaatsanwalt der, -anwältin die.

**district council** n Br ADMIN Bezirksverwaltung die.

**district nurse** n Br Gemeindeschwester die.

**distrust** [dɪsˈtrʌst] n Misstrauen das ◇ vt misstrauen (+ D).

**distrustful** [dɪsˈtrʌstfʊl] adj misstrauisch.

**disturb** [dɪˈstɜːb] vt - **1.** [interrupt] stören - **2.** [upset, worry] beunruhigen - **3.** [alter - surface of water] bewegen; [ - papers] durcheinander bringen.

**disturbance** [dɪˈstɜːbəns] n - **1.** [fight] Krawall der - **2.** (U) [interruption, disruption] Störung die; ~ **of the peace** LAW öffentliche Ruhestörung.

**disturbed** [dɪˈstɜːbd] adj - **1.** [upset, ill] gestört - **2.** [worried] beunruhigt.

**disturbing** [dɪˈstɜːbɪŋ] adj beunruhigend.

**disunity** [ˌdɪsˈjuːnətɪ] n Uneinigkeit die.

**disuse** [ˌdɪsˈjuːs] n: **to fall into ~** [regulation] außer Gebrauch kommen; [building, mine] nicht mehr genutzt werden.

**disused** [ˌdɪsˈjuːzd] adj stillgelegt.

**ditch** [dɪtʃ] n Graben der ◇ vt inf - **1.** [boyfriend, girlfriend] abservieren - **2.** [plan] fallen lassen - **3.** [old car] (einfach) zurücklassen.

**dither** [ˈdɪðəʳ] vi zaudern.

**ditto** [ˈdɪtəʊ] adv dito.

**diuretic** [ˌdaɪjʊˈretɪk] n harntreibendes Mittel.

**diva** [ˈdiːvə] (pl -**s**) n Diva die.

**divan** [dɪˈvæn] n Diwan der.

**divan bed** n Liege die.

**dive** [daɪv] (Br pt & pp -**d**, Am pt & pp -**d** OR **dove**) vi - **1.** [goalkeeper] hechten; [bird, aircraft] einen Sturzflug machen; [submarine] abltauchen - **2.** [as sport - from board] einen Kopfsprung machen [ - underwater] tauchen; **he ~d**

into the water er sprang kopfüber ins Wasser - **3.** [rush] stürzen - **4.** [into pocket, bag]: **to ~ into sthg** in etw *(D)* wühlen ◇ n - **1.** [of swimmer] Kopfsprung *der;* **to go into a ~** [bird, aircraft] einen Sturzflug machen; [submarine] abtauchen; **to make a ~ for the ball** nach dem Ball hechten - **2.** *inf pej* [bar, restaurant] Kaschemme *die.*

**dive-bomb** *vt* im Sturzflug bombardieren.

**diver** ['daɪvə'] *n* [from board] Springer *der,* -in *die;* [underwater] Taucher *der,* -in *die.*

**diverge** [daɪ'vɜːdʒ] *vi* - **1.** [opinions, interests] voneinander abweichen; **to ~ from sthg** von etw abweichen - **2.** [roads, paths] sich trennen.

**divergence** [daɪ'vɜːdʒəns] *n* Auseinandergehen *das.*

**divergent** [daɪ'vɜːdʒənt] *adj* auseinander gehend.

**diverse** [daɪ'vɜːs] *adj* [opinions, people] unterschiedlich; [topics, nationalities] verschiedenartig.

**diversification** [daɪ‚vɜːsɪfɪ'keɪʃn] *n* Diversifikation *die.*

**diversify** [daɪ'vɜːsɪfaɪ] (*pt & pp* -**ied**) *vt & vi* diversifizieren.

**diversion** [daɪ'vɜːʃn] *n* - **1.** [distraction] Ablenkung *die* - **2.** [of traffic, river] Umleitung *die* - **3.** [of funds] Umverteilung *die.*

**diversionary** [daɪ'vɜːʃnrɪ] *adj:* **~ tactic** Ablenkungstaktik *die.*

**diversity** [daɪ'vɜːsətɪ] *n* Mannigfaltigkeit *die.*

**divert** [daɪ'vɜːt] *vt* - **1.** [traffic, river] umlleiten - **2.** [funds] umlverteilen - **3.** [person, attention] ablenken.

**divest** [daɪ'vest] *vt fml:* **to ~ sb of sthg** jn einer Sache *(G)* berauben; **to ~ o.s. of sthg** sich einer Sache *(G)* entledigen.

**divide** [dɪ'vaɪd] *vt* - **1.** [form barrier between] trennen - **2.** [share out, distribute] auflteilen; **to ~ sthg between** OR **among** etw auflteilen zwischen (+ *D*) OR unter (+ *D*) - **3.** [split up]: **to ~ sthg into** etw auflteilen in (+ *A*) - **4.** MATH: **to ~ 9 by 3, to ~ 3 into 9** 9 durch 3 teilen OR dividieren - **5.** [disunite] spalten ◇ *vi* - **1.** [split into two] sich teilen - **2.** [disagree]: **to ~ over sthg** geteilter Meinung über etw *(A)* sein ◇ *n* [difference] Kluft *die.*

◆ **divide up** *vt sep* - **1.** [split up] teilen - **2.** [share out, distribute] auflteilen.

**divided** [dɪ'vaɪdɪd] *adj* geteilt.

**dividend** ['dɪvɪdend] *n* Dividende *die;* **to pay ~s** sich bezahlt machen.

**dividers** [dɪ'vaɪdəz] *npl* Zirkel *der.*

**dividing line** [dɪ'vaɪdɪŋ-] *n* Trennungslinie *die.*

**divine** [dɪ'vaɪn] *adj lit & fig* göttlich ◇ *vt*

- **1.** [truth, meaning] erraten; [future] weissagen - **2.** [water] auf lspüren.

**diving** ['daɪvɪŋ] *n* [from board] Springen *das;* [underwater] Tauchen *das.*

**divingboard** ['daɪvɪŋbɔːd] *n* Sprungbrett *das.*

**diving suit** *n* Taucheranzug *der.*

**divinity** [dɪ'vɪnətɪ] (*pl* -**ies**) *n* - **1.** [godliness] Göttlichkeit *die* - **2.** [study] Theologie *die* - **3.** [god, goddess] Gottheit *die.*

**divisible** [dɪ'vɪzəbl] *adj* MATH: **~ (by)** teilbar (durch).

**division** [dɪ'vɪʒn] *n* - **1.** [barrier] Trennung *die;* [of country, group] Teilung *die;* **~ between** Trennung zwischen (+ *D*) - **2.** [sharing out, distribution] Teilung *die* - **3.** MATH Division *die* - **4.** [disagreement] Uneinigkeit *die;* **~ of opinion** Meinungsverschiedenheit *die* - **5.** [department] Abteilung *die* - **6.** *Br* [in sports league] Liga *die.*

**division sign** *n* Teilungszeichen *das.*

**divisive** [dɪ'vaɪsɪv] *adj* Uneinigkeit schaffend.

**divorce** [dɪ'vɔːs] *n* LAW Scheidung *die* ◇ *vt* - **1.** LAW [husband, wife] sich scheiden lassen von - **2.** [separate]: **to ~ sthg from sthg** etw von etw trennen.

**divorced** [dɪ'vɔːst] *adj* - **1.** LAW geschieden; **to get ~** sich scheiden lassen - **2.** *fig* [separated]: **to be ~ from sthg** keine Beziehung haben zu etw.

**divorcee** [dɪvɔː'siː] *n* geschiedener Mann, geschiedene Frau.

**divulge** [daɪ'vʌldʒ] *vt* preislgeben.

**DIY** *n Br abbr of* **do-it-yourself.**

**dizziness** ['dɪzɪnɪs] *n* Schwindel *der.*

**dizzy** ['dɪzɪ] (*compar* -**ier**; *superl* -**iest**) *adj* - **1.** [person] schwind(e)lig - **2.** *fig* [height, speed] Schwindel erregend.

**DJ** *n* - **1.** *abbr of* **disc jockey** - **2.** *abbr of* **dinner jacket.**

**DJIA** (*abbr of* **Dow-Jones industrial average**) *n Am* ▷ **Dow Jones average.**

**dl** (*abbr of* **decilitre**) dl.

**DMZ** (*abbr of* **demilitarized zone**) *n entmilitarisierte Zone.*

**DNA** (*abbr of* **deoxyribonucleic acid**) *n* DNS *die.*

**do¹** [duː] *abbr of* **ditto.**

**do²** [duː] (*pt* **did**; *pp* **done**; *pl* **dos** OR **do's**) *aux vb* - **1.** (*in negatives*): **don't ~ that!** tu das nicht!; **she didn't listen** sie hat nicht zugehört; **don't park your car there** stell dein Auto nicht dort ab - **2.** (*in questions*): **did he like it?** hat es ihm gefallen?; **how ~ you ~ it?** wie machst du das?; **what did he want?** was wollte er? - **3.** (*referring back to previous verb*): **I eat more than you ~** ich esse mehr als du; **no I didn't!**

nein, habe ich nicht!; **so ~ I** ich auch - **4.** *(in question tags):* **so, you like Denver, ~ you?** Sie mögen Denver, nicht wahr?; **you come from Ireland, don't you?** Sie kommen aus Irland, oder?; **I like coffee – ~ you?** ich mag Kaffee – du auch? - **5.** *(for emphasis):* **I ~ like this bedroom** das Schlafzimmer gefällt mir wirklich; **~ come in!** kommen Sie doch herein! ◇ *vt -* **1.** [perform] machen, tun; **I've a lot to ~** ich habe viel zu tun; **to ~ one's homework** seine Hausaufgaben machen; **what is she ~ing?** was macht sie?; **what can I ~ for you?** was kann ich für Sie tun?; **to ~ aerobics/gymnastics** Aerobic/Gymnastik machen; **to ~ the cooking** kochen; **to ~ sums** rechnen; **to ~ one's duty** seine Pflicht tun; **well done!** bravo! - **2.** [clean, brush, cook *etc*]: **to ~ one's make-up** sich schminken; **to ~ one's teeth** sich *(D)* die Zähne putzen; **how would you like the steak done?** wie möchten Sie Ihr Steak (haben)? - **3.** [take action] tun, machen; **he couldn't ~ anything about it** er konnte nichts dagegen tun *OR* machen; **we'll have to ~ something about that tree** wir müssen etwas mit diesem Baum machen; **I'll ~ my best to help** ich helfe, so gut ich kann - **4.** [cause]: **the storm did a lot of damage** der Sturm hat viel Schaden angerichtet; **to ~ sb good** jm gut tun; **to ~ more harm than good** mehr schaden als nützen - **5.** [have as job]: **what ~ you ~?** was machen Sie beruflich?; **what ~ you want to ~ when you leave school?** was willst du machen, wenn du mit der Schule fertig bist? - **6.** [provide, offer]: **do you ~ vegetarian food?** haben Sie vegetarisches Essen?; **we ~ pizzas for under £4** wir bieten Pizzas für weniger als 4 Pfund an - **7.** [study] studieren, machen; **I did physics at school** ich habe Physik in der Schule gehabt *OR* gemacht; **she's ~ing Spanish at Oxford** sie studiert Spanisch in Oxford - **8.** [subj: vehicle] fahren; **the car can ~ 110 mph** das Auto schafft 175 km/h - **9.** inf [visit]: **we did Switzerland in a week** wir haben uns in einer Woche die Schweiz angesehen - **10.** [be good enough for] genügen (+ *D)*; **that'll ~ me nicely** das genügt mir - **11.** inf [cheat]: **to ~ sb** jn übers Ohr hauen ◇ *vi* - **1.** [behave, act] tun; **~ as I say** tu, was ich sage; **you would ~ well to reconsider** Sie sollten es sich lieber noch einmal überlegen - **2.** [progress, get on]: **to ~ well/badly** gut/schlecht vorankommen; [in exam] gut/schlecht abschneiden; **he will ~ well** er wird Erfolg haben - **3.** [be sufficient] reichen, genügen; **will £5 ~?** genügen 5 Pfund *OR* sind 5 Pfund genug?; **that will ~ (nicely)** das genügt *OR* reicht; **that will ~!** [showing annoyance] das reicht! - **4.** phr: **how ~ you ~?** Guten Tag!; **how are you ~ing?** wie geht's? ◇ *n* [party] Party die.

◆ **dos** npl: **~s and don'ts** was man tun und lassen sollte.

◆ **do away with** vt fus [law, practice] abschaffen; **it enables us to ~ away with a lot of red tape** das macht einen Großteil unserer Bürokratie überflüssig.

◆ **do down** vt sep: **to ~ sb/o.s. down** jn/sich schlecht machen.

◆ **do for** vt fus inf [kill]: **these kids will ~ for me** diese Kinder bringen mich noch um; **I thought I was done for** ich dachte, ich sei erledigt.

◆ **do in** vt sep - **1.** inf [kill] kaltlmachen - **2.** [beat up]: **to ~ sb** jm eine reinlhauen - **3.** [tire]: **I'm done in** ich bin völlig fertig.

◆ **do out of** vt sep: **to ~ sb out of £10** jn um 10 Pfund betrügen.

◆ **do up** vt sep - **1.** [fasten] zumachen; **~ your shoes up** binde dir die Schuhe - **2.** [decorate] renovieren - **3.** [wrap up] einpacken; **it was done up with green ribbon** es war mit einem grünen Band verziert.

◆ **do with** vt fus - **1.** [need]: **I could ~ with a drink** ich könnte einen Drink gebrauchen; **the floor could ~ with a wash** der Boden könnte mal (wieder) geputzt werden - **2.** [have connection with]: **what has that got to ~ with it?** was hat das damit zu tun?; **that has nothing to ~ with you** das geht dich gar nichts an; **it's something to ~ with the way he speaks** es liegt an seiner Aussprache.

◆ **do without** vt fus: **to ~ without sthg** ohne etw auskommen; **I can ~ without your sarcasm** [expressing annoyance] Sie können sich Ihren Sarkasmus sparen ◇ vi: **we'll just have to ~ without then** dann müssen wir eben so auskommen

**DOA** *(abbr of* **dead on arrival***) adj* auf dem Weg ins Krankenhaus gestorben.

**doable** ['du:əbl] *adj inf* [schedule] einhaltbar; [work] machbar.

**dob** *abbr of* date of birth.

**Doberman** ['dəʊbəmən] *(pl -s) n:* **~ (pinscher)** Dobermann(pinscher) *der.*

**docile** [Br 'dəʊsaɪl, Am 'dɒsəl] *adj* fügsam.

**dock** [dɒk] *n* - **1.** [in harbour] Dock *das* - **2.** [in court] Anklagebank *die* ◇ *vt* [wages] kürzen ◇ *vi* [ship] anlegen.

**docker** ['dɒkəʳ] *n* Hafenarbeiter *der,* -in *die.*

**docket** ['dɒkɪt] *n Br* Warenbegleitschein *der.*

**docklands** ['dɒkləndz] *npl Br* Hafenviertel *das.*

**dockworker** ['dɒkwɜːkəʳ] *n =* docker.

**dockyard** ['dɒkjɑːd] *n* Werft *die.*

**doctor** ['dɒktəʳ] *n* - **1.** [of medicine] Arzt *der,* Ärztin *die;* **to go to the ~'s** zum Arzt gehen - **2.** [holder of PhD] Doktor *der* ◇ *vt* - **1.** [tamper with - results] fälschen; [ - text] verfälschen; **her drink had been ~ed** ihrem Getränk war etwas beigemischt worden - **2.** *Br* [neuter] kastrieren.

**doctorate** ['dɒktərət], **doctor's degree** n Doktorwürde die; ~ **in physics** Doktor(titel) der in Physik.

**Doctor of Medicine** n Doktor der Medizin der.

**doctrinaire** [ˌdɒktrɪ'neəʳ] adj doktrinär.

**doctrine** ['dɒktrɪn] n Doktrin die, Lehre die.

**docudrama** [ˌdɒkjʊ'drɑːmə] (pl -s) n TV Dokumentarspiel das.

**document** [n 'dɒkjʊmənt, vt 'dɒkjʊment] n Dokument das <> vt dokumentieren.

**documentary** [ˌdɒkjʊ'mentərɪ] (pl -ies) adj dokumentarisch <> n Dokumentarfilm der.

**documentation** [ˌdɒkjʊmen'teɪʃn] n Dokumentation die.

**DOD** (abbr of Department of Defense) n Verteidigungsministerium das.

**doddering** ['dɒdərɪŋ], **doddery** ['dɒdərɪ] adj inf tatterig.

**doddle** ['dɒdl] n Br inf Kinderspiel das.

**Dodecanese** [ˌdəʊdɪkə'niːz] npl: **the** ~ die Südlichen Sporaden.

**dodge** [dɒdʒ] n inf Trick der <> vt [avoid] ausl-weichen <> vi: **to** ~ **out of the way/to one side** zur Seite springen; **he** ~**d behind the fence** er verschwand schnell hinter dem Zaun.

**Dodgems**® ['dɒdʒəmz] npl Br Autoskooter der.

**dodgy** ['dɒdʒɪ] adj Br inf [business, deal] windig; [plan] dubios.

**doe** [dəʊ] n - **1.** [female deer - roe deer] Ricke die; [ - red deer] Hirschkuh die - **2.** [female rabbit] Kaninchenweibchen das.

**DOE** n - **1.** (abbr of Department of the Environment) Umweltministerium das - **2.** (abbr of Department of Energy) Energieministerium das.

**doer** ['duːəʳ] n inf Macher der.

**does** [weak form dəz, strong form dʌz] vb ⊳ **do.**

**doesn't** ['dʌznt] = **does not.**

**dog** [dɒg] (pt & pp -**ged**; cont -**ging**) n - **1.** [animal] Hund der; **it's a** ~**'s life** es ist ein Hundeleben; **to go to the** ~**s** inf vor die Hunde gehen - **2. Am** [hot dog] Hotdog der <> vt - **1.** [follow closely] auf den Fersen sein (+ D) - **2.** [subj: problems, bad luck]: ~**ged by problems** von Problemen geplagt; ~**ged by bad luck** von Pech verfolgt.

**dog biscuit** n Hundekuchen der.

**dog collar** n - **1.** [of dog] Halsband das - **2.** [of clergyman] steifer weißer Kragen.

**dog-eared** [-ɪəd] adj mit Eselsohren.

**dog-eat-dog** adj: **it's** ~ jeder kämpft gegen jeden.

**dog-end** n inf [of cigarette] Kippe die.

**dogfight** ['dɒgfaɪt] n - **1.** [between dogs] Hundekampf der - **2.** [between aircraft] Luftkampf der.

**dogfish** (pl inv) n Katzenhai der.

**dog food** n Hundefutter das.

**dogged** ['dɒgɪd] adj beharrlich.

**doggone** ['dɒgɒn], **doggoned** ['dɒgɒnd] adj **Am** inf verflixt.

**doggy** ['dɒgɪ] (pl -ies) n Wauwau der.

**doggy bag** n Tütchen für Essensreste, die vom Restaurant nach Hause mitgenommen werden.

**dogma** ['dɒgmə] n Dogma das.

**dogmatic** [dɒg'mætɪk] adj dogmatisch.

**do-gooder** [-'gʊdəʳ] n pej Weltverbesserer der.

**dog paddle** n: **to do the** ~ [person] (in Hundemanier) paddeln.

**dogsbody** ['dɒgzˌbɒdɪ] (pl -ies) n Br inf Mädchen das für alles.

**dog tag** n Erkennungsmarke die.

**doing** ['duːɪŋ] n: **is this your** ~? ist das dein Werk?

➡ **doings** npl [activities] Taten pl.

**do-it-yourself** n Heimwerken das, Do-it-yourself das.

**doldrums** ['dɒldrəmz] npl: **to be in the** ~ fig [industry] in einer Flaute stecken; [person] Trübsal blasen.

**dole** [dəʊl] n Br [unemployment benefit] Arbeitslosenunterstützung die; **to be on the** ~ Arbeitslosenunterstützung beziehen.

➡ **dole out** vt sep ausfteilen.

**doleful** ['dəʊlfʊl] adj traurig.

**doll** [dɒl] n Puppe die.

**dollar** ['dɒləʳ] n Dollar der.

**dolled up** [dɒld-] adj inf aufgedonnert.

**dollhouse** n Am = **doll's house.**

**dollop** ['dɒləp] n inf Klacks der.

**doll's house** Br, **dollhouse** [dɒlhaʊs] Am n Puppenhaus das.

**dolly** ['dɒlɪ] (pl -ies) n - **1.** [doll] Püppi die - **2.** TECH [for TV or film camera] Dolly der.

**Dolomites** ['dɒləmaɪts] npl: **the** ~ die Dolomiten pl.

**dolphin** ['dɒlfɪn] n Delfin der.

**domain** [də'meɪn] n - **1.** [sphere of interest] Gebiet das - **2.** [land - owned by state] Domäne die; [ - owned by person] Gut das.

**dome** [dəʊm] n ARCHIT Kuppel die.

**domestic** [də'mestɪk] adj - **1.** [internal - flight] Inland-; [ - policy] Innen- - **2.** [household, home-loving] häuslich; **the** ~ **water supply** die Wasserversorgung der Privathaushalte - **3.** [not wild] Haus- <> n Hausangestellte der, die.

**domestic appliance** *n* Haushaltsgerät *das*.

**domesticated** [dəˈmestɪkeɪtɪd] *adj* - **1.** [animal] domestiziert, gezähmt - **2.** *hum* [person] häuslich.

**domesticity** [ˌdəʊmeˈstɪsətɪ] *n* häusliches Leben.

**domestic science** *n* Hauswirtschaftslehre *die*.

**domicile** [ˈdɒmɪsaɪl] *n fml* Wohnsitz *der*.

**dominance** [ˈdɒmɪnəns] *n* - **1.** [control, power - of country] Vorherrschaft *die*; [ - of person] Dominanz *die* - **2.** [importance] Vorrangstellung *die*.

**dominant** [ˈdɒmɪnənt] *adj* [personality] dominant; [nation, group, colour] dominierend.

**dominate** [ˈdɒmɪneɪt] *vt* dominieren.

**dominating** [ˈdɒmɪneɪtɪŋ] *adj* dominant.

**domination** [ˌdɒmɪˈneɪʃn] *n* Vorherrschaft *die*; **under Roman ~** unter römischer Herrschaft.

**domineering** [ˌdɒmɪˈnɪərɪŋ] *adj* herrisch.

**dominion** [dəˈmɪnjən] *n* - **1.** [power] Herrschaft *die* - **2.** [land] Herrschaftsgebiet *das*.

**domino** [ˈdɒmɪnəʊ] (*pl* -**es**) *n* Dominostein *der*.

➤ **dominoes** *npl* [game] Domino *das*.

**domino effect** *n* Domino-Effekt *der*.

**don** [dɒn] (*pt & pp* -**ned**; *cont* -**ning**) *n Br* UNIV Universitätsdozent *der*, -in *die* ◇ *vt* anl-ziehen; [hat] aufsetzen.

**donate** [dəˈneɪt] *vt* spenden.

**donation** [dəˈneɪʃn] *n* - **1.** [act] Spenden *das* - **2.** [sum] Spende *die*.

**done** [dʌn] *pp* ▷ **do** ◇ *adj* - **1.** [finished] erledigt; **I'm nearly ~** ich bin fast fertig - **2.** [cooked] gar - **3.** [socially acceptable]: **it's not the ~ thing** das tut man nicht ◇ *excl* [to conclude deal] abgemacht!

**donkey** [ˈdɒŋkɪ] (*pl* -**s**) *n* Esel *der*.

**donkey jacket** *n Br* dicke blaue Jacke, die traditionell im Straßenbau getragen wird.

**donkeywork** [ˈdɒŋkɪwɜːk] *n (U) Br inf* Drecksarbeit *die*.

**donor** [ˈdəʊnəʳ] *n* Spender *der*, -in *die*.

**donor card** *n* Organspenderausweis *der*.

**don't** [dəʊnt] = **do not**.

**doodle** [ˈduːdl] *n* Kritzelei *die* ◇ *vi* vor sich hin kritzeln.

**doom** [duːm] *n (U)* Verhängnis *das*.

**doomed** [duːmd] *adj* zum Scheitern verurteilt; **to be ~ to sthg** zu etw verurteilt sein; **we were ~ to die** wir waren dem Tode geweiht.

**door** [dɔːʳ] *n* Tür *die*; **to open the ~ to sthg** *fig* etw in greifbare Nähe rücken.

**doorbell** [ˈdɔːbel] *n* Türklingel *die*, Türglocke *die*.

**doorhandle** [ˈdɔːhændl] *n* Türklinke *die*.

**doorknob** [ˈdɔːnɒb] *n* Türknauf *der*.

**doorknocker** [ˈdɔːˌnɒkəʳ] *n* Türklopfer *der*.

**doorman** [ˈdɔːmən] (*pl* -**men** [-mən]) *n* Portier *der*.

**doormat** [ˈdɔːmæt] *n lit & fig* Fußabtreter *der*.

**doorstep** [ˈdɔːstep] *n* Eingangsstufe *die*; **the supermarket's right at her ~** sie hat den Supermarkt direkt vor der Tür.

**doorstop** [ˈdɔːstɒp] *n* Türstopper *der*.

**door-to-door** *adj* [selling] von Haus zu Haus; **~ salesman** Vertreter *der*.

**doorway** [ˈdɔːweɪ] *n* Eingang *der*.

**dope** [dəʊp] *n* - **1.** *drugs sl* [cannabis] Hasch *das* - **2.** [for athlete, horse] Aufputschmittel *das* - **3.** *inf* [fool] Trottel *der* ◇ *vt* dopen.

**dope test** *n* SPORT Dopingkontrolle *die*.

**dopey** [ˈdəʊpɪ] (*compar* -**ier**; *superl* -**iest**) *adj inf* - **1.** [groggy] benommen - **2.** [stupid] blöd.

**dormant** [ˈdɔːmənt] *adj* - **1.** [volcano] untätig - **2.** [law] (zur Zeit) nicht wirksam; **to lie ~** [talents] schlummern.

**dormer (window)** [ˈdɔːməʳ-] *n* Mansardenfenster *das*.

**dormice** [ˈdɔːmaɪs] *pl* ▷ **dormouse**.

**dormitory** [ˈdɔːmətrɪ] (*pl* -**ies**) *n* - **1.** [room] Schlafsaal *der* - **2.** *Am* [in university] Wohnheim *das*.

**Dormobile**® [ˈdɔːməˌbiːl] *n* Campingbus *der*.

**dormouse** [ˈdɔːmaʊs] (*pl* -**mice**) *n* Haselmaus *die*.

**DOS** [dɒs] (*abbr of* **disk operating system**) *n* DOS *das*.

**dosage** [ˈdəʊsɪdʒ] *n* Dosis *die*.

**dose** [dəʊs] *n* - **1.** [of medicine, drug] Dosis *die* - **2.** [of illness] Anfall *der* ◇ *vt*: **to ~ sb with sthg** jm etw verabreichen.

**doss** [dɒs] ➤ **doss down** *vi Br inf* sich hinlhauen.

**dosser** [ˈdɒsəʳ] *n Br inf* Penner *der*, -in *die*.

**dosshouse** [ˈdɒshaʊs, *pl* -haʊzɪz] *n Br inf* Obdachlosenheim *das*.

**dossier** [ˈdɒsɪeɪ] *n* Dossier *das*.

**dot** [dɒt] (*pt & pp* -**ted**; *cont* -**ting**) *n* Punkt *der* ◇ *vt* verstreuen; **the meadow was ~ted with flowers** auf der Weide sprossen hier und da Blumen.

➤ **on the dot** *adv*: **at four on the ~** Punkt vier Uhr; **to arrive on the ~** auf die Minute pünktlich (an)kommen.

**DOT** (*abbr of* **Department of Transportation**) *n* Verkehrsministerium *das*.

**dotage** ['dəʊtɪdʒ] *n:* **to be in one's ~** senil sein.

**dote** ◆ **dote upon** *vt fus* vernarrt sein in *(+ A)*.

**doting** ['dəʊtɪŋ] *adj:* **his ~ parents** seine ihn vergötternden Eltern.

**dot-matrix printer** *n* Matrixdrucker *der.*

**dotted line** ['dɒtɪd-] *n* punktierte Linie; **to sign on the ~** auf der punktierten Linie unterschreiben.

**dotty** ['dɒtɪ] *(compar* **-ier;** *superl* **-iest)** *adj inf* schrullig.

**double** ['dʌbl] *adj* doppelt; [row, door] Doppel-; **to have a ~ meaning** doppeldeutig sein; **two ~ one** zwei eins eins; **Susanne with a ~ "n"** Susanne mit zwei „n" ◇ *adv* **- 1.** [twice]: **~ the amount/number** doppelt so viel/viele **- 2.** [two of the same] doppelt; **to see ~** doppelt sehen **- 3.** [in two - fold] einmal; **to bend ~ sich** zusammen|krümmen ◇ *n* **- 1.** [twice the amount] Doppelte *das* **- 2.** [of alcohol] Doppelter *der* **- 3.** [look-alike] Ebenbild *das* **- 4.** CINEMA Double *das* ◇ *vt* [increase twofold] verdoppeln ◇ *vi* **- 1.** [increase twofold] verdoppeln **- 2.** [serve two purposes]: **to ~ as** [thing] zugleich dienen als; [person] zugleich die Funktion *(+ G)* haben.

◆ **doubles** *npl* TENNIS Doppel *das.*

◆ **double up** *vt sep:* **she was ~d up in pain** sie krümmte sich vor Schmerzen; **she was ~d up with laughter** sie bog sich vor Lachen ◇ *vi* [bend over] sich krümmen.

**double act** *n* zwei Komödianten, die als Paar auftreten.

**double agent** *n* Doppelagent *der,* -in *die.*

**double-barrelled** *Br,* **double-barreled** *Am* [-'bærəld] *adj* **- 1.** [shotgun] doppelläufig **- 2.** [name] Doppel-.

**double bass** [-beɪs] *n* Kontrabass *der.*

**double bed** *n* Doppelbett *das.*

**double-breasted** [-'brestɪd] *adj* zweireihig.

**double-check** *vt* noch einmal überprüfen.

**double chin** *n* Doppelkinn *das.*

**double cream** *n Br* Schlagsahne *die.*

**double-cross** *vt* doppeltes Spiel treiben mit.

**double-dealer** *n* Betrüger *der,* -in *die.*

**double-decker** [-'dekəʳ] *n* Doppeldecker *der.*

**double-declutch** [-di:'klʌtʃ] *vi Br* AUT mit Zwischengas schalten.

**double-density** *adj* COMPUT [disk] mit doppelter Dichte.

**double-dutch** *n Br hum* Kauderwelsch *das.*

**double-edged** [-'edʒd] *adj* zweischneidig.

**double entendre** [ˌdu:blɑ̃'tɑ̃dr] *n* Zweideutigkeit *die.*

**double fault** *n* TENNIS Doppelfehler *der.*

**double figures** *npl* zweistellige Zahlen *pl.*

**double-glazing** [-'gleɪzɪŋ] *n* Doppelverglasung *die.*

**double-jointed** [-'dʒɔɪntɪd] *adj* [person] sehr gelenkig.

**double-park** *vi* AUT in der zweiten Reihe parken.

**double-quick** *inf adj* sehr schnell; **in ~ time** im Nu ◇ *adv* im Nu.

**double room** *n* Doppelzimmer *das.*

**double-sided** *adj* COMPUT [disk] zweiseitig.

**double standards** *npl:* **to have ~** mit zweierlei Maß messen.

**double take** *n:* **to do a ~** erst nach einer kurzen Pause reagieren.

**double-talk** *n* [deceitful] doppelzüngiges Gerede.

**double time** *n* doppelter Stundenlohn.

**double vision** *n* doppeltes Sehen.

**double whammy** [-'wæmɪ] *n inf* doppelter Schlag.

**doubly** ['dʌblɪ] *adv:* **~ difficult/important/**etc umso schwieriger/wichtiger/etc; **to be ~ mistaken** in zweierlei Hinsicht Unrecht haben.

**doubt** [daʊt] *n* Zweifel *der;* **there is no ~ that ...** es besteht kein Zweifel, dass ...; **to cast ~ on sthg** etw in Zweifel ziehen; **no ~** ohne Zweifel, zweifelsohne; **without (a) ~, beyond (all) ~** ohne Zweifel; **to be in ~** ungewiss sein ◇ *vt* **- 1.** [distrust] zweifeln an *(+ D)* **- 2.** [consider unlikely] bezweifeln.

**doubtful** ['daʊtfʊl] *adj* **- 1.** [unlikely, dubious] zweifelhaft **- 2.** [uncertain] ungewiss; **to be ~ about** OR **of sthg** in Bezug auf etw Zweifel haben.

**doubtless** ['daʊtlɪs] *adv* ohne Zweifel, zweifelsohne.

**dough** [dəʊ] *n (U)* **- 1.** [for baking] Teig *der* **- 2.** *vinf* [money] Knete *die.*

**doughnut** ['dəʊnʌt] *n* ≃ Berliner *der.*

**dour** [dʊəʳ] *adj* mürrisch.

**douse** [daʊs] *vt* **- 1.** [fire, light] löschen **- 2.** [person] übergießen.

**dove**[1] [dʌv] *n* [bird] Taube *die.*

**dove**[2] [dəʊv] *pt Am* ⊏➤ **dive.**

**dovecot(e)** ['dʌvkɒt] *n* Taubenschlag *der.*

**dovetail** ['dʌvteɪl] *vt* [arrangements] koordinieren ◇ *vi* [arrangements] aufeinander abgestimmt sein.

**dovetail joint** *n* Schwalbenschwanzverbindung *die.*

**dowager** ['daʊədʒəʳ] *n literary* [old lady] *ehrwürdige und wohlhabende alte Dame.*

D

**dowdy** [ˈdaʊdɪ] (*compar* -**ier**; *superl* -**iest**) *adj* ohne jeden Schick.

**Dow-Jones average** [ˌdaʊˈdʒəʊnz-] *n:* **the ~** der Dow-Jones-Index.

**down** [daʊn] *adv* - **1.** [towards the bottom] nach unten, hinunter/herunter; **~ here/there** hier/dort unten; **to fall ~** [person] hinlfallen; [thing] herunterlfallen; **to bend ~** sich bücken; **head ~** mit gesenktem Kopf - **2.** [along]: **I'm going ~ to the shops** ich gehe einkaufen - **3.** [downstairs] herunter, nach unten; **I'll come ~ later** ich komme später herunter - **4.** [southwards] hinunter/herunter; **we're going ~ to London** wir fahren hinunter nach London; **they're coming ~ from Manchester** sie kommen von Manchester herunter - **5.** [in writing]: **to write sthg ~** etw auf lschreiben; **did you get that ~?** hast du alles mitschreiben können? - **6.** [as deposit]: **to pay £5 ~** 5 Pfund anlzahlen - **7.** [reduced]: **prices are coming ~** die Preise fallen - **8.** [as far as]: **~ to the last detail** bis ins letzte Detail; **~ to the present** bis in die heutige Zeit ◇ *prep* - **1.** [towards the bottom of]: **they ran ~ the hill** sie liefen den Hügel hinunter; **to fall ~ the stairs** die Treppe hinunterlfallen - **2.** [along] entlang; **I was walking ~ the street when ...** ich lief gerade die Straße entlang, als ... ◇ *adj* - **1.** *inf* [depressed] down; **to be ~ in the mouth** bedrückt sein - **2.** [behind]: **we're two goals ~** wir liegen zwei Tore zurück - **3.** [lower in amount]: **prices are ~** die Preise sind gefallen - **4.** [not in operation]: **the computers are ~ again** die Computer tun es wieder (mal) nicht ◇ *n* - **1.** (*U*) [feathers] Daunen *pl* - **2.** *phr:* **to have a ~ on sb** *inf* jn nicht leiden können - **3.** [in American football] Down *der* ◇ *vt* - **1.** [knock over] niederlschlagen - **2.** [swallow] hastig trinken - **3.** *phr:* **to ~ tools** die Arbeit niederllegen.

➤ **downs** *npl Br* Hügelland *das.*

➤ **down with** *excl:* **~ with the King!** nieder mit dem König!

**down-and-out** *adj* heruntergekommen ◇ *n* Landstreicher *der*, -in *die.*

**down-at-heel** *adj esp Br* heruntergekommen.

**downbeat** [ˈdaʊnbiːt] *adj inf* [ending] undramatisch.

**downcast** [ˈdaʊnkɑːst] *adj fml* niedergeschlagen.

**downer** [ˈdaʊnəʳ] *n inf* - **1.** [drug] Beruhigungsmittel *das* - **2.** *inf* [depressing event or person]: **he's/it's a real ~** er/das kann einen wirklich die Stimmung verderben; **to be on a ~** niedergeschlagen sein.

**downfall** [ˈdaʊnfɔːl] *n* - **1.** (*U*) [ruin - of dictator] Sturz *der*; [ - of business] Ruin *der* - **2.** [cause of ruin] Ruin *der.*

**downgrade** [ˈdaʊngreɪd] *vt* herunterlstufen.

**downhearted** [ˌdaʊnˈhɑːtɪd] *adj* niedergeschlagen.

**downhill** [ˌdaʊnˈhɪl] *adj* - **1.** [path] bergab führend - **2.** *fig* [easy]: **it's ~ all the way now** jetzt wird es leichter - **3.** SKIING [skier] Abfahrts- ◇ *adv* - **1.** [downwards] bergab, abwärts - **2.** *fig:* **her career went ~ after that** mit ihrer Karriere ging es danach bergab ◇ *n* SKIING Abfahrtslauf *der.*

**Downing Street** [ˈdaʊnɪŋ-] *n* Straße, in der sich der offizielle Wohnsitz des britischen Premierministers und des Schatzkanzlers befindet.

**DOWNING STREET**

Diese Straße in London ist berühmt durch den Sitz des britischen Premierministers (Hausnummer 10) und des Schatzkanzlers (Hausnummer 11). Der Begriff wird manchmal als Synonym für die britische Regierung benutzt.

**download** [ˌdaʊnˈləʊd] *vt* COMPUT laden.

**down-market** *adj* [area] weniger anspruchsvoll; [product] von geringer Qualität.

**down payment** *n* Anzahlung *die.*

**downplay** [ˈdaʊnpleɪ] *vt* herunterlspielen.

**downpour** [ˈdaʊnpɔːʳ] *n* Platzregen *der.*

**downright** [ˈdaʊnraɪt] *adj* [fool, cheat, cheek] ausgesprochen; [lie] glatt; [insult] grob ◇ *adv* ausgesprochen.

**downside** [ˈdaʊnsaɪd] *n* Nachteil *der.*

**downsize** [ˈdaʊnsaɪz] *vi* sich verkleinern.

**Down's syndrome** *n* (*U*) Down-Syndrom *das.*

**downstairs** [ˌdaʊnˈsteəz] *adj:* **a ~ flat** eine Parterre- OR Erdgeschosswohnung ◇ *adv* [be, live] unten; **to go ~** (die Treppe) hinunterlgehen; **to come ~** (die Treppe) herunterlkommen.

**downstream** [ˌdaʊnˈstriːm] *adv* flussabwärts, stromabwärts.

**downtime** [ˈdaʊntaɪm] *n* (*U*) Ausfallzeit *die.*

**down-to-earth** *adj* sachlich, nüchtern.

**downtown** [ˌdaʊnˈtaʊn] *esp Am adj:* **~ New York** im Stadtzentrum von New York ◇ *adv* [go] ins Stadtzentrum; [live] im Stadtzentrum.

**downtrodden** [ˈdaʊnˌtrɒdn] *adj* unterdrückt.

**downturn** [ˈdaʊntɜːn] *n:* **~ (in sthg)** Abnahme *die* (von etw).

**down under** *adv Br* [live] in Australien/Neuseeland; [go] nach Australien/Neuseeland.

**downward** [ˈdaʊnwəd] *adj* - **1.** [towards ground] abwärts gerichtet; **~ glance** Blick nach unten; **~ movement** Abwärtsbewegung *die*

**- 2.** [decreasing] abnehmend, fallend ◇ *adv Am* = **downwards.**

**downwards** ['daʊnwədz] *adv* **- 1.** [look, move] nach unten **- 2.** [in hierarchy] abwärts.

**downwind** [ˌdaʊn'wɪnd] *adv* in Windrichtung.

**dowry** ['daʊərɪ] (*pl* **-ies**) *n* Mitgift *die.*

**doz.** *abbr of* **dozen.**

**doze** [dəʊz] *n* Nickerchen *das* ◇ *vi* dösen.
◆ **doze off** *vi* einlnicken.

**dozen** ['dʌzn] *n* Dutzend *das*; **a ~ eggs** ein Dutzend Eier ◇ *n* Dutzend *das.*
◆ **dozens** *npl inf:* **~s of** Dutzende (von); **~s of times** x-mal.

**dozy** ['dəʊzɪ] (*compar* **-ier;** *superl* **-iest**) *adj*
**- 1.** [sleepy] schläfrig **- 2.** *Br inf* [stupid] blöd.

**DP** *n abbr of* **data processing.**

**DPh, DPhil** [ˌdiː'fɪl] (*abbr of* **Doctor of Philosophy**) *n* Dr. phil.

**DPP** *n abbr of* **Director of Public Prosecutions.**

**DPT** (*abbr of* **diphtheria, pertussis, tetanus**) *n* DPT.

**Dr. - 1.** *abbr of* **Drive - 2.** *abbr of* **Doctor.**

**drab** [dræb] (*compar* **-ber;** *superl* **-best**) *adj*
**- 1.** [colour, buildings] trist; [clothes] langweilig; [place] trostlos **- 2.** [life] eintönig, farblos.

**draconian** [drə'kəʊnjən] *adj fml* drakonisch.

**draft** [drɑːft] *n* **- 1.** [early version] Entwurf *der;* [picture, plan] Skizze *die* **- 2.** [money order] Zahlungsanweisung *die* **- 3.** *Am* MIL: **the ~** die Einberufung **- 4.** *Am* = **draught** ◇ *vt* **- 1.** [write] entwerfen **- 2.** *Am* MIL einlberufen, einlziehen **- 3.** [recruit] rekrutieren.

**draft dodger** [-dɒdʒə<sup>r</sup>] *n Am* Wehrdienstverweigerer *der.*

**draftee** [ˌdrɑːf'tiː] *n Am* Einberufene *der.*

**draftsman** *n Am* = **draughtsman.**

**draftsmanship** *n Am* = **draughtsmanship.**

**drafty** *adj Am* = **draughty.**

**drag** [dræg] (*pt* & *pp* **-ged;** *cont* **-ging**) *vt*
**- 1.** [pull] ziehen; **she ~ged the dog along behind her** sie zog den Hund hinter sich her; **she ~ged herself to the door** sie schleppte sich zur Tür; **she ~ged me to the hairdresser** sie hat mich zum Friseur geschleift **- 2.** [lake, river] (mit dem Schleppnetz) ablsuchen ◇ *vi*
**- 1.** [trail]: **to ~ on the ground** auf dem Boden schleifen **- 2.** [pass slowly] sich in die Länge ziehen ◇ *n* **- 1.** *inf* [bore] langweilige Sache/Person; **what a ~!** wie öde!; **the guy's a real ~** der Typ ist ein totaler Langweiler **- 2.** *inf* [on cigarette] Zug *der* **- 3.** [wind resistance] Luftwiderstand *der* **- 4.** [cross-dressing]: **in ~** in Frauenkleidern, als Frau gekleidet.
◆ **drag down** *vt sep fig* ruinieren; **they ~ged him down with them** sie zogen ihn mit nach unten.

◆ **drag in** *vt sep* [involve] (mit) hineinlziehen; **don't ~ me into this!** zieh mich da nicht mit rein!; **he was ~ged into the affair** er wurde in die Affäre hineingezogen.
◆ **drag on** *vi* sich in die Länge ziehen.
◆ **drag out** *vt sep* **- 1.** [protract] hinauslziehen **- 2.** [extract]: **to ~ sthg out of sb** etw aus jm herauslbekommen.

**dragnet** ['drægnet] *n* **- 1.** [net] Schleppnetz *das* **- 2.** *fig* [to catch criminal] Netz *das.*

**dragon** ['drægən] *n lit* & *fig* Drache *der.*

**dragonfly** ['drægnflaɪ] (*pl* **-ies**) *n* Libelle *die.*

**dragoon** [drə'guːn] *n* Dragoner *der* ◇ *vt:* **to ~ sb into doing sthg** jn dazu zwingen, etw zu tun.

**drag racing** *n* Beschleunigungsrennen *das.*

**dragster** ['drægstə<sup>r</sup>] *n* Dragster *der, für Beschleunigungsrennen konstruiertes Fahrzeug.*

**drain** [dreɪn] *n* **- 1.** [pipe] Abflussrohr *das;* [grating in street] Gully *der;* **that's £50 down the ~** *fig* die 50 Pfund sind zum Fenster rausgeworfen **- 2.** [depletion]: **~ on sthg** [resources, funds] Belastung *die* für etw; [energy, time] Verlust *der* von etw ◇ *vt* **- 1.** [remove water from - vegetables] ablgießen; [ - marsh, field] entwässern **- 2.** [deplete - funds, resources] erschöpfen; [ - strength, energy] entziehen; **to feel ~ed** sich ausgelaugt fühlen **- 3.** [drink, glass] ausltrinken ◇ *vi*
**- 1.** [dry] abltropfen **- 2.** [disappear]: **the blood/colour ~ed from her face** sie wurde kreidebleich (im Gesicht).

**drainage** ['dreɪnɪdʒ] *n* **- 1.** [ditches, channels] Entwässerungssystem *das;* [in city] Kanalisation *die* **- 2.** [draining] Entwässerung *die.*

**draining board** *Br* ['dreɪnɪŋ-], **drainboard** *Am* ['dreɪnbɔːrd] *n* Abtropfbrett *das.*

**drainpipe** ['dreɪnpaɪp] *n* Abflussrohr *das.*
◆ **drainpipes** *npl* = **drainpipe trousers.**

**drainpipe trousers** *npl Br* Röhrenhosen *pl.*

**drake** [dreɪk] *n* Erpel *der.*

**dram** [dræm] *n* [of whisky] Schlückchen *das.*

**drama** ['drɑːmə] *n* **- 1.** [play, genre, event] Drama *das* **- 2.** [dramatic quality] Dramatik *die* ◇ *comp* Schauspiel-.

**dramatic** [drə'mætɪk] *adj* dramatisch.

**dramatically** [drə'mætɪklɪ] *adv* dramatisch.

**dramatist** ['dræmətɪst] *n* Dramatiker *der,* -in *die.*

**dramatization** [ˌdræmətaɪ'zeɪʃn] *n* [for theatre, film, television] Dramatisierung *die;* **a stage ~** eine Bühnenbearbeitung.

**dramatize, -ise** ['dræmətaɪz] *vt* dramatisieren.

**drank** [dræŋk] *pt* ▷ **drink.**

**drape** [dreɪp] *vt* drapieren; **to be ~d with** *OR* **in sthg** mit etw drapiert sein.

**D**

**drapes** *npl Am* Vorhänge *pl.*

**draper** ['dreɪpə'] *n:* ~'s (shop) Textilgeschäft *das.*

**drastic** ['dræstɪk] *adj* drastisch.

**drastically** ['dræstɪklɪ] *adv* drastisch.

**draught** *Br,* **draft** *Am* [drɑːft] *n* - **1.** [air current] Luftzug *der;* **there's a ~ in here** hier zieht es - **2.** *literary* [of water] Schluck *der* - **3.** [from barrel]: **on ~** [beer] vom Fass.

**draughts** *n Br* Damespiel *das;* **to play ~s** Dame spielen.

**draught beer** *n Br* Fassbier *das,* Bier *das* vom Fass.

**draughtboard** ['drɑːftbɔːd] *n Br* Damebrett *das.*

**draught excluder** *n* Dichtvorrichtung *die.*

**draughtsman** *Br,* **draftsman** *Am* ['drɑːftsmən] (*pl* **-men** [-mən]) *n* technischer Zeichner.

**draughtsmanship** *Br,* **draftsmanship** *Am* ['drɑːftsmənʃɪp] *n* - **1.** [of artist] Zeichentalent *das* - **2.** [of work] Zeichenkunst *die.*

**draughtswoman** *Br,* **draftswoman** *Am* ['drɑːftswʊmən] (*pl* **-women** [-wɪmɪn]) *n* technische Zeichnerin.

**draughty** *Br,* **drafty** *Am* ['drɑːftɪ] (*compar* **-ier;** *superl* **-iest**) *adj* zugig.

**draw** [drɔː] (*pt* **drew;** *pp* **drawn**) *vt* - **1.** [sketch] zeichnen - **2.** [pull, pull out] ziehen; **to ~ the curtains** [open] die Vorhänge auf|ziehen; [close] die Vorhänge zulziehen - **3.** [breath]: **to ~ breath** ein|atmen - **4.** [conclusion, comparison, distinction] ziehen - **5.** [criticism, support] hervor|rufen; **to be** *or* **feel ~n to** sich hingezogen fühlen zu; **to ~ sb's attention to sthg** js Aufmerksamkeit auf etw *(A)* lenken <> *vi* - **1.** [sketch] zeichnen - **2.** [move]: **to ~ away** weglziehen, davon|führen; **to ~ near** heran|ziehen; **to ~ to an end** *or* **a close** zu Ende gehen - **3.** *sport* unentschieden spielen; **to ~ with sb** gegen jn unentschieden spielen <> *n* - **1.** *sport* [result] Unentschieden *das* - **2.** [lottery] Ziehung *die,* Verlosung *die* - **3.** [attraction] Anziehungspunkt *der.*

**draw in** *vi* [days] kürzer werden.

**draw into** *vt sep:* **to ~ sb into sthg** [quarrel, plot] jn in etw *(A)* hinein|ziehen; [conversation] jn in etw *(A)* ein|beziehen.

**draw on** *vt fus* - **1.** = draw upon - **2.** [smoke] ziehen an *(+ D).*

**draw out** *vt sep* - **1.** [encourage] aus der Reserve locken - **2.** [prolong] in die Länge ziehen - **3.** [withdraw] ab|heben.

**draw up** *vt sep* [draft] auf|setzen, entwerfen; [list] auf|stellen <> *vi* [stop] an|halten, halten.

**draw upon** *vt fus* Gebrauch machen von.

**drawback** ['drɔːbæk] *n* Nachteil *der.*

**drawbridge** ['drɔːbrɪdʒ] *n* Zugbrücke *die.*

**drawer** [drɔː'] *n* Schublade *die.*

**drawing** ['drɔːɪŋ] *n* - **1.** [picture] Zeichnung *die* - **2.** [skill, act] Zeichnen *das.*

**drawing board** *n* Reißbrett *das;* **back to the ~!** *inf* versuchen wir was Anderes *or* Neues!

**drawing pin** *n Br* Reißzwecke *die.*

**drawing room** *n* Salon *der.*

**drawl** [drɔːl] *n* gedehntes Sprechen <> *vi* gedehnt sprechen.

**drawn** [drɔːn] *pp* ⊳ **draw** <> *adj* - **1.** [closed] zugezogen - **2.** [tired, ill] abgespannt.

**drawn-out** *adj* in die Länge gezogen.

**drawstring** ['drɔːstrɪŋ] *n* Durchziehschnur *die.*

**dread** [dred] *n* Furcht *die* <> *vt* fürchten; **to ~ doing sthg** es schrecklich finden, etw tun zu müssen; **I ~ to think** ich wage kaum, daran zu denken.

**dreaded** ['dredɪd] *adj* gefürchtet.

**dreadful** ['dredfʊl] *adj* schrecklich, furchtbar; **I feel ~** [guilty] es ist mir sehr peinlich.

**dreadfully** ['dredfʊlɪ] *adv* - **1.** [badly] furchtbar, fürchterlich - **2.** [extremely] schrecklich, furchtbar.

**dreadlocks** ['dredlɒks] *npl* Dreadlocks *pl.*

**dream** [driːm] (*pt* & *pp* **-ed** *or* **dreamt**) *n* Traum *der* <> *adj* Traum- <> *vt* [during sleep] träumen; **I never ~ed this would happen** ich habe nicht im Traum daran gedacht, dass das passieren könnte <> *vi:* **to ~ (of** *or* **about sthg)** (von etw) träumen; **I wouldn't ~ of it** *fig* das würde mir nicht im Traum ein|fallen; **to ~ of doing sthg** davon träumen, etw zu tun.

**dream up** *vt sep* sich *(D)* einfallen lassen *or* aus|denken.

**dreamer** ['driːmə'] *n* Träumer *der,* -in *die.*

**dreamily** ['driːmɪlɪ] *adv* verträumt, träumerisch.

**dreamlike** ['driːmlaɪk] *adj* traumhaft.

**dreamt** [dremt] *pt* & *pp* ⊳ **dream.**

**dream world** *n* Traumwelt *die,* Fantasiewelt *die.*

**dreamy** ['driːmɪ] (*compar* **-ier;** *superl* **-iest**) *adj* - **1.** [distracted] verträumt - **2.** [languorous] traumhaft.

**dreary** ['drɪərɪ] (*compar* **-ier;** *superl* **-iest**) *adj* - **1.** [gloomy, depressing] trostlos - **2.** [dull, boring] langweilig, öde.

**dredge** [dredʒ] *vt* aus|baggern.

**dredge up** *vt sep* - **1.** [from lake, river] herauf|holen, heraus|holen - **2.** *fig* [from past] aus|graben.

**dredger** ['dredʒə'] *n* Bagger *der.*

**dregs** [dregz] *npl* - **1.** [of liquid] (Boden)satz *der* - **2.** *fig* [of society] Abschaum *der*.

**drench** [drentʃ] *vt* durchlnässen; **to be ~ed in** OR **with sweat** in Schweiß gebadet sein.

**dress** [dres] *n* - **1.** [frock] Kleid *das* - **2.** [type of clothing] Kleidung *die* ⬦ *vt* - **1.** [clothe] anlziehen; **to be ~ed** angezogen sein; **to be ~ed in** gekleidet sein in (+ *A*); **to get ~ed** sich anlziehen - **2.** [wound] verbinden - **3.** [salad] anlmachen ⬦ *vi* sich anlziehen, sich kleiden.
➨ **dress up** *vt sep* - **1.** [in costume] verkleiden - **2.** [in nice clothes] feinlmachen; [in formal clothes] festlich anlziehen - **3.** [facts, story] auslschmücken ⬦ *vi* - **1.** [in costume] sich verkleiden - **2.** [in best clothes] sich festlich anlziehen.

**dressage** [ˈdresɑːʒ] *n* (*U*) Dressur *die*.

**dress circle** *n* THEATRE erster Rang.

**dresser** [ˈdresəʳ] *n* - **1.** [for dishes] Küchenbüffet *das* (mit Tellerbord) - **2.** *Am* [chest of drawers] Frisiertisch *der*, Frisierkommode *die* - **3.** [person]: **he is a smart ~** er zieht sich elegant an - **4.** THEATRE Garderobier *der*, -e *die*.

**dressing** [ˈdresɪŋ] *n* - **1.** [bandage] Verband *der* - **2.** [for salad] Dressing *das*, Salatsoße *die* - **3.** *Am* [for turkey *etc*] Füllung *die*.

**dressing gown** *n* Bademantel *der*.

**dressing room** *n* - **1.** SPORT Umkleidekabine *die* - **2.** THEATRE Garderobe *die*.

**dressing table** *n* Frisiertisch *der*, Frisierkommode *die*.

**dressmaker** [ˈdresˌmeɪkəʳ] *n* Schneider *der*, -in *die*.

**dressmaking** [ˈdresˌmeɪkɪŋ] *n* Schneidern *das*.

**dress rehearsal** *n* Generalprobe *die*.

**dress shirt** *n* Smokinghemd *das*.

**dressy** [ˈdresɪ] (*compar* -**ier**; *superl* -**iest**) *adj* elegant.

**drew** [druː] *pt* ⬅ draw.

**dribble** [ˈdrɪbl] *n* [trickle] Rinnsal *das* ⬦ *vt* SPORT [ball] dribbeln ⬦ *vi* - **1.** [drool] sabbern - **2.** [spill] tropfen - **3.** SPORT [ball] dribbeln.

**dribs** [drɪbz] *npl*: **in ~ and drabs** kleckerweise.

**dried** [draɪd] *pt* & *pp* ⬅ dry ⬦ *adj* getrocknet; **~ milk** Trockenmilch *die*.

**dried fruit** *n* Trockenobst *das*, Dörrobst *das*.

**dried-up** *adj* ausgetrocknet.

**drier** [ˈdraɪəʳ] *n* = dryer.

**drift** [drɪft] *n* - **1.** [of people] Strom *der*; **the ~ back to traditional values** die Rückbesinnung auf traditionelle Werte - **2.** [mass - of snow, leaves, sand] Verwehung *die* - **3.** [meaning]: **I get her general ~** ich verstehe, worauf sie hinauslwill ⬦ *vi* - **1.** [boat, snow, sand, leaves] treiben - **2.** [person] sich treiben lassen; **to**

**~ into sthg** [job, marriage] in etw (*A*) hineinlrutschen; **to ~ apart** sich fremd werden.
➨ **drift off** *vi* einlschlummern.

**drifter** [ˈdrɪftəʳ] *n*: **he is a ~** er lässt sich treiben.

**driftwood** [ˈdrɪftwʊd] *n* Treibholz *das*.

**drill** [drɪl] *n* - **1.** [tool] Bohrer *der* - **2.** [exercise, training] Übung *die* (für den Ernstfall) ⬦ *vt* - **1.** [metal, wood, hole] bohren - **2.** [instruct] drillen; **to ~ sthg into sb** jm etw einlbläuen ⬦ *vi*: **to ~ (into sthg)** bohren (in etw (*A*)); **to ~ for sthg** nach etw bohren.

**drilling platform** [ˈdrɪlɪŋ-] *n* Bohrinsel *die*.

**drily** [ˈdraɪlɪ] *adv* = dryly.

**drink** [drɪŋk] (*pt* **drank**; *pp* **drunk**) *n* - **1.** [gen] Getränk *das*; **a ~ of water** ein Glas Wasser - **2.** [alcoholic beverage] Drink *der*; **to have a ~** etwas trinken - **3.** [alcohol] Alkohol *der* ⬦ *vt* trinken ⬦ *vi* trinken; **to ~ to sb/sthg** auf jn/etw anlstoßen.

**drinkable** [ˈdrɪŋkəbl] *adj* trinkbar.

**drink-driving** *Br*, **drunk-driving** *Am n* Trunkenheit *die* am Steuer.

**drinker** [ˈdrɪŋkəʳ] *n* Trinker *der*, -in *die*.

**drinking** [ˈdrɪŋkɪŋ] *adj*: **he's not much of a ~ man** er trinkt nicht viel Alkohol ⬦ *n* Trinken *das*.

**drinking companion** *n* Trinkbruder *der*.

**drinking fountain** *n* Trinkbrunnen *der*.

**drinking-up time** *n Br* Zeitpunkt kurz vor dem Schließen einer Bar, zu dem die Gäste ihre Getränke austrinken müssen.

**drinking water** *n* Trinkwasser *das*

**drip** [drɪp] (*pt* & *pp* -**ped**; *cont* -**ping**) *n* - **1.** [drop] Tropfen *der* - **2.** MED Tropf *der*, Infusion *die*; **to be on a ~** am Tropf hängen - **3.** *inf* [wimp] Niete *die* ⬦ *vt* tropfen ⬦ *vi* tropfen; **to be ~ping with** [diamonds, furs] behangen sein mit; **I'm ~ping with sweat** mir läuft der Schweiß nur so herunter.

**drip-dry** *adj* bügelfrei.

**drip-feed** *n* intravenöse Ernährung ⬦ *vt* intravenös ernähren.

**dripping** [ˈdrɪpɪŋ] *adj* - **1.** [person, clothes, hair]: **~ (wet)** klatschnass - **2.** [tap] tropfend ⬦ *n* CU-LIN [from meat] Brat(en)fett *das*.

**drive** [draɪv] (*pt* **drove**; *pp* **driven**) *n* - **1.** [journey] Fahrt *die*; **an hour's ~** eine Stunde Fahrt; **to go for a ~** spazieren fahren - **2.** [urge] Trieb *der* - **3.** [campaign] Aktion *die* - **4.** (*U*) [energy] Energie *die* - **5.** [in front of house] Einfahrt *die* - **6.** [stroke - in golf] Treibschlag *der*; [ - in tennis] Drive *der* - **7.** AUT: **left-/right-hand ~** Links-/Rechtslenkung *die* - **8.** COMPUT Laufwerk *das* ⬦ *vt* - **1.** [vehicle, passenger] fahren; **he ~s a taxi** er ist Taxifahrer; **to ~ sb home** jn nach Hause fahren - **2.** TECH [operate] anltreiben; **~n by**

electricity mit elektrischem Antrieb
- **3.** [chase - cattle, clouds, people] treiben; **they
were ~n from** their homeland sie wurden aus
ihrer Heimat vertrieben - **4.** [motivate]: **~ n by
greed/ambition** von Gier/Ehrgeiz getrieben
- **5.** [force]: **to ~ sb to do sthg** jn dazu treiben,
etw zu tun; **to ~ sb hard** jn schinden; **to ~ sb
mad** OR **crazy** jn verrückt machen - **6.** [hammer] schlagen - **7.** SPORT [hit] schlagen; [kick]
schießen ⬦ *vi* fahren; **can you ~?** kannst du
Auto fahren?

➤ **drive at** *vt fus*: **what are you driving at?** worauf willst du hinaus?

➤ **drive out** *vt sep* [person, evil spirit] vertreiben.

**drive-in** *esp Am adj* Drive-in- ⬦ *n* - **1.** [restaurant] Drive-in-Restaurant *das* - **2.** [cinema] Autokino *das.*

**drivel** ['drɪvl] *n inf* Quatsch *der.*

**driven** ['drɪvn] *pp* ⊨ **drive.**

**driver** ['draɪvə'] *n* - **1.** [of vehicle] Fahrer *der*, -in
*die* - **2.** COMPUT Treiber *der.*

**driver's license** *n Am* = **driving licence.**

**drive shaft** *n* Antriebswelle *die.*

**driveway** ['draɪvweɪ] *n* Auffahrt *die.*

**driving** ['draɪvɪŋ] *adj* [rain] strömend; [wind]
stürmisch ⬦ *n* Fahren *das.*

**driving force** *n* treibende Kraft.

**driving instructor** *n* Fahrlehrer *der*, -in
*die.*

**driving lesson** *n* Fahrstunde *die.*

**driving licence** *Br*, **driver's license** *Am n*
Führerschein *der.*

**driving mirror** *n* Rückspiegel *der.*

**driving school** *n* Fahrschule *die.*

**driving test** *n* Fahrprüfung *die.*

**drizzle** ['drɪzl] *n* Sprühregen *der* ⬦ *v impers*:
**it's drizzling** es nieselt.

**drizzly** ['drɪzlɪ] (*compar* **-ier;** *superl* **-iest**) *adj*
Niesel-; **it's ~** es nieselt.

**droll** [drəʊl] *adj* drollig.

**dromedary** ['drɒmədrɪ] (*pl* **-ies**) *n* Dromedar
*das.*

**drone** [drəʊn] *n* - **1.** [sound - of machine, engine,
loudspeaker] Dröhnen *das;* [ - of insect] Summen
*das* - **2.** [male bee] Drohne *die* ⬦ *vi* dröhnen,
brummen.

➤ **drone on** *vi* monoton sprechen; **to ~ on
about sthg** über etw (A) (stundenlang) labern.

**drool** [druːl] *vi* - **1.** [dribble] sabbern - **2.** *fig* [admire]: **he stood there ~ing over the sports car** er
konnte sich an dem Sportwagen nicht satt
sehen; **they sat there ~ing over their favourite
recipes** sie schwärmten von ihren Lieblingsrezepten.

**droop** [druːp] *vi* - **1.** [hang down] herunterl-

hängen; [flower] den Kopf hängen lassen
- **2.** *fig* [spirits]: **his spirits ~ed** sein Mut sank.

**drop** [drɒp] (*pt & pp* **-ped;** *cont* **-ping**) *n* - **1.** [of
liquid] Tropfen *der* - **2.** [sweet] Drops *der* OR *das*
- **3.** [decrease]: **~ (in sthg)** Rückgang *der* (von
etw); [in salary] Minderung *die* (von etw)
- **4.** [vertical distance] Höhenunterschied *der;*
**there's a 50 m ~** hier geht es 50 m (senkrecht) hinunter ⬦ *vt* - **1.** [gen] fallen lassen;
**to ~ (sb) a hint** (jm gegenüber) eine Anspielung machen - **2.** [decrease, lower] senken
- **3.** [leave out] weglassen - **4.** [let out of car] absetzen - **5.** TENNIS [lose] verlieren - **6.** [write]: **to
~ sb a line** OR **note** jm ein paar Zeilen schreiben ⬦ *vi* - **1.** [fall] fallen; [with exhaustion] umlfallen - **2.** [decrease] sinken - **3.** [voice] leiser
werden.

➤ **drops** *npl* MED Tropfen *pl.*

➤ **drop by** *vi inf* vorbeilkommen.

➤ **drop in** *vi inf*: **to ~ in (on sb)** vorbeilkommen
(bei jm).

➤ **drop off** *vt sep* [person] ablsetzen; [letter, package] ablschicken ⬦ *vi* - **1.** [fall asleep] einlnicken - **2.** [grow less] zurücklgehen.

➤ **drop out** *vi*: **to ~ out (of** OR **from sthg)** auslsteigen (aus etw).

**drop-in centre** *n* soziale Beratungs- und Begegnungsstätte, die jedem offen steht.

**droplet** ['drɒplɪt] *n* Tröpfchen *das.*

**dropout** ['drɒpaʊt] *n* - **1.** [from society] Aussteiger *der*, -in *die* - **2.** [from university] Studienabbrecher *der*, -in *die.*

**dropper** ['drɒpə'] *n* Pipette *die.*

**droppings** ['drɒpɪŋz] *npl* Kot *der;* [of horses] Äpfel *pl.*

**drop shot** *n* [in tennis] Stoppball *der.*

**dross** [drɒs] *n* (U) - **1.** TECH [waste material] Schlacke *die* - **2.** *fig inf* [rubbish] Mist *der.*

**drought** [draʊt] *n* Dürre *die.*

**drove** [drəʊv] *pt* ⊨ **drive** ⬦ *n* [of people]
Schar *die.*

**drown** [draʊn] *vt* - **1.** [person, animal] ertränken
- **2.** [sound]: **to ~ sb/sthg (out)** jn/etw übertönen ⬦ *vi* ertrinken.

**drowsy** ['draʊzɪ] (*compar* **-ier;** *superl* **-iest**) *adj*
schläfrig.

**drudge** [drʌdʒ] *n* Schwerarbeiter *der;* **I'm not
your household ~!** ich bin nicht dein Dienstmädchen!

**drudgery** ['drʌdʒərɪ] *n* Schinderei *die*,
Schufterei *die.*

**drug** [drʌg] (*pt & pp* **-ged;** *cont* **-ging**) *n*
- **1.** [medication] Arzneimittel *das*, Medikament *das* - **2.** [illegal substance] Droge *die*,
Rauschgift *das;* **to be on ~s** drogen- OR
rauschgiftabhängig sein ⬦ *vt* [person, animal]
Drogen verabreichen (+ D), betäuben; [food,
drink] mit Drogen versetzen.

**drug abuse** n Drogenmissbrauch der.

**drug addict** n Drogensüchtige der, die.

**drug addiction** n Drogensucht die, Rauschgiftsucht die.

**drug dealer** n Drogenhändler der, -in die.

**druggist** ['drʌgɪst] n Am Apotheker der, -in die.

**drugstore** ['drʌgstɔːr] n Am Drugstore der.

**druid** ['druːɪd] n Druide der.

**drum** [drʌm] (pt & pp -med; cont -ming) n - **1.** [instrument, cylinder] Trommel die - **2.** [container] Tonne die <> vt & vi trommeln.
◆ **drums** npl Schlagzeug das.
◆ **drum into** vt sep: to ~ sthg into sb jm etw einlpauken OR einlhämmern.
◆ **drum up** vt sep [people] zusammenltrommeln; [business] anlkurbeln.

**drumbeat** ['drʌmbiːt] n Trommelschlag der.

**drum brake** n Trommelbremse die.

**drummer** ['drʌmər] n Schlagzeuger der, -in die.

**drumming** ['drʌmɪŋ] n Trommeln das.

**drum roll** n Trommelwirbel der.

**drumstick** ['drʌmstɪk] n - **1.** [for drum] Trommelschlägel der - **2.** [of chicken] Keule die.

**drunk** [drʌŋk] pp ⊳ **drink** <> adj - **1.** [on alcohol] betrunken; ~ **and disorderly** betrunken und renitent - **2.** fig [excited]: **to be ~ with** OR **on sthg** berauscht von etw sein <> n [on one occasion] Betrunkene der, die; [habitual] Trinker der, -in die.

**drunkard** ['drʌŋkəd] n Trinker der, -in die.

**drunk-driving** n Am = drink-driving.

**drunken** ['drʌŋkn] adj [person] betrunken; a ~ **evening** ein feuchtfröhlicher Abend; **in a ~ stupor** sinnlos betrunken.

**drunken driving** n = drink-driving.

**drunkenness** ['drʌŋkənɪs] n Trunkenheit die.

**dry** [draɪ] (compar -ier; superl -iest; pt & pp dried) adj - **1.** [gen] trocken - **2.** [river, lake] ausgetrocknet - **3.** [thirsty] durstig; **to feel** OR **be ~** durstig sein, Durst haben <> vt & vi trocknen.
◆ **dry out** vt sep trocknen (lassen) <> vi ausltrocknen.
◆ **dry up** vt sep [dishes] abltrocknen <> vi - **1.** [river, lake, well] ausltrocknen, versiegen - **2.** [supplies, inspiration] zur Neige gehen - **3.** [actor, speaker] stecken bleiben - **4.** [dry dishes] abltrocknen.

**dry-clean** vt chemisch reinigen.

**dry cleaner** n: ~'s chemische Reinigung.

**dry cleaning** n chemische Reinigung.

**dry dock** n Trockendock das.

**dryer** ['draɪər] n [for clothes] Trockner der.

**dry goods** npl Textilwaren pl.

**dry ice** n Trockeneis das.

**dry land** n Festland das.

**dryly** ['draɪlɪ] adv [wryly] trocken.

**dryness** ['draɪnɪs] n - **1.** [lack of water] Trockenheit die - **2.** [wryness] (trockene) Ironie.

**dry rot** n Trockenfäule die.

**dry run** n Probelauf der.

**dry ski slope** n Sommerskihang der.

**drystone wall** ['draɪstəʊn-] n Trockenmauerwerk das.

**DSc** (abbr of Doctor of Science) n Doktorgrad in Naturwissenschaften oder dessen Inhaber.

**DSS** (abbr of Department of Social Security) n britisches Sozialamt.

**DST** abbr of daylight saving time.

**DTI** (abbr of Department of Trade and Industry) n Handels- und Industrieministerium das.

**DTP** (abbr of desktop publishing) n DTP das.

**DT's** [ˌdiːˈtiːz] (abbr of delirium tremens) npl inf: **to have the ~** im Delirium sein.

**dual** ['djuːəl] adj doppelt, Doppel-; ~ **personality** gespaltene Persönlichkeit.

**dual carriageway** n Br vierspurige Straße.

**dual control** n [in car] doppelte Pedale pl.

**dual nationality** n doppelte Staatsbürgerschaft.

**dual-purpose** adj Mehrzweck-.

**dubbed** [dʌbd] adj - **1.** CINEMA synchronisiert - **2.** [nicknamed] genannt.

**dubious** ['djuːbjəs] adj - **1.** [suspect, questionable] dubios, zweifelhaft - **2.** [uncertain, undecided]: **to be ~ about doing sthg** nicht wissen, ob man etw tun soll.

**Dublin** ['dʌblɪn] n Dublin nt.

**Dubliner** ['dʌblɪnər] n Dubliner der, -in die.

**duchess** ['dʌtʃɪs] n Herzogin die.

**duchy** ['dʌtʃɪ] (pl -ies) n Herzogtum das.

**duck** [dʌk] n Ente die; **to take to sthg like a ~ to water** bei etw sofort in seinem Element sein <> vt - **1.** [head] ducken, einlziehen - **2.** [responsibility, duty] auslweichen (+ D) - **3.** [person] unterltauchen <> vi sich ducken.
◆ **duck out** vi: **to ~ out (of sthg)** sich (aus etw) zurücklziehen, (aus etw) auslsteigen.

**duckling** ['dʌklɪŋ] n - **1.** [animal] Entenküken das - **2.** (U) [food] junge Ente.

**duct** [dʌkt] n - **1.** [pipe] Leitung die, Rohr das - **2.** ANAT Kanal der.

**dud** [dʌd] adj - **1.** [false] falsch, gefälscht - **2.** [useless] wertlos - **3.**: a ~ **bomb/shell** ein Blindgänger <> n - **1.** [person] Niete die, Ver-

sager *der*, -in *die* - **2.** [note] Blüte *die*; [cheque]
ungedeckter Scheck - **3.** [bomb, shell] Blindgänger *der*.

**dude** [dju:d] *n Am inf* Typ *der*.

**dude ranch** *n Am* Touristenranch *die*.

**due** [dju:] *adj* - **1.** [expected] fällig; **the book's
~ (out) in May** das Buch soll im Mai erschei-
nen - **2.** [proper] ordnungsgemäß, nötig; **in
~ course** zu gegebener Zeit - **3.** [owed, owing]
fällig <> *n:* **to give him his ~,** ... das muss man
ihm lassen, ... <> *adv:* **~ west** genau nach
Westen.

➤ **dues** *npl* Abgaben *pl*, Gebühren *pl*.

➤ **due to** *prep* wegen (+ *G*, *D*).

**due date** *n* Fällingkeitsdatum *das*.

**duel** ['dju:əl] *n* Duell *das*.

**duet** [dju:'et] *n* Duett *das*.

**duff** [dʌf] *adj Br inf* nutzlos, wertlos.

➤ **duff up** *vt sep Br inf:* **to ~ sb up** jm verprügeln.

**duffel bag** ['dʌfl-] *n* Seesack *der*.

**duffel coat** ['dʌfl-] *n* Dufflecoat *der*.

**duffle bag** ['dʌfl-] *n* = **duffel bag.**

**duffle coat** ['dʌfl-] *n* = **duffel coat.**

**dug** [dʌg] *pt* & *pp* ⊳ **dig.**

**dugout** ['dʌgaʊt] *n* - **1.** [canoe] Einbaum *der*
- **2.** SPORT Unterstand *der*.

**duke** [dju:k] *n* Herzog *der*.

**dull** [dʌl] *adj* - **1.** [boring] langweilig - **2.** [colour,
light] matt - **3.** [day, weather] trüb - **4.** [noise, pain]
dumpf <> *vt* - **1.** [senses] abstumpfen; [pain]
dämpfen - **2.** [make less bright - metal] stumpf
werden lassen; [ - colour] verblassen lassen.

**duly** ['dju:lɪ] *adv* - **1.** [properly] ordnungsgemäß
- **2.** [as expected] erwartungsgemäß.

**dumb** [dʌm] *adj* - **1.** [unable to speak] stumm; **to
be struck ~** sprachlos sein - **2.** *esp Am inf* [stu-
pid] dumm.

**dumbbell** ['dʌmbel] *n* Hantel *die*.

**dumbfound** [dʌm'faʊnd] *vt* verblüffen; **to be
~ed** verblüfft sein, sprachlos sein.

**dumbstruck** ['dʌmstrʌk] *adj* völlig verblüfft
sein, völlig sprachlos sein.

**dumbwaiter** [,dʌm'weɪtə'] *n* Speiseaufzug
*der*.

**dumdum (bullet)** ['dʌmdʌm-] *n* Dumdum-
geschoss *das*.

**dummy** ['dʌmɪ] (*pl* **-ies**) *adj* unecht; **a ~ gun** eine Spielzeugpistole <> *n* - **1.** [model of human
figure - for tailoring] Schneiderpuppe *die*; [ - for
crash testing] Dummy *der*; [ - in shop] Schaufensterpuppe *die* - **2.** [copy, fake object] Attrappe *die*
- **3.** *Br* [for baby] Schnuller *der*.

**dummy run** *n* Probe *die*, Probelauf *der*.

**dump** [dʌmp] *n* - **1.** [for rubbish] Müllhalde *die*
- **2.** [for ammunition] Munitionslager *das* - **3.** *inf*

*pej* [ugly place - house, flat] Loch *das*; [ - hotel] Absteige *die*; [ - town] schäbiges Kaff <> *vt* - **1.** *inf*
[put down] abladen, hinschmeißen; [load] ab-
laden - **2.** [dispose of - waste, rubbish] weg-
werfen; [ - car] zurücklassen - **3.** COMM zu
Schleuderpreisen OR Dumpingpreisen
verkaufen - **4.** COMPUT löschen - **5.** *inf* [jilt] in die
Wüste schicken.

➤ **dumps** *npl:* **to be (down) in the ~s** ziemlich
down sein.

**dumper (truck)** ['dʌmpə'-] *Br*, **dump truck**
*Am n* Kipper *der*, Kipplaster *der*.

**dumping** ['dʌmpɪŋ] *n* [of waste] Abladen *das*;
**'no ~'** 'Schutt abladen verboten'.

**dumping ground** *n* Abladeplatz *der*; [for
waste] Müllkippe *die*.

**dumpling** ['dʌmplɪŋ] *n* CULIN Kloß *der*, Knödel
*der*.

**dumpster** *n Am* Müllcontainer *der*.

**dump truck** *n Am* = **dumper truck.**

**dumpy** ['dʌmpɪ] (*compar* **-ier**; *superl* **-iest**) *adj inf*
dicklich, untersetzt.

**dunce** [dʌns] *n* Ignorant *der*, Dummkopf *der*.

**dune** [dju:n] *n* Düne *die*.

**dung** [dʌŋ] *n* Dung *der*, Mist *der*.

**dungarees** [,dʌŋgə'ri:z] *npl* - **1.** *Br* [for work] Ar-
beitshose *die*; [fashion garment] Segeltuch *das*
- **2.** *Am* [heavy jeans] Latzhose *die*.

**dungeon** ['dʌndʒən] *n* Verlies *das*, Kerker
*der*.

**dunk** [dʌŋk] *vt inf* eintauchen.

**Dunkirk** [dʌn'kɜːk] *n* Dünkirchen *nt*.

**duo** ['dju:əʊ] *n* - **1.** [of singers, musicians] Duett *das*;
[on stage] Duo *das* - **2.** [couple] Duo *das*.

**duodenal ulcer** [,dju:əʊ'di:nl-] *n* Zwölffin-
gerdarmgeschwür *das*.

**dupe** [dju:p] *n* Dumme *der*, *die* <> *vt* hereinlegen; **to ~ sb into doing sthg** jn (auf betrüge-
rische Weise) dazu bringen, etw zu tun.

**duplex** ['dju:pleks] *n Am* - **1.** [apartment] Doppe-
lapartment *das* - **2.** [house] Zweifamilien-
haus *das*.

**duplicate** [*adj* & *n* 'dju:plɪkət, *vb* 'dju:plɪkeɪt] *adj*
[document] kopiert; **a ~ key** ein Nachschlüssel
<> *n* Duplikat *das*, Kopie *die*; **in ~** in doppel-
ter Ausfertigung <> *vt* - **1.** [copy - document]
kopieren, vervielfältigen; [ - key] nachl-
machen - **2.** [repeat] doppelt tun.

**duplication** [,dju:plɪ'keɪʃn] *n (U)* - **1.** [copying]
Kopieren *das*, Vervielfältigen *das* - **2.** [repeti-
tion] Wiederholung *die*.

**duplicity** [dju:'plɪsətɪ] *n fml* Falschheit *die*.

**Dur** *abk für Durham*, in Postanschrift verwendet.

**durability** [,djʊərə'bɪlətɪ] *n* Haltbarkeit *die*;
[of relationship] Dauerhaftigkeit *die*.

**durable** ['djʊərəbl] adj strapazierfähig, haltbar.

**duration** [djʊ'reɪʃn] n Dauer die; **for the ~ of** für die Dauer von.

**duress** [djʊ'res] n: **under ~** unter Zwang.

**Durex**® ['djʊəreks] n Kondom das.

**during** ['djʊərɪŋ] prep während (+ G).

**dusk** [dʌsk] n Abenddämmerung die.

**dusky** ['dʌskɪ] (compar **-ier;** superl **-iest**) adj literary [skin] dunkel(häutig).

**dust** [dʌst] n Staub der; **to gather ~** [get dusty] Staub anlsetzen <> vt **- 1.** [clean] ablstauben **- 2.** [cover]: **to ~ sthg with sthg** etw mit etw bestäuben.
◆ **dust off** vt sep **- 1.** [clean] ablklopfen **- 2.** fig [reuse] entstauben.

**dustbin** ['dʌstbɪn] n Br Mülltonne die.

**dustbowl** ['dʌstbəʊl] n GEOL Trockengebiet das.

**dustcart** ['dʌstkɑːt] n Br Müllwagen der.

**dust cover** n = dust jacket.

**duster** ['dʌstər] n **- 1.** [cloth] Staubtuch das, Staublappen der **- 2.** Am [overall] Staubmantel der.

**dust jacket** n [on book] Schutzumschlag der.

**dustman** ['dʌstmən] (pl **-men** [-mən]) n Br Müllmann der.

**dust mite** n Staubmilbe die.

**dustpan** ['dʌstpæn] n Kehrschaufel die.

**dustsheet** ['dʌstʃiːt] n Br Staublaken das.

**dust storm** n Sandsturm der.

**dustup** ['dʌstʌp] n inf Handgemenge das, Gerangel das.

**dusty** ['dʌstɪ] (compar **-ier;** superl **-iest**) adj staubig, verstaubt.

**Dutch** [dʌtʃ] adj niederländisch, holländisch <> n [language] Niederländisch(e) das <> npl: **the ~** die Niederländer, die Holländer <> adv: **to go ~** getrennt bezahlen.

**Dutch auction** n Br Auktion, bei der der Preis gesenkt wird, bis sich ein Käufer findet.

**Dutch barn** n Br Scheune mit doppelt geknicktem Dach, niedrigen Seitenwänden und breiten Doppeltüren.

**Dutch cap** n Br Pessar das.

**Dutch courage** n angetrunkener Mut.

**Dutch elm disease** n (U) Ulmensterben das.

**Dutchman** ['dʌtʃmən] (pl **-men** [-mən]) n Niederländer der, Holländer der.

**Dutchwoman** ['dʌtʃˌwʊmən] (pl **-women** [-ˌwɪmɪn]) n Niederländerin die, Holländerin die.

**dutiable** ['djuːtjəbl] adj zollpflichtig.

**dutiful** ['djuːtɪfʊl] adj pflichtbewusst.

**duty** ['djuːtɪ] (pl **-ies**) n **- 1.** (U) [responsibility] Pflicht die; **to do one's ~** seine Pflicht tun **- 2.** (U) [work] Dienst der; **to be on ~** Dienst haben; **to be off ~** dienstfrei haben **- 3.** [tax] Zoll der.
◆ **duties** npl [tasks] Aufgaben pl.

**duty bound** adj: **to be ~ (to do sthg)** verpflichtet sein (etw zu tun).

**duty-free** adj zollfrei <> n (U) [goods] zollfreie Waren pl.

**duty-free shop** n Duty-free-Shop der.

**duty officer** n MIL diensthabender Offizier; [in police station] diensthabender Beamter, diensthabende Beamtin.

**duvet** ['duːveɪ] n Br Daunendecke die.

**duvet cover** n Br Bettbezug der (für eine Daunendecke).

**DVD** (abbr of **Digital Versatile Disk**) n DVD die.

**DVLC** (abbr of **Driver and Vehicle Licensing Centre**) n britische Führerschein- und Kraftfahrzeugzulassungsstelle.

**dwarf** [dwɔːf] (pl **-s** OR **dwarves** [dwɔːvz]) adj [plant, animal] Zwerg- <> n Zwerg der, -in die <> vt [tower over] winzig erscheinen lassen.

**dwell** [dwel] (pt & pp **dwelt** OR **-ed**) vi literary [live] wohnen.
◆ **dwell on** vt fus [talk about] sich lange befassen mit; [think about] lange nachldenken über (+ A).

**-dweller** ['dwelər] suffix Bewohner der, -in die.

**dwelling** ['dwelɪŋ] n literary Wohnung die.

**dwelt** [dwelt] pt & pp ⊏> dwell.

**dwindle** ['dwɪndl] vi dahinlschwinden.

**dwindling** ['dwɪndlɪŋ] adj schwindend.

**dye** [daɪ] n Farbstoff der <> vt färben.

**dyed** [daɪd] adj gefärbt.

**dying** ['daɪɪŋ] cont ⊏> die <> adj **- 1.** [person, animal] sterbend **- 2.** fig [tradition, language] aussterbend <> npl: **the ~** die Sterbenden pl.

**dyke** [daɪk] n = dike.

**dynamic** [daɪ'næmɪk] adj dynamisch.
◆ **dynamics** npl Dynamik die.

**dynamism** ['daɪnəmɪzm] n Dynamik die.

**dynamite** ['daɪnəmaɪt] n (U) **- 1.** [explosive] Dynamit das **- 2.** inf fig [story, news]: **to be ~** viel Zündstoff enthalten **- 3.** inf fig [excellent]: **to be ~** eine Wucht sein <> vt sprengen.

**dynamo** ['daɪnəməʊ] (pl **-s**) n TECH Dynamo der; AUT Lichtmaschine die.

**dynasty** [Br 'dɪnəstɪ, Am 'daɪnəstɪ] (pl **-ies**) n Dynastie die.

**dysentery** ['dɪsntrɪ] n (U) Ruhr die.

**dyslexia** [dɪs'leksɪə] n (U) Legasthenie die.

D

**dyslexic** [dɪs'leksɪk] *adj* legasthenisch; **to be ~** Legastheniker/Legasthenikerin sein.

**dyspepsia** [dɪs'pepsɪə] *n (U)* MED Verdauungsstörung *die.*

**dystrophy** ['dɪstrəfɪ] *n* ▷ muscular dystrophy.

**e** (*pl* **e's** OR **es**), **E** (*pl* **E's** OR **Es**) [i:] *n* [letter] e *das,* E *das.*
◆ **E** *n* - **1.** MUS E *das* - **2.** *abbr of* **east** - **3.** *inf* (*abbr of* **ecstasy**) E *das.*

**E111** *n* E111.

**ea.** *abbr of* **each.**

**each** [i:tʃ] *adj* jede, -r, -s ◇ *pron:* **~ (one)** jede, -r, -s; **~ other** einander; **separated from ~** other voneinander getrennt; **they know ~** other sie kennen sich; **they kissed ~** other on the cheek sie küssten sich auf die Wange; **there's one ~** es ist für jeden eins da; **I'd like one of ~** ich möchte von jedem/jeder eins; **they cost £10 ~** sie kosten je 10 Pfund.

**eager** ['i:gəʳ] *adj* [person] eifrig; [expression] erwartungsvoll; **to be ~ for sthg** auf etw (A) erpicht sein; **to be ~ to do sthg** etw unbedingt tun wollen.

**eagerly** ['i:gəlɪ] *adv* eifrig.

**eagle** ['i:gl] *n* Adler *der.*

**eagle-eyed** [-aɪd] *adj:* **an ~ person** eine Person mit Adleraugen.

**E and OE** (*abbr of* **errors and omissions excepted**) *Fehler und Auslassungen ausgenommen.*

**ear** [ɪəʳ] *n* - **1.** [of person, animal] Ohr *das;* **to play by ~** MUS nach Gehör spielen; **to go in one ~ and out the other** *inf* zu einem Ohr rein und zum anderen wieder raus gehen; **to have** OR **keep one's ~ to the ground** *inf* die Ohren offen halten; **to have sb's ~** Einfluss auf jn haben; **to have an ~ for sthg** ein Gehör für etw haben; **I'll play it by ~** ich werde es auf mich zukommen lassen - **2.** [of corn] Ähre *die.*

**earache** ['ɪəreɪk] *n* Ohrenschmerzen *pl.*

**eardrum** ['ɪədrʌm] *n* Trommelfell *das.*

**earl** [ɜ:l] *n* Graf *der.*

**earlier** ['ɜ:lɪəʳ] *adj & adv* früher; **~ on** früher.

**earliest** ['ɜ:lɪəst] *adj* - **1.** [first] frühstmöglich; **at the ~ opportunity** so bald wie möglich - **2.** [most early] frühest ◇ *adv:* **she'll not be back till four o'clock at the ~** sie wird frühestens um vier Uhr wieder hier sein.

**earlobe** ['ɪələʊbl] *n* Ohrläppchen *das.*

**early** ['ɜ:lɪ] (*compar* **-ier;** *superl* **-iest**) *adj* früh; **~ death** vorzeitiger Tod; **at an ~ hour** zu früher Stunde; **at an ~ age** [early in life] schon früh; [as a child] im Kindesalter; **in the ~ afternoon** am frühen Nachmittag; **to have an ~ breakfast/night** früh frühstücken/zu Bett gehen ◇ *adv* früh; **to leave ~** [person] früher gehen; [bus, train] zu früh abfahren; **as ~ as next week** schon nächste Woche; **~ on** früh.

**early closing** *n:* **today is ~** heute schließen die Geschäfte früher.

**early retirement** *n:* **to take ~** in den vorzeitigen Ruhestand gehen.

**early warning system** *n* MIL Frühwarnsystem *das.*

**earmark** ['ɪəmɑ:k] *vt:* **to be ~ed for sthg** für etw vorgesehen sein.

**earn** [ɜ:n] *vt* - **1.** [gen] verdienen - **2.** COMM erwirtschaften.

**earned income** [ɜ:nd-] *n* erarbeitetes Einkommen.

**earner** ['ɜ:nəʳ] *n* - **1.** [person] Verdiener *der,* -in *die* - **2.** *Br inf* [deal]: **a nice little ~** eine nette Einnahmequelle.

**earnest** ['ɜ:nɪst] *adj* ernsthaft.
◆ **in earnest** *adj:* **I'm in ~** ich meine es ernst; **to begin in ~** richtig anlfangen ◇ *adv* ernsthaft.

**earnestly** ['ɜ:nɪstlɪ] *adv* ernsthaft.

**earnings** ['ɜ:nɪŋz] *npl* [of person] Einkommen *das;* [of business] Ertrag *der.*

**earnings-related** *adj* einkommensabhängig.

**ear, nose and throat specialist** *n* Hals-, Nasen-, Ohrenarzt *der,* -ärztin *die.*

**earphones** ['ɪəfəʊnz] *npl* Kopfhörer *der.*

**earpiece** *n* [of telephone] Hörmuschel *die;* [of radio, mobile phone] ≈ Kopfhörer *der.*

**earplugs** ['ɪəplʌgz] *npl* Ohropax® *pl.*

**earring** ['ɪərɪŋ] *n* Ohrring *der.*

**earshot** ['ɪəʃɒt] *n:* **within/out of ~** in/außer Hörweite.

**earsplitting** ['ɪəsplɪtɪŋ] *adj* ohrenbetäubend.

**earth** [ɜ:θ] *n* [gen] *Br* ELEC Erde *die;* **how/what/where/why on ~ ...?** wie/was/wo/warum um Himmels willen ...?; **to cost the ~** *Br* ein Vermögen kosten ◇ *vt Br:* **to be ~ed** geerdet sein.

**earthenware** [ˈɜːθnweəʳ] *adj* aus Ton ◇ *n (U)* Töpferwaren *pl*.

**earthling** [ˈɜːθlɪŋ] *n* Erdling *der*.

**earthly** [ˈɜːθlɪ] *adj* - **1.** [of material world] irdisch - **2.** *inf* [reason] erdenklich; **for no ~ reason** ohne den geringsten Grund.

**earthquake** [ˈɜːθkweɪk] *n* Erdbeben *das*.

**earthshattering** [ˈɜːθˌʃætərɪŋ] *adj Br inf* weltbewegend.

**earth tremor** *n* Erdstoß *der*.

**earthward(s)** [ˈɜːθwəd(z)] *adv* auf die Erde zu.

**earthworks** [ˈɜːθwɜːks] *npl* ARCHAEOL Erdwälle *pl*.

**earthworm** [ˈɜːθwɜːm] *n* Regenwurm *der*.

**earthy** [ˈɜːθɪ] (*compar* **-ier;** *superl* **-iest**) *adj* - **1.** [humour, person] derb - **2.** [taste, smell] erdig.

**earwax** [ˈɪəwæks] *n* Ohrenschmalz *der*.

**earwig** [ˈɪəwɪg] *n* Ohrwurm *der*.

**ease** [iːz] *n* - **1.** [in doing sthg] Leichtigkeit *die;* **it is designed for ~ of use** es ist so konzipiert, dass es einfach zu gebrauchen ist; **to do sthg with ~** etw mit Leichtigkeit tun - **2.** [comfort]: **a life of ~** ein komfortables Leben; **to put sb at ~** jm die Befangenheit nehmen; **I feel at ~ (with him)** ich fühle mich (in seiner Gegenwart) wohl; **ill at ~** unbehaglich ◇ *vt* - **1.** [make less severe - pain] lindern; [ - restriction, problem] verringern - **2.** [move carefully]: **she ~d herself out of the armchair** sie erhob sich behutsam aus dem Sessel; **she ~d the window open** sie öffnete behutsam das Fenster ◇ *vi* [pain, rain] nachlassen; [grip] sich lockern; [problem] sich verringern.

➤ **ease off** *vi* [pain, rain] nachlassen; [problem] sich verringern.

➤ **ease up** *vi* - **1.** [rain] nachlassen - **2.** [relax] sich *(D)* mehr Ruhe gönnen; **to ~ up on sb** *inf* mit jm weniger streng umgehen.

**easel** [ˈiːzl] *n* Staffelei *die*.

**easily** [ˈiːzɪlɪ] *adv* - **1.** [without difficulty] leicht - **2.** [undoubtedly] zweifellos - **3.** [in a relaxed manner] entspannt.

**easiness** [ˈiːzɪnɪs] *n* Leichtigkeit *die*.

**east** [iːst] *adj* Ost-, östlich; **~ wind** Ostwind *der* ◇ *adv* [travel, face] ostwärds, nach Osten; **~ of** östlich von ◇ *n* - **1.** [direction] Osten *der* - **2.** [region]: **the ~** der Osten.

➤ **East** *n:* **the East** [Asia & POL] der Osten.

**East Anglia** [-ˈæŋglɪə] *n Region im Osten Englands.*

**eastbound** [ˈiːstbaʊnd] *adj* (in) Richtung Osten.

**East End** *n:* **the ~** der Londoner Osten nördlich der Themse.

**Easter** [ˈiːstəʳ] *n* Ostern *pl*.

**Easter egg** *n* Osterei *das*.

**easterly** [ˈiːstəlɪ] *adj* östlich; **~ wind** Ostwind *der;* **in an ~ direction** in östlicher Richtung.

**eastern** [ˈiːstən] *adj* Ost-.

➤ **Eastern** *adj* - **1.** [from Asia] östlich - **2.** POL Ost-.

**Eastern bloc** [-blɒk] *n:* **the ~** der Ostblock.

**Eastern Europe** *n* Osteuropa *nt*.

**Eastern Seaboard** *n* Ostküste *die (der USA).*

**Easter Sunday** *n* Ostersonntag *der*.

**East German** *adj* ostdeutsch ◇ *n* Ostdeutsche *der, die*.

**East Germany** *n:* (the former) ~ Ostdeutschland *nt*.

**eastward** [ˈiːstwəd] *adj* (in) Richtung Osten ◇ *adv* = **eastwards**.

**eastwards** [ˈiːstwədz] *adv* ostwärts.

**easy** [ˈiːzɪ] (*compar* **-ier;** *superl* **-iest**) *adj* - **1.** [not difficult] leicht; [route] einfach - **2.** [comfortable] leicht, einfach; **an ~ life** ein bequemes Leben - **3.** [relaxed] ungezwungen ◇ *adv:* **to go ~ on sb** *inf* [treat kindly] netter zu jm sein; **to go ~ on sthg** *inf* [not use too much] sparsam mit etw sein; **to take it** OR **things ~** *inf* [ease up] sich *(D)* mehr Ruhe gönnen; [have a rest] eine ruhige Kugel schieben.

**easy chair** *n* [armchair] Sessel *der*.

**easygoing** [ˌiːzɪˈgəʊɪŋ] *adj* [person] unbekümmert; [manner] lässig.

**eat** [iːt] (*pt* **ate;** *pp* **eaten**) *vt* [subj: person] essen; [subj: animal] fressen ◇ *vi* [person] essen; [animal] fressen.

➤ **eat away** *vt sep*, **eat into** *vt fus* - **1.** [subj: rust, acid] zerfressen - **2.** [savings] auf lzehren.

➤ **eat out** *vi* [at restaurant] essen gehen.

➤ **eat up** *vt sep* - **1.** [food - subj: person] auf lessen; [ - subj: animal] auf lfressen - **2.** *fig* [money, time] fressen.

**eatable** [ˈiːtəbl] *adj* essbar, genießbar.

**eaten** [ˈiːtn] *pp* ▻ **eat**.

**eater** [ˈiːtəʳ] *n* Esser *der*, -in *die*.

**eatery** [ˈiːtərɪ] (*pl* **-ies**) *n Am* Esslokal *das*.

**eating apple** [ˈiːtɪŋ-] *n* Essapfel *der*.

**eau de cologne** [ˌəʊdəkəˈləʊn] *n* Eau de Cologne *das*, Kölnischwasser *das*.

**eaves** [ˈiːvz] *npl* [of house] Dachvorsprung *der*.

**eavesdrop** [ˈiːvzdrɒp] (*pt* & *pp* **-ped;** *cont* **-ping**) *vi* lauschen; **to ~ on sb** jn belauschen.

**ebb** [eb] *n* Ebbe *die;* **the ~ and flow of sthg** *fig* das Auf und Ab von etw; **at a low ~** *fig* auf einem Tiefstand ◇ *vi* - **1.** [tide, sea] zurück lgehen - **2.** *literary* [strength, pain, feeling]: **to ~ (away)** dahinschwinden.

**ebb tide** *n* Ebbe *die*.

**ebony** [ˈebənɪ] *adj literary* schwarz wie Ebenholz ◇ *n* Ebenholz *das*.

**ebullient** [ɪˈbʌljənt] *adj* [person] ausgelassen;

[manner] überschwenglich; [wit] übersprudelnd.

**EC** (*abbr of* **European Community**) *n* EG *die*.

**e-cash** *n* COMPUT elektronisches Geld.

**ECB** (*abbr of* **European Central Bank**) *n* EZB *die*.

**eccentric** [ɪk'sentrɪk] *adj* exzentrisch <> *n* Exzentriker *der*, -in *die*.

**eccentricity** [ˌeksen'trɪsətɪ] (*pl* -ies) *n* Exzentrizität *die*.

**ecclesiastic(al)** [ɪˌkliːzɪ'æstɪk(l)] *adj* kirchlich.

**ECG** *n* - **1.** (*abbr of* **electrocardiogram**) EKG *das* - **2.** (*abbr of* **electrocardiograph**) EKG *das*.

**ECH** (*abbr of* **electric central heating**) *Br* elektrische Zentralheizung.

**echelon** ['eʃəlɒn] *n fml* [rank] Rang *der*.

**echo** ['ekəʊ] (*pl* -es; *pt* & *pp* -ed; *cont* -ing) *n* - **1.** [sound] Echo *das* - **2.** [reminder] Reminiszenz *die* <> *vt* [repeat - opinion] wiederlgeben; **he ~ed my words** er sagte genau dasselbe <> *vi* widerlhallen.

**éclair** [eɪ'kleə'] *n* Eclair *das*.

**eclectic** [ɪ'klektɪk] *adj* eklektisch.

**eclipse** [ɪ'klɪps] *n* - **1.** [of sun, moon] Eklipse *die*, Finsternis *die* - **2.** *fig* [decline] Niedergang *der* <> *vt fig* [overshadow] in den Schatten stellen.

**eco-friendly** *adj* umweltfreundlich.

**ecological** [ˌiːkə'lɒdʒɪkl] *adj* ökologisch; **an ~ group** eine Gruppe von Umweltschützern.

**ecologically** [ˌiːkə'lɒdʒɪklɪ] *adv* ökologisch; **~ friendly** umweltfreundlich.

**ecologist** [ɪ'kɒlədʒɪst] *n* - **1.** [scientist] Ökologe *der*, -gin *die* - **2.** [conservationist] Umweltschützer *der*, -in *die*.

**ecology** [ɪ'kɒlədʒɪ] *n* Ökologie *die*.

**economic** [ˌiːkə'nɒmɪk] *adj* - **1.** [growth, system, policy] Wirtschafts- - **2.** [business] wirtschaftlich.

**economical** [ˌiːkə'nɒmɪkl] *adj* wirtschaftlich; [person] sparsam.

**economics** [ˌiːkə'nɒmɪks] *n (U)* [study] Wirtschaftswissenschaften *pl* <> *npl* [of plan, business, trade] Wirtschaftlichkeit *die*.

**economist** [ɪ'kɒnəmɪst] *n* Wirtschaftswissenschaftler *der*, -in *die*.

**economize, -ise** [ɪ'kɒnəmaɪz] *vi* sparen; **to ~ on sthg** an etw (*D*) sparen.

**economy** [ɪ'kɒnəmɪ] (*pl* -ies) *n* - **1.** [system] Wirtschaft *die* - **2.** [saving]: **it is a false ~** es hilft nicht zu sparen; **to make economies** Sparmaßnahmen treffen; **economies of scale** Einsparungen durch Massenproduktion; **~ measure** Sparmaßnahme *die*.

**economy class** *n* Touristenklasse *die*.

**economy drive** *n* Sparmaßnahmen *pl*.

**economy-size(d)** *adj:* **~ pack** Haushaltspackung *die*.

**ecosystem** ['iːkəʊˌsɪstəm] *n* Ökosystem *das*.

**ECSC** (*abbr of* **European Coal & Steel Community**) *n* EGKS *die*.

**ecstasy** ['ekstəsɪ] (*pl* -ies) *n* - **1.** [great happiness] Ekstase *die;* **to go into ecstasies about sthg** über etw (*A*) in Verzückung geraten - **2.** (*U*) [drug] Ecstasy *das*.

**ecstatic** [ek'stætɪk] *adj* ekstatisch.

**ecstatically** [ek'stætɪklɪ] *adv* ekstatisch; [happy] über alle Maßen.

**ECT** (*abbr of* **electroconvulsive therapy**) *n* Elektrokrampftherapie *die*.

**Ecuador** ['ekwədɔː'] *n* Ecuador *nt*.

**Ecuadoran** [ˌekwə'dɔːrən], **Ecuadorian** [ˌekwə'dɔːrɪən] *adj* ecuadorianisch <> *n* Ecuadorianer *der*, -in *die*.

**ecumenical** [ˌiːkjuː'menɪkl] *adj* ökumenisch.

**eczema** ['eksɪmə] *n (U)* Ekzem *das*.

**ed. - 1.** (*abbr of* **edited**) hrsg. - **2.** *abbr of* **edition** - **3.** *abbr of* **editor**.

**eddy** ['edɪ] (*pl* -ies; *pt* & *pp* -ied) *n* [of water] Strudel *der* <> *vi* [water] strudeln.

**Eden** ['iːdn] *n* Eden *das;* **the Garden of ~** der Garten Eden.

**edge** [edʒ] *n* - **1.** [of cliff, path, forest] Rand *der;* [of table, coin, book] Kante *die;* **to be on the ~ of madness** am Rande des Wahnsinns sein; **to be on the ~ of war** kurz vor einem Krieg stehen - **2.** [of blade] Schneide *die* - **3.** [advantage]: **to have an ~ over sb, to have the ~ on sb** jm gegenüber einen Vorteil haben; **to have an ~ over sthg, to have the ~ on sthg** etw (*D*) überlegen sein - **4.** *fig* [in voice] Schärfe *die* <> *vi* [move slowly]: **to ~ forwards** sich Stück für Stück vorwärtslbewegen; **to ~ away** sich langsam zurücklziehen.

➡ **on edge** *adj:* **to be on ~** [person] nervös sein; [nerves] gereizt sein.

**edged** [edʒd] *adj:* **~ with** [with gold] eingefasst in (+ *D*); [with trees] umrandet von; [with lace] eingefasst mit.

**edgeways** ['edʒweɪz], **edgewise** ['edʒwaɪz] *adv* seitwärts.

**edging** ['edʒɪŋ] *n* Einfassung *die*.

**edgy** ['edʒɪ] (*compar* -ier; *superl* -iest) *adj* nervös.

**edible** ['edɪbl] *adj* essbar.

**edifice** ['edɪfɪs] *n fml* Bau *der*.

**edify** ['edɪfaɪ] (*pt* & *pp* -ied) *vt fml* erbauen.

**edifying** ['edɪfaɪɪŋ] *adj fml* erbaulich.

**Edinburgh** ['edɪnbrə] *n* Edinburgh *nt*.

**Edinburgh Festival** *n:* **the ~** das Edinburgh Festival.

**edit** ['edɪt] *vt* - **1.** [correct, select material for] redigieren - **2.** CINEMA & RADIO & TV schneiden - **3.** [newspaper, magazine] herauslgeben - **4.** COMPUT editieren.

➠ **edit out** vt sep [remove] streichen.

**edition** [ɪ'dɪʃn] n - **1.** [of book, newspaper] Ausgabe die - **2.** [broadcast] Sendung die.

**editor** ['edɪtəʳ] n - **1.** [of newspaper, magazine, book] Herausgeber der, -in die - **2.** [of section of newspaper, programme] Redakteur der, -in die - **3.** [copy editor] Lektor der, -in die - **4.** CINEMA & RADIO & TV Cutter der, -in die - **5.** COMPUT Editor der.

**editorial** [ˌedɪ'tɔːrɪəl] adj redaktionell; ~ **department/staff** Redaktion die <> n Redaktion die.

**EDP** (abbr of **electronic data processing**) n EDV die.

**EDT** (abbr of **Eastern Daylight Time**) n Sommerzeit in der östlichen Zeitzone der USA.

**educate** ['edʒʊkeɪt] vt - **1.** SCH & UNIV auslbilden; [subj: parents] erziehen - **2.** [inform] informieren.

**educated** ['edʒʊkeɪtɪd] adj [cultured] gebildet.

**education** [ˌedʒʊ'keɪʃn] n Ausbildung die; [by parents] Erziehung die.

**educational** [ˌedʒʊ'keɪʃənl] adj - **1.** [establishment, policy] Bildungs-; ~ **background** Ausbildung die - **2.** [toy] didaktisch; [experience] lehrreich.

**educationalist** [ˌedʒʊ'keɪʃnəlɪst] n Pädagoge der, -gin die.

**educator** ['edʒʊkeɪtəʳ] n esp Am fml [teacher] Pädagoge der, -gin die.

**Edwardian** [ed'wɔːdɪən] adj aus der Zeit Eduards VII; ~ **society** die Gesellschaft zur Zeit Eduards VII.

**EEC** (abbr of **European Economic Community**) n EWG die.

**EEG** n - **1.** (abbr of **electroencephalogram**) EEG das - **2.** (abbr of **electroencephalograph**) EEG das.

**eel** [iːl] n Aal der.

**EENT** (abbr of **eye, ear, nose and throat**) n: ~ **specialist** Augen- und HNO-Arzt der.

**EEOC** (abbr of **Equal Employment Opportunity Commission**) n Kommission in den USA zur Wahrung der Chancengleichheit im Berufsleben.

**eerie** ['ɪərɪ] adj unheimlich.

**EET** (abbr of **Eastern European Time**) n OEZ.

**efface** [ɪ'feɪs] vt [mark, inscription] entfernen; [memory] ausllöschen.

**effect** [ɪ'fekt] n - **1.** [result] Wirkung die; **to have an ~ on sb/sthg** eine Wirkung auf jn/etw haben; **to take ~** [law, rule] in Kraft treten; [drug] wirken; **to put sthg into ~** etw in Kraft setzen - **2.** [impression] Wirkung die, Effekt der; **for ~** aus Effekthascherei - **3.** [meaning]: **a statement to the ~ that** eine Aussage, die besagt, dass; **to that ~** in diesem Sinne <> vt bewirken.

➠ **effects** npl - **1.**: (special) ~s (Spezial)effekte pl - **2.** [property] Habe die.

➠ **in effect** adv in Wirklichkeit.

**effective** [ɪ'fektɪv] adj - **1.** [successful] effektiv - **2.** [actual] eigentlich - **3.** [in operation] wirksam.

**effectively** [ɪ'fektɪvlɪ] adv - **1.** [successfully] effektiv - **2.** [in fact] in Wirklichkeit.

**effectiveness** [ɪ'fektɪvnɪs] n [success] Effektivität die.

**effeminate** [ɪ'femɪnət] adj pej weibisch.

**effervescent** [ˌefə'vesənt] adj sprudelnd.

**effete** [ɪ'fiːt] adj pej verweichlicht.

**efficacious** [efɪ'keɪʃəs] adj fml wirksam.

**efficacy** ['efɪkəsɪ] n Wirksamkeit die.

**efficiency** [ɪ'fɪʃənsɪ] n [of person] Tüchtigkeit die; [of machine] Leistungsfähigkeit die; [of system] Effizienz die.

**efficient** [ɪ'fɪʃənt] adj [person] tüchtig; [machine] leistungsfähig; [method] effizient.

**efficiently** [ɪ'fɪʃəntlɪ] adv effizient.

**effigy** ['efɪdʒɪ] (pl -ies) n Bildnis das.

**effluent** ['efluənt] n Abwasser das.

**effort** ['efət] n - **1.** [exertion] Anstrengung die; **it's not worth the** ~ es ist nicht der Mühe wert; **to make the** ~ **to do sthg** sich bemühen, etw zu tun; **with** ~ mit Mühe - **2.** [attempt] Versuch der; **to make an/no** ~ **to do sthg** sich anlstrengen/sich nicht anlstrengen, etw zu tun.

**effortless** ['efətlɪs] adj mühelos.

**effortlessly** ['efətlɪslɪ] adv mühelos.

**effrontery** [ɪ'frʌntərɪ] n Unverfrorenheit die.

**effusive** [ɪ'fjuːsɪv] adj überschwenglich.

**effusively** [ɪ'fjuːsɪvlɪ] adv überschwenglich.

**EFL** ['efəl] (abbr of **English as a foreign language**) n Englisch als Fremdsprache.

**EFTA** ['eftə] (abbr of **European Free Trade Association**) n EFTA die.

**EFTS** [efts] (abbr of **electronic funds transfer system**) n elektronisches Überweisungssystem.

**e.g.** (abbr of **exempli gratia**) adv z. B.

**EGA** (abbr of **enhanced graphics adapter**) n EGA.

**egalitarian** [ɪˌɡælɪ'teərɪən] adj egalitär.

**egg** [eɡ] n Ei das.

➠ **egg on** vt sep anlstacheln.

**eggcup** ['eɡkʌp] n Eierbecher der.

**eggplant** ['eɡplɑːnt] n Am Aubergine die.

**E**

**eggshell** ['egʃel] n Eierschale die.

**egg timer** n Eieruhr die.

**egg whisk** n Schneebesen der.

**egg white** n Eiweiß das.

**egg yolk** n Eigelb das.

**EGM** (abbr of **extraordinary general meeting**) n aoHV die.

**ego** ['i:gəʊ] (pl **-s**) n [opinion of self] Selbstbewusstsein das; PSYCH Ego das.

**egocentric** [ˌi:gəʊ'sentrɪk] adj fml & pej egozentrisch.

**egoism** ['i:gəʊɪzm] n Egoismus der.

**egoist** ['i:gəʊɪst] n Egoist der, -in die.

**egoistic** [ˌi:gəʊ'ɪstɪk] adj egoistisch.

**egotism** ['i:gətɪzml] n Egoismus der.

**egotist** ['i:gətɪst] n Egoist der, -in die.

**egotistic(al)** [ˌi:gə'tɪstɪk(l)] adj egoistisch.

**ego trip** n inf Egotrip der.

**Egypt** ['i:dʒɪpt] n Ägypten nt.

**Egyptian** [ɪ'dʒɪpʃn] adj ägyptisch ◇ n Ägypter der, -in die.

**eh** [eɪ] excl Br inf **- 1.** [inviting agreement] nicht? **- 2.** [what did you say?] was?

**eiderdown** ['aɪdədaʊn] n esp Br [bed cover] Daunendecke die.

**eight** [eɪt] num acht; see also **six**.

**eighteen** [ˌeɪ'ti:n] num achtzehn; see also **six**.

**eighteenth** [ˌeɪ'ti:nθ] num achtzehnte, -r, -s; see also **sixth**.

**eighth** [eɪtθ] num achte, -r, -s; see also **sixth**.

**eightieth** ['eɪtɪɪθ] num achtzigste, -r, -s; see also **sixth**.

**eighty** ['eɪtɪ] (pl **-ies**) num achtzig; see also **sixty**.

**Eire** ['eərə] n Irland nt.

**either** ['aɪðər, 'i:ðər] adj **- 1.** [one or the other]: ~ **will do** es ist egal, welches (von beiden); ~ **way I will lose** wie ich es auch mache, ich werde dabei verlieren **- 2.** [each] beide; **on** ~ **side** auf beiden Seiten ◇ pron: **I'll take ~ (of them)** ich nehme einen/eine/eins (von beiden); **I don't like ~ (of them)** ich mag keinen/keine/keins (von beiden) ◇ adv (in negatives): **I can't ~** ich auch nicht ◇ conj: ~ ... **or ...** entweder ... oder; **I don't like ~ him or her** ich mag weder ihn noch sie; **without ~ writing or phoning** ohne zu schreiben oder anzurufen.

**ejaculate** [ɪ'dʒækjʊleɪt] vt [exclaim] auslrufen ◇ vi [have orgasm] ejakulieren.

**eject** [ɪ'dʒekt] vt **- 1.** [object] auslstoßen **- 2.** [person]: **to ~ sb (from)** jn hinauslwerfen (aus).

**ejector seat** Br [ɪ'dʒektə'-], **ejection seat** Am [ɪ'dʒekʃn-] n Schleudersitz der.

**eke** ➡ **eke out** vt sep strecken ◇ vt fus: **to** ~ **out a living** sich mit Müh und Not durchlschlagen.

**EKG** (abbr of **electrocardiogram**) n Am EKG das.

**el** [el] (abbr of **elevated railroad**) n Am inf Hochbahn die.

**elaborate** [adj ɪ'læbrət, vb ɪ'læbəreɪt] adj [explanation] ausführlich; [plan] ausgefeilt; [carving] kunstvoll; [ceremony] kompliziert ◇ vi: **to** ~ **(on sthg)** (etw) näher erläutern.

**elaborately** [ɪ'læbərətlɪ] adv [plan] ausgefeilt; [decorate] kunstvoll.

**elapse** [ɪ'læps] vi [time] verstreichen.

**elastic** [ɪ'læstɪk] adj **- 1.** [stretchy] elastisch **- 2.** fig [flexible] flexibel ◇ n (U) [material] Gummiband das.

**elasticated** [ɪ'læstɪkeɪtɪd] adj [waistband] mit Gummizug.

**elastic band** n Br Gummiband das.

**elasticity** [ˌelæ'stɪsətɪ] n Elastizität die.

**elated** [ɪ'leɪtɪd] adj in Hochstimmung.

**elation** [ɪ'leɪʃn] n Hochstimmung die.

**elbow** ['elbəʊ] n Ellbogen der ◇ vt: **to** ~ **sb aside** jn beiseite stoßen.

**elbow grease** n inf: **to use some** ~ Kraft anlwenden.

**elbowroom** ['elbəʊrʊm] n inf Bewegungsfreiheit die.

**elder** ['eldər] adj ältere, -r, -s ◇ n **- 1.** [older person]: **show respect to your ~s** zeige Respekt gegenüber älteren Menschen **- 2.** [of tribe] Älteste der, die **- 3.** [of church] Presbyter der **- 4.** BOT Holunder der.

**elderberry** ['eldəˌberɪ] (pl **-ies**) n Holunderbeere die.

**elderly** ['eldəlɪ] adj ältere, -r, -s ◇ npl: **the** ~ ältere Menschen pl.

**elder statesman** n erfahrener Staatsmann.

**eldest** ['eldɪst] adj älteste, -r, -s.

**elect** [ɪ'lekt] adj: **president** ~ designierter Präsident ◇ vt **- 1.** [by voting] wählen; **he was** ~**ed (as) party leader** er wurde zum Parteivorsitzenden gewählt **- 2.** fml [choose]: **to ~ to do sthg** sich dafür entscheiden, etw zu tun.

**elected** [ɪ'lektɪd] adj gewählt.

**election** [ɪ'lekʃn] n Wahl die; **to have** OR **hold an** ~ eine Wahl ablhalten.

**election campaign** n Wahlkampf der.

**electioneering** [ɪˌlekʃə'nɪərɪŋ] n pej Wahlpropaganda die.

**elective** [ɪ'lektɪv] n SCH & UNIV Wahlfach das.

**elector** [ɪ'lektər] n [voter] Wähler der, -in die.

**electoral** [ɪ'lektərəl] adj Wahl-.

**electoral college** n POL Wahlgremium das.

**electoral register, electoral roll** *n:* the ~ das Wählerverzeichnis.

**electorate** [ɪ'lektərət] *n:* the ~ die Wählerschaft.

**electric** [ɪ'lektrɪk] *adj* - **1.** [gen] elektrisch - **2.** *fig* [atmosphere] elektrisiert.
➤ **electrics** *npl Br inf* [in car, machine] Elektrik *die.*

**electrical** [ɪ'lektrɪkl] *adj* elektrisch; ~ **goods** Elektrowaren *pl.*

**electrical engineer** *n* Elektrotechniker *der, -in die.*

**electrical engineering** *n* Elektrotechnik *die.*

**electrically** [ɪ'lektrɪklɪ] *adv* elektrisch.

**electrical shock** *n Am* = electric shock.

**electric blanket** *n* Heizdecke *die.*

**electric chair** *n:* the ~ der elektrische Stuhl.

**electric cooker** *n* Elektroherd *der.*

**electric current** *n* elektrischer Strom.

**electric drill** *n* Bohrmaschine *die.*

**electric fence** *n* Elektrozaun *der.*

**electric fire** *n* Heizstrahler *der.*

**electric guitar** *n* elektrische Gitarre.

**electrician** [ˌɪlek'trɪʃn] *n* Elektriker *der, -in die.*

**electricity** [ˌɪlek'trɪsətɪ] *n* - **1.** [current] Strom *der;* [in physics] Elektrizität *die* - **2.** *fig* [excitement] Spannung *die.*

**electric light** *n* elektrisches Licht.

**electric shock** *Br,* **electrical shock** *Am n* Stromschlag *der.*

**electric shock therapy** *n* Elektroschocktherapie *die.*

**electric storm** *n* Gewitter *das.*

**electrify** [ɪ'lektrɪfaɪ] (*pt & pp* **-ied**) *vt* - **1.** [railway line] elektrifizieren - **2.** *fig* [excite] elektrisieren.

**electrifying** [ɪ'lektrɪfaɪɪŋ] *adj fig* elektrisierend.

**electro-** [ɪ'lektrəʊ] *prefix* Elektro-.

**electrocardiograph** [ɪˌlektrəʊ'kɑːdɪəgrɑːf] *n* MED Elektrokardiograf *der.*

**electrocute** [ɪ'lektrəkjuːt] *vt:* to ~ o.s., to be ~d sich durch Stromschlag töten; to be ~d [executed] auf dem elektrischen Stuhl hingerichtet werden.

**electrode** [ɪ'lektrəʊd] *n* Elektrode *die.*

**electroencephalograph** [ɪˌlektrəʊen-'sefələgrɑːf] *n* Elektroenzephalograf *der.*

**electrolysis** [ˌɪlek'trɒləsɪs] *n* Elektrolyse *die.*

**electromagnet** [ɪˌlektrəʊ'mægnɪt] *n* Elektromagnet *der.*

**electromagnetic** [ɪˌlektrəʊmæg'netɪk] *adj* elektromagnetisch.

**electron** [ɪ'lektrɒn] *n* Elektron *das.*

**electronic** [ˌɪlek'trɒnɪk] *adj* elektronisch.
➤ **electronics** *n (U)* [technology] Elektronik *die* ◇ *npl* [of car, machine] Elektronik *die.*

**electronic data processing** *n* elektronische Datenverarbeitung.

**electronic mail** *n* elektronische Post, E-mail *die.*

**electroplated** [ɪ'lektrəʊpleɪtɪd] *adj* galvanisiert.

**elegance** ['elɪgəns] *n* Eleganz *die.*

**elegant** ['elɪgənt] *adj* elegant.

**elegantly** ['elɪgəntlɪ] *adv* elegant.

**elegy** ['elɪdʒɪ] (*pl* **-ies**) *n* Elegie *die.*

**element** ['elɪmənt] *n* - **1.** [gen] Element *das;* [component] Bestandteil *der;* an ~ of truth ein Körnchen Wahrheit; an ~ of jealousy eine Spur von Eifersucht - **2.** [of heater, kettle] Heizelement *das* - **3.** *phr:* to be in one's ~ in seinem Element sein.
➤ **elements** *npl* - **1.** [basics] Grundlagen *pl* - **2.** [weather]: the ~s die Elemente *pl.*

**elementary** [ˌelɪ'mentərɪ] *adj* [precautions, mistake, question] simpel; [education, maths] Elementar-.

**elementary school** *n Am* Grundschule *die.*

**elephant** ['elɪfənt] (*pl inv OR* **-s**) *n* Elefant *der.*

**elevate** ['elɪveɪt] *vt* - **1.** [raise] heben - **2.** [give importance to] erheben; [promote] befördern; to ~ **sb to the peerage** jn in den Adelsstand erheben.

**elevated** ['elɪveɪtɪd] *adj fml* - **1.** [important] bedeutend - **2.** [idea, feelings] erhaben - **3.** [raised - land] hochgelegen; [ - platform] erhöht.

**elevated railway** *n* Hochbahn *die.*

**elevation** [ˌelɪ'veɪʃn] *n fml* - **1.** [promotion] Beförderung *die* - **2.** [height] Höhe *die* (über dem Meeresspiegel).

**elevator** ['elɪveɪtər] *n Am* Fahrstuhl *der.*

**eleven** [ɪ'levn] *num* elf; *see also* six.

**elevenses** [ɪ'levnzɪz] *n Br* zweites Frühstück.

**eleventh** [ɪ'levnθ] *num* elfte, -r, -s; *see also* sixth.

**eleventh hour** *n fig:* at the ~ in letzter Minute.

**elf** [elf] (*pl* **elves**) *n* Elf *der, -e die.*

**elicit** [ɪ'lɪsɪt] *vt fml:* to ~ sthg (from sb) (jm) etw entlocken.

**eligibility** [ˌelɪdʒə'bɪlətɪ] *n* [suitability] Eignung *die;* [for grant] berechtiger Anspruch.

**eligible** ['elɪdʒəbl] *adj* - **1.** [suitable, qualified] geeignet; to be ~ for sthg für etw in Frage kommen; **to be ~ to join the team** für die Mannschaft in Frage kommen; **to be ~ for a pension** pensionsberechtigt sein **- 2.** *dated* [marriageable]: **~ bachelor** begehrter Junggeselle.

**eliminate** [ɪ'lɪmɪneɪt] *vt* **- 1.** [remove] ausschließen; [disease, poverty] eliminieren **- 2.** [from competition]: **to be ~d from sthg** aus etw ausⅼscheiden.

**elimination** [ɪ,lɪmɪ'neɪʃn] *n* **- 1.** [removal] Ausschluss *der;* [of disease, poverty] Elimination *die* **- 2.** [from competition] Ausscheiden *das.*

**elite** [ɪ'liːt] *adj* Elite- ⬦ *n* Elite *die.*

**elitist** [ɪ'liːtɪst] *adj* elitär.

**elixir** [ɪ'lɪksəʳ] *n* Elixier *das.*

**Elizabethan** [ɪ,lɪzə'biːθn] *adj* elisabethanisch.

**elk** [elk] *(pl inv OR -s)* *n* Elch *der;* [Canadian] Elk *der.*

**ellipse** [ɪ'lɪps] *n* Ellipse *die.*

**elliptical** [ɪ'lɪptɪkl] *adj* elliptisch.

**elm** [elm] *n:* **~ (tree)** Ulme *die.*

**elocution** [,elə'kjuːʃn] *n* Sprechtechnik *die.*

**elongated** ['iːlɒŋɡeɪtɪd] *adj* [face, shape] lang gezogen.

**elope** [ɪ'ləʊp] *vi* durchⅼbrennen.

**elopement** [ɪ'ləʊpmənt] *n* Durchbrennen *das.*

**eloquence** ['eləkwəns] *n* [of speaker] Wortgewandtheit *die;* [of speech] Wohlgesetztheit *die.*

**eloquent** ['eləkwənt] *adj* **- 1.** [speaker] wortgewandt **- 2.** [speech, words] wohlgesetzt.

**eloquently** ['eləkwəntlɪ] *adv* wortgewandt.

**El Salvador** [,el'sælvədɔːʳ] *n* El Salvador *nt.*

**else** [els] *adv:* **I don't want anything ~** ich will nichts mehr; **anything ~?** sonst noch etwas?; **everyone ~** alle anderen; **nobody ~** niemand anders; **nothing ~** sonst nichts; **somebody ~** [additional person] noch jemand anders; [different person] jemand anders; **anybody ~ (but you) would have given up** jeder andere (außer dir) hätte aufgegeben; **something ~** [additional thing] noch etwas; [different thing] etwas anderes; **somewhere ~** woanders; **to go somewhere ~** woandershin gehen; **what ~?** [in addition] was (sonst) noch?; [instead] was sonst?; **who ~?** [in addition] wer (sonst) noch?; [instead] wer sonst?

➤ **or else** *conj* **- 1.** [or if not] sonst, oder; **come in or ~ go out** komm entweder herein oder geh hinaus **- 2.** [as threat]: **do what I say, or ~!** tu, was ich sage, sonst passiert was!

**elsewhere** [els'weəʳ] *adv* woanders, anderswo.

**ELT** *(abbr of* **English language teaching)** *n* englischer Sprachunterricht.

**elucidate** [ɪ'luːsɪdeɪt] *vt fml* erläutern.

**elude** [ɪ'luːd] *vt* **- 1.** [police, pursuers] entwischen **- 2.** [subj: fact, name] entfallen sein *(+ D).*

**elusive** [ɪ'luːsɪv] *adj* [quality] schwer fassbar; [success] schwer erreichbar; **he is very ~** er ist selten anzutreffen.

**elves** [elvz] *pl* ⬅ **elf.**

**'em** [əm] *inf* = **them.**

**emaciated** [ɪ'meɪʃɪeɪtɪd] *adj* stark abgemagert.

**e-mail** *n* E-Mail *die;* **by ~** per E-Mail ⬦ *vt:* **to ~ sb** jm eine E-mail schicken, jm mailen.

**e-mail address** *n COMPUT* E-Mail-Adresse *die.*

**emanate** ['emaneɪt] *fml vt* ausⅼstrahlen ⬦ *vi:* **to ~ from** [idea] stammen von; [smell] kommen von/aus.

**emancipate** [ɪ'mænsɪpeɪt] *vt* befreien; [women] emanzipieren.

**emancipation** [ɪ,mænsɪ'peɪʃn] *n* Befreiung *die;* [of women] Emanzipation *die.*

**emasculate** [ɪ'mæskjʊleɪt] *vt fml* [weaken] schwächen.

**embalm** [ɪm'bɑːm] *vt* einⅼbalsamieren.

**embankment** [ɪm'bæŋkmənt] *n* **- 1.** [along road, path] Böschung *die* **- 2.** [along river] Damm *der;* [along railway] Bahndamm *der.*

**embargo** [em'bɑːɡəʊ] *(pl -es; pt & pp -ed; cont -ing)* *n* **- 1.** COMM & POL Embargo *das;* **to put an ~ on sthg** etw mit einem Embargo belegen **- 2.** *fig* [ban] Sperre *die* ⬦ *vt* **- 1.** COMM & POL mit einem Embargo belegen **- 2.** *fig* [ban] sperren.

**embark** [ɪm'bɑːk] *vi* **- 1.** [board ship] sich einⅼschiffen **- 2.** [start]: **to ~ (up)on sthg** mit etw beginnen.

**embarkation** [,embɑː'keɪʃn] *n* Einschiffung *die.*

**embarkation card** *n Br* Bordkarte *die.*

**embarrass** [ɪm'bærəs] *vt* in Verlegenheit bringen.

**embarrassed** [ɪm'bærəst] *adj* verlegen.

**embarrassing** [ɪm'bærəsɪŋ] *adj* peinlich.

**embarrassment** [ɪm'bærəsmənt] *n* Verlegenheit *die;* **to be an ~ to sb** jn in Verlegenheit bringen.

**embassy** ['embəsɪ] *(pl -ies)* *n* Botschaft *die.*

**embattled** [ɪm'bætld] *adj:* **the ~ government** die Regierung, die in Schwierigkeiten ist.

**embedded** [ɪm'bedɪd] *adj* **- 1.** [in rock, wood, mud]: **to be ~ in sthg** in etw *(D)* festⅼstecken **- 2.** *fig* [feeling] fest verwurzelt.

**embellish** [ɪm'belɪʃ] *vt* **- 1.** [decorate]: **to ~ sthg with sthg** etw mit etw schmücken **- 2.** *fig* [story] ausⅼschmücken.

**embers** ['embəz] *npl* Glut *die.*

**embezzle** [ɪm'bezl] *vt* unterschlagen.

**embezzlement** [ɪm'bezlmənt] n Unterschlagung die.

**embittered** [ɪm'bɪtəd] adj verbittert.

**emblazoned** [ɪm'bleɪzn̩d] adj: **to be ~ on** sthg auf etw (D) prangen; **to be ~ with** sthg mit etw geschmückt sein.

**emblem** ['embləm] n Emblem das.

**embodiment** [ɪm'bɒdɪmənt] n Verkörperung die.

**embody** [ɪm'bɒdɪ] (pt & pp **-ied**) vt **- 1.** [epitomize] verkörpern **- 2.** [include] enthalten.

**embolism** ['embəlɪzm] n Embolie die.

**embossed** [ɪm'bɒst] adj geprägt.

**embrace** [ɪm'breɪs] n Umarmung die ⋄ vt **- 1.** [hug] umarmen **- 2.** fml [belief, religion] an|nehmen **- 3.** fml [include] umfassen ⋄ vi sich umarmen.

**embroider** [ɪm'brɔɪdə'] vt **- 1.** [design] sticken; [tablecloth, blouse] besticken **- 2.** [story] aus|schmücken.

**embroidered** [ɪm'brɔɪdəd] adj bestickt.

**embroidery** [ɪm'brɔɪdərɪ] n **- 1.** [skill] Sticken das **- 2.** [designs] Stickerei die.

**embroil** [ɪm'brɔɪl] vt: **to get ~ed (in** sthg) (in etw (A)) verwickelt werden.

**embryo** ['embrɪəʊ] (pl **-s**) n Embryo der; **fig to be in ~** noch in den Kinderschuhen stecken.

**embryonic** [ˌembrɪ'ɒnɪk] adj fig: **to be at an ~ stage** noch in den Kinderschuhen stecken.

**emcee** [ˌem'siː] n Am abbr of master of ceremonies.

**emend** [ɪ'mend] vt verbessern.

**emerald** ['emərəld] adj: **~ (green)** smaragdgrün ⋄ n Smaragd der.

**emerge** [ɪ'mɜːdʒ] vi **- 1.** [come out] auf|tauchen; **to ~ from** sthg aus etw heraus|kommen **- 2.** [facts, truth] heraus|kommen ⋄ vt: **it ~d that ...** es stellte sich heraus, dass ...

**emergence** [ɪ'mɜːdʒəns] n Auftauchen das; [of new organization] Entstehen das.

**emergency** [ɪ'mɜːdʒənsɪ] (pl **-ies**) adj Not- ⋄ n Notfall der; **in an ~** im Notfall.

**emergency brake** n Am Notbremse die.

**emergency exit** n Notausgang der.

**emergency landing** n Notlandung die.

**emergency room** n Am Unfallstation die.

**emergency services** npl Hilfsdienste pl.

**emergency stop** n Vollbremsung die.

**emergent** [ɪ'mɜːdʒənt] adj aufstrebend.

**emery board** ['emərɪ-] n Papiernagelfeile die.

**emetic** [ɪ'metɪk] adj emetisch ⋄ n Brechmittel das.

**emigrant** ['emɪgrənt] n Auswanderer der.

**emigrate** ['emɪgreɪt] vi aus|wandern.

**emigration** [ˌemɪ'greɪʃn̩] n Auswanderung die.

**émigré** ['emɪgreɪ] n fml Emigrant der.

**eminence** ['emɪnəns] n [prominence] hohes Ansehen.

**eminent** ['emɪnənt] adj berühmt und anerkannt.

**eminently** ['emɪnəntlɪ] adv fml [extremely] ausgesprochen.

**emissary** ['emɪsərɪ] (pl **-ies**) n fml Abgesandte der, die.

**emission** [ɪ'mɪʃn̩] n fml [of light] Ausstrahlung die; [of fumes] Emission die; [of heat, sound] Abgabe die.

**emit** [ɪ'mɪt] (pt & pp **-ted;** cont **-ting**) vt fml [light] aus|strahlen; [radiator, smoke] emittieren; [sound, heat] ab|geben.

**emolument** [ɪ'mɒljʊmənt] n fml Vergütung die.

**emoticon** [ɪ'məʊtɪkɒn] n COMPUT Emoticon das, Gefühlssymbol das.

**emotion** [ɪ'məʊʃn̩] n **- 1.** [particular feeling] Gefühl das, Emotion die **- 2.** (U) [strength of feeling] Gemütsbewegung die; **she showed no ~** sie blieb vollkommen unbewegt; **to speak with ~** ergriffen sprechen.

**emotional** [ɪ'məʊʃənl̩] adj **- 1.** [person - by nature] gefühlsbetont; [ - temporarily] emotional; **to get ~** emotional werden **- 2.** [scene, farewell] emotionsgeladen; [music] gefühlvoll; [appeal, speech] gefühlsbetont **- 3.** [problems, needs, reaction] emotional.

**emotionally** [ɪ'məʊʃnəlɪ] adv [react, disturbed] emotional; [speak] gefühlvoll.

**emotionless** [ɪ'məʊʃnlɪs] adj ausdruckslos.

**emotive** [ɪ'məʊtɪv] adj [speech, language] gefühlsbetont; [issue] emotionsgeladen.

**empathy** ['empəθɪ] n Einfühlungsvermögen das, Empathie die.

**emperor** ['empərə'] n Kaiser der.

**emphasis** ['emfəsɪs] (pl **-ases** [-əsiːz]) n Betonung die; **to lay** OR **place ~ on** sthg großen Wert auf etw (A) legen.

**emphasize, -ise** ['emfəsaɪz] vt betonen; [point, feature] hervor|heben.

**emphatic** [ɪm'fætɪk] adj [forceful] entschieden.

**emphatically** [ɪm'fætɪklɪ] adv **- 1.** [with emphasis] mit Nachdruck **- 2.** [deny] entschieden.

**emphysema** [ˌemfɪ'siːmə] n Emphysem das.

**empire** ['empaɪə'] n **- 1.** POL Reich das **- 2.** COMM Imperium das.

**empirical** [ɪm'pɪrɪkl] *adj* empirisch.

**empiricism** [ɪm'pɪrɪsɪzm] *n* Empirismus *der*.

**employ** [ɪm'plɔɪ] *vt* - **1.** [give work to] beschäftigen; [recruit] anstellen; **to be ~ed as a secretary** als Sekretär(in) arbeiten - **2.** *fml* [use] anwenden.

**employable** [ɪm'plɔɪəbl] *adj* anstellbar.

**employee** [ɪm'plɔɪiː] *n* Angestellte *der, die*.

**employer** [ɪm'plɔɪə'] *n* Arbeitgeber *der*, -in *die*.

**employment** [ɪm'plɔɪmənt] *n* (U) Arbeit *die*; [recruitment] Anstellung *die*; **to be in ~** eine Stelle haben.

**employment agency** *n* Stellenvermittlung *die*.

**employment office** *n* Arbeitsamt *das*.

**emporium** [em'pɔːrɪəm] *n* großes Kaufhaus.

**empower** [ɪm'paʊə'] *vt fml*: **to be ~ed to do sthg** ermächtigt sein, etw zu tun.

**empress** ['emprɪs] *n* Kaiserin *die*.

**emptiness** ['emptɪnɪs] *n* Leere *die*.

**empty** ['emptɪ] (*compar* **-ier;** *superl* **-iest;** *pt* & *pp* **-ied;** *pl* **-ies**) *adj* leer; **on an ~ stomach** MED auf nüchternen Magen ⟨⟩ *vt* leeren; [bin] ausleeren; [room] ausräumen; **to ~ sthg into/out of sthg** [pour] etw in etw (A) /aus etw schütten ⟨⟩ *vi* [room, theatre] sich leeren ⟨⟩ *n inf* [bottle] leere Flasche; [glass] leeres Glas.

**empty-handed** [-'hændɪd] *adv* unverrichteter Dinge.

**empty-headed** [-'hedɪd] *adj pej* strohdumm.

**emu** ['iːmjuː] (*pl inv* OR **-s**) *n* Emu *der*.

**EMU** (*abbr of* **European Monetary Union**) *n* WWU *die*.

**emulate** ['emjʊleɪt] *vt* [person, example] nacheifern (+ D); [system] nachlahmen.

**emulsion** [ɪ'mʌlʃn] *n* - **1.:** **~ (paint)** Dispersionsfarbe *die* - **2.** PHOT Emulsion *die*.

**enable** [ɪ'neɪbl] *vt:* **to ~ sb to do sthg** es jm möglich machen, etw zu tun.

**enact** [ɪ'nækt] *vt* - **1.** LAW erlassen - **2.** [scene, play] auflführen.

**enactment** [ɪ'næktmənt] *n* - **1.** LAW Erlassung *die* - **2.** [of scene, play] Aufführung *die*.

**enamel** [ɪ'næml] *n* - **1.** [on metal, glass] Email *das* - **2.** [on tooth] Zahnschmelz *der* - **3.** [paint] Emaillack *der*.

**enamelled** *Br*, **enameled** *Am* [ɪ'næmld] *adj* emailliert.

**enamel paint** *n* Emaillack *der*.

**enamoured** *Br*, **enamored** *Am* [ɪ'næməd] *adj*: **to be ~ of sb/sthg** von jm/etw angetan sein.

**enc.** - **1.** (*abbr of* **enclosure**) Anlage *die* - **2.** (*abbr of* **enclosed**) anbei, als Anlage.

**encamp** [ɪn'kæmp] *vi* kampieren.

**encampment** [ɪn'kæmpmənt] *n* Lager *das*.

**encapsulate** [ɪn'kæpsjʊleɪt] *vt fig* zusammenlfassen.

**encase** [ɪn'keɪs] *vt:* **to be ~d in concrete** einbetoniert sein.

**encash** [ɪn'kæʃ] *vt Br* einllösen.

**enchanted** [ɪn'tʃɑːntɪd] *adj* - **1.** [delighted]: **to be ~ by** OR **with sthg** von etw OR über etw (A) entzückt sein - **2.** *literary* [magical] verzaubert.

**enchanting** [ɪn'tʃɑːntɪŋ] *adj* bezaubernd.

**encircle** [ɪn'sɜːkl] *vt* umgeben; [subj: troops] umringen.

**enclave** ['enkleɪv] *n* Enklave *die*.

**enclose** [ɪn'kləʊz] *vt* - **1.** [surround] umgeben; **~d space** abgeschlossener Raum; **to be ~d by** OR **with sthg** von etw umgeben sein - **2.** [put in envelope] beillegen; **please find ~d ... als Anlage senden wir Ihnen ...**

**enclosure** [ɪn'kləʊʒə'] *n* - **1.** [place] eingezäuntes Grundstück; [for animals] Gehege *das* - **2.** [in letter] Anlage *die*.

**encompass** [ɪn'kʌmpəs] *vt fml* umfassen.

**encore** ['ɒŋkɔː'] *n* Zugabe *die* ⟨⟩ *excl* Zugabe!

**encounter** [ɪn'kaʊntə'] *n* Begegnung *die*; [battle] Kampf *der* ⟨⟩ *vt fml* - **1.** [meet] begegnen (+ D) - **2.** [experience] stoßen auf (+ A).

**encourage** [ɪn'kʌrɪdʒ] *vt* - **1.** [person] ermutigen, ermuntern; **to ~ sb to do sthg** jn ermutigen OR ermuntern, etw zu tun - **2.** [foster] fördern.

**encouragement** [ɪn'kʌrɪdʒmənt] *n* Ermutigung *die*; [support] Förderung *die*.

**encouraging** [ɪn'kʌrɪdʒɪŋ] *adj* ermutigend; **she was very ~** sie machte mir/uns viel Mut.

**encroach** [ɪn'krəʊtʃ] *vi:* **to ~ (up)on sthg** [on territory] in etw (A) vorldringen; [on rights, privacy] in etw (A) einlgreifen.

**encrusted** [ɪn'krʌstɪd] *adj* [with mud] verkrustet; **~ with diamonds** mit Diamanten dicht besetzt.

**encumber** [ɪn'kʌmbə'] *vt fml:* **to be ~ed with sthg** mit etw beladen sein; [with debts] mit etw belastet sein.

**encyclop(a)edia** [ɪn,saɪklə'piːdjə] *n* Lexikon *das*, Enzyklopädie *die*.

**encyclop(a)edic** [ɪn,saɪkləʊ'piːdɪk] *adj* enzyklopädisch.

**end** [end] *n* - **1.** [finish] Ende *das*; **from beginning to ~** von vorn bis hinten; **at the ~ of May** Ende Mai; **at an ~** zu Ende; **to come to an ~** enden; **to put an ~ to sthg** etw (D) ein Ende setzen; **at the ~ of the day** *fig* schließlich und endlich; **in the ~** [finally] schließlich - **2.** [extremity] Ende *das*; [of box] Seite *die*; [of finger, stick] Spitze *die*; **~ to ~** mit den Enden aneinander; **to make ~s meet** [financially] zurechtkommen - **3.** [leftover part] Rest der; [of candle] Stummel der - **4.** fml [purpose] Ziel das; **it is an ~ in itself** das ist reiner Selbstzweck - **5.** literary [death] Ende das ◇ vt beenden ◇ vi enden; **to ~ in failure** in einem Misserfolg enden.

 **on end** adv - **1.** [upright] hoch kant - **2.** [continuously]: **for days on ~** tagelang.

 **no end** adv inf [a lot] irrsinnig.

 **no end of** prep inf: **no ~ of problems** irrsinnig viele Probleme; **it will do you no ~ of good** das wird dir unheimlich gut tun.

 **end up** vi: **to ~ up in prison** im Gefängnis landen; **to ~ up as president** schließlich Präsident werden; **to ~ up doing sthg** schließlich etw tun.

**endanger** [ɪnˈdeɪndʒəʳ] vt gefährden.

**endangered species** [ɪnˈdeɪndʒəd-] n von Aussterben bedrohte Art.

**endear** [ɪnˈdɪəʳ] vt: **to ~ sb to sb** jn bei jm beliebt machen; **to ~ o.s. to sb** sich bei jm beliebt machen.

**endearing** [ɪnˈdɪərɪŋ] adj liebenswert.

**endearment** [ɪnˈdɪəmənt] n fml [word] zärtliches Wort.

**endeavour** Br, **endeavor** Am [ɪnˈdevəʳ] fml n Bemühung die; **human ~** menschliches Streben ◇ vt: **to ~ to do sthg** sich bemühen, etw zu tun.

**endemic** [enˈdemɪk] adj - **1.** MED endemisch - **2.** [problem, poverty, racism] ausgeprägt.

**ending** [ˈendɪŋ] n - **1.** [of story, film] Ende das, Schluss der - **2.** GRAMM Endung die.

**endive** [ˈendaɪv] n - **1.** [salad vegetable] Endivie die, Endiviensalat der - **2.** [chicory] Chicorée die OR der.

**endless** [ˈendlɪs] adj endlos; [possibilities, desert] unendlich.

**endlessly** [ˈendlɪslɪ] adv endlos; [patient, kind] unendlich.

**endorse** [ɪnˈdɔːs] vt - **1.** [approve] billigen - **2.** [cheque] auf der Rückseite unterschreiben, indossieren - **3.** Br [driving licence] eine Strafe vermerken auf (+ D).

**endorsement** [ɪnˈdɔːsmənt] n - **1.** [approval] Billigung die - **2.** [of cheque] Indossament das - **3.** Br [on driving licence] Strafvermerk der (auf dem Führerschein).

**endow** [ɪnˈdaʊ] vt - **1.** [equip]: **to be ~ed with sthg** mit etw ausgestattet sein; **to be ~ed with charm/talent** Charme/Talent haben - **2.** [donate money to] eine Stiftung machen an (+ A).

**endowment** [ɪnˈdaʊmənt] n - **1.** [talent] Begabung die - **2.** [gift of money] Stiftung die.

**endowment insurance** n Erlebensfallversicherung die.

**endowment mortgage** n Hypothek die mit Lebensversicherung.

**end product** n Endprodukt das.

**end result** n Endergebnis das.

**endurable** [ɪnˈdjʊərəbl] adj erträglich.

**endurance** [ɪnˈdjʊərəns] n Durchhaltevermögen das; **it was beyond ~** es war nicht auszuhalten.

**endurance test** n Belastungsprobe die.

**endure** [ɪnˈdjʊəʳ] vt ertragen ◇ vi fml Bestand haben.

**enduring** [ɪnˈdjʊərɪŋ] adj fml dauerhaft.

**end user** n Endverbraucher der.

**endways** Br [ˈendweɪz], **endwise** Am [ˈendwaɪz] adv - **1.** [lengthways] mit dem Ende nach vorn - **2.** [end to end] mit den Enden aneinander.

**enema** [ˈenəmə] n Einlauf der.

**enemy** [ˈenɪmɪ] (pl -ies) n Feind der ◇ comp feindlich.

**energetic** [ˌenəˈdʒetɪk] adj - **1.** [lively] energiegeladen, sehr aktiv; **to feel/be ~** viel Energie haben - **2.** [game, activity] viel Energie erfordernd - **3.** [supporter, campaigner] tatkräftig.

**energy** [ˈenədʒɪ] (pl -ies) n - **1.** [gen] Energie die - **2.** [effort] Energie die, Kraft die.

**energy-saving** adj energiesparend.

**enervating** [ˈenəveɪtɪŋ] adj fml strapazierend.

**enfold** [ɪnˈfəʊld] vt literary einlhüllen; **she ~ed him in her arms** sie schloss ihn in ihre Arme.

**enforce** [ɪnˈfɔːs] vt [high standards, discipline] sorgen für; **to ~ a law** für die Einhaltung eines Gesetzes sorgen.

**enforceable** [ɪnˈfɔːsəbl] adj durchsetzbar.

**enforced** [ɪnˈfɔːst] adj aufgezwungen.

**enforcement** [ɪnˈfɔːsmənt] n [of law] Durchsetzung die.

**enfranchise** [ɪnˈfræntʃaɪz] vt - **1.** [give vote to] das Wahlrecht geben (+ D) - **2.** [set free] freillassen.

**engage** [ɪnˈgeɪdʒ] vt - **1.** [attract - attention] in Anspruch nehmen; [ - interest] fesseln; **to ~ sb in conversation** jn in ein Gespräch verwickeln - **2.** TECH [wheels] ineinander greifen lassen; [gear] einllegen; **to ~ the clutch** kuppeln - **3.** fml [employ] anlstellen; **to be ~d in** OR **on sthg** mit etw beschäftigt sein; **to be ~d in negotiations** Verhandlungen führen ◇ vi: **to ~ in sthg** sich mit etw befassen.

**engaged** [ɪnˈgeɪdʒd] adj - **1.** [couple]: **~ (to sb)** (mit jm) verlobt; **to get ~** sich verloben - **2.** [busy] beschäftigt - **3.** [toilet, telephone, number] besetzt.

**engaged tone** n Br Besetztzeichen das.

**engagement** [ɪnˈgeɪdʒmənt] n - **1.** [of couple]

Verlobung *die* **- 2.** [appointment - gen] Verpflichtung *die;* [ - business] Termin *der.*

**engagement ring** *n* Verlobungsring *der.*

**engaging** [ɪn'geɪdʒɪŋ] *adj* [manner, personality] einnehmend; [smile] gewinnend.

**engender** [ɪn'dʒendər] *vt fml* erzeugen.

**engine** ['endʒɪn] *n* **- 1.** [of car, plane] Motor *der;* [of ship] Maschine *die* **- 2.** RAIL Lokomotive *die.*

**engine driver** *n Br* Lokomotivführer *der.*

**engineer** [ˌendʒɪ'nɪər] *n* **- 1.** [of roads, machines, bridges] Techniker *der,* -in *die;* [with degree] Ingenieur *der,* -in *die* **- 2.** [on ship] Maschinist *der,* -in *die* **- 3.** *Am* [engine driver] Lokomotivführer *der* ◇ *vt* **- 1.** [construct] konstruieren **- 2.** [arrange] arrangieren.

**engineering** [ˌendʒɪ'nɪərɪŋ] *n* (U) Technik *die;* [mechanical] Maschinenbau *der;* **a superb piece of** ~ eine meisterhafte Konstruktion.

**England** ['ɪŋglənd] *n* England *nt.*

**English** ['ɪŋglɪʃ] *adj* englisch ◇ *n* Englisch(e) *das* ◇ *npl:* **the** ~ die Engländer *pl.*

**English breakfast** *n* englisches Frühstück.

**English Channel** *n:* **the** ~ der Ärmelkanal.

**Englishman** ['ɪŋglɪʃmən] (*pl* **-men** [-mən]) *n* Engländer *der.*

**English muffin** *n Am kleines rundes Stück Brot, das vor dem Verzehr getoastet wird.*

**Englishwoman** ['ɪŋglɪʃˌwʊmən] (*pl* **-women** [-wɪmɪn]) *n* Engländerin *die.*

**engrave** [ɪn'greɪv] *vt* [metal, glass] gravieren; [design] eingravieren; *fig:* **it's ~d on my memory** es hat sich mir tief eingeprägt.

**engraver** [ɪn'greɪvər] *n* Graveur *der,* -in *die.*

**engraving** [ɪn'greɪvɪŋ] *n* **- 1.** [design] Gravierung *die;* [print] Stich *der* **- 2.** [skill] Gravieren *das.*

**engrossed** [ɪn'grəʊst] *adj:* **to be** ~ **(in sthg)** (in etw (A)) vertieft sein.

**engrossing** [ɪn'grəʊsɪŋ] *adj* fesselnd.

**engulf** [ɪn'gʌlf] *vt* [subj: fire, water] verschlingen; [subj: panic, fear] überwältigen.

**enhance** [ɪn'hɑːns] *vt* verbessern; [value, chances] steigern, erhöhen; [beauty] betonen.

**enhancement** [ɪn'hɑːnsmənt] *n* Verbesserung *die.*

**enigma** [ɪ'nɪgmə] *n* Rätsel *das.*

**enigmatic** [ˌenɪg'mætɪk] *adj* rätselhaft.

**enjoy** [ɪn'dʒɔɪ] *vt* **- 1.** [like] genießen; **she ~ed the film/book** der Film/das Buch hat ihr gefallen; **did you** ~ **it?** hast du es genossen?, hat es dir gefallen?; **to** ~ **doing sthg** etw gern(e) tun; **I** ~ **going to the cinema** ich gehe gern(e) ins Kino; **to** ~ **o.s.** sich amüsieren; ~ **yourself!** viel Spaß! **- 2.** *fml* [possess] genießen; **to** ~ **good health** sich guter Gesund-

heit erfreuen ◇ *vi Am:* ~! [enjoy yourself] viel Spaß!; [before meal] guten Appetit!

**enjoyable** [ɪn'dʒɔɪəbl] *adj* [job, work, experience] angenehm; [holiday, day] schön; [film, book] unterhaltsam.

**enjoyment** [ɪn'dʒɔɪmənt] *n* **- 1.** [gen] Vergnügen *das* **- 2.** [possession] Genuss *der.*

**enlarge** [ɪn'lɑːdʒ] *vt* vergrößern; [scope, interest, circle of friends] erweitern.

◆ **enlarge (up)on** *vt fus* sich genauer äußern über (+ A).

**enlargement** [ɪn'lɑːdʒmənt] *n* Vergrößerung *die;* [of scope, programme] Erweiterung *die.*

**enlighten** [ɪn'laɪtn] *vt fml* aufklären.

**enlightened** [ɪn'laɪtnd] *adj* [person] aufgeklärt; [approach] fortschrittlich.

**enlightening** [ɪn'laɪtnɪŋ] *adj* aufschlussreich.

**enlightenment** [ɪn'laɪtnmənt] *n* Aufklärung *die.*

◆ **Enlightenment** *n* HIST: **the Enlightenment** die Aufklärung.

**enlist** [ɪn'lɪst] *vt* **- 1.** MIL [recruit] einziehen **- 2.** [support, help] in Anspruch nehmen ◇ *vi* MIL: **to** ~ **(in)** sich melden (zu).

**enlisted man** [ɪn'lɪstɪd-] *n Am* gemeiner Soldat.

**enliven** [ɪn'laɪvn] *vt* beleben.

**en masse** [ɒn'mæs] *adv* alle zusammen.

**enmeshed** [ɪn'meʃt] *adj:* **to be** ~ **in sthg** in etw (+ D) verstrickt sein.

**enmity** ['enmətɪ] (*pl* **-ies**) *n* Feindschaft *die.*

**ennoble** [ɪ'nəʊbl] *vt* adeln.

**enormity** [ɪ'nɔːmətɪ] *n* ungeheueres Ausmaß.

**enormous** [ɪ'nɔːməs] *adj* ungeheuer groß, riesig.

**enormously** [ɪ'nɔːməslɪ] *adv* ungeheuer.

**enough** [ɪ'nʌf] *adj* genug; ~ **time** Zeit genug; **have you got** ~ **money?** hast du genügend Geld? ◇ *pron* genug; **is that** ~? reicht das?; **to have had** ~ **(of sthg)** genug (von etw) haben; **I've had** ~! [expressing annoyance] jetzt reichts mir aber!; **that's** ~ **of that!** das reicht!; **more than** ~ mehr als genug; ~ **is** ~ was zuviel ist, ist zuviel; **it's** ~ **to drive you crazy!** es ist zum Verrücktwerden! ◇ *adv* **- 1.** [sufficiently] genug; **good** ~ gut genug; **would you be good** ~ **to open the door for me?** *fml* wärst du so gut und öffnest mir die Tür?; **I was stupid** ~ **to believe him** ich war dumm genug, ihm zu glauben **- 2.** [rather] **he seems a nice** ~ **chap** er scheint ganz nett zu sein; **strangely** ~ merkwürdigerweise; **sure** ~ tatsächlich.

**enquire** [ɪn'kwaɪər] *vt* & *vi* = **inquire.**

**enquiry** [ɪn'kwaɪərɪ] (*pl* **-ies**) *n* = **inquiry.**

**enraged** [ɪnˈreɪdʒd] *adj* wütend.

**enrich** [ɪnˈrɪtʃ] *vt* - **1.** [make wealthy] wohlhabender machen - **2.** [improve - life, mind] bereichern; [ - soil] anlreichern.

**enrol** (*pt* & *pp* **-led**; *cont* **-ling**), **enroll** *Am* [ɪnˈrəʊl] *vt* einlschreiben; scʜ anlmelden <> *vi:* **to ~ (on** oʀ **in)** sich einlschreiben (für).

**enrolment** *Br*, **enrollment** *Am* [ɪnˈrəʊlmənt] *n* Einschreibung *die.*

**en route** [ɒnˈruːt] *adv:* **~ (from/to)** unterwegs (von/nach).

**ensconced** [ɪnˈskɒnst] *adj fml:* **to be ~ (in)** sich niedergelassen haben (auf *(+ D)*).

**enshrine** [ɪnˈʃraɪn] *vt:* **to be ~d in sthg** durch etw bewahrt werden.

**ensign** [ˈensaɪn] *n* - **1.** [flag] Nationalflagge *die* - **2.** *Am* [sailor] Fähnrich *der* zur See.

**enslave** [ɪnˈsleɪv] *vt* versklaven.

**ensue** [ɪnˈsjuː] *vi fml* folgen.

**ensuing** [ɪnˈsjuːɪŋ] *adj fml* folgend.

**ensure** [ɪnˈʃʊəʳ] *vt* sicherlstellen; [safety, privacy] gewährleisten; **to ~ (that)** ... dafür sorgen, dass ...

**ENT** (*abbr of* **Ear, Nose & Throat**) HNO.

**entail** [ɪnˈteɪl] *vt* mit sich bringen.

**entangled** [ɪnˈtæŋgld] *adj* - **1.** [ensnared]: **to be ~ in sthg** in etw *(D)* verfangen sein - **2.** [involved]: **to be ~ in sthg** in etw *(D)* verwickelt sein; **to be ~ with sb** [romantically] sich mit jm eingelassen haben.

**entanglement** [ɪnˈtæŋglmənt] *n* [romantic] Techtelmechtel *das.*

**enter** [ˈentəʳ] *vt* - **1.** [house, room] einlltreten in *(+ A)*, betreten; [car, bus, train] einlsteigen in *(+ A)*; [subj: vehicle] fahren in *(+ A)*; [subj: ship] einllaufen in *(+ A)*; [country] einllreisen in *(+ A)* - **2.** [army] einltreten in *(+ A)*; [competition, race] teillnehmen an *(+ D)*; **to ~ politics** in die Politik gehen; **to ~ the church** Geistlicher werden; **to ~ university** zur Universität gehen - **3.** [horse, competitor] anlmelden; [poem, story] einlreichen - **4.** [write down] einltragen - **5.** coᴍᴘᴜᴛ einlgeben <> *vi* - **1.** [come or go in] einltreten; [enter bus, train] einlsteigen; [enter country] einllreisen - **2.** [register]: **to ~ (for sthg)** sich (für etw) anlmelden.

➤ **enter into** *vt fus* [negotiations] treten in *(+ A)*; **to ~ into an agreement with sb** mit jm ein Abkommen schließen; **to ~ into conversation with sb** mit jm ins Gespräch kommen.

**enteritis** [ˌentəˈraɪtɪs] *n (U)* Enteritis *die.*

**enter key** *n* coᴍᴘᴜᴛ Eingabetaste *die.*

**enterprise** [ˈentəpraɪz] *n* - **1.** [company, project] Unternehmen *das;* **private ~** Privatwirtschaft *die* - **2.** *(U)* [initiative] Initiative *die.*

**enterprising** [ˈentəpraɪzɪŋ] *adj* [person] einfallsreich; [plan, idea] innovativ.

**entertain** [ˌentəˈteɪn] *vt* - **1.** [amuse] unterhalten - **2.** [dinner guest] bewirten - **3.** *fml* [idea, proposal] erwägen; [hopes] nähren; [suspicion, ambition] hegen <> *vi* [have guests] Gäste haben.

**entertainer** [ˌentəˈteɪnəʳ] *n* Unterhalter *der,* -in *die,* Entertainer *der,* -in *die.*

**entertaining** [ˌentəˈteɪnɪŋ] *adj* unterhaltsam <> *n:* **she does a lot of ~** sie hat oft Gäste.

**entertainment** [ˌentəˈteɪnmənt] *n* - **1.** [amusement] Unterhaltung *die* - **2.** [show] Darbietung *die.*

**entertainment allowance** *n* Auslagenpauschale *die.*

**enthral** (*pt* & *pp* **-led**; *cont* **-ling**), **enthrall** *Am* [ɪnˈθrɔːl] *vt* fesseln.

**enthralling** [ɪnˈθrɔːlɪŋ] *adj* fesselnd.

**enthrone** [ɪnˈθrəʊn] *vt fml* inthronisieren.

**enthuse** [ɪnˈθjuːz] *vi:* **to ~ (about)** schwärmen (von).

**enthusiasm** [ɪnˈθjuːzɪæzm] *n* - **1.** [eagerness] Begeisterung *die,* Enthusiasmus *der* - **2.** [hobby] Leidenschaft *die.*

**enthusiast** [ɪnˈθjuːzɪæst] *n* Enthusiast *der,* -in *die.*

**enthusiastic** [ɪnˌθjuːzɪˈæstɪk] *adj* begeistert, enthusiastisch.

**enthusiastically** [ɪnˌθjuːzɪˈæstɪklɪ] *adv* begeistert, enthusiastisch.

**entice** [ɪnˈtaɪs] *vt* locken; **to ~ sb away from sthg** jn von etw weglocken.

**enticing** [ɪnˈtaɪsɪŋ] *adj* verlockend.

**entire** [ɪnˈtaɪəʳ] *adj* ganz; [amount, population] gesamt; [confidence, attention] voll.

**entirely** [ɪnˈtaɪəlɪ] *adv* ganz; **I agree ~** ich stimme voll und ganz zu.

**entirety** [ɪnˈtaɪrətɪ] *n fml:* **in its ~** in seiner Gesamtheit.

**entitle** [ɪnˈtaɪtl] *vt* [allow]: **to ~ sb to sthg** jn zu etw berechtigen; **to ~ sb to do sthg** jn dazu berechtigen, etw zu tun.

**entitled** [ɪnˈtaɪtld] *adj* - **1.** [allowed] berechtigt; **to be ~ to sthg** das Recht auf etw *(A)* haben - **2.** [called]: **to be ~d** den Titel haben.

**entitlement** [ɪnˈtaɪtlmənt] *n* Berechtigung *die;* [to compensation, holiday] Anspruch *der.*

**entity** [ˈentətɪ] (*pl* **-ies**) *n* Wesen *das.*

**entomology** [ˌentəˈmɒlədʒɪ] *n* Entomologie *die.*

**entourage** [ˌɒntuˈrɑːʒ] *n* Gefolge *das.*

**entrails** [ˈentreɪlz] *npl* Eingeweide *pl.*

**entrance** [*n* ˈentrəns, *vt* ɪnˈtrɑːns] *n* - **1.** [way in]: **~ (to)** Eingang *der* (zu) - **2.** [arrival] Eintritt *der;* [of actor] Auftritt *der* - **3.** [admission] Eintritt *der;* **to gain ~ to sthg** *fml* [building] Zutritt zu etw erhalten; [society, university] die Zulassung zu

E

etw erhalten; 'no ~' 'Zutritt verboten' <> *vt* [delight] bezaubern.

**entrance examination** *n* Aufnahmeprüfung *die.*

**entrance fee** *n* Eintrittsgeld *das;* [for club] Aufnahmegebühr *die.*

**entrancing** [ɪn'trɑːnsɪŋ] *adj* bezaubernd.

**entrant** ['entrənt] *n* - **1.** [in competition, exam, race] Teilnehmer *der,* -in *die* - **2.** [to university] Neuzugang *der;* [to profession] Berufsanfänger *der,* -in *die.*

**entreat** [ɪn'triːt] *vt:* **to ~ sb to do sthg** jn inständig bitten, etw zu tun; [plead with] jn anflehen, etw zu tun.

**entreaty** [ɪn'triːtɪ] (*pl* -**ies**) *n* dringende Bitte.

**entrenched** [ɪn'trentʃt] *adj* (fest) verwurzelt.

**entrepreneur** [ˌɒntrəprə'nɜːr] *n* Unternehmer *der,* -in *die.*

**entrepreneurial** [ˌɒntrəprə'nɜːrɪəl] *adj* unternehmerisch.

**entrust** [ɪn'trʌst] *vt:* **to ~ sthg to sb** jm etw anvertrauen; **to ~ sb with sthg** jn mit etw betrauen.

**entry** ['entrɪ] (*pl* -**ies**) *n* - **1.** [entrance, arrival]: **~ (into)** Eingang *der* (in (+ A)) - **2.** (U) [admission]: **~ (to)** [to country] Einreise *die* (in (+ A)); [to building] Zutritt *der* (zu); [to event] Einlass *der* (in (+ A)); **to gain ~ to** [house] gelangen in (+ A); [organization] beitreten (+ D); **'no ~'** 'Zutritt verboten'; AUT 'Durchfahrt verboten' - **3.** *fig* [joining] Beitritt *der* - **4.** [for race] Nennung *die;* [for competition] Einsendung *die* - **5.** [in diary, dictionary, ledger] Eintragung *die* - **6.** COMPUT Eingabe *die* - **7.** *esp Am* [gate, door] Eingang *der.*

**entry fee** *n* Nenngeld *das.*

**entry form** *n* Anmeldeformular *das.*

**entry phone** *n* Türsprechanlage *die.*

**entryway** ['entrɪˌweɪ] *n Am* Flur *der;* [between buildings, yards] Durchgang *der.*

**entwine** [ɪn'twaɪn] *vt:* **their arms/fingers were ~d** ihre Arme/Finger waren ineinander verschlungen <> *vi* sich ineinander schlingen.

**E number** *n* E-Nummer *die.*

**enumerate** [ɪ'njuːməreɪt] *vt* auf lzählen; [on list] auf llisten.

**enunciate** [ɪ'nʌnsɪeɪt] *vt* - **1.** [words] artikulieren - **2.** [ideas] formulieren <> *vi* [speak clearly] artikulieren.

**envelop** [ɪn'veləp] *vt:* **to ~ sb/sthg in sthg** jn/etw in etw (A) (ein)hüllen.

**envelope** ['envələʊp] *n* Briefumschlag *der.*

**enviable** ['envɪəbl] *adj* beneidenswert.

**envious** ['envɪəs] *adj:* **~ (of sb/sthg)** neidisch (auf jn/etw); **she was very ~ of his success** sie beneidete ihn um seinen Erfolg.

**enviously** ['envɪəslɪ] *adv* neidisch, neiderfüllt.

**environment** [ɪn'vaɪərənmənt] *n* - **1.** [surroundings] Umgebung *die* - **2.** [natural world]: **the ~** die Umwelt; **Department of the Environment** *Br* ≃ Umweltministerium *das.*

**environmental** [ɪnˌvaɪərən'mentl] *adj* Umwelt-.

**environmentalist** [ɪnˌvaɪərən'mentəlɪst] *n* Umweltschützer *der,* -in *die.*

**environmentally** [ɪnˌvaɪərən'mentəlɪ] *adv* umwelt-; **~ friendly** umweltfreundlich.

**Environmental Protection Agency** *n Am:* **the ~** *Umweltschutzbehörde der US-amerikanischen Regierung.*

**environs** [ɪn'vaɪrənz] *npl* Umgebung *die.*

**envisage** [ɪn'vɪzɪdʒ], **envision** *Am* [ɪn'vɪʒn] *vt* sich vorlstellen.

**envoy** ['envɔɪ] *n* Gesandte *der,* *die.*

**envy** ['envɪ] (*pt & pp* -**ied**) *n* Neid *der;* **to be the ~ of** beneidet werden von; **to be green with ~** grün sein vor Neid <> *vt* beneiden; **to ~ sb sthg** jn um etw beneiden.

**enzyme** ['enzaɪm] *n* Enzym *das.*

**EOC** *n abbr of* **Equal Opportunities Commission.**

**eon** *n Am* = **aeon.**

**EPA** *n abbr of* **Environmental Protection Agency.**

**epaulet(te)** [ˌepə'let] *n* Schulterstück *das.*

**ephemeral** [ɪ'femərəl] *adj* kurzlebig; [happiness] von kurzer Dauer.

**epic** ['epɪk] *adj* [poetry] episch; [journey] lang und abenteuerlich; [story] monumental <> *n* [book, film] Epos *das.*

**epicentre** *Br,* **epicenter** *Am* ['epɪsentər] *n* Epizentrum *das.*

**epidemic** [ˌepɪ'demɪk] *n* Epidemie *die.*

**epidural** [ˌepɪ'djʊərəl] *n* Epiduralanästhesie *die.*

**epigram** ['epɪɡræm] *n* Epigramm *das.*

**epilepsy** ['epɪlepsɪ] *n* Epilepsie *die.*

**epileptic** [ˌepɪ'leptɪk] *adj* epileptisch <> *n* Epileptiker *der,* -in *die.*

**epilogue** *Br,* **epilog** *Am* ['epɪlɒɡ] *n* Epilog *der.*

**Epiphany** [ɪ'pɪfənɪ] *n:* **(the) ~** das Dreikönigsfest.

**episcopal** [ɪ'pɪskəpl] *adj* bischöflich, episkopal.

**episode** ['epɪsəʊd] *n* - **1.** [event] Episode *die* - **2.** [broadcast] Folge *die.*

**episodic** [ˌepɪ'sɒdɪk] *adj* episodenhaft.

**epistle** [ɪ'pɪsl] *n literary* Epistel *die,* Brief *der.*

**epitaph** ['epɪtɑːf] *n* Epitaph *das,* Grabinschrift *die.*

**epithet** ['epɪθet] n Beiname der.

**epitome** [ɪ'pɪtəmɪ] n: the ~ of der Inbegriff (+ G).

**epitomize, -ise** [ɪ'pɪtəmaɪz] vt beispielhaft zeigen.

**epoch** ['iːpɒk] n Epoche die.

**eponymous** [ɪ'pɒnɪməs] adj namengebend.

**EPOS** ['iːpɒs] (abbr of electronic point of sale) n elektronisches Kassenterminal.

**equable** ['ekwəbl] adj [calm, reasonable] ausgeglichen.

**equal** ['iːkwəl] (Br pt & pp -led; cont -ling, Am pt & pp -ed; cont -ing) adj - 1. [of the same quantity, size, shape, degree] gleich; they're of ~ size sie sind gleich groß; to divide sthg into two ~ parts etw in zwei gleiche Hälften teilen; to be ~ to sthg [sum] etw (D) entsprechen - 2. [in status] gleich(berechtigt); ~ rights Gleichberechtigung die; on ~ terms als Gleichgestellte, zu gleichen Bedingungen - 3. [capable]: to be ~ to sthg etw (D) gewachsen sein <> n [person] Gleichgestellte der, die <> vt - 1. MATH gleichen - 2. [in standard] gleichlkommen (+ D).

**equality** [iː'kwɒlətɪ] n Gleichheit die.

**equalize, -ise** ['iːkwəlaɪz] vt & vi SPORT auslgleichen.

**equalizer** ['iːkwəlaɪzə'], **-iser** n SPORT Ausgleich der.

**equally** ['iːkwəlɪ] adv - 1. [to the same extent] ebenso - 2. [divide, share] in gleiche Teile, gleichmäßig - 3. [by the same token] gleichzeitig.

**equal opportunities** npl Chancengleichheit die.

**Equal Opportunities Commission** n Br: the ~ ≃ der Gleichstellungsausschuss.

**equal(s) sign** n Gleichheitszeichen das.

**equanimity** [ˌekwə'nɪmətɪ] n Gelassenheit die.

**equate** [ɪ'kweɪt] vt: to ~ sthg with sthg etw mit etw gleichlsetzen.

**equation** [ɪ'kweɪʒn] n MATH Gleichung die.

**equator** [ɪ'kweɪtə'] n: the ~ der Äquator.

**equatorial** [ˌekwə'tɔːrɪəl] adj äquatorial.

**equestrian** [ɪ'kwestrɪən] adj [talent, event] Reit-; [statue] Reiter-.

**equidistant** [ˌiːkwɪ'dɪstənt] adj: ~ (from) gleich weit entfernt (von).

**equilateral triangle** [ˌiːkwɪ'lætərəl-] n gleichseitiges Dreieck.

**equilibrium** [ˌiːkwɪ'lɪbrɪəm] n Gleichgewicht das.

**equine** ['ekwaɪn] adj Pferde-.

**equinox** ['ekwɪnɒks] n Tagundnachtgleiche die.

**equip** [ɪ'kwɪp] (pt & pp -ped; cont -ping) vt - 1. [provide with equipment] auslstatten; to ~ sb/sthg with sthg jn/etw mit etw auslrüsten - 2. [prepare mentally]: to ~ sb for sthg jn für etw vorlbereiten; he's well ~ped for the job er bringt die nötigen Voraussetzungen für die Stelle mit.

**equipment** [ɪ'kwɪpmənt] n (U) Ausrüstung die, Ausstattung die; electrical ~ Elektrogeräte pl.

**equitable** ['ekwɪtəbl] adj gerecht.

**equity** n (U) FIN [market value] Eigenkapital das.
➡ **equities** npl ST EX Stammaktien pl.

**equivalent** [ɪ'kwɪvələnt] adj entsprechend, äquivalent; to be ~ to sthg etw (D) entsprechen <> n Gegenstück das.

**equivocal** [ɪ'kwɪvəkl] adj - 1. [statement, remark] zweideutig - 2. [behaviour, event] zweifelhaft.

**equivocate** [ɪ'kwɪvəkeɪt] vi zweideutige Aussagen machen.

**er** [ɜːʳ] excl äh.

**ER** (abbr of Elizabeth Regina) Emblem der britischen Königin.

**era** ['ɪərə] (pl -s) n Ära die.

**ERA** (abbr of Equal Rights Amendment) n Gesetz zur Gleichstellung von Frauen in den USA.

**eradicate** [ɪ'rædɪkeɪt] vt auslrotten.

**eradication** [ɪˌrædɪ'keɪʃn] n Ausrottung die.

**erase** [ɪ'reɪz] vt - 1. [rub out] auslradieren; [tape, recording] löschen - 2. fig [memory] (aus dem Gedächtnis) tilgen; [hunger, poverty] beseitigen.

**eraser** [ɪ'reɪzə'] n esp Am Radiergummi der.

**erect** [ɪ'rekt] adj - 1. [person, posture] aufrecht - 2. [penis] erigiert <> vt - 1. [building, statue] errichten, bauen - 2. [tent] auflbauen; [roadblock, sign] auflstellen.

**erection** [ɪ'rekʃn] n - 1. (U) [of building, statue] Errichtung die, Bau der - 2. [erect penis] Erektion die; to get/have an ~ eine Erektion bekommen/haben.

**ergonomic** [ˌɜːgə'nɒmɪk] adj ergonomisch.

**ergonomics** [ˌɜːgə'nɒmɪks] n Ergonomie die.

**ERM** (abbr of Exchange Rate Mechanism) n WUM der.

**ermine** ['ɜːmɪn] n Hermelin der.

**erode** [ɪ'rəʊd] vt - 1. GEOL erodieren - 2. fig [destroy] unterlgraben <> vi - 1. GEOL abgetragen werden, verwittern - 2. fig [be destroyed] untergraben werden.

**erogenous zone** [ɪ'rɒdʒɪnəs-] n erogene Zone.

**erosion** [ɪ'rəʊʒn] n - 1. GEOL Erosion die - 2. fig [destruction] Untergrabung die.

**erotic** [ɪ'rɒtɪk] adj erotisch.

**eroticism** [ɪ'rɒtɪsɪzm] n Erotik die.

**err** [ɜːr] vi sich irren; **to ~ on the side of caution** auf Nummer sicher gehen; **to ~ is human** Irren ist menschlich.

**errand** ['erənd] n Besorgung die; **to go on** OR **run an ~ (for sb)** (für jn) eine Besorgung OR einen Botengang machen.

**errand boy** n Botenjunge der.

**erratic** [ɪ'rætɪk] adj wechselhaft; [movement, bus service] unregelmäßig; [performance] variabel; [player] unberechenbar.

**erroneous** [ɪ'rəʊnjəs] adj fml falsch, irrig.

**error** ['erəʳ] n - **1.** [mistake] Fehler der; **~ of judgement** Fehleinschätzung die - **2.** (U) [making mistakes] Irrtum der; **in ~** aus Versehen, irrtümlicherweise.

**error message** n COMPUT Fehlermeldung die.

**erstwhile** ['ɜːstwaɪl] adj literary einstig.

**erudite** ['eruːdaɪt] adj gelehrt.

**erupt** [ɪ'rʌpt] vi auslbrechen.

**eruption** [ɪ'rʌpʃn] n Ausbruch der.

**ESA** (abbr of **European Space Agency**) n ESA die.

**escalate** ['eskəleɪt] vi eskalieren.

**escalation** [ˌeskə'leɪʃn] n - **1.** [worsening] Eskalation die - **2.** [rapid growth] sprunghafter Anstieg.

**escalator** ['eskəleɪtəʳ] n Rolltreppe die.

**escalator clause** n Gleitklausel die.

**escapade** [ˌeskə'peɪd] n Eskapade die.

**escape** [ɪ'skeɪp] n - **1.** [from person, place, situation]: **~ (from sb/sthg)** Flucht die (vor jn/vor OR aus etw); **there was no ~** es gab kein Entkommen; **to make an** OR **one's ~ (from)** flüchten (aus) - **2.** [from danger]: **to have a narrow ~** mit knapper Not entkommen - **3.** [leakage] Ausströmen das - **4.** COMPUT Escape das ◇ vt - **1.** [avoid] entkommen (+ D), entgehen (+ D); **to ~ notice** unbemerkt bleiben - **2.** [subj: fact, name] entfallen; **her name ~s me just now** ihr Name fällt mir momentan nicht ein ◇ vi - **1.** [from person, place, situation]: **to ~ (from sb)** fliehen OR flüchten (vor jm); **to ~ (from sthg)** fliehen OR flüchten (vor OR aus etw); **to ~ from prison** aus dem Gefängnis fliehen - **2.** [from danger] davonlkommen - **3.** [leak] auslströmen.

**escape clause** n Ausweichklausel die.

**escape key** n COMPUT Escape-Taste die.

**escape route** n Fluchtweg der.

**escapism** [ɪ'skeɪpɪzm] n Realitätsflucht die.

**escapist** [ɪ'skeɪpɪst] adj Aussteiger-.

**escapologist** [ˌeskə'pɒlədʒɪst] n Entfesselungskünstler der, -in die.

**escarpment** [ɪ'skɑːpmənt] n Böschung die.

**eschew** [ɪs'tʃuː] vt fml meiden.

**escort** [n 'eskɔːt, vb ɪ'skɔːt] n - **1.** [guard] Geleitschutz der, Eskorte die; **under ~** unter Bewachung - **2.** [companion] Begleiter der, -in die ◇ vt [accompany] begleiten; [for protection] eskortieren, Geleitschutz geben (+ D).

**escort agency** n Begleitagentur die.

**Eskimo** ['eskɪməʊ] (pl **-s**) adj Eskimo- ◇ n - **1.** [person] Eskimo der, -frau die - **2.** [language] Eskimoisch(e) das.

**ESL** (abbr of **English as a Second Language**) n Englisch als Zweitsprache.

**esophagus** n Am = oesophagus.

**esoteric** [ˌesə'terɪk] adj esoterisch.

**esp.** (abbr of **especially**) bes.

**ESP** n - **1.** (abbr of **extrasensory perception**) ASW die - **2.** (abbr of **English for special purposes**) Englisch für besondere Zwecke.

**espadrille** [ˌespə'drɪl] n Espadrille die.

**especial** [ɪ'speʃl] adj besondere, -r, -s.

**especially** [ɪ'speʃəlɪ] adv - **1.** [in particular, more than usually] besonders - **2.** [specifically] speziell.

**Esperanto** [ˌespə'ræntəʊ] n Esperanto das.

**espionage** ['espɪəˌnɑːʒ] n Spionage die.

**esplanade** [ˌesplə'neɪd] n (Strand)promenade die.

**espouse** [ɪ'spaʊz] vt einltreten für.

**espresso** [e'spresəʊ] (pl **-s**) n Espresso der.

**Esq.** n abbr of **Esquire**.

**Esquire** [ɪ'skwaɪəʳ] n ≃ Herr/Herrn, britische Höflichkeitsanrede in der Postanschrift.

**essay** ['eseɪ] n - **1.** SCH Aufsatz der - **2.** LITERATURE & UNIV Essay der.

**essayist** ['eseɪɪst] n Essayist der.

**essence** ['esns] n - **1.** [nature] Wesentliche das, Kern der; **in ~** im Wesentlichen - **2.** (U) CULIN Essenz die.

**essential** [ɪ'senʃl] adj - **1.** [necessary]: **~ (to** OR **for sthg)** (unbedingt) notwendig (für etw) - **2.** [basic] wesentlich, grundlegend.

◆ **essentials** npl - **1.** [basic commodities] Notwendigste das - **2.** [most important elements] Grundlagen pl.

**essentially** [ɪ'senʃəlɪ] adv im Grunde.

**est. - 1.** (abbr of **established**) gegr. - **2.** (abbr of **estimated**) geschätzt.

**EST** (abbr of **Eastern Standard Time**) n Standardzeit in der östlichen Zeitzone der USA.

**establish** [ɪ'stæblɪʃ] vt - **1.** [create - company, organization] gründen; [- system, law, post] schaffen - **2.** [initiate]: **to ~ contact with sb** Kontakt mit jm auflnehmen - **3.** [ascertain] festlstellen, ermitteln - **4.** [cause to be accepted] bestätigen; **to ~ o.s. (as)** sich (D) einen Namen machen (als), sich etablieren (als).

**established** [ɪ'stæblɪʃt] adj - **1.** [accepted] etabliert; [author] anerkannt - **2.** [founded] gegründet.

**establishment** [ɪ'stæblɪʃmənt] n - **1.** (U) [creation, foundation] Gründung die, Errichtung die - **2.** [shop, business] Unternehmen das.
➡ **Establishment** n: the Establishment das Establishment.

**estate** [ɪ'steɪt] n - **1.** [land, property] Gut das - **2.** [for housing] Wohnsiedlung die; [for industry] Industriegebiet das - **3.** LAW [inheritance] Besitz der, Besitztümer pl.

**estate agency** n Br Immobilienagentur die.

**estate agent** n Br Grundstücksmakler der, -in die; ~'s Immobilienbüro das.

**estate car** n Br Kombiwagen der.

**estd., est'd.** (abbr of established) gegr.

**esteem** [ɪ'stiːm] n Achtung die, Wertschätzung die; to hold sb/sthg in high ~ große Achtung vor jm/etw haben <> vt schätzen, achten.

**esthetic** etc adj Am = aesthetic etc.

**estimate** [n 'estɪmət, vb 'estɪmeɪt] n - **1.** [calculation, reckoning] Schätzung die - **2.** COMM Kostenvoranschlag der <> vt schätzen, einlschätzen <> vi COMM: to ~ for sthg veranschlagen für etw.

**estimated** ['estɪmeɪtɪd] adj geschätzt.

**estimation** [ˌestɪ'meɪʃn] n (U) - **1.** [opinion] Urteil das, Einschätzung die; to go up/down in one's ~ in js Achtung steigen/sinken - **2.** [calculation] Schätzung die.

**Estonia** [e'stəʊnɪə] n Estland nt.

**Estonian** [e'stəʊnɪən] adj estnisch <> n - **1.** [person] Este der, -tin die - **2.** [language] Estnisch(e) das.

**estranged** [ɪ'streɪndʒd] adj getrennt lebend.

**estrogen** n Am = oestrogen.

**estuary** ['estjʊərɪ] (pl -ies) n Flußmündung die.

**ETA** (abbr of estimated time of arrival) n voraussichtliche Ankunftszeit.

**et al.** ['et ˌæl] (abbr of et alii) et al.

**etc.** (abbr of etcetera) usw.

**etcetera** [ɪt'setərə] adv und so weiter.

**etch** [etʃ] vt - **1.** [engrave] radieren - **2.** fig [imprint]: to be ~ed on sb's memory in js Gedächtnis eingegraben sein.

**etching** ['etʃɪŋ] n Radierung die.

**ETD** (abbr of estimated time of departure) n voraussichtliche Abfahrtszeit.

**eternal** [ɪ'tɜːnl] adj ewig.

**eternally** [ɪ'tɜːnəlɪ] adv ewig.

**eternity** [ɪ'tɜːnətɪ] n Ewigkeit die.

**eternity ring** n Br ringsherum mit Steinen besetzter Ring, den ein Ehemann seiner Frau nach einer bestimmten Ehezeit als Treueversprechen gibt.

**ether** ['iːθəʳ] n Äther der.

**ethereal** [iː'θɪərɪəl] adj literary ätherisch.

**ethic** ['eθɪk] n Ethik die, Ethos das.
➡ **ethics** n [study] Ethik die <> npl [morals] Moral die.

**ethical** ['eθɪkl] adj ethisch.

**Ethiopia** [ˌiːθɪ'əʊpɪə] n Äthiopien nt.

**Ethiopian** [ˌiːθɪ'əʊpɪən] adj äthiopisch <> n Äthiopier der, -in die.

**ethnic** ['eθnɪk] adj - **1.** [traditions, groups, conflict] ethnisch - **2.** [clothes] folkloristisch; [food] einheimisch.

**ethnic cleansing** [-'klenzɪŋ] n ethnische Säuberung.

**ethnic minority** n ethnische Minderheit.

**ethnology** [eθ'nɒlədʒɪ] n Ethnologie die.

**ethos** ['iːθɒs] n Ethos das, Gesinnung die.

**etiquette** ['etɪket] n Etikette die, Verhaltensregeln pl.

**etymology** [ˌetɪ'mɒlədʒɪ] (pl -ies) n Etymologie die.

**EU** (abbr of European Union) n EU die.

**eucalyptus** [ˌjuːkə'lɪptəs] (pl -tuses) n Eukalyptus der.

**eulogize, -ise** ['juːlədʒaɪz] vt rühmen.

**eulogy** ['juːlədʒɪ] (pl -ies) n Lobrede die.

**eunuch** ['juːnək] n Eunuch der.

**euphemism** ['juːfəmɪzm] n Euphemismus der.

**euphemistic** [ˌjuːfə'mɪstɪk] adj euphemistisch.

**euphoria** [juː'fɔːrɪə] n Euphorie die.

**euphoric** [juː'fɒrɪk] adj euphorisch.

**Eurasia** [jʊə'reɪʒə] n Eurasien nt.

**Eurasian** [jʊə'reɪʒən] adj [of Europe and Asia] eurasisch <> n Eurasier der, -in die.

**eureka** [jʊə'riːkə] excl heureka.

**Euro** ['jʊərəʊ] n Euro der.

**Eurocheque** ['jʊərəʊˌtʃek] n Euroscheck der.

**euro cent** n Eurocent der.

**Eurocrat** ['jʊərəˌkræt] n Eurokrat der, -in die.

**Eurocurrency** ['jʊərəʊˌkʌrənsɪ] (pl -ies) n Eurowährung die.

**Eurodollar** ['jʊərəʊˌdɒləʳ] n Eurodollar der.

**Euro-elections** npl Europawahlen pl.

**Euroland** n Euroland das.

**Euro MP** n Europaabgeordnete der, die.

**Europe** ['jʊərəp] n Europa nt.

**European** [ˌjʊərə'piːən] adj europäisch <> n Europäer der, -in die.

**European Community** n: the ~ die Europäische Gemeinschaft.

**European Court of Human Rights** *n:* the ~ der Europäische Hof für Menschenrechte.

**European Court of Justice** *n:* the ~ der Europäische Gerichtshof.

**European Currency Unit** *n* Europäische Währungseinheit *die.*

**Europeanism** [ˌjʊərə'piːənɪzm] *n* Europäertum *das,* europäischer Gedanke.

**Europeanize, -ise** [ˌjʊərə'piːənaɪz] *vt* europäisieren.

**European Monetary System** *n:* the ~ das Europäische Währungssystem.

**European Parliament** *n:* the ~ das Europäische Parlament.

**European Union** *n:* the ~ die Europäische Union.

**euro zone** *n* Eurozone *die.*

**euthanasia** [ˌjuːθə'neɪzjə] *n* Euthanasie *die.*

**evacuate** [ɪ'vækjʊeɪt] *vt* evakuieren.

**evacuation** [ɪˌvækjʊ'eɪʃn] *n* Evakuierung *die.*

**evacuee** [ɪˌvækjʊ'iː] *n* Evakuierte *der, die.*

**evade** [ɪ'veɪd] *vt* - **1.** [pursuers, capture] sich entziehen (+ D), entkommen (+ D) - **2.** [issue, question] auslweichen (+ D), (ver)meiden - **3.** [subj: love, success]: **love/success has always ~d him** ihm ist die Liebe/der Erfolg immer versagt geblieben.

**evaluate** [ɪ'væljʊeɪt] *vt* bewerten.

**evaluation** [ɪˌvæljʊ'eɪʃn] *n* Bewertung *die.*

**evangelical** [ˌiːvæn'dʒelɪkl] *adj* evangelisch.

**evangelism** [ɪ'vændʒəlɪzm] *n* Missionstätigkeit *die.*

**evangelist** [ɪ'vændʒəlɪst] *n* Evangelist *der;* [preacher] Prediger *der,* -in *die.*

**evangelize, -ise** [ɪ'vændʒəlaɪz] *vt* missionieren.

**evaporate** [ɪ'væpəreɪt] *vi* - **1.** [liquid] verdunsten - **2.** *fig* [feeling] schwinden, sich in Luft auf lösen.

**evaporated milk** [ɪ'væpəreɪtɪd-] *n* Kondensmilch *die.*

**evaporation** [ɪˌvæpə'reɪʃn] *n* - **1.** [of liquid] Verdunstung *die* - **2.** *fig* [of feeling] Schwinden *das.*

**evasion** [ɪ'veɪʒn] *n* - **1.** [of responsibility, payment etc] Ausweichen *das,* Umgehen *das* - **2.** [lie] Ausflucht *die.*

**evasive** [ɪ'veɪsɪv] *adj* - **1.** [to avoid question, subject] ausweichend - **2.** [to avoid being hit]: **to take ~ action** ein Ausweichmanöver machen.

**evasiveness** [ɪ'veɪsɪvnɪs] *n* Ausweichen *das.*

**eve** [iːv] *n* [day before] Vortag *der.*

**even** [ɪ'iːvn] *adj* - **1.** [rate, speed] gleichmäßig - **2.** [calm] ausgeglichen - **3.** [level, flat] eben - **4.** [teams] gleich stark; **the scores were ~** es

herrschte Gleichstand; **to get ~ with sb** es jm heimlzahlen - **5.** [number] gerade ◇ *adv* - **1.** [for emphasis] sogar; **not ~** nicht einmal; **without ~ thinking** ohne auch nur einen Moment nachzudenken; **~ now** sogar jetzt; **~ then** selbst dann - **2.** [in comparisons] noch; **~ better** noch besser; **~ more stupid** (sogar) noch dümmer.

➤ **even as** *conj* [while] gerade als; **~ as we speak** ... in diesem Augenblick ...

➤ **even if** *conj* selbst *or* auch wenn.

➤ **even out** *vt sep* - **1.** [gen] auslgleichen; **to ~ things out** das Kräfteverhältnis auslgleichen - **2.** [surface] ebnen ◇ *vi* sich auslgleichen.

➤ **even so** *adv* trotzdem.

➤ **even though** *conj* obwohl.

**even-handed** [-'hændɪd] *adj* gerecht.

**evening** [ɪ'iːvnɪŋ] *n* Abend *der;* **in the ~s** am Abend, abends.

➤ **evenings** *adv Am* am Abend, abends.

**evening class** *n* Abendkurs *der.*

**evening dress** *n* - **1.** [formal clothes] Abendkleidung *die* - **2.** [woman's garment] Abendkleid *das.*

**evening star** *n:* the ~ der Abendstern.

**evenly** [ɪ'iːvnlɪ] *adv* - **1.** [regularly, equally] gleichmäßig; **to be ~ spaced** den gleichen Abstand voneinander haben - **2.** [calmly] gelassen.

**evenness** [ɪ'iːvnnɪs] *n* - **1.** [regularity] Gleichmäßigkeit *die* - **2.** [equality] Ausgeglichenheit *die.*

**evensong** [ɪ'iːvnsɒŋ] *n* Abendandacht *die.*

**event** [ɪ'vent] *n* - **1.** [happening] Ereignis *das* - **2.** sport Wettkampf *der* - **3.** [case] Fall *der;* **in the ~ of** im Falle (+ G); **in the ~ of rain** bei Regen; **in the ~ that** falls.

➤ **in any event** *adv* [all the same] wie dem auch sei, wie auch immer.

➤ **in the event** *adv Br* letztlich.

**even-tempered** [-'tempəd] *adj* ausgeglichen.

**eventful** [ɪ'ventfʊl] *adj* ereignisreich; [life] bewegt.

**eventing** [ɪ'ventɪŋ] *n (U) Br* sport: **(three-day) ~** Pferdesportveranstaltung *die.*

**eventual** [ɪ'ventʃʊəl] *adj:* **the ~ winner/outcome was** ... der Sieger/das Resultat war schließlich ...

**eventuality** [ɪˌventʃʊ'ælətɪ] *(pl* -ies) *n* (möglicher) Fall, Eventualität *die.*

**eventually** [ɪ'ventʃʊəlɪ] *adv* schließlich, am Ende.

**ever** [ɪ'evə'] *adv* - **1.** [at any time] je, jemals; **the worst film I've ~ seen** der schlimmste Film, den ich je gesehen habe; **have you ~ been to Chicago?** sind Sie jemals in Chicago gewesen?; **don't ~ speak to me like that again!** so redest du nicht noch einmal mit mir!; **hardly** ~ **fast nie; if** ~ wenn überhaupt - **2.** [all the time] immer; **for** ~ [eternally] für immer; [for a long time] seit Ewigkeiten; **I'll love you for** ~ ich werde dich immer lieben; **as** ~ wie immer; ~ **larger** immer größer - **3.** [for emphasis]: **why/ how** ~ **did you do it?** warum/wie hast du das bloß gemacht?; **what** ~ **is the matter with you?** was ist denn mit dir los?; **he was** ~ **so angry** er war sehr verärgert; ~ **such a mess** ein fürchterliches Durcheinander.

▪ **ever since** adv seitdem ⬦ prep & conj seit.

**Everest** ['evərɪst] n Mount Everest der.

**Everglades** ['evəˌgleɪdz] npl: **the** ~ die Everglades pl, sumpfiges Flussgebiet in den USA.

**evergreen** ['evəgriːn] adj immergrün ⬦ n [plant] immergrüne Pflanze; [tree] immergrüner Baum.

**everlasting** [ˌevə'lɑːstɪŋ] adj ewig; [peace] immer während.

**every** ['evrɪ] adj - **1.** [each] jede, -r, -s; ~ **day** jeden Tag; ~ **few days** alle paar Tage; **one in** ~ **ten** eine, -r, -s von zehn - **2.** [all]: **we make** ~ **effort ...** wir geben uns alle Mühe ...; **to have** ~ **confidence** volles Vertrauen haben.

▪ **every now and then, every so often** adv dann und wann, ab und zu.

▪ **every other** adj: ~ **other day/car** jeden zweiten Tag/Wagen.

▪ **every which way** adv Am überallhin.

**everybody** ['evrɪˌbɒdɪ] pron = **everyone.**

**everyday** ['evrɪdeɪ] adj [all]täglich, Alltags-.

**everyone** ['evrɪwʌn] pron alle; [each person] jeder; **as** ~ **knows** wie jeder weiß.

**everyplace** adv Am = **everywhere.**

**everything** ['evrɪθɪŋ] pron alles; **money isn't** ~ Geld ist nicht alles.

**everywhere** ['evrɪweəʳ], **everyplace** Am ['evrɪˌpleɪs] adv überall; [go] überallhin.

**evict** [ɪ'vɪkt] vt: **to** ~ **sb (from a house)** jn zur Räumung zwingen (eines Hauses).

**eviction** [ɪ'vɪkʃn] n - **1.** (U) [act of evicting] Vertreibung die - **2.** [fact of being evicted] Zwangsräumung die.

**eviction notice** n Räumungsbescheid der.

**evidence** ['evɪdəns] n (U) - **1.** [proof] Beweis der - **2.** LAW Beweismaterial das; **piece of** ~ Beweisstück das; **to give** ~ (als Zeuge/Zeugin) auslsagen.

▪ **in evidence** adj [noticeable]: **to be in** ~ in Erscheinung treten.

**evident** ['evɪdənt] adj offensichtlich.

**evidently** ['evɪdəntlɪ] adv offensichtlich.

**evil** ['iːvl] adj [morally bad] böse, schlecht; [practice] übel ⬦ n - **1.** [wickedness] Böse das - **2.** [wicked thing] Übel das.

**evil-minded** [-'maɪndɪd] adj bösartig.

**evince** [ɪ'vɪns] vt fml an den Tag legen.

**evocation** [ˌevəʊ'keɪʃn] n Heraufbeschwören das.

**evocative** [ɪ'vɒkətɪv] adj: **to be** ~ **of sthg** an etw (A) erinnern.

**evoke** [ɪ'vəʊk] vt hervorlrufen.

**evolution** [ˌiːvə'luːʃn] n - **1.** BIOL Evolution die - **2.** [development] Entwicklung die.

**evolve** [ɪ'vɒlv] vt entwickeln ⬦ vi - **1.** BIOL: **to** ~ **(into/from)** sich entwickeln (in (+ D)/aus) - **2.** [develop] sich entwickeln.

**ewe** [juː] n Mutterschaf das.

**ex-** [eks] prefix Ex-, ehemalige, -r, -s.

**exacerbate** [ɪg'zæsəbeɪt] vt verschlimmern.

**exact** [ɪg'zækt] adj genau; **to be** ~ um genau zu sein ⬦ vt: **to** ~ **sthg (from sb)** etw (von jm) erzwingen OR erpressen.

**exacting** [ɪg'zæktɪŋ] adj - **1.** [demanding, tiring] anspruchsvoll - **2.** [rigorous] streng.

**exactitude** [ɪg'zæktɪtjuːd] n (U) fml Genauigkeit die.

**exactly** [ɪg'zæktlɪ] adv genau, exakt; **not** ~ [not really] nicht gerade; [as reply] nicht wirklich ⬦ excl genau!

**exaggerate** [ɪg'zædʒəreɪt] vt & vi übertreiben.

**exaggerated** [ɪg'zædʒəreɪtɪd] adj übertrieben.

**exaggeration** [ɪgˌzædʒə'reɪʃn] n Übertreibung die.

**exalted** [ɪg'zɔːltɪd] adj [important - person] hoch gestellt; [ - position] hoch.

**exam** [ɪg'zæm] (abbr of **examination**) n Prüfung die; **to take** OR **sit an** ~ eine Prüfung machen OR ablegen.

**examination** [ɪgˌzæmɪ'neɪʃn] n - **1.** [test, inspection, consideration] Prüfung die - **2.** MED Untersuchung die - **3.** LAW [of witness, suspect] Vernehmung die, Verhör das.

**examination board** n Prüfungsbehörde die.

**examination paper** n Br schriftliche Prüfung.

**examine** [ɪg'zæmɪn] vt - **1.** [look at, inspect] überprüfen - **2.** MED untersuchen - **3.** [consider, test knowledge of] prüfen - **4.** LAW vernehmen.

**examiner** [ɪg'zæmɪnəʳ] n Prüfer der, -in die; **internal/external** ~ interner/externer Prüfer, interne/externe Prüferin.

**example** [ɪg'zɑːmpl] n - **1.** [instance] Beispiel das; **for** ~ zum Beispiel - **2.** [model] Vorbild das; **to follow sb's** ~ js Beispiel folgen; **to make an** ~ **of sb** ein Exempel an jm statuieren.

**exasperate** [ɪg'zæspəreɪt] vt zum Verzweifeln bringen.

**exasperating** [ɪg'zæspəreɪtɪŋ] *adj:* to be ~ zum Verzweifeln sein.

**exasperation** [ɪg,zæspə'reɪʃn] *n* Verzweiflung *die.*

**excavate** ['ekskəveɪt] *vt* - **1.** ARCHAEOL auslgraben - **2.** CONSTR auslheben.

**excavation** [,ekskə'veɪʃn] *n* - **1.** *(U)* [act of excavating - archaeology] Ausgraben *das;* [ - construction] Graben *der* - **2.** ARCHAEOL [instance] Ausgrabung *die.*

**excavator** ['ekskə,veɪtər] *n Br* [machine] Bagger *der.*

**exceed** [ɪk'siːd] *vt* - **1.** [be bigger than] übersteigen - **2.** [go beyond, go over] übersteigen; [limit] überschreiten; [expectations] übertreffen.

**exceedingly** [ɪk'siːdɪŋlɪ] *adv* äußerst, ausgesprochen.

**excel** [ɪk'sel] (*pt* & *pp* **-led;** *cont* **-ling**) *vi:* to ~ (in OR at sthg) sich hervorltun (in etw *(D)*); to ~ in playing tennis hervorragend Tennis spielen ◇ *vt:* to ~ o.s. *Br* sich selbst übertreffen.

**excellence** ['eksələns] *n* [high quality] hervorragende Qualität; [high performance] hervorragende Leistung.

**Excellency** ['eksələnsɪ] (*pl* **-ies**) *n* Exzellenz *die.*

**excellent** ['eksələnt] *adj* ausgezeichnet.

**except** [ɪk'sept] *prep* außer; **everyone ~ her** alle außer ihr ◇ *conj:* **he does nothing ~ sleep** er tut nichts anderes als schlafen; **I'll do anything ~ typing** ich mache alles, nur nicht Maschine schreiben ◇ *vt:* **present company ~ed** Anwesende ausgenommen.
➤ **except for** *prep* & *conj* abgesehen von.

**excepted** [ɪk'septɪd] *prep* ausgenommen.

**excepting** [ɪk'septɪŋ] *prep* & *conj* = **except.**

**exception** [ɪk'sepʃn] *n* - **1.** [exclusion] Ausnahme *die;* **an ~ to the rule** die Ausnahme von der Regel; **with the ~ of** mit Ausnahme von; **without ~** ohne Ausnahme - **2.** [offence]: **to take ~ to sthg** an etw *(D)* Anstoß nehmen

**exceptional** [ɪk'sepʃənl] *adj* außergewöhnlich.

**exceptionally** [ɪk'sepʃnəlɪ] *adv* außergewöhnlich.

**excerpt** ['eksɜːpt] *n:* ~ (from) [from text] Auszug *der* (aus); [from film, play, piece of music] Ausschnitt *der* (aus).

**excess** [ɪk'ses, *before nouns* 'ekses] *adj* [fat in diet] überschüssig; [weight] über- ◇ *n* Übermaß *das;* **in ~ of** über (+ *D);* **to ~** übermäßig.

**excess baggage** *n* Übergewicht *das.*

**excess fare** *n Br* Nachlösegebühr *die.*

**excessive** [ɪk'sesɪv] *adj* übermäßig; [price] überhöht.

**excess luggage** *n* = **excess baggage.**

**exchange** [ɪks'tʃeɪndʒ] *n* - **1.** [of information, students] Austausch *der;* **to be on an ~** [student] Austauschstudent, **-in sein** - **2.** [swap] Tausch *der;* **in ~ dafür; in ~ for** im Tausch gegen - **3.** TELEC **(telephone)** ~ Fernmeldeamt *das* - **4.** *fml* [conversation] Wortwechsel *der* ◇ *vt* [houses, seats, jobs] tauschen; [addresses] ausltauschen; [in shop] umltauschen; **to ~ letters** einen Briefwechsel führen; **to ~ sthg for sthg** etw gegen etw einltauschen; [foreign currency] etw in etw *(A)* umltauschen; [in shop] etw gegen etw umltauschen; **to ~ sthg with sb** etw mit jm (aus)ltauschen.

**exchange rate** *n* FIN Wechselkurs *der.*

**Exchequer** [ɪks'tʃekər] *n Br:* **the ~** das Schatzamt.

**excise** ['eksaɪz] *n (U)* Verbrauchssteuer *die* ◇ *vt fml* herauslschneiden.

**excise duties** *npl* Verbrauchssteuern *pl.*

**excitable** [ɪk'saɪtəbl] *adj* leicht erregbar.

**excite** [ɪk'saɪt] *vt* - **1.** [person] begeistern - **2.** [interest, curiosity, feeling] erregen.

**excited** [ɪk'saɪtɪd] *adj* aufgeregt.

**excitement** [ɪk'saɪtmənt] *n* Aufregung *die.*

**exciting** [ɪk'saɪtɪŋ] *adj* aufregend; [story, race, film] spannend.

**excl.** *abbr of* **excluding.**

**exclaim** [ɪk'skleɪm] *vt* auslrufen ◇ *vi:* to ~ in delight/horror vor Freude/Entsetzen auflschreien.

**exclamation** [,eksklə'meɪʃn] *n* Ausruf *der.*

**exclamation mark** *Br,* **exclamation point** *Am n* Ausrufezeichen *das.*

**exclude** [ɪk'skluːd] *vt* - **1.** [not include]: **to ~ sb/ sthg (from sthg)** jn/etw (von etw) auslnehmen - **2.** [prevent from entering]: **to ~ sb (from)** jm den Zutritt verweigern (zu) - **3.** [reject, rule out] auslschließen

**excluding** [ɪk'skluːdɪŋ] *prep* außer (+ *D).*

**exclusion** [ɪk'skluːʒn] *n:* ~ (from) Ausschluss *der* (von); **she plays the violin, to the ~ of all other instruments** sie spielt ausschließlich Geige.

**exclusion clause** *n* COMM Haftungsausschlussklausel *die.*

**exclusive** [ɪk'skluːsɪv] *adj* - **1.** [high-class] exklusiv - **2.** [sole] ausschließlich - **3.** PRESS Exklusiv- ◇ *n* [interview] Exklusivinterview *das;* [reports] Exklusivbericht *der.*
➤ **exclusive of** *prep* exklusive (+ *G).*

**exclusively** [ɪk'skluːsɪvlɪ] *adv* ausschließlich.

**excommunicate** [,ekskə'mjuːnɪkeɪt] *vt* exkommunizieren.

**excommunication** ['ekskə,mjuːnɪ'keɪʃn] *n* Exkommunizierung *die.*

**excrement** ['ekskrɪmənt] n (U) fml Exkremente pl.

**excrete** [ɪk'skriːt] vt [urine, waste matter] auslscheiden.

**excruciating** [ɪk'skruːʃieɪtɪŋ] adj - 1. [pain, headache] schrecklich - 2. [embarrassment, experience] unerträglich.

**excursion** [ɪk'skɜːʃn] n Ausflug der.

**excusable** [ɪk'skjuːzəbl] adj entschuldbar.

**excuse** [n ɪk'skjuːs, vb ɪk'skjuːz] n: ~ (for) Entschuldigung die (für); **that's just an ~** das ist nur eine Ausrede <> vt - 1. [justify] entschuldigen; **to ~ o.s.** sich entschuldigen; **she ~d herself for arriving late** sie entschuldigte sich dafür, dass sie zu spät gekommen war - 2. [forgive] verzeihen; **to ~ sb for sthg** jm etw verzeihen - 3. [let off]: **to ~ sb (from sthg)** jn (von etw) befreien - 4. phr: **~ me!** [to attract attention] entschuldigen Sie bitte!; [forgive me] Entschuldigung!; Am [sorry] Verzeihung!; **~ me for phoning so late** entschuldigen Sie bitte, dass ich so spät anrufe.

**ex-directory** adj Br: **to be ~** nicht im Telefonbuch stehen.

**exec** [ɪg'zek] abbr of **executive.**

**execrable** ['eksɪkrəbl] adj fml [performance] miserabel; [taste, cooking] abscheulich.

**execute** ['eksɪkjuːt] vt - 1. [kill] hinlrichten - 2. fml [order, plan, movement] auslführen.

**execution** [,eksɪ'kjuːʃn] n - 1. [killing] Hinrichtung die - 2. fml [of movement, order, plan] Ausführung die.

**executioner** [,eksɪ'kjuːʃnəʳ] n Scharfrichter der.

**executive** [ɪg'zekjutɪv] adj: **~ position** leitende Position; **~ power** Entscheidungsbefugnis die <> n - 1. COMM leitende Angestellte der, die - 2. [of government] Exekutive die - 3. [of political party] Vorstand der.

**executor** [ɪg'zekjutəʳ] n Testamentsvollstrecker der.

**exemplary** [ɪg'zemplərɪ] adj beispielhaft, vorbildlich.

**exemplify** [ɪg'zemplɪfaɪ] (pt & pp **-ied**) vt - 1. [typify] ein typisches Beispiel sein für - 2. [give example of] veranschaulichen.

**exempt** [ɪg'zempt] adj: **~ (from)** befreit (von) <> vt: **to ~ sb/sthg from** jn/etw befreien von.

**exemption** [ɪg'zempʃn] n: **~ (from)** Befreiung die (von).

**exercise** ['eksəsaɪz] n - 1. (U) [physical movement] Bewegung die; **to take ~** sich bewegen - 2. [series of movements] gymnastische Übung; **to do ~s** Gymnastik machen - 3. MIL & SCH Übung die - 4. [activity]: **it's a pointless ~** das ist eine sinnlose Übung - 5. [of right] Wahrnehmung die <> vt - 1. [horse] bewegen; [dog] ausl-

führen - 2. fml [power] auslüben; [right] wahrlnehmen; [caution] walten lassen - 3. [trouble]: **to ~ sb's mind** js Gedanken beschäftigen <> vi sich bewegen.

**exercise bike** n Heimtrainer der (Fahrrad).

**exercise book** n Heft das.

**exert** [ɪg'zɜːt] vt auslüben; **to ~ o.s.** sich anlstrengen.

**exertion** [ɪg'zɜːʃn] n - 1. [of influence, power] Ausübung die - 2. [effort] Anstrengung die.

**ex gratia** [eks'greɪʃə] adj Br Sonder-.

**exhale** [eks'heɪl] vt & vi auslatmen.

**exhaust** [ɪg'zɔːst] n - 1. (U) [fumes] Abgase pl - 2. [on car]: **~ (pipe)** Auspuff der <> vt - 1. [tire] erschöpfen - 2. [use up] auflbrauchen; [subject] erschöpfen; **my patience is ~ed** meine Geduld ist zu Ende.

**exhausted** [ɪg'zɔːstɪd] adj erschöpft.

**exhausting** [ɪg'zɔːstɪŋ] adj anstrengend.

**exhaustion** [ɪg'zɔːstʃn] n Erschöpfung die.

**exhaustive** [ɪg'zɔːstɪv] adj [search, study] eingehend; [list] erschöpfend.

**exhibit** [ɪg'zɪbɪt] n - 1. ART Ausstellungsstück das - 2. LAW Beweisstück das <> vt - 1. fml [demonstrate] zeigen - 2. ART auslstellen <> vi ART auslstellen.

**exhibition** [,eksɪ'bɪʃn] n - 1. ART Ausstellung die - 2. [demonstration]: **it was a fine ~ of skill** er/sie zeigte viel Geschick - 3. phr: **to make an ~ of o.s.** Br sich lächerlich machen.

**exhibitionist** [,eksɪ'bɪʃnɪst] n: **to be an ~** sich gerne zur Schau stellen.

**exhibitor** [ɪg'zɪbɪtəʳ] n Aussteller der, -in die.

**exhilarating** [ɪg'zɪləreɪtɪŋ] adj aufregend.

**exhort** [ɪg'zɔːt] vt fml: **to ~ sb to do sthg** jn ermahnen, etw zu tun.

**exhume** [eks'hjuːm] vt fml exhumieren.

**exile** ['eksaɪl] n - 1. [condition] Exil das; **in ~** im Exil - 2. [person] Person die, die im Exil lebt <> vt: **to ~ sb (to)** jn auslweisen or verbannen (nach).

**exiled** ['eksaɪld] adj exiliert.

**exist** [ɪg'zɪst] vi existieren.

**existence** [ɪg'zɪstəns] n - 1. [state of being] Existenz die; **to be in ~** existieren, bestehen; **to come into ~** entstehen - 2. [life] Dasein das, Leben das.

**existentialism** [,egzɪ'stenʃəlɪzm] n Existenzialismus der.

**existing** [ɪg'zɪstɪŋ] adj bestehend; [government] gegenwärtig.

**exit** ['eksɪt] n - 1. [way out] Ausgang der; [from motorway] Ausfahrt die - 2. [departure]: **to make an ~** hinauslgehen <> vi [from building] hinauslgehen; [from stage] ablgehen; [from motorway] ablfahren.

**exit poll** *n* Br POL *Umfrage bei Wählern unmittelbar nachdem sie das Wahllokal verlassen haben.*

**exit visa** *n* Ausreisevisum *das.*

**exodus** ['eksədəs] *n* Auszug *der.*

**ex officio** [eksə'fɪʃɪəʊ] *fml adj* von Amts wegen ◇ *adv* kraft seines Amtes.

**exonerate** [ɪg'zɒnəreɪt] *vt:* **to ~ sb (from)** jn entlasten (von).

**exorbitant** [ɪg'zɔːbɪtənt] *adj* [cost, price] übertrieben hoch; [demands] übertrieben.

**exorcism** ['eksɔːsɪzm] *n* Exorzismus *der.*

**exorcize, -ise** ['eksɔːsaɪz] *vt* - **1.** [ghost] austreiben - **2.** [place, person] von Geistern befreien.

**exotic** [ɪg'zɒtɪk] *adj* exotisch.

**expand** [ɪk'spænd] *vt* [department, influence, area] vergrößern; [business, production, knowledge] erweitern ◇ *vi* sich vergrößern; [business] erweitern; [metal] sich ausdehnen.

➜ **expand (up)on** *vt fus* weiter ausführen.

**expanse** [ɪk'spæns] *n:* **an ~ of water/sand** eine Wasserfläche/Sandfläche; **she gazed at the vast ~ of the sky** sie blickte in die Weite des Himmels.

**expansion** [ɪk'spænʃn] *n* [of business, production, knowledge] Erweiterung *die;* [of department, influence, area] Vergrößerung *die;* [of metal, gas] Ausdehnung *die.*

**expansion card** *n* COMPUT Erweiterungskarte *die.*

**expansionist** [ɪk'spænʃənɪst] *adj* expansionistisch.

**expansion slot** *n* COMPUT Erweiterungssteckplatz *der.*

**expansive** [ɪk'spænsɪv] *adj* [relaxed, talkative] mitteilsam.

**expatriate** [eks'pætrɪət] *adj:* **~ community** Auslandsgemeinde *die* ◇ *n* im Ausland Lebende *der, die.*

**expect** [ɪk'spekt] *vt* - **1.** [anticipate] erwarten; [count on] rechnen mit; **to ~ sthg from sb** etw von jm erwarten; **I didn't ~ it to be so boring** ich habe nicht damit gerechnet, dass es so langweilig ist; **to ~ to do sthg** damit rechnen, etw zu tun; **I ~ to be treated with respect** ich erwarte, dass ich mit Respekt behandelt werde; **to ~ sb to do sthg** erwarten, dass jd etw tut; **what do you expect?** was willst du denn? - **2.** [suppose]: **to ~ (that)** ... glauben, dass ..., denken, dass ...; **I ~ so** ich denke schon - **3.** [be pregnant with]: **to be ~ing a baby** ein Kind erwarten ◇ *vi* [be pregnant]: **to be ~ing** in anderen Umständen sein.

**expectancy** *n* ▷ **life expectancy**.

**expectant** [ɪk'spektənt] *adj* [crowd, person] erwartungsvoll.

**expectantly** [ɪk'spektəntlɪ] *adv* erwartungsvoll.

**expectant mother** *n* werdende Mutter.

**expectation** [ˌekspek'teɪʃn] *n:* **they have no ~ of winning** sie erwarten nicht, dass sie gewinnen; **against** OR **contrary to all ~(s)** wider Erwarten.

**expectorant** [ɪk'spektərənt] *n* Expektorans *das.*

**expedient** [ɪk'spiːdjənt] *adj fml* angebracht.

**expedite** ['ekspɪdaɪt] *vt fml* beschleunigen.

**expedition** [ˌekspɪ'dɪʃn] *n* - **1.** [organized journey] Expedition *die* - **2.** [short trip] Tour *die.*

**expeditionary force** ['ekspɪ'dɪʃnərɪ-] *n* Expeditionskorps *das.*

**expel** [ɪk'spel] (*pt & pp* **-led;** *cont* **-ling**) *vt* - **1.** [person]: **to ~ sb (from)** [country] jn ausweisen (aus); [school] jn verweisen (von) - **2.** [liquid, gas] ausstoßen.

**expend** [ɪk'spend] *vt:* **to ~ sthg (on)** etw aufwenden (auf (+ A)).

**expendable** [ɪk'spendəbl] *adj* [person] entbehrlich.

**expenditure** [ɪk'spendɪtʃəʳ] *n* (*U*) - **1.** [of money] Ausgaben *pl* - **2.** [of energy] Aufwand *der.*

**expense** [ɪk'spens] *n* - **1.** [amount spent] Ausgabe *die* - **2.** (*U*) [cost] Kosten *pl;* **to go to great ~ (to do sthg)** sich in hohe Unkosten stürzen (, um etw zu tun); **at the ~ of** auf Kosten (+ *G*); **at his ~** auf seine Kosten.

➜ **expenses** *npl* COMM Spesen *pl;* **to put sthg on ~s** etw auf die Spesenrechnung schreiben.

**expense account** *n* Spesenkonto *das.*

**expensive** [ɪk'spensɪv] *adj* - **1.** [financially] teuer - **2.** *fig* [mistake] schwerwiegend.

**experience** [ɪk'spɪərɪəns] *n* - **1.** (*U*) [knowledge, practice] Erfahrung *die* - **2.** [event] Erlebnis *das* ◇ *vt* erfahren; [change] erleben.

**experienced** [ɪk'spɪərɪənst] *adj:* **~ (at** OR **in)** erfahren (in (+ *D*)).

**experiment** [ɪk'sperɪmənt] *n* - **1.** [science] Experiment *das;* **to carry out an ~** ein Experiment durchführen - **2.** [exploratory attempt] Versuch *der* ◇ *vi lit & fig:* **to ~ (with)** experimentieren (mit); **to ~ on sb/sthg** Versuche an jm/etw durchführen.

**experimental** [ɪkˌsperɪ'mentl] *adj* experimentell.

**expert** ['ekspɜːt] *adj* [player] ausgezeichnet; [advice] fachmännisch; **to be ~ at sthg** sachkundig in etw (*D*) sein ◇ *n* Fachmann *der,* -frau *die.*

**expertise** [ˌekspɜː'tiːz] *n* Sachkenntnis *die.*

**expert system** *n* COMPUT Expertensystem *das.*

**expiate** ['ekspɪeɪt] *vt fml* sühnen.

**expire** [ɪk'spaɪəʳ] *vi* [licence, passport] ablaufen.

**expiry** [ɪk'spaərɪ] n Ablauf der.

**expiry date** n Ablaufdatum das; ~: **15/4/02** gültig bis 15/4/02.

**explain** [ɪk'spleɪn] vt erklären; "my car broke down", she ~ed „mein Auto ist kaputtgegangen", sagte sie; **to ~ o.s.** [justify o.s.] sich rechtfertigen; [clarify one's meaning] sich klar ausldrücken; **to ~ sthg to sb** jm etw erklären ◇ vi erklären.

➤ **explain away** vt sep: **to ~ sthg away** eine Erklärung/Erklärungen für etw anlführen.

**explanation** [ˌeksplə'neɪʃn] n: ~ **(for)** Erklärung die (für).

**explanatory** [ɪk'splænətrɪ] adj: ~ **notes** Anmerkungen pl zur Erläuterung; ~ **leaflet** Informationsbroschüre die.

**expletive** [ɪk'spliːtɪv] n fml Kraftausdruck der.

**explicit** [ɪk'splɪsɪt] adj - **1.** [clearly expressed] explizit - **2.** [graphic] eindeutig.

**explode** [ɪk'spləʊd] vt - **1.** [bomb] explodieren - **2.** fig [argument] widerlegen; [theory] umlstoßen ◇ vi - **1.** [bomb] explodieren - **2.** fig [with feeling]: **to ~ in anger** (vor Wut) explodieren; **he ~d with laughter** er brach in schallendes Gelächter aus.

**exploit** [n 'eksplɔɪt, vb ɪk'splɔɪt] n Heldentat die ◇ vt - **1.** [workers] auslbeuten; [friend] auslnutzen - **2.** [resources] auslschöpfen; [opportunity] nutzen.

**exploitation** [ˌeksplɔɪ'teɪʃn] n - **1.** [of workers] Ausbeutung die; [of friend] Ausnutzung die - **2.** [of resources] Ausschöpfung die.

**exploration** [ˌeksplə'reɪʃn] n - **1.** [of place] Erforschung die - **2.** [of idea, theory] Untersuchung die.

**exploratory** [ɪk'splɒrətrɪ] adj: ~ **talks** Sondierungsgespräche pl; ~ **operation** Explorationsoperation die.

**explore** [ɪk'splɔːr] vt - **1.** [place] erforschen - **2.** [idea, theory] untersuchen ◇ vi auf Erkundungstour gehen.

**explorer** [ɪk'splɔːrər] n Erforscher der, -in die.

**explosion** [ɪk'spləʊʒn] n lit & fig Explosion die; ~ **of crime** rapider Anstieg der Verbrechensrate.

**explosive** [ɪk'spləʊsɪv] adj [material, situation] explosiv; [question] heikel; [temper] explosiv ◇ n Sprengstoff der.

**explosive device** n Sprengsatz der.

**exponent** [ɪk'spəʊnənt] n - **1.** [supporter - of theory] Vertreter der, -in die; [ - of plan] Befürworter der, -in die; - **2.** MATH Exponent der.

**exponential** [ˌekspə'nenʃl] adj fml [growth] exponenziell.

**export** [n & comp 'ekspɔːt, vb ɪk'spɔːt] n Export

der, Ausfuhr die ◇ comp Export- ◇ vt lit & fig exportieren.

➤ **exports** npl [goods] Exportgüter pl.

**exportable** [ɪk'spɔːtəbl] adj exportfähig.

**exportation** [ˌekspɔː'teɪʃn] n (U) Export der, Ausfuhr die.

**exporter** [ek'spɔːtər] n Exporteur der; [country] Exportland das.

**export licence** n Br COMM Exportlizenz die.

**expose** [ɪks'pəʊz] vt - **1.** [uncover - skin] entblößen; [ - underlying layer] freillegen; **to be ~d to sthg** einer Sache (D) ausgesetzt sein; **to ~ o.s.** sich entblößen - **2.** [crime] aufldecken; [criminal] entlarven - **3.** PHOT belichten.

**exposé** [ek'spəʊzeɪ] n Exposé das.

**exposed** [ɪk'spəʊzd] adj [place] ungeschützt.

**exposition** [ˌekspə'zɪʃn] n - **1.** fml [explanation] Darlegung die - **2.** [exhibition] Ausstellung die.

**exposure** [ɪk'spəʊʒər] n - **1.** [to light, sun, radiation]: ~ **(to)** Ausgesetztsein das (+ D) - **2.**: **to die from ~** [hypothermia] erfrieren - **3.** [of crime] Aufdeckung die; [of criminal] Entlarvung die - **4.** [PHOT - time] Belichtung die; [ - photograph] Aufnahme die - **5.** [publicity] Publicity die.

**exposure meter** n Belichtungsmesser der.

**expound** [ɪk'spaʊnd] fml vt darllegen ◇ vi: **to ~ on sthg** etw darllegen.

**express** [ɪk'spres] adj - **1.** Br [letter, delivery] Eil- - **2.** fml [request] ausdrücklich; [purpose] bestimmt ◇ adv [send] per Express ◇ n: ~ **(train)** D-Zug der ◇ vt - **1.** [feeling, opinion] ausldrücken; **to ~ o.s.** sich ausldrücken - **2.** MATH darlstellen.

**expression** [ɪk'spreʃn] n - **1.** [gen] Ausdruck der - **2.** [of feeling, opinion] Äußerung die - **3.** [look on face] Gesichtsausdruck der.

**expressionism** [ɪk'spreʃənɪzm] n Expressionismus der.

**expressionist** [ɪk'spreʃənɪst] adj expressionistisch ◇ n Expressionist der, -in die.

**expressionless** [ɪk'spreʃənlɪs] adj ausdruckslos.

**expressive** [ɪk'spresɪv] adj ausdrucksvoll.

**expressively** [ɪk'spresɪvlɪ] adv ausdrucksvoll.

**expressly** [ɪk'spreslɪ] adv ausdrücklich.

**expressway** [ɪk'spresweɪ] n Am Schnellstraße die.

**expropriate** [eks'prəʊprɪeɪt] vt fml enteignen.

**expropriation** [eksˌprəʊprɪ'eɪʃn] n fml Enteignung die.

**expulsion** [ɪk'spʌlʃn] n - **1.** [from school]: ~ **(from)** Verweisung die (von) - **2.** [from country]: ~ **(from)** Ausweisung die (aus).

**exquisite** [ɪk'skwɪzɪt] adj [object, jewellery] exquisit; [food] köstlich; [painting] ausgezeichnet; [taste] erlesen; [manners] ausgezeichnet.

**exquisitely** [ɪk'skwɪzɪtlɪ] adv [decorated, arranged] ausgezeichnet; [dressed] exquisit.

**ex-serviceman** n Br ehemaliger Soldat.

**ex-servicewoman** n Br ehemalige Soldatin.

**ext., extn.** (abbr of **extension**) App.

**extant** [ek'stænt] adj noch vorhanden.

**extemporize, -ise** [ɪk'stempəraɪz] vi fml aus dem Stegreif sprechen.

**extend** [ɪk'stend] vt - **1.** [road, building] auslbauen - **2.** [visit, visa, deadline] verlängern - **3.** [authority, law] ausldehnen - **4.** fml [head, arm] auslstrecken - **5.** [offer - credit, help] gewähren; **to ~ a welcome to sb** jn willkommen heißen <> vi - **1.** [stretch - in space] sich erstrecken; [ - in time] anldauern - **2.** [rule, law]: **to ~ to sb/sthg** sich auf jn/etw erstrecken - **3.** [protrude] ablstehen.

**extendable** [ɪk'stendəbl] adj [ladder] ausziehbar.

**extended-play** [ɪk'stendɪd-] adj Langspiel-.

**extension** [ɪk'stenʃn] n - **1.** [new room, building] Anbau der - **2.** [of visit, visa, deadline] Verlängerung die - **3.** [of authority, law] Ausdehnung die - **4.** TELEC Nebenanschluss der - **5.** ELEC Verlängerungskabel das - **6.** COMPUT: **filename ~** Dateinamenendung die.

**extension lead** n [lead] Verlängerungsschnur die.

**extensive** [ɪk'stensɪv] adj - **1.** [damage] beträchtlich - **2.** [land, area] ausgedehnt - **3.** [discussions, tests] ausgedehnt; [use] häufig.

**extensively** [ɪk'stensɪvlɪ] adv - **1.** [modify, damage] beträchtlich - **2.** [discuss] ausführlich; [read] viel.

**extent** [ɪk'stent] n - **1.** [of land, area] Ausdehnung die - **2.** [of knowledge, damage] Umfang der; [of problem] Größe die - **3.** [degree]: **to what ~ ...?** inwieweit ...?; **to the ~ that** [in that, in so far as] insofern dass; [to the point where] derart ..., dass; **to a certain ~** in gewissem Maße; **to a large** OR **great ~** in hohem Maße; **to some ~** bis zu einem gewissen Grade.

**extenuating circumstances** [ɪk'stenjʊeɪtɪŋ-] npl mildernde Umstände pl.

**exterior** [ɪk'stɪərɪər] adj [wall, lights] Außen-; **~ paintwork** äußerer Anstrich <> n [of house, car, person] Äußere das.

**exterminate** [ɪk'stɜːmɪneɪt] vt auslrotten.

**extermination** [ɪk,stɜːmɪ'neɪʃn] n Ausrottung die.

**external** [ɪk'stɜːnl] adj - **1.** [outside] äußere, -r, -s; **for ~ use only** nur äußerlich anzuwenden - **2.** [foreign - debt] Auslands-; [ - affairs] auswärtig.

➡ **externals** npl Äußerlichkeiten pl.

**externally** [ɪk'stɜːnəlɪ] adv äußerlich; [located] außen.

**extinct** [ɪk'stɪŋkt] adj - **1.** [species] ausgestorben - **2.** [volcano] erloschen.

**extinction** [ɪk'stɪŋkʃn] n [of species] Aussterben das.

**extinguish** [ɪk'stɪŋgwɪʃ] vt - **1.** fml [fire] löschen; [cigarette] ausldrücken - **2.** fig [memory, feeling] ausllöschen.

**extinguisher** [ɪk'stɪŋgwɪʃər] n: **(fire) ~** Feuerlöscher der.

**extol** (pt & pp **-led;** cont **-ling**), **extoll** Am [ɪk'stəʊl] vt rühmen.

**extort** [ɪk'stɔːt] vt: **to ~ sthg from sb** etw von jm erpressen.

**extortion** [ɪk'stɔːʃn] n Erpressung die.

**extortionate** [ɪk'stɔːʃnət] adj [price] Wucher-; [demand] ungeheuer.

**extra** ['ekstrə] adj [additional] zusätzlich; **~ charge** Zuschlag der <> n - **1.** [addition] Extra das - **2.** CINEMA & THEATRE Statist der, -in die <> adv [to pay, charge] extra.

➡ **extras** npl [in price] zusätzliche Kosten pl.

**extra-** ['ekstrə] prefix besonders; **an ~special present** ein ganz besonderes Geschenk.

**extract** [n 'ekstrækt, vb ɪk'strækt] n - **1.** [from book] Auszug der; [from film, piece of music] Ausschnitt der - **2.** [substance] Extrakt der <> vt - **1.** [pull out]: **to ~ sthg (from)** etw ziehen (aus) - **2.** [information, confession]: **to ~ sthg (from sb)** etw (aus jm) herauslholen - **3.** [coal, oil]: **to ~ sthg (from)** etw gewinnen (aus).

**extraction** [ɪk'strækʃn] n - **1.** [descent] Herkunft die - **2.** [of coal, oil] Gewinnung die; [of tooth] Ziehen das.

**extractor (fan)** [ɪk'stræktər-] n Br Entlüfter der.

**extracurricular** [,ekstrəkə'rɪkjʊlər] adj außerhalb des Stundenplans.

**extradite** ['ekstrədaɪt] vt: **to ~ sb (from/to)** jn ausliefern (von/an).

**extradition** [,ekstrə'dɪʃn] n Auslieferung die.

**extramarital** [,ekstrə'mærɪtl] adj außerehelich.

**extramural** [,ekstrə'mjʊərəl] adj UNIV: **~ studies** Studium für Teilzeitstudenten.

**extraneous** [ɪk'streɪnjəs] adj - **1.** [irrelevant] irrelevant - **2.** [outside] von außen.

**extraordinary** [ɪk'strɔːdnrɪ] adj - **1.** [very special] außergewöhnlich - **2.** [strange] merkwürdig - **3.** [meeting] außerordentlich.

**extraordinary general meeting** n außerordentliche Hauptversammlung.

**extrapolate** [ɪk'stræpəleɪt] vt - **1.** MATH: **to ~ sthg from sthg** etw aus etw extrapolieren

**- 2.** [deduce]: **to ~ sthg from sthg** etw aus etw erschließen.

**extrasensory perception** [ˌekstrə'sensərɪ-] n außersinnliche Wahrnehmung.

**extraterrestrial** [ˌekstrətə'restrɪəl] adj außerirdisch.

**extra time** n (U) Br sport Verlängerung die.

**extravagance** [ɪk'strævəgəns] n - **1.** [excessive spending] Verschwendung die - **2.** [luxury] Extravaganz die.

**extravagant** [ɪk'strævəgənt] adj - **1.** [wasteful - person, use] verschwenderisch; [ - tastes] kostspielig - **2.** [gift, party, behaviour] extravagant - **3.** [claim] übertrieben.

**extravaganza** [ɪkˌstrævə'gænzə] n aufwendig gestaltete Vorführung.

**extreme** [ɪk'striːm] adj - **1.** [gen] äußerste, -r, -s; **~ heat** extreme Hitze - **2.** [conditions, views, politician] extrem <> n [furthest limit] Extrem das; **in the ~** äußerst; **to go to ~s** es zu weit treiben.

**extremely** [ɪk'striːmlɪ] adv [very] äußerst.

**extremism** [ɪk'striːmɪzm] n Extremismus der.

**extremist** [ɪk'striːmɪst] adj extremistisch <> n Extremist der, -in die.

**extremity** [ɪk'stremətɪ] (pl -ies) n - **1.** (U) fml [extreme adversity] Extremsituation die - **2.** fml [end] äußerstes Ende.

➤ **extremities** npl [of body] Hände und Füße.

**extricate** ['ekstrɪkeɪt] vt: **to ~ sthg (from)** etw befreien (aus); **to ~ o.s. (from)** sich herauswinden (aus); fig sich befreien (aus).

**extrovert** ['ekstrəvɜːt] adj extrovertiert <> n extrovertierter Mensch.

**exuberance** [ɪg'zjuːbərəns] n Ausgelassenheit die.

**exuberant** [ɪg'zjuːbərənt] adj ausgelassen.

**exude** [ɪg'zjuːd] vt - **1.** [smell] absondern; [liquid] ausscheiden - **2.** fig [confidence] ausstrahlen; **to ~ charm** seinen Charme versprühen.

**exult** [ɪg'zʌlt] vi: **to ~ (at** OR **in)** [at sb's defeat, a victory] jubeln (über (+ A)); [at sb's discomfiture] frohlocken (über (+ A)).

**exultant** [ɪg'zʌltənt] adj [person, crowd] jubelnd; [smile] triumphierend.

**eye** [aɪ] (cont **eyeing** OR **eying**) n - **1.** [gen] Auge das; **before my (very) ~s** vor meinen eigenen Augen; **in my ~s** meiner Ansicht nach; **to cast** OR **run one's ~ over sthg** etw überfliegen; **the advertisement caught my ~** die Anzeige stach mir ins Auge; **to catch the waiter's ~** die Aufmerksamkeit des Kellners erregen; **to clap** OR **lay** OR **set ~s on sb** jn zu Gesicht bekommen; **to cry one's ~s out** inf sich (D) die Augen ausheulen; **to feast one's ~s on sthg** sich am Anblick von etw weiden; **to have an ~ for sthg** ein Auge für etw haben; **to have one's ~ on sb/sthg** ein Auge auf jn/etw haben; **to keep one's ~s open for, to keep an ~ out for** Ausschau halten nach (+ D); **to keep an ~ on** auf jn passen auf (+ A); **there is more to this than meets the ~** da steckt mehr dahinter als auf den ersten Blick ersichtlich ist; **to open sb's ~s (to)** jm die Augen öffnen (über (+ A)); **not to see ~ to ~ with sb** mit jm nicht einer Meinung sein; **to close** OR **shut one's ~s to sthg** die Augen vor etw (D) verschließen; **to turn a blind ~ to sthg** über etw (A) hinwegsehen; **to be up to one's ~s in sthg** Br inf bis über beide Ohren in etw (D) stecken - **2.** [of needle] Öhr das - **3.** [of potato] Auge das - **4.** [of hurricane] Auge das <> vt [suspiciously] beäugen; [with desire] sehnsüchtig anschauen.

➤ **eye up** vt sep Br [person] anmachend anschauen.

**eyeball** ['aɪbɔːl] n Augapfel der <> vt Am inf herausfordernd anschauen.

**eyebath** ['aɪbɑːθ] n Augenbad das.

**eyebrow** ['aɪbraʊ] n Augenbraue die; **to raise one's ~s at sthg** fig [in disapproval] über etw (A) die Stirn runzeln; [in surprise] über etw (A) verwundert sein.

**eyebrow pencil** n Augenbrauenstift der.

**eye-catching** adj auffallend.

**eye contact** n: **to make/avoid ~ (with sb)** Blickkontakt (mit jm) herstellen/vermeiden.

**eyedrops** ['aɪdrɒps] npl Augentropfen pl.

**eyeglasses** ['aɪˌglɑːsɪz] npl Am Brille die.

**eyelash** ['aɪlæʃ] n Augenwimper die.

**eyelet** ['aɪlɪt] n Öse die.

**eye-level** adj in Augenhöhe.

**eyelid** ['aɪlɪd] n Augenlid das; **she didn't bat an ~** inf sie zuckte nicht mal mit der Wimper.

**eyeliner** ['aɪˌlaɪnər] n Eyeliner der.

**eye-opener** n inf: **it was an ~ for me** das hat mir die Augen geöffnet.

**eyepatch** ['aɪpætʃ] n Augenklappe die.

**eye shadow** n Lidschatten der.

**eyesight** ['aɪsaɪt] n (U) Sehkraft die; **to have good/bad ~** gute/schlechte Augen haben.

**eyesore** ['aɪsɔːr] n Schandfleck der.

**eyestrain** ['aɪstreɪn] n Überanstrengung die der Augen.

**eyetooth** ['aɪtuːθ] (pl -teeth) n: **to give one's eyeteeth to do sthg** alles darum geben, etw zu tun.

**eyewash** ['aɪwɒʃ] n inf [nonsense] Unsinn der.

**eyewitness** [ˌaɪ'wɪtnɪs] n Augenzeuge der, -gin die.

**eyrie** ['aɪərɪ] n Horst der.

**f** (pl **f's** OR **fs**), **F** (pl **F's** OR **Fs**) [ef] n [letter] f das, F das.
◆ **F** n - **1.** MUS F das - **2.** (abbr of **Fahrenheit**) F.

**FA** (abbr of **Football Association**) n Fußballverband in England und Wales.

**FAA** (abbr of **Federal Aviation Administration**) n amerikanische Flugaufsichtsbehörde.

**fable** ['feɪbl] n Fabel die.

**fabled** ['feɪbld] adj sagenhaft.

**fabric** ['fæbrɪk] n - **1.** [cloth] Stoff der - **2.** [of building] Bausubstanz die - **3.** [of society] Gefüge das.

**fabricate** ['fæbrɪkeɪt] vt - **1.** [invent] erfinden - **2.** [manufacture] herstellen, fabrizieren.

**fabrication** [ˌfæbrɪ'keɪʃn] n - **1.** (U) [lying] Erfindung die - **2.** [lie] Lüge die - **3.** (U) [manufacture] Herstellung die, Fabrikation die.

**fabulous** ['fæbjʊləs] adj - **1.** inf [excellent] toll - **2.** fml [wealth, beauty] unglaublich - **3.** fml [fairytale] sagenhaft; ~ **beast** Fabeltier das.

**fabulously** ['fæbjʊləslɪ] adv unglaublich.

**facade** [fə'sɑːd] n lit & fig Fassade die.

**face** [feɪs] n - **1.** [of person] Gesicht das; ~ **to ~** [with person] von Angesicht zu Angesicht; **to come ~ to ~ with sthg** mit etw konfrontiert werden; **to fall flat on one's ~** auf die Nase fallen; **to look sb in the ~** jm in die Augen sehen; **to say sthg to sb's ~** jm etw offen ins Gesicht sagen; **to show one's ~** sich sehen lassen; **it was staring me in the ~** es war direkt unter meiner Nase - **2.** [expression] Gesicht das, Gesichtsausdruck der; **to make** OR **pull a ~** ein Gesicht ziehen, das Gesicht verziehen; **her ~ fell** sie machte ein langes Gesicht - **3.** [of cliff] Wand die; [of coin] Vorderseite die; [of building] Fassade die; **the ~ of British politics** das Erscheinungsbild britischer Politik; **the species was wiped off the ~ of the earth** die Spezies wurde von der Erdoberfläche gefegt; **on the ~ of it** auf den ersten Blick - **4.** [of clock, watch] Zifferblatt das - **5.** [respect]: **to lose ~** das Gesicht verlieren; **to save ~** das Gesicht wahren - **6.** phr: **to fly in the ~ of sthg** etw (D) entgegenlaufen ◇ vt - **1.** [look towards] gegenüberstehen (+ D); **my house ~s south** mein Haus liegt nach Süden; **the hotel ~s the harbour** das Hotel liegt gegenüber vom Hafen - **2.** [confront] sich stellen (+ D); **to be ~d with sthg** [problem, decision] mit etw konfrontiert werden - **3.** [facts, truth] ins Auge sehen (+ D); **let's ~ it!** machen wir uns nichts vor! - **4.** inf [cope with]: **I can't ~ another omelette** ich kann kein Omelett mehr sehen!; **I can't ~ it!** ich bringe es einfach nicht über mich.

◆ **face down** adv [person] mit dem Gesicht nach unten; [book] mit der aufgeschlagenen Seite nach unten; [playing card] mit der Bildseite nach unten.

◆ **face up** adv [person] mit dem Gesicht nach oben; [book] mit der aufgeschlagenen Seite nach oben; [playing card] mit der Bildseite nach oben.

◆ **in the face of** prep [in spite of] trotz (+ G).

◆ **face up to** vt fus [responsibility] auf sich (A) nehmen; [problem] sich stellen (+ D).

**facecloth** ['feɪsklɒθ] n Br Waschlappen der.

**face cream** n Gesichtscreme die.

**faceless** ['feɪslɪs] adj anonym.

**face-lift** n - **1.** [on face] Gesichtsstraffung die - **2.** fig [on building]: **to give sthg a ~** etw verschönern.

**face pack** n Gesichtspackung die.

**face powder** n Gesichtspuder das.

**face-saving** [-ˌseɪvɪŋ] adj: **a ~ agreement/measure** eine Vereinbarung/Maßnahme, um das Gesicht zu wahren.

**facet** ['fæsɪt] n - **1.** [aspect] Seite die - **2.** [of jewel] Facette die.

**facetious** [fə'siːʃəs] adj leicht spöttisch.

**facetiously** [fə'siːʃəslɪ] adv leicht spöttisch.

**face-to-face** adj persönlich.

**face value** n [of coin, stamp] Nennwert der; **to take sthg at ~** fig etw für bare Münze nehmen.

**facial** ['feɪʃl] adj Gesichts- ◇ n kosmetische Gesichtsbehandlung.

**facile** [Br 'fæsaɪl, Am 'fæsl] adj pej trivial.

**facilitate** [fə'sɪlɪteɪt] vt fml erleichtern.

**facility** [fə'sɪlətɪ] (pl **-ies**) n - **1.** [ability]: **to have a ~ for sthg** eine Begabung für etw haben - **2.** [feature] Einrichtung die.
◆ **facilities** npl [amenities] Ausstattung die; **cooking facilities** Kochgelegenheiten pl.

**facing** ['feɪsɪŋ] adj [opposite] gegenüber befindlich.

**facsimile** [fæk'sɪmɪlɪ] n - **1.** [message] Fax das - **2.** [exact copy] Faksimile das.

**facsimile machine** n fml Faxgerät das.

**fact** [fækt] n Tatsache die; **it is a ~ that ...** es steht fest, dass ...; **the ~ is, ...** die Wahrheit ist, dass ...; **the ~ remains that ...** Tatsache bleibt, dass ...; **to know sthg for a ~** etw genau wissen.

◆ **in fact** adv [in reality] tatsächlich; [moreover] sogar.

**fact-finding** [-'faɪndɪŋ] adj [trip] Informations-; [mission] Erkundungs-.

**faction** ['fækʃn] n Splittergruppe die.

**fact of life** n Tatsache die (mit der man sich abfinden muss).

➡ **facts of life** npl euphemism: **to tell sb the ~s of life** jn auflklären.

**factor** ['fæktəʳ] n Faktor der.

**factory** ['fæktərɪ] (pl -ies) n Fabrik die.

**factory farming** n Massentierhaltung die.

**factory ship** n Fabrikschiff das.

**factotum** [fæk'təʊtəm] (pl -s) n Faktotum das.

**fact sheet** n Br Informationsblatt das.

**factual** ['fæktʃʊəl] adj [account] auf Tatsachen beruhend.

**faculty** ['fækltɪ] (pl -ies) n - **1.** [ability] Fähigkeit die; **the ~ of sight** das Sehvermögen; **he was still in control of his faculties** er war (immer) noch im Vollbesitz seiner Kräfte - **2.** UNIV [section] Fakultät die; [staff] Lehrkörper der.

**FA Cup** n Br: **the ~** Pokalwettbewerb des englischen Fußballbundes.

**fad** [fæd] n Tick der.

**fade** [feɪd] vi - **1.** [material, colour] verbleichen; [flower] verwelken - **2.** [light] nachllassen - **3.** [sound] verklingen - **4.** [feeling, interest, smile] schwinden; [memory] verblassen ◇ vt [material, colour] auslbleichen.

➡ **fade away, fade out** vi [sound] verklingen; [image] verschwinden.

**faded** ['feɪdɪd] adj verblichen.

**faeces** Br, **feces** Am ['fiːsiːz] npl Fäkalien pl.

**Faeroe** ['feərəʊ] n: **the ~ Islands, the ~s** die Färöer Inseln pl, die Färöer pl; **in the ~ Islands** auf den Färöer Inseln.

**faff** ➡ **faff about, faff around** vi Br inf herumlwursteln.

**fag** [fæg] n - **1.** Br inf [cigarette] Glimmstengel der - **2.** Br inf [chore] Schinderei die - **3.** Am pej [homosexual] Schwuler der.

**fag end** n Br inf Kippe die.

**fagged out** [fægd-] adj Br inf völlig K.O.

**faggot** ['fægət] n Br CULIN Frikadelle die.

**fagot** ['fægət] n Am inf pej [homosexual] Schwuler der.

**Fahrenheit** ['færənhaɪt] adj Fahrenheit.

**fail** [feɪl] vt - **1.** [not succeed in]: **to ~ to do sthg** etw nicht tun können; **you can't ~ to notice it** du kannst es nicht übersehen; **he ~ed to persuade her** es gelang ihm nicht, sie zu überreden; **I ~ to see what's so funny** ich verstehe nicht, was daran so komisch ist - **2.** [exam, test] durchlfallen; [candidate] durchfallen lassen - **3.** [let down] im Stich lassen ◇ vi - **1.** [not succeed] scheitern - **2.** [in exam, test] durchlfallen - **3.** [brakes, engine, heart] versagen; [lights]

auslfallen - **4.** [eyesight] nachllassen; [health] sich verschlechtern.

**failed** [feɪld] adj [singer, writer etc] gescheitert.

**failing** ['feɪlɪŋ] n [weakness] Schwäche die ◇ prep wenn ... nicht; **~ any renewed fighting** wenn es keine neuen Kampfhandlungen gibt; **~ that** andernfalls.

**fail-safe** adj [device, system] so beschaffen, dass ein auftretender Fehler keine gravierenden Schäden verursachen kann.

**failure** ['feɪljəʳ] n - **1.** [gen] Misserfolg der - **2.** [person] Versager der - **3.** [to attend, appear, act]: **I was surprised by her ~ to attend the meeting** ich war überrascht, dass sie nicht an der Besprechung teilnahm - **4.** [of engine, brakes, heart] Versagen das; [of lights] Ausfall der.

**faint** [feɪnt] adj - **1.** [slight] schwach; [image] kaum sichtbar; [chance] gering; **I haven't the ~est idea** ich habe keinen blassen Schimmer - **2.** [dizzy] schwindelig; **to be ~ with hunger** sich schwach vor Hunger fühlen ◇ vi ohnmächtig werden.

**faint-hearted** [-'hɑːtɪd] adj zaghaft.

**faintly** ['feɪntlɪ] adv - **1.** [shine] schwach; [speak, ring] leise; **~ visible** kaum sichtbar - **2.** [slightly] ein wenig.

**faintness** ['feɪntnɪs] n - **1.** [dizziness] Ohnmachtsgefühl das - **2.** [dimness - of sound, hope, memory] Schwäche die; **because of the ~ of the image** weil das Bild kaum sichtbar ist.

**fair** [feəʳ] adj - **1.** [just - judge, person] gerecht; [- result, decision, trial] fair; **it's not ~!** das ist ungerecht!; **to be ~, he did try to apologize** fairerweise muss man sagen, dass er versucht hat, sich zu entschuldigen - **2.** [quite large] ziemlich groß - **3.** [quite good] ziemlich gut - **4.** [hair, person] blond - **5.** [skin, complexion] hell - **6.** [weather] schön ◇ n - **1.** Br [funfair] Jahrmarkt der - **2.** [trade fair] Messe die ◇ adv [play, fight] fair.

➡ **fair enough** excl Br inf na gut!

**fair copy** n Reinschrift die.

**fair game** n fig leichte Beute, Freiwild das.

**fairground** ['feəgraʊnd] n Rummelplatz der.

**fair-haired** [-'heəd] adj blond.

**fairly** ['feəlɪ] adv - **1.** [rather] ziemlich - **2.** [treat, distribute] gerecht; [describe, fight, play] fair.

**fair-minded** [-'maɪndɪd] adj gerecht.

**fairness** ['feənɪs] n [of judgement, person] Gerechtigkeit die; [of decision, trial, result] Fairness die; **in ~ to him** OR **in all ~, he did try to apologize** fairerweise, muss man sagen, dass er versucht hat, sich zu entschuldigen.

**fair play** n (U) Fairplay das.

**fairway** ['feəweɪ] n Fairway das.

**fairy** ['feərɪ] (pl -ies) n Fee die.

**fairy lights** npl Br Lichterkette die.

**fairy tale** n Märchen das.

**fait accompli** [‚feɪtə'kɒmpli:] (pl **faits accomplis**) n vollendete Tatsache.

**faith** [feɪθ] n - **1.** [trust]: ~ **(in)** Vertrauen das (zu); **I have** ~ **in her ability to win** ich glaube, dass sie gut genug ist zu gewinnen; **in good** ~ in gutem Glauben; **in bad** ~ mit böser Absicht; **I told you that in good** ~ ich habe dir das im Vertrauen gesagt - **2.** [particular religion] Religion die - **3.** (U) [religious belief] Glaube der.

**faithful** ['feɪθfʊl] adj - **1.** [friend, dog, lover] treu - **2.** [account, translation] getreu, genau <> npl REⲖⲓⲅ: **the** ~ die Gläubigen.

**faithfully** ['feɪθfʊlɪ] adv [support] treu; [promise] fest; **Yours** ~ Br [in letter] hochachtungsvoll.

**faithfulness** ['feɪθfʊlnɪs] n - **1.** [loyalty] Treue die - **2.** [accuracy] Genauigkeit die.

**faith healer** n Gesundbeter der, -in die.

**faithless** ['feɪθlɪs] adj treulos.

**fake** [feɪk] adj [painting, passport] gefälscht; [gun, jewellery] unecht <> n - **1.** [of painting, passport] Fälschung die; [of gun, jewellery] Imitation die - **2.** [person] Schwindler der, -in die <> vt - **1.** [signature, results] fälschen - **2.** [simulate] vorⲁtäuschen; [illness] simulieren <> vi: **he's faking** er tut nur so.

**falcon** ['fɔːlkən] n Falke der.

**Falkland Islands** ['fɔːklənd-], **Falklands** ['fɔːkləndz] npl: **the** ~ die Falkland Inseln pl; **in the** ~ auf den Falkland Inseln.

**fall** [fɔːl] (pt **fell**; pp **fallen**) vi - **1.** [gen] fallen; [person] hinⲁfallen; [from great height, heavily, in sport] stürzen; [thing to ground] herunter-/hinunterⲁfallen; **the city fell to the enemy troops** die Stadt fiel in die Hände der feindlichen Truppen; **to** ~ **flat** [joke] daneben gehen - **2.** [decrease - temperature] fallen; [ - number] abⲁnehmen; [ - demand, wind] nachⲁlassen - **3.** [become - ill, silent, vacant] werden; **to** ~ **asleep** einⲁschlafen; **to** ~ **in love** sich verlieben; **to** ~ **under suspicion** in Verdacht geraten; **to** ~ **open** sich öffnen; **to** ~ **to bits** OR **pieces** auseinander fallen - **4.** [government, leader] gestürzt werden - **5.** [occur]: **to** ~ **(on)** fallen (auf (+ D)); **they** ~ **into two groups** sie lassen sich zwei Gruppen zuordnen - **6.** [silence] sich ausⲁbreiten; [night] hereinⲁbrechen <> n - **1.** [accident, from power] Sturz der; **to have a** ~ stürzen - **2.**: ~ **of snow** Schneefall der - **3.** [of city, country] Eroberung die - **4.** [decrease]: ~ (in) Abnahme die (+ G) - **5.** Am [autumn] Herbst der.

**falls** npl [waterfall] Wasserfall der.

**fall about** vi Br inf: **to** ~ **about (laughing)** sich krankⲁlachen.

**fall apart** vi - **1.** [book, chair] auseinander fallen - **2.** fig [country, person] zusammenⲁbrechen.

**fall away** vi - **1.** [plaster, paint] abⲁbröckeln - **2.** [land, slope] abⲁfallen.

**fall back** vi - **1.** [retreat] zurückⲁweichen - **2.** [lag behind] zurückⲁfallen.

**fall back on** vt fus [resort to] zurückⲁgreifen auf (+ A).

**fall behind** vi - **1.** [in race] zurückⲁfallen - **2.** [with rent, work] in Rückstand geraten.

**fall down** vi - **1.** [picture] herunter-/hinunterⲁfallen; [person] hinⲁfallen; [building] einⲁstürzen - **2.** [fail]: **the plan** ~**s down on three points** der Plan funktioniert an drei Stellen nicht; **this is where your argument** ~**s down** an dieser Stelle ist dein Argument nicht stichhaltig.

**fall for** vt fus - **1.** inf [fall in love with] sich verlieben in (+ A) - **2.** [trick] hereinⲁfallen auf (+ A).

**fall in** vi - **1.** [roof, ceiling] einⲁstürzen - **2.** MIL (in Reih und Glied) anⲁtreten.

**fall in with** vt fus [suggestion, request] akzeptieren.

**fall off** vi - **1.** [drop off] herunter-/hinunterⲁfallen - **2.** [diminish] zurückⲁgehen.

**fall on** vt fus - **1.** [subj: eyes, gaze] fallen auf (+ A) - **2.** [attack] herⲁfallen über (+ A).

**fall out** vi - **1.** [hair, tooth] ausⲁfallen - **2.** [quarrel]: **to** ~ **out (with sb)** sich (mit jm) zerstreiten - **3.** MIL wegⲁtreten.

**fall over** vt fus [step, obstacle] fallen über (+ A); **to** ~ **ing over o.s. to do sthg** inf sich fast überschlagen, etw zu tun <> vi [lose balance - person] hinⲁfallen; [ - chair, jug] umⲁkippen.

**fall through** vi [plan, deal] fehlⲁschlagen.

**fall to** vt fus [subj: duty] zuⲁfallen (+ D); **it** ~**s to me to ...** es obliegt mir ...

**fallacious** [fə'leɪʃəs] adj fml irrig.

**fallacy** ['fæləsɪ] (pl -ies) n Irrtum der.

**fallen** ['fɔːln] pp ▷ **fall**.

**fall guy** n Am inf [scapegoat] Sündenbock der.

**fallible** ['fæləbl] adj [person] fehlbar; [method, plan] nicht unfehlbar.

**falling** ['fɔːlɪŋ] adj [decreasing] sinkend.

**fallopian tube** [fə'ləʊpɪən-] n Eileiter der.

**fallout** ['fɔːlaʊt] n [radiation] radioaktiver Niederschlag.

**fallow** ['fæləʊ] adj [land] brach; **to lie** ~ brachⲁliegen.

**false** [fɔːls] adj - **1.** [gen] falsch - **2.** [fake - nose, eyelashes] künstlich; [ - passport] gefälscht; [ - smile] gekünstelt; ~ **ceiling** Einschubdecke die.

**false alarm** n falscher Alarm.

**falsehood** ['fɔːlshʊd] n fml [lie] Unwahrheit die.

**falsely** ['fɔːlslɪ] adv - **1.** [accused, imprisoned] zu Unrecht; ~ **stated** fälschlicherweise angegeben - **2.** [laugh] gekünstelt.

**false start** n Fehlstart der.

**false teeth** npl künstliches Gebiss.

**falsetto** [fɔ:l'setəʊ] (pl **-s**) n MUS Falsett das ◇ adv im Falsett.

**falsify** ['fɔ:lsɪfaɪ] (pt & pp **-ied**) vt [facts, accounts] verfälschen.

**falter** ['fɔ:ltər'] vi **- 1.** [move unsteadily] wankend **- 2.** [voice] stocken **- 3.** [hesitate] zögern.

**faltering** ['fɔ:ltərɪŋ] adj [steps] wankend; [voice] stockend.

**fame** [feɪm] n Ruhm der.

**familiar** [fə'mɪljər'] adj **- 1.** [known] vertraut; **to be ~ to sb** jm bekannt vorlkommen **- 2.** [conversant]: **to be ~ with sthg** sich mit etw auslkennen; **to be on ~ terms with sb** mit jm auf vertrautem Fuße stehen **- 3.** pej [overly informal] vertraulich.

**familiarity** [fə,mɪlɪ'ærətɪ] n **- 1.** [gen] Vertrautheit die **- 2.** pej [excessive informality] Vertraulichkeit die.

**familiarize, -ise** [fə'mɪljəraɪz] vt: **to ~ o.s. with sthg** sich mit etw vertraut machen; **to ~ sb with sthg** jn mit etw vertraut machen.

**family** ['fæmlɪ] (pl **-ies**) n Familie die ◇ comp Familien-; **~ entertainment/programme** Unterhaltung die Sendung/die für die ganze Familie.

**family business** n Familienunternehmen das.

**family credit** n (U) Br staatlicher Zuschuss an einkommensschwache Familien.

**family doctor** n Hausarzt der, -ärztin die.

**family life** n Familienleben das.

**family planning** n Familienplanung die.

**family tree** n Stammbaum der.

**famine** ['fæmɪn] n Hungersnot die.

**famished** ['fæmɪʃt] adj inf [very hungry]: **I'm ~** ich sterbe vor Hunger.

**famous** ['feɪməs] adj: **~ (for)** berühmt (für).

**famously** ['feɪməslɪ] adv dated: **they get on** OR **along ~** sie kommen prima miteinander aus.

**fan** [fæn] (pt & pp **-ned**; cont **-ning**) n **- 1.** [held in hand] Fächer der **- 2.** [electric] Ventilator der **- 3.** [enthusiast] Fan der ◇ vt **- 1.** [cool]: **to ~ one's face** sich (D) das Gesicht fächeln; **to ~ o.s.** sich (D) Luft zulfächeln **- 2.** [stimulate - fire, flames] anlfachen; [ - feelings] entfachen; [ - fears] schüren.

➤ **fan out** vi [army, search party] auslschwärmen.

**fanatic** [fə'nætɪk] n Fanatiker der, -in die.

**fanatical** [fə'nætɪkl] adj fanatisch.

**fanaticism** [fə'nætɪsɪzm] n Fanatismus der.

**fan belt** n Keilriemen der.

**fanciful** ['fænsɪfʊl] adj **- 1.** [odd] abstrus **- 2.** [elaborate] fantastisch.

**fan club** n Fanklub der.

**fancy** ['fænsɪ] (compar **-ier**; superl **-iest**; pl **-ies**; pt & pp **-ied**) adj **- 1.** [elaborate - clothes, design, restaurant, hotel] ausgefallen; [ - food, cakes] fein **- 2.** [expensive] exklusiv ◇ n **- 1.** [liking] Lust die; **to take a ~ to** angetan sein von; **to take sb's ~** jm gefallen, jn anlsprechen **- 2.** [whim] Laune die **- 3.** [fantasy] Fantasie die ◇ vt **- 1.** inf [want] Lust haben auf (+ A); **to ~ doing sthg** Lust dazu haben, etw zu tun **- 2.** [person] scharf sein auf (+ A); **to ~ o.s.** von sich eingenommen sein **- 3.** [imagine]: **~ that!** wer hätte das gedacht!; **~ meeting you here!** wer hätte das gedacht, dass wir uns hier treffen; **to ~ o.s. as a painter/writer** sich für einen Maler/Schriftsteller halten.

**fancy dress** n (Masken)kostüm das.

**fancy-dress party** n Kostümfest das.

**fancy goods** npl Geschenkartikel pl.

**fanfare** ['fænfeər'] n MUS Fanfare die.

**fang** [fæŋ] n **- 1.** [of snake] Giftzahn der **- 2.** [of wolf] Reißzahn der.

**fan heater** n Heizlüfter der.

**fanlight** ['fænlaɪt] n Br Oberlicht das.

**fan mail** n (U) Fanpost die.

**fanny** ['fænɪ] n Am inf [buttocks] Po der.

**fanny pack** n Am Gürteltasche die.

**fantasize, -ise** ['fæntəsaɪz] vi fantasieren; **~ about sthg** sich etw vorlstellen; **to ~ about doing sthg** sich vorlstellen, etw zu tun.

**fantastic** [fæn'tæstɪk] adj **- 1.** inf [gen] fantastisch **- 2.** [bizarre - story] fantastisch; [ - animal] Fantasie-.

**fantastically** [fæn'tæstɪklɪ] adv **- 1.** [extremely] unwahrscheinlich **- 2.** [bizarrely] fantastisch.

**fantasy** ['fæntəsɪ] (pl **-ies**) n Fantasie die ◇ comp Fantasie-.

**fanzine** ['fænziːn] n Fan-Magazin das.

**fao** (abbr of **for the attention of**) z. H. (von).

**FAO** (abbr of **Food and Agriculture Organization**) n FAO die.

**FAQ** (abbr of **free alongside quay**) FAQ.

**far** [fɑːr] (compar **farther** OR **further**; superl **farthest** OR **furthest**) adv **- 1.** [in distance, time] weit; **have you come ~?** sind Sie von weit her gekommen?; **how ~ is it (to London)?** wie weit ist es (bis London)?; **as ~ as** [town, country] bis nach; [station, school] bis zu; **as ~ back as 1900** schon (im Jahre) 1900; **so ~** [until now] bisher; **~ and wide** überall; **he will go ~** fig er wird es weit bringen **- 2.** [in degree]: **~ better/quicker** weitaus besser/schneller; **you're not ~ wrong** OR **out** da liegst du nicht ganz falsch; **as ~ as I'm concerned** was mich betrifft; **as ~ as I know** so weit ich weiß; **~ and away, by ~** bei weitem; **~ from it** keineswegs; **so ~ so good** so weit, so gut; **I wouldn't go so ~ as to say I liked it** ich würde nicht gerade sagen, dass es mir gefallen hat; **that's going too ~** das geht zu weit ◇ adj: **at the ~ end** am anderen Ende; **the ~ right/left** [in politics] die extreme Rechte/Linke.

**faraway** ['fɑːrəweɪ] *adj* - **1.** [place, country] weit entfernt - **2.** [look] abwesend.

**farce** [fɑːs] *n* THEATRE & *fig* Farce *die.*

**farcical** ['fɑːsɪkl] *adj* lächerlich.

**fare** [feəʳ] *n* - **1.** [payment] Fahrpreis *der;* [for flight] Flugpreis *der* - **2.** *fml* [food] Kost *die* ⟨⟩ *vi:* **he is faring ~ well/badly** es geht ihm gut/ schlecht.

**Far East** *n:* **the ~** der Ferne Osten.

**farewell** [ˌfeə'wel] *n* Lebewohl *das;* **they said their ~s** sie verabschiedeten sich ⟨⟩ *excl literary* lebe wohl!

**farfetched** [ˌfɑː'fetʃt] *adj* weithergeholt.

**far-flung** *adj* [remote] abgelegen; [extensive] ausgedehnt.

**farm** [fɑːm] *n* Bauernhof *der* ⟨⟩ *vt* bewirtschaften ⟨⟩ *vi* Landwirtschaft betreiben.
➤ **farm out** *vt sep* [work] vergeben.

**farmer** ['fɑːməʳ] *n* Bauer *der,* Bäuerin *die.*

**farmhand** ['fɑːmhænd] *n* Landarbeiter *der,* -in *die.*

**farmhouse** ['fɑːmhaʊs, *pl* -haʊzɪz] *n* Bauernhaus *das.*

**farming** ['fɑːmɪŋ] *n* Landwirtschaft *die;* **crop ~** Ackerbau *der;* **sheep ~** Schafzucht *die.*

**farmland** ['fɑːmlænd] *n (U)* Ackerland *das.*

**farmstead** ['fɑːmsted] *n Am* Gehöft *das.*

**farmyard** ['fɑːmjɑːd] *n* Hof *der.*

**Faroe** *n* = Faeroe.

**far-off** *adj* fern.

**far-reaching** [-'riːtʃɪŋ] *adj* weitreichend.

**farrier** ['færɪəʳ] *n* Hufschmied *der.*

**farsighted** [ˌfɑː'saɪtɪd] *adj* - **1.** [person] weitblickend; [plan] auf weite Sicht konzipiert - **2.** *Am* [longsighted] weitsichtig.

**fart** [fɑːt] *inf n* - **1.** [wind] Furz *der* - **2.** [person] Scheißer *der* ⟨⟩ *vi* furzen.

**farther** ['fɑːðəʳ] *compar* ⟮⟯ **far.**

**farthest** ['fɑːðəst] *superl* ⟮⟯ **far.**

**fascia** ['feɪʃə] *n* - **1.** [on shop] Ladenschild *das* - **2.** [in car] Armaturenbrett *das.*

**fascinate** ['fæsɪneɪt] *vt* faszinieren.

**fascinating** ['fæsɪneɪtɪŋ] *adj* faszinierend.

**fascination** [ˌfæsɪ'neɪʃn] *n* Faszination *die;* **he watched in ~** er schaute fasziniert zu.

**fascism** ['fæʃɪzm] *n* Faschismus *der.*

**fascist** ['fæʃɪst] *adj* faschistisch ⟨⟩ *n* Faschist *der,* -in *die.*

**fashion** ['fæʃn] *n* - **1.** [current style] Mode *die;* **the latest ~s** die neueste Mode; **it's the ~ to wear your hair long** es ist jetzt Mode, das Haar lang zu tragen; **to be in/out of ~** modern/

unmodern sein - **2.** [manner] Art *die;* **after a ~** so einiger maßen ⟨⟩ *vt fml* [shape] formen.

**fashionable** ['fæʃnəbl] *adj* [clothes, hairstyle] modisch; **a ~ restaurant/opinion** ein Restaurant, das/eine Meinung, die gerade „in" ist.

**fashion-conscious** *adj* modebewusst.

**fashion designer** *n* Modedesigner *der,* -in *die.*

**fashion show** *n* Modeschau *die.*

**fast** [fɑːst] *adj* - **1.** [rapid] schnell; [journey] kurz; **to be in the ~ track** [in career] einen steilen Aufstieg vor sich *(D)* haben; **to pull a ~ one on sb** *inf* jn reinlegen - **2.** [clock, watch]: **to be ~** vorlgehen - **3.** [dye] farbecht ⟨⟩ *adv* - **1.** [rapidly] schnell - **2.** [firmly] fest; **to hold ~ to sthg** [grip firmly] an etw *(D)* festlhalten; **to be ~ asleep** fest schlafen ⟨⟩ *n* [act] Fasten *das;* [period] Fastenzeit *die* ⟨⟩ *vi* fasten.

**fast breeder reactor** *n* schneller Brüter.

**fasten** ['fɑːsn] *vt* - **1.** [coat, door, bag, window] zumachen; **to ~ one's seat belt** sich anlschnallen - **2.** [attach]: **to ~ sthg to sthg** etw an etw *(D)* befestigen - **3.** [grasp]: **to ~ one's hands around sthg** etw mit den Händen umgreifen ⟨⟩ *vi:* **to ~ on to sthg** an etw *(D)* befestigt werden.

**fastener** ['fɑːsnəʳ] *n* Verschluss *der.*

**fastening** ['fɑːsnɪŋ] *n* Verschluss *der.*

**fast food** *n* Fastfood *das.*

**fast-forward** *n* [button] Vorspultaste *die;* **to put a tape on ~** eine Kassette vorspulen ⟨⟩ *vt* & *vi* vorspulen.

**fastidious** [fə'stɪdɪəs] *adj* sehr genau.

**fast lane** *n* Überholspur *die.*

**fat** [fæt] (*compar* **-ter;** *superl* **-test**) *adj* - **1.** [gen] dick; **to get ~** dick werden - **2.** [meat] fett - **3.** *iron* [small]: **a ~ lot of good that did you!** einen schönen Nutzen hat es dir gebracht!; **~ chance!** wers glaubt wird selig! ⟨⟩ *n* Fett *das.*

**fatal** ['feɪtl] *adj* - **1.** [mistake, decision] fatal - **2.** [accident, illness] tödlich.

**fatalism** ['feɪtəlɪzm] *n* Fatalismus *der.*

**fatalistic** [ˌfeɪtə'lɪstɪk] *adj* fatalistisch.

**fatality** [fə'tælətɪ] (*pl* -**ies**) *n* - **1.** [accident victim] Todesopfer *das* - **2.** = fatalism.

**fatally** ['feɪtəlɪ] *adv* [wounded] tödlich; **the plan is ~ flawed** der Plan ist fehlerhaft und daher zum Scheitern verurteilt.

**fate** [feɪt] *n* Schicksal *das;* **to tempt ~** das Schicksal herauslfordern.

**fated** ['feɪtɪd] *adj* - **1.**: **to be ~ to do sthg** dazu bestimmt sein, etw zu tun - **2.** [doomed] zum Scheitern verurteilt.

**fateful** ['feɪtfʊl] *adj* verhängnisvoll.

**fathead** ['fæthed] *n inf* Dummkopf *der.*

**father** ['fɑːðəʳ] n Vater der ◇ vt [child] zeugen.
➤ **Father** n - 1. [priest] Vater der - 2. [God]: **our Father** unser Vater.

**Father Christmas** n Br Weihnachtsmann der.

**fatherhood** ['fɑːðəhʊd] n Vaterschaft die.

**father-in-law** (pl **father-in-laws** OR **fathers-in-law**) n Schwiegervater der.

**fatherly** ['fɑːðəlɪ] adj väterlich.

**Father's Day** n Vatertag der.

**fathom** ['fæðəm] n Faden der ◇ vt: **to ~ sb/sthg (out)** jn/etw ergründen.

**fatigue** [fə'tiːg] n - 1. [exhaustion] Erschöpfung die - 2. [in metal] Ermüdung die ◇ vt [weary] erschöpfen.
➤ **fatigues** npl Arbeitsuniform die.

**fatless** ['fætlɪs] adj fettfrei.

**fatten** ['fætn] vt mästen.
➤ **fatten up** vt sep mästen.

**fattening** ['fætnɪŋ] adj dick machend; **to be ~** dick machen.

**fatty** ['fætɪ] (compar **-ier**; superl **-iest**; pl **-ies**) adj - 1. [food, meat] fett - 2. BIOL [tissue, acid] Fett- ◇ n inf pej Dickwanst der.

**fatuous** ['fætjʊəs] adj albern.

**fatuously** ['fætjʊəslɪ] adv albern.

**faucet** ['fɔːsɪt] n Am Wasserhahn der.

**fault** ['fɔːlt] n - 1. [responsibility] Schuld die; **it's my ~** es ist meine Schuld; **whose ~ is it?** wer ist schuld daran? - 2. [error, defect, in tennis] Fehler der; **to find ~ with sb/sthg** etw an jm/etw auszusetzen haben; **at ~** im Unrecht; **through no ~ of my own** ohne mein Verschulden - 3. GEOL Verwerfung die ◇ vt: **to ~ sb (on sthg)** jm widerlegen (in Bezug auf etw (A)).

**faultless** ['fɔːltlɪs] adj fehlerfrei.

**faulty** ['fɔːltɪ] (compar **-ier**; superl **-iest**) adj fehlerhaft.

**fauna** ['fɔːnə] n Fauna die.

**favour** Br, **favor** Am ['feɪvəʳ] n - 1. (U) [approval] Gunst die; **in sb's ~** zu js Gunsten; **to be in/out of ~ (with sb)** (bei jm) beliebt/unbeliebt sein; **to curry ~ with sb** sich bei jm einlschmeicheln - 2. [kind act] Gefallen der, Gefälligkeit die; **to do sb a ~** jm einen Gefallen tun - 3. [favouritism]: **to show ~ to sb** jn bevorzugen - 4. [advantage]: **to rule in sb's ~** zu js Vorteil OR Gunsten entscheiden ◇ vt - 1. [prefer] bevorzugen - 2. [benefit] begünstigen - 3. iron [honour]: **to ~ sb with sthg** jn mit etw beehren.
➤ **in favour** adv [in agreement]: **to be in ~** dafür sein.
➤ **in favour of** prep - 1. [in preference to] zugunsten (+ G) - 2. [in agreement with]: **to be in ~ of sthg**

für etw sein; **to be in ~ of doing sthg** dafür sein, etw zu tun.

**favourable** Br, **favorable** Am ['feɪvrəbl] adj - 1. [conditions, weather] günstig - 2. [review, impression] positiv.

**favourably** Br, **favorably** Am ['feɪvrəblɪ] adv: **to be ~ impressed** einen positiven Eindruck haben; **to speak ~ of sb** sich lobend über jn äußern.

**favourite** Br, **favorite** Am ['feɪvrɪt] adj Lieblings- ◇ n - 1. [person] Liebling der; **this jacket is my ~** das ist meine Lieblingsjacke - 2. [in race, contest] Favorit der, -in die.

**favouritism** Br, **favoritism** Am ['feɪvrɪtɪzm] n Günstlingswirtschaft die.

**fawn** [fɔːn] adj rehbraun ◇ n [animal] Hirschkalb das; [of roe deer] Rehkitz das ◇ vi: **to ~ on sb** sich bei jm einlschmeicheln.

**fax** [fæks] n - 1. [device] Faxgerät das - 2. [message] Fax das ◇ vt [document] faxen; **to ~ sb sthg** jm etw faxen.

**fax machine** n Faxgerät das.

**fax modem** n COMPUT Faxmodem das.

**fax number** n Faxnummer die.

**faze** [feɪz] vt esp Am inf aus der Fassung bringen.

**FBI** (abbr of **Federal Bureau of Investigation**) n FBI das.

**FC** (abbr of **Football Club**) n FC der.

**FCO** (abbr of **Foreign and Commonwealth Office**) n ≃ AA, Ministerium für Auswärtiges und das Commonwealth.

**FD** (abbr of **Fire Department**) n abbr of **Fire Department**.

**FDA** n - 1. (abbr of **Food and Drug Administration**) US-Bundesbehörde für Lebens- und Arzneimittelüberwachung - 2. (abbr of **Association of First Division Civil Servants**) britische Gewerkschaft für hochgestellte Mitarbeiter des öffentlichen Dienstes.

**FE** n abbr of **Further Education**.

**fear** [fɪəʳ] n - 1. [gen] Angst die, Furcht die - 2. [risk] Gefahr die; **there's no ~ of him coming back** es besteht keine Gefahr, dass er zurückkommt; **for ~ of waking him** aus Angst, dass er aufwachen könnte; **no ~!** inf auf keinen Fall! ◇ vt Angst haben vor (+ D), sich fürchten vor (+ D); **to ~ the worst** das Schlimmste befürchten ◇ vi: **to ~ for** fürchten um.

**fearful** ['fɪəfʊl] adj - 1. fml: **to be ~ of sthg** vor etw (D) Angst haben - 2. [noise, temper] furchterregend.

**fearless** ['fɪələs] adj furchtlos.

**fearlessly** ['fɪələslɪ] adv furchtlos.

**fearsome** ['fɪəsəm] adj furchterregend.

**feasibility** [ˌfiːzəˈbɪlətɪ] n [of plan] Durchführbarkeit die.

**feasibility study** n Durchführbarkeitsanalyse die.

**feasible** [ˈfiːzəbl] adj [plan] durchführbar.

**feast** [fiːst] n Festessen das ⬦ vi: **to ~ on** OR **off sthg** etw ausgiebig genießen.

**feat** [fiːt] n Meisterleistung die.

**feather** [ˈfeðəʳ] n Feder die; **that's a ~ in his cap!** darauf kann er stolz sein.

**feather bed** n Federbett das.

**featherbrained** [ˈfeðəbreɪnd] adj: **he's ~** er hat ein Spatzenhirn.

**featherweight** [ˈfeðəweɪt] n Federgewicht das.

**feature** [ˈfiːtʃəʳ] n - **1.** [characteristic - gen] Merkmal das; [ - of personality] Charakterzug der - **2.** [facial] Gesichtszug der - **3.** [article] Reportage die, Feature das - **4.** RADIO & TV [programme] Feature das - **5.** CINEMA Kinofilm der ⬦ vt: **the film ~s Brad Pitt** Brad Pitt spielt in dem Film mit; **the exhibition ~s the work of two young artists** die Ausstellung zeigt das Werk zweier junger Künstler ⬦ vi: **to ~ (in)** vorˈkommen (in (+ D)).

**feature film** n Spielfilm der.

**featureless** [ˈfiːtʃəlɪs] adj ohne herausragende Merkmale.

**Feb.** [feb] (abbr of **February**) Feb.

**February** [ˈfebruərɪ] n Februar der; see also **September.**

**feces** npl Am = **faeces.**

**feckless** [ˈfeklɪs] adj nutzlos.

**fed** [fed] pt & pp ⊳ **feed.**

**Fed** [fed] n inf (abbr of **Federal Reserve Board**) Kontrollorgan der Zentralbank der USA ⬦ - **1.** abbr of **federal** - **2.** abbr of **federation.**

**federal** [ˈfedrəl] adj Bundes-.

**federalism** [ˈfedrəlɪzml] n Föderalismus der.

**federation** [ˌfedəˈreɪʃn] n - **1.** [country] Föderation die - **2.** [association] Zusammenschluss der.

**fed up** adj: **to be ~ with sb/sthg** etw/jn satt haben; **I'm (feeling) ~** ich habe keine Lust mehr.

**fee** [fiː] n [for service] Gebühr die; [for membership] Beitrag der; [for doctor] Honorar das; **school ~s** Schulgeld das; **the entrance ~ is five pounds** der Eintritt kostet fünf Pfund.

**feeble** [ˈfiːbl] adj - **1.** [weak] schwach - **2.** [excuse, joke] lahm.

**feebleminded** [ˌfiːblˈmaɪndɪd] adj dümmlich.

**feebleness** [ˈfiːblnɪs] n - **1.** [weakness] Schwäche die - **2.** [of excuse, joke] Lahmheit die.

**feebly** [ˈfiːblɪ] adv - **1.** [smile, speak, shine] schwach - **2.** [explain] wenig überzeugend.

**feed** [fiːd] (pt & pp **fed**) vt - **1.** [baby, animal] füttern - **2.** fig [rumour] nähren; [fear] schüren - **3.** [insert]: **to ~ sthg into sthg** etw in etw (A) einführen; [coins] etw in etw (A) einlwerfen ⬦ vi - **1.** [baby] essen; [animal] fressen - **2.** fig [prejudice, fear]: **to ~ on** OR **off sthg** von etw leben ⬦ n - **1.** [for baby] Mahlzeit die - **2.** [for animal] Futter das.

**feedback** [ˈfiːdbæk] n (U) - **1.** [reaction] Feedback das - **2.** ELEC Rückkopplung die.

**feedbag** [ˈfiːdbæg] n Am Futtersack der.

**feeder road** n Zuführungsstraße die.

**feeding bottle** [ˈfiːdɪŋ-] n Br Saugflasche die.

**feel** [fiːl] (pt & pp **felt**) vt - **1.** [touch] fühlen; [examine] befühlen - **2.** [be aware of - tension, presence] spüren; **I can ~ it in my bones** ich spüre es in den Knochen - **3.** [think]: **to ~ that** glauben, dass; **she felt herself to be a failure** sie glaubte, eine Versagerin zu sein; **he felt it (to be) his duty** er hielt es für seine Pflicht - **4.** [experience - sensation] spüren, fühlen; [ - emotion] empfinden; **I ~ the cold a lot** ich leide sehr unter der Kälte; **I felt myself blushing** ich fühlte, wie ich rot wurde - **5.** phr: **I'm not ~ing myself today** ich bin heute nicht ich selbst ⬦ vi - **1.** [happy, angry, sleepy] sein; [lonely, fit, uncomfortable] sich fühlen; **I ~ cold** mir ist kalt; **I ~ stupid** ich komme mir blöd vor; **I ~ ill** ich fühle mich nicht gut; **to ~ like sthg** Lust haben auf etw (A); **I don't ~ like it** ich habe keine Lust dazu - **2.** [seem - light, heavy, soft etc] sich anlfühlen - **3.** [by touch]: **to ~ for sthg** nach etw (D) tasten ⬦ n - **1.** [of material]: **it has a soft ~** es fühlt sich weich an - **2.** [atmosphere] Atmosphäre die - **3.** phr: **to get/have a ~ for sthg** ein Gefühl für etw bekommen/haben.

**feeler** [ˈfiːləʳ] n - **1.** [of insect, snail] Fühler der - **2.** [of octopus] Tentakel der.

**feeling** [ˈfiːlɪŋ] n - **1.** [gen] Gefühl das; **bad ~** Verstimmung die - **2.** [impression] Eindruck der; [opinion] Meinung die.
↪ **feelings** npl Gefühle pl; **to hurt sb's ~s** jn verletzen; **no hard ~s!** nichts für ungut!

**fee-paying** [-ˈpeɪɪŋ] adj Br [pupil] Schulgeld zahlend; [school] schulgeldpflichtig.

**feet** [fiːt] pl ⊳ **foot.**

**feign** [feɪn] vt fml vorˈtäuschen.

**feint** [feɪnt] n Finte die ⬦ vi eine Finte anlwenden.

**feisty** [ˈfaɪstɪ] (compar **-ier**; superl **-iest**) adj esp Am inf kämpferisch.

**felicitous** [fɪˈlɪsɪtəs] adj fml [choice] glücklich; [combination] passend.

**feline** [ˈfiːlaɪn] adj Katzen-; [appearance] katzenhaft ⬦ n fml Katze die.

**fell** [fel] *pt* ⊳ **fall** ⬦ *vt* - **1.** [tree] fällen - **2.** [person] niederlstrecken.

**fellow** ['feləʊ] *adj* Mit-; ~ **passenger** Mitreisende *der, die;* ~ **sufferer** Leidensgenosse *der,* -sin *die;* ~ **student** Kommilitone *der,* -nin *die* ⬦ *n* - **1.** *dated* [man] Kerl *der* - **2.** [comrade] Kamerad *der* - **3.** [of society] Mitglied *das;* [of college] Fellow *der.*

**fellowship** ['feləʊʃɪp] *n* - **1.** [comradeship] Kameradschaftlichkeit *die* - **2.** [organization] Vereinigung *die* - **3.** [UNIV - scholarship] Stipendium *das;* [ - post] Stellung *die* eines Fellows.

**felony** ['feləniː] (*pl* -**ies**) *n* LAW schweres Verbrechen.

**felt** [felt] *pt* & *pp* ⊳ **feel** ⬦ *n* Filz *der.*

**felt-tip pen** *n* Filzstift *der.*

**female** ['fiːmeɪl] *adj* weiblich; ~ **worker** Arbeiterin *die;* ~ **student** Studentin *die* ⬦ *n* - **1.** [animal] Weibchen *das* - **2.** *pej inf* [woman] Weib *das.*

**feminine** ['femɪnɪn] *adj* feminin ⬦ *n* GRAMM Femininum *das.*

**femininity** [femɪ'nɪnətɪ] *n* Weiblichkeit *die.*

**feminism** ['femɪnɪzm] *n* Feminismus *der.*

**feminist** ['femɪnɪst] *n* Feminist *der,* -in *die.*

**fence** [fens] *n* Zaun *der;* to sit on the ~ *fig* nicht Partei ergreifen ⬦ *vt* einlzäunen.
  ➤ **fence in** *vt sep* - **1.** [garden] einlzäunen - **2.** *fig* [person] einlengen.
  ➤ **fence off** *vt sep* ablzäunen.

**fencing** ['fensɪŋ] *n* - **1.** SPORT Fechten *das* - **2.** [fences] Zäune *pl.*

**fend** [fend] *vi:* to ~ for o.s. für sich selbst sorgen.
  ➤ **fend off** *vt sep* ablwehren.

**fender** ['fendəʳ] *n* - **1.** [round fireplace] Kamingitter *das* - **2.** [on boat] Fender *der* - **3.** *Am* [over car wheel] Kotflügel *der.*

**fennel** ['fenl] *n* Fenchel *der.*

**Fens** [fenz] *npl Br:* the ~ *sumpfiges Flachlandgebiet in der Region East Anglia.*

**feral** ['ferəl] *adj* [cat, pigeon] verwildert.

**ferment** [*n* 'fɜːment, *vb* fə'ment] *n* [unrest] Aufruhr *der* ⬦ *vi* [beer, wine] gären.

**fermentation** [fɜːmən'teɪʃn] *n* Gärung *die.*

**fermented** [fə'mentɪd] *adj* fermentiert.

**fern** [fɜːn] *n* Farn *der.*

**ferocious** [fə'rəʊʃəs] *adj* [animal] wild; [attack, criticism] heftig.

**ferociously** [fə'rəʊʃəslɪ] *adv* heftig.

**ferocity** [fə'rɒsɪtɪ] *n* [of attack] Heftigkeit *die;* [of animal] Wildheit *die.*

**ferret** ['ferɪt] *n* Frettchen *das.*
  ➤ **ferret about, ferret around** *vi inf* herumlstöbern.
  ➤ **ferret out** *vt sep inf* auf lstöbern.

**ferris wheel** ['ferɪs-] *n* Riesenrad *das.*

**ferry** ['ferɪ] (*pl* -**ies;** *pt* & *pp* -**ied**) *n* Fähre *die* ⬦ *vt* transportieren.

**ferryboat** ['ferɪbəʊt] *n* = **ferry.**

**ferryman** ['ferɪmən] (*pl* -**men** [-mən]) *n* Fährmann *der.*

**fertile** ['fɜːtaɪl] *adj* - **1.** [gen] fruchtbar - **2.** [imagination] reich.

**fertility** [fɜː'tɪlətɪ] *n* Fruchtbarkeit *die.*

**fertility drug** *n* Hormonpräparat zur Steigerung der Fruchtbarkeit.

**fertilization** [fɜːtɪlaɪ'zeɪʃn] *n* - **1.** [of land] Düngung *die* - **2.** [of egg, seed] Befruchtung *die.*

**fertilize, -ise** ['fɜːtɪlaɪz] *vt* - **1.** [land] düngen - **2.** [egg, seed] befruchten.

**fertilizer** ['fɜːtɪlaɪzəʳ] *n* Dünger *der.*

**fervent** ['fɜːvənt] *adj* leidenschaftlich.

**fervour** *Br,* **fervor** *Am* ['fɜːvəʳ] *n* Leidenschaftlichkeit *die;* [of belief] Inbrunst *die.*

**fester** ['festəʳ] *vi* - **1.** [wound, sore] eitern - **2.** *fig* [anger, bitterness] wachsen; [quarrel] sich verschlimmern.

**festival** ['festəvl] *n* - **1.** [series of organized events] Festival *das* - **2.** [holiday] Feiertag *der.*

**festive** ['festɪv] *adj* festlich.

**festive season** *n:* the ~ die Weihnachtszeit.

**festivities** [fes'tɪvətɪz] *npl* Feierlichkeiten *pl.*

**festoon** [fe'stuːn] *vt* schmücken; to be ~ed with sthg mit etw geschmückt sein.

**fetal** ['fiːtl] *adj* = **foetal.**

**fetch** [fetʃ] *vt* - **1.** [go and get] holen; [person from station, school *etc*] ablholen - **2.** [sell for] einlbringen; to ~ a high price einen hohen Preis erzielen.

**fetching** ['fetʃɪŋ] *adj* attraktiv.

**fete, fête** [feɪt] *n* Wohltätigkeitsbasar *der* ⬦ *vt* durch Feiern ehren.

**fetid** ['fetɪd] *adj* übel riechend.

**fetish** ['fetɪʃ] *n* - **1.** [sexual obsession] Fetisch *der* - **2.** [mania] Manie *die.*

**fetishism** ['fetɪʃɪzm] *n* Fetischismus *der.*

**fetlock** ['fetlɒk] *n* Fessel *die.*

**fetter** ['fetəʳ] *vt* [person] fesseln.
  ➤ **fetters** *npl lit* & *fig* Fesseln *pl.*

**fettle** ['fetl] *n:* in fine ~ [person] in Hochform.

**fetus** ['fiːtəs] *n* = **foetus.**

**feud** [fjuːd] *n* Fehde *die* ⬦ *vi* in Fehde liegen.

**feudal** ['fjuːdl] *adj* feudal; [system, lord] Feudal-.

**fever** ['fiːvəʳ] *n lit* & *fig* Fieber *das;* in a ~ of excitement höchst aufgeregt.

**fevered** ['fiːvəd] *adj* - **1.** [brow] fiebrig - **2.** [imagination] aufgewühlt.

F

**feverish** ['fiːvərɪʃ] adj - **1.** MED fiebrig - **2.** [frenzied] fieberhaft.

**fever pitch** n Siedepunkt der.

**few** [fjuː] adj wenige; **the first ~ times** die ersten paar Male; **in a ~ minutes** in einigen Minuten <> pron: **a ~** ein paar; **a ~ more** noch ein paar; **quite a ~, a good ~** eine ganze Menge; **~ and far between** dünn gesät.

**fewer** ['fjuːə'] adj weniger; **there were ~ visitors this year** dieses Jahr kamen weniger Besucher <> pron weniger; **I got ~ than last time** ich habe weniger bekommen als das letzte Mal; **no ~ than ten times** nicht weniger als zehn Mal; **there are far ~ (of them) now** heute gibt es weit weniger.

**fewest** ['fjuːəst] adj: **(the) ~** die wenigsten.

**FH** Br abbr of **fire hydrant**.

**fiancé** [fɪ'ɒnseɪ] n Verlobte der.

**fiancée** [fɪ'ɒnseɪ] n Verlobte die.

**fiasco** [fɪ'æskəʊ] (Br pl **-s**, Am pl **-s** OR **-es**) n Fiasko das.

**fib** [fɪb] (pt & pp **-bed**; cont **-bing**) inf n Schwindelei die; **to tell ~s** schwindeln <> vi schwindeln.

**fibber** ['fɪbə'] n inf Schwindler der, -in die.

**fibre** Br, **fiber** Am ['faɪbə'] n - **1.** [gen] Faser die - **2.** (U) [roughage] Ballaststoffe pl - **3.** [strength]: **moral ~** Charakterstärke die.

**fibreboard** Br, **fiberboard** Am ['faɪbəbɔːd] n (U) Faserplatte die.

**fibreglass** Br, **fiberglass** Am ['faɪbəɡlɑːs] n Fiberglas das <> comp Fiberglas-, aus Fiberglas.

**fibre optics** n (Glas)faseroptik die.

**fickle** ['fɪkl] adj wankelmütig.

**fiction** ['fɪkʃn] n - **1.** (U) [literature] Belletristik die - **2.** [lie] Fiktion die.

**fictional** ['fɪkʃənl] adj [work] erzählend; [character] fiktiv; [event] erfunden.

**fictionalize, -ise** ['fɪkʃənəlaɪz] vt erfinden.

**fictitious** [fɪk'tɪʃəs] adj frei erfunden.

**fiddle** ['fɪdl] n - **1.** [violin] Geige die; **(as) fit as a ~** kerngesund; **to play second ~ to sb** in js Schatten stehen - **2.** Br inf [fraud] Schiebung die; **tax ~** Steuermanipulation die <> vt Br inf frisieren <> vi - **1.** [fidget]: **to ~ (about** OR **around)** (herum)zappeln; **to ~ (about** OR **around) with sthg** an etw (D) OR mit etw (herum)spielen - **2.** [waste time]: **to ~ about** OR **around** herum|trödeln.

**fiddler** ['fɪdlə'] n [violinist] Geiger der, -in die.

**fiddly** ['fɪdlɪ] (compar **-ier**; superl **-iest**) adj Br inf knifflig.

**fidelity** [fɪ'delətɪ] n - **1.** [loyalty] Treue die - **2.** [accuracy] originalgetreue Wiedergabe.

**fidget** ['fɪdʒɪt] vi zappeln.

**fidgety** ['fɪdʒɪtɪ] adj inf zapp(e)lig.

**field** [fiːld] n - **1.** [gen] Feld das; **in the ~** in der Praxis; **~ of vision** Gesichtsfeld das - **2.** [for sports] Spielfeld das - **3.** [of knowledge] Gebiet das - **4.** COMPUT Datenfeld das <> vt [question] parieren <> vi [in cricket, baseball] als Fänger spielen.

**field day** n: **to have a ~** fig seinen großen Tag haben.

**fielder** ['fiːldə'] n Fänger der, -in die.

**field event** n Sportart, die nicht auf der Aschenbahn ausgeübt wird.

**field glasses** npl Feldstecher der.

**field marshal** n Feldmarschall der.

**field mouse** n Feldmaus die.

**field trip** n Exkursion die.

**fieldwork** ['fiːldwɜːk] n Arbeit die im Gelände.

**fiend** [fiːnd] n - **1.** [cruel person] Teufel der - **2.** inf [fanatic] Fanatiker der, -in die.

**fiendish** ['fiːndɪʃ] adj - **1.** [evil] teuflisch - **2.** inf [very difficult, complex] verteufelt schwer.

**fierce** [fɪəs] adj [dog] bissig; [lion, warrior] aggressiv; [storm, temper] heftig; [competition] hart; [criticism] scharf; [heat] glühend.

**fiercely** ['fɪəslɪ] adv - **1.** [attack, rage] heftig; [fight, defend] erbittert - **2.** [critical, independent] äußerst.

**fiery** ['faɪərɪ] (compar **-ier**; superl **-iest**) adj - **1.** [burning] brennend - **2.** [food] sehr scharf - **3.** [speech] feurig; [temper] hitzig - **4.** [sunset, hair] feuerrot.

**FIFA** ['fiːfə] (abbr of **Fédération Internationale de Football Association**) n FIFA die.

**fifteen** [fɪf'tiːn] num fünfzehn; see also **six**.

**fifteenth** [fɪf'tiːnθ] num fünfzehnte, -r, -s; see also **sixth**.

**fifth** [fɪfθ] num fünfte, -r, -s; see also **sixth**.

**Fifth Amendment** n Am: **to take the ~** die Aussage verweigern.

**fifth column** n fünfte Kolonne.

**fiftieth** ['fɪftɪəθ] num fünfzigste, -r, -s; see also **sixth**.

**fifty** ['fɪftɪ] (pl **-ies**) num fünfzig; see also **sixty**.

**fifty-fifty** adj & adv fifty-fifty.

**fig** [fɪɡ] n Feige die.

**fight** [faɪt] (pt & pp **fought**) n - **1.** [brawl] Schlägerei die; [between boxers] Kampf der; **to have a ~ with sb** sich mit jm schlagen; **to put up a ~** sich heftig zur Wehr setzen - **2.** fig [struggle] Kampf der - **3.** [argument] Streit der; **to have a ~ (with sb)** Streit (mit jm) haben - **4.** [fighting spirit]: **there was no ~ left in him** er war kampfmüde <> vt - **1.** [physically] sich schlagen mit; [in battle, war] kämpfen mit OR gegen - **2.** [battle] aus|tragen; [war] führen - **3.** [prejudice, racism]

**bekämpfen** ◇ *vi* - **1.** [physically] sich schlagen; [in war] kämpfen - **2.** *fig* [struggle]: **to ~ for/against** sthg für/gegen etw kämpfen - **3.** [argue] sich streiten; **to ~ about** *OR* **over** sthg sich um *OR* über etw (A) streiten.

➤ **fight back** *vt fus* [tears, anger] zurücklhalten ◇ *vi* sich zur Wehr setzen.

➤ **fight off** *vt sep* - **1.** [attacker] sich zur Wehr setzen gegen - **2.** *fig* [feeling, illness] anlkämpfen gegen.

➤ **fight out** *vt sep:* **to ~ it out** ausltragen.

**fighter** ['faɪtər] *n* - **1.** [plane] Jagdflugzeug *das* - **2.** [soldier] Kämpfer *der* - **3.** [combative person] Kämpfernatur *die.*

**fighting** ['faɪtɪŋ] *n (U)* [in war] Kämpfe *pl;* [brawling] Schlägereien *pl.*

**fighting chance** *n:* **to have a ~** gute Chancen haben.

**figment** ['fɪgmənt] *n:* **a ~ of your/his imagination** ein Hirngespinst von dir/ihm.

**figurative** ['fɪgərətɪv] *adj* - **1.** [language] bildlich - **2.** ART gegenständlich.

**figuratively** ['fɪgərətɪvlɪ] *adv* bildlich.

**figure** [*Br* 'fɪgər, *Am* 'fɪgjər] *n* - **1.** [number] Zahl *die;* [digit] Ziffer *die;* **in single/double ~s** in ein-/zweistelligen Zahlen; **to put a ~ on** sthg [cost] Zahlen für etw anlgeben; [value] den Wert für etw anlgeben - **2.** [outline of person] Gestalt *die* - **3.** [personality] Persönlichkeit *die;* **a father ~** eine Vaterfigur - **4.** [shape of body] Figur *die* - **5.** [diagram] Abbildung *die* ◇ *vt esp Am* [suppose] schätzen ◇ *vi* - **1.** [feature] auf ltauchen; **to ~ prominently** eine wichtige Rolle spielen - **2.** *Am* [make sense]: **that ~s** das war ja klar.

➤ **figure out** *vt sep* [answer] herauslbekommen; [puzzle, problem] lösen.

**figure eight** *n Am* = figure of eight.

**figurehead** ['fɪgəhed] *n lit* & *fig* Galionsfigur *die.*

**figure of eight** *Br*, **figure eight** *Am n:* **to be (in) a ~** die Form einer Acht haben.

**figure of speech** *n* Redensart *die.*

**figure skating** *n* Eiskunstlauf *der.*

**figurine** [*Br* 'fɪgəri:n, *Am* ˌfɪgjə'ri:n] *n* Figurine *die.*

**Fiji** ['fi:dʒi:] *n* Fidschiinseln *pl;* **in ~** auf den Fidschiinseln.

**Fijian** [ˌfi:'dʒɪən] *adj* fidschianisch ◇ *n* Fidschiinsulaner *der*, -in *die.*

**filament** ['fɪləmənt] *n* [in bulb] Glühfaden *der.*

**filch** [fɪltʃ] *vt inf* klauen.

**file** [faɪl] *n* - **1.** [folder] Aktenordner *der* - **2.** [report] Akte *die;* **on ~, on the ~s** in der Akte, in den Akten - **3.** COMPUT Datei *die* - **4.** [tool] Feile *die* - **5.** [line]: **in single ~** hintereinander ◇ *vt* - **1.** [put in folder] ablheften - **2.** [complaint, petition, lawsuit] einlreichen - **3.** [wood, metal] feilen; **to ~ one's fingernails** sich (D) die Finger-

nägel feilen ◇ *vi* - **1.** [walk in single file]: **to ~ in/out** nacheinander hinein-/hinauslgehen - **2.** LAW: **to ~ for divorce** die Scheidung einlreichen.

**file clerk** *n Am* = filing clerk.

**filename** ['faɪlˌneɪm] *n* COMPUT Dateiname *der.*

**filet** *n Am* = fillet.

**filibuster** ['fɪlɪbʌstər] *vi esp Am* POL durch Marathonreden die Verabschiedung eines Gesetzes aufzuhalten versuchen.

**filigree** ['fɪlɪgri:] *n* Filigran *das.*

**filing cabinet** ['faɪlɪŋ-] *n* Aktenschrank *der.*

**filing clerk** *Br* ['faɪlɪŋ-], **file clerk** *Am n* Registraturangestellte *der*, *die.*

**Filipino** [ˌfɪlɪ'pi:nəʊ] (*pl* -**s**) *adj* philippinisch ◇ *n* Filipino *der*, -na *die.*

**fill** [fɪl] *vt* - **1.** [gen] füllen; **crowds ~ed the streets** Menschenmengen bevölkerten die Straßen - **2.** [repair - crack] zulspachteln; [ - hole in ground] zulschütten - **3.** [fulfil - role] spielen; [ - vacancy] besetzen; [ - need] befriedigen ◇ *vi* sich füllen ◇ *n:* **to have had one's ~ of** sthg genug von etw gehabt haben; **to eat one's ~** sich satt essen.

➤ **fill in** *vt sep* - **1.** [form, questionnaire] auslfüllen; [name, address] einlsetzen - **2.** [inform]: **to ~ sb in (on** sthg) jn (über etw (A)) ins Bild setzen ◇ *vt fus:* **I'm just ~ing in time** ich überbrücke nur die Zeit ◇ *vi:* **to ~ in for** sb für jn einlspringen.

➤ **fill out** *vt sep* [form, questionnaire] auslfüllen ◇ *vi* [get fatter] fülliger werden.

➤ **fill up** *vt sep* voll füllen ◇ *vi* sich füllen.

**filler** ['fɪlər] *n* [for cracks] Spachtelmasse *die.*

**fillet** *Br*, **filet** *Am* ['fɪlɪt] *n* Filet *das.*

**fillet steak** *n* Filetsteak *das.*

**filling** ['fɪlɪŋ] *adj* [food] sättigend ◇ *n* Füllung *die.*

**filling station** *n* Tankstelle *die.*

**fillip** ['fɪlɪp] *n:* **to give sb a ~** jm neuen Schwung geben; **to give sthg a ~** neuen Schwung in etw (A) bringen.

**filly** ['fɪlɪ] (*pl* -**ies**) *n* Stutfohlen *das.*

**film** [fɪlm] *n* - **1.** [movie, for camera] Film *der* - **2.** [layer] Schicht *die* ◇ *vt* filmen; [book, play] verfilmen ◇ *vi* drehen.

**filming** ['fɪlmɪŋ] *n* [of event] Filmen *das;* [of book] Verfilmung *die;* **the ~ lasted six months** die Dreharbeiten dauerten sechs Monate.

**film-maker** *n* Filmemacher *der*, -in *die.*

**film star** *n* Filmstar *der.*

**film studio** *n* Filmstudio *das.*

**Filofax®** ['faɪləʊfæks] *n* Filofax® *der.*

**filter** ['fɪltər] *n* Filter *der* ◇ *vt* filtern ◇ *vi* [people]: **to ~ in** einer nach dem anderen hineinlgehen/hineinlkommen.

➤ **filter out** *vt sep* [impurities] herauslfiltern.

F

**filter through** vi durchlsickern.
**filter coffee** n Filterkaffee der.
**filter lane** n Br Abbiegespur die.
**filter paper** n Filterpapier das.
**filter-tipped** [-'tɪpt] adj mit Filter.
**filth** [fɪlθ] n (U) - **1.** [dirt] Dreck der - **2.** [obscenity] Obszönitäten pl.
**filthy** ['fɪlθɪ] (compar -ier; superl -iest) adj - **1.** [very dirty] dreckig - **2.** [obscene] obszön; **to have a ~ mind** er hat eine schmutzige Fantasie.
**fin** [fɪn] n - **1.** [on fish] Flosse die - **2.** Am [for swimmer] Schwimmflosse die.
**final** ['faɪnl] adj - **1.** [last] letzte, -r, -s - **2.** [at end]: **the ~ score** der Schlussstand - **3.** [decision, version, defeat] endgültig; **I said no, and that's ~!** ich sagte nein, und damit basta! ◇ n [of ball games] Endspiel das; [of races] Endrunde die.
**finals** npl UNIV Examen das.
**final demand** n letzte Zahlungsaufforderung.
**finale** [fɪ'nɑːlɪ] n Finale das.
**finalist** ['faɪnəlɪst] n Finalist der, -in die.
**finalize, -ise** ['faɪnəlaɪz] vt [arrangements, details, dates] endgültig festlegen; [deal] zum Abschluss bringen.
**finally** ['faɪnəlɪ] adv - **1.** [at last] schließlich; [with relief] endlich - **2.** [lastly] zum Schluss.
**finance** [n 'faɪnæns, vb faɪ'næns] n (U) - **1.** [money] Geldmittel pl - **2.** [money management] Finanzwesen das ◇ vt finanzieren.
**finances** npl Finanzen pl.
**financial** [fɪ'nænʃl] adj finanziell.
**financial adviser** n Finanzberater der, -in die.
**financially** [fɪ'nænʃəlɪ] adv finanziell.
**financial services** npl Finanzdienstleistungen pl.
**financial year** Br, **fiscal year** Am n Geschäftsjahr das.
**financier** [fɪ'nænsɪər] n Br Finanzier der.
**finch** [fɪntʃ] n Fink der.
**find** [faɪnd] (pt & pp **found**) vt - **1.** [gen] finden; **to ~ the time to do sthg** die Zeit finden, etw zu tun; **did you ~ your way here all right?** haben Sie gut hierher gefunden?; **I ~ him fascinating** ich finde ihn faszinierend - **2.** [discover]: **to ~ that** festlstellen, dass; **I found myself back where I started** ich stellte fest, dass ich wieder da angekommen war, wo ich angefangen hatte - **3.** LAW: **to be found guilty/not guilty** für schuldig/nicht schuldig befunden werden ◇ n Fund der.
**find out** vi herauslfinden ◇ vt fus [information, truth] herauslfinden ◇ vt sep [person] auf die Schliche kommen (+ D).
**findings** ['faɪndɪŋz] npl Ergebnis das.

**fine** [faɪn] adj - **1.** [good - food, work] ausgezeichnet; [ - building] prächtig; [ - weather, day] schön; **how are you? - ~, thanks** wie gehts? - gut, danke - **2.** [satisfactory] in Ordnung, gut; **everything OK? - yes, ~!** ist alles OK? - ja, alles in Ordnung!; **more tea? - no, I'm ~, thanks** noch mehr Tee? - danke, ich habe genug; **it's ~ by me** ich habe nichts dagegen - **3.** [hair] fein; [thread, wire] dünn - **4.** [sand, powder, sandpaper] fein - **5.** [small, exact - detail] klein; **~ tuning** genaue Einstellung - **6.** [grand - clothes, people] vornehm ◇ adv - **1.** [quite well] gut; **that suits me ~** das passt mir gut - **2.** [thinly] fein ◇ n Geldstrafe die ◇ vt zu einer Geldstrafe verurteilen.
**fine arts** npl schöne Künste pl.
**finely** ['faɪnlɪ] adv - **1.** [sliced] dünn; [chopped] fein; [ground] fein - **2.** [tuned] genau; [balanced] gut.
**fineness** ['faɪnnɪs] n - **1.** [high quality] Güte die - **2.** [of hair, sand, powder] Feinheit die; [of thread] Dünnheit die - **3.** [of distinction] Feinheit die.
**finery** ['faɪnərɪ] n Staat der.
**finesse** [fɪ'nes] n Geschick das.
**fine-tooth comb** n: **to go over sthg with a ~** etw genau unter die Lupe nehmen.
**fine-tune** vt lit & fig fein ablstimmen.
**finger** ['fɪŋgər] n Finger der; **to keep one's ~s crossed** die Daumen drücken; **she didn't lay a ~ on him** sie hat ihm kein Haar gekrümmt; **he didn't lift a ~ to help** er rührte keinen Finger(, um zu helfen); **to point a** OR **the ~ at sb** mit dem Finger auf jn zeigen; **to put one's ~ on sthg** etw genau auslmachen; **to twist sb round one's little ~** jn um den (kleinen) Finger wickeln ◇ vt [feel] anlfassen.
**fingermark** ['fɪŋgəmɑːk] n Fingerabdruck der.
**fingernail** ['fɪŋgəneɪl] n Fingernagel der.
**fingerprint** ['fɪŋgəprɪnt] n Fingerabdruck der; **to take sb's ~s** jm Fingerabdrücke ablnehmen.
**fingertip** ['fɪŋgətɪp] n Fingerspitze die; **to have sthg at one's ~s** etw parat haben.
**finicky** ['fɪnɪkɪ] adj pej [eater] wählerisch; [person] pingelig; [task] knifflig.
**finish** ['fɪnɪʃ] n - **1.** [end] Ende das; [of race] Finish das - **2.** [on furniture, pottery] Oberfläche die ◇ vt - **1.** [complete] beenden; **to ~ doing the ironing/eating breakfast/**etc mit dem Bügeln/dem Frühstück/etc fertig sein; **to ~ writing a letter** einen Brief zu Ende schreiben - **2.** [food] auf lessen; [drink] auslltrinken; [supplies] auf lbrauchen; [cigarette] zu Ende rauchen; [book] ausllesen - **3.** [work, school]: **I ~ work at half past five** ich mache um halb sechs Feierabend; **I ~ school at half past three** ich habe um halb vier Schule aus ◇ vi - **1.** [end] zu Ende sein; **when does the film ~?**

wann ist der Film zu Ende?; **when do you ~?**
[stop work] wann machst du Feierabend?
**- 2.** [complete task] fertig werden; **I haven't ~ed**
**yet** ich bin noch nicht fertig **- 3.** [in race, competition]: **to ~ top of the league** Tabellenführer
werden; **to ~ fifth** Fünfter werden.

➤ **finish off** vt sep **- 1.** [complete] beenden
**- 2.** [food] auflessen; [drink] ausltrinken
**- 3.** [kill - subj: person] umlbringen *(jn, der bereits schwach oder verwundet ist);* **the pneumonia ~ed him off** die Lungenentzündung
bedeutete für ihn das Ende.

➤ **finish up** vi: **we ~ed up in a pub** wir sind
schließlich in einer Kneipe gelandet; **she**
**~ed up running her own company** zum Schluss
leitete sie ihre eigene Firma.

➤ **finish with** vt fus **- 1.** [boyfriend, girlfriend]
Schluss machen mit **- 2.** [stop using]: **have you**
**~ed with the newspaper?** brauchst du die
Zeitung noch?

**finished** ['fɪnɪʃt] adj **- 1.** [completed] fertig
**- 2.** [no longer interested]: **to be ~ with sthg** mit
etw fertig sein **- 3.** [programme, trial, meeting]
vorbei; **the wine's ~** der Wein ist alle.

**finishing line** ['fɪnɪʃɪŋ-] n Ziellinie die.

**finite** ['faɪnaɪt] adj **- 1.** [limited] begrenzt
**- 2.** GRAMM finit.

**Finland** ['fɪnlənd] n Finnland nt.

**Finn** [fɪn] n Finne der, -nin die.

**Finnish** ['fɪnɪʃ] adj finnisch <> n [language] Finnisch(e) das.

**fiord** [fjɔːd] n = fjord.

**fir** [fɜːr] n Tanne die.

**fire** ['faɪər] n **- 1.** [gen] Feuer das; **to be on ~**
brennen; **to catch ~** Feuer fangen; [forest,
building] in Brand geraten; **to set ~ to sthg** etw
anlzünden; [deliberately] etw in Brand setzen
**- 2.** [in forest, of building] Brand der **- 3.** Br [heater]
Ofen der **- 4.** (U) [shooting]: **under ~** unter Beschuss; **to open ~ (on sb)** das Feuer eröffnen
(auf jn) <> vt **- 1.** [shoot - bullet, missile] ablfeuern; [ - gun] ablschießen **- 2.** [shout - accusation] überhäufen mit; **to ~ questions at sb** jn
mit Fragen bombardieren **- 3.** [from job] feuern **- 4.** [imagination] beflügeln **- 5.** [pottery]
brennen <> vi: **to ~ (on OR at sb/sthg)** (auf jn/
etw) schießen OR feuern.

**fire alarm** n Feueralarm der.

**firearm** ['faɪərɑːm] n Schusswaffe die.

**fireball** ['faɪəbɔːl] n Feuerball der.

**firebomb** ['faɪəbɒm] n Brandbombe die <> vt
einen Brandanschlag verüben auf (+ A).

**firebreak** ['faɪəbreɪk] n Feuerschneise die.

**fire brigade** Br, **fire department** Am n
Feuerwehr die.

**firecracker** ['faɪəˌkrækər] n Knallkörper der.

**fire-damaged** adj durch Brand beschädigt.

**fire department** n Am = fire brigade.

**fire door** n Feuerschutztür die.

**fire drill** n Probealarm der.

**fire-eater** n Feuerschlucker der, -in die.

**fire engine** n Feuerwehrauto das.

**fire escape** n [stairs] Feuertreppe die; [ladder]
Feuerleiter die.

**fire extinguisher** n Feuerlöscher der.

**fire fighter** n Feuerwehrmann der.

**fireguard** ['faɪəgɑːd] n Kamingitter das.

**fire hazard** n: **to be a ~** feuergefährlich
sein.

**fire hydrant** [-'haɪdrənt], **fireplug** Am
['faɪəplʌg] n Hydrant der.

**firelight** ['faɪəlaɪt] n Schein der des Feuers.

**firelighter** ['faɪəlaɪtər] n Feueranzünder der.

**fireman** ['faɪəmən] (pl -men [-mən]) n Feuerwehrmann der.

**fireplace** ['faɪəpleɪs] n Kamin der.

**fireplug** n Am = fire hydrant.

**firepower** ['faɪəˌpaʊər] n Waffenkontingent
das.

**fireproof** ['faɪəpruːf] adj feuerfest.

**fire-raiser** [-ˌreɪzər] n Br Brandstifter der, -in
die.

**fire regulations** npl Brandschutzbestimmungen pl.

**fire service** n Br Feuerwehr die.

**fireside** ['faɪəsaɪd] n: **by the ~** am Kamin.

**fire station** n Feuerwache die.

**firewood** ['faɪəwʊd] n Brennholz das.

**firework** ['faɪəwɜːk] n Feuerwerkskörper
der; **~s** Feuerwerk das.

➤ **fireworks** npl fig: **there will be ~s** da werden
die Fetzen fliegen.

**firework display** n Feuerwerk das.

**firing squad** n Exekutionskommando das.

**firm** [fɜːm] adj **- 1.** [in texture] fest **- 2.** [structure,
shelf] stabil **- 3.** [forceful, strong - pressure, hold, control] fest; [ - leader, voice] energisch; **you must be**
**~ with him** Sie müssen ihm gegenüber bestimmt auftreten; **to stand ~** standhaft bleiben **- 4.** [belief] unerschütterlich; [answer] entschieden; [evidence] sicher <> n Firma die.

➤ **firm up** vt sep **- 1.** [body, muscles] straffen
**- 2.** [agreement] zum Abschluss bringen.

**firmly** ['fɜːmlɪ] adv **- 1.** [hold, attach, push] fest
**- 2.** [forcefully - rule] entschlossen; [ - answer] in
entschiedenem Ton **- 3.** [believe] unerschütterlich.

**firmness** ['fɜːmnɪs] n **- 1.** [of texture, fruit] Festigkeit die **- 2.** [in dealing with person] Standfestigkeit die.

**first** [fɜːst] adj erste, -r, -s; **my ~ concern** meine
größte Sorge; **for the ~ time** zum ersten

**F**

Mal; **I'll do it ~ thing (in the morning)** das ist das Erste, was ich morgen tun werde; **at ~ sight** auf den ersten Blick; **in the ~ place,** ... zunächst einmal ...; **~ things ~** eins nach dem anderen; **I don't know the ~ thing about it** ich habe keine Ahnung davon <> *adv* **- 1.** [firstly] zuerst; [arrive, speak etc] als erste, -r, -s; **~ of all** zuallererst; **what should I do ~?** was soll ich zuerst tun? **- 2.** [for the first time] zum ersten Mal <> *pron* Erste der, die, das; **the ~ of January** der erste Januar <> *n* **- 1.** [event]: **the balloon race was a world ~** der Ballonweltflug war der erste seiner Art auf der Welt **- 2.** *Br* UNIV *Abschluss mit „Sehr gut"* **- 3.** AUT: **~ (gear)** erster Gang.

➡ **at first** *adv* zuerst.

➡ **at first hand** *adv* aus erster Hand.

**first aid** *n* Erste Hilfe.

**first-aider** [-'eɪdəʳ] *n* Sanitäter der, -in die.

**first-aid kit** *n* Verbandskasten der.

**first-class** *adj* **- 1.** [excellent] erstklassig **- 2.** [ticket] erster Klasse; **~ compartment** Erste-Klasse-Abteil das; [stamp] *für Briefe, die innerhalb Großbritanniens schneller befördert werden sollen.*

**first course** *n* erster Gang.

**first cousin** *n* Cousin der, -e die (ersten Grades).

**first-day cover** *n* Ersttagsbrief der.

**first-degree** *adj* **- 1.** MED: **~ burn** Verbrennung die ersten Grades **- 2.** *Am* LAW: **~ murder** Mord der.

**first floor** *n* **- 1.** *Br* [above ground level] erster Stock **- 2.** *Am* [at ground level] Erdgeschoss das.

**firsthand** [fɜːst'hænd] *adj* & *adv* aus erster Hand.

**first lady** *n* POL First Lady die, Frau des US-Präsidenten.

**first language** *n* Muttersprache die.

**first lieutenant** *n* Oberleutnant der.

**firstly** ['fɜːstlɪ] *adv* zuerst; [followed by "secondly"] erstens.

**first mate** *n* Erster Offizier.

**first name** *n* Vorname der.

➡ **first-name** *adj*: **to be on first-name terms with sb** jn mit Vornamen anreden.

**first night** *n* Premiere die.

**first offender** *n* Ersttäter der, -in die.

**first officer** *n* = first mate.

**first-past-the-post system** *n Br* ≃ Mehrheitswahlrecht das.

**first-rate** *adj* erstklassig.

**First World War** *n*: **the ~** der erste Weltkrieg.

**firtree** ['fɜːtriː] *n* = fir.

**fiscal** ['fɪskl] *adj* fiskalisch; [policy] Fiskal-.

**fiscal year** *n Am* = financial year.

**fish** [fɪʃ] (*pl inv OR* **-es**) *n* Fisch der <> *vt*: **to ~ a river** in einem Fluss fischen; [with rod] in einem Fluss angeln <> *vi*: **to ~ (for)** fischen; [with rod] angeln; **to ~ for compliments** *fig* auf Komplimente aus sein.

➡ **fish out** *vt sep inf* [bring out] herausIfischen.

**fish and chips** *npl Br frittierter Fisch mit Pommes frites.*

> **FISH AND CHIPS**
>
> Ein traditionelles englisches Gericht, das aus frittiertem Fisch in Panade und Pommes frites besteht und das man in den „fish and chip shops" (einer Art Imbissstube) zum Mitnehmen in braunes Packpapier oder Zeitungspapier eingepackt bekommt. „Fish and chip shops" sind landauf, landab zu finden und bieten neben „fish and chips" auch eine Auswahl an anderen fritierten Schnellgerichten, zum Beispiel Würstchen, Hähnchen, Blutwurst und „meat pies" (Fleischpasteten) an. „Fish and chips" werden oft auf der Straße direkt aus der Hand gegessen.

**fish and chip shop** *n Br Imbissstube, die hauptsächlich frittierten Fisch mit Pommes frites verkauft.*

**fishbowl** ['fɪʃbəʊl] *n* (Gold)fischglas das.

**fishcake** ['fɪʃkeɪk] *n* Fischfrikadelle die.

**fisherman** ['fɪʃəmən] (*pl* **-men** [-mən]) *n* Fischer der; [angler] Angler der, -in die.

**fishery** ['fɪʃərɪ] (*pl* **-ies**) *n* [area] Fischereigewässer das.

**fish-eye lens** *n* Fischauge das.

**fish farm** *n* Fischzuchtanlage die.

**fish fingers** *Br*, **fish sticks** *Am npl* Fischstäbchen das.

**fishhook** ['fɪʃhʊk] *n* Angelhaken der.

**fishing** ['fɪʃɪŋ] *n* Fischen das; [with rod] Angeln das; [industry] Fischerei die; **to go ~** auf Fischfang gehen; [with rod] angeln gehen.

**fishing boat** *n* Fischerboot das.

**fishing line** *n* Angelschnur die.

**fishing rod** *n* Angelrute die.

**fishmonger** ['fɪʃ,mʌŋgəʳ] *n esp Br* Fischhändler der, -in die; **~'s (shop)** Fischgeschäft das.

**fishnet** ['fɪʃnet] *n* **- 1.** [for fishing] Netz das **- 2.** [material]: **~ stockings** Netzstrümpfe pl; **~ tights** Netzstrumpfhose die.

**fish pond** *n* Fischteich der.

**fish shop** *n* Fischgeschäft das.

**fish slice** *n Br* Bratenwender der.

**fish sticks** *npl Am* = fish fingers.

**fish tank** *n* [in house] Aquarium das.

**fishwife** ['fɪʃwaɪf] (*pl* **-wives** [-waɪvz]) *n pej* Marktweib das.

**fishy** ['fɪʃɪ] (compar **-ier;** superl **-iest**) adj
- **1.** [smell, taste] Fisch- - **2.** fig [suspicious]: **there's
something ~ about it** daran ist etwas faul.

**fissure** ['fɪʃəʳ] n Spalte die.

**fist** [fɪst] n Faust die.

**fit** [fɪt] (pt & pp **-ted;** cont **-ting**) adj - **1.** [suitable]:
**~ (for)** geeignet (für); **to be ~ to do sthg** die
richtige Person sein, um etw zu tun; **he's
not ~ to drive** [drunk] er ist nicht mehr in der
Lage, Auto zu fahren; **~ to eat** essbar; **to see
OR think ~ to do sthg** es für richtig halten, etw
zu tun - **2.** [healthy] fit; **to keep/get ~** fit
bleiben/werden ◇ - **2.** [of clothes, shoes etc]:
**to be a good ~** gut passen - **2.** [epileptic, of anger,
coughing] Anfall der; **to have a ~** MED einen Anfall haben OR erleiden; fig [be angry] einen
Wutanfall kriegen; **in ~s and starts** [move]
ruckartig, ruckweise; **to work in ~s and starts**
die Arbeit mehrmals unterbrechen ◇ vt
- **1.** [subj: clothes, shoes] passen (+ D); [subj: key]
passen in (+ A) - **2.** [insert]: **to ~ sthg into sthg**
etw in etw (A) stecken - **3.** [install] einlbauen;
**to ~ sthg with sthg** etw mit etw auslstatten
- **4.** [correspond to] entsprechen (+ D); **he ~s the
description** die Beschreibung passt auf ihn
- **5.** [for clothes]: **he was ~ted for a suit** der
Schneider hat bei ihm Maß genommen
◇ vi passen.
➤ **fit in** vt sep [find time for - person] dazwischen|-
schieben; [- task] zusätzlich erledigen ◇ vi
[belong]: **he's never ~ted in here** er hat hier nie
hingepasst; **to learn to ~ in** lernen, sich anl-
zupassen.
➤ **fit out** vt sep [ship, person] auslstatten.
➤ **fit together** vt sep [assemble] zusammen|-
bauen ◇ vi [make sense] zusammen|passen.

**fitful** ['fɪtful] adj [sleep] unruhig.

**fitment** ['fɪtmənt] n Einrichtungsgegen-
stand der.

**fitness** ['fɪtnəs] n - **1.** [health] Fitness die, Kondition die - **2.** [suitability - for job]: **~ (for)** Eignung
die (für).

**fitted** ['fɪtəd] adj - **1.** [suited]: **~ for** OR **to sthg** für
etw geeignet - **2.** [skirt, jacket] auf Taille gearbeitet - **3.** Br [shelves] eingebaut; [cupboard] Ein-
bau-.

**fitted carpet** n Teppichboden der.

**fitted kitchen** n Br Einbauküche die.

**fitted sheet** n Spannbetttuch das.

**fitter** ['fɪtəʳ] n [mechanic] Monteur der, -in die,
Installateur der, -in die.

**fitting** ['fɪtɪŋ] adj fml angemessen ◇ n
- **1.** [part] Zubehörteil das - **2.** [for clothing] An-
probe die.
➤ **fittings** npl Ausstattung die; [electrical, pipes]
Installation die.

**fitting room** n Umkleidekabine die.

**five** [faɪv] num fünf; see also **six.**

**fiver** ['faɪvəʳ] n inf - **1.** Br [amount] fünf britische

Pfund pl; [note] Fünfpfundschein der - **2.** Am
[amount] fünf Dollar pl; [note] Fünfdollar-
schein der.

**five-star** adj Fünf-Sterne-.

**fix** [fɪks] vt - **1.** [attach] befestigen; **to ~ sthg to
sthg** etw an etw (D) befestigen; **to ~ one's eyes
on sthg** seine Augen auf etw (A) heften
- **2.** [decide - date, amount, price] festlsetzen; **I've
~ed it with him** ich habe es mit ihm abge-
macht; **how are you ~ed for money?** wie sieht
es bei dir mit dem Geld aus? - **3.** [repair] reparieren - **4.** inf [rig - race, fight] manipulieren
- **5.** esp Am [food, drink] machen ◇ n - **1.** inf [dif-
ficult situation]: **to be in a ~** in der Patsche
sitzen - **2.** drugs sl Fix der.
➤ **fix up** vt sep - **1.** [provide]: **to ~ sb up with sthg**
jm etw besorgen - **2.** [arrange] arrangieren.

**fixation** [fɪk'seɪʃn] n Fixierung die.

**fixed** [fɪkst] adj - **1.** [attached] fest - **2.** [charge,
rate] festgesetzt - **3.** [smile, stare, belief] starr.

**fixed assets** npl Anlagevermögen das.

**fixture** ['fɪkstʃəʳ] n - **1.** [in building] festes Inventar; **~s and fittings** zu einer Wohnung gehörende Ausstattung und Installationen; **he's
become a ~** fig er gehört schon zum Inventar - **2.** [sports event] Spiel das.

**fizz** [fɪz] vi [drink] sprudeln; [champagne] perlen
◇ n [of drink] Sprudeln das; [of champagne] Perlen die.

**fizzle** ['fɪzl] ➤ **fizzle out** vi [fire, enthusiasm] ver-
puffen.

**fizzy** ['fɪzɪ] (compar **-ier;** superl **-iest**) adj kohlensäurehaltig.

**fjord** [fjɔːd] n Fjord der.

**FL** abk für Florida, in Postanschrift verwendet.

**flab** [flæb] n Speck der.

**flabbergasted** ['flæbəgɑːstɪd] adj platt.

**flabby** ['flæbɪ] (compar **-ier;** superl **-iest**) adj
wabbelig.

**flaccid** ['flæsɪd] adj schlaff.

**flag** [flæg] (pt & pp **-ged;** cont **-ging**) n Fahne
die; [of country] Flagge die, Fahne die ◇ vi [per-
son] ermüden; [enthusiasm, energy] nachllassen.
➤ **flag down** vt sep anlhalten.

**Flag Day** n 14. Juni, Feiertag, an dem überall
in den USA die amerikanische Flagge gehisst
wird.

**flag of convenience** n Billigflagge die.

**flagon** ['flægən] n - **1.** [bottle] Flasche die
- **2.** [jug] Krug der.

**flagpole** ['flægpəʊl] n Fahnenstange die.

**flagrant** ['fleɪgrənt] adj himmelschreiend.

**flagship** ['flægʃɪp] n lit & fig Flaggschiff das.

**flagstone** ['flægstəʊn] n Steinplatte die; [on
floors] Fliese die.

**flail** [fleɪl] vt: **to ~ one's arms about** mit den Ar-

**F**

men fuchteln; **to ~ one's legs about** mit den Beinen in der Luft strampeln ◇ *vi* herumlfuchteln.

**flair** [fleə'] *n* - **1.** [talent]: **~ (for)** Talent *das* (für) - **2.** [stylishness - of person] Ausstrahlung *die*.

**flak** [flæk] *n* - **1.** [gunfire] Flakfeuer *das* - **2.** *inf* [criticism]: **to get a lot of ~** unter schweren Beschuss geraten.

**flake** [fleɪk] *n* [of snow] Flocke *die;* [of skin] Schuppe *die;* **some ~s of paint/rust** ein bisschen Farbe/Rost ◇ *vi* [paint] ablblättern; [skin] sich schuppen.

◆ **flake out** *vi inf* zusammenlklappen.

**flaky** [ˈfleɪkɪ] (*compar* **-ier;** *superl* **-iest**) *adj* - **1.** [skin] schuppig; [paintwork] bröckelig; [texture] flockig - **2.** *Am inf* [person] verrückt.

**flaky pastry** *n* Blätterteig *der*.

**flambé** [ˈflɒmbeɪ] (*pt* & *pp* **-ed;** *cont* **-ing**) *adj* flambiert ◇ *vt* flambieren.

**flamboyant** [flæmˈbɔɪənt] *adj* extravagant; [design, decoration] üppig.

**flame** [fleɪm] *n* Flamme *die;* **to be in ~s** in Flammen stehen; **to burst into ~s** in Brand geraten ◇ *vi* brennen ◇ *vt* COMPUT Flames schicken (+ D).

**flameproof** [ˈfleɪmpruːf] *adj* feuerbeständig.

**flame-thrower** [-ˌθrəʊə'] *n* Flammenwerfer *der*.

**flaming** [ˈfleɪmɪŋ] *adj* - **1.** [red] flammend - **2.** *Br* [argument] heftig - **3.** *Br inf* [for emphasis] verflixt.

**flamingo** [fləˈmɪŋgəʊ] (*pl* **-s** OR **-es**) *n* Flamingo *der*.

**flammable** [ˈflæməbl] *adj* leicht entflammbar.

**flan** [flæn] *n* [sweet] Torte *die;* [savoury] Quiche *die*.

**Flanders** [ˈflɑːndəz] *n* Flandern *nt*.

**flange** [flændʒ] *n* Flansch *der;* [on wheel] Spurkranz *der*.

**flank** [flæŋk] *n* Flanke *die* ◇ *vt*: **to be ~ed by sb/sthg** von jm/etw flankiert sein.

**flannel** [ˈflænl] *n* - **1.** [fabric] Flannel *der* - **2.** *Br* [facecloth] Waschlappen *der*.

◆ **flannels** *npl* Flannelhose *die*.

**flannelette** [flænəˈlet] *n* Flanell *der (aus Baumwolle)*.

**flap** [flæp] (*pt* & *pp* **-ped;** *cont* **-ping**) *n* - **1.** [of pocket] Klappe *die;* [of envelope] Lasche *die;* [of table] hochklappbarer Teil; **a ~ of skin** ein Hautfetzen - **2.** *inf* [panic]: **in a ~** in Panik ◇ *vt* [wings] schlagen mit; [arms] wedeln mit ◇ *vi* - **1.** [wings] schlagen; [sail, flag, clothes] flattern - **2.** *inf* [panic] in Panik geraten.

**flapjack** [ˈflæpdʒæk] *n* - **1.** *Br* [biscuit] Haferflo-

ckenkeks *der* - **2.** *Am* [pancake] Pfannkuchen *der*.

**flare** [fleə'] *n* [distress signal] Leuchtsignal *das* ◇ *vi* - **1.** [fire]: **to ~ (up)** (auf l)lodern - **2.:** **to ~ (up)** [war, violence, disease] auslbrechen - **3.** [trousers, skirt] ausgestellt sein - **4.** [nostrils] sich blähen.

◆ **flares** *npl Br* [trousers] Hose *die* mit Schlag.

**flared** [fleəd] *adj* [trousers, skirt] ausgestellt.

**flash** [flæʃ] *adj* - **1.** PHOT Blitz- - **2.** *inf* [car, watch, person] protzig ◇ *n* - **1.** [of light - bright] Aufblitzen *das;* **a ~ of lightning** ein Blitz; **a ~ of inspiration** *fig* ein Geistesblitz; **in a ~** blitzartig; **quick as a ~** blitzschnell - **2.** PHOT Blitz *der* ◇ *vt* - **1.** [torch]: **to ~ a torch on sthg** etw anlleuchten; **to ~ one's headlights** die Lichthupe benutzen; **to ~ sb a look/smile** jn plötzlich (kurz) anlschauen/anllächeln - **2.** [show briefly - passport, image] kurz zeigen ◇ *vi* [light] auf lblinken; **to ~ by** OR **past** vorbeilsausen.

**flashback** [ˈflæʃbæk] *n* [in film] Rückblende *die*.

**flashbulb** [ˈflæʃbʌlb] *n* Blitzlicht *das*.

**flasher** [ˈflæʃə'] *n* - **1.** *Br* [light] Lichthupe *die* - **2.** *Br inf* [man] Exhibitionist *der*.

**flash flood** *n* flutartige Überschwemmung.

**flashgun** [ˈflæʃgʌn] *n* Blitzgerät *das*.

**flashlight** [ˈflæʃlaɪt] *n* [torch] Taschenlampe *die*.

**flash point** *n* [place] Krisenherd *der*.

**flashy** [ˈflæʃɪ] (*compar* **-ier;** *superl* **-iest**) *adj inf* protzig.

**flask** [flɑːsk] *n* - **1.** [Thermos] Thermosflasche *die* - **2.** [in chemistry] Glaskolben *der* - **3.** [hip flask] Flachmann *der*.

**flat** [flæt] (*compar* **-ter;** *superl* **-test**) *adj* - **1.** [gen] flach; [feet, tyre] platt; **~ roof** Flachdach *das* - **2.** [refusal, denial] glatt - **3.** [voice] monoton - **4.** [MUS - singer, instrument] zu tief; **C ~** Ces *das;* **D ~** Des *das;* **A ~** As *das;* **B ~** B *das* - **5.** COMM [fare, fee] Pauschal- - **6.** [drink] abgestanden - **7.** [battery] leer ◇ *adv* - **1.** [level] flach - **2.** [absolutely]: **~ broke** völlig pleite - **3.** [refuse, deny] rundweg - **4.** [exactly]: **in five minutes ~** in ganzen fünf Minuten - **5.** [MUS - sing, play] zu tief ◇ *n* - **1.** *Br* [apartment] Wohnung *die* - **2.** [MUS - note] erniedrigter Ton; [-symbol] Erniedrigungszeichen *das* - **3.** *inf* [flat tyre] Platte *die*.

◆ **flat out** *adv* [work] auf Hochtouren.

**flat-chested** [-ˈtʃestɪd] *adj* flachbrüstig.

**flatfish** [ˈflætfɪʃ] (*pl inv*) *n* Plattfisch *der*.

**flat-footed** [-ˈfʊtɪd] *adj* plattfüßig.

**flatly** [ˈflætlɪ] *adv* - **1.** [refuse, deny] rundweg - **2.** [speak] monoton.

**flatmate** [ˈflætmeɪt] *n Br* Mitbewohner *der,* -in *die*.

**flat-packed** *adj* [furniture] zum Zusammenbauen.

**flat racing** *n* Flachrennen *das.*

**flat rate** *n* Pauschalpreis *der.*

**flatten** ['flætn] *vt* - **1.** [surface] glätten; [paper] glatt streichen; **to ~ o.s. against sthg** sich gegen etw drücken - **2.** [destroy] dem Erdboden gleich machen - **3.** *inf* [knock out] umhauen.
➡ **flatten out** *vi* eben(er) werden ⬦ *vt sep* [surface] glätten; [paper] glatt streichen.

**flatter** ['flætəʳ] *vt* schmeicheln (+ D); **to ~ o.s. on having/being sthg** sich einlbilden etw zu haben/sein.

**flatterer** ['flætərəʳ] *n* Schmeichler *der*, -in *die.*

**flattering** ['flætərɪŋ] *adj* schmeichelhaft.

**flattery** ['flætəri] *n* (U) Schmeicheleien *pl.*

**flatulence** ['flætjʊləns] *n* (U) Blähungen *pl.*

**flatware** ['flætweəʳ] *n* Am Besteck *das.*

**flaunt** [flɔːnt] *vt* zur Schau stellen.

**flautist** Br ['flɔːtɪst], **flutist** Am ['fluːtɪst] *n* Flötist *der*, -in *die.*

**flavour** Br, **flavor** Am ['fleɪvəʳ] *n* - **1.** [taste] Geschmack *der* - **2.** *fig* [atmosphere] Touch *der* ⬦ *vt* [food, drink] Geschmack verleihen (+ D).

**flavouring** Br, **flavoring** Am ['fleɪvərɪŋ] *n* Aroma *das.*

**flaw** [flɔː] *n* Fehler *der.*

**flawed** [flɔːd] *adj* fehlerhaft.

**flawless** ['flɔːlɪs] *adj* fehlerlos.

**flax** [flæks] *n* - **1.** [plant] Flachs *der* - **2.** [fibre] Flachsfaser *die.*

**flay** [fleɪ] *vt* [skin] ablziehen.

**flea** [fliː] *n* Floh *der;* **to send sb away with a ~ in his/her ear** jm eine Abfuhr erteilen.

**flea market** *n* Flohmarkt *der.*

**fleck** [flek] *n* Tupfen *der* ⬦ *vt:* **~ed (with)** besprenkelt (mit).

**fled** [fled] *pt & pp* ⬧ **flee.**

**fledg(e)ling** ['fledʒlɪŋ] *adj* [industry, democracy] jung ⬦ *n* Vogeljunge *das.*

**flee** [fliː] (*pt & pp* **fled**) *vt* [country] fliehen aus; [enemy] fliehen vor (+ D) ⬦ *vi* fliehen.

**fleece** [fliːs] *n* - **1.** [of sheep] Schaffell *das* - **2.** [material] Fleece *das;* [jacket] Fleecejacke *die* ⬦ *vt inf* [cheat] abzocken.

**fleet** [fliːt] *n* - **1.** [of ships] Flotte *die* - **2.** [of cars, buses] Fuhrpark *der.*

**fleeting** ['fliːtɪŋ] *adj* flüchtig; **a ~ visit** eine Stippvisite.

**Fleet Street** *n* früherer Stammsitz der britischen Presse.

**Fleming** ['flemɪŋ] *n* Flame *der*, Flämin *die.*

**Flemish** ['flemɪʃ] *adj* flämisch ⬦ *n* [language] Flämisch(e) *das* ⬦ *npl:* **the ~** die Flamen *pl.*

**flesh** [fleʃ] *n* Fleisch *das;* [of fruit] Fruchtfleisch *das;* [of vegetable] Mark *das;* **~ and blood** [family] Fleisch und Blut; **in the ~** leibhaftig.
➡ **flesh out** *vt sep* ausgestalten.

**flesh wound** *n* Fleischwunde *die.*

**fleshy** ['fleʃi] (*compar* **-ier;** *superl* **-iest**) *adj* [arms] fleischig; [cheeks, person] dick.

**flew** [fluː] *pt* ⬧ **fly.**

**flex** [fleks] *n* ELEC Kabel *das* ⬦ *vt* [arm, knee] beugen.

**flexibility** ['fleksə'bɪlətɪ] *n* - **1.** [of material, bar] Biegsamkeit *die* - **2.** [of person, system] Flexibilität *die.*

**flexible** ['fleksəbl] *adj* - **1.** [material, bar] biegsam - **2.** [person, system] flexibel.

**flexitime** ['fleksɪtaɪm] *n* Gleitzeit *die.*

**flick** [flɪk] *n* - **1.** [of whip] Schnalzen *das* - **2.** [with finger] Schnippen *das* ⬦ *vt* - **1.** [whip] schnalzen mit - **2.** [with finger] schnippen - **3.** [switch - turn on] anlknipsen; [ - turn off] auslknipsen.
➡ **flicks** *npl inf:* **the ~s** das Kino.
➡ **flick through** *vt fus* durchlblättern.

**flicker** ['flɪkəʳ] *n* [of light, candle] Flackern *das;* [of TV, screen] Flimmern *das;* **a ~ of hope** ein Hoffnungsschimmer ⬦ *vi* [light, candle] flackern; [TV, screen] flimmern; [shadow, eyelids] zucken.

**flick knife** *n* Br Klappmesser *das.*

**flier** ['flaɪəʳ] *n* - **1.** [pilot] Flieger *der*, -in *die* - **2.** [leaflet] Flugblatt *das.*

**flight** [flaɪt] *n* - **1.** [of plane, bird] Flug *der* - **2.:** **a ~ (of steps/stairs)** eine Treppe - **3.** [escape] Flucht *die.*

**flight attendant** *n* Flugbegleiter *der*, -in *die.*

**flight crew** *n* Flugbesatzung *die.*

**flight deck** *n* - **1.** [of aircraft carrier] Flugdeck *das* - **2.** [of aircraft] Cockpit *das.*

**flight path** *n* Flugbahn *die.*

**flight recorder** *n* Flugschreiber *der.*

**flighty** ['flaɪtɪ] (*compar* **-ier;** *superl* **-iest**) *adj* flatterhaft.

**flimsy** ['flɪmzɪ] (*compar* **-ier;** *superl* **-iest**) *adj* - **1.** [material, clothes, shoes] dünn; [paper] hauchdünn; [structure] nicht sehr stabil - **2.** [excuse] schwach; [argument] fadenscheinig.

**flinch** [flɪntʃ] *vi* zurücklzucken; **to ~ from sthg** *fig* vor etw zurücklschrecken.

**fling** [flɪŋ] (*pt & pp* **flung**) *n* [affair] Affäre *die* ⬦ *vt* [throw] schleudern; **to ~ o.s. into an armchair/onto the ground** sich in den Sessel/auf den Boden werfen.

**flint** [flɪnt] *n* Feuerstein *der.*

**flip** [flɪp] (*pt & pp* **-ped;** *cont* **-ping**) *vt* - **1.** [omelette, steak etc] wenden; **to ~ a coin** eine Münze werfen; **to ~ open** auflklappen; **to ~ over** umldrehen; **to ~ through** [magazine] durchlblättern - **2.** [switch - turn on] anlknipsen; [ - turn off] auslknipsen - **3.** [with finger] schnippen mit <> *vi inf* [become angry] auslflippen <> *n* - **1.** [of coin]: **it was decided on the ~ of a coin** wir haben eine Münze geworfen, um zu entscheiden - **2.** [somersault] Salto *der* - **3.** *phr:* at the ~ of a switch auf Knopfdruck.

**flipchart** [ˈflɪpˌtʃɑːt] *n* Flipchart *das.*

**flip-flops** *n Br* [shoes] Badelatschen *pl.*

**flippant** [ˈflɪpənt] *adj* leichtfertig.

**flippantly** [ˈflɪpəntlɪ] *adv* leichtfertig.

**flipper** [ˈflɪpəʳ] *n* - **1.** [of animal] Flosse *die* - **2.** [for swimmer, diver] Schwimmflosse *die.*

**flipping** [ˈflɪpɪŋ] *adj Br inf* verflixt.

**flip side** *n* [of record] B-Seite *die.*

**flirt** [flɜːt] *n:* **he's a terrible ~** er flirtet mit allen <> *vi* - **1.** [with person]: **to ~ (with)** flirten (mit) - **2.** [with idea]: **to ~ with sthg** mit etw liebäugeln.

**flirtation** [flɜːˈteɪʃn] *n* - **1.** *(U)* [flirting] Flirt *der* - **2.** [love affair] Affäre *die.*

**flirtatious** [flɜːˈteɪʃəs] *adj* kokett.

**flit** [flɪt] *(pt & pp* -**ted***; cont* -**ting***) vi* [bird] flattern; **a look of surprise ~ted across her face** ein Ausdruck der Überraschung huschte über ihr Gesicht.

**float** [fləʊt] *n* - **1.** [for fishing] Schwimmer *der;* [for swimming] Schwimmbrett *das* - **2.** [in procession] Festwagen *der* - **3.** [money] Wechselgeld *das* - **4.** [drink] *alkoholfreies Getränk mit einer Kugel Speiseeis* <> *vt* - **1.** [on water - logs] flößen; [ - boat] zu Wasser lassen - **2.** [idea, project] zur Debatte stellen <> *vi* - **1.** [on water - not sink] schwimmen; [ - move] treiben - **2.** [through air] schweben.

**floating** [ˈfləʊtɪŋ] *adj* [on water - restaurant, hotel] schwimmend; [ - log] treibend.

**floating voter** *n Br* Wechselwähler *der,* -in *die.*

**flock** [flɒk] *n* [of birds] Schwarm *der;* [of sheep] Herde *die;* [of people] Schar *die* <> *vi:* **to ~ to** strömen zu *or* nach.

**floe** [fləʊ] *n* Eisscholle *die.*

**flog** [flɒg] *(pt & pp* -**ged***; cont* -**ging***) vt* - **1.** [whip] auslpeitschen - **2.** *Br inf* [sell] verkloppen.

**flood** [flʌd] *n* Flut *die* <> *vt* - **1.** [gen] überschwemmen; [kitchen] unter Wasser setzen; **to ~ the market** den Markt überschwemmen - **2.** [with light] durchfluten - **3.** *AUT* [engine] ablwürgen <> *vi* - **1.** [river] über die Ufer treten - **2.** [street, land] überschwemmt werden - **3.** *fig:* **to ~ in** hereinlströmen; **to ~ back** [memories, feelings] unvermittelt mit großer Stärke zurücklkommen.

➤ **floods** *npl* [from river, rain] Überschwemmung *die;* **to be in ~s of tears** in Tränen aufgelöst sein.

**floodgates** [ˈflʌdgeɪts] *npl:* **to open the ~ (to sthg)** *fig* (einer Sache *(D)*) Tür und Tor öffnen.

**flooding** [ˈflʌdɪŋ] *n* Überschwemmung *die.*

**floodlight** [ˈflʌdlaɪt] *n* Scheinwerfer *der.*

**floodlit** [ˈflʌdlɪt] *adj* [stadium] mit Flutlicht beleuchtet; [building] angestrahlt.

**flood tide** *n* Flut *die.*

**floor** *n* - **1.** [of room] Fußboden *der* - **2.** [of valley, sea] Boden *der* - **3.** [storey] Stock *der* - **4.** [at meeting, debate] Publikum *das* - **5.** [for dancing] Tanzfläche *die* - **6.** [of stock exchange] Parkett *das* <> *vt* - **1.** [knock down] zu Boden schlagen - **2.** [subj: comment, question]: **to ~ sb** jm die Sprache verschlagen.

**floorboard** [ˈflɔːbɔːd] *n* Diele *die.*

**floor cloth** *n Br* Scheuertuch *das.*

**floor lamp** *n Am* Stehlampe *die.*

**floorwalker** [ˈflɔːˌwɔːkəʳ] *n* Ladenaufsicht *die.*

**floozy** [ˈfluːzɪ] *(pl* -**ies***) n dated & pej* Flittchen *das.*

**flop** [flɒp] *(pt & pp* -**ped***; cont* -**ping***) inf n* [failure] Flop *der* <> *vi* - **1.** [fail] ein Flop sein - **2.** [into chair, onto bed] sich fallen lassen.

**floppy** [ˈflɒpɪ] *(compar* -**ier***; superl* -**iest***) adj* schlaff herunterhängend.

**floppy (disk)** *n* Diskette *die.*

**flora** [ˈflɔːrə] *n* Flora *die;* **~ and fauna** Flora und Fauna.

**floral** [ˈflɔːrəl] *adj* - **1.** [arrangement, tribute] Blumen- - **2.** [pattern, material] geblümt.

**Florence** [ˈflɒrəns] *n* Florenz *nt.*

**Florentine** [ˈflɒrəntaɪn] *adj* florentinisch.

**floret** [ˈflɒrɪt] *n* [of cauliflower, broccoli] Röschen *das.*

**florid** [ˈflɒrɪd] *adj* - **1.** [face, complexion] gerötet - **2.** [style] blumig.

**florist** [ˈflɒrɪst] *n* Florist *der,* -in *die;* **~'s (shop)** Blumengeschäft *das.*

**floss** [flɒs] *n* [dental floss] Zahnseide *die* <> *vt* [teeth] mit Zahnseide reinigen.

**flotation** [fləʊˈteɪʃn] *n ST EX:* **since the ~ of the company** seit die Firma an der Börse notiert ist.

**flotilla** [fləˈtɪlə] *n* Flotille *die.*

**flotsam** [ˈflɒtsəm] *n:* **~ and jetsam** Treibgut und Strandgut.

**flounce** [flaʊns] *n* [in cloth] Rüsche *die* <> *vi* [move] stolzieren.

**flounder** [ˈflaʊndəʳ] *(pl inv or* -**s***) n* [fish] Flunder *die* <> *vi* - **1.** [in water] sich ablstrampeln; **to ~ in the mud** sich durch den Schlamm quälen - **2.** [in conversation, speech] ins Schwimmen kommen.

**flour** [ˈflaʊəʳ] *n* Mehl *das.*

**flourish** [ˈflʌrɪʃ] *vi* - **1.** [plant, flower] prächtig gedeihen **- 2.** [company, business] florieren; [music etc] eine Blütezeit erleben ⬦ vt schwenken ⬦ n: **to do sthg with a ~** etw mit einer schwungvollen Bewegung tun.

**flourishing** ['flʌrɪʃɪŋ] adj **- 1.** [plant] prächtig gedeihend **- 2.** [company, sector] florierend.

**flout** [flaʊt] vt missachten.

**flow** [fləʊ] n **- 1.** [river, of liquid] Fluss der; [of words] Redefluss der; **~ of lava/people** Lava-/Menschenstrom der; **~ of information/traffic** Informations-/Verkehrsfluss **- 2.** [of tide] Flut die ⬦ vi **- 1.** [gen] fließen; [air, people] strömen **- 2.** [tide] steigen **- 3.** [hair, dress] wallen **- 4.** [result]: **to ~ from sthg** aus etw folgen.

**flowchart** [fləʊtʃɑːt], **flow diagram** n Flussdiagramm das.

**flower** ['flaʊəʳ] n [plant] Blume die; [blossom] Blüte die; **in ~** in Blüte ⬦ comp Blumen- ⬦ vi blühen; fig [music etc] eine Blütezeit erleben.

**flowerbed** ['flaʊəbed] n Blumenbeet das.

**flowering** ['flaʊərɪŋ] adj [plant] Blüten-; [shrub] Zier- ⬦ n fig [of artistic movement, talents] Blütezeit die.

**flowerpot** ['flaʊəpɒt] n Blumentopf der.

**flowery** ['flaʊərɪ] (compar **-ier;** superl **-iest**) adj **- 1.** [dress, material] geblümt **- 2.** pej [language] blumig **- 3.** [perfume] süß.

**flowing** ['fləʊɪŋ] adj fig [writing, style] flüssig; [hair, robe] wallend.

**flown** [fləʊn] pp ⬦ **fly.**

**fl. oz.** abbr of **fluid ounce** = 28,41 cm³.

**flu** [fluː] n (U) Grippe die; **to have ~** (eine OR die) Grippe haben.

**fluctuate** ['flʌktʃʊeɪt] vi schwanken.

**fluctuation** [ˌflʌktʃʊ'eɪʃn] n Schwankung die.

**flue** [fluː] n Rauchfang der.

**fluency** ['fluːənsɪ] n **- 1.** [in a foreign language] Gewandtheit die **- 2.** [in speaking, writing] Flüssigkeit die.

**fluent** ['fluːənt] adj **- 1.** [in a foreign language] fließend; **to be ~ in German** fließend Deutsch sprechen **- 2.** [writing] flüssig; [speaker] gewandt.

**fluently** ['fluːəntlɪ] adv **- 1.** [speak a foreign language] fließend **- 2.** [speak, write, read] flüssig.

**fluff** [flʌf] n (U) **- 1.** [down] Flaum der **- 2.** [on clothes] Fussel die ⬦ vt **- 1.** [cushion]: **to ~ sthg (up)** etw auf schütteln **- 2.** inf [do badly] vermasseln.

**fluffy** ['flʌfɪ] (compar **-ier;** superl **-iest**) adj [animal] flaumweich; [jumper] flauschig.

**fluid** ['fluːɪd] n Flüssigkeit die ⬦ adj **- 1.** [movement] fließend; [style] flüssig **- 2.** [situation] Veränderungen unterworfen.

**fluid ounce** n = 28,41 cm³.

**fluke** [fluːk] n inf [chance]: **it was a ~** das war reiner Dusel.

**flummox** ['flʌməks] vt esp Br inf durcheinander bringen.

**flung** [flʌŋ] pt & pp ⬦ **fling.**

**flunk** [flʌŋk] Am inf vt [SCH & UNIV - exam, test] fallen durch; [ - student] durchfallen lassen ⬦ vi durch fallen.

**fluorescent** [flʊə'resənt] adj fluoreszierend.

**fluorescent light** n Neonlampe die.

**fluoridate** ['flʊərɪdeɪt] vt mit Fluor versetzen.

**fluoride** ['flʊəraɪd] n Fluorid das.

**fluorine** ['flʊəriːn] n Fluor das.

**flurry** ['flʌrɪ] (pl **-ies**) n [of rain] Guss der; [of snow] Gestöber das; [of wind] Stoß der; **there was a ~ of activity** es herrschte rege Betriebsamkeit.

**flush** [flʌʃ] adj **- 1.** [level]: **to be ~ with sthg** bündig mit etw abschließen **- 2.** inf [rich]: **to be ~** gut bei Kasse sein ⬦ n **- 1.** [in toilet] Spülung die **- 2.** [blush] Röte die **- 3.** [of anger] Aufwallung die; **in the first ~ of youth** literary in der ersten Blüte der Jugend ⬦ vt **- 1.** [with water]: **to ~ the toilet** spülen; **to ~ sthg down the toilet** etw die Toilette hinunter spülen **- 2.** fig [force out of hiding]: **to ~ sb out** jn auf stöbern ⬦ vi **- 1.** [toilet] spülen **- 2.** [blush] erröten.

**flushed** [flʌʃt] adj **- 1.** [face] gerötet **- 2.** [excited]: **to be ~ with sthg** über etw (A) aufgeregt und glücklich sein.

**fluster** ['flʌstəʳ] n: **to be in a ~** konfus sein ⬦ vt konfus machen.

**flustered** ['flʌstəd] adj konfus.

**flute** [fluːt] n MUS Querflöte die.

**fluted** ['fluːtɪd] adj [column] kanneliert.

**flutist** n Am = **flautist.**

**flutter** ['flʌtəʳ] n **- 1.** [of wings, heart] Flattern das **- 2.** inf: **in a ~ (of excitement)** in großer Aufregung ⬦ vt [wings] flattern mit; [eyelashes] klimpern mit ⬦ vi flattern.

**flux** [flʌks] n: **to be in a state of ~** im Fluss sein.

**fly** [flaɪ] (pl **flies;** pt **flew;** pp **flown**) n **- 1.** [insect] Fliege die; **the ~ in the ointment was that ...** fig der Haken an der Sache war, dass ... **- 2.** [of trousers] Hosenschlitz der ⬦ vt **- 1.** [plane] fliegen; [kite] steigen lassen; [model aircraft] fliegen lassen; [passengers, goods] fliegen; [airline] fliegen mit **- 2.** [flag] gehisst haben ⬦ vi **- 1.** [gen] fliegen; **the days flew by** OR **past** die Tage sind schnell verflogen; **time flies** die Zeit verfliegt **- 2.** [attack]: **to ~ at sb** auf jn losl gehen **- 3.** [flag] wehen.

➤ **fly away** vi weg fliegen.

➤ **fly in** vt sep [troops, supplies] ein fliegen ⬦ vi an kommen; [person] mit dem Flugzeug an kommen.

**fly into** *vt fus:* **to ~ into a rage** einen Wutanfall bekommen.

**fly out** *vt sep* [troops, supplies] auslfliegen ◇ *vi* fliegen.

**flyby** ['flaɪˌbaɪ] *n Am* = flypast.

**fly-drive** *n* Fly-drive-Urlaub *der.*

**fly-fishing** *n* Fliegenfischen *das.*

**fly half** *n Br* Halbspieler *der.*

**flying** ['flaɪɪŋ] *adj* [animal] Flug-; **~ leap** großer Sprung ◇ *n* Fliegen *das.*

**flying colours** *npl:* **to pass (sthg) with ~** (etw) glänzend bestehen.

**flying doctor** *n* ein Arzt (vor allem in Australien), der seine Patienten per Flugzeug besucht.

**flying officer** *n Br* Oberleutnant *der.*

**flying picket** *n* mobiler Streikposten.

**flying saucer** *n* fliegende Untertasse.

**flying squad** *n Br* Bereitschaftsdienst *der.*

**flying start** *n:* **to get off to a ~** einen glänzenden Start haben.

**flying visit** *n* Stippvisite *die.*

**flyleaf** ['flaɪliːf] *(pl* **-leaves)** *n* Vorsatzblatt *das.*

**flyover** ['flaɪˌəʊvə'] *n Br* Überführung *die.*

**flypast** *Br* ['flaɪˌpɑːst], **flyby** *Am n* Luftparade *die.*

**flysheet** ['flaɪʃiːt] *n* Überzelt *das.*

**flyweight** ['flaɪweɪt] *n* Fliegengewicht *das.*

**flywheel** ['flaɪwiːl] *n* Schwungrad *das.*

**FM - 1.** *(abbr of* **frequency modulation)** UKW **- 2.** *abbr of* **field marshal.**

**FO** *n abbr of* **Foreign Office.**

**foal** [fəʊl] *n* Fohlen *das.*

**foam** [fəʊm] *n* **- 1.** [bubbles] Schaum *der* **- 2.** [material]: **~ (rubber)** Schaumgummi *der* ◇ *vi* schäumen.

**foamy** ['fəʊmɪ] *(compar* **-ier;** *superl* **-iest)** *adj* [drink, sea] schäumend.

**fob** [fɒb] *(pt & pp* **-bed;** *cont* **-bing)** **fob off** *vt sep:* **to ~ sthg off on sb** jm etw anldrehen; **to ~ sb off with sthg** jn mit etw ablspeisen.

**fob watch** *n* Taschenuhr *die.*

**foc** *(abbr of* **free of charge)** gebührenfrei.

**focal point** ['fəʊkl-] *n fig* Mittelpunkt *der.*

**focus** ['fəʊkəs] *(pl* **-cuses** OR **-ci** [-kaɪ]) *n* **- 1.** PHOT Fokus *der;* [of rays] Brennpunkt *der;* [of discussion] Mittelpunkt *der;* **in ~** [image] scharf; **out of ~** [image] unscharf **- 2.: to be the ~ of attention** im Mittelpunkt der Aufmerksamkeit stehen ◇ *vt* **- 1.** [lens, camera]: **to ~ sthg (on)** etw einlstellen (auf (+ A)) **- 2.** [mentally]: **to ~ one's attention on sb/sthg** seine Aufmerksamkeit auf jn/etw richten ◇ *vi:* **to ~ on** [with eyes] den Blick richten auf (+ A); [with camera] mit der Kamera scharf stellen auf (+ A); *fig* [mentally] konzentrieren auf (+ A).

**focused, focussed** ['fəʊkəst] *adj* [mentally] konzentriert; **to stay ~** bei der Sache bleiben.

**fodder** ['fɒdə'] *n* Futter *das.*

**foe** [fəʊ] *n literary* Feind *der.*

**foetal** ['fiːtl] *adj* fötal.

**foetus** ['fiːtəs] *n* Fötus *der.*

**fog** [fɒg] *n* Nebel *der.*

**fogbound** ['fɒgbaʊnd] *adj* durch Nebel behindert.

**fogey** ['fəʊgɪ] *n* = fogy.

**foggiest** ['fɒgɪəst] *n inf:* **I haven't the ~** ich habe keinen blassen Dunst.

**foggy** ['fɒgɪ] *(compar* **-ier;** *superl* **-iest)** *adj* neblig.

**foghorn** ['fɒghɔːn] *n* Nebelhorn *das.*

**fog lamp** *n* Nebelscheinwerfer *der.*

**fogy** ['fəʊgɪ] *(pl* **-ies)** *n inf:* **old ~** alter Spießer.

**foible** ['fɔɪbl] *n* Eigenheit *die.*

**foil** [fɔɪl] *n (U)* [material] Folie *die* ◇ *vt* [criminal] einen Strich durch die Rechnung machen (+ D); [plot, plan] vereiteln.

**foist** [fɔɪst] *vt:* **to ~ sthg on sb** [goods] jm etw anldrehen; [responsibility, work] etw auf jn ablwälzen.

**fold** [fəʊld] *vt* **- 1.** [sheet, blanket, paper] falten; **to ~ one's arms** die Arme verschränken **- 2.** [wrap] einlwickeln; **he ~ed her in his arms** er schloss sie in die Arme ◇ *vi* **- 1.** [bed, chair, bicycle] sich zusammenklappen lassen **- 2.** *inf* [business] einlgehen ◇ *n* **- 1.** [in material, paper] Falte *die* **- 2.** [for animals] Pferch *der;* **to return to the ~** *fig* in den Schoß der Gemeinde zurücklkehren.

**fold up** *vt sep* **- 1.** [sheet, blanket, paper] zusammenlfalten **- 2.** [chair, bed, bicycle] zusammenlklappen ◇ *vi* **- 1.** [sheet, blanket, paper] sich zusammenfalten lassen **- 2.** [chair, bed, bicycle] sich zusammenklappen lassen.

**foldaway** ['fəʊldəˌweɪ] *adj* Klapp-, zusammenklappbar.

**folder** ['fəʊldə'] *n* **- 1.** [for papers] Mappe *die* **- 2.** COMPUT Ordner *der.*

**folding** ['fəʊldɪŋ] *adj* [chair, table] Klapp-.

**foliage** ['fəʊlɪɪdʒ] *n (U)* Blätter *pl.*

**folk** [fəʊk] *adj* Volks- ◇ *n* [music - popular] Folk *der;* [ - traditional] Volksmusik *die* ◇ *npl* [people] Leute *pl.*

**folks** *npl inf* **- 1.** [relatives]: **my ~s** meine Leute **- 2.** [everyone]: **hi ~s!** hi Leute!

**folklore** ['fəʊklɔː'] *n* Folklore *die.*

**folk music** *n* [popular] Folk *der;* [traditional] Volksmusik *die.*

**folk singer** *n* Folksänger *der,* **-in** *die.*

**folk song** n [popular] Folksong der; [traditional] Volkslied das.

**folksy** ['fəʊksɪ] (compar **-ier;** superl **-iest**) adj Am inf gemütlich.

**follicle** ['fɒlɪkl] n Follikel das.

**follow** ['fɒləʊ] vt **- 1.** [gen] folgen (+ D); **a presentation, ~ed by a discussion** ein Vortrag, gefolgt von einer Diskussion **- 2.** [pursue] verfolgen **- 3.** [advice, instructions] befolgen **- 4.** [news, sb's career] verfolgen; [fashion] sich interessieren für <> vi folgen; **as ~s** wie folgt; **it ~s that ...** daraus folgt, dass ...; **I don't quite ~** [understand] da komm ich nicht ganz mit.

➤ **follow up** vt sep **- 1.** [complaint] nachlgehen (+ D); [suggestion] auf lgreifen **- 2.** [supplement]: **to ~ sthg up with sthg** etw auf etw (A) folgen lassen.

**follower** ['fɒləʊəʳ] n [disciple, believer] Anhänger der, -in die.

**following** ['fɒləʊɪŋ] adj folgend; **the ~ day** am nächsten Tag <> n [supporters] Anhängerschaft die <> prep [after] nach.

**follow-up** adj: **a ~ visit** ein zweiter Besuch <> n [to programme] Fortsetzung die; [to treatment] Nachuntersuchung die.

**folly** ['fɒlɪ] n [foolishness] Torheit die.

**foment** [fəʊ'ment] vt fml schüren.

**fond** [fɒnd] adj **- 1.** [affectionate] liebevoll; **to be ~ of sthg** gerne haben; **they're ~ of each other** sie haben sich gern; **to be ~ of sthg/of doing sthg** etw gerne haben/tun **- 2.** fml [hope, wish] kühn.

**fondle** ['fɒndl] vt streicheln.

**fondly** ['fɒndlɪ] adv **- 1.** [affectionately] liebevoll; [remember] gern(e) **- 2.** [naively] unrealistischerweise.

**fondness** ['fɒndnɪs] n: **~ (for)** Schwäche die (für).

**fondue** ['fɒnduː] n CULIN Fondue das.

**font** [fɒnt] n **- 1.** [in church] Taufstein der **- 2.** COMPUT & TYPO Schrift die.

**food** [fuːd] n Essen das; [for animals] Futter das; **health ~s** Reformkost die; **~ for thought** Stoff der zum Nachdenken.

**food chain** n Nahrungskette die.

**food poisoning** [-,pɔɪznɪŋ] n Lebensmittelvergiftung die.

**food processor** [-,prəʊsesəʳ] n Küchenmaschine die.

**food stamp** n Am Lebensmittelgutschein, den die US-Regierung an Arme ausgibt.

**foodstuffs** ['fuːdstʌfs] npl Nahrungsmittel pl.

**fool** [fuːl] n **- 1.** [idiot] Narr der, Trottel der; **to make a ~ of sb** jn zum Narren machen; **to make a ~ of o.s.** sich zum Narren machen; **to act** OR **play the ~** herumlalbern **- 2.** Br [dessert] Cremespeise aus Sahne und Obst <> vt täuschen; **to ~ sb into doing sthg** jn durch Tricks dazu bringen, etw zu tun.

➤ **fool about, fool around** vi **- 1.** [behave foolishly]: **to ~ about (with sthg)** (mit etw) herumlalbern **- 2.** [be unfaithful]: **to ~ about (with sb)** (mit jm) eine Affäre haben **- 3.** Am [tamper]: **to ~ around with sthg** mit etw Blödsinn machen.

**foolhardy** ['fuːl,hɑːdɪ] adj tollkühn.

**foolish** ['fuːlɪʃ] adj **- 1.** [unwise, silly] töricht **- 2.** [laughable, undignified] dumm; **to look ~** albern auslsehen; **to feel ~** sich (D) albern vorlkommen.

**foolishly** ['fuːlɪʃlɪ] adv **- 1.** [behave] töricht **- 2.** [laugh, smile] blöd.

**foolishness** ['fuːlɪʃnɪs] n Dummheit die.

**foolproof** ['fuːlpruːf] adj absolut sicher.

**foolscap** ['fuːlzkæp] n britisches Papierformat, 33cm x 20cm.

**foot** [fʊt] (pl sense 1 **feet;** pl sense 2 inv OR **feet**) n **- 1.** [gen] Fuß der; [of sheep, cow] Huf der; [of bed] Fußende das; [of page] Ende das; **to be on one's feet** auf den Beinen sein; **to get to one's feet** auf lstehen; **on** OR **by ~** zu Fuß; **it's wet under ~** der Boden ist nass; **to be back on one's feet** wieder auf den Beinen sein; **to find one's feet** Fuß fassen; **to have/get cold feet** kalte Füße bekommen; **to have itchy feet** weg wollen; **to put one's ~ down** [insist] ein Machtwort sprechen; AUT aufs Gas treten; **to put one's ~ in it** ins Fettnäpfchen treten; **to put one's feet up** die Beine hochllegen; **to be rushed off one's feet** dauernd auf Trab sein; **to set ~ in sthg** etw betreten; **to stand on one's own two feet** auf eigenen Füßen stehen **- 2.** [measurement] Fuß der, = 30,48 cm <> vt inf: **to ~ the bill (for sthg)** die Rechnung (für etw) bezahlen.

**foot-and-mouth (disease)** n Maul- und Klauenseuche die.

**football** ['fʊtbɔːl] n **- 1.** Br [soccer] Fußball der **- 2.** Am [American football] Football der **- 3.** [ball - in soccer] Fußball der; [ - in American football] Ball der.

**football club** n Br Fußballmannschaft die.

**footballer** ['fʊtbɔːləʳ] n Br Fußballspieler der, -in die.

**football game** n Am [American football] Footballspiel das.

**football ground** n Br Fußballplatz der.

**football match** n Br Fußballspiel das.

**football player** n Fußballspieler der, -in die.

**football pools** npl Br Fußballtoto das.

**football supporter** n Fußballfan der.

**footbrake** ['fʊtbreɪk] n Fußbremse die.

**footbridge** ['fʊtbrɪdʒ] n Fußgängerbrücke die.

**footer** ['fʊtəʳ] n COMPUT Fußzeile die.

**F**

**foot fault** *n* TENNIS Fußfehler *der.*

**foothills** ['fʊthɪlz] *npl* Gebirgsausläufer *pl.*

**foothold** ['fʊthəʊld] *n* Halt *der;* **to get a ~** [on mountain, rockface] mit den Füßen Halt gewinnen; [in organization, company] Fuß fassen.

**footing** ['fʊtɪŋ] *n* - **1.** [foothold] Halt *der;* **to lose one's ~** den Halt verlieren - **2.** [basis] Basis *die;* **to be on an equal ~ (with sb)** (jm) gleichgestellt sein; **to be on a war ~** auf einen Krieg vorbereitet sein.

**footlights** ['fʊtlaɪts] *npl* Rampenlicht *das.*

**footman** ['fʊtmən] (*pl* -men [-mən]) *n* Lakai *der.*

**footmark** ['fʊtmɑːk] *n* Fußabdruck *der.*

**footmen** *pl* ⊏> **footman.**

**footnote** ['fʊtnəʊt] *n* Fußnote *die.*

**footpath** ['fʊtpɑːθ, *pl* -pɑːðz] *n* Fußweg *der.*

**footprint** ['fʊtprɪnt] *n* Fußabdruck *der.*

**Footsie** ['fʊtsɪ] *n Br inf* Footsie *der, britischer Aktienindex der 100 bedeutendsten britischen Firmen.*

**footsore** ['fʊtsɔːʳ] *adj* mit wunden Füßen.

**footstep** ['fʊtstep] *n* - **1.** [sound] Schritt *der* - **2.** [footprint] Fußabdruck *der;* **to follow in sb's ~s** in js Fußstapfen treten.

**footwear** ['fʊtweəʳ] *n* Schuhwerk *das.*

**footwork** ['fʊtwɜːk] *n* SPORT Beinarbeit *die.*

**for** [fɔːʳ] *prep* - **1.** [expressing purpose, reason, destination] für; **this is ~ you** dieses Buch ist für dich; **a ticket ~ Manchester** eine Fahrkarte nach Manchester; **~ this reason** aus diesem Grund; **a cure ~ sore throats** ein Mittel gegen Halsschmerzen; **what did you do that ~?** wozu OR warum hast du das getan?; **to jump ~ joy** vor Freude an die Decke springen; **~ fear of failing** aus Angst, zu versagen; **what's it ~?** wofür ist das?; **to go ~ a walk** spazieren gehen; **it's time ~ bed** es ist Zeit schlafen OR ins Bett zu gehen; **'~ sale'** 'zu verkaufen' - **2.** [during] seit; **I've lived here ~ ten years** ich lebe seit zehn Jahren hier; **we talked ~ hours** wir redeten stundenlang - **3.** [by, before] für; **be there ~ 8 p.m.** sei um acht Uhr abends da; **I'll do it ~ tomorrow** ich mache es bis morgen; **be there at 7.30 ~ 8 o'clock** versucht um 19.30 Uhr da zu sein, damit wir um 20.00 Uhr anfangen können - **4.** [on the occasion of] **I got socks ~ Christmas** ich habe Socken zu Weihnachten bekommen; **what's ~ dinner?** was gibt's zum Abendessen? - **5.** [on behalf of] für; **to do sthg ~ for sb** etw für jn tun; **the MP ~ Barnsley** der Parlamentsabgeordnete für Barnsley - **6.** [with time and space] für; **there's no room ~ it** dafür ist kein Platz; **to have time ~ sthg** für etw Zeit haben - **7.** [expressing distance]: **we drove ~ miles** wir fuhren meilenweit; **road works ~ 20 miles** Straßenarbeiten auf 20 Meilen - **8.** [express-

ing price] für; **I bought it ~ five pounds** ich habe es für fünf Pfund gekauft; **~ free** gratis - **9.** [expressing meaning]: **what's the German ~ "boy"?** wie heißt „boy" auf Deutsch?; **P ~ Peter** P wie Peter - **10.** [with regard to] für; **it's warm ~ November** es ist warm für November; **it's too far ~ him to walk** zum Gehen ist es für ihn zu weit; **it's not ~ me to say** ich kann dazu nichts sagen; **it's all very well ~ him** er hat gut reden; **to feel sorry ~ sb** jn bemitleiden; **to be glad ~ sb** sich für jn freuen - **11.** [in favour of] für; **is she ~ or against it?** ist sie dafür oder dagegen?; **to vote ~ sthg** für etw stimmen; **I'm all ~ doing it** ich bin sehr dafür, dass wir das tun - **12.** [in ratios] für; **~ every person who passes the test there are five who fail** auf jede Person, die die Prüfung besteht, kommen fünf, die durchfallen - **13.** *phr:* **you'll be ~ it when ...** du kannst dich auf etwas gefasst machen, wenn ... ◇ *conj literary* denn.

◂ **for all** *prep* - **1.** [in spite of] trotz; **~ all that** trotzdem - **2.** [considering how little]: **~ all the good it's done me** so wenig, wie es mir genützt hat ◇ *conj:* **~ all he promised to do it, he never actually did** trotz all seiner Versprechen hat er es dann doch nie getan; **~ all I care** meinetwegen, von mir aus; **~ all I know** so viel ich weiß.

**forage** ['fɒrɪdʒ] *vi* [search] herumstöbern; **to ~ for sthg** nach etw stöbern.

**foray** ['fɒreɪ] *n* (Raub)überfall *der;* **to make a ~ into politics/publishing** *fig* einen Ausflug in die Politik/das Verlagswesen machen.

**forbad** [fə'bæd], **forbade** [fə'beɪd] *pt* ⊏> **forbid.**

**forbearing** [fɔː'beərɪŋ] *adj* nachsichtig.

**forbid** [fə'bɪd] (*pt* -**bade** OR -**bad**; *pp* **forbid** OR -**bidden**; *cont* -**bidding**) *vt* verbieten; **to ~ sb to do sthg** jm verbieten, etw zu tun; **God** OR **Heaven ~!** Gott bewahre!, der Himmel bewahre!

**forbidden** [fə'bɪdn] *pp* ⊏> **forbid** ◇ *adj* [activity] verboten; **~ subject** Tabuthema *das.*

**forbidding** [fə'bɪdɪŋ] *adj* [person] abweisend; [landscape] unwirtlich.

**force** [fɔːs] *n* - **1.** [strength, magnitude] Stärke *die;* [of explosion, blow] Wucht *die;* **a ~ ten gale** ein Sturm mit Windstärke zehn - **2.** [violence] Gewalt *die;* **by ~** mit Gewalt - **3.** PHYSICS Kraft *die* - **4.** [powerful person, influence] Macht *die;* **by ~ of habit** aus Gewohnheit - **5.** [group]: **armed ~s** Streitkräfte *pl;* **the police ~** die Polizei; **sales ~** Verkaufspersonal *das;* **security ~s** Sicherheitskräfte *pl;* **in ~** [arrive] in großer Anzahl - **6.** [effect]: **to be in/come into ~** in Kraft sein/treten ◇ *vt* - **1.** [compel] zwingen; **to ~ sb to do sthg** jn zwingen, etw zu tun; **to ~ sthg on sb** jm etw auf lzwingen; **to ~ o.s.** sich zwingen; **go on, ~ yourself!** mach schon! - **2.** [lock, door] auf lbrechen - **3.** [push] pressen; **to ~ sthg open** etw auf lbrechen; **to ~ one's way through/into** sich gewaltsam einen Weg bahnen durch/in (+ A) - **4.: to ~ a smile** sich zu einem Lächeln zwingen.

➤ **forces** npl: **the ~s** die Streitkräfte pl; **to join ~s (with sb)** sich (mit jm) zusammenltun.

➤ **by force of** prep mittels (+ G).

➤ **force back** vt sep - **1.** [crowd] zurücklldrängen - **2.** [emotion, tears] unterdrücken.

➤ **force down** vt sep - **1.** [food] hinunterllzwingen - **2.** [aeroplane] zur Landung zwingen.

**forced** [fɔːst] adj - **1.** [labour] Zwangs-; [march] Gewalt- - **2.** [smile, conversation] gezwungen.

**forced landing** n Notlandung die.

**force-feed** vt zwangsernähren.

**forceful** [ˈfɔːsfʊl] adj [person] energisch; [words] eindringlich; [speech] überzeugend.

**forcemeat** [ˈfɔːsmiːt] n esp Br Fleischfüllung die.

**forceps** [ˈfɔːseps] npl Zange die.

**forcible** [ˈfɔːsəbl] adj - **1.** [entry] gewaltsam - **2.** [example, argument] überzeugend.

**forcibly** [ˈfɔːsəblɪ] adv - **1.** [seize, enter, remove] gewaltsam - **2.** [argue, express] überzeugend.

**ford** [fɔːd] n Furt die ⟨⟩ vt (an einer Furt) durchqueren.

**fore** [fɔːr] adj NAUT vordere, -r, -s; **~ deck** Vordeck das ⟨⟩ n: **to come to the ~** fig [become well-known] bekannt werden; [become important] bedeutend werden.

**forearm** [ˈfɔːrɑːm] n Unterarm der.

**forebear** n fml Ahne der, -nin die.

**foreboding** [fɔːˈbəʊdɪŋ] n Vorahnung die; **to view sthg with ~** etw (D) mit einem unguten Gefühl entgegenlsehen.

**forecast** [ˈfɔːkɑːst] (pt & pp forecast OR -ed) n Prognose die; **(weather) ~** (Wetter)vorhersage die ⟨⟩ vt vorherlsagen.

**forecaster** [ˈfɔːkɑːstər] n Prognostiker der, -in die; [of weather] Meteorologe der, -gin die.

**foreclose** [fɔːˈkləʊz] vt & vi: **to ~ (on) a mortgage** eine (durch eine Hypothek gesicherte) Schuldforderung geltend machen.

**foreclosure** [fɔːˈkləʊʒər] n Zwangsvollstreckung die.

**forecourt** [ˈfɔːkɔːt] n Vorhof der.

**forefathers** [ˈfɔːˌfɑːðəz] npl Vorväter pl.

**forefinger** [ˈfɔːˌfɪŋgər] n Zeigefinger der.

**forefront** [ˈfɔːfrʌnt] n: **to be in** OR **at the ~ of sthg** [campaign, movement] an der Spitze einer Sache (G) stehen; **to be in** OR **at the ~ of his mind** im Zentrum seiner Aufmerksamkeit stehen.

**forego** [fɔːˈgəʊ] vt = forgo.

**foregoing** [fɔːˈgəʊɪŋ] adj vorhergehend ⟨⟩ n fml: **the ~** das Vorhergehende.

**foregone conclusion** [ˈfɔːgɒn-] n: **it's a ~** es stand von vornherein fest.

**foreground** [ˈfɔːgraʊnd] n Vordergrund der; **in the ~** im Vordergrund.

**forehand** [ˈfɔːhænd] n Vorhand die.

**forehead** [ˈfɔːhed] n Stirn die.

**foreign** [ˈfɒrən] adj - **1.** [gen] ausländisch; **~ person** Ausländer der, -in die; **~ holiday** Urlaub der im Ausland; **~ country** fremdes Land; **~ countries** das Ausland; **she must be ~** sie muss Ausländerin sein; [correspondent, debt] Auslands-; [policy] Außen- - **2.** [alien]: **~ matter/object** Fremdkörper der; **it is ~ to her nature** es ist ihrem Wesen fremd.

**foreign affairs** npl Außenpolitik die.

**foreign aid** n (U) Entwicklungshilfe die.

**foreign body** n Fremdkörper der.

**foreign currency** n (U) Devisen pl.

**foreigner** [ˈfɒrənər] n Ausländer der, -in die.

**foreign exchange** n (U) Devisen pl; **~ market** Devisenmarkt der.

**foreign language** n Fremdsprache die.

**foreign minister** n Außenminister der, -in die.

**Foreign Office** n Br: **the ~** das Außenministerium.

**Foreign Secretary** n Br Außenminister der, -in die.

**foreleg** [ˈfɔːleg] n Vorderbein das.

**foreman** [ˈfɔːmən] (pl -men [-mən]) n - **1.** [of workers] Vorarbeiter der - **2.** [of jury] Obmann der, -männin die.

**foremost** [ˈfɔːməʊst] adj führend ⟨⟩ adv: **first and ~** vor allem.

**forename** [ˈfɔːneɪm] n Vorname der.

**forensic** [fəˈrensɪk] adj [examination] gerichtsmedizinisch.

**forensic medicine** n Gerichtsmedizin die.

**forensic science** n Kriminaltechnik die.

**forerunner** [ˈfɔːˌrʌnər] n [precursor] Vorläufer der, -in die.

**foresee** [fɔːˈsiː] (pt -saw [-ˈsɔː], pp -seen) vt vorherlsehen, vorauslsehen.

**foreseeable** [fɔːˈsiːəbl] adj vorhersehbar; **for the ~ future** in absehbarer Zeit.

**foreseen** [fɔːˈsiːn] pp ⟹ foresee.

**foreshadow** [fɔːˈʃædəʊ] vt ahnen lassen.

**foresight** [ˈfɔːsaɪt] n (U) Weitsicht die.

**foreskin** [ˈfɔːskɪn] n Vorhaut die.

**forest** [ˈfɒrɪst] n Wald der.

**forestall** [fɔːˈstɔːl] vt zuvorlkommen (+ D).

**forestry** [ˈfɒrɪstrɪ] n Forstwirtschaft die; [science] Forstwissenschaft die.

**F**

**Forestry Commission** *n Br:* the ~ die Forstverwaltung.

**foretaste** ['fɔːteɪst] *n* Vorgeschmack *der.*

**foretell** [fɔː'tel] (*pt* & *pp* -told) *vt* vorherlsagen.

**forethought** ['fɔːθɔːt] *n:* to have the ~ to do sthg so vorausschauend sein, etw zu tun.

**foretold** [fɔː'təʊld] *pt* & *pp* ⊏> foretell.

**forever** [fə'revə'] *adv* - **1.** [eternally] ewig; [disappear, exile] für immer - **2.** *inf* [incessantly] ständig - **3.** *inf* [a long time] ewig; I've been waiting ~! ich warte schon seit Ewigkeiten!

**forewarn** [fɔː'wɔːn] *vt* vorlwarnen.

**foreword** ['fɔːwɜːd] *n* Vorwort *das.*

**forfeit** ['fɔːfɪt] *n* Strafe *die* <> *vt* [deposit, chance] einlbüßen; [right] verwirken.

**forgave** [fə'geɪv] *pt* ⊏> forgive.

**forge** [fɔːdʒ] *n* [place] Schmiede *die* <> *vt* - **1.** [metal] schmieden - **2.** [friendship, alliance] schließen; [relationship] knüpfen - **3.** [signature, passport, banknotes] fälschen.

➥ **forge ahead** *vi* voranlkommen.

**forger** ['fɔːdʒə'] *n* Fälscher *der,* -in *die.*

**forgery** ['fɔːdʒərɪ] (*pl* -ies) *n* Fälschung *die.*

**forget** [fə'get] (*pt* -got; *pp* -gotten; *cont* -getting) *vt* vergessen; to ~ to do sthg vergessen, etw zu tun; to ~ o.s. sich vergessen; to ~ how to dance das Tanzen verlernen; ~ it! vergiss es! <> *vi* es vergessen; to ~ about sthg etw vergessen.

**forgetful** [fə'getfʊl] *adj* vergesslich.

**forgetfulness** [fə'getfʊlnɪs] *n* Vergesslichkeit *die.*

**forget-me-not** *n* Vergissmeinnicht *das.*

**forgive** [fə'gɪv] (*pt* -gave, *pp* -given [-'gɪvən]) *vt* [person] verzeihen *(+ D);* [sins] vergeben; ~ my ignorance but ... entschuldigen Sie bitte meine Unkenntnis, aber ...; to ~ sb for sthg jm etw verzeihen.

**forgiveness** [fə'gɪvnɪs] *n* Verzeihung *die.*

**forgiving** [fə'gɪvɪŋ] *adj* versöhnlich.

**forgo** [fɔː'gəʊ] (*pt* -went, *pp* -gone [-'gɒn]) *vt* verzichten auf *(+ A).*

**forgot** [fə'gɒt] *pt* ⊏> forget.

**forgotten** [fə'gɒtn] *pp* ⊏> forget.

**fork** [fɔːk] *n* - **1.** [for food, gardening] Gabel *die* - **2.** [in road, path, river] Gabelung *die* <> *vi* [road, river] sich gabeln; to ~ left/right [driver] nach links/rechts abbiegen.

➥ **fork out** *inf vt fus* blechen; to ~ out money on OR for sthg für etw blechen müssen <> *vi:* to ~ out (for sthg) (für etw) blechen.

➥ **forks** *npl* [of bike, motorbike] Gabel *die.*

**forklift truck** ['fɔːklɪft-] *n* Gabelstapler *der.*

**forlorn** [fə'lɔːn] *adj* - **1.** [expression] betrübt; [cry] verzweifelt - **2.** [desolate - person] einsam und unglücklich; [ - place] trostlos - **3.** [hope] schwach; [attempt] verzweifelt.

**form** [fɔːm] *n* - **1.** [shape, type] Form *die;* [shape of person] Gestalt *die;* in the ~ of in Form von; to take ~ [plan, idea] Gestalt anlnehmen; the programme took the ~ of a series of interviews die Sendung bestand aus einer Reihe von Interviews - **2.** [health & SPORT] Form *die;* on ~ *Br,* in ~ *Am* in Form; off ~ nicht in Form; according to ~, true to ~ wie erwartet - **3.** [piece of paper] Formular *das;* [application form] Bewerbungsbogen *der* - **4.** *Br SCH* [class] Klasse *die* - **5.** *esp Br* [bench] Bank *die (ohne Rückenlehne)* - **6.** [etiquette]: it is bad ~ to arrive late es ist schlechtes Benehmen, zu spät zu kommen; for ~'s sake der Form halber <> *vt* - **1.** [plan] entwerfen; [friendship] schließen; [character] formen; to ~ an idea of sthg sich *(D)* eine Vorstellung von etw machen - **2.** [circle, sentence, plural, government] bilden - **3.** [constitute] sein; to ~ part of sthg ein Teil von etw sein <> *vi* sich bilden.

**formal** ['fɔːml] *adj* - **1.** [language] formell; [person] förmlich - **2.** [event] feierlich; ~ clothes Gesellschaftskleidung *die* - **3.** [offer, decision] offiziell; ~ education Ausbildung *die* in einer Institution.

**formality** [fɔː'mælətɪ] (*pl* -ies) *n* - **1.** (*U*) [correctness] Förmlichkeit *die* - **2.** [convention] Formalität *die.*

**formalize, -ise** ['fɔːməlaɪz] *vt* [plan] offiziell machen; [thoughts] Form geben *(+ D).*

**formally** ['fɔːməlɪ] *adv* - **1.** [behave, write] förmlich; to be ~ dressed Gesellschaftskleidung tragen - **2.** [offer, decide] offiziell.

**format** ['fɔːmæt] (*pt* & *pp* -ted; *cont* -ting) *n* - **1.** [size & COMPUT] Format *das* - **2.** [structure, arrangement] Struktur *die* <> *vt* COMPUT formatieren.

**formation** [fɔː'meɪʃn] *n* - **1.** (*U*) [of company] Gründung *die;* [of government] Bildung *die* - **2.** [arrangement] Formation *die* - **3.** [of plan] Entwurf *der;* [of character] Formung *die.*

**formative** ['fɔːmətɪv] *adj* prägend; ~ years entscheidende Jahre.

**former** ['fɔːmə'] *adj* - **1.** [previous] früher, ehemalig; in ~ times früher - **2.** [first] erstere, -r, -s <> *n:* the ~ der/die/das Erstere.

**formerly** ['fɔːməlɪ] *adv* früher.

**form feed** *n* Papiervorschub *der.*

**Formica®** [fɔː'maɪkəl] *n* Resopal® *das.*

**formidable** ['fɔːmɪdəbl] *adj* Respekt einflößend; [task] gewaltig

**formula** ['fɔːmjʊlə] (*pl* -as OR -ae [-iːl]) *n* - **1.** [gen] Formel *die* - **2.** *fig* [for success] Rezept *das* - **3.** [baby milk] *Milchpulverpräparat für Säuglinge, das mit Wasser gemischt wird.*

**formulate** ['fɔːmjʊleɪt] *vt* - **1.** [express] formulieren - **2.** [plan] auslarbeiten.

**formulation** [ˌfɔːmjʊ'leɪʃn] n - **1.** [expression] Formulierung die - **2.** [planning] Ausarbeitung die.

**fornicate** ['fɔːnɪkeɪt] vi fml Unzucht treiben.

**forsake** [fə'seɪk] (pt -sook; pp -saken) vt literary [person] verlassen; [habit] auflgeben.

**forsook** [fə'sʊk] pt ⊳ forsake.

**fort** [fɔːt] n Fort das; to hold the ~ die Stellung halten.

**forte** ['fɔːtɪ] n Stärke die.

**forth** [fɔːθ] adv literary - **1.** [outwards, onwards]: to go/send ~ fortlgehen/-schicken; to bring ~ hervorlbringen - **2.** [into future]: from that day ~ von jenem Tag an; and so ~ und so weiter.

**forthcoming** [fɔːθ'kʌmɪŋ] adj - **1.** [future - election, events] bevorstehend; [ - book] in Kürze erscheinend - **2.** [available - help, answer, money]: to be ~ kommen - **3.** [willing to talk] mitteilsam.

**forthright** ['fɔːθraɪt] adj [person, manner] direkt; [opinions] unverblümt.

**forthwith** [ˌfɔːθ'wɪθ] adv fml unverzüglich.

**fortieth** ['fɔːtɪɪθ] num vierzigste, -r, -s; see also sixth.

**fortification** [ˌfɔːtɪfɪ'keɪʃn] n Befestigung die.

**fortified wine** ['fɔːtɪfaɪd-] n mit zusätzlichem Alkohol angereicherter Wein.

**fortify** ['fɔːtɪfaɪ] (pt & pp -ied) vt - **1.** [place] befestigen - **2.** fig [person, resolve] bestärken.

**fortitude** ['fɔːtɪtjuːd] n (U) innere Stärke.

**fortnight** ['fɔːtnaɪt] n vierzehn Tage pl, zwei Wochen pl.

**fortnightly** ['fɔːtˌnaɪtlɪ] adj [visit, meeting] alle zwei Wochen stattfindend; [magazine] alle zwei Wochen erscheinend ⊳ adv alle vierzehn Tage, alle zwei Wochen.

**fortress** ['fɔːtrɪs] n Festung die.

**fortuitous** [fɔː'tjuːɪtəs] adj fml zufällig.

**fortunate** ['fɔːtʃuːnət] adj glücklich; to be ~ Glück haben; it's ~ that ... es ist ein Glück, dass ...

**fortunately** ['fɔːtʃnətlɪ] adv zum Glück.

**fortune** ['fɔːtʃuːn] n - **1.** [money] Vermögen das; it costs a ~ inf es kostet ein Vermögen - **2.** [luck] Glück das - **3.** [fate] Schicksal das - **4.** [future]: to tell sb's ~ jm die Zukunft vorauslsagen.

**fortune-teller** [-ˌtelər] n Wahrsager der, -in die.

**forty** ['fɔːtɪ] num vierzig; see also sixty.

**forum** ['fɔːrəm] (pl -s) n Forum das.

**forward** ['fɔːwəd] adj - **1.** [movement] vorwärts- - **2.** [planning] Voraus-; we're no further ~ now than we were last year wir sind jetzt nicht weiter als letztes Jahr - **3.** [impudent] dreist ⊳ adv - **1.** [in space - go, move] vorwärts; [- look,

lean] nach vorn; [- fall] vornüber - **2.** [in time]: to bring a meeting ~ ein Treffen vorlverlegen; from this time ~ [now] von jetzt an; [then] seitdem; to put a clock ~ eine Uhr vorlstellen ⊳ n sport Stürmer der, -in die ⊳ vt - **1.** [letter, parcel] nachlsenden; 'please ~' 'bitte nachsenden' - **2.** [career] voranlbringen.

**forwarding address** ['fɔːwədɪŋ-] n Nachsendeadresse die.

**forward-looking** [-'lʊkɪŋ] adj fortschrittlich.

**forwardness** ['fɔːwədnɪs] n [boldness] Dreistigkeit die.

**forwards** ['fɔːwədz] adv = forward.

**forwent** [fɔː'went] pt ⊳ forgo.

**fossil** ['fɒsɪl] n Fossil das.

**fossil fuel** n fossile Brennstoffe pl.

**fossilized, -ised** ['fɒsɪlaɪzd] adj [animal, remains] versteinert.

**foster** ['fɒstər] adj [family, mother] Pflege- ⊳ vt - **1.** [child] in Pflege nehmen - **2.** [idea, hope] hegen; [relations] fördern.

**foster child** n Pflegekind das.

**foster parents** npl Pflegeeltern pl.

**fought** [fɔːt] pt & pp ⊳ fight.

**foul** [faʊl] adj - **1.** [water] faulig; [air] verpestet; [food] verdorben; [smell, taste] übel; ~ breath Mundgeruch der - **2.** [very unpleasant] schrecklich; what ~ weather! was für ein scheußliches Wetter!; she's in a ~ mood today sie ist heute in sehr schlechter Stimmung - **3.** [language] unflätig - **4.** phr: to fall ~ of sb mit jm in Konflikt geraten ⊳ n sport Foul das ⊳ vt - **1.** [make dirty] verunreinigen - **2.** sport foulen - **3.** [entangle]: the net ~ed the propeller das Netz hat sich im Propeller verheddert.

➤ **foul up** vt sep inf [plans, day] vermasseln; [life] kaputt machen.

**foul-mouthed** [-'maʊðd] adj unflätig.

**foul play** n (U) - **1.** sport Foulspiel das - **2.** [criminal act]: the police suspect ~ die Polizei vermutet, dass es Mord war.

**found** [faʊnd] pt & pp ⊳ find ⊳ vt - **1.** [organization, town] gründen; [hospital, school] errichten - **2.** [base]: to be ~ed on sth auf etw (D) basieren.

**foundation** [faʊn'deɪʃn] n - **1.** [of organization, town] Gründung die; [of hospital, school] Errichtung die - **2.** [basis] Grundlage die; without ~ unbegründet - **3.** [organization] Stiftung die - **4.** [cosmetic]: ~ (cream) Grundierungscreme die.

➤ **foundations** npl constr Fundament das.

**foundation stone** n Grundstein der.

**founder** ['faʊndər] n [person] Gründer der, -in die ⊳ vi - **1.** [sink] sinken - **2.** fig [fail - plan, arrangement] scheitern; [ - hope] sich zerschlagen.

**founder member** n Gründungsmitglied das.

**foundry** ['faundrɪ] (pl **-ies**) n Gießerei die.

**fountain** ['fauntɪn] n [man-made] Springbrunnen der.

**fountain pen** n Füllfederhalter der, Füller der.

**four** [fɔːʳ] num vier; **on all ~s** auf allen vieren; see also **six.**

**four-letter word** n Vulgärausdruck der.

**four-poster (bed)** n Himmelbett das.

**foursome** ['fɔːsəm] n Quartett das.

**four-star (petrol)** n Super das.

**fourteen** [ˌfɔːˈtiːn] num vierzehn; see also **six.**

**fourteenth** [ˌfɔːˈtiːnθ] num vierzehnte, -r, -s; see also **sixth.**

**fourth** [fɔːθ] num vierte, -r, -s; see also **sixth.**

**Fourth of July** n: **the ~** der vierte Juli, Nationalfeiertag (Unabhängigkeitstag) in den USA.

**four-way stop** n Am Kreuzung, an der in allen vier Richtungen angehalten werden muss.

**four-wheel drive** n - **1.** [vehicle] Fahrzeug das mit Allradantrieb - **2.** [system] Allradantrieb der.

**fowl** [faul] (pl inv OR **-s**) n [chicken] Huhn das; [turkey] Truthahn der.

**fox** [fɒks] n Fuchs der <> vt - **1.** [outwit] täuschen - **2.** [baffle] vor ein Rätsel stellen.

**foxcub** ['fɒkskʌb] n Fuchswelpe der.

**foxglove** ['fɒksglʌv] n Fingerhut der.

**foxhole** ['fɒkshəul] n Fuchsbau der.

**foxhound** ['fɒkshaund] n Foxhound der.

**foxhunting** ['fɒksˌhʌntɪŋ] n (U) Fuchsjagd die.

**fox terrier** n Foxterrier der.

**foxy** ['fɒksɪ] adj inf [sexy] scharf.

**foyer** ['fɔɪeɪ] n - **1.** [of hotel, theatre] Foyer das - **2.** Am [of house] Diele die.

**FP** n - **1.** (abbr of **former pupil**) ehemaliger Schüler - **2.** Am abbr of **fireplug.**

**fr.** (abbr of **franc**) F.

**Fr.** (abbr of **Father**) P.

**fracas** ['fræka:, Am 'freɪkəs] (Br pl inv, Am pl **fracases**) n Tumult der.

**fraction** ['frækʃn] n - **1.** MATH Bruch der - **2.** [small part] Bruchteil der; **lift it up a ~** heb es eine Spur höher.

**fractionally** ['frækʃnəlɪ] adv geringfügig.

**fracture** ['fræktʃəʳ] n Bruch der <> vt brechen; **to ~ one's arm** sich (D) den Arm brechen.

**fragile** ['frædʒaɪl] adj zerbrechlich; [health] anfällig; **to feel ~** sich angeschlagen fühlen.

**fragility** [frə'dʒɪlətɪ] n Zerbrechlichkeit die; [of health] Anfälligkeit die.

**fragment** [n 'frægmənt, vb fræg'ment] n - **1.** [of china, glass] Scherbe die - **2.** [of text] Fragment das; [of conversation] Fetzen der <> vi [organization, society] zersplittern.

**fragmented** [fræg'mentɪd] adj [account] unzusammenhängend; [organization, society] zersplittert.

**fragrance** ['freɪgrəns] n Duft der.

**fragrant** ['freɪgrənt] adj duftend.

**frail** [freɪl] adj - **1.** [person, health] zart - **2.** [structure] brüchig.

**frailty** ['freɪltɪ] (pl **-ies**) n - **1.** [of person, health] Zartheit die - **2.** [of structure] Brüchigkeit die - **3.** [imperfection] Schwäche die.

**frame** [freɪm] n - **1.** [gen] Rahmen der; [of glasses, bed] Gestell das; [of house, boat] Gerippe das - **2.** [physique] Körper der - **3.** phr: **~ of mind** Gemütsverfassung die <> vt - **1.** [painting, photograph] rahmen - **2.** fig [surround] umrahmen - **3.** [thoughts, answer] formulieren - **4.** inf [falsely incriminate]: **to ~ sb** jm eine Sache anhängen.

**framework** ['freɪmwɜːk] n - **1.** [of boat, house] Gerippe das - **2.** [of society, democracy] (Grund)struktur die; [of essay] Gliederung die; **a ~ for negotiations** eine Basis für Verhandlungen; **within the ~ of** im Rahmen (+ G).

**France** [frɑːns] n Frankreich nt.

**franchise** ['fræntʃaɪz] n - **1.** POL Wahlrecht das - **2.** COMM Lizenz die.

**franchisee** [ˌfræntʃaɪˈziː] n Lizenznehmer der, -in die.

**franchisor** ['fræntʃaɪzəʳ] n Lizenzgeber der, -in die.

**frank** [fræŋk] adj offen; **to be ~, ...** offen gestanden, ... <> vt [letter] (frei)stempeln.

**Frankfurt** ['fræŋkfət] n: **~ (am Main)** Frankfurt (am Main) nt.

**frankfurter** ['fræŋkfɜːtəʳ] n Wiener Würstchen das, Wiener die.

**frankincense** ['fræŋkɪnsens] n Weihrauch der.

**franking machine** ['fræŋkɪŋ-] n Freistempler der.

**frankly** ['fræŋklɪ] adv - **1.** [talk] offen - **2.** [to be honest] offen gestanden.

**frankness** ['fræŋknɪs] n Offenheit die.

**frantic** ['fræntɪk] adj - **1.** [person] außer sich - **2.** [activity, day, pace] hektisch.

**frantically** ['fræntɪklɪ] adv [search] verzweifelt; [run around, work] wie wild.

**fraternal** [frə'tɜːnl] adj brüderlich; **~ twins** zweieiige Zwillinge.

**fraternity** [frə'tɜːnətɪ] (*pl* -ies) *n* - **1.** [community]: **the medical/banking ~** die Mediziner/Bankfachleute - **2.** *Am* [of students] Studentenverbindung *die* - **3.** [friendship] Brüderlichkeit *die*.

**fraternize, -ise** ['frætənaɪz] *vi:* **to ~ (with sb)** sich (mit jm) verbrüdern; **to ~ with the enemy** mit dem Feind fraternisieren.

**fraud** [frɔːd] *n* - **1.** (*U*) [crime] Betrug *der* - **2.** [deceitful act] Schwindel *der* - **3.** *pej* [impostor] Betrüger *der*, -in *die*.

**fraudulent** ['frɔːdjʊlənt] *adj* [means] betrügerisch; [charge, promise] falsch.

**fraught** [frɔːt] *adj* - **1.** [full]: **~ with danger** gefährlich; **~ with problems** voller Probleme - **2.** *Br* [frantic - person] gestresst; [ - time] stressig.

**fray** [freɪ] *vi* - **1.** [clothing, fabric] auslfransen; [rope] sich durchlscheuern - **2.** *fig*: **tempers began to ~** die Gemüter erhitzten sich ◇ *n literary* [brawl] Kampf *der*; [quarrel] Streit *der*; **to join in the ~** sich in den Kampf/Streit einlmischen.

**frayed** [freɪd] *adj* - **1.** [clothing, fabric] ausgefranst; [rope] durchgescheuert - **2.** *fig* [nerves] strapaziert; **tempers were ~** Gemüter waren erhitzt.

**frazzled** ['fræzld] *adj inf* [harassed] angegriffen.

**FRB** (*abbr of* **Federal Reserve Board**) *n* Kontrollorgan der Zentralbank der USA.

**FRCP** (*abbr of* **Fellow of the Royal College of Physicians**) *Mitglied des britischen Ärzteverbandes.*

**FRCS** (*abbr of* **Fellow of the Royal College of Surgeons**) *Mitglied des britischen Chirurgenverbandes.*

**freak** [friːk] *adj* außergewöhnlich ◇ *n* - **1.** [strange creature - in appearance] Missgeburt *die*; [ - in behaviour] Irre *der*, *die*; **~ of nature** Laune *die* der Natur - **2.** [unusual event] außergewöhnliche Begebenheit - **3.** *inf* [fanatic]: **a fitness ~** ein Fitnessfanatiker; **a computer ~** ein Computerfreak.

➡ **freak out** *inf vi* - **1.** [get angry] auslflippen - **2.** [panic] durchdrehen ◇ *vt sep:* **it ~ed him out** er ist dabei durchgedreht.

**freakish** ['friːkɪʃ] *adj* [strange] sehr sonderbar.

**freckle** ['frekl] *n* Sommersprosse *die*.

**free** [friː] (*compar* **freer**; *superl* **freest**; *pt & pp* **freed**) *adj* - **1.** [gen] frei; **~ period** scн Freistunde *die*; **she is ~ to leave** es steht ihr frei, zu gehen; **feel ~ to disagree** sie sind nicht gezwungen, zuzustimmen; **feel ~!** nur zu!; **to set sb/an animal ~** jn/ein Tier freillassen; **if you have a ~ moment** wenn Sie einen Moment Zeit haben - **2.** [costing nothing] kostenlos; **'admission ~'** Eintritt frei'; **~ of charge** umsonst, kostenlos - **3.** [unattached] lose - **4.** [without]: **~ from blame** frei von Schuld;

**~ from worry/pain** sorgen-/schmerzfrei - **5.** [generous]: **to be ~ with one's money** freigebig mit seinem Geld sein; **to be ~ with one's advice** nicht mit Ratschlägen geizen ◇ *adv* - **1.** [without payment] kostenlos; **for ~** umsonst - **2.** [without restraint]: **to cut ~** losIschneiden; [from wrecked vehicle] befreien; **to work ~** sich lockern ◇ *vt* - **1.** [prisoner, animal] freillassen; [country, city] befreien - **2.** [make available] zur Verfügung stellen - **3.** [extricate - person] befreien; [ - object] herausIkriegen.

**-free** [friː] *suffix inf* -frei.

**freebie** ['friːbɪ] *n inf* Gratisgeschenk *das*.

**freedom** ['friːdəm] *n* Freiheit *die;* **~ of speech** Redefreiheit *die*.

**freedom fighter** *n* Freiheitskämpfer *der*, -in *die*.

**free enterprise** *n* freies Unternehmertum.

**free-fall** *n* freier Fall.

**freefone** ['friːfəʊn] *adj Br:* **a ~ number** eine gebührenfreie Telefonnummer.

**free-for-all** *n* - **1.** [brawl] allgemeine Schlägerei - **2.** [argument] allgemeine lautstarke Auseinandersetzung.

**free gift** *n* Gratisgabe *die*.

**freehand** ['friːhænd] *adj* [drawing] Freihand- ◇ *adv* aus der Hand.

**freehold** ['friːhəʊld] *adv:* **to own sthg ~** etw besitzen; **to buy sthg ~** etw kaufen ◇ *n:* **to buy the ~ of one's house** das Haus, in dem man wohnt, kaufen.

**free house** *n* Wirtshaus, das keiner bestimmten Brauerei gehört und daher Bier verschiedener Marken ausschenken darf.

**free kick** *n* Freistoß *der*.

**freelance** ['friːlɑːns] *adj* [work] freiberuflich; [translator, journalist] freiberuflich tätig ◇ *adv* freiberuflich ◇ *n* Freiberufler *der*, -in *die* ◇ *vi* freiberuflich arbeiten.

**freeloader** ['friːləʊdə'] *n inf* Schmarotzer *der*, -in *die*.

**freely** ['friːlɪ] *adv* - **1.** [available, move] frei; [admit, talk] offen; [travel] ungehindert - **2.** [generously] großzügig.

**freeman** ['friːmən] (*pl* -men [-mən]) *n* [citizen] Ehrenbürger *der*.

**free-market economy** *n* freie Marktwirtschaft.

**Freemason** ['friː‚meɪsn] *n* Freimaurer *der*.

**Freemasonry** ['friː‚meɪsnrɪ] *n* Freimaurerei *die*.

**freemen** ['friːmən] *pl* ▷ **freeman**.

**freephone** ['friːfəʊn] *n* = **freefone**.

**freepost** ['friːpəʊst] *adv* [send] portofrei.

**free-range** *adj Br* [eggs] von frei laufenden Hühnern; [hens] frei laufend.

**free sample** n Gratisprobe die.

**free speech** n Redefreiheit die.

**freestanding** [‚friːˈstændɪŋ] adj frei stehend.

**freestyle** [ˈfriːstaɪl] n [in swimming] Freistil der.

**freethinker** [friːˈθɪŋkəʳ] n Freidenker der, -in die.

**free time** n Freizeit die.

**free trade** n Freihandel der.

**freeware** [ˈfriːweəʳ] n COMPUT Freeware die.

**freeway** [ˈfriːweɪ] n Am Autobahn die.

**freewheel** [‚friːˈwiːl] vi [cyclist] (mit dem Fahr-rad) rollen; [motorist] im Leerlauf fahren.

**freewheeling** [‚friːˈwiːlɪŋ] adj inf [style, attitude] locker.

**free will** n freier Wille; **to do sthg of one's own ~** etw aus freien Stücken tun.

**free world** n: **the ~** die freie Welt.

**freeze** [friːz] (pt **froze**; pp **frozen**) vt einfrieren; [pond, river] zufrieren lassen; [lock, pipes] einfrieren lassen ⟨⟩ vi - **1.** [pond, river] zufrieren; [pipes] einfrieren - **2.** METEOR frieren - **3.** [stop moving] in der Bewegung erstarren; **freeze!** keine Bewegung! ⟨⟩ n - **1.** [cold weather] Frost der - **2.**: **wage/price ~** Lohn-/Preisstopp der.

◆ **freeze over** vi zufrieren.

◆ **freeze up** vi [pond, river] zufrieren.

**freeze-dried** [-ˈdraɪd] adj gefriergetrock-net.

**freeze frame** n Standbild das.

**freezer** [ˈfriːzəʳ] n [upright] Tiefkühlschrank der; [chest] Tiefkühltruhe die; [part of fridge] Gefrierfach das.

**freezing** [ˈfriːzɪŋ] adj eiskalt; **I'm ~** mir ist eiskalt ⟨⟩ n inf: **above/below ~** über/unter dem Gefrierpunkt.

**freezing point** n Gefrierpunkt der.

**freight** [freɪt] n [goods] Fracht die.

**freight train** n Güterzug der.

**French** [frentʃ] adj französisch ⟨⟩ n Franzose der, -zösin die ⟨⟩ npl: **the ~** die Franzosen pl.

**French bean** n grüne Bohne.

**French Canadian** adj frankokanadisch ⟨⟩ n Frankokanadier der, -in die.

**French doors** npl = French windows.

**French dressing** n - **1.** [in UK] Vinaigrette die - **2.** [in US] Salatsoße mit Majonäse und Ketschup.

**French fries** npl esp Am Pommes frites pl.

**French kiss** n Zungenkuss der.

**Frenchman** [ˈfrentʃmən] (pl **-men** [-mən]) n Franzose der.

**French Riviera** n: **the ~** die französische Riviera.

**French stick** n Br Baguette das.

**French toast** n Weißbrot, das in Ei und Milch gewendet und gebraten wird, ≃ arme Ritter pl.

**French windows** npl große zweiflügelige Glastür.

**Frenchwoman** [ˈfrentʃˌwʊmən] (pl **-women** [-ˌwɪmɪn]) n Französin die.

**frenetic** [frəˈnetɪk] adj [activity] hektisch; [pace] rasend.

**frenzied** [ˈfrenzɪd] adj [activity] hektisch; [attack] wild; [crowd] rasend.

**frenzy** [ˈfrenzɪ] (pl **-ies**) n: **in a ~** hektisch; **the office was in a ~ of activity** im Büro herrschte große Betriebsamkeit.

**frequency** [ˈfriːkwənsɪ] (pl **-ies**) n - **1.** [rate] Häufigkeit die - **2.** [radio wave] Frequenz die.

**frequency modulation** n Frequenzmodulation die.

**frequent** [adj ˈfriːkwənt, vb frɪˈkwent] adj häufig; **she is a ~ visitor** sie kommt häufig zu Besuch ⟨⟩ vt häufig besuchen.

**frequently** [ˈfriːkwəntlɪ] adv häufig.

**fresco** [ˈfreskəʊ] (pl **-es** OR **-s**) n Fresko das.

**fresh** [freʃ] adj - **1.** [gen] frisch; **~ water** Süßwasser das - **2.** [new] neu; **to make a ~ pot of tea** noch einmal eine Kanne Tee machen; **to give sthg a ~ coat of paint** etw neu streichen; **to make a ~ start** einen neuen Anfang machen - **3.** [refreshing] erfrischend; **to get some ~ air** an die frische Luft gehen - **4.** [original] originell - **5.** inf dated [cheeky] frech; **to get ~ with sb** jm frech kommen ⟨⟩ adv [recently] frisch; **I'm ~ out of milk** inf mir ist die Milch ausgegangen.

**freshen** [ˈfreʃn] vt: **to ~ (the air in) a room** [by airing] einen Raum lüften; [with air freshener] die Luft in einem Raum verbessern ⟨⟩ vi [wind] auflfrischen.

◆ **freshen up** vt sep - **1.** [person]: **to ~ o.s. up** sich frisch machen - **2.** [room, house] auflfrischen ⟨⟩ vi [person] sich frisch machen.

**fresher** [ˈfreʃəʳ] n Br inf Erstsemester das.

**freshly** [ˈfreʃlɪ] adv frisch.

**freshman** [ˈfreʃmən] (pl **-men** [-mən]) n Erstsemester das.

**freshness** [ˈfreʃnɪs] n - **1.** [of food, air, taste] Frische die - **2.** [originality] Originalität die.

**freshwater** [ˈfreʃˌwɔːtəʳ] adj Süßwasser-.

**fret** [fret] (pt & pp **-ted**; cont **-ting**) vi [worry] sich (D) Sorgen machen.

**fretful** [ˈfretfʊl] adj [baby] quengelig; [sleep] unruhig.

**fretsaw** [ˈfretsɔː] n Laubsäge die.

**Freudian slip** [ˈfrɔɪdɪən-] n freudscher Versprecher.

**FRG** (abbr of **Federal Republic of Germany**) n BRD die.

**Fri.** (*abbr of* **Friday**) Fr.

**friar** ['fraɪəʳ] *n* Mönch *der*.

**friction** ['frɪkʃn] *n* (U) - **1.** [force] Reibung *die* - **2.** [rubbing] Reiben *das* - **3.** [conflict] Reibereien *pl*.

**Friday** ['fraɪdɪ] *n* Freitag *der; see also* **Saturday.**

**fridge** [frɪdʒ] *n esp Br* Kühlschrank *der*.

**fridge-freezer** *n Br* Kühlgefrierkombination *die*.

**fried** [fraɪd] *pt & pp* ⊏> **fry** <> *adj* gebraten; **~ egg** Spiegelei *das*.

**friend** [frend] *n* - **1.** [gen] Freund *der*, -in *die;* **to be ~s (with sb)** (mit jm) befreundet sein; **to make ~s (with sb)** sich (mit jm) an|freunden - **2.** [of theatre, orchestra *etc*] Freund und Förderer *der*.

**friendless** ['frendlɪs] *adj* ohne Freunde.

**friendly** ['frendlɪ] (*compar* -**ier;** *superl* -**iest;** *pl* -**ies**) *adj* freundlich; [country] befreundet; **to be ~ with sb** mit jm befreundet sein <> *n esp Br* SPORT Freundschaftsspiel *das*.

**friendship** ['frendʃɪp] *n* Freundschaft *die*.

**fries** [fraɪz] *npl* = **French fries.**

**Friesian (cow)** ['friːʒən-] *n* schwarzbunte Kuh.

**frieze** [friːz] *n* ARCHIT Fries *der;* [on wallpaper] Bordüre *die*.

**frigate** ['frɪgət] *n* Fregatte *die*.

**fright** [fraɪt] *n* - **1.** (U) [fear] Angst *die;* **to take ~** es mit der Angst zu tun bekommen - **2.** [shock] Schreck *der;* **to give sb a ~** jn erschrecken, jm einen Schreck ein|jagen.

**frighten** ['fraɪtn] *vt* Angst machen (*+ D*), erschrecken.

━➤ **frighten away** *vt sep* verscheuchen.

━➤ **frighten off** *vt sep* verscheuchen.

**frightened** ['fraɪtnd] *adj* [person] verängstigt; [voice, expression] angsterfüllt; **to be ~ (of)** Angst haben (vor (*+ D*)).

**frightening** ['fraɪtnɪŋ] *adj* beängstigend.

**frightful** ['fraɪtfʊl] *adj* schrecklich.

**frigid** ['frɪdʒɪd] *adj* [sexually] frigide.

**frill** [frɪl] *n* - **1.** [on clothes] Rüsche *die* - **2.** *inf* [extra]: **with no ~s** ohne Extras.

**frilly** ['frɪlɪ] (*compar* -**ier;** *superl* -**iest**) *adj* [blouse] Rüschen-; [skirt] mit Rüschen.

**fringe** [frɪndʒ] *n* - **1.** [on clothes, curtain] Fransen *pl* - **2.** *Br* [of hair] Pony *der* - **3.** [edge] Rand *der* <> *vt* [border] säumen.

**fringe benefits** *npl* zusätzliche Leistungen *pl*.

**fringe group** *n* Randgruppe *die*.

**fringe theatre** *n Br alternatives Theater, welches vom großen kommerziellen Theaterbetrieb unabhängig ist*.

**Frisbee**® ['frɪzbɪ] *n* Frisbee® *das*.

**frisk** [frɪsk] *vt* [search] durchsuchen.

**frisky** ['frɪskɪ] (*compar* -**ier;** *superl* -**iest**) *adj inf* quicklebendig.

**fritter** ['frɪtəʳ] *n* CULIN in Pfannkuchenteig getauchtes und gebratenes Obst-, Gemüseoder Fleischstück.

━➤ **fritter away** *vt sep* vergeuden; **to ~ money/time away on sthg** Geld/Zeit für etw vergeuden.

**frivolity** [frɪˈvɒlətɪ] (*pl* -**ies**) *n:* **such ~ is out of place** solche Leichtfertigkeit ist fehl am Platze; **I've no time for frivolities** ich habe keine Zeit für belanglose Dinge.

**frivolous** ['frɪvələs] *adj* frivol.

**frizzy** ['frɪzɪ] (*compar* -**ier;** *superl* -**iest**) *adj* kraus.

**fro** [frəʊ] ⊏> **to.**

**frock** [frɒk] *n dated* Kleid *das*.

**frog** [frɒg] *n* [animal] Frosch *der;* **to have a ~ in one's throat** einen Frosch im Hals haben.

**frogman** ['frɒgmən] (*pl* -**men**) *n* Froschmann *der*.

**frogmarch** ['frɒgmɑːtʃ] *vt* im Polizeigriff ab|führen.

**frogmen** ['frɒgmən] *pl* ⊏> **frogman.**

**frogspawn** ['frɒgspɔːn] *n* (U) Froschlaich *der*.

**frolic** ['frɒlɪk] (*pt & pp* -**ked;** *cont* -**king**) *vi* herum|tollen.

**from** [*weak form* frəm, *strong form* frɒm] *prep* - **1.** [expressing origin, source] von; **where did you get that ~?** woher hast du das?; **I'm ~ England** ich bin aus England; **I bought it ~ a supermarket** ich habe es in einem Supermarkt gekauft; **the train ~ Manchester** der Zug aus Manchester; **we moved ~ Boston to Denver** wir sind von Boston nach Denver umgezogen - **2.** [expressing removal, deduction] von; **away ~ home** weg von zu Hause; **to take sthg away ~ sb** jm etw weg|nehmen; **take 5 (away) ~ 9** ziehe 5 von 9 ab; **he took a notebook ~ his pocket** er nahm ein Notizbuch aus der Tasche; **to drink ~ a cup** aus einer Tasse trinken - **3.** [expressing distance] von; **five miles ~ London** fünf Meilen von London entfernt; **it's not far ~ here** es ist nicht weit von hier - **4.** [expressing position] von; **~ here you can see the valley** von hier aus kann man das Tal sehen - **5.** [expressing starting time] von ... an; **open ~ nine to five** von neun bis fünf geöffnet; **~ next year** ab nächstem Jahr; **~ the moment I met him ...** schon bei unserer ersten Begegnung ...; **~ now on** von nun an, ab jetzt - **6.** [expressing change] von; **the price has gone up ~ one to two pounds** der Preis ist von einem Pfund auf zwei Pfund gestiegen - **7.** [expressing range]: **tickets cost ~ $10** Karten gibt es ab 10 Dollar; **it could take ~ two to six months** es könnte zwischen zwei und sechs Monaten dauern - **8.** [as a result of] von; **I'm tired ~ walk-**

ing ich bin vom Gehen müde; **to suffer ~ asthma** an Asthma leiden **- 9.** [expressing protection] vor (+ D); **sheltered ~ the wind** windgeschützt **- 10.** [in comparisons]: **different ~ anders als; to distinguish good ~ bad** gut und böse auseinander halten **- 11.** [indicating material]: **made ~ wood/plastic** aus Holz/Kunststoff (gemacht) **- 12.** [on the evidence of]: **to speak ~ experience** aus Erfahrung sprechen; **~ what I can see** so wie ich es verstehe; **to judge ~ appearances** nach dem Äußeren urteilen.

**frond** [frɒnd] n Wedel der.

**front** [frʌnt] n **- 1.** [most forward part] Vorderseite die; [of house] Vorderfront die; **at the ~** vorne; **at the ~ of the train** vorne im Zug; **on the ~ of her dress** vorn auf ihrem Kleid; **to lie on one's ~** auf dem Bauch liegen; **at the ~ of the book** auf den ersten Seiten **- 2.** MIL & METEOR Front die **- 3.** [by the sea] (Strand)promenade die **- 4.** [outward appearance]: **it's all a ~** es ist alles nur Fassade; **she tried to put a brave ~ on things** sie versuchte, sich nach außen hin tapfer zu zeigen ⟨⟩ adj Vorder-, vordere, -r, -s; [row, page] erste, -r, -s; **~ garden** Vorgarten der ⟨⟩ vt [TV programme] moderieren; [organization] repräsentieren ⟨⟩ vi: **to ~ onto the lake/road** zum See/zur Straße hinausgehen.

➤ **in front** adv vorne; **the people in ~** die vorne sitzenden/stehenden Leute.

➤ **in front of** prep vor (+ D).

**frontage** [ˈfrʌntɪdʒ] n Front die.

**frontal** [ˈfrʌntl] adj [attack] Frontal-.

**frontbench** [ˌfrʌntˈbentʃ] n POL führende Mitglieder der Regierung oder der Opposition.

**front desk** n Rezeption die.

**front door** n [of house] Haustür die.

**frontier** [ˈfrʌntɪəʳ, Am frʌnˈtɪər] n lit & fig Grenze die.

**frontispiece** [ˈfrʌntɪspiːs] n Titelbild das.

**front line** n: **the ~** die Frontlinie.

**front man** n **- 1.** [of pop group] Frontmann der **- 2.** [of programme] Moderator der.

**front room** n Wohnzimmer das.

**front-runner** n SPORT Läufer der, -in die an der Spitze; fig Spitzenkandidat der, -in die.

**front-wheel drive** n **- 1.** [vehicle] Fahrzeug das mit Vorderradantrieb **- 2.** (U) [system] Vorderradantrieb der.

**frost** [frɒst] n **- 1.** (U) [layer of ice] Frost der, Reif der **- 2.** [weather] Frost der ⟨⟩ vi: **to ~ over** OR **up** [window] vereisen.

**frostbite** [ˈfrɒstbaɪt] n (U) Erfrierungen pl.

**frostbitten** [ˈfrɒstˌbɪtn] adj [toes, fingers] erfroren.

**frosted** [ˈfrɒstɪd] adj **- 1.** [opaque]: **~ glass** Milchglas das **- 2.** Am CULIN mit Zuckerguss überzogen.

**frosting** [ˈfrɒstɪŋ] n Am CULIN Zuckerguss der.

**frosty** [ˈfrɒstɪ] (compar **-ier**; superl **-iest**) adj **- 1.** lit & fig [cold] frostig **- 2.** [field] bereift; [ground] gefroren.

**froth** [frɒθ] n Schaum der ⟨⟩ vi schäumen.

**frothy** [ˈfrɒθɪ] (compar **-ier**; superl **-iest**) adj schäumend.

**frown** [fraʊn] n: **to give a ~** die Stirn runzeln ⟨⟩ vi die Stirn runzeln.

➤ **frown (up)on** vt fus missbilligen.

**froze** [frəʊz] pt ⟩ **freeze**.

**frozen** [ˈfrəʊzn] pp ⟩ **freeze** ⟨⟩ adj **- 1.** [ground] gefroren; [pipes] eingefroren; [lake] zugefroren **- 2.** [food] tiefgefroren **- 3.** [very cold] eiskalt; **I'm ~** mir ist eiskalt **- 4.** fig [rigid]: **~ with fear** starr vor Angst.

**FRS** n **- 1.** (abbr of **Fellow of the Royal Society**) Mitglied der britischen Akademie der Wissenschaften **- 2.** (abbr of **Federal Reserve System**) Notenbanksystem der USA.

**frugal** [ˈfruːgl] adj **- 1.** [meal] einfach **- 2.** [person] sparsam.

**fruit** [fruːt] (pl inv OR **- s**) n **- 1.** [food] Obst das; [variety of fruit] Frucht die **- 2.** fig [result] Frucht die; **to bear ~** Früchte tragen ⟨⟩ comp: **~ tree** Obstbaum der; **~ bowl** Obstschale die; **~ cocktail** Obstsalat der.

**fruitcake** [ˈfruːtkeɪk] n Kuchen mit Trockenfrüchten.

**fruiterer** [ˈfruːtərəʳ] n Br Obsthändler der, -in die.

**fruitful** [ˈfruːtfʊl] adj fruchtbar.

**fruition** [fruːˈɪʃn] n: **to come to ~** [hopes] in Erfüllung gehen; [plans] Wirklichkeit werden.

**fruit juice** n Fruchtsaft der.

**fruitless** [ˈfruːtlɪs] adj fruchtlos.

**fruit machine** n Br Spielautomat der.

**fruit salad** n Obstsalat der.

**frumpy** [ˈfrʌmpɪ] (compar **-ier**; superl **-iest**) adj inf [clothes] unmodisch; [person] unmodisch gekleidet.

**frustrate** [frʌˈstreɪt] vt **- 1.** [person] frustrieren **- 2.** [plan, attempt] vereiteln.

**frustrated** [frʌˈstreɪtɪd] adj **- 1.** [person] frustriert **- 2.** [poet, artist] gescheitert **- 3.** [plan, attempt] vereitelt.

**frustrating** [frʌˈstreɪtɪŋ] adj frustrierend.

**frustration** [frʌˈstreɪʃn] n Frustration die.

**fry** [fraɪ] (pt & pp **fried**) vt [food] braten; **to ~ an egg** ein Spiegelei machen ⟨⟩ vi [food] braten.

**frying pan** [ˈfraɪɪŋ-] n Bratpfanne die; **to jump out of the ~ into the fire** vom Regen in die Traufe kommen.

**ft.** (abbr of **foot** OR **feet**) ft.

**FTSE** (abbr of **Financial Times Stock Exchange**): the ~ **(index)** britischer Aktienindex der 100 bedeutendsten britischen Firmen.

**fuchsia** ['fju:ʃə] n Fuchsie die.

**fuck** [fʌk] vulg vt & vi ficken ◇ excl Scheiße! ◆ **fuck off** vulg vi sich verpissen ◇ excl verpiss dich!

**fucking** ['fʌkɪŋ] vulg adj [for emphasis] Scheiß- ◇ adv verdammt.

**fuddy-duddy** ['fʌdɪ,dʌdɪ] (pl **fuddy-duddies**) n inf Fossil das.

**fudge** [fʌdʒ] n (U) [sweet] weiches Bonbon aus Milch, Zucker und Butter ◇ vt inf [issue] auslweichen (+ D).

**fuel** [fjʊəl] (Br pt & pp **-led**; cont **-ling**, Am pt & pp **-ed**; cont **-ing**) n [for fire] Brennmaterial das; [for aircraft, ship] Treibstoff der; [for vehicle] Benzin das; **to add ~ to the fire** fig Öl ins Feuer gießen ◇ vt **- 1.** [furnace, boiler] mit Brennstoff versorgen **- 2.** [argument, violence] anlheizen ◇ vi auflanken.

**fuel injection** n Benzineinspritzung die.

**fuel pump** n Kraftstoffpumpe die.

**fuel tank** n Benzintank der.

**fugitive** ['fju:dʒətɪv] n: **to be a ~ from justice** vor der Justiz auf der Flucht sein.

**fulcrum** ['fʊlkrəm] (pl **-crums** OR **-cra** [-krə]) n Angelpunkt der.

**fulfil** (pt & pp **-led**; cont **-ling**), **fulfill** Am [fʊl'fɪl] vt **- 1.** [carry out - duty] erfüllen; [- promise] halten; [- role] auslfüllen **- 2.** [satisfy - need] befriedigen; [- requirement] entsprechen (+ D); [- hope, ambition] erfüllen; **to ~ o.s.** sich selbst verwirklichen.

**fulfilling** [fʊl'fɪlɪŋ] adj [life] erfüllt; **a ~ job** eine Arbeit, in der man Erfüllung findet.

**fulfilment**, **fulfillment** Am [fʊl'fɪlmənt] n (U) **- 1.** [satisfaction] Befriedigung die **- 2.** [carrying through - of ambition, dream] Erfüllung die; [- of need] Befriedigung die

**full** [fʊl] adj **- 1.** [filled] voll; **I'm ~ (up)** [after meal] ich bin satt; **the bus is ~** der Bus ist voll besetzt; **the room was ~ of furniture** das Zimmer war voll mit Möbeln; **his pockets were ~ of sweets** er hatte die Taschen voller Süßigkeiten **- 2.** [complete - day, amount] ganz; [- details] genau; [- report] ausführlich **- 3.** [plump - face] voll; [- figure] mollig **- 4.** [skirt, sleeve] weit **- 5.** [flavour] voll ◇ adv **- 1.** [directly] voll **- 2.** [very]: **he knows ~ well that ...** er weiß ganz genau, dass ... **- 3.** [at maximum]: **the sound was turned up ~** die Lautstärke war voll aufgedreht ◇ n: **in ~** vollständig; **to enjoy sthg to the ~** etw in vollen Zügen genießen.

**fullback** ['fʊlbæk] n Verteidiger der, -in die.

**full-blooded** [-'blʌdɪd] adj **- 1.** [pure-blooded]

reinblütig **- 2.** [whole-hearted - argument] hitzig; [- support] voll.

**full-blown** [-'bləʊn] adj [heart attack] groß; [war] richtig; **~ Aids** Vollbild-Aids das.

**full board** n (U) Vollpension die.

**full-bodied** [-'bɒdɪd] adj vollmundig.

**full dress** n (U) Gesellschaftskleidung die.

**full-face** adj: **~ portrait** bildliche Darstellung, die das Gesicht von vorne zeigt.

**full-fashioned** adj Am = **fully-fashioned**.

**full-fledged** adj Am = **fully-fledged**.

**full-frontal** adj: **why is there so much ~ nudity in films?** warum werden in Filmen so viele Nackte gezeigt?

**full-grown** adj ausgewachsen.

**full house** n [at show, event] ausverkauftes Haus.

**full-length** adj **- 1.**: **~ mirror** hoher Spiegel (in dem man sich vollständig sehen kann); **~ portrait** Ganzporträt das **- 2.** [dress] lang; [curtains] bodenlang **- 3.**: **a ~ novel/film** ein Roman/Film normaler Länge ◇ adv [lie] ausgestreckt.

**full moon** n Vollmond der.

**fullness** ['fʊlnɪs] n [of details, information] Vollständigkeit die; **in the ~ of time** wenn die Zeit dafür gekommen ist.

**full-page** adj ganzseitig.

**full-scale** adj **- 1.** [life-size] in Originalgröße **- 2.** [thorough - inquiry] umfassend; [- war] total.

**full-size(d)** adj **- 1.** [life-size] in Originalgröße **- 2.** [adult] normalgroß.

**full stop** n Punkt der ◇ adv Br: **I don't want to do it, ~** ich will es nicht machen und damit basta.

**full time** n Br SPORT Spielende das. ◆ **full-time** adj [job, employment] Ganztags-; [worker] Vollzeit- ◇ adv ganztags.

**full up** adj **- 1.** [after meal] satt **- 2.** [bus, train] voll.

**fully** ['fʊlɪ] adv **- 1.** [completely] vollkommen; **~ trained/automatic** vollausgebildet/-automatisch **- 2.** [in detail - answer] ausführlich; [- describe] detailliert.

**fully-fashioned** Br, **full-fashioned** Am [-'fæʃnd] adj mit Passform.

**fully-fledged** Br, **full-fledged** Am [-'fledʒd] adj fig [doctor, lawyer] vollausgebildet.

**fulness** ['fʊlnɪs] n = **fullness**.

**fulsome** ['fʊlsəm] adj übertrieben.

**fumble** ['fʌmbl] vt [ball] nicht richtig fangen ◇ vi [in bag, pocket] wühlen; **to ~ for sthg** [for light switch] nach etw tasten; [for words] nach etw suchen; **he ~d for his keys** er wühlte nach seinen Schlüsseln.

**fume** [fju:m] vi [with anger] kochen.

➡ **fumes** *npl* Dämpfe *pl;* [from car] Abgase *pl;* [from fire] Rauch *der.*

**fumigate** ['fjuːmɪɡeɪt] *vt* [room, building] auslräuchern.

**fun** [fʌn] *n* - **1.** [gen] Spaß *der;* **it's good ~** es macht viel Spaß; **to have ~** sich amüsieren; **for ~, for the ~ of it** aus *OR* zum Spaß - **2.** [ridicule]: **to make ~ of sb, to poke ~ at sb** sich über jn lustig machen ◇ *adj* lustig; **to have a ~ time** Spaß haben.

**function** ['fʌŋkʃn] *n* - **1.** [gen] Funktion *die* - **2.** [social event] Veranstaltung *die* ◇ *vi* - **1.** [work] funktionieren - **2.** [serve]: **to ~ as** dienen als.

**functional** ['fʌŋkʃnəl] *adj* - **1.** [practical] funktionell - **2.** [operational] funktionsfähig.

**function key** *n* COMPUT Funktionstaste *die.*

**fund** [fʌnd] *n* - **1.** [amount of money] Fonds *der* - **2.** *fig* [of knowledge, experience] Fundus *der* ◇ *vt* finanzieren.

➡ **funds** *npl* Gelder *pl;* **public ~s** öffentliche Mittel *pl.*

**fundamental** [ˌfʌndə'mentl] *adj* - **1.** [basic - idea] grundlegend; [ - principle, change, error] fundamental; [ - inability] generell - **2.** [vital]: **to be ~ (to)** von fundamentaler Bedeutung sein (für).

➡ **fundamentals** *npl* Grundlagen *pl.*

**fundamentalism** [ˌfʌndə'mentəlɪzm] *n* Fundamentalismus *der.*

**fundamentally** [ˌfʌndə'mentəlɪ] *adv* - **1.** [basically] grundsätzlich - **2.** [radically] fundamental; **to disagree ~ with sthg** mit etw überhaupt nicht übereinstimmen.

**funding** ['fʌndɪŋ] *n* Gelder *pl.*

**fund-raising** [-ˌreɪzɪŋ] *n* Geldbeschaffung *die* ◇ *comp:* **~ event** Veranstaltung *die* zur Geldbeschaffung.

**funeral** ['fjuːnərəl] *n* Beerdigung *die.*

**funeral director** *n* Bestattungsunternehmer *der,* -in *die.*

**funeral parlour** *n* Beerdigungsinstitut *das.*

**funeral service** *n* Trauergottesdienst *der.*

**funereal** [fjuː'nɪərɪəl] *adj* [music] düster; [tone] trauervoll.

**funfair** ['fʌnfeəʳ] *n* Kirmes *die.*

**fungus** ['fʌŋɡəs] (*pl* -gi [-gaɪ] *OR* -guses) *n* BOT Pilz *der.*

**funk** [fʌŋk] *n* - **1.** MUS Funk *der* - **2.** *dated* [fear] Bammel *der.*

**funky** ['fʌŋkɪ] (*compar* -ier; *superl* -iest) *adj* - **1.** [music] funky - **2.** *inf* [great] cool.

**funnel** ['fʌnl] (*Br pt* & *pp* -led; *cont* -ling; *Am pt* & *pp* -ed; *cont* -ing) *n* - **1.** [tube] Trichter *der* - **2.** [on ship] Schornstein *der* ◇ *vt* - **1.** [liquid] leiten - **2.** [crowd, money] schleusen.

**funnily** ['fʌnɪlɪ] *adv* [strangely] komisch; **~ enough** komischerweise.

**funny** ['fʌnɪ] (*compar* -ier; *superl* -iest) *adj* - **1.** [amusing] lustig - **2.** [odd] komisch - **3.** [ill]: **I feel ~** mir ist komisch.

➡ **funnies** *npl Am* Cartoons *pl.*

**funny bone** *n* Musikantenknochen *der.*

**funny farm** *n esp Am inf hum* Klapsmühle *die.*

**fun run** *n Langstreckenlauf, dessen Erlös Wohltätigkeitszwecken zugute kommt.*

**fur** [fɜːʳ] *n* - **1.** [on animal] Fell *das* - **2.** [garment] Pelz *der.*

**fur coat** *n* Pelzmantel *der.*

**furious** ['fjʊərɪəs] *adj* - **1.** [very angry] wütend - **2.** [violent] heftig; **at a ~ pace/speed** mit rasender Geschwindigkeit.

**furiously** ['fjʊərɪəslɪ] *adv* - **1.** [angrily] wütend - **2.** [fight] heftig; [drive] mit rasender Geschwindigkeit; [work] wie wild.

**furl** *vt* [sail, flag] einlrollen; [umbrella] zusammenlrollen.

**furlong** ['fɜːlɒŋ] *n* Achtelmeile *die.*

**furnace** ['fɜːnɪs] *n* [for melting metal] Schmelzofen *der.*

**furnish** ['fɜːnɪʃ] *vt* - **1.** [room, house] einlrichten - **2.** *fml* [provide - proof, explanation] liefern; **to ~ sb with sthg** jm etw liefern.

**furnished** ['fɜːnɪʃt] *adj* möbliert.

**furnishings** ['fɜːnɪʃɪŋz] *npl* Einrichtungsgegenstände *pl.*

**furniture** ['fɜːnɪtʃəʳ] *n (U)* Möbel *pl;* **a piece of ~** ein Möbelstück *das.*

**furniture polish** *n* Möbelpolitur *die.*

**furore** *Br* ['fjʊərɔːrɪ], **furor** *Am* ['fjʊrɔːr] *n* Aufruhr *der.*

**furrier** ['fʌrɪəʳ] *n* [dealer] Pelzhändler *der,* -in *die;* [craftsman] Kürschner *der,* -in *die.*

**furrow** ['fʌrəʊ] *n* - **1.** [in field] Furche *die* - **2.** [on forehead] Runzel *die.*

**furrowed** ['fʌrəʊd] *adj* - **1.** [field, land] gefurcht - **2.** [brow] gerunzelt.

**furry** ['fɜːrɪ] (*compar* -ier; *superl* -iest) *adj* - **1.** [animal] mit dichtem Fell - **2.** [material] flauschig; **~ toy** Plüschtier *das.*

**further** ['fɜːðəʳ] *compar* ▷ **far** ◇ *adv* - **1.** [gen] weiter; **~ back** weiter hinten; [in time] weiter zurück; **~ on** weiter; **the police decided not to take the matter any ~** die Polizei entschied, die Angelegenheit nicht weiterzuverfolgen; **this mustn't go any ~** das darf nicht weitergetragen werden - **2.** [in addition] darüber hinaus ◇ *adj* [additional] weitere, -r, -s; **until ~ notice** bis auf weiteres ◇ *vt* [career] voranlbringen; [aim] unterstützen.

➡ **further to** *prep fml* Bezug nehmend auf (+ A).

**further education** n Br Erwachsenenbildung die.

**furthermore** [ˌfɜ:ðə'mɔ:ʳ] adv außerdem.

**furthermost** ['fɜ:ðəməʊst] adj am weitesten entfernt.

**furthest** ['fɜ:ðɪst] superl ⊳ **far** ⟨⟩ adj am weitesten entfernt ⟨⟩ adv am weitesten.

**furtive** ['fɜ:tɪv] adj [glance] verstohlen; [behaviour] heimlichtuerisch.

**furtively** ['fɜ:tɪvlɪ] adv [look] verstohlen; [behave] heimlichtuerisch.

**fury** ['fjʊərɪ] n Wut die; **in a ~** wütend.

**fuse** Br, **fuze** Am [fju:z] n - **1.** [of plug] Sicherung die - **2.** [of bomb, firework] Zünder der ⟨⟩ vt - **1.** [metal, plastic] verschmelzen - **2.** [ideas, styles] verbinden ⟨⟩ vi - **1.** ELEC: **the lights have ~d** die Sicherung (für das Licht) ist durchgebrannt - **2.** [metal, plastic] verschmelzen.

**fusebox** ['fju:zbɒks] n Sicherungskasten der.

**fused** [fju:zd] adj [plug] gesichert.

**fuselage** ['fju:zəlɑ:ʒ] n (Flugzeug)rumpf der.

**fuse wire** n Sicherungsdraht der.

**fusillade** [ˌfju:zə'leɪd] n Salve die.

**fusion** ['fju:ʒn] n - **1.** [of ideas, styles] Verbindung die - **2.** PHYSICS Fusion die.

**fuss** [fʌs] n Theater das; **to make a ~** Aufhebens machen; **to kick up** OR **to make a ~ about** sthg Krach schlagen wegen etw (D); **to make a ~ of sb** Br viel Wirbel um jn machen ⟨⟩ vi sich aufIregen.

➡ **fuss over** vt fus viel Wirbel machen um.

**fusspot** ['fʌspɒt] n inf: **to be a ~** pingelig sein.

**fussy** ['fʌsɪ] (compar **-ier;** superl **-iest**) adj - **1.** [person] pingelig - **2.** [design, dress] verspielt.

**fusty** ['fʌstɪ] (compar **-ier;** superl **-iest**) adj - **1.** [room] muffig - **2.** [old-fashioned] altmodisch.

**futile** ['fju:taɪl] adj zwecklos.

**futility** [fju:'tɪlətɪ] n Zwecklosigkeit die.

**futon** ['fu:tɒn] n Futon der.

**future** ['fju:tʃəʳ] n - **1.** [time ahead] Zukunft die; **in ~** in Zukunft; **in the ~** in der Zukunft - **2.** GRAMM: **~ (tense)** Futur das ⟨⟩ adj künftig; **at a ~ date** zu einem späteren Zeitpunkt.

➡ **futures** npl COMM Termingeschäfte pl.

**futuristic** [ˌfju:tʃə'rɪstɪk] adj futuristisch.

**fuze** n, vt & vi Am = **fuse**.

**fuzz** [fʌz] n - **1.** [hair] Flaum der - **2.** inf [police]: **the ~** die Bullen pl.

**fuzzy** ['fʌzɪ] (compar **-ier;** superl **-iest**) adj - **1.** [hair] kraus - **2.** [image, photo] unscharf - **3.** [ideas] wirr.

**fwd.** abbr of **forward**.

**FYI** (abbr of **for your information**) zur Kenntnisnahme.

**g¹** (pl **g's** OR **gs**), **G** (pl **G's** OR **Gs**) [dʒi:] n [letter] g das, G das.

➡ **G** n MUS G das ⟨⟩ - **1.** abbr of **good** - **2.** Am (abbr of **general (audience)**) jugendfrei.

**g²** [dʒi:] - **1.** (abbr of **gram**) g - **2.** (abbr of **gravity**) g.

**GA** abk für Georgia, in Postanschrift verwendet.

**gab** [gæb] n ⊳ **gift**.

**gabardine** [ˌgæbə'di:n] n Gabardine der.

**gabble** ['gæbl] vt herunterIrasseln ⟨⟩ vi brabbeln ⟨⟩ n Gebrabbel das.

**gable** ['geɪbl] n Giebel der.

**Gabon** [gæ'bɒn] n Gabun nt.

**gad** ➡ **gad about** (pt & pp **-ded;** cont **-ding**) vi inf herumIziehen.

**gadget** ['gædʒɪt] n Gerät das.

**Gaelic** ['geɪlɪk] adj gälisch ⟨⟩ n Gälisch(e) das.

**gaffe** [gæf] n Fauxpas der.

**gaffer** ['gæfəʳ] n Br inf [boss] Chef der.

**gag** [gæg] (pt & pp **-ged;** cont **-ging**) n - **1.** [for mouth] Knebel der - **2.** inf [joke] Gag der ⟨⟩ vt knebeln ⟨⟩ vi - **1.** [joke] Witze machen - **2.** [retch] würgen.

**gage** n & vt Am = **gauge**.

**gaiety** ['geɪətɪ] n Fröhlichkeit die.

**gaily** ['geɪlɪ] adv - **1.** [cheerfully] fröhlich; [dressed] in leuchtenden Farben; **~ coloured** farbenfroh - **2.** [thoughtlessly] unbekümmert.

**gain** [geɪn] n - **1.** [profit] Gewinn der; [advantage] Vorteil der - **2.** [increase] Zunahme die ⟨⟩ vt - **1.** [support] gewinnen; [advantage] sich verschaffen; [reputation] erwerben; [victory] erringen - **2.** [increase]: **to ~ weight** zunehmen; **to ~ speed** schneller werden; **to ~ strength/popularity** an Stärke/Beliebtheit gewinnen - **3.** [subj: watch, clock] vorIgehen um ⟨⟩ vi - **1.** [increase]: **to ~ in sthg** an etw (D) gewinnen - **2.** [profit]: **to ~ (from/by sthg)** (von/durch etw) profitieren - **3.** [watch, clock] vorIgehen.

➡ **gain on** vt fus: **to ~ on sb** jm (immer) näher kommen.

**gainful** ['geɪnfʊl] adj fml bezahlt; **~ employment** Erwerbstätigkeit die.

**gainfully** ['geɪnfʊlɪ] adv fml: **~ employed** erwerbstätig.

**gainsay** [ˌgeɪn'seɪ] (pt & pp -said) vt fml leugnen; [person] widersprechen (+ D).

**gait** [geɪt] n Gang der.

**gaiters** ['geɪtəz] npl Gamaschen pl.

**gala** ['gɑːlə] n - **1.** [celebration] Festveranstaltung die - **2.** Br SPORT: **swimming ~** Schwimmfest das ⟷ comp [performance, occasion] Gala-.

**galaxy** ['gæləksɪ] (pl -ies) n Galaxis die.

**gale** [geɪl] n Sturm der.

**Galicia** [gə'lɪʃɪə] n - **1.** [in Central Europe] Galizien nt - **2.** [in Spain] Galicien nt.

**gall** [gɔːl] n: **to have the ~ to do sthg** die Frechheit haben, etw zu tun ⟷ vt: **it ~s me to have to admit it** es ärgert mich, dass ich es zugeben muss.

**gal(l).** (abbr of gallon) Gal.

**gallant** [sense 1 'gælənt, sense 2 gə'lænt, 'gælənt] adj - **1.** [courageous] mutig - **2.** [polite to women] galant.

**gallantry** ['gæləntrɪ] n - **1.** [courage] Mut der - **2.** [politeness to women] Galanterie die.

**gall bladder** n Gallenblase die.

**galleon** ['gælɪən] n Galeone die.

**gallery** ['gælərɪ] (pl -ies) n - **1.** [gen] Galerie die - **2.** THEATRE dritter Rang.

**galley** ['gælɪ] (pl -s) n - **1.** [ship] Galeere die - **2.** [kitchen - of ship] Kombüse die; [ - of aircraft] Bordküche die - **3.** PRESS: **~ (proof)** Fahne die.

**Gallic** ['gælɪk] adj gallisch.

**galling** ['gɔːlɪŋ] adj ärgerlich.

**gallivant** [ˌgælɪ'vænt] vi inf sich herumltreiben.

**gallon** ['gælən] n Gallone die.

**gallop** ['gæləp] n - **1.** [pace of horse] Galopp der - **2.** [horse ride] Galoppritt der ⟷ vi - **1.** [horse] galoppieren - **2.** fig [person] sausen.

**galloping** ['gæləpɪŋ] adj fig [inflation] galoppierend.

**gallows** ['gæləʊz] (pl inv) n Galgen der.

**gallstone** ['gɔːlstəʊn] n Gallenstein der.

**Gallup poll** ['gæləp-] n Br Meinungsumfrage die.

**galore** [gə'lɔːr] adv in Hülle und Fülle.

**galoshes** [gə'lɒʃɪz] npl Galoschen pl.

**galvanize, -ise** ['gælvənaɪz] vt - **1.** TECH galvanisieren - **2.** [impel]: **to ~ sb into action** jn dazu veranlassen, aktiv zu werden.

**Gambia** ['gæmbɪə] n: **(the) ~** Gambia nt.

**Gambian** ['gæmbɪən] adj gambisch ⟷ n Gambier der, -in die.

**gamble** ['gæmbl] n [risk] Risiko das; **to take a ~** ein Risiko einlgehen ⟷ vi - **1.** [bet] (um Geld) spielen; **to ~ on the horses** auf Pferde wetten; **to ~ on the stock exchange** an der Börse spekulieren - **2.** [take risk]: **to ~ on sthg** sich auf etw (A) verlassen.

**gambler** ['gæmblər] n Spieler der, -in die.

**gambling** ['gæmblɪŋ] n Spielen das (um Geld).

**gambol** ['gæmbl] (Br pt & pp -led; cont -ling; Am pt & pp -ed; cont -ing) vi herumltollen.

**game** [geɪm] n - **1.** [gen] Spiel das; **fancy a ~ of chess/cards?** hast du Lust auf eine Partie Schach/Karten? - **2.** [hunted animals, meat] Wild das - **3.** phr: **to beat sb at their own ~** jn mit den eigenen Waffen schlagen; **the ~'s up** das Spiel ist aus; **to give the ~ away** alles verderben; **to play ~s with sb** sein Spiel mit jm treiben; **what's his ~?** was führt er im Schilde?; **two can play at that ~** wie du mir, so ich dir ⟷ adj - **1.** [brave] mutig - **2.** [willing]: **to be ~ for sthg** für etw bereit sein; **to be ~ to do sthg** bereit sein, etw zu tun.
➤ **games** n SCH Sport der ⟷ npl [sporting event] Spiele pl.

**gamekeeper** ['geɪmˌkiːpər] n Wildhüter der.

**gamely** ['geɪmlɪ] adv [bravely] mutig.

**game reserve** n Wildreservat das.

**gamesmanship** ['geɪmzmənʃɪp] n Gerissenheit die.

**gamma rays** ['gæmə-] npl Gammastrahlen pl.

**gammon** ['gæmən] n geräucherter und gekochter Vorderschinken.

**gammy** ['gæmɪ] (compar -ier; superl -iest) adj Br inf lahm.

**gamut** ['gæmət] n Skala die; **to run the ~ of sthg** die ganze Bandbreite von etw kennen lernen.

**gander** ['gændər] n Gänserich der, Ganter der.

**gang** [gæŋ] n [of criminals] Bande die, Gang die; [of young people] Clique die.
➤ **gang up** vi inf sich zusammenltun; **to ~ up on sb** sich gegen jn verbünden.

**Ganges** ['gændʒiːz] n: **the ~** der Ganges.

**gangland** ['gæŋlænd] adj: **~ crime** organisiertes Verbrechen; **~ killer** professioneller Killer.

**gangling** ['gæŋglɪŋ], **gangly** ['gæŋglɪ] (compar -ier; superl -iest) adj schlaksig.

**gangplank** ['gæŋplæŋk] n Gangway die.

**gangrene** ['gæŋgriːn] n Wundbrand der.

**gangrenous** ['gæŋgrɪnəs] adj brandig.

**gangster** ['gæŋstər] n Gangster der.

**gangway** ['gæŋweɪ] n - **1.** Br [aisle] Gang der - **2.** [gangplank] Gangway die.

**gannet** ['gænɪt] (pl inv OR -s) n [bird] Tölpel der.

**gantry** ['gæntrɪ] (pl -ies) n [for crane] Portal das.

**gaol** [dʒeɪl] n & vt Br = jail.

**gap** [gæp] n - **1.** [empty space, omission] Lücke die - **2.** [in time] Abstand der - **3.** fig [disparity] Kluft die.

**gape** [geɪp] vi - **1.** [person] gaffen; **to ~ at sb/sthg** jn/etw begaffen - **2.** [hole, shirt, wound] klaffen.

**gaping** ['geɪpɪŋ] adj - **1.** [person] gaffend - **2.** [hole, shirt, wound] klaffend.

**garage** [Br 'gæraːʒ, 'gærɪdʒ, Am gə'rɑːʒ] n - **1.** [for keeping car] Garage die - **2.** Br [for fuel] Tankstelle die - **3.** [for car repair] Werkstatt die - **4.** [for selling cars] Autohändler der.

**garage sale** n Am im Vorgarten oder in der Garage stattfindender privater Verkauf von nicht mehr benötigten Dingen.

**garb** [gɑːb] n (U) fml Gewand das.

**garbage** ['gɑːbɪdʒ] n esp Am - **1.** [refuse] Müll der - **2.** inf [nonsense] Unsinn der, Quatsch der.

**garbage can** n Am Mülltonne die.

**garbage collector** n Am Müllmann der.

**garbage truck** n Am Müllauto das, Müllwagen der.

**garbled** ['gɑːbld] adj entstellt, verstümmelt.

**Garda (Síochána)** ['gɑːdə (ʃɪ'kɔːnə)] n Irish: **the ~** die Polizei der Republik Irland.

**garden** ['gɑːdn] n - **1.** [private] Garten der - **2.** [public] Grünanlage die ⟨⟩ comp Garten- ⟨⟩ vi gärtnern, im Garten arbeiten.
◆ **gardens** npl Grünanlagen pl, Park der.

**garden centre** n Gartencenter das.

**garden city** n Br Gartenstadt die.

**gardener** ['gɑːdnəʳ] n - **1.** [professional] Gärtner der, -in die - **2.** [amateur] Hobbygärtner der, -in die.

**gardenia** [gɑː'diːnjə] n Gardenie die.

**gardening** ['gɑːdnɪŋ] n Gartenarbeit die ⟨⟩ comp Garten-.

**garden party** n Gartenparty die.

**gargantuan** [gɑː'gæntjʊən] adj gewaltig, riesig.

**gargle** ['gɑːgl] vi gurgeln.

**gargoyle** ['gɑːgɔɪl] n Wasserspeier der.

**garish** ['geərɪʃ] adj grell.

**garland** ['gɑːlənd] n Girlande die.

**garlic** ['gɑːlɪk] n Knoblauch der.

**garlic bread** n (U) Knoblauchbrot das.

**garlicky** ['gɑːlɪkɪ] adj inf Knoblauch-; **to taste ~** nach Knoblauch schmecken.

**garment** ['gɑːmənt] n Kleidungsstück das.

**garner** ['gɑːnəʳ] vt fml sammeln.

**garnet** ['gɑːnɪt] n Granat der.

**garnish** ['gɑːnɪʃ] culn n Garnierung die ⟨⟩ vt garnieren.

**garret** ['gærət] n Dachstube die.

**garrison** ['gærɪsn] n Garnison die ⟨⟩ vt in Garnison legen.

**garrulous** ['gærələs] adj geschwätzig, schwatzhaft.

**garter** ['gɑːtəʳ] n - **1.** [around leg] Strumpfband das - **2.** Am [suspender] Strumpfhalter der.

**gas** [gæs] (pl gases OR gasses; pt & pp gassed; cont gassing) n - **1.** [gen] Gas das - **2.** Am [fuel for vehicle] Benzin das; **to step on the ~** inf aufs Gas treten OR steigen ⟨⟩ vt [poison] vergasen.

**gas chamber** n Gaskammer die.

**gas cooker** n Br Gasherd der.

**gas cylinder** n Gasflasche die.

**gaseous** ['gæsɪəs] adj TECH gasförmig.

**gas fire** n Br Gasofen der.

**gas fitter** n Gasinstallateur der.

**gas gauge** n Am Benzinuhr die.

**gash** [gæʃ] n tiefe Schnittwunde ⟨⟩ vt: **to ~ one's hand/arm** sich in die Hand/den Arm schneiden.

**gasket** ['gæskɪt] n Dichtung die.

**gasman** ['gæsmæn] (pl -men [-men]) n Gasmann der.

**gas mask** n Gasmaske die.

**gasmen** pl ⟹ gasman.

**gas meter** n Gaszähler der, Gasuhr die.

**gasoline** ['gæsəliːn] n Am Benzin das.

**gasometer** [gæ'sɒmɪtəʳ] n Gasometer der.

**gas oven** n - **1.** [for cooking] Gasherd der - **2.** [gas chamber] Gaskammer die.

**gasp** [gɑːsp] n Keuchen das ⟨⟩ vi - **1.** [breathe quickly] keuchen - **2.** [in shock, surprise] nach Luft schnappen.

**gas pedal** n Am Gaspedal das.

**gasping** ['gɑːspɪŋ] adj Br inf [thirsty] durstig.

**gas pump attendant** n Am Tankwart der, -in die.

**gas station** n Am Tankstelle die.

**gas stove** n = gas cooker.

**gassy** ['gæsɪ] (compar -ier; superl -iest) adj pej kohlensäurehaltig; **this beer is very ~** in dem Bier ist zu viel Kohlensäure.

**gas tank** n Am Benzintank der.

**gas tap** n Gashahn der.

**gastric** ['gæstrɪk] adj Magen-, gastrisch.

**gastric ulcer** n Magengeschwür das.

**gastritis** [gæs'traɪtɪs] n Gastritis die.

**gastroenteritis** ['gæstrəʊ͵entə'raɪtɪs] n Magen-Darm-Katarrh der.

**gastronomic** [͵gæstrə'nɒmɪk] adj gastronomisch.

**gastronomy** [gæs'trɒnəmɪ] n Gastronomie die.

**gasworks** ['gæswɜːks] (pl inv) n Gaswerk das.

**gate** [geɪt] *n* - **1.** [in wall, fence] Tor *das* - **2.** [at airport] Flugsteig *der*.

-GATE

Dieses Suffix wird zur Bezeichnung eines öffentlichen, meist politischen Skandals gebraucht. Es ist von dem Namen des Gebäudes abgeleitet, in welchem sich die „Watergate"-Affäre abspielte, die zum Sturz von US-Präsident Nixon führte. Andere Beispiele sind „Irangate" (Waffengeschäfte der US-Regierung mit dem Iran, deren Erlös zur Finanzierung der Contra-Rebellen in Nicaragua diente) und „Monicagate" (Präsident Clintons Sexaffäre mit Monica Lewinsky und ihre politischen Folgen).

**gâteau** (*pl* -**x**) *n Br* Torte *die*.

**gatecrash** [ˈgeɪtkræʃ] *inf vt* hereinlplatzen <> *vi* uneingeladen erscheinen *(auf einer Party)*.

**gatecrasher** [ˈgeɪtˌkræʃəʳ] *n inf* ungebetener Gast.

**gatehouse** [ˈgeɪthaʊs] *n* Pförtnerhäuschen *das*.

**gatekeeper** [ˈgeɪtˌkiːpəʳ] *n* Pförtner *der*.

**gatepost** [ˈgeɪtpəʊst] *n* Torpfosten *der*.

**gateway** [ˈgeɪtweɪ] *n* Tor *das*.

**gather** [ˈgæðəʳ] *vt* - **1.** [collect] sammeln; **to ~ together** sich versammeln, zusammenlkommen - **2.** [speed]: **to ~ speed** schneller werden - **3.** [understand]: **to ~ that** annehmen, dass; **as far as I can ~** soweit ich weiß - **4.** [into folds] raffen, kräuseln <> *vi* [come together - people] sich versammeln; [ - crowd] sich anl sammeln; [ - clouds] sich zusammenlziehen; **I ~ from what he says, that ...** seinen Worten entnehme ich, dass ...
◆ **gather up** *vt sep* einlsammeln.

**gathering** [ˈgæðərɪŋ] *n* Versammlung *die*.

**GATT** [gæt] (*abbr of* **General Agreement on Tariffs and Trade**) *n* GATT *das*.

**gauche** [gəʊʃ] *adj* linkisch.

**gaudy** [ˈgɔːdɪ] (*compar* -**ier**; *superl* -**iest**) *adj* grell.

**gauge, gage** *Am* [geɪdʒ] *n* - **1.** [measuring instrument] Messinstrument *das* - **2.** [calibre] Kaliber *das* - **3.** RAIL Spurweite *die* <> *vt* - **1.** [measure, calculate] messen - **2.** [judge, predict] beurteilen.

**gaunt** [gɔːnt] *adj* hager.

**gauntlet** [ˈgɔːntlɪt] *n* [medieval glove] Panzerhandschuh *der*; [for motorcyclist] Stulpenhandschuh *der*; **to run the ~** Spießbruten laufen; **to throw down the ~ (to sb)** (jm) den Fehdehandschuh hinlwerfen.

**gauze** [gɔːz] *n* Gaze *die*.

**gave** [geɪv] *pt* ⊳ **give**.

**gawky** [ˈgɔːkɪ] (*compar* -**ier**; *superl* -**iest**) *adj* unbeholfen.

**gawp** [gɔːp] *vi* gaffen; **to ~ at sb/sthg** jn/etw anlgaffen.

**gay** [geɪ] *adj* - **1.** [homosexual] schwul - **2.** [cheerful, lively] fröhlich - **3.** [brightly coloured] bunt <> *n* [homosexual] Schwule *der*.

**gay rights** *npl* Rechte *pl* von Homosexuellen.

**Gaza Strip** [ˈgɑːzə-] *n:* **the ~** der Gazastreifen.

**gaze** [geɪz] *n* Blick *der* <> *vi:* **to ~ (at sb/sthg)** (jn/etw) anlstarren.

**gazebo** [gəˈziːbəʊ] (*pl* -**s**) *n* Gartenlaube *die*.

**gazelle** [gəˈzel] (*pl inv OR* -**s**) *n* Gazelle *die*.

**gazette** [gəˈzet] *n* Anzeiger *der*.

**gazetteer** [ˌgæzɪˈtɪəʳ] *n* geografisches Namensverzeichnis.

**gazump** [gəˈzʌmp] *vt Br inf* jn um die Möglichkeit bringen, ein Haus zu kaufen, indem man es trotz mündlicher Zusage einem Höherbietenden verkauft.

**GB** (*abbr of* **Great Britain**) *n* GB.

**GBH** *n abbr of* **grievous bodily harm**.

**GC** *n abbr of* **George Cross**.

**GCE** (*abbr of* **General Certificate of Education**) *n* ehemalige Abschlussprüfung an weiterführenden Schulen in England, Wales und Nordirland.

**GCH** *Br* (*abbr of* **gas central heating**) ZH.

**GCHQ** (*abbr of* **Government Communications Headquarters**) *n* Zentrale des britischen Nachrichtendienstes.

**GCSE** (*abbr of* **General Certificate of Secondary Education**) *n* Abschlussprüfung an weiterführenden Schulen in England, Wales und Nordirland.

GCSE

Das „GCSE" wurde 1988 eingeführt und ersetzt die bis dahin üblichen „O level"-Prüfungen. Es handelt sich um Schulabschlussprüfungen in verschiedenen Fächern, die im Alter von 15 oder 16 Jahren abgelegt werden müssen. Will der Schüler eine weiterführende Schule besuchen und seine „A level"-Prüfungen machen, muss er sie in mindestens fünf Schulfächern ablegen. Im Gegensatz zu den „O levels" fließen beim GCSE neben dem Prüfungsergebnis auch die im Laufe des Schuljahres erzielten Ergebnisse in die Endnote mit ein.

**Gdns** *abbr of* **Gardens**.

**GDP** (*abbr of* **gross domestic product**) *n* BIP *das*.

**GDR** (*abbr of* **German Democratic Republic**) *n* DDR *die*.

**gear** [gɪəʳ] *n* - **1.** TECH [mechanism] Zahnrad *das*

**- 2.** [on car, bicycle] Gang *der;* **out of ~** im Leerlauf; **in ~** mit eingelegtem Gang **- 3.** *(U)* [equipment, clothes] Ausrüstung *die* <> *vt:* **to ~ sthg to sb/sthg** etw auf jn/etw ausrichten.

**⇒ gear up** *vi:* **to ~ up for sthg** sich für etw rüsten; **to ~ up to do sthg** sich dafür rüsten, etw zu tun.

**gearbox** ['gɪəbɒks] *n* Getriebegehäuse *das;* **six-speed ~** Sechsganggetriebe *das.*

**gearing** ['gɪərɪŋ] *n* Getriebe *das.*

**gear lever, gear stick** *Br,* **gear shift** *Am n* Schaltknüppel *der.*

**gear wheel** *n* Zahnrad *das.*

**gee** [dʒiː] *excl* **- 1.** [to horse]: **~ up!** hüh!, hühott! **- 2.** *Am inf* [expressing surprise, excitement]: **~ (whizz)!** na so was!

**geese** [giːs] *pl* ⊳ **goose.**

**Geiger counter** ['gaɪgə'-] *n* Geigerzähler *der.*

**geisha (girl)** ['geɪʃə-] *n* Geisha *die.*

**gel** [dʒel] (*pt* & *pp* **-led;** *cont* **-ling**) *n* Gel *das* <> *vi* **- 1.** *fig* [idea, plan] Gestalt anInehmen **- 2.** [thicken] gelieren.

**gelatin** ['dʒelətɪn], **gelatine** [ˌdʒelə'tiːn] *n* Gelatine *die.*

**gelding** ['geldɪŋ] *n* Wallach *der.*

**gelignite** ['dʒelɪgnaɪt] *n* Plastiksprengstoff *der.*

**gem** [dʒem] *n* **- 1.** [jewel] (geschliffener) Edelstein **- 2.** *fig* [person] Juwel *das.*

**Gemini** ['dʒemɪnaɪ] *n* **- 1.** [sign] Zwillinge *pl* **- 2.** [person] Zwilling *der;* **I'm (a) ~** ich bin Zwilling.

**gemstone** ['dʒemstəʊn] *n* Edelstein *der.*

**gen** [dʒen] (*pt* & *pp* **-ned;** *cont* **-ning**) *n (U) Br inf* Informationen *pl.*

**⇒ gen up** *vi Br inf:* **to ~ up (on sthg)** sich (über etw *(A)*) informieren.

**gen. - 1.** (*abbr of* **general**) allg. **- 2.** (*abbr of* **generally**) allg.

**Gen.** (*abbr of* **General**) Gen.

**gender** ['dʒendə'] *n* Geschlecht *das.*

**gene** [dʒiːn] *n* Gen *das.*

**genealogist** [ˌdʒiːnɪ'ælədʒɪst] *n* Genealoge *der,* -gin *die.*

**genealogy** [ˌdʒiːnɪ'ælədʒɪ] (*pl* **-ies**) *n* **- 1.** [study] Genealogie *die* **- 2.** [family history] Stammbaumforschung *die.*

**genera** ['dʒenərə] *pl* ⊳ **genus.**

**general** ['dʒenərəl] *adj* [gen] allgemein <> *n MIL* General *der.*

**⇒ in general** *adv* **- 1.** [as a whole] im Allgemeinen **- 2.** [usually] gewöhnlich.

**general anaesthetic** *n* Vollnarkose *die.*

**general delivery** *adv Am* postlagernd.

**general election** *n* Parlamentswahlen *pl.*

**generality** [ˌdʒenə'rælətɪ] (*pl* **-ies**) *n* **- 1.** [generalization] Verallgemeinerung *die* **- 2.** [majority] Mehrheit *die.*

**generalization** [ˌdʒenərəlaɪ'zeɪʃn] *n* Verallgemeinerung *die.*

**generalize, -ise** ['dʒenərəlaɪz] *vi:* **to ~ (about sthg)** (etw) verallgemeinern.

**general knowledge** *n* Allgemeinbildung *die.*

**generally** ['dʒenərəlɪ] *adv* **- 1.** [usually] im Allgemeinen **- 2.** [in a general way] allgemein.

**general manager** *n* Hauptgeschäftsführer *der,* -in *die.*

**general practice** *n* Allgemeinmedizin *die.*

**general practitioner** *n* Arzt *der,* Ärztin *die* für Allgemeinmedizin.

**general public** *n:* **the ~** die breite Öffentlichkeit.

**general-purpose** *adj* Allzweck-.

**general store** *n* Gemischtwarenhandlung *die.*

**general strike** *n* Generalstreik *der.*

**generate** ['dʒenəreɪt] *vt* **- 1.** [energy, power, heat] erzeugen **- 2.** [interest, excitement] hervorrufen; [jobs, employment] schaffen.

**generation** [ˌdʒenə'reɪʃn] *n* **- 1.** [gen] Generation *die;* **a second ~ American** ein Amerikaner der zweiten Generation **- 2.** [of jobs] Schaffung *die;* [of interest, excitement] Hervorrufen *das* **- 3.** [of energy, power, heat] Erzeugung *die.*

**generation gap** *n* Generationsunterschied *der.*

**generator** ['dʒenəreɪtə'] *n* Generator *der.*

**generic** [dʒɪ'nerɪk] *adj* Gattungs-.

**generosity** [ˌdʒenə'rɒsətɪ] *n* Freigebigkeit *die,* Großzügigkeit *die.*

**generous** ['dʒenərəs] *adj* großzügig.

**generously** ['dʒenərəslɪ] *adv* großzügig.

**genesis** ['dʒenəsɪs] (*pl* **-eses** [-əsiːz]) *n* Entstehung *die.*

**genetic** [dʒɪ'netɪk] *adj* genetisch.

**⇒ genetics** *n* Genetik *die,* Vererbungslehre *die.*

**genetically modified** *adj* genmanipuliert, gentechnisch verändert.

**genetic engineering** *n* Gentechnologie *die.*

**genetic fingerprinting** [-'fɪŋgəprɪntɪŋ] *n* DNA-Fingerprintmethode *die.*

**Geneva** [dʒɪ'niːvə] *n* Genf *nt.*

**Geneva convention** *n:* **the ~** die Genfer Konvention.

**genial** ['dʒiːnjəl] *adj* jovial.

G

**genie** ['dʒi:nɪ] (pl **-s** OR **genii** ['dʒi:nɪaɪ]) n Dschinn der, Flaschengeist der.

**genitals** ['dʒenɪtlz] npl Genitalien pl.

**genius** ['dʒi:njəs] (pl **-es**) n Genie das; **to have a ~ for sthg** ein Talent für etw haben; **to have a ~ for doing sthg** ein Talent haben, etw zu tun; **he has a ~ for turning up late** iron er hat das Talent, zu spät zu kommen.

**Genoa** ['dʒenəʊə] n Genua nt.

**genocide** ['dʒenəsaɪd] n Völkermord der.

**genre** ['ʒɑrə] n Genre das, Gattung die.

**gent** [dʒent] n Br inf Gentleman der.
➤ **gents** n Br [toilets] Herrentoilette die.

**genteel** [dʒen'ti:l] adj - **1.** [refined] vornehm - **2.** [affected] geziert.

**gentile** ['dʒentaɪl] adj nichtjüdisch <> n Nichtjude der.

**gentle** ['dʒentl] adj - **1.** [person] sanftmütig; [smile, manner] freundlich - **2.** [rain, breeze, movement] sanft, leicht - **3.** [slope, curve] sanft - **4.** [hint] zart.

**gentleman** ['dʒentlmən] (pl **-men** [-mən]) n - **1.** [well-bred man] Gentleman der; **~'s agreement** Vereinbarung die auf Treu und Glauben - **2.** [man] Herr der.

**gentlemanly** ['dʒentlmənlɪ] adj vornehm.

**gentlemen** pl ⟵ gentleman.

**gentleness** ['dʒentlnɪs] n - **1.** [of person] Sanftmütigkeit die; [of smile, manner] Freundlichkeit die - **2.** [of rain, breeze, movement, slope, curve] Sanftheit die.

**gently** ['dʒentlɪ] adv - **1.** [speak] sanft; [behave, smile] freundlich - **2.** [blow] leicht; [move, heat] behutsam - **3.** [slope, curve] allmählich.

**gentry** ['dʒentrɪ] n (niederer) Adel.

**genuflect** ['dʒenju:flekt] vi fml knicksen; RELIG eine Kniebeuge machen.

**genuine** ['dʒenjʊɪn] adj - **1.** [real] echt - **2.** [sincere] aufrichtig.

**genuinely** ['dʒenjʊɪnlɪ] adv [sincerely] wirklich; **I was ~ pleased for him** ich freute mich aufrichtig für ihn.

**genus** ['dʒi:nəs] (pl **genera**) n Gattung die.

**geographer** [dʒɪ'ɒɡrəfər] n Geograf der, -in die.

**geographical** [dʒɪə'ɡræfɪkl] adj geografisch.

**geography** [dʒɪ'ɒɡrəfɪ] n - **1.** [science] Geografie die; [in school] Erdkunde die - **2.** [layout] Anordnung die.

**geological** [dʒɪə'lɒdʒɪkl] adj geologisch.

**geologist** [dʒɪ'ɒlədʒɪst] n Geologe der, -gin die.

**geology** [dʒɪ'ɒlədʒɪ] n Geologie die.

**geometric(al)** [dʒɪə'metrɪk(l)] adj geometrisch.

**geometry** [dʒɪ'ɒmətrɪ] n Geometrie die.

**geophysics** [dʒi:əʊ'fɪzɪks] n Geophysik die.

**Geordie** ['dʒɔːdɪ] n [person] Einwohner von Tyneside, der Region um Newcastle im Nordosten Englands.

**George Cross** ['dʒɔːdʒ-] n Br nichtmilitärisches britisches Verdienstkreuz, das für mutige Taten vergeben wird und hohes Ansehen genießt.

**geranium** [dʒɪ'reɪnjəm] (pl **-s**) n Geranie die.

**gerbil** ['dʒɜːbɪl] n Rennmaus die.

**geriatric** [dʒerɪ'ætrɪk] adj - **1.** [of old people] geriatrisch - **2.** pej [very old, inefficient] veraltet, altersschwach.

**germ** [dʒɜːm] n lit & fig Keim der.

**German** ['dʒɜːmən] adj deutsch <> n - **1.** [person] Deutsche der, die - **2.** [language] Deutsch(e) das.

**Germanic** [dʒɜː'mænɪk] adj - **1.** [architecture, style] germanisch - **2.** [characteristics, humour] deutsch.

**German measles** n Röteln die.

**German shepherd (dog)** n deutscher Schäferhund.

**Germany** ['dʒɜːmənɪ] (pl **-ies**) n Deutschland nt.

**germicide** ['dʒɜːmɪsaɪd] n keimtötendes Mittel.

**germinate** ['dʒɜːmɪneɪt] vt - **1.** [seed] zum Keimen bringen - **2.** fig [idea, feeling] auf keimen <> vi lit & fig keimen.

**germination** [dʒɜːmɪ'neɪʃn] n - **1.** [of seed] Keimung die - **2.** fig [of idea, feeling] Aufkeimen das.

**germ warfare** n bakteriologische Kriegsführung.

**gerrymandering** ['dʒerɪmændərɪŋ] n die willkürliche Vergrößerung bestimmter Wahlkreise zum Vorteil eines Kandidaten oder einer Partei.

**gerund** ['dʒerənd] n GRAMM Gerundium das.

**gestation** [dʒe'steɪʃn] n - **1.** [of animal] Trächtigkeit die; [of woman] Schwangerschaft die - **2.** fig Reifwerden das, Heranreifen das.

**gestation period** n Reifezeit die.

**gesticulate** [dʒes'tɪkjʊleɪt] vi gestikulieren.

**gesticulation** [dʒeˌstɪkjʊ'leɪʃn] n [gesture] Gebärde die.

**gesture** ['dʒestʃər] n Geste die <> vi: **to ~ to** OR **towards sb** auf jn deuten.

**get** [get] (pt & pp **got**, Am pp **gotten**; cont **-ting**) vt - **1.** [obtain] bekommen, kriegen; **she got a job** sie hat eine Stelle gefunden; **he got us two tickets** er hat uns zwei Karten besorgt; **to ~ one's own way** seinen Willen durchsetzen - **2.** [receive] bekommen; **I got a book for Christmas** ich habe zu Weihnachten ein Buch bekommen; **when did you ~ the news?** wann haben Sie die Nachricht bekommen?; **to ~ ten years** [criminal] zehn Jahre bekommen **- 3.** [train, plane, bus] nehmen; **let's ~ a taxi** lass uns ein Taxi nehmen **- 4.** [fetch] holen; **could you ~ me the manager?** [on phone] könnten Sie mir den Geschäftsführer geben?; **can I ~ you something to eat/drink?** möchtest du etwas essen/trinken? **- 5.** [illness] bekommen; **I got this cold while I was on holiday** ich habe mir diese Erkältung im Urlaub zugezogen **- 6.** [catch] fangen; **the police have got the killer** die Polizei hat den Mörder gefasst **- 7.** [cause to be done]: **to ~ sthg done** etw machen lassen; **can I ~ my car repaired here?** kann ich mein Auto hier reparieren lassen? **- 8.** [cause to become]: **she got the children ready for school** sie machte die Kinder für die Schule fertig; **I can't ~ the car started** ich kriege das Auto nicht an; **to ~ lunch** das Mittagessen zubereiten **- 9.** [ask, tell]: **to ~ sb to do sthg** jn bitten, etw zu tun **- 10.** [move]: **I can't ~ it through the door** ich bekomme es nicht durch die Tür **- 11.** [understand] verstehen; **I don't ~ it** inf das verstehe ich nicht, da komme ich nicht mit **- 12.** [time, chance] haben; **we didn't ~ the chance to see everything** wir hatten nicht die Gelegenheit, uns alles anzuschauen; **I haven't got (the) time** ich habe keine Zeit **- 13.** [idea, feeling] haben; **I ~ a lot of enjoyment from it** ich habe viel Spaß daran **- 14.** [answer - phone]: **could you ~ the phone?** könntest du ans Telefon gehen? **- 15.** inf [annoy]: **what really ~s me is his smugness** am meisten nervt mich seine Selbstgefälligkeit **- 16.** phr: **we ~ a lot of German tourists here** zu uns kommen viele deutsche Touristen; **we ~ a lot of rain here in winter** hier regnet es viel im Winter; ⊏⟩ **have** ◇ vi **- 1.** [become] werden; **it's getting late** es wird spät; **to ~ lost** sich verirren; **~ lost!** inf hau ab!, verschwinde!; **to ~ ready** sich fertig machen **- 2.** [into particular state, position]: **to ~ into trouble** in Schwierigkeiten geraten; **how do you ~ to the river from here?** wie kommt man von hier zum Fluss?; **to ~ dressed** sich anziehen; **to ~ married** heiraten; **to ~ into the car** ins Auto steigen **- 3.** [arrive] anlkommen; **when does the train ~ here?** wann kommt der Zug hier an? **- 4.** [eventually succeed]: **I finally got to meet him last week** letzte Woche habe ich ihn endlich getroffen; **did you ~ to see him?** hast du ihn gesehen?; **she got to like the class** allmählich gefiel ihr der Kurs; **to ~ to know sb** jn kennen lernen **- 5.** [progress]: **how far have you got?** wie weit bist du gekommen?; **we're ~ting nowhere** so kommen wir nicht weiter ◇ aux vb werden; **to ~ delayed** aufgehalten werden; **to ~ killed** getötet werden; **to ~ excited** aufgeregt werden; **let's ~ going** OR **moving!** also los!, auf gehts!

➤ **get about** vi **- 1.** [move from place to place] herumlkommen; **he ~s about a lot** er kommt viel herum **- 2.** [news, rumour] sich verbreiten.

➤ **get across** vt sep: **to ~ sthg across (to sb)** (jm) etw klarlmachen.

➤ **get ahead** vi voranlkommen.

➤ **get along** vi **- 1.** [manage]: **to ~ along (without sb/sthg)** (ohne jn/etw) zurechtlkommen **- 2.** [progress]: **how are you ~ting along?** wie kommst du voran? **- 3.** [in relationship]: **to ~ along (with sb)** (mit jm) auslkommen **- 4.** [leave] gehen; **I must be ~ting along** ich muss jetzt gehen.

➤ **get around, get round** vt fus [problem] umlgehen ◇ vi **- 1.** [move from place to place] herumlkommen **- 2.** [circulate - news] sich verbreiten **- 3.** [eventually do]: **to ~ around to sthg/to doing sthg** dazu kommen, etw zu tun.

➤ **get at** vt fus **- 1.** [reach] heranlkommen an (+ A); [truth] herauslbekommen **- 2.** [imply]: **what are you ~ting at?** worauf willst du hinaus? **- 3.** inf [nag]: **stop ~ting at me!** nörgel nicht dauernd an mir rum!

➤ **get away** vt sep: **~ him away from here** bring ihn von hier weg ◇ vi **- 1.** [leave] weglkommen; **I need to ~ away by five** ich muss um fünf Uhr weg **- 2.** [escape] entkommen **- 3.** [go on holiday]: **we like to ~ away at the weekend** wir fahren am Wochenende gerne weg; **to ~ away from it all** dem Alltag entfliehen.

➤ **get away with** vt fus durchkommen mit; **she lets him ~ away with everything** sie lässt ihm alles durchgehen.

➤ **get back** vt sep **- 1.** [recover, regain] zurücklbekommen; **to ~ one's strength back** wieder zu Kräften kommen **- 2.** [take revenge on]: **to ~ sb back for sthg** jm etw heimlzahlen; **to ~ one's own back** sich revanchieren ◇ vi **- 1.** [return] zurücklkommen **- 2.** [move away] zurückltreten.

➤ **get back to** vt fus **- 1.** [return to previous state, activity]: **to ~ back to sleep** wieder einlschlafen; **to ~ back to work** zur Arbeit zurücklkehren **- 2.** [phone back]: **I'll ~ back to you later** ich rufe Sie später zurück.

➤ **get by** vi [manage, survive] zurechtlkommen; **to ~ by on sthg** mit etw auslkommen.

➤ **get down** vt sep **- 1.** [depress] deprimieren; **don't let it ~ you down** lass dich davon nicht unterlkriegen **- 2.** [fetch from higher level] herunterlholen **- 3.** [write] auflschreiben.

➤ **get down to** vt fus: **to ~ down to doing sthg** sich daran machen, etw zu tun; **to ~ down to sthg** an etw (A) machen; **to ~ down to work** sich an die Arbeit machen; **to ~ down to business** zur Sache kommen.

➤ **get in** vi **- 1.** [arrive] anlkommen **- 2.** [into car, bus] einlsteigen **- 3.** [be elected] gewählt werden ◇ vt sep **- 1.** [bring in - washing] hereinl-

holen - **2.** [interject]: **to ~ a word in** zu Wort
kommen.

◆ **get into** vt fus - **1.** [car] einlsteigen in (+ A)
- **2.** [become involved in] geraten in (+ A); **to ~ into
an argument with sb** mit jm in Streit geraten
- **3.** [enter into a particular situation, state] geraten in
(+ A); **to ~ into a panic** in Panik geraten; **to
~ into trouble** in Schwierigkeiten geraten;
**she has got into the habit of getting up early** sie
hat sich daran gewöhnt, früh aufzustehen
- **4.** [college]: **she managed to ~ into Oxford** sie
hat es geschafft, einen Studienplatz in Oxford zu bekommen - **5.** inf [affect]: **what's got
into you?** was ist bloß in dich gefahren?

◆ **get off** vt sep [remove - clothes, shoes] ausziehen; [- stain] herauslbekommen; [- lid] ab-
bekommen; **to ~ sb/sthg off one's hands** jn/
etw loslwerden; **to ~ sthg off one's chest** sich
(D) etw von der Seele reden ◇ vt fus [bus,
train] auslsteigen aus; [bicycle] ablsteigen von;
**~ off my land!** verschwinde von meinem
Grundstück! ◇ vi - **1.** [from train, bus] aussteigen; [from bicycle] ablsteigen - **2.** [leave] losgehen; [in car] loslfahren - **3.** [escape punishment]
davonlkommen; **he got off lightly/with a
warning** er ist glimpflich/mit einer Verwarnung davongekommen.

◆ **get off with** vt fus inf Br: **to ~ off with sb** jn
auflreißen.

◆ **get on** vt sep [put on - clothes] anlziehen ◇ vt
fus [bus, train] einlsteigen in (+ A); [bicycle] steigen auf (+ A) ◇ vi - **1.** [on train, bus] einlsteigen; [on bicycle] auflsteigen - **2.** [in relation-
ship] sich verstehen; **how do you ~ on with his
family?** wie kommst du mit seiner Familie
aus? - **3.** [progress]: **how are you ~ting on?** wie
kommst du voran? - **4.** [proceed]: **to ~ on (with
sthg)** (mit etw) weiterlmachen - **5.** [have suc-
cess] Erfolg haben - **6.** [grow old, late]: **he's ~ting
on** er wird langsam alt; **time's ~ting on** es
wird langsam spät.

◆ **get on for** vt fus: **she's ~ting on for 65** sie
geht auf die 65 zu; **it's ~ting on for 5 o'clock** es
ist fast 5 Uhr.

◆ **get on to** vt fus - **1.** [begin to talk about]: **how did
we ~ on to this subject?** wie sind wir auf das
Thema gekommen? - **2.** [contact] sich in
Verbindung setzen mit; **I'll ~ on to them right
away** [by telephone] ich werde sie sofort anlrufen.

◆ **get out** vt sep - **1.** [take out] herauslnehmen; **she got a pen out of her bag** sie
nahm einen Kuli aus der Handtasche; **to
~ a book out of the library** sich (D) ein Buch
aus der Bibliothek auslleihen - **2.** [remove]:
**how do you ~ wine stains out?** wie bekommt
man Weinflecken heraus? ◇ vi - **1.** [from car,
bus] auslsteigen - **2.** [become known - news]
herauslkommen.

◆ **get out of** vt fus - **1.** [car, bus, train] auslsteigen aus - **2.** [escape from] herauslkommen aus; **to ~ out of a difficult situation**

sich aus einer schwierigen Lage befreien
- **3.** [avoid]: **to ~ out of sthg** um etw herumlkommen; **to ~ out of doing sthg** darum
herumlkommen, etw zu tun ◇ vt sep: **to
~ sb out of jail** jn aus dem Gefängnis herauslholen; **I got nothing out of him** ich habe
nichts aus ihm herauslbekommen.

◆ **get over** vt fus - **1.** [recover from] hinweglkommen über (+ A); **she can't ~ over her disappointment** sie kommt nicht über ihre Enttäuschung hinweg - **2.** [overcome] überwinden ◇ vt sep [communicate] verständlich
machen.

◆ **get over with** vt sep: **to ~ sthg over with** etw
hinter sich (A) bringen.

◆ **get round** vt fus & vi = **get around.**

◆ **get through** vt fus - **1.** [work, task] erledigen
- **2.** [exam] bestehen - **3.** [food, drink] verbrauchen - **4.** [survive] überstehen ◇ vi - **1.** [on
phone] durchlkommen; **I couldn't ~ through to
her** ich konnte sie nicht erreichen - **2.** [make
oneself understood]: **I couldn't ~ through to her** ich
konnte es ihr nicht verständlich machen.

◆ **get to** vt fus inf [annoy] auf die Nerven gehen; **don't let him ~ to you** lass dich von ihm
nicht ärgern.

◆ **get together** vt sep - **1.** [organize - team, report]
zusammenlstellen; [ - demonstration] organisieren - **2.** [gather - people] zusammenlbringen; [ - belongings] zusammenlpacken
◇ vi zusammenlkommen; **they ~ together
every Friday evening** sie trafen sich jeden
Freitagabend; **they got together to campaign
against it** sie taten sich zusammen, um eine
Kampagne dagegen zu führen.

◆ **get up** vi auflstehen ◇ vt fus - **1.** [organ-
ize - petition etc] organisieren - **2.** [gather - speed]
in Fahrt kommen.

◆ **get up to** vt fus inf anlstellen; **I wonder what
they're ~ting up to** ich frage mich, was die da
treiben.

**getaway** ['getəweɪ] n Flucht die.

**getaway car** n Fluchtauto das.

**get-together** n inf Zusammenkunft die,
Treffen das.

**getup** ['getʌp] n inf Aufmachung die.

**get-up-and-go** n inf Schwung der, Elan der.

**get-well card** n Karte mit Wünschen zur guten Besserung.

**geyser** ['giːzər] n - **1.** [hot spring] Geysir der
- **2.** Br [water heater] Durchlauferhitzer der.

**Ghana** ['gɑːnə] n Ghana nt.

**Ghan(a)ian** [gɑːˈneɪən] adj ghanaisch ◇ n
Ghanaer der, -in die.

**ghastly** ['gɑːstlɪ] (compar -**ier**; superl -**iest**) adj
- **1.** inf [very bad, unpleasant] scheußlich, grässlich - **2.** [horrifying, macabre] schrecklich,
schauerlich - **3.** [ill] grässlich.

**gherkin** ['gɜːkɪn] *n* Gewürzgurke *die*, Essiggurke *die*.

**ghetto** ['getəʊl] (*pl* **-s** *or* **-es**) *n* Ghetto *das*, Getto *das*.

**ghetto blaster** [-ˌblɑːstə<sup>r</sup>] *n inf* Ghettoblaster *der*.

**ghost** [gəʊst] *n* Geist *der*, Gespenst *das;* **he doesn't have a ~ of a chance** er hat nicht die Spur einer Chance ⬦ *vt* = **ghostwrite.**

**ghostly** ['gəʊstlɪ] (*compar* **-ier;** *superl* **-iest**) *adj* gespenstisch.

**ghost town** *n* Geisterstadt *die*.

**ghostwrite** ['gəʊstraɪt] (*pt* **-wrote;** *pp* **-written**) *vt:* **to ~ a book** ein Buch anonym für jn schreiben.

**ghostwriter** ['gəʊstˌraɪtə<sup>r</sup>] *n* Ghostwriter *der*.

**ghostwritten** ['gəʊstˌrɪtn] *pp* ▷ **ghostwrite.**

**ghostwrote** ['gəʊstrəʊt] *pt* ▷ **ghostwrite.**

**ghoul** [guːl] *n* **- 1.** [spirit] böser Geist **- 2.** *pej* [ghoulish person] makabrer Mensch.

**ghoulish** ['guːlɪʃ] *adj* makaber.

**GHQ** (*abbr of* **general headquarters**) *n* HQ *das*.

**GI** (*abbr of* **government issue**) *n* GI *der*.

**giant** ['dʒaɪənt] *adj* riesig ⬦ *n* **- 1.** [very tall man] Riese *der* **- 2.** [talented person] Größe *die* **- 3.** [business, organization] Gigant *der*.

**giant-size(d)** *adj* Riesen-.

**gibber** ['dʒɪbə<sup>r</sup>] *vi* stammeln.

**gibberish** ['dʒɪbərɪʃ] *n* [meaningless] Unsinn *der*, Quatsch *der;* [hard to understand] Kauderwelsch *das*.

**gibbon** ['gɪbən] *n* Gibbon *der*.

**gibe** [dʒaɪb] *n* Seitenhieb *der* ⬦ *vi:* **to ~ at sb/ sthg** jn/etw verhöhnen *or* verspotten.

**giblets** ['dʒɪblɪts] *npl* Geflügelklein *das*.

**Gibraltar** [dʒɪ'brɔːltə<sup>r</sup>] *n* Gibraltar *nt;* **in ~** auf Gibraltar; **the Rock of ~** der Fels von Gibraltar.

**giddy** ['gɪdɪ] (*compar* **-ier;** *superl* **-iest**) *adj* [dizzy] schwindelig.

**gift** [gɪft] *n* **- 1.** [present] Geschenk *das* **- 2.** [talent] Talent *das*, Begabung *die;* **to have a ~ for sthg** ein Talent *or* eine Begabung für etw haben; **to have a ~ for doing sthg** ein Talent *or* eine Begabung haben, etw zu tun; **the ~ of the gab** die Überzeugungsgabe.

**gift certificate** *n Am* = **gift token.**

**gifted** ['gɪftɪd] *adj* talentiert, begabt.

**gift token, gift voucher** *Br*, **gift certificate** *Am n* Geschenkgutschein *der*.

**gift wrap** *n* Geschenkpapier *das*.

**gift-wrapped** [-ræpt] *adj* als Geschenk verpackt.

**gig** [gɪg] *n inf* Gig *der*, Konzert *das*.

**gigabyte** ['gɪgəbaɪt] *n* COMPUT Gigabyte *das*.

**gigantic** [dʒaɪ'gæntɪk] *adj* gigantisch, riesig.

**giggle** ['gɪgl] *n* **- 1.** [laugh] Gekicher *das* **- 2.** *Br inf* [fun] Spaß *der;* **it was a real ~!** es war sehr amüsant! ⬦ *vi* [laugh] kichern.

**giggly** ['gɪglɪ] (*compar* **-ier;** *superl* **-iest**) *adj* albern.

**GIGO** ['gaɪgəʊ] (*abbr of* **garbage in, garbage out**) COMPUT *inf* unsinnige Eingabe erzeugt unsinnnige Ausgabe.

**gigolo** ['ʒɪgələʊ] (*pl* **-s**) *n pej* Gigolo *der*.

**gigot** ['ʒiːgəʊ] *n* Lammkeule *die*.

**gilded** ['gɪldɪd] *adj* = **gilt.**

**gill** [dʒɪl] *n* Viertelpint *das*.

**gills** [gɪlz] *npl* Kiemen *pl*.

**gilt** [gɪlt] *adj* vergoldet ⬦ *n* [gold layer] Vergoldung *die*.
➤ **gilts** *npl* FIN öffentliche Schuldverschreibungen.

**gilt-edged** [-edʒd] *adj* FIN: **~ stocks or securities** öffentliche Schuldverschreibung.

**gimme** ['gɪmɪ] *inf* = **give me.**

**gimmick** ['gɪmɪk] *n pej* Spielerei *die*.

**gin** [dʒɪn] *n* Gin *der;* **~ and tonic** Gin Tonic *der*.

**ginger** ['dʒɪndʒə<sup>r</sup>] *adj Br* [colour - hair] rotblond; [- cat] rötlichbraun ⬦ *n* Ingwer *der*.

**ginger ale** *n* Ginger Ale *die*.

**ginger beer** *n* Ingwerbier *das*.

**gingerbread** ['dʒɪndʒəbred] *n* (U) **- 1.** [cake] *Kuchen mit Ingwergeschmack* **- 2.** [biscuit] *Pfefferkuchen mit Ingwergeschmack.*

**ginger-haired** [-'heəd] *adj* rothaarig.

**gingerly** ['dʒɪndʒəlɪ] *adv* vorsichtig, sachte.

**gingham** ['gɪŋəm] *n* Gingan *der*.

**gingivitis** [ˌdʒɪndʒɪ'vaɪtɪs] *n* (U) Zahnfleischentzündung *die*.

**ginseng** ['dʒɪnseŋ] *n* Ginseng *der*.

**gipsy** ['dʒɪpsɪ] (*pl* **-ies**) *adj* Zigeuner- ⬦ *n* Zigeuner *der*, -in *die*.

**giraffe** [dʒɪ'rɑːf] (*pl inv or* **-s**) *n* Giraffe *die*.

**gird** [gɜːd] (*pt & pp* **-ed** *or* **girt**) *vt* ▷ **loin.**

**girder** ['gɜːdə<sup>r</sup>] *n* Träger *der*.

**girdle** ['gɜːdl] *n* [corset] Mieder *das*.

**girl** [gɜːl] *n* Mädchen *das;* [daughter] Tochter *die*, Mädchen *das;* **I'm going out with the ~s tonight** ich gehe heute Abend mit meinen Freundinnen aus; **the ~s at work** die Kolleginnen.

**girl Friday** *n* Allround-Büroangestellte *die*.

**girlfriend** ['gɜːlfrend] *n* Freundin *die*.

**girl guide** *Br*, **girl scout** *Am n* Pfadfinderin *die*.

**girlie magazine** ['gɜːlɪː-] *n inf* Zeitschrift mit Bildern nackter Mädchen.

**girlish** ['gɜːlɪʃ] *adj* mädchenhaft.

**girl scout** *n Am* = girl guide.

**giro** ['dʒaɪrəʊ] (*pl* -s) *n Br* [system] Giro *das;* ~ (**cheque**) Giroscheck für Sozialhilfeempfänger.

**girt** [gɜːt] *pt* & *pp* ⊳ **gird.**

**girth** [gɜːθ] *n* - **1.** [circumference] Umfang *der* - **2.** [of horse] (Sattel)gurt *der.*

**gist** [dʒɪst] *n* Wesentliche *das;* **to get the** ~ **(of sthg)** das Wesentliche (einer Sache (G)) mitlbekommen.

**give** [gɪv] (*pt* **gave;** *pp* **given**) *vt* - **1.** [gen] geben; **to** ~ **sb/sthg jm** etw geben; **to** ~ **sb a push/kiss** jm einen Schubs/Kuss geben; **to** ~ **sb a look/ smile** jn anlsehen/anllächeln; **to** ~ **a cry** auf lschreien - **2.** [as present]: **to** ~ **sb sthg** jm etw schenken; [as donation] jm etw spenden - **3.** [speech] halten - **4.** [attention, time]: **he ~s the issue a lot of attention** er widmet der Sache viel Aufmerksamkeit - **5.** [communicate] geben; **when will you** ~ **me your decision?** wann werden Sie mir Ihre Entscheidung mitteilen?; **I'll** ~ **him the message** ich werde es ihm ausrichten; ~ **her my regards** grüß sie schön von mir - **6.** [produce] machen; **to** ~ **sb a surprise** jm eine Überraschung bereiten; **to** ~ **sb pleasure/trouble** jm Freude/Probleme bereiten *OR* machen; **does it** ~ **you much pain?** tut es sehr weh?; **to** ~ **sb a fright** jn erschrecken; **what gave you that idea?** wie bist du auf diese Idee gekommen? - **7.** *phr:* '~ **way**' 'Vorfahrt beachten'; **he gave me to believe** *OR* **understand that** ... *fml* er gab mir zu verstehen, dass ...; ~**n the choice, I would** ... wenn ich die Wahl hätte, würde ich ...; **I'll** ~ **it a go** ich werde es (mal) versuchen ⟨> *vi* [yield] nachlgeben ⟨> *n* [elasticity] Nachgiebigkeit *die.*

◆ **give or take** *prep:* **5,000 people,** ~ **or take a few hundred** schätzungsweise 5000 Leute.

◆ **give away** *vt sep* - **1.** [hand over] weglgeben - **2.** [reveal] verraten; **to** ~ **the game away** alles verraten.

◆ **give back** *vt sep* zurücklgeben.

◆ **give in** *vi* - **1.** [agree unwillingly] nachlgeben; **to** ~ **in to sb/sthg** jm/etw nachlgeben - **2.** [admit defeat] sich geschlagen geben.

◆ **give off** *vt fus* ablgeben.

◆ **give out** *vt sep* [distribute] auslteilen ⟨> *vi* [fail - legs, machine] versagen; [- strength, supply] zu Ende gehen.

◆ **give over** *vt sep* [dedicate]: **this building was ~n over to the church** das Gebäude wurde der Kirche übergeben; **the evening was ~n over to playing football** der Abend wurde mit Fußballspielen verbracht ⟨> *vi Br inf:* ~ **over!** hör auf!

◆ **give up** *vt sep* - **1.** [stop, abandon] auflgeben; **to** ~ **up doing sthg** aufhören, etw zu

tun - **2.** [surrender]: **to** ~ **o.s. up (to sb)** sich (jm) ergeben ⟨> *vi* [admit defeat] auf lgeben.

◆ **give up on** *vt fus* [abandon] auf lgeben.

**give-and-take** *n* Kompromissbereitschaft *die.*

**giveaway** ['gɪvə,weɪ] *adj* - **1.** [sign, comment] verräterisch - **2.** [price] Schleuder- ⟨> *n* [telltale sign]: **it was a (dead)** ~ es hat sie/ihn/*etc* verraten.

**given** ['gɪvn] *pp* ⊳ **give** ⟨> *adj* - **1.** [fixed] bestimmt; **at any** ~ **time** zu jeder beliebigen Zeit - **2.** [prone]: **to be** ~ **to sthg** zu etw neigen; **to be** ~ **to doing sthg** die Angewohnheit haben, etw zu tun ⟨> *prep* [taking into account] angesichts (+ G); ~ **that** ... angesichts der Tatsache, dass ...

**given name** *n Am* Vorname *der.*

**glacial** ['gleɪsjəl] *adj* - **1.** [of glacier] Gletscher- - **2.** *fig* [unfriendly] eisig.

**glacier** ['glæsjəʳ] *n* Gletscher *der.*

**glad** [glæd] (*compar* **-der;** *superl* **-dest**) *adj* - **1.** [happy] froh, erfreut; **to be** ~ **about sthg** sich über etw (A) freuen; **I would be** ~ **to help you** ich würde Ihnen sehr gerne helfen - **2.** [grateful]: **to be** ~ **of sthg** dankbar für etw sein.

**gladden** ['glædn] *vt literary* erfreuen.

**glade** [gleɪd] *n literary* Lichtung *die.*

**gladioli** [ˌglædɪ'əʊlaɪ] *npl* Gladiolen *pl.*

**gladly** ['glædlɪ] *adv* [willingly, eagerly] gern(e).

**glamor** *n Am* = glamour.

**glamorize, -ise** ['glæməraɪz] *vt* idealisieren; [war, crime] glorifizieren.

**glamorous** ['glæmərəs] *adj* [film star, lifestyle] glamourös; [job] Traum-.

**glamour** *Br,* **glamor** *Am* ['glæməʳ] *n* [of film star, lifestyle] Glamour *der;* [of job] Reiz *der.*

**glance** [glɑːns] *n* Blick *der;* **to cast** *OR* **take a** ~ **at sthg** einen Blick auf etw (A) werfen; **at a** ~ auf einen Blick; **at first** ~ auf den ersten Blick ⟨> *vi:* **to** ~ **at sb** jn kurz anlsehen; **to** ~ **at sthg** einen Blick auf etw (A) werfen; **to** ~ **at** *OR* **through sthg** [newspaper, book] etw überfliegen.

◆ **glance off** *vt fus* [subj: ball, bullet] ablprallen an (+ D); [subj: light] reflektiert werden von.

**glancing** ['glɑːnsɪŋ] *adj:* **to strike sb a** ~ **blow** jn nur streifen.

**gland** [glænd] *n* Drüse *die.*

**glandular fever** [ˌglændjʊləʳ-] *n* Drüsenfieber *das.*

**glare** [gleəʳ] *n* - **1.** [scowl] langer wütender Blick - **2.** (*U*) [of light, sun] greller Schein; **the** ~ **of publicity** das Rampenlicht der Öffentlichkeit ⟨> *vi* - **1.** [scowl] böse blicken; **to** ~ **at sb/sthg** jn/etw böse anlstarren - **2.** [light, sun] grell scheinen.

**glaring** ['gleərɪŋ] adj - **1.** [error, example] eklatant - **2.** [light, sun] grell.

**Glasgow** ['glɑːzgəʊ] n Glasgow nt.

**glass** [glɑːs] n - **1.** [gen] Glas das; a ~ of wine ein Glas Wein - **2.** (U) [glassware] Glaswaren pl ◇ comp Glas-.

➡ **glasses** npl [spectacles] Brille die; [binoculars] Fernglas das; a pair of ~es eine Brille.

**glassblowing** ['glɑːs‚bləʊɪŋ] n Glasbläserei die.

**glass fibre** n (U) Br Glasfaser die.

**glasshouse** ['glɑːshaʊs‚ pl -haʊzɪz] n Br [greenhouse] Gewächshaus das.

**glassware** ['glɑːsweəʳ] n (U) Glaswaren pl.

**glassy** ['glɑːsɪ] (compar -ier; superl -iest) adj - **1.** [surface, sea] spiegelglatt - **2.** [stare, eye] glasig.

**Glaswegian** [glæz'wiːdʒjən] adj Glasgower- ◇ n Glasgower der, -in die.

**glaucoma** [glɔː'kəʊmə] n (U) grüner Star.

**glaze** [gleɪz] n Glasur die ◇ vt [pottery & CULIN] glasieren.

➡ **glaze over** vi [eyes] glasig werden.

**glazed** [gleɪzd] adj - **1.** [eyes] glasig; [expression] starr - **2.** [pottery & CULIN] glasiert - **3.** [door, window] verglast.

**glazier** ['gleɪzjəʳ] n Glaser der, -in die.

**GLC** (abbr of **Greater London Council**) n ehemalige Stadtregierung des Großraums London.

**gleam** [gliːml] n [of surface] Schimmer der; [of light, sunset] Schein der; a ~ of hope ein Hoffnungsschimmer ◇ vi [surface, object] schimmern; [gold, brass] glänzen; [light] scheinen; [eyes] funkeln.

**gleaming** ['gliːmɪŋ] adj [surface, object] schimmernd; [gold, brass] glänzend; [light] scheinend; [eyes] funkelnd.

**glean** [gliːn] vt [gather] zusammenltragen.

**glee** [gliː] n [joy] Freude die; [gloating] Schadenfreude die.

**gleeful** ['gliːfʊl] adj [joyful] freudig; [gloating] schadenfroh.

**glen** [glen] n Irish & Scot enges Tal.

**glib** [glɪb] (compar -ber; superl -best) adj pej - **1.** [answer, excuse] leichthin gesagt - **2.** [person] aalglatt.

**glibly** ['glɪblɪ] adv pej [talk, reply] leichthin.

**glide** [glaɪd] vi - **1.** [move smoothly - boat] gleiten; [ - dancer] schweben - **2.** [fly] schweben.

**glider** ['glaɪdəʳ] n Segelflugzeug das.

**gliding** ['glaɪdɪŋ] n Segelfliegen das.

**glimmer** ['glɪməʳ] n - **1.** [faint light] schwacher Schein - **2.** fig: ~ of hope Hoffnungsschimmer der; **she didn't show a ~ of interest/ understanding** sie zeigte nicht die leiseste

Spur von Interesse/Verständnis ◇ vi schwach scheinen.

**glimpse** [glɪmps] n - **1.** [look] flüchtiger Blick; **to catch a ~ of sb/sthg** jn/etw flüchtig zu sehen bekommen - **2.** [insight]: **we got a ~ of his true character** wir haben einen Eindruck davon bekommen, wie er wirklich war ◇ vt - **1.** [catch sight of] flüchtig or kurz sehen - **2.** [perceive]: **to ~ sb's true feelings** einen Eindruck von js wahren Gefühlen bekommen.

**glint** [glɪnt] n - **1.** [of metal, sunlight] Glitzern das - **2.** [in eyes]: **there was a ~ of anger in his eyes** seine Augen funkelten böse ◇ vi - **1.** [metal, sunlight] glitzern - **2.** [eyes] funkeln.

**glisten** ['glɪsn] vi [gold, lips] glänzen; [lake, raindrops] glitzern.

**glitch** [glɪtʃ] n inf [in plan] Fehler der.

**glitter** ['glɪtəʳ] n - **1.** [of object, light] Glitzern das; [of diamonds, stars] Funkeln das - **2.** [decoration, make-up] Glitzerstaub der ◇ vi glitzern; [diamonds, stars] funkeln.

**glittering** ['glɪtərɪŋ] adj - **1.** [object, light] glitzernd; [diamonds, stars] funkelnd - **2.** [glamorous - career] glänzend; [ - party] glanzvoll.

**glitzy** ['glɪtsɪ] (compar -ier; superl -iest) adj inf [dress, party] glamourös.

**gloat** [gləʊt] vi: **to ~ (over sthg)** [over sb's misfortune] sich hämisch (über etw (A)) freuen; [over one's own success] sich selbstzufrieden (über etw (A)) freuen.

**global** ['gləʊbl] adj global; [economy, peace] Welt-.

**globally** ['gləʊbəlɪ] adv - **1.** [worldwide] global, weltweit - **2.** [generally] allgemein.

**global warming** [-'wɔːmɪŋ] n Erwärmung die der Erdatmosphäre.

**globe** [gləʊb] n - **1.** [Earth]: **the ~** die Erde - **2.** [sphere representing world] Globus der.

**globetrotter** ['gləʊb‚trɒtəʳ] n inf Globetrotter der, -in die.

**globule** ['glɒbjuːl] n [of blood, water] Tröpfchen das; [of wax] Kügelchen das.

**gloom** [gluːm] n - **1.** [darkness] Düsterkeit die - **2.** [unhappiness] Trübsinn der.

**gloomy** ['gluːmɪ] (compar -ier; superl -iest) adj - **1.** [place, landscape, weather] düster - **2.** [person, atmosphere] trübsinnig - **3.** [outlook] düster; [news] bedrückend.

**glorification** [‚glɔːrɪfɪ'keɪʃn] n Verherrlichung die.

**glorified** ['glɔːrɪfaɪd] adj pej: **air hostesses are just ~ waitresses** Stewardessen sind nichts weiter als bessere Kellnerinnen.

**glorify** ['glɔːrɪfaɪ] (pt & pp -ied) vt verherrlichen.

**glorious** [ˈglɔːrɪəs] *adj* - **1.** [illustrious] glorreich - **2.** [wonderful] herrlich.

**glory** [ˈglɔːrɪ] (*pl* -**ies**) *n* - **1.** [fame, honour] Ruhm *der* - **2.** [splendour] Herrlichkeit *die* - **3.** [best feature] Stolz *der*.
➤ **glories** *npl* [successes] Erfolge *pl*.
➤ **glory in** *vt fus* [success] sich sonnen in (+ D); [freedom] genießen.

**Glos** *abk für* Gloucestershire, *in Postanschrift verwendet.*

**gloss** [glɒs] *n* - **1.** [shine] Glanz *der* - **2.:** ~ (**paint**) Lackfarbe *die*.
➤ **gloss over** *vt fus* [treat briefly] nur ganz kurz erwähnen; [hide] unter den Teppich kehren.

**glossary** [ˈglɒsərɪ] (*pl* -**ies**) *n* Glossar *das*.

**glossy** [ˈglɒsɪ] (*compar* -**ier**; *superl* -**iest**) *adj* glänzend; [photo, paper] Glanz-.

**glossy magazine** *n* Hochglanzmagazin *das*.

**glove** [glʌv] *n* Handschuh *der;* **to fit like a ~** [garment] wie angegossen passen.

**glove compartment** *n* Handschuhfach *das*.

**glove puppet** *n Br* Handpuppe *die*.

**glow** [gləʊ] *n* - **1.** [of fire, light, sunset] Schein *der* - **2.** [flush]: **there was a healthy ~ in her cheeks** ihre Wangen hatten eine blühende Farbe - **3.** [feeling]: **he felt a ~ of pride in his achievement** seine Leistung erfüllte ihn mit großem Stolz; **she felt a ~ of pleasure** sie empfand eine tiefe Freude ◇ *vi* - **1.** [light] scheinen; [fire, sky] glühen - **2.** [with colour] leuchten - **3.** [person]: **to ~ with pleasure** vor Freude strahlen; **he was ~ing with health** er strotzte vor Gesundheit.

**glower** [ˈglaʊəʳ] *vi* wütend dreinblicken; **to ~ at sb/sthg** jn/etw wütend anblicken.

**glowing** [ˈgləʊɪŋ] *adj* [report, description] begeistert.

**glow-worm** *n* Glühwürmchen *das*.

**glucose** [ˈgluːkəʊs] *n* Glukose *die*.

**glue** [gluː] (*cont* **glueing** *OR* **gluing**) *n* Klebstoff *der* ◇ *vt* kleben; **to ~ sthg to sthg** etw an etw (A) kleben; **to be ~d to the TV** unentwegt vor dem Fernseher hocken.

**glue-sniffing** [-ˌsnɪfɪŋ] *n* (Klebstoff)schnüffeln *das*.

**glum** [glʌm] (*compar* -**mer**; *superl* -**mest**) *adj* trübsinnig.

**glut** [glʌt] *n:* ~ (**of sthg**) Überangebot *das* (an etw (D)).

**gluten** [ˈgluːtən] *n* Gluten *die*.

**glutinous** [ˈgluːtɪnəs] *adj* klebrig.

**glutton** [ˈglʌtn] *n* Vielfraß *der;* **to be a ~ for punishment** ein Masochist sein.

**gluttony** [ˈglʌtənɪ] *n* Völlerei *die*.

**glycerin** [ˈglɪsərɪn], **glycerine** [ˈglɪsəriːn] *n* Glyzerin *das*.

**gm** (*abbr of* **gram**) g.

**GM** *adj abbr of* **genetically modified**.

**GMB** (*abbr of* **General, Municipal, and Boilermakers**) *n britische Industriegewerkschaft*.

**GMO** (*abbr of* **genetically modified organism**) *n* GVO *der*.

**GMT** (*abbr of* **Greenwich Mean Time**) *n* WEZ, GMT.

**gnarled** [nɑːld] *adj* knorrig.

**gnash** [næʃ] *vt:* **to ~ one's teeth** mit den Zähnen knirschen.

**gnat** [næt] *n* Mücke *die*.

**gnaw** [nɔː] *vt* nagen an (+ D); [fingernails] kauen an (+ D); **to ~ a hole in sthg** ein Loch in etw (A) nagen ◇ *vi* [worry]: **to ~ (away) at sb** jn quälen.

**gnome** [nəʊm] *n* Gnom *der;* [in garden] Gartenzwerg *der*.

**GNP** (*abbr of* **gross national product**) *n* BSP *das*.

**gnu** [nuː] (*pl inv OR* -**s**) *n* Gnu *das*.

**go** [gəʊ] (*pt* **went**; *pp* **gone**; *pl* **goes**) *vi* - **1.** [move] gehen; [by vehicle, travel] fahren; [by plane] fliegen; **to ~ shopping/for a walk** einkaufen/spazieren gehen; **I'll ~ and collect the cases** ich gehe die Koffer abholen; **to ~ home/to school** nach Hause/in die Schule gehen; **to ~ to Austria** nach Österreich fahren; **to ~ by bus** mit dem Bus fahren; **to ~ by plane** fliegen; **to ~ to work** zur Arbeit gehen; **where do we ~ from here?** *fig* was machen wir nun? - **2.** [leave] gehen; [in vehicle] fahren; **it's time we went** es wird Zeit, dass wir gehen; **let's ~!** gehen wir!; **when does the bus ~?** wann fährt der Bus ab?; **~ away!** geh weg! - **3.** [lead]: **where does this path ~?** wohin führt dieser Weg? - **4.** [time] vergehen - **5.** [progress - negotiations, preparations, business] laufen; **how are your studies ~ing?** wie läuft es mit deinem Studium?; **how did the party ~?** wie war die Party?; **to ~ well** gut gehen; **how's it ~ing?** wie geht's? - **6.** [become] werden; **she went pale** sie wurde bleich; **the milk has gone sour** die Milch ist sauer geworden; **to ~ bankrupt** Bankrott machen - **7.** [be]: **our cries went unheard** unsere Rufe blieben ungehört; **to ~ hungry** hungern; **to allow sb to ~ free** jn freilassen - **8.** [expressing future tense]: **to be ~ing to do sthg** etw tun werden; **it's ~ing to rain tomorrow** morgen wird es regnen; **we're ~ing to go to Switzerland** wir fahren in die Schweiz; **she's ~ing to have a baby** sie bekommt ein Baby - **9.** [function - gear] laufen; [ - watch, clock] gehen - **10.** [become damaged] kaputtgehen; **the fuse has gone** die Sicherung ist herausgesprungen; **her sight is ~ing** ihre Sehkraft lässt nach - **11.** [bell, alarm] losgehen; **the bell went** es klingelte - **12.** [match]

zusammenǀpassen; **to ~ with** passen zu; **red wine doesn't ~ with fish** Rotwein passt nicht zu Fisch **- 13.** [fit] passen, gehen; **it won't ~ into my case** es geht OR passt nicht in meinen Koffer **- 14.** [belong] kommen; **the plates ~ in the cupboard** die Teller kommen in den Schrank **- 15.** [be sold] verkauft werden; 'everything must ~' 'alles muss weg' **- 16.** [be spent]: **all my money goes on rent** mein ganzes Geld geht für die Miete drauf **- 17.** [be given]: **to ~ to sb/sthg** an jn/etw gehen; **the contract/prize went to X** der Vertrag/Preis ging an X **- 18.** [in division] gehen; **three into two won't ~** zwei durch drei geht nicht **- 19.** [referring to story, song etc] gehen; **how does that song ~?** wie geht das Lied?; **as the saying goes** wie man so sagt **- 20.** inf [with negative - giving advice]: **now, don't ~ catching cold** erkälte dich bloß nicht **- 21.** inf [expressing irritation]: **he's gone and broken my computer!** er hat doch tatsächlich meinen Computer kaputtgemacht!; **now what's he gone and done?** was hat er jetzt wieder gemacht?; **you've gone and done it now!** jetzt hast du es geschafft! **- 22.** phr: **to let ~ of sthg** [drop] etw losǀlassen; **to ~ it alone** es allein versuchen ◇ vt **- 1.** [make noise] machen; **the dog went "woof"** der Hund machte „Wuff" **- 2.** inf [say] sagen ◇ n **- 1.** [turn]: **it's your ~** du bist dran **- 2.** inf [attempt] Versuch der; **to have a ~ at sthg** etw versuchen, etw probieren, **to have a ~ on sthg** etw ausǀ probieren; **'50p a ~'** 'jede Runde 50 Pence' **- 3.** inf [success]: **at** OR **in one ~** auf einmal; **to make a ~ of sthg** aus etw einen Erfolg machen **- 4.** phr: **to have a ~ at sb** inf [criticize] jn zur Schnecke machen; **to be on the ~** inf auf Trab sein.

‣ **to go** adv **- 1.** [remaining]: **how long is there to ~ until Christmas?** wie lange ist es noch bis Weihnachten?; **with five minutes to ~ they were winning** fünf Minuten vor dem Abpfiff führten sie **- 2.** Am [to take away] zum Mitnehmen.

‣ **go about** vt fus **- 1.** [perform]: **to ~ about one's business** seinen Geschäften nachǀ gehen **- 2.** [tackle]: **I don't know how to ~ about doing it** ich weiß nicht, wie ich das anfangen soll; **how do you intend ~ing about it?** wie willst du das machen? ◇ vi = **go around**.

‣ **go after** vt fus [aim for] aus sein auf (+ A).

‣ **go against** vt fus **- 1.** [be in conflict with] gehen gegen **- 2.** [disregard] missachten; **she went against our wishes** sie hat unsere Wünsche missachtet **- 3.** [be unfavourable to]: **the vote went against us** wir haben die Wahl verloren; **the verdict went against us** das Urteil fiel gegen uns aus.

‣ **go ahead** vi **- 1.**: **to ~ ahead (with sthg)** (mit etw) anǀfangen OR beginnen; **the government is ~ing ahead with its plans** die Regierung wird die Pläne nun doch in die Tat umset-

zen; **~ ahead!** bitte! **- 2.** [take place] stattǀ finden.

‣ **go along** vi: **we were ~ing along when the engine died** während der Fahrt starb plötzlich der Motor ab; **he was making it up as he went along** er sagte einfach, was ihm gerade im Sinn kam.

‣ **go along with** vt fus [idea, plan] zuǀstimmen (+ D).

‣ **go around** vi **- 1.** inf [behave in a certain way]: **you can't ~ around telling lies** du kannst nicht einfach Lügen erzählen **- 2.** [associate]: **to ~ around with sb** mit jm herumǀziehen **- 3.** [joke, illness, story] herumǀgehen; [rumour] umǀgehen.

‣ **go away** vi wegǀgehen; [by vehicle] wegǀ fahren; **~ away!** geh weg!; **we're ~ing away for the weekend** wir fahren übers Wochenende weg.

‣ **go back** vi **- 1.** [return] zurückǀgehen; [by vehicle] zurückǀfahren **- 2.** [to activity]: **to ~ back to work** [after interruption] die Arbeit wieder aufǀ nehmen; [after holiday] wieder arbeiten gehen; **to ~ back to sleep** wieder einǀ schlafen **- 3.** [to previous topic]: **to ~ back to sthg** auf etw (A) zurückǀkommen **- 4.** [date from]: **their friendship goes back to 1955** sie sind schon seit 1955 befreundet.

‣ **go back on** vt fus: **to ~ back on one's word** sein Wort nicht halten.

‣ **go before** vi [precede]: **to ~ before sb/sthg** jm/ einer Sache voranǀgehen.

‣ **go by** vi [time] vergehen ◇ vt fus **- 1.** [be guided by - instincts] folgen (+ D); [ - instructions] befolgen **- 2.** [judge by - appearances] gehen nach; **~ing by her accent, I'd say she was French** ihrem Akzent nach ist sie Französin.

‣ **go down** vi **- 1.** [decrease - prices, value, temperature] sinken, fallen **- 2.** [sun] unterǀgehen **- 3.** [tyre] platt werden **- 4.** [be accepted]: **to ~ down well/badly** gut schlecht anǀkommen ◇ vt fus [stairs, road] hinunterǀgehen.

‣ **go down with** vt fus [illness] bekommen.

‣ **go for** vt fus **- 1.** [choose] wählen; [buy] nehmen **- 2.** [be attracted to]: **to ~ for sb/sthg** jn/etw bevorzugen **- 3.** [attack]: **to ~ for sb** auf jn losǀ gehen **- 4.** [try to obtain] aus sein auf (+ A); **just ~ for it and ask her out!** frag sie einfach, ob sie mit dir ausgehen will! **- 5.** [be valid] gelten; **does that ~ for me too?** gilt das auch für mich?

‣ **go in** vi hineinǀgehen.

‣ **go in for** vt fus **- 1.** [enter - competition] mitǀ machen bei; [ - exam] machen **- 2.** inf [activity]: **he goes in for sports in a big way** er ist ein großer Sportfan; **I don't really ~ in for classical music** ich mache mir nicht viel aus klassischer Musik.

‣ **go into** vt fus **- 1.** [describe]: **to ~ into sthg (in detail)** auf etw (A) (näher) einǀgehen **- 2.** [investigate] sich befassen mit **- 3.** [take up as a profession]: **to ~ into teaching** Lehrer werden

**G**

- **4.** [subj: effort, money]: **a lot of hard work went into that book** das Buch hat viel Arbeit gekostet - **5.** [begin]: **the plane went into a spin** das Flugzeug geriet ins Trudeln; **to ~ into a rage** wütend werden.

◆ **go off** *vi* - **1.** [alarm] loslgehen; [bomb] explodieren - **2.** [food] schlecht werden - **3.** [light, heating] auslgehen - **4.** [happen] verlaufen; **everything went off well** alles ist gut verlaufen ◇ *vt fus inf* [lose interest in] nicht mehr mögen.

◆ **go on** *vi* - **1.** [happen] los sein; **what's ~ing on next door?** was ist nebenan los? - **2.** [light, heating] anlgehen - **3.** [continue]: **to ~ on doing sthg** etw weiter tun; **I can't ~ on!** ich kann nicht mehr!; **~ on!** [continue talking] weiter!; **we went on to a disco afterwards** anschließend gingen wir in eine Disko; **he went on to become president** später wurde er Präsident - **4.** [go in advance] vorauslgehen; **you ~ on, I'll wait here** geh nur, ich bleibe hier - **5.** [pass - time] vergehen - **6.** [talk for too long]: **she doesn't half ~ on** *inf* sie ist eine Quasselstrippe; **to ~ on (and on) about sthg** auf etw (D) herumlreiten; **don't ~ on about it!** hör doch mal (damit) auf! ◇ *vt fus* [be guided by]: **I've got nothing to ~ on** ich habe keine Anhaltspunkte ◇ *excl* [expressing encouragement]: **~ on!** komm schon!; **~ on, have another chocolate** nimm doch noch eine Praline.

◆ **go on at** *vt fus* [nag]: **to ~ on at sb** an jm herumlnörgeln.

◆ **go out** *vi* - **1.** [light, heating] auslgehen - **2.** [move outside] hinauslgehen; **to ~ out for a meal** essen gehen; **to ~ out for a walk** einen Spaziergang machen - **3.** [have relationship]: **to ~ out with sb** mit jm zusammen sein; **we've been ~ing out for six years** wir sind seit sechs Jahren zusammen; **he's ~ing out with a Frenchwoman** er ist mit einer Französin zusammen, seine Freundin ist Französin - **4.** [tide]: **the tide is ~ing out** die Ebbe hat eingesetzt.

◆ **go over** *vt fus* - **1.** [check] überprüfen, durchlgehen - **2.** [repeat]: **to ~ over sthg again** etw wiederholen.

◆ **go over to** *vt fus* - **1.** [change to]: **we're ~ing over to gas** wir steigen auf Gas um - **2.** [change sides]: **to ~ over to the enemy** zum Feind überlaufen; **to ~ over to the Labour Party** zur Labourpartei überlwechseln - **3.** TV & RADIO: **we're now ~ing over to Washington/our New York correspondent** wir schalten jetzt nach Washington/zu unserem Korrespondenten in New York.

◆ **go round** *vi* - **1.** [revolve] sich drehen - **2.** [be enough] auslreichen; **there isn't enough to ~ round** es reicht nicht für alle; *see also* **go around**.

◆ **go through** *vt fus* - **1.** [experience] durchlmachen - **2.** [use up - money] auslgeben; [ - inheritance] durchlbringen; **I went through five packets of cigarettes** ich habe fünf Schach-

teln Zigaretten geraucht - **3.** [search] durchlsuchen - **4.** [read] durchlsehen ◇ *vi* [bill] durchlkommen; **the deal didn't ~ through** das Geschäft kam nicht zustande; **my divorce has gone through** meine Scheidung ist durch.

◆ **go through with** *vt fus*: **the government is ~ing through with the plan** die Regierung setzt den Plan in die Tat um; **she couldn't ~ through with it** sie brachte es nicht fertig.

◆ **go towards** *vt fus* [contribute to] bestimmt sein für.

◆ **go under** *vi lit* & *fig* unterlgehen.

◆ **go up** *vi* - **1.** [increase] steigen - **2.** [move upwards - balloon] auflsteigen; [ - person] auflsteigen - **3.** [be built] gebaut werden - **4.** [explode] in die Luft gehen; **to ~ up in flames** in Flammen auflgehen ◇ *vt fus* [stairs, hill] hinauflsteigen.

◆ **go with** *vt fus* - **1.** [be included with] gehören zu - **2.** [match] passen zu.

◆ **go without** *vt fus*: **to ~ without sthg** ohne etw auslkommen.

**goad** [gəʊd] *vt* [provoke] provozieren; **to ~ sb into doing sthg** jn so lange provozieren, bis er/sie etw tut.

**go-ahead** *adj* fortschrittlich ◇ *n* Erlaubnis *die*; **to give sb the ~ (for sthg)** jm grünes Licht (für etw) geben.

**goal** [gəʊl] *n* - **1.** SPORT Tor *das*; **to score a ~** ein Tor erzielen - **2.** [aim] Ziel *das*.

**goalie** [ˈgəʊlɪ] *n inf* Torwart *der*.

**goalkeeper** [ˈgəʊlˌkiːpəʳ] *n* Torwart *der*, Torhüter *der*, -in *die*.

**goalless** [ˈgəʊllɪs] *adj*: **to end in a ~ draw** Null zu Null enden.

**goalmouth** [ˈgəʊlmaʊθ, *pl* -maʊðz] *n unmittelbarer Torbereich*.

**goalpost** [ˈgəʊlpəʊst] *n* Torpfosten *der*.

**goat** [gəʊt] *n* Ziege *die*; **to act the ~** *Br* herumlalbern.

**goatee (beard)** [ˈgəʊtɪ-] *n* Ziegenbärtchen *das*.

**goat's cheese** *n* Ziegenkäse *der*.

**gob** [gɒb] (*pt* & *pp* -**bed**; *cont* -**bing**) *inf n Br* [mouth] Maul *das*, Schnauze *die* ◇ *vi* [spit] spucken.

**gobble** [ˈgɒbl] *vt* hinunterlschlingen.

◆ **gobble down, gobble up** *vt sep* hinunterlschlingen.

**gobbledygook** [ˈgɒbldɪguːk] *n* - **1.** [official language] Kauderwelsch *das* - **2.** *inf* [nonsense] Unsinn *der*.

**go-between** *n* Vermittler *der*, -in *die*.

**Gobi Desert** [ˈgəʊbɪ-] *n*: **the ~** die Wüste Gobi.

**goblet** [ˈgɒblɪt] *n* Kelch *der*.

**goblin** [ˈgɒblɪn] *n* Kobold *der*.

**gobsmacked** [ˈgɒbsmækt] *adj Br inf* platt.

**go-cart** n = go-kart.

**god** [gɒd] n Gott der.
➤ **God** n Gott der; **God knows** keine Ahnung; **God knows the money I've spent on those kids** ich habe weiß Gott viel Geld für diese Kinder ausgegeben; **for God's sake!** um Gottes willen!; **thank God!** Gott sei Dank! ◇ excl: **(my) God!** (mein) Gott!
➤ **gods** npl Br inf: **the ~s** THEATRE der Olymp.

**godchild** ['gɒdtʃaɪld] (pl -children [-ˌtʃɪldrən]) n Patenkind das.

**goddam(n)** ['gɒdæm] esp Am adj vinf verdammt ◇ excl verdammt noch mal!

**goddaughter** ['gɒdˌdɔːtəʳ] n Patentochter die.

**goddess** ['gɒdɪs] n Göttin die.

**godfather** ['gɒdˌfɑːðəʳ] n Pate der, Patenonkel der.

**godforsaken** ['gɒdfəˌseɪkn] adj gottverlassen.

**godmother** ['gɒdˌmʌðəʳ] n Patin die, Patentante die.

**godparents** ['gɒdˌpeərənts] npl Paten pl.

**godsend** ['gɒdsend] n Geschenk das des Himmels.

**godson** ['gɒdsʌn] n Patensohn der.

**goes** [gəʊz] vb ⊳ go.

**gofer** ['gəʊfəʳ] n Am inf Mädchen das für alles.

**go-getter** [-ˈgetəʳ] n dynamischer Mensch.

**goggle** ['gɒgl] vi: **to ~ at** sb/sthg auf jn/etw mit weit aufgerissenen Augen starren.

**goggles** ['gɒglz] npl [in industry] Schutzbrille die; [for diving] Taucherbrille die; [for skiing] Skibrille die.

**going** ['gəʊɪŋ] adj - **1.** [rate, salary] üblich - **2.** Br [available]: **any jobs ~?** gibt es freie Stellen?; **she's the biggest fool ~** sie ist der größte Dummkopf, den es gibt ◇ n - **1.** [progress]: **have you finished already? – that's good ~** bist du schon fertig? – du bist gut OR schnell vorangekommen; **it was slow ~** es ging nur langsam voran - **2.** [in horse racing] Geläuf das; **the ~ is good** die Bahn ist gut; **this novel is heavy ~** dieser Roman liest sich schwer.

**going concern** n gut gehendes Unternehmen.

**goings-on** npl inf: **strange ~** seltsame Dinge pl.

**go-kart** [-kɑːt] n Br Go-Kart der.

**gold** [gəʊld] adj [gold-coloured] golden ◇ n - **1.** [gen] Gold das; **to be as good as ~** sehr brav sein - **2.** [medal] Goldmedaille die ◇ comp [made of gold] Gold-.

**golden** ['gəʊldən] adj - **1.** [made of gold] Gold- - **2.** [gold-coloured] golden.

**golden age** n goldenes Zeitalter.

**golden eagle** n Steinadler der.

**golden handshake** n hohe Geldsumme, die leitenden Angestellten beim Verlassen ihrer Firma in Anerkennung ihrer Dienste gezahlt wird.

**golden opportunity** n ideale Gelegenheit.

**golden retriever** n Golden Retriever der.

**golden rule** n goldene Regel.

**golden wedding** n goldene Hochzeit.

**goldfish** ['gəʊldfɪʃ] (pl inv) n Goldfisch der.

**goldfish bowl** n Goldfischglas das.

**gold leaf** n Blattgold das.

**gold medal** n Goldmedaille die.

**goldmine** ['gəʊldmaɪn] n - **1.** [mine] Goldmine die - **2.** [profitable business] Goldgrube die.

**gold-plated** [-ˈpleɪtɪd] adj vergoldet.

**goldsmith** ['gəʊldsmɪθ] n Goldschmied der, -in die.

**golf** [gɒlf] n Golf das.

**golf ball** n - **1.** [for golf] Golfball der - **2.** [for typewriter] Kugelkopf der.

**golf club** n - **1.** [place, society] Golfklub der - **2.** [equipment] Golfschläger der.

**golf course** n Golfplatz der.

**golfer** ['gɒlfəʳ] n Golfspieler der, -in die.

**golly** ['gɒlɪ] excl inf dated Menschenskind!

**gondola** ['gɒndələ] n Gondel die.

**gone** [gɒn] pp ⊳ go ◇ adj [no longer here] weg ◇ prep [past] nach; **it's ~ twelve (o'clock)** es ist zwölf Uhr vorbei.

**gong** [gɒŋ] n Gong der.

**gonna** ['gɒnə] inf = going to.

**gonorrh(o)ea** [ˌgɒnəˈrɪə] n Tripper der, Gonorrhö die.

**goo** [guː] n (U) inf klebriges Zeug.

**good** [gʊd] (compar **better**; superl **best**) adj - **1.** [gen] gut; **it's ~ to see you again** schön, Sie wieder zu sehen; **to have a ~ time** sich gut amüsieren; **to feel ~** sich wohl fühlen; **it tastes/smells ~** es schmeckt/riecht gut; **is this meat still ~?** kann man das Fleisch noch essen?; **it's ~ for you** [beneficial] das wird dir gut tun; [food] das ist gesund; **a ~ opportunity** eine günstige Gelegenheit; **to be ~ at sthg** etw gut können; **~ at French** gut in Französisch; **she's ~ with her hands** sie ist geschickt mit den Händen; **she's very ~ with children** sie kann sehr gut mit Kindern umgehen - **2.** [suitable] geeignet; **he would make a ~ president** er eignet sich zum Präsidenten - **3.** [kind] lieb; **that's very ~ of you** das ist sehr nett von Ihnen; **to be ~ to sb** gut zu jm sein; **would you be ~ enough to open the door?** wären Sie so liebenswürdig, mir die Tür zu öffnen? - **4.** [well-behaved] artig, brav; **be ~!** sei brav! - **5.** [thorough] gründlich - **6.** [considerable]: a ~ while/deal ziemlich lange/viel; a ~ ten minutes gute zehn Minuten - **7.** *phr*: in ~ time beizeiten; to make sthg ~ [damage, loss] etw wieder gutImachen; it's a ~ job OR thing (that) ... zum Glück ...; ~ for you! wie schön für Dich!; to give as ~ as one gets Gleiches mit Gleichem vergelten <> *n* - **1.** [moral correctness] Gute *das*; to be up to no ~ nichts Gutes im Schilde führen - **2.** [use]: it's no ~ [there's no point] es hat keinen Zweck; what's the ~ of worrying (about it)? was nützt es, wenn man sich deswegen Sorgen macht?; will this be any ~? nützt das was? - **3.** [benefit]: for the ~ of zum Wohle (+ G); for your own ~ zu deinem Besten; it will do him ~ es wird ihm gut tun.

➤ **goods** *npl* Waren *pl*; to come up with OR deliver the ~s *Br inf* Wort halten.

➤ **as good as** *adv* so gut wie; as ~ as new so gut wie neu.

➤ **for good** *adv* für immer.

➤ **good afternoon** *excl* guten Tag!

➤ **good evening** *excl* guten Abend!

➤ **good morning** *excl* guten Morgen!

➤ **good night** *excl* gute Nacht!

**goodbye** [ˌgʊd'baɪ] *excl* auf Wiedersehen!; [on phone] auf Wiederhören! <> *n*: to say ~ auf Wiedersehen sagen; to wave ~ zum Abschied winken.

**good deed** *n* gute Tat.

**good-for-nothing** *adj* nichtsnutzig <> *n* Taugenichts *der*.

**good fortune** *n* Glück *das*.

**Good Friday** *n* Karfreitag *der*.

**GOOD FRIDAY AGREEMENT**

So genannt, weil es am Karfreitag 1998 (nach einem Volkentscheid) unterzeichnet wurde, ist dieses Abkommen zwischen der Bevölkerung Irlands und der britischen Regierung ein Meilenstein des Friedensprozesses in Nordirland. In diesem Abkommen erklärt die britische Regierung ihre Bereitschaft, die Verfassung so zu ändern, dass Nordirland, falls die Mehrheit der dortigen Bevölkerung dies wünscht, sich mit Irland vereinigen kann, während die Republik Irland sich bereit erklärt, ihre territorialen Ansprüche auf Nordirland aufzugeben. Das Abkommen enthält darüber hinaus weitere wichtige Aussagen zu Fragen der Regierung, der gemeinsamen Verantwortung für das Rechtswesen usw, darunter auch die Übereinkunft, alle paramilitärischen Organisationen zu entwaffnen.

**good-humoured** [-'hjuːməd] *adj* [person - temporarily] gut gelaunt; [ - by nature] gutmütig; [rivalry] freundschaftlich.

**good-looking** [-'lʊkɪŋ] *adj* gut aussehend.

**good manners** *npl* gute Manieren *pl*.

**good-natured** [-'neɪtʃəd] *adj* [person] gutmütig; [rivalry] freundschaftlich; [argument] friedlich.

**goodness** ['gʊdnɪs] *n* - **1.** [kindness] Güte *die* - **2.** [of food] Nährgehalt *der* <> *excl*: (my) ~! meine Güte!; for ~' sake! um Himmels willen!; thank ~! Gott sei Dank!

**goods train** *n Br* Güterzug *der*.

**good-tempered** [-'tempəd] *adj* [person] ausgeglichen; [meeting] harmonisch.

**good turn** *n*: to do sb a ~ jm einen Gefallen tun.

**goodwill** [ˌgʊd'wɪl] *n (U)* guter Wille; [between countries & COMM] Goodwill *der*.

**goody** ['gʊdɪ] (*pl* -ies) *n inf* [in story] Gute *der, die* <> *excl* toll!, prima!

➤ **goodies** *npl inf* - **1.** [delicious food] Leckerbissen *pl* - **2.** [desirable objects] schöne Dinge *pl*.

**gooey** ['guːɪ] (*compar* **gooier**; *superl* **gooiest**) *adj inf* [sticky] klebrig.

**goof** [guːf] *Am inf n* [mistake] Patzer *der* <> *vi* Mist bauen.

➤ **goof off** *vi Am inf* [waste time] herumltrödeln; [do nothing] auf der faulen Haut liegen.

**goofy** ['guːfɪ] (*compar* -**ier**; *superl* -**iest**) *adj inf* albern.

**goose** [guːs] (*pl* **geese**) *n* Gans *die*.

**gooseberry** ['gʊzbərɪ] (*pl* -ies) *n* Stachelbeere *die*; to play ~ *Br inf* das fünfte Rad am Wagen sein.

**gooseflesh** ['guːsfleʃ] *n*, **goose pimples** *Br npl*, **goosebumps** *Am* ['guːsbʌmps] *npl* Gänsehaut *die*.

**goosestep** ['guːsˌstep] (*pt & pp* -**ped**; *cont* -**ping**) *n* Stechschritt *der* <> *vi* im Stechschritt marschieren.

**GOP** (*abbr* of **Grand Old Party**) *n Partei der Republikaner in den USA*.

**gopher** ['gəʊfəʳ] *n* Taschenratte *die*.

**gore** [gɔːʳ] *n (U) literary* [blood] Blut *das* <> *vt* [subj: bull] mit den Hörnern verletzen.

**gorge** [gɔːdʒ] *n* Schlucht *die* <> *vt*: to ~ o.s. on OR with sthg sich mit etw vollIstopfen.

**gorgeous** ['gɔːdʒəs] *adj* - **1.** [place, present, weather] herrlich, wunderschön - **2.** *inf* [person] toll aussehend; to be ~ toll ausIsehen.

**gorilla** [gə'rɪlə] *n* Gorilla *der*.

**gormless** ['gɔːmlɪs] *adj Br inf* dämlich.

**gorse** [gɔːs] *n* Stechginster *der*.

**gory** ['gɔːrɪ] (*compar* -**ier**; *superl* -**iest**) *adj* [story, film] blutrünstig.

**gosh** [gɒʃ] *excl inf* mein Gott!, Mensch!

**go-slow** *n Br* Bummelstreik *der*.

**gospel** ['gɒspl] *n* - **1.** [doctrine] Lehre *die* - **2.** (*U*): to take sthg as ~ (truth) etw für bare Münze

nehmen; **it's the ~ truth** es ist die reine Wahrheit <> *comp* [music, song] Gospel-.
➤ **Gospel** *n* [in Bible] Evangelium *das.*

**gossip** ['gɒsɪp] *n* - **1.** [conversation] Klatsch *der;* **to have a ~** klatschen - **2.** [person] Klatschbase *die* <> *vi* klatschen.

**gossip column** *n* Klatschspalte *die.*

**got** [gɒt] *pt* & *pp* ⊳ **get.**

**Gothic** ['gɒθɪk] *adj* - **1.** [architecture, script] gotisch - **2.** [novel, story] Schauer-.

**gotta** ['gɒtə] *inf* = got to.

**gotten** ['gɒtn] *pp Am* ⊳ **get.**

**gouge** [gaʊdʒ] ➤ **gouge out** *vt sep* [hole] machen; [eyes] auslstechen.

**goulash** ['guːlæʃ] *n* Gulasch *das.*

**gourd** [gʊəd] *n* - **1.** [fruit] Flaschenkürbis *der* - **2.** [container] Kürbisflasche *die.*

**gourmet** ['gʊəmeɪ] *n* Feinschmecker *der,* -in *die* <> *comp* [food, restaurant] Feinschmecker-.

**gout** [gaʊt] *n* Gicht *die.*

**govern** ['gʌvən] *vt* - **1.** POL regieren - **2.** [determine] bestimmen <> *vi* POL regieren.

**governess** ['gʌvənɪs] *n* Gouvernante *die.*

**governing** ['gʌvənɪŋ] *adj* POL regierend; **~ party** Regierungspartei *die.*

**government** ['gʌvənmənt] *n* Regierung *die* <> *comp* [policy, official] Regierungs-; **~ spending** Staatsausgaben *pl;* **~ department** Ministerium *das.*

**governmental** [ˌgʌvn'mentl] *adj* Regierungs-.

**governor** ['gʌvənə] *n* - **1.** POL Gouverneur *der,* -in *die* - **2.** [of school] Mitglied *das* des Schulbeirats; [of bank] Mitglied *das* des Direktoriums - **3.** [of prison] Direktor *der,* -in *die.*

**govt** (*abbr of* **government**) Rg., Reg.

**gown** [gaʊn] *n* - **1.** [dress] Kleid *das;* [evening gown] Abendkleid *das* - **2.** UNIV & LAW Talar *der* - **3.** MED Kittel *der.*

**GP** *n abbr of* **general practitioner.**

**GPO** (*abbr of* **General Post Office**) *n* Post *die.*

**grab** [græb] (*pt* & *pp* **-bed**; *cont* **-bing**) *vt* - **1.** [with hands]: **to ~ (hold of)** [person] packen; [object] schnappen; **to ~ (hold of) sb's arm** jn am Arm packen - **2.** *fig* [opportunity] (beim Schopf) ergreifen; [sandwich, lunch] schnell essen; **to ~ a few hours' sleep** ein paar Stunden Schlaf kriegen - **3.** *inf* [appeal to]: **how does that ~ you?** wie findest du das? <> *vi:* **to ~ at sthg** [with hands] nach etw greifen <> *n:* **make a ~ at** OR **for sthg** nach etw greifen.

**grace** [greɪs] *n* - **1.** (U) [elegance] Grazie *die,* Anmut *die* - **2.** [graciousness]: **to have the ~ to do sthg** den Anstand haben, etw zu tun; **to do sthg with good ~** etw anstandslos tun - **3.** [extra time]: **ten days' ~** zehn Tage Aufschub

- **4.** [prayer] Tischgebet *das* <> *vt* - **1.** *fml* [honour] beehren - **2.** [adorn] schmücken.
➤ **Grace** *n* [title]: **Your Grace** Euer Gnaden.

**graceful** ['greɪsfʊl] *adj* - **1.** [beautiful] graziös, anmutig; [line, curve] gefällig - **2.** [gracious]: **he was ~ enough to say he was sorry** er war so anständig, sich zu entschuldigen.

**graceless** ['greɪslɪs] *adj* - **1.** [lacking charm] reizlos - **2.** [ill-mannered] unhöflich.

**gracious** ['greɪʃəs] *adj* - **1.** [polite] höflich - **2.** [elegant] mondän <> *excl:* **(good) ~!** ach du meine Güte!

**graciously** ['greɪʃəslɪ] *adv* [politely] höflich.

**gradation** [grə'deɪʃn] *n* Abstufung *die.*

**grade** [greɪd] *n* - **1.** [quality] Güteklasse *die;* **high-~** hochwertig - **2.** [in company, organization]: **(salary) ~** Gehaltsstufe *die;* **to make the ~** es schaffen - **3.** *Am* [class] Klasse *die* - **4.** [in exam, test] Note *die* - **5.** *Am* [gradient] Gefälle *das* <> *vt* - **1.** [classify] klassifizieren - **2.** [test, exam] benoten.

**grade crossing** *n Am* Bahnübergang *der.*

**grade school** *n Am* Grundschule *die.*

**grade school teacher** *n Am* Grundschullehrer *der,* -in *die.*

**gradient** ['greɪdjənt] *n* [of road - upward] Steigung *die;* [ - downward] Gefälle *das.*

**gradual** ['grædjʊəl] *adj* allmählich.

**gradually** ['grædjʊəlɪ] *adv* allmählich.

**graduate** [*n* 'grædjʊət, *vb* 'grædjʊeɪt] *n* - **1.** [person with a degree] Graduierte *der, die;* **he is an English ~** er hat einen Hochschulabschluss in Englisch - **2.** *Am* [of high school] ≃ Abiturient *der,* -in *die* (*mit bestandenem Abitur*) <> *vi* - **1.** [with a degree]: **to ~ (from)** seinen Hochschulabschluss machen (an (+ *D*)) - **2.** *Am* [from high school]: **to ~ (from)** ≃ das Abitur machen (an (+ *D*)) - **3.** [progress]: **to ~ from sthg to sthg** sich von etw zu etw hochlarbeiten.

**graduated** ['grædjʊeɪtɪd] *adj* [pension, tax, colours] abgestuft; [measuring jug, thermometer] mit Maßeinteilung.

**graduate school** *n Am* Hochschule oder College, an dem man sein Studium nach dem ersten akademischen Grad weiterführen kann.

**graduation** [ˌgrædjʊ'eɪʃn] *n* - **1.** [completion of course] Abschluss *der* des Studiums; *Am* [at high school] ≃ Abitur *das* - **2.** [university or school ceremony] Abschlussfeier *die.*

**graffiti** [grə'fiːtɪ] *n* (U) Graffiti *pl.*

**graft** [grɑːft] *n* - **1.** [from plant] Pfropfreis *das* - **2.** MED Transplantat *das* - **3.** *Br inf* [hard work] Plackerei *die* - **4.** *Am inf* [corruption] Schiebung *die* <> *vt* - **1.** [plant]: **to ~ sthg (onto)** etw pfropfen (auf (+ *A*)) - **2.** MED: **to ~ sthg (onto)** etw

G

transplantieren (in *(+ A))* - **3.** [idea, system]: **to ~ sthg onto** etw einlbringen in *(+ A)*.

**grain** [greɪn] *n* - **1.** [of corn, rice, salt, sand] Korn *das* - **2.** *(U)* [crops] Getreide *das*, Korn *das* - **3.** *fig* [of truth] Körnchen *das* - **4.** [in wood] Maserung *die;* [in rock] Korn *das;* **to go against the ~** *fig* gegen den Strich gehen.

**gram** [græm] *n* Gramm *das*.

**grammar** [ˈgræməʳ] *n* Grammatik *die;* **her ~ is appalling** sie macht entsetzlich viele Grammatikfehler.

**grammar school** *n* - **1.** [in UK] ≃ Gymnasium *das* - **2.** [in US] ≃ Grundschule *die*.

**GRAMMAR SCHOOL**

> „Grammar Schools" (in England und Wales) sind staatlich geförderte oder private weiterführende Schulen, die am ehesten dem traditionellen Gymnasium entsprechen. Sie bieten eine Ausbildung vom mehr traditionellen, akademischen Typ, die die Schüler auf ein Hochschulstudium vorbereiten soll. Die Aufnahme ist an eine Aufnahmeprüfung oder sonstige schriftliche Leistungsnachweise gebunden. Heute besuchen nur noch ca. 5% aller Schüler eine „Grammar School".

**grammatical** [grəˈmætɪkl] *adj* grammatisch; **it's not ~** es ist nicht grammatikalisch richtig.

**gramme** [græm] *n Br* = **gram**.

**gramophone** [ˈgræməfəʊn] *n dated* Grammofon *das*.

**gran** [græn] *n Br inf* Oma *die*, Omi *die*.

**grand** [grænd] *(pl inv) adj* - **1.** [house, style] prachtvoll; [design, plan] ehrgeizig; [person, job] bedeutend - **2.** *inf dated* [excellent] fantastisch ◇ *n inf* [thousand pounds] tausend Pfund *pl;* [thousand dollars] tausend Dollar *pl*.

**grandad** *n inf* Opa *der*, Opi *der*.

**Grand Canyon** *n:* **the ~** der Grand Canyon.

**grandchild** [ˈgræntʃaɪld] *(pl* -**children** [-ˌtʃɪldrən]) *n* Enkelkind *das*.

**granddad** [ˈgrændæd] *n inf* = **grandad**.

**granddaughter** [ˈgrænˌdɔːtəʳ] *n* Enkelin *die*.

**grand duchess** *n* Großherzogin *die*.

**grand duke** *n* Großherzog *der*.

**grandeur** [ˈgrændʒəʳ] *n* [of building] Pracht *die;* [of scenery] Herrlichkeit *die*.

**grandfather** [ˈgrændˌfɑːðəʳ] *n* Großvater *der*.

**grandfather clock** *n* Standuhr *die*.

**grandiose** [ˈgrændɪəʊz] *adj pej* [building, style] bombastisch; [plan, idea] hochfliegend.

**grand jury** *n Am* Geschworenengericht in den USA, das darüber entscheidet, ob jemand für ein Verbrechen vor Gericht gestellt wird.

**grandma** [ˈgrænmɑː] *n inf* Oma *die*, Omi *die*.

**grandmother** [ˈgrænˌmʌðəʳ] *n* Großmutter *die*.

**Grand National** *n:* **the ~** berühmtes Pferderennen in England.

**grandpa** [ˈgrænpɑː] *n inf* Opa *der*, Opi *der*.

**grandparents** [ˈgrænˌpeərənts] *npl* Großeltern *pl*.

**grand piano** *n* Flügel *der*.

**grand slam** *n sport* Grand Slam *der*.

**grandson** [ˈgrænsʌn] *n* Enkel *der*.

**grandstand** [ˈgrændstænd] *n* (überdachte) Tribüne *die*.

**grand total** *n* Endsumme *die*.

**granite** [ˈgrænɪt] *n* Granit *der*.

**granny** [ˈgrænɪ] *(pl* -**ies**) *n inf* Oma *die*, Omi *die*.

**granny flat** *n Br* Einliegerwohnung *die*.

**granola** [grəˈnəʊlə] *n Am* ≃ Müsli *das*.

**grant** [grɑːnt] *n* [money] Zuschuss *der;* [for study] Stipendium *das* ◇ *vt fml* - **1.** [request, right] gewähren; [appeal] nachlkommen *(+ D);* [wish] erfüllen - **2.** [admit] zulgeben; **I ~ that ...** ich gebe zu, dass ... - **3.** *phr:* **to take sthg for ~ed** etw als selbstverständlich betrachten; **he takes his wife for ~ed** er weiß nicht zu schätzen, was seine Frau für ihn tut; **to take it for ~ed that ...** es als selbstverständlich betrachten, dass ...

**granulated sugar** [ˈgrænjʊleɪtɪd-] *n* Kristallzucker *der*.

**granule** [ˈgrænjuːl] *n* Körnchen *das*.

**grape** [greɪp] *n* (Wein)traube *die*.

**grapefruit** [ˈgreɪpfruːt] *(pl inv or* -**s**) *n* Grapefruit *die*, Pampelmuse *die*.

**grape picking** [-ˈpɪkɪŋ] *n (U)* Weinlese *die*.

**grapevine** [ˈgreɪpvaɪn] *n* Weinstock *der;* **we heard on the ~ that ...** *fig* wir haben gehört, dass ...

**graph** [grɑːf] *n* Diagramm *das*.

**graphic** [ˈgræfɪk] *adj* - **1.** [vivid] anschaulich - **2.** ART grafisch.

➤ **graphics** *npl* [pictures] grafische Darstellungen *pl;* **computer ~s** (Computer)grafik *die*.

**graphic artist** *n* Grafiker *der*, -in *die*.

**graphic design** *n* Grafikdesign *das*.

**graphic designer** *n* Grafikdesigner *der*, -in *die*.

**graphic equalizer** *n* Graphic-Equalizer *der*.

**graphics card** *n* COMPUT Grafikkarte *die*.

**graphite** [ˈgræfaɪt] *n* Graphit *das*.

**graphology** [græˈfɒlədʒɪ] *n* Graphologie *die*.

**graph paper** *n* Millimeterpapier *das*.

**grapple** [ˈgræpl] ➤ **grapple with** *vt fus lit* & *fig* ringen mit.

**grappling iron** [ˈgræplɪŋ-] *n* Draggen *der*.

**grasp** [grɑːsp] n - **1.** [grip] Griff der; **success is now within their ~** der Erfolg ist nun in greifbarer Nähe - **2.** [understanding]: **to have a good ~ of sthg** [language] etw gut beherrschen; [situation] etw verstehen; **this is beyond her ~** das ist zu hoch für sie ◇ vt - **1.** [with hands] ergreifen - **2.** [understand] begreifen.

**grasping** ['grɑːspɪŋ] adj pej [greedy] habgierig.

**grass** [grɑːs] n - **1.** [on ground] Gras das; [lawn] Rasen der - **2.** drugs sl [marijuana] Gras das ◇ vi Br crime sl: **to ~ on sb** jn verpfeifen.

**grasshopper** ['grɑːsˌhɒpəʳ] n Heuschrecke die.

**grassland** ['grɑːslænd] n Grasland das.

**grass roots** npl [ordinary people] Basis die ◇ comp: **~ opinion/support** Meinung/Unterstützung der Basis; **at ~ level** an der Basis.

**grass snake** n Ringelnatter die.

**grassy** ['grɑːsɪ] (compar -ier; superl -iest) adj mit Gras bewachsen.

**grate** [greɪt] n [in fireplace] (Kamin)rost der ◇ vt [cheese, carrots] reiben ◇ vi [irritate]: **to ~ (on sb's nerves)** jm auf die Nerven gehen.

**grateful** ['greɪtfʊl] adj: **to be ~ to sb (for sthg)** jm (für etw) dankbar sein.

**gratefully** ['greɪtfʊlɪ] adv dankbar.

**grater** ['greɪtəʳ] n Reibe die.

**gratification** [ˌgrætɪfɪˈkeɪʃn] n - **1.** [pleasure] Genugtuung die - **2.** [of desire] Befriedigung die.

**gratify** ['grætɪfaɪ] (pt & pp -ied) vt - **1.** [please]: **to be gratified to hear/discover that ...** mit Genugtuung hören/entdecken, dass ... - **2.** [desire] befriedigen.

**gratifying** ['grætɪfaɪɪŋ] adj [pleasing] erfreulich.

**grating** ['greɪtɪŋ] adj nervend ◇ n [grille] Gitter das.

**gratitude** ['grætɪtjuːd] n: **~ (to sb)** Dankbarkeit die (gegenüber jm).

**gratuitous** [grəˈtjuːɪtəs] adj fml unnötig.

**gratuity** [grəˈtjuːɪtɪ] (pl -ies) n fml [tip] Trinkgeld das.

**grave** [greɪv] adj - **1.** [solemn] ernst - **2.** [serious - situation, threat, illness] ernst; [ - news] schlimm ◇ n Grab das; **to turn in one's ~** sich im Grab umldrehen.

**gravedigger** ['greɪvˌdɪgəʳ] n Totengräber der, -in die.

**gravel** ['grævl] n Kies der.

**gravestone** ['greɪvstəʊn] n Grabstein der.

**graveyard** ['greɪvjɑːd] n Friedhof der.

**gravitate** ['grævɪteɪt] vi: **to ~ towards** fig [be attracted to] sich hingezogen fühlen zu.

**gravity** ['grævətɪ] n (U) - **1.** [force] Schwerkraft die - **2.** fml [seriousness] Ernst der.

**gravy** ['greɪvɪ] n (U) - **1.** [meat juice] Bratensaft der; [sauce] Soße die - **2.** Am inf [easy money] leichtes Geld.

**gravy boat** n Sauciere die.

**gravy train** n inf: **to get on the ~** leichtes Geld machen.

**gray** adj & n Am = grey.

**graze** [greɪz] vt - **1.** [field - subj: cattle] ablgrasen, ablweiden; [cattle] grasen OR weiden lassen - **2.** [knee, elbow] auf Ischürfen - **3.** [touch lightly] streifen ◇ vi [animals] grasen, weiden ◇ n [wound] Schürfwunde die.

**grease** [griːs] n (U) - **1.** [animal fat] Fett das - **2.** [lubricant] Schmiere die ◇ vt [engine, machine] schmieren; [baking tray] einlfetten.

**grease gun** n Fettpresse die.

**greasepaint** ['griːspeɪnt] n (Fett)schminke die (für Schauspieler).

**greaseproof paper** [ˌgriːspruːf-] n Br Pergamentpapier das.

**greasy** ['griːsɪ] (compar -ier; superl -iest) adj - **1.** [food, hair, hands] fettig - **2.** [clothes] schmierig.

**greasy spoon** n [cafe] kleines, billiges Lokal, das gebratenes und fritiertes Essen serviert.

**great** [greɪt] adj - **1.** [large] groß; **to a ~ extent** in hohem Maße; **the ~ majority** die überwiegende Mehrheit; **a ~ deal of money** eine Menge OR sehr viel Geld - **2.** [very good] großartig; **we had a ~ time** wir haben uns toll amüsiert ◇ n [person] Größe die ◇ excl: **(that's) ~!** (das ist) toll!

**Great Barrier Reef** n: **the ~** großes Korallenriff vor der Nordostküste Australiens.

**Great Bear** n: **the ~** der Große Bär.

**Great Britain** n Großbritannien nt.

**greatcoat** ['greɪtkəʊt] n langer schwerer Mantel.

**Great Dane** n Deutsche Dogge.

**Great Depression** n: **the ~** die Weltwirtschaftskrise.

**great-grandchild** n Urenkel der, -in die.

**great-grandfather** n Urgroßvater der.

**great-grandmother** n Urgroßmutter die.

**Great Lakes** npl: the ~ die Großen Seen.

**greatly** ['greɪtlɪ] adv sehr.

**greatness** ['greɪtnɪs] n [importance] Bedeutung die; [size] Größe die.

**Great Wall of China** n: the ~ die Chinesische Mauer.

**Great War** n: the ~ der Erste Weltkrieg.

**Greece** [griːs] n Griechenland nt.

**greed** [griːd] n - **1.** [for food] Gefräßigkeit die - **2.** fig [for money, power] Gier die; ~ **for money/power** Geld-/Machtgier die.

**greedily** ['griːdɪlɪ] adv gierig.

**greedy** ['griːdɪ] (compar -ier; superl -iest) adj - **1.** [for food] gefräßig - **2.** fig [for money, power]: ~ **for money/power** geld-/machtgierig.

**Greek** [griːk] adj griechisch; the ~ Islands die griechischen Inseln <> n - **1.** [person] Grieche der, -chin die - **2.** [language] Griechisch(e) das.

**green** [griːn] adj grün; ~ **(with envy)** blass OR grün (vor Neid) <> n - **1.** [colour] Grün das - **2.** [in village]: **(village)** ~ (Dorf)wiese die - **3.** GOLF Grün das.

➤ **Green** n POL Grüne der, die; the Greens die Grünen.

➤ **greens** npl [vegetables] Grüngemüse das.

**greenback** ['griːnbæk] n Am inf [banknote] Dollarschein der.

**green bean** n grüne Bohne.

**green belt** n Br Grüngürtel der.

**Green Beret** n Am inf: the ~s amerikanische Kommandotruppe.

**green card** n - **1.** Br [for insuring vehicle] grüne Versicherungskarte - **2.** Am [resident's permit] Aufenthaltserlaubnis die.

**greenery** ['griːnərɪ] n Grün das.

**green fingers** npl Br fig: to have ~ einen grünen Daumen haben.

**greenfly** ['griːnflaɪ] (pl inv OR -ies) n (grüne) Blattlaus.

**greengage** ['griːngeɪdʒ] n Reneklode die.

**greengrocer** ['griːnˌgrəʊsə'] n Obst- und Gemüsehändler der, -in die; ~'s **(shop)** Obst- und Gemüsegeschäft das.

**greenhorn** ['griːnhɔːn] n Am [novice] Greenhorn das.

**greenhouse** ['griːnhaʊs, pl -haʊzɪz] n Gewächshaus das, Treibhaus das.

**greenhouse effect** n: the ~ der Treibhauseffekt.

**greenish** ['griːnɪʃ] adj grünlich.

**Greenland** ['griːnlənd] n Grönland nt.

**Greenlander** ['griːnləndə'] n Grönländer der, -in die.

**green light** n: to give sb the ~ jm grünes Licht geben.

**green paper** n POL von der Regierung vorgelegtes Papier, mit dem Vorschläge zu bestimmten politischen Fragen im Parlament zur Diskussion gestellt werden.

**Green Party** n: the ~ die Grünen.

**green salad** n grüner Salat.

**green thumb** n Am fig: to have a ~ einen grünen Daumen haben.

**greet** [griːt] vt lit & fig begrüßen; [say hello to in passing] grüßen.

**greeting** ['griːtɪŋ] n Gruß der; to exchange ~s sich grüßen.

➤ **greetings** npl [on card]: **Christmas** ~s Weihnachtsgrüße; **birthday** ~s Glückwünsche zum Geburtstag.

**greetings card** Br, **greeting card** Am n Glückwunschkarte die.

**gregarious** [grɪ'geərɪəs] adj [animal] Herden-; [person] gesellig.

**gremlin** ['gremlɪn] n inf imaginärer böser Geist, der für unerklärliche Defekte an Maschinen verantwortlich gemacht wird.

**Grenada** [grə'neɪdə] n Grenada nt.

**grenade** [grə'neɪd] n: **(hand)** ~ (Hand)granate die.

**grew** [gruː] pt ⊳ **grow.**

**grey** Br, **gray** Am [greɪ] adj grau; [life] trostlos; **to go** ~ grau werden, ergrauen <> n Grau das.

**grey area** n Grauzone die.

**grey-haired** [-'heəd] adj grauhaarig.

**greyhound** ['greɪhaʊnd] n Windhund der.

**greying** Br, **graying** Am ['greɪɪŋ] adj: **his hair/he is** ~ sein Haar/er ergraut langsam.

**grey matter** n (U) inf graue Zellen pl.

**grey squirrel** n Grauhörnchen das.

**grid** [grɪd] n - **1.** [grating] Gitter das - **2.** [for maps] Gitternetz das; ELEC Überlandleitungsnetz das.

**griddle** ['grɪdl] n gusseiserne Platte zum Backen von Pfannkuchen.

**gridiron** ['grɪdˌaɪən] n - **1.** [in cooking] Bratrost der - **2.** Am [game] American Football der; [field] Spielfeld das.

**gridlock** ['grɪdlɒk] n [in traffic] Zusammenbruch der des Verkehrs.

**grid reference** n Positionsangabe die.

**grief** [griːf] n - **1.** [sorrow] Trauer die - **2.** inf [trouble] Ärger der - **3.** phr: **to come to** ~ [in an accident] verunglücken; [plan] scheitern; **good** ~! ach du lieber Himmel!

**grief-stricken** *adj* schmerzerfüllt.

**grievance** ['griːvns] *n* [complaint] Beschwerde *die.*

**grieve** [griːv] *vt fml:* it ~s me to ... es bekümmert mich, zu ... <> *vi:* **to ~ (for sb/sthg)** (um jn/etw) trauern.

**grieving** ['griːvɪŋ] *n* Trauern *das.*

**grievous** ['griːvəs] *adj fml* [wound] schlimm; [mistake] schwer wiegend.

**grievous bodily harm** *n* schwere Körperverletzung.

**grievously** ['griːvəslɪ] *adv fml* [wounded, ill] schwer.

**grill** [grɪl] *n* - **1.** [of cooker] Grill *der;* [over fire] Bratrost *der* - **2.** [food] Grillgericht *das* <> *vt* - **1.** [cook] grillen - **2.** *inf* [interrogate - interviewee] auslquetschen; [ - prisoner, suspect] ins Verhör nehmen.

**grille** [grɪl] *n* Gitter *das;* **radiator** ~ AUT Kühlergrill *der.*

**grim** [grɪm] (*compar* **-mer;** *superl* **-mest**) *adj* - **1.** [face, smile] grimmig; [determination] eisern - **2.** [place, situation] trostlos; [prospect] düster; [news] grauenvoll.

**grimace** ['grɪməs] *n* Grimasse *die* <> *vi* Grimassen schneiden; **to ~ with pain** vor Schmerz das Gesicht verziehen.

**grime** [graɪm] *n* Schmutz *der,* [soot] Ruß *der.*

**grimly** ['grɪmlɪ] *adv* - **1.** [say, smile] grimmig - **2.** [struggle, defend] verbissen.

**grimy** ['graɪmɪ] (*compar* **-ier;** *superl* **-iest**) *adj* schmutzig; [soot] verrußt.

**grin** [grɪn] (*pt* & *pp* **-ned;** *cont* **-ning**) *n* Grinsen *das* <> *vi* grinsen; **to ~ at sb/sthg** jn/etw anlgrinsen; **to ~ and bear it** gute Miene zum bösen Spiel machen.

**grind** [graɪnd] (*pt* & *pp* **ground**) *vt* - **1.** [coffee, pepper, flour] mahlen - **2.** [press] **to ~ sthg into sthg** [knee, foot] etw in etw (A) bohren - **3.** [metal, glass] schleifen; **to ~ one's teeth** mit den Zähnen knirschen <> *vi* [car, gears] knirschen <> *n* - **1.** [hard, boring work] Schinderei *die;* **the daily ~** der tägliche Trott - **2.** *Am inf* [hard worker] Arbeitstier *das.*
➤ **grind down** *vt sep* [oppress] unterdrücken.
➤ **grind up** *vt sep* zermahlen.

**grinder** ['graɪndəʳ] *n* [for coffee, pepper] Mühle *die.*

**grinding** ['graɪndɪŋ] *adj* [poverty] drückend.

**grinning** ['grɪnɪŋ] *adj* grinsend.

**grip** [grɪp] (*pt* & *pp* **-ped;** *cont* **-ping**) *n* - **1.** [physical hold] **to release one's ~ on sb/sthg** jn/etw loslassen; **he couldn't get a ~ on the rope** er konnte keinen Halt am Seil finden - **2.** [control] **to have a (good) ~ on a situation** eine Situation im Griff haben; **to be in the ~ of fear** von Angst ergriffen sein; **to get to ~s with**

sthg etw in den Griff bekommen; **to get a ~ on o.s.** sich zusammenlreißen; **to lose one's ~** *fig* nachllassen - **3.** [of tyres] Haftung *die;* [of shoes] Halt *der* - **4.** [handle] Griff *der* - **5.** *dated* [bag] Reisetasche *die* <> *vt* - **1.** [grasp] festlhalten - **2.** [subj: tyres] haften auf (+ D) - **3.** [imagination, attention, audience] fesseln; **panic ~ped the country** das Land wurde von Panik ergriffen.

**gripe** [graɪp] *n inf* [complaint] Gemecker *das* <> *vi:* **to ~ (about sthg)** (über etw (A)) meckern.

**gripping** ['grɪpɪŋ] *adj* [story, film] fesselnd.

**grisly** ['grɪzlɪ] (*compar* **-ier;** *superl* **-iest**) *adj* grausig.

**gristle** ['grɪsl] *n* Knorpel *der.*

**gristly** ['grɪslɪ] (*compar* **-ier;** *superl* **-iest**) *adj* knorpelig.

**grit** [grɪt] (*pt* & *pp* **-ted;** *cont* **-ting**) *n* (*U*) - **1.** [for roads, in winter] Streusand *der;* **I've got some ~ in my eye** ich habe etwas im Auge - **2.** *inf* [courage] Schneid *der* <> *vt* [road, steps] streuen.
➤ **grits** *npl Am* Maisgrieß *der.*

**gritter** ['grɪtəʳ] *n* Streufahrzeug *das.*

**gritty** ['grɪtɪ] (*compar* **-ier;** *superl* **-iest**) *adj:* **~ determination** Verbissenheit *die.*

**grizzled** ['grɪzld] *adj* ergraut.

**grizzly** ['grɪzlɪ] (*pl* **-ies**) *n:* **~ (bear)** Grislibär *der.*

**groan** [grəʊn] *n* Stöhnen *das* <> *vi* - **1.** [moan] stöhnen - **2.** [door, table] ächzen - **3.** [complain] sich beklagen.

**grocer** ['grəʊsəʳ] *n* Lebensmittelhändler *der,* -in *die;* **~'s (shop)** Lebensmittelgeschäft *das.*

**groceries** ['grəʊsərɪz] *npl* Lebensmittel *pl.*

**groggy** ['grɒgɪ] (*compar* **-ier;** *superl* **-iest**) *adj* geschwächt.

**groin** [grɔɪn] *n* Leiste *die.*

**groom** [gruːm] *n* - **1.** [of horses] Stallbursche *der,* Stallgehilfin *die* - **2.** [bridegroom] Bräutigam *der* <> *vt* - **1.** [horse] striegeln; [dog] bürsten - **2.** [candidate] **to ~ sb (for)** jn vorlbereiten (auf (+ A)).

**groomed** [gruːmd] *adj:* **well ~** gepflegt; **badly ~** ungepflegt.

**groove** [gruːv] *n* Rille *die.*

**grope** [grəʊp] *vt* - **1.** [sexually] befummeln - **2.** [try to find] **to ~ one's way** sich vorwärts tasten <> *vi:* **to ~ (about) for sthg** [object] nach etw tasten; *fig* [solution, remedy] nach etw suchen.

**gross** [grəʊs] (*pl inv* OR **-es**) *adj* - **1.** [weight, income] Brutto- - **2.** *fml* [error, misconduct] grob; [exaggeration] krass - **3.** *inf* [coarse, vulgar - person, behaviour] ordinär; [ - food] widerlich - **4.** *inf* [obese] fett <> *n* Gros *das* <> *vt* [subj: person] brutto verdienen; [subj: store, film] brutto einlnehmen.

**gross domestic product** *n* Bruttoinlandsprodukt *das*.

**grossly** ['grəʊslı] *adv* [for emphasis] äußerst.

**gross national product** *n* Bruttosozialprodukt *das*.

**gross profit** *n* Bruttogewinn *der*.

**grotesque** [grəʊ'tesk] *adj* grotesk.

**grotto** ['grɒtəʊ] (*pl* -es OR -s) *n* Grotte *die*.

**grotty** ['grɒtı] (*compar* -ier; *superl* -iest) *adj Br inf* mies.

**grouchy** ['graʊtʃı] (*compar* -ier; *superl* -iest) *adj inf* grantig.

**ground** [graʊnd] *pt & pp* ⊳ **grind** ◇ *n* - **1.** [gen] Boden *der;* **low ~** niedriges Gelände; **above ~** über der Erde; **below ~** unter der Erde; **on the ~** auf dem Boden; *fig* vor Ort; **thin on the ~** dünn gesät; **to get sthg off the ~** *fig* [company] etw zum Florieren bringen; **to be on dangerous ~** sich auf gefährlichem Boden bewegen; **to cover a lot of ~** [in discussion] einen weiten Themenkreis behandeln; **to break new ~** Neuland betreten; **to gain/lose ~** an Boden gewinnen/verlieren; **to cut the ~ from under sb's feet** jm den Boden unter den Füßen weglziehen; **to go to ~** unterltauchen; **to run sb/sthg to ~** jn/etw ausfindig machen; **to stand one's ~** nicht von der Stelle weichen; *fig* auf seinem Standpunkt beharren - **2.** SPORT Sportplatz *der;* [stadium] Stadion *das;* **football ~** Fußballplatz *der;* [stadium] Fußballstadion *das* ◇ *vt* - **1.** [base]: **to be ~ed on** OR **in sthg** basieren auf etw (*D*) - **2.** [aircraft, pilot] *inf* nicht fliegen lassen - **3.** *esp Am* [child]: **to be ~ed** Hausarrest haben - **4.** *Am* ELEC: **to be ~ed** geerdet sein.

◆ **grounds** *npl* - **1.** [reason] Grund *der;* **to have ~s for doing sthg** einen Grund dafür haben, etw zu tun; **on health ~s** aus gesundheitlichen Gründen; **on the ~s of** aufgrund (+ G); **on the ~s that ...** mit der Begründung, dass ... - **2.** [building] Gelände *das* - **3.:** **coffee ~s** Kaffeesatz *der*.

**ground cover** *n* Bodenvegetation *die*.

**ground crew** *n* Bodenpersonal *das*.

**ground floor** *n* Erdgeschoss *das*.

**grounding** ['graʊndıŋ] *n:* **to have a ~ in sthg** die Grundkenntnisse in etw (+ D) haben.

**groundless** ['graʊndlıs] *adj* grundlos, unbegründet.

**ground level** *n:* **at ~** ebenerdig; [in house] im Erdgeschoss.

**groundnut** ['graʊndnʌt] *n* Erdnuss *die*.

**ground plan** *n* [of building] Grundriss *der*.

**ground rent** *n* Pachtzins *der (für ein Grundstück)*.

**ground rules** *npl* Grundregeln *pl*.

**groundsheet** ['graʊndʃiːt] *n* Bodenplane *die*.

**groundsman** ['graʊndzmən] (*pl* -men [-mən]) *n Br* [at sports ground] Platzwart *der*.

**ground staff** *n Br* [at airport] Bodenpersonal *das*.

**groundswell** ['graʊndswel] *n* Zunahme *die;* **there was a ~ of opinion in his favour** er erhielt zunehmend Zuspruch von der Öffentlichkeit.

**groundwork** ['graʊndwɜːk] *n (U)* Vorarbeit *pl*.

**group** [gruːp] *n* - **1.** [gen] Gruppe *die;* **a ~ of trees** eine Baumgruppe - **2.** COMM Gruppe *die*, Konzern *der* ◇ *vt* gruppieren; [classify] klassifizieren ◇ *vi:* **to ~ (together)** sich zusammenltun.

**group captain** *n Br* Oberst *der*.

**groupie** ['gruːpı] *n inf* Groupie *das*.

**group practice** *n* Gemeinschaftspraxis *die*.

**grouse** [graʊs] (*pl inv* OR -s) *n* [bird] Schottisches Moorschneehuhn ◇ *vi inf* meckern.

**grove** [grəʊv] *n* Hain *der*.

**grovel** ['grɒvl] (*Br pt & pp* -led; *cont* -ling, *Am pt & pp* -ed; *cont* -ing) *vi* kriechen; **to ~ to sb** vor jm kriechen.

**grow** [grəʊ] (*pt* grew; *pp* grown) *vi* - **1.** [gen] wachsen; [problem] sich vergrößern; [love] stärker werden; [idea] Formen anlnehmen; **to ~ in popularity** an Beliebtheit gewinnen - **2.** [become] werden; **to ~ old** alt werden; **to ~ to do sthg** allmählich etw tun; **she grew to hate her mother** sie begann, ihre Mutter zu hassen ◇ *vt* [crops, vegetables] anlbauen; [flowers] züchten; **to ~ one's hair/a beard** sich (*D*) die Haare/einen Bart wachsen lassen.

◆ **grow apart** *vi* [friends] sich auseinander leben.

◆ **grow into** *vt fus* [clothes, shoes] hineinlwachsen in (+ A).

◆ **grow on** *vt fus inf* [subj: music, idea]: **it'll ~ on you** es wird dir mit der Zeit immer besser gefallen.

◆ **grow out** *vi* [perm, dye] herauslwachsen.

◆ **grow out of** *vt fus* - **1.** [clothes, shoes] herauslwachsen aus - **2.** [habit] abllegen.

◆ **grow up** *vi* - **1.** [person] auflwachsen; [become adult] erwachsen werden; **~ up!** werd endlich erwachsen! - **2.** [feeling, city] entstehen.

**grower** ['grəʊə'] *n* [of flowers] Züchter *der*, -in *die;* [of crops, vegetables] Anbauer *der*, -in *die*.

**growl** [graʊl] *n* Knurren *das;* [of bear, engine] Brummen *das* ◇ *vi* knurren; [bear, engine] brummen.

**grown** [grəʊn] *pp* ⊳ **grow** ◇ *adj* erwachsen.

**grown-up** adj [fully grown] ausgewachsen; [mature] erwachsen ◇ n Erwachsene der, die.

**growth** [grəʊθ] n - **1.** [increase - of economy, company, population] Wachstum das; [ - of research, opposition, nationalism] Zunahme die - **2.** [development - of person] Entwicklung die - **3.** MED Geschwulst die.

**growth rate** n Wachstumsrate die.

**grub** [grʌb] n - **1.** [insect] Larve die - **2.** inf [food] Futter das.

**grubby** ['grʌbɪ] (compar -ier; superl -iest) adj [clothes] schmuddelig; [hands, child] schmutzig.

**grudge** [grʌdʒ] n Groll der; **to bear sb a ~, to have a ~ against sb** einen Groll gegen jn hegen ◇ vt: **to ~ sb sthg** jm etw missgönnen; **I don't ~ her her success** ich gönne ihr ihren Erfolg; **to ~ doing sthg** etw widerwillig tun.

**grudging** ['grʌdʒɪŋ] adj widerwillig.

**grudgingly** ['grʌdʒɪŋlɪ] adv widerwillig.

**gruelling** Br, **grueling** Am ['grʊəlɪŋ] adj strapaziös.

**gruesome** ['gru:səm] adj grausig.

**gruff** [grʌf] adj - **1.** [voice] rau - **2.** [person, manner] barsch.

**grumble** ['grʌmbl] n - **1.** [complaint] Klage die - **2.** [of stomach] Knurren das ◇ vi - **1.** [complain]: **to ~ (about)** murren (über (+ A)) - **2.** [stomach] knurren.

**grumbling** ['grʌmblɪŋ] n [complaining] Klagen das.

**grumpy** ['grʌmpɪ] (compar -ier; superl -iest) adj inf mürrisch.

**grunt** [grʌnt] n Grunzen das ◇ vi grunzen.

**G-string** n - **1.** MUS G-Saite die - **2.** [clothing] Tangaslip der.

**GU** abk für Guam, in Postanschrift verwendet.

**guarantee** [ˌgærən'ti:] n Garantie die; [document] Garantieschein der; **it is still under ~** es hat noch Garantie; **to give sb a ~ that ...** jm garantieren, dass ... ◇ vt - **1.** COMM Garantie geben auf (+ A); **it is ~d for one year** es hat ein Jahr Garantie - **2.** [promise] garantieren.

**guarantor** [ˌgærən'tɔ:ʳ] n Bürge der, -gin die.

**guard** [gɑ:d] n - **1.** [person] Wachposten der; [for prisoner] Gefängniswärter der, -in die; [group of guards] Wache die - **2.** [supervision] Überwachung die; **to be on ~** Wache haben; **to stand ~** Wache halten; **to be on (one's) ~ (against sthg)** auf der Hut (vor etw (D)) sein; **to catch sb off ~** jn überrumpeln - **3.** Br RAIL Schaffner der, -in die - **4.** [protective device] Schutz der; [for machine] Schutzvorrichtung die; [for fire] Schutzgitter das - **5.** [in boxing] Deckung die ◇ vt bewachen.

◆ **guard against** vt fus vorbeugen (+ D); [bad habit] sich hüten vor (+ D).

**guard dog** n Wachhund der.

**guarded** ['gɑ:dɪd] adj [reply, statement] vorsichtig.

**guardian** ['gɑ:djən] n - **1.** LAW [of child] Vormund der - **2.** [protector] Wächter der, -in die.

**guardian angel** n Schutzengel der.

**guardrail** ['gɑ:dreɪl] n Geländer das.

**guardsman** ['gɑ:dzmən] (pl -men [-mən]) n Gardist der.

**guard's van** n Br Schaffnerabteil das.

**Guatemala** [ˌgwætə'mɑ:lə] n Guatemala nt.

**Guatemalan** [ˌgwætə'mɑ:lən] adj guatemaltekisch ◇ n Guatemalteke der, -kin die.

**guerilla** [gə'rɪlə] n = guerrilla.

**Guernsey** ['gɜ:nzɪ] n - **1.** [place] Guernsey nt; **in ~** auf Guernsey - **2.** [cow] Guernseyrind das.

**guerrilla** [gə'rɪlə] n Guerillakämpfer der, -in die.

**guerrilla warfare** n (U) Guerillakrieg der.

**guess** [ges] n - **1.** [at facts, figures] Schätzung die; **to take a ~ raten; at a ~** schätzungsweise - **2.** [hypothesis] Vermutung die; **it's anybody's ~** das wissen die Götter ◇ vt [answer, name] raten; [correctly] erraten, richtig raten; [figure, weight] schätzen; **~ what!** stell dir vor! ◇ vi - **1.** [gen] raten; **to ~ at sthg** etw zu erraten versuchen; **to keep sb ~ing** jn im Ungewissen lassen - **2.** [suppose] glauben, denken; **I ~ (so)** ich glaube (schon).

**guesstimate** ['gestɪmət] n inf grobe Schätzung.

**guesswork** ['geswɜ:k] n (U) (reine) Vermutung.

**guest** [gest] n Gast der; **we've got ~s** wir haben Besuch; **be my ~!** nur zu!

**guesthouse** ['gesthaʊs, pl -haʊzɪz] n Pension die.

**guest of honour** n Ehrengast der.

**guestroom** ['gestrʊm] n Gästezimmer das.

**guest star** n Gaststar der.

**guffaw** [gʌ'fɔ:] n schallendes Gelächter ◇ vi schallend lachen.

**GUI** (abbr of graphical user interface) n COMPUT grafische Benutzeroberfläche.

**Guiana** [gaɪ'ɑ:nə] n Guayana nt.

**guidance** ['gaɪdəns] n (U) - **1.** [help from teacher, parents] Anleitung die; [counselling] Beratung die - **2.** [leadership] Führung die.

**guide** [gaɪd] n - **1.** [for tourists] Fremdenführer der, -in die; **tour ~** Reiseleiter der, -in die - **2.** [guide book] Führer der; [manual] Handbuch das; **user's ~** Gebrauchsanleitung die; [indication] Orientierungshilfe die; **to use sthg as a ~** etw als Vorbild nehmen - **4.** = girl guide ◇ vt - **1.** [lead] führen; [influenced]: **to be ~d by**

sb/sthg sich von jm/etw leiten lassen
- **2.** [plane, missile] lenken.

**guide book** n Führer der.

**guided missile** [ˈgaɪdɪd-] n Lenkflugkörper
der.

**guide dog** n Blindenhund der.

**guided tour** [ˈgaɪdɪd-] n Führung die.

**guideline** [ˈgaɪdlaɪn] n Richtlinie die.

**guiding** [ˈgaɪdɪŋ] adj: ~ principle Richtschnur
die; ~ influence bestimmender Einfluss.

**guild** [gɪld] n - **1.** HIST Zunft die - **2.** [association]
Vereinigung die.

**guile** [gaɪl] n literary List die.

**guileless** [ˈgaɪlləs] adj literary arglos.

**guillotine** [ˈgɪləˌtiːn] n - **1.** [for executions] Guillotine die - **2.** [for paper] Papierschneidema-
schine die - **3.** Br POL zeitliche Begrenzung der
Debatte zur Verabschiedung eines Gesetzes-
vorschlags <> vt [execute] guillotinieren.

**guilt** [gɪlt] n Schuld die.

**guiltily** [ˈgɪltɪlɪ] adv schuldbewusst.

**guilty** [ˈgɪltɪ] (compar -ier; superl -iest) adj
- **1.** [gen] schuldig; [smile, look] schuldbewusst;
to have a ~ conscience ein schlechtes Gewissen haben - **2.**: to be found ~/not ~ LAW für
schuldig/nicht schuldig befunden werden; to be ~ of neglect/a mistake der Ver-
nachlässigung/eines Fehlers schuldig
sein.

**guinea** [ˈgɪnɪ] n Guinee die.

**Guinea** [ˈgɪnɪ] n Guinea nt.

**guinea fowl** n Perlhuhn das.

**guinea pig** [ˈgɪnɪ-] n - **1.** [animal] Meerschweinchen das - **2.** [subject of experiment] Ver-
suchskaninchen das.

**guise** [gaɪz] n fml: to present sthg in a new ~ etw
anders darstellen; under the ~ of friendship
unter dem Deckmantel der Freundschaft.

**guitar** [gɪˈtɑːʳ] n Gitarre die.

**guitarist** [gɪˈtɑːrɪst] n Gitarrist der, -in die.

**gulch** [gʌltʃ] n Am Felsschlucht die.

**gulf** [gʌlf] n - **1.** [sea] Golf der, Meerbusen der
- **2.** lit & fig [gap] Kluft die.
➤ **Gulf** n: the Gulf der Golf; the Gulf of Mexico
der Golf von Mexiko.

**Gulf States** npl: the ~ die Golfstaaten.

**Gulf Stream** n: the ~ der Golfstrom.

**gull** [gʌl] n Möwe die.

**gullet** [ˈgʌlɪt] n Speiseröhre die.

**gullible** [ˈgʌləbll] adj leichtgläubig.

**gully** [ˈgʌlɪ] (pl -ies) n - **1.** [valley] Schlucht die
- **2.** [ditch] Graben der.

**gulp** [gʌlp] n Schluck der <> vt hinunterschlucken <> vi schlucken.
➤ **gulp down** vt sep hinunterschlucken.

**gum** [gʌm] (pt & pp -med; cont -ming) n
- **1.** [chewing gum] Kaugummi der - **2.** [adhesive]
Klebstoff der - **3.** ANAT Zahnfleisch das <> vt
[stick] kleben.

**gumboil** [ˈgʌmbɔɪl] n Zahnfleischgeschwür
das.

**gumboots** [ˈgʌmbuːts] npl Br Gummistiefel
pl.

**gummed** adj gummiert.

**gumption** [ˈgʌmpʃn] n inf Grips der.

**gumshoe** [ˈgʌmʃuː] n Am crime sl Schnüffler
der.

**gun** [gʌn] (pt & pp -ned; cont -ning) n - **1.** [weap-
on - revolver] Pistole die, Revolver der; [ - rifle,
shotgun] Gewehr das; [ - cannon] Kanone die,
Geschütz das; to stick to one's ~s seiner
Überzeugung treu bleiben - **2.** SPORT [starting
pistol] Startpistole die; to jump the ~ fig vorschnell OR voreilig handeln - **3.** [for paint,
spraying] Pistole die.
➤ **gun down** vt sep [person, animal] nieder-
schießen.

**gunboat** [ˈgʌnbəʊt] n Kanonenboot das.

**gundog** [ˈgʌndɒg] n Jagdhund der.

**gunfire** [ˈgʌnfaɪəʳ] n (U) MIL Geschützfeuer das;
[of small arms] Schießerei die.

**gunge** [gʌndʒ] n Br inf schmieriges OR klebriges Zeug.

**gunk** [gʌŋk] n inf schmieriges OR klebriges
Zeug.

**gunman** [ˈgʌnmən] (pl -men [-mən]) n (mit einer Schußwaffe) bewaffneter Mann.

**gunner** [ˈgʌnəʳ] n MIL Artillerist der.

**gunpoint** [ˈgʌnpɔɪnt] n: to hold sb at ~ jn mit
einer Pistole/einem Gewehr bedrohen.

**gunpowder** [ˈgʌnˌpaʊdəʳ] n Schießpulver
das.

**gunrunning** [ˈgʌnˌrʌnɪŋ] n Waffenschmug-
gel der.

**gunshot** [ˈgʌnʃɒt] n Schuss der.

**gunsmith** [ˈgʌnsmɪθ] n Büchsenmacher der.

**gurgle** [ˈgɜːgl] vi - **1.** [water] gluckern - **2.** [baby]
glucksen <> n - **1.** [of water] Gluckern das
- **2.** [of baby] Glucksen das.

**guru** [ˈguru:] n Guru der.

**gush** [gʌʃ] n Strahl der <> vt: sthg ~es blood/
oil/etc Blut/Öl/etc schießt aus etw heraus
<> vi - **1.** [flow out] herausschießen - **2.** pej
[enthuse] schwärmen.

**gushing** [ˈgʌʃɪŋ] adj pej überspannt.

**gusset** [ˈgʌsɪt] n [sewing] Zwickel der.

**gust** [gʌst] n Windstoß der, Böe die <> vi böig
wehen.

**gusto** [ˈgʌstəʊ] n: with ~ mit Genuss.

**gusty** [ˈgʌstɪ] (compar -ier; superl -iest) adj stürmisch.

**gut** [gʌt] (*pt* & *pp* -ted; *cont* -ting) *n* - **1.** MED Darm *der* - **2.** *inf* [stomach] Bauch *der* ◇ *vt* - **1.** [animal, fish] auslnehmen - **2.** [building]: **the fire ~ted the house** das Haus brannte völlig aus.

➡ **guts** *npl inf* - **1.** [intestines] Eingeweide *pl;* **to hate sb's ~s** jn absolut nicht ausstehen können - **2.** [courage] Mumm *der;* **to have ~s** Mumm haben.

**gut feeling** *n* instinktives Gefühl.

**gut reaction** *n* instinktive Reaktion.

**gutter** ['gʌtəʳ] *n* - **1.** [beside road] Rinnstein *der* - **2.** [on roof] Dachrinne *die.*

**gutter press** *n pej* Regenbogenpresse *die.*

**guttural** ['gʌtərəl] *adj* guttural.

**guv** [gʌv] *n Br inf* Chef *der.*

**guy** [gaɪ] *n* - **1.** *inf* [man] Typ *der* - **2.** *esp Am* [person]: **are you ready, ~s?** seid ihr fertig? - **3.** *Br* [dummy] *Puppe, die Guy Fawkes darstellt und in der „Guy Fawkes Night" verbrannt wird.*

**Guyana** [gaɪˈɑːnə] *n* Guyana *nt.*

**Guy Fawkes' Night** *n* Nacht des 5. November, Jahrestag der Pulververschwörung 1605.

**GUY FAWKES' NIGHT**

An diesem Tag, dem 5. November (auch „Bonfire Night" genannt), wird alljährlich mit Feuerwerken und Freudenfeuern die rechtzeitige Entdeckung des „Gunpowder Plot" gefeiert. Dabei handelte es sich um eine katholische Verschwörung im Jahre 1605, bei der König James I. und die Parlamentsgebäude in die Luft gesprengt werden sollten. Der Brauch will es, dass die Kinder zu dieser Gelegenheit eine Stoff- oder Strohpuppe basteln, die „Guy Fawkes", den Hauptverschwörer, verkörpert. Diese wird zum Geldsammeln für Feuerwerkskörper benutzt und dann am 5. November im Freudenfeuer verbrannt.

**guy rope** *n* Spannleine *die.*

**guzzle** ['gʌzl] *vt* [food] hinunterlschlingen; [drink] hinunterlkippen ◇ *vi* [eat] sich volllfressen.

**gym** [dʒɪm] *n inf* - **1.** [gymnasium - in school] Turnhalle *die;* [ - in hotel] Fitnessraum *der;* [ - health club] Fitnessstudio *das* - **2.** [exercises] Turnen *das.*

**gymkhana** [dʒɪmˈkɑːnə] *n* Reitwettbewerb *mit Rennen und Sprungreiten.*

**gymnasium** [dʒɪmˈneɪzjəm] (*pl* -iums OR -ia [-jə]) *n* [in school] Turnhalle *die;* [in hotel] Fitnessraum *der;* [health club] Fitnessstudio *das.*

**gymnast** ['dʒɪmnæst] *n* Turner *der,* -in *die.*

**gymnastics** [dʒɪmˈnæstɪks] *n* (U) [exercises] Gymnastik *die;* [discipline] Turnen *das.*

**gym shoes** *npl* Turnschuhe *pl.*

**gymslip** ['dʒɪmˌslɪp] *n Br* Trägerrock *einer Schuluniform.*

**gynaecological** *Br,* **gynecological** *Am* [ˌgaɪnəkəˈlɒdʒɪkl] *adj* gynäkologisch.

**gynaecologist** *Br,* **gynecologist** *Am* [ˌgaɪnəˈkɒlədʒɪst] *n* Gynäkologe *der,* -gin *die,* Frauenarzt *der,* -ärztin *die.*

**gynaecology, gynecology** *Am* [ˌgaɪnəˈkɒlədʒɪ] *n* Gynäkologie *die,* Frauenheilkunde *die.*

**gypsy** ['dʒɪpsɪ] (*pl* -ies) *adj* & *n* = gipsy.

**gyrate** [dʒaɪˈreɪt] *vi* sich schnell drehen; [disco dancer] ausgelassen tanzen.

**gyroscope** ['dʒaɪrəskəʊp] *n* Kreisel *der.*

**h** (*pl* h's OR hs), **H** (*pl* H's OR Hs) [eɪtʃ] *n* [letter] h *das,* H *das.*

**ha** [hɑː] *excl* ha!

**haberdashery** ['hæbədæʃərɪ] (*pl* -ies) *n* - **1.** (U) [goods] Kurzwaren *pl* - **2.** [shop] Kurzwarengeschäft *das.*

**habit** ['hæbɪt] *n* - **1.** [usual practice] Gewohnheit *die;* **to be in the ~ of doing sthg** die Angewohnheit haben, etw zu tun; **I don't make a ~ of it** das mache ich nur ausnahmsweise; **to get into the ~ of doing sthg** sich (D) daran gewöhnen, etw zu tun - **2.** [drug addiction] Abhängigkeit *die* - **3.** [garment] Habit *das.*

**habitable** ['hæbɪtəbl] *adj* bewohnbar.

**habitat** ['hæbɪtæt] *n* Lebensraum *der.*

**habitation** [hæbɪˈteɪʃn] *n* - **1.** [occupation]: **unfit for human ~** unbewohnbar - **2.** *fml* [house] Behausung *die.*

**habit-forming** [-ˌfɔːmɪŋ] *adj* [drug] abhängig machend.

**habitual** [həˈbɪtʃʊəl] *adj* - **1.** [customary] gewohnt - **2.** [offender, smoker, drinker] Gewohnheits-.

**habitually** [həˈbɪtʃʊəlɪ] *adv* ständig, aus Gewohnheit.

**hack** [hæk] *n* - **1.** *pej* [writer] Schreiberling *der* - **2.** *Am inf* [taxi] Taxi *das* ◇ *vt* - **1.** [cut] hacken; **to ~ sthg to pieces** etw zerhacken - **2.** *inf* [cope

**H**

with]: **he can't ~ it** er packt es nicht ◇ *vi* [cut] hacken.

→ **hack into** *vt fus* COMPUT einldringen in (+ *A*).

→ **hack through** *vt fus* hacken; **to ~ (one's way) through sthg** sich (seinen Weg) durch etw schlagen.

**hacker** ['hækə'] *n* COMPUT Hacker *der*.

**hackie** ['hækı] *n Am inf* Taxifahrer *der*.

**hacking** ['hækıŋ] *n* COMPUT Hacken *das*.

**hacking cough** *n* trockener Husten.

**hackles** ['hæklz] *npl* [of animal] Nackenfell *das*; [of bird] Nackengefieder *das*; **to make sb's ~ rise** jn auf die Palme bringen.

**hackney cab, hackney carriage** ['hæknı-] *n fml* [taxi] Taxi *das*.

**hackneyed** ['hæknıd] *adj pej* abgedroschen.

**hacksaw** ['hæksɔ:] *n* Metallsäge *die*.

**had** [weak form həd, strong form hæd] *pt* & *pp* ⊳ have.

**haddock** ['hædək] (*pl inv*) *n* Schellfisch *der*.

**hadn't** ['hædnt] = had not.

**haematology** [ˌhi:mə'tɒlədʒı] *n* = hematology.

**haemoglobin** [ˌhi:mə'gləubın] *n* = hemoglobin.

**haemophilia** [ˌhi:mə'fılıə] *n* = hemophilia.

**haemophiliac** [ˌhi:mə'fılıæk] *n* = hemophiliac.

**haemorrhage** ['hemərıdʒ] *n* & *vi* = hemorrhage.

**haemorrhoids** ['heməroıdz] *npl* = hemorrhoids.

**hag** [hæg] *n pej* Hexe *die*.

**haggard** ['hægəd] *adj* verhärmt.

**haggis** ['hægıs] *n schottische Spezialität aus Schafsinnereien, im Schafsmagen gekocht*.

**haggle** ['hægl] *vi*: **to ~ (over** OR **about)** feilschen (um).

**haggling** ['hæglıŋ] *n* Feilschen *das*.

**Hague** [heıg] *n*: **The ~** Den Haag *nt*.

**hail** [heıl] *n lit* & *fig* Hagel *der*; **a ~ of bullets** ein Kugelhagel ◇ *vt* - **1.** [call] rufen; [taxi] heranlwinken, anlhalten - **2.** [acclaim]: **to ~ sb/sthg as sthg** jn/etw als etw feiern ◇ *v impers* METEOR hageln.

**hailstone** ['heılstəun] *n* Hagelkorn *das*.

**hailstorm** ['heılstɔ:m] *n* Hagelsturm *der*.

**hair** [heə'] *n* - **1.** (U) [on human head] Haare *pl*, Haar *das*; [single hair] Haar *das*; **to have one's ~ cut** sich (D) die Haare schneiden lassen; **to do one's ~** sich (D) die Haare machen, sich frisieren; **keep your ~ on!** nur ruhig Blut!; **to let one's ~ down** aus sich herauslgehen; **it makes your ~ stand on end** da stehen einem die Haare zu Berge; **to split ~s** Haare spal-

ten - **2.** [on animal, insect, plant] Haar *das* - **3.** [on human skin] Haar *das*; **body ~** Körperbehaarung *die* ◇ *comp* Haar-.

**hairbrush** ['heəbrʌʃ] *n* Haarbürste *die*.

**haircut** ['heəkʌt] *n* Haarschnitt *der*; **to get a ~** sich (D) die Haare schneiden lassen.

**hairdo** ['heədu:] (*pl* -**s**) *n inf* Frisur *die*.

**hairdresser** ['heəˌdresə'] *n* Friseur *der*, -euse *die*; **~'s (salon)** Friseur *der*.

**hairdressing** ['heəˌdresıŋ] *n* Frisieren *das*.

**hairdryer** ['heəˌdraıə'] *n* [handheld] Föhn *der*, Haartrockner *der*; [with hood] Trockenhaube *die*.

**hair gel** *n* Haargel *das*.

**hairgrip** ['heəgrıp] *n Br* Haarklammer *die*.

**hairline** ['heəlaın] *n* [of hair] Haaransatz *der*.

**hairline fracture** *n* Haarriss *der*.

**hairnet** ['heənet] *n* Haarnetz *das*.

**hairpiece** ['heəpi:s] *n* Haarteil *das*.

**hairpin** ['heəpın] *n* Haarnadel *die*.

**hairpin bend** *n* Haarnadelkurve *die*.

**hair-raising** [-ˌreızıŋ] *adj* haarsträubend.

**hair remover** [-rıˌmu:və'] *n* Enthaarungscreme *die*.

**hair-restorer** *n* Haarwuchsmittel *das*.

**hair's breadth** *n*: **by a ~** um Haaresbreite.

**hair slide** *n Br* Haarspange *die*.

**hair-splitting** *n pej* Haarspalterei *die*.

**hairspray** ['heəspreı] *n* Haarspray *das*.

**hairstyle** ['heəstaıl] *n* Frisur *die*.

**hairstylist** ['heəˌstaılıst] *n* Coiffeur *der*, -euse *die*.

**hairy** ['heərı] (*compar* -**ier**; *superl* -**iest**) *adj* - **1.** [animal, person, body] behaart - **2.** *inf* [dangerous] haarig.

**Haiti** ['heıtı] *n* Haiti *nt*; **in ~** auf Haiti.

**Haitian** ['heıʃn] *adj* haitianisch ◇ *n* Haitier *der*, -in *die*.

**hake** [heık] (*pl inv* OR -**s**) *n* Seehecht *der*.

**halcyon** ['hælsıən] *adj literary*: **~ days** glückliche Tage.

**hale** [heıl] *adj*: **~ and hearty** gesund und munter.

**half** [*Br* hɑ:f, *Am* hæf] (*pl senses 1, 2 and 3* **halves**; *pl senses 4, 5 and 6* **halves** OR **halfs**) *adj* halb, -e, -er, -es; **~ my life** mein halbes Leben (lang); **~ a dozen** ein halbes Dutzend; **~ an hour** eine halbe Stunde ◇ *adv* halb; **~ as big** halb so groß; **~ as much again** noch einmal halb soviel; **~ past ten** *Br*, **~ after ten** *Am* halb elf; **it's ~ past** es ist halb; **not ~!** *Br inf* und wie!; **it isn't ~ cold** *Br inf* es ist unheimlich kalt; **~-and-~** halb und halb ◇ *n* - **1.** [50%] Hälfte *die*; **~ of it** die Hälfte davon; **by ~** um die Hälfte; **in**

~ [cut, tear] in zwei Hälften; **to be too clever by ~** neunmalklug sein; **he doesn't do things by halves** er macht keine halben Sachen; **to go halves (with sb)** (mit jm) halbe-halbe machen - **2.** [fraction] Halbe(s) *das;* **four and a ~** viereinhalb - **3.** SPORT [of sports match] Spielhälfte *die* - **4.** SPORT [halfback] Läufer *der*, -in *die* - **5.** [of beer] kleines Bier - **6.** [child's ticket] Fahrkarte *die* zum halben Preis; **one and a ~** ein Erwachsener und ein Kind.

**halfback** ['hɑːfbæk] *n* Läufer *der*, -in *die.*

**half-baked** [-'beɪkt] *adj inf* unausgegoren.

**half board** *n (U) esp Br* Halbpension *die.*

**half-breed** *adj* Halbblut- ⟨> *n* Mischling *der.*

**half-brother** *n* Halbbruder *der.*

**half-caste** [-kɑːst] *adj* Halbblut- ⟨> *n* Mischling *der.*

**half cock** *n:* **to go off (at) ~** ein Reinfall sein.

**half-day** *n* [at school] halber Schultag; [at work] halber Tag.

**half-fare** *n* halber Fahrpreis.

**half-hearted** [-'hɑːtɪd] *adj* halbherzig.

**half-heartedly** [-'hɑːtɪdlɪ] *adv* halbherzig.

**half hour** *n* halbe Stunde.
➥ **half-hour** *adj* = **half-hourly.**

**half-hourly** *adj* halbstündlich.

**half-light** *n (U)* Dämmerlicht *das.*

**half-mast** *n Br:* **at ~** [flag] auf halbmast.

**half measures** *npl* Halbheiten *pl.*

**half moon** *n* Halbmond *der.*

**half note** *n Am* MUS halbe Note.

**halfpenny** ['heɪpnɪ] (*pl* **-pennies** OR **-pence**) *n* halber Penny.

**half-price** *adj* & *adv* zum halben Preis.

**half-sister** *n* Halbschwester *die.*

**half term** *n Br* kurze Schulferien in der Mitte des Trimesters.

**half time** *n* Halbzeit *die.*

**half tone** *n Am* MUS Halbton *der.*

**half-truth** *n* Halbwahrheit *die.*

**halfway** [hɑːf'weɪ] *adj:* **at the ~ stage** OR **point of sthg** in der Mitte von etw ⟨> *adv:* **to go ~** die Hälfte des Weges zurücklegen; **I was ~ up the street before I noticed** ich war schon halb die Straße hinunter, als ich es bemerkte; **~ through the holidays** mitten im Urlaub; **to meet sb ~** *fig* [compromise] jm auf halbem Weg entgegenkommen.

**half-wit** *n* Einfaltspinsel *der.*

**half-yearly** *adj* & *adv* halbjährlich.

**halibut** ['hælɪbət] (*pl inv* OR **-s**) *n* Heilbutt *der.*

**halitosis** [ˌhælɪ'təʊsɪs] *n (U)* Mundgeruch *der.*

**hall** [hɔːl] *n* - **1.** [in house] Diele *die*, Flur *der* - **2.** [meeting room] Saal *der* - **3.** [public building]

Halle *die* - **4.** *Br* UNIV [hall of residence] Studentenwohnheim *das* - **5.** [country house] Herrensitz *der.*

**halleluja** [ˌhælɪ'luːjə] *excl* halleluja!

**hallmark** ['hɔːlmɑːk] *n* - **1.** [typical feature] Kennzeichen *das* - **2.** [on metal] Feingehaltsstempel *der.*

**hallo** [hə'ləʊ] *excl* = **hello.**

**hall of residence** (*pl* **halls of residence**) *n Br* UNIV Studentenwohnheim *das.*

**hallowed** ['hæləʊd] *adj* [respected] heilig.

**Hallowe'en, Halloween** [ˌhæləʊ'iːn] *n Abend vor Allerheiligen, an dem sich Kinder oft als Gespenster verkleiden.*

---

**HALLOWEEN**

Der 31. Oktober, „Halloween" oder auch „All Hallows Eve" genannt, ist der Tradition zufolge die Nacht, in der Geister und Hexen umgehen. Die Kinder verkleiden sich, machen die Runde in der Nachbarschaft und spielen „trick or treat" (Trick oder Belohnung). Das heißt, sie drohen einen bösen Streich an, wenn sie keine Belohnung in Form von Süßigkeiten oder Geld bekommen. Es ist auch üblich, Laternen zu basteln, indem man einen Kürbis aushöhlt, eine Kerze hineinsteckt und ein Gesicht in eine Seite schnitzt.

---

**hallucinate** [hə'luːsɪneɪt] *vi* halluzinieren.

**hallucination** [ˌhəluːsɪ'neɪʃn] *n* Halluzination *die.*

**hallucinogenic** [həˌluːsɪnə'dʒenɪk] *adj* halluzinogen.

**hallway** ['hɔːlweɪ] *n* Diele *die*, Flur *der.*

**halo** ['heɪləʊ] (*pl* **-es** OR **-s**) *n* - **1.** [of saint, angel] Heiligenschein *der* - **2.** [round sun, moon] Hof *der.*

**halogen** ['hælədʒen] *n* Halogen *das.*

**halt** [hɔːlt] *n:* **to come to a ~** *lit* & *fig* zum Stillstand kommen; **to call a ~ to sthg** etw *(D)* Einhalt gebieten ⟨> *vt* [person] anlhalten; [development, activity] zum Stillstand bringen ⟨> *vi* [vehicle] anlhalten, halten; [person] stehen bleiben; [development, activity] stilllstehen.

**halter** ['hɔːltəʳ] *n* Halfter *das.*

**halterneck** ['hɔːltənek] *adj* rückenfrei.

**halting** ['hɔːltɪŋ] *adj* zögernd.

**halve** [*Br* hɑːv, *Am* hæv] *vt* - **1.** [reduce by half] halbieren - **2.** [divide] teilen.

**halves** [*Br* hɑːvz, *Am* hævz] *pl* ⊏> **half.**

**ham** [hæm] (*pt* & *pp* **-med;** *cont* **-ming**) *n* - **1.** [meat] Schinken *der* - **2.** *pej* [actor] Schmierenkomödiant *der*, -in *die* - **3.** [radio fanatic: (**radio**) ~ Funkamateur *der*, -in *die* ⟨> *comp* [salad, sandwich] Schinken- ⟨> *vt:* **to ~ it up** THEATRE übertrieben spielen.

**Hamburg** [ˈhæmbɜːg] n Hamburg nt.

**hamburger** [ˈhæmbɜːgəʳ] n - **1.** [burger] Hamburger der - **2.** (U) Am [mince] Hackfleisch das.

**ham-fisted** [-ˈfɪstɪd] adj ungeschickt.

**hamlet** [ˈhæmlɪt] n kleines Dorf.

**hammer** [ˈhæməʳ] n Hammer der <> vt - **1.** [with tool - nail] einlschlagen; [ - panel] hämmern - **2.** inf fig [fact, order]: **to ~ sthg into sb** jm etw einlbläuen - **3.** inf fig [team, player] ablservieren <> vi: **to ~ (on)** hämmern (an (+ A)).

➡ **hammer out** vt fus [agreement, solution] auslarbeiten <> vt sep [metal] auslhämmern; [dent] auslbeulen.

**hammock** [ˈhæmək] n Hängematte die.

**hamper** [ˈhæmpəʳ] n - **1.** [for picnic] Picknickkorb der - **2.** Am [for laundry] Wäschekorb der <> vt [impede] behindern.

**hamster** [ˈhæmstəʳ] n Hamster der.

**hamstring** [ˈhæmstrɪŋ] n ANAT Kniesehne die <> vt fig [thwart] vereiteln.

**hand** [hænd] n - **1.** [part of body] Hand die; **to hold ~s** Händchen halten; **by ~** von Hand; **~ in ~** lit & fig Hand in Hand; **with one's bare ~s** mit bloßen Händen; **at the ~s of** vonseiten (+ G); **~s up!** Hände hoch!; **to change ~s** den Besitzer wechseln; **to force sb's ~** auf jn Druck auslösen; **to get or lay one's ~s on sb/ sthg** an jn/etw heranlkommen; **to give sb a free ~** jm freie Hand lassen; **to have one's ~s full** alle Hände voll zu tun haben; **to try one's ~ at sthg** sich in etw (D) versuchen; **to wait on sb ~ and foot** von vorne bis hinten bedienen; **to take sb in ~** [discipline] jn an die Hand nehmen; **to have a ~ in sthg** [be involved] an etw (D) beteiligt sein; **I wash my ~s of it** ich will nichts (mehr) damit zu tun haben - **2.** [help] Hilfe die; **do you need a ~?** kann ich dir helfen?; **to give or lend sb a ~** jm helfen - **3.** [worker] Arbeiter der, -in die; [on ship] Besatzungsmitglied das - **4.** [of clock, watch] Zeiger der - **5.** [handwriting] Handschrift die - **6.** [of cards] Blatt das - **7.** inf [applause] Beifall der, Applaus der <> vt: **to ~ sthg to sb, to ~ sb sthg** jm etw geben OR reichen.

➡ **(close) at hand** adv nah in Reichweite.

➡ **in hand** adv - **1.** [time, money]: **I have ten pounds in ~** ich habe zehn Pfund übrig; **we have an hour in ~** es bleibt uns noch eine Stunde - **2.** [problem, situation]: **to have sthg in ~** etw in Bearbeitung haben.

➡ **on hand** adv zur Stelle.

➡ **on the one hand** adv einerseits.

➡ **on the other hand** adv andererseits.

➡ **out of hand** adj [situation]: **to get out of ~** außer Kontrolle geraten <> adv [completely] rundweg.

➡ **to hand** adv zur Hand.

➡ **hand down** vt sep [heirloom] hinterlassen; [knowledge] weiterlgeben.

➡ **hand in** vt sep [lost property] ablgeben; [essay, application] einlreichen.

➡ **hand on** vt sep weiterlgeben.

➡ **hand out** vt sep auslteilen.

➡ **hand over** vt sep - **1.** [gen] übergeben - **2.** TELEC: **I'll ~ you over to the manager** ich gebe Ihnen (mal) den Manager <> vi: **to ~ over (to sb)** (an jn) übergeben.

**handbag** [ˈhændbæg] n Handtasche die.

**handball** [ˈhændbɔːl] n [game] Handball der.

**handbill** [ˈhændbɪl] n Flugblatt das.

**handbook** [ˈhændbʊk] n Handbuch das.

**handbrake** [ˈhændbreɪk] n Handbremse die.

**handclap** [ˈhændklæp] n: **slow ~** langsames Klatschen.

**handcuff** [ˈhændkʌf] vt Handschellen anllegen (+ D).

**handcuffs** [ˈhændkʌfs] npl Handschellen pl.

**handful** [ˈhændfʊl] n - **1.** [gen] Hand die voll; [of grass, hair] Büschel das - **2.** inf [difficult person, animal]: **to be a ~** anstrengend sein.

**handgun** [ˈhændgʌn] n Handfeuerwaffe die.

**handicap** [ˈhændɪkæp] (pt & pp -ped; cont -ping) n - **1.** [disability] Behinderung die - **2.** fig [disadvantage] Nachteil der - **3.** SPORT Handicap das <> vt [hinder] behindern.

**handicapped** [ˈhændɪkæpt] adj [disabled] behindert.

**handicraft** [ˈhændɪkrɑːft] n [skill] Handwerk das.

**handiwork** [ˈhændɪwɜːk] n (U) Handarbeit die.

**handkerchief** [ˈhæŋkətʃɪf] (pl -chiefs OR -chieves [-tʃiːvz]) n Taschentuch das (aus Stoff).

**handle** [ˈhændl] n Griff der; [of door] Klinke die; [of broom, spade, frying pan] Stiel der; [of jug, cup] Henkel der; **to fly off the ~** aus der Haut fahren <> vt - **1.** [with hands] anlfassen - **2.** [control - tool, machine, words] handhaben; [ - car, ship] steuern - **3.** [process - orders, complaints] bearbeiten; [ - stolen goods] verschieben - **4.** [cope with - situation, crisis, death] umlgehen mit <> vi [vehicle, ship] sich steuern lassen.

**handlebars** [ˈhændlbɑːz] npl Lenker der.

**handler** [ˈhændləʳ] n - **1.**: **dog ~** Hundeführer der, -in die - **2.**: **(baggage) ~** Gepäckabfertiger der, -in die - **3.** [of stolen goods] Schieber der, -in die.

**handling charges** [ˈhændlɪŋ-] npl [at bank] Bearbeitungsgebühren pl.

**hand lotion** n Handlotion die.

**hand luggage** n (U) Br Handgepäck das.

**handmade** [ˌhænd'meɪd] adj in Handarbeit hergestellt.

**hand-me-downs** *npl inf* abgelegte Kleidung.

**handout** ['hændaʊt] *n* - **1.** [of money, food] Almosen *das* - **2.** [leaflet] Flugblatt *das* - **3.** [for lecture, discussion] Handout *das*.

**handover** ['hændəʊvəʳ] *n* Übergabe *die*.

**handpicked** [ˌhænd'pɪkt] *adj* handverlesen.

**handrail** ['hændreɪl] *n* Geländer *das*.

**handset** ['hændset] *n* TELEC Hörer *der*.

**handshake** ['hændʃeɪk] *n* Händedruck *der*.

**hands-off** *adj*: **to adopt a ~ approach** sich heraushalten.

**handsome** ['hænsəm] *adj* - **1.** [man] gut aussehend - **2.** *literary* [woman] schön - **3.** [reward] großzügig; [profit] groß.

**handsomely** ['hænsəmlɪ] *adv* [generously] großzügig.

**hands-on** *adj* [training, experience] aktiv.

**handstand** ['hændstænd] *n* Handstand *der*.

**hand-to-mouth** *adj*: **they lead a ~ existence** sie leben von der Hand in den Mund.

**hand towel** *n* Händehandtuch *das*.

**handwriting** ['hændˌraɪtɪŋ] *n* Handschrift *die*.

**handwritten** ['hændˌrɪtn] *adj* handgeschrieben.

**handy** ['hændɪ] (*compar* -**ier**; *superl* -**iest**) *adj inf* - **1.** [useful] praktisch; **to come in ~** nützlich sein - **2.** [person] geschickt - **3.** [near]: **the newsagent's is very ~** der Zeitungshändler ist gleich um die Ecke; **to keep sthg ~** etw in Reichweite haben.

**handyman** ['hændɪmæn] (*pl* -**men** [-men]) *n* Heimwerker *der*.

**hang** [hæŋ] (*pt* & *pp sense 1* **hung**; *pt* & *pp sense 2* **hung** OR **hanged**) *vt* - **1.** [suspend] aufhängen; **to ~ sthg on sthg** etw an etw (*A*) hängen - **2.** [execute] hängen ◇ *vi* hängen ◇ *n*: **to get the ~ of sthg** *inf* kapieren, wie etw funktioniert.

➡ **hang about, hang around** *vi* - **1.** [loiter] herumhängen - **2.** [wait] warten.

➡ **hang down** *vi* herunterhängen.

➡ **hang on** *vt fus* [depend on] abhängen von ◇ *vi* - **1.** [keep hold]: **to ~ on (to)** sich festhalten (an (+ *D*)) - **2.** *inf* [continue waiting] warten; **~ on!** Moment mal!; [on telephone] bleiben Sie am Apparat! - **3.** [persevere] aushalten, durchhalten.

➡ **hang onto** *vt fus* [rope, ledge, branch] sich festhalten an (+ *D*), sich festklammern an (+ *D*); [job] behalten; **to ~ onto power** an der Macht bleiben.

➡ **hang out** *vt sep* [washing] aufhängen ◇ *vi inf* [spend time] herumhängen.

➡ **hang round** *vi* = hang about.

➡ **hang together** *vi* [argument] schlüssig OR zusammenhängend sein.

➡ **hang up** *vt sep* [suspend] aufhängen ◇ *vi* [on telephone] auflegen, auflegen.

➡ **hang up on** *vt fus* TELEC: **he hung up on me** er hat einfach aufgelegt.

**hangar** ['hæŋəʳ] *n* Hangar *der*.

**hangdog** ['hæŋdɒg] *adj* zerknirscht.

**hanger** ['hæŋəʳ] *n* [coat hanger] Kleiderbügel *der*.

**hangers-on** *npl* Gefolgsleute *pl*.

**hang glider** *n* [apparatus] Drachen *der*.

**hang gliding** *n* Drachenfliegen *das*.

**hanging** ['hæŋɪŋ] *n* - **1.** [punishment] Erhängen *das;* [execution] Hinrichtung *die* - **2.** [for wall] Vorhang *der*.

**hangman** ['hæŋmən] (*pl* -**men** [-mən]) *n* Henker *der*.

**hangover** ['hæŋˌəʊvəʳ] *n* - **1.** [from drinking] Kater *der* - **2.** [from past]: **~ (from)** Überbleibsel *das* (von).

**hang-up** *n inf* PSYCH Komplex *der*.

**hank** [hæŋk] *n* [of wool] Strang *der*.

**hanker** ['hæŋkəʳ] ➡ **hanker after, hanker for** *vt fus* sich sehnen nach.

**hankering** ['hæŋkərɪŋ] *n*: **~ after** OR **for** Sehnsucht *die* nach.

**hankie, hanky** ['hæŋkɪ] (*pl* -**ies**) *n inf abbr of* handkerchief.

**hanky-panky** *n* (*U*) *inf* [sexual behaviour] Knutscherei *die*, Gefummel *das*.

**Hansard** ['hænsɑːd] *n britisches Parlamentsprotokoll.*

**Hants** [hænts] *abk für* Hampshire, *in Postanschrift verwendet.*

**haphazard** [ˌhæp'hæzəd] *adj* willkürlich, planlos.

**haphazardly** [ˌhæp'hæzədlɪ] *adv* willkürlich, planlos.

**hapless** ['hæplɪs] *adj literary* unglückselig.

**happen** ['hæpən] *vi* - **1.** [occur] geschehen, passieren; **to ~ to sb** jm passieren - **2.** [chance]: **to ~ to do sthg** zufällig etw tun; **as it ~s** zufälligerweise; **as it ~s, I HAVE read the book** ich habe das Buch sehr wohl gelesen.

**happening** ['hæpənɪŋ] *n* Ereignis *das*.

**happily** ['hæpɪlɪ] *adv* - **1.** [contentedly]: **the children were playing ~** die Kinder spielten vergnügt; **she smiled ~** sie lächelte glücklich - **2.** [fortunately] glücklicherweise - **3.** [willingly] gern.

**happiness** ['hæpɪnɪs] *n* Glück *das*.

**happy** ['hæpɪ] (*compar* -**ier**; *superl* -**iest**) *adj* - **1.** [contented] glücklich - **2.** [causing contentment - life, day] glücklich; [ - story] erfreulich; **Happy Christmas!** frohe OR fröhliche Weih-

H

nachten!; **Happy New Year!** frohes neues Jahr!; **Happy Birthday!** herzlichen Glückwunsch zum Geburtstag! - **3.** [satisfied] zufrieden; **to be ~ with** OR **about sthg** glücklich OR zufrieden mit etw sein - **4.** [fortunate] glücklich; **by a ~ coincidence** durch einen glücklichen Zufall - **5.** [willing]: **to be ~ to do sthg** etw gerne tun.

**happy event** n freudiges Ereignis.

**happy-go-lucky** adj inf unbeschwert.

**happy hour** n eine vorher festgelegte Zeit, zu der alkoholische Getränke in einer Bar zu einem Sonderpreis verkauft werden.

**happy medium** n goldene Mitte.

**harangue** [həˈræŋ] n Standpauke die <> vt: **to ~ sb** jm eine Standpauke halten.

**harass** [ˈhærəs] vt belästigen.

**harassed** [ˈhærəst] adj abgekämpft.

**harassment** [ˈhærəsmənt] n [persecution] Schikanierung die.

**harbinger** [ˈhɑːbɪndʒəʳ] n literary Vorbote der.

**harbour** Br, **harbor** Am [ˈhɑːbəʳ] n Hafen der <> vt - **1.** [feeling] hegen - **2.** [person] versteckt halten.

**harbour master** n Hafenmeister der.

**hard** [hɑːd] adj - **1.** [gen] hart; **to be ~ on sb** streng mit jm sein; **walking downhill is ~ on your knees** bergab gehen belastet die Knie; **to be as ~ as nails** ein zäher Typ sein - **2.** [difficult, strenuous] schwer; **~ times** schwere Zeiten; **he learnt not to trust people the ~ way** er hat auf schmerzliche Weise lernen müssen, dass man Menschen nicht trauen kann; **it is ~ to believe that ...** es ist kaum zu glauben, dass ...; **~ of hearing** schwerhörig - **3.** [kick, push] heftig - **4.** [fact] nackt - **5.** Br POL: **the ~ left/right** der linke/rechte Flügel der Partei <> adv - **1.** [work, hit] hart; **to try ~** sich (D) viel Mühe geben; **to listen ~** genau hinlhören - **2.** [rain] heftig - **3.** phr: **to be ~ pushed** OR **put** OR **pressed to do sthg** Schwierigkeiten haben, etw zu tun; **to feel ~ done by** sich benachteiligt fühlen.

**hard-and-fast** adj eisern.

**hardback** [ˈhɑːbæk] adj gebunden <> n [book] gebundene Ausgabe.

**hard-bitten** adj hartgesotten.

**hardboard** [ˈhɑːbɔːd] n Pressspanplatte die.

**hard-boiled** adj - **1.** [egg] hart gekocht - **2.** [person] hartgesotten.

**hard cash** n Bargeld das.

**hard cider** n Am Cidre der.

**hard copy** n COMPUT Papierausdruck der, Hardcopy die.

**hard-core** adj [pornography] hart.

➡ **hard core** n [of group] harter Kern.

**hard court** n Hartplatz der.

**hard currency** n harte Währung.

**hard disk** n Festplatte die.

**hard drugs** npl harte Drogen pl.

**harden** [ˈhɑːdn] vt - **1.** [steel] härten; [arteries] verhärten - **2.** fig [person] abhärten - **3.**: **to ~ sb's opinion/attitude** jn in seiner Meinung/Einstellung bestärken <> vi - **1.** [glue, concrete] härten, hart werden; [arteries] sich verhärten - **2.** fig [person] abhärten - **3.** [attitude, ideas, opinion] sich verhärten.

**hardened** [ˈhɑːdnd] adj - **1.** [steel] gehärtet; [arteries] verhärtet - **2.** [criminal] verroht - **3.** [accustomed]: **~ to sthg** abgehärtet gegen etw.

**hardening** [ˈhɑːdnɪŋ] n (U) [of steel] Härtung die; [of arteries] Verhärtung die.

**hard hat** n [for protection] Schutzhelm der.

**hardheaded** adj nüchtern.

**hard-hearted** [-ˈhɑːtɪd] adj hartherzig.

**hard-hitting** [-ˈhɪtɪŋ] adj [reporting] aggressiv; [photographs] schonungslos.

**hard labour** n Zwangsarbeit die.

**hard line** n: **to take a ~ on sthg** in etw (A) unnachgiebig sein.

➡ **hard-line** adj kompromisslos; [Communist, Tory] überzeugt.

➡ **hard lines** excl Br Pech!

**hard-liner** n Hardliner der, -in die.

**hardly** [ˈhɑːdlɪ] adv - **1.** [scarcely, not really] kaum; **~ ever** fast nie, kaum jemals; **~ anything** fast nichts, kaum etwas; **I can ~ move** ich kann mich kaum bewegen - **2.** [only just] gerade erst.

**hardness** [ˈhɑːdnɪs] n - **1.** [of water, firmness] Härte die - **2.** [difficulty] Schwierigkeit die - **3.** [of heart, person] Strenge die.

**hard-nosed** [-ˈnəʊzd] adj abgebrüht.

**hard return** n COMPUT harter Zeilenumbruch, Absatzzeichen das.

**hard sell** n aggressive Verkaufsmethoden.

**hardship** [ˈhɑːdʃɪp] n Entbehrung die, Not die; **a life of many ~s** ein Leben voller Entbehrungen.

**hard shoulder** n Br AUT Standspur die.

**hard up** adj inf knapp bei Kasse; **~ for sthg** knapp an etw (D).

**hardware** [ˈhɑːdweəʳ] n (U) - **1.** [tools, equipment] Eisenwaren pl - **2.** COMPUT Hardware die.

**hardware shop** n Eisenwarenhandlung die.

**hardwearing** [ˌhɑːdˈweərɪŋ] adj Br strapazierfähig.

**hardwood** [ˈhɑːdwʊd] n Hartholz das.

**hardworking** [ˌhɑːdˈwɜːkɪŋ] adj fleißig.

**hardy** [ˈhɑːdɪ] (compar -ier; superl -iest) adj

**- 1.** [person, animal] abgehärtet **- 2.** [plant] mehrjährig.

**hare** [heə'] *n* Hase *der*, Feldhase *der* ◇ *vi Br inf:* **to ~ off** losrasen.

**harebell** ['heəbell] *n* Glockenblume *die*.

**harebrained** ['heə,breɪnd] *adj inf* hirnverbrannt.

**harelip** [,heə'lɪp] *n* Hasenscharte *die*.

**harem** [*Br* ha:'ri:m, *Am* 'hærəm] *n* Harem *der*.

**haricot (bean)** ['hærɪkəʊ-] *n* weiße Bohne.

**hark** [ha:k] ➤ **hark back** *vi:* **to ~ back to sthg** auf etw *(A)* zurückIkommen.

**harlequin** ['ha:lǝkwɪn] *n* Harlekin *der* ◇ *comp* Harlekin-.

**Harley Street** ['ha:lɪ-] *n* Straße in London, in der viele Spezialärzte ihre Praxis haben.

**harm** [ha:m] *n* [physical] Verletzung *die;* [psychological] Schaden *der;* **to do ~ to sb/sthg, to do sb/ sthg ~** jm/etw Schaden zufügen, jm/etw schaden; **she means no ~ by it** sie meint es nicht böse; **there's no ~ in it** es kann nichts schaden; **to be out of ~'s way** [person] in Sicherheit sein; [thing] aus dem Weg sein; **to come to no ~** [person] nicht zu Schaden kommen; [thing] nicht beschädigt werden ◇ *vt* [physically] verletzen; [psychologically] schädigen.

**harmful** ['ha:mfʊl] *adj* schädlich.

**harmless** ['ha:mlɪs] *adj* harmlos; [substance] unschädlich.

**harmlessly** ['ha:mlɪslɪ] *adv* harmlos.

**harmonic** [ha:'mɒnɪk] *adj* harmonisch.

**harmonica** [ha:'mɒnɪkə] *n* Mundharmonika *die*.

**harmonious** [ha:'məʊnjəs] *adj* harmonisch.

**harmonium** [ha:'məʊnjəm] *(pl* **-s)** *n* Harmonium *das*.

**harmonize, -ise** ['ha:mǝnaɪz] *vt* [views, policies] in Einklang bringen ◇ *vi* **- 1.** [sounds, colours]: **to ~ (with sthg)** harmonieren (mit etw) **- 2.** MUS harmonisieren.

**harmony** ['ha:mǝnɪ] *(pl* **-ies)** *n* Harmonie *die;* **in ~ with sthg** in Harmonie mit etw.

**harness** ['ha:nɪs] *n* **- 1.** [for horse] Geschirr *das* **- 2.** [for person, child] Gurt *der* ◇ *vt* **- 1.** [horse] anlschirren **- 2.** [energy, solar power] nutzbar machen.

**harp** [ha:p] *n* MUS Harfe *die*.
➤ **harp on** *vi:* **to ~ on (about sthg)** immer wieder anlfangen (von etw).

**harpist** ['ha:pɪst] *n* Harfenist *der*, -in *die*.

**harpoon** [ha:'pu:n] *n* Harpune *die* ◇ *vt* harpunieren.

**harpsichord** ['ha:psɪkɔ:d] *n* Cembalo *das*.

**harrowing** ['hærǝʊɪŋ] *adj* grauenvoll.

**harry** ['hærɪ] *(pt & pp* **-ied)** *vt* **- 1.** [pester] verfolgen, plagen; **to ~ sb for sthg** jn mit etw belästigen **- 2.** MIL [attack] wiederholt anlgreifen.

**harsh** [ha:ʃ] *adj* **- 1.** [person, criticism, treatment, words] hart, streng **- 2.** [conditions, weather] rau **- 3.** [voice] barsch; [cry] schrill **- 4.** [colour, contrast, light] grell **- 5.** [landscape] trostlos **- 6.** [taste] streng.

**harshly** ['ha:ʃlɪ] *adv* **- 1.** [treat, punish, judge] hart **- 2.** [cry, shout] rau **- 3.** [shine] grell.

**harshness** ['ha:ʃnɪs] *n* **- 1.** [of person, criticism, treatment, words] Härte *die* **- 2.** [of conditions, weather, taste] Strenge *die* **- 3.** [of voice] Barschheit *die;* [of cry] schriller Klang **- 4.** [of colour, contrast, light] Grelle *die*, Grellheit *die* **- 5.** [of landscape] Trostlosigkeit *die*.

**harvest** ['ha:vɪst] *n* Ernte *die* ◇ *vt* ernten.

**harvest festival** *n* Erntedankfest *das*.

**has** [*weak form* həz, *strong form* hæz] *vb* ▷ **have.**

**has-been** *n inf pej* vergessene Größe.

**hash** [hæʃ] *n* **- 1.** [meat] Haschee *das* **- 2.** *inf* [mess]: **to make a ~ of sthg** etw vermasseln **- 3.** *drugs sl* [hashish] Hasch *das*.
➤ **hash up** *vt sep Br inf* [make a mess of] vermasseln, verpfuschen.

**hash browns** *npl Am* Reibekuchen *pl*, Kartoffelpuffer *pl*.

**hashish** ['hæʃi:ʃ] *n* Haschisch *das*.

**hasn't** ['hæznt] = **has not.**

**hassle** ['hæsl] *inf* Ärger *der* ◇ *vt* ärgern.

**haste** [heɪst] *n* **- 1.** [rush] Eile *die*, Hast *die;* **to do sthg in ~** etw in Eile tun, etw hastig tun **- 2.** [speed] Eile *die;* **to make ~** *dated* eilen, sich sputen.

**hasten** ['heɪsn] *vt* beschleunigen ◇ *vi:* **to ~ (to do sthg)** sich beeilen(, etw zu tun).

**hastily** ['heɪstɪlɪ] *adv* **- 1.** [rashly] übereilt **- 2.** [quickly] hastig.

**hasty** ['heɪstɪ] *(compar* **-ier;** *superl* **-iest)** *adj* **- 1.** [rash] übereilt **- 2.** [quick] hastig.

**hat** [hæt] *n* Hut *der;* **keep it under your ~** behalte es für dich!; **to be talking through one's ~** dummes Zeug reden; **old ~** alter Hut, alte Kamellen.

**hatbox** ['hæt,bɒks] *n* Hutschachtel *die*.

**hatch** [hætʃ] *vt* **- 1.** [egg] auslbrüten **- 2.** *fig* [scheme, plot] auslhecken ◇ *vi* [chick] auslschlüpfen ◇ *n* [for serving food] Durchreiche *die*.

**hatchback** ['hætʃ,bæk] *n* Schräghecklimousine *die*.

**hatchet** ['hætʃɪt] *n* Beil *das;* **to bury the ~** das Kriegsbeil begraben.

**hatchet job** *n inf:* to do a ~ on sb jn fertig machen.

**hatchway** ['hætʃˌweɪ] *n* Luke *die.*

**hate** [heɪt] *n* [emotion] Hass *der* <> *vt* hassen, verabscheuen; **to ~ doing sthg** es hassen, etw zu tun.

**hateful** ['heɪtfʊl] *adj* abscheulich.

**hatred** ['heɪtrɪd] *n* Hass *der.*

**hat trick** *n* SPORT Hattrick *der.*

**haughty** ['hɔːtɪ] (*compar* -ier; *superl* -iest) *adj* hochmütig.

**haul** [hɔːl] *n* - **1.** [of drugs, stolen goods] Beute *die* - **2.** [distance]: **a long ~** ein langer Weg <> *vt* - **1.** [pull] ziehen; **I'm tired of ~ing these bags around** ich bin es leid, diese Taschen mit mir herumzuschleppen - **2.** [by lorry] transportieren, befördern.

**haulage** ['hɔːlɪdʒ] *n* (U) - **1.** [business] Transportunternehmen *das* - **2.** [act] Transport *der* - **3.** [cost] Transportkosten *pl.*

**haulage contractor** *n* Spediteur *der.*

**haulier** *Br* ['hɔːlɪəʳ], **hauler** *Am* ['hɔːlər] *n* - **1.** [business] Spedition *die* - **2.** [owner] Spediteur *der.*

**haunch** [hɔːntʃ] *n* - **1.** [of person] Gesäß *das* - **2.** [of animal] Keule *die.*

**haunt** [hɔːnt] *n* [place] Lieblingsort *der;* [pub] Stammlokal *das* <> *vt* - **1.** [subj: ghost] spuken in (+ D), umlgehen in (+ D) - **2.** [subj: memory, fear, problem] verfolgen.

**haunted** ['hɔːntɪd] *adj* - **1.** [house, castle] Spuk-, Geister-; **this place is ~** hier spukt es - **2.** [look] gehetzt.

**haunting** ['hɔːntɪŋ] *adj* immer wiederkehrend.

**have** [hæv] (*pt & pp* **had**) *aux vb* (to form perfect tenses) haben/sein; **I ~ burnt it** ich habe es verbrannt; **he has come** er ist gekommen; **I ~ finished** ich bin fertig; **I ~ lived here for three years** ich wohne hier seit drei Jahren; **~ you seen the film?** hast du den Film gesehen?; **~ you been there? - no, I haven't/yes I ~** warst du schon mal dort? – nein, noch nie/ja; **she hasn't gone yet, has she?** sie ist noch nicht gegangen, oder?; **we had already left** wir waren schon gegangen; **I would never ~ gone if I'd known** ich wäre nie gegangen, wenn ich das gewusst hätte; **I was out of breath, having run all the way** ich war außer Atem, weil ich den ganzen Weg gerannt war <> *modal vb* [be obliged]: **to ~ (got) to do sthg** etw tun müssen; **do you ~ to go, ~ you got to go?** musst du wirklich gehen?; **I've got to go to work** ich muss arbeiten gehen; **do you ~ to pay?** muss man bezahlen? <> *vt* - **1.** [possess]: **to ~ (got)** haben; **I ~ no money, I haven't got any money** ich habe kein Geld; **she has (got) brown hair** sie hat braunes Haar; **do you ~ a double**

room? haben Sie ein Doppelzimmer? - **2.** [illness] haben; **to ~ a cold** eine Erkältung haben - **3.** [need to deal with]: **to ~ (got)** haben; **I've got things to do** ich habe einiges zu erledigen - **4.** [receive - news, letter] bekommen; **we don't ~ many visitors** wir haben *OR* bekommen wenig Besuch - **5.** [instead of another verb] haben; **to ~ a read of sthg** etw lesen; **to ~ an operation** sich operieren lassen; **to ~ a bath** ein Bad nehmen; **to ~ breakfast** frühstücken; **to ~ a cigarette** eine Zigarette rauchen; **to ~ a drink** etwas trinken; **to ~ a game of chess** eine Partie Schach spielen; **to ~ lunch/dinner** zu Mittag/zu Abend essen; **to ~ a shower** duschen; **to ~ a swim** schwimmen; **to ~ a walk** spazierenlgehen; **I had another piece of cake** ich nahm noch ein Stück Kuchen; **I've had a bad day** heute ist alles schief gegangen; **to ~ no choice** keine Wahl haben; **I ~ no doubt about it** ich habe keine Zweifel daran - **6.** [give birth to]: **to ~ a baby** ein Kind bekommen - **7.** [cause to be done]: **to ~ sb do sthg** jn etw tun lassen; **to ~ sthg done** etw machen lassen; **I'm having the house decorated** ich lasse das Haus tapezieren; **to ~ one's hair cut** sich (D) die Haare schneiden lassen - **8.** [be treated in a certain way]: **I've had my wallet stolen** mir ist mein Geldbeutel gestohlen worden - **9.** [experience, suffer - accident] haben; **I had a nasty surprise** ich erlebte eine böse Überraschung; **to ~ a good time** sich großartig amüsieren - **10.** [organize - party] machen; [ - meeting] abhalten - **11.** *inf* [cheat]: **you've been had!** du bist reingelegt worden! - **12.** *phr:* **to ~ it in for sb** es auf jn abgesehen haben; **to ~ had it** [car, machine, clothes] hinüber sein; **I've had it** [be tired] ich kann nicht mehr; [be in trouble] ich bin geliefert.

➤ **haves** *npl* the **~s and the ~ nots** die Reichen und die Armen.

➤ **have on** *vt sep* - **1.** [be wearing] anlhaben - **2.** [tease] anlführen; **you're having me on!** du willst mich wohl auf den Arm nehmen! - **3.:** **to ~ (got) sthg on** [have to do] etw zu tun haben; [have planned] etw vorlhaben; **I've got a lot of work on** ich habe viel zu tun.

➤ **have out** *vt sep* - **1.** [appendix, tonsils] herausgenommen bekommen; **to ~ a tooth out** einen Zahn gezogen bekommen - **2.** [discuss frankly]: **to ~ it out with sb** sich mit jm ausIsprechen.

➤ **have up** *vt sep Br inf* [take to court]: **to be had up for sthg** wegen etw vor Gericht kommen.

**haven** ['heɪvn] *n* Zufluchtsort *der;* **a safe ~** ein sicherer Hafen.

**haven't** ['hævnt] = have not.

**haversack** ['hævəsæk] *n dated* Rucksack *der.*

**havoc** ['hævək] *n* Chaos *das,* Verwüstung *die;* **to play ~ with sthg** [health] etw ruinieren; [plans] etw über den Haufen werfen.

**Hawaii** [həˈwaɪiː] *n* Hawaii *nt.*

**Hawaiian** [hə'waɪjən] *adj* hawaiisch ⬦ *n* Hawaiianer *der*, -in *die*.

**hawk** [hɔːk] *n lit* & *fig* Falke *der*; **to watch sb like a ~** jn mit Argusaugen beobachten ⬦ *vt* [in the street] feilbieten; [door to door] hausieren gehen mit.

**hawker** ['hɔːkə'] *n* - **1.** [street vendor] Straßenhändler *der*, -in *die* - **2.** [door-to-door] Hausierer *der*, -in *die*.

**hawthorn** ['hɔːθɔːn] *n* Hagedorn *der*.

**hay** [heɪ] *n* Heu *das*; **to make ~ while the sun shines** die Gunst der Stunde nutzen.

**hay fever** *n* Heuschnupfen *der*.

**haymaking** ['heɪˌmeɪkɪŋ] *n* Heumachen *das*.

**haystack** ['heɪˌstæk] *n* Heuschober *der*.

**haywire** ['heɪˌwaɪə'] *adj inf*: **to go ~** [person] durchdrehen; [machine] verrückt spielen.

**hazard** ['hæzəd] *n* [danger] Gefahr *die*; [risk] Risiko *das* ⬦ *vt* - **1.** [life, reputation] riskieren, aufs Spiel setzen - **2.** [guess, suggestion] wagen.

**hazardous** ['hæzədəs] *adj* [risky] riskant; [dangerous] gefährlich.

**hazard warning lights** *npl Br* Warnblinkanlage *die*.

**haze** [heɪz] *n* - **1.** [mist] Dunst *der* - **2.** [state of confusion] Verwirrtheit *die*.

**hazel** ['heɪzl] *adj* haselnussbraun ⬦ *n* [tree] Haselnussstrauch *der*.

**hazelnut** ['heɪzlˌnʌt] *n* Haselnuss *die*.

**hazy** ['heɪzɪ] (*compar* **-ier**; *superl* **-iest**) *adj* - **1.** [misty] dunstig - **2.** [vague, confused] verwirrt.

**H-bomb** *n* H-Bombe *die*, Wasserstoffbombe *die*.

**h & c** *abbr of* **hot and cold (water)**.

**he** [hiː] *pers pron* er; **~'s tall** er ist groß; **~ doesn't care** ihm ist es egal; **there ~ is** dort ist er; HE **can't do it** den kann das nicht tun ⬦ *n inf*: **it's a ~** [animal] es ist ein Er ⬦ *comp*: **~-goat** Ziegenbock *der*.

**HE** - **1.** (*abbr of* **high explosive**) hochexplosiver Stoff - **2.** (*abbr of* **His (or Her) Excellency**) Seine/Ihre Exzellenz.

**head** [hed] *n* - **1.** [part of body] Kopf *der*; **a or per ~** pro Kopf; **off the top of one's ~** aus dem Stegreif; **to bite or snap sb's ~ off** jm den Kopf abreißen; **to laugh one's ~ off** sich totlachen; **to sing/shout one's ~ off** aus vollem Halse singen/schreien; **to be banging one's ~ against a brick wall** gegen eine Wand reden; **I can't make ~ nor tail of it** ich werde daraus nicht schlau; **on your own ~ be it** auf deine Verantwortung - **2.** [mind, brain] Verstand *der*; **to have a ~ for figures** eine Begabung für Zahlen haben; **to have a ~ for heights** schwindelfrei sein; **to be off one's ~ *Br*, to be out of one's ~ *Am*** [mad] verrückt or

durchgedreht sein; *inf* [drunk] besoffen sein; **we put our ~s together** wir haben uns zusammengesetzt; **to go to sb's ~** [alcohol, success, praise] jm zu Kopf steigen; **to keep one's ~** den Kopf nicht verlieren, die Ruhe bewahren; **to lose one's ~** den Kopf verlieren; **to be soft in the ~** schwachsinnig sein - **3.** [top, extremity - of stairs] oberer Absatz; [ - of queue] Anfang *der*; [ - of table, bed] Kopfende *das*; [ - of procession, arrow] Spitze *die* - **4.** [of flower, cabbage] Kopf *der* - **5.** [leader - gen] Leiter *der*, -in *die*; [ - of family] Oberhaupt *das* - **6.** [head teacher] Schulleiter *der*, -in *die* - **7.** *phr*: **to come to a ~** sich zu|spitzen ⬦ *vt* - **1.** [procession, queue, list] an|führen - **2.** [organization, delegation] leiten - **3.** FTBL köpfen ⬦ *vi* [gen] gehen *nj* [by car, bus] fahren; **where are you ~ing?** wohin gehst/fährst du?; **to ~ home** nach Hause gehen/fahren.

➤ **heads** *npl* [on coin] Kopf *der*; **~s or tails?** Kopf oder Zahl?

➤ **head for** *vt fus* - **1.** [place]: **to ~ for Glasgow** Richtung Glasgow fahren; **to ~ for the bar** auf die Bar zu|steuern - **2.** *fig* [trouble, disaster] zu|steuern auf (+ *A*).

➤ **head off** *vt sep* - **1.** [enemy, escapees] ab|fangen - **2.** [threat, risk, disaster] ab|wenden ⬦ *vi* [leave] gehen.

**headache** ['hedeɪk] *n* Kopfschmerzen *pl*; **to have a ~** Kopfschmerzen haben.

**headband** ['hedbænd] *n* Stirnband *das*.

**headboard** ['hedˌbɔːd] *n* Kopfteil *das*.

**head boy** *n Br* Schulsprecher *der*.

**head cold** *n* Kopfgrippe *die*.

**head count** *n* Kopfzahl *die*.

**headdress** ['hedˌdres] *n* Kopfschmuck *der*.

**header** ['hedə'] *n* - **1.** FTBL Kopfball *der*, Kopfstoß *der* - **2.** [at top of page] Kopfzeile *die*.

**headfirst** [ˌhed'fɜːst] *adv* kopfüber.

**headgear** ['hedˌgɪə'] *n (U)* Kopfbedeckung *die*.

**head girl** *n Br* Schulsprecherin *die*.

**headhunt** ['hedhʌnt] *vt* ab|werben.

**headhunter** ['hedˌhʌntə'] *n* jemand, der Führungskräfte abwirbt.

**heading** ['hedɪŋ] *n* Überschrift *die*.

**headlamp** ['hedlæmp] *n Br* Scheinwerfer *der*.

**headland** ['hedlənd] *n* Landspitze *die*.

**headlight** ['hedlaɪt] *n* Scheinwerfer *der*.

**headline** ['hedlaɪn] *n* - **1.** [in newspaper] Schlagzeile *die* - **2.** [of news broadcast]: **the news ~s** die Kurznachrichten *pl*.

**headlong** ['hedlɒŋ] *adv* - **1.** [at great speed] halsbrecherisch - **2.** [impetuously] blindlings - **3.** [dive, fall] kopfüber ⬦ *adj* [impetuous] unüberlegt.

**headmaster** [ˌhed'mɑːstə'] *n* Schulleiter *der*.

**headmistress** [ˌhedˈmɪstrɪs] n Schulleiterin die.

**head office** n Hauptsitz der.

**head-on** adj [collision] frontal; [confrontation] direkt <> adv frontal; [meet] direkt.

**headphones** [ˈhedfəʊnz] npl Kopfhörer der.

**headquarters** [ˌhedˈkwɔːtəz] npl [of business, organization] Hauptniederlassung die; [of armed forces] Hauptquartier das.

**headrest** [ˈhedrest] n Kopfstütze die.

**headroom** [ˈhedrʊm] n [in car] Kopfraum der; [below bridge] lichte Höhe.

**headscarf** [ˈhedskɑːf] (pl -s OR -scarves [-skɑːvz]) n Kopftuch das.

**headset** [ˈhedset] n Kopfhörer der.

**headship** [ˈhedʃɪp] n Schulleiterstelle die.

**headstand** [ˈhedstænd] n Kopfstand der.

**head start** n: ~ (on OR over sb) Vorsprung der (vor OR gegenüber jm).

**headstone** [ˈhedstəʊn] n Grabstein der.

**headstrong** [ˈhedstrɒŋ] adj eigenwillig.

**head teacher** n Schulleiter der, -in die.

**head waiter** n Oberkellner der.

**headway** [ˈhedweɪ] n: to make ~ voran|kommen.

**headwind** [ˈhedwɪnd] n Gegenwind der.

**headword** [ˈhedwɜːd] n Stichwort das.

**heady** [ˈhedɪ] (compar -ier; superl -iest) adj - **1.** [exciting] aufregend - **2.** [causing giddiness] berauschend.

**heal** [hiːl] vt - **1.** [person, wound] heilen - **2.** fig [breach, division] schlichten, beillegen <> vi heilen.

➤ **heal up** vi verheilen.

**healing** [ˈhiːlɪŋ] adj heilend <> n (U) Heilung die.

**health** [helθ] n Gesundheit die; **to be in good/poor ~** bei guter/schlechter Gesundheit sein; **to drink (to) sb's ~** auf js Gesundheit OR Wohl trinken.

**health centre** n Ärztezentrum das.

**health-conscious** adj gesundheitsbewusst.

**health farm** n Gesundheitsfarm die.

**health food** n Reformkost die.

**health food shop** n Reformhaus das.

**health hazard** n Gesundheitsrisiko das.

**health service** n Gesundheitsdienst der.

**health visitor** n Br Pflegekraft, die im Auftrag der Gesundheitsbehörden Bürger informiert und berät.

**healthy** [ˈhelθɪ] (compar -ier; superl -iest) adj - **1.** [gen] gesund - **2.** [profit, sum] ordentlich - **3.** [attitude] vernünftig; [respect] angebracht.

**heap** [hiːp] n Haufen der; **in a ~** auf einem Haufen <> vt - **1.** [pile up] auf|häufen; **to ~ sthg on(to) stho** etw auf etw (A) häufen - **2.** fig [lavish]: **to ~ sthg on sb** jn mit etw überhäufen OR überschütten.

➤ **heaps** npl inf: **~s of money/people/books** ein Haufen Geld/Leute/Bücher; **~s of time** eine Menge Zeit.

**hear** [hɪəʳ] (pt & pp heard [hɜːd]) vt - **1.** [perceive] hören - **2.** [learn of] hören, erfahren; **to ~ (that) ...** hören, dass ..., erfahren, dass ... - **3.** LAW [listen to] an|hören <> vi - **1.** [gen] hören; **to ~ from sb** von jm hören - **2.** [know]: **to' ~ about sthg** etw erfahren - **3.** phr: **to have heard of sb/sthg** von jm/etw gehört haben; **I won't ~ of it!** ich möchte nichts davon hören!

➤ **hear out** vt sep ausreden lassen.

**hearing** [ˈhɪərɪŋ] n - **1.** [sense] Gehör das; **don't say this in her ~** lass sie das nicht hören; **hard of ~** schwerhörig - **2.** LAW [trial] Verhandlung die; **to get a fair ~** fig in Ruhe angehört werden.

**hearing aid** n Hörgerät das.

**hearsay** [ˈhɪəseɪ] n Hörensagen das.

**hearse** [hɜːs] n Leichenwagen der.

**heart** [hɑːt] n - **1.** [gen] Herz das; **to have a ~ of gold** ein Herz aus Gold haben; **his ~ isn't in it** er ist nicht mit ganzem Herzen dabei; **it's a subject close to my ~** es liegt mir sehr am Herzen; **from the ~** von Herzen; **from the bottom of my ~** aus tiefstem Herzen; **I believe in my ~ of ~s that ...** im Grunde meines Herzens glaube ich, dass ...; **to do sthg to one's ~'s content** etw nach Herzenslust tun; **my ~ sank** mir rutschte das Herz in die Hose; **my ~ leapt** mein Herz schlug höher; **to break sb's ~** jm das Herz brechen; **to set one's ~ on sthg** sein Herz an etw (A) hängen; **to set one's ~ on doing sthg** etw unbedingt tun wollen; **to take sthg to ~** sich (D) etw zu Herzen nehmen - **2.** (U) [courage] Mut der; **to lose ~** den Mut verlieren - **3.** [core - of city] Herz das; [ - of problem] Kern der.

➤ **hearts** npl [playing cards] Herz das; **the six of ~s** die Herz Sechs.

➤ **at heart** adv im Grunde.

➤ **by heart** adv auswendig.

**heartache** [ˈhɑːteɪk] n Kummer der.

**heart attack** n Herzanfall der.

**heartbeat** [ˈhɑːtbiːt] n Herzschlag der.

**heartbreaking** [ˈhɑːtˌbreɪkɪŋ] adj herzzerreißend.

**heartbroken** [ˈhɑːtˌbrəʊkn] adj untröstlich.

**heartburn** [ˈhɑːtbɜːn] n Sodbrennen das.

**heart disease** n Herzkrankheit die, Herzleiden das.

**heartening** [ˈhɑːtnɪŋ] adj ermutigend.

**heart failure** n Herzversagen das.

**heartfelt** ['hɑːtfelt] adj tief empfunden.

**hearth** [hɑːθ] n Kamin der.

**heartland** ['hɑːtlænd] n Herzland das.

**heartless** ['hɑːtlɪs] adj herzlos.

**heartrending** ['hɑːt,rendɪŋ] adj herzzerreißend.

**heart-searching** [-,sɜːtʃɪŋ] n Gewissenserforschung die.

**heartthrob** ['hɑːtθrɒb] n Idol das.

**heart-to-heart** adj offen ◇ n offene Aussprache.

**heart transplant** n Herztransplantation die, Herzverpflanzung die.

**heartwarming** ['hɑːt,wɔːmɪŋ] adj herzerfreuend.

**hearty** ['hɑːtɪ] (compar **-ier**; superl **-iest**) adj - **1.** [laughter, praise, welcome] herzlich - **2.** [meal, appetite] herzhaft - **3.** [dislike, distrust] tief.

**heat** [hiːt] n - **1.** [warmth] Wärme die - **2.** (U) [specific temperature] Temperatur die - **3.** (U) [fire, source of heat] Feuer das - **4.** (U) [hot weather] Hitze die - **5.** fig [pressure]: **in the ~ of the moment** in der Hitze des Gefechts - **6.** [eliminating round - in race] Vorlauf der; [ - in competition] Vorrunde die - **7.** ZOOL: **on ~** Br, **in ~** Am brünstig; [dog, cat] läufig; [horse] rossig ◇ vt heiß machen, erhitzen; [house, pool] heizen.

➤ **heat up** vt sep heiß machen, auflwärmen ◇ vi sich erwärmen, warm werden.

**heated** ['hiːtɪd] adj - **1.** [room, swimming pool] beheizt - **2.** [argument, discussion, person] hitzig.

**heater** ['hiːtə'] n [in car] Heizung die; [in room, water tank] Heizgerät das.

**heath** [hiːθ] n Heide die.

**heathen** ['hiːðn] adj heidnisch ◇ n Heide der, -din die.

**heather** ['heðə'] n Heidekraut das.

**heating** ['hiːtɪŋ] n Heizung die.

**heat rash** n Hitzeausschlag der.

**heat-resistant** adj hitzebeständig.

**heat-seeking** [-,siːkɪŋ] adj auf Wärme ansprechend.

**heatstroke** ['hiːtstrəʊk] n Hitzschlag der.

**heat wave** n Hitzewelle die.

**heave** [hiːv] vt - **1.** [pull] hieven, wuchten, schleppen; [push] schieben - **2.** inf [throw] schmeißen - **3.** [give out]: **to ~ a sigh** einen Seufzer auslstoßen ◇ vi - **1.** [pull] ziehen - **2.** [rise and fall] sich heben und senken - **3.** [retch] brechen ◇ n [pull] kräftiger Ruck.

**heaven** ['hevn] n - **1.** [Paradise] Himmel der; **~ (alone) knows!** weiß der Himmel! - **2.** [something delightful]: **it was ~ at the swimming pool** es war himmlisch am Swimmingpool.

➤ **heavens** npl: **the ~s** literary der Himmel ◇ excl: **(good) ~s!** du lieber Himmel!

**heavenly** ['hevnlɪ] adj - **1.** inf [delightful] himmlisch, herrlich - **2.** literary [of the skies] Himmels-.

**heavily** ['hevɪlɪ] adv - **1.** [smoke, drink] stark; [rain] heftig - **2.** [built] solide - **3.** [breathe, sigh] schwer, laut - **4.** [fall, land] schwerfällig - **5.** [sleep] tief.

**heaviness** ['hevɪnɪs] n - **1.** [of object] Gewicht das - **2.** [of sleep] Tiefe die - **3.** [of movement] Schwerfälligkeit die.

**heavy** ['hevɪ] (compar **-ier**; superl **-iest**) adj - **1.** [in weight] schwer - **2.** [fighting, losses] schwer; [rain] heftig; [traffic, smoker, drinker] stark; **to be a ~ sleeper** immer tief und fest schlafen; **to be ~ on sthg** inf einen hohen Verbrauch an etw (D) haben - **3.** [person - fat] dick, schwergewichtig; [ - solidly built] untersetzt, kräftig - **4.** [laden]: **a tree ~ with fruit** ein Baum voller Früchte; **her eyes were ~ with sleep** ihr fielen fast die Augen zu - **5.** [coat, sweater] dick - **6.** [food, responsibility] schwer - **7.** [breathing, step, fall] schwerfällig - **8.** [schedule, week] arbeitsreich - **9.** [work, job] anstrengend - **10.** [weather, air] schwül; [sky] wolkenverhangen - **11.** [sad]: **with a ~ heart** schweren Herzens.

**heavy cream** n Am Schlagsahne die.

**heavy-duty** adj [machine] Hochleistungs-; [material] strapazierfähig.

**heavy goods vehicle** n Br Schwertransporter der.

**heavy-handed** [-'hændɪd] adj ungeschickt, schwerfällig.

**heavy industry** n Schwerindustrie die.

**heavy metal** n MUS Heavy Metal das.

**heavyweight** ['hevɪweɪt] adj SPORT Schwergewichts- ◇ n - **1.** [SPORT - class] Schwergewicht das; [ - boxer] Schwergewichtler der - **2.** [intellectual] Größe die.

**Hebrew** ['hiːbruː] adj hebräisch ◇ n - **1.** [person] Hebräer der, -in die - **2.** [language] Hebräisch(e) das.

**Hebrides** ['hebrɪdiːz] npl: **the ~** die Hebriden; **in the ~** auf den Hebriden.

**heck** [hek] excl: **what/where/why the ~ ...?** was/wo/warum zum Teufel ...?; **a ~ of a nice guy** ein wahnsinnig netter Kerl; **a ~ of a lot of people** wahnsinnig viele Leute.

**heckle** ['hekl] vt (durch Zwischenrufe) unterbrechen ◇ vi zwischenlrufen.

**heckler** ['heklə'] n Zwischenrufer der, -in die.

**hectare** ['hekteə'] n Hektar der OR das.

**hectic** ['hektɪk] adj hektisch.

**hector** ['hektə'] vt tyrannisieren.

**he'd** [hiːd] = he had, he would.

**hedge** [hedʒ] n [shrub] Hecke die ◇ vi [prevari-cate] Ausflüchte machen.

**hedgehog** ['hedʒhɒg] n Igel der.

**hedgerow** ['hedʒrəʊ] n Naturhecke die.

**hedonism** ['hi:dənɪzml] n Hedonismus der.

**hedonist** ['hi:dənɪst] n Hedonist der, -in die.

**heed** [hi:d] n: **to pay ~ to sb** jm Beachtung schenken; **to take ~ of sthg** etw (D) Beach-tung schenken ◇ vt fml beachten.

**heedless** ['hi:dlɪs] adj: **to be ~ of sthg** etw nicht beachten.

**heel** [hi:l] n - **1.** [of foot] Ferse die; **to dig one's ~s in** fig sich auf die Hinterbeine stellen; **to fol-low hard on the ~s (of sb/sthg)** (jm/etw) dicht auf den Fersen sein; **to take to one's ~s** die Beine in die Hand nehmen; **to turn on one's ~** auf dem Absatz kehrtlmachen - **2.** [of shoe] Absatz der.

**hefty** ['heftɪ] (compar -ier; superl -iest) adj inf - **1.** [person] kräftig - **2.** [fee, fine] saftig; [salary] dick.

**heifer** ['hefə'] n Färse die.

**height** [haɪt] n - **1.** [gen] Höhe die; [of person] Größe die; **5 metres in ~** 5 Meter hoch; **what ~ is it?** wie hoch ist es?; **what ~ are you?** wie groß sind Sie?; **to gain/lose ~** an Höhe gewinnen/verlieren - **2.** [zenith] Höhepunkt der; **the ~ of stupidity/audacity** der Gipfel der Dummheit/Dreistigkeit.

➤ **heights** npl [high places] Höhen pl; **are you afraid of ~s?** haben Sie Höhenangst?

**heighten** ['haɪtn] vt [feeling, awareness] verstär-ken; [anxiety] steigern ◇ vi sich verstärken.

**heinous** ['heɪnəs] adj fml ruchlos.

**heir** [eə'] n Erbe der, -bin die.

**heir apparent** (pl heirs apparent) n gesetz-licher Erbe, gesetzliche Erbin.

**heiress** ['eərɪs] n Erbin die.

**heirloom** ['eəlu:m] n Erbstück das.

**heist** [haɪst] n inf Raubüberfall der.

**held** [held] pt & pp ▷ hold.

**helices** ['helɪsi:z] pl ▷ helix.

**helicopter** ['helɪkɒptə'] n Hubschrauber der.

**heliport** ['helɪpɔ:t] n Hubschrauberlande-platz der.

**helium** ['hi:lɪəm] n Helium das.

**helix** ['hi:lɪks] (pl -es OR helices) n Spirale die; CHEM Helix die.

**hell** [hel] n - **1.** [gen] Hölle die - **2.** inf [for empha-sis]: **what/where/why the ~ ...?** was/wo/ warum zum Teufel ...?; **one** OR **a ~ of a mess** ein wahnsinniges Durcheinander; **one** OR **a ~ of a nice guy** ein wahnsinnig netter Kerl; **we ran like ~** wir rannten so schnell wir konnten; **it hurts like ~** es tut höllisch weh; **like ~ you will!** von wegen!; **to get the ~ out**

ablhauen, sich zum Teufel scheren - **3.** phr: **to ~ with him!** inf er kann mir gestohlen blei-ben!; **to ~ with the expense!** inf (es ist mir) egal, was es kostet!; **all ~ broke loose** inf da war der Teufel los; **to do sthg for the ~ of it** inf etw aus Jux machen; **to give sb ~** inf jm die Hölle heiß machen; **go to ~!** inf hau ab!, scher dich zum Teufel!; **this damp weather plays ~ with my knees** das feuchte Wetter macht meinen Knien zu schaffen ◇ excl inf verdammt!

**he'll** [hi:l] = he will.

**hell-bent** adj: **to be ~ on sthg** auf etw (A) ver-sessen sein; **to be ~ on doing sthg** darauf ver-sessen sein, etw zu tun.

**hellish** ['helɪʃ] adj inf höllisch, schrecklich.

**hello** [hə'ləʊ] excl hallo.

**helm** [helm] n lit & fig Ruder das; **at the ~** am Ruder.

**helmet** ['helmɪt] n Helm der.

**helmsman** ['helmzmən] (pl -men [-mən]) n NAUT Steuermann der.

**help** [help] n Hilfe die; **to be of ~** behilflich sein; **to be a ~** eine Hilfe sein; **with sb's ~** mit js Hilfe; **with the ~ of sthg** mit Hilfe einer Sa-che (G) ◇ vt - **1.** [assist] helfen (+ D); **to ~ sb (to) do sthg** jm helfen, etw zu tun; **to ~ sb with sthg** jm bei etw helfen; **can I ~ you?** [in shop, at reception] kann ich Ihnen behilflich sein? - **2.** [make easier for] erleichtern; **to ~ sb (to) do sthg** es jm erleichtern, etw zu tun - **3.** [con-tribute to]: **to ~ (to) do sthg** helfen, etw zu tun - **4.** [avoid]: **I can't ~ it** ich kann nichts dafür; **I couldn't ~ laughing** ich mußte einfach la-chen - **5.** phr: **to ~ o.s.** sich bedienen; **to ~ o.s. to sthg** sich (D) etw nehmen ◇ vi helfen; **to ~ with sthg** bei etw helfen ◇ excl Hilfe!

➤ **help out** vt sep auslhelfen (+ D) ◇ vi auslhelfen.

**helper** ['helpə'] n - **1.** [on any task] Helfer der, -in die - **2.** Am [to do housework] Hausgehilfe der, -fin die.

**helpful** ['helpfʊl] adj - **1.** [willing to help] hilfsbe-reit - **2.** [useful] nützlich, hilfreich.

**helping** ['helpɪŋ] n Portion die.

**helping hand** n: **to give sb a ~ (with sthg)** jm (bei etw) helfen.

**helpless** ['helplɪs] adj hilflos.

**helplessly** ['helplɪslɪ] adv hilflos.

**helpline** ['helplaɪn] n Servicenummer die; COM-PUT Hotline die.

**Helsinki** ['helsɪŋkɪ] n Helsinki nt.

**helter-skelter** ['heltə'skeltə'] Br n Rutsch-bahn die ◇ adv [run, fall] Hals über Kopf.

**hem** [hem] (pt & pp -med; cont -ming) n Saum der ◇ vt säumen.

➤ **hem in** vt sep einlengen.

**he-man** *n inf hum:* a real ~ ein echter OR ganzer Mann.

**hematology** [ˌhiːməˈtɒlədʒɪ] *n* Hämatologie *die.*

**hemisphere** [ˈhemɪˌsfɪəʳ] *n* Hemisphäre *die.*

**hemline** [ˈhemlaɪn] *n* Saum *der.*

**hemoglobin** [ˌhiːməˈgləʊbɪn] *n* Hämoglobin *das.*

**hemophilia** [ˌhiːməˈfɪlɪə] *n* Bluterkrankheit *die,* Hämophilie *die.*

**hemophiliac** [ˌhiːməˈfɪlɪæk] *n* Bluter *der,* -in *die.*

**hemorrhage** [ˈhemərɪdʒ] *n* Blutung *die* <> *vi* bluten.

**hemorrhoids** [ˈhemərɔɪdz] *npl* Hämorrhoiden *pl.*

**hemp** [hemp] *n* Hanf *der.*

**hen** [hen] *n* - **1.** [female chicken] Huhn *das,* Henne *die* - **2.** [female bird] Weibchen *das.*

**hence** [hens] *adv fml* - **1.** [therefore] folglich, daher - **2.** [from now]: **ten years ~** in zehn Jahren.

**henceforth** [ˌhensˈfɔːθ] *adv fml* fortan.

**henchman** [ˈhentʃmən] *(pl* -men [-mən]) *n pej* Helfershelfer *der.*

**henna** [ˈhenə] *n* Henna *die* OR *das* <> *vt* mit Henna färben.

**hen party** *n Br inf letzte für die Braut vor der Hochzeit arrangierte Damenparty.*

**henpecked** [ˈhenpekt] *adj pej:* **to be ~** unter dem Pantoffel stehen; **a ~ husband** ein Pantoffelheld.

**hepatitis** [ˌhepəˈtaɪtɪs] *n* Hepatitis *die.*

**her** [hɜːʳ] *pers pron (accusative)* sie; *(dative)* ihr; **I know ~** ich kenne sie; **it's ~** sie ist es; **send it to ~** schick es ihr; **tell ~ ...** sag ihr ...; **he's worse than ~** er ist schlimmer als sie; **she took her luggage with ~** sie nahm ihr Gepäck mit <> *poss adj* ihr; **~ friend** ihr Freund/ihre Freundin; **~ children** ihre Kinder; **she washed ~ hair** sie hat sich die Haare gewaschen.

**herald** [ˈherəld] *vt fml* an|künd(ig)en <> *n* [messenger] Bote *der.*

**heraldry** [ˈherəldrɪ] *n* Wappenkunde *die,* Heraldik *die.*

**herb** [hɜːb] *n* Kraut *das.*

**herbaceous border** [hɜːˌbeɪʃəs-] *n:* Staudenrabatte *die.*

**herbal** [ˈhɜːbl] *adj* Kräuter-.

**herbalist** [ˈhɜːbəlɪst] *n* [seller] Herbalist *der,* -in *die.*

**herbicide** [ˈhɜːbɪsaɪd] *n* Unkrautvernichtungsmittel *das,* Herbizid *das.*

**herbivore** [ˈhɜːbɪvɔːʳ] *n* Pflanzenfresser *der.*

**herb tea** *n* Kräutertee *der.*

**herd** [hɜːd] *n lit* & *fig* Herde *die* <> *vt* treiben.

**herdsman** [ˈhɜːdzmən] *(pl* -men [-mən]) *n* Hirte *der.*

**here** [hɪəʳ] *adv* hier; **come ~!** komm her!; **~ you are!** [when giving sthg] bitte!; [greeting sb] da bist du ja!; **~ we are** da sind wir; **~ and there** hier und da; **~ and now** sofort; **~'s to you!** [in toast] auf Ihr Wohl!; **~ goes!** *inf* los gehts!

**hereabouts** *Br* [ˌhɪərəˈbaʊts], **hereabout** *Am* [ˌhɪərəˈbaʊt] *adv* in dieser Gegend.

**hereafter** [ˌhɪərˈɑːftəʳ] *adv fml* im Folgenden <> *n:* **the ~** das Jenseits.

**hereby** [ˌhɪəˈbaɪ] *adv fml* hiermit.

**hereditary** [hɪˈredɪtrɪ] *adj* erblich, Erb-.

**heredity** [hɪˈredətɪ] *n* Vererbung *die.*

**heresy** [ˈherəsɪ] *(pl* -ies) *n* Ketzerei *die,* Häresie *die.*

**heretic** [ˈherətɪk] *n* Ketzer *der,* -in *die.*

**herewith** [ˌhɪəˈwɪð] *adv fml* anbei.

**heritage** [ˈherɪtɪdʒ] *n* Erbe *das.*

**heritage centre** *n* Besucherzentrum oder Museum an historisch interessanter Stelle.

**hermaphrodite** [hɜːˈmæfrədaɪt] ZOOL *adj* zwittrig, hermaphroditisch <> *n* Zwitter *der,* Hermaphrodit *der.*

**hermetic** [hɜːˈmetɪk] *adj* luftdicht.

**hermetically** [hɜːˈmetɪklɪ] *adv:* **~ sealed** hermetisch verschlossen.

**hermit** [ˈhɜːmɪt] *n* Einsiedler *der,* -in *die,* Eremit *der,* -in *die.*

**hernia** [ˈhɜːnɪə] *n* Bruch *der,* Hernie *die.*

**hero** [ˈhɪərəʊ] *(pl* -es) *n* - **1.** [gen] Held *der* - **2.** [idol] Idol *das.*

**heroic** [hɪˈrəʊɪk] *adj* [person, deed] heldenhaft, heroisch.
➥ **heroics** *npl pej* Heldenstücke *pl.*

**heroin** [ˈherəʊɪn] *n* Heroin *das.*

**heroine** [ˈherəʊɪn] *n* Heldin *die.*

**heroism** [ˈherəʊɪzm] *n* Heldentum *das.*

**heron** [ˈherən] *(pl inv* OR *-s) n* Reiher *der.*

**hero worship** *n* Heldenverehrung *die.*

**herpes** [ˈhɜːpiːz] *n* Herpes *der.*

**herring** [ˈherɪŋ] *(pl inv* OR *-s) n* Hering *der.*

**herringbone** [ˈherɪŋbəʊn] *n:* **~ pattern** Fischgrätenmuster *das.*

**hers** [hɜːz] *poss pron* ihre, -r, -s; **a friend of ~** ein Freund von ihr; **these shoes are ~** diese Schuhe gehören ihr; **she ate my portion and ~** sie aß meine und ihre Portion.

**herself** [hɜːˈself] *pron* - **1.** *(reflexive)* sich; **she hurt ~** sie hat sich verletzt - **2.** *(after prep)* sich selbst; **she did it ~** [stressed] sie hat es selbst getan; **by ~** allein.

**Herts** *abk für Hertfordshire, in Postanschrift verwendet.*

**he's** [hiːz] = he is, he has.

**hesitant** ['hezɪtənt] adj [person] unentschlossen, zögerlich; **she was ~ about coming** sie war sich nicht sicher, ob sie kommen sollte.

**hesitate** ['hezɪteɪt] vi zögern; **to ~ to do sthg** Bedenken haben, etw zu tun.

**hesitation** [ˌhezɪ'teɪʃn] n Zögern das; **without ~** ohne zu zögern; **to have no ~ in doing sthg** keine Bedenken haben, etw zu tun.

**hessian** ['hesɪən] n Br Sackleinen das.

**heterogeneous** [ˌhetərə'dʒiːnɪəs] adj fml heterogen.

**heterosexual** [ˌhetərəʊ'sekʃʊəl] adj heterosexuell ◇ n Heterosexuelle der, die.

**het up** [ˌhet-] adj inf aufgeregt.

**hew** [hjuː] (pt -ed; pp -ed OR hewn [hjuːn]) vt literary [stone, wood] behauen.

**hex** [heks] n [curse] Fluch der.

**hexagon** ['heksəgən] n Sechseck das, Hexagon das.

**hexagonal** [hek'sægənl] adj sechseckig, hexagonal.

**hey** [heɪ] excl he!

**heyday** ['heɪdeɪ] n Glanzzeit die.

**hey presto** [-'prestəʊ] excl simsalabim!

**HF** (abbr of high frequency) HF.

**HGV** (abbr of heavy goods vehicle) n LKW der.

**hi** [haɪ] excl inf hallo!

**HI** abk für Hawaii, in Postanschrift verwendet.

**hiatus** [haɪ'eɪtəs] (pl -es) n fml Unterbrechung die.

**hibernate** ['haɪbəneɪt] vi Winterschlaf halten

**hibernation** [ˌhaɪbə'neɪʃn] n Winterschlaf der.

**hiccough, hiccup** ['hɪkʌp] (pt & pp -ped; cont -ping) n - **1.** [sound] Schluckauf der; **to have ~s** (den) Schluckauf haben - **2.** fig [difficulty] kleines Problem; **without a ~** wie geschmiert ◇ vi schlucksen.

**hick** [hɪk] n esp Am inf pej Hinterwäldler der, -in die.

**hid** [hɪd] pt ⊳ hide.

**hidden** ['hɪdn] pp ⊳ hide ◇ adj versteckt; **~ costs** verdeckte Unkosten.

**hide** [haɪd] (pt hid; pp hidden) vt - **1.** [conceal - person, item] verstecken; [ - emotions, facts] verbergen; **to ~ sthg (from sb)** etw (vor jm) verstecken/verbergen - **2.** [cover] verdecken ◇ vi sich verstecken ◇ n - **1.** [animal skin] Haut die - **2.** [for watching birds, animals] Versteck das.

**hide-and-seek** n Versteckspiel das.

**hideaway** ['haɪdəweɪ] n inf Versteck das.

**hidebound** ['haɪdbaʊnd] adj pej engstirnig.

**hideous** ['hɪdɪəs] adj grässlich.

**hideout** ['haɪdaʊt] n Versteck das.

**hiding** ['haɪdɪŋ] n - **1.** [concealment]: **to be in ~** sich verstecken - **2.** inf [beating]: **to give sb a (good) ~** jm eine (ordentliche) Abreibung verpassen; **to get a (good) ~** eine (ordentliche) Abreibung bekommen.

**hiding place** n Versteck das.

**hierarchical** [ˌhaɪə'rɑːkɪkl] adj hierarchisch.

**hierarchy** ['haɪərɑːkɪ] (pl -ies) n Hierarchie die.

**hieroglyphics** [ˌhaɪərə'glɪfɪks] npl Hieroglyphen pl.

**hi-fi** ['haɪfaɪ] n Hi-Fi das.

**higgledy-piggledy** [ˌhɪgldɪ'pɪgldɪ] adv inf wie Kraut und Rüben.

**high** [haɪ] adj - **1.** [gen] hoch; (before noun) hohe, -r, -s; **to be ~** [building, mountain] hoch sein; **how ~ is it?** wie hoch ist es?; **it's 10 metres ~** es ist 10 Meter hoch; **~ winds** starker Wind; **at ~ altitudes** in größeren Höhenlagen; **~ and mighty** [person] hochmütig; **it's ~ time he started school** es ist höchste Zeit, dass er in die Schule kommt; **to have a ~ opinion of sb/sthg** eine hohe Meinung von jm/etw haben - **2.** inf [from drugs] high ◇ n - **1.** [weather front] Hoch das - **2.** [highest point] Höchststand der; **inflation has reached a new ~** die Inflation hat einen neuen Höchststand erreicht ◇ adv hoch; **to aim ~** hoch hinauswollen; **to search ~ and low for sthg** etw überall suchen; **feelings were running ~** die Gemüter erhitzten sich.

**highball** ['haɪbɔːl] n Am Highball der.

**highbrow** ['haɪbraʊ] adj intellektuell; [literature, tastes] anspruchsvoll.

**high chair** n (Kinder)hochstuhl der.

**high-class** adj [superior - hotel, restaurant] vornehm; [ - performance] hochwertig.

**high command** n Oberkommando das.

**high commissioner** n Hochkommissar der (Botschafter eines Commonwealthstaates).

**High Court** n Br LAW oberster Gerichtshof.

**high-density** adj COMPUT: **~ disk** HD-Diskette die.

**higher** ['haɪəʳ] adj [exam, qualification] höher.

➤ **Higher** n: SCH **Higher (Grade)** schottischer Abiturabschluss in einem Fach.

**higher education** n Hochschulbildung die.

**high explosive** n hochexplosiver Sprengstoff.

**high-fidelity** adj Highfidelity-.

**high finance** n Hochfinanz die.

**high-flier** n Senkrechtstarter der.

**high-handed** [-'hændɪd] adj überheblich.

**high-heeled** [-hiːld] adj Stöckel-.

**high horse** n inf: **to get on one's ~** sich aufs hohe Ross setzen.

**high jump** n SPORT Hochsprung der; **to be for the ~** Br inf dran sein.

**Highland Games** ['haɪlənd-] npl schottisches Volksfest mit unterschiedlichen Wettbewerben.

**Highlands** ['haɪləndz] npl: **the ~** [of Scotland] das schottische Hochland, die Highlands.

**high-level** adj - **1.** [talks, discussions] auf höchster Ebene - **2.** [diplomats, officials] hochrangig.

**high life** n: **the ~** das Highlife.

**highlight** ['haɪlaɪt] n [of event, occasion] Höhepunkt der ◇ vt hervorlheben.

➤ **highlights** npl [in hair] Strähnchen pl.

**highlighter (pen)** ['haɪlaɪtər-] n Textmarker der.

**highly** ['haɪlɪ] adv - **1.** [very, extremely] höchst - **2.** [very well] sehr gut - **3.** [at an important level]: **~ placed** hoch plaziert; **~ connected** mit guten Verbindungen - **4.** [favourably] sehr gut; **I ~ recommend it** ich kann es sehr empfehlen.

**highly-strung** [-'strʌŋ] adj nervös.

**high mass** n Hochamt das.

**high-minded** [-'maɪndɪd] adj [principles] hehr; [person] mit hehren Prinzipien.

**Highness** ['haɪnɪs] n: **His/Her/Your (Royal) ~** Seine/Ihre/Eure (Königliche) Hoheit; **Their (Royal) ~es** Ihre (Königlichen) Hoheiten.

**high-octane** adj mit hoher Oktanzahl.

**high-pitched** [-'pɪtʃt] adj [voice] hoch; [shout, scream] schrill.

**high point** n Höhepunkt der.

**high-powered** [-'pauəd] adj - **1.** [powerful - engine] stark; [ - car] stark motorisiert - **2.** [dynamic - activity, place] anspruchsvoll, leistungsorientiert; [ - person] dynamisch.

**high-pressure** adj - **1.** [air, gas] Hochdruck- - **2.** [salesman, selling techniques] aggressiv.

**high priest** n RELIG Hohepriester der.

**high-ranking** [-'ræŋkɪŋ] adj ranghoch.

**high-resolution** adj COMPUT mit hoher Auflösung.

**high-rise** adj: **~ building** Hochhaus das.

**high-risk** adj hochriskant; [group] Risiko-.

**high school** n höhere Schule, Oberschule die.

**high seas** npl: **on the ~** auf hoher See.

**high season** n Hochsaison die.

**high-speed** adj - **1.** [train] Schnell- - **2.** PHOT [film] hochempfindlich.

**high-spirited** [-'spɪrɪtəd] adj [person] ausgelassen.

**high spot** n Höhepunkt der.

**high street** n Br Hauptstraße die.

**hightail** ['haɪteɪl] vt esp Am inf: **to ~ it** sich aus dem Staub machen.

**high tea** n Br Abendmahlzeit mit Tee und Gebäck.

**high-tech** [-'tek] adj Hightech- ◇ n (abbr of high technology) Hochtechnologie die.

**high technology** n Hochtechnologie die.

**high-tension** adj Hochspannungs-.

**high tide** n Flut die.

**high treason** n Hochverrat der.

**high water** n Hochwasser das.

**highway** ['haɪweɪ] n - **1.** Am [main road between cities] Schnellstraße die - **2.** Br [any main road] Landstraße die.

**Highway Code** n Br: **the ~** die Straßenverkehrsordnung.

**high wire** n Drahtseil das.

**hijack** ['haɪdʒæk] n Entführung die ◇ vt entführen.

**hijacker** ['haɪdʒækər] n [of aircraft] Flugzeugentführer der, -in die; [of vehicle] Entführer der, -in die.

**hike** [haɪk] n Wanderung die ◇ vi wandern.

**hiker** ['haɪkər] n Wanderer der, -in die.

**hiking** ['haɪkɪŋ] n Wandern das; **to go ~** wandern gehen.

**hilarious** [hɪ'leərɪəs] adj urkomisch.

**hilarity** [hɪ'lærətɪ] n fml Heiterkeit die.

**hill** [hɪl] n - **1.** [mound] Hügel der - **2.** [slope] Hang der.

**hillbilly** ['hɪlˌbɪlɪ] (pl -ies) n Am inf pej Hinterwäldler der, -in die.

**hillock** ['hɪlək] n Anhöhe die, Hügel der.

**hillside** ['hɪlsaɪd] n Hang der.

**hill start** n: **to do a ~** an Berg anlfahren.

**hilltop** ['hɪltɒp] n: **on the ~** auf dem Berg.

**hilly** ['hɪlɪ] (compar -ier; superl -iest) adj hügelig.

**hilt** [hɪlt] n Heft das; **to support/defend sb to the ~** jn voll und ganz unterstützen/verteidigen; **to be mortgaged to the ~** total verschuldet sein.

**him** [hɪm] pers pron (accusative) ihn; (dative) ihm; **I know ~** ich kenne ihn; **it's ~** er ist es; **send it to ~** schick es ihm; **tell ~** sag ihm; **she's worse than ~** sie ist schlimmer als er; **he took his luggage with ~** er nahm sein Gepäck mit.

**Himalayan** [ˌhɪmə'leɪən] adj Himalaja-.

**Himalayas** [ˌhɪmə'leɪəz] npl: **the ~** der Himalaja.

**himself** [hɪm'self] pron - **1.** (reflexive) sich; **he**

hurt ~ er hat sich verletzt **- 2.** *(after prep)* sich selbst; **he did it ~** [stressed] er hat es selbst getan; **by ~** allein.

**hind** [haɪnd] *(pl inv OR* **-s***) adj:* **~ legs** Hinterbeine *pl* ◇ *n* Hirschkuh *die.*

**hinder** ['hɪndə'] *vt* behindern.

**Hindi** ['hɪndɪ] *n* [language] Hindi *das.*

**hindmost** ['haɪndməʊst] *adj* hinterste, -r, -s.

**hindquarters** ['haɪnd,kwɔːtəz] *npl* Hinterteil *das.*

**hindrance** ['hɪndrəns] *n* **- 1.** [obstacle] Hindernis *das* **- 2.** (U) [delay] Behinderung *die.*

**hindsight** ['haɪndsaɪt] *n (U):* **with the benefit of ~** im Nachhinein.

**Hindu** ['hɪnduː] *(pl* **-s***) adj* Hindu-, hinduistisch ◇ *n* Hindu *der.*

**Hinduism** ['hɪnduːɪzml] *n* Hinduismus *der.*

**hinge** [hɪndʒ] *(cont* **hinging***) n* [on door, window] Angel *die;* [on lid] Scharnier *das.*

- **hinge (up)on** *vt fus* [depend on] ablhängen von.

**hint** [hɪnt] *n* **- 1.** [indirect suggestion] Andeutung *die,* Wink *der;* **to drop a ~** eine Andeutung machen, einen Wink geben; **to take the ~** den Wink verstehen **- 2.** [useful suggestion, tip] Tipp *der* **- 3.** [small amount, trace] Spur *die* ◇ *vi:* **to ~ at sthg** etw anldeuten ◇ *vt:* **to ~ that** anldeuten, dass.

**hinterland** ['hɪntəlænd] *n* Hinterland *das.*

**hip** [hɪp] *adj inf* [fashionable] in, angesagt ◇ *n* [part of body] Hüfte *die.*

**hipbath** ['hɪpbɑːθ] *n* Sitzbad *das.*

**hipbone** ['hɪpbəʊn] *n* Hüftknochen *der.*

**hip flask** *n* Flachmann *der.*

**hip-hop** *n* [music] Hip-Hop *der.*

**hippie** ['hɪpɪ] *n* Hippie *der.*

**hippo** ['hɪpəʊ] *(pl* **-s***) n* Nilpferd *das.*

**hippopotamus** [,hɪpə'pɒtəməs] *(pl* **-muses** OR **-mi** [-maɪ]) *n* Nilpferd *das.*

**hippy** ['hɪpɪ] *(pl* **-ies***) n* = **hippie.**

**hire** ['haɪə'] *n (U)* [of car, television, venue] Mieten *das;* [of suit] Leihen *das;* **'for ~'** 'zu vermieten'; [taxi sign] 'frei'; **on ~** [car, television, venue] gemietet; [suit] geliehen ◇ *vt* **- 1.** [rent - car, television, venue] mieten; [ - suit] leihen **- 2.** [employ] anlstellen.

- **hire out** *vt sep* [car, television, venue] vermieten; [suit] verleihen; **to ~ out one's services** seine Dienste anlbieten.

**hire car** *n Br* Mietwagen *der.*

**hired help** [,haɪəd-] *n* [domestic staff] Dienstboten *pl.*

**hire purchase** *n* Ratenkauf *der;* **to buy sthg on ~** etw auf Raten kaufen.

**his** [hɪz] *poss adj* sein; **~ friend** sein Freund/

seine Freundin; **~ children** seine Kinder; **he washed ~ hair** er hat sich die Haare gewaschen ◇ *poss pron* seine, -r, -s; **a friend of ~** ein Freund von ihm; **these shoes are ~** diese Schuhe gehören ihm; **he ate my portion and ~** er aß meine und seine Portion.

**Hispanic** [hɪ'spænɪk] *adj* hispanoamerikanisch ◇ *n esp Am* Hispanoamerikaner *der,* -in *die.*

**hiss** [hɪs] *n* Zischen *das;* [of cat] Fauchen *das* ◇ *vt* [actor, performance] auslpfeifen ◇ *vi* zischen; [cat] fauchen.

**histogram** ['hɪstəgræm] *n* Histogramm *das.*

**historian** [hɪ'stɔːrɪən] *n* Historiker *der,* -in *die.*

**historic** [hɪ'stɒrɪk] *adj* historisch.

**historical** [hɪ'stɒrɪkəl] *adj* historisch.

**history** ['hɪstərɪ] *(pl* **-ies***) n* **- 1.** [gen] Geschichte *die;* **to go down in ~** in die Geschichte einlgehen; **to make ~** Geschichte machen **- 2.** [past record] Vorgeschichte *die,* Hintergrund *der.*

**histrionics** [hɪstrɪ'ɒnɪks] *npl pej* theatralisches Getue.

**hit** [hɪt] *(pt* & *pp* **hit***; cont* **-ting***) n* **- 1.** [blow] Schlag *der* **- 2.** [successful strike] Treffer *der* **- 3.** [success] Erfolg *der;* [record] Hit *der;* **she was a big ~ with the audience** sie kam beim Publikum sehr gut an **- 4.** COMPUT [of website] Treffer *der* ◇ *comp* Erfolgs-; [record] Hit- ◇ *vt* **- 1.** [strike] schlagen **- 2.** [subj: stones, bullet] treffen, erwischen; [subj: vehicle - tree, wall] fahren gegen; [ - person] erwischen **- 3.** [score, affect] treffen **- 4.** [reach] erreichen **- 5.** *phr:* **to ~ it off (with sb)** sich gut (mit jm) verstehen.

- **hit back** *vi:* **to ~ back (at sb/sthg)** *fig* sich (gegen jn/etw) wehren.

- **hit on** *vt fus* **- 1.** = **hit upon - 2.** *Am inf* [chat up] anlmachen.

- **hit out** *vi:* **to ~ out at sb/sthg** [physically] auf jn/etw loslschlagen OR einlschlagen; [in speech, writing] jn/etw attackieren.

- **hit upon** *vt fus* [think of] stoßen auf *(+ A).*

**hit-and-miss** *adj* = **hit-or-miss.**

**hit-and-run** *n:* **~ (accident)** Unfall *der* mit Fahrerflucht ◇ *adj* [driver] unfallflüchtig.

**hitch** [hɪtʃ] *n* [problem, snag] Problem *das;* **a technical ~** eine Panne ◇ *vt* **- 1.** [solicit]: **to ~ a lift** trampen, per Anhalter fahren **- 2.** [fasten]: **to ~ sthg on(to) sthg** etw an etw (D) befestigen ◇ *vi* [hitchhike] trampen, per Anhalter fahren.

- **hitch up** *vt sep* [skirt, trousers] hochlziehen.

**hitchhike** ['hɪtʃhaɪk] *vi* trampen, per Anhalter fahren.

**hitchhiker** ['hɪtʃhaɪkə'] *n* Anhalter *der,* -in *die,* Tramper *der,* -in *die.*

**hi-tech** [,haɪ'tek] *adj* = **high-tech.**

**hither** ['hɪðə'] adv literary hierher; ~ and thither hierhin und dorthin.

**hitherto** [ˌhɪðə'tu:] adv fml bisher.

**hit list** n [of people to be attacked] Abschussliste die.

**hit man** n Killer der.

**hit-or-miss** adj willkürlich.

**hit parade** n dated Hitparade die.

**HIV** (abbr of human immunodeficiency virus) n HIV; to be ~-positive HIV-positiv sein.

**hive** [haɪv] n [for bees] Bienenstock der; to be a ~ of activity fig der reinste Bienenstock sein.

➡ **hive off** vt sep [separate] ablspalten, auslgliedern.

**hl** (abbr of hectolitre) hl.

**HM** (abbr of His (or Her) Majesty) S.M./I.M.

**HMI** (abbr of His (or Her) Majesty's Inspector) n Schulinspektor der britischen Regierung.

**HMO** (abbr of health maintenance organization) n US-Gesundheitsbehörde.

**HMS** (abbr of His (or Her) Majesty's Ship) Bezeichnung aller Schiffe der britischen Marine.

**HMSO** (abbr of His (or Her) Majesty's Stationery Office) n Druckerei für staatliche Publikationen.

**HNC** (abbr of Higher National Certificate) n britische Qualifikation in technischen Fächern.

**HND** (abbr of Higher National Diploma) n britische Hochschulqualifikation in technischen Fächern.

**hoard** [hɔ:d] n Vorrat der ⬥ vt horten.

**hoarding** ['hɔ:dɪŋ] n Br Plakatwand die.

**hoarfrost** ['hɔ:frɒst] n Raureif der.

**hoarse** [hɔ:s] adj heiser.

**hoax** [həʊks] n [joke] Streich der; [threat, alarm] blinder Alarm.

**hoaxer** ['həʊksə'] n jemand, der einen Streich spielt oder einen blinden Alarm auslöst.

**hob** [hɒb] n Br [on cooker] Kochfläche die.

**hobble** ['hɒbl] vi humpeln.

**hobby** ['hɒbɪ] (pl -ies) n Hobby das.

**hobbyhorse** ['hɒbɪhɔ:s] n - 1. [toy] Steckenpferd das - 2. [favourite topic] Lieblingsthema das.

**hobnob** ['hɒbnɒb] (pt & pp -bed; cont -bing) vi: to ~ with sb mit jm gut Freund sein.

**hobo** ['həʊbəʊ] (pl -es OR -s) n Am Landstreicher der, Penner der.

**Ho Chi Minh City** [ˌhəʊˌtʃi:'mɪn-] n Ho-Chi-Minh-Stadt die.

**hock** [hɒk] n [wine] (weißer) Rheinwein.

**hockey** ['hɒkɪ] n - 1. [on grass] Hockey das - 2. Am [ice hockey] Eishockey das.

**hockey stick** n Hockeyschläger der.

**hocus-pocus** [ˌhəʊkəs'pəʊkəs] n faule Tricks pl, Hokuspokus der.

**hod** [hɒd] n Tragmulde die.

**hodgepodge** n Am = hotchpotch.

**hoe** [həʊ] n Hacke die ⬥ vt hacken.

**hog** [hɒg] (pt & pp -ged; cont -ging) n - 1. Am [pig] Schwein das - 2. inf [greedy person] Vielfraß der - 3. phr: to go the whole ~ aufs Ganze gehen ⬥ vt inf [monopolize - road] in Beschlag nehmen; [- attention] mit Beschlag belegen; don't ~ the sweets! nimm dir nicht alle Süßigkeiten!

**Hogmanay** ['hɒgməneɪ] n Scot Silvester der OR das.

**hoi-polloi** [ˌhɔɪpə'lɔɪ] npl pej: the ~ das (gemeine) Volk, der Pöbel.

**hoist** [hɔɪst] n [device for lifting] Lastenaufzug der ⬥ vt - 1. [load, person] heben, hieven - 2. [sail, flag] hissen.

**hokum** ['həʊkəm] n Am inf Quatsch der.

**hold** [həʊld] (pt & pp held) vt - 1. [gen] halten; to ~ sb prisoner/hostage jn gefangen halten/als Geisel festlhalten - 2. [position, responsibility, title, driving licence] haben; [belief, principle] vertreten - 3. [meeting, talks] ablhalten; [conversation] führen - 4. fml [consider]: to ~ sthg to be necessary/important etw für notwendig/wichtig erachten OR halten; to ~ that der Meinung sein, dass; to ~ sb responsible for sthg jn für etw verantwortlich machen; she held her reputation dear ihr Ruf war ihr sehr teuer - 5. [on telephone]: please ~ the line bitte bleiben Sie am Apparat - 6. [attention, interest] fesseln - 7. [support] tragen - 8. [contain] enthalten; what does the future ~ for him? was birgt die Zukunft für ihn? - 9. [have space for] Platz haben für - 10. phr: ~ it!, ~ everything! halt!; to ~ one's own sich behaupten können ⬥ vi - 1. [promise, objection] gelten; [weather] sich halten; his luck held das Glück blieb ihm treu; to ~ still OR steady still halten - 2. [on phone] am Apparat bleiben ⬥ n - 1. [grip] Griff der; to keep ~ of sthg [with hand] etw festlhalten; [save] etw behalten; to take OR lay ~ of sthg etw fassen OR packen; to get ~ of sthg [obtain] etw bekommen; to get ~ of sb [find] jn erreichen - 2. [of ship, aircraft] Laderaum der, Frachtraum der - 3. [control, influence]: to have a ~ over sb [person] jn in der Hand haben; [feeling, idea] von jm Besitz ergreifen; to take ~ [fire] um sich greifen.

➡ **hold against** vt sep: to ~ sthg against sb fig jm etw übel nehmen.

➡ **hold back** vi sich zurücklhalten; to ~ back from doing sthg darauf verzichten, etw zu tun ⬥ vt sep - 1. [gen] zurücklhalten - 2. [prevent progress of]: to ~ sb back (from doing sthg) jn davon ablhalten(, etw zu tun).

➤ **hold down** *vt sep:* **to ~ down a job** sich in einer Stelle halten.

➤ **hold off** *vt sep* [fend off] ablwehren ◇ *vi* [rain] auslbleiben.

➤ **hold on** *vi* **- 1.** [wait, on phone] warten; **~ on!** [on phone] einen Moment, bitte! **- 2.** [grip]: **to ~ on (to sthg)** sich (an etw (D)) festlhalten; **~ on tight!** gut festlhalten!

➤ **hold onto** *vt fus* [retain] behalten; [power] nicht auf lgeben.

➤ **hold out** *vt sep* [hand] auslstrecken; [arms] auslbreiten ◇ *vi* **- 1.** [last] reichen **- 2.** [resist]: **to ~ out (against sb/sthg)** sich (gegen jn/etw) behaupten.

➤ **hold out for** *vt fus* bestehen auf (+ D).

➤ **hold up** *vt sep* **- 1.** [raise] hochlheben **- 2.** [delay - traffic, production] auf lhalten; [ - plans] verzögern **- 3.** *inf* [rob] überfallen.

➤ **hold with** *vt fus* [approve of] billigen.

**holdall** ['həʊldɔːl] *n Br* Reisetasche *die.*

**holder** ['həʊldəʳ] *n* **- 1.** [container] Halter *der;* [for cigarette] Spitze *die* **- 2.** [owner] Inhaber *der*, -in *die.*

**holding** ['həʊldɪŋ] *n* **- 1.** [investment] Aktienbesitz *der* **- 2.** [farm] Gut *das* ◇ *adj:* **~ operation** *Aktion zur Erhaltung des Status quo, bis eine bessere Lösung gefunden werden kann.*

**holding company** *n* Holdinggesellschaft *die.*

**holdup** ['həʊldʌp] *n* **- 1.** [robbery] bewaffneter Raubüberfall **- 2.** [delay] Verzögerung *die;* [of traffic] stockender Verkehr.

**hole** [həʊl] *n* **- 1.** [gen] Loch *das;* **~ in one** [in golf] As *das;* **to pick ~s in sthg** [criticize] etw auseinander nehmen **- 2.** *inf* [horrible place] Loch *das;* [town] Kaff *das* **- 3.** *inf* [predicament]: **to get o.s. into a ~** in die Bredouille kommen; **to be in a ~** in der Bredouille sein.

➤ **hole up** *vi* sich verkriechen.

**holiday** ['hɒlɪdeɪ] *n* **- 1.** [vacation] Urlaub *der;* **~s** Urlaub *der;* sch Ferien *pl;* **to be on ~** im Urlaub sein; **to go on ~** in Urlaub fahren **- 2.** [public holiday] Feiertag *der.*

**holiday camp** *n Br* ≈ Feriendorf *das.*

**holidaymaker** ['hɒlɪdɪ,meɪkəʳ] *n Br* Urlauber *der*, -in *die.*

**holiday pay** *n Br* Urlaubsgeld *das.*

**holiday resort** *n Br* Ferienort *der.*

**holiday season** *n Br* Urlaubszeit *die;* sch Ferienzeit *die.*

**holiness** ['həʊlɪnɪs] *n* Heiligkeit *die.*
➤ **Holiness** *n:* **His/Your Holiness** Seine/Eure Heiligkeit.

**holistic** [həʊ'lɪstɪk] *adj* holistisch.

**Holland** ['hɒlənd] *n* Holland *nt.*

**hollandaise sauce** [ˌhɒlən'deɪz-] *n* Sauce Hollandaise *die.*

**holler** ['hɒləʳ] *vt & vi inf* brüllen.

**hollow** ['hɒləʊ] *adj* hohl; [cheeks] eingefallen; [victory, success] wertlos; [promise] leer ◇ *n* **- 1.** [in tree] Höhlung *die* **- 2.** [in ground, pillow] Mulde *die;* **the ~ of one's hand/back** die hohle Hand/das Kreuz.

➤ **hollow out** *vt sep* auslhöhlen.

**holly** ['hɒlɪ] *n* Stechpalme *die.*

**hollyhock** ['hɒlɪhɒk] *n* Malve *die.*

**Hollywood** ['hɒlɪwʊd] *n* Hollywood *nt* ◇ *comp* Hollywood-.

**holocaust** ['hɒləkɔːst] *n:* **a nuclear ~** ein atomarer Holocaust.
➤ **Holocaust** *n:* **the Holocaust** der Holocaust.

**hologram** ['hɒləɡræm] *n* Hologramm *das.*

**hols** [hɒlz] *npl Br inf* Ferien *pl.*

**holster** ['həʊlstəʳ] *n* Pistolenhalfter *das.*

**holy** ['həʊlɪ] (*compar* -**ier**; *superl* -**iest**) *adj* heilig; [ground] geweiht.

**Holy Communion** *n* Heilige Kommunion.

**Holy Ghost** *n:* **the ~** der Heilige Geist.

**Holy Grail** [-'ɡreɪl] *n:* **the ~** der Heilige Gral.

**Holy Land** *n:* **the ~** das Heilige Land.

**holy orders** *npl:* **to take ~** Priester werden.

**Holy Spirit** *n:* **the ~** der Heilige Geist.

**homage** ['hɒmɪdʒ] *n fml* **- 1.** [respect]: **to pay ~ to sb/sthg** jm/etw huldigen **- 2.** [tribute]: **~ (to)** Hommage *die* (an (+ A)).

**home** [həʊm] *n* **- 1.** [place of residence, institution] Heim *das;* **Manchester's my ~ now** ich bin nun in Manchester zu Hause; **to make one's ~ somewhere** sich irgendwo niederllassen; **it's a ~ from ~** *Br,* **it's a ~ away from ~** *Am* es ist wie zu Hause **- 2.** [place of origin] Heimat *die* **- 3.** [family unit] Zuhause *das;* **to be from a broken ~** aus zerrütteten Familienverhältnissen kommen; **to leave ~** von zu Hause weglgehen ◇ *adj* **- 1.** [market, product] inländisch **- 2.** sport Heim- ◇ *adv* **- 1.**: **to go ~** nach Hause gehen; [from abroad] zurücklfahren/zurücklfliegen; **to be ~** zu Hause sein **- 2.** *phr:* **to bring sthg ~ to sb** jm etw klarlmachen; **to drive** or **hammer sthg ~ to sb** jm etw einlbläuen.

➤ **at home** *adv* **- 1.** [in one's house, flat] daheim, zu Hause **- 2.** [comfortable]: **to feel at ~** somewhere sich irgendwo wohl fühlen; **I feel at ~ with this work** diese Arbeit bereitet mir keine Probleme; **to make o.s. at ~** es sich (D) bequem machen **- 3.** [in one's own country]: **at ~ the shops close at five** bei uns machen die Geschäfte um fünf zu **- 4.** sport: **to play at ~** ein Heimspiel haben.

➤ **home in** *vi:* **to ~ in on sthg** [target] auf etw (A) zulsteuern; [detail, problem] sich auf etw (A) konzentrieren.

**home address** *n* Privatadresse *die.*

**home banking** *n* Homebanking *das.*

**home brew** *n (U)* selbstgebrautes Bier.

**homecoming** ['hǝʊmˌkʌmɪŋ] *n* - **1.** [return] Heimkehr *die* - **2.** *Am* SCH & UNIV *alljährliches Zusammentreffen von derzeitigen und ehemaligen Studenten eines Colleges/einer Universität.*

**home computer** *n* Heimcomputer *der.*

**home cooking** *n* bürgerliche Küche.

**Home Counties** *npl Br:* the ~ *die London umgebenden Grafschaften.*

**home economics** *n (U)* Hauswirtschaft(slehre) *die.*

**home fries** *npl Am ungeschälte, fritierte Kartoffelstücke.*

**home ground** *n:* to be on ~ *lit* & *fig* sich auslkennen.

**homegrown** [ˌhǝʊm'grǝʊn] *adj* selbstgezogen.

**home help** *n Br* Haushaltshilfe *die.*

**home improvements** *npl Renovierungsarbeiten am Eigenheim.*

**homeland** ['hǝʊmlænd] *n* - **1.** [country of birth] Heimatland *das* - **2.** [in South Africa] Homeland *das.*

**homeless** ['hǝʊmlɪs] *adj* obdachlos <> *npl:* the ~ die Obdachlosen.

**homelessness** ['hǝʊmlɪsnǝs] *n* Obdachlosigkeit *die.*

**home loan** *n Darlehen für Renovierungsarbeiten am Eigenheim.*

**homely** ['hǝʊmlɪ] *adj* - **1.** [simple, unpretentious - place] schlicht; ~ fare Hausmannskost *die* - **2.** [ugly] unattraktiv.

**homemade** [ˌhǝʊm'meɪd] *adj* selbstgemacht; [bread] selbstgebacken; [food] hausgemacht.

**home movie** *n* selbstgedrehter Film.

**Home Office** *n Br:* the ~ das Innenministerium.

**homeopathic** [ˌhǝʊmɪǝʊ'pæθɪk] *adj* homöopathisch.

**homeopathy** [ˌhǝʊmɪ'ɒpǝθɪ] *n* Homöopathie *die.*

**homeowner** ['hǝʊmˌǝʊnǝ'] *n* Hausbesitzer *der,* -in *die.*

**home page** *n* COMPUT Homepage *die.*

**home rule** *n* Autonomie *die.*

**home run** *n Am Lauf um alle vier Male im Baseball.*

**Home Secretary** *n Br* Innenminister *der,* -in *die.*

**homesick** ['hǝʊmsɪk] *adj* heimwehkrank; to be/feel ~ Heimweh haben.

**homesickness** ['hǝʊmˌsɪknɪs] *n* Heimweh *das.*

**homespun** ['hǝʊmspʌn] *adj* [unsophisticated] einfach.

**homestead** ['hǝʊmstedl] *n Am* Gehöft *das.*

**home straight** *n:* the ~ [of race] die Zielgerade; we're on the ~ now *fig* das Ende ist in Sicht.

**hometown** ['hǝʊmtaʊn] *n* Heimatstadt *die.*

**home truth** *n:* to tell sb a few ~s jm die Meinung sagen.

**homeward** ['hǝʊmwǝdl] *adj* Heim- <> *adv* = homewards.

**homewards** ['hǝʊmwǝdz] *adv* nach Hause.

**homework** ['hǝʊmwɜːk] *n (U)* - **1.** SCH Hausaufgaben *pl* - **2.** *inf* [preparation] he's really done his ~ er hat sich gut vorbereitet.

**homey, homy** ['hǝʊmɪ] (*compar* -ier; *superl* -iest) *adj* [place, atmosphere] heimelig.

**homicidal** ['hɒmɪsaɪdl] *adj* [person] gemeingefährlich; [rage] mörderisch.

**homicide** ['hɒmɪsaɪd] *n* Mord *der.*

**homily** ['hɒmɪlɪ] (*pl* -ies) *n* Predigt *die.*

**homing** ['hǝʊmɪŋ] *adj* - **1.** [instinct] Heimfinde- - **2.** [device] Zielsuch-.

**homing pigeon** *n* Brieftaube *die.*

**homoeopathy** *etc* [ˌhǝʊmɪ'ɒpǝθɪ] *n* = homeopathy *etc.*

**homogeneous** [ˌhɒmǝ'dʒiːnɪǝs] *adj* homogen.

**homogenize, -ise** [hǝ'mɒdʒǝnaɪz] *vt Br* homogenisieren.

**homophobic** [ˌhɒmǝ'fǝʊbɪk] *adj* homosexuellenfeindlich, homophob.

**homosexual** [ˌhɒmǝ'sekʃʊǝl] *adj* homosexuell <> *n* Homosexuelle *der, die.*

**homosexuality** [ˌhɒmǝˌseksjʊ'ælǝtɪ] *n* Homosexualität *die.*

**homy** *adj Am* = homey.

**Hon.** *abbr of* **Honourable.**

**hone** [hǝʊn] *vt* - **1.** [knife, sword] schleifen, wetzen - **2.** [intellect, wit] schärfen.

**honest** ['ɒnɪst] *adj* - **1.** [trustworthy, legal] redlich; to make an ~ living seinen Lebensunterhalt auf ehrliche Weise verdienen - **2.** [truthful] ehrlich; to be ~, ... ehrlich gesagt, ... <> *adv inf* ehrlich.

**honestly** ['ɒnɪstlɪ] *adv* - **1.** [in a trustworthy manner] redlich - **2.** [truthfully] ehrlich <> *excl* also wirklich!

**honesty** ['ɒnɪstɪ] *n* - **1.** [trustworthiness] Redlichkeit *die* - **2.** [truthfulness] Ehrlichkeit *die.*

**honey** ['hʌnɪ] *n* - **1.** [food] Honig *der* - **2.** *esp Am* [dear] Liebling *der.*

**honeybee** ['hʌnɪbiː] *n* Honigbiene *die.*

**honeycomb** ['hʌnɪkǝʊm] *n* - **1.** [in wax] Bienenwabe *die* - **2.** [pattern] Wabenmuster *das.*

**honeymoon** ['hʌnɪmuːn] n - 1. [after wedding] Flitterwochen pl; [trip] Hochzeitsreise die; **they went on their ~ to** Majorca sie machten ihre Hochzeitsreise nach Mallorca - 2. fig [initial trouble-free period] Schonzeit die ◇ vi Hochzeitsreise machen.

**honeysuckle** ['hʌnɪˌsʌkl] n Geißblatt das.

**Hong Kong** [ˌhɒŋ'kɒŋ] n Hongkong nt.

**honk** [hɒŋk] vi - 1. [motorist] hupen - 2. [goose] schreien ◇ vt: **to ~ one's horn** auf die Hupe drücken, hupen ◇ n - 1. [of horn] Hupen das - 2. [of goose] Schrei der.

**honky** ['hɒŋkɪ] (pl -ies) n Am vinf offensive Weiße der, die.

**Honolulu** [ˌhɒnə'luːluː] n Honolulu nt.

**honor** etc Am = **honour** etc.

**honorary** [Br 'ɒnərərɪ, Am ɒnə'reərɪl] adj - 1. [given as an honour] Ehren-; **~ degree** ehrenhalber verliehener akademischer Grad - 2. [unpaid] ehrenamtlich.

**honor roll** n Am SCH & UNIV Liste der besten Schüler einer Schule/Studenten in einer College.

**honour** Br, **honor** Am ['ɒnəʳ] n Ehre die; **a man of ~** ein Ehrenmann; **in her ~** zu ihren Ehren; **in ~ of his achievements** zu Ehren seiner Leistungen ◇ vt - 1. [fulfil - debt] begleichen; [ - promise, agreement] erfüllen; [ - cheque] akzeptieren - 2. fml [bring honour to] ehren.

➤ **Honour** n: **His/Her Honour** das Gericht; **Your Honour** Euer Ehren.

➤ **honours** npl - 1. [tokens of respect] Ehren pl; **with full military ~s** mit militärischen Ehren - 2. UNIV der erste erreichbare akademische Grad, der in ein oder zwei Fächern erlangt wird - 3. phr: **to do the ~s** [serve drinks] einlschenken; [serve food] servieren; [make introductions] die Honneurs machen.

**honourable** Br, **honorable** Am ['ɒnrəbl] adj ehrenhaft.

➤ **Honourable** adj [in titles]: **the Honourable ...** der ehrenwerte ..., die ehrenwerte ...; **the Honourable Member for Southend** [in House of Commons] der Herr/die Frau Abgeordnete für den Wahlkreis Southend.

**honourably** Br, **honorably** Am ['ɒnrəblɪ] adv ehrenhaft.

**honour bound** adj: **to be ~ to do sthg** moralisch dazu verpflichtet sein, etw zu tun.

**honours list** n Br Liste der Titel- und Rangverleihungen.

**hooch** [huːtʃ] n (U) inf Fusel der (illegal hergestellt).

**hood** [hʊd] n - 1. [on cloak, jacket] Kapuze die; [of robber] Maske die - 2. [of cooker] Abzugshaube die; [of pram, convertible car] Verdeck das - 3. Am [car bonnet] Motorhaube die.

**hooded** ['hʊdɪd] adj - 1. [wearing a hood] mit ei-

ner Kapuze; [robber] maskiert - 2. [eyes] mit schweren Lidern.

**hoodlum** ['huːdləm] n Am inf [youth] Rowdy der; [gangster] Gangster der.

**hoodwink** ['hʊdwɪŋk] vt reinllegen.

**hooey** ['huːɪ] n Am inf Quatsch der.

**hoof** [huːf, hʊf] (pl -s OR hooves) n Huf der.

**hook** [hʊk] n Haken der; **~ and eye** Haken und Öse ◇ vt - 1. [fasten with hook]: **to ~ sthg on to sthg** etw an etw (D) festlhaken - 2. [fish] an die Angel bekommen - 3.: **to ~ one's arm/leg round sthg** den Arm/das Bein um etw schlingen.

➤ **off the hook** adv - 1. TELEC: **the telephone is off the ~** der Hörer ist abgenommen; **to leave the phone off the ~** den Hörer nicht aufllegen - 2. [out of trouble]: **to be off the ~** aus dem Schneider sein; **to get sb off the ~** jn aus der Klemme helfen.

➤ **hook up** vt sep: **to ~ sthg up to sthg** COMPUT & TELEC etw an etw (A) anlschließen.

**hooked** [hʊkt] adj - 1. [shaped like a hook] gebogen; **~ nose** Hakennase die - 2. inf [addicted]: **to be ~ on sthg** [on drugs] von etw abhängig sein; [on music, money, art] auf etw (A) ganz versessen sein.

**hooker** ['hʊkəʳ] n Am inf Nutte die.

**hook(e)y** ['hʊkɪ] n Am inf: **to play ~** (die Schule) schwänzen

**hooligan** ['huːlɪɡən] n Rowdy der.

**hooliganism** ['huːlɪɡənɪzm] n Rowdytun das.

**hoop** [huːp] n Reifen der.

**hoop-la** ['huːplɑː] n [game] Ringwerfen das.

**hooray** [hʊ'reɪ] excl = **hurray.**

**hoot** [huːt] n - 1. [of owl] Schrei der - 2. [of horn] Hupen das - 3. inf [of laughter] schallendes Gelächter - 4. Br inf [amusing thing, person]: **to be a ~** zum Schießen sein ◇ vi - 1. [owl] schreien - 2. [horn] hupen - 3. inf: **to ~ with laughter** in schallendes Gelächter auslbrechen ◇ vt [horn]: **to ~ one's horn** hupen.

**hooter** ['huːtəʳ] n - 1. [horn - of car] Hupe die; [ - of factory] Sirene die - 2. Br inf [nose] Zinken der.

**Hoover®** ['huːvəʳ] n Br Staubsauger der.

➤ **hoover** vt & vi (staub)saugen.

**hooves** [huːvz] pl ⊳ **hoof.**

**hop** [hɒp] (pt & pp -ped; cont -ping) n - 1. [of person, animal, bird] Hüpfer der - 2. inf [trip] Trip der ◇ vi - 1. [jump] hüpfen - 2. inf [move nimbly] springen; **to ~ on a bus/train/plane** kurz entschlossen den Bus/den Zug/das Flugzeug nehmen ◇ vt inf - 1. Am [bus, train]: **to ~ a bus/ train** (kurzerhand) in einen Bus/Zug einl steigen - 2. phr: **~ it!** verschwinde!

➤ **hops** npl [for making beer] Hopfen der.

**hope** [həʊp] vi hoffen; **to ~ for sthg** auf etw (A) hoffen; **I ~ so** hoffentlich; **I ~ not** hoffentlich nicht; **to ~ for the best** das Beste hoffen ◇ *vt:* **to ~ (that)** hoffen, dass; **to ~ to do sthg** hoffen, etw zu tun ◇ *n* - **1.** *(U)* [belief, optimism] Hoffnung *die;* **to be beyond ~** [situation] aussichtslos OR hoffnungslos sein; **I don't hold out much ~** ich habe wenig Hoffnung - **2.** [expectation, chance] Hoffnung *die;* **in the ~ of doing sthg** in der Hoffnung, etw zu tun; **to pin one's ~s on sb/sthg** seine Hoffnungen auf jn/etw setzen; **to raise sb's ~s** jn Hoffnung machen.

**hope chest** *n* Am Aussteuertruhe *die.*

**hopeful** ['həʊpfʊl] *adj* - **1.** [person] hoffnungsvoll; **to be ~ that** zuversichtlich sein, dass; **to be ~ of doing sthg** zuversichtlich sein, etw zu tun - **2.** [sign, future] vielversprechend ◇ *n:* **a young ~** ein hoffnungsvoller Mensch.

**hopefully** ['həʊpfəlɪ] *adv* - **1.** [in a hopeful way] hoffnungsvoll - **2.** [with luck] hoffentlich.

**hopeless** ['həʊplɪs] *adj* - **1.** [despairing, impossible] hoffnungslos - **2.** *inf* [useless] miserabel.

**hopelessly** ['həʊplɪslɪ] *adv* hoffnungslos.

**hopper** ['hɒpəʳ] *n* [bin] Einfülltrichter *der.*

**hopping** ['hɒpɪŋ] *adv:* **to be ~ mad** fuchsteufelswild sein.

**hopscotch** ['hɒpskɒtʃ] *n* *(U)* Himmel-und-Hölle(-Spiel) *das.*

**horde** [hɔːd] *n* [of people] Horde *die;* [of insects] Schwarm *der.*
➤ **hordes** *npl:* **~s of** Horden *pl* von; [of letters] Massen *pl* von.

**horizon** [hə'raɪzn] *n* [of sky] Horizont *der;* **on the ~** *lit* & *fig* am Horizont.
➤ **horizons** *npl* Horizont *der.*

**horizontal** [ˌhɒrɪ'zɒntl] *adj* horizontal ◇ *n:* **the ~** die Horizontale.

**hormone** ['hɔːməʊn] *n* Hormon *das.*

**hormone replacement therapy** *n* Hormonersatztherapie *die.*

**horn** [hɔːn] *n* - **1.** [gen] Horn *das* - **2.** [on car] Hupe *die;* [on ship] Signalhorn *das.*

**hornet** ['hɔːnɪt] *n* Hornisse *die.*

**horn-rimmed** [-'rɪmd] *adj:* **~ glasses** Hornbrille *die.*

**horny** ['hɔːnɪ] (*compar* **-ier;** *superl* **-iest**) *adj* - **1.** [scale, body] hornig; [hand] schwielig - **2.** *vinf* [sexually excited] geil.

**horoscope** ['hɒrəskəʊp] *n* Horoskop *das.*

**horrendous** [hɒ'rendəs] *adj* - **1.** [horrific] entsetzlich - **2.** *inf* [unpleasant - bill, amount] horrend; [ - weather] scheußlich.

**horrible** ['hɒrəbl] *adj* schrecklich, fürchterlich.

**horribly** ['hɒrəblɪ] *adv lit* & *fig* schrecklich.

**horrid** ['hɒrɪd] *adj esp Br* fürchterlich; **don't be so ~** sei nicht so gemein.

**horrific** [hɒ'rɪfɪk] *adj* entsetzlich.

**horrify** ['hɒrɪfaɪ] (*pt* & *pp* **-ied**) *vt* entsetzen.

**horrifying** ['hɒrɪfaɪɪŋ] *adj* entsetzlich.

**horror** ['hɒrəʳ] *n* - **1.** [alarm, fear] Entsetzen *das;* **the ~ of terrorism** der Schrecken des Terrorismus; **to my/his ~** zu meinem/seinem Entsetzen - **2.** [strong dislike]: **to have a ~ of sthg** einen Horror vor etw *(D)* haben - **3.** [horrifying thing] Schrecken *der;* **the ~s of war** die Gräuel des Krieges.

**horror film** *n* Horrorfilm *der.*

**horror-struck** *adj* vor Schreck gelähmt.

**hors d'oeuvre** [ɔː'dɜːvr] (*pl* **-s**) *n* Hors d'oeuvre *das,* Vorspeise *die.*

**horse** [hɔːs] *n* Pferd *das.*

**horseback** ['hɔːsbæk] *adj:* **~ riding** Am Reiten *das* ◇ *n:* **on ~** zu Pferd.

**horsebox** Br ['hɔːsbɒks], **horsecar** Am ['hɔːskɑːr] *n* Pferdetransporter *der.*

**horse chestnut** *n* [tree, nut] Rosskastanie *die.*

**horse-drawn** *adj* Pferde-.

**horsehair** ['hɔːsheəʳ] *n* Rosshaar *das.*

**horseman** ['hɔːsmən] (*pl* **-men** [-mən]) *n* Reiter *der.*

**horseplay** ['hɔːspleɪ] *n* *(U)* Balgerei *die.*

**horsepower** ['hɔːsˌpaʊəʳ] *n* *(U)* Pferdestärke *die.*

**horse racing** *n* Pferderennen *das.*

**horseradish** ['hɔːsˌrædɪʃ] *n* *(U)* [plant] Meerrettich *der.*

**horse riding** *n* Reiten *das.*

**horseshoe** ['hɔːsʃuː] *n* Hufeisen *das.*

**horse show** *n* Reitturnier *das.*

**horse-trading** [-ˌtreɪdɪŋ] *n* *fig* & *pej* Kuhhandel *der.*

**horse trials** *npl* Military *die.*

**horsewhip** ['hɔːswɪp] (*pt* & *pp* **-ped;** *cont* **-ping**) *vt* auspeitschen.

**horsewoman** ['hɔːsˌwʊmən] (*pl* **-women** [-ˌwɪmɪn]) *n* Reiterin *die.*

**horticultural** [ˌhɔːtɪ'kʌltʃərəl] *adj* [skill] gärtnerisch; [society] Gartenbau-.

**horticulture** ['hɔːtɪˌkʌltʃəʳ] *n* Gartenbau *der.*

**hose** [həʊz] *n* [hosepipe] Schlauch *der* ◇ *vt* [garden] sprengen.
➤ **hose down** *vt sep* ablspritzen.

**hosepipe** ['həʊzpaɪp] *n* Schlauch *der.*

**hosiery** ['həʊzɪərɪ] *n* *(U)* Strumpfwaren *pl.*

**hospice** ['hɒspɪs] *n* Sterbeklinik *die.*

**hospitable** [hɒ'spɪtəbl] *adj* gastfreundlich.

**hospital** ['hɒspɪtl] *n* Krankenhaus *das.*

**hospitality** [ˌhɒspɪ'tælətɪ] *n* Gastfreundschaft *die.*

H

**hospitality suite** n Gesellschaftsräume pl.

**hospitalize, -ise** [ˈhɒspɪtəlaɪz] vt ins Krankenhaus einlweisen.

**host** [həʊst] n - **1.** [gen] Gastgeber der; ~ **city** gastgebende Stadt; ~ **country** Gastland das - **2.** [compere] Moderator der - **3.** literary [large number]: **a ~ of sthg** eine Schar von etw ◇ vt moderieren.
➡ **Host** n RELIG: **the Host** die Hostie.

**hostage** [ˈhɒstɪdʒ] n Geisel die; **to be taken/ held ~** als Geisel genommen/festgehalten werden.

**hostel** [ˈhɒstl] n Wohnheim das; **(youth) ~** Jugendherberge die.

**hostelry** [ˈhɒstəlrɪ] (pl -ries) n hum Gastwirtschaft die.

**hostess** [ˈhəʊstes] n [at party] Gastgeberin die.

**hostile** [Br ˈhɒstaɪl, Am ˈhɒstl] adj - **1.** [antagonistic, unfriendly]: ~ **(to sb/sthg)** feindselig (gegenüber jm/etw) - **2.** [weather conditions] widrig; [climate] unwirtlich - **3.** MIL [territory, forces] feindlich.

**hostility** [hɒˈstɪlətɪ] n (U) Feindseligkeit die.
➡ **hostilities** npl Feindseligkeiten pl.

**hot** [hɒt] (compar -ter; superl -test; pt & pp -ted; cont -ting) adj - **1.** [gen] heiß; **I'm ~** mir ist heiß - **2.** [cooked] warm - **3.** [spicy] scharf - **4.** inf [expert] stark; **to be ~ on** OR **at sthg** super in etw (D) sein - **5.** [recent]: **a ~ piece of news** das Neueste vom Neuesten - **6.** [temper] hitzig.
➡ **hot up** vi inf [situation] sich verschärfen; [party] in Schwung kommen; **the pace is ~ting up** das Tempo steigert sich.

**hot-air balloon** n Heißluftballon der.

**hotbed** [ˈhɒtbed] n Brutstätte die.

**hotchpotch** Br [ˈhɒtʃpɒtʃ], **hodgepodge** Am [ˈhɒdʒpɒdʒ] n inf Mischmasch der.

**hot-cross bun** n Rosinenbrötchen mit kleinem Teigkreuz, wird um Ostern gegessen.

**hot dog** n Hot Dog der OR das.

**hotel** [həʊˈtel] n Hotel das ◇ comp Hotel-.

**hotelier** [həʊˈtelɪə] n Hotelier der.

**hot flush** Br, **hot flash** Am n Hitzewallung die; **~es** fliegende Hitze.

**hotfoot** [ˌhɒtˈfʊt] adv literary eilends.

**hotheaded** [ˌhɒtˈhedɪd] adj hitzköpfig.

**hothouse** [ˈhɒthaʊs, pl -haʊzɪz] n [greenhouse] Treibhaus das ◇ comp Treibhaus-.

**hot line** n - **1.** [between government heads] heißer Draht - **2.** [for crisis, disaster] Hotline die.

**hotly** [ˈhɒtlɪ] adv - **1.** [argue, debate, deny] heftig - **2.** [pursue]: **they were ~ pursued by a policeman** ein Polizist war ihnen dicht auf den Fersen.

**hotplate** [ˈhɒtpleɪt] n Kochplatte die.

**hotpot** [ˈhɒtpɒt] n Br Eintopf der.

**hot potato** n inf fig heißes Eisen.

**hot rod** n AUT frisiertes Auto.

**hot seat** n inf: **to be in the ~** aufgrund einer verantwortungsvollen Position schwierige Entscheidungen treffen müssen.

**hot spot** n - **1.** [exciting place]: **the ~s of the Costa Brava** die Nachtklubs und Kasinos der Costa Brava - **2.** [politically unsettled area] Krisenherd der.

**hot-tempered** [-ˈtempəd] adj jähzornig.

**hot water** n inf fig: **to get into/be in ~** in Schwulitäten kommen/sein.

**hot-water bottle** n Wärmflasche die.

**hot-wire** vt inf kurzlschließen.

**hound** [haʊnd] n Jagdhund der ◇ vt verfolgen; **to ~ sb out (of a place)** jn (aus einem Ort) vertreiben.

**hour** [ˈaʊə] n Stunde die; **half an ~** eine halbe Stunde; **per** OR **an ~** pro OR die Stunde; **it's an ~'s drive away** es ist eine Stunde mit dem Auto von hier entfernt; **on the ~** zur vollen Stunde; **every ~, on the ~** jede volle Stunde; **in the small ~s** früh morgens; **in my ~ of need** literary in der Stunde der Not.
➡ **hours** npl - **1.** [of business] Geschäftszeiten pl; [of pub, museum etc] Öffnungszeiten pl; [of doctor] Sprechstunde die; **after ~s** [in pub] nach der Polizeistunde; [in office] nach Dienstschluss - **2.** [routine]: **to keep regular/irregular ~s** [work] regelmäßig/unregelmäßig arbeiten; **to work long ~s** lange arbeiten.

**hourly** [ˈaʊəlɪ] adj - **1.** [happening every hour] stündlich - **2.** [per hour] Stunden- ◇ adv - **1.** [every hour] stündlich - **2.** [per hour] pro Stunde - **3.** fig [constantly] ständig.

**house** [n & adj haʊs, pl ˈhaʊzɪz, vb haʊz] n - **1.** [gen] Haus das; **to put** OR **set one's ~ in order** vor seiner eigenen Tür kehren; **to move ~** umlziehen; **on the ~** auf Kosten des Hauses; **to play to a full ~** vor vollem Haus spielen; **to bring the ~ down** das Publikum zum Toben bringen; **this ~ believes that ...** [in debate] wir glauben, dass ... - **2.** SCH eine der traditionellen Schülergemeinschaften innerhalb einer Schule, die untereinander Wettbewerbe veranstalten ◇ vt [subj: person] unterlbringen; **the building ~s three families/offices** in dem Gebäude sind drei Familien/Büros untergebracht ◇ adj Haus-; ~ **style** hauseigener Stil; ~ **red/white** [wine] Hausmarke die (Rot-/ Weißwein).

**house arrest** n: **under ~** unter Hausarrest.

**houseboat** [ˈhaʊsbəʊt] n Hausboot das.

**housebound** [ˈhaʊsbaʊnd] adj ans Haus gefesselt.

**housebreaking** ['haʊsˌbreɪkɪŋ] *n (U)* Einbruch *der*.

**housebroken** ['haʊsˌbrəʊkn] *adj Am* [pet] stubenrein.

**housecoat** ['haʊskəʊt] *n* Morgenrock *der*.

**household** ['haʊshəʊld] *adj* - **1.** [domestic] Haushalts-; ~ **work** Hausarbeit *die* - **2.** [familiar]: **to be a** ~ **name** ein Begriff sein ◇ *n* Haushalt *der*.

**householder** ['haʊsˌhəʊldəʳ] *n* Hausinhaber *der*, -in *die*; [of flat] Wohnungsinhaber *der*, -in *die*.

**househunting** ['haʊsˌhʌntɪŋ] *n* Haussuche *die*.

**house husband** *n* Hausmann *der*.

**housekeeper** ['haʊsˌkiːpəʳ] *n* Haushälterin *die*.

**housekeeping** ['haʊsˌkiːpɪŋ] *n* - **1.** [work] Haushaltsführung *die* - **2.** [budget]: ~ **(money)** Haushaltsgeld *das*.

**houseman** ['haʊsmən] (*pl* -**men** [-mən]) *n Br* Assistenzarzt *der*, -ärztin *die*.

**house martin** *n* Mehlschwalbe *die*.

**housemen** ['haʊsmən] *pl* ⊳ **houseman**.

**house music** *n* Hausmusik *die*.

**House of Commons** *n Br*: **the** ~ das britische Unterhaus.

**House of Lords** *n Br*: **the** ~ das britische Oberhaus.

**House of Representatives** *n Am*: **the** ~ das Repräsentantenhaus.

**house-owner** *n* Hauseigentümer *der*, -in *die*.

**houseplant** ['haʊsplɑːnt] *n* Zimmerpflanze *die*.

**house-proud** *adj* penibel (im Haushalt).

**Houses of Parliament** *npl Br*: **the** ~ Sitz *des britischen Parlaments*.

**house-to-house** *adj*: ~ **collection** Haussammlung *die*; **to conduct a** ~ **search** jedes Haus durchsuchen.

**house-train** *vt Br* stubenrein machen; ~**ed** stubenrein.

**housewarming (party)** ['haʊsˌwɔːmɪŋ-] *n* Einzugsparty *die*.

**housewife** ['haʊswaɪf] (*pl* -**wives** [-waɪvz]) *n* Hausfrau *die*.

**housework** ['haʊswɜːk] *n* Hausarbeit *die*.

**housing** ['haʊzɪŋ] *n* - **1.** (*U*) [accommodation] Wohnungen *pl*; [act] Unterbringung *die* - **2.** TECH Gehäuse *das* ◇ *comp* Wohnungs-; ~ **conditions** Wohnverhältnisse *pl*.

**housing association** *n Br* Wohnungsbaugesellschaft *die*.

**housing benefit** *n (U) Br* Wohngeld *das*.

**housing development** *n* Wohnsiedlung *die*.

**housing estate** *Br*, **housing project** *Am n* Wohnsiedlung *die*.

**hovel** ['hɒvl] *n* armselige Hütte.

**hover** ['hɒvəʳ] *vi* - **1.** [fly] schweben - **2.** [linger - person] herumstehen.

**hovercraft** ['hɒvəkrɑːft] (*pl inv* OR -**s**) *n* Luftkissenfahrzeug *das*.

**hoverport** ['hɒvəpɔːt] *n* Anlegestelle für Luftkissenfahrzeuge.

**how** [haʊ] *adv* - **1.** [referring to way, manner] wie; ~ **do you get there?** wie kommt man dahin?; **tell me** ~ **to do it** sag mir, wie man das macht - **2.** [referring to health, general state] wie; ~ **are you?** wie gehts dir?; ~ **are you doing?**, ~ **are things?** wie gehts dir?; ~ **is your room?** wie ist dein Zimmer?; ~ **do you do?** guten Tag! - **3.** [referring to degree, amount] wie; ~ **far?** wie weit?;

~ **long?** wie lang?; ~ **many?** wie viele?; ~ **much?** wie viel?; ~ **much is it?** wie viel kostet es?; ~ **old are you?** wie alt bist du? - **4.** [in exclamations] wie; ~ **nice/awful!** wie schön/schrecklich!; ~ **I wish I could!** wenn ich doch nur könnte! - **5.** [expressing surprise, outrage]: ~ **can you say that?** wie kannst du das sagen?; ~ **can you be so rude?** wie kannst du mir so unhöflich sein?

◆ **how about** *adv:* ~ **about a drink?** wie wäre es mit einem Drink?; **I fancy a game of cards,** ~ **about it?** ich habe Lust, Karten zu spielen, wie wärs?; **I could do with a night off,** ~ **about you?** ich könnte einen freien Abend gebrauchen, du auch?

**howdy** ['haʊdɪ] *excl Am inf* Tag!

**however** [haʊ'evəʳ] *conj* [in whatever way] wie (immer) <> *adv* - **1.** [nevertheless] jedoch; ~, **it was not to be** es sollte jedoch nicht sein - **2.** [no matter how] wie ... auch, egal wie; ~ **difficult/good it is** wie schwierig/gut es auch ist, egal wie schwierig/gut es ist; ~ **many/much you have** wie viele/viel du auch hast - **3.** [how] wie ... bloß; ~ **did you know?** woher hast du das bloß gewusst?

**howl** [haʊl] *n* [of person] Schrei *der;* [of animal, wind] Heulen *das* <> *vi* - **1.** [animal, wind] heulen - **2.** [person] schreien; **to** ~ **with laughter** brüllen vor Lachen.

**howler** ['haʊləʳ] *n inf* [mistake] Schnitzer *der.*

**howling** ['haʊlɪŋ] *adj inf* [success] Riesen-.

**hp** (*abbr of* **horsepower**) *n* PS.

**HP** *n* - **1.** (*abbr of* **hire purchase**): **to buy sthg on** ~ etw auf Raten kaufen - **2.** = **hp.**

**HQ** (*abbr of* **headquarters**) *n* HQ *das.*

**hr** (*abbr of* **hour**) Std.

**HRH** (*abbr of* **His (or Her) Royal Highness**) S.M./I.M.

**hrs** (*abbr of* **hours**) Std.

**HRT** (*abbr of* **hormone replacement therapy**) *n* Hormonsubstitionstherapie *die.*

**HST** (*abbr of* **Hawaiian Standard Time**) *Zeit in der Zeitzone Hawaiis.*

**ht** *abbr of* **height.**

**HTML** (*abbr of* **hypertext markup language**) HTML *das, Programmiersprache zur Formatierung von elektronischen Textdokumenten.*

**hub** [hʌb] *n* - **1.** [of wheel] (Rad)nabe *die* - **2.** [of activity] Zentrum *das.*

**hub airport** *n* zentraler Flughafen.

**hubbub** ['hʌbʌb] *n* Lärm *der;* ~ **of voices** Stimmengewirr *das.*

**hubcap** ['hʌbkæp] *n* Radkappe *die.*

**huddle** ['hʌdl] *vi* - **1.** [crouch, curl up] kauern - **2.** [crowd together]: **to** ~ **(together)** sich (zusammen)drängen <> *n* [of people] Grüppchen *das.*

**hue** [hjuː] *n* [colour] Farbton *der.*

**huff** [hʌf] *n:* **in a** ~ beleidigt <> *vi:* **to** ~ **and puff** *fig* großes Trara machen.

**huffy** ['hʌfɪ] (*compar* **-ier;** *superl* **-iest**) *adj inf* - **1.** [offended] eingeschnappt - **2.** [touchy] empfindlich.

**hug** [hʌg] (*pt* & *pp* **-ged;** *cont* **-ging**) *n* Umarmung *die;* **to give sb a** ~ jn umarmen <> *vt* - **1.** [embrace] umarmen - **2.** [hold - one's knees] umfassen; **to** ~ **sthg to o.s.** etw an sich (A) drücken - **3.** [stay close to]: **to** ~ **the coast/kerb** dicht an der Küste/am Straßenrand entlangfahren.

**huge** [hjuːdʒ] *adj* riesig; [subject] vielfältig.

**huh** [hʌ] *excl* - **1.** [expressing surprise, asking for repeat] was? - **2.** [after questions]: **you must be tired,** ~? du bist bestimmt müde, ne? - **3.** [expressing scorn] pah!

**hulk** [hʌlk] *n* - **1.** [of ship] (Schiffs)rumpf *der* - **2.** [person] Koloss *der.*

**hulking** ['hʌlkɪŋ] *adj* [building] klobig; [person] ungeschlacht.

**hull** [hʌl] *n* [of ship] Schiffskörper *der.*

**hullabaloo** [ˌhʌləbə'luː] *n inf* Spektakel *der.*

**hullo** [hə'ləʊ] *excl* = **hello.**

**hum** [hʌm] (*pt* & *pp* **-med;** *cont* **-ming**) *vi* - **1.** [bee] summen; [car, machine] brummen - **2.** [sing] summen - **3.** [be busy - place] voller Leben sein; [ - office] voller Aktivität sein - **4.** *phr:* **to** ~ **and haw** herumdrucksen <> *vt* [tune] summen <> *n* (U) [buzz - of bee] Summen *das;* [ - of car, machine] Brummen *das;* [ - of conversation] Gemurmel *das.*

**human** ['hjuːmən] *adj* menschlich <> *n:* ~ **(being)** Mensch *der.*

**humane** [hjuː'meɪn] *adj* [compassionate] human.

**humanely** [hjuː'meɪnlɪ] *adv* human.

**human error** *n* (U) menschliches Versagen.

**humanist** ['hjuːmənɪst] *n* PHILOSOPHY Humanist *der,* -**in** *die.*

**humanitarian** [hjuːˌmænɪ'teərɪən] *adj* humanitär <> *n* Anhänger *der,* -**in** *die* des Humanitätsgedankens.

**humanity** [hjuː'mænətɪ] *n* - **1.** [kindness, sympathy] Humanität *die* - **2.** [mankind] Menschheit *die.*

◆ **humanities** *npl:* **the humanities** die Geisteswissenschaften.

**humanly** ['hjuːmənlɪ] *adv:* **all that is** ~ **possible** alles, was menschenmöglich ist; **as far as is** ~ **possible** so weit wie irgend möglich.

**human nature** *n* die menschliche Natur.

**human race** *n:* **the** ~ die menschliche Rasse.

**human resources** *npl* Humankapital *das.*

**human rights** npl Menschenrechte pl.

**humble** ['hʌmbl] adj [position, job, origins] niedrig; [clerk] einfach; [home, room, opinion] bescheiden; [person] demütig ⋄ vt demütigen; **to ~ o.s.** sich demütigen OR erniedrigen.

**humbly** ['hʌmblɪ] adv [say, suggest] demütig; [live] bescheiden.

**humbug** ['hʌmbʌg] n - **1.** dated [hypocrisy] Heuchelei die - **2.** Br [sweet] Pfefferminzbonbon der OR das.

**humdrum** ['hʌmdrʌm] adj [life] eintönig.

**humid** ['hju:mɪd] adj feucht.

**humidity** [hju:'mɪdətɪ] n (Luft)feuchtigkeit die.

**humiliate** [hju:'mɪlɪeɪt] vt demütigen.

**humiliating** [hju:'mɪlɪeɪtɪŋ] adj demütigend.

**humiliation** [hju:ˌmɪlɪ'eɪʃn] n Demütigung die.

**humility** [hju:'mɪlətɪ] n Domut die.

**hummingbird** ['hʌmɪŋbɜ:d] n Kolibri der.

**humor** n & vt Am = humour.

**humorist** ['hju:mərɪst] n Humorist der.

**humorous** ['hju:mərəs] adj [remark, story] lustig; [person] humorvoll.

**humour** Br, **humor** Am ['hju:mə<sup>r</sup>] n - **1.** [comedy] Humor der; [of situation, remark] Komik die - **2.** dated [mood] Stimmung die, Laune die ⋄ vt: **to ~ sb** jm seinen Willen lassen.

**hump** [hʌmp] n - **1.** [hill] Hügel der - **2.** [of camel] Höcker der; [of person] Buckel der ⋄ vt inf [carry] schleppen.

**humpbacked bridge** [ˌhʌmpbækt-] n gewölbte Brücke.

**humus** ['hju:məs] n Humus der.

**hunch** [hʌntʃ] n inf Gefühl das, Ahnung die ⋄ vt [shoulders] hochziehen ⋄ vi: **she sat ~ed over a book** sie saß über ein Buch gebeugt.

**hunchback** ['hʌntʃbæk] n Bucklige der, die.

**hundred** ['hʌndrəd] num hundert; **a** OR **one ~** (ein)hundert; see also **six**.
➡ **hundreds** npl Hunderte pl.

**hundredth** ['hʌndrəθ] num hundertste, -r, -s; see also **sixth**.

**hundredweight** ['hʌndrədweɪt] n - **1.** [in UK] ≈ Zentner der, 50,8 kg - **2.** [in US] ≈ Zentner der, 45,36 kg.

**hung** [hʌŋ] pt & pp ⊳ hang ⋄ adj POL: **a ~ parliament** ein Parlament ohne klare Mehrheitsverhältnisse.

**Hungarian** [hʌŋ'geərɪən] adj ungarisch ⋄ n - **1.** [person] Ungar der, -in die - **2.** [language] Ungarisch(e) das.

**Hungary** ['hʌŋgərɪ] n Ungarn nt.

**hunger** ['hʌŋgə<sup>r</sup>] n lit & fig Hunger der.

➡ **hunger after, hunger for** vt fus literary hungern nach.

**hunger strike** n Hungerstreik der.

**hung over** adj inf verkatert.

**hungry** ['hʌŋgrɪ] (compar **-ier**; superl **-iest**) adj hungrig; **to be ~** Hunger haben; **to go ~** hungern; **to be ~ for sthg** fig sich nach etw sehnen; **to be ~ for power** machthungrig sein.

**hung up** adj inf: **to be ~ (on** OR **about)** sich verrückt machen (wegen (+ G)).

**hunk** [hʌŋk] n - **1.** [of bread, cheese] Stück das - **2.** inf [attractive man]: **he's a real ~** er ist ein richtiger Mann.

**hunky-dory** [ˌhʌŋkɪ'dɔ:rɪ] adj inf: **everything is ~** es ist alles in Butter.

**hunt** [hʌnt] n - **1.** SPORT Jagd die; Br [for foxes] Fuchsjagd die; [hunters] Jagdgesellschaft die - **2.** [search] Suche die; **a murder ~** eine Mörderjagd ⋄ vi - **1.** [for food, sport] jagen - **2.** Br [for foxes] auf die Fuchsjagd gehen - **3.** [search]: **to ~ (for)** suchen (nach) ⋄ vt - **1.** [animals, birds] jagen - **2.** [criminal] fahnden nach.

➡ **hunt down** vt sep [catch] zur Strecke bringen; [chase] Jagd machen auf.

**hunter** ['hʌntə<sup>r</sup>] n - **1.** [of animals, birds] Jäger der - **2.** [of things]: **autograph ~** Autogrammjäger; **bargain ~** Schnäppchenjäger.

**hunting** ['hʌntɪŋ] n (U) - **1.** SPORT Jagd die - **2.** Br [foxhunting] Fuchsjagd die - **3.** [searching] Suche die ⋄ comp [dog, clothes] Jagd-.

**huntsman** ['hʌntsmən] (pl **-men** [-mən]) n Jäger der.

**hurdle** ['hɜ:dl] n lit & fig Hürde die ⋄ vt [jump over] überspringen.

➡ **hurdles** npl SPORT Hürdenlauf der.

**hurl** [hɜ:l] vt schleudern; **to ~ abuse at sb** jm Beschimpfungen an den Kopf werfen.

**hurrah** [hʊ'rɑ:] excl dated hurra!

**hurray** [hʊ'reɪ] excl hurra!

**hurricane** ['hʌrɪkən] n Orkan der, [tropical] Hurrikan der.

**hurried** ['hʌrɪd] adj [meal] hastig; [departure] überstürzt; [glance] flüchtig; [note] eilig geschrieben.

**hurriedly** ['hʌrɪdlɪ] adv [eat] hastig; [leave, write] eilig.

**hurry** ['hʌrɪ] (pt & pp **-ied**) vt [person] (zur Eile) anltreiben; [process] beschleunigen; **don't ~ me** hetz mich nicht; **to ~ to do sthg** sich beeilen, etw zu tun ⋄ vi sich beeilen ⋄ n Eile die; **to be in a ~** in Eile sein, es eilig haben; **to do sthg in a ~** etw in Eile tun; **to be in no ~ to do sthg** [unwilling] es nicht eilig haben, etw zu tun.

➡ **hurry off** vi schnell weglgehen.
➡ **hurry up** vi sich beeilen ⋄ vt sep [person]

(zur Eile) an|treiben; [process] beschleunigen.

**hurt** [hɜːt] (*pt* & *pp* **hurt**) *vt* - **1.** [cause physical pain to] wehtun (+ *D*); **to ~ one's leg/arm** sich (*D*) am Bein/Arm wehtun; **to ~ o.s.** sich (*D*) wehtun - **2.** [injure, upset] verletzen; **to ~ sb's feelings** js Gefühle verletzen - **3.** [harm] schaden (+ *D*) ◇ *vi* - **1.** [gen] wehtun; **that ~s!** das tut weh! - **2.** [harm] schaden; **I suppose it won't ~** ich denke, es kann nicht schaden ◇ *adj* [leg, arm, feelings] verletzt; [look, voice] gekränkt ◇ *n* (*U*) [emotional pain] Schmerz *der*.

**hurtful** [ˈhɜːtfʊl] *adj* verletzend.

**hurtle** [ˈhɜːtl] *vi* sausen.

**husband** [ˈhʌzbənd] *n* Ehemann *der;* **my ~** mein Mann.

**hush** [hʌʃ] *n* Schweigen *das;* **a deathly ~** eine Totenstille ◇ *vt* [crowd, person] zum Schweigen bringen ◇ *excl* still!
➔ **hush up** *vt sep* [affair] vertuschen.

**hush money** *n inf* Schweigegeld *das*.

**husk** [hʌsk] *n* [of seed] Hülse *die;* [of grain] Spelze *die*.

**husky** [ˈhʌski] (*compar* -**ier;** *superl* -**iest**) *adj* [voice] rau; [laugh] heiser ◇ *n* [dog] Husky *der*, Eskimohund *der*.

**hustings** [ˈhʌstɪŋz] *npl Br* [campaign] Wahlkampf *der;* [meetings] Wahlveranstaltungen *pl*.

**hustle** [ˈhʌsl] *vt* - **1.** [hurry] **he ~d her out of the room** er drängte sie schnell aus dem Raum - **2.** *Am* [persuade] **to ~ sb into doing sthg** jn dazu bringen wollen, etw zu tun ◇ *n:* **~ and bustle** geschäftiges Treiben.

**hut** [hʌt] *n* Hütte *die;* [temporary building] Baracke *die*.

**hutch** [hʌtʃ] *n* Stall *der*.

**hyacinth** [ˈhaɪəsɪnθ] *n* Hyazinthe *die*.

**hybrid** [ˈhaɪbrɪd] *adj* - **1.** [plant, animal] hybrid - **2.** [system, organization] Misch- ◇ *n* - **1.** [plant, animal] Hybride *der* OR *die* - **2.** [mixture] Mischung *die*.

**hydrangea** [haɪˈdreɪndʒə] *n* Hortensie *die*.

**hydrant** [ˈhaɪdrənt] *n* Hydrant *der*.

**hydraulic** [haɪˈdrɔːlɪk] *adj* hydraulisch.
➔ **hydraulics** *n* (*U*) Hydraulik *die*.

**hydrocarbon** [ˌhaɪdrəˈkɑːbən] *n* Kohlenwasserstoff *der*.

**hydrochloric acid** [ˌhaɪdrəˌklɔːrɪk-] *n* Salzsäure *die*.

**hydroelectric** [ˌhaɪdrəʊˈlektrɪk] *adj* hydroelektrisch; **~ power** durch Wasserkraft erzeugte Energie.

**hydrofoil** [ˈhaɪdrəfɔɪl] *n* Tragflächenboot *das*.

**hydrogen** [ˈhaɪdrədʒən] *n* Wasserstoff *der*.

**hydrogen bomb** *n* Wasserstoffbombe *die*.

**hydrophobia** [ˌhaɪdrəˈfəʊbɪə] *n fml* [rabies] Tollwut *die*.

**hydroplane** [ˈhaɪdrəpleɪn] *n* - **1.** [speedboat] Gleitboot *das* - **2.** [hydrofoil] Tragflächenboot *das*, Tragflügelboot *das*.

**hyena** [haɪˈiːnə] *n* Hyäne *die*.

**hygiene** [ˈhaɪdʒiːn] *n* Hygiene *die;* **personal ~** Körperpflege *die*.

**hygienic** [haɪˈdʒiːnɪk] *adj* hygienisch.

**hygienist** [haɪˈdʒiːnɪst] *n* Zahnhygieniker *der*, -in *die*.

**hymn** [hɪm] *n* Kirchenlied *das*.

**hymn book** *n* Gesangbuch *das*.

**hype** [haɪp] *inf n* Publicity *die* ◇ *vt* Publicity machen für.

**hyped up** [ˌhaɪpt-] *adj inf* aufgeregt.

**hyper** [ˈhaɪpə·] *adj inf* überdreht.

**hyperactive** [ˌhaɪpərˈæktɪv] *adj* überaktiv.

**hyperinflation** [ˌhaɪpərɪnˈfleɪʃn] *n* sehr hohe Inflation.

**hyperlink** [ˈhaɪpəlɪŋk] *n* COMPUT Hyperlink *das*.

**hypermarket** [ˈhaɪpəˌmɑːkɪt] *n* Großmarkt *der*.

**hypersensitive** [ˌhaɪpəˈsensɪtɪv] *adj* überempfindlich.

**hypertension** [ˌhaɪpəˈtenʃn] *n* MED Hypertonie *die*, Bluthochdruck *der*.

**hypertext** [ˈhaɪpətekst] *n* COMPUT Hypertext *der*.

**hyperventilate** [ˌhaɪpəˈventɪleɪt] *vi* hyperventilieren.

**hyphen** [ˈhaɪfn] *n* Bindestrich *der;* [at end of line] Trennungsstrich *der*.

**hyphenate** [ˈhaɪfəneɪt] *vt* mit Bindestrich schreiben.

**hypnosis** [hɪpˈnəʊsɪs] *n* Hypnose *die;* **to be under ~** unter Hypnose stehen.

**hypnotic** [hɪpˈnɒtɪk] *adj* hypnotisch.

**hypnotism** [ˈhɪpnətɪzm] *n* Hypnotik *die*, Hypnose *die*.

**hypnotist** [ˈhɪpnətɪst] *n* Hypnotiseur *der*, -euse *die*.

**hypnotize, -ise** [ˈhɪpnətaɪz] *vt* hypnotisieren.

**hypoallergenic** [ˈhaɪpəʊˌælə'dʒenɪk] *adj* antiallergisch.

**hypochondriac** [ˌhaɪpəˈkɒndriæk] *n* Hypochonder *der*, -in *die*.

**hypocrisy** [hɪˈpɒkrəsɪ] *n* Heuchelei *die*.

**hypocrite** [ˈhɪpəkrɪt] *n* Heuchler *der*, -in *die*.

**hypocritical** [ˌhɪpəˈkrɪtɪkl] *adj* heuchlerisch.

**hypodermic needle** [ˌhaɪpəˈdɜːmɪk-] *n* Kanüle *die*.

**hypodermic syringe** [ˌhaɪpə'dɜːmɪk-] n Injektionsspritze die.

**hypothermia** [ˌhaɪpəʊ'θɜːmɪə] n Unterkühlung die.

**hypothesis** [haɪ'pɒθɪsɪs] (pl **-theses** [-θɪsiːz]) n Hypothese die.

**hypothetical** [ˌhaɪpə'θetɪkl] adj hypothetisch.

**hysterectomy** [ˌhɪstə'rektəmɪ] (pl **-ies**) n Hysterektomie die.

**hysteria** [hɪs'tɪərɪə] n Hysterie die.

**hysterical** [hɪs'terɪkl] adj **- 1.** [gen] hysterisch **- 2.** inf [very funny] urkomisch.

**hysterics** [hɪs'terɪks] npl [panic] hysterischer Anfall; **to be in ~** inf [with laughter] sich ausslschütten vor Lachen; **he had us in ~** er war so lustig, dass wir uns (halb) totgelacht haben.

**Hz** (abbr of **hertz**) Hz.

**i** (pl **i's** OR **is**), **I** (pl **I's** OR **Is**) [aɪ] n [letter] i das, I das.

**I¹** abbr of **Island, Isle.**

**I²** [aɪ] pers pron ich; **I'm tall** ich bin groß; **she and I were at college together** ich war mit ihr zusammen im College; **it is I** fml ich bins.

**IA** abk für Iowa, in Postanschrift verwendet.

**IAEA** (abbr of **International Atomic Energy Agency**) n IAEA die.

**Iberian** [aɪ'bɪərɪən] adj iberisch.

**Iberian peninsula** n: **the ~** die Iberische Halbinsel.

**ibid** (abbr of **ibidem**) ibd.

**i/c** (abbr of **in charge**) ⊳ **charge.**

**ICA** (abbr of **Institute of Contemporary Art**) n Zentrum für moderne Kunst in London.

**ICBM** n abbr of **intercontinental ballistic missile.**

**ICC** n **- 1.** (abbr of **International Chamber of Commerce**) IHK die, Internationale Handelskammer **- 2.** (abbr of **Interstate Commerce Commission**) Regulierungsbehörde für den Handel zwischen US-Staaten.

**ice** [aɪs] n **- 1.** (U) [gen] Eis das; [on pond] Eisschicht die; [on road] Glatteis das; **to break the ~** fig das Eis brechen; **to put sthg on ~** fig etw auf Eis legen **- 2.** Br [ice cream] (Speise)eis das, Eiskrem die ⋄ vt Br [cake] glasieren, mit Zuckerguss überziehen.

➤ **ice over, ice up** vi [windscreen] vereisen; [lake] zulfrieren.

**ice age** n Eiszeit die.

**iceberg** ['aɪsbɜːg] n Eisberg der.

**iceberg lettuce** n Eisbergsalat der.

**icebox** ['aɪsbɒks] n **- 1.** Br [in refrigerator] Eisfach das **- 2.** Am [refrigerator] Eisschrank der.

**ice bucket** n Eiskühler der.

**ice cap** n Eiskappe die.

**ice-cold** adj eiskalt.

**ice cream** n Eis das, Eiskrem die.

**ice cream van** n Br leuchtend bunter Wagen eines fahrenden Eisverkäufers.

**ice cube** n Eiswürfel der.

**iced** [aɪst] adj **- 1.** [drink] eisgekühlt; **~ coffee** Eiskaffee der; **~ tea** Eistee der **- 2.** [cake] glasiert, mit Zuckerguss überzogen.

**ice floe** n Eisscholle die.

**ice hockey** n Eishockey das.

**Iceland** ['aɪslənd] n Island nt.

**Icelander** ['aɪsləndəʳ] n Isländer der, -in die.

**Icelandic** [aɪs'lændɪk] adj isländisch ⋄ n [language] Isländisch(e) das.

**ice lolly** n Br Eis das am Stiel.

**ice pick** n Eispickel der.

**ice rink** n Schlittschuhbahn die, Eisbahn die.

**ice skate** n Schlittschuh der.

➤ **ice-skate** vi Schlittschuh laufen, Eis laufen.

**ice-skater** n Schlittschuhläufer der, -in die, Eisläufer der, -in die.

**ice-skating** n Schlittschuhlaufen das, Eislaufen das; [sport] Eiskunstlauf der; **to go ~** Schlittschuh laufen gehen.

**icicle** ['aɪsɪkl] n Eiszapfen der.

**icily** ['aɪsɪlɪ] adv [in unfriendly way] eisig.

**icing** ['aɪsɪŋ] n [of cake] Zuckerguss der; **the ~ on the cake** fig das Tüpfelchen auf dem i.

**icing sugar** n Br Puderzucker der.

**ICJ** (abbr of **International Court of Justice**) n IGH der.

**icon** ['aɪkɒn] n **- 1.** RELIG Ikone die **- 2.** COMPUT Icon das.

**ICR** (abbr of **Institute for Cancer Research**) n Krebsforschungsinstitut in den USA.

**ICU** (abbr of **intensive care unit**) n Intensivstation die.

**icy** ['aɪsɪ] (compar **-ier;** superl **-iest**) adj **- 1.** [wind,

cold, weather] eisig; **it's ~ cold** es ist eiskalt
**- 2.** [road, pavement] vereist **- 3.** *fig* [welcome, at-
mosphere] eisig.

**I'd** [aɪd] = **I would, I had.**

**ID** *n* (*abbr of* **identification**) Ausweis *der*
◇ *abk für Idaho, in Postanschrift verwendet.*

**ID card** *n* = **identity card.**

**IDD** (*abbr of* **international direct dialling**) *n* internationales Selbstwählen.

**idea** [aɪ'dɪə] *n* **- 1.** [plan, suggestion] Idee *die;* **the
very ~!** der bloße Gedanke! **- 2.** [notion] Vorstellung *die;* **you have no ~ how difficult it is** du
kannst dir nicht vorstellen, wie schwer es
ist; **can you give me an ~ of the price?** können
Sie mir eine ungefähren Preis nennen?;
**I've got the general ~** ich habe ungefähr verstanden, worum es geht; **to get the ~ that ...**
den Eindruck bekommen, dass ...; **to have
an ~ of sthg** eine Vorstellung von etw haben; **to have an ~ that ...** glauben, dass ...; **to
have no ~** keine Ahnung haben **- 3.** [intention]
Absicht *die;* **the ~ is to ...** es ist beabsichtigt,
zu ...; **what's the big ~?** *inf* was soll das
(heißen)?

**ideal** [aɪ'dɪəl] *adj* ideal ◇ *n* Ideal *das.*

**idealism** [aɪ'dɪəlɪzm] *n* Idealismus *der.*

**idealist** [aɪ'dɪəlɪst] *n* Idealist *der*, -in *die.*

**idealize, -ise** [aɪ'dɪəlaɪz] *vt* idealisieren.

**ideally** [aɪ'dɪəlɪ] *adv* **- 1.** [located] ideal; **he was
~ suited to the job** er war perfekt geeignet
für die Stelle **- 2.** [preferably] idealerweise,
im Idealfall.

**identical** [aɪ'dentɪkl] *adj* identisch; **this is the
~ restaurant we ate in last month** das ist dasselbe Restaurant, in dem wir letzten Monat gegessen haben.

**identical twins** *npl* eineiige Zwillinge *pl.*

**identifiable** [aɪ'dentɪfaɪəbl] *adj* erkennbar.

**identification** [aɪ,dentɪfɪ'keɪʃn] *n* **- 1.** [gen]
Identifizierung *die;* [of cause, need] Erkennen
*das* **- 2.** (*U*) [documentation] Ausweispapiere *pl;*
**do you have any ~?** können Sie sich ausweisen?

**identify** [aɪ'dentɪfaɪ] (*pt & pp* **-ied**) *vt* **- 1.** [gen]
identifizieren; [cause, need] erkennen; **to ~
o.s.** sich ausweisen **- 2.** [connect]: **to ~ sb with
sthg** jn mit etw in Verbindung bringen ◇ *vi*
[empathize]: **to ~ with sb/sthg** sich mit jm/etw
identifizieren.

**Identikit picture®** [aɪ,dentɪkɪt-] *n* Phan-
tombild *das.*

**identity** [aɪ'dentətɪ] (*pl* **-ies**) *n* Identität *die.*

**identity card** *n* Personalausweis *der.*

**identity parade** *n* Gegenüberstellung *die.*

**ideological** [,aɪdɪə'lɒdʒɪkl] *adj* weltanschau-
lich; *pej* ideologisch.

**ideology** [,aɪdɪ'ɒlədʒɪ] (*pl* **-ies**) *n* Weltanschauung *die;* *pej* Ideologie *die.*

**idiom** ['ɪdɪəm] *n* **- 1.** [phrase] Redewendung *die*
**- 2.** *fml* [style] Idiom *das.*

**idiomatic** [,ɪdɪə'mætɪk] *adj* idiomatisch.

**idiosyncrasy** [,ɪdɪə'sɪŋkrəsɪ] (*pl* **-ies**) *n* [of per-
son] Eigenheit *die;* [of thing] Besonderheit *die.*

**idiot** ['ɪdɪət] *n* Idiot *der.*

**idiotic** [,ɪdɪ'ɒtɪk] *adj* idiotisch.

**idle** ['aɪdl] *adj* **- 1.** [person - inactive] untätig,
müßig; [ - lazy] faul **- 2.** [machine, factory] stillste-
hend; [workers] unbeschäftigt **- 3.** [threat] leer;
**an ~ boast** eine Prahlerei, hinter der nichts
ist **- 4.** [glance] flüchtig; **out of ~ curiosity** aus
reiner Neugier **- 5.** [futile] sinnlos ◇ *vi* [en-
gine] im Leerlauf sein.

➤ **idle away** *vt sep* [time] vertrödeln.

**idleness** ['aɪdlnɪs] *n* [laziness] Faulheit *die.*

**idler** ['aɪdlər] *n* Faulenzer *der*, -in *die.*

**idly** ['aɪdlɪ] *adv* **- 1.** [lazily] faul; **to stand ~ by** untätig herumstehen **- 2.** [glance] flüchtig.

**idol** ['aɪdl] *n* **- 1.** [hero] Idol *das* **- 2.** RELIG Götze
*der.*

**idolize, -ise** ['aɪdəlaɪz] *vt* vergöttern.

**idyl(l)** ['ɪdɪl] *n* Idylle *die.*

**idyllic** [ɪ'dɪlɪk] *adj* idyllisch.

**i.e.** (*abbr of* **id est**) d. h.

**if** [ɪf] *conj* wenn, falls; (*in indirect questions after
"know", "wonder"*) ob; **~ I were you** wenn ich
du wäre; **pleasant weather, ~ rather cold** schönes Wetter, wenn auch ziemlich kalt; **as ~**
als ob ◇ *n*: **~s and buts** Wenn und Aber *das.*

➤ **if not** *conj* wenn nicht, falls nicht.

➤ **if only** *conj* **- 1.** [expressing regret] wenn ...
nur; **~ only I had known** wenn ich das nur OR
bloß gewusst hätte **- 2.** [providing a reason]
(und) sei es nur; **go and see him, ~ only to
please me** geh ihn besuchen, und sei es nur
mir zuliebe ◇ *excl*: **~ only!** das wäre schön!

**iffy** ['ɪfɪ] (*compar* **-ier**; *superl* **-iest**) *adj inf* [uncer-
tain] ungewiss.

**igloo** ['ɪgluː] (*pl* **-s**) *n* Iglu *der* OR *das.*

**ignite** [ɪg'naɪt] *vt* entzünden; AUT zünden ◇ *vi*
sich entzünden; AUT zünden.

**ignition** [ɪg'nɪʃn] *n* **- 1.** [act of igniting] Entzünden *das* **- 2.** [in car] Zündung *die.*

**ignition key** *n* Zündschlüssel *der.*

**ignoble** [ɪg'nəubl] *adj fml* [person] niederträchtig; [thought, action] schändlich.

**ignominious** [,ɪgnə'mɪnɪəs] *adj fml* schmach-
voll.

**ignominy** ['ɪgnəmɪnɪ] *n* (*U*) *fml* Schmach *die.*

**ignoramus** [,ɪgnə'reɪməs] (*pl* **-es**) *n* Ignorant
*der*, -in *die.*

**ignorance** ['ɪgnərəns] *n* Unwissenheit *die;* [of
particular subject, information *etc*] Unkenntnis *die.*

**ignorant** [ˈɪgnərənt] *adj* - **1.** [uneducated] ungebildet; [lacking information] unwissend; **I'm ~
about politics** ich weiß nichts über Politik
- **2.** *fml* [unaware]: **to be ~ of sthg** von etw nichts
wissen - **3.** *inf* [rude] ungehobelt.

**ignore** [ɪgˈnɔːˈ] *vt* ignorieren.

**iguana** [ɪˈgwɑːnə] (*pl inv OR* -**s**) *n* Leguan *der*.

**ikon** [ˈaɪkɒn] *n* = **icon**.

**IL** *abk für Illinois, in Postanschrift verwendet.*

**ilk** [ɪlk] *n:* **people of that ~** solche Leute; **and
others of that ~** und seines-/ihresgleichen.

**ill** [ɪl] *adj* - **1.** [sick] krank; **to feel ~** sich unwohl
*OR* krank fühlen; **to be taken ~, to fall ~** krank
werden - **2.** [bad - omen, treatment] schlecht;
[ - effects] nachteilig; **~ luck** Pech *das;* **~ at ease**
unbehaglich ⟨⟩ *adv* schlecht; **to speak/think
~ of sb** schlecht über jn reden/denken.
➡ **ills** *npl* Missstände *pl.*

**ill.** (*abbr of* **illustration**) Abb.

**I'll** [aɪl] = **I will, I shall.**

**ill-advised** [-əd'vaɪzd] *adj* unklug; **they would
be ~ to do this** sie wären schlecht beraten,
wenn sie dies täten.

**ill-bred** [-'bred] *adj* ungezogen.

**ill-considered** [-kən'sɪdəd] *adj* unüberlegt.

**ill-disposed** [-dɪ'spəʊzd] *adj:* **to be ~ towards
sb** jm übel gesinnt sein.

**illegal** [ɪ'liːgl] *adj* [action] gesetzwidrig; [organ-
ization] illegal; **it is ~ to drive without a licence** es
ist verboten, ohne Führerschein Auto zu
fahren; **an ~ immigrant** ein illegaler Einwanderer, eine illegale Einwanderin.

**illegally** [ɪ'liːgəlɪ] *adv* [park, enter] unerlaubt;
[act] gesetzwidrig; [enter a country] illegal.

**illegible** [ɪ'ledʒəbl] *adj* unleserlich.

**illegitimate** [ˌɪlɪ'dʒɪtɪmət] *adj* - **1.** [child] unehelich - **2.** [activity] unzulässig, unrechtmäßig.

**ill-equipped** [-ɪ'kwɪpt] *adj:* **to be ~ to do sthg**
[unsuited] nicht dafür geeignet sein, etw zu
tun.

**ill-fated** [-'feɪtɪd] *adj* unglückselig.

**ill feeling** *n* Feindseligkeit *die.*

**ill-founded** [-'faʊndɪd] *adj* unbegründet.

**ill health** *n* schwache Gesundheit.

**illicit** [ɪ'lɪsɪt] *adj* illegal.

**illicitly** [ɪ'lɪsɪtlɪ] *adv* illegal.

**ill-informed** *adj* [person] schlecht informiert.

**illiteracy** [ɪ'lɪtərəsɪ] *n* Analphabetentum *das.*

**illiterate** [ɪ'lɪtərət] *adj* - **1.** [unable to read] des
Lesens und Schreibens unkundig; **to be ~**
Analphabet, -in sein - **2.** [uneducated] unge-
bildet ⟨⟩ *n* Analphabet *der*, -in *die.*

**ill-mannered** *adj* [impolite] unhöflich; [rude]
ungehobelt.

**illness** [ˈɪlnɪs] *n* Krankheit *die.*

**illogical** [ɪ'lɒdʒɪkl] *adj* unlogisch.

**ill-suited** *adj* nicht zusammenpassend; **to
be ~ to sthg** für etw ungeeignet sein.

**ill-tempered** *adj* [by nature] griesgrämig; [on
particular occasion] schlecht gelaunt.

**ill-treat** *vt* misshandeln; [worker] schlecht
behandeln.

**ill-treatment** *n* Misshandlung *die;* [of
workers] schlechte Behandlung.

**illuminate** [ɪ'luːmɪneɪt] *vt* - **1.** [light up] beleuchten - **2.** [problem, subject] erhellen.

**illuminated** [ɪ'luːmɪneɪtɪd] *adj* - **1.** [sign, notice]
beleuchtet - **2.** [book, manuscript] illuminiert.

**illuminating** [ɪ'luːmɪneɪtɪŋ] *adj* [book] instruktiv; [talk, experience] aufschlussreich.

**illumination** [ɪˌluːmɪ'neɪʃn] *n* [lighting] Beleuchtung *die.*
➡ **illuminations** *npl Br* festliche Beleuchtung.

**illusion** [ɪ'luːʒn] *n* Illusion *die;* **to have no ~s
about sb/sthg** sich über jm/etw keine Illusionen machen; **to be under the ~ that** sich
einbilden, dass; **optical ~** optische Täuschung.

**illusionist** [ɪ'luːʒənɪst] *n fml* Illusionist *der.*

**illusory** [ɪ'luːsərɪ] *adj fml* illusionär.

**illustrate** [ˈɪləstreɪt] *vt* illustrieren.

**illustration** [ˌɪlə'streɪʃn] *n* - **1.** [picture] Illustration *die*, Abbildung *die* - **2.** [example] Beispiel *das.*

**illustrator** [ˈɪləstreɪtəʳ] *n* Illustrator *der*, -in
*die.*

**illustrious** [ɪ'lʌstrɪəs] *adj fml* berühmt; [career]
glanzvoll.

**ill will** *n* böses Blut; **he didn't bear anyone any
~** er war niemandem feindlich gesinnt.

**ill wind** *n:* **it's an ~ (that blows nobody any
good)** *proverb* so hat alles auch seine guten
Seiten.

**ILO** (*abbr of* **International Labour Organization**) *n* IAA *das*, *Internationales Arbeitsamt.*

**I'm** [aɪm] = **I am.**

**image** [ˈɪmɪdʒ] *n* - **1.** [gen] Bild *das;* [in mirror]
Spiegelbild *das* - **2.** [in mind] Vorstellung *die*
- **3.** [of company, public figure] Image *das* - **4.** [like-
ness]: **to be the ~ of sb** js Ebenbild sein.

**imagery** [ˈɪmɪdʒrɪ] *n* [in writing] Metaphorik
*die;* [in visual arts] Bildersymbolik *die.*

**imaginable** [ɪ'mædʒɪnəbl] *adj* denkbar.

**imaginary** [ɪ'mædʒɪnrɪ] *adj* imaginär.

**imagination** [ɪˌmædʒɪ'neɪʃn] *n* - **1.** [ability, fantasy] Fantasie *die* - **2.** [mind] Einbildung *die; it's all in her ~* das bildet sie sich nur ein.

**imaginative** [ɪˈmædʒɪnətɪv] *adj* fantasievoll; [concerning new ideas] einfallsreich.

**imagine** [ɪˈmædʒɪn] *vt* - **1.** [visualize] sich (D) vorstellen, sich (D) denken; *to ~ doing sthg* sich (D) vorstellen, etw zu tun; *~ (that)!* stell dir das mal vor! - **2.** [dream] sich (D) einbilden; *you ~d it* du hast es dir (nur) eingebildet - **3.** [suppose] an|nehmen, vermuten.

**imbalance** [ˌɪmˈbæləns] *n* Ungleichgewicht *das*.

**imbecile** [ˈɪmbɪsiːl] *n* Idiot *der*, Schwachkopf *der*.

**imbue** [ɪmˈbjuː] *vt fml: to be ~d with sthg* von etw durchdrungen sein.

**IMF** (*abbr of* **International Monetary Fund**) *n* IWF *der*.

**imitate** [ˈɪmɪteɪt] *vt* nachlahmen, imitieren.

**imitation** [ˌɪmɪˈteɪʃn] *n* - **1.** [gen] Nachahmung *die*, Imitation *die* - **2.** [copy] Kopie *die* <> *adj* unecht, imitiert; *~ leather* Kunstleder *das*.

**imitator** [ˈɪmɪteɪtəʳ] *n* Nachahmer *der*, -in *die*.

**immaculate** [ɪˈmækjʊlət] *adj* - **1.** [clean and tidy] makellos - **2.** [behaviour] tadellos; [timing] perfekt.

**immaculately** [ɪˈmækjʊlətlɪ] *adv* - **1.** [cleanly, tidily] makellos - **2.** [behave] tadellos; [timed] perfekt.

**immaterial** [ˌɪməˈtɪərɪəl] *adj* [irrelevant] unwichtig.

**immature** [ˌɪməˈtjʊəʳ] *adj* - **1.** [person, behaviour] unreif; *don't be so ~!* sei nicht so kindisch! - **2.** BOT & ZOOL noch nicht voll entwickelt.

**immaturity** [ˌɪməˈtjʊərətɪ] *n* Unreife *die*.

**immeasurable** [ɪˈmeʒrəbl] *adj* unermesslich.

**immediacy** [ɪˈmiːdjəsɪ] *n* Unmittelbarkeit *die*; [of need, problem] Dringlichkeit *die*.

**immediate** [ɪˈmiːdjət] *adj* - **1.** [response, attention] unverzüglich; [need, problem] dringend; *to take ~ action* sofort OR unverzüglich handeln - **2.** [future, neighbourhood] unmittelbar; *in the ~ aftermath of the riots* unmittelbar nach den Krawallen; *the ~ area* das Gebiet in unmittelbarer Nähe; *the ~ family* die engste Familie.

**immediately** [ɪˈmiːdjətlɪ] *adv* - **1.** [at once] sofort - **2.** [directly] unmittelbar, direkt <> *conj* [as soon as] sobald.

**immemorial** [ˌɪmɪˈmɔːrɪəl] *adj: from time ~* seit undenklichen Zeiten.

**immense** [ɪˈmens] *adj* enorm.

**immensely** [ɪˈmenslɪ] *adv* ungemein.

**immensity** [ɪˈmensətɪ] *n* Unermesslichkeit *die*.

**immerse** [ɪˈmɜːs] *vt* - **1.** [in liquid]: *to ~ sthg in sthg* etw in etw (A) eintauchen - **2.** *fig* [involve]: *to ~ o.s. in sthg* sich in etw (A) stürzen.

**immersion heater** [ɪˈmɜːʃn-] *n* Heißwasserbereiter *der*.

**immigrant** [ˈɪmɪgrənt] *n* Einwanderer *der*, -derin *die* <> *comp: ~ children* Kinder von Einwanderern.

**immigration** [ˌɪmɪˈgreɪʃn] *n* Einwanderung *die*.

**imminent** [ˈɪmɪnənt] *adj* [danger] drohend; [death, disaster] unmittelbar bevorstehend.

**immobile** [ɪˈməʊbaɪl] *adj* unbeweglich.

**immobilize, -ise** [ɪˈməʊbɪlaɪz] *vt* [machine, lift] lahm legen; [vehicle] gegen Wegfahren sichern.

**immobilizer, -iser** [ɪˈməʊbɪlaɪzəʳ] *n* AUT Wegfahrsperre *die*.

**immodest** [ɪˈmɒdɪst] *adj* - **1.** [vain] unbescheiden - **2.** [indecent] unanständig.

**immoral** [ɪˈmɒrəl] *adj* unmoralisch.

**immorality** [ˌɪməˈrælətɪ] *n* Unmoral *die*.

**immortal** [ɪˈmɔːtl] *adj* unsterblich <> *n* Unsterbliche *der*, *die*.

**immortality** [ˌɪmɔːˈtælətɪ] *n* Unsterblichkeit *die*.

**immortalize, -ise** [ɪˈmɔːtəlaɪz] *vt* unsterblich machen.

**immovable** [ɪˈmuːvəbl] *adj* - **1.** [fixed] unbeweglich - **2.** [obstinate] unnachgiebig.

**immune** [ɪˈmjuːn] *adj* - **1.** MED: *~ (to)* immun (gegen) - **2.** *fig: to ~ to criticism* gegen Kritik unempfindlich sein; *to be ~ from prosecution* vor Strafverfolgung geschützt sein.

**immune system** *n* Immunsystem *das*.

**immunity** [ɪˈmjuːnətɪ] *n* - **1.** MED: *~ (to)* Immunität *die* (gegen) - **2.** *fig: ~ to criticism* Unempfindlichkeit *die* gegen Kritik; *~ from prosecution* Schutz *der* vor Strafverfolgung.

**immunization** [ˌɪmjuːnaɪˈzeɪʃn] *n* MED Immunisierung *die*.

**immunize, -ise** [ˈɪmjuːnaɪz] *vt: to ~ sb (against)* MED jn immunisieren (gegen).

**immunology** [ˌɪmjuːˈnɒlədʒɪ] *n* Immunologie *die*.

**imp** [ɪmp] *n* - **1.** [creature] Kobold *der* - **2.** [naughty child] Racker *der*.

**impact** [*n* ˈɪmpækt, *vb* ɪmˈpækt] *n* - **1.** [force of contact] Aufprall *der*; [of two moving objects] Zusammenprall *der* - **2.** [effect] Auswirkung *die*; *to make an ~ on sb* Eindruck auf jn machen; *to make an ~ on sthg* einen Einfluss auf etw (A) haben <> *vt* - **1.** [collide with] auf|prallen auf (+ A) - **2.** [influence] sich aus|wirken auf (+ A).

**impair** [ɪm'peəʳ] *vt* beeinträchtigen.

**impale** [ɪm'peɪl] *vt* auf lspießen.

**impart** [ɪm'pɑːt] *vt fml* - **1.** [knowledge, skills]: **to ~ sthg to sb** jm etw vermitteln - **2.** [feeling, quality]: **to ~ sthg to sthg** etw *(D)* etw verleihen.

**impartial** [ɪm'pɑːʃl] *adj* [person] unparteiisch; [news report] objektiv.

**impartiality** [ɪm,pɑːʃɪ'ælətɪ] *n* [of person] Unparteilichkeit *die;* [of news report] Objektivität *die.*

**impassable** [ɪm'pɑːsəbl] *adj* unpassierbar.

**impasse** [æm'pɑːs] *n* Sackgasse *die;* **to reach an ~** in eine Sackgasse geraten.

**impassioned** [ɪm'pæʃnd] *adj* leidenschaftlich.

**impassive** [ɪm'pæsɪv] *adj* unbewegt.

**impatience** [ɪm'peɪʃns] *n* Ungeduld *die.*

**impatient** [ɪm'peɪʃnt] *adj* ungeduldig; **to be ~ to do sthg** es nicht erwarten können, etw zu tun.

**impatiently** [ɪm'peɪʃntlɪ] *adv* ungeduldig.

**impeach** [ɪm'piːtʃ] *vt* LAW des Amtsmissbrauchs anlklagen.

**impeachment** [ɪm'piːtʃmənt] *n (U)* LAW Anklage *die* wegen Amtsmissbrauchs, Impeachment *das.*

**impeccable** [ɪm'pekəbl] *adj* untadelig.

**impeccably** [ɪm'pekəblɪ] *adv* tadellos.

**impede** [ɪm'piːd] *vt* [person] hindern; [progress, activity] behindern.

**impediment** [ɪm'pedɪmənt] *n* - **1.** [obstacle] Hindernis *das* - **2.** [disability] Behinderung *die.*

**impel** [ɪm'pel] (*pt* & *pp* -**led**; *cont* -**ling**) *vt*: **to ~ sb to do sthg** jn (dazu) nötigen, etw zu tun.

**impending** [ɪm'pendɪŋ] *adj* [doom, disaster] drohend; [interview, test] bevorstehend.

**impenetrable** [ɪm'penɪtrəbl] *adj* - **1.** [forest] undurchdringlich - **2.** [text] unverständlich.

**imperative** [ɪm'perətɪv] *adj* dringend notwendig ◇ *n* - **1.** [necessity] dringende Notwendigkeit - **2.** GRAMM Imperativ *der.*

**imperceptible** [,ɪmpə'septəbl] *adj* unmerklich.

**imperfect** [ɪm'pɜːfɪkt] *adj* [work, copy] fehlerhaft; [knowledge] mangelhaft ◇ *n* GRAMM: **~ (tense)** Imperfekt *das.*

**imperfection** [,ɪmpə'fekʃn] *n* - **1.** [state] Unvollkommenheit *die* - **2.** [fault] Makel *der.*

**imperial** [ɪm'pɪərɪəl] *adj* - **1.** [of an empire] imperial; [of an emperor] kaiserlich - **2.** [measurement] britisch.

**imperialism** [ɪm'pɪərɪəlɪzm] *n* Imperialismus *der.*

**imperialist** [ɪm'pɪərɪəlɪst] *adj* imperialistisch.

**imperil** [ɪm'perɪl] (*Br pt* & *pp* -**led**; *cont* -**ling**, *Am pt* & *pp* -**ed**; *cont* -**ing**) *vt fml* gefährden.

**imperious** [ɪm'pɪərɪəs] *adj* gebieterisch.

**impersonal** [ɪm'pɜːsnl] *adj* - **1.** [unemotional] unpersönlich - **2.** GRAMM: **~ verb** unpersönlich gebrauchtes Verb.

**impersonate** [ɪm'pɜːsəneɪt] *vt* - **1.** [mimic] imitieren, nachlahmen - **2.** [pretend to be] sich auslgeben als.

**impersonation** [ɪm,pɜːsə'neɪʃn] *n* [by mimic] Imitation *die*, Nachahmung *die;* **to do ~s of sb** jn imitieren OR nachlahmen.

**impersonator** [ɪm'pɜːsəneɪtəʳ] *n* [mimic] Imitator *der*, -in *die.*

**impertinence** [ɪm'pɜːtɪnəns] *n* Unverschämtheit *die.*

**impertinent** [ɪm'pɜːtɪnənt] *adj* unverschämt.

**imperturbable** [,ɪmpə'tɜːbəbl] *adj* unerschütterlich.

**impervious** [ɪm'pɜːvɪəs] *adj*: **to be ~ to charm** für Charme unempfänglich sein; **to be ~ to criticism** von Kritik unberührt sein.

**impetuous** [ɪm'petʃʊəs] *adj* impulsiv.

**impetus** ['ɪmpɪtəs] *n* - **1.** *(U)* [momentum] Schwung *der* - **2.** [stimulus] Impuls *der.*

**impinge** [ɪm'pɪndʒ] *vi*: **to ~ on sb/sthg** sich auf jn/etw auslwirken.

**impish** ['ɪmpɪʃ] *adj* [behaviour] spitzbübisch; [grin] verschmitzt.

**implacable** [ɪm'plækəbl] *adj* unerbittlich.

**implant** [*n* 'ɪmplɑːnt, *vb* ɪm'plɑːnt] *n* Implantat *das* ◇ *vt* - **1.** [instil]: **to ~ sthg in sb** jm etw einlimpfen - **2.** MED: **to ~ sthg in(to) sb** jm etw implantieren.

**implausible** [ɪm'plɔːzəbl] *adj* [story] unglaubwürdig.

**implement** [*n* 'ɪmplɪmənt, *vb* 'ɪmplɪment] *n* [tool] Werkzeug *das;* [piece of equipment] Gerät *das* ◇ *vt* [plan] auslführen; [law] vollziehen; [policy] in die Praxis umlsetzen.

**implementation** [,ɪmplɪmen'teɪʃn] *n* [of policy] Umsetzung *die* in die Praxis; [of law] Vollzug *der.*

**implicate** ['ɪmplɪkeɪt] *vt*: **to ~ sb in sthg** jn in etw *(A)* verwickeln.

**implication** [,ɪmplɪ'keɪʃn] *n* - **1.** *(U)* [involvement] Verwicklung *die* - **2.** [inference] Auswirkung *die;* **by ~** implizit.

**implicit** [ɪm'plɪsɪt] *adj* - **1.** [inferred] implizit; [acknowledgement] stillschweigend; [criticism] unausgesprochen - **2.** [inherent]: **to be ~ in sthg** durch etw impliziert werden - **3.** [faith, belief] blind.

**implicitly** [ɪm'plɪsɪtlɪ] *adv* - **1.** [by inference] implizit; [condone] stillschweigend; [criticize] unausgesprochen - **2.** [believe] absolut; [trust] blind.

**implied** [ɪm'plaɪd] *adj* [criticism] unausgesprochen; [threat] indirekt.

**implode** [ɪm'pləʊd] *vi* implodieren.

**implore** [ɪm'plɔːr] *vt*: **to ~ sb (to do sthg)** jn inständig bitten(, etw zu tun).

**imply** [ɪm'plaɪ] (*pt* & *pp* -**ied**) *vt* - **1.** [suggest]: **I'm not ~ing that ...** ich will damit nicht sagen, dass ...; **what are you ~ing?** was wollen Sie damit sagen?; **his words ~ no criticism** seine Worte sind nicht als Kritik gemeint - **2.** [responsibility] mit einlschließen.

**impolite** [ˌɪmpə'laɪt] *adj* unhöflich.

**import** [*n* 'ɪmpɔːt, *vb* ɪm'pɔːt] *n* - **1.** [product] Importware *die* - **2.** (*U*) [act of importing] Import *der*, Einfuhr *die* - **3.** *fml* [meaning] Bedeutung *die* - **4.** (*U*) *fml* [importance] Wichtigkeit *die* ◇ *comp* Einfuhr-, Import- ◇ *vt* - **1.** [goods] importieren, einlführen - **2.** COMPUT importieren.

**importance** [ɪm'pɔːtns] *n* (*U*) Wichtigkeit *die;* [significance] Bedeutung *die*.

**important** [ɪm'pɔːtnt] *adj* wichtig; [significant] bedeutend; [person] einflussreich; **to be ~ to sb** für jn wichtig sein.

**importantly** [ɪm'pɔːtntlɪ] *adv*: **more ~** was noch wichtiger ist.

**importation** [ˌɪmpɔː'teɪʃn] *n* Import *der*, Einfuhr *die*.

**imported** [ɪm'pɔːtɪd] *adj* [goods] importiert, eingeführt.

**importer** [ɪm'pɔːtər] *n* [person, firm] Importeur *der;* [country] Importland *das*.

**impose** [ɪm'pəʊz] *vt*: **to ~ sthg (on sb/sthg)** (jm/ etw) etw auf lerlegen; **to ~ a tax on sb** jn besteuern; **to ~ one's beliefs on sb** jm seine Überzeugungen auf lzwingen ◇ *vi*: **to ~ (on sb)** (jm) zur Last fallen.

**imposing** [ɪm'pəʊzɪŋ] *adj* beeindruckend.

**imposition** [ˌɪmpə'zɪʃn] *n* - **1.** [enforcement - gen] Auferlegung *die;* [ - of tax] Erhebung *die;* [ - of opinions, beliefs] Aufzwingen *das* - **2.** [burden] Zumutung *die*.

**impossibility** [ɪmˌpɒsə'bɪlətɪ] (*pl* -**ies**) *n* Unmöglichkeit *die*.

**impossible** [ɪm'pɒsəbl] *adj* unmöglich ◇ *n*: **to do the ~** [in general] Unmögliches tun; [in a specific case] das Unmögliche tun.

**impostor, imposter** *Am* [ɪm'pɒstər] *n* Hochstapler *der*, -in *die*.

**impotence** ['ɪmpətəns] *n* - **1.** [sexual] Impotenz *die* - **2.** [lack of power] Machtlosigkeit *die*.

**impotent** ['ɪmpətənt] *adj* - **1.** [sexually] impotent - **2.** [powerless] machtlos.

**impound** [ɪm'paʊnd] *vt* beschlagnahmen.

**impoverished** [ɪm'pɒvərɪʃt] *adj lit* & *fig* verarmt.

**impracticable** [ɪm'præktɪkəbl] *adj* [idea] undurchführbar.

**impractical** [ɪm'præktɪkl] *adj* praxisfern.

**imprecation** [ˌɪmprɪ'keɪʃn] *n fml* Verwünschung *die*.

**imprecise** [ɪmprɪ'saɪs] *adj* ungenau, unpräzise.

**impregnable** [ɪm'pregnəbl] *adj* [fortress, defences] uneinnehmbar; *fig* [person] unangreifbar; [position, argument] unanfechtbar.

**impregnate** ['ɪmpregneɪt] *vt* - **1.** [saturate]: **to ~ sthg with sthg** etw mit etw tränken; [to protect material] etw mit etw imprägnieren - **2.** *fml* [fertilize] befruchten.

**impresario** [ˌɪmprɪ'sɑːrɪəʊ] (*pl* -**s**) *n* Impresario *der*.

**impress** [ɪm'pres] *vt* - **1.** [make impression on] beeindrucken; [deliberately] imponieren (+ *D*); **to be favourably/unfavourably ~ed** einen guten/ schlechten Eindruck haben - **2.** [make clear]: **to ~ sthg on sb** jm etw einlschärfen ◇ *vi* Eindruck machen.

**impression** [ɪm'preʃn] *n* - **1.** [gen] Eindruck *der;* **to make an ~** Eindruck machen; **to give sb the ~ that ...** jm den Eindruck vermitteln, dass ...; **to be under the ~ (that)** ... den Eindruck haben, dass ... - **2.** [impersonation] Nachahmung *die*, Imitation *die;* **to do an ~ of sb** jn imitieren OR nachlahmen - **3.** [of book] Nachdruck *der*.

**impressionable** [ɪm'preʃnəbl] *adj* leicht zu beeindrucken; **to be at an ~ age** in einem Alter sein, in dem man leicht zu beeinflussen ist.

**Impressionism** [ɪm'preʃənɪzml] *n* Impressionismus *der*.

**impressionist** [ɪm'preʃənɪst] *n* [entertainer] Imitator *der*, -in *die*.

**impressive** [ɪm'presɪv] *adj* beeindruckend.

**imprint** [*n* 'ɪmprɪnt, *vb* ɪm'prɪnt] *n* - **1.** [mark] Abdruck *der* - **2.** [publisher's name] Impressum *das* ◇ *vt* [mark] prägen; [on paper] auf ldrucken; **it's ~ed on my mind** *fig* es hat sich unauslöschlich in mein Gedächtnis eingeprägt.

**imprison** [ɪm'prɪzn] *vt* inhaftieren, in Haft nehmen.

**imprisonment** [ɪm'prɪznmənt] *n* (*U*) Haft *die;* **to sentence sb to seven years' ~** jn zu sieben Jahren Freiheitsstrafe OR Gefängnis verurteilen.

**improbable** [ɪm'prɒbəbl] *adj* - **1.** [unlikely] unwahrscheinlich - **2.** [strange] komisch.

**impromptu** [ɪm'prɒmptjuː] *adj* improvisiert.

**improper** [ɪm'prɒpər] *adj* - **1.** [unsuitable - treatment] unangebracht; [ - behaviour] unpassend

- **2.** [dishonest - actions] unehrenhaft; [ - dealings] unlauter - **3.** [rude] unanständig.

**impropriety** [ˌɪmprəˈpraɪətɪ] n - **1.** [unsuitable behaviour] unpassendes Verhalten - **2.** [dishonest behaviour] Unredlichkeit die - **3.** [rude behaviour] Unanständigkeit die.

**improve** [ɪmˈpruːv] vi [weather, work, student] besser werden; [delinquent, health] sich bessern; [productivity] sich steigern; **to ~ (up)on** übertreffen; [offer] überbieten ◇ vt - **1.** [make better] verbessern - **2.** [increase - vocabulary, knowledge] erweitern; [ - productivity] erhöhen, steigern - **3.** [cultivate]: **to ~ one's mind** sich (weiter!)bilden; **to ~ o.s.** an sich (D) arbeiten.

**improved** [ɪmˈpruːvd] adj verbessert.

**improvement** [ɪmˈpruːvmənt] n Verbesserung die; [in health, sb's behaviour, weather] Besserung die; [in productivity, sports] Steigerung die; **there has been no ~ in the patient's condition** der Zustand des Patienten hat sich nicht gebessert; **we've made some ~s to the house** wir haben einige Renovierungsarbeiten am Haus durchgeführt.

**improvisation** [ˌɪmprəvaɪˈzeɪʃn] n Improvisation die.

**improvise** [ˈɪmprəvaɪz] vt improvisieren; [shelter] notdürftig erstellen ◇ vi improvisieren.

**imprudent** [ɪmˈpruːdənt] adj unklug.

**impudence** [ˈɪmpjʊdəns] n Unverschämtheit die.

**impudent** [ˈɪmpjʊdənt] adj unverschämt.

**impugn** [ɪmˈpjuːn] vt fml in Zweifel ziehen.

**impulse** [ˈɪmpʌls] n Impuls der; **to do sthg on ~** etw aus einem Impuls heraus tun.

**impulse buying** [-ˌbaɪɪŋ] n (U) Spontankäufe pl.

**impulsive** [ɪmˈpʌlsɪv] adj impulsiv.

**impunity** [ɪmˈpjuːnətɪ] n: **with ~** ungestraft.

**impure** [ɪmˈpjʊəʳ] adj - **1.** [not clean] unrein - **2.** [sinful - thoughts, acts] unsittlich; [ - person] verdorben.

**impurity** [ɪmˈpjʊərətɪ] (pl -ies) n Unreinheit die.

**in** [ɪn] prep - **1.** [indicating place, position] in (+ D); (with verbs of motion) in (+ A); **it's ~ the box/garden** es ist in der Schachtel/im Garten; **put it ~ the box/garden** leg es in die Schachtel/in den Garten; **~ the street/world** auf der Straße/Welt; **~ the country** auf dem Lande; **~ the sky** am Himmel; **~ Paris/Belgium** in Paris/Belgien; **to be ~ hospital/prison** im Krankenhaus/Gefängnis sein; **~ here/there** hier/dort drinnen - **2.** [wearing] in (+ D); **she was still ~ her nightclothes** sie war noch im Nachthemd; **(dressed) ~ red** rot gekleidet; **the man ~ the top hat** der Mann mit dem Zylinder - **3.** [appearing in, included in] in (+ D);

there's a mistake **~ this paragraph** in diesem Abschnitt ist ein Fehler; **who's ~ the play?** wer spielt in dem Stück? - **4.** [at a particular time, during] in (+ D); **~ April** im April; **she was born ~ 1999** sie wurde 1999 geboren; **~ (the) spring/winter** im Frühling/Winter; **~ the afternoon/morning** am Nachmittag/Morgen; **ten o'clock ~ the morning** zehn Uhr morgens; **~ the future** in Zukunft - **5.** [within, after] in (+ D); **he learned to type ~ two weeks** lernte in zwei Wochen Maschine schreiben; **it'll be ready ~ an hour** es ist in einer Stunde fertig - **6.** [expressing time passed] seit; **it's my first decent meal ~ weeks** das ist meine erste anständige Mahlzeit seit Wochen - **7.** [indicating situation, circumstances]: **~ the sun/rain** in der Sonne/im Regen; **you shouldn't drive ~ this fog** sie sollten bei diesem Nebel nicht fahren; **~ ruins** in Trümmern; **to be ~ pain** Schmerzen haben; **~ danger/difficulty** in Gefahr/Schwierigkeiten; **to live/die ~ poverty** in Armut leben/sterben; **~ these circumstances** unter diesen Umständen - **8.** [indicating manner]: **to write ~ ink** mit Tinte schreiben; **~ a soft voice** mit sanfter Stimme; **they were talking ~ English** sie sprachen Englisch; **~ writing** schriftlich - **9.** [indicating emotional state]: **~ anger/delight/amazement/despair** wütend/entzückt/erstaunt/verzweifelt; **~ my excitement** in meiner Aufregung - **10.** [specifying area of activity]: **advances ~ medicine** Fortschritte in der Medizin; **he's ~ computers** er ist in der Computerbranche - **11.** [referring to quantity]: **to buy sthg ~ large/small quantities** etw in großen/kleinen Mengen kaufen; **~ (their) thousands** zu Tausenden - **12.** [referring to age]: **she's ~ her twenties** sie ist in den Zwanzigern - **13.** [describing arrangement] in (+ D); **~ a circle/line** im Kreis/in einer Reihe; **to stand ~ twos** zu zweit dastehen - **14.** [indicating colour] in (+ D); **it comes ~ green or blue** es gibt es in grün oder blau - **15.** [as regards]: **a rise ~ prices** ein Preisanstieg; **to be 3 metres ~ length** 3 Meter lang sein; **a change ~ direction** ein Richtungswechsel - **16.** [in ratios]: **one ~ ten** jeder Zehnte; **an increase of five pence ~ the pound** eine Preiserhöhung von fünf Prozent - **17.** (after superl) in (+ D); **the best ~ the world** der/die/das Beste in der Welt - **18.** (+ present participle): **she made a mistake ~ accepting the offer** sie machte einen Fehler, indem sie das Angebot annahm ◇ adv - **1.** [inside] herein/hinein; **come ~!** herein!; **you can go ~ now** du kannst jetzt hineingehen; **put the clothes ~** leg die Kleider hinein - **2.** [at home, work] da; **is Judith ~?** ist Judith da?; **to stay ~** zu Hause bleiben - **3.** [of train, boat, plane]: **to get ~** ankommen; **the train isn't ~ yet** der Zug ist noch nicht angekommen - **4.** [in shop]: **is my new TV ~ yet?** ist mein neuer Fernseher schon da? - **5.** [of tide]: **the tide is ~** es ist Flut

**- 6.** *phr:* you're ~ for a surprise du wirst eine Überraschung erleben; he's ~ for it *inf* der kann sich auf etwas gefasst machen; to be ~ on sthg an etw *(D)* beteiligt sein; my luck is ~ das Glück ist auf meiner Seite ◇ *adj inf* in; short skirts are ~ this year kurze Röcke sind dieses Jahr in.

➧ **ins** *npl:* she knows the ~s and outs of the matter sie ist mit allen Feinheiten der Sache vertraut.

➧ **in that** *conj* insofern als.

**in.** *abbr of* **inch.**

**IN** *abk für* Indiana, *in Postanschrift verwendet.*

**inability** [ˌɪnə'bɪlətɪ] *n* Unfähigkeit *die;* his ~ to sympathize seine Unfähigkeit, Mitleid zu empfinden.

**inaccessible** [ˌɪnək'sesəbl] *adj* **- 1.** [place] unzugänglich **- 2.** [book, film, music] schwer verständlich.

**inaccuracy** [ɪn'ækjʊrəsɪ] *(pl* -ies) *n* Ungenauigkeit *die.*

**inaccurate** [ɪn'ækjʊrət] *adj* [imprecise] ungenau; [incorrect] inkorrekt.

**inaction** [ɪn'ækʃn] *n* Untätigkeit *die.*

**inactive** [ɪn'æktɪv] *adj* inaktiv; [person] untätig.

**inactivity** [ˌɪnæk'tɪvətɪ] *n* Untätigkeit *die.*

**inadequacy** [ɪn'ædɪkwəsɪ] *(pl* -ies) *n* **- 1.** [insufficiency] Unzulänglichkeit *die* **- 2.** [weakness] Schwäche *die.*

**inadequate** [ɪn'ædɪkwət] *adj* unzureichend; to feel ~ sich der Situation nicht gewachsen fühlen.

**inadmissible** [ˌɪnəd'mɪsəbl] *adj* unzulässig.

**inadvertent** [ˌɪnəd'vɜːtnt] *adj* [mistake] unbeabsichtigt; [discovery] zufällig.

**inadvertently** [ˌɪnəd'vɜːtəntlɪ] *adv* [forget, break] aus Versehen; [discover] zufällig.

**inadvisable** [ˌɪnəd'vaɪzəbl] *adj* nicht ratsam.

**inalienable** [ɪn'eɪljənəbl] *adj fml* unveräußerlich.

**inane** [ɪ'neɪn] *adj* dumm.

**inanely** [ɪ'neɪnlɪ] *adv* dumm.

**inanimate** [ɪn'ænɪmət] *adj* leblos.

**inanity** [ɪ'nænətɪ] *n* Dummheit *die.*

**inapplicable** [ɪnə'plɪkəbl] *adj* [rule] nicht anwendbar; [question] unzutreffend.

**inappropriate** [ˌɪnə'prəʊprɪət] *adj* unpassend.

**inarticulate** [ˌɪnɑː'tɪkjʊlət] *adj* **- 1.** [person]: to be ~ sich nicht gut ausdrücken können **- 2.** [words, sounds] inartikuliert.

**inasmuch** [ˌɪnəz'mʌtʃ] ➧ **inasmuch as** *conj fml* [because] da; [to the extent that] insofern als.

**inattention** [ˌɪnə'tenʃn] *n* Unaufmerksamkeit *die.*

**inattentive** [ˌɪnə'tentɪv] *adj* unaufmerksam.

**inaudible** [ɪ'nɔːdɪbl] *adj* unhörbar.

**inaugural** [ɪ'nɔːgjʊrəl] *adj* [meeting] Eröffnungs-; [speech] Antritts-.

**inaugurate** [ɪ'nɔːgjʊreɪt] *vt* **- 1.** [leader, president] in sein/ihr Amt einlführen **- 2.** [building] einlweihen; [system] einlführen.

**inauguration** [ɪˌnɔːgjʊ'reɪʃn] *n* **- 1.** [of leader, president] Amtseinführung *die* **- 2.** [of building] Einweihung *die;* [of system] Einführung *die.*

**inauspicious** [ˌɪnɔː'spɪʃəs] *adj* Unheil verkündend; the meeting got off to an ~ start schon der Beginn des Treffens verhieß nichts Gutes.

**inboard motor** [ˌɪnbɔːd-] *n* Innenbordmotor *der.*

**inborn** [ˌɪn'bɔːn] *adj* angeboren.

**inbound** ['ɪnbaʊnd] *adj* ankommend.

**inbred** [ˌɪn'bred] *adj* **- 1.** [family]: an ~ family eine Familie, in der Inzucht herrscht **- 2.** [characteristic, quality] angeboren.

**inbreeding** ['ɪnˌbriːdɪŋ] *n* Inzucht *die.*

**inbuilt** [ˌɪn'bɪlt] *adj* **- 1.** [device] integriert **- 2.** [quality, defect] angeboren.

**inc.** *(abbr of* **inclusive)** inkl.

**Inc.** [ɪŋk] *abbr of* **incorporated.**

**Inca** ['ɪŋkə] *n* Inka *der.*

**incalculable** [ɪn'kælkjʊləbl] *adj* [very great] unabsehbar

**incandescent** [ˌɪnkæn'desnt] *adj:* ~ with rage vor Wut schäumend.

**incantation** [ˌɪnkæn'teɪʃn] *n* Zauberspruch *der.*

**incapable** [ɪn'keɪpəbl] *adj* **- 1.** [unable]: to be ~ of sthg zu etw nicht fähig sein; to be ~ of doing sthg nicht fähig sein, etw zu tun **- 2.** [incompetent] unfähig.

**incapacitate** [ˌɪnkə'pæsɪteɪt] *vt* [for work] arbeitsunfähig machen.

**incapacitated** [ˌɪnkə'pæsɪteɪtɪd] *adj* [for work] arbeitsunfähig.

**incapacity** [ˌɪnkə'pæsətɪ] *n* Unfähigkeit *die;* ~ for work Arbeitsunfähigkeit *die.*

**incarcerate** [ɪn'kɑːsəreɪt] *vt fml* einlkerkern.

**incarceration** [ɪnˌkɑːsə'reɪʃn] *n fml* Einkerkerung *die;* [time in prison] Kerkerhaft *die.*

**incarnate** [ɪn'kɑːneɪt] *adj* in Person.

**incarnation** [ˌɪnkɑː'neɪʃn] *n* Verkörperung *die;* in a previous ~ in einem früheren Leben.

**incendiary device** [ɪn'sendjərɪ-] *n* Brandsatz *der.*

**incense** [*n* 'ɪnsens, *vb* ɪn'sens] *n* Weihrauch *der* ◇ *vt* [anger] erbosen, erzürnen.

**incentive** [ɪn'sentɪv] *n* Anreiz *der.*

**incentive scheme** *n* Anreizsystem *das.*

**inception** [ɪn'sepʃn] n *fml* Beginn *der;* [of institution] Gründung *die;* [of system] Einführung *die.*

**incessant** [ɪn'sesnt] adj unaufhörlich, unablässig.

**incessantly** [ɪn'sesntlɪ] adv unaufhörlich, unablässig.

**incest** ['ɪnsest] n Inzest *der.*

**incestuous** [ɪn'sestjʊəs] adj inzestuös; theatre people are a rather ~ group *fig* Theaterleute sind sehr aufeinander fixiert.

**inch** [ɪntʃ] n = 2,54 cm, Zoll *der* <> vi: to ~ forward/through sich zentimeterweise vorwärts bewegen/hindurchbewegen.

**incidence** ['ɪnsɪdəns] n Häufigkeit *die;* a high ~ of child mortality eine hohe Sterblichkeitsrate bei Kindern.

**incident** ['ɪnsɪdənt] n - 1. [event] Vorfall *der;* the meeting went off without ~ das Treffen verlief ohne Zwischenfälle - 2. POL Zwischenfall *der.*

**incidental** [ˌɪnsɪ'dentl] adj [minor] nebensächlich; ~ expenses Nebenausgaben *pl.*

**incidentally** [ˌɪnsɪ'dentəlɪ] adv [by the way] übrigens.

**incidental music** n Begleitmusik *die.*

**incinerate** [ɪn'sɪnəreɪt] vt verbrennen.

**incinerator** [ɪn'sɪnəreɪtəʳ] n [large] Müllverbrennungsanlage *die;* [smaller] Verbrennungsofen *der.*

**incipient** [ɪn'sɪpɪənt] adj *fml* beginnend.

**incision** [ɪn'sɪʒn] n *fml* Schnitt *der.*

**incisive** [ɪn'saɪsɪv] adj [person] scharfsinnig; [comment, writing] pointiert.

**incisor** [ɪn'saɪzəʳ] n Schneidezahn *der.*

**incite** [ɪn'saɪt] vt auf lhetzen; to ~ sb to do sthg jn dazu auf lstacheln, etw zu tun.

**incitement** [ɪn'saɪtmənt] n Aufhetzung *die.*

**incl.** (*abbr of* inclusive) inkl.

**inclement** [ɪn'klemənt] adj *fml* [weather] unfreundlich.

**inclination** [ˌɪnklɪ'neɪʃn] n - 1. [desire, slope] Neigung *die;* she showed no ~ to go sie machte keine Anstalten zu gehen - 2. [tendency]: to have an ~ to do sthg die Neigung (dazu) haben, etw zu tun.

**incline** [n 'ɪnklaɪn, vb ɪn'klaɪn] n [slope] Hang *der;* [angle] Neigung *die* <> vt [head, body] neigen <> vi: to ~ to sthg zu etw neigen.

**inclined** [ɪn'klaɪnd] adj - 1. [tending] geneigt; I'm not that way ~ es sagt mir nicht zu; to be ~ to sthg zu etw neigen; to be ~ to do sthg dazu neigen, etw zu tun - 2. [wanting]: to be ~ to do sthg Lust haben, etw zu tun - 3. [sloping] geneigt.

**include** [ɪn'kluːd] vt - 1. [gen] (mit) einl-

schließen; [contain] enthalten - 2. [add, count] mitlrechnen.

**included** [ɪn'kluːdɪd] adj eingeschlossen; service is not ~ die Bedienung ist nicht inbegriffen.

**including** [ɪn'kluːdɪŋ] prep einschließlich (+ G); the band played several songs, ~ some of my favourites die Band spielte mehrere Lieder, darunter einige meiner Lieblingslieder; up to and ~ last month bis einschließlich des letzten Monats.

**inclusion** [ɪn'kluːʒn] n Aufnahme *die.*

**inclusive** [ɪn'kluːsɪv] adj einschließlich, inklusive; ~ price Pauschalpreis *der;* from the 8th to the 16th ~ vom 8. bis einschließlich 16.; ~ of einschließlich (+ G).

**incognito** [ˌɪnkɒg'niːtəʊ] adv inkognito.

**incoherent** [ˌɪnkəʊ'hɪərənt] adj [speech] zusammenhanglos; he was ~ er drückte sich unklar aus.

**income** ['ɪŋkʌm] n Einkommen *das.*

**income support** n *Br* Sozialhilfe *die.*

**income tax** n Einkommensteuer *die.*

**incoming** ['ɪnˌkʌmɪŋ] adj - 1. [plane] landend; [passengers] ankommend; [mail, report, phone call] eingehend; the ~ tide die Flut - 2. [government, official] neu.

**incommunicado** [ˌɪnkəmjuːnɪ'kɑːdəʊ] adv von der Außenwelt abgeschnitten.

**incomparable** [ɪn'kɒmpərəbl] adj unvergleichlich.

**incompatible** [ˌɪnkəm'pætɪbl] adj [ideas, jobs, characters] unvereinbar; [computers] inkompatibel; to be ~ with sb nicht zu jm passen; Linda and John are ~ Linda und John passen nicht zueinander.

**incompetence** [ɪn'kɒmpɪtəns] n Unfähigkeit *die,* Inkompetenz *die.*

**incompetent** [ɪn'kɒmpɪtənt] adj unfähig, inkompetent; [work] unzulänglich.

**incomplete** [ˌɪnkəm'pliːt] adj unvollständig; [story] nicht abgeschlossen.

**incomprehensible** [ɪnˌkɒmprɪ'hensəbl] adj unverständlich.

**inconceivable** [ˌɪnkən'siːvəbl] adj undenkbar, unvorstellbar.

**inconclusive** [ˌɪnkən'kluːsɪv] adj [meeting, debate] ergebnislos; [evidence, argument] nicht schlüssig.

**incongruous** [ɪn'kɒŋgrʊəs] adj [clothes, behaviour] unpassend.

**inconsequential** [ˌɪnkɒnsɪ'kwenʃl] adj [insignificant] unbedeutend.

**inconsiderable** [ˌɪnkən'sɪdərəbl] adj: not ~ nicht unbeträchtlich.

**inconsiderate** [ˌɪnkən'sɪdərət] *adj* rücksichtslos.

**inconsistency** [ˌɪnkən'sɪstənsɪ] (*pl* -ies) *n* Widersprüchlichkeit *die*.

**inconsistent** [ˌɪnkən'sɪstənt] *adj* widersprüchlich; [performance] schwankend; [work] unbeständig; [behaviour] inkonsequent; **to be ~ with sthg** mit etw nicht übereinlstimmen, zu etw im Widerspruch stehen.

**inconsolable** [ˌɪnkən'səʊləbl] *adj* untröstlich.

**inconspicuous** [ˌɪnkən'spɪkjʊəs] *adj* unauffällig.

**incontinence** [ɪn'kɒntɪnəns] *n* Inkontinenz *die*.

**incontinent** [ɪn'kɒntɪnənt] *adj:* **to be ~** an Inkontinenz leiden.

**incontrovertible** [ˌɪnkɒntrə'vɜːtəbl] *adj* [evidence] unwiderlegbar; [fact] unbestreitbar.

**inconvenience** [ˌɪnkən'viːnjəns] *n* Unannehmlichkeit *die* ◇ *vt* Unannehmlichkeiten *OR* Umstände bereiten.

**inconvenient** [ˌɪnkən'viːnjənt] *adj* ungünstig; **to be ~ for sb** jm ungelegen kommen.

**incorporate** [ɪn'kɔːpəreɪt] *vt* einlschließen; **to ~ sb/sthg in(to) sthg** jn/etw in etw (A) auflnehmen.

**incorporated company** *n* COMM (im Handelsregister) eingetragene Gesellschaft.

**incorrect** [ˌɪnkə'rekt] *adj* falsch; [behaviour] inkorrekt.

**incorrigible** [ɪn'kɒrɪdʒəbl] *adj* unverbesserlich.

**incorruptible** [ˌɪnkə'rʌptəbl] *adj* [person] unbestechlich.

**increase** [*n* 'ɪnkriːs, *vb* ɪn'kriːs] *n:* **~ (in)** [number, unemployment] Zunahme *die* (+ G); [price, demand, speed] Erhöhung *die* (+ G); [output] Steigerung *die* (+ G); **to be on the ~** (ständig) zunehmen ◇ *vt* [price, wages, speed] erhöhen; [output] steigern; [fear, efforts] verstärken ◇ *vi* steigen; [unemployment, pain] zulnehmen; [anxiety] wachsen.

**increased** [ɪn'kriːst] *adj* [efficiency, effort] gesteigert; [demand] erhöht.

**increasing** [ɪn'kriːsɪŋ] *adj* [number, use, frequency] zunehmend; [anxiety, demand] wachsend.

**increasingly** [ɪn'kriːsɪŋlɪ] *adv* zunehmend.

**incredible** [ɪn'kredəbl] *adj* - **1.** [wonderful] sagenhaft - **2.** [very large, unbelievable] unglaublich.

**incredulous** [ɪn'kredjʊləs] *adj* ungläubig, skeptisch.

**increment** ['ɪnkrɪmənt] *n* Zuwachs *der;* [of salary] Gehaltserhöhung *die*.

**incriminate** [ɪn'krɪmɪneɪt] *vt* belasten; **to ~ o.s.** sich selbst belasten.

**incriminating** [ɪn'krɪmɪneɪtɪŋ] *adj* belastend.

**incrusted** [ɪn'krʌstɪd] *adj* = **encrusted.**

**incubate** ['ɪnkjʊbeɪt] *vt* [egg] auslbrüten ◇ *vi* [egg] ausgebrütet werden.

**incubation** [ˌɪnkjʊ'beɪʃn] *n* - **1.** [of egg] Ausbrüten *das* - **2.** MED: **~ period** Inkubationszeit *die*.

**incubator** ['ɪnkjʊbeɪtə'] *n* [for baby] Brutkasten *der*.

**inculcate** ['ɪnkʌlkeɪt] *vt fml:* **to ~ sthg in(to) sb** jm etw einlschärfen.

**incumbent** [ɪn'kʌmbənt] *fml adj:* **to be ~ (up)on sb to do sthg** jm obliegen, etw zu tun ◇ *n* [postholder] Amtsinhaber *der*, -in *die*.

**incur** [ɪn'kɜː'] (*pt* & *pp* -**red**; *cont* -**ring**) *vt* [loss] erleiden; [expenses] haben; [debts] machen.

**incurable** [ɪn'kjʊərəbl] *adj* - **1.** [disease] unheilbar - **2.** *fig* [romantic, cynic] unverbesserlich.

**incursion** [*Br* ɪn'kɜːʃn, *Am* ɪn'kɜːʒn] *n* MIL Einfall *der; fig* Eindringen *das*.

**indebted** [ɪn'detɪd] *adj* - **1.** [grateful]: **to be ~ to sb** jm zu Dank verpflichtet sein - **2.** [owing money]: **to be ~ to sb** bei jm Schulden haben.

**indecency** [ɪn'diːsnsɪ] *n* Unanständigkeit *die*.

**indecent** [ɪn'diːsnt] *adj* unanständig; **~ haste** ungebührliche Eile.

**indecent assault** *n* Notzucht *die*.

**indecent exposure** *n* exhibitionistische Handlung.

**indecipherable** [ˌɪndɪ'saɪfərəbl] *adj* nicht entzifferbar.

**indecision** [ˌɪndɪ'sɪʒn] *n* Unentschlossenheit *die*.

**indecisive** [ˌɪndɪ'saɪsɪv] *adj* - **1.** [person] unentschlossen - **2.** [result] unklar.

**indeed** [ɪn'diːd] *adv* wirklich, tatsächlich; [certainly] natürlich; **very big ~** wirklich sehr groß; **thank you very much ~** vielen herzlichen Dank; **~?** [in surprise] wirklich?, so?

**indefatigable** [ˌɪndɪ'fætɪgəbl] *adj* unermüdlich.

**indefensible** [ˌɪndɪ'fensəbl] *adj* [behaviour] unentschuldbar; [argument] unhaltbar.

**indefinable** [ˌɪndɪ'faɪnəbl] *adj* undefinierbar.

**indefinite** [ɪn'defɪnɪt] *adj* - **1.** [period, number] unbestimmt - **2.** [answer] unklar.

**indefinitely** [ɪn'defɪnətlɪ] *adv* [wait] unbegrenzt lange; [closed] bis auf weiteres; [postpone] auf unbestimmte Zeit.

**indelible** [ɪn'deləbl] *adj* - **1.** [mark, stain] nicht zu entfernen - **2.** [ink] wasserunlöslich; **~ pencil** Kopierstift *der* - **3.** [memory] unauslöschlich.

**indelicate** [ɪn'delɪkət] adj [behaviour, remark] ungehörig.

**indemnify** [ɪn'demnɪfaɪ] (pt & pp -ied) vt - **1.** [insure]: **to ~ sb for** OR **against sthg** jn gegen etw versichern - **2.** [compensate]: **to ~ sb for sthg** jn für etw entschädigen.

**indemnity** [ɪn'demnətɪ] n - **1.** [insurance] Versicherung die - **2.** [compensation] Entschädigung die.

**indent** [ɪn'dent] vt - **1.** [text] einlrücken - **2.** [edge, surface] einlkerben.

**indentation** [ˌɪnden'teɪʃn] n - **1.** [in text] Einrückung die - **2.** [in edge, surface] Einkerbung die.

**independence** [ˌɪndɪ'pendəns] n - **1.** [gen] Unabhängigkeit die - **2.** [in character] Selbstständigkeit die.

**Independence Day** n (amerikanischer) Unabhängigkeitstag (4. Juli).

**independent** [ˌɪndɪ'pendənt] adj - **1.** [gen]: ~ **(of)** unabhängig (von) - **2.** [person - in character] selbstständig.

**independently** [ˌɪndɪ'pendəntlɪ] adv - **1.** [gen]: ~ **(of)** unabhängig (von) - **2.** [live, think, act] selbstständig.

**independent school** n Br nichtstaatliche Schule.

**in-depth** adj eingehend.

**indescribable** [ˌɪndɪ'skraɪbəbl] adj unbeschreiblich.

**indestructible** [ˌɪndɪ'strʌktəbl] adj unzerstörbar.

**indeterminate** [ˌɪndɪ'tɜːmɪnət] adj unbestimmt.

**index** ['ɪndeks] (pl senses 1 and 2 -es; pl sense 3 -es OR indices) n - **1.** [of book] Register das, Index der - **2.** [in library] Kartei die - **3.** ECON Index der <> vt [book] mit einem Register OR Index versehen.

**index card** n Karteikarte die.

**index finger** n Zeigefinger der.

**index-linked** [-ˌlɪŋkt] adj der Inflationsrate angepasst.

**India** ['ɪndɪə] n Indien nt.

**India ink** n Am = Indian ink.

**Indian** ['ɪndɪən] adj - **1.** [from India] indisch - **2.** [from the Americas] indianisch, Indianer- <> n - **1.** [from India] Inder der, -in die - **2.** [from the Americas] Indianer der, -in die.

**Indian ink** Br, **India ink** Am n (U) Tusche die.

**Indian Ocean** n: **the ~** der Indische Ozean.

**Indian summer** n Altweibersommer der.

**india rubber** n (U) Gummi das OR der.

**indicate** ['ɪndɪkeɪt] vt - **1.** [with finger, pointer] zeigen auf (+ A); [subj: dial, arrow, gauge] anlzeigen - **2.** [intention, fact] anldeuten - **3.** [mention - desire, preference] zum Ausdruck bringen - **4.** [suggest] hinldeuten auf (+ A); **the symptoms ~ thrombosis** die Symptome deuten auf eine Thrombose hin <> vi [when driving] blinken.

**indication** [ˌɪndɪ'keɪʃn] n - **1.** [suggestion]: **can you give me an ~ of when you will arrive?** können nen Sie mir ungefähr sagen, wann Sie ankommen? - **2.** [sign] (An)zeichen das; [hint] Hinweis der.

**indicative** [ɪn'dɪkətɪv] adj: **to be ~ of sthg** auf etw (A) hinldeuten, auf etw (A) schließen lassen <> n GRAMM Indikativ der.

**indicator** ['ɪndɪkeɪtə'] n - **1.** [sign] Indikator der - **2.** [on car] Blinker der.

**indices** ['ɪndɪsiːz] pl ⊏> **index.**

**indict** [ɪn'daɪt] vt: **to ~ sb (for)** jn anlklagen (wegen (+ G)).

**indictable** [ɪn'daɪtəbl] adj [offence] strafbar.

**indictment** [ɪn'daɪtmənt] n - **1.** LAW Anklageerhebung die - **2.** [criticism]: **an ~ of ein** Armutszeugnis für.

**indie** ['ɪndɪ] adj inf: **an ~ band** eine Independent-Band.

**indifference** [ɪn'dɪfrəns] n Gleichgültigkeit die.

**indifferent** [ɪn'dɪfrənt] adj - **1.** [uninterested] gleichgültig; **to be ~ to sthg** sich für etw nicht interessieren - **2.** [mediocre] mittelmäßig.

**indigenous** [ɪn'dɪdʒɪnəs] adj [culture, traditions] einheimisch, landeseigen.

**indigestible** [ˌɪndɪ'dʒestəbl] adj lit & fig schwer verdaulich.

**indigestion** [ˌɪndɪ'dʒestʃn] n (U) Magenverstimmung die; **to have ~** eine Magenverstimmung haben.

**indignant** [ɪn'dɪgnənt] adj: **to be ~ (at)** empört sein (über (+ A)).

**indignantly** [ɪn'dɪgnəntlɪ] adv empört.

**indignation** [ˌɪndɪg'neɪʃn] n Empörung die.

**indignity** [ɪn'dɪgnətɪ] (pl -ies) n Demütigung die.

**indigo** ['ɪndɪgəʊ] adj indigoblau <> n Indigo das OR der.

**indirect** [ˌɪndɪ'rekt] adj indirekt; **an ~ route** ein Umweg; **to make an ~ reference to sb** auf jn anlspielen.

**indirect costs** npl Betriebskosten pl.

**indirectly** [ˌɪndɪ'rektlɪ] adv indirekt.

**indirect speech** n indirekte Rede.

**indiscreet** [ˌɪndɪ'skriːt] adj indiskret; [tactless] taktlos.

**indiscretion** [ˌɪndɪ'skreʃn] n Indiskretion die; [tactless behaviour] Taktlosigkeit die.

**indiscriminate** [ˌɪndɪ'skrɪmɪnət] adj wahllos; [treatment] willkürlich; [person] unkritisch.

**indiscriminately** [ˌɪndɪˈskrɪmɪnətlɪ] *adv* wahllos; [treat] willkürlich.

**indispensable** [ˌɪndɪˈspensəbl] *adj* unentbehrlich.

**indisposed** [ˌɪndɪˈspəʊzd] *adj fml* [unwell] unpässlich.

**indisputable** [ˌɪndɪˈspjuːtəbl] *adj* unbestreitbar; [evidence] unanfechtbar.

**indistinct** [ˌɪndɪˈstɪŋkt] *adj* undeutlich; [picture, photo] verschwommen.

**indistinguishable** [ˌɪndɪˈstɪŋgwɪʃəbl] *adj:* to be ~ (from sb/sthg) (von jm/etw) nicht zu unterscheiden sein.

**individual** [ˌɪndɪˈvɪdʒʊəl] *adj* - **1.** [single] einzeln; [tuition] Einzel-; ~ case Einzelfall *der* - **2.** [distinctive] individuell ◇ *n* Einzelne *der*, *die*, Individuum *das*; who's that strange ~? wer ist dieses komische Individuum?

**individualistic** [ˈɪndɪˌvɪdʒʊəˈlɪstɪk] *adj* individualistisch.

**individuality** [ˈɪndɪˌvɪdʒʊˈælətɪ] *n* Individualität *die*.

**individually** [ˌɪndɪˈvɪdʒʊəlɪ] *adv* einzeln.

**indivisible** [ˌɪndɪˈvɪzəbl] *adj* unteilbar.

**Indochina** [ˌɪndəʊˈtʃaɪnə] *n* Indochina *nt*.

**indoctrinate** [ɪnˈdɒktrɪneɪt] *vt* indoktrinieren.

**indolent** [ˈɪndələnt] *adj fml* träge.

**indomitable** [ɪnˈdɒmɪtəbl] *adj* [will] unbeugsam; [spirit, person] unbezwingbar.

**Indonesia** [ˌɪndəˈniːzɪə] *n* Indonesien *nt*.

**Indonesian** [ˌɪndəˈniːzɪən] *adj* indonesisch ◇ *n* - **1.** [person] Indonesier *der*, -in *die* - **2.** [language] Indonesisch(e) *das*.

**indoor** [ˈɪndɔːʳ] *adj* [swimming pool, sports] Hallen-; [plant] Zimmer-.

**indoors** [ˌɪnˈdɔːz] *adv* [stay] drinnen; [go] nach drinnen.

**indubitably** [ɪnˈdjuːbɪtəblɪ] *adv* zweifellos.

**induce** [ɪnˈdjuːs] *vt* - **1.** [persuade]: to ~ sb to do sthg jn dazu bringen, etw zu tun - **2.** MED [labour] einleiten - **3.** [cause - sleep] herbeiführen.

**inducement** [ɪnˈdjuːsmənt] *n* [incentive] Anreiz *der*.

**induction** [ɪnˈdʌkʃn] *n* - **1.** [of leader, bishop] Amtseinführung *die* - **2.** (U) MED [of labour] Einleitung *die* - **3.** [introduction to job] Einführung *die* - **4.** ELEC Induktion *die*.

**induction course** *n* Einführungskurs *der*.

**indulge** [ɪnˈdʌldʒ] *vt* - **1.** [whim] nachlgeben (+ D); [passion] frönen (+ D) - **2.** [child, person] verwöhnen; to ~ o.s. sich verwöhnen ◇ *vi:* to ~ in sthg etw (D) frönen.

**indulgence** [ɪnˈdʌldʒəns] *n* - **1.** (U) [tolerance, kindness] Nachsicht *die* - **2.** [special treat] Luxus *der*.

**indulgent** [ɪnˈdʌldʒənt] *adj* nachsichtig; [giving way] nachgiebig.

**industrial** [ɪnˈdʌstrɪəl] *adj* industriell; [city, area, society] Industrie-.

**industrial action** *n:* to take ~ in den Ausstand treten.

**industrial estate** *Br*, **industrial park** *Am n* Industriegebiet *das*.

**industrialist** [ɪnˈdʌstrɪəlɪst] *n* Industrielle *der*, *die*.

**industrialization** [ɪnˌdʌstrɪəlaɪˈzeɪʃn] *n* Industrialisierung *die*.

**industrialize, -ise** [ɪnˈdʌstrɪəlaɪz] *vt* & *vi* industrialisieren.

**industrial park** *n Am* = industrial estate.

**industrial relations** *npl* Beziehungen *pl* zwischen Arbeitgebern und Gewerkschaften.

**industrial revolution** *n* Industrielle Revolution.

**industrial tribunal** *n* Arbeitsgericht *das*.

**industrious** [ɪnˈdʌstrɪəs] *adj* fleißig, arbeitsam.

**industry** [ˈɪndəstrɪ] (*pl* -ies) *n* - **1.** [gen] Industrie *die;* the tourist ~ die Tourismusbranche - **2.** [hard work] Fleiß *der*.

**inebriated** [ɪˈniːbrɪeɪtɪd] *adj fml* betrunken.

**inedible** [ɪnˈedɪbl] *adj* - **1.** [unpleasant to eat] ungenießbar - **2.** [poisonous] nicht essbar.

**ineffective** [ˌɪnɪˈfektɪv] *adj* unwirksam, ineffektiv.

**ineffectual** [ˌɪnɪˈfektʃʊəl] *adj* [person] unfähig; [plan] ineffizient.

**inefficiency** [ˌɪnɪˈfɪʃnsɪ] *n* [of person] Unfähigkeit *die;* [of process] Unproduktivität *die;* [of machine] Unwirtschaftlichkeit *die*.

**inefficient** [ˌɪnɪˈfɪʃnt] *adj* [person] unfähig, ineffizient; [process] unproduktiv; [machine] unwirtschaftlich.

**inelegant** [ɪnˈelɪgənt] *adj* nicht elegant.

**ineligible** [ɪnˈelɪdʒəbl] *adj:* to be ~ for sthg [promotion] für etw nicht in Frage kommen; [benefits] auf etw (A) keinen Anspruch haben.

**inept** [ɪˈnept] *adj* [person] unfähig; [comment] unpassend; [performance, attempt] ungeschickt.

**ineptitude** [ɪˈneptɪtjuːd] *n* (U) [incompetence] Unfähigkeit *die*.

**inequality** [ˌɪnɪˈkwɒlətɪ] (*pl* -ies) *n* - **1.** [gen] Ungleichheit *die* - **2.** [difference] Unterschied *der*.

**inequitable** [ɪnˈekwɪtəbl] *adj fml* ungerecht.

**inert** [ɪ'nɜːt] adj [person] reglos; ~ **gas** Edelgas das.

**inertia** [ɪ'nɜːʃə] n - **1.** [gen] Trägheit die - **2.** [of process] Stillstand der.

**inertia-reel seat belt** n Automatikgurt der.

**inescapable** [ˌɪnɪ'skeɪpəbl] adj unausweichlich.

**inessential** [ˌɪnɪ'senʃl] adj: ~ **(to sthg)** (für etw) unwesentlich.

**inestimable** [ɪn'estɪməbl] adj fml unschätzbar.

**inevitable** [ɪn'evɪtəbl] adj unvermeidlich <> n: **the** ~ das Unvermeidliche.

**inevitably** [ɪn'evɪtəblɪ] adv zwangsläufig.

**inexact** [ˌɪnɪg'zækt] adj ungenau.

**inexcusable** [ˌɪnɪk'skjuːzəbl] adj unverzeihlich, unentschuldbar.

**inexhaustible** [ˌɪnɪg'zɔːstəbl] adj unerschöpflich.

**inexorable** [ɪn'eksərəbl] adj fml unaufhaltsam.

**inexorably** [ɪn'eksərəblɪ] adv unaufhaltsam.

**inexpensive** [ˌɪnɪk'spensɪv] adj preiswert.

**inexperience** [ˌɪnɪk'spɪərɪəns] n Unerfahrenheit die, Mangel der an Erfahrung.

**inexperienced** [ˌɪnɪk'spɪərɪənst] adj unerfahren; **to be** ~ **in sthg** mit etw wenig vertraut sein.

**inexpert** [ɪn'ekspɜːt] adj [attempt] unfachmännisch; [person] ungeschult.

**inexplicable** [ˌɪnɪk'splɪkəbl] adj unerklärlich.

**inexplicably** [ˌɪnɪk'splɪkəblɪ] adv unerklärlicherweise.

**inextricably** [ˌɪnek'strɪkəblɪ] adv untrennbar.

**infallible** [ɪn'fæləbl] adj unfehlbar.

**infamous** ['ɪnfəməs] adj berüchtigt.

**infamy** ['ɪnfəmɪ] n fml Verrufenheit die.

**infancy** ['ɪnfənsɪ] n frühe Kindheit; **to be in its** ~ fig (noch) in den Kinderschuhen stecken.

**infant** ['ɪnfənt] n - **1.** [baby] Säugling der - **2.** [young child] Kleinkind das.

**infantile** ['ɪnfəntaɪl] adj - **1.** [of, for infants] Kinder- - **2.** pej [childish] kindisch, infantil.

**infant mortality** n Säuglingssterblichkeit die.

**infantry** ['ɪnfəntrɪ] n Infanterie die.

**infantryman** ['ɪnfəntrɪmən] (pl -men [-mən]) n Infanterist der.

**infant school** n Br Vorschule die (für 5- bis 7-jährige).

**infatuated** [ɪn'fætjʊeɪtɪd] adj: **to be** ~ **(with sb/ sthg)** (in jn/etw) vernarrt sein.

**infatuation** [ɪnˌfætjʊ'eɪʃn] n: ~ **(with sb/sthg)** Vernarrtheit die (in jn/etw).

**infect** [ɪn'fekt] vt MED infizieren; **to** ~ **sb with sthg** jn mit etw infizieren.

**infected** [ɪn'fektɪd] adj MED: ~ **(with sthg)** (mit etw) infiziert.

**infection** [ɪn'fekʃn] n MED Infektion die; **ear** ~ Ohrenentzündung die.

**infectious** [ɪn'fekʃəs] adj lit & fig ansteckend.

**infer** [ɪn'fɜːʳ] (pt & pp -**red**; cont -**ring**) vt - **1.** [deduce]: **to** ~ **that** folgern, dass; **to** ~ **sthg (from sthg)** etw (aus etw) folgern - **2.** inf [imply] andeuten.

**inference** ['ɪnfrəns] n - **1.** [conclusion] Schluss der, Schlussfolgerung die - **2.** [deduction]: **by** ~ somit; **the film was shorter and by** ~ **more bearable** der Film war kürzer und somit leichter erträglich.

**inferior** [ɪn'fɪərɪəʳ] adj - **1.** [lower in status] untergeordnet; **to be** ~ **(to sb/sthg)** (jm/etw) untergeordnet sein - **2.** [lower in quality] minderwertig; **to feel** ~ sich unterlegen fühlen; **to be** ~ **to sthg** von geringerer Qualität als etw sein <> n [in status] Untergebene der, die.

**inferiority** [ɪnˌfɪərɪ'ɒrətɪ] n - **1.** [in status] untergeordnete Stellung - **2.** [in quality] Minderwertigkeit die.

**inferiority complex** n Minderwertigkeitskomplex der.

**infernal** [ɪn'fɜːnl] adj inf dated grässlich; [noise] höllisch.

**inferno** [ɪn'fɜːnəʊ] (pl -s) n Flammenmeer das.

**infertile** [ɪn'fɜːtaɪl] adj unfruchtbar.

**infertility** [ˌɪnfə'tɪlətɪ] n Unfruchtbarkeit die.

**infestation** [ˌɪnfe'steɪʃn] n Plage die.

**infested** [ɪn'festɪd] adj: ~ **with sthg** [vermin, insects] von etw befallen; [weeds] von etw überwuchert.

**infidelity** [ˌɪnfɪ'delətɪ] n [of partner] Untreue die.

**infighting** ['ɪnˌfaɪtɪŋ] n (U) [rivalry] interne Machtkämpfe pl; [quarrelling] interne Querelen pl.

**infiltrate** ['ɪnfɪltreɪt] vt [territory] infiltrieren; [party, organization] unterwandern; **to** ~ **sb into sthg** jn in etw (A) einschleusen <> vi: **to** ~ **into sthg** [enter secretly] sich in etw (A) einlschleusen.

**infinite** ['ɪnfɪnət] adj unendlich.

**infinitely** ['ɪnfɪnətlɪ] adv [large, wide] unendlich; [more, better] unendlich viel.

**infinitesimal** [ˌɪnfɪnɪ'tesɪml] adj äußerst gering.

**infinitive** [ɪnˈfɪnɪtɪv] n Infinitiv der.

**infinity** [ɪnˈfɪnətɪ] n - **1.** [unreachable point] Unendlichkeit die - **2.** MATH Unendliche das.

**infirm** [ɪnˈfɜːm] adj gebrechlich ◇ npl: **the ~** die Gebrechlichen.

**infirmary** [ɪnˈfɜːmərɪ] (pl **-ies**) n - **1.** [hospital] Krankenhaus das - **2.** [room] Krankenzimmer das.

**infirmity** [ɪnˈfɜːmətɪ] (pl **-ies**) n - **1.** [individual weakness or illness] Gebrechen das - **2.** [state of being weak or ill] Gebrechlichkeit die.

**inflamed** [ɪnˈfleɪmd] adj MED entzündet; **to become ~** sich entzünden.

**inflammable** [ɪnˈflæməbl] adj leicht entzündlich.

**inflammation** [ˌɪnfləˈmeɪʃn] n MED Entzündung die.

**inflammatory** [ɪnˈflæmətrɪ] adj aufrührerisch.

**inflatable** [ɪnˈfleɪtəbl] adj aufblasbar; **~ mattress** Luftmatratze die.

**inflate** [ɪnˈfleɪt] vt - **1.** [fill with air - tyre] auf lpumpen; [ - life-jacket, balloon] auf lblasen - **2.** ECON [increase] in die Höhe treiben.

**inflated** [ɪnˈfleɪtɪd] adj - **1.** [filled with air - tyre] aufgepumpt; [ - life jacket, balloon] aufgeblasen - **2.** pej [exaggerated]: **to have an ~ opinion of oneself** eine zu hohe Meinung von sich haben - **3.** ECON [unreasonably high] überhöht.

**inflation** [ɪnˈfleɪʃn] n ECON Inflation die.

**inflationary** [ɪnˈfleɪʃnrɪ] adj [ECON - policy, spiral] Inflations-; [ - trend, wage rise] inflationär.

**inflationary spiral** n Inflationsspirale die.

**inflation-proof** adj inflationssicher.

**inflation rate** n ECON Inflationsrate die.

**inflection** [ɪnˈflekʃn] n GRAMM Flexion die.

**inflexible** [ɪnˈfleksəbl] adj - **1.** [unbendable] unbiegsam - **2.** pej [unyielding - person, attitude] unflexibel; [ - will] unbeugsam - **3.** [fixed - decision, arrangement] unabänderlich; [ - working hours] festgelegt.

**inflict** [ɪnˈflɪkt] vt: **to ~ sthg on sb** [pain] jm etw zufügen; [responsibility] jm etw übertragen; [problem] jn mit etw belasten; [punishment] jn mit etw belegen.

**in-flight** adj [magazine] Bord-.

**inflow** [ˈɪnfləʊ] n [of information] Zufluss der; [of immigrants, capital] Zustrom der.

**influence** [ˈɪnfluəns] n: **~ (on sb/sthg)**, **~ (over sb/sthg)** Einfluss der (auf jn/etw); **he is a bad ~ on her** er hat einen schlechten Einfluss auf sie; **under the ~ of** unter dem Einfluss von ◇ vt beeinflussen.

**influential** [ˌɪnfluˈenʃl] adj einflussreich.

**influenza** [ˌɪnfluˈenzə] n fml Grippe die.

**influx** [ˈɪnflʌks] n Zustrom der.

**info** [ˈɪnfəʊ] (abbr of **information**) n (U) inf Info die.

**inform** [ɪnˈfɔːm] vt benachrichtigen, informieren; [police] verständigen; **to ~ sb of/about sthg** jm etw mitteilen, jn über etw (A) informieren.

➝ **inform on** vt fus anlzeigen.

**informal** [ɪnˈfɔːml] adj - **1.** [casual, relaxed - party, clothes] zwanglos; [ - language] informell - **2.** [non-official] inoffiziell.

**informally** [ɪnˈfɔːməlɪ] adv - **1.** [casually - dress] zwanglos; [ - talk] ungezwungen - **2.** [non-officially] inoffiziell.

**informant** [ɪnˈfɔːmənt] n Informant der, -in die.

**information** [ˌɪnfəˈmeɪʃn] n (U): **~ (on OR about sthg)** Informationen pl (über etw (A)); **to get ~** sich informieren; **a piece of ~** eine Auskunft, eine Information; '**Information**' ['Information', 'Auskunft']; **for your ~** COMM zu Ihrer Kenntnisnahme OR Information.

**information desk** n Auskunftsschalter der.

**information office** n Auskunftsbüro das.

**information retrieval** n Informationsbeschaffung die.

**information technology** n Informationstechnologie die.

**informative** [ɪnˈfɔːmətɪv] adj [person] auskunftsfreudig; [book, film] informativ.

**informed** [ɪnˈfɔːmd] adj - **1.** [having information] informiert - **2.** [based on information] kundig.

**informer** [ɪnˈfɔːməʳ] n [denouncer] Informant der, -in die.

**infrared** [ˌɪnfrəˈred] adj Infrarot-.

**infrastructure** [ˈɪnfrəˌstrʌktʃəʳ] n Infrastruktur die.

**infrequent** [ɪnˈfriːkwənt] adj selten; **he's an ~ visitor** er kommt ab und zu zu Besuch; **the buses are ~** die Busse verkehren nur selten.

**infringe** [ɪnˈfrɪndʒ] (cont **infringing**) vt - **1.** [right] verletzen - **2.** [law, agreement] verstoßen gegen ◇ vi - **1.: to ~ on sb's rights** js Rechte verletzen - **2.** [on law, agreement]: **to ~ on sthg** gegen etw verstoßen.

**infringement** [ɪnˈfrɪndʒmənt] n - **1.** [of right] Verletzung die - **2.** [of law, agreement] Verstoß der.

**infuriate** [ɪnˈfjʊərɪeɪt] vt sehr wütend OR rasend machen.

**infuriating** [ɪnˈfjʊərɪeɪtɪŋ] adj: **he/his behaviour is ~!** er/sein Benehmen macht mich rasend!

**infuse** [ɪnˈfjuːz] vt: **to ~ sb with sthg** [courage,

ideas] jm etw einlflößen <> vi [tea, herbs] ziehen.

**infusion** [ɪn'fjuːʒn] n - **1.** (U) [of courage, ideas] Einflößen das - **2.** [of tea, herbs] Aufguss der.

**ingenious** [ɪn'dʒiːnjəs] adj genial; [device, method] raffiniert; [person] einfallsreich, erfinderisch.

**ingenuity** [ˌɪndʒɪ'njuːətɪ] n [of person] Genialität die, Einfallsreichtum der; [of device, method] Raffiniertheit die.

**ingenuous** [ɪn'dʒenjʊəs] adj fml naiv.

**ingest** [ɪn'dʒest] vt fml auf lnehmen.

**ingot** ['ɪŋgət] n [of gold, silver] Barren der; [of metal] Block der.

**ingrained** [ˌɪn'greɪnd] adj - **1.** [dirt] tief sitzend - **2.** [belief] unerschütterlich; [hatred] tief.

**ingratiate** [ɪn'greɪʃɪeɪt] vt: to ~ o.s. with sb sich bei jm einlschmeicheln.

**ingratiating** [ɪn'greɪʃɪeɪtɪŋ] adj [smile] zuckersüß; [person, manner] schmeichlerisch.

**ingratitude** [ɪn'grætɪtjuːd] n Undankbarkeit die.

**ingredient** [ɪn'griːdɪənt] n - **1.** [in cooking] Zutat die - **2.** [element] Element das.

**ingrowing** ['ɪnˌgrəʊɪŋ], **ingrown** ['ɪnˌgrəʊn] adj eingewachsen.

**inhabit** [ɪn'hæbɪt] vt bewohnen.

**inhabitant** [ɪn'hæbɪtənt] n [of country, city] Einwohner der, -in die; [of house] Bewohner der, -in die.

**inhalation** [ˌɪnhə'leɪʃn] n Inhalation die.

**inhale** [ɪn'heɪl] vt einlatmen <> vi [breathe in] einlatmen; [smoker] Lungenzüge machen.

**inhaler** [ɪn'heɪlə'] n MED Inhalationsapparat der.

**inherent** [ɪn'hɪərənt, ɪn'herənt] adj her ~ laziness die ihr eigene Faulheit; **the dangers ~ in this sport** die mit diesem Sport verbundenen Gefahren.

**inherently** [ɪn'hɪərəntlɪ, ɪn'herəntlɪ] adv von Natur aus.

**inherit** [ɪn'herɪt] vt: to ~ sthg (from sb) etw (von jm) erben <> vi erben.

**inheritance** [ɪn'herɪtəns] n Erbe das.

**inheritor** [ɪn'herɪtə'] n Erbe der, Erbin die.

**inhibit** [ɪn'hɪbɪt] vt hemmen.

**inhibited** [ɪn'hɪbɪtɪd] adj gehemmt.

**inhibition** [ˌɪnhɪ'bɪʃn] n Hemmung die.

**inhospitable** [ˌɪnhɒ'spɪtəbl] adj - **1.** [person] ungastlich - **2.** [climate, area] unwirtlich.

**in-house** adj hausintern; ~ **staff** festangestellte Mitarbeiter <> adv im Hause.

**inhuman** [ɪn'hjuːmən] adj - **1.** [cruel] unmenschlich - **2.** [not human] nicht menschlich.

**inhumane** [ˌɪnhjuː'meɪn] adj unmenschlich.

**inimitable** [ɪ'nɪmɪtəbl] adj unnachahmlich.

**iniquitous** [ɪ'nɪkwɪtəs] adj fml ungerecht.

**iniquity** [ɪ'nɪkwətɪ] (pl -ies) n - **1.** (U) fml Ungerechtigkeit die; **a den of ~** eine Lästerhöhle - **2.** [wicked act] Missetat die; [unjust act] Ungerechtigkeit die.

**initial** [ɪ'nɪʃl] (Br pt & pp -led; cont -ling, Am pt & pp -ed; cont -ing) adj - **1.** [early] anfänglich - **2.**: ~ **letter** Initiale die <> vt mit seinen Initialen unterschreiben; [as authorization] ablzeichnen.
⟳ **initials** npl Initialen pl.

**initialize, -ise** [ɪ'nɪʃəlaɪz] vt COMPUT initialisieren.

**initially** [ɪ'nɪʃəlɪ] adv anfangs, am OR zu Anfang.

**initiate** [vb ɪ'nɪʃɪeɪt, n ɪ'nɪʃɪət] vt - **1.** [start] initiieren; [talks, scheme] in die Wege leiten - **2.** [teach]: to ~ sb (into sthg) [into skill] jn (in etw (A)) einlführen; [into mystery, secret] jn (in etw (A)) einlweihen; [into group] jn (in etw (A)) feierlich auf lnehmen <> n eingeweihtes neues Mitglied.

**initiation** [ɪˌnɪʃɪ'eɪʃn] n (U) - **1.** [start] Initiierung die - **2.** [introduction, teaching - into skill] Einführung die; [ - into mystery, secret] Einweihung die; [ - into group] feierliche Aufnahme; ~ **ceremony** Aufnahmezeremonie die.

**initiative** [ɪ'nɪʃətɪv] n Initiative die; **to take the ~** die Initiative ergreifen; **to use one's ~** selber Initiative entfalten; **on one's own ~** aus eigener Initiative.

**inject** [ɪn'dʒekt] vt - **1.** MED: to ~ sb with sthg, to ~ sthg into sb jm etw spritzen OR injizieren - **2.** fig [add]: to ~ sthg into sthg [fun, excitement] etw in etw (A) bringen; [money, funds] etw in etw (A) pumpen; [resources] etw zu etw beilsteuern.

**injection** [ɪn'dʒekʃn] n - **1.** MED Spritze die, Injektion die - **2.** [of funds] Zuschuss der.

**injudicious** [ˌɪndʒuː'dɪʃəs] adj fml unklug.

**injunction** [ɪn'dʒʌŋkʃn] n LAW gerichtliche Verfügung.

**injure** ['ɪndʒə'] vt - **1.** [hurt physically, offend] verletzen; to ~ o.s. sich verletzen - **2.** [reputation] schaden (+ D); [chances] beeinträchtigen.

**injured** [ɪn'dʒəd] adj - **1.** [physically hurt, offended] verletzt - **2.** [reputation] geschädigt; [chances] beeinträchtigt <> npl: **the ~** die Verletzten.

**injurious** [ɪn'dʒʊərɪəs] adj fml schädlich; **to be ~ to sb/sthg** jm/etw schaden.

**injury** ['ɪndʒərɪ] (pl -ies) n - **1.** (U) [physical harm] Verletzungen pl - **2.** [wound, to one's feelings] Verletzung die; **to do o.s. an ~** sich verletzen - **3.** (U) [to one's reputation] Schädigung die.

**injury time** n (U) Nachspielzeit die.

**injustice** [ɪnˈdʒʌstɪs] n Ungerechtigkeit die; **to do sb an ~** jm unrecht tun.

**ink** [ɪŋk] n (U) [for writing] Tinte die; [for drawing] Tusche die; [for printing] Druckfarbe die ⟨⟩ comp Tinten-.

**ink-jet printer** n Tintenstrahldrucker der.

**inkling** [ˈɪŋklɪŋ] n: **to have an ~ of sthg** etw ahnen; **he had no ~ of what was going on** er hatte nicht die leiseste Ahnung, was vorging; **to have an ~ that** ... ahnen, dass ...

**inkpad** [ˈɪŋkpæd] n Stempelkissen das.

**INLA** (abbr of **Irish National Liberation Army**) n paramilitärische, pro-irische Organisation.

**inlaid** [ˌɪnˈleɪd] adj: **~ (with sthg)** (mit etw) eingelegt.

**inland** [adj ˈɪnlənd, adv ɪnˈlænd] adj Binnen-; **it's far ~** es liegt weit im Landesinneren ⟨⟩ adv landeinwärts

**Inland Revenue** n Br: **the ~** ≈ das Finanzamt.

**in-laws** npl inf angeheiratete Verwandte pl; [parents-in-law] Schwiegereltern pl.

**inlet** [ˈɪnlet] n - **1.** [stretch of water - from lake] (schmale) Bucht; [ - from sea] Meeresarm der - **2.** [way in] Zuleitung die.

**inmate** [ˈɪnmeɪt] n Insasse der, -sin die.

**inmost** [ˈɪnməʊst] adj literary [feelings, secrets] tiefst; [thoughts] innerst.

**inn** [ɪn] n Wirtshaus das.

**innards** [ˈɪnədz] npl - **1.** [internal organs] Eingeweide pl - **2.** [of engine, machine] Innereien pl.

**innate** [ɪˈneɪt] adj angeboren.

**inner** [ˈɪnəʳ] adj - **1.** [most central] innere, -r, -s; [room] innen liegend; [courtyard] Innen-; **~ ear** Innenohr das; **Inner London** Innenstadt die Londons - **2.** [unexpressed, secret] innere.

**inner city** n: **the ~** die Innenstadt, die Innenbezirke einer Stadt, in denen es oft soziale Probleme gibt ⟨⟩ comp: **~ problems** Probleme der Innenstadt/der Innenstädte.

**innermost** [ˈɪnəməʊst] adj = **inmost**.

**inner tube** n Schlauch der.

**inning** [ˈɪnɪŋ] n [in baseball] Inning das

**innings** [ˈɪnɪŋz] (pl inv) n Br [in cricket] Durchgang der; **to have had a good ~** fig ein langes, erfülltes Leben gehabt haben.

**innocence** [ˈɪnəsəns] n (U) Unschuld die.

**innocent** [ˈɪnəsənt] adj unschuldig; **to be ~ of sthg** an etw (D) unschuldig sein ⟨⟩ n [naive person] Unschuld die.

**innocuous** [ɪˈnɒkjʊəs] adj harmlos.

**innovation** [ˌɪnəˈveɪʃn] n Innovation die.

**innovative** [ˈɪnəvətɪv] adj innovativ.

**innovator** [ˈɪnəveɪtəʳ] n Neuerer der, -rin die.

**innuendo** [ˌɪnjuːˈendəʊ] (pl **-es** OR **-s**) n

**- 1.** [individual remark] versteckte Andeutung, Anspielung die - **2.** (U) [style of speaking] Anspielungen pl.

**innumerable** [ɪˈnjuːmərəbl] adj unzählig, zahllos.

**inoculate** [ɪˈnɒkjʊleɪt] vt impfen; **to ~ sb with/against sthg** jn mit/gegen etw impfen.

**inoculation** [ɪˌnɒkjʊˈleɪʃn] n Impfung die.

**inoffensive** [ˌɪnəˈfensɪv] adj [person, remark] harmlos; [manner] nicht verletzend; [smell] unaufdringlich.

**inoperable** [ɪnˈɒprəbl] adj - **1.** MED inoperabel - **2.** fml [unworkable - plan, reforms] undurchführbar; [ - method] nicht verwendbar.

**inoperative** [ɪnˈɒprətɪv] adj - **1.** [unworkable - rule, tax] ungültig, außer Kraft; [ - principle, method, plan] nicht anwendbar - **2.** [not working] außer Betrieb.

**inopportune** [ɪnˈɒpətjuːn] adj fml [moment, visit] ungelegen; [remark] unpassend.

**inordinate** [ɪˈnɔːdɪnət] adj fml ungeheuer.

**inordinately** [ɪˈnɔːdɪnətlɪ] adv fml außerordentlich.

**inorganic** [ˌɪnɔːˈgænɪk] adj anorganisch.

**in-patient** n stationärer Patient, stationäre Patientin.

**input** [ˈɪnpʊt] (pt & pp **input** OR **-ted;** cont **-ting**) n (U) - **1.** [contribution - money, resources] Investition die; [ - labour, effort] Beitrag der - **2.** COMPUT Eingabe die - **3.** ELEC Energiezufuhr die ⟨⟩ vt COMPUT einlgeben.

**input/output** n COMPUT Eingabe/Ausgabe.

**inquest** [ˈɪnkwest] n LAW gerichtliche Untersuchung der Todesursache.

**inquire** [ɪnˈkwaɪəʳ] vt: **to ~ when/whether** OR **if/how ...** sich erkundigen wann/ob/wie ... ⟨⟩ vi [ask for information] sich erkundigen; **to ~ about sthg** sich nach etw erkundigen, nach etw fragen.

➣ **inquire after** vt fus sich erkundigen nach.

➣ **inquire into** vt fus untersuchen.

**inquiring** [ɪnˈkwaɪərɪŋ] adj [mind] forschend; [look, tone] fragend.

**inquiry** [ɪnˈkwaɪərɪ] (pl **-ies**) n - **1.** [question] Anfrage die; **to make inquiries** Erkundigungen einlziehen; [police] Nachforschungen anlstellen; **'Inquiries'** 'Auskunft', 'Information' - **2.** [investigation] Untersuchung die.

**inquiry desk** n Auskunftsschalter der.

**inquisition** [ˌɪnkwɪˈzɪʃn] n pej Verhör das.

➣ **Inquisition** n: **the Inquisition** die Inquisition.

**inquisitive** [ɪnˈkwɪzɪtɪv] adj [curious] neugierig; [for knowledge] wissbegierig.

**inroads** [ˈɪnrəʊdz] npl: **to make ~ into sthg** [savings, supplies] etw an|greifen; [field of knowledge] in etw *(A)* vor|dringen.

**insane** [ɪn'seɪn] *adj* **- 1.** MED [mad] geisteskrank **- 2.** *fig* [person, idea, jealousy] verrückt, irrsinnig ⬦ *npl*: the ~ die Geisteskranken.

**insanitary** [ɪn'sænɪtrɪ] *adj* unhygienisch.

**insanity** [ɪn'sænətɪ] *n (U)* **- 1.** MED [madness] Geisteskrankheit *die* **- 2.** *fig* [of person, idea] Irrsinn *der*, Wahnsinn *der*.

**insatiable** [ɪn'seɪʃəbl] *adj* unersättlich.

**inscribe** [ɪn'skraɪb] *vt* **- 1.** [on wall, headstone] ein|meißeln; [on plaque] ein|gravieren; to ~ sthg (on sthg) [on wall, headstone] etw (in etw *(A)*) ein|meißeln; [on plaque] etw (in etw *(A)*) ein|gravieren **- 2.** [in book]: to ~ sthg (in sthg) etw (als Widmung) (in etw *(A)*) schreiben.

**inscription** [ɪn'skrɪpʃn] *n* **- 1.** [on wall, headstone, plaque - written] Aufschrift *die*; [ - cut] Inschrift *die* **- 2.** [in book] Widmung *die*.

**inscrutable** [ɪn'skruːtəbl] *adj* unergründlich; [smile] geheimnisvoll; [look] undurchdringlich.

**insect** ['ɪnsekt] *n* Insekt *das*.

**insect bite** *n* Insektenstich *der*.

**insecticide** [ɪn'sektɪsaɪd] *n (U)* Insektizid *das*.

**insect repellent** *n (U)* Insektenschutzmittel *das*.

**insecure** [ˌɪnsɪ'kjʊəʳ] *adj* unsicher.

**insecurity** [ˌɪnsɪ'kjʊərətɪ] *n* Unsicherheit *die*.

**insensible** [ɪn'sensəbl] *adj* **- 1.** [unconscious] bewusstlos **- 2.** [unaware]: to be ~ of sthg sich etw *(G)* nicht bewusst sein **- 3.** [to pain, cold]: to be ~ to sthg gegen etw unempfindlich sein.

**insensitive** [ɪn'sensətɪv] *adj* **- 1.** [unkind, thoughtless] unsensibel **- 2.** [unresponsive]: ~ to sthg unempfänglich für etw **- 3.** [to pain, cold]: ~ to sthg unempfindlich gegen etw.

**insensitivity** [ɪnˌsensə'tɪvətɪ] *n (U)* **- 1.** [unkindness, thoughtlessness] mangelnde Sensibilität **- 2.** [lack of sensation]: ~ to cold/pain Kälte-/Schmerzunempfindlichkeit *die*.

**inseparable** [ɪn'seprəbl] *adj* **- 1.** [subjects, facts]: to be ~ (from sthg) (mit etw) untrennbar verbunden sein **- 2.** [people] unzertrennlich.

**insert** [*vb* ɪn'sɜːt, *n* 'ɪnsɜːt] *vt* **- 1.** [put inside]: to ~ sthg (in OR into sthg) etw (in etw *(A)*) ein|führen **- 2.** [include, add]: to ~ sthg (in OR into sthg) etw (in etw *(A)*) ein|fügen ⬦ *n* Einlage *die*.

**insertion** [ɪn'sɜːʃn] *n* **- 1.** [act of inserting] Einführen *das* **- 2.** [thing inserted - in text] Einfügung *die*.

**in-service training** *n Br* (berufsbegleitende) Fortbildung.

**inset** ['ɪnset] *n* [picture, diagram] Nebenbild *das*; [map] Nebenkarte *die*.

**inshore** [*adj* 'ɪnʃɔː, *adv* ɪn'ʃɔː] *adj* Küsten- ⬦ *adv* [be situated] in Küstennähe; [sail, swim] auf die Küste zu.

**inside** [ɪn'saɪd] *prep* **- 1.** [indicating place, position] in (+ D); (with verbs of motion) in (+ A); it's ~ the box es ist in der Schachtel; put it ~ the box leg es in die Schachtel; come ~ the house! komm ins Haus!; the baby moved ~ her das Baby bewegte sich in ihr; despair was growing ~ him Verzweiflung wuchs in ihm **- 2.** [indicating time, limit]: ~ three weeks in weniger als drei Wochen; he was just ~ the record er lag knapp unter der Rekordzeit ⬦ *adv* **- 1.** [referring to place, object, building] innen; to be ~ drinnen sein; to come ~ herein|kommen; to go ~ hinein|gehen; there was something ~ es war etwas drin **- 2.** [referring to body, mind] innerlich **- 3.** *prison sl inf* im Kitchen OR Knast; to be ~ sitzen ⬦ *adj* Innen-; an ~ toilet eine Toilette im Haus; ~ information vertrauliche Information ⬦ *n* **- 1.** [interior, inner part]: the ~ das Innere; lock the door from the ~ schließ die Tür von innen ab; on the ~ innen; ~ out [clothes] links (herum); to turn sthg ~ out etw auf links drehen; to know sthg ~ out *fig* etw in- und auswendig kennen **- 2.** AUT: the ~ lane [in UK] die linke Fahrspur; [in Europe, US *etc*] die rechte Fahrspur.

➤ **insides** *npl inf* [intestines] Eingeweide *pl*.

➤ **inside of** *prep Am* [building, object] in.

**inside information** *n (U)* Insider-Informationen *pl*.

**inside job** *n inf* Werk *das* von Insidern.

**inside lane** *n* AUT [in UK] linke Fahrspur; [in Europe, US *etc*] rechte Fahrspur.

**insider** [ˌɪn'saɪdəʳ] *n* Insider *der*.

**insider dealing, insider trading** *n* Insiderhandel *der*.

**inside story** *n* wahre Geschichte.

**insidious** [ɪn'sɪdɪəs] *adj* heimtückisch.

**insight** ['ɪnsaɪt] *n* **- 1.** *(U)* [wisdom]: ~ (into sthg) Verständnis *das* (für etw) **- 2.** [glimpse]: ~ (into sthg) Einblick *das* (in etw *(A)*).

**insignia** [ɪn'sɪgnɪə] (*pl inv*) *n* Abzeichen *das*; [royal] Insignien *pl*.

**insignificance** [ˌɪnsɪg'nɪfɪkəns] *n (U)* Bedeutungslosigkeit *die*.

**insignificant** [ˌɪnsɪg'nɪfɪkənt] *adj* unbedeutend.

**insincere** [ˌɪnsɪn'sɪəʳ] *adj* [person, remark] unaufrichtig; [smile] falsch.

**insincerity** [ˌɪnsɪn'serətɪ] *n* [of person, remark] Unaufrichtigkeit *die*; [of smile, person] Falschheit *die*.

**insinuate** [ɪn'sɪnjʊeɪt] *vt pej* [imply]: to ~ (that) an|deuten (dass).

**insinuation** [ɪnˌsɪnjʊ'eɪʃn] *n pej* Anspielung *die*.

**insipid** [ɪnˈsɪpɪd] *adj pej* - **1.** [taste, colour, music] fade; [person, character] geistlos - **2.** [food, drink] fade, geschmacklos.

**insist** [ɪnˈsɪst] *vt* - **1.** [state firmly]: **to ~ that** darauf beharren, dass - **2.** [demand]: **to ~ that** darauf bestehen, dass ◇ *vi*: **to ~ on sthg** auf etw (D) bestehen; **to ~ on doing sthg** darauf bestehen, etw zu tun.

**insistence** [ɪnˈsɪstəns] *n:* **~ (on sthg/on doing sthg)** Bestehen *das* (auf etw (D)/darauf, etw zu tun); **I came at his ~** ich kam, weil er darauf bestand.

**insistent** [ɪnˈsɪstənt] *adj* - **1.** [determined] beharrlich, hartnäckig; **to be ~ on sthg** auf etw (D) beharren OR bestehen - **2.** [continual] anhaltend.

**in situ** [ˌɪnˈsɪtjuː] *adv* an Ort und Stelle.

**insofar** [ˌɪnsəʊˈfɑːr] ➡ **insofar as** *conj* insofern als.

**insole** [ˈɪnsəʊl] *n* Einlegesohle *die.*

**insolence** [ˈɪnsələns] *n* Frechheit *die,* Unverschämtheit *die.*

**insolent** [ˈɪnsələnt] *adj* frech, unverschämt.

**insoluble** Br [ɪnˈsɒljʊbl], **insolvable** Am [ɪnˈsɒlvəbl] *adj* - **1.** [which cannot be solved] unlösbar - **2.** [which cannot be dissolved] unauflösbar.

**insolvency** [ɪnˈsɒlvənsɪ] *n* Zahlungsunfähigkeit *die,* Insolvenz *die.*

**insolvent** [ɪnˈsɒlvənt] *adj* zahlungsunfähig, insolvent.

**insomnia** [ɪnˈsɒmnɪə] *n* Schlaflosigkeit *die.*

**insomniac** [ɪnˈsɒmnɪæk] *n:* **to be an ~** an Schlaflosigkeit leiden.

**insomuch** [ˌɪnsəʊˈmʌtʃ] ➡ **insomuch as** *conj* insofern als.

**inspect** [ɪnˈspekt] *vt* - **1.** [letter, person] genau betrachten - **2.** [factory, troops, premises] inspizieren; [machine] prüfen.

**inspection** [ɪnˈspekʃn] *n* - **1.** [examination] Prüfung *die;* **on closer ~** bei näherer Betrachtung - **2.** [of factory, troops, premises] Inspektion *die;* [of machine] Prüfung *die.*

**inspector** [ɪnˈspektər] *n* - **1.** [official] Inspektor *der,* -in *die;* [on bus, train] Kontrolleur *der,* -in *die* - **2.** [of police] ≈ Kommissar *der,* -in *die.*

**inspector of taxes** *n* Steuerinspektor *der,* -in *die.*

**inspiration** [ˌɪnspəˈreɪʃn] *n* - **1.** (U) [source of ideas] Inspiration *die;* **to get ~ from sthg** sich von etw inspirieren lassen; **to be the ~ for sthg** die Inspiration für etw sein - **2.** [brilliant idea] Eingebung *die.*

**inspire** [ɪnˈspaɪər] *vt* inspirieren; **to ~ sb with sthg, to ~ sthg in sb** [confidence, passion, enthusiasm] in jm etw wecken; [respect] jm etw einflößen.

**inspired** [ɪnˈspaɪəd] *adj* genial; **that was an ~ guess** das war toll erraten.

**inspiring** [ɪnˈspaɪərɪŋ] *adj* inspirierend.

**instability** [ˌɪnstəˈbɪlətɪ] *n* [political] Instabilität *die;* [mental] Labilität *die.*

**install** Br, **instal** Am [ɪnˈstɔːl] *vt* - **1.** [machinery, equipment] installieren - **2.** [appoint]: **to ~ sb in a post** jn in ein Amt einlsetzen; **to ~ sb as managing director** jn in das Amt des Geschäftsführers/der Geschäftsführerin einlsetzen - **3.** [settle] unterlbringen; **to ~ o.s. in front of the fire** sich vor dem Kaminfeuer niederllassen.

**installation** [ˌɪnstəˈleɪʃn] *n* - **1.** [base, site] Anlage *die* - **2.** (U) [act of fitting] Installation *die.*

**installment** *n* Am = instalment.

**installment plan** *n* Am Ratenzahlung *die;* **to buy sthg on the ~** etw auf Raten kaufen.

**instalment** Br, **installment** Am [ɪnˈstɔːlmənt] *n* - **1.** [payment] Rate *die;* **to pay in ~s** in Raten zahlen - **2.** [episode - of story] Fortsetzung *die;* [ - of TV, radio programme] Folge *die.*

**instance** [ˈɪnstəns] *n* Fall *der;* **for ~** zum Beispiel; **in the first ~** *fml* zunächst.

**instant** [ˈɪnstənt] *adj* - **1.** [immediate] sofort, unmittelbar - **2.** [food]: **~ coffee** Instant- OR Pulverkaffee *der;* **~ mashed potato** fertiger Kartoffelpüree ◇ *n* [moment] Augenblick *der,* Moment *der;* **the ~ (that) ...** in dem Augenblick, in dem ...; **at that** OR **the same ~** im selben Augenblick; **this ~** sofort, auf der Stelle.

**instantaneous** [ˌɪnstənˈteɪnɪəs] *adj* unmittelbar; **her reaction was ~** sie reagierte sofort.

**instantly** [ˈɪnstəntlɪ] *adv* sofort.

**instead** [ɪnˈsted] *adv* stattdessen; **~ of** statt (+ G), anstelle (+ G); **~ of him** an seiner Stelle.

**instep** [ˈɪnstep] *n* Spann *der,* Fußrücken *der.*

**instigate** [ˈɪnstɪgeɪt] *vt* [discussions] den Anstoß geben zu; [meeting] in die Wege leiten; [investigation] einlleiten; [strike, revolt] anlstiften zu.

**instigation** [ˌɪnstɪˈgeɪʃn] *n:* **at sb's ~** auf js Betreiben.

**instigator** [ˈɪnstɪgeɪtər] *n* [of discussions, meeting, investigation] Initiator *der,* -in *die;* [of strike, revolt] Anstifter *der,* -in *die.*

**instil** Br (*pt* & *pp* -led; *cont* -ling), **instill** Am [ɪnˈstɪl] *vt:* **to ~ sthg in(to) sb** jm etw beilbringen.

**instinct** [ˈɪnstɪŋkt] *n* - **1.** (U) [natural ability] Instinkt *der;* **by ~** instinktiv - **2.** [impulse] Impuls *der;* **the survival ~** der Überlebenstrieb; **my first ~ was to run away** meine spontane Reaktion war, wegrennen zu wollen.

**instinctive** [ɪnˈstɪŋktɪv] *adj* instinktiv.

**instinctively** [ɪn'stɪŋktɪvlɪ] *adv* instinktiv.

**institute** ['ɪnstɪtjuːt] *n* Institut *das* <> *vt* - **1.** [establish] einlführen - **2.** [proceedings] anlstrengen.

**institution** [ˌɪnstɪ'tjuːʃn] *n* - **1.** [tradition, system, organization] Institution *die* - **2.** [home] Heim *das*, Anstalt *die*.

**institutional** [ˌɪnstɪ'tjuːʃənl] *adj* - **1.** [of organization] institutionell - **2.: to be in ~ care** [in psychiatric hospital] in der Psychiatrie sein; [in old folk's home] im Altenheim sein.

**institutionalized, -ised** [ˌɪnstɪ'tjuːʃnəˌlaɪzd] *adj* [established] institutionalisiert.

**instruct** [ɪn'strʌkt] *vt* - **1.** [tell, order]: **to ~ sb to do sthg** jn anlweisen, etw zu tun - **2.** [teach] unterrichten; **to ~ sb in sthg** jn in etw *(D)* unterrichten.

**instruction** [ɪn'strʌkʃn] *n* - **1.** [order] Anweisung *die* - **2.** (U) [teaching] Unterricht *der*.
➤ **instructions** *npl* [for use] Gebrauchsanleitung *die*.

**instruction manual** *n* Bedienungsanleitung *die*.

**instructive** [ɪn'strʌktɪv] *adj* lehrreich; [talk] aufschlussreich.

**instructor** [ɪn'strʌktə'] *n* Lehrer *der*, -in *die*.

**instrument** ['ɪnstrʊmənt] *n* - **1.** [gen] Instrument *das* - **2.** *literary* [means] Mittel *das*.

**instrumental** [ˌɪnstrʊ'mentl] *adj* - **1.** [important, helpful]: **to be ~ in sthg** eine entscheidende Rolle bei etw spielen - **2.** [music] Instrumental- <> *n* MUS Instrumentalstück *das*.

**instrumentalist** [ˌɪnstrʊ'mentəlɪst] *n* MUS Instrumentalist *der*, -in *die*.

**instrument panel** *n* Armaturenbrett *das*.

**insubordinate** [ˌɪnsə'bɔːdɪnət] *adj fml* aufsässig; MIL ungehorsam.

**insubordination** ['ɪnsəˌbɔːdɪ'neɪʃn] *n fml* Aufsässigkeit *die*; MIL Gehorsamsverweigerung *die*.

**insubstantial** [ˌɪnsəb'stænʃl] *adj* - **1.** [fragile] zerbrechlich - **2.** [unsatisfying - meal] dürftig; [ - book] ohne Substanz.

**insufferable** [ɪn'sʌfərəbl] *adj* unerträglich.

**insufficient** [ˌɪnsə'fɪʃnt] *adj fml*: **~ (for sthg)** unzureichend (für etw); **to be ~ to do sthg** nicht dafür auslreichen, um etw zu tun.

**insular** ['ɪnsjʊlə'] *adj* - **1.** [narrow-minded] engstirnig - **2.** [isolated] isoliert.

**insulate** ['ɪnsjʊleɪt] *vt* - **1.** [house, tank & ELEC] isolieren - **2.** [protect] schützen; **to ~ sb against OR from sthg** jn gegen etw ablschirmen.

**insulating tape** ['ɪnsjʊleɪtɪŋ-] *n (U) Br* Isolierband *das*.

**insulation** [ˌɪnsjʊ'leɪʃn] *n (U)* [material] Isolierung *die*.

**insulin** ['ɪnsjʊlɪn] *n* Insulin *das*.

**insult** [*vb* ɪn'sʌlt, *n* 'ɪnsʌlt] *vt* beleidigen <> *n* Beleidigung *die;* **and to add ~ to injury** und um das Ganze noch schlimmer zu machen.

**insulting** [ɪn'sʌltɪŋ] *adj* beleidigend.

**insuperable** [ɪn'suːprəbl] *adj fml* unüberwindlich.

**insurance** [ɪn'ʃʊərəns] *n lit & fig*: **~ (against sthg)** Versicherung (gegen etw) <> *comp* Versicherungs-.

**insurance broker** *n* Versicherungsmakler *der*, -in *die*.

**insurance policy** *n* Versicherungspolice *die*.

**insurance premium** *n* Versicherungsprämie *die*.

**insure** [ɪn'ʃʊə'] *vt* - **1.** [against fire, accident, theft]: **to ~ sb/sthg against sthg** jn/etw gegen etw versichern - **2.** *Am* [make certain] sicher stellen <> *vi* [protect]: **to ~ against sthg** sich gegen etw ablsichern.

**insured** [ɪn'ʃʊəd] *adj* - **1.** [against fire, accident, theft]: **~ (against OR for sthg)** versichert (gegen etw) - **2.** *Am* [certain] sicher <> *n*: **the ~** der Versicherungsnehmer, die Versicherungsnehmerin.

**insurer** [ɪn'ʃʊərə'] *n* Versicherungsgeber *der*, -in *die*.

**insurgent** [ɪn'sɜːdʒənt] *n* Aufständische *der*, *die*.

**insurmountable** [ˌɪnsə'maʊntəbl] *adj* unüberwindlich.

**insurrection** [ˌɪnsə'rekʃn] *n* Aufstand *der*.

**intact** [ɪn'tækt] *adj* unversehrt, intakt.

**intake** ['ɪnteɪk] *n* - **1.** [amount consumed] Aufnahme *die* - **2.** [people recruited]: **this year's ~ includes several overseas students** dieses Jahr wurden einige ausländische Studenten aufgenommen - **3.** [inlet] Einlass *der*.

**intangible** [ɪn'tændʒəbl] *adj* [quality] unbestimmbar; [ideas] nicht greifbar.

**integral** ['ɪntɪɡrəl] *adj* [part, feature] wesentlich; **to be ~ to sthg** für etw wesentlich sein.

**integrate** ['ɪntɪɡreɪt] *vi*: **to ~ (with OR into sthg)** sich (in etw *(A)*) integrieren <> *vt* - **1.** [include in a larger unit, combine] integrieren; **to ~ sb/sthg with OR into sthg** jn/etw in etw *(A)* integrieren - **2.** [end segregation of] für Vertreter aller Rassen zugänglich machen.

**integrated** ['ɪntɪɡreɪtɪd] *adj* [multiracial] für Vertreter aller Rassen zugänglich.

**integrated circuit** *n* integrierter Schaltkreis.

**integration** [ˌɪntɪ'greɪʃn] *n:* ~ **(with** OR **into sthg)** Integration *die* (in etw *(A)).*

**integrity** [ɪn'tegrətɪ] *n* - **1.** [honour] Integrität *die* - **2.** *fml* [wholeness] Einheit *die.*

**intellect** ['ɪntəlekt] *n* - **1.** [ability to reason] Verstand *der* - **2.** [mind, intelligence] Intellekt *der.*

**intellectual** [ˌɪntə'lektjʊəl] *adj* intellektuell ◇ *n* Intellektuelle *der, die.*

**intelligence** [ɪn'telɪdʒəns] *n (U)* - **1.** [ability to reason] Intelligenz *die* - **2.** [information service] Nachrichtendienst *der* - **3.** [information] Information *die.*

**intelligence quotient** *n* Intelligenzquotient *der.*

**intelligence test** *n* Intelligenztest *der.*

**intelligent** [ɪn'telɪdʒənt] *adj* intelligent; ~ **life** vernunftbegabte Lebewesen *pl.*

**intelligently** [ɪn'telɪdʒəntlɪ] *adv* intelligent.

**intelligentsia** [ɪnˌtelɪ'dʒentsɪə] *n:* **the** ~ die Intelligenz.

**intelligible** [ɪn'telɪdʒəbl] *adj* verständlich.

**intemperate** [ɪn'tempərət] *adj fml* - **1.** [drinking] übermäßig - **2.** [behaviour] zügellos - **3.** [climate] extrem.

**intend** [ɪn'tendl] *vt* beabsichtigen; **to be ~ed as sthg** als etw gemeint sein; **it was ~ed to be a surprise** es sollte eine Überraschung sein; **to ~ doing** OR **to do sthg** beabsichtigen, etw zu tun.

**intended** [ɪn'tendɪd] *adj* [result] beabsichtigt.

**intense** [ɪn'tens] *adj* - **1.** [competition, pain, emotion] heftig; [concentration] äußerst; [colour, light] intensiv; [heat] stark - **2.** [person - serious] ernsthaft; [ - emotional] heftig.

**intensely** [ɪn'tenslɪ] *adv* äußerst.

**intensify** [ɪn'tensɪfaɪ] *(pt & pp* -**ied)** *vt* intensivieren ◇ *vi* [cold, heat] zulnehmen; [pressure, problem] sich verschärfen.

**intensity** [ɪn'tensətɪ] *n* - **1.** [of competition, pain, emotion] Heftigkeit *die;* [of colour, light, concentration] Intensität *die;* [of heat] Stärke *die* - **2.** [of person - seriousness] Ernsthaftigkeit *die;* [ - of emotional nature] Heftigkeit *die.*

**intensive** [ɪn'tensɪv] *adj* intensiv; **an ~ course in German** ein Intensivkurs in Deutsch.

**intensive care** *n:* **to be in** ~ auf der Intensivstation sein.

**intensive care unit** *n* Intensivstation *die.*

**intent** [ɪn'tent] *adj* - **1.** [expression] gespannt - **2.** [determined]: **to be ~ (up)on doing sthg** fest entschlossen sein, etw zu tun ◇ *n fml* Absicht *die;* **to all ~s and purposes** im Grunde, so gut wie.

**intention** [ɪn'tenʃn] *n* Absicht *die.*

**intentional** [ɪn'tenʃənl] *adj* absichtlich.

**intentionally** [ɪn'tenʃənəlɪ] *adv* absichtlich.

**intently** [ɪn'tentlɪ] *adv* konzentriert.

**inter** [ɪn'tɜːr] *(pt & pp* -**red;** *cont* -**ring)** *vt fml* bestatten.

**interact** [ˌɪntər'ækt] *vi* - **1.** [people]: **to ~ (with sb)** (mit jm) Kontakt haben - **2.** [forces, ideas]: **to ~ (with sthg)** (mit etw) in Wechselwirkung stehen.

**interaction** [ˌɪntər'ækʃn] *n* - **1.** [of people]: **there needs to be more ~ between them** sie müssen engeren Kontakt haben - **2.** [of forces, ideas] Wechselwirkung *die.*

**interactive** [ˌɪntər'æktɪv] *adj* COMPUT interaktiv.

**intercede** [ˌɪntə'siːd] *vi fml:* **to ~ (with sb)** sich einlsetzen (bei jm).

**intercept** [ˌɪntə'sept] *vt* ablfangen.

**interception** [ˌɪntə'sepʃn] *n* Abfangen *das.*

**interchange** [*n* 'ɪntətʃeɪndʒ, *vb* ˌɪntə'tʃeɪndʒ] *n* - **1.** [exchange] Austausch *der* - **2.** [road junction] Kreuzung *die* ◇ *vt* ausltauschen; **to ~ sthg with sb/sthg** etw mit jm/gegen etw ausltauschen.

**interchangeable** [ˌɪntə'tʃeɪndʒəbl] *adj:* ~ **(with sb/ sthg)** austauschbar (mit jm/etw).

**intercity** [ˌɪntə'sɪtɪ] *adj* Br Intercity- ◇ *n:* **Intercity 125®** Intercity 125® *der.*

**intercom** ['ɪntəkɒm] *n* Gegensprechanlage *die.*

**interconnect** [ˌɪntəkə'nekt] *vi* sich miteinander verbinden; **to ~ with sthg** mit etw verbinden.

**interconnecting** [ˌɪntəkə'nektɪŋ] *adj* miteinander verbunden.

**intercontinental** ['ɪntəˌkɒntɪ'nentl] *adj* Interkontinental-.

**intercontinental ballistic missile** *n* Interkontinentalrakete *die.*

**intercourse** ['ɪntəkɔːs] *n:* **(sexual)** ~ (Geschlechts)verkehr *der.*

**interdenominational** ['ɪntədɪˌnɒmɪ'neɪʃənl] *adj* interkonfessionell.

**interdepartmental** ['ɪntəˌdiːpɑːt'mentl] *adj* abteilungsübergreifend.

**interdependent** [ˌɪntədɪ'pendənt] *adj* wechselseitig voneinander abhängig.

**interdict** ['ɪntədɪkt] *n* - **1.** LAW Verbot *das* - **2.** RELIG Interdikt *das.*

**interest** ['ɪntrəst] *n* - **1.** [enthusiasm, appeal, advantage] Interesse *das;* ~ **in sb/sthg** Interesse an jm/etw; **in the ~s of** im Interesse (+ G) - **2.** [hobby] Hobby *das* - **3.** *(U)* [financial charge] Zinsen *pl* - **4.** [share in company] Anteil *der* ◇ *vt* interessieren; **to ~ sb in sthg** jn für etw interessieren; **can I ~ you in buying my car?** wären Sie interessiert, mein Auto zu kaufen?

**interested** ['ɪntrəstɪd] *adj* - **1.** [enthusiastic, curious] interessiert; **to be ~ in sthg** [in job] Interesse haben an etw *(+ D);* [in butterflies, films] sich für etw *(A)* interessieren; **to be ~ in doing sthg** interessiert sein, etw zu tun - **2.** [concerned] beteiligt; **I'm only ~ in your money** mir ist nur an deinem Geld gelegen.

**interest-free** *adj* zinslos.

**interesting** ['ɪntrəstɪŋ] *adj* interessant.

**interest rate** *n* Zinssatz *der.*

**interface** [*n* 'ɪntəfeɪs, *vb* ˌɪntə'feɪs] *n* COMPUT Schnittstelle *die* <> *vt* COMPUT koppeln.

**interfere** [ˌɪntə'fɪəʳ] *vi* - **1.** [meddle]: **to ~ (in sthg)** sich (in etw *(A)*) ein|mischen - **2.** [cause disruption]: **to ~ with sthg** etw stören.

**interference** [ˌɪntə'fɪərəns] *n (U)* - **1.** [meddling]: **~ (with OR in sthg)** Einmischung *die* (in etw *(A)*) - **2.** RADIO & TV Störung *die.*

**interfering** [ˌɪntə'fɪərɪŋ] *adj pej:* he's an ~ busybody er mischt sich ständig ein.

**intergalactic** [ˌɪntəgə'læktɪk] *adj* intergalaktisch.

**interim** ['ɪntərɪm] *adj* [measure] Übergangs-; [report] Zwischen- <> *n:* **in the ~** in der Zwischenzeit.

**interior** [ɪn'tɪərɪəʳ] *adj* Innen- <> *n* - **1.** [inside] Innere *das* - **2.** [of country]: **the ~** das Landesinnere.

**interior decorator** *n* Innenausstatter *der,* -in *die.*

**interior designer** *n* Innenarchitekt *der,* -in *die.*

**interject** [ˌɪntə'dʒekt] *fml vt* - **1.** [add] ein|werfen - **2.** [interrupt]: **"I don't understand,"** he **~ed** „ich verstehe nicht", rief er dazwischen <> *vi* dazwischen|rufen.

**interjection** [ˌɪntə'dʒekʃn] *n* - **1.** [remark] Einwurf *der* - **2.** GRAMM Ausruf *der.*

**interlock** [ˌɪntə'lɒk] *vi* - **1.** TECH ineinander greifen; **to ~ with sthg** in etw *(A)* greifen - **2.** [fingers] einander umschließen <> *vt* - **1.** TECH ineinander|stecken; **to ~ sthg with sthg** etw in etw *(A)* stecken - **2.** [fingers] verschränken.

**interloper** ['ɪntələʊpəʳ] *n* Eindringling *der.*

**interlude** ['ɪntəluːd] *n* - **1.** [period of time] Zwischenzeit *die* - **2.** CINEMA & THEATRE Pause *die* - **3.** MUS Interludium *das.*

**intermarry** [ˌɪntə'mærɪ] *(pt & pp* **-ied)** *vi:* **to ~** [races] Mischehen eingehen; [tribes, family members] untereinander heiraten.

**intermediary** [ˌɪntə'miːdjərɪ] *(pl* **-ies)** *n* Mittelsmann *der,* -person *die.*

**intermediate** [ˌɪntə'miːdjət] *adj* - **1.** [transitional] Zwischen- - **2.** [post-beginner] fortgeschritten.

**interminable** [ɪn'tɜːmɪnəbl] *adj* endlos.

**intermingle** [ˌɪntə'mɪŋgl] *vi:* **to ~ (with sb/ sthg)** sich (mit jm/etw) vermischen.

**intermission** [ˌɪntə'mɪʃn] *n* Pause *die.*

**intermittent** [ˌɪntə'mɪtənt] *adj* in Abständen auftretend.

**intern** [*vb* ɪn'tɜːn, *n* 'ɪntɜːn] *vt* internieren <> *n esp Am* [trainee - teacher] Assistent *der,* -in *die;* [ - doctor] Assistenzarzt *der,* -ärztin *die.*

**internal** [ɪn'tɜːnl] *adj* - **1.** [within the body] innere, -r, -s - **2.** [within a country - flight] Inlands-; [ - trade] Binnen-; **~ affairs** innere Angelegenheiten - **3.** [within an organization] intern.

**internal-combustion engine** *n* Verbrennungsmotor *der.*

**internally** [ɪn'tɜːnəlɪ] *adv* - **1.** [within the body] innerlich - **2.** [within a country] landesintern - **3.** [within an organization] intern.

**Internal Revenue** *n Am:* **the ~** das Finanzamt.

**international** [ˌɪntə'næʃənl] *adj* international <> *n Br* SPORT - **1.** [match] Länderspiel *das* - **2.** [player] Nationalspieler *der,* -in *die.*

**international date line** *n:* **the ~** die Datumsgrenze.

**internationally** [ˌɪntə'næʃnəlɪ] *adv* international.

**International Monetary Fund** *n:* **the ~** der Internationale Währungsfond.

**international relations** *npl* international Beziehungen *pl.*

**internee** [ˌɪntɜː'niː] *n* Internierte *der, die.*

**Internet** ['ɪntənet] *n:* **the ~** das Internet.

**Internet service provider** *n* COMPUT Internetprovider *der.*

**internment** [ɪn'tɜːnmənt] *n* Internierung *die.*

**interpersonal** [ˌɪntə'pɜːsənl] *adj* zwischenmenschlich.

**interplay** ['ɪntəpleɪ] *n (U):* **~ (of/between)** Zusammenspiel (von/zwischen *(+D)*).

**Interpol** ['ɪntəpɒl] *n* Interpol *die.*

**interpolate** [ɪn'tɜːpəleɪt] *vt fml* - **1.** [add]: **to ~ sthg (into sthg)** etw (in etw *(A)*) ein|fügen - **2.** [interrupt]: **"just a moment,"** she **~d** „Moment mal," warf sie ein.

**interpose** [ˌɪntə'pəʊz] *vt fml* - **1.** [add] ein|werfen - **2.** [interrupt]: **"just a moment,"** he **~d** „Moment mal", rief er dazwischen.

**interpret** [ɪn'tɜːprɪt] *vt* - **1.** [understand] auslegen, interpretieren; **to ~ sthg as** etw interpretieren als - **2.** [translate] dolmetschen - **3.** *fml* [perform] interpretieren <> *vi* dolmetschen.

**interpretation** [ɪnˌtɜːprɪ'teɪʃn] *n* Interpretation *die.*

**interpreter** [ɪn'tɜːprɪtəʳ] *n* [person] Dolmetscher *der,* -in *die.*

**interpreting** [ɪn'tɜ:prɪtɪŋ] n [occupation] Dolmetschen das.

**interracial** [ˌɪntə'reɪʃl] adj zwischen den Rassen.

**interrelate** [ˌɪntərɪ'leɪt] vt in Beziehung bringen <> vi: **to ~ (with sthg)** (mit etw) in Beziehung stehen.

**interrogate** [ɪn'terəgeɪt] vt - **1.** [question] verhören - **2.** COMPUT befragen.

**interrogation** [ɪnˌterə'geɪʃn] n Verhör das.

**interrogation mark** n Am Fragezeichen das.

**interrogative** [ˌɪntə'rɒgətɪv] GRAMM adj Frage- <> n - **1.** [form]: **the ~** die Frageform - **2.** [word] Fragefürwort das.

**interrogator** [ɪn'terəgeɪtə'] n Vernehmungsbeamte der, die.

**interrupt** [ˌɪntə'rʌpt] vt & vi unterbrechen.

**interrupter** n ELEC Unterbrecher der.

**interruption** [ˌɪntə'rʌpʃn] n Unterbrechung die.

**intersect** [ˌɪntə'sekt] vi sich kreuzen <> vt kreuzen.

**intersection** [ˌɪntə'sekʃn] n [junction] Kreuzung die.

**intersperse** [ˌɪntə'spɜ:s] vt: **to be ~d with sthg** von etw unterbrochen OR durchsetzt sein.

**interstate (highway)** ['ɪntəsteɪt-] n Am Interstate Highway der, Autobahn zwischen den US-Bundesstaaten.

**interval** ['ɪntəvl] n - **1.** [period of time]: **~ (between)** Abstand (zwischen (+ D)); **at ~s** in Abständen von; **at monthly/yearly ~s** in monatlichen/jährlichen Abständen - **2.** Br [at play, concert] Pause die - **3.** MUS Intervall der.

**intervene** [ˌɪntə'vi:n] vt: **"that's enough!"** she ~d „das reicht!", rief sie dazwischen <> vi - **1.** [person, government] ein|greifen, ein|schreiten; **to ~ in sthg** in etw (A) ein|greifen - **2.** [event] dazwischen|kommen.

**intervening** [ˌɪntə'vi:nɪŋ] adj [period of time] dazwischenliegend.

**intervention** [ˌɪntə'venʃn] n Eingreifen das.

**interventionist** [ˌɪntə'venʃənɪst] adj interventionistisch <> n Interventionist der, -in die.

**interview** ['ɪntəvju:] n - **1.** [for job] Vorstellungsgespräch das - **2.** PRESS Interview das <> vt - **1.** [for job] ein Vorstellungsgespräch führen mit - **2.** PRESS interviewen.

**interviewee** [ˌɪntəvju:'i:] n - **1.** [for job] Kandidat der, -in die - **2.** PRESS Interviewte der, die.

**interviewer** ['ɪntəvju:ə'] n - **1.** [for job] Leiter der, -in die des Vorstellungsgesprächs - **2.** PRESS Interviewer der, -in die.

**interweave** [ˌɪntə'wi:v] (pt **-wove;** pp **-woven**) fig vt verweben <> vi sich verweben.

**intestate** [ɪn'testeɪt] adj: **to die ~** ohne Testament sterben.

**intestine** [ɪn'testɪn] n Darm der.
➤ **intestines** npl Gedärm das.

**intimacy** ['ɪntɪməsɪ] (pl **-ies**) n [closeness]: **~ (between/with)** Vertrautheit die (zwischen (+D)/mit).
➤ **intimacies** npl Vertraulichkeiten pl.

**intimate** [adj & n 'ɪntɪmət, vb 'ɪntɪmeɪt] adj - **1.** [friend, relationship] vertraut; **to be on ~ terms with sb** mit jm auf vertrautem Fuße stehen - **2.** [place, atmosphere, dinner] intim - **3.** fml [sexually]: **to be ~ with sb** intim mit jm sein - **4.** [thoughts, details] persönlich - **5.** [thorough - knowledge] gründlich - **6.** [direct - link] direkt <> n fml Vertraute der, die <> vt fml an|deuten; **to ~ that** an|deuten, dass.

**intimately** ['ɪntɪmətlɪ] adv - **1.** [directly] direkt - **2.** [as close friends] vertraulich; **to know sb ~** jn gut kennen - **3.** [thoroughly] gründlich.

**intimation** [ˌɪntɪ'meɪʃn] n fml Andeutung die.

**intimidate** [ɪn'tɪmɪdeɪt] vt ein|schüchtern.

**intimidation** [ɪnˌtɪmɪ'deɪʃn] n Einschüchterung die.

**into** ['ɪntʊ] prep - **1.** [inside] in (+ A); **to put sthg ~ sthg** [lying down] etw in etw (A) legen; [upright] etw in etw (A) stellen; **to put sthg ~ one's pocket** etw in die Tasche stecken; **to go ~ the house** ins Haus hineingehen - **2.** [against]: **to bump/crash into sthg** gegen etw stoßen/knallen - **3.** [indicating transformation, change] in (+ A); **to change ~ sthg** [become] zu etw werden; [clothes] sich (D) etw an|ziehen; **to translate ~ German** ins Deutsche übersetzen - **4.** [concerning, about] über (+ A); **research ~ the causes of the First World War** Forschung die über die Ursachen des Ersten Weltkriegs - **5.** MATH: **4 ~ 20 goes 5 (times)** 20 (geteilt) durch 4 ist 5 - **6.** [indicating elapsed time]: **I was a week ~ my holiday when ...** in meiner zweiten Urlaubswoche ...; **late ~ the night** bis tief in die Nacht hinein - **7.** inf [interested in]: **to be ~ sthg** etw mögen; **she's ~ jazz** sie ist ein Jazzfan.

**intolerable** [ɪn'tɒlrəbl] adj unerträglich.

**intolerance** [ɪn'tɒlərəns] n Intoleranz die.

**intolerant** [ɪn'tɒlərənt] adj intolerant; **to be ~ of sb/sthg** jm/etw gegenüber intolerant sein.

**intonation** [ˌɪntə'neɪʃn] n Intonation die.

**intone** [ɪn'təʊn] vt literary intonieren.

**intoxicated** [ɪn'tɒksɪkeɪtɪd] adj - **1.** [drunk]: **to be ~** berauscht sein - **2.** fig [excited]: **to be ~ by** OR **with sthg** von etw berauscht sein.

**intoxicating** [ɪn'tɒksɪkeɪtɪŋ] adj - **1.** [alcoholic] alkoholisch - **2.** fig [exciting] berauschend.

**intoxication** [ɪnˌtɒksɪ'keɪʃn] n fml - **1.** [drunkenness] Trunkenheit die - **2.** [excitement] Rausch der.

**intractable** [ɪn'træktəbl] adj fml - **1.** [stubborn] unnachgiebig - **2.** [insoluble] hartnäckig.

**intramural** [ˌɪntrə'mjʊərəl] adj innerhalb der Universität.

**intranet** ['ɪntrənet] n COMPUT Intranet das.

**intransigent** [ɪn'trænzɪdʒənt] adj fml unnachgiebig.

**intransitive** [ɪn'trænzətɪv] adj intransitiv.

**intrauterine device** [ˌɪntrə'juːtəraɪn-] n Intrauterinpessar das.

**intravenous** [ˌɪntrə'viːnəs] adj intravenös.

**in-tray** n Eingangsablage die.

**intrepid** [ɪn'trepɪd] adj literary kühn

**intricacy** ['ɪntrɪkəsɪ] (pl -ies) n - **1.** (U) [complexity] Kniffligkeit die - **2.** [detail]: **intricacies** feine Details.

**intricate** ['ɪntrɪkət] adj knifflig.

**intrigue** [n 'ɪntriːg, vb ɪn'triːg] n Intrige die ⬦ vt faszinieren ⬦ vi: **to ~ against sb** gegen jn intrigieren.

**intriguing** [ɪn'triːgɪŋ] adj faszinierend.

**intrinsic** [ɪn'trɪnsɪk] adj immanent.

**intro** ['ɪntrəʊ] (pl -s) (abbr of **introduction**) n inf MUS Intro das, Einleitung die.

**introduce** [ˌɪntrə'djuːs] vt - **1.** [one person to another] vorstellen; **to ~ sb to sb** jm jn vorstellen - **2.** RADIO & TV [programme] vorstellen - **3.** [animal, plant, method]: **to ~ sthg (to** OR **into)** etw (in (+ D)) einführen - **4.** [to new experience]: **to ~ sb to sthg** jn in etw (A) einführen - **5.** [signal start of] einleiten.

**introduction** [ˌɪntrə'dʌkʃn] n - **1.** [of method, technology] Einführung die - **2.** [first experience]: **~ to sthg** Bekanntschaft mit etw - **3.** [preface]: **~ to sthg** Einleitung zu etw - **4.** [book] Einführung die.

**introductory** [ˌɪntrə'dʌktrɪ] adj einleitend; **an ~ offer** ein Eröffnungsangebot.

**introspective** [ˌɪntrə'spektɪv] adj introspektiv.

**introvert** ['ɪntrəvɜːt] n introvertierter Mensch.

**introverted** ['ɪntrəvɜːtɪd] adj introvertiert.

**intrude** [ɪn'truːd] vi stören; **to ~ (up)on sb/sthg** jn/etw stören.

**intruder** [ɪn'truːdər] n Eindringling der.

**intrusion** [ɪn'truːʒn] n Störung die; [into private life] Eindringen das.

**intrusive** [ɪn'truːsɪv] adj aufdringlich.

**intuition** [ˌɪntjuː'ɪʃn] n - **1.** (U) [sense] Intuition die - **2.** [hunch] Vorahnung die.

**intuitive** [ɪn'tjuːɪtɪv] adj [feeling, understanding] instinktiv; [person] intuitiv.

**Inuit** ['ɪnʊɪt] adj eskimoisch ⬦ n Eskimo der, die.

**inundate** ['ɪnʌndeɪt] vt - **1.** fml [flood] überschwemmen - **2.** [overwhelm]: **to be ~d with sthg** von etw überschwemmt werden.

**inured** [ɪ'njʊəd] adj fml: **to become ~ to sthg** sich an etw (A) gewöhnen.

**invade** [ɪn'veɪd] vt - **1.** MIL einmarschieren in (+ A) - **2.** [subj: shoppers, fans] einfallen - **3.** [privacy, calm] stören; **the village was ~d by tourists** das Dorf war von Touristen überlaufen.

**invader** [ɪn'veɪdər] n MIL Invasor der.

**invading** [ɪn'veɪdɪŋ] adj - **1.** MIL Invasions- - **2.** [tourists, insects, fans] einfallend.

**invalid** [adj ɪn'vælɪd, n & vb 'ɪnvəlɪd] adj - **1.** [ticket, contract, vote] ungültig - **2.** [argument, theory] nicht schlüssig ⬦ n Invalide der, -din die
➡ **invalid out** vt sep: **to be ~ed out (of)** wegen Dienstuntauglichkeit entlassen werden (aus (+ D)).

**invalidate** [ɪn'vælɪdeɪt] vt - **1.** [claim, theory] entkräften - **2.** [contract, agreement] ungültig machen.

**invalid chair** ['ɪnvəlɪd-] n Rollstuhl der.

**invaluable** [ɪn'væljʊəbl] adj: **~ (to sb/sthg)** unschätzbar (für jn/etw).

**invariable** [ɪn'veərɪəbl] adj unveränderlich.

**invariably** [ɪn'veərɪəblɪ] adv stets.

**invasion** [ɪn'veɪʒn] n - **1.** MIL Invasion die - **2.** fig [intrusion] Eingriff der.

**invective** [ɪn'vektɪv] n (U) fml Schmähung die.

**inveigle** [ɪn'veɪgl] vt: **to ~ sb into doing sthg** jn dazu verleiten, etw zu tun.

**invent** [ɪn'vent] vt erfinden.

**invention** [ɪn'venʃn] n - **1.** [creation, untruth] Erfindung die - **2.** (U) [inventiveness] Vorstellungsgabe die.

**inventive** [ɪn'ventɪv] adj einfallsreich.

**inventor** [ɪn'ventər] n Erfinder der, -in die.

**inventory** ['ɪnvəntrɪ] (pl -ies) n - **1.** [list] Inventar das - **2.** Am [goods] Bestand der.

**inverse** [ɪn'vɜːs] adj umgekehrt ⬦ n fml Gegenteil das.

**invert** [ɪn'vɜːt] vt fml umdrehen.

**invertebrate** [ɪn'vɜːtɪbreɪt] n wirbelloses Tier.

**inverted commas** [ɪnˌvɜːtɪd-] npl Br Anführungszeichen die.

**invest** [ɪn'vest] vt - **1.** [money]: **to ~ sthg (in sthg)** etw (in etw (A)) investieren - **2.** [time, energy]: **to ~ sthg in sthg** etw in etw (A) investieren - **3.** fml [endow]: **to ~ sb with sthg** jm etw verleihen ⬦ vi - **1.** [financially]: **to ~ (in sthg)** (in etw

(A)) investieren - **2.** *fig* [in sthg useful]: **to ~ in sthg** in etw (A) investieren.

**investigate** [ɪn'vestɪgeɪt] *vt* untersuchen ◇ *vi* ermitteln.

**investigation** [ɪn͵vestɪ'geɪʃn] *n* Untersuchung *die*; **an ~ into sthg** eine Untersuchung von etw.

**investigative** [ɪn'vestɪgətɪv] *adj* Enthüllungs-.

**investigator** [ɪn'vestɪgeɪtə<sup>r</sup>] *n* Ermittler *der*, -in *die*; **private ~** (Privat)detektiv *der*, -in *die*.

**investiture** [ɪn'vestɪtʃə<sup>r</sup>] *n* Amtseinführung *die*.

**investment** [ɪn'vestmənt] *n* - **1.** [gen] Investition *die* - **2.** [financial product, purchase] Anlage *die*.

**investment analyst** *n* Investitionsanalytiker *der*, -in *die*.

**investment trust** *n* Investmenttrust *der*.

**investor** [ɪn'vestə<sup>r</sup>] *n* Anleger *der*, -in *die*.

**inveterate** [ɪn'vetərət] *adj* - **1.** [dislike, hatred] abgrundtief - **2.** [liar, gambler] unverbesserlich.

**invidious** [ɪn'vɪdɪəs] *adj* - **1.** [unfair] ungerecht - **2.** [unpleasant] unangenehm.

**invigilate** [ɪn'vɪdʒɪleɪt] *Br vt* Aufsicht führen bei ◇ *vi* Aufsicht führen.

**invigilator** [ɪn'vɪdʒɪleɪtə<sup>r</sup>] *n Br* Aufsichtführende *der*, *die*.

**invigorating** [ɪn'vɪgəreɪtɪŋ] *adj* erfrischend, belebend.

**invincible** [ɪn'vɪnsɪbl] *adj* unschlagbar.

**inviolate** [ɪn'vaɪələt] *adj* unbeschadet.

**invisible** [ɪn'vɪzɪbl] *adj* unsichtbar.

**invisible assets** *npl* unsichtbares Vermögen.

**invisible earnings** *npl* unsichtbare Einkünfte *pl*.

**invisible ink** *n (U)* unsichtbare Tinte.

**invitation** [͵ɪnvɪ'teɪʃn] *n* - **1.** [request to attend] Einladung *die* - **2.** [encouragement]: **an ~ to do sthg** eine Aufforderung, etw zu tun; **that's an ~ to thieves** das ist eine Aufforderung zum Diebstahl.

**invite** [ɪn'vaɪt] *vt* - **1.** [request to attend] einladen; **to ~ sb to sthg** jn zu etw einladen - **2.** [ask politely]: **to ~ sb to do sthg** jn ersuchen, etw zu tun - **3.** [questions, suggestions, donations] bitten um - **4.** [trouble, criticism] herausfordern.

**inviting** [ɪn'vaɪtɪŋ] *adj* einladend.

**in vitro fertilization** [͵ɪn'viːtrəʊ-] *n* künstliche Befruchtung.

**invoice** ['ɪnvɔɪs] *n* Rechnung *die* ◇ *vt*

- **1.** [customer] eine Rechnung schicken an (+ A) - **2.** [goods] in Rechnung stellen.

**invoke** [ɪn'vəʊk] *vt* - **1.** *fml* [quote as justification] sich berufen auf - **2.** [feeling] hervor[rufen.

**involuntary** [ɪn'vɒləntrɪ] *adj* [movement] unwillkürlich.

**involve** [ɪn'vɒlv] *vt* - **1.** [entail, require - work, travelling] mit sich bringen; [ - special equipment, knowledge] erfordern; **the job ~s working late** der Job bringt es mit sich, lange arbeiten zu müssen - **2.** [concern, affect] betreffen - **3.** [make part of sthg]: **to ~ sb in sthg** jn in etw (A) hineinziehen; **to ~ o.s. in sthg** sich an etw (D) aktiv beteiligen.

**involved** [ɪn'vɒlvd] *adj* - **1.** [complex] kompliziert - **2.** [participating]: **to be ~ in sthg** an etw (D) beteiligt sein - **3.** [in a relationship]: **to be/get ~ with sb** mit jm eine enge Beziehung haben/eingehen - **4.** [entailed]: **what is ~ (in it)?** worum geht es (dabei)?

**involvement** [ɪn'vɒlvmənt] *n* - **1.** [participation]: **~ (in sthg)** Beteiligung (an etw (D)) - **2.** [commitment]: **~ (in sthg)** Engagement (für etw).

**invulnerable** [ɪn'vʌlnərəbl] *adj:* **to be ~ to sthg** [disease, criticism] immun sein gegen etw; **the fortress is ~ to attack** die Festung ist uneinnehmbar.

**inward** ['ɪnwəd] *adj* - **1.** [feelings, satisfaction] innerlich - **2.** [flow, movement] nach innen gehend ◇ *adv Am* = **inwards**.

**inward investment** *n (U)* Investitionen *pl* aus dem Ausland.

**inwardly** ['ɪnwədlɪ] *adv* innerlich.

**inwards** ['ɪnwədz], **inward** *Am adv* nach innen.

**I/O** (*abbr of* **input/output**) Ein-/Ausgabe *die*.

**IOC** (*abbr of* **International Olympic Committee**) *n* IOC *das*.

**iodine** [*Br* 'aɪədiːn, *Am* 'aɪədaɪn] *n (U)* Jod *das*.

**IOM** *abk für* Isle of Man, *in Postanschrift verwendet*.

**ion** ['aɪən] *n* Ion *das*.

**Ionian Sea** [aɪ͵əʊnɪən-] *n:* **the ~** das Ionische Meer.

**iota** [aɪ'əʊtə] *n* Jota *das*.

**IOU** (*abbr of* **I owe you**) *n* Schuldschein *der*.

**IOW** *abk für* Isle of Wight, *in Postanschrift verwendet*.

**IPA** (*abbr of* **International Phonetic Alphabet**) *n* IPA *das*.

**IQ** (*abbr of* **intelligence quotient**) *n* IQ *der*.

**IRA** *n* - **1.** (*abbr of* **Irish Republican Army**) IRA *die* - **2.** (*abbr of* **individual retirement account**) *Rentenprogramm in den USA*.

**Iran** [ɪ'rɑːn] *n* Iran *der*.

**Iranian** [ɪ'reɪnɪən] *adj* iranisch ◇ *n* [person] Iraner *der*, -in *die*.

**Iraq** [ɪ'rɑːk] *n* Irak *der*.

**Iraqi** [ɪ'rɑːkɪ] *adj* irakisch ◇ *n* [person] Iraker *der*, -in *die*.

**irascible** [ɪ'ræsəbl] *adj* reizbar.

**irate** [aɪ'reɪt] *adj* zornig.

**Ireland** ['aɪələnd] *n* Irland *nt;* **the Republic of ~** die Republik Irland.

**iris** ['aɪərɪs] (*pl* **-es**) *n* **- 1.** [flower] Schwertlilie *die*, Iris *die* **- 2.** [of eye] Iris *die*.

**Irish** ['aɪrɪʃ] *adj* irisch ◇ *n* [language] Irisch(e) *das* ◇ *npl:* **the ~** die Iren.

**Irish coffee** *n* Irish Coffee *der*.

**Irishman** ['aɪrɪʃmən] (*pl* **-men** [-mən]) *n* Ire *der*.

**Irish Sea** *n:* **the ~** die Irische See.

**Irish setter** [-'setər] *n* Irish Setter *der*.

**Irish stew** *n* Eintopf aus verschiedenen Gemüsesorten, Kartoffeln und Lammfleisch.

**Irish wolfhound** *n* irischer Wolfshund.

**Irishwoman** ['aɪrɪʃˌwumən] (*pl* **-women** [-ˌwɪmɪn]) *n* Irin *die*.

**irk** [ɜːk] *vt* ärgern.

**irksome** ['ɜːksəm] *adj* lästig.

**IRN** (*abbr of* **Independent Radio News**) *n* britische Nachrichtenagentur für private Radiosender.

**iron** ['aɪən] *adj* **- 1.** [made of iron] eisern, aus Eisen; **~ bar** Eisenstange *die* **- 2.** *fig* [very strict] eisern ◇ *n* **- 1.** [metal, golf club] Eisen *das* **- 2.** [for clothes] Bügeleisen *das* ◇ *vt* bügeln.
➤ **iron out** *vt sep* [problems] auslbügeln.

**Iron Age** *n:* **the ~** die Eisenzeit ◇ *comp* Eisenzeit-.

**Iron Curtain** *n:* **the ~** der Eiserne Vorhang.

**ironic(al)** [aɪ'rɒnɪk(l)] *adj* **- 1.** [using irony] ironisch **- 2.** [paradoxical] paradox.

**ironically** [aɪ'rɒnɪklɪ] *adv* **- 1.** [in an ironic way] ironisch **- 2.** [paradoxically] paradoxerweise.

**ironing** ['aɪənɪŋ] *n* **- 1.** [work] Bügeln *das;* **to do the ~** bügeln **- 2.** [clothes] Bügelwäsche *die*.

**ironing board** *n* Bügelbrett *das*.

**iron lung** *n* eiserne Lunge.

**ironmonger** ['aɪənˌmʌŋgə'] *n Br* Eisenwarenhändler *der*, -in *die;* **~'s (shop)** Eisenwarenhandlung *die*.

**ironworks** ['aɪənwɜːks] (*pl inv*) *n* Eisenhütte *die*.

**irony** ['aɪərənɪ] (*pl* **-ies**) *n* Ironie *die*.

**irradiate** [ɪ'reɪdɪeɪt] *vt* bestrahlen.

**irrational** [ɪ'ræʃənl] *adj* irrational.

**irreconcilable** [ɪˌrekən'saɪləbl] *adj* [views, differences] unvereinbar.

**irredeemable** [ˌɪrɪ'diːməbl] *adj fml* **- 1.** [loss] unwiederbringlich **- 2.** [situation] hoffnungslos.

**irrefutable** [ɪ'refjʊtəbl] *adj fml* unwiderlegbar.

**irregular** [ɪ'regjʊlə'] *adj* **- 1.** [gen & GRAMM] unregelmäßig; [surface] uneben **- 2.** *fml* [unorthodox] ungehörig.

**irregularity** [ɪˌregjʊ'lærətɪ] (*pl* **-ies**) *n* **- 1.** [gen] Unregelmäßigkeit *die;* [of surface] Unebenheit *die* **- 2.** [anomaly] Ungesetzlichkeit *die*.

**irregularly** [ɪ'regjʊləlɪ] *adv* unregelmäßig.

**irrelevance** [ɪ'reləvəns], **irrelevancy** [ɪ'reləvənsɪ] (*pl* **-ies**) *n* **- 1.** (*U*) [state of being irrelevant] Unwichtigkeit *die* **- 2.** [irrelevant thing] Nichtigkeit *die*.

**irrelevant** [ɪ'reləvənt] *adj* unwichtig.

**irreligious** [ˌɪrɪ'lɪdʒəs] *adj* unreligiös.

**irremediable** [ˌɪrɪ'miːdɪəbl] *adj fml* [damage] nicht behebbar; [loss] nicht ersetzbar; **the situation is ~** die Situation ist nicht zu retten.

**irreparable** [ɪ'repərəbl] *adj* irreparabel.

**irreplaceable** [ˌɪrɪ'pleɪsəbl] *adj* unersetzlich.

**irrepressible** [ˌɪrɪ'presəbl] *adj* unerschütterlich; **he's ~** er ist nicht unterzukriegen.

**irreproachable** [ˌɪrɪ'prəʊtʃəbl] *adj* einwandfrei.

**irresistible** [ˌɪrɪ'zɪstəbl] *adj* unwiderstehlich.

**irresolute** [ɪ'rezəluːt] *adj fml* unentschlossen.

**irrespective** [ˌɪrɪ'spektɪv] ➤ **irrespective of** *prep* ungeachtet (+ G).

**irresponsible** [ˌɪrɪ'spɒnsəbl] *adj* unverantwortlich.

**irretrievable** [ˌɪrɪ'triːvəbl] *adj* [loss] unwiederbringlich; [computer data] nicht abrufbar; **the situation is ~** die Situation ist nicht zu retten.

**irreverent** [ɪ'revərənt] *adj* respektlos.

**irreversible** [ˌɪrɪ'vɜːsəbl] *adj* [judgement, decision] unwiderruflich; [damage] bleibend.

**irrevocable** [ɪ'revəkəbl] *adj* unwiderruflich.

**irrigate** ['ɪrɪgeɪt] *vt* [land] bewässern.

**irrigation** [ˌɪrɪ'geɪʃn] *n* [of land] Bewässerung *die* ◇ *comp* Bewässerungs-.

**irritable** ['ɪrɪtəbl] *adj* [person, mood] reizbar; [voice, reply] gereizt.

**irritant** ['ɪrɪtənt] *n* **- 1.** [irritating situation, person] Ärgernis *das* **- 2.** [substance] Reizerreger *der*.

**irritate** ['ɪrɪteɪt] *vt* **- 1.** [make angry] ärgern **- 2.** [make sore] reizen.

**irritated** ['ɪrɪteɪtɪd] *adj* [angry, sore] gereizt.

**irritating** ['ɪrɪteɪtɪŋ] *adj* - **1.** [person, noise] ärgerlich - **2.** [substance, material] reizend.

**irritation** [ɪrɪ'teɪʃn] *n* - **1.** [anger] Ärger *der* - **2.** [cause of anger] Ärgernis *das* - **3.** [soreness] Reizung *die*.

**IRS** (*abbr of* **Internal Revenue Service**) *n Am:* the ~ das Finanzamt.

**is** [ɪz] *vb* ➪ **be.**

**ISBN** (*abbr of* **International Standard Book Number**) *n* ISBN *die*.

**Islam** ['ɪzlɑːm] *n* [religion] Islam *der*.

**Islamic** [ɪz'læmɪk] *adj* islamisch.

**island** ['aɪlənd] *n lit* & *fig* Insel *die*.

**islander** ['aɪləndəʳ] *n* Inselbewohner *der*, -in *die*.

**isle** [aɪl] *n* Insel *die*.

**Isle of Man** *n:* the ~ die Insel Man.

**Isle of Wight** [-'waɪt] *n:* the ~ Wight.

**Isles of Scilly** *npl* = Scilly Isles.

**isn't** ['ɪznt] = is not.

**isobar** ['aɪsəbɑːʳ] *n* METEOR Isobare *die*.

**isolate** ['aɪsəleɪt] *vt* isolieren; to ~ sb/sthg from sb/sthg jn/etw von jm/etw isolieren.

**isolated** ['aɪsəleɪtɪd] *adj* - **1.** [place] abgelegen - **2.** [person] isoliert - **3.** [example, incident] einzeln.

**isolation** [aɪsə'leɪʃn] *n* [solitariness] Isolation *die*; **in** ~ [live, happen, consider] isoliert.

**isolationism** [aɪsə'leɪʃənɪzm] *n* Isolationismus *der*.

**isosceles triangle** [aɪ,sɒsɪliːz-] *n* gleichschenkliges Dreieck.

**isotope** ['aɪsətəʊp] *n* Isotop *das*.

**ISP** (*abbr of* **Internet service provider**) *n* ISP *der*.

**Israel** ['ɪzreɪəl] *n* Israel *nt*.

**Israeli** [ɪz'reɪlɪ] *adj* israelisch ⬦ *n* Israeli *der*, *die*.

**Israelite** ['ɪz,rɪəlaɪt] *adj* israelitisch ⬦ *n* Israelit *der*, -in *die*.

**issue** ['ɪʃuː] *n* - **1.** [important subject] Frage *die*; the point at ~ der zur Debatte stehende Punkt; to make an ~ of sthg ein Problem aus etw machen - **2.** [edition] Ausgabe *die* - **3.** [of stamps, bank notes, shares] Ausgabe *die* ⬦ *vt* - **1.** [statement] ablgeben; [decree] erlassen; [warning] auslsprechen - **2.** [stamps, bank notes, shares] auslgeben - **3.** [passport, documents] auslstellen; [uniforms] auslgeben; **to ~ sthg to sb, to ~ sb with sthg** jm etw auslstellen, jm mit etw auslstatten ⬦ *vi fml* [come out, go out]: **to ~ from** strömen aus.

**isthmus** ['ɪsməs] *n* Landenge *die*.

**it** [ɪt] *pron* - **1.** [referring to specific person or thing] (*subj*) er/sie/es; (*direct object*) ihn/sie/es; (*indi-*

*rect object*) ihm/ihr; ~'s **big** er/sie/es ist groß; **she hit** ~ sie hat ihn/sie/es getroffen; **get the cat/dog and give** ~ **a drink** hole die Katze/den Hund und gib ihr/ihm etwas zu trinken; **if the jar won't open, give** ~ **a shake** wenn das Glas nicht aufgeht, schüttel es - **2.** (*with prepositions*): **tell me about** ~ erzähl mir davon; **you're good at** ~ du kannst das gut; **a table with a chair beside** ~ ein Tisch mit einem Stuhl daneben; **what did you learn from** ~? was hast du daraus gelernt?; **put your hand in** ~ steck deine Hand hinein; **stand on top of** ~ stell dich darauf; **put the books on** ~ leg die Bücher darauf; **it had a sheet over** ~ darüber lag ein Tuch; **shall we go to** ~? sollen wir hinlgehen?; **put the box under** ~ stell die Schachtel darunter; **a free book came with** ~ es war ein kostenloses Buch dabei - **3.** (*impersonal use*) es; ~'s **hot** es ist heiß; ~'s **raining** es regnet; ~'s **Sunday** es ist Sonntag; ~'s **six o'clock** es ist sechs Uhr; ~'s **the children that worry me most** am meisten mache ich mir um die Kinder Sorgen; ~'s **said that ...** man sagt, dass ... - **4.** (*nonspecific*) es; ~'s **easy** es ist einfach; ~'s **a difficult question** das ist eine schwierige Frage; **who is** ~? – ~'s **Mary/me** wer ist da? – Mary/ich bins.

**IT** *abbr of* **information technology.**

**Italian** [ɪ'tæljən] *adj* italienisch ⬦ *n* - **1.** [person] Italiener *der*, -in *die* - **2.** [language] Italienisch(e) *das*.

**italic** [ɪ'tælɪk] *adj* kursiv.
➪ **italics** *npl* Kursivschrift *die*.

**Italy** ['ɪtəlɪ] *n* Italien *nt*.

**ITC** (*abbr of* **Independent Television Commission**) *n britischer Rundfunkrat für die privaten Fernsehanstalten.*

**itch** [ɪtʃ] *n* Juckreiz *der* ⬦ *vi* [part of body] jucken; **I'm ~ing** es juckt mich; **I'm ~ing to do it** es juckt mich, das zu tun.

**itchy** ['ɪtʃɪ] (*compar* -**ier**; *superl* -**iest**) *adj* juckend; **to be** ~ [part of body] jucken; **I feel** ~ es juckt mich.

**it'd** ['ɪtəd] = it would, it had.

**item** ['aɪtəm] *n* - **1.** [object] Gegenstand *der*; [in shop] Artikel *der*; [on agenda] Punkt *der*; COMM Posten *der*; ~ **of clothing** Kleidungsstück *das* - **2.** [of news] Meldung *die*.

**itemize, -ise** ['aɪtəmaɪz] *vt* auf einer Liste einzeln auf lführen.

**itemized bill** [,aɪtəmaɪzd-] *n* Rechnung *die* mit Einzelaufstellung der Posten.

**itinerant** [ɪ'tɪnərənt] *adj* umherziehend; ~ **preacher** Wanderprediger *der*.

**itinerary** [aɪ'tɪnərərɪ] (*pl* -**ies**) *n* Reiseroute *die*.

**it'll** [ɪtl] = it will.

**ITN** (abbr of **Independent Television News**) n britische Nachrichtenagentur für private Fernsehsender.

**its** [ɪts] poss adj [masculine, neuter subject] sein; [feminine subject] ihr; **the dog wagged ~ tail** der Hund wedelte mit dem Schwanz.

**it's** [ɪts] = **it is**, **it has**.

**itself** [ɪt'self] pron - **1.** (reflexive) sich - **2.** (after prep) sich selbst; **by ~** allein; **in ~** an sich - **3.** (stressed) selbst; **the house ~ is fine** das Haus selbst ist in Ordnung.

**ITV** (abbr of **Independent Television**) n britischer Fernsehsender.

**IUCD** (abbr of **intrauterine contraceptive device**) n Intrauterinpessar das.

**IUD** (abbr of **intrauterine device**) n Intrauterinpessar das.

**I've** [aɪv] = **I have**.

**IVF** (abbr of **in vitro fertilization**) n IVF die.

**ivory** ['aɪvərɪ] adj [colour] elfenbeinfarben ◇ n Elfenbein das ◇ comp [made of ivory] Elfenbein-.

**Ivory Coast** n: **the ~** die Elfenbeinküste.

**ivory tower** n fig Elfenbeinturm der.

**ivy** ['aɪvɪ] n Efeu der.

**Ivy League** n Am Gruppe von alten, angesehenen Universitäten im Osten der USA.

**J**

**j** (pl **j's** OR **js**), **J** (pl **J's** OR **Js**) [dʒeɪ] n [letter] j das, J das.

**J/A** (abbr of **joint account**) Gemeinschaftskonto das.

**jab** [dʒæb] (pt & pp -**bed**; cont -**bing**) n - **1.** [push] Stoß der; [with needle, knife] Stich der - **2.** Br inf [injection] Spritze die ◇ vt [with sthg] stechen; **to ~ one's finger at sb/sthg** mit dem Finger auf jn/etw zeigen; **to ~ sthg into sb/sthg** etw in jn/etw (hinein)stoßen ◇ vi: **to ~ (at)** stoßen (nach (+ D)).

**jabber** ['dʒæbər] vt brabbeln ◇ vi plappern.

**jack** [dʒæk] n - **1.** [for car] Wagenheber der - **2.** [playing card] Bube der.

➤ **jack in** vt sep Br inf (auf)stecken.
➤ **jack up** vt sep - **1.** [car] auf (bocken - **2.** [price] in die Höhe treiben.

**jackal** ['dʒækəl] n Schakal der.

**jackdaw** ['dʒækdɔ:] n Dohle die.

**jacket** ['dʒækɪt] n - **1.** [garment] Jacke die; [of suit] Jacket das - **2.** [of potato] Schale die - **3.** [of book] Schutzumschlag der - **4.** Am [of record] Plattenhülle die - **5.** [of boiler] Mantel der.

**jacket potato** n in der Schale gebackene Kartoffel.

**jackhammer** ['dʒæk,hæmər] n Am Pressluftbohrer der.

**jack-in-the-box** n Kastenteufel der.

**jack knife** n Klappmesser das.
➤ **jack-knife** vi [lorry] sich quer (stellen.

**jack-of-all-trades** (pl **jacks-of-all-trades**) n Alleskönner der.

**jack plug** n Bananenstecker der.

**jackpot** ['dʒækpɒt] n Jackpot der.

**Jacobean** [,dʒækə'bɪən] adj aus der Zeit Jakobs I. (von England).

**Jacuzzi**® [dʒə'ku:zɪ] n Whirlpool der.

**jade** [dʒeɪd] n - **1.** [stone] Jade der OR die - **2.** [colour] Jadegrün das ◇ comp [made of jade] Jade-.

**jaded** ['dʒeɪdɪd] adj abgestumpft.

**jagged** ['dʒægɪd] adj [metal] schartig; [edge] ausgezackt; [rocks] zerklüftet.

**jaguar** ['dʒægjʊər] n Jaguar der.

**jail** [dʒeɪl] n Gefängnis das; **in ~** im Gefängnis; **to go to ~** ins Gefängnis kommen ◇ vt ein (sperren.

**jailbird** ['dʒeɪlbɜ:d] n inf Knastbruder der.

**jailbreak** ['dʒeɪlbreɪk] n Ausbruch der (aus dem Gefängnis).

**jailer** ['dʒeɪlər] n Gefängniswärter der, -in die.

**jam** [dʒæm] (pt & pp -**med**; cont -**ming**) n - **1.** [preserve] Marmelade die - **2.** [of traffic] Stau der - **3.** inf [difficult situation] Klemme die, Patsche die; **to get into a ~** in eine Patsche geraten ◇ vt - **1.** [cause to stick]: **to ~ shut** [window, door] fest zulmachen; [mechanism, brakes] blockieren; **to get one's finger ~med** sich (D) den Finger einlquetschen - **2.** [cram]: **to ~ sthg into sthg** etw in etw (A) stopfen - **3.** [streets, town] verstopfen - **4.** TELEC: **thousands of callers ~med the switchboard** Tausende von Anrufern blockierten die Leitungen der (Telefon)zentrale - **5.** RADIO stören ◇ vi [stick - window, door] klemmen; [- brakes, lever] sich verklemmen.

➤ **jam on** vt sep: **to ~ the brakes on** eine Vollbremsung machen.

**Jamaica** [dʒə'meɪkə] n Jamaika nt; **in ~** auf Jamaika.

**Jamaican** [dʒə'meɪkn] *adj* jamaikanisch ◇ *n* Jamaikaner *der*, -in *die*.

**jamb** [dʒæm] *n* (Fenster-/Tür)pfosten *der*.

**jamming** ['dʒæmɪŋ] *n* (U) RADIO Störung *die*.

**jam-packed** [-'pækt] *adj inf* proppenvoll.

**jam session** *n* Jamsession *die*.

**Jan.** (*abbr of* **January**) Jan.

**jangle** ['dʒæŋgl] *n* [of bells] Bimmeln *das;* [of keys] Klimpern *das* ◇ *vt* [bells] bimmeln lassen; [keys] klimpern mit ◇ *vi* [bells] bimmeln; [keys] klimpern.

**janitor** ['dʒænɪtə'] *n Am* & *Scot* [caretaker] Hausmeister *der*.

**January** ['dʒænjʊərɪ] *n* Januar *der; see also* **September.**

**Japan** [dʒə'pæn] *n* Japan *nt*.

**Japanese** [ˌdʒæpə'niːz] (*pl inv*) *adj* japanisch ◇ *n* [language] Japanisch(e) *das* ◇ *npl* [people]: the ~ die Japaner *pl*.

**jape** [dʒeɪp] *n dated* Streich *der*.

**jar** [dʒɑː'] (*pt* & *pp* -**red**; *cont* -**ring**) *n* Glas *das* ◇ *vt* [shake] durchlschütteln ◇ *vi* - **1.** [noise, voice]: **to ~ (on sb)** unangenehm sein (für jn) - **2.** [colours] sich beißen.

**jargon** ['dʒɑːgən] *n* Fachsprache *die*.

**jarring** ['dʒɑːrɪŋ] *adj* - **1.** [noise, voice] unangenehm - **2.** [colours] sich beißend.

**jasmine** ['dʒæzmɪn] *n* Jasmin *der*.

**jaundice** ['dʒɔːndɪs] *n* Gelbsucht *die*.

**jaundiced** ['dʒɔːndɪst] *adj fig* [attitude, view] verbittert.

**jaunt** [dʒɔːnt] *n* Ausflug *der*.

**jaunty** ['dʒɔːntɪ] (*compar* -**ier**; *superl* -**iest**) *adj* [hat, wave] flott; [person] munter.

**Java** ['dʒɑːvə] *n* Java *nt*; **in ~** auf Java.

**javelin** ['dʒævlɪn] *n* Speer *der*.

**jaw** [dʒɔː] *n* - **1.** [of person, animal] Kiefer *der* - **2.** [of vice] Klemmbacke *die* ◇ *vi inf* quatschen.

**jawbone** ['dʒɔːbəʊn] *n* Kieferknochen *der*.

**jay** [dʒeɪ] *n* Eichelhäher *der*.

**jaywalk** ['dʒeɪwɔːk] *vi* als Fußgänger im Straßenverkehr unachtsam sein.

**jaywalker** ['dʒeɪwɔːkə'] *n* im Straßenverkehr unachtsamer Fußgänger.

**jazz** [dʒæz] *n* - **1.** MUS Jazz *der* - **2.** Am inf [insincere talk] Geschwätz *das*.
◆ **jazz up** *vt sep inf* auflpeppen.

**jazzy** ['dʒæzɪ] (*compar* -**ier**; *superl* -**iest**) *adj* - **1.** [colour, clothes] poppig - **2.** [music] jazzig.

**JCR** (*abbr of* **junior common room**) *n* Aufenthaltsraum für Studenten.

**jealous** ['dʒeləs] *adj* - **1.** [envious]: **to be ~ (of)**

neidisch sein (auf (+ A)) - **2.** [possessive]: **to be ~ (of)** eifersüchtig sein (auf (+ A)).

**jealously** ['dʒeləslɪ] *adv* - **1.** [enviously] neidisch - **2.** [possessively] eifersüchtig.

**jealousy** ['dʒeləsɪ] *n* - **1.** [envy] Neid *der* - **2.** [possessiveness] Eifersucht *die*.

**jeans** [dʒiːnz] *npl* Jeans *pl*.

**Jeep®** [dʒiːp] *n* Jeep® *der*.

**jeer** [dʒɪə'] *vt* verhöhnen ◇ *vi* [crowd, fans] höhnisch johlen; **to ~ at sb** jn verhöhnen.
◆ **jeers** *npl* höhnische Johlen.

**jeering** ['dʒɪərɪŋ] *adj* [crowd] höhnisch johlend ◇ *n* (U) höhnisches Johlen.

**Jello®** ['dʒeləʊ] *n Am* Wackelpudding *der*.

**jelly** ['dʒelɪ] (*pl* -**ies**) *n* - **1.** [dessert] Wackelpudding *der* - **2.** [jam] Gelee *das*.

**jelly baby** *n Br* in verschiedenen Farben erhältliches kleines Gummibonbon in der Form eines Babys.

**jelly bean** *n* bohnenförmiges Gummibonbon, das in vielen verschiedenen Farben und Geschmacksrichtungen angeboten wird.

**jellyfish** ['dʒelɪfɪʃ] (*pl inv* OR -**es**) *n* Qualle *die*.

**jemmy** *Br* ['dʒemɪ], **jimmy** *Am* ['dʒɪmɪ] (*pl* -**ies**) *n* Stemmeisen *das*.

**jeopardize, -ise** ['dʒepədaɪz] *vt* gefährden.

**jeopardy** ['dʒepədɪ] *n:* **in ~** in Gefahr.

**jerk** [dʒɜːk] *n* - **1.** [movement] Ruck *der* - **2.** *inf pej* [fool] Trottel *der* ◇ *vt* reißen ◇ *vi* einen Satz machen; **to ~ to a stop** ruckweise zum Stehen kommen.

**jerkily** ['dʒɜːkɪlɪ] *adv* ruckartig.

**jerkin** ['dʒɜːkɪn] *n* Wams *das*.

**jerky** ['dʒɜːkɪ] (*compar* -**ier**; *superl* -**iest**) *adj* ruckartig.

**jerry-built** ['dʒerɪ-] *adj* schlampig gebaut.

**jerry can** ['dʒerɪ-] *n* großer Blechkanister.

**jersey** ['dʒɜːzɪ] (*pl* -**s**) *n* - **1.** [sweater] Pullover *der* - **2.** (U) [cloth] Jersey *der*.

**Jersey** ['dʒɜːzɪ] *n* Jersey *nt*; **in ~** auf Jersey.

**Jerusalem** [dʒə'ruːsələm] *n* Jerusalem *nt*.

**Jerusalem artichoke** *n* Topinambur *der*.

**jest** [dʒest] *n* Scherz *der*; **in ~** im Spaß.

**jester** ['dʒestə'] *n* Narr *der*.

**Jesuit** ['dʒezjʊɪt] *n* Jesuit *der*.

**Jesus (Christ)** ['dʒiːzəs-] *n* Jesus (Christus) ◇ *interj inf* Menschenskind!

**jet** [dʒet] (*pt* & *pp* -**ted**; *cont* -**ting**) *n* - **1.** [aircraft] Jet *der*, Düsenflugzeug *das* - **2.** [of liquid, gas, steam] Strahl *der* - **3.** [nozzle] Düse *die* ◇ *vi* [travel by jet] jetten.

**jet-black** *adj* pechschwarz.

**jet engine** *n* Düsentriebwerk *das*.

**jetfoil** ['dʒetfɔɪl] *n* Tragflügelboot *das*.

**jet lag** n Jetlag der.

**jet-propelled** [-prə'peld] adj mit Düsenantrieb.

**jetsam** ['dʒetsəm] n ⊳ flotsam.

**jet set** n: the ~ der Jetset.

**jettison** ['dʒetɪsən] vt - **1.** [cargo, bombs - from plane] ablwerfen; [ - from ship] über Bord werfen - **2.** fig [discard - ideas, hope] über Bord werfen; [ - unwanted possession] weglwerfen.

**jetty** ['dʒetɪ] (pl -ies) n Landungssteg der.

**Jew** [dʒu:] n Jude der, Jüdin die.

**jewel** ['dʒu:əl] n Edelstein der; [in watch] Stein der; ~s [jewellery] Schmuck der ⟨> comp Juwelen-.

**jeweller** Br, **jeweler** Am ['dʒu:ələ'] n Juwelier der; ~'s (shop) Juweliergeschäft das.

**jewellery** Br, **jewelry** Am ['dʒu:əlrɪ] n Schmuck der; piece of ~ Schmuckstück das.

**Jewish** ['dʒu:ɪʃ] adj jüdisch.

**JFK** (abbr of John Fitzgerald Kennedy International Airport) n Flughafen in New York.

**jib** [dʒɪb] (pt & pp -bed; cont -bing) n - **1.** [NAUT - beam] Klüver der; [ - sail] Fock die - **2.** [of crane] Ausleger der ⟨> vi: to ~ at sthg sich gegen etw sträuben.

**jibe** [dʒaɪb] n spöttische Bemerkung.

**jiffy** ['dʒɪfɪ] n inf: in a ~ sofort.

**Jiffy bag**® n Versandtasche die.

**jig** [dʒɪg] (pt & pp -ged; cont -ging) n [dance] lebhafter Schreittanz, vor allem auf dem Land früher beliebt ⟨> vi [jump] springen.

**jiggle** ['dʒɪgl] vt [door handle, key in door] rütteln an (+ D); [bunch of keys] klappern mit; [pencil] wackeln mit.

**jigsaw (puzzle)** ['dʒɪgsɔ:-] n Puzzle(spiel) das.

**jilt** [dʒɪlt] vt sitzen lassen.

**jimmy** n Am = jemmy.

**jingle** ['dʒɪŋgl] n - **1.** [of bells] Bimmeln das; [of keys] Klimpern das - **2.** [in advertising] Jingle der ⟨> vi [bells] bimmeln; [keys] klimpern.

**jingoism** ['dʒɪŋgəʊɪzm] n Chauvinismus der.

**jinx** [dʒɪŋks] n: there's a ~ on it es ist verhext.

**jinxed** [dʒɪŋkst] adj verhext.

**jitters** ['dʒɪtəz] npl inf: the ~ das große Zittern.

**jittery** ['dʒɪtərɪ] adj inf rappelig.

**jive** [dʒaɪv] n - **1.** [dance] Jive der - **2.** Am inf [glib talk] Schmalz der ⟨> vi Jive tanzen.

**job** [dʒɒb] n - **1.** [paid work] Stelle die; to lose one's ~ entlassen werden - **2.** [task] Arbeit die, Aufgabe die; on the ~ bei der Arbeit; to do a good ~ gute Arbeit leisten; to make a good ~ of sthg etw gut machen - **3.** [difficult time]: to have a ~ doing sthg (große) Mühe ha-

ben, etw zu tun - **4.** [function] Aufgabe die - **5.** inf [plastic surgery]: to have a nose ~ sich die Nase operieren lassen - **6.** inf [crime] Ding das - **7.** phr: that's just the ~ Br inf das ist genau das Richtige; it's a good ~ you came ich hatte/wir hatten Glück, dass du gekommen bist.

**jobbing** ['dʒɒbɪŋ] adj Br Gelegenheits-.

**job centre** n Br Arbeitsamt das.

**job creation scheme** n Arbeitsbeschaffungsprogramm das.

**job description** n Tätigkeitsbeschreibung die.

**jobless** ['dʒɒblɪs] adj arbeitslos ⟨> npl: the ~ die Arbeitslosen pl.

**job lot** n mehrere Waren geringer Qualität, die billig zusammen verkauft werden.

**job satisfaction** n Zufriedenheit die mit seiner Arbeit.

**job security** n Sicherheit die des Arbeitsplatzes.

**jobsharing** ['dʒɒbʃeərɪŋ] n Jobsharing das

**Joburg, Jo'burg** ['dʒəʊbɜ:g] n inf Johannesburg nt.

**jockey** ['dʒɒkɪ] (pl -s) n Jockey der ⟨> vi: to ~ for position um eine gute Position kämpfen.

**jockstrap** ['dʒɒkstræp] n Suspensorium das.

**jocular** ['dʒɒkjʊlə'] adj witzig, lustig.

**jodhpurs** ['dʒɒdpəz] npl Reithose die.

**Joe Public** [,dʒəʊ-] n Otto Normalverbraucher der.

**jog** [dʒɒg] (pt & pp -ged; cont -ging) n [run]: to go for a ~ joggen gehen ⟨> vt [nudge - person] anlstoßen; [ - table, sb's arm, elbow] stoßen gegen; to ~ sb's memory js Gedächtnis nachlhelfen ⟨> vi [run] joggen.

**jogger** ['dʒɒgə'] n Jogger der, -in die.

**jogging** ['dʒɒgɪŋ] n Joggen das; to go ~ joggen gehen.

**joggle** ['dʒɒgl] vt [baby] hin- und herwiegen.

**Johannesburg** [dʒə'hænɪsbɜ:g] n Johannesburg nt.

**john** [dʒɒn] n Am inf [toilet] Klo das.

**John Hancock** [-,hæŋkɒk] n Am inf Unterschrift die.

**join** [dʒɔɪn] n Naht(stelle) die ⟨> vt - **1.** [connect] verbinden; to ~ sthg to sthg etw mit etw verbinden - **2.** [other people] sich anlschließen (+ D); do ~ us for lunch iss doch mit uns zusammen zu Mittag; I'll ~ you in a moment [follow you] ich komme gleich nach - **3.** [club, organization] beiltreten (+ D); [company] anlfangen bei; [army] gehen zu - **4.** [take part in] teillnehmen an (+ D); to ~ the queue Br, to ~ the line Am sich in die Schlange einlreihen

◇ vi - **1.** [connect - rivers] ineinander fließen; [ - edges, pieces] miteinander verbunden sein - **2.** [become a member] Mitglied werden.

➤ **join in** vt fus mitlmachen bei ◇ vi mitlmachen.

➤ **join up** vi MIL zum Militär gehen.

**joiner** ['dʒɔɪnəʳ] n Tischler der, -in die.

**joinery** ['dʒɔɪnərɪ] n (U) Tischlerei die.

**joint** [dʒɔɪnt] adj [effort] vereint; [responsibility] gemeinsam; [owner] Mit- ◇ n - **1.** ANAT Gelenk das - **2.** [in structure] Verbindungsstelle die; [in carpentry] Fuge die - **3.** Br [of meat] Braten der - **4.** inf pej [place] Laden der - **5.** drugs sl [cannabis cigarette] Joint der.

**joint account** n gemeinsames Konto.

**Joint Chiefs of Staff** npl: **the ~** die Stabschefs der vier Hauptdivisionen der US-Armee.

**jointly** ['dʒɔɪntlɪ] adv gemeinsam.

**joint ownership** n Miteigentum das.

**joint-stock company** n Aktiengesellschaft die.

**joint venture** n Jointventure das.

**joist** [dʒɔɪst] n Balken der.

**joke** [dʒəʊk] n Witz der; **it's gone beyond a ~** da hört der Spaß auf; **to play a ~ on sb** jm einen Streich spielen; **it's no ~** [not easy] das ist keine Kleinigkeit; **to be a ~** [person] eine Witzfigur sein ◇ vi Witze machen; **to ~ about sthg** über etw (A) Witze machen; **to ~ with sb** mit jm scherzen; **you must be joking!** das meinst du doch nicht im Ernst!

**joker** ['dʒəʊkəʳ] n - **1.** [person] Spaßvogel der - **2.** [playing card] Joker der.

**jollity** ['dʒɒlɪtɪ] n Fröhlichkeit die.

**jolly** ['dʒɒlɪ] (compar **-ier;** superl **-iest**) adj lustig, fröhlich ◇ adv Br [very] super.

**jolt** [dʒəʊlt] n - **1.** [jerk] Ruck der - **2.** [shock]: **to give sb a ~** jm einen Schock versetzen ◇ vt - **1.** [jerk] durchlschütteln - **2.** [shock]: **to ~ sb into doing sthg** jn so auf lrütteln, dass er etw tut ◇ vi holpern.

**Joneses** ['dʒəʊnzɪz] npl: **to keep up with the ~** mit den Nachbarn mitlhalten.

**Jordan** ['dʒɔːdn] n Jordanien nt; **the (River) ~** der Jordan.

**Jordanian** [dʒɔːˈdeɪnɪən] adj jordanisch ◇ n Jordanier der, -in die.

**joss stick** ['dʒɒs-] n Räucherstäbchen das.

**jostle** ['dʒɒsl] vt anlrempeln ◇ vi drängeln.

**jot** [dʒɒt] (pt & pp **-ted;** cont **-ting**) n: **there isn't a ~ of truth in it** es ist kein Funken Wahrheit darin; **I don't care a ~ what the rest of you think** es interessiert mich kein bisschen was ihr anderen denkt.

➤ **jot down** vt sep sich (D) notieren.

**jotter** ['dʒɒtəʳ] n Notizheft das.

**jottings** ['dʒɒtɪŋz] npl Notizen pl.

**journal** ['dʒɜːnl] n - **1.** [magazine] Zeitschrift die - **2.** [diary] Tagebuch das.

**journalese** [ˌdʒɜːnəˈliːz] n pej Zeitungsjargon der.

**journalism** ['dʒɜːnəlɪzm] n Journalismus der.

**journalist** ['dʒɜːnəlɪst] n Journalist der, -in die.

**journey** ['dʒɜːnɪ] (pl **-s**) n Reise die; **to go on a ~** verreisen; **an hour's ~** eine Stunde Fahrt.

**joust** [dʒaʊst] n Turnierkampf der ◇ vi (im) Turnier kämpfen.

**jovial** ['dʒəʊvɪəl] adj fröhlich.

**jowls** [dʒaʊlz] npl Kinnbacken pl.

**joy** [dʒɔɪ] n Freude die.

**joyful** ['dʒɔɪfʊl] adj [person] froh; [shout] freudig; [news, scene] erfreulich.

**joyfully** ['dʒɔɪfʊlɪ] adv freudig.

**joyous** ['dʒɔɪəs] adj literary [song] fröhlich; [occasion] freudig.

**joyously** ['dʒɔɪəslɪ] adv literary fröhlich.

**joypad** ['dʒɔɪpæd] n COMPUT Joypad der.

**joyride** ['dʒɔɪraɪd] n Spritztour die (mit einem gestohlenen Auto).

**joyrider** ['dʒɔɪraɪdəʳ] n Person, die mit einem (gestohlenen) Auto eine Spritztour macht.

**joystick** ['dʒɔɪstɪk] n - **1.** [in aircraft] Steuerknüppel der - **2.** [for computers] Joystick der.

**JP** n abbr of **Justice of the Peace.**

**Jr.** (abbr of **Junior**) jun.

**jubilant** ['dʒuːbɪlənt] adj [person, fans] überglücklich; [shout] Jubel-.

**jubilation** [ˌdʒuːbɪˈleɪʃn] n Jubel der.

**jubilee** ['dʒuːbɪliː] n Jubiläum das.

**Judaism** [dʒuːˈdeɪɪzm] n Judaismus der.

**judder** ['dʒʌdəʳ] vi Br rucken.

**judge** [dʒʌdʒ] n - **1.** LAW Richter der, -in die - **2.** SPORT Schiedsrichter der, -in die; [of competition] Preisrichter der, -in die ◇ vt - **1.** LAW [case] verhandeln - **2.** [competition] beurteilen - **3.** [estimate] (einl)schätzen ◇ vi [decide] (be)urteilen; **to ~ from** OR **by sthg, judging from** OR **by sthg** nach etw zu urteilen.

**judg(e)ment** ['dʒʌdʒmənt] n - **1.** LAW Urteil das; **to pass ~ (on sb)** das Urteil sprechen (über jn) - **2.** [opinion] Urteil das, Beurteilung die; **to pass ~ (on sb/sthg)** ein Urteil (über jn/ etw) ablgeben; **to reserve ~** mit einem Urteil zurücklhalten - **3.** [ability to form opinion] Urteilsvermögen das; **against my better ~** gegen mein besseres Wissen - **4.** [punishment] Strafe die.

**judg(e)mental** [dʒʌdʒˈmentl] adj pej zu vorschneller Kritik neigend.

**judicial** [dʒuː'dɪʃl] *adj* Gerichts-.

**judiciary** [dʒuː'dɪʃərɪ] *n:* **the ~** das Gerichtswesen.

**judicious** [dʒuː'dɪʃəs] *adj* klug.

**judo** ['dʒuːdəʊ] *n* Judo *das.*

**jug** [dʒʌg] *n* Krug *der.*

**juggernaut** ['dʒʌgənɔːt] *n* [truck] Laster *der.*

**juggle** ['dʒʌgl] *vt & vi* **- 1.** [throw] jonglieren **- 2.: to ~ (with) figures** die Zahlen so hinldrehen, wie man sie haben will.

**juggler** ['dʒʌglə'] *n* Jongleur *der,* -in *die.*

**jugular (vein)** ['dʒʌgjʊlə'-] *n* Jugularvene *die.*

**juice** [dʒuːs] *n* Saft *der.*
➠ **juices** *npl* [in stomach] (Magen)säfte *pl.*

**juicy** ['dʒuːsɪ] (*compar* **-ier;** *superl* **-iest**) *adj* **- 1.** [fruit] saftig **- 2.** *inf* [story, details] pikant **- 3.** *inf* [role] toll; [contract] fett.

**jukebox** ['dʒuːkbɒks] *n* Musikbox *die.*

**Jul.** (*abbr of* July) Jul.

**July** [dʒuː'laɪ] *n* Juli *der; see also* **September.**

**jumble** ['dʒʌmbl] *n* [mixture] Durcheinander *das* ◇ *vt:* **to ~ (up)** [objects] durcheinander werfen; [words] durcheinander bringen.

**jumble sale** *n Br* in Pfarrsälen oder Gemeinde- und Stadthallen abgehaltene Trödelmärkte, deren Erlös wohltätigen Vereinen zugute kommt.

**jumbo jet** ['dʒʌmbəʊ-] *n* Jumbojet *der.*

**jumbo-sized** [-saizd] *adj* Riesen-.

**jump** [dʒʌmp] *n* **- 1.** [leap] Sprung *der* **- 2.** [fence in horse-jumping] Hindernis *das* **- 3.** [rapid increase] Sprung *der* **- 4.** *phr:* **to keep one ~ ahead of sb** jm einen Schritt voraus sein ◇ *vt* **- 1.** [fence, stream] überspringen; **to ~ the rails** [train] entgleisen; **to ~ the queue** sich vorldrängen **- 2.** *inf* [attack] überfallen **- 3.** *Am* [train, bus] schwarzlfahren in (+ *D*) ◇ *vi* **- 1.** [gen] springen **to ~ over sthg** über etw (*A*) springen; **- 2.** [with fright, surprise] einen Satz machen; **you made me ~!** du hast mich erschreckt! **- 3.** [increase] sprunghaft anlsteigen.
➠ **jump at** *vt fus fig* [opportunity] ergreifen.
➠ **jump in** *vi* hereinlspringen; **~ in!** [get in car] spring rein!
➠ **jump out** *vi* herauslspringen; **to ~ out (of) the window** aus dem Fenster springen.
➠ **jump up** *vi* [get up quickly] auf lspringen.

**jumped-up** ['dʒʌmpt-] *adj Br inf pej* aufgeblasen.

**jumper** ['dʒʌmpə'] *n* **- 1.** *Br* [pullover] Pullover *der* **- 2.** *Am* [dress] Trägerkleid *das.*

**jump jet** *n* Senkrechtstarter *der.*

**jump leads** *npl* Starthilfekabel *pl.*

**jump-start** *vt* mit Starthilfe zünden.

**jumpsuit** ['dʒʌmpsuːt] *n* Overall *der.*

**jumpy** ['dʒʌmpɪ] (*compar* **-ier;** *superl* **-iest**) *adj* nervös.

**Jun. - 1.** (*abbr of* June) Jun. **- 2.** = **Junr.**

**junction** ['dʒʌŋkʃn] *n* [of roads] Kreuzung *die;* [of railway lines, pipes] Knotenpunkt *der;* [on motorway] Anschlussstelle *die.*

**junction box** *n* Verteilerkasten *der.*

**juncture** ['dʒʌŋktʃə'] *n fml:* **at this ~** zu diesem Zeitpunkt.

**June** [dʒuːn] *n* Juni *der; see also* **September.**

**jungle** ['dʒʌŋgl] *n lit & fig* Dschungel *der.*

**jungle gym** *n Am* Klettergerüst *das.*

**junior** ['dʒuːnɪə'] *adj* **- 1.** [younger] jünger **- 2.** [lower in rank] untergeordnet; **~ partner** Juniorpartner *der* **- 3.** *Am* [after name] junior ◇ *n* **- 1.** [person of lower rank] *Person niedrigeren Ranges* **- 2.** [younger person] Jüngere *der, die;* **he is two years my ~** er ist zwei Jahre jünger als ich **- 3.** *Am* SCH & UNIV *Schüler/Student im vorletzten Jahr.*

**junior doctor** *n* Assistenzarzt *der,* -ärztin *die.*

**junior high school** *n Am Schule zwischen Grund- und Oberschule.*

**junior school** *n Br* Grundschule *die* (für 7- bis 11-jährige).

**juniper** ['dʒuːnɪpə'] *n* Wacholder *der.*

**junk** [dʒʌŋk] *n* **- 1.** *inf* [unwanted things] Ramsch *der* **- 2.** [boat] Dschunke *die* ◇ *vt inf* [car, appliance] verschrotten.

**junket** ['dʒʌŋkɪt] *n* **- 1.** [pudding] *süße Nachspeise aus Dickmilch* **- 2.** *inf pej* [trip] *Vergnügungsreise auf Staatskosten.*

**junk food** *n pej* ungesundes Essen wie Fast Food, Chips, Süßigkeiten.

**junkie** ['dʒʌŋkɪ] *n drugs sl* Junkie *der,* Fixer *der,* -in *die.*

**junk mail** *n (U) pej* Reklamemüll *der (der mit der Post kommt).*

**junk shop** *n* Trödelladen *der.*

**Junr** (*abbr of* Junior) jun.

**Jupiter** ['dʒuːpɪtə'] *n* [planet] Jupiter *der.*

**jurisdiction** [ˌdʒʊərɪs'dɪkʃn] *n* [of court] Zuständigkeitsbereich *der.*

**juror** ['dʒʊərə'] *n* Geschworene *der, die.*

**jury** ['dʒʊərɪ] (*pl* **-ies**) *n* **- 1.** [in court of law]: **the ~** die Geschworenen *pl* **- 2.** [in contest] Jury *die.*

**jury box** *n* Geschworenenbank *die.*

**jury service** *n:* **to do ~** das Amt eines/einer Geschworenen auslüben.

**just** [dʒʌst] *adv* **- 1.** [recently] gerade; **to have ~ done sthg** gerade etw getan haben; **he has ~ left** [gen] er ist gerade weggegangen; [in car] er ist gerade losgefahren **- 2.** [at this or that moment] gerade; **I was ~ about to pick up the**

phone, when ... ich wollte gerade den Hörer abnehmen, als ...; **we were ~ leaving, when ...** wir wollten gerade gehen, als ...; **~ as he was leaving** gerade als er wegging; **I'm ~ coming** ich komme schon - **3.** [exactly] genau; **~ what I need** genau das was, ich brauche; **it's ~ as good** es ist genauso gut - **4.** [only] nur; **~ a bit** nur ein bisschen; **~ over an hour** etwas über eine Stunde; **~ a minute!** einen Moment! - **5.** [simply] einfach; '**~ add water**' 'nur Wasser zugeben' - **6.** [almost not]: **(only) ~** gerade (noch) - **7.** [for emphasis]: **~ look what you've done!** sieh nur, was du gemacht hast!; **that's ~ marvellous** das ist einfach großartig - **8.** [in requests]: **could you ~ open your mouth?** können Sie mal den Mund auf lmachen? <> adj [fair] gerecht; **it's only ~** es ist nur recht und billig.

➤ **just about** adv [almost] fast.

➤ **just now** adv - **1.** [a short time ago] gerade; **I was speaking to her ~ now** ich habe gerade mit ihr gesprochen - **2.** [at this moment] im Moment.

**justice** ['dʒʌstɪs] n (U) - **1.** [fairness] Gerechtigkeit die - **2.** LAW [power of law] Justiz die; **to bring sb to ~** jn vor Gericht bringen - **3.** [of cause, claim] Rechtmäßigkeit die - **4.** [judge] Richter der, -in die - **5.** phr: **to do ~ to sthg** [to job] etw (D) gerecht werden; [to meal] etw (D) gebührend zulsprechen; **to do ~ to sb** jm gerecht werden; **to do o.s. ~** zeigen, was man kann.

**Justice of the Peace** (pl **Justices of the Peace**) n Friedensrichter der, -in die.

**justifiable** ['dʒʌstɪfaɪəbl] adj berechtigt.

**justifiably** ['dʒʌstɪfaɪəblɪ] adv zu Recht.

**justification** [ˌdʒʌstɪfɪ'keɪʃn] n Rechtfertigung die.

**justify** ['dʒʌstɪfaɪ] (pt & pp -ied) vt - **1.** [gen] rechtfertigen; **how can you ~ spending so much money?** wie kannst du es rechtfertigen, so viel Geld ausgegeben zu haben? - **2.** TYPO justieren; COMPUT ausIrichten; **right/left justified** rechts-/linksbündig.

**justly** ['dʒʌstlɪ] adv zu Recht, mit Recht.

**justness** ['dʒʌstnɪs] n Gerechtigkeit die.

**jut** [dʒʌt] (pt & pp **-ted**; cont **-ting**) vi: **to ~ (out)** (her)vorIragen.

**juvenile** ['dʒuːvənaɪl] adj - **1.** LAW jugendlich; **~ crime** die Jugendkriminalität - **2.** pej [childish] infantil <> n LAW Jugendliche der, die.

**juvenile court** n Jugendgericht das.

**juvenile delinquent** n jugendlicher Straftäter, jugendliche Straftäterin.

**juxtapose** [ˌdʒʌkstə'pəʊz] vt: **to ~ sthg with sthg** etw neben etw (A) stellen.

**juxtaposition** [ˌdʒʌkstəpə'zɪʃn] n Nebeneinanderstellung die.

**k** (pl **k's** OR **ks**), **K** (pl **K's** OR **Ks**) [keɪ] n [letter] k das, K das.

➤ **K** n - **1.** (abbr of **kilobyte**) Kb das - **2.** (abbr of **thousand**) Tsd.

**kaftan** ['kæftæn] n Kaftan der.

**Kalahari Desert** [ˌkælə'hɑːrɪ-] n: **the ~** die Kalahari-Wüste.

**kale** [keɪl] n Grünkohl der.

**kaleidoscope** [kə'laɪdəskəʊp] n Kaleidoskop das.

**Kampuchea** [ˌkæmpuː'tʃɪə] n Kamputschea nt.

**kangaroo** [ˌkæŋgə'ruː] n Känguruh das.

**kaolin** ['keɪəlɪn] n Kaolin das.

**kaput** [kə'pʊt] adj inf kaputt.

**karaoke** [kærɪ'əʊkiː] n Karaoke das.

**karat** ['kærət] n Am Karat das.

**karate** [kə'rɑːtɪ] n Karate das.

**Kashmir** [kæʃ'mɪəʳ] n Kaschmir nt.

**kayak** ['kaɪæk] n Kajak der OR das.

**KB** (abbr of **kilobyte(s)**) n COMPUT Kb das.

**KC** (abbr of **King's Counsel**) n Anwalt der, -wältin die der Krone.

**kcal** (abbr of **kilocalorie**) kcal.

**kebab** [kɪ'bæb] n: **(shish) ~** Kebab der; **(doner) ~** Gyros der.

**kedgeree** [ˌkedʒə'riː] n Br Gericht aus Reis, Fisch und Eiern.

**keel** [kiːl] n Kiel der; **to get sthg back on an even ~** etw wieder auf die Beine bringen.

➤ **keel over** vi [ship] kentern; [person] umlkippen.

**keen** [kiːn] adj - **1.** [enthusiastic] begeistert; **to be ~ on sthg** etw sehr mögen; **to be ~ to do** OR **on doing sthg** etw unbedingt tun wollen; **she wasn't ~ on the idea** sie war von der Sache nicht angetan - **2.** [interest, desire, competition] stark - **3.** [edge] scharf; [eyesight, hearing] gut - **4.** [wind] scharf.

**keenly** ['kiːnlɪ] adv - **1.** [interested] stark; **~ contested** hart umkämpft - **2.** [watch, listen] scharf.

**keenness** ['kiːnnɪs] n - **1.** [enthusiasm] Begeisterung die - **2.** [of interest, competition] Stärke die - **3.** [of wind, blade] Schärfe die; **the ~ of his eyesight** sein gutes Sehvermögen.

**keep** [ki:p] (*pt* & *pp* **kept**) *vt* - **1.** [retain] behalten; **please ~ the change** bitte behalten Sie das Wechselgeld; **to ~ a seat for sb** einen Platz für jn freihalten - **2.** [store] aufl-bewahren - **3.** [maintain] halten; **to ~ sb waiting** jn warten lassen; **to ~ sb awake** jn wach halten - **4.** [promise, appointment] einlhalten - **5.** [secret] für sich behalten; **to ~ sthg from sb** etw vor jm geheim halten - **6.** [delay]: **what kept you?** wo bist du denn so lang gewesen? - **7.** [record, diary] führen; **to ~ a note of sthg** etw auf lschreiben - **8.** [prevent]: **to ~ sb from doing sthg** jn davon abhalten, etw zu tun; **the noise kept me from sleeping** der Lärm ließ mich nicht schlafen - **9.** [own - farm animals] halten - **10.** *phr:* **they ~ themselves to themselves** sie bleiben für sich ◇ *vi* - **1.** [remain] bleiben; **to ~ fit** fit bleiben; **to ~ silent** schweigen; **to ~ warm** sich warm halten; **to ~ clear of sthg** sich von etw fern halten - **2.** [continue]: **to ~ doing sthg** [continuously] etw weiter tun; [repeatedly] etw dauernd tun; **to ~ going** [walking] weiterlgehen; [driving] weiterlfahren; [working] weiterlmachen; '**~ left**' 'links fahren'; **~ straight on** [walking] gehen Sie immer geradeaus; [driving] fahren Sie immer geradeaus - **3.** [food] sich halten - **4.** *Br* [in health]: **how are you ~ing?** wie geht es dir? ◇ *n* [food, lodging] Unterhalt *der;* **to earn one's ~** sein eigenes Brot verdienen.

➤ **for keeps** *adv* für immer.

➤ **keep at** *vt fus:* **to ~ at it** am Ball bleiben; **~ at it!** mach weiter!

➤ **keep back** *vt sep* - **1.** [information] verschweigen - **2.** [money] zurücklbehalten ◇ *vi* [stand back] zurücklbleiben.

➤ **keep down** *vt sep* - **1.** [prices] niedrig halten - **2.** [food] bei sich behalten.

➤ **keep off** *vt fus* [subject, food, drink] vermeiden; '**~ off the grass**' 'Rasen betreten verboten'.

➤ **keep on** *vi* - **1.** [continue]: **to ~ on doing sthg** [continuously] etw weiter tun; [repeatedly] etw dauernd tun - **2.** [talk incessantly]: **to ~ on (about sthg)** dauernd (über etw (A)) reden.

➤ **keep on at** *vt fus Br:* **to ~ on at sb** dauernd an jm herumlnörgeln.

➤ **keep out** *vt sep* nicht hereinllassen ◇ *vi:* '**~ out!**' 'Betreten verboten!'; **~ out of this!** misch dich nicht ein!

➤ **keep to** *vt fus* - **1.** [rule, promise, plan]: **to ~ to sthg** sich an etw (A) halten - **2.** [not deviate from]: **to ~ to the point** bei der Sache bleiben; **~ to the path!** auf dem Weg bleiben!

➤ **keep up** *vt sep* - **1.** [prevent from falling] halten; **a belt to ~ my trousers up** ein Gürtel, damit meine Hose nicht herunterlrutscht - **2.** [maintain - standards, friendship] aufrechtl-erhalten; [ - house, garden] instand halten; **~ it up!** weiter so! - **3.** [prevent from going to bed]: **to ~ sb up** jn vom Schlafen ablhalten ◇ *vi* - **1.** [maintain pace, level] mitlhalten; **to ~ up with sb/sthg** mit jm/etw mithalten können; **to**

**~ up with the news** sich auf dem Laufenden halten - **2.** [stay in contact]: **to ~ up with sb** mit jm in Kontakt bleiben.

**keeper** ['ki:pə'] *n* - **1.** [in zoo] Wärter *der*, -in *die* - **2.** [of museum] Kustos *der*.

**keep-fit** *Br n* Fitness *die* ◇ *comp* Fitness-.

**keeping** ['ki:pɪŋ] *n* - **1.** [care]: **in safe ~** sicher verwahrt; **for safe ~** zur Verwahrung - **2.** [conformity]: **to be in ~ with sthg** [regulations, decision] etw (D) entsprechen; [clothes, furniture, style] zu etw passen.

**keepsake** ['ki:pseɪk] *n* Andenken *das*.

**keg** [keg] *n* kleines Fass.

**ken** [ken] *n:* **it's beyond our ~** es entzieht sich unserer Kenntnis.

**kennel** ['kenl] *n* - **1.** [for dog] Hundehütte *die;* [for many dogs] Zwinger *der* - **2.** *Am* = **kennels**.

➤ **kennels** *npl Br* [for boarding pets] Tierpension *die.*

**Kenya** ['kenjə] *n* Kenia *nt.*

**kept** [kept] *pt* & *pp* ▷ **keep.**

**kerb** [kɜ:b] *n Br* Bordsteinkante *die.*

**kerb crawler** [-ˌkrɔ:lə'] *n Br* Freier, *der* langsam an der Straßenseite entlangfährt, um sich eine Prostituierte auszusuchen.

**kerbstone** ['kɜ:bstəʊn] *n Br* Bordstein *der.*

**kerfuffle** [kəˈfʌfl] *n Br inf* [noise] Lärm *der;* [fight] Rangelei *die.*

**kernel** ['kɜ:nl] *n* [of nut] Kern *der.*

**kerosene** ['kerəsi:n] *n* Petroleum *das.*

**kestrel** ['kestrəl] *n* Turmfalke *der.*

**ketchup** ['ketʃəp] *n* Ketschup *das* OR *der.*

**kettle** ['ketl] *n* Kessel *der;* **to put the ~ on** Wasser auf lsetzen.

**kettledrum** ['ketldrʌm] *n* (Kessel)pauke *die.*

**key** [ki:] *n* - **1.** [gen] Schlüssel *der* - **2.** [of typewriter, computer, piano] Taste *die* - **3.** MUS Tonart *die* ◇ *adj* [main] Schlüssel-, wichtigste, -r, -s.

➤ **key in** *vt sep* eingeben.

**keyboard** ['ki:bɔ:d] *n* - **1.** [of typewriter, computer] Tastatur *die*, Keyboard *das* - **2.** [of piano] Klaviatur *die*, Tastatur *die;* [of organ] Manual *das;* [of electric organ] Keyboard *das* ◇ *vt* einlgeben.

**keyed up** [ˌki:d-] *adj* aufgeregt, nervös.

**keyhole** ['ki:həʊl] *n* Schlüsselloch *das.*

**keynote** ['ki:nəʊt] *n* [main point] Hauptgedanke *der.*

**keypad** ['ki:pæd] *n* COMPUT Tastenfeld *das.*

**key ring** *n* Schlüsselring *der.*

**keystone** ['ki:stəʊn] *n* - **1.** [stone] Schlussstein *der* - **2.** [essential idea] Grundprinzip *das.*

**keystroke** ['ki:strəʊk] *n* COMPUT Drücken *das* (einer Taste).

**kg** (*abbr of* **kilogram**) kg.

**KGB** *n* KGB *der.*

**khaki** [ˈkɑːkɪ] *adj* kakifarben ◇ *n* - **1.** [colour] Kaki *das* - **2.** [cloth] Kaki *der.*

**kHz** (*abbr of* **kilohertz**) *n* kHz.

**kibbutz** [kɪˈbʊts] (*pl* **kibbutzim** [kɪbʊˈtsiːm] OR -**es**) *n* Kibbuz *der.*

**kick** [kɪk] *n* - **1.** [with foot] (Fuß)tritt *der* - **2.** *inf* [excitement]: **to do sthg for ~s** etw aus Spaß tun; **to get a ~ from sthg** an etw (D) Spaß haben - **3.** [of gun] Rückstoß *der;* **a drink that's got a ~** ein Drink, der es in sich hat ◇ *vt* - **1.** [with foot - gen] treten; [ - ball] kicken; **I could have ~ed myself!** ich hätte mich ohrfeigen können! - **2.** *inf* [habit] auf |geben ◇ *vi* [person] treten; [baby] strampeln; [animal] aus|schlagen, treten.

◆ **kick about, kick around** *vi Br inf* [lie around] herum|hängen.

◆ **kick off** *vi* - **1.** FTBL an|stoßen - **2.** *inf fig* [start] an|fangen.

◆ **kick out** *vt sep inf* raus|schmeißen.

◆ **kick up** *vt fus inf*: **to ~ up a fuss** Ärger OR Theater machen.

**kickoff** [ˈkɪkɒf] *n* [in soccer] Anstoß *der;* [in American football] Kick-off *der.*

**kick-start** *vt* [motorbike] (mit dem Kickstarter) an|treten.

**kid** [kɪd] (*pt & pp* -**ded;** *cont* -**ding**) *n* - **1.** *inf* [child] Kind *das* - **2.** [young goat] Zicklein *das* - **3.** [leather] Glacéleder *das* ◇ *comp inf* [brother, sister] kleine, -r, jüngere, -r ◇ *vt inf* - **1.** [tease] veralbern - **2.** [delude]: **to ~ o.s.** sich (D) etwas vor|machen ◇ *vi inf*: **to be ~ding** Spaß machen; **you're ~ding!** das ist nicht dein Ernst!; **no ~ding!** im Ernst!, wirklich!

**kiddie, kiddy** [ˈkɪdɪ] (*pl* -**ies**) *n inf* Kleine *der, die.*

**kid gloves** *npl*: **to treat** OR **handle sb with ~** jn mit Samthandschuhen an|fassen.

**kidnap** [ˈkɪdnæp] (*Br pt & pp* -**ped;** *cont* -**ping,** *Am pt & pp* -**ed;** *cont* -**ing**) *vt* entführen, kid- nappen.

**kidnapper** *Br*, **kidnaper** *Am* [ˈkɪdnæpəʳ] *n* Kidnapper *der*, -in *die*, Entführer *der*, -in *die.*

**kidnapping** *Br*, **kidnaping** *Am* [ˈkɪdnæpɪŋ] *n* Kidnapping *das*, Entführung *die.*

**kidney** [ˈkɪdnɪ] (*pl* **kidneys**) *n* Niere *die.*

**kidney bean** *n* Kidneybohne *die.*

**kidney machine** *n* künstliche Niere.

**Kilimanjaro** [ˌkɪlɪmənˈdʒɑːrəʊ] *n* Kiliman- dscharo *der.*

**kill** [kɪl] *vt* - **1.** [person, animal] töten; [murder] um| bringen; [plant] eingehen lassen; **to ~ o.s.** sich um|bringen; **my feet are ~ing me** *inf* meine Füße bringen mich um - **2.** *fig* [hope] zerstören; [conversation, desire] zum Erliegen bringen; [pain] ab|töten, betäuben; **to ~ time** Zeit tot|schlagen ◇ *vi* töten ◇ *n* - **1.** [killing]: **the lion made its ~** der Löwe erlegte sein Op-

fer; **to move in for the ~** *fig* zum entscheiden- den Schlag aus|holen - **2.** [dead animal] Beute *die.*

◆ **kill off** *vt sep* - **1.** [cause death of] vernichten - **2.** *fig* [chances, hope] zunichte machen.

**killer** [ˈkɪləʳ] *n* - **1.** [person] Mörder *der*, -in *die* - **2.** [disease] tödliche Krankheit.

**killer whale** *n* Schwertwal *der.*

**killing** [ˈkɪlɪŋ] *adj inf* [very funny] urkomisch ◇ *n* - **1.** [murder] Tötung *die* - **2.** *inf* [profit]: **to make a ~** ein Riesengeschäft machen.

**killjoy** [ˈkɪldʒɔɪ] *n* Spielverderber *der.*

**kiln** [kɪln] *n* [for bricks, pottery] Brennofen *der;* [for hops] Darrofen *der.*

**kilo** [ˈkiːləʊ] (*pl* -**s**) (*abbr of* **kilogram**) *n* Kilo *das.*

**kilo-** [ˈkɪlə] *prefix* Kilo-.

**kilobyte** [ˈkɪləbaɪt] *n* Kilobyte *das.*

**kilocalorie** [ˈkɪləˌkælərɪ] *n* Kilokalorie *die.*

**kilogram(me)** [ˈkɪləgræm] *n* Kilogramm *das.*

**kilohertz** [ˈkɪləhɜːts] (*pl inv*) *n* Kilohertz *das.*

**kilojoule** [ˈkɪlədʒuːl] *n* Kilojoule *das.*

**kilometre** *Br* [ˈkɪləˌmiːtəʳ], **kilometer** *Am* [kɪˈlɒmɪtər] *n* Kilometer *der.*

**kilowatt** [ˈkɪləwɒt] *n* Kilowatt *das.*

**kilt** [kɪlt] *n* Kilt *der*, Schottenrock *der.*

**kimono** [kɪˈməʊnəʊ] (*pl* -**s**) *n* Kimono *der.*

**kin** [kɪn] *n* ⊳ **kith.**

**kind** [kaɪnd] *adj* nett; **that's very ~ of you** es ist sehr nett von dir; **would you be so ~ as to …?** könnten Sie bitte …? ◇ *n* Art *die;* [of cheese, wine etc] Sorte *die;* **what ~ of music do you like?** welche Musik magst du?; **what ~ of car do you drive?** was für ein Auto hast du?; **~ of** *inf* irgendwie; **they're two of a ~** sie sind vom gleichen Schlag; **all ~s of animals** allerlei Tie- re; **in ~** [payment] in Naturalien.

**kindergarten** [ˈkɪndəˌgɑːtn] *n* Kindergarten *der.*

**kind-hearted** [-ˈhɑːtɪd] *adj* gutherzig.

**kindle** [ˈkɪndl] *vt* - **1.** [fire] an|zünden - **2.** *fig* [idea, feeling] entfachen.

**kindling** [ˈkɪndlɪŋ] *n* Anmachholz *das.*

**kindly** [ˈkaɪndlɪ] (*compar* -**ier;** *superl* -**iest**) *adj* gütig, wohltätig ◇ *adv* - **1.** [speak, smile] freundlich; **to look ~ on sb/sthg** auf jn/etw freundlich blicken - **2.** [please] freundlicher- weise - **3.** *phr*: **not to take ~ to sthg** etw nicht gut auf |nehmen.

**kindness** [ˈkaɪndnɪs] *n* - **1.** [gentleness] Freund- lichkeit *die* - **2.** [helpful act] Gefälligkeit *die.*

**kindred** [ˈkɪndrɪd] *adj* ähnlich; **~ spirit** ver- wandte Seele.

**kinetic** [kɪˈnetɪk] *adj* kinetisch.

**kinfolk(s)** [ˈkɪnfəʊk(s)] *npl Am* = **kinsfolk.**

**king** [kɪŋ] *n* König *der.*

**kingdom** ['kɪŋdəm] n - **1.** [country] Königreich das - **2.** [of animals, plants] Reich das.
**kingfisher** ['kɪŋ,fɪʃəʳ] n Eisvogel der.
**kingpin** ['kɪŋpɪn] n - **1.** TECH Achsschenkelbolzen der - **2.** fig [person] Hauptperson die.
**king prawn** n Riesengarnele die.
**king-size(d)** [-saɪz(d)] adj Kingsize-.
**kink** [kɪŋk] n [in rope] Knick der.
**kinky** ['kɪŋkɪ] (compar -ier; superl -iest) adj inf abartig.
**kinsfolk** ['kɪnzfəʊk], **kinfolk(s)** Am npl (Bluts)verwandte pl.
**kinship** ['kɪnʃɪp] n Verwandtschaft die.
**kiosk** ['kiːɒsk] n - **1.** [small shop] Kiosk der - **2.** Br [telephone box] Telefonzelle die.
**kip** [kɪp] (pt & pp -ped; cont -ping) Br inf n: to have a ~ eine Runde schlafen ⬦ vi eine Runde schlafen.
**kipper** ['kɪpəʳ] n Räucherhering der.
**kiss** [kɪs] n Kuss der; to give sb a ~ jm einen Kuss geben ⬦ vt küssen; to ~ sb goodbye jn zum Abschied küssen ⬦ vi sich küssen.
**kiss of death** n fig: to be the ~ for sthg etw (D) den Todesstoß versetzen.
**kiss of life** n: the ~ die Mund-zu-Mund Beatmung.
**kit** [kɪt] (pt & pp -ted; cont -ting) n - **1.** [set] Ausrüstung die, Satz der; repair ~ Flickzeug das - **2.** (U) [sports clothes] Sportsachen pl - **3.** [to be assembled] Bausatz der.
⬦ **kit out** vt sep Br komplett OR vollständig ausrüsten.
**kit bag** n [of soldier] Sturmgepäck das; [of seaman] Seesack der.
**kitchen** ['kɪtʃɪn] n Küche die.
**kitchenette** [,kɪtʃɪ'net] n Kochnische die.
**kitchen garden** n Gemüsegarten der.
**kitchen roll** n Küchenrolle der.
**kitchen sink** n Spülbecken das.
**kitchen unit** n Küchenelement das.
**kite** [kaɪt] n - **1.** [toy] Drachen der - **2.** [bird] Milan der.
**Kite-mark** n Br ≃ GS-Siegel das, Prüfsiegel des Britischen Instituts für Normung auf Waren, welches deren Konformität mit Sicherheits- und Qualitätsstandards zertifiziert.
**kith** [kɪθ] n: ~ and kin Kind und Kegel.
**kitten** ['kɪtn] n Kätzchen das.
**kitty** ['kɪtɪ] (pl -ies) n - **1.** [for bills, drinks] Gemeinschaftskasse die; [in card games] Bank die - **2.** inf [cat] Kätzchen das.
**kiwi** ['kiːwiː] n - **1.** [bird] Kiwi der - **2.** inf [New Zealander] Neuseeländer der, -in die.
**kiwi fruit** n Kiwi die.

**KKK** n abbr of Ku Klux Klan.
**klaxon** ['klæksn] n Mehrklanghorn das.
**Kleenex®** ['kliːneks] n Tempo® das.
**kleptomaniac** [,kleptə'meɪnɪæk] n Kleptomane der, -nin die.
**km** (abbr of kilometre) km.
**km/h** (abbr of kilometres per hour) km/h.
**knack** [næk] n Trick der; to have a OR the ~ of doing sthg [ability] den Dreh rauslhaben, etw zu tun; he has a OR the ~ of turning up late er hat das Talent, (immer) zu spät zu kommen.
**knacker** ['nækəʳ] Br n [horse slaughterer] Pferdeschlächter der, Abdecker der ⬦ vt inf kaputt machen.
**knackered** ['nækəd] adj Br inf kaputt.
**knapsack** ['næpsæk] n Rucksack der; MIL Tornister der.
**knave** [neɪv] n [playing card] Bube der.
**knead** [niːd] vt [dough, clay] kneten.
**knee** [niː] n Knie das; to be on one's ~s knien; to go down on one's ~s niederlknien; to bring sb to their ~s jn in die Knie zwingen.
**kneecap** ['niːkæp] n Kniescheibe die.
**knee-deep** adj knietief.
**knee-high** adj kniehoch.
**kneel** [niːl] (Br pt & pp knelt, Am pt & pp knelt OR -ed) vi knien.
⬦ **kneel down** vi niederlknien.
**knee-length** adj knielang.
**knees-up** n Br inf [party] wilde Party.
**knell** [nel] n Totengeläute das; to sound the ~ of sthg fig das Ende einer Sache (G) einläuten.
**knelt** [nelt] pt & pp ⊳ kneel.
**knew** [njuː] pt ⊳ know.
**knickers** ['nɪkəz] npl - **1.** Br [underwear] Schlüpfer der - **2.** Am [knickerbockers] Knickerbockers pl.
**knick-knacks** ['nɪknæks] npl Nippes pl.
**knife** [naɪf] (pl knives) n Messer das ⬦ vt einlstechen auf (+ A).
**knight** [naɪt] n - **1.** [gen] Ritter der - **2.** [in chess] Springer der ⬦ vt in den Adelsstand erheben.
**knighthood** ['naɪthʊd] n: to get OR be given a ~ in den Adelsstand erhoben werden.
**knit** [nɪt] (pt & pp knit OR -ted; cont -ting) adj: closely OR tightly ~ fig eng verbunden ⬦ vt stricken ⬦ vi - **1.** [with wool] stricken - **2.** [join] zusammenlwachsen.
**knitted** ['nɪtɪd] adj [scarf, hat] gestrickt.
**knitting** ['nɪtɪŋ] n (U) - **1.** [activity] Stricken das - **2.** [thing being knitted] Strickzeug das.
**knitting needle** n Stricknadel die.

K

**knitting pattern** *n* Strickmuster *das.*

**knitwear** ['nɪtweəʳ] *n (U)* Strickwaren *pl.*

**knives** [naɪvz] *pl* ⊏> **knife.**

**knob** [nɒb] *n* - **1.** [handle] Griff *der,* Knauf *der* - **2.** [on TV, radio] Knopf *der.*

**knobbly** *Br* ['nɒblɪ] (*compar* **-ier;** *superl* **-iest**), **knobby** *Am* ['nɒbɪ] (*compar* **-ier;** *superl* **-iest**) *adj* [surface] knorrig; [knees] knochig

**knock** [nɒk] *n* - **1.** [hit - on body] Schlag *der;* [ - on door] Klopfen *das* - **2.** *inf* [piece of bad luck] Schlag *der* <> *vt* - **1.** [hit] (an)schlagen, (an)stoßen - **2.** *inf* [criticize] stark kritisieren <> *vi* - **1.** [on door]: **to ~ (at** OR **on)** klopfen (auf OR an (+ A)) - **2.** [car engine] klopfen.

◆ **knock about, knock around** *inf* *vt sep* [beat up] verprügeln <> *vi* - **1.** [wander about] sich herumltreiben - **2.** [spend time]: **to ~ about with sb** mit jm herumlhängen.

◆ **knock back** *vt sep* *inf* [drink] trinken; [drink quickly] herunterlstürzen.

◆ **knock down** *vt sep* - **1.** [pedestrian] anlfahren - **2.** [building] niederlreißen - **3.** [price] herunterlhandeln.

◆ **knock off** *vt sep* - **1.** [lower price by]: **he ~ed £5 off (the price)** er ließ 5 Pfund (vom Preis) nach - **2.** *Br inf* [steal] klauen <> *vi inf* [stop working] Feierabend machen.

◆ **knock out** *vt sep* - **1.** [make unconscious - subj: person, punch] k.o. schlagen; [ - subj: drug] bewusstlos werden lassen - **2.** [from competition] auslscheiden.

◆ **knock over** *vt sep* - **1.** [push over] umlstoßen; [person] umlwerfen - **2.** [pedestrian] überfahren.

◆ **knock up** *vt sep* [produce hurriedly] schnell zusammenlschustern <> *vi* TENNIS sich *(D)* einlspielen.

**knocker** ['nɒkəʳ] *n* [on door] Türklopfer *der.*

**knocking** ['nɒkɪŋ] *n* - *(U)* [noise] Klopfen *das* - **2.** *inf* [criticism]: **to get** OR **take a ~** stark kritisiert werden.

**knock-kneed** [-'niːd] *adj* X-beinig.

**knock-on effect** *n* *Br* Auswirkung *die.*

**knockout** ['nɒkaʊt] *n* - **1.** [in boxing] Knockout *der,* K.O. *der* - **2.** *inf* [sensation]: **she's a ~** sie ist toll.

**knockout competition** *n* *Br* Ausscheidungs(wett)kampf *der.*

**knot** [nɒt] (*pt* & *pp* **-ted;** *cont* **-ting**) *n* - **1.** [in rope, string] Knoten *der;* **to tie/untie a ~** einen Knoten machen/lösen - **2.** [of people] (Menschen)knäuel *das* - **3.** [in wood] Ast *der* - **4.** [ship's speed] Knoten *der* <> *vt* [rope, string] knoten.

**knotted** ['nɒtɪd] *adj* - **1.** [rope, handkerchief] geknotet - **2.** *phr:* **get ~!** *inf* vergiss es!

**knotty** ['nɒtɪ] (*compar* **-ier;** *superl* **-iest**) *adj* [difficult] verzwickt, knifflig.

**know** [nəʊl] (*pt* **knew;** *pp* **known**) *vt* - **1.** [fact, information] wissen; **as far as I ~** so viel ich weiß; **to let sb ~ sthg** jn etw wissen lassen - **2.** [person, place] kennen; **to get to ~ sb** jn kennen lernen - **3.** [language, skill] können; **to ~ how to do sthg** etw tun können - **4.** [recognize] erkennen - **5.** [call]: **to be ~n as** bekannt sein als - **6.** [distinguish] unterscheiden können; **to ~ right from wrong** Gut und Böse unterscheiden können <> *vi:* **I ~** das weiß ich; **to ~ about sthg** [understand] sich mit etw auslkennen; [have heard about] etw wissen; **to ~ of** kennen, wissen von; **you ~** [for emphasis] weißt du; **there is no ~ing** ... niemand kann sagen ...; **you should have ~n better** das hättest du wissen müssen <> *n:* **to be in the ~** im Bilde sein.

**know-all** *n* *Br* Besserwisser *der,* -in *die.*

**know-how** *n* Know-how *das.*

**knowing** ['nəʊɪŋ] *adj* [look, smile] wissend.

**knowingly** ['nəʊɪŋlɪ] *adv* - **1.** [look, smile] wissend - **2.** [act] wissentlich.

**know-it-all** *n* = **know-all.**

**knowledge** ['nɒlɪdʒ] *n (U)* - **1.** [learning] Kenntnisse *pl,* Wissen *das;* **it's common ~ that** ... es ist allgemein bekannt, dass ... - **2.** [awareness] Wissen *das;* **I had no ~ of it** ich wusste nichts davon; **not to my ~** nicht, dass ich wüsste; **to the best of my ~** soweit OR soviel ich weiß.

**knowledgeable** ['nɒlɪdʒəbl] *adj* sachkundig; **to be ~ about sthg** in etw *(D)* bewandert sein.

**known** [nəʊn] *pp* ⊏> **know** <> *adj* bekannt.

**knuckle** ['nʌkl] *n* - **1.** ANAT (Finger)knöchel *der* - **2.** [of meat] Haxe *die.*

◆ **knuckle down** *vi* sich dahinter klemmen; **to ~ down to sthg** sich hinter *(A)* etw klemmen.

◆ **knuckle under** *vi* sich unterwerfen.

**knuckle-duster** *n* Schlagring *der.*

**KO** (*abbr of* **knockout**) *n* K.O. *der.*

**koala (bear)** [kəʊˈɑːlə-] *n* Koala(bär) *der.*

**kooky** ['kuːkɪ] (*compar* **-ier;** *superl* **-iest**) *adj* *Am* *inf* verrückt.

**Koran** [kɒˈrɑːn] *n:* **the ~** der Koran.

**Korea** [kəˈrɪə] *n* Korea *nt.*

**Korean** [kəˈrɪən] *adj* koreanisch <> *n* - **1.** [person] Koreaner *der,* -in *die* - **2.** [language] Koreanisch(e) *das.*

**kosher** ['kəʊʃəʳ] *adj* koscher.

**kowtow** [ˌkaʊˈtaʊ] *vi:* **to ~ (to sb)** [behave humbly] (vor jm) kriechen.

**Kremlin** ['kremlɪn] *n:* **the ~** der Kreml.

**KS** *abk für Kansas, in Postanschrift verwendet.*

**Kuala Lumpur** [ˌkwɑːləˈlʊmpʊəʳ] *n* Kuala Lumpur *nt.*

**kudos** ['kjuːdɒs] *n* Prestige *das.*

**Ku Klux Klan** [ˌkuːklʌks'klæn] *n:* the ~ der Ku-Klux-Klan.

**kung fu** [ˌkʌŋ'fuː] *n* Kung-Fu *das.*

**Kurd** [kɜːd] *n* Kurde *der,* -din *die.*

**Kurdish** ['kɜːdɪʃ] *adj* kurdisch.

**Kurdistan** [ˌkɜːdɪ'stɑːn] *n* Kurdistan *nt.*

**Kuwait** [ku'weɪt] *n* - **1.** [country] Kuwait *nt* - **2.** [city] Kuwait-City *nt.*

**Kuwaiti** [ku'weɪtɪ] *adj* kuwaitisch ⬦ *n* Kuwaiter *der,* -in *die.*

**kW** (*abbr of* **kilowatt**) kW.

**kWh** (*abbr of* **kilowatt-hour**) kWh.

**KY** *abk für* Kentucky, *in Postanschrift verwendet.*

**l**[1] (*pl* **l's** *OR* **ls**), **L** (*pl* **L's** *OR* **Ls**) [el] *n* [letter] l *das,* L *das.*

➡ **L** - **1.** *abbr of* **lake** - **2.** *abbr of* **large** - **3.** *abbr of* **left** - **4.** *abbr of* **learner.**

> **L**
>
> Im Vereinigten Königreich zeigt ein rotes „L" am Kraftfahrzeug an, dass der Fahrer oder die Fahrerin die Fahrprüfung noch nicht absolviert hat und daher nur in Begleitung einer Person mit Führerschein ans Steuer darf.

**l**[2] (*abbr of* **litre**)l.

**LA** *n* (*abbr of* **Los Angeles**) Los Angeles *nt,* LA *nt* ⬦ *abk für* Louisiana, *in Postanschrift verwendet.*

**lab** [læb] *n inf* Labor *das.*

**label** ['leɪbl] (*Br pt* & *pp* -**led**; *cont* -**ling**, *Am pt* & *pp* -**ed**; *cont* -**ing**) *n* - **1.** [on bottle, clothing] Etikett *das;* [tied on] Anhänger *der;* [stuck on] Aufkleber *der* - **2.** [of record] Label *das* ⬦ *vt* - **1.** [fix label to - bottle, clothing] etikettieren; [ - with tied-on label] mit Anhänger versehen; [ - with stuck-on label] mit Aufkleber versehen - **2.** [describe]: **to ~ sb (as) sthg** jn als etw ein|stufen.

**labor** *etc n Am* = **labour** *etc.*

**laboratory** [*Br* lə'bɒrətrɪ, *Am* 'læbrəˌtɔːrɪ] (*pl* -**ies**) *n* Labor(atorium) *das* ⬦ *comp* Labor-.

**Labor Day** *n Am* Tag der Arbeit *der (am ersten Montag im September).*

**laborious** [lə'bɔːrɪəs] *adj* mühsam.

**labor union** *n Am* (Arbeiter)gewerkschaft *die.*

**labour** *Br,* **labor** *Am* ['leɪbə'] *n* - **1.** [work] Arbeit *die* - **2.** (*U*) [workers] Arbeiterschaft *die,* Arbeiter *pl* - **3.** MED (Geburts)wehen *pl;* **to go into ~** in den Wehen liegen ⬦ *vt:* **to ~ the point** darauf herum|reiten ⬦ *vi* - **1.** [work] arbeiten - **2.** [struggle]: **to ~ at** *OR* **over sthg** sich mit etw plagen; **to ~ under a delusion** sich einer Täuschung hingeben.

➡ **Labour** *Br* POL *adj* Labour- ⬦ *n* Labour Party *die.*

**labour camp** *n* Arbeitslager *das.*

**labour costs** *npl* Arbeitskosten *pl.*

**laboured** *Br,* **labored** *Am* ['leɪbəd] *adj* [breathing] schwer; [style] schwerfällig.

**labourer** *Br,* **laborer** *Am* ['leɪbərə'] *n* Arbeiter *der* -in *die.*

**labour force** *n* Arbeiterschaft *die.*

**labour-intensive** *adj* arbeitsintensiv.

**labour market** *n* Arbeitsmarkt *der.*

**labour of love** *n:* **it was a ~** das habe ich aus Liebe zur Sache gemacht.

**labour pains** *npl* (Geburts)wehen *pl.*

**Labour Party** *n Br:* **the ~** die Labour Party.

**labour relations** *npl* Arbeitsbeziehungen *pl.*

**laboursaving** *Br,* **laborsaving** *Am* ['leɪbəˌseɪvɪŋ] *adj:* **~ device** arbeitssparende Vorrichtung.

**Labrador** ['læbrədɔː'] *n* [dog] Labrador *der.*

**laburnum** [lə'bɜːnəm] *n* Goldregen *der.*

**labyrinth** ['læbərɪnθ] *n* Labyrinth *das.*

**lace** [leɪs] *n* - **1.** (*U*) [material] Spitze *die* - **2.** [for shoe] Schnürsenkel *der* ⬦ *comp* Spitzen- ⬦ *vt* - **1.** [shoe, boot] (zu)schnüren - **2.** [drink] mit einem Schuss Alkohol versetzen.

➡ **lace up** *vt sep* zu|schnüren.

**laceration** [ˌlæsə'reɪʃn] *n fml* & MED Fleischwunde *die.*

**lace-up** *adj* [shoes] Schnür-, zum Schnüren ⬦ *n Br* Schnürschuh *der.*

**lack** [læk] *n:* **~ (of)** Mangel *der* (an (+ *D*)); **for ~ of money** aus Geldmangel; **there is no ~ of es** mangelt nicht an (+ *D*) ⬦ *vt:* **he ~s confidence/intelligence** es mangelt ihm an Selbstvertrauen/Intelligenz ⬦ *vi:* **to be ~ing** fehlen; **he is ~ing in confidence/intelligence** es mangelt ihm an Selbstvertrauen/Intelligenz.

**lackadaisical** [ˌlækə'deɪzɪkl] *adj pej* lustlos.

**lackey** ['lækɪ] (*pl* **lackeys**) *n pej* Lakai *der*.

**lacklustre** *Br*, **lackluster** *Am* ['læk‚lʌstəʳ] *adj* [performance] glanzlos; [person, party] langweilig.

**laconic** [lə'kɒnɪk] *adj* lakonisch.

**lacquer** ['lækəʳ] *n* - **1.** [for wood, metal] Lack *der* - **2.** [for hair] Haarspray *das* ◇ *vt* - **1.** [wood, metal] lackieren - **2.** [hair] mit Haarspray einl sprühen.

**lacrosse** [lə'krɒs] *n* Lacrosse *das*.

**lacy** ['leɪsɪ] (*compar* **-ier**; *superl* **-iest**) *adj* Spitzen-.

**lad** [læd] *n inf* - **1.** [young boy] Junge *der* - **2.** [male friend] Kumpel *der*.

**ladder** ['lædəʳ] *n* - **1.** [for climbing] Leiter *die* - **2.** *Br* [in tights] Laufmasche *die* ◇ *vt Br*: **I've ~ed my tights** ich habe eine Laufmasche ◇ *vi Br* [tights] eine Laufmasche bekommen.

**laden** ['leɪdn] *adj*: **~ (with)** beladen (mit).

**la-di-da** [‚lɑːdɪ'dɑː] *adj inf pej* affektiert.

**ladies** *Br* ['leɪdɪz], **ladies room** *Am n* Damentoilette *die*.

**ladle** ['leɪdl] *n* (Schöpf)kelle *die* ◇ *vt* (ausl)schöpfen.

**lady** ['leɪdɪ] (*pl* **-ies**) *n* - **1.** [woman] Dame *die* - **2.** [by birth or upbringing] Lady *die* - **3.** *Am inf* [to address woman]: **watch out, ~!** passen Sie auf! ◇ *comp*: **~ doctor** Ärztin; **~ dentist** Zahnärztin.

➤ **Lady** *n* - **1.** [member of nobility] Lady *die* - **2.** RELIG: **Our Lady** Unsere Liebe Frau.

**ladybird** *Br* ['leɪdɪbɜːd], **ladybug** *Am* ['leɪdɪbʌg] *n* Marienkäfer *der*.

**lady-in-waiting** [-'weɪtɪŋ] (*pl* **ladies-in-waiting**) *n* Hofdame *die*.

**lady-killer** *n inf* Frauenheld *der*.

**ladylike** ['leɪdɪlaɪk] *adj* damenhaft.

**Ladyship** ['leɪdɪʃɪp] *n*: **Her/Your ~** Ihre Ladyschaft.

**lag** [læg] (*pt* & *pp* **-ged**; *cont* **-ging**) *vi*: **to ~ (behind)** zurücklbleiben ◇ *vt* isolieren ◇ *n* [time lag] zeitliche Verzögerung.

**lager** ['lɑːgəʳ] *n* helles Bier.

**lagging** ['lægɪŋ] *n* (U) [material] Isoliermaterial *das*.

**lagoon** [lə'guːn] *n* Lagune *die*.

**lah-di-dah** *adj* = **la-di-da**.

**laid** [leɪd] *pt* & *pp* ▷ **lay**.

**laid-back** *adj inf* gelassen.

**lain** [leɪn] *pp* ▷ **lie**.

**lair** [leəʳ] *n* Lager *das*.

**laissez-faire** [‚leɪseɪ'feəʳ] *adj* Laissez-faire-.

**laity** ['leɪətɪ] *n* RELIG: **the ~** der Laienstand.

**lake** [leɪk] *n* See *der*.

**Lake Constance** [-'kɒnstəns] *n* Bodensee *der*.

**Lake District** *n*: **the ~** der Lake District, *Seenlandschaft in Nordwestengland*.

**Lake Geneva** *n* Genfer See.

**lama** ['lɑːmə] (*pl* **-s**) *n* [animal] Lama *das*.

**lamb** [læm] *n* Lamm *das*.

**lambast** [læm'bæst], **lambaste** [læm'beɪst] *vt* scharf kritisieren.

**lamb chop** *n* Lammkotelett *das*.

**lambing** ['læmɪŋ] *n* Lammen *das*.

**lambskin** ['læmskɪn] *n* Lammfell *das*.

**lambswool** ['læmzwʊl] *n* Lambswool *die*.

**lame** [leɪm] *adj lit* & *fig* lahm.

**lame duck** *n* - **1.** *fig* [person] lahme Ente; [business] unrentables Unternehmen - **2.** *Am* [president] US-Präsident, *der nicht wiedergewählt werden kann bzw. die Wahlen verloren hat und bis zur Wahl eines Nachfolgers im Amt bleibt.*

**lamely** ['leɪmlɪ] *adv* [unconvincingly] nicht überzeugend.

**lament** [lə'ment] *n* Klage *die*; [song] Klagelied *das* ◇ *vt* beklagen.

**lamentable** ['læməntəbl] *adj* beklagenswert.

**laminated** ['læmɪneɪtɪd] *adj* geschichtet; **~ glass** Verbundglas *das*.

**lamp** [læmp] *n* Lampe *die*; [on street] Laterne *die*.

**lamplight** ['læmplaɪt] *n* (U): **by ~** [read] bei Lampenlicht; **in the ~** [in street] im Schein der Laterne.

**lampoon** [læm'puːn] *n* Spottschrift *die* ◇ *vt* verspotten.

**lamppost** ['læmppəʊst] *n* Laternenpfahl *der*.

**lampshade** ['læmpʃeɪd] *n* Lampenschirm *der*.

**lance** [lɑːns] *n* [spear] Lanze *die* ◇ *vt* MED aufl schneiden.

**lance corporal** *n* Hauptgefreite *der*, *die*.

**lancet** ['lɑːnsɪt] *n* MED Lanzette *die*.

**Lancs** [læŋks] *abk für* Lancashire, *in Postanschrift verwendet*.

**land** [lænd] *n* - **1.** [gen] Land *das* - **2.** [property] Land *das*, Boden *der* ◇ *vt* - **1.** [plane] landen - **2.** [cargo] löschen; [passengers] ablsetzen - **3.** [fish] an Land ziehen - **4.** *inf* [job, contract] kriegen - **5.** *inf* [put]: **to ~ sb in trouble/jail** jn in Schwierigkeiten/ins Gefängnis bringen - **6.** *inf* [encumber]: **to ~ sb with sb/sthg** jm jn/etw auf lhalsen ◇ *vi* - **1.** [plane, passenger] landen; [from ship] an Land gehen - **2.** [fall] fallen.

➤ **land up** *vi inf* [in place] landen; [in situation] enden.

**landed gentry** [‚lændɪd-] *npl* Landadel *der*.

**landing** ['lændɪŋ] *n* - **1.** [between stairs] Treppenabsatz der - **2.** [of aeroplane] Landung die - **3.** [of goods from ship] Löschung die.

**landing card** n Einreisekarte die.

**landing craft** n Landungsboot das.

**landing gear** n (U) Fahrgestell das.

**landing stage** n Landungsbrücke die.

**landing strip** n Landebahn die.

**landlady** ['lænd,leɪdɪ] (pl -**ies**) n - **1.** [of pub] Wirtin die - **2.** [of lodgings] Vermieterin die.

**landlocked** ['lændlɒkt] adj: ~ **country** Binnen-staat der; **to be** ~ vom Land umschlossen sein.

**landlord** ['lændlɔːd] n - **1.** [of pub] Wirt der - **2.** [of lodgings] Vermieter der.

**landmark** ['lændmɑːk] n - **1.** [prominent feature] Wahrzeichen das - **2.** fig [in history] Meilen-stein der.

**landmine** ['lændmaɪn] n Landmine die.

**landowner** ['lænd,əʊnər] n Grundbesitzer der, -in die.

**Land Rover**® [-,rəʊvər] n Land Rover® der.

**landscape** ['lændskeɪp] n - **1.** [scenery] Land-schaft die - **2.** [painting] Landschaftsbild das ◇ vt gärtnerisch gestalten.

**landscape gardener** n Landschaftsgärt-ner der, -in die.

**landslide** ['lændslaɪd] n lit & fig Erdrutsch der ◇ comp POL [victory] Erdrutsch-.

**landslip** ['lændslɪp] n Erdrutsch der.

**lane** [leɪn] n - **1.** [country road] (enge) Land-straße - **2.** [division of road] Fahrspur die, Fahr-streifen der; '**get in** ~' 'Bitte einordnen'; '**keep in** ~' 'Auf der Fahrspur bleiben' - **3.** [in swimming pool, on racetrack] Bahn die - **4.** [for shipping] Schifffahrtsweg der; [for aircraft] Flug-route die.

**language** ['læŋgwɪdʒ] n Sprache die; **bad** ~ Kraftausdrücke pl.

**language laboratory** n Sprachlabor das.

**languid** ['læŋgwɪd] adj [gesture] lässig; [person] träge.

**languish** ['læŋgwɪʃ] vi - **1.** [suffer] schmachten - **2.** [become weak - person, plant] verkümmern.

**languorous** ['læŋgərəs] adj literary [feeling] wohlig; [person] träge.

**lank** [læŋk] adj [hair] strähnig.

**lanky** ['læŋkɪ] (compar -**ier**; superl -**iest**) adj schlaksig.

**lanolin(e)** ['lænəlɪn] n (U) Lanolin(fett) das.

**lantern** ['læntən] n Laterne die.

**Laos** [laʊs] n Laos nt.

**lap** [læp] (pt & pp -**ped**; cont -**ping**) n - **1.** [knees] Schoß der - **2.** SPORT Runde die ◇ vt - **1.** [subj:

animal] (auf)schlecken - **2.** SPORT [runner, car] überrunden ◇ vi [water, waves] plätschern.

◆ **lap up** vt sep - **1.** [subj: animal] (auf)schlecken - **2.** fig [compliments] genießen.

**laparoscopy** [,læpə'rɒskəpɪ] (pl -**ies**) n Lapa-roskopie die.

**lapdog** ['læpdɒg] n [dog] Schoßhündchen das.

**lapel** [lə'pel] n Revers das.

**Lapland** ['læplænd] n Lappland nt.

**Lapp** [læp] adj lappländisch ◇ n - **1.** [person] Lappe der, Läppin die - **2.** [language] Lappländ-isch(e) das.

**lapse** [læps] n - **1.** [failing]: ~ **of concentration** Konzentrationsschwäche die; **memory** ~ Gedächtnislücke die - **2.** [in behaviour] Lapsus der - **3.** [of time]: **after a** ~ **of three years** nach drei Jahren ◇ vi - **1.** [licence, passport] abl-laufen; [law] nicht mehr gelten; [custom] ausl-sterben - **2.** [standards] verfallen; [quality] sich verschlechtern - **3.** [subj: person]: **to** ~ **into sthg** in etw (A) verfallen; [coma] in etw (A) fallen.

**lapsed** [læpst] adj [Catholic, Jew] (vom Glauben) abgefallen.

**lap-top (computer)** n Laptop der.

**larceny** ['lɑːsənɪ] n (U) Diebstahl der.

**larch** [lɑːtʃ] n Lärche die.

**lard** [lɑːd] n Schweineschmalz das.

**larder** ['lɑːdər] n [room] Vorratsraum der; [cup-board] Vorratsschrank der.

**large** [lɑːdʒ] adj groß; [person] korpulent.

◆ **at large** adj: **to be at** ~ [prisoner] auf freiem Fuß sein; [animal] frei herumlaufen ◇ adv [as a whole]: **society-the world at** ~ die ganze Gesellschaft/Welt.

**largely** ['lɑːdʒlɪ] adv zum größten Teil.

**larger-than-life** ['lɑːdʒər-] adj: **a** ~ **character** eine auffallende Persönlichkeit.

**large-scale** adj - **1.** [wide-ranging - operation] großangelegt; [ - investment] in großem Rah-men - **2.** [map, diagram] in großem Maßstab.

**largesse, largess** Am [lɑː'dʒes] n (U) Großzügigkeit die.

**lark** [lɑːk] n - **1.** [bird] Lerche die - **2.** inf [joke] Jux der; **for a** ~ (nur) aus Jux.

◆ **lark about** vi herumalbern.

**larva** ['lɑːvə] (pl -**vae** [-viː]) n Larve die.

**laryngitis** [,lærɪn'dʒaɪtɪs] n (U) Kehlkopfent-zündung die.

**larynx** ['lærɪŋks] (pl -**es**) n Kehlkopf der.

**lasagna, lasagne** [lə'zænjə] n (U) Lasagne pl.

**lascivious** [lə'sɪvɪəs] adj lüstern.

**laser** ['leɪzər] n Laser der.

**laser beam** n Laserstrahl der.

**laser printer** n Laserdrucker der.

**laser show** n Lasershow die.

**lash** [læʃ] *n* - **1.** [eyelash] Wimper *die* - **2.** [part of whip] Peitschenriemen *der* - **3.** [blow with whip] Peitschenhieb *der* <> *vt* - **1.** [whip as punishment] auslpeitschen - **2.** [subj: wind, rain, waves] peitschen gegen - **3.** [tie]: **to ~ sthg to sthg** etw an etw *(D)* festlbinden.

➤ **lash out** *vi* - **1.** [physically] um sich schlagen; **to ~ out at** OR **against sb** auf jn einlschlagen OR loslschlagen - **2.** [verbally]: **to ~ out at** OR **against sb** Schimpftiraden auf jn losllassen, jn beschimpfen - **3.** Br inf [spend money]: **to ~ out (on sthg)** sich (wegen etw) in Unkosten stürzen.

**lass** [læs] *n* Mädel *das*.

**lasso** [læ'su:] *(pl -s; pt & pp -ed; cont -ing) n* Lasso *das* <> *vt* mit dem Lasso einlfangen.

**last** [lɑ:st] *adj* letzte, -r, -s; **~ Tuesday** letzten Dienstag; **~ but one** vorletzte, -r, -s; **you're the ~ person I expected to see** du bist der Letzte, den ich hier zu sehen erwartet habe; **that's the ~ thing I want** das ist das Letzte, was ich will <> *adv* zuletzt <> *pron:* **to be the ~ to arrive/sit down**/etc als Letzte(r) anlkommen/sich hinlsetzen/etc; **I'm always the ~ to be told** ich bin immer der Letzte, der etwas erfährt; **to leave sthg till ~** etw bis zuletzt auflschieben; **the Saturday before ~** vorletzten Samstag; **the ~ but one** der/die/das Vorletzte <> *n* [final thing]: **the ~ I saw/heard of him** das Letzte, was ich von ihm sah/hörte <> *vi* - **1.** [continue to exist or function] dauern; [shoes] halten; [luck, feeling] anlhalten - **2.** [keep fresh] sich halten - **3.** [be enough for]: **this will ~ a week** das wird für eine Woche reichen <> *vt* - **1.** [be enough for]: **this will ~ us till Friday** das wird bis Freitag reichen - **2.** [survive]: **she won't ~ the week** [dying person] sie wird die Woche nicht überleben; [incompetent worker] sie wird sich nicht länger als eine Woche halten können.

➤ **at (long) last** *adv* endlich.

**last-ditch** *adj* allerletzte, -r, -s.

**lasting** ['lɑ:stɪŋ] *adj* [peace] dauerhaft; [effect, mistrust] anhaltend.

**lastly** ['lɑ:stlɪ] *adv* zum Schluss.

**last-minute** *adj* in letzter Minute; [flight, ticket] Last-Minute-.

**last name** *n* Familienname *der*.

**last post** *n* - **1.** [postal collection] letzte Leerung - **2.** MIL Zapfenstreich *der*.

**last rites** *npl* Sterbesakramente *pl*.

**last straw** *n:* it was the **~** das brachte das Fass zum Überlaufen.

**Last Supper** *n:* the **~** das letzte Abendmahl.

**last word** *n:* to have the **~** das letzte Wort haben.

**latch** [lætʃ] *n* Riegel *der;* **on the ~** (nur) eingeklinkt, nicht verschlossen.

➤ **latch onto** *vt fus inf* [idea] ablfahren auf; [person] sich hängen an.

**latchkey** ['lætʃki:] *(pl -s) n* [of house] Hausschlüssel *der;* [of apartment] Wohnungsschlüssel *der*.

**late** [leɪt] *adj* - **1.** [not on time]: **to be ~** [person] zu spät dran sein; [train, bus] Verspätung haben; **to be ~ for sthg** zu etw zu spät kommen - **2.** [near end of]: **in the ~ evening/afternoon/morning** am späten Abend/Nachmittag/Vormittag; **he arrived in ~ December** er kam Ende Dezember - **3.** [later than normal] spät - **4.** [dead] verstorben - **5.** [former] vorige <> *adv* - **1.** [not on time]: **to arrive (20 minutes) ~** [bus, train] (20 Minuten) Verspätung haben; [person] (20 Minuten) zu spät kommen - **2.** [later than normal, near end of period] spät; **~ in the afternoon** am späten Nachmittag; **~ in August** Ende August; **I worked ~** ich habe lange gearbeitet.

➤ **of late** *adv* in letzter Zeit.

**latecomer** ['leɪt,kʌmər] *n* Zuspätkommende *der*, *die*.

**lately** ['leɪtlɪ] *adv* in letzter Zeit.

**lateness** ['leɪtnɪs] *n (U)* - **1.** [of person] Zuspätkommen *das;* [of train] Verspätung *die* - **2.** [advanced hour]: **the ~ of the meeting** der späte Beginn des Treffens.

**late-night** *adj* nächtlich; [television programme] Nacht-; **~ chemist** Nachtapotheke *die;* **Thursday is ~ opening** donnerstags haben die Geschäfte länger geöffnet.

**latent** ['leɪtənt] *adj* latent vorhanden.

**later** ['leɪtər] *adj* später <> *adv:* **~ (on)** später.

**lateral** ['lætərəl] *adj* seitlich.

**latest** ['leɪtɪst] *adj* [most recent] neueste, -r, -s <> *n:* **at the ~** spätestens.

**latex** ['leɪteks] *n (U)* Latex *der* <> *comp* Latex-.

**lath** [lɑ:θ] *n* Latte *die*.

**lathe** [leɪð] *n* Drehbank *die*.

**lather** ['lɑ:ðər] *n* (Seifen)schaum *der* <> *vt* einlseifen <> *vi* schäumen.

**Latin** ['lætɪn] *adj* - **1.** [temperament] südländisch - **2.** [studies, student] Latein- <> *n* [language] Latein(ische) *das*.

**Latin America** *n* Lateinamerika *nt*.

**Latin American** *adj* lateinamerikanisch <> *n* [person] Lateinamerikaner *der*, -in *die*.

**latitude** ['lætɪtju:d] *n* - **1.** GEOGR Breite *die* - **2.** fml [freedom] Freiheit *die*.

**latrine** [lə'tri:n] *n* Latrine *die*.

**latter** ['lætər] *adj* - **1.** [later - years] spätere; **in the ~ part of the century** in der zweiten Hälfte des Jahrhunderts - **2.** [second] zweite, -r, -s; [opposed to former] letzte, -r, -s <> *n:* **the ~** der/die/das Letztere.

**latter-day** *adj* modern.

**latterly** ['lætəlɪ] *adv* in letzter Zeit.

**lattice** ['lætɪs] *n* Gitter *das*.

**lattice window** *n* Gitterfenster *das*.

**Latvia** ['lætvɪə] *n* Lettland *nt*.

**Latvian** ['lætvɪən] *adj* lettisch ◇ *n* - **1.** [person] Lette *der*, -tin *die* - **2.** [language] Lettisch(e) *das*.

**laudable** ['lɔ:dəbl] *adj* lobenswert.

**laugh** [lɑ:f] *n* - **1.** [sound] Lachen *das;* **to have the last** ~ der sein, der zuletzt lacht - **2.** *inf* [fun, joke] Spaß *der;* **to do sthg for** ~**s** OR **a** ~ etw aus OR zum Spaß machen ◇ *vi* lachen.

⭢ **laugh at** *vt fus* [mock] sich lustig machen über (+ A).

⭢ **laugh off** *vt sep* [dismiss] mit einem Lachen abltun.

**laughable** ['lɑ:fəbl] *adj pej* lächerlich.

**laughing gas** ['lɑ:fɪŋ-] *n* (U) Lachgas *das*.

**laughingstock** ['lɑ:fɪŋstɒk] *n* Zielscheibe *die* des Spotts.

**laughter** ['lɑ:ftə'] *n* Gelächter *das*.

**launch** [lɔ:ntʃ] *n* - **1.** [of new ship] Stapellauf *der* - **2.** [into air - of missile] Abschuss *der;* **when is the (rocket)** ~**?** wann wird die Rakete in den Weltraum geschossen? - **3.** [start] Beginn *der* - **4.** COMM [of new book, product] Lancieren *das* - **5.** [boat] Barkasse *die* ◇ *vt* - **1.** [into water - boat] zu Wasser lassen; [ - new ship] vom Stapel lassen - **2.** [into air - space rocket, satellite] in den Weltraum schießen; [ - missile] ablschießen - **3.** [start - campaign] beginnen; **to** ~ **an attack** einen Angriff durchlführen - **4.** COMM [new book, product] lancieren.

⭢ **launch into** *vt fus*: **to** ~ **into an explanation** plötzlich Erklärungen ablgeben; **to** ~ **into an argument** plötzlich anlfangen, sich zu streiten.

**launch(ing) pad** ['lɔ:ntʃ(ɪŋ)-] *n* [for rocket, missile, satellite] Abschussrampe *die*.

**launder** ['lɔ:ndə'] *vt* - **1.** [clothes] waschen und bügeln - **2.** *inf* [money] waschen.

**laund(e)rette** [lɔ:n'dret], **Laundromat**® Am ['lɔ:ndrəmæt] *n* Waschsalon *der*.

**laundry** ['lɔ:ndrɪ] (*pl* -**ies**) *n* - **1.** (U) [clothes] Wäsche *die* - **2.** [business] Wäscherei *die*.

**laundry basket** *n* Wäschekorb *der*.

**laureate** ['lɔ:rɪət] *n* ▷ **poet laureate**.

**laurel** ['lɒrəl] *n* Lorbeer *der*.

⭢ **laurels** *npl*: **to rest on one's** ~**s** sich auf seinen Lorbeeren auslruhen.

**lava** ['lɑ:və] *n* Lava *die*.

**lavatory** ['lævətrɪ] (*pl* -**ies**) *n* Toilette *die*.

**lavatory paper** *n Br* Toilettenpapier *das*.

**lavender** ['lævəndə'] *adj* [colour] lavendelblau ◇ *n* - **1.** [plant] Lavendel *der* - **2.** [colour] Lavendelblau *das*.

**lavish** ['lævɪʃ] *adj* - **1.** [generous] großzügig; **to be** ~ **with sthg** [with money, time] mit etw großzügig sein; **she's** ~ **with her praise** sie spart nicht mit ihrem Lob - **2.** [sumptuous - decoration] aufwendig; [ - banquet] üppig ◇ *vt*: **to** ~ **sthg on sb/sthg** [praise, attention, money] jn mit etw förmlich überhäufen.

**lavishly** ['lævɪʃlɪ] *adv* - **1.** [generously - praise] überschwenglich; [- entertain] üppig - **2.** [sumptuously] aufwendig.

**law** [lɔ:] *n* - **1.** [legislation, rule, natural or scientific principle] Gesetz *das;* **to become** ~ rechtskräftig werden; **to break the** ~ das Gesetz brechen; **against the** ~ gesetzeswidrig; ~ **and order** Recht und Ordnung; **the** ~ **of the jungle** das Gesetz des Dschungels - **2.** (U) [legal system]: **(the)** ~ das Recht - **3.** [subject studied] Jura - **4.** (U) *inf* [police]: **the** ~ die Polente - **5.** *phr:* **he's been laying down the** ~ **again** er musste uns mal wieder sagen, was wir zu tun haben ◇ *comp* Jura-; **a** ~ **firm** eine Anwaltskanzlei.

**law-abiding** [-ə'baɪdɪŋ] *adj* gesetzestreu.

**law-breaker** [-,breɪkə'] *n* Rechtsbrecher *der*, -in *die*.

**law court** *n* Gericht *das*.

**lawful** ['lɔ:fʊl] *adj fml* rechtmäßig.

**lawfully** ['lɔ:fʊlɪ] *adv fml* auf legalem Wege.

**lawless** ['lɔ:lɪs] *adj* - **1.** *fml* [illegal] gesetzeswidrig - **2.** [without laws] gesetzlos.

**Law Lords** *npl Br* LAW: **the** ~ *Mitglieder des britischen Oberhauses, die den Obersten Gerichtshof repräsentieren, ähnlich dem Deutschen Bundesgerichtshof.*

**lawmaker** ['lɔ:,meɪkə'] *n* Gesetzgeber *der*.

**lawn** [lɔ:n] *n* Rasen *der*.

**lawnmower** ['lɔ:n,məʊə'] *n* Rasenmäher *der*.

**lawn party** *n Am* Gartenparty *die*.

**lawn tennis** *n* Rasentennis *das*.

**law school** *n* juristische Fakultät.

**lawsuit** ['lɔ:su:t] *n* Klage *die*.

**lawyer** ['lɔ:jə'] *n* (Rechts)anwalt *der*, -anwältin *die*.

**lax** [læks] *adj* lax; [discipline] lasch; [behaviour] locker.

**laxative** ['læksətɪv] *n* Abführmittel *das*.

**laxity** ['læksɪtɪ], **laxness** ['læksnɪs] *n* (U) Laxheit *die*; [in work] Nachlässigkeit *die*.

**lay** [leɪ] (*pt* & *pp* **laid**) *pt* ▷ **lie** ◇ *vt* - **1.** [in specified position] legen - **2.** [prepare - trap, snare] auf lstellen; [ - plans] schmieden; **to** ~ **the table** den Tisch decken - **3.** [carpet, cable, pipes] verlegen; [bricks, foundations] legen - **4.** [egg] legen - **5.**: **to** ~ **the blame (for sthg) on sb** jm die Schuld (für etw) geben; **to** ~ **emphasis on sthg** Wert auf etw (A) legen ◇ *adj* - **1.** RELIG Laien-

L

**- 2.** [untrained, unqualified] laienhaft; **~ person** Laie *der.*

◆ **lay aside** *vt sep* **- 1.** [save - food, money] zur Seite legen **- 2.** [knitting, book] wegllegen; [plans] auf Eis legen.

◆ **lay before** *vt sep* [present]: **to ~ sthg before sb** jm etw vorllegen.

◆ **lay down** *vt sep* **- 1.** [regulations] auf lstellen, festlsetzen; **the guidelines lay down that ...** die Richtlinien schrieben vor, dass ... **- 2.** [arms, tools] niederllegen.

◆ **lay into** *vt fus inf* [attack - physically] loslgehen auf (+ A); [ - verbally] herunterlputzen.

◆ **lay off** *vt sep* [workers] entlassen ◇ *vt fus inf* **- 1.** [leave alone] in Ruhe lassen **- 2.** [stop, give up]: **to ~ off alcohol/cigarettes** mit dem Trinken/Rauchen auf lhören; **~ off kicking that chair!** hör auf, gegen den Stuhl zu treten!

◆ **lay on** *vt sep Br* [provide, supply] sorgen für.

◆ **lay out** *vt sep* **- 1.** [clothes, tools, ingredients] bereitllegen **- 2.** [garden, house, town] planen.

◆ **lay over** *vi Am* einen Zwischenstopp einllegen.

**layabout** ['leɪəbaʊt] *n Br inf* Faulenzer *der.*

**lay-by** (*pl* **-s**) *n Br* [small] Parkbucht *die;* [large] Rastplatz *der.*

**layer** ['leɪəʳ] *n* **- 1.** [of substance, material] Schicht *die;* **she wore several ~s of clothes** sie trug mehrere Kleider übereinander **- 2.** *fig* [level] Ebene *die.*

**layette** [leɪ'et] *n* Babyausstattung *die.*

**layman** ['leɪmən] (*pl* **-men** [-mən]) *n* RELIG & *fig* Laie *der.*

**lay-off** *n:* **there will be ~s at the factory** es wird in den Fabrik zu Entlassungen kommen.

**layout** ['leɪaʊt] *n* [of house] Raumaufteilung *die;* [of garden] Anlage *die;* [of text] Layout *das.*

**layover** ['leɪəʊvəʳ] *n Am* Zwischenstopp *der.*

**laze** [leɪz] *vi:* **to ~ (about OR around)** faulenzen.

**lazily** ['leɪzɪlɪ] *adv* [sit] faul; [yawn, speak, stroll] träge.

**laziness** ['leɪzɪnɪs] *n (U)* Faulheit *die.*

**lazy** ['leɪzɪ] (*compar* **-ier;** *superl* **-iest**) *adj* **- 1.** [person] faul **- 2.** [action] träge.

**lazybones** ['leɪzɪbəʊnz] (*pl inv*) *n* Faulpelz *der.*

**lb** *abbr of* **pound.**

**L/C** (*abbr of* **letter of credit**) Kreditbrief *der.*

**LCD** (*abbr of* **liquid crystal display**) *n* LCD *das;* **~ display** LCD-Anzeige *die.*

**L-driver** *n Br abbr of* **learner driver.**

**LEA** (*abbr of* **local education authority**) *n* ≈ Schulamt *das.*

**lead¹** [liːd] (*pt* & *pp* **led**) *n* **- 1.** *(U)* [winning position] Führung *die;* **to be in OR have the ~** in Führung liegen **- 2.** [amount ahead] Vorsprung *der*

**- 3.** *(U)* [initiative, example]: **to take the ~** [do sthg first] mit gutem Beispiel voranlgehen; **I followed his ~** ich folgte seinem Beispiel **- 4.** *(U)* [stage or film role]: **the ~** die Hauptrolle **- 5.** [clue] Anhaltspunkt *der* **- 6.** [for dog] Leine *die* **- 7.** [wire, cable] Kabel *das* ◇ *adj* [most important]: **~ singer** Leadsänger *der,* -in *die;* **~ actor** Hauptdarsteller *der;* **~ story** Leitartikel *der* ◇ *vt* **- 1.** [procession, parade] anlführen **- 2.** [person, existence] führen; **to ~ the way** *lit* voranlgehen; **America ~s the way in space technology** Amerika ist führend im Bereich der Weltraumtechnologie **- 3.** [team, investigation] leiten; [political party] führen **- 4.** [strike, campaign] organisieren **- 5.** [cause, influence]: **to ~ sb to do sthg** jn veranlassen, etw zu tun ◇ *vi* **- 1.** [go] führen **- 2.** [give access to]: **to ~ to/into sthg** zu etw/in etw *(A)* führen **- 3.** [be winning] führen **- 4.** [result in]: **to ~ to sthg** zu etw führen.

◆ **lead off** *vi* **- 1.** [diverge]: **several streets ~ off (from) the main road** mehrere Straßen gehen von der Hauptstraße ab; **three bedrooms ~ off (from) the corridor** der Korridor führt zu drei Zimmern **- 2.** [begin] anlfangen.

◆ **lead up to** *vt fus* **- 1.** [precede]: **the events that led up to the disaster** die Ereignisse, die der Katastrophe vorausgingen **- 2.** [in conversation - topic] zulsteuern auf (+ A); **what are you ~ing up to?** worauf willst du hinaus?

**lead²** [led] *n* **- 1.** [metal] Blei *das* **- 2.** [in pencil] Mine *die* ◇ *comp* Blei-.

**leaded** ['ledɪd] *adj* **- 1.** [petrol] verbleit **- 2.** [window] Bleiglas-.

**leaden** ['ledn] *adj* **- 1.** *literary* [sky] bleiern; [step, heart] schwer **- 2.** [very dull - conversation] schleppend.

**leader** ['liːdəʳ] *n* **- 1.** [head - of organization] Leiter *der,* -in *die;* [ - of political party] Vorsitzende *der, die;* [ - of gang] Anführer *der,* -in *die* **- 2.** [in race, competition] Führende *der, die;* **to be the ~** in Führung liegen **- 3.** *Br* [in newspaper] Leitartikel *der.*

**leadership** ['liːdəʃɪp] *n* [position, people in charge] Führung *die;* [quality] Führungsqualitäten *pl.*

**lead-free** [led-] *adj* bleifrei.

**leading** ['liːdɪŋ] *adj* **- 1.** [prominent] führend **- 2.** [main]: **~ part OR role** THEATRE & *fig* Hauptrolle *die,* führende Rolle **- 3.** SPORT [at front]: **the ~ runner** der in Führung liegende.

**leading article** *n Br* Leitartikel *der.*

**leading lady** *n* Hauptdarstellerin *die.*

**leading light** *n* herausragende Persönlichkeit.

**leading man** *n* Hauptdarsteller *der.*

**leading question** *n* Suggestivfrage *die.*

**lead pencil** [led-] *n* Bleistift *der.*

**lead poisoning** [led-] n (U) Bleivergiftung die.

**lead time** ['li:d-] n COMM [for delivery] Lieferzeit die.

**leaf** [li:f] (pl **leaves**) n **- 1.** [of tree, plant, book] Blatt das **- 2.** [of table] Platte die (zur Vergrößerung eines Tisches).
➤ **leaf through** vt fus durchlblättern.

**leaflet** ['li:flɪt] n Broschüre die; [commercial] Prospekt der; [political] Flugblatt das ⟨⟩ vt Broschüren/Prospekte/Flugblätter verteilen in (+ D).

**leafy** ['li:fɪ] (compar **-ier**; superl **-iest**) adj **- 1.** [tree, branch] belaubt; [vegetable] Blatt- **- 2.** [lane] von Bäumen gesäumt; [suburb] mit viel Grün.

**league** [li:g] n **- 1.** [group - of people, countries] Bündnis das; **to be in ~ with sb** mit jm verbündet sein **- 2.** SPORT Liga die.

**league table** n Tabelle die.

**leak** [li:k] n **- 1.** [in pipe, tank, roof] undichte Stelle; [in boat] Leck das **- 2.** [disclosure]: **there has been a ~** es ist etwas durchgesickert ⟨⟩ vt [make known] durchlsickern lassen ⟨⟩ vi [pipe, tank, roof, shoe] undicht sein; [boat] lecken; [gas] auslströmen; [liquid] auslaufen; **to ~ (out) from sthg** aus etw auslaufen OR auslströmen.
➤ **leak out** vi **- 1.** [liquid] durchlsickern; [gas] auslströmen **- 2.** [news, secret] durchlsickern.

**leakage** ['li:kɪdʒ] n [of water, oil] Auslaufen das; [of gas] Ausströmen das.

**leaky** ['li:kɪ] (compar **-ier**; superl **-iest**) adj [bucket, roof] undicht; [boat] leck.

**lean** [li:n] (pt & pp **leant** OR **-ed**) adj **- 1.** [person - thin] dünn; [ - slim] schlank **- 2.** [meat, harvest, year] mager ⟨⟩ vt: **to ~ sthg against sthg** etw gegen OR an etw (A) lehnen ⟨⟩ vi **- 1.** [bend, slope - person] sich beugen; [ - wall] sich neigen; **to ~ forward** sich vorlbeugen **- 2.** [rest]: **to ~ on/against sthg** sich an etw (A)/gegen etw (A) lehnen.
➤ **lean back** vi sich zurückllehnen.

**leaning** ['li:nɪŋ] n: **~ (towards sthg)** Neigung die (zu etw); **to have Communist ~s** zum Kommunismus tendieren.

**leant** [lent] pt & pp ⊳ **lean**.

**lean-to** (pl **-s**) n angebauter Schuppen.

**leap** [li:p] (pt & pp **leapt** OR **-ed**) n **- 1.** [jump] Sprung der **- 2.** [increase] sprunghafter Anstieg ⟨⟩ vi **- 1.** [jump] springen **- 2.** [increase] sprunghaft anlsteigen.
➤ **leap at** vt fus fig [invitation] sich förmlich stürzen auf (+ A); **to ~ at the chance** OR **opportunity** die Gelegenheit beim Schopf packen.

**leapfrog** ['li:pfrɒg] (pt & pp **-ged**; cont **-ging**) n (U) Bockspringen das ⟨⟩ vt fig überlspringen

⟨⟩ vi [jump]: **to ~ over sthg** über etw (A) einen Bocksprung machen.

**leapt** [lept] pt & pp ⊳ **leap**.

**leap year** n Schaltjahr das.

**learn** [lɜ:n] (pt & pp **-ed** OR **learnt**) vt **- 1.** [acquire knowledge, skill of] (er)lernen; **to ~ (how) to cook/read/**etc kochen/lesen/etc lernen **- 2.** [memorize] (auswendig) lernen **- 3.** [hear] erfahren; **to ~ that** erfahren, dass ⟨⟩ vi **- 1.** [acquire knowledge, skill] lernen **- 2.** [hear]: **to ~ of** OR **about sthg** von etw erfahren.

**learned** ['lɜ:nɪd] adj **- 1.** [person] gelehrt **- 2.** [journal, paper, book] wissenschaftlich.

**learner** ['lɜ:nə'] n: **she's a quick ~** sie lernt schnell; **~s of English** Englischlerner pl.

**learner (driver)** n Fahrschüler der, -in die.

**learning** ['lɜ:nɪŋ] n (U) [process] Lernen das; [knowledge] Wissen das; [result] Gelehrsamkeit die.

**learning curve** n Lernkurve die.

**learnt** [lɜ:nt] pt & pp ⊳ **learn**.

**lease** [li:s] n LAW [of premises] Pacht die; [contract] Pachtvertrag der; [of car] Leasing das; [contract] Leasingvertrag der; **a new ~ of life** Br, **a new ~ on life** Am [for person] neue Lebenskraft; [for thing] eine neue Lebensspanne ⟨⟩ vt [premises - to sb] verpachten; [ - from sb] pachten; [ - car] leasen.

**leaseback** ['li:sbæk] n der Verkauf von Dingen mit weiterbestehendem Mietrecht durch den früheren Eigentümer.

**leasehold** ['li:shəʊld] adj [property] Pacht-.

**leaseholder** ['li:s ˌhəʊldə'] n Pächter der, -in die.

**leash** [li:ʃ] n (Hunde)leine die.

**least** [li:st] (superl of **little**) adj wenigste, -r, -s; **he earns the ~ money** er verdient am wenigsten; **that's the ~ of my worries** das soll meine geringste Sorge sein ⟨⟩ pron: **(the) ~** das Wenigste; **it's the ~ I can do** das ist das Mindeste, was ich tun kann; **not in the ~** nicht im Geringsten; **to say the ~** gelinde gesagt ⟨⟩ adv am wenigsten.
➤ **at least** adv wenigstens.
➤ **least of all** adv am allerwenigsten.

**leather** ['leðə'] n Leder das ⟨⟩ comp Leder-.
➤ **leathers** npl [of motorbike rider] Motorradkleidung die (aus Leder).

**leatherette** [ˌleðə'ret] n Kunstleder das.

**leave** [li:v] (pt & pp **left**) vt **- 1.** [gen] verlassen; **~ the door open** lass die Tür offen; **it ~s me cold** es lässt mich kalt; **let's ~ it at that** lassen wir es dabei **- 2.** [not take away] lassen **- 3.** [not use, not eat] übrig lassen **- 4.** [a mark, scar, message, etc] hinterlassen; **to ~ sb's money to sb** jm sein Geld hinterlassen **- 5.** [space, gap] lassen **- 6.** [entrust] überlassen; **he left it to her**

**to decide** er hat ihr die Entscheidung über-lassen; ⊳ **left** ◇ *vi* gehen; [train, bus] ab-fahren ◇ *n (U)* - **1.** [time off work] Urlaub *der;* **on ~** auf Urlaub - **2.** *fml* [permission] Erlaubnis *die.*

◂ **leave behind** *vt sep* zurücklassen.

◂ **leave off** *vt sep* [omit]: **to ~ sb's name off a list** js Namen nicht in eine Liste ein-tragen ◇ *vt fus* [stop]: **to ~ off doing sthg** aufhören, etw zu tun ◇ *vi* aufhören.

◂ **leave out** *vt sep* ausllassen; **to feel left out** sich ausgeschlossen fühlen.

**leave of absence** *n* Urlaub *der.*

**leaves** [li:vz] *pl* ⊳ **leaf.**

**Lebanese** [ˌlebəˈni:z] *(pl inv)* adj libanesisch ◇ *n* [person] Libanese *der,* -sin *die.*

**Lebanon** [ˈlebənən] *n* Libanon *der;* **in (the) ~** im Libanon.

**lecherous** [ˈletʃərəs] *adj* lüstern.

**lechery** [ˈletʃəri] *n (U)* Lüsternheit *die.*

**lectern** [ˈlektən] *n* Lesepult *das.*

**lecture** [ˈlektʃəʳ] *n* - **1.** [talk - at university] Vorle-sung *die;* [ - at conference] Vortrag *der;* **to give a ~ (on sthg)** eine Vorlesung/einen Vortrag (über etw *(A)*) halten - **2.** [criticism, reprimand] Strafpredigt *die;* **to give sb a ~** jm eine Straf-predigt halten ◇ *vt* [scold]: **to ~ sb** jm eine Strafpredigt halten ◇ *vi* [give talk]: **to ~ (on/in sthg)** eine Vorlesung/einen Vortrag (über etw *(A)*) halten.

**lecture hall** *n* Hörsaal *der.*

**lecturer** [ˈlektʃərəʳ] *n* - **1.** [teacher] Dozent *der,* -in *die* - **2.** [speaker] Redner *der,* -in *die.*

**lecture theatre** *n* Hörsaal *der.*

**led** [led] *pt* & *pp* ⊳ **lead¹.**

**LED** *(abbr of* **light-emitting diode)** *n* LED *die.*

**ledge** [ledʒ] *n* - **1.** [of window - outside] Fenster-sims *der;* [ - inside] Fensterbrett *das* - **2.** [of mountain] Felsvorsprung *der.*

**ledger** [ˈledʒəʳ] *n* Hauptbuch *das.*

**lee** [li:] *n:* **in the ~ of sthg** im Windschatten von etw.

**leech** [li:tʃ] *n* - **1.** [creature] Blutegel *der* - **2.** *fig* & *pej* [person] Schmarotzer *der.*

**leek** [li:k] *n:* **a ~** eine Stange Lauch; **a pound of ~s** ≈ 500 g Lauch.

**leer** [lɪəʳ] *n* lüsterner Blick ◇ *vi:* **to ~ at sb** jm einen Lüsternen Blick zulwerfen.

**leeway** [ˈli:weɪ] *n* - **1.** [room to manoeuvre] Spiel-raum *der* - **2.** [time lost]: **to make up ~** Ver-säumtes nachlholen.

**left** [left] *pt* & *pp* ⊳ **leave** ◇ *adj* - **1.** [remain-ing] übrig; **to be ~** übrig geblieben sein - **2.** [side, hand, foot] linke, -r, -s ◇ *adv* links ◇ *n* [direction]: **on the ~** auf der linken Sei-te; **to the ~** [position] auf der linken Seite;

[movement] auf die linke Seite; **to keep to the ~** sich links halten.

◂ **Left** *n* POL: **the Left** die Linke; **parties of the Left** politisch links orientierte Parteien.

**left-hand** *adj* linke, -r, -s; **the ~ side** die linke Seite.

**left-hand drive** *adj* mit Linkssteuer ◇ *n* [steering] Linkssteuerung *die;* [car] Auto *das* mit Linkssteuerung.

**left-handed** [-ˈhændɪd] *adj* - **1.** [person] links-händig - **2.** [implement] für Linkshänder - **3.** *Am* [compliment] zweifelhaft ◇ *adv* mit der linken Hand.

**left-hander** [-ˈhændəʳ] *n* Linkshänder *der,* -in *die.*

**Leftist** [ˈleftɪst] POL *adj* linksgerichtet ◇ *n* Linke *der, die.*

**left luggage (office)** *n Br* Gepäckaufbe-wahrung *die.*

**leftover** [ˈleftəʊvəʳ] *adj* übrig geblieben.

◂ **leftovers** *npl* Reste *pl.*

**left wing** *n* POL linker Flügel.

◂ **left-wing** *adj* POL linke, -r, -s.

**left-winger** *n* POL Linke *der, die.*

**lefty** [ˈleftɪ] *(pl* **-ies)** *n* - **1.** *Br inf pej* POL Linke *der, die* - **2.** *Am* [left-handed person] Linkshänder *der,* -in *die.*

**leg** [leg] *n* - **1.** [gen] Bein *das;* **to be on one's last ~s** in den letzten Zügen liegen; **you don't have a ~ to stand on** du hast keine Beweise mehr; **to pull sb's ~** jn auf den Arm nehmen - **2.** CULIN [of chicken] Schenkel *der;* [of lamb, pork] Keule *die* - **3.** [of journey] Etappe *die;* [of tourna-ment] Runde *die.*

**legacy** [ˈlegəsɪ] *(pl* **-ies)** *n* - **1.** [gift of money] Erb-schaft *die* - **2.** *fig* [consequence] Erbe *das.*

**legal** [ˈli:gl] *adj* - **1.** [concerning the law - system] Rechts-; [ - advice] juristisch; **the ~ profession** die Juristenschaft - **2.** [lawful] legal, gesetz-lich erlaubt.

**legal action** *n:* **to take ~ against sb** gegen jn gerichtlich vorlgehen.

**legal aid** *n* Prozesskostenhilfe *die.*

**legality** [li:ˈgælətɪ] *n (U)* Legalität *die;* [of claim] Rechtmäßigkeit *die.*

**legalize, -ise** [ˈli:gəlaɪz] *vt* legalisieren.

**legally** [ˈli:gəlɪ] *adv* [married, adopted] recht-mäßig; **~ binding** rechtsverbindlich; **to be ~ responsible for sb** vor dem Gesetz für jn verantwortlich sein.

**legal tender** *n (U)* legales Zahlungsmittel.

**legation** [lɪˈgeɪʃn] *n* Gesandtschaft *die.*

**legend** [ˈledʒənd] *n* - **1.** [myth] Sage *die* - **2.** *fig* [person] Legende *die.*

**legendary** [ˈledʒəndrɪ] *adj* - **1.** [mythical] sagen-haft - **2.** [very famous] legendär.

**leggings** ['legɪŋz] npl Leggings pl.

**legible** ['ledʒəbl] adj lesbar.

**legibly** ['ledʒəblɪ] adv leserlich.

**legion** ['liːdʒən] n - 1. MIL Legion die - 2. fig [large number] Legion die ⟨⟩ adj fml: to be ~ Legion sein.

**legionnaire's disease** [ˌliːdʒə'neəz-] n (U) Legionärskrankheit die.

**legislate** ['ledʒɪsleɪt] vi: to ~ (against) ein Gesetz/Gesetze erlassen (gegen).

**legislation** [ˌledʒɪs'leɪʃn] n (U) [laws] Gesetze pl.

**legislative** ['ledʒɪslətɪv] adj [body, powers] gesetzgebend; [process] gesetzgeberisch.

**legislator** ['ledʒɪsleɪtə'] n Gesetzgeber der.

**legislature** ['ledʒɪsleɪtʃə'] n Legislative die.

**legitimacy** [lɪ'dʒɪtɪməsɪ] n (U) - 1. [of government, court judgement] Rechtmäßigkeit die - 2. [of argument] Stichhaltigkeit die; [of complaint] Berechtigung die - 3. [of child] Ehelichkeit die.

**legitimate** [lɪ'dʒɪtɪmət] adj - 1. [government] rechtmäßig; [business, action] legal - 2. [argument] stichhaltig; [complaint, question] berechtigt - 3. [child] ehelich.

**legitimately** [lɪ'dʒɪtɪmətlɪ] adv - 1. [lawfully] legal - 2. [reasonably] mit Recht.

**legitimize, -ise** [lɪ'dʒɪtəmaɪz] vt [make legal] legitimieren.

**legless** ['leglɪs] adj Br inf [drunk] sternhagelvoll.

**legroom** ['legruml] n Beinfreiheit die.

**leg-warmers** [-ˌwɔːməz] npl Legwärmer pl.

**legwork** ['legwɜːk] n (U): to do the ~ die Lauferei erledigen.

**leisure** [Br 'leʒə', Am 'liːʒər] n Freizeit die; do it at (your) ~ machen Sie es, wenn Sie Zeit haben.

**leisure centre** n Freizeitzentrum das.

**leisurely** [Br 'leʒəlɪ, Am 'liːʒərlɪ] adj & adv gemächlich.

**leisure time** n Freizeit die.

**lemming** ['lemɪŋ] n - 1. [animal] Lemming der - 2. fig [person] Schaf das.

**lemon** ['lemən] n - 1. [fruit] Zitrone die - 2. (U) [drink] Zitronensaftgetränk das.

**lemonade** [ˌlemə'neɪd] n - 1. Br [fizzy] Limonade die - 2. [made with fresh lemons] Zitronensaftgetränk (aus Zitronen, Zucker und Wasser bestehend).

**lemon curd** n (U) Br Brotaufstrich gelblicher Farbe, der nach Zitronen schmeckt.

**lemon juice** n (U) Zitronensaft der.

**lemon sole** n Seezunge die.

**lemon squash** n (U) Br Zitronengetränk das.

**lemon squeezer** [-ˌskwiːzə'] n Zitronenpresse die.

**lemon tea** n Zitronentee der.

**lend** [lend] (pt & pp lent) vt - 1. [money, book]: to ~ sb sthg, to ~ sthg to sb jm etw leihen; I don't like ~ing money ich verleihe nicht gerne Geld - 2. [support, assistance]: to ~ one's support to sb jn unterstützen; to ~ one's assistance to sb jm helfen - 3. [credibility, quality]: to ~ sthg to sb/sthg jm/einer Sache (D) etw verleihen - 4. phr: the novel doesn't ~ itself to being filmed der Roman eignet sich nicht als Vorlage für einen Film.

**lender** ['lendə'] n [of money] Kreditgeber der.

**lending library** ['lendɪŋ-] n Leihbücherei die.

**lending rate** ['lendɪŋ-] n Darlehenszinssatz der.

**length** [leŋθ] n - 1. [gen] Länge die; in ~ in der Länge, lang - 2. [whole distance]: we walked the ~ of the street wir gingen die ganze Straße entlang; the ~ and breadth of the country das ganze Land - 3. [of swimming pool] Länge die, Bahn die - 4. [of string, wood, cloth] Stück das - 5. phr: he went to great ~s to achieve his goal er tat alles Mögliche, um sein Ziel zu erreichen; he would go to any ~s to meet her er würde alles tun, um sie zu treffen.

◆ **at length** adv - 1. [eventually] endlich - 2. [in detail] ausführlich.

**lengthen** ['leŋθən] vt verlängern ⟨⟩ vi länger werden.

**lengthways** ['leŋθweɪz] adv der Länge nach, längs.

**lengthy** ['leŋθɪ] (compar -ier; superl -iest) adj lang, langwierig; [stay, visit] ausgedehnt; [discussions] langwierig.

**leniency** ['liːnɪənsɪ] n Nachsicht die; [of verdict, sentence] Milde die.

**lenient** ['liːnɪənt] adj [person] nachsichtig; [verdict, sentence] mild.

**lens** [lenz] n - 1. PHOT & ANAT Linse die; [of glasses] Glas das - 2. [contact lens] Kontaktlinse die.

**lent** [lent] pt & pp ⟩ lend.

**Lent** [lent] n Fastenzeit die.

**lentil** ['lentɪl] n Linse die.

**Leo** ['liːəʊ] n Löwe der.

**leopard** ['lepəd] n Leopard der.

**leotard** ['liːətɑːd] n einteiliger Anzug für Artisten und Showtänzer.

**leper** ['lepə'] n Leprakranke der, die.

**leprechaun** ['leprəkɔːn] n Kobold der.

**leprosy** ['leprəsɪ] n Lepra die.

**lesbian** ['lezbɪən] adj lesbisch ⟨⟩ n Lesbe die, Lesbierin die.

**lesbianism** ['lezbɪənɪzml] n lesbische Liebe.

L

**lesion** ['li:ʒn] n MED Läsion die.

**less** [les] (compar of little) adj weniger; ~ ... than weniger ... als; of ~ value von geringerem Wert ◇ pron weniger; ~ than 20 weniger als 20 ◇ adv weniger; ~ and ~ immer weniger ◇ prep [minus] weniger; purchase price ~ 10% Kaufpreis abzüglich 10%.

**lessee** [le'si:] n fml Mieter der, -in die.

**lessen** ['lesn] vt [risk, chances, effect] verringern; [pain] lindern ◇ vi nachlassen.

**lesser** ['lesə'] adj geringer; to a ~ extent OR degree in geringerem Umfang.

**lesson** ['lesn] n - **1.** [class] (Unterrichts)stunde die; to give/take ~s (in sthg) (Unterrichts)stunden (in etw (D)) erteilen/nehmen - **2.** [example]: that was a ~ to me das war mir eine Lehre; to teach sb a ~ jm eine Lektion erteilen.

**lessor** [le'sɔ:'] n fml Vermieter der, -in die.

**lest** [lest] conj fml damit ... nicht; she wrote it down, ~ she forget sie schrieb es nieder, um es nicht zu vergessen.

**let** [let] (pt & pp let; cont -ting) vt - **1.** [allow] lassen; to ~ sb do sthg jn etw tun lassen; she ~ her hair grow sie ließ sich (D) die Haare wachsen; to ~ go of sthg etw loslassen; to ~ sb go [release] jn loslassen; to ~ o.s. go [neglect] sich gehen lassen; to ~ sb have sthg [permanently] jm etw überlassen; he wouldn't ~ me have the book er wollte mir das Buch nicht geben; to ~ sb know sthg jn etw wissen lassen; ~ me know as soon as possible sagen Sie mir so bald wie möglich Bescheid - **2.** [in verb forms]: ~'s go! gehen wir!; ~ me see lass mich überlegen - **3.** [rent out] vermieten; 'to ~' 'zu vermieten'.

◆ **let alone** conj geschweige denn.

◆ **let down** vt sep - **1.** [let air out of]: to ~ sb's tyres down jm die Luft aus den Reifen lassen - **2.** [person - disappoint] enttäuschen; [- not help] im Stich lassen.

◆ **let in** vt sep hereinlassen; to ~ o.s. in for sthg sich auf etw (A) einlassen; to ~ sb in on sthg [secret, plan] jn in etw (A) einweihen.

◆ **let off** vt sep - **1.** [excuse] davonkommen lassen - **2.** [from vehicle] aussteigen lassen; can you ~ me off at the station? kannst du mich am Bahnhof aussteigen lassen? - **3.** [cannon, missile] ablfeuern; [firework] loslassen.

◆ **let on** vi: to ~ on about sthg etw verraten.

◆ **let out** vt sep heraus-/hinauslassen; ~ me out! lass mich heraus!; to ~ out a scream einen Schrei auslstoßen.

◆ **let up** vi nachlassen.

**letdown** ['letdaʊn] n inf Enttäuschung die.

**lethal** ['li:θl] adj tödlich.

**lethargic** [lə'θɑ:dʒɪk] adj träge, lethargisch.

**lethargy** ['leθədʒɪ] n (U) Trägheit die, Lethargie die.

**let's** [lets] = let us.

**letter** ['letə'] n - **1.** [written message] Brief der - **2.** [of alphabet] Buchstabe der.

◆ **letters** npl fml [literature] Literatur die.

**letter bomb** n Briefbombe die.

**letterbox** ['letəbɒks] n Br Briefkasten der.

**letterhead** ['letəhed] n Briefkopf der.

**lettering** ['letərɪŋ] n Beschriftung die.

**letter of credit** n Akkreditiv das.

**letter opener** n Brieföffner der.

**lettuce** ['letɪs] n Kopfsalat der.

**letup** ['letʌp] n Pause die.

**leuk(a)emia** [lu:'ki:mɪə] n Leukämie die.

**levee** ['levɪ] n Am Uferdamm der.

**level** ['levl] (Br pt & pp -led; cont -ling, Am pt & pp -ed; cont -ing) adj - **1.** [equal in height]: to be ~ (with sthg) (mit etw) auf gleicher Höhe sein, (mit etw) bündig sein - **2.** [equal in standard] ebenbürtig - **3.** [flat] waagerecht; [teaspoon] gestrichen ◇ adv: to draw ~ with sb mit jm gleichziehen ◇ n - **1.** [amount - gen] Niveau das; [- of noise] Pegel der; [- of temperature] Höhe die; high ~s of unemployment hohe Arbeitslosigkeit - **2.** [of liquid] Stand der; to be on a ~ (with sthg) (mit etw) auf gleichem Niveau sein - **3.** [standard] Niveau das - **4.** Am [spirit level] Wasserwaage die - **5.** [storey] Geschoss das, Stock der; [of multistorey car park] Ebene die - **6.** phr: to be on the ~ inf ehrlich sein ◇ vt - **1.** [make flat] ebnen, nivellieren - **2.** [demolish] dem Erdboden gleichmachen - **3.** [aim]: to ~ a gun at sb/sthg ein Gewehr auf jn/etw richten; to ~ an accusation at OR against sb eine Anklage gegen jn richten.

◆ **level off, level out** vi - **1.** [unemployment, inflation] aufhören zu steigen - **2.** AERON [aircraft] ablfangen.

◆ **level with** vt fus inf ehrlich sein mit.

**level crossing** n Br ebener Bahnübergang.

**level-headed** [-'hedɪd] adj vernünftig, ausgeglichen.

**level pegging** [-'pegɪŋ] adj Br: to be ~ gleichauf liegen.

**lever** [Br 'li:və', Am 'levər] n - **1.** [handle, bar] Hebel der - **2.** fig [tactic] (taktisches) Manöver.

**leverage** [Br 'li:vərɪdʒ, Am 'levərɪdʒ] n (U) - **1.** fig [influence] Einfluss der - **2.** [principle] Hebelwirkung die; [force] Hebelkraft die.

**leviathan** [lɪ'vaɪəθn] n [large body, organization] Gigant der.

**levitation** [levɪ'teɪʃn] n Levitation die.

**levity** ['levətɪ] n Leichtfertigkeit die.

**levy** ['levɪ] (pl levies; pt & pp -ied) n: ~ (on sthg) Steuer die (auf etw (A)), Abgabe die (auf etw (A)) ◇ vt erheben.

**lewd** [lju:d] *adj* [joke, song] unanständig; [remark] anzüglich.

**lexical** ['leksɪkl] *adj* lexikalisch.

**LI** *abk für* Long Island, *in Postanschrift verwendet.*

**liability** [ˌlaɪə'bɪlətɪ] (*pl* -ies) *n* - 1. [hindrance] Belastung *die* - 2. LAW [legal responsibility]: ~ (for sthg) Haftung *die* (für etw).

➥ **liabilities** *npl* FIN Verbindlichkeiten *pl*, Schulden *pl*.

**liable** ['laɪəbl] *adj* - 1. [likely]: to be ~ to do sthg die Neigung haben, etw zu tun; if you don't remind him, he's ~ to forget wenn du ihn nicht daran erinnerst, vergisst er es wahrscheinlich - 2. [prone]: to be ~ to sthg für etw anfällig OR empfänglich sein - 3. LAW: to be ~ (for sthg) [debt, accident, damage] (für etw) verantwortlich sein; to be ~ to sthg [fine, arrest, imprisonment] für etw haftbar sein; to be ~ to a fine mit einer Geldstrafe belegt werden können.

**liaise** [lɪ'eɪz] *vi*: to ~ with Kontakt auflnehmen mit; to ~ between als Verbindungsperson agieren zwischen (+D).

**liaison** [lɪ'eɪzɒn] *n* - 1.: ~ (with/between) [contact] Verbindung *die* (mit/zwischen (+D)); [cooperation] Zusammenarbeit *die* (mit/zwischen (+D)) - 2. [affair, relationship]: ~ (with) Verhältnis *das* (mit).

**liar** ['laɪə'] *n* Lügner *der*, -in *die*.

**Lib.** [lɪb] *abbr of* Liberal.

**libel** ['laɪbl] (*Br pt* & *pp* -led; *cont* -ling, *Am pt* & *pp* -ed; *cont* -ing) *n* (schriftliche) Verleumdung <> *vt* (schriftlich) verleumden.

**libellous** *Br*, **libelous** *Am* ['laɪbələs] *adj* verleumderisch.

**liberal** ['lɪbərəl] *adj* - 1. [tolerant] liberal, aufgeschlossen - 2. [generous] großzügig <> *n* großzügiger Mensch.

➥ **Liberal** POL *adj* liberal <> *n* Liberale *der*, die.

**liberal arts** *npl esp Am* Geisteswissenschaften *pl*.

**Liberal Democrat** *adj* liberaldemokratisch <> *n* Liberaldemokrat *der*, -in die.

**liberalize, -ise** ['lɪbərəlaɪz] *vt* liberalisieren.

**liberal-minded** [-'maɪndɪd] *adj* aufgeschlossen.

**liberate** ['lɪbəreɪt] *vt* befreien.

**liberation** [ˌlɪbə'reɪʃn] *n* Befreiung *die*.

**liberator** ['lɪbəreɪtə'] *n* Befreier *der*.

**Liberia** [laɪ'bɪərɪə] *n* Liberia *nt*.

**Liberian** [laɪ'bɪərɪən] *adj* liberianisch <> *n* Liberianer *der*, -in die.

**liberty** ['lɪbətɪ] (*pl* -ies) *n* Freiheit *die*; at ~ auf freiem Fuß; you are at ~ to leave es steht dir frei zu gehen; to take liberties (with

sb) sich (D) (jm gegenüber) Freiheiten herauslnehmen.

**libido** [lɪ'bi:dəʊ] (*pl* -s) *n* Libido *die*.

**Libra** ['li:brə] *n* Waage *die*.

**librarian** [laɪ'breərɪən] *n* Bibliothekar *der*, -in die.

**librarianship** [laɪ'breərɪənʃɪp] *n* Bibliothekswesen *das*.

**library** ['laɪbrərɪ] (*pl* -ies) *n* Bibliothek *die*, Bücherei *die*.

**library book** *n* Leihbuch *das*.

**libretto** [lɪ'bretəʊ] (*pl* -s) *n* Libretto *das*.

**Libya** ['lɪbɪə] *n* Libyen *nt*.

**Libyan** ['lɪbɪən] *adj* libysch <> *n* Libyer *der*, -in die.

**lice** [laɪs] *pl* ⊳ louse.

**licence** ['laɪsəns] *n* - 1. [permit - for dog] Genehmigung *die*; [ - for TV] Anmeldung *die*; [ - for driver] Führerschein *der*; [ - for marriage] Erlaubnis *die*, Lizenz *die*; [ - for bar, pub] Konzession *die*; [ - for pilot] Pilotenschein *der* - 2. COMM Lizenz *die*; under ~ in Lizenz <> *vt Am* = license.

**license** ['laɪsəns] *vt* COMM: to ~ sb to do sthg jm eine Lizenz erteilen, etw zu tun; to ~ sthg eine Lizenz OR Konzession für etw erteilen <> *n Am* = licence.

**licensed** ['laɪsənst] *adj* - 1. [person]: to be ~ to do sthg die Genehmigung haben, etw zu tun; to be ~ to drive eine Fahrerlaubnis besitzen; he is ~d to sell alchohol er hat eine Verkaufslizenz für Alkohol - 2. [object] zugelassen - 3. *Br* [premises] mit Schankerlaubnis OR Schankkonzession.

**licensee** [ˌlaɪsən'si:] *n* Lizenznehmer *der*, -in die; [of bar] Konzessionsinhaber *der*, -in die.

**license plate** *n Am* Nummernschild *das*.

**licensing hours** ['laɪsənsɪŋ-] *npl Br* Ausschankzeiten *pl*.

**licensing laws** ['laɪsənsɪŋ-] *npl Br* Gesetze *pl* zum Ausschank von Alkohol.

**licentious** [laɪ'senʃəs] *adj fml* & *pej* unzüchtig.

**lichen** ['laɪkən] *n* Flechte *die*.

**lick** [lɪk] *n* - 1. [act of licking] Lecken *das*; to give sthg a ~ an etw (D) lecken - 2. *inf* [small amount]: a ~ of paint ein bisschen Farbe <> *vt* - 1. [with tongue] lecken; to ~ one's lips sich (D) die Lippen lecken - 2. *fig* [subj: flames] emporzüngeln an (+ D); [subj: waves] (uml)spülen - 3. *inf* [defeat] ablziehen.

**licorice** ['lɪkərɪs] *n* = liquorice.

**lid** [lɪd] *n* - 1. [cover] Deckel *der* - 2. [eyelid] Augenlid *das*.

**lido** ['li:dəʊ] (*pl* -s) *n* - 1. *Br* [swimming pool] Freibad *das* - 2. [beach] Strandbad *das*.

**lie** [laɪ] (*pt sense 1* lied; *pt senses 2-5* lay; *pp sense 1*

**lied;** pp senses 2-5 **lain;** cont all senses **lying**) n Lüge die; **to tell ~s** lügen ⬦ vi - **1.** [tell lie] lügen; **to ~ to sb** jn anlügen; **to ~ about sthg** über etw (A) nicht die Wahrheit sagen - **2.** [be horizontal, be situated] liegen; **to ~ in wait for sb** jm auf llauern; **to ~ idle** [machine] stilllstehen; **here ~s...** [buried] hier ruht ... - **3.** [lie down] sich legen - **4.** [difficulty, answer, responsibility etc] liegen - **5.** phr: **to ~ low** sich versteckt halten.

⬦ **lie about, lie around** vi herumlliegen.

⬦ **lie down** vi sich hinllegen.

⬦ **lie in** vi Br im Bett bleiben.

**Liechtenstein** ['lɪktənstaɪn] n Liechtenstein nt.

**lie detector** n Lügendetektor der.

**lie-down** n Br Nickerchen das; **to have a ~** sich (kurz) hinllegen.

**lie-in** n Br: **to have a ~** richtig auslschlafen.

**lieu** [lju:, lu:] ⬦ **in lieu** adv stattdessen; **in ~ of** anstelle (+ G), anstatt (+ G).

**Lieut.** abbr of **lieutenant**.

**lieutenant** [Br lef'tenənt, Am lu:'tenənt] n [in army] Oberleutnant der; [in navy] Kapitänleutnant der.

**lieutenant colonel** n Oberstleutnant der.

**life** [laɪf] (pl **lives**) n - **1.** [gen] Leben das; **to breathe ~ into** sthg einer Sache (D) Leben einlhauchen, einer Sache (D) beleben; **to come to ~** zum Leben erwachen; **that's ~!** so ist das Leben!; **he was sent to prison for ~** er wurde zu einer lebenslänglichen Haftstrafe verurteilt; **marriage is a commitment for ~** die Ehe ist ein Bund fürs Leben; **for the ~ of me** inf beim besten Willen; **to lay down one's ~** sein Leben opfern; **to risk ~ and limb to do sthg** Kopf und Kragen riskieren, um etw zu tun; **to scare the ~ out of sb** jn zu Tode erschrecken; **to take sb's/one's own ~** jm/sich das Leben nehmen - **2.** [of product, machine] Lebensdauer die - **3.** inf [life imprisonment] lebenslängliche Freiheitsstrafe; **to get ~** inf lebenslänglich kriegen ⬦ comp lebenslang.

**life-and-death** adj [fight] um Leben und Tod; **a ~ struggle** ein Kampf um Leben und Tod; **a ~ decision** eine lebenswichtige Entscheidung.

**life annuity** n Leibrente die.

**life assurance** n = **life insurance**.

**life belt** n Rettungsring der.

**lifeblood** ['laɪfblʌd] n fig [source of strength] Herzblut das.

**lifeboat** ['laɪfbəʊt] n Rettungsboot das.

**life buoy** n Rettungsboje die.

**life cycle** n Lebenszyklus der.

**life expectancy** [-ɪk'spektənsɪ] n Lebenserwartung die.

**lifeguard** ['laɪfgɑːd] n Rettungsschwimmer der, -in die.

**life imprisonment** [-ɪm'prɪznmənt] n lebenslängliche Freiheitsstrafe.

**life insurance** n Lebensversicherung die.

**life jacket** n Schwimmweste die, Rettungsweste die.

**lifeless** ['laɪflɪs] adj leblos.

**lifelike** ['laɪflaɪk] adj lebensecht.

**lifeline** ['laɪflaɪn] n - **1.** [rope] Rettungsleine die - **2.** fig [with outside] Verbindung die mit der Außenwelt.

**lifelong** ['laɪflɒŋ] adj lebenslang.

**life peer** n Br durch Geburtsrecht bestimmtes Mitglied des britischen Hochadels auf Lebenszeit.

**life preserver** [-prɪˌzɜːvəʳ] n Am - **1.** [belt] Rettungsring der - **2.** [jacket] Schwimmweste die, Rettungsweste die.

**life raft** n Rettungsfloß das.

**lifesaver** ['laɪfˌseɪvəʳ] n Lebensretter der.

**life sentence** n lebenslange Freiheitsstrafe.

**life-size(d)** [-saɪz(d)] adj lebensgroß.

**lifespan** ['laɪfspæn] n - **1.** [of person, animal] Lebenserwartung die - **2.** [of product, machine] Lebensdauer die.

**lifestyle** ['laɪfstaɪl] n Lebensstil der.

**life-support system** n lebenserhaltende Apparaturen.

**lifetime** ['laɪftaɪm] n Lebenszeit die.

**lift** [lɪft] n - **1.** [ride]: **to give sb a ~** jn (im Auto) mitlnehmen - **2.** Br [elevator] Fahrstuhl der ⬦ vt - **1.** [hand, arm, leg] heben - **2.** [object] hochlheben - **3.**: **to ~ sb's spirits** jn auflmuntern - **4.** [ban, embargo] auflheben - **5.** [plagiarize - idea] stehlen; [ - writing] ablschreiben - **6.** inf [steal] klauen ⬦ vi - **1.** [lid, top] sich heben - **2.** [mist, fog, clouds] sich lichten - **3.** [heart, spirits] neuen Auftrieb bekommen.

⬦ **lift up** vt sep hochlheben, hochlnehmen ⬦ vi sich heben.

**lift-off** n Abheben das.

**ligament** ['lɪgəmənt] n ANAT Band das

**light** [laɪt] (pt & pp **lit** OR **-ed**) adj - **1.** [gen] leicht - **2.** [pale, bright] hell; **~ blue** hellblau ⬦ n - **1.** (U) [brightness] Licht das - **2.** [device - lamp] Lampe die; [ - on car] Scheinwerfer der; [ - in street] Laterne die; **to put** OR **turn the ~ on** das Licht anlschalten - **3.** [for cigarette, pipe] Feuer das, Streichholz das; **to set ~ to sthg** etw anlzünden - **4.** [perspective]: **in the ~ of** Br, **in ~ of** Am angesichts (+ G); **to see sb/sthg in a different ~** jn/etw in einem anderen Licht sehen - **5.** literary [in sb's eyes] Leuchten das, Glanz der - **6.** phr: **to come to ~** ans Licht kommen; **to**

**see the ~** klar sehen; **to throw** OR **cast** OR **shed ~ on sthg** Licht in etw *(A)* bringen ◇ *vt* - **1.** [ignite] anlzünden - **2.** [illuminate] erleuchten ◇ *adv:* **to travel ~** mit wenig Gepäck reisen.

➤ **light out** *vi Am inf* ablhauen.

➤ **light up** *vt sep* - **1.** [sky, room, stage] erleuchten; **a smile lit up his face** ein Lächeln erhellte sein Gesicht - **2.** [cigarette, cigar, pipe] anlzünden ◇ *vi* - **1.** [face, eyes] auflleuchten - **2.** *inf* [start smoking] sich *(D)* eine anlzünden.

**light aircraft** *(pl inv)* n kleines Flugzeug.

**light ale** n *Br* leichtes Ale, *englische Biersorte.*

**light bulb** n Glühbirne *die.*

**light cream** n *Am* kalorienarme Sahne.

**lighted** ['laɪtɪd] *adj* - **1.** [illuminated] erleuchtet - **2.** [on fire] angezündet.

**light-emitting diode** [-ɪˌmɪtɪŋ-] n Leuchtdiode *die.*

**lighten** ['laɪtn] *vt* - **1.** [make brighter - gen] heller machen; [ - hair] auflhellen - **2.** [make less heavy - load] leichter machen; [ - workload] erleichtern ◇ *vi* - **1.** [sky] sich auflhellen - **2.** [mood, atmosphere] lockerer OR entspannter werden.

➤ **lighten up** *vi inf* lockerer werden.

**lighter** ['laɪtəʳ] n Feuerzeug *das.*

**light-fingered** [-'fɪŋɡəd] *adj inf* langfing(e)rig.

**light-headed** [-'hedɪd] *adj* schwindlig.

**light-hearted** [-'hɑːtɪd] *adj* - **1.** [cheerful] heiter, unbeschwert - **2.** [amusing] fröhlich.

**lighthouse** ['laɪthaʊs, *pl* -haʊzɪz] n Leuchtturm *der.*

**light industry** n Leichtindustrie *die.*

**lighting** ['laɪtɪŋ] n Beleuchtung *die.*

**lighting-up time** n *Zeitpunkt, zu dem Fahrzeug- und Straßenbeleuchtung eingeschaltet werden müssen.*

**lightly** ['laɪtlɪ] *adv* - **1.** [tap, knock] leise - **2.** [cook, grill] leicht - **3.** [remark, say] leichten Herzens.

**light meter** n Lichtmesser *der;* PHOT Belichtungsmesser *der.*

**lightning** ['laɪtnɪŋ] n (U) Blitz *der.*

**lightning conductor** *Br,* **lightning rod** *Am* n Blitzableiter *der.*

**lightning strike** n *Br* spontane Arbeitsniederlegung.

**light opera** n Operette *die.*

**light pen** n Lichtstift *der.*

**lightship** ['laɪtʃɪp] n Feuerschiff *das.*

**lightweight** ['laɪtweɪt] *adj* - **1.** [object] leicht - **2.** *fig* & *pej* [person] Schmalspur- ◇ n Leichtgewicht *das;* **political ~s** Schmalspurpolitiker *der.*

**light year** n Lichtjahr *das.*

**likable** ['laɪkəbl] *adj* sympathisch.

**like** [laɪk] *prep* wie; **~ this/that** so; **what's it ~?** wie ist es?; **to look ~ sb/sthg** jm/etw ähnlich sehen; **it looks ~ rain** es sieht nach Regen aus ◇ *vt* mögen; **to ~ doing sthg** etw gern tun; **do you ~ it?** gefällt es dir?; **as you ~** wie Sie wollen/wie du willst; **I don't ~ to bother her** ich will sie nicht stören; **I'd ~ to sit down** ich würde mich gern hinsetzen; **I'd ~ a drink** ich würde gern etwas trinken; **I'd ~ a kilo of apples** ich hätte gern ein Kilo Äpfel; **we'd ~ you to come for dinner** wir möchten Sie zum Essen einladen ◇ *adj* ähnlich; **people of ~ mind** Gleichgesinnte *pl* ◇ n: **and the ~** und dergleichen.

**likeable** ['laɪkəbl] *adj* = likable.

**likelihood** ['laɪklɪhʊd] n Wahrscheinlichkeit *die;* **in all ~** aller Wahrscheinlichkeit nach.

**likely** ['laɪklɪ] *adj* - **1.** [probable] wahrscheinlich; **they're ~ to win** sie werden wahrscheinlich gewinnen; **a ~ story!** *iron* na klar!, höchstwahrscheinlich! - **2.** [suitable] geeignet.

**like-minded** [-'maɪndɪd] *adj* gleichgesinnt.

**liken** ['laɪkn] *vt:* **to ~ sb/sthg to** jn/etw vergleichen mit.

**likeness** ['laɪknɪs] n - **1.** [resemblance]: **~ (to sb/ sthg)** Ähnlichkeit *die* (mit jm/etw) - **2.** [portrait] Bildnis *das,* Porträt *das.*

**likewise** ['laɪkwaɪz] *adv* gleichfalls, ebenfalls; **to do ~** das Gleiche tun.

**liking** ['laɪkɪŋ] n: **~ for sb/sthg** Vorliebe *die* für jn/etw; **to have a ~ for sb/sthg** für jn/etw eine Vorliebe haben; **that's not to my ~** das ist nicht nach meinem Geschmack; **too ... for ~** zu ... für Geschmack; **he's too cheeky for my ~** er ist etwas zu frech für meinen Geschmack.

**lilac** ['laɪlək] *adj* [colour] lila ◇ n - **1.** [tree] Flieder *der* - **2.** [colour] Lila *das.*

**Lilo**® ['laɪləʊ] *(pl* -s) n *Br* Luftmatratze *die.*

**lilt** [lɪlt] n [in voice] singender Tonfall.

**lilting** ['lɪltɪŋ] *adj* beschwingt.

**lily** ['lɪlɪ] *(pl* -ies) n Lilie *die.*

**lily of the valley** *(pl* lilies of the valley) n Maiglöckchen *das.*

**limb** [lɪm] n - **1.** [of body] Glied *das;* **~s** Glieder *pl,* Gliedmaßen *pl* - **2.** [of tree] Ast *der* - **3.** *phr:* **to be out on a ~** völlig allein dalstehen.

**limber** ['lɪmbəʳ] ➤ **limber up** *vi* sich auf llockern, Lockerungsübungen machen.

**limbo** ['lɪmbəʊ] *(pl* -s) n - **1.** [uncertain state]: **to be in ~** in der Schwebe sein - **2.** [dance]: **the ~** der Limbo.

**lime** [laɪm] n - **1.** [fruit] Limone *die;* **~ juice** Limonensaft *der* - **2.** [linden tree] Linde *die* - **3.** [for

**L**

making cement, fertilizer] Kalk der - **4.** [for painting walls] Kalkfarbe die.

**lime cordial** n Limonensirup der.

**lime-green** adj hellgrün.

**limelight** ['laɪmlaɪt] n: **the ~** das Rampenlicht.

**limerick** ['lɪmərɪk] n Limerick der.

**limestone** ['laɪmstəʊn] n Kalkstein der.

**limey** ['laɪmɪ] (pl -s) n Am inf pej Engländer der, -in die.

**limit** ['lɪmɪt] n - **1.** [restriction] Begrenzung die - **2.** [boundary, greatest extent] Grenze die; '**off ~s**' esp Am 'Zutritt verboten'; **that subject is off ~s** das Thema ist tabu; **within ~s** [to a certain extent] innerhalb bestimmter Grenzen; **he's/she's the ~!** inf er/sie ist unmöglich! ◇ vt begrenzen; **to ~ o.s. to sthg** sich auf etw (A) beschränken.

**limitation** [ˌlɪmɪ'teɪʃn] n - **1.** [restriction, control] Begrenzung die - **2.** [shortcoming]: **~s** Grenzen pl.

**limited** ['lɪmɪtɪd] adj begrenzt; **to be ~ to sthg** auf etw (A) beschränkt sein.

**limited company** n Gesellschaft die mit beschränkter Haftung.

**limited edition** n limitierte Auflage.

**limited liability company** n = limited company.

**limitless** ['lɪmɪtlɪs] adj grenzenlos.

**limo** ['lɪməʊ] (pl -s) n inf luxuriöse Limousine.

**limousine** ['lɪməziːn] n luxuriöse Limousine.

**limp** [lɪmp] adj schlaff; [lettuce, flowers] welk ◇ n Hinken das; **to walk with a ~** hinken ◇ vi hinken.

**limpet** ['lɪmpɪt] n Napfschnecke die.

**limpid** ['lɪmpɪd] adj literary klar.

**limply** ['lɪmplɪ] adv - **1.** [lie, hang] schlaff - **2.** [reply] schwach.

**linchpin** ['lɪntʃpɪn] n fig [person] Hauptfigur die; [thing] wichtigstes Element.

**Lincs.** [lɪŋks] abk für Lincolnshire, in Postanschrift verwendet.

**linctus** ['lɪŋktəs] n Br Hustensirup der.

**line** [laɪn] n - **1.** [mark] Linie die; **to draw the ~ at sthg** fig bei etw den Schlussstrich ziehen - **2.** [row] Reihe die - **3.** [queue] Schlange die; **to stand** OR **wait in ~** Schlange stehen OR anstehen; **to be in ~ for promotion** Aussicht auf Beförderung haben - **4.** [direction of movement] Gerade, die; gerade Linie; **he can't walk in a straight ~** er kann nicht (mehr) geradeaus gehen - **5.** [alignment]: **in ~ (with)** in einer Linie (mit); **to step out of ~** [misbehave] aus der Reihe tanzen - **6.** [RAIL - railway track] Gleise pl; [ - route] Bahnlinie die; **the ~ was blocked die**

Strecke war blockiert - **7.** NAUT: **shipping ~** Schifffahrtslinie die - **8.** [of poem, song, text] Zeile die; **to read between the ~s** zwischen den Zeilen lesen - **9.** [wrinkle] Falte die - **10.** [outline] Konturen pl, Linienführung die - **11.** [rope] Leine die; [wire] Kabel das; [string] Schnur die - **12.** TELEC [telephone connection] Leitung die; **hold the ~** bleiben Sie am Apparat - **13.** inf [short letter] kurze Nachricht; **to drop sb a ~** jm ein paar Zeilen schreiben - **14.**: **~ of argument** Argumentation die; **we are pursuing several ~s of enquiry** wir ermitteln in verschiedenen Richtungen; **along the same ~s** in gleicher Weise; **to be on the right ~s** auf dem richtigen Weg sein - **15.** inf [field of activity] Branche die - **16.** MIL: **enemy ~s** feindliche Linien - **17.** [lineage, ancestry] Linie die - **18.** [limit, borderline] Grenze die - **19.** COMM [type of product] Modell das; [group of products] Kollektion die ◇ vt - **1.** [form rows along] säumen - **2.** [cover inside surface of - drawer] auslschlagen; [ - garment, curtains] füttern.

➤ **lines** npl - **1.** SCH Strafarbeit die; **to get fifty ~s** etwas fünfzigmal aufschreiben müssen - **2.** [actor's words] Text der.

➤ **on the line** adv: **he's put his career on the ~** er hat seine Karriere aufs Spiel gesetzt.

➤ **out of line** adj fehl am Platz.

➤ **line up** vt sep - **1.** [in rows] auf lstellen - **2.** inf [organize] arrangieren ◇ vi - **1.** [in a row] sich auf lstellen - **2.** [in a queue] sich anlstellen.

**lineage** ['lɪnɪɪdʒ] n fml Abstammung die.

**linear** ['lɪnɪə'] adj - **1.** [made of lines] linear - **2.** [in a straight line] geradlinig.

**lined** [laɪnd] adj - **1.** [paper] liniert - **2.** [face] faltig.

**line drawing** n Strichzeichnung die.

**line feed** n COMPUT zeilenweiser Blatteinzug.

**linen** ['lɪnɪn] n (U) - **1.** [cloth] Leinen das - **2.** [tablecloths] Wäsche die ◇ comp - **1.** [suit, napkins] Leinen- - **2.** [cupboard, drawer] Wäsche-.

**linen basket** n Wäschekorb der.

**lineout** ['laɪnaʊt] n RUGBY Gasse die.

**line printer** n Zeilendrucker der.

**liner** ['laɪnə'] n [ship] Linienschiff das.

**linesman** ['laɪnzmən] (pl -men [-mən]) n SPORT Linienrichter der.

**lineup** ['laɪnʌp] n - **1.** [of players, competitors] Aufstellung die - **2.** Am [identification parade] Aufstellung von Verdächtigen zur Identifizierung durch Zeugen bei der Polizei.

**linger** ['lɪŋgə'] vi - **1.** [dawdle]: **we ~ed over our meal** wir aßen in aller Gemütlichkeit; **she ~ed behind after school** sie blieb nach Schulschluss noch da - **2.** [persist] zurücklbleiben.

**lingerie** ['læŋʒərɪ] n Damenunterwäsche die.

**lingering** ['lɪŋgrɪŋ] adj - **1.** [feeling, hope, doubt] zurückbleibend - **2.** [death] langsam - **3.** [kiss, look, farewell, illness] lang.

**lingo** ['lɪŋgəʊ] (pl **-es**) n inf - **1.** [language] Sprache die - **2.** [specialist jargon] (Fach)jargon der.

**linguist** ['lɪŋgwɪst] n - **1.** [person good at languages] Sprachkundige der, die - **2.** [student or teacher of linguistics] Linguist der, -in die.

**linguistic** [lɪŋ'gwɪstɪk] adj [of language] sprachlich; [of linguistics] sprachwissenschaftlich, linguistisch.

→ **linguistics** n Sprachwissenschaft die, Linguistik die.

**liniment** ['lɪnɪmənt] n Einreibemittel das.

**lining** ['laɪnɪŋ] n - **1.** [of garment, curtains, box] Futter das - **2.** [of stomach, nose] Schleimhaut die - **3.** (U) AUT [of brakes] Belag der.

**link** [lɪŋk] n - **1.** [of chain] Glied das - **2.** [connection]: ~ **(between/with)** Verbindung die (zwischen (+ D))/mit OR zu) ⟨⟩ vt verbinden; **to ~ arms with sb** sich bei jm unterhaken.

→ **link up** vt sep verbinden, anlschließen; **to ~ sthg up with sthg** etw mit etw verbinden, etw an etw (A) anlschließen ⟨⟩ vi: **to ~ up (with sb/sthg)** TV & TELEC schalten (zu jm/etw).

**linkage** ['lɪŋkɪdʒ] n [connection] Verbindung die; [system of bars] Gestänge das.

**linked** [lɪŋkt] adj verbunden; **the crimes seem to be ~** die Verbrechen scheinen miteinander in Verbindung zu stehen.

**links** [lɪŋks] (pl inv) n SPORT Golfplatz der.

**linkup** ['lɪŋkʌp] n Anschluss der.

**lino** ['laɪnəʊ], **linoleum** [lɪ'nəʊliəm] n Linoleum das.

**linseed oil** [ˌlɪnsiːd-] n Leinöl das.

**lint** [lɪnt] n (U) - **1.** [dressing] Mull der - **2.** Am [fluff] Fussel die.

**lintel** ['lɪntl] n Fenstersturz der.

**lion** ['laɪən] n Löwe der.

**lion cub** n Löwenjunge das.

**lip** [lɪp] n - **1.** [of mouth] Lippe die; **to keep a stiff upper ~** die Ohren steif lhalten; **my ~s are sealed** ich sage kein Wort - **2.** [of container] Rand der.

**liposuction** ['lɪpəʊˌsʌkʃən] n Fettabsaugen das.

**lip-read** vi von den Lippen lesen.

**lip-reading** n Ablesen das von den Lippen.

**lip salve** [-sælv] n Br Lippenbalsam der.

**lip service** n: **to pay ~ to sthg** ein Lippenbekenntnis zu etw ablegen.

**lipstick** ['lɪpstɪk] n Lippenstift der.

**liquefy** ['lɪkwɪfaɪ] (pt & pp **-ied**) vt verflüssigen ⟨⟩ vi sich verflüssigen.

**liqueur** [lɪ'kjʊəʳ] n Likör der.

**liquid** ['lɪkwɪd] adj flüssig ⟨⟩ n Flüssigkeit die.

**liquid assets** npl verfügbare Vermögenswerte pl.

**liquidate** ['lɪkwɪdeɪt] vt liquidieren.

**liquidation** [ˌlɪkwɪ'deɪʃn] n Liquidation die.

**liquidator** ['lɪkwɪdeɪtəʳ] n Liquidator der.

**liquid crystal display** n Flüssigkristallanzeige die.

**liquidity** [lɪ'kwɪdətɪ] n - **1.** [having money] Liquidität die - **2.** [being liquid] Flüssigkeit die.

**liquidize, -ise** ['lɪkwɪdaɪz] vt Br CULIN mit dem Mixer pürieren.

**liquidizer, -iser** ['lɪkwɪdaɪzəʳ] n Br (elektrischer) Mixer.

**liquor** ['lɪkəʳ] n esp Am [alcoholic drink] Alkohol der; [spirits] Spirituosen pl.

**liquorice** ['lɪkərɪʃ, 'lɪkərɪs] n Lakritze die.

**liquor store** n Am Wein- und Spirituosenhandlung die.

**lira** ['lɪərə] n Lira die.

**Lisbon** ['lɪzbən] n Lissabon nt.

**lisp** [lɪsp] n Lispeln das ⟨⟩ vi lispeln.

**lissom(e)** ['lɪsəm] adj literary geschmeidig.

**list** [lɪst] n Liste die ⟨⟩ vt - **1.** [in writing] auflisten, (in eine Liste) einltragen - **2.** [in speech] auflführen, auflzählen ⟨⟩ vi NAUT Schlagseite haben.

**listed building** [ˌlɪstɪd-] n Br unter Denkmalschutz stehendes Gebäude.

**listed company** [ˌlɪstɪd-] n Br eingetragene Firma OR Gesellschaft.

**listen** ['lɪsn] vi - **1.** [give attention] zulhören, hinlhören; **to ~ to sb/sthg** jm/etw zulhören; **to ~ for sthg** auf etw (A) horchen - **2.** [heed advice] hören; **to ~ to sb/sthg** auf jn/etw hören.

→ **listen in** vi - **1.** RADIO: **I ~ in to his show every afternoon** ich höre jeden Nachmittag seine Sendung - **2.** [eavesdrop] mitlhören; **to ~ in on sthg** bei etw mitlhören.

→ **listen up** vi Am inf auf lpassen.

**listener** ['lɪsnəʳ] n Zuhörer der, -in die; [of radio] Hörer der, -in die.

**listing** ['lɪstɪŋ] n [COMPUT - result] Ausdruck eines Listing-Protokolls.

→ **listings** npl [of events] Veranstaltungskalender der.

**listless** ['lɪstlɪs] adj apathisch.

**list price** n Listenpreis der.

**lit** [lɪt] pt & pp ⊳ **light.**

**litany** ['lɪtənɪ] (pl **-ies**) n Litanei die.

**liter** n Am = litre.

**literacy** ['lɪtərəsɪ] n (U) Lese- und Schreibfähigkeit die.

**literal** ['lɪtərəl] adj wörtlich.

**literally** ['lɪtərəlɪ] adv - **1.** [for emphasis] im

wahrsten Sinne des Wortes, buchstäblich - **2.** [not figuratively] wörtlich; **to take sthg ~** etw wörtlich nehmen.

**literary** ['lɪtərərɪ] *adj* literarisch; **a ~ critic** ein Literaturkritiker.

**literate** ['lɪtərət] *adj* - **1.** [able to read and write] des Lesens und Schreibens kundig - **2.** [well-read] gebildet.

**literature** ['lɪtrətʃəʳ] *n* - **1.** [novels, plays, poetry] Literatur *die* - **2.** [printed information] Informationsmaterial *das*.

**lithe** [laɪð] *adj* geschmeidig.

**lithium** ['lɪθɪəm] *n* Lithium *das*.

**lithograph** ['lɪθəgrɑːf] *n* Lithografie *die*.

**lithography** [lɪ'θɒgrəfɪ] *n (U)* Lithografie *die*.

**Lithuania** [ˌlɪθjʊ'eɪnɪə] *n* Litauen *nt*.

**Lithuanian** [ˌlɪθjʊ'eɪnɪən] *adj* litauisch <> *n* - **1.** [person] Litauer *der*, -in *die* - **2.** [language] Litauisch(e) *das*.

**litigant** ['lɪtɪgənt] *n fml* Prozesspartei *die*.

**litigate** ['lɪtɪgeɪt] *vi fml* prozessieren.

**litigation** [ˌlɪtɪ'geɪʃn] *n (U) fml* Prozess *der*, Rechtsstreit *der*.

**litmus paper** ['lɪtməs-] *n* Lackmuspapier *das*.

**litre** *Br*, **liter** *Am* ['liːtəʳ] *n* Liter *der*.

**litter** ['lɪtəʳ] *n* - **1.** [waste material] Abfall *der*, Müll *der* - **2.** [newborn animals] Wurf *der* - **3.** [for litter tray]: **(cat) ~** (Katzen)streu *die* <> *vt*: **to be ~ed with sthg** mit etw übersät sein.

**litterbin** ['lɪtəˌbɪn] *n Br* Mülleimer *der*.

**litterlout** *Br* ['lɪtəlaʊt], **litterbug** ['lɪtəbʌg] *n inf* Schmutzfink *der*.

**litter tray** *n* Katzenklo *das*.

**little** ['lɪtl] (*compar sense 3* **less**; *superl sense 3* **least**) *adj* - **1.** [small, younger] klein; **the ~ ones** die Kleinen *pl* - **2.** [in distance, time] kurz - **3.** [not much] wenig; **he speaks ~ English** er spricht wenig Englisch; **he speaks a ~ English** er spricht ein bisschen Englisch <> *pron* wenig; **a ~** ein bisschen <> *adv* wenig; **~ by ~** nach und nach; **as ~ as possible** so wenig wie möglich.

**little finger** *n* kleiner Finger *der*.

**little-known** *adj* kaum bekannt.

**liturgy** ['lɪtədʒɪ] (*pl* **-ies**) *n* Liturgie *die*.

**live¹** [lɪv] *vi* - **1.** [have home] wohnen - **2.** [be alive] leben; **long ~ the queen!** es lebe die Königin!; **to ~ to a great age** ein hohes Alter erreichen - **3.** [survive] überleben <> *vt* führen; **to ~ a happy life** ein glückliches Leben führen; **to ~ it up** *inf* in Saus und Braus leben.

➤ **live down** *vt sep*: **she'll never ~ this down** das wird ihr auf ewig anhängen.

➤ **live for** *vt fus* leben für.

➤ **live in** *vi* [nanny, servant] im Hause wohnen; [student] im Studentenheim wohnen.

➤ **live off** *vt fus* [savings, land] leben von.

➤ **live on** *vt fus* [savings] leben von; [food] sich ernähren von; **I have enough to ~ on** ich habe genug zum Leben <> *vi* [continue] weiterleben.

➤ **live out** *vt sep* [life] verbringen <> *vi* [student] außerhalb (des Studentenheims) wohnen.

➤ **live together** *vi* zusammenwohnen.

➤ **live up to** *vt fus* [reputation] gerecht werden (+ *D*); [expectations] entsprechen (+ *D*).

➤ **live with** *vt fus* - **1.** [in same house] zusammenwohnen mit - **2.** *inf* [problem, situation] sich abfinden mit.

**live²** [laɪv] *adj* - **1.** [alive] lebendig - **2.** [programme, performance] Live-; ELEC [wire] geladen - **3.** [burning] glühend - **4.** [ammunition] scharf <> *adv* [broadcast] live.

**live-in** [lɪv-] *adj* im Haus wohnend.

**livelihood** ['laɪvlɪhʊd] *n* Lebensunterhalt *der*.

**liveliness** ['laɪvlɪnɪs] *n* Lebhaftigkeit *die*, Lebendigkeit *die*.

**lively** ['laɪvlɪ] (*compar* **-ier**; *superl* **-iest**) *adj* lebhaft.

**liven** ['laɪvn] ➤ **liven up** *vt sep* beleben, in Stimmung bringen <> *vi* [person] aufleben, in Stimmung kommen.

**liver** ['lɪvəʳ] *n* Leber *die*.

**Liverpudlian** [ˌlɪvə'pʌdlɪən] *adj* Liverpooler <> *n* Liverpooler *der*, -in *die*.

**liver sausage** *Br*, **liverwurst** *Am* ['lɪvəwɜːst] *n (U)* Leberwurst *die*.

**livery** ['lɪvərɪ] (*pl* **-ies**) *n* Livree *die*.

**lives** [laɪvz] *pl* ➤ **life**.

**livestock** ['laɪvstɒk] *n* Nutzvieh *das*.

**live wire** [laɪv-] *n* - **1.** [wire] stromführendes Kabel - **2.** *inf* [person] Energiebündel *das*.

**livid** ['lɪvɪd] *adj* - **1.** *inf* [angry] wütend, stinksauer - **2.** [bruise] blau.

**living** ['lɪvɪŋ] *adj* - **1.** [person] lebend - **2.** [language] lebendig <> *n* - **1.** [means of earning money] Lebensunterhalt *der*; **what do you do for a ~?** was machen Sie beruflich? - **2.** [lifestyle] Leben *das*.

**living conditions** *npl* Lebensbedingungen *pl*.

**living expenses** *npl* Lebenshaltungskosten *pl*.

**living room** *n* Wohnzimmer *das*.

**living standards** *npl* Lebensstandard *der*.

**living wage** *n* zum Leben ausreichender Lohn.

**lizard** ['lɪzəd] *n* Eidechse *die*.

**llama** ['lɑːmə] (pl inv OR -s) n Lama das.

**lo** [ləʊ] excl: ~ **and behold!** siehe da!

**load** [ləʊd] n - 1. [something carried] Ladung die - 2. [burden] Last die - 3. [large amount]: ~s of, a ~ of inf eine Menge, eine ganze Menge; **what a ~ of rubbish!** inf was für ein Blödsinn! ⬦ vt - 1. [container, vehicle, person] beladen; **to ~ sthg with sthg** etw mit etw beladen; **she was ~ed with shopping bags** sie war mit Einkaufstüten beladen - 2. [gun, cannon]: **to ~ sthg (with sthg)** etw (mit etw) laden - 3. [camera]: **to ~ a camera with a film** einen Film in eine Kamera einllegen - 4. COMPUT [program] laden.
➤ **load up** vt sep beladen ⬦ vi auf lladen.

**loaded** ['ləʊdɪd] adj - 1. [question, statement] gewichtig - 2. [gun] geladen; [camera] mit eingelegtem Film - 3. inf [rich] stinkreich.

**loading bay** ['ləʊdɪŋ-] n Ladeplatz der.

**loaf** [ləʊf] (pl **loaves**) n Laib der.
➤ **loaf about** vi herumllungern, herumlhängen.

**loafer** ['ləʊfə'] n [shoe] mokassinartiger Freizeitschuh; [lazy person] Faulenzer der, -in die.

**loan** [ləʊn] n - 1. [something lent] Leihgabe die; [money lent] Darlehen das, Kredit der - 2. [act of lending] Ausleihen das; **on ~** ausgeliehen ⬦ vt: **to ~ sthg (to sb), to ~ (sb) sthg** etw (an jn) verleihen, (jm) etw leihen.

**loan account** n Darlehenskonto das.

**loan capital** n Darlehenskapital das.

**loan shark** n inf pej Kredithai der.

**loath** [ləʊθ] adj: **to be ~ to do sthg** etw nur ungern tun.

**loathe** [ləʊð] vt verabscheuen, nicht ausllstehen können; **to ~ doing sthg** es verabscheuen, etw zu tun.

**loathing** ['ləʊðɪŋ] n Abscheu der.

**loathsome** ['ləʊðsəm] adj abscheulich.

**loaves** [ləʊvz] pl ⬅ **loaf.**

**lob** [lɒb] (pt & pp -**bed**; cont -**bing**) n TENNIS Lob der ⬦ vt - 1. [throw] (in hohem Bogen) werfen - 2. TENNIS lobben.

**lobby** ['lɒbɪ] (pl -**ies**; pt & pp -**ied**) n - 1. [anteroom] Vorraum der; [in hotel] Empfangshalle die, Lobby die; [in theatre] Foyer das - 2. [pressure group] Lobby die, Interessengruppe die ⬦ vt Einfluss nehmen auf (A).

**lobbyist** ['lɒbɪɪst] n Lobbyist der, -in die.

**lobe** [ləʊb] n ANAT [of brain] Lappen der; [of ear] Ohrläppchen das.

**lobotomy** [lə'bɒtəmɪ] (pl -**ies**) n Lobotomie die.

**lobster** ['lɒbstə'] n Hummer der.

**lobster pot** n Hummerkorb der.

**local** ['ləʊkl] adj - 1. [of the immediate area - tradition] örtlich, einheimisch; [ - phone call] Orts-; [ - hospital, shop, inhabitants] örtlich - 2. ADMIN & POL [services, council] Kommunal-, kommunal ⬦ n inf - 1. [person]: **the ~s** die Einheimischen pl - 2. Br [pub] Stammkneipe die - 3. Am [bus] Nahverkehrsbus der; [train] Nahverkehrszug der.

**local anaesthetic** n örtliche Betäubung.

**local area network** n COMPUT lokales Netzwerk.

**local authority** n Br Kommunalverwaltung die.

**local call** n Ortsgespräch das.

**local colour** n Lokalkolorit das.

**local derby** n Br Lokalderby das.

**locale** [ləʊ'kɑːl] n fml Ort der; [of film, crime] Schauplatz der.

**local government** n Kommunalverwaltung die.

**locality** [ləʊ'kælətɪ] (pl -**ies**) n Gegend die.

**localized, -ised** ['ləʊkəlaɪzd] adj örtlich begrenzt.

**locally** ['ləʊkəlɪ] adv [in region] am Ort; [in neighbourhood] in der Nachbarschaft.

**local time** n Ortszeit die.

**locate** [Br ləʊ'keɪt, Am 'ləʊkeɪt] vt - 1. [find] ausfindig machen, lokalisieren - 2. [situate]: **to be ~d** sich befinden ⬦ vi Am [settle] sich anlsiedeln.

**location** [ləʊ'keɪʃn] n - 1. [place] Ort der - 2. CINEMA: **the film was shot on ~ in China** die Außenaufnahmen zu diesem Film wurden in China gemacht.

**loc. cit.** [lɒk'sɪt] (abbr of loco citato) l.c.

**loch** [lɒk, lɒx] n Scot See der; **Loch Lomond** Loch Lomond.

**lock** [lɒk] n - 1. [of door, window, box] Schloss das; **under ~ and key** [money, object] unter Verschluss; [person] hinter Schloss und Riegel - 2. [on canal] Schleuse die - 3. AUT [steering lock] Einschlag der - 4. [of hair] Locke die - 5. phr: ~, **stock and barrel** mit allem, was dazugehört; **we have to sell the company ~, stock and barrel** wir müssen die gesamte Firma verkaufen ⬦ vt - 1. [fasten securely] abllschließen; [bicycle] anllschließen - 2. [keep safely]: **to ~ sthg in sthg** etw in etw (A) einllschließen - 3. [immobilize] sperren, blockieren - 4. [hold firmly]: **to be ~ed in an embrace** sich eng umschlungen halten; **to be ~ed in combat** lit (miteinander) im Kampf verschlungen sein; fig (miteinander) im Kampf stehen ⬦ vi - 1. [fasten securely] verschließen - 2. [become immobilized] blockieren.
➤ **locks** npl literary [hair] Locken pl.
➤ **lock away** vt sep wegllschließen.
➤ **lock in** vt sep einllschließen.
➤ **lock out** vt sep ausllsperren.

➤ **lock up** vt sep - **1.** [person] einlsperren - **2.** [house] ablschließen - **3.** [valuables] weglschließen ⬦ vi ablschließen.

**lockable** ['lɒkəbl] adj abschließbar.

**locker** ['lɒkə'] n [at gym, work] Spind der; [at station] Schließfach das.

**locker room** n Am Umkleideraum der.

**locket** ['lɒkɪt] n Medaillon das.

**lockjaw** ['lɒkdʒɔː] n (U) Wundstarrkrampf der.

**lockout** ['lɒkaut] n Aussperrung die.

**locksmith** ['lɒksmɪθ] n Schlosser der, -in die.

**lockup** ['lɒkʌp] n - **1.** [prison] Zelle die - **2.** Br [garage] Mietgarage, die zum Abstellen eines Autos oder verschiedener Gegenstände verwendet wird.

**loco** ['ləʊkəʊ] adj Am inf verrückt, bekloppt.

**locomotive** [,ləʊkə'məʊtɪv] n Lokomotive die.

**locum** ['ləʊkəm] (pl -s) n Stellvertreter der, -in die.

**locust** ['ləʊkəst] n Heuschrecke die, Wanderheuschrecke die.

**lodge** [lɒdʒ] n - **1.** [caretaker's room, of Freemasons] Loge die - **2.** [of manor house] Pförtnerhaus das - **3.** [for hunting] Jagdhütte die ⬦ vi - **1.** [stay, live]: **to ~ with sb** bei jm (zur Untermiete) wohnen - **2.** [become stuck] steckenlbleiben, festlsitzen - **3.** fig [in mind] sich festlsetzen ⬦ vt fml [register] einlreichen.

**lodger** ['lɒdʒə'] n Untermieter der, -in die.

**lodging** ['lɒdʒɪŋ] n ⊳ board.
➤ **lodgings** npl möblierte Zimmer pl.

**loft** [lɒft] n Dachboden der.

**lofty** ['lɒftɪ] (compar -ier; superl -iest) adj - **1.** [noble] hoch; [feelings] erhaben; [aims] hoch gesteckt - **2.** pej [haughty] hochmütig - **3.** literary [high] hoch.

**log** [lɒg] (pt & pp -ged; cont -ging) n - **1.** [of wood] Holzscheit das - **2.** [written record - of ship] Logbuch das; [ - of plane] Bordbuch das ⬦ vt - **1.** [information - on paper] einltragen; [ - in computer] einlgeben - **2.** [speed, distance, time] zurückllegen.
➤ **log in** vi COMPUT (sich) einlloggen.
➤ **log out** vi COMPUT (sich) auslloggen.

**loganberry** ['ləʊgənbərɪ] (pl -ies) n Loganbeere die.

**logarithm** ['lɒgərɪðm] n Logarithmus der.

**logbook** ['lɒgbʊk] n - **1.** [ship] Logbuch das; [plane] Bordbuch das - **2.** [of car] Fahrtenbuch das.

**log cabin** n Holzhütte die, Blockhütte die.

**log fire** n Kaminfeuer das.

**loggerheads** ['lɒgəhedz] n: **to be at ~** sich (D) in den Haaren liegen.

**logic** ['lɒdʒɪk] n Logik die.

**logical** ['lɒdʒɪkl] adj logisch.

**logically** ['lɒdʒɪklɪ] adv logisch.

**logistical** [lə'dʒɪstɪkl] adj logistisch.

**logistics** [lə'dʒɪstɪks] n (U) Logistik die.

**logjam** ['lɒgdʒæm] n esp Am [impasse] toter Punkt.

**logo** ['ləʊgəʊ] (pl -s) n Logo das, Firmenzeichen das.

**logrolling** ['lɒgrəʊlɪŋ] n Am gegenseitige Hilfe OR Unterstützung; POL gegenseitige Unterstützung zwischen Politikern im Wahlkampf und bei der Wahl.

**logy** ['ləʊgɪ] adj Am inf faul, träge (nach üppiger Mahlzeit).

**loin** [lɔɪn] n Lende die.
➤ **loins** npl ANAT Lenden pl; **to gird one's ~s** fig sich bereitlmachen.

**loincloth** ['lɔɪnklɒθ] n Lendenschurz der.

**loiter** ['lɔɪtə'] vi - **1.** [hang about] herumllungern - **2.** [dawdle] trödeln, bummeln.

**loll** [lɒl] vi - **1.** [sit, lie about] (sich) lümmeln, herumllümmeln - **2.** [hang down - tongue] herauslhängen; [ - head] herunterlhängen.

**lollipop** ['lɒlɪpɒp] n Lutscher der, Lolli der.

**lollipop lady** n Br meist ältere Dame in der Funktion eines Schülerlotsen.

**lollipop man** n Br meist älterer Herr in der Funktion eines Schülerlotsen.

**lolly** ['lɒlɪ] (pl -ies) n - **1.** [lollipop] Lutscher der, Lolli der - **2.** (U) Br inf [money] Piepen pl.

**London** ['lʌndən] n London nt.

**Londoner** ['lʌndənə'] n Londoner der, -in die.

**lone** [ləʊn] adj [lonely] einsam; [only] einzig.

**loneliness** ['ləʊnlɪnɪs] n Einsamkeit die.

**lonely** ['ləʊnlɪ] (compar -ier; superl -iest) adj einsam.

**lone parent** n Br alleinerziehende Mutter, alleinerziehender Vater.

**loner** ['ləʊnə'] n Einzelgänger der, -in die.

**lonesome** ['ləʊnsəm] adj Am inf einsam.

**long** [lɒŋ] adj lang; **it's 2 metres ~** es ist 2 Meter lang; **it's two hours ~** es dauert zwei Stunden; **the book is 500 pages ~** das Buch hat 500 Seiten; **how ~ is it?** [in distance] wie lang ist es?; [in time] wie lange dauert es?; **a ~ time** lange ⬦ adv lange; **I won't be ~** ich komme gleich wieder; **how ~ will it take?** wie lange dauert es?; **all day ~** den ganzen Tag; **for ~** lange; **before ~** bald; **no ~er** nicht mehr; **so ~!** inf tschüs! ⬦ n: **the ~ and the short of it is that ...** kurzum ..., mit einem Wort ... ⬦ vt: **to ~ to do sthg** sich danach sehnen, etw zu tun.
➤ **as long as, so long as** conj [if] solange.
➤ **long for** vt fus sich sehnen nach.

**long.** *abbr of* **longitude**.

**long-awaited** [-ə'weɪtɪd] *adj* lang erwartet.

**long-distance** *adj:* **a ~ race** ein Langstreckenrennen; **he's a ~ lorry driver** er ist Fernfahrer.

**long-distance call** *n* Ferngespräch *das.*

**long division** *n längere, schriftlich durchgeführte Division.*

**long-drawn-out** *adj* in die Länge gezogen.

**long drink** *n* Longdrink *der.*

**longevity** [lɒn'dʒevətɪ] *n* Langlebigkeit *die.*

**longhaired** [ˌlɒŋ'heəd] *adj* [person] langhaarig; [animal] Langhaar-.

**longhand** ['lɒŋhænd] *n* Langschrift *die.*

**long-haul** *adj:* **~ flight** Langstreckenflug *der.*

**longing** ['lɒŋɪŋ] *adj* sehnsüchtig, sehnsuchtsvoll <> *n:* **~ (for sthg)** Sehnsucht *die* (nach etw), Verlangen *das* (nach etw).

**longingly** ['lɒŋɪŋlɪ] *adv* sehnsüchtig, sehnsuchtsvoll.

**Long Island** *n* Long Island *nt.*

**longitude** ['lɒndʒɪtjuːd] *n* GEOGR (geografische) Länge.

**long johns** *npl* lange Unterhosen *pl.*

**long jump** *n* Weitsprung *der.*

**long-lasting** *adj* [effect] lang anhaltend; [material] haltbar.

**long-life** *adj* [battery] mit langer Lebensdauer; **~ milk** H-Milch *die.*

**long-lost** *adj* lang(e) verschollen.

**long-playing record** [-ˌpleɪŋ-] *n* Langspielplatte *die,* LP *die.*

**long-range** *adj* **- 1.** [missile, bomber] Langstrecken- **- 2.** [plan, forecast] langfristig.

**long-running** *adj* (schon) lange laufend.

**longshoreman** ['lɒŋʃɔːmən] (*pl* **-men** [-mən]) *n Am* Hafenarbeiter *der.*

**long shot** *n fig:* **it's a ~,** **but it might work** es ist ein gewagtes Unternehmen, aber es könnte klappen.

**longsighted** [ˌlɒŋ'saɪtɪd] *adj* weitsichtig.

**long-standing** *adj* (schon) lange bestehend.

**longsuffering** [ˌlɒŋ'sʌfərɪŋ] *adj* geduldig, langmütig.

**long term** *n:* **in the ~** auf lange Sicht, langfristig gesehen.

**~ long-term** *adj* langfristig.

**long vacation** *n Br* UNIV Sommerferien *pl.*

**long wave** *n* Langwelle *die.*

**longways** ['lɒŋweɪz] *adv* der Länge nach.

**longwearing** [ˌlɒŋ'weərɪŋ] *adj Am* langanhaltend, dauerhaft.

**long weekend** *n* langes Wochenende.

**longwinded** [ˌlɒŋ'wɪndɪd] *adj* langatmig, langwierig.

**loo** [luː] (*pl* **-s**) *n Br inf* Klo *das.*

**loofa(h)** ['luːfə] *n* Luffaschwamm *der.*

**look** [lʊk] *n* **- 1.** [with eyes] Blick *der;* **to give sb a ~** jm einen Blick zuwerfen; **to have a ~ at sthg** sich (D) etw ansehen; **let me have a ~!** lass mich mal sehen!; **come and have a ~!** schau dir das mal an! **- 2.** [search]: **to have a ~ (for sthg)** (etw) suchen **- 3.** [appearance] Aussehen *das;* **by the ~** OR **~s of sthg** allem Anschein nach <> *vi* **- 1.** [with eyes] sehen, schauen; **to ~ at sb/sthg** jn/etw ansehen; **I'm just ~ing** [in shop] ich wollte mich nur umsehen; **~ here!** *inf* na hör mal! **- 2.** [search] suchen **- 3.** [building, room]: **to ~ onto** gehen auf (+ A) **- 4.** [seem] auslsehen; **he ~s as if he hasn't slept** er sieht aus, als hätte er nicht geschlafen; **it ~s like rain** es sieht nach Regen aus; **she ~s like her mother** sie sieht wie ihre Mutter aus, sie sieht ihrer Mutter ähnlich <> *vt* **- 1.** [look at] sehen; **~ what you've done!** schau, was du gemacht hast!; **~ where you're going!** pass auf, wohin du trittst!; **to ~ sb in the face** jm in die Auge sehen **- 2.** [appear] **she ~s her age** man sieht ihr ihr Alter an; **to ~ one's best** fabelhaft auslsehen.

**~ looks** *npl:* **(good) ~s** gutes Aussehen.

**~ look after** *vt fus* [take care of] sich kümmern um.

**~ look at** *vt fus* anlsehen; **he ~ed at his watch** er sah OR schaute auf seine Uhr.

**~ look back** *vi* [reminisce] zurückblicken; **she's never ~ed back** sie hat es nie bereut.

**~ look down on** *vt fus* [condescend to] herablsehen auf (+ A).

**~ look for** *vt fus* suchen.

**~ look forward to** *vt fus* sich freuen auf (+ A).

**~ look into** *vt fus* [examine] untersuchen; **I'll ~ into it** ich werde der Sache nachlgehen.

**~ look on** *vt fus* = **look upon** <> *vi* [watch] zulsehen, zulschauen.

**~ look out** *vi* auflpassen; **~ out!** Vorsicht!

**~ look out for** *vt fus* [person, place] Ausschau halten nach; [opportunity] suchen nach.

**~ look round** *vt fus* [city, museum] besichtigen; **to ~ round the shops** einen Einkaufsbummel machen <> *vi* **- 1.** [look at surroundings] sich umlsehen **- 2.** [turn] sich umldrehen.

**~ look through** *vt fus* [report, document] durchlsehen; [examine] überprüfen.

**~ look to** *vt fus* **- 1.** [depend on] sich verlassen auf (+ A); **they ~ed to her for help** sie verließen sich darauf, dass sie ihnen helfen würde **- 2.** [think about] planen.

**~ look up** *vt sep* **- 1.** [in dictionary] nachlschlagen; [in phone book] herauslsuchen **- 2.** [visit]: **to ~ sb up** jn auflsuchen <> *vi* sich bessern.

**look upon** *vt fus* [consider]: **to ~ upon sb/sthg as sthg** jn/etw als etw betrachten.

**look up to** *vt fus* [admire]: **to ~ up to sb** zu jm aufIsehen.

**look-alike** *n* Doppelgänger *der*, -in *die*.

**look-in** *n Br*: **to get a ~** eine Chance (aùf Erfolg) haben.

**lookout** ['lʊkaʊt] *n* - **1.** [place] Ausguck *der*, Beobachtungsposten *der* - **2.** [person] Wachposten *der*, Wache *die* - **3.** [search]: **to be on the ~ for sthg** nach etw Ausschau halten.

**loom** [luːm] *n* Webstuhl *der* ⋄ *vi* - **1.** [rise up] (plötzlich) aufItauchen - **2.** *fig* [be imminent - date] bevorIstehen; [ - threat, difficulties] sich abIzeichnen; **to ~ large** drohend bevorIstehen.

**loom up** *vi* (plötzlich) aufItauchen.

**looming** ['luːmɪŋ] *adj* bevorstehend.

**loony** ['luːnɪ] (*compar* **-ier**; *superl* **-iest**; *pl* **-ies**) *inf adj* bekloppt, verrückt ⋄ *n* Bekloppte *der*, *die*, Verrückte *der*, *die*.

**loop** [luːp] *n* - **1.** [shape] Schleife *die*, Schlinge *die* - **2.** [contraceptive] Spirale *die* - **3.** COMPUT Loop *der*, Schleife *die* ⋄ *vt* [rope, string] (um)schlingen; **to ~ sthg around sthg** etw um etw schlingen ⋄ *vi* [road, river] sich krümmen.

**loophole** ['luːphəʊl] *n fig* Schlupfloch *das*.

**loo roll** *n Br inf* [one roll] Rolle *die* Klopapier; [paper] Klopapier *das*.

**loose** [luːs] *adj* - **1.** [not firmly fixed - joint, tooth, handle] lose, locker - **2.** [unpackaged - sweets, nails, paper] lose - **3.** [not tight-fitting - clothes, fit] locker sitzend, leger - **4.** [animal - free, not restrained] frei laufend; [ - which has escaped] entlaufen; [hair] offen - **5.** *pej* & *dated* [promiscuous] freizügig - **6.** [translation, definition] frei - **7.** [association, structure] locker - **8.** *Am inf* [relaxed]: **to stay ~** locker bleiben ⋄ *n*: **on the ~** [prisoner] auf freiem Fuß; [animal] entlaufen.

**loose change** *n* Kleingeld *das*.

**loose end** *n*: **to tie up ~s** noch ausstehende Probleme lösen; **to be at a ~** *Br*, **to be at ~s** *Am* nichts zu tun haben.

**loose-fitting** *adj* locker sitzend, locker fallend.

**loose-leaf binder** *n* Ringbuch *das*.

**loosely** ['luːslɪ] *adv* - **1.** [hold, connect, tie] locker - **2.** [translate, define] frei.

**loosen** ['luːsn] *vt* lockern ⋄ *vi* sich lockern.

**loosen up** *vi* - **1.** [before game, race] sich aufIwärmen - **2.** *inf* [relax] sich entspannen, locker werden.

**loot** [luːt] *n* Beute *die* ⋄ *vt* ausIplündern, ausIrauben.

**looter** ['luːtəʳ] *n* Plünderer *der*, -in *die*.

**looting** ['luːtɪŋ] *n* Plündern *das*.

**lop** [lɒp] (*pt* & *pp* **-ped**; *cont* **-ping**) *vt* stutzen, beschneiden.

**lop off** *vt sep* abIschneiden, abIsägen.

**lope** [ləʊp] *vi* (in großen Sprüngen) rennen.

**lop-sided** [-'saɪdɪd] *adj* - **1.** [uneven] schief - **2.** *fig* [biased] voreingenommen, parteiisch.

**lord** [lɔːd] *n Br* Lord *der* ⋄ *vt*: **to ~ it (over sb)** sich (gegenüber jm) aufIspielen.

**Lord** *n* - **1.** RELIG: **the Lord** [God] der Herr; **good Lord!** *Br* Grundgütiger!, oh mein Gott! - **2.** [in titles] Lord *der*; [as form of address]: **my Lord** Mylord.

**Lords** *npl Br* POL: **the (House of) Lords** das Oberhaus.

**Lord Chancellor** *n Br* Lordkanzler *der*, *Vorsitzender des Oberhauses*.

**lordly** ['lɔːdlɪ] (*compar* **-ier**; *superl* **-iest**) *adj* - **1.** [noble] vornehm, herrschaftlich - **2.** *pej* [arrogant] überheblich, arrogant.

**Lord Mayor** *n Br* Oberbürgermeister *der*.

**Lordship** ['lɔːdʃɪp] *n*: **your/his ~** Eure/Seine Lordschaft, Eure/Seine Gnaden.

**Lord's Prayer** *n*: **the ~** das Vaterunser.

**lore** [lɔːʳ] *n* Wissen *das*, Lehre *die*.

**lorry** ['lɒrɪ] (*pl* **-ies**) *n Br* Lastkraftwagen *der*, LKW *der*.

**lorry driver** *n Br* Lastkraftwagenfahrer *der*, LKW-Fahrer *der*.

**lose** [luːz] (*pt* & *pp* **lost**) *vt* - **1.** [gen] verlieren; **to ~ sight of sb/sthg** jn/etw aus den Augen verlieren; **to ~ one's way** sich verirren - **2.** [waste - time] verschwenden, vergeuden; [ - opportunity] versäumen, verpassen - **3.** [subj: clock, watch] nachIgehen; **my watch ~s five minutes every day** meine Uhr geht jeden Tag fünf Minuten nach - **4.** [pursuers] abIschütteln, abIhängen ⋄ *vi* verlieren.

**lose out** *vi*: **to ~ out (on sthg)** (bei etw) den Kürzeren ziehen, (bei etw) verlieren.

**loser** ['luːzəʳ] *n* - **1.** [of competition] Verlierer *der*, -in *die*; **a good/bad ~** ein guter/schlechter Verlierer - **2.** *pej* [unsuccessful person] Loser *der*.

**losing** ['luːzɪŋ] *adj* Verlierer-.

**loss** [lɒs] *n* - **1.** [gen] Verlust *der*; **to make a ~** Verlust machen - **2.** [of match, competition] Niederlage *die* - **3.** *phr*: **I'm at a ~ to explain it** ich weiß nicht, wie ich es erklären soll; **he was at a ~ for words** ihm fehlten die Worte; **to cut one's ~es** Schlimmeres verhindern.

**loss adjuster** [-ə‚dʒʌstəʳ] *n* [of insurance company] Schadensregulierer *der*, -in *die*.

**loss leader** *n* COMM Lockangebot *das*.

**lost** [lɒst] *pt* & *pp* ⟼ **lose** ⋄ *adj* - **1.** [unable to find way] verirrt; **to get ~** sich verirren, sich verlieren; **get ~!** *inf* verschwinde!, hau ab! - **2.** [keys, wallet] verloren - **3.** [wasted] verschwendet, versäumt; **my advice was ~ on**

**him** er wusste meinen Rat überhaupt nicht zu würdigen.

**lost-and-found office** n Am Fundbüro das.

**lost cause** n verlorene Sache.

**lost property** n Fundsache die.

**lost property office** n Br Fundbüro das.

**lot** [lɒt] n - **1.** [large amount]: a ~ of, ~s of eine Menge - **2.** inf [group of things]: put this ~ in my office bring das hier in mein Büro - **3.** inf [group of people] Gesellschaft die, Truppe die - **4.** [destiny] Los das - **5.** [at auction] Posten der - **6.** [entire amount]: the ~ alles, das Ganze - **7.** Am [of land] Parzelle die; [car park] Stellfläche die, Parkplatz der - **8.** phr: to draw ~s losen.

➤ **a lot** adv (sehr) viel.

**loth** [ləʊθ] adj = loath.

**lotion** ['ləʊʃn] n Lotion die.

**lottery** ['lɒtərɪ] (pl -ies) n - **1.** [raffle] Lotterie die - **2.** [risky venture] Glücksspiel das, Glückssache die.

**lotus position** ['ləʊtəs-] n Lotussitz der.

**loud** [laʊd] adj - **1.** [not quiet, noisy] laut - **2.** [emphatic]: to be ~ in one's criticism of sthg etw lautstark kritisieren - **3.** [garish] grell, auffallend <> adv laut, lautstark; out ~ laut.

**loudhailer** [ˌlaʊd'heɪlər] n Br Megafon das.

**loudly** ['laʊdlɪ] adv - **1.** [noisily] laut - **2.** [garishly] grell.

**loudmouth** ['laʊdmaʊθ, pl -maʊðz] n inf Großmaul das, Angeber der.

**loudness** ['laʊdnɪs] n Lautstärke die.

**loudspeaker** [ˌlaʊd'spiːkər] n Lautsprecher der.

**lough** [lɒk, lɒx] n Irish See der.

**lounge** [laʊndʒ] (cont lounging) n - **1.** [in house] Wohnzimmer das - **2.** [in airport, hotel] Lounge die - **3.** Br = lounge bar <> vi sich lümmeln, sich rekeln.

➤ **lounge about, lounge around** vi herumlümmeln.

**lounge bar** n Br abgetrennter, meist gemütlicherer Teil eines Pubs, in dem die Getränke teurer sind.

**lounge lizard** n Salonlöwe der.

**lounge suit** n Br Straßenanzug der.

**louse** [laʊs] (pl sense 1 lice; pl sense 2 -s) n - **1.** [insect] Laus die - **2.** fig [person] Laus die.

➤ **louse up** vt sep Am inf verpfuschen, versauen.

**lousy** ['laʊzɪ] (compar -ier; superl -iest) adj inf - **1.** [poor-quality] lausig, miserabel - **2.** [ill]: to feel ~ sich miserabel fühlen.

**lout** [laʊt] n Flegel der, Lümmel der.

**louvre** Br, **louver** Am ['luːvər] n: a ~ window ein Jalousiefenster; a ~ door eine Jalousietür.

**lovable** ['lʌvəbl] adj liebenswert.

**love** [lʌv] n - **1.** [gen] Liebe die; a ~ of OR for sthg eine Liebe zu OR für etw; give her my ~ grüße sie herzlich von mir; a ~-hate relationship eine Hassliebe; ~ from [at end of letter] alles Liebe von, liebe Grüße von; to be in ~ verliebt sein; to fall in ~ (with sb) sich (in jn) verlieben; to make ~ miteinander schlafen - **2.** inf [term of address] Schatz der, Liebste der, die - **3.** TENNIS Null <> vt lieben; to ~ to do sthg OR doing sthg etw sehr OR wahnsinnig gern tun.

**love affair** n Affäre die.

**lovebite** ['lʌvbaɪt] n Knutschfleck der.

**loveless** ['lʌvlɪs] adj [marriage] ohne Liebe.

**love letter** n Liebesbrief der.

**love life** n Liebesleben das.

**lovely** ['lʌvlɪ] (compar -ier; superl -iest) adj - **1.** [in looks - child] reizend; [ - person] sehr hübsch; [in character] reizend - **2.** [good, nice] wunderschön; it was ~ to meet you es war sehr nett, Sie kennen zu lernen.

**lovemaking** ['lʌvˌmeɪkɪŋ] n Miteinanderschlafen das.

**lover** ['lʌvər] n - **1.** [sexual partner] Geliebte der, die - **2.** [enthusiast]: a ~ of ein Liebhaber, eine Liebhaberin (+ G); a ~ of literature/art ein Literatur-/Kunstliebhaber.

**lovesick** ['lʌvsɪk] adj liebeskrank.

**love song** n Liebeslied das.

**love story** n Liebesgeschichte die.

**loving** ['lʌvɪŋ] adj liebevoll.

**lovingly** ['lʌvɪŋlɪ] adv liebevoll.

**low** [ləʊ] adj - **1.** [gen] niedrig; a ~ trick eine Gemeinheit; to keep a ~ profile sich unauffällig benehmen - **2.** [standard, quality, opinion] schlecht - **3.** [level, sound, note, neckline] tief - **4.** [light, heat] schwach - **5.** [supplies] knapp; we're ~ on petrol wir haben nicht mehr viel Benzin - **6.** [voice] leise - **7.** [depressed] niedergeschlagen; in ~ spirits in gedrückter Stimmung <> adv [fly, bend, sink] tief <> n - **1.** [low point] Tiefstand der - **2.** [area of low pressure] Tief das.

**low-alcohol** adj mit geringem Alkoholgehalt.

**lowbrow** ['ləʊbraʊ] adj geistig anspruchslos.

**low-calorie** adj kalorienarm.

**Low Church** n Teilgruppe der Anglikanischen Kirche, die Einfachheit bei der Pflege christlicher Traditionen predigt.

**Low Countries** npl: the ~ die Beneluxstaaten.

**low-cut** adj tief ausgeschnitten.

L

**low-down** *adj inf* gemein.

➤ **lowdown** *n inf*: **to give sb the lowdown (on sthg)** jn (über etw *(A)*) auf lklären.

**lower**¹ [ˈləʊəʳ] *adj* untere, -r, -s; [lip] Unter-~ **leg** Unterschenkel *der* <> *vt* - **1.** [move downwards - drawbridge, car window] herunterllassen; [ - flag] einlholen; [ - head, eyes] senken - **2.** [reduce] senken; [resistance] schwächen - **3.** [voice]: **to ~ one's voice** leiser sprechen.

**lower**² [ˈlaʊəʳ] *vi* - **1.** [sky] dunkel sein - **2.** [frown]: **to ~ at sb** jn finster anlblicken.

**Lower Chamber** [ˌləʊəʳ-] *n* POL Unterhaus *das*.

**lower class** [ˌləʊəʳ-] *n*: **the ~(es)** die unteren Klassen *OR* Schichten *pl*.

**Lower House** [ˌləʊəʳ-] *n* POL Unterhaus *das*.

**lowest common denominator** [ˌləʊɪst-] *n*: **the ~** der kleinste gemeinsame Nenner.

**low-fat** *adj* fettarm.

**low-flying** *adj*: **~ plane** Tiefflieger *der*.

**low frequency** *n* Niederfrequenz *die*.

**low gear** *n* niedriger Gang.

**low-key** *adj* [negotiations] informell; [approach] zurückhaltend.

**Lowlands** [ˈləʊləndz] *npl*: **the ~** [of Scotland] das schottische Tiefland.

**low-level language** *n* COMPUT einfache Programmiersprache.

**low-loader** [-ˈləʊdəʳ] *n* Tieflader *der*.

**lowly** [ˈləʊlɪ] (*compar* **-ier**; *superl* **-iest**) *adj* [status] niedrig; [person] einfach.

**low-lying** *adj* tief gelegen.

**Low Mass** *n* stille Messe.

**low-necked** [-ˈnekt] *adj* tief ausgeschnitten.

**low-paid** *adj* schlecht bezahlt.

**low-rise** *adj* niedrig.

**low season** *n* Nebensaison *die*.

**low tide** *n* Ebbe *die*.

**loyal** [ˈlɔɪəl] *adj*: **to be ~ to sb** [friend, supporter] jm treu sein; [king, boss] gegenüber jm loyal sein.

**loyalist** [ˈlɔɪəlɪst] *n* Loyalist *der*, -in *die*.

➤ **Loyalist** *n* POL [in Northern Ireland] *Anhänger der britischen Regierung in Nordirland.*

**loyalty** [ˈlɔɪəltɪ] (*pl* **-ies**) *n* [of friend, supporter] Treue *die*; [to government] Loyalität *die*.

**lozenge** [ˈlɒzɪndʒ] *n* - **1.** [tablet] Pastille *die* - **2.** [shape] Raute *die*.

**LP** (*abbr of* **long-playing record**) *n* LP *die*.

**L-plate** *n Br* Schild mit einem L, welches anzeigt, dass der Fahrer des Wagens Fahrschüler ist.

**LSD** *n* - **1.** (*abbr of* **lysergic acid diethylamide**) LSD *das* - **2.** (*abbr of* **pounds, shillings and pence - librae, solidi, denarii**) *britisches Wäh-*

*rungssysten vor der Einführung der Dezimaleinteilung 1971.*

**LSE** (*abbr of* **London School of Economics**) *n renomierte Wirtschaftshochschule in London.*

**LSO** (*abbr of* **London Symphony Orchestra**) *n* Londoner Sinfonieorchester *das*.

**Lt.** *abbr of* **lieutenant.**

**Ltd, ltd** (*abbr of* **limited**) GmbH.

**lubricant** [ˈluːbrɪkənt] *n* Schmiermittel *das*.

**lubricate** [ˈluːbrɪkeɪt] *vt* schmieren.

**lubrication** [ˌluːbrɪˈkeɪʃn] *n* Schmieren *das*.

**Lucerne** [luːˈsɜːn] *n* Luzern *nt*.

**lucid** [ˈluːsɪd] *adj* - **1.** [easily understood] klar - **2.** [clear-headed]: **~ moments** lichte Augenblicke; **the patient isn't ~** der Patient ist nicht bei klarem Verstand.

**lucidly** [ˈluːsɪdlɪ] *adv* klar und verständlich.

**luck** [lʌk] *n*: **(good) ~** Glück *das*; **good ~!** viel Glück!; **bad ~ Pech** *das*; **bad ~!, hard ~!** so ein Pech!; **to be in ~** Glück haben; **to try one's ~ at sthg** sein Glück mit etw versuchen; **with (any) ~** mit (ein bisschen) Glück.

➤ **luck out** *vi Am inf* Schwein haben.

**luckily** [ˈlʌkɪlɪ] *adv* glücklicherweise.

**luckless** [ˈlʌklɪs] *adj* glücklos.

**lucky** [ˈlʌkɪ] (*compar* **-ier**; *superl* **-iest**) *adj* - **1.** [fortunate] glücklich; **to be ~** Glück haben; **it was a ~ guess** das war gut geraten; **she had a ~ escape** sie ist noch einmal davongekommen - **2.** [bringing good luck] Glück bringend; [number] Glücks-.

**lucky charm** *n* Glücksbringer *der*.

**lucky dip** *n Br* Spiel, bei dem man mit der Hand einen Preis aus einem Behälter herausgreift ohne hinzuzuschauen.

**lucrative** [ˈluːkrətɪv] *adj* lukrativ.

**ludicrous** [ˈluːdɪkrəs] *adj* lächerlich.

**ludo** [ˈluːdəʊ] *n Br* Mensch ärgere dich nicht *das*.

**lug** [lʌg] (*pt & pp* **-ged**; *cont* **-ging**) *vt inf* schleppen.

**luggage** [ˈlʌgɪdʒ] *n Br* Gepäck *das*.

**luggage rack** *n Br* [in train] Gepäckablage *die*; [on car] Dachgepäckträger *der*.

**luggage van** *n Br* Gepäckwagen *der*.

**lugubrious** [luːˈguːbrɪəs] *adj fml* [person] trübselig; [music, look] düster.

**lukewarm** [ˈluːkwɔːm] *adj* - **1.** [tepid] lauwarm - **2.** [unenthusiastic] lau.

**lull** [lʌl] *n* Pause *die*; **a ~ in the fighting** eine Kampfpause; **the ~ before the storm** *fig* die Ruhe vor dem Sturm <> *vt* - **1.** [make sleepy]: **to ~ sb to sleep** jn in den Schlaf lullen - **2.** [reassure]: **to ~ sb into a false sense of security** jn in Sicherheit wiegen.

**lullaby** [ˈlʌləbaɪ] (pl -ies) n Schlaflied das, Wiegenlied das.

**lumbago** [lʌmˈbeɪgəʊl n Hexenschuss der.

**lumber** [ˈlʌmbəʳ] n (U) - **1.** Am [timber] Bauholz das - **2.** Br [bric-a-brac] Gerümpel das ◇ vi [person, animal] schwerfällig gehen; [vehicle] sich schwerfällig voranbewegen.
➡ **lumber with** vt sep Br inf: **to ~ sb with sthg** jm etw auf lhalsen.

**lumbering** [ˈlʌmbərɪŋ] adj [gait] schwerfällig.

**lumberjack** [ˈlʌmbədʒækl n Holzfäller der.

**lumbermill** [ˈlʌmbə͵mɪl] n Am Sägemühle die.

**lumber-room** n Br Abstellkammer die.

**lumberyard** [ˈlʌmbəjɑːd] n Holzlager das.

**luminous** [ˈluːmɪnəs] adj [armband] leuchtend; [dial, paint] Leucht-.

**lump** [lʌmp] n - **1.** [piece - of earth, in sauce] Klumpen der; [ - of coal, cheese] Stück das - **2.** [MED - bump] Beule die; [ - tumour] Knoten der - **3.** [of sugar] Stück das ◇ vt: **to ~ together** [not differentiate between] in einem Topf werfen; **you'll just have to ~ it** inf du musst dich damit abfinden.

**lump sum** n Pauschalbetrag der.

**lumpy** [ˈlʌmpɪ] (compar -ier; superl -iest) adj [sauce] klumpig; [mattress] mit klumpiger Füllung.

**lunacy** [ˈluːnəsɪ] n Wahnsinn der.

**lunar** [ˈluːnəʳ] adj Mond-.

**lunatic** [ˈluːnətɪk] adj pej wahnwitzig ◇ n Wahnsinnige der, die, Irre der, die.

**lunatic asylum** n Irrenanstalt die.

**lunatic fringe** n Extremisten pl.

**lunch** [lʌntʃ] n Mittagessen das; **to have ~** zu Mittag essen ◇ vi zu Mittag essen.

**luncheon** [ˈlʌntʃən] n fml Mittagessen das.

**luncheonette** [͵lʌntʃəˈnet] n Am Imbissstube die.

**luncheon meat** n Frühstücksfleisch das.

**luncheon voucher** n Br Essensbon der.

**lunch hour** n Mittagspause die.

**lunchtime** [ˈlʌntʃtaɪm] n Mittagszeit die.

**lung** [lʌŋ] n Lunge die.

**lung cancer** n Lungenkrebs der.

**lunge** [lʌndʒ] vi: **to ~ forward** nach vorn springen; **to ~ at sb** sich auf jn stürzen.

**lupin** Br [ˈluːpɪn], **lupine** Am [ˈluːpaɪn] n Lupine die.

**lurch** [lɜːtʃ] n: **to give a ~** [person] taumeln; [ship] schlingern; [car] rucken; **to leave sb in the ~** jn im Stich lassen ◇ vi [person] taumeln; [drunkard] torkeln; [ship] schlingern; [car] sich ruckartig bewegen.

**lure** [ljʊəʳ] n [attraction] Reiz der ◇ vt [tempt] locken.

**lurid** [ˈljʊərɪd] adj - **1.** [brightly coloured] grell; [clothes] in grellen Farben - **2.** [sensational] reißerisch.

**lurk** [lɜːk] vi [person, danger] lauern.

**lurking** [ˈlɜːkɪŋ] adj [doubts] heimlich.

**luscious** [ˈlʌʃəs] adj - **1.** [fruit] saftig; [colour] satt - **2.** fig [woman] üppig.

**lush** [lʌʃ] adj - **1.** [grass] saftig; [vegetation] üppig - **2.** inf [decorations] üppig; [apartment] luxuriös ◇ n Am inf [drunkard] Säufer der, -in die.

**lust** [lʌst] n - **1.** (U) [sexual desire] (sexuelle) Begierde - **2.** [greed]: **~ for sthg** Gier die nach etw; **~ for power** Machtgier die.
➡ **lust after, lust for** vt fus - **1.** [money, power] gieren nach - **2.** [person] begehren.

**luster** n Am = lustre.

**lustful** [ˈlʌstfʊl] adj lüstern.

**lustre** Br, **luster** Am [ˈlʌstəʳ] n [brightness] schimmernder Glanz.

**lusty** [ˈlʌstɪ] (compar -ier; superl -iest) adj [blow, cry] kräftig; [person] gesund und munter.

**lute** [luːt] n Laute die.

**Luxembourg** [ˈlʌksəmbɜːg] n Luxemburg nt.

**luxuriant** [lʌgˈzjʊərɪənt] adj [vegetation] üppig; [hair, beard] dicht.

**luxuriate** [lʌgˈzjʊərɪeɪt] vi: **to ~ in sthg** [in the sun] sich in etw (D) aalen; [in bath] sich genüsslich in etw (D) rekeln.

**luxurious** [lʌgˈzjʊərɪəs] adj - **1.** [expensive] luxuriös - **2.** [voluptuous] üppig.

**luxury** [ˈlʌkʃərɪ] (pl -ies) n Luxus der; [expensive item] Luxusartikel der ◇ comp Luxus-.

**luxury goods** npl Luxusartikel pl.

**LV** n abbr of **luncheon voucher.**

**LW** (abbr of **long wave**) LW.

**lychee** [͵laɪˈtʃiː] n Litschi die.

**Lycra**® [ˈlaɪkrə] n (U) Lycra® das ◇ comp aus Lycra®.

**lying** [ˈlaɪɪŋ] adj lügnerisch, verlogen ◇ n [dishonesty] Lügen das.

**lymph gland** [ˈlɪmf-l n Lymphknoten der.

**lynch** [lɪntʃ] vt lynchen.

**lynx** [lɪŋks] (pl inv OR -es) n Luchs der.

**lyre** [ˈlaɪəʳ] n Leier die.

**lyric** [ˈlɪrɪk] adj: **~ poetry** Lyrik die; **~ poet** Lyriker der, -in die.
➡ **lyrics** npl [of song] Text der.

**lyrical** [ˈlɪrɪkl] adj - **1.** [poetic] lyrisch - **2.** [enthusiastic]: **to wax ~ about sthg** von etw schwärmen.

L

**m¹** (*pl* **m's** *OR* **ms**), **M** (*pl* **M's** *OR* **Ms**) [em] *n* [letter] m *das*, M *das*.
➤ **M** - **1.** *Br abbr of* **motorway** - **2.** *abbr of* **medium**.

**m²** - **1.** *abbr of* **metre** - **2.** *abbr of* **million** - **3.** *abbr of* **mile**.

**ma** [mɑ:] *n esp Am inf* Mutti *die*, Mama *die*.

**MA** *n abbr of* **Master of Arts** ⟨⟩ *abk. für Massachusetts, in Postanschrift verwendet.*

**ma'am** [mɑ:m] *n* gnä' Frau *die*.

**mac** [mæk] *n Br inf abbr of* **mackintosh**.

**macabre** [mə'kɑ:brə] *adj* makaber.

**macaroni** [ˌmækə'rəʊnɪ] *n* (U) Makkaroni *pl*.

**macaroni cheese** *n* (U) Makkaroni *pl* mit Käsesauce.

**macaroon** [ˌmækə'ru:n] *n* Makrone *die*.

**mace** [meɪs] *n* - **1.** [ornamental rod] Amtsstab *der* - **2.** (U) [spice] Muskatblüte *die*.

**Macedonia** [ˌmæsɪ'dəʊnɪə] *n* Mazedonien *nt*.

**Macedonian** [ˌmæsɪ'dəʊnɪən] *adj* mazedonisch ⟨⟩ *n* Mazedonier *der*, -in *die*.

**machete** [mə'ʃetɪ] *n* Machete *die*.

**Machiavellian** [ˌmækɪə'velɪən] *adj* machiavellistisch.

**machinations** [ˌmækɪ'neɪʃnz] *npl* Machenschaften *pl*.

**machine** [mə'ʃi:n] *n* - **1.** [device] Maschine *die* - **2.** [organization] Apparat *der* ⟨⟩ *vt* - **1.** SEWING mit der Maschine nähen - **2.** [TECH - make] maschinell her|stellen; [ - work on] maschinell bearbeiten.

**machine code** *n* COMPUT Maschinencode *der*.

**machinegun** [mə'ʃi:ngʌn] (*pt* & *pp* **-ned**; *cont* **-ning**) *n* Maschinengewehr *das* ⟨⟩ *vt* mit dem Maschinengewehr schießen auf (+ A).

**machine language** *n* COMPUT Maschinensprache *die*.

**machine-readable** *adj* COMPUT maschinenlesbar.

**machinery** [mə'ʃi:nərɪ] *n* (U) - **1.** [machines] Maschinen *pl* - **2.** *fig* [system] Maschinerie *die*.

**machine shop** *n* Maschinenhalle *die*.

**machine tool** *n* Werkzeugmaschine *die*.

**machine-washable** *adj* waschmaschinenfest.

**machinist** [mə'ʃi:nɪst] *n* - **1.** SEWING (Maschinen)näherin *die* - **2.** TECH [operator] Maschinist *der*, -in *die*.

**machismo** [mə'tʃɪzməʊ] *n* Machismo *der*.

**macho** ['mætʃəʊ] *adj inf* machohaft; ~ **man** Macho *der*.

**mackerel** ['mækrəl] (*pl inv OR* **-s**) *n* Makrele *die*.

**mackintosh** ['mækɪntɒʃ] *n Br* Regenmantel *der*.

**macramé** [mə'krɑ:mɪ] *n* Makramee *das*.

**macro** ['mækrəʊ] *n* COMPUT Makro *das*.

**macrocosm** ['mækrəʊkɒzm] *n* Makrokosmos *der*.

**macroeconomics** ['mækrəʊˌi:kə'nɒmɪks] *n* (U) Makroökonomie *die*.

**mad** [mæd] (*compar* **-der**; *superl* **-dest**) *adj* - **1.** [insane, foolish] verrückt; **to go** ~ verrückt werden - **2.** [furious] wütend; **to go** ~ **at sb** auf jn sehr wütend werden - **3.** [hectic]: **there was a** ~ **rush for the door** alle stürzten zur Tür; **like** ~ wie verrückt - **4.** [very enthusiastic]: **to be** ~ **about sb/sthg** nach jm/auf etw (A) ganz verrückt sein.

**Madagascar** [ˌmædə'gæskəʳ] *n* Madagaskar *nt*.

**madam** ['mædəm] *n fml* [form of address] gnädige Frau; **Dear Madam** [in letter] Sehr geehrte gnädige Frau.

**madcap** ['mædkæp] *adj* verrückt.

**mad cow disease** *n* Rinderwahnsinn *der*.

**madden** ['mædn] *vt* wahnsinnig machen.

**maddening** ['mædnɪŋ] *adj* [noise, pain] unerträglich; [problem] äußerst ärgerlich; **she's** ~ sie macht mich wahnsinnig.

**made** [meɪd] *pt* & *pp* ⟹ **make**.

**-made** [meɪd] *suffix*: **factory**~ maschinell hergestellt; **French**~ in Frankreich hergestellt; **hand**~ handgefertigt.

**Madeira** [mə'dɪərə] *n* - **1.** (U) [wine] Madeira *der* - **2.** GEOGR Madeira *nt*; **in** ~ auf Madeira.

**made-to-measure** *adj* maßgeschneidert.

**made-up** *adj* - **1.** [face, eyes] geschminkt - **2.** [mixture, solution] fertig - **3.** [story, excuse] erfunden.

**madhouse** ['mædhaʊs] *n fig* Tollhaus *das*.

**madly** ['mædlɪ] *adv* [frantically] wie verrückt; **to be** ~ **in love (with sb)** bis über beide Ohren (in jn) verliebt sein.

**madman** ['mædmən] (*pl* **-men** [-mən]) *n* Verrückte *der*, Irre *der*.

**madness** ['mædnɪs] *n* Wahnsinn *der*.

**Madonna** [mə'dɒnə] n - **1.** RELIG: the ~ die Muttergottes - **2.** ART Madonna die.

**Madrid** [mə'drɪd] n Madrid nt.

**madrigal** ['mædrɪgl] n Madrigal das.

**madwoman** ['mæd,wʊmən] (pl -women [-,wɪmɪn]) n Verrückte die, Irre die.

**maestro** ['maɪstrəʊ] (pl -tros OR -tri [-triː]) n MUS Maestro der; fig Meister der.

**Mafia** ['mæfɪə] n: the ~ die Mafia.

**mag** [mæg] n inf abbr of magazine.

**magazine** [,mægə'ziːn] n - **1.** [periodical] Zeitschrift die, Magazin das - **2.** [news programme, of gun] Magazin das.

**magenta** [mə'dʒentə] adj purpurrot.

**maggot** ['mægət] n Made die.

**magic** ['mædʒɪk] adj - **1.** [potion, spell, trick] Zauber- - **2.** inf [moment, feeling] wundervoll <> n - **1.** [sorcery] Magie die - **2.** [conjuring] Zauberei die - **3.** [special quality] Zauber der.

**magical** ['mædʒɪkl] adj magisch.

**magic carpet** n fliegender Teppich.

**magician** [mə'dʒɪʃn] n Zauberer der, Magier der.

**magic wand** n Zauberstab der.

**magisterial** [,mædʒɪ'stɪərɪəl] adj - **1.** fml [authoritative] gebieterisch - **2.** LAW eines Friedensrichters.

**magistrate** ['mædʒɪstreɪt] n Friedensrichter der, -in die.

**magistrates' court** n Br Gerichtshof in England und Wales, der sich mit kleineren Vergehen und Straftaten beschäftigt.

**Magna Carta** [,mægnə'kɑːtə] n: the ~ die Magna Charta.

**magnanimous** [mæg'nænɪməs] adj großmütig.

**magnate** ['mægneɪt] n Magnat der.

**magnesium** [mæg'niːzɪəm] n Magnesium das.

**magnet** ['mægnɪt] n lit & fig Magnet der.

**magnetic** [mæg'netɪk] adj - **1.** [force, object] magnetisch - **2.** fig: to have a ~ personality ein sehr anziehendes Wesen haben.

**magnetic disk** n Magnetscheibe die.

**magnetic field** n Magnetfeld das.

**magnetic tape** n (U) Magnetband das.

**magnetism** ['mægnɪtɪzm] n - **1.** PHYSICS Magnetismus der - **2.** [of person] Anziehungskraft die.

**magnification** [,mægnɪfɪ'keɪʃn] n (U) Vergrößerung die.

**magnificence** [mæg'nɪfɪsəns] n (U) Herrlichkeit die, Pracht die.

**magnificent** [mæg'nɪfɪsənt] adj [building, gown] prächtig; [idea, book] großartig.

**magnify** ['mægnɪfaɪ] (pt & pp -ied) vt - **1.** [TECH - image] vergrößern; [- sound] verstärken - **2.** fig [exaggerate] überbewerten.

**magnifying glass** ['mægnɪfaɪɪŋ-] n Lupe die.

**magnitude** ['mægnɪtjuːd] n (U) - **1.** [size] Größe die - **2.** [importance] Bedeutung die; a problem of this ~ ein Problem dieser Größenordnung.

**magnolia** [mæg'nəʊlɪə] n Magnolie die.

**magnum** ['mægnəm] (pl -s) n ≃ Eineinhalbliterflasche die.

**magpie** ['mægpaɪ] n Elster die.

**maharaja(h)** [,mɑːhə'rɑːdʒə] n Maharadscha der.

**mahogany** [mə'hɒgənɪ] n [wood] Mahagoni das.

**maid** [meɪd] n [servant] Dienstmädchen das; [in hotel] Zimmermädchen das.

**maiden** ['meɪdn] adj [voyage, flight] Jungfern- <> n literary [young girl] Maid die; [virgin] Jungfrau die.

**maiden aunt** n unverheiratete Tante.

**maiden name** n Mädchenname der.

**maiden speech** n POL Jungfernrede die.

**mail** [meɪl] n (U) Post die; by ~ mit der Post <> vt esp Am (mit der Post) (ver)schicken OR senden.

**mailbag** ['meɪlbæg] n Postsack der.

**mailbox** ['meɪlbɒks] n - **1.** Am [for letters] Briefkasten der - **2.** COMPUT Mailbox die.

**mailing list** ['meɪlɪŋ-] n Adressenliste die.

**mailman** ['meɪlmən] (pl -men [-mən]) n Am Postbote der, Briefträger der.

**mail order** n Versandhandel der.

**mailshot** ['meɪlʃɒt] n - **1.** [material] Postwurfsendung die - **2.** [activity]: to do a ~ Postwurfsendungen verschicken.

**mail train** n Postzug der.

**mail truck** n Am Postauto das.

**mail van** n [using road] Postauto das; [using rail] Postwagen der.

**maim** [meɪm] vt verstümmeln.

**main** [meɪn] adj Haupt- <> n Hauptleitung die; a gas ~ eine Hauptgasleitung.
- **mains** npl: to turn the water/gas off at the ~s den Haupthahn für das Wasser/Gas abldrehen; to turn the electricity off at the ~s den Strom am Hauptschalter abschalten.
- **in the main** adv im Allgemeinen.

**main course** n Hauptgericht das.

**mainframe (computer)** ['meɪnfreɪm-] n Großrechner der.

M

**mainland** ['meɪnlənd] *adj:* ~ **Britain** das britische Festland <> *n:* **the** ~ das Festland

**main line** *n* RAIL Hauptstrecke *die.*

⮞ **mainline** *adj* [train] Schnell-; [station] an der Hauptstrecke liegend <> *vt* **drugs** *sl* spritzen <> *vi* **drugs** *sl* fixen.

**mainly** ['meɪnlɪ] *adv* hauptsächlich.

**main road** *n* Hauptstraße *die.*

**mainsail** ['meɪnseɪl, 'meɪnsəl] *n* Großsegel *das.*

**mainstay** ['meɪnsteɪ] *n* [person] wichtigste Stütze; **tourism is the ~ of the economy** der Tourismus ist der Hauptpfeiler der Wirtschaft.

**mainstream** ['meɪnstriːm] *adj* vorherrschend; [music] Mainstream- <> *n:* **the** ~ die Hauptrichtung; **the ~ of public opinion** die allgemeine öffentliche Meinung.

**maintain** [meɪn'teɪn] *vt* - **1.** [friendship, order, image] aufrecht erhalten - **2.** [speed, temperature] beibehalten - **3.** [family, children] unterhalten - **4.** [vehicle, building] instand halten - **5.** [assert - one's innocence] beteuern; **to ~ (that)** ... behaupten, dass ...

**maintenance** ['meɪntənəns] *n (U)* - **1.** [of vehicle, building] Instandhaltung *die* - **2.** [paid to ex-wife] Unterhalt *der* - **3.** [of law and order] Aufrechterhaltung *die.*

**maisonette** [ˌmeɪzə'net] *n* Maisonette *die.*

**maize** [meɪz] *n* Mais *der.*

**Maj.** *abbr of* Major.

**majestic** [mə'dʒestɪk] *adj* majestätisch.

**majestically** [mə'dʒestɪklɪ] *adv* majestätisch.

**majesty** ['mædʒəstɪ] *(pl* **-ies)** *n* Erhabenheit *die.*

⮞ **Majesty** *n:* **His/Her/Your Majesty** Seine/Ihre/Eure Majestät.

**major** ['meɪdʒəʳ] *adj* - **1.** [important] bedeutend; [problem] groß; **a ~ operation** eine größere Operation - **2.** [main] Haupt- - **3.** MUS [key, scale] Dur-; **C** ~ C-Dur <> *n* Major *der* <> *vi* **Am** UNIV: **to ~ in sthg** etw als Hauptfach studieren.

**Majorca** [mə'dʒɔːkə, mə'jɔːkəl] *n* Mallorca *nt;* **in ~** auf Mallorca.

**majorette** [ˌmeɪdʒə'ret] *n* Tambourmajorette *die.*

**major general** *n* Generalmajor *der.*

**majority** [mə'dʒɒrətɪ] *(pl* **-ies)** *n* Mehrheit *die;* **in a** OR **the** ~ in der Mehrzahl.

**majority shareholder** *n* Hauptaktionär *der,* **-in** *die.*

**make** [meɪk] *(pt* & *pp* **made)** *vt* - **1.** [produce] machen; [manufacture] herstellen; **to ~ a lot of noise** eine Menge Lärm machen; **to be made of sthg** aus etw (gemacht) sein; **it's made of wood** es ist aus Holz; **made in Taiwan** in Taiwan hergestellt - **2.** [prepare] machen; **to ~ lunch** das Mittagessen machen; **to ~ some tea** Tee kochen - **3.** [perform, do] machen; **to ~ a decision** eine Entscheidung treffen; **to ~ an effort** sich anstrengen; **to ~ a mistake** einen Fehler machen; **to ~ a phone call** telefonieren; **to ~ a request** eine Bitte vorbringen; **to ~ a speech** eine Rede halten - **4.** [bed] machen - **5.** [cause to be] machen; **to ~ sb happy/sad** jn glücklich/traurig machen; **she made him a manager** sie machte ihn zum Geschäftsführer; **to ~ sthg into sthg** etw zu etw machen; **he made the house into a museum** er machte aus dem Haus ein Museum; **to ~ o.s. heard** sich *(D)* Gehör verschaffen; **to ~ sthg known** etw bekannt geben - **6.** [cause to do]: **to ~ sb/sthg do sthg** jn/etw dazulbringen OR veranlassen, etw zu tun; **it made her laugh/cry** das brachte sie zum Lachen/Weinen; **you made me jump!** du hast mich vielleicht erschreckt!; **what made him do it?** was hat ihn dazu veranlasst? - **7.** [force] zwingen; **to ~ sb do sthg** jn zwingen, etw zu tun; **we were made to wait in the hall** wir mussten in der Halle warten - **8.** [add up to] machen; **two and two ~** OR **~s four** zwei und zwei macht vier; **that ~s £5** das macht 5 Pfund - **9.** [calculate]: **I ~ it 50** ich komme auf 50; **what time do you ~ it?** wie spät hast du?; **I ~ it six o'clock** nach meiner Uhr ist es sechs Uhr - **10.** [earn] verdienen; **to ~ a profit/loss** einen Gewinn/Verlust machen - **11.** [have the right qualities for] abgeben; **he ~s a good doctor** er gibt einen guten Arzt ab; **books ~ excellent presents** Bücher sind gute Geschenke; **this would ~ a lovely bedroom** das wäre ein hübsches Schlafzimmer - **12.** [reach, be able to attend]: **we didn't ~ the train** wir haben den Zug nicht geschafft; **can you ~ lunch tomorrow?** schaffen Sie es morgen zum Mittagessen? - **13.** [cause to be a success] erfolgreich machen; **she really ~s the film** der Film lebt praktisch von ihr; **that's made my day!** das hat meinen Tag gerettet!; **it will ~ or break him** es wird sein Glück oder Verderben sein - **14.** [gain - friend, enemy] machen; **to ~ friends with sb** mit jm Freundschaft schließen - **15.** *phr:* **to ~ it** es schaffen; **I won't be able to ~ it tonight** ich schaffe es heute Abend nicht; **to have it made** es geschafft haben; **to ~ do with sthg** mit etw auslkommen <> *n* - **1.** [brand] Marke *die;* **what ~ is your car?** was fahren Sie? - **2.** *inf pej:* **to be on the ~** [act selfishly] profitieren wollen.

⮞ **make for** *vt fus* - **1.** [move towards] zulhalten auf *(+ A)* - **2.** [contribute to, enable] fördern.

⮞ **make of** *vt sep* halten von; **I can't ~ anything of his latest book** ich kann mit seinem neuesten Buch nichts anfangen.

⮞ **make off** *vi* sich davonlmachen.

⮞ **make off with** *vt fus inf:* **he made off with the**

**money** er ist mit dem Geld durchgebrannt.

➤ **make out** *vt sep* - **1.** *inf* [see] ausmachen; [hear, understand] verstehen - **2.** [cheque, receipt] ausstellen; [application form] ausfüllen; [list] auf lstellen ◇ *vt fus* [pretend, claim]: **to ~ out (that)** ... vorlgeben, dass ...

➤ **make up** *vt sep* - **1.** [compose, constitute] bilden; **to be made up of sthg** aus etw bestehen - **2.** [invent] erfinden, sich *(D)* ausldenken; **she made it up** sie hat es erfunden - **3.** [face] schminken; **to ~ o.s. up** sich schminken - **4.** [prepare - parcel] packen; [ - prescription] zulbereiten; [ - bed] herlrichten - **5.** [make complete]: **they made up the amount to £50** sie rundeten den Betrag auf £50 auf; **to ~ up the difference** den Unterschied auslgleichen - **6.** [quarrel]: **to ~ it up with sb** sich mit jm versöhnen ◇ *vi* [become friends again]: **to ~ up with sb** sich mit jm versöhnen.

➤ **make up for** *vt fus* wettlmachen; **to ~ up for lost time** verlorene Zeit auflholen.

➤ **make up to** *vt sep*: **I'll try to ~ it up to you** ich werde versuchen, es wieder gutzumachen.

**make-believe** *n (U)* Fantasie *die*.

**maker** ['meɪkə'] *n* [of product] Hersteller *der*, -in *die*; [producer - of film] Produzent *der*, -in *die*.

**makeshift** ['meɪkʃɪft] *adj* behelfsmäßig.

**make-up** *n* - **1.** [cosmetics] Make-up *das*; ~ **bag** Schminktäschen *das*; ~ **remover** Makeup-Entferner *der* - **2.** [person's character] Charakter *der* - **3.** [composition] Beschaffenheit *die*; [of team] Zusammensetzung *die*.

**making** ['meɪkɪŋ] *n* [of product] Herstellung *die*; [of cake] Backen *das*; **during the ~ of the film** während des Dreharbeiten; **she's a pianist in the ~** sie ist eine angehende Pianistin; **his problems are of his own ~** seine Probleme hat er sich selbst zuzuschreiben; **going to America was the ~ of him** dank seiner Auswanderung nach Amerika wurde er zu dem, was er heute ist; **to have the ~s of** das Zeug *OR* das Talent haben zu.

**maladjusted** [ˌmælə'dʒʌstɪd] *adj* verhaltensgestört.

**malaise** [mæ'leɪz] *n fml* [unease] Unbehagen *das*.

**malaria** [mə'leərɪə] *n* Malaria *die*.

**Malay** [mə'leɪ] *n* Malaiisch(e) *das*.

**Malaysia** [mə'leɪzɪə] *n* Malaysia *nt*.

**Malaysian** [mə'leɪzɪən] *adj* malayisch ◇ *n* Malaysier *der*, -in *die*.

**malcontent** ['mælkənˌtent] *n fml* Unzufriedene *der*, *die*.

**Maldives** ['mɔːldaɪvz] *npl*: **the ~** die Malediven *pl*; **in the ~** auf den Malediven.

**male** [meɪl] *adj* - **1.** [staff, members] männ

lich; ~ **monkey/hamster** Affen-/Hamstermännchen *das*; ~ **cat** Kater *der* - **2.** [concerning men - problems] Männer-; [ - hormone] männlich; ~ **unemployment** Arbeitslosigkeit *die* unter Männern ◇ *n* - **1.** [animal] Männchen *das* - **2.** [human] Mann *der*.

**male chauvinist** *n pej* Chauvinist *der*; ~ **pig** Chauvinistenschwein *das*.

**male nurse** *n* (Kranken)pfleger *der*.

**malevolent** [mə'levələnt] *adj* boshaft; [intention, action] böswillig.

**malformed** [mæl'fɔːmd] *adj* missgebildet.

**malfunction** [mæl'fʌŋkʃn] *n* Fehlfunktion *die* ◇ *vi* nicht richtig funktionieren.

**malice** ['mælɪs] *n* Boshaftigkeit *die*; **without ~** ohne Groll.

**malicious** [mə'lɪʃəs] *adj* boshaft; [act, intention] böswillig.

**malign** [mə'laɪn] *adj* [influence] schädlich; [behaviour] Unheil bringend ◇ *vt* verleumden.

**malignant** [mə'lɪgnənt] *adj* - **1.** [full of hate] boshaft; [plan, behaviour] böswillig - **2.** MED bösartig.

**malinger** [mə'lɪŋgə'] *vi pej* sich krank stellen.

**malingerer** [mə'lɪŋgərə'] *n pej* Simulant *der*, -in *die (einer Krankheit)*.

**mall** [mɔːl] *n esp Am*: (shopping) ~ Einkaufszentrum *das*.

**mallard** ['mælədl] *n* Stockente *die*.

**malleable** ['mælɪəbl] *adj lit & fig* formbar.

**mallet** ['mælɪt] *n* [tool] Holzhammer *der*.

**malnourished** [ˌmæl'nʌrɪʃt] *adj* unterernährt.

**malnutrition** [ˌmælnjuː'trɪʃn] *n* Unterernährung *die*.

**malpractice** [ˌmæl'præktɪs] *n* LAW Amtsmissbrauch *der*.

**malt** [mɔːlt] *n* - **1.** [grain] Malz *das* - **2.** [whisky] Malt Whisky *der*.

**Malta** ['mɔːltə] *n* Malta *nt*; **in ~** auf Malta.

**Maltese** [ˌmɔːl'tiːz] *(pl inv) adj* maltesisch ◇ *n* - **1.** [person] Malteser *der*, -in *die* - **2.** [language] Maltesisch(e) *das*.

**maltreat** [ˌmæl'triːt] *vt* schlecht behandeln; [violently] misshandeln.

**maltreatment** [ˌmæl'triːtmənt] *n (U)* schlechte Behandlung; [violent] Misshandlung *die*.

**malt whisky** *n* Malt Whisky *der*.

**mammal** ['mæml] *n* Säugetier *das*.

**Mammon** ['mæmən] *n* Mammon *der*.

**mammoth** ['mæməθ] *adj* ungeheuer groß ◇ *n* Mammut *das*.

**man** [mæn] *(pl* **men** [men], *pt & pp* **-ned**; *cont* **-ning**) *n* - **1.** [gen] Mann *der*; **the ~ in the street** der Mann auf der Straße; **to talk ~ to ~** sich

**M**

von Mann zu Mann unterhalten; **to be ~ enough to do sthg** Manns genug sein, etw zu tun - **2.** [type] **he's not a betting ~** er macht sich nicht viel aus Wetten; **he's not a ~ to give up easily** er ist nicht der Typ, der leicht aufgibt - **3.** (U) [human beings] Mensch der <> vt [ship, spaceship] bemannen; [machine] bedienen; [switchboard] besetzen; **to ~ the telephone(s)** Telefondienst machen.

**manacles** ['mænəklz] npl Handschellen pl.

**manage** ['mænɪdʒ] vi zurechtlkommen; **thanks, I can ~!** danke, ich komme schon zurecht! <> vt - **1.** [succeed] **to ~ to do sthg** es schaffen, etw zu tun - **2.** [control - company, organization] leiten; [ - popstar, boxer, football team] managen; [ - one's money, time] einteilen - **3.** [be available for]: **I can ~ a few hours on Friday** Freitag hätte ich für ein paar Stunden Zeit; **I can't ~ four o'clock** vier Uhr kann ich nicht schaffen.

**manageable** ['mænɪdʒəbl] adj [task] zu bewältigen; [child] fügsam; [hair] leicht frisierbar.

**management** ['mænɪdʒmənt] n - **1.** (U) [control - of company, organization] Leitung die; [ - of popstar, boxer, football team] Managen die; [ - of one's money, time] Einteilung die; **bad ~** schlechtes Management - **2.** [people in control - of business] Geschäftsführung die; [ - of operation] Leitung die; [ - of theatre] Direktion die.

**management consultant** n Unternehmensberater der, -in die.

**manager** ['mænɪdʒə'] n [of company, shop] Geschäftsführer der, -in die; [of organization] Leiter der, -in die; [of popstar, boxer, football team] Manager der, -in die.

**manageress** [,mænɪdʒə'res] n Br Geschäftsführerin die.

**managerial** [,mænɪ'dʒɪərɪəl] adj [post] leitend; **~ skills** Führungsqualitäten pl.

**managing director** [,mænɪdʒɪŋ-] n Geschäftsführer der, -in die.

**Mancunian** [mæŋ'kjuːnɪən] adj [people] aus Manchester <> n [person] Einwohner der, -in die von Manchester.

**mandarin** ['mændərɪn] n - **1.** [fruit] Mandarine die - **2.** [civil servant] hoher Staatsbeamte, hohe Staatsbeamtin.

**mandate** ['mændeɪt] n - **1.** [elected right or authority] Mandat das - **2.** [task] Auftrag der.

**mandatory** ['mændətrɪ] adj obligatorisch; **to be ~** Pflicht sein.

**mandolin** [,mændə'lɪn] n Mandoline die.

**mane** [meɪn] n Mähne die.

**man-eating** [-,iːtɪŋ] adj Menschenfressend.

**maneuver** n, vt & vi Am = manoeuvre.

**manfully** ['mænfʊlɪ] adv tapfer.

**manganese** ['mæŋgəniːz] n Mangan das.

**mange** [meɪndʒ] n Räude die.

**manger** ['meɪndʒə'] n Krippe die.

**mangetout (pea)** [,mɒnˈʒtuː-] n Br Zuckererbse die.

**mangle** ['mæŋgl] n Mangel die <> vt - **1.** [body, car] (übel) zurichten - **2.** fig [text] entstellen.

**mango** ['mæŋgəʊ] (pl -es OR -s) n Mango die.

**mangrove** ['mæŋgrəʊv] n Mangrovenbaum der.

**mangy** ['meɪndʒɪ] (compar -ier; superl -iest) adj [animal] räudig.

**manhandle** ['mæn,hændl] vt [person] grob behandeln.

**Manhattan** [mæn'hætən] n Manhattan nt.

**manhole** ['mænhəʊl] n Kanalschacht der.

**manhood** ['mænhʊd] n (U) - **1.** [age] Mannesalter das - **2.** [virility] Männlichkeit die.

**manhour** ['mæn,aʊə'] n Arbeitsstunde die.

**manhunt** ['mænhʌnt] n Fahndung die.

**mania** ['meɪnɪə] n - **1.** [excessive liking]: **~ (for)** Leidenschaft die (für) - **2.** PSYCH Manie die.

**maniac** ['meɪnɪæk] n - **1.** [madman] Wahnsinnige der, die - **2.** [fanatic]: **a football ~** ein Fußballfanatiker, eine Fußballfanatikerin; **a TV/sex ~** ein Fernseh-/Sexbesessener, eine Fernseh-/Sexbesessene.

**manic** ['mænɪk] adj - **1.** [overexcited - person] aufgedreht - **2.** PSYCH manisch.

**manic-depressive** adj manisch-depressiv <> n Manisch-Depressive der, die.

**manicure** ['mænɪ,kjʊə'] n Maniküre die; **to have a ~** zur Maniküre gehen <> vt maniküren.

**manifest** ['mænɪfest] fml adj offenkundig <> vt bekunden, zum Ausdruck bringen; **to ~ itself** sich zeigen.

**manifestation** [,mænɪfes'teɪʃn] n fml [of doubt, revolt] Ausdruck der; [of change] Zeichen das.

**manifestly** ['mænɪfestlɪ] adv fml [obvious, irrelevant] völlig; [stupid, vital] offensichtlich.

**manifesto** [,mænɪ'festəʊ] (pl -s OR -es) n Manifest das.

**manifold** ['mænɪfəʊld] adj literary mannigfaltig <> n AUT: **inlet ~** Ansaugrohr das; **exhaust ~** Auspuffrohr das.

**manila** [mə'nɪlə] adj [envelope] aus braunem festen Papier.

**Manila** [mə'nɪlə] n Manila nt.

**manilla** [mə'nɪlə] adj = manila.

**manipulate** [mə'nɪpjʊleɪt] vt - **1.** [people] manipulieren - **2.** [machine, controls] bedienen.

**manipulation** [mə,nɪpjʊ'leɪʃn] n - **1.** [of people] Manipulation die - **2.** [of machine, controls] Bedienung die.

**manipulative** [mə'nɪpjʊlətɪv] *adj* manipulativ.

**mankind** [mæn'kaɪnd] *n* Menschheit *die*.

**manly** ['mænlɪ] (*compar* -ier; *superl* -iest) *adj* [voice, bearing] männlich; [behaviour] mannhaft.

**man-made** *adj* [fibre] Kunst-; [environment] von Menschen geschaffen; [problem, disaster] von Menschen verursacht.

**manned** [mænd] *adj* bemannt.

**mannequin** ['mænɪkɪn] *n* - **1.** *dated* [woman] Mannequin *das* - **2.** [dummy] Schaufensterpuppe *die*.

**manner** ['mænə'] *n* - **1.** [method] Art *die*, Weise *die*; **in this ~** auf diese Art und Weise; **in a ~ of speaking** sozusagen, gewissermaßen - **2.** [attitude] Auftreten *das*; **I don't like your ~!** mir gefällt nicht, wie Sie mit mir reden! - **3.** *literary* [type]: **all ~ of** alle möglichen.
➡ **manners** *npl* Manieren *pl*; **it's bad ~s to point at people** es gehört sich nicht, auf Leute zu zeigen.

**mannered** ['mænəd] *adj* *fml* manieriert, gekünstelt.

**mannerism** ['mænərɪzm] *n* [of behaviour, speech] Angewohnheit *die*.

**mannish** ['mænɪʃ] *adj* [woman] maskulin.

**manoeuvrable** *Br*, **maneuverable** *Am* [mə'nu:vrəbl] *adj* [vehicle] wendig.

**manoeuvre** *Br*, **maneuver** *Am* [mə'nu:və'] *n* - **1.** [movement] Manöver *das* - **2.** *fig* [clever move] Manöver *das* ◇ *vt* [car, ship] manövrieren ◇ *vi* [move]: **he ~d into the parking space** er manövrierte das Auto in die Parklücke.
➡ **manoeuvres** *npl* MIL Manöver *das*; **to be on ~s** im Manöver sein.

**manor** ['mænə'] *n* Herrenhaus *das*.

**manpower** ['mæn,paʊə'] *n (U)* Arbeitskräfte *pl*.

**manservant** ['mænsɜ:vənt] (*pl* **menservants**) *n* *dated* Diener *der*.

**mansion** ['mænʃn] *n* Villa *die*.

**man-size(d)** [-saɪz(d)] *adj* groß.

**manslaughter** ['mæn,slɔ:tə'] *n (U)* Totschlag *der*.

**mantelpiece** ['mæntlpi:s] *n* Kaminsims *der*.

**mantle** ['mæntl] *n*: **~ of snow** Schneedecke *die*; **the ~ of leadership** die Führungsrolle.

**man-to-man** *adj* von Mann zu Mann.

**manual** ['mænjʊəl] *adj* [work, system] manuell; [device] manuell zu bedienen ◇ *n* [handbook] Handbuch *das*.

**manually** ['mænjʊəlɪ] *adv* manuell, von Hand.

**manual worker** *n* Handarbeiter *der*, -in *die*.

**manufacture** [,mænjʊ'fæktʃə'] *n (U)* Herstel-lung *die* ◇ *vt* - **1.** [make] herlstellen; **~d goods** Fertigprodukte *pl* - **2.** [invent] erfinden.

**manufacturer** [,mænjʊ'fæktʃərə'] *n* Hersteller *der*.

**manufacturing** [,mænjʊ'fæktʃərɪŋ] *n (U)* industrielle Produktion.

**manufacturing industries** *npl* verarbeitende Industrie.

**manure** [mə'njʊə'] *n* Dung *der*.

**manuscript** ['mænjʊskrɪpt] *n* - **1.** [untyped copy] Manuskript *das* - **2.** [old document] Handschrift *die*.

**Manx** [mæŋks] *adj* der Insel Man ◇ *n* [language] Manx *das*.

**many** ['menɪ] (*compar* **more**; *superl* **most**) *adj* viele; **~ people** viele Leute; **(a good) ~ times** (sehr) oft ◇ *pron* viele; **how ~?** wie viele?; **a good OR great ~** eine ganze Reihe; **~ a time** oft; **as ~ again** doppelt so viele; **one too ~** eine, -r, -s zu viel.

**Maori** ['maʊrɪ] *adj* maorisch ◇ *n* Maori *der*, *die*.

**map** [mæp] (*pt & pp* **-ped**; *cont* **-ping**) *n* (Land)karte *die*; [of town] Stadtplan *der*.
➡ **map out** *vt sep* [project, plan] genau auslarbeiten.

**maple** ['meɪpl] *n* Ahorn *der*.

**maple syrup** *n* Ahornsirup *der*.

**mar** [ma:'] (*pt & pp* **-red**; *cont* **-ring**) *vt* [performance, victory] verderben; [appearance, chances, success] beeinträchtigen; [beauty] mindern.

**Mar.** *abbr of* March.

**marathon** ['mærəθn] *adj* [speech] endlos lang; [task] ungeheuer langwierig ◇ *n* Marathon(lauf) *der*.

**marathon runner** *n* Marathonläufer *der*, -in *die*.

**marauder** [mə'rɔ:də'] *n* Plünderer *der*.

**marauding** [mə'rɔ:dɪŋ] *adj* - **1.** [human] plündernd - **2.** [animal] Beute suchend.

**marble** ['ma:bl] *n* - **1.** [stone] Marmor *der* - **2.** [glass ball] Murmel *die*.
➡ **marbles** *n (U)* [game] Murmelspiel *das*.

**march** [ma:tʃ] *n* - **1.** MIL Marsch *der* - **2.** [of demonstrators] Protestmarsch *der* ◇ *vi* - **1.** [soldiers, protesters] marschieren - **2.** [walk briskly]: **to ~ up to sb** schnurstracks auf jn zulmarschieren ◇ *vt*: **to ~ sb out of the door** jn zur Tür hinauslbefördern.

**March** [ma:tʃ] *n* März *der*; *see also* **September**.

**marcher** ['ma:tʃə'] *n* [protester] Demonstrant *der*, -in *die*.

**marching orders** ['ma:tʃɪŋ-] *npl*: **to give sb his/her ~** [employee] jn feuern; [lover] jm den Laufpass geben.

**marchioness** ['ma:ʃənes] *n* Marquise *die*.

**march-past** n Defilee das.

**Mardi Gras** [ˌmɑːdɪˈgrɑː] n [carnival] Karneval der.

**mare** [meəʳ] n Stute die.

**margarine** [ˌmɑːdʒəˈriːn, ˌmɑːgəˈriːn] n Margarine die.

**marge** [mɑːdʒ] n inf Margarine die.

**margin** [ˈmɑːdʒɪn] n - **1.** [in contest] Spielraum der; **by a narrow** ~ mit knappem Vorsprung; ~ **of error** Spielraum für Fehler - **2.** COMM: **profit** ~ Gewinnspanne die - **3.** [edge - of page, wood] Rand der.

**marginal** [ˈmɑːdʒɪnl] adj - **1.** [unimportant] von geringer Bedeutung; [effect, adjustment] geringfügig - **2.** Br POL: ~ **seat** nur mit knapper Mehrheit gewonnener Sitz.

**marginally** [ˈmɑːdʒɪnəlɪ] adv geringfügig.

**marigold** [ˈmærɪgəʊld] n Ringelblume die.

**marihuana, marijuana** [ˌmærɪˈwɑːnə] n Marihuana das.

**marina** [məˈriːnə] n Jachthafen der.

**marinade** [ˌmærɪˈneɪd] n Marinade die ◇ vt & vi = **marinate**.

**marinate** [ˈmærɪneɪt] vt marinieren ◇ vi: **leave it to** ~ weichen Sie es in Marinade ein.

**marine** [məˈriːn] adj [plant] im Meer lebend; ~ **life** Meeresflora und -fauna die ◇ n Marineinfanterist der.

**marionette** [ˌmærɪəˈnet] n Marionette die.

**marital** [ˈmærɪtl] adj [happiness, crisis] Ehe-; [sex, rights] ehelich.

**marital status** n Familienstand der.

**maritime** [ˈmærɪtaɪm] adj See-.

**marjoram** [ˈmɑːdʒərəm] n Majoran der.

**mark** [mɑːk] n - **1.** [stain] Fleck der; [scratch] Kratzer der; [on person's skin] Mal das - **2.** [sign] Zeichen das; **as a** ~ **of respect** als Zeichen des Respekts - **3.** SCH & UNIV Note die; **nine ~s out of ten** neun von zehn Punkten - **4.** [stage, level]: **we've reached the halfway** ~ wir haben die Hälfte hinter uns; **debts beyond the billion** ~ Schulden, die über die Milliardenmarke hinausgehen - **5.** [currency] Mark die - **6.** CULIN: **(gas)** ~ **6** Stufe 6 - **7.** phr: **to make one's** ~ sich (D) einen Namen machen; **to be quick/slow off the** ~ fix/langsam sein; **you are wide of the** ~ du liegst mit deiner Schätzung völlig daneben ◇ vt - **1.** [stain] fleckig machen; [scratch] zerkratzen - **2.** [label] kennzeichnen - **3.** SCH & UNIV korrigieren - **4.** [identify] markieren - **5.** [commemorate] begehen - **6.** SPORT [player] decken.

➤ **mark down** vt sep - **1.** COMM herablsetzen - **2.** [student]: **to** ~ **sb down** js Note herunterlsetzen.

➤ **mark off** vt sep [cross off] ablhaken.

➤ **mark up** vt sep COMM heraufl setzen.

**marked** [mɑːkt] adj [noticeable] merklich.

**markedly** [ˈmɑːkɪdlɪ] adv [noticeably] merklich.

**marker** [ˈmɑːkəʳ] n - **1.** [sign] Markierung die - **2.** SPORT [player] Manndecker der - **3.** [of exam] Korrektor der, -in die.

**marker pen** n Markierstift der, Marker der.

**market** [ˈmɑːkɪt] n Markt der; **to put on the** ~ [product] auf den Markt bringen; [house] zum Verkauf anlbieten ◇ vt vermarkten; [distribute] vertreiben ◇ vi Am [shop]: **to go ~ing** einkaufen gehen.

**marketable** [ˈmɑːkɪtəbl] adj vermarktbar.

**market day** n Markttag der.

**market forces** npl COMM Kräfte pl des Marktes.

**market garden** n esp Br Obst- und Gemüseanbaubetrieb der.

**marketing** [ˈmɑːkɪtɪŋ] n COMM Marketing das.

**marketplace** [ˈmɑːkɪtpleɪs] n - **1.** [in a town] Marktplatz der - **2.** COMM Markt der.

**market price** n COMM Marktpreis der.

**market research** n Marktforschung die.

**market town** n kleine Stadt, in der regelmäßig Markt abgehalten wird.

**market value** n COMM Marktwert der.

**marking** [ˈmɑːkɪŋ] n SCH & UNIV Korrigieren das.

➤ **markings** npl [of animal] Zeichnung die; [on road] Markierungen pl.

**marksman** [ˈmɑːksmən] (pl **-men** [-mən]) n Scharfschütze der.

**marksmanship** [ˈmɑːksmənʃɪp] n Treffsicherheit die.

**markup** [ˈmɑːkʌp] n Handelsspanne die.

**marmalade** [ˈmɑːməleɪd] n (U): **(orange)** ~ Orangenmarmelade die.

**maroon** [məˈruːn] adj kastanienbraun.

**marooned** [məˈruːnd] adj: **to be** ~ festlsitzen.

**marquee** [mɑːˈkiː] n Festzelt das.

**marquess** [ˈmɑːkwɪs] n = **marquis**.

**marquis** [ˈmɑːkwɪs] n Marquis der.

**marriage** [ˈmærɪdʒ] n - **1.** [wedding] Hochzeit die, Heirat die; [ceremony] Trauung die - **2.** [state] Ehe die.

**marriage bureau** n Br Ehevermittlungsinstitut das.

**marriage certificate** n Heiratsurkunde die.

**marriage guidance** n Eheberatung die.

**marriage guidance counsellor** n Eheberater der, -in die.

**married** [ˈmærɪd] adj - **1.** [man, woman] verheiratet; **to be** ~ **to sb** mit jm verheiratet sein - **2.** [life, name] Ehe-.

**marrow** ['mærəʊ] *n* - **1.** *Br* [vegetable] Speise-kürbis *der* - **2.** *(U)* [in bones] (Knochen)mark *das*.

**marry** ['mærɪ] (*pt* & *pp* -**ied**) *vt* - **1.** [become spouse of] heiraten; **to get married** heiraten - **2.** [subj: priest, minister, registrar] trauen ⋄ *vi* heiraten.

**Mars** [mɑːz] *n* [planet] Mars *der*.

**marsh** [mɑːʃ] *n* Sumpf *der*.

**marshal** ['mɑːʃl] (*Br pt* & *pp* -**led**; *cont* -**ling**, *Am pt* & *pp* -**ed**; *cont* -**ing**) *n* - **1.** MIL Marschall *der* - **2.** [at march, concert, race] Ordner *der* - **3.** *Am* [law officer] Sheriff *der* ⋄ *vt* - **1.** [people] für Ordnung sorgen unter (+ *D*) - **2.** [thoughts] ordnen; [support] sichern.

**marshalling yard** ['mɑːʃlɪŋ-] *n* Rangier-bahnhof *der*.

**marshland** ['mɑːʃlænd] *n (U)* Sumpfgebiet *das*.

**marshmallow** [*Br* ˌmɑːʃ'mæləʊ, *Am* 'mɑːrʃˌmeləʊ] *n* Marshmallow *das*.

**marshy** ['mɑːʃɪ] (*compar* -**ier**; *superl* -**iest**) *adj* sumpfig.

**marsupial** [mɑː'suːpɪəl] *n* Beuteltier *das*.

**martial** ['mɑːʃl] *adj* [music] kriegerisch.

**martial arts** [ˌmɑːʃl-] *npl* Kampfsportarten *pl*.

**martial law** [ˌmɑːʃl-] *n* Kriegsrecht *das*.

**Martian** ['mɑːʃn] *n* Marsmensch *der*.

**martini** [mɑː'tiːnɪ] *n* Martini *der*.

**martyr** ['mɑːtər] *n* Märtyrer *der*, -in *die*.

**martyrdom** ['mɑːtədəm] *n* [suffering] Martyri-um *das;* [death] Märtyrertod *der*.

**martyred** ['mɑːtəd] *adj:* **a ~ expression** eine Duldermiene.

**marvel** ['mɑːvl] (*Br pt* & *pp* -**led**; *cont* -**ling**, *Am pt* & *pp* -**ed**; *cont* -**ing**) *n* Wunder *das;* **you're a ~!** du bist ja unglaublich! ⋄ *vt:* **to ~ that** sich wundern, dass ⋄ *vi:* **to ~ (at sthg)** staunen (über etw (*A*)).

**marvellous** *Br*, **marvelous** *Am* ['mɑːvələs] *adj* wunderbar.

**Marxism** ['mɑːksɪzm] *n* Marxismus *der*.

**Marxist** ['mɑːksɪst] *adj* marxistisch ⋄ *n* Marxist *der*, -in *die*.

**marzipan** ['mɑːzɪpæn] *n* Marzipan *das*.

**mascara** [mæs'kɑːrə] *n* Wimperntusche *die*.

**mascot** ['mæskət] *n* Maskottchen *das*.

**masculine** ['mæskjʊlɪn] *adj* - **1.** [typically male] männlich - **2.** GRAMM & [woman] maskulin.

**masculinity** [ˌmæskjʊ'lɪnətɪ] *n* Männlichkeit *die*.

**mash** [mæʃ] *vt* (zu Brei) zerdrücken.

**MASH** [mæʃ] (*abbr of* **mobile army surgical hospital**) *n Am* mobiles Lazarett.

**mashed potatoes** [mæʃt-] *npl* Kartoffel-brei *der*.

**mask** [mɑːsk] *n* - **1.** [covering face] Maske *die* - **2.** *fig:* **behind a ~ of** hinter der Maske (+ *G*) ⋄ *vt* - **1.** [truth, feelings] verbergen - **2.** [smell, flavour] überdecken.

**masked** [mɑːskt] *adj* [face, man] maskiert.

**masking tape** ['mɑːskɪŋ-] *n (U)* Abklebe-band *das*.

**masochism** ['mæsəkɪzm] *n* Masochismus *der*.

**masochist** ['mæsəkɪst] *n* Masochist *der*, -in *die*.

**masochistic** [ˌmæsə'kɪstɪk] *adj* masochis-tisch.

**mason** ['meɪsn] *n* - **1.** [stonemason] Steinmetz *der* - **2.** [Freemason] Freimaurer *der*.

**masonic** [mə'sɒnɪk] *adj* [lodge] Freimaurer-.

**masonry** ['meɪsnrɪ] *n* Mauerwerk *das*.

**masquerade** [ˌmæskə'reɪd] *vi:* **to ~ as** sich auslgeben als.

**mass** [mæs] *n* - **1.** [gen & PHYS] Masse *die* - **2.** [large quantity] Unmenge *die;* **a ~ of people** eine große Menschenmenge; **a ~ of hair** eine Fülle von Haaren; **he was a ~ of bruises** er hatte überall blaue Flecken ⋄ *adj* [unemployment, protest *etc*] Massen- ⋄ *vt* [troops] zusammen|ziehen ⋄ *vi* [troops, clouds] sich zusammen|ziehen; [protesters] sich versam-meln.

➥ **Mass** *n* RELIG Messe *die*.

➥ **masses** *npl* - **1.** *inf* [lots] eine Masse; **~es of money/people** eine Masse Geld/von Leuten - **2.** [ordinary people]: **the ~es** die (breite) Masse.

**massacre** ['mæsəkər] *n* Massaker *das* ⋄ *vt* nieder|metzeln.

**massage** [*Br* 'mæsɑːʒ, *Am* mə'sɑːʒ] *n* Massage *die* ⋄ *vt* massieren.

**massage parlour** *n* Massageinstitut *das*.

**masseur** [mæ'sɜːr] *n* Masseur *der*.

**masseuse** [mæ'sɜːz] *n* Masseurin *die*.

**massive** ['mæsɪv] *adj* riesig; [dose] sehr groß.

**massively** ['mæsɪvlɪ] *adv* enorm.

**mass-market** *adj* [product] für die (breite) Masse.

**mass media** *n* OR *npl:* **the ~** die Massenme-dien *pl*.

**mass-produce** *vt* in Massenproduktion her|stellen.

**mass production** *n* Massenproduktion *die*.

**mast** [mɑːst] *n* - **1.** [on boat] Mast *der* - **2.** RADIO & TV Sendemast *der*.

**mastectomy** [mæs'tektəmɪ] (*pl* -**ies**) *n* Mas-tektomie *die*.

**master** ['mɑːstər] *n* - **1.** [gen] Herr *der;* **to be**

M

**one's own ~** sein eigener Herr sein; **he is ~ of the situation** er ist Herr der Lage **- 2.** *Br* [teacher] Lehrer der **- 3.** [of ship] Kapitän der **- 4.** [original copy] Original das ◇ *adj* **- 1.** [in trade]: **~ builder** Baumeister der **- 2.** [copy, tape] Original- ◇ *vt* **- 1.** [control - situation] meistern; [ - temper] zügeln **- 2.** [job, skill, language] beherrschen.

**master bedroom** *n größtes Schlafzimmer in einem Haus.*

**masterful** ['mɑːstəfʊl] *adj* [person] herrisch.

**master key** *n* Generalschlüssel der.

**masterly** ['mɑːstəlɪ] *adj* meisterhaft.

**mastermind** ['mɑːstəmaɪnd] *n* führender Kopf ◇ *vt* der führende Kopf sein bei.

**Master of Arts** (*pl* Masters of Arts) *n* **- 1.** [degree] ≃ Magister Artium der **- 2.** [person] Inhaber des „Master of Arts".

**master of ceremonies** (*pl* masters of ceremonies) *n* [at formal occasion] Zeremonienmeister der; [in variety show] Conférencier der.

**Master of Science** (*pl* Masters of Science) *n* **- 1.** [degree] ≃ Magister rerum naturalium der **- 2.** [person] Inhaber des „Master of Science".

**masterpiece** ['mɑːstəpiːs] *n* lit & fig Meisterwerk das.

**master plan** *n* Gesamtplan der.

**master's degree** *n* Magister(titel) der.

**masterstroke** ['mɑːstəstrəʊk] *n* Geniestreich der.

**masterwork** ['mɑːstəwɜːk] *n* Meisterwerk das.

**mastery** ['mɑːstərɪ] *n* (U) **- 1.** [thorough grasp] Beherrschung die **- 2.** [control - of country] Herrschaft die; [ - of feelings] Kontrolle die.

**mastic** ['mæstɪk] *n* Mastix der.

**masticate** ['mæstɪkeɪt] *fml* vt & vi kauen.

**mastiff** ['mæstɪf] *n* Mastiff der.

**masturbate** ['mæstəbeɪt] *vi* masturbieren.

**masturbation** [,mæstə'beɪʃn] *n* Masturbation die.

**mat** [mæt] *n* [on table] Untersetzer der; [on floor] (Fuß)matte die; [in sport] Matte die.

**match** [mætʃ] *n* **- 1.** [game] Spiel das; [in boxing, wrestling] Kampf der **- 2.** [for lighting] Streichholz das **- 3.** [equal]: **to be no ~ for sb** jm nicht gewachsen sein; **to meet one's ~** seinen Meister finden ◇ *vt* **- 1.** [views, feelings, ideas] übereinstimmen mit **- 2.** [in colour, design] passen zu (+ D) **- 3.** [be as good as] gleichkommen (+ D); **they can't be ~ed for quality** in puncto Qualität kann es keiner mit ihnen auf|nehmen ◇ *vi* **- 1.** [views, ideas] übereinstimmen **- 2.** [in colour, design] zusammen|passen.

**matchbox** ['mætʃbɒks] *n* Streichholzschachtel die.

**matched** [mætʃt] *adj*: **to be well ~** [well suited] gut zueinander passen; [equal in strength] sich (D) ebenbürtig sein.

**matching** ['mætʃɪŋ] *adj* (dazu) passend; **three ~ armchairs** drei zueinander passende Sessel.

**matchless** ['mætʃlɪs] *adj literary* unvergleichlich.

**matchmaker** ['mætʃˌmeɪkəʳ] *n* Ehestifter der, -in die.

**match point** *n* TENNIS Matchball der.

**matchstick** ['mætʃstɪk] *n* Streichholz das.

**mate** [meɪt] *n* **- 1.** inf [friend] Kumpel der **- 2.** Br inf [term of address] Kumpel der **- 3.** [of animal - male] Männchen das; [ - female] Weibchen das **- 4.** NAUT: (first) **~** Maat der ◇ *vi* [animals]: **to ~ (with)** sich paaren (mit)

**material** [mə'tɪərɪəl] *adj* **- 1.** [physical] materiell **- 2.** [important] wesentlich ◇ *n* **- 1.** [substance] Material das **- 2.** [fabric] Stoff der **- 3.** (U) [ideas, information] Stoff der, Material das.

➡ **materials** *npl*: **building ~s** Baumaterialien pl; **writing ~s** Schreibzeug das; **cleaning ~s** Putzzeug das.

**materialism** [mə'tɪərɪəlɪzm] *n* Materialismus der.

**materialistic** [mə,tɪərɪə'lɪstɪk] *adj* materialistisch.

**materialize, -ise** [mə'tɪərɪəlaɪz] *vi* **- 1.** [happen - crisis] ein|treten; [ - threat] in die Tat umgesetzt werden; **the promised funds failed to ~** aus den versprochenen Geldern ist nichts geworden **- 2.** [appear] auf|tauchen.

**materially** [mə'tɪərɪəlɪ] *adv* **- 1.** [physically] materiell **- 2.** [importantly] grundlegend.

**maternal** [mə'tɜːnl] *adj* **- 1.** [instinct] Mutter-; [person] mütterlich **- 2.** [on mother's side]: **~ grandparents** Großeltern mütterlicherseits.

**maternity** [mə'tɜːnətɪ] *n* Mutterschaft die.

**maternity benefit** *n* Mutterschaftsgeld das.

**maternity dress** *n* Umstandskleid das.

**maternity leave** *n* (U) Mutterschaftsurlaub der.

**maternity ward** *n* Entbindungsstation die.

**math** *n* Am = maths.

**mathematical** [,mæθə'mætɪkl] *adj* mathematisch.

**mathematician** [,mæθəmə'tɪʃn] *n* Mathematiker der, -in die.

**mathematics** [,mæθə'mætɪks] *n* (U) Mathematik die.

**maths** *Br* [mæθs], **math** *Am* [mæθ] (*abbr of*

**mathematics)** *inf n (U)* Mathe *die* <> *comp* Mathe-.

**maths coprocessor** [-ˌkəʊ'prəʊsesəʳ] *n* COMPUT Arithmetikprozessor *der.*

**matinée** ['mætɪneɪ] *n* Nachmittagsvorstellung *die.*

**mating call** ['meɪtɪŋ-] *n* Paarungsruf *der.*

**mating season** ['meɪtɪŋ-] *n* Paarungszeit *die.*

**matriarch** ['meɪtrɪɑːk] *n literary* [of a family] weibliches Familienoberhaupt.

**matrices** ['meɪtrɪsiːz] *pl* ⊳ **matrix.**

**matriculate** [mə'trɪkjʊleɪt] *vi* UNIV sich immatrikulieren.

**matriculation** [məˌtrɪkjʊ'leɪʃn] *n* UNIV Immatrikulation *die.*

**matrimonial** [ˌmætrɪ'məʊnɪəl] *adj* [problems, dispute] Ehe-; [harmony] ehelich.

**matrimony** ['mætrɪmənɪ] *n* Ehestand *der.*

**matrix** ['meɪtrɪks] (*pl* **matrices** OR **-es**) *n* - **1.** [context] Kontext *der* - **2.** TECH [mould] Matrize *die* - **3.** MATH Matrix *die.*

**matron** ['meɪtrən] *n* - **1.** *Br* [in hospital] Oberschwester *die* - **2.** [in school] Schwester *die.*

**matronly** ['meɪtrənlɪ] *adj euphemism* matronenhaft.

**matt** *Br,* **matte** *Am* [mæt] *adj* matt.

**matted** ['mætɪd] *adj* verfilzt.

**matter** ['mætəʳ] *n* - **1.** [question, situation] Angelegenheit *die;* **it's a ~ of life and death** es geht um Leben und Tod; **the fact** OR **truth of the ~ is ...** die Sache ist die dass ...; **that's quite another** OR **a different ~** das ist etwas ganz anderes; **that's a ~ of opinion** das ist Ansichtssache; **a ~ of time** eine Frage der Zeit; **to make ~s worse** die Sache noch schlimmer machen; **and to make ~s worse, ...** zu allem Unglück ..., und obendrein ...; **as a ~ of course** selbstverständlich; **as a ~ of principle** aus Prinzip; **within a ~ of hours** innerhalb von wenigen Stunden - **2.** [trouble]: **there's something the ~ with my radio** etwas stimmt nicht mit dem Radio; **what's the ~?** was ist (denn) los?; **what's the ~ with it/her?** was ist (los) damit/mit ihr? - **3.** [substance] Materie *die* - **4.** (U) [material] Stoff *der;* **reading ~** Lesestoff *der* <> *vi* von Bedeutung sein; **it doesn't ~ das macht nichts; it doesn't ~ what I do, ...** ganz gleich, was ich tue, ...; **nothing else ~s** alles andere ist unwichtig.

➤ **as a matter of fact** *adv* sogar.
➤ **for that matter** *adv* eigentlich.
➤ **no matter** *adv:* **no ~ how ...** ganz gleich wie ...; **no ~ what** ganz egal was.

**matter-of-fact** *adj* sachlich, nüchtern.

**matting** ['mætɪŋ] *n (U)* Matten *pl.*

**mattress** ['mætrɪs] *n* Matratze *die.*

**mature** [mə'tjʊəʳ] *adj* - **1.** [person] reif - **2.** [cheese] reif; [wine] ausgereift <> *vi* - **1.** [child] erwachsen werden; [animal] zur vollen Größe heranlwachsen; [plant] die volle Größe erreichen - **2.** *fig* [grow up] reifer werden - **3.** [cheese] reifen; [wine] auslreifen - **4.** [insurance policy] fällig werden.

**mature student** *n Br* UNIV Person, die erst einige Jahre nach dem Schulabschluss ein Studium aufnimmt.

**maturity** [mə'tjʊərətɪ] *n* Reife *die;* **to reach ~** [person] erwachsen werden; [animal] ausgewachsen sein.

**maudlin** ['mɔːdlɪn] *adj* sentimental.

**maul** [mɔːl] *vt* übel zulrichten.

**Mauritius** [mə'rɪʃəs] *n* Mauritius *nt;* **in ~** auf Mauritius.

**mausoleum** [ˌmɔːsə'lɪəm] (*pl* **-s**) *n* Mausoleum *das.*

**mauve** [məʊv] *adj* mauve <> *n* Mauvein *das.*

**maverick** ['mævərɪk] *n* Alleingänger *der,* -in *die.*

**mawkish** ['mɔːkɪʃ] *adj* [sentimentality, poetry] rührselig; [person, behaviour] sentimental.

**max.** *abbr of* maximum.

**maxim** ['mæksɪm] (*pl* **-s**) *n* Maxime *die.*

**maxima** ['mæksɪmə] *pl* ⊳ **maximum.**

**maximize, -ise** ['mæksɪmaɪz] *vt* maximieren.

**maximum** ['mæksɪməm] (*pl* **maxima** OR **-s**) *adj* maximal; [speed, weight, temperature] Höchst- <> *n* Maximum *das.*

**may** [meɪ] *aux vb* - **1.** [expressing possibility] können; **it ~ be done as follows** man kann wie folgt vorgehen; **it ~ rain** es könnte regnen; **they ~ have got lost** sie haben sich vielleicht verirrt; **be that as it ~** wie dem auch sei; **come what ~** komme, was wolle - **2.** [expressing permission] können; **~ I smoke?** darf ich rauchen?; **you ~ sit, if you wish** Sie können sich hinsetzen, wenn Sie Wollen - **3.** [when conceding a point]: **it ~ be a long walk, but it's worth it** es ist vielleicht ein langer Weg, aber es lohnt sich - **4.** *fml* [expressing wish, hope]: **~ you be very happy!** ich wünsche dir, dass du glücklich wirst!; ⊳ **might.**

**May** [meɪ] *n* Mai *der; see also* **September.**

**Maya** ['maɪə] *n:* **the ~** die Mayas.

**maybe** ['meɪbɪ] *adv* vielleicht.

**mayday** ['meɪdeɪ] *n* [SOS] Mayday *das.*

**May Day** *n* der 1. Mai.

**mayfly** ['meɪflaɪ] (*pl* **-flies**) *n* Eintagsfliege *die.*

**mayhem** ['meɪhem] *n* Chaos *das.*

**mayn't** [meɪənt] = may not.

**mayonnaise** [ˌmeɪə'neɪz] *n* Majonäse *die.*

**mayor** [meəʳ] *n* Bürgermeister *der.*

**M**

**mayoress** ['meərɪs] n [female mayor] Bürgermeisterin die; [mayor's wife] Frau die des Bürgermeisters.

**maypole** ['meɪpəʊl] n Maibaum der.

**may've** ['meɪəv] = may have.

**maze** [meɪz] n - **1.** [system of paths] Irrgarten der - **2.** fig [of ideas] Wirrwarr der; [of streets] Labyrinth das.

**MB** - **1.** (abbr of **megabyte**) Mb das - **2.** abk für Manitoba, in Postanschrift verwendet.

**MBA** (abbr of **Master of Business Administration**) n akademischer Grad in Betriebswirtschaft oder dessen Inhaber.

**MBE** (abbr of **Member of the Order of the British Empire**) n Auszeichnung des britischen Königreichs oder deren Inhaber.

**MC** abbr of **master of ceremonies**.

**McCoy** [mə'kɔɪ] n inf: it's the real ~ es ist eine Echte/ein Echter/ein Echtes.

**MCP** n inf abbr of **male chauvinist pig**.

**MD** n - **1.** (abbr of **Doctor of Medicine**) Dr. med. - **2.** abbr of **managing director** ◇ abk für Maryland, in Postanschrift verwendet.

**MDT** (abbr of **Mountain Daylight Time**) n Sommerzeit in der Gebirgszeitzone der USA.

**me** [miː] pers pron (accusative) mich; (dative) mir; **she knows** ~ sie kennt mich; **it's** ~ ich bins; **send it to** ~ schick es mir; **tell** ~ sagen Sie mal, sag mal; **he's worse than** ~ er ist schlechter als ich.

**ME** n (abbr of **myalgic encephalomyelitis**) myalgische Enzephalomyelitis ◇ abk für Maine, in Postanschrift verwendet.

**meadow** ['medəʊ] n Wiese die.

**meagre** Br, **meager** Am ['miːgəʳ] adj dürftig.

**meal** [miːl] n - **1.** [occasion] Mahlzeit die; **to go out for a** ~ essen gehen - **2.** [food] Essen das, Gericht das; **to make a** ~ **of sthg** Br fig & pej viel Umstände mit etw machen.

**meals on wheels** npl Br Essen das auf Rädern.

**mealtime** ['miːltaɪm] n Essenszeit die; **at** ~s während des Essens.

**mealy-mouthed** ['miːlɪ'maʊðd] adj pej unaufrichtig.

**mean** [miːn] (pt & pp **meant**) vt - **1.** [signify] bedeuten; **the name** ~**s nothing to me** der Name sagt mir nichts - **2.** [intend] beabsichtigen; **to** ~ **to do sthg** vorhaben, etw zu tun; **the bus was meant to leave at eight** der Bus hätte eigentlich um acht Uhr abfahren sollen; **it's meant to be good** das soll gut sein; **he** ~**s well** er meint es gut - **3.** [with remark] meinen; **what do you** ~ **by that?** was meinst du damit? - **4.** [be serious about] ernst meinen; **I didn't** ~ **it!** ich habe es nicht so gemeint!; **I** ~ **it!** es ist mein Ernst!, ich meine es ernst! - **5.** phr: Paul,

**I** ~ **Peter** [when correcting o.s.] Paul, ich meine (natürlich) Peter ◇ adj - **1.** [miserly] geizig - **2.** [unkind] gemein; **to be** ~ **to sb** gemein zu jm sein - **3.** [average] durchschnittlich - **4.** iron: **she's no** ~ **singer** [excellent] sie singt wirklich gut; **that's no** ~ **feat** [difficult] das ist keine geringe Leistung ◇ n [average] Durchschnitt der; ⊳ **means**.

**meander** [mɪ'ændəʳ] vi - **1.** [river, road] sich schlängeln - **2.** [person] schlendern.

**meaning** ['miːnɪŋ] n Bedeutung die; [of film, work of art, life] Sinn der; **what's the** ~ **of this?** was soll denn das?

**meaningful** ['miːnɪŋfʊl] adj - **1.** [look, comment] vielsagend - **2.** [discussion, relationship] ernsthaft.

**meaningless** ['miːnɪŋlɪs] adj - **1.** [word, lyrics] ohne Sinn - **2.** [futile] sinnlos.

**meanness** ['miːnnɪs] n - **1.** [stinginess - of person] Geiz der; [ - of gift] Schäbigkeit die - **2.** [unkindness] Gemeinheit die.

**means** [miːnz] (pl inv) n [method] Mittel das; ~ **of transport** Verkehrsmittel das; **we have no** ~ **of contacting her** wir haben keine Möglichkeit, sie zu erreichen; **a** ~ **to an end** ein Mittel zum Zweck; **by** ~ **of** mittels (+ G), durch ◇ npl [money] Mittel pl; **it is beyond my** ~ das kann ich mir nicht leisten; **can I have one?** – **by all** ~! darf ich eins haben? – (aber) selbstverständlich!; **by all** ~ **try it out, but ...** probiere es ruhig aus, aber ...

➡ **by no means** adv keineswegs.

**means test** n esp Br Überprüfung die der Bedürftigkeit.

**meant** [ment] pt & pp ⊳ **mean**.

**meantime** ['miːn,taɪm] n: **in the** ~ in der Zwischenzeit.

**meanwhile** ['miːn,waɪl] adv inzwischen.

**measles** ['miːzlz] n: **(the)** ~ Masern pl.

**measly** ['miːzlɪ] (compar **-ier**; superl **-iest**) adj inf mick(e)rig.

**measurable** ['meʒərəbl] adj merklich.

**measurably** ['meʒərəblɪ] adv merklich.

**measure** ['meʒəʳ] n - **1.** [step, action] Maßnahme die - **2.** (U) [amount]: **a** ~ **of success/responsibility** ein gewisses Maß an Erfolg/Verantwortung; **for good** ~ sicherheitshalber; [as an additional item] zusätzlich noch; **to get the** ~ **of sb** jn (richtig) einschätzen - **3.** [of alcohol] ausgeschenkte Menge - **4.** [indication]: **to be a** ~ **of sthg** ein Zeichen für etw sein - **5.** [device] Maß das ◇ vt messen; [room] ausImessen; [damage, harm] abIschätzen ◇ vi: **it** ~**s three metres by two** das misst drei mal zwei Meter.

➡ **measure up** vi [be good enough] gut genug sein; **to** ~ **up to sthg** etw (D) entsprechen.

**measured** ['meʒədl adj literary [voice, steps] bedächtig.

**measurement** ['meʒəmənt] n - **1.** [figure] Maß das - **2.** (U) [act of measuring] Messung die.
➡ **measurements** npl [of sb's body] Maße pl; **to take sb's ~s** bei jm Maß nehmen.

**measuring jug** ['meʒərɪŋ] n Messbecher der.

**measuring tape** ['meʒərɪŋ-] n Maßband das.

**meat** [mi:t] n Fleisch das.

**meatball** ['mi:tbɔ:l] n Fleischklößchen das.

**meat pie** n Br Fleischpastete die.

**meaty** ['mi:tɪ] (compar -ier; superl -iest) adj fig [full of ideas] aussagehaltig.

**Mecca** ['mekə] n - **1.** GEOGR Mekka nt - **2.** fig [paradise]: **a ~ for** ein Mekka für.

**mechanic** [mɪ'kænɪk] n Mechaniker der, -in die.
➡ **mechanics** n (U) [study] Mechanik die ◇ npl [way sthg works] Funktionsweise die.

**mechanical** [mɪ'kænɪkl] adj - **1.** [device, action, smile] mechanisch - **2.** [good at mechanics - person] technisch begabt; [-skills] technisch.

**mechanical engineering** n Maschinenbau der.

**mechanism** ['mekənɪzml] n - **1.** [of machine, behaviour] Mechanismus der - **2.** [procedure] Verfahren das.

**mechanization** [ˌmekənaɪ'zeɪʃn] n Mechanisierung die.

**mechanize, -ise** ['mekənaɪz] vt & vi mechanisieren.

**MEd** [ˌem'ed] (abbr of **Master of Education**) n akademischer Grad in Erziehungswissenschaft oder dessen Inhaber.

**medal** ['medl] n Medaille die.

**medallion** [mɪ'dæljən] n Medaillon das.

**medallist** Br, **medalist** Am ['medəlɪst] n Medaillengewinner der, -in die.

**meddle** ['medl] vi: **to ~ (in/with sthg)** sich (in etw (A)) einlmischen; **to ~ with sb** sich mit jm einllassen.

**meddlesome** ['medlsəml adj: **don't be so ~** misch dich nicht in alles ein.

**media** ['mi:dɪə] pl ▷ **medium** ◇ n OR npl: **the ~ die Medien** pl.

**mediaeval** [ˌmedɪ'i:vl] adj = **medieval**.

**media event** n Medienereignis das.

**median** ['mi:dɪən] adj MATH Mittel-, mittlere, -r, -s; **~ value** Zentralwert der ◇ n Am [of road] Mittelstreifen der.

**mediate** ['mi:dɪeɪt] vt auslhandeln, herbeilführen ◇ vi: **to ~ (for/between)** vermitteln (für/zwischen (+ D)).

**mediation** [ˌmi:dɪ'eɪʃn] n (U) Vermittlung die.

**mediator** ['mi:dɪeɪtə'] n Vermittler der, -in die.

**medic** ['medɪk] n inf - **1.** [medical student] Medizinstudent der, -in die - **2.** [doctor] Mediziner der, -in die.

**Medicaid** ['medɪkeɪd] n Am staatliche Gesundheitsfürsorge für einkommensschwache US-Bürger.

**medical** ['medɪkl] adj medizinisch ◇ n ärztliche Untersuchung.

**medical certificate** n - **1.** [result of medical exam] Gesundheitszeugnis das - **2.** [for sickness] ärztliches Attest.

**medical insurance** n (U) Krankenversicherung die.

**medical student** n Medizinstudent der, -in die.

**Medicare** ['medɪkeə'] n Am staatliche Gesundheitsfürsorge für ältere US-Bürger.

**medicated** ['medɪkeɪtɪd] adj medizinisch.

**medication** [ˌmedɪ'keɪʃn] n - **1.** (U) [use of medicines] medikamentöse Behandlung - **2.** [medicine] Medikamente pl; **to be on ~** Medikamente einlnehmen.

**medicinal** [me'dɪsɪnl] adj [tea] Heilkräuter-; **~ herbs** Heilkräuter.

**medicine** ['medsɪn] n - **1.** [treatment of illness] Medizin die - **2.** [substance] Medikament das.

**medicine man** n Medizinmann der.

**medieval** [ˌmedɪ'i:vl] adj mittelalterlich.

**mediocre** [ˌmi:dɪ'əʊkə'] adj mittelmäßig.

**mediocrity** [ˌmi:dɪ'ɒkrətɪ] n [poor quality] Mittelmäßigkeit die.

**meditate** ['medɪteɪt] vi - **1.** [reflect, ponder]: **to ~ (on OR upon)** nachldenken (über (+ A)) - **2.** [practise meditation] meditieren.

**meditation** [ˌmedɪ'teɪʃn] n Meditation die.

**Mediterranean** [ˌmedɪtə'reɪnɪən] n - **1.** [sea]: **the ~ (Sea)** das Mittelmeer - **2.** [area around sea]: **the ~** der Mittelmeerraum ◇ adj Mittelmeer-, mediterran.

**medium** ['mi:dɪəml] adj mittlere, -r, -s ◇ n Medium das.

**medium-dry** adj halbtrocken.

**medium-size(d)** [-saɪz(d)] adj mittelgroß, von mittlerer Größe.

**medium wave** n Mittelwelle die.

**medley** ['medlɪ] (pl **medleys**) n - **1.** [mixture] Gemisch das - **2.** [selection of music] Medley das, Potpourri das.

**meek** [mi:k] adj sanftmütig; [voice] sanft.

**meekly** ['mi:klɪ] adv sanftmütig.

**meet** [mi:t] (pt & pp met) vt - **1.** [by arrangement] sich treffen mit; [by chance] treffen; [get to know] kennen lernen; **to arrange to ~ sb** sich

M

mit jm verabreden; **pleased to ~ you!** sehr erfreut! **- 2.** [go to collect] ablholen **- 3.** [need, requirement] erfüllen **- 4.** [cost, expense] begleichen **- 5.** [experience, deal with - difficulty etc] begegnen (+ D) **- 6.** [hit] treffen; **to ~ sb's eye** jm in die Augen blicken **- 7.** [join - subj: road, river] treffen auf (+ A) <> vi **- 1.** [by arrangement, by chance] sich treffen; [committee etc] zusammenlkommen; **their eyes met** ihre Blicke trafen sich **- 2.** [get to know each other] sich kennen lernen **- 3.** [intersect] aufeinander treffen **- 4.** [join] zusammenlkommen <> n Am [sports meeting] Sportfest das.

- **meet up** vi: **to ~ up (with sb)** sich (mit jm) treffen.

- **meet with** vt fus **- 1.** [problems, resistance] stoßen auf (+ A); **to ~ with success** Erfolg haben **- 2.** [by arrangement] sich treffen mit.

**meeting** ['miːtɪŋ] n **- 1.** [for discussions, business] Meeting das, Sitzung die **- 2.** (U) [people attending meeting] Versammlung die **- 3.** [coming together - by chance] Begegnung die; [ - by arrangement] Treffen das.

**meeting place** n Treffpunkt der.

**mega-** ['megə] prefix Mega-.

**megabit** ['megəbɪt] n COMPUT Megabit das.

**megabyte** ['megəbaɪt] n COMPUT Megabyte das.

**megahertz** ['megəhɜːts] n RADIO Megahertz das.

**megalomania** [ˌmegələ'meɪnɪə] n Größenwahn der, Megalomanie die.

**megalomaniac** [ˌmegələ'meɪnɪæk] n Größenwahnsinnige der, die.

**megaphone** ['megəfəʊn] n Megafon das.

**megaton** ['megətʌn] n Megatonne die.

**megawatt** ['megəwɒt] n Megawatt das.

**melamine** ['meləmiːn] n Melamin das.

**melancholy** ['melənkəlɪ] adj melancholisch; [facts, news] traurig <> n Melancholie die.

**mellow** ['meləʊ] adj **- 1.** [a light] warm **- 2.** [smooth, pleasant] angenehm; [sound, tones] lieblich, sanft; [wine] ausgereift; [whisky] mild **- 3.** [gentle, relaxed] milde, sanft <> vt: **to be ~ed by sthg** [by age, experience] gereift sein durch etw <> vi [person] abgeklärt werden.

**melodic** [mɪ'lɒdɪk] adj melodisch.

**melodious** [mɪ'ləʊdɪəs] adj melodiös.

**melodrama** ['melədrɑːmə] n Melodrama das.

**melodramatic** [ˌmelədrə'mætɪk] adj melodramatisch.

**melody** ['melədɪ] (pl -ies) n Melodie die.

**melon** ['melən] n Melone die.

**melt** [melt] vt **- 1.** [make liquid - chocolate, snow] schmelzen; [butter] zerlassen **- 2.** fig: **to ~ sb's heart** js Herz übergehen lassen <> vi **- 1.** [become liquid] schmelzen **- 2.** fig [soften - person] dahinlschmelzen; [ - heart] überlgehen

**- 3.** fig [disappear]: **to ~ into the crowd** in der Menge unterltauchen; **to ~ away** [savings, anger] dahinlschmelzen, weglschmelzen.

- **melt down** vt sep einlschmelzen.

**meltdown** ['meltdaʊn] n Kernschmelze die.

**melting point** ['meltɪŋ-] n Schmelzpunkt der.

**melting pot** ['meltɪŋ-] n fig Schmelztiegel der.

**member** ['membə'] adj Mitglieds- <> n Mitglied das; **a ~ of staff** ein Firmenangehöriger, eine Firmenangehörige.

**Member of Congress** (pl **Members of Congress**) n Am Kongressmitglied das.

**Member of Parliament** (pl **Members of Parliament**) n Parlamentsabgeordnete der, die.

**membership** ['membəʃɪp] n (U) **- 1.** [fact of belonging] Mitgliedschaft die **- 2.** [number of members] Mitgliederzahl die **- 3.** [people]: **the ~** die Mitglieder.

**membership card** n Mitgliedskarte die, Mitgliedsausweis der.

**membrane** ['membreɪn] n ANAT Membran die.

**memento** [mɪ'mentəʊ] (pl **-s**) n Andenken das.

**memo** ['meməʊ] (pl **-s**) n Mitteilung die, Notiz die.

**memoirs** ['memwɑːz] npl Memoiren pl.

**memo pad** n Notizblock der.

**memorabilia** [ˌmemərə'bɪlɪə] npl Memorabilien pl.

**memorable** ['memərəbl] adj [occasion, lecture, day] denkwürdig; [journey] unvergesslich.

**memorandum** [ˌmemə'rændəm] (pl **-da** [-də] OR **-dums**) n fml Memorandum das, Mitteilung die.

**memorial** [mɪ'mɔːrɪəl] adj Gedenk- <> n Denkmal das.

**memorize, -ise** ['meməraɪz] vt auswendig lernen.

**memory** ['memərɪ] (pl **-ies**) n **- 1.** [ability to remember] Gedächtnis das **- 2.** (U) [things remembered] Erinnerung die; **I have no ~ of it** ich kann mich nicht daran erinnern; **to lose one's ~** sein Gedächtnis verlieren; **from ~** auswendig; **within living ~** seit Menschengedenken **- 3.** [event, experience remembered] Erinnerung die **- 4.** (U) [of dead person] Andenken das; **in ~ of** zum Andenken OR zur Erinnerung an (+ A) **- 5.** COMPUT Speicher der, Memory das.

**memory card** n COMPUT Speicherkarte die.

**men** [men] pl [> **man**.

**menace** ['menəs] n **- 1.** [threat] Drohung die; [danger] drohende Gefahr **- 2.** (U) [threatening

quality] Bedrohung *die* - **3.** *inf* [nuisance, pest]
Plage *die* ⬦ *vt* bedrohen.

**menacing** ['menəsɪŋ] *adj* bedrohlich.

**menacingly** ['menəsɪŋlɪ] *adv* bedrohlich.

**menagerie** [mɪ'nædʒərɪ] *n* Menagerie *die*.

**mend** [mend] *n inf:* **to be on the ~** auf dem Weg
der Besserung sein ⬦ *vt* [repair] reparieren;
[clothes] flicken; **to ~ one's ways** sich bessern.

**mending** ['mendɪŋ] *n (U)* - **1.** [repairing of clothes]:
**to do the ~** die Flickarbeit erledigen
- **2.** [clothes] Flickarbeit *die*.

**menfolk** ['menfəʊk] *npl* Männer *pl*.

**menial** ['miːnɪəl] *adj* niedrig.

**meningitis** [ˌmenɪn'dʒaɪtɪs] *n* MED Hirnhaut-
entzündung *die*, Meningitis *die*.

**menopause** ['menəpɔːz] *n (U):* **the ~** die
Wechseljahre, die Menopause.

**menservants** ['mensɜːvənts] *pl* ⟶ **manservant**.

**men's room** *n Am:* **the ~** die Herrentoilette.

**menstrual** ['menstrʊəl] *adj* Menstruations-.

**menstruate** ['menstrʊeɪt] *vi* menstruieren.

**menstruation** [ˌmenstrʊ'eɪʃn] *n (U)* Menstruation *die*, Periode *die*.

**menswear** ['menzweəʳ] *n (U)* Herrenbeklei-
dung *die*.

**mental** ['mentl] *adj* - **1.** [intellectual] geistig
- **2.** [psychiatric] psychiatrisch; **~ illness** Geisteskrankheit *die;* **her ~ health** ihr Geisteszustand - **3.** [performed in the mind] im Kopf;
**~ arithmetic** Kopfrechnen *das*.

**mental age** *n:* **to have a ~ of eight** auf dem
geistigen Entwicklungsstand eines Acht-
jährigen sein.

**mental block** *n:* **I have a ~ about it** ich habe
da eine geistige Blockade.

**mental hospital** *n* Nervenklinik *die*, psychiatrische Klinik.

**mentality** [men'tælətɪ] *n (U)* Mentalität *die*.

**mentally** ['mentəlɪ] *adv* geistig.

**mentally handicapped** *npl:* **the ~** die geistig Behinderten.

➣ **mentally-handicapped** *adj* geistig behindert *pl*.

**mental note** *n:* **I must make a ~ to tell him** ich
darf nicht vergessen, es ihm zu sagen.

**menthol** ['menθɒl] *n* Menthol *das*.

**mentholated** ['menθəleɪtɪd] *adj* Menthol-.

**mention** ['menʃn] *vt* erwähnen; **to ~ sthg to sb**
etw jm gegenüber erwähnen; **not to ~ ...**
ganz zu schweigen von ...; **don't ~ it!** gern
geschehen! ⬦ *n* Erwähnung *die;* **to get a ~**
erwähnt werden; **to make no ~ of sthg** etw
nicht erwähnen.

**mentor** ['mentɔːʳ] *n fml* Mentor *der*.

**menu** ['menjuː] *n* - **1.** [in restaurant - card] Speise-
karte *die;* [ - dishes] Menü *das* - **2.** COMPUT Menü
*das*.

**menu-driven** *adj* COMPUT menügesteuert.

**meow** *n & vi Am* = miaow.

**MEP** (*abbr of* **Member of the European Parliament**) *n* MdEP *das*.

**mercantile** ['mɜːkəntaɪl] *adj* Handels-.

**mercenary** ['mɜːsɪnrɪ] (*pl* -ies) *adj* - **1.** [only interested in money] gewinnsüchtig, geldgierig
- **2.** MIL Söldner- ⬦ *n* [soldier] Söldner *der*.

**merchandise** ['mɜːtʃəndaɪz] *n (U)* Ware *die*.

**merchant** ['mɜːtʃənt] *adj* Handels- ⬦ *n*
Händler *der*, -in *die*.

**merchant bank** *n Br* Handelsbank *die*.

**merchant navy** *Br*, **merchant marine**
*Am n* Handelsmarine *die*.

**merciful** ['mɜːsɪfʊl] *adj* [person] barmherzig;
**her death was a ~ release** ihr Tod war eine Erlösung.

**mercifully** ['mɜːsɪfʊlɪ] *adv* - **1.** [fortunately]
glücklicherweise, zum Glück - **2.** [with clem-
ency] barmherzig.

**merciless** ['mɜːsɪlɪs] *adj* gnadenlos.

**mercilessly** ['mɜːsɪlɪslɪ] *adv* gnadenlos.

**mercury** ['mɜːkjʊrɪ] *n* Quecksilber *das*.

**Mercury** ['mɜːkjʊrɪ] *n* [planet] Merkur *der*.

**mercy** ['mɜːsɪ] (*pl* -ies) *n* - **1.** [kindness, pity] Gnade *die*, Erbarmen *das;* **to be at the ~ of sb/sthg**
*fig* jm/etw ausgeliefert sein - **2.** [blessing] Segen *der*, Glück *das*.

**mercy killing** *n* Euthanasie *die*.

**mere** [mɪəʳ] *adj:* **a ~ £10 is all it costs** es kostet
bloß OR nur 10 Pfund; **it took him a ~ two
hours** er brauchte bloß OR nur zwei Stunden; **she's a ~ child!** sie ist ja noch ein Kind!;
**the ~ mention of her name infuriates him** er gerät schon außer sich, wenn nur ihr Name
erwähnt wird.

**merely** ['mɪəlɪ] *adv* bloß, nur.

**merge** [mɜːdʒ] *vt* - **1.** COMM fusionieren - **2.** COM-
PUT mischen ⬦ *vi* - **1.** COMM: **to ~ (with)** fusionieren (mit) - **2.** [roads, lines] zusammenl-
laufen - **3.** [blend] ineinander über|gehen; **to
~ into the landscape/background** mit der
Landschaft/dem Hintergrund verschmelzen ⬦ *n* COMPUT: **to do a ~** Dateien mischen.

**merger** ['mɜːdʒəʳ] *n* COMM Fusion *die*.

**meridian** [mə'rɪdɪən] *n* GEOGR Meridian *der*.

**meringue** [mə'ræŋ] *n* Baiser *das*.

**merino** [mə'riːnəʊ] *adj* Merino-.

**merit** ['merɪt] *n (U)* [value] Wert *der;* **she was
chosen for the post on ~** sie bekam die Stelle
aufgrund ihrer guten Leistungen ⬦ *vt*
verdienen.

➣ **merits** *npl* Vorteile *pl*, Vorzüge *pl;* **to judge**

**M**

**sth**g **on its ~s** etw nach seinen Vorzügen OR Vorteilen beurteilen.

**meritocracy** [ˌmerɪ'tɒkrəsɪ] (pl -ies) n Leistungsgesellschaft die.

**mermaid** ['mɜːmeɪd] n Meerjungfrau die.

**merrily** ['merɪlɪ] adv - **1.** iron [unwittingly, blithely] vergnügt, munter - **2.** literary [laugh, twinkle] vergnügt.

**merriment** ['merɪmənt] n (U) literary [laughter] Gelächter das.

**merry** ['merɪ] (compar -ier; superl -iest) adj - **1.** literary [laugh, joke, person] lustig - **2.** [party] fröhlich, munter; **Merry Christmas!** frohe OR fröhliche Weihnachten! - **3.** inf [tipsy] angeheitert, beschwipst.

**merry-go-round** n Karussell das.

**merrymaking** ['merɪˌmeɪkɪŋ] n (U) literary Feiern das.

**mesh** [meʃ] n (U) [netting]: **(wire) ~** Maschendraht der <> vi [gears] ineinander greifen; [ideas] sich vereinbaren lassen.

**mesmerize, -ise** ['mezməraɪz] vt: **to be ~d by sb/sth**g fasziniert OR gebannt sein von jm/etw.

**mess** [mes] n - **1.** [untidy state] Durcheinander das, Unordnung die; **to be (in) a ~** unordentlich sein, durcheinander sein - **2.** [sth spilt, knocked over] Schweinerei die - **3.** [muddle] Durcheinander das; [problematic situation] Schlamassel der - **4.** MIL Messe die.

◆ **mess about, mess around** inf vt sep an der Nase herumlführen <> vi - **1.** [fool around, waste time] herumlgammeln - **2.** [interfere]: **to ~ about with** [machine] herumlbasteln an (+ D); [sb's papers] durcheinander bringen.

◆ **mess up** vt sep inf - **1.** [make dirty] verdrecken, schmutzig machen; [make untidy] in Unordnung bringen - **2.** [plan, evening] verderben, ruinieren.

◆ **mess with** vt fus inf: **to ~ with sb** sich mit jm einllassen OR ablgeben.

**message** ['mesɪdʒ] n - **1.** [piece of information] Nachricht die; **I get the ~** inf ich kapiere - **2.** [idea, moral] Botschaft die.

**message switching** [-ˌswɪtʃɪŋ] n (U) COMPUT Speichervermittlung die.

**messenger** ['mesɪndʒəʳ] n Bote der; **by ~** per Bote.

**Messiah** [mɪ'saɪə] n: **the ~** der Messias.

**Messrs, Messrs.** ['mesəz] (abbr of **messieurs**): **~ Wilson and Williams** die Herren Wilson und Williams.

**messy** ['mesɪ] (compar -ier; superl -iest) adj - **1.** [untidy] unordentlich; [dirty] dreckig - **2.** inf [complicated, confused] kompliziert.

**met** [met] pt & pp ▷ **meet.**

**Met** [met] (abbr of **Metropolitan Opera**) n: **the ~** die Met.

**metabolism** [mɪ'tæbəlɪzm] n BIOL Stoffwechsel der, Metabolismus der.

**metal** ['metl] n Metall das <> adj Metall-, metallen.

**metallic** [mɪ'tælɪk] adj - **1.** [sound] metallisch - **2.** [shiny]: **~ paint** Metalliclackierung die; **~ blue** metallicblau - **3.** TECH [ore, alloy] Metall-.

**metallurgist** [me'tælədʒɪst] n Metallurg der, -in die.

**metallurgy** [me'tælədʒɪ] n Metallurgie die.

**metalwork** ['metəlwɜːk] n (U) [craft] Metallarbeit die.

**metalworker** ['metəlˌwɜːkəʳ] n Metallarbeiter der, -in die.

**metamorphose** [ˌmetə'mɔːfəuz] vi: **to ~ (into sth**g) sich verwandeln OR umlwandeln (in etw (A)).

**metamorphosis** [ˌmetə'mɔːfəsɪs, ˌmetəmɔː'fəusɪs] (pl -phoses [-'fəusɪːz]) n Metamorphose die.

**metaphor** ['metəfəʳ] n - **1.** [symbolism, imagery] Metaphorik die - **2.** [symbol, image] Metapher die.

**metaphorical** [ˌmetə'fɒrɪkl] adj metaphorisch.

**metaphysical** [ˌmetə'fɪzɪkl] adj metaphysisch.

**metaphysics** [ˌmetə'fɪzɪks] n (U) Metaphysik die.

**mete** [miːt] ◆ **mete out** vt sep: **to ~ sth**g **out to sb** jm etw zulmessen.

**meteor** ['miːtɪəʳ] n Meteor der.

**meteoric** [miːtɪ'ɒrɪk] adj [rapid] kometenhaft.

**meteorite** ['miːtɪəraɪt] n Meteorit der.

**meteorological** [ˌmiːtɪərə'lɒdʒɪkl] adj meteorologisch, Wetter-.

**meteorologist** [miːtɪə'rɒlədʒɪst] n Meteorologe der, -gin die.

**meteorology** [miːtɪə'rɒlədʒɪ] n Meteorologie die.

**meter** ['miːtəʳ] n - **1.** [device - for gas, electricity] Zähler der; [- in taxi] Uhr die; [- for parking] Parkuhr die - **2.** Am = **metre** <> vt messen.

**methadone** ['meθədəun] n Methadon das.

**methane** ['miːθeɪn] n Methan das.

**method** ['meθəd] n Methode die.

**methodical** [mɪ'θɒdɪkl] adj methodisch.

**methodically** [mɪ'θɒdɪklɪ] adv methodisch.

**Methodist** ['meθədɪst] adj Methodisten- <> n Methodist der, -in die.

**methodology** [ˌmeθə'dɒlədʒɪ] (pl -ies) n fml Methodologie die.

**meths** [meθs] n (U) Br inf Brennspiritus der.

**methylated spirits** [ˌmeθɪleɪtɪd-] n (U) Brennspiritus der.

**meticulous** [mɪ'tɪkjʊləs] adj genau, sorgfältig.

**meticulously** [mɪ'tɪkjʊləslɪ] adv sorgfältig.

**Met Office** (abbr of **Meteorological Office**) n britischer Wetterdienst.

**metre** Br, **meter** Am ['miːtəʳ] n - **1.** [unit of measurement] Meter der - **2.** [in poetry] Versmaß das.

**metric** ['metrɪk] adj metrisch.

**metrication** [ˌmetrɪ'keɪʃn] n (U) Br Übergang der zum Dezimalsystem.

**metric system** n: the ~ das metrische System.

**metric ton** n metrische Tonne.

**metro** ['metrəʊ] (pl -s) n U-Bahn die.

**metronome** ['metrənəʊm] n Metronom das.

**metropolis** [mɪ'trɒpəlɪs] (pl -es) n [large city] Metropole die.

**metropolitan** [ˌmetrə'pɒlɪtn] adj Stadt-.

**Metropolitan Police** npl: the ~ die Stadtpolizei von London.

**mettle** ['metl] n (U): to be on one's ~ sein Bestes geben; to show one's ~ zeigen, was man kann.

**mew** [mjuː] n & vi = miaow.

**mews** [mjuːz] (pl inv) n Br [stables] Stallungen pl; [street] Gasse mit ehemaligen Stallungen.

**Mexican** ['meksɪkn] adj mexikanisch ◇ n Mexikaner der, -in die.

**Mexico** ['meksɪkəʊ] n Mexiko nt

**mezzanine** ['metsəniːn] n - **1.** [floor] Mezzanin das, Zwischengeschoss das - **2.** Am [in theatre] Balkon der.

**mfr** abbr of **manufacturer.**

**mg** (abbr of **milligram**) mg.

**MHz** (abbr of **megahertz**) MHz.

**MI** abk für Michigan, in Postanschrift verwendet.

**MI5** (abbr of **Military Intelligence 5**) n MI5 der, britische Spionageabwehr.

**MI6** (abbr of **Military Intelligence 6**) n MI6 der, britischer Nachrichtendienst.

**MIA** (abbr of **missing in action**) vermißt im Kampf.

**miaow** Br [miː'aʊ], **meow** Am [mɪ'aʊ] n Miau das ◇ vi miauen.

**mice** [maɪs] pl ▷ **mouse.**

**Mich.** abk für Michigan, in Postanschrift verwendet.

**mickey** ['mɪkɪ] n: to take the ~ out of sb Br inf jn auf den Arm nehmen.

**micro-** ['maɪkrəʊ] prefix [in noun] Mikro-; [in adjective] mikro-.

**microbe** ['maɪkrəʊb] n Mikrobe die.

**microbiologist** [ˌmaɪkrəʊbaɪ'ɒlədʒɪst] n Mikrobiologe der, -gin die.

**microbiology** [ˌmaɪkrəʊbaɪ'ɒlədʒɪ] n Mikrobiologie die.

**microchip** ['maɪkrəʊtʃɪp] n Mikrochip der.

**microcircuit** ['maɪkrəʊˌsɜːkɪt] n Mikroschaltkreis der.

**microclimate** ['maɪkrəʊˌklaɪmət] n Mikroklima das.

**microcomputer** [ˌmaɪkrəʊkəm'pjuːtəʳ] n Mikrocomputer der.

**microcosm** ['maɪkrəkɒzm] n Mikrokosmos der.

**microfiche** ['maɪkrəʊfiːʃ] (pl inv OR -s) n Mikrofiche der OR das.

**microfilm** ['maɪkrəʊfɪlm] n Mikrofilm der.

**microlight** ['maɪkrəlaɪt] n Ultraleichtflugzeug das.

**micron** ['maɪkrɒn] n Mikron das.

**microorganism** [ˌmaɪkrəʊ'ɔːgənɪzm] n Mikroorganismus der.

**microphone** ['maɪkrəfəʊn] n Mikrofon das.

**microprocessor** [ˌmaɪkrəʊ'prəʊsesəʳ] n Mikroprozessor der.

**microscope** ['maɪkrəskəʊp] n Mikroskop das.

**microscopic** [ˌmaɪkrə'skɒpɪk] adj - **1.** [very small] mikroskopisch - **2.** [detailed] detailliert.

**microsecond** ['maɪkrəʊˌsekənd] n Mikrosekunde die.

**microsurgery** [ˌmaɪkrə'sɜːdʒərɪ] n Mikrochirurgie die.

**microwave (oven)** [ˌmaɪkrəweɪv-] n Mikrowellenherd der.

**mid-** [mɪd] prefix: in ~June Mitte Juni; a ~morning snack ein zweites Frühstück; he is in his ~fifties er ist Mitte fünfzig; in the ~20th century Mitte des 20. Jahrhunderts.

**midair** [ˌmɪd'eəʳ] adj: ~ collision Zusammenstoß in der Luft ◇ n. in ~ in der Luft.

**midday** [ˌmɪd'deɪ] n Mittag der; at ~ mittags.

**middle** ['mɪdl] adj - **1.** [central] Mittel-, mittlere, -r, -s - **2.** [in time]: he's in his ~ forties er ist Mitte vierzig ◇ n - **1.** [gen] Mitte die; in the ~ (of sthg) in der Mitte (von etw); in the ~ of nowhere am Ende der Welt; in the ~ of the night mitten in der Nacht; to be in the ~ of doing sthg gerade dabei sein, etw zu tun - **2.** [waist] Taille die.

**middle age** n mittleres Alter.

**middle-aged** [-'eɪdʒd] adj im mittleren Alter, mittleren Alters.

**Middle Ages** npl: the ~ das Mittelalter.

**middle-class** adj Mittelklasse-.

**middle classes** npl: the ~ die Mittelklasse.

M

**middle distance** n: in the ~ in mittlerer Entfernung.

**Middle East** n: the ~ der Nahe Osten.

**Middle Eastern** adj nahöstlich.

**middle finger** n Mittelfinger der.

**middleman** ['mɪdlmæn] (pl -men [-menl]) n - **1.** COMM Zwischenhändler der - **2.** [in negotiations] Vermittler der.

**middle management** n (U) mittleres Management.

**middle name** n zweiter Vorname.

**middle-of-the-road** adj - **1.** [politics] gemäßigt - **2.** [music, tastes] herkömmlich.

**middle school** n Br Schule für Kinder im Alter zwischen 8 und 12 Jahren.

**middleweight** ['mɪdlweɪt] n [boxer] Mittelgewicht das, Mittelgewichtler der.

**middling** ['mɪdlɪŋ] adj mittelmäßig; **how are you? - oh, ~** wie gehts? - so einigermaßen.

**midfield** [mɪd'fiːld] n FTBL Mittelfeld das.

**midge** [mɪdʒ] n Mücke die.

**midget** ['mɪdʒɪt] n Zwerg der.

**Midlands** ['mɪdləndz] npl: the ~ Region im Zentrum von England.

**midnight** ['mɪdnaɪt] n Mitternacht die; at ~ um Mitternacht <> comp Mitternachts-.

**midriff** ['mɪdrɪf] n Bauch der.

**midst** [mɪdst] n: in the ~ of mitten in (+ D); to be in the ~ of doing sthg gerade dabei sein, etw zu tun; in our ~ in unserer Mitte.

**midstream** [mɪd'striːm] n [of river]: in ~ in der Mitte des Flusses OR Stromes; [when talking] mitten im Redefluss.

**midsummer** ['mɪdˌsʌmər] n (U) Hochsommer der.

**Midsummer Day** n Johannistag der.

**midway** [mɪd'weɪ] adv - **1.** [in space]: ~ (between) auf halbem Wege (zwischen) - **2.** [in time] in der Mitte; ~ through mitten in (+ D).

**midweek** [adj 'mɪdwiːk, adv ˌmɪd'wiːk] adj: a ~ meeting/match ein Mitte der Woche stattfindendes Treffen/Spiel <> adv Mitte der Woche.

**Midwest** [mɪd'west] n: the ~ der Mittelwesten (von Amerika).

**midwife** ['mɪdwaɪf] (pl -wives [-waɪvz]) n Hebamme die.

**midwifery** ['mɪdˌwɪfərɪ] n Geburtshilfe die.

**miffed** [mɪft] adj inf eingeschnappt.

**might** [maɪt] modal vb - **1.** [expressing possibility] können; **they ~ still come** sie könnten noch kommen; **they ~ have been killed** sie sind vielleicht umgekommen - **2.** [expressing suggestion]: **you ~ have told me!** das hättest du mir doch sagen können!; **it ~ be better to**

**wait** sie sollten vielleicht lieber warten - **3.** fml [asking permission]: ~ **I have a few words?** könnte ich Sie mal sprechen?; **he asked if he** ~ **leave the room** er fragte, ob er das Zimmer verlassen dürfte - **4.** [when conceding a point]: **it** ~ **be expensive, but it's good quality** es ist zwar teuer, aber es ist eine gute Qualität - **5.** [would]: **I'd hoped you** ~ **come too** ich hatte gehofft, du würdest auch mitkommen - **6.** phr: **I** ~ **have known** OR **guessed** das hätte ich eigentlich wissen/mir eigentlich denken können <> n (U) Macht die; **with all one's** ~ mit aller Macht/Kraft.

**mightn't** ['maɪtənt] = might not.

**might've** ['maɪtəv] = might have.

**mighty** ['maɪtɪ] (compar -ier; superl -iest) adj - **1.** [powerful] mächtig - **2.** [very large] gewaltig <> adv Am inf mächtig.

**migraine** ['miːgreɪn, 'maɪgreɪn] n Migräne die.

**migrant** ['maɪgrənt] adj - **1.** [bird] Zug- - **2.** [worker] Wander- <> n - **1.** [bird] Zugvogel der - **2.** [worker] Wanderarbeiter der, -in die.

**migrate** [Br maɪ'greɪt, Am 'maɪgreɪt] vi - **1.** [bird] in den Süden ziehen - **2.** [person] abwandern.

**migration** [maɪ'greɪʃn] n - **1.** [of birds] Zug der - **2.** [of people] Abwanderung die.

**migratory** ['maɪgrətrɪ] adj [bird] Zug-.

**mike** [maɪk] (abbr of **microphone**) n inf Mikro das.

**Milan** [mɪ'læn] n Mailand nt.

**Milanese** [ˌmɪlə'niːz] n Mailänder der, -in die.

**mild** [maɪld] adj - **1.** [gen] mild; [sedative, illness] leicht - **2.** [person, manner] sanft <> n leichtes, dunkles Bier.

**mildew** ['mɪldjuː] n [on books, walls] Schimmel der.

**mildly** ['maɪldlɪ] adv milde; **to put it** ~ gelinde gesagt.

**mild-mannered** adj sanftmütig.

**mildness** ['maɪldnɪs] n (U) - **1.** [gen] Milde die - **2.** [of person, manner] Sanftheit die, Sanftmütigkeit die.

**mile** [maɪl] n Meile die; **for ~s** meilenweit; **to be ~s away** [distracted] (mit seinen Gedanken) ganz woanders sein.

➤ **miles** adv (in comparisons) weit; ~**s better** weit besser.

**mileage** ['maɪlɪdʒ] n - **1.** [recorded] Meilenzahl die, Meilenstand der; **unlimited** ~ [allowed on hire car] unbegrenzte Kilometerzahl; **what is your weekly** ~? wie viele Kilometer fahren Sie pro Woche? - **2.** (U) inf [advantage] Vorteil der.

**mileage allowance** n ≃ Kilometerpauschale die.

**mileometer** [maɪˈlɒmɪtəʳ] *n* ≃ Kilometer-zähler *der*.

**milestone** [ˈmaɪlstəʊn] *n lit* & *fig* Meilenstein *der*.

**milieu** [*Br* ˈmiːljɜː, *Am* miːlˈjuː] (*pl* -s *OR* -x [*Br* -jɜː *OR* -jɜːz, *Am* -ˈjuː *OR* -ˈjuːz]) *n* Milieu *das*.

**militant** [ˈmɪlɪtənt] *adj* militant ◇ *n* militanter Student/Arbeiter/*etc*.

**militarism** [ˈmɪlɪtərɪzm] *n* Militarismus *der*.

**militarist** [ˈmɪlɪtərɪst] *n* Militarist *der*, -in *die*.

**militarized zone, militarised zone** [ˈmɪlɪtəraɪzd-] *n* militarisierte Zone.

**military** [ˈmɪlɪtrɪ] *adj* Militär-, militärisch ◇ *n*: the ~ das Militär.

**military police** *npl* Militärpolizei *die*.

**militate** [ˈmɪlɪteɪt] *vi fml*: to ~ against sthg gegen etw wirken.

**militia** [mɪˈlɪʃə] *n* Miliz *die*.

**milk** [mɪlk] *n* Milch *die* ◇ *vt* - **1**. [cow, goat] melken - **2**. [company] schröpfen; *fig* [situation, scandal] ausInutzen.

**milk chocolate** *n* Milchschokolade *die* ◇ *comp* Milchschokoladen-.

**milk float** *Br*, **milk truck** *Am n* elektrischer Milchwagen.

**milking** [ˈmɪlkɪŋ] *n* Melken *das*.

**milkman** [ˈmɪlkmən] (*pl* -men [-mən]) *n* Milchmann *der*.

**milk round** *n Br* - **1**. [by milkman] *Runde des Milchmanns* - **2**. UNIV [recruitment drive] *Reihe von Besuchen, die große Firmen alljährlich den Universitäten abstatten, um potentielle Arbeitskräfte zu finden.*

**milk shake** *n* Milchshake *der*.

**milk tooth** *n* Milchzahn *der*.

**milk truck** *n Am* = milk float.

**milky** [ˈmɪlkɪ] (*compar* -ier; *superl* -iest) *adj* - **1**. *Br* [coffee] Milch-, mit Milch; [tea] mit Milch - **2**. [complexion] milchig.

**Milky Way** *n*: the ~ die Milchstraße.

**mill** [mɪl] *n* - **1**. [flour mill, grinder] Mühle *die* - **2**. [cloth factory] Weberei *die* ◇ *vt* [grain] mahlen.

➤ **mill about, mill around** *vi* umherlaufen.

**millennium** [mɪˈlenɪəm] (*pl* -nnia [-nɪə]) *n* Millennium *das*; the ~ bug das Jahr-2000-Computerproblem.

**miller** [ˈmɪləʳ] *n* Müller *der*.

**millet** [ˈmɪlɪt] *n* (U) Hirse *die*.

**milli-** [ˈmɪlɪ] *prefix* Milli-.

**millibar** [ˈmɪlɪbɑːʳ] *n* Millibar *das*.

**milligram(me)** [ˈmɪlɪgræm] *n* Milligramm *das*.

**millilitre** *Br*, **milliliter** *Am* [ˈmɪlɪˌliːtəʳ] *n* Milliliter *der*.

**millimetre** *Br*, **millimeter** *Am* [ˈmɪlɪˌmiːtəʳ] *n* Millimeter *der*.

**millinery** [ˈmɪlɪnrɪ] *n* (U) Damenhüte *pl*.

**million** [ˈmɪljən] *n* - **1**. [1,000,000] Million *die* - **2**. [enormous number]: a ~, ~s of zig, tausende von.

**millionaire** [ˌmɪljəˈneəʳ] *n* Millionär *der*, -in *die*.

**millionairess** [ˌmɪljəˈneərɪs] *n* Millionärin *die*.

**millipede** [ˈmɪlɪpiːd] *n* Tausendfüßler *der*.

**millisecond** [ˈmɪlɪˌsekənd] *n* Millisekunde *die*.

**millstone** [ˈmɪlstəʊn] *n* [for grinding] Mühlstein *der*; he's (like) a ~ round my neck *fig* er hängt mir wie ein Klotz am Bein.

**millwheel** [ˈmɪlwiːl] *n* Mühlrad *das*.

**milometer** [maɪˈlɒmɪtəʳ] *n* = mileometer.

**mime** [maɪm] *n* - **1**. [acting, act] Pantomime *die* - **2**. [actor]: ~ (artist) Pantomime *der*, -min *die* ◇ *vt* mimen.

**mimic** [ˈmɪmɪk] (*pt* & *pp* -ked; *cont* -king) *n* Imitator *der*, -in *die* ◇ *vt* nachlahmen.

**mimicry** [ˈmɪmɪkrɪ] *n* (U) Nachahmung *die*.

**mimosa** [mɪˈməʊzə] *n* Mimose *die*.

**min.** - **1**. *abbr of* minute - **2**. *abbr of* minimum.

**Min.** (*abbr of* ministry) Min.

**mince** [mɪns] *n* (U) *Br* Hackfleisch *das* ◇ *vt* - **1**. [meat] durchIdrehen - **2.**: not to ~ one's words kein Blatt vor den Mund nehmen ◇ *vi* [walk] trippeln.

**mincemeat** [ˈmɪnsmiːt] *n* (U) - **1**. [fruit] *Mischung aus Äpfeln, Rosinen, Fett und Gewürzen, die im Teigmantel gebacken wird* - **2**. *Am* [minced meat] Hackfleisch *das*.

**mince pie** *n* mit Mincemeat gefüllte Pastete.

**mincer** [ˈmɪnsəʳ] *n* Fleischwolf *der*.

**mind** [maɪnd] *n* - **1**. [reason] Verstand *der*; to be out of one's ~ nicht bei Sinnen *OR* verrückt sein; no one in their right ~ would do that kein vernünftiger Mensch würde das tun; state of ~ Geisteszustand *der* - **2**. [thoughts] Gedanken *pl*; I can't get her out of my ~ sie geht mir nicht aus dem Kopf; to come into/cross sb's ~ jm in den Sinn kommen; to have sthg on one's ~ etw auf dem Herzen haben; to take sb's ~ off sthg jn von etw abIlenken; to take a load *OR* weight off one's ~ eine Last von den Schultern nehmen; to put *OR* set sb's ~ at rest jn beruhigen - **3**. [intellect] Geist *der*; to broaden one's ~ seinen geistigen Horizont erweitern - **4**. [attention]: to keep one's ~ on sthg sich auf etw (A) konzentrieren; if you put your ~ to it wenn du dich anstrengst; to slip one's ~ jm entfallen - **5**. [opinion]: to my ~ meiner Ansicht *OR* Meinung nach; to change one's ~ seine Meinung ändern; to keep an open ~ sich nicht festllegen; **to make one's ~ up** sich entschließen; **to speak one's ~** seine Meinung frei äußern; **to be in two ~s about sthg** hinsichtlich einer Sache *(G)* unentschlossen sein - **6.** [memory] Gedächtnis *das;* **to bear sthg in ~** etw nicht vergessen; **to call sthg to ~** sich an etw *(A)* erinnern; **to cast one's ~ back** zurückldenken - **7.** [intention]: **to have sthg in ~** an etw *(A)* denken; **to have a ~ to do sthg** die Absicht haben, etw zu tun - **8.** [intelligent person, thinker] Geist *der;* **he is one of the greatest ~s of the 19th century** er ist einer der größten Köpfe des 19. Jahrhunderts ◇ *vi* - **1.** [object]: **I don't ~** ich habe nichts dagegen; **do you ~ if ...?** macht es Ihnen etwas aus, wenn ...?, stört es Sie, wenn ...? - **2.** [care, worry]: **I don't ~ if ...** es macht mir nichts aus, wenn ...; **never ~** [don't worry] mach dir nichts draus; [it's not important] es macht nichts - **3.** [be careful]: **~ out!** *Br* pass auf! ◇ *vt* - **1.** [object to]: **I don't ~ it/him** ich habe nichts dagegen/gegen ihn; **do you ~ waiting?** macht es dir etwas aus, zu warten?; **I wouldn't ~ a beer** ich hätte nichts gegen ein Bier - **2.** [bother about]: **I don't ~ what he says** es ist mir gleichgültig, was er sagt - **3.** [pay attention to] achten auf *(+ A)* - **4.** [take care of] sich kümmern um.

◆ **mind you** *adv* allerdings.

**minder** ['maɪndə'] *n* - **1.** [of child] Kindermädchen *das*, Babysitter *der* - **2.** *Br* [bodyguard] Leibwächter *der*, -in *die*.

**mindful** ['maɪndfʊl] *adj:* **to be ~ of sthg** sich *(D)* einer Sache *(G)* bewusst sein.

**mindless** ['maɪndlɪs] *adj* - **1.** [stupid] sinnlos - **2.** [not requiring thought] geistlos, anspruchslos.

**mind reader** *n* Gedankenleser *der*, -in *die;* **I'm not a ~!** ich kann keine Gedanken lesen!

**mindset** ['maɪndset] *n* Einstellung *die*.

**mind's eye** *n:* **in one's ~** vor seinem geistigen Auge.

**mine¹** [maɪn] *n* - **1.** [for excavating minerals] Bergwerk *das;* [for gold, diamond] Mine *die* - **2.** [bomb] Mine *die* - **3.** [source]: **a ~ of information** eine unerschöpfliche Informationsquelle ◇ *vt* - **1.** [coal, gold] fördern, ablbauen - **2.** [lay mines in] verminen.

**mine²** [maɪn] *poss pron* meine, -r, -s; **it's ~** es gehört mir; **a friend of ~** ein Freund von mir; **she ate her portion and ~** sie aß ihre Portion und meine.

**mine detector** *n* Minensuchgerät *das*.

**minefield** ['maɪnfiːld] *n lit* & *fig* Minenfeld *das*.

**minelayer** ['maɪn,leɪə'] *n* Minenleger *der*.

**miner** ['maɪnə'] *n* Bergarbeiter *der*, -in *die*.

**mineral** ['mɪnərəl] GEOL *adj* mineralisch ◇ *n* Mineral *das*.

**mineralogy** [,mɪnə'rælədʒɪ] *n* Mineralogie *die*.

**mineral water** *n (U)* Mineralwasser *das*.

**minestrone** [,mɪnɪ'strəʊnɪ] *n (U)* Minestrone *die*.

**minesweeper** ['maɪn,swiːpə'] *n* Minensuchboot *das*.

**mingle** ['mɪŋgl] *vt:* **to ~ sthg with sthg** etw mit etw vermischen ◇ *vi* - **1.** [combine] **to ~ (with)** sich mischen (mit) - **2.** [at party]: **to ~ (with the guests)** sich unter die Gäste mischen.

**mini** ['mɪnɪ] *n* [skirt] Minirock *der;* [dress] Minikleid *das*.

**miniature** ['mɪnətʃə'] *adj* Miniatur- ◇ *n* - **1.** [painting] Miniatur *die* - **2.** [of alcohol] Miniflasche *die* - **3.** [small scale]: **in ~** im Kleinen, Miniatur-.

**minibus** ['mɪnɪbʌs] *(pl* -es*) n* Kleinbus *der*.

**minicab** ['mɪnɪkæb] *n Br* Kleintaxi *das*.

**minicomputer** [,mɪnɪkəm'pjuːtə'] *n* Minicomputer *der*.

**minim** ['mɪnɪm] *n* MUS halbe Note.

**minima** ['mɪnɪmə] *pl* ▷ **minimum**.

**minimal** ['mɪnɪml] *adj* minimal.

**minimize, -ise** ['mɪnɪmaɪz] *vt* [reduce] minimieren, reduzieren.

**minimum** ['mɪnɪməm] *(pl* -mums *OR* -ma*) adj* Mindest- ◇ *n* Minimum *das*.

**minimum wage** *n* Mindestlohn *der*.

**mining** ['maɪnɪŋ] *n* Bergbau *der* ◇ *adj* Bergbau-; [accident] Gruben-.

**minion** ['mɪnjən] *n hum OR pej* Untergebene *der*, *die*.

**miniseries** ['mɪnɪ,sɪəriːz] *(pl inv) n* Miniserie *die*.

**miniskirt** ['mɪnɪskɜːt] *n* Minirock *der*.

**minister** ['mɪnɪstə'] *n* - **1.** POL: **(of** *OR* **for sthg)** Minister *der*, -in *die* (für etw) - **2.** RELIG Pastor *der*, -in *die*.

◆ **minister to** *vt fus* sich kümmern um; **to ~ to sb's needs** js Bedürfnisse befriedigen.

**ministerial** [,mɪnɪ'stɪərɪəl] *adj* POL Ministerial-, ministerial.

**minister of state** *n:* **~ (for sthg)** Staatsminister *der*, -in *die* (für etw).

**ministry** ['mɪnɪstrɪ] *(pl* -ies*) n* - **1.** POL Ministerium *das;* **Ministry of Defence** Verteidigungsministerium *das* - **2.** RELIG: **the ~** das geistliche Amt.

**mink** [mɪŋk] *(pl inv) n* [fur, animal] Nerz *der*.

**mink coat** *n* Nerzmantel *der*.

**minnow** ['mɪnəʊ] *n* [fish] Elritze *die*.

**minor** ['maɪnə'] *adj* - **1.** [unimportant] unbedeutend, klein(er) - **2.** MUS [key] Moll-; **in B ~** in H-Moll <> n [in age] Minderjährige der, die.

**Minorca** [mɪ'nɔːkə] n Menorca nt.

**minority** [maɪ'nɒrətɪ] (pl **-ies**) n Minderheit die; **to be in a** OR **the ~** in der Minderheit sein.

**minority government** n Minderheitsregierung die.

**minor road** n Nebenstraße die.

**minster** ['mɪnstəʳ] n Münster das.

**minstrel** ['mɪnstrəl] n Spielmann der.

**mint** [mɪnt] n - **1.** (U) [herb] Minze die - **2.** [sweet] Pfefferminzbonbon das - **3.** [for coins]: **the Mint** die Münze; **in ~ condition** in neuwertigem OR tadellosem Zustand <> vt [coins] prägen.

**mint sauce** n (U) Mintsoße die.

**minuet** [ˌmɪnjʊ'et] n Menuett das.

**minus** ['maɪnəs] (pl **-es**) prep - **1.** MATH minus, weniger - **2.** [in temperatures] minus <> adj - **1.** MATH negativ - **2.** SCH [in grades] minus <> n - **1.** MATH Minus das - **2.** [disadvantage] Nachteil der.

**minuscule** ['mɪnəskjuːl] adj winzig.

**minus sign** n Minuszeichen das.

**minute¹** [mɪnɪt] n - **1.** [period of 60 seconds] Minute die - **2.** [moment] Moment der, Augenblick der; **at any ~** jederzeit; **at the last ~** in letzter Minute; **this ~** sofort, auf der Stelle; **up to the ~** allerneueste, -r, -s; **wait a ~!** Moment mal!

↪ **minutes** npl [of meeting] Protokoll das.

**minute²** [maɪ'njuːt] adj [tiny] winzig.

**minutiae** [maɪ'njuːʃɪaɪ] npl genaue Einzelheiten pl.

**miracle** ['mɪrəkl] n Wunder das.

**miraculous** [mɪ'rækjʊləs] adj - **1.** RELIG wundersam - **2.** fig [recovery, escape] wunderbar.

**miraculously** [mɪ'rækjʊləslɪ] adv: **~, no one was hurt** wie durch ein Wunder wurde niemand verletzt.

**mirage** [mɪ'rɑːʒ] n - **1.** [in desert] Fata Morgana die - **2.** fig [unrealizable hope] Illusion die.

**mire** [maɪəʳ] n Morast der, Schlamm der.

**mirror** ['mɪrəʳ] n Spiegel der <> vt - **1.** [copy] widerlspiegeln - **2.** literary [reflect] spiegeln.

**mirror image** n Spiegelbild das.

**mirth** [mɜːθ] n Heiterkeit die.

**misadventure** [ˌmɪsəd'ventʃəʳ] n [unfortunate accident] Missgeschick das; **death by ~** LAW Tod durch Unglücksfall.

**misanthropist** [mɪ'sænθrəpɪst] n Menschenfeind der, -in die.

**misapplication** [ˌmɪsæplɪ'keɪʃn] n falsche Anwendung.

**misapprehension** [ˌmɪsæprɪ'henʃn] n Missverständnis das; **they were under the ~ that ...**

sie hatten fälschlicherweise angenommen, dass ...

**misappropriate** [ˌmɪsə'prəʊprɪeɪt] vt veruntreuen.

**misappropriation** [ˌmɪsəprəʊprɪ'eɪʃn] n Veruntreuung die.

**misbehave** [ˌmɪsbɪ'heɪv] vi sich schlecht benehmen.

**misbehaviour** Br, **misbehavior** Am [ˌmɪsbɪ'heɪvjəʳ] n schlechtes Benehmen.

**misc** (abbr of **miscellaneous**) Verschiedenes.

**miscalculate** [ˌmɪs'kælkjʊleɪt] vt - **1.** [amount, time, distance] falsch berechnen - **2.** fig [misjudge] falsch einschätzen <> vi - **1.** MATH sich verrechnen - **2.** fig [misjudge] sich verschätzen.

**miscalculation** [ˌmɪskælkjʊ'leɪʃn] n - **1.** (U) MATH Rechenfehler der - **2.** fig [mistake] Fehlkalkulation die, Fehleinschätzung die.

**miscarriage** [ˌmɪs'kærɪdʒ] n Fehlgeburt die.

**miscarriage of justice** n Justizirrtum der.

**miscarry** [ˌmɪs'kærɪ] (pt & pp **-ied**) vi - **1.** [woman] eine Fehlgeburt haben - **2.** [plan] fehlschlagen.

**miscellaneous** [ˌmɪsə'leɪnɪəs] adj verschieden.

**miscellany** [Br mɪ'selənɪ, Am 'mɪsəleɪnɪ] (pl **-ies**) n Sammlung die.

**mischance** [ˌmɪs'tʃɑːns] n: **by ~** durch einen unglücklichen Zufall.

**mischief** ['mɪstʃɪf] n (U) - **1.** [playfulness] Schalkhaftigkeit die - **2.** [naughty behaviour] Unfug der, Unartigkeit die - **3.** [harm] Schaden der.

**mischievous** ['mɪstʃɪvəs] adj - **1.** [playful] schelmisch, verschmitzt - **2.** [naughty] unartig.

**misconceived** [ˌmɪskən'siːvd] adj [plan, idea] falsch aufgefasst.

**misconception** [ˌmɪskən'sepʃn] n falsche Vorstellung, falsche Auffassung.

**misconduct** [ˌmɪs'kɒndʌkt] n [bad behaviour] schlechtes Benehmen.

**misconstrue** [ˌmɪskən'struː] vt fml falsch ausllegen.

**miscount** [ˌmɪs'kaʊnt] vt falsch zählen <> vi sich verzählen.

**misdeed** [ˌmɪs'diːd] n literary Missetat die.

**misdemeanour** Br, **misdemeanor** Am [ˌmɪsdɪ'miːnəʳ] n LAW Vergehen das.

**misdirected** [ˌmɪsdɪ'rektɪd] adj - **1.** [letter] falsch zugestellt - **2.** [efforts, energy] falsch eingesetzt, vergeudet.

**miser** ['maɪzəʳ] n Geizhals der.

**miserable** ['mɪzrəbl] adj - **1.** [person, life] elend; **don't look so ~** guck nicht so jämmerlich

**M**

- **2.** [conditions, pay, weather] miserabel; [evening, holiday] schrecklich - **3.** [failure] kläglich.

**miserably** ['mızrəblı] *adv* - **1.** [die] elend - **2.** [paid] miserabel - **3.** [fail] kläglich.

**miserly** ['maızəlı] *adj* geizig.

**misery** ['mızərı] (*pl* **-ies**) *n* - **1.** [unhappiness] Kummer *der* - **2.** [poverty] Elend *das*, Armut *die* - **3.** [gloomy person] Miesepeter *der*.

**misfire** [,mıs'faıəʳ] *vi* - **1.** [gun, car engine] fehllzünden - **2.** [plan] fehllschlagen.

**misfit** ['mısfıt] *n* Außenseiter *der*, -in *die*.

**misfortune** [mıs'fɔːtʃuːn] *n* - **1.** [bad luck] Pech *das* - **2.** [piece of bad luck] Unglück *das*.

**misgivings** [mıs'gıvıŋz] *npl* Bedenken *pl*.

**misguided** [,mıs'gaıdıd] *adj* [opinion] töricht.

**mishandle** [,mıs'hændl] *vt* - **1.** [person, animal] schlecht behandeln - **2.** [negotiations, business] falsch handhaben.

**mishap** ['mıshæp] *n* - **1.** [accident]: **without ~** ohne Zwischenfall - **2.** [unfortunate event] Missgeschick *das*.

**mishear** [,mıs'hıəʳ] (*pt* & *pp* **-heard** [-'hɜːd]) *vt* falsch hören ◇ *vi* sich verhören.

**mishmash** ['mıʃmæʃ] *n inf* Mischmasch *der*.

**misinform** [,mısın'fɔːm] *vt* falsch informieren *OR* unterrichten.

**misinformation** [,mısınfə'meıʃn] *n* (*U*) falsche Informationen *pl*.

**misinterpret** [,mısın'tɜːprıt] *vt* falsch ausllegen *OR* deuten.

**misjudge** [,mıs'dʒʌdʒ] *vt* - **1.** [calculate wrongly] falsch einlschätzen - **2.** [appraise wrongly] falsch beurteilen.

**misjudg(e)ment** [,mıs'dʒʌdʒmənt] *n* Fehleinschätzung *die;* [of person] falsche Beurteilung.

**mislay** [,mıs'leı] (*pt* & *pp* **-laid** [-'leıd]) *vt* verlegen.

**mislead** [,mıs'liːd] (*pt* & *pp* **-led**) *vt* irrelführen.

**misleading** [,mıs'liːdıŋ] *adj* irreführend.

**misled** [,mıs'led] *pt* & *pp* ⊳ **mislead.**

**mismanage** [,mıs'mænıdʒ] *vt* [affairs] schlecht ablwickeln; [finances, budget] schlecht verwalten; [project] schlecht organisieren.

**mismanagement** [,mıs'mænıdʒmənt] *n* (*U*) Missmanagement *das*.

**mismatch** [,mıs'mætʃ] *vt:* **to be ~ed** [colours, two people] nicht zusammenlpassen.

**misnomer** [,mıs'nəʊməʳ] *n* unzutreffende Bezeichnung.

**misogynist** [mı'sɒdʒınıst] *n* Frauenfeind *der*.

**misplace** [,mıs'pleıs] *vt* verlegen.

**misplaced** [,mıs'pleıst] *adj* [trust, confidence] unangebracht.

**misprint** ['mısprınt] *n* Druckfehler *der*.

**mispronounce** [,mısprə'naʊns] *vt* falsch auslsprechen.

**misquote** [,mıs'kwəʊt] *vt* falsch zitieren.

**misread** [,mıs'riːd] (*pt* & *pp* **-read** [-'red]) *vt* - **1.** [read wrongly] falsch lesen - **2.** [misinterpret] falsch verstehen.

**misrepresent** [,mısreprı'zent] *vt* falsch darlstellen.

**misrepresentation** [,mısreprızen'teıʃn] *n* falsche Darstellung.

**misrule** [,mıs'ruːl] *n* (*U*) [misgovernment] schlechte Regierung.

**miss** [mıs] *vt* - **1.** [person in crowd, film, turning, opportunity, train, flight] verpassen - **2.** [subj: bullet, ball, footballer] verfehlen - **3.** [wife, family, home] vermissen; **I ~ reading English newspapers** ich vermisse es, englische Zeitungen zu lesen - **4.** [meeting, appointment, school] versäumen - **5.** [disaster] entkommen (+ *D*); **I just ~ed being run over** ich wäre beinahe überfahren worden ◇ *vi* [fail to hit] nicht treffen ◇ *n:* **to give sthg a ~** *inf* sich (*D*) etw verkneifen.
◆ **miss out** *vt sep* [omit - by accident] übersehen; [ - deliberately] ausllassen ◇ *vi:* **to ~ out on sthg** etw verpassen.

**Miss** [mıs] *n* Fräulein *nt*.

**misshapen** [,mıs'ʃeıpn] *adj* [hands, fingers, toes] missgebildet; [biscuits, cake] missraten.

**missile** [*Br* 'mısaıl, *Am* 'mısəl] *n* - **1.** [weapon] Rakete *die*, Flugkörper *der* - **2.** [thrown object] Wurfgeschoss *das*.

**missile launcher** [-,lɔːntʃəʳ] *n* Abschussrampe *die*, Startrampe *die*.

**missing** ['mısıŋ] *adj* - **1.** [lost] verschwunden; **~ in action** vermisst; **sixty people are still ~** sechzig Personen werden immer noch vermisst; **to go ~** verschwinden, verloren gehen - **2.** [not present] fehlend; **who's ~?** wer fehlt?

**missing link** *n* fehlendes Glied.

**missing person** *n* Vermisste *der*, *die*.

**mission** ['mıʃn] *n* - **1.** [task, duty] Auftrag *der* - **2.** [delegation] Delegation *die*, Gesandtschaft *die* - **3.** ASTRON & MIL Mission *die* - **4.** [RELIG - building, teaching] Mission *die*.

**missionary** ['mıʃənrı] (*pl* **-ies**) *n* Missionar *der*, -in *die*.

**Mississippi** [,mısı'sıpı] *n* [river]: **the ~** der Mississippi.

**missive** ['mısıv] *n* Schreiben *das*.

**misspell** [,mıs'spel] (*pt* & *pp* **-spelt** *OR* **-spelled**) *vt* falsch schreiben.

**misspelling** [,mıs'spelıŋ] *n:* **to be a ~** falsch geschrieben sein.

**misspelt** [,mıs'spelt] *pt* & *pp* ⊳ **misspell.**

**misspend** [ˌmɪs'spend] (*pt* & *pp* **-spent** [-'spent]) *vt* [money, talent, youth] vergeuden.

**mist** [mɪst] *n* Nebel *der.*

◆ **mist over, mist up** *vi* beschlagen; **her eyes ~ed over** ihre Augen füllten sich mit Tränen.

**mistake** [mɪ'steɪk] (*pt* **-took;** *pp* **-taken**) *n* Fehler *der;* **to make a ~** [in writing, work] einen Fehler machen; [be mistaken] sich irren; **by ~** irrtümlich ⟨> *vt* **- 1.** [misunderstand] falsch verstehen, missverstehen **- 2.** [fail to distinguish]: **to ~ sb/sthg for** jn/etw verwechseln mit.

**mistaken** [mɪ'steɪkn] *pp* ▷ **mistake** ⟨> *adj* **- 1.** [person]: **to be ~** sich irren; **to be ~ about sb/ sthg** sich in jm/etw irren **- 2.** [belief, idea] irrig, falsch.

**mistaken identity** *n:* **a case of ~** eine Personenverwechslung.

**mistakenly** [mɪs'teɪknlɪ] *adv* fälschlicherweise, irrtümlicherweise.

**mister** ['mɪstər] *n inf:* **hey mister!** he, Chef.

**mistime** [ˌmɪs'taɪm] *vt* [shot in tennis] falsch timen; [announcement] den falschen Zeitpunkt wählen für.

**mistletoe** ['mɪsltəʊ] *n (U)* Mistel *die.*

**mistook** [mɪ'stʊk] *pt* ▷ **mistake.**

**mistranslation** [ˌmɪstræns'leɪʃn] *n* falsche Übersetzung.

**mistreat** [ˌmɪs'triːt] *vt* schlecht behandeln.

**mistreatment** [ˌmɪs'triːtmənt] *n (U)* schlechte Behandlung.

**mistress** ['mɪstrɪs] *n* **- 1.** [of house, situation] Herrin *die* **- 2.** [female lover] Geliebte *die* **- 3.** [schoolteacher] Lehrerin *die.*

**mistrial** ['mɪstraɪəl] *n* Prozess *der* mit Verfahrensmängeln.

**mistrust** [ˌmɪs'trʌst] *n* Misstrauen *das* ⟨> *vt* misstrauen (+ *D*).

**mistrustful** [ˌmɪs'trʌstfʊl] *adj* misstrauisch; **to be ~ of sb/sthg** jm/etw gegenüber misstrauisch sein.

**misty** ['mɪstɪ] (*compar* **-ier;** *superl* **-iest**) *adj* neblig.

**misunderstand** [ˌmɪsʌndə'stænd] (*pt* & *pp* **-stood**) *vt* missverstehen ⟨> *vi* falsch verstehen.

**misunderstanding** [ˌmɪsʌndə'stændɪŋ] *n* **- 1.** [lack of understanding, wrong interpretation] Missverständnis *das* **- 2.** [disagreement] Meinungsverschiedenheit *die.*

**misunderstood** [ˌmɪsʌndə'stʊd] *pt* & *pp* ▷ **misunderstand.**

**misuse** [*n* ˌmɪs'juːs, *vb* ˌmɪs'juːz] *n* Missbrauch *der;* [of funds] Zweckentfremdung *die* ⟨> *vt*

**- 1.** [abuse] missbrauchen; [funds] zweckentfremden **- 2.** [waste] vergeuden.

**MIT** (*abbr of* Massachusetts Institute of Technology) *n* MIT *das.*

**mite** [maɪt] *n* **- 1.** [insect] Milbe *die* **- 2.** *inf* [small amount]: **a ~** ein bisschen **- 3.** *inf* [small child] Würmchen *das.*

**miter** *n Am* = **mitre.**

**mitigate** ['mɪtɪgeɪt] *vt fml* lindern.

**mitigating** ['mɪtɪgeɪtɪŋ] *adj fml:* **~ circumstances** mildernde Umstände *pl.*

**mitigation** [ˌmɪtɪ'geɪʃn] *n (U) fml:* **he pleaded in ~ that ...** er sagte zu seiner Verteidigung, dass ...

**mitre** *Br,* **miter** *Am* ['maɪtər] *n* **- 1.** [hat] Mitra *die* **- 2.** [joint]: **~ (joint)** Gehrfuge *die.*

**mitt** [mɪt] *n* **- 1.** = **mitten - 2.** [in baseball] Handschuh *der.*

**mitten** ['mɪtn] *n* Fausthandschuh *der.*

**mix** [mɪks] *vt* **- 1.** [substances] mischen; [activities] miteinander verbinden; **to ~ sthg with sthg** etw mit etw vermischen **- 2.** [drink, song] mixen; [cement] mischen ⟨> *vi* **- 1.** [substances] sich vermischen; **business and pleasure don't ~** Geschäft und Vergnügen gehen nicht zusammen *OR* sollte man trennen **- 2.** [socially]: **to ~ with sb** mit jm verkehren, Umgang pflegen mit jm ⟨> *n* **- 1.** [combination] Mischung *die* **- 2.** *MUS* Mix *der.*

◆ **mix up** *vt sep* **- 1.** [confuse] verwechseln **- 2.** [disorder] durcheinander bringen.

**mixed** [mɪkst] *adj* gemischt.

**mixed-ability** *adj Br:* **a ~ class** *eine Schulklasse, in der Schüler mit unterschiedlichen Fähigkeiten zusammen unterrichtet werden.*

**mixed blessing** *n* zweischneidiges Schwert.

**mixed doubles** *n (U)* gemischtes Doppel.

**mixed economy** *n* gemischte Wirtschaftsform.

**mixed grill** *n* gemischter Grillteller.

**mixed marriage** *n* Mischehe *die.*

**mixed up** *adj* **- 1.** [confused] verwirrt **- 2.** [involved]: **to be ~ in sthg** in etw (*A*) verwickelt sein.

**mixer** ['mɪksər] *n* **- 1.** [device] Mixer *der;* [cement] Mischer *der* **- 2.** [soft drink] *alkoholfreies Getränk, wie z. B. Fruchtsaft, das zum Mischen mit Spirituosen verwendet wird.*

**mixer tap** *n Br* Mischbatterie *die.*

**mixing bowl** ['mɪksɪŋ-] *n* Rührschüssel *die.*

**mixture** ['mɪkstʃər] *n* Mischung *die.*

**mix-up** *n inf* Verwechslung *die.*

**mk, MK** *abbr of* **mark.**

**mkt** *abbr of* **market.**

**M**

**ml** (abbr of **millilitre**) ml.

**MLitt** [em'lɪt] (abbr of **Master of Literature, Master of Letters**) n akademischer Grad in Literaturwissenschaft oder dessen Inhaber.

**MLR** abbr of **minimum lending rate**.

**mm** (abbr of **millimetre**) mm.

**MMR** (abbr of **measles, mumps, rubella**) n Masern, Mumps und Röteln.

**MN** abk für Minnesota, in Postanschrift verwendet.

**mnemonic** [nɪ'mɒnɪk] n Eselsbrücke die, Gedächtnisstütze die.

**m.o.** abbr of **money order**.

**MO** n (abbr of **medical officer**) Amts- oder Betriebsarzt ⬦ abk für Missouri, in Postanschrift verwendet.

**moan** [məʊn] n - **1.** [of pain] Stöhnen das; [of sadness] Seufzer der - **2.** inf [complaint] Gejammer das ⬦ vi - **1.** [in pain] stöhnen; [in sadness] seufzen - **2.** inf [complain] jammern; **to ~ about sb/sthg** jammern OR sich beklagen über jn/etw.

**moaning** ['məʊnɪŋ] n (U) [complaining] Gejammer das.

**moat** [məʊt] n [around castle] Burggraben der; [in zoo] Wassergraben der.

**mob** [mɒb] (pt & pp **-bed**; cont **-bing**) n Mob der ⬦ vt belagern.

**mobile** ['məʊbaɪl] adj - **1.** [able to move] beweglich - **2.** inf [having transport] motorisiert ⬦ n - **1.** [phone] Handy das - **2.** [decoration] Mobile das.

**mobile home** n Wohnmobil das.

**mobile library** n Fahrbücherei die.

**mobile phone** n Mobiltelefon das, Handy das.

**mobile shop** n Verkaufswagen der.

**mobility** [mə'bɪlətɪ] n - **1.** [physical - of person] Beweglichkeit die; [ - of troops] Mobilität die - **2.** [social] Mobilität die.

**mobility allowance** n Br Mobilitätsbeihilfe die.

**mobilization** [ˌməʊbɪlaɪ'zeɪʃn] n - **1.** [of support, workforce] Mobilisierung die - **2.** MIL Mobilmachung die.

**mobilize, -ise** ['məʊbɪlaɪz] vt - **1.** [support, workforce] mobilisieren - **2.** MIL mobil machen ⬦ vi MIL mobil machen.

**moccasin** ['mɒkəsɪn] n Mokassin der.

**mock** [mɒk] adj [surprise] gespielt; [Georgian house] Pseudo-; [exam] Übungs- ⬦ vt [deride] verspotten ⬦ vi sich mokieren.

**mockery** ['mɒkərɪ] n - **1.** [scorn] Spott der - **2.** [travesty] Farce die; **to make a ~ of sthg** etw zur Farce machen.

**mocking** ['mɒkɪŋ] adj spöttisch.

**mockingbird** ['mɒkɪŋbɜːd] n Spottdrossel die.

**mock-up** n Modell in Originalgröße.

**MoD** (abbr of **Ministry of Defence**) n das Verteidigungsministerium.

**mode** [məʊd] n [manner] Art (und Weise) die; **~ of life** Lebensweise die; **~ of transport** Transportmittel das.

**model** ['mɒdl] (Br pt & pp **-led**; cont **-ling**, Am pt & pp **-ed**; cont **-ing**) n - **1.** [gen] Modell das - **2.** [basis for imitation] Vorlage die; [person, society] Vorbild das - **3.** [best example] Musterbeispiel das ⬦ adj - **1.** [miniature] Modell- - **2.** [exemplary] Muster-, musterhaft ⬦ vt - **1.** [shape] modellieren - **2.** [in fashion show] vorführen - **3.** [copy]: **to ~ o.s. on sb** sich (D) jn zum Vorbild nehmen ⬦ vi [in fashion show] als Modell arbeiten, modeln.

**modem** ['məʊdem] n COMPUT Modem das.

**moderate** [adj & n 'mɒdərət, vb 'mɒdəreɪt] adj - **1.** [views, habits] gemäßigt; [demands] bescheiden - **2.** [heat] mäßig; [quantity] angemessen; **of ~ height/size** mittelgroß - **3.** [success, ability] mittelmäßig, bescheiden ⬦ n POL Gemäßigte der, die ⬦ vt mäßigen ⬦ vi sich mäßigen; [views] gemäßigter werden.

**moderately** ['mɒdərətlɪ] adv mäßig; **~ expensive** etwas teuer.

**moderation** [ˌmɒdə'reɪʃn] n Mäßigung die; **in ~** in Maßen.

**moderator** ['mɒdəreɪtər] n [of exam] Prüfungsvorsitzende der, die.

**modern** ['mɒdən] adj modern.

**modern-day** adj modern.

**modernism** ['mɒdənɪzm] n Modernismus der.

**modernization** [ˌmɒdənaɪ'zeɪʃn] n Modernisierung die.

**modernize, -ise** ['mɒdənaɪz] vt & vi modernisieren.

**modern languages** npl neue Sprachen pl, moderne Sprachen pl.

**modest** ['mɒdɪst] adj bescheiden.

**modestly** ['mɒdɪstlɪ] adv bescheiden.

**modesty** ['mɒdɪstɪ] n Bescheidenheit die.

**modicum** ['mɒdɪkəm] n fml: **a ~ of** ein bisschen; **a ~ of truth** ein Körnchen Wahrheit; **a ~ of intelligence** ein Minimum an Intelligenz.

**modification** [ˌmɒdɪfɪ'keɪʃn] n Änderung die.

**modify** ['mɒdɪfaɪ] (pt & pp **-ied**) vt - **1.** [alter] ändern, abländern - **2.** [tone down] mäßigen.

**modular** ['mɒdjʊlər] adj - **1.** [furniture] Baustein- - **2.** SCH & UNIV [course] aus verschiedenen Unterrichtseinheiten bestehend.

**modulated** ['mɒdjʊleɪtɪd] adj [voice] moduliert.

**modulation** [ˌmɒdjʊ'leɪʃn] n RADIO Modulation die.

**module** ['mɒdjuːl] n - 1. [unit] Modul das, Bauteil das; SCH & UNIV zu einem Kurs gehörende Unterrichtseinheit - 2. [of spacecraft] Raumkapsel die.

**moggy** ['mɒgɪ] (pl -ies) n Br inf Mieze die.

**mogul** ['məʊgl] n [magnate] Mogul der.

**mohair** ['məʊheəʳ] n (U) Mohair der ◇ comp Mohair-.

**Mohammedan** [mə'hæmɪdn] adj mohammedanisch ◇ n Mohammedaner der, -in die.

**Mohican** [məʊ'hiːkən, 'məʊɪkən] n [haircut] Irokesenschnitt der.

**moist** [mɔɪst] adj feucht.

**moisten** ['mɔɪsn] vt befeuchten, anfeuchten.

**moisture** ['mɔɪstʃəʳ] n Feuchtigkeit die.

**moisturize, -ise** ['mɔɪstʃəraɪz] vt Feuchtigkeitscreme auftragen auf (+ A).

**moisturizer, -iser** ['mɔɪstʃəraɪzəʳ] n Feuchtigkeitscreme die.

**molar** ['məʊləʳ] n Backenzahn der.

**molasses** [mə'læsɪz] n (U) Melasse die.

**mold** etc n & vt Am = **mould.**

**Moldavia** [mɒl'deɪvɪə] n Moldawien nt.

**mole** [məʊl] n - 1. [animal] Maulwurf der - 2. [on skin] Muttermal das, Leberfleck der - 3. [spy] Spion der.

**molecular** [mə'lekjʊləʳ] adj molekular.

**molecule** ['mɒlɪkjuːl] n Molekül das.

**molehill** ['məʊlhɪl] n Maulwurfshügel der.

**molest** [mə'lest] vt - 1. [attack sexually] sexuell belästigen - 2. [bother] belästigen.

**molester** [mə'lestəʳ] n: child ~ Kinderschänder der, -in die.

**mollify** ['mɒlɪfaɪ] (pt & pp -ied) vt fml besänftigen.

**mollusc, mollusk** Am ['mɒləsk] n Weichtier das.

**mollycoddle** ['mɒlɪˌkɒdl] vt inf verhätscheln, verzärteln.

**Molotov cocktail** [ˌmɒlətɒf-] n Molotowcocktail der.

**molt** vt & vi Am = **moult.**

**molten** ['məʊltn] adj geschmolzen.

**mom** [mɒm] n Am inf Mutter die; [within speaker's family] Mutti die.

**moment** ['məʊmənt] n - 1. [very short period of time] Moment der, Augenblick der; for one ~ einen Moment lang - 2. [particular point in time] Zeitpunkt der; the ~ of truth die Stunde der Wahrheit; at any ~ jeden Moment; at the ~ im Moment; at the last ~ im letzten Moment; for the ~ vorerst - 3. [importance] Bedeutung die.

**momentarily** ['məʊməntərɪlɪ] adv - 1. [for a short time] momentan, für einen Moment - 2. Am [immediately] jeden Moment OR Augenblick.

**momentary** ['məʊməntrɪ] adj kurz.

**momentous** [mə'mentəs] adj bedeutsam, wichtig.

**momentum** [mə'mentəm] n [speed] Schwung der; to gain OR gather ~ [object, campaign] in Fahrt kommen.

**momma** ['mɒmə], **mommy** ['mɒmɪ] n Am Mama die, Mami die.

**Mon.** (abbr of Monday) Mo.

**Monaco** ['mɒnəkəʊ] n Monaco nt.

**monarch** ['mɒnək] n Monarch der, -in die.

**monarchist** ['mɒnəkɪst] n Monarchist der, -in die.

**monarchy** ['mɒnəkɪ] (pl -ies) n Monarchie die.

**monastery** ['mɒnəstrɪ] (pl -ies) n Kloster das.

**monastic** [mə'næstɪk] adj klösterlich.

**Monday** ['mʌndɪ] n Montag der; see also **Saturday.**

**monetarism** ['mʌnɪtərɪzm] n Monetarismus der.

**monetarist** ['mʌnɪtərɪst] n Monetarist der, -in die.

**monetary** ['mʌnɪtrɪ] adj Währungs-.

**money** ['mʌnɪ] n (U) Geld das; to make ~ Geld machen; to get one's ~'s worth etw für sein Geld geboten bekommen.

**moneybox** ['mʌnɪbɒks] n Sparbüchse die.

**moneyed** ['mʌnɪd] adj fml begütert, wohlhabend.

**moneylender** ['mʌnɪˌlendəʳ] n Geld(ver)leiher der, -in die.

**moneymaker** ['mʌnɪˌmeɪkəʳ] n [product] Kassenschlager der.

**moneymaking** ['mʌnɪˌmeɪkɪŋ] adj profitabel, einträglich.

**money market** n Geldmarkt der.

**money order** n Zahlungsanweisung die.

**money-spinner** [-ˌspɪnəʳ] n esp Br inf Kassenschlager der.

**money supply** n Geldvolumen das.

**mongol** ['mɒŋgəl] dated & offensive adj mongoloid ◇ n Mongoloide der, die.
➥ **Mongol** adj & n = **Mongolian.**

**Mongolia** [mɒŋ'gəʊlɪə] n Mongolei die.

**Mongolian** [mɒŋ'gəʊlɪən] adj mongolisch

◇ *n* - **1.** [person] Mongole *der*, -lin *die* - **2.** [language] Mongolisch(e) *das*.

**mongoose** ['mɒŋguːs] (*pl* -**s**) *n* Mungo *der*.

**mongrel** ['mʌŋgrəl] *n* [dog] Mischling *der*.

**monitor** ['mɒnɪtə'] *n* Monitor *der* ◇ *vt* - **1.** [check] überwachen, kontrollieren - **2.** [listen in to] abhören, mithören.

**monk** [mʌŋk] *n* Mönch *der*.

**monkey** ['mʌŋkɪ] (*pl* **monkeys**) *n* [animal] Affe *der*.

**monkey nut** *n* Erdnuss *die*.

**monkey wrench** *n* Engländer *der*.

**monkfish** (*pl inv OR* -**es**) *n* Seeteufel *der*.

**mono** ['mɒnəʊ] *adj* [with noun] Mono-; [with adj] mono- ◇ *n inf* - **1.** [sound] Mono *das* - **2.** *Am* [glandular fever] Drüsenfieber *das*.

**monochrome** ['mɒnəkrəʊm] *adj* monochrom, schwarzweiß.

**monocle** ['mɒnəkl] *n* Monokel *das*.

**monogamous** [mɒ'nɒgəməs] *adj* monogam.

**monogamy** [mɒ'nɒgəmɪ] *n* Monogamie *die*.

**monogrammed** ['mɒnəgræmd] *adj* mit Monogramm (bestickt).

**monolingual** [‚mɒnə'lɪŋgwəl] *adj* einsprachig.

**monolithic** [‚mɒnə'lɪθɪk] *adj* - **1.** *pej* [organization] starr; [building] riesig - **2.** [rock] monolithisch.

**monologue, monolog** *Am* ['mɒnəlɒg] *n* Monolog *der*.

**mononucleosis** ['mɒnəʊ‚njuːklɪ'əʊsɪs] *n Am* Drüsenfieber *das*.

**monoplane** ['mɒnəpleɪn] *n* Eindecker *der*.

**monopolize, -ise** [mə'nɒpəlaɪz] *vt* monopolisieren; [conversation] beherrschen, an sich (*A*) reißen; [person] in Beschlag nehmen.

**monopoly** [mə'nɒpəlɪ] (*pl* -**ies**) *n*: ~ (**on** *OR* **of**) Monopol *das* (auf (+ *A*)); **the Monopolies and Mergers Commission** *Br britisches Kartellamt*.

**monorail** ['mɒnəreɪl] *n* Einschienenbahn *die*.

**monosodium glutamate** [‚mɒnə‚səʊdɪəm-'gluːtəmeɪt] *n* Mononatriumglutamat *das*.

**monosyllabic** [‚mɒnəsɪ'læbɪk] *adj* einsilbig.

**monosyllable** ['mɒnə‚sɪləbl] *n* Einsilber *der*, einsilbiges Wort.

**monotone** ['mɒnətəʊn] *n* monotoner Klang; **he speaks in a** ~ er spricht mit monotoner Stimme.

**monotonous** [mə'nɒtənəs] *adj* monoton.

**monotonously** [mə'nɒtənəslɪ] *adv* monoton.

**monotony** [mə'nɒtənɪ] *n* Monotonie *die*.

**monoxide** [mɒ'nɒksaɪd] *n* Monoxyd *das*.

**Monsignor** [‚mɒn'siːnjə'] *n* Monsignore *der*.

**monsoon** [mɒn'suːn] *n* Monsun *der*.

**monster** ['mɒnstə'] *n* Monster *das* ◇ *adj* Monster-, Riesen-.

**monstrosity** [mɒn'strɒsətɪ] (*pl* -**ies**) *n* Monstrosität *die*, Ungeheuerlichkeit *die*.

**monstrous** ['mɒnstrəs] *adj* - **1.** [appalling] abscheulich - **2.** [hideous] scheußlich - **3.** [very large] riesig.

**montage** ['mɒntɑːʒ] *n* Montage *die*.

**Mont Blanc** [‚mɔ̃'blɑ̃] *n* Montblanc *der*.

**Montenegro** [‚mɒntɪ'niːgrəʊ] *n* Montenegro *nt*.

**month** [mʌnθ] *n* Monat *der*.

**monthly** ['mʌnθlɪ] (*pl* -**ies**) *adj* monatlich; [magazine] Monats- ◇ *adv* monatlich ◇ *n* [magazine] Monatsmagazin *das*.

**monument** ['mɒnjʊmənt] *n* - **1.** [memorial] Monument *das* - **2.** [historic building] Denkmal *das*.

**monumental** [‚mɒnjʊ'mentl] *adj* - **1.** [very large] monumental - **2.** [important] bedeutend - **3.** [extremely bad] ungeheuerlich.

**moo** [muː] (*pl* -**s**) *n* Muhen *das* ◇ *vi* muhen.

**mooch** [muːtʃ] ◆ **mooch about, mooch around** *vi inf* herumlungern, herumgammeln.

**mood** [muːd] *n* Stimmung *die*; [of person] Laune *die*; **to be in a (bad)** ~ schlechte Laune haben, schlecht gelaunt sein; **to be in a good** ~ gute Laune haben, gut gelaunt sein.

**moody** ['muːdɪ] (*compar* -**ier**; *superl* -**iest**) *adj pej* - **1.** [changeable] launisch - **2.** [bad-tempered] schlecht gelaunt.

**moon** [muːn] *n* Mond *der*; **to be over the** ~ *inf* überglücklich sein.

**moonbeam** ['muːnbiːm] *n* Mondstrahl *der*.

**moonlight** ['muːnlaɪt] (*pt* & *pp* -**ed**) *n* Mondlicht *das* ◇ *vi inf* [have second job - legally] einen Nebenjob haben; [ - illegally] schwarzarbeiten.

**moonlighting** ['muːnlaɪtɪŋ] *n* [illegal work] Schwarzarbeit *die*.

**moonlit** ['muːnlɪt] *adj* [place] mondbeschienen; [night] mondhell.

**moon shot** *n* Mondflug *der*.

**moonstone** ['muːnstəʊn] *n* Mondstein *der*.

**moonstruck** ['muːnstrʌk] *adj inf* mondsüchtig.

**moor** [mɔː'] *n esp Br* Heide *die* ◇ *vt* vertäuen ◇ *vi* anlegen.

**Moor** [mɔː'] *n* Maure *der*, -rin *die*.

**moorhen** ['mɔːhen] *n* Teichhuhn *das*.

**moorings** ['mɔːrɪŋz] *npl* [ropes, chains] Vertäuung *die*; [place] Anlegestelle *die*.

**Moorish** ['mɔːrɪʃ] *adj* maurisch.

**moorland** ['mɔːlənd] *n esp Br* Heideland *das*.

**moose** [muːs] (*pl inv*) *n* Elch *der*.

**moot** [muːt] vt zur Debatte stellen.

**moot point** n: it's a ~ darüber lässt sich streiten.

**mop** [mɒp] (pt & pp **-ped**; cont **-ping**) n **- 1.** [for cleaning] Mopp der **- 2.** inf [of hair]: ~ **of curls** Wuschelkopf der; ~ **of hair** (Haar)mähne die ◇ vt wischen; **to ~ the sweat from one's brow** sich den Schweiß von der Stirn wischen.
➤ **mop up** vt sep [liquid, dirt] auf [wischen.

**mope** [məʊp] vi pej Trübsal blasen.
➤ **mope about, mope around** vi pej Trübsal blasen.

**moped** ['məʊped] n Moped das.

**moral** ['mɒrəl] adj **- 1.** [relating to morals] moralisch **- 2.** [behaving correctly] moralisch einwandfrei; ~ **support** moralische Unterstützung ◇ n [lesson] Moral die.
➤ **morals** npl [principles] Moral die.

**morale** [məˈrɑːl] n Moral die.

**moralistic** [ˌmɒrəˈlɪstɪk] adj pej moralistisch.

**morality** [məˈrælətɪ] (pl **-ies**) n Moralität die.

**moralize, -ise** ['mɒrəlaɪz] vi pej moralisieren.

**morally** ['mɒrəlɪ] adv **- 1.** [with regard to morals] moralisch **- 2.** [correctly] moralisch einwandfrei.

**Moral Majority** n moralische Mehrheit.

**morass** [məˈræs] n: a ~ **of detail** ein Wust von Details.

**moratorium** [ˌmɒrəˈtɔːrɪəm] (pl **-ria** [-rɪə]) n fml: ~ **(on sthg)** Moratorium das (für etw).

**morbid** ['mɔːbɪd] adj morbid.

**more** [mɔː] adv **- 1.** (in comparatives): ~ **difficult (than)** schwieriger (als); **speak** ~ **clearly** sprich deutlicher; **much** ~ **quickly** viel schneller **- 2.** [to a greater degree] mehr; **we ought to go to the cinema** ~ wir sollten öfters ins Kino gehen; **I couldn't agree** ~ ich stimme dem völlig zu; **she's** ~ **like a mother to me than a sister** sie ist mehr eine Mutter als eine Schwester für mich; **we were** ~ **hurt than angry** wir waren eher verletzt als zornig; **we'd be** ~ **than happy to help** wir würden sehr gerne helfen; **he's little** ~ **than a child** er ist fast noch ein Kind; ~ **than ever** mehr denn je **- 3.** [referring to time]: **once/twice** ~ noch einmal/zweimal; **I don't go there any** ~ ich gehe da nicht mehr hin ◇ adj **- 1.** [larger number, amount of] mehr; **there are** ~ **tourists than usual** es sind mehr Touristen als gewöhnlich da; ~ **than ten men** mehr als zehn Männer; **I got many** ~ **presents than last time** ich bekam viel mehr Geschenke als letztes Mal; **the** ~ **money he has, the** ~ **he wants** je mehr Geld er hat, desto mehr will er haben **- 2.** [additional] mehr; **we need** ~ **money/time** wir brauchen mehr Geld/Zeit; **two** ~ **bottles** noch zwei Flaschen; **is there any** ~ **cake?**

ist noch mehr Kuchen da?; **there's no** ~ **wine** es ist kein Wein mehr da; **have some** ~ **tea** nehmen Sie noch etwas Tee ◇ pron **- 1.** [larger number, amount] mehr; **I've got** ~ **than you** ich habe mehr als du; ~ **than 20** mehr als 20 **- 2.** [additional amount] mehr; **we need** ~ wir brauchen mehr; **I'd like two** ~ ich möchte noch zwei; **to see** ~ **of sb** jn öfter sehen; **is there any** ~? ist noch mehr da?; **there's no** ~ es ist nichts mehr da; **I have no** ~ **(of them)** ich habe keine mehr; nimm mir noch; **(and) what's** ~ außerdem; **the** ~ **he has, the** ~ **he wants** je mehr er hat, desto mehr will er haben; **what** ~ **do you want?** was wollen Sie noch mehr?
➤ **more and more** adv **- 1.** [increasingly] immer mehr; ~ **and** ~ **depressed/difficult** immer deprimierter/schwieriger **- 2.** [increasingly often] immer mehr oR öfter ◇ adj immer mehr; **there are** ~ **and** ~ **cars on the roads** es gibt immer mehr Autos auf den Straßen ◇ pron immer mehr; **we are spending** ~ **and** ~ **on petrol** wir geben immer mehr für Benzin aus.
➤ **more or less** adv [almost] mehr oder weniger; **she** ~ **or less suggested I had stolen it** sie hat mehr oder weniger behauptet, dass ich es gestohlen hätte; **it cost $500,** ~ **or less** es kostete um die $500.

**moreover** [mɔːˈrəʊvə] adv fml außerdem, überdies.

**morgue** [mɔːg] n Leichenhalle die.

**MORI** ['mɒrɪ] (abbr of **Market and Opinion Research Institute**) n britisches Meinungsforschungsinstitut.

**moribund** ['mɒrɪbʌnd] adj fml [business, magazine] zum Scheitern verurteilt; [tradition] aussterbend.

**Mormon** ['mɔːmən] n Mormone der, -nin die.

**morning** ['mɔːnɪŋ] n **- 1.** [first part of day] Morgen der, Vormittag der; **in the** ~ [before lunch] morgens, vormittags; [tomorrow morning] morgen **- 2.** [between midnight and noon] Morgen der.
➤ **mornings** adv Am morgens.

**morning-after pill** n Pille danach die.

**morning dress** n (U) esp Br Cutaway der.

**morning sickness** n (U) morgendliche Übelkeit.

**Moroccan** [məˈrɒkən] adj marokkanisch ◇ n Marokkaner der, -in die.

**Morocco** [məˈrɒkəʊ] n Marokko nt.

**moron** ['mɔːrɒn] n inf Bekloppte der, die.

**moronic** [məˈrɒnɪk] adj idiotisch.

**morose** [məˈrəʊs] adj griesgrämig, mürrisch.

**morphine** ['mɔːfiːn] n Morphium das.

**morris dancing** ['mɒrɪs-] n (U) traditioneller

**M**

*englischer Tanz, bei dem mit Glöckchen versehene Kostüme getragen werden.*

**Morse (code)** [mɔːs-] *n (U)* Morsezeichen *pl.*

**morsel** [ˈmɔːsl] *n* Bissen *der,* Happen *der.*

**mortal** [ˈmɔːtl] *adj* - **1.** [not eternal] sterblich - **2.** [causing death] tödlich - **3.** [danger, fear] Todes-; ~ **enemy** Todfeind *der;* ~ **combat** Kampf *der* um Leben und Tod ⬦ *n* Sterbliche *der, die.*

**mortality** [mɔːˈtælətɪ] *n* Sterblichkeit *die.*

**mortality rate** *n* Sterblichkeitsrate *die.*

**mortally** [ˈmɔːtəlɪ] *adv* tödlich.

**mortar** [ˈmɔːtəˈ] *n* - **1.** [cement mixture] Mörtel *der* - **2.** [gun, bowl] Mörser *der.*

**mortarboard** [ˈmɔːtəbɔːd] *n* - **1.** CONSTR Mörtelbrett *das* - **2.** UNIV Doktorhut *der.*

**mortgage** [ˈmɔːgɪdʒ] *n* Hypothek *die* ⬦ *comp* Hypotheken- ⬦ *vt* mit einer Hypothek belasten.

**mortgagee** [ˌmɔːgɪˈdʒiː] *n* Hypothekengläubiger *der.*

**mortgagor** [ˌmɔːgɪˈdʒɔːˈ] *n* Hypothekenschuldner *der.*

**mortician** [mɔːˈtɪʃn] *n* Am Leichenbestatter *der,* -in *die.*

**mortified** [ˈmɔːtɪfaɪd] *adj* beschämt.

**mortise lock** [ˈmɔːtɪs-] *n* Einsteckschloss *das.*

**mortuary** [ˈmɔːtʃʊərɪ] *(pl* **-ies)** *n* Leichenhalle *die.*

**mosaic** [məˈzeɪɪk] *n* Mosaik *das.*

**Moscow** [ˈmɒskəʊ] *n* Moskau *nt.*

**Moslem** [ˈmɒzləm] *adj* & *n* = **Muslim.**

**mosque** [mɒsk] *n* Moschee *die.*

**mosquito** [məˈskiːtəʊ] *(pl* **-es** OR **-s)** *n* Moskito *der.*

**mosquito net** *n* Moskitonetz *das.*

**moss** [mɒs] *n (U)* Moos *das.*

**mossy** [ˈmɒsɪ] *(compar* **-ier;** *superl* **-iest)** *adj* moosbewachsen.

**most** [məʊst] *(superl of* **many** & **much)** *adj* - **1.** [the majority of] die meisten; ~ **people agree** die meisten Leute sind dieser Meinung - **2.** [the largest amount of] der/die/das meiste; **I drank (the)** ~ **beer** ich habe das meiste Bier getrunken ⬦ *adv* - **1.** [in superlatives]: **she spoke (the)** ~ **clearly** sie sprach am deutlichsten; **the** ~ **expensive hotel in town** das teuerste Hotel in der Stadt - **2.** [to the greatest degree] am meisten; **I like this one** ~ mir gefällt dieses am besten - **3.** *fml* [very] äußerst, höchst; **it was a** ~ **pleasant evening** es war ein äußerst angenehmer Abend ⬦ *pron* - **1.** [the majority] die meisten *pl;* ~ **of the villages** die meisten Dörfer; ~ **of the time** die meiste Zeit; ~ **of the work** der größte Teil der Arbeit - **2.** [the lar-

gest amount] das meiste; **she earns (the)** ~ sie verdient am meisten - **3.** *phr:* **at** ~ höchstens; **to make the** ~ **of sthg** das Beste aus etw machen; **to make the** ~ **of an opportunity** eine Gelegenheit voll ausnutzen.

**mostly** [ˈməʊstlɪ] *adv* hauptsächlich, meistens.

**MOT** *n (abbr of* **Ministry of Transport (test))** ≃ TÜV *der* ⬦ *vt:* **to have one's car** ~'**d** sein Auto durch den TÜV bringen.

**motel** [məʊˈtel] *n* Motel *das.*

**moth** [mɒθ] *n* Nachtfalter *der;* [eating clothes] Motte *die.*

**mothball** [ˈmɒθbɔːl] *n* Mottenkugel *die.*

**moth-eaten** *adj* mottenzerfressen.

**mother** [ˈmʌðəˈ] *n* Mutter *die* ⬦ *vt pej* [spoil] bemuttern.

**motherboard** [ˈmʌðəbɔːd] *n* COMPUT Hauptplatine *die,* Motherboard *das.*

**motherhood** [ˈmʌðəhʊd] *n* Mutterschaft *die.*

**Mothering Sunday** [ˈmʌðərɪŋ-] *n* Muttertag *der.*

**mother-in-law** *(pl* **mothers-in-law** OR **mother-in-laws)** *n* Schwiegermutter *die.*

**motherland** [ˈmʌðəlænd] *n* Vaterland *das,* Heimat *die.*

**motherless** [ˈmʌðəlɪs] *adj* mutterlos.

**motherly** [ˈmʌðəlɪ] *adj* mütterlich.

**Mother Nature** *n* Mutter Natur *die.*

**mother-of-pearl** *n* Perlmutt *das* ⬦ *comp* Perlmutt-.

**Mother's Day** *n* Muttertag *der.*

**mother ship** *n* Mutterschiff *das.*

**mother superior** *n* Mutter Oberin *die.*

**mother-to-be** *(pl* **mothers-to-be)** *n* werdende Mutter.

**mother tongue** *n* Muttersprache *die.*

**motif** [məʊˈtiːf] *n* - **1.** [pattern] Muster *das* - **2.** MUS Motiv *das.*

**motion** [ˈməʊʃn] *n* - **1.** [movement] Bewegung *die;* **to set sthg in** ~ etw in Bewegung setzen; **I went through the** ~**s** [acted insincerely] ich habe es der Form halber getan - **2.** [proposal] Antrag *der* ⬦ *vt* & *vi:* **to** ~ **(to) sb to do sthg** jm durch Zeichen zu verstehen geben, etw zu tun.

**motionless** [ˈməʊʃənlɪs] *adj* bewegungslos.

**motion picture** *n* Am Film *der.*

**motivate** [ˈməʊtɪveɪt] *vt* motivieren; **to** ~ **sb to do sthg** jn dazu motivieren, etw zu tun.

**motivated** [ˈməʊtɪveɪtɪd] *adj* motiviert.

**motivation** [ˌməʊtɪˈveɪʃn] *n* Motivation *die.*

**motive** [ˈməʊtɪv] *n* Motiv *das.*

**motley** ['mɒtlɪ] *adj pej* bunt gemischt, bunt zusammengewürfelt.

**motocross** ['məʊtəkrɒs] *n* Motocross *das.*

**motor** ['məʊtəʳ] *adj Br* [relating to cars] Auto- ⬦ *n* [engine] Motor *der* ⬦ *vi dated* (mit dem Auto) fahren.

**Motorail®** ['məʊtəreɪl] *n Br britischer Autorei-sezug.*

**motorbike** ['məʊtəbaɪk] *n inf* Motorrad *das.*

**motorboat** ['məʊtəbəʊt] *n* Motorboot *das.*

**motorcade** ['məʊtəkeɪd] *n* Fahrzeugkolon-ne *die.*

**motorcar** ['məʊtəkɑːʳ] *n Br fml* Automobil *das.*

**motorcycle** ['məʊtəˌsaɪkl] *n* Motorrad *das.*

**motorcyclist** ['məʊtəˌsaɪklɪst] *n* Motorrad-fahrer *der*, -in *die.*

**motoring** ['məʊtərɪŋ] *adj Br* [offence] Verkehrs-; [magazine] Auto- ⬦ *n dated* Auto-fahren *das.*

**motorist** ['məʊtərɪst] *n* Autofahrer *der*, -in *die.*

**motorize, -ise** ['məʊtəraɪz] *vt* motorisieren.

**motor lodge** *n Am* Motel *das.*

**motor racing** *n* Autorennen *das.*

**motor scooter** *n* Motorroller *der.*

**motor vehicle** *n* Kraftfahrzeug *das.*

**motorway** ['məʊtəweɪ] *n Br* Autobahn *die* ⬦ *comp* Autobahn-.

**mottled** ['mɒtld] *adj* [leaf] gesprenkelt; [skin, face] fleckig.

**motto** ['mɒtəʊ] (*pl* -s *OR* -es) *n* [maxim] Motto *das.*

**mould, mold** *Am* [məʊld] *n* - **1.** [growth] Schimmel *der* - **2.** [shape] Form *die* ⬦ *vt* for-men.

**moulding, molding** *Am* ['məʊldɪŋ] *n* [decor-ation] Fries *der.*

**mouldy, moldy** *Am* ['məʊldɪ] (*compar* -ier; *superl* -iest) *adj* schimmelig.

**moult, molt** *Am* [məʊlt] *vi* [bird] sich mau-sern; [animal] im Fellwechsel *OR* Haarwech-sel sein.

**mound** [maʊnd] *n* - **1.** [small hill] Hügel *der* - **2.** [untidy pile] Haufen *der;* [of papers, blankets] Stapel *der.*

**mount** [maʊnt] *n* - **1.** [support, frame - for photo-graph] Rahmen *der;* [ - for jewel] Fassung *die;* [ - for machine] Sockel *der* - **2.** [horse, pony] Reit-tier *das* - **3.** [mountain]: **Mount Everest** Mount Everest; **Mount Etna** Etna ⬦ *vt* - **1.** [climb onto] besteigen - **2.** *fml* [climb up - stairs] hoch-steigen; [ - hill] besteigen - **3.** [organize] organi-sieren, vor|bereiten; **to ~ guard over sb/sthg** eine Wache für jn/etw auf |stellen - **4.** [fix in place - jewel] ein|fassen; [ - photographic slide] rah-men; **to ~ sthg on the wall** etw an die Wand

hängen ⬦ *vi* - **1.** [increase] sich erhöhen - **2.** [climb on horse] auf |sitzen.

⬦ **mount up** *vi* sich häufen, sich an-sammeln.

**mountain** ['maʊntɪn] *n lit & fig* Berg *der;* **to make a ~ out of a molehill** aus einer Mücke ei-nen Elefanten machen.

**mountain bike** *n* Mountainbike *das.*

**mountaineer** [ˌmaʊntɪ'nɪəʳ] *n* Bergsteiger *der*, -in *die.*

**mountaineering** [ˌmaʊntɪ'nɪərɪŋ] *n* Berg-steigen *das.*

**mountainous** ['maʊntɪnəs] *adj* [full of mountains] bergig.

**mountain range** *n* Gebirgszug *der*, Ge-birgskette *die.*

**mountain rescue** *n* Bergwacht *die.*

**mounted** ['maʊntɪd] *adj* [on horseback] beritten.

**Mountie** ['maʊntɪ] *n inf* Abkürzung für ein Mit-glied der kanadischen berittenen Polizei (Royal Canadian Mounted Police).

**mourn** [mɔːn] *vt* trauern um ⬦ *vi* trauern; **to ~ for sb** um jn trauern.

**mourner** ['mɔːnəʳ] *n* Trauernde *der*, *die.*

**mournful** ['mɔːnfʊl] *adj* traurig.

**mourning** ['mɔːnɪŋ] *n* [period] Trauerzeit *die;* **to be in ~** [mourn] trauern; [wear mourning clothes] Trauerkleidung tragen.

**mouse** [maʊs] (*pl* mice) *n* [animal & COMPUT] Maus *die.*

**mouse mat, mouse pad** *n* COMPUT Mouse-pad *das.*

**mousetrap** ['maʊstræp] *n* Mausefalle *die.*

**moussaka** [muːˈsɑːkə] *n* Moussaka *die.*

**mousse** [muːs] *n* - **1.** [food] Mousse *die* - **2.** [for hair] Schaumfestiger *der.*

**moustache** *Br* [məˈstɑːʃ], **mustache** *Am* ['mʌstæʃ] *n* Schnurrbart *der.*

**mouth** [*n* maʊθ, *vt* maʊð] *n* - **1.** [of person] Mund *der;* **to keep one's ~ shut** *inf* den Mund *OR* die Klappe halten - **2.** [entrance - of cave, tunnel] Eingang *der;* [ - of river] Mündung *die* ⬦ *vt* - **1.** [silently] lautlos mit Lippensprache aus|drücken - **2.** [platitudes, insults] von sich geben.

**mouthful** ['maʊθfʊl] *n* - **1.** [amount - of food] Bis-sen *der*, Happen *der;* [ - of drink] Schluck *der* - **2.** *inf* [difficult word] Zungenbrecher *der.*

**mouthorgan** ['maʊθˌɔːgən] *n* Mundharmo-nika *die.*

**mouthpiece** ['maʊθpiːs] *n* - **1.** [of telephone] Sprechmuschel *die* - **2.** [of musical instrument] Mundstück *das* - **3.** [spokesperson] Sprachrohr *das.*

**mouth-to-mouth** *adj:* **~ resuscitation** Mund-zu-Mund-Beatmung *die.*

M

**mouthwash** ['maʊθwɒʃ] n (U) Mundwasser das.

**mouth-watering** [-ˌwɔːtərɪŋ] adj appetitlich, appetitanregend.

**movable** ['muːvəbl] adj beweglich.

**move** [muːv] n - 1. [movement] Bewegung die; **to be on the ~** [travelling around] unterwegs sein; [beginning to move] sich in Bewegung setzen; **to get a ~ on** inf sich beeilen - 2. [to new house] Umzug der; [to higher position in company] Aufstieg der - 3. [in board game] Zug der; **it's your ~** du bist am Zug - 4. [course of action]: **it would be a good ~** es wäre klug ⟨⟩ vt - 1. [arm, head] bewegen; [piece of furniture] rücken; [car] weglfahren; [piece in board game] einen Zug machen mit - 2. [change]: **to ~ house** umlziehen; **to ~ sb to another job** jn versetzen - 3. [affect emotionally] bewegen, rühren - 4. [in debate]: **to ~ that ...** beantragen, dass ... - 5. fml [cause]: **to ~ sb to do sthg** jn dazu bewegen, etw zu tun ⟨⟩ vi - 1. [shift] sich bewegen - 2. [act] handeln - 3. [to new house] umlziehen.

◆ **move about** vi - 1. [fidget] sich unruhig (hin und her) bewegen - 2. [travel] unterwegs sein.

◆ **move along** vt sep [person, crowds] zum Weitergehen veranlassen ⟨⟩ vi weiterlgehen; [in car] weiterlfahren.

◆ **move around** vi = move about.

◆ **move away** vi [go in opposite direction] weglgehen; [car] weglfahren.

◆ **move in** vt sep [troops] einrücken lassen ⟨⟩ vi - 1. [to new house] umlziehen - 2. [troops] einlrücken; [competitors] auf den Plan treten.

◆ **move off** vi [train, bus, car] ablfahren, loslfahren.

◆ **move on** vt sep [person, crowds] zum Weitergehen veranlassen ⟨⟩ vi - 1. [after stopping] weiterlgehen; [in car] weiterlfahren - 2. [in discussion] fortlfahren.

◆ **move out** vt sep [troops] ablziehen ⟨⟩ vi [from house] auslziehen.

◆ **move over** vi zur Seite rutschen OR rücken.

◆ **move up** vi [on seat] auflrutschen, auflrücken.

**moveable** ['muːvəbl] adj = movable.

**movement** ['muːvmənt] n - 1. [motion, gesture, group] Bewegung die - 2. [transportation] Beförderung die - 3. [trend] Trend der - 4. MUS Satz der.

**movie** ['muːvɪ] n esp Am Film der; **to go to the ~** ins Kino gehen.

**movie camera** n Filmkamera die.

**moviegoer** ['muːvɪˌɡəʊər] n Am Kinogänger der, -in die.

**movie star** n Am Filmstar der.

**movie theater** n Am Kino das.

**moving** ['muːvɪŋ] adj - 1. [touching] bewegend - 2. [not fixed] beweglich.

**moving staircase** n Rolltreppe die.

**mow** [məʊ] (pt -ed; pp -ed OR mown) vt mähen.

◆ **mow down** vt sep niederlmähen.

**mower** ['məʊər] n [lawnmower] Rasenmäher der.

**mown** [məʊn] pp ▷ mow.

**Mozambique** [ˌməʊzæm'biːk] n Mosambik nt, Mosambique nt.

**MP** n - 1. abbr of **Military Police** - 2. Br abbr of **Member of Parliament** - 3. Can (abbr of **Mounted Police**) kanadische Polizei.

**mpg** (abbr of **miles per gallon**) n: 31 ~ ≈ 9,1 l auf 100 km.

**mph** (abbr of **miles per hour**) n: he was doing 50 ~ ≈ er fuhr 80 km/h (schnell).

**MPhil** [ˌem'fɪl] (abbr of **Master of Philosophy**) n akademischer Grad in Philosophie oder dessen Inhaber.

**Mr** ['mɪstər] n - 1. [before man's name] Herr - 2. [before title] Hr.

**MRC** (abbr of **Medical Research Council**) n medizinische Forschungsrat in Großbritannien.

**MRCP** (abbr of **Member of the Royal College of Physicians**) n Mitglied einer britischen Ärztevereinigung.

**MRCS** (abbr of **Member of the Royal College of Surgeons**) n Mitglied des britischen Chirurgenverbandes.

**MRCVS** (abbr of **Member of the Royal College of Veterinary Surgeons**) n Mitglied einer britischen Vereinigung der Veterinärmediziner.

**Mrs** ['mɪsɪz] n Frau, Fr.

**ms.** (abbr of **manuscript**) n Mskr.

**Ms** [mɪz] n Frau, Fr.

**MS**

Titel und Anrede für Frauen („Ms Smith"), der nicht angibt, ob die Betreffende verheiratet ist oder nicht. Vor allem in Briefen und Dokumenten wird „Ms" zunehmend an Stelle des traditionellen „Mrs" (verheiratet) und „Miss" (unverheiratet) gebraucht.

**MS** n - 1. (abbr of **manuscript**) = ms. - 2. (abbr of **multiple sclerosis**) MS ⟨⟩ abk für Mississippi, in Postanschrift verwendet.

**MSc** n abbr of **Master of Science**.

**MSF** (abbr of **Manufacturing Science and Finance**) n bedeutende britische Gewerkschaft.

**MSG** (abbr of **monosodium glutamate**) n Natriumglutamat das, Geschmacksverstärker.

**MSP** (abbr of **Member of the Scottish Parliament**) n Mitglied des schottischen Parlaments.

**MST** (*abbr of* **Mountain Standard Time**) *n Winterzeit in der Gebirgszeitzone der USA*

**Mt** *abbr of* **mount.**

**MT** *abk für Montana, in Postanschrift verwendet.*

**much** [mʌtʃ] (*compar* **more;** *superl* **most**) *adj* viel; **I haven't got ~ money** ich habe nicht viel Geld; **as ~ food as you can eat** so viel du essen kannst/Sie essen können; **how ~ time is left?** wie viel Zeit bleibt noch?; **we have too ~ work** wir haben zu viel Arbeit ◇ *adv* - **1.** [to a great extent] viel; **it's ~ better** es ist viel besser; **I like it very ~** es gefällt mir sehr gut; **it's not ~ good** *inf* es ist nicht Besonders; **nothing ~** nichts Besonderes; **thank you very ~** vielen Dank; **as I like him** so gern ich ihn auch mag; **~ to my surprise** sehr zu meiner Überraschung; **~ the same** ziemlich das Gleiche; **he's not so ~ stupid as lazy** er ist weniger dumm als faul; **he left without so ~ as a goodbye** er hat sich nicht einmal verabschiedet - **2.** [often] oft; **we don't go there ~** wir gehen da nicht oft hin ◇ *pron* viel; **I haven't got ~** ich habe nicht viel; **as ~ as you like** so viel Sie wollen/du willst; **how ~ is it?** wie viel kostet es?; **you've got too ~** du hast zu viel; **I don't think ~ of him** ich halte nicht viel von ihm; **I thought as ~** das habe ich mir gedacht; **it's not up to ~** *inf* es ist nicht besonders; **I'm not ~ of a cook** ich bin kein großer Koch; **so ~ for his friendship!** und das nennt sich Freundschaft!

**muchness** [mʌtʃnɪs] *n:* **to be much of a ~** so ziemlich das Gleiche sein.

**muck** [mʌk] *n inf* - **1.** [dirt] Dreck *der* - **2.** [manure] Mist *der.*

➤ **muck about, muck around** *Br inf vt sep* an der Nase herumlführen ◇ *vi* herumlalbern.

➤ **muck in** *vi Br inf* mit anlpacken.

➤ **muck out** *vt sep* auslmisten.

➤ **muck up** *vt sep Br inf* vermasseln.

**muckraking** [mʌkreɪkɪŋ] *n* Sensationsmache *die.*

**mucky** [mʌkɪ] (*compar* -**ier;** *superl* -**iest**) *adj inf* dreckig.

**mucus** [mju:kəs] *n* (U) Schleim *der.*

**mud** [mʌd] *n* Schlamm *der.*

**muddle** [mʌdl] *n* - **1.** [disorder] Durcheinander *das;* **to be in a ~** durcheinander sein - **2.** [confusion]: **to be in a ~** [person] verwirrt *OR* durcheinander sein ◇ *vt* - **1.** [put into disorder] durcheinander bringen - **2.** [confuse - person] verwirren, durcheinander bringen.

➤ **muddle along** *vi* vor sich (A) hin wursteln.

➤ **muddle through** *vi* sich durchlwursteln *OR* durchschlagen.

➤ **muddle up** *vt sep* durcheinander bringen.

**muddle-headed** [-'hedɪd] *adj* verwirrt.

**muddy** [mʌdɪ] (*compar* -**ier;** *superl* -**iest;** *pt & pp* -**ied**) *adj* [floor, boots] schmutzig; [river] schlammig ◇ *vt fig* [issue, situation] verworren machen.

**mudflap** [mʌdflæp] *n* Schmutzfänger *der.*

**mudflat** [mʌdflæt] *n* Wattenmeer *das,* Watt *das.*

**mudguard** [mʌdgɑːd] *n* [on car] Kotflügel *der;* [on motorcycle] Schutzblech *das.*

**mudpack** [mʌdpæk] *n* Schlammpackung *die.*

**mudslinging** [mʌd‚slɪŋɪŋ] *n* (U) Verleumdung *die.*

**muesli** [mju:zlɪ] *n Br* Müsli *das.*

**muff** [mʌf] *n* [for hands] Muff *der;* [for ears] Ohrenwärmer *der* ◇ *vt inf* verpatzen.

**muffin** [mʌfɪn] *n* - **1.** *Br* [bread roll] *kleines flaches Milchbrötchen, das warm und mit Butter gegessen wird* - **2.** *Am* [cake] *kleiner Kuchen.*

**muffle** [mʌfl] *vt* [quieten] dämpfen.

**muffled** [mʌfld] *adj* - **1.** [sound] gedämpft - **2.** [wrapped up warmly]: **~ (up)** eingemummelt.

**muffler** [mʌflər] *n Am* [for car] Auspuff *der.*

**mug** [mʌg] (*pt & pp* -**ged;** *cont* -**ging**) *n* - **1.** [cup, mugful] Tasse *die* - **2.** *inf* [fool] Trottel *der* ◇ *vt* [attack and rob] überfallen und berauben.

**mugger** [mʌgər] *n* Straßenräuber *der,* -in *die.*

**mugging** [mʌgɪŋ] *n* Straßenraub *der.*

**muggy** [mʌgɪ] (*compar* -**ier;** *superl* -**iest**) *adj* schwül.

**mugshot** [mʌgʃɒt] *n inf* Verbrecherfoto *das.*

**mujaheddin** [‚mu:dʒəhəˈdiːn] *npl* Mudschaheddin *pl.*

**mulatto** [mjuːˈlætəʊ] (*pl* -**s** *OR* -**es**) *n* Mulatte *der,* -tin *die.*

**mule** [mjuːl] *n* - **1.** [animal] Maultier *das* - **2.** [slipper] Schlappen *der.*

**mull** [mʌl] ➤ **mull over** *vt sep* gründlich durchdenken.

**mullah** [mʌlə] *n* Mullah *der.*

**mulled** [mʌld] *adj:* **~ wine** Glühwein *der.*

**mullet** [mʌlɪt] (*pl inv* *OR* -**s**) *n* [fish] Meeräsche *die.*

**mulligatawny** [‚mʌlɪgəˈtɔːnɪ] *n* Currysuppe *die.*

**mullioned** [mʌlɪəndl] *adj* längs unterteilt.

**multicoloured** *Br,* **multicolored** *Am* [mʌltɪ‚kʌləd] *adj* bunt, mehrfarbig.

**multicultural** [‚mʌltɪˈkʌltʃərəl] *adj* multikulturell.

**multifarious** [‚mʌltɪˈfeərɪəs] *adj* vielfältig.

**multilateral** [‚mʌltɪˈlætərəl] *adj* multilateral.

**M**

**multilingual** [ˌmʌltɪˈlɪŋgwəl] *adj* mehrsprachig.

**multimedia** [ˌmʌltɪˈmiːdɪə] *adj* - **1.** [involving different media] multimedial - **2.** COMPUT Multimedia-.

**multimillionaire** [ˈmʌltɪˌmɪljəˈneəʳ] *n* Multimillionär *der*, -in *die*.

**multinational** [ˌmʌltɪˈnæʃənl] *adj* multinational <> *n* multinationales Unternehmen.

**multiple** [ˈmʌltɪpl] *adj* vielfach; ~ birth Mehrlingsgeburt *die* <> *n* MATH Vielfache *das*.

**multiple-choice** *adj* Multiple-Choice-.

**multiple injuries** *npl* zahlreiche Verletzungen *pl*.

**multiple pileup** *n* Massenkarambolage *die*.

**multiple sclerosis** [-sklɪˈrəʊsɪs] *n (U)* multiple Sklerose.

**multiplex (cinema)** [ˈmʌltɪpleks-] *n großes Kino mit mehreren Vorführsälen.*

**multiplication** [ˌmʌltɪplɪˈkeɪʃn] *n (U)* - **1.** MATH Multiplikation *die* - **2.** [increase] Vervielfachung *die*, Vermehrung *die*.

**multiplication sign** *n* Multiplikationszeichen *das*, Malzeichen *das*.

**multiplication table** *n* Multiplikationstabelle *die;* to say one's ~s das Einmaleins auf l- sagen.

**multiplicity** [ˌmʌltɪˈplɪsətɪ] *n* Vielzahl *die.*

**multiply** [ˈmʌltɪplaɪ] *(pt & pp -ied) vt* - **1.** MATH multiplizieren, mallnehmen - **2.** [increase] vermehren, vervielfachen <> *vi* - **1.** MATH multiplizieren - **2.** [increase] sich vervielfältigen, zulnehmen - **3.** [breed] sich vermehren.

**multipurpose** [ˌmʌltɪˈpɜːpəs] *adj* Mehrzweck-.

**multiracial** [ˌmʌltɪˈreɪʃl] *adj* gemischtrassig.

**multiscreen cinema** [ˌmʌltɪskriːn-] *n großes Kino mit mehreren Vorführsälen.*

**multistorey** *Br*, **multistory** *Am* [ˌmʌltɪˈstɔːrɪ] *adj* mehrstöckig; ~ car park Parkhaus *das* <> *n* [car park] Parkhaus *das.*

**multitude** [ˈmʌltɪtjuːd] *n* - **1.** [large number] Vielzahl *die* - **2.** [crowd] Menschenmenge *die.*

**mum** [mʌm] *Br inf* *n* Mutter *die;* [within speaker's family] Mutti *die* <> *adj:* to keep ~ den Mund halten.

**mumble** [ˈmʌmbl] *vt* [response] murmeln; [words] nuscheln <> *vi* vor sich *(A)* hin murmeln; **stop mumbling** hör auf zu nuscheln.

**mumbo jumbo** [ˈmʌmbəʊˈdʒʌmbəʊ] *n pej* Hokuspokus *der.*

**mummify** [ˈmʌmɪfaɪ] *(pt & pp -ied) vt* mumifizieren.

**mummy** [ˈmʌmɪ] *(pl -ies) n* - **1.** *Br inf* [mother] Mami *die*, Mama *die* - **2.** [preserved body] Mumie *die.*

**mumps** [mʌmps] *n (U)* Mumps *der*, Ziegenpeter *der.*

**munch** [mʌntʃ] *vt & vi* mampfen.

**mundane** [mʌnˈdeɪn] *adj* [ordinary] alltäglich.

**mung bean** [mʌŋ-] *n* Mungobohne *die.*

**Munich** [ˈmjuːnɪk] *n* München *nt.*

**municipal** [mjuːˈnɪsɪpl] *adj* städtisch; [park, administration] Stadt-.

**municipality** [mjuːˌnɪsɪˈpælɪtɪ] *(pl -ies) n* Stadt *die*, Gemeinde *die.*

**munificent** [mjuːˈnɪfɪsənt] *adj fml* großzügig.

**munitions** [mjuːˈnɪʃnz] *npl* Kriegsmaterial *das.*

**mural** [ˈmjuːərəl] *n* Wandgemälde *das.*

**murder** [ˈmɜːdəʳ] *n* Mord *der;* to get away with ~ *fig* sich *(D)* alles erlauben können <> *vt* ermorden.

**murderer** [ˈmɜːdərəʳ] *n* Mörder *der*, -in *die.*

**murderess** [ˈmɜːdərɪs] *n* Mörderin *die.*

**murderous** [ˈmɜːdərəs] *adj* [thugs] mordgierig; [attack] mörderisch.

**murky** [ˈmɜːkɪ] *(compar -ier; superl -iest) adj* - **1.** [dark - place] düster; [ - water] trüb - **2.** [shameful] dunkel, finster.

**murmur** [ˈmɜːməʳ] *n* - **1.** [low sound - of voices] Gemurmel *das;* [ - of disapproving voices] Murmeln *das* - **2.** MED [of heart] Herzgeräusch *das* <> *vt & vi* murmeln.

**MusB** [mjuːzˈbiː], **MusBac** [mjuːzˈbæk] *(abbr of Bachelor of Music) n akademischer Grad in Musikwissenschaft oder dessen Inhaber.*

**muscle** [ˈmʌsl] *n* - **1.** [organ] Muskel *der* - **2.** *(U)* MED [tissue] Muskelgewebe *das* - **3.** *(U) fig* [power] Macht *die.*

➨ **muscle in** *vi* mitlmischen.

**muscleman** [ˈmʌslmən] *(pl -men* [-men]*) n* Muskelmann *der.*

**Muscovite** [ˈmʌskəvaɪt] *adj* Moskauer <> *n* Moskauer *der*, -in *die.*

**muscular** [ˈmʌskjʊləʳ] *adj* - **1.** [of muscles] Muskel- - **2.** [strong] muskulös.

**muscular dystrophy** [-ˈdɪstrəfɪ] *n* Muskeldystrophie *die.*

**MusD** [mjuːzˈdiː], **MusDoc** [mjuːzˈdɒk] *(abbr of Doctor of Music) n Doktorgrad in Musikwissenschaft oder dessen Inhaber.*

**muse** [mjuːz] *n* Muse *die* <> *vi* sinnieren.

**museum** [mjuːˈzɪəm] *n* Museum *das.*

**mush** [mʌʃ] *n inf* - **1.** [substance] Brei *der* - **2.** [sentimental] Schmalz *der.*

**mushroom** [ˈmʌʃrʊm] *n* [cultivated] Pilz *der*, Champignon *der* <> *vi* [grow quickly - organization, movement] sehr schnell wachsen; [ - houses] wie Pilze aus dem Boden schießen; **the peace movement ~ed all over Europe** die Friedensbewegung breitete sich sehr schnell über ganz Europa aus.

**mushroom cloud** n Atompilz der.

**mushy** ['mʌʃi] (compar **-ier;** superl **-iest**) adj - **1.** [very soft] breiig - **2.** [over-sentimental] schmalzig.

**music** ['mjuːzɪk] n - **1.** [gen] Musik die; **a piece of ~** ein Musikstück - **2.** [subject studied] Musik die - **3.** [written] Noten pl; **to read ~** Noten lesen.

**musical** ['mjuːzɪkl] adj - **1.** [education, director] Musik-; **~ career** Laufbahn als Musiker - **2.** [talented in music] musikalisch - **3.** [voice, sound] melodiös ◇ n Musical das.

**musical box** Br, **music box** Am n Spieldose die.

**musical chairs** n Reise die nach Jerusalem.

**musical instrument** n Musikinstrument das.

**music box** n Am = musical box.

**music centre** n Kompaktanlage die.

**music hall** n Br Varieté das.

**musician** [mjuːˈzɪʃn] n Musiker der, -in die.

**music stand** n Notenständer der.

**musk** [mʌsk] n Moschus der.

**musket** ['mʌskɪt] n Muskete die.

**muskrat** ['mʌskræt] n Bisamratte die.

**Muslim** ['muzlɪm] adj moslemisch ◇ n Moslem der, Moslime die.

**muslin** ['mʌzlɪn] n Musselin der.

**musquash** ['mʌskwɒʃ] n - **1.** [animal] Bisamratte die - **2.** [fur] Bisam der.

**muss** [mʌs] vt Am: **to ~ sthg (up)** etw in Unordnung bringen.

**mussel** ['mʌsl] n Miesmuschel die.

**must** [mʌst] aux vb müssen; [with negative] dürfen; **I ~ go** ich muss gehen; **you ~n't be late** du darfst nicht zu spät kommen; **do it, if you ~** tu es, wenn es sein muss; **the room ~ be vacated by ten** das Zimmer ist bis zehn Uhr zu räumen; **you ~ have seen it** du musst es doch gesehen haben; **you ~ see that film** du musst dir diesen Film ansehen; **you ~ be joking!** das kann doch nicht dein Ernst sein! ◇ n: **it's a ~** inf das ist ein Muss.

**mustache** n Am = moustache.

**mustard** ['mʌstəd] n Senf der.

**muster** ['mʌstər] vt - **1.** [summon - strength, courage] zusammennehmen; [ - support] zusammenbekommen - **2.** [assemble - volunteers, helpers] versammeln; [ - troops] zusammen-

ziehen ◇ vi [volunteers] sich versammeln; [troops] sich sammeln.

◆ **muster up** vt fus [courage, strength] zusammennehmen; [support] zusammenbekommen.

**mustn't** [mʌsnt] = must not.

**must've** ['mʌstəv] = must have.

**musty** ['mʌsti] (compar **-ier;** superl **-iest**) adj [smell, room, air] muffig; [books] moderig.

**mutant** ['mjuːtənt] adj mutiert ◇ n Mutante die.

**mutate** [mjuːˈteɪt] vi mutieren; **to ~ into sthg** zu etw mutieren.

**mutation** [mjuːˈteɪʃn] n Mutation die.

**mute** [mjuːt] adj - **1.** [person] stumm - **2.** [amazement] sprachlos; [admiration] stumm ◇ n [person] Stumme der, die ◇ vt [sound] dämpfen.

**muted** ['mjuːtɪd] adj - **1.** [sound, colour] gedämpft - **2.** [protest] schwach.

**mutilate** ['mjuːtɪleɪt] vt - **1.** [maim] verstümmeln - **2.** [damage, spoil] ruinieren.

**mutilation** [ˌmjuːtɪˈleɪʃn] n - **1.** [maiming] Verstümmelung die - **2.** [damaging, spoiling]: **he was fined for the ~ of a book** er musste eine Strafe dafür bezahlen, dass er ein Buch ruiniert hatte.

**mutineer** [ˌmjuːtɪˈnɪər] n Meuterer der.

**mutinous** ['mjuːtɪnəs] adj rebellisch; [ship's crew] meuternd.

**mutiny** ['mjuːtɪnɪ] (pl **-ies;** pt & pp **-ied**) n Meuterei die ◇ vi meutern.

**mutt** [mʌt] n inf - **1.** [fool] Dussel der - **2.** Am [dog] Mischling der.

**mutter** ['mʌtər] vt murmeln ◇ vi murmeln; [grumble] murren; **to ~ to o.s.** vor sich hin murmeln.

**muttering** ['mʌtərɪŋ] n - **1.** [remark] Gemurre das - **2.** (U) [sound] Gemurmel das.

**mutton** ['mʌtn] n Hammelfleisch das; **she's ~ dressed as lamb** Br sie ist wie eine junge Frau aufgetakelt.

**mutual** ['mjuːtʃʊəl] adj - **1.** [aid] gegenseitig; **the feeling was ~** das Gefühl beruhte auf Gegenseitigkeit; **by ~ consent** in gegenseitigem Einverständnis - **2.** [friend, interest] gemeinsam.

**mutual fund** n Am Investmentfonds der.

**mutually** ['mjuːtʃʊəlɪ] adv [reciprocally - beneficial, convenient] für beide Seiten; [ - agreed] von beiden Seiten; **to be ~ exclusive** einander ausschließen.

**Muzak**® ['mjuːzæk] n Hintergrundmusik die.

**muzzle** ['mʌzl] n - **1.** [dog's nose and jaws] Schnauze die - **2.** [for dog] Maulkorb der - **3.** [of gun] Mündung die ◇ vt - **1.** [dog] einen

Maulkorb anlegen *(+ D)* - **2.** *fig* [press, opposition] knebeln.

**MVP** *(abbr of* **most valuable player)** *n in den USA die Bezeichnung für den besten Spieler oder die beste Spielerin einer Mannschaft.*

**MW** *(abbr of* **medium wave)** MW.

**my** [maɪ] *poss adj* mein; **~ friend** mein Freund, meine Freundin; **~ children** meine Kinder; **I washed ~ hair** ich habe mir die Haare gewaschen ◇ *excl:* **(oh) ~!** meine Güte!

**Myanmar** [ˌmaɪæn'mɑːʳ] *n* Myanmar *nt.*

**mynah bird** ['maɪnə-] *n* Beo *der.*

**myopic** [maɪ'ɒpɪk] *adj* kurzsichtig.

**myriad** ['mɪrɪəd] *literary adj* unzählig ◇ *n* Myriade *die.*

**myrrh** [mɜːʳ] *n* Myrrhe *die.*

**myrtle** ['mɜːtl] *n* Myrte *die.*

**myself** [maɪ'self] *pron* - **1.** *(reflexive: accusative)* mich; *(reflexive: dative)* mir; **I have hurt ~** ich habe mich verletzt; **I bought ~ some new clothes** ich habe mir neue Kleider gekauft - **2.** *(after prep: accusative)* mich selbst; *(after prep: dative)* mir selbst; **I did it ~** ich habe es selbst gemacht; **by ~** allein.

**mysterious** [mɪ'stɪərɪəs] *adj* - **1.** [puzzling - illness, sound] rätselhaft; [ - disappearance] mysteriös - **2.** [secretive] geheimnisvoll; **to be ~ about sthg** ein Geheimnis aus etw machen.

**mysteriously** [mɪ'stɪərɪəslɪ] *adv* - **1.** [inexplicably - change] auf rätselhafte Weise; [ - disappear] auf mysteriöse Weise - **2.** [secretively] geheimnisvoll.

**mystery** ['mɪstərɪ] *(pl* **-ies)** *adj* unbekannt ◇ *n* - **1.** [puzzle] Rätsel *das* - **2.** [secret] Geheimnis *das.*

**mystery story** *n* Kriminalgeschichte *die.*

**mystery tour** *n* Fahrt *die* ins Blaue.

**mystic** ['mɪstɪk] *adj* mystisch ◇ *n* Mystiker *der,* -in *die.*

**mystical** ['mɪstɪkl] *adj* mystisch.

**mysticism** ['mɪstɪsɪzml] *n* Mystik *die.*

**mystified** ['mɪstɪfaɪd] *adj* verwirrt; **I was ~ by the case** der Fall stellte mich vor ein Rätsel.

**mystifying** ['mɪstɪfaɪɪŋ] *adj* [action] rätselhaft; [decision] unerklärlich.

**mystique** [mɪ'stiːk] *n (U)* geheimnisvoller Nimbus.

**myth** [mɪθ] *n* - **1.** [legend] Mythos *der* - **2.** [false belief] Irrglauben *der;* **it's a ~ that Elvis is still alive** es ist ein Märchen, dass Elvis noch am Leben ist.

**mythic** ['mɪθɪk] *adj* mythisch.

**mythical** ['mɪθɪkl] *adj* - **1.** [legendary] mythisch - **2.** [imaginary - place, time] fiktiv; [ - beliefs] irrig.

**mythological** [ˌmɪθə'lɒdʒɪkl] *adj* mythologisch.

**mythology** [mɪ'θɒlədʒɪ] *(pl* **-ies)** *n* Mythologie *die.*

**myxomatosis** [ˌmɪksəmə'təʊsɪs] *n* Myxomatose *die.*

**n** *(pl* **n's** *or* **ns)**, **N** *(pl* **N's** *or* **Ns)** [en] *n* [letter] n *das,* N *das.*
➡ **N** *(abbr of* **north)** N.

**n/a, N/A** - **1.** *(abbr of* **not applicable)** entf. - **2.** *(abbr of* **not available)** n. bez.

**NAACP** *(abbr of* **National Association for the Advancement of Colored People)** *n Vereinigung zur Unterstützung und Förderung Farbiger.*

**NAAFI** ['næfɪ] *(abbr of* **Navy, Army & Air Force Institute)** *n Betreiberorganisation der Kantinen und Geschäfte für die britischen Truppen.*

**nab** [næb] *(pt* & *pp* **-bed;** *cont* **-bing)** *vt inf* - **1.** [arrest] schnappen - **2.** [claim quickly] sich *(D)* schnappen.

**NACU** *(abbr of* **National Association of Colleges and Universities)** *n Vereinigung US-amerikanischer Colleges und Universitäten.*

**nadir** ['neɪdɪəʳ] *n* - **1.** ASTRON Nadir *der* - **2.** *fig* [low point] Tiefpunkt *der.*

**naff** [næf] *adj Br inf* - **1.** [untrendy] uncool - **2.** [mediocre] platt - **3.** [stupid] blöd.

**NAFTA** *(abbr of* **North American Free Trade Agreement)** *n* Nordamerikanisches Freihandelsabkommen *das,* NAFTA *das.*

**nag** [næg] *(pt* & *pp* **-ged;** *cont* **-ging)** *vt* [pester] keine Ruhe lassen *(+ D);* [find fault with] herumlnörgeln an *(+ D);* **to ~ sb to do sthg** jm zulsetzen, damit er etw tut ◇ *vi* - **1.** [person]: **to ~** [pester] keine Ruhe geben; [find fault with] herumlnörgeln; **to ~ at sb** [pester] jm keine Ruhe lassen; [find fault with] an jm herumlnörgeln - **2.** [thought, doubt]: **to ~ at sb** jn quälen ◇ *n inf* - **1.** [sb who pesters] Quälgeist *der;* [sb who finds fault] Nörgler *der,* -in *die* - **2.** *Br* [horse] Klepper *der.*

**nagging** ['nægɪŋ] *adj* - **1.** [thought, doubt, pain] quälend - **2.** [person - pestering] ständig drängend; [ - finding fault] nörglerisch.

**nail** [neɪl] *n* - **1.** [for fastening] Nagel *der;* **to hit the ~ on the head** den Nagel auf den Kopf treffen - **2.** [of finger, toe] Nagel *der* <> *vt:* **to ~ sthg to sthg** etw an etw *(A)* nageln.
➤ **nail down** *vt sep lit* & *fig* festlnageln.
➤ **nail up** *vt sep* - **1.** [picture, notice] anlnageln - **2.** [box] zulnageln.

**nail-biting** [-ˌbaɪtɪŋ] *adj* [conclusion] spannend; [match, contest] nervenaufpeitschend.

**nailbrush** ['neɪlbrʌʃ] *n* Nagelbürste *die.*

**nail clippers** [-ˌklɪpəz] *npl* Nagelknipser *der.*

**nail file** *n* Nagelfeile *die.*

**nail polish** *n* Nagellack *der.*

**nail scissors** *npl* Nagelschere *die.*

**nail varnish** *n* Nagellack *der.*

**nail varnish remover** [-rɪ'muːvəʳ] *n* Nagellackentferner *der.*

**Nairobi** [naɪ'rəubɪ] *n* Nairobi *nt.*

**naive, naïve** [naɪ'iːv] *adj* naiv.

**naivety, naïvety** [naɪ'iːvtɪ] *n* Naivität *die.*

**naked** ['neɪkɪd] *adj* - **1.** [nude] nackt - **2.** [flame] offen; [light bulb] nackt; **with the ~ eye** mit bloßem Auge - **3.** [truth, aggression] nackt.

**Nam** [næm] *n Am abbr of* Vietnam.

**name** [neɪm] *n* - **1.** [gen] Name *der;* **what's your ~?** wie heißen Sie/heißt du?; **my ~ is ...** ich heiße ...; **to know sb by ~** jn mit Namen kennen; **to know sb only by ~** jn nur dem Namen nach kennen; **by the ~ of** namens; **in the ~ of** im Namen *(+ G);* **the account is in her ~** das Konto läuft auf ihren Namen; **in ~ only** nur auf dem Papier; **to call sb ~s** jn beschimpfen - **2.** [reputation] Name *der,* Ruf *der;* **to clear one's ~** seine Unschuld beweisen; **to make a ~ for o.s.** sich *(D)* einen Namen machen <> *vt* - **1.** [baby, place, ship] einen Namen geben *(+ D);* **they ~d their daughter Kate** sie nannten ihre Tochter Kate; **I ~ this ship "Bounty"** ich taufe das Schiff auf den Namen „Bounty"; **to ~ sb after sb** *Br,* **to ~ sb for sb** *Am* jn nach jm nennen; **to ~ sthg after sthg** *Br,* **to ~ sthg for sthg** *Am* etw nach etw benennen - **2.** [reveal identity of]: **to ~ sb** js Namen nennen - **3.** [choose - price, date] nennen; [ - successor] ernennen.

**namedropping** ['neɪmdrɒpɪŋ] *n (U) geschicktes Einflechten der Namen berühmter Persönlichkeiten in eine Unterhaltung, um Eindruck zu machen.*

**nameless** ['neɪmlɪs] *adj* - **1.** [unknown] unbekannt; [having no name] namenlos; **one candidate, who shall remain ~** ... ein Kandidat, der ungenannt bleiben soll, ... - **2.** [indescribable] unbeschreiblich.

**namely** ['neɪmlɪ] *adv* nämlich.

**nameplate** ['neɪmpleɪt] *n* Namensschild *das;* [of company] Firmenschild *das.*

**namesake** ['neɪmseɪk] *n* Namensvetter *der,* -in *die.*

**Namibia** [nə'mɪbɪə] *n* Namibia *nt.*

**nan(a)** [næn(ə)] *n Br inf* Omi *die.*

**nan bread** [naːn-] *n fladenförmiges Brot, das zu indischem Curry serviert wird.*

**nanny** ['nænɪ] *n (pl* **-ies)** *n* [childminder] Kindermädchen *das.*

**nanny goat** *n* Ziege *die.*

**nap** [næp] *(pt* & *pp* **-ped;** *cont* **-ping)** *n* [sleep] Nickerchen *das;* **to take** *OR* **have a ~** ein Nickerchen machen <> *vi* [sleep] ein Nickerchen machen; **to be caught ~ping** *inf* überrumpelt werden.

**nape** [neɪp] *n:* **~ (of the neck)** Nacken *der.*

**napkin** ['næpkɪn] *n* [serviette] Serviette *die.*

**nappy** ['næpɪ] *n (pl* **-ies)** *n Br* Windel *die.*

**narcissi** [naː'sɪsaɪ] *pl* ⊏> **narcissus.**

**narcissism** ['naːsɪsɪzm] *n* Narzissmus *der.*

**narcissistic** [ˌnaːsɪ'sɪstɪk] *adj* narzisstisch.

**narcissus** [naː'sɪsəs] *(pl* **-cissuses** *OR* **-cissi)** *n* Narzisse *die.*

**narcotic** [naː'kɒtɪk] *n* Betäubungsmittel *das.*
➤ **narcotics** *npl* Rauschgift *das.*

**nark** [naːk] *Br inf n* [police informer] Spitzel *der* <> *vt* ärgern; **to be ~ed** sauer sein.

**narky** ['naːkɪ] *(compar* **-ier;** *superl* **-iest)** *adj Br inf* gereizt.

**narrate** [*Br* nə'reɪt, *Am* 'næreɪt] *vt* [story] erzählen; [documentary] kommentieren.

**narration** [*Br* nə'reɪʃn, *Am* næ'reɪʃn] *n* [product - of story] Erzählung *die;* [ - of documentary] Kommentierung *die;* [action - of story] Erzählen *das;* [ - of documentary] Kommentieren *das.*

**narrative** ['nærətɪv] *adj* [ability, skill] erzählerisch; [poem] narrativ <> *n* - **1.** [account] Schilderung *die* - **2.** *(U)* [art of narrating] Erzählkunst *die.*

**narrator** [*Br* nə'reɪtəʳ, *Am* 'næreɪtəʳ] *n* [in book] Erzähler *der,* -in *die;* [of documentary] Kommentator *der,* -in *die.*

**narrow** ['nærəu] *adj* - **1.** [not wide] schmal; [valley, lane] eng - **2.** [attitude, beliefs] engstirnig - **3.** [victory, defeat, majority] knapp <> *vt* - **1.** [almost shut]: **to ~ one's eyes** die Augen zu Schlitzen verengen - **2.** [difference, gap] verringern <> *vi* - **1.** [become less wide] sich verengen - **2.** [eyes] zu Schlitzen werden - **3.** [difference, gap] sich verringern.
➤ **narrow down** *vt sep* [restrict - choice] einlschränken; [ - possibilities] beschränken.

**narrow-gauge** *adj* RAIL Schmalspur-.

**narrowly** ['nærəulɪ] *adv* [just] knapp; [escape] mit knapper Not.

**narrow-minded** [-'maɪndɪd] *adj* engstirnig.

**N**

**NASA** ['næsəl (abbr of **National Aeronautics and Space Administration**) n NASA die.

**nasal** ['neızl] adj - **1.** [sound] näselnd - **2.** ANAT Nasen-.

**nastily** ['nɑːstɪlɪ] adv - **1.** [unkindly - act] gemein; [ - say] gehässig - **2.** [painfully - injure oneself] schlimm.

**nastiness** ['nɑːstɪnɪs] n [unkindness - of person, behaviour] Gemeinheit die; [ - of remark] Gehässigkeit die.

**nasturtium** [nəˈstɜːʃəm] (pl -s) n Kapuzinerkresse die.

**nasty** ['nɑːstɪ] (compar -ier; superl -iest) adj - **1.** [unkind - person, behaviour] gemein; [ - remark] gehässig - **2.** [smell, taste, weather] scheußlich - **3.** [problem, question] schwierig - **4.** [injury, accident, fall] schlimm.

**NAS/UWT** (abbr of **National Association of Schoolmasters/Union of Women Teachers**) n Lehrer- und Lehrerinnengewerkschaft in England und Wales.

**Natal** [nəˈtæl] n Natal nt.

**nation** ['neɪʃn] n Nation die; [people] Volk das.

**national** ['næʃənl] adj - **1.** [nationwide - strike] national, landesweit; [ - newspaper] überregional; [ - library, debt] Staats- - **2.** [typical of nation] landestypisch; [custom] Volks- <> n Staatsbürger der, -in die.

**national anthem** n Nationalhymne die.

**national curriculum** n Programm, das die Fächer und zu erreichenden Standards in den staatlichen Schulen in England und Wales festlegt.

**national debt** n Staatsverschuldung die.

**national dress** n Landestracht die.

**National Front** n rechtsradikale Partei in Großbritannien.

**national grid** n Br nationales Verbundnetz (für Elektrizität).

**National Guard** n Am: the ~ die Nationalgarde.

**National Health Service** n staatlicher britischer Gesundheitsdienst.

**National Insurance** n (U) Br - **1.** [system] Sozialversicherung die - **2.** [payments] Sozialversicherungsbeiträge pl.

**nationalism** ['næʃnəlɪzm] n Nationalismus der.

**nationalist** ['næʃnəlɪst] adj nationalistisch <> n Nationalist der, -in die.

**nationality** [ˌnæʃəˈnælətɪ] (pl -ies) n Nationalität die; dual ~ doppelte Staatsbürgerschaft.

**nationalization, -isation** [ˌnæʃnəlaɪˈzeɪʃn] n Verstaatlichung die.

**nationalize, -ise** ['næʃnəlaɪz] vt verstaatlichen.

**nationalized, -ised** ['næʃnəlaɪzd] adj verstaatlicht.

**National Lottery** n ≃ Lotto das, Lotto, das von einem britischen Privatunternehmen veranstaltet wird, dessen Gewinne teilweise einem guten Zweck zugeführt werden.

**national park** n Nationalpark der.

**national service** n Wehrdienst der.

**National Trust** n britische Organisation, die im Besitz historischer Bauwerke ist und diese unterhält.

**nation state** n Nationalstaat der.

**nationwide** ['neɪʃənwaɪd] adj & adv landesweit.

**native** ['neɪtɪv] adj [customs, population, plant] einheimisch; ~ **country** Heimatland das; **a ~ Italian** ein gebürtiger Italiener; ~ **speaker** Muttersprachler der; ~ **language** Muttersprache die; ~ **to** [plant, animal] beheimatet in (+ D) <> n [person] Einheimische der, die; offensive [of colony] Eingeborene der, die.

**Native American** adj indianisch <> n Indianer der, -in die.

**Nativity** [nəˈtɪvətɪ] n: **the** ~ die Geburt Christi.

**nativity play** n Krippenspiel das.

**NATO** ['neɪtəʊ] (abbr of **North Atlantic Treaty Organization**) n NATO die.

**natter** ['nætəʳ] Br inf n: **to have a** ~ ein Schwätzchen halten <> vi quasseln.

**natty** ['nætɪ] (compar -ier; superl -iest) adj inf [smart] schick.

**natural** ['nætʃrəl] adj - **1.** [gen] natürlich - **2.** [inborn - instinct, skill] angeboren; [ - footballer, musician etc] geboren - **3.** [disaster, phenomenon] Natur-; **to die of** ~ **causes** eines natürlichen Todes sterben - **4.** [mother, father] leiblich <> n: **she's a** ~ sie ist ein Naturtalent.

**natural childbirth** n natürliche Geburt.

**natural gas** n Erdgas das.

**natural history** n (U) Naturkunde die.

**naturalist** ['nætʃrəlɪst] n Naturforscher der, -in die.

**naturalize, -ise** ['nætʃrəlaɪz] vt [make citizen] einbürgern; **to be ~d** eingebürgert werden.

**naturally** ['nætʃrəlɪ] adv - **1.** [of course] natürlich - **2.** [behave, speak] natürlich - **3.** [cheerful, talented] von Natur aus; **to come ~ to sb** jm leicht fallen.

**naturalness** ['nætʃrəlnɪs] n Natürlichkeit die.

**natural resources** npl natürliche Ressourcen pl.

**natural science** n Naturwissenschaft die.

**natural yoghurt** *n* Naturjoghurt *der* OR *das.*

**nature** ['neɪtʃə'] *n* - **1.** [gen] Natur *die;* **matters of a serious** ~ ernste Angelegenheiten - **2.** [temperament] Wesen *das;* **by** ~ von Natur aus - **3.** [type] Art *die.*

**nature reserve** *n* Naturschutzgebiet *das.*

**nature trail** *n* Naturlehrpfad *der.*

**naturist** ['neɪtʃərɪst] *n* Anhänger *der,* -in *die* der Freikörperkultur; ~ **beach** FKK-Strand *der.*

**naughty** ['nɔːtɪ] (*compar* -**ier;** *superl* -**iest**) *adj* - **1.** [child] ungezogen; [animal] schlecht erzogen - **2.** [word, story] unanständig.

**nausea** ['nɔːzɪə] *n* Übelkeit *die.*

**nauseam** ['nɔːzɪæm] ⊳ **ad nauseam.**

**nauseate** ['nɔːzɪeɪt] *vt:* **to** ~ **sb** in jm Übelkeit erregen; **fig** jn anwidern.

**nauseating** ['nɔːzɪeɪtɪŋ] *adj* - **1.** [sickening] Übelkeit erregend - **2.** **fig** [disgusting] abscheulich.

**nauseous** ['nɔːʒəs] *adj* - **1.** [sick] übel; **I feel** ~ mir ist übel - **2.** **fig** [revolting] scheußlich.

**nautical** ['nɔːtɪkl] *adj* nautisch; [map] See-; [term] seemännisch.

**nautical mile** *n* Seemeile *die.*

**naval** ['neɪvl] *adj* Marine-; [battle, forces] See-.

**naval officer** *n* Marineoffizier *der.*

**nave** [neɪv] *n* Kirchenschiff *das.*

**navel** ['neɪvl] *n* Nabel *der.*

**navigate** ['nævɪgeɪt] *vt* - **1.** [steer - plane, ship] navigieren - **2.** [sea] befahren ⟨⟩ *vi* [in plane, ship] navigieren; **I'll drive, and you** ~ ich fahre, und du dirigierst mich.

**navigation** [ˌnævɪ'geɪʃn] *n* Navigation *die.*

**navigator** ['nævɪgeɪtə'] *n* Navigator *der.*

**navvy** ['nævɪ] (*pl* -**ies**) *n* Br inf Bauarbeiter *der.*

**navy** ['neɪvɪ] (*pl* -**ies**) *n* - **1.** [armed force] (Kriegs)marine *die* - **2.** [colour] Marineblau *das* ⟨⟩ *adj* [in colour] marineblau.

**navy blue** *adj* marineblau ⟨⟩ *n* Marineblau *das.*

**Nazareth** ['næzərɪθ] *n* Nazareth *nt.*

**Nazi** ['nɑːtsɪ] (*pl* -**s**) *adj* [supporter] Nazi-; [ideas, beliefs] nazistisch ⟨⟩ *n* Nazi *der.*

**NB** - **1.** (*abbr of* **nota bene**) NB - **2.** *abbr of* **New Brunswick.**

**NBA** *n* - **1.** (*abbr of* **National Basketball Association**) NBA *die* - **2.** (*abbr of* **National Boxing Association**) NBA *die.*

**NBC** (*abbr of* **National Broadcasting Company**) *n* NBC *die.*

**NC** - **1.** (*abbr of* **no charge**) gebührenfrei - **2.** *abk für* **North Carolina**, *in Postanschrift verwendet.*

**NCO** (*abbr of* **noncommissioned officer**) *n* Uffz. *der.*

**ND** *abk für* **North Dakota**, *in Postanschrift verwendet.*

**NE** - **1.** *abk für* **Nebraska**, *in Postanschrift verwendet* - **2.** *abk für* **New England**, *in Postanschrift verwendet* - **3.** (*abbr of* **northeast**) NO.

**Neanderthal** [nɪ'ændətɑːl] *n* Neandertaler *der.*

**neap tide** [niːp-] *n* Nippflut *die*

**near** [nɪə'] *adj* nahe; **in the** ~ **future** demnächst; **the** ~**est hospital** das nächste Krankenhaus; **a** ~ **disaster** beinahe ein Unglück; **it was a** ~ **thing (for us)** wir sind gerade noch davongekommen ⟨⟩ *adv* nahe; ~ **at hand** (ganz) in der Nähe; **to come** OR **draw** ~ **to sb/ sthg** sich jm/etw nähern; **a** ~ **impossible task** eine nahezu unmögliche Aufgabe ⟨⟩ *prep:* ~ **(to)** nahe an (+ D); ~ **the door** bei der Tür; **bring your chair** ~**er to the fire** rück deinen Stuhl näher ans Feuer; ~ **to death/despair** dem Tode/der Verzweiflung nahe; **that's nowhere** ~ **enough** das ist bei weitem nicht genug; **to be** ~ **(to) the truth** an die Wahrheit herankommen ⟨⟩ *vt* sich nähern (+ D); **they** ~**ed their destination** sie kamen ihren Ziel näher; **the road is** ~**ing completion** die Straße ist fast fertig ⟨⟩ *vi* sich nähern.

**nearby** [nɪə'baɪ] *adj* nahe gelegen ⟨⟩ *adv* in der Nähe.

**Near East** *n:* **the** ~ der Nahe Osten.

**nearly** ['nɪəlɪ] *adv* [almost] fast, beinahe; **I** ~ **fell** ich bin fast OR beinahe gefallen; **not** ~ bei weitem nicht; **not** ~ **enough** bei weitem nicht genug.

**near miss** *n* [between aircraft] Beinahezusammenstoß *der.*

**nearness** ['nɪənɪs] *n* Nähe *die.*

**nearside** ['nɪəsaɪd] *adj* auf der Beifahrerseite ⟨⟩ *n* Beifahrerseite *die.*

**nearsighted** [ˌnɪə'saɪtɪd] *adj* Am kurzsichtig.

**neat** [niːt] *adj* - **1.** [tidy] ordentlich; [sb's appearance] adrett - **2.** [skilful - solution] elegant; [ - manoeuvre] geschickt - **3.** [whisky, vodka *etc*] pur - **4.** Am inf [very good] super.

**neatly** ['niːtlɪ] *adv* - **1.** [tidily] ordentlich; [dress] adrett - **2.** [skilfully] geschickt.

**neatness** ['niːtnɪs] *n* (U) [tidiness] Ordentlichkeit *die;* [of appearance] Adrettheit *die.*

**NEC** (*abbr of* **National Exhibition Centre**) *n* Messe- und Veranstaltungszentrum in Birmingham.

**necessarily** [ˌnesə'serɪlɪ, Br 'nesəsrəlɪ] *adv* notwendigerweise; **not** ~ nicht unbedingt.

**necessary** ['nesəsrɪ] *adj* - **1.** [required] notwendig, nötig; **to make it** ~ **for sb to do sthg** es erforderlich machen, dass jd etw tut - **2.** [inevitable] unausweichlich.

**necessitate** [nɪ'sesɪteɪt] *vt fml* erforderlich machen.

**necessity** [nɪ'sesətɪ] (*pl* -ies) *n* - **1.** [need] Notwendigkeit *die;* the basic necessities of life das Lebensnotwendige; of ~ notwendigerweise - **2.** [necessary thing] Notwendigkeit *die.*

**neck** [nek] *n* - **1.** [gen] Hals *der;* to be up to one's ~ in sthg bis zum Hals in etw (*D*) stecken; to breathe down sb's ~ [subj: boss] jm dauernd auf die Finger sehen; [subj: competitors] jm im Nacken sitzen; she didn't want to stick her ~ out sie hatte Angst, etwas zu riskieren - **2.** [of shirt] Kragen *der;* [of dress] Ausschnitt *der* <> *vi inf* knutschen.

➤ neck and neck *adj* gleichauf; the two horses are ~ and ~ zwischen den beiden Pferden gibt es ein Kopf-an-Kopf-Rennen.

**neckerchief** ['nekətʃɪf] (*pl* -chiefs OR -chieves [-tʃiːvz]) *n* Halstuch *das.*

**necklace** ['neklɪs] *n* (Hals)kette *die.*

**neckline** ['neklaɪn] *n* Ausschnitt *der.*

**necktie** ['nektaɪ] *n Am* Krawatte *die.*

**nectar** ['nektəʳ] *n* Nektar *der.*

**nectarine** ['nektərɪn] *n* Nektarine *die.*

**née** [neɪ] *adj* geborene.

**need** [niːd] *n* - **1.** [requirement, necessity] Bedürfnis *das;* to be in OR have ~ of sthg etw brauchen; in ~ of repair reparaturbedürftig; there is no ~ (for you) to cry du brauchst nicht zu weinen; if ~ be notfalls - **2.** [distress, poverty] Not *die* <> *vt* brauchen; to ~ to do sthg etw tun müssen; you don't ~ to wait for me du brauchst nicht auf mich zu warten; that's all I ~! *fig* das hat mir gerade noch gefehlt! <> *aux vb:* ~ we go? müssen wir gehen?; it ~ not happen es muss nicht dazu kommen.

➤ needs *adv:* if ~s must wenn unbedingt notwendig.

**needle** ['niːdl] *n* Nadel *die;* it's like looking for a ~ in a haystack es ist, als ob man eine Stecknadel im Heuhafen suchen würde <> *vt inf* ärgern.

**needless** ['niːdlɪs] *adj* unnötig; ~ to say ... selbstverständlich ...

**needlessly** ['niːdlɪslɪ] *adv* unnötigerweise.

**needlework** ['niːdlwɜːk] *n* (*U*) Handarbeit *die.*

**needn't** ['niːdnt] = need not.

**needy** ['niːdɪ] (*compar* -ier; *superl* -iest) *adj* bedürftig <> *npl:* the ~ die Bedürftigen *pl.*

**nefarious** [nɪ'feərɪəs] *adj fml* ruchlos.

**negate** [nɪ'geɪt] *vt fml* [cancel out] zunichte machen.

**negative** ['negətɪv] *adj* - **1.** [not affirmative] negativ - **2.** [pessimistic] pessimistisch <> *n*

- **1.** PHOT Negativ *das* - **2.** LING Verneinung *die;* [word] Verneinungswort *das;* to answer in the ~ mit „Nein" antworten.

**neglect** [nɪ'glekt] *n* Vernachlässigung *die* <> *vt* - **1.** [not take care of] vernachlässigen - **2.** [not do - duty] versäumen; [ - task, work] unerledigt lassen; to ~ to do sthg es versäumen, etw zu tun.

**neglected** [nɪ'glektɪd] *adj* [child] vernachlässigt; [garden] verwahrlost.

**neglectful** [nɪ'glektfʊl] *adj:* ~ parents ihr(e) Kind(er) vernachlässigende Eltern; to be ~ of sb/sthg jn/etw vernachlässigen.

**negligee** ['neglɪʒeɪ] *n* Negligee *das.*

**negligence** ['neglɪdʒəns] *n* Nachlässigkeit *die;* [causing danger & LAW] Fahrlässigkeit *die.*

**negligent** ['neglɪdʒənt] *adj* nachlässig; [causing danger & LAW] fahrlässig.

**negligently** ['neglɪdʒəntlɪ] *adv* nachlässig; [causing danger & LAW] fahrlässig.

**negligible** ['neglɪdʒəbl] *adj* unerheblich.

**negotiable** [nɪ'gəʊʃəbl] *adj* verhandlungsfähig; the salary is ~ über das Gehalt kann verhandelt werden.

**negotiate** [nɪ'gəʊʃɪeɪt] *vt* - **1.** [agreement, deal] aushandeln - **2.** [obstacle] überwinden; [bend] nehmen; [hill, rapids] passieren <> *vi* verhandeln; to ~ with sb for sthg mit jm über etw (*A*) verhandeln.

**negotiation** [nɪˌgəʊʃɪ'eɪʃn] *n* Verhandlung *die.*

**negotiator** [nɪ'gəʊʃɪeɪtəʳ] *n* Unterhändler *der,* -in *die.*

**Negress** ['niːgrɪs] *n* Negerin *die.*

**Negro** ['niːgrəʊ] (*pl* -es) *n* Neger *der.*

**neigh** [neɪ] *vi* wiehern.

**neighbor** *etc n Am* = neighbour *etc.*

**neighbour** *Br,* **neighbor** *Am* ['neɪbəʳ] *n* Nachbar *der,* -in *die;* [at table] Tischnachbar *der,* -in *die;* [country] Nachbarland *das.*

**neighbourhood** *Br,* **neighborhood** *Am* ['neɪbəhʊd] *n* [small area of town] Gegend *die;* [people] Nachbarschaft *die;* in the ~ in der Nachbarschaft; [approximately]: it costs in the ~ of £3,000 es kostet so um die 3000 Pfund.

**neighbourhood watch** *n Br* Programm *zur Verbrechensbekämpfung, bei dem die Bewohner einer Gegend die Nachbarschaft überwachen und Vorfälle der Polizei melden.*

**neighbouring** *Br,* **neighboring** *Am* ['neɪbərɪŋ] *adj* angrenzend.

**neighbourly** *Br,* **neighborly** *Am* ['neɪbəlɪ] *adj* [relations, deed] gutnachbarlich; a ~ person ein guter Nachbar.

**neither** ['naɪðəʳ, 'niːðəʳ] *adj:* ~ bag is big enough keine der beiden Taschen ist groß genug

◇ *pron:* ~ **of us** keiner von uns beiden ◇ *conj:* ~ **do** I ich auch nicht; ~ ... **nor** ... weder ... noch ...; **that's** ~ **here nor there** *fig* das hat nichts mit der Sache zu tun.

**neo-** ['ni:əʊ] *prefix* Neo-, neo-.

**neoclassical** [,ni:əʊ'klæsɪkl] *adj* klassizistisch.

**neolithic** [,ni:ə'lɪθɪk] *adj* neolithisch.

**neologism** [ni:'ɒlədʒɪzm] *n* Neologismus *der.*

**neon** ['ni:ɒn] *n* Neon *das.*

**neon light** *n* Neonlicht *das.*

**neon sign** *n* [name] Neonschild *das;* [advertisement] Neonreklame *die.*

**Nepal** [nɪ'pɔːl] *n* Nepal *nt.*

**Nepalese** [,nepə'liːz] (*pl inv*) *adj* nepalesisch ◇ *n* [person] Nepalese *der,* -sin *die.*

**Nepali** [nɪ'pɔːlɪ] *n* Nepali *das.*

**nephew** ['nefjuː] *n* Neffe *der.*

**nepotism** ['nepətɪzm] *n* Vetternwirtschaft *die.*

**Neptune** ['neptjuːn] *n* [planet] Neptun *der.*

**nerd** [nɜːd] *n inf:* **computer** ~ Computerfreak *der.*

**nerve** [nɜːv] *n* - **1.** ANAT Nerv *der* - **2.** [courage] Mut *der;* **to lose/keep one's** ~ seine Nerven verlieren/behalten - **3.** [cheek] Frechheit *die.*

➡ **nerves** *npl* Nerven *pl;* **to get on sb's** ~**s** jm auf die Nerven gehen.

**nerve centre** *n* - **1.** ANAT Nervenzentrum *das* - **2.** *fig* [headquarters] Schaltstelle *die.*

**nerve-racking** [-,rækɪŋ] *adj* nervenaufreibend.

**nervous** ['nɜːvəs] *adj* [condition, twitch] nervös; [tissue, illness] Nerven-; **to be** ~ **of** Angst haben vor; **to be** ~ **about sthg** nervös wegen etw *(D)* sein.

**nervous breakdown** *n* Nervenzusammenbruch *der.*

**nervously** ['nɜːvəslɪ] *adv* nervös.

**nervousness** ['nɜːvəsnɪs] *n* - **1.** [apprehension] Nervosität *die* - **2.** [tension] Angespanntheit *die.*

**nervous system** *n* Nervensystem *das.*

**nervous wreck** *n:* **to be a** ~ mit den Nerven völlig am Ende sein.

**nervy** ['nɜːvɪ] (*compar* -ier; *superl* -iest) *adj inf* - **1.** [nervous] nervös - **2.** *Am* [cheeky] frech.

**nest** [nest] *n* - **1.** [gen] Nest *das* - **2.** [of tables] Satz *der* ◇ *vi* [bird] nisten.

**nest egg** *n* [money] Notgroschen *der.*

**nestle** ['nesl] *vi* [make o.s. comfortable] es sich bequem machen; **to** ~ **(down) among the cushions** sich in die Kissen kuscheln.

**nestling** ['neslɪŋ] *n* Nestling *der.*

**net** [net] *n* (*pt* & *pp* **-ted;** *cont* **-ting**) *adj* - **1.** [profit, weight] Netto-, netto - **2.** [final] End- ◇ *n* - **1.** [gen] Netz *das* - **2.** *(U)* [type of fabric] Tüll *der* ◇ *vt* - **1.** [catch] mit dem Netz fangen - **2.** *fig* [husband] sich *(D)* angeln; [criminal] fangen; [fortune] verdienen - **3.** [profit, sum - subj: deal] netto einIbringen; [ - subj: person] netto einInehmen.

➡ **Net** *n* COMPUT: **the Net** das Internet.

**netball** ['netbɔːl] *n* Korbball *der.*

**net curtains** *npl* Tüllgardinen *pl.*

**Netherlands** ['neðələndz] *npl:* **the** ~ die Niederlande *pl.*

**net profit** *n* Nettogewinn *der.*

**nett** [net] *adj* = **net.**

**netting** ['netɪŋ] *n (U)* - **1.** [gen] Netz *das;* [metal] Maschendraht *der* - **2.** [fabric] Tüll *der.*

**nettle** ['netl] *n* Nessel *die* ◇ *vt* [irritate] ärgern.

**network** ['netwɜːk] *n* - **1.** [gen] Netz *das* - **2.** RADIO & TV [station] Sendenetz *das* - **3.** COMPUT Netzwerk *das* ◇ *vt* - **1.** RADIO & TV [broadcast] ausIstrahlen - **2.** COMPUT vernetzen ◇ *vi* COMM Kontakte knüpfen.

**networking** ['netwɜːkɪŋ] *n (U)* COMM Kontaktpflege *die.*

**neuralgia** [njʊə'rældʒə] *n* Neuralgie *die.*

**neurological** [,njʊərə'lɒdʒɪkl] *adj* neurologisch.

**neurologist** [,njʊə'rɒlədʒɪst] *n* Neurologe *der,* -gin *die.*

**neurology** [,njʊə'rɒlədʒɪ] *n* Neurologie *die.*

**neurosis** [,njʊə'rəʊsɪs] (*pl* **-ses** [siːz]) *n* Neurose *die.*

**neurosurgery** [,njʊərəʊ's3ːdʒərɪ] *n* Neurochirurgie *die.*

**neurotic** [,njʊə'rɒtɪk] *adj* neurotisch ◇ *n* Neurotiker *der,* -in *die.*

**neuter** ['njuːtə'] *adj* GRAMM sächlich ◇ *vt* [animal] kastrieren.

**neutral** ['njuːtrəl] *adj* - **1.** POL & ELEC neutral - **2.** [inexpressive] ausdruckslos - **3.** [pale grey-brown] naturfarben - **4.** [colourless] farblos ◇ *n* - **1.** *(U)* AUT Leerlauf *der;* **in** ~ im Leerlauf - **2.** POL [country] neutrales Land; [person] Neutrale *der,* *die.*

**neutrality** [njuː'trælətɪ] *n* POL Neutralität *die.*

**neutralize, -ise** ['njuːtrəlaɪz] *vt* [effects] neutralisieren.

**neutron** ['njuːtrɒn] *n* Neutron *das.*

**neutron bomb** *n* Neutronenbombe *die.*

**never** ['nevə'] *adv* nie; *(simple negative)* nicht; **she's** ~ **late** sie kommt nie zu spät; **he** ~ **said a word about it** er hat gar nichts davon gesagt; ~ **mind!** macht nichts!; **you've** ~ **asked him to dinner!** [in disbelief] hast du ihn wirklich zum Essen eingeladen?; **well** I ~! na so was!

**N**

**never-ending** *adj* endlos.

**never-never** *n Br inf:* on the ~ auf Pump, auf Raten.

**nevertheless** [ˌnevəðə'les] *adv* trotzdem, nichtsdestoweniger.

**new** [*adj* njuː, *n* njuːz] *adj* neu; **as good as** ~ so gut wie neu; **to be** ~ **to sthg** neu in etw *(D)* sein.

➤ **news** *n (U)* - **1.** [information] Nachricht *die*, Neuigkeit *die;* **that's ~s to me** das ist mir neu; **who will break the ~s to him?** wer wird es ihm beibringen? - **2.** RADIO & TV Nachrichten *pl*.

**New Age** *n* New Age *das*.

**new blood** *n (U) fig* junges Blut.

**newborn** ['njuːbɔːn] *adj* neugeboren.

**newcomer** ['njuːˌkʌməʳ] *n:* ~ **(to sthg)** Neuling *der* (in etw *(D)*).

**New England** *n* Neuengland *nt*.

**newfangled** [ˌnjuː'fæŋgld] *adj inf pej* neumodisch.

**new-found** *adj* [confidence, strength] neu gefunden.

**Newfoundland** ['njuːfəndlənd] *n* Neufundland *nt*.

**newly** ['njuːlɪ] *adv* neu; ~ **painted** frisch gestrichen.

**newlyweds** ['njuːlɪwedz] *npl* Frischvermählte *pl*.

**new moon** *n* Neumond *der*.

**news agency** *n* Nachrichtenagentur *die*.

**newsagent** *Br* ['njuːzeɪdʒənt], **newsdealer** *Am* ['njuːzdiːlər] *n* Zeitungshändler *der*, -in *die;* ~'**s (shop)** Zeitungshändler *der*.

**news bulletin** *n* Bulletin *das*.

**newscast** ['njuːzkɑːst] *n* Nachrichtensendung *die*.

**newscaster** ['njuːzkɑːstəʳ] *n* Nachrichtensprecher *der*, -in *die*.

**news conference** *n* Pressekonferenz *die*.

**newsdealer** *n Am* = newsagent.

**newsflash** ['njuːzflæʃ] *n* Kurzmeldung *die*.

**newsletter** ['njuːzˌletəʳ] *n* Rundschreiben *das*, Mitteilungsblatt *das*.

**newsman** ['njuːzmæn] *(pl* -men [-mən]) *n* Reporter *der*.

**newspaper** ['njuːzˌpeɪpəʳ] *n* - **1.** [publication, company] Zeitung *die* - **2.** [paper] Zeitungspapier *das*.

**newspaperman** ['njuːzˌpeɪpəmæn] *(pl* -men [-men]) *n* - **1.** [journalist] Journalist *der* - **2.** [seller] Zeitungsverkäufer *der*.

**newsprint** ['njuːzprɪnt] *n* Zeitungspapier *das*.

**newsreader** ['njuːzˌriːdəʳ] *n* Nachrichtensprecher *der*, -in *die*.

**newsroom** ['njuːzruːm] *n* Nachrichtenredaktion *die*.

**newssheet** ['njuːzʃiːt] *n* Informationsblatt *das*.

**newsstand** ['njuːzstænd] *n* Zeitungskiosk *der*.

**newsworthy** ['njuːzˌwɜːðɪ] *adj* berichtenswert.

**newt** [njuːt] *n* Wassermolch *der*.

**New Testament** *n:* the ~ das Neue Testament.

**new town** *n Br* vollständig neu erbaute Stadt.

**new wave** *n* - **1.** CINEMA neue Welle - **2.** [in pop music] New Wave *die*.

**New World** *n:* the ~ die Neue Welt.

**New Year** *n* Neujahr *das;* **Happy ~!** frohes neues Jahr!

**New Year's Day** *n* Neujahrstag *der*.

**New Year's Eve** *n* Silvester *der OR das*.

**New York** [-'jɔːk] *n* New York *nt*.

**New Yorker** [-'jɔːkəʳ] *n* New Yorker *der*, -in *die*.

**New Zealand** [-'ziːlənd] *n* Neuseeland *nt*.

**New Zealander** [-'ziːləndəʳ] *n* Neuseeländer *der*, -in *die*.

**next** [nekst] *adj* nächste, -r, -s; **when does the** ~ **bus leave?** wann fährt der nächste Bus ab? ◇ *adv* - **1.** [afterwards] als nächstes, danach - **2.** [on next occasion] das nächste Mal; **the week after** ~ übernächste Woche - **3.** *(with superlatives):* **the** ~ **most expensive** der/die/das nächstteuerste; **the** ~ **best thing to do would be to ...** das nächstbeste wäre, zu ... ◇ *pron:* ~ **please!** der Nächste bitte!

➤ **next to** *prep* - **1.** [near] neben - **2.** [in comparisons]: ~ **to music I like the theatre best** nach Musik mag ich Theater am liebsten - **3.** [almost] fast; ~ **to nothing** fast nichts; **I got it for** ~ **nothing** ich habe es fast umsonst bekommen.

**next door** *adv* nebenan.

➤ **next-door** *adj:* **next-door neighbour** direkter Nachbar, direkte Nachbarin.

**next of kin** *n* nächste Angehörige *der*, nächste Angehörige *die*.

**NF** *n abbr of* **National Front** ◇ *abk für Newfoundland, in Postanschrift verwendet*.

**NFL** *(abbr of* **National Football League**) *n höchste American Football-Liga in den USA*.

**NFU** *(abbr of* **National Farmers' Union**) *n britische Bauerngewerkschaft*.

**NG** *n abbr of* **National Guard**.

**NGO** *(abbr of* **non-governmental organization**) *n* NRO *die*, *Nichtregierungsorganisation*.

**NH** *abk für New Hampshire, in Postanschrift verwendet.*

**NHL** (*abbr of* **National Hockey League**) *n Natio-nale Eishockeyliga in den USA.*

**NHS** *n abbr of* **National Health Service.**

**NI** *n abbr of* **National Insurance** <> *abk für Northern Ireland, in Postanschrift verwendet.*

**Niagara** [naɪˈægrə] *n:* ~ **Falls** Niagarafälle *pl.*

**nib** [nɪb] *n* Feder *die.*

**nibble** [ˈnɪbl] *vt* knabbern <> *vi:* **to ~ at sthg** an etw (D) knabbern.

**Nicaragua** [ˌnɪkəˈrægjʊə] *n* Nicaragua *nt.*

**Nicaraguan** [ˌnɪkəˈrægjʊən] *adj* nicaragua-nisch <> *n* Nicaraguaner *der,* -in *die.*

**nice** [naɪs] *adj* **- 1.** [car, picture, weather] schön; [dress] hübsch; [food] gut; **to have a ~ time** Spaß haben; **it's ~ and warm** es ist schön warm **- 2.** [kind, pleasant] nett, sympathisch; **to be ~ to sb** nett zu jm sein.

**nice-looking** [-ˈlʊkɪŋ] *adj* [person] gut ausse-hend; [car, house] schön.

**nicely** [ˈnaɪslɪ] *adv* **- 1.** [well, attractively - dressed, decorated] hübsch; [ - made] schön **- 2.** [politely - ask] höflich; [ - behave] gut **- 3.** [satisfactorily] gut; **that will do ~** das ist genau richtig.

**niceties** [ˈnaɪsətɪz] *npl* Feinheiten *pl.*

**niche** [niːʃ] *n* **- 1.** [in wall] Nische *die* **- 2.** [in life]: **she's found her ~ in life** sie hat ihren Platz ge-funden.

**nick** [nɪk] *n* **- 1.** [cut] Kerbe *die,* Einkerbung *die* **- 2.** *Br inf* [jail]: **the ~** der Knast **- 3.** *Br inf* [condi-tion]: **to be in good/bad ~** [object] gut/schlecht erhalten sein; [person] in guter/schlechter Verfassung sein **- 4.** *phr:* **in the ~ of time** in letzter Minute <> *vt* **- 1.** [cut - wood] einl-kerben; **to ~ one's chin** sich am Kinn schnei-den **- 2.** *Br inf* [steal] klauen **- 3.** *Br inf* [arrest] schnappen.

**nickel** [ˈnɪkl] *n* **- 1.** [metal] Nickel *das* **- 2.** *Am* [coin] Fünfcentstück *das.*

**nickname** [ˈnɪkneɪm] *n* Spitzname *der* <> *vt:* **they ~d him One Eye** sie gaben ihm den Spitznamen Einäugiger.

**nicotine** [ˈnɪkətiːn] *n* Nikotin *das.*

**niece** [niːs] *n* Nichte *die.*

**nifty** [ˈnɪftɪ] (*compar* **-ier**; *superl* **-iest**) *adj inf* [gadget] raffiniert, ausgeklügelt; [car] klasse, prima.

**Niger** [ˈnaɪdʒəʳ] *n* **- 1.** [country] Niger *nt* **- 2.** [river]: **the ~** der Niger.

**Nigeria** [naɪˈdʒɪərɪə] *n* Nigeria *nt.*

**Nigerian** [naɪˈdʒɪərɪən] *adj* nigerianisch <> *n* Nigerianer *der,* -in *die.*

**niggardly** [ˈnɪgədlɪ] *adj* [person] knauserig; [amount] spärlich.

**niggle** [ˈnɪgl] *n* Besorgnis *die* <> *vt* **- 1.** [worry]

zu schaffen machen (+D) **- 2.** [criticize] heruml-kritisieren an (+ D) <> *vi* **- 1.** [worry]: **to ~ at sb** nagen an jm **- 2.** [criticize] heruml-kritisieren.

**nigh** [naɪ] *adv* **- 1.** *literary* [near] nah **- 2.: well ~** [almost] nahezu.

**night** [naɪt] *n* **- 1.** [not day] Nacht *die;* **at ~** nachts; **~ and day, day and ~** tagein tagaus **- 2.** [evening] Abend *der;* **at ~** abends **- 3.** *phr:* **to have an early/a late ~** früh/spät ins Bett ge-hen.

➤ **nights** *adv* **- 1.** *Am* [at night] nachts **- 2.** *Br* [night shift]: **to work ~s** Nachtschicht arbeiten.

**nightcap** [ˈnaɪtkæp] *n* **- 1.** [drink] Schlummer-trunk *der* **- 2.** [hat] Nachtmütze *die.*

**nightclub** [ˈnaɪtklʌb] *n* Nightclub *der.*

**nightdress** [ˈnaɪtdres] *n* Nachthemd *das.*

**nightfall** [ˈnaɪtfɔːl] *n:* **at ~** bei Einbruch der Dunkelheit.

**nightgown** [ˈnaɪtgaʊn] *n* Nachthemd *das.*

**nightie** [ˈnaɪtɪ] *n inf* Nachthemd *das.*

**nightingale** [ˈnaɪtɪŋgeɪl] *n* Nachtigall *die.*

**nightlife** [ˈnaɪtlaɪf] *n* Nachtleben *das.*

**nightlight** [ˈnaɪtlaɪt] *n* Nachtlicht *das.*

**nightly** [ˈnaɪtlɪ] *adj* nächtlich <> *adv* [every evening] jeden Abend; [every night] jede Nacht.

**nightmare** [ˈnaɪtmeəʳ] *n lit* & *fig* Albtraum *der.*

**nightmarish** [ˈnaɪtmeərɪʃ] *adj* grauenhaft.

**night owl** *n fig* Nachteule *die.*

**night porter** *n* Nachtportier *der.*

**night safe** *n* Nachttresor *der.*

**night school** *n (U)* Abendschule *die.*

**night shift** *n* Nachtschicht *die.*

**nightshirt** [ˈnaɪtʃɜːt] *n* Nachthemd *das (für Herren).*

**nightstick** [ˈnaɪtˌstɪk] *n Am* Schlagstock *der.*

**nighttime** [ˈnaɪttaɪm] *n (U)* Nacht *die.*

**night watchman** *n* Nachtwächter *der.*

**nihilism** [ˈnaɪəlɪzm] *n* Nihilismus *der.*

**nil** [nɪl] *n* **- 1.** [nothing] null **- 2.** *Br* SPORT: **two ~** zwei zu null.

**Nile** [naɪl] *n:* **the ~** der Nil.

**nimble** [ˈnɪmbl] *adj* **- 1.** [person] wendig, be-weglich; [fingers] geschickt **- 2.** [mind] beweg-lich, wach.

**nimbly** [ˈnɪmblɪ] *adv* flink.

**nine** [naɪn] *num* neun; *see also* **six.**

**nineteen** [ˌnaɪnˈtiːn] *num* neunzehn; *see also* **six.**

**nineteenth** [naɪnˈtiːnθ] *num* neunzehnte, -r, -s; *see also* **sixth.**

**ninetieth** ['naɪntɪəθ] *num* neunzigste, -r, -s; *see also* **sixth.**

**ninety** ['naɪntɪ] *num* neunzig; *see also* **sixty.**

**ninny** ['nɪnɪ] (*pl* **-ies**) *n inf* Trottel *der.*

**ninth** [naɪnθ] *num* neunte, -r, -s; *see also* **sixth.**

**nip** [nɪp] (*pt* & *pp* **-ped;** *cont* **-ping**) *n* - **1.** [bite] leichter Biss; [pinch] Kniff *der* - **2.** [of drink] Schluck *der* ◇ *vt* [bite] beißen; [pinch] kneifen ◇ *vi Br inf:* **I'm just ~ping to the shops/pub** ich gehe mal kurz einkaufen/in die Kneipe.

**nipper** ['nɪpəʳ] *n Br inf* Kleine *der, die.*

**nipple** ['nɪpl] *n* - **1.** [of breast] Brustwarze *die* - **2.** [of baby's bottle] Schnuller *der,* Sauger *der.*

**nippy** ['nɪpɪ] (*compar* **-ier;** *superl* **-iest**) *adj* - **1.** [cold] frisch - **2.** [quick - car] flott; [ - person] flink.

**Nissen hut** ['nɪsn-] *n* Nissenhütte *die.*

**nit** [nɪt] *n* - **1.** [in hair] Nisse *die* - **2.** *Br inf* [idiot] Blödmann *der.*

**nitpicking** ['nɪtpɪkɪŋ] *inf adj* spitzfindig ◇ *n* (*U*) Spitzfindigkeit *die.*

**nitrate** ['naɪtreɪt] *n* Nitrat *das.*

**nitric acid** [ˌnaɪtrɪk-] *n* Salpetersäure *die.*

**nitrogen** ['naɪtrədʒən] *n* Stickstoff *der.*

**nitroglycerin(e)** [ˌnaɪtrəʊ'glɪsəriːn] *n* Nitroglyzerin *das.*

**nitty-gritty** [ˌnɪtɪ'grɪtɪ] *n inf:* **to get down to the ~** zur Sache kommen.

**nitwit** ['nɪtwɪt] *n inf* Trottel *der.*

**nix** [nɪks] *Am inf n* [nothing] nix ◇ *adv* [no] nein ◇ *vt* [say no to] über den Haufen werfen.

**NJ** *abk für New Jersey, in Postanschrift verwendet.*

**NLRB** (*abbr of* **National Labor Relations Board**) *n US-Vermittlungsstelle zur Beilegung von Konflikten in der Industrie.*

**NM** *abk für New Mexico, in Postanschrift verwendet.*

**no** [nəʊ] (*pl* **-es**) *adv* nein; **to answer ~** mit einem Nein antworten; **I am ~ richer than he is** ich bin nicht reicher als er ◇ *adj* kein; **I have ~ money left** ich habe kein Geld übrig; **it's ~ easy job** es ist keine leichte Aufgabe; **it's ~ good** *OR* **use** es nützt nichts; **in ~ time** im Nu; **'~ smoking'** 'Rauchen verboten'; **~ way!** *inf* auf keinen Fall!, nie im Leben! ◇ *n* Nein *das;* **she won't take ~ for an answer** sie lässt sich nicht davon abbringen.

**No., no.** (*abbr of* **number**) Nr.

**Noah's ark** [ˌnəʊəz-] *n* Arche Noah *die.*

**nobble** ['nɒbl] *vt Br inf* - **1.** [racehorse] lahm legen - **2.** [bribe] bestechen - **3.** [grab, catch] sich (*D*) schnappen.

**Nobel prize** [ˌnəʊˌbel-] *n* Nobelpreis *der.*

**nobility** [nə'bɪlətɪ] *n* - **1.** [aristocracy]: **the ~** der Adel - **2.** [nobleness] Vornehmheit *die.*

**noble** ['nəʊbl] *adj* - **1.** [aristocratic] adlig - **2.** [fine, distinguished] edel, nobel - **3.** [brave] heldenhaft ◇ *n* Adlige *der, die.*

**nobleman** ['nəʊblmən] (*pl* **-men** [-mən]) *n* Edelmann *der.*

**noblewoman** ['nəʊblˌwʊmən] (*pl* **-women** [-ˌwɪmɪn]) *n* Edelfrau *die.*

**nobly** ['nəʊblɪ] *adv* [generously] großmütig.

**nobody** ['nəʊbədɪ] (*pl* **-ies**) *pron* niemand; **~ else can do it** das kann sonst keiner ◇ *n pej* Niemand *der.*

**no-claim(s) bonus** *n* Schadenfreiheitsrabatt *der.*

**nocturnal** [nɒk'tɜːnl] *adj* - **1.** [at night] nächtlich - **2.** [animal] Nacht-.

**nod** [nɒd] (*pt* & *pp* **-ded;** *cont* **-ding**) *n* Nicken *das;* **to give a ~** nicken ◇ *vt:* **to ~ one's head** mit dem Kopf nicken ◇ *vi* nicken; **to ~ to sb** jm zulnicken.
➣ **nod off** *vi* einlnicken.

**node** [nəʊd] *n* Knoten *der.*

**nodule** ['nɒdjuːl] *n* Knötchen *das.*

**no-go area** *n Br* Sperrgebiet *das.*

**noise** [nɔɪz] *n* - **1.** [sound] Geräusch *das* - **2.** (*U*) [unpleasant sound] Krach *der,* Lärm *der.*

**noiseless** ['nɔɪzlɪs] *adj* geräuschlos, lautlos.

**noiselessly** ['nɔɪzlɪslɪ] *adv* geräuschlos, lautlos.

**noisily** ['nɔɪzɪlɪ] *adv* laut.

**noisy** ['nɔɪzɪ] (*compar* **-ier;** *superl* **-iest**) *adj* laut.

**nomad** ['nəʊmæd] *n* Nomade *der,* -din *die.*

**nomadic** [nə'mædɪk] *adj* nomadisch, Nomaden-.

**no-man's-land** *n* Niemandsland *das.*

**nominal** ['nɒmɪnl] *adj* - **1.** [in name only] nominell - **2.** [very small] gering.

**nominally** ['nɒmɪnəlɪ] *adv* nominell.

**nominate** ['nɒmɪneɪt] *vt* - **1.** [propose]: **to ~ sb (for/as sthg)** jn (für/als etw) nominieren - **2.** [appoint]: **to ~ sb to sthg** jn zu etw ernennen.

**nomination** [ˌnɒmɪ'neɪʃn] *n* - **1.** [proposal] Nominierung *die* - **2.** (*U*) [appointment]: **~ to sthg** Ernennung *die.*

**nominee** [ˌnɒmɪ'niː] *n* Kandidat *der,* -in *die.*

**non-** [nɒn] *prefix* [with noun] Nicht-; [with adj] nicht-.

**nonaddictive** [ˌnɒnə'dɪktɪv] *adj* nicht abhängig machend.

**nonaggression** [ˌnɒnə'greʃn] *n* (*U*) Nichtangriff *der.*

**nonalcoholic** [ˌnɒnælkə'hɒlɪk] adj nichtalkoholisch, ohne Alkohol.

**nonaligned** [ˌnɒnə'laɪnd] adj blockfrei.

**nonbeliever** [ˌnɒnbɪ'liːvəʳ] n Ungläubige der, die.

**nonchalant** [Br 'nɒnʃələnt, Am ˌnɒnʃə'lɑːnt] adj nonchalant, lässig.

**nonchalantly** [Br 'nɒnʃələntlɪ, Am ˌnɒnʃə'lɑːntlɪ] adv nonchalant, lässig.

**noncommissioned officer** [ˌnɒnkə'mɪʃənd-] n Unteroffizier der, -in die.

**noncommittal** [ˌnɒnkə'mɪtl] adj [reply, attitude] unverbindlich; **he was ~** er legte sich nicht fest.

**noncompetitive** [ˌnɒnkəm'petɪtɪv] adj wettbewerbsfrei.

**nonconformist** [ˌnɒnkən'fɔːmɪst] adj nonkonformistisch <> n Nonkonformist der, -in die.

**noncontributory** [ˌnɒnkən'trɪbjʊtərɪ] adj beitragsfrei.

**noncooperation** ['nɒnkəʊˌɒpə'reɪʃn] n (U) unkooperative Haltung.

**nondescript** [Br 'nɒndɪskrɪpt, Am ˌnɒndɪ'skrɪpt] adj unscheinbar.

**nondrinker** [ˌnɒn'drɪŋkəʳ] n Nichttrinker der, -in die.

**nondrip** [ˌnɒn'drɪp] adj nicht tropfend.

**nondriver** [ˌnɒn'draɪvəʳ] n Nichtfahrer der, -in die.

**none** [nʌn] pron [not any] keine, -r, -s; **~ of us** keiner von uns; **~ of the money** nichts von dem Geld; **I'll have ~ of your nonsense** ich will nichts von dem Unsinn hören; **it is ~ of his business** es geht ihn gar nichts an <> adv: **I'm ~ the wiser** ich bin um nichts schlauer geworden; **I like him ~ the worse for it** ich mag ihn deshalb nicht weniger.

➤ **none too** adv: **~ too soon** keine Minute zu früh.

**nonentity** [nɒ'nentətɪ] (pl -ies) n Null die.

**nonessential** [ˌnɒnɪ'senʃl] adj unnötig.

**nonetheless** [ˌnʌnðə'les] adv nichtsdestoweniger.

**non-event** n Reinfall der.

**nonexecutive director** [nɒnɪgˌzekjʊtɪv-] n Direktor, der eine beratende Funktion, jedoch keine Entscheidungsbefugnis hat.

**nonexistent** [ˌnɒnɪg'zɪstənt] adj nicht existierend; **to be ~** nicht existieren.

**nonfattening** [ˌnɒn'fætnɪŋ] adj fettreduziert, fettarm.

**nonfiction** [ˌnɒn'fɪkʃn] n (U) Sachliteratur die.

**nonflammable** [ˌnɒn'flæməbl] adj nicht brennbar.

**noninfectious** [ˌnɒnɪn'fekʃəs] adj nicht ansteckend.

**noninflammable** [ˌnɒnɪn'flæməbl] adj nicht brennbar.

**noninterference** [ˌnɒnɪntə'fɪərəns], **nonintervention** [ˌnɒnɪntə'venʃn] n Nichteinmischung die.

**non-iron** adj bügelfrei.

**nonmalignant** [ˌnɒnmə'lɪgnənt] adj gutartig.

**nonmember** [ˌnɒn'membəʳ] n Nichtmitglied das.

**nonnegotiable** [ˌnɒnnɪ'gəʊʃjəbl] adj nicht verhandelbar.

**no-no** n inf: **it's a ~** das macht man nicht.

**no-nonsense** adj sachlich.

**nonoperational** [ˌnɒnɒpə'reɪʃənl] adj [machine, factory] nicht in Betrieb; [troops] nicht im Einsatz.

**nonparticipation** [ˌnɒnpɑːtɪsɪ'peɪʃn] n Nichtteilnahme die.

**nonpayment** [ˌnɒn'peɪmənt] n (U) Nichtzahlung die.

**nonplussed, nonplused** Am [ˌnɒn'plʌst] adj verblüfft.

**non-profit-making** Br, **non-profit** Am adj gemeinnützig.

**nonproliferation** ['nɒnprəˌlɪfə'reɪʃn] n Nichtverbreitung die.

**nonrenewable** [ˌnɒnrɪ'njuːəbl] adj - **1.** [contract, agreement] nicht verlängerbar - **2.** [natural resources, fossil fuels] nicht erneuerbar.

**nonresident** [ˌnɒn'rezɪdənt] n - **1.** [of country] Nichtansässige der, die - **2.** [of hotel]: **the restaurant is open to ~s** das Restaurant ist für Nichthotelgäste offen.

**nonreturnable** [ˌnɒnrɪ'tɜːnəbl] adj [bottle] Einweg-.

**nonsense** ['nɒnsəns] n (U) - **1.** [meaningless words, foolish idea] Unsinn der - **2.** [foolish behaviour] Dummheiten pl; **to make (a) ~ of sthg** etw unsinnig OR sinnlos machen <> excl Unsinn!

**nonsensical** [nɒn'sensɪkl] adj unsinnig.

**non sequitur** [-'sekwɪtəʳ] n unlogische Schlussfolgerung.

**nonshrink** [ˌnɒn'ʃrɪŋk] adj nicht einlaufend.

**nonskid** [ˌnɒn'skɪd] adj rutschfest.

**nonslip** [ˌnɒn'slɪp] adj rutschfest.

**nonsmoker** [ˌnɒn'sməʊkəʳ] n Nichtraucher der, -in die.

**nonstarter** [ˌnɒn'stɑːtəʳ] n Br inf [plan] Blindgänger der.

**nonstick** [ˌnɒn'stɪk] adj antihaftbeschichtet.

**nonstop** [ˌnɒn'stɒp] adj [flight, race] Nonstop-; [activity, rain] ohne Unterbrechung <> adv ununterbrochen.

**nontaxable** [ˌnɒnˈtæksəbl] *adj* nicht steuerpflichtig.

**nontoxic** [ˌnɒnˈtɒksɪk] *adj* ungiftig.

**nontransferable** [ˌnɒntrænsˈfɜːrəbl] *adj* nicht übertragbar.

**non-U** [nɒnˈjuː] *adj Br dated* unfein.

**nonviolence** [ˌnɒnˈvaɪələns] *n* Gewaltlosigkeit *die.*

**nonvoter** [ˌnɒnˈvəʊtəʳ] *n* Nichtwähler *der*, -in *die.*

**nonvoting** [ˌnɒnˈvəʊtɪŋ] *adj* - **1.** [member] nicht wählend - **2.** FIN [shares] nicht stimmberechtigt.

**nonwhite** [ˌnɒnˈwaɪt] *adj* farbig ◇ *n* Farbige *der, die.*

**noodles** [ˈnuːdlz] *npl* Nudeln *pl.*

**nook** [nʊk] *n* [of room] Winkel *der*, Ecke *die;* in every ~ and cranny in allen Ecken OR Winkeln.

**noon** [nuːn] *n* Mittag *der* ◇ *comp* Mittags-.

**noonday** [ˈnuːndeɪ] *comp* Mittags-.

**no one** *pron* = nobody.

**noose** [nuːs] *n* Schlinge *die.*

**no-place** *adv Am* = nowhere.

**nor** [nɔːʳ] *conj* auch nicht; ~ do I ich auch nicht; I don't know, ~ do I care das weiß ich nicht, und es ist mir auch egal.

**Nordic** [ˈnɔːdɪk] *adj* nordisch.

**Norf** *abk für* Norfolk, *in Postanschrift verwendet.*

**Norfolk Broads** [ˌnɔːfək-] *npl:* **the ~** die Norfolk Broads, *sumpfreiche Seenlandschaft in Norfolk, ein beliebtes Feriengebiet und Seglerparadies.*

**norm** [nɔːm] *n* Norm *die.*

**normal** [ˈnɔːml] *adj* normal.

**normality** [nɔːˈmælɪtɪ] *n* Normalität *die.*

**normalize, -ise** [ˈnɔːməlaɪz] *vt* normalisieren ◇ *vi* sich normalisieren.

**normally** [ˈnɔːməlɪ] *adv* - **1.** [usually] normalerweise - **2.** [in a normal way] normal.

**Norman** [ˈnɔːmən] *adj* normannisch ◇ *n* Normanne *der*, -nin *die.*

**Norse** [nɔːs] *adj* altnordisch.

**north** [nɔːθ] *adj* Nord-, nördlich ◇ *adv* nach Norden, nordwärts; ~ of nördlich von ◇ *n* Norden *der.*

**North Africa** *n* Nordafrika *nt.*

**North America** *n* Nordamerika *nt.*

**North American** *adj* nordamerikanisch ◇ *n* Nordamerikaner *der*, -in *die.*

**northbound** [ˈnɔːθbaʊnd] *adj* in nördlicher Richtung, in Richtung Norden.

**North Country** *n:* **the ~** *Br* Nordengland *nt.*

**northeast** [ˌnɔːθˈiːst] *n* Nordosten *der* ◇ *adj* nordöstlich, Nordost- ◇ *adv* nordostwärts, nach Nordosten; ~ of nordöstlich von.

**northeasterly** [ˌnɔːθˈiːstəlɪ] *adj* [direction] nordöstlich; [area] im Nordosten; [wind] Nordost-.

**northerly** [ˈnɔːðəlɪ] *adj* [direction] nördlich; [area] im Norden; [wind] Nord-.

**northern** [ˈnɔːðən] *adj* [region, dialect] nördlich; [Europe] Nord-.

**Northerner** [ˈnɔːðənəʳ] *n* [from North England] Nordengländer *der*, -in *die.*

**Northern Ireland** *n* Nordirland *nt.*

**Northern Lights** *npl:* **the ~** das Nordlicht.

**northernmost** [ˈnɔːðənməʊst] *adj* nördlichste, -r, -s.

**North Korea** *n* Nordkorea *nt.*

**North Pole** *n:* **the ~** der Nordpol.

**North Sea** *n:* **the ~** die Nordsee ◇ *comp* Nordsee-.

**North Star** *n:* **the ~** der Nordstern.

**northward** [ˈnɔːθwəd] *adj* [migration] nördlich, nach Norden ◇ *adv* = **northwards.**

**northwards** [ˈnɔːθwədz] *adv* nach Norden.

**northwest** [ˌnɔːθˈwest] *n* Nordwesten *der* ◇ *adj* nordwestlich, Nordwest- ◇ *adv* nordwestwärts, nach Nordwesten; ~ of nordwestlich von.

**northwesterly** [ˌnɔːθˈwestəlɪ] *adj* [direction] nordwestlich; [area] im Nordwesten; [wind] Nordwest-.

**Norway** [ˈnɔːweɪ] *n* Norwegen *nt.*

**Norwegian** [nɔːˈwiːdʒən] *adj* norwegisch ◇ *n* - **1.** [person] Norweger *der*, -in *die* - **2.** [language] Norwegisch(e) *das.*

**Nos., nos.** (*abbr of* numbers) Nm.

**nose** [nəʊz] *n* - **1.** [of person] Nase *die;* it's under your ~ es ist vor deiner Nase; to cut one's ~ off to spite one's face sich ins eigene Fleisch schneiden; to have a ~ for sthg eine Nase OR ein Gespür für etw haben; he gets up my ~ *inf* er geht mir auf die Nerven; to keep one's ~ out of sthg sich aus etw heraushalten; to look down one's ~ at sb/sthg *fig* von oben herabschauen auf jn/etw; to pay through the ~ viel zu viel zahlen; to poke OR stick one's ~ into sthg *inf* seine Nase in etw (A) stecken; to turn up one's ~ at sthg seine Nase über etw (A) rümpfen - **2.** [of plane] Nase *die;* [of car] Schnauze *die.*

➤ **nose about, nose around** *vi* herumschnüffeln.

**nosebag** [ˈnəʊzbæg] *n* Futtersack *der.*

**nosebleed** [ˈnəʊzbliːd] *n* Nasenbluten *das.*

**nosecone** [ˈnəʊzkəʊn] *n* Spitze *die.*

**nosedive** ['nəʊzdaɪv] n [of plane] Sturzflug der ◇ vi - **1.** [plane] in den Sturzflug gehen - **2.** fig [prices, popularity] rapide ablsinken.

**nosey** ['nəʊzɪ] adj = nosy.

**nosh** [nɒʃ] n Br inf [food] Futter das.

**nosh-up** n Br inf Schlemmergelage das.

**nostalgia** [nɒ'stældʒə] n (U) Nostalgie die; ~ for sthg Sehnsucht die nach etw.

**nostalgic** [nɒ'stældʒɪk] adj [feeling, film] nostalgisch; to feel ~ wehmütig sein.

**nostril** ['nɒstrəl] n Nasenloch das.

**nosy** ['nəʊzɪ] (compar -ier; superl -iest) adj neugierig.

**not** [nɒt] adv nicht; she's ~ there sie ist nicht da; ~ any kein; ~ yet noch nicht; ~ at all [pleased, interested] überhaupt nicht; [in reply to thanks] gern geschehen; ~ that I'm afraid of him nicht etwa, dass ich Angst vor ihm habe; ~ to worry! keine Sorge!, das macht nichts!

**notable** ['nəʊtəbl] adj [person] bedeutend; [success] bemerkenswert; [improvement] beachtlich, beträchtlich; to be ~ for sthg durch etw auf lfallen; with the ~ exception of mit Ausnahme von ◇ n bedeutende Persönlichkeit.

**notably** ['nəʊtəblɪ] adv - **1.** [in particular] vor allem - **2.** [noticeably] deutlich.

**notary** ['nəʊtərɪ] (pl -ies) n: ~ (public) Notar der, -in die.

**notation** [nəʊ'teɪʃn] n mus Notenschrift die; math Zeichensystem das.

**notch** [nɒtʃ] n - **1.** [cut] Kerbe die - **2.** fig: she's gone up a ~ in my estimation sie ist in meiner Achtung gestiegen.

◆ **notch up** vt fus erzielen.

**note** [nəʊt] n - **1.** [short letter] Zettel der - **2.** [written reminder, record] Notiz die; to take ~ of sthg etw bemerken, Notiz von etw nehmen; to compare ~s sich ausltauschen - **3.** [paper money] Geldschein der, Banknote die; a £5 ~ eine Fünfpfundnote, ein Fünfpfundschein - **4.** [mus - symbol] Note die; [ - sound] Klang der - **5.** [tone] Ton der - **6.** [importance]: of ~ von Bedeutung ◇ vt - **1.** [observe] bemerken - **2.** [mention] erwähnen.

◆ **notes** npl [in book] Anmerkungen pl.

◆ **note down** vt sep auf lschreiben.

**notebook** ['nəʊtbʊk] n - **1.** [for writing in] Notizbuch das - **2.** comput Notebook das.

**noted** ['nəʊtɪd] adj: ~ (for sthg) bekannt (für etw).

**notepad** ['nəʊtpæd] n Notizblock der.

**notepaper** ['nəʊtpeɪpə'] n Briefpapier das.

**noteworthy** ['nəʊt,wɜːðɪ] (compar -ier; superl -iest) adj bemerkenswert.

**nothing** ['nʌθɪŋ] pron nichts; ~ new/interesting nichts Neues/Interessantes; there's ~ to it es ist ganz einfach; for ~ [for free] umsonst; [in vain] vergeblich; she is ~ if not discreet diskret ist sie auf jeden Fall; ~ but nichts als; he does ~ but complain er beschwert sich dauernd; he thinks ~ of walking ten miles es macht ihm nichts aus, zehn Meilen zu gehen ◇ adv: ~ like [very unlike] ganz anders als; ~ like enough lange nicht genug; ~ like as good längst nicht so gut.

**nothingness** ['nʌθɪŋnɪs] n (U) Nichts das.

**notice** ['nəʊtɪs] n - **1.** [piece of paper - announcing sthg] Ankündigung die; [ - informing of sthg] Mitteilung die - **2.** [attention]: to come to one's ~ jm auf lfallen; it escaped her ~ es entging ihrer Aufmerksamkeit; to take ~/no ~ of sb/sthg jn/etw beachten/nicht beachten; he/she didn't take a blind bit of ~ er/sie nahm nicht die geringste Notiz - **3.** (U) [warning] Bescheid der; at short ~ kurzfristig; until further ~ bis auf weiteres - **4.** [at work]: to be given one's ~ gekündigt werden; to hand in one's ~ seine Kündigung einlreichen ◇ vt bemerken ◇ vi: I've never ~d es ist mir nie aufgefallen.

**noticeable** ['nəʊtɪsəbl] adj deutlich.

**noticeably** ['nəʊtɪsəblɪ] adv deutlich.

**notice board** n Anschlagbrett das.

**notification** [,nəʊtɪfɪ'keɪʃn] n (U) Benachrichtigung die, Mitteilung die.

**notify** ['nəʊtɪfaɪ] (pt & pp -ied) vt: to ~ sb (of sthg) jn benachrichtigen (über etw (A)).

**notion** ['nəʊʃn] n [concept, idea] Idee die, Vorstellung die.

◆ **notions** npl Am [haberdashery] Kurzwaren pl.

**notional** ['nəʊʃənl] adj [hypothetical] fiktiv.

**notoriety** [,nəʊtə'raɪətɪ] n traurige Berühmtheit, schlechter Ruf.

**notorious** [nəʊ'tɔːrɪəs] adj [person] berühmt; [criminal, event] berühmt-berüchtigt; [place] verrufen; ~ (for sthg) berüchtigt (für etw).

**notoriously** [nəʊ'tɔːrɪəslɪ] adv notorisch.

**Notts** [nɒts] abk für Nottinghamshire, in Postanschrift verwendet.

**notwithstanding** [,nɒtwɪθ'stændɪŋ] fml prep trotz (+ G), ungeachtet (+ G) ◇ adv trotzdem, dennoch.

**nougat** ['nuːgɑː] n Nugat der oR das.

**nought** [nɔːt] num Null die; ~s and crosses Kreuzchen- und Kringelspiel das.

**noun** [naʊn] n Substantiv das.

**nourish** ['nʌrɪʃ] vt - **1.** [feed] ernähren - **2.** [entertain, foster] nähren, hegen.

**nourishing** ['nʌrɪʃɪŋ] adj nahrhaft.

**nourishment** ['nʌrɪʃmənt] n Nahrung die.

**N**

**nouveau riche** [ˌnuːvəʊˈriːʃ] adj neureich ◇ n Neureiche der, die.

**Nov.** (abbr of **November**) Nov.

**novel** [ˈnɒvl] adj neuartig ◇ n Roman der.

**novelist** [ˈnɒvəlɪst] n Romanschriftsteller der, -in die.

**novelty** [ˈnɒvltɪ] (pl -ies) n - 1. [quality] Neuartigkeit die - 2. [unusual object, event] Neuheit die - 3. [cheap object] Krimskrams der.

**November** [nəˈvembəʳ] n November der; see also **September**.

**novice** [ˈnɒvɪs] n - 1. [inexperienced person] Neuling der - 2. RELIG Novize der, -zin die.

**now** [naʊ] adv - 1. [gen] jetzt; **just ~** gerade eben; **right ~** [at the moment] im Moment; [immediately] sofort; **by ~** inszwischen; **they should be here by ~** sie sollten inzwischen hier sein; **from ~ on** von jetzt an; **three days from ~** heute in drei Tagen; **any day/time ~** jeden Tag/Moment; **(every) ~ and then** OR **again** hin und wieder; **for ~** erst einmal - 2. [introducing statement]: **~ (then), ... also ... ◇ conj: ~ (that) ...** jetzt, wo ...

**NOW** [naʊ] (abbr of **National Organization for Women**) n feministische Vereinigung in den USA.

**nowadays** [ˈnaʊədeɪz] adv heutzutage, heute.

**nowhere** Br [ˈnəʊweəʳ], **no-place** Am adv nirgendwo, nirgends; **to appear out of** OR **from ~** aus heiterem Himmel auf |tauchen; **~ near** nicht annähernd; **dinner is ~ near ready** das Abendessen ist noch lange nicht fertig; **to be getting ~** zu nichts kommen; **this is getting us ~** das bringt uns nicht weiter.

**no-win situation** n ausweglose Situation.

**noxious** [ˈnɒkʃəs] adj schädlich.

**nozzle** [ˈnɒzl] n Düse die.

**NS** abk für Nova Scotia, in Postanschrift verwendet.

**NSC** (abbr of **National Security Council**) n Nationaler Sicherheitsrat der USA.

**NSPCC** (abbr of **National Society for the Prevention of Cruelty to Children**) n ≈ Kinderschutzbund der.

**NSU** (abbr of **nonspecific urethritis**) n nichtspezifische Harnleiterentzündung.

**NSW** abk für New South Wales, in Postanschrift verwendet.

**NT** n - 1. (abbr of **New Testament**) NT das - 2. abbr of **National Trust**.

**nth** [enθ] adj inf [umpteenth]: **for the ~ time** zum x-ten Mal.

**nuance** [njuːˈɒːns] n Nuance die.

**nub** [nʌb] n Kernpunkt der.

**nubile** [Br ˈnjuːbaɪl, Am ˈnuːbəl] adj fml OR hum heiratsfähig.

**nubuck** [ˈnjuːbʌk] n Nubuk das.

**nuclear** [ˈnjuːklɪəʳ] adj nuklear, Nuklear-.

**nuclear bomb** n Atombombe die.

**nuclear disarmament** n nukleare Abrüstung.

**nuclear energy** n Atomenergie die, Kernenergie die.

**nuclear family** n Kernfamilie die.

**nuclear fission** n Kernspaltung die.

**nuclear-free zone** n atomwaffenfreie Zone.

**nuclear fusion** n Kernfusion die.

**nuclear physics** n Kernphysik die.

**nuclear power** n Atomkraft die, Kernkraft die; **~ station** Atomkraftwerk das.

**nuclear reactor** n Atomreaktor der, Kernreaktor der.

**nuclear war** n Atomkrieg der.

**nuclear winter** n nuklearer Winter.

**nucleus** [ˈnjuːklɪəs] (pl -lei [-lɪaɪ]) n Kern der; **atomic ~** Atomkern der.

**nude** [njuːd] adj nackt ◇ n [figure, painting] Akt der; **in the ~** nackt.

**nudge** [nʌdʒ] n - 1. [with elbow] Stups der - 2. fig [to encourage] Ermunterung die ◇ vt - 1. [with elbow] an|stupsen - 2. fig [to encourage] ermuntern.

**nudist** [ˈnjuːdɪst] adj Nudisten-; **~ beach** Nacktbadestrand der ◇ n Nudist der, -in die.

**nudity** [ˈnjuːdətɪ] n Nacktheit die.

**nugget** [ˈnʌgɪt] n - 1. [of gold] Nugget das, Goldklümpchen das - 2. fig: **a ~ of information** ein wertvolles Stück Information.

**nuisance** [ˈnjuːsns] n - 1. [annoying thing, situation] Ärgernis das; **what a ~!** wie ärgerlich!, wie lästig! - 2. [annoying person] Nervensäge die; **to make a ~ of o.s.** lästig werden.

**NUJ** (abbr of **National Union of Journalists**) n britische Journalistengewerkschaft.

**nuke** [njuːk] inf n Kernwaffe die ◇ vt mit Kernwaffen an|greifen.

**null** [nʌl] adj: **~ and void** null und nichtig.

**nullify** [ˈnʌlɪfaɪ] (pt & pp -ied) vt - 1. LAW [declare null] für nichtig erklären - 2. [negate] nichtig machen.

**NUM** (abbr of **National Union of Mineworkers**) n britische Bergarbeitergewerkschaft.

**numb** [nʌm] adj [shoulder, hand] taub, gefühllos; [person] benommen; **to be ~ with sthg** [with cold, fear, shock] starr vor etw (D) sein; [with grief] benommen vor etw *(D)* sein ⬦ *vt* [subj: cold, anaesthetic] betäuben.

**number** [ˈnʌmbəʳ] *n* - **1.** [numeral] Zahl *die*, Ziffer *die* - **2.** [of telephone, house, car] Nummer *die* - **3.** [quantity] Anzahl *die*, Zahl *die*; **a ~ of** mehrere; **any ~ of** unzählig - **4.** [song] Nummer *die* ⬦ *vt* - **1.** [amount to] zählen - **2.** [give a number to] nummerieren - **3.** [include]: **to ~ sb/sthg among** jn/etw zählen zu; **he is ~ed among the greatest politicians of this century** er zählt zu den größten Politikern dieses Jahrhunderts.

**numberless** [ˈnʌmbəlɪs] *adj* unzählig.

**number one** *adj* [main] vorrangig ⬦ *n* - **1.** [priority] Vorrang *der* - **2.** *inf* [oneself] Nummer eins.

**numberplate** [ˈnʌmbəpleɪt] *n Br* Nummernschild *das*.

**Number Ten** *n*: **~ (Downing Street)** Sitz des britischen Premierministers.

**numbness** [ˈnʌmnɪs] *n (U)* - **1.** [with cold] Taubheit *die*, Gefühllosigkeit *die*; [with anaesthetic] Betäubtheit *die* - **2.** *fig* [with shock, fear] Starrheit *die*, Benommenheit *die*.

**numbskull** [ˈnʌmskʌl] *n* = **numskull.**

**numeracy** [ˈnjuːmərəsɪ] *n (U) Br* rechnerische Fähigkeiten *pl*.

**numeral** [ˈnjuːmərəl] *n* Ziffer *die*.

**numerate** [ˈnjuːmərət] *adj Br* rechenkundig.

**numerical** [njuːˈmerɪkl] *adj* numerisch.

**numerous** [ˈnjuːmərəs] *adj* zahlreich.

**numskull** [ˈnʌmskʌl] *n inf* Schwachkopf *der*.

**nun** [nʌn] *n* Nonne *die*.

**nuptial** [ˈnʌpʃl] *adj fml* ehelich, Ehe-.

**NURMTW** *(abbr of* **National Union of Rail, Maritime and Transport Workers)** *n britische Gewerkschaft der Eisenbahner und Seeleute.*

**nurse** [nɜːs] *n* Krankenschwester *die*; [male] Krankenpfleger *der* ⬦ *vt* - **1.** MED [person] pflegen - **2.** [desire, dream, hope] hegen, nähren - **3.** [breast-feed] stillen.

**nursemaid** [ˈnɜːsmeɪd] *n* Kindermädchen *das*.

**nursery** [ˈnɜːsərɪ] *(pl* **-ies)** *adj* Kindergarten-, Vorschul- ⬦ *n* - **1.** [for children] Kinderzimmer *das* - **2.** [for plants] Gärtnerei *die*.

**nursery nurse** *n Br* Kinderschwester *die*, Kinderpflegerin *die*.

**nursery rhyme** *n* Kinderreim *der*, Kinderlied *das*.

**nursery school** *n* Kindergarten *der*, Vorschule *die*.

**nursery slope** *n* Idiotenhügel *der*.

**nursing** [ˈnɜːsɪŋ] *n (U)* - **1.** [profession] Krankenpflege *die* - **2.** [care] Pflege *die*.

**nursing auxiliary** *n* Schwesternhelferin *die*; [male] Hilfspfleger *der*.

**nursing home** *n* - **1.** [for old people] Pflegeheim *das* - **2.** [for childbirth] Entbindungsklinik *die*.

**nurture** [ˈnɜːtʃəʳ] *vt* - **1.** [children] nähren; [plants] hegen - **2.** [hope, desire, plan] hegen, nähren.

**NUS** *(abbr of* **National Union of Students)** *n britischer Verband der Studierenden.*

**nut** [nʌt] *n* - **1.** [to eat] Nuss *die* - **2.** TECH Schraubenmutter *die*; **~s and bolts** *fig* [basics] Grundlagen *pl* - **3.** *inf* [mad person] Spinner *der*, -in *die* - **4.** *inf* [enthusiast] Fan *der* - **5.** *inf* [head] Birne *die*.

⬗ **nuts** *inf adj*: **to be ~s** verrückt sein, eine Schraube locker haben ⬦ *excl Am* verdammt!

**NUT** *(abbr of* **National Union of Teachers)** *n britische Lehrer- und Lehrerinnengewerkschaft.*

**nutcase** [ˈnʌtkeɪs] *n inf* Spinner *der*, -in *die*.

**nutcrackers** [ˈnʌtˌkrækəz] *npl* Nussknacker *der*.

**nutmeg** [ˈnʌtmeg] *n* Muskatnuss *die*.

**nutrient** [ˈnjuːtrɪənt] *n* Nährstoff *der*.

**nutrition** [njuːˈtrɪʃn] *n* Ernährung *die*.

**nutritional** [njuːˈtrɪʃənl] *adj* Nähr-.

**nutritionist** [njuːˈtrɪʃənɪst] *n* Ernährungswissenschaftler *der*, -in *die*.

**nutritious** [njuːˈtrɪʃəs] *adj* nahrhaft.

**nutshell** [ˈnʌtʃel] *n*: **in a ~** kurz gefasst, kurz und bündig.

**nutter** [ˈnʌtəʳ] *n Br inf* Spinner *der*, -in *die*.

**nuzzle** [ˈnʌzl] *vt* beschnüffeln, beschnuppern ⬦ *vi*: **to ~ (up) against sb/sthg** sich an jn/etw anschmiegen OR drücken.

**NV** *abk für Nevada, in Postanschrift verwendet.*

**NW** *(abbr of* **northwest)** NW.

**NWT** *abbr of* **Northwest Territories.**

**NY** *abbr of* **New York.**

**Nyasaland** [naɪˈæsəlænd] *n* Njassaland *nt*.

**NYC** *(abbr of* **New York City)** *New York City.*

**nylon** [ˈnaɪlɒn] *n* [fabric] Nylon *das* ⬦ *comp* Nylon-.

⬗ **nylons** *npl dated* [stockings] Nylonstrümpfe *pl*.

**nymph** [nɪmf] *n* Nymphe *die*.

**nymphomaniac** [ˌnɪmfəˈmeɪnɪæk] *n* Nymphomanin *die*.

**NYSE** *(abbr of* **New York Stock Exchange)** *n Börse in New York.*

**NZ** *abbr of* **New Zealand.**

**N**

**o** (pl **o's** OR **os**), **O** (pl **O's** OR **Os**) [əʊ] n - **1.** [letter] o das, O das - **2.** [zero] Null die.

**oaf** [əʊf] n Tölpel der.

**oak** [əʊk] n - **1.** [tree] Eiche die - **2.** (U) [wood] Eichenholz das <> comp Eichenholz-.

**OAP** n abbr of **old age pensioner.**

**oar** [ɔːʳ] n Ruder das; **to put** OR **stick one's ~ in** fig sich einlmischen.

**oarsman** [ˈɔːzmən] (pl **-men** [-mən]) n Ruderer der.

**oarswoman** [ˈɔːzˌwʊmən] (pl **-women** [-ˌwɪmɪn]) n Ruderin die.

**OAS** (abbr of **Organization of American States**) n OAS die.

**oasis** [əʊˈeɪsɪs] (pl **oases** [əʊˈeɪsiːz]) n lit & fig Oase die.

**oatcake** [ˈəʊtkeɪk] n Haferplätzchen das.

**oath** [əʊθ] n - **1.** [promise] Eid der, Schwur der; **on** OR **under ~** unter Eid - **2.** [swearword] Fluch der.

**oatmeal** [ˈəʊtmiːl] n [food] Hafermehl das <> comp Hafer-.

**oats** [əʊts] npl Hafer der.

**OAU** (abbr of **Organization of African Unity**) n OAE die.

**OB** (abbr of **outside broadcast**) n Außenübertragung die.

**obdurate** [ˈɒbdjʊrət] adj fml starrköpfig.

**OBE** (abbr of **Order of the British Empire**) n Auszeichnung des britischen Königreichs oder deren Inhaber.

**obedience** [əˈbiːdɪəns] n: **~ (to sb)** Gehorsam der (gegenüber jm).

**obedient** [əˈbiːdɪənt] adj gehorsam.

**obediently** [əˈbiːdɪəntlɪ] adv gehorsam.

**obelisk** [ˈɒbəlɪsk] n Obelisk der.

**obese** [əʊˈbiːs] adj fettleibig.

**obesity** [əʊˈbiːsətɪ] n Fettleibigkeit die.

**obey** [əˈbeɪ] vt [person] gehorchen (+ D); [orders, command, law] befolgen <> vi gehorchen.

**obituary** [əˈbɪtʃʊərɪ] (pl **-ies**) n Nachruf der.

**object** [n ˈɒbdʒɪkt, vb ɒbˈdʒekt] n - **1.** [thing] Gegenstand der - **2.** [aim] Ziel das; **the ~ of the exercise** der Zweck der Übung - **3.** [focus] &

GRAMM Objekt das <> vt: **to ~ that ...** einlwenden, dass ...<> vi dagegen sein; **to ~ to sthg** gegen etw sein; **to ~ to doing sthg** etwas dagegen haben, etw zu tun.

**objection** [əbˈdʒekʃn] n Einwand der; **to have no ~ to sthg** keinen Einwand gegen etw haben; **to have no ~ to doing sthg** nichts dagegen haben, etw zu tun.

**objectionable** [əbˈdʒekʃənəbl] adj [behaviour, language] anstößig; [person] unausstehlich, widerwärtig.

**objective** [əbˈdʒektɪv] adj objektiv <> n Ziel das.

**objectively** [əbˈdʒektɪvlɪ] adv objektiv.

**objectivity** [ˌɒbdʒekˈtɪvətɪ] n Objektivität die.

**object lesson** [ˈɒbdʒɪkt-] n: **an ~ in sthg** ein Musterbeispiel für etw.

**objector** [əbˈdʒektəʳ] n Gegner der, -in die.

**obligate** [ˈɒblɪgeɪt] vt fml verpflichten; **to ~ sb to do sthg** jn verpflichten, etw zu tun.

**obligation** [ˌɒblɪˈgeɪʃn] n - **1.** [compulsion] Zwang der - **2.** [duty] Verpflichtung die, Pflicht die.

**obligatory** [əˈblɪgətrɪ] adj obligatorisch; **to be ~** Pflicht sein.

**oblige** [əˈblaɪdʒ] vt - **1.** [force]: **to ~ sb to do sthg** jn zwingen, etw zu tun - **2.** fml [do a favour for]: **to ~ sb** jm einen Gefallen tun <> vi gefällig sein.

**obliging** [əˈblaɪdʒɪŋ] adj zuvorkommend.

**oblique** [əˈbliːk] adj - **1.** [look, compliment] indirekt; [hint] versteckt - **2.** [line] Schräg-, schräg <> n TYPO Schrägstrich der.

**obliquely** [əˈbliːklɪ] adv [indirectly] indirekt.

**obliterate** [əˈblɪtəreɪt] vt ausllöschen.

**obliteration** [əˌblɪtəˈreɪʃn] n Auslöschung die.

**oblivion** [əˈblɪvɪən] n - **1.** [unconsciousness] Bewusstlosigkeit die - **2.** [state of being forgotten] Vergessenheit die, Vergessen das.

**oblivious** [əˈblɪvɪəs] adj: **to be ~ to** OR **of sthg** sich (D) einer Sache (G) nicht bewusst sein.

**oblong** [ˈɒblɒŋ] adj rechteckig <> n Rechteck das.

**obnoxious** [əbˈnɒkʃəs] adj [smell] widerlich; [remark] gemein; [person] unausstehlich.

**o.b.o.** (abbr of **or best offer**) ⟹ o. n. o.

**oboe** [ˈəʊbəʊ] n Oboe die.

**oboist** [ˈəʊbəʊɪst] n Oboist der, -in die.

**obscene** [əbˈsiːn] adj obszön.

**obscenity** [əbˈsenətɪ] (pl **-ies**) n - **1.** (U) [obscene behaviour] Obszönität die - **2.** [swearword] Fluch der.

**obscure** [əbˈskjʊəʳ] adj - **1.** [not well-known] un-

bekannt - **2.** [difficult to understand, see] unklar
◇ *vt* - **1.** [make difficult to understand] unklar machen - **2.** [hide] verdecken.

**obscurity** [əb'skjʊərətɪ] *n* - **1.** [state of being un-
known] Unbekanntheit *die* - **2.** [difficulty] Un-
klarheit *die*, Verworrenheit *die* - **3.** [darkness]
Dunkelheit *die*, Finsternis *die*.

**obsequious** [əb'siːkwɪəs] *adj fml* & *pej* unterwürfig.

**observance** [əb'zɜːvəns] *n* (U) Einhaltung *die*.

**observant** [əb'zɜːvnt] *adj* aufmerksam.

**observation** [ˌɒbzə'veɪʃn] *n* - **1.** (U) [action of
watching] Beobachtung *die* - **2.** [remark] Bemerkung *die*, Äußerung *die*.

**observation post** *n* Beobachtungsposten
*der*.

**observatory** [əb'zɜːvətrɪ] (*pl* -ies) *n* Observa-
torium *das*, Sternwarte *die*.

**observe** [əb'zɜːv] *vt* - **1.** *fml* [notice] bemerken
- **2.** [watch carefully] beobachten - **3.** [obey] einhalten - **4.** [remark] bemerken, äußern.

**observer** [əb'zɜːvəʳ] *n* - **1.** [watcher] Zuschauer
*der*, -in *die* - **2.** [commentator] Beobachter *der*,
-in *die*.

**obsess** [əb'ses] *vt*: **to be ~ed by sb/sthg, to be
~ed with sb/sthg** von jm/etw besessen sein.

**obsession** [əb'seʃn] *n* Besessenheit *die*.

**obsessional** [əb'seʃənl] *adj* obsessiv, zwanghaft.

**obsessive** [əb'sesɪv] *adj* obsessiv, zwanghaft.

**obsolescence** [ˌɒbsə'lesns] *n* Veralten *das*,
Überholtsein *das*.

**obsolescent** [ˌɒbsə'lesnt] *adj* veraltend.

**obsolete** ['ɒbsəliːt] *adj* veraltet, überholt.

**obstacle** ['ɒbstəkl] *n* Hindernis *das*.

**obstacle race** *n* Hindernisrennen *das*.

**obstetrician** [ˌɒbstə'trɪʃn] *n* Geburtshelfer
*der*, -in *die*.

**obstetrics** [ɒb'stetrɪks] *n* Geburtshilfe *die*.

**obstinacy** ['ɒbstɪnəsɪ] *n* Verbohrtheit *die*,
Störrigkeit *die*.

**obstinate** ['ɒbstənət] *adj* - **1.** [person] verbohrt
- **2.** [cough, resistance] hartnäckig.

**obstinately** ['ɒbstənətlɪ] *adv* hartnäckig.

**obstreperous** [əb'strepərəs] *adj fml* OR *hum*
aufsässig.

**obstruct** [əb'strʌkt] *vt* - **1.** [road, path] blockieren, versperren - **2.** [progress, justice, traffic] behindern.

**obstruction** [əb'strʌkʃn] *n* - **1.** [in road, pipe]
Blockierung *die* - **2.** [of justice] Behinderung
*die* - **3.** SPORT Behinderung *die*, Sperren *das*.

**obstructive** [əb'strʌktɪv] *adj* obstruktiv, hinderlich.

**obtain** [əb'teɪn] *vt* erhalten.

**obtainable** [əb'teɪnəbl] *adj* erhältlich.

**obtrusive** [əb'truːsɪv] *adj* [person, behaviour] aufdringlich; [colour] auffällig; [smell] penetrant.

**obtrusively** [əb'truːsɪvlɪ] *adv* aufdringlich.

**obtuse** [əb'tjuːs] *adj* - **1.** *fml* [person] begriffsstutzig - **2.** GEOM [angle] stumpf.

**obverse** ['ɒbvɜːs] *n* - **1.** [front side] Vorderseite
*die* - **2.** [opposite] andere Seite, Kehrseite *die*.

**obviate** ['ɒbvɪeɪt] *vt fml* beseitigen; **to ~ the
need to do sthg** es unnötig machen, etw zu
tun.

**obvious** ['ɒbvɪəs] *adj* offensichtlich ◇ *n*: **to
state the ~** längst Bekanntes sagen.

**obviously** ['ɒbvɪəslɪ] *adv* - **1.** [of course] selbstverständlich - **2.** [clearly] eindeutig, offensichtlich.

**obviousness** ['ɒbvɪəsnɪs] *n* Offensichtlich-
keit *die*, Eindeutigkeit *die*.

**occasion** [ə'keɪʒn] *n* - **1.** [circumstance, time] Gelegenheit *die*; **on one ~** einmal; **on ~** *fml* bei
Gelegenheit, gelegentlich - **2.** [important
event] Anlass *der*; **special ~** besonderer Anlass; **to rise to the ~** sich der Lage gewachsen zeigen - **3.** *fml* [reason, motive] Grund *der*
◇ *vt fml* [cause] hervorrufen, verursachen.

**occasional** [ə'keɪʒənl] *adj* gelegentlich.

**occasionally** [ə'keɪʒnəlɪ] *adv* gelegentlich.

**occasional table** *n* Beistelltisch *der*.

**occult** [ɒ'kʌlt] *adj* okkult ◇ *n*: **the ~** das Ok-
kulte.

**occupancy** ['ɒkjʊpənsɪ] *n* (U) *fml* [of land] Nutzung *die*; [of house, flat] Bewohnen *das*.

**occupant** ['ɒkjʊpənt] *n* - **1.** [of building, room]
Bewohner *der*, -in *die* - **2.** [of chair] Inhaber
*der*, -in *die*; [of vehicle] Insasse *der*, -sin *die*.

**occupation** [ˌɒkjʊ'peɪʃn] *n* - **1.** [job] Beruf *der*
- **2.** [pastime] Beschäftigung *die* - **3.** MIL Besetzung *die*, Okkupation *die*.

**occupational** [ˌɒkjʊ'peɪʃənl] *adj* berufsbe-
dingt, beruflich; [pension scheme] betrieblich.

**occupational disease** *n* Berufskrankheit
*die*.

**occupational hazard** *n* Berufsrisiko *das*.

**occupational therapist** *n* Beschäfti-
gungstherapeut *der*, -in *die*.

**occupational therapy** *n* Beschäftigungs-
therapie *die*.

**occupied** ['ɒkjʊpaɪd] *adj* - **1.** [taken] belegt
- **2.** MIL besetzt, okkupiert.

**occupier** ['ɒkjʊpaɪəʳ] *n* Bewohner *der*, -in *die*.

**occupy** ['ɒkjʊpaɪ] (*pt* & *pp* -ied) *vt* - **1.** [house,
room] bewohnen; [seat] belegen - **2.** MIL besetzen, okkupieren - **3.** [role, rank] innehaben
- **4.** [keep busy]: **to ~ o.s.** sich beschäftigen
- **5.** [time, space] in Anspruch nehmen; **how do**

you ~ your evenings? wie füllst du deine Abende aus?

**occur** [ə'kɜːʳ] (*pt* & *pp* **-red**; *cont* **-ring**) *vi* - **1.** [happen] sich ereignen; [change] statt-finden; [difficulty] auf ltreten - **2.** [exist, be found] vor|kommen - **3.** [come to mind]: **to ~ to sb** jm in den Sinn kommen.

**occurrence** [ə'kʌrəns] *n* - **1.** [event] Vor-kommnis *das*, Ereignis *das* - **2.** [fact or instance of occurring] Vorkommen *das*, Auftreten *das*

**ocean** ['əʊʃn] *n* - **1.** [in names] Ozean *der* - **2.** *Am* [sea] Meer *das*.

**oceangoing** ['əʊʃn̩ˌgəʊɪŋ] *adj* Hochsee-, hochseetauglich.

**Oceania** [ˌəʊʃɪ'eɪnɪə] *n* Ozeanien *nt*.

**Oceanian** [ˌəʊʃɪ'eɪnɪən] *adj* ozeanisch ⟨⟩ *n* Ozeanier *der*, -in *die*.

**ochre** *Br*, **ocher** *Am* ['əʊkəʳ] *adj* ockerfarben.

**o'clock** [ə'klɒk] *adv* Uhr; **five ~** fünf Uhr.

**OCR** *n abbr of* **optical character reader**.

**Oct.** (*abbr of* **October**) Okt.

**octagon** ['ɒktəgən] *n* Achteck *das*, Oktagon *das*.

**octagonal** [ɒk'tægən̩l] *adj* achteckig, okta-gonal.

**octane** ['ɒkteɪn] *n* Oktan *das*.

**octane number, octane rating** *n* Oktan-zahl *die*.

**octave** ['ɒktɪv] *n* MUS Oktave *die*.

**octet** [ɒk'tet] *n* MUS Oktett *das*.

**October** [ɒk'təʊbəʳ] *n* Oktober *der*; *see also* September.

**octogenarian** [ˌɒktəʊdʒɪ'neərɪən] *n* Achtzi-ger *der*, -in *die*.

**octopus** ['ɒktəpəs] (*pl* **-puses** OR **-pi** [-paɪ]) *n* Tintenfisch *der*.

**OD** - **1.** *abbr of* **overdose** - **2.** *abbr of* **over-drawn**.

**odd** [ɒd] *adj* - **1.** [strange] seltsam, eigenartig - **2.** [not part of pair] einzeln - **3.** [number] ungerade - **4.** [leftover] überzählig, übrig - **5.** [occasional] gelegentlich - **6.** *inf* [approxi-mately] ungefähr, etwa; **twenty ~ years** mehr als zwanzig Jahre.

◆ **odds** *npl* - **1.** [probability] Wahrscheinlich-keit *die*, Chancen *pl*; **the ~s are that ...** aller Wahrscheinlichkeit nach ..., es ist wahr-scheinlich, dass ...; **against all** OR **the ~s** wider Erwarten - **2.** [bits]: **~s and ends** Krimskrams *der* - **3.** *phr*: **to be at ~s with** sb/sthg sich mit jm/etw uneinig sein.

**oddball** ['ɒdbɔːl] *n inf* seltsamer Kauz.

**oddity** ['ɒdɪtɪ] (*pl* **-ies**) *n* - **1.** [strange person] Son-derling *der*; [strange thing] Kuriosität *die* - **2.** [strangeness] Eigenartigkeit *die*.

**odd-job man** *Br*, **odd-jobber** *Am* [-'dʒɒbəʳ] *n* Gelegenheitsarbeiter *der*.

**odd jobs** *npl* Gelegenheitsarbeiten *pl*.

**oddly** ['ɒdlɪ] *adv* seltsam.

**oddments** ['ɒdmənts] *npl* Einzelstücke *pl*.

**odds-on** ['ɒdz-] *adj inf*: **the ~ favourite** der kla-re Favorit; **it's ~ that ...** es ist sehr wahr-scheinlich, dass ...

**ode** [əʊd] *n* Ode *die*.

**odious** ['əʊdɪəs] *adj* [person] abstoßend; [action] abscheulich.

**odometer** [əʊ'dɒmɪtəʳ] *n* Kilometerzähler *der*.

**odor** *n Am* = **odour**.

**odorless** *adj Am* = **odourless**.

**odour** *Br*, **odor** *Am* ['əʊdəʳ] *n* Geruch *der*.

**odourless** *Br*, **odorless** *Am* ['əʊdəlɪs] *adj* ge-ruchlos.

**odyssey** ['ɒdɪsɪ] (*pl* **odysseys**) *n literary* Odys-see *die*.

**OECD** (*abbr of* **Organization for Economic Co-operation and Development**) *n* OECD *die*.

**oesophagus** *Br*, **esophagus** *Am* [ɪ'sɒfəgəs] *n* Ösophagus *der*.

**oestrogen** *Br*, **estrogen** *Am* ['iːstrədʒən] *n* Östrogen *das*.

**of** [*unstressed* əv, *stressed* ɒv] *prep* - **1.** [gen] von *(the genitive case is often used instead of "von")*; **the cover ~ the book** der Umschlag des Buches; **the colour ~ the car** die Farbe des Autos; **the handle ~ the door** der Türgriff; **a friend ~ mine** ein Freund von mir; **the works ~ Shakespeare** die Werke Shakespeares OR von Shake-speare; **the Queen ~ England** die Königin von England; **the University ~ Leeds** die Universi-tät Leeds; **south ~ Boston/the river** südlich von Boston/des Flusses - **2.** [expressing quan-tity, contents, age]: **a pound ~ sweets** ein Pfund Bonbons; **a piece ~ cake** ein Stück Kuchen; **a cup ~ coffee** eine Tasse Kaffee; **a group ~ women** eine Gruppe Frauen; **a rise ~ 20%** ein Anstieg um 20%; **a town ~ 50,000 people** eine Stadt mit 50 000 Einwohnern; **thousands ~ people** Tausende von Leuten; **a girl ~ six** ein sechsjähriges Mädchen; **both/one ~ us** beide/einer von uns; **a man ~ cour-age** ein mutiger Mann - **3.** [made from] aus; **a house ~ stone** ein Haus aus Stein; **it's made ~ wood** es ist aus Holz - **4.** [with emotions]: **a love ~ France** eine Liebe zu Frankreich; **a fear ~ flying** Angst vor dem Fliegen - **5.** [on the part of] von; **that was very kind ~ you** das war sehr nett von Ihnen - **6.** [referring to place names]: **the city ~ Birmingham** die Stadt Birmingham - **7.** [indicating resemblance] von; **it was the size ~ a pea** es war so groß wie eine Erbse; es hatte die Größe einer Erbse - **8.** [with dates, periods of time]: **the 26th ~ April** der

26. April; **the night** ~ **the murder** die Mordnacht; **the summer** ~ **1969** der Sommer 1969; **in September** ~ **last year** im September letzten Jahres **- 9.** [indicating cause of death]: **to die** ~ **sthg** an etw *(D)* sterben **- 10.** *Am* [in telling the time] vor; **it's ten** ~ **four** es ist zehn vor vier.

**off** [ɒf] *adv* **- 1.** [away] weg; **to get** ~ [from bus, train, plane] auslsteigen; **we're** ~ **to Austria next week** wir fahren nächste Woche nach Österreich; **I must be** ~ ich muss gehen; **to go** OR **drop** ~ **to sleep** einlschlafen **- 2.** [expressing removal] ab; **to take sthg** ~ [clothes, shoes] etw auslziehen; [lid, wrapper] etw ablnehmen; **with his shoes** ~ ohne Schuhe **- 3.** [not working]: **to turn sthg** ~ [TV, radio, engine] etw auslschalten; [tap] etw zuldrehen **- 4.** [expressing distance or time away]: **it's 10 miles** ~ es sind noch 10 Meilen bis dahin; **it's two months** ~ **yet** es sind noch zwei Monate bis dahin; **it's a long way** ~ [in distance] es ist noch ein weiter Weg bis dahin; [in time] bis dahin ist es noch lange hin **- 5.** [not at work]. **I'm taking a week** ~ ich nehme mir eine Woche frei **- 6.** [financially]: **well/badly** ~ gut/schlecht daran <> *prep* **- 1.** [away from] von; **to get** ~ **sthg** aus etw auslsteigen; ~ **the coast** vor der Küste; **it's just** ~ **the main road** es ist gleich in der Nähe der Hauptstraße **- 2.** [indicating removal] von … ab; **take the lid** ~ **the jar** mach den Deckel von dem Glas ab; **they've taken £20** ~ **the price** sie haben es um 20 Pfund billiger gemacht; **to take sthg** ~ **the table** etw vom Tisch nehmen; **take your hands** ~ **me!** nimm die Hände weg! **- 3.** [absent from]: **to be** ~ **work** frei haben **- 4.** *inf* [from] von; **I bought it** ~ **her** ich habe es von ihr gekauft **- 5.** *inf* [no longer liking or needing]: **I'm** ~ **my food at the moment** ich habe zur Zeit keinen Appetit; **she's** ~ **drugs now** sie nimmt keine Drogen mehr <> *adj* **- 1.** [meat, cheese, milk, beer] schlecht **- 2.** [not working] aus; [tap] zu **- 3.** [cancelled] abgesagt; **the deal is** ~ die Sache ist abgeblasen **- 4.** [not available]: **the soup's** ~ es ist keine Suppe mehr da **- 5.** *inf* [offhand] schroff.

**offal** [ˈɒfl] *n* Innereien *pl.*

**off-balance** *adv* **- 1.** [not standing firmly]: **he pushed me** ~ er brachte mich aus dem Gleichgewicht **- 2.** [unprepared] unvorbereitet.

**offbeat** [ˈɒfbiːt] *adj inf* [person] unkonventionell; [sense of humour] merkwürdig.

**off-centre** *adj* & *adv* nicht mittig.

**off-chance** *n:* **on the** ~ auf gut Glück.

**off colour** *adj* kränklich.

**offcut** [ˈɒfkʌt] *n* Verschnitt *der.*

**off-day** *n inf* schlechter Tag.

**off duty** *adv* außer Dienst, dienstfrei.
⬤ **off-duty** *adj* außer Dienst.

**offence** *Br,* **offense** *Am* [əˈfens] *n* **- 1.** [crime]

Verbrechen *das* **- 2.** [displeasure, hurt] Beleidigung *die,* Kränkung *die;* **to take** ~ beleidigt sein, gekränkt sein.

**offend** [əˈfend] *vt* beleidigen <> *vi* **- 1.** [contravene]: **to** ~ **against sthg** gegen etw verstoßen **- 2.** [commit a crime] ein Verbrechen begehen.

**offended** [əˈfendɪd] *adj* beleidigt, gekränkt.

**offender** [əˈfendər] *n* **- 1.** [criminal] Straftäter *der,* -in *die* **- 2.** [culprit] Schuldige *der, die.*

**offending** [əˈfendɪŋ] *adj* [newspaper article, word, statement] beleidigend; [object] anstößig.

**offense** [sense 2 ˈɒfens] *n Am* **- 1.** = offence **- 2.** SPORT Angriff *der.*

**offensive** [əˈfensɪv] *adj* **- 1.** [causing offence] beleidigend, kränkend; [behaviour] anstößig **- 2.** [aggressive] Angriffs-, aggressiv <> *n* **- 1.** MIL Offensive *die,* Angriff *der* **- 2.** *fig* [attack]: **to go on** OR **take the** ~ in die Offensive gehen.

**offensiveness** [əˈfensɪvnɪs] *n* Anstößigkeit *die.*

**offer** [ˈɒfər] *n* Angebot *das;* **on** [available] verkäuflich; [at a special price] im Angebot <> *vt* anlbieten; **to** ~ **sthg to sb, to** ~ **sb sthg** jm etw anlbieten; **to** ~ **to do sthg** anlbieten, etw zu tun <> *vi* sich anlbieten.

**OFFER** [ˈɒfər] (*abbr of* **Office of Electricity Regulation**) *n Regulierungsbehörde für den britischen Elektrizitätsmarkt.*

**offering** [ˈɒfərɪŋ] *n* **- 1.** [something offered] Gabe *die* **- 2.** RELIG [sacrifice] Opfer *das,* Opfergabe *die.*

**off guard** *adv* unvorbereitet.

**offhand** [ˌɒfˈhænd] *adj* lässig <> *adv* auf Anhieb.

**office** [ˈɒfɪs] *n* **- 1.** [gen] Büro *das* **- 2.** [government department] Behörde *die* **- 3.** [position of authority] Amt *das;* **in** ~ im Amt; **to take** ~ sein Amt anltreten.

**office automation** *n* Büroautomation *die.*

**office block** *n* Bürogebäude *das.*

**office boy** *n* Laufbursche *der.*

**officeholder** [ˈɒfɪsˌhəʊldər] *n* Amtsinhaber *der,* -in *die.*

**office hours** *npl* Bürostunden *pl.*

**office junior** *n Br* Bürogehilfe *der,* -fin *die.*

**Office of Fair Trading** *n staatliche Verbraucherschutzorganisation in Großbritannien.*

**officer** [ˈɒfɪsər] *n* **- 1.** MIL Offizier *der* **- 2.** [in organization] Vertreter *der,* -in *die* **- 3.** [in police force] Polizeibeamte *der,* -tin *die.*

**office work** *n (U)* Büroarbeit *die.*

**office worker** *n* Büroangestellte *der, die.*

**official** [əˈfɪʃl] *adj* offiziell <> *n* Beamte *der,* -tin *die;* SPORT Funktionär *der,* -in *die.*

**officialdom** [əˈfɪʃəldəm] *n* Beamtentum *das,* Bürokratie *die.*

**officially** [ə'fɪʃəlɪ] *adv* offiziell.

**official receiver** *n* Konkursverwalter *der*.

**officiate** [ə'fɪʃɪeɪt] *vi* amtieren; **to ~ at sthg** bei etw fungieren.

**officious** [ə'fɪʃəs] *adj pej* übereifrig.

**offing** ['ɒfɪŋ] *n*: **in the ~** in Sicht.

**off-key** *adj* & *adv* MUS falsch.

**off-licence** *n Br* Wein- und Spirituosen- handlung *die*.

**off limits** *adj esp Am* verboten.

**off-line** *adj* COMPUT offline.

**offload** [ɒf'ləʊd] *vt inf*: **to ~ sthg (on to sb)** etw (auf jn) abschieben OR abwälzen.

**off-peak** *adj*: **~ electricity** Nachtstrom *der*; **~ fares** verbilligter Tarif; **during ~ hours** außerhalb der Stoßzeiten <> *adv* [travel] außerhalb der Hauptreisezeit.

**off-putting** [-ˌpʊtɪŋ] *adj* abstoßend.

**off sales** *npl Br* Verkauf von Spirituosen zum Mitnehmen in einem Pub.

**off season** *n*: **the ~** die Nebensaison.
◆ **off-season** *adj* außerhalb der Saison.

**offset** ['ɒfset] (*pt* & *pp* offset; *cont* -ting) *vt* ausgleichen.

**offshoot** ['ɒfʃuːt] *n* Ableger *der*; **to be an ~ of sthg** ein Ableger von etw sein.

**offshore** [ˌɒf'ʃɔːʳ] *adj* - **1.** [in or on the sea] Offshore- - **2.** [near coast] in Küstennähe; **~ waters** Küstengewässer *pl* <> *adv* - **1.** [out at sea] offshore, im offenen Meer - **2.** [near coast] in Küstennähe.

**offside** [*adj* & *adv* ˌɒf'saɪd, *n* 'ɒfsaɪd] *adj* - **1.** [part of vehicle] auf der Fahrerseite - **2.** SPORT Abseits- <> *adv* SPORT im Abseits <> *n* [of vehicle] Fahrerseite *die*.

**offspring** ['ɒfsprɪŋ] (*pl inv*) *n* - **1.** *fml* OR *hum* [of people] Nachwuchs *der* - **2.** [of animals] Junge(s) *das*.

**offstage** [ˌɒf'steɪdʒ] *adj* & *adv* hinter der Bühne, hinter den Kulissen.

**off-the-cuff** *adj* & *adv* unüberlegt, spon- tan.

**off-the-peg** *adj Br*: **~ suit** Anzug *der* von der Stange.

**off-the-record** *adj* & *adv* inoffiziell.

**off-the-wall** *adj* verrückt.

**off-white** *adj* gebrochen weiß.

**OFGAS** ['ɒfgæs] (*abbr of* Office of Gas Supply) *n* Regulierungsbehörde für den britischen Gasmarkt.

**OFSTED** ['ɒfsted] (*abbr of* Office for Standards in Education) *n* britische Schulaufsichtsbe- hörde.

**OFT** *n abbr of* Office of Fair Trading.

**OFTEL** ['ɒftel] (*abbr of* Office of Telecommuni-

cations) *n* Regulierungsbehörde für den briti- schen Telefonmarkt.

**often** ['ɒfn, 'ɒftn] *adv* oft; **how ~ do the buses run?** wie oft fährt der Bus?; **every so ~** gele- gentlich; **as ~ as not, more ~ than not** meis- tens.

**OFWAT** ['ɒfwɒt] (*abbr of* Office of Water Ser- vices) *n* Regulierungsbehörde für den briti- schen Wassermarkt.

**ogle** ['əʊgl] *vt pej* begaffen.

**ogre** ['əʊgəʳ] *n* Menschenfresser *der*.

**oh** [əʊ] *excl* - **1.** [to introduce comment] ach! - **2.** [ex- pressing hesitation, joy, surprise, fear] oh!; **~ no!** oh nein!

**OH** *abk für* Ohio, *in Postanschrift verwendet*.

**ohm** [əʊm] *n* Ohm *das*.

**OHMS** (*abbr of* On His (or Her) Majesty's Ser- vice) *Aufdruck auf amtlichen Briefsachen*.

**oil** [ɔɪl] *n* Öl *das* <> *vt* ölen, schmieren.
◆ **oils** *npl* ART Ölmalerei *die*.

**oilcan** ['ɔɪlkæn] *n* Ölkanne *die*.

**oil change** *n* Ölwechsel *der*.

**oilcloth** ['ɔɪlklɒθ] *n* Wachstuch *das*.

**oilfield** ['ɔɪlfiːld] *n* Ölfeld *das*.

**oil filter** *n* Ölfilter *der*.

**oil-fired** [-ˌfaɪəd] *adj* ölbefeuert; **~ central heating** Ölheizung *die*.

**oil industry** *n*: **the ~** die Erdölindustrie.

**oil paint** *n* Ölfarbe *die*.

**oil painting** *n* - **1.** [picture] Ölgemälde *das* - **2.** [art] Ölmalerei *die*.

**oilrig** ['ɔɪlrɪg] *n* Ölbohrinsel *die*.

**oilskins** ['ɔɪlskɪnz] *npl* Ölzeug *das*.

**oil slick** *n* Ölteppich *der*.

**oil tanker** *n* - **1.** [ship] Öltanker *der* - **2.** [lorry] Tankwagen *der*.

**oil well** *n* Ölquelle *die*.

**oily** ['ɔɪlɪ] (*compar* -ier; *superl* -iest) *adj* - **1.** [rag, clothes] ölig; [food] fettig - **2.** *pej* [smarmy] schlei- mig.

**ointment** ['ɔɪntmənt] *n* Salbe *die*.

**oiro** (*abbr of* offers in the region of) ≃ VB.

**OK¹** (*pl* OKs, *pt* & *pp* OKed; *cont* OKing), **okay** [ˌəʊ'keɪ] *inf adj* in Ordnung; **are you ~?** ist al- les in Ordnung?; **is that ~ with you?** ist dir das recht? <> *adv* [well] gut <> *n*: **to give (sb) the ~** (jm) sein Okay geben <> *excl* - **1.** [ex- pressing agreement] okay!, in Ordnung! - **2.** [to introduce new topic]: **~, let's get started** Okay, fangen wir an <> *vt* sein Okay geben zu.

**OK²** *abk für* Oklahoma, *in Postanschrift ver- wendet*.

**okra** ['əʊkrə] *n* (U) Okra *die*.

**old** [əʊld] *adj* - **1.** [gen] alt; **how ~ are you?** wie alt bist du?; **I'm 36 years ~** ich bin 36 (Jahre alt); **to get ~** alt werden; **in the ~ days** früher **- 2.** [for emphasis]: **any ~ thing** das erste beste, das Erstbeste; **good ~ George!** der gute alte Georg! <> *npl:* **the ~** ältere Leute.

**old age** *n (U)* Alter *das.*

**old age pension** *n Br* Rente *die.*

**old age pensioner** *n Br* Rentner *der,* -in *die.*

**Old Bailey** [-'beɪlɪ] *n:* **the ~** *oberster Strafgerichtshof in London.*

**olden** ['əʊldn] *adj:* **in the ~ days** früher.

**old-fashioned** [-'fæʃnd] *adj* [person, clothes] altmodisch; [ideas] überholt.

**old flame** *n* alte Flamme.

**old maid** *n pej* [spinster] alte Jungfer.

**old master** *n* alter Meister.

**old people's home** *n* Altersheim *das.*

**Old Testament** *n:* **the ~** das Alte Testament.

**old-time** *adj* im alten Stil.

**old-timer** *n* [old man] Alte *der.*

**old wives' tale** *n* Ammenmärchen *das.*

**Old World** *n:* **the ~** die Alte Welt.

**O level** (*abbr of* **ordinary level**) *n Br* ≃ mittlere Reife, *früherer Schulabschluss in England und Wales, 1988 durch das GCSE ersetzt.*

**oligarchy** ['ɒlɪgɑːkɪ] (*pl* **-ies**) *n* Oligarchie *die.*

**olive** ['ɒlɪv] *adj* oliv <> *n* Olive *die;* **~ (tree)** Olivenbaum *der.*

**olive green** *adj* olivgrün.

**olive oil** *n* Olivenöl *das.*

**Olympic** [ə'lɪmpɪk] *adj* olympisch.
➥ **Olympics** *npl:* **the ~s** die Olympischen Spiele.

**Olympic Games** *npl:* **the ~** die Olympischen Spiele.

**Oman** [əʊ'mɑːn] *n* Oman *nt.*

**ombudsman** ['ɒmbʊdzmən] (*pl* **-men** [-mən]) *n* Ombudsmann *der.*

**omelet(te)** ['ɒmlɪt] *n* Omelett *das.*

**omen** ['əʊmən] *n* Omen *das.*

**ominous** ['ɒmɪnəs] *adj* ominös.

**ominously** ['ɒmɪnəslɪ] *adv* bedrohlich; [speak] in einem unheilverkündenden Ton.

**omission** [ə'mɪʃn] *n* Auslassung *die.*

**omit** [ə'mɪt] (*pt & pp* **-ted**; *cont* **-ting**) *vt* auslassen; **to ~ to do sthg** es unterlassen, etw zu tun; [unintentionally] es versäumen, etw zu tun.

**omnibus** ['ɒmnɪbəs] *n* **- 1.** [book] Sammelband *der* **- 2.** *Br* RADIO & TV *erneute Ausstrahlung mehrerer Folgen einer Serie zusammen in einer Sendung.*

**omnipotent** [ɒm'nɪpətənt] *adj fml* allmächtig.

**omnipresent** [ˌɒmnɪ'prezənt] *adj fml* allgegenwärtig.

**omniscient** [ɒm'nɪsɪənt] *adj fml* allwissend.

**omnivorous** [ɒm'nɪvərəs] *adj:* **~ animal** Allesfresser *der.*

**on** [ɒn] *prep* **- 1.** [indicating position, location] auf (+ D); (with verbs of motion) auf (+ A); **it's ~ the table** es ist auf dem Tisch; **put it ~ the table** leg es auf den Tisch; **~ the wall/ceiling** an der Wand/der Decke; **~ page four** auf Seite vier; **~ my left/right** zu meiner Linken/Rechten; **~ the left/right** auf der linken/rechten Seite, links/rechts; **we stayed ~ a farm** wir übernachteten auf einem Bauernhof; **~ the Rhine** am Rhein; **~ the main road** an der Hauptstraße; **he had a scar ~ his face** er hatte eine Narbe im Gesicht; **do you have any money ~ you?** hast du Geld bei dir? **- 2.** [indicating means] auf (+ D); **recorded ~ tape** auf Band; **~ TV/the radio** im Radio/Fernsehen; **it runs ~ unleaded petrol** es fährt mit bleifreiem Benzin; **he lives ~ fruit and yoghurt** er lebt von Obst und Joghurt; **to cut o.s. ~ sthg** sich an etw (D) schneiden **- 3.** [indicating mode of transport]: **to be ~ the train/plane** im Zug/Flugzeug sein; **to travel ~ the bus/train** mit dem Bus/Zug fahren; **to get ~ a bus** in einen Bus einsteigen; **~ foot** zu Fuß **- 4.** [using, supported by]: **to stand ~ one leg** auf einem Bein stehen; **he was lying ~ his back** er lag auf dem Rücken; **he's ~ medication** er muss Medikamente nehmen; **to be ~ drugs** [addicted] drogensüchtig sein, Drogen nehmen; **to be ~ social security** Sozialhilfe bekommen **- 5.** [about] über (+ A); **a book ~ Germany** ein Buch über Deutschland **- 6.** [indicating time] an (+ D); **~ Tuesday** am Dienstag; **~ Tuesdays** dienstags; **~ 25 August** am 25. August; **~ my birthday** an meinem Geburtstag; **~ arrival** bei Ankunft; **~ my return, ~ returning** bei meiner Rückkehr, als ich zurückkam **- 7.** [indicating activity]: **to work ~ sthg** an etw (D) arbeiten; **he's here ~ business** er ist geschäftlich hier; **~ holiday** im Urlaub, in Ferien; **she's ~ the telephone** [talking] sie telefoniert gerade; **to be ~ night shift** Nachtschicht haben; **to be ~ fire** brennen **- 8.** [according to]: **~ good authority** aus guter Quelle; **~ this evidence ...** aufgrund dieser Beweise ... **- 9.** [indicating influence, effect] auf (+ A); **the effect ~ Britain** die Auswirkungen auf Großbritannien; **a tax ~ imports** eine Steuer auf Importe **- 10.** [indicating membership] in (+ D); **to be ~ a committee** Mitglied eines Ausschusses sein **- 11.** [earning]: **she's ~ £25,000 a year** sie verdient £25.000 pro Jahr; **to be ~ a low income** ein niedriges Einkommen haben **- 12.** [obtained from]: **interest ~ investments** Zinsen aus Investitionen **- 13.** [referring to musical instrument] auf (+ D); **~ the violin/flute** auf der Geige/Flöte **- 14.**: **~ the cheap** billig; **~ the sly**

**O**

hintenherum - **15.** inf [paid by]: **the drinks are ~ me** die Drinks gehen auf mich ◇ adv - **1.** [in place, covering]: **to have sthg ~** [clothes, hat] etw anlhaben; **put the lid ~** mach den Deckel drauf; **to put one's clothes ~** sich (D) (seine Kleider) anlziehen - **2.** [taking place]: **to be ~** stattlfinden; **how long is the festival ~?** wie lange geht das Festival?; **when the war was ~** während des Krieges; **to have sthg ~** [planned] etw vorlhaben - **3.** [film, play, programme]: **the news is ~** die Nachrichten laufen; **what's ~ at the cinema?** was läuft im Kino?; **there's nothing ~ tonight** heute abend kommt nichts - **4.** [working]: **you left the heater ~** du hast das Heizgerät angelassen; **to turn sthg ~** [TV, radio, engine] etw einlschalten; [tap] etw auf ldrehen - **5.** [indicating continuing action] weiter; **to work ~** weiterlarbeiten; **we talked ~ into the night** wir redeten noch bis in die Nacht hinein; **he kept ~ walking** er ging immer weiter - **6.** [forward]: **send my mail ~ (to me)** senden Sie mir die Post nach - **7.** [with transport]: **to get ~** einlsteigen; **is everyone ~?** sind alle eingestiegen? - **8.** phr: **earlier ~** früher; **later ~** später; **it's just not ~!** inf das geht einfach nicht!; **to be** OR **go ~ at sb (to do sthg)** [pester] jm zulsetzen(, etw zu tun).

◆ **from ... on** adv: **from that moment ~** von dem Moment an; **from now ~** von jetzt an, ab jetzt; **from then ~** von da an.

◆ **on and off** adv ab und zu.

◆ **on and on** adv: **to go ~ and ~ (about sthg)** (über etw (A)) unaufhörlich sprechen.

◆ **on to, onto** prep (only written as onto for senses 4 and 5) - **1.** [to a position on top of] auf (+ A); **she jumped ~ to the chair** sie sprang auf den Stuhl - **2.** [into a vehicle] in (+ A); **she got ~ to the bus** sie stieg in den Bus ein - **3.** [wall, door] an (+ A); **stick the photo ~ to the page** kleb das Foto auf die Seite - **4.** [aware of]: **to be ~ to sb** [subj: police] jm auf der Spur sein; **she's ~to something** sie hat etwas entdeckt - **5.** [into contact with]: **to get ~to sb** sich an jn wenden.

**ON** abk für Ontario, in Postanschrift verwendet.

**once** [wʌns] adv einmal; **not ~** kein einziges Mal; **for ~** ausnahmsweise; **~ more** [one more time] noch einmal; [again] wieder; **~ and for all** ein für allemal; **this ~** dieses eine Mal; **~ (upon a time) there was ...** es war einmal ... ◇ conj wenn.

◆ **at once** adv - **1.** [immediately] sofort - **2.** [at the same time] gleichzeitig; **all at ~** auf einmal.

**once-over** n inf: **to give sb/sthg the ~** jn/etw kurz in Augenschein nehmen.

**oncoming** ['ɒnˌkʌmɪŋ] adj: **~ traffic** Gegenverkehr der.

**one** [wʌn] num - **1.** [the number 1] eins; **~, two, three eins**, zwei, drei; **a ~ followed by three twos** eine Eins und drei Zweien; **thirty-~** einunddreißig; **at ~/~ thirty** [time] um eins/

halb zwei; **in ~s and twos** vereinzelt - **2.** (with masculine and neuter nouns) ein; (with feminine nouns) eine; **~ brother and ~ sister** ein Bruder und eine Schwester; **~ hundred/thousand** (ein)hundert/(ein)tausend; **page ~** Seite eins; **~-fifth** ein Fünftel; **~ or two** einige ◇ adj - **1.** [only] einzige, -r, -s; **it's her ~ ambition** das ist ihr einziger Ehrgeiz - **2.** [indefinite]: **~ day** [in past, future] eines Tages; **~ of these days** irgendwann einmal; **~ afternoon/night** an einem Nachmittag/Abend - **3.** fml [a certain] ein gewisser, eine gewisse; **~ James Smith** ein gewisser James Smith - **4.** inf [a]: **~ awful hangover** ein Mordskater; **~ hell of a bang** ein Mordsknall ◇ pron - **1.** [referring to a particular thing or person]: **the red/blue ~** der/die/das Rote/Blaue; **the best ~s** die besten; **the ~ on the table** der/die/das auf dem Tisch; **the ~ I told you about** der/die/das, von dem/der/dem ich dir erzählt habe; **the ~s you want** die OR diejenigen, die du willst; **I like that ~** ich mag den/die/das (da); **which ~?** welche, -r, -s?; **a red dot and a blue ~** ein roter Punkt und ein blauer; **I'm not** OR **I've never been ~ to ...** ich bin nicht einer, der ... - **2.** [indefinite] eine/einer/eins; **there's only ~ left** es ist nur eine/einer/eins übrig; **have you got ~?** hast du eine/einen/eins?; **~ of my friends** einer meiner Freunde; **~ of them** keiner (von ihnen); **~ by ~** einer nach dem anderen - **3.** [referring to money]: **~ fifty, please** eins fünfzig, bitte - **4.** fml [you, anyone] man; **~ never knows** man weiß nie; **to give ~'s opinion** seine Meinung sagen; **to cut ~'s finger** sich (D) in den Finger schneiden - **5.** inf [blow]: **she thumped him ~** sie hat ihm eine geschmiert.

◆ **at one** adj: **to be at ~ with sb** sich (D) mit jm einig sein; **to be at ~ with sthg** mit etw im Einklang sein.

◆ **for one** adv: **I for ~ will come** ich jedenfalls werde kommen.

◆ **one up on** adj: **to be** OR **have ~ up on sb** [have advantage] jm etwas vorauslhaben.

**one-armed bandit** [-ɑːmd-] n einarmiger Bandit.

**one-liner** n witziger Einzeiler.

**one-man** adj Einmann-.

**one-man band** n - **1.** [musician] Einmannband die - **2.** [business] Einmannbetrieb der.

**one-night stand** n - **1.** [performance] einmaliges Gastspiel - **2.** inf [sexual relationship] One-Night-Stand der.

**one-off** inf adj [event, offer, concert] einmalig; **~ object/product** Einzelstück das ◇ n - **1.** [unique event] einmalige Sache; [person] Original das - **2.** [unique object, product] Einzelstück das.

**one-on-one** adj Am = one-to-one.

**one-parent family** n Einelternfamilie die.

**one-piece swimsuit** n Einteiler der.

**onerous** ['ɔʊnərəs] adj [task] mühevoll; [responsibility] schwer.

**oneself** [wʌn'self] pron fml - **1.** (reflexive) sich; **to make ~ comfortable** es sich (D) bequem machen - **2.** (after prep) sich selbst; **to look at ~ in the mirror** sich (selbst) im Spiegel betrachten - **3.** (stressed) selbst; **to do sthg ~** etw selbst tun.

**one-sided** [-'saɪdɪd] adj einseitig.

**onetime** ['wʌntaɪm] adj [former] ehemalig.

**one-to-one** Br, **one-on-one** Am adj: **~ discussion** Diskussion die unter vier Augen; **~ tuition** Einzelunterricht der.

**one-way** adj: **~ street** Einbahnstraße die; **~ traffic** Einbahnverkehr der; **~ ticket** einfache Fahrkarte.

**ongoing** ['ɒn.gəʊɪŋ] adj [situation] andauernd; [project] laufend; [discussions] im Gang befindlich.

**onion** ['ʌnjən] n Zwiebel die.

**online** [adj 'ɒnlaɪn, adv .ɒn'laɪn,] COMPUT adj On-line- ⬦ adv online.

**onlooker** ['ɒn.lʊkə'] n Zuschauer der, -in die; [at accident scene] Schaulustige der, die.

**only** ['əʊnlɪ] adj einzige, -r, -s; **an ~ child** ein Einzelkind ⬦ adv nur; **I ~ want one** ich möchte nur einen/eine/eines; **I ~ wish I could** ich würde es wirklich gern tun; **~ yesterday** erst gestern; **we've ~ just arrived** wir sind gerade erst angekommen; **there's ~ just enough** es ist gerade noch genug da; **not ~** nicht nur ⬦ conj aber; **I would go, ~ I'm too tired** ich würde gehen, aber ich bin zu müde.

**o.n.o., ono** (abbr of or near(est) offer) ≈ VB oder gegen Verbot.

**onrush** ['ɒnrʌʃ] n [of feeling] Ansturm der.

**on-screen** COMPUT adj & adv auf dem Bildschirm.

**onset** ['ɒnset] n Beginn der; [of war, illness] Ausbruch der.

**onshore** [.ɒn'ʃɔ:'] adj [oil production] an Land stattfindend; **~ wind** Seewind der ⬦ adv an Land; [blow] landwärts.

**onside** [ɒn'saɪd] adj SPORT: **to be ~** nicht im Abseits sein.

**onslaught** ['ɒnslɔ:t] n - **1.** [physical] (heftiger) Angriff - **2.** [verbal] (verbale) Attacke.

**Ont.** abk für Ontario, in Postanschrift verwendet.

**on-the-job** adj [training] innerbetrieblich.

**on-the-spot** adj: **~ interview/reporter** Interview das/Reporter der, -in die vor Ort.

**onto** [unstressed before consonant 'ɒntə, un-

stressed before vowel 'ɒntʊ, stressed 'ɒntu:] prep ▷ **on.**

**onus** ['əʊnəs] n: **the ~ is on him to convince us** es liegt an ihm, uns zu überzeugen.

**onward** ['ɒnwəd] adj: **~ journey** Weiterreise die ⬦ adv = **onwards.**

**onwards** ['ɒnwədz] adv [forwards] vorwärts; **to travel ~** weiterlreisen; **from now ~** von jetzt an; **from October ~** ab Oktober.

**onyx** ['ɒnɪks] n Onyx der.

**oodles** ['u:dlz] npl inf: **~ of money/chocolate/etc** jede Menge Geld/Schokolade/etc.

**ooh** [u:] excl inf oh!

**oops** [ʊps, u:ps] excl inf huch!; [after mistake] oh!

**ooze** [u:z] vt fig [charm] auslstrahlen; [confidence] strotzen vor (+ D) ⬦ vi [liquid, blood] triefen; [mud] (herausl)quellen ⬦ n [mud] Schlamm der.

**opal** ['əʊpl] n Opal der.

**opaque** [əʊ'peɪk] adj - **1.** [not transparent] undurchsichtig - **2.** fig [text, meaning] unverständlich.

**OPEC** ['əʊpek] (abbr of **Organization of Petroleum-Exporting Countries**) n OPEC die.

**open** ['əʊpn] adj - **1.** [gen] offen; **wide ~** weit offen - **2.** [receptive - mind, person]: **to be ~ to sthg** [ready to accept] für etw offen sein; **~ to question** fraglich; **to lay o.s. ~ to criticism** sich der Kritik auslsetzen; **two options are ~ to us** zwei Möglichkeiten stehen uns offen - **3.** [shop, office, library] geöffnet; **are you ~ at the weekend?** haben Sie am Wochenende geöffnet?; **~ to the public** der Öffentlichkeit zugänglich - **4.** [inaugurated] eröffnet - **5.** [unobstructed - road, passage] frei; [- view] weit - **6.** [not enclosed]: **~ country** freies Land; **in the ~ air** im Freien ⬦ n: **in the ~** [in the fresh air] im Freien; **to bring sthg out into the ~** etw ans Licht bringen ⬦ vt - **1.** [gen] öffnen, auflmachen; **to ~ fire** das Feuer eröffnen - **2.** [bank account, meeting, event, new building] eröffnen ⬦ vi - **1.** [door, window, eyes, flower] sich öffnen, auflgehen - **2.** [begin business] öffnen, auflmachen - **3.** [commence] beginnen, anlfangen.

➤ **open on to** vt fus [subj: door] führen auf (+ A).

➤ **open out** vi - **1.** [bud, petals] sich öffnen, auflgehen - **2.** [road, path, river] breiter werden - **3.** [valley] sich öffnen; [view] sich erstrecken.

➤ **open up** vt sep - **1.** [gen] öffnen, auflmachen - **2.** [for development - country, market] erschließen ⬦ vi - **1.** [unlock door] auflschließen - **2.** [for business] öffnen, auflmachen - **3.** [become available - possibilities, chances] sich eröffnen, sich auflltun - **4.** [become less reserved] offener werden.

**open-air** adj [concert] Openair-; **~ swimming pool** Freibad das.

**o**

**open-and-shut** *adj:* an ~ case ein klarer Fall.

**open day** *n* Tag der der offenen Tür.

**open-ended** [-'endıd] *adj* [without time limitation] ohne Zeitbeschränkung.

**opener** ['əʊpnəʳ] *n* Öffner der.

**open-handed** [-'hændıd] *adj* großzügig.

**open-heart surgery** *n* (U) Eingriff der am offenen Herzen.

**opening** ['əʊpnıŋ] *adj* [speech, scene] Eröffnungs- ◇ *n* - **1.** [beginning] Anfang der - **2.** [gap] Öffnung die - **3.** [opportunity, business possibility] Möglichkeit die - **4.** [job vacancy] freie Stelle.

**opening hours** *npl* Öffnungszeiten *pl*.

**opening night** *n* Premiere die.

**opening time** *n* Br [of pub] Ausschankzeit die.

**open letter** *n* offener Brief.

**openly** ['əʊpənlı] *adv* [frankly] offen; [publicly] öffentlich; **to be ~ gay** offen zeigen, dass man schwul ist.

**open market** *n* freier Markt.

**open-minded** [-'maındıd] *adj* aufgeschlossen.

**open-mouthed** [-'maʊðd] *adv* mit offenem Mund.

**open-necked** [-'nekt] *adj* mit offenem Kragen.

**openness** ['əʊpənnıs] *n* [frankness] Offenheit die.

**open-plan** *adj* [office] Großraum-.

**open prison** *n* offene Anstalt.

**open sandwich** *n* belegtes Brot.

**open season** *n* [for hunting] Jagdzeit die; [for fishing] Fangzeit die.

**Open University** *n* Br: **the ~** britische Fernuniversität.

**OPEN UNIVERSITY**

Die britische „OU", wie sie auch abgekürzt wird, ist eine Fernuniversität, deren Vorlesungen in Radio und Fernsehen ausgestrahlt werden und die es Erwachsenen ermöglicht, von zu Hause aus Studienabschlüsse zu erwerben. Zur Vertiefung dienen schriftliche Hausaufgaben, die korrigiert zurückgeschickt werden, monatliche Seminartreffen und jährliche „summer schools", die meist etwa eine Woche dauern. Die OU steht allen offen und ist an keine Qualifikationen gebunden. Für die Kurse wird eine Gebühr erhoben.

**opera** ['ɒpərə] *n* Oper die.

**opera glasses** *npl* Opernglas das.

**opera house** *n* Opernhaus das.

**opera singer** *n* Opernsänger der, -in die.

**operate** ['ɒpəreıt] *vt* - **1.** [machine] bedienen - **2.** COMM [business] leiten, führen ◇ *vi* - **1.** [law] sich auswirken; [system] funktionieren; [machine - function] funktionieren; [ - be in operation] in Betrieb sein - **2.** COMM [business] arbeiten; **where do you ~ from?** wo haben Sie Ihren Geschäftssitz? - **3.** MED: **to ~ (on sb/sthg)** (jn/etw) operieren.

**operatic** [‚ɒpə'rætık] *adj* Opern-.

**operating room** ['ɒpəreıtıŋ-] *n* Am = operating theatre.

**operating system** ['ɒpəreıtıŋ-] *n* COMPUT Betriebssystem das.

**operating theatre** Br, **operating room** Am ['ɒpəreıtıŋ-] *n* Operationssaal der.

**operation** [‚ɒpə'reıʃn] *n* - **1.** [planned activity - MIL] Operation die; [ - of police force] Einsatz der; **rescue ~** Rettungsaktion die; **relief ~** Hilfsaktion die - **2.** (U) [COMM - management] Leitung die; [ - company, business] Unternehmen das - **3.** (U) [of machine - running] Betrieb der; [ - control] Bedienung die; **to be in ~** [machine] in Betrieb sein; [law] in Kraft sein; [system] angewendet werden - **4.** MED Operation die; **to have an ~** operiert werden.

**operational** [‚ɒpə'reıʃənl] *adj* - **1.** [machine]: **to be ~** [ready for use] betriebsbereit sein; [in use] in Betrieb sein - **2.** [costs, problem] Betriebs-.

**operative** ['ɒprətıv] *adj:* **to become ~** [law] in Kraft treten; [system] eingeführt werden ◇ *n* [in factory] Maschinenarbeiter der, -in die.

**operator** ['ɒpəreıtəʳ] *n* - **1.** [TELEC - at telephone exchange] Vermittlung die; [ - at switchboard] Telefonist der, -in die - **2.** [of machine] Maschinenarbeiter der, -in die; [of computer] Operator der, -in die - **3.** COMM [person in charge] Unternehmer der, -in die.

**operetta** [‚ɒpə'retə] *n* Operette die.

**ophthalmic optician** [ɒf'θælmık-] *n* Augenoptiker der, -in die.

**ophthalmologist** [‚ɒfθæl'mɒlədʒıst] *n* Augenarzt der, -ärztin die.

**opinion** [ə'pınjən] *n* Meinung die, Ansicht die; MED Gutachten das; **what's your ~ of him?** was halten Sie von ihm?; **to be of the ~ that** ... der Meinung OR Ansicht sein, dass ...; **to have a high/low ~ of sb** eine hohe/schlechte Meinung von jm haben; **in my ~** meiner Meinung OR Ansicht nach; **public ~** die öffentliche Meinung.

**opinionated** [ə'pınjəneıtıd] *adj pej* rechthaberisch.

**opinion poll** *n* Meinungsumfrage die.

**opium** ['əʊpıəm] *n* Opium das.

**opponent** [ə'pəʊnənt] *n* Gegner der, -in die.

**opportune** [ˈɒpətjuːn] *adj* [moment] günstig.

**opportunist** [ˌɒpəˈtjuːnɪst] *n* Opportunist *der*, -in *die*.

**opportunity** [ˌɒpəˈtjuːnətɪ] (*pl* -ies) *n* Gelegenheit *die;* **to get the ~ (to do sthg)** die Chance bekommen(, etw zu tun); **to take the ~ to do** OR **of doing sthg** die Gelegenheit ergreifen, um etw zu tun.

**oppose** [əˈpəʊz] *vt* [resist] sich widersetzen *(+ D);* [ideas, views] ablehnen.

**opposed** [əˈpəʊzd] *adj:* **to be ~ to sthg** gegen etw sein; **as ~ to** im Gegensatz zu.

**opposing** [əˈpəʊzɪŋ] *adj* [points of view] entgegengesetzt; [teams] gegnerisch.

**opposite** [ˈɒpəzɪt] *adj* - **1.** [facing] gegenüberliegend; **the houses ~** die Häuser gegenüber - **2.** [very different] entgegengesetzt ⟨⟩ *adv* gegenüber ⟨⟩ *prep* [facing] gegenüber *(+ D)* ⟨⟩ *n* Gegenteil *das*.

**opposite number** *n* Pendant *das*.

**opposite sex** *n:* **the ~** das andere Geschlecht.

**opposition** [ˌɒpəˈzɪʃn] *n* - **1.** [disapproval] Widerstand *der*, Opposition *die* - **2.** [opposing team] Gegner *pl*.
➨ **Opposition** *n* Br POL: **the Opposition** die Opposition.

**oppress** [əˈpres] *vt* - **1.** [persecute] unterdrücken - **2.** [subj: anxiety, atmosphere] bedrücken.

**oppressed** [əˈprest] *adj* unterdrückt ⟨⟩ *npl:* **the ~** die Unterdrückten *pl*.

**oppression** [əˈpreʃn] *n* - **1.** [persecution] Unterdrückung *die* - **2.** [despondency] Bedrücktheit *die*.

**oppressive** [əˈpresɪv] *adj* - **1.** [regime, government, society] repressiv - **2.** [heat, weather] drückend - **3.** [situation, silence] bedrückend.

**oppressor** [əˈpresər] *n* Unterdrücker *der*, -in *die*.

**opt** [ɒpt] *vt:* **to ~ to do sthg** sich dafür entscheiden, etw zu tun ⟨⟩ *vi:* **to ~ for sthg** sich für etw entscheiden.
➨ **opt in** *vi:* **to ~ in to sthg** etw *(D)* beitreten.
➨ **opt out** *vi:* **to ~ out (of)** [scheme, system] austreten (aus).

**optic** [ˈɒptɪk] *adj* optisch; **~ nerve** Sehnerv *die*.
➨ **optics** *n (U)* Optik *die*.

**optical** [ˈɒptɪkl] *adj* optisch.

**optical character reader** *n* COMPUT Klarschriftleser *der*.

**optical fibre** *n* TELEC Glasfaserkabel *das*.

**optical illusion** *n* optische Täuschung.

**optician** [ɒpˈtɪʃn] *n* Optiker *der*, -in *die;* **to go to the ~'s** zum Optiker gehen.

**optimism** [ˈɒptɪmɪzm] *n* Optimismus *der*.

**optimist** [ˈɒptɪmɪst] *n* Optimist *der*, -in *die*.

**optimistic** [ˌɒptɪˈmɪstɪk] *adj:* **~ (about)** optimistisch (in Bezug auf *(+ A)*); **she's ~ about passing her driving test** sie ist optimistisch, dass sie die Fahrprüfung bestehen wird.

**optimize, -ise** [ˈɒptɪmaɪz] *vt* optimieren.

**optimum** [ˈɒptɪməm] *adj* optimal.

**option** [ˈɒpʃn] *n* [choice] Wahl *die;* [alternative to be chosen] (Wahl)möglichkeit *die;* **she had no ~ but to go** ihr blieb nichts anderes übrig, als zu gehen; **to have the ~ to do** OR **of doing sthg** die Möglichkeit haben, etw zu tun.

**optional** [ˈɒpʃənl] *adj* [subject] Wahl-; [course] fakultativ; **~ extra** Extra *das*.

**opulence** [ˈɒpjʊləns] *n* - **1.** [wealth] Reichtum *der* - **2.** [of decor] Üppigkeit *die*.

**opulent** [ˈɒpjʊlənt] *adj* - **1.** [wealthy] reich - **2.** [decor] üppig.

**or** [ɔːr] *conj* - **1.** [linking alternatives] oder; **either one ~ the other** entweder das eine oder das andere; **~ (else)** [otherwise] sonst; **ten kilometres ~ so** [approximately] ungefähr zehn Kilometer - **2.** (*after negatives*) noch; **he cannot read ~ write** er kann weder lesen noch schreiben.

**OR** *abk für Oregon, in Postanschrift verwendet.*

**oral** [ˈɔːrəl] *adj* - **1.** [exam] mündlich - **2.** MED [medicine] zum Einnehmen; [hygiene] Mund-; **~ vaccine** Schluckimpfung *die* ⟨⟩ *n* mündliche Prüfung.

**orally** [ˈɔːrəlɪ] *adv* MED oral; **to take sthg ~** etw einnehmen.

**orange** [ˈɒrɪndʒ] *adj* [colour] orange ⟨⟩ *n* - **1.** [fruit] Orange *die*, Apfelsine *die* - **2.** (*U*) [colour] Orange *das*.

**orange juice** *n* Orangensaft *der*.

**orangutang** [ɔːˌræŋuːˈtæŋ] *n* Orang-Utan *der*.

**oration** [ɔːˈreɪʃn] *n fml* Rede *die*.

**orator** [ˈɒrətər] *n* Redner *der*, -in *die*.

**oratorio** [ˌɒrəˈtɔːrɪəʊ] (*pl* -s) *n* Oratorium *das*.

**orb** [ɔːb] *n* - **1.** [sphere] Kugel *die* - **2.** [of ruler] Reichsapfel *der*.

**orbit** [ˈɔːbɪt] *n* - **1.** [in space] Umlaufbahn *die;* **to go into ~** in die Umlaufbahn eintreten - **2.** [sphere of influence] Einflusssphäre *die* ⟨⟩ *vt* umkreisen.

**orbital motorway** [ˌɔːbɪtl-] *n Br* Ringautobahn *die*.

**orchard** [ˈɔːtʃəd] *n* Obstgarten *der*.

**orchestra** [ˈɔːkɪstrə] *n* Orchester *das*.

**orchestral** [ɔːˈkestrəl] *adj* Orchester-.

**orchestra pit** *n* Orchestergraben *der*.

**orchestrate** [ˈɔːkɪstreɪt] *vt* - **1.** MUS orchestrieren - **2.** *fig* [organize] sorgfältig organisieren.

**orchestration** [ˌɔːkeˈstreɪʃn] n - **1.** mus Orchestrierung die - **2.** fig [organization] sorgfältige Organisation.

**orchid** [ˈɔːkɪd] n Orchidee die.

**ordain** [ɔːˈdeɪn] vt - **1.** fml [decree - subj: ruler] verfügen; [ - subj: God, law] bestimmen - **2.** relig: **to be ~ed** (zum Priester) geweiht werden.

**ordeal** [ɔːˈdiːl] n Tortur die.

**order** [ˈɔːdər] n - **1.** [instruction] Anweisung die; mil Befehl der; **until further ~s** bis auf weiteren Befehl; **to be under ~s to do sthg** mil den Befehl haben, etw zu tun - **2.** comm [request, in restaurant] Bestellung die; [contract to manufacture or supply goods] Auftrag der; **to place an ~ with sb for sthg** bei jm eine Bestellung für etw auflgeben, jm für etw einen Auftrag erteilen; **to ~ auf** Bestellung - **3.** (U) [sequence] Reihenfolge die; **arranged in ~ of importance** nach Wichtigkeit geordnet; **in the right ~** in der richtigen Reihenfolge; **out of ~, in the wrong ~** in der falschen Reihenfolge; **in alphabetical ~** in alphabetischer Reihenfolge - **4.** (U) [neatness, discipline, system] Ordnung die - **5.** [fitness for use]: **in ~** [valid] in Ordnung; **in working ~** funktionstüchtig; **out of ~** [machine, lift] außer Betrieb; **you're out of ~!** inf pass auf, was du sagst/machst!; **to keep ~** die Disziplin aufrechterhalten - **6.** relig Orden der - **7.** Am [portion] Portion die ◇ vt - **1.** [command] anlordnen; mil befehlen (+ D); [subj: court] verfügen; **to ~ sb to do sthg** jn anlweisen, etw zu tun; mil jm befehlen, etw zu tun; **to ~ that** anlordnen, dass; mil befehlen, dass - **2.** comm [request] bestellen; [to be manufactured: suit, aircraft, ship] in Auftrag geben ◇ vi [in restaurant] bestellen.

➤ **orders** npl relig: **(holy) ~s** (Priester)weihe die; **to take holy ~s** die Weihen empfangen.

➤ **in the order of** Br, **on the order of** Am adv etwa.

➤ **in order that** conj damit.

➤ **in order to** conj um … zu; **in ~ to get a better view** um eine bessere Sicht zu bekommen.

➤ **order about, order around** vt sep herumlkommandieren.

**order book** n Auftragsbuch das.

**order form** n Bestellschein der.

**orderly** [ˈɔːdəlɪ] (pl -ies) adj ordentlich ◇ n [in hospital] Pfleger der, -in die.

**order number** n Auftragsnummer die.

**ordinal** [ˈɔːdɪnl] n Ordnungszahl die.

**ordinarily** [ˈɔːdənrəlɪ] adv [normally] gewöhnlich, normalerweise.

**ordinary** [ˈɔːdənrɪ] adj - **1.** [normal] gewöhnlich, normal; **~ people** einfache Leute - **2.** pej [unexceptional] gewöhnlich ◇ n: **out of the ~** außergewöhnlich.

**ordinary seaman** n Br Leichtmatrose der.

**ordinary shares** npl Br fin Stammaktien pl.

**ordination** [ˌɔːdɪˈneɪʃn] n (U) Ordination die.

**ordnance** [ˈɔːdnəns] n mil [artillery] Artillerie die.

**Ordnance Survey** n britisches Landesvermessungsamt.

**ore** [ɔːr] n Erz das.

**oregano** [ˌɒrɪˈɡɑːnəʊ] n Oregano der.

**organ** [ˈɔːɡən] n - **1.** anat Organ das - **2.** mus Orgel die - **3.** fig [newspaper, magazine] Organ das.

**organic** [ɔːˈɡænɪk] adj - **1.** [of animals, plants] organisch - **2.** [food] biodynamisch.

**organically** [ɔːˈɡænɪklɪ] adv [grown] biodynamisch.

**organism** [ˈɔːɡənɪzm] n Organismus der.

**organist** [ˈɔːɡənɪst] n Organist der, -in die.

**organization** [ˌɔːɡənaɪˈzeɪʃn] n - **1.** [gen] Organisation die - **2.** (U) [arrangement] Ordnung die.

**organizational** [ˌɔːɡənaɪˈzeɪʃnl] adj [structure] Organisations-; [skills] organisatorisch.

**organize, -ise** [ˈɔːɡənaɪz] vt organisieren; [affairs, thoughts] ordnen ◇ vi sich organisieren.

**organized, -ised** [ˈɔːɡənaɪzd] adj organisiert; **she's not very ~** bei ihr geht alles durcheinander.

**organized crime** n (U) organisiertes Verbrechen.

**organizer, -iser** [ˈɔːɡənaɪzər] n [person] Organisator der, -in die.

**orgasm** [ˈɔːɡæzm] n Orgasmus der.

**orgy** [ˈɔːdʒɪ] (pl -ies) n Orgie die.

**orient** [ˈɔːrɪənt] vt esp Am = orientate.

**Orient** [ˈɔːrɪənt] n: **the ~** der Orient.

**oriental** [ˌɔːrɪˈentl] adj orientalisch ◇ n Orientale der, -lin die.

**orientate** [ˈɔːrɪənteɪt] vt: **to be ~d towards** ausgerichtet sein auf (+ A); **to ~ o.s.** sich orientieren.

**orientation** [ˌɔːrɪənˈteɪʃn] n [of organization, system] Ausrichtung die.

**orienteering** [ˌɔːrɪənˈtɪərɪŋ] n Orientierungslauf der.

**orifice** [ˈɒrɪfɪs] n Öffnung die.

**origami** [ˌɒrɪˈɡɑːmɪ] n Origami das.

**origin** [ˈɒrɪdʒɪn] n - **1.** [starting point] Ursprung der - **2.** (U) [birth] Herkunft die; **country of ~** Herkunftsland das.

➤ **origins** npl Herkunft die.

**original** [əˈrɪdʒənl] adj - **1.** [first] ursprünglich - **2.** [document] Original-; **~ painting** Original das - **3.** [new, unusual] originell ◇ n Original das.

**originality** [əˌrɪdʒəˈnælətɪ] n Originalität die.

**originally** [ə'rɪdʒənəlɪ] *adv* [initially] ursprünglich.

**original sin** *n* Erbsünde *die*.

**originate** [ə'rɪdʒəneɪt] *vt* [scheme, policy] ins Leben rufen; [new style] begründen ◇ *vi:* **to ~ in/ from** seinen Ursprung haben in (+ *D*); **how did this belief ~?** wie ist dieser Glaube entstanden?

**originator** [ə'rɪdʒəneɪtəʳ] *n* [of idea] Urheber *der*, -in *die*; [of new style] Begründer *der*, -in *die*.

**Orkney Islands** ['ɔːknɪ-], **Orkneys** ['ɔːknɪz] *npl:* **the ~** die Orkneyinseln; **in the ~** auf den Orkney Inseln.

**ornament** ['ɔːnəmənt] *n* **- 1.** [object] Ziergegenstand *der* **- 2.** (*U*) [decoration] Verzierungen *pl*.

**ornamental** [ˌɔːnə'mentl] *adj* dekorativ; **~ garden** Ziergarten *der*.

**ornate** [ɔː'neɪt] *adj* reich verziert; [language] blumig.

**ornately** [ɔː'neɪtlɪ] *adv* kunstvoll; [written] blumig.

**ornery** ['ɔːnərɪ] *adj Am inf* übellaunig.

**ornithologist** [ˌɔːnɪ'θɒlədʒɪst] *n* Ornithologe *der*, -gin *die*.

**ornithology** [ˌɔːnɪ'θɒlədʒɪ] *n* Ornithologie *die*.

**orphan** ['ɔːfn] *n* Waise *die*, Waisenkind *das* ◇ *vt:* **to be ~ed** (zur) Waise werden.

**orphanage** ['ɔːfənɪdʒ] *n* Waisenhaus *das*.

**orthodontist** [ˌɔːθə'dɒntɪst] *n* Kieferorthopäde *der*, -din *die*.

**orthodox** ['ɔːθədɒks] *adj* **- 1.** [conventional] konventionell **- 2.** RELIG orthodox.

**Orthodox Church** *n:* **the ~** die Orthodoxe Kirche.

**orthodoxy** ['ɔːθədɒksɪ] *n* Orthodoxie *die*.

**orthopaedic** [ˌɔːθə'piːdɪk] *adj* orthopädisch.

**orthopaedics** [ˌɔːθə'piːdɪks] *n* (*U*) Orthopädie *die*.

**orthopedic** *etc* [ˌɔːθə'piːdɪk] *adj* = **orthopaedic** *etc*.

**OS** *n abbr of* **Ordnance Survey** ◇ (*abbr of* **outsize**) *in* Übergröße.

**O/S** (*abbr of* **out of stock**) nicht vorrätig.

**oscillate** ['ɒsɪleɪt] *vi* [pendulum] schwingen; [needle on dial] sich hin und her bewegen; **to ~ between** *fig* schwanken zwischen.

**oscilloscope** [ɒ'sɪləskəʊp] *n* Oszilloskop *das*.

**Oslo** ['ɒzləʊ] *n* Oslo *nt*.

**osmosis** [ɒz'məʊsɪs] *n* Osmose *die*.

**osprey** ['ɒsprɪ] (*pl* **ospreys**) *n* Fischadler *der*.

**ostensible** [ɒ'stensəbl] *adj* angeblich.

**ostensibly** [ɒ'stensəblɪ] *adv* angeblich.

**ostentation** [ˌɒstən'teɪʃn] *n* [display of knowledge, skill] Prahlerei *die*; [display of wealth] Pomp *der*.

**ostentatious** [ˌɒstən'teɪʃəs] *adj* [person] protzenhaft; [behaviour] betont auffällig.

**osteopath** ['ɒstɪəpæθ] *n* Osteopath *der*, -in *die*.

**ostracize, -ise** ['ɒstrəsaɪz] *vt* ächten.

**ostrich** ['ɒstrɪtʃ] *n* Strauß *der*.

**OT** *n* **- 1.** (*abbr of* **Old Testament**) AT *das* **- 2.** *abbr of* **occupational therapy**.

**OTC** (*abbr of* **Officers' Training Corps**) *n* Militärschule für die Offizierausbildung.

**other** ['ʌðəʳ] *adj* andere, -r, -s; **the ~ one** der/ die/das andere; **the ~ day** neulich; **every ~ day** jeden zweiten Tag; **any ~ questions?** sonst noch Fragen? ◇ *pron* andere, -r, -s; **one or ~ (of us)** der eine oder andere (von uns); **one after the ~** hintereinander ◇ *adv:* **~ than** außer; **it was none ~ than the king** es war kein anderer als der König.

**otherwise** ['ʌðəwaɪz] *adv* **- 1.** [apart from that] ansonsten, sonst **- 2.** [differently] anders; **to be ~ engaged** anderweitig beschäftigt sein; **~ known as** auch bekannt als ◇ *conj* [or else] sonst, andernfalls.

**other world** *n:* **the ~** das Jenseits.

**otherworldly** [ˌʌðə'wɜːldlɪ] *adj* [person] vergeistigt; [attitude] weltfern.

**OTT** (*abbr of* **over the top**) *adj Br inf* übertrieben.

**otter** ['ɒtəʳ] *n* Otter *der*.

**OU** *abbr of* **Open University**.

**ouch** [aʊtʃ] *excl* au!, aua!

**ought** [ɔːt] *aux vb:* **I ~ to go now** ich sollte jetzt gehen; **you ~ not to have said that** du hättest das nicht sagen sollen; **you ~ to see a doctor** du solltest zum Arzt gehen; **the car ~ to be ready by Friday** das Auto sollte Freitag fertig sein; **that ~ to be enough for three** das dürfte für drei Personen genügen.

**oughtn't** ['ɔːtnt] = **ought not**.

**ounce** [aʊns] *n* **- 1.** [unit of measurement] Unze *die*, = 28,35 *g* **- 2.** *fig* [of truth, intelligence] Funken *der*.

**our** ['aʊəʳ] *poss adj* unser; **~ children** unsere Kinder; **we washed ~ hair** wir haben uns die Haare gewaschen; **a home of ~ own** ein eigenes Haus.

**ours** ['aʊəz] *poss pron* unsere, -r, -s; **this suitcase is ~** dieser Koffer gehört uns; **a friend of ~** ein Freund von uns.

**ourselves** [aʊə'selvz] *pron* (*reflexive, after prep*) uns; **we did it ~** wir haben es selbst gemacht; **(all) by ~** (ganz) allein.

**O**

**oust** [aʊst] vt fml: **to ~ sb from sthg** [position, job] jn aus etw verdrängen.

**ouster** ['aʊstə'] n Am **- 1.** [from country] Ausweisung die **- 2.** [from office] Verdrängung die.

**out** [aʊt] adj [light, cigarette] aus <> adv **- 1.** [outside] draußen; **to come ~ (of)** herauskommen (aus); **to get ~ (of)** auslsteigen (aus); **it's cold ~ today** es ist heute kalt draußen; **~ you go!** raus mit dir!; **~ here/ there** hier/dort draußen **- 2.** [not at home, work]: **she's ~** sie ist nicht da; **to go ~** auslgehen; **to go ~ for a walk** einen Spaziergang machen **- 3.** [so as to be extinguished] aus; **put your cigarette ~!** mach deine Zigarette aus! **- 4.** [of tides]: **the tide is ~** es ist Ebbe **- 5.** [expressing removal]: **to take sthg ~ (of)** etw herauslnehmen (aus); [money] etw ablheben (von); **he poured the water ~** er schüttete das Wasser aus **- 6.** [outwards]: **to stick ~** herauslstehen **- 7.** [expressing distribution]: **to hand sthg ~** etw auslteilen **- 8.** [wrong]: **the bill's £10 ~** die Rechnung stimmt um 10 Pfund nicht **- 9.** [published, known]: **the book is just ~** das Buch ist soeben erschienen; **the secret is ~** das Geheimnis ist gelüftet **- 10.** [in flower] aufgeblüht; **the roses are ~** die Rosen blühen **- 11.** [visible]: **the moon is ~** der Mond scheint **- 12.** [out of fashion] aus der Mode **- 13.** inf [on strike]: **they've been ~ for months now** sie streiken schon seit Monaten **- 14.** [not possible] ausgeschlossen; **sorry, that's ~** tut mir leid, das ist nicht drin **- 15.** [determined]: **to be ~ for revenge** auf Rache aus sein; **I'm not ~ to make money** ich bin nicht darauf aus, Geld zu verdienen.

◆ **out of** prep **- 1.** [away from, outside]: **stay ~ of the sun** bleib aus der Sonne; **I was ~ of the country** ich war im Ausland **- 2.** [indicating cause, origin] aus (+ D); **~ of respect/curiosity** aus Respekt/Neugierde; **made ~ of wood** aus Holz (gemacht) **- 3.** [without]: **I'm ~ of** OR **I've run ~ of cigarettes** ich habe keine Zigaretten mehr **- 4.** [to indicate proportion]: **five ~ of ten** fünf von zehn **- 5.** phr: **~ of danger/control** außer Gefahr/Kontrolle.

◆ **out of doors** adv im Freien.

**out-and-out** adj [liar, fool, crook] ausgemacht; **an ~ disgrace** ein bodenlose Schande.

**outback** ['aʊtbæk] n: **the ~** weit abseits der Städte gelegener Teil Australiens.

**outbid** [aʊt'bɪd] (pt & pp outbid; cont -ding) vt: **to ~ sb (for sthg)** mehr bieten als jd (für etw).

**outboard (motor)** ['aʊtbɔːd-] n Außenbordmotor der.

**outbound** ['aʊtbaʊnd] adj [flight, journey] Hin-.

**outbreak** ['aʊtbreɪk] n [of war, disease] Ausbruch der; **~ of crime** plötzliches Auftreten von Verbrechen.

**outbuildings** ['aʊtbɪldɪŋz] npl Nebengebäude pl.

**outburst** ['aʊtbɜːst] n [of emotion, violence] Ausbruch der; **~ of anger** Wutanfall der.

**outcast** ['aʊtkɑːst] n [socially] Außenseiter der, -in die; [from family, group] Verstoßene der, die.

**outclass** [ˌaʊt'klɑːs] vt in den Schatten stellen.

**outcome** ['aʊtkʌm] n Ergebnis das.

**outcrop** ['aʊtkrɒp] n aus dem Boden hoch ragende Felsmasse.

**outcry** ['aʊtkraɪ] (pl -ies) n Aufschrei der der Empörung.

**outdated** [ˌaʊt'deɪtɪd] adj [belief, concept, method] überholt; [language] antiquiert.

**outdid** [ˌaʊt'dɪd] pt [⇒ outdo.

**outdistance** [ˌaʊt'dɪstəns] vt **- 1.** [in race] weit hinter sich (D) lassen **- 2.** fig [in business, development] überflügeln.

**outdo** [ˌaʊt'duː] (pt -did; pp -done [-'dʌn]) vt übertreffen.

**outdoor** ['aʊtdɔː'] adj [life, activity] im Freien; **~ swimming pool** Freibad das; **~ clothes** Straßenkleidung die.

**outdoors** [aʊt'dɔːz] adv draußen, im Freien; [go] nach draußen.

**outer** ['aʊtə'] adj [wall] Außen-; [layer] äußere, -r, -s; **~ suburbs** Außenbezirke pl; **Outer London** die Peripherie Londons.

**outermost** ['aʊtəməʊst] adj äußerste, -r, -s.

**outer space** n Weltraum der.

**outfit** ['aʊtfɪt] n **- 1.** [clothes] Kleider pl; [fancy dress] Kostüm das **- 2.** inf [organization] Laden der, Verein der.

**outfitters** ['aʊtˌfɪtəz] n Br dated: **gents' ~** Herrenausstatter der.

**outflank** [ˌaʊt'flæŋk] vt **- 1.** MIL von der Flanke OR den Flanken anlgreifen **- 2.** fig [in argument, business] auslmanövrieren.

**outgoing** ['aʊtˌgəʊɪŋ] adj **- 1.** [from job] (aus dem Amt) scheidend **- 2.** [from place - trains] abgehend; [- mail] ausgehend **- 3.** [friendly, sociable] kontaktfreudig.

◆ **outgoings** npl Br Ausgaben pl.

**outgrow** [ˌaʊt'grəʊ] (pt -grew [-'gruː]; pp -grown [-'grəʊn]) vt **- 1.** [grow too big for] herauslwachsen aus **- 2.** [habit] abllegen.

**outhouse** ['aʊthaʊs, pl -haʊzɪz] n Nebengebäude das.

**outing** ['aʊtɪŋ] n **- 1.** [trip] Ausflug der **- 2.** (U) [of homosexuals] Outing das.

**outlandish** [aʊt'lændɪʃ] adj sonderbar.

**outlast** [ˌaʊt'lɑːst] vt [subj: person] überdauern, überleben.

**outlaw** ['aʊtlɔː] n Geächtete der, die; [in the Wild West] Bandit der <> vt **- 1.** [make illegal] verbieten **- 2.** [declare an outlaw] ächten.

**outlay** ['aʊtleɪ] n Kostenaufwand der.

**outlet** ['aʊtlet] n - **1.** [for feelings] Ventil das - **2.** [hole, pipe] Auslass der - **3.** [shop] Verkaufsstelle die - **4.** Am ELEC Steckdose die.

**outline** ['aʊtlaɪn] n - **1.** [brief description] Abriss der; **in ~** in Grundzügen - **2.** [silhouette] Umriss der <> vt - **1.** [describe briefly] umreißen, skizzieren - **2.** [silhouette]: **the figure was ~d against the setting sun** die Umrisse der Gestalt zeichneten sich gegen die untergehende Sonne ab.

**outlive** [ˌaʊt'lɪv] vt - **1.** [subj: person] überleben - **2.** fig [subj: idea, object] überdauern; **it has ~d its usefulness** es hat ausgedient.

**outlook** ['aʊtlʊk] n - **1.** [attitude, disposition] Einstellung die; **~ on life** Lebensauffassung die - **2.** [prospect] Aussichten pl.

**outlying** ['aʊtˌlaɪɪŋ] adj [villages] abgelegen; **~ district** Außenbezirk der.

**outmanoeuvre** Br, **outmaneuver** Am [ˌaʊtmə'nu:vəʳ] vt auslmanövrieren.

**outmoded** [ˌaʊt'məʊdɪd] adj überholt.

**outnumber** [ˌaʊt'nʌmbəʳ] vt zahlenmäßig überlegen sein (+ D).

**out-of-date** adj [passport, season ticket] abgelaufen; [clothes] altmodisch; [belief] überholt.

**out of doors** adv draußen, im Freien; [go] nach draußen.

**out-of-the-way** adj [isolated] abgelegen.

**outpatient** ['aʊtˌpeɪʃnt] n ambulanter Patient, ambulante Patientin; **~s (department)** Ambulanz die.

**outplay** [ˌaʊt'pleɪ] vt SPORT besser spielen als.

**outpost** ['aʊtpəʊst] n fig [bastion] Vorposten der.

**output** ['aʊtpʊt] n (U) - **1.** [production - of factory, writer] Produktion die; [ - in agriculture] Ertrag der - **2.** [COMPUT - printing out] Ausdrucken das; [ - printout] Ausdruck der <> vt COMPUT ausldrucken.

**outrage** ['aʊtreɪdʒ] n - **1.** (U) [anger, shock] Empörung die - **2.** [atrocity] Verbrechen das <> vt empören; [sense of morality] zuwiderllaufen (+ D).

**outraged** ['aʊtreɪdʒd] adj empört.

**outrageous** [aʊt'reɪdʒəs] adj - **1.** [offensive, shocking - crime] verabscheuungswürdig; [ - language] unflätig; [ - behaviour] unerhört - **2.** [extravagant, wild - outfit, idea] exzentrisch.

**outran** [ˌaʊt'ræn] pt ▷ **outrun**.

**outrank** [aʊt'ræŋk] vt rangmäßig stehen über (+ D).

**outright** [adj 'aʊtraɪt, adv ˌaʊt'raɪt] adj [refusal, denial] kategorisch; [disaster] total; [winner, victory] klar; [lie] glatt <> adv [ask] ohne Umschweife; [deny] kategorisch; [win, fail] klar; **to be killed ~** sofort tot sein.

**outrun** [ˌaʊt'rʌn] (pt -ran; pp -run; cont -ning) vt [runners] schneller laufen als; [attackers] davonllaufen (+ D).

**outsell** [ˌaʊt'sell] (pt & pp -sold) vt [product] sich besser verkaufen als.

**outset** ['aʊtset] n: **at the ~** zu OR am Anfang; **from the ~** von Anfang an.

**outshine** [ˌaʊt'ʃaɪn] (pt & pp -shone [-'ʃɒn]) vt [do better than] in den Schatten stellen.

**outside** [adv ˌaʊt'saɪd, adj, prep & n 'aʊtsaɪd] adv draußen; **to go ~** nach draußen gehen <> prep - **1.** [gen] außerhalb (+ G); **we live just ~ London** wir wohnen gleich außerhalb Londons; **~ (office) hours** außerhalb der Dienststunden - **2.** [in front of] vor (+ A, D); **~ the door** vor der Tür <> adj - **1.** [exterior] Außen- - **2.** [help, advice] von außen; **~ influence** äußere Einflüsse - **3.** [unlikely]: **there's an ~ chance** es besteht eine geringe Chance <> n - **1.** [of building, car, container] Außenseite die; **to open the door from the ~** die Tür von außen öffnen - **2.** AUT: **the ~** [in UK] rechts; [in Europe, US] links - **3.** fig [limit]: **at the ~** höchstens.

➡ **outside of** prep - **1.** Am [on the outside of] außerhalb (+ G) - **2.** [apart from] außer.

**outside broadcast** n Br RADIO & TV nicht im Studio produzierte Sendung.

**outside lane** n Überholspur die.

**outside line** n Amtsleitung die.

**outsider** [ˌaʊt'saɪdəʳ] n Außenseiter der, -in die.

**outsize** ['aʊtsaɪz] adj - **1.** [book, portion] überdimensional - **2.**: **~ clothes** Kleidung die in Übergröße.

**outsized** ['aʊtsaɪzd] adj überdimensional.

**outskirts** ['aʊtskɜ:ts] npl: **the ~** die Außenbezirke pl; **on the ~** am Stadtrand.

**outsmart** [ˌaʊt'smɑ:t] vt überlisten.

**outsold** [ˌaʊt'səʊld] pt & pp ▷ **outsell**.

**outspoken** [ˌaʊt'spəʊkn] adj freimütig.

**outspread** [ˌaʊt'spred] adj ausgebreitet.

**outstanding** [ˌaʊt'stændɪŋ] adj - **1.** [excellent - person] außergewöhnlich; [ - performance, achievement] hervorragend - **2.** [very obvious, important] bemerkenswert - **3.** [not paid - money] ausstehend; [ - bill] unbezahlt - **4.** [still to be done - work] unerledigt; [ - problem] ungeklärt.

**outstay** [ˌaʊt'steɪ] vt: **to ~ one's welcome** länger bleiben als erwünscht.

**outstretched** [ˌaʊt'stretʃt] adj ausgestreckt.

**outstrip** [ˌaʊt'strɪp] (pt & pp -ped; cont -ping) vt - **1.** [do better than] übertreffen - **2.** [run faster than] überholen.

**out-take** n CINEMA & TV Filmsequenz, die in der fertigen Sendung bzw. im fertigen Film nicht verwendet wird.

**out-tray** n Ablage die für Ausgänge.

**O**

**outvote** [ˌaʊt'vəʊt] *vt:* **to be ~d** überstimmt werden.

**outward** ['aʊtwəd] *adj* - **1.** [going away]: **~ journey** Hinreise *die* - **2.** [external, visible]: **she maintained her ~ composure** sie blieb äußerlich ruhig; **he shows no ~ sign of his grief** nach außen hin zeigt er nichts von seinem Kummer ◇ *adv Am* = **outwards.**

**outwardly** ['aʊtwədlɪ] *adv* nach außen hin.

**outwards** *Br* ['aʊtwədz], **outward** *Am adv* nach außen.

**outweigh** [ˌaʊt'weɪ] *vt* überwiegen.

**outwit** [ˌaʊt'wɪt] (*pt* & *pp* **-ted;** *cont* **-ting**) *vt* überlisten.

**outworker** ['aʊtˌwɜːkəʳ] *n* Heimarbeiter *der*, -in *die.*

**oval** ['əʊvl] *adj* oval ◇ *n* Oval *das.*

**Oval Office** *n:* **the ~** Büro *des US-Präsidenten im Weißen Haus.*

**ovarian** [əʊ'veərɪən] *adj* der Eierstöcke; **~ cancer** Eierstockkrebs *der.*

**ovary** ['əʊvərɪ] (*pl* **-ies**) *n* ANAT Eierstock *der.*

**ovation** [əʊ'veɪʃn] *n* Ovation *die,* begeisterter Beifall; **to give a standing ~** jm stehende Ovationen darlbringen.

**oven** ['ʌvn] *n* [for cooking] Backofen *der.*

**oven glove** *n* Topfhandschuh *der.*

**ovenproof** ['ʌvnpruːf] *adj* feuerfest, hitzebeständig.

**oven-ready** *adj* backfertig; [chicken] bratfertig.

**ovenware** ['ʌvnweəʳ] *n* feuerfestes Geschirr.

**over** ['əʊvəʳ] *prep* - **1.** [directly above] über (+ D); **a bridge ~ the road** eine Brücke über der Straße - **2.** [indicating place, position] über (+ D); [indicating direction] über (+ A); **she wore a veil ~ her face** sie trug einen Schleier vor dem Gesicht; **put your coat ~ the chair** leg deinen Mantel über den Stuhl; **put a plaster ~ the cut** klebe ein Pflaster auf die Wunde - **3.** [across] über (+ A); **to walk ~ sthg** über etw laufen; **he threw it ~ the wall** er warf es über die Mauer; **it's just ~ the road** es ist gleich gegenüber; **it's ~ the river** es ist auf der anderen Seite des Flusses; **with a view ~ the gardens** mit Blick auf die Gärten - **4.** [more than] über (+ A); **it cost ~ $1,000** es hat über 1000 Dollar gekostet; **~ and above this amount** über den Betrag hinaus - **5.** [indicating control] über (+ A); **to rule ~ a country** über ein Land herrschen - **6.** [about] über (+ A); **an argument ~ the price** ein Streit über den Preis - **7.** [during]: **~ New Year** über Neujahr; **~ the weekend** übers Wochenende; **~ the past two years** in den letzten zwei Jahren; **to discuss sthg ~ lunch/a cup of coffee** etw beim Essen/bei einer Tasse Kaffee besprechen - **8.** [to do]:

**he took a long time ~ it** er hat lange dazu gebraucht - **9.** [recovered from] über (+ A); **to be ~ sthg** über etw (A) hinweg sein - **10.** [by means of] über (+ A); **~ the phone** am Telefon; **~ the radio** im Radio ◇ *adv* - **1.** [referring to distance away]: **~ by the gate** drüben beim Tor; **~ here/there** hier/da drüben - **2.** [across] herüber/hinüber; **to drive ~** herüberlfahren/hinüberlfahren - **3.** [downwards]: **to fall ~** umlfallen; **to lean ~** sich vornüber lehnen; **to knock sthg ~** etw umlwerfen - **4.** [round to other side]: **to turn sthg ~** etw umldrehen; **to roll ~** sich umldrehen - **5.** [more]: **children aged 12 and ~** Kinder ab 12; **sums of £100 and ~** Summen von 100 Pfund und mehr - **6.** [remaining] übrig; **to be (left) ~** übrig bleiben - **7.** [at/to sb's house]: **to invite sb ~ for dinner** jn zu sich zum Essen einlladen; **I was ~ at my mum's yesterday** ich war gestern bei meiner Mutter - **8.** RADIO over; **~ and out!** over and out! - **9.** [involving repetitions]: **(all) ~ again** wieder von vorne; **~ and ~ (again)** immer wieder ◇ *adj* [finished]: **to be ~** zu Ende sein.

➤ **all over** *prep:* **all ~ his/her face** im ganzen Gesicht; **all ~ the floor** auf dem ganzen Boden; **all ~ the world** in der ganzen Welt ◇ *adv* [everywhere] überall ◇ *adj* [finished] zu Ende.

**over-** ['əʊvəʳ] *prefix* [with adjective, verb] überl-; [with noun] Über-.

**overabundance** [ˌəʊvərə'bʌndəns] *n* (U): **~ (of)** Überschuss *der* (an (+ D)).

**overact** [ˌəʊvər'ækt] *vi pej* [in play] übertreiben.

**overactive** [ˌəʊvər'æktɪv] *adj* [child] hyperaktiv; [imagination] zu lebhaft.

**overall** [*adj* & *n* 'əʊvərɔːl, *adv* ˌəʊvər'ɔːl] *adj* - **1.** [total] Gesamt- - **2.** [general] allgemein ◇ *adv* - **1.** [in total] insgesamt - **2.** [in general] im Großen und Ganzen ◇ *n* - **1.** [coat] Kittel *der* - **2.** *Am* [with trousers] Overall *der.*

➤ **overalls** *npl* - **1.** [with long sleeves] Overall *der* - **2.** *Am* [with bib] Latzhose *die.*

**overambitious** [ˌəʊvəræm'bɪʃəs] *adj* zu ehrgeizig.

**overanxious** [ˌəʊvər'æŋkʃəs] *adj* übertrieben besorgt.

**overarm** ['əʊvərɑːm] *adj* & *adv* mit erhobenem Arm, über Kopf.

**overate** [ˌəʊvər'et] *pt* ▷ **overeat.**

**overawe** [ˌəʊvər'ɔː] *vt* [subj: person - make feel fear] einlschüchtern; [ - make feel respect] Ehrfurcht einlflößen (+ D); [subj: surroundings] überwältigen.

**overbalance** [ˌəʊvə'bæləns] *vi* das Gleichgewicht verlieren.

**overbearing** [ˌəʊvə'beərɪŋ] *adj pej* herrisch.

**overblown** [ˌəʊvə'bləʊn] *adj pej* übertrieben.

**overboard** ['əʊvəbɔːd] *adv* - **1.** NAUT: **to fall ~**

über Bord gehen **- 2.: to go ~ (about sthg)** *inf* [be overenthusiastic about] (bei etw) vollkommen aus dem Häuschen geraten.

**overbook** [ˌəʊvə'bʊk] *vt* überbuchen.

**overburden** [ˌəʊvə'bɜːdn] *vt*: **to be ~ed with work** mit Arbeit überlastet sein

**overcame** [ˌəʊvə'keɪm] *pt* ⊳ **overcome**.

**overcast** [ˌəʊvə'kɑːst] *adj* bedeckt.

**overcharge** [ˌəʊvə'tʃɑːdʒ] *vt*: **to ~ sb (for sthg)** jm zu viel berechnen (für etw) ⟨⟩ *vi*: **to ~ (for sthg)** zu viel verlangen (für etw).

**overcoat** ['əʊvəkəʊt] *n* Mantel *der*.

**overcome** [ˌəʊvə'kʌm] (*pt* **-came**; *pp* **-come**) *vt* **- 1.** [control, deal with] überwinden **- 2.** [overwhelm]: **to be ~ with emotion** gerührt sein; **to be ~ by fear** von Furcht ergriffen werden; **he was ~ by the fumes** die Dämpfe machten ihn bewusstlos.

**overconfident** [ˌəʊvə'kɒnfɪdənt] *adj* übertrieben selbstsicher.

**overcooked** [ˌəʊvə'kʊkt] *adj* [meat] verbraten; [vegetables] verkocht.

**overcrowded** [ˌəʊvə'kraʊdɪd] *adj* [room, pub, prison] überfüllt; [town] übervölkert.

**overcrowding** [ˌəʊvə'kraʊdɪŋ] *n* [of room, pub, prison] Überfüllung *die*; [of town] Übervölkerung *die*.

**overdeveloped** [ˌəʊvədɪ'veləpt] *adj* PHOT überentwickelt.

**overdo** [ˌəʊvə'duː] (*pt* **-did** [-'dɪd]; *pp* **-done** [-'dʌn]) *vt* **- 1.** [exaggerate, do too much] es übertreiben mit; **to ~ it** es übertreiben; [work too hard] sich übernehmen **- 2.** [overcook - vegetables] verkochen; [ - steak] verbraten.

**overdose** [*n* 'əʊvədəʊs, *vb* ˌəʊvə'dəʊs] *n* Überdosis *die* ⟨⟩ *vi*: **to ~ on sleeping pills** eine Überdosis Schlaftabletten nehmen.

**overdraft** ['əʊvədrɑːft] *n* Kontoüberziehung *die*; **I've got a £200 ~** ich habe mein Konto um 200 Pfund überzogen.

**overdrawn** [ˌəʊvə'drɔːn] *adj* [account] überzogen; **I'm (£200) ~** mein Konto ist (um 200 Pfund) überzogen.

**overdress** [ˌəʊvə'dres] *vi* sich zu fein anlziehen.

**overdrive** ['əʊvədraɪv] *n*: **to go into ~** [work intensely] sich in die Arbeit stürzen.

**overdue** [ˌəʊvə'djuː] *adj* **- 1.** [late - library, book] überfällig; **the train is 20 minutes ~** der Zug hat 20 Minuten Verspätung; **I'm ~ for a dental checkup** ich hätte schon längst zum Zahnarzt gemusst **- 2.** [reform, rent, bill] überfällig.

**overeager** [ˌəʊvər'iːgə¹] *adj* übereifrig.

**overeat** [ˌəʊvər'iːt] (*pt* **-ate**; *pp* **-eaten** [-'iːtn]) *vi* zu viel essen.

**overemphasize, -ise** [ˌəʊvər'emfəsaɪz] *vt*: **its significance cannot be ~d** man kann nicht genug betonen, wie wichtig das ist.

**overenthusiastic** ['əʊvərɪnˌθjuːzɪ'æstɪk] *adj* übertrieben begeistert.

**overestimate** [ˌəʊvər'estɪmeɪt] *vt* **- 1.** [guess too high a value for] zu hoch (ein)lschätzen **- 2.** [overrate] überschätzen.

**overexcited** [ˌəʊvərɪk'saɪtɪd] *adj* zu aufgedreht.

**overexpose** [ˌəʊvərɪk'spəʊz] *vt* PHOT überbelichten.

**overfeed** [ˌəʊvə'fiːd] (*pt* & *pp* **-fed** [-'fed]) *vt* überfüttern.

**overfill** [ˌəʊvə'fɪl] *vt* zu voll machen.

**overflow** [*vb* ˌəʊvə'fləʊ, *n* 'əʊvəfləʊ] *vi* **- 1.** [bath] überlaufen; [river] über die Ufer treten **- 2.** [people]: **there were so many people at the party that some ~ed into the kitchen** es waren so viele Leute auf der Party, dass einige in die Küche ausweichen mussten **- 3.** [place, container]: **to be ~ing (with sthg)** [room] überfüllt sein (mit etw); [drawer, box] überquellen (vor etw); **full to ~ing** [place] vollkommen überfüllt ⟨⟩ *vt* [spill over]: **the river ~ed its banks** der Fluss trat über die Ufer ⟨⟩ *n* [pipe, hole] Überlauf *der*.

**overgrown** [ˌəʊvə'grəʊn] *adj* [garden, path] überwuchert.

**overhang** [*n* 'əʊvəhæŋ, *vb* ˌəʊvə'hæŋ] (*pt* & *pp* **-hung**) *n* Überhang *der* ⟨⟩ *vt* hinauslragen über (+ A).

**overhaul** [*n* 'əʊvəhɔːl, *vb* ˌəʊvə'hɔːl] *n* **- 1.** [service] Überholung *die* **- 2.** [revision] Überarbeitung *die* ⟨⟩ *vt* **- 1.** [service] überholen **- 2.** [revise] überarbeiten.

**overhead** [*adv* ˌəʊvə'hed, *adj* & *n* 'əʊvəhed] *adj*: **~ cable** ELEC Hochspannungsleitung *die*; **~ lighting** Deckenbeleuchtung *die* ⟨⟩ *adv* über uns/ihm/*etc*; **the clouds ~** die Wolken am Himmel ⟨⟩ *n* (*U*) *Am* Gemeinkosten *pl*. ➣ **overheads** *npl* *Br* Gemeinkosten *pl*.

**overhead projector** *n* Overheadprojektor *der*.

**overhear** [ˌəʊvə'hɪə¹] (*pt* & *pp* **-heard** [-'hɜːd]) *vt* [remark] zufällig hören; [conversation] zufällig mitlhören; **I overheard them talking about me** ich hörte zufällig, wie sie über mich redeten.

**overheat** [ˌəʊvə'hiːt] *vt* [engine] überhitzen; [room] überheizen ⟨⟩ *vi* [engine, car] heißlaufen; [photocopier, transistor] zu heiß werden.

**overhung** [ˌəʊvə'hʌŋ] *pt* & *pp* ⊳ **overhang**.

**overindulge** [ˌəʊvərɪn'dʌldʒ] *vt* zu nachsichtig sein mit ⟨⟩ *vi* es sich (*D*) zu gut gehen lassen; **to ~ in sthg** etw übermäßig genießen.

**overjoyed** [ˌəuvə'dʒɔɪd] *adj:* to be ~ (at sthg) (über etw (A)) überglücklich sein.

**overkill** ['əuvəkɪl] *n* [excess]: to be ~ zu viel des Guten sein.

**overladen** [ˌəuvə'leɪdn] *pp* ▷ **overload** <> *adj* zu schwer beladen.

**overlaid** [ˌəuvə'leɪd] *pt* & *pp* ▷ **overlay**.

**overland** ['əuvəlænd] *adj* & *adv* auf dem Landweg.

**overlap** [*n* 'əuvəlæp, *vb* ˌəuvə'læp] (*pt* & *pp* **-ped;** *cont* **-ping**) *n* - **1.** (U) [similarity - of ideas, systems] teilweise Deckung; [ - of timetable, holidays] Überschneidung *die* - **2.** [overlapping part, amount] Überlappung *die* <> *vt* [cover] teilweise liegen über (+ D) <> *vi* - **1.** [cover each other] einander teilweise überdecken - **2.** [be similar]: to ~ (with sthg) [ideas, systems] sich teilweise decken (mit etw); [timetable, holiday] sich überschneiden (mit etw).

**overlay** [ˌəuvə'leɪ] (*pt* & *pp* **-laid**) *vt:* to be overlaid with sthg mit etw überzogen sein.

**overleaf** [ˌəuvə'liːf] *adv* auf der Rückseite.

**overload** [ˌəuvə'ləud] (*pp* **-loaded** OR **-laden**) *vt* - **1.** [put too much in] überladen - **2.** ELEC überlasten - **3.** [with work, problems]: to be ~ed (with sthg) überlastet sein (mit etw).

**overlook** [ˌəuvə'luk] *vt* - **1.** [look over] eine Aussicht haben auf (+ A); a room ~ing the square ein Zimmer mit Blick auf den Platz - **2.** [disregard, miss] übersehen - **3.** [excuse] hinwegsehen über (+ A).

**overly** ['əuvəlɪ] *adv* übermäßig.

**overmanning** [ˌəuvə'mænɪŋ] *n* (U) personelle Übersetzung.

**overnight** [*adj* 'əuvənaɪt, *adv* ˌəuvə'naɪt] *adj:* ~ stay Übernachtung *die;* ~ bag kleine Reisetasche; to be an ~ success [person] über Nacht großen Erfolg haben; [play] über Nacht ein großer Erfolg sein <> *adv* über Nacht.

**overpaid** [ˌəuvə'peɪd] *pt* & *pp* ▷ **overpay** <> *adj* überbezahlt.

**overpass** ['əuvəpɑːs] *n Am* Überführung *die.*

**overpay** [ˌəuvə'peɪ] (*pt* & *pp* **-paid**) *vt* überbezahlen.

**overplay** [ˌəuvə'pleɪ] *vt* hochspielen; to ~ one's hand den Bogen überspannen.

**overpopulated** [ˌəuvə'pɒpjuleɪtɪd] *adj* überbevölkert.

**overpower** [ˌəuvə'pauəʳ] *vt* überwältigen.

**overpowering** [ˌəuvə'pauərɪŋ] *adj* [feeling] überwältigend; [heat] unerträglich; [smell] penetrant; [person] einschüchternd.

**overpriced** [ˌəuvə'praɪst] *adj* zu teuer.

**overproduction** [ˌəuvəprə'dʌkʃn] *n* Überproduktion *die.*

**overprotective** [ˌəuvəprə'tektɪv] *adj* zu fürsorglich.

**overran** [ˌəuvə'ræn] *pt* ▷ **overrun**.

**overrated** [ˌəuvə'reɪtɪd] *adj:* to be ~ überschätzt werden.

**overreach** [ˌəuvə'riːtʃ] *vt:* to ~ o.s. sich übernehmen.

**overreact** [ˌəuvərɪ'ækt] *vi:* to ~ (to sthg) übertrieben reagieren (auf etw (A)).

**override** [ˌəuvə'raɪd] (*pt* **-rode;** *pp* **-ridden** [-'rɪdn] ) *vt* - **1.** [be more important than] Vorrang haben vor (+ D) - **2.** [overrule - decision] auf lheben.

**overriding** [ˌəuvə'raɪdɪŋ] *adj* vorrangig.

**overripe** [ˌəuvə'raɪp] *adj* überreif.

**overrode** [ˌəuvə'rəud] *pt* ▷ **override**.

**overrule** [ˌəuvə'ruːl] *vt* [person] überstimmen; [decision] auf lheben; [objection] ablweisen.

**overrun** [ˌəuvə'rʌn] (*pt* **-ran;** *pp* **-run;** *cont* **-running**) *vt* - **1.** MIL [occupy] einlfallen in (+ A) - **2.** *fig:* to be ~ with [insects, rats] wimmeln von; [weeds] überwuchert sein von; [tourists] überlaufen sein von <> *vi* [last too long] länger als vorgesehen dauern.

**oversaw** [ˌəuvə'sɔː] *pt* ▷ **oversee**.

**overseas** [*adj* 'əuvəsiːz, *adv* ˌəuvə'siːz] *adj* - **1.** [in or to foreign countries] Auslands-; ~ aid Entwicklungshilfe *die* - **2.** [from abroad] aus dem Ausland <> *adv* [travel] nach Übersee, ins Ausland; [study, live] in Übersee, im Ausland.

**oversee** [ˌəuvə'siː] (*pt* **-saw;** *pp* **-seen** [-'siːn] ) *vt* beaufsichtigen.

**overseer** ['əuvəˌsɪəʳ] *n* [foreman] Vorarbeiter *der,* -in *die.*

**overshadow** [ˌəuvə'ʃædəu] *vt* - **1.** [make darker] überschatten - **2.** *fig* [outweigh, eclipse]: to be ~ed by sb/sthg von jm/etw in den Schatten gestellt werden - **3.** *fig* [mar, cloud]: to be ~ed by sthg [subj: party, victory] von etw überschattet werden; [subj: happiness, peace of mind] durch etw stark beeinträchtigt werden.

**overshoot** [ˌəuvə'ʃuːt] (*pt* & *pp* **-shot** [-'ʃɒt] ) *vt* [go past - turning] vorbeilfahren an (+ D); [ - runway] hinauslrollen über (+ A).

**oversight** ['əuvəsaɪt] *n* Versehen *das;* through an ~ aus Versehen.

**oversimplification** ['əuvəˌsɪmplɪfɪ'keɪʃn] *n* (zu) starke Vereinfachung.

**oversimplify** [ˌəuvə'sɪmplɪfaɪ] (*pt* & *pp* **-ied**) *vt* (zu) stark vereinfachen <> *vi* die Dinge (zu) stark vereinfachen.

**oversleep** [ˌəuvə'sliːp] (*pt* & *pp* **-slept** [-'slept] ) *vi* verschlafen.

**overspend** [ˌəuvə'spend] (*pt* & *pp* **-spent** [-'spent] ) *vi* zu viel auslgeben.

**overstaffed** [ˌəʊvə'stɑːft] *adj* überbesetzt; **to be ~** zu viel Personal haben.

**overstate** [ˌəʊvə'steɪt] *vt* [case] übertrieben darlstellen; [importance] zu stark betonen.

**overstay** [ˌəʊvə'steɪ] *vt:* **to ~ one's welcome** länger bleiben als erwünscht.

**overstep** [ˌəʊvə'step] (*pt* & *pp* **-ped**; *cont* **-ping**) *vt* überschreiten; **to ~ the mark** zu weit gehen.

**oversubscribed** [ˌəʊvəsʌb'skraɪbd] *adj* [share offer] überzeichnet.

**overt** ['əʊvɜːt] *adj* unverhohlen.

**overtake** [ˌəʊvə'teɪk] (*pt* **-took**; *pp* **-taken** [-'teɪkn]) *vt* **- 1.** AUT überholen **- 2.** [subj: disaster, misfortune] ereilen ◇ *vi* überholen.

**overtaking** [ˌəʊvə'teɪkɪŋ] *n* (*U*) Überholen *das;* 'no ~' 'Überholen verboten'.

**overthrow** [*n* 'əʊvəθrəʊ, *vb* ˌəʊvə'θrəʊ] (*pt* **-threw** [-'θruː]; *pp* **-thrown** [-'θrəʊn]) *n* [of government] Sturz *der* ◇ *vt* **- 1.** [government, president] stürzen **- 2.** [concept, idea] zunichte machen.

**overtime** ['əʊvətaɪm] *n* (*U*) **- 1.** [extra time worked] Überstunden *pl* **- 2.** *Am* SPORT Verlängerung *die* ◇ *adv:* **to work ~** Überstunden machen.

**overtly** [əʊ'vɜːtlɪ] *adv:* **to be ~ jealous/hostile** seine Eifersucht/Feindseligkeit offen zeigen.

**overtones** ['əʊvətəʊnz] *npl* Untertöne *pl;* **there were ~ of anger in her voice** Ärger schwang in ihrer Stimme mit.

**overtook** [ˌəʊvə'tʊk] *pt* ⊳ **overtake**.

**overture** ['əʊvəˌtjʊəʳ] *n* MUS Ouvertüre *die.*

➤ **overtures** *npl:* **to make ~s to sb** Kontakt zu jm aufzunehmen versuchen.

**overturn** [ˌəʊvə'tɜːn] *vt* **- 1.** [turn over] umlwerfen **- 2.** [overrule] auf lheben **- 3.** [overthrow] stürzen ◇ *vi* [boat] kentern; [lorry] umlstürzen.

**overuse** [ˌəʊvə'juːz] *vt* zu oft verwenden.

**overview** ['əʊvəvjuː] *n:* **~ (of)** Überblick *der* (über (+ *A*)).

**overweening** [ˌəʊvə'wiːnɪŋ] *adj* maßlos.

**overweight** [ˌəʊvə'weɪt] *adj* [person] übergewichtig; **to be three kilos ~** drei Kilo zu viel wiegen.

**overwhelm** [ˌəʊvə'welm] *vt* überwältigen.

**overwhelming** [ˌəʊvə'welmɪŋ] *adj* **- 1.** [feeling, quality] überwältigend **- 2.** [victory, majority] überwältigend; [defeat] vernichtend.

**overwhelmingly** [ˌəʊvə'welmɪŋlɪ] *adv* [vote] mit überwältigender Mehrheit.

**overwork** [ˌəʊvə'wɜːk] *n* (*U*) Überlastung *die* ◇ *vt* **- 1.** [give too much work to] mit Arbeit überlasten **- 2.** *fig* [overuse] überstrapazieren ◇ *vi* sich überarbeiten.

**overwrought** [ˌəʊvə'rɔːt] *adj* überreizt.

**ovulate** ['ɒvjʊleɪt] *vi* ovulieren.

**ovulation** [ˌɒvjʊ'leɪʃn] *n* (*U*) Eisprung *der.*

**ow** [aʊ] *excl* au!

**owe** [əʊ] *vt:* **to ~ sthg to sb, to ~ sb sthg** [money, respect, gratitude] jm etw schulden; [good looks, success] jm etw verdanken.

**owing** ['əʊɪŋ] *adj:* **the amount ~** der ausstehende Betrag; **to be ~** auslstehen.

➤ **owing to** *prep* wegen (+ *G*).

**owl** [aʊl] *n* Eule *die.*

**own** [əʊn] *adj* eigen; **I have my ~ bedroom** ich habe ein eigenes Zimmer; **she makes her ~ clothes** sie näht ihre Kleider selbst ◇ *pron:* **it has a taste all of its ~** es hat einen ganz eigenen Geschmack; **on my ~** allein; **to get one's ~ back** *inf* sich revanchieren; **he can hold his ~** er kann sich behaupten ◇ *vt* [possess] besitzen; **who ~s this car?** wem gehört dieses Auto?

➤ **own up** *vi:* **to ~ up (to sthg)** (etw) zulgeben.

**own brand** *n* COMM Hausmarke *die.*

**owner** ['əʊnəʳ] *n* Besitzer *der,* -in *die;* [of firm, shop] Inhaber *der,* -in *die.*

**owner-occupier** *n esp Br* Eigenheimbesitzer *der,* -in *die.*

**ownership** ['əʊnəʃɪp] *n* Besitz *der.*

**own goal** *n esp Br* lit & fig Eigentor *das;* **to score an ~** ein Eigentor schießen.

**ox** [ɒks] (*pl* **oxen**) *n* Ochse *der.*

**Oxbridge** ['ɒksbrɪdʒ] *n* die Universitäten Oxford und Cambridge.

**oxen** ['ɒksn] *pl* ⊳ **ox**.

**Oxfam** ['ɒksfæm] *n britischer karitativer Verein zur Unterstützung von Projekten in der Dritten Welt.*

**oxide** ['ɒksaɪd] *n* Oxid *das.*

**oxidize, -ise** ['ɒksɪdaɪz] *vi* oxidieren.

**Oxon.** (*abbr of* **Oxoniensis**) (*von*) *der Universität Oxford.*

**oxtail soup** [ˌɒksteɪl-] *n* Ochsenschwanzsuppe *die.*

**oxyacetylene** [ˌɒksɪə'setɪliːn] *comp:* **~ torch** Schweißbrenner *der;* **~ welding** Autogenschweißen *das.*

**oxygen** ['ɒksɪdʒən] *n* Sauerstoff *der.*

**oxygenate** ['ɒksɪdʒəneɪt] *vt* oxygenieren.

**oxygen mask** *n* Sauerstoffmaske *die.*

**oxygen tent** *n* Sauerstoffzelt *das.*

**oyster** ['ɔɪstəʳ] *n* Auster *die.*

**oz.** *abbr of* **ounce**.

**ozone** ['əʊzəʊn] *n* Ozon *das.*

**ozone-friendly** *adj* FCKW-frei.

**ozone layer** *n* Ozonschicht *die.*

**O**

# P

**p¹** (pl **p's** OR **ps**), **P** (pl **P's** OR **Ps**) [piː] n [letter] p das, P das.

➤ **P - 1.** (abbr of **president**) Präs. **- 2.** (abbr of **prince**) Prz.

**p²** [piː] **- 1.** abbr of **page - 2.** abbr of **penny**, **pence**.

**P45** [ˌpiːfɔːtɪˈfaɪv] n Br Steuerbescheinigung, die bei einem Arbeitsplatzwechsel dem neuen Arbeitgeber vorgelegt werden muss, ≃ Lohnsteuerkarte die.

**P60** [ˌpiːˈsɪkstɪ] n Br Bescheinigung des Arbeitgebers über die Einkünfte des Arbeitnehmers innerhalb eines Steuerjahres.

**pa** [pɑː] n inf esp Am Papa der, Vati der.

**p.a.** (abbr of **per annum**) p. a.

**PA** n **- 1.** Br abbr of **personal assistant - 2.** (abbr of **public address system**) Lautsprecheranlage die **- 3.** (abbr of **Press Association**) britische Presseagentur ⇔ abk für Pennsylvania, in Postanschrift verwendet.

**PAC** (abbr of **political action committee**) n US-Organisation, die Spenden für politische Zwecke sammelt.

**pace** [peɪs] n **- 1.** [speed, rate] Tempo das; **at one's own ~** in seinem eigenen Tempo; **to keep ~ (with sb/sthg)** (mit jm/etw) Schritt halten **- 2.** [step] Schritt der ⇔ vt [walk up and down in] auf und ab gehen in (+ D) ⇔ vi [walk up and down] auf und ab gehen.

**pacemaker** [ˈpeɪsˌmeɪkəʳ] n **- 1.** MED Herzschrittmacher der **- 2.** [in race] Schrittmacher der, -in die.

**pacesetter** [ˈpeɪsˌsetəʳ] n Am SPORT Schrittmacher der, -in die.

**Pacific** [pəˈsɪfɪk] adj pazifisch; [coast] Pazifik- ⇔ n: **the ~ (Ocean)** der Pazifik, der Pazifische Ozean.

**Pacific Rim** n: **the ~** die pazifischen Anrainerstaaten.

**pacifier** [ˈpæsɪfaɪəʳ] n Am [for child] Schnuller der.

**pacifism** [ˈpæsɪfɪzm] n Pazifismus der.

**pacifist** [ˈpæsɪfɪst] n Pazifist der, -in die.

**pacify** [ˈpæsɪfaɪ] (pt & pp **-ied**) vt **- 1.** [person] beruhigen **- 2.** [country, region] befriedigen.

**pack** [pæk] n **- 1.** [bag - on back] Rucksack der; [ - carried by animal] Last die **- 2.** [packet of cigarettes, tissues] Packung die; [ - of washing powder] Paket das **- 3.** [of cards] (Karten)spiel das **- 4.** [group - of wolves] Rudel das; [ - of hounds] Meute die; [ - of thieves] Bande die **- 5.** RUGBY Stürmer pl **- 6.** phr: **that's a ~ of lies!** das ist alles erstunken und erlogen! ⇔ vt **- 1.** [for journey, holiday - bag, suitcase] packen; [ - clothes, toothbrush] einlpacken **- 2.** [put in container, parcel] einlpacken; [product] verpacken **- 3.** [crowd into] füllen; **to be ~ed into sthg** in etw (A) gezwängt sein ⇔ vi **- 1.** [for journey, holiday] packen **- 2.** [crowd] sich drängen.

➤ **pack in** vt sep Br inf [job] hinlschmeißen; [boyfriend] sausen lassen; [smoking] auflhören mit; **~ it in!** [stop annoying me, shut up] hör (doch) auf damit! ⇔ vi inf [break down] den Geist auflgeben.

➤ **pack off** vt sep inf fortlschicken.

➤ **pack up** vt sep zusammenlpacken ⇔ vi **- 1.** [pack one's suitcase] packen **- 2.** inf [finish work] Feierabend machen **- 3.** Br inf [break down] den Geist auflgeben.

**package** [ˈpækɪdʒ] n **- 1.** [gen & COMPUT] Paket das **- 2.** esp Am [packet - of cigarettes, tissues] Packung die; [ - of washing powder] Paket das ⇔ vt [wrap up, pack up] verpacken.

**package deal** n Paket das.

**package holiday** n Pauschalreise die.

**package tour** n Pauschalreise die.

**packaging** [ˈpækɪdʒɪŋ] n (U) [wrapping] Verpackung die.

**packed** [pækt] adj **- 1.** [place]: **~ (with)** (über)voll (mit) **- 2.** [magazine, information pack]: **~ with** voll mit.

**packed lunch** n Br Lunchpaket das.

**packed out** adj Br inf: **to be ~** gerammelt voll sein.

**packet** [ˈpækɪt] n **- 1.** [box, bag, contents - of biscuits, cigarettes] Packung die; [ - of washing powder] Paket das **- 2.** [parcel] Päckchen das **- 3.** Br inf [lot of money] **a ~** ein Haufen Geld.

**packhorse** [ˈpækhɔːs] n Packpferd das.

**pack ice** n Packeis das.

**packing** [ˈpækɪŋ] n (U) **- 1.** [protective material] Verpackungsmaterial das **- 2.** [for journey, holiday] Packen das.

**packing case** n Kiste die.

**pact** [pækt] n Pakt der.

**pad** [pæd] (pt & pp **-ded**; cont **-ding**) n **- 1.** [for garment] Polster das **- 2.** [for protection] Schützer der **- 3.** [notepad] Block der **- 4.** [for absorbing liquid]: **~ of cotton wool** Wattebausch der; **sanitary ~** Damenbinde die **- 5.** SPACE: **(launch) ~** Abschussrampe die **- 6.** inf dated [home] Bude die ⇔ vt **- 1.** [furniture] polstern; [clothing] wattieren **- 2.** [wound] eine Kompresse aufllegen auf (+ A) **- 3.** fig [letter, essay] länger machen; [speech] ausldehnen ◇ *vi* [walk softly] tappen.

➡ **pad out** *vt sep* - **1.** [furniture] polstern; [clothing] wattieren - **2.** [letter, essay] länger machen; [speech] ausldehnen.

**padded** ['pædɪd] *adj* [chair] gepolstert; [jacket, shoulders] wattiert.

**padded cell** *n* Gummizelle *die*.

**padding** ['pædɪŋ] *n* (U) - **1.** [protective material] Polsterung *die* - **2.** [in speech, essay, letter] Füllwerk *das*.

**paddle** ['pædl] *n* - **1.** [for canoe, dinghy] Paddel *das* - **2.** [wade]: **to have a ~** durchs Wasser waten ◇ *vt* paddeln mit ◇ *vi* - **1.** [in canoe, dinghy] paddeln - **2.** [wade] waten.

**paddle boat, paddle steamer** *n* Raddampfer *der*.

**paddling pool** ['pædlɪŋ-] *n* - **1.** [in park] Plantschbad *das* - **2.** [inflatable] Plantschbecken *das*.

**paddock** ['pædək] *n* - **1.** [small field] Koppel *die* - **2.** [at racecourse] Sattelplatz *der*.

**paddy field** ['pædɪ-] *n* Reisfeld *das*.

**paddy wagon** ['pædɪ-] *n Am* [police vehicle] grüne Minna.

**padlock** ['pædlɒk] *n* Vorhängeschloss *das* ◇ *vt* (mit einem Vorhängeschloss) verschließen.

**paederast** ['pedəræst] *n* = pederast.

**paediatric** [ˌpiːdɪˈætrɪk] *adj* = pediatric.

**paediatrician** [ˌpiːdɪəˈtrɪʃn] *n* = pediatrician.

**paediatrics** [ˌpiːdɪˈætrɪks] *n* = pediatrics.

**paedophile** ['piːdəfaɪl] *n* = pedophile.

**paella** [paɪˈelə] *n* Paella *die*.

**paeony** ['piːənɪ] (*pl* -ies) *n* = peony.

**pagan** ['peɪɡən] *adj* heidnisch ◇ *n* Heide *der*, -din *die*.

**paganism** ['peɪɡənɪzm] *n* Heidentum *das*.

**page** [peɪdʒ] *n* - **1.** [side of paper] Seite *die* - **2.** [leaf, sheet of paper] Blatt *das* ◇ *vt* [call out name of] ausrufen lassen; **paging Miss Smith!** Miss Smith, bitte!

**pageant** ['pædʒənt] *n* [show] historisches Schauspiel; [parade] Festumzug *der*.

**pageantry** ['pædʒəntrɪ] *n* Prunk *der*, Pomp *der*.

**page boy** *n* - **1.** *Br* [at wedding] *kleiner Junge, der bei der Hochzeitszeremonie hilft* - **2.** [hairstyle] Pagenkopf *der*.

**page break** *n* COMPUT Seitenumbruch *der*.

**pager** ['peɪdʒə'] *n* Piepser *der*.

**pagination** [ˌpædʒɪˈneɪʃn] *n* (U) Paginierung *die*.

**pagoda** [pəˈɡəʊdə] *n* Pagode *die*.

**paid** [peɪd] *pt* & *pp* ▷ **pay** ◇ *adj* bezahlt; **badly/well ~** schlecht/gut bezahlt.

**paid-up** *adj Br*: **a fully ~ member** ein Mitglied, das alle Beiträge bezahlt hat.

**pail** [peɪl] *n* Eimer *der*.

**pain** [peɪn] *n* - **1.** [ache] Schmerz *der*; **he's a real ~ (in the neck)** *inf* er ist eine richtige Nervensäge; **it's a ~ in the neck** *inf* es geht mir auf den Geist - **2.** (U) [physical suffering] Schmerzen *pl*; **to be in ~** Schmerzen haben - **3.** (U) [mental suffering] Qualen *pl* ◇ *vt fml* schmerzen, wehtun (+ D).

➡ **pains** *npl* [effort] Mühe *die*; **to be at ~s to do sthg** sich (D) große Mühe geben, etw zu tun; **to take ~s to do sthg** sich (D) Mühe geben, etw zu tun; **she got nothing for her ~s** ihre Mühe war umsonst.

**pained** [peɪnd] *adj* [expression] gequält.

**painful** ['peɪnfʊl] *adj* - **1.** [physically] schmerzhaft; **to be ~** wehtun, schmerzen - **2.** [distressing] schmerzlich.

**painfully** ['peɪnfʊlɪ] *adv* - **1.** [physically] unter Schmerzen - **2.** [distressingly] schmerzlich - **3.** [for emphasis]: **~ boring** schrecklich OR furchtbar langweilig; **she made it ~ obvious that ...** sie machte klar deutlich, dass ...

**painkiller** ['peɪnˌkɪlə'] *n* schmerzstillendes Mittel.

**painless** ['peɪnlɪs] *adj* - **1.** [physically] schmerzlos - **2.** [unproblematic] unproblematisch; [exam, decision] leicht.

**painlessly** ['peɪnlɪslɪ] *adv* - **1.** [without hurting] schmerzlos - **2.** [unproblematically] problemlos.

**painstaking** ['peɪnzˌteɪkɪŋ] *adj* sorgfältig.

**painstakingly** ['peɪnzˌteɪkɪŋlɪ] *adv* sorgfältig.

**paint** [peɪnt] *n* Farbe *die*; [on car, furniture] Lack *der* ◇ *vt* - **1.** [picture, portrait] malen; **he ~ed a gloomy picture of the holiday** *fig* er schilderte den Urlaub in düsteren Farben - **2.** [wall, room] streichen; [car, fingernails] lackieren; [lips, face] schminken ◇ *vi* - **1.** ART malen - **2.** [decorate] streichen.

**paintbox** ['peɪntbɒks] *n* Farbkasten *der*.

**paintbrush** ['peɪntbrʌʃ] *n* Pinsel *der*.

**painted** ['peɪntɪd] *adj* bemalt.

**painter** ['peɪntə'] *n* Maler *der*, -in *die*.

**painting** ['peɪntɪŋ] *n* - **1.** [picture] Gemälde *das*, Bild *das* - **2.** [artistic] Malen *das*; [activity] Malerei *die* - **3.** [by decorator] Anstreichen *das*.

**paintwork** ['peɪntwɜːk] *n* (U) [on wall] Anstrich *der*; [on car] Lack *der*.

**pair** [peə'] *n* Paar *das*; **in ~s** paarweise; **a ~ of pliers** eine Zange; **a ~ of scissors** eine Schere; **a ~ of shorts** Shorts *pl*; **a ~ of spectacles** eine

P

Brille; **a ~ of tights** eine Strumpfhose; **a ~ of trousers** eine Hose.

➤ **pair off** *vt sep* zu Paaren *OR* paarweise zusammenlstellen ◇ *vi* Zweiergruppen bilden.

**paisley (pattern)** ['peɪzlɪ-] *n* Paisleymuster *das* ◇ *comp* Paisley-.

**pajamas** [pə'dʒɑːməz] *npl Am* = **pyjamas.**

**Paki** ['pækɪ] *n Br vinf abwertende und rassistische Bezeichnung für einen Pakistaner oder eine Pakistanerin.*

**Pakistan** [*Br* ˌpɑːkɪ'stɑːn, *Am* ˌpækɪ'stæn] *n* Pakistan *nt.*

**Pakistani** [*Br* ˌpɑːkɪ'stɑːnɪ, *Am* 'pækɪstænɪ] *adj* pakistanisch ◇ *n* Pakistaner *der*, -in *die.*

**pal** [pæl] *n inf* Kumpel *der*; **be a ~!** sei so nett!

**PAL** (*abbr of* **phase alternation line**) *n* PAL.

**palace** ['pælɪs] *n* Palast *der*; [of bishop, aristocracy] Palais *das*; [grand house] Schloss *das.*

**palaeontology** *Br*, **paleontology** *Am* [ˌpælɪɒn'tɒlədʒɪ] *n* Paläontologie *die.*

**palatable** ['pælətəbl] *adj* - **1.** [food] wohlschmeckend - **2.** [suggestion, idea] annehmbar.

**palate** ['pælət] *n* Gaumen *der.*

**palatial** [pə'leɪʃl] *adj* palastartig.

**palaver** [pə'lɑːvər] *n inf* - **1.** [talk] Palaver *das* - **2.** [fuss] Theater *das.*

**pale** [peɪl] *adj* [colour, face] blass; [clothes] hell; [light] fahl ◇ *vi* bleich *OR* blass werden; **to ~ into insignificance (beside)** völlig bedeutungslos werden (neben).

**pale ale** *n Br* helleres Dunkelbier.

**paleness** ['peɪlnɪs] *n* [of colour, face] Blässe *die*; [of clothes] Bleichheit *die*; [of light] Fahlheit *die.*

**paleontology** *n Am* = **palaeontology.**

**Palestine** ['pæləˌstaɪn] *n* Palästina *nt.*

**Palestinian** [ˌpælə'stɪnɪən] *adj* palästinensisch ◇ *n* [person] Palästinenser *der*, -in *die.*

**palette** ['pælət] *n ART* Palette *die.*

**palette knife** *n* Palettenmesser *das.*

**palimony** ['pælɪmənɪ] *n Unterhaltszahlung von ehemaligen Lebensgefährten.*

**palings** ['peɪlɪŋz] *npl* Lattenzaun *der.*

**pall** [pɔːl] *n* - **1.** : **a ~ of smoke** eine Rauchglocke - **2.** *Am* [over coffin] Sargtuch *das* ◇ *vi* an Reiz verlieren.

**pallbearer** ['pɔːlˌbeərər] *n* Sargträger *der*, -in *die.*

**pallet** ['pælɪt] *n* Palette *die.*

**palliative** ['pælɪətɪv] *adj fml* lindernd.

**pallid** ['pælɪd] *adj literary* blass.

**pallor** ['pælər] *n literary* Blässe *die.*

**palm** [pɑːm] *n* - **1.** [tree] Palme *die* - **2.** [of hand]

Handfläche *die*; **to read sb's ~** jm aus der Hand lesen.

➤ **palm off** *vt sep inf*: **to ~ sthg off on sb** jm etw anldrehen; **to ~ sb off with sthg** jn mit etw ablspeisen.

**palmistry** ['pɑːmɪstrɪ] *n* Handlesekunst *die.*

**Palm Sunday** *n* Palmsonntag *der.*

**palmtop** ['pɑːmtɒp] *n COMPUT* Palmtopcomputer *der.*

**palm tree** *n* Palme *die.*

**palomino** [ˌpælə'miːnəʊ] (*pl* -**s**) *n* Palomino *das.*

**palpable** ['pælpəbl] *adj* [obvious] offensichtlich.

**palpably** ['pælpəblɪ] *adv* eindeutig.

**palpitate** ['pælpɪteɪt] *vi* [heart] heftig klopfen.

**palpitations** [ˌpælpɪ'teɪʃənz] *npl* Herzklopfen *das.*

**palsy** ['pɔːlzɪ] *n* Lähmung *die.*

**paltry** ['pɔːltrɪ] (*compar* -**ier**; *superl* -**iest**) *adj* armselig.

**pamper** ['pæmpər] *vt* verhätscheln.

**pamphlet** ['pæmflɪt] *n* [for information] Broschüre *die*; [for publicity] (Werbe)prospekt *der*; [political] Pamphlet *das.*

**pan** [pæn] (*pt* & *pp* -**ned**; *cont* -**ning**) *n* - **1.** [for frying] Pfanne *die*; [saucepan] Topf *der* - **2.** *Am* [for baking] Backform *die* - **3.** [of scales] Schale *die* - **4.** [of toilet] Becken *das* ◇ *vt inf* [criticize] verreißen ◇ *vi* - **1.** **to ~ for gold** Gold waschen - **2.** CINEMA schwenken.

**panacea** [ˌpænə'sɪə] *n* Allheilmittel *das.*

**panache** [pə'næʃ] *n* (*U*) Schwung *der.*

**panama** [ˌpænə'mɑː] *n*: **~ (hat)** Panamahut *der.*

**Panama** ['pænəmɑː] *n* Panama *nt.*

**Panama Canal** *n*: **the ~** der Panamakanal.

**pan-American** *adj* panamerikanisch.

**pancake** ['pænkeɪk] *n* Pfannkuchen *der.*

**Pancake Day** *n Br* Fastnachtsdienstag *der.*

**pancake roll** *n* Frühlingsrolle *die.*

**Pancake Tuesday** *n* Fastnachtsdienstag *der.*

**pancreas** ['pæŋkrɪəs] *n* Bauchspeicheldrüse *die.*

**panda** ['pændə] (*pl inv OR* -**s**) *n* Panda *der.*

**pandemonium** [ˌpændɪ'məʊnɪəm] *n* Chaos *das.*

**pander** ['pændər] *vi*: **to ~ to sb/sthg** jm/etw nachlgeben.

**pane** [peɪn] *n* Scheibe *die.*

**panel** ['pænl] *n* - **1.** [of experts, interviewers] Gremium *das*; [on TV and radio programmes] Diskussionsrunde *die*; **a ~ of experts** ein

Sachverständigengremium **- 2.** [of wood] Platte *die* **- 3.** [of machine] Schalttafel *die.*

**panel game** *n Br* Quizsendung *die.*

**panelling** *Br,* **paneling** *Am* ['pænəlɪŋ] *n* Täfelung *die.*

**panellist** *Br,* **panelist** *Am* ['pænəlɪst] *n* Diskussionsteilnehmer *der,* -in *die.*

**panel pin** *n Br* Stift *der.*

**pang** [pæŋ] *n* [of guilt, fear, regret] Anfall *der;* ~s of conscience Gewissensbisse *pl.*

**panic** ['pænɪk] (*pt* & *pp* **-ked;** *cont* **-king**) *n* Panik *die* <> *vi* in Panik geraten; **don't ~!** keine Panik!

**panicky** ['pænɪkɪ] *adj* [feeling] panisch; **to feel ~** Angst bekommen.

**panic stations** *n inf:* **it was ~** alles war am Rotieren.

**panic-stricken** *adj* von Panik erfasst *OR* ergriffen.

**pannier** ['pænɪəʳ] *n* Satteltasche *die.*

**panoply** ['pænəplɪ] *n (U) fml* Palette *die.*

**panorama** [ˌpænə'rɑːmə] *n* Panorama *das.*

**panoramic** [ˌpænə'ræmɪk] *adj* Panorama-.

**pansy** ['pænzɪ] (*pl* **-ies**) *n* **- 1.** [flower] Stiefmütterchen *das* **- 2.** *inf pej* [man] Tunte *die.*

**pant** [pænt] *vi* keuchen; [dog] hecheln.

➡ **pants** *npl* **- 1.** *Br* [underpants - for men] Unterhose *die;* [ - for women] Schlüpfer *der* **- 2.** *Am* [trousers] Hose *die.*

**panther** ['pænθəʳ] (*pl inv OR* **-s**) *n* Panther *der.*

**panties** ['pæntɪz] *npl inf* Schlüpfer *der.*

**pantihose** ['pæntɪhəʊz] *npl Am* = **panty hose.**

**panto** ['pæntəʊ] (*pl* **-s**) *n Br inf* = **pantomime.**

**pantomime** ['pæntəmaɪm] *n Br meist um die Weihnachtszeit aufgeführtes Märchenspiel;* ~ **dame** *von einem Mann gespielte Figur einer alten Dame in einer „pantomime".*

**pantry** ['pæntrɪ] (*pl* **-ies**) *n* Speisekammer *die.*

**panty hose** ['pæntɪhəʊz] *npl Am* Strumpfhose *die.*

**papa** [*Br* pə'pɑː, *Am* 'pæpə] *n dated* [father] Papa *der.*

**papacy** ['peɪpəsɪ] (*pl* **-ies**) *n* **- 1.** [period] Amtszeit *die* als Papst **- 2.** [institution]: **the ~** das Papsttum.

**papadum** ['pæpədəm] *n* = **popadum.**

**papal** ['peɪpl] *adj* päpstlich.

**paparazzi** [ˌpæpə'rætsɪ] *npl pej* Paparazzi *pl.*

**papaya** [pə'paɪə] *n* [fruit] Papaya *die;* [tree] Papayabaum *der.*

**paper** ['peɪpəʳ] *n* **- 1.** [for writing on] Papier *das;* **a piece of ~** [scrap] ein Stück Papier; [sheet] ein Blatt Papier; **on ~** [written down] schriftlich; [in theory] auf dem Papier **- 2.** [newspaper] Zei-

tung *die* **- 3.** [exam] Klausur *die* **- 4.** [essay] Arbeit *die* **- 5.** [at conference] Referat *das* <> *adj* **- 1.** [cup, napkin, hat] Papier-, aus Papier **- 2.** [qualifications] auf dem Papier; [profits] nominell <> *vt* [with wallpaper] tapezieren.

➡ **papers** *npl* **- 1.** [identity papers] Papiere *pl* **- 2.** [documents] Dokumente *pl,* Unterlagen *pl.*

➡ **paper over** *vt fus fig* übertünchen.

**paperback** ['peɪpəbæk] *n:* ~ **(book)** Taschenbuch *das.*

**paper bag** *n* Papiertüte *die.*

**paperboy** ['peɪpəbɔɪ] *n* Zeitungsjunge *der.*

**paper clip** *n* Büroklammer *die.*

**papergirl** ['peɪpəgɜːl] *n* Zeitungsausträgerin *die.*

**paper handkerchief** *n* Papiertaschentuch *das.*

**paper knife** *n* Brieföffner *der.*

**paper mill** *n* Papierfabrik *die*

**paper shop** *n Br* Zeitungsgeschäft *das.*

**paperweight** ['peɪpəweɪt] *n* Briefbeschwerer *der.*

**paperwork** ['peɪpəwɜːk] *n (U)* Schreibarbeit *die.*

**papier-mâché** [ˌpæpjeɪ'mæʃeɪ] *n (U)* Pappmaschee *das* <> *comp* auf Pappmaschee.

**paprika** ['pæprɪkə] *n* Paprika *der.*

**Papua New Guinea** [ˌpæpʊə] *n* Papua-Neuguinea *nt.*

**par** [pɑːʳ] *n* **- 1.: to be on a ~ with sb/sthg** [person] sich mit jm/etw messen können; [company, country] mit jm/etw vergleichbar sein **- 2.** [in golf] Par *das;* **under/over ~** unter/über Par; **above/below ~** *fig* über/unter dem Durchschnitt **- 3.** [good health]: **to feel below** *OR* **under ~** nicht ganz auf dem Posten *OR* Damm sein **- 4.** FIN Nennwert *der;* **to be above/below ~** über/unter Pari stehen.

**para** ['pærə] *n Br inf* Fallschirmjäger *der.*

**parable** ['pærəbl] *n* REL Gleichnis *das;* [moral story] Parabel *die.*

**parabola** [pə'ræbələ] *n* Parabel *die.*

**paracetamol** [ˌpærə'siːtəmɒl] *n* **- 1.** *(U)* [substance] Paracetamol *das* **- 2.** [pill] Paracetamoltablette *die.*

**parachute** ['pærəʃuːt] *n* Fallschirm *der* <> *vi* mit dem Fallschirm abspringen.

**parade** [pə'reɪd] *n* **- 1.** [procession] Umzug *der* **- 2.** MIL Parade *die;* **to be on ~** eine Parade abhalten **- 3.** *Br:* **a shopping ~** eine Reihe von Läden *OR* Geschäften **- 4.** [street, path] Promenade *die* <> *vt* **- 1.** [people - soldiers] marschieren lassen; [ - captives] zur Schau stellen **- 2.** [object] vor sich *(D)* hertragen **- 3.** *fig* [flaunt] zur Schau stellen ◇ vi paradieren; [soldiers] marschieren.

**parade ground** n Exerzierplatz der.

**paradigm** ['pærədaım] n [example] Musterbeispiel das.

**paradigmatic** [ˌpærədɪg'mætɪk] adj beispielhaft.

**paradise** ['pærədaɪs] n Paradies das.

**paradox** ['pærədɒks] n Paradox(on) das.

**paradoxical** [ˌpærə'dɒksɪkl] adj paradox.

**paradoxically** [ˌpærə'dɒksɪklɪ] adv paradoxerweise.

**paraffin** ['pærəfɪn] n Paraffin das.

**paragon** ['pærəgən] n Muster das; a ~ of virtue ein Muster an Tugendhaftigkeit; a ~ of beauty der Inbegriff der Schönheit.

**paragraph** ['pærəgrɑːf] n Absatz der.

**Paraguay** ['pærəgwaɪ] n Paraguay nt.

**parakeet** ['pærəkiːt] n Sittich der.

**paralegal** [ˌpærə'liːgəl] n Rechtsassistent der, -in die.

**parallel** ['pærəlel] (Br pt & pp -ed OR -led; cont -ing OR -ling; Am pt & pp -ed; cont -ing) adj lit & fig: ~ (to OR with) parallel (zu) ◇ n - **1.** [gen] Parallele die; to have no ~ keine Parallele haben OR auflweisen - **2.** GEOGR Breitenkreis der; the 38th ~ der 38. Breitengrad ◇ vt gleichen (+ D).

**parallel bars** npl Barren der.

**paralyse** Br, **paralyze** Am ['pærəlaɪz] vt - **1.** MED lähmen - **2.** fig [immobilize] lahm legen.

**paralysed** Br, **paralyzed** Am ['pærəlaɪzd] adj - **1.** MED gelähmt - **2.** fig [immobilized] lahm gelegt.

**paralysis** [pə'rælɪsɪs] (pl -lyses [-lɪsiːz]) n - **1.** MED Lähmung die - **2.** [of industry, traffic] Lahmlegung die.

**paralytic** [ˌpærə'lɪtɪk] adj - **1.** MED gelähmt - **2.** Br inf [drunk] sternhagelvoll ◇ n Gelähmte der, die.

**paralyze** vt Am = paralyse.

**paralyzed** adj Am = paralysed.

**paramedic** [ˌpærə'medɪk] n Sanitäter der, -in die.

**parameter** [pə'ræmɪtər] n Parameter der.

**paramilitary** [ˌpærə'mɪlɪtrɪ] adj paramilitärisch.

**paramount** ['pærəmaunt] adj: to be ~ Vorrang OR Priorität haben; of ~ importance von äußerster Wichtigkeit.

**paranoia** [ˌpærə'nɔɪə] n Paranoia die.

**paranoiac** [ˌpærə'nɔɪæk] MED adj paranoisch ◇ n Paranoiker der, -in die.

**paranoid** ['pærənɔɪd] adj - **1.** MED paranoid - **2.** [worried, suspicious]: she's ~ about being on time sie hat ständig Angst, zu spät zu kommen; you're getting ~! dein Misstrauen ist ja krankhaft!

**paranormal** [ˌpærə'nɔːml] adj paranormal.

**parapet** ['pærəpɪt] n Brüstung die.

**paraphernalia** [ˌpærəfə'neɪlɪə] n Drum und Dran das.

**paraphrase** ['pærəfreɪz] n Paraphrase die ◇ vt paraphrasieren.

**paraplegic** [ˌpærə'pliːdʒɪk] adj doppelseitig gelähmt ◇ n Paraplegiker der, -in die.

**parapsychology** [ˌpærəsaɪ'kɒlədʒɪ] n Parapsychologie die.

**parasite** ['pærəsaɪt] n lit & fig Schmarotzer der, Parasit der.

**parasitic** [ˌpærə'sɪtɪk] adj parasitär.

**parasol** ['pærəsɒl] n Sonnenschirm der.

**paratrooper** ['pærətruːpər] n Fallschirmjäger der.

**parboil** ['pɑːbɔɪl] vt ankochen.

**parcel** ['pɑːsl] (Br pt & pp -led; cont -ling, Am pt & pp -ed; cont -ing) n Paket das.

◆ **parcel up** vt sep als Paket verpacken.

**parcel post** n Paketpost die.

**parched** [pɑːtʃt] adj - **1.** [very dry - grass, plain] ausgetrocknet, verdorrt; [ - throat, lips] trocken - **2.** inf [very thirsty]: I'm ~ ich habe riesigen Durst.

**parchment** ['pɑːtʃmənt] n Pergament das.

**pardon** ['pɑːdn] n - **1.** LAW Begnadigung die - **2.** [forgiveness] Vergebung die; I beg your ~? [showing surprise or offence] erlauben Sie mal!; [what did you say?] (wie) bitte?; I beg your ~! [apologizing] Entschuldigung!, Verzeihung! ◇ vt - **1.** LAW begnadigen - **2.** [forgive] verzeihen, vergeben; to ~ sb for sthg jm etw verzeihen; pardon? [what did you say?] wie bitte?; ~ me! Entschuldigung!, Verzeihung!

**pardonable** ['pɑːdnəbl] adj entschuldbar.

**pare** [peər] vt [apple, potato, stick] schälen; [fingernail] schneiden.

◆ **pare down** vt sep [costs, spending] kürzen; [personnel] einlsparen.

**parent** ['peərənt] n [father] Vater der; [mother] Mutter die; ~s Eltern pl.

**parentage** ['peərəntɪdʒ] n Herkunft die.

**parental** [pə'rentl] adj elterlich; ~ approval Zustimmung die der Eltern.

**parent company** n Muttergesellschaft die.

**parenthesis** [pə'renθɪsɪs] (pl -theses [-θɪsiːz]) n: in parentheses in Klammern.

**parenthood** ['peərənthʊd] n Elternschaft die.

**parenting** ['peərəntɪŋ] n elterliche Sorgepflicht.

**parent-teacher association** n Eltern-Lehrer-Vertretung die.

**pariah** [pə'raɪə] n pej Paria der.

**Paris** ['pærɪs] n Paris nt.

**parish** ['pærɪʃ] n Gemeinde die.

**parish council** n Br Gemeinderat der.

**parishioner** [pə'rɪʃənər] n Gemeindemitglied das.

**parish priest** n Gemeindepfarrer der.

**Parisian** [pə'rɪzɪən] adj Pariser <> n Pariser der, -in die.

**parity** ['pærətɪ] n [state] Gleichheit die; [action] Gleichstellung die.

**park** [pɑːk] n Park der <> vt parken; [bicycle] abstellen <> vi parken.

**parka** ['pɑːkə] n Parka der.

**parking** ['pɑːkɪŋ] n (U) - **1.** [act] Parken das; 'no ~' 'Parken verboten' - **2.** [space] Parkplätze pl.

**parking garage** n Am Parkhaus das.

**parking light** n Am Parkleuchte die.

**parking lot** n Am Parkplatz der.

**parking meter** n Parkuhr die.

**parking place** n Parkplatz der.

**parking ticket** n Strafzettel der.

**Parkinson's (disease)** ['pɑːkɪnsnz-] n (U) Parkinsonkrankheit die.

**park keeper** n Br Parkwächter der, -in die.

**parkland** ['pɑːklænd] n (U) Parklandschaft die.

**parkway** ['pɑːkweɪ] n Am Allee die.

**parky** ['pɑːkɪ] (compar -ier; superl -iest) adj Br inf kühl, frisch.

**parlance** ['pɑːləns] n: in common/legal ~ im allgemeinen/juristischen Sprachgebrauch.

**parliament** ['pɑːləmənt] n Parlament das.

**parliamentarian** [,pɑːləmen'teərɪən] n Parlamentarier der, -in die.

**parliamentary** [,pɑːlə'mentərɪ] adj Parlaments-, parlamentarisch; [monarchy, system] parlamentarisch.

**parlour** Br, **parlor** Am ['pɑːlər] n - **1.** dated [in house] Salon der - **2.** [cafe]: **ice cream ~** Eisdiele die.

**parlour game** n Gesellschaftsspiel das.

**parlous** ['pɑːləs] adj fml kritisch.

**Parmesan (cheese)** [,pɑːmɪ'zæn-] n Parmesan(käse) der.

**parochial** [pə'rəukɪəl] adj pej [person] engstirnig; [view, approach] eng, beschränkt.

**parochial school** n Am Konfessionsschule die.

**parody** ['pærədɪ] (pl -ies; pt & pp -ied) n Parodie die; **a ~ of** eine Parodie auf (+ A) <> vt parodieren.

**parole** [pə'rəul] n (U) Bewährung die; **on ~** auf Bewährung <> vt auf Bewährung entlassen.

**paroxysm** ['pærəksɪzm] n Anfall der; **~s of laughter** ein Lachkrampf.

**parquet** ['pɑːkeɪ] n Parkett das.

**parrot** ['pærət] n Papagei der.

**parrot fashion** adv [repeat] wie ein Papagei, papageienhaft; [learn] stur auswendig.

**parry** ['pærɪ] (pt & pp -ied) vt lit & fig abwehren.

**parsimonious** [,pɑːsɪ'məunɪəs] adj fml & pej geizig.

**parsley** ['pɑːslɪ] n Petersilie die.

**parsnip** ['pɑːsnɪp] n Pastinak der, Pastinake die.

**parson** ['pɑːsn] n Pfarrer der, -in die.

**parson's nose** n Br Bürzel der.

**part** [pɑːt] n - **1.** [gen] Teil der; **in this ~ of Germany** in dieser Gegend Deutschlands; **in ~** teilweise, zum Teil; **to be ~ and parcel of sthg** fester Bestandteil einer Sache (G) sein; **that's only ~ of the story** das ist noch nicht alles; **for the better ~ of two hours** fast zwei Stunden; **for the most ~** zum größten Teil - **2.** [of TV serial] Fortsetzung die - **3.** [component] Teil das; **spare ~s** Ersatzteile; **to form ~ of sthg** Teil von etw sein - **4.** [acting role] Rolle die, Part der; fig [involvement] Anteil der, Rolle die; **his ~ in the crime** seine Rolle bei dem Verbrechen; **to play an important ~ in sthg** eine wichtige Rolle bei etw spielen; **to want no ~ in sthg** mit etw nichts zu tun haben wollen; **to take ~ in sthg** an etw (D) teilnehmen, sich an etw (D) beteiligen; **for my/his/etc ~** was mich/ihn/etc anbetrifft; **on my ~** meinerseits; **on the ~ of** vonseiten (+ G), seitens (+ G) - **5.** Am [hair parting] Scheitel der - **6.** MUS Stimme die <> adv teils <> vt - **1.** [separate] trennen - **2.** [curtains] öffnen, zur Seite schieben; [branches] zur Seite schieben; [legs] auf l-machen; [hair] scheiteln <> vi - **1.** [people] sich trennen - **2.** [curtains, lips, legs] sich öffnen; [crowd, branches] sich teilen.

➤ **parts** npl: **in these ~s** in dieser Gegend; **in foreign ~s** in fremden Ländern.

➤ **part with** vt fus sich trennen von.

**partake** [pɑː'teɪk] (pt -took; pp -taken [pɑː'teɪkn]) vi fml: **to ~ of sthg** etw zu sich nehmen.

**part exchange** n: **in ~ (for)** in Zahlung (für).

**partial** ['pɑːʃl] adj - **1.** [incomplete] Teil-, teilweise - **2.** [biased] parteiisch - **3.** [fond]: **to be ~ to sthg** eine Schwäche für etw haben.

**partiality** [ˌpɑːʃɪˈælətɪ] *n* - **1.** [bias] Parteilichkeit *die* - **2.** [fondness]: ~ **(for)** Schwäche *die* (für).

**partially** [ˈpɑːʃəlɪ] *adv* [partly] zum Teil, teilweise.

**partially sighted** [-ˈsaɪtɪd] *adj* eingeschränkt sehfähig.

**participant** [pɑːˈtɪsɪpənt] *n* Teilnehmer *der*, -in *die*.

**participate** [pɑːˈtɪspeɪt] *vi*: to ~ **(in)** teillnehmen (an (+ D)).

**participation** [pɑːˌtɪsɪˈpeɪʃən] *n* Teilnahme *die*.

**participle** [ˈpɑːtɪsɪpl] *n* Partizip *das*.

**particle** [ˈpɑːtɪkl] *n* - **1.** [tiny piece] Teilchen *das* - **2.** GRAMM Partikel *die*.

**particular** [pəˈtɪkjʊlə‍ʳ] *adj* - **1.** [specific] bestimmt, speziell; **for no ~ reason** aus keinem bestimmten Grund - **2.** [special] besondere, -r, -s - **3.** [fussy] eigen.

➣ **particulars** *npl* Einzelheiten *pl*.
➣ **in particular** *adv* besonders, vor allem; **nothing in ~** nichts Besonderes.

**particularly** [pəˈtɪkjʊləlɪ] *adv* - **1.** [in particular] besonders, vor allem - **2.** [very] besonders.

**parting** [ˈpɑːtɪŋ] *n* - **1.** [farewell] Abschied *der* - **2.** Br [in hair] Scheitel *der*.

**parting shot** *n* Schlussbemerkung *die*.

**partisan** [ˌpɑːtɪˈzæn] *adj* parteiisch ⟨> *n* [freedom fighter] Partisan *der*, -in *die*.

**partition** [pɑːˈtɪʃn] *n* - **1.** [wall, screen] Trennwand *die* - **2.** (U) [of country] Teilung *die* ⟨> *vt* teilen.

**partly** [ˈpɑːtlɪ] *adv* zum Teil, teilweise.

**partner** [ˈpɑːtnə‍ʳ] *n* - **1.** [gen] Partner *der*, -in *die* - **2.** [in a business] Geschäftspartner *der*, -in *die* - **3.** [in crime] Komplize *der*, -zin *die* ⟨> *vt*: **to ~ sb** js Partner sein; **to ~ sb with sb** jn mit jm zusammenlbringen.

**partnership** [ˈpɑːtnəʃɪp] *n* - **1.** [relationship] Partnerschaft *die* - **2.** [business] (Personen)gesellschaft *die*.

**partook** [pɑːˈtʊk] *pt* ⊳ **partake**.

**partridge** [ˈpɑːtrɪdʒ] (*pl inv* OR **-s**) *n* Rebhuhn *das*.

**part-time** *adj* Teilzeit- ⟨> *adv*: **to work ~** Teilzeit arbeiten.

**part-timer** *n* Teilzeitbeschäftigte *der*, *die*.

**party** [ˈpɑːtɪ] (*pl* **-ies**; *pt* & *pp* **-ied**) *n* - **1.** POL & LAW Partei *die* - **2.** [social gathering] Party *die*; **to have a ~** eine Party geben - **3.** [group of people] Gruppe *die* - **4.** [involved person]: **to be a ~ to sthg** beteiligt sein an etw (D) ⟨> *vi inf* feiern.

**party line** *n* - **1.** POL Parteilinie *die* - **2.** TELEC Gemeinschaftsanschluss *der*.

**party political broadcast** *n* Br parteipolitische Sendung.

**party politics** *n* Parteipolitik *die*.

**pass** [pɑːs] *vt* - **1.** [walk past] vorbeigehen an (+ D); [drive past] vorbeilfahren an (+ D) - **2.** AUT [overtake] überholen - **3.** [hand over] reichen; **to ~ sthg to sb, to ~ sb sthg** jm etw reichen - **4.** [in football, hockey etc]: **to ~ sb the ball, to ~ the ball to sb** jm den Ball zulspielen OR passen - **5.** [exam, test] bestehen - **6.** [candidate] bestehen lassen - **7.** [approve - law] verabschieden; [- motion] anlnehmen; **this product has been ~ed as fit for sale** dieses Produkt ist für den Verkauf freigegeben worden - **8.** [life, time] verbringen - **9.** [exceed] überschreiten - **10.** [judgement] fällen; [sentence] verhängen ⟨> *vi* - **1.** [walk past] vorbeigehen; [drive past] vorbeilfahren; **to let sb ~** jn vorbeilassen; **if you're ~ing this way** falls Sie hier vorbeilkommen - **2.** AUT [overtake] überholen - **3.** [road, river, path] führen; [pipe, cable] verlaufen - **4.** [time, holiday, lesson] vergehen - **5.** [in test, exam] bestehen - **6.** [in football, hockey etc] einen Pass spielen - **7.** [occur] verlaufen; **to ~ unnoticed** unbemerkt bleiben ⟨> *n* - **1.** [document] Ausweis *der* - **2.** Br [in exam] Bestehen *das*; **to get a ~** bestehen - **3.** [between mountains] Pass *der* - **4.** [in football, hockey etc] Pass *der*; [in tennis] Passierschlag *der* - **5.** *phr*: **to make a ~ at sb** *inf* bei jm Annäherungsversuche machen.

➣ **pass around** *vt sep* = **pass round**.
➣ **pass as** *vt fus* durchlgehen.
➣ **pass away** *vi* entschlafen.
➣ **pass by** *vt fus* [walk past] vorbeigehen an (+ D); [drive past] vorbeilfahren an (+ D) ⟨> *vt sep fig* [subj: news, events] vorbeigehen an (+ D) ⟨> *vi* [walk past] vorbeigehen; [drive past] vorbeilfahren.
➣ **pass for** *vt fus* = **pass as**.
➣ **pass off** *vt sep*: **to ~ o.s./sb/sthg off as sthg** sich/jn/etw als etw auslgeben ⟨> *vi* [occur] verlaufen.
➣ **pass on** *vt sep lit* & *fig*: **to ~ sthg on (to sb)** etw (an jn) weiterlgeben ⟨> *vi* - **1.** [move on] weiterlmachen; **let's ~ on to the next question** gehen wir zur nächsten Frage über - **2.** = **pass away**.
➣ **pass out** *vi* - **1.** [faint] ohnmächtig werden - **2.** Br MIL ernannt werden.
➣ **pass over** *vt fus* [subject, problem] übergehen; **to be ~ed over for promotion** bei der Beförderung übergangen werden.
➣ **pass round** *vt sep* herumlreichen.
➣ **pass through** *vi* durchlkommen; **we're just ~ing through** wir sind nur auf der Durchreise.
➣ **pass to** *vt fus* [as part of inheritance] überlgehen auf (+ A).
➣ **pass up** *vt sep* [opportunity] vorübergehen lassen; [invitation, offer] abllehnen.

**passable** [ˈpɑːsəbl] *adj* - **1.** [satisfactory] passabel - **2.** [road, path] passierbar.

**passably** ['pɑːsəblɪ] *adv* [satisfactorily] ganz passabel.

**passage** ['pæsɪdʒ] *n* - **1.** [corridor] Gang *der*; [between houses] Durchgang *der* - **2.** [through crowd] Weg *der* - **3.** ANAT Gang *der* - **4.** [in book, music] Passage *die* - **5.** (U) *fml* [transition] Übergang *der*; **the ~ of time** der Strom der Zeit - **6.** [sea journey] Überfahrt *die*.

**passageway** ['pæsɪdʒweɪ] *n* Gang *der*; [between houses] Durchgang *der*.

**passbook** ['pɑːsbʊk] *n* Sparbuch *das*.

**passé** ['pæseɪ] *adj pej* überholt, passé.

**passenger** ['pæsɪndʒəʳ] *n* [gen] Passagier *der*; [in taxi] Fahrgast *der*; [in car] Insasse *der*, -sin *die*.

**passerby** [ˌpɑːsə'baɪ] (*pl* **passersby** [ˌpɑːsəz'baɪ]) *n* Passant *der*, -in *die*.

**passing** ['pɑːsɪŋ] *adj* [remark] beiläufig; [fashion, mood] vorübergehend ◇ *n* - **1.** [of time] Lauf *der*; **with the ~ of the years** im Lauf(e) der Jahre - **2.** [death] Hinscheiden *das*.
➠ **in passing** *adv* [mention] beiläufig.

**passion** ['pæʃn] *n* Leidenschaft *die*.
➠ **Passion** *n:* **the Passion** die Passion.

**passionate** ['pæʃənət] *adj* leidenschaftlich.

**passionately** ['pæʃənətlɪ] *adv* - **1.** [kiss, embrace] leidenschaftlich - **2.** [care, speak, write] voller Leidenschaft.

**passionfruit** ['pæʃənfruːt] *n* Passionsfrucht *die*.

**passive** ['pæsɪv] *adj* - **1.** [person] passiv - **2.** GRAMM passivisch, Passiv- ◇ *n:* **the ~** das Passiv.

**passively** ['pæsɪvlɪ] *adv* [accept] widerspruchslos; [watch] tatenlos.

**passive resistance** *n* passiver Widerstand.

**passive smoking** *n* passives Rauchen.

**passivity** [pæ'sɪvətɪ] *n* Passivität *die*.

**passkey** ['pɑːskiː] *n* Hausschlüssel *der*.

**Passover** ['pɑːsˌəʊvəʳ] *n* Passah *das*.

**passport** ['pɑːspɔːt] *n* (Reise)pass *der*; **a ~ to power/success** *fig* ein Schlüssel zur Macht/ zum Erfolg.

**passport control** *n* Passkontrolle *die*.

**password** ['pɑːswɜːd] *n* Passwort *das*.

**past** [pɑːst] *adj* - **1.** [former] ehemalig - **2.** [earlier] vergangene, -r, -s; **in ~ times** in früheren Zeiten - **3.** [most recent, last] letzte, -r, -s; **the ~ month** der letzte Monat - **4.** [finished] vorbei ◇ *n* - **1.** [time]: **the ~** die Vergangenheit; **in the ~** früher - **2.** [personal history] Vergangenheit *die* - **3.** GRAMM Vergangenheit *die* ◇ *adv* - **1.** [telling the time] nach; **it's ten/a quarter ~** es ist zehn/viertel nach - **2.** [by] vorbei; **to run ~** vorbeilaufen ◇ *prep* - **1.** [telling the time]

nach; **twenty ~ four** zwanzig nach vier; **at half/a quarter ~ eight** um halb/viertel neun - **2.** [by] an (+ *D*) ... vorbei; **he drove ~ the house** er fuhr am Haus vorbei - **3.** [beyond] hinter (+ *D*); **to be ~ it** *inf* zu alt sein; **I wouldn't put it ~ him** *inf* ich würde es ihm zutrauen.

**pasta** ['pæstə] *n* (U) Nudeln *pl*, Teigwaren *pl*.

**paste** [peɪst] *n* - **1.** [smooth mixture] Brei *der*, Teig *der* - **2.** (U) CULIN Brotaufstrich *der*, Paste *die* - **3.** [glue] Kleister *der* - **4.** [jewellery] Strass *der* ◇ *vt* kleben; COMPUT einlfügen.

**pastel** ['pæstl] *adj* pastellfarben ◇ *n* - **1.** [colour] Pastell *das* - **2.** ART [drawing] Pastellmalerei *die*.

**pasteurize, -ise** ['pɑːstʃəraɪz] *vt* pasteurisieren.

**pastiche** [pæ'stiːʃ] *n* - **1.** [imitation] Persiflage *die* - **2.** [mixture of styles] Pastiche *der*.

**pastille** ['pæstɪl] *n* Pastille *die*.

**pastime** ['pɑːstaɪm] *n* Hobby *das*.

**pasting** ['peɪstɪŋ] *n inf*: **to give sb a ~** [beat up] jm eins überbraten; [defeat] jn fertiglmachen.

**pastor** ['pɑːstəʳ] *n* Pfarrer *der*, -in *die*.

**pastoral** ['pɑːstərəl] *adj* - **1.** RELIG pastoral; **~ care** Seelsorge *die* - **2.** [scene, life] ländlich; [in literature, art, music] pastoral.

**past participle** *n* Partizip Perfekt *das*.

**pastrami** [pə'strɑːmɪ] *n* (U) *geräuchertes, stark gewürztes Rindfleisch.*

**pastry** ['peɪstrɪ] (*pl* **-ies**) *n* - **1.** [mixture] Teig *der* - **2.** [cake] Teilchen *das*.

**past tense** *n* Vergangenheit *die*.

**pasture** ['pɑːstʃəʳ] *n* [field] Weide *die*.

**pastureland** ['pɑːstʃələænd] *n* Weideland *das*.

**pasty**[1] ['peɪstɪ] (*compar* **-ier**; *superl* **-iest**) *adj* [face] bleich.

**pasty**[2] ['pæstɪ] (*pl* **-ies**) *n Br* CULIN Pastete *die*.

**pasty-faced** ['peɪstɪˌfeɪst] *adj* bleichgesichtig.

**pat** [pæt] (*compar* **-ter**; *superl* **-test**; *pt* & *pp* **-ted**; *cont* **-ting**) *adj* präpariert ◇ *adv:* **to have sthg off ~** etw parat haben ◇ *n* - **1.** [light stroke] Klaps *der* - **2.** [of butter] Portion *die* ◇ *vt* [dog, hand] tätscheln; [back, shoulder] (leicht) klopfen auf (+ *A*).

**Patagonia** [ˌpætə'gəʊnɪə] *n* Patagonien *nt*.

**patch** [pætʃ] *n* - **1.** [piece of material] Flicken *der* - **2.** [over eye] Augenklappe *die* - **3.** [small area] Fleck *der*; **there were still ~es of snow** es lag vereinzelt *OR* stellenweise noch Schnee; **a bald ~** eine kahle Stelle - **4.** [of land] Stück (Land) *das*; **vegetable ~** Gemüsebeet *das* - **5.** [period of time]: **to be going through a difficult ~** eine schwierige Zeit durchmachen - **6.** *phr:* **not to be a ~ on sb/sthg** *inf* nichts gegen jn/etw sein ◇ *vt* flicken.

**P**

**patch together** *vt sep* [agreement] zusammenlschustern; [government] (in aller Eile) zusammenlstellen.

**patch up** *vt sep* - **1.** [mend] zusammenlflicken - **2.** *fig* [quarrel] beilegen; [marriage] kitten.

**patchwork** l'pætʃwɜːkl *adj* Patchwork- ◇ *n*: a ~ of fields ein bunter Teppich von Feldern.

**patchy** l'pætʃıl (*compar* -**ier**; *superl* -**iest**) *adj* - **1.** [fog, sunshine] vereinzelt; [colour] fleckig - **2.** [knowledge] lückenhaft - **3.** [performance, game] unterschiedlich (in der Qualität).

**pâté** l'pæteɪl *n (U)* Pastete *die*.

**patent** [*Br* 'peɪtənt, *Am* 'pætənt] *adj* [obvious] offensichtlich ◇ *n* Patent *das* ◇ *vt* patentieren lassen.

**patented** [*Br* 'peɪtəntɪd, *Am* 'pætəntɪd] *adj* patentiert.

**patentee** [*Br* ˌpeɪtən'tiː, *Am* ˌpætən'tiːl *n* Patentinhaber *der*, -in *die*.

**patent leather** *n* Lackleder *das*.

**patently** [*Br* 'peɪtntlɪ, *Am* 'pætəntlɪl *adv* offensichtlich; ~ **obvious** ganz offensichtlich.

**Patent Office** *n*: the ~ das Patentamt.

**paternal** [pə'tɜːnl] *adj* - **1.** [love, attitude] väterlich - **2.** [on father's side] ~ **grandmother/grandfather** Großmutter *die*/Großvater *der* väterlicherseits.

**paternalistic** [pəˌtɜːnə'lɪstɪk] *adj pej* patriarchalisch.

**paternity** [pə'tɜːnətɪ] *n* [fatherhood] Vaterschaft *die*.

**paternity leave** *n* Vaterschaftsurlaub *der*.

**paternity suit** *n* Vaterschaftsprozess *der*.

**path** [pɑːθ, *pl* pɑːðz] *n* - **1.** [track] Weg *der*; [narrower] Pfad *der* - **2.** [way ahead, course of action] Weg *der*; **our ~s had crossed before** unsere Wege hatten sich schon vorher gekreuzt - **3.** [trajectory] Bahn *die*.

**pathetic** [pə'θetɪk] *adj* - **1.** [causing pity] Mitleid erregend; **to be a ~ sight** ein Bild des Jammers bieten - **2.** [useless - attempt, effort] erbärmlich; **she's ~** sie ist ein hoffnungsloser Fall.

**pathetically** [pə'θetɪklɪ] *adv* - **1.** [causing pity] Mitleid erregend - **2.** [uselessly] erbärmlich.

**pathological** [ˌpæθə'lɒdʒɪkl] *adj* - **1.** MED pathologisch - **2.** [uncontrollable] krankhaft.

**pathologist** [pə'θɒlədʒɪst] *n* Pathologe *der*, -gin *die*.

**pathology** [pə'θɒlədʒɪ] *n* Pathologie *die*.

**pathos** l'peɪθɒsl *n* Pathos *das*.

**pathway** l'pɑːθweɪl *n* Weg *der*; [narrower] Pfad *der*.

**patience** l'peɪʃnsl *n* - **1.** [quality] Geduld *die*; **to**

**try sb's ~** js Geduld auf die Probe stellen - **2.** [card game] Patience *die*.

**patient** l'peɪʃntl *adj* geduldig ◇ *n* Patient *der*, -in *die*.

**patiently** l'peɪʃntlɪl *adv* geduldig.

**patina** l'pætɪnəl *n* Patina *die*.

**patio** l'pætɪəʊl (*pl* -**s**) *n* Terrasse *die*.

**patisserie** [pə'tiːsərɪ] *n* Konditorei *die*.

**Patna rice** l'pætnə-l *n* Patnareis *der*.

**patriarch** l'peɪtrɪɑːkl *n* Patriarch *der*.

**patriarchy** l'peɪtrɪɑːkɪl (*pl* -**ies**) *n* Patriarchat *das*.

**patrimony** [*Br* 'pætrɪmənɪ, *Am* 'pætrɪməʊnɪ] *n (U) fml* Patrimonium *das*.

**patriot** [*Br* 'pætrɪət, *Am* 'peɪtrɪət] *n* Patriot *der*, -in *die*.

**patriotic** [*Br* ˌpætrɪ'ɒtɪk, *Am* ˌpeɪtrɪ'ɒtɪk] *adj* patriotisch.

**patriotism** [*Br* 'pætrɪətɪzm, *Am* 'peɪtrɪətɪzm] *n* Patriotismus *der*.

**patrol** [pə'trəʊl] (*pt* & *pp* -**led**; *cont* -**ling**) *n* [of police] Streife *die*; [of soldiers] Patrouille *die*; **on ~** auf Streife/Patrouille ◇ *vt* [subj: police - in vehicle] Streife fahren in (+ *D*); [ - on foot] seine Runden machen in (+ *D*); [subj: soldiers] patrouillieren.

**patrol car** *n* Streifenwagen *der*.

**patrolman** [pə'trəʊlmən] (*pl* -**men** [-mən]) *n Am* (Streifen)polizist *der*.

**patrol wagon** *n Am* Gefangenenwagen *der*.

**patrolwoman** [pə'trəʊlˌwʊmən] (*pl* -**women** [-ˌwɪmɪn]) *n Am* (Streifen)polizistin *die*.

**patron** l'peɪtrənl *n* - **1.** [sponsor] Förderer *der*, -derin *die* - **2.** *Br* [of charity, campaign] Schirmherr *der*, -in *die* - **3.** *fml* [of shop] Kunde *der*, -din *die*; [of cinema] Besucher *der*, -in *die*; [of pub, hotel] Gast *der*; **for ~s only** nur für Kunden/Gäste.

**patronage** l'peɪtrənɪdʒl *n* [sponsorship - of organization] Schirmherrschaft *die*; [ - of activity] (finanzielle) Förderung.

**patronize, -ise** l'pætrənaɪzl *vt* - **1.** *pej* [talk down to] von oben herab behandeln - **2.** *fml* [be a customer of - shop] einlkaufen bei; [ - business] Kunde/Kundin sein von - **3.** *fml* [back financially] fördern.

**patronizing -ising** l'pætrənaɪzɪŋl *adj pej* gönnerhaft.

**patron saint** *n* Schutzpatron *der*, -in *die*.

**patter** l'pætəˈl *n* - **1.** [of feet] Getrappel *das*; [of raindrops] Platschen *das* - **2.** [talk] Sprüche *pl* ◇ *vi* [dog, feet] trappeln; [rain] platschen.

**pattern** l'pætənl *n* - **1.** [design] Muster *das* - **2.** [of life, work] Ablauf *der*; **behaviour ~** Verhaltensmuster *das* - **3.** [of distribution] Schema *das* - **4.** [for sewing] Schnittmuster *das;* [for knitting] Strickanleitung *die* - **5.** [model] Vorbild *das.*

**patterned** ['pætənd] *adj* gemustert.

**patty** ['pætɪ] (*pl* -ies) *n* - **1.** [pasty] Pastete *die* - **2.** [savoury meat cake] Frikadelle *die.*

**paucity** ['pɔːsətɪ] *n fml:* ~ of sthg Mangel *der* an etw *(D).*

**paunch** [pɔːntʃ] *n* Bauch *der.*

**pauper** ['pɔːpəʳ] *n* Arme *der, die.*

**pause** [pɔːz] *n* Pause *die;* without a ~ ohne Unterbrechung <> *vi* - **1.** [stop speaking] innelhalten - **2.** [stop doing sthg] eine Pause machen OR einllegen.

**pave** [peɪv] *vt* pflastern; to ~ the way for sb/sthg jm/etw den Weg ebnen.

**paved** [peɪvd] *adj* gepflastert.

**pavement** ['peɪvmənt] *n* - **1.** *Br* [at side of road] Bürgersteig *der* - **2.** *Am* [road surface] Fahrbahnbelag *der.*

**pavement artist** *n Br* Pflastermaler *der,* -in *die.*

**pavilion** [pə'vɪljən] *n* - **1.** [at sports field] Klubhaus *das* - **2.** [at exhibition] Pavillon *der.*

**paving** ['peɪvɪŋ] *n (U)* - **1.** [material] Belag *der* - **2.** [paved surface] Pflaster *das.*

**paving stone** *n* Pflasterstein *der.*

**paw** [pɔː] *n* Pfote *die;* [of lion, bear] Tatze *die* <> *vt* - **1.** [subj: animal]: to ~ the ground am Boden scharren - **2.** *pej* [subj: person] betatschen.

**pawn** [pɔːn] *n* - **1.** [chesspiece] Bauer *der* - **2.** [unimportant person] Schachfigur *die* <> *vt* verpfänden.

**pawnbroker** ['pɔːn,brəʊkəʳ] *n* Pfandleiher *der,* -in *die.*

**pawnshop** ['pɔːnʃɒp] *n* Pfandhaus *das.*

**pay** [peɪ] (*pt* & *pp* **paid**) *vt* - **1.** [bill, debt, person] bezahlen; [fine, taxes, fare, sum of money] zahlen; to ~ sb for sthg jm das Geld für etw geben; how much did you ~ for it? wie viel hast du dafür gezahlt?; to ~ money into an account *Br* Geld auf ein Konto einlzahlen; to ~ one's way für alles selber auf lkommen - **2.** [be profitable, advantageous to]: it won't ~ you to sell the house just now es wird sich für dich nicht lohnen, das Haus jetzt zu verkaufen; it will ~ you to keep quiet es wird für dich von Vorteil sein, wenn du schweigst - **3.**: to ~ sb a compliment jm ein Kompliment machen; to ~ a visit to sb/a place jn/einen Ort besuchen <> *vi* - **1.** [for services, work, goods] (be)zahlen; to ~ for sthg etw bezahlen - **2.** [be profitable - crime] sich lohnen; [ - work] sich rentieren - **3.** *fig* [suffer] bezahlen; to ~ dearly for sthg teuer für etw bezahlen <> *n* [wages] Lohn *der;* [salary] Gehalt *das.*

◆ **pay back** *vt sep* - **1.** [return money to]: I'll ~ you

back (the money) tomorrow ich zahle dir morgen das Geld zurück - **2.** [revenge o.s. on]: I'll ~ you back for that! das werde ich dir heimlzahlen!

◆ **pay off** *vt sep* - **1.** [debt] ablbezahlen; [loan] tilgen - **2.** [employee] auslzahlen - **3.** [informer, blackmailer] Schweigegeld zahlen (+ D) <> *vi* [be successful] sich auslzahlen.

◆ **pay out** *vt sep* - **1.** [money] auslgeben - **2.** [rope] ablaufen lassen <> *vi* bezahlen.

◆ **pay up** *vi* zahlen.

**payable** ['peɪəbl] *adj* - **1.** [debt, loan]: to be ~ fällig sein - **2.** [cheque]: to be ~ to sb an jn zu zahlen sein; to make a cheque ~ to sb einen Scheck auf jn auslstellen.

**pay as you earn** *n Br* britisches Steuersystem, bei dem die Lohnsteuer direkt vom Gehalt abgezogen wird.

**paybed** ['peɪbed] *n Br* Privatbett *das.*

**paycheck** ['peɪtʃek] *n Am* [cheque] Lohnscheck *der;* [money] Lohn *der.*

**payday** ['peɪdeɪ] *n* Zahltag *der.*

**PAYE** *abbr of* pay as you earn

**payee** [peɪ'iː] *n* Zahlungsempfänger *der,* -in *die.*

**pay envelope** *n Am* Lohntüte *die.*

**payer** ['peɪəʳ] *n* Zahler *der,* -in *die.*

**paying guest** [,peɪŋ-] *n* zahlender Gast.

**paying-in book** [,peɪŋ-] *n Br* Heft mit Einzahlungsformularen.

**payload** ['peɪləʊd] *n* - **1.** [load] Nutzlast *die* - **2.** [explosive in missile] Sprengstoffmenge *die.*

**paymaster general** [,peɪmɑːstəʳ] *n Br* britisches Kabinettsmitglied, zuständig für Lohn- und Gehaltszahlungen im öffentlichen Dienst in Großbritannien.

**payment** ['peɪmənt] *n* - **1.** [act of paying] Bezahlung *die* - **2.** [amount of money] Zahlung *die.*

**payoff** ['peɪɒf] *n* - **1.** [result] Lohn *der* - **2.** *Br* [redundancy payment] Abfindung *die.*

**payola** [peɪ'əʊlə] *n esp Am inf* - **1.** [bribing] Bestechung *die* - **2.** [bribe] Bestechungsgeld *das.*

**pay packet** *n Br* - **1.** [envelope] Lohntüte *die* - **2.** [wages] Lohn *der.*

**pay-per-view** *adj* Pay-per-View-.

**pay phone, pay station** *Am n* Münzfernsprecher *der.*

**payroll** ['peɪrəʊl] *n:* to be on the ~ angestellt sein.

**payslip** *Br* ['peɪslɪp], **paystub** *Am* ['peɪstʌb] *n* [for wages] Lohnstreifen *der;* [for salary] Gehaltsstreifen *der.*

**pay station** *n Am* = pay phone.

**paystub** *n Am* = payslip.

**PBS** (*abbr of* **Public Broadcasting Service**) *n Am*

*alle öffentlich-rechtlichen Fernsehstationen umfassende Rundfunkgesellschaft.*

**pc** *n abbr of* **postcard** ◇ *abbr of* **per cent.**

**p/c** *abbr of* **petty cash.**

**PC** *n* - **1.** (*abbr of* **personal computer**) PC *der* - **2.** *abbr of* **police constable** ◇ *adj abbr of* **politically correct.**

**pcm** (*abbr of* **per calendar month**) p. M.

**pd** (*abbr of* **paid**) bez.

**PD** (*abbr of* **police department**) *Polizeiwache in den USA.*

**pdq** (*abbr of* **pretty damn quick**) *adv inf* verdammt schnell.

**PDSA** (*abbr of* **People's Dispensary for Sick Animals**) *n kostenlose Behandlungseinrichtung für Haustiere in Großbritannien.*

**PDT** (*abbr of* **Pacific Daylight Time**) *n Sommerzeit in der pazifischen Zeitzone der USA.*

**PE** *n abbr of* **physical education.**

**pea** [piː] *n* Erbse *die*

**peace** [piːs] *n* - **1.** [tranquillity] Ruhe *die;* ~ **of mind** Seelenfrieden *der;* **to be at** ~ **with sb/sthg** mit jm/etw in Frieden leben; **to be at** ~ **with o.s.** mit sich selbst im Reinen sein - **2.** [no war] Frieden *der;* **to make (one's)** ~ **with sb/sthg** mit jm/etw Frieden schließen - **3.** [law and order] Ruhe *die* und Ordnung.

**peaceable** ['piːsəbl] *adj* [people] friedfertig.

**peaceably** ['piːsəbli] *adv* friedlich.

**Peace Corps** *n* Friedenskorps *das.*

**peaceful** ['piːsfʊl] *adj* friedlich.

**peacefully** ['piːsfʊli] *adv* friedlich.

**peacefulness** ['piːsfʊlnɪs] *n* [tranquillity] Ruhe *die.*

**peacekeeping force** ['piːsˌkiːpɪŋ-] *n* Friedenstruppe *die.*

**peacemaker** ['piːsˌmeɪkəʳ] *n* Friedensstifter *der,* -in *die.*

**peace offering** *n inf* Friedensangebot *das.*

**peacetime** ['piːstaɪm] *n (U)* Friedenszeiten *pl.*

**peach** [piːtʃ] *adj* [in colour] pfirsichfarben ◇ *n* - **1.** [fruit] Pfirsich *der* - **2.** [colour] Pfirsichton *der* ◇ *comp* Pfirsich-.

**Peach Melba** [-'melbə] *n* Pfirsich Melba *der.*

**peacock** ['piːkɒk] *n* Pfau *der.*

**peahen** ['piːhen] *n* Pfauenhenne *die.*

**peak** [piːk] *n* - **1.** [mountain top] Gipfel *der* - **2.** [highest point] Höhepunkt *der;* **to be at one's** ~ auf dem Höhepunkt seiner Leistungen sein - **3.** [of cap] Schirm *der* ◇ *adj:* **in** ~ **condition** in Höchstform ◇ *vi* den Höchststand erreichen.

**peaked** [piːkt] *adj:* ~ **cap** Schirmmütze *die.*

**peak hour** *n* TELEC & ELEC Hauptbelastungszeit *die;* [for traffic] Hauptverkehrszeit *die.*

**peak period** *n* Hochsaison *die.*

**peak rate** *n* Höchsttarif *der.*

**peaky** ['piːkɪ] (*compar* -ier; *superl* -iest) *adj Br inf:* **to look** ~ schlecht auslsehen; **to feel** ~ sich nicht gut fühlen.

**peal** [piːl] *n* - **1.** [of bells] Glockenläuten *das* - **2.:** ~**s of laughter** schallendes Gelächter; ~ **of thunder** Donnerschlag *der* ◇ *vi* [bells] läuten.

**peanut** ['piːnʌt] *n* Erdnuss *die.*

**peanut butter** *n* Erdnussbutter *die.*

**pear** [peəʳ] *n* Birne *die.*

**pearl** [pɜːl] *n* Perle *die.*

**peasant** ['peznt] *n* - **1.** [in countryside] (armer) Bauer, (arme) Bäuerin - **2.** *pej* [ignorant person] Banause *der,* -sin *die.*

**peasantry** ['pezntrɪ] *n:* **the** ~ die Bauernschaft.

**peashooter** ['piːˌʃuːtəʳ] *n* Blasrohr *das.*

**peat** [piːt] *n* Torf *der.*

**peaty** ['piːtɪ] (*compar* -ier; *superl* -iest) *adj* torfig.

**pebble** ['pebl] *n* Kiesel(stein) *der.*

**pebbledash** [ˌpebl'dæʃ] *n Br* Kieselrauputz *der.*

**pecan (nut)** [pɪ'kæn-] *n* Pekannuss *die.*

**pecan pie** *n* Pekannusstorte *die.*

**peck** [pek] *n* [kiss] Küsschen *das* ◇ *vt* - **1.** [with beak - hand] picken nach - **2.** [kiss] ein Küsschen geben (+ *D*) ◇ *vi* picken; **to** ~ **at corn** Maiskörner picken.

**pecking order** ['pekɪŋ-] *n* Hackordnung *die.*

**peckish** ['pekɪʃ] *adj Br inf* (etwas) hungrig.

**pectin** ['pektɪn] *n* Pektin *das.*

**pectoral** ['pektərəl] *adj* pektoral.

**peculiar** [pɪ'kjuːlɪəʳ] *adj* - **1.** [odd] seltsam, eigenartig - **2.** [slightly ill]: **to feel** ~ sich komisch fühlen - **3.** [characteristic]: **to be** ~ **to sb/sthg** jm/etw eigentümlich sein.

**peculiarity** [pɪˌkjuːlɪ'ærətɪ] (*pl* -ies) *n* - **1.** [strange habit] Eigenheit *die* - **2.** [individual characteristic] Charakteristikum *das* - **3.** [oddness] Eigenartigkeit *die.*

**peculiarly** [pɪ'kjuːlɪəlɪ] *adv* - **1.** [especially] besonders - **2.** [oddly] seltsam, eigenartig - **3.** [characteristically] typisch.

**pecuniary** [pɪ'kjuːnɪərɪ] *adj* finanziell.

**pedagogical** [ˌpedə'gɒdʒɪkl] *adj* pädagogisch.

**pedagogy** ['pedəgɒdʒɪ] *n* Pädagogik *die.*

**pedal** ['pedl] (*Br pt* & *pp* -led; *cont* -ling, *Am pt* & *pp* -ed; *cont* -ing) *n* Pedal *das* ◇ *vi* - **1.** (turn pedals] in die Pedale treten - **2.** [cycle] mit dem Fahrrad fahren.

**pedal bin** n Treteimer der.

**pedalo** ['pedələʊ] (pl **-s** OR **-es**) n Br Tretboot das.

**pedant** ['pedənt] n pej Pedant der, -in die.

**pedantic** [pɪ'dæntɪk] adj pej pedantisch.

**pedantry** ['pedəntrɪ] n pej Pedanterie die.

**peddle** ['pedl] vt - **1.** [drugs] handeln mit - **2.** [rumour, gossip] verbreiten.

**peddler** ['pedlə'] n - **1.** [drug dealer] Drogenhändler der, -in die - **2.** Am = **pedlar.**

**pederast** ['pedəræst] n Päderast der.

**pedestal** ['pedɪstl] n Sockel der; **to put sb on a** ~ jn in den Himmel heben.

**pedestrian** [pɪ'destrɪən] adj pej langweilig ◇ n Fußgänger der, -in die.

**pedestrian crossing** n Br Fußgängerüberweg der.

**pedestrianize, -ise** [pɪ'destrɪənaɪz] vt in eine Fußgängerzone umlwandeln.

**pedestrian precinct** Br, **pedestrian zone** Am n Fußgängerzone die.

**pediatric** [ˌpiːdɪ'ætrɪk] adj Kinder-, pädiatrisch.

**pediatrician** [ˌpiːdɪə'trɪʃn] n Kinderarzt der, -ärztin die.

**pediatrics** [ˌpiːdɪ'ætrɪks] n Kinderheilkunde die, Pädiatrie die.

**pedicure** ['pedɪˌkjʊə'] n Pediküre die.

**pedigree** ['pedɪgriː] adj mit einem Stammbaum ◇ n Stammbaum der.

**pedlar** Br, **peddler** Am ['pedlə'] n: (drug) ~ Drogenhändler der, -in die.

**pedophile** ['pedʒəfaɪl] n Pädophile der, die.

**pee** [piː] inf n - **1.** [act of urinating]: **to have a** ~ pinkeln; **to go for a** ~ pinkeln gehen - **2.** [urine] Urin die ◇ vi pinkeln.

**peek** [piːk] inf n kurzer Blick; **to have** OR **take a** ~ **at sthg** einen kurzen Blick auf etw (A) werfen ◇ vi gucken.

**peel** [piːl] n (U) Schale die ◇ vt schälen ◇ vi [walls, paint] abllblättern; [wallpaper] sich lösen; [skin, nose, back] sich schälen.
➥ **peel off** vt sep - **1.** [label] abllziehen - **2.** [sweater] abllstreifen.

**peeler** ['piːlə'] n [implement] Schälmesser das.

**peelings** ['piːlɪŋz] npl Schalen pl.

**peep** [piːp] n - **1.** [look] kurzer Blick; **to have** OR **take a** ~ **at sthg** einen kurzen Blick auf etw (A) werfen - **2.** inf [sound] Piep(s) der; **I haven't heard a** ~ **from them** ich habe keinen Pieps von ihnen gehört ◇ vi [look] gucken.
➥ **peep out** vi [person] herauslgucken.

**peephole** ['piːpˌhəʊl] n [in door] Spion der.

**peeping Tom** [ˌpiːpɪŋ'tɒm] n Spanner der.

**peep show** n Peepshow die.

**peer** [pɪə'] n - **1.** [noble] Angehöriger des hohen Adels in Großbritannien - **2.** [equal]: **he is respected by his** ~**s** er ist sehr anerkannt bei seinesgleichen ◇ vi angestrengt schauen.

**peerage** ['pɪərɪdʒ] n - **1.** [rank]: **to give sb a** ~ jn in den Adelsstand erheben - **2.** [group]: **the** ~ Angehörige des hohen Adels in Großbritannien.

**peer group** n Peergroup die.

**peer pressure** n Gruppenzwang der.

**peeved** [piːvd] adj inf eingeschnappt.

**peevish** ['piːvɪʃ] adj [remark, mood] gereizt; [person - as characteristic] reizbar; [ - temporarily] gereizt.

**peg** [peg] (pt & pp **-ged;** cont **-ging**) n - **1.** [hook] Haken der - **2.** [for washing line] (Wäsche)klammer die - **3.** [for tent] Hering der ◇ vt [price] festlsetzen.
➥ **peg out** vt sep [washing] (draußen) auflhängen ◇ vi Br inf [die] den Löffel abllgeben.

**PEI** n abk für Prince Edward Island, in Postanschrift verwendet.

**pejorative** [pɪ'dʒɒrətɪv] adj abwertend, pejorativ.

**pekinese** [ˌpiːkə'niːz] (pl inv OR **-s**) n Pekinese der.

**Peking** [piː'kɪŋ] n Peking nt.

**pekingese** [ˌpiːkɪŋ'iːz] (pl inv OR **-s**) n = pekinese.

**pelican** ['pelɪkən] (pl inv OR **-s**) n Pelikan der.

**pelican crossing** n Br Ampelübergang der.

**pellet** ['pelɪt] n - **1.** [of mud, food, paper] Kügelchen das - **2.** [for gun] Schrotkugel die.

**pell-mell** [ˌpel'mel] adv durcheinander.

**pelmet** ['pelmɪt] n Br Blende die; [of cloth] Schabracke die.

**Peloponnese** [ˌpeləpə'niːz] npl: **the** ~ der Peloponnes.

**pelt** [pelt] n - **1.** [of sheep, hare etc] Fell das; [of bear] Pelz der - **2.** [speed]: **(at) full** ~ mit Karacho ◇ vt: **to** ~ **sb (with sthg)** jn (mit etw) bewerfen ◇ vi - **1.** [rain]: **it's** ~**ing (with rain)** es schüttet - **2.** [run very fast] rasen.

**pelves** ['pelviːz] pl ⊳ **pelvis.**

**pelvic** ['pelvɪk] adj Becken-.

**pelvis** ['pelvɪs] (pl **-vises** OR **-ves**) n Becken das.

**pen** [pen] (pt & pp **-ned;** cont **-ning**) n - **1.** [for writing]: **(ballpoint)** ~ Kugelschreiber der; **(fountain)** ~ Füllfederhalter der; **(felt-tipped)** ~ Filzstift der - **2.** [enclosure] Pferch der ◇ vt - **1.** literary [letter] verfassen; [reply, note] schreiben - **2.** [enclose] einlpferchen.

P

**penal** ['pi:nl] *adj* LAW: ~ **system** Strafrecht *das;* ~ **reform** Strafrechtsreform *die.*

**penalize, -ise** ['pi:nəlaız] *vt* - **1.** [punish & SPORT] bestrafen - **2.** [put at a disadvantage] benachteiligen.

**penalty** ['penltı] (*pl* **-ies**) *n* - **1.** [punishment] Strafe *die;* **to pay the ~ (for sthg)** *fig* (für etw) büßen müssen - **2.** [fine] Geldstrafe *die* - **3.** SPORT: ~ **(kick)** FTBL Strafstoß *der*, Elfmeter *der;* RUGBY Straftritt *der.*

**penalty area, penalty box** *n* Br FTBL Strafraum *der.*

**penalty clause** *n* Strafklausel *die.*

**penalty goal** *n* RUGBY Straftor *das.*

**penalty kick** *n* ▷ **penalty.**

**penance** ['penəns] *n* (*U*) - **1.** RELIG Buße *die* - **2.** *fig* [punishment] Strafe *die.*

**pen-and-ink drawing** *n* Federzeichnung *die.*

**pence** [pens] Br *pl* ▷ **penny.**

**penchant** [Br pãʃã, Am 'pentʃənt] *n:* **to have a ~ for sthg** eine Schwäche OR Vorliebe für etw haben.

**pencil** ['pensl] (Br *pt* & *pp* **-led**; *cont* **-ling**, Am *pt* & *pp* **-ed**; *cont* **-ing**) *n* Bleistift *der;* **in ~** mit Bleistift.
▶ **pencil in** *vt sep* [person] vorlmerken; [date] vorläufig festlhalten.

**pencil case** *n* Federmäppchen *das.*

**pencil sharpener** [-ˌʃɑ:pnə<sup>r</sup>] *n* (Bleistift)spitzer *der.*

**pendant** ['pendənt] *n* [jewel on chain] Anhänger *der.*

**pending** ['pendıŋ] *fml adj:* **to be ~** [about to happen] bevorlstehen; LAW [waiting to be dealt with] noch anhängig sein ◇ *prep* bis zu; **~ further inquiries** bis weitere Untersuchungen durchgeführt worden sind.

**pending tray** *n* Br Ablage für noch unerledigte Dinge.

**pendulum** ['pendjʊləm] (*pl* **-s**) *n* Pendel *das.*

**penetrate** ['penıtreıt] *vt* - **1.** [get into - subj: person] vorldringen in (+ A); [ - subj: wind, rain, light] durchldringen; [ - subj: sharp object, bullet] einldringen in (+ A) - **2.** [infiltrate] sich einlschleusen in (+ A) ◇ *vi inf* [be understood]: **it didn't ~** er/sie hat es nicht kapiert.

**penetrating** ['penıtreıtıŋ] *adj* durchdringend.

**penetration** [ˌpenıˈtreıʃn] *n* - **1.** [in sex] Penetration *die* - **2.** *fml* [insight] Scharfsinn *der.*

**pen friend** *n* Brieffreund *der*, -in *die.*

**penguin** ['peŋgwın] *n* Pinguin *der.*

**penicillin** [ˌpenıˈsılın] *n* Penizillin *das.*

**peninsula** [pəˈnınsjʊlə] (*pl* **-s**) *n* Halbinsel *die.*

**penis** ['pi:nıs] (*pl* **penises** ['pi:nısızl]) *n* Penis *der.*

**penitent** ['penıtənt] *adj fml* reuig.

**penitentiary** [ˌpenıˈtenʃərı] (*pl* **-ies**) *n* Am Gefängnis *das.*

**penknife** ['pennaıf] (*pl* **-knives** [-naıvz]) *n* Taschenmesser *das.*

**pen name** *n* Pseudonym *das.*

**pennant** ['penənt] *n* Wimpel *der.*

**penniless** ['penılıs] *adj* mittellos.

**Pennines** ['penaınz] *npl:* **the ~** Gebirgszug in Nordengland.

**penny** ['penı] (*pl senses 1 & 2* **-ies**; *pl sense 3* **pence**) *n* - **1.** Br [coin] Penny *der* - **2.** Am [coin] Centstück *das* - **3.** Br [value]: **30 pence** 30 Pence - **4.** *phr:* **a ~ for your thoughts** was denkst du gerade?; **the ~ dropped** Br *inf* der Groschen ist gefallen; **to spend a ~** Br *inf* mal eben verschwinden; **two** OR **ten a ~** Br *inf* wie Sand am Meer.

**penny-pinching** [-ˌpıntʃıŋ] *adj* knaus(e)rig ◇ *n* Knauserei *die.*

**pen pal** *n inf* Brieffreund *der*, -in *die.*

**pension** ['penʃn] *n* - **1.** Rente *die* - **2.** [disability pension] Erwerbsunfähigkeitsrente *die.*
▶ **pension off** *vt sep* vorzeitig pensionieren.

**pensionable** ['penʃənəbl] *adj:* **of ~ age** im Rentenalter.

**pension book** *n* Br Rentenausweis *der.*

**pensioner** ['penʃənə<sup>r</sup>] *n* Br: **(old-age) ~** Rentner *der*, -in *die.*

**pension fund** *n* Rentenfonds *der.*

**pension plan, pension scheme** *n* Rentenversicherung *die.*

**pensive** ['pensıv] *adj* nachdenklich.

**pentagon** ['pentəgən] *n* Fünfeck *das.*
▶ **Pentagon** *n* Am: **the Pentagon** das Pentagon.

> **PENTAGON**
>
> Das Pentagon in Washington D.C. ist ein riesiges fünfeckiges Gebäude, das das Verteidigungsministerium (Defense Department) der USA beherbergt. Im weiteren Sinne bezeichnet „Pentagon" auch das US-Militär allgemein.

**pentathlon** [pen'tæθlən] (*pl* **-s**) *n* Fünfkampf *der.*

**Pentecost** ['pentıkɒst] *n* - **1.** [Christian] Pfingsten *das* - **2.** [Jewish] Ernte(dank)fest *das.*

**penthouse** ['penthaʊs, *pl* **-hauzız**] *n* Penthouse *das.*

**pent up** ['pent-] *adj* [emotions] unterdrückt; [energy] angestaut.

**penultimate** [pe'nʌltɪmət] *adj* vorletzte, -r, -s.

**penury** ['penjʊrɪ] *n fml* Armut *die.*

**peony** ['pi:ənɪ] (*pl* -ies) *n* Pfingstrose *die.*

**people** ['pi:pl] *n* [nation, race] Volk *das* ◇ *npl* - 1. [persons] Menschen *pl*, Leute *pl;* a lot of ~ viele Menschen *or* Leute; five ~ fünf Personen *or* Leute - 2. [in indefinite uses] Leute *die;* ~ say that ... man sagt *or* es heißt, dass ... - 3. [inhabitants - of country] Bevölkerung *die;* [ - of town, city] Einwohner *pl* - 4. POL: the ~ das Volk ◇ *vt:* to be ~d by *or* with bevölkert sein von.

**pep** [pep] (*pt* & *pp* -ped; *cont* -ping) *n inf* Schwung *der.*

➤ **pep up** *vt sep inf* - 1. [person] munter machen - 2. [party, event] in Schwung bringen.

**PEP** [pep] (*abbr of* personal equity plan) *n* britischer Sparvertrag mit Steuervorteilen.

**pepper** ['pepə'] *n* - 1. [spice] Pfeffer *der;* black/ white ~ schwarzer/weißer Pfeffer - 2. [vegetable] Paprika *der;* red/green ~ roter/ grüner Paprika.

**pepperbox** *n Am* = pepper pot.

**peppercorn** ['pepəkɔ:n] *n* Pfefferkorn *das.*

**peppered** ['pepəd] *adj:* to be ~ with mistakes/ holes voller Fehler/Löcher sein.

**pepper mill** *n* Pfeffermühle *die.*

**peppermint** ['pepəmɪnt] *n* - 1. [sweet] Pfefferminz(bonbon) *das* - 2. [herb] Pfefferminze *die.*

**pepper pot** *Br,* **pepperbox** *Am* ['pepəbɒks] *n* Pfefferstreuer *der.*

**peppery** ['pepərɪ] *adj* [food] nach Pfeffer schmeckend.

**pep talk** *n inf:* to give sb a ~ jm ein paar aufmunternde Worte sagen.

**peptic ulcer** [,peptɪk-] *n* Magengeschwür *das.*

**per** [pɜ:'] *prep* [expressing rate, ratio] pro; as ~ instructions gemäß Anweisung.

**per annum** [pər'ænəm] *adv* pro Jahr.

**P-E ratio** (*abbr of* price-earnings ratio) *n* Preis-Einkommen-Verhältnis *das.*

**per capita** [pə'kæpɪtə] *adv* pro Kopf.

**perceive** [pə'si:v] *vt* - 1. [see] wahr|nehmen - 2. [notice, realize] erkennen - 3. [conceive, consider]: to ~ sb/sthg as jn/etw betrachten als.

**percent** [pə'sent] *n* Prozent *das.*

**percentage** [pə'sentɪdʒ] *n* Prozentsatz *der.*

**perceptible** [pə'septəbl] *adj* [sound] wahr-nehmbar; [change, difference, improvement] spür-bar.

**perception** [pə'sepʃn] *n* - 1. [of colour, sound, time] Wahrnehmung *die* - 2. [insight] Auffas-sungsvermögen *das* - 3. [opinion] Einschät-zung *die.*

**perceptive** [pə'septɪv] *adj* scharfsinnig.

**perceptively** [pə'septɪvlɪ] *adv* scharfsinnig.

**perch** [pɜ:tʃ] (*pl sense 3 only inv or* -es) *n* - 1. [for bird] (Sitz)stange *die* - 2. [high position] Sitz-platz *der* hoch oben - 3. [fish] Flussbarsch *der* ◇ *vi* - 1. [bird]: to ~ (on sthg) sich (auf etw (*D*)) nieder|lassen - 2. [person]: to ~ on (the edge of) a desk sich auf die Kante eines Schreibti-sches setzen.

**percolate** ['pɜ:kəleɪt] *vi* - 1. [coffee] durch|laufen - 2. [water, news] durch|sickern.

**percolator** ['pɜ:kəleɪtə'] *n* Kaffeemaschine *die.*

**percussion** [pə'kʌʃn] *n* MUS: the ~ (section) das Schlagzeug; ~ instrument Schlaginstru-ment *das.*

**percussionist** [pə'kʌʃənɪst] *n* Schlagzeuger *der,* -in *die.*

**peremptory** [pə'remptərɪ] *adj* gebieterisch.

**perennial** [pə'renɪəl] *adj* - 1. [continual] immer wieder auftretend - 2. BOT perennierend ◇ *n* BOT perennierende Pflanze.

**perfect** [*adj* & *n* 'pɜ:fɪkt, *vb* pə'fekt] *adj* - 1. [ideal, faultless] perfekt, vollkommen; that would be ~! das wäre ideal! - 2. [for emphasis - nuisance] ausgesprochen; ~ strangers wildfremde Leute ◇ *n* GRAMM: ~ (tense) Perfekt *das* ◇ *vt* vervollkommnen, perfektionieren.

**perfection** [pə'fekʃn] *n* - 1. [making perfect] Per-fektionierung *die* - 2. [faultlessness] Perfektion *die;* to do sthg to ~ etw perfekt machen.

**perfectionist** [pə'fekʃənɪst] *n* Perfektionist *der,* -in *die.*

**perfectly** ['pɜ:fɪktlɪ] *adv* - 1. [for emphasis - hon-est, frank, ridiculous] absolut; you know ~ well ... du weißt ganz genau ... - 2. [to perfection] exakt, genau; to speak English ~ perfekt Englisch sprechen.

**perforate** ['pɜ:fəreɪt] *vt* [paper - with one hole] lo-chen; [ - with row of holes] perforieren; [lung, ear-drum] durchstechen.

**perform** [pə'fɔ:m] *vt* - 1. [carry out - operation] durch|führen; [ - miracle] vollbringen; [ - service, function] erfüllen - 2. [play, concert] auf|führen; [part] spielen; [dance] vor|tanzen ◇ *vi* - 1. [car, machine] laufen; [in exam] ab|schneiden; he is ~ing well [employee] er leistet gute Arbeit; [sportsman] er ist in Hochform - 2. [actor, singer] auf|treten.

**performance** [pə'fɔ:məns] *n* - 1. [of task, duty] Erfüllung *die;* [of operation] Durchführung *die* - 2. [at cinema] Vorstellung *die;* [of play, concert] Aufführung *die* - 3. [by actor, singer, of car, engine] Leistung *die.*

**performance car** *n* leistungsstarkes Au-to.

**performer** [pə'fɔ:mə'] *n* Künstler *der,* -in *die.*

**performing arts** [pə‚fɔːmɪŋ-] npl: **the ~** die darstellenden Künste.

**perfume** ['pɜːfjuːm] n - **1.** [for woman] Parfüm das - **2.** [pleasant smell] Duft der.

**perfumed** [Br 'pɜːfjuːmd, Am pər'fjuːmd] adj [air, skin] parfümiert; [flowers] duftend.

**perfunctory** [pə'fʌŋktərɪ] adj [search, read] oberflächlich; [kiss, glance] flüchtig; [explanation, apology] der Form halber.

**perhaps** [pə'hæps] adv vielleicht; **~ so** (das) mag sein; **~ not** vielleicht nicht.

**peril** ['perɪl] n (U) literary Gefahr die; **at one's ~** auf eigene Gefahr.

**perilous** ['perələs] adj literary gefährlich.

**perilously** ['perələslɪ] adv gefährlich.

**perimeter** [pə'rɪmɪtəʳ] n Begrenzung die; **around the ~ of the field** um das Feld herum; **~ fence** Umzäunung die.

**period** ['pɪərɪəd] n - **1.** [of time] Zeit die; **over a ~ of several years** über einen Zeitraum von mehreren Jahren - **2.** HIST Zeitalter das, Epoche die; **the Elizabethan ~** die elisabethanische Zeit - **3.** SCH (Schul)stunde die; **free ~** Freistunde die - **4.** [menstruation] Periode die - **5.** Am [full stop] Punkt der <> comp [dress, furniture] zeitgenössisch.

**periodic** [‚pɪərɪ'ɒdɪk] adj [events] regelmäßig wiederkehrend; [visits] regelmäßig.

**periodical** [‚pɪərɪ'ɒdɪkl] adj = **periodic** <> n [magazine] Zeitschrift die.

**periodic table** n Periodensystem das.

**period pains** npl Regelschmerzen pl.

**period piece** n zeitgenössisches Stück.

**peripatetic** [‚perɪpə'tetɪk] adj umherreisend.

**peripheral** [pə'rɪfərəl] adj - **1.** [of little importance] nebensächlich - **2.** [vision] peripher; [region, group] Rand- <> n COMPUT Peripheriegerät das.

**periphery** [pə'rɪfərɪ] (pl -ies) n - **1.** [edge - of vision] Peripherie die; [ - of area, crowd] Rand der - **2.** [unimportant area] Randgebiet das.

**periscope** ['perɪskəʊp] n Periskop das.

**perish** ['perɪʃ] vi - **1.** [die] umlkommen - **2.** [food] verderben; [rubber] verschleißen.

**perishable** ['perɪʃəbl] adj verderblich.
◆ **perishables** npl verderbliche Waren pl.

**perishing** ['perɪʃɪŋ] adj Br inf - **1.** [cold] eiskalt, saukalt - **2.** [for emphasis] verflixt.

**peritonitis** [‚perɪtə'naɪtɪs] n (U) Bauchfellentzündung die.

**perjure** ['pɜːdʒəʳ] vt LAW: **to ~ o.s.** einen Meineid leisten.

**perjury** ['pɜːdʒərɪ] n (U) LAW Meineid der.

**perk** [pɜːk] n inf Vergünstigung die.

◆ **perk up** vi [become more energetic] munter werden; [become more cheerful] auflleben.

**perky** ['pɜːkɪ] (compar -ier; superl -iest) adj inf munter.

**perm** [pɜːm] n Dauerwelle die <> vt: **to have one's hair ~ed** sich (D) eine Dauerwelle machen lassen.

**permanence** ['pɜːmənəns] n Dauerhaftigkeit die.

**permanent** ['pɜːmənənt] adj - **1.** [not temporary] dauerhaft; [job] fest - **2.** [continuous] ständig; [constant] konstant <> n Am [perm] Dauerwelle die.

**permanently** ['pɜːmənəntlɪ] adv - **1.** [forever] auf Dauer - **2.** [constantly] ständig.

**permeable** ['pɜːmɪəbl] adj durchlässig.

**permeate** ['pɜːmɪeɪt] vt lit & fig durchldringen.

**permissible** [pə'mɪsəbl] adj erlaubt, zulässig.

**permission** [pə'mɪʃn] n (U) Erlaubnis die; [official] Genehmigung die.

**permissive** [pə'mɪsɪv] adj nachgiebig; **~ society** permissive Gesellschaft.

**permissiveness** [pə'mɪsɪvnɪs] n Nachgiebigkeit die.

**permit** [vb pə'mɪt, n 'pɜːmɪt] (pt & pp -ted; cont -ting) vt - **1.** [allow] erlauben, gestatten; **to ~ sb to do sthg** jm erlauben, etw zu tun; **to ~ sb sthg** jm etw gestatten - **2.** [enable] zullassen <> vi [allow] zullassen; **weather ~ting** wenn es das Wetter zulässt <> n Genehmigung die.

**permutation** [‚pɜːmjuː'teɪʃn] n Permutation die.

**pernicious** [pə'nɪʃəs] adj fml [harmful] schädlich.

**pernickety** [pə'nɪkətɪ] adj inf [fussy] pingelig.

**peroxide** [pə'rɒksaɪd] n Peroxid das.

**peroxide blonde** n Wasserstoffblondine die.

**perpendicular** [‚pɜːpən'dɪkjʊləʳ] adj: **~ (to)** senkrecht (zu) <> n MATH Senkrechte die.

**perpetrate** ['pɜːpɪtreɪt] vt fml [crime, murder] begehen.

**perpetration** [‚pɜːpɪ'treɪʃn] n fml Begehen das.

**perpetrator** ['pɜːpɪtreɪtəʳ] n fml Täter der, -in die.

**perpetual** [pə'petʃʊəl] adj - **1.** pej [continuous] ständig - **2.** [everlasting] ewig.

**perpetually** [pə'petʃʊəlɪ] adv - **1.** pej [continuously] ständig - **2.** [forever] ewig.

**perpetual motion** n (U) unaufhörliche Bewegung.

**perpetuate** [pə'petʃʊeɪt] *vt* [myth] aufrechtlerhalten; [practice] beilbehalten.

**perpetuation** [pə,petʃʊ'eɪʃn] *n* [of myth] Aufrechterhaltung *die;* [of practice] Beibehaltung *die.*

**perpetuity** [,pɜːpɪ'tjuːətɪ] *n:* **in ~** *fml* auf ewig.

**perplex** [pə'pleks] *vt* verblüffen.

**perplexed** [pə'plekst] *adj* verblüfft, perplex.

**perplexing** [pə'pleksɪŋ] *adj* verblüffend.

**perplexity** [pə'pleksətɪ] *n* Verblüffung *die.*

**perquisite** ['pɜːkwɪzɪt] *n* *fml* Vergünstigung *die.*

**per se** [pɜː'seɪ] *adv* an sich.

**persecute** ['pɜːsɪkjuːt] *vt* verfolgen.

**persecution** [,pɜːsɪ'kjuːʃn] *n* Verfolgung *die.*

**persecutor** ['pɜːsɪkjuːtə'] *n* Verfolger *der, -in die.*

**perseverance** [,pɜːsɪ'vɪərəns] *n* Beharrlichkeit *die.*

**persevere** [,pɜːsɪ'vɪə'] *vi* - **1.** [with difficulty] durchlhalten; **to ~ with sthg** [studies, job] mit etw weiterlmachen; [search] etw nicht auflgeben - **2.** [with determination]: **to ~ in doing sthg** darauf beharren, etw zu tun.

**Persia** ['pɜːʃə] *n* Persien *nt.*

**Persian** ['pɜːʃn] *adj* persisch ◇ *n* - **1.** [person] Perser *der, -in die* - **2.** [language] Persisch(e) *das.*

**Persian cat** *n* Perserkatze *die.*

**Persian Gulf** *n:* **the ~** der Persische Golf.

**persist** [pə'sɪst] *vi* - **1.** [problem, situation, rain] anlhalten, fortldauern - **2.** [person]: **to ~ in doing sthg** etw unaufhörlich tun.

**persistence** [pə'sɪstəns] *n* - **1.** [continuation] Fortdauer *die,* Anhalten *das* - **2.** [determination] Beharrlichkeit *die.*

**persistent** [pə'sɪstənt] *adj* - **1.** [constant] fortdauernd, anhaltend - **2.** [determined] hartnäckig.

**persistently** [pə'sɪstəntlɪ] *adv* - **1.** [constantly] fortdauernd - **2.** [determinedly] hartnäckig.

**persnickety** [pə'snɪkɪtɪ] *adj Am* pingelig.

**person** ['pɜːsn] (*pl* people *OR* persons *fml*) *n* - **1.** [man or woman] Mensch *der;* **in ~** persönlich; **in the ~ of** in Gestalt von - **2.** [body]: **about my ~** bei mir - **3.** GRAMM Person *die.*

**persona** [pə'səʊnə] (*pl* -s *OR* -nae) *n* Rolle *die.*

**personable** ['pɜːsnəbl] *adj* von angenehmem Äußeren.

**personae** [pə'səʊniː] *pl* ⊳ persona.

**personage** ['pɜːsənɪdʒ] *n* *fml* Persönlichkeit *die.*

**personal** ['pɜːsənl] *adj* - **1.** [gen] persönlich - **2.** [letter, message] privat ◇ *n Am* [advert] Privatanzeige *die.*

**personal account** *n* [at bank] Privatkonto *das.*

**personal allowance** *n* FIN persönlicher Steuerfreibetrag.

**personal assistant** *n* persönlicher Assistent, persönliche Assistentin.

**personal call** *n* Privatgespräch *das.*

**personal column** *n* Privatanzeigen *pl.*

**personal computer** *n* Personalcomputer *der.*

**personal hygiene** *n* (U) Körperpflege *die.*

**personality** [,pɜːsə'nælətɪ] (*pl* -ies) *n* Persönlichkeit *die.*

**personalize, -ise** ['pɜːsənəlaɪz] *vt* - **1.** [stationery, clothes] mit Namen versehen - **2.** *pej* [issue, argument] in etw (D) persönlich werden.

**personalized, -ised** ['pɜːsənəlaɪzd] *adj* - **1.** [stationery, clothes] mit Namen versehen - **2.** [for one person] individuell.

**personally** ['pɜːsnəlɪ] *adv* persönlich.

**personal organizer, -iser** *n* Terminplaner *der.*

**personal pension plan** *n* private Altersversorgung.

**personal pronoun** *n* Personalpronomen *das.*

**personal property** *n* (U) LAW Privateigentum *das.*

**personal stereo** *n* Walkman® *der.*

**personify** [pə'sɒnɪfaɪ] (*pt & pp* -ied) *vt* [represent] verkörpern; **she's evil personified** sie ist das Böse in Person.

**personnel** [,pɜːsə'nel] *n* (U) [department] Personalabteilung *die* ◇ *npl* [staff] Personal *das.*

**personnel department** *n* Personalabteilung *die.*

**perspective** [pə'spektɪv] *n* Perspektive *die;* **to get sthg in ~** *fig* etw sachlich betrachten.

**Perspex**® ['pɜːspeks] *n Br* Plexiglas® *das.*

**perspicacious** [,pɜːspɪ'keɪʃəs] *adj fml* scharfsinnig.

**perspiration** [,pɜːspə'reɪʃn] *n* - **1.** [sweat] Schweiß *der* - **2.** [sweating] Schwitzen *das.*

**perspire** [pə'spaɪə'] *vi* schwitzen.

**persuade** [pə'sweɪd] *vt* [convince] überzeugen; **to ~ sb to do sthg** jn überreden, etw zu tun; **to ~ sb that ...** jn davon überzeugen, dass ...; **to ~ sb of sthg** jn von etw überzeugen.

**persuasion** [pə'sweɪʒn] *n* - **1.** (U) [act of persuading] Überredung *die* - **2.** [belief] Überzeugung *die.*

**persuasive** [pə'sweɪsɪv] *adj* überzeugend.

**persuasively** [pə'sweɪsɪvlɪ] *adv* überzeugend.

**pert** [pɜːt] *adj* kess, keck.

P

**pertain** [pəˈteɪn] *vi fml:* **to ~ to** gehören zu.

**pertinence** [ˈpɜːtɪnəns] *n* Relevanz *die.*

**pertinent** [ˈpɜːtɪnənt] *adj* relevant.

**perturb** [pəˈtɜːb] *vt fml* beunruhigen.

**perturbed** [pəˈtɜːbd] *adj fml* beunruhigt.

**Peru** [pəˈruː] *n* Peru *nt.*

**perusal** [pəˈruːzl] *n* [reading - thorough] Durchlesen *das;* [ - quick] Überfliegen *das;* **to give sthg a brief ~** etw kurz überfliegen.

**peruse** [pəˈruːz] *vt* [read - thoroughly] sorgfältig durchllesen; [ - quickly] überfliegen.

**Peruvian** [pəˈruːvɪən] *adj* peruanisch ⬦ *n* Peruaner *der,* -in *die.*

**pervade** [pəˈveɪd] *vt* durchdringen.

**pervasive** [pəˈveɪsɪv] *adj* durchdringend.

**perverse** [pəˈvɜːs] *adj* pervers.

**perversely** [pəˈvɜːslɪ] *adv* pervers.

**perversion** [*Br* pəˈvɜːʃn, *Am* pərˈvɜːrʒn] *n* - **1.** [sexual deviation] Perversion *die* - **2.** *(U)* [distortion - of truth] Verzerrung *die.*

**perversity** [pəˈvɜːsətɪ] *n (U)* [contrariness] Böswilligkeit *die.*

**pervert** [*n* ˈpɜːvɜːt, *vb* pəˈvɜːt] *n* Perverse *der, die* ⬦ *vt* - **1.** [distort - truth] verzerren; [ - course of justice] behindern - **2.** [corrupt morally - person, mind] verderben.

**perverted** [pəˈvɜːtɪd] *adj* - **1.** [sexually] pervers - **2.** [distorted] verzerrt.

**peseta** [pəˈseɪtə] *n* Peseta *die.*

**peso** [ˈpeɪsəʊ] *(pl* -s) *n* Peso *der.*

**pessary** [ˈpesərɪ] *(pl* -ies) *n* [device] Pessar *das;* [substance] Vaginalzäpfchen *das.*

**pessimism** [ˈpesɪmɪzm] *n* Pessimismus *der.*

**pessimist** [ˈpesɪmɪst] *n* Pessimist *der,* -in *die.*

**pessimistic** [ˌpesɪˈmɪstɪk] *adj* pessimistisch.

**pest** [pest] *n* - **1.** [in garden, on farm] Schädling *der* - **2.** *inf* [annoying person, thing] Pest *die,* Plage *die.*

**pester** [ˈpestəʳ] *vt* belästigen; **to ~ sb** jm keine Ruhe lassen.

**pesticide** [ˈpestɪsaɪd] *n* Schädlingsbekämpfungsmittel *das.*

**pestle** [ˈpesl] *n* Stößel *der.*

**pet** [pet] *(pt & pp* -**ted;** *cont* -**ting)** *adj* [favourite] Lieblings- ⬦ *n* - **1.** [animal] Haustier *das* - **2.** [favourite person] Liebling *der* ⬦ *vt* [stroke] streicheln ⬦ *vi* [sexually] Petting machen.

**petal** [ˈpetl] *n* Blütenblatt *das.*

**peter** [ˈpiːtəʳ] ⬥ **peter out** *vi* [supply] versiegen; [interest] schwinden; [path] auslaufen.

**petit bourgeois** [pəˌtiːˈbʊəʒwɑː] *adj* kleinbürgerlich.

**petite** [pəˈtiːt] *adj* zierlich.

**petit four** [ˌpetiˈfɔːʳ] *(pl* **petits fours** [ˌpetiˈfɔːz]) *n* Petit Four *das.*

**petition** [pɪˈtɪʃn] *n* - **1.** [supporting campaign] Petition *die* - **2.** LAW: **~ for divorce** Scheidungsantrag *der* ⬦ *vt* [lobby]: **to ~ sb** eine Petition bei jm einlreichen ⬦ *vi* - **1.** [campaign]: **to ~ for/ against sthg** eine Petition für/gegen etw einlreichen - **2.** LAW: **to ~ for divorce** die Scheidung einlreichen.

**petitioner** [pɪˈtɪʃənəʳ] *n* - **1.** LAW Kläger *der,* -in *die* - **2.** [on petition] Bittsteller *der,* -in *die.*

**pet name** *n* Kosename *der.*

**petrified** [ˈpetrɪfaɪd] *adj* [terrified] verängstigt, gelähmt vor Angst.

**petrify** [ˈpetrɪfaɪ] *(pt & pp* -**ied)** *vt* [terrify] verängstigen.

**petrochemical** [ˌpetrəʊˈkemɪkl] *adj* petrochemisch.

**petrodollar** [ˈpetrəʊˌdɒləʳ] *n* FIN Petrodollar *der.*

**petrol** [ˈpetrəl] *n Br* Benzin *das*

**petrolatum** [ˌpetrəˈleɪtəm] *n Am* Vaseline *die.*

**petrol bomb** *n Br* Benzinbombe *die.*

**petrol can** *n Br* Benzinkanister *der.*

**petrol cap** *n* Tankverschluss *der.*

**petroleum** [pɪˈtrəʊlɪəm] *n* Petroleum *das.*

**petroleum jelly** *n Br* Vaseline *die.*

**petrol pump** *n Br* Zapfsäule *die.*

**petrol pump attendant** *n Br* Tankwart *der.*

**petrol station** *n Br* Tankstelle *die.*

**petrol tank** *n Br* Benzintank *der.*

**pet shop** *n* Tierhandlung *die.*

**petticoat** [ˈpetɪkəʊt] *n* Unterrock *der.*

**pettiness** [ˈpetɪnɪs] *n* [small-mindedness] Kleinlichkeit *die.*

**petty** [ˈpetɪ] *(compar* -**ier;** *superl* -**iest)** *adj* - **1.** [small-minded] kleinlich - **2.** [trivial] geringfügig.

**petty cash** *n* Portokasse *die.*

**petty officer** *n* Fähnrich *der* zur See.

**petulant** [ˈpetjʊlənt] *adj* mürrisch; [child] bockig.

**petunia** [pɪˈtjuːnɪə] *n* Petunie *die.*

**pew** [pjuː] *n* Kirchenbank *die.*

**pewter** [ˈpjuːtəʳ] *n* Zinn *das.*

**PG** *(abbr of* **parental guidance)** *britische Einstufung von Kinofilmen als bedingt jugendfrei.*

**PGA** *(abbr of* **Professional Golfers' Association)** *n* PGA *die.*

**pH** *(abbr of* **potential of hydrogen)** *n* CHEM pH-Wert *der.*

**PHA** (*abbr of* **Public Housing Administration**) *n* US-*Baugesellschaft für sozialen Wohnungsbau.*

**phalli** ['fælaɪ] *pl* ⊳ **phallus.**

**phallic** ['fælɪk] *adj* phallisch; ~ **symbol** Phallussymbol *das.*

**phallus** ['fæləs] (*pl* -**es** OR **phalli** *n* Phallus *der.*

**phantom** ['fæntəm] *adj* [imaginary] Phantom- ⬦ *n* [ghost] Phantom *das*, Geist *der.*

**phantom pregnancy** *n* Scheinschwangerschaft *die.*

**pharaoh** ['feərəʊ] *n* Pharao *der.*

**pharmaceutical** [ˌfɑːmə'sjuːtɪkl] *adj* pharmazeutisch; ~ **industry** Pharmaindustrie *die.*
➥ **pharmaceuticals** *npl* Arzneimittel *pl.*

**pharmacist** ['fɑːməsɪst] *n* [in shop] Apotheker *der*, -in *die.*

**pharmacology** [ˌfɑːmə'kɒlədʒɪ] *n* Pharmakologie *die.*

**pharmacy** ['fɑːməsɪ] (*pl* -**ies**) *n* [shop] Apotheke *die.*

**phase** [feɪz] *n* Phase *die* ⬦ *vt* [introduce gradually] schrittweise durchlführen.
➥ **phase in** *vt sep* schrittweise OR allmählich einlführen.
➥ **phase out** *vt sep* ausllaufen lassen.

**PhD** (*abbr of* **Doctor of Philosophy**) *n* Dr. Phil.

**pheasant** ['feznt] (*pl inv* OR -**s**) *n* Fasan *der.*

**phenomena** [fɪ'nɒmɪnə] *pl* ⊳ **phenomenon.**

**phenomenal** [fɪ'nɒmɪnl] *adj* [remarkable] phänomenal.

**phenomenon** [fɪ'nɒmɪnən] (*pl* -**mena**) *n* Phänomen *das.*

**phew** [fjuː] *excl* puh!

**phial** ['faɪəl] *n* Fläschchen *das.*

**philanderer** [fɪ'lændərəʳ] *n* Schürzenjäger *der.*

**philanthropic** [ˌfɪlən'θrɒpɪk] *adj* menschenfreundlich.

**philanthropist** [fɪ'lænθrəpɪst] *n* Philanthrop *der*, Menschenfreund *der.*

**philately** [fɪ'lætəlɪ] *n* Briefmarkenkunde *die.*

**philharmonic** [ˌfɪlɑː'mɒnɪk] *adj* philharmonisch.

**Philippine** ['fɪlɪpiːn] *adj* philippinisch.
➥ **Philippines** *npl:* the ~**s** die Philippinen *pl.*

**philistine** [Br 'fɪlɪstaɪn, Am 'fɪlɪstiːn] *n* Kulturbanause *der.*

**Phillips**® ['fɪlɪps] *comp:* ~ **screw** Kreuzschraube *die;* ~ **screwdriver** Kreuzschraubenzieher *der.*

**philosopher** [fɪ'lɒsəfəʳ] *n* Philosoph *der*, -in *die.*

**philosophical** [ˌfɪlə'sɒfɪkl] *adj* - **1.** [gen] philosophisch - **2.** [stoical] gelassen.

**philosophize, -ise** [fɪ'lɒsəfaɪz] *vi* philosophieren.

**philosophy** [fɪ'lɒsəfɪ] (*pl* -**ies**) *n* Philosophie *die.*

**phlegm** [flem] *n* (U) [mucus] Schleim *der.*

**phlegmatic** [fleg'mætɪk] *adj* phlegmatisch.

**phobia** ['fəʊbɪə] *n* Phobie *die;* **to have a ~ about** sthg eine Phobie vor etw (D) haben.

**phoenix** ['fiːnɪks] *n* Phönix *der.*

**phone** [fəʊn] *n* Telefon *das;* **to be on the** ~ [speaking] telefonieren, am Telefon sein; Br [connected to network] Telefon haben ⬦ *comp* Telefon- ⬦ *vt* & *vi* anlrufen.
➥ **phone back** *vt sep* & *vi* zurücklrufen.
➥ **phone up** *vt sep* & *vi* anlrufen.

**phone book** *n* Telefonbuch *das.*

**phone booth** *n* Br Telefonkabine *die.*

**phone box** *n* Br Telefonzelle *die.*

**phone call** *n* Telefonanruf *der*, Telefongespräch *das;* **to make a ~** telefonieren.

**phonecard** ['fəʊnkɑːd] *n* Telefonkarte *die.*

**phone-in** *n* Radio- *oder* TV-Programm, bei dem Zuhörer bzw. Zuschauer anrufen können, um ihre Meinung zu äußern.

**phone line** *n* Telefonleitung *die.*

**phone number** *n* Telefonnummer *die.*

**phone-tapping** [-ˌtæpɪŋ] *n* Anzapfen *das* von Telefonleitungen.

**phonetics** [fə'netɪks] *n* (U) Fonetik *die.*

**phoney** Br, **phony** Am ['fəʊnɪ] (*compar* -**ier**; *superl* -**iest**; *pl* -**ies**) *inf adj* - **1.** [false] falsch - **2.** [insincere] unaufrichtig ⬦ *n* [person] Hochstapler *der*, -in *die;* [doctor] Scharlatan *der.*

**phoney war** *n* Scheinkrieg *der.*

**phony** *adj* & *n* Am = **phoney.**

**phosphate** ['fɒsfeɪt] *n* CHEM Phosphat *das;* AGRIC Phosphatdünger *der.*

**phosphorus** ['fɒsfərəs] *n* Phosphor *der.*

**photo** ['fəʊtəʊ] *n* Foto *das;* **to take a ~ (of)** ein Foto machen (von).

**photo booth** *n* Fotoautomat *der.*

**photocall** ['fəʊtəʊkɔːl] *n* Fototermin *der.*

**photocopier** ['fəʊtəʊˌkɒpɪəʳ] *n* Fotokopierer *der.*

**photocopy** ['fəʊtəʊˌkɒpɪ] (*pl* -**ies**; *pt* & *pp* -**ied**) *n* Fotokopie *die* ⬦ *vt* fotokopieren.

**photo finish** *n* SPORT Fotofinish *das.*

**photogenic** [ˌfəʊtəʊ'dʒenɪk] *adj* fotogen.

**photograph** ['fəʊtəgrɑːf] *n* Fotografie *die*,

**P**

Aufnahme *die;* **to take a ~ (of sb/sthg)** jn/etw fotografieren ⟷ *vt* fotografieren.

**photographer** [fə'tɒɡrəfə'] *n* Fotograf *der,* -in *die.*

**photographic** [ˌfəʊtə'ɡræfɪk] *adj* Foto-.

**photographic memory** *n* fotografisches Gedächtnis.

**photography** [fə'tɒɡrəfɪ] *n (U)* Fotografie *die.*

**photojournalism** [ˌfəʊtəʊ'dʒɜːnəlɪzm] *n (U)* Bildjournalismus *der.*

**photon** ['fəʊtɒn] *n* Photon *das.*

**photosensitive** [ˌfəʊtəʊ'sensɪtɪv] *adj* lichtempfindlich.

**Photostat®** ['fəʊtəstæt] (*pt* & *pp* **-ted;** *cont* **-ting**) *n* Fotokopie *die.*
↪ **photostat** *vt* fotokopieren.

**photosynthesis** [ˌfəʊtəʊ'sɪnθəsɪs] *n* Fotosynthese *die.*

**phrasal verb** [ˌfreɪzl-] *n* Verb *das* mit Präposition.

**phrase** [freɪz] *n* - **1.** [part of sentence] Satzglied *das* - **2.** [expression] Wendung *die* ⟷ *vt* [express] ausldrücken.

**phrasebook** ['freɪzbʊk] *n* Sprachführer *der.*

**physical** ['fɪzɪkl] *adj* - **1.** [relating to the body] körperlich - **2.** [world, object] fassbar, materiell - **3.** [relating to physics] physikalisch ⟷ *n* ärztliche Untersuchung.

**physical chemistry** *n* physikalische Chemie.

**physical education** *n* Sportunterricht *der.*

**physical examination** *n* ärztliche Untersuchung.

**physically** ['fɪzɪklɪ] *adv* - **1.** [bodily] körperlich - **2.** [materially] materiell, physisch.

**physically handicapped** *adj* körperbehindert ⟷ *npl:* **the ~** die Körperbehinderten *pl.*

**physical science** *n (U) Physik, Chemie und Geologie.*

**physical training** *n* Sportunterricht *der.*

**physician** [fɪ'zɪʃn] *n* Arzt *der,* Ärztin *die.*

**physicist** ['fɪzɪsɪst] *n* Physiker *der,* -in *die.*

**physics** ['fɪzɪks] *n (U)* Physik *die.*

**physio** ['fɪzɪəʊ] (*pl* **-s**) *n inf* - **1.** [physiotherapist] Physiotherapeut *der,* -in *die* - **2.** [physiotherapy] Physiotherapie *die.*

**physiognomy** [ˌfɪzɪ'ɒnəmɪ] (*pl* **-ies**) *n fml* Physiognomie *die.*

**physiology** [ˌfɪzɪ'ɒlədʒɪ] *n* Physiologie *die.*

**physiotherapist** [ˌfɪzɪəʊ'θerəpɪst] *n* Physiotherapeut *der,* -in *die.*

**physiotherapy** [ˌfɪzɪəʊ'θerəpɪ] *n* Physiotherapie *die.*

**physique** [fɪ'ziːk] *n* Körperbau *der.*

**pianist** ['pɪənɪst] *n* Pianist *der,* -in *die.*

**piano** [pɪ'ænəʊ] (*pl* **-s**) *n* Klavier *das.*

**piccalilli** [ˌpɪkə'lɪlɪ] *n (U)* Piccalilli *pl.*

**piccolo** ['pɪkələʊ] (*pl* **-s**) *n* Pikkoloflöte *die.*

**pick** [pɪk] *n* - **1.** [tool] Spitzhacke *die* - **2.** [selection]: **take your ~** such dir eine/einen/eins aus - **3.** [best]: **the ~ of** das Beste von ⟷ *vt* - **1.** [choose] auslsuchen; [winner] auslwählen; [team] auflstellen; **to ~ one's way across/through sthg** vorsichtig seinen Weg über/durch etw *(A)* suchen - **2.** [fruit, flowers] pflücken - **3.** [remove] entfernen - **4.** [nose, teeth]: **to ~ one's nose** in der Nase bohren; **to ~ one's teeth** in seinen Zähnen stochern - **5.** [provoke]: **to ~ a fight (with sb)** (mit jm) einen Streit anlfangen - **6.** [lock] knacken ⟷ *vi* [choose] auslsuchen; **to ~ and choose** wählerisch sein.
↪ **pick at** *vt fus* [food] herumlstochern in (+ *D*).
↪ **pick on** *vt fus* auf dem Kieker haben.
↪ **pick out** *vt sep* - **1.** [recognize] erkennen - **2.** [select] auslsuchen; [winner] auslwählen; [team] auflstellen.
↪ **pick up** *vt sep* - **1.** [lift up] hochlheben; [after dropping] auflheben; **to ~ up the pieces** *fig* wieder neu anlfangen - **2.** [collect - gen] ablholen; [ - hitchhiker] mitlnehmen - **3.** [acquire - habit] anlnehmen; [ - tips] bekommen; [ - skill, language] lernen; **to ~ up speed** schneller werden - **4.** [subj: police]: **to ~ sb up for sthg** jn wegen etw *(D)* hochnehmen - **5.** *inf* [man, woman] anlmachen - **6.** RADIO & TELEC [signal] empfangen - **7.** [conversation, work] wieder auflnehmen ⟷ *vi* - **1.** [improve] sich verbessern - **2.** [resume] weiterlmachen.

**pickaxe** *Br,* **pickax** *Am* ['pɪkæks] *n* Spitzhacke *die.*

**picker** ['pɪkə'] *n* [of fruit] Pflücker *der,* -in *die.*

**picket** ['pɪkɪt] *n* [at place of work] Streikposten *der* ⟷ *vt* [place of work] Streikposten auflstellen vor (+ *D*).

**picketing** ['pɪkətɪŋ] *n* Aufstellen *das* von Streikposten.

**picket line** *n* Streikpostenkette *die.*

**pickings** ['pɪkɪŋz] *npl:* **easy/rich ~** leichte/reiche Ausbeute.

**pickle** ['pɪkl] *n* - **1.** *(U)* [food] Pickles *pl* - **2.** *inf* [difficult situation]: **to be in a ~** in der Tinte sitzen ⟷ *vt* einlegen.

**pickled** ['pɪkld] *adj* [food] eingelegt.

**pick-me-up** *n inf* Muntermacher *der.*

**pickpocket** ['pɪkˌpɒkɪt] *n* Taschendieb *der,* -in *die.*

**pick-up** *n* - **1.** [of record player] Tonabnehmer *der* - **2.** [truck] Pick-up *der.*

**pick-up truck** *n* Pick-up *der.*

**picky** ['pɪkɪ] (compar -ier; superl -iest) adj [about food] wählerisch; [finding fault] pingelig.

**picnic** ['pɪknɪk] (pt & pp -ked; cont -king) n Picknick das ◇ vi picknicken.

**pictorial** [pɪk'tɔ:rɪəl] adj [illustrated] bebildert.

**picture** ['pɪktʃə'] n - 1. [gen] Bild das; [painting] Gemälde das; as pretty as a ~ bildhübsch - 2. [movie] Film der - 3. [in one's mind] Vorstellung die - 4. [prospect] Aussicht die - 5. [epitome]: he was the ~ of misery er war ein Bild des Jammers - 6. phr: to get the ~ inf kapieren; to put sb in the ~ jn ins Bild setzen; to be in the ~ im Bilde sein ◇ vt - 1. [in mind] sich (D) vorlstellen - 2. [in photo] fotografieren; [in painting, drawing] darlstellen.

→ **pictures** npl Br: the ~s [cinema] das Kino.

**picture book** n Bilderbuch das.

**picture rail** n Bilderleiste die.

**picturesque** [,pɪktʃə'resk] adj malerisch.

**picture window** n Aussichtsfenster das.

**piddling** ['pɪdlɪŋ] adj inf pej lächerlich.

**pidgin** ['pɪdʒɪn] n Mischsprache die ◇ comp: ~ English Pidgin-Englisch.

**pie** [paɪ] n - 1. [sweet] Obstkuchen der - 2. [savoury] Pastete die; it's just ~ in the sky das sind nur Luftschlösser.

**piebald** ['paɪbɔ:ld] adj gescheckt.

**piece** [pi:s] n - 1. [gen] Stück das; [component] Teil das; a ~ of news eine Neuigkeit; a ~ of advice ein Rat; a ~ of furniture ein Möbelstück; a fifty pence ~ ein Fünfzigpencestück; to be smashed to ~s [car, aeroplane] zerschmettert werden; [mirror, vase] in tausend Stücke zerspringen; to fall to ~s auseinanderlfallen; to pull sb to ~s [criticize] jn in Stücke reißen; to pull sthg to ~s etw scharf kritisieren; to take sthg to ~s etw auseinander nehmen; in one ~ [intact, unharmed] heil; to go to ~s fig zerbrechen - 2. [in chess] Figur die; [in backgammon, draughts] Stein der - 3. [of journalism] Artikel der.

→ **piece together** vt sep [facts] zusammenlfügen.

**pièce de résistance** [pi:,esdərezi:'stɑ:ns] (pl pièces de résistance [pi:,esdərezi:'stɑ:ns] ) n Krönung die.

**piecemeal** ['pi:smi:l] adj & adv stückweise.

**piecework** ['pi:swɜ:k] n (U) Akkordarbeit die.

**pie chart** n Kreisdiagramm das.

**pied-à-terre** [,pjeɪdæ'teə'] (pl pieds-à-terre [,pjeɪdæ'teə'] ) n Zweitwohnung die.

**pie-eyed** [-'aɪd] adj inf sternhagelvoll.

**pier** [pɪə'] n [at seaside] Pier der.

**pierce** [pɪəs] vt [subj: bullet, noise, light] durchldringen; [subj: needle] durchlstechen; to have one's ears ~d sich (D) Ohrlöcher stechen lassen.

**pierced** [pɪəst] adj [ears, navel] durchstochen.

**piercing** ['pɪəsɪŋ] adj [sound, voice] durchdringend; [wind] schneidend; [look, eyes] stechend ◇ n Piercing das.

**piety** ['paɪətɪ] n Pietät die, Frömmigkeit die.

**piffle** ['pɪfl] n inf Quatsch der.

**piffling** ['pɪflɪŋ] adj inf lächerlich.

**pig** [pɪg] (pt & pp -ged; cont -ging) n - 1. [animal] Schwein das - 2. inf pej [greedy eater] Vielfraß der; to make a ~ of o.s. sich voll fressen - 3. inf pej [unkind person] Schwein das.

→ **pig out** vi inf sich (D) den Bauch voll schlagen.

**pigeon** ['pɪdʒɪn] (pl inv OR -s) n Taube die.

**pigeon-chested** [-'tʃestɪd] adj hühnerbrüstig.

**pigeonhole** ['pɪdʒɪnhəʊl] n [compartment] Fach das ◇ vt fig [classify] in eine Kategorie einlordnen.

**pigeon-toed** [-,təʊd] adj mit einwärts gerichteten Füßen.

**piggy** ['pɪgɪ] (compar -ier; superl -iest; pl -ies) adj Schweins- ◇ n inf [piglet] Ferkel das.

**piggyback** ['pɪgɪbæk] n: to give sb a ~ jn huckepack nehmen.

**piggybank** ['pɪgɪbæŋk] n Sparschwein das.

**pigheaded** [,pɪg'hedɪd] adj stur, starrköpfig.

**piglet** ['pɪglɪt] n Ferkel das.

**pigment** ['pɪgmənt] n Pigment das.

**pigmentation** [,pɪgmən'teɪʃn] n Pigmentation die.

**pigmy** ['pɪgmɪ] (pl -ies) n = pygmy.

**pigpen** n Am = pigsty.

**pigskin** ['pɪgskɪn] n Schweinsleder das ◇ comp Schweinsleder-.

**pigsty** ['pɪgstaɪ] (pl -ies), **pigpen** Am ['pɪgpen] n lit & fig Schweinestall der.

**pigswill** ['pɪgswɪl] n - 1. [pig food] Schweinefutter das - 2. fig [tasteless food] Schweinefraß der.

**pigtail** ['pɪgteɪl] n Zopf der.

**pike** [paɪk] (pl sense 1 only inv OR -s) n - 1. [fish] Hecht der - 2. [spear] Pike die.

**pikestaff** ['paɪkstɑ:f] n: as plain as a ~ glasklar.

**pilchard** ['pɪltʃəd] n Sardine die.

**pile** [paɪl] n - 1. [heap] Haufen der; a ~ OR ~s of money/work inf ein Haufen Geld/Arbeit - 2. [neat stack] Stapel der, Stoß der - 3. [of carpet, fabric] Flor der ◇ vt stapeln; to be ~d high with sthg mit etw voll gestapelt sein.

→ **piles** npl MED Hämorrhoiden pl.

→ **pile in** vi inf hineinldrängen.

→ **pile into** vt fus inf [car] sich zwängen in (+ A); [room] drängen in (+ A).

**P**

**pile out** *vi inf:* to ~ out (of) [room, car] drängen aus *(+ A)*.

**pile up** *vt sep* [books, boxes] aufstapeln; [snow] auflhäufen <> *vi* [accumulate] sich anlhäufen.

**pile driver** *n* Ramme *die*.

**pileup** ['paɪlʌp] *n* Massenkarambolage *die*.

**pilfer** ['pɪlfə<sup>r</sup>] *vt & vi* stehlen.

**pilgrim** ['pɪlɡrɪm] *n* Pilger *der*, -in *die*.

**PILGRIM FATHERS**

Bezeichnung für eine Gruppe puritanischer Siedler, die 1620 auf der „Mayflower" von England nach Amerika segelten, um dort eine Gesellschaft zu gründen, in der sie frei von Verfolgung ihren Glauben praktizieren konnten. Die Pilgerväter landeten bei dem heutigen Plymouth (Massachusetts), wo die meisten von ihnen sich niederließen.

**pilgrimage** ['pɪlɡrɪmɪdʒ] *n* Pilgerfahrt *die*.

**pill** [pɪl] *n* Pille *die*, Tablette *die;* [contraceptive]: the ~ die Pille; to be on the ~ die Pille nehmen.

**pillage** ['pɪlɪdʒ] *n* Plünderung *die* <> *vt* plündern.

**pillar** ['pɪlə<sup>r</sup>] *n* Pfeiler *der*, Säule *die;* a ~ of the community *fig* eine Stütze der Gesellschaft.

**pillar box** *n Br* Briefkasten *der*.

**pillbox** ['pɪlbɒks] *n* - **1.** [box for pills] Pillendose *die* - **2.** MIL MG-Unterstand *der*.

**pillion** ['pɪljən] *n* Soziussitz *der;* to ride ~ auf dem Soziussitz mitlfahren.

**pillock** ['pɪlək] *n Br inf* Schwachkopf *der*.

**pillory** ['pɪlərɪ] *(pt & pp -ied) vt fig:* to be pilloried an den Pranger gestellt werden.

**pillow** ['pɪləʊ] *n* - **1.** [for bed] Kopfkissen *das* - **2.** *Am* [on sofa, chair] Kissen *das*.

**pillowcase** ['pɪləʊkeɪs], **pillowslip** ['pɪləʊslɪp] *n* Kopfkissenbezug *der*.

**pilot** ['paɪlət] *n* - **1.** [of plane] Pilot *der*, -in *die* - **2.** NAUT Lotse *der* - **3.** TV Pilotfilm *der* <> *comp* [trial] Pilot- <> *vt* - **1.** [plane] führen, fliegen - **2.** NAUT lotsen - **3.** [scheme] testen.

**pilot light** *n* Zündflamme *die*.

**pilot scheme** *n* Pilotprojekt *das*.

**pilot study** *n* Pilotstudie *die*.

**pimento** [pɪ'mentəʊ] *(pl inv OR -s) n* - **1.** Piment *der OR das* - **2.** Paprikaschote *die*.

**pimp** [pɪmp] *n inf* Zuhälter *der*.

**pimple** ['pɪmpl] *n* Pickel *der*.

**pimply** ['pɪmplɪ] *(compar -ier; superl -iest) adj* pickelig.

**pin** [pɪn] *(pt & pp -ned; cont -ning) n* - **1.** [for sewing] Nadel *die;* I've got ~s and needles in my feet *fig* meine Füße sind eingeschlafen; to be on

~s and needles *Am* (wie) auf glühenden Kohlen sitzen - **2.** [drawing pin] Reißzwecke *die;* [safety pin] Sicherheitsnadel *die* - **3.** [of plug] Kontaktstift *der* - **4.** TECH Bolzen *der*, Stift *der* - **5.** *Am* [brooch] Brosche *die;* [badge] Anstecknadel *die* - **6.** [in grenade] Sicherungsstift *der* - **7.** GOLF: the ~ der Flaggenstock <> *vt:* to ~ sthg to OR on etw heften an *(+ A);* to ~ sb to the wall/ground jn gegen die Wand/auf den Boden drücken; to ~ the blame for sthg on sb jm die Schuld an etw zulschieben.

**pin down** *vt sep* - **1.** [identify] bestimmen - **2.** [force to make a decision] festllegen.

**pin up** *vt sep* [with drawing pin] auflhängen; [hem, hair] hochlstecken.

**PIN** [pɪn] *(abbr of* personal identification number*) n* PIN(-Nummer) *die*.

**pinafore** ['pɪnəfɔː<sup>r</sup>] *n* - **1.** [apron] Schürze *die* - **2.** *Br* [dress] Trägerkleid *das*.

**pinball** ['pɪnbɔːl] *n (U)* Flipper *der*.

**pinball machine** *n* Flipper(automat) *der*.

**pincers** ['pɪnsəz] *npl* - **1.** [tool] Kneifzange *die* - **2.** [of crab, lobster] Schere *die*.

**pinch** [pɪntʃ] *n* - **1.** [nip] Kneifen *das;* to feel the ~ die schlechte Lage zu spüren bekommen - **2.** [of salt, herbs etc] Prise *die* <> *vt* - **1.** [nip] kneifen - **2.** *inf* [steal] klauen.

**at a pinch** *Br,* **in a pinch** *Am adv* zur Not.

**pinched** [pɪntʃt] *adj* - **1.** [face] verhärmt - **2.** [short of]: to be ~ for time keine Zeit haben; to be ~ for money knapp bei Kasse sein.

**pincushion** ['pɪnˌkʊʃn] *n* Nadelkissen *das*.

**pine** [paɪn] *n* - **1.** [tree] Kiefer *die* - **2.** [wood] Kiefernholz *das* <> *comp* [furniture] Kiefernholz- <> *vi:* to ~ for sich sehnen nach.

**pine away** *vi* vergehen (vor Grauen).

**pineapple** ['paɪnæpl] *n* Ananas *die*.

**pinecone** ['paɪnkəʊn] *n* Kiefernzapfen *der*.

**pine needle** *n* Kiefernnadel *die*.

**pinetree** ['paɪntriː] *n* Kiefer *die*.

**ping** [pɪŋ] *n* [sound] Ping *das* <> *vi* ping machen.

**Ping-Pong®** ['pɪŋpɒŋ] *n* Pingpong *das*.

**pinhole** ['pɪnhəʊl] *n* Loch *das*.

**pinion** ['pɪnjən] *n* TECH Ritzel *das* <> *vt* festlhalten.

**pink** [pɪŋk] *adj* rosa; to go ~ erröten <> *n* - **1.** [colour] Rosa *das* - **2.** [flower] Nelke *die*.

**pinkie** ['pɪŋkɪ] *n Am & Scot* kleiner Finger.

**pinking** ['pɪŋkɪŋ] *n Br* AUT Klopfen *das*.

**pin money** *n* Taschengeld *das*.

**pinnacle** ['pɪnəkl] *n* - **1.** *fig* [of career, success] Höhepunkt *der* - **2.** [mountain peak] Gipfel *der* - **3.** ARCHIT [spire] Spitzturm *der*.

**pinny** ['pɪnɪ] *(pl -ies) n inf* Schürze *die*.

**pinpoint** ['pɪnpɔɪnt] *vt* bestimmen.

**pinprick** ['pınprık] n fig Kleinigkeit die; a ~ of light ein Lichtpunkt.

**pin-striped** [-ˌstraıpt] adj Nadelstreifen-.

**pint** [paınt] n - **1.** Am [unit of measurement] Pint das, = 0,568 l. - **2.** Am [unit of measurement] Pint das, = 0,473 l. - **3.** Br [beer]: **let's go for a** ~ lass uns ein Bier trinken gehen; **a** ~ **of Guinness** ein großes (Glas) Guinness.

**pint-size(d)** [saız(d)] adj inf winzig.

**pin-up** ['pınʌp] n Pinup-Foto das.

**pioneer** [ˌpaıə'nıəʳ] n Pionier der <> vt: **the company have ~ed a new type of engine** die Firma hat ein bahnbrechendes Motorkonzept entwickelt.

**pioneering** [ˌpaıə'nıərıŋ] adj Pionier-.

**pious** ['paıəs] adj - **1.** [religious] fromm - **2.** pej [sanctimonious] scheinheilig.

**piously** ['paıəslı] adv - **1.** [religiously] fromm - **2.** pej [sanctimoniously] scheinheilig.

**pip** [pıp] n - **1.** [seed] Kern der - **2.** Br: **the ~s** [on radio] das Zeitzeichen; [on public telephone] Warnton, der ertönt, wenn Geld nachgeworfen werden muss.

**pipe** [paıp] n - **1.** [for gas, water] Rohr das, Leitung die - **2.** [for smoking] Pfeife die - **3.** mus Flöte die; [of organ] Pfeife die <> vt [liquid, gas] leiten.
➤ **pipes** npl mus [bagpipes] Dudelsack der.
➤ **pipe down** vi inf still sein.
➤ **pipe up** vi inf sich (spontan) zu Wort melden.

**pipe cleaner** n Pfeifenreiniger der.

**piped music** [paıpt-] n Br Hintergrundmusik die.

**pipe dream** n Wunschtraum der.

**pipeline** ['paıplaın] n Pipeline die; **to be in the** ~ fig in Vorbereitung sein.

**piper** ['paıpəʳ] n mus Flötenspieler der, -in die; [on bagpipes] Dudelsackspieler der, -in die.

**piping hot** [ˌpaıpıŋ-] adj siedend heiß.

**pipsqueak** ['pıpskwiːk] n pej Niemand der.

**piquant** ['piːkənt] adj lit & fig pikant.

**pique** [piːk] n: **a fit of** ~ ein Anfall von Wut.

**piracy** ['paırəsı] n Piraterie die.

**piranha** [pı'rɑːnə] n Piranha der.

**pirate** ['paırət] adj [video, copy etc] Piraten-, Raub- <> n - **1.** [sailor] Pirat der - **2.** [illegal copy] Raubkopie die <> vt [copy illegally] Raubkopien machen von.

**pirate radio** n Br Piratensender der.

**pirouette** [ˌpıru'et] n Pirouette die <> vi Pirouetten drehen.

**Pisces** ['paısiːz] n Fische pl; **I'm (a)** ~ ich bin Fisch.

**piss** [pıs] vinf n [urine] Pisse die; **to have a** ~ pissen gehen; **to take the** ~ **out of sb** jn verar-

schen; **to take the** ~ **out of sthg** sich über etw (A) lustig machen <> vi pissen; **it's** ~ **ing with rain** es schifft.
➤ **piss down** vi Br vinf [rain] schiffen.
➤ **piss off** vinf vt sep: **to be** ~**ed off with sb/sthg** stocksauer auf jn über/etw sein; **you really** ~ **me off sometimes!** du gehst mir manchmal furchtbar auf den Keks! <> vi Br sich verpissen; ~ **off!** verpiss dich!

**pissed** [pıst] adj vinf - **1.** Br [drunk] voll, besoffen - **2.** Am [annoyed] stocksauer.

**pissed off** adj vinf stocksauer.

**pistachio** [pı'stɑːʃıəʊ] (pl -s) n Pistazie die.

**piste** [piːst] n skiing Piste die.

**pistol** ['pıstl] n Pistole die.

**piston** ['pıstən] n Kolben der.

**pit** [pıt] (pt & pp -ted; cont -ting) n - **1.** [large hole, coalmine] Grube die - **2.** [small hole - in glass] Vertiefung die; [ - on skin, metal] Narbe die - **3.** [for orchestra] Orchestergraben der - **4.** [quarry] Steinbruch der - **5.** Am [of fruit] Kern der - **6.** phr: **in the** ~ **of one's stomach** in der Magengrube <> vt: **to be** ~**ted against sb** [in game] gegen jn spielen (müssen); [in fight] gegen jn kämpfen (müssen); **to** ~ **one's wits against sb/ sthg** sich intellektuell mit jm/etw messen.
➤ **pits** npl - **1.** [in motor racing]: **the** ~**s** die Boxen pl - **2.** inf [awful]: **the** ~**s** die Höhe, das Letzte.

**pit bull (terrier)** n Pitbull(terrier) der.

**pitch** [pıtʃ] n - **1.** sport Feld das, Platz der - **2.** mus Tonhöhe die; [of voice] Stimmlage die; [of instrument] Tonlage die - **3.** [level, degree] Ausmaß das - **4.** [in market, on street] Standplatz der - **5.** inf [sales talk] Verkaufsvortrag der - **6.** [of ship, aircraft] Absacken das - **7.** [of slope] Gefälle das; [of roof] Neigung die - **8.** [throw] Wurf der - **9.** [tar] Pech das <> vt - **1.** [throw] werfen - **2.** [set level of] anlegen - **3.** [camp, tent] auf lschlagen <> vi - **1.** [fall] fallen; **to** ~ **forward** nach vorne fallen - **2.** [ship] stampfen; [plane] ablsacken.
➤ **pitch in** vi inf [lend a hand] helfen.

**pitch-black** adj stockfinster.

**pitched** [pıtʃt] adj: ~ **roof** Giebeldach das.

**pitcher** ['pıtʃəʳ] n Am - **1.** [jug] Krug der - **2.** [in baseball] Pitcher der.

**pitchfork** ['pıtʃfɔːk] n Mistgabel die, Heugabel die.

**piteous** ['pıtıəs] adj Mitleid erregend.

**piteously** ['pıtıəslı] adv Mitleid erregend.

**pitfall** ['pıtfɔːl] n [hazard] Falle die.

**pith** [pıθ] n [of fruit] weiße Haut.

**pithead** ['pıthed] n Grubeneingang der.

**pith helmet** n Tropenhelm der.

**pithy** ['pıθı] (compar -ier; superl -iest) adj prägnant.

**P**

**pitiable** ['pɪtɪəbl] *adj* - **1.** [arousing pity] Mitleid erregend - **2.** [arousing contempt] jämmerlich.

**pitiful** ['pɪtɪfʊl] *adj* - **1.** [arousing pity] Mitleid erregend - **2.** [arousing contempt] jämmerlich.

**pitifully** ['pɪtɪfʊlɪ] *adv* - **1.** [arousing pity] Mitleid erregend - **2.** [arousing contempt] jämmerlich.

**pitiless** ['pɪtɪlɪs] *adj* erbarmungslos.

**pit stop** *n* Boxenstopp *der.*

**pitta bread** ['pɪtə-] *n* Fladenbrot *das.*

**pittance** ['pɪtəns] *n* Hungerlohn *der.*

**pitted** ['pɪtɪd] *adj* - **1.** [olives] entsteint - **2.** [skin] narbig.

**pituitary** [pɪ'tjuːɪtrɪ] (*pl* -ies) *n:* ~ **(gland)** Hirnanhangdrüse *die.*

**pity** ['pɪtɪ] (*pt* & *pp* -ied) *n* - **1.** [compassion] Mitleid *das;* **to take** OR **have** ~ **on sb** Mitleid mit jm haben - **2.** [shame]: **it's a** ~ **(that)** ... (es ist) schade(, dass) ...; **what a** ~! wie schade! ⋄ *vt* bemitleiden.

**pitying** ['pɪtɪɪŋ] *adj* mitleidig.

**pivot** ['pɪvət] *n* - **1.** TECH [joint] Drehgelenk *das* - **2.** *fig* [crux] Dreh- und Angelpunkt *der* ⋄ *vi* sich drehen.

**pixel** ['pɪksl] *n* COMPUT Pixel *das.*

**pixie, pixy** ['pɪksɪ] (*pl* -ies) *n* Kobold *der.*

**pizza** ['piːtsə] *n* Pizza *die.*

**pizzazz** [pɪ'zæz] *n inf* Schwung *der.*

**Pk** *abbr of* park.

**Pl.** *abbr of* Place.

**P & L** (*abbr of* profit and loss) *n Gewinn und Verlust.*

**placard** ['plækɑːd] *n* Plakat *das.*

**placate** [plə'keɪt] *vt* beschwichtigen.

**placatory** [plə'keɪtərɪ] *adj* beschwichtigend

**place** [pleɪs] *n* - **1.** [location] Ort *der;* [spot, place in text & MATH] Stelle *die;* ~ **of birth** Geburtsort; **to two decimal** ~**s** bis auf zwei Stellen nach dem Komma - **2.** [proper position, seat, rank]: **to fall into** ~ klar werden; **to put sb in their** ~ jn zurechtlweisen - **3.** [home] Zuhause *das;* **let's go to my** ~ gehen wir zu mir - **4.** [post, vacancy] Stelle *die* - **5.** [role, function] Rolle *die* - **6.** [table setting] Gedeck *das* - **7.** [instance]: **in the first** ~ am Anfang; **why didn't you say so in the first** ~? warum hast du das nicht gleich OR direkt gesagt?; **in the first** ~ ..., **and in the second** ~ ... erstens ..., zweitens ... - **8.** *phr:* **to take** ~ stattlfinden; **to take sb's** ~ js Platz einlnehmen ⋄ *vt* - **1.** [put] stellen; [put flat] legen; **to** ~ **the blame on sb** jm die Schuld zulschieben; **to** ~ **emphasis on sthg** Betonung auf etw legen; **to** ~ **an ad in the paper** eine Anzeige in die Zeitung setzen - **2.** [identify] einlordnen - **3.** [make]: **to** ~ **an order** COMM eine Bestellung auf lgeben; **to** ~ **a bet on sthg** auf etw (D) wetten - **4.** [be situated]: **the house is well**

~**d for the tube** das Haus liegt ganz in der Nähe der U-Bahn; **how are we** ~**d for money/time?** wie viel Geld/Zeit haben wir? - **5.** [in race]: **to be** ~**d** sich platzieren.

→ **all over the place** *adv* überall.

→ **in place** *adv* - **1.** [in proper position] an seinem Platz - **2.** [established, set up] eingerichtet.

→ **in place of** *prep* anstatt (+ G).

→ **out of place** *adv* - **1.** [in wrong position] nicht an seinem Platz - **2.** [unsuitable] unpassend.

**placebo** [plə'siːbəʊ] (*pl* -s OR -es) *n* Plazebo *das.*

**place card** *n* Platzkarte *die.*

**place mat** *n* Platzset *das.*

**placement** ['pleɪsmənt] *n* - **1.** [positioning] Platzierung *die* - **2.** [work experience] Praktikum *das.*

**placenta** [plə'sentə] (*pl* -s OR -tae [-tiːl]) *n* Plazenta *die.*

**place setting** *n* Gedeck *das.*

**placid** ['plæsɪd] *adj* - **1.** [person, child, animal] ausgeglichen - **2.** [place] ruhig.

**placidly** ['plæsɪdlɪ] *adv* ruhig.

**plagiarism** ['pleɪdʒərɪzm] *n* Plagiarismus *der.*

**plagiarist** ['pleɪdʒərɪst] *n* Plagiarist *der.*

**plagiarize, -ise** ['pleɪdʒəraɪz] *vt* plagiieren.

**plague** [pleɪg] *n* - **1.** MED Seuche *die;* (U) [specific disease] Pest *die;* **to avoid sb/sthg like the** ~ jn/etw wie die Pest meiden - **2.** [nuisance] Plage *die* ⋄ *vt* plagen; **to be** ~**d by bad luck** vom Pech verfolgt sein.

**plaice** [pleɪs] (*pl inv*) *n* Scholle *die.*

**Plaid Cymru** [ˌplaɪd'kʌmrɪ] *n Br* POL *walisische nationalistische Partei.*

**plain** [pleɪn] *adj* - **1.** [simple] einfach, schlicht; [paper] unliniert; [in colour] einfarbig; [unpatterned] uni; [yoghurt] Natur-; **in** ~ **clothes** in Zivil - **2.** [clear] klar; **to make sthg** ~ **to sb** jm etw klar machen - **3.** [blunt - statement, answer] unverblümt; **the** ~ **truth** die reine Wahrheit - **4.** [absolute - madness, stupidity] absolut, schier - **5.** [not pretty] unattraktiv ⋄ *adv inf* [completely] einfach ⋄ *n* GEOGR Ebene *die.*

**plain chocolate** *n Br* Bitterschokolade *die.*

**plain-clothes** *adj* in Zivil.

**plainly** ['pleɪnlɪ] *adv* - **1.** [upset, angry] sichtlich; [remember, hear] deutlich - **2.** [frankly] offen, geradeheraus - **3.** [simply] einfach, schlicht.

**plain sailing** *n:* **it should be** ~ **from here** ab jetzt müsste (eigentlich) alles glatt gehen.

**plainspoken** [ˌpleɪn'spəʊkən] *adj* geradeheraus.

**plaintiff** ['pleɪntɪf] *n* Kläger *der,* -in *die.*

**plaintive** ['pleɪntɪv] *adj* klagend.

**plait** [plæt] *n* Zopf *der* ⋄ *vt* flechten.

**plan** [plæn] (*pt* & *pp* -ned; *cont* -ning) *n* - **1.** [gen]

Plan *der;* **to make ~s** Pläne machen; **have you got any ~s for tonight?** hast du heute Abend etwas vor?; **to go according to ~** nach Plan verlaufen **- 2.** [of story, project] Konzept *das,* Entwurf *der* <> *vt* **- 1.** [organize] planen **- 2.** [intend]: **to ~ to do sthg** vor|haben, etw zu tun **- 3.** [design] entwerfen <> *vi* planen; **to ~ for sthg** Pläne für etw machen.

➡ **plan on** *vt fus:* **to ~ on doing sthg** vor|haben, etw zu tun.

➡ **plan out** *vt sep* vor|bereiten.

**plane** [pleɪn] *adj* GEOM eben <> *n* **- 1.** [aircraft] Flugzeug *das* **- 2.** GEOM Ebene *die* **- 3.** *fig* [level] Niveau *das,* Ebene *die* **- 4.** [tool] Hobel *der* **- 5.** [tree] Platane *die* <> *vt* [wood] hobeln.

**planet** [ˈplænɪt] *n* Planet *der.*

**planetarium** [ˌplænɪˈteərɪəm] (*pl* **-riums** OR **-ria** [-rɪəl]) *n* Planetarium *das.*

**planetary** [ˈplænɪtrɪ] *adj* planetar.

**plane tree** *n* Platane *die.*

**plank** [plæŋk] *n* **- 1.** [piece of wood] (langes) Brett **- 2.** POL [main policy] Programmpunkt *der.*

**plankton** [ˈplæŋktən] *n* Plankton *das.*

**planner** [ˈplænəʳ] *n* Planer *der,* -in *die.*

**planning** [ˈplænɪŋ] *n* Planung *die.*

**planning permission** *n* (U) Baugenehmigung *die.*

**plan of action** *n* Vorgehensplan *der.*

**plant** [plɑːnt] *n* **- 1.** BOT Pflanze *die* **- 2.** [factory] Werk *das,* Fabrik *die* **- 3.** (U) [heavy machinery] Maschinen *pl* <> *vt* **- 1.** [tree, vegetable] pflanzen, an|pflanzen; [seed] säen, aus|säen; [field, garden] bepflanzen **- 2.** [place firmly] auf|stellen; **she ~ed a blow on his chin** sie versetzte ihm einen Kinnhaken; **he ~ed a kiss on her cheek** er gab ihr einen Kuss auf die Wange **- 3.** [bomb, microphone, spy] platzieren, an|bringen; [thought, idea] pflanzen, setzen; **to ~ sthg on sb** jdm etw unter|schieben.

➡ **plant out** *vt sep* aus|pflanzen.

**plantain** [ˈplæntɪn] *n* [fruit] Kochbanane *die.*

**plantation** [plænˈteɪʃn] *n* **- 1.** [piece of land] Plantage *die* **- 2.** [of trees] Anpflanzung *die.*

**planter** [ˈplɑːntəʳ] *n* **- 1.** [farmer] Pflanzer *der,* -in *die* **- 2.** [container] Blumenkübel *der.*

**plant pot** *n* Blumentopf *der.*

**plaque** [plɑːk] *n* **- 1.** [plate] Gedenktafel *die* **- 2.** (U) [on teeth] Zahnbelag *der.*

**plasma** [ˈplæzmə] *n* Plasma *das.*

**plaster** [ˈplɑːstəʳ] *n* **- 1.** [for wall, ceiling] Putz *der* **- 2.** [for broken bones] Gips *der;* **in ~** in Gips **- 3.** *Br* [for cut]: **(sticking) ~** Pflaster *das* <> *vt* **- 1.** [wall, ceiling] verputzen **- 2.** [cover] pflastern; **she's always ~ed with make-up** sie kleistert sich immer mit Make-up zu.

**plasterboard** [ˈplɑːstəbɔːd] *n* (U) Gipskartonplatte *die.*

**plaster cast** *n* **- 1.** [for broken bones] Gipsverband *der* **- 2.** [model, statue] Gipsform *die.*

**plastered** [ˈplɑːstəd] *adj inf* [drunk] besoffen.

**plasterer** [ˈplɑːstərəʳ] *n* Putzer *der,* -in *die.*

**plaster of paris** *n* Gips *der.*

**plastic** [ˈplæstɪk] *adj* Plastik-, Kunststoff- <> *n* **- 1.** [material] Plastik *das,* Kunststoff *der* **- 2.** (U) *inf* [credit cards] Kreditkarten *pl;* **to pay with ~** mit (der) Kreditkarte bezahlen.

**plastic bullet** *n* Kunststoffgeschoss *das.*

**plastic explosive** *n* Plastiksprengstoff *der.*

**Plasticine®** *Br* [ˈplæstɪsiːn], **play dough** *Am* *n* Plastilin *das.*

**plastic surgeon** *n* plastischer Chirurg, plastische Chirurgin.

**plastic surgery** *n* plastische Chirurgie.

**plate** [pleɪt] *n* **- 1.** [dish] Teller *der;* **to have a lot on one's ~** *fig* viel um die Ohren haben; **to be handed sthg on a ~** *fig* etw auf einem silbernen Tablett präsentiert bekommen **- 2.** [of metal, glass] Platte *die* **- 3.** [plaque] Schild *das* **- 4.** [silverware] Tafelsilber *das;* [goldware] Tafelgold *das* **- 5.** [illustration] Tafel *die* **- 6.** [in dentistry] Gaumenplatte *die* **- 7.** [in baseball] Schlagmal *das* <> *vt:* **to be ~d with silver/gold** versilbert/ vergoldet sein.

**Plate** [pleɪt] *n:* **the River ~** Rio de la Plata.

**plateau** [ˈplætəʊ] (*pl* **-s** OR **-x** [-z]) *n* **- 1.** GEOGR Plateau *das* **- 2.** *fig* [steady level]: **prices have reached a ~** die Preise haben sich stabilisiert.

**plateful** [ˈpleɪtfʊl] *n:* **a ~ of chips** ein Teller (voll) Pommes frites.

**plate-glass** *adj* Spiegelglas-.

**platelet** [ˈpleɪtlɪt] *n* Plättchen *das.*

**plate rack** *n* Geschirrständer *der.*

**platform** [ˈplætfɔːm] *n* **- 1.** [gen & COMPUT] Plattform *die;* [for speaker, performer] Podium *das* **- 2.** [at railway station] Bahnsteig *der;* **~ 12** Gleis 12 **- 3.** [of bus] Trittfläche *die.*

**platinum** [ˈplætɪnəm] *adj* Platin- <> *n* Platin *das.*

**platinum blonde** *n* Platinblonde *die.*

**platitude** [ˈplætɪtjuːd] *n* Plattitüde *die.*

**platonic** [pləˈtɒnɪk] *adj* platonisch.

**platoon** [pləˈtuːn] *n* Zug *der.*

**platter** [ˈplætəʳ] *n* [dish] Platte *die.*

**platypus** [ˈplætɪpəs] (*pl* **-es**) *n* Schnabeltier *das.*

**plaudits** [ˈplɔːdɪts] *npl* Beifall *der.*

**plausible** [ˈplɔːzəbl] *adj* [reason, excuse] plausibel; [person] überzeugend.

**plausibly** [ˈplɔːzəblɪ] *adv* [lie, argue] plausibel.

**play** [pleɪ] *n* **- 1.** [gen] Spiel *das;* **in ~** SPORT im Spiel; **out of ~** SPORT im Aus; **to come into ~** *fig* eine Rolle spielen; **~ on words** Wortspiel *das*

**- 2.** [in theatre] Schauspiel *das*, Stück *das;* [on radio] Hörspiel *das;* [on television] Fernsehspiel *das* <> *vt* spielen; [opposing player or team] spielen gegen; **to ~ the piano** Klavier spielen; **to ~ a trick on sb** jm einen Streich spielen; **to ~ a part** OR **role in sthg** *fig* eine Rolle in etw *(D)* spielen; **to ~ it cool** so tun, als sei nichts gewesen <> *vi* spielen; **to ~ for time** versuchen, Zeit zu gewinnen; **to ~ safe** auf Nummer Sicher gehen.

◆ **play along** *vi:* **to ~ along (with sb)** sich (jm) vorübergehend fügen.

◆ **play at** *vt fus:* **what do you think you're ~ing at?** *inf* was soll denn das?

◆ **play back** *vt sep* ab|spielen.

◆ **play down** *vt sep* herunter|spielen.

◆ **play off** *vt sep:* **to ~ sb/sthg off (against)** jn/etw aus|spielen (gegen) <> *vi* SPORT um die Entscheidung spielen.

◆ **play on** *vt fus* [fears, weaknesses] aus|nutzen.

◆ **play up** *vt sep* [emphasize] betonen <> *vi* [machine, part of body] Schwierigkeiten machen; [children] sich wie wild gebärden.

◆ **play upon** *vt fus:* play on.

**playable** ['pleɪəbl] *adj* [pitch] bespielbar.

**play-act** *vi* schauspielern.

**playboy** ['pleɪbɔɪ] *n* Playboy *der*.

**play dough** *n Am* = **Plasticine**®.

**player** ['pleɪəʳ] *n* - **1.** [gen] Spieler *der*, -in *die* - **2.** *dated* THEATRE Schauspieler *der*, -in *die*.

**playful** ['pleɪful] *adj* [comment] neckisch; [person, animal] verspielt.

**playfully** ['pleɪfulɪ] *adv* [teasingly] neckisch; [enthusiastically] spielerisch, ausgelassen.

**playground** ['pleɪgraund] *n* [at school] Schulhof *der;* [in park] Spielplatz *der*.

**playgroup** ['pleɪgruːp] *n* Krabbelgruppe *die*.

**playhouse** ['pleɪhaus, *pl* -hauzɪz] *n* - **1.** *Am* [toy house] Spielhaus *das* - **2.** *dated* [theatre] Schauspielhaus *das*.

**playing card** ['pleɪɪŋ-] *n* Spielkarte *die*.

**playing field** ['pleɪɪŋ-] *n* Sportplatz *der*.

**playmate** ['pleɪmeɪt] *n* Spielkamerad *der*, -in *die*.

**play-off** *n* Entscheidungsspiel *das*.

**playpen** ['pleɪpen] *n* Laufstall *der*.

**playroom** ['pleɪrum] *n* Spielzimmer *das*.

**playschool** ['pleɪskuːl] *n* Krabbelgruppe *die*.

**plaything** ['pleɪθɪŋ] *n lit* & *fig* Spielzeug *das*.

**playtime** ['pleɪtaɪm] *n (U)* [at school]: **at ~** in der großen Pause.

**playwright** ['pleɪraɪt] *n* Dramatiker *der*, -in *die*.

**plaza** ['plɑːzə] *n* - **1.** [public square] Platz *der* - **2.** [shopping centre] Einkaufszentrum *das*.

**plc** (*abbr of* **public limited company**) AG *die*.

**plea** [pliː] *n* - **1.** [appeal] Appell *der* - **2.** LAW Plädoyer *das;* **what's your ~?** wie plädieren Sie?

**plea bargain** *n* Verhandlung zwischen Anklage und Verteidigung über die Möglichkeit, im Falle eines Teilgeständnisses eine Strafminderung zu erreichen.

**plead** [pliːd] (*pt* & *pp* **-ed** OR **pled**) *vt* - **1.** LAW plädieren; **to ~ guilty/not guilty** sich schuldig/nicht schuldig bekennen - **2.** sich berufen auf *(+ A)* <> *vi* - **1.** [beg] flehen; **to ~ with sb to do sthg** jn an|flehen, etw zu tun; **to ~ for sthg** um etw flehen - **2.** LAW: **to ~ sb's case** jn in einer Sache vertreten.

**pleading** ['pliːdɪŋ] *adj* flehend <> *n* Flehen *das*.

**pleasant** ['pleznt] *adj* angenehm; [smile] freundlich; [day] schön.

**pleasantly** ['plezntlɪ] *adv* angenehm; [smile, reply] freundlich.

**pleasantry** ['plezntrɪ] (*pl* **-ies**) *n:* **to exchange pleasantries** Nettigkeiten aus|tauschen.

**please** [pliːz] *vt* gefallen *(+ D);* **there's no pleasing him** man kann ihm nichts recht machen; **he's hard to ~** er ist nicht leicht zufrieden zu stellen; **~ yourself!** wie du willst! <> *vi* gefallen; **may I? - ~ do!** darf ich? - bitte sehr!; **he does as he ~s** er macht, was ihm gefällt; **if you ~** [making request] bitte; [expressing disgust] erlauben Sie mal! <> *adv* bitte; **yes, ~!** ja, bitte!

**pleased** [pliːzd] *adj* [happy] erfreut; [satisfied] zufrieden; **to be ~ about sthg** sich über etw *(A)* freuen; **to be ~ with sb/sthg** mit jm/etw zufrieden sein; **~ to meet you!** angenehm!

**pleasing** ['pliːzɪŋ] *adj* erfreulich.

**pleasingly** ['pliːzɪŋlɪ] *adv* erfreulich.

**pleasurable** ['pleʒərəbl] *adj* angenehm.

**pleasure** ['pleʒəʳ] *n* - **1.** [gen] Freude *die;* **with ~** gern(e); **it's a ~!, my ~!** gern geschehen! - **2.** *(U)* [enjoyment] Vergnügen *das*.

**pleat** [pliːt] *n* Falte *die* <> *vt* fälteln.

**pleated** ['pliːtɪd] *adj* gefältelt.

**plebiscite** ['plebɪsaɪt] *n* Volksentscheid *der*.

**plectrum** ['plektrəm] (*pl* **-s**) *n* Plektrum *das*.

**pled** [pled] *pt* & *pp* ▷ **plead**.

**pledge** [pledʒ] *n* - **1.** [promise] Versprechen *das* - **2.** [token] Pfand *das* <> *vt* - **1.** [promise] versprechen - **2.** [commit]: **to be ~d to sthg** zu etw verpflichtet werden; **to ~ o.s. to sthg** sich zu etw verpflichten - **3.** [pawn] verpfänden.

**plenary session** ['pliːnərɪ-] *n* Plenarsitzung *die*.

**plentiful** ['plentɪful] *adj* reichlich.

**plenty** ['plentɪ] *n (U)* Überfluss *der* <> *pron:* **we've got ~** wir haben mehr als genug; **five**

will be ~ fünf sind mehr als genug; ~ of viel, eine Menge ◇ adv Am [very] sehr.

**plethora** ['pleθərə] n Übermaß das.

**pleurisy** ['pluərəsɪ] n (U) Rippenfellentzündung die.

**Plexiglas®** ['pleksɪglɑːs] n Am Plexiglas® das.

**pliable** ['plaɪəbl], **pliant** ['plaɪənt] adj - 1. [metal] biegsam; [material] geschmeidig - 2. [person] anpassungsfähig.

**pliers** ['plaɪəz] npl Zange die.

**plight** [plaɪt] n Elend das.

**plimsoll** ['plɪmsəl] n Br Turnschuh der.

**Plimsoll line** ['plɪmsəl-] n Höchstlademarkierung die (an der Außenwand von Schiffen).

**plinth** [plɪnθ] n Plinthe die.

**PLO** (abbr of Palestine Liberation Organization) n PLO die.

**plod** [plɒd] (pt & pp -ded; cont -ding) vi - 1. [walk slowly] schwerfällig gehen - 2. [work slowly] sich abmühen.

**plodder** ['plɒdə'] n pej: he's a bit of a ~ er arbeitet eher langsam und ohne Begeisterung.

**plonk** [plɒŋk] n (U) Br inf [wine] billiger Wein.
➤ **plonk down** vt sep inf hinlknallen; **she ~ed herself down on the sofa** sie warf sich aufs Sofa.

**plop** [plɒp] (pt & pp -ped; cont -ping) n Platsch der ◇ vi [liquid] platschen; [land heavily] plumpsen.

**plot** [plɒt] (pt & pp -ted; cont -ting) n - 1. [conspiracy] Komplott das; **the ~ thickens** die Geschichte wird immer undurchsichtiger - 2. [of story, film, play] Handlung die - 3. [of land] Stück das Land; [allotment] Parzelle die - 4. Am [house plan] Grundriss der ◇ vt - 1. [conspire] planen; **to ~ to do sthg** gemeinsam planen, etw zu tun - 2. [chart] einlzeichnen; MATH auflzeichnen ◇ vi: **to ~ (against)** sich verschwören (gegen).

**plotter** ['plɒtə'] n Verschwörer der, -in die.

**plough** Br, **plow** Am [plaʊ] n Pflug der ◇ vt pflügen; **to ~ money into sthg** Geld in etw (A) stecken ◇ vi [crash]: **to ~ into sthg** in etw (A) rasen.
➤ **plough on** vi [on journey] sich voranlkämpfen; [in work] weiterlmachen.
➤ **plough up** vt sep auflwühlen; [field] umlpflügen.

**ploughman's** ['plaʊmənz] (pl inv) n Br: ~ (lunch) Pubmahlzeit aus Käse, Brot und Pickles.

**ploughshare** Br, **plowshare** Am ['plaʊʃeə'] n Pflugschar die.

**plow** etc n & vb Am = plough etc.

**ploy** [plɔɪ] n Trick der.

**pls** abbr of please.

**pluck** [plʌk] vt - 1. [flower, fruit] pflücken - 2. [pull] ziehen; **to be ~ed to safety** geborgen werden - 3. [chicken] rupfen - 4. [eyebrows, guitar, harp] zupfen ◇ n (U) dated Mut der.
➤ **pluck up** vt sep: **to ~ up the courage to do sthg** den Mut auf lbringen, etw zu tun.

**plucky** ['plʌkɪ] (compar -ier; superl -iest) adj dated mutig.

**plug** [plʌg] (pt & pp -ged; cont -ging) n - 1. ELEC Stecker der; [socket] Steckdose die - 2. [for bath, sink] Stöpsel der - 3. inf [publicity] Schleichwerbung die; **to give sthg a ~** Schleichwerbung für etw machen ◇ vt - 1. [hole, ears] zulstopfen, verstopfen - 2. inf [advertise] Schleichwerbung machen für.
➤ **plug in** vt sep ELEC einlstecken, anlschließen.

**plughole** ['plʌghəʊl] n Abfluss der.

**plum** [plʌm] adj - 1. [colour] pflaumenfarben - 2. [choice]: **a ~ job** ein Traumjob ◇ n - 1. [fruit] Pflaume die - 2. [colour] Pflaumenblau das.

**plumage** ['pluːmɪdʒ] n Gefieder das.

**plumb** [plʌm] adv - 1. Br [exactly] genau; **~ in the middle** genau in der/die Mitte - 2. Am [completely] völlig, komplett ◇ vt: **to ~ the depths of sthg** den Tiefpunkt von etw erreichen.
➤ **plumb in** vt sep Br anlschließen.

**plumber** ['plʌmə'] n Klempner der, Installateur der.

**plumbing** ['plʌmɪŋ] n (U) - 1. [fittings] Leitungen pl - 2. [work] Installieren das von Sanitäranlagen.

**plumb line** n Lot das.

**plume** [pluːm] n - 1. [on bird, hat] Feder die; [on helmet] Federbusch der - 2. [column]: **a ~ of smoke** eine Rauchfahne.

**plummet** ['plʌmɪt] vi - 1. [plane, bird] (senkrecht) hinuntrlstürzen - 2. [prices, value, shares] rapide fallen.

**plummy** ['plʌmɪ] (compar -ier; superl -iest) adj Br inf pej [accent] affektiert.

**plump** [plʌmp] adj rundlich, mollig ◇ vi: **to ~ for sthg** sich für etw entscheiden.
➤ **plump up** vt sep auf lschütteln.

**plum tree** n Pflaumenbaum der.

**plunder** ['plʌndə'] n (U) - 1. [pillaging] Plündern das - 2. [booty] Beute die ◇ vt plündern.

**plunge** [plʌndʒ] n - 1. [rapid decrease] Sturz der - 2. [dive] Sprung der; [head-on] Kopfsprung der; **to take the ~** den Schritt wagen ◇ vt - 1. [immerse]: **to ~ sthg into sthg** etw in etw (A) werfen - 2. [thrust]: **to ~ sthg into sthg** etw in etw (A) treiben; **~d into darkness** in Dunkelheit getaucht ⬦ *vi* - **1.** [dive] springen; [out of control] stürzen - **2.** [prices, value] fallen.

**plunger** ['plʌndʒəʳ] *n* [for sinks, drains] Saugglocke *die*.

**plunging** ['plʌndʒɪŋ] *adj* [neckline] tief ausgeschnitten.

**pluperfect** [,pluː'pɜːfɪkt] *n:* ~ **(tense)** Plusquamperfekt *das*.

**plural** ['pluərəl] *adj* - **1.** GRAMM im Plural - **2.** [society] pluralistisch ⬦ *n* Plural *der*, Mehrzahl *die;* in the ~ im Plural.

**pluralistic** [,pluərə'lɪstɪk] *adj* pluralistisch.

**plurality** [plu'rælətɪ] *n* - **1.** [large number]: a ~ of eine Vielzahl von - **2.** Am [majority] Mehrheit *die*.

**plus** [plʌs] (*pl* -es OR -ses) *adj* - **1.** [over, more than]: 30 ~ mehr als 30, über 30 - **2.** [in school marks] plus ⬦ *n* - **1.** MATH [sign] Pluszeichen *das* - **2.** *inf* [bonus] Plus *das* ⬦ *prep* - **1.** MATH plus, und - **2.** [as well as] und ⬦ *conj* [moreover] und (außerdem).

**plus fours** *npl* Knickerbocker *pl*.

**plush** [plʌʃ] *adj* luxuriös.

**plus sign** *n* Pluszeichen *das*.

**Pluto** ['pluːtəʊ] *n* [planet] Pluto *der*.

**plutonium** [pluː'təʊnɪəm] *n* Plutonium *das*.

**ply** [plaɪ] (*pt* & *pp* **plied**) *vt* - **1.** [work at]: **to ~ a trade** ein Gewerbe betreiben - **2.:** **to ~ sb with drink** jm Alkohol auf|drängen; **to ~ sb with questions** jn mit Fragen bedrängen ⬦ *vi* [boat]: **to ~ between** verkehren zwischen.

**-ply** [plaɪ] *adj:* **four~** [wood] vierschichtig; [wool] vierfädig.

**plywood** ['plaɪwʊd] *n* Sperrholz *das*.

**p.m., pm** (*abbr of* **post meridiem**) nachmittags; **at 9 ~** um 21 Uhr OR 9 Uhr abends.

**PM** *n abbr of* **prime minister**.

**PMS** *n abbr of* **premenstrual syndrome**.

**PMT** *n abbr of* **premenstrual tension**.

**pneumatic** [njuː'mætɪk] *adj* pneumatisch.

**pneumatic drill** *n* Pressluftbohrer *der*.

**pneumonia** [njuː'məʊnɪə] *n (U)* Lungenentzündung *die*.

**po** *n abbr of* **postal order**.

**PO** *n* - **1.** *abbr of* **Post Office** - **2.** *abbr of* **postal order**.

**POA** (*abbr of* **Prison Officers' Association**) *n* Gewerkschaft der Arbeitnehmer im britischen Strafvollzug.

**poach** [pəʊtʃ] *vt* - **1.** [hunt illegally] wildern - **2.** [idea] kopieren - **3.** [egg] pochieren ⬦ *vi* wildern.

**poacher** ['pəʊtʃəʳ] *n* - **1.** [person] Wilderer *der* - **2.** [for eggs] Pochierpfanne *die*.

**poaching** ['pəʊtʃɪŋ] *n* Wildern *das*.

**PO Box** *n abbr of* **Post Office Box**.

**pocket** ['pɒkɪt] *n* - **1.** [in clothes] Tasche *die;* **to live in each other's ~s** ständig zusammen sein; **to be out of ~** drauf|zahlen; **to pick sb's ~** jm etwas (aus der Tasche) stehlen - **2.** [of warm air, mineral] Einschluss *der;* **~ of resistance** Widerstandsnest *das* - **3.** [of snooker, pool table] Loch *das* ⬦ *adj* Taschen- ⬦ *vt* ein|stecken.

**pocketbook** ['pɒkɪtbʊk] *n* - **1.** [notebook] Notizbuch *das* - **2.** Am [handbag] Handtasche *die*.

**pocket calculator** *n* Taschenrechner *der*.

**pocketful** ['pɒkɪtfʊl] *n:* **a ~ of sweets** eine Tasche voller Süßigkeiten.

**pocket-handkerchief** *n* Taschentuch *das*.

**pocketknife** ['pɒkɪtnaɪf] (*pl* -**knives** [-naɪvz]) *n* Taschenmesser *das*.

**pocket money** *n* Taschengeld *das*.

**pocket-size(d)** [saɪz(d)] *adj* im Taschenformat.

**pockmark** ['pɒkmɑːk] *n* Pockennarbe *die*.

**pod** [pɒd] *n* - **1.** [of plants] Hülse *die*, Schote *die* - **2.** [of spacecraft] Kapsel *die*.

**podgy** ['pɒdʒɪ] (*compar* -**ier**; *superl* -**iest**) *adj* *inf* pummelig.

**podia** ['pəʊdɪə] *pl* ⬭ **podium**.

**podiatrist** [pə'daɪətrɪst] *n* Am Fußpfleger *der*, -in *die*.

**podium** ['pəʊdɪəm] (*pl* -**diums** OR -**dia**) *n* Podium *das*.

**poem** ['pəʊɪm] *n* Gedicht *das*.

**poet** ['pəʊɪt] *n* Dichter *der*, -in *die*.

**poetic** [pəʊ'etɪk] *adj* poetisch.

**poetic justice** *n* ausgleichende Gerechtigkeit.

**poet laureate** *n* Hofdichter *der*.

**poetry** ['pəʊɪtrɪ] *n (U)* - **1.** [poems] Dichtung *die* - **2.** *fig* [beauty] Poesie *die*.

**pogo stick** ['pəʊgəʊ-] *n* Springstock *der*.

**poignancy** ['pɔɪnjənsɪ] *n* [of moving nature] Ergriffenheit *die*.

**poignant** ['pɔɪnjənt] *adj* [moving] ergreifend.

**poinsettia** [pɔɪn'setɪə] *n* Weihnachtsstern *der*, Poinsettie *die*.

**point** [pɔɪnt] *n* - **1.** [tip] Spitze *die* - **2.** [place, dot, moment] Punkt *der;* **the ~s of the compass** die Himmelsrichtungen; **at this ~ in time** zum jetzigen Zeitpunkt; **~ of no return** Zeitpunkt, ab dem es kein Zurück mehr gibt - **3.** [in discussion, debate] Punkt *der;* **you may have a ~ there** da hast du vielleicht Recht; **to make a ~** eine Anmerkung machen; **to make one's ~** seinen Standpunkt deutlich machen; **a sore ~** ein wunder Punkt - **4.** [meaning] Sinn *der;* **you've missed the ~ of what he is**

trying to say du hast nicht verstanden, worauf er hinauswill; **to get** OR **come to the ~** zur Sache kommen; **that's beside the ~** das tut hier nichts zur Sache; **to the ~** präzise - **5.** [feature]: **good** OR **strong ~** Stärke die; **bad** OR **weak ~** Schwäche die - **6.** [purpose] Zweck der; **there's no ~** es hat keinen Sinn - **7.** MATH Komma das; **five ~ seven** fünf Komma sieben - **8.** [in scores] Punkt der - **9.** Br ELEC Steckdose die - **10.** Am [full stop] Punkt der - **11.** phr: **to make a ~ of doing sthg** etw bewusst tun ◇ vt: **to ~ sthg (at)** etw richten (auf (+ A)); **to ~ the way (to sthg)** den Weg (zu etw) zeigen ◇ vi - **1.** [person]: **to ~ at** OR **to** zeigen auf (+ A) - **2.** [needle on dial]: **to ~ to sthg** etw anzeigen; **the sign is ~ing to the stadium** [road sign] das Schild zeigt in Richtung Stadion - **3.** [gun, camera, light] gerichtet sein; **to ~ at sthg** auf etw gerichtet sein - **4.** fig [evidence, facts]: **to ~ to sb/sthg** auf jn/etw hin!weisen.

➡ **points** npl Br RAIL Weiche die.

➡ **on the point of** prep: **to be on the ~ of doing sthg** im Begriff sein, etw zu tun; **I was on the ~ of going** ich wollte gerade gehen.

➡ **up to a point** adv bis zu einem gewissen Punkt.

➡ **point out** vt sep - **1.** [indicate] zeigen - **2.** [call attention to] hin!weisen auf (+ A).

**point-blank** adj - **1.** [refusal] glatt - **2.**: **at ~ range** aus nächster Nähe ◇ adv - **1.** [directly] direkt; [ask] geradeheraus; [refuse] rundweg - **2.** [shoot] aus nächster Nähe.

**point duty** n Br Verkehrsdienst der.

**pointed** ['pɔɪntɪd] adj - **1.** [sharp] spitz - **2.** [meaningful] betont; [remark] spitz.

**pointedly** ['pɔɪntɪdlɪ] adv [meaningfully] betont; [remark] spitz.

**pointer** ['pɔɪntə'] n - **1.** [tip] Hinweis der - **2.** [needle on dial] Zeiger der - **3.** [stick] Zeigestock der - **4.** [dog] Vorstehhund der - **5.** COMPUT Mauszeiger der.

**pointing** ['pɔɪntɪŋ] n [of wall] Ausfugung die.

**pointless** ['pɔɪntlɪs] adj zwecklos, sinnlos.

**point of sale** (pl **points of sale**) n COMM Verkaufsstelle die.

**point of view** (pl **points of view**) n [attitude] Standpunkt der; [visual angle] Blickwinkel der.

**poise** [pɔɪz] n (U) [composure] Selbstsicherheit die.

**poised** [pɔɪzd] adj - **1.** [ready] bereit; **to be ~ to do sthg** bereit sein, etw zu tun; **to be ~ for sthg** bereit sein für etw OR zu etw - **2.** [composed] gefasst.

**poison** ['pɔɪzn] n Gift das ◇ vt - **1.** [gen] vergiften - **2.** fig [corrupt] verschmutzen - **3.** [atmosphere, water] verderben.

**poisoning** ['pɔɪznɪŋ] n Vergiftung die.

**poisonous** ['pɔɪznəs] adj - **1.** [gen] giftig - **2.** fig [corrupting] zersetzend.

**poison-pen letter** n anonymer Brief.

**poke** [pəʊk] n [with finger, stick] Stoß der ◇ vt - **1.** [with finger, stick] stoßen; **to ~ sb in the ribs** jm einen Stoß in die Rippen geben - **2.** [thrust] stecken; **to ~ a hole in sthg** ein Loch in etw stechen OR bohren; **he ~d his head round the door** er steckte den Kopf zur Tür herein - **3.** [fire] schüren ◇ vi: **to ~ out of** hervor!schauen aus.

➡ **poke about, poke around** vi inf herum!stochern.

➡ **poke at** vt fus an!stoßen.

**poker** ['pəʊkə'] n - **1.** [game] Poker das - **2.** [for fire] Schürhaken der.

**poker-faced** [-ˌfeɪst] adj mit einem Pokerface.

**poky** ['pəʊkɪ] (compar -**ier**; superl -**iest**) adj pej eng; **a ~ flat** eine winzige Wohnung.

**Poland** ['pəʊlənd] n Polen nt.

**polar** ['pəʊlə'] adj GEOGR polar.

**polar bear** n Eisbär der.

**polarity** [pəʊ'lærətɪ] n Polarität die.

**polarization, -isation** [ˌpəʊləraɪ'zeɪʃn] n Polarisierung die.

**polarize, -ise** ['pəʊləraɪz] vt polarisieren.

**Polaroid**® ['pəʊlərɔɪd] n - **1.** [camera] Polaroidkamera® die - **2.** [photograph] Polaroidfoto das.

**Polaroids**® ['pəʊlərɔɪdz] npl [sunglasses] mit Polaroidmaterial beschichtete Sonnenbrille.

**pole** [pəʊl] n - **1.** Stange die; [for electricity] Pfahl der; [for flag] Mast der; [for skiing] Stock der - **2.** GEOGR & ELEC Pol der; **~s apart** völlig entgegengesetzt.

**Pole** [pəʊl] n Pole der, -lin die.

**poleaxe** ['pəʊlæks] vt: **I was ~d to hear that ...** es hat mich umgehauen, als ich hörte, dass ...

**polecat** ['pəʊlkæt] n Iltis der.

**polemic** [pə'lemɪk] n fml Polemik die.

**pole position** n SPORT erste Startposition.

**Pole Star** n: **the ~** der Polarstern.

**pole vault** n: **the ~** der Stabhochsprung.

➡ **pole-vault** vi stabhochspringen.

**pole-vaulter** [-ˌvɔːltə'] n Stabhochspringer der, -in die.

**police** [pə'liːs] npl - **1.** [police force]: **the ~** die Polizei - **2.** [policemen] Polizisten pl ◇ vt [area] kontrollieren.

**police car** n Streifenwagen der.

**police constable** n Br Wachtmeister der, -in die.

**police department** n Am Polizei die.

P

**police dog** n Polizeihund der.

**police force** n Polizei die.

**policeman** [pə'liːsmən] (pl -men [-mən]) n Polizist der.

**police officer** n Polizeibeamte der, -tin die

**police record** n: to have a ~ vorbestraft sein.

**police state** n Polizeistaat der.

**police station** n Br Polizeiwache die.

**policewoman** [pə'liːs‿wumən] (pl -women [-‿wɪmɪn]) n Polizistin die.

**policy** ['pɒləsɪ] (pl -ies) n - 1. [plan] Politik die; what's your ~ on refunds? wie lauten Ihre Umtauschbedingungen? - 2. [for insurance] Police die.

**policy-holder** [-‿həuldəʳ] n Versicherungsnehmer der, -in die.

**polio** ['pəuliəu] n (U) Kinderlähmung die.

**polish** ['pɒlɪʃ] n - 1. [cleaning material] Politur die; window ~ Glasreiniger der - 2. [shine] Glanz der; [of furniture] Politur die - 3. fig [of performance] Brillianz die; [of style, manners] Schliff der <> vt - 1. [shine] polieren - 2. fig [perfect]: to ~ sthg (up) etw verfeinern.

➡ **polish off** vt sep inf - 1. [meal] verputzen - 2. [job] schnell erledigen; [book] verschlingen.

**Polish** ['pəulɪʃ] adj polnisch <> n [language] Polnisch(e) das <> npl: the ~ die Polen pl.

**polished** ['pɒlɪʃt] adj - 1. [surface] poliert - 2. [person, manners] geschliffen - 3. [performance] brilliant.

**polite** [pə'laɪt] adj höflich.

**politely** [pə'laɪtlɪ] adv höflich.

**politeness** [pə'laɪtnɪs] n Höflichkeit die.

**politic** ['pɒlətɪk] adj fml klug.

**political** [pə'lɪtɪkl] adj politisch.

**political asylum** n politisches Asyl.

**political geography** n politische Geografie.

**politically** [pə'lɪtɪklɪ] adv politisch.

**politically correct** adj politisch korrekt.

**POLITICALLY CORRECT** ▬▬▬

„Political correctness" ist ein intellektueller Sprachregelungstrend (am stärksten in den USA), der beansprucht, durch das Ausmerzen von als diskriminierend empfundenen Bezeichnungen für mehr gesellschaftliche Gerechtigkeit zu sorgen. Typische „PC"-Ausdrücke sind z. B. „Native American" (an Stelle von „American Indian") oder „differently abled" (für „disabled").

**political prisoner** n politischer Gefangene, politische Gefangene.

**political science** n Politikwissenschaft die.

**politician** [‿pɒlɪ'tɪʃn] n Politiker der, -in die.

**politicize, -ise** [pə'lɪtɪsaɪz] vt politisieren.

**politics** ['pɒlətɪks] n (U) Politik die <> npl - 1. [personal beliefs] politische Ansichten - 2. [of a group, area] Politik die.

**polka** ['pɒlkə] n Polka die.

**polka dot** n Tupfen der.

**poll** [pəul] n - 1. [election] Wahl die - 2. [survey] Umfrage die <> vt - 1. [people] befragen - 2. [votes] erhalten.

➡ **polls** npl: to go to the ~s wählen gehen.

**pollen** ['pɒlən] n Blütenstaub der.

**pollen count** n Pollenzahl die.

**pollinate** ['pɒləneɪt] vt bestäuben.

**pollination** [‿pɒlɪ'neɪʃn] n Bestäubung die.

**polling** ['pəulɪŋ] n (U) Stimmabgabe die.

**polling booth** n Wahlkabine die.

**polling day** n Br Wahltag der.

**polling station** n Wahllokal das.

**poll tax** n Kopfsteuer die.

➡ **Poll Tax** n Br Gemeindesteuer die.

**pollutant** [pə'luːtnt] n Schadstoff der.

**pollute** [pə'luːt] vt verschmutzen.

**pollution** [pə'luːʃn] n Verschmutzung die.

**polo** ['pəuləu] n Polo das.

**polo neck** n Br - 1. [collar] Rollkragen der - 2. [jumper] Rollkragenpullover der.

➡ **polo-neck** adj Br Rollkragen-.

**polo shirt** n Polohemd das.

**poltergeist** ['pɒltəgaɪst] n Poltergeist der.

**poly** ['pɒlɪ] (pl polys) n inf abbr of polytechnic.

**polyanthus** ['pɒləsɪ] ['pɒləsɪ] (pl -thuses OR -thi [-θaɪ]) n Gartenprimel die.

**polyester** [‿pɒlɪ'estəʳ] n Polyester der.

**polyethylene** n Am = polythene.

**polygamist** [pə'lɪgəmɪst] n Polygamist der.

**polygamy** [pə'lɪgəmɪ] n Polygamie die.

**polygon** ['pɒlɪgɒn] n Polygon das.

**polymer** ['pɒlɪməʳ] n Polymer das.

**polyp** ['pɒlɪp] n Polyp der.

**polystyrene** [‿pɒlɪ'staɪriːn] n Styropor® das.

**polytechnic** [‿pɒlɪ'teknɪk] n Br Polytechnikum das, ≈ technische Hochschule.

**polythene** Br ['pɒlɪθiːn], **polyethylene** Am [‿pɒlɪ'eθɪliːn] n Polyethylen das.

**polythene bag** n Br Plastiktüte die.

**polyunsaturated** [‿pɒlɪʌn'sætʃəreɪtɪd] adj mehrfach ungesättigt.

**polyurethane** [‿pɒlɪ'juərəθeɪn] n Polyurethan das.

**pom** [pɒm] n Austr offensive beleidigender,

*manchmal auch liebevoll-belustigter Ausdruck für „Engländer".*

**pomander** [pə'mændəʳ] n Duftkugel *die.*

**pomegranate** ['pɒmɪˌgrænɪt] n Granatapfel *der.*

**pommel** ['pɒml] n - **1.** [on saddle] Sattelknauf *der* - **2.** [on sword] Schwertknauf *der.*

**pomp** [pɒmp] n Pomp *der.*

**pompom** ['pɒmpɒm] n Pompon *der.*

**pompous** ['pɒmpəs] adj [pretentious] aufgeblasen; [speech] geschwollen.

**ponce** [pɒns] n *Br vinf pej* - **1.** [effeminate man] Weichei *das* - **2.** [pimp] Zuhälter *der.*

**poncho** ['pɒntʃəʊ] (pl -s) n Poncho *der.*

**pond** [pɒnd] n Teich *der.*

**ponder** ['pɒndəʳ] vt & vi nachldenken; **to ~ on** OR **over sthg** über etw (A) nachldenken.

**ponderous** ['pɒndərəs] adj schwerfällig.

**pong** [pɒŋ] *Br inf* n Gestank *der,* Mief *der* <> vi stinken, miefen.

**pontiff** ['pɒntɪf] n Pontifex *der.*

**pontificate** [pɒn'tɪfɪkeɪt] vi *pej* dozieren.

**pontoon** [pɒn'tuːn] n - **1.** [bridge] Ponton *der* - **2.** *Br* [game] Siebzehnundvier *das.*

**pony** ['pəʊnɪ] (pl -ies) n Pony *das.*

**ponytail** ['pəʊnɪteɪl] n Pferdeschwanz *der.*

**pony-trekking** [-ˌtrekɪŋ] n Ponyreiten *das.*

**poodle** ['puːdl] n Pudel *der.*

**poof** [pʊf] n *Br vinf pej* Schwuchtel *die.*

**pooh** [puː] excl puh!

**pooh-pooh** vt inf verächtlich abllehnen.

**pool** [puːl] n - **1.** [of water, blood] Lache *die;* [of light] Lichtkegel *der;* [of rain] Pfütze *die* - **2.** [swimming pool] Swimmingpool *der;* [small pond] Teich *der* - **3.** [game] Poolbillard *das* <> vt zusammenllegen.
➡ **pools** npl *Br:* **the ~s** das Fußballtoto.

**pooped** [puːpt] adj inf völlig fertig.

**poor** [pɔːʳ] adj - **1.** [impoverished, unfortunate] arm - **2.** [not very good] schlecht <> npl: **the ~** die Armen pl.

**poorhouse** ['pɔːhaʊs, pl -haʊzɪz] n Armenhaus *das.*

**poorly** ['pɔːlɪ] adj *Br inf* krank <> adv [badly] schlecht.

**poor relation** n fig Stiefkind *das.*

**pop** [pɒp] (pt & pp -**ped**; cont -**ping**) n - **1.** [music] Pop *der* - **2.** inf [fizzy drink] Brause *die* - **3.** esp Am inf [father] Papa *der* - **4.** [noise] Knall *der* <> vt - **1.** [balloon, bubble] platzen, zerplatzen - **2.** [put] stecken <> vi - **1.** [balloon] platzen; [cork] knallen; **my ears are ~ping** ich habe Druck auf den Ohren; **her eyes were ~ping** sie machte große Augen - **2.** [go quickly]: **I'm**

**just ~ping to the shops** ich gehe (nur) schnell einkaufen.
➡ **pop in** vi [visit] vorbeilschauen.
➡ **pop up** vi auf ltauchen.

**popadum** ['pɒpədəm] n *Indisches Fladenbrot mit dünnem knusprigem Teig.*

**pop concert** n Popkonzert *das.*

**popcorn** ['pɒpkɔːn] n Popcorn *das.*

**pope** [pəʊp] n Papst *der.*

**pop group** n Popgruppe *die.*

**poplar** ['pɒpləʳ] n Pappel *die.*

**poplin** ['pɒplɪn] n Popelin *der.*

**popper** ['pɒpəʳ] n *Br* Druckknopf *der.*

**poppy** ['pɒpɪ] (pl -**ies**) n Mohn *der.*

**poppycock** ['pɒpɪkɒk] n inf pej Quatsch *der.*

**Poppy Day** n *Br* ≃ Volkstrauertag *der.*

**Popsicle®** ['pɒpsɪkl] n *Am* Eis *das* am Stiel.

**pop singer** n Popsänger *der,* -in *die.*

**populace** ['pɒpjʊləs] n: **the ~** die breite Bevölkerung.

**popular** ['pɒpjʊləʳ] adj - **1.** [well-liked] populär, beliebt - **2.** [common] weit verbreitet - **3.** [newspaper, politics] volksnah; [entertainment] volkstümlich; [debate] öffentlich.

**popularity** [ˌpɒpjʊ'lærətɪ] n Popularität *die,* Beliebtheit *die.*

**popularize, -ise** ['pɒpjʊləraɪz] vt - **1.** [make popular] popularisieren - **2.** [simplify] vereinfachen.

**popularly** ['pɒpjʊləlɪ] adv [commonly] gemeinhin, allgemein.

**populate** ['pɒpjʊleɪt] vt bevölkern.

**populated** ['pɒpjʊleɪtɪd] adj bevölkert.

**population** [ˌpɒpjʊ'leɪʃn] n - **1.** [gen] Bevölkerung *die* - **2.** [particular group] Bevölkerungsgruppe *die.*

**population explosion** n Bevölkerungsexplosion *die.*

**populist** ['pɒpjʊlɪst] n Populist *der,* -in *die.*

**pop-up** adj - **1.** [toaster] automatisch - **2.**: **~ book** Hochklappbuch *das.*

**porcelain** ['pɔːsəlɪn] n Porzellan *das.*

**porch** [pɔːtʃ] n - **1.** [entrance] Windfang *der* - **2.** *Am* [veranda] Veranda *die.*

**porcupine** ['pɔːkjʊpaɪn] n Stachelschwein *das.*

**pore** [pɔːʳ] n Pore *die.*
➡ **pore over** vt fus (eingehend) studieren.

**pork** [pɔːk] n Schweinefleisch *das.*

**pork chop** n Schweinekotelett *das.*

**pork pie** n Schweinefleischpastete *die.*

**porn** [pɔːn] n inf Porno *der;* **hard ~** Hardcoreporno *der;* **soft ~** Softporno *der.*

P

**pornographic** [ˌpɔːnəˈgræfɪk] *adj* pornografisch.

**pornography** [pɔːˈnɒgrəfɪ] *n* Pornografie *die*.

**porous** [ˈpɔːrəs] *adj* porös.

**porpoise** [ˈpɔːpəs] *n* Tümmler *der*.

**porridge** [ˈpɒrɪdʒ] *n* Haferbrei *der*.

**port** [pɔːt] *n* - **1.** [coastal town] Hafenstadt *die;* [harbour] Hafen *der* - **2.** NAUT Backbord *das;* **to ~** nach Backbord - **3.** [drink] Portwein *der* - **4.** COMPUT Anschluss *der* ⬦ *comp* - **1.** [relating to a harbour] Hafen- - **2.** NAUT Backbord-.

**portable** [ˈpɔːtəbl] *adj* tragbar.

**Portacrib**® [ˈpɔːtəˌkrɪb] *n* Am Babytragetasche *die*.

**portal** [ˈpɔːtl] *n literary* & COMPUT Portal *das*.

**portcullis** [ˌpɔːtˈkʌlɪs] *n* Fallgitter *das*.

**portend** [pɔːˈtend] *vt literary* vorherlsagen.

**portent** [ˈpɔːtənt] *n literary* Vorzeichen *das*.

**porter** [ˈpɔːtəʳ] *n* - **1.** Br [at hotel, museum] Pförtner *der*, Portier *der* - **2.** [at station, airport] Gepäckträger *der* - **3.** Am [on train] Schlafwagenschaffner *der*.

**portfolio** [ˌpɔːtˈfəʊlɪəʊ] (*pl* -s) *n* - **1.** [case] Aktentasche *die* - **2.** [sample of work] Mappe *die* - **3.** FIN Portefeuille *das*.

**porthole** [ˈpɔːthəʊl] *n* Bullauge *das*.

**portion** [ˈpɔːʃn] *n* - **1.** [part, share] Teil *der* - **2.** [of food] Portion *die*.

**portly** [ˈpɔːtlɪ] (*compar* -ier; *superl* -iest) *adj* beleibt.

**port of call** *n* - **1.** NAUT Anlaufhafen *der* - **2.** *fig* [on journey] Ziel *das*.

**portrait** [ˈpɔːtreɪt] *n lit* & *fig* Porträt *das*.

**portraitist** [ˈpɔːtreɪtɪst] *n* Porträtmaler *der*, -in *die*.

**portray** [pɔːˈtreɪ] *vt* - **1.** [gen] darlstellen - **2.** [subj: artist] porträtieren.

**portrayal** [pɔːˈtreɪəl] *n* Darstellung *die*.

**Portugal** [ˈpɔːtʃʊgl] *n* Portugal *nt*.

**Portuguese** [ˌpɔːtʃʊˈgiːz] (*pl inv*) *adj* portugiesisch ⬦ *n* - **1.** [person] Portugiese *der*, -sin *die* - **2.** [language] Portugiesisch(e) *das* ⬦ *npl*: **the ~** die Portugiesen *pl*.

**pose** [pəʊz] *n* - **1.** [position] Haltung *die* - **2.** *pej* [pretence] Pose *die* ⬦ *vt* - **1.** [problem, danger, threat] darlstellen - **2.** [a question] stellen ⬦ *vi* - **1.** [for photo] posieren; [for painting] Modell stehen - **2.** *pej* [behave affectedly] posieren - **3.** [pretend to be]: **to ~ as a tourist** sich als Tourist auslgeben.

**poser** [ˈpəʊzəʳ] *n* - **1.** *pej* [person] Angeber *der*, -in *die* - **2.** *inf* [question] knifflige Frage.

**poseur** [pəʊˈzɜːʳ] *n pej* Angeber *der*, -in *die*.

**posh** [pɒʃ] *adj inf* nobel.

**posit** [ˈpɒzɪt] *vt fml* auflstellen.

**position** [pəˈzɪʃn] *n* - **1.** [place, situation] Lage *die* - **2.** [of plane, ship] Position *die* - **3.** [of body] Haltung *die* - **4.** [setting, rank] Stellung *die* - **5.** [in race, combat] Platz *der* - **6.** [job] Stelle *die;* **to be in a/no ~ to do sthg** in der Lage/nicht in der Lage sein, etw zu tun - **7.** [stance, opinion]: **~ on sthg** Haltung *die* gegenüber etw *(D)* ⬦ *vt* positionieren; **to ~ o.s.** sich stellen.

**positive** [ˈpɒzətɪv] *adj* - **1.** [gen] positiv - **2.** [sure, certain] sicher; **to be ~ about sthg** sich einer Sache *(G)* sicher sein - **3.** [evidence, fact] definitiv, eindeutig - **4.** [for emphasis] total.

**positive discrimination** *n* Bevorzugung *die* von Minderheiten.

**positively** [ˈpɒzətɪvlɪ] *adv* - **1.** [gen] positiv - **2.** [prove, identify] definitiv - **3.** [for emphasis] wirklich.

**posse** [ˈpɒsɪ] *n* - **1.** Am [of sheriff] Hilfstrupp *der* - **2.** *inf* [gang] Clique *die*.

**possess** [pəˈzes] *vt* besitzen; **what ~ed you to do that?** was ist in Sie gefahren, dass Sie das gemacht haben?

**possessed** [pəˈzest] *adj* [mad] besessen.

**possession** [pəˈzeʃn] *n* Besitz *der;* **to have sthg in one's ~, to be in ~ of sthg** im Besitz von etw sein.

➡ **possessions** *npl* Habe *die;* **his personal ~s** all seine Sachen.

**possessive** [pəˈzesɪv] *adj* - **1.** *pej* [person] besitzergreifend - **2.** GRAMM Possessiv- ⬦ *n* GRAMM Possessivfunktion *die*.

**possessively** [pəˈzesɪvlɪ] *adv* besitzergreifend.

**possessor** [pəˈzesəʳ] *n fml* Besitzer *der*, -in *die*.

**possibility** [ˌpɒsəˈbɪlətɪ] (*pl* -ies) *n* Möglichkeit *die;* **there's a ~ that I'll be a little late** ich komme vielleicht etwas später.

**possible** [ˈpɒsəbl] *adj* möglich; **would it be ~ for me to ...?** könnte ich vielleicht ...?; **as soon as ~** so bald wie möglich; **as much as ~** so viel wie möglich; **if ~** wenn möglich.

**possibly** [ˈpɒsəblɪ] *adv* - **1.** [perhaps] möglicherweise - **2.** [conceivably] möglich; **I'll do all I ~ can** ich werde mein Möglichstes tun; **I can't ~ do that** das kann ich unmöglich tun.

**possum** [ˈpɒsəm] (*pl inv* OR -s) *n* Am Opossum *das*.

**post** [pəʊst] *n* - **1.** [service, letters, delivery] Post *die;* **by ~** per Post; **in the ~** in der Post - **2.** [pole] Pfosten *der;* **to pip sb at the ~** [in race] jn knapp schlagen; *fig* jm etw vor der Nase weglschnappen - **3.** [job & MIL] Posten *der* ⬦ *vt* - **1.** [by mail] per OR mit der Post schicken - **2.** [employee] versetzen - **3.** *phr*: **to keep sb ~ed** jn auf dem Laufenden halten.

**post-** [pəʊst] *prefix* post-, Nach-.

**postage** ['pəʊstɪdʒ] *n* Porto *das;* ~ **and packing** Porto und Verpackung.

**postage stamp** *n fml* Briefmarke *die.*

**postal** ['pəʊstl] *adj* Post-, postalisch.

**postal order** *n* Postanweisung *die.*

**postbag** ['pəʊstbæg] *n* Postsack *der;* **the programme makers received a large** ~ die Programmverantwortlichen erhielten viel Zuschauerpost.

**postbox** ['pəʊstbɒks] *n Br* Briefkasten *der.*

**postcard** ['pəʊstkɑːd] *n* Postkarte *die.*

**postcode** ['pəʊstkəʊd] *n Br* Postleitzahl *die.*

**postdate** [ˌpəʊst'deɪt] *vt* vorldatieren.

**poster** ['pəʊstər] *n* Poster *das*, Plakat *das.*

**poste restante** [ˌpəʊst'restɑːnt] *n (U) esp Br:* **to send sthg** ~ etw postlagernd schicken.

**posterior** [pɒ'stɪərɪər] *adj* [rear] hintere, -r, -s <> *n hum* Hinterteil *das.*

**posterity** [pɒ'sterətɪ] *n* Nachwelt *die.*

**poster paint** *n* Plakatmalfarbe *die.*

**post-free** *adj esp Br* portofrei.

**postgraduate** [ˌpəʊst'grædʒʊət] *adj* [studies, course] Aufbau- <> *n:* ~ **(student)** *Student, der ein Aufbaustudium absolviert.*

**posthaste** [ˌpəʊst'heɪst] *adv dated* schnellstens.

**posthumous** ['pɒstjʊməs] *adj* postum.

**posthumously** ['pɒstjʊməslɪ] *adv* postum.

**post-industrial** *adj* postindustriell.

**posting** ['pəʊstɪŋ] *n* [assignment] Versetzung *die.*

**postman** ['pəʊstmən] (*pl* -**men** [-mən]) *n* Briefträger *der*, Postbote *der.*

**postmark** ['pəʊstmɑːk] *n* Poststempel *der* <> *vt* stempeln; **the letter is** ~**ed Berlin** der Brief ist in Berlin abgestempelt.

**postmaster** ['pəʊstˌmɑːstər] *n* Postamtsleiter *der.*

**Postmaster General** (*pl* **Postmasters General**) *n* Postminister *der*, -in *die.*

**postmistress** ['pəʊstˌmɪstrɪs] *n* Postamtsleiterin *die.*

**postmortem** [ˌpəʊst'mɔːtəm] *n* - **1.** [autopsy]: ~ **(examination)** Obduktion *die*, Autopsie *die* - **2.** *fig* [analysis] Analyse *die*, Untersuchung *die.*

**postnatal** [ˌpəʊst'neɪtl] *adj* [care, depression] postnatal, nach der Geburt.

**post office** *n* Post *die.*

**post office box** *n* Postfach *das.*

**postoperative** [ˌpəʊst'ɒpərətɪv] *adj* postoperativ, nach der Operation.

**postpaid** [ˌpəʊst'peɪd] *adj* portofrei.

**postpone** [ˌpəʊst'pəʊn] *vt* verschieben; [decision] auf lschieben; **the meeting was** ~**d until Friday** das Treffen wurde auf Freitag verschoben.

**postponement** [ˌpəʊst'pəʊnmənt] *n* Verschiebung *die;* [decision] Aufschub *der.*

**postscript** ['pəʊstskrɪpt] *n* - **1.** [to letter] Postskriptum *das* - **2.** *fig* [additional information] (zusätzlicher) Kommentar.

**postulate** ['pɒstjʊleɪt] *vt fml* [theory] auf lstellen.

**posture** ['pɒstʃər] *n lit* & *fig* Haltung *die;* **his** ~ **on the issue** seine Haltung zu der Frage <> *vi:* sich in Szene *(A)* setzen; *pej* scheinheilig übertreiben.

**posturing** ['pɒstʃərɪŋ] *n (U) pej* scheinheilige Übertreibung.

**postwar** [ˌpəʊst'wɔːr] *adj* Nachkriegs-.

**posy** ['pəʊzɪ] (*pl* -**ies**) *n* Blumensträußchen *das.*

**pot** [pɒt] (*pt* & *pp* -**ted;** *cont* -**ting**) *n* - **1.** [for cooking, flowers] Topf *der* - **2.** [for tea, coffee] Kanne *die* - **3.** [for paint] Büchse *die;* [for jam] Glas *das* - **4.** *(U) drugs sl* [cannabis] Hasch *das* <> *vt* [plant] einltopfen.

**potash** ['pɒtæʃ] *n* Pottasche *die*, Kaliumkarbonat *das.*

**potassium** [pə'tæsɪəm] *n* Kalium *das.*

**potato** [pə'teɪtəʊ] (*pl* -**es**) *n* Kartoffel *die.*

**potato crisps** *Br*, **potato chips** *Am npl* Kartoffelchips *pl.*

**potato peeler** [-ˌpiːlər] *n* Kartoffelschäler *der.*

**potbellied** [pɒt'belɪd] *adj* - **1.** [from overeating, overdrinking] dickbäuchig - **2.** [from malnutrition] mit aufgeblähtem Bauch.

**potboiler** ['pɒtˌbɔɪlər] *n pej künstlerische Arbeit, die nur dem Gelderwerb dient und daher oft sehr einfach und billig in der Ausführung ist.*

**potency** ['pəʊtənsɪ] *n (U)* - **1.** [of argument] Stichhaltigkeit *die* - **2.** [of drink, drug] Stärke *die* - **3.** [of man] Potenz *die.*

**potent** ['pəʊtənt] *adj* - **1.** [argument] stichhaltig - **2.** [drink, drug] stark - **3.** [male] potent.

**potentate** ['pəʊtənteɪt] *n* Potentat *der.*

**potential** [pə'tenʃl] *adj* potenziell <> *n (U)* [of person] Potenzial *das;* **to have** ~ [person] das Potenzial haben; [scheme, plan, company, business] entwicklungsfähig sein.

**potentially** [pə'tenʃəlɪ] *adv* potenziell.

**pothole** ['pɒthəʊl] *n* - **1.** [in road] Schlagloch *das* - **2.** [underground] Höhle *die.*

**P**

**potholer** [ˈpɒtˌhəʊləʳ] n Br Höhlenforscher der, -in die.

**potholing** [ˈpɒtˌhəʊlɪŋ] n Br Höhlenforschung die; **to go ~** eine Höhle erforschen (gehen).

**potion** [ˈpəʊʃn] n Trank der.

**potluck** [ˌpɒtˈlʌk] n: **to take ~** aufs Geratewohl auswählen; [at meal] mit dem vorlieb nehmen, was gerade da ist.

**pot plant** n Topfpflanze die.

**potpourri** [ˌpəʊˈpʊərɪ] n (U) [dried flowers] Potpourri das.

**pot roast** n Schmorbraten der.

**potshot** [ˈpɒtˌʃɒt] n: **to take a ~ at sthg** aufs Geratewohl auf etw (A) schießen.

**potted** [ˈpɒtɪd] adj - **1.** [grown in pot] Topf- - **2.** [meat] eingemacht - **3.** Br fig [condensed] (stark) gekürzt.

**potter** [ˈpɒtəʳ] n [craftsperson] Töpfer der, -in die.
➤ **potter about, potter around** vi Br [do minor work] herumlwerkeln; [work slowly] herumltrödeln.

**Potteries** [ˈpɒtərɪz] npl: **the ~** Region im Westen Mittelenglands, in der die Keramik- und Porzellanproduktion konzentriert ist.

**potter's wheel** n Töpferscheibe die.

**pottery** [ˈpɒtərɪ] (pl -**ies**) n - **1.** (U) [clay objects] Töpferwaren pl - **2.** [craft] Töpfern das - **3.** [factory] Töpferei die.

**potting compost** [ˈpɒtɪŋ-] n (U) Blumenerde die.

**potty** [ˈpɒtɪ] (compar -**ier**; superl -**iest**; pl -**ies**) Br inf adj verrückt; **to be ~ about sb/sthg** nach jm/etw verrückt sein ◇ n Töpfchen das.

**potty-trained** [-ˌtreɪnd] adj: **is he ~ yet?** geht er schon aufs Töpfchen?

**pouch** [paʊtʃ] n Beutel der.

**pouffe** [puːf] n Br [seat] Polstersitz der, Puff der.

**poultice** [ˈpəʊltɪs] n Breipackung die.

**poultry** [ˈpəʊltrɪ] n [meat] Geflügel das ◇ npl [birds] Geflügel das.

**pounce** [paʊns] vi: **to ~ on** OR **upon** sich stürzen auf (+ A).

**pound** [paʊnd] n - **1.** Br [unit of money, currency system] Pfund das - **2.** [unit of weight] ≈ Pfund das (= 454 g) - **3.** [for cars] Abstellplatz der (für abgeschleppte Fahrzeuge); [for dogs] Asyl das ◇ vt - **1.** [strike loudly - on door] hämmern an OR gegen (+ A); [ - on table] hämmern auf (+ A) - **2.** [pulverize] pulverisieren ◇ vi - **1.** [strike loudly]: **to ~ on sthg** [wall, door] an OR gegen etw (A) hämmern; [table] auf etw (A) hämmern - **2.** [beat, throb - heart] pochen, klopfen; [ - head] brummen, dröhnen.

**pound coin** n Einpfundmünze die.

**pounding** [ˈpaʊndɪŋ] n (U) - **1.** [of drums] Schlagen das - **2.** [of heart] Pochen das, Klopfen das - **3.** phr: **to get** OR **take a ~** [be severely damaged] schwer zerstört werden; [be heavily defeated] schwer einstecken müssen.

**pound sterling** n Pfund das Sterling.

**pour** [pɔːʳ] vt - **1.** [cause to flow]: **to ~ sthg (into sthg)** [liquid] etw (in etw (A)) gießen; [grain, sugar] etw (in etw (A)) schütten; **to ~ sb a drink, to ~ a drink for sb** jm einen Drink einlgießen - **2.** fig [invest]: **to ~ money into sthg** Geld in etw (A) fließen lassen ◇ vi lit & fig strömen; **sweat was ~ing off him** ihm lief der Schweiß herunter ◇ v impers [rain hard] (wie aus Eimern) gießen.
➤ **pour in** vi [in großen Mengen) einltreffen.
➤ **pour out** vt sep - **1.** [from container] auslschütten - **2.** [drink] einlschenken - **3.** fig [emotions]: **she ~ed out her heart to me** sie hat mir ihr Herz ausgeschüttet.

**pouring** [ˈpɔːrɪŋ] adj [rain] strömend.

**pout** [paʊt] n Schmollmund der ◇ vi schmollen.

**poverty** [ˈpɒvətɪ] n (U) - **1.** [hardship] Armut die - **2.** [lack]: **~ of sthg** Mangel an etw (D).

**poverty line** n Armutsgrenze die.

**poverty-stricken** [-ˌstrɪkən] adj verarmt.

**poverty trap** n Br Situation eines Empfängers von staatlichen Sozialleistungen, dessen Einkünfte sich durch Aufnahme einer Erwerbstätigkeit verringern würden.

**pow** [paʊ] excl inf peng!

**POW** n abbr of **prisoner of war**.

**powder** [ˈpaʊdəʳ] n [for baking, washing] Pulver das; [for face, body] Puder der ◇ vt [face, body] pudern.

**powder compact** n Puderdose die.

**powdered** [ˈpaʊdəd] adj - **1.** [in powder form]: **~ milk** Trockenmilch die; **~ sugar** Puderzucker der; **~ eggs** Trockenei das - **2.** [covered in powder] gepudert.

**powder puff** n Puderquaste die.

**powder room** n Damentoilette die.

**powdery** [ˈpaʊdərɪ] adj [like powder] pulvrig; **~ snow** Pulverschnee der.

**power** [ˈpaʊəʳ] n - **1.** (U) [control, influence] Macht die; **to be in ~** an der Macht sein; **to come to ~** an die Macht kommen; **to have ~ over sb** Macht über jn haben; **to take ~** die Macht übernehmen - **2.** [ability, capacity] Vermögen das, Fähigkeit die; **mental ~s** geistige Fähigkeiten; **to have great ~s of persuasion** ein Überredungskünstler sein; **to be (with)in one's ~ to do sthg** in js Macht liegen, etw zu tun - **3.** [legal authority] Macht die; **to have the ~ to do sthg** das Recht haben, etw zu tun - **4.** (U) [strength] Stärke die - **5.** (U) TECH [energy]

Energie *die* - **6.** *(U)* [electricity] Strom *der*
- **7.** [powerful person, group] Macht *die;* **the ~s that
be** die Obrigkeit <> *vt* [machine] an|treiben;
**~ed by solar energy** mit Solarenergie betrieben.

**power base** *n* Machtgrundlage *die.*

**powerboat** ['paʊəbəʊt] *n* Rennboot *das.*

**power cut** *n* Stromsperre *die.*

**power failure** *n* Stromausfall *der.*

**powerful** ['paʊəfʊl] *adj* - **1.** [influential] mächtig
- **2.** [strong] kräftig; [drug, smell] stark; [blow, kick]
kraftvoll; [machine] leistungsstark - **3.** [very
convincing, very moving - piece of writing, speech]
überzeugend; [ - work of art] überwältigend.

**powerhouse** ['paʊəhaʊs, *pl* -haʊzɪz] *n* [energetic
person] Energiebündel *das.*

**powerless** ['paʊəlɪs] *adj* machtlos; **he was
~ to help** es stand nicht in seiner Macht zu
helfen.

**power line** *n* Starkstromkabel *das.*

**power of attorney** *n* Vollmacht *die.*

**power plant** *n* [generator] Generator *der.*

**power point** *n Br* Steckdose *die.*

**power-sharing** [-ˌʃeərɪŋ] *n* (U) POL Koalition
*die.*

**power station** *n* Kraftwerk *das.*

**power steering** *n* Servolenkung *die.*

**pp** (*abbr of* **per procurationem**) pp.

**p & p** (*abbr of* **postage and packing**) *n Post-
und Verpackungsgebühr.*

**PPE** (*abbr of* **philosophy, politics and economics**) *n* Universitätsstudiengang mit der Fä-
cherkombination Philosophie, Politik und
Wirtschaftswissenschaft.

**ppm** (*abbr of* **parts per million**) ppm.

**PQ** *abk für Province of Quebec, in Postanschrift verwendet.*

**Pr.** *abbr of* **prince.**

**PR** *n* - **1.** *abbr of* **proportional representation**
- **2.** *abbr of* **public relations** <> *abk für Puerto
Rico, in Postanschrift verwendet.*

**practicable** ['præktɪkəbl] *adj* durchführbar,
umsetzbar.

**practical** ['præktɪkl] *adj* - **1.** [gen] praktisch
- **2.** [practicable] durchführbar, umsetzbar
<> *n* Praktikum *das.*

**practicality** [ˌpræktɪ'kælətɪ] *n* Praxisbezo-
genheit *die.*
⇒ **practicalities** *npl:* **the practicalities of the plan**
die praktische Seite des Plans.

**practical joke** *n* Streich *der.*

**practically** ['præktɪklɪ] *adv* - **1.** [sensibly] praktisch - **2.** [almost] fast.

**practice, practise** *Am* ['præktɪs] *n* - **1.** *(U)*

[training] Übung *die;* [for sport] Training *das;* [for
music] Üben *das;* **~ makes perfect** Übung
macht den Meister; **to be out of ~** aus der
Übung sein - **2.** [training session - of choir] Probe
*die;* [ - of sport] Training *das* - **3.** [implementation]:
**to put sthg into ~** etw in die Praxis um-
setzen; **in ~** [in fact] in Wirklichkeit, tatsächlich - **4.** [habit, regular activity - of group] Brauch
*der;* [ - of person] Gewohnheit *die* - **5.** [carrying out
of profession] Praktizieren *das* - **6.** [business]
Praxis *die.*

**practiced** *adj Am* = **practised.**

**practicing** *adj Am* = **practising.**

**practise, practice** *Am* ['præktɪs] *vt* - **1.** [musical
instrument, movement in sport] üben; [foreign lan-
guage] sprechen - **2.** [safe sex, magic] praktizieren; **to ~ what one preaches** selbst tun, was
man anderen predigt - **3.** [customs, beliefs]
aus|üben - **4.** [do as profession] praktizieren
<> *vi* - **1.** [train] üben - **2.** [doctor, lawyer] prakti-
zieren.

**practised, practiced** *Am* ['præktɪst] *adj* geübt; **to be ~ at doing sthg** geübt sein, etw zu
tun.

**practising, practicing** *Am* ['præktɪsɪŋ] *adj*
praktizierend.

**practitioner** [præk'tɪʃnər] *n* MED praktischer
Arzt, praktische Ärztin.

**pragmatic** [præg'mætɪk] *adj* pragmatisch.

**pragmatism** ['prægmətɪzml] *n* Pragmatis-
mus *der.*

**pragmatist** ['prægmətɪst] *n* Pragmatiker *der,*
-in *die.*

**Prague** [prɑːɡ] *n* Prag *nt.*

**prairie** ['preərɪ] *n* Prärie *die.*

**praise** [preɪz] *n* Lob *das;* **~ be to God!** gepriesen OR gelobt sei Gott!; **to sing sb's ~s** ein
Loblied auf jn singen <> *vt* loben.

**praiseworthy** ['preɪzˌwɜːðɪ] *adj* lobenswert.

**pram** [præm] *n Br* Kinderwagen *der.*

**prance** [prɑːns] *vi* - **1.** [vain person] (herum]-
stolzieren; [child] herum|hüpfen - **2.** [horse]
tänzeln.

**prang** [præŋ] *Br inf dated n* [of car] Unfall *der*
<> *vt* [car] einen Unfall bauen mit.

**prank** [præŋk] *n* Streich *der.*

**prat** [præt] *n Br vinf* Arsch *der.*

**prattle** ['prætl] *pej n* (U) Gequassel *das* <> *vi*
quasseln; **to ~ on about sthg** über etw (A)
quasseln.

**prawn** [prɔːn] *n* Garnele *die.*

**prawn cocktail** *n* Krabbencocktail *der.*

**prawn crackers** *npl* Krabbenchips *pl.*

**pray** [preɪ] *vi* - **1.** RELIG beten; **to ~ to God** zu Gott

**P**

beten - **2.** *fig* [hope]: **to ~ for** sthg auf etw *(A)* hoffen.

**prayer** [preə<sup>r</sup>] *n* - **1.** *(U)* [act of praying] Beten *das*, Gebet *das* - **2.** [set of words] Gebet *das;* **to say one's ~s** sein Gebet sprechen - **3.** *fig* [strong hope] starke Hoffnung.

➤ **prayers** *npl* [service] Andacht *die*.

**prayer book** *n* Gebetsbuch *das*.

**prayer meeting** *n* Gebetsstunde *die*.

**pre-** [pri:] *prefix* vor-, prä-.

**preach** [pri:tʃ] *vt lit* & *fig* predigen ◇ *vi* - **1.** RELIG predigen - **2.** *pej* [pontificate]: **to ~ (at sb)** (jm) eine Predigt halten.

**preacher** ['pri:tʃə<sup>r</sup>] *n* Prediger *der*, -in *die*.

**preamble** [pri:'æmbl] *n* Einleitung *die*.

**prearranged** [ˌpri:ə'reɪndʒd] *adj* vorher vereinbart.

**precarious** [prɪ'keərɪəs] *adj* wackelig; [situation] prekär.

**precariously** [prɪ'keərɪəslɪ] *adv* unsicher.

**precast** [ˌpri:'kɑːst] *adj:* **~ concrete** Fertigbeton *der*.

**precaution** [prɪ'kɔːʃn] *n* Vorsichtsmaßnahme *die;* **as a ~ against** sthg als eine Vorsichtsmaßnahme gegen etw.

**precautionary** [prɪ'kɔːʃənərɪ] *adj* [measure] Vorsichts-.

**precede** [prɪ'si:d] *vt* vorausgehen *(+ D)*.

**precedence** ['presɪdəns] *n:* **to take ~ over** sb/ sthg den Vorrang vor jm/gegenüber etw haben.

**precedent** ['presɪdənt] *n* Präzedenzfall *der*.

**preceding** [prɪ'si:dɪŋ] *adj* - **1.** [month] vorige, -r, -s; [day] Vor- - **2.** [chapter, paragraph] vorhergehend.

**precept** ['pri:sept] *n* Gebot *das*.

**precinct** ['pri:sɪŋkt] *n* - **1.** *Br* [for pedestrians] Fußgängerzone *die;* [for shopping] verkehrsfreies Einkaufsviertel - **2.** *Am* [district] Bezirk *der;* **police ~** Polizeirevier *das*.

➤ **precincts** *npl* [around building] Umgebung *die*, Bereich *der*.

**precious** ['preʃəs] *adj* - **1.** [gen] kostbar - **2.** *inf iron* [damned] verflixt, verdammt; **~ little** herzlich wenig - **3.** [affected] affektiert.

**precious metal** *n* Edelmetall *das*.

**precious stone** *n* Edelstein *der*.

**precipice** ['presɪpɪs] *n* Steilwand *die*, Abgrund *der*.

**precipitate** [*adj* prɪ'sɪpɪtət, *vb* prɪ'sɪpɪteɪt] *fml adj* übereilt, voreilig ◇ *vt* [provoke] (plötzlich) verursachen.

**precipitation** [prɪˌsɪpɪ'teɪʃn] *n (U)* - **1.** CHEM & METEOR Niederschlag *der* - **2.** *fml* [extreme haste] Übereile *die*, Überstürztheit *die*.

**precipitous** [prɪ'sɪpɪtəs] *adj* - **1.** [very steep] abschüssig - **2.** [hasty] jäh, übereilt.

**précis** ['preɪsi:] *(pl inv* ['preɪsi:z]) *n* Zusammenfassung *die*.

**precise** [prɪ'saɪs] *adj* genau; **or, to be ~,** ... oder, um genau zu sein, ...

**precisely** [prɪ'saɪslɪ] *adv* genau.

**precision** [prɪ'sɪʒn] *n (U)* Genauigkeit *die*, Präzision *die* ◇ *comp* [instrument] Präzisions-; **~ bombing** Punktzielbombardement *das*.

**preclude** [prɪ'klu:d] *vt fml* [possibility, misunderstanding] ausIschließen; [event, action] unmöglich machen; **to ~ sb from doing** sthg es jm unmöglich machen, etw zu tun.

**precocious** [prɪ'kəʊʃəs] *adj* frühreif.

**precocity** [prɪ'kɒsətɪ] *n (U)* Frühreife *die*.

**preconceived** [ˌpri:kən'si:vd] *adj* vorgefasst.

**preconception** [ˌpri:kən'sepʃn] *n* vorgefasste Meinung.

**precondition** [ˌpri:kən'dɪʃn] *n fml* (Vor)bedingung *die;* **to be a ~ for** OR **of** sthg eine (Vor)bedingung für etw sein.

**precooked** [ˌpri:'kʊkt] *adj* Fertig-.

**precursor** [ˌpri:'kɜ:sə<sup>r</sup>] *n fml* Vorläufer *der;* **to be a ~ of** sthg ein Vorläufer von etw sein.

**predate** [ˌpri:'deɪt] *vt* vorausIgehen *(+ D)*.

**predator** ['predətə<sup>r</sup>] *n* [animal] Raubtier *das;* [bird] Raubvogel *der*.

**predatory** ['predətrɪ] *adj* räuberisch.

**predecease** [ˌpri:dɪ'si:s] *vt fml:* **to ~ sb** vor jm sterben.

**predecessor** ['pri:dɪsesə<sup>r</sup>] *n* - **1.** [person] Vorgänger *der*, -in *die* - **2.** [thing] Vorläufer *der*.

**predestination** [pri:ˌdestɪ'neɪʃn] *n (U)* RELIG Vorbestimmung *die*, Prädestination *die*.

**predestine** [ˌpri:'destɪn] *vt:* **to be ~d to** fail zum Scheitern verurteilt sein; **they were ~d to meet** es war Schicksal, dass sie sich getroffen haben.

**predetermine** [ˌpri:dɪ'tɜ:mɪn] *vt* [predestine] vorherIbestimmen.

**predetermined** [ˌpri:dɪ'tɜ:mɪnd] *adj* im Voraus festgelegt.

**predicament** [prɪ'dɪkəmənt] *n* missliche Lage; **to be in a ~** in einer misslichen Lage sein.

**predicate** ['predɪkət] *n* GRAMM Prädikat *das*.

**predict** [prɪ'dɪkt] *vt* vorherIsagen.

**predictable** [prɪ'dɪktəbl] *adj* [result, reaction] vorhersehbar; [person, behaviour] berechenbar.

**predictably** [prɪ'dɪktəblɪ] *adv* - **1.** [in an expected way]: **she reacted ~** sie reagierte, wie es vorauszusehen war - **2.** [as was expected] wie es vorauszusehen war.

**prediction** [prɪ'dɪkʃn] n - **1.** [something foretold] Voraussage die - **2.** [foretelling] Voraussagen das.

**predictor** [prɪ'dɪktəʳ] n [indication] Anzeichen das.

**predigest** [ˌpriːdaɪ'dʒest] vt fig vorverdauen.

**predilection** [ˌpriːdɪ'lekʃn] n: ~ for sthg Vorliebe die für etw.

**predispose** [ˌpriːdɪs'pəʊz] vt: to be ~d to do sthg dazu neigen, etw zu tun; to be ~d to sthg zu etw neigen.

**predisposition** [ˈpriːˌdɪspə'zɪʃn] n: ~ to sthg Neigung die zu etw.

**predominance** [prɪ'dɒmɪnəns] n - **1.** [preponderance]: there is a ~ of old people in this area in dieser Gegend wohnen überwiegend alte Leute - **2.** [control] Vorherrschaft die.

**predominant** [prɪ'dɒmɪnənt] adj vorherrschend.

**predominantly** [prɪ'dɒmɪnəntlɪ] adv überwiegend.

**predominate** [prɪ'dɒmɪneɪt] vi - **1.** [be greater in number] überwiegen - **2.** [prevail] vorlherrschen.

**preeminent** [priː'emɪnənt] adj herausragend.

**preempt** [ˌpriː'empt] vt zuvorlkommen (+ D).

**preemptive strike** [priːˌemptɪv-] n Präventivschlag der.

**preen** [priːn] vt - **1.** [subj: bird] putzen - **2.** fig [subj: person]: to ~ o.s. sich zurechtlmachen.

**preexist** [ˌpriːɪg'zɪst] vi vorher existieren.

**prefab** ['priːfæb] n inf Fertighaus das.

**prefabricate** [ˌpriː'fæbrɪkeɪt] vt [part] vorlfertigen; [house, ship] aus Fertigteilen bauen oʀ herlstellen.

**preface** ['prefɪs] n [in book] Vorwort das; ~ to sthg [to text] Vorwort einer Sache (G); [to speech] Einleitung die einer Sache (G) ⟨⟩ vt: to ~ sthg (with sthg) etw (mit etw) einleiten.

**prefect** ['priːfekt] n Br [pupil] Aufsichtsschüler der, -in die.

**prefer** [prɪ'fɜːʳ] (pt & pp -red; cont -ring) vt vorlziehen, bevorzugen; to ~ sthg to sthg etw etw (D) vorlziehen; to ~ to do sthg es vorlziehen, etw zu tun.

**preferable** ['prefrəbl] adj: to be ~ (to sthg) (etw (D)) vorzuziehen sein.

**preferably** ['prefrəblɪ] adv vorzugsweise, am besten.

**preference** ['prefərəns] n - **1.** [liking]: ~ (for sthg) Vorliebe die (für etw) - **2.** [precedence]: to

give sb/sthg ~, to give ~ to sb/sthg jm/etw den Vorzug geben.

**preference shares** Br npl, **preferred stock** Am n (U) Vorzugsaktien pl.

**preferential** [ˌprefə'renʃl] adj [treatment] bevorzugt; ~ terms Sonderkonditionen.

**preferred** [prɪ'fɜːd] adj bevorzugt.

**preferred stock** n (U) Am = **preference shares.**

**prefigure** [ˌpriː'fɪgəʳ] vt fml anldeuten.

**prefix** ['priːfɪks] n ɢʀᴀᴍᴍ Präfix das.

**pregnancy** ['pregnənsɪ] (pl -ies) n Schwangerschaft die.

**pregnancy test** n Schwangerschaftstest der.

**pregnant** ['pregnənt] adj - **1.** [woman] schwanger; [animal] trächtig - **2.** fig [significant] bedeutungsschwer.

**preheated** [ˌpriː'hiːtɪd] adj vorgeheizt.

**prehistoric** [ˌpriːhɪ'stɒrɪk] adj prähistorisch, vorgeschichtlich.

**prehistory** [ˌpriː'hɪstərɪ] n (U) Prähistorie die, Vorgeschichte die.

**pre-industrial** adj vorindustriell.

**prejudge** [ˌpriː'dʒʌdʒ] vt vorschnell urteilen über (+ A).

**prejudice** ['predʒʊdɪs] n - **1.** [bias]: ~ (against) Vorurteil das (gegen) - **2.** (U) [harm]: to be to the ~ of sthg etw (D) schaden ⟨⟩ vt - **1.** [bias]: to ~ sb in favour of/against sthg jn für/gegen etw einlnehmen - **2.** [jeopardize] schaden (+ D).

**prejudiced** ['predʒʊdɪst] adj voreingenommen; to be ~ in favour of/against sb/sthg für/gegen jn/etw voreingenommen sein.

**prejudicial** [ˌpredʒʊ'dɪʃl] adj: to be ~ to sb für jn schädlich sein; to be ~ to sthg einer Sache (D) abträglich sein.

**prelate** ['prelɪt] n ʀᴇʟɪɢ Prälat der.

**preliminary** [prɪ'lɪmɪnərɪ] (pl -ies) adj [activity] vorbereitend; [talks, investigation] Vor-; [report, results] vorläufig.

➡ **preliminaries** npl - **1.** [at start of meeting] Präliminarien pl - **2.** [eliminating contests] Vorausscheidungen pl.

**prelims** ['priːlɪmz] npl Br [exams] Vorprüfungen pl, Zwischenprüfungen pl.

**prelude** ['preljuːd] n [event]: ~ to sthg Auftakt der zu etw.

**premarital** [ˌpriː'mærɪtl] adj vor der Ehe.

**premature** ['premətjʊəʳ] adj - **1.** [death, baldness] vorzeitig - **2.:** ~ birth/child Frühgeburt die - **3.** pej [decision, action] übereilt, verfrüht.

**prematurely** ['premətjʊəlɪ] adv - **1.** [die] vorzeitig; [be born] zu früh - **2.** *pej* [decide, act] übereilt, verfrüht.

**premeditated** [ˌpriːˈmedɪteɪtɪd] *adj* vorsätzlich.

**premenstrual syndrome, premenstrual tension** [priːˌmenstruəl-] *n* prämenstruelles Syndrom.

**premier** [ˈpremjəʳ] *adj* führend; **of ~ importance** von äußerster Wichtigkeit ⟨⟩ *n* Premierminister *der*, -in *die*.

**premiere** [ˈpremɪeəʳ] *n* Premiere *die*, Uraufführung *die*.

**premiership** [ˈpremɪəʃɪp] *n* [office] Amt *das* des Premierministers; [term] Amtszeit *die* des Premierministers.

➤ **Premiership** *n* FTBL *Liga der führenden britischen Fußballvereine, entspricht in etwa der deutschen 1. Bundesliga.*

**premise** [ˈpremɪs] *n* Voraussetzung *die;* **on the ~ that** unter der Voraussetzung, dass.

➤ **premises** *npl* Räumlichkeiten *pl;* **on the ~s** im Hause.

**premium** [ˈpriːmɪəm] *n* - **1.:** **to sell sthg at a ~** [above usual value] etw über Wert verkaufen; **to be at a ~** [in great demand] sehr gefragt sein - **2.** [insurance payment] Prämie *die* - **3.** *phr:* **to put** OR **place a high ~ on sthg** etw für sehr wichtig erachten.

**premium bond** *n* Br Prämienanleihe *die, britische Staatsanleihe, die eine monatliche Verlosungsteilnahme beinhaltet.*

**premonition** [ˌpreməˈnɪʃn] *n* Vorahnung *die.*

**prenatal** [ˌpriːˈneɪtl] *adj* Am Schwangerschafts-.

**preoccupation** [priːˌɒkjʊˈpeɪʃn] *n* Hauptbeschäftigung *die.*

**preoccupied** [priːˈɒkjʊpaɪd] *adj* in Gedanken vertieft OR versunken; **to be ~ with sthg** mit etw beschäftigt sein.

**preoccupy** [priːˈɒkjʊpaɪ] (*pt* & *pp* **-ied**) *vt* beschäftigen.

**preordain** [ˌpriːɔːˈdeɪn] *vt* vorherbestimmen; **he was ~ed to fail** es war ihm vorherbestimmt zu scheitern.

**prep** [prep] *n* (*U*) Br inf [homework]: **to do one's ~** seine Hausaufgaben machen.

**prepacked** [ˌpriːˈpækt] *adj* abgepackt.

**prepaid** [ˈpriːpeɪd] *adj* [envelope] portofrei; [items] im Voraus bezahlt.

**preparation** [ˌprepəˈreɪʃn] *n* - **1.** (*U*) [act of preparing] Vorbereitung *die;* **in ~ for sthg** in Vorbereitung auf etw (A) - **2.** [prepared mixture - food] Fertigmischung *die;* [ - medicine, cosmetics] Präparat *die.*

➤ **preparations** *npl* [plans] Vorbereitungen *pl;* **to make ~s for sthg** Vorbereitungen für etw treffen.

**preparatory** [prɪˈpærətrɪ] *adj* vorbereitend.

**preparatory school** *n* - **1.** [in UK] *private Grundschule, die auf die Aufnahme in eine Public School vorbereitet* - **2.** [in US] *private höhere Schule, die auf die Aufnahme in eine Hochschule vorbereitet.*

**prepare** [prɪˈpeəʳ] *vt* - **1.** [make ready] vorbereiten; **to ~ to do sthg** sich anschicken, etw zu tun - **2.** [make, assemble] zubereiten ⟨⟩ *vi:* **to ~ for sthg** sich auf etw (A) vorbereiten.

**prepared** [prɪˈpeəd] *adj* - **1.** [organized, done beforehand] vorbereitet - **2.** [willing]: **to be ~ to do sthg** bereit sein, etw zu tun - **3.** [ready]: **to be ~ for sthg** auf etw (A) vorbereitet sein.

**preponderance** [prɪˈpɒndərəns] *n* (überwiegende) Mehrheit.

**preponderantly** [prɪˈpɒndərəntlɪ] *adv* überwiegend.

**preposition** [ˌprepəˈzɪʃn] *n* Präposition *die.*

**prepossessing** [ˌpriːpəˈzesɪŋ] *adj* fml anziehend.

**preposterous** [prɪˈpɒstərəs] *adj* absurd, grotesk.

**preppy** [ˈprepɪ] (*pl* **-ies**) *adj* Am inf *bezeichnet den konservativen Kleidungsstil eines wohlhabenden Schülers einer privaten höheren Schule.*

**prep school** *n abbr of* **preparatory school**.

**Pre-Raphaelite** [ˌpriːˈræfəlaɪt] *adj* präraffaelitisch ⟨⟩ *n* Präraffaelit *der.*

**prerecorded** [ˌpriːrɪˈkɔːdɪd] *adj* vorher aufgezeichnet.

**prerequisite** [ˌpriːˈrekwɪzɪt] *n:* **~ (of** OR **for)** Voraussetzung *die* (für).

**prerogative** [prɪˈrɒgətɪv] *n* Vorrecht *das.*

**presage** [ˈpresɪdʒ] *vt fml* ankündigen.

**Presbyterian** [ˌprezbɪˈtɪərɪən] *adj* presbyterianisch ⟨⟩ *n* Presbyterianer *der*, -in *die.*

**presbytery** [ˈprezbɪtrɪ] *n* [residence] (katholische) Pfarrei.

**preschool** [ˌpriːˈskuːl] *adj* Vorschul-.

**prescient** [ˈpresɪənt] *adj fml* voraussehend, weitsichtig.

**prescribe** [prɪˈskraɪb] *vt* - **1.** MED verschreiben - **2.** [order] vorschreiben.

**prescription** [prɪˈskrɪpʃn] *n* MED Rezept *das;* **on ~** auf Rezept.

**prescription charge** *n* Br Rezeptgebühr *die.*

**prescriptive** [prɪˈskrɪptɪv] *adj* GRAMM normativ.

**presence** [ˈprezns] *n* - **1.** [being present] Anwesenheit *die*, Gegenwart *die;* **in his ~** in seiner Gegenwart - **2.** (*U*) [personality, charisma] Ausstrahlung *die;* **to have ~** Ausstrahlung haben - **3.** [entity]: **I felt a ghostly ~ around me** ich spürte, dass etwas Geisterhaftes im Zimmer war.

**presence of mind** n Geistesgegenwart die.

**present** [adj & n 'preznt, vb prı'zent] adj - **1.** [current] gegenwärtig, derzeitig - **2.** [in attendance] anwesend; **to be ~ at sthg** bei etw anwesend sein ⟨> n - **1.** [current time]: **the ~** die Gegenwart; **at ~** zur Zeit; **for the ~** zur Zeit - **2.** [gift] Geschenk das - **3.** GRAMM: **~ (tense)** Präsens das, Gegenwart die ⟨> vt - **1.** [gift, award] überreichen; **to ~ sb with sthg, to ~ sthg to sb** jm etw überreichen, etw an jn überreichen - **2.** [opportunity] bieten; [problem] auflwerfen; **this job will ~ her with a challenge** diese Arbeit wird eine Herausforderung für sie sein - **3.** [introduce - person] vorlstellen; **to ~ sb to sb** jm jn vorlstellen - **4.** [TV, radio programme] moderieren - **5.** [facts, figures, report] vorllegen - **6.** [portray] darlstellen; **the article ~s her as a liar** der Artikel stellt sie als Lügnerin hin - **7.** [arrive, go]: **to ~ o.s.** [at reception] sich melden; [for interview] erscheinen - **8.** [perform] darlbieten.

**presentable** [prı'zentəbl] adj präsentabel, vorzeigbar.

**presentation** [ˌprezn'teıʃn] n - **1.** (U) [publication, broadcasting] Präsentation die - **2.** (U) [of product] Aufmachung die; [of policy, text] Präsentation die - **3.** [ceremony] Verleihung die - **4.** [talk] Präsentation die - **5.** [performance] Darbietung die.

**presentation copy** n Widmungsexemplar das.

**present day** n: **the ~** der heutige Tag, jetzt.
⮞ **present-day** adj heutig.

**presenter** [prı'zentə'] n Br Moderator der, -in die.

**presentiment** [prı'zentımənt] n fml (böse) Vorahnung.

**presently** ['prezntlı] adv - **1.** [soon] bald - **2.** [now] gegenwärtig, jetzt.

**preservation** [ˌprezə'veıʃn] n (U) - **1.** [of democracy, law and order] Aufrechterhaltung die; [of building, wildlife, countryside] Erhaltung die - **2.** [of food] Konservierung die.

**preservation order** n esp Br: **to be under a ~** [building] unter Denkmalschutz stehen.

**preservative** [prı'zɜːvətıv] n [in food] Konservierungsmittel das; [for wood] Schutzmittel das.

**preserve** [prı'zɜːv] vt - **1.** [democracy, peace, situation] aufrechterhalten; [building, wildlife, way of life] erhalten; [food] konservieren; [fruit] einlwecken ⟨> n [jam] Konfitüre die.

**preserved** [prı'zɜːvd] adj [food] konserviert; [fruit] eingeweckt.

**preset** [ˌpriː'set] (pt & pp preset; cont -ting) vt [oven] vorlheizen; [VCR] programmieren.

**preshrunk** [ˌpriː'ʃrʌŋk] adj vorgewaschen.

**preside** [prı'zaıd] vi den Vorsitz haben OR führen; **to ~ over OR at sthg** den Vorsitz bei etw haben OR führen.

**presidency** ['prezıdənsı] (pl -ies) n - **1.** [position] Präsidentschaft die - **2.** [period of time] Präsidentschaftszeit die, Amtszeit die.

**president** ['prezıdənt] n Präsident der, -in die.

**President-elect** n (neu) gewählter Präsident, *Titel des US-Präsidenten zwischen seiner Wahl im November und der Amtseinführung im Januar.*

**presidential** [ˌprezı'denʃl] adj [decision] des Präsidenten; [campaign, election] Präsidentschafts-; [staff, limousine] Präsidenten-.

**press** [pres] n - **1.** [push]: **to give sthg a ~** etw drücken; **at the ~ of a button** auf Knopfdruck - **2.** [journalism]: **the ~** die Presse; **to get a good/bad ~** eine gute/schlechte Presse bekommen - **3.** [printing machine, pressing machine] Presse die ⟨> vt - **1.** [push firmly] drücken; **to ~ sthg against sthg** etw gegen etw pressen - **2.** [squeeze] drücken; [grapes] keltern; [flowers] pressen - **3.** [iron] bügeln - **4.** [urge, force] drängen; **to ~ sb for sthg** jn zu etw drängen; **to ~ sb to do sthg OR into doing sthg** jn drängen OR zwingen, etw zu tun; **to ~ sthg (up)on sb** jm etw auf ldrängen - **5.** [pursue - claim, point] beharren auf (+ D) - **6.** LAW: **to ~ charges (against sb)** (gegen jn) Anklage erheben ⟨> vi - **1.** [push hard]: **to ~ (on)** drücken (auf (+ A)) - **2.** [surge] drängen.
⮞ **press on** vi [continue]: **to ~ on with** weiterlmachen (mit).

**press agency** n Presseagentur die.

**press agent** n Presseagent der, -in die.

**press baron** n Br Zeitungsbaron der, Zeitungsmagnat der.

**press box** n Reporterkabine die.

**press conference** n Pressekonferenz die.

**press corps** n Am Berichterstatter pl, Korrespondenten pl.

**press cutting** [-ˌkʌtıŋ] n Br Zeitungsausschnitt der.

**pressed** [prest] adj: **to be ~ for time/money** unter Zeitdruck/finanziellem Druck stehen.

**press fastener** n Br Druckknopf der.

**press gallery** n Pressetribüne die.

**pressgang** ['presgæŋ] n Anwerbetrupp der ⟨> vt Br: **to ~ sb into doing sthg** jn drängen OR zwingen, etw zu tun.

**pressing** ['presıŋ] adj [urgent] dringend, drängend.

**pressman** ['presmæn] (pl -men [-men]) n Br [journalist] Journalist der.

**press officer** n Pressesprecher der, -in die.

**press release** n Pressemitteilung die.

**press-stud** n Br Druckknopf der.

**press-up** n Br Liegestütz der.

**pressure** ['preʃə'] n (U) lit & fig Druck der; to put ~ on sb (to do sthg) auf jn Druck auslüben(, etw zu tun) ⬦ vt: to ~ sb to do OR into doing sthg jn (dazu) drängen, etw zu tun.

**pressure cooker** n Schnellkochtopf der.

**pressure gauge** n Druckmesser der.

**pressure group** n Interessengruppe die.

**pressurize, -ise** ['preʃəraɪz] vt - 1. TECH unter Druck setzen - 2. Br [force]: to ~ sb to do OR into doing sthg jn (dazu) drängen, etw zu tun.

**prestige** [pre'stiːʒ] n Prestige das ⬦ comp Prestige-.

**prestigious** [pre'stɪdʒəs] adj angesehen.

**presumably** [prɪ'zjuːməblɪ] adv vermutlich.

**presume** [prɪ'zjuːm] vt [assume] anlnehmen; to ~ (that) anlnehmen, dass; he is ~d dead es wird davon ausgegangen, dass er tot ist.

**presumption** [prɪ'zʌmpʃn] n - 1. [assumption] Annahme die - 2. (U) [audacity] Vermessenheit die.

**presumptuous** [prɪ'zʌmptʃʊəs] adj anmaßend.

**presuppose** [ˌpriːsə'pəʊz] vt vorauslsetzen.

**pretax** [ˌpriː'tæks] adj vor Steuern.

**pretence, pretense** Am [prɪ'tens] n: he made no ~ of being interested er gab nicht vor, interessiert zu sein; under false ~s unter Vortäuschung falscher Tatsachen.

**pretend** [prɪ'tend] vt - 1. [make believe]: to ~ to do sthg vorgeben, etw zu tun; to ~ (that) so tun, als ob - 2. [claim]: to ~ to do sthg behaupten, dass man etw tut ⬦ vi [feign] nur so tun.

**pretense** n Am = pretence.

**pretension** [prɪ'tenʃn] n [claim] Anspruch der; she has OR makes no ~s to being a musician sie hat nicht den Anspruch, eine Musikerin zu sein.

**pretentious** [prɪ'tenʃəs] adj [person] wichtigtuerisch; [film, book] prätentiös.

**pretentiously** [prɪ'tenʃəslɪ] adv [behave] wichtigtuerisch; [talk, write] hochtrabend.

**pretentiousness** [prɪ'tenʃəsnɪs] n (U) [of person] Wichtigtuerei die.

**preterite** ['pretərət] n Präteritum das.

**pretext** ['priːtekst] n Vorwand der; on OR under the ~ that unter dem Vorwand, dass; on OR under the ~ of doing sthg unter dem Vorwand, etw zu tun.

**prettily** ['prɪtɪlɪ] adv [dress] hübsch; [smile] nett.

**pretty** ['prɪtɪ] (compar -ier; superl -iest) adj hübsch ⬦ adv [quite, rather] ziemlich; ~ much OR well so ziemlich.

**pretzel** ['pretsl] n (Laugen)brezel die.

**prevail** [prɪ'veɪl] vi - 1. [be widespread] vorherrschen; [custom] weit verbreitet sein - 2. [triumph] sich durchlsetzen; to ~ over sb/sthg sich gegen jn/etw durchlsetzen - 3. [persuade]: to ~ (up)on sb to do sthg jn dazu bringen, etw zu tun.

**prevailing** [prɪ'veɪlɪŋ] adj - 1. [belief, opinion] vorherrschend; [fashion] aktuell - 2. [wind] vorherrschend.

**prevalence** ['prevələns] n Vorherrschen das; [of illness] weite Verbreitung.

**prevalent** ['prevələnt] adj vorherrschend; [illness] weit verbreitet.

**prevaricate** [prɪ'værɪkeɪt] vi Ausflüchte machen.

**prevent** [prɪ'vent] vt verhindern; [illness] vorlbeugen (+ D); to ~ sb (from) doing sthg jn daran hindern, etw zu tun; they couldn't ~ the fire from spreading sie konnten die Ausbreitung des Feuers nicht verhindern.

**preventable** [prɪ'ventəbl] adj: to be ~ verhindert werden können.

**preventative** [prɪ'ventətɪv] adj = preventive.

**prevention** [prɪ'venʃn] n (U) [of disease] Vorbeugung die; accident/crime ~ Unfall-/Verbrechensverhütung die.

**preventive** [prɪ'ventɪv] adj vorbeugend; [measures, medicine] Präventiv-.

**preview** ['priːvjuː] n - 1. [early showing - of film, play] Voraufführung die; [ - of exhibition] Vorbesichtigung die - 2. [trailer for films] Vorschau die.

**previous** ['priːvɪəs] adj - 1. [earlier, prior] früher; ~ conviction Vorstrafe die; do you have any ~ experience? haben Sie schon Berufserfahrung? - 2. [with days and dates] vorhergehend; in ~ years in früheren Jahren - 3. [former] vorherig, früher.

**previously** ['priːvɪəslɪ] adv - 1. [formerly] vorher - 2. [with days and dates] zuvor.

**prewar** [ˌpriː'wɔː'] adj Vorkriegs-.

**prewash** ['priːwɒʃ] n Vorwäsche die.

**prey** [preɪ] n (U) Beute die; to fall ~ to sb/sthg jm/etw zum Opfer fallen.

➤ **prey on** vt fus - 1. [subj: animal, bird] Beute machen auf (+ A) - 2. [trouble]: to ~ on sb's mind jn bedrücken.

**price** [praɪs] n - 1. [cost] Preis der - 2. [value] Wert der; to be without ~ (mit Geld) nicht zu bezahlen sein - 3. fig: they reached an agreement, but at a ~ sie sind zu einer Einigung gekommen, aber für einen hohen Preis; **at any ~** um jeden Preis; **to pay the ~ for sthg** den Preis für etw bezahlen ◇ *vt* [set cost of] den Preis festlsetzen von; **it was ~d at £100** es sollte 100 Pfund kosten.

**price-cutting** [-ˈkʌtɪŋ] *n (U)* Preissenkungen *pl.*

**price-fixing** [-ˌfɪksɪŋ] *n (U)* Preisabsprachen *pl.*

**priceless** [ˈpraɪslɪs] *adj* - **1.** [very valuable] von unschätzbarem Wert - **2.** *inf* [funny] wahnsinnig komisch.

**price list** *n* Preisliste *die.*

**price tag** *n* [label] Preisschild *das.*

**price war** *n* Preiskrieg *der.*

**pricey** [ˈpraɪsɪ] (*compar* **-ier;** *superl* **-iest**) *adj inf* teuer.

**prick** [prɪk] *n* - **1.** [scratch, wound] Stich *der* - **2.** *vulg* [penis] Schwanz *der* - **3.** *vulg* [stupid person] Arschloch *das* ◇ *vt* [jab, pierce] stechen in (+ A); **to ~ one's finger** sich (D) in den Finger stechen.

➤ **prick up** *vt sep:* **to ~ up one's ears** *lit & fig* seine Ohren spitzen.

**prickle** [ˈprɪkl] *n* - **1.** [thorn] Stachel *der* - **2.** [sensation] Prickeln *das* ◇ *vi* prickeln.

**prickly** [ˈprɪklɪ] (*compar* **-ier;** *superl* **-iest**) *adj* - **1.** [thorny] stachelig - **2.** *fig* [touchy] reizbar.

**prickly heat** *n* Hitzeausschlag *der.*

**pride** [praɪd] *n* Stolz *der;* **to take ~ in sthg** auf etw (A) stolz sein; **his ~ and joy** sein ganzer Stolz; **to have ~ of place** einen Ehrenplatz haben; **to swallow one's ~** seinen Stolz überwinden ◇ *vt:* **to ~ o.s. on sthg** auf etw (A) stolz sein.

**priest** [priːst] *n* Priester *der.*

**priestess** [ˈpriːstɪs] *n* Priesterin *die.*

**priesthood** [ˈpriːsthʊd] *n (U)* - **1.** [position, office]: **the ~** das Priesteramt - **2.** [priests collectively]: **the ~** die Priesterschaft.

**prig** [prɪg] *n* Tugendbold *der.*

**prim** [prɪm] (*compar* **-mer;** *superl* **-mest**) *adj* [person, behaviour] sittsam.

**primacy** [ˈpraɪməsɪ] *n* [preeminence] Vorrang *der.*

**prima donna** [ˌpriːməˈdɒnə] (*pl* **-s**) *n lit & fig* Primadonna *die.*

**primaeval** [praɪˈmiːvəl] *adj* = **primeval**.

**prima facie** [ˌpraɪməˈfeɪʃiː] *adj* LAW: **~ evidence** Anscheinsbeweis *der;* **we have ~ evidence that ...** wir haben glaubhafte Beweise, dass ...

**primal** [ˈpraɪml] *adj* - **1.** [original] Ur- - **2.** [most important - need] Grund-; [ - concern] Haupt-.

**primarily** [ˈpraɪmərɪlɪ] *adv* in erster Linie.

**primary** [ˈpraɪmərɪ] (*pl* **-ies**) *adj* - **1.** [main - concern, aim, reason] Haupt- - **2.** SCH Grundschul- ◇ *n* Am POL Vorwahl *die (zur Bestimmung der Präsidentschaftskandidaten einer Partei).*

**PRIMARIES**

Die amerikanischen „Primaries" sind Wahlen (je nach Einzelstaat direkt oder indirekt), bei denen die Kandidaten einer Partei für öffentliche Ämter und Parlamentssitze gewählt werden. Sie fungieren auch als Vorwahlen zur Bestimmung der Delegierten, die später den Präsidentschaftskandidaten nominieren.

**primary colour** *n* Grundfarbe *die.*

**primary election** *n* Am Vorwahl *die (zur Bestimmung der Präsidentschaftskandidaten einer Partei).*

**primary school** *n* Grundschule *die.*

**primary teacher** *n* [in UK] Grundschullehrer *der,* -in *die.*

**primate** [ˈpraɪmeɪt] *n* - **1.** ZOOL Primat *der* - **2.** RELIG Primas *der.*

**prime** [praɪm] *adj* - **1.** [main - concern, aim, reason] Haupt- - **2.** [excellent] erstklassig ◇ *n* [peak]: **to be in one's ~** in den besten Jahren sein ◇ *vt* - **1.** [inform]: **to ~ sb about sthg** jn über etw (A) instruieren - **2.** [paint] grundieren - **3.** [make ready - gun] laden; [ - bomb] scharf machen.

**prime minister** *n* Premierminister *der,* -in *die.*

**prime mover** [-ˈmuːvəʳ] *n fig* [person] treibende Kraft.

**prime number** *n* Primzahl *die.*

**primer** [ˈpraɪməʳ] *n* - **1.** [paint] Grundierung *die* - **2.** [textbook] Fibel *die.*

**prime time** *n (U)* Hauptsendezeit *die.*

➤ **prime-time** *adj:* **~ television** Hauptsendezeit *die* im Fernsehen.

**primeval** [praɪˈmiːvl] *adj* [ancestor] Ur-; **~ forest** Urwald *der.*

**primitive** [ˈprɪmɪtɪv] *adj* primitiv.

**primordial** [praɪˈmɔːdɪəl] *adj fml* ursprünglich.

**primrose** [ˈprɪmrəʊz] *n* Himmelschlüssel *der.*

**Primus stove®** [ˈpraɪməs-] *n* Campingkocher *der.*

**prince** [prɪns] *n* - **1.** [son of king, queen] Prinz *der;* **Prince of Wales** Prince of Wales - **2.** [ruler] Fürst *der.*

**Prince Charming** [-ˈtʃɑːmɪŋ] *n hum* Märchenprinz *der.*

**princely** [ˈprɪnslɪ] (*compar* **-ier;** *superl* **-iest**) *adj lit & fig* fürstlich.

**princess** [prɪnˈses] *n* Prinzessin *die;* **Princess**

P

Royal *(Titel für die)* älteste Tochter eines Monarchen.

**principal** [ˈprɪnsəpl] *adj* Haupt-; **the ~ rivers** die wichtigsten Flüsse ◇ *n* [of school, college] Direktor *der*, -in *die*.

**principality** [ˌprɪnsɪˈpælətɪ] *(pl* -ies) *n* Fürstentum *das;* **the Principality** [Wales] das Fürstentum Wales, *Fürstentum, das dem britischen Thronfolger untersteht.*

**principally** [ˈprɪnsəplɪ] *adv* hauptsächlich.

**principle** [ˈprɪnsəpl] *n* - **1.** [gen] Prinzip *das* - **2.** [integrity] Prinzipien *pl;* **to do sthg on ~** OR **as a matter of ~** etw aus Prinzip tun.

➤ **in principle** *adv* im Prinzip.

**principled** [ˈprɪnsəpld] *adj* [person] mit Prinzipien; [behaviour] von Prinzipien geleitet.

**print** [prɪnt] *n* - **1.** *(U)* [printed characters] Schrift *die;* [printed matter] Gedrucktes *das;* **in large/small ~** groß/klein gedruckt; **in ~** [available] erhältlich; [in newspaper] gedruckt; **to be out of ~** vergriffen sein - **2.** ART Druck *der* - **3.** [photograph] Abzug *der* - **4.** [fabric] bedruckter Stoff - **5.** [footprint, fingerprint] Abdruck *der* ◇ *vt* - **1.** [gen] drucken - **2.** [write clearly] in Druckschrift schreiben ◇ *vi* - **1.** [in handwriting] in Druckschrift schreiben - **2.** [printer] drucken.

➤ **print out** *vt sep* COMPUT ausldrucken.

**printed circuit** [ˌprɪntɪd-] *n* gedruckte Schaltung.

**printed matter** [ˈprɪntɪd-] *n (U)* Drucksache *die.*

**printer** [ˈprɪntəʳ] *n* [person & COMPUT] Drucker *der;* [firm] Druckerei *die.*

**printing** [ˈprɪntɪŋ] *n (U)* - **1.** [act] Drucken *das* - **2.** [trade] Druckereigewerbe *das.*

**printing press** *n* Druckerpresse *die.*

**printout** [ˈprɪntaʊt] *n* Ausdruck *der.*

**prior** [ˈpraɪəʳ] *adj* - **1.** [previous - agreement] vorherig; [ - warning] Vor-; **a ~ engagement** eine anderweitige Verpflichtung - **2.** [more important] vorrangig ◇ *n* [monk] Prior *der.*

➤ **prior to** *prep* vor (+ *D*); **~ to leaving** bevor ich/er/etc ging.

**prioritize, -ise** [praɪˈɒrɪtaɪz] *vt* [give priority to] den Vorrang geben (+ *D*); [put in order of importance] nach Dringlichkeit ordnen.

**priority** [praɪˈɒrɪtɪ] *(pl* -ies) *adj* vorrangig ◇ *n* - **1.** Vorrang *der* - **2.: to have** OR **take ~ (over sthg)** Vorrang (vor etw *(D)*) haben; **to have top ~** absolute Priorität haben.

➤ **priorities** *npl* Prioritäten *pl;* **we must get our priorities right** wir müssen unsere Prioritäten setzen.

**priory** [ˈpraɪərɪ] *(pl* -ies) *n* Priorat *das.*

**prise** [praɪz] *vt:* **to ~ sthg open** etw auflbrechen.

**prism** [ˈprɪzm] *n* Prisma *das.*

**prison** [ˈprɪzn] *n* Gefängnis *das.*

**prison camp** *n* Gefangenenlager *das.*

**prisoner** [ˈprɪznəʳ] *n* Gefangene *der*, *die;* **to be taken ~** gefangen genommen werden.

**prisoner of war** *(pl* **prisoners of war)** *n* Kriegsgefangene *der*, *die.*

**prissy** [ˈprɪsɪ] *(compar* -ier; *superl* -iest) *adj* spießig.

**pristine** [ˈprɪstiːn] *adj* makellos.

**privacy** [Br ˈprɪvəsɪ, Am ˈpraɪvəsɪ] *n (U)* Privatsphäre *die;* **in the ~ of one's own home** in den eigenen vier Wänden.

**private** [ˈpraɪvɪt] *adj* - **1.** [gen] privat; [hospital, house, industry, life] Privat- - **2.** [confidential] vertraulich - **3.** [personal - belongings, plans] persönlich - **4.** [secluded] abgelegen - **5.** [reserved] in sich zurückgezogen ◇ *n* - **1.** [soldier] einfacher Soldat; **Private Smith** Soldat Smith - **2.** [secrecy]: **in ~** [of conversation between two people] unter vier Augen; [of meeting] hinter geschlossenen Türen.

➤ **privates** *npl inf* ANAT Geschlechtsteile *pl.*

**private company** *n* Privatunternehmen *das.*

**private detective** *n* Privatdetektiv *der*, -in *die.*

**private enterprise** *n (U)* freies Unternehmertum.

**private eye** *n* Privatdetektiv *der*, -in *die.*

**private income** *n Br* private Einkünfte *pl.*

**private investigator** *n* Privatdetektiv *der*, -in *die.*

**private limited company** *n* COMM Gesellschaft *die* mit beschränkter Haftung.

**privately** [ˈpraɪvɪtlɪ] *adv* - **1.** [not by the state] privat; **~ owned** in Privatbesitz - **2.** [confidentially - discuss between two people] unter vier Augen; [ - discuss in meeting] hinter verschlossenen Türen; [ - meet, agree] insgeheim - **3.** [personally] persönlich.

**private member's bill** *n Br* Gesetzentwurf *eines Abgeordneten, der kein Ministeramt hat.*

**private parts** *npl inf* Geschlechtsteile *pl.*

**private practice** *n (U) Br:* **to be in ~** eine Privatpraxis haben.

**private property** *n (U)* Privatgrundstück *das.*

**private school** *n* Privatschule *die.*

**private sector** *n (U):* **the ~** der private Sektor.

**privation** [praɪˈveɪʃn] *n:* **a life of ~** ein Leben voller Entbehrungen.

**privatization, -isation** [ˌpraɪvɪtaɪˈzeɪʃn] *n (U)* Privatisierung *die.*

**privatize, -ise** [ˈpraɪvɪtaɪz] *vt* privatisieren.

**privet** [ˈprɪvɪt] *n (U)* Liguster *der.*

**privilege** ['prɪvɪlɪdʒ] n - 1. [special advantage]
Privileg das - 2. [honour] Ehre die.

**privileged** ['prɪvɪlɪdʒd] adj [person, position] privilegiert.

**privy** ['prɪvɪ] adj: to be ~ to sthg fml in etw (A)
eingeweiht sein.

**Privy Council** n Br: the ~ der Geheime
Staatsrat.

**Privy Purse** n: the ~ von der britischen Regierung zur Verfügung gestelltes Geld für die
persönlichen Ausgaben des Monarchen

**prize** [praɪz] adj - 1. [prizewinning] preisgekrönt
- 2. [perfect] perfekt; ~ **idiot** Vollidiot der
- 3. [valued] wertvoll <> n Preis der <> vt [value]
(hoch)schätzen.

**prize day** n Br Tag, an dem an britischen
Schulen Preise für besondere Leistungen vergeben werden.

**prizefight** ['praɪzfaɪt] n Preisboxkampf der.

**prize-giving** [-ˌgɪvɪŋ] n Br Preisverleihung
die.

**prize money** n (U) Preisgeld das.

**prizewinner** ['praɪzˌwɪnəʳ] n Preisträger der,
-in die.

**pro** [prəʊ] (pl -s) n - 1. inf [professional] Profi der
- 2. [advantage]: the ~s and cons das Für und
Wider.

**pro-** [prəʊ] prefix pro-; ~**government** für die
Regierung.

**pro-am** [ˌprəʊ'æm] adj für Profis und Amateure <> n Wettkampf/Turnier für Profis
und Amateure.

**probability** [ˌprɒbə'bɪlətɪ] (pl -ies) n - 1. [gen]
Wahrscheinlichkeit die; in all ~ aller Wahrscheinlichkeit nach - 2. [probable thing, event]:
war is a real ~ es ist sehr wahrscheinlich,
dass Krieg ausbrechen wird.

**probable** ['prɒbəbl] adj wahrscheinlich.

**probably** ['prɒbəblɪ] adv wahrscheinlich.

**probate** ['prəʊbeɪt] LAW n (U) gerichtliche Tes-
tamentsbestätigung <> vt Am: to ~ a will die
Echtheit eines Testaments bestätigen.

**probation** [prə'beɪʃn] n (U) - 1. [of prisoner] Bewährung die; to put sb on ~ jm Bewährung
geben - 2. [trial period] Probezeit die; I'm on ~
ich bin in der Probezeit; to be on ~ for two
years zwei Jahre Probezeit haben.

**probationary** [prə'beɪʃnrɪ] adj [teacher, nurse] in
der Probezeit; [year] Probe-; ~ period Probezeit die.

**probationer** [prə'beɪʃnəʳ] n - 1. [employee] Angestellte der, die auf Probe - 2. [offender] auf
Bewährung Freigelassene der, auf Bewährung Freigelassene die.

**probation officer** n Bewährungshelfer
der, -in die.

**probe** [prəʊb] n - 1. [investigation]: ~ (into) Untersuchung die (+ G) - 2. MED & TECH Sonde die
<> vt - 1. [investigate] sondieren; [mystery] erfor-
schen - 2. [prod - with stick] suchend herumlstochern in (+ D) <> vi: to ~ for evidence nach
Beweisen suchen; to ~ into sb's affairs in js
Angelegenheiten heruml schnüffeln.

**probing** ['prəʊbɪŋ] adj [question] bohrend; [look]
forschend.

**probity** ['prəʊbətɪ] n fml Redlichkeit die.

**problem** ['prɒbləm] n Problem das; no ~! inf
kein Problem! <> comp Problem-.

**problematic(al)** [ˌprɒblə'mætɪk(l)] adj problematisch.

**problem page** n Kummerkasten-Seite die.

**procedural** [prə'siːdʒərəl] adj verfahrens-
technisch.

**procedure** [prə'siːdʒəʳ] n Verfahren das.

**proceed** [vb prə'siːd, npl 'prəʊsiːdz] vt: to ~ to do
sthg dazu übergehen, etw zu tun <> vi
- 1. [continue] fortlfahren; [activity] fortgesetzt
werden; [event] weiterl gehen; to ~ with sthg
mit etw fortlfahren - 2. fml [go, advance - on foot]
gehen; [- in vehicle] fahren; to ~ somewhere
sich irgendwohin begeben.

➡ **proceeds** npl Erlös der.

**proceedings** [prə'siːdɪŋz] npl - 1. [series of ac-
tions] Vorgänge pl; [event] Veranstaltung die
- 2. [legal action] Verfahren das.

**process** ['prəʊses] n - 1. [series of actions] Prozess der; electoral ~ Wahlverfahren das; in the
~ dabei; to be in the ~ of doing sthg dabei
sein, etw zu tun - 2. [method] Verfahren das
<> vt - 1. [treat - materials] verarbeiten; [- food]
behandeln - 2. [examine, deal with - application]
bearbeiten; [- information, data] verarbeiten.

**processed cheese** [ˌprəʊsest-] n Schmelz-
käse der.

**processing** ['prəʊsesɪŋ] n (U) - 1. [treating - of ma-
terials] Verarbeitung die; [- of food] Behandeln
das - 2. [examining - of applications] Bearbeitung
die; [- of information, data] Verarbeitung die.

**procession** [prə'seʃn] n Zug der; funeral ~
Trauerzug der; in ~ in einem langen Zug.

P

**processor** [ˈprəʊsesəʳ] n - 1. COMPUT Prozessor der - 2. CULIN Küchenmaschine die.

**pro-choice** adj: ~ group Gruppe, die für die Entscheidungsfreiheit bei Abtreibungen eintritt.

**proclaim** [prəˈkleɪm] vt [independence] proklamieren; [innocence, loyalty] beteuern; **to ~ sb king** jn zum König ernennen.

**proclamation** [ˌprɒkləˈmeɪʃn] n [of independence, ruler] Proklamation die; [of innocence, loyalty] Beteuerung die.

**proclivity** [prəˈklɪvətɪ] (pl -ies) n fml: ~ (to OR towards) Neigung die (zu).

**procrastinate** [prəˈkræstɪneɪt] vi: **I should stop procrastinating** ich darf es nicht länger hinauslschieben.

**procrastination** [prəˌkræstɪˈneɪʃn] n Hinausschieben das.

**procreate** [ˈprəʊkrɪeɪt] vi sich fortlpflanzen.

**procreation** [ˌprəʊkrɪˈeɪʃn] n Fortpflanzung die.

**procurator fiscal** [ˌprɒkjʊereɪtəʳ-] n Scot ≃ Staatsanwalt der, -anwältin die.

**procure** [prəˈkjʊəʳ] vt [tickets, supplies] beschaffen; [somebody's release] bewirken.

**procurement** [prəˈkjʊəmənt] n [of tickets, supplies] Beschaffung die; [of release] Bewirkung die.

**prod** [prɒd] (pt & pp **-ded**; cont **-ding**) n - 1. [push, poke] Stupser der - 2. fig [reminder]: **you'll need to give him a ~** du musst ihn noch mal daran erinnern <> vt - 1. [push, poke - person] anlstupsen; [ - ground, food] herumlstochern in (+ D) - 2. [remind, prompt]: **to ~ sb (into doing sthg)** jn dazu bringen(, etw zu tun).

**prodigal** [ˈprɒdɪgl] adj verschwenderisch; **the ~ son** der verlorene Sohn.

**prodigious** [prəˈdɪdʒəs] adj unglaublich.

**prodigy** [ˈprɒdɪdʒɪ] (pl -ies) n Wunderkind das.

**produce** [n ˈprɒdjuːs, vb prəˈdjuːs] n (U) - 1. [goods] Erzeugnisse pl - 2. [fruit and vegetables] Obst und Gemüse das <> vt - 1. [manufacture, make] produzieren, herlstellen; [work of art] schaffen - 2. [yield - raw materials] liefern; [ - heat, crop, gas] erzeugen; [ - interest, profit] einlbringen - 3. [cause - results, agreements] erzielen; [ - disaster] hervorlrufen - 4. [give birth to - subj: woman] gebären; [ - subj: animal] werfen - 5. [leaves, flowers] hervorlbringen - 6. [present, show - evidence, argument] liefern; [ - passport, letter] vorlzeigen - 7. [film, TV programme] produzieren; [play] inszenieren.

**producer** [prəˈdjuːsəʳ] n - 1. [of film, TV programme] Produzent der, -in die; [of play] Regisseur der, -in die - 2. [manufacturer] Hersteller der, -in die.

**product** [ˈprɒdʌkt] n - 1. [thing manufactured or grown] Produkt das - 2. [result]: **to be a ~ of sthg** [of situation, process] das Ergebnis einer Sache sein; [subj: person] das Produkt einer Sache sein.

**production** [prəˈdʌkʃn] n - 1. (U) [process - of goods] Produktion die, Herstellung die; [ - of electricity, heat] Erzeugung die; [ - of blood cells] Bildung die; **to put sthg into ~** die Produktion von etw auf lnehmen; **to go into ~** in Produktion gehen - 2. (U) [output] Produktion die - 3. CINEMA, THEATRE & TV Produktion die.

**production line** n Fertigungsstraße die.

**production manager** n Produktionsleiter der, -in die.

**productive** [prəˈdʌktɪv] adj - 1. [worker] produktiv; [land] ertragreich; [business] leistungsfähig - 2. [meeting, relationship, experience] Gewinn bringend.

**productively** [prəˈdʌktɪvlɪ] adv - 1. [work, use land] produktiv - 2. [spend time] Gewinn bringend.

**productivity** [ˌprɒdʌkˈtɪvətɪ] n Produktivität die.

**productivity deal** n Produktivitätsvereinbarung die.

**Prof.** abbr of Professor.

**profane** [prəˈfeɪn] adj [vulgar] gotteslästerlich.

**profanity** [prəˈfænətɪ] (pl -ies) n - 1. (U) [of language, behaviour] Gotteslästerlichkeit die - 2. [word] Fluch der; [invoking God] Gotteslästerung die.

**profess** [prəˈfes] vt - 1. [claim - innocence] beteuern; [ - support] kundtun; **to ~ to do sthg** behaupten, etw zu tun - 2. [declare] bekunden.

**professed** [prəˈfest] adj - 1. [avowed] erklärt; **a ~ Christian** ein bekennender Christ - 2. [alleged] angeblich.

**profession** [prəˈfeʃn] n - 1. [career] Beruf der; **by ~** von Beruf - 2. [body of people] Berufsstand der; **the medical/teaching ~** die Ärzteschaft/Lehrerschaft.

**professional** [prəˈfeʃənl] adj - 1. [relating to a profession - qualifications] beruflich; [ - advice, help, opinion] fachmännisch; **in his ~ capacity as a lawyer** in seiner Eigenschaft als Anwalt; **~ people** hochqualifizierte Personen - 2. [full-time, of high standard] professionell; [army, actor] Berufs-; [footballer] Profi- <> n - 1. [full-time sportsperson] Profi der; [full-time actor] Berufsschauspieler der - 2. [skilled person]: **he's a real ~** er ist ein echter Profi.

**professional foul** n absichtliches Foul.

**professionalism** [prəˈfeʃnəlɪzm] n [high quality] Professionalität die.

**professionally** [prəˈfeʃnəlɪ] adv - 1. [as profession]: **to be ~ qualified/trained** eine (abgeschlossene) Berufsausbildung haben; **he**

**acts/plays** ~ er ist Berufsschauspieler/ Profispieler - **2.** [skilfully] professionell.

**professor** [prə'fesə'] n - **1.** Br [head of department] Professor der, -in die - **2.** Am & Can [teacher, lecturer] Dozent der, -in die.

**professorship** [prə'fesəʃɪp] n Br Professur die; Am Dozentur die.

**proffer** ['prɒfə'] vt: **to ~ sthg (to sb)** (jm) etw anlbieten.

**proficiency** [prə'fɪʃənsɪ] n (U): ~ **(in)** Kompetenz die (in (+ D)).

**proficient** [prə'fɪʃənt] adj kompetent; **to be ~ in** OR **at sthg** in etw (D) kompetent sein.

**profile** ['prəʊfaɪl] n - **1.** [outline of face] Profil das; **in ~** im Profil; **to keep a low ~** fig sich unauffällig verhalten - **2.** [biography] Porträt das.

**profit** ['prɒfɪt] n - **1.** [financial gain] Gewinn der, Profit der; **to make a ~** einen Gewinn machen; **to sell sthg at a ~** etw mit Gewinn verkaufen - **2.** [advantage]: **you may learn something to your ~** du könntest etwas lernen, was nützlich für dich ist ⬦ vi: **to ~ (from** OR **by sthg)** (von etw) profitieren.

**profitability** [ˌprɒfɪtə'bɪlətɪ] n Rentabilität die.

**profitable** ['prɒfɪtəbl] adj Gewinn bringend.

**profitably** ['prɒfɪtəblɪ] adv - **1.** [at a profit] Gewinn bringend - **2.** [usefully]: **to use one's time ~** seine Zeit gut nutzen.

**profiteering** [ˌprɒfɪ'tɪərɪŋ] n (U) Wucher der.

**profit-making** [-ˌmeɪkɪŋ] adj Gewinn bringend ⬦ n Einbringen das von Gewinnen OR Profit.

**profit margin** n Gewinnspanne die.

**profit sharing** [-ˌʃeərɪŋ] n (U) Gewinnbeteiligung die.

**profligate** ['prɒflɪgɪt] adj - **1.** [extravagant] verschwenderisch - **2.** [immoral] lasterhaft.

**pro forma** [-'fɔːmə] adj: ~ **invoice** Pro-Forma-Rechnung die.

**profound** [prə'faʊnd] adj - **1.** [intense - feeling, silence] tief; [ - change] tief greifend; [ - effect] nachhaltig - **2.** [penetrating, wise - idea, book] tiefgründig.

**profoundly** [prə'faʊndlɪ] adv - **1.** [intensely]: ~ **significant** äußerst bedeutsam; ~ **sad** tieftraurig - **2.** [wisely - say, remark] tiefsinnig.

**profuse** [prə'fjuːs] adj - **1.** [bleeding] sehr stark - **2.** [praise] überschwenglich; **to offer ~ apologies** sich vielmals entschuldigen.

**profusely** [prə'fjuːslɪ] adv - **1.** [bleed, sweat] sehr stark - **2.** [thank] überschwenglich; **to apologize ~** sich vielmals entschuldigen.

**profusion** [prə'fjuːʒn] n: ~ **(of)** (Über)fülle die (von).

**progeny** ['prɒdʒənɪ] n (U) fml Nachkommen pl.

**progesterone** [prə'dʒestərəʊn] n Progesteron das.

**prognosis** [prɒg'nəʊsɪs] (pl -noses [-'nəʊsiːz]) n Prognose die.

**prognostication** [prɒgˌnɒstɪ'keɪʃn] n Voraussage die.

**program** ['prəʊgræm] (pt & pp -med OR -ed; cont -ming OR -ing) n - **1.** COMPUT Programm das - **2.** Am = **programme** ⬦ vt - **1.** COMPUT programmieren - **2.** Am = **programme**.

**programer** n Am = **programmer**.

**programmable** [prəʊ'græməbl] adj programmierbar.

**programme** Br, **program** Am ['prəʊgræm] n - **1.** [gen] Programm das - **2.** RADIO & TV Sendung die ⬦ vt programmieren.

**programmer** Br, **programer** Am ['prəʊgræmə'] n COMPUT Programmierer der, -in die.

**programming** ['prəʊgræmɪŋ] n COMPUT Programmieren das.

**programming language** n Programmiersprache die.

**progress** [n 'prəʊgres, vb prə'gres] n - **1.** [physical movement] Vorwärtskommen das - **2.** [headway] Voranschreiten das; **to make ~ (in sthg)** (bei etw) Fortschritte machen; **in ~** im Gange - **3.** [evolution] Fortschritt der ⬦ vi - **1.** [improve - science, technology, work] voranlkommen; [ - patient, student] Fortschritte machen - **2.** [continue]: **as the journey/meeting ~ed** im Laufe der Reise/des Treffens - **3.** [move forward]: vorldringen; **to ~ to sthg** zu etw vordringen.

**progression** [prə'greʃn] n - **1.** [advance] Übergang der - **2.** [series] Folge die.

**progressive** [prə'gresɪv] adj - **1.** [forward-looking] fortschrittlich - **2.** [gradual] fortschreitend.

**progressively** [prə'gresɪvlɪ] adv [gradually] zunehmend.

**progress report** n [on pupil, student] Bericht der über die Lernerfolge; [on patient] Bericht der über den Krankheitsverlauf; [on project] Tätigkeitsbericht der.

**prohibit** [prə'hɪbɪt] vt verbieten; **to ~ sb from doing sthg** jm verbieten, etw zu tun.

**prohibition** [ˌprəʊɪ'bɪʃn] n Verbot das.

**prohibitive** [prə'hɪbətɪv] adj [cost] untragbar; [tax, laws] prohibitiv.

**project** [n 'prɒdʒekt, vb prə'dʒekt] n - **1.** [plan, idea] Vorhaben das, Projekt das - **2.** SCH [study] Projekt das; ~ **(on)** Projekt das (über (+ A)) ⬦ vt - **1.** [plan] planen - **2.** [estimate] voraussagen; [costs] überschlagen - **3.** [film, light] projizieren; **to ~ sthg on to sthg** etw auf etw (A) projizieren - **4.** [present] darlstellen; [image] vermitteln ⬦ vi [jut out] hervorlragen.

**projectile** [prə'dʒektaɪl] n Geschoss das.

**projection** [prə'dʒekʃn] n - **1.** [estimate] Vor-

P

**aussage** *die;* [of costs] Überschlagen *das* - **2.** [protrusion] Vorsprung *der* - **3.** *(U)* [of film, light] Projektion *die.*

**projectionist** [prə'dʒekʃənɪst] *n* Filmvorführer *der,* -in *die.*

**projection room** *n* Vorführraum *der.*

**projector** [prə'dʒektər] *n* Projektor *der.*

**proletarian** [ˌprəʊlɪ'teərɪən] *adj* proletarisch; [class, party] Arbeiter-.

**proletariat** [ˌprəʊlɪ'teərɪət] *n* Proletariat *das.*

**pro-life** *adj* gegen Abtreibung eingestellt.

**proliferate** [prə'lɪfəreɪt] *vi* [animals] sich vermehren; [vegetation] sich rasch auslbreiten; [ideas] um sich greifen.

**prolific** [prə'lɪfɪk] *adj* sehr produktiv.

**prologue, prolog** *Am* ['prəʊlɒg] *n* - **1.** [introduction] Prolog *der* - **2.** *fig* [preceding event]: **to be the ~ to sthg** die Vorstufe für etw sein.

**prolong** [prə'lɒŋ] *vt* verlängern.

**prom** [prɒm] *n* - **1.** (*abbr of* **promenade**) *Br inf* [at seaside] Strandpromenade *die* - **2.** *Am* [ball - at high school] Schulball *der;* [ - at college] Studentenball *der.*

---

**PROMS**

Eine Tradition seit 1871, sind die „Proms" (Abkürzung für „Promenade Concerts") eine Serie von Sommerkonzerten, die einem größeren Publikum vorwiegend klassische Musik zugänglich machen sollen und über mehrere Wochen in der Royal Albert Hall in London stattfinden. Für Besucher mit schmalem Geldbeutel gibt es sehr preiswerte Stehplätze (ursprünglich stand man nicht, sondern lief während des Konzerts umher; daher der Name „Proms"). Die Proms werden vom BBC gesponsort und über Radio 3 ausgestrahlt, einige, vor allem die berühmte „last night of the proms", auch über BBC 2 (Fernsehen).

---

**promenade** [ˌprɒmə'nɑːd] *n Br* [at seaside] Strandpromenade *die.*

**prominence** ['prɒmɪnəns] *n (U)* - **1.** [importance - person] Berühmtheit *die;* [ - of ideas, issues] Bedeutung *die* - **2.** [conspicuousness] exponierte Lage.

**prominent** ['prɒmɪnənt] *adj* - **1.** [important - person] prominent; [ - ideas, issues] wichtig - **2.** [noticeable - building, landmark] exponiert; [ - features] markant.

**prominently** ['prɒmɪnəntlɪ] *adv* [display, place] deutlich sichtbar.

**promiscuity** [ˌprɒmɪs'kjuːətɪ] *n* Promiskuität *die.*

**promiscuous** [prɒ'mɪskjʊəs] *adj* promiskuitiv.

**promise** ['prɒmɪs] *n* - **1.** [vow] Versprechen *das;* **to make (sb) a ~** (jm) ein Versprechen

geben - **2.** *(U)* [hope, prospect]: **~ (of)** Aussicht *die* (auf (+ A)); **to show ~** zu großen Hoffnungen Anlass geben <> *vt* versprechen; **to ~ sb sthg** jm etw versprechen; **to ~ (sb) to do sthg** (jm) versprechen, etw zu tun <> *vi* versprechen.

**promising** ['prɒmɪsɪŋ] *adj* vielversprechend.

**promissory note** ['prɒmɪsərɪ-] *n* Schuldschein *der.*

**promo** ['prəʊməʊ] (*pl* **-s**) *n inf* Werbeaktion *die.*

**promontory** ['prɒməntrɪ] (*pl* **-ies**) *n* Kap *das.*

**promote** [prə'məʊt] *vt* - **1.** [foster] fördern - **2.** [push, advertise] Werbung machen für - **3.** [in job] befördern; **she was ~d to Head of Department** sie wurde zur Abteilungsleiterin befördert - **4.** *sport:* **to be ~d** auf lsteigen.

**promoter** [prə'məʊtər] *n* - **1.** [of event, concert] Veranstalter *der,* -in *die* - **2.** [of cause, idea] Förderer *der.*

**promotion** [prə'məʊʃn] *n* - **1.** [in job] Beförderung *die;* **to get** *OR* **be given ~** befördert werden - **2.** [advertising] Werbung *die* - **3.** [campaign] Werbekampagne *die.*

**prompt** [prɒmpt] *adj* - **1.** [quick] prompt; [action] sofortig - **2.** [punctual] pünktlich <> *adv:* **at nine o'clock ~** Punkt 9 Uhr <> *vt* - **1.** [provoke, persuade]: **to ~ sb to do sthg** jn dazu veranlassen, etw zu tun - **2.** *theatre* soufflieren (+ D) <> *n* [theatre - person] Souffleur *der,* -euse *die;* [ - line]: **to give sb a ~** jm soufflieren.

**prompter** ['prɒmptər] *n* Souffleur *der,* -euse *die.*

**promptly** ['prɒmptlɪ] *adv* - **1.** [quickly] prompt - **2.** [punctually] pünktlich.

**promptness** ['prɒmptnɪs] *n* - **1.** [quickness] Promptheit *die* - **2.** [punctuality] Pünktlichkeit *die.*

**promulgate** ['prɒmlgeɪt] *vt* - **1.** [law, decree] verkünden - **2.** [belief, idea] verbreiten.

**prone** [prəʊn] *adj* - **1.** [susceptible]: **to be ~ to sthg** zu etw neigen; **to be ~ to do sthg** dazu neigen, etw zu tun - **2.** [lying flat]: **to lie/be ~** auf dem Bauch liegen.

**prong** [prɒŋ] *n* Zinke *die.*

**pronoun** ['prəʊnaʊn] *n* Pronomen *das.*

**pronounce** [prə'naʊns] *vt* - **1.** [say aloud] auslsprechen - **2.** [declare, state - verdict, opinion] verkünden; **to ~ sb fit for work/dead** jn für arbeitsfähig/tot erklären <> *vi:* **to ~ on sthg** eine Meinung zu etw ablgeben.

**pronounced** [prə'naʊnst] *adj* [accent] stark; [improvement, deterioration] deutlich.

**pronouncement** [prə'naʊnsmənt] *n* Erklärung *die.*

**pronto** ['prɒntəʊ] *adv inf* ganz fix.

**pronunciation** [prəˌnʌnsɪ'eɪʃn] *n* Aussprache *die.*

**proof** [pruːf] *n* - **1.** [evidence] Beweis *der* - **2.** PRESS [first copy] Korrekturfahne *die* - **3.** [of alcohol] Alkoholgehalt *der*.

**proofread** ['pruːfriːd] (*pt* & *pp* -**read** [-red]) *vt* Korrektur lesen.

**proofreader** ['pruːfˌriːdəʳ] *n* Korrektor *der*, -in *die*.

**prop** [prɒp] (*pt* & *pp* -**ped;** *cont* -**ping**) *n lit* & *fig* Stütze *die* ◇ *vt:* **to ~ sthg against sthg** etw gegen etw lehnen.

➭ **props** *npl* [in film, play] Requisiten *pl.*

➭ **prop up** *vt sep* - **1.** [support physically - wall] ablstützen; [ - ladder] anlehnen - **2.** *fig* [sustain - regime] stützen; [ - organization] unterstützen; [ - company] vor dem Konkurs bewahren.

**Prop.** *abbr of* proprietor.

**propagate** ['prɒpəgeɪt] *vt* - **1.** BOT züchten - **2.** [spread] verbreiten ◇ *vi* sich vermehren.

**propagation** [ˌprɒpəˈgeɪʃn] *n (U)* - **1.** BOT Vermehrung *die* - **2.** [dissemination] Verbreitung *die*.

**propane** ['prəʊpeɪn] *n* Propan *das*.

**propel** [prəˈpel] (*pt* & *pp* -**led;** *cont* -**ling**) *vt* anltreiben.

**propeller** [prəˈpeləʳ] *n* [of plane] Propeller *der;* [of ship] Schraube *die*.

**propelling pencil** [prəˈpelɪŋ-] *n Br* Drehbleistift *der*.

**propensity** [prəˈpensətɪ] (*pl* -**ies**) *n fml:* **~ for** OR **to sthg** Hang *der* zu etw; **to have a ~ to do sthg** dazu neigen, etw zu tun.

**proper** ['prɒpəʳ] *adj* - **1.** [real] richtig - **2.** [correct] korrekt - **3.** [decent] anständig - **4.** [specifically]: **I live in the city ~** ich lebe direkt in der Stadt - **5.** *inf* [for emphasis] richtig; **he's a ~ idiot** er ist ein Vollidiot.

**properly** ['prɒpəlɪ] *adv* - **1.** [satisfactorily, correctly] richtig - **2.** [decently] anständig.

**proper noun** *n* Eigenname *der*.

**property** ['prɒpətɪ] (*pl* -**ies**) *n* - **1.** [possession] Eigentum *das* - **2.** [specific building] Haus *das;* [piece of land] Grundstück *das* - **3.** *(U)* [buildings, land] Immobilien *pl* - **4.** [quality] Eigenschaft *die*.

**property developer** [-ˌdɪveləpəʳ] *n Bauunternehmer, der Gebäude bzw. Land zum Bebauen kauft, um das erschlossene Gebiet oder die Gebäude anschließend Gewinn bringend zu verkaufen oder zu verpachten.*

**property owner** *n* [of house] Hausbesitzer *der*, -in *die;* [of land] Grundbesitzer *der*, -in *die*.

**property tax** *n* Vermögenssteuer *die*.

**prophecy** ['prɒfɪsɪ] (*pl* -**ies**) *n* Prophezeiung *die*.

**prophesy** ['prɒfɪsaɪ] (*pt* & *pp* -**ied**) *vt* prophezeien.

**prophet** ['prɒfɪt] *n* - **1.** RELIG Prophet *der* - **2.** [predictor] Prophet *der*, -in *die*.

**prophetic** [prəˈfetɪk] *adj* prophetisch.

**propitious** [prəˈpɪʃəs] *adj fml* günstig.

**proponent** [prəˈpəʊnənt] *n* Befürworter *der*, -in *die*.

**proportion** [prəˈpɔːʃn] *n* - **1.** [part] Teil *der*, Anteil *der* - **2.** [ratio, comparison] Verhältnis *das;* **in ~ to** im Verhältnis zu; **out of all ~ to** in keinem Verhältnis zu - **3.** *(U)* ART: **in ~** in den richtigen Proportionen; **out of ~** mit verschobenen Proportionen; **a sense of ~** *fig* ein vernünftiger Maßstab; **to get sthg out of ~** *fig* bei etw den vernünftigen Maßstab verlieren.

**proportional** [prəˈpɔːʃənl] *adj* im Verhältnis stehend; MATH proportional; **to be ~ to sthg** zu etw im Verhältnis stehen; MATH zu etw proportional sein.

**proportional representation** *n (U)* Verhältniswahlsystem *das*.

**proportionate** [prəˈpɔːʃnət] *adj:* **~ (to sthg)** im Verhältnis (zu etw).

**proposal** [prəˈpəʊzl] *n* - **1.** [plan, suggestion] Vorschlag *der* - **2.** [offer of marriage] Heiratsantrag *der*.

**propose** [prəˈpəʊz] *vt* - **1.** [plan, solution, person] vorlschlagen; [toast] auslbringen; **to ~ marriage** einen Heiratsantrag machen - **2.** [motion] einlbringen, stellen - **3.** [intend]: **to ~ doing** OR **to do sthg** vorlhaben OR beabsichtigen, etw zu tun ◇ *vi:* **to ~ (to sb)** (jm) einen Heiratsantrag machen.

**proposed** [prəˈpəʊzd] *adj* beabsichtigt, geplant.

**proposition** [ˌprɒpəˈzɪʃn] *n* - **1.** [statement of theory] These *die* - **2.** [suggestion] Vorschlag *der;* **to make sb a ~** jm einen Vorschlag machen ◇ *vt fml:* **he ~ed her** er fragte sie, ob sie mit ihm schlafen würde.

**propound** [prəˈpaʊnd] *vt fml* darllegen.

**proprietary** [prəˈpraɪətrɪ] *adj* COMM: **~ name** Markenbezeichnung *die;* **~ product** Markenartikel *der*.

**proprietor** [prəˈpraɪətəʳ] *n* Besitzer *der*, -in *die*.

**proprietorial** [prəˌpraɪəˈtɔːrɪəl] *adj* [possessive] besitzergreifend.

**propriety** [prəˈpraɪətɪ] *n fml* [moral correctness] Anstand *der*.

**propulsion** [prəˈpʌlʃn] *n* Antrieb *der*.

**pro rata** [-ˈrɑːtə] *adj* & *adv* anteilig.

**prosaic** [prəʊˈzeɪɪk] *adj* prosaisch.

**proscenium** [prəˈsiːnɪəm] (*pl* -**niums** OR -**nia** [-nɪə]) *n:* **~ (arch)** Proszenium *das*.

**proscribe** [prəʊˈskraɪb] *vt fml* verbieten.

**prose** [prəʊz] *n* Prosa *die* ◇ *comp* Prosa-.

**prosecute** ['prɒsɪkjuːt] *vt* LAW strafrechtlich verfolgen; **to be ~d for sthg** wegen etw strafrechtlich verfolgt werden ◇ *vi* - **1.** [bring a

**P**

charge] vor Gericht gehen - **2.** [represent in court] die Anklage vertreten.

**prosecution** [ˌprɒsɪ'kju:ʃn] *n* - **1.** [criminal charge] strafrechtliche Verfolgung - **2.** [lawyers]: **the ~** die Anklage(vertretung).

**prosecutor** ['prɒsɪkju:təʳ] *n esp Am* Ankläger *der*, -in *die*.

**prospect** [*n* 'prɒspekt, *vb* prə'spekt] *n* Aussicht *die* <> *vi*: **to ~ (for sthg)** [gold] schürfen (nach etw); [oil] bohren (nach etw).

➠ **prospects** *npl*: **~s (for sthg)** Aussichten *pl* (auf etw (A)); **he has good ~s** er hat gute Erfolgschancen.

**prospecting** [prə'spektɪŋ] *n* [for gold] Schürfen *das;* [for oil] Bohren *das*.

**prospective** [prə'spektɪv] *adj* voraussichtlich.

**prospector** [prə'spektəʳ] *n* [for gold] Goldschürfer *der*.

**prospectus** [prə'spektəs] (*pl* -es) *n* (Werbe)prospekt *der*.

**prosper** ['prɒspəʳ] *vi* [business, country] blühen; [person] Erfolg haben.

**prosperity** [prɒ'sperətɪ] *n* Wohlstand *der*.

**prosperous** ['prɒspərəs] *adj* [person] wohlhabend; [business, place] blühend.

**prostate (gland)** ['prɒsteɪt-] *n* Prostata *die*.

**prosthesis** [prɒs'θiːsɪs] (*pl* -theses [-'θiːsiːz]) *n* Prothese *die*.

**prostitute** ['prɒstɪtjuːt] *n* Prostituierte *die;* **(male) ~** Stricher *der*, Strichjunge *der*.

**prostitution** [ˌprɒstɪ'tjuːʃn] *n* Prostitution *die*.

**prostrate** [*adj* 'prɒstreɪt, *vb* prɒ'streɪt] *adj* - **1.** [lying flat] (auf dem Bauch) ausgestreckt - **2.** *fig* [with grief] gebrochen, niedergeschmettert <> *vt*: **to ~ o.s. (before sb)** sich (vor jm) in den Staub werfen, sich (vor jm) auf den Boden werfen.

**protagonist** [prə'tægənɪst] *n* Hauptfigur *die*, Protagonist *der*, -in *die*.

**protect** [prə'tekt] *vt* schützen; **to ~ sb/sthg from/against** jn/etw schützen vor (+ D) /gegen.

**protection** [prə'tekʃn] *n*: **~ (from/against)** Schutz *der* (vor (+ D) /gegen).

**protectionism** [prə'tekʃənɪzm] *n* (U) Protektionismus *der*.

**protectionist** [prə'tekʃənɪst] *adj* protektionistisch.

**protection money** *n* Schutzgeld *das*.

**protective** [prə'tektɪv] *adj* - **1.** [layer, clothing] Schutz-, schützend - **2.** [feelings, instinct] Beschützer-; **to be ~ towards sb** fürsorglich gegenüber jm sein.

**protective custody** *n* Schutzhaft *die*.

**protector** [prə'tektəʳ] *n* - **1.** [person] Beschüt-

zer *der*, -in *die* - **2.** [on machine] Schutzvorrichtung *die*.

**protectorate** [prə'tektərət] *n* Protektorat *das*.

**protégé** ['prəʊtəʒeɪ] *n* Protégé *der*, Schützling *der*.

**protein** ['prəʊtiːn] *n* Protein *das*, Eiweiß *das*.

**protest** [*n* 'prəʊtest, *vb* prə'test] *n* - **1.** [complaint] Protest *der* - **2.** [demonstration] Protestkundgebung *die* <> *vt* - **1.** [one's innocence] beteuern - **2.** *Am* [protest against] protestieren gegen <> *vi* [complain]: **to ~ (about/against sthg)** protestieren (gegen etw).

**Protestant** ['prɒtɪstənt] *adj* protestantisch <> *n* Protestant *der*, -in *die*.

**Protestantism** ['prɒtɪstəntɪzm] *n* Protestantismus *der*.

**protestation** [ˌprɒte'steɪʃn] *n fml* - **1.** [declaration] Beteuerung *die* - **2.** [protest] Protest *der*.

**protester** [prə'testəʳ] *n* [demonstrator] Protestierende *der*, *die*.

**protest march** *n* Protestmarsch *der*.

**protocol** ['prəʊtəkɒl] *n* (U) Protokoll *das*.

**proton** ['prəʊtɒn] *n* Proton *das*.

**prototype** ['prəʊtətaɪp] *n* Prototyp *der*.

**protracted** [prə'træktɪd] *adj* langwierig.

**protractor** [prə'træktəʳ] *n* Winkelmesser *der*.

**protrude** [prə'truːd] *vi*: **to ~ (from sthg)** (aus etw) hervorlstehen.

**protrusion** [prə'truːʒn] *n* [protruding part] hervorstehender Teil.

**protuberance** [prə'tjuːbərəns] *n* Auswuchs *der*.

**proud** [praʊd] *adj* stolz; **to be ~ of sb/sthg** auf jn/etw stolz sein; **to be ~ to do sthg** stolz (darauf) sein, etw zu tun.

**proudly** ['praʊdlɪ] *adv* stolz.

**provable** ['pruːvəbl] *adj* beweisbar.

**prove** [pruːv] (*pp* -**d** OR **proven**) *vt* - **1.** [show to be true] beweisen - **2.** [show o.s. to be]: **to ~ (to be) sthg** sich als etw erweisen; **to ~ o.s. to be sthg** sich als etw erweisen.

**proven** ['pruːvn, 'prəʊvn] *pp* ▷ **prove** <> *adj* [fact] erwiesen, bewiesen; [liar] ausgewiesen; **he is a businessman of ~ ability** er hat sich als Geschäftsmann bewährt.

**proverb** ['prɒvɜːb] *n* Sprichwort *das*.

**proverbial** [prə'vɜːbɪəl] *adj lit* & *fig* sprichwörtlich.

**provide** [prə'vaɪd] *vt* [food, money, information] zur Verfügung stellen; [opportunity] bieten; **to ~ sb with sthg, to ~ sthg for sb** jm etw zur Verfügung stellen, jn mit etw versorgen.

➠ **provide for** *vt fus* - **1.** [support] sorgen für - **2.** *fml* [make arrangements for] vorlsorgen für.

**provided** [prə'vaɪdɪd] ➠ **provided (that)** *conj* vorausgesetzt, dass.

**providence** ['prɒvɪdəns] n Vorsehung die.
**providential** [ˌprɒvɪ'denʃl] adj fml: it was ~ (that) es war ein Glück(, dass).
**provider** [prə'vaɪdər] n Versorger der, -in die.
**providing** [prə'vaɪdɪŋ] ◆ **providing (that)** conj vorausgesetzt, dass.
**province** ['prɒvɪns] n - **1.** [part of country] Provinz die - **2.** [specialist subject] Fachgebiet das; [area of responsibility] Aufgabenbereich der.
◆ **provinces** npl: the ~s die Provinz.
**provincial** [prə'vɪnʃl] adj - **1.** [of a province] Provinz- - **2.** pej [narrow-minded] provinziell.
**provision** [prə'vɪʒn] n - **1.** [act of supplying] Bereitstellung die - **2.** (U) [arrangement] Vorkehrung die; **to make ~ for sb/sthg** Vorkehrungen für jn/etw treffen - **3.** [in agreement, law] Bestimmung die.
◆ **provisions** npl [supplies] Vorräte pl.
**provisional** [prə'vɪʒənl] adj provisorisch.
**Provisional IRA** n: the ~ die IRA.
**provisional licence** n Br vorläufiger Führerschein.
**provisionally** [prə'vɪʒnəlɪ] adv provisorisch.
**proviso** [prə'vaɪzəʊ] (pl -s) n Vorbehalt der; **with the ~ that** unter dem Vorbehalt, dass.
**provocation** [ˌprɒvə'keɪʃn] n Provokation die.
**provocative** [prə'vɒkətɪv] adj - **1.** [controversial] provokativ - **2.** [sexy] aufreizend.
**provocatively** [prə'vɒkətɪvlɪ] adv - **1.** [controversially] provokativ - **2.** [sexily] aufreizend.
**provoke** [prə'vəʊk] vt - **1.** [annoy] provozieren - **2.** [cause - criticism, reaction] hervorlrufen, erregen; [ - argument] provozieren.
**provoking** [prə'vəʊkɪŋ] adj provokant.
**provost** ['prɒvəst] n - **1.** Br [head of college] Rektor der, -in die - **2.** Scot [head of town council] Bürgermeister der, -in die.
**prow** [praʊ] n Bug der.
**prowess** ['praʊɪs] n (U) fml Erfahrenheit die, Tüchtigkeit die.
**prowl** [praʊl] n: **to be on the ~** (auf Beutezug) herumlstreifen <> vt durchstreifen <> vi herumlstreifen, umherlstreifen.
**prowl car** n Am Streifenwagen der.
**prowler** ['praʊlər] n Herumtreiber der, -in die.
**proximity** [prɒk'sɪmətɪ] n (U) fml: ~ **(to sthg)** Nähe die (zu etw); **in the ~ of** in der Nähe (+ G).
**proxy** ['prɒksɪ] (pl -ies) n: **by ~** in Vertretung.
**prude** [pruːd] n Prüde der, die; **to be a ~** prüde sein.
**prudence** ['pruːdns] n fml Umsicht die, Vorsicht die.
**prudent** ['pruːdnt] adj [person] umsichtig; [action] überlegt; **it would be ~ not to mention her name** es wäre unklug, ihren Namen zu erwähnen.
**prudently** ['pruːdntlɪ] adv umsichtig, überlegt.
**prudish** ['pruːdɪʃ] adj prüde.
**prune** [pruːn] n [fruit] Backpflaume die, Dörrpflaume die <> vt [hedge, tree] beschneiden, stutzen.
**prurient** ['prʊərɪənt] adj fml lüstern.
**Prussian** ['prʌʃn] adj preußisch <> n Preuße der, -ßin die.
**pry** [praɪ] (pt & pp pried) vi neugierig sein; **to ~ into sthg** seine Nase in etw stecken, in etw herumlschnüffeln.
**PS** (abbr of postscript) n PS das.
**psalm** [sɑːm] n Psalm der.
**pseud** [sjuːd] n Br inf Pseudointellektuelle der, die.
**pseudo-** [ˌsjuːdəʊ] prefix [with adj] pseudo-; [with noun] Pseudo-.
**pseudonym** ['sjuːdənɪm] n Pseudonym das.
**psi** (abbr of pounds per square inch) psi, veraltete britische Druckeinheit.
**psoriasis** [sɒ'raɪəsɪs] n Schuppenflechte die.
**psst** [pst] excl st!
**PST** (abbr of Pacific Standard Time) n Standardzeit in der pazifischen Zeitzone der USA.
**psych** [saɪk] ◆ **psych up** vt sep inf motivieren; **to ~ o.s. up** sich motivieren.
**psyche** ['saɪkɪ] n Psyche die.
**psychedelic** [ˌsaɪkɪ'delɪk] adj psychedelisch.
**psychiatric** [ˌsaɪkɪ'ætrɪk] adj [hospital, department] psychiatrisch; [illness, problem] psychisch.
**psychiatric nurse** n psychiatrische Krankenschwester, psychiatrischer Krankenpfleger.
**psychiatrist** [saɪ'kaɪətrɪst] n Psychiater der, -in die.
**psychiatry** [saɪ'kaɪətrɪ] n (U) Psychiatrie die.
**psychic** ['saɪkɪk] adj - **1.** [clairvoyant - powers] übersinnlich; **she is ~** sie hat übersinnliche Kräfte - **2.** [mental] psychisch <> n Person die mit übersinnlichen Kräften.
**psychoanalyse, psychoanalyze** Am [ˌsaɪkəʊ'ænəlaɪz] vt psychoanalytisch behandeln.
**psychoanalysis** [ˌsaɪkəʊə'næləsɪs] n Psychoanalyse die.
**psychoanalyst** [ˌsaɪkəʊ'ænəlɪst] n Psychoanalytiker der, -in die.
**psychoanalyze** vt Am = psychoanalyse.
**psychological** [ˌsaɪkə'lɒdʒɪkl] adj psychologisch.
**psychological warfare** n psychologische Kriegführung.

P

**psychologist** [saɪ'kɒlədʒɪst] *n* Psychologe *der*, -gin *die*.

**psychology** [saɪ'kɒlədʒɪ] *n* Psychologie *die*.

**psychopath** ['saɪkəpæθ] *n* Psychopath *der*, -in *die*.

**psychosis** [saɪ'kəʊsɪs] (*pl* -choses [-'kəʊsiːz]) *n* Psychose *die*.

**psychosomatic** [ˌsaɪkəʊsə'mætɪk] *adj* psychosomatisch.

**psychotherapy** [ˌsaɪkəʊ'θerəpɪ] *n* Psychotherapie *die*.

**psychotic** [saɪ'kɒtɪk] *adj* psychotisch ◇ *n* Psychotiker *der*, -in *die*.

**pt - 1.** *abbr of* **pint - 2.** (*abbr of* **point**) Pkt.

**Pt.** (*abbr of* **Point**) [on map] *Landzunge.*

**PT** *n abbr of* **physical training**.

**PTA** *n abbr of* **parent-teacher association**.

**Pte.** *abbr of* **Private**.

**PTO** *n* (*abbr of* **parent-teacher organization**) = **PTA** ◇ (*abbr of* **please turn over**) b.w.

**pub** [pʌb] *n* Pub *der*, Bierlokal *das*.

---

**PUB**

In Großbritannien spielt sich ein großer Teil des sozialen Lebens, ganz besonders in den ländlichen Gegenden, in den „Pubs" ab, einer Mischung aus Gasthaus und Kneipe. Bis vor wenigen Jahren waren die Öffnungszeiten streng reguliert, doch heute sind „Pubs" meist von 11 bis 23 Uhr durchgehend geöffnet. Auch das Pubverbot für Kinder unter 16 gilt heute generell nicht mehr. Dies wird jedoch von Gegend zu Gegend und von Pub zu Pub unterschiedlich gehandhabt. Außer Getränken wird in den meisten Pubs auch eine Auswahl an leichten Mahlzeiten angeboten.

---

**pub.** *abbr of* **published**.

**pub-crawl** *n Br* Kneipentour *die;* **to go on a ~** eine Kneipentour machen.

**puberty** ['pjuːbətɪ] *n* Pubertät *die*.

**pubescent** [pjuː'besnt] *adj* pubertierend.

**pubic** ['pjuːbɪk] *adj* Scham-

**public** ['pʌblɪk] *adj* - **1.** [of people in general, open to all] öffentlich - **2.** [of, by the state] staatlich, Staats- - **3.** [known to everyone]: **~ figure** bekannte Persönlichkeit; **to retire from ~ life** sich aus der Öffentlichkeit zürucklziehen; **it's ~ knowledge that ...** es ist allgemein bekannt, dass ...; **to go ~ about sthg** *inf* etw herauslposaunen; **to make sthg ~** etw öffentlich bekanntlgeben, mit etw an die Öffentlichkeit gehen - **4.** comm: **to go ~** an die Börse gehen ◇ *n*: **the ~** die Öffentlichkeit; **in ~** in der Öffentlichkeit.

**public-address system** *n* Lautsprecheranlage *die*.

**publican** ['pʌblɪkən] *n Br* Wirt *der*, -in *die*.

**publication** [ˌpʌblɪ'keɪʃn] *n* - **1.** (U) [act of publishing] Veröffentlichung *die* - **2.** [book, article] Publikation *die;* **this magazine is a monthly ~** diese Zeitschrift erscheint monatlich.

**public bar** *n Br* schlicht eingerichteter Teil eines Pubs, in dem die Getränke billiger als in der „Lounge-Bar" sind.

**public company** *n* Aktiengesellschaft *die*.

**public convenience** *n Br* öffentliche Toilette.

**public domain** *n:* **to be in the ~** [information] öffentlich zugänglich sein.

**public holiday** *n* gesetzlicher Feiertag.

**public house** *n Br fml* Gaststätte *die*.

**publicist** ['pʌblɪsɪst] *n* [publicity agent] PR-Agent *der*, -in *die*.

**publicity** [pʌb'lɪsɪtɪ] *n* (U) - **1.** [media attention] Publicity *die* - **2.** [information] Werbung *die*, Reklame *die* ◇ *comp* Werbe-.

**publicity stunt** *n:* **it's only a ~** es ist nur ein Werbetrick.

**publicize, -ise** ['pʌblɪsaɪz] *vt* bekannt machen.

**public limited company** *n* ≈ Aktiengesellschaft *die*.

**publicly** ['pʌblɪklɪ] *adv* öffentlich.

**public office** *n:* **to stand for ~** für ein öffentliches Amt kandidieren.

**public opinion** *n* (U) öffentliche Meinung.

**public ownership** *n* Staatsbesitz *der*.

**public prosecutor** *n* Staatsanwalt *der*, -anwältin *die*.

**public relations** *n* (U) [work] Öffentlichkeitsarbeit *die*, Public Relations *pl* ◇ *npl*: **it would be good for ~** es wäre gut für unser öffentliches Ansehen.

**public relations officer** *n* PR-Manager *der*, -in *die*.

**public school** *n* - **1.** *Br* [private school] höhere Privatschule - **2.** *Am* & *Scot* [state school] staatliche Schule.

---

**PUBLIC SCHOOL**

In England und Wales ist eine Public School eine traditionelle Privatschule (meist Internat). Einige Public Schools (z. B. Eton und Harrow) sind sehr bekannt und gelten als begehrte Eliteschmieden. In den USA dagegen und zum Teil auch in Schottland bezeichnet der Ausdruck „public school" eine staatliche Schule.

---

**public sector** *n* öffentliches Sektor.

**public servant** *n* Staatsbeamte *der*, *die*.

**public-spirited** ['spɪrɪtɪd] *adj*: **to be ~** Gemeinschaftssinn haben.

**public transport** n (U) öffentliche Verkehrsmittel pl.

**public utility** n öffentlicher Versorgungsbetrieb.

**public works** npl staatliche Bauvorhaben.

**publish** ['pʌblɪʃ] vt veröffentlichen.

**publisher** ['pʌblɪʃər] n - 1. [company] Verlag der - 2. [person] Verleger der, -in die.

**publishing** ['pʌblɪʃɪŋ] n Verlagswesen das.

**publishing company, publishing house** n Verlag der.

**pub lunch** n Mittagessen das im Pub.

**puck** [pʌk] n ICE HOCKEY Puck der.

**pucker** ['pʌkər] vt [lips for kissing] spitzen ⬦ vi [material] Falten werfen.

**pudding** ['pudɪŋ] n - 1. [sweet food] Nachspeise die; milk ~ Pudding der - 2. (U) Br [part of meal] Nachtisch der, Dessert das.

**puddle** ['pʌdl] n Pfütze die.

**pudgy** ['pʌdʒɪ] adj = podgy.

**puerile** ['pjʊəraɪl] adj fml kindisch, infantil.

**Puerto Rican** [ˌpwɜːtəʊ'riːkən] adj puertoricanisch ⬦ n Puertoricaner der, -in die.

**Puerto Rico** [ˌpwɜːtəʊ'riːkəʊ] n Puerto Rico nt.

**puff** [pʌf] n - 1. [of cigarette, pipe] Zug der - 2.: ~ of wind Windhauch der; ~ of smoke Rauchwölkchen das ⬦ vt paffen ⬦ vi - 1. [smoke]: to ~ at OR on sthg an etw (D) paffen - 2. [pant] keuchen, schnaufen.

⬦ **puff out** vt sep [cheeks] auf lblasen; [chest] anschwellen lassen; [feathers] auf lplustern.

⬦ **puff up** vi [eyes, skin] an lschwellen.

**puffed** [pʌft] adj - 1. [swollen]: ~ up angeschwollen - 2. Br inf [out of breath]: ~ (out) außer Atem.

**puffed sleeve** n Puffärmel der.

**puffin** ['pʌfɪn] n Papageientaucher der.

**puff pastry, puff paste** Am n (U) Blätterteig der.

**puffy** ['pʌfɪ] (compar -ier; superl -iest) adj aufgedunsen, angeschwollen.

**pug** [pʌg] n Mops der.

**pugnacious** [pʌg'neɪʃəs] adj fml kampflustig.

**puke** [pjuːk] vi vinf kotzen.

**pull** [pʊl] vt - 1. [rope, hair] ziehen an (+ D); [cart] ziehen; to ~ sthg to pieces etw in Stücke reißen, fig etw scharf kritisieren - 2. [curtains - open] auf lziehen; [ - close] zulziehen - 3. [trigger] drücken; [lever] ziehen - 4. [take out - cork] herauslziehen; [ - gun, tooth] ziehen; she ~ed herself out of the water sie rettete sich aus dem Wasser - 5. [muscle, hamstring] sich (D) zerren - 6. [crowd, voters] anlziehen ⬦ vi [tug with hand] ziehen ⬦ n - 1. [tug with hand] Ziehen das, Zug der; to give the rope a ~ am Seil ziehen - 2. (U) [influence] Einfluss der.

⬦ **pull ahead** vi: to ~ ahead (of sb/sthg) (jm/etw) davon lziehen.

⬦ **pull apart** vt sep [separate] auseinander ziehen.

⬦ **pull at** vt fus ziehen an (+ D).

⬦ **pull away** vi - 1. [from roadside]: to ~ away (from) weglziehen (von) - 2. [in race]: to ~ away (from) sich ablsetzen (von).

⬦ **pull back** vi [step backwards] (nach hinten) auslweichen, zurückltreten.

⬦ **pull down** vt sep [demolish] ablreißen.

⬦ **pull in** vi [car, bus] anlhalten; [train] einlfahren.

⬦ **pull off** vt sep - 1. [take off] auslziehen - 2. [succeed in - coup, robbery] landen; [ - deal] an Land ziehen.

⬦ **pull on** vt sep [clothes, shoes] anlziehen.

⬦ **pull out** vt sep [withdraw] zurücklziehen ⬦ vi - 1. [train] ablfahren - 2. [vehicle - from kerb] ablfahren; [ - from lane] auslscheren - 3. [withdraw] sich zurücklziehen.

⬦ **pull over** vi [vehicle, driver] an den Straßenrand fahren.

⬦ **pull through** vi [patient] durchlkommen ⬦ vt sep [subj: doctor] durchlbringen, durchlbekommen.

⬦ **pull together** vt sep: to ~ o.s. together sich zusammenlreißen, sich zusammenlnehmen ⬦ vi [combine efforts] am gleichen Strang ziehen.

⬦ **pull up** vt sep - 1. [raise] hochlziehen, herauf|ziehen - 2. [move closer] heranlziehen - 3. [stop]: to ~ sb up short jn zum Nachdenken bringen ⬦ vi anlhalten.

**pull-down menu** n COMPUT Pull-down-Menü das.

**pulley** ['pʊlɪ] (pl pulleys) n [wheel] Rolle die; [whole system] Flaschenzug der.

**pullout** ['pʊlaʊt] n - 1. [of troops] Abzug der - 2. [in magazine]: ~ (section) herausnehmbarer Teil.

**pullover** ['pʊlˌəʊvər] n Pullover der.

**pulp** [pʌlp] adj: ~ novel Schundroman der; ~ fiction Schundliteratur die ⬦ n - 1. [soft mass] Brei der - 2. [of fruit] Fruchtfleisch das - 3. [for paper] Papierbrei der ⬦ vt [books] einlstampfen.

**pulpit** ['pʊlpɪt] n Kanzel die.

**pulsar** ['pʌlsɑːr] n Pulsar der.

**pulsate** [pʌl'seɪt] vi pulsieren; [air, sound] vibrieren.

**pulse** [pʌls] n - 1. [in body] Puls der; to take sb's ~ jm den Puls messen - 2. TECH Impuls der ⬦ vi [blood, music] pulsieren.

⬦ **pulses** npl [food] Hülsenfrüchte pl.

**pulverize, -ise** ['pʌlvəraɪz] vt - 1. [crush] pulverisieren, zermahlen - 2. fig [person] fertig machen; [argument] vom Tisch wischen.

**puma** ['pjuːmə] (pl inv OR -s) n Puma der.

P

**pumice (stone)** ['pʌmɪs-] *n (U)* Bimsstein
der.

**pummel** ['pʌml] (*Br pt* & *pp* -led; *cont* -ling, *Am
pt* & *pp* -ed; *cont* -ing) *vt* mit den Fäusten bearbeiten, einschlagen auf (+ A).

**pump** [pʌmp] *n* - **1.** [machine] Pumpe *die* - **2.** [for
petrol] Zapfsäule *die*, Tanksäule *die* <> *vt*
- **1.** [convey by pumping] pumpen - **2.** *inf* [invest]: **to
~ money into sthg** Geld in etw fließen lassen
*OR* stecken - **3.** *inf* [interrogate]: **to ~ sb for information** aus jm Informationen herauslholen
<> *vi* [machine, person, heart] pumpen.
⬥ **pumps** *npl* [shoes] Pumps *pl*.

**pumpernickel** ['pʌmpənɪkl] *n* Pumpernickel *das*.

**pumpkin** ['pʌmpkɪn] *n* Kürbis *der*.

**pumpkin pie** *n* Kürbiskuchen *der*.

**pun** [pʌn] *n* Wortspiel *das*.

**punch** [pʌntʃ] *n* - **1.** [blow] (Faust)schlag *der*
- **2.** [for making holes in paper] Locher *der* - **3.** *(U)*
[drink - cold] Bowle *die;* [ - hot] Punsch *der* <> *vt*
- **1.** [hit] (mit der Faust) schlagen - **2.** [per-
forate - ticket] lochen; **to ~ a hole in sthg** ein
Loch in etw machen.
⬥ **punch in** *vi Am* stechen, stempeln (bei Arbeitsbeginn).
⬥ **punch out** *vi Am* stechen, stempeln (bei Arbeitsende).

**Punch-and-Judy show** [,pʌntʃən'dʒuːdɪ-] *n*
Kasperletheater *das*.

PUNCH-AND-JUDY SHOW

Die Punch and Judy show, die oft im Sommer am Strand aufgeführt wird, ist das
britische Kasperletheater, komplett mit
Krokodilen, gestohlenen Würstchen, lus-
tigen Prügeleien (mit dem „Slapstick", der
zum Markennamen für das Genre des ko-
mischen Klamaukstücks wurde), schreien-
den Babys, nörgelnden Ehefrauen (Judy)
und schlagkräftigen Ehemännern (Mr
Punch). Nach wie vor ein Renner bei Kindern, ähnlich wie Cartoons wie „Tom and
Jerry".

**punch-bag, punching bag** *Am* ['pʌntʃɪŋ-] *n*
Sandsack *der*.

**punch ball** *n* Punchingball *der*.

**punch bowl** *n* Bowlegefäß *das*.

**punch-drunk** *adj* [groggy] benommen.

**punch(ed) card** [pʌntʃ(t)-] *n* Lochkarte *die*.

**punching bag** *n Am* = **punch-bag**.

**punch line** *n* Pointe *die*.

**punch-up** *n Br inf* Schlägerei *die*.

**punchy** ['pʌntʃɪ] (*compar* -ier; *superl* -iest) *adj inf*
[style] prägnant; [slogan] durchschlagend.

**punctilious** [pʌŋk'tɪlɪəs] *adj fml* äußerst korrekt.

**punctual** ['pʌŋktʃʊəl] *adj* pünktlich.

**punctually** ['pʌŋktʃʊəlɪ] *adv* pünktlich.

**punctuate** ['pʌŋktʃʊeɪt] *vt* - **1.** [add punctuation
to] Satzzeichen setzen in (+ D) - **2.** [interrupt]:
**to be ~d by** *OR* **with sthg** von *OR* mit etw unterbrochen werden.

**punctuation** [,pʌŋktʃʊ'eɪʃn] *n* Zeichenset-
zung *die*, Interpunktion *die*.

**punctuation mark** *n* Satzzeichen *das*.

**puncture** ['pʌŋktʃəʳ] *n* [in tyre, ball] (kleines)
Loch; **I had a ~** ich hatte einen Platten <> *vt*
- **1.** [tyre, ball] ein Loch machen in (+ A)
- **2.** [lung, skin] punktieren.

**pundit** ['pʌndɪt] *n* Experte *der*, -tin *die*.

**pungent** ['pʌndʒənt] *adj* - **1.** [smell] stechend,
beißend; [taste] scharf - **2.** *fig* [criticism, remark]
scharf.

**punish** ['pʌnɪʃ] *vt* bestrafen; **to ~ sb for sthg** jn
für etw bestrafen.

**punishable** ['pʌnɪʃəbl] *adj* strafbar; **to be ~ by
life imprisonment** mit lebenslänglicher Haft
bestraft werden.

**punishing** ['pʌnɪʃɪŋ] *adj* [work, schedule] strapaziös.

**punishment** ['pʌnɪʃmənt] *n* - **1.** *(U)* [act of pun-
ishing] Bestrafung *die* - **2.** [means of punishment]
Strafe *die* - **3.** [heavy use]: **the car takes a lot of ~**
das Auto wird ganz schön strapaziert.

**punitive** ['pjuːnətɪv] *adj* [measures] Straf-; [taxes]
sehr hoch.

**Punjab** [,pʌn'dʒɑːb] *n:* **the ~** das Pandschab.

**Punjabi** [,pʌn'dʒɑːbɪ] *adj* Pandschabi- <> *n*
- **1.** [person] Pandschabi *der*, *die* - **2.** [language]
Pandschabi *das*.

**punk** [pʌŋk] *adj* Punker- <> *n* - **1.** [music]:
**~ (rock)** Punk(rock) *der* - **2.** [person]: **~ (rocker)**
Punker *der*, -in *die* - **3.** *Am inf* [lout] Rowdy *der*,
Randalierer *der*.

**punnet** ['pʌnɪt] *n Br* Schale *die*, Körbchen *das*.

**punt** [pʌnt] *n* - **1.** [boat] Stechkahn *der* - **2.** [Irish
currency] Punt *das* <> *vi* [in boat] staken.

**punter** ['pʌntəʳ] *n* - **1.** [someone who bets] Wetter
*der*, -in *die* - **2.** *Br inf* [customer] Kunde *der*, -din
*die*.

**puny** ['pjuːnɪ] (*compar* -ier; *superl* -iest) *adj* [per-
son] kümmerlich; [limbs] schwächlich; [effort]
erbärmlich.

**pup** [pʌp] *n* - **1.** [young dog] Hundejunge *das*,
Welpe *der* - **2.**: **seal ~** Robbenjunge *das*.

**pupil** ['pjuːpl] *n* - **1.** [student, follower] Schüler
*der*, -in *die* - **2.** [of eye] Pupille *die*.

**puppet** ['pʌpɪt] *n* - **1.** [string puppet] & *fig* Marionette *die* - **2.** [glove puppet] Handpuppe *die*.

**puppet government** *n* Marionettenre-
gierung *die*.

**puppet show** *n* [with string puppets] Marionet-
tentheater *das;* [with glove puppets] Puppen-
spiel *das*.

**puppy** ['pʌpɪ] (pl -ies) n Hundejunge das, Welpe der.

**puppy fat** n (U) inf Babyspeck der.

**purchase** ['pɜːtʃəs] fml n - **1.** (U) [act of buying] Kauf der - **2.** [thing bought]: ~s Einkäufe pl; **this was a good** ~ das war ein guter Kauf - **3.** (U) [grip] Halt der ◇ vt kaufen.

**purchase order** n Auftragsbestätigung die.

**purchase price** n Kaufpreis der.

**purchaser** ['pɜːtʃəsəʳ] n Käufer der, -in die.

**purchasing power** ['pɜːtʃəsɪŋ-] n (U) Kaufkraft die.

**purdah** ['pɜːdə] n (U) RELIG moslemischer Brauch, nach dem sich Frauen in abgeteilten Räumen aufhalten oder einen Schleier tragen müssen, um den Blicken fremder Männer zu entgehen.

**pure** [pjʊəʳ] adj - **1.** [unadulterated, untainted] rein - **2.** [voice, sound] klar - **3.** literary [chaste] rein - **4.** [science, maths] theoretisch - **5.** [for emphasis] pur.

**purebred** ['pjʊəbred] adj reinrassig.

**puree** ['pjʊəreɪ] n Püree das ◇ vt pürieren.

**purely** ['pjʊəlɪ] adv rein.

**pureness** ['pjʊənɪs] n Reinheit die; [of sound, voice] Klarheit die.

**purgative** ['pɜːgətɪv] n Abführmittel das.

**purgatory** ['pɜːgətrɪ] n (U) hum [suffering] Quälerei die.
◆ **Purgatory** n [place] Fegefeuer das.

**purge** [pɜːdʒ] n POL Säuberungsaktion die ◇ vt - **1.** POL säubern - **2.** [rid]: **to** ~ **sthg/o.s. of** sthg etw/sich von etw befreien.

**purification** [ˌpjʊərɪfɪˈkeɪʃn] n (U) [of air, water] Reinigung die.

**purifier** ['pjʊərɪfaɪəʳ] n [for air] Luftreiniger der; [for water] Wasserreiniger der.

**purify** ['pjʊərɪfaɪ] (pt & pp -ied) vt [air, water] reinigen.

**purist** ['pjʊərɪst] n Purist der, -in die.

**puritan** ['pjʊərɪtən] adj puritanisch ◇ n Puritaner der, -in die.

**puritanical** [ˌpjʊərɪˈtænɪkl] adj pej puritanisch.

**purity** ['pjʊərətɪ] n (U) - **1.** [of air, water] Reinheit die - **2.** [of sound, voice] Klarheit die - **3.** literary [chastity] Reinheit die.

**purl** [pɜːl] n: ~ **(stitch)** linke Masche ◇ vt [stitch] links stricken.

**purloin** [pɜːˈlɔɪn] vt fml OR hum entwenden.

**purple** ['pɜːpl] adj violett, lila ◇ n Violett das, Lila das.

**purport** [pəˈpɔːt] vi fml: **to** ~ **to do/be sthg** vorgeben, etw zu tun/sein.

**purpose** ['pɜːpəs] n - **1.** [objective, reason] Zweck der - **2.** [use]: **to no** ~ umsonst - **3.** [determination] Entschlossenheit die.
◆ **on purpose** adv absichtlich, mit Absicht.

**purpose-built** adj zu diesem Zweck gebaut.

**purposeful** ['pɜːpəsfʊl] adj zielbewusst, entschlossen.

**purposely** ['pɜːpəslɪ] adv absichtlich, mit Absicht.

**purr** [pɜːʳ] n - **1.** [of cat] Schnurren das - **2.** [of engine] Summen das ◇ vi - **1.** [cat, person] schnurren - **2.** [engine, machine] summen.

**purse** [pɜːs] n - **1.** [for money] Portmonee das - **2.** Am [handbag] Handtasche die ◇ vt [lips] auflwerfen, schürzen.

**purser** ['pɜːsəʳ] n Zahlmeister der, -in die.

**purse snatcher** [-ˌsnætʃəʳ] n Am (Hand)taschendieb der, -in die.

**purse strings** npl: **to hold the** ~ über das Geld bestimmen.

**pursue** [pəˈsjuː] vt - **1.** [criminal, car] verfolgen - **2.** [hobby, interest] nachlgehen (+ D); [aim] verfolgen - **3.** [matter] weiterlverfolgen.

**pursuer** [pəˈsjuːəʳ] n Verfolger der, -in die.

**pursuit** [pəˈsjuːt] n - **1.** (U) fml [attempt to obtain, achieve]: **the** ~ **of sthg** das Streben nach etw - **2.** [chase] Verfolgung die; **to set off in** ~ **of sb** jm nachjagen; **in hot** ~ dicht auf den Fersen - **3.** SPORT Verfolgung die - **4.** [occupation, activity] Beschäftigung die, Betätigung die.

**purveyor** [pəˈveɪəʳ] n fml Lieferant der.

**pus** [pʌs] n Eiter der.

**push** [pʊʃ] vt - **1.** [press, move - button] drücken; [ - bicycle, person] schieben; **to** ~ **the door open/to** die Tür auf l-/zulmachen - **2.** [encourage] (nachdrücklich) ermutigen; **to** ~ **sb to do sthg** jn (nachdrücklich) ermutigen, etw zu tun - **3.** [force] drängen; **to** ~ **sb into doing sthg** jn drängen, etw zu tun - **4.** inf [promote] Werbung machen für - **5.** drugs sl [sell illegally] handeln mit, dealen mit - **6.** inf [approach]: **he's** ~**ing forty** er geht auf die vierzig zu; **we were** ~**ing ninety miles an hour** wir fuhren fast neunzig Meilen pro Stunde ◇ vi - **1.** [shove] schieben; [in crowd] drängen - **2.** [on button, bell] drücken - **3.** [campaign]: **to** ~ **for sthg** auf etw (A) drängen, es auf etw (A) anllegen ◇ n - **1.** [shove] Stoß der, Schubs der - **2.** [on button, bell]: **to give sthg a** ~ etw drücken - **3.** [campaign] (großangelegte) Aktion - **4.** phr: **to give sb the** ~ Br inf [end relationship] mit jm Schluss machen; [dismiss] jn rauslschmeißen.
◆ **push ahead** vi: **to** ~ **ahead (with sthg)** (mit etw) weiterlmachen.
◆ **push around** vt sep inf fig [bully] herumlschubsen.
◆ **push in** vi [in queue] (sich) vorldrängen, sich reinldrängen.

◆ **push off** *vi inf* [go away] verschwinden, ablhauen.

◆ **push on** *vi* [continue] weiterlmachen.

◆ **push over** *vt sep* umlstürzen, umlschmeißen.

◆ **push through** *vt sep* [new law, reform] durchlbringen, durchlsetzen.

**pushbike** ['pʊʃbaɪk] *n Br* Fahrrad *das.*

**push-button** *adj* [phone] Tasten-.

**pushcart** ['pʊʃkɑːt] *n* Schubwagen *der,* Karren *der.*

**pushchair** ['pʊʃtʃeəʳ] *n Br* Sportwagen *der.*

**pushed** [pʊʃt] *adj inf:* to be ~ for time unter Zeitdruck stehen; to be ~ for money in Geldnöten sein; to be hard ~ to do sthg es schwer finden, etw zu tun.

**pusher** ['pʊʃəʳ] *n drugs sl* Dealer *der,* -in *die.*

**pushover** ['pʊʃˌəʊvəʳ] *n inf* [sucker]: he's a ~ er lässt sich leicht reinlegen.

**push-start** *vt* anlschieben.

**push-up** *n esp Am* Liegestütz *der.*

**pushy** ['pʊʃɪ] (*compar* -ier; *superl* -iest) *adj pej* aufdringlich, aggressiv.

**puss** [pʊs], **pussy (cat)** ['pʊsɪ-] *n inf* Miezelkatze) *die.*

**put** [pʊt] (*pt & pp* put; *cont* -ting) *vt* - **1.** [place] tun; [place upright] stellen; [lay flat] legen; **to ~ sthg into sthg** etw in etw *(A)* hineinltun/hineinlstellen/hineinllegen; he ~ his arm round her shoulder er legte ihr den Arm um die Schulter; I ~ the children first bei mir kommen die Kinder zuerst; he ~ his hand in his pocket er steckte die Hand in die Tasche; that ~s me in a difficult position das bringt mich in eine schwierige Lage - **2.** [send]: **to ~ sb in prison/hospital** jn ins Gefängnis stecken/ins Krankenhaus schicken; **to ~ a child to bed** ein Kind ins Bett bringen - **3.** [express] sagen; I ~ **it to you that ...** bedenken Sie, dass ... - **4.** [ask]: **to ~ a question (to sb)** (jm) eine Frage stellen - **5.** [make]: **to ~ a proposal to sb** jm einen Vorschlag machen - **6.** [write] schreiben - **7.** [cause]: **to ~ sb to a lot of trouble** jm viel Mühe machen - **8.** [estimate]: **to ~ sthg at** etw schätzen auf *(+ A)* - **9.** [invest - money, time, energy]: **to ~ sthg into sthg** etw in etw *(A)* investieren, etw für etw auflwenden - **10.** [apply]: **to ~ pressure on sb,** **to ~ sb under pressure** jn unter Druck setzen; **to ~ the blame on sb** jm die Schuld geben.

◆ **put across** *vt sep* [ideas] verständlich machen.

◆ **put aside** *vt sep* - **1.** [gen] beiseite legen - **2.** [money] zur Seite legen.

◆ **put away** *vt sep* - **1.** [tidy away] weglräumen - **2.** *inf* [lock up] einlsperren - **3.** *inf* [eat] verdrücken; [drink] schlucken; he can really ~ it away der kann wirklich was wegstecken.

◆ **put back** *vt sep* - **1.** [replace] zurückllegen;

[upright] zurücklstellen; ~ it back in the bag stecke es wieder in die Tasche - **2.** [postpone] verschieben - **3.** [clock, watch] zurücklstellen.

◆ **put by** *vt sep* [money] zurückllegen.

◆ **put down** *vt sep* - **1.** [place] setzen; [place upright] (hin)lstellen; [lay flat] (hin)llegen - **2.** [passenger] ablsetzen - **3.** [deposit] anlzahlen - **4.** [riot, rebellion] niederlschlagen - **5.** *inf* [criticize] schlecht machen - **6.** [write down] auflschreiben; **to ~ sthg down in writing** etw schriftlich niederllegen - **7.** *Br* [animal] einlschläfern.

◆ **put down to** *vt sep:* **to ~ sthg down to sthg** etw einer Sache *(D)* zulschreiben.

◆ **put forward** *vt sep* - **1.** [plan, theory, name] vorlschlagen; [proposal] machen - **2.** [meeting, date] vorlverlegen - **3.** [clock, watch] vorlstellen.

◆ **put in** *vt sep* - **1.** [spend - time] verwenden - **2.** [submit] einlreichen - **3.** [install] einlbauen.

◆ **put in for** *vt fus* [request] sich bewerben um.

◆ **put off** *vt sep* - **1.** [postpone] verschieben; **to ~ off doing sthg** es verschieben, etw zu tun - **2.** [switch off] auslschalten, auslmachen - **3.** [cause to wait] hinlhalten - **4.** [discourage]: **to ~ sb off doing sthg** jn davon ablbringen, etw zu tun - **5.** [distract] ablenken - **6.** [cause to dislike]: **to ~ sb off doing sthg** es jm verleiden, etw zu tun - **7.** [passenger] ablsetzen.

◆ **put on** *vt sep* - **1.** [clothes] anlziehen; [hat, glasses] auflsetzen; [make-up] aufllegen; ~ **your clothes on!** zieh dich an! - **2.** [play, show] auflführen; [exhibition] veranstalten - **3.** [gain in weight]: **to ~ on weight** zulnehmen; I've ~ **on two kilos** ich habe zwei Kilo zugenommen - **4.** [TV, radio, light] anlschalten; [handbrake] anlziehen - **5.** [CD, record] auffllegen; [tape] einllegen; [music] anlstellen - **6.** [start cooking] auflstellen; **to ~ the kettle on** Wasser auflsetzen - **7.** [feign] vorltäuschen - **8.** [bet]: **to ~ money on a horse** Geld auf ein Pferd setzen - **9.** [add] auflschlagen - **10.** [provide - bus, train] einlsetzen - **11.** *inf* [tease] auf Schippe nehmen.

◆ **put onto** *vt sep:* **to ~ sb onto sb/sthg** jn mit jm/etw in Verbindung setzen.

◆ **put out** *vt sep* - **1.** [place outside - milk bottles] hinauslstellen; [ - rubbish] hinauslbringen; [ - cat] hinauslsetzen - **2.** [issue - book, record] veröffentlichen; [ - statement] ablgeben - **3.** [cigarette, fire, light] auslmachen - **4.** [hand, arm, leg] auslstrecken - **5.** *inf* [injure]: **to ~ one's back out** sich *(D)* den Rücken verrenken - **6.** [annoy]: **to be ~ out** verärgert sein, sich ärgern - **7.** [inconvenience]: **to ~ sb out** jm Umstände machen; **to ~ o.s. out for sb** sich *(D)* wegen jm viel Mühe machen.

◆ **put over** *vt sep* = **put across.**

◆ **put through** *vt sep* [phonecall] durchlstellen; **to ~ sb through to sb** jn mit jm verbinden.

◆ **put together** *vt sep* - **1.** [assemble - machine, tool] zusammenlsetzen; [ - team, report]

zusammenlstellen - **2.** [combine] zusammenlstellen; **she's better than all the others ~
together** sie ist besser als alle anderen zusammen - **3.** [organize - exhibition]
zusammenlstellen; [ - campaign, event] auf
die Beine stellen.

◆ **put up** *vt sep* - **1.** [tent, statue, building]
auflstellen, errichten - **2.** [umbrella] auf lspannen; [flag] hochlziehen - **3.** [notice]
anlschlagen; [sign] anlbringen; [curtains] auf lhängen - **4.** [provide - money] stellen - **5.** [propose - candidate] auf lstellen - **6.** [increase - price,
cost] hochltreiben - **7.** [provide accommodation for]
unterlbringen ◇ *vt fus* [resistance] leisten; **to
~ up a fight** sich wehren ◇ *vi Br* [in hotel]
unterlkommen.

◆ **put upon** *vt fus Br:* **to be ~ upon** ausgenutzt
werden.

◆ **put up to** *vt sep:* **to ~ sb up to sthg** jn zu etw
anlstiften.

◆ **put up with** *vt fus* dulden.

**putative** ['pjuːtətɪv] *adj fml* mutmaßlich.

**put-down** *n inf* Abfuhr *die.*

**putrefaction** [ˌpjuːtrɪ'fækʃn] *n* Verwesung
*die.*

**putrefy** ['pjuːtrɪfaɪ] (*pt & pp* **-ied**) *vi fml* verwesen.

**putrid** ['pjuːtrɪd] *adj fml* [decayed] faulig.

**putsch** [pʊtʃ] *n* Putsch *der.*

**putt** [pʌt] *n* Schlag *der* ◇ *vt & vi* putten, einllochen.

**putter** ['pʌtə'] *n* [club] Putter *der.*

◆ **putter about, putter around** *Am vi* = **potter
about.**

**putting green** ['pʌtɪŋ-] *n* [for practising] *Rasenfläche zum Putten.*

**putty** ['pʌtɪ] *n* Kitt *der.*

**put-up job** *n inf* abgekartetes Spiel.

**put-upon** *adj inf* ausgenutzt.

**puzzle** ['pʌzl] *n* - **1.** [game] Rätsel *das;* [toy] Geduldsspiel *das;* **(jigsaw) ~** Puzzle *das* - **2.** [mystery] Rätsel *das* ◇ *vt* verblüffen ◇ *vi:* **to
~ over sthg** sich *(D)* über etw *(A)* den Kopf
zerbrechen.

◆ **puzzle out** *vt sep* herauslfinden.

**puzzled** ['pʌzld] *adj* verblüfft.

**puzzling** ['pʌzlɪŋ] *adj* verblüffend.

**PVC** *n* PVC *das.*

**Pvt.** *abbr of* **Private.**

**Pygmy** ['pɪgmɪ] (*pl* **-ies**) *n* [in Africa] Pygmäe *der,*
-äin *die.*

**pyjama** [pə'dʒɑːmə] *comp* Schlafanzug-,
Pyjama-.

**pyjamas** [pə'dʒɑːməz] *npl* Schlafanzug *der,*
Pyjama *der.*

**pylon** ['paɪlən] *n* ELEC Mast *der.*

**PYO** (*abbr of* **pick your own**) *auf Schildern verwendeter Hinweis, dass man bei diesen Bauern Früchte und Gemüse selbst pflücken und
kaufen kann.*

**pyramid** ['pɪrəmɪd] *n* Pyramide *die.*

**pyramid selling** [-ˌselɪŋ] *n (U)* Schneeballsystem *das.*

**pyre** ['paɪə'] *n* Scheiterhaufen *der.*

**Pyrenean** [ˌpɪrə'niːən] *adj* pyrenäisch.

**Pyrenees** [ˌpɪrə'niːz] *npl:* **the ~** die Pyrenäen.

**Pyrex**® ['paɪreks] *n (U)* ≃ Jenaer Glas® *das*
◇ *comp* ≃ aus Jenaer Glas®.

**pyromaniac** [ˌpaɪrə'meɪnɪæk] *n* Pyromane
*der,* -nin *die.*

**pyrotechnics** [ˌpaɪrəʊ'tekniks] *n (U)* [science]
Pyrotechnik *die* ◇ *npl* **fig** [show of brilliance]
Feuerwerk *das.*

**python** ['paɪθn] (*pl inv OR* **-s**) *n* Pythonschlange *die.*

**q** (*pl* **q's** *OR* **qs**), **Q** (*pl* **Q's** *OR* **Qs**) [kjuː] *n* q *das,* Q
*das.*

**QC** *n abbr of* **Queen's Counsel.**

**QED** (*abbr of* **quod erat demonstrandum**)
q. e. d.

**QM** *n abbr of* **quartermaster.**

**q.t., QT** (*abbr of* **quiet**) *inf:* **on the ~** heimlich.

**Q-tip**® *n esp Am* Wattestäbchen *das.*

**qty** *abbr of* **quantity.**

**quack** [kwæk] *n* - **1.** [noise] Quaken *das* - **2.** *inf
pej* [doctor] Quacksalber *der,* Kurpfuscher *der*
◇ *vi* quaken.

**quad** [kwɒd] *n* - **1.** *abbr of* **quadruplet** - **2.** *abbr
of* **quadrangle.**

**quadrangle** ['kwɒdræŋgl] *n* - **1.** [figure] Viereck *das* - **2.** [courtyard] (viereckiger) Hof.

**quadrant** ['kwɒdrənt] *n* [instrument] Quadrant
*der.*

**quadraphonic** [ˌkwɒdrə'fɒnɪk] *adj* quadrofonisch.

**quadrilateral** [ˌkwɒdrɪ'lætərəl] *adj* vierseitig
◇ *n* Viereck *das.*

**quadruped** [ˈkwɒdrʊped] n Vierfüßler der.

**quadruple** [kwɒˈdruːpl] adj vierfach; **sales are ~ last year's figures** die Verkaufszahlen haben sich im Vergleich zum Vorjahr vervierfacht ◇ vt vervierfachen ◇ vi sich vervierfachen.

**quadruplets** [ˈkwɒdrʊplɪts] npl Vierlinge pl.

**quads** [kwɒdz] npl inf Vierlinge pl.

**quaff** [kwɒf] vt dated trinken.

**quagmire** [ˈkwægmaɪəʳ] n Sumpf der.

**quail** [kweɪl] (pl inv OR -s) n Wachtel die ◇ vi literary beben, zittern.

**quaint** [kweɪnt] adj [cottage] urig; [tradition] kurios.

**quake** [kweɪk] n inf (abbr of **earthquake**) Beben das ◇ vi beben, zittern.

**Quaker** [ˈkweɪkəʳ] n Quäker der, -in die.

**qualification** [ˌkwɒlɪfɪˈkeɪʃn] n - 1. [examination, certificate, skill] Qualifikation die - 2. [qualifying statement] Einschränkung die.

**qualified** [ˈkwɒlɪfaɪd] adj - 1. [trained] ausgebildet - 2. [able]: **to be ~ to do sthg** qualifiziert sein, etw zu tun - 3. [limited] eingeschränkt.

**qualify** [ˈkwɒlɪfaɪ] (pt & pp -ied) vt - 1. [statement] einlschränken - 2. [entitle]: **to ~ sb to do sthg** jn berechtigen, etw zu tun ◇ vi - 1. [pass exams & SPORT] sich qualifizieren - 2. [be entitled]: **to ~ for sthg** zu etw berechtigt sein.

**qualifying** [ˈkwɒlɪfaɪŋ] adj - 1. [statement] einlschränkend - 2. [entitling]: **~ exam** Zulassungsprüfung die - 3. SPORT Qualifikations-; **~ round** Qualifikationsrunde die.

**qualitative** [ˈkwɒlɪtətɪv] adj qualitativ.

**quality** [ˈkwɒlətɪ] (pl -ies) n - 1. [gen] Qualität die - 2. [characteristic] Eigenschaft die ◇ comp Qualitäts-.

**quality control** n Qualitätskontrolle die.

**quality press** n Br: **the ~** die seriöse Presse.

**qualms** [kwɑːmz] npl Skrupel pl.

**quandary** [ˈkwɒndərɪ] (pl -ies) n Zwickmühle die; **to be in a ~ about** OR **over sthg** in einer Zwickmühle stecken wegen etw OR in Bezug auf etw (A).

**quango** [ˈkwæŋgəʊ] (pl -s) (abbr of **quasi-autonomous non-governmental organization**) n Br usu pej in Großbritannien ein vom Staat eingesetzte Behörde zum Betrieb eines öffentlichen Dienstes.

**quantifiable** [kwɒntɪˈfaɪəbl] adj quantifizierbar.

**quantify** [ˈkwɒntɪfaɪ] (pt & pp -ied) vt in Zahlen ausldrücken.

**quantitative** [ˈkwɒntɪtətɪv] adj quantitativ.

**quantity** [ˈkwɒntətɪ] (pl -ies) n Menge die; **in ~** in großer Menge; **to be an unknown ~** eine unbekannte Größe sein.

**quantity surveyor** n Baukostenkalkulator der, -in die.

**quantum leap** [ˌkwɒntəm-] n fig Riesenschritt der.

**quantum theory** [ˈkwɒntəm-] n Quantentheorie die.

**quarantine** [ˈkwɒrəntiːn] n Quarantäne die; **to be in ~** in Quarantäne sein; **to put in ~** unter Quarantäne stellen ◇ vt unter Quarantäne stellen.

**quark** [kwɑːk] n - 1. PHYS Quarks pl - 2. CULIN Quark der.

**quarrel** [ˈkwɒrəl] (Br pt & pp -led; cont -ling, Am pt & pp -ed; cont -ing) n Streit der; **to have no ~ with sb/sthg** nichts gegen jn/etw haben ◇ vi sich streiten; **to ~ with sb** sich mit jm streiten; **to ~ with sthg** an etw (D) etwas auszusetzen haben.

**quarrelsome** [ˈkwɒrəlsəm] adj streitsüchtig.

**quarry** [ˈkwɒrɪ] (pl -ies; pt & pp -ied) n - 1. [place] Steinbruch der - 2. [prey] Beute die ◇ vt [stone] brechen.

**quart** [kwɔːt] n [unit of measurement] Br Quart das (= 1,14 l); Am Quart das (= 0,95 l).

**quarter** [ˈkwɔːtəʳ] n - 1. [fraction, area in town] Viertel das - 2. [in telling time]: **a ~ past (two)** Br, **a ~ after (two)** Am Viertel nach (zwei); **a ~ to (two)** Br, **a ~ of (two)** Am Viertel vor (zwei) - 3. [of year] Vierteljahr das, Quartal das - 4. Am [coin] Vierteldollar der - 5. [four ounces] ≈ Viertelpfund das - 6. [direction] Richtung die; **from all ~s of the globe** aus allen Himmelsrichtungen; **from an unexpected ~** von unerwarteter Seite.
◆ **quarters** npl [rooms] Quartier das.
◆ **at close quarters** adv aus der Nähe.

**quarterback** [ˈkwɔːtəbæk] n Am Quarterback der.

**quarterdeck** [ˈkwɔːtədek] n Achterdeck das.

**quarterfinal** [ˌkwɔːtəˈfaɪnl] n Viertelfinalspiel das.

**quarter-hour** adj viertelstündlich.

**quarter light** n Br kleines dreieckiges ausstellbares Seitenfenster.

**quarterly** [ˈkwɔːtəlɪ] (pl -ies) adj & adv vierteljährlich ◇ n Vierteljahresschrift die.

**quartermaster** [ˈkwɔːtəˌmɑːstəʳ] n MIL Quartiermeister der.

**quarter note** n Am MUS Viertelnote die.

**quartet** [kwɔːˈtet] n Quartett das.

**quarto** [ˈkwɔːtəʊ] (pl -s) n Quartformat das.

**quartz** [kwɔːts] n (U) Quarz der.

**quartz watch** n Quarzuhr die.

**quasar** [ˈkweɪzɑːʳ] n Quasar der.

**quash** [kwɒʃ] *vt* - **1.** [decision, sentence] auf l-heben, widerrufen - **2.** [rebellion] unterdrü-cken, niederlschlagen.

**quasi-** ['kweɪzaɪ] *prefix* quasi-.

**quaver** ['kweɪvə'] *n* - **1.** MUS Achtelnote *die* - **2.** [in voice] Zittern *das* ◇ *vi* zittern.

**quavering** ['kweɪvərɪŋ] *adj* zitternd.

**quay** [ki:] *n* Kai *der*.

**quayside** ['ki:saɪd] *n* Kai *der*.

**queasy** ['kwi:zɪ] (*compar* **-ier;** *superl* **-iest**) *adj* unwohl.

**queen** [kwi:n] *n* - **1.** [royalty, bee] Königin *die* - **2.** [in chess, playing card] Dame *die*.

**queen bee** *n* Bienenkönigin *die*.

**queen mother** *n:* the ~ die Königinmutter.

**Queen's Counsel** *n Br* Anwalt *der*, -wältin *die* der Krone.

**Queen's English** *n Br:* the ~ die englische Hochsprache.

**queen's evidence** *n Br:* to turn ~ als Kron-zeuge auf ltreten.

**queer** [kwɪə'] *adj* [odd] seltsam, eigenartig; **I'm feeling a bit** ~ mir ist nicht ganz wohl ◇ *n inf pej* [homosexual] Schwule *der*.

**quell** [kwel] *vt* unterdrücken.

**quench** [kwentʃ] *vt* stillen.

**querulous** ['kwerʊləs] *adj fml* nörglerisch.

**query** ['kwɪərɪ] (*pl* **-ies;** *pt* & *pp* **-ied**) *n* Frage *die* ◇ *vt* [decision] in Frage stellen; [invoice] be-anstanden.

**quest** [kwest] *n literary:* ~ **(for sthg)** Suche *die* (nach etw).

**question** ['kwestʃn] *n* Frage *die;* **to ask (sb) a** ~ (jm) eine Frage stellen; **to bring** OR **call sthg into** ~ etw in Frage stellen; **to be beyond** ~ außer Zweifel OR Frage stehen; **it's open to** ~ **whether ...** es ist zweifelhaft, ob ...; **without** ~ ohne Zweifel, ohne Frage; **there's no** ~ **of doing it** es kommt nicht in Frage, es zu tun ◇ *vt* - **1.** [interrogate] befragen - **2.** [express doubt about] bezweifeln.
  ➥ **in question** *adv:* the ... in ~ der/die/das be-treffende ...
  ➥ **out of the question** *adj* ausgeschlossen.

**questionable** ['kwestʃənəbl] *adj* - **1.** [uncertain] fraglich - **2.** [not right, not honest] fragwürdig.

**questioner** ['kwestʃənə'] *n* Fragesteller *der*, -in *die*.

**questioning** ['kwestʃənɪŋ] *adj* [look] fragend ◇ *n (U)* Befragung *die*.

**question mark** *n* Fragezeichen *das*.

**question master** *esp Br,* **quizmaster** *esp Am* ['kwɪz,mɑ:stə'] *n* Quizmaster *der*.

**questionnaire** [,kwestʃə'neə'] *n* Fragebogen *der*.

**question time** *n (U) Br* POL Fragestunde *die*.

**queue** [kju:] *Br n* Schlange *die;* **to jump the** ~ sich vorldrängeln ◇ *vi* Schlange stehen; **to** ~ **(up) for sthg** für etw anlstehen.

**queue-jump** *vi Br* sich vorldrängeln.

**quibble** ['kwɪbl] *pej n* Spitzfindigkeit *die* ◇ *vi* spitzfindig sein; **to** ~ **over** OR **about sthg** über etw *(A)* streiten.

**quiche** [ki:ʃ] *n* Quiche *die*

**quick** [kwɪk] *adj* & *adv* schnell.

**quicken** ['kwɪkn] *vt* [make faster] beschleuni-gen ◇ *vi* [get faster] schneller werden.

**quickly** ['kwɪklɪ] *adv* schnell.

**quickness** ['kwɪknɪs] *n* Schnelligkeit *die*.

**quicksand** ['kwɪksænd] *n* Treibsand *der*.

**quicksilver** ['kwɪk,sɪlvə'] *n dated* Quecksil-ber *das*.

**quickstep** ['kwɪkstep] *n* Quickstepp *der*.

**quick-tempered** [-'tempəd] *adj* aufbrau-send.

**quick-witted** [-'wɪtɪd] *adj* [person] geistesge-genwärtig; [response] schlagkräftig.

**quid** [kwɪd] (*pl inv*) *n Br inf* Pfund *das*.

**quid pro quo** [-'kwəʊ] (*pl* **quid pro quos**) *n* Gegenleistung *die*.

**quiescent** [kwaɪ'esnt] *adj fml* still, ruhig.

**quiet** ['kwaɪət] *adj* - **1.** [not noisy, calm] ruhig - **2.** [not talkative, silent] still; **to keep** ~ **about sthg** über etw *(A)* nichts sagen; **be** ~! sei/seid still! - **3.** [discreet - clothes, colours] dezent; **to have a** ~ **word with sb** mit jm unter vier Au-gen reden; **to use** ~ **diplomacy** diplomatisch vorlgehen - **4.** [wedding] im kleinen Kreis ◇ *n* Ruhe *die;* **on the** ~ *inf* heimlich ◇ *vt Am* zum Schweigen bringen.
  ➥ **quiet down** *Am vt sep* beruhigen ◇ *vi* sich beruhigen.

**quieten** ['kwaɪətn] *vt* beruhigen.
  ➥ **quieten down** *vt sep* beruhigen ◇ *vi* sich beruhigen.

**quietly** ['kwaɪətlɪ] *adv* - **1.** [without noise] leise - **2.** [without excitement] ruhig - **3.** [without fuss] in aller Stille.

**quietness** ['kwaɪətnɪs] *n* - **1.** [silence] Stille *die* - **2.** [peacefulness] Ruhe *die*.

**quiff** [kwɪf] *n Br* Tolle *die*.

**quill (pen)** [kwɪl-] *n* Feder *die*.

**quilt** [kwɪlt] *n* Steppdecke *die*.

**quilted** ['kwɪltɪd] *adj* gesteppt.

**quince** [kwɪns] *n* Quitte *die*.

**quinine** [kwɪ'ni:n] *n* Chinin *das*.

**quins** *Br* [kwɪnz], **quints** *Am* [kwɪnts] *npl inf* Fünflinge *pl*.

**quintessential** [kwɪntə'senʃl] *adj* typisch.

**quintet** [kwɪn'tet] *n* Quintett *das*.

Q

**quints** npl Am = **quins.**

**quintuplets** [kwɪn'tjuːplɪts] npl Fünflinge pl.

**quip** [kwɪp] (pt & pp **-ped;** cont **-ping**) n geistreiche Bemerkung ◇ vt witzeln.

**quirk** [kwɜːk] n **- 1.** [habit] Marotte die **- 2.** [strange event]: **a ~ of fate** eine Laune des Schicksals.

**quirky** ['kwɜːkɪ] (compar **-ier;** superl **-iest**) adj schrullig.

**quit** [kwɪt] (Br pt & pp **quit** OR **-ted;** cont **-ting,** Am pt & pp **quit;** cont **-ting**) vt **- 1.** [resign from - job] auflgeben, kündigen; [ - army] verlassen **- 2.** [stop] auflhören mit ◇ vi **- 1.** [resign] kündigen **- 2.** [stop] auflhören.

**quite** [kwaɪt] adv **- 1.** [fairly] ziemlich; **~ a lot** ziemlich viel; **~ a few** ziemlich viele **- 2.** [completely] ganz; **I ~ agree** das finde ich auch **- 3.** [after negative]: **not ~ big enough** nicht groß genug; **I don't ~ understand** ich verstehe nicht ganz **- 4.** [for emphasis]: **it was ~ a surprise** es war eine ziemliche Überraschung; **she's ~ a singer** sie singt ganz gut **- 5.** [to express agreement]: **~ (so)!** richtig!, genau!

**quits** [kwɪts] adj inf: **to be ~ (with sb)** (mit jm) quitt sein; **we'll call it ~** [forget the debt] es ist schon in Ordnung; [stop doing sthg] lassen Sie uns jetzt auflhören.

**quitter** ['kwɪtəʳ] n inf pej: **he's a ~** er gibt leicht auf.

**quiver** ['kwɪvəʳ] n **- 1.** [shiver] Zittern das **- 2.** [for arrows] Köcher der ◇ vi zittern.

**quivering** ['kwɪvərɪŋ] adj zitternd.

**quixotic** [kwɪk'sɒtɪk] adj literary idealistisch.

**quiz** [kwɪz] (pl **-zes;** pt & pp **-zed;** cont **-zing**) n **- 1.** [competition, game] Quiz das **- 2.** Am SCH Prüfung die ◇ vt: **to ~ sb (about sthg)** jn (über etw (A)) auslfragen.

**quizmaster** n esp Am = **question master.**

**quizzical** ['kwɪzɪkl] adj fragend.

**quoits** [kwɔɪts] n Wurfringspiel das.

**Quonset hut®** ['kwɒnsɪt-] n Am Nissenhütte die.

**quorate** ['kwɔːreɪt] adj Br: **to be ~** beschlussfähig sein.

**quorum** ['kwɔːrəm] n Quorum das.

**quota** ['kwəʊtə] n Quote die.

**quotation** [kwəʊ'teɪʃn] n **- 1.** [citation] Zitat das **- 2.** COMM Kostenvoranschlag der.

**quotation marks** npl Anführungszeichen pl; **in ~** in Anführungszeichen.

**quote** [kwəʊt] n **- 1.** [citation] Zitat das **- 2.** COMM Kostenvoranschlag der ◇ vt **- 1.** [cite] zitieren **- 2.** COMM: **to ~ sb a price for sthg** jm einen Preis für etw nennen ◇ vi **- 1.** [cite] zitieren; **to ~ from sthg** zitieren aus etw **- 2.** COMM: **to**

**~ for sthg** einen Kostenvoranschlag für etw machen.

**quotes** npl inf Anführungszeichen pl; **single/double ~s** einfache/doppelte Anführungszeichen; **in ~s** in Anführungszeichen.

**quoted company** [ˌkwəʊtɪd-] n Br börsennotiertes Unternehmen.

**quotient** ['kwəʊʃnt] n Quotient der.

**qv** (abbr of **quod vide**) siehe.

**qwerty keyboard** [ˌkwɜːtɪ-] n Br Qwerty-Tastatur die.

# R

**r** (pl **r's** OR **rs**), **R** (pl **R's** OR **Rs**) [ɑːʳ] n r das, R das.

**R - 1.** abbr of **right - 2.** abbr of **River - 3.** (abbr of **Réaumur**) R. **- 4.** abbr of **restricted - 5.** Am abbr of **Republican - 6.** Br (abbr of **Rex**) König der **- 7.** Br (abbr of **Regina**) Königin die.

**RA** (abbr of **Royal Academy**) n königliche Akademie der Künste oder eines ihrer Mitglieder.

**rabbi** ['ræbaɪ] n Rabbiner der.

**rabbit** ['ræbɪt] n Kaninchen das.

**rabbit hole** n Kaninchenbau der.

**rabbit hutch** n Kaninchenstall der.

**rabbit warren** n **- 1.** [for rabbits] Kaninchenbau der **- 2.** fig [building] Labyrinth das.

**rabble** ['ræbl] n **- 1.** [disorderly crowd] aufwieglerische Menge **- 2.** [riffraff]: **the ~** der Pöbel.

**rabble-rousing** [-ˌraʊzɪŋ] adj aufwieglerisch.

**rabid** ['ræbɪd, 'reɪbɪd] adj **- 1.** [infected with rabies] tollwütig **- 2.** pej [fanatical] fanatisch.

**rabies** ['reɪbiːz] n Tollwut die.

**RAC** (abbr of **Royal Automobile Club**) n ≈ ADAC der.

**raccoon** [rə'kuːn] n Waschbär der.

**race** [reɪs] n **- 1.** [competition] Rennen das **- 2.** fig [for power, control] Wettlauf der; **arms ~** Wettrüsten das **- 3.** [people, ethnic background] Rasse die ◇ vt **- 1.** [compete against]: **to ~ sb** mit jm um die Wette laufen/fahren/etc **- 2.** [animal, vehicle] antreten lassen ◇ vi **- 1.** [compete]: **to ~ against sb** gegen jn anltreten **- 2.** [rush] ren-

nen **- 3.** [heart, pulse] rasen **- 4.** [engine] durchldrehen.

**race car** n Am = racing car.

**racecourse** ['reɪskɔːs] n Rennbahn die.

**race driver** n Am = racing driver.

**racehorse** ['reɪshɔːs] n Rennpferd das.

**race meeting** n Rennveranstaltung die.

**race relations** npl Beziehungen pl zwischen den Rassen.

**race riots** npl Rassenunruhen pl.

**racetrack** ['reɪstræk] n Rennbahn die.

**racial** ['reɪʃəl] adj Rassen-.

**racial discrimination** n Rassendiskrimi-
nierung die.

**racialism** etc ['reɪʃəlɪzml] n = racism etc.

**racing** ['reɪsɪŋ] n [motor racing] Rennsport der;
[horse racing] Pferderennsport die.

**racing car** Br, **race car** Am n Rennwagen
der.

**racing driver** Br, **race driver** Am n Renn-
fahrer der, -in die.

**racism** ['reɪsɪzm] n Rassismus der.

**racist** ['reɪsɪst] adj rassistisch <> n Rassist
der, -in die.

**rack** [ræk] n **- 1.** [frame] Ständer der **- 2.** [for lug-
gage] Ablage die <> vt literary: to be ~ed by OR
with sthg von etw gequält werden.

**racket** ['rækɪt] n **- 1.** [noise] Krach der **- 2.** [illegal
activity] Gaunerei die **- 3.** SPORT Schläger der.

**racketeering** [ˌrækə'tɪərɪŋ] n (U) pej Gaune-
reien pl.

**raconteur** [ˌrækɒn'tɜːˀ] n: he is a well-known ~
er ist ein bekannter Geschichtenerzähler.

**racoon** [rə'kuːn] n = raccoon.

**racquet** ['rækɪt] n Schläger der.

**racy** ['reɪsɪ] (compar -ier; superl -iest) adj feurig.

**RADA** ['rɑːdə] (abbr of Royal Academy of Dramatic Art) n königliche Schauspielakademie.

**radar** ['reɪdɑːˀ] n Radar der.

**radar trap** n Radarfalle die.

**radial (tyre)** ['reɪdɪəl-] n Radialreifen der.

**radiance** ['reɪdɪəns] n Strahlen das.

**radiant** ['reɪdɪənt] adj strahlend; ~ **heat**
Strahlungswärme die.

**radiate** ['reɪdɪeɪt] vt ausIstrahlen <> vi
**- 1.** [heat, light] ausgestrahlt werden **- 2.** [roads,
lines] strahlenförmig ausIgehen.

**radiation** [ˌreɪdɪ'eɪʃn] n (U) [radioactive] radio-
aktive Strahlung.

**radiation sickness** n Strahlenkrankheit
die.

**radiator** ['reɪdɪeɪtəˀ] n **- 1.** [in house] Heizkör-
per der **- 2.** AUT Kühler der.

**radiator grille** n Kühlergrill der.

**radical** ['rædɪkl] adj **- 1.** POL radikal **- 2.** [funda-
mental] fundamental <> n POL Radikale der,
die.

**radically** ['rædɪklɪ] adv radikal.

**radii** ['reɪdɪaɪ] pl ▷ radius.

**radio** ['reɪdɪəʊ] (pl -s) n **- 1.** [system of communica-
tion] Rundfunk der **- 2.** [broadcasting, equipment]
Radio das <> comp Radio- <> vt [message] funken; [person] anIfunken.

**radioactive** [ˌreɪdɪəʊ'æktɪv] adj radioaktiv.

**radioactive waste** n radioaktiver Müll.

**radioactivity** [ˌreɪdɪəʊæk'tɪvətɪ] n Radioak-
tivität die.

**radio alarm** n Radiowecker der.

**radio-controlled** [-kən'trəʊld] adj ferngе-
steuert.

**radio frequency** n Radiofrequenz die.

**radiogram** ['reɪdɪəʊˌgræm] n [message] Funk-
spruch der.

**radiographer** [ˌreɪdɪ'ɒgrəfəˀ] n Röntgenas-
sistent der, -in die.

**radiography** [ˌreɪdɪ'ɒgrəfɪ] n Röntgenogra-
fie die.

**radiology** [ˌreɪdɪ'ɒlədʒɪ] n Radiologie die.

**radiopaging** ['reɪdɪəʊˌpeɪdʒɪŋ] n (U) Funkruf
der.

**radiotelephone** [ˌreɪdɪəʊ'telɪfəʊn] n Funk-
sprechgerät das.

**radiotherapist** [ˌreɪdɪəʊ'θerəpɪst] n Strah-
lentherapeut der, -in die.

**radiotherapy** [ˌreɪdɪəʊ'θerəpɪ] n Strahlen-
therapie die.

**radish** ['rædɪʃ] n Radieschen das.

**radium** ['reɪdɪəm] n Radium das.

**radius** ['reɪdɪəs] (pl radii) n **- 1.** MATH Radius der
**- 2.** ANAT Speiche die.

**radon** ['reɪdɒn] n Radon das.

**RAF** [ɑːreɪ'ef, ræf] n abbr of Royal Air Force.

**raffia** ['ræfɪə] n Bast der.

**raffish** ['ræfɪʃ] adj verwegen.

**raffle** ['ræfl] n Tombola die <> vt verlosen.

**raffle ticket** n Los das.

**raft** [rɑːft] n Floß das; **a whole ~ of policies** POL eine ganze Reihe von politischen Maßnah-
men.

**rafter** ['rɑːftəˀ] n Dachsparren der.

**rag** [ræg] n **- 1.** [piece of cloth] Lumpen der; **to be
like a red ~ to a bull to sb** ein rotes Tuch für jn
sein **- 2.** pej [newspaper] Käseblatt das.
➡ **rags** npl [clothes] Lumpen pl; **he went from ~s
to riches** er hat es vom Tellerwäscher zum
Millionär gebracht.

R

**ragamuffin** [ˈræɡəˌmʌfɪn] *n* [rascal] Frechdachs *der*.

**rag-and-bone man** *n* Lumpensammler *der*.

**ragbag** [ˈræɡbæɡ] *n fig* Sammelsurium *das*.

**rag doll** *n* Flickenpuppe *die*.

**rage** [reɪdʒ] *n* - **1.** [fury] Wut *die;* **to fly into a ~** in Rage geraten - **2.** *inf* [fashion]: **to be all the ~** der letzte Schrei sein ⬦ *vi* toben; [disease] wüten.

**ragged** [ˈræɡɪd] *adj* - **1.** [person, clothes] zerlumpt - **2.** [coastline] zerklüftet - **3.** [performance] stümperhaft.

**raging** [ˈreɪdʒɪŋ] *adj* [headache] rasend; [storm] tobend; [thirst] schrecklich.

**ragout** [ˈræɡuː] *n* Ragout *das*.

**rag trade** *n inf:* **the ~** die Modebranche.

**rag week** *n Br Woche, in der Studenten durch originelle Aktionen Geld für Wohltätigkeitsorganisationen eintreiben.*

**raid** [reɪd] *n* - **1.** MIL [attack] Angriff *der* - **2.** [forced entry - by thieves] Überfall *der;* [ - by police] Razzia *die* ⬦ *vt* - **1.** MIL [attack] anlgreifen - **2.** [enter by force - subj: thieves] einlbrechen in (+ A); [ - subj: police] eine Razzia machen in (+ D).

**raider** [ˈreɪdə<sup>r</sup>] *n* - **1.** [attacker] Angreifer *der*, -in *die* - **2.** [thief] Einbrecher *der*, -in *die*.

**rail** [reɪl] *n* - **1.** [fence] Geländer *das;* [on ship] Reling *die* - **2.** [bar, of railway] Schiene *die* - **3.** (U) [form of transport] (Eisen)bahn *die* ⬦ *comp* Eisenbahn-, Bahn-.

**railcard** [ˈreɪlkɑːd] *n Br* ≃ Bahncard *die*.

**railing** [ˈreɪlɪŋ] *n* Geländer *das;* [on ship] Reling *die*.

**railway** *Br* [ˈreɪlweɪ], **railroad** *Am* [ˈreɪlrəʊd] *n* - **1.** [track] Gleis *das* - **2.** [company, system] (Eisen)bahn *die*.

**railway engine** *n* Lokomotive *die*.

**railway line** *n* - **1.** [route] (Eisen)bahnlinie *die* - **2.** [track] Gleis *das*.

**railwayman** [ˈreɪlweɪmən] (*pl* -men [-mən]) *n Br* Eisenbahner *der*.

**railway station** *n* Bahnhof *der*.

**railway track** *n* Gleis *das*.

**rain** [reɪn] *n* Regen *der* ⬦ *v impers* & *vi* regnen; **it's ~ing** es regnet.
⬧ **rain down** *vi* regnen.
⬧ **rain off** *Br*, **rain out** *Am vt sep:* **to be ~ed off** *Br OR* **out** *Am* wegen Regen abgesagt werden.

**rainbow** [ˈreɪnbəʊ] *n* Regenbogen *der*.

**rainbow trout** *n* Regenbogenforelle *die*.

**rain check** *n Am:* **to take a ~ on sthg** etw auf ein andermal verschieben.

**raincoat** [ˈreɪnkəʊt] *n* Regenmantel *der*.

**raindrop** [ˈreɪndrɒp] *n* Regentropfen *der*.

**rainfall** [ˈreɪnfɔːl] *n* (U) Niederschlag *der*.

**rain forest** *n* Regenwald *der*.

**rain gauge** *n* Regenmesser *der*.

**rainproof** [ˈreɪnpruːf] *adj* wasserdicht.

**rainstorm** [ˈreɪnstɔːm] *n* strömender Regen.

**rainwater** [ˈreɪnˌwɔːtə<sup>r</sup>] *n* Regenwasser *das*.

**rainy** [ˈreɪnɪ] (*compar* -**ier**; *superl* -**iest**) *adj* regnerisch.

**raise** [reɪz] *vt* - **1.** [lift up] heben; [window] hochlziehen; **to ~ o.s.** sich auflrichten - **2.** [increase, improve] anlheben; **to ~ one's voice** [make louder] seine Stimme heben; [in protest] seine Stimme erheben - **3.** [obtain - from donations] auflbringen; [ - by selling, borrowing] auf ltreiben - **4.** [evoke] (herauf)beschwören - **5.** [child, animal] auf lziehen - **6.** [crop] anlbauen - **7.** [mention] auf lwerfen - **8.** [build] errichten ⬦ *n Am* Erhöhung *die*.

**raisin** [ˈreɪzn] *n* Rosine *die*.

**Raj** [rɑːdʒ] *n:* **the (British) ~** britische Herrschaft *in Indien bis 1947.*

**rajah** [ˈrɑːdʒə] *n* Radscha *der*.

**rake** [reɪk] *n* - **1.** [implement] Harke *die*, Rechen *der* - **2.** *dated* & *literary* [immoral man] Lebemann *der* ⬦ *vt* - **1.** [smooth] harken, rechen - **2.** [gather] zusammenlrechen.
⬧ **rake in** *vt sep inf* scheffeln.
⬧ **rake up** *vt sep* [past] auf lwärmen.

**rake-off** *n inf* Anteil *der*.

**rakish** [ˈreɪkɪʃ] *adj* - **1.** [dissolute] ausschweifend - **2.** [jaunty] flott, verwegen.

**rally** [ˈrælɪ] (*pl* -**ies**; *pt* & *pp* -**ied**) *n* - **1.** [meeting] Versammlung *die* - **2.** [car race] Rallye *die* - **3.** SPORT [exchange of shots] Ballwechsel *der* ⬦ *vt* sammeln ⬦ *vi* - **1.** [come together] sich sammeln - **2.** [recover] sich erholen.
⬧ **rally round** *vt fus* sich scharen um ⬦ *vi* sich seiner/ihrer/*etc* anlnehmen.

**rallying** [ˈrælɪŋ] *n* [rally driving] Rallyefahren *das*.

**rallying cry** *n* anspornender Ruf.

**rallying point** *n* Sammelpunkt *der*, Sammelstelle *die*.

**ram** [ræm] (*pt* & *pp* -**med**; *cont* -**ming**) *n* [animal] Widder *der* ⬦ *vt* rammen; **we'll have to ~ the message home to them** wir müssen es ihnen klar machen.

**RAM** [ræm] (*abbr of* **random access memory**) *n* RAM.

**Ramadan** [ˌræməˈdæn] *n* Ramadan *der*.

**ramble** [ˈræmbl] *n* Wanderung *die* ⬦ *vi* - **1.** [walk] wandern - **2.** [talk] schwafeln.

**rambler** [ˈræmblə<sup>r</sup>] *n* [walker] Spaziergänger *der*, -in *die*.

**rambling** [ˈræmblɪŋ] *adj* - **1.** [building] weitläufig - **2.** [conversation, book] weitschweifig.

**RAMC** (*abbr of* **Royal Army Medical Corps**) *n* Sanitätsdienst der britischen Armee.

**ramekin** ['ræmɪkɪn] *n* Auflaufförmchen das.

**ramification** [ˌræmɪfɪ'keɪʃn] *n* [implication] Implikation die.

**ramp** [ræmp] *n* Rampe die.

**rampage** [ræm'peɪdʒ] *n:* **to go on the ~** randalieren ⇔ *vi* wüten.

**rampant** ['ræmpənt] *adj* - **1.** [unrestrained] wuchernd; **to be ~** wüten - **2.** [widespread] weit verbreitet.

**ramparts** ['ræmpɑːts] *npl* Schutzwall der.

**ramshackle** ['ræmˌʃækl] *adj* heruntergekommen.

**ran** [ræn] *pt* ▷ **run**.

**ranch** [rɑːntʃ] *n* Ranch die.

**rancher** ['rɑːntʃəʳ] *n* Viehzüchter der, -in die.

**ranch house** *n Am* - **1.** [house on ranch] Farmhaus das - **2.** [ranch-style house] Bungalow der.

**rancid** ['rænsɪd] *adj* ranzig.

**rancour** *Br*, **rancor** *Am* ['ræŋkəʳ] *n* Bitterkeit die.

**random** ['rændəm] *adj* willkürlich; **~ sample** Stichprobe die ⇔ *n:* **at ~** [choose, sample] willkürlich; [fire, hit out] ziellos.

**random access memory** *n (U)* COMPUT Arbeitsspeicher der.

**randomly** ['rændəmlɪ] *adv* [choose] willkürlich; [shoot, hit out] ziellos.

**R and R** (*abbr of* **rest and recreation**) *n Am* Urlaub vom Militärdienst.

**randy** ['rændɪ] (*compar* **-ier**; *superl* **-iest**) *adj inf* scharf.

**rang** [ræŋ] *pt* ▷ **ring**.

**range** [reɪndʒ] *n* - **1.** [distance covered] Reichweite die; **to be out of ~** außer Reichweite sein; **to be within ~ of sthg** innerhalb der Reichweite von etw sein; **at close ~** auf kurze Entfernung - **2.** [variety] Auswahl die; **there was a wide ~ of people there** es waren ganz unterschiedliche Leute da - **3.** [bracket] Klasse die - **4.** [of mountains, hills] Kette die - **5.** [shooting area] Platz der - **6.** MUS [of voice] Stimmumfang der ⇔ *vt* [place in row] auf Istellen ⇔ *vi* - **1.** [vary]: **to ~ from ... to ...** reichen von ... bis ...; **to ~ between ... and ...** liegen zwischen ... und ... - **2.** [deal with, include]: **to ~ over sthg** sich erstrecken auf etw (A).

**ranger** ['reɪndʒəʳ] *n* [of park] Aufseher der, -in die; [of forest] Förster der, -in die.

**rank** [ræŋk] *adj* - **1.** [utter, absolute] ausgesprochen - **2.** [offensive] übel ⇔ *n* - **1.** [in army, police] Rang der; **the ~ and file** MIL die Mannschaft; [of political party, organization] die Basis; **to pull ~** seinen Rang hervorIkehren; **to close ~s** *fig* die Reihen schließen - **2.** [social class] Stand der

- **3.** [row, line] Reihe die; **taxi ~** Taxistand der ⇔ *vt* - **1.** [classify]: **to ~ sb among the great writers** jn zu den großen Schriftstellern zählen; **he is ~ed fourth in the world** er steht an vierter Stelle in der Weltrangliste - **2.** *Am:* **out~** rangüberlegen (+ *D*) sein ⇔ *vi:* **to ~ as** gelten als; **to ~ among** zählen zu.

➡ **ranks** *npl* - **1.** MIL: **the ~s** die einfachen Soldaten - **2.** *fig* [members] Reihen *pl*.

**ranking** ['ræŋkɪŋ] *n* [rating] Rang der ⇔ *adj Am* [highest-ranking]: **~ officer** ranghöchster Offizier, ranghöchste Offizierin.

**rankle** ['ræŋkl] *vi:* **it still ~s with me** es wurmt mich noch immer.

**ransack** ['rænsæk] *vt* - **1.** [plunder] plündern - **2.** [search] durchlwühlen.

**ransom** ['rænsəm] *n* Lösegeld das; **to hold sb to ~** [keep prisoner] jn als Geisel halten; *fig* [put in impossible position] jn erpressen.

**rant** [rænt] *vi* schwadronieren.

**ranting** ['ræntɪŋ] *n* Schwadronieren das.

**rap** [ræp] (*pt* & *pp* **-ped**; *cont* **-ping**) *n* - **1.** [knock] Klopfen das - **2.** MUS Rap der - **3.** *phr:* **to take the ~** den Kopf hinlhalten ⇔ *vt* [on table] klopfen auf (+ *A*); **to ~ sb on the knuckles** jm auf die Finger klopfen ⇔ *vi* - **1.** [knock]: **to ~ on sthg** [on door] an etw (*A*) klopfen; [on table] auf etw (*A*) klopfen - **2.** MUS rappen.

**rapacious** [rə'peɪʃəs] *adj fml* habgierig.

**rape** [reɪp] *n* - **1.** [crime, attack] Vergewaltigung die - **2.** *fig* [destruction]: **the ~ of the countryside** der Raubbau an der Landschaft - **3.** [plant] Raps der ⇔ *vt* vergewaltigen.

**rapeseed** ['reɪpsiːd] *n* Rapssamen der.

**rapid** ['ræpɪd] *adj* rapide, schnell.

➡ **rapids** *npl* Stromschnelle die.

**rapid-fire** *adj* - **1.** MIL Schnellfeuer- - **2.** *fig:* **he was subjected to ~ questioning** eine Unzahl von Fragen stürmte auf ihn ein.

**rapidity** [rə'pɪdətɪ] *n* Schnelligkeit die.

**rapidly** ['ræpɪdlɪ] *adv* schnell.

**rapidness** ['ræpɪdnɪs] *n* = **rapidity**.

**rapist** ['reɪpɪst] *n* Vergewaltiger der.

**rapper** ['ræpəʳ] *n* MUS Rapper der, -in die.

**rapport** [ræ'pɔːʳ] *n:* **a (good) ~ with/between** ein gutes Verhältnis mit/zwischen (+ *D*).

**rapprochement** [ræ'prɒʃmɑ̃] *n* Annäherung die.

**rapt** [ræpt] *adj* gespannt.

**rapture** ['ræptʃəʳ] *n:* **to go into ~s over** OR **about sb/sthg** über jn/etw in Verzückung geraten.

**rapturous** ['ræptʃərəs] *adj* begeistert.

**rare** [reəʳ] *adj* - **1.** [scarce, infrequent] selten - **2.** [exceptional] rar - **3.** CULIN [underdone] blutig.

**R**

**rarefied** ['reərɪfaɪd] adj - **1.** [air, atmosphere] dünn - **2.** [refined] exklusiv.

**rarely** ['reəlɪ] adv selten.

**rareness** ['reənɪs] n [scarcity, infrequency] Seltenheit die.

**raring** ['reərɪŋ] adj: to be ~ to go in den Startlöchern sein.

**rarity** ['reərətɪ] (pl -ies) n - **1.** [unusual object, person] Rarität die - **2.** (U) [scarcity] Seltenheit die.

**rascal** ['rɑːskl] n [mischievous child] Frechdachs der.

**rash** [ræʃ] adj [person] unbesonnen; [action, decision, promise] voreilig <> n - **1.** MED Ausschlag der - **2.** [spate] Serie die.

**rasher** ['ræʃəʳ] n Streifen der.

**rashly** ['ræʃlɪ] adv [behave] unbesonnen; [promise, decide] voreilig.

**rashness** ['ræʃnɪs] n [of behaviour] Unbesonnenheit die; [of promise, decision] Voreiligkeit die.

**rasp** [rɑːsp] n [of tool] Kratzen das <> vi [person, voice] krächzen.

**raspberry** ['rɑːzbərɪ] (pl -ies) n - **1.** [fruit] Himbeere die - **2.** [rude noise]: to blow a ~ einen abfälligen Ton erzeugen, der dadurch verursacht wird, dass man die Zunge zwischen die Lippen steckt und Luft hindurch bläst.

**rasping** ['rɑːspɪŋ] adj [voice, cough] krächzend.

**rasta** ['ræstə] n inf Rasta der, die.

**rastafarian** [ˌræstəˈfeərɪən] n Rastafarier der, -in die.

**rat** [ræt] n - **1.** [animal] Ratte die; to smell a ~ fig Verdacht schöpfen - **2.** pej [person] Schwein das.

**ratbag** ['rætbæg] n Br inf pej [man] Blödmann der; [woman] dumme Kuh.

**ratchet** ['rætʃɪt] n Ratsche die.

**rate** [reɪt] n - **1.** [speed] Tempo das; at this ~ bei diesem Tempo - **2.** [ratio, proportion] Rate die - **3.** [of taxation, interest] Satz der; what's the (going) ~ for it? wie viel kostet es? <> vt - **1.** [consider]: to ~ sb/sthg (as) jn/etw einlschätzen (als); to ~ sb/sthg among jn/etw zählen zu - **2.** [deserve] verdienen.

➤ **rates** npl Br dated Gemeindesteuern pl.

➤ **at any rate** adv auf jeden Fall.

**rateable value** [ˌreɪtəbl-] n Br steuerbarer Wert.

**rate of exchange** n Wechselkurs der.

**ratepayer** ['reɪtˌpeɪəʳ] n Br Steuerzahler der, -in die.

**rather** ['rɑːðəʳ] adv - **1.** [slightly, a bit] ziemlich; he's had ~ too much to drink er hat ziemlich viel getrunken - **2.** [for emphasis] recht; I ~ thought so das habe ich mir fast gedacht; I ~ like him ich mag ihn recht gern - **3.** [ex-pressing a preference] lieber; would you ~ ...? möchtest du lieber ...?; I'd ~ not lieber nicht - **4.** [more exactly]: or ~ vielmehr... - **5.** [on the contrary]: (but) ~ vielmehr...

➤ **rather than** conj statt.

**ratification** [ˌrætɪfɪˈkeɪʃn] n Ratifizierung die.

**ratify** ['rætɪfaɪ] (pt & pp -ied) vt ratifizieren.

**rating** ['reɪtɪŋ] n - **1.** [standing]: popularity ~ Beliebtheitsgrad der; what is her ~ in the polls? wie hoch ist ihr Beliebtheitsgrad? - **2.** Br [sailor] Matrose der.

➤ **ratings** npl TV Einschaltquoten pl.

**ratio** ['reɪʃɪəʊ] (pl -s) n Verhältnis das.

**ration** ['ræʃn] n Ration die <> vt [goods] rationieren.

➤ **rations** npl Rationen pl.

**rational** ['ræʃənl] adj - **1.** [reasonable] rational - **2.** [capable of reason] vernünftig.

**rationale** [ˌræʃəˈnɑːl] n Gründe pl.

**rationalization** [ˌræʃənəlaɪˈzeɪʃn] n Rationalisierung die.

**rationalize, -ise** ['ræʃənəlaɪz] vt rationalisieren.

**rationing** ['ræʃənɪŋ] n Rationierung die.

**rat race** n ständiger Konkurrenzkampf.

**rattle** ['rætl] n - **1.** [noise] Klappern das; [of machine-gun] Knattern das; [of bottles] Klirren das - **2.** [toy] Klapper die, Rassel die <> vt - **1.** [make rattling noise with - keys] klimpern mit; [subj: wind - windows] rütteln an (+ D) - **2.** [unsettle] durcheinander bringen <> vi [make rattling noise] klappern; [gunfire] knattern; [bottles] klirren.

➤ **rattle off** vt sep herunterlrasseln.

➤ **rattle on** vi: to ~ on (about sthg) quasseln (über etw (A)).

➤ **rattle through** vt fus [speech, list] herunterlrasseln; [work] schnell hinter sich (A) bringen.

**rattlesnake** ['rætlsneɪk], **rattler** Am ['rætləʳ] n Klapperschlange die.

**ratty** ['rætɪ] (compar -ier; superl -iest) adj inf - **1.** Br [in bad mood] gereizt - **2.** Am [in bad condition] verlottert.

**raucous** ['rɔːkəs] adj [voice, laughter] rau; [behaviour] wüst.

**raunchy** ['rɔːntʃɪ] (compar -ier; superl -iest) adj sexy.

**ravage** ['rævɪdʒ] vt verheeren, verwüsten.

➤ **ravages** npl Verheerung die.

**rave** [reɪv] adj glänzend <> n Br inf [event] Rave der OR das <> vi - **1.** [talk angrily]: to ~ at sb jn anl brüllen; to ~ about/against sthg über etw (A)/gegen etw wettern - **2.** [talk enthusiastically]: to ~ about sthg von etw schwärmen.

**raven** ['reɪvn] n Rabe der.

**ravenous** ['rævənəs] adj ausgehungert; [appetite] gewaltig; **I'm ~!** ich habe einen Bären-hunger!

**raver** ['reɪvəʳ] n Br inf [partygoer] Raver der, -in die.

**rave-up** n Br inf wilde Party.

**ravine** [rə'viːn] n Schlucht die.

**raving** ['reɪvɪŋ] adj: **he's a ~ lunatic** er ist total verrückt.

➡ **ravings** npl Fantasterei die.

**ravioli** [ˌrævɪ'əʊlɪ] n (U) Ravioli pl.

**ravish** ['rævɪʃ] vt - **1.** literary [rape] schänden - **2.** [delight] hinlreißen.

**ravishing** ['rævɪʃɪŋ] adj hinreißend.

**raw** [rɔː] adj - **1.** [uncooked] roh - **2.** [untreated] roh, Roh- - **3.** [painful - wound] offen; [ - skin] wund - **4.** [inexperienced] unerfahren - **5.** [cold] rau.

**raw deal** n: **to get a ~** schlecht weglkommen.

**Rawlplug**® ['rɔːlplʌg] n Dübel der.

**raw material** n - **1.** [natural substance] Rohstoff der - **2.** (U) fig [basis] Grundlage die.

**ray** [reɪ] n - **1.** [beam] Strahl der - **2.** fig [glimmer] Schimmer der.

**rayon** ['reɪɒn] n Reyon das.

**raze** [reɪz] vt zerstören; **the house was ~d to the ground** das Haus wurde dem Erdboden gleichgemacht.

**razor** ['reɪzəʳ] n Rasierapparat der.

**razor blade** n Rasierklinge die.

**razor-sharp** adj - **1.** [very sharp] (messer)scharf - **2.** fig [person] scharfsinnig; [mind, wit] messerscharf.

**razzle** ['ræzl] n Br inf: **to go on the ~** einen drauflmachen.

**razzmatazz** ['ræzmətæz] n (U) inf Rummel der.

**R & B** (abbr of **rhythm and blues**) n R & B der.

**RC** (abbr of **Roman Catholic**) adj röm.-kath.

**RCMP** (abbr of **Royal Canadian Mounted Police**) n kanadische Polizei.

**Rd** (abbr of **Road**) Str.

**R & D** (abbr of **research and development**) n F & E.

**re** [riː] prep betreffs (+ G).

**RE** n - **1.** (abbr of **religious education**) Religionsunterricht der - **2.** (abbr of **Royal Engineers**) Einheit der britischen Armee.

**reach** [riːtʃ] vt - **1.** [arrive at] anlkommen in (+ D) - **2.** [be able to touch] heranlkommen an (+ A) - **3.** [contact, extend as far as, attain, achieve] erreichen ⟨⟩ vi - **1.** [person, arm, hand] greifen; **to ~ (out) for sthg** nach etw greifen - **2.** [land] reichen ⟨⟩ n [of boxer] Reichweite die; **within sb's ~** [easily touched] innerhalb js Reichweite; **within easy ~ of the station** vom Bahnhof leicht zu erreichen; **out of** OR **beyond sb's ~** [not easily touched] außerhalb js Reichweite; **they were beyond the ~ of the rescue team** die Rettungsmannschaften konnten sie nicht erreichen.

➡ **reaches** npl [area] Gebiet das; **upper/lower ~es** [of river] Ober-/Unterlauf der.

**reachable** ['riːtʃəbl] adj erreichbar.

**react** [rɪ'ækt] vi - **1.** [respond]: **to ~ (to sthg)** (auf etw (A)) reagieren - **2.** [rebel]: **to ~ against sthg** sich gegen etw auf llehnen - **3.** CHEM: **to ~ with sthg** auf etw (A) reagieren - **4.** MED: **to ~ to sthg** auf etw (A) reagieren.

**reaction** [rɪ'ækʃn] n - **1.** [response & MED]: **~ (to sthg)** Reaktion die (auf etw (A)) - **2.** [rebellion]: **~ (against sthg)** Gegenreaktion die (auf etw (A)) - **3.** [reflex] Reaktionsfähigkeit die; **she's got very quick ~s** sie hat sehr gute Reflexe - **4.** POL & CHEM Reaktion die.

**reactionary** [rɪ'ækʃənrɪ] adj reaktionär ⟨⟩ n Reaktionär der, -in die.

**reactivate** [rɪ'æktɪveɪt] vt reaktivieren.

**reactor** [rɪ'æktəʳ] n [nuclear reactor] Reaktor der.

**read** [riːd] (pt & pp **read** [red]) vt - **1.** [book, magazine, music] lesen; **to ~ music** Noten lesen - **2.** [say aloud]: **to ~ sb sthg** jm etw vorllesen - **3.** [subj: sign, notice] besagen; [subj: gauge, meter, barometer] anlzeigen - **4.** [take reading from - meter, gauge] ablesen - **5.** [interpret] verstehen; [sb's thoughts] lesen - **6.** Br UNIV studieren ⟨⟩ vi - **1.** [in book, magazine] lesen; **to ~ about sthg** von etw lesen - **2.** [out loud]: **to ~ to sb (from)** jm vorllesen (aus) - **3.** [text]: **to ~ well/badly** sich gut/schlecht lesen ⟨⟩ n: **to be a good ~** guter Lesestoff sein.

➡ **read into** vt sep: **I wouldn't ~ too much into it** ich würde zu nicht zu viel hineinllesen.

➡ **read out** vt sep vorllesen.

➡ **read over, read through** vt sep durchllesen.

➡ **read up on** vt fus nachllesen über (+ A).

**readable** ['riːdəbl] adj - **1.** [book] lesenswert - **2.** COMPUT [disk] lesbar.

**readdress** [ˌriːə'dres] vt umladressieren.

**reader** ['riːdəʳ] n [person who reads] Leser der, -in die.

**readership** ['riːdəʃɪp] n [total number of readers] Leser pl.

**readily** ['redɪlɪ] adv - **1.** [willingly] bereitwillig - **2.** [easily] leicht.

**readiness** ['redɪnɪs] n - **1.** [preparedness] Bereitschaft die - **2.** [willingness]: **~ (to do sthg)** Bereitwilligkeit die (, etw zu tun).

**reading** ['riːdɪŋ] n - **1.** [act of reading] Lesen das - **2.** [reading material] Lektüre die; **her autobiography makes good ~** ihre Autobiografie liest sich gut - **3.** [recital] Lesung die - **4.** [taken from meter] Zählerstand der; [taken from thermometer]

**R**

Thermometerstand *der* - **5.** [POL - of bill] Lesung *die*.

**reading lamp** *n* Leselampe *die*.

**reading room** *n* Lesesaal *der*.

**readjust** [ˌriːə'dʒʌst] *vt* [mechanism, instrument] nachlstellen; [mirror] einlstellen; [policy] neu anlpassen ◇ *vi*: **to ~ to sthg** sich wieder an etw *(A)* gewöhnen.

**readmit** [ˌriːəd'mɪt] *vt* [to hospital] wieder einlweisen; [to club] wieder auflnehmen.

**readout** ['riːdaʊt] *n* COMPUT Anzeige *die*.

**read-through** [riːd-] *n*: **to give sthg a quick ~** etw rasch durchllesen.

**ready** ['redɪ] (*pt* & *pp* **-ied**) *adj* - **1.** [prepared] fertig; **to be ~ to do sthg** bereit sein, etw zu tun; **to be ~ for sthg** für etw bereit sein; **to get ~** sich fertig machen; **to get sthg ~** etw fertig machen - **2.** [willing]: **to be ~ to do sthg** bereit sein, etw zu tun - **3.** [in need of]: **to be ~ for sthg** etw gebrauchen können; **I'm ~ for bed** ich bin bettreif - **4.** [likely]: **to be ~ to collapse** zum Umfallen müde sein; **she was ~ to cry** sie war den Tränen nahe ◇ *vt* vorlbereiten.

**ready cash** *n* Bargeld *das*.

**ready-made** *adj* - **1.** [product] Fertig-; **~ clothes** Konfektionskleidung *die*, Kleidung *die* von der Stange - **2.** *fig* [reply, excuse] vorgefertigt.

**ready money** *n* Bargeld *das*.

**ready-to-wear** *adj*: **~ clothes** Konfektionskleidung *die*, Kleidung *die* von der Stange.

**reaffirm** [ˌriːə'fɜːm] *vt* bekräftigen.

**reafforest** [ˌriːə'fɒrɪst] *vt* wiederlaufforsten.

**reafforestation** ['riːəˌfɒrɪ'steɪʃn] *n* Wiederaufforstung *die*.

**real** ['rɪəl] *adj* - **1.** [authentic, for emphasis] echt; **this is the ~ thing!** [marvellous] das ist unglaublich toll!; **this time it's for ~** diesmal ist es echt - **2.** [actually existing] real - **3.** [cost, value] tatsächlich; **in ~ terms** real ◇ *adv Am* wirklich.

**real ale** *n Br nach traditioneller Weise gebrautes Ale*.

**real estate** *n (U)* Immobilien *pl*.

**realign** [ˌriːə'laɪn] *vt* [brakes] nachlstellen.

**realignment** [ˌriːə'laɪnmənt] *n* - **1.** POL Neuordnung *die* - **2.** [of brakes] Nachstellen *das*.

**realism** ['rɪəlɪzm] *n* Realismus *der*.

**realist** ['rɪəlɪst] *n* Realist *der*, -in *die*.

**realistic** [ˌrɪə'lɪstɪk] *adj* realistisch; **to be ~ about sthg** in Bezug auf etw *(A)* realistisch sein.

**realistically** [ˌrɪə'lɪstɪklɪ] *adv* realistisch.

**reality** [rɪ'ælətɪ] (*pl* **-ies**) *n* Realität *die*; **in ~** [in fact] in Wirklichkeit; [in real life] wirklich.

**realization** [ˌrɪəlaɪ'zeɪʃn] *n (U)* - **1.** [awareness, recognition] Realisation *die* - **2.** [achievement] Realisierung *die*.

**realize, -ise** ['rɪəlaɪz] *vt* - **1.** [become aware of, understand] begreifen, realisieren - **2.** [achieve] verwirklichen - **3.** COMM erzielen.

**reallocate** [ˌriː'æləkeɪt] *vt* umlverteilen.

**really** ['rɪəlɪ] *adv* - **1.** [for emphasis] wirklich; **~ good/bad** wirklich gut/schlecht; **you ~ ought to see this film** du solltest dir den Film unbedingt ansehen - **2.** [actually] eigentlich; **not ~** eigentlich nicht - **3.** [honestly] wirklich - **4.** [to sound less negative] eigentlich ◇ *excl* - **1.** [expressing doubt, surprise]: **really? wirklich? - 2.** [expressing disapproval]: **really!** also wirklich!

**realm** [relm] *n* - **1.** [field] Bereich *der* - **2.** [kingdom] Reich *das*.

**real-time** *adj* COMPUT Echtzeit-.

**realtor** ['rɪəltər] *n Am* Grundstücksmakler *der*, -in *die*.

**ream** [riːm] *n 500 Blatt*.

⟐ **reams** *npl fig* [a lot]: **he's written ~s on the subject** er hat ganze Bände zu diesem Thema geschrieben.

**reap** [riːp] *vt lit* & *fig* ernten.

**reappear** [ˌriːə'pɪər] *vi* wieder erscheinen.

**reappearance** [ˌriːə'pɪərəns] *n* Wiedererscheinen *das*.

**reapply** [ˌriːə'plaɪ] (*pt* & *pp* **-ied**) *vi*: **to ~ (for sthg)** sich von neuem (um etw) bewerben.

**reappraisal** [ˌriːə'preɪzl] *n* Neueinschätzung *die*.

**reappraise** [ˌriːə'preɪz] *vt* neu einlschätzen.

**rear** [rɪər] *adj* [wheel] Hinter-; **~ window** [of car] Heckscheibe *die* ◇ *n* - **1.** [back] Rückseite *die*; **to be at the ~** [of queue, line of traffic] am hinteren Ende sein; **to bring up the ~** die Nachhut bilden - **2.** *inf* [buttocks] Hintern *der* ◇ *vt* - **1.** [children, animals, plants] auf lziehen - **2.** *fig*: **racism has ~ed its head again** der Rassismus ist wieder zum Leben erwacht ◇ *vi*: **to ~ (up)** sich auflbäumen.

**rear admiral** *n* Konteradmiral *der*.

**rearguard action** ['rɪəɡɑːd-] *n lit* & *fig* Nachhutgefecht *das*.

**rear light** *n* Rücklicht *das*.

**rearm** [riː'ɑːm] *vt* wieder bewaffnen ◇ *vi* wieder auf lrüsten.

**rearmament** [rɪ'ɑːməmənt] *n* Wiederaufrüstung *die*.

**rearmost** ['rɪəməʊst] *adj* hinterste, -r, -s.

**rearrange** [ˌriːə'reɪndʒ] *vt* - **1.** [arrange differently] umlstellen - **2.** [reschedule] verlegen.

**rearview mirror** ['rɪəvjuː-] *n* Rückspiegel *der*.

**reason** ['riːzn] *n* - **1.** [cause]: **~ (for sthg)** Grund *der* (für etw); **by ~ of** *fml* aufgrund *(+ G);* **for some ~** aus irgendeinem Grund - **2.** [justification]: **to have ~ to do sthg** Grund haben, etw zu tun - **3.** [common sense] Vernunft *die;* **to listen to ~** auf die Stimme der Vernunft hören; **it stands to ~** es ist logisch ◇ *vt* [conclude]: **to ~ that** folgern, dass ◇ *vi* vernünftig denken.

◆ **reason with** *vt fus* vernünftig reden mit.

**reasonable** ['ri:znəbl] *adj* - **1.** [sensible] vernünftig - **2.** [acceptable - decision, explanation] angemessen; [ - work] ganz gut; [ - offer] akzeptabel; [ - price] vernünftig - **3.** [fairly large]: **a ~ amount/number** ziemlich viel/viele.

**reasonably** ['ri:znəbli] *adv* - **1.** [quite] ziemlich - **2.** [sensibly] vernünftig.

**reasoned** ['ri:znd] *adj* durchdacht.

**reasoning** ['ri:znɪŋ] *n* (U) Argumentation *die.*

**reassemble** [ˌri:ə'sembl] *vt* - **1.** [machinery] wieder zusammenlbauen - **2.** [people] wieder versammeln ◇ *vi* sich wieder versammeln.

**reassess** [ˌri:ə'ses] *vt* [position, opinion] neu einlschätzen.

**reassessment** [ˌri:ə'sesmənt] *n* [of position, opinion] Neueinschätzung *die.*

**reassurance** [ˌri:ə'ʃʊərəns] *n* - **1.** [comfort] Beruhigung *die* - **2.** [promise] Versicherung *die.*

**reassure** [ˌri:ə'ʃʊəʳ] *vt* beruhigen; **he ~d me that ...** er versicherte mir, dass ...

**reassuring** [ˌri:ə'ʃʊərɪŋ] *adj* beruhigend.

**reawaken** [ˌri:ə'weɪkn] *vt* wieder erwecken.

**rebate** ['ri:beɪt] *n* Nachlass *der.*

**rebel** [*n* 'rebl, *vb* rɪ'bel] *(pt & pp* -**led;** *cont* -**ling**) *n* Rebell *der,* -in *die* ◇ *vi:* **to ~ (against)** rebellieren (gegen).

**rebellion** [rɪ'beljən] *n* Rebellion *die.*

**rebellious** [rɪ'beljəs] *adj* rebellisch.

**rebirth** [ˌri:'bɜ:θ] *n* Wiedergeburt *die.*

**rebound** [*n* 'ri:baʊnd, *vb* rɪ'baʊnd] *n:* **to catch a ball on the ~** einen abgeprallten Ball fangen; **she married him on the ~** sie hat ihn geheiratet, nachdem ihre vorige Beziehung in die Brüche gegangen ist ◇ *vi* - **1.** [ball] ablprallen - **2.** [harm]: **to ~ (up)on sb** auf jn zurücklfallen.

**rebuff** [rɪ'bʌf] *n* Abfuhr *die* ◇ *vt* ablweisen.

**rebuild** [ˌri:'bɪld] *(pt & pp* -**built** [ˌri:'bɪlt]) *vt* wieder auflbauen.

**rebuke** [rɪ'bju:k] *n* Tadel *der* ◇ *vt:* **to ~ sb (for sthg)** jn (für etw) tadeln.

**rebut** [ri:'bʌt] *(pt & pp* -**ted;** *cont* -**ting**) *vt* widerlegen.

**rebuttal** [ri:'bʌtl] *n* Widerlegung *die.*

**rec.** *abbr of* **received.**

**recalcitrant** [rɪ'kælsɪtrənt] *adj* aufsässig.

**recall** [rɪ'kɔ:l] *n* - **1.** (U) [memory] Erinnerung *die* - **2.** [change]: **to be beyond ~** nicht umkehrbar sein ◇ *vt* - **1.** [remember] sich erinnern an *(+ A)* - **2.** [summon back] zurücklrufen.

**recant** [rɪ'kænt] *vt & vi* widerrufen.

**recap** [*n* 'ri:kæp, *vb* ˌri:'kæp] *(pt & pp* -**ped;** *cont* -**ping**) *inf n* Zusammenfassung *die* ◇ *vt* - **1.** [summarize] zusammenlfassen - **2.** *Am:* **to ~ a tire** die Laufflächen eines Reifens erneuern ◇ *vi* [summarize] zusammenlfassen.

**recapitulate** [ˌri:kə'pɪtjʊleɪt] *vt & vi* zusammenlfassen.

**recapture** [ˌri:'kæptʃəʳ] *n* [of animal] Wiedereinfangen *das;* [of prisoner] Wiederergreifen *das;* [of territory, town] Wiedereroberung *die* ◇ *vt* - **1.** [animal] wieder einlfangen; [prisoner] wieder ergreifen; [territory, town] wiederlerobern - **2.** [mood, feeling] auferstehen lassen.

**recd, rec'd** *abbr of* **received.**

**recede** [rɪ'si:d] *vi* - **1.** [move away] zurücklweichen; **his hair is receding** er bekommt eine leichte Stirnglatze - **2.** *fig* [disappear, fade] schwinden.

**receding** [rɪ'si:dɪŋ] *adj* [chin] fliehend; [hairline] zurückweichend.

**receipt** [rɪ'si:t] *n* - **1.** [piece of paper] Quittung *die* - **2.** (U) [act of receiving] Empfang *der.*

◆ **receipts** *npl* [money taken] Einnahmen *pl.*

**receivable** [rɪ'si:vəbl] *adj* [liable for payment] ausstehend.

**receive** [rɪ'si:v] *vt* - **1.** [gift, letter] erhalten, bekommen - **2.** [news] erfahren, hören - **3.** [setback] erfahren; **to ~ criticism** kritisiert werden; **to ~ an injury** verletzt werden - **4.** [visitor, guest] empfangen - **5.** [greet]: **to be well/badly ~d** gut/schlecht aufgenommen werden ◇ *vi* [in tennis etc] rücklschlagen.

**receiver** [rɪ'si:vəʳ] *n* - **1.** [of telephone] Hörer *der* - **2.** [radio, TV set] Empfänger *der* - **3.** [criminal] Hehler *der,* -in *die* - **4.** FIN [official] Konkursverwalter *der,* -in *die.*

**receivership** [rɪ'si:vəʃɪp] *n:* **to go into ~** Konkurs anlmelden.

**receiving end** [rɪ'si:vɪŋ-] *n:* **to be on the ~ of sthg** etw ablkriegen.

**recent** ['ri:snt] *adj* neueste, -r, -s.

**recently** ['ri:sntli] *adv* kürzlich, vor kurzem.

**receptacle** [rɪ'septəkl] *n* Behälter *der.*

**reception** [rɪ'sepʃn] *n* Empfang *der.*

**reception centre** *n Br* [for refugees] Aufnahmelager *das.*

**reception class** *n* Anfängerklasse *die.*

**reception desk** *n* Empfang *der,* Rezeption *die.*

**receptionist** [rɪ'sepʃənɪst] *n* Empfangschef *der,* Empfangsdame *die.*

R

**reception room** n [in house] Wohnzimmer das.

**receptive** [rɪ'septɪv] adj aufnahmefähig, empfänglich; **to be ~ to sthg** für etw empfänglich sein.

**receptiveness** [rɪ'septɪvnɪs] n Empfänglichkeit die.

**recess** ['riːses, Br rɪ'ses] n - **1.** [vacation] Ferien pl; **to be in/go into ~** eine Sitzungspause haben/beginnen - **2.** [alcove] Nische die - **3.** [of mind, memory] Winkel der - **4.** Am sch Pause die.

**recessed** ['riːsest, Br rɪ'sest] adj versenkt.

**recession** [rɪ'seʃn] n Rezession die.

**recessive** [rɪ'sesɪv] adj bɪoʟ rezessiv.

**recharge** [ˌriː'tʃɑːdʒ] vt (auf)laden.

**rechargeable** [ˌriː'tʃɑːdʒəbl] adj wieder aufladbar.

**recipe** ['resɪpɪ] n lit & fig Rezept das.

**recipient** [rɪ'sɪpɪənt] n Empfänger der, -in die.

**reciprocal** [rɪ'sɪprəkl] adj wechselseitig.

**reciprocate** [rɪ'sɪprəkeɪt] vt erwidern ◇ vi: **she smiled at me and I ~d** sie lächelte mich an und ich lächelte zurück.

**recital** [rɪ'saɪtl] n [of poetry] Vortrag der; [of music] Konzert das.

**recitation** [ˌresɪ'teɪʃn] n Vortrag der.

**recite** [rɪ'saɪt] vt - **1.** [perform aloud] vor|tragen - **2.** [list] auf|zählen.

**reckless** ['reklɪs] adj leichtsinnig.

**recklessness** ['reklɪsnɪs] n Leichtsinnigkeit die.

**reckon** ['rekn] vt - **1.** inf [think]: **to ~ (that)** ... schätzen, dass ... - **2.** [consider, judge]: **to be ~ed to be sthg** als etw eingeschätzt werden - **3.** [expect]: **to ~ to do sthg** erwarten, etw zu tun - **4.** [calculate] schätzen.
➤ **reckon on** vt fus zählen auf (+ A).
➤ **reckon with** vt fus - **1.** [expect] rechnen mit - **2.** [deal with]: **he is a force to be ~ed with** er ist jemand, mit dem man rechnen muss.
➤ **reckon without** vt fus nicht rechnen mit.

**reckoning** ['rekənɪŋ] n (U) [calculation] Schätzung die; **the day of ~** der Tag der Abrechnung.

**reclaim** [rɪ'kleɪm] vt - **1.** [claim back - lost item, luggage] ab|holen; [ - tax, expenses] zurück|erlangen - **2.** [make fit for use] gewinnen.

**reclamation** [ˌreklə'meɪʃn] n [of land] Gewinnung die.

**recline** [rɪ'klaɪn] vi [lie back] sich zurück|lehnen.

**reclining** [rɪ'klaɪnɪŋ] adj verstellbar.

**recluse** [rɪ'kluːs] n Einsiedler der, -in die.

**reclusive** [rɪ'kluːsɪv] adj zurückgezogen.

**recognition** [ˌrekəg'nɪʃn] n (U) - **1.** [identification] Erkennen das; **to have changed beyond** or **out of all ~** nicht wiederzuerkennen sein - **2.** [acknowledgement] Anerkennung die; **in ~ of** in Anerkennung (+ G).

**recognizable** ['rekəgnaɪzəbl] adj erkennbar.

**recognize, -ise** ['rekəgnaɪz] vt - **1.** [gen] erkennen; **I ~ that I was wrong** ich gebe zu, dass ich im Unrecht war - **2.** [officially accept, approve] anerkennen.

**recoil** [vb rɪ'kɔɪl, n 'riːkɔɪl] vi - **1.** [draw back] zurück|weichen - **2.** fig [shrink from]: **to ~ from/ at sthg** vor etw (D) zurück|schrecken ◇ n [of gun] Rückstoß der.

**recollect** [ˌrekə'lekt] vt sich erinnern an (+ A).

**recollection** [ˌrekə'lekʃn] n Erinnerung die.

**recommence** [ˌriːkə'mens] vt wieder auf|nehmen ◇ vi von neuem beginnen.

**recommend** [ˌrekə'mend] vt - **1.** [commend, speak in favour of]: **to ~ sb/sthg (to sb)** (jm) jn/etw empfehlen - **2.** [advise] raten zu.

**recommendation** [ˌrekəmen'deɪʃn] n - **1.** [personal commendation] Empfehlung die - **2.** [advice] Rat der.

**recommended retail price** [ˌrekə'mendɪd-] n unverbindliche Preisempfehlung.

**recompense** ['rekəmpens] n: **~ (for sthg)** Entschädigung die (für etw) ◇ vt: **to ~ sb (for sthg)** jn (für etw) entschädigen.

**reconcile** ['rekənsaɪl] vt - **1.** [beliefs, ideas] (miteinander) vereinbaren; **to ~ sthg with sthg** etw mit etw vereinbaren - **2.** [people] versöhnen; **to be ~d with sb** mit jm ausgesöhnt or versöhnt sein - **3.** [resign]: **to ~ o.s. to sthg** sich mit etw aus|söhnen.

**reconciliation** [ˌrekənsɪlɪ'eɪʃn] n - **1.** [of beliefs, ideas] Vereinbarung die - **2.** [of people] Versöhnung die.

**recondite** ['rekəndaɪt] adj fml abstrus.

**reconditioned** [ˌriːkən'dɪʃnd] adj überholt.

**reconnaissance** [rɪ'kɒnɪsəns] n (U) Erkundung die.

**reconnect** [ˌriːkə'nekt] vt wieder an|schließen.

**reconnoitre** Br, **reconnoiter** Am [ˌrekə'nɔɪtər] vt aus|kundschaften ◇ vi das Gelände erkunden.

**reconsider** [ˌriːkən'sɪdər] vt neu überdenken ◇ vi: **it's not too late to ~** Sie können es sich noch einmal überlegen.

**reconstitute** [ˌriː'kɒnstɪtjuːt] vt - **1.** [organization, group] neu bilden - **2.** [dried food] zu|bereiten (durch Zufügen von Wasser).

**reconstruct** [ˌriːkən'strʌkt] vt - **1.** [building, bridge, country] wieder auf|bauen - **2.** [event, crime] rekonstruieren.

**reconstruction** [ˌriːkən'strʌkʃn] n - **1.** [of building, bridge, country] Wiederaufbau *der* - **2.** [of event, crime] Rekonstruktion *die.*

**reconvene** [ˌriːkən'viːn] *vt* von neuem einlberufen.

**record** [*n & adj* 'rekɔːd, *vb* rɪ'kɔːd] *n* - **1.** [written account] Aufzeichnung *die;* **off the ~** inoffiziell; **on ~** [on file] im Archiv; **these are the worst sales figures on ~** das sind die schlechtesten Verkaufszahlen, die je erzielt wurden; **he was on ~ as saying ...** es ist belegt, dass er sagte ... - **2.** [vinyl disc] (Schall)platte *die* - **3.** [best achievement] Rekord *der* - **4.** [history]: **to have a good ~** gute Leistungen aufweisen können; **to have a criminal ~** vorbestraft sein - **5.** *phr:* **to set** OR **put the ~ straight** für klare Verhältnisse sorgen ⬦ *adj* Rekord- ⬦ *vt* - **1.** [write down] auf|zeichnen - **2.** [put on tape *etc*] auf|nehmen.

**record-breaker** *n* Rekordbrecher *der,* -in *die.*

**record-breaking** *adj* rekordebrechend.

**recorded delivery** [rɪ'kɔːdɪd-] *n:* **to send sthg by ~** etw per Einschreiben schicken.

**recorder** [rɪ'kɔːdəʳ] *n* - **1.** [machine]: **(tape) ~** Tonbandgerät *das;* **(cassette) ~** Kassettenrekorder *der;* **(video) ~** Videorekorder *der* - **2.** [musical instrument] Blockflöte *die.*

**record holder** *n* Rekordinhaber *der,* -in *die.*

**recording** [rɪ'kɔːdɪŋ] *n* - **1.** [individual recording] Aufnahme *die* - **2.** (U) [process of recording] Aufzeichnung *die.*

**recording studio** *n* Aufnahmestudio *das.*

**record library** *n* (Schall)plattenverleih *der.*

**record player** *n* Plattenspieler *der.*

**recount** [*n* 'riːkaʊnt, *vt sense 1* rɪ'kaʊnt, *sense 2* ˌriː'kaʊnt] *n* Nachzählung *die* ⬦ *vt* - **1.** [narrate] erzählen - **2.** [count again] nachlzählen.

**recoup** [rɪ'kuːp] *vt* [recover] wieder einlbringen.

**recourse** [rɪ'kɔːs] *n fml:* **to have ~ to sthg** Zuflucht zu etw nehmen.

**recover** [rɪ'kʌvəʳ] *vt* - **1.** [stolen goods, money] zurücklbekommen; **to ~ sthg from sb/ somewhere** etw von jm/irgendwo zurücklbekommen - **2.** [one's strength, balance, senses] wiederlgewinnen; **to ~ consciousness** wieder zu Bewusstsein kommen; **to ~ one's breath** wieder zu Atem kommen; **to ~ o.s.** sich erholen ⬦ *vi* [from illness]: **to ~ (from)** genesen (von).

**recoverable** [rɪ'kʌvrəbl] *adj* FIN rückerstattbar.

**recovery** [rɪ'kʌvərɪ] (*pl* -ies) *n* - **1.** [from illness]: **~ (from)** Genesung *die* (von) - **2.** *fig* [of currency, economy] Erholung *die* - **3.** [of stolen goods, money] Wiedererlangung *die.*

**recovery vehicle** *n* Br Abschleppwagen *der.*

**recreate** [ˌriːkrɪ'eɪt] *vt* [reproduce] wieder auf|leben lassen.

**recreation** [ˌrekrɪ'eɪʃn] *n* [leisure] Erholung *die.*

**recreational** [ˌrekrɪ'eɪʃənl] *adj* Freizeit-.

**recreation room** *n* - **1.** [in public building] Aufenthaltsraum *der* - **2.** Am [in house] Freizeitraum *der.*

**recrimination** [rɪˌkrɪmɪ'neɪʃn] *n* (U) Gegenbeschuldigung *die.*
➣ **recriminations** *npl* gegenseitige Beschuldigungen *pl.*

**recruit** [rɪ'kruːt] *n* [in armed forces] Rekrut *der,* -in *die;* [in company, organization] neues Mitglied ⬦ *vt* - **1.** [find, employ - in armed forces] rekrutieren; [ - in company, organization] einlstellen - **2.** [persuade to join] werben; **they ~ed her to help out** sie haben sie zur Hilfe herangezogen ⬦ *vi* [look for new staff] einlstellen.

**recruitment** [rɪ'kruːtmənt] *n* (U) [of staff] Einstellung *die;* [of soldiers] Rekrutierung *die.*

**rectangle** ['rek,tæŋgl] *n* Rechteck *das.*

**rectangular** [rek'tæŋgjʊləʳ] *adj* rechteckig.

**rectify** ['rektɪfaɪ] (*pt & pp* -ied) *vt fml* berichtigen.

**rectitude** ['rektɪtjuːd] *n fml* Rechtschaffenheit *die.*

**rector** ['rektəʳ] *n* - **1.** [priest] Pfarrer *der* - **2.** Scot [head - of school] Direktor *der,* -in *die;* [ - of college, university] Rektor *der,* -in *die.*

**rectory** ['rektərɪ] (*pl* -ies) *n* Pfarrhaus *das.*

**rectum** ['rektəm] (*pl* -s) *n* Rektum *das.*

**recuperate** [rɪ'kuːpəreɪt] *vi fml:* **to ~ (from)** genesen (von).

**recuperation** [rɪˌkuːpə'reɪʃn] *n* Genesung *die.*

**recur** [rɪ'kɜːʳ] (*pt & pp* -red; *cont* -ring) *vi* wiederlkehren; [problem, error] wieder auf|treten.

**recurrence** [rɪ'kʌrəns] *n fml* Wiederkehr *die;* [of problem, error] Wiederauf|treten *das.*

**recurrent** [rɪ'kʌrənt] *adj* immer wiederkehrend; [problem, error] immer wieder auftretend.

**recurring** [rɪ'kɜːrɪŋ] *adj* - **1.** = recurrent - **2.** MATH: 3.3 ~ 3,3 Periode.

**recyclable** [ˌriːˈsaɪkləbl] *adj* recycelbar, wieder verwertbar.

**recycle** [ˌriːˈsaɪkl] *vt* recyceln, wieder verwerten.

**recycling** [ˌriːˈsaɪklɪŋ] *n* Recycling *das.*

**red** [red] (*compar* -der; *superl* -dest) *adj* rot ⬦ *n* [colour] Rot *das;* **to be in the ~** *inf* in den roten Zahlen sein; **to see ~** rotlsehen.
➣ **Red** *pej adj* [left-wing, communist] rot ⬦ *n* [left-winger, communist] Rote *der, die.*

**red alert** n - **1.** [state of readiness]: **to be on ~ in** höchster Alarmbereitschaft sein - **2.** [order to be ready] Alarmstufe *die* rot.

**red blood cell** n rotes Blutkörperchen.

**red-blooded** [-'blʌdɪd] adj hum heißblütig.

**red-brick** adj Br [building] Backstein-.

➤ **redbrick** adj Br UNIV: **redbrick university** *Ende des 19. Jahrhunderts in Opposition zu den Traditionsuniversitäten gegründete moderne Universität.*

**red card** n FTBL: **to be shown the ~, to get a ~** die rote Karte gezeigt bekommen, die rote Karte kriegen.

**red carpet** n: **to roll out the ~ for sb** für jn den roten Teppich auslrollen.

➤ **red-carpet** adj: **to give sb the red-carpet treatment** für jn den roten Teppich auslrollen.

**Red Crescent** n: **the ~** der Rote Halbmond.

**Red Cross** n: **the ~** das Rote Kreuz.

**redcurrant** [ˌred'kʌrənt] n (rote) Johannisbeere.

**red deer** n [one] Rothirsch *der;* [many] Rotwild *das.*

**redden** ['redn] vt rot färben <> vi [person, face] erröten.

**redecorate** [ˌri:'dekəreɪt] vt & vi renovieren.

**redeem** [rɪ'di:m] vt - **1.** [save, rescue] retten; **she tried to ~ herself for her faux pas** sie versuchte, ihren Fehltritt wettzumachen - **2.** [from pawnbroker] einllösen.

**redeeming** [rɪ'di:mɪŋ] adj: **her one ~ feature is** ... ihre einzige positive Eigenschaft ist ...

**redefine** [ˌri:dɪ'faɪn] vt neu definieren.

**redemption** [rɪ'dempʃn] n RELIG Erlösung *die;* **to be beyond OR past ~** fig nicht mehr zu retten sein.

**redeploy** [ˌri:dɪ'plɔɪ] vt [troops] umverlegen; [workers, staff] an anderer Stelle einlsetzen.

**redeployment** [ˌri:dɪ'plɔɪmənt] n (U) [of troops] Umverlegung *die;* [of workers, staff] Einsatz *der* an anderer Stelle.

**redesign** [ˌri:dɪ'zaɪn] vt - **1.** [replan, redraw] neu entwerfen - **2.** [reorganize, rethink] neu strukturieren.

**redevelop** [ˌri:dɪ'veləp] vt sanieren.

**redevelopment** [ˌri:dɪ'veləpmənt] n (U) Sanierung *die.*

**red-faced** [-'feɪst] adj - **1.** [after exercise, with heat] gerötet - **2.** [with embarrassment] mit rotem Kopf.

**red-haired** [-'heəd] adj rothaarig.

**red-handed** [-'hændɪd] adj: **to catch sb ~** jn auf frischer Tat ertappen.

**redhead** ['redhed] n Rotkopf *der.*

**red herring** n fig falsche Spur.

**red-hot** adj - **1.** [extremely hot] rot glühend - **2.** [very enthusiastic] glühend - **3.** inf [very good] klasse, super.

**redid** [ˌri:'dɪd] pt ⊳ redo.

**Red Indian** n Indianer *der,* -in *die.*

**redirect** [ˌri:dɪ'rekt] vt - **1.** [mail] nachlsenden - **2.** [aircraft, aid] umlleiten; [one's energies] anders einlsetzen.

**rediscover** [ˌri:dɪ'skʌvər] vt - **1.** [re-experience] wieder entdecken - **2.** [make popular, famous again]: **to be ~ed** wieder entdeckt werden.

**redistribute** [ˌri:dɪ'strɪbju:t] vt umlverteilen.

**red-letter day** n Tag, an dem etwas sehr Positives passiert.

**red light** n [traffic signal] rote Ampel.

**red-light district** n Rotlichtviertel *das.*

**red meat** n Fleisch vom Rind, vom Lamm, und vom Reh.

**red mullet** n Rote Meeräsche.

**redness** ['rednɪs] n Röte *die.*

**redo** [ˌri:'du:] (pt -did; pp -done) vt - **1.** [do again] noch einmal machen; [letter, essay] noch einmal schreiben - **2.** inf [redecorate] renovieren.

**redolent** ['redələnt] adj: **to be ~ of sthg** literary [reminiscent] an etw (A) erinnern; [smelling] nach etw duften.

**redone** [ˌri:'dʌn] pp ⊳ redo.

**redouble** [ˌri:'dʌbl] vt: **to ~ one's efforts (to do sthg)** seine Anstrengungen verdoppeln (, etw zu tun).

**redoubtable** [rɪ'daʊtəbl] adj fml Ehrfurcht gebietend.

**redraft** [ˌri:'drɑːft] vt neu abfassen.

**redraw** [ˌri:'drɔ:] (pt -drew; pp -drawn) vt neu zeichnen.

**redress** [rɪ'dres] fml n: **to have no ~ against sb** keinen Rechtsanspruch gegenüber jm haben <> vt: **to ~ the balance** das Gleichgewicht wiederherlstellen.

**redrew** [ˌri:'dru:] pt ⊳ redraw.

**Red Sea** n: **the ~** das Rote Meer.

**red setter** n (Roter) Setter.

**Red Square** n Roter Platz.

**red squirrel** n Eichhörnchen *das.*

**red tape** n fig Bürokratie *die.*

**reduce** [rɪ'dju:s] vt - **1.** [make smaller, less] reduzieren; **to ~ sthg to a pulp** etw zu Brei schlagen - **2.** CULIN einlkochen - **3.** [force, bring]: **to be ~d to doing sthg** dazu gezwungen sein, etw zu tun; **to be ~d to tears** zum Weinen gebracht werden; **to be ~d to a nervous wreck** zu einem Nervenbündel gemacht werden <> vi Am [lose weight] ablnehmen.

**reduced** [rɪ'dju:st] adj [size] verkleinert; [risk] reduziert; [price] herabgesetzt; **in ~ circum-**

stances in finanziell eingeschränkten Verhältnissen.

**reduction** [rɪ'dʌkʃn] n **- 1.** [decrease]: **~ (in sth)** Reduzierung die (einer Sache (G)) **- 2.** [amount of decrease]: **~ (of)** Ermäßigung die (um).

**redundancy** [rɪ'dʌndənsɪ] (pl **-ies**) n Br **- 1.** [job loss]: **redundancies** Entlassungen pl **- 2.** [jobless state] Arbeitslosigkeit die.

**redundancy payment** n Br Abfindung die.

**redundant** [rɪ'dʌndənt] adj **- 1.** Br [jobless]: **to be made ~** den Arbeitsplatz verlieren **- 2.** [superfluous] überflüssig.

**redwood** ['redwʊd] n: **~ (tree)** Redwoodbaum der.

**reecho** [ˌriː'ekəʊ] vt wiederholen.

**reed** [riːd] n **- 1.** [plant] Schilfrohr das **- 2.** [of musical instrument] Rohrblatt das <> comp [made of reeds] aus Schilfrohr.

**reeducate** [ˌriː'edjʊkeɪt] vt umlerziehen.

**reedy** ['riːdɪ] (compar **-ier;** superl **-iest**) adj [voice] durchdringend.

**reef** [riːf] n [in sea] Riff das.

**reek** [riːk] n Gestank der <> vi: **to ~ (of sth)** (nach etw) stinken.

**reel** [riːl] n **- 1.** [roll] Spule die **- 2.** [on fishing rod] Rolle die <> vi [stagger] torkeln; **my head ~ed** mir schwirrte der Kopf; **to ~ from sth** von etw schwindlig sein.

➤ **reel in** vt sep [fishing line] einlrollen; [fish] einlholen.

➤ **reel off** vt sep [list] ablspulen.

**reelect** [ˌriːɪ'lekt] vt: **to ~ sb (as) sth** jn als etw wiederlwählen.

**reelection** [ˌriːɪ'lekʃn] n Wiederwahl die.

**reemphasize** [ˌriː'emfəsaɪz] vt von neuem unterstreichen.

**reenact** [ˌriːɪ'nækt] vt nachlspielen.

**reenter** [ˌriː'entəʳ] vt **- 1.** [room] wieder hineinlgehen/hereinlkommen in (+ A); [country] wieder einlreisen in (+ A) **- 2.** comput [data] von neuem eingeben.

**reentry** [ˌriː'entrɪ] n **- 1.** [into country] Wiedereinreise die **- 2.** comput [of data] Neueingabe die.

**reexamine** [ˌriːɪg'zæmɪn] vt **- 1.** [question, case] nochmals prüfen **- 2.** [witness] nochmals vernehmen.

**reexport** [ˌriː'ekspɔːt] comm n Wiederausfuhr die <> vt wieder auslführen.

**ref** n **- 1.** inf (abbr of **referee**) sport Schiri der **- 2.** admin abbr of **reference**.

**refectory** [rɪ'fektərɪ] (pl **-ies**) n **- 1.** [in school, college] Speisesaal der **- 2.** [in monastery] Refektorium das.

**refer** [rɪ'fɜːʳ] (pt & pp **-red;** cont **-ring**) vt **- 1.** [person]: **to ~ sb to sb** jn an jn verweisen; **to**

**~ sb to sthg** [document, article] jn auf etw (A) verweisen **- 2.** [report, case, decision]: **to ~ sthg to sb/sthg** etw an jn/etw weiterleiten.

➤ **refer to** vt fus **- 1.** [mention] erwähnen; [as support for argument] sich beziehen auf (+ A); **Charles II is often ~red to as the Merry Monarch** Charles II. wird oft als der lustige Monarch bezeichnet **- 2.** [apply to, concern] betreffen; **to which noun does the adjective ~?** auf welches Substantiv bezieht sich das Adjektiv? **- 3.** [consult] zu Rate ziehen.

**referee** [ˌrefə'riː] n **- 1.** sport Schiedsrichter der, -in die **- 2.** Br [for job application] Referenz die <> vt sport leiten <> vi sport Schiedsrichter sein.

**reference** ['refrəns] n **- 1.** [act of mentioning]: **to make ~ to sb/sthg** jn/etw erwähnen; **with ~ to** fml mit Bezug auf (+ A) **- 2.** [mention]: **~ (to)** Anspielung die (auf (+ A)) **- 3.** [for information]: **for future ~** für späteren Gebrauch **- 4.** [in catalogue, on map] Verweis der **- 5.** comm [in letter, for job application] Referenz die.

**reference book** n Nachschlagewerk das.

**reference library** n Präsenzbibliothek die.

**reference number** n [for customer] Kundennummer die; [for member] Mitgliedsnummer die; [on file] Aktenzeichen das.

**referendum** [ˌrefə'rendəm] (pl **-s** or **-da** [-də]) n pol Referendum das.

**referral** [rɪ'fɜːrəl] n fml **- 1.** [act of referring] Weiterleitung die **- 2.** [case referred] Überweisung die.

**refill** [n 'riːfɪl, vb ˌriː'fɪl] n **- 1.** [for pen, lighter] Nachfüllpatrone die **- 2.** inf [drink]: **would you like a ~?** möchten Sie nachgeschenkt haben? <> vt nachlfüllen.

**refillable** [ˌriː'fɪləbl] adj nachfüllbar.

**refine** [rɪ'faɪn] vt **- 1.** [oil, food] raffinieren **- 2.** [details, speech] verfeinern.

**refined** [rɪ'faɪnd] adj **- 1.** [genteel] fein **- 2.** [highly developed, purified] raffiniert.

**refinement** [rɪ'faɪnmənt] n **- 1.** [improvement]: **~ (on sthg)** Verfeinerung die (von etw) **- 2.** (U) [gentility] Feinheit die.

**refinery** [rɪ'faɪnərɪ] (pl **-ies**) n Raffinerie die.

**refit** [n 'riːfɪt, vb ˌriː'fɪt] (pt & pp **-ted;** cont **-ting**) n [of ship] Überholung die <> vt [ship] überholen.

**reflate** [ˌriː'fleɪt] vt econ anlkurbeln.

**reflation** [ˌriː'fleɪʃn] n (U) econ Ankurbelung die der Konjunktur.

**reflationary** [riː'fleɪʃənrɪ] adj econ reflationär.

**reflect** [rɪ'flekt] vt **- 1.** [show, be a sign of] widerlspiegeln **- 2.** [throw back - light, heat] reflektieren; [ - image] spiegeln, reflektieren; **to be ~ed in sthg** in etw reflektiert werden **- 3.** [think, consider]: **to ~ that ...** daran denken, dass ... <> *vi* [think, consider]: **to ~ (on** OR **upon sthg)** reflektieren (über etw (A)), nachldenken (über etw (A)).

**reflection** [rɪˈflekʃn] *n* - **1.** [sign, consequence] Widerspiegelung *die* - **2.** [criticism]: **this is no ~ on your judgement** das ist keine Kritik an Ihrem Urteil - **3.** [image] Spiegelung *die* - **4.** *(U)* [of light, heat] Reflexion *die* - **5.** *(U)* *literary* [thinking] Reflexion *die;* **on ~** bei näherer Überlegung - **6.** *literary* [thought]: **~s (on sthg)** Reflexionen *pl* (über etw (A)).

**reflective** [rɪˈflektɪv] *adj* - **1.** [thoughtful] nachdenklich - **2.** [shiny] reflektierend.

**reflector** [rɪˈflektəʳ] *n* Rückstrahler *der.*

**reflex** [ˈriːfleks] *n:* **~ (action)** Reflex *der.*
➤ **reflexes** *npl* Reflexe *pl.*

**reflex camera** *n* Spiegelreflexkamera *die.*

**reflexive** [rɪˈfleksɪv] *adj* GRAMM reflexiv.

**reflexology** [ˌriːflekˈsɒlədʒɪ] *n* Reflexzonenmassage *die.*

**reforest** [ˌriːˈfɒrɪst] *vt esp Am* = reafforest.

**reforestation** [riːˌfɒrɪˈsteɪʃn] *n esp Am* = reafforestation.

**reform** [rɪˈfɔːm] *n* Reform *die* <> *vt* - **1.** [change] reformieren - **2.** [improve behaviour of] bessern <> *vi* [behave better] sich bessern.

**reformat** [ˌriːˈfɔːmæt] *(pt* & *pp* **-ted;** *cont* **-ting)** *vt* COMPUT neu formatieren.

**Reformation** [ˌrefəˈmeɪʃn] *n:* **the ~** die Reformation.

**reformatory** [rɪˈfɔːmətrɪ] *(pl* **-ies)** *n Am* Besserungsanstalt *die.*

**reformed** [rɪˈfɔːmd] *adj* [drug addict, alcoholic] ehemalig; **he is a ~ character** er hat sich gebessert.

**reformer** [rɪˈfɔːməʳ] *n* Reformer *der,* -in *die.*

**reformist** [rɪˈfɔːmɪst] *adj* reformistisch <> *n* Reformist *der,* -in *die.*

**refract** [rɪˈfrækt] *vt* brechen <> *vi* sich brechen.

**refrain** [rɪˈfreɪn] *n* Refrain *der* <> *vi fml:* **to ~ from doing sthg** es unterlassen, etw zu tun.

**refresh** [rɪˈfreʃ] *vt* erfrischen; **to ~ sb's memory** js Gedächtnis auf lfrischen.

**refresher course** [rɪˈfreʃəʳ-] *n* Auffrischungskurs *der.*

**refreshing** [rɪˈfreʃɪŋ] *adj* erfrischend.

**refreshments** [rɪˈfreʃmənts] *npl* Erfrischungen *pl.*

**refrigerate** [rɪˈfrɪdʒəreɪt] *vt* kühlen.

**refrigeration** [rɪˌfrɪdʒəˈreɪʃn] *n (U)* Kühlung *die.*

**refrigerator** [rɪˈfrɪdʒəreɪtəʳ] *n* Kühlschrank *der.*

**refuel** [ˌriːˈfjʊəl] *(Br pt* & *pp* **-led;** *cont* **-ling,** *Am pt* & *pp* **-ed;** *cont* **-ing)** *vt* & *vi* auf ltanken.

**refuge** [ˈrefjuːdʒ] *n* - **1.** [place of safety] Zuflucht *die* - **2.** [safety]: **to seek** OR **take ~** [hide] Zuflucht suchen; **to seek** OR **take ~ in sthg** *fig* in etw (D) Zuflucht suchen.

**refugee** [ˌrefjʊˈdʒiː] *n* Flüchtling *der.*

**refugee camp** *n* Flüchtlingslager *das.*

**refund** [*n* ˈriːfʌnd, *vb* rɪˈfʌnd] *n* Rückzahlung *die* <> *vt:* **to ~ sthg to sb, to ~ sb sthg** etw an jn zurücklzahlen, jm etw zurücklzahlen.

**refurbish** [ˌriːˈfɜːbɪʃ] *vt* renovieren.

**refurbishment** [ˌriːˈfɜːbɪʃmənt] *n* Renovierung *die.*

**refurnish** [ˌriːˈfɜːnɪʃ] *vt* neu einlrichten.

**refusal** [rɪˈfjuːzl] *n:* **~ (to do sthg)** Weigerung *die* (etw zu tun); **she met with a ~** sie erhielt eine Absage; **to give sb first ~** jm das Vorkaufsrecht einlräumen.

**refuse**[1] [rəˈfjuːz] *vt* - **1.** [withhold, deny]: **to ~ sb sthg, to ~ sthg to sb** jm etw verweigern - **2.** [decline] abllehnen; **to ~ to do sthg** sich weigern, etw zu tun <> *vi* sich weigern.

**refuse**[2] [ˈrefjuːs] *n* Müll *der.*

**refuse collection** [ˈrefjuːs-] *n* Müllabfuhr *die.*

**refuse collector** [ˈrefjuːs-] *n* Müllmann *der.*

**refuse dump** [ˈrefjuːs-] *n* Müllabladeplatz *der.*

**refute** [rɪˈfjuːt] *vt fml* widerlegen.

**reg.** *(abbr of* **registered):** **~ trademark** eingetr. Warenzeichen.

**regain** [rɪˈgeɪn] *vt* [recover] wiederlgewinnen; **to ~ consciousness** wieder zu Bewusstsein kommen; **to ~ one's health** wieder gesund werden.

**regal** [ˈriːgl] *adj* majestätisch.

**regale** [rɪˈgeɪl] *vt:* **to ~ sb with sthg** jn mit etw unterhalten.

**regalia** [rɪˈgeɪljə] *n (U)* Insignien *pl.*

**regard** [rɪˈgɑːd] *n* - **1.** *(U) fml* [respect, esteem]: **~ (for sb/sthg)** Achtung *die* (vor jm/etw); **to have the greatest ~ for sb/sthg** vor jm/etw Hochachtung haben; **to hold sb/sthg in high/low ~** jn/etw hoch/gering achten - **2.** [aspect]: **in this/that ~** in dieser/jener Hinsicht <> *vt:* **to ~ o.s./sb/sthg as** sich/jn/etw halten für; **he ~ed her with admiration/suspicion** er bewunderte sie/misstraute ihr; **to be highly ~ed** hoch geachtet sein.
➤ **regards** *npl* [in greetings] Grüße *pl;* **send her my ~s** grüße sie von mir.
➤ **as regards** *prep* in Bezug auf (+ A).
➤ **in regard to, with regard to** *prep* bezüglich (+ G).

**regarding** [rɪˈgɑːdɪŋ] *prep* in Bezug auf (+ A).

**regardless** [rɪ'gɑːdlɪs] *adv* trotzdem.
➤ **regardless of** *prep* ohne Rücksicht auf (+ A).

**regatta** [rɪ'gætə] *n* Regatta *die*.

**regd.** = reg.

**Regency** ['riːdʒənsɪ] *adj* Regency-.

**regenerate** [rɪ'dʒenəreɪt] *vt* [economy, area] wieder beleben.

**regeneration** [rɪˌdʒenə'reɪʃn] *n* [of economy, area] Wiederbelebung *die*.

**regent** ['riːdʒənt] *adj*: prince ~ Prinzregent *der* ⬦ *n* Regent *der*, -in *die*.

**reggae** ['regeɪ] *n* Reggae *der*.

**regime** [reɪ'ʒiːm] *n pej* Regime *das*.

**regiment** ['redʒɪmənt] *n* MIL Regiment *das*.

**regimental** [ˌredʒɪ'mentl] *adj* MIL Regiments-.

**regimented** ['redʒɪmentɪd] *adj pej* [workforce, system] reglementiert.

**region** ['riːdʒən] *n* - **1.** [of country] Gebiet *das*, Region *die* - **2.** [of body] Bereich *der* - **3.** [range]: in the ~ of ungefähr.

**regional** ['riːdʒənl] *adj* regional.

**register** ['redʒɪstə'] *n* [of school class] Klassenbuch *das;* **electoral** ~ Wählerverzeichnis *das;* ~ **of companies** Handelsregister *das* ⬦ *vt* - **1.** [record officially, show, measure] registrieren - **2.** [express] zeigen ⬦ *vi* - **1.** [enrol]: **to** ~ **as/for** sthg sich als/für etw (an)melden - **2.** [book in] sich eintragen - **3.** *inf* [be properly understood]: **it didn't** ~ **(with her)** sie registrierte es gar nicht.

**registered** ['redʒɪstəd] *adj* - **1.** [officially listed - company, charity] eingetragen; **are you** ~ **disabled?** haben Sie einen Schwerbehindertenausweis? - **2.** [letter, parcel] eingeschrieben.

**registered nurse** *n* staatlich geprüfter Krankenpfleger, staatlich geprüfte Krankenschwester.

**registered post** *Br,* **registered mail** *Am* *n*: **to send sthg by** ~ etw per Einschreiben schicken.

**registered trademark** *n* eingetragenes Warenzeichen.

**registrar** [ˌredʒɪ'strɑː'] *n* - **1.** [keeper of records] Standesbeamte *der*, -tin *die* - **2.** UNIV [administrator] Kanzler *der*, -in *die* - **3.** *Br* [doctor] Krankenhausarzt *der*, -ärztin *die*.

**registration** [ˌredʒɪ'streɪʃn] *n* - **1.** [in records] Eintragung *die* - **2.** [on course] Anmeldung *die* - **3.** AUT = registration number.

**registration document** *n* Kraftfahrzeugbrief *der*.

**registration number** *n* AUT Kennzeichen *das*.

**registry** ['redʒɪstrɪ] (*pl* -ies) *n* Registratur *die*.

**registry office** *n* Standesamt *das*.

**regress** [rɪ'gres] *vi fml*: **to** ~ **(to sthg)** sich (zu etw) zurücklentwickeln.

**regression** [rɪ'greʃn] *n (U) fml* rückläufige Entwicklung.

**regressive** [rɪ'gresɪv] *adj fml* rückschrittlich.

**regret** [rɪ'gret] (*pt* & *pp* **-ted**; *cont* **-ting**) *n* Bedauern *das;* **I have no** ~**s about it** ich bedauere es nicht ⬦ *vt* bedauern; **to** ~ **doing sthg** bedauern, etw getan zu haben; **we** ~ **to announce that ...** wir bedauern, Ihnen mitteilen zu müssen, dass ...

**regretful** [rɪ'gretfʊl] *adj* [look] bedauernd.

**regretfully** [rɪ'gretfʊlɪ] *adv* mit Bedauern.

**regrettable** [rɪ'gretəbl] *adj* bedauerlich.

**regrettably** [rɪ'gretəblɪ] *adv* [unfortunately] bedauerlicherweise, leider.

**regroup** [ˌriː'gruːp] *vi* sich neu gruppieren; [soldiers] sich neu formieren.

**regt** (*abbr of* **regiment**).

**regular** ['regjʊlə'] *adj* - **1.** [gen & GRAMM] regelmäßig - **2.** [usual] üblich - **3.** *Am* [in size] klein - **4.** *Am* [pleasant]: **he's a** ~ **guy** er ist O.K. - **5.** *Am* [normal] normal, gewöhnlich ⬦ *n* [customer, client] Stammkunde *der*, -din *die*.

**regular army** *n* Berufsarmee *die*.

**regularity** [ˌregjʊ'lærətɪ] *n* Regelmäßigkeit *die*.

**regularly** ['regjʊləlɪ] *adv* regelmäßig.

**regulate** ['regjʊleɪt] *vt* - **1.** [control] regulieren - **2.** [adjust] regeln.

**regulation** [ˌregjʊ'leɪʃn] *adj* [standard] vorgeschrieben ⬦ *n* - **1.** [rule] Vorschrift *die* - **2.** *(U)* [control] Regulierung *die*.

**regurgitate** [rɪ'gɜːdʒɪteɪt] *vt* - **1.** [bring up] wieder hochlbringen - **2.** *fig* & *pej* [repeat] wiederlkäuen.

**rehabilitate** [ˌriːə'bɪlɪteɪt] *vt* rehabilitieren.

**rehabilitation** ['riːəˌbɪlɪ'teɪʃn] *n* Rehabilitation *die*.

**rehash** [*vb* ˌriː'hæʃ, *n* 'riːhæʃ] *pej inf vt* auflwärmen ⬦ *n* Aufguss *der*.

**rehearsal** [rɪ'hɜːsl] *n* Probe *die*.

**rehearse** [rɪ'hɜːs] *vt* & *vi* proben.

**reheat** [ˌriː'hiːt] *vt* auflwärmen.

**rehouse** [ˌriː'haʊz] *vt*: **to be** ~**d** umquartiert werden.

**reign** [reɪn] *n lit* & *fig* Herrschaft *die* ⬦ *vi* - **1.** [rule]: **to** ~ **(over)** herrschen (über (+ A)) - **2.** [prevail]: **to** ~ **over** sich auslbreiten über (+ D).

**reigning** ['reɪnɪŋ] *adj* [champion] amtierend.

**reimburse** [ˌriːɪm'bɜːs] *vt* [person] entschädigen; [expenses] zurücklerstatten; **to** ~ **sb for sthg** jm etw zurücklerstatten.

R

**reimbursement** [ˌriːɪmˈbɜːsmənt] n (U) fml [of expenses] Rückerstattung die; [of person] Entschädigung die.

**rein** [reɪn] n fig: **to give sb (a) free ~** jm freie Hand lassen; **to keep a tight ~ on sb/sthg** bei jm/etw die Zügel kurz halten.

➤ **reins** npl - **1.** [for horse] Zügel pl - **2.** [for child] Laufgurt der.

➤ **rein in** vt sep [horse] zügeln.

**reincarnation** [ˌriːɪnkɑːˈneɪʃn] n - **1.** [life after death] Wiedergeburt die - **2.** [reborn person, animal] Reinkarnation die.

**reindeer** [ˈreɪnˌdɪəʳ] (pl inv) n Rentier das.

**reinforce** [ˌriːɪnˈfɔːs] vt - **1.** [ceiling, frame, cover]: **to ~ sthg (with sthg)** etw (mit etw) verstärken - **2.** [dislike, prejudice] bestärken - **3.** [argument, claim] stützen.

**reinforced concrete** [ˌriːɪnˈfɔːst-] n Stahlbeton der.

**reinforcement** [ˌriːɪnˈfɔːsmənt] n [in construction] Verstärkung die.

➤ **reinforcements** npl MIL Verstärkung die.

**reinstate** [ˌriːɪnˈsteɪt] vt - **1.** [employee] wieder einlstellen - **2.** [payment, policy] wieder auflnehmen.

**reinstatement** [ˌriːɪnˈsteɪtmənt] n - **1.** [of employee] Wiedereinstellung die - **2.** [of payment, policy] Wiederaufnahme die.

**reinterpret** [ˌriːɪnˈtɜːprɪt] vt neu interpretieren.

**reintroduce** [ˈriːˌɪntrəˈdjuːs] vt wieder einlführen.

**reintroduction** [ˌriːɪntrəˈdʌkʃn] n Wiedereinführung die.

**reissue** [riːˈɪʃuː] n Neuausgabe die; [of book] Neuauflage die ◇ vt neu herauslgeben; [book] neu aufllegen.

**reiterate** [riːˈɪtəreɪt] vt fml wiederholen.

**reiteration** [riːˌɪtəˈreɪʃn] n fml Wiederholung die.

**reject** [n ˈriːdʒekt, vb rɪˈdʒekt] n: **~s** [from factory] Ausschuss der; **it's a ~** [in shop] es ist zweite Wahl ◇ vt abllehnen; **the machine keeps on ~ing the coin** die Maschine nimmt die Münze nicht an.

**rejection** [rɪˈdʒekʃn] n - **1.** [of offer, values, religion] Ablehnung die - **2.** [for job] Absage die.

**rejig** [ˌriːˈdʒɪg] (pt & pp -ged; cont -ging) vt Br inf umlkrempeln.

**rejoice** [rɪˈdʒɔɪs] vi: **to ~ (at OR in sthg)** sich freuen (über etw (A)).

**rejoicing** [rɪˈdʒɔɪsɪŋ] n: **~ (at OR over sthg)** Freude die (über etw (A)).

**rejoin** [rɪˈdʒɔɪn] vt - **1.** [group, regiment, club] sich wieder anlschließen (+ D); [motorway] wieder auflfahren auf (+ A) - **2.** [reply] erwidern.

**rejoinder** [rɪˈdʒɔɪndəʳ] n Erwiderung die.

**rejuvenate** [rɪˈdʒuːvəneɪt] vt verjüngen.

**rekindle** [ˌriːˈkɪndl] vt fig wieder entflammen.

**relapse** [rɪˈlæps] n Rückfall der; **to have a ~** einen Rückfall haben ◇ vi: **to ~ into sthg** in etw (A) zurücklfallen.

**relate** [rɪˈleɪt] vt - **1.** [connect]: **to ~ sthg to sthg** etw zu etw in Beziehung bringen OR setzen - **2.** [tell] erzählen ◇ vi - **1.** [connect]: **to ~ to sthg** mit etw zusammenlhängen - **2.** [concern]: **to ~ to sb/sthg** jn/etw betreffen - **3.** [empathize]: **to ~ to sb/sthg** einen Bezug zu jm/ etw haben.

➤ **relating to** prep im Zusammenhang mit.

**related** [rɪˈleɪtɪd] adj - **1.** [in same family] verwandt; **to be ~ to sb** mit jm verwandt sein - **2.** [connected] zusammenhängend; **to be ~ to sthg** mit etw zusammenlhängen.

**relation** [rɪˈleɪʃn] n - **1.** (U) [connection]: **~ to/ between** Beziehung die zu/zwischen (+ D); **in ~ to** [state, size] im Verhältnis zu; [position] im Vergleich zu - **2.** [family member] Verwandte der, die.

➤ **relations** npl [relationship]: **~s (between/with)** Beziehungen pl (zwischen (+ D)/mit).

**relational** [rɪˈleɪʃənl] adj COMPUT relational.

**relationship** [rɪˈleɪʃnʃɪp] n Beziehung die.

**relative** [ˈrelətɪv] adj - **1.** [gen] relativ; **he is a ~ newcomer to the firm** er ist noch relativ neu in der Firma - **2.** [respective] jeweilig ◇ n Verwandte der, die.

➤ **relative to** prep fml - **1.** [compared to] im Vergleich zu - **2.** [connected with] sich beziehend auf (+ A).

**relatively** [ˈrelətɪvlɪ] adv relativ.

**relativity** [ˌreləˈtɪvətɪ] n Relativität die.

**relax** [rɪˈlæks] vt - **1.** [mind, muscle, person] entspannen - **2.** [grip, discipline, regulation] lockern ◇ vi - **1.** [person, body, muscle] sich entspannen - **2.** [grip] sich lockern.

**relaxation** [ˌriːlækˈseɪʃn] n (U) - **1.** [rest] Entspannung die - **2.** [of regulation, discipline] Lockerung die.

**relaxed** [rɪˈlækst] adj entspannt.

**relaxing** [rɪˈlæksɪŋ] adj entspannend.

**relay** [n & vb senses 1 & 2 ˈriːleɪ, vb sense 3 ˌriːˈleɪ] (pt & pp senses 1 & 2 -ed; pt & pp sense 3 relaid) n - **1.** SPORT: **~ (race)** Staffellauf der; **to work in ~s** fig sich (bei der Arbeit) abllösen - **2.** RADIO & TV Relais das ◇ vt - **1.** RADIO & TV [broadcast] übertragen - **2.** [message, news]: **to ~ sthg (to sb)** (jm) etw auslrichten - **3.** [cable, carpet, tiles] neu verlegen.

**release** [rɪˈliːs] n - **1.** (U) [from captivity] Freilassung die - **2.** (U) [from pain, suffering] Erlösung die - **3.** [statement] Verlautbarung die - **4.** [of gas, fumes] Freisetzen das - **5.** [of film, video, CD] Freigabe die; **the movie is on ~ from Friday** der

Film ist von Freitag an im Kino (zu sehen)
- **6.** [video, CD]: **new ~** Neuerscheinung *die;*
[film] neuer Film ◇ *vt* - **1.** [set free] freilassen;
**to ~ sb from prison/captivity** jm aus dem
Gefängnis/der Gefangenschaft entlassen;
**to ~ sb from sthg** [promise, contract] jn von etw
befreien - **2.** [make available] freisetzen
- **3.** [from control, grasp] loslassen - **4.** [brake,
lever, handle] lösen - **5.** [let out, emit]: **to be ~d
(from/into sthg)** freigesetzt werden (aus
etw/in etw *(A)*) - **6.** [film, video, CD] herausl
bringen; [statement, news story] veröffentli
chen.

**relegate** ['relɪgeɪt] *vt* - **1.** [lower status of]: **to ~ sb/
sthg (to)** jn/etw verbannen (in *(+ A)*) - **2.** *Br*
SPORT: **to be ~d** absteigen.

**relegation** [ˌrelɪ'geɪʃn] *n (U)* - **1.** [lowering of sta
tus]: **~ (to)** Verbannung *die* (in *(+ A)*) - **2.** *Br* SPORT:
**~ (to)** Abstieg *der* (in *(+ A)*).

**relent** [rɪ'lent] *vi* [person] nachlgeben; [wind,
storm] nachllassen.

**relentless** [rɪ'lentlɪs] *adj* erbarmungslos.

**relentlessly** [rɪ'lentlɪslɪ] *adv* erbarmungslos.

**relevance** ['reləvəns] *n (U)* - **1.** [connection]:
**~ (to)** Relevanz *die* (für) - **2.** [significance]: **~ (to/
for)** Bedeutung *die* (für).

**relevant** ['reləvənt] *adj* - **1.** [connected]: **~ (to)**
relevant (für) - **2.** [important]: **~ (to)** wichtig
(für) - **3.** [appropriate] entsprechend.

**reliability** [rɪˌlaɪə'bɪlətɪ] *n* Zuverlässigkeit
*die.*

**reliable** [rɪ'laɪəbl] *adj* zuverlässig.

**reliably** [rɪ'laɪəblɪ] *adv* zuverlässig.

**reliance** [rɪ'laɪəns] *n (U):* **~ (on)** Abhängigkeit
*die* (von).

**reliant** [rɪ'laɪənt] *adj:* **~ on** abhängig von *(+ D).*

**relic** ['relɪk] *n* - **1.** [old object, custom - still in use]
Überbleibsel *das;* [ - no longer in use] Relikt *das*
- **2.** RELIG Reliquie *die.*

**relief** [rɪ'liːf] *n* - **1.** [comfort] Erleichterung *die*
- **2.** *(U)* [for poor, refugees] Hilfe *die* - **3.** *Am* [social
security] Fürsorge *die.*

**relief map** *n* Reliefkarte *die.*

**relief road** *n Br* Ausweichstraße *die.*

**relieve** [rɪ'liːv] *vt* - **1.** [ease, lessen] lindern; **to
~ sb of sthg** jn von etw befreien - **2.** [take over
from]: **to ~ sb of sthg** jn einer Sache *(G)* enthe
ben - **3.** [give help to] helfen *(+ D).*

**relieved** [rɪ'liːvd] *adj* erleichtert.

**religion** [rɪ'lɪdʒn] *n* - **1.** [belief in a god] Glaube
*der* - **2.** [system of belief] Religion *die.*

**religious** [rɪ'lɪdʒəs] *adj* religiös.

**reline** [ˌriː'laɪn] *vt* [skirt] neu füttern; [brakes]
neu belegen.

**relinquish** [rɪ'lɪŋkwɪʃ] *vt* auflgeben.

**relish** ['relɪʃ] *n* - **1.** [enjoyment]: **with (great) ~** ge

nüsslich - **2.** [pickle] Soße *die* ◇ *vt* [enjoy] ge
nießen; **to ~ the idea** *OR* **thought of doing sthg**
sich darauf freuen, etw zu tun.

**relive** [ˌriː'lɪv] *vt* noch einmal durchleben.

**relocate** [ˌriːləʊ'keɪt] *vt* verlegen ◇ *vi* den
Standort wechseln.

**relocation** [ˌriːləʊ'keɪʃn] *n* [of business, staff]
Standortwechsel *der.*

**relocation expenses** *npl* Umzugskosten
*pl.*

**reluctance** [rɪ'lʌktəns] *n* Widerwille *der;* **with
~** widerwillig.

**reluctant** [rɪ'lʌktənt] *adj* widerwillig; **to be
~ to do sthg** abgeneigt sein, etw zu tun.

**reluctantly** [rɪ'lʌktəntlɪ] *adv* widerwillig.

**rely** [rɪ'laɪ] *(pt & pp -ied)* ⇒ **rely on** *vt fus*
- **1.** [count on] sich verlassen auf *(+ A);* **I'm ~ing
on you to do this work** ich verlasse mich da
rauf, dass du diese Arbeit erledigst - **2.** [be
dependent on]: **to ~ on sb/sthg for sthg** wegen
etw auf jn/etw angewiesen sein.

**REM** *(abbr of* **rapid eye movement)** *n:* **~ sleep**
REM-Phase *die.*

**remain** [rɪ'meɪn] *vt:* **that ~s to be done** das
bleibt (noch) zu tun; **it ~s to be seen ...** es
wird sich zeigen ... ◇ *vi* bleiben.
⇒ **remains** *npl* - **1.** [of meal, ancient civilization, build
ing] Überreste *pl* - **2.** [corpse] menschliche
Überreste *pl.*

**remainder** [rɪ'meɪndə*ʳ*] *n* Rest *der.*

**remaining** [rɪ'meɪnɪŋ] *adj* verbleibend; **last ~**
letzte, -r, -s.

**remake** [*n* 'riːmeɪk, *vb* ˌriː'meɪk] CINEMA *n* Re
make *das,* Neuverfilmung *die* ◇ *vt* neu ver
filmen.

**remand** [rɪ'mɑːnd] LAW *n:* **on ~** in Untersu
chungshaft ◇ *vt* in Untersuchungshaft
behalten; **to be ~ed in custody** in Untersu
chungshaft verbleiben.

**remand centre** *n Br Untersuchungsgefäng
nis, in dem jugendliche Straftäter zwischen
14 und 21 Jahren inhaftiert sind.*

**remark** [rɪ'mɑːk] *n* Bemerkung *die* ◇ *vt:* **to
~ that ...** bemerken, dass ... ◇ *vi:* **to ~ on sthg**
über etw *(A)* eine Bemerkung machen.

**remarkable** [rɪ'mɑːkəbl] *adj* bemerkens
wert.

**remarkably** [rɪ'mɑːkəblɪ] *adv* bemerkens
wert.

**remarry** [ˌriː'mærɪ] *(pt & pp -ied)* *vi* wieder
heiraten.

**remedial** [rɪ'miːdjəl] *adj* - **1.** SCH Förder
- **2.** [corrective - action] abhelfend; **~ therapy** Re
habilitationsbehandlung *die.*

**remedy** ['remədɪ] *(pl -ies; pt & pp -ied)* *n:* **~ (for
sthg)** [for ill health] Heilmittel *das* (für *OR* gegen

**R**

etw); [solution] Lösung *die* (für etw) <> *vt* abl helfen (+ D).

**remember** [rɪ'membə'] *vt* - **1.** [recollect] sich erinnern an (+ A); **to ~ doing sthg** sich daran erinnern, etw getan zu haben - **2.** [not forget] denken an (+ A); **to ~ to do sthg** daran denken, etw zu tun - **3.** [as greeting]: **~ me to your wife** grüßen Sie Ihre Frau von mir <> *vi* sich erinnern.

**remembrance** [rɪ'membrəns] *n fml*: **in ~ of** zur Erinnerung an (+ A).

**Remembrance Day** *n nationaler britischer Trauertag zum Gedenken an die in den beiden Weltkriegen gefallenen Soldaten. Er wird am dem 11. November nächstliegenden Sonntag begangen.*

**remind** [rɪ'maɪnd] *vt* - **1.** [tell]: **to ~ sb about sthg** jn an etw (A) erinnern; **to ~ sb to do sthg** jn daran erinnern, etw zu tun - **2.** [be reminiscent of]: **to ~ sb of sb/sthg** jn an jn/etw erinnern.

**reminder** [rɪ'maɪndə'] *n* - **1.** [to jog memory]: **to give sb a ~ to do sthg** jn daran erinnern, etw zu tun - **2.** [for bill, membership, licence] Mahnung *die*.

**reminisce** [,remɪ'nɪs] *vi*: **to ~ (about sthg)** in Erinnerungen (an etw (A)) schwelgen.

**reminiscences** [,remɪ'nɪsənsɪz] *npl* (nostalgische) Erinnerungen *pl*.

**reminiscent** [,remɪ'nɪsnt] *adj*: **to be ~ of sb/ sthg** an jn/etw erinnern.

**remiss** [rɪ'mɪs] *adj* nachlässig.

**remission** [rɪ'mɪʃn] *n* (U) - **1.** LAW Straferlass *der* - **2.** MED: **to be in ~** [disease] vorübergehend zum Stillstand gekommen sein.

**remit** [*n* 'ri:mɪt, *vb* rɪ'mɪt] (*pt* & *pp* -ted; *cont* -ting) *n Br* Aufgabenbereich *der* <> *vt* [send] überweisen.

**remittance** [rɪ'mɪtns] *n* Überweisung *die*.

**remnant** ['remnənt] *n* Rest *der*.

**remodel** [,ri:'mɒdl] (*Br pt* & *pp* -led; *cont* -ling, *Am pt* & *pp* -ed; *cont* -ing) *vt* umgestalten.

**remold** *n Am* = remould.

**remonstrate** ['remənstreɪt] *vi fml*: **to ~ with sb (about sthg)** jm (wegen etw) Vorhaltungen machen.

**remorse** [rɪ'mɔːs] *n* Reue *die*.

**remorseful** [rɪ'mɔːsfʊl] *adj* reuig, reumütig.

**remorseless** [rɪ'mɔːslɪs] *adj* - **1.** [pitiless] unbarmherzig - **2.** [unstoppable] unaufhaltsam.

**remorselessly** [rɪ'mɔːslɪslɪ] *adv* - **1.** [pitilessly] unbarmherzig - **2.** [unstoppably] unaufhaltsam.

**remote** [rɪ'məʊt] *adj* - **1.** [distant - place] abgelegen; [ - time] entfernt - **2.** [aloof] unnahbar; **~ from reality** realitätsfern - **3.** [unconnected, irrelevant]: **~ from** entfernt von - **4.** [slight - resemblance] entfernt; [ - chance, possibility] gering.

**remote control** *n* - **1.** (U) [system] Fernsteuerung *die* - **2.** [machine, device] Fernbedienung *die*.

**remote-controlled** [-kən'trəʊld] *adj* ferngesteuert.

**remotely** [rɪ'məʊtlɪ] *adv* - **1.** [slightly]: **not ~** nicht im Entferntesten, nicht im Geringsten - **2.** [distantly] entfernt.

**remoteness** [rɪ'məʊtnɪs] *n* (U) - **1.** [in space, time] Ferne *die* - **2.** [aloofness] Unnahbarkeit *die*.

**remoulds** *Br*, **remolds** *Am* ['ri:məʊldz] *npl* runderneuerte Reifen *pl*.

**removable** [rɪ'muːvəbl] *adj* [detachable] abnehmbar.

**removal** [rɪ'muːvl] *n* - **1.** *Br* [change of house] Umzug *der* - **2.** [act of removing] Entfernen *das*.

**removal man** *n Br* Möbelpacker *der*.

**removal van** *n Br* Möbelwagen *der*.

**remove** [rɪ'muːv] *vt* - **1.** [take away, clean]: **~ sthg (from)** etw entfernen (aus/von) - **2.** [clothes, hat] ablegen - **3.** [from a job]: **to ~ sb (from)** jn entfernen (von) - **4.** [problem] beseitigen; [suspicion] zerstreuen.

**removed** [rɪ'muːvd] *adj*: **to be far ~ from** weit entfernt sein von.

**remover** [rɪ'muːvə'] *n* Entferner *der*.

**remuneration** [rɪ,mjuːnə'reɪʃn] *n fml* - **1.** [pay] Bezahlung *die* - **2.** [amount of money] Vergütung *die*.

**Renaissance** [rə'neɪsəns] *n*: **the ~** die Renaissance <> *comp* Renaissance-.

**rename** [,ri:'neɪm] *vt* umbenennen.

**rend** [rend] (*pt* & *pp* rent) *vt* zerreißen.

**render** ['rendə'] *vt* - **1.** [make] machen - **2.** [give - help, service] leisten.

**rendering** ['rendərɪŋ] *n* - **1.** [performance] Interpretation *die* - **2.** [translation] Übersetzung *die*.

**rendezvous** ['rɒndɪvuː] (*pl inv*) *n* - **1.** [meeting] Rendezvous *das* - **2.** [place] Treffpunkt *der*.

**rendition** [ren'dɪʃn] *n* [of poem, piece of music] Vortrag *der*.

**renegade** ['renɪgeɪd] *adj* abtrünnig <> *n* Abtrünnige *der, die*.

**renege** [rɪ'neɪg] *vi fml*: **to ~ on sthg** etw brechen.

**renegotiate** [,ri:nɪ'gəʊʃɪeɪt] *vt* & *vi* von neuem verhandeln.

**renew** [rɪ'njuː] *vt* - **1.** [repeat, restart] wieder aufnehmen - **2.** [extend validity of] verlängern - **3.** [increase]: **with ~ed enthusiasm/interest** mit neuem Enthusiasmus/Interesse.

**renewable** [rɪ'njuːəbl] *adj* - **1.** [resources] erneuerbar - **2.** [contract, licence, membership] verlängerbar.

**renewal** [rɪ'njuːəl] *n* - **1.** [of activity] Wiederaufnahme *die* - **2.** *(U)* [of contract, licence, membership] Verlängerung *die*.

**rennet** [ˈrenɪt] *n (U)* Lab *das*.

**renounce** [rɪˈnaʊns] *vt* - **1.** [reject] ablschwören (+ D) - **2.** *fml* [relinquish] verzichten auf (+ A).

**renovate** [ˈrenəveɪt] *vt* renovieren.

**renovation** [ˌrenəˈveɪʃn] *n (U)* Renovierung *die*.

➡ **renovations** *npl* Renovierung *die*.

**renown** [rɪˈnaʊn] *n* Ruf *der*.

**renowned** [rɪˈnaʊnd] *adj*: ~ (for sthg) berühmt (für etw).

**rent** [rent] *pt* & *pp* ▷ **rend** ◇ *n* Miete *die* ◇ *vt* - **1.** [subj: tenant, hirer] mieten - **2.** [subj: owner] vermieten.

➡ **rent out** *vt sep* vermieten.

**rental** [ˈrentl] *adj* Miet- ◇ *n* [money] Leihgebühr *die*; [for house] Miete *die*.

**rent book** *n* Mietbuch *das*.

**rent boy** *n Br inf* Strichjunge *der*.

**rent-free** *adj* & *adv* mietfrei.

**renumber** [ˌriːˈnʌmbəʳ] *vt* umlnummerieren.

**renunciation** [rɪˌnʌnsɪˈeɪʃn] *n (U)* - **1.** [relinquishing]: ~ of sthg Verzicht *der* auf etw (A) - **2.** [rejection]: ~ of sthg Abschwörung *die* von etw.

**reoccurrence** [ˌriːəˈkʌrəns] *n* Wiederauftreten *das*.

**reopen** [ˌriːˈəʊpn] *vt* - **1.** [shop, theatre] wieder eröffnen; [border, route] wieder öffnen - **2.** [case, talks] wieder auflnehmen ◇ *vi* - **1.** [shop, theatre] wieder eröffnen - **2.** [case, talks] von neuem beginnen - **3.** [wound] sich wieder öffnen.

**reorganization** [ˈriːˌɔːgənaɪˈzeɪʃn] *n (U)* Neuorganisation *die*.

**reorganize, -ise** [ˌriːˈɔːgənaɪz] *vt* neu organisieren ◇ *vi* sich neu organisieren.

**rep** [rep] *n* - **1.** *abbr of* **representative** - **2.** *abbr of* **repertory company**.

**Rep.** *Am* - **1.** *abbr of* **Representative** - **2.** *abbr of* **Republican**.

**repaid** [ˌriːˈpeɪd] *pt* & *pp* ▷ **repay**.

**repaint** [ˌriːˈpeɪnt] *vt* neu streichen.

**repair** [rɪˈpeəʳ] *n* Reparatur *die*; in good/bad ~ in gutem/schlechtem Zustand ◇ *vt* - **1.** [fix, mend] reparieren; [puncture, crack] auslbessern - **2.** [make amends for] wieder gutlmachen.

**repair kit** *n* Flickzeug *das*.

**repaper** [ˌriːˈpeɪpəʳ] *vt* neu tapezieren.

**reparations** [ˌrepəˈreɪʃnz] *npl* Reparationen *pl*.

**repartee** [ˌrepɑːˈtiː] *n (U)* Schlagabtausch *der*.

**repatriate** [ˌriːˈpætrɪeɪt] *vt* repatriieren.

**repay** [ˌriːˈpeɪ] *(pt* & *pp* **repaid)** *vt* - **1.** [money]

zurücklzahlen; to ~ sb sthg, to ~ sthg to sb jm etw zurücklzahlen - **2.** [kindness] vergelten; to ~ sb for sthg jm etw vergelten.

**repayment** [riːˈpeɪmənt] *n* Rückzahlung *die*.

**repeal** [rɪˈpiːl] *n* Aufhebung *die* ◇ *vt* auflheben.

**repeat** [rɪˈpiːt] *vt* wiederholen; to ~ o.s. sich wiederholen ◇ *n* [broadcast] Wiederholung *die*.

**repeated** [rɪˈpiːtɪd] *adj* wiederholt.

**repeatedly** [rɪˈpiːtɪdlɪ] *adv* wiederholt.

**repel** [rɪˈpel] *(pt* & *pp* **-led;** *cont* **-ling)** *vt* - **1.** [disgust] ablstoßen - **2.** [drive away] ablwehren.

**repellent** [rɪˈpelənt] *adj* abstoßend ◇ *n*: (insect) ~ Insektenabwehrmittel *das*.

**repent** [rɪˈpent] *vt* bereuen ◇ *vi*: to ~ of sthg über etw (A) Reue empfinden.

**repentance** [rɪˈpentəns] *n* Reue *die*.

**repentant** [rɪˈpentənt] *adj* reuevoll.

**repercussions** [ˌriːpəˈkʌʃnz] *npl* Auswirkungen *pl*.

**repertoire** [ˈrepətwɑːʳ] *n* Repertoire *das*.

**repertory** [ˈrepətrɪ] *n* [repertoire] Repertoire *das*.

**repertory company** *n* Repertoireensemble *das*.

**repetition** [ˌrepɪˈtɪʃn] *n* Wiederholung *die*.

**repetitious** [ˌrepɪˈtɪʃəs], **repetitive** [rɪˈpetɪtɪv] *adj* monoton.

**rephrase** [ˌriːˈfreɪz] *vt* anders formulieren.

**replace** [rɪˈpleɪs] *vt* - **1.** [gen] ersetzen; to ~ sb/sthg with sb/sthg jn/etw durch jn/etw ersetzen - **2.** [put back - upright] zurücklstellen; [- lying flat] zurückllegen.

**replacement** [rɪˈpleɪsmənt] *n* - **1.** [act of replacing] Ersetzen *das* - **2.** [new person, object]: ~ (for sthg) Ersatz *der* (für etw); ~ (for sb) [in job - temporary] Vertretung *die* (von jm); [- permanent] Nachfolger *der*, -in *die* (von jm); he came on as a ~ for the injured player er wurde gegen den verletzten Spieler ausgewechselt.

**replacement part** *n* Ersatzteil *das*.

**replay** [*n* ˈriːpleɪ, *vb* ˌriːˈpleɪ] *n* - **1.** [recording]: (action) ~ Wiederholung *die* - **2.** [game] Wiederholungsspiel *das* ◇ *vt* - **1.** [match, game] wiederholen - **2.** [film, tape] nochmals ablspielen.

**replenish** [rɪˈplenɪʃ] *vt fml*: to ~ sthg (with sthg) etw (mit etw) wieder auflfüllen.

**replete** [rɪˈpliːt] *adj fml* [person] gesättigt.

**replica** [ˈreplɪkə] *n* Kopie *die*.

**replicate** [ˈreplɪkeɪt] *vt fml* reproduzieren

**reply** [rɪˈplaɪ] *(pl* **-ies;** *pt* & *pp* **-ied)** *n*: ~ (to sthg) Antwort *die* (auf etw (A)); in ~ (to sthg) als Antwort (auf etw (A)) ◇ *vt* antworten ◇ *vi* antworten; **to ~ to sb/sthg** jm/auf etw *(A)* antworten.

**reply coupon** *n* Antwortschein *der.*

**reply-paid** *adj* [postcard, envelope] Frei-.

**report** [rɪ'pɔːt] *n* - **1.** [description, account] Bericht *der* - **2.** PRESS Reportage *die* - **3.** *Br* SCH Zeugnis *das* <> *vt* - **1.** [news, crime] melden - **2.** [make known]: **to ~ that ...** berichten, dass ...; **to ~ sthg (to sb)** (jm) etw berichten - **3.** [complain about]: **to ~ sb (to sb)** jn (bei jm) an|zeigen ; **to ~ sb for sthg** jn wegen etw an|zeigen <> *vi* - **1.** [give account]: **to ~ (on sthg)** (über etw) berichten - **2.** PRESS: **this is John Smith, ~ing from Moscow** John Smith (mit einem Bericht) aus Moskau; **to ~ on sthg** über etw *(A)* berichten - **3.** [present o.s.]: **to ~ to** sich melden bei; **to ~ for duty** sich zum Dienst melden.

➤ **report back** *vi:* **to ~ back (to sb)** (jm) Bericht erstatten.

**reportage** [ˌrepɔːˈtɑːʒ] *n (U)* Berichterstattung *die.*

**report card** *n Am* SCH Zeugnis *das.*

**reportedly** [rɪ'pɔːtɪdlɪ] *adv* angeblich.

**reported speech** [rɪˈpɔːtɪd-] *n (U)* indirekte Rede.

**reporter** [rɪ'pɔːtəʳ] *n* [in TV, radio, press] Reporter *der,* Reporterin *die.*

**repose** [rɪ'pəʊz] *n literary* Ruhe *die.*

**repository** [rɪ'pɒzɪtrɪ] *(pl* **-ies)** *n* [store] Lager *das.*

**repossess** [ˌriːpəˈzes] *vt* wieder in Besitz nehmen.

**repossession** [ˌriːpəˈzeʃn] *n* Wiederinbesitznahme *die.*

**repossession order** *n gerichtliche Anweisung zur Wiederinbesitznahme.*

**reprehensible** [ˌreprɪˈhensəbl] *adj fml* verwerflich.

**represent** [ˌreprɪˈzent] *vt* - **1.** [act for] vertreten - **2.** [constitute, symbolize] darlstellen - **3.** [describe]: **to ~ sb/sthg as** jn/etw darlstellen als - **4.** *phr:* **to be well** OR **strongly ~ed** gut OR stark vertreten sein.

**representation** [ˌreprɪzen'teɪʃn] *n* - **1.** *(U)* POL [having a say] Repräsentation *die* - **2.** [depiction] Darstellung *die.*

➤ **representations** *npl fml:* **to make ~s to sb** sich mit einem Anliegen an jn wenden.

**representative** [ˌreprɪˈzentətɪv] *adj* - **1.** [acting for main group] stellvertretend - **2.** [typical]: **~ (of)** repräsentativ (für) <> *n* - **1.** [of company, organization, group] Vertreter *der,* -in *die* - **2.** *Am* POL Abgeordnete *der, die.*

**repress** [rɪ'pres] *vt* unterdrücken.

**repressed** [rɪ'prest] *adj* unterdrückt.

**repression** [rɪ'preʃn] *n (U)* Unterdrückung *die.*

**repressive** [rɪ'presɪv] *adj* repressiv.

**reprieve** [rɪ'priːv] *n* - **1.** [of death sentence] Begnadigung *die* - **2.** [respite] Gnadenfrist *die* <> *vt* begnadigen.

**reprimand** ['reprɪmɑːnd] *n* Tadel *der* <> *vt* tadeln.

**reprint** [*n* 'riːprɪnt, *vb* ˌriː'prɪnt] *n* Neuauflage *die* <> *vt* neu auf|legen.

**reprisal** [rɪ'praɪzl] *n* - **1.** [counterblow] Vergeltungsmaßnahme *die* - **2.** [revenge]: **in ~ (for)** als Vergeltung (für).

**reproach** [rɪ'prəʊtʃ] *n* Vorwurf *der;* **to be beyond ~** über jeden Vorwurf erhaben sein <> *vt:* **to ~ sb (for** OR **with sthg)** jm (wegen etw) Vorwürfe machen.

**reproachful** [rɪ'prəʊtʃfʊl] *adj* vorwurfsvoll.

**reprobate** ['reprəbeɪt] *n hum* Schuft *der.*

**reproduce** [ˌriːprə'djuːs] *vt* [copy] reproduzieren <> *vi* BIOL sich fort|pflanzen.

**reproduction** [ˌriːprə'dʌkʃn] *n* - **1.** [replica] Reproduktion *die;* **~ furniture** Stilmöbel *pl* - **2.** *(U)* [copying, simulation] Reproduktion *die;* **sound ~** Tonwiedergabe *die* - **3.** BIOL Fortpflanzung *die.*

**reproductive** [ˌriːprə'dʌktɪv] *adj* BIOL Fortpflanzungs-.

**reprogram** [ˌriː'prəʊgræm] *(pt & pp* **-ed** OR **-med;** *cont* **-ing** OR **-ming)** *vt* neu programmieren.

**reproof** [rɪ'pruːf] *n* Tadel *der.*

**reprove** [rɪ'pruːv] *vt:* **to ~ sb (for sthg)** jn (wegen etw) tadeln.

**reptile** ['reptaɪl] *n* Reptil *das.*

**Repub.** *n Am abbr of* **Republican.**

**republic** [rɪ'pʌblɪk] *n* Republik *die.*

**republican** [rɪ'pʌblɪkən] *adj* republikanisch <> *n* Republikaner *der,* -in *die.*

➤ **Republican** *adj* - **1.** [in USA] republikanisch; **the Republican Party** die Republikanische Partei - **2.** [in Northern Ireland] *bezeichnet einen Befürworter einer vereinten unabhängigen Republik Irland bzw. dessen Ideen* <> *n* - **1.** [in USA] Republikaner *der,* -in *die* - **2.** [in Northern Ireland] *Befürworter einer vereinten unabhängigen Republik Irland.*

**repudiate** [rɪ'pjuːdɪeɪt] *vt fml* zurück|weisen; [person] verstoßen.

**repudiation** [rɪˌpjuːdɪ'eɪʃn] *n (U) fml* Zurückweisung *die;* [of person] Verstoßung *die.*

**repugnant** [rɪ'pʌgnənt] *adj fml* abstoßend.

**repulse** [rɪ'pʌls] *vt* - **1.** [refuse] zurück|weisen; [person] verstoßen - **2.** MIL [drive back] ab|wehren.

**repulsion** [rɪ'pʌlʃn] *n* Widerwille *der.*

**repulsive** [rɪ'pʌlsɪv] *adj* abstoßend.

**reputable** ['repjʊtəbl] *adj* seriös.

**reputation** [ˌrepjʊ'teɪʃn] n Ruf der; **to have a ~ for being sthg** den Ruf haben, etw zu sein.

**repute** [rɪ'pju:t] n fml - **1.** [reputation]: **of good/ill ~** von gutem/schlechtem Ruf - **2.** [distinction]: **of ~** von Ruf.

**reputed** [rɪ'pju:tɪd] adj: **he is a ~ expert/ millionaire** er soll ein Fachmann/Millionär sein; **to be ~ to be** etw als etw gelten.

**reputedly** [rɪ'pju:tɪdlɪ] adv: **he is ~ the best surgeon** er gilt als der beste Chirurg.

**reqd** abbr of **required.**

**request** [rɪ'kwest] n: **~ (for sthg)** Bitte die (um etw); **on ~** auf Wunsch; **at her ~** auf ihren Wunsch ⟨> vt bitten um; **to ~ sb to do sthg** jn bitten, etw zu tun.

**request stop** n Br Bedarfshaltestelle die.

**requiem (mass)** ['rekwɪəm-] n Requiem das.

**require** [rɪ'kwaɪəʳ] vt erfordern; **to be ~d to do sthg** aufgefordert werden, etw zu tun.

**required** [rɪ'kwaɪəd] adj erforderlich.

**requirement** [rɪ'kwaɪəmənt] n - **1.** [condition] Erfordernis das - **2.** [need] Bedarf der.

**requisite** ['rekwɪzɪt] adj fml erforderlich.

**requisition** [ˌrekwɪ'zɪʃn] vt beschlagnahmen.

**reran** [ˌri:'ræn] pt ⟩ **rerun.**

**reread** [ˌri:'ri:d] (pt & pp **reread** [ˌri:'red]) vt wieder lesen.

**rerecord** [ˌri:rɪ'kɔ:d] vt neu auf Inehmen.

**reroute** [ˌri:'ru:t] vt umleiten.

**rerun** [n 'ri:rʌn, vb ˌri:'rʌn] (pt **reran**; pp **rerun**; cont **-ning**) n Wiederholung die ⟨> vt - **1.** [gen] wiederholen - **2.** [tape] wieder ablspielen.

**resale price maintenance** ['ri:seɪl-] n (U) Br FIN Preisbindung die.

**resat** [ˌri:'sæt] pt & pp ⟩ **resit.**

**reschedule** [Br ˌri:'ʃedjʊl, Am ˌri:'skedʒʊl] vt FIN [loan] umlschulden.

**rescind** [rɪ'sɪnd] vt LAW annulieren.

**rescue** ['reskju:] n Rettung die; **to go/come to sb's ~** jm zur Hilfe eilen/kommen ⟨> vt retten; **to ~ sb/sthg from sb/sthg** jn/etw vor jm/ aus etw retten.

**rescue operation** n Rettungsaktion die.

**rescuer** ['reskjʊəʳ] n Retter der, -in die.

**reseal** [ˌri:'si:l] vt wiederverschließen.

**resealable** [ˌri:'si:ləbl] adj wiederverschließbar.

**research** [rɪ'sɜ:tʃ] n (U): **~ (on OR into sthg)** Forschung die (über etw (A)); **~ and development** Forschung und Entwicklung ⟨> vt erforschen; [article, book] recherchieren ⟨> vi: **to ~ into sthg** etw erforschen.

**researcher** [rɪ'sɜ:tʃəʳ] n Forscher der, -in die.

**research work** n (U) Forschungsarbeit die.

**resell** [ˌri:'sell] (pt & pp **resold**) vt weiterlverkaufen.

**resemblance** [rɪ'zembləns] n: **~ (to/between)** Ähnlichkeit die (mit/zwischen (+ D)).

**resemble** [rɪ'zembl] vt ähneln.

**resent** [rɪ'zent] vt sich ärgern über (+ A); **I ~ that!** das ärgert mich!

**resentful** [rɪ'zentfʊl] adj verärgert.

**resentfully** [rɪ'zentfʊlɪ] adv ärgerlich.

**resentment** [rɪ'zentmənt] n Groll der.

**reservation** [ˌrezə'veɪʃn] n - **1.** [booking] Reservierung die - **2.** [doubt]: **without ~** ohne Vorbehalt - **3.** Am [for Native Americans] Reservat das.

↪ **reservations** npl [doubts] Vorbehalte pl.

**reserve** [rɪ'zɜ:v] n - **1.** [supply] Reserve die; **in ~** in Reserve - **2.** SPORT [substitute] Reservespieler der, -in die - **3.** [sanctuary] Reservat das - **4.** (U) [restraint, shyness] Reserve die ⟨> vt - **1.** [keep for particular purpose]: **to ~ sthg for sb/ sthg** etw für jn/etw reservieren - **2.** [book] reservieren - **3.** [retain]: **to ~ the right to do sthg** sich das Recht vorbehalten, etw zu tun.

**reserve bank** n Am Reservenbank die.

**reserve currency** n Leitwährung die. .

**reserved** [rɪ'zɜ:vd] adj reserviert.

**reserve price** n Br Mindestpreis der.

**reserve team** n Br Reservemannschaft die.

**reservist** [rɪ'zɜ:vɪst] n Reservist der, -in die.

**reservoir** ['rezəvwɑ:ʳ] n - **1.** [lake] Reservoir das - **2.** [large supply] Vorrat der.

**reset** [ˌri:'set] (pt & pp **reset**; cont **-ting**) vt - **1.** [clock] neu stellen; [meter] zurücklstellen - **2.** [bone] wieder einlrichten - **3.** COMPUT rücksetzen ⟨> vi COMPUT rücksetzen.

**resettle** [ˌri:'setl] vt - **1.** [land] neu besiedeln - **2.** [people] umlsiedeln ⟨> vi [people] umlsiedeln.

**resettlement** [ˌri:'setlmənt] n (U) - **1.** [of land] Neubesiedlung die - **2.** [of people] Umsiedlung die.

**reshape** [ˌri:'ʃeɪp] vt [policy, thinking] umlformen.

**reshuffle** [ˌri:'ʃʌfl] POL n Umbildung die; **cabinet ~** Kabinettsumbildung die ⟨> vt umlbilden.

**reside** [rɪ'zaɪd] vi fml - **1.** [live] seinen Wohnsitz haben - **2.** [be located, found]: **to ~ in sthg** in etw (D) liegen.

**residence** ['rezɪdəns] n - **1.** [house] Wohnsitz der - **2.** [state of residing]: **to be in ~** anwesend sein; **to take up ~** sich niederllassen.

**residence permit** n Aufenthaltserlaubnis die.

**resident** ['rezɪdənt] adj - **1.** [settled, living] wohn-

R

haft - **2.** [on-site, live-in] Haus- $\diamond$ n [of town, street] Bewohner der, -in die; [in hotel] Gast der.

**residential** [,rezɪ'denʃl] adj: ~ **course** Kurs, bei dem die Teilnehmer auf dem Schulgelände untergebracht werden; ~ **care** Pflege die im Haus.

**residential area** n Wohngebiet das.

**residents' association** n Bürgerinitiative die.

**residual** [rɪ'zɪdjʊəl] adj restlich.

**residue** ['rezɪdjuː] n CHEM Rückstand der.

**resign** [rɪ'zaɪn] vt - **1.** [give up - job] kündigen; [ - post] zurückltreten von - **2.** [accept calmly]: **to ~ o.s. to sthg** sich mit etw abfinden $\diamond$ vi [from job] kündigen; [from post] zurückltreten; **to ~ from one's job** seine Stelle kündigen.

**resignation** [,rezɪg'neɪʃn] n - **1.** [from job] Kündigung die; [from post] Rücktritt der - **2.** [calm acceptance] Resignation die.

**resigned** [rɪ'zaɪnd] adj: **to be ~ to sthg** sich mit etw abgefunden haben.

**resilience** [rɪ'zɪlɪəns] n [of person] Unverwüstlichkeit die.

**resilient** [rɪ'zɪlɪənt] adj - **1.** [material] elastisch - **2.** [person] unverwüstlich.

**resin** ['rezɪn] n (U) Harz das.

**resist** [rɪ'zɪst] vt Widerstand leisten gegen; [temptation, offer] widerstehen (+ D).

**resistance** [rɪ'zɪstəns] n (U): ~ **(to sthg)** Widerstand der (gegen etw).

**resistant** [rɪ'zɪstənt] adj - **1.** [opposed]: **to be ~ to sthg** sich einer Sache (D) widersetzen - **2.** MED [immune]: ~ **to sthg** immun gegen etw.

**resistor** [rɪ'zɪstəʳ] n ELEC Widerstand der.

**resit** [n 'riːsɪt, vb ,riː'sɪt] (pt & pp resat; cont -ting) Br n Wiederholungsprüfung die $\diamond$ vt wiederholen.

**resold** [,riː'səʊld] pt & pp $\triangleright$ resell.

**resolute** ['rezəluːt] adj energisch.

**resolutely** ['rezəluːtlɪ] adv entschlossen.

**resolution** [,rezə'luːʃn] n - **1.** [motion, decision] Resolution die - **2.** [vow, promise] Vorsatz der - **3.** [determination] Entschlossenheit die - **4.** (U) [solution - of problem] Lösung die; [ - of dispute, argument] Beilegung die.

**resolve** [rɪ'zɒlv] n [determination] Entschlossenheit die $\diamond$ vt - **1.** [vow, promise]: **to ~ that ...** beschließen, dass ...; **to ~ to do sthg** sich entschließen, etw zu tun - **2.** [solve - problem] lösen; [ - dispute, argument] beilegen.

**resonance** ['rezənəns] n (U) [of voice, sound] Resonanz die.

**resonant** ['rezənənt] adj [voice, sound] voll.

**resonate** ['rezəneɪt] vi widerlhallen.

**resort** [rɪ'zɔːt] n - **1.** [for holidays] Urlaubsort der

- **2.** [solution]: **as a last ~** als letzte Möglichkeit; **in the last ~** im schlimmsten Fall.

$\rightarrow$ **resort to** vt fus [lying, begging] sich verlegen auf (+ A); [violence] anlwenden.

**resound** [rɪ'zaʊnd] vi - **1.** [noise] schallen - **2.** [place]: **to ~ with** widerlhallen von.

**resounding** [rɪ'zaʊndɪŋ] adj - **1.** [noise, voice] schallend - **2.** [success, victory] gewaltig.

**resource** [rɪ'zɔːs] n [asset] Resourcen pl; **natural ~s** Naturschätze pl.

**resourceful** [rɪ'zɔːsfʊl] adj einfallsreich.

**resourcefulness** [rɪ'zɔːsfʊlnɪs] n Einfallsreichtum der.

**respect** [rɪ'spekt] n - **1.** (U) [admiration]: ~ **(for)** Respekt der (vor (+ D)); **with ~, ...** bei allem Respekt, ... - **2.** (U) [observance]: ~ **for sthg** Achtung die vor etw (D) - **3.** [aspect] Hinsicht die; **in this/that ~** in dieser/jener Hinsicht $\diamond$ vt - **1.** [admire] anlerkennen; **to ~ sb for sthg** jn für etw respektieren - **2.** [observe] achten.

$\rightarrow$ **respects** npl Grüße pl; **give my ~s to your wife** grüßen Sie Ihre Frau von mir; **to pay one's last ~s to sb** jm die letzte Ehre erweisen.

$\rightarrow$ **with respect to** prep in Bezug auf (+ A).

**respectability** [rɪ,spektə'bɪlətɪ] n Ehrbarkeit die.

**respectable** [rɪ'spektəbl] adj - **1.** [morally correct] ehrbar - **2.** [adequate, quite good] ansehnlich.

**respectably** [rɪ'spektəblɪ] adv [correctly] anständig.

**respected** [rɪ'spektɪd] adj angesehen.

**respectful** [rɪ'spektfʊl] adj respektvoll.

**respectfully** [rɪ'spektfʊlɪ] adv respektvoll.

**respective** [rɪ'spektɪv] adj jeweilig.

**respectively** [rɪ'spektɪvlɪ] adv beziehungsweise; **Jill and John are four and six years old ~** Jill and John sind vier beziehungsweise sechs Jahre alt.

**respiration** [,respə'reɪʃn] n Atmung die.

**respirator** ['respəreɪtəʳ] n - **1.** [gas mask] Atemschutzmaske die - **2.** [machine] Respirator der.

**respiratory** [Br rɪ'spɪrətrɪ, Am 'respərətɔːrɪ] adj [system, function] Atmungs-; [disease] Atemweg(s)-.

**respite** ['respaɪt] n - **1.** [pause] Atempause die; **without ~** ohne Unterbrechung - **2.** [delay] Aufschub der.

**resplendent** [rɪ'splendənt] adj literary prachtvoll.

**respond** [rɪ'spɒnd] vt antworten $\diamond$ vi: **to ~ (to sthg)** antworten (auf etw (A)); **they ~ed by ignoring us completely** ihre Reaktion war, uns völlig zu ignorieren.

**response** [rɪ'spɒns] n Antwort die; **in ~ (to)** als Antwort (auf (+ A)).

**responsibility** [rɪˌspɒnsə'bɪlətɪ] (pl -ies) n - **1.** [charge, blame]: ~ **(for sthg)** Verantwortung die (für etw) - **2.** [duty - of job, position] Aufgabe die; [ - to sb else]: ~ **(to sb)** Verantwortung die (jm gegenüber).

**responsible** [rɪ'spɒnsəbl] adj - **1.** [in charge, to blame]: ~ **(for sthg)** verantwortlich (für etw) - **2.** [answerable]: ~ **to sb** jm (gegenüber) verantwortlich - **3.** [sensible] vernünftig - **4.** [position, task] verantwortungsvoll.

**responsibly** [rɪ'spɒnsəblɪ] adv verantwortungsbewusst.

**responsive** [rɪ'spɒnsɪv] adj: **to be** ~ [audience] mitlgehen; [class] mitlmachen; **to be** ~ **to sthg** [to criticism, praise] für etw empfänglich sein; [to sb's needs] gegenüber etw aufmerksam sein.

**respray** [n 'riːspreɪ, vb ˌriː'spreɪ] n Umspritzen das <> vt umspritzen.

**rest** [rest] n - **1.** [remainder]: **the** ~ der Rest; **the** ~ **of the cake/customers** der Rest des Kuchens/der Kunden - **2.** [relaxation] Ruhe die - **3.** [break] Pause die - **4.** [support] Stütze die - **5.** phr: **to come to** ~ zum Stillstand kommen <> vt - **1.** [relax] auslruhen - **2.** [support, lean]: **to** ~ **sthg on/against sthg** etw auf (+ A)/gegen etw lehnen - **3.** phr: ~ **assured (that) ...** seien Sie versichert, dass ... <> vi - **1.** [relax, be still] sich auslruhen - **2.** [depend]: **to** ~ **(up)on sb/sthg** von jm/etw abhängen - **3.** [duty, responsibility, decision]: **to** ~ **with sb** bei jm liegen - **4.** [be supported]: **to** ~ **on sthg** auf etw (D) ruhen; **to** ~ **against sthg** an etw (D) lehnen.

**rest area** n Am & Austr Rastplatz der.

**restart** [n 'riːstɑːt, vb ˌriː'stɑːt] n COMPUT Neustart der <> vt - **1.** [vehicle, engine] wieder anllassen - **2.** [work] wieder auflnehmen <> vi - **1.** [play, film] weiterlgehen - **2.** [vehicle, engine] wieder anlspringen.

**restate** [ˌriː'steɪt] vt [one's position] erneut vorltragen; [problem] neu darlstellen.

**restaurant** ['restərɒnt] n Restaurant das.

**restaurant car** n Br Speisewagen der.

**rest cure** n Liegekur die.

**rested** ['restɪd] adj ausgeruht.

**restful** ['restfʊl] adj ruhig.

**rest home** n Pflegeheim das.

**resting place** ['restɪŋ-] n: **(final)** ~ (letzte) Ruhestätte.

**restitution** [ˌrestɪ'tjuːʃn] n fml Rückgabe die.

**restive** ['restɪv] adj unruhig.

**restless** ['restlɪs] adj - **1.** [bored, fidgety] rastlos - **2.** [sleepless] schlaflos.

**restlessly** ['restlɪslɪ] adv - **1.** [impatiently] rastlos - **2.** [sleeplessly] schlaflos.

**restock** [ˌriː'stɒk] vt wieder auflfüllen <> vi [in shop] die Bestände erneuen.

**restoration** [ˌrestə'reɪʃn] n (U) - **1.** [reestablish-ment] Wiederherstellung die - **2.** [renovation] Restaurierung die.

**restorative** [rɪ'stɒrətɪv] adj fml stärkend.

**restore** [rɪ'stɔːʳ] vt - **1.** [reestablish] wieder herlstellen; **I feel completely** ~**d to health** ich fühle mich komplett wiederhergestellt; **the palace has been** ~**d to its former glory** dem Palast ist seine alte Pracht wiedergegeben worden - **2.** [renovate] restaurieren - **3.** [give back] zurücklgeben.

**restorer** [rɪ'stɔːrəʳ] n - **1.** [person] Restaurator der, -in die - **2.** [substance]: **hair** ~ Haarwuchsmittel das.

**restrain** [rɪ'streɪn] vt - **1.** [hold back] zurücklhalten; **to** ~ **o.s. from doing sthg** sich zurücklhalten (davon), etw zu tun - **2.** [dog, attacker] bändigen - **3.** [repress] unterdrücken.

**restrained** [rɪ'streɪnd] adj - **1.** [person] beherrscht - **2.** [tone] verhalten.

**restraint** [rɪ'streɪnt] n - **1.** [rule, check] Beschränkung die - **2.** [self-control] Selbstbeherrschung die.

**restrict** [rɪ'strɪkt] vt [limit] einlschränken; **to** ~ **sb/sthg to sthg/sb** jn/etw auf jn/etw beschränken; **to** ~ **o.s. to sthg** sich auf etw (A) beschränken.

**restricted** [rɪ'strɪktɪd] adj - **1.** [limited, small] eingeschränkt - **2.** [classified, not public] geheim; ~ **area** Sperrgebiet das.

**restriction** [rɪ'strɪkʃn] n [limitation, regulation] Einschränkung die; **import** ~**s** Importbeschränkungen; **to place** ~**s on sthg** etw einlschränken.

**restrictive** [rɪ'strɪktɪv] adj einschränkend.

**restrictive practices** npl wettbewerbsbeschränkende Geschäftspraktiken pl.

**rest room** n Am Toilette die.

**restructure** [ˌriː'strʌktʃəʳ] vt umlstrukturieren.

**result** [rɪ'zʌlt] n - **1.** [gen] Ergebnis das - **2.** [consequence] Folge die; **as a** ~ folglich; **as a** ~ **of sthg** als Folge von etw <> vi: **to** ~ **in sthg** zu etw führen; **to** ~ **from sthg** aus etw folgen.

**resultant** [rɪ'zʌltənt] adj fml resultierend.

**resume** [rɪ'zjuːm] vt - **1.** [activity] wieder auflnehmen - **2.** fml: **to** ~ **one's seat** seinen Platz einlnehmen <> vi wieder beginnen.

**résumé** ['rezjuːmeɪ] n - **1.** [summary] Resümee das, Zusammenfassung die - **2.** Am [of career, qualifications] Lebenslauf der.

**resumption** [rɪ'zʌmpʃn] n Wiederaufnahme die.

**resurface** [ˌriː'sɜːfɪs] vt neu belegen <> vi wieder aufltauchen.

**resurgence** [rɪ'sɜːdʒəns] n Wiederaufleben das.

R

**resurrect** [ˌrezə'rekt] vt [policy, festival, legal case] wieder beleben.

**resurrection** [ˌrezə'rekʃn] n [of policy, festival, legal case] Wiederbelebung die.
◆ **Resurrection** n RELIG: **the Resurrection** die Auferstehung.

**resuscitate** [rɪ'sʌsɪteɪt] vt wieder beleben.

**resuscitation** [rɪˌsʌsɪ'teɪʃn] n Wiederbelebung die.

**retail** ['riːteɪl] n Einzelhandel der ◇ adv im Einzelhandel ◇ vi: **it ~s at £10** es kostet im Einzelhandel 10 Pfund.

**retailer** ['riːteɪləʳ] n Einzelhändler der, -in die.

**retail outlet** n Einzelhandelsgeschäft das.

**retail price** n Einzelhandelspreis der.

**retail price index** n Br Einzelhandelspreisindex der.

**retain** [rɪ'teɪn] vt - **1.** [pride, power, independence] behalten - **2.** [heat] speichern.

**retainer** [rɪ'teɪnəʳ] n - **1.** [fee] Vorschuss der - **2.** [servant] Faktotum das.

**retaining wall** [rɪ'teɪnɪŋ-] n Stützmauer die.

**retaliate** [rɪ'tælɪeɪt] vi zurücklschlagen.

**retaliation** [rɪˌtælɪ'eɪʃn] n Vergeltung die.

**retarded** [rɪ'tɑːdɪd] adj offensive [child] zurückgeblieben.

**retch** [retʃ] vi würgen.

**retention** [rɪ'tenʃn] n - **1.** [of pride, power, independence] Beibehaltung die - **2.** [of heat] Speicherung die.

**retentive** [rɪ'tentɪv] adj [memory] aufnahmefähig.

**rethink** [n ˈriːθɪŋk, vb ˌriː'θɪŋk] (pt & pp -thought [-'θɔːt]) n: **to have a ~ about** sthg etw noch einmal überdenken ◇ vt überdenken ◇ vi umldenken.

**reticence** ['retɪsəns] n Zurückhaltung die.

**reticent** ['retɪsənt] adj zurückhaltend.

**retina** ['retɪnə] (pl -nas OR -nae [-niː]) n Netzhaut die, Retina die.

**retinue** ['retɪnjuː] n Gefolge das.

**retire** [rɪ'taɪəʳ] vi - **1.** [from work] in den Ruhestand treten - **2.** fml [to another place, to bed] sich zurücklziehen.

**retired** [rɪ'taɪəd] adj pensioniert; **to be ~** im Ruhestand sein.

**retirement** [rɪ'taɪəmənt] n (U) - **1.** [act of retiring] Pensionierung die - **2.** [life after work] Ruhestand der.

**retirement age** n Rentenalter das.

**retirement pension** n Altersruhegeld das.

**retiring** [rɪ'taɪərɪŋ] adj [shy] zurückhaltend.

**retort** [rɪ'tɔːt] n [sharp reply] (scharfe) Erwiderung ◇ vt: **to ~ that ...** erwidern, dass ...

**retouch** [ˌriː'tʌtʃ] vt retuschieren.

**retrace** [rɪ'treɪs] vt: **to ~ one's steps** denselben Weg zurücklgehen.

**retract** [rɪ'trækt] vt - **1.** [take back] zurücknehmen - **2.** [draw in] einlziehen ◇ vi - **1.** [recant] einen Rückzieher machen - **2.** [be drawn in] eingezogen werden.

**retractable** [rɪ'træktəbl] adj einziehbar.

**retraction** [rɪ'trækʃn] n [written apology] Zurücknahme die.

**retrain** [ˌriː'treɪn] vt umlschulen ◇ vi sich umschulen lassen.

**retraining** [ˌriː'treɪnɪŋ] n Umschulung die.

**retread** ['riːtred] n runderneuerter Reifen.

**retreat** [rɪ'triːt] n - **1.** MIL [withdrawal]: **~ (from)** Rückzug der (aus) - **2.** fig [departure]: **to beat a (hasty) ~** sich (hastig) zurücklziehen - **3.** [refuge] Zuflucht die ◇ vi - **1.** [withdraw]: **to ~ (to)** sich zurücklziehen (in (+ A)); **she ~ed hastily** sie wich hastig zurück - **2.** MIL: **to ~ (from)** den Rückzug anltreten (aus) - **3.** [from principle, policy, lifestyle]: **to ~ from** sthg etw auf lgeben; **to ~ from public life** sich aus der Öffentlichkeit zurücklziehen.

**retrenchment** [ˌriː'trentʃmənt] n fml [of spending] Einsparung die.

**retrial** ['riːtraɪəl] n Wiederaufnahmeverfahren das.

**retribution** [ˌretrɪ'bjuːʃn] n Vergeltung die.

**retrieval** [rɪ'triːvl] n COMPUT Wiederauffinden das.

**retrieve** [rɪ'triːv] vt - **1.** [get back] zurücklbekommen - **2.** COMPUT wiederauffinden - **3.** [situation] retten.

**retriever** [rɪ'triːvəʳ] n [dog] Apportierhund der; [of specific breed] Retriever der.

**retroactive** [ˌretrəʊ'æktɪv] adj fml rückwirkend.

**retrograde** ['retrəgreɪd] adj fml: **~ step** Rückschritt der.

**retrogressive** [ˌretrə'gresɪv] adj fml: **~ step** Rückschritt der.

**retrospect** ['retrəspekt] n: **in ~** im Nachhinein.

**retrospective** [ˌretrə'spektɪv] adj - **1.** [mood] (zu)rückblickend; **~ look** Blick der zurück - **2.** [law, pay rise] rückwirkend ◇ n Retrospektive die.

**retrospectively** [ˌretrə'spektɪvlɪ] adv - **1.** [describe, feel] rückblickend - **2.** [come into force, pay] rückwirkend.

**return** [rɪ'tɜːn] n - **1.** [arrival back]: **~ (to)** Rückkehr die (nach); **~ to sthg** fig Rückkehr die zu etw - **2.** [giving back] Rückgabe die - **3.** TENNIS Return der - **4.** Br [ticket] Rückfahrkarte die; [for plane] Rückflugticket das - **5.** [profit] Ertrag der - **6.** COMPUT [on keyboard] Eingabetaste die

◇ comp [journey] Rück- ◇ vt - **1.** [give back] zurücklgeben; [loan] zurücklzahlen - **2.** [visit, compliment, love] erwidern - **3.** [replace] zurücklstellen - **4.** LAW [verdict] fällen - **5.** POL [candidate] wählen ◇ vi [come back] zurücklkommen; [go back] zurücklgehen; [pain] wiederlkehren; **to ~ from Germany** aus Deutschland zurücklkehren OR zurücklkommen; **to ~ to London** nach London zurücklkehren OR zurücklkommen; **to ~ to work** wieder arbeiten; **to ~ to a subject** auf ein Thema zurücklkommen.

➼ **returns** npl - **1.** COMM Gewinn der - **2.** [on birthday]: **many happy ~s (of the day)!** herzlichen Glückwunsch (zum Geburtstag)!

➼ **in return** adv dafür.

➼ **in return for** prep für.

**returnable** [rɪˈtɜːnəbl] adj [reusable] Mehrweg-.

**returning officer** [rɪˈtɜːnɪŋ-] n Br Wahlleiter der, -in die.

**return key** n COMPUT Eingabetaste die.

**return match** n Rückspiel das.

**return ticket** n Br Rückfahrkarte die.

**reunification** [ˌriːjuːnɪfɪˈkeɪʃn] n Wiedervereinigung die.

**reunion** [ˌriːˈjuːnjən] n - **1.** [party] Treffen das - **2.** (U) [meeting again] Wiedersehen das.

**reunite** [ˌriːjuːˈnaɪt] vt wieder vereinigen; **to be ~d with sb/sthg** mit jm/etw wieder vereint sein.

**reusable** [riːˈjuːzəbl] adj wieder verwendbar.

**reuse** [n ˌriːˈjuːs, vb ˌriːˈjuːz] n Wiederverwendung die ◇ vt wieder verwenden.

**rev** [rev] (pt & pp -**ved**; cont -**ving**) inf n (abbr of revolution) Umdrehung die ◇ vt: **to ~ the engine (up)** den Motor hoch drehen lassen ◇ vi: **to ~ (up)** [driver] den Motor aufheulen lassen; [engine] hoch drehen.

**revalue** [ˌriːˈvæljuː] vt - **1.** [house, painting] neu schätzen - **2.** FIN [currency] auf lwerten.

**revamp** [ˌriːˈvæmp] vt inf - **1.** [reorganize] auf Vordermann bringen - **2.** [redecorate] auf lmöbeln.

**rev counter** n Drehzahlmesser der.

**reveal** [rɪˈviːl] vt enthüllen.

**revealing** [rɪˈviːlɪŋ] adj - **1.** [dress, blouse] offenherzig - **2.** [comment] aufschlussreich.

**reveille** [Br rɪˈvælɪ, Am ˈrevəlɪ] n Wecksignal das, Reveille die.

**revel** [ˈrevl] (Br pt & pp -**led**; cont -**ling**, Am pt & pp -**ed**; cont -**ing**) vi: **to ~ in sthg** [freedom, success] etw in vollen Zügen genießen; [gossip] in etw (D) schwelgen.

**revelation** [ˌrevəˈleɪʃn] n - **1.** [surprising fact] Enthüllung die - **2.** [surprising experience] Offen-

barung die; **to be a ~ to sb** jm die Augen öffnen.

**reveller** Br, **reveler** Am [ˈrevələr] n Feiernde der, die.

**revelry** [ˈrevlrɪ] n Feiern das.

**revenge** [rɪˈvendʒ] n Rache die; [in game] Revanche die; **to take ~ (on sb)** sich (an jm) rächen ◇ comp Rache-; **~ match** Revanche die ◇ vt rächen; **to ~ o.s. on sb/sthg** sich an jm/ etw rächen.

**revenue** [ˈrevənjuː] n [income] Einnahmen pl; [of State] Staatseinnahmen pl.

**reverberate** [rɪˈvɜːbəreɪt] vi - **1.** [re-echo] widerlhallen; [shock wave] sich fortlsetzen - **2.** [have repercussions] Auswirkungen haben.

**reverberations** [rɪˌvɜːbəˈreɪʃnz] npl - **1.** [echoes] Widerhall der - **2.** [repercussions] Auswirkungen pl.

**revere** [rɪˈvɪər] vt fml verehren.

**reverence** [ˈrevərəns] n fml Ehrfurcht die.

**Reverend** [ˈrevərənd] n: **(the) ~ Peter James** Pfarrer Peter James.

**Reverend Mother** n Mutter Oberin die.

**reverent** [ˈrevərənt] adj ehrfürchtig.

**reverential** [ˌrevəˈrenʃl] adj fml ehrerbietig.

**reverie** [ˈrevərɪ] n fml Träumerei die.

**reversal** [rɪˈvɜːsl] n - **1.** [of order, position, trend] Umkehrung die; [of decision] Umstoßung die; [of roles] Vertauschung die; **~ of policy** Umschwung der in der Politik - **2.** [piece of ill luck] Rückschlag der.

**reverse** [rɪˈvɜːs] adj umgekehrt; [side] Rück- ◇ n - **1.** AUT: **~ (gear)** Rückwärtsgang der; **to be in ~** im Rückwärtsgang sein; **to go into ~** den Rückwärtsgang einlegen - **2.** [opposite]: **the ~** das Gegenteil - **3.** [back]: **the ~** die Rückseite; [of coin] die Kehrseite ◇ vt - **1.** AUT rückwärts fahren mit - **2.** [order, position, trend] umlkehren; [decision] umlstoßen; [roles] tauschen; **to ~ one's policy** eine entgegengesetzte Politik einlschlagen - **3.** [turn over] umldrehen - **4.** Br TELEC: **to ~ the charges** ein R-Gespräch führen ◇ vi AUT rückwärts fahren.

**reverse-charge call** n Br R-Gespräch das.

**reversible** [rɪˈvɜːsəbl] adj - **1.** [jacket, coat] Wende- - **2.** [process] umkehrbar; [decision] umstoßbar.

**reversing light** [rɪˈvɜːsɪŋ-] n Br Rückfahrscheinwerfer der.

**revert** [rɪˈvɜːt] vi: **to ~ to sthg** zu etw zurücklkehren; **to ~ to type** fig wieder in die alten Gewohnheiten verfallen.

**review** [rɪˈvjuː] n - **1.** [examination] Überprüfung die; **it comes up for ~ next month** es soll nächsten Monat überprüft werden; **to be under ~** überprüft werden - **2.** [critique] Be-

R

sprechung *die*, Rezension *die* ◇ *vt* - **1.** [reassess] überprüfen - **2.** [write critique of] besprechen - **3.** [troops] inspizieren, mustern - **4.** *Am* [study] wiederlholen.

**reviewer** [rɪ'vjuːəʳ] *n* Rezensent *der*, -in *die*.

**revile** [rɪ'vaɪl] *vt literary* schmähen.

**revise** [rɪ'vaɪz] *vt* - **1.** [alter] revidieren - **2.** [rewrite] überarbeiten - **3.** *Br* [study] wiederholen ◇ *vi Br:* **to ~ (for sthg)** den Stoff (für etw) wiederholen.

**revised** [rɪ'vaɪzd] *adj* [estimate, figures] revidiert; [version] überarbeitet.

**revision** [rɪ'vɪʒn] *n* - **1.** [alteration] Revision *die* - **2.** *Br* [study]: **to do some ~** den Stoff wiederholen.

**revisionist** [rɪ'vɪʒnɪst] *adj* revisionistisch ◇ *n* Revisionist *der*, -in *die*.

**revisit** [ˌriː'vɪzɪt] *vt* wieder OR nochmals besuchen.

**revitalize, -ise** [ˌriː'vaɪtəlaɪz] *vt* wieder beleben.

**revival** [rɪ'vaɪvl] *n* [of economy, interest] Wiederbelebung *die*.

**revive** [rɪ'vaɪv] *vt* wieder beleben; [tradition, memories] wieder aufleben lassen; [play] wieder auflführen ◇ *vi* - **1.** [regain consciousness] wieder zu sich kommen - **2.** [plant, economy, interest] wieder aufleben, wieder erblühen.

**revoke** [rɪ'vəʊk] *vt fml* widerrufen.

**revolt** [rɪ'vəʊlt] *n* Aufstand *der*, Revolte *die* ◇ *vt* anlwidern ◇ *vi:* **to ~ (against)** revoltieren (gegen).

**revolting** [rɪ'vəʊltɪŋ] *adj* widerlich.

**revolution** [ˌrevə'luːʃn] *n* - **1.** POL & *fig* Revolution *die* - **2.** TECH [circular movement] Umdrehung *die*.

**revolutionary** [ˌrevə'luːʃnərɪ] (*pl* -ies) *adj lit* & *fig* revolutionär ◇ *n* POL Revolutionär *der*, -in *die*.

**revolutionize, -ise** [ˌrevə'luːʃənaɪz] *vt* revolutionieren.

**revolve** [rɪ'vɒlv] *vi* sich drehen; **to ~ (a)round** *lit* & *fig* sich drehen um.

**revolver** [rɪ'vɒlvəʳ] *n* Revolver *der*.

**revolving** [rɪ'vɒlvɪŋ] *adj* Dreh-.

**revolving door** *n* Drehtür *die*.

**revue** [rɪ'vjuː] *n* Revue *die*.

**revulsion** [rɪ'vʌlʃn] *n* Ekel *der*.

**reward** [rɪ'wɔːd] *n* Belohnung *die* ◇ *vt* belohnen; **to ~ sb for/with sthg** jn für/mit etw belohnen.

**rewarding** [rɪ'wɔːdɪŋ] *adj* lohnend; **it is a ~ book** es lohnt sich, das Buch zu lesen.

**rewind** [ˌriː'waɪnd] (*pt* & *pp* **rewound**) *vt* [tape] zurücklspulen.

**rewire** [ˌriː'waɪəʳ] *vt* [house] neu verkabeln; [plug] neu anlschließen.

**reword** [ˌriː'wɜːd] *vt* neu formulieren.

**rework** [ˌriː'wɜːk] *vt* überarbeiten.

**rewound** [ˌriː'waʊnd] *pt* & *pp* ⊳ **rewind.**

**rewrite** [ˌriː'raɪt] (*pt* **rewrote** [ˌriː'rəʊt]; *pp* **rewritten** [ˌriː'rɪtn]) *vt* neu schreiben.

**Reykjavik** ['rekjəvɪk] *n* Reykjavik *nt*.

**RFC** (*abbr of* **Rugby Football Club**) *n* Kürzel *von* Rugbyvereinen.

**RGN** (*abbr of* **registered general nurse**) *n* examinierte Krankenschwester *oder* examinierter Krankenpfleger in Großbritannien.

**Rh** *abbr of* **rhesus.**

**rhapsody** ['ræpsədɪ] (*pl* -ies) *n* - **1.** MUS Rhapsodie *die* - **2.** [strong approval]: **to go into rhapsodies over sthg** von etw zu schwärmen beginnen.

**Rhesus** ['riːsəs] *n:* **~ positive/negative** Rhesus positiv/negativ.

**rhetoric** ['retərɪk] *n* (*U*) [effective speech, writing] Rhetorik *die*.

**rhetorical question** [rɪ'tɒrɪkl-] *n* rhetorische Frage.

**rheumatic** [ruː'mætɪk] *adj* rheumatisch.

**rheumatism** ['ruːmətɪzm] *n* Rheuma *das*.

**rheumatoid arthritis** ['ruːmətɔɪd-] *n* chronischer Gelenkrheumatismus.

**Rhine** [raɪn] *n:* **the ~** der Rhein.

**rhinestone** ['raɪnstəʊn] *n* Rheinkiesel *der*.

**rhino** ['raɪnəʊ] (*pl inv* OR -s) *n inf* Nashorn *das*, Rhinozeros *das*.

**rhinoceros, rhinoceros** [raɪ'nɒsərəs] (*pl inv* OR -es) *n* Nashorn *das*, Rhinozeros *das*.

**Rhodes** [rəʊdz] *n* Rhodos *nt*.

**rhododendron** [ˌrəʊdə'dendrən] *n* Rhododendron *der* OR *das*.

**rhubarb** ['ruːbɑːb] *n* Rhabarber *der*.

**rhyme** [raɪm] *n* Reim *der;* **to be in ~** gereimt sein ◇ *vi:* **to ~ (with sthg)** sich (mit etw) reimen.

**rhyming slang** ['raɪmɪŋ-] *n Br* Slang, *der vorwiegend von den Sprechern des Cockney-Englisch verwendet wird, bei dem ein Wort durch ein sich darauf reimendes ersetzt wird.*

**RHYMING SLANG**

Bei dem für den Londoner Cockney-Dialekt typischen Rhyming Slang, ursprünglich eine Art Geheimsprache unter Straßenhändlern, werden an Stelle des gemeinten Wortes Worte oder Wortgruppen benutzt, die sich damit reimen (z. B. „pork pie" für „lie"/Lüge). Oft wird der Reim auf das erste Wort verkürzt („porkie" für „lie").

**rhythm** ['rɪðm] *n* Rhythmus *der*.

**rhythm and blues** n Rhythm and Blues der.

**rhythmic(al)** ['rɪðmɪk(l)] adj rhythmisch.

**RI** n (abbr of **religious instruction**) Religionsunterricht der <> abk für Rhode Island, in Postanschrift verwendet.

**rib** [rɪb] n [of body, framework] Rippe die.

**ribald** ['rɪbəld] adj [remark] zotig; [humour, laughter] derb.

**ribbed** [rɪbd] adj gerippt.

**ribbon** ['rɪbən] n - **1.** [for decoration] Band das - **2.** [for typewriter] Farbband das.

**rib cage** n Brustkorb der.

**rice** [raɪs] n Reis der.

**rice field** n Reisfeld das.

**rice paper** n (U) Reispapier das.

**rice pudding** n Milchreis der.

**rich** [rɪtʃ] adj - **1.** [gen] reich; **to be ~ in sthg** reich an etw (D) sein - **2.** [soil] fruchtbar - **3.** [food, cake] schwer - **4.** [colour] satt; [sound] voll, satt - **5.** [fabric, clothes] prächtig <> npl: **the ~** die Reichen pl.
➡ **riches** npl Reichtümer pl.

**richly** ['rɪtʃlɪ] adv - **1.** [well - rewarded] reich; **~ deserved** reichlich verdient - **2.** [abundantly] reichlich - **3.** [sumptuously, expensively] reich.

**richness** ['rɪtʃnɪs] n (U) - **1.** [of deposit] Reichtum der - **2.** [of soil] Fruchtbarkeit die - **3.** [of food] Schwere die - **4.** [of colour, sound] Sattheit die - **5.** [of fabric, clothes] Pracht die.

**Richter scale** ['rɪktə'-] n: **the ~** die Richterskala.

**rickets** ['rɪkɪts] n (U) Rachitis die.

**rickety** ['rɪkətɪ] adj wackelig.

**rickshaw** ['rɪkʃɔː] n Rikscha die.

**ricochet** ['rɪkəʃeɪ] (pt & pp **-ed** OR **-ted**; cont **-ing** OR **-ting**) n Abprall der <> vi: **to ~ (off sthg)** (von etw) abprallen.

**rid** [rɪd] (pt rid OR **-ded**; pp rid; cont **-ding**) adj: **to be/get ~ of sb/sthg** jn/etw los sein/loswerden <> vt: **to ~ sb/sthg of sthg** jn/etw von etw befreien; **to ~ o.s. of sthg** sich von etw befreien.

**riddance** ['rɪdəns] n inf: **good ~!** den/die/das sind wir glücklich los!

**ridden** ['rɪdn] pp ⊳ ride.

**riddle** ['rɪdl] n Rätsel das.

**riddled** ['rɪdld] adj: **to be ~ with holes** ganz durchlöchert sein; **to be ~ with errors** voller Fehler sein.

**ride** [raɪd] (pt rode; pp ridden) n - **1.** [on horseback] Ritt der; **to go for a ~** reiten gehen - **2.** [on bicycle, motorbike, in car] Fahrt die; **to go for a ~** eine Fahrt/Tour machen - **3.** phr: **to take sb for a ~** inf [trick] jn reinllegen <> vt - **1.** [horse] reiten - **2.** [bicycle, motorbike] fahren; **to ~ a bicycle/**

**motorbike** Rad/Motorrad fahren - **3.** [distance - on horse] reiten; [ - on bicycle, motorbike] fahren - **4.** Am [train, bus, elevator] fahren mit <> vi - **1.** [on horseback] reiten - **2.** [on bicycle, motorbike] fahren - **3.** [in car, bus]: **to ~ in sthg** mit etw fahren.
➡ **ride up** vi [skirt] hoch rutschen.

**rider** ['raɪdə'] n - **1.** [on horseback] Reiter der, -in die - **2.** [on bicycle, motorbike] Fahrer der, -in die.

**ridge** [rɪdʒ] n - **1.** [on mountain] Kamm der, Rücken der - **2.** [on flat surface] Riffel die.

**ridicule** ['rɪdɪkjuːl] n Spott der <> vt lächerlich machen, verspotten.

**ridiculous** [rɪ'dɪkjʊləs] adj lächerlich.

**ridiculously** [rɪ'dɪkjʊləslɪ] adv lächerlich.

**riding** ['raɪdɪŋ] n Reiten das <> comp Reit-.

**riding crop** n Reitgerte die.

**riding habit** n Reitkostüm das.

**riding school** n Reitschule die.

**rife** [raɪf] adj: **to be ~** grassieren; **to be ~ with sthg** von etw voll sein, voller einer Sache (G) sein.

**riffraff** ['rɪfræf] n Gesindel das.

**rifle** ['raɪfl] n Gewehr das.
➡ **rifle through** vt fus durchwühlen.

**rifle range** n Schießstand der.

**rift** [rɪft] n - **1.** GEOL Spalt der - **2.** [quarrel]: **a ~ between** eine Kluft zwischen (+ D); **a ~ in their friendship** ein Riss in ihrer Freundschaft.

**rig** [rɪg] (pt & pp **-ged**; cont **-ging**) n: **(oil) ~** Bohrinsel die <> vt [fix outcome of] manipulieren.
➡ **rig up** vt sep auf lstellen, montieren.

**rigging** ['rɪgɪŋ] n (U) [on ship] Takelung die.

**right** [raɪt] adj - **1.** [gen] richtig; **have you got the ~ time?** haben Sie die genaue Zeit?; **to be ~ (about sthg)** (bezüglich etw) Recht haben; **to be ~ to do sthg** Recht haben, etw zu tun; **to get the answer ~** die richtige Antwort geben - **2.** [going well]: **things aren't ~ between them** sie kommen nicht gut miteinander aus; **a cup of tea will soon put you ~** eine Tasse Tee wird dir gut tun - **3.** [not left] rechte, -r, -s - **4.** Br inf [idiot, mess] richtig, total <> n - **1.** [moral correctness, entitlement] Recht das; **to be in the ~** im Recht sein; **human ~s** Menschenrechte pl; **by ~s** rechtmäßig, von Rechts wegen; **in one's own ~** selbst - **2.** [right-hand side] rechte Seite; **on your ~** zu Ihrer Rechten; **on the ~** rechts <> adv - **1.** [correctly] richtig - **2.** [not left] rechts - **3.** [emphatic use] ganz; **stay ~ here** bleib hier; **to turn ~ round** sich ganz herumldrehen - **4.** [immediately] gleich; **~ now** [immediately] (jetzt) gleich; [at this very moment] (jetzt) gerade; **~ away** sofort <> vt - **1.** [correct] wieder gutlmachen - **2.** [make upright] auf lrichten <> excl gut!, O. K.!
➡ **Right** n POL: **the Right** die Rechte.

**right angle** n rechter Winkel; at ~s to sthg im rechten Winkel zu etw.

**righteous** ['raɪtʃəs] adj [person] rechtschaffen; [anger] selbstgerecht.

**righteousness** ['raɪtʃəsnɪs] n Rechtschaffenheit die.

**rightful** ['raɪtfʊl] adj rechtmäßig.

**rightfully** ['raɪtfʊlɪ] adv rechtmäßig; **the house is ~ mine** ich bin der rechtmäßige Eigentümer des Hauses.

**right-hand** adj [on the right] rechte, -r, -s.

**right-hand drive** adj rechts gesteuert.

**right-handed** [-'hændɪd] adj rechtshändig.

**right-hand man** n rechte Hand.

**rightly** ['raɪtlɪ] adv - **1.** [correctly, without error] ganz richtig - **2.** [appropriately, aptly] korrekt, richtig - **3.** [justifiably] mit Recht.

**right-minded** [-'maɪndɪd] adj vernünftig.

**rightness** ['raɪtnɪs] n Richtigkeit die.

**righto** ['raɪtəʊ] excl inf O. K.!

**right of way** n - **1.** AUT Vorfahrt die - **2.** [access] Durchgangsrecht das.

**right-thinking** [-'θɪŋkɪŋ] adj vernünftig.

**right wing** n: **the ~** der rechte Flügel.
⇒ **right-wing** adj rechtsgerichtet.

**right-winger** n POL Rechte der, die.

**rigid** ['rɪdʒɪd] adj - **1.** [hard, stiff, inflexible] starr - **2.** [strict] strikt.

**rigidity** [rɪ'dʒɪdətɪ] n - **1.** [hardness, stiffness] Starrheit die - **2.** [strictness] Striktheit die.

**rigidly** ['rɪdʒɪdlɪ] adv - **1.** [fixedly] starr - **2.** [strictly] strikt.

**rigmarole** ['rɪgmərəʊl] n (U) inf pej Zirkus der.

**rigor** n Am = rigour.

**rigor mortis** [-'mɔːtɪs] n Totenstarre die.

**rigorous** ['rɪgərəs] adj streng.

**rigorously** ['rɪgərəslɪ] adv streng.

**rigour** Br, **rigor** Am ['rɪgəʳ] n Strenge die.
⇒ **rigours** npl Unbilden pl.

**rig-out** n Br inf Aufmachung die.

**rile** [raɪl] vt ärgern.

**rim** [rɪm] n Rand der; [of spectacles] Fassung die; [of wheel] Felge die.

**rind** [raɪnd] n [of fruit] Schale die; [of cheese] Rinde die; [of bacon] Schwarte die.

**ring** [rɪŋ] (pt rang; pp vt senses 1 & 2 & vi rung; pt & pp vt senses 3 & 4 only -ed) n - **1.** [telephone call]: **to give sb a ~** jn anlrufen - **2.** [sound of bell] Klingeln das - **3.** [quality, tone]: **her excuse had a familiar ~ (about it)** ihre Ausrede kam mir bekannt vor; **there's a ~ of truth about it** es klingt sehr wahrscheinlich - **4.** [object, jewellery, for boxing] Ring der - **5.** [of people, trees] Kreis der - **6.** [people working together] Ring der; **crime ~**

Verbrecherring der - **7.** phr: **to run ~s round sb** fig jn in die Tasche stecken ⇔ vt - **1.** Br [phone] anlrufen - **2.** [bell] läuten; **to ~ the doorbell** (an der Tür) klingeln OR läuten - **3.** [draw a circle round] einlkreisen - **4.** [surround] umringen; **to be ~ed with sthg** von etw umringt sein ⇔ vi - **1.** Br [phone] klingeln - **2.** [doorbell, person at door] klingeln, läuten - **3.** [to attract attention]: **to ~ (for sb)** (nach jm) läuten - **4.** [resound]: **the hall rang with their laughter** der Saal hallte von ihrem Lachen wider - **5.** phr: **to ~ true** wahr klingen.
⇒ **ring back** vt sep & vi Br zurücklrufen.
⇒ **ring off** vi Br auf lhängen.
⇒ **ring out** vi [sound] ertönen, erklingen; [bells] läuten.
⇒ **ring up** vt sep Br anlrufen.

**ring binder** n Ringbuch das.

**ringer** ['rɪŋəʳ] n: **to be a dead ~ for sb** jm zum Verwechseln ähnlich sehen.

**ring finger** n Ringfinger der.

**ringing** ['rɪŋɪŋ] adj [clear, loud] schallend; **in ~ tones** mit tönender OR schallender Stimme ⇔ n [of bell] Läuten das; [of telephone] Klingeln das; [in ears] Klingen das.

**ringing tone** n Br TELEC Freizeichen das.

**ringleader** ['rɪŋ,liːdəʳ] n Anführer der, -in die.

**ringlet** ['rɪŋlɪt] n Ringellocke die.

**ringmaster** ['rɪŋ,mɑːstəʳ] n Zirkusdirektor der.

**ring road** n Br Umgehungsstraße die.

**ringside** ['rɪŋsaɪd] n: **at the ~** am Ring; **~ seat** Ringplatz der.

**ringworm** ['rɪŋwɜːm] n (U) Haarpilzflechte die.

**rink** [rɪŋk] n [for ice-skating] Eisbahn die; [for roller-skating] Rollschuhbahn die.

**rinse** [rɪns] n: **to give sthg a ~** [clothes] etw spülen; [vegetables] etw waschen; **to give one's hands a ~** die Hände abspülen ⇔ vt [clothes] spülen; [vegetables] waschen; **to ~ one's hands** die Hände abspülen; **to ~ one's mouth out** sich (D) den Mund auslspülen.

**Rio (de Janeiro)** [ˌriːəʊ(dədʒəˈnɪərəʊ)] n Rio (de Janeiro) nt.

**riot** ['raɪət] n Aufruhr der; **to run ~** [hooligans] randalieren; [children] außer Rand und Band sein; [plants] wuchern ⇔ vi einen Aufruhr machen.

**rioter** ['raɪətəʳ] n Aufrührer der, -in die.

**rioting** ['raɪətɪŋ] n (U) Unruhen pl, Krawalle pl.

**riotous** ['raɪətəs] adj [mob] randalierend; [party, behaviour] ausgelassen, wild.

**riot police** npl Bereitschaftspolizei die.

**riot shield** n Schutzschild der.

**rip** [rɪp] (pt & pp -ped; cont -ping) n Riss der

◇ *vt* - **1.** [tear, shred] zerreißen - **2.** [remove]: **to ~ sthg from** *or* **off sthg** etw von etw ablreißen ◇ *vi* reißen.

➤ **rip off** *vt sep inf* - **1.** [cheat] übers Ohr hauen - **2.** [steal] klauen, mitgehen lassen.

➤ **rip up** *vt sep* zerreißen.

**RIP** (*abbr of* **rest in peace**) R. I. P.

**ripcord** ['rɪpkɔːd] *n* Reißleine *die*.

**ripe** [raɪp] *adj* [ready to eat] reif; **to be ~ for sthg** *fig* für etw reif sein.

**ripen** ['raɪpn] *vt* reifen lassen ◇ *vi* reifen.

**ripeness** ['raɪpnɪs] *n* Reife *die*.

**rip-off** *n inf* [excessive charge] Wucher *der*.

**ripple** ['rɪpl] *n* - **1.** [in water] kleine Welle - **2.** [sound]: **a ~ of laughter** sanftes Gelächter; **a ~ of applause** kurzer Applaus ◇ *vt* kräuseln.

**rise** [raɪz] (*pt* **rose**; *pp* **risen** ['rɪzn]) *n* - **1.** *Br* [increase in amount]: **~ (in sthg)** Anstieg *der* (einer Sache (G)) - **2.** *Br* [increase in salary] Gehaltserhöhung *die* - **3.** [to power, fame] Aufstieg *der* - **4.** [slope] Steigung *die* - **5.** *phr*: **to give ~ to sthg** zu etw führen ◇ *vi* - **1.** [go upwards, become higher, increase] steigen - **2.** [sun, bread] auflgehen - **3.** [stand up, get out of bed] auflstehen - **4.** [slope upwards] (an)lsteigen - **5.** [become louder - voice] lauter werden - **6.** [become higher in pitch] höher werden - **7.** [prove o.s.]: **to ~ to the occasion** der Lage gewachsen sein; **to ~ to the challenge** die Herausforderung anlnehmen - **8.** [rebel] sich erheben - **9.** [in status] auflsteigen; **to ~ to power** an die Macht kommen.

➤ **rise above** *vt fus* [difficulty, problem] stehen über (+ *D*).

**riser** ['raɪzəʳ] *n*: **she is an early ~** sie ist eine Frühaufsteherin; **he is a late ~** er ist ein Langschläfer.

**risible** ['rɪzəbl] *adj fml* lächerlich.

**rising** ['raɪzɪŋ] *adj* - **1.** [sloping upwards] (an)lsteigend - **2.** [increasing, tide] steigend - **3.** [increasingly successful] aufsteigend ◇ *n* [rebellion] Aufstand *der*, Erhebung *die*.

**rising damp** *n* Bodenfeuchtigkeit *die*.

**risk** [rɪsk] *n* Risiko *das*; **to run the ~ of doing sthg** Gefahr laufen, etw zu tun; **to take a ~** ein Risiko einlgehen; **at one's own ~** auf eigenes Risiko; **at ~** in Gefahr; **to put at ~** gefährden; **at the ~ of sounding rude** ... auf die Gefahr hin, unhöflich zu sein ... ◇ *vt* - **1.** [put in danger] riskieren - **2.** [take the chance of]: **to ~ doing sthg** riskieren, etw zu tun; **to ~ it** es riskieren.

**risk capital** *n* (*U*) Risikokapital *das*.

**risk-taking** *n* (*U*) Risiko *das*.

**risky** ['rɪskɪ] (*compar* **-ier**; *superl* **-iest**) *adj* riskant.

**risotto** [rɪ'zɒtəʊ] (*pl* **-s**) *n* Risotto *der or das*.

**risqué** [rɪ'skeɪ] *adj* gewagt, schlüpfrig.

**rissole** ['rɪsəʊl] *n Br* Frikadelle *die*.

**rite** [raɪt] *n* Ritus *der*.

**ritual** ['rɪtʃʊəl] *adj* rituell ◇ *n* Ritual *das*.

**rival** ['raɪvl] (*Br pt* & *pp* **-led**; *cont* **-ling**, *Am pt* & *pp* **-ed**; *cont* **-ing**) *adj* Konkurrenz-, konkurrierend ◇ *n* Rivale *der*, -lin *die*; *comm* Konkurrent *der*, -in *die* ◇ *vt* sich messen mit, konkurrieren mit.

**rivalry** ['raɪvlrɪ] *n* Rivalität *die*.

**river** ['rɪvəʳ] *n* Fluss *der*; **the River Thames** *Br*, **the Thames River** *Am* die Themse.

**river bank** *n* Flussufer *das*.

**riverbed** ['rɪvəbed] *n* Flussbett *das*.

**riverside** ['rɪvəsaɪd] *n*: **the ~** das Flussufer.

**rivet** ['rɪvɪt] *n* Niete *die* ◇ *vt* - **1.** [fasten with rivets] nieten - **2.** *fig* [fascinate]: **to be ~ed by sthg** von etw gefesselt sein.

**riveting** ['rɪvɪtɪŋ] *adj* fesselnd.

**Riviera** [ˌrɪvɪ'eərə] *n*: **the French/Italian ~** die französische/italienische Riviera.

**RN** *n* - **1.** *abbr of* **Royal Navy** - **2.** (*abbr of* **registered nurse**) = RGN.

**RNA** (*abbr of* **ribonucleic acid**) *n* RNS *die*.

**RNLI** (*abbr of* **Royal National Lifeboat Institution**) *n* freiwilliger Seerettungsdienst in Großbritannien und Irland.

**roach** [rəʊtʃ] (*pl sense 1 inv or* **-es**; *pl sense 2* **-es**) *n* - **1.** [fish] Plötze *die* - **2.** *Am* [cockroach] Schabe *die*.

**road** [rəʊd] *n* Straße *die*; **by ~** [send] per Spedition; [travel] mit dem Auto/Bus/*etc*; **on the ~** [on the way] unterwegs; **on the ~ to victory/success/recovery** auf dem Weg zum Sieg/zum Erfolg/der Besserung.

**road atlas** *n* Autoatlas *der*.

**roadblock** ['rəʊdblɒk] *n* Straßensperre *die*.

**road haulage** *n* (*U*) Spedition *die*.

**road hog** *n inf pej* Verkehrsrowdy *der*.

**roadholding** ['rəʊdˌhəʊldɪŋ] *n* Straßenlage *die*.

**roadie** ['rəʊdɪ] *n inf* Roadie *der*.

**road map** *n* Straßenkarte *die*.

**road roller** [-ˌrəʊləʳl] *n* Straßenwalze *die*.

**road safety** *n* Verkehrssicherheit *die*.

**roadside** ['rəʊdsaɪd] *n*: **by the ~** am Straßenrand ◇ *comp* Straßen-.

**road sign** *n* Verkehrszeichen *das*.

**roadsweeper** ['rəʊdˌswiːpəʳ] *n* [vehicle] (Straßen)kehrmaschine *die*; [person] Straßenfeger *der*, -in *die*.

**road tax** *n* Kraftfahrzeugsteuer *die*.

**road test** *n* Straßentest *der*.

**R**

➤ **road-test** *vt* einen Straßentest machen mit.

**roadway** ['rəudweɪ] *n* Fahrbahn *die*.

**road works** *npl* (Straßen)bauarbeiten *pl*.

**roadworthy** ['rəud‚wɜːðɪ] *adj* fahrtüchtig.

**roam** [rəum] *vt* [countryside] durchstreifen; [streets] herumlziehen in (+ D) ⬦ *vi* [in countryside] wandern; [in streets] herumlziehen.

**roar** [rɔːʳ] *vi* - **1.** [lion, person] brüllen; **to ~ with laughter** vor Lachen brüllen - **2.** [wind, engine] heulen ⬦ *vt* brüllen ⬦ *n* - **1.** [of lion, person] Brüllen *das* - **2.** [of wind, engine] Heulen *das;* [of traffic] Lärm *der*.

**roaring** ['rɔːrɪŋ] *adj* - **1.** [traffic] lärmend; [wind, engine] heulend - **2.** [fire] prasselnd - **3.** [for emphasis]: **a ~ success** ein Riesenerfolg; **to do a ~ trade** ein Riesengeschäft machen ⬦ *adv:* **~ drunk** sternhagelvoll.

**roast** [rəust] *adj:* **~ beef** Rinderbraten *der*, Roastbeef *das;* **~ chicken** Brathähnchen *das;* **~ pork** Schweinebraten *der;* **~ potatoes** *im Ofen in Fett gebackene Kartoffeln* ⬦ *n* Braten *der* ⬦ *vt* - **1.** [meat] braten; [potatoes] *im Ofen in Fett backen* - **2.** [coffee beans, nuts] rösten.

**roasting** ['rəustɪŋ] *adj* & *adv inf:* **I'm/it's ~ (hot)!** mir/es ist fürchterlich heiß!

**roasting tin** *n* Blech *zum Braten von Fleisch oder Kartoffeln im Ofen*.

**rob** [rɒb] (*pt* & *pp* -**bed;** *cont* -**bing**) *vt* [person] bestehlen; [bank, house] auslrauben; **to ~ sb of sthg** [of money, goods] jm etw stehlen; *fig* [of opportunity, glory] jn einer Sache (G) berauben.

**robber** ['rɒbəʳ] *n* Räuber *der*, -in *die*.

**robbery** ['rɒbərɪ] (*pl* -**ies**) *n* Raub *der*.

**robe** [rəub] *n* - **1.** [of priest, judge, monarch] Robe *die* - **2.** *Am* [dressing gown] Morgenrock *der*.

**robin** ['rɒbɪn] *n* Rotkehlchen *das*.

**robot** ['rəubɒt] *n* Roboter *der*.

**robotics** [rəu'bɒtɪks] *n* (*U*) Robotertechnik *die*.

**robust** [rəu'bʌst] *adj* [person, health] robust; [economy] stabil; [criticism, defence] stark.

**robustly** [rəu'bʌstlɪ] *adv* robust; [defend] stark.

**rock** [rɒk] *n* - **1.** (*U*) [substance] Stein *der* - **2.** [boulder] Fels(en) *der* - **3.** *Am* [pebble] Stein *der* - **4.** [music] Rock *der* - **5.** *Br* [sweet]: **stick of ~** Zuckerstange *die* ⬦ *comp* [band, concert, singer] Rock- ⬦ *vt* - **1.** [cause to move] schaukeln; [baby] wiegen - **2.** [shock] erschüttern ⬦ *vi* [boat, cradle, in chair] schaukeln.

➤ **on the rocks** *adv* - **1.** [drink] mit Eis - **2.** [marriage, relationship] kaputt.

**rock and roll** *n* Rock and Roll *der*.

**rock bottom** *n:* **to be at ~** auf dem Tiefpunkt sein; **to hit ~** den Tiefpunkt erreichen.

➤ **rock-bottom** *adj* [prices] Schleuder-.

**rock cake** *n Br* kleiner Rosinenkuchen.

**rock climber** *n* Kletterer *der*, -in *die*.

**rock-climbing** *n* Klettern *das*.

**rocker** ['rɒkəʳ] *n* [chair] Schaukelstuhl *der;* **to be off one's ~** *inf* übergeschnappt sein.

**rockery** ['rɒkərɪ] (*pl* -**ies**) *n* Steingarten *der*.

**rocket** ['rɒkɪt] *n* Rakete *die* ⬦ *vi* hoch schießen.

**rocket launcher** [-‚lɔːntʃəʳ] *n* Raketenwerfer *der*.

**rock face** *n* Felswand *die*.

**rockfall** ['rɒkfɔːl] *n* Steinschlag *der*.

**rock-hard** *adj* steinhart.

**Rockies** ['rɒkɪz] *npl:* **the ~** die Rocky Mountains.

**rocking chair** ['rɒkɪŋ-] *n* Schaukelstuhl *der*.

**rocking horse** ['rɒkɪŋ-] *n* Schaukelpferd *das*.

**rock music** *n* Rockmusik *die*.

**rock 'n' roll** *n* = rock and roll.

**rock pool** *n* Felstümpel *der*.

**rock salt** *n* Steinsalz *das*.

**rocky** ['rɒkɪ] (*compar* -**ier;** *superl* -**iest**) *adj* - **1.** [full of rocks] steinig - **2.** [unsteady] wackelig.

**Rocky Mountains** *npl:* **the ~** die Rocky Mountains.

**rococo** [rə'kəukəu] *adj* Rokoko-.

**rod** [rɒd] *n* Stange *die;* [for fishing] Angel *die*.

**rode** [rəud] *pt* ⬲ ride.

**rodent** ['rəudənt] *n* Nagetier *das*.

**rodeo** ['rəudɪəu] (*pl* -**s**) *n* Rodeo *das*.

**roe** [rəu] *n* [of fish] Rogen *der*.

**roe deer** *n* Reh *das*.

**rogue** [rəug] *adj* [elephant] Einzelgänger- ⬦ *n* - **1.** [likable rascal] Frechdachs *der* - **2.** *dated* [dishonest person] Schurke *der*.

**roguish** ['rəugɪʃ] *adj* schelmisch.

**role** [rəul] *n* Rolle *die*.

**roll** [rəul] *n* - **1.** [of material, paper, film] Rolle *die* - **2.** [of bread] Brötchen *das;* **a cheese ~** ein Käsebrötchen - **3.** [list] Liste *die;* **electoral ~** Wählerverzeichnis *das* - **4.** [sound - of thunder] Rollen *das;* [- of drums] Wirbel *der* ⬦ *vt* - **1.** [turn over] rollen; **to ~ one's eyes** die Augen verdrehen - **2.** [make into cylinder] auf lrollen; [umbrella] zusammenlrollen; **~ed into one** *fig* in einem - **3.** [cigarette] drehen ⬦ *vi* - **1.** [gen] rollen - **2.** [ship] schlingern - **3.** [make loud noise - thunder] rollen; [- drums] wirbeln.

➤ **roll about, roll around** *vi* herumlrollen; [person] sich wälzen.

➤ **roll back** *vt sep Am* [prices] reduzieren.

**roll in** *vi inf* - **1.** [money] herein|strömen - **2.** [person] ein|trudeln.

**roll over** *vi* [person] sich um|drehen.

**roll up** *vt sep* - **1.** [make into cylinder] auf|-rollen, zusammen|rollen - **2.** [sleeves] hoch|-krempeln ⋄ *vi* - **1.** [vehicle] vor|fahren - **2.** *inf* [person] auf|kreuzen.

**roll bar** *n* [in car] Überrollbügel *der.*

**roll call** *n* Namensaufruf *der;* MIL Appell *der;* **to take a ~** die Namen auf|rufen; MIL einen Appell ab|halten.

**rolled gold** [rǝʊld-] *n (U)* Dubleegold *das.*

**roller** ['rǝʊlǝ'] *n* - **1.** [cylinder] Walze *die* - **2.** [curler] (Locken)wickler *der.*

**roller blades** *npl* Rollerblades *pl.*

**roller blind** *n* Rollo *das.*

**roller coaster** *n* Achterbahn *die.*

**roller skate** *n* Rollschuh *der.*

**roller-skate** *vi* Rollschuh laufen.

**roller towel** *n* Rollhandtuch *das.*

**rollicking** ['rɒlɪkɪŋ] *adj:* **we had a ~ (good) time** wir hatten einen Mordsspaß.

**rolling** ['rǝʊlɪŋ] *adj* - **1.** [hills] wellig - **2.** [gait] schaukelnd - **3.** *phr:* **to be ~ in it** *inf* im Geld schwimmen.

**rolling pin** *n* Nudelholz *das.*

**rolling stock** *n (U)* rollendes Material, Schienenfahrzeuge *pl.*

**rollneck** ['rǝʊlnek] *adj* Rollkragen-.

**roll of honour** *n* Ehrenliste *die (der Gefallenen).*

**roll-on** *adj & n:* ~ **(deodorant)** Deoroller *der.*

**roll-on roll-off** *adj Br* Roll-on-roll-off-.

**roly-poly** [ˌrǝʊlɪ'pǝʊlɪ] *(pl* -ies) *n Br:* ~ **(pudding)** *mit Rindertalg hergestellter und mit Marmelade gefüllter Strudel.*

**ROM** [rɒm] *(abbr of* read only memory) *n* ROM.

**romaine lettuce** [rǝʊ'meɪn-] *n Am* römischer Salat.

**Roman** ['rǝʊmǝn] *adj* römisch ⋄ *n* Römer *der,* -in *die.*

**Roman Catholic** *adj* römisch-katholisch ⋄ *n* Katholik *der,* -in *die.*

**romance** [rǝʊ'mæns] *n* - **1.** [romantic quality] Romantik *die* - **2.** [love affair] Romanze *die* - **3.** [novel] Liebesroman *der.*

**Romanesque** [ˌrǝʊmǝ'nesk] *adj* romanisch.

**Romani** ['rǝʊmǝnɪ] *adj & n* = **Romany.**

**Romania** [ru:'meɪnjǝ] *n* Rumänien *nt.*

**Romanian** [ru:'meɪnjǝn] *adj* rumänisch ⋄ *n* - **1.** [person] Rumäne *der,* -nin *die* - **2.** [language] Rumänisch(e) *das.*

**Roman numerals** *npl* römische Ziffern *pl.*

**romantic** [rǝʊ'mæntɪk] *adj* - **1.** [gen] romantisch - **2.** [novel, film, play] Liebes-.

**romanticism** [rǝʊ'mæntɪsɪzm] *n* Romantik *die.*

**romanticize, -ise** [rǝʊ'mæntɪsaɪz] *vt* romantisieren ⋄ *vi* fantasieren.

**Romany** ['rǝʊmǝnɪ] *(pl* -ies) *adj* Roma-; **the ~ people** die Roma *pl* ⋄ *n* - **1.** [person] Rom *der;* **Romanies** Roma *pl* - **2.** [language] Romani *das.*

**Rome** [rǝʊm] *n* Rom *nt.*

**romp** [rɒmp] *n:* **to have a ~** herum|toben, herum|tollen ⋄ *vi* [play noisily] herum|toben, herum|tollen.

**rompers** ['rɒmpǝz] *npl,* **romper suit** ['rɒmpǝ'-] *n* Strampelhose *die.*

**roof** [ru:f] *n* - **1.** [of building, vehicle] Dach *das;* **under the same ~** unter einem Dach; **to have a ~ over one's head** ein Dach über dem Kopf haben; **to go through** OR **hit the ~** an die Decke gehen - **2.** [upper part - of cave] Gewölbe *das;* ~ **of the mouth** Gaumen *der.*

**roof garden** *n* Dachgarten *der.*

**roofing** ['ru:fɪŋ] *n (U)* [material] Deckung *die.*

**roof rack** *n* Dachträger *der.*

**rooftop** ['ru:ftɒp] *n* Dach *das.*

**rook** [rʊk] *n* - **1.** [bird] Krähe *die* - **2.** [chess piece] Turm *der.*

**rookie** ['rʊkɪ] *n Am inf* Grünschnabel *der.*

**room** [ru:m, rʊm] *n* - **1.** [in house, hotel] Zimmer *das;* [in office, public building *etc*] Raum *der* - **2.** *(U)* [space] Platz *der;* **to make ~ for sb/sthg** für jn/etw Platz machen - **3.** *(U)* [opportunity, possibility]: **there is ~ for improvement** es könnte besser sein; **there is no ~ for sentimentality in politics** Sentimentalität hat in der Politik nichts zu suchen; ~ **to** OR **for manoeuvre** Spielraum *der.*

**rooming house** ['ru:mɪŋ-] *n Am* Logierhaus *das.*

**roommate** ['ru:mmeɪt] *n* Zimmergenosse *der,* -sin *die.*

**room service** *n (U)* Zimmerservice *der.*

**room temperature** *n* Zimmertemperatur *die.*

**roomy** ['ru:mɪ] *(compar* -ier; *superl* -iest) *adj* [house, car] geräumig; [garment] weit.

**roost** [ru:st] *n* Hühnerstange *die;* **to rule the ~** Herr im Haus sein ⋄ *vi* [hens] auf der Stange sitzen.

**rooster** ['ru:stǝ'] *n* Hahn *der.*

**root** [ru:t] *adj* [cause] eigentlich ⋄ *n lit & fig* Wurzel *die;* **to put down ~s** [person] Wurzeln schlagen; **to take ~** [plant] Wurzel fassen; [idea] Fuß fassen; **the ~ of the problem** die Ursache des Problems ⋄ *vi* [search] wühlen.

**roots** *npl* [origins] Wurzeln *pl.*

**root for** *vt fus esp Am inf* an|feuern.

**root out** *vt sep* [eradicate] aus|rotten.

**R**

**root beer** n Am leicht würzig schmeckende Limonade.

**root crop** n Wurzelgemüse das.

**rooted** ['ruːtɪd] adj: **to be ~ to the spot** wie angewurzelt dastehen.

**rootless** ['ruːtlɪs] adj wurzellos.

**root vegetable** n Wurzelgemüse das.

**rope** [rəʊp] n Seil das; **to know the ~s** sich auslkennen ⬦ vt: **to ~ together** zusammenlbinden; [climbers] anlseilen.

➤ **rope in** vt sep inf [involve] ranlkriegen.

➤ **rope off** vt sep mit einem Seil ablsperren.

**rop(e)y** ['rəʊpɪ] (compar -**ier**; superl -**iest**) adj Br inf - **1.** [poor-quality] mies; **these shoes are ~** diese Schuhe taugen nichts - **2.** [unwell - feel] mies; [ - look] mitgenommen.

**rosary** ['rəʊzərɪ] (pl -**ies**) n Rosenkranz der.

**rose** [rəʊz] pt ⬥ **rise** ⬦ adj [pink] rosa ⬦ n [flower] Rose die.

**rosé** ['rəʊzeɪ] n Rosé der.

**rosebed** ['rəʊzbed] n Rosenbeet das.

**rosebud** ['rəʊzbʌd] n Rosenknospe die.

**rose bush** n Rosenstrauch der.

**rose hip** n Hagebutte die.

**rosemary** ['rəʊzmərɪ] n Rosmarin der.

**rosette** [rəʊ'zet] n Rosette die.

**rosewater** ['rəʊz,wɔːtər] n Rosenwasser das.

**rosewood** ['rəʊzwʊd] n Rosenholz das.

**ROSPA** ['rɒspə] (abbr of **Royal Society for the Prevention of Accidents**) n britischer Gesellschaft zur Unfallverhütung.

**roster** ['rɒstər] n Dienstplan der.

**rostrum** ['rɒstrəm] (pl -**trums** OR -**tra** [-trə]) n [for speaker, conductor] Pult das

**rosy** ['rəʊzɪ] (compar -**ier**; superl -**iest**) adj lit & fig rosig.

**rot** [rɒt] (pt ⬥ pp -**ted**; cont -**ting**) n - **1.** (U) [decay - of wood, food] Fäulnis die; [ - in society, organization] Verfall der; **dry ~** Trockenfäule die; **to stop the ~** den Verfall auflhalten; **the ~ set in** es ging abwärts - **2.** Br dated [nonsense] Quatsch der ⬦ vt faulen lassen ⬦ vi faulen.

**rota** ['rəʊtə] n Dienstplan der.

**rotary** ['rəʊtərɪ] adj rotierend, Rotations- ⬦ n Am [roundabout] Kreisverkehr der.

**Rotary Club** n: **the ~** der Rotary Club.

**rotate** [rəʊ'teɪt] vt - **1.** [turn] drehen - **2.** [in sequence - crops] im Wechsel anlbauen; **to ~ the presidency** turnusmäßig die Präsidentschaft übernehmen ⬦ vi - **1.** [turn] sich drehen, rotieren - **2.** [in sequence - job] turnusmäßig wechseln; [ - crops] im Wechsel angebaut werden.

**rotation** [rəʊ'teɪʃn] n - **1.** [turning movement] Drehung die, Rotation die - **2.** (U) [sequence]:

**~ of crops** Fruchtwechsel der; **in ~** turnusmäßig.

**rote** [rəʊt] n: **by ~** auswendig.

**rote learning** n Auswendiglernen das.

**rotor** ['rəʊtər] n Rotor der.

**rotten** ['rɒtn] adj - **1.** [decayed] verfault - **2.** inf [poor-quality, unskilled] lausig - **3.** inf [mean] gemein - **4.** inf [unpleasant, unenjoyable] mies - **5.** inf [unwell]: **to feel ~** sich mies fühlen - **6.** [unhappy, bad]: **I feel ~ about sending him away** ich habe ein schlechtes Gewissen, weil ich ihn weggeschickt habe.

**rotund** [rəʊ'tʌnd] adj fml rundlich.

**rouble** ['ruːbl] n Rubel der.

**rouge** [ruːʒ] n Rouge das.

**rough** [rʌf] adj - **1.** [not smooth - surface] rau; [ - road] uneben, holprig - **2.** [violent] grob, rau - **3.** [crude, basic - shelter, conditions] primitiv; [ - people, manners] rau - **4.** [not detailed, not exact] grob; **~ draft** Rohentwurf der; **at a ~ guess** grob geschätzt; **can you give me a ~ idea of the cost?** können Sie mir sagen, wie viel es ungefähr kostet? - **5.** [unpleasant, tough - life, time] hart; [ - journey] anstrengend; [ - area] rau; **to be ~ on sb** hart für jn sein - **6.** [stormy] stürmisch - **7.** [harsh - voice] rau; [ - wine] sauer - **8.** [tired, ill - feel] mies; [ - look] mitgenommen ⬦ adv: **to sleep ~** im Freien übernachten ⬦ n - **1.** GOLF: **the ~** das Rough - **2.** [draft]: **to write sthg in ~** ein Konzept für etw machen ⬦ vt phr: **to ~ it** primitiv leben.

➤ **rough out** vt sep grob entwerfen.

➤ **rough up** vt sep verprügeln.

**roughage** ['rʌfɪdʒ] n (U) Ballaststoffe pl.

**rough and ready** adj primitiv; [person] rau(beinig).

**rough-and-tumble** n (U) [playing] Balgerei die; **the ~ of politics** das bewegte Leben in der Politik.

**roughcast** ['rʌfkɑːst] n Rauputz der.

**rough diamond** n Br fig: **he is a ~** bei ihm gilt auch: raue Schale, weicher Kern.

**roughen** ['rʌfn] vt [surface] auflrauen.

**rough justice** n (U): **that's ~!** das ist ein unangemessen hartes Urteil!

**roughly** ['rʌflɪ] adv - **1.** [gen] grob - **2.** [approximately] etwa.

**roughneck** ['rʌfnek] n - **1.** [oilrig worker] Arbeiter auf einer Ölbohrinsel - **2.** Am inf [ruffian] Rowdy der.

**roughness** ['rʌfnɪs] n (U) - **1.** [lack of smoothness] Rauheit die - **2.** [lack of gentleness] Grobheit die.

**roughshod** ['rʌfʃɒd] adv: **to ride ~ over sb/sthg** jn/etw rücksichtslos übergehen.

**roulette** [ruː'let] n Roulette das.

**round** [raʊnd] adj rund ⬦ prep - **1.** [surrounding]

um ... herum; **there were soldiers all ~ the building** rund um das Gebäude waren Soldaten - **2.** [near]: **~ here/there** hier/dort in der Nähe; **is there a bank anywhere ~ here?** gibt es hier irgendwo eine Bank? - **3.** [all over]: **150 offices ~ the world** 150 Büros in der ganzen Welt; **all ~ the country** im ganzen Land; **to go ~ a museum** ein Museum besuchen; **to go ~ a town** sich *(D)* eine Stadt anlsehen; **to show sb ~ sthg** jn in etw *(D)* herumlführen - **4.** [in a circle]: **we walked ~ the lake** wir gingen um den See herum; **to go/drive ~ sthg** um etw herumlgehen/herumlfahren; **~ the clock** *fig* rund um die Uhr - **5.** [in circumference]: **she measures 30 inches ~ the waist** um die Taille misst sie 75 cm - **6.** [on or to the other side of]: **to be/go ~ the corner** um die Ecke sein/gehen - **7.** [so as to avoid] um ... herum; **to get ~ an obstacle** um ein Hindernis herumlgehen; **to find a way ~ a problem** einen Ausweg für ein Problem finden ⬦ *adv* - **1.** [on all sides] herum; **all ~** auf allen Seiten, rundherum - **2.** [near]: **~ about** [in distance] in der Nähe; [approximately] rund; **~ about ten o'clock** gegen zehn Uhr - **3.** [here and there] herum; **to travel ~** herumlreisen - **4.** [in a circle]: **to spin ~ (and ~)** sich im Kreis drehen - **5.** [to the other side]: **to go ~** herumlgehen; **to turn ~** sich umldrehen; **to look ~** sich umlsehen; **it's a long way ~** das ist ein Umweg - **6.** [on a visit]: **why don't you come ~?** warum kommst du nicht vorbei?; **to ask some friends ~** ein paar Freunde zu sich einladen; **I spent the day ~ at her house** ich war den ganzen Tag bei ihr (zu Hause) - **7.** [when sharing]: **to hand sthg ~** etw herumlreichen - **8.** [continuously]: **all year ~** das ganze Jahr über ⬦ *n* - **1.** [gen & SPORT] Runde *die;* **a ~ of applause** eine Runde Applaus - **2.** [of ammunition] Schuss *der* - **3.** [of drinks] Runde *die;* **it's my ~** es ist meine Runde - **4.** **: a ~ of sandwiches** ein Sandwich - **5.** [of toast] Scheibe *die* ⬦ *vt* [turn]: **to ~ a bend** um eine Kurve fahren.

➧ **rounds** *npl* [of doctor, milkman, postman]: **to do one's ~s** *fig* seine Runde machen; **to do** OR **go the ~s** [joke, rumour, illness] umlgehen.

➧ **round off** *vt sep* ablrunden.

➧ **round up** *vt sep* - **1.** [animals] zusammenltreiben - **2.** [number] auf lrunden.

**roundabout** ['raʊndəbaʊt] *adj* umständlich ⬦ *n Br* - **1.** [on road] Kreisverkehr *der* - **2.** [at fairground, playground] Karussell *das.*

**rounded** ['raʊndɪd] *adj* [in shape] abgerundet.

**rounders** ['raʊndəz] *n (U) Br* Schlagball *der.*

**Roundhead** ['raʊndhed] *n* HIST Rundkopf *der.*

**roundly** ['raʊndlɪ] *adv* [criticize] scharf; [defeated] vernichtend.

**round-neck** *adj* [jumper] mit rundem Ausschnitt.

**round-shouldered** [-'ʃəʊldəd] *adj* mit hängenden Schultern.

**round-table** *adj:* **~ talks/negotiations** Gespräche/Verhandlungen am runden Tisch.

**round the clock** *adv* rund um die Uhr.

➧ **round-the-clock** *adj:* round-the-clock surveillance/activity Überwachung/Aktivität rund um die Uhr.

**round trip** *adj Am:* **~ ticket** Rückfahrkarte *die;* [for plane] Rückflugticket *das* ⬦ *n* Rundreise *die.*

**roundup** ['raʊndʌp] *n* [summary] Zusammenfassung *die.*

**rouse** [raʊz] *vt* - **1.** [wake up] wecken - **2.** [impel]: **to ~ o.s. to do sthg** sich dazu auflraffen, etw zu tun; **to ~ sb to action** jn zum Handeln bewegen - **3.** [subj: orator] in Erregung versetzen - **4.** [give rise to] hervorlrufen; [emotions, interest] wecken, wachlrufen.

**rousing** ['raʊzɪŋ] *adj* [speech] mitreißend; [cheer] stürmisch.

**rout** [raʊt] *n* Niederlage *die* ⬦ *vt* in die Flucht schlagen.

**route** [ru:t] *n* - **1.** [line of travel] Strecke *die,* Route *die* - **2.** [fixed itinerary]: **air/bus/shipping ~** Flug-/Bus-/Schifffahrtslinie *die* - **3.** *fig* [to achievement] Weg *der* ⬦ *vt* [flight, traffic] legen; [goods] schicken.

**route map** *n* [for public transport] Streckenkarte *die;* [for holiday route] Tourenplan *der.*

**route march** *n* Übungsmarsch *der.*

**routine** [ru:'ti:n] *adj* routinemäßig, Routine- ⬦ *n* Routine *die.*

**routinely** [ru:'ti:nlɪ] *adv* routinemäßig.

**rove** [rəʊv] *literary vt* durchlziehen, streifen durch ⬦ *vi:* **to ~ around** umherlziehen, umherlstreifen.

**roving** ['rəʊvɪŋ] *adj:* **to have a ~ eye** ständig auf der Suche nach Abenteuern mit anderen Frauen/Männern sein; **"our ~ reporter"** „unser rasender Reporter".

**row**[1] [rəʊ] *n* Reihe *die;* **in a ~** nacheinander ⬦ *vt & vi* rudern.

**row**[2] [raʊ] *n* - **1.** [quarrel] Streit *der,* Krach *der* - **2.** *inf* [noise] Krach *der,* Krawall *der* ⬦ *vi* [quarrel] sich streiten.

**rowboat** ['rəʊbəʊt] *n Am* Ruderboot *das.*

**rowdy** ['raʊdɪ] *(compar* -ier; *superl* -iest) *adj* [person] wild, randalierend; [party, atmosphere] laut.

**rower** ['rəʊə'] *n* Ruderer, -in *die.*

**row house** [rəʊ-] *n Am* Reihenhaus *das.*

**rowing** ['rəʊɪŋ] *n* Rudern *das.*

**rowing boat** *n Br* Ruderboot *das.*

**rowing machine** *n* Rudermaschine *die.*

**royal** ['rɔɪəl] *adj* [regal] königlich ⬦ *n inf* Angehörige *der*, *die* der königlichen Familie.

**Royal Air Force** *n*: the ~ die Königliche Luftwaffe.

**royal blue** *adj* königsblau.

**royal family** *n* königliche Familie.

**royalist** ['rɔɪəlɪst] *n* Royalist *der*, -in *die*.

**royal jelly** *n* Gelée royale *das*.

**Royal Mail** *n Br*: the ~ die Königliche Post.

**Royal Marines** *n Br*: the ~ die Königliche Marineinfanterie.

**Royal Navy** *n*: the ~ die Königliche Marine.

**royalty** ['rɔɪəltɪ] *n* (U) [persons] Königshaus *das*; she is ~ sie gehört zum Königshaus.
⮞ **royalties** *npl* Tantiemen *pl*.

**RP** (*abbr of* received pronunciation) *n* englische Standardaussprache.

**RPI** (*abbr of* retail price index) *n* Verbraucherpreisindex *der*.

**rpm** (*abbr of* revolutions per minute) *npl* U/min.

**RRP** (*abbr of* recommended retail price) *n* VVP *die*, unverbindliche Preisempfehlung.

**RSC** (*abbr of* Royal Shakespeare Company) *n* britisches Theaterensemble.

**RSI** (*abbr of* repetitive strain injury) *n* RSI, chronisches Überlastungssyndrom.

**RSPB** (*abbr of* Royal Society for the Protection of Birds) *n* britischer Vogelschutzbund.

**RSPCA** (*abbr of* Royal Society for the Prevention of Cruelty to Animals) *n* britischer Tierschutzverein.

**RSVP** (*abbr of* répondez s'il vous plaît) u. A.w.g.

**Rt Hon** (*abbr of* Right Honourable) Anrede für Parlamentsabgeordnete.

**Rt Rev** (*abbr of* Right Reverend) Anrede für Bischöfe der anglikanischen Kirche.

**rub** [rʌb] (*pt & pp* -bed; *cont* -bing) *vt* reiben; to ~ one's hands together sich (*D*) die Hände reiben; to ~ sthg against *OR* on sthg etw an etw (*D*) /auf etw (*A*) reiben; he ~bed sun cream into her back er rieb ihren Rücken mit Sonnencreme ein; don't ~ it in *inf fig* du brauchst es mir nicht unter die Nase zu reiben; to ~ sb up the wrong way *Br*, to ~ sb the wrong way *Am fig* jn verstimmen ⬦ *vi*: to ~ against *OR* on sthg an etw (*D*) reiben; [person, animal] sich an etw (*D*) reiben; to ~ together sich reiben.
⮞ **rub off on** *vt fus* [subj: quality] abfärben auf (+ *A*).
⮞ **rub out** *vt sep* [erase] ausradieren.

**rubber** ['rʌbə'] *adj* [made of rubber] Gummi- ⬦ *n* - **1.** [substance] Gummi *der* - **2.** *Br* [eraser] Radiergummi *der* - **3.** [in cards] Robber *der* - **4.** *Am inf* [condom] Gummi *der* - **5.** *Am* [overshoe] Gummiüberschuh *der*.

**rubber band** *n* Gummiband *das*.

**rubber boot** *n Am* Gummistiefel *der*.

**rubber dinghy** *n* Schlauchboot *das*.

**rubberize, -ise** ['rʌbəraɪz] *vt* gummieren.

**rubberneck** ['rʌbənek] *vi Am inf* [stare] gaffen.

**rubber plant** *n* Gummibaum *der*.

**rubber stamp** *n* Stempel *der*.
⮞ **rubber-stamp** *vt* stempeln.

**rubber tree** *n* Kautschukbaum *der*.

**rubbery** ['rʌbərɪ] *adj* wie Gummi; [meat] zäh.

**rubbing** ['rʌbɪŋ] *n*: brass ~ (Anfertigung einer) Pauszeichnung, die durch Auflegen von Papier auf eine Messingtafel und Durchrubbeln des Bildmotivs entsteht.

**rubbish** ['rʌbɪʃ] *n* (U) - **1.** [refuse] Abfall *der*, Müll *der* - **2.** *inf fig* [worthless thing] Mist *der* - **3.** *inf* [nonsense] Quatsch *der*, Blödsinn *der* ⬦ *vt inf* [person, opinion] lächerlich machen; [play, book] verreißen ⬦ *excl inf* Quatsch!

**rubbish bag** *n Br* Müllsack *der*.

**rubbish bin** *n Br* Mülleimer *der*.

**rubbish dump, rubbish tip** *n Br* Müllabladeplatz *der*.

**rubbishy** ['rʌbɪʃɪ] *adj inf* mies; [idea] blödsinnig; these shoes are ~ diese Schuhe taugen nichts.

**rubble** ['rʌbl] *n* Schutt *der*.

**rubella** [ruː'belə] *n* (U) Röteln *pl*.

**ruby** ['ruːbɪ] (*pl* -ies) *n* [gem] Rubin *der*.

**RUC** (*abbr of* Royal Ulster Constabulary) *n* Polizei in Nordirland.

**ruck** [rʌk] *n* RUGBY offenes Gedränge.

**rucksack** ['rʌksæk] *n* Rucksack *der*.

**ructions** ['rʌkʃnz] *npl inf* Krach *der*.

**rudder** ['rʌdə'] *n* Ruder *das*.

**ruddy** ['rʌdɪ] (*compar* -ier; *superl* -iest) *adj* - **1.** [reddish] rot; [complexion] gesund - **2.** *Br dated* [for emphasis] verdammt.

**rude** [ruːd] *adj* - **1.** [impolite] unhöflich - **2.** [dirty, naughty] unanständig - **3.** [unexpected]: ~ awakening böses Erwachen - **4.** *literary* [primitive] einfach.

**rudely** ['ruːdlɪ] *adv* - **1.** [impolitely] unhöflich - **2.** [dirtily, naughtily] unanständig - **3.** [unexpectedly] jäh.

**rudeness** ['ruːdnɪs] *n* - **1.** [impoliteness] Unhöflichkeit *die* - **2.** [dirtiness, naughtiness] Unanständigkeit *die*.

**rudimentary** [ˌruːdɪ'mentərɪ] *adj* [basic] elementar.

**rudiments** ['ruːdɪmənts] *npl* Grundlagen *pl*.

**rue** [ruː] *vt* bereuen; **to ~ the day when …** den Tag verwünschen, an dem …

**rueful** ['ruːfʊl] *adj* reumütig; [smile] wehmütig.

**ruff** [rʌf] *n* [collar] Halskrause *die.*

**ruffian** ['rʌfjən] *n* Grobian *der.*

**ruffle** ['rʌfl] *n* [frill] Rüsche *die* ◇ *vt* - **1.** [hair, fur] zersausen; [water] kräuseln - **2.** [pride] verletzen; **to ~ sb's composure** jn aus der Ruhe bringen.

**rug** [rʌg] *n* - **1.** [carpet] kleiner Teppich; [by bed] Bettvorleger *der* - **2.** [blanket] Decke *die.*

**rugby** ['rʌgbɪ] *n* Rugby *das.*

**Rugby League** *n* Rugby mit dreizehn Spielern je Mannschaft.

**Rugby Union** *n* Rugby mit fünfzehn Spielern je Mannschaft.

**rugged** ['rʌgɪd] *adj* - **1.** [rocky, uneven - landscape] wild; [ - cliffs] zerklüftet - **2.** [sturdy] stabil - **3.** [roughly handsome]: **his ~ good looks** seine markanten Gesichtszüge.

**ruggedness** ['rʌgɪdnɪs] *n* [of landscape] Wildheit *die.*

**rugger** ['rʌgər] *n Br inf* Rugby *das.*

**ruin** ['ruːɪn] *n* - **1.** [financial downfall] Ruin *der* - **2.** [ruined building] Ruine *die* ◇ *vt* ruinieren; [chances, atmosphere] verderben.

➤ **in ruins** *adv*: **to be in ~s** [town, country] in Ruinen liegen; [building] eine Ruine sein; [marriage, career, plans] ruiniert sein.

**ruinous** ['ruːɪnəs] *adj* [expensive] ruinös.

**rule** [ruːl] *n* - **1.** [regulation, guideline] Regel *die;* **to bend the ~s** die Regeln frei ausllegen; [by turning a blind eye] ein Auge zuldrücken - **2.** [norm]: **the ~** die Regel; **as a ~** in der Regel - **3.** (*U*) [control] Herrschaft *die* - **4.** [ruler] Lineal *das* ◇ *vt* - **1.** [control, guide] beherrschen - **2.** [govern] regieren - **3.** [decide]: **to ~ that …** entscheiden, dass … ◇ *vi* - **1.** [give decision] entscheiden - **2.** *fml* [be paramount] herrschen - **3.** [govern] regieren.

➤ **rule out** *vt sep* auslschließen.

**rulebook** ['ruːlbʊk] *n:* **the ~** das Regelheft.

**ruled** [ruːld] *adj* [lined] liniert.

**ruler** ['ruːlər] *n* - **1.** [for measurement] Lineal *das* - **2.** [leader] Herrscher *der*, -in *die.*

**ruling** ['ruːlɪŋ] *adj* [in control] herrschend ◇ *n* [decision] Entscheidung *die.*

**rum** [rʌm] (*compar* **-mer;** *superl* **-mest**) *n* Rum *der* ◇ *adj Br dated* komisch; [person] kauzig.

**Rumania** [ruːˈmeɪnjə] *n* = **Romania.**

**Rumanian** [ruːˈmeɪnjən] *adj & n* = **Romanian.**

**rumba** ['rʌmbə] *n* Rumba *der* OR *die.*

**rumble** ['rʌmbl] *n* - **1.** [of thunder] Grollen *das;* [of lorry, train] Rumpeln *das;* [of stomach] Knurren *das* - **2.** *Am inf* [fight] Keilerei *die* ◇ *vt Br inf*

[discover] auf ldecken ◇ *vi* [thunder] grollen; [train] rumpeln; [stomach] knurren.

**rumbustious** [rʌmˈbʌstʃəs] *adj Br* wild und ausgelassen.

**ruminate** ['ruːmɪneɪt] *vi fml* [think]: **to ~ (about** OR **on sthg)** (über etw (*A*)) grübeln.

**rummage** ['rʌmɪdʒ] *vi* wühlen, stöbern.

**rummage sale** *n Am* Ramschverkauf *der.*

**rummy** ['rʌmɪ] *n* Rommé *das.*

**rumour** *Br*, **rumor** *Am* ['ruːmər] *n* Gerücht *das.*

**rumoured** *Br*, **rumored** *Am* ['ruːməd] *adj:* **he is ~ to be married already** er soll angeblich schon verheiratet sein.

**rump** [rʌmp] *n* - **1.** [of animal] Hinterteil *das* - **2.** *inf* [of person] Hinterteil *das* - **3.** POL Rumpf *der.*

**rumple** ['rʌmpl] *vt* [clothes] zerknittern; [hair] zerzausen.

**rump steak** *n* Rumpsteak *das.*

**rumpus** ['rʌmpəs] *n inf* Spektakel *das*, Krach *der.*

**rumpus room** *n Am* Spielzimmer *das.*

**run** [rʌn] (*pt* **ran;** *pp* **run;** *cont* **-ning**) *n* - **1.** [on foot] Lauf *der;* **to go for a ~** laufen gehen; **at a ~** im Lauf; **on the ~** auf der Flucht; **to make a ~ for it** rennen - **2.** [in car] Fahrt *die;* **to go for a ~** eine Fahrt machen - **3.** [series] Reihe *die;* **a ~ of successes** eine Erfolgsserie; **a ~ of bad luck** eine Pechsträhne - **4.** THEATRE: **it had an eight-week ~ on Broadway** es wurde für acht Wochen am Broadway gespielt - **5.** [great demand]: **a ~ on sthg** ein Ansturm auf etw (*A*) - **6.** [in tights] Laufmasche *die* - **7.** [in cricket, baseball] Lauf *der* - **8.** [for skiing] Abfahrt *die;* [for bobsleigh] Bahn *die* - **9.** [term, period]: **in the long/ short ~** auf lange/kurze Sicht (gesehen) - **10.** [free use]: **to have the ~ of the house** das Haus für sich haben ◇ *vt* - **1.** [on foot] rennen, laufen; **to ~ a race** ein Rennen laufen - **2.** [business, hotel] führen; [course, event] leiten - **3.** [operate - machine, film, computer program] laufen lassen; [ - experiment] durchlführen - **4.** [have and use - car] halten - **5.** [water, tap] laufen lassen; **to ~ a bath** ein Bad einlassen - **6.** [article, headline] veröffentlichen - **7.** *inf* [drive] fahren; **I'll ~ you home** ich fahre dich nach Hause - **8.** [move, pass]: **to ~ one's hand along sthg/over sthg** mit der Hand an etw (*D*) entlang/über etw (*A*) fahren - **9.** [put on - bus, train]: **we're ~ning a special bus to the airport** wir setzen einen Sonderbus zum Flughafen ein ◇ *vi* - **1.** [on foot, in race] laufen; [fast] rennen; **we had to ~ for the bus** wir mussten rennen, um den Bus zu erwischen; **to ~ for it** rennen - **2.** [road, track] führen, verlaufen; [river] fließen; [pipe, cable] verlaufen; **the path ~s along the coast** der Weg verläuft entlang der Küste - **3.** [in election]: **to ~ (for)** kandidieren

**R**

(für) **- 4.** [progress, develop] laufen; **to ~ smoothly** gut laufen **- 5.** [operate - machine, engine] laufen; [ - factory] arbeiten; **to ~ on unleaded petrol** mit bleifreiem Benzin fahren; **to ~ off mains electricity** mit Netzstrom laufen **- 6.** [bus, train] fahren; **the bus ~s every hour** der Bus fährt jede Stunde; **to be ~ning (an hour) late** (eine Stunde) Verspätung haben **- 7.** [liquid, tears, tap] laufen **- 8.** [eyes] tränen; **my nose is ~ning** mir läuft die Nase **- 9.** [colour] auslaufen; [clothes] ablfärben **- 10.** [continue - contract] gültig sein, laufen; [ - play] laufen; **the offer ~s until July** das Angebot gilt bis Juli **- 11.** *phr:* **to ~ dry** [river, well] ausltrocknen; [tank] leer werden; **to ~ low** knapp werden; **feelings are ~ning high** es herrscht große Aufregung.

◆ **run about** *vi* herumllaufen.

◆ **run across** *vt fus* [meet] zufällig treffen.

◆ **run along** *vi dated:* **~ along now!** fort mit dir/euch!

◆ **run around** *vi* = **run about.**

◆ **run away** *vi* [flee]: **to ~ away (from)** wegllaufen (von); [fast] weglrennen (von).

◆ **run away with** *vt fus* [subj: enthusiasm, emotions] durchlgehen mit; **he tends to let his enthusiasm ~ away with him** sein Enthusiasmus geht gern mit ihm durch.

◆ **run down** *vt sep* **- 1.** [in vehicle] überfahren **- 2.** [criticize] herunterlmachen **- 3.** [allow to decline] ablbauen ⬦ *vi* [battery] leer werden; [clock] abllaufen.

◆ **run in** *vt sep* [car] einlfahren.

◆ **run into** *vt fus* **- 1.** [meet - person] zufällig treffen **- 2.** [encounter - problem] stoßen auf (+ A); **to ~ into debt** in Schulden geraten **- 3.** [in vehicle] laufen *or* fahren gegen **- 4.** [amount to] sich belaufen auf (+ A).

◆ **run off** *vt sep* [copy] drucken ⬦ *vi:* **to ~ off (with sthg)** sich (mit etw) davonlmachen; **to ~ off with sb** mit jm durchlbrennen.

◆ **run on** *vi* [continue for longer than planned - story, meeting] sich hinlziehen; **time is ~ning on** die Zeit läuft.

◆ **run out** *vi* **- 1.** [supply, fuel] ausllgehen; **time is ~ning out** die Zeit wird knapp **- 2.** [licence, contract] abllaufen.

◆ **run out of** *vt fus:* **we've ~ out of petrol/money** wir haben kein Benzin/Geld mehr.

◆ **run over** *vt sep* [knock down] überfahren.

◆ **run through** *vt fus* **- 1.** [be present throughout] durchlaufen **- 2.** [practise] durchlgehen **- 3.** [read through] schnell durchllesen.

◆ **run to** *vt fus* **- 1.** [amount to] sich belaufen auf (+ A) **- 2.** [subj: budget] reichen für; **I can't ~ to that** das kann ich mir nicht leisten.

◆ **run up** *vt sep* [debt] machen; [bill] zusammenkommen lassen.

◆ **run up against** *vt fus* stoßen auf (+ A).

**run-around** *n inf:* **to give sb the ~** jn an der Nase herumlführen.

**runaway** ['rʌnǝweɪ] *adj* [child] ausgerissen;

[horse] durchgegangen; [inflation] galoppierend; [victory] sehr überzeugend ⬦ *n* [escapee] Ausreißer *der*, **-in** *die*.

**rundown** ['rʌndaʊn] *n* **- 1.** [report] Bericht *der* **- 2.** [decline] Abbau *der*.

◆ **run-down** *adj* **- 1.** [dilapidated] heruntergekommen **- 2.** [tired] erschöpft.

**rung** [rʌŋ] *pp* ▷ **ring** ⬦ *n lit* & *fig* Sprosse *die.*

**run-in** *n inf:* **to have a ~ with sb** mit jm aneinander geraten; **to have a ~ with the law** mit dem Gesetz in Konflikt geraten.

**runner** ['rʌnǝʳ] *n* **- 1.** [athlete] Läufer *der*, **-in** *die* **- 2.** [smuggler] Schmuggler *der*, **-in** *die*; **gun ~** Waffenschmuggler *der*, **-in** *die* **- 3.** [of sledge, skate] Kufe *die;* [of drawer] Schiene *die.*

**runner bean** *n Br* Stangenbohne *die.*

**runner-up** (*pl* **runners-up**) *n* Zweite *der, die.*

**running** ['rʌnɪŋ] *adj* **- 1.** [continuous] ständig **- 2.** [consecutive] hintereinander; **three weeks ~** drei Wochen hintereinander **- 3.** [water] fließend ⬦ *n* **- 1.** *sport* Laufen *das* **- 2.** [management, control] Leitung *die* **- 3.** [of machine] Betrieb *der* **- 4.** *phr:* **to make the ~** das Rennen machen; **to be in the ~ (for sthg)** im Rennen (für etw) liegen; **to be out of the ~ (for sthg)** aus dem Rennen (für etw) sein ⬦ *comp sport* [shoes, shorts] Lauf-; **~ track** Aschenbahn *die.*

**running commentary** *n* laufender Kommentar.

**running costs** *npl* Betriebskosten *pl.*

**running mate** *n* *Am* Kandidat für die Vizepräsidentschaft.

**running repairs** *npl* laufende Reparaturen *pl.*

**runny** ['rʌnɪ] (*compar* **-ier;** *superl* **-iest**) *adj* **- 1.** [food] flüssig **- 2.** [nose] laufend; [eyes] wässerig; **he had a ~ nose** ihm lief die Nase.

**run-of-the-mill** *adj* durchschnittlich, nullachtfünfzehn.

**runt** [rʌnt] *n* **- 1.** [animal] *kleinstes Tier eines Wurfs* **- 2.** *pej* [person] mickriger Kerl.

**run-through** *n* Probe *die.*

**run-up** *n* **- 1.** [preceding time]: **in the ~** to in der Zeit vor (+ D) **- 2.** *sport* Anlauf *der.*

**runway** ['rʌnweɪ] *n* Start- und Landebahn *die;* [for takeoff] Startbahn *die;* [for landing] Landebahn *die.*

**rupture** ['rʌptʃǝʳ] *n* **- 1.** *med* Bruch *der* **- 2.** [of relationship] (Ab)bruch *der.*

**rural** ['rʊǝrǝl] *adj* ländlich.

**ruse** [ruːz] *n* List *die.*

**rush** [rʌʃ] *n* **- 1.** [hurry] Eile *die;* **to be in a ~** es sehr eilig haben; **there's no ~** es eilt nicht; **to make a ~ for sthg** auf etw (A) zulstürzen *or* zulleilen **- 2.** [demand]: **~ (for *or* on sthg)** Ansturm *der* (auf etw (A)) **- 3.** [busiest period]

Stoßzeit *die* - **4.** [surge - of blood] Andrang *der;* [ - of water] Schwall *der* ◇ *vt* - **1.** [hurry - work] hastig erledigen; [ - meal] hastig essen; [ - person] drängen; **to ~ sb into sthg/into doing sthg** jn zu etw drängen/dazu drängen, etw zu tun - **2.** [send quickly - people] schnell bringen; [ - supplies, troops] schnell schicken; **to ~ sb to hospital** jn schnell ins Krankenhaus bringen - **3.** [attack suddenly] zulstürmen auf *(+ A);* [enemy, position] stürmen ◇ *vi* - **1.** [hurry] sich beeilen; **don't ~ into it!** [don't be hasty] handle nicht überstürzt! - **2.** [crowd] stürzen; [air, blood, water] schießen.

➼ **rushes** *npl* - **1.** BOT Binsen *pl* - **2.** CINEMA Musterkopie *die.*

**rushed** [rʌʃt] *adj* [person] unter Zeitdruck; [piece of work] schludrig.

**rush hour** *n* Hauptverkehrszeit *die,* Stoßzeit *die.*

**rush job** *n* - **1.** [urgent job] eilige Arbeit - **2.** [bad work] schludrige Arbeit.

**rusk** [rʌsk] *n* Zwieback *der.*

**russet** ['rʌsɪt] *adj* rostbraun.

**Russia** ['rʌʃə] *n* Russland *nt.*

**Russian** ['rʌʃn] *adj* russisch ◇ *n* - **1.** [person] Russe *der,* -sin *die* - **2.** [language] Russisch(e) *das.*

**Russian roulette** *n* russisches Roulett.

**rust** [rʌst] *n* [on metal] Rost *der* ◇ *vi* rosten.

**rustic** ['rʌstɪk] *adj* ländlich; [furniture, person] rustikal.

**rustle** ['rʌsl] *n* Rascheln *das* ◇ *vt* - **1.** [paper] rascheln mit; [subj: wind - leaves] rascheln lassen - **2.** *Am* [cattle] stehlen ◇ *vi* [paper, leaves] rascheln.

**rustproof** ['rʌstpruːf] *adj* rostfrei.

**rusty** ['rʌstɪ] (*compar* -ier; *superl* -iest) *adj* - **1.** [metal] rostig - **2.** *fig* [skill] eingerostet; **I'm ~** ich bin aus der Übung.

**rut** [rʌt] *n* [furrow] Furche *die;* **to get into a ~** in einen Trott kommen.

**rutabaga** [ˌruːtəˈbeɪɡə] *n Am* Steckrübe *die.*

**ruthless** ['ruːθlɪs] *adj* [person] rücksichtslos; [investigation, destruction] schonungslos; [murder] brutal.

**ruthlessly** ['ruːθlɪslɪ] *adv* rücksichtslos; [investigate] schonungslos.

**ruthlessness** ['ruːθlɪsnɪs] *n* Rücksichtslosigkeit *die;* [of investigation] Schonungslosigkeit *die.*

**RV** *n* - **1.** (*abbr of* revised version) *englische Bibelübersetzung aus dem 19. Jahrhundert* - **2.** *Am* (*abbr of* recreational vehicle) Wohnmobil *das.*

**Rwanda** [rʊˈændə] *n* Ruanda *nt.*

**Rwandan** [rʊˈændən] *adj* ruandisch ◇ *n* Ruander *der,* -in *die.*

**rye** [raɪ] *n* [grain] Roggen *der.*

**rye bread** *n* (U) Roggenbrot *das.*

**rye whiskey** *n* Ryewhiskey *der.*

## S

**s** (*pl* ss OR s's), **S** (*pl* Ss OR S's) [es] *n* [letter] s *das,* S *das.*

➼ **S** (*abbr of* south) S.

**SA** - **1.** *abbr of* South Africa - **2.** *abbr of* South America.

**Sabbath** ['sæbəθ] *n:* **the ~** der Sabbat.

**sabbatical** [səˈbætɪkl] *n* akademischer Urlaub; **to be on ~** akademischen Urlaub haben.

**saber** *n Am* = sabre.

**sable** *n* - **1.** (U) [fur] Zabel *der* - **2.** [coat] Zabelpelz *der.*

**sabotage** ['sæbətɑːʒ] *n* Sabotage *die* ◇ *vt* sabotieren.

**saboteur** [ˌsæbəˈtɜːʳ] *n* Saboteur *der,* -in *die.*

**sabre** *Br,* **saber** *Am* ['seɪbəʳ] *n* Säbel *der.*

**saccharin(e)** ['sækərɪn] *n* Saccharin *das.*

**sachet** ['sæʃeɪ] *n* [of shampoo, cream] Einzelpackung *die;* [of sugar, coffee] Portionspackung *die.*

**sack** [sæk] *n* - **1.** [bag] Sack *der* - **2.** *Br inf* [dismissal]: **to get** OR **be given the ~** rausgeschmissen werden ◇ *vt Br inf* [dismiss] rauslschmeißen.

**sackful** ['sækfʊl] *n* Sack *der.*

**sacking** ['sækɪŋ] *n* [fabric] Sackleinen *das.*

**sacrament** ['sækrəmənt] *n* Sakrament *das.*

**sacred** ['seɪkrɪd] *adj lit* & *fig* heilig.

**sacrifice** ['sækrɪfaɪs] *n lit* & *fig* Opfer *das* ◇ *vt lit* & *fig* opfern.

**sacrilege** ['sækrɪlɪdʒ] *n lit* & *fig* Sakrileg *das.*

**sacrilegious** [ˌsækrɪˈlɪdʒəs] *adj* sakrilegisch; *fig* frevelhaft.

**sacrosanct** ['sækrəʊsæŋkt] *adj lit* & *fig* sakrosankt.

**sad** [sæd] (*compar* -der; *superl* -dest) *adj* traurig.

**SAD** (*abbr of* seasonal affective disorder) *n saisonabhängige Depressionen.*

**S**

**sadden** ['sædn] *vt* traurig machen; I was ~ed to hear of her death die Nachricht von ihrem Tod machte mich sehr traurig.

**saddle** ['sædl] *n* Sattel *der* <> *vt* - **1.** [put saddle on] satteln - **2.** *fig* [burden]: **to ~ sb with sthg** jm etw auf lhalsen; **to be ~d with sthg** etw am Hals haben.

➤ **saddle up** *vt sep* & *vi* auf lsatteln.

**saddlebag** ['sædlbæg] *n* Satteltasche *die*.

**saddler** ['sædlə'] *n* Sattler *der*, -in *die*.

**sadism** ['seɪdɪzm] *n* Sadismus *der*.

**sadist** ['seɪdɪst] *n* Sadist *der*, -in *die*.

**sadistic** [sə'dɪstɪk] *adj* sadistisch.

**sadly** ['sædlɪ] *adv* - **1.** [sorrowfully] traurig - **2.** [regrettably] leider; ~ **neglected** stark vernachlässigt.

**sadness** ['sædnɪs] *n* - **1.** [sorrow] Trauer *die* - **2.** [distressing nature] Traurigkeit *die*.

**sadomasochistic** [,seɪdəʊmæsə'kɪstɪk] *adj* sadomasochistisch.

**s.a.e., sae** *n abbr of* **stamped addressed envelope.**

**safari** [sə'fɑːrɪ] *n* Safari *die;* **to go on ~** auf Safari gehen.

**safari park** *n* Safaripark *der*.

**safe** [seɪf] *adj* sicher; [product] ungefährlich; **it's not ~ for young children** es ist gefährlich für kleine Kinder; **have a ~ journey!** gute Reise!; **in ~ hands** in guten Händen; **~ and sound** wohlbehalten; **it's ~ to say that ...** man kann mit Sicherheit sagen, dass ...; **to be on the ~ side** um sicher zu gehen <> *n* Safe *der*.

**safebreaker** ['seɪf,breɪkə'] *n* Safeknacker *der*, -in *die*.

**safe-conduct** *n* - **1.** [document giving protection] Geleitbrief *der* - **2.** [protection] sicheres Geleit.

**safe-deposit box** *n* Banksafe *der*.

**safeguard** ['seɪfɡɑːd] *n:* ~ **(against sthg)** Schutz *der* (gegen etw) <> *vt:* **to ~ sb/sthg (against sthg)** jn/etw (vor etw (D)) schützen.

**safe haven** *n* sicherer Ort *or* Hafen.

**safe house** *n* Unterschlupf *der*.

**safekeeping** [,seɪf'kiːpɪŋ] *n* (sichere) Aufbewahrung.

**safely** ['seɪflɪ] *adv* sicher; [arrive] wohlbehalten; **I can ~ say (that)** ... ich kann mit Sicherheit sagen, dass ...

**safe sex** *n* Safersex *der*.

**safety** ['seɪftɪ] *n* Sicherheit *die* <> *comp* Sicherheits-.

**safety belt** *n* Sicherheitsgurt *der*.

**safety catch** *n* [on door] Sicherheitsverschluss *der;* [on gun] Abzugssicherung *die*.

**safety curtain** *n* eiserner Vorhang.

**safety-deposit box** *n* = **safe-deposit box.**

**safety island** *n Am* Verkehrsinsel *die*.

**safety match** *n* Sicherheitszündholz *das*.

**safety net** *n lit* & *fig* Sicherheitsnetz *das*.

**safety pin** *n* Sicherheitsnadel *die*.

**safety valve** *n* - **1.** TECH Sicherheitsventil *das* - **2.** *fig* [for emotions] Ventil *das*.

**saffron** ['sæfrən] *n* - **1.** [spice] Safran *der* - **2.** [colour] Safrangelb *das*.

**sag** [sæg] (*pt* & *pp* -**ged;** *cont* -**ging**) *vi* - **1.** [sink downwards] durchhängen - **2.** *fig* [demand, interest] ablflauen.

**saga** ['sɑːɡə] *n* - **1.** LITERATURE Sage *die;* [novel] Familienroman *der* - **2.** *pej* [drawn-out account] Roman *der*, Story *die*.

**sage** [seɪdʒ] *adj* [wise] weise <> *n* - **1.** [herb] Salbei *der* - **2.** [wise man] Weise *der*.

**Sagittarius** [,sædʒɪ'teərɪəs] *n* Schütze *der*.

**Sahara** [sə'hɑːrə] *n:* **the ~ (Desert)** die (Wüste) Sahara.

**said** [sed] *pt* & *pp* ▷ **say.**

**sail** [seɪl] *n* - **1.** [of boat] Segel *das;* **to set ~** loslfahren - **2.** [journey by boat]: **to go for a ~** segeln gehen <> *vt* - **1.** [ship] steuern; [sailing boat] segeln mit - **2.** [sea] befahren <> *vi* - **1.** [person - travel] mit dem Schiff fahren; [ - leave] ablfahren; SPORT segeln - **2.** [ship - move] fahren; [ - leave] ablfahren - **3.** [sailing boat] segeln - **4.** *fig* [through air] segeln.

➤ **sail through** *vt fus* [exam] spielend bestehen.

**sailboard** ['seɪlbɔːd] *n* Surfbrett *das*.

**sailboat** *n Am* = **sailing boat.**

**sailcloth** ['seɪlklɒθ] *n* Segeltuch *das*.

**sailing** ['seɪlɪŋ] *n* - **1.** SPORT Segeln *das;* **plain ~** ganz einfach - **2.** [trip by ship]: **there are ten ~s a day** das Schiff fährt zehnmal am Tag.

**sailing boat** *Br*, **sailboat** *Am* ['seɪlbəʊt] *n* Segelboot *das*.

**sailing dinghy** *n* (kleines) Segelboot.

**sailing ship** *n* Segelschiff *das*.

**sailor** ['seɪlə'] *n* Seemann *der;* [in navy] Matrose *der;* SPORT Segler *der*, -in *die;* **to be a good ~** [not seasick] seefest sein.

**saint** [seɪnt] *n* - **1.** RELIG Heilige *der*, *die* - **2.** *inf* [very good person]: **you'd need to be a ~ to put up with him** du müsstest eine Engelsgeduld haben, um mit ihm auszukommen.

**saintly** ['seɪntlɪ] (*compar* -**ier;** *superl* -**iest**) *adj* [person] gütig.

**sake** [seɪk] *n* - **1.** [benefit, advantage]: **for the ~ of sb** jm zuliebe; **for my/your ~** mir/dir zuliebe - **2.** [purpose]: **for the ~ of peace/your health** um des Friedens/deiner Gesundheit willen; **let us say, for the ~ of argument, that ...** sagen wir spaßeshalber, dass ...; **for the ~ of a few pounds** wegen ein paar Pfund - **3.** *phr:* **he likes to argue for its own ~** er streitet einfach gern; **for God's** OR **Heaven's ~!** um Gottes willen!

**salad** ['sæləd] *n* Salat *der*.

**salad bowl** *n* Salatschüssel *die*.

**salad cream** *n* Br *majonäseartige Salatsoße*.

**salad dressing** *n* Salatsoße *die*, Dressing *das*.

**salad oil** *n* Salatöl *das*.

**salamander** ['sæləˌmændəʳ] *n* Salamander *der*.

**salami** [sə'lɑːmɪ] *n* Salami *die*.

**salaried** ['sælərɪd] *adj*: **~ employee** Gehaltsempfänger *der*, -in *die*; **~ job** Angestelltenposten *der*.

**salary** ['sælərɪ] (*pl* -ies) *n* Gehalt *das*.

**salary scale** *n* Gehaltsskala *die*.

**sale** [seɪl] *n* - **1.** [instance of selling] Verkauf *der;* **to make a ~** etwas verkaufen - **2.** (U) [selling] Verkauf *der;* **to be on ~** verkauft werden; **to be for ~** zu verkaufen sein - **3.** [at reduced prices] Ausverkauf *der* - **4.** [auction] Auktion *die*.

➤ **sales** *npl* - **1.** [quantity sold] Absatz *der* - **2.** [at reduced prices]: **the ~s** der Schlussverkauf; **the January/summer ~s** der Winter-/Sommerschlussverkauf ⬥ *comp* Verkaufs-.

**saleroom** Br ['seɪlruːm], **salesroom** Am ['seɪlzruːm] *n* [for auction] Auktionsraum *der*.

**sales assistant** ['seɪlz-], **salesclerk** ['seɪlzklɜːrk] Am *n* Verkäufer *der*, -in *die*.

**sales drive** *n* verstärkter Werbeeinsatz.

**salesman** ['seɪlzmən] (*pl* -men [-mən]) *n* Verkäufer *der*; [representative] Vertreter *der*.

**sales pitch** *n* Verkaufstechnik *die*.

**sales rep** *n inf* Vertreter *der*, -in *die*.

**sales representative** *n* Vertreter *der*, -in *die*.

**salesroom** *n* Am = saleroom.

**sales slip** *n* Am [receipt] Kassenzettel *der*, Kassenbon *der*.

**sales tax** *n* Umsatzsteuer *die*.

**sales team** *n* Verkaufsteam *das*.

**saleswoman** ['seɪlzˌwumən] (*pl* -women [-ˌwɪmɪn]) *n* Verkäuferin *die*; [representative] Vertreterin *die*.

**salient** ['seɪljənt] *adj fml* Haupt-.

**saline** ['seɪlaɪn] *adj* salzig; **to be on a ~ drip** MED eine Tropfinfusion bekommen.

**saliva** [sə'laɪvə] *n* Speichel *der*.

**salivate** ['sælɪveɪt] *vi* Speichel produzieren.

**sallow** ['sæləʊ] *adj* fahl.

**sally** ['sælɪ] (*pl* -ies; *pt* & *pp* -ied) *n* [clever remark] geistreiche Bemerkung.

➤ **sally forth** *vi hum* OR *literary* los|ziehen.

**salmon** ['sæmən] (*pl inv* OR **-s**) *n* Lachs *der*.

**salmonella** [ˌsælmə'nelə] *n* (U): **~ (poisoning)** Salmonellenvergiftung *die*.

**salmon pink** *adj* lachsfarben.

**salon** ['sælɒn] *n* Salon *der*.

**saloon** [sə'luːn] *n* - **1.** Br [car] Limousine *die* - **2.** Am [bar] Wirtschaft *die;* [in the Wild West] Saloon *der* - **3.** Br [in pub]: **~ (bar)** *vornehmerer Teil eines Pubs, in dem die Getränke teurer sind* - **4.** [on ship] Salon *der*.

**salopettes** [ˌsælə'pets] *npl* Skihose *die*.

**salt** [sɔːlt, sɒlt] *n* Salz *das;* **the ~ of the earth** das Salz der Erde; **to rub ~ into sb's wounds** jm Salz in die Wunde streuen; **to take sthg with a pinch of ~** etw nicht wörtlich nehmen ⬥ *comp* Salz- ⬥ *vt* - **1.** [food] salzen - **2.** [roads] streuen.

➤ **salt away** *vt sep inf* [money] auf die hohe Kante legen.

**SALT** [sɔːlt] (*abbr of* **Strategic Arms Limitation Talks/Treaty**) *n* SALT.

**saltcellar** Br, ['sɔːlt,seləʳ], **salt shaker** Am, [-ˌʃeɪkəʳ] *n* Salzstreuer *der*.

**salted** ['sɔːltɪd] *adj* gesalzen; [water, herring] Salz-.

**saltpetre** Br, **saltpeter** Am [ˌsɔːlt'piːtəʳ] *n* Salpeter *der*.

**salt shaker** *n* Am = saltcellar.

**saltwater** ['sɔːlt,wɔːtəʳ] *n* Salzwasser *das* ⬥ *adj* Meeres-.

**salty** ['sɔːltɪ] (*compar* -ier; *superl* -iest) *adj* [tasting of salt] salzig.

**salubrious** [sə'luːbrɪəs] *adj*: **a not very ~ area** eine ziemlich heruntergekommene Gegend.

**salutary** ['sæljutrɪ] *adj* [warning] nützlich; [experience] heilsam.

**salute** [sə'luːt] *n* - **1.** MIL [with hand] Gruß *der;* **to give a ~** salutieren - **2.** MIL [firing of guns] Salut *der* - **3.** [formal acknowledgement]: **~ (to sthg)** Würdigung *die* (von etw) ⬥ *vt* - **1.** MIL salutieren vor (+ *D*) - **2.** [acknowledge formally, honour] würdigen; [person] ehren ⬥ *vi* MIL salutieren.

**salvage** ['sælvɪdʒ] *n* (U) - **1.** [rescue of ship] Bergung *die* - **2.** [property rescued] Bergungsgut *das* ⬥ *vt* - **1.** [rescue]: **to ~ sthg (from)** etw bergen (aus) - **2.** *fig:* **to ~ one's reputation** seinen Ruf retten.

**salvage vessel** *n* Bergungsschiff *das*.

**salvation** [sæl'veɪʃn] *n* (U) - **1.** [saviour] Rettung *die* - **2.** RELIG Erlösung *die*.

**Salvation Army** *n:* **the ~** die Heilsarmee.

**salve** [sælv] *vt:* **to ~ one's conscience** sein Gewissen beruhigen.

**salver** ['sælvəʳ] *n* Tablett *das*.

S

**salvo** ['sælvəʊ] (pl -s OR -es) n Salve die.

**Samaritan** [sə'mærɪtn] n: good ~ barmherziger Samariter.

**samba** ['sæmbə] n Samba die.

**same** [seɪm] adj - **1.** [identical]: **the ~** derselbe/dieselbe/dasselbe, dieselben pl; **you've got the ~ book as me** du hast das gleiche Buch wie ich; **the ~ thing** dasselbe; **the ~ ones** dieselben; **at the ~ time** [simultaneously] zur gleichen Zeit; [nevertheless] andererseits; **one and the ~** ein und derselbe/dieselbe/dasselbe - **2.** [unchanged]: **the ~** der/die/das Gleiche, die Gleichen pl; **the ~ ones** die Gleichen <> pron - **1.** [identical]: **the ~** derselbe/dieselbe/dasselbe, dieselben pl; **I'll have the ~ as her** ich möchte das Gleiche wie sie; **all** OR **just the ~** [nevertheless] trotzdem; **it's all the ~ to me** es ist mir gleich; **they are all the ~** sie sind alle gleich; **the ~ to you** gleichfalls; **(the) ~ again, please** noch einen/eine/eins, bitte; **it's not the ~** es ist nicht dasselbe - **2.** [unchanged]: **the ~** der/die/das Gleiche, die Gleichen pl; **her views are still the ~** sie hat immer noch die gleichen Ansichten <> adv [identically]: **to dress/feel the ~** sich gleich anziehen/fühlen; **they look the ~** sie sehen gleich aus.

**sameness** ['seɪmnɪs] n [similarity] Gleichheit die.

**samosa** [sə'məʊsə] n indische dreieckige Teigtasche mit würziger Gemüse- oder Fleischfüllung.

**sample** ['sɑːmpl] n - **1.** [of product] Probe die; [of fabric] Muster das - **2.** [for analysis] Probe die - **3.** [representative portion - of work] Musterbeispiel das; [ - of people in survey] Auswahl die <> vt - **1.** [taste] kosten - **2.** [try out, test] auslprobieren - **3.** MUS sampeln.

**sampler** ['sɑːmplə'] n SEWING Stickmustertuch das.

**sanatorium, sanitorium** Am [ˌsænə'tɔːrɪəm] (pl -riums OR -ria [-rɪə]) n Sanatorium das.

**sanctify** ['sæŋktɪfaɪ] (pt & pp -ied) vt - **1.** RELIG heiligen - **2.** [approve] sanktionieren.

**sanctimonious** [ˌsæŋktɪ'məʊnjəs] adj pej frömmlerisch.

**sanction** ['sæŋkʃn] n - **1.** [formal approval] Billigung die - **2.** [punishment] Strafe die <> vt [authorize] billigen.
➡ **sanctions** npl POL Sanktionen pl.

**sanctity** ['sæŋktətɪ] n [holiness] Heiligkeit die.

**sanctuary** ['sæŋktʃʊərɪ] (pl -ies) n - **1.** [for birds, wildlife] Schutzgebiet das - **2.** [safety, place of safety] Zufluchtsort der - **3.** [holy place] Heiligtum das.

**sanctum** ['sæŋktəm] (pl -s) n inf [private place]: **inner ~** Allerheiligste das.

**sand** [sænd] n Sand der <> vt [make smooth] schmirgeln.
➡ **sands** npl [beach] Sandstrand der.
➡ **sand down** vt sep ablschmirgeln.

**sandal** ['sændl] n Sandale die.

**sandalwood** ['sændlwʊd] n Sandelholz das.

**sandbag** ['sændbæg] n Sandsack der.

**sandbank** ['sændbæŋk] n Sandbank die.

**sandblast** ['sændblɑːst] vt sandstrahlen.

**sandbox** n Am = sandpit.

**sandcastle** ['sændˌkɑːsl] n Sandburg die.

**sand dune** n Sanddüne die.

**sander** ['sændə'] n [device] Abschleifgerät das.

**sandpaper** ['sændˌpeɪpə'] n Sandpapier das <> vt mit Sandpapier ablschmirgeln.

**sandpit** Br ['sændpɪt], **sandbox** Am ['sændbɒks] n Sandkasten der.

**sandstone** ['sændstəʊn] n Sandstein der.

**sandstorm** ['sændstɔːm] n Sandsturm der.

**sand trap** n Am GOLF Bunker der.

**sandwich** ['sænwɪdʒ] n Sandwich das; **ham/cheese ~** Schinken-/Käsebrot das <> vt fig: **to be ~ed between** eingeklemmt sein zwischen (+ D).

**sandwich board** n zweiteilige Reklametafel zum Umhängen.

**sandwich course** n Br Kurs, bei dem sich Studium und Praktikum abwechseln.

**sandy** ['sændɪ] (compar -ier; superl -iest) adj - **1.** [beach] sandig - **2.** [sand-coloured] sandfarben.

**sane** [seɪn] adj - **1.** [not mad] normal, bei Verstand - **2.** [sensible] vernünftig.

**sang** [sæŋ] pt ▷ sing.

**sanguine** ['sæŋgwɪn] adj: **to be ~ about sthg** zuversichtlich hinsichtlich einer Sache (G) sein.

**sanitary** ['sænɪtrɪ] adj - **1.** [connected with health - officer, system] Gesundheits-; [ - procedures] sanitär - **2.** [clean, hygienic] hygienisch.

**sanitary towel, sanitary napkin** Am n Damenbinde die.

**sanitation** [ˌsænɪ'teɪʃn] n (U) sanitäre Einrichtungen pl.

**sanitation worker** n Am Stadtreiniger der, -in die.

**sanitize, -ise** ['sænɪtaɪz] vt: **a ~d version of sthg** eine von den kompromittierenden Stellen gesäuberte Version einer Sache (G).

**sanitorium** n Am = sanatorium.

**sanity** ['sænətɪ] n (U) - **1.** [saneness] Verstand der - **2.** [good sense] Vernunft die.

**sank** [sæŋk] pt ▷ sink.

**Sanskrit** ['sænskrɪt] n Sanskrit das.

**Santa (Claus)** [ˈsæntə(ˌklɔːz)] n der Weih-nachtsmann.

**sap** [sæp] (pt & pp **-ped;** cont **-ping**) n **- 1.** (U) [of plant] Saft der **- 2.** Am inf [gullible person] Trottel der ◇ vt [weaken] schwächen.

**sapling** [ˈsæplɪŋ] n junger Baum.

**sapphire** [ˈsæfaɪəʳ] n Saphir der.

**Sarajevo** [ˌsærəˈjeɪvəʊ] n Sarajevo nt.

**sarcasm** [ˈsɑːkæzm] n Sarkasmus der.

**sarcastic** [sɑːˈkæstɪk] adj sarkastisch.

**sarcophagus** [sɑːˈkɒfəgəs] (pl **-gi** [-gaɪ] OR **-guses**) n Sarkophag der.

**sardine** [sɑːˈdiːn] n Sardine die.

**Sardinia** [sɑːˈdɪnjə] n Sardinien nt.

**sardonic** [sɑːˈdɒnɪk] adj [smile, look] hämisch.

**sari** [ˈsɑːrɪ] n Sari der.

**sarong** [səˈrɒŋ] n Sarong der.

**sarsaparilla** [ˌsɑːspəˈrɪlə] n **- 1.** [plant] Sarsa-parille die **- 2.** [drink] nichtalkoholisches koh-lensäurehaltiges Getränk aus Sarsaparillen-wurzeln.

**sartorial** [sɑːˈtɔːrɪəl] adj fml: his ~ elegance die Eleganz seiner Kleidung.

**SAS** (abbr of Special Air Service) n Spezialein-heit der britischen Armee.

**SASE** n Am abbr of self-addressed stamped en-velope.

**sash** [sæʃ] n [strip of cloth] Schärpe die.

**sash window** n Schiebefenster das.

**sassy** [ˈsæsɪ] adj Am inf frech.

**sat** [sæt] pt & pp ▷ sit.

**Sat.** (abbr of Saturday) Sa.

**SAT** [sæt] n **- 1.** (abbr of Standard Assessment Test) Eignungstest für Schulkinder in Eng-land und Wales **- 2.** (abbr of Scholastic Apti-tude Test) Zulassungsprüfung an US-Universitäten.

SAT
> Der SAT („Scholastic Aptitude Test") ist ei-ne in den USA übliche, aus zwei Teilen be-stehende Aufnahmeprüfung für die Univer-sität, die die sprachlichen (Lesen und Schreiben) und mathematischen Fertigkei-ten der Schüler im letzten Jahr der High School testet. Anders als die englischen „A-level"-Prüfungen ist sie nicht auf bestimm-te Leistungskurse bezogen.

**Satan** [ˈseɪtn] n Satan der.

**satanic** [səˈtænɪk] adj satanisch.

**satchel** [ˈsætʃəl] n Schultasche die.

**sated** [ˈseɪtɪd] adj fml: to be ~ with sthg von etw übersättigt sein.

**satellite** [ˈsætəlaɪt] n lit & fig Satellit der ◇ comp Satelliten-.

**satellite TV** n Satellitenfernsehen das.

**satiate** [ˈseɪʃɪeɪt] vt fml sättigen.

**satin** [ˈsætɪn] n Satin der ◇ comp **- 1.** [made of satin] Satin- **- 2.** [wallpaper, paint, finish] seiden-matt.

**satire** [ˈsætaɪəʳ] n Satire die.

**satirical** [səˈtɪrɪkl] adj satirisch.

**satirist** [ˈsætərɪst] n Satiriker der, -in die.

**satirize, -ise** [ˈsætəraɪz] vt satirisch dar-stellen.

**satisfaction** [ˌsætɪsˈfækʃn] n **- 1.** [pleasure] Be-friedigung die; to do sthg to sb's ~ etw zu js Zufriedenheit tun **- 2.** [something that pleases]: the job has few ~s die Arbeit ist nicht sehr befriedigend **- 3.** [fulfilment - of need, demand] Befriedigung die; [ - of criteria] Erfüllung die; to get ~ from sb Genugtuung von jm erhalten.

**satisfactory** [ˌsætɪsˈfæktərɪ] adj befriedi-gend.

**satisfied** [ˈsætɪsfaɪd] adj **- 1.** [happy] zufrieden; to be ~ with sthg mit etw zufrieden sein **- 2.** [convinced] überzeugt; to be ~ that ... über-zeugt sein, dass ...

**satisfy** [ˈsætɪsfaɪ] (pt & pp **-ied**) vt **- 1.** [make hap-py] zufrieden stellen **- 2.** [convince] überzeu-gen; to ~ sb/o.s. that ... jn/sich davon über-zeugen, dass ... **- 3.** [fulfil - need, demand] befriedigen; [ - requirements] genügen (+ D).

**satisfying** [ˈsætɪsfaɪŋ] adj befriedigend.

**satsuma** [ˌsætˈsuːmə] n Satsuma die.

**saturate** [ˈsætʃəreɪt] vt **- 1.** [drench] tränken; [subj: rain] durchnässen **- 2.** [fill completely, swamp - area, town] überschwemmen; [ - market] sättigen.

**saturated** adj **- 1.** [drenched] getränkt; [with rain] durchnässt **- 2.** [fat] gesättigt.

**saturation** [ˌsætʃəˈreɪʃn] comp: ~ bombing Bombenteppich der; ~ (television) coverage erschöpfende Berichterstattung im Fern-sehen.

**saturation point** n: to reach ~ den Sätti-gungspunkt erreichen.

**Saturday** [ˈsætədɪ] n Samstag der; what day is it? – it's ~ was ist heute? – es ist Samstag; are you going ~? inf gehst du (am) Samstag?; see you ~! inf bis Samstag!; on ~ am Samstag; on ~s samstags; to work ~s samstags arbeiten; last/this/next ~ letzten/diesen/nächsten Samstag; every ~ jeden Samstag; every other ~ jeden zweiten Samstag; the ~ before den Samstag davor, am vorhergehenden Samstag; the ~ before last vorletzten Sams-tag; the ~ after next, ~ week, a week on ~ über-nächsten Samstag, Samstag in einer Wo-che ◇ comp Samstags-; ~ morning/afternoon/evening/night Samstagmorgen der/-nachmittag der/-abend der/-nacht die; a ~ job ein Samstagsjob.

S

**Saturn** ['sætən] n [planet] Saturn der.

**sauce** [sɔːs] n - 1. CULIN Soße die, Sauce die; **apple ~** Apfelmus das - 2. Br inf [cheek] Frechheit die; **none of your ~!** sei nicht so frech!

**sauce boat** n Sauciere die.

**saucepan** ['sɔːspən] n Kochtopf der.

**saucer** ['sɔːsəʳ] n Untertasse die.

**saucy** ['sɔːsɪ] (compar **-ier**; superl **-iest**) adj inf frech.

**Saudi Arabia** ['saʊdɪ-] n Saudi-Arabien nt.

**sauna** ['sɔːnə] n Sauna die; **to have a ~** in die Sauna gehen.

**saunter** ['sɔːntəʳ] vi schlendern.

**sausage** ['sɒsɪdʒ] n Wurst die.

**sausage roll** n Br Würstchen in Blätterteig.

**sauté** [Br 'saʊteɪ, Am sʊ'teɪ] (pt & pp **sautéed** OR **sautéd**) adj [potatoes] Röst-, Brat- <> vt [potatoes] rösten, braten; [meat] sautieren.

**savage** ['sævɪdʒ] adj [attack, criticism, person] brutal; [dog] bissig <> n Wilde der, die <> vt - 1. [attack physically] anfallen - 2. [criticize] verreißen.

**savageness** ['sævɪdʒnɪs], **savagery** ['sævɪdʒrɪ] n [of attack, criticism] Brutalität die.

**savanna(h)** [sə'vænə] n Savanne die.

**save** [seɪv] vt - 1. [rescue] retten; **to ~ sb from sthg** jn vor etw (D) retten; **to ~ sb's life** jm das Leben retten - 2. [money, time, space] sparen - 3. [reserve] auf lheben; **to ~ a seat for sb** jm einen Platz freihalten; **to ~ one's strength/voice** seine Kräfte/Stimme schonen - 4. [make unnecessary - trouble, work] ersparen; [ - expense] vermeiden; **to ~ sb from doing sthg** es jm ersparen, etw zu tun - 5. SPORT ablwehren - 6. COMPUT speichern <> vi [save money] sparen; **to ~ with a bank** ein Sparkonto bei einer Bank haben <> n SPORT Parade die <> prep fml: **~ (for)** außer (+ D).
➤ **save on** vt fus sparen.
➤ **save up** vi: **to ~ up (for sthg)** (auf etw (A)) sparen.

**save as you earn** n Br Sparförderungsprogramm, bei dem monatlich direkt vom Einkommen abgezogene Beiträge steuerfreie Zinsen erbringen.

**saveloy** ['sævəlɔɪ] n Br Zervelatwurst die.

**saver** ['seɪvəʳ] n - 1. [object]: **to be a time/money ~** Zeit/Geld sparen - 2. [at bank, building society] Sparer der, -in die.

**saving grace** n [of person] positiver Zug; **the book's (one) ~** das einzig Positive an dem Buch.

**savings** ['seɪvɪŋz] npl Ersparnisse pl.

**savings account** n Am Sparkonto das.

**savings and loan association** n Am Bausparkasse die.

**savings bank** n Sparkasse die.

**saviour** Br, **savior** Am ['seɪvjəʳ] n Retter der, -in die.
➤ **Saviour** n: **the Saviour** der Erlöser OR Heiland.

**savoir-faire** [ˌsævwɑː'feəʳ] n Gewandtheit die.

**savour** Br, **savor** Am ['seɪvəʳ] vt genießen.

**savoury** Br, **savory** Am ['seɪvərɪ] (pl **-ies**) adj - 1. [not sweet] pikant - 2. [respectable, pleasant] angenehm <> n (pikantes) Häppchen.

**savoy (cabbage)** [sə'vɔɪ-] n Wirsing der.

**saw** [sɔː] (Br pt **-ed**; pp **sawn**, Am pt & pp **-ed**) pt ▷ **see** <> n Säge die <> vt sägen.
➤ **saw up** vt sep zersägen.

**sawdust** ['sɔːdʌst] n Sägemehl das.

**sawed-off shotgun** n Am = sawn-off shotgun.

**sawmill** ['sɔːmɪl] n Sägewerk das.

**sawn** [sɔːn] pp Br ▷ **saw**.

**sawn-off shotgun** Br, **sawed-off shotgun** ['sɔːd-] Am n Gewehr mit abgesägtem Lauf.

**sax** [sæks] n inf Saxofon das.

**Saxon** ['sæksn] adj sächsisch <> n Sachse der, Sächsin die.

**saxophone** ['sæksəfəʊn] n Saxofon das.

**saxophonist** [Br sæk'sɒfənɪst, Am 'sæksəˌfəʊnɪst] n Saxofonist der, -in die.

**say** [seɪ] (pt & pp **said**) vt - 1. [gen] sagen; **to ~ sthg again** etw nochmal sagen, etw wiederholen; **to ~ sthg to o.s.** sich (D) etw sagen; **who should I ~ it is?** wen darf ich melden?; **to ~ nothing of ...** von ... ganz zu schweigen; **he's said to be good** er soll gut sein - 2. [subj: clock, meter] anlzeigen; [subj: sign] besagen; **the letter ~s ...** in dem Brief steht ...; **it ~s here that ...** hier heißt es, dass ... - 3. [assume]: **I'd ~** he's lying meiner Meinung nach lügt er; **(let's) ~ you were to lose** nehmen wir an, du verlierst; **shall we ~ nine (o'clock)?** sagen wir um neun? - 4. phr: **that goes without ~ing** das versteht sich von selbst; **that's not ~ing much** das will nicht viel heißen; **I'll ~ this for him/ her ...** das muss ich aber doch zu seinen/ ihren Gunsten sagen ...; **it has a lot to be said for it** es spricht vieles dafür; **she doesn't have much to ~ for herself** inf sie sagt nicht viel <> n: **to have a/no ~ (in sthg)** etw/nichts (bei etw) zu sagen haben; **to have one's ~** seine Meinung äußern.
➤ **that is to say** adv das heißt.

**SAYE** abbr of save as you earn.

**saying** ['seɪɪŋ] n Redensart die; **as the ~ goes** wie man so sagt.

**say-so** n inf - 1. [unproven statement]: **don't believe it just on her ~** glaube es nicht einfach, nur

weil sie es sagt - **2.** [permission] Zustimmung
die.

**s/c** abbr of **self-contained.**

**scab** [skæb] n - **1.** [of wound] Schorf der - **2.** pej
[non-striker] Streikbrecher der, -in die.

**scabby** ['skæbɪ] (compar **-ier**; superl **-iest**) adj
schorfig.

**scabies** ['skeɪbiːz] n Krätze die, Skabies die.

**scaffold** ['skæfəʊld] n - **1.** [frame] Gerüst das
- **2.** [for executions] Schafott das.

**scaffolding** ['skæfəldɪŋ] n (U) Gerüst das.

**scalawag** n Am = **scallywag.**

**scald** [skɔːld] n Verbrühung die ◇ vt [burn]
verbrühen.

**scalding** ['skɔːldɪŋ] adj: ~ **(hot)** siedend
(heiß).

**scale** [skeɪl] n - **1.** [set of numbers] Skala die; [of
pay] Tarif der - **2.** [of ruler, thermometer] Einteilung die - **3.** [size] Größe die; [extent] Ausmaß
das; **on a small/large** ~ im Kleinen/Großen;
**the project is on a large** ~ das Projekt ist groß
angelegt - **4.** [size ratio] Maßstab der; **to** ~
maßstab(s)getreu - **5.** MUS Tonleiter die
- **6.** [of fish, snake] Schuppe die - **7.** Am = **scales**
◇ vt - **1.** [climb] erklimmen - **2.** [remove scales
from] schuppen.

➡ **scales** npl Waage die.

➡ **scale down** vt sep [industry] ablbauen; [invest-
ment] reduzieren; [production] drosseln.

**scale diagram** n maßstabgetreues Diagramm.

**scale model** n maßstabgetreues Modell.

**scallion** ['skæljən] n Am & Irish [spring onion]
Frühlingszwiebel die.

**scallop** ['skɒləp] n [shellfish] Kammmuschel
die; CULIN Jakobsmuschel die ◇ vt [decorate] mit
einem Bogenrand verzieren.

**scallywag** Br ['skælɪwæg], **scalawag** Am
['skæləwæg] n inf Frechdachs der.

**scalp** [skælp] n - **1.** ANAT Kopfhaut die - **2.** [re-
moved from head] Skalp der ◇ vt skalpieren.

**scalpel** ['skælpəl] n Skalpell das.

**scalper** ['skælpər] n Am Kartenschwarzhänd-
ler der, -in die.

**scam** [skæm] n inf Betrug der.

**scamp** [skæmp] n inf Frechdachs der.

**scamper** ['skæmpər] vi [children, dog] flitzen;
[mouse] huschen; **to** ~ **around** [children] herumltollen.

**scampi** ['skæmpɪ] n (U) Scampi pl.

**scan** [skæn] (pt & pp **-ned**; cont **-ning**) n MED &
TECH Scan der; [on pregnant woman] Ultraschall-
untersuchung die ◇ vt - **1.** [examine carefully
- map] studieren; [ - area] ablsuchen; [ - crowd]
mit den Augen ablsuchen - **2.** [glance at]
überfliegen - **3.** MED computertomografisch

untersuchen - **4.** COMPUT & TECH scannen ◇ vi
- **1.** LITERATURE dem Versmaß entsprechen
- **2.** COMPUT scannen.

**scandal** ['skændl] n - **1.** [scandalous event, outrage]
Skandal der - **2.** (U) [rumours] Skandalge-
schichten pl.

**scandalize, -ise** ['skændəlaɪz] vt schockieren.

**scandalous** ['skændələs] adj skandalös.

**Scandinavia** [ˌskændɪˈneɪvjə] n Skandinavi-
en nt.

**Scandinavian** [ˌskændɪˈneɪvjən] adj skandinavisch ◇ n [person] Skandinavier der, -in
die.

**scanner** ['skænər] n Scanner der.

**scant** [skænt] adj wenig.

**scanty** ['skæntɪ] (compar **-ier**; superl **-iest**) adj
[amount, resources] dürftig, spärlich; [dress]
knapp.

**scapegoat** ['skeɪpgəʊt] n Sündenbock der.

**scar** [skɑːr] (pt & pp **-red**; cont **-ring**) n lit & fig
Narbe die ◇ vt - **1.** [physically - skin, face]
Narben/eine Narbe hinterlassen auf (+ D);
[ - landscape] Spuren hinterlassen in (+ D)
- **2.** fig [mentally] zeichnen.

**scarce** ['skeəs] adj knapp; **to make o.s.** ~ sich
davonlschleichen.

**scarcely** ['skeəslɪ] adv kaum; **the prospects
were** ~ **promising** iron die Aussichten waren
nicht gerade vielversprechend.

**scarcity** ['skeəsətɪ] n Knappheit die.

**scare** [skeər] n - **1.** [sudden fright] Schreck(en)
der; **to give sb a** ~ jn erschrecken - **2.** [public
panic] Panik die; **a bomb** ~ ein Bombenalarm
◇ vt [frighten] erschrecken.

➡ **scare away, scare off** vt sep verscheuchen.

**scarecrow** ['skeəkrəʊ] n Vogelscheuche die.

**scared** ['skeəd] adj - **1.** [very frightened] verängstigt; **to be** ~ Angst haben; **to be** ~ **stiff** OR **to
death** fürchterliche Angst haben - **2.** [nerv-
ous, worried]: **to be** ~ **that** ... befürchten, dass ...

**scaremonger** ['skeəmʌŋgər] n Panikmacher
der, -in die.

**scarey** ['skeərɪ] adj = **scary.**

**scarf** [skɑːf] (pl **-s** OR **scarves**) n Schal der; [head-
scarf] Kopftuch das.

**scarlet** ['skɑːlət] adj scharlachrot.

**scarlet fever** n Scharlach der.

**scarper** ['skɑːpər] vi Br inf ablhauen.

**scarves** [skɑːvz] pl ➡ **scarf.**

**scary** ['skeərɪ] (compar **-ier**; superl **-iest**) adj inf
[story, film] gruselig.

**scathing** ['skeɪðɪŋ] adj [remark, criticism] scharf;
**to be** ~ **about sb/sthg** scharfe Bemerkungen
über jn/etw machen.

**S**

**scatter** ['skætə'] *vt* [spread out] verstreuen; [seed] streuen ⬦ *vi* [crowd] sich zerstreuen; [birds] auf lfliegen.

➤ **scatter about, scatter around** *vt sep* verstreuen.

**scatterbrained** ['skætəbreɪnd] *adj inf* zerstreut.

**scattered** ['skætəd] *adj* verstreut; [showers] vereinzelt.

**scattering** ['skætərɪŋ] *n:* a ~ of houses vereinzelte Häuser; a ~ of snow eine dünne Schneedecke.

**scatty** ['skætɪ] (*compar* -ier; *superl* -iest) *adj Br inf* schusselig.

**scavenge** ['skævɪndʒ] *vt* ergattern ⬦ *vi:* to ~ for sthg nach etw suchen.

**scavenger** ['skævɪndʒə'] *n* - 1. [animal] Aasfresser *der* - 2. *fig* [person]: he's a ~ er lebt von dem, was andere weglwerfen.

**scenario** [sɪ'nɑːrɪəʊ] (*pl* -s) *n* Szenario *das.*

**scene** [siːn] *n* Szene *die;* [location] Ort *der;* behind the ~s hinter den Kulissen; the police were quickly on the ~ die Polizei war schnell zur Stelle; to need a change of ~ einen Tapetenwechsel brauchen; it's not my ~ das ist nicht mein Fall; to set the ~ [give background information] Hintergrundinformationen geben; to set the ~ for sthg den Nährboden für etw bilden.

**scenery** ['siːnərɪ] *n* (U) - 1. [of countryside] Landschaft *die* - 2. [in theatre] Kulissen *pl.*

**scenic** ['siːnɪk] *adj* [view] schön; a ~ tour of the Highlands eine Tour durch die schöne Landschaft der Highlands.

**scenic route** *n* landschaftlich schöne Strecke.

**scent** [sent] *n* - 1. [smell - of flowers] Duft *der;* [ - of animal] Witterung *die* - 2. *fig* [track] Fährte *die;* to throw sb off the ~ jn von der Fährte ablbringen - 3. [perfume] Parfüm *das* ⬦ *vt* [subj: animal, person] wittern.

**scented** ['sentɪd] *adj* parfümiert; [flower] duftend.

**scepter** *n Am* = sceptre.

**sceptic** *Br*, **skeptic** *Am* ['skeptɪk] *n* Skeptiker *der*, -in *die.*

**sceptical** *Br*, **skeptical** *Am* ['skeptɪkl] *adj* skeptisch; to be ~ about sthg bezüglich etw (G) skeptisch sein.

**scepticism** *Br*, **skepticism** *Am* ['skeptɪsɪzm] *n* Skepsis *die.*

**sceptre** *Br*, **scepter** *Am* ['septə'] *n* Zepter *das.*

**schedule** [*Br* 'ʃedjuːl, *Am* 'skedʒʊl] *n* - 1. [plan] Plan *der*, Programm *das;* **(according) to** ~ planmäßig; ahead of/behind ~ früher/ später als geplant; on ~ pünktlich, plan-

mäßig - 2. [written list] Verzeichnis *das* ⬦ *vt:* to ~ sthg (for) etw planen *or* anlsetzen (für).

**scheduled flight** [*Br* 'ʃedjuːld-, *Am* 'skedjʊld-] *n* Linienflug *der.*

**schematic** [skɪ'mætɪk] *adj* schematisch.

**scheme** [skiːm] *n* - 1. [plan] Programm *das;* pension ~ Altersversorgung *die* - 2. *pej* [dishonest plan] raffinierter Plan - 3. [arrangement, decoration - of room] Einrichtung *die;* colour ~ Farbzusammenstellung *die* - 4. *phr:* in the (grand) ~ of things gesamt betrachtet ⬦ *vt pej:* to ~ to do sthg planen, etw zu tun ⬦ *vi pej* Pläne schmieden.

**scheming** ['skiːmɪŋ] *adj* raffiniert; [politician] intrigant.

**schism** ['sɪzm, 'skɪzm] *n* Spaltung *die.*

**schizophrenia** [ˌskɪtsə'friːnjə] *n* Schizophrenie *die.*

**schizophrenic** [ˌskɪtsə'frenɪk] *adj* schizophren ⬦ *n* Schizophrene *der*, *die.*

**schlepp** [ʃlep] *Am inf vt* schleppen ⬦ *vi* sich schleppen.

**schmal(t)z** [ʃmɔːlts] *n inf* Schmalz *der.*

**schmuck** [ʃmʌk] *n Am inf* Dussel *der.*

**scholar** ['skɒlə'] *n* - 1. [expert] Gelehrte *der*, *die* - 2. *dated* [school student] Schüler *der*, -in *die* - 3. [holder of scholarship] Stipendiat *der*, -in *die.*

**scholarship** ['skɒləʃɪp] *n* - 1. [grant] Stipendium *das* - 2. [learning] Gelehrsamkeit *die.*

**scholastic** [skə'læstɪk] *adj fml* [educational] schulisch.

**school** [skuːl] *n* - 1. [gen] Schule *die;* to go to ~ in die Schule gehen; at ~ in der Schule - 2. UNIV [department] Fachbereich *der;* ~ of medicine/ law medizinische/juristische Fakultät - 3. *Am* [university] Universität *die* - 4. [group of fish, dolphins] Schule *der.*

**school age** *n* Schulalter *das*, schulpflichtiges Alter.

**schoolbook** ['skuːlbʊk] *n* Schulbuch *das.*

**schoolboy** ['skuːlbɔɪ] *n* Schuljunge *der*, Schüler *der.*

**schoolchild** ['skuːltʃaɪld] (*pl* -children [-tʃɪldrən]) *n* Schulkind *das.*

**schooldays** ['skuːldeɪz] *npl* Schulzeit *die.*

**school dinner** *n* Schulessen *das.*

**school district** *n Am* Schulbezirk *der.*

**school friend** *n* Schulfreund *der*, -in *die.*

**schoolgirl** ['skuːlgɜːl] *n* Schulmädchen *das*, Schülerin *die.*

**schooling** ['skuːlɪŋ] *n* [education] Ausbildung *die.*

**schoolkid** ['skuːlkɪd] *n inf* Schulkind *das.*

**school-leaver** [-ˌliːvə'] *n Br* Schulabgänger *der*, -in *die.*

**school-leaving age** [-'liːvɪŋ-] *n Br* Schulabgangsalter *das*.

**schoolmarm** ['skuːlmɑːm] *n Am* Schulmeisterin *die*.

**schoolmaster** ['skuːlˌmɑːstəʳ] *n dated* Schulmeister *der*.

**schoolmistress** ['skuːlˌmɪstrɪs] *n dated* Schulmeisterin *die*.

**school of thought** *n* Denkart *die*.

**school report** *n* (Schul)zeugnis *das*.

**schoolroom** ['skuːlrʊm] *n dated* Klassenzimmer *das*.

**schoolteacher** ['skuːlˌtiːtʃəʳ] *n* Lehrer *der*, -in *die*.

**school uniform** *n* Schuluniform *die*.

**schoolwork** ['skuːlwɜːk] *n (U)* Schularbeiten *pl*.

**school year** *n* Schuljahr *das*.

**schooner** ['skuːnəʳ] *n* - **1.** [ship] Schoner *der* - **2.** *Br* [sherry glass] großes Sherryglas.

**sciatica** [saɪ'ætɪkə] *n* Ischias *der*.

**science** ['saɪəns] *n* - **1.** *(U)* [system of knowledge] Wissenschaft *die* - **2.** [branch of knowledge] Naturwissenschaft *die* ◇ *comp* [course, book] naturwissenschaftlich; [degree] in Naturwissenschaften.

**science fiction** *n* Sciencefiction *die*.

**science park** *n* Wissenschaftspark *der*.

**scientific** [ˌsaɪən'tɪfɪk] *adj* wissenschaftlich.

**scientist** ['saɪəntɪst] *n* Wissenschaftler *der*, -in *die*; [of physical or natural sciences] Naturwissenschaftler *der*, -in *die*.

**sci-fi** [ˌsaɪ'faɪ] *n inf abbr of* science fiction.

**Scilly Isles** ['sɪlɪ-], **Scillies** ['sɪlɪz] *npl*: the ~ die Scilly-Inseln; in the ~ auf den Scilly-Inseln.

**scintillating** ['sɪntɪleɪtɪŋ] *adj* [conversation, speaker] vor Geist sprühend.

**scissors** ['sɪzəz] *npl* Schere *die*; a pair of ~ eine Schere.

**sclerosis** [sklɪ'rəʊsɪs] *n* ▷ **multiple sclerosis**.

**scoff** [skɒf] *vt Br inf* verputzen ◇ *vi* [mock] spotten; to ~ at sb/sthg über jn/etw spotten.

**scold** [skəʊld] *vt* auslschimpfen.

**scone** [skɒn, skəʊn] *n* kleiner brötchenartiger Kuchen, der mit Butter oder Marmelade und Schlagsahne bestrichen gegessen wird.

**scoop** [skuːp] *n* - **1.** [kitchen implement] Schaufel *die*; [for potato, ice-cream] Portionierer *der* - **2.** [scoopful] Kugel *die* - **3.** [news report] Exklusivbericht *der* ◇ *vt* schaufeln; [liquid] schöpfen.

◆ **scoop out** *vt sep* [remove] herauslöffeln.

**scoot** [skuːt] *vi inf* sausen.

**scooter** ['skuːtəʳ] *n* - **1.** [toy] (Tret)roller *der* - **2.** [motorcycle] (Motor)roller *der*.

**scope** [skəʊp] *n (U)* - **1.** [opportunity] Möglichkeit *die* - **2.** [range] Umfang *der*.

**scorch** [skɔːtʃ] *vt* - **1.** [clothes] versengen; [food] anlbrennen; [skin] verbrennen - **2.** [grass, fields] versengen.

**scorched earth policy** [skɔːtʃt-] *n* Politik *die* der verbrannten Erde.

**scorcher** ['skɔːtʃəʳ] *n inf* [very hot day] knallheißer Tag.

**scorching** ['skɔːtʃɪŋ] *adj inf*: ~ (hot) [day, weather] knallheiß; [sun] sengend.

**score** [skɔːʳ] *n* - **1.** SPORT Spielstand *der*; [at end of game] Ergebnis *das*; the ~ is 4–3 es steht 4 zu 3 - **2.** [in test, competition] Punkte *pl* - **3.** *dated* [twenty] zwanzig; three ~ years and ten siebzig Jahre - **4.** MUS Noten *pl* - **5.** [subject]: on that ~ in dieser Hinsicht ◇ *vt* - **1.** SPORT [goal] schießen; [achieve - success] erzielen; [ - victory] erringen; [ - hit] landen - **2.** [win in an argument]: to ~ a point over sb jn auslstechen - **4.** [cut - surface] einlkerben; [ - line] einlritzen ◇ *vi* - **1.** SPORT Punkte erzielen; to ~ a goal [in football] ein Tor schießen; [in handball] ein Tor werfen - **2.** [in an argument]: to ~ over sb jn auslstechen.

◆ **scores** *npl* [lots]: ~s of letters/phone calls/etc jede Menge Briefe/Anrufe/etc.

◆ **score out** *vt sep Br* durchlstreichen.

**scoreboard** ['skɔːbɔːd] *n* Anzeigetafel *die*.

**scorecard** ['skɔːkɑːd] *n* Punktkarte *die*.

**score-draw** *n* FTBL Erzielen von Punkten beim Toto, von mindestens 1:1.

**scorer** ['skɔːrəʳ] *n* - **1.** [official] Anschreiber *der*, -in *die* - **2.** [player]: (goal) ~ Torschütze *der*, -zin *die*.

**scorn** [skɔːn] *n (U)* Verachtung *die*; to pour ~ on sb/sthg jn/etw verhöhnen ◇ *vt* - **1.** [despise] verachten - **2.** *fml* [refuse to accept] verschmähen.

**scornful** ['skɔːnfʊl] *adj* [laugh, remark] verächtlich; he's always very ~ about my work er beltrachtet meine Arbeit mit Verachtung; to be ~ of sthg etw verachten.

**Scorpio** ['skɔːpɪəʊ] (*pl* -**s**) *n* Skorpion *der*.

**scorpion** ['skɔːpjən] *n* Skorpion *der*.

**Scot** [skɒt] *n* Schotte *der*, -tin *die*.

**scotch** [skɒtʃ] *vt* [idea, rumour] ein Ende setzen (+ *D*).

**Scotch** [skɒtʃ] *adj* schottisch ◇ *n* [whisky] Scotch *der*.

**Scotch egg** *n Br* hartgekochtes Ei, das mit einer Mischung aus Wurst- und Brotstückchen paniert wird.

**Scotch (tape)**® *n Am* Tesafilm® *der*.

**S**

**scot-free** *adj inf:* **to get off ~** ungeschoren davonlkommen.

**Scotland** ['skɒtlənd] *n* Schottland *nt.*

**Scotland Yard** *n* Scotland Yard *der, Sitz der Londoner Polizei.*

**Scots** [skɒts] *adj* schottisch ◇ *n* [dialect] Schottisch *das.*

**Scotsman** ['skɒtsmən] *(pl* **-men** [-mən]) *n* Schotte *der.*

**Scotswoman** ['skɒtswʊmən] *(pl* **-women** [-ˌwɪmɪn]) *n* Schottin *die.*

**Scottish** ['skɒtɪʃ] *adj* schottisch.

**Scottish National Party** *n:* **the ~** die Schottische Nationale Partei.

**scoundrel** ['skaʊndrəl] *n dated* Schurke *der.*

**scour** [skaʊəʳ] *vt* - **1.** [clean] scheuern - **2.** [search] durchkämmen.

**scourer** ['skaʊərəʳ] *n* Topfkratzer *der.*

**scourge** [skɜːdʒ] *n* Geißel *die.*

**Scouse** [skaʊs] *n inf* - **1.** [person] Liverpooler *der,* -in *die* - **2.** [accent] Liverpooler Dialekt.

**scout** [skaʊt] *n* MIL Kundschafter *der,* -in *die.* ◆ **Scout** *n* [boy scout] Pfadfinder *der.* ➧ **scout around** *vi:* **to ~ around (for sthg)** (nach etw) herumlsuchen.

**scoutmaster** ['skaʊtˌmɑːstəʳ] *n* Gruppenführer *der.*

**scowl** [skaʊl] *n* finsterer OR böser Blick ◇ *vi* ein finsteres OR böses Gesicht machen; **to ~ at sb** jn finster OR böse anlsehen.

**SCR** *(abbr of* **senior common room)** *n Br* Aufenthaltsraum für Lehrkräfte an Universitäten.

**scrabble** ['skræbl] *vi* - **1.** [scramble] klettern - **2.** [feel around] herumlwühlen; **to ~ around for sthg** nach etw wühlen.

**scraggy** ['skrægɪ] *(compar* **-ier;** *superl* **-iest)** *adj inf* [animal] mager; [neck, meat] sehnig.

**scram** [skræm] *(pt & pp* **-med;** *cont* **-ming)** *vi inf* verduften.

**scramble** ['skræmbl] *n* [rush] Gedrängel *das* ◇ *vi* - **1.** [climb] klettern - **2.** [struggle]: **to ~ for sthg** um etw kämpfen.

**scrambled eggs** ['skræmbld-] *npl* Rührei *das.*

**scrambler** ['skræmbləʳ] *n* COMPUT Scrambler *der.*

**scrap** [skræp] *(pt & pp* **-ped;** *cont* **-ping)** *n* - **1.** [small piece] Stückchen *das;* [of paper, material, conversation] Fetzen *der;* **not a ~ of evidence** kein einziger Beweis; **it won't make a ~ of difference** das macht überhaupt keinen Unterschied - **2.** [metal] Schrott *der* - **3.** *inf* [fight] Rauferei *die;* [quarrel] Streit *der* ◇ *vt* [plan, system] auflgeben; [car, ship] verschrotten. ➧ **scraps** *npl* [food] (Essens)reste *pl.*

**scrapbook** ['skræpbʊk] *n* Erinnerungsalbum *das.*

**scrap dealer** *n* Schrotthändler *der,* -in *die.*

**scrape** [skreɪp] *n* - **1.** [scraping noise] Kratzen *das* - **2.** *dated* [difficult situation]: **to get into a ~** in die Klemme geraten ◇ *vt* - **1.** [remove]: **to ~ sthg off sthg** etw von etw ablschaben - **2.** [peel] schaben - **3.** [rub against - car, bumper] schrammen; [ - glass] verkratzen; [ - knee, skin] aufl-schürfen ◇ *vi* [rub]: **to ~ against sthg** etw streifen. ➧ **scrape through** *vt fus* [exam, test] mit knapper Not bestehen. ➧ **scrape together** *vt sep* [money] zusammenlkratzen; [sponsors, team] zusammenlbekommen.

**scraper** ['skreɪpəʳ] *n* [for paint] Spachtel *der.*

**scrap heap** *n* - **1.** [of waste metal] Schrotthaufen *der* - **2.** *fig:* **to be thrown on the ~** [people] zum alten Eisen geworfen werden; [ideas] ausrangiert werden.

**scrapings** ['skreɪpɪŋz] *npl* [bits] Reste *pl;* [peelings] Schalen *pl.*

**scrap merchant** *n Br* Schrotthändler *der,* -in *die.*

**scrap metal** *n* Schrott *der.*

**scrap paper** *Br,* **scratch paper** *Am n* Schmierpapier *das.*

**scrappy** ['skræpɪ] *(compar* **-ier;** *superl* **-iest)** *adj pej* [piece of work] zusammengestückelt; [knowledge] lückenhaft.

**scrapyard** ['skræpjɑːd] *n* Schrottplatz *der.*

**scratch** [skrætʃ] *n* - **1.** [on skin, surface] Kratzer *der* - **2.** *phr:* **to start sthg from ~** etw ganz von vorne anlfangen; **to be up to ~** den Erwartungen entsprechen ◇ *vt* - **1.** [skin] kratzen; **to ~ o.s.** sich kratzen - **2.** [surface] verkratzen ◇ *vi* - **1.** [branch, knife, thorn]: **to ~ at/against sthg** an etw *(D)*/gegen etw kratzen - **2.** [person, animal] sich kratzen.

**scratch card** *n* Rubbellos *das.*

**scratchpad** ['skrætʃpæd] *n Am* Notizblock *der.*

**scratch paper** *n Am* = scrap paper.

**scratchy** ['skrætʃɪ] *(compar* **-ier;** *superl* **-iest)** *adj* - **1.** [sound] kratzend; [record] verkratzt - **2.** [material, garment] kratzig.

**scrawl** [skrɔːl] *n* [scribble] Kritzelei *die* ◇ *vt* [scribble] hinlkritzeln.

**scrawny** ['skrɔːnɪ] *(compar* **-ier;** *superl* **-iest)** *adj* [person, legs, arms] dürr; [animal] mager.

**scream** [skriːm] *n* - **1.** [of person] Schrei *der* - **2.** [of tyres] Quietschen *das;* [of siren, machine] Heulen *das* - **3.** *inf* [funny person]: **to be a ~** zum Schreien sein ◇ *vt* schreien ◇ *vi* - **1.** [person] schreien - **2.** [tyres] quietschen; [machine, jet] heulen.

**scree** [skriː] *n* Geröll *das.*

**screech** [skriːtʃ] *n* - **1.** [of person, bird] Kreischen *das* - **2.** [of tyres, brakes] Quietschen *das* ◇ *vt* kreischen ◇ *vi* - **1.** [person, bird] kreischen

- **2.** [tyres] quietschen; **to ~ to a halt** mit quietschenden Bremsen anlhalten.

**screen** [skri:n] *n* - **1.** [viewing surface] Bildschirm *der;* [in cinema] Leinwand *die* - **2.** [films]: **the (big) ~** der Film - **3.** [protective panel] Wandschirm *der* <> *vt* - **1.** [in cinema] zeigen - **2.** [on TV] auslstrahlen - **3.** [hide] ablschirmen; **~ed from view** vor Blicken geschützt - **4.** [shield]: **to ~ sthg (from sb/sthg)** etw (gegen jn/etw) ablschirmen - **5.** [candidate, luggage] überprüfen - **6.** MED [examine] untersuchen; **to ~ sb for sthg** jn auf etw (A) untersuchen.

▸ **screen off** *vt sep* abltrennen.

**screening** ['skri:nɪŋ] *n* - **1.** [in cinema] Vorführrung *die* - **2.** [on TV] Ausstrahlung *die* - **3.** (U) [for security] Überprüfung *die* - **4.** (U) MED [examination] Untersuchung *die.*

**screenplay** ['skri:npleɪ] *n* Drehbuch *das.*

**screen print** *n* Siebdruck *der.*

**screen saver** *n* COMPUT Bildschirmschoner *der.*

**screen test** *n* Probeaufnahmen *pl.*

**screenwriter** ['skri:n̩raɪtəʳ] *n* Filmautor *der,* -in *die.*

**screw** [skru:] *n* [nail] Schraube *die* <> *vt* - **1.** [fix with screws]: **to ~ sthg to sthg** etw an etw (A) schrauben - **2.** [lid]: **to ~ sthg on/off** etw zu-/auf lschrauben - **3.** vulg [have sex with] bumsen, vögeln <> *vi* - **1.** [lid]: **to ~ on/off** sich zu-/auf lschrauben lassen; **to ~ together** sich zusammenschrauben lassen - **2.** vulg [have sex] bumsen, vögeln.

▸ **screw up** *vt sep* - **1.** [crumple up] zusammenlknüllen - **2.** [contort, twist - eyes] zusammenlkneifen; [ - face] verziehen - **3.** vinf [ruin] vermasseln.

**screwball** ['skru:bɔ:l] *n* Am inf [person] Spinner *der,* -in *die.*

**screwdriver** ['skru:draɪvəʳ] *n* [tool] Schraubenzieher *der.*

**screwtop jar** ['skru:tɒp-] *n* Glas *das* mit Schraubverschluss.

**screwy** ['skru:ɪ] *adj Am inf* verrückt.

**scribble** ['skrɪbl] *n* Gekritzel *das* <> *vt* hinlkritzeln <> *vi* [write] vor sich hinlschreiben; [messily] kritzeln.

**scribe** [skraɪb] *n fml* Schreiber *der,* -in *die.*

**scrimp** [skrɪmp] *vi:* **to ~ and save** geizen und sparen.

**script** [skrɪpt] *n* - **1.** [of film] Skript *das* - **2.** [system of writing] Schrift *die* - **3.** [handwriting] Handschrift *die.*

**scripted** ['skrɪptɪd] *adj* schriftlich ausgearbeitet.

**Scriptures** ['skrɪptʃəz] *npl:* **the ~** die (Heilige) Schrift.

**scriptwriter** ['skrɪptˌraɪtəʳ] *n* Textautor *der,* -in *die;* [of film] Filmautor *der,* -in *die.*

**scroll** [skrəʊl] *n* [roll of paper] Schriftrolle *die.*

▸ **scroll down** *vi* COMPUT hinunterlscrollen.

▸ **scroll up** *vi* COMPUT hinauf lscrollen.

**scroll bar** *n* COMPUT Scrollbar *die.*

**scrooge** [skru:dʒ] *n inf pej* Geizhals *der.*

**scrotum** ['skrəʊtəm] (*pl* -ta [-tə] OR -tums) *n* Hodensack *der,* Skrotum *das.*

**scrounge** [skraʊndʒ] *inf vt:* **to ~ sthg (off sb)** etw (bei jm) ablstauben OR schnorren <> *vi* schnorren; **to ~ off sb** Br jm auf der Tasche liegen.

**scrounger** ['skraʊndʒəʳ] *n inf* Schnorrer *der,* -in *die.*

**scrub** [skrʌb] (*pt* & *pp* -**bed;** *cont* -**bing**) *n* - **1.** [rub]: **to give sthg a (good) ~** etw (gründlich) schrubben - **2.** [undergrowth] Gestrüpp *das* <> *vt* schrubben.

**scrubbing brush** Br ['skrʌbɪŋ-], **scrub brush** Am *n* Schrubbbürste *die.*

**scruff** [skrʌf] *n:* **by the ~ of the neck** am Genick.

**scruffy** ['skrʌfɪ] (*compar* -**ier;** *superl* -**iest**) *adj* [person, clothes] ungepflegt; [part of town] heruntergekommen.

**scrum(mage)** ['skrʌm(ɪdʒ)] *n* RUGBY Gedränge *das.*

**scrumptious** ['skrʌmpʃəs] *adj inf* lecker.

**scrumpy** ['skrʌmpɪ] *n* (U) Br starker Apfelmost.

**scrunch** [skrʌntʃ] *inf vt* [paper] zusammenlknüllen; [can] zusammenlquetschen <> *vi* knirschen.

**scrunchy** ['skrʌntʃɪ] (*pl* -**ies**) *n* Zopfband *das.*

**scruples** ['skru:plz] *npl* Skrupel *pl.*

**scrupulous** ['skru:pjʊləs] *adj* - **1.** [fair] gewissenhaft - **2.** [thorough] peinlich genau.

**scrupulously** ['skru:pjʊləslɪ] *adv* - **1.** [fairly] gewissenhaft - **2.** [thoroughly - honest, fair] äußerst; [ - clean] peinlich.

**scrutinize, -ise** ['skru:tɪnaɪz] *vt* genau untersuchen; [face] prüfend anlsehen.

**scrutiny** ['skru:tɪnɪ] *n* (U) (genaue) Untersuchung OR Prüfung.

**scuba diving** ['sku:bə-] *n* (Sport)tauchen *das.*

**scud** [skʌd] (*pt* & *pp* -**ded;** *cont* -**ding**) *vi literary* jagen.

**scuff** [skʌf] *vt* - **1.** [drag]: **to ~ one's feet** schlurfen - **2.** [damage - shoes, floor] ablwetzen; [ - furniture] ablnutzen.

**scuffle** ['skʌfl] *n* Rauferei *die* <> *vi* sich raufen; **to ~ with sb** mit jm raufen.

**scull** [skʌl] *n* [oar] Skull *das* <> *vi* skullen.

**S**

**scullery** ['skʌlərɪ] (pl **-ies**) n Spülküche die.

**sculpt** [skʌlpt] vt: **to ~ a figure in wood/marble** eine Figur in Holz schnitzen/in Marmor meißeln.

**sculptor** ['skʌlptəʳ] n Bildhauer der, -in die.

**sculpture** ['skʌlptʃəʳ] n - **1.** [work of art] Skulptur die, Plastik die - **2.** (U) [art] Bildhauerei die, Skulptur die ⋄ vt formen; [in stone, wood] hauen.

**scum** [skʌm] n - **1.** [froth] Schaum der - **2.** vinf pej [worthless people] Abschaum der.

**scupper** ['skʌpəʳ] vt - **1.** NAUT [sink] versenken - **2.** Br fig [plan] zerschlagen; [chance] ruinieren.

**scurf** [skɜːf] n (U) Schuppen pl.

**scurrilous** ['skʌrələs] adj fml verleumderisch.

**scurry** ['skʌrɪ] (pt & pp **-ied**) vi hasten; [mouse] huschen.

**scurvy** ['skɜːvɪ] n Skarbut der.

**scuttle** ['skʌtl] n: **(coal) ~** Kohleneimer der ⋄ vi [rush] hasten; [mouse] huschen.

**scuzzy** ['skʌzɪ] (compar **-ier**; superl **-iest**) adj inf schmutzig.

**scythe** [saɪð] n Sense die ⋄ vt (mit der Sense) mähen.

**SD** abk für South Dakota, in Postanschrift verwendet.

**SDLP** (abbr of **Social Democratic and Labour Party**) n gemäßigte pro-irische Partei Nordirlands.

**SDP** (abbr of **Social Democratic Party**) n Sozialdemokratische Partei in Großbritannien.

**SE** (abbr of **southeast**) SO.

**sea** [siː] n - **1.** [ocean] Meer das, See die; **to be at ~** [ship, sailor] auf See sein; **to be all at ~** fig [person] verwirrt sein; **by ~** [send] auf dem Seeweg; [travel] mit dem Schiff fahren; **by the ~** am Meer; **out to ~** aufs Meer hinaus - **2.** fig [large number] Meer das ⋄ comp See-.
 ⟿ **seas** npl: **the ~s** die Meere.

**sea air** n Seeluft die.

**sea anemone** n Seeanemone die.

**seabed** ['siːbed] n: **the ~** der Meeresgrund.

**seabird** ['siːbɜːd] n Seevogel der.

**seaboard** ['siːbɔːd] n fml Küste die.

**sea breeze** n Seewind der.

**seafaring** ['siːˌfeərɪŋ] adj: **a ~ man** ein Seefahrer; **a ~ nation** eine Seefahrernation.

**seafood** ['siːfuːd] n (U) Meeresfrüchte pl; **~ restaurant** Fischrestaurant das.

**seafront** ['siːfrʌnt] n Strandpromenade die.

**seagoing** ['siːˌgəʊɪŋ] adj seetüchtig.

**seagull** ['siːgʌl] n Möwe die.

**seahorse** ['siːhɔːs] n Seepferdchen das.

**seal** [siːl] (pl sense 1 only inv OR **-s**) n - **1.** [animal] Robbe die - **2.** [official mark] Siegel das; **~ of approval** offizielle Zustimmung; **to put** OR **set the ~ on sthg** etw besiegeln - **3.** [official fastening] Versiegelung die; [on letter] Siegel das; [of metal] Plombe die - **4.** TECH Verschluss der; [washer] Dichtung die ⋄ vt - **1.** [stick down] zukleben - **2.** [block up] abdichten.
 ⟿ **seal off** vt sep abriegeln.

**sealable** ['siːləbl] adj [container] (luftdicht) verschließbar.

**sea lane** n Schifffahrtsstraße die.

**sealant** ['siːlənt] n Versiegeler der.

**sea level** n Meeresspiegel der.

**sealing wax** ['siːlɪŋ-] n Siegelwachs das.

**sea lion** (pl inv OR **-s**) n Seelöwe der.

**sealskin** ['siːlskɪn] n (U) Robben das.

**seam** [siːm] n - **1.** SEWING Naht die; **to be bursting at the ~s** aus allen Nähten platzen - **2.** [of coal] Flöz das.

**seaman** ['siːmən] (pl **-men** [-mən]) n Seemann der.

**seamanship** ['siːmənʃɪp] n Seemannschaft die.

**sea mist** n Seenebel die.

**seamless** ['siːmlɪs] adj - **1.** [stockings] nahtlos - **2.** fig [logic, story] kohärent.

**seamstress** ['semstrɪs] n Näherin die.

**seamy** ['siːmɪ] (compar **-ier**; superl **-iest**) adj anrüchig; **the ~ side of life** die Schattenseite des Lebens.

**séance** ['seɪɒns] n spiritistische Sitzung.

**seaplane** ['siːpleɪn] n Wasserflugzeug das.

**seaport** ['siːpɔːt] n Seehafen der.

**search** [sɜːtʃ] n - **1.** [for lost person, object]: **~ (for)** Suche die (nach); **in ~ of** auf der Suche nach - **2.** [of person, luggage, house] Durchsuchung die ⋄ vt durchsuchen; [city] absuchen; [one's mind, memory] durchforschen; **to ~ sthg for sthg** in etw (D) nach etw suchen ⋄ vi: **~ (for)** suchen (nach).
 ⟿ **search out** vt sep [facts, weakness] herausfinden; [books] herausuchen; [person] ausfindig machen.

**search engine** n COMPUT Suchmaschine die.

**searcher** ['sɜːtʃəʳ] n Suchende der, die.

**searching** ['sɜːtʃɪŋ] adj [look] prüfend, forschend; [question] tiefschürfend; [examination] gründlich.

**searchlight** ['sɜːtʃlaɪt] n Suchscheinwerfer der.

**search party** n Suchmannschaft die.

**search warrant** n Durchsuchungsbefehl der.

**searing** ['sɪərɪŋ] adj - **1.** [intense] stechend, brennend - **2.** [highly critical] scharf.

**sea salt** n Meersalz das.

**seashell** ['siːʃel] n Muschel die.

**seashore** ['siːʃɔːʳ] n: **the ~** der Strand.

**seasick** ['siːsɪk] adj seekrank.

**seaside** ['siːsaɪd] n: **the ~** das Meer.

**seaside resort** n Seebad das.

**season** ['siːzn] n **- 1.** [time of year] Jahreszeit die **- 2.** [for particular activity] Zeit die **- 3.** [of holiday] Saison die; **out of ~** außerhalb der Saison **- 4.** [of food]: **strawberries are out of ~** zu dieser Jahreszeit gibt es keine Erdbeeren; **the strawberry ~** die Erdbeerzeit **- 5.** [series - of films] Saison die; [ - of lectures] Reihe die <> vt [food] würzen.

**seasonal** ['siːzənl] adj [change] saisonal; [work] Saison-.

**seasoned** ['siːznd] adj [experienced] erfahren.

**seasoning** ['siːznɪŋ] n [for food] Gewürz das.

**season ticket** n Dauerkarte die; [for train] Zeitkarte die; [for theatre] Abonnement das.

**seat** [siːt] n **- 1.** [chair, part of chair, in parliament] Sitz der **- 2.** [place to sit] (Sitz)platz der; **take** OR **have a ~** nehmen Sie Platz **- 3.** [of skirt] Sitz der; [of trousers] Hosenboden der <> vt **- 1.** [person, guests] setzen; **to ~ o.s.** sich setzen **- 2.** [subj: building, vehicle] Sitzplätze haben für.

**seat belt** n Sicherheitsgurt der.

**seated** ['siːtɪd] adj: **to be ~** [sitting] sitzen; **please be ~** bitte, setzen Sie sich.

**-seater** ['siːtəʳ] suffix -sitzer der; **a two~** (car) ein Zweisitzer.

**seating** ['siːtɪŋ] n (U) [capacity] Sitzgelegenheiten pl <> comp Sitz-.

**sea urchin** n Seeigel der.

**seawall** [ˌsiːˈwɔːl] n Deich der.

**seawater** ['siːˌwɔːtəʳ] n Meerwasser das, Seewasser das.

**seaweed** ['siːwiːd] n Seetang der.

**seaworthy** ['siːˌwɜːðɪ] adj seetüchtig.

**sebaceous gland** [sɪˈbeɪʃəs -] n Talgdrüse die.

**sec.** (abbr of **second**) n sek.

**secateurs** [ˌsekəˈtɜːz] npl Br Gartenschere die.

**secede** [sɪˈsiːd] vi fml: **to ~ (from sthg)** sich (von etw) abspalten.

**secession** [sɪˈseʃn] n (U) fml Abspaltung die.

**secluded** [sɪˈkluːdɪd] adj abgelegen, versteckt.

**seclusion** [sɪˈkluːʒn] n Abgeschiedenheit die.

**second**[1] ['sekənd] n **- 1.** [of time, of angle] Sekunde die **- 2.** Br UNIV Note an britischen Universitäten, die dem deutschen „Gut" entspricht **- 3.** [moment] Moment der; **can I see you for a ~?**

kann ich Sie kurz sprechen?; **wait a ~!** einen Moment! **- 4.** AUT: **~ (gear)** zweiter Gang <> num zweite, -r, -s; **the ~** der/die/das Zweite; **on the ~ (of March)** am zweiten (März); **she's ~ only to him** nur er ist besser als sie; **to come ~** den zweiten Platz belegen; see also **sixth** <> vt [support] befürworten.

➤ **seconds** npl **- 1.** COMM Waren pl zweiter Wahl **- 2.** [of food] zweite Portion.

**second**[2] [sɪˈkɒnd] vt Br [send] einstweilig versetzen.

**secondary** ['sekəndrɪ] adj **- 1.** SCH: **~ education** höhere Schulbildung; **~ teacher** Lehrer der, -in die an einer höheren Schule **- 2.** [less important - road, cause] Neben-; [ - issue] nebensächlich; **to be ~ to sthg** weniger wichtig als etw sein.

**secondary modern** n Br ≈ Realschule die.

**secondary picketing** n solidarisches Aufstellen von Streikposten vor einem Unternehmen, dem die Streikposten selbst nicht angehören.

**secondary school** n höhere Schule.

**second best** ['sekənd-] adj zweitbeste, -r, -s; **to come off ~** das Nachsehen haben.

**second-class** ['sekənd-] adj **- 1.** pej [less important] zweitklassig; [citizen] zweiter Klasse **- 2.** [ticket, seat] Zweite-Klasse- **- 3.** [postage]: **~ stamp** billigere Briefmarke für Post, die weniger schnell befördert wird **- 4.** Br UNIV Note an britischen Universitäten, die dem deutschen „Gut" entspricht.

**second cousin** ['sekənd-] n Cousin der, -e die zweiten Grades.

**second-degree burn** ['sekənd-] n Verbrennung die zweiten Grades.

**seconder** ['sekəndəʳ] n [in meeting] Befürworter der, -in die.

**second floor** ['sekənd-] n **- 1.** Br [third storey] zweiter Stock **- 2.** Am [second storey] erster Stock.

**second-guess** ['sekənd-] vt **- 1.** [predict] vorauslagen; **to ~ sb** vorauslagen, was jd tun/sagen wird **- 2.** Am [with hindsight] im Nachhinein kritisieren.

**second-hand** ['sekənd-] adj **- 1.** [goods] gebraucht; [clothes] Secondhand- **- 2.** [shop] Gebrauchtwaren-; [selling clothes] Secondhand- **- 3.** fig [indirect] aus zweiter Hand <> adv **- 1.** [not new] gebraucht **- 2.** fig [indirectly]: **to hear sthg ~** etw aus zweiter Hand hören.

**second hand** ['sekənd-] n [of clock] Sekundenzeiger der.

**second-in-command** ['sekənd-] n MIL stellvertretender Kommandeur, stellvertretende Kommandeurin; fig Stellvertreter der, -in die.

**secondly** ['sekəndlɪ] adv zweitens.

**S**

**secondment** [sɪ'kɒndmənt] *n Br* einstweilige Versetzung.

**second nature** ['sekənd-] *n* zweite Natur.

**second-rate** ['sekənd-] *adj pej* zweitklassig, zweitrangig.

**second thought** ['sekənd-] *n:* **to have ~s about sthg** sich *(D)* etw anders überlegen; **on ~s** *Br,* **on ~** *Am* nach nochmaligem Überlegen.

**secrecy** ['siːkrəsɪ] *n (U)* - **1.** [being kept secret] Geheimhaltung *die* - **2.** [secretiveness] Heimlichtuerei *die.*

**secret** ['siːkrɪt] *adj* geheim; [admirer] heimlich ◇ *n* Geheimnis *das;* **in ~** im Geheimen.

**secret agent** *n* Geheimagent *der,* -in *die.*

**secretarial** [ˌsekrə'teərɪəl] *adj:* **~ staff** Büroangestellte *pl;* **~ training** Sekretärinnenausbildung *die.*

**secretariat** [ˌsekrə'teərɪət] *n* Sekretariat *das.*

**secretary** [*Br* 'sekrətrɪ, *Am* 'sekrəˌterɪ] *(pl* -ies) *n* - **1.** [clerical worker] Sekretär *der,* -in *die* - **2.** [head of organization] Geschäftsführer *der,* -in *die* - **3.** POL [minister] Minister *der,* -in *die.*

**secretary-general** *(pl* **secretaries-general)** *n* Generalsekretär *der,* -in *die.*

**Secretary of State** *n* - **1.** *Br* [minister]: **~ (for sthg)** Minister *der,* -in *die* (für etw) - **2.** *Am* [in charge of foreign affairs] Außenminister *der,* -in *die.*

**secrete** [sɪ'kriːt] *vt* - **1.** [produce] ablsondern - **2.** *fml* [hide] verbergen.

**secretion** [sɪ'kriːʃn] *n* [liquid secreted] Sekret *das.*

**secretive** ['siːkrətɪv] *adj* [person] heimlichtuerisch; **the organization is very ~ about their members** die Organisation hält Informationen über ihre Mitglieder geheim.

**secretly** ['siːkrɪtlɪ] *adv* [privately] heimlich.

**secret police** *n* Geheimpolizei *die.*

**secret service** *n* Geheimdienst *der.*

**sect** [sekt] *n* Sekte *die.*

**sectarian** [sek'teərɪən] *adj* konfessionsbedingt; [war, quarrel] Konfessions-.

**section** ['sekʃn] *n* - **1.** [portion] Teil *der;* [of book, road] Abschnitt *der;* [of law] Absatz *der;* [of community] Gruppe *die;* [of fruit] Stück *das;* **the sports ~ of the newspaper** der Sportteil der Zeitung - **2.** GEOM Schnitt *der.*

**sector** ['sektər] *n* Sektor *der.*

**secular** ['sekjʊlər] *adj* säkular, weltlich; [music] profan.

**secure** [sɪ'kjʊər] *adj* - **1.** [gen] sicher - **2.** [building] einbruchssicher, sicher OR fest verschlossen ◇ *vt* - **1.** [obtain] sich *(D)* sichern; [agreement] erzielen - **2.** [make safe] sichern

- **3.** [fasten] festlmachen; [door, window, lid] sicher verschließen.

**securely** [sɪ'kjʊəlɪ] *adv* [firmly] sicher.

**security** [sɪ'kjʊərətɪ] *(pl* -ies) *n* Sicherheit *die;* **~ of tenure** Kündigungsschutz *der* ◇ *comp* Sicherheits-.
◆ **securities** *npl* FIN Wertpapiere *pl.*

**security blanket** *n* [of child] Schmusedecke *die.*

**Security Council** *n:* **the ~** der Sicherheitsrat.

**security forces** *npl* Sicherheitstruppen *pl.*

**security guard** *n* Wache *die.*

**security risk** *n* Sicherheitsrisiko *das.*

**sedan** [sɪ'dæn] *n Am* Limousine *die.*

**sedan chair** *n* Sänfte *die.*

**sedate** [sɪ'deɪt] *adj* ruhig ◇ *vt* Beruhigungsmittel geben *(+ D).*

**sedation** [sɪ'deɪʃn] *n:* **they've got him under ~** er hat Beruhigungsmittel bekommen.

**sedative** ['sedətɪv] *adj* beruhigend ◇ *n* Beruhigungsmittel *das.*

**sedentary** ['sedntrɪ] *adj* [job] sitzend.

**sediment** ['sedɪmənt] *n* (Boden)satz *der;* CHEM & GEOL Sediment *das.*

**sedition** [sɪ'dɪʃn] *n* Aufwiegelung *die.*

**seditious** [sɪ'dɪʃəs] *adj* aufwiegelnd.

**seduce** [sɪ'djuːs] *vt* verführen; **to ~ sb into doing sthg** jn dazu verleiten, etw zu tun.

**seduction** [sɪ'dʌkʃn] *n* Verführung *die.*

**seductive** [sɪ'dʌktɪv] *adj* verführerisch.

**see** [siː] *(pt* saw, *pp* seen) *vt* - **1.** [gen] sehen; **as I ~ it** wie ich es sehe; **what do you ~ in him?** was findest du bloß an ihm?; **I'll ~ what I can do** ich will sehen, was ich tun kann; **~ p. 10** siehe S. 10; **do you ~ what I mean?** verstehst du, was ich meine? - **2.** [visit] besuchen; [doctor, solicitor] gehen zu; **to ~ sb about sthg** jn wegen etw sprechen; **~ you!** tschüs!; **~ you soon/ later!** bis bald!; **~ you tomorrow/on Thursday!** bis morgen/Donnerstag! - **3.** [accompany] begleiten - **4.** [make sure]: **to ~ that ...** dafür sorgen, dass ... - **5.** [subj: day, date] today saw the release of his new film/the end of an era heute kam sein neuer Film heraus/ging eine Ära zu Ende ◇ *vi* - **1.** [with eyes] sehen; **let me ~** [have a look] lass mich mal sehen - **2.** [understand] verstehen; **I ~** ich verstehe; **you ~, it's not that far at all** du siehst ja, es ist gar nicht weit; **I had a deprived childhood, you ~** ich war nämlich als Kind benachteiligt - **3.** [find out]: **to ~ if one can do sthg** sehen, ob man was tun kann; **I'll go and ~** ich sehe mal nach; **~ for yourself** überzeugen Sie sich selbst; **let's ~, let me ~** [when thinking] warten Sie mal, also - **4.** [decide]: **I'll (have to) ~** ich muss es mir überlegen.

⟳ **seeing as, seeing that** *conj inf* da.

⟳ **see about** *vt fus* - **1.** [organize] sich kümmern um - **2.** [expressing doubt]: **we'll ~ about that** das werden wir sehen.

⟳ **see off** *vt sep* - **1.** [say goodbye to] verabschieden - **2.** *Br* [chase away] verjagen.

⟳ **see through** *vt fus* [person, scheme] durchschauen ⟳ *vt sep* - **1.** [not abandon - deal, project] zu Ende bringen - **2.** [help to survive] durchlbringen.

⟳ **see to** *vt fus* [deal with] sich kümmern um; [repair] reparieren; **I'll ~ to it that he gets it** ich sorge dafür, dass er es bekommt.

**seed** [si:d] *n* - **1.** [of plant] Samen *der;* [pip] Kern *der* - **2.** SPORT: **to be the top/fourth ~** als Nummer eins/vier gesetzt sein ⟳ *vt:* **to be ~ed** gesetzt *or* plaziert sein; **to be ~ed third** als Nummer drei gesetzt sein.

⟳ **seeds** *npl* **fig** [beginnings] Keim *der.*

**seedless** ['si:dlɪs] *adj* kernlos.

**seedling** ['si:dlɪŋ] *n* Sämling *der.*

**seedy** ['si:dɪ] (*compar* **-ier;** *superl* **-iest**) *adj* [shabby] schäbig; [disreputable] zwielichtig.

**seek** [si:k] (*pt* & *pp* **sought**) *vt fml* suchen; **to ~ sb's advice/help** jm um Rat fragen/Hilfe bitten; **to ~ to do sthg** danach streben, etw zu tun.

⟳ **seek out** *vt sep* ausfindig machen.

**seem** [si:m] *vi* scheinen; **he ~s better** es scheint ihm besser zu gehen; **I can't ~ to shake off this cold** ich kann die Erkältung einfach nicht loswerden; **they ~ to believe that ...** sie glauben anscheinend, dass ...; **I ~ to remember his name was John** ich glaube, er hieß John ⟳ *v impers* scheinen; **it ~s (that) ...** anscheinend ...; **it ~s to me (that) you're right** mir scheint, du hast Recht; **so it would ~** so scheint es wenigstens.

**seeming** ['si:mɪŋ] *adj fml* scheinbar.

**seemingly** ['si:mɪŋlɪ] *adv* scheinbar.

**seemly** ['si:mlɪ] (*compar* **-ier;** *superl* **-iest**) *adj* **dated** & **literary** schicklich.

**seen** [si:n] *pp* ➭ **see.**

**seep** [si:p] *vi* sickern.

**seesaw** ['si:sɔ:] *n* Wippe *die.*

**seethe** [si:ð] *vi* - **1.** [person] vor Wut schäumen - **2.** [place]: **to be seething with sthg** von etw wimmeln.

**seething** ['si:ðɪŋ] *adj* [mass of people] wimmelnd.

**see-through** *adj* durchsichtig.

**segment** ['segmənt] *n* - **1.** [of report, audience] Teil *der;* [of market] Segment *das* - **2.** [of fruit] Stück *das.*

**segregate** ['segrɪgeɪt] *vt* trennen.

**segregation** [ˌsegrɪ'geɪʃn] *n* Segregation *die;* [of races] Rassentrennung *die.*

**seismic** ['saɪzmɪk] *adj* seismisch; **~ activity** Erdbebentätigkeit *die.*

**seize** [si:z] *vt* - **1.** [grab] packen, greifen - **2.** [win - control, power] übernehmen; [ - town] einlnehmen - **3.** [arrest] festlnehmen - **4.** [chance, opportunity] ergreifen.

⟳ **seize (up)on** *vt fus* [suggestion, idea] sich stützen auf (+ A).

⟳ **seize up** *vi* - **1.** [body] versagen - **2.** [engine] sich festlfressen.

**seizure** ['si:ʒə'] *n* - **1.** MED Anfall *der* - **2.** (U) [taking - of town] Einnahme *die;* [ - of control, power] Übernahme *die;* [ - of goods by customs] Beschlagnahme *die.*

**seldom** ['seldəm] *adv* selten.

**select** [sɪ'lekt] *adj* - **1.** [carefully chosen] auserlesen - **2.** [exclusive] exklusiv ⟳ *vt* auslwählen.

**select committee** *n* Sonderausschuss *der.*

**selected** [sɪ'lektɪd] *adj* ausgewählt.

**selection** [sɪ'lekʃn] *n* [choice, assortment, range] Auswahl *die.*

**selective** [sɪ'lektɪv] *adj* - **1.** [not general, limited] selektiv - **2.** [choosy] wählerisch.

**selector** [sɪ'lektə'] *n* SPORT Angehöriger eines Kommitees, das die Mannschaftsaufstellung vornimmt.

**self** [self] (*pl* **selves**) *n* Selbst *das;* **she's her old ~ again** sie ist wieder ganz die Alte.

**self-** [self] *prefix* [in adjectives] selbst-; [in nouns] Selbst-.

**self-addressed envelope** [-ə'drest-] *n* adressierter Rückumschlag.

**self-addressed stamped envelope** [-ə'drest-] *n* **Am** adressierter und frankierter Rückumschlag.

**self-adhesive** *adj* selbstklebend.

**self-appointed** [-ə'pɔɪntɪd] *adj* **pej** selbst ernannt.

**self-assembly** *adj* **Br** zum Zusammenbauen.

**self-assertive** *adj* selbstbewusst.

**self-assurance** *n* Selbstbewusstsein *das.*

**self-assured** *adj* selbstbewusst.

**self-catering** *adj* mit Selbstversorgung.

**self-centred** [-'sentəd] *adj* egozentrisch.

**self-cleaning** *adj* selbstreinigend.

**self-coloured** *adj* **Br** einfarbig.

**self-confessed** [-kən'fest] *adj* erklärt.

**self-confidence** *n* Selbstbewusstsein *das.*

**self-confident** *adj* selbstbewusst.

**self-conscious** *adj* verlegen, befangen.

**self-contained** [-kən'teɪnd] *adj* - **1.** [person - independent] unabhängig; [ - reserved] reserviert - **2.** [flat] abgeschlossen.

**self-control** *n* Selbstbeherrschung *die.*

S

**self-controlled** *adj* beherrscht.

**self-defence** *n* Selbstverteidigung *die;* **in ~** in Notwehr.

**self-denial** *n (U)* Entsagung *die.*

**self-destruct** [-dɪs'trʌkt] *adj* Selbstzerstörungs- <> *vi* sich selbst zerstören.

**self-determination** *n* Selbstbestimmung *die.*

**self-discipline** *n* Selbstdisziplin *die.*

**self-doubt** *n (U)* Selbstzweifel *pl.*

**self-drive** *adj Br* für Selbstfahrer.

**self-educated** *adj* autodidaktisch; **he's ~** er ist Autodidakt.

**self-effacing** [-ɪ'feɪsɪŋ] *adj* zurückhaltend.

**self-employed** [-ɪm'plɔɪd] *adj* selbstständig.

**self-esteem** *n* Selbstachtung *die.*

**self-evident** *adj* offensichtlich.

**self-explanatory** *adj* aus sich heraus verständlich.

**self-focusing** [-'fəʊkəsɪŋ] *adj* mit Autofokus.

**self-government** *n* Selbstverwaltung *die.*

**self-help** *n* Selbsthilfe *die.*

**self-important** *adj pej* überheblich.

**self-imposed** [-ɪm'pəʊzd] *adj* selbst auferlegt.

**self-indulgent** *adj pej* [person] genusssüchtig.

**self-inflicted** [-ɪn'flɪktɪd] *adj* [problem, pain] selbst verursacht; [wound] selbst beigebracht.

**self-interest** *n pej* Eigennutz *der.*

**selfish** ['selfɪʃ] *adj* selbstsüchtig, egoistisch.

**selfishness** ['selfɪʃnɪs] *n* Selbstsucht *die,* Egoismus *der.*

**selfless** ['selflɪs] *adj* selbstlos.

**self-locking** [-'lɒkɪŋ] *adj* selbstschließend.

**self-made** *adj* [man] Selfmade-; **she's a ~** millionaire sie hat es aus eigener Kraft bis zur Millionärin geschafft.

**self-opinionated** *adj pej* rechthaberisch.

**self-perpetuating** [-pə'petʃʊeɪtɪŋ] *adj* sich selbst erhaltend.

**self-pity** *n pej* Selbstmitleid *das.*

**self-portrait** *n* Selbstporträt *das.*

**self-possessed** *adj* beherrscht.

**self-preservation** *n* Selbsterhaltung *die;* **instinct for ~** Selbsterhaltungstrieb *der.*

**self-proclaimed** [-prə'kleɪmd] *adj pej* selbst ernannt.

**self-raising flour** *Br* [-ˌreɪzɪŋ-], **self-rising flour** *Am n (U)* Mehl *das* mit Backpulverzusatz.

**self-regulating** [-'regjʊleɪtɪŋ] *adj* sich selbst verwaltend.

**self-reliant** *adj* selbstständig.

**self-respect** *n* Selbstachtung *die.*

**self-respecting** [-rɪs'pektɪŋ] *adj:* **no ~ parent** would dress their child so badly Eltern, die etwas auf sich halten, würden ihr Kind nicht so furchtbar anziehen.

**self-restraint** *n* Selbstbeherrschung *die.*

**self-righteous** *adj pej* selbstgerecht.

**self-rising flour** *n Am* = self-raising flour.

**self-rule** *n* Selbstverwaltung *die.*

**self-sacrifice** *n* Selbstaufopferung *die,* Selbstlosigkeit *die.*

**selfsame** ['selfseɪm] *adj:* **the ~** genau derselbe/dieselbe/dasselbe.

**self-satisfied** *adj pej* selbstzufrieden.

**self-sealing** [-'siːlɪŋ] *adj* [envelope] selbstklebend.

**self-seeking** [-'siːkɪŋ] *pej adj* selbstsüchtig.

**self-service** *n* Selbstbedienung *die* <> *comp* Selbstbedienungs-.

**self-starter** *n* - **1.** AUT Anlasser *der* - **2.** [in job advert]: **you should be an ambitious ~** Sie sollten ambitioniert sein und selbstständig arbeiten können.

**self-styled** [-'staɪld] *adj pej* selbst ernannt.

**self-sufficient** *adj* [person, community]: **to be ~ (in sthg)** sich selbst (mit etw) versorgend; **Great Britain is ~ in coal** Großbritannien deckt seinen Kohlebedarf selbst.

**self-supporting** [-sə'pɔːtɪŋ] *adj* [business, industry] unabhängig.

**self-tanning** *adj* (Selbst)bräunungs-.

**self-taught** *adj* autodidaktisch; **where did you learn Gaelic? – I'm ~** wo hast du Gälisch gelernt? – ich habe es mir selbst beigebracht.

**self-test** *vi* COMPUT einen Selbsttest durchführen.

**self-willed** *adj pej* eigensinnig.

**sell** [sel] (*pt & pp* **sold**) *vt* - **1.** [goods] verkaufen; **to ~ sthg to sb, to ~ sb sthg** etw an jn verkaufen, jm etw verkaufen; **I sold it for fifty pounds** ich habe es für fünfzig Pfund verkauft - **2.** [promote sale of]: **such a cover will ~ the magazine** mit so einem Titelbild verkauft sich die Zeitschrift garantiert gut; **to ~ o.s.** *fig* sich verkaufen - **3.** *fig* [make enthusiastic about]: **to ~ sthg to sb, to ~ sb sthg** jm etw schmackhaft machen; **I'm not sold on the idea** ich bin von der Idee nicht begeistert <> *vi* - **1.** [person] verkaufen - **2.** [product] sich verkaufen; **to ~ for** OR **at** verkauft werden für OR zu.

➡ **sell off** *vt sep* verkaufen.

**sell out** vt sep [performance]: **to be sold out** ausverkauft sein ◇ vi - **1.** [shop, ticket office]: **we've sold out** wir sind ausverkauft; **we've sold out of bread** wir haben kein Brot mehr - **2.** [betray one's principles] sich verkaufen.

**sell up** vi seine ganze Habe verkaufen, alles verkaufen.

**sell-by date** n Br Verfallsdatum das.

**seller** ['selər] n [vendor] Verkäufer der, -in die.

**seller's market** n Verkäufermarkt der.

**selling** ['selɪŋ] n Verkaufen das.

**selling price** n Verkaufspreis der.

**Sellotape®** ['seləteɪp] n Br Tesafilm® der, Klebeband das.

**sellotape** vt mit Klebeband OR Tesafilm® kleben.

**sell-out** n [performance, match]: **to be a ~** ausverkauft sein.

**seltzer** ['seltsər] n Am Selterswasser das.

**selves** [selvz] pl ⊳ self.

**semantic** [sɪ'mæntɪk] adj semantisch.

**semantics** n (U) Semantik die.

**semaphore** ['seməfɔːr] n (U) Flaggenzeichen pl.

**semblance** ['sembləns] n fml Anschein der.

**semen** ['siːmen] n (U) Samen der.

**semester** [sɪ'mestər] n Semester das.

**semi** ['semɪ] n - **1.** Br inf [house] Doppelhaushälfte die - **2.** Am [truck] Sattelzug der.

**semi-** [semɪ] prefix [in adjectives] halb-; [in nouns] Halb-.

**semiautomatic** [semɪ ɔːtə'mætɪk] adj halbautomatisch.

**semicircle** ['semɪ sɜːkl] n Halbkreis der.

**semicircular** [semɪ'sɜːkjʊlər] adj halbkreisförmig.

**semicolon** [semɪ'kəʊlən] n Semikolon das.

**semiconscious** [semɪ'kɒnʃəs] adj halb bei Bewusstsein.

**semidetached** [semɪdɪ'tætʃt] adj & n Br: **~ (house)** Doppelhaushälfte die.

**semifinal** [semɪ'faɪnl] n Halbfinale das.

**semifinalist** [semɪ'faɪnəlɪst] n Halbfinalist der, -in die.

**seminal** ['semɪnl] adj - **1.** [important] wegweisend - **2.** [of semen] Samen-.

**seminar** ['semɪnɑːr] n Seminar das.

**seminary** ['semɪnərɪ] (pl -ies) n RELIG Priesterseminar das.

**semiotics** [semɪ'ɒtɪks] n (U) Semiotik die.

**semiprecious** ['semɪ preʃəs] adj: **~ stone** Halbedelstein der.

**semiskilled** [semɪ'skɪld] adj angelernt.

**semiskimmed** [semɪ'skɪmd] adj: **~ milk** Halbfettmilch die.

**semitrailer** [semɪ'treɪlər] n - **1.** [trailer] Sattelanhänger der - **2.** Am [truck] Sattelzug der.

**semolina** [semə'liːnə] n Grieß der.

**Sen.** - **1.** abbr of senator - **2.** abbr of Senior.

**SEN** (abbr of State Enrolled Nurse) n frühere Bezeichnung für eine geprüfte Krankenschwester/einen geprüften Krankenpfleger.

**Senate** ['senɪt] n POL: **the ~** der Senat; **the United States ~** der Senat der Vereinigten Staaten.

**SENATE**

Der Senat bildet zusammen mit dem „House of Representatives" den Kongress, das oberste Gesetzgebungsorgan der USA. Seine 100 Mitglieder werden in unmittelbarer, geheimer Wahl in den Einzelstaaten gewählt; jeder Staat entsendet zwei Abgeordnete. Zur Ernennung von Kabinettsmitgliedern und sonstigen Regierungsmitarbeitern benötigt der Präsident die Zustimmung des Senats.

**senator** ['senətər] n Senator der, -in die.

**send** [send] (pt & pp sent) vt - **1.** [letter, message, money] schicken; [signal] senden; **to ~ sb sthg, to ~ sthg to sb** jm etw schicken, etw an jn schicken - **2.** [tell to go]: **to ~ sb (to)** jn schicken (zu); **to ~ sb for sthg** jn nach etw schicken - **3.** [propel, to cause to move]: **the fire sent sparks into the night** das Feuer warf Funken in die Nacht; **to ~ sthg crashing to the ground** etw zusammenstürzen lassen; **the explosion sent glass flying everywhere** durch die Explosion flogen Glassplitter in alle Richtungen - **4.** [into a specific state]: **to ~ sb to sleep** jn zum Einschlafen bringen; **to ~ sb into a rage** jn wütend machen.

**send back** vt sep zurücklschicken.

**send down** vt sep inf [send to prison] ins Gefängnis stecken.

**send for** vt fus - **1.** [person] holen lassen - **2.** [by post] anlfordern.

**send in** vt sep - **1.** [visitor] hereinlschicken - **2.** [troops, police] entsenden, schicken - **3.** [submit] einlreichen.

**send off** vt sep - **1.** [by post] ablschicken - **2.** SPORT [player] vom Platz verweisen.

**send off for** vt fus [by post] schriftlich anlfordern.

**send up** vt sep inf - **1.** Br [imitate] parodieren - **2.** Am [send to prison] ins Gefängnis stecken.

**sender** ['sendər] n Absender der, -in die.

**send-off** n Verabschiedung die.

**send-up** n Br inf Parodie die.

**Senegal** [senɪ'gɔːl] n Senegal nt.

**senile** ['siːnaɪl] adj senil.

**senile dementia** n Altersschwachsinn der.

**senility** [sɪ'nɪlətɪ] n Senilität die.

**senior** ['siːnjəʳ] adj - **1.** [high-ranking - position, manager] leitend; [ - official] höher; [ - nurse, doctor] Ober-; [ - police officer] ranghoch - **2.** [higher-ranking]: **to be ~ to sb** höher als jn gestellt sein - **3.** SCH [classes] höher; [pupils] älter; **~ year** Am letztes Jahr an einer Highschool, einem College oder einer Universität ◇ n - **1.** [older person]: **I'm five years his ~, I'm his ~ by five years** ich bin fünf Jahre älter als er - **2.** SCH Schüler/Student im letzten Schul- /Studienjahr.

**senior citizen** n Senior der, -in die.

**senior high school** n Am ≈ Oberstufe die.

**seniority** [ˌsiːnɪ'ɒrətɪ] n (U) [in rank] höhere Position.

**sensation** [sen'seɪʃn] n - **1.** [feeling] Gefühl das - **2.** [cause of excitement] Sensation die.

**sensational** [sen'seɪʃənl] adj - **1.** [news, victory, show] sensationell; [person, appearance] toll - **2.** [sensationalist] Sensations-.

**sensationalist** [sen'seɪʃnəlɪst] adj pej Sensations-.

**sense** [sens] n - **1.** [faculty] Sinn der - **2.** [feeling, sensation] Gefühl das; **~ of guilt** Schuldgefühl das; **~ of justice** Gerechtigkeitssinn der - **3.** [natural ability] Gefühl das; **business ~** Geschäftssinn der; **a ~ of humour** Humor der - **4.** [wisdom, reason] Vernunft die; **she had the ~ to warn us beforehand** sie war so vernünftig, uns vorher zu warnen; **to talk ~** vernünftig sein; **there's no ~ in arguing/fighting/** etc es hat keinen Sinn zu streiten/ kämpfen/etc - **5.** [meaning] Bedeutung die; **to make ~** [have clear meaning] Sinn haben; [be logical] sinnvoll sein; **to make no ~** keinen Sinn machen; **to make ~ of sthg** etw verstehen - **6.** phr: **to come to one's ~s** [be sensible again] (wieder) zur Vernunft kommen; [regain consciousness] (wieder) zu Bewusstsein kommen ◇ vt [feel] spüren; **to ~ (that)** ... spüren, dass ...

➨ **in a sense** adv in gewissem Sinne.

**senseless** ['senslɪs] adj - **1.** [stupid] sinnlos - **2.** [unconscious] bewusstlos.

**sensibilities** [ˌsensɪ'bɪlətɪz] npl [delicate feelings] Empfindlichkeit die.

**sensible** ['sensəbl] adj vernünftig.

**sensibly** ['sensəblɪ] adv vernünftig.

**sensitive** ['sensɪtɪv] adj - **1.** [eyes, skin] empfindlich; **~ to heat/light** hitze-/lichtempfindlich - **2.** [understanding, aware]: **to be ~ (to sthg)** (gegenüber etw) aufmerksam sein - **3.** [easily hurt, touchy]: **to be ~ to sthg** gegenüber etw empfindlich sein; **to be ~ about sthg** wegen etw empfindlich sein - **4.** [controversial] heikel - **5.** [instrument] empfindlich.

**sensitivity** [ˌsensɪ'tɪvətɪ] n (U) - **1.** [gen] Empfindlichkeit die - **2.** [understanding] Aufmerksamkeit die.

**sensor** ['sensəʳ] n Sensor der.

**sensual** ['sensjʊəl] adj sinnlich.

**sensuous** ['sensjʊəs] adj sinnlich.

**sent** [sent] pt & pp ⊳ send.

**sentence** ['sentəns] n - **1.** [group of words] Satz der - **2.** LAW [decision] Urteil das; **a ~ of five years** eine fünfjährige Haftstrafe ◇ vt: **to ~ sb (to sthg)** jn (zu etw) verurteilen.

**sententious** [sen'tenʃəs] adj pej schulmeisterlich.

**sentiment** ['sentɪmənt] n - **1.** [feeling] Gefühl das; [opinion] Meinung die - **2.** pej [sentimentality] Sentimentalität die.

**sentimental** [ˌsentɪ'mentl] adj sentimental.

**sentimentality** [ˌsentɪmen'tælətɪ] n Sentimentalität die.

**sentinel** ['sentɪnl] n Wache die.

**sentry** ['sentrɪ] (pl -ies) n Wache die.

**Seoul** [səʊl] n Seoul nt.

**separable** ['seprəbl] adj: **~ (from sthg)** trennbar (von etw).

**separate** [adj & n 'seprət, vb 'sepəreɪt] adj - **1.** [not joined, apart]: **~ (from sthg)** getrennt (von etw) - **2.** [individual, distinct] verschieden; **write on a ~ piece of paper** schreiben Sie auf ein neues Blatt ◇ vt - **1.** [keep or set apart]: **to ~ (from)** trennen (von); **to ~ sb/sthg into** jn/ etw einteilen in (+ A) - **2.** [distinguish] unterscheiden; **to ~ sb/sthg from** jn/etw unterscheiden von ◇ vi - **1.** [go different ways]: **to ~ (from)** sich trennen (von) - **2.** [come apart, divide] auseinander gehen; **to ~ (into sthg)** sich teilen (in etw (A)) - **3.** [couple] sich trennen.

➨ **separates** npl Br Kombinationskleidung die.

**separated** ['sepəreɪtɪd] adj [not living together] getrennt.

**separately** ['seprətlɪ] adv getrennt.

**separation** [ˌsepə'reɪʃn] n Trennung die; [division] Einteilung die.

**separatism** ['seprətɪzm] n Separatismus der.

**separatist** ['seprətɪst] n Separatist der, -in die.

**sepia** ['siːpɪə] adj Sepia-.

**Sept.** (abbr of September) Sept.

**September** [sep'tembəʳ] n September der; **in ~** im September; **last/this/next ~** letzten/ diesen/nächsten September; **by ~** bis September; **every ~** jeden September, jedes Jahr im September; **during ~** im September; **at the beginning/end of ~** Anfang/Ende

September; **in the middle of** ~ Mitte September- ber <> *comp* September-.

**septet** [sep'tet] *n* Septett *das*.

**septic** ['septɪk] *adj* eitrig; MED septisch.

**septicaemia** *Br*, **septicemia** *Am* [septɪ'siːmɪə] *n (U)* Blutvergiftung *die*.

**septic tank** *n* Klärgrube *die*.

**sequel** ['siːkwəl] *n* - **1.** [book, film]: ~ **(to sthg)** Fortsetzung *die* (von etw) - **2.** [consequence]: ~ **to sthg** Folge *die* von etw.

**sequence** ['siːkwəns] *n* - **1.** [series] Reihe *die* - **2.** *(U)* [order] Reihenfolge *die;* **in** ~ der Reihenfolge nach - **3.** [of film] Sequenz *die*.

**sequester** [sɪ'kwestə<sup>r</sup>], **sequestrate** [sɪ'kwestreɪt] *vt* LAW zwangsverwalten.

**sequin** ['siːkwɪn] *n* Paillette *die*.

**sera** *pl* <> **serum**.

**Serb** [sɜːb] *adj* & *n* = **Serbian**.

**Serbia** ['sɜːbjə] *n* Serbien *nt*.

**Serbian** ['sɜːbjən] *adj* serbisch <> *n* [person] Serbe *der*, -bin *die*.

**Serbo-Croat** [ˌsɜːbəʊ'krəʊæt], **Serbo-Croatian** [ˌsɜːbəʊkrəʊ'eɪʃn] *adj* serbokroatisch <> *n* [language] Serbokroatisch(e) *das*.

**serenade** [ˌserə'neɪd] *n* - **1.** [to lover] Ständchen *das* - **2.** [orchestral] Serenade *die* <> *vt* ein Ständchen bringen *(+ D)*.

**serene** [sɪ'riːn] *adj* [person] gelassen.

**serenely** [sɪ'riːnlɪ] *adv* gelassen.

**serenity** [sɪ'renətɪ] *n* Gelassenheit *die*.

**serf** [sɜːf] *n* HIST Leibeigene *der*, *die*.

**serge** [sɜːdʒ] *n (U)* Serge *die*, Sersche *die*.

**sergeant** ['sɑːdʒənt] *n* - **1.** [in the army] Feldwebel *der* - **2.** [in the police] Wachtmeister *der*, -in *die*.

**sergeant major** *n* Hauptfeldwebel *der*.

**serial** ['sɪərɪəl] *n* [on TV] Serie *die;* [on radio] Sendereihe *die;* [in newspaper] Fortsetzungsroman *der*.

**serialize, -ise** ['sɪərɪəlaɪz] *vt* [book] in Fortsetzungen veröffentlichen.

**serial killer** *n* Serienmörder *der*, -in *die*.

**serial number** *n* Seriennummer *die*.

**series** ['sɪəriːz] *(pl inv)* *n* - **1.** [sequence] Reihe *die* - **2.** RADIO & TV Serie *die*.

**serious** ['sɪərɪəs] *adj* - **1.** [gen] ernst; [situation, problem, illness, loss] schwer; [shortage] groß - **2.** [newspaper] seriös; **are you ~?** ist das dein Ernst?

**serious crime** *n (U)* schwere Straftaten *pl*.

**seriously** ['sɪərɪəslɪ] *adv* - **1.** [earnestly] ernsthaft; **to take sb/sthg** ~ jn/etw ernst nehmen - **2.** [very badly - ill] schwer; [ - lacking] sehr.

**seriousness** ['sɪərɪəsnɪs] *n* - **1.** [of person, expres-sion, situation] Ernst *der;* **in all** ~ allen Ernstes - **2.** [of illness, loss] Schwere *die*.

**sermon** ['sɜːmən] *n* - **1.** [in church] Predigt *die* - **2.** *fig* & *pej* [lecture] Moralpredigt *die*.

**serpent** ['sɜːpənt] *n literary* Schlange *die*.

**serrated** [sɪ'reɪtɪd] *adj* gezackt.

**serum** ['sɪərəm] *(pl* **serums** OR **sera)** *n* Serum *das*.

**servant** ['sɜːvənt] *n* [in household] Diener *der*, -in *die*.

**serve** [sɜːv] *vt* - **1.** [work for] dienen *(+ D)* - **2.** [have effect]: **this only ~d to make him more angry** das führte nur dazu, dass er noch ärgerlicher wurde; **to ~ a purpose** einem Zweck dienen - **3.** [provide - with gas, electricity, water] versorgen; **which motorways ~ Birmingham?** welche Autobahnen führen nach Birmingham? - **4.** [food or drink]: **to ~ sthg to sb, to ~ sb sthg** jm etw servieren; **this recipe ~s four** das Rezept ergibt vier Portionen - **5.** [customer] bedienen - **6.** LAW: **to ~ sb with a writ** jn vor Gericht laden - **7.** [complete, carry out - prison sentence] verbüßen; [ - apprenticeship] absolvieren; **to ~ a term of office** im Amt sein - **8.** SPORT auf|schlagen - **9.** *phr:* **it ~s you right** das geschieht dir recht <> *vi* - **1.** [be employed - as soldier] dienen; [ - in profession] arbeiten; **to ~on** [committee] an|gehören *(+ D)* - **2.** [function]: **to ~ as sthg** als etw dienen - **3.** [with food, drink] servieren - **4.** [in shop, bar etc] bedienen - **5.** SPORT auf|schlagen <> *n* SPORT Aufschlag *der*.

➤ **serve out, serve up** *vt sep* [food] servieren.

**server** ['sɜːvə<sup>r</sup>] *n* COMPUT Server *der*.

**service** ['sɜːvɪs] *n* - **1.** [organization, system] Dienst *der;* **bus/train** ~ Bus-/Zugverbindung *die* - **2.** [amenity] Dienstleistung *die*, Service *der* - **3.** [employment - length of time] Dienstzeit *die* - **4.** *(U)* [in shop, bar etc] Bedienung *die*, Service *der;* '~ **not included'** 'Trinkgeld nicht inbegriffen' - **5.** MIL Militärdienst *der* - **6.** [mechanical check - of car] Durchsicht *die;* [ - of machine] Wartung *die* - **7.** RELIG Gottesdienst *der* - **8.** [set of tableware] Service *das* - **9.** [operation] Betrieb *der;* **in/out of** ~ in/außer Betrieb - **10.** SPORT Aufschlag *der* - **11.** [help]: **to be of** ~ **to sb** [person] jm behilflich sein; [thing] jm von Nutzen sein <> *vt* - **1.** [car, machine] warten - **2.** FIN [debt, loan] bedienen.

➤ **services** *npl* - **1.** [on motorway] Raststätte *die (mit Tankstelle)* - **2.** [armed forces]: **the ~s** das Militär - **3.** [help] Hilfe *die*, Dienste *pl*.

**serviceable** ['sɜːvɪsəbl] *adj* praktisch.

**service area** *n* Raststätte *die (mit Tankstelle)*.

**service charge** *n* Bedienungszuschlag *der*, Service *der*.

**service industries** *npl* Dienstleistungssektor *der*.

S

**serviceman** ['sɜːvɪsmən] (pl **-men** [-mən]) n MIL Militärangehörige der.

**service provider** n COMPUT Internetprovider der.

**service station** n Raststätte die (mit Tankstelle).

**servicewoman** ['sɜːvɪsˌwʊmən] (pl **-women** [-ˌwɪmɪn]) n MIL Militärangehörige die.

**serviette** [ˌsɜːvɪ'et] n Serviette die.

**servile** ['sɜːvaɪl] adj unterwürfig.

**servility** [sɜː'vɪlətɪ] n Unterwürfigkeit die.

**serving** ['sɜːvɪŋ] adj - 1. [spoon, dish, fork] Servier- - 2. [member, chairman] amtierend ◇ n [portion] Portion die.

**sesame** ['sesəmɪ] n (U) Sesam der; **open ~!** Sesam öffne dich!

**session** ['seʃn] n - 1. [of court, parliament] Sitzung die; **to be in ~** tagen - 2. [meeting] Treffen das; **we had a ~ to discuss the problem** wir sind zusammengekommen, um das Problem zu diskutieren; **recording ~** Aufnahme die - 3. Am [school term] Semester das.

**set** [set] (pt & pp **set**; cont **-ting**) adj - 1. [specified, prescribed] festgelegt, festgesetzt; [book, text] vorgeschrieben - 2. [fixed - phrase, expression] fest; [ - ideas, routine] starr; **to be ~ in one's ways** ein Gewohnheitsmensch sein - 3. [ready]: **to be (all) ~ (to do sthg)** startbereit sein(, etw zu tun) - 4. [determined]: **to be ~ on doing sthg** entschlossen sein, etw zu tun; **to be dead ~ against sthg** völlig gegen etw sein ◇ n - 1. [collection, group] Satz der; **~ of teeth** Gebiss das; **chess ~** Schachspiel das - 2. [television, radio] Apparat der - 3. [of film] Filmkulisse die; [of play] Kulisse die - 4. TENNIS Satz der ◇ vt - 1. [put in specified position, place] stellen; [lying down] legen - 2. [fix, insert]: **to ~ sthg in(to) sthg** etw in etw (A) einlassen - 3. [indicating change of state or activity]: **to ~ sb free** jn befreien; **to ~ sb's mind at rest** jn beruhigen; **to ~ sthg on fire** etw anlzünden; **her remark ~ me thinking** ihre Bemerkung brachte mich zum Nachdenken - 4. [prepare in advance - trap] auflstellen; [ - table] decken - 5. [clock, meter] stellen - 6. [time, deadline, minimum wage] festlsetzen, festllegen - 7. [create - trend] setzen; [ - example] geben; [ - precedent] schaffen; [ - record] auflstellen - 8. [assign - target] setzen; [ - essay, homework] auflgeben; [ - exam] auslarbeiten - 9. MED [bone, broken leg] richten - 10. MUS: **to ~ sthg to music** etw vertonen - 11. [story, film] spielen - 12. [hair] legen ◇ vi - 1. [sun] unterlgehen - 2. [jelly, cement] fest werden.

➤ **set about** vt fus [start]: **to ~ about sthg** etw in Angriff nehmen; **to ~ about doing sthg** sich daranmachen, etw zu tun.

➤ **set against** vt sep - 1. [compare] gegenüberlstellen (+ D) - 2. [put in opposition] gegeneinanderlstellen - 3. FIN: **to ~ sthg against tax** etw von der Steuer ablsetzen.

➤ **set ahead** vt sep Am [clock] vorlstellen.

➤ **set apart** vt sep [distinguish]: **to ~ sb/sthg apart from** jn/etw unterscheiden von.

➤ **set aside** vt sep - 1. [keep, save - food] auflheben; [ - money] beiseite legen; [ - time] einlplanen - 2. [not consider] außer Acht lassen.

➤ **set back** vt sep - 1. [delay] zurücklwerfen - 2. inf [cost]: **it ~ me back £300** es hat mich 300 Pfund gekostet.

➤ **set down** vt sep - 1. [write down] niederlschreiben - 2. [put down] ablsetzen.

➤ **set in** vi [cold, rain] einlsetzen; [infection] kommen zu; [winter] Einzug halten; **he walked for twenty miles before exhaustion ~ in** nachdem er zwanzig Meilen gewandert war, kamen seine Kräfte zum Erliegen.

➤ **set off** vt sep - 1. [initiate, cause] ausllösen - 2. [trigger - bomb] zünden; [ - alarm] ausllösen ◇ vi [on journey] auflbrechen.

➤ **set on** vt sep [dog] hetzen auf (+ A); **to ~ the police on sb** jm die Polizei auf den Hals hetzen.

➤ **set out** vt sep - 1. [arrange, spread out] zurechtllegen; [chairs] auflstellen; [food] anlrichten - 2. [clarify, explain] darllegen ◇ vt fus [intend]: **to ~ out to do sthg** sich (D) vorlnehmen, etw zu tun ◇ vi [on journey] auflbrechen.

➤ **set up** vt sep - 1. [establish, arrange - fund, organization] gründen; [ - interview, meeting] anlsetzen; **to ~ o.s. up** sich etablieren; **to ~ up house** OR **home** einen (eigenen) Haushalt gründen - 2. [erect - roadblock] errichten; **to ~ up camp** Zelte auflschlagen - 3. [install] auflstellen - 4. inf [incriminate] als Schuldigen hinlstellen ◇ vi [in business] sich selbstständig machen.

**setback** ['setbæk] n Rückschlag der.

**set menu** n Menü das.

**setsquare** ['setskweəʳ] n Br Zeichendreieck das.

**settee** [se'tiː] n Sofa das, Couch die.

**setter** ['setəʳ] n [dog] Setter der.

**setting** ['setɪŋ] n - 1. [surroundings] Umgebung die - 2. [of dial, control] Einstellung die.

**settle** ['setl] vt - 1. [argument, differences] beillegen - 2. [pay - bill, debt] begleichen; [ - account] auslgleichen - 3. [make comfortable]: **she ~d herself in an armchair** sie machte es sich in einem Sessel bequem - 4. [nerves, stomach] beruhigen ◇ vi - 1. [go to live] sich niederllassen - 2. [make o.s. comfortable] es sich (D) bequem machen - 3. [come to rest - dust] sich legen; [ - sediment] sich setzen; **to ~ on sthg** [bird, butterfly] sich auf etw (D) niederllassen.

➤ **settle down** vi - 1. [give one's attention]: **to ~ down to work** sich an die Arbeit machen; **to ~ down to doing sthg** sich daranlmachen, etw zu tun - **2.** [assume stable lifestyle] sesshaft werden - **3.** [make o.s. comfortable] es sich *(D)* bequem machen - **4.** [become calm] sich beruhigen.

◆ **settle for** *vt fus* sich zufrieden|geben mit.

◆ **settle in** *vi* [in house] sich ein|leben; [in job] sich ein|gewöhnen.

◆ **settle on** *vt fus* [choose] sich entscheiden für.

◆ **settle up** *vi* [financially]: **to ~ up (with sb)** ab|rechnen (mit jm).

**settled** ['setld] *adj* [weather] beständig.

**settlement** ['setlmənt] *n* - **1.** [agreement] Übereinkunft *die*, Einigung *die* - **2.** [village] (An)siedlung *die* - **3.** [payment] Begleichung *die*, Bezahlung *die*.

**settler** ['setlə'] *n* Siedler *der*, -in *die*.

**set-to** *n inf* [fight] Schlägerei *die;* [quarrel] Streit *der*.

**set-up** *n inf* - **1.** [system] System *das;* [organization] Organisation *die* - **2.** [deception to incriminate] Falle *die*.

**seven** ['sevn] *num* sieben; *see also* **six**.

**seventeen** [ˌsevn'tiːn] *num* siebzehn; *see also* **six**.

**seventeenth** [ˌsevn'tiːnθ] *num* siebzehnte, -r, -s; *see also* **sixth**.

**seventh** ['sevnθ] *num* siebte, -r, -s; *see also* **sixth**.

**seventh heaven** *n:* **to be in ~** im siebenten Himmel sein.

**seventieth** ['sevntjəθ] *num* siebzigste, -r, -s; *see also* **sixth**.

**seventy** ['sevntɪ] *num* siebzig; *see also* **sixty**.

**sever** ['sevə'] *vt* - **1.** [limb] ab|trennen; [rope] durch|schneiden; [ligament] reißen - **2.** [relationship, ties] ab|brechen; [agreement] brechen.

**several** ['sevrəl] *adj* [some] mehrere, einige ⟨⟩ *pron* mehrere, einige.

**severance pay** *n (U)* Abfindung *die*.

**severe** [sɪ'vɪə'] *adj* - **1.** [shock, pain, gale] stark; [illness, injury] schwer; [problem] ernst - **2.** [stern - person] streng; [ - criticism] heftig.

**severely** [sɪ'vɪəlɪ] *adv* - **1.** [extremely, badly] stark; [injured] schwer - **2.** [sternly] streng.

**severity** [sɪ'verətɪ] *n (U)* - **1.** [of storm] Stärke *die;* [of illness] Schwere *die;* [of problem] Ernst *der* - **2.** [sternness - of person] Strenge *die;* [ - of criticism] Heftigkeit *die*.

**sew** [səʊ] *(Br pp* **sewn**, *Am pp* **sewed** OR **sewn)** *vt & vi* nähen.

◆ **sew up** *vt sep* - **1.** [join] zusammen|nähen - **2.** *inf* [arrange, fix] in der Hand haben.

**sewage** ['suːɪdʒ] *n* Abwasser *das*.

**sewage works** *n* Klärwerk *das*.

**sewer** ['suə'] *n* Abwasserkanal *der*.

**sewerage** ['suərɪdʒ] *n (U)* [sewers] Kanalisation *die*.

**sewing** ['səʊɪŋ] *n (U)* - **1.** [activity] Nähen *das* - **2.** [items] Näharbeit *die*.

**sewing machine** *n* Nähmaschine *die*.

**sewn** [səʊn] *pp* ⊳ **sew**.

**sex** [seks] *n* - **1.** [gender] Geschlecht *das* - **2.** [sexual intercourse] Sex *der;* **to have ~ (with sb)** (mit jm) Sex haben.

**sex appeal** *n* Sexappeal *der*.

**sex education** *n* Sexualerziehung *die*.

**sexism** ['seksɪzml] *n* Sexismus *der*.

**sexist** ['seksɪst] *adj* sexistisch ⟨⟩ *n* Sexist *der*, -in *die*.

**sex life** *n* Sex(ual)leben *das*.

**sex object** *n* Sexobjekt *das*, Lustobjekt *das*.

**sex shop** *n* Sexshop *der*.

**sextet** [seks'tet] *n* Sextett *das*.

**sextuplet** [seks'tjuːplɪt] *n* Sechsling *der*.

**sexual** ['sekʃʊəl] *adj* - **1.** [of sexuality, sexual intercourse] sexuell; [disease, organ] Geschlechts- - **2.** [of gender]: **~ equality/rivalry** Gleichheit/Rivalität zwischen den Geschlechtern.

**sexual assault** *n* Notzucht *die*.

**sexual discrimination** *n* Diskriminierung *die* aufgrund des Geschlechts.

**sexual harassment** *n (U)* sexuelle Belästigung.

**sexual intercourse** *n (U)* Geschlechtsverkehr *der*.

**sexuality** [ˌsekʃʊ'ælətɪ] *n* Sexualität *die*.

**sexually transmitted disease** *n* sexuell übertragbare Krankheit.

**sexy** ['seksɪ] *(compar* **-ier**; *superl* **-iest**) *adj inf* sexy.

**Seychelles** [seɪ'ʃelz] *npl:* **the ~** die Seychellen *pl;* **in the ~** auf den Seychellen.

**sf, SF** *n abbr of* **science fiction**.

**SFO** *(abbr of* **Serious Fraud Office***) n britisches Betrugsdezernat*.

**Sgt** *abbr of* **sergeant**.

**sh** [ʃ] *excl* pst!

**shabby** ['ʃæbɪ] *(compar* **-ier**; *superl* **-iest**) *adj* schäbig; [street] heruntergekommen.

**shack** [ʃæk] *n* Hütte *die*.

**shackle** ['ʃækl] *vt* - **1.** [chain] fesseln - **2.** *literary* [restrict] (be)hindern.

◆ **shackles** *npl* - **1.** [metal restraints] Ketten *pl* - **2.** *literary* [restrictions] Behinderungen *pl*.

**shade** [ʃeɪd] *n* - **1.** *(U)* [shadow] Schatten *der* - **2.** [lampshade] Lampenschirm *der* - **3.** [colour] Farbton *der* - **4.** [nuance] Schattierung *die* ⟨⟩ *vt* - **1.** [from light] beschatten; **to ~ one's eyes** seine Augen ab|schirmen - **2.** [in drawing]

**S**

schattieren ◇ vi [merge]: **to ~ into sthg** in etw (A) über|gehen.

◆ **shades** npl inf [sunglasses] Sonnenbrille die.

**shading** ['ʃeɪdɪŋ] n [darker area] Schattierung die.

**shadow** ['ʃædəʊ] n Schatten der; **to be a ~ of one's former self** (nur noch) ein Schatten seiner selbst sein; **there's not a** OR **the ~ of a doubt** es gibt nicht den geringsten Zweifel ◇ adj Br POL Schatten-.

**shadow cabinet** n Schattenkabinett das.

**shadowy** ['ʃædəʊɪ] adj - **1.** [dark] dunkel - **2.** [hard to see] schattenhaft - **3.** [unknown, sinister] mysteriös.

**shady** ['ʃeɪdɪ] (compar -ier; superl -iest) adj - **1.** [place] schattig - **2.** [tree] Schatten spendend - **3.** inf [dishonest, sinister] zweifelhaft.

**shaft** [ʃɑːft] n - **1.** [vertical passage] Schacht der - **2.** [rod - of tool] Stiel der; [ - of column] Schaft der; [ - of propeller] Welle die - **3.** [of light] Strahl der ◇ vt vinf - **1.** [dupe] an|schmieren - **2.** Am [treat unfairly] mies behandeln.

**shaggy** ['ʃægɪ] (compar -ier; superl -iest) adj [hair, beard, dog] struppig; [carpet] verfilzt.

**shaggy-dog story** n langatmige Anekdote ohne Höhepunkt.

**shake** [ʃeɪk] (pt **shook**; pp **shaken**) vt - **1.** [move vigorously] schütteln; **to ~ hands** sich (D) die Hände schütteln; **to ~ sb's hand, to ~ hands with sb** jm die Hand schütteln, js Hand schütteln; **to ~ one's head** den Kopf schütteln - **2.** [upset, undermine] erschüttern ◇ vi zittern ◇ n: **to give sthg a ~** etw schütteln.

◆ **shake down** vt sep Am inf - **1.** [extort] erpressen - **2.** [search] gründlich durchsuchen.

◆ **shake off** vt sep [police, pursuer] ab|schütteln; [illness] los|werden.

◆ **shake up** vt sep [upset] stark mit|nehmen.

**shakedown** ['ʃeɪkdaʊn] n Am inf - **1.** [extortion] Erpressung die - **2.** [search] gründliche Durchsuchung.

**shaken** ['ʃeɪkn] pp ⊳ shake.

**shakeout** ['ʃeɪkaʊt] n [shake-up] radikale Umstrukturierung.

**Shakespearean** [ʃeɪk'spɪərɪən] adj Shakespearisch; **in ~ times** zu Zeiten Shakespeares.

**shake-up** n inf radikale Umstrukturierung.

**shaky** ['ʃeɪkɪ] (compar -ier; superl -iest) adj - **1.** [unsteady - chair, table] wackelig; [ - hand, writing, voice] zitternd; [ - person] zitterig - **2.** [weak, uncertain] schwach; [finances] unsicher.

**shall** [weak form ʃəl, strong form ʃæl] aux vb - **1.** (1st person sg & 1st person pl) [to express future tense] werden; **I ~ be late tomorrow** morgen werde ich später kommen; **I ~ be ready soon** ich bin bald fertig; **will you be there? - we ~** werdet ihr dort sein? - ja - **2.** (esp 1st person sg & 1st person pl) [in questions] sollen; **~ I buy some wine?** soll ich Wein kaufen?; **where ~ we go?** wo gehen wir hin?; **I'll tell her too, ~ I?** ich sag es ihr auch, OK? - **3.** [will definitely] werden; **we ~ overcome!** wir werden siegen! - **4.** [in orders] sollen; **you ~ tell me what happened!** du wirst mir erzählen, was passiert ist!; **the committee ~ decide on this** der Ausschuss entscheidet hierüber; **payment ~ be made within a week** die Zahlung muss innerhalb einer Woche erfolgen.

**shallot** [ʃə'lɒt] n Schalotte die

**shallow** ['ʃæləʊ] adj - **1.** [in size] flach - **2.** pej [superficial] seicht - **3.** [breathing] flach.

◆ **shallows** npl Untiefe die.

**sham** [ʃæm] (pt & pp -med; cont -ming) adj [feeling] vorgetäuscht ◇ n [piece of deceit] Schein der ◇ vi [pretend to be ill] simulieren; [pretend to feel sthg] heucheln.

**shambles** ['ʃæmblz] n - **1.** [disorder] Chaos das - **2.** [fiasco] Disaster das.

**shame** [ʃeɪm] n - **1.** [remorse] Scham die - **2.** [dishonour]: **to bring ~ (up)on sb** Schande über jn bringen - **3.** [pity]: **it's a ~ (that)** ... schade, dass ...; **what a ~!** (wie) schade! ◇ vt beschämen; **to ~ sb into doing sthg** jn moralisch zwingen, etw zu tun.

**shamefaced** [ʃeɪm'feɪst] adj beschämt.

**shameful** ['ʃeɪmfʊl] adj schändlich.

**shameless** ['ʃeɪmlɪs] adj schamlos.

**shammy** ['ʃæmɪ] (pl -ies) n inf: **~ (leather)** Fensterleder das.

**shampoo** [ʃæm'puː] (pl -s; pt & pp -ed; cont -ing) n - **1.** [liquid] Shampoo das; **carpet ~** Teppichreiniger der - **2.** [act of shampooing]: **to give one's hair a ~** sich (D) das Haar schampunieren ◇ vt [hair] schampunieren; [carpet] reinigen.

**shamrock** ['ʃæmrɒk] n Klee der.

**shandy** ['ʃændɪ] (pl -ies) n [in Northern Germany] Alsterwasser das; [in Southern Germany] Radler das.

**shan't** [ʃɑːnt] = shall not.

**shantytown** ['ʃæntɪtaʊn] n Slum der.

**shape** [ʃeɪp] n - **1.** [outer form] Form die - **2.** [figure, abstract structure] Gestalt die; **to take ~** Gestalt an|nehmen - **3.** [guise]: **in the ~ of** in Form von; **not in any ~ or form** in keiner Weise - **4.** [form, health]: **to be in good/bad ~** [person] in guter/schlechter Form sein; **his business is in bad ~** seine Geschäfte laufen schlecht; **to lick** OR **knock sb into ~** jn in Form bringen ◇ vt - **1.** [mould physically]: **to ~ sthg (into)** etw formen (in (+ A)); **~d like a star** sternenförmig - **2.** [influence - person, character] formen; [ - ideas, life, future] beeinflussen.

◆ **shape up** vi [develop] sich entwickeln.

**-shaped** ['ʃeɪpt] suffix -förmig; **egg~** eiförmig.

**shapeless** [ˈʃeɪplɪs] adj formlos.

**shapely** [ˈʃeɪplɪ] (compar -ier; superl -iest) adj [legs] wohlproportioniert; [woman] wohlgeformt.

**shard** [ʃɑːd] n Scherbe die.

**share** [ʃeəʳ] n: ~ (of/in sthg) Anteil der (von/an etw (D)); **to have one's ~ of sthg** seinen Anteil an etw (D) haben; **to do one's ~ of sthg** seinen Beitrag zu etw leisten <> vt teilen; **to ~ sthg (with sb)** etw (mit jm) teilen <> vi [share book] zusammen hineinlschauen; **there's only one room left – we'll have to ~** es gibt nur noch ein Zimmer – wir müssen es teilen; **to ~ in sthg** sich an etw (D) beteiligen.

➣ **shares** npl FIN Aktien pl.

➣ **share out** vt sep verteilen.

**share capital** n (U) Aktienkapital das.

**share certificate** n Aktienzertifikat das.

**shareholder** [ˈʃeəˌhəʊldəʳ] n Aktionär der, -in die.

**share index** n Aktienindex der.

**share-out** n Verteilung die.

**shareware** [ˈʃeəweəʳ] n COMPUT Shareware die.

**shark** [ʃɑːk] (pl inv OR -s) n - **1.** [fish] Hai der - **2.** fig [dishonest person] Gauner der.

**sharp** [ʃɑːp] adj - **1.** [not blunt] scharf; [needle, pencil] spitz - **2.** [well-defined] scharf - **3.** [intelligent, keen - person, mind] scharfsinnig; [ - eyesight, hearing] scharf - **4.** [sudden - increase, fall] abrupt; [ - turn] scharf; [ - slope] steil - **5.** [angry, severe] scharf; **she was rather ~ with me** sie war recht schroff zu mir - **6.** [piercing, loud] schrill - **7.** [painful] schneidend - **8.** [bitter] herb - **9.** [MUS - raised a semitone] um einen Halbton erhöht; **C ~ Cis** das; **D ~ Dis** das; **A ~ Ais** das <> adv - **1.** [punctually] pünktlich; **at eight o'clock ~ Punkt acht Uhr - 2.** [quickly, suddenly]: **to turn ~ right/left** scharf nach rechts/links ablbiegen <> n [MUS - note] erhöhter Ton; [ - symbol] Kreuz das.

**sharpen** [ˈʃɑːpn] vt - **1.** [make sharp] schärfen; [pencil] (anl)spitzen - **2.** [heighten - sense, mind] anlstrengen; [ - conflict, contrast] verschärfen <> vi [pain, wind, conflict] sich verschärfen.

**sharp end** n Br fig: **to be at the ~** an vorderster Front stehen.

**sharpener** [ˈʃɑːpnəʳ] n [for pencil] Spitzer der; [for knife] Messerschärfer der.

**sharp-eyed** [-ˈaɪd] adj scharfsichtig.

**sharply** [ˈʃɑːplɪ] adv - **1.** [distinctly] scharf - **2.** [suddenly - increase, fall] abrupt; [ - turn] scharf; [ - slope] steil - **3.** [harshly] scharf.

**sharpness** [ˈʃɑːpnɪs] n Schärfe die; [of point, pencil] Spitzheit die; [of pain] Heftigkeit die; [of voice] Schrillheit die; [of wine] herber Geschmack.

**sharpshooter** [ˈʃɑːpˌʃuːtəʳ] n Scharfschütze der.

**sharp-tongued** [-ˈtʌŋd] adj scharfzüngig.

**sharp-witted** [-ˈwɪtɪd] adj scharfsinnig.

**shat** [ʃæt] pt & pp ⊳ shit.

**shatter** [ˈʃætəʳ] vt - **1.** [glass, window] zerschmettern - **2.** fig [beliefs, hopes, dreams] zerschlagen; **to be ~ed (by sthg)** (wegen etw) niedergeschmettert sein <> vi [glass, window] zerspringen.

**shattered** [ˈʃætəd] adj - **1.** [shocked, upset] niedergeschmettert - **2.** Br inf [very tired] völlig fertig.

**shattering** [ˈʃætərɪŋ] adj - **1.** [shocking, upsetting] niederschmetternd - **2.** Br inf [very tiring] ermüdend.

**shatterproof** [ˈʃætəpruːf] adj bruchsicher.

**shave** [ʃeɪv] n [with razor] Rasur die; **to have a ~** sich rasieren; **that was a close ~!** fig das war knapp! <> vt - **1.** [with razor] rasieren - **2.** [wood] ablhobeln <> vi sich rasieren.

➣ **shave off** vt scp [with razor] ablrasieren.

**shaven** [ˈʃeɪvn] adj rasiert.

**shaver** [ˈʃeɪvəʳ] n Rasierapparat der.

**shaving brush** [ˈʃeɪvɪŋ-] n Rasierpinsel der.

**shaving cream** [ˈʃeɪvɪŋ-] n Rasiercreme die.

**shaving foam** [ˈʃeɪvɪŋ-] n Rasierschaum der.

**shavings** [ˈʃeɪvɪŋz] npl Späne pl.

**shaving soap** [ˈʃeɪvɪŋ-] n Rasierseife die.

**shawl** [ʃɔːl] n Schultertuch das.

**she** [ʃiː] pers pron - **1.** [referring to woman, girl, animal] sie; **~'s tall** sie ist groß; **there ~ is** da ist sie; **SHE can't do it** SIE kann es nicht tun; **if I were** OR **was ~** fml wenn ich sie wäre - **2.** [referring to boat, car, country] es; **~ sails tomorrow** es fährt morgen ab <> n inf: **it's a ~** es ist eine Sie <> comp: **~-bear** Bärin die.

**sheaf** [ʃiːf] (pl sheaves) n - **1.** [of papers, letters] Bündel das - **2.** [of corn, grain] Garbe die.

**shear** [ʃɪəʳ] (pt -ed; pp -ed OR shorn) vt scheren.

➣ **shears** npl - **1.** [for garden] Heckenschere die - **2.** [for dressmaking] große Schere.

➣ **shear off** vt sep ablschneiden <> vi ablbrechen.

**sheath** [ʃiːθ] (pl -s [ʃiːðz]) n - **1.** [for knife] Scheide die - **2.** [for cable] Umhüllung die, Ummantelung die - **3.** Br [condom] Kondom das.

**sheathe** vt - **1.** [sword, dagger] in die Scheide stecken - **2.** [cable, pipe]: **~d in sthg** mit etw umlmantelt.

**sheath knife** n Fahrtenmesser das.

**sheaves** [ʃiːvz] pl ⊳ sheaf.

**shed** [ʃed] (pt & pp shed; cont -ding) n Schuppen der <> vt - **1.** [gen] verlieren - **2.** [employees] entlassen; [inhibitions] überwinden - **3.** [tears, blood] vergießen.

**S**

**she'd** [weak form ʃɪd, strong form ʃiːd] = **she had, she would.**

**sheen** [ʃiːn] n Glanz der.

**sheep** [ʃiːp] (pl inv) n Schaf das.

**sheepdog** ['ʃiːpdɒg] n Hütehund der.

**sheepfold** ['ʃiːpfəʊld] n Schafhürde die.

**sheepish** ['ʃiːpɪʃ] adj verlegen.

**sheepishly** ['ʃiːpɪʃlɪ] adv verlegen.

**sheepskin** ['ʃiːpskɪn] n Schaffell das.

**sheepskin jacket** n Schaffelljacke die.

**sheepskin rug** n Schaffellteppich der.

**sheer** [ʃɪəʳ] adj - **1.** [absolute] rein - **2.** [very steep] senkrecht - **3.** [delicate] hauchdünn.

**sheet** [ʃiːt] n - **1.** [for bed] Bettuch das, Laken das; **as white as a ~** totenbleich - **2.** [of paper] Blatt das - **3.** [of glass] Scheibe die; [of metal] Blech das; [of wood] Platte die.

**sheet feed** n COMPUT Einzelblatteinzug der.

**sheet ice** n Eisschicht die.

**sheeting** ['ʃiːtɪŋ] n Abdeckung die.

**sheet lightning** n Wetterleuchten das.

**sheet metal** n (U) Blech das.

**sheet music** n (U) Notenblätter pl.

**sheik(h)** [ʃeɪk] n Scheich der.

**shelf** [ʃelf] (pl **shelves**) n Regal das.

**shelf life** n Haltbarkeit die.

**shell** [ʃel] n - **1.** [of egg, nut] Schale die - **2.** [of tortoise] Panzer der; [of snail] Haus das - **3.** [on beach] Muschel die - **4.** [of building] Rohbau der; [of car] Karosserie die; [of boat] Rumpf der - **5.** MIL Granate die ⇔ vt - **1.** [remove covering from] schälen; [peas] enthülsen - **2.** MIL beschießen.

➤ **shell out** inf vt sep blechen ⇔ vi: **to ~ out for sthg** für etw blechen müssen.

**she'll** [ʃiːl] = **she will, she shall.**

**shellfish** ['ʃelfɪʃ] (pl inv) n - **1.** [creature] Schalentier das - **2.** (U) [food] Meeresfrüchte pl.

**shelling** ['ʃelɪŋ] n MIL Beschuss der.

**shellshock** ['ʃelʃɒk] n (U) Kriegstrauma das.

**shell suit** n Br Jogginganzug der (aus Nylon).

**shelter** ['ʃeltəʳ] n - **1.** [building, structure] Unterstand der; [against air raids] (Luftschutz)bunker der; [in mountains] Berghütte die - **2.** [cover, protection] Schutz der - **3.** [accommodation] Obdach das ⇔ vt - **1.** [from rain, sun, bombs]: **to be ~ed by/from sthg** von/vor etw (D) geschützt sein - **2.** [give asylum to - refugee] Obdach geben (+ D); [ - fugitive, criminal] Unterschlupf gewähren (+ D) ⇔ vi: **to ~ from/in sthg** vor/in etw (D) Schutz suchen.

**sheltered** ['ʃeltəd] adj - **1.** [place] geschützt - **2.** [life, childhood] behütet - **3.** [accommodation, housing] betreut.

**shelve** [ʃelv] vt [plan] auf|schieben ⇔ vi [ground, beach] sich (sanft) neigen.

**shelves** [ʃelvz] pl ➢ **shelf.**

**shelving** ['ʃelvɪŋ] n (U) [shelves] Regale pl.

**shenanigans** [ʃɪ'nænɪgənz] npl inf - **1.** [trickery] Tricks pl - **2.** [mischief] Dummheiten pl.

**shepherd** ['ʃepəd] n Schäfer der ⇔ vt fig führen.

**shepherd's pie** ['ʃepədz-] n mit Kartoffelbrei überbackenes Hackfleisch.

**sherbet** ['ʃɜːbət] n - **1.** (U) Br [sweet powder] Brausepulver das - **2.** Am [sorbet] Sorbet das.

**sheriff** ['ʃerɪf] n - **1.** Am [law officer] Sheriff der - **2.** Scot [judge] (oberster) Richter einer Grafschaft.

**sherry** ['ʃerɪ] (pl **-ies**) n Sherry der.

**she's** [ʃiːz] = **she is, she has.**

**Shetland** ['ʃetlənd] n: **~, the ~ Islands** die Shetlandinseln pl; **in ~, in the ~ Islands** auf den Shetlandinseln.

**shh** [ʃ] excl = **sh.**

**shield** [ʃiːld] n - **1.** [armour] Schild der - **2.** Br [sports trophy] Trophäe die - **3.** [protection]: **~ against sthg** Schutz der gegen etw ⇔ vt: **to ~ sb/o.s. (from sthg)** jn/sich (vor etw (D)) schützen.

**shift** [ʃɪft] n - **1.** [slight change] Veränderung die - **2.** [period of work, workers] Schicht die ⇔ vt - **1.** [move, put elsewhere] verschieben - **2.** [change slightly] ändern - **3.** fig [blame, responsibility]: **to ~ sthg onto sb** jm etw in die Schuhe schieben - **4.** Am AUT: **to ~ gear** schalten - **5.** [stain] entfernen ⇔ vi - **1.** [move] sich bewegen; [move up - person] rutschen; [ - thing] verrutschen; **he ~ed about in his chair** er rutschte auf seinem Stuhl herum - **2.** [change slightly - attitude, opinion] sich ändern; [ - wind] umschlagen - **3.** Am AUT schalten - **4.** [stain] sich entfernen lassen.

**shift key** n Umschalttaste die, Shift-Taste die.

**shiftless** ['ʃɪftlɪs] adj träge.

**shift stick** n Am Schaltknüppel der.

**shifty** ['ʃɪftɪ] (compar **-ier;** superl **-iest**) adj inf verschlagen.

**Shiite** ['ʃiːaɪt] adj schiitisch ⇔ n Schiite der, -tin die.

**shilling** ['ʃɪlɪŋ] n Br Shilling der.

**shilly-shally** ['ʃɪlɪ ˌʃælɪ] (pt & pp **-ied**) vi unentschlossen sein.

**shimmer** ['ʃɪməʳ] n Schimmer der; [in heat] Flimmern das ⇔ vi schimmern; [in heat] flimmern.

**shin** [ʃɪn] (pt & pp **-ned;** cont **-ning**) n Schienbein das.

➤ **shin up** Br, **shinny up** Am vt fus hinauf|-klettern.

**shinbone** ['ʃɪnbəʊn] n Schienbein das.

**shine** [ʃaɪn] (pt & pp **shone**) n Glanz der ⇔ vt

**- 1.** [torch, lamp]: **to ~ sthg on sthg** mit etw auf etw (A) leuchten **- 2.** [polish] polieren ⟨⟩ vi **- 1.** [moon, sun] scheinen; [stars, light] leuchten; [eyes, metal, shoes] glänzen **- 2.** [excel]: **to ~ at sthg in etw** glänzen.

**shingle** ['ʃɪŋgl] n [on beach] Strandkies der.
➤ **shingles** (U) n MED Gürtelrose die.

**shining** ['ʃaɪnɪŋ] adj **- 1.** [gleaming] glänzend **- 2.** [outstanding] hervorragend.

**shinny** ➤ **shinny up** vt fus Am = shin up.

**shin pads** npl Schienbeinschoner pl.

**shiny** ['ʃaɪnɪ] (compar **-ier**; superl **-iest**) adj glänzend.

**ship** [ʃɪp] (pt & pp **-ped**; cont **-ping**) n Schiff das ⟨⟩ vt [send] versenden; [send by ship - people] befördern; [ - goods] verschiffen.

**shipbuilder** ['ʃɪpˌbɪldə<sup>r</sup>] n Schiffbauer der.

**shipbuilding** ['ʃɪpˌbɪldɪŋ] n Schiffbau der.

**ship canal** n Seekanal der.

**shipment** ['ʃɪpmənt] n **- 1.** [cargo] Sendung die; [in ship] Ladung die **- 2.** [act of shipping] Versand der; [by ship] Verschiffung die.

**shipper** ['ʃɪpə<sup>r</sup>] n Spediteur der.

**shipping** ['ʃɪpɪŋ] n (U) **- 1.** [transport] Versand der; [by ship] Verschiffung die **- 2.** [ships] Schiffe pl.

**shipping agent** n Schiffsmakler der.

**shipping company** n Reederei die.

**shipping forecast** n Seewetterbericht der.

**shipping lane** n Schifffahrtsstraße die.

**shipshape** ['ʃɪpʃeɪp] adj tipptopp in Ordnung.

**shipwreck** ['ʃɪprek] n **- 1.** [destruction of ship] Schiffbruch der **- 2.** [wrecked ship] Schiffswrack das ⟨⟩ vt: **to be ~ed** Schiffbruch erleiden.

**shipwrecked** ['ʃɪprekt] adj schiffbrüchig.

**shipyard** ['ʃɪpjɑːd] n (Schiffs)werft die.

**shire** [ʃaɪə<sup>r</sup>] n [county] Grafschaft die.
➤ **Shire** n: **the Shires** Sammelbegriff für die Grafschaften in Mittelengland.

**shire horse** n Zugpferd das.

**shirk** [ʃɜːk] vt sich drücken vor (+ D).

**shirker** ['ʃɜːkə<sup>r</sup>] n Drückeberger der, -in die.

**shirt** [ʃɜːt] n Hemd das.

**shirtsleeves** ['ʃɜːtsliːvz] npl: **to be in (one's) ~** in Hemdsärmeln sein.

**shirttail** ['ʃɜːteɪl] n Hemdschoß der.

**shirty** ['ʃɜːtɪ] (compar **-ier**; superl **-iest**) adj Br inf sauer.

**shit** [ʃɪt] (pt & pp **shit** OR **-ted** OR **shat**; cont **-ting**) vulg n **- 1.** [excrement, nonsense] Scheiße die **- 2.** [person] Scheißkerl der ⟨⟩ vi scheißen ⟨⟩ excl Scheiße!

**shiver** ['ʃɪvə<sup>r</sup>] n Schauder der; **to give sb the ~s** jn schaudern lassen ⟨⟩ vi: **to ~ (with sthg)** (vor etw (D)) zittern.

**shoal** [ʃəʊl] n [of fish] Schwarm der.

**shock** [ʃɒk] n **- 1.** [surprise, reaction] Schock der **- 2.** MED: **to be suffering from ~, to be in (a state of) ~** unter Schock stehen **- 3.** [impact] Wucht die **- 4.** ELEC Schlag der **- 5.** [thick mass]: **~ of hair** Haarschopf ⟨⟩ vt & vi [upset] schockieren.

**shock absorber** [-əbˌzɔːbə<sup>r</sup>] n Stoßdämpfer der.

**shocked** [ʃɒkt] adj schockiert.

**shocking** ['ʃɒkɪŋ] adj **- 1.** [very bad] miserabel **- 2.** [scandalous, horrifying] schockierend.

**shockproof** ['ʃɒkpruːf] adj stoßfest.

**shock tactics** npl **- 1.** MIL Überraschungsschlag der **- 2.** fig [surprising manoeuvre] Schocktherapie die.

**shock therapy, shock treatment** n (U) MED Schocktherapie die.

**shock troops** npl Stoßtruppen pl.

**shock wave** n **- 1.** [intense pressure] Druckwelle die **- 2.** fig [strong reaction] Welle die des Entsetzens.

**shod** [ʃɒd] pt & pp ⟼ **shoe** ⟨⟩ adj: **well/poorly ~** gut/schlecht beschuht.

**shoddy** ['ʃɒdɪ] (compar **-ier**; superl **-iest**) adj schäbig.

**shoe** [ʃuː] (pt & pp **-d** OR **shod**; cont **-ing**) n **- 1.** [for person] Schuh der **- 2.** [for horse] Hufeisen das **- 3.** [for brake] Bremsbacke die ⟨⟩ vt [horse] beschlagen.

**shoebrush** ['ʃuːbrʌʃ] n Schuhbürste die.

**shoehorn** ['ʃuːhɔːn] n Schuhanzieher der.

**shoelace** ['ʃuːleɪs] n Schnürsenkel der.

**shoemaker** ['ʃuːˌmeɪkə<sup>r</sup>] n Schuhmacher der, -in die.

**shoe polish** n (U) Schuh(putz)creme die.

**shoe repairer** [-rɪˌpeərə<sup>r</sup>] n Schuster der, -in die.

**shoe shop** n Schuhgeschäft das.

**shoestring** ['ʃuːstrɪŋ] adj [budget] knapp ⟨⟩ fig: **on a ~** mit minimalen (finanziellen) Mitteln.

**shoetree** ['ʃuːtriː] n Schuhspanner der.

**shone** [ʃɒn] pt & pp ⟼ **shine**.

**shoo** [ʃuː] vt verscheuchen ⟨⟩ excl husch!

**shook** [ʃʊk] pt ⟼ **shake**.

**shoot** [ʃuːt] (pt & pp **shot**) vt **- 1.** [fire gun at - killing] erschießen; [ - wounding] anschießen; **to ~ o.s.** [kill o.s.] sich erschießen **- 2.** Br [hunt] jagen **- 3.** [arrow] abschießen **- 4.** [direct]: **to ~ sb a look** jm einen Blick zuwerfen; **to ~ questions at sb** jn mit Fragen bombardieren **- 5.** CINEMA drehen **- 6.** Am: **to ~ pool** Billard spielen ⟨⟩ vi **- 1.** [fire gun]: **to ~ (at sb/sthg)** (auf

S

jn/etw) schießen - **2.** *Br* [hunt] jagen - **3.** [move quickly]: **to ~ in/out/past** herein-/heraus-/vorbeischießen - **4.** CINEMA drehen - **5.** SPORT schießen ◇ *n* - **1.** *Br* [hunting expedition] Jagd *die* - **2.** [of plant] Trieb *der* ◇ *excl Am inf* - **1.** [go ahead] schieß los! - **2.** [damn] Mist!

➤ **shoot down** *vt sep* - **1.** [plane, helicopter] ablschießen; [person] niederlschießen - **2.** *fig* [reject] neiderlmachen.

➤ **shoot up** *vi* - **1.** [grow quickly] schnell wachsen - **2.** [increase quickly] in die Höhe schießen - **3.** *drugs sl* [take drugs] sich *(D)* Drogen spritzen.

**shooting** [ˈʃuːtɪŋ] *n* - **1.** [killing] Schießerei *die* - **2.** [hunting] Jagd *die*.

**shooting range** *n* Schießplatz *der*.

**shooting star** *n* Sternschnuppe *die*.

**shooting stick** *n* Sitzstock *der*.

**shoot-out** *n* Schießerei *die*.

**shop** [ʃɒp] (*pt* & *pp* -**ped**; *cont* -**ping**) *n* - **1.** [store] Geschäft *das*, Laden *der;* **to talk ~** fachsimpeln - **2.** [workshop] Werkstatt *die* ◇ *vi* einlkaufen; **to go ~ping** einkaufen gehen.

➤ **shop around** *vi* Preisvergleich machen.

**shop assistant** *n Br* Verkäufer *der*, -in *die*.

**shop floor** *n:* **the ~** [workers] die Arbeiter *pl;* **on the ~** bei den Arbeitern.

**shopkeeper** [ˈʃɒpˌkiːpəʳ] *n* Ladenbesitzer *der*, -in *die*.

**shoplifter** [ˈʃɒpˌlɪftəʳ] *n* Ladendieb *der*, -in *die*.

**shoplifting** [ˈʃɒpˌlɪftɪŋ] *n (U)* Ladendiebstahl *der*.

**shopper** [ˈʃɒpəʳ] *n* Käufer *der*, -in *die*.

**shopping** [ˈʃɒpɪŋ] *n (U)* - **1.** [purchases] Einkäufe *pl* - **2.** [act of shopping] Einkaufen *das;* **to do the ~** einkaufen (gehen).

**shopping bag** *n* Einkaufstasche *die*.

**shopping centre** *Br*, **shopping mall** *Am*, **shopping plaza** *Am* [-ˌplɑːzə] *n* Einkaufszentrum *das*.

**shopping list** *n* Einkaufsliste *die*.

**shopping mall, shopping plaza** *n Am* = shopping centre.

**shopsoiled** *Br* [ˈʃɒpsɔɪld], **shopworn** *Am* [ˈʃɒpwɔːn] *adj* angestaubt.

**shop steward** *n* gewerkschaftliche Vertrauensperson.

**shopwalker** [ˈʃɒpˌwɔːkəʳ] *n Br* Aufsicht *die*.

**shopwindow** [ˌʃɒpˈwɪndəʊ] *n* Schaufenster *das*.

**shopworn** *adj Am* = shopsoiled.

**shore** [ʃɔːʳ] *n* Ufer *das;* **on ~** [not at sea] an Land.

➤ **shore up** *vt sep* - **1.** [prop up] ablstützen - **2.** *fig* [sustain] stützen.

**shore leave** *n* Landurlaub *der*.

**shoreline** [ˈʃɔːlaɪn] *n* Uferlinie *die*.

**shorn** [ʃɔːn] *pp* ▷ **shear** ◇ *adj* [head, sheep] geschoren; [hair] kurz geschoren.

**short** [ʃɔːt] *adj* - **1.** [gen] kurz - **2.** [in height] klein - **3.** [curt]: **to be ~ (with sb)** (zu jm) schroff OR barsch sein - **4.** [lacking] knapp; **we're £10 ~** uns fehlen 10 Pfund; **he is ~ on intelligence/money** es mangelt ihm an Intelligenz/Geld; **to be ~ of breath** [permanently] kurzatmig sein; [temporarily] außer Atem sein - **5.** [abbreviated]: **to be ~ for sthg** die Kurzform von etw sein ◇ *adv* - **1.** [lacking]: **we're running ~ of food** unsere Lebensmittelvorräte gehen langsam zur Neige - **2.** [suddenly, abruptly]: **to cut sthg ~** etw vorzeitig ablbrechen; **to stop ~** plötzlich stehenlbleiben; **to bring** OR **pull sb up ~** jn zum Nachdenken bringen ◇ *n* - **1.** *Br* [alcoholic drink] Schnaps *der* - **2.** CINEMA Kurzfilm *der*.

➤ **shorts** *npl* - **1.** [short trousers] Shorts *pl* - **2.** *Am* [underwear] Boxershorts *pl*.

➤ **for short** *adv:* **he's called Bob for ~** er wird kurz Bob genannt.

➤ **in short** *adv* kurz gesagt.

➤ **nothing short of** *prep* nichts anderes als.

➤ **short of** *prep* [apart from]: **~ of ringing up, I don't see how I can find out** ich kann es nur herausfinden, wenn ich anrufe.

**shortage** [ˈʃɔːtɪdʒ] *n* Mangel *der*, Knappheit *die*.

**short back and sides** *n Br* Fassonschnitt *der*.

**shortbread** [ˈʃɔːtbred] *n (U)* Buttergebäck *das*.

**short-change** *vt* - **1.** [in shop, restaurant] zu wenig herauslgeben (+ *D*) - **2.** *fig* [reward unfairly] übers Ohr gehauen werden.

**short circuit** *n* Kurzschluss *der*.

➤ **short-circuit** *vt* kurzlschließen ◇ *vi* einen Kurzschluss haben.

**shortcomings** [ˈʃɔːtˌkʌmɪŋz] *npl* Unzulänglichkeiten *pl*.

**shortcrust pastry** [ˈʃɔːtkrʌst-] *n (U)* Mürbeteig *der*.

**short cut** *n* - **1.** [quick route] Abkürzung *die* - **2.** [quick method] schneller Weg.

**shorten** [ˈʃɔːtn] *vt* - **1.** [in time] verkürzen - **2.** [in length] kürzen ◇ *vi* [days, nights] kürzer werden.

**shortening** [ˈʃɔːtnɪŋ] *n (U)* CULIN Backfett *das*.

**shortfall** [ˈʃɔːtfɔːl] *n:* **~ (in/of sthg)** Defizit *das* (bei/von etw).

**shorthand** [ˈʃɔːthænd] *n (U)* - **1.** [writing system] Stenografie *die*, Kurzschrift *die* - **2.** [euphemism]: **to be ~ for sthg** etw im Klartext heißen.

**shorthanded** [ˌʃɔːtˈhændɪd] *adj:* **to be ~** an Personalmangel leiden.

**shorthand typist** n Br Stenotypist der, -in die.

**short-haul** adj Kurzstrecken-.

**short list** n Br engere Wahl.

◆ **short-list** vt Br: **to be short-listed (for sthg)** (für etw) in die engere Wahl gezogen werden.

**short-lived** [-'lɪvd] adj kurzlebig.

**shortly** ['ʃɔːtlɪ] adv - **1.** [soon] bald; **~ before/ after our arrival** kurz vor/nach unserer Ankunft - **2.** [curtly, abruptly] schroff, barsch.

**shortness** ['ʃɔːtnɪs] n (U) Kürze die; [in height] (geringe) Größe.

**short-range** adj - **1.** [missile, weapon] Kurzstrecken- - **2.** [forecast - economic] kurzfristig; [ - weather] für die nächsten Tage.

**short shrift** [-'ʃrɪft] n: **to give sb ~** jn kurz abfertigen.

**shortsighted** [ ˌʃɔːt'saɪtɪd] adj lit & fig kurzsichtig.

**short-staffed** [-'stɑːft] adj: **to be ~** an Personalmangel leiden.

**short-stay car park** n Kurzzeitparkplatz der.

**short story** n Kurzgeschichte die.

**short-tempered** [-'tempəd] adj reizbar.

**short-term** adj kurzfristig.

**short time** n Br: **on ~** auf Kurzarbeit.

**short wave** n Kurzwelle die.

**shot** [ʃɒt] pt & pp ⊳ **shoot** ⊳ n - **1.** [gunshot, injection, drink] Schuss der; **like a ~** [quickly] wie der Blitz - **2.** [marksman] Schütze der, -zin die - **3.** [SPORT - in football] Schuss der; [ - in golf, tennis] Schlag der - **4.** [photograph] Aufnahme die - **5.** CINEMA Einstellung die - **6.** inf [try, go] Versuch der.

**shotgun** ['ʃɒtɡʌn] n Schrotflinte die.

**shot put** n: **the ~** das Kugelstoßen.

**should** [ʃʊd] aux vb - **1.** [expressing desirability]: **we ~ leave now** wir sollten jetzt gehen; **you ~ have seen her!** du hättest sie sehen sollen! - **2.** [asking for advice, permission]: **~ I go too?** soll ich auch gehen?; **~ I do it now?** soll ich es jetzt tun? - **3.** [as suggestion]: **I ~ deny everything** ich würde alles abstreiten; **I ~n't take too much notice** kümmern Sie sich nicht zu sehr darum - **4.** [expressing probability]: **she ~ be home soon** sie müsste bald zu Hause sein - **5.** [ought to]: **they ~ have won the match** sie hätten das Spiel gewinnen müssen; **that ~ do das** dürfte genügen - **6.** fml [expressing wish]: **I ~ like to come with you** ich würde gerne mit dir mitkommen - **7.** (as conditional): **~ you need anything, call reception** fml sollten Sie irgendetwas brauchen, rufen Sie die Rezeption an; **how ~ I know?** wie soll ich das wissen? - **8.** (in subordinate clauses): **we decided that you ~ meet him** wir beschlossen, dass

du ihn kennenlernen solltest - **9.** [expressing uncertain opinion]: **I ~ imagine he's about 50** meiner Meinung nach ist er etwa 50 - **10.** (after "who" or "what") [expressing surprise]: **and who ~ I run into but Ann!** ausgerechnet Ann ist mir über den Weg gelaufen!

**shoulder** ['ʃəʊldə'] n Schulter die; **to look over one's ~** über seine Schulter sehen; **a ~ to cry on** jemand zum Ausweinen; **to rub ~s with sb** mit jm zusammenkommen ⟨⟩ vt - **1.** [load] auf die Schulter(n) nehmen - **2.** [responsibility] übernehmen.

**shoulder bag** n Umhängetasche die.

**shoulder blade** n Schulterblatt das.

**shoulder-length** adj schulterlang.

**shoulder pad** n Schulterpolster das.

**shoulder strap** n - **1.** [on dress] Träger der - **2.** [on bag] Schulterriemen der.

**shouldn't** ['ʃʊdnt] = should not.

**should've** ['ʃʊdəv] = should have.

**shout** [ʃaʊt] n Schrei der ⟨⟩ vt schreien ⟨⟩ vi schreien; **to ~ at sb** jn anschreien.

◆ **shout down** vt sep niederschreien.

◆ **shout out** vt sep herausschreien.

**shouting** ['ʃaʊtɪŋ] n Geschrei das.

**shove** [ʃʌv] inf n: **to give sb a ~** jm einen Schubs geben; **to give sthg a ~** etw rücken; [car] etw anschieben ⟨⟩ vt [push - person] schubsen; [ - thing] schieben; [stuff] stopfen.

◆ **shove off** vi - **1.** [in boat] (vom Ufer) abstoßen - **2.** inf [go away] verschwinden.

**shovel** ['ʃʌvl] (Br pt & pp -led; cont -ling, Am pt & pp -ed; cont -ing) n Schaufel die ⟨⟩ vt - **1.** [with a shovel] schaufeln - **2.** fig: **to ~ ice cream into one's mouth** Eis in sich hineinschaufeln.

**show** [ʃəʊ] (pt -ed; pp shown OR -ed) n - **1.** [entertainment] Show die - **2.** CINEMA Vorstellung die - **3.** [exhibition] Ausstellung die; **on ~** ausgestellt - **4.** [display - of strength] Zurschaustellen das; [ - of temper] Anfall der, Ausbruch der; **for ~** nur fürs Auge - **5.** [pretence]: **~ of indifference** vorgetäuschte Gleichgültigkeit; **it's all ~** es ist alles Show ⟨⟩ vt zeigen; [subj: thermometer, dial] anzeigen; [profit, loss] auf|weisen; [work of art] aus|stellen; **to ~ sb sthg, to ~ sthg to sb** jm etw zeigen; **he has nothing to ~ for his hard work** man sieht nichts von der Arbeit, die er hineingesteckt hat; **to ~ o.s.** sich zeigen; **it just goes to ~ (that)** ... das zeigt OR beweist mal wieder, dass ...; **to ~ sb how to do sthg** jm zeigen, wie man etw tut; **to ~ sb to the door/ his table** jn zur Tür bringen/zu seinem Tisch führen ⟨⟩ vi - **1.** [indicate, make clear] zeigen - **2.** [be visible] zu sehen sein - **3.** CINEMA: **what's ~ing tonight?** welcher Film läuft heute Abend?

◆ **show around** vt sep = **show round**.

◆ **show in** vt sep herein|führen.

**show off** vt sep vorlführen ◇ vi anlgeben.

**show out** vt sep herauslführen.

**show round** vt sep herumlführen.

**show up** vt sep [embarrass] blamieren ◇ vi - **1.** [stand out] hervorlstehen, hervorltreten - **2.** [arrive] auf ltauchen.

**showbiz** ['ʃəʊbɪz] n inf Showbusiness das, Showgeschäft das.

**show business** n Showbusiness das, Showgeschäft das.

**showcase** ['ʃəʊkeɪs] n - **1.** [glass case] Vitrine die, Schaukasten der - **2.** fig [advantageous setting] Schaufenster das.

**showdown** ['ʃəʊdaʊn] n: to have a ~ with sb mit jm eine klärende Auseinandersetzung haben.

**shower** ['ʃaʊə'] n - **1.** [device] Dusche die - **2.** [wash]: to have OR take a ~ duschen - **3.** [of rain] Schauer der - **4.** [of confetti, sparks] Regen der; [of insults, abuse] Flut der - **5.** Am [party] Party für eine Frau, die bald heiraten oder ein Kind bekommen wird, zu der jeder Gast ein Geschenk mitbringt ◇ vt: to ~ sb with sthg jn mit etw überschütten; the police were ~ed with stones Steine hagelten auf die Polizisten nieder; they ~ed insults upon him sie überschütteten ihn mit Beleidigungen ◇ vi [wash] duschen.

**shower cap** n Duschhaube die.

**showerproof** ['ʃaʊəpruːf] adj wasserfest.

**showery** ['ʃaʊərɪ] adj regnerisch.

**showing** ['ʃəʊɪŋ] n CINEMA Vorstellung die.

**show jumping** [-ˌdʒʌmpɪŋ] n Springreiten das.

**showman** ['ʃəʊmən] (pl -men [-mən]) n - **1.** [at fair, circus] Schausteller der - **2.** fig [publicity-seeker] Showman der.

**showmanship** ['ʃəʊmənʃɪp] n (U) Unterhaltungstalent das.

**shown** [ʃəʊn] pp ▷ show.

**show-off** n inf Angeber der, -in die.

**show of hands** n Handzeichen das.

**showpiece** ['ʃəʊpiːs] n [main attraction] Paradestück das.

**showroom** ['ʃəʊrʊm] n Ausstellungsraum der.

**showy** ['ʃəʊɪ] (compar -ier; superl -iest) adj auffällig.

**shrank** [ʃræŋk] pt ▷ shrink.

**shrapnel** ['ʃræpnl] n (U) Granatsplitter pl.

**shred** [ʃred] (pt & pp -ded; cont -ding) n - **1.** [of paper] Schnitzel der; [of fabric] Fetzen der - **2.** fig [of truth] Funken der; [of evidence] Hauch der ◇ vt - **1.** CULIN [cabbage, lettuce] in Streifen schneiden - **2.** [paper in shredder] in den Reißwolf stecken.

**shredder** ['ʃredə'] n - **1.** CULIN [in food processor] Zerkleinerer der - **2.** [for documents] Aktenvernichter der.

**shrew** [ʃruː] n [animal] Spitzmaus die.

**shrewd** [ʃruːd] adj scharfsinnig; [person] klug; [action, judgement, move] klug.

**shrewdness** ['ʃruːdnɪs] n Scharfsinnigkeit die.

**shriek** [ʃriːk] n Schrei der ◇ vt schreien ◇ vi: to ~ (with/in) auf lschreien (vor (+ D)).

**shrill** [ʃrɪl] adj [high-pitched] schrill.

**shrimp** [ʃrɪmp] n Garnele die.

**shrine** [ʃraɪn] n Schrein der.

**shrink** [ʃrɪŋk] (pt shrank; pp shrunk) vt eingehen lassen ◇ vi - **1.** [become smaller] schrumpfen; [person] kleiner werden; [clothing] einlgehen - **2.** fig [contract, diminish] zusammenlschrumpfen; [of trade] zurücklgehen - **3.** [recoil]: to ~ away from sb/sthg vor jm/etw zurücklweichen - **4.** [be reluctant]: to ~ from a task sich vor einer Aufgabe scheuen ◇ n inf [psychoanalyst] Nervenklempner der.

**shrinkage** ['ʃrɪŋkɪdʒ] n (U) - **1.** [of clothing] Eingehen das - **2.** fig [contraction] Zusammenschrumpfen das; [of trade] Zurückgehen das.

**shrink-wrap** vt einlschweißen.

**shrivel** ['ʃrɪvl] (Br pt & pp -led; cont -ling, Am pt & pp -ed; cont -ing) vt: to ~ (up) [plant] welken lassen; [skin] runzelig werden lassen ◇ vi: to ~ (up) [plant] welken; [skin] runzelig werden.

**shroud** [ʃraʊd] n [cloth] Leichentuch das ◇ vt: to be ~ed in sthg in etw (A) eingehüllt sein.

**Shrove Tuesday** ['ʃraʊv-] n Faschingsdienstag der, Fastnachtsdienstag der.

**shrub** [ʃrʌb] n Strauch der, Busch der.

**shrubbery** ['ʃrʌbərɪ] (pl -ies) n Gebüsch das.

**shrug** [ʃrʌg] (pt & pp -ged; cont -ging) n Achselzucken das; to give a ~ mit den Achseln zucken ◇ vt: to ~ one's shoulders mit den Achseln zucken ◇ vi mit den Achseln zucken.

**shrug off** vt sep beiseite schieben.

**shrunk** [ʃrʌŋk] pp ▷ shrink.

**shrunken** ['ʃrʌŋkn] adj [fruit] verschrumpelt; [old person] zusammengeschrumpft.

**shucks** [ʃʌks] excl Am inf - **1.** [it was nothing] schon gut! - **2.** [damn] Mist!

**shudder** ['ʃʌdə'] n [of fear, horror] Schauer der, Schauder der ◇ vi - **1.** [person]: to ~ (with sthg) (vor etw (D)) schauern OR schaudern; I ~ to think what might have happened ich denke mit Schaudern daran, was hätte passieren können - **2.** [machine, vehicle] beben.

**shuffle** ['ʃʌfl] n - **1.** [of feet] Schlurfen das - **2.** [of cards]: to give the cards a ~ die Karten mischen ◇ vt - **1.**: to ~ one's feet mit den

Füßen scharren; [when walking] schlurfen
- **2.** [cards] mischen - **3.** [papers] durchl-
sortieren ◇ *vi* - **1.** [walk]: **to ~ in/out/along**
herein-/heraus-/entlangschlurfen
- **2.** [fidget] herumlrutschen.

**shun** [ʃʌn] (*pt* & *pp* -**ned**; *cont* -**ning**) *vt* meiden
(+ D).

**shunt** [ʃʌnt] *vt* - **1.** RAIL rangieren - **2.** *fig* [move]
herumlschieben.

**shush** [ʃʊʃ] *excl* pst!

**shut** [ʃʌt] (*pt* & *pp* **shut**; *cont* -**ting**) *adj* geschlossen ◇ *vt* schließen, zulmachen;
**~ your mouth** OR **face!** *vinf* halt den Mund!
◇ *vi* schließen; [eyes] zulfallen.
➥ **shut away** *vt sep* - **1.** [criminal] einlsperren;
**to ~ o.s. away** sich einlschließen - **2.** [valuables]
einlschließen.
➥ **shut down** *vt sep* & *vi* [factory, business]
schließen.
➥ **shut in** *vt sep* einlschließen; **to ~ o.s. in** sich
einlschließen.
➥ **shut out** *vt sep* - **1.** [person, cat] auslsperren;
[light, noise] am Eindringen hindern
- **2.** [thought, feeling] verbannen.
➥ **shut up** *vt sep* - **1.** [lock up] ablschließen
- **2.** [silence] zum Schweigen bringen ◇ *vi*
- **1.** *inf* [be quiet] den Mund halten; **~ up!** halt
den Mund! - **2.** [close] schließen.

**shutter** [ʃʌtəʳ] *n* - **1.** [on window] Fensterladen
*der* - **2.** [in camera] Blende *die*.

**shuttle** [ʃʌtl] *adj*: **~ service** Shuttle-Service
*der*, Pendelverkehr *der* ◇ *n* [service] Shuttle-
Service *der*, Pendelverkehr *der;* [plane] Pen-
delflugzeug *das;* [train] Pendelzug *der;* [bus]
Pendelbus *der* ◇ *vi* [vehicle] hin- und herlfahren; [commuter] pendeln ◇ *vt* hin- und
herlbringen.

**shuttlecock** [ʃʌtlkɒk] *n* Federball *der*.

**shy** [ʃaɪ] (*pt* & *pp* **shied**) *adj* [timid] schüchtern;
**he was too ~ to ask her** er getraute sich nicht,
sie zu fragen ◇ *vi* scheuen.
➥ **shy away from** *vt fus*: **to ~ away from doing**
**sthg** sich scheuen, etw zu tun.

**shyly** [ʃaɪlɪ] *adv* schüchtern.

**shyness** [ʃaɪnɪs] *n* Schüchternheit *die*.

**Siamese** [ˌsaɪəˈmiːz] (*pl inv*) *adj* siamesisch
◇ *n* - **1.** [person] Siamese *der*, -sin *die* - **2.**:
**~ (cat)** Siamkatze *die*.

**Siamese twins** *npl* siamesische Zwillinge
*pl*.

**SIB** (*abbr of* **Securities and Investment Board**)
*n Regulierungsstelle für den Finanzplatz Lon-
don.*

**Siberia** [saɪˈbɪərɪə] *n* Siberien *nt*.

**siblings** [ˈsɪblɪŋs] *npl* Geschwister *pl*.

**Sicily** [ˈsɪsɪlɪ] *n* Sizilien *nt*.

**sick** [sɪk] *adj* - **1.** [unwell] krank; **she's off ~ this
week** sie fehlt diese Woche wegen Krank-

heit - **2.** [nauseous]: **she felt ~** ihr war schlecht
OR übel - **3.** [vomiting]: **to be ~** Br sich übergeben (müssen) - **4.** [fed up]: **to be ~ of sthg** etw
satt haben; **to be ~ of doing sthg** es satt haben, etw zu tun - **5.** [angry, disgusted]: **to make sb
~** *fig* jn krank machen - **6.** [offensive - joke] makaber; [ - humour] schwarz.

**sickbay** [ˈsɪkbeɪ] *n* Krankenstation *die*.

**sickbed** [ˈsɪkbed] *n* Krankenbett *das*.

**sicken** [ˈsɪkn] *vt* [disgust] krank machen ◇ *vi*
Br: **to be ~ing for sthg** etw auslbrüten.

**sickening** [ˈsɪknɪŋ] *adj* - **1.** [disgusting] widerlich - **2.** *hum* [infuriating] unerträglich.

**sickle** [ˈsɪkl] *n* Sichel *die*.

**sick leave** *n*: **to be on ~** krankgeschrieben
sein.

**sickly** [ˈsɪklɪ] (*compar* -**ier**; *superl* -**iest**) *adj*
- **1.** [unhealthy] kränklich - **2.** [nauseating] widerlich.

**sickness** [ˈsɪknɪs] *n* - **1.** [illness] Krankheit *die*
- **2.** Br [nausea] Übelkeit *die;* [vomiting] Erbrechen *das*.

**sickness benefit** *n* Krankengeld *das*.

**sick pay** *n* (U) Lohnfortzahlung *die* im
Krankheitsfall.

**sickroom** [ˈsɪkrʊm] *n* Krankenzimmer *das*.

**side** [saɪd] *n* - **1.** [gen] Seite *die;* **on every ~, on all
~s** auf allen Seiten; **from ~ to ~** von einer
Seite auf die andere, hin und her; **to put
sthg to** OR **on one ~** etw beiseite legen; [money]
etw auf die hohe Kante legen; **at** OR **by sb's ~**
an js Seite; **~ by ~** Seite an Seite; **on one's
mother's** mütterlicherseits; **on one's father's
~** väterlicherseits - **2.** [inner surface - of cave,
crate, bathtub] Wand *die* - **3.** [of river, lake] Ufer
*das;* [of road] Rand *der* - **4.** [team] Mannschaft
*die* - **5.** [of argument] Standpunkt *der;* **to take
sb's ~** für jn Partei ergreifen; **to be on sb's ~**
auf js Seite stehen - **6.** [aspect - of character, per-
sonality] Seite *die;* [ - of situation] Aspekt *der;* **to be
on the safe ~** um sicherzugehen - **7.** *phr:* **on
the large/small ~** zu groß/klein; **to do sthg on
the ~** etw nebenbei tun; **to keep** OR **stay on the
right ~ of sb** sich mit jm gut stellen ◇ *adj* [sit-
uated on side] Seiten-.
➥ **side with** *vt fus* Partei ergreifen für.

**sideboard** [ˈsaɪdbɔːd] *n* Anrichte *die*, Büfett
*das*.

**sideboards** Br [ˈsaɪdbɔːdz], **sideburns** Am
[ˈsaɪdbɜːnz] *npl* Koteletten *pl*.

**sidecar** [ˈsaɪdkɑːʳ] *n* Beiwagen *der*.

**side dish** *n* Beilage *die*.

**side effect** *n* - **1.** MED [secondary effect] Neben-
wirkung *die* - **2.** [unplanned result] Nebeneffekt
*der*.

**sidekick** [ˈsaɪdkɪk] *n inf* Handlanger *der*.

**sidelight** [ˈsaɪdlaɪt] *n* Seitenlicht *das*.

S

**sideline** ['saɪdlaɪn] n - **1.** [extra business] Neben-beschäftigung die - **2.** SPORT [painted line] Seiten-linie die - **3.** [periphery]: **on the ~s** im Hinter-grund.

**sidelong** ['saɪdlɒŋ] adj Seiten- ⋄ adv: **to look ~ at sb/sthg** jn/etw aus dem Augenwinkel anlschauen.

**side-on** adj & adv seitlich.

**side plate** n kleiner Teller.

**side road** n Nebenstraße die, Seitenstraße die.

**sidesaddle** ['saɪd,sædl] adv: **to ride ~** im Damensitz reiten.

**sideshow** ['saɪdʃəʊl] n Nebenattraktion die.

**sidestep** ['saɪdstep] (pt & pp **-ped**; cont **-ping**) vt lit & fig auslweichen (+ D).

**side street** n Nebenstraße die, Seiten-straße die.

**sidetrack** ['saɪdtræk] vt: **to be ~ed** abgelenkt werden.

**sidewalk** ['saɪdwɔːk] n Am Bürgersteig der.

**sideways** ['saɪdweɪz] adj [movement] zur Seite; [look] Seiten- ⋄ adv seitwärts.

**siding** ['saɪdɪŋ] n Abstellgleis das.

**sidle** ['saɪdl] ➤ **sidle up** vi: **to ~ up to sb** sich an jn heranlschleichen.

**SIDS** (abbr of **sudden infant death syndrome**) n plötzlicher Kindstod.

**siege** [siːdʒ] n - **1.** [by army] Belagerung die - **2.** [by police] Umstellen das.

**Sierra Leone** [sɪ'erəli'əʊn] n Sierra Leone nt.

**siesta** [sɪ'estə] n Siesta die, Mittagsschläf-chen das.

**sieve** [sɪv] n Sieb das; **to have a head** OR **memory like a ~** ein Gedächtnis wie ein Sieb haben ⋄ vt sieben.

**sift** [sɪft] vt - **1.** [sieve] sieben - **2.** fig [examine care-fully] sichten, durchlsehen ⋄ vi: **to ~ through sthg** etw durchlsehen OR durchlgehen.

**sigh** [saɪ] n Seufzer der; **to heave a ~ of relief** er-leichtert auflatmen ⋄ vi seufzen.

**sight** [saɪt] n - **1.** [vision] Sehvermögen das; **he has good/poor ~** er sieht gut/schlecht - **2.** [act of seeing]: **it was their first ~ of their grandchild** sie haben ihr Enkelkind zum ersten Mal gesehen; **in ~** in Sicht; **out of ~** außer Sicht; **to catch ~ of sb/sthg** jn/etw erspähen; **to know sb by ~** jn vom Sehen kennen; **to lose ~ of sb/sthg** jn/etw aus den Augen verlie-ren; **to shoot on ~** ohne Vorwarnung schießen; **at first ~** auf den ersten Blick - **3.** [spectacle] Anblick der - **4.** [on gun] Visier das; **to set one's ~s on doing sthg** sich (D) vorl-nehmen, etw zu tun - **5.** [a lot]: **a ~ better/worse** wesentlich besser/schlechter ⋄ vt [see] erspähen; [land] sichten.

➤ **sights** npl [on tour] Sehenswürdigkeiten pl.

**sighting** ['saɪtɪŋ] n: **there has been a ~ of the es-caped prisoner** der entflohene Gefangene ist gesichtet worden.

**sightseeing** ['saɪt,siːɪŋ] n Sightseeing das; **to do some** OR **go ~** Sehenswürdigkeiten be-sichtigen.

**sightseer** ['saɪt,siːəʳ] n Tourist der, -in die.

**sign** [saɪn] n - **1.** [written symbol, gesture] Zeichen das - **2.** [notice] Schild das - **3.** [indication] Anzei-chen das; **there's no ~ of him yet** von ihm ist noch nichts zu sehen ⋄ vt - **1.** [letter] unter-schreiben; [document] unterzeichnen; [paint-ing] signieren; **to ~ one's name** unterschrei-ben - **2.** SPORT [player] verpflichten.

➤ **sign away** vt sep übertragen.

➤ **sign for** vt fus - **1.** [sign receipt for] quittieren - **2.** [subj: sportsman] (einen Vertrag) unter-schreiben bei.

➤ **sign in** vi [at hotel, club] sich einltragen.

➤ **sign on** vi - **1.** [enrol - for course] sich einl-schreiben; MIL sich verpflichten - **2.** [register as unemployed] sich beim Arbeitsamt melden.

➤ **sign out** vi [at hotel] sich ablmelden; [at club] sich ausltragen.

➤ **sign up** vt sep [employee] einlstellen; [recruit] verpflichten ⋄ vi [enrol]: [for course] sich einl-schreiben; MIL sich verpflichten.

**signal** ['sɪgnl] (Br pt & pp **-led**; cont **-ling**, Am pt & pp **-ed**; cont **-ing**) n Signal das ⋄ vt: **to ~ sb to do sthg** jm ein Zeichen geben, etw zu tun ⋄ adj fml [failure] schwerwiegend; [success] außerordentlich ⋄ vi - **1.** AUT blinken - **2.** [in-dicate]: **to ~ sb to do sthg** jm ein Zeichen ge-ben, etw zu tun.

**signal box** Br, **signal tower** Am n Stell-werk das.

**signalman** ['sɪgnlmən] (pl **-men** [-mən]) n RAIL Stellwerkswärter der.

**signal tower** n Am = **signal box**.

**signatory** ['sɪgnətrɪ] (pl **-ies**) n Unterzeich-nende der, die; [country] Unterzeichnerstaat der.

**signature** ['sɪgnətʃəʳ] n [name] Unterschrift die.

**signature tune** n Erkennungsmelodie die.

**signet ring** ['sɪgnɪt-] n Siegelring der.

**significance** [sɪg'nɪfɪkəns] n (U) Bedeutung die.

**significant** [sɪg'nɪfɪkənt] adj - **1.** [large, impor-tant] bedeutend - **2.** [full of hidden meaning] be-deutsam.

**significantly** [sɪg'nɪfɪkəntlɪ] adv - **1.** [improve, increase, change] bedeutend - **2.** [smile, nod, wink] bedeutungsvoll.

**signify** ['sɪgnɪfaɪ] (pt & pp **-ied**) vt bedeuten.

**signing** ['saɪnɪŋ] n Br SPORT [player] Einkauf der.

**sign language** n Zeichensprache die.

**signpost** ['saɪnpəʊst] n Wegweiser der.

**Sikh** [siːk] *adj* Sikh- <> *n* Sikh *der, die.*

**silage** ['saɪlɪdʒ] *n* Silage *die,* Gärfutter *das.*

**silence** ['saɪləns] *n* - **1.** [of person, on topic] Schweigen *das;* **in ~** schweigend - **2.** [of place] Stille *die,* Ruhe *die* <> *vt* zum Schweigen bringen.

**silencer** ['saɪlənsəʳ] *n* Schalldämpfer *der.*

**silent** ['saɪlənt] *adj* - **1.** [speechless] still - **2.** [taciturn] schweigsam - **3.** [not revealing anything]: **to be ~ about sthg** über etw *(A)* schweigen - **4.** [noiseless] ruhig, leise - **5.** CINEMA Stumm- - **6.** LING stumm.

**silently** ['saɪləntlɪ] *adv* - **1.** [without speaking] schweigend - **2.** [noiselessly] ruhig, leise.

**silent partner** *n Am* stiller Teilhaber, stille Teilhaberin.

**silhouette** [ˌsɪluːˈet] *n* Silhouette *die* <> *vt:* **to be ~d against sthg** sich gegen etw abⁱzeichnen.

**silicon** ['sɪlɪkən] *n* Silizium *das.*

**silicon chip** *n* Siliziumchip *der.*

**silicone** ['sɪlɪkəʊn] *n* Silikon *das.*

**Silicon Valley** *n* Silicon Valley *das.*

**silk** [sɪlk] *n* Seide *die* <> *comp* Seiden-.

**silk screen printing** *n (U)* Siebdruck *der.*

**silkworm** ['sɪlkwɜːm] *n* Seidenraupe *die.*

**silky** ['sɪlkɪ] (*compar* -**ier;** *superl* -**iest**) *adj* seidig; [voice] samtig.

**sill** [sɪl] *n* [of window] (Fenster)sims *der.*

**silliness** ['sɪlɪnɪs] *n* Dummheit *die.*

**silly** ['sɪlɪ] (*compar* -**ier;** *superl* -**iest**) *adj* - **1.** [foolish] dumm - **2.** [comical] komisch - **3.** [childish, ridiculous]: **don't be so ~!** sei nicht so albern!

**silo** ['saɪləʊ] (*pl* -**s**) *n* Silo *das.*

**silt** [sɪlt] *n* Schlick *der,* Schlamm *der.*
> **silt up** *vi* verschlammen.

**silver** ['sɪlvəʳ] *adj* [greyish-white] silbern <> *n (U)* - **1.** [metal, silverware] Silber *das* - **2.** [coins] Silbermünzen *pl* <> *comp* [made of silver] Silber-.

**silver foil, silver paper** *n (U)* Alufolie *die.*

**silver-plated** [-ˈpleɪtɪd] *adj* versilbert.

**silver screen** *n inf:* **the ~** die Leinwand.

**silversmith** ['sɪlvəsmɪθ] *n* Silberschmied *der,* -in *die.*

**silverware** ['sɪlvəweəʳ] *n* - **1.** [objects made of silver] Silber *das* - **2.** *Am* [cutlery] Besteck *das.*

**silver wedding** *n* silberne Hochzeit, Silberhochzeit *die.*

**silvery** ['sɪlvərɪ] *adj* [colour, sheen] silbrig.

**similar** ['sɪmɪləʳ] *adj* ähnlich; **to be ~ to sthg** so ähnlich wie etw sein.

**similarity** [ˌsɪmɪˈlærətɪ] (*pl* -**ies**) *n:* **~ (between/ to)** [person, place] Ähnlichkeit *die* (zwischen (+ D)/mit); **there's no ~ between my experience**

**and yours** unsere Erfahrungen sind völlig verschieden.

**similarly** ['sɪmɪləlɪ] *adv* ebenso.

**simile** ['sɪmɪlɪ] *n* Gleichnis *das,* Vergleich *der.*

**simmer** ['sɪməʳ] *vt* & *vi* auf kleiner Flamme kochen.
> **simmer down** *vi inf* sich beruhigen.

**simper** ['sɪmpəʳ] *n* albernes Lächeln <> *vi* albern lächeln.

**simpering** ['sɪmpərɪŋ] *adj* [person] albern lächelnd; [smile] albern.

**simple** ['sɪmpl] *adj* - **1.** [easy] einfach - **2.** [plain - clothing, furniture, style] schlicht; [ - fact, truth] rein; [ - way of life] einfach - **3.** [mentally retarded] einfältig.

**simple-minded** [-ˈmaɪndɪd] *adj* [person] einfältig; [view] vereinfacht.

**simpleton** ['sɪmpltən] *n dated* Einfaltspinsel *der.*

**simplicity** [sɪmˈplɪsətɪ] *n* Einfachheit *die;* [plainness - of clothing, furniture, style] Schlichtheit *die.*

**simplification** [ˌsɪmplɪfɪˈkeɪʃn] *n* Vereinfachung *die.*

**simplify** ['sɪmplɪfaɪ] (*pt* & *pp* -**ied**) *vt* vereinfachen.

**simplistic** [sɪmˈplɪstɪk] *adj* stark vereinfacht.

**simply** ['sɪmplɪ] *adv* - **1.** [merely] einfach - **2.** [for emphasis]: **you ~ must go** du musst unbedingt gehen; **the weather is ~ dreadful** das Wetter ist einfach scheußlich - **3.** [in an uncomplicated way - live] einfach; [ - dress] schlicht.

**simulate** ['sɪmjʊleɪt] *vt* - **1.** [feign - gen] vorⁱtäuschen; [ - illness] simulieren - **2.** [produce effect, appearance of] simulieren.

**simulation** [ˌsɪmjʊˈleɪʃn] *n* - **1.** [feigning] Vortäuschung *die* - **2.** [simulated appearance, effect & COMPUT] Simulation *die.*

**simulator** ['sɪmjʊleɪtəʳ] *n* Simulator *der.*

**simultaneous** [*Br* ˌsɪmʊlˈteɪnjəs, *Am* ˌsaɪməlˈteɪnjəs] *adj* gleichzeitig; [broadcast] direkt; [interpreting] Simultan-.

**simultaneously** [*Br* ˌsɪmʊlˈteɪnjəslɪ, *Am* ˌsaɪməlˈteɪnjəslɪ] *adv* gleichzeitig.

**sin** [sɪn] (*pt* & *pp* -**ned;** *cont* -**ning**) *n* Sünde *die;* **to live in ~** in wilder Ehe leben <> *vi:* **to ~ (against)** sündigen (gegen).

**sin bin** *n inf* SPORT Strafbank *die.*

**since** [sɪns] *adv* seitdem; **I haven't seen them ~** ich habe sie seitdem nicht mehr gesehen; **she has ~ moved to London** inzwischen ist sie nach London umgezogen; **~ then** seitdem; **long ~** (schon) längst <> *prep* seit; **I've been here ~ six o'clock** ich bin hier seit sechs Uhr; **~ when do you give the orders?** seit wann bestimmst du hier? <> *conj* - **1.** [in time] seit; **it's ages ~ I saw her** ich habe sie schon seit langem nicht mehr gesehen; **it's a week ~ he**

**S**

came er ist vor einer Woche gekommen
- **2.** [because] da.

**sincere** [sɪn'sɪəʳ] *adj* aufrichtig.

**sincerely** [sɪn'sɪəlɪ] *adv* aufrichtig; **Yours ~** [at end of letter] mit freundlichen Grüßen.

**sincerity** [sɪn'serətɪ] *n* Aufrichtigkeit *die*.

**sinecure** ['saɪnɪˌkjʊəʳ] *n* [easy job] Ruheposten *der*.

**sinew** ['sɪnjuː] *n* Sehne *die*.

**sinewy** ['sɪnjuːɪ] *adj* sehnig.

**sinful** ['sɪnfʊl] *adj* sündig.

**sing** [sɪŋ] (*pt* **sang**; *pp* **sung**) *vt* singen; **to ~ sb a song, to ~ a song to sb** jm ein Lied vorlsingen ◇ *vi* singen.

**Singapore** [ˌsɪŋə'pɔːʳ] *n* Singapur *nt*.

**singe** [sɪndʒ] (*cont* **-ing**) *vt* versengen.

**singer** ['sɪŋəʳ] *n* Sänger *der*, -in *die*.

**Singhalese** [ˌsɪŋhə'liːz] *adj* singhalesisch ◇ *n* - **1.** [person] Singhalese *der*, -sin *die* - **2.** [language] Singhalesisch(e) *das*.

**singing** ['sɪŋɪŋ] *adj* [voice] Sing-; [lesson] Gesangs- ◇ *n* (*U*) Gesang *der*.

**single** ['sɪŋgl] *adj* - **1.** [sole] einzig; **every ~** jede/jeder/jedes einzelne - **2.** [unmarried] ledig - **3.** *Br* [one-way] einfach ◇ *n* - **1.** *Br* [one-way ticket] einfache Fahrkarte - **2.** MUS Single *die*.
➤ **singles** *npl* TENNIS Einzel *das*.
➤ **single out** *vt sep*: **to ~ sb out (for sthg)** jn (für etw) auslsuchen OR auslwählen.

**single bed** *n* Einzelbett *das*.

**single-breasted** [-'brestɪd] *adj* einreihig.

**single cream** *n* (*U*) *Br* Sahne mit niedrigem Fettgehalt.

**single-decker (bus)** [-'dekəʳ-] *n* *Br* Eindeckerbus *der*.

**Single European Market** *n*: **the ~** der europäische Binnenmarkt.

**single file** *n*: **in ~** im Gänsermarsch.

**single-handed** [-'hændɪd] *adv* eigenhändig.

**single-minded** [-'maɪndɪd] *adj* zielstrebig; **to be ~ about sthg** in etw (*D*) zielstrebig sein.

**single parent** *n* [mother] alleinerziehende Mutter; [father] alleinerziehender Vater.

**single-parent family** *n* Familie *die* mit nur einem Elternteil.

**single room** *n* Einzelzimmer *das*.

**singles bar** *n* Singlebar *die*.

**singlet** ['sɪŋglɪt] *n* - **1.** *Br* [underwear] Unterhemd *das* - **2.** SPORT ärmelloses Trikot.

**single ticket** *n* *Br* einfache Fahrkarte.

**singsong** ['sɪŋsɒŋ] *adj*: **he has a ~ voice** er hat einen Singsang in der Stimme ◇ *n* *Br* gemeinsames Singen.

**singular** ['sɪŋgjʊləʳ] *adj* - **1.** GRAMM im Singular, in der Einzahl - **2.** [unusual] eigentümlich;

[unique] einzigartig ◇ *n* Singular *der*, Einzahl *die*.

**singularly** ['sɪŋgjʊləlɪ] *adv* [remarkably] außerordentlich.

**Sinhalese** ['sɪnəliːz] *adj* & *n* = **Singhalese.**

**sinister** ['sɪnɪstəʳ] *adj* finster, unheimlich.

**sink** [sɪŋk] (*pt* **sank**; *pp* **sunk**) *n* - **1.** [in kitchen] Spülbecken *das* - **2.** [in bathroom] Waschbecken *das* ◇ *vt* - **1.** [in water] versenken - **2.** [teeth, claws]: **to ~ sthg into sthg** etw in etw (*A*) graben ◇ *vi* - **1.** [gen] sinken; [person - in water] unterlgehen; **to ~ to one's knees** auf die Knie sinken - **2.** *fig* [heart, spirits]: **my heart sank when I heard the news** meine Stimmung sank, als ich die Nachricht hörte - **3.** [building, ground] sich senken - **4.** *fig* [slip]: **to ~ into sthg** [despair, depression] in etw (*A*) versinken; [coma, sleep] in etw (*A*) fallen.
➤ **sink in** *vi*: **it hasn't sunk in yet** ich habe/er hat/*etc* es noch nicht realisiert.

**sinking** ['sɪŋkɪŋ] *n* [of ship] Versenken *das*.

**sink unit** *n* Spüle *die*.

**sinner** ['sɪnəʳ] *n* Sünder *der*, -in *die*.

**Sinn Fein** [ʃɪn'feɪn] *n* Sinn Fein *die*, *der politische Flügel der IRA.*

**sinuous** ['sɪnjʊəs] *adj* gewunden; [movement, dancing] schlängelnd.

**sinus** ['saɪnəs] (*pl* **-es**) *n* Stirnhöhle *die*.

**sinusitis** [ˌsaɪnə'saɪtəs] *n* (*U*) Nebenhöhlenentzündung *die*.

**sip** [sɪp] (*pt* & *pp* **-ped**; *cont* **-ping**) *n* kleiner Schluck ◇ *vt* nippen an (+ *D*), in kleinen Schlucken trinken.

**siphon** ['saɪfn] *n*: **(soda) ~** Siphon *der* ◇ *vt* - **1.**: **to ~ (off)** ablsaugen - **2.** *fig* [transfer] verlagern.

**sir** [sɜːʳ] *n* - **1.** [form of address] mein Herr - **2.** [in titles] Sir *der*.

**siren** ['saɪərən] *n* Sirene *die*.

**sirloin (steak)** ['sɜːlɔɪn-] *n* Lendensteak *das*.

**sissy** ['sɪsɪ] (*pl* **-ies**) *n inf* Waschlappen *der*.

**sister** ['sɪstəʳ] *adj* Schwester- ◇ *n* - **1.** [gen] Schwester *die* - **2.** *Br* [senior nurse] Oberschwester *die*.

**sister-in-law** (*pl* **sisters-in-law** OR **sister-in-laws**) *n* Schwägerin *die*.

**sisterly** ['sɪstəlɪ] *adj* schwesterlich.

**sit** [sɪt] (*pt* & *pp* **sat**; *cont* **-ting**) *vt* - **1.** [place] setzen - **2.** *Br* [examination] abllegen ◇ *vi* - **1.** [be in seated position] sitzen - **2.** [sit down] sich hinlsetzen - **3.** [be member]: **to ~ on sthg** in etw (*D*) sitzen - **4.** [be in session] tagen - **5.** [be situated] sich befinden; [building] stehen; **the letter sat unopened on the desk** der Brief lag ungeöffnet auf dem Schreibtisch - **6.** *phr*: **to ~ tight** geduldig ablwarten.
➤ **sit about, sit around** *vi* herumlsitzen.

➡ **sit back** *vi lit* & *fig* sich zurückllehnen.

➡ **sit down** *vt sep* setzen ⬦ *vi* sich setzen.

➡ **sit in on** *vt fus* beilwohnen (+ D).

➡ **sit out** *vt sep* - **1.** [tolerate] bis zum Ende durchlhalten - **2.** [a dance] ausllassen.

➡ **sit through** *vt fus* bis zum Ende durchlhalten.

➡ **sit up** *vi* - **1.** [be sitting upright] aufrecht sitzen; [move into upright position] sich auf lsetzen - **2.** [stay up] auf lbleiben.

**sitcom** ['sɪtkɒm] *n inf* Situationskomödie *die*.

**sit-down** *adj* [protest, strike] Sitz- ⬦ *n Br:* **to have a ~** sich auslruhen.

**site** [saɪt] *n* - **1.**: **archaeological ~** Ausgrabungsstätte *die;* **building ~** Baustelle *die;* **camping ~** Campingplatz *der;* **missile ~** Raketenstellung *die* - **2.** [location, place] Ort *der,* Stelle *die* ⬦ *vt:* **to be ~d** gelegen sein.

**sit-in** *n* Sit-in *das*.

**sitter** ['sɪtəʳ] *n* - **1.** ART Modell *das* - **2.** [baby-sitter] Babysitter *der,* -in *die*.

**sitting** ['sɪtɪŋ] *n* - **1.**: **dinner is served in two ~s** das Abendessen wird in zwei Schichten serviert - **2.** [session] Sitzung *die*.

**sitting duck** *n inf* leichte Beute.

**sitting room** *n* Wohnzimmer *das*.

**sitting tenant** *n Br* Mieter *der,* -in *die (mit bleibendem Mietrecht, wenn der Eigentümer wechselt)*.

**situate** ['sɪtjʊeɪt] *vt* - **1.** [building] hinlstellen - **2.** [put in context] einlordnen.

**situated** ['sɪtjʊeɪtɪd] *adj* [located]: **to be ~** sich befinden.

**situation** [ˌsɪtjʊ'eɪʃn] *n* - **1.** [circumstances] Lage *die,* Situation *die* - **2.** [location] Lage *die* - **3.** [job] Stelle *die;* **'Situations Vacant'** *Br* 'Stellenangebote'.

**situation comedy** *n* Situationskomödie *die*.

**sit-up** *n* Rumpfbeuge *die*.

**six** [sɪks] *num adj* - **1.** [numbering six] sechs - **2.** [referring to age]: **she's ~ (years old)** sie ist sechs (Jahre alt) ⬦ *num pron* sechs; **I want ~** ich möchte sechs (Stück); **there were ~ of us** wir waren zu sechst; **groups of ~** [people] Sechsergruppen; [objects] Gruppen von jeweils sechs ⬦ *num n* - **1.** [the number six] Sechs *die;* **two hundred and ~** zweihundertsechs - **2.** [six o'clock]: **at ~** um sechs (Uhr) - **3.** [six degrees]: **it's ~ below (zero)** es sind minus sechs Grad - **4.** [in addresses]: **~ Peyton Place** Peyton Place sechs - **5.** [group of six]: **the batteries come in ~es** die Batterien werden im Sechserpack verkauft; **we need one more person to make a ~** wir brauchen noch eine Person, um eine Sechsergruppe zu bilden - **6.** [in scores] sechs; **~-zero** sechs zu null - **7.** [in cards] Sechs *die;* **the ~ of hearts** die Herzsechs.

**six-shooter** [-'ʃuːtəʳ] *n Am* sechsschüssiger Revolver.

**sixteen** [ˌsɪks'tiːn] *num* sechzehn; *see also* **six**.

**sixteenth** [ˌsɪks'tiːnθ] *num* sechzehnte, -r, -s; *see also* **sixth**.

**sixth** [sɪksθ] *num adj* sechste, -r, -s ⬦ *num adv* [on list] an sechster Stelle; **he came ~** er wurde Sechster ⬦ *num pron* [in series] Sechste, -r, -s ⬦ *n* - **1.** [fraction] Sechstel *das* - **2.** [in dates] Sechste *der;* **the ~ of March** der sechste März.

**sixth form** *n Br* SCH ≈ Oberstufe *die*.

**sixth form college** *n Br* zu den A-Levels *führende Schule für Schüler ab 16 Jahren*.

**sixth sense** *n* sechster Sinn.

**sixtieth** ['sɪkstɪəθ] *num* sechzigste, -r, -s; *see also* **sixth**.

**sixty** ['sɪkstɪ] (*pl* -**ies**) *num* sechzig; *see also* **six**.

➡ **sixties** *npl* - **1.** [decade]: **the sixties** die Sechzigerjahre - **2.** [in ages]: **to be in one's sixties** in den Sechzigern sein - **3.** [in temperatures]: **in the sixties** über sechzig Grad Fahrenheit.

**size** [saɪz] *n* Größe *die;* **to cut sb down to ~** jn zurechtlstutzen.

➡ **size up** *vt sep* sich (D) eine Meinung bilden über (+ A).

**sizeable** ['saɪzəbl] *adj* ziemlich groß.

**-sized** [-saɪzd] *suffix* -groß; **medium~** mittelgroß.

**sizzle** ['sɪzl] *vi* brutzeln.

**SK** *abk für Saskatchewan, in Postanschrift verwendet*.

**skate** [skeɪt] (*pl sense 3 only inv OR* -**s**) *n* - **1.** [ice skate] Schlittschuh *der* - **2.** [roller skate] Rollschuh *der* - **3.** [fish] Rochen *der* ⬦ *vi* - **1.** [on ice skates] Schlittschuh laufen - **2.** [on roller skates] Rollschuh laufen.

➡ **skate over, skate round** *vt fus* [avoid] hinweglgehen über (+ A).

**skateboard** ['skeɪtbɔːd] *n* Skateboard *das*.

**skateboarder** ['skeɪtbɔːdəʳ] *n* Skateboarder *der,* -in *die*.

**skater** ['skeɪtəʳ] *n* - **1.** [on ice] Schlittschuhläufer *der,* -in *die* - **2.** [on roller skates] Rollschuhläufer *der,* -in *die*.

**skating** ['skeɪtɪŋ] *n* - **1.** [on ice] Schlittschuhlaufen *das* - **2.** [on roller skates] Rollschuhlaufen *das*.

**skating rink** *n* - **1.** [for ice skating] Eis(lauf)bahn *die* - **2.** [for roller skating] Rollschuhbahn *die*.

**skein** [skeɪn] *n* [length of thread] Strang *der*.

**skeletal** ['skelɪtl] *adj* [emaciated] ausgemergelt.

**skeleton** ['skelɪtn] *n* Skelett *das;* **to have a ~ in the cupboard** *Br OR* **closet** *Am fig* eine Leiche im Keller haben.

S

**skeleton key** *n* Dietrich *der.*

**skeleton staff** *n* Minimalbelegschaft *die.*

**skeptic** *etc n Am* = sceptic *etc.*

**sketch** [sketʃ] *n* - **1.** [drawing] Skizze *die* - **2.** [brief description] kurze Darstellung - **3.** [on TV, radio, stage] Sketch *der* <> *vt* - **1.** [draw] skizzieren - **2.** [describe] kurz darllegen <> *vi* Skizzen machen.

➡ **sketch in** *vt sep* [facts] kurz darllegen.

➡ **sketch out** *vt sep* [situation] umlreißen.

**sketchbook** [ˈsketʃbʊk] *n* Skizzenbuch *das.*

**sketchpad** [ˈsketʃpæd] *n* Skizzenblock *der.*

**sketchy** [ˈsketʃɪ] *(compar* -ier; *superl* -iest) *adj* oberflächlich.

**skew** [skju:] *n Br*: on the ~ schief <> *vt* verfälschen <> *vi* [vehicle] schräg rutschen.

**skewer** [ˈskjʊəʳ] *n* Spieß *der* <> *vt* auflspießen.

**skew-whiff** [ˌskju:ˈwɪf] *adj Br inf* schief.

**ski** [ski:] *(pt & pp* skied; *cont* skiing) *n* Ski *der* <> *comp* Ski- <> *vi* Ski fahren.

**ski boots** *npl* Skistiefel *pl.*

**skid** [skɪd] *(pt & pp* -ded; *cont* -ding) *n* Schleudern *das;* to go into a ~ ins Schleudern geraten <> *vi* schleudern.

**skid mark** *n* Bremsspur *die.*

**skid row** *n Am inf*: to be on ~ heruntergekommen sein.

**skier** [ˈski:əʳ] *n* Skiläufer *der,* -in *die.*

**skiing** [ˈski:ɪŋ] *n* Skifahren *das* <> *comp* Ski-.

**ski instructor** *n* Skilehrer *der,* -in *die.*

**ski jump** *n* - **1.** [slope] Sprungschanze *die* - **2.** [sporting event] Skispringen *das.*

**skilful, skillful** *Am* [ˈskɪlfʊl] *adj* geschickt.

**skilfully, skillfully** *Am* [ˈskɪlfʊlɪ] *adv* geschickt.

**ski lift** *n* Skilift *der.*

**skill** [skɪl] *n* - **1.** [expertise] Geschicklichkeit *die* - **2.** [craft, technique] Fertigkeit *die.*

**skilled** [skɪld] *adj* - **1.** [skilful] geschickt; ~ in OR at doing sthg geschickt darin sein, etw zu tun - **2.** [trained - worker] ausgebildet; [ - work, labour] fachmännisch.

**skillet** [ˈskɪlɪt] *n Am* Bratpfanne *die.*

**skillful** *etc Am* = skilful *etc.*

**skim** [skɪm] *(pt & pp* -med; *cont* -ming) *vt* - **1.** [remove] ablschöpfen - **2.** [glide over] hinweglgleiten über *(+ A)* - **3.** [glance through] überfliegen <> *vi* - **1.** [bird]: to ~ over sthg hinweglgleiten über *(+ A)* - **2.** [read]: to ~ through sthg etw überfliegen.

**skim(med) milk** [skɪm(d)-] *n* Magermilch *die.*

**skimp** [skɪmp] *vt* sparen an *(+ D)* <> *vi*: to ~ on sthg an etw *(D)* sparen.

**skimpy** [ˈskɪmpɪ] *(compar* -ier; *superl* -iest) *adj* dürftig; [clothes] knapp.

**skin** [skɪn] *(pt & pp* -ned; *cont* -ning) *n* - **1.** [of person, on liquid] Haut *die;* to do sthg by the ~ of one's teeth etw mit knapper Not tun; to jump out of one's ~ *Br* zusammenlzucken; he/it makes my ~ crawl er/es ist abstoßend; to save one's own ~ seine Haut retten - **2.** [of animal] Fell *das* - **3.** [of fruit, vegetable] Schale *die* <> *vt* - **1.** [animal] häuten - **2.** [graze] auflschürfen.

**skin-deep** *adj* oberflächlich.

**skin diver** *n* Sporttaucher *der,* -in *die.*

**skin diving** *n* Sporttauchen *das.*

**skinflint** [ˈskɪnflɪnt] *n* Geizkragen *der.*

**skin graft** *n* Hauttransplantation *die.*

**skinhead** [ˈskɪnhed] *n Br* Skinhead *der.*

**skinny** [ˈskɪnɪ] *(compar* -ier; *superl* -iest) *adj inf* dürr.

**skint** [skɪnt] *adj Br vinf* pleite.

**skin test** *n* Hauttest *der.*

**skin-tight** *adj* hauteng.

**skip** [skɪp] *(pt & pp* -ped; *cont* -ping) *n* - **1.** [little jump] Hüpfer *der* - **2.** *Br* [large container] Sperrmüllcontainer *der* <> *vt* [miss - page] überspringen; [ - meal] ausllassen; to ~ school die Schule schwänzen <> *vi* - **1.** [move in little jumps] hüpfen - **2.** *Br* [jump over rope] seillspringen.

**ski pants** *npl* Skihosen *pl.*

**ski pole** *n* Skistock *der.*

**skipper** [ˈskɪpəʳ] *n* Kapitän *der.*

**skipping** [ˈskɪpɪŋ] *n Br* [game] Seilspringen *das.*

**skipping rope** *n Br* Springseil *das.*

**ski resort** *n* Skiort *der.*

**skirmish** [ˈskɜ:mɪʃ] *n* - **1.** MIL Gefecht *das* - **2.** *fig* [disagreement] Auseinandersetzung *die* <> *vi* - **1.** MIL sich *(D)* ein Gefecht liefern - **2.** *fig* [argue] eine Auseinandersetzung haben.

**skirt** [skɜ:t] *n* [garment] Rock *der* <> *vt lit & fig* umlgehen.

➡ **skirt round** *vt fus lit & fig* umlgehen.

**skirting board** [ˈskɜ:tɪŋ-] *n Br* Fußleiste *die.*

**ski stick** *n* Skistock *der.*

**skit** [skɪt] *n*: a ~ on sthg eine Parodie auf etw *(A).*

**ski tow** *n* Skilift *der.*

**skittish** [ˈskɪtɪʃ] *adj* - **1.** [person - playful] ausgelassen - **2.** [animal] scheu.

**skittle** [ˈskɪtl] *n Br* Kegel *der;* to have a game of ~s kegeln (gehen).

**skive** [skaɪv] *vi Br inf*: to ~ (off) [from school] schwänzen; [from work] blau machen.

**skivvy** [ˈskɪvɪ] *(pl* -ies; *pt & pp* -ied) *Br inf n*

Dienstmädchen *das* <> *vi:* **to ~ (for sb)** (für jn) Dienstmädchen spielen.

**skulduggery** [skʌl'dʌgərɪ] *n (U)* Machenschaften *pl.*

**skulk** [skʌlk] *vi* - **1.** [hide] sich verstecken - **2.** [prowl] herumlschleichen.

**skull** [skʌl] *n* Schädel *der.*

**skullcap** ['skʌlkæp] *n* Scheitelkäppchen *das.*

**skunk** [skʌŋk] *n* Stinktier *das.*

**sky** [skaɪ] *(pl* **skies)** *n* Himmel *der.*

**skycap** ['skaɪkæp] *n Am* Gepäckträger *der,* -in *die (auf Flugplätzen).*

**skydiver** ['skaɪˌdaɪvəʳ] *n* Skydiver *der,* -in *die.*

**skydiving** ['skaɪˌdaɪvɪŋ] *n* Skydiving *das.*

**sky-high** *inf adj* sehr hoch <> *adv:* **to blow sthg ~** [bridge, building] etw in die Luft jagen; *fig* [argument, theory] etw völlig über den Haufen werfen; **to go ~** in die Höhe schießen.

**skylark** ['skaɪlɑːk] *n* Feldlerche *die.*

**skylight** ['skaɪlaɪt] *n* Dachfenster *das.*

**skyline** ['skaɪlaɪn] *n* [horizon] Horizont *der;* [of city, buildings] Skyline *die.*

**skyscraper** ['skaɪˌskreɪpəʳ] *n* Wolkenkratzer *der.*

**slab** [slæb] *n* - **1.** [of concrete, stone] Platte *die;* [of wood] Tafel *die* - **2.** [of meat, chocolate, cake] großes Stück.

**slack** [slæk] *adj* - **1.** [not taut] locker - **2.** [not busy] flau - **3.** [careless] nachlässig <> *n:* **there is too much ~ in the rope** das Seil ist nicht straff genug.
➤ **slacks** *npl dated* Hose *die.*

**slacken** ['slækn] *vt* - **1.** [make slower] verlangsamen - **2.** [make looser] lockern <> *vi* [become slower] langsamer werden.
➤ **slacken off** *vi* - **1.** [rain, storm] nachllassen - **2.** [work] ablnehmen.

**slag** [slæg] *n (U)* [waste material] Schlacke *die.*

**slagheap** ['slæghiːp] *n* Halde *die.*

**slain** [sleɪn] *pp* ▷ **slay.**

**slalom** ['slɑːləm] *n* Slalom *der.*

**slam** [slæm] *(pt &  pp* **-med;** *cont* **-ming)** *vt* - **1.** [shut] zulknallen - **2.** [criticize] scharf kritisieren - **3.** [place roughly]: **to ~ sthg on(to)** etw auf etw *(A)* knallen <> *vi* [shut] zulknallen.

**slander** ['slɑːndəʳ] *n (U)* Verleumdung *die* <> *vt* verleumden.

**slanderous** ['slɑːndrəs] *adj* verleumderisch.

**slang** [slæŋ] *adj* Slang- <> *n* Slang *der.*

**slant** [slɑːnt] *n* - **1.** [diagonal angle] Schräge *die;* **on** *OR* **at a ~** schräg - **2.** [point of view] Blickwinkel *der* <> *vt* [bias] zurechtlbiegen <> *vi* schräg sein.

**slanting** ['slɑːntɪŋ] *adj* schräg.

**slap** [slæp] *(pt &  pp* **-ped;** *cont* **-ping)** *n* Schlag *der;* [in face] Ohrfeige *die;* [on back] Klaps *der;* **a ~ in the face** *fig* ein Schlag ins Gesicht <> *vt* - **1.** [person] schlagen; **to ~ sb's face** jm eine Ohrfeige geben; **to ~ sb on the back** jm auf den Rücken klopfen - **2.** [put]: **to ~ sthg on(to)** sthg etw auf etw *(A)* knallen <> *adv inf* [directly] direkt.

**slapdash** ['slæp,dæʃ], **slaphappy** ['slæp-,hæpɪ] *adj inf* schlampig.

**slapstick** ['slæpstɪk] *n* Slapstick *der.*

**slap-up** *adj Br inf* Super-.

**slash** [slæʃ] *n* - **1.** [long cut] Schnitt *der* - **2.** *esp Am* [oblique stroke] Schrägstrich *der* <> *vt* - **1.** [cut - material] (zer)schneiden; [ - tyres] zerschlitzen, auflschlitzen; **to ~ one's wrists** sich die Pulsadern auflschneiden - **2.** *inf* [reduce drastically] stark reduzieren.

**slat** [slæt] *n* [in blind] Lamelle *die;* [in bench] Latte *die.*

**slate** [sleɪt] *n* - **1.** *(U)* [rock] Schiefer *der* - **2.** [on roof] Schieferplatte *die* <> *vt* [criticize] verreißen.

**slatted** ['slætɪd] *adj* [blind] Lamellen-.

**slaughter** ['slɔːtəʳ] *n* - **1.** [of animals] Schlachten *das* - **2.** [of people] Abschlachten *das* <> *vt* - **1.** [animals] schlachten - **2.** [people] ablschlachten.

**slaughterhouse** ['slɔːtəhaʊs, *pl* -haʊzɪz] *n* Schlachthof *der.*

**Slav** [slɑːv] *adj* slawisch <> *n* Slawe *der,* -win *die.*

**slave** [sleɪv] *n* - **1.** [servant] Sklave *der,* -vin *die* - **2.** *fig* [captive]: **to be a ~ to sthg** Sklave einer Sache *(G)* sein <> *vi:* **to ~ (over sthg)** sich (mit etw) ablplagen.

**slaver** ['sleɪvəʳ] *vi* sabbern.

**slavery** ['sleɪvərɪ] *n* Sklaverei *die.*

**slave trade** *n:* **the ~ der** Sklavenhandel.

**Slavic** ['slɑːvɪk] *adj* slawisch <> *n* [language] Slawisch(e) *das.*

**slavish** ['sleɪvɪʃ] *adj pej* sklavisch.

**Slavonic** [slə'vɒnɪk] *adj & n* = **Slavic.**

**slay** [sleɪ] *(pt* **slew;** *pp* **slain)** *vt literary* töten.

**sleaze** ['sliːz] *n* Korruption *die.*

**sleazy** ['sliːzɪ] *(compar* **-ier;** *superl* **-iest)** *adj* [area, bar] schäbig; [behaviour] korrupt.

**sledge** [sledʒ], **sled** *Am* [sled] *n* Schlitten *der.*

**sledgehammer** ['sledʒ,hæməʳ] *n* Vorschlaghammer *der.*

**sleek** [sliːk] *adj* - **1.** [hair, fur] seidig glänzend - **2.** [car, plane] schnittig.

**sleep** [sliːp] *(pt &  pp* **slept)** *n* Schlaf *der;* **to go to ~** [doze off, go numb] einlschlafen; **to put to ~** [patient] ein Schlafmittel geben *(+ D);* [animal] einlschläfern <> *vi* schlafen.

**S**

➧ **sleep around** *vi inf pej* mit jedem ins Bett gehen.

➧ **sleep in** *vi* [oversleep] verschlafen.

➧ **sleep off** *vt sep* auslschlafen.

➧ **sleep through** *vt fus* verschlafen.

➧ **sleep together** *vi euphemism* miteinander schlafen.

➧ **sleep with** *vt fus euphemism* schlafen mit.

**sleeper** ['sli:pə'] *n* - **1.** [person]: **to be a heavy/ light ~** einen tiefen/leichten Schlaf haben - **2.** [sleeping compartment] Schlafwagenabteil *das* - **3.** [train] Schlafwagenzug *der* - **4. Br** [on railway track] Schwelle *die*.

**sleepily** ['sli:pɪlɪ] *adv* schläfrig.

**sleeping bag** ['sli:pɪŋ-] *n* Schlafsack *der*.

**sleeping car** ['sli:pɪŋ-] *n* Schlafwagen *der*.

**sleeping partner** ['sli:pɪŋ-] *n Br* stiller Teilhaber, stille Teilhaberin.

**sleeping pill** ['sli:pɪŋ-] *n* Schlaftablette *die*.

**sleeping policeman** ['sli:pɪŋ-] *n Br inf* Geschwindigkeitsschwelle *die*.

**sleeping tablet** ['sli:pɪŋ-] *n* Schlaftablette *die*.

**sleepless** ['sli:plɪs] *adj* schlaflos.

**sleeplessness** ['sli:plɪsnɪs] *n* Schlaflosigkeit *die*.

**sleepwalk** ['sli:pwɔ:k] *vi* schlaflwandeln.

**sleepy** ['sli:pɪ] (*compar* **-ier;** *superl* **-iest**) *adj* - **1.** [person] schläfrig - **2.** [place] verschlafen.

**sleet** [sli:t] *n* Schneeregen *der* <> *v impers*: **it's ~ing** es fällt Schneeregen.

**sleeve** [sli:v] *n* - **1.** [of garment] Ärmel *der*; **to have sthg up one's ~** noch etw in der Hinterhand haben - **2.** [for record] Hülle *die*.

**sleeveless** ['sli:vlɪs] *adj* ärmellos.

**sleigh** [sleɪ] *n* Schlitten *der*.

**sleight of hand** [ˌslaɪt-] *n* (*U*) - **1.** [skill with hands] Fingerfertigkeit *die* - **2.** *fig* [deception] Trick *der*.

**slender** ['slendə'] *adj* - **1.** [thin] schlank - **2.** [scarce - resources] knapp; [ - hope, chance] gering.

**slept** [slept] *pt* & *pp* ▷ **sleep.**

**sleuth** [slu:θ] *n inf hum* Spürhund *der*.

**slew** [slu:] *pt* ▷ **slay** <> *vi* [vehicle] schleudern.

**slice** [slaɪs] *n* - **1.** [thin piece] Scheibe *die;* [of pizza] Stück *das* - **2.** [proportion] Teil *der* - **3.** SPORT Slice *der* <> *vt* - **1.** [cut into slices] in Scheiben schneiden - **2.** SPORT slicen, mit Unterschnitt spielen <> *vi* [move]: **to ~ through sthg** etw durchlschneiden.

➧ **slice off** *vt sep* [sever] abltrennen.

➧ **slice up** *vt sep* [food] auf lschneiden.

**sliced bread** [ˌslaɪst-] *n* (*U*) Brot *das* in Scheiben.

**slick** [slɪk] *adj* - **1.** [smoothly efficient] geschickt gemacht - **2.** *pej* [person] aalglatt; [answer, argument] glatt <> *n:* (oil) **~** Ölteppich *der*.

**slicker** ['slɪkə'] *n Am* [raincoat] Regenmantel *der*.

**slide** [slaɪd] (*pt* & *pp* slid [slɪd]) *n* - **1.** PHOT Dia(positiv) *das* - **2.** [in playground] Rutsche *die* - **3.** [for microscope] Objektträger *der* - **4. Br** [for hair] Haarspange *die* - **5.** [decline - of person] Abrutschen *das;* [ - in prices, standards] Absinken *das* <> *vt* gleiten lassen <> *vi* - **1.** [on ice, slippery surface] schlittern - **2.** [move quietly] gleiten - **3.** [decline - person] ablrutschen; [ - prices, standards] ablsinken; **to let things ~** die Dinge schleifen lassen.

**slide projector** *n* Diaprojektor *der*.

**slide rule** *n* Rechenschieber *der*.

**sliding door** [ˌslaɪdɪŋ-] *n* Schiebetür *die*.

**sliding scale** [ˌslaɪdɪŋ-] *n* gleitende Skala.

**slight** [slaɪt] *adj* - **1.** [minor] leicht; **not the ~est interest** nicht das geringste Interesse; **not in the ~est** nicht im Geringsten - **2.** [slender] schmal <> *n* [insult] Kränkung *die* <> *vt* [offend] kränken.

**slightly** ['slaɪtlɪ] *adv* - **1.** [to small extent] etwas - **2.** [slenderly]: **~ built** schmal.

**slim** [slɪm] (*compar* **-mer;** *superl* **-mest;** *pt* & *pp* **-med;** *cont* **-ming**) *adj* - **1.** [person] schlank - **2.** [object] schmal - **3.** [chance, possibility] gering <> *vi* [lose weight] abl nehmen; [diet] eine Diät machen.

**slime** [slaɪm] *n* Schleim *der*.

**slimline** ['slɪmlaɪn] *adj* [drink] kalorienarm.

**slimmer** ['slɪmə'] *n Person, die abnehmen will;* [on diet] *Person, die eine Diät macht.*

**slimming** ['slɪmɪŋ] *n* Abnehmen *das* <> *adj* [club, magazine] Diät-; [product] Schlankheits-.

**slimness** ['slɪmnɪs] *n* Schlankheit *die*.

**slimy** ['slaɪmɪ] (*compar* **-ier;** *superl* **-iest**) *adj lit* & *fig* schleimig.

**sling** [slɪŋ] (*pt* & *pp* slung) *n* - **1.** [for injured arm] Armschlinge *die* - **2.** [for carrying things] Trageriemen *der* <> *vt* - **1.** [hang roughly]: **she slung the bag over her shoulder** sie hängte sich die Tasche über die Schulter - **2.** *inf* [throw] schleudern - **3.** [hang by both ends] spannen.

**slingback** ['slɪŋbæk] *n* Slingpumps *der*.

**slingshot** ['slɪŋʃɒt] *n Am* Schleuder *die*.

**slink** [slɪŋk] (*pt* & *pp* slunk) *vi:* **to ~ away** OR **off** davonlschleichen.

**slip** [slɪp] (*pt* & *pp* **-ped;** *cont* **-ping**) *n* - **1.** [mistake] Versehen *das;* **a ~ of the pen** ein Schreibfehler; **a ~ of the tongue** ein Versprecher - **2.** [form] Abschnitt *der* - **3.** [of paper]: **~ (of paper)** Zettel *der* - **4.** [underwear] Unterrock *der* - **5.** *phr:* **to give sb the ~** *inf* jm entkommen <> *vt* - **1.** [put, slide] stecken

**- 2.** [clothes]: **to ~ sthg on/off** etw überlziehen/ auslziehen **- 3.** [escape]: **it ~ped my mind** ich habe es vergessen ◇ vi **- 1.** [lose balance] auslrutschen **- 2.** [move unexpectedly - hand, foot] rutschen; **it ~ped out of my hand** es rutschte mir aus der Hand; **to ~ into a coma** ins Koma fallen; **I let it ~** [revealed it] es ist mir herausgerutscht **- 3.** [decline] sinken; **to let things ~** die Dinge schleifen lassen **- 4.** [move discreetly] schlüpfen; **to ~ into/out of sthg** [clothes] in etw (A)/aus etw schlüpfen **- 5.** AUT [clutch] schleifen.

➡ **slip away** vi [leave] sich davonlschleichen.

➡ **slip on** vt sep [clothes] überlziehen; [shoes] anlziehen.

➡ **slip up** vi sich vertun.

**slip-on** adj: **~ shoes** Slipper pl.

➡ **slip-ons** npl [shoes] Slipper pl.

**slipped disc** [ˌslɪpt-] n Bandscheibenvorfall der.

**slipper** ['slɪpə] n Hausschuh der.

**slippery** ['slɪpərɪ] adj **- 1.** [surface, soap] rutschig **- 2.** [person] windig.

**slip road** n Br [onto motorway] Auffahrt die; [leaving motorway] Ausfahrt die.

**slipshod** ['slɪpʃɒd] adj schlampig.

**slipstream** ['slɪpstriːm] n [of car] Windschatten der; [of plane] Sog der.

**slip-up** n inf Versehen das.

**slipway** ['slɪpweɪ] n Helling die.

**slit** [slɪt] (pt & pp **slit**; cont **-ting**) n Schlitz der ◇ vt auflschlitzen.

**slither** ['slɪðə] vi **- 1.** [car, person] rutschen **- 2.** [snake] gleiten.

**sliver** ['slɪvə] n **- 1.** [splinter] Splitter der **- 2.** [slice] hauchdünne Scheibe.

**slob** [slɒb] n inf Dreckschwein das.

**slobber** ['slɒbə] vi [dribble] sabbern.

**slog** [slɒg] (pt & pp **-ged**; cont **-ging**) inf n **- 1.** [tiring work] Schinderei die **- 2.** [tiring walk] Quälerei die ◇ vi **- 1.** [work]: **to ~ (away) at sthg** sich mit etw ablplagen **- 2.** [walk, move] sich quälen.

**slogan** ['sləʊgən] n Slogan der.

**slop** [slɒp] (pt & pp **-ped**; cont **-ping**) vt verschütten ◇ vi überlschwappen.

**slope** [sləʊp] n **- 1.** [of roof, ground] Neigung die **- 2.** [hill] Hang der **- 3.** phr: **to be on a slippery ~** auf die schiefe Bahn geraten sein ◇ vi [shelf, table] schräg sein; **the garden ~s down to the river** der Garten fällt zum Fluss hin ab.

**sloping** ['sləʊpɪŋ] adj schräg; [land] abfallend.

**sloppy** ['slɒpɪ] (compar **-ier**; superl **-iest**) adj **- 1.** [careless] schlampig **- 2.** inf [sentimental] rührselig.

**slosh** [slɒʃ] vt **- 1.** [spill] verschütten **- 2.** [pour] schütten **- 3.** [apply] schmieren ◇ vi **- 1.** [liquid] herumlschwappen **- 2.** [through liquid, mud] patschen.

**sloshed** [slɒʃt] adj Br inf besoffen.

**slot** [slɒt] (pt & pp **-ted**; cont **-ting**) n **- 1.** [opening] Schlitz der **- 2.** [groove] Nut die **- 3.** [place in broadcasting schedule] Sendezeit die.

➡ **slot in** vt sep einlfügen ◇ vi hineinlpassen.

**sloth** [sləʊθ] n **- 1.** [animal] Faultier das **- 2.** literary [laziness] Faulheit die.

**slot machine** n **- 1.** [vending machine] Münzautomat der **- 2.** [arcade machine] Spielautomat der.

**slot meter** n Br Münzzähler der.

**slouch** [slaʊtʃ] n: **to be no ~ at sthg** in etw (D) gut sein ◇ vi [when sitting] sich hinllümmeln; [when standing] schlaff dalstehen.

**slough** [slʌf] vt sep [skin] ablstreifen.

➡ **slough off** vt sep [get rid of] ablwerfen.

**Slovak** ['sləʊvæk] adj slowakisch ◇ n **- 1.** [person] Slowake der, -kin die **- 2.** [language] Slowakisch(e) das.

**Slovakia** [slə'vækɪə] n Slowakei die; **in ~** in der Slowakei.

**Slovakian** [slə'vækɪən] adj slowakisch ◇ n Slowake der, -kin die.

**Slovenia** [slə'viːnjə] n Slowenien das.

**Slovenian** [slə'viːnjən] adj slowenisch ◇ n Slowene der, -nin die.

**slovenly** ['slʌvnlɪ] adj schlampig.

**slow** [sləʊ] adj **- 1.** [not fast] langsam **- 2.** [clock, watch]: **to be ~** nachlgehen **- 3.** [not busy - business] flau; [ - place] ruhig **- 4.** [not intelligent] langsam ◇ adv: **to go ~** [driver] langsam fahren; [workers] Bummelstreik machen ◇ vt verlangsamen ◇ vi [person] langsam werden; [car] langsamer fahren; [increase, progress] sich verlangsamen.

➡ **slow down, slow up** vt sep verlangsamen ◇ vi langsamer werden; [car] langsamer fahren; [walker] langsamer gehen.

**slow-acting** adj langsam wirkend.

**slowcoach** ['sləʊkəʊtʃ], **slowpoke** Am ['sləʊpəʊk] n inf Trantüte die.

**slowdown** ['sləʊdaʊn] n Verlangsamung die.

**slow handclap** n langsames rhythmisches Klatschen zum Ausdruck des Missfallens.

**slowly** ['sləʊlɪ] adv langsam; **~ but surely** langsam, aber sicher.

**slow motion** n Zeitlupe die.

➡ **slow-motion** adj Zeitlupen-.

**slowpoke** n Am = slowcoach.

**SLR** (abbr of **single-lens reflex**) n Spiegelreflexkamera die.

**sludge** [slʌdʒ] n Schlamm der.

**slug** [slʌg] (pt & pp **-ged**; cont **-ging**) n **- 1.** ZOOL Nacktschnecke die **- 2.** inf [of alcohol] Schluck

**S**

der **- 3. Am** inf [bullet] Kugel die <> vt inf [hit] einen Faustschlag versetzen (+ D).

**sluggish** ['slʌgɪʃ] adj träge; [business] flau.

**sluice** [sluːs] n Schleuse die <> vt [rinse]: **to
~ sthg down/out** etw ab-/auslspülen.

**slum** [slʌm] (pt & pp **-med;** cont **-ming)** n [area]
Slum der <> vt: **to ~ it** inf wie die einfachen
Leute leben/essen/etc.

**slumber** ['slʌmbəʳ] literary n Schlummer der
<> vi schlummern.

**slump** [slʌmp] n **- 1.** [decline]: **~ (in sthg)** Abfall
der (einer Sache (G)) **- 2.** [period of economic de-
pression] Konjunkturabschwung der <> vi
**- 1.** [business, market] plötzlich zurücklgehen;
[prices] stürzen **- 2.** [person] sich fallen lassen.

**slung** [slʌŋ] pt & pp ➡ sling.

**slunk** [slʌŋk] pt & pp ➡ slink.

**slur** [slɜːʳ] (pt & pp **-red;** cont **-ring)** n **- 1.** [in
voice]: **to speak with a ~** mit schwerer Zunge
sprechen **- 2.** [insult]: **~ (on sb/sthg)** Schande
die (für jn/etw) <> vt [speech]: **to ~ one's words**
mit schwerer Zunge sprechen.

**slurp** [slɜːp] vt schlürfen.

**slurred** [slɜːd] adj [voice] undeutlich.

**slurry** ['slʌrɪ] n [liquid manure] Gülle die.

**slush** [slʌʃ] n Schneematsch der.

**slush fund, slush money Am** n Schmier-
gelder pl.

**slut** [slʌt] n inf Schlampe die.

**sly** [slaɪ] (compar **slyer** OR **slier;** superl **slyest** OR
**sliest)** adj **- 1.** [look, smile, grin] wissend **- 2.** [cun-
ning] listig **- 3.** [secretive] heimlich <> n: **on the
~** heimlich.

**slyness** ['slaɪnɪs] n [deceitfulness] Hinterlistig-
keit die.

**S & M** (abbr of **sadism and masochism)** n S/M.

**smack** [smæk] n [slap] Klaps der; [on face] Ohrfeige die <> vt **- 1.** [slap] einen Klaps geben (+
D); [in the face] ohrfeigen; **to ~ one's lips** mit
den Lippen schmatzen **- 2.** [put] knallen
<> vi: **to ~ of sthg** [actions] nach etw auslsehen;
[words] nach etw klingen <> adv inf [directly] direkt.

**small** [smɔːl] adj klein; **a ~ number** eine geringe Anzahl; **a ~ matter** eine Kleinigkeit; **a
~ business** ein Kleinbetrieb; **in a ~ way** in be-
scheidenem Maße; **to feel ~** sich schämen
<> adv: **to chop sthg up ~** etw kleinl-
schneiden <> n: **the ~ of the back** das Kreuz.
➡ **smalls** npl Br inf Unterwäsche pl.

**small ads** [-ædz] npl Br Kleinanzeigen pl.

**small arms** npl Handfeuerwaffen pl.

**small change** n Kleingeld das.

**small fry** n (U) kleine Fische pl.

**smallholder** ['smɔːl,həʊldəʳ] n Br Kleinbauer
der, -bäuerin die.

**smallholding** ['smɔːl,həʊldɪŋ] n Br landwirt-
schaftlicher Kleinbetrieb.

**small hours** npl frühe Morgenstunden pl.

**small letters** npl: in ~ in Kleinbuchstaben.

**smallness** ['smɔːlnɪs] n (U) geringe Größe; [of
amount, income] Bescheidenheit die.

**smallpox** ['smɔːlpɒks] n (U) Pocken pl.

**small print** n: the ~ das Kleingedruckte.

**small-scale** adj [map] in verkleinertem
Maßstab; [venture] Klein-.

**small talk** n Smalltalk der.

**small-time** adj: **~ criminal** Kleinkriminelle
der, die.

**smarmy** ['smɑːmɪ] (compar **-ier;** superl **-iest)** adj
schleimig.

**smart** [smɑːt] adj **- 1.** [elegant] elegant **- 2.** esp
**Am** [clever] klug **- 3.** [fashionable, exclusive] exklusiv **- 4.** [rapid] flott **- 5.** [impertinent] frech <> vi
**- 1.** [sting] brennen **- 2.** [feel anger and humiliation]
verletzt sein.

**smart card** n Chipkarte die.

**smarten** ['smɑːtn] ➡ **smarten up** vt sep [room]
auflräumen; **to ~ up one's appearance** sich
herlrichten.

**smash** [smæʃ] n **- 1.** [sound] Krach der **- 2.** inf [car
crash] Unfall der **- 3.** inf [success] Bombenerfolg
der **- 4.** TENNIS Schmetterball der <> vt **- 1.** [break
into pieces] zerschlagen **- 2.** [hit]: **she ~ed her fist
into his face** sie schmetterte ihm ihre Faust
ins Gesicht **- 3.** fig [defeat] zerschlagen <> vi
**- 1.** [break into pieces] zerbrechen **- 2.** [crash, col-
lide]: **to ~ through sthg** durch etw rasen; **the
car ~ed into the tree** das Auto krachte gegen
den Baum.
➡ **smash up** vt sep zertrümmern; [car] zu
Schrott fahren.

**smash-and-grab (raid)** n Br Schaufens-
tereinbruch der.

**smashed** [smæʃt] adj inf stockbesoffen.

**smash hit** n Superhit der.

**smashing** ['smæʃɪŋ] adj inf klasse, toll.

**smash-up** n Zusammenstoß der.

**smattering** ['smætərɪŋ] n: **to have a ~ of sthg**
Grundkenntnisse in etw (D) haben; **I have a
~ of German** ich kann ein bisschen Deutsch.

**SME** (abbr of **small and medium-sized enterprise)** n KMU das.

**smear** [smɪəʳ] n **- 1.** [dirty mark] Fleck der **- 2.** MED
Abstrich der **- 3.** [slander] Verleumdung die
<> vt **- 1.** [smudge - page, painting] verschmie-
ren; [ - paint, ink] verwischen **- 2.** [spread]: **to
~ sthg onto sthg** etw auf etw (A) schmieren;
**she ~ed her skin with suncream** sie schmierte
ihre Haut mit Sonnencreme ein **- 3.** [slander]
verleumden.

**smear campaign** n Verleumdungskam-
pagne die.

**smear test** *n* Abstrich *der.*

**smell** [smell] (*pt* & *pp* **-ed** OR **smelt**) *n* - **1.** [odour] Geruch *der;* [unpleasant] Gestank *der* - **2.** (U) [sense of smell] Geruchssinn *der* - **3.** [sniff]: **to have a ~ of sthg** an atw (D) riechen ◇ *vt* - **1.** [notice an odour of, sense] riechen - **2.** [sniff at] riechen an (+ D); [subj: dog] schnuppern an (+ D) ◇ *vi* - **1.** [have sense of smell] riechen - **2.** [have particular smell]: **to ~ of sthg** nach etw riechen; **to ~ like sthg** wie etw riechen; **to ~ good/bad** gut/schlecht riechen - **3.** [smell unpleasantly] übel riechen.

**smelling salts** ['smelɪŋ-] *npl* Riechsalz *das.*

**smelly** ['smelɪ] (*compar* **-ier;** *superl* **-iest**) *adj* übel riechend.

**smelt** [smelt] *pt* & *pp* ▷ **smell** ◇ *vt* TECH [ore] verhütten; [metal] erschmelzen.

**smile** [smaɪl] *n* Lächeln *das* ◇ *vi* lächeln.

**smiley** ['smaɪlɪ] *n* COMPUT Smiley *der.*

**smiling** ['smaɪlɪŋ] *adj* lächelnd.

**smirk** [smɜːk] *n* Grinsen *das* ◇ *vi* grinsen.

**smithereens** [ˌsmɪðəˈriːnz] *npl inf*: **to be smashed to ~** in tausend Stücke zerspringen.

**smitten** ['smɪtn] *adj inf hum*: **to be ~ with sb/sthg** in jn/etw (ganz) verliebt sein.

**smock** [smɒk] *n* Kittel *der.*

**smog** [smɒg] *n* Smog *der.*

**smoke** [sməʊk] *n* - **1.** [from fire] Rauch *der* - **2.** [act of smoking] Rauchen *das;* **to have a ~** eine rauchen ◇ *vt* - **1.** [cigarette, cigar] rauchen - **2.** [fish, meat, cheese] räuchern ◇ *vi* rauchen.

**smoked** [sməʊkt] *adj* [food] geräuchert.

**smokeless fuel** ['sməʊklɪs-] *n* rauchloser Brennstoff.

**smokeless zone** ['sməʊklɪs-] *n* Gebiet, in dem die Verwendung von umweltschädigenden Brennstoffen verboten ist.

**smoker** ['sməʊkər] *n* - **1.** [person who smokes] Raucher *der* - **2.** RAIL [compartment] Raucherabteil *das.*

**smokescreen** ['sməʊkskriːn] *n fig*: **to be a ~ for sthg** etw verschleiern.

**smoke shop** *n Am* Tabakladen *der.*

**smokestack** ['sməʊkstæk] *n* Schornstein *der.*

**smokestack industries** *npl Am* traditionelle Industriezweige *pl.*

**smoking** ['sməʊkɪŋ] *n* Rauchen *das;* 'no ~' 'Rauchen verboten'.

**smoking compartment** *Br,* **smoking car** *Am n* Raucherabteil *das.*

**smoky** ['sməʊkɪ] (*compar* **-ier;** *superl* **-iest**) *adj* rauchig.

**smolder** *vi Am* = smoulder.

**smooch** [smuːtʃ] *vi inf* knutschen.

**smooth** [smuːð] *adj* - **1.** [surface] glatt - **2.** [sauce, paste] sämig - **3.** [flow, pace, supply] gleichmäßig - **4.** [taste] weich - **5.** [flight, ride] ruhig; [takeoff,

landing] weich; [engine] ruhig laufend - **6.** *pej* [person, manner] aalglatt - **7.** [trouble-free] glatt verlaufend; [transition] reibungslos ◇ *vt* - **1.** [hair, skirt, tablecloth] glatt streichen; **to ~ the way for sthg** etw (D) den Weg ebnen - **2.** [rub]: **~ the oil into your skin** reiben Sie ihre Haut mit dem Öl ein.

➤ **smooth out** *vt sep* - **1.** [skirt, sheet, crease] glatt streichen - **2.** [difficulties] aus dem Weg räumen.

➤ **smooth over** *vt fus* einlenken.

**smoothly** ['smuːðlɪ] *adv* - **1.** [easily, steadily] ruhig - **2.** [without problems] reibungslos.

**smoothness** ['smuːðnɪs] *n* - **1.** [of surface] Glätte *die* - **2.** [of texture] Sämigkeit *die* - **3.** [of flow, pace, supply] Gleichmäßigkeit *die* - **4.** [of flight, ride] ruhiger Verlauf.

**smooth-talking** [-ˌtɔːkɪŋ] *adj* schönrednerisch.

**smother** ['smʌðər] *vt* - **1.** [cover thickly]: **to ~ sthg in** OR **with sthg** etw mit etw bedecken - **2.** [suffocate, extinguish] ersticken - **3.** *fig* [repress] unterdrücken - **4.** [suffocate with love] (mit Liebe) erdrücken.

**smoulder** *Br,* **smolder** *Am* ['sməʊldər] *vi lit* & *fig* schwelen.

**SMS** (*abbr of* **Short Message System**) *n* SMS *die.*

**smudge** [smʌdʒ] *n* [dirty mark] Fleck *der;* [of ink] verwischte Stelle ◇ *vt* [spoil - by blurring] verschmieren; [ - outline, ink] verwischen; [ - by dirtying] beschmutzen.

**smug** [smʌg] (*compar* **-ger;** *superl* **-gest**) *adj pej* selbstzufrieden.

**smuggle** ['smʌgl] *vt* schmuggeln; **to ~ sthg in/ out** etw herein-/herausschmuggeln.

**smuggler** ['smʌglər] *n* Schmuggler *der,* -in *die.*

**smuggling** ['smʌglɪŋ] *n* Schmuggel *der.*

**smugness** ['smʌgnɪs] *n pej* Selbstzufriedenheit *die.*

**smut** [smʌt] *n* - **1.** [piece of soot] Rußflocke *die* - **2.** *inf pej* [lewd matter] Schund *der.*

**smutty** ['smʌtɪ] (*compar* **-ier;** *superl* **-iest**) *adj inf pej* [lewd] schmutzig.

**snack** [snæk] *n* Snack *der,* Imbiss *der* ◇ *vi Am* zwischendurch essen.

**snack bar** *n* Snackbar *die,* Imbissstube *die.*

**snag** [snæg] (*pt* & *pp* **-ged;** *cont* **-ging**) *n* [problem] Haken *der* ◇ *vt* [garment] zerreißen ◇ *vi*: **to ~ on sthg** an etw (D) hängen bleiben.

**snail** [sneɪl] *n* Schnecke *die.*

**snake** [sneɪk] *n* Schlange *die* ◇ *vi* sich schlängeln.

**snap** [snæp] (*pt* & *pp* **-ped;** *cont* **-ping**) *adj* spontan; [election] Spontan- ◇ *n* - **1.** [of twig, branch] Knacken *das;* [of whip] Knallen *das* - **2.** *inf* [photograph] Schnappschuss *der* - **3.** [card game]

**S**

**Schnippschnappschnurr** das <> vt - **1.**
[break - rope] zerreißen; **to ~ one's fingers** mit
den Fingern schnippen - **2.** [say sharply]
hervorlstoßen - **3.** *inf* [photograph] knipsen
<> vi - **1.** [break] (zer)brechen; [rope] (zer)-
reißen - **2.** [make cracking sound - whip] knallen;
[ - twig, branch] knacken; **the part ~s into place**
das Teil schnappt ein - **3.** [attempt to bite]: **to
~ (at sb/sthg)** (nach jm/etw) schnappen
- **4.** [speak sharply]: **to ~ at sb** jn an-
fahren - **5.** *phr:* **to ~ out of it** sich zusammen-
reißen.

➥ **snap up** *vt sep* zulschlagen bei *(+ D).*

**snap fastener** *n* Druckknopf *der.*

**snappy** ['snæpɪ] (*compar* **-ier;** *superl* **-iest**) *adj inf*
[stylish, quick] flott; **make it ~!** mach hin!

**snapshot** ['snæpʃɒt] *n* Schnappschuss *der.*

**snare** [sneər] *n* Falle *die* <> *vt* in einer Falle
fangen.

**snarl** [snɑːl] *n* Knurren *das* <> *vi* knurren.

**snarl-up** *n* [in traffic] Stau *der.*

**snatch** [snætʃ] *n* [of song, conversation] Bruchstück *das* <> *vt* - **1.** [grab] schnappen - **2.** *fig*
[sleep] kriegen; [opportunity] ergreifen; [look] er-
haschen <> *vi:* **to ~ (at sthg)** (nach etw)
schnappen.

**snazzy** ['snæzɪ] (*compar* **-ier;** *superl* **-iest**) *adj inf*
schick.

**sneak** [sniːk] (**Am** *pt* **snuck**) *n* **Br** *inf* Petze *die*
<> *vt* [bring secretly] schmuggeln; **to ~ a look at
sb/sthg** jn/etw heimlich anlsehen <> *vi* [move
quietly] schleichen; **to ~ up on sb** sich an jn
heranlschleichen.

**sneakers** ['sniːkəz] *npl* **Am** Sportschuhe *pl.*

**sneaking** ['sniːkɪŋ] *adj* [feeling, suspicion] heimlich.

**sneak preview** *n* [of film, play] Voraufführung *die.*

**sneaky** ['sniːkɪ] (*compar* **-ier;** *superl* **-iest**) *adj inf*
hinterhältig.

**sneer** [snɪər] *n* spöttisches Lächeln <> *vi*
- **1.** [smile unpleasantly] spöttisch lächeln
- **2.** [ridicule]: **to ~ (at sthg)** (über etw *(A)*) spotten.

**sneeze** [sniːz] *n* Niesen *das* <> *vi* niesen; **it's
not to be ~d at** *inf* es ist nicht zu verachten.

**snicker** ['snɪkər] *vi* **Am** hämisch kichern.

**snide** [snaɪd] *adj* abfällig.

**sniff** [snɪf] *n:* **to have a ~ of sthg** an etw *(D)*
schnuppern <> *vt* - **1.** [smell] riechen an *(+ D)*
- **2.** [drug] schnüffeln <> *vi* schniefen.

➥ **sniff out** *vt sep* - **1.** [detect by sniffing] auf l-
spüren - **2.** *inf* [seek out] herauslkriegen.

**sniffer dog** ['snɪfə‿] *n* Spürhund *der.*

**sniffle** ['snɪfl] *vi* schniefen.

**snigger** ['snɪgər] *n* hämisches Kichern <> *vi*
hämisch kichern.

**snip** [snɪp] (*pt* & *pp* **-ped;** *cont* **-ping**) *n inf* [bar-
gain] Schnäppchen *das* <> *vt* [cut] schnippeln.

**snipe** [snaɪp] *vi* - **1.** [shoot]: **to ~ (at sb/sthg)** aus
dem Hinterhalt (auf jn/etw) schießen
- **2.** [criticize]: **to ~ at sb** jn attackieren.

**sniper** ['snaɪpər] *n* Heckenschütze *der.*

**snippet** ['snɪpɪt] *n* Bruchstück *das.*

**snivel** ['snɪvl] (**Br** *pt* & *pp* **-led;** *cont* **-ling**, **Am** *pt*
& *pp* **-ed;** *cont* **-ing**) *vi* jammern.

**snob** [snɒb] *n* Snob *der.*

**snobbery** ['snɒbərɪ] *n* Snobismus *der.*

**snobbish** ['snɒbɪʃ], **snobby** ['snɒbɪ] (*compar*
**-ier;** *superl* **-iest**) *adj* snobistisch.

**snog** (*pt* & *pp* **-ged;** *cont* **-ging**) *vi* **Br** *inf* knutschen.

**snooker** ['snuːkər] *n* Snooker *das* <> *vt* **Br** *inf*
[thwart - plan] vereiteln; **we're ~ed!** wir sitzen
in der Klemme!

**snoop** [snuːp] *vi inf* (herum)schnüffeln.

**snooper** ['snuːpər] *n inf* Schnüffler *der*, **-in** *die.*

**snooty** ['snuːtɪ] (*compar* **-ier;** *superl* **-iest**) *adj*
hochnäsig.

**snooze** [snuːz] *n* Nickerchen *das;* **to have a ~**
ein Nickerchen machen <> *vi* ein Nicker-
chen machen.

**snore** [snɔːr] *n* Schnarchen *das* <> *vi* schnarchen.

**snoring** ['snɔːrɪŋ] *n* Schnarchen *das.*

**snorkel** ['snɔːkl] *n* Schnorchel *der.*

**snorkelling** **Br**, **snorkeling** **Am** ['snɔːklɪŋ] *n*
Schnorcheln *das.*

**snort** [snɔːt] *n* Schnauben *das* <> *vi* schnauben <> *vt drugs sl* schnüffeln.

**snotty** ['snɒtɪ] (*compar* **-ier;** *superl* **-iest**) *adj inf*
[snooty] hochnäsig.

**snout** [snaʊt] *n* Schnauze *die.*

**snow** [snəʊ] *n* Schnee *der* <> *v impers:* **it's ~ing**
es schneit.

➥ **snow in** *vt sep:* **to be ~ed in** eingeschneit
sein.

➥ **snow under** *vt sep:* **to be ~ed under with sthg**
*fig* mit etw überhäuft sein.

**snowball** ['snəʊbɔːl] *n* Schneeball *der* <> *vi fig*
lawinenartig anlwachsen.

**snow blindness** *n* Schneeblindheit *die.*

**snowbound** ['snəʊbaʊnd] *adj* eingeschneit.

**snow-capped** [-kæpt] *adj* schneebedeckt.

**snowdrift** ['snəʊdrɪft] *n* Schneewehe *die.*

**snowdrop** ['snəʊdrɒp] *n* Schneeglöckchen
*das.*

**snowfall** ['snəʊfɔːl] *n* Schneefall *der.*

**snowflake** ['snəʊfleɪk] *n* Schneeflocke *die.*

**snowman** ['snəʊmæn] (*pl* **-men** [-men]) *n*
Schneemann *der.*

**snow pea** *n Am* Zuckererbse *die.*

**snowplough** *Br*, **snowplow** *Am* [ˈsnəʊplaʊ] *n* [vehicle] Schneepflug *der.*

**snowshoe** [ˈsnəʊʃuː] *n* Schneeschuh *der.*

**snowstorm** [ˈsnəʊstɔːm] *n* Schneesturm *der.*

**snowy** [ˈsnəʊɪ] (*compar* **-ier**; *superl* **-iest**) *adj* [peak, road] schneebedeckt.

**SNP** (*abbr of* **Scottish National Party**) *n* nationalistische Partei in Schottland.

**Snr, snr** (*abbr of* **senior**) sen.

**snub** [snʌb] (*pt* & *pp* **-bed**; *cont* **-bing**) *n* Abfuhr *die* ⋄ *vt:* **to ~ sb** jm eine Abfuhr erteilen.

**snuck** [snʌk] *pt Am* ▷ **sneak.**

**snuff** [snʌf] *n* Schnupftabak *der* ⋄ *vt:* **to ~ it** *inf* abkratzen.

**snuffle** [ˈsnʌfl] *vi* schniefen.

**snug** [snʌg] (*compar* **-ger**; *superl* **-gest**) *adj* - **1.** [person, feeling, place] gemütlich - **2.** [close-fitting] gut sitzend.

**snuggle** [ˈsnʌgl] *vi:* **to ~ up to sb** sich an jn kuscheln; **to ~ down in bed** sich ins Bett kuscheln.

**so** [səʊ] *adv* - **1.** [to such a degree] so; **it's ~ difficult that ...** es ist so schwierig, dass ...; **don't be ~ stupid!** sei nicht so dumm!; **I (do) ~ hope you can come** ich hoffe so sehr, dass du kommen kannst; **~ much money/many cars** so viel Geld/viele Autos; **I liked it ~ much that ...** es gefiel mir so sehr *OR* gut, dass ...; **~ much ~ that ...** dermaßen, dass ... - **2.** [referring back]: **~ what's the point then?** was soll das also?; **~ you knew already?** du hast es also schon gewusst?; **I think ~** ich glaube (schon); **I don't think ~** ich glaube nicht; **I'm afraid ~** leider ja; **I told you ~** das habe ich dir gleich gesagt; **if ~** falls ja; **is that ~?** tatsächlich? - **3.** [also] auch; **~ can I** ich auch; **~ do I** ich auch; **he is clever and ~ is she** er ist intelligent und sie auch; **as with children, ~ with adults** bei Kindern wie bei Erwachsenen; **just as some people like family holidays, ~ others prefer to holiday alone** während manche Leute Familienurlaub mögen, ziehen andere es vor, alleine Ferien zu machen - **4.** [in this way] so; **hold your arm out, (like) ~** strecken Sie Ihren Arm so aus; **~ be it!** na gut! - **5.** [in expressing agreement]: **~ there is** ja, stimmt; **that's her car - ~ it is!** das ist ihr Auto - tatsächlich!; **~ I see** das sehe ich - **6.** [referring to unspecified amount, limit]: **there's only ~ much incompetence you can put up with** man kann nur ein bestimmtes Maß an Inkompetenz ertragen; **they pay us ~ much a week** sie zahlen uns so viel die Woche; **it's not ~ much the money as the time involved** es ist weniger das Geld als die Zeit; **or ~** oder so; **a week or ~ ago** vor ungefähr einer Woche ⋄ *conj* - **1.** [consequently] also; **he said yes and ~ we got married** er sagte ja, also heirateten wir; **I'm away next week**

**~ I won't be there** ich bin nächste Woche weg, also werde ich nicht kommen - **2.** [to introduce a statement] also; **~ what have you been up to?** na, was treibst du so?; **~ that's who she is!** das ist sie also!; **~ what?** *inf* na und?; **~ there!** *inf* das wars!

➡ **and so on, and so forth** *adv* und so weiter.

➡ **so as** *conj* um; **we didn't knock ~ as not to disturb them** wir klopften nicht an, um sie nicht zu stören.

➡ **so that** *conj* damit.

➡ **SO** *abbr of* **standing order.**

**soak** [səʊk] *vt* - **1.** [leave immersed] einweichen - **2.** [wet thoroughly] durchnässen; **to be ~ed with sthg** mit etw durchtränkt sein ⋄ *vi* - **1.** [become thoroughly wet]: **to leave sthg to ~**, **to let sthg ~** etw einweichen - **2.** [spread]: **to ~ into sthg** in etw (*A*) einsickern; **to ~ through sthg** durch etw (hindurch)sickern.

➡ **soak up** *vt sep* [liquid] auf saugen.

**soaked** [səʊkt] *adj* durchnässt; **to be ~ through** völlig durchnässt sein.

**soaking** [ˈsəʊkɪŋ] *adj:* **to be ~ (wet)** durchnässt sein.

**so-and-so** *n inf* - **1.** [to replace a name]: **Mr So-and-so** Herr Soundso - **2.** [annoying person]: **you little ~!** du Biest!

**soap** [səʊp] *n* - **1.** (*U*) [for washing] Seife *die* - **2.** ⲧⲱ Seifenoper *die* ⋄ *vt* einseifen.

**soap bubble** *n* Seifenblase *die.*

**soap dish** *n* Seifenschale *die.*

**soap flakes** *npl* Seifenflocken *pl.*

**soap opera** *n* Seifenoper *die.*

**SOAP OPERA**

Diese groß angelegten Fernseh- und Radiosendungen mit ihren oft melodramatischen Beschreibungen des Alltagslebens werden heute in aller Welt ausgestrahlt. Der Name ist dem Umstand zu verdanken, dass solche Serien früher oft von der Waschmittelindustrie gesponsort wurden. „Seifenopern" haben ein erstaunlich langes Leben: die in Manchester spielende britische Serie „Coronation Street" gibt es seit mehr als 40 Jahren.

**soap powder** *n* Seifenpulver *das.*

**soapsuds** [ˈsəʊpsʌdz] *npl* Seifenschaum *der.*

**soapy** [ˈsəʊpɪ] (*compar* **-ier**; *superl* **-iest**) *adj* seifig.

**soar** [sɔːʳ] *vi* - **1.** [bird, kite, rocket] auf steigen - **2.** [increase rapidly] rapide ansteigen - **3.** *literary* [be impressively high] hoch auf ragen - **4.** [rise in volume] lauter werden; [rise in pitch] höher werden.

**soaring** [ˈsɔːrɪŋ] *adj* - **1.** [rapidly increasing] rapide ansteigend - **2.** [spire, tower] hoch aufragend - **3.** [rising in volume] lauter werdend; [rising in pitch] höher werdend.

**sob** [sɒb] (*pt* & *pp* -bed; *cont* -bing) *n* Schluchzer *der* <> *vt* & *vi* schluchzen.

**sobbing** ['sɒbɪŋ] *n* Schluchzen *das*.

**sober** ['səʊbə<sup>r</sup>] *adj* - **1.** [not drunk] nüchtern - **2.** [serious] ernsthaft - **3.** [plain] einfach.

<> **sober up** *vi* nüchtern werden.

**sobering** ['səʊbərɪŋ] *adj* ernüchternd.

**Soc.** *abbr of* Society.

**so-called** [-kɔːld] *adj* so genannt.

**soccer** ['sɒkə<sup>r</sup>] *n* (*U*) Fußball *der*.

**sociable** ['səʊʃəbl] *adj* gesellig.

**social** ['səʊʃl] *adj* - **1.** [behaviour, background, conditions] sozial, gesellschaftlich - **2.** [gathering, drinking] gesellig - **3.** ZOOL [animals, insects] in einer Gemeinschaft lebend.

**social climber** *n pej* Emporkömmling *der*.

**social conscience** *n* soziales Bewusstsein.

**social democracy** *n* Sozialdemokratie *die*.

**social event** *n* - **1.** [at work *etc*] geselliges Treffen - **2.** [in village *etc*] gesellschaftliches Ereignis.

**social fund** *n* Sozialfond *der*.

**socialism** ['səʊʃəlɪzml] *n* Sozialismus *der*.

**socialist** ['səʊʃəlɪst] *adj* sozialistisch <> *n* Sozialist *der*, -in *die*.

**socialite** ['səʊʃəlaɪt] *n* Prominente *der*, *die*.

**socialize, -ise** ['səʊʃəlaɪz] *vi:* to ~ with sb mit jm gesellschaftlich verkehren; she ~s a lot sie geht viel aus.

**socialized medicine** ['səʊʃəlaɪzd-] *n Am* kostenlose staatliche Gesundheitsfürsorge.

**social life** *n* gesellschaftliches Leben; he hasn't much of a ~ er geht nicht viel aus.

**socially** ['səʊʃəlɪ] *adv* - **1.** [towards society] sozial, gesellschaftlich - **2.** [outside business] privat.

**social order** *n* Gesellschaftsordnung *die*.

**social science** *n* - **1.** [in general] Sozialwissenschaften *pl* - **2.** [individual science] Sozialwissenschaft *die*.

**social security** *n* (*U*) Sozialversicherung *die*.

**social services** *npl* Sozialeinrichtungen *pl*.

**social studies** *n* Gemeinschaftskunde *die*.

**social work** *n* Sozialarbeit *die*.

**social worker** *n* Sozialarbeiter *der*, -in *die*.

**society** [sə'saɪətɪ] (*pl* -ies) *n* - **1.** [mankind, community] Gesellschaft *die* - **2.** [club, organization] Verein *der*, Klub *der*.

**socioeconomic** ['səʊsɪəʊˌiːkə'nɒmɪk] *adj* POL sozioökonomisch.

**sociological** [ˌsəʊsjə'lɒdʒɪkl] *adj* soziologisch.

**sociologist** [ˌsəʊsɪ'ɒlədʒɪst] *n* Soziologe *der*, -gin *die*.

**sociology** [ˌsəʊsɪ'ɒlədʒɪl] *n* Soziologie *die*.

**sock** [sɒk] *n* Socke *die*, Socken *der;* **to pull one's ~s up** *inf fig* sich am Riemen reißen.

**socket** ['sɒkɪt] *n* - **1.** ELEC Steckdose *die* - **2.** ANAT [of joint] Gelenkpfanne *die;* [of eye] Augenhöhle *die*.

**sod** [sɒd] *n* - **1.** [of turf] Sode *die* - **2.** *vinf* [man] Scheißkerl *der;* [woman] Miststück *das*.

**soda** ['səʊdə] *n* - **1.** CHEM Soda *das*, Natron *das* - **2.** [soda water] Soda *das* - **3.** *Am* [fizzy drink] Limonade *die*.

**soda syphon** *n* Siphon *der*.

**soda water** *n* Sodawasser *das*.

**sodden** ['sɒdn] *adj* durchnässt.

**sodium** ['səʊdɪəm] *n* Natrium *das*.

**sofa** ['səʊfə] *n* Sofa *das*.

**sofabed** ['səʊfəbed] *n* Schlafcouch *die*.

**Sofia** ['səʊfjə] *n* Sofia *nt*.

**soft** [sɒft] *adj* - **1.** [gen] weich - **2.** [breeze, sound, knock, nature] sanft - **3.** [light, colour, music] gedämpft - **4.** [not strict] mild.

**softball** ['sɒftbɔːll] *n* SPORT Softball *der*.

**soft-boiled** *adj* weich gekocht.

**soft drink** *n* alkoholfreies Getränk.

**soft drugs** *npl* weiche Drogen *pl*.

**soften** ['sɒfn] *vt* - **1.** [substance] weich machen; [water] enthärten - **2.** [punch, impact, effect, light] dämpfen; [blow, attitude] mildern <> *vi* - **1.** [substance] weich werden - **2.** [attitude] his attitude towards foreigners has ~ed er ist Ausländern gegenüber toleranter geworden - **3.** [eyes, voice, expression] sanft werden.

<> **soften up** *vt sep inf* [make amenable] weich klopfen.

**soft focus** *n* Weichzeichner *der;* in ~ mit Weichzeichner.

**soft furnishings** *npl Br* Raumtextilien *pl*.

**softhearted** [ˌsɒft'hɑːtɪd] *adj* weichherzig.

**softly** ['sɒftlɪ] *adv* - **1.** [move, touch] sanft - **2.** [speak, sing, shine] leise - **3.** [smile, look] sanft.

**softness** ['sɒftnɪs] *n* - **1.** [gen] Weichheit *die* - **2.** [gentleness] Sanftheit *die;* [voice, music, light, colour] Gedämpftheit *die*.

**soft return** *n* COMPUT weicher Zeilenumbruch.

**soft sell** *n inf* Verkauf *der* durch sanfte Überredung.

**soft-spoken** *adj* [person] mit sanfter Stimme.

**soft toy** *n* Stofftier *das*.

**software** ['sɒftweə<sup>r</sup>] *n* COMPUT Software *die*.

**software package** *n* COMPUT Softwarepaket *das*.

**softwood** ['spftwud] n Weichholz das.

**softy** ['spftɪ] (pl -ies) n inf - 1. pej [weak person] Weichling der - 2. [sensitive person] Softie der.

**soggy** ['spgɪ] (compar -ier; superl -iest) adj durchnässt; [ground] matschig.

**soil** [sɔɪl] n - 1. [earth] Erde die; [ground & GEOGR] Boden der - 2. fig [territory] Boden der ⟨⟩ vt [dirty] beschmutzen.

**soiled** [sɔɪld] adj schmutzig.

**solace** ['spləs] n Trost der.

**solar** ['səʊlər] adj Sonnen-.

**solar energy** n Solarenergie die.

**solarium** [sə'leərɪəm] (pl -riums OR -ria [-rɪəl]) n Solarium das.

**solar panel** n [on roof] Sonnenkollektor der; [of satellite] Sonnensegel das.

**solar plexus** [-'pleksəs] n Solarplexus der.

**solar system** n Sonnensystem das.

**sold** [səʊld] pt & pp ⊳ sell.

**solder** ['səʊldər] n (U) TECH Lot das ⟨⟩ vt löten.

**soldering iron** ['səʊldərɪŋ-] n Lötkolben der.

**soldier** ['səʊldʒər] n Soldat der.
◆ **soldier on** vi Br verbissen weitermachen.

**sold out** adj ausverkauft.

**sole** [səʊl] (pl sense 2 only inv OR -s) adj - 1. [only] einzig - 2. [exclusive] alleinig ⟨⟩ n - 1. [of foot] Sohle die - 2. [fish] Seezunge die.

**solely** ['səʊllɪ] adv (einzig und) allein.

**solemn** ['spləm] adj - 1. [person, face, voice] ernst - 2. [agreement, promise, occasion, music] feierlich.

**solemnly** ['spləmlɪ] adv - 1. [speak, behave] ernsthaft - 2. [agree, promise] feierlich.

**sole trader** n Br COMM selbstständiger Händler.

**solicit** [sə'lɪsɪt] vt fml [request] werben um ⟨⟩ vi [prostitute] sich anbieten.

**solicitor** [sə'lɪsɪtər] n Br Rechtsanwalt der, -anwältin die.

**solicitous** [sə'lɪsɪtəs] adj - 1. [caring] besorgt - 2. [anxious]: ~ of OR for sthg um etw bemüht.

**solid** ['splɪd] adj - 1. [not liquid or gas] fest - 2. [gold, silver, wood] massiv; ~ tyre Vollgummireifen der - 3. [building, base, relationship, person] solide - 4. [support] einmütig; [evidence] handfest; [majority] solide - 5. [line] ununterbrochen, durchgängig; **two hours** ~, **two** ~ **hours** zwei volle Stunden ⟨⟩ adv: **to be packed** ~ brechend voll sein ⟨⟩ n [not liquid or gas] fester Stoff.
◆ **solids** npl [food] feste Nahrung.

**solidarity** [,splɪ'dærətɪ] n Solidarität die.

**solid fuel** n fester Brennstoff.

**solidify** [sə'lɪdɪfaɪ] (pt & pp -ied) vi fest werden.

**solidly** ['splɪdlɪ] adv - 1. [sturdily] massiv, solide

**soliloquy** [sə'lɪləkwɪ] (pl -ies) n LITERATURE Monolog der.

**solitaire** [,splɪ'teər] n - 1. [jewel] Solitär der - 2. [board game] Solitaire das - 3. Am [card game] Patience die.

**solitary** ['splɪtrɪ] adj - 1. [involving one person, single] einzeln - 2. [enjoying solitude] einsam; **I've always been rather** ~ ich war immer schon eher ein Einzelgänger.

**solitary confinement** n Einzelhaft die.

**solitude** ['splɪtjuːd] n Einsamkeit die.

**solo** ['səʊləʊ] (pl -s) adj - 1. MUS Solo- - 2. [attempt, flight] Allein- ⟨⟩ n MUS Solo das ⟨⟩ adv - 1. MUS solo - 2. [fly, climb] allein.

**soloist** ['səʊləʊɪst] n Solist der, -in die.

**solstice** ['splstɪs] n Sonnenwende die.

**soluble** ['spljʊbl] adj - 1. [substance] löslich - 2. [problem] lösbar.

**solution** [sə'luːʃn] n Lösung die; **a** ~ **to sthg** eine Lösung für etw.

**solve** [splv] vt lösen.

**solvency** ['splvənsɪ] n FIN Solvenz die.

**solvent** ['splvənt] adj FIN solvent ⟨⟩ n [substance] Lösungsmittel das.

**solvent abuse** n Schnüffeln das (von Lösungsmitteln).

**Somali** [sə'mɑːlɪ] adj somalisch ⟨⟩ n - 1. [person] Somali der, die - 2. [language] Somali das.

**Somalia** [sə'mɑːlɪə] n Somalia nt.

**sombre** Br, **somber** Am ['spmbər] adj düster.

**some** [sʌm] adj - 1. [a certain amount of] etwas; ~ **money** etwas Geld; ~ **meat** ein bisschen Fleisch; **I bought** ~ **coffee** ich habe Kaffee gekauft; **would you like** ~ **(more) tea?** möchtest du (noch) Tee?; **I had** ~ **difficulty getting here** es war ziemlich schwierig für mich, hierher zu kommen; **for** ~ **time** seit einiger Zeit; [in future] für einige Zeit - 2. [a certain number of] einige; ~ **people** einige Leute; **I bought** ~ **sweets** ich habe Bonbons gekauft; **can I have** ~ **sweets?** kann ich Bonbons haben?; **I've known her for** ~ **years** ich kenne sie schon seit einigen Jahren - 3. (contrastive use) [certain] manche; ~ **jobs are better paid than others** manche Jobs sind besser bezahlt als andere - 4. [in imprecise statements] irgendein, -e; **she married** ~ **Italian (or other)** sie hat irgend so einen Italiener geheiratet; **there must be** ~ **mistake** das muss ein Irrtum sein - 5. inf [very good]: **that was** ~ **welcome** das war vielleicht ein toller Empfang - 6. inf iron [not very good]: ~ **welcome that was!** das war vielleicht ein enttäuschender Empfang!; ~ **friend you are!** du bist mir vielleicht ein Freund! ⟨⟩ pron - 1. [a certain amount] etwas;

I've read ~ of the article ich habe einen Teil des Artikels gelesen; ~ of it is mine ein Teil davon gehört mir; **can I have ~?** [milk] kann ich ein bisschen haben?; [coffee] kann ich einen haben?; [money] kann ich welches haben?; **take ~ bread - I've already got ~** nimm dir Brot - ich habe schon - **2.** [a certain number] einige; **can I have ~?** [books, pens, potatoes *etc*] kann ich welche haben?; **have ~ strawberries - I've already got ~** nimm dir Erdbeeren - ich habe schon welche; ~ **(of them) left early** einige (von ihnen) gingen vorher - **3.** [some people] manche; ~ **say he lied** manche sagen, dass er gelogen hat <> *adv* ungefähr; **there were ~ 7,000 people there** es waren ungefähr *OR* um die 7 000 Leute da.

**somebody** ['sʌmbədɪ] *pron* jemand; **ask ~ else** frag jemand anders; ~ **or other** irgend jemand; **he really thinks he's ~** [important person] er glaubt wirklich, er ist wer.

**someday** ['sʌmdeɪ] *adv* eines Tages.

**somehow** ['sʌmhaʊ], **someway** *Am* ['sʌmweɪ] *adv* irgendwie.

**someone** ['sʌmwʌn] *pron* = somebody.

**someplace** *adv Am* = somewhere.

**somersault** ['sʌməsɔːlt] *n* Purzelbaum *der;* sport Salto *der* <> *vi* einen Purzelbaum schlagen; sport einen Salto machen.

**something** ['sʌmθɪŋ] *pron* etwas; **I saw ~ moving** ich sah, wie sich etwas bewegte; ~ **nice** etwas Schönes; **there's ~ about him I don't like** er hat etwas an sich, das mir nicht gefällt; ~ **else** sonst etwas; ~ **or other** irgend etwas; **or ~** *inf* oder so etwas; **well, at least that's ~** nun, das ist immerhin etwas; **there's ~ in what you say** es ist schon etwas Wahres an dem, was du sagst; **it's really ~!** es ist ganz toll!; **it came as ~ of a surprise to me** es war schon irgendwie eine Überraschung für mich <> *adv* [in approximations] ~ **like/in the region of** ungefähr; **it looks ~ like a rose** es sieht so ähnlich wie eine Rose aus.

**sometime** ['sʌmtaɪm] *adj* ehemalig <> *adv* irgendwann.

**sometimes** ['sʌmtaɪmz] *adv* manchmal.

**someway** *adv Am* = somehow.

**somewhat** ['sʌmwɒt] *adv* ziemlich.

**somewhere** *Br* ['sʌmweə'], **someplace** *Am* ['sʌmpleɪs] *adv* - **1.** [gen - with verbs of position] irgendwo; [ - with verbs of motion] irgendwohin; ~ **else** irgendwo anders/irgendwo anders-hin; ~ **or other** irgendwo/irgendwohin - **2.** [in approximations] ungefähr; ~ **around** *OR* **in the region of 50** ungefähr 50 - **3.** *phr:* **to be getting ~** Fortschritte machen.

**son** [sʌn] *n* Sohn *der.*

**sonar** ['səʊnɑː'] *n* Sonar *das.*

**sonata** [sə'nɑːtə] *n* Sonate *die.*

**song** [sɒŋ] *n* Lied *das;* [of bird] Gesang *der;* **to**

burst into ~ ein Lied anstimmen; **for a** ~ [cheaply] für einen Apfel und ein Ei; **to make a ~ and dance about sthg** *inf* ein Theater um etw machen.

**songbook** ['sɒŋbʊk] *n* Liederbuch *das.*

**sonic** ['sɒnɪk] *adj* Schall-.

**sonic boom** *n* Überschallknall *der.*

**son-in-law** (*pl* sons-in-law *OR* son-in-laws) *n* Schwiegersohn *der.*

**sonnet** ['sɒnɪt] *n* Sonett *das.*

**soon** [suːn] *adv* - **1.** [in a short time] bald; ~ **after** *OR* **afterwards** kurz danach - **2.** [early]: **how ~ can you be ready?** wie schnell kannst du fertig sein?; **too** ~ zu früh; **not a minute too** ~ keine Minute zu früh; **as ~ as** sobald; **as ~ as possible** so bald wie möglich - **3.** *phr:* **I'd just as ~ ...** ich würde ebenso gern ...

**sooner** ['suːnə'] *adv* - **1.** [earlier] früher; **no ~ ... than ... kaum ... als** (auch schon) ...; ~ **or later** früher oder später; **the ~ the better** je früher, desto besser - **2.** [expressing preference] lieber.

**soot** [sʊt] *n* Ruß *der.*

**soothe** [suːð] *vt* - **1.** [pain] lindern - **2.** [person, fear] beruhigen.

**soothing** ['suːðɪŋ] *adj* - **1.** [pain-relieving] schmerzlindernd - **2.** [calming] beruhigend.

**sooty** ['sʊtɪ] (*compar* -ier; *superl* -iest) *adj* rußig.

**sop** [sɒp] *n pej:* ~ **(to sb/sthg)** Zugeständnis *das* (an jn/etw).

**sophisticated** [sə'fɪstɪkeɪtɪd] *adj* - **1.** [stylish] hochelegant - **2.** [intelligent] kultiviert - **3.** [complicated] hoch entwickelt.

**sophistication** [sə,fɪstɪ'keɪʃn] *n* (*U*) - **1.** [stylishness] große Eleganz - **2.** [intelligence] Kultiviertheit *die* - **3.** [complexity] hoher Entwicklungsgrad.

**sophomore** ['sɒfəmɔː'] *n Am* Student *der,* -in *die* im zweiten Studienjahr.

**soporific** [,sɒpə'rɪfɪk] *adj* einschläfernd.

**sopping** ['sɒpɪŋ] *adj:* ~ **(wet)** klatschnass.

**soppy** ['sɒpɪ] (*compar* -ier; *superl* -iest) *adj inf pej* rührselig.

**soprano** [sə'prɑːnəʊ] (*pl* -s) *n* - **1.** [person] Sopranistin *die* - **2.** [voice] Sopran *der.*

**sorbet** ['sɔːbeɪ] *n* Sorbet *das.*

**sorcerer** ['sɔːsərə'] *n* Zauberer *der.*

**sordid** ['sɔːdɪd] *adj* [desires, thoughts, past] schmutzig.

**sore** [sɔː'] *adj* - **1.** [painful] wund, entzündet; **to have a ~ throat/head** Halsschmerzen/ Kopfschmerzen haben - **2.** *Am inf* [angry] sauer <> *n* MED wunde *OR* entzündete Stelle.

**sorority** [sə'rɒrɪtɪ] (*pl* -ies) *n Am* Studentinnenverbindung *die.*

**sorrel** ['sɒrəl] *n* Sauerampfer *der.*

**sorrow** ['sɒrəʊ] *n* - **1.** [feeling of sadness] Kummer *der* - **2.** [cause of sadness] Leid *das*.

**sorrowful** ['sɒrəʊfʊl] *adj* bekümmert, sorgenvoll.

**sorry** ['sɒrɪ] (*compar* -**ier;** *superl* -**iest**) *adj* - **1.** [expressing apology]: **I'm ~** es tut mir leid; **I'm ~ about the mess** entschuldige bitte die Unordnung; **I'm ~ for what I did** was ich getan habe, tut mir leid; **I'm ~ to bother you, but could you ...** Verzeihung, könnten Sie ... - **2.** [expressing disappointment]: **I'm ~ you couldn't come** schade, dass du nicht kommen konntest; **we were ~ about his resignation** wir bedauern seinen Rücktritt; **we're ~ to see you go** wir finden es schade, dass du gehst - **3.** [expressing regret]: **I'm ~ I ever came here** ich bereue, jemals hierhergekommen zu sein; **I'm ~ to have to announce ...** ich muss Ihnen leider mitteilen ... - **4.** [expressing sympathy]: **to be** OR **feel ~ for sb** jn bedauern OR bemitleiden; **to be** OR **feel ~ for o.s.** sich selbst bedauern OR bemitleiden - **5.** [expressing polite disagreement]: **I'm ~, but ...** Entschuldigung OR Verzeihung, aber ... - **6.** [poor, pitiable] bedauernswert; **in a ~ state** in einem erbärmlichen Zustand ⬦ *excl* - **1.** [expressing apology] Entschuldigung!, Verzeihung! - **2.** [asking for repetition] wie bitte? - **3.** [to correct o.s.] ich meine (natürlich).

**sort** [sɔːt] *n* - **1.** [kind, type] Sorte *die;* **what ~ of car have you got?** was für ein Auto hast du?; **a ~ of** eine Art (von) - **2.** [person]: **a good ~** ein feiner Kerl ⬦ *vt* [classify, separate] sortieren.

⬤ **sorts** *npl*: **she's a singer of ~s** sie hält sich für eine Sängerin; **to be out of ~s** [in health] nicht ganz fit sein; [in mood] schlecht gelaunt sein.

⬤ **sort of** *adv* [rather] irgendwie.

⬤ **sort out** *vt sep* - **1.** [into groups] sortieren - **2.** [tidy up - papers, clothes] wegräumen; [ - room] aufräumen; [ - affairs, finances] regeln; **she needs to ~ out her life** sie muss ihr Leben in Ordnung bringen - **3.** [work out, arrange] sich (D) überlegen.

**sortie** ['sɔːtiː] *n* [MIL - by troops] Ausfall *der;* [ - by aircraft] Feindflug *der* eines einzelnen Flugzeugs.

**sorting office** ['sɔːtɪŋ-] *n* Verteilerpostamt *das*.

**SOS** (*abbr of* save our souls) *n* SOS *das*.

**so-so** *adj* & *adv inf* so la la.

**soufflé** ['suːfleɪ] *n* Soufflee *das*.

**sought** [sɔːt] *pt* & *pp* ⊏➤ **seek.**

**sought-after** *adj* gesucht.

**soul** [səʊl] *n* - **1.** [gen] Seele *die* - **2.** [perfect example] Inbegriff *der;* **I'm the ~ of discretion** ich bin die Verschwiegenheit in Person - **3.** [music] Soul *der*.

**soul-destroying** [-dɪˌstrɔɪɪŋ] *adj* [boring] geisttötend; [discouraging] sehr entmutigend.

**soul food** *n* Am Soul Food *das, die traditionelle Küche der Afroamerikaner.*

**soulful** ['səʊlfʊl] *adj* gefühlvoll.

**soulless** ['səʊllɪs] *adj* seelenlos.

**soul mate** *n* Seelenverwandte *der, die*.

**soul music** *n* Soulmusik *die*.

**soul-searching** *n* Selbstreflektion *die*.

**sound** [saʊnd] *adj* - **1.** [mind, body] gesund - **2.** [building, structure] intakt - **3.** [advice, investment] vernünftig - **4.** [thorough] ordentlich ⬦ *adv*: **to be ~ asleep** tief OR fest schlafen ⬦ *n* - **1.** [noise] Geräusch *das;* [of music, voice, instrument] Klang *der;* [of person, animal] Laut *der* - **2.** (U) PHYS Schall *der;* **the speed of ~** die Schallgeschwindigkeit - **3.** [volume] Lautstärke *die* - **4.** [impression, idea] Gedanke *der;* **I don't like the ~ of this new plan** der neue Plan behagt mir nicht; **by the ~ of it** allem Anschein nach ⬦ *vt* ertönen lassen; [alarm] auslösen; [bell] läuten; [horn] hupen ⬦ *vi* - **1.** [make a noise] ertönen; **to ~ like sthg** wie etw klingen - **2.** [seem] klingen, zu sein scheinen; **she ~s nice** sie scheint nett zu sein; **it ~s like a good investment** das hört sich nach einer guten Investition an.

⬤ **sound out** *vt sep*: **to ~ sb out** bei jm vorfühlen; [furtively] jn auslorchen.

**sound barrier** *n* Schallmauer *die*.

**sound bite** *n* prägnantes Zitat.

**sound card** *n* COMPUT Soundkarte *die*.

**sound effects** *npl* Klangeffekte *pl*.

**sounding** ['saʊndɪŋ] *n* - **1.** NAUT [measurement] Loten *das* - **2.** *fig* [investigation] Sondierung *die*.

**sounding board** *n fig* [person] Sprachrohr *das*.

**soundly** ['saʊndlɪ] *adv* - **1.** [beat, defeat] vernichtend - **2.** [sleep] tief, fest.

**soundness** ['saʊndnɪs] *n* [reliability - of argument] Stichhaltigkeit *die;* [ - of method] Zuverlässigkeit *die*.

**soundproof** ['saʊndpruːf] *adj* schalldicht.

**soundtrack** ['saʊndtræk] *n* Soundtrack *der*.

**sound wave** *n* Schallwelle *die*.

**soup** [suːp] *n* Suppe *die*.

⬤ **soup up** *vt sep inf* [car] frisieren, tunen.

**soup kitchen** *n* Volksküche *die*.

**soup plate** *n* Suppenteller *der*.

**soup spoon** *n* Suppenlöffel *der*.

**sour** ['saʊə<sup>r</sup>] *adj* sauer; **to go** OR **turn ~** [milk] sauer werden; [relationship] erkalten ⬦ *vt* [person] verbittern; [relationship] erkalten lassen ⬦ *vi* [person] verbittern; [relationship] erkalten.

**source** [sɔːs] *n* Quelle *die*.

**soured cream** ['saʊəd-] *n* saure Sahne.

S

**sour grapes** n etwas, dessen Wert man herunterspielt, weil man es nicht haben kann.

**sourness** ['sauənɪs] n (U) - **1.** [gen] Säure die - **2.** [ill humour] Bitterkeit die - **3.** [of relations] ruinierter Zustand.

**south** [sauθ] adj Süd-, südlich ◇ adv nach Süden, südwärts; ~ **of** südlich von; **in the** ~ **of England** im Süden Englands ◇ n - **1.** [direction] Süden der - **2.** [region]: **the** ~ der Süden.

**South Africa** n Südafrika nt; **the Republic of** ~ die Republik Südafrika.

**South America** n Südamerika nt.

**southbound** ['sauθbaund] adj in südlicher Richtung, in Richtung Süden.

**southeast** [ˌsauθ'iːst] adj südöstlich, Südost- ◇ adv südostwärts, nach Südosten; ~ **of** südöstlich von ◇ n [direction] Südosten der.

**Southeast Asia** n Südostasien das.

**southeasterly** [ˌsauθ'iːstəlɪ] adj [direction, area] südöstlich; [wind] Südost-.

**southerly** ['sʌðəlɪ] adj - **1.** [direction] südlich; [area] im Süden - **2.** [wind] Süd-.

**southern** ['sʌðən] adj [region, dialect] südlich; [Europe] Süd-.

**Southern Africa** n südliches Afrika.

**Southerner** ['sʌðənəʳ] n Bewohner der, -in die des Südens

**South Korea** n Südkorea nt.

**South Korean** adj südkoreanisch ◇ n Südkoreaner der, -in die.

**South Pole** n: **the** ~ der Südpol.

**southward** ['sauθwəd] adj südlich, nach Süden ◇ adv = **southwards**.

**southwards** ['sauθwədz] adv nach Süden.

**southwest** [ˌsauθ'west] adj südwestlich, Südwest- ◇ adv südwestwärts, nach Südwesten; ~ **of** südwestlich von ◇ n Südwesten der.

**southwesterly** [ˌsauθ'westəlɪ] adj [direction] südwestlich; [area] im Südwesten; [wind] Südwest-.

**southwestern** [ˌsauθ'westən] adj südwestlich; ~ **Scotland** Südwestschottland.

**souvenir** [ˌsuːvə'nɪəʳ] n Souvenir das, Andenken das.

**sou'wester** [sau'westəʳ] n [hat] Südwester der.

**sovereign** ['sɒvrɪn] adj [state, territory] souverän ◇ n - **1.** [ruler] Herrscher der, -in die - **2.** [coin] Sovereign der.

**sovereignty** ['sɒvrɪntɪ] n [supreme power] Staatshoheit die.

**soviet** ['sauvɪət] n Sowjet der.
➤ **Soviet** adj sowjetisch ◇ n [person] Sowjetbürger der, -in die.

**Soviet Union** n: **the (former)** ~ die (ehemalige) Sowjetunion.

**sow**[1] [sau] (pt -ed; pp sown OR -ed) vt - **1.** [seeds] säen, auslsäen - **2.** fig [doubt] säen.

**sow**[2] [sau] n [pig] Sau die.

**sown** [saun] pp ▷ **sow**[1].

**sox** [sɒks] npl Am = **socks**.

**soya** ['sɔɪə] n Soja das.

**soy(a) bean** ['sɔɪ(ə)-] n Sojabohne die.

**soy sauce** [sɔɪ-] n Sojasoße die.

**sozzled** ['sɒzld] adj Br inf besoffen.

**spa** [spɑː] n [spring] Mineralquelle die; [place] Bad das.

**space** [speɪs] n - **1.** (U) [room] Raum der; **there isn't enough** ~ **in here** hier ist nicht genug Platz; **I need more** ~, **I feel too confined** ich brauche mehr Raum, ich fühle mich zu beengt - **2.** [outer space] Weltraum der; **to stare into** ~ ins Leere starren OR blicken - **3.** [gap] Zwischenraum der - **4.** [area] Fläche die, Raum der - **5.** TYPO Leerzeichen das - **6.** [period of time] Zeitraum der; **within the** ~ **of ten minutes** innerhalb von zehn Minuten; **in a short** ~ **of time** [in future] in Kürze; [in past] nach kurzer Zeit - **7.** [seat, place] Platz der ◇ comp Weltraum- ◇ vt in regelmäßigen Abständen anlordnen.
➤ **space out** vt sep [arrange] in regelmäßigen Abständen anlordnen.

**space age** n: **the** ~ das Raumfahrtzeitalter.
➤ **space-age** adj inf futuristisch.

**space bar** n Leertaste die.

**space capsule** n Raumkapsel die.

**spacecraft** ['speɪskrɑːft] (pl inv) n Raumschiff das.

**spaceman** ['speɪsmæn] (pl -men [-men]) n [astronaut] Raumfahrer der.

**space probe** n Raumsonde die.

**spaceship** ['speɪsʃɪp] n Raumschiff das.

**space shuttle** n Spaceshuttle das.

**space station** n Raumstation die.

**spacesuit** ['speɪssuːt] n Raumanzug der.

**spacewoman** ['speɪsˌwumən] (pl -women [-ˌwɪmɪn]) n Raumfahrerin die.

**spacing** ['speɪsɪŋ] n TYPO Zeilenabstand der.

**spacious** ['speɪʃəs] adj geräumig.

**spade** [speɪd] n - **1.** [tool] Spaten der - **2.** [playing card] Pik das.
➤ **spades** npl Pik das; **the jack of** ~ **s** Pik Bube.

**spadework** ['speɪdwɜːk] n (U) inf (mühsame) Vorarbeit, Kleinarbeit die.

**spaghetti** [spə'getɪ] n (U) Spaghetti pl.

**Spain** [speɪn] n Spanien nt.

**spam** n (U) COMPUT Reklame-E-Mails pl ◇ vt Reklame-E-Mails verschicken (+ D).

**span** [spæn] (pt & pp **-ned**; cont **-ning**) pt ▷
**spin** ◇ n - **1.** [in time] Zeitraum der, Zeitspanne die - **2.** [range] Reihe die - **3.** [of hands, arms, wings, bridge] Spannweite die ◇ vt - **1.** [encompass] umfassen - **2.** [cross] überspannen.

**spandex** ['spændeks] n Spandex das.

**spangled** ['spæŋgld] adj literary: ~ with sthg mit etw übersät.

**Spaniard** ['spænjəd] n Spanier der, -in die.

**spaniel** ['spænjəl] n Spaniel der.

**Spanish** ['spænɪʃ] adj spanisch ◇ n [language] Spanisch(e) das ◇ npl: the ~ die Spanier pl.

**spank** [spæŋk] n Klaps der auf den Hintern ◇ vt: to ~ sb [once] jm einen Klaps auf den Hintern geben; [several times] jm den Hintern versohlen.

**spanner** ['spænəʳ] n Schraubenschlüssel der.

**spar** [spɑːʳ] (pt & pp **-red**; cont **-ring**) vi - **1.** BOXING sparren - **2.** [verbally]: to ~ (with sb) sich (mit jm) ein Wortgefecht liefern.

**spare** [speəʳ] adj - **1.** [surplus] zusätzlich, Ersatz-; have you got a ~ pencil? hast du einen Bleistift übrig? - **2.** [free] frei ◇ n inf - **1.** [wheel] Ersatzrad das - **2.** [part] Ersatzteil das ◇ vt - **1.** [make available] entbehren können, übrig haben; can you ~ five minutes? hast du (mal) fünf Minuten Zeit?; to ~ [extra] übrig, zur Verfügung; we had an hour to ~ wir hatten (noch) eine Stunde Zeit - **2.** [not harm] verschonen - **3.** [effort, trouble] scheuen; to ~ no expense keine Kosten scheuen - **4.** [save, protect from]: to ~ sb sthg jm etw ersparen.

**spare part** n AUT Ersatzteil das.

**spare room** n Gästezimmer das.

**spare time** n Freizeit die.

**spare tyre** n - **1.** AUT Ersatzreifen der - **2.** hum [roll of fat] Rettungsring der, Speckrolle die.

**spare wheel** n Ersatzrad das.

**sparing** ['speərɪŋ] adj: to be ~ with sthg mit etw sparsam sein.

**sparingly** ['speərɪŋlɪ] adv sparsam.

**spark** [spɑːk] n - **1.** [from fire, electricity] Funke der - **2.** fig [of understanding, interest, humour] Funken der ◇ vt [trigger] auslösen.

**sparkle** ['spɑːkl] n [of jewel, frost, stars, sea] Glitzern das; [of eyes] Funkeln das ◇ vi - **1.** [jewel, frost, stars, sea] glitzern; [eyes] funkeln - **2.** [person, in performance] glänzen.

**sparkler** ['spɑːkləʳ] n [firework] Wunderkerze die.

**sparkling** ['spɑːklɪŋ] adj - **1.** [mineral water] sprudelnd - **2.** [wit] sprühend.

**sparkling wine** n Schaumwein der, Sekt der.

**spark plug** n Zündkerze die.

**sparrow** ['spærəʊ] n Spatz der, Sperling der.

**sparse** ['spɑːs] adj spärlich; [hair] schütter, dünn.

**spartan** ['spɑːtn] adj spartanisch.

**spasm** ['spæzml] n - **1.** MED [muscular contraction] Krampf der - **2.** [fit] Anfall der.

**spasmodic** [spæz'mɒdɪk] adj unregelmäßig, schubweise.

**spastic** ['spæstɪk] MED adj spastisch ◇ n Spastiker der, -in die.

**spat** [spæt] pt & pp ▷ spit.

**spate** [speɪt] n Flut die.

**spatial** ['speɪʃl] adj fml räumlich.

**spatter** ['spætəʳ] vt bespritzen ◇ vi spritzen.

**spatula** ['spætjʊlə] n - **1.** CULIN Spachtel der - **2.** MED Spatel der.

**spawn** [spɔːn] n Laich der ◇ vt fig [produce] erzeugen ◇ vi ZOOL laichen.

**spay** [speɪ] vt sterilisieren.

**SPCA** (abbr of **Society for the Prevention of Cruelty to Animals**) n britischer Tierschutzverein.

**SPCC** (abbr of **Society for the Prevention of Cruelty to Children**) n britischer Kinderschutzbund.

**speak** [spiːk] (pt spoke; pp spoken) vt sprechen; to ~ ill of sb schlecht von jm or über jn sprechen ◇ vi - **1.** [say words] sprechen; to ~ to OR with sb mit jm sprechen OR reden; to ~ to sb about sthg mit jm über etw (A) sprechen OR reden; to ~ about sb/sthg über jn/etw sprechen OR reden; nobody to ~ of niemand Besonderes - **2.** [make a speech] sprechen, reden; to ~ on sthg über etw (A) sprechen - **3.** [in giving an opinion]: generally ~ing im Allgemeinen, im Großen und Ganzen; personally ~ing meiner Ansicht nach; ~ing as a foreigner I doubt ... ich als Ausländer bezweifle ...; ~ing of [on the subject of] apropos.

◆ **so to speak** adv sozusagen.

◆ **speak for** vt fus [represent] sprechen für; it ~s for itself es spricht für sich selbst; ~ for yourself! du vielleicht – ich nicht!

◆ **speak out** vi offen seine Meinung sagen; to ~ out against sb/sthg sich gegen jn/etw auslsprechen.

◆ **speak up** vi - **1.** [say something] sprechen; to ~ up for sb/sthg für jn/etw einltreten - **2.** [speak louder] lauter sprechen.

**speaker** ['spiːkəʳ] n - **1.** [person talking] Sprecher der, -in die - **2.** [in lecture] Redner der, -in die - **3.** [of a language]: a German ~ ein Sprecher, eine Sprecherin des Deutschen - **4.** [loudspeaker, in hi-fi] Lautsprecher der.

◆ **Speaker** n Br [in House of Commons] Präsident der, -in die des Unterhauses.

**speaking** ['spiːkɪŋ] n Sprechen das, Reden das.

**speaking clock** n Br Zeitansage die.

**spear** [spɪəʳ] n Speer der <> vt (mit dem Speer) durchlbohren.

**spearhead** ['spɪəhed] n Speerspitze die; MIL Angriffsspitze die <> vt anlführen.

**spec** [spek] n Br inf: on ~ aufs Geratewohl.

**special** ['speʃl] adj - **1.** [specific, out of the ordinary] besondere, -r, -s, spezielle, -r, -s - **2.** [valued]: to be ~ to sb jm viel bedeuten <> n - **1.** [on menu] Spezialität die des Tages - **2.** [on TV] Sondersendung die, Special das - **3.** [train] Sonderzug der.

**special agent** n Spezialagent der, -in die.

**special constable** n Br Hilfspolizist der, -in die.

**special correspondent** n Sonderkorrespondent der, -in die.

**special delivery** n Eilzustellung die.

**special effects** npl Spezialeffekte pl; [in film] Special Effects pl.

**specialist** ['speʃəlɪst] adj Fach- <> n [expert] Spezialist der, -in die; [doctor] Facharzt der, -ärztin die.

**speciality** [ˌspeʃɪ'ælətɪ] (pl -ies), **specialty** Am ['speʃltɪ] (pl -ies) n - **1.** [field of knowledge] Spezialgebiet das - **2.** [service, product] Spezialität die.

**specialize, -ise** ['speʃəlaɪz] vi: to ~ (in sthg) sich (auf etw (A)) spezialisieren; [have special qualifications] (auf etw (A)) spezialisiert sein.

**specially** ['speʃəlɪ] adv - **1.** [on purpose, specifically] speziell - **2.** [really] besonders; **do you want to buy it? - not ~** möchtest du es kaufen? - nicht unbedingt.

**special offer** n Sonderangebot das.

**special school** n Sonderschule die.

**specialty** n Am = speciality.

**species** ['spi:ʃi:z] (pl inv) n Spezies die, Art die.

**specific** [spə'sɪfɪk] adj bestimmt, spezifisch; to be ~ to sb/sthg jm/etw eigen sein.
➤ **specifics** npl [details] Einzelheiten die.

**specifically** [spə'sɪfɪklɪ] adv - **1.** [explicitly] ausdrücklich - **2.** [particularly, precisely] im Besonderen.

**specification** [ˌspesɪfɪ'keɪʃn] ➤ **specifications** npl TECH technische Daten pl.

**specify** ['spesɪfaɪ] (pt & pp -ied) vt spezifizieren, herauslstellen; to ~ that ... deutlich machen, dass ..., herauslstellen, dass....

**specimen** ['spesɪmən] n - **1.** [example] Exemplar das - **2.** [sample] Probe die.

**specimen copy** n Probeexemplar das; [of book] Probedruck der.

**specimen signature** n Vergleichsunterschrift die.

**speck** [spek] n - **1.** [small stain] Fleck der; [of paint, mud] Spritzer der - **2.** [small particle - of dust] Körnchen das; [ - of soot] Flocke die.

**speckled** ['spekld] adj: ~ (with sthg) gesprenkelt (mit etw).

**specs** [speks] npl inf Brille die.

**spectacle** ['spektəkl] n - **1.** [sight] Anblick der; to make a ~ of o.s. sich unmöglich benehmen - **2.** [event] Spektakel das.
➤ **spectacles** npl Br [glasses] Brille die.

**spectacular** [spek'tækjʊləʳ] adj spektakulär <> n Spektakel das.

**spectate** [spek'teɪt] vi zulschauen.

**spectator** [spek'teɪtəʳ] n Zuschauer der, -in die.

**spectator sport** n Publikumssport der.

**spectre** Br, **specter** Am ['spektəʳ] n - **1.** fml [ghost] Gespenst das - **2.** fig [frightening prospect] Schreckgespenst das.

**spectrum** ['spektrəm] (pl -tra [-trə]) n PHYSICS & fig Spektrum das.

**speculate** ['spekjʊleɪt] vt: to ~ that ... vermuten, dass ... <> vi spekulieren.

**speculation** [ˌspekjʊ'leɪʃn] n Spekulation die.

**speculative** ['spekjʊlətɪv] adj - **1.** [based on guesswork] spekulativ - **2.** [contemplative] grüblerisch - **3.** FIN Spekulations-.

**speculator** ['spekjʊleɪtəʳ] n FIN Spekulant der, -in die.

**sped** [sped] pt & pp ▷ **speed.**

**speech** [spi:tʃ] n - **1.** (U) [ability to speak, dialect] Sprache die - **2.** [formal talk] Rede die; **to give OR make a ~ (on sthg)** eine Rede (über etw (A)) halten; **to give OR make a ~ to sb** eine Rede vor jm halten - **3.** THEATRE Text der - **4.** [manner of speaking] Sprechweise die; **his ~ is clear and precise** er spricht klar und deutlich - **5.** GRAMM: direct/indirect ~ direkte/indirekte Rede.

**speech day** n Br jährliche Schulfeier.

**speech impediment** n Sprachstörung die.

**speechless** ['spi:tʃlɪs] adj: to be ~ (with sthg) (vor etw (D)) sprachlos sein.

**speech processing** n COMPUT Sprachverarbeitung die.

**speech therapist** n Sprachtherapeut der, -in die.

**speech therapy** n (U) Sprachtherapie die.

**speed** [spi:d] (pt & pp -ed OR sped) n - **1.** [pace, rapid rate] Geschwindigkeit die, Tempo das; ~ of light/sound Licht-/Schallgeschwindigkeit die; **at high/low** ~ mit hoher/ niedriger Geschwindigkeit; **at top OR full** ~ mit Höchstgeschwindigkeit - **2.** [gear] Gang der; **five-~ bike** Fahrrad das mit Fünfgangschaltung - **3.** PHOT [of film] Lichtempfindlichkeit die; **shutter** ~ Belichtungszeit die <> vi

- **1.** [move fast]: **to ~ along/away/by** entlang-/davon-/vorbeijagen - **2.** AUT [go too fast] zu schnell fahren.

◆ **speed up** vt sep beschleunigen; [person] auf Trab bringen ◇ vi [worker] sich beeilen; [driver, vehicle] beschleunigen; [production] sich erhöhen.

**speedboat** ['spi:dbəʊt] n Rennboot das.

**speeding** ['spi:dɪŋ] n zu schnelles Fahren; LAW Geschwindigkeitsüberschreitung die.

**speed limit** n Geschwindigkeitsbeschränkung die; **what's the ~ here?** wie schnell darf man hier fahren?

**speedo** ['spi:dəʊ] (pl -s) n Br inf Tacho der.

**speedometer** [spɪ'dɒmɪtəʳ] n Tachometer der OR das.

**speed trap** n Geschwindigkeitskontrolle die.

**speedway** ['spi:dweɪ] n - **1.** SPORT Speedwayrennen das - **2.** Am [road] Schnellstraße die.

**speedy** ['spi:dɪ] (compar -ier; superl -iest) adj schnell.

**spell** [spel] (Br pt & pp spelt OR -ed, Am pt & pp -ed) n - **1.** [period of time] Weile die; **with some sunny ~s** mit sonnigen Abschnitten; **for a ~** eine Weile - **2.** [enchantment] Zauber der; **to cast** OR **put a ~ on sb** jn verzaubern - **3.** [magic word] Zauberspruch der ◇ vt - **1.** [word, name] schreiben; [aloud] buchstabieren - **2.** fig [signify] bedeuten; [aloud] buchstabieren; **it ~s disaster** das bedeutet Unglück ◇ vi: **to be able to ~** fehlerfrei schreiben können.

◆ **spell out** vt sep - **1.** [read aloud] buchstabieren - **2.** [explain]: **to ~ sthg out (for** OR **to sb)** (jm) etw klarmachen.

**spellbound** ['spelbaʊnd] adj gebannt; **she can hold her readers ~** sie kann ihre Leser fesseln.

**spelling** ['spelɪŋ] n - **1.** [of a particular word] Schreibweise die - **2.** [ability to spell] Rechtschreibung die.

**spelt** [spelt] pt & pp Br ▷ spell.

**spend** [spend] (pt & pp spent) vt - **1.** [pay out] ausgeben; **she ~s a lot of money on clothes** sie gibt viel Geld für Kleidung aus - **2.** [time, life] verbringen; **he spent two hours shopping** er ist zwei Stunden lang einkaufen gewesen.

**spender** ['spendəʳ] n: **she is a big ~** bei ihr sitzt das Geld locker.

**spending** ['spendɪŋ] n (U) Ausgaben pl.

**spending money** n Taschengeld das.

**spending power** n Kaufkraft die.

**spendthrift** ['spendθrɪft] n Verschwender der, -in die.

**spent** [spent] pt & pp ▷ spend ◇ adj [fuel, matches] verbraucht; [ammunition] verschossen; [patience, energy] erschöpft.

**sperm** [spɜ:m] (pl inv OR -s) n - **1.** [cell] Spermium das - **2.** (U) [fluid] Sperma das.

**spermicidal cream** [ˌspɜ:mɪ'saɪdl-] n Spermizid das.

**sperm whale** n Pottwal der.

**spew** [spju:] vt [flames, lava] speien ◇ vi: **to ~ (out) from sthg** aus etw hervorschießen.

**sphere** [sfɪəʳ] n - **1.** [globe] Kugel die - **2.** [of interest, activity] Bereich der; **~ of influence** Einflussbereich der.

**spherical** ['sferɪkl] adj kugelförmig.

**sphinx** [sfɪŋks] (pl -es) n Sphinx die.

**spice** [spaɪs] n - **1.** CULIN Gewürz das - **2.** (U) fig [excitement] Würze die ◇ vt - **1.** CULIN: **to ~ sthg (with sthg)** etw (mit etw) würzen - **2.** fig [add excitement to]: **to ~ sthg (up)** etw auf|peppen.

**spick-and-span** [ˌspɪkən'spæn] adj blitzblank.

**spicy** ['spaɪsɪ] (compar -ier; superl -iest) adj pikant.

**spider** ['spaɪdəʳ] n Spinne die.

**spider's web, spiderweb** Am ['spaɪdəweb] n Spinnennetz das.

**spidery** ['spaɪdərɪ] adj [handwriting] krakelig.

**spiel** [ʃpi:l] n Gerede das.

**spike** [spaɪk] n - **1.** [on railings] Spitze die; [on shoe] Spike der - **2.** [on plant] Stachel der ◇ vt [drink] einen Schuss (Alkohol) zulgeben; **~d with whisky** mit einem Schuss Whisky.

◆ **spikes** npl Br Spikes pl.

**spiky** ['spaɪkɪ] (compar -ier; superl -iest) adj [plant, hair] stach(e)lig.

**spill** [spɪl] (Br pt & pp spilt OR -ed, Am pt & pp -ed) vt - **1.** [liquid, salt] verschütten - **2.** [blood] vergießen ◇ vi - **1.** [liquid, salt] sich ergießen - **2.** [crowd]: **to ~ out of/into sthg** aus etw/in etw (A) strömen.

**spillage** ['spɪlɪdʒ] n: (oil) **~** ausgelaufenes Öl; **measures to prevent (oil) ~s** Maßnahmen, um das Auslaufen von Öl zu verhindern.

**spilt** [spɪlt] pt & pp Br ▷ spill.

**S**

**spin** [spɪn] (pt span OR spun; pp spun; cont -ning) n - **1.** [turn] Drehung die - **2.** AERON Trudeln das; **the plane went into a ~** das Flugzeug begann zu trudeln - **3.** inf [in car] Spritztour die; **to go for a ~** eine Spritztour machen - **4.** SPORT [on ball] Effet der ◇ vt - **1.** [gen] schnell drehen - **2.** [in spin-dryer] schleudern; [coin in the air] hochlwerfen - **3.** [thread, cloth, wool] spinnen - **4.** SPORT [ball] einen Effet geben (+ D) ◇ vi - **1.** [gen] sich schnell drehen; [plane] trudeln - **2.** [feel dizzy]: **my head is ~ning** mir dreht sich alles - **3.** [spinner of thread] spinnen - **4.** [in spin-dryer] schleudern.

◆ **spin out** vt sep [story, explanation] in die Länge ziehen; [money, food] strecken.

**spina bifida** [ˌspaɪnəˈbɪfɪdə] n Wirbelsäulenspaltbildung die.

**spinach** [ˈspɪnɪdʒ] n Spinat der.

**spinal column** [ˈspaɪnl-] n Wirbelsäule die.

**spinal cord** [ˈspaɪnl-] n Rückenmark das.

**spindle** [ˈspɪndl] n - 1. [machine rod] Achse die - 2. [for spinning] Spindel die.

**spindly** [ˈspɪndlɪ] (compar -ier; superl -iest) adj [arms, legs] spindeldürr; [plant] zierlich.

**spin doctor** n pej Pressebeauftragter eines Politikers oder einer Partei, der Informationen an die Öffentlichkeit weitergibt, die die jeweiligen Handlungen in ein positives Licht rücken.

**spin-dry** vt Br schleudern.

**spin-dryer** n Br Wäscheschleuder die.

**spine** [spaɪn] n - 1. ANAT Wirbelsäule die - 2. [of book] Rücken der - 3. [of hedgehog, plant] Stachel der.

**spine-chilling** adj gruselig, schaurig.

**spineless** [ˈspaɪnlɪs] adj [feeble] ohne Rückgrat.

**spinner** [ˈspɪnəʳ] n [of thread] Spinner der, -in die.

**spinning** [ˈspɪnɪŋ] n [of thread] Spinnen das.

**spinning top** n Kreisel der.

**spin-off** n [by-product] Nebenprodukt das.

**spinster** [ˈspɪnstəʳ] n Unverheiratete die.

**spiral** [ˈspaɪərəl] (Br pt & pp -led; cont -ling, Am pt & pp -ed; cont -ing) adj spiralförmig <> n lit & fig Spirale die <> vi - 1. [move in spiral curve - staircase, path] sich (hoch) winden; [ - smoke] spiralförmig auf   steigen - 2. [increase rapidly] stark steigen - 3. [decrease rapidly]: **to ~ downwards** stark fallen.

**spiral staircase** n Wendeltreppe die.

**spire** [ˈspaɪəʳ] n Turmspitze die.

**spirit** [ˈspɪrɪt] n - 1. [soul, ghost] Geist der; **to be with sb in ~** in Gedanken bei jm sein - 2. (U) [courage] Mut der - 3. (U) [attitude] Geist der; [mood] Stimmung die; **fighting ~** Kampfgeist der; **~ of optimism** optimistische Stimmung; **to enter into the ~ of sthg** sich mit ganzem Herzen an etw (D) beteiligen - 4. [essence] Geist der, Sinn der <> vt: **to ~ sb into/out of sthg** jn in etw (A) /aus etw schleusen.

➡ **spirits** npl - 1. [mood] Stimmung die, Laune die; **to be in high/low ~s** guter/schlechter Laune sein - 2. [alcohol] Spirituosen pl.

**spirited** [ˈspɪrɪtɪd] adj [action, defence] beherzt; [performance] lebendig; [debate] lebhaft.

**spirit level** n Wasserwaage die.

**spiritual** [ˈspɪrɪtʃʊəl] adj - 1. [of the spirit] geistig, spirituell; **~ life** Seelenleben das - 2. [religious] geistlich.

**spiritualism** [ˈspɪrɪtʃʊəlɪzm] n Spiritismus der.

**spiritualist** [ˈspɪrɪtʃʊəlɪst] n Spiritist der, -in die.

**spit** [spɪt] (Br pt & pp spat; cont -ting, Am pt & pp spit; cont -ting) n - 1. [saliva] Spucke die - 2. [skewer] Spieß der <> vi [from mouth] spucken <> v impers Br [rain lightly] tröpfeln.

➡ **spit out** vt sep - 1. [food, liquid] aus   spucken - 2. [say angrily] aus   stoßen; **~ it out!** spucks aus!

**spite** [spaɪt] n (U) Bosheit die; **to do sthg out of OR from ~** etw aus reiner Bosheit tun <> vt ärgern.

➡ **in spite of** prep trotz (+ G); **to do sthg in ~ of o.s.** [unintentionally] etw tun, ohne es zu wollen.

**spiteful** [ˈspaɪtfʊl] adj boshaft.

**spitting image** [ˈspɪtɪŋ-] n: **to be the ~ of sb** jm wie aus dem Gesicht geschnitten sein.

**spittle** [ˈspɪtl] n Spucke die.

**splash** [splæʃ] n - 1. [sound] Platschen das; **it fell into the water with a ~** es platschte ins Wasser - 2. [small quantity of drink] Schuss der; [ - of paint, mud] Spritzer der - 3. [patch - of colour] Tupfen der; [ - of light] Fleck der <> vt - 1. [subj: person] bespritzen - 2. [subj: water] spritzen auf (+ A) - 3. [apply haphazardly] klatschen <> vi - 1. [person]: **to ~ about OR around** herum   spritzen - 2. [water, liquid]: **to ~ on/against sthg** an etw (A)/gegen etw klatschen.

➡ **splash down** vi [space shuttle] wassern.

➡ **splash out** inf vt sep & vi: **I ~ed out (£500) on a suit** ich habe mir (für 500 Pfund) einen Anzug geleistet.

**splash guard** n Am Schmutzfänger der.

**splay** [spleɪ] vt spreizen.

**spleen** [spliːn] n - 1. ANAT Milz die - 2. (U) fig [anger]: **to vent one's ~ on sb** seine Wut OR schlechte Laune an jm aus   lassen.

**splendid** [ˈsplendɪd] adj - 1. [very good] großartig - 2. [magnificent, beautiful] prachtvoll.

**splendidly** [ˈsplendɪdlɪ] adv - 1. [perform, write, behave] großartig - 2. [design, dress, entertain] prächtig.

**splendour** Br, **splendor** Am [ˈsplendəʳ] n - 1. [beauty, magnificence] Pracht die - 2. [magnificent feature]: **~s** Herrlichkeiten pl.

**splice** [splaɪs] vt [ropes] spleißen; [film, tape] zusammen   kleben.

**splint** [splɪnt] n Schiene die.

**splinter** [ˈsplɪntəʳ] n Splitter der <> vt: **to be ~ed** zersplittert sein <> vi [glass, bone, wood] splittern.

**splinter group** n Splittergruppe die.

**split** [splɪt] (pt & pp split; cont -ting) n - 1. [crack] Spalt der - 2. [tear] Riss der - 3. [division, schism]

Spaltung *die*, Riss *der* <> *vt* - **1.** [crack, divide] spalten; **the collision ~ the ship in two** bei dem Zusammenstoß zerbrach das Schiff in zwei Teile - **2.** [tear] zerreißen - **3.** [share] teilen; **we'll ~ the costs** wir werden uns die Kosten teilen; **to ~ the difference** sich in der Mitte treffen <> *vi* - **1.** [crack - wood, stone] sich spalten; [ - ship] auseinanderlbrechen - **2.** [tear - fabric] reißen; [ - seam, trousers] platzen; **the bag ~ open** die Tasche platzte auf - **3.** [divide] sich teilen - **4.** *Am inf* [leave] ablhauen.

➤ **splits** *npl*: **to do the ~s** einen Spagat machen.

➤ **split off** *vt sep* [snap off]: **to ~ sthg off (from sthg)** etw (von etw) ablbrechen <> *vi* - **1.** [snap off]: **to ~ off (from sthg)** ablbrechen (von etw) - **2.** [separate]: **to ~ off (from sb)** sich (von jm) trennen.

➤ **split up** *vt sep*: **to ~ sthg up (into sthg)** etw (in etw *(A)*) (auf l)teilen; **he intervened and ~ the boys up** er griff ein und trennte die Jungen <> *vi* sich trennen; **to ~ up with sb** sich von jm trennen.

**split ends** *npl* Spliss *der*.

**split-level** *adj* [building, room] mit verschiedenen Wohnebenen.

**split peas** *npl getrocknete halbe Erbsen*.

**split personality** *n* gespaltene Persönlichkeit.

**split screen** *n* geteilter Bildschirm.

**split second** *n* Bruchteil *der* einer Sekunde.

**splitting** ['splɪtɪŋ] *adj*: **~ headache** rasende Kopfschmerzen *pl*.

**splutter** ['splʌtəʳ] *vi* - **1.** [person speaking, engine] stottern - **2.** [fire, flames] zischen.

**spoil** [spɔɪl] (*pt* & *pp* **-ed** *OR* **spoilt**) *vt* - **1.** [ruin] verderben; **to ~ sb's fun** jm den Spaß verderben - **2.** [pamper] verwöhnen; **to be ~t for choice** die Qual der Wahl haben; **to ~ o.s.** sich verwöhnen.

➤ **spoils** *npl* Beute *die*.

**spoiled** [spɔɪld] *adj* = **spoilt**.

**spoiler** ['spɔɪləʳ] *n AUT* Spoiler *der*.

**spoilsport** ['spɔɪlspɔːt] *n* Spielverderber *der*, -in *die*.

**spoilt** [spɔɪlt] *pt* & *pp* ⊳ **spoil** <> *adj* - **1.** [child] verzogen - **2.** [food, dinner] verdorben.

**spoke** [spəʊk] *pt* ⊳ **speak** <> *n* Speiche *die*.

**spoken** ['spəʊkn] *pp* ⊳ **speak**.

**spokesman** ['spəʊksmən] (*pl* **-men** [-mən]) *n* Sprecher *der*.

**spokesperson** ['spəʊks,pɜːsn] (*pl* **spokespeople**) *n* Sprecher *der*, -in *die*.

**spokeswoman** ['spəʊks,wʊmən] (*pl* **-women** [-,wɪmɪn]) *n* Sprecherin *die*.

**sponge** [spʌndʒ] (*Br cont* **spongeing**, *Am cont* **sponging**) *n* - **1.** [for cleaning, washing] Schwamm *der* - **2.** [cake] Biskuitkuchen *der* <> *vt* [face] ablwischen; [wall, car] mit einem Schwamm ablwaschen <> *vi inf*: **to ~ off sb** jm auf der Tasche liegen.

**sponge bag** *n Br* Kulturbeutel *der*.

**sponge cake** *n* Biskuitkuchen *der*.

**sponger** ['spʌndʒəʳ] *n inf pej* Schmarotzer *der*, -in *die*.

**spongy** ['spʌndʒɪ] (*compar* **-ier**; *superl* **-iest**) *adj* [head, ground] locker; [material] schwammig.

**sponsor** ['spɒnsəʳ] *n* - **1.** [of team, film, TV programme] Sponsor *der* - **2.** [of student, museum, for charity] Förderer *der*, -in *die* <> *vt* - **1.** [team, film, TV programme] sponsern - **2.** [student, museum, for charity] finanziell unterstützen - **3.** [bill, appeal, proposal] unterstützen.

**sponsored walk** [,spɒnsəd-] *n* Wohltätigkeitsmarsch *der*.

**sponsorship** ['spɒnsəʃɪp] *n (U)* finanzielle Unterstützung.

**spontaneity** [,spɒntə'neɪətɪ] *n* Sponta-n(e)ität *die*.

**spontaneous** [spɒn'teɪnjəs] *adj* spontan.

**spontaneously** [spɒn'teɪnjəslɪ] *adv* spontan.

**spoof** [spuːf] *n*: **~ (of** *OR* **on sthg)** Parodie *die* (auf etw *(A)*).

**spook** [spuːk] *vt Am*: **to ~ sb** jm einen Schreck einljagen.

**spooky** ['spuːkɪ] (*compar* **-ier**; *superl* **-iest**) *adj inf* unheimlich.

**spool** [spuːl] *n* Spule *die* <> *vi* spulen.

**spoon** [spuːn] *n* Löffel *der* <> *vt* löffeln.

**spoon-feed** *vt* - **1.** [feed with spoon] füttern - **2.** *fig* [students, pupils] gängeln.

**spoonful** ['spuːnfʊl] (*pl* **-s** *OR* **spoonsful**) *n* Löffel *der*; **a ~ of salt** ein Löffel Salz.

**sporadic** [spə'rædɪk] *adj* sporadisch; [showers, shooting] vereinzelt.

**sport** [spɔːt] *n* - **1.** [games] Sport *der*; [type of sport] Sportart *die*; **she's good at ~** sie ist sportlich - **2.** *dated* [cheerful person]: **he's a (good) ~** er ist in Ordnung <> *vt* [wear] tragen.

➤ **sports** *npl Br* [sports day] Sportfest *das* <> *comp* Sport-.

**sporting** ['spɔːtɪŋ] *adj* - **1.** [relating to sport] sportlich; **~ event** Wettkampf *der* - **2.** [generous, fair] anständig, fair.

**sports car** ['spɔːts-] *n* Sportwagen *der*.

**sports day** ['spɔːts-] *n Br* Sportfest *das*.

**sports jacket** ['spɔːts-] *n* sportliches Sakko.

**sportsman** ['spɔːtsmən] (*pl* **-men** [-mən]) *n* Sportler *der*.

**S**

**sportsmanship** [ˈspɔːtsmənʃɪp] n sportliche Fairness.

**sports pages** [ˈspɔːts-] npl Sportseiten pl.

**sportswear** [ˈspɔːtsweəʳ] n (U) [in sport] Sportbekleidung die; [for leisure] Freizeitkleidung die.

**sportswoman** [ˈspɔːtsˌwʊmən] (pl -women [-ˌwɪmɪn]) n Sportlerin die.

**sporty** [ˈspɔːtɪ] (compar -ier; superl -iest) adj inf sportlich.

**spot** [spɒt] (pt & pp -ted; cont -ting) n - **1.** [of blood, ink, paint] Fleck der; **a white blouse with blue ~s** eine weiße Bluse mit blauen Punkten - **2.** [pimple] Pickel der - **3.** inf [small amount]: **a few ~s of rain** ein paar Regentropfen; **~ of** ein bisschen, etwas; **to have a ~ of lunch** eine Kleinigkeit zu Mittag essen; **to do a ~ of work** ein bisschen arbeiten - **4.** [place] Stelle die; **what a lovely ~!** was für ein schönes Plätzchen!; **to do sthg on the ~** etw auf der Stelle tun - **5.** RADIO & TV: **to have a (regular) ~ on a show** regelmäßiger Gast in einer Fernsehshow sein - **6.** phr: **to have a soft ~ for sb** eine Schwäche für jn haben; **to put sb on the ~** jn in Verlegenheit bringen ⬦ vt [notice] sehen; [mistake] finden.

**spot check** n Stichprobe die.

**spotless** [ˈspɒtlɪs] adj [clean] blitzsauber.

**spotlight** [ˈspɒtlaɪt] n [in theatre, TV] Scheinwerfer der; [at home] Spot der; **to be in the ~** fig im Rampenlicht stehen.

**spot-on** adj Br inf [guess, answer] exakt; **he was ~** er lag genau richtig.

**spot price** n Kassakurs der.

**spotted** [ˈspɒtɪd] adj [material, garment] gepunktet.

**spotty** [ˈspɒtɪ] (compar -ier; superl -iest) adj - **1.** Br [skin] pick(e)lig - **2.** Am [patchy] von wechselnder Qualität.

**spouse** [spaʊs] n Gatte der, -tin die.

**spout** [spaʊt] n - **1.** [of kettle, watering can] Schnabel der - **2.** [of water - from fountain, geyser] Strahl der ⬦ vt pej [nonsense] von sich geben; [statistics] herunter|rasseln ⬦ vi: **to ~ from** OR **out of sthg** [liquid] aus etw hervor|spritzen; [flames] aus etw hervor|schießen.

**sprain** [spreɪn] n Verstauchung die ⬦ vt: **to ~ one's ankle/wrist** sich (D) den Knöchel/das Handgelenk verstauchen.

**sprang** [spræŋ] pt ▷ spring.

**sprawl** [sprɔːl] n: **urban ~** unkontrollierte Ausdehnung des städtischen Raumes ⬦ vi - **1.** [person] sich aus|strecken - **2.** [city, suburbs] sich unkontrolliert aus|breiten.

**sprawling** [ˈsprɔːlɪŋ] adj [city, suburbs] wuchernd.

**spray** [spreɪ] n - **1.** [droplets] Sprühnebel der; [of sea] Gischt die - **2.** [pressurized liquid] Spray das - **3.** [can, container] Sprühdose die - **4.** [of flowers] Strauß der ⬦ vt - **1.** [plant, field] besprühen; [crops] spritzen; **to ~ one's hair** sich das Haar mit Haarspray stylen - **2.** [paint, perfume] sprühen ⬦ vi spritzen.

**spray can** n Sprühdose die.

**spray paint** n Sprühfarbe die.

**spread** [spred] (pt & pp **spread**) n - **1.** CULIN [paste] Brotaufstrich der; **cheese ~** Streichkäse der - **2.** [diffusion, growth] Ausbreitung die - **3.** [range] Umfang der - **4.** PRESS: **a two-page ~** ein zweiseitiger Bericht - **5.** [buffet] Festessen das - **6.** Am [bedspread] Decke die ⬦ vt - **1.** [open out - map, tablecloth, arms] aus|breiten; [ - fingers, legs] spreizen - **2.** [apply]: **to ~ sthg with butter** etw mit Butter bestreichen; **to ~ butter/jam on one's bread** Butter/Marmelade aufs Brot streichen - **3.** [diffuse, disseminate] verbreiten - **4.** [over a period of time]: **to be ~ over sthg** sich über etw (A) erstrecken - **5.** [over a surface, share evenly] verteilen ⬦ vi - **1.** [disease, fire, rumour, news] sich aus|breiten - **2.** [water, cloud] sich aus|dehnen.

◆ **spread out** vt sep - **1.:** **to be ~ out** [far apart] verteilt sein; [sprawling] sich aus|dehnen - **2.** [open out, unfold - map, tablecloth, arms] aus|breiten; [ - fingers, legs] spreizen ⬦ vi [disperse] sich verteilen; **the searchers ~ out** die Suchmannschaft schwärmte aus.

**spread-eagled** [-ˌiːgld] adj: **to be** OR **lie ~** aus-gestreckt da|liegen.

**spreadsheet** [ˈspredʃiːt] n COMPUT Tabelle die; **~ program** Tabellenkalkulationsprogramm das.

**spree** [spriː] n: **to go on a spending/shopping ~** groß einkaufen gehen.

**sprig** [sprɪg] n Zweig der.

**sprightly** [ˈspraɪtlɪ] (compar -ier; superl -iest) adj [old person] rüstig.

**spring** [sprɪŋ] (pt **sprang**; pp **sprung**) n - **1.** [season] Frühling der, Frühjahr das; **in (the) ~** im Frühling, im Frühjahr - **2.** [coil] Feder die - **3.** [leap] Satz der - **4.** [water source] Quelle die ⬦ comp - **1.** [rain, weather, colours] Frühlings- - **2.** [mattress] Federkern- - **3.** [water] Quell- ⬦ vt - **1.** [make known suddenly]: **to ~ sthg on sb** jm mit etw konfrontieren; **to ~ a surprise on sb** jn völlig überraschen - **2.** [develop]: **to ~ a leak** [ship] plötzlich lecken; [container] undicht werden ⬦ vi - **1.** [leap] springen; **to ~ to one's feet** auf |springen; **to ~ into action** in Aktion treten; **the engine sprang to life** der Motor sprang an - **2.** [be released]: **the branch sprang back** der Zweig schnellte zurück; **to ~ shut** zu|fallen; **to ~ open** auf|springen - **3.** [originate]: **to ~ from sthg** aus etw entstehen.

◆ **spring up** vi - **1.** [get up] auf|springen - **2.** [grow in size, height] wachsen - **3.** [appear - building] aus dem Boden schießen;

[ - wind] auf lkommen; [ - problem] auf ltauchen.

**springboard** ['sprɪŋbɔːd] *n lit* & *fig* Sprungbrett *das.*

**spring-clean** *vt:* to ~ the house Frühjahrsputz machen <> *vi* Frühjahrsputz machen.

**spring-loaded** *adj* mit einer Sprungfeder.

**spring onion** *n Br* Frühlingszwiebel *die.*

**spring roll** *n Br* Frühlingsrolle *die.*

**spring tide** *n* Springflut *die.*

**springtime** ['sprɪŋtaɪm] *n:* in (the) ~ im Frühling.

**springy** ['sprɪŋɪ] (*compar* -ier; *superl* -iest) *adj*
[carpet, mattress, step] federnd; [ground, rubber]
elastisch.

**sprinkle** ['sprɪŋkl] *vt* [liquid] sprenkeln, sprengen; [powder, salt] streuen; to ~ sthg with sthg
[liquid] etw mit etw (be)sprengen; [powder, salt]
etw mit etw bestreuen.

**sprinkler** ['sprɪŋklər] *n* - 1. [for gardens] Rasensprenger *der* - 2. [for extinguishing fires]: a ~ system Sprinkleranlage *die.*

**sprinkling** ['sprɪŋklɪŋ] *n:* we had only a ~ of
snow bei uns fiel nur ganz wenig Schnee;
there was only a ~ of people on the beach es waren nur ein paar vereinzelte Menschen
am Strand.

**sprint** [sprɪnt] *n* sport [race] Lauf *der*, Sprint *der;*
to break into OR put on a ~ loslspurten <> *vi*
rennen; sport sprinten.

**sprinter** ['sprɪntər] *n* Sprinter *der*, -in *die.*

**sprite** [spraɪt] *n* Geist *der.*

**spritzer** ['sprɪtsər] *n:* (white wine) ~ Weiß-
weinschorle *die.*

**sprocket** ['sprɒkɪt] *n* [wheel] Zahnrad *das.*

**sprout** [spraʊt] *n* - 1. cuLIN: (brussels) ~s Rosenkohl *der* - 2. [shoot] Trieb *der* <> *vt* - 1. [germi-
nate] keimen lassen - 2. [grow - leaves, shoots]
(aus)treiben; [ - beard, moustache] sich (D)
wachsen lassen <> *vi* - 1. [germinate] keimen
- 2. [grow] wachsen, sprießen - 3. [appear]: to
~ (up) wie Pilze aus dem Boden schießen.

**spruce** [spruːs] *adj* gepflegt <> *n* [tree] Fichte
*die.*

➡ **spruce up** *vt sep* [room, house] auf Vordermann bringen; to ~ o.s. up sich zurechtlmachen.

**sprung** [sprʌŋ] *pp* ⮕ spring.

**spry** [spraɪ] (*compar* -ier; *superl* -iest) *adj* rüstig.

**SPUC** (*abbr of* Society for the Protection of the
Unborn Child) *n* britische Anti-Abtrei-
bungsvereinigung.

**spud** [spʌd] *n inf* Kartoffel *die.*

**spun** [spʌn] *pt* & *pp* ⮕ spin.

**spur** [spɜːr] (*pt* & *pp* -red; *cont* -ring) *n* - 1. [in-
centive]: ~ (to sthg) Ansporn *der* OR Antrieb *der*

(für etw) - 2. [on rider's boot] Sporn *der* <> *vt*
- 1. [horse] die Sporen geben (+ D) - 2. [encour-
age]: to ~ sb to do sthg jn anlspornen, etw zu
tun.

➡ **on the spur of the moment** *adv* ganz spontan.

➡ **spur on** *vt sep* [encourage] anlspornen.

**spurious** ['spjʊərɪəs] *adj* - 1. [not genuinely felt]
gespielt - 2. [based on false reasoning - argument]
fadenscheinig; [ - claim] unberechtigt.

**spurn** [spɜːn] *vt* verschmähen.

**spurt** [spɜːt] *n* - 1. [of water, steam] Strahl *der*
- 2. [of energy] Anfall *der* - 3. [burst of speed]
Spurt *der;* to put on a ~ [while running, cycling] einen Spurt einllegen; [while working] sich sehr
beeilen <> *vi* - 1.: to ~ (out of OR from sthg)
[water, steam, flames] herauslschießen (aus
etw) - 2. [run] spurten.

**sputter** ['spʌtər] *vi* - 1. [engine] stottern
- 2. [person] stammeln - 3. [oil in pan] spritzen.

**spy** [spaɪ] (*pl* spies; *pt* & *pp* spied) *n* Spion *der*,
-in *die* <> *vt* sichten <> *vi* - 1. [work as spy]
spionieren - 2. [watch secretly]: to ~ on sb jm
nachlspionieren.

**spying** ['spaɪɪŋ] *n* Spionage *die.*

**spy satellite** *n* Spionagesatellit *der.*

**Sq., sq.** *abbr of* square.

**squabble** ['skwɒbl] *n* Zank *der* <> *vi:* to
~ (about OR over sthg) sich (wegen etw) zanken.

**squad** [skwɒd] *n* - 1. [police department] Dezernat *das* - 2. MIL Trupp *der* - 3. sport Mannschaft
*die.*

**squad car** *n* Streifenwagen *der.*

**squadron** ['skwɒdrən] *n* [of fighter planes] Staffel
*die;* [of warships] Geschwader *das.*

**squadron leader** *n Br* Major *der* der Luftwaffe.

**squalid** ['skwɒlɪd] *adj* - 1. [filthy - place] dreckig
und verkommen; [ - conditions] erbärmlich
- 2. [base, dishonest] schmutzig.

**squall** [skwɔːl] *n* [storm] Bö(e) *die.*

**squalor** ['skwɒlər] *n* Schmutz *der.*

**squander** ['skwɒndər] *vt* [money] verschwenden; [opportunity] vertun.

**square** [skweər] *adj* - 1. [in shape] quadratisch;
[face, brackets] eckig - 2. *Br* [MATH - referring to area]
Quadrat-; [ - when each side is of same length] im
Quadrat - 3. [not owing money]: to be ~ quitt
sein - 4. *inf* [unfashionable]: he's ~ er ist von
(vor)gestern <> *n* - 1. [shape] Quadrat *das*
- 2. [in town, city] Platz *der* - 3. *inf* [unfashionable
person] Spießer *der*, -in *die* - 4. *phr:* they were
back to ~ one sie waren wieder da, wo sie
angefangen hatten <> *vt* - 1. MATH [multiply by it-
self] quadrieren; 4 ~d is 16 4 hoch 2 ist 16, 4
(zum) Quadrat ist 16 - 2. [balance, reconcile]: to

**S**

~ **sthg with sthg** etw mit etw in Einklang bringen.

⇒ **square up** *vi* - **1.** [settle up]: **to ~ up with sb** mit jm ablrechnen - **2.** [confront]: **to ~ up to sb/sthg** sich jm/etw stellen.

**squared** ['skweədl] *adj* [paper] kariert.

**square dance** *n* Squaredance *der.*

**square deal** *n* faires Geschäft.

**squarely** ['skweəlɪ] *adv* - **1.** [directly] genau - **2.** [honestly] offen und ehrlich.

**square meal** *n* anständige Mahlzeit.

**square root** *n* Quadratswurzel *die.*

**squash** [skwɒʃ] *n* - **1.** sport Squash *das* - **2.** *Br* [drink]: **lemon/orange ~** Fruchtsaftgetränk mit Zitronen-/Orangengeschmack - **3.** *Am* [vegetable] Kürbis *der* ◇ *vt* [hat] zerdrücken; [box] zusammenldrücken; [fruit] zerquetschen.

**squat** [skwɒt] (*compar* -**ter**; *superl* -**test**; *pt* & *pp* -**ted**; *cont* -**ting**) *adj* gedrungen ◇ *n Br* [building] besetztes Haus ◇ *vi* - **1.** [crouch]: **to ~ (down)** sich (hinl)hocken; **he was ~ting** er hockte - **2.** *Br* [be a squatter] in einem besetzten Haus leben.

**squatter** ['skwɒtər] *n Br* [in empty building] Hausbesetzer *der*, -in *die.*

**squawk** [skwɔːk] *n* [of bird] Kreischen *das* ◇ *vi* [bird] kreischen.

**squeak** [skwiːk] *n* - **1.** [of animal] Quieken *das* - **2.** [of door, hinge] Quietschen *das* ◇ *vi* - **1.** [animal] quieken - **2.** [floorboard, bed, hinge] quietschen.

**squeaky** ['skwiːkɪ] (*compar* -**ier**; *superl* -**iest**) *adj* - **1.** [floorboard, bed, hinge] quietschend - **2.** [voice] piepsig.

**squeal** [skwiːl] *n* - **1.** [of person] Kreischen *das*; [of animal] Quieken *das* - **2.** [of brakes, tyres] Quietschen *das* ◇ *vi* - **1.** [person] kreischen; [animal] quieken - **2.** [brakes, tyres] quietschen.

**squeamish** ['skwiːmɪʃ] *adj* zart besaitet; **I'm ~ about the sight of blood** ich kann kein Blut sehen.

**squeeze** [skwiːz] *n* - **1.** [pressure]: **to give sthg a ~** etw drücken - **2.** *inf* [crush of people] Gedränge *das* ◇ *vt* - **1.** [press firmly] drücken; [orange, lemon] auslpressen - **2.** [extract, press out - juice] herauslpressen; **to ~ sthg out of sthg** etw aus etw drücken - **3.** [cram]: **to ~ sthg into sthg** etw in etw *(A)* hineinlpressen *or* zwängen - **4.** *fig* [information]: **to ~ sthg out of sb** etw aus jm herauslpressen ◇ *vi:* **to ~ into/past/through sthg** sich in etw *(A)* /vorbei an etw *(D)* /durch etw zwängen.

**squeezer** ['skwiːzər] *n* Presse *die.*

**squelch** [skweltʃ] *vi* [through mud] patschen.

**squib** [skwɪb] *n:* **damp ~** Reinfall *der.*

**squid** [skwɪd] (*pl inv OR* -**s**) *n* Tintenfisch *der.*

**squiggle** ['skwɪgl] *n* Schnörkel *der.*

**squint** [skwɪnt] *n* MED: **to have a ~** schielen ◇ *vi* - **1.** MED schielen - **2.** [half-close one's eyes]: **to ~ at sthg** etw blinzelnd anlsehen.

**squire** ['skwaɪər] *n* [landowner] Gutsherr *der.*

**squirm** [skwɜːm] *vi lit* & *fig* sich winden.

**squirrel** [*Br* 'skwɪrəl, *Am* 'skwɜːrəl] *n* Eichhörnchen *das.*

**squirt** [skwɜːt] *vt* - **1.** [force out] spritzen - **2.** [cover with liquid]: **to ~ sb/sthg with sthg** jn/ etw mit etw bespritzen ◇ *vi:* **to ~ (out of sthg)** (herausl)spritzen (aus etw).

**Sr** - **1.** *abbr of* **senior** - **2.** *abbr of* **sister.**

**SRC** *n* (*abbr of* **Science Research Council**) wissenschaftlicher Forschungsrat in Großbritannien.

**Sri Lanka** [ˌsriː'læŋkə] *n* Sri Lanka *nt;* **in ~** auf Sri Lanka.

**Sri Lankan** [ˌsriː'læŋkn] *adj* sri-lankisch ◇ *n* Sri-Lanker *der*, -in *die.*

**SRN** (*abbr of* **State Registered Nurse**) *n* examinierte Krankenschwester/examinierter Krankenpfleger in Großbritannien.

**SS** (*abbr of* **steamship**) MS.

**SSSI** (*abbr of* **Site of Special Scientific Interest**) *n* unter Natur- oder Denkmalschutz stehendes Areal in Großbritannien.

**St** - **1.** *abbr of* **saint** - **2.** *abbr of* **street.**

**stab** [stæb] (*pt* & *pp* -**bed**; *cont* -**bing**) *n* - **1.** [with knife] Stich *der* - **2.** *inf* [attempt]: **to have a ~ at sthg** etw probieren - **3.** [twinge]: **a ~ of pain** ein stechender Schmerz ◇ *vt* - **1.** [with knife] einlstechen (auf *(+ A)*); **to ~ sb to death** jn erstechen; **to ~ sb in the back** *fig* jm in den Rücken fallen - **2.** [with fork] auf lspießen ◇ *vi:* **to ~ at sthg** [with knife] auf etw *(A)* einlstechen.

**stabbing** ['stæbɪŋ] *adj* [pain] stechend ◇ *n* Messerstecherei *die.*

**stability** [stə'bɪlətɪ] *n* Stabilität *die.*

**stabilize, -ise** ['steɪbəlaɪz] *vt* stabilisieren ◇ *vi* sich stabilisieren.

**stabilizer** ['steɪbəlaɪzər] *n* Stabilisator *der;* [on bicycle] Stützrad *das.*

**stable** ['steɪbl] *adj* - **1.** [steady, unchanging] stabil; [job] sicher - **2.** [solid, anchored - ladder, shelf] stabil; [ - ship, aircraft] sicher - **3.** [person, personality]: **(mentally) ~** innerlich gefestigt ◇ *n* [building] Reitstall *der;* [horses] Rennstall *der.*

**stable lad** *n* Stallbursche *der.*

**staccato** [stə'kɑːtəʊ] *adj* & *adv* staccato.

**stack** [stæk] *n* - **1.** [pile] Stoß *der*, Stapel *der* - **2.** *inf* [a lot, lots]: **~s** *OR* **a ~ of** ein Haufen *(+ G)* ◇ *vt* - **1.** [pile up] stapeln - **2.** [fill]: **to be ~ed with sthg** mit etw vollgestapelt sein.

**stadium** ['steɪdjəm] (*pl* -**diums** *OR* -**dia** [-djəl) *n* Stadion *das.*

**staff** [stɑːf] *n* [employees] Personal *das;* **(teach-**

**ing)** ~ Lehrkräfte pl <> vt mit Personal auslstatten.

**staffing** ['stɑːfɪŋ] n Stellenbesetzung die.

**staff nurse** n Br ≈ stellvertretende Oberschwester.

**staff room** n Lehrerzimmer das.

**stag** [stæg] (pl inv OR -s) n [deer] Hirsch der.

**stage** [steɪdʒ] n - **1.** [period, phase] Stadium das, Phase die; **at this** ~ zu diesem Zeitpunkt - **2.** [platform] Bühne die; **on** ~ auf der Bühne; **to set the** ~ **for sthg** den Weg für etw bereiten - **3.** [acting profession]: **the** ~ die Bühne <> vt - **1.** THEATRE auf lführen, inszenieren - **2.** [organize] veranstalten.

**stagecoach** ['steɪdʒkəʊtʃ] n Postkutsche die.

**stage door** n Bühneneingang der.

**stage fright** n Lampenfieber das.

**stagehand** ['steɪdʒhænd] n Bühnenarbeiter der, -in die.

**stage-manage** vt - **1.** THEATRE Inspizient/Inspizientin sein bei - **2.** fig [orchestrate] inszenieren.

**stage manager** n Inspizient der, -in die.

**stage name** n Künstlername der.

**stagflation** [stæg'fleɪʃn] n POL Stagflation die.

**stagger** ['stægər] vt - **1.** [astound] die Sprache verschlagen (+ D); **he ~ed me with his revelations** seine Enthüllungen haben mir die Sprache verschlagen - **2.** [arrange at different times] staffeln <> vi [totter] schwanken.

**staggering** ['stægərɪŋ] adj [news] erschütternd; [amount] Schwindel erregend.

**staging** ['steɪdʒɪŋ] n - **1.** THEATRE Inszenierung die - **2.** [organizing] Inszenieren das.

**stagnant** ['stægnənt] adj - **1.** [water] stehend; [air] verbraucht - **2.** [business, career, economy] stagnierend.

**stagnate** [stæg'neɪt] vi - **1.** [water] stehen; [air] verbraucht werden - **2.** [business, career, economy] stagnieren.

**stag night, stag party** n feucht-fröhlicher Männerabend, mit dem ein Bräutigam am Abend vor der Hochzeit sein Jungesellendasein beschließt.

**staid** [steɪd] adj [person] seriös, gesetzt; [appearance, attitude] bieder.

**stain** [steɪn] n [mark] Fleck der <> vt [discolour] Flecken hinterlassen auf (+ D).

**stained** [steɪnd] adj - **1.** [soiled, marked] fleckig - **2.** [wood] gebeizt.

**stained glass** n farbiges Glas.

**stained-glass window** n farbiges Glasfenster.

**stainless steel** ['steɪnlɪs-] n Edelstahl der.

**stain remover** [-ˌrɪmuːvəʳ] n Fleckenentferner der.

**stair** [steəʳ] n [step] Stufe die.
➤ **stairs** npl Treppe die.

**staircase** ['steəkeɪs] n Treppe die.

**stairway** ['steəweɪ] n Treppenaufgang der, Treppe die.

**stairwell** ['steəwel] n Treppenhaus das.

**stake** [steɪk] n - **1.** [share]: **to have a** ~ **in sthg** einen Anteil an etw (D) haben - **2.** [wooden post] Pfahl der - **3.** [in gambling] Einsatz der <> vt - **1.** [risk]: **to** ~ **sthg on sthg** etw auf etw (A) setzen - **2.** [in gambling] setzen - **3.** [state]: **to** ~ **a claim to sthg** Ansprüche auf etw (A) anlmelden.
➤ **stakes** npl - **1.** [prize] Gewinn der - **2.** [contest] Preis der.
➤ **to be at stake** adv auf dem Spiel stehen.

**stakeout** ['steɪkaʊt] n esp Am [police surveillance] Überwachung die.

**stalactite** ['stæləktaɪt] n Stalaktit der.

**stalagmite** ['stæləgmaɪt] n Stalagmit der.

**stale** [steɪl] adj - **1.** [bread] altbacken; [cake] trocken; [water, beer, air] abgestanden - **2.** [news, ideas] überholt; [joke] abgedroschen.

**stalemate** ['steɪlmeɪt] n - **1.** [deadlock] Sackgasse die - **2.** CHESS Patt das.

**stalk** [stɔːk] n Stiel der; [of cabbage] Strunk der <> vt [animal] sich heranlpirschen an (+ A); [person] nachlstellen (+ D) <> vi [walk] stolzieren.

**stall** [stɔːl] n - **1.** [table] Stand der - **2.** [in stable] Box die <> vt - **1.** AUT ablwürgen - **2.** [delay - person] hinlhalten; [ - event] verzögern <> vi - **1.** AUT ablsterben - **2.** [delay]: **to** ~ **for time** versuchen, Zeit zu schinden.
➤ **stalls** npl Br [in theatre, cinema] Parkett das.

**stallholder** ['stɔːlˌhəʊldəʳ] n Br Standinhaber der, -in die.

**stallion** ['stæljən] n Hengst der.

**stalwart** ['stɔːlwət] adj [loyal] treu <> n treuer Anhänger, treue Anhängerin.

**stamen** ['steɪmən] n Staubgefäß das.

**stamina** ['stæmɪnə] n Ausdauer die.

**stammer** ['stæməʳ] n Stottern das; **to have a** ~ stottern <> vi stottern.

**stamp** [stæmp] n - **1.** [postage stamp] Briefmarke die - **2.** [rubber stamp] Stempel der - **3.** fig [hallmark]: **to have the** ~ **of authenticity** den Echtheitsstempel tragen <> vt - **1.** [produce by stamping] auf lstempeln - **2.** [stomp]: **to** ~ **one's foot** auf lstampfen (mit dem Fuß) - **3.** [stick stamp on] frankieren, freilmachen - **4.** fig [with characteristic quality]: **the project had failure ~ed all over it** es war klar, dass das Projekt nicht erfolgreich sein würde <> vi - **1.** [walk]

stampfen, trampeln - **2.** [with one foot]: **to ~ on sthg** auf etw (A) treten.

➤ **stamp out** vt sep [fire] ausltreten; [crime, disease] auslrotten; [opposition] zunichte machen.

**stamp album** n Briefmarkenalbum das.

**stamp-collecting** [-kəˌlektɪŋ] n Briefmarkensammeln das.

**stamp collector** n Briefmarkensammler der, -in die.

**stamp duty** n (U) Br Stempelgebühr die.

**stamped addressed envelope** [ˈstæmptəˌdrest-] n Br frankierter Rückumschlag.

**stampede** [stæmˈpiːd] n - **1.** [of animals] panische Flucht - **2.** [of people] Massenandrang der ◇ vi [animals] panisch die Flucht ergreifen.

**stamp machine** n Briefmarkenautomat der.

**stance** [stɑːns] n - **1.** [posture] Haltung die - **2.** [attitude]: ~ **(on)** Einstellung die (zu).

**stand** [stænd] (pt & pp **stood**) n - **1.** [stall] Stand der - **2.** [for umbrellas, coats, bicycle] Ständer der - **3.** [at sports stadium] Tribüne die - **4.** MIL & fig: **to make a ~** Widerstand leisten - **5.** [position] Standpunkt der; **to take a ~ on sthg** Stellung zu etw beziehen - **6.** Am LAW Zeugenstand der; **to take the ~** in den Zeugenstand treten ◇ vt - **1.** [place] stellen - **2.** [withstand - pressure, heat] ertragen; **I can't ~ him** ich kann ihn nicht ausstehen - **3.** [put up with] auslhalten - **4.** [treat]: **to ~ sb a drink/meal** jm ein Getränk/Essen spendieren - **5.** LAW: **to ~ trial** angeklagt sein ◇ vi - **1.** [gen] stehen; **to be ~ing** stehen - **2.** [rise to one's feet] auf lstehen - **3.** [on issue]: **where do you ~ on ...?** wie stehen Sie zu ...? - **4.** Br POL [be a candidate] kandidieren - **5.** [be likely]: **we ~ to gain £200 on the deal** wir können bei dem Geschäft 200 Pfund gewinnen - **6.** Am [stop]: 'no **~ing**' 'Halten verboten'.

➤ **stand aside** vi [move aside] zur Seite treten.

➤ **stand back** vi zurückltreten.

➤ **stand by** vt fus - **1.** [person] halten zu - **2.** [promise] halten; [decision, offer] bleiben bei ◇ vi - **1.** [in readiness] sich bereitlhalten - **2.** [not intervene] daneben stehen.

➤ **stand for** vt fus - **1.** [signify] stehen für - **2.** [tolerate] hinlnehmen.

➤ **stand in** vi: **to ~ in for sb** für jn einlspringen.

➤ **stand out** vi - **1.** [be clearly visible] herauslstechen - **2.** [be superior] sich ablheben.

➤ **stand up** vt sep inf [boyfriend, girlfriend etc] versetzen ◇ vi - **1.** [be on one's feet] stehen - **2.** [rise to one's feet] auf lstehen - **3.** [be upright] aufrecht stehen - **4.** [claim, evidence] bestehen.

➤ **stand up for** vt fus einltreten für.

➤ **stand up to** vt fus - **1.** [bad treatment] sich wehren gegen; [weather, heat] trotzen (+ D) - **2.** [person, boss] sich behaupten gegenüber.

**standard** [ˈstændəd] adj Standard-; [spelling, pronunciation] korrekt ◇ n - **1.** [level] Niveau das; **up to ~** der Norm entsprechend - **2.** [point of reference] Maßstab der - **3.** [flag] Fahne die.

➤ **standards** npl [principles] Wertvorstellungen pl.

**standard-bearer** n fig führender Kopf.

**standardize, -ise** [ˈstændədaɪz] vt vereinheitlichen.

**standard lamp** n Br Stehlampe die.

**standard of living** (pl **standards of living**) n Lebensstandard der.

**standby** [ˈstændbaɪ] (pl **standbys**) n [substitute] Ersatz der; **on ~** in Bereitschaft ◇ comp [ticket] Standby-.

**stand-in** n - **1.** [replacement] Vertretung die - **2.** [stunt person] Double das.

**standing** [ˈstændɪŋ] adj [permanent] ständig; [army] stehend ◇ n - **1.** [reputation] Ruf der - **2.** [duration] Dauer die.

**standing charge** n Grundgebühr die.

**standing order** n Dauerauftrag der.

**standing ovation** n stehende Ovation.

**standing room** n (U) Stehplätze pl.

**standoffish** [ˌstændˈɒfɪʃ] adj kühl.

**standpipe** [ˈstændpaɪp] n Steigrohr das.

**standpoint** [ˈstændpɔɪnt] n Standpunkt der.

**standstill** [ˈstændstɪl] n: **to be at a ~** [car, train] stehen; [traffic] stilllstehen; fig ruhen; **to come to a ~** [stop moving] stehen bleiben; fig zum Erliegen kommen.

**stand-up** adj: **~ comedian** Komiker der, -in die; **~ comedy** Comedyshow die.

**stank** [stæŋk] pt ▷ **stink**.

**Stanley knife®** [ˈstænlɪ-] n Teppichmesser das.

**stanza** [ˈstænzə] n Strophe die.

**staple** [ˈsteɪpl] adj [principal] Haupt- ◇ n - **1.** [for paper] (Heft)klammer die - **2.** [principal commodity] Grundnahrungsmittel das ◇ vt zusammenheften.

**staple diet** n Hauptnahrung die.

**staple gun** n Tacker der.

**stapler** [ˈsteɪplər] n Hefter der.

**star** [stɑːr] (pt & pp **-red**; cont **-ring**) n - **1.** [gen] Stern der - **2.** [celebrity] Star der - **3.** [asterisk] Sternchen das ◇ comp [performer] Star-; **~ attraction** Spitzenattraktion die ◇ vt [subj: film, play]: **the film ~s Kevin Costner** in diesem Film spielt Kevin Costner die Hauptrolle ◇ vi [actor]: **to ~ (in)** die Hauptrolle spielen (in (+ D)).

**stars** *npl* [horoscope] Sterne *pl.*

**starboard** ['stɑːbəd] *adj* Steuerbord- ◇ *n:* to ~ nach Steuerbord.

**starch** [stɑːtʃ] *n* Stärke *die.*

**starched** [stɑːtʃt] *adj* gestärkt.

**starchy** ['stɑːtʃɪ] (*compar* -ier; *superl* -iest) *adj* [food] stärkehaltig.

**stardom** ['stɑːdəm] *n* Ruhm *der.*

**stare** [steəʳ] *n* starrer Blick ◇ *vi* starren; to ~ at sb/sthg jn/etw anlstarren.

**starfish** ['stɑːfɪʃ] (*pl inv* OR -es) *n* Seestern *der.*

**stark** [stɑːk] *adj* - 1. [landscape, room] kahl - 2. [fact, truth] nackt; [contrast] scharf ◇ *adv:* ~ naked splitternackt.

**starlet** ['stɑːlət] *n pej* Starlet *das.*

**starlight** ['stɑːlaɪt] *n* Sternenlicht *das.*

**starling** ['stɑːlɪŋ] *n* Star *der.*

**starlit** ['stɑːlɪt] *adj* [night] sternenklar.

**starry** ['stɑːrɪ] (*compar* -ier; *superl* -iest) *adj* sternenklar.

**starry-eyed** [-'aɪd] *adj* [naive] naiv.

**Stars and Stripes** *n:* the ~ das Sternenbanner.

**star sign** *n* Sternzeichen *das.*

**star-studded** *adj:* ~ cast Starbesetzung *die.*

**start** [stɑːt] *n* - 1. [beginning] Anfang *der,* Beginn *der;* for a ~ erstens - 2. [jump] Schreck(en) *der* - 3. SPORT Start *der* - 4. [lead, advantage] Vorsprung *der* ◇ *vt* - 1. [begin] anlfangen, beginnen; to ~ work anfangen zu arbeiten; to ~ a race ein Rennen starten; to ~ doing OR to do sthg anlfangen, etw zu tun; it ~ed me thinking es gab mir zu denken - 2. [engine, car] starten; [cassette player] einlschalten; to ~ a fire [arson] Feuer legen; [for warmth] Feuer machen - 3. [business] gründen; [shop] auflmachen; [society] ins Leben rufen ◇ *vi* - 1. [begin] beginnen, anlfangen; to ~ with sb/sthg mit jm/etw beginnen; ~ing from next week ab nächster Woche; to ~ in business ins Geschäftsleben eintreten; to ~ with [at first] zuerst; [in the first place] erstens; [when ordering meal] als Vorspeise - 2. [car, engine] starten; [tape] laufen - 3. [on journey] auf l-brechen - 4. [jump] zusammenlschrecken.

◆ **start off** *vt sep* [meeting, discussion] beginnen; [rumour] in Umlauf bringen; this should be enough to ~ you off das sollte für den Anfang reichen ◇ *vi* - 1. [begin] beginnen, anlfangen - 2. [on journey] auf lbrechen.

◆ **start on** *vt fus* [begin] beginnen mit.

◆ **start out** *vi* - 1. [in life, career] anlfangen; to ~ out as sthg ursprünglich etw sein - 2. [on journey] auf lbrechen.

◆ **start up** *vt sep* - 1. [business] gründen; [shop] auf lmachen; [society] ins Leben rufen - 2. [car, engine] starten ◇ *vi* - 1. [guns, music,

noise] loslgehen - 2. [car, engine] starten - 3. [set up business] anlfangen.

**starter** ['stɑːtəʳ] *n* - 1. *Br* [of meal] Vorspeise *die* - 2. AUT Anlasser *der* - 3. SPORT [official] Starter *der,* -in *die;* [competitor] Teilnehmer *der,* -in *die.*

**starter motor** *n* Anlasser *der.*

**starting block** ['stɑːtɪŋ-] *n* Startblock *der.*

**starting point** ['stɑːtɪŋ-] *n* Ausgangspunkt *der.*

**startle** ['stɑːtl] *vt* erschrecken.

**startling** ['stɑːtlɪŋ] *adj* überraschend.

**starvation** [stɑː'veɪʃn] *n* Hunger *der;* to die of ~ verhungern.

**starve** [stɑːv] *vt* - 1. [deprive of food] ausl-hungern - 2. [deprive]: to ~ sb of sthg jm etw vorenthalten ◇ *vi* [have no food] hungern; [die of hunger] verhungern; I'm starving! ich habe einen Mordshunger.

**starving** ['stɑːvɪŋ] *adj* [without food] hungernd.

**state** [steɪt] *n* - 1. [condition] Zustand *der;* not to be in a fit ~ to do sthg nicht im Stande sein, etw zu tun - 2.: to get into a ~ sich auf lregen - 3. [country, region] Staat *der* ◇ *comp* Staats- ◇ *vt* [declare] erklären; [specify] anlgeben.

◆ **State** *n* [government]: the State der Staat.

◆ **States** *npl* [USA]: the States die Vereinigten Staaten *pl.*

**state-controlled** *adj* staatlich kontrolliert.

**State Department** *n Am* Außenministerium *das.*

**state education** *n Br* staatliches Bildungswesen.

**stateless** ['steɪtlɪs] *adj* staatenlos.

**stately** ['steɪtlɪ] (*compar* -ier; *superl* -iest) *adj* [building] stattlich; [person] würdevoll.

**stately home** *n Br* herrschaftliches Anwesen.

**statement** ['steɪtmənt] *n* - 1. [declaration & LAW] Aussage *die* - 2. [from bank] Kontoauszug *der.*

**state of affairs** *n* Lage *die* der Dinge.

**state of emergency** *n* Notstand *der.*

**state of mind** (*pl* states of mind) *n* [mood] Verfassung *die.*

**state-of-the-art** *adj* hochmodern.

**state-owned** [-'əʊnd] *adj* staatseigen.

**state school** *n* staatliche Schule.

---

**STATE SCHOOL**

Die meisten Schulen in Großbritannien sind staatlich; sie stehen allen offen, und ihr Besuch ist kostenlos. In den USA werden staatliche Schulen „public schools" genannt. In beiden Ländern haben Eltern auch die Möglichkeit, ihre Kinder auf Privatschulen zu schicken.

**S**

**state secret** n Staatsgeheimnis das.

**state's evidence** n Am: to turn ~ als Kronzeuge auftreten.

**stateside** ['steɪtsaɪd] adj & adv in den (Vereinigten) Staaten.

**statesman** ['steɪtsmən] (pl -men [-mən]) n Staatsmann der.

**static** ['stætɪk] adj [unchanging] konstant <> n [on TV, radio] Empfangsstörung die.

**static electricity** n Reibungselektrizität die.

**station** ['steɪʃn] n - 1. [for trains] Bahnhof der; [for buses] Busbahnhof der - 2. RADIO Sender der - 3. [police or fire station] Wache die - 4. [position] Platz der - 5. fml [rank] Stand der <> vt - 1. [position] auf lstellen - 2. MIL stationieren.

**stationary** ['steɪʃnərɪ] adj stehend.

**stationer** ['steɪʃnəʳ] n Schreibwarenhändler der, -in die; ~'s (shop) Schreibwarenhandlung die.

**stationery** ['steɪʃnərɪ] n (U) Schreibwaren pl.

**station house** n Am Polizeiwache die.

**stationmaster** ['steɪʃn,mɑːstəʳ] n Bahnhofsvorsteher der, -in die.

**station wagon** n Am Kombiwagen der.

**statistic** [stə'tɪstɪk] n [number] statistisches Ergebnis; ~s Statistik die.
→ **statistics** n (U) [science] Statistik die.

**statistical** [stə'tɪstɪkl] adj statistisch.

**statistician** [,stætɪ'stɪʃn] n Statistiker der, -in die.

**statue** ['stætʃuː] n Statue die.

**statuesque** [,stætjʊ'esk] adj wie eine Statue.

**statuette** [,stætjʊ'et] n Statuette die.

**stature** ['stætʃəʳ] n - 1. [height, size] Statur die - 2. [importance] Format das.

**status** ['steɪtəs] n - 1. [legal or social position] Status der - 2. [prestige] Prestige das.

**status quo** [-'kwəʊ] n: the ~ der Status quo.

**status symbol** n Statussymbol das.

**statute** ['stætjuːt] n - 1. [law] Gesetz das - 2. [of organization] Statut das.

**statute book** n: the ~ das Gesetzbuch.

**statutory** ['stætjʊtrɪ] adj gesetzlich.

**staunch** [stɔːntʃ] adj treu <> vt [blood] stillen; [flow] stauen.

**stave** [steɪv] (pt & pp -d OR stove) n MUS Notenlinien pl.
→ **stave off** vt sep [danger, disaster] ablwenden; [hunger] lindern.

**stay** [steɪ] vi - 1. [gen] bleiben; [as guest] übernachten; I'm ~ing at the hotel/with friends ich wohne im Hotel/bei Freunden; to ~ for dinner zum Abendessen bleiben; to ~ the night übernachten; to ~ put liegen-/stehen-/sitzen bleiben - 2. Scot [reside] wohnen <> n [visit] Aufenthalt der.
→ **stay away** vi fernlhalten.
→ **stay in** vi [stay at home] zu Hause bleiben.
→ **stay on** vi bleiben.
→ **stay out** vi - 1. [not come home]: he ~ed out last night er ist letzte Nacht nicht nach Hause gekommen - 2. [strikers] weiterlstreiken - 3. [not get involved]: to ~ out of sthg sich aus etw rauslhalten.
→ **stay up** vi - 1. [not go to bed] auflbleiben - 2. [shelf, picture] hängen bleiben; [socks] oben bleiben.

**staying power** ['steɪŋ-] n Stehvermögen das.

**St Bernard** [Br -'bɜːnəd, Am -bərˈnɑːrd] n [dog] Bernhardiner der.

**STD** n (abbr of sexually transmitted disease) Geschlechtskrankheit die.

**stead** [sted] n: to stand sb in good ~ jm zustatten kommen.

**steadfast** ['stedfɑːst] adj - 1. [supporter] treu - 2. [resolve] unerschütterlich - 3. [gaze] unverwandt.

**steadily** ['stedɪlɪ] adv - 1. [improve, increase] stetig - 2. [breathe, move] gleichmäßig - 3. [look, say] ruhig.

**steady** ['stedɪ] (compar -ier; superl -iest; pt & pp -ied) adj - 1. [gradual] stetig - 2. [regular, constant] konstant - 3. [not shaking, calm] ruhig - 4. [boyfriend, job] fest - 5. [worker] zuverlässig <> vt - 1. [boat, camera] ins Gleichgewicht bringen; to ~ o.s. Halt finden - 2. [voice, nerves] beruhigen; to ~ o.s. sich beruhigen.

**steak** [steɪk] n - 1. [meat] Steak das - 2. [fish] Fischsteak das.

**steakhouse** ['steɪkhaʊs, pl -haʊzɪz] n Steakhaus das.

**steal** [stiːl] (pt stole; pp stolen) vt lit & fig stehlen; to ~ sthg from sb jm etw stehlen <> vi - 1. [take illegally] stehlen - 2. [move stealthily] schleichen.

**stealing** ['stiːlɪŋ] n Stehlen das.

**stealth** [stelθ] n List die.

**stealthy** ['stelθɪ] (compar -ier; superl -iest) adj verstohlen.

**steam** [stiːm] n Dampf der; to let off ~ Dampf abllassen; to run out of ~ Schwung verlieren <> comp Dampf- <> vt CULIN dämpfen <> vi dampfen.
→ **steam up** vt sep - 1. [window] beschlagen lassen - 2. fig [get angry]: to get ~ed up about sthg sich über etw (A) auflregen <> vi [window, glasses] beschlagen.

**steamboat** ['stiːmbəʊt] n Dampfer der.

**steam engine** n Dampflok die.

**steamer** ['stiːməʳ] n - 1. [ship] Dampfer der - 2. CULIN Dampfkochtopf der.

**steam iron** n Dampfbügeleisen das.

**steamroller** ['sti:mˌrəʊləʳ] n Dampfwalze die.

**steam shovel** n Am Bagger der.

**steamy** ['sti:mɪ] (compar -ier; superl -iest) adj - **1.** [room] voll Dampf - **2.** inf [erotic] heiß.

**steel** [sti:l] n Stahl der <> comp Stahl- <> vt: to ~ o.s. (for sthg) sich (für etw) stählen.

**steel industry** n Stahlindustrie die.

**steel wool** n Stahlwolle die.

**steelworker** ['sti:lˌwɜ:kəʳ] n Stahlarbeiter der, -in die.

**steelworks** ['sti:lwɜ:ks] (pl inv) n Stahlwerk das.

**steely** ['sti:lɪ] (compar -ier; superl -iest) adj [determination, look] stählern.

**steep** [sti:p] adj - **1.** [gen] steil - **2.** inf [expensive] gesalzen - **3.** inf [unreasonable]: it's a bit ~ expecting us to do that! es ist ganz schön unverschämt, das von uns zu erwarten! <> vt [soak] einlweichen.

**steeped** [sti:pt] adj fig: ~ in tradition/history traditionsreich/geschichtsträchtig.

**steeple** ['sti:pl] n Kirchturm der.

**steeplechase** ['sti:plˌtʃeɪs] n - **1.** [horse race] Hindernisrennen das - **2.** [athletics race] Hindernislauf der.

**steeply** ['sti:plɪ] adv steil.

**steer** ['stɪəʳ] n [bullock] junger Ochse <> vt - **1.** [boat] steuern; [car] lenken - **2.** [person] lotsen; he ~ed the conversation round to ... er lenkte das Gespräch auf (+ A) ... <> vi steuern; to ~ clear of sb/sthg fig einen großen Bogen um jn/etw machen.

**steering** ['stɪərɪŋ] n Lenkung die.

**steering column** n Lenksäule die.

**steering committee** n Lenkungsausschuss der.

**steering lock** n Lenkradschloss das.

**steering wheel** n Lenkrad das.

**stem** [stem] (pt & pp -med; cont -ming) n - **1.** [of plant, glass] Stiel der - **2.** [of pipe] Hals der - **3.** GRAMM Stamm der <> vt [stop] einldämmen.
◆ **stem from** vt fus herlrühren von.

**stench** [stentʃ] n Gestank der.

**stencil** ['stensl] (Br pt & pp -led; cont -ling, Am pt & pp -ed; cont -ing) n Schablone die <> vt [design, pattern] mit einer Schablone zeichnen; [words] mit einer Schablone schreiben.

**stenographer** [stəˈnɒgrəfəʳ] n Stenograf der, -in die.

**stenography** [stəˈnɒgrəfɪ] n Stenografie die.

**step** [step] (pt & pp -ped; cont -ping) n - **1.** [pace, stage] Schritt der; to be in ~/out of ~ with public opinion fig im Einklang/nicht im Einklang mit der öffentlichen Meinung sein; to keep in ~ with sthg mit etw Schritt halten; to watch one's ~ lit & fig sich vorlsehen; ~ by ~ Schritt für Schritt - **2.** [measure] Maßnahme die; it's a ~ in the right direction das ist immerhin ein Anfang - **3.** [of staircase, ladder] Stufe die - **4.** Am MUS Tonschritt der <> vi treten; ~ this way folgen Sie mir bitte; she ~ped off the bus sie stieg aus dem Bus; to ~ on/in sthg auf/in etw (A) treten; to ~ on it inf [drive fast] aufs Gas drücken; [hurry up] hinlmachen.
◆ **steps** npl - **1.** [stairs] Stufen pl - **2.** Br [stepladder] Trittleiter die.
◆ **step aside** vi - **1.** [move to one side] zur Seite treten - **2.** [resign] zurückltreten.
◆ **step back** vi zurückltreten.
◆ **step down** vi [resign] zurückltreten.
◆ **step in** vi [intervene] einlschreiten.
◆ **step up** vt sep [increase] steigern.

**step aerobics** n Stepaerobic das.

**stepbrother** ['stepˌbrʌðəʳ] n Stiefbruder der.

**stepchild** ['steptʃaɪld] (pl -children [-ˌtʃɪldrən]) n Stiefkind das.

**stepdaughter** ['stepˌdɔ:təʳ] n Stieftochter die.

**stepfather** ['stepˌfɑ:ðəʳ] n Stiefvater der.

**stepladder** ['stepˌlædəʳ] n Trittleiter die.

**stepmother** ['stepˌmʌðəʳ] n Stiefmutter die.

**stepping-stone** ['stepɪŋ-] n - **1.** [in river] Trittstein der - **2.** fig [way to success] Sprungbrett das.

**stepsister** ['stepˌsɪstəʳ] n Stiefschwester die.

**stepson** ['stepsʌn] n Stiefsohn der.

**stereo** ['sterɪəʊ] (pl -s) adj Stereo- <> n - **1.** [stereo system] Stereoanlage die - **2.** [stereo sound] Stereo das.

**stereophonic** [ˌsterɪəˈfɒnɪk] adj stereofon.

**stereotype** ['sterɪətaɪp] n Klischee das <> vt in ein Klischee einlordnen.

**sterile** ['steraɪl] adj - **1.** [germ-free] steril - **2.** [man, woman, animal] unfruchtbar - **3.** pej [discussion] fruchtlos; [ideas] abgenutzt.

**sterility** [steˈrɪlətɪ] n - **1.** [lack of germs] Sterilität die - **2.** [of man, woman, animal] Unfruchtbarkeit die.

**sterilization** [ˌsterəlaɪˈzeɪʃn] n Sterilisierung die.

**sterilize, -ise** ['sterəlaɪz] vt sterilisieren.

**sterilized milk** ['sterəlaɪzd-] n sterilisierte Milch.

**sterling** ['stɜ:lɪŋ] adj - **1.** [pound]: £100 ~ 100 Pfund Sterling - **2.** [excellent] gediegen <> n (U) Pfund das Sterling.

**sterling silver** n Sterlingsilber das.

**stern** [stɜ:n] adj streng <> n Heck das.

**sternly** ['stɜ:nlɪ] adv streng.

**steroid** ['stɪərɔɪd] n Steroid das.

**S**

**stethoscope** ['steθəskəʊp] n Stethoskop das.

**stetson** ['stetsn] n Cowboyhut der.

**stew** [stju:] n Eintopf der ◇ vt schmoren ◇ vi: **to let sb ~** fig jn schmoren lassen.

**steward** ['stjʊəd] n - **1.** Br [on plane, ship] Steward der - **2.** Br [at public event] Ordner der, -in die.

**stewardess** ['stjʊədɪs] n Stewardess die.

**stewing steak** Br ['stju:ɪŋ-], **stewbeef** Am ['stju:bi:f] n Rinderschmorfleisch das.

**St. Ex.** (abbr of **stock exchange**) Börse die.

**stick** [stɪk] (pt & pp **stuck**) n - **1.** [piece of wood] Stock der - **2.** [of dynamite, celery, cinnamon, rhubarb] Stange die; [of chewing gum, chalk] Stück das - **3.** SPORT Schläger der - **4.** phr: **to get the wrong end of the ~** es falsch verstehen ◇ vt - **1.** [with adhesive] kleben; **to ~ sthg on** OR **to sthg** etw an etw (A) kleben - **2.** [push, insert] stecken; **to ~ sthg in(to) sthg** etw in etw (A) stechen - **3.** inf [put] tun - **4.** Br inf [tolerate] ertragen; **to ~ it** es auslhalten ◇ vi - **1.** [arrow, dart, spear] stecken - **2.** [adhere]: **to ~ (to)** kleben (an OR auf (+ D)) - **3.** [become jammed] klemmen - **4.** [remain]: **to ~ in sb's mind** jm im Gedächtnis bleiben.

➣ **sticks** npl pej: **in the ~s** in der Provinz.

➣ **stick around** vi inf dalbleiben.

➣ **stick at** vt fus weiterlmachen mit; **to ~ at it** dranlbleiben.

➣ **stick by** vt fus - **1.** [person] halten zu - **2.** [decision] stehen zu.

➣ **stick out** vt sep - **1.** [extend - tongue, head] herauslstrecken; [ - hand] auslstrecken - **2.** inf [endure]: **to ~ it out** es durchlhalten ◇ vi - **1.** [protrude] vorlstehen; [ears] ablstehen - **2.** inf [be noticeable] auf lfallen.

➣ **stick out for** vt fus Br sich einlsetzen für.

➣ **stick to** vt fus [person, decision] bleiben bei; [path] bleiben auf (+ D); [promise] halten.

➣ **stick together** vi zusammenlkleben; [people] zusammenlhalten.

➣ **stick up** vt sep - **1.** [sign, notice, postcard] auf lhängen - **2.** [with gun]: **~ 'em up!** Hände hoch! ◇ vi vorlstehen; [hair] hochlstehen.

➣ **stick up for** vt fus einltreten für.

➣ **stick with** vt fus bleiben bei.

**sticker** ['stɪkər] n Aufkleber der.

**sticking plaster** ['stɪkɪŋ-] n Heftpflaster das.

**stick insect** n Stabheuschrecke die.

**stick-in-the-mud** n inf Spießer der, -in die.

**stickleback** ['stɪklbæk] n Stichling der.

**stickler** ['stɪklər] n: **to be a ~ for sthg** ein Pedant in Bezug auf etw (A) sein.

**stick-on** adj Klebe-.

**stickpin** ['stɪkpɪn] n Am Krawattennadel die.

**stick shift** n Am - **1.** [gear lever] Schalthebel der - **2.** [car] Auto das mit Handschaltung.

**sticky** ['stɪkɪ] (compar **-ier**; superl **-iest**) adj

- **1.** [hands] klebrig; **~ tape** Klebeband das; **~ label** Aufkleber der - **2.** inf [awkward] heikel - **3.** [weather, day] schwül.

**stiff** [stɪf] adj - **1.** [gen] steif; [rod, brush] hart; [shoes] fest; [drawer, door] widerspenstig - **2.** [resistance, drink] stark; [penalty] hart - **3.** [difficult] schwer ◇ adv inf: **to be bored ~** sich zu Tode langweilen; **to be scared ~** starr vor Angst sein.

**stiffen** ['stɪfn] vt - **1.** [material] steif machen - **2.** [resistance, resolve] verstärken ◇ vi - **1.** [gen] steif werden; [with horror] erstarren - **2.** [resistance, resolve] sich verstärken - **3.** [breeze] auflfrischen.

**stiffener** ['stɪfnər] n [in collar] Kragenstäbchen das.

**stiffness** ['stɪfnɪs] n - **1.** [gen] Steifheit die - **2.** [of hinge, handle, door] Widerstand der - **3.** [of sentence, punishment] Härte die; [of resistance, resolve] Stärke die - **4.** [of exam] Schwierigkeit die.

**stifle** ['staɪfl] vt - **1.** [suffocate] ersticken - **2.** [suppress] unterdrücken ◇ vi [suffocate] ersticken.

**stifling** ['staɪflɪŋ] adj drückend.

**stigma** ['stɪgmə] n - **1.** [social disgrace] Schande die - **2.** BOT Stigma das.

**stigmatize, -ise** ['stɪgmətaɪz] vt brandmarken.

**stile** [staɪl] n Zaunübertritt der.

**stiletto** [stɪ'letəʊ] n Br [shoe] Stöckelschuh der.

**still** [stɪl] adv - **1.** [gen] noch; **we've ~ got ten minutes** wir haben noch zehn Minuten; **I ~ haven't seen it** ich habe es noch nicht gesehen; **~ bigger/more important** noch größer/wichtiger; **~ more money** noch mehr Geld - **2.** [even now] immer noch; **she could ~ change her mind** sie könnte es sich immer noch anders überlegen - **3.** [nevertheless] trotzdem; **you ~ have to pay** Sie müssen trotzdem zahlen; **the train was half an hour late – ~, what do you expect?** der Zug hatte eine halbe Stunde Verspätung – na ja, was haben Sie erwartet? - **4.** [motionless]: **to stand ~** stilllstehen; **sit ~!** sitz still! ◇ adj - **1.** [motionless] bewegungslos; **please be ~!** sitz/steh bitte still! - **2.** [calm, quiet] ruhig - **3.** [not windy] windstill - **4.** [not fizzy] ohne Kohlensäure ◇ n - **1.** PHOT Standfoto das - **2.** [for making alcohol] Destillierapparat der.

**stillborn** ['stɪlbɔːn] adj tot geboren.

**still life** (pl **-s**) n Stillleben das.

**stillness** ['stɪlnɪs] n - **1.** [lack of motion] Bewegungslosigkeit die - **2.** [calm] Stille die.

**stilted** ['stɪltɪd] adj gespreizt.

**stilts** ['stɪlts] npl - **1.** [for person] Stelzen pl - **2.** [for building] Pfähle pl.

**stimulant** ['stɪmjʊlənt] n - **1.** [drug] Aufputschmittel das - **2.** [incentive] Anreiz der.

**stimulate** ['stɪmjʊleɪt] vt - **1.** [interest] anlregen; [growth, economy] anlkurbeln - **2.** [person - physically] erregen; [- mentally] stimulieren.

**stimulating** ['stɪmjʊleɪtɪŋ] adj - **1.** [physically] belebend - **2.** [mentally] stimulierend.

**stimulation** [ˌstɪmjʊ'leɪʃn] n (U) - **1.** [of growth, economy] Ankurbeln das - **2.** [mental] Stimulierung die.

**stimulus** ['stɪmjʊləs] (pl -li [-laɪ]) n - **1.** [gen] Anreiz der - **2.** BIOL Reiz der.

**sting** [stɪŋ] (pt & pp stung) n - **1.** [wound, pain, mark] Stich der; to take the ~ out of sthg fig etw entschärfen - **2.** [part of bee, wasp, scorpion] Stachel der ◇ vt - **1.** [subj: bee, wasp, scorpion] stechen; smoke stung her eyes Rauch brannte in ihren Augen; I was stung by the nettles ich habe mich an den Brennnesseln verbrannt - **2.** fig [subj: remark, criticism] schmerzen ◇ vi [bee, wasp, scorpion] stechen; [nettle, smoke, eyes, skin] brennen.

**stinging nettle** ['stɪŋɪŋ-] n Br Brennnessel die.

**stingy** ['stɪndʒɪ] (compar -ier; superl -iest) adj inf geizig.

**stink** [stɪŋk] (pt stank OR stunk; pp stunk) n Gestank der ◇ vi - **1.** [smell] stinken - **2.** inf fig [be worthless] echt Scheiße sein.

**stink-bomb** n Stinkbombe die.

**stinking** ['stɪŋkɪŋ] inf adj fig [for emphasis] Scheiß- ◇ adv: ~ rich stinkreich.

**stint** [stɪnt] n [period of time] Zeit die; he did a two-year ~ as editor er arbeitete zwei Jahre lang als Redakteur ◇ vi: to ~ on sthg mit etw sparen.

**stipend** ['staɪpend] n [for priest] Gehalt das.

**stipulate** ['stɪpjʊleɪt] vt festlegen.

**stipulation** [ˌstɪpjʊ'leɪʃn] n - **1.** [stating] Festsetzung die - **2.** [condition] Bedingung die.

**stir** [stɜːʳ] (pt & pp -red) n - **1.** [act of mixing]: to give sthg a ~ etw umlrühren - **2.** [excitement] Aufsehen das ◇ vt - **1.** [mix] umlrühren - **2.** [subj: wind] spielen mit; to ~ o.s. sich bewegen - **3.** [excite] bewegen ◇ vi - **1.** [move] sich bewegen - **2.** [emotion] wach werden.

➤ **stir up** vt sep - **1.** [dust, mud] auflwühlen - **2.** [trouble, feelings, memories] wachrufen.

**stir-fry** vt kurz anlbraten.

**stirring** ['stɜːrɪŋ] adj bewegend ◇ n [of emotion, interest] Erwachen das.

**stirrup** ['stɪrəp] n Steigbügel der.

**stitch** [stɪtʃ] n - **1.** [in sewing, for wound] Stich der; [in knitting] Masche die - **2.** [pain]: to have a ~ Seitenstechen haben - **3.** phr: to be in ~es sich halb totlachen ◇ vt nähen.

**stitching** ['stɪtʃɪŋ] n (U) Naht die.

**stoat** [stəʊt] n Hermelin das.

**stock** [stɒk] n - **1.** [supply] Vorrat der - **2.** (U) COMM [of shop] Lagerbestand der; in ~ vorrätig; out of ~ nicht vorrätig - **3.** FIN: ~s and shares Wertpapiere und Aktien - **4.** (U) [ancestry] Herkunft die - **5.** CULIN Brühe die - **6.** [livestock] Nutzvieh das - **7.** [of gun] Schaft der - **8.** phr: to take ~ (of) Bilanz ziehen (über (+ A)) ◇ adj [typical] stereotyp ◇ vt - **1.** [have in stock] auf Lager haben - **2.** [shelves] auflfüllen; [lake with fish] bestücken.

➤ **stock up** vi: to ~ up (on OR with) sich einldecken (mit).

**stockade** [stɒ'keɪd] n Palisade die.

**stockbroker** ['stɒkˌbrəʊkəʳ] n Börsenmakler der, -in die.

**stockcar** ['stɒkkɑːʳ] n Stockcar der.

**stock company** n Am Aktiengesellschaft die.

**stock control** n Lagerbestandskontrolle die.

**stock cube** n Br Brühwürfel der.

**stock exchange** n Börse die.

**stockholder** ['stɒkˌhəʊldəʳ] n Am Aktionär der, -in die.

**Stockholm** ['stɒkhəʊm] n Stockholm nt.

**stocking** ['stɒkɪŋ] n Strumpf der.

**stock-in-trade** n Repertoire das.

**stockist** ['stɒkɪst] n Br Fachhändler der.

**stock market** n Börse die.

**stock phrase** n Floskel die.

**stockpile** ['stɒkpaɪl] n Lager das ◇ vt horten; to ~ weapons ein Waffenlager anllegen.

**stockroom** ['stɒkrʊm] n Lager das.

**stock-still** adv stocksteif.

**stocktaking** ['stɒkˌteɪkɪŋ] n (U) Inventur die.

**stocky** ['stɒkɪ] (compar -ier; superl -iest) adj stämmig.

**stodgy** ['stɒdʒɪ] (compar -ier; superl -iest) adj - **1.** [food] schwer - **2.** pej [uninteresting] fade.

**stoic** ['stəʊɪk] adj stoisch ◇ n Stoiker der, -in die.

**stoical** ['stəʊɪkl] adj stoisch.

**stoicism** ['stəʊɪsɪzm] n Gleichmut der.

**stoke** [stəʊk] vt [fire] schüren.

**stole** [stəʊl] pt ⊏▷ steal ◇ n [shawl] Stola die.

**stolen** ['stəʊln] pp ⊏▷ steal.

**stolid** ['stɒlɪd] adj stur.

**stomach** ['stʌmək] n - **1.** [organ] Magen der; on a full/an empty ~ auf vollen/leeren Magen - **2.** [belly] Bauch der ◇ vt [tolerate] ertragen.

**stomachache** ['stʌməkeɪk] n Magenschmerzen pl.

**S**

**stomach pump** n Magenpumpe die.

**stomach ulcer** n Magengeschwür das.

**stomach upset** n Magenverstimmung die.

**stomp** [stɒmp] vi stampfen.

**stone** [stəʊn] (pl sense 3 only inv OR -s) n - **1.** [gen] Stein der; a ~'s throw from einen Steinwurf von - **2.** [jewel] Edelstein der - **3.** [unit of measurement] = 6,35 kg ⟷ comp aus Stein; [bridge, wall] Stein- ⟷ vt mit Steinen bewerfen.

**Stone Age** n: the ~ die Steinzeit.

**stone-cold** adj eiskalt.

**stoned** [stəʊnd] adj inf - **1.** [drunk] stockbesoffen - **2.** [on drugs] stoned.

**stonemason** ['stəʊnˌmeɪsn] n Steinmetz der, -in die.

**stonewall** [ˌstəʊn'wɔːl] vi auslweichen.

**stoneware** ['stəʊnweəʳ] n Steingut das.

**stonework** ['stəʊnwɜːk] n Mauerwerk das.

**stony** ['stəʊnɪ] (compar -ier; superl -iest) adj - **1.** [ground, soil] steinig - **2.** [expression] steinern; [silence] eisig.

**stood** [stʊd] pt & pp ⊳ stand.

**stooge** [stuːdʒ] n inf Marionette die; [in comedy act] Stichwortgeber der, -in die.

**stool** [stuːl] n [seat] Hocker der.

**stoop** [stuːp] n - **1.** [bent back]: to walk with a ~ gebeugt gehen - **2.** Am [of house] Treppe die ⟷ vi - **1.** [bend forwards] sich bücken - **2.** [have a stoop] gebeugt gehen - **3.** fig [debase o.s.]: to ~ to sthg sich zu etw herablassen; to ~ to doing sthg sich dazu erniedrigen, etw zu tun.

**stop** [stɒp] (pt & pp -ped; cont -ping) n - **1.** [of bus] Haltestelle die; [of train] Station die - **2.** [in journey] Halt der; [longer] Aufenthalt der - **3.** [standstill]: to come to a ~ anlhalten; to put a ~ to sthg einer Sache (D) ein Ende machen - **4.** [in punctuation] Punkt der - **5.** TECH Anschlag der - **6.** phr: to pull out all the ~s fig alle Register ziehen ⟷ vt - **1.** [halt - person, car] anlhalten; [ - machine, engine] ablstellen; [ - ball] stoppen; to ~ doing sthg auflhören, etw zu tun; to ~ smoking mit dem Rauchen auflhören - **2.** [prevent] verhindern; to ~ sb from doing sthg jn daran hindern, etw zu tun; to ~ sthg from happening verhindern, dass etw geschieht - **3.** [payment] einlstellen; [cheque] sperren; [game - finish] ablbrechen - **4.** [hole, gap] stopfen ⟷ vi - **1.** [come to an end] auflhören - **2.** [halt] anlhalten; [walker, machine, watch] stehen bleiben; [on journey] Halt machen; to ~ at nothing (to do sthg) vor nichts Halt machen(, um etw zu tun) - **3.** [stay] bleiben.

➤ **stop off** vi Halt machen.

➤ **stop over** vi Zwischenstation machen.

➤ **stop up** vt sep [block] zulstopfen.

**stopcock** ['stɒpkɒk] n Absperrhahn der.

**stopgap** ['stɒpgæp] n Notlösung die.

**stopover** ['stɒpˌəʊvəʳ] n Zwischenstation die.

**stoppage** ['stɒpɪdʒ] n - **1.** [strike] Streik der - **2.** Br [deduction] Abzug der.

**stopper** ['stɒpəʳ] n Pfropfen der, Stöpsel der.

**stopping** ['stɒpɪŋ] adj Br: ~ train Nahverkehrszug der.

**stop press** n letzte Meldungen pl.

**stop sign** n AUT Stoppschild das.

**stopwatch** ['stɒpwɒtʃ] n Stoppuhr die.

**storage** ['stɔːrɪdʒ] n - **1.** [act of storing] Lagerung die - **2.** COMPUT Speichern das.

**storage heater** n Br Nachtspeicherofen der.

**store** [stɔːʳ] n - **1.** esp Am [shop] Laden der, Geschäft das; [department store] Kaufhaus das - **2.** [supply]: ~ of sthg Vorrat der an etw (D) - **3.** [storage place] Lager das - **4.** phr: to set great ~ by OR on sthg großen Wert auf etw (A) legen ⟷ vt - **1.** [keep, save - address, details] auflbewahren; [ - goods, provisions] lagern; [ - furniture] einlstellen - **2.** COMPUT speichern.

➤ **in store** adv [imminent]: who knows what the future has in ~ for us? wer weiß, was die Zukunft bringt?

➤ **store up** vt sep [information] anlsammeln; to ~ food Lebensmittelvorräte anlegen.

**store detective** n Kaufhausdetektiv der, -in die.

**storehouse** ['stɔːhaʊs, pl -haʊzɪz] n - **1.** esp Am [warehouse] Lagerhaus das - **2.** fig [treasury] Fundgrube die.

**storekeeper** ['stɔːˌkiːpəʳ] n Am Ladenbesitzer der, -in die.

**storeroom** ['stɔːrʊm] n Lagerraum der.

**storey** Br (pl -s), **story** Am (pl -ies) ['stɔːrɪ] n Stockwerk das.

**stork** [stɔːk] n Storch der.

**storm** [stɔːm] n - **1.** [bad weather] Sturm der; a ~ in a teacup ein Sturm im Wasserglas - **2.** [violent reaction - of abuse, tears] Flut die; [ - of protest] Sturm der; a ~ of applause stürmischer Applaus ⟷ vt - **1.** MIL stürmen - **2.** [say angrily] toben ⟷ vi [go angrily] stürmen.

**storm cloud** n Gewitterwolke die.

**storming** ['stɔːmɪŋ] n: the ~ of a fortress der Sturm einer Festung.

**stormy** ['stɔːmɪ] (compar -ier; superl -iest) adj lit & fig stürmisch.

**story** ['stɔːrɪ] (pl -ies) n - **1.** [tale, history] Geschichte die; it's the (same) old ~ es ist das alte Lied; to cut a long ~ short … um es kurz zu machen … - **2.** [article - in newspaper] Artikel der; [ - on TV/radio news] Bericht der - **3.** euphemism [lie] Märchen das - **4.** Am = storey.

**storybook** ['stɔːrɪbʊk] adj wie im Märchen.

**storyteller** ['stɔːrɪˌteləʳ] n - **1.** [teller of story] Geschichtenerzähler der, -in die - **2.** euphemism [liar] Lügner der, -in die.

**stout** [staʊt] adj - **1.** [corpulent] korpulent - **2.** [strong] kräftig; [boots] fest - **3.** [brave] tapfer ◇ n Starkbier das.

**stoutness** ['staʊtnɪs] n [corpulence] Korpulenz die.

**stove** [staʊv] pt & pp ⊳ **stave** ◇ n - **1.** [for cooking] Herd der - **2.** [for heating] Ofen der.

**stow** [staʊ] vt: **to ~ sthg (away)** etw verstauen.
➤ **stow away** vi [on ship, plane] blinder Passagier sein.

**stowaway** ['staʊəweɪ] n blinder Passagier.

**straddle** ['strædl] vt - **1.** [subj: person - chair] rittlings sitzen auf (+ D); [ - gap] breitbeinig stehen über (+ D) - **2.** [subj: bridge] überspannen; **the town ~s the border** der Ort erstreckt sich zu beiden Seiten der Grenze.

**strafe** [strɑːf] vt MIL unter Beschuss nehmen.

**straggle** ['strægl] vi - **1.** [buildings] verstreut liegen; [plant] wuchern - **2.** [person, group] zurücklbleiben.

**straggler** ['strægləʳ] n Nachzügler der, -in die.

**straggly** ['stræglɪ] (compar -ier; superl -iest) adj [hair] zottelig; [shrub] wuchernd.

**straight** [streɪt] adj - **1.** [not curved, level, upright] gerade - **2.** [not curly] glatt - **3.** [honest, frank] ehrlich, offen - **4.** [tidy] ordentlich; **to put a room ~** ein Zimmer auf lräumen - **5.** [simple - exchange] einfach; [ - choice] klar - **6.** [undiluted] pur - **7.** inf [conventional] konventionell - **8.** gay sl [heterosexual] hetero - **9.** [quits] quitt - **10.** phr: **to get sthg ~** etw klarlstellen ◇ adv - **1.** [in a straight line, upright] gerade - **2.** [directly, immediately] direkt - **3.** [honestly, frankly] offen - **4.** [undiluted] pur - **5.** phr: **to go ~** [criminal] keine krummen Sachen mehr machen ◇ n SPORT: **the ~** die Gerade.
➤ **straight off** adv sofort.
➤ **straight out** adv rundheraus.

**straightaway** [ˌstreɪtəˈweɪ] adv sofort.

**straighten** ['streɪtn] vt - **1.** [tidy - dress] gerade ziehen; [ - room, desk] auflräumen - **2.** [make straight] begradigen - **3.** [make level] auslrichten ◇ vi: **to ~ (up)** sich auflrichten.
➤ **straighten out** vt sep [sort out] klären.

**straight face** n: **to keep a ~** ernst bleiben.

**straightforward** [ˌstreɪtˈfɔːwəd] adj - **1.** [easy] einfach - **2.** [honest, frank] offen, ehrlich.

**strain** [streɪn] n - **1.** [gen] Belastung die - **2.** MED [of muscle] Zerrung die; [of back] Überanstrengung die - **3.** [type, variety] Art die ◇ vt - **1.** [work hard - eyes] überanstrengen; **don't ~ yourself!** iron überanstrenge dich nicht! - **2.** MED [injure]: **to ~ a muscle/one's back** sich einen Muskel zerren/seinen Rücken überanstrengen - **3.** [overtax - resources] überbeanspruchen;

[ - patience] auf die Probe stellen - **4.** [drain] durch ein Sieb gießen - **5.** TECH [rope, girder, ceiling] belasten ◇ vi: **to ~ to do sthg** sich anlstrengen, etw zu tun.
➤ **strains** npl literary [of music] Klänge pl.

**strained** [streɪnd] adj - **1.** [forced] angestrengt - **2.** [tense] angespannt - **3.** MED [sprained] gezerrt - **4.** CULIN [liquid] durch ein Sieb gegossen.

**strainer** ['streɪnəʳ] n Sieb das.

**strait** [streɪt] n GEOGR Meerenge die.
➤ **straits** npl: **in dire** OR **desperate ~s** in einer Notlage.

**straitened** ['streɪtnd] adj fml: **in ~ circumstances** in beschränkten Verhältnissen.

**straitjacket** ['streɪtˌdʒækɪt] n Zwangsjacke die.

**straitlaced** [ˌstreɪt'leɪst] adj pej spießig.

**Strait of Gibraltar** n: **the ~** die Straße von Gibraltar.

**strand** [strænd] n Faden der; [of hair] Strähne die.

**stranded** ['strændɪd] adj [person, car] festsitzend.

**strange** [streɪndʒ] adj - **1.** [unusual, unexpected] seltsam - **2.** [unfamiliar] fremd.

**strangely** ['streɪndʒlɪ] adv seltsam; **~ (enough)** seltsamerweise.

**stranger** ['streɪndʒəʳ] n - **1.** [unknown person] Unbekannte der, die; **she's a complete ~ to me** ich kenne sie überhaupt nicht; **to be no ~ to sthg** etw gut kennen - **2.** [person from elsewhere] Fremde der, die.

**strangle** ['stræŋgl] vt - **1.** [kill] erwürgen - **2.** fig [stifle] ersticken.

**stranglehold** ['stræŋglhəʊld] n - **1.** [around neck] Würgegriff der - **2.** fig [strong influence]: **to have a ~ on sb** jm in der Zange haben; **to have a ~ on sthg** etw beherrschen.

**strangulation** [ˌstræŋgjʊ'leɪʃn] n [act of killing] Erwürgen das.

**strap** [stræp] (pt & pp -ped; cont -ping) n - **1.** [for carrying] Riemen der - **2.** [for fastening - of dress, bra] Träger der; [ - of watch] Armband das ◇ vt [fasten]: **to ~ sthg (on)to sthg** etw auf etw (A) schnallen.

**strapless** ['stræplɪs] adj trägerlos.

**strapping** ['stræpɪŋ] adj stramm.

**Strasbourg** ['stræzbɜːg] n Straßburg nt.

**strata** ['strɑːtə] pl ⊳ **stratum**.

**stratagem** ['strætədʒəm] n List die.

**strategic** [strə'tiːdʒɪk] adj strategisch.

**strategist** ['strætɪdʒɪst] n MIL Stratege der, -gin die.

**strategy** ['strætɪdʒɪ] (pl -ies) n Strategie die.

**stratified** ['strætɪfaɪd] adj - **1.** GEOL in Schich-

**S**

ten gelagert, geschichtet - **2.** *fig* [society] vielschichtig.

**stratosphere** [ˈstrætəˌsfɪəʳ] *n:* **the ~** die Stratosphäre.

**stratum** [ˈstrɑːtəm] (*pl* **-ta**) *n* GEOL & *fig* Schicht *die*.

**straw** [strɔː] *n* - **1.** [dried corn] Stroh *das* - **2.** [for drinking] Strohhalm *der* - **3.** *phr:* **to clutch at ~s** sich an einen Strohhalm klammern; **that's the last ~!** das ist der Gipfel! ⬦ *comp* Stroh-.

**strawberry** [ˈstrɔːbərɪ] (*pl* **-ies**) *n* Erdbeere *die* ⬦ *comp* Erdbeer-.

**straw poll** *n* Probeabstimmung *die*.

**stray** [streɪ] *adj* - **1.** [cat, dog] streunend - **2.** [bullet] verirrt ⬦ *n* [animal] streunendes Tier ⬦ *vi* - **1.** [person, animal] herumlstreunen; **to ~ from the path** vom Weg ablweichen - **2.** [thoughts, mind] ablschweifen.

**streak** [striːk] *n* - **1.** [mark, line] Streifen *der;* **she's had blond ~s put in her hair** sie hat sich blonde Strähnchen machen lassen; **a ~ of lightning** ein Blitz(strahl) - **2.** [in character] Zug *der* - **3.** [period]: **a winning/losing ~** eine Glückssträhne/Pechsträhne ⬦ *vi* [move quickly] sausen.

**streaked** [striːkt] *adj:* **~ with sthg** mit etw beschmiert; **her hair was ~ with grey** ihr Haar hatte graue Strähnen.

**streaky** [ˈstriːkɪ] (*compar* **-ier;** *superl* **-iest**) *adj* [surface] verschmiert.

**streaky bacon** *n* *Br* durchwachsener Speck.

**stream** [striːm] *n* - **1.** [gen] Strom *der* - **2.** [brook] Bach *der* - **3.** [of abuse, complaints] Flut *die* - **4.** *Br* SCH Leistungsgruppe *die* ⬦ *vt* *Br* SCH in Leistungsgruppen einlteilen ⬦ *vi* strömen.

**streamer** [ˈstriːməʳ] *n* [for party] Luftschlange *die*.

**streamline** [ˈstriːmlaɪn] *vt* - **1.** [make aerodynamic] stromlinienförmig machen - **2.** [make efficient] rationalisieren.

**streamlined** [ˈstriːmlaɪnd] *adj* - **1.** [aerodynamic] stromlinienförmig - **2.** [efficient] rationalisiert.

**street** [striːt] *n* Straße *die;* **that's right up my ~** *Br inf* das ist genau mein Fall; **to be ~s ahead of sb** *Br* jm haushoch überlegen sein.

**streetcar** [ˈstriːtkɑːʳ] *n* *Am* Straßenbahn *die*.

**street-cred(ibility)** *n* (U) *inf* Image *das*.

**street lamp, street light** *n* Straßenlaterne *die*.

**street lighting** *n* (U) Straßenbeleuchtung *die*.

**street map** *n* Stadtplan *der*.

**street market** *n* Straßenmarkt *der*.

**street plan** *n* Stadtplan *der*.

**street value** *n* Verkaufswert *der*.

**streetwise** [ˈstriːtwaɪz] *adj:* **to be ~** wissen, wie es läuft.

**strength** [streŋθ] *n* - **1.** [gen] Stärke *die;* **on the ~ of** auf der Basis von; **to go from ~ to ~** einen Erfolg nach dem anderen erzielen - **2.** (U) [confidence, courage] Kraft *die* - **3.** [solidity] Stabilität *die* - **4.** [number]: **at full ~** vollzählig; **below ~** nicht vollzählig; **in ~** zahlreich.

**strengthen** [ˈstreŋθn] *vt* - **1.** [gen] stärken - **2.** [team, structure, resolve] verstärken - **3.** [friendship, ties, bond] festigen - **4.** [make braver, more confident] bestärken ⬦ *vi* - **1.** [gen] stärker werden - **2.** [friendship, ties, bond] sich festigen.

**strenuous** [ˈstrenjʊəs] *adj* [exercise] anstrengend; [effort] gewaltig.

**stress** [stres] *n* - **1.** [emphasis]: **to lay** *OR* **put ~ on sthg** etw besonders betonen - **2.** [tension, anxiety] Stress *der;* **to be under ~** unter Stress stehen - **3.** TECH [physical pressure]: **~ (on sthg)** Druck *der* (auf etw (A)) - **4.** LING [on word, syllable] Betonung *die* ⬦ *vt* [emphasize & LING] betonen.

**stressed** [strest] *adj* [tense, anxious] gestresst.

**stressful** [ˈstresfʊl] *adj* stressig.

**stretch** [stretʃ] *n* - **1.** [area] Stück *das* - **2.** [period of time] Zeitspanne *die;* **for a five-year ~** für fünf Jahre - **3.** [effort]: **by no ~ of the imagination** beim besten Willen nicht ⬦ *vt* - **1.** [pull longer or wider] dehnen - **2.** [pull taut] spannen - **3.** [extend to fullest] auslstrecken - **4.** [rules, meaning, truth]: **to ~ the rules** eine Ausnahme machen; **to ~ the truth** übertreiben - **5.** [budget, resources] strecken - **6.** [provide challenge for] fordern ⬦ *vi* - **1.** [area]: **to ~ over sich** ausldehnen über (+ *A*); **to ~ from ... to** reichen von ... bis - **2.** [person, animal] sich strecken - **3.** [material, elastic] sich dehnen ⬦ *adj* Stretch-.

➤ **at a stretch** *adv:* **for five hours at a~** fünf Stunden ohne Unterbrechung.

➤ **stretch out** *vt sep* [hold out] auslstrecken ⬦ *vi* [lie down] sich auslstrecken.

**stretcher** [ˈstretʃəʳ] *n* Trage *die*.

**stretcher party** *n* Gruppe *die* von Krankenträgern.

**stretchmarks** [ˈstretʃmɑːks] *npl* Schwangerschaftsstreifen *pl*.

**stretchy** [ˈstretʃɪ] (*compar* **-ier;** *superl* **-iest**) *adj* elastisch.

**strew** [struː] (*pt* **-ed;** *pp* **strewn** [struːn] *OR* **-ed**) *vt* [scatter untidily]: **to be ~n on** *OR* **over sthg** auf etw (D) oder etw (A) verstreut sein; **to be ~n with sthg** [freckles, confetti] mit etw übersät sein; **the streets were ~n with litter** die Straßen waren voller Müll.

**stricken** [ˈstrɪkn] *adj:* **to be ~ by** *OR* **with sthg** [doubt, horror, panic] von etw erfüllt sein; [illness] an etw (D) leiden.

**strict** [strɪkt] *adj* - **1.** [severe] streng - **2.** [inflexible] strikt - **3.** [exact, precise] genau; **in the ~est sense of a word** im engsten Sinne des Wortes.

**strictly** ['strɪktlɪ] *adv* - **1.** [severely, rigidly, absolutely] streng - **2.** [precisely, exactly] genau; **~ speaking** genau genommen - **3.** [exclusively] ausschließlich.

**strictness** ['strɪktnɪs] *n* - **1.** [severity] Strenge *die* - **2.** [rigidity] Striktheit *die*.

**stride** [straɪd] (*pt* **strode;** *pp* **stridden** ['strɪdn]) *n* [step] Schritt *der;* **to take sthg in one's ~** *fig* mit etw leicht fertig werden ◇ *vi* schreiten.
➧ **strides** *npl* [progress]: **to make (great) ~s** (große) Fortschritte machen.

**strident** ['straɪdnt] *adj* - **1.** [voice, sound] durchdringend - **2.** [demand] lautstark.

**strife** [straɪf] *n fml* Zwietracht *die*.

**strike** [straɪk] (*pt* & *pp* **struck**) *n* - **1.** [refusal to work, do sthg] Streik *der;* **to be (out) on ~** streiken; **to go on ~** in Streik treten - **2.** MIL [attack] Angriff *der* - **3.** [find] Fund *der* ◇ *comp* Streik- ◇ *vt* - **1.** [hit deliberately] schlagen; [hit accidentally - car] fahren gegen; [ - boat] auflaufen auf (+ A) - **2.** [subj: hurricane, disaster, lightning] treffen - **3.** [subj: thought]: **it ~s me that ...** mir fällt auf, dass ...; **the thought had never struck me before** der Gedanke ist mir vorher nie gekommen; **he ~s me as very capable** er scheint mir sehr fähig zu sein - **4.** [impress]: **to be struck by** OR **with sthg** von etw beeindruckt sein - **5.** [bargain] aushandeln - **6.** [match] anzünden - **7.** [find] finden; **to ~ a balance (between)** die goldene Mitte finden (zwischen (+D)); **to ~ a serious/happy note** einen ernsten/heiteren Ton anschlagen - **8.** [chime] schlagen - **9.** *phr:* **to be struck dumb** sprachlos sein; **to ~ fear** OR **terror into sb** jm Furcht OR Schrecken einjagen; **to ~ (it) lucky** einen Glückstreffer landen; **to ~ it rich** das große Los ziehen ◇ *vi* - **1.** [stop working] streiken - **2.** [happen suddenly - disaster, hurricane] losbrechen; [ - lightning] einschlagen - **3.** [attack] angreifen - **4.** [chime] schlagen.
➧ **strike back** *vi* zurückschlagen.
➧ **strike down** *vt sep* niederschlagen.
➧ **strike off** *vt sep:* **to be struck off** [doctor, lawyer] die Zulassung entzogen bekommen.
➧ **strike out** *vt sep* durchstreichen ◇ *vi* - **1.** [head out] losziehen - **2.** [do sthg different]: **to ~ out on one's own** eigene Wege gehen.
➧ **strike up** *vt fus* - **1.** [friendship, conversation] anfangen - **2.** [music] anfangen zu spielen ◇ *vi* [band] anfangen zu spielen.

**strikebound** ['straɪkbaʊnd] *adj* durch einen Streik gelähmt.

**strikebreaker** ['straɪk,breɪkə<sup>r</sup>] *n* Streikbrecher *der*, -in *die*.

**strike pay** *n* Streikgeld *das*.

**striker** ['straɪkə<sup>r</sup>] *n* - **1.** [person on strike] Streikende *der*, *die* - **2.** FTBL Stürmer *der*, -in *die*.

**striking** ['straɪkɪŋ] *adj* - **1.** [noticeable, unusual] auffallend - **2.** [attractive] umwerfend.

**striking distance** *n:* **within ~ (of sthg)** [close] ganz in der Nähe (von etw).

**string** [strɪŋ] (*pt* & *pp* **strung**) *n* - **1.** [gen] Schnur *die;* **(with) no ~s attached** ohne Bedingungen; **to pull ~s** Beziehungen spielen lassen - **2.** [of onions] Zopf *der;* **~ of pearls** [necklace] Perlenkette *die* - **3.** [series] Reihe *die;* **she owns a ~ of racehorses** sie besitzt mehrere Rennpferde - **4.** [for musical instrument, tennis racket] Saite *die;* [for bow] Sehne *die* ◇ *comp* [vest] Netz-; **~ bag** Einkaufsnetz *das*.
➧ **strings** *npl* MUS: **the ~s** die Streicher *pl.*
➧ **string along** *vt sep inf* [deceive] zum Narren halten.
➧ **string out** *vt sep* [disperse]: **to be strung out** verteilt sein.
➧ **string together** *vt sep fig* [words, sentences] aneinander fügen.
➧ **string up** *vt sep inf* [kill by hanging] aufhängen.

**string bean** *n* Stangenbohne *die*.

**stringed instrument** [strɪŋd-] *n* Saiteninstrument *das*.

**stringent** ['strɪndʒənt] *adj* streng.

**string quartet** *n* Streichquartett *das*.

**stringy** ['strɪŋɪ] (*compar* **-ier;** *superl* **-iest**) *adj* [beans, meat] faserig.

**strip** [strɪp] (*pt* & *pp* **-ped;** *cont* **-ping**) *n* - **1.** [of fabric, paper, land, water] Streifen *der;* **to tear a ~ off sb** *Br* jn zusammenstauchen - **2.** *Br* SPORT [clothes] Trikot *das* ◇ *vt* - **1.** [undress] ausziehen; **~ped to the waist** mit freiem Oberkörper - **2.** [remove - paint] abkratzen; [ - wallpaper] abziehen - **3.** [take away from]: **to ~ sb of sthg** jm etw aberkennen ◇ *vi* - **1.** [undress] sich ausziehen - **2.** [do a striptease] strippen.
➧ **strip off** *vt sep* [clothes] ausziehen ◇ *vi* sich ausziehen.

**strip cartoon** *n Br* Comic *der*.

**stripe** [straɪp] *n* - **1.** [band of colour] Streifen *der* - **2.** [sign of rank] Ärmelstreifen *der*.

**striped** [straɪpt] *adj* gestreift.

**strip lighting** *n* (U) Neonbeleuchtung *die*.

**stripper** ['strɪpə<sup>r</sup>] *n* - **1.** [performer of striptease] Stripper *der*, -in *die* - **2.** [liquid] Entferner *der;* [tool] Spachtel *der*.

**strip-search** *n* Leibesvisitation *die* ◇ *vt* einer Leibesvisitation unterziehen.

**strip show** *n* Stripteaseshow *die*.

**striptease** ['striptiːz] *n* Striptease *der*.

**stripy** ['straɪpɪ] (*compar* **-ier;** *superl* **-iest**) *adj* gestreift.

**strive** [straɪv] (*pt* **strove;** *pp* **striven** ['strɪvn]) *vi*

**S**

*fml:* to ~ for sthg nach etw streben; to ~ to do sthg bemüht sein, etw zu tun.

**strobe (light)** ['strəub-] *n* Stroboskoplicht *das.*

**strode** [strəud] *pt* ⊳ **stride.**

**stroke** [strəuk] *n* - **1.** MED Schlaganfall *der* - **2.** [of pen, brush] Strich *der* - **3.** [in swimming - movement] Zug *der;* [ - style] Stil *der* - **4.** [in rowing, in ball game, of clock] Schlag *der* - **5.** Br TYPO [oblique] Schrägstrich *der* - **6.** [piece]: **a ~ of genius** ein Geniestreich; **a ~ of luck** ein Glücksfall; **not to do a ~ of work** keinen Finger rühren; **at a ~** mit einem Streich ⋄ *vt* streicheln.

**stroll** [strəul] *n* Spaziergang *der* ⋄ *vi* spazieren gehen.

**stroller** ['strəulə'] *n* Am [for baby] Sportwagen *der.*

**strong** [strɒŋ] *adj* - **1.** [gen] stark; **to be ~ in sthg** gut in etw *(D)* sein; **~ point** Stärke *die* - **2.** [physically powerful, healthy] kräftig - **3.** [solid, sturdy] stabil; [measures] energisch - **4.** [argument, case, evidence] überzeugend ⋄ *adv:* **to be still going ~** [person, group] immer noch gut dabei sein; [machine] immer noch funktionieren.

**strongarm** ['strɒŋɑːm] *adj:* **~ tactics** brutale Taktiken *pl.*

**strongbox** ['strɒŋbɒks] *n* Tresor *der.*

**stronghold** ['strɒŋhəuld] *n fig* Hochburg *die.*

**strong language** *n (U)* Kraftausdrücke *pl.*

**strongly** ['strɒŋlɪ] *adv* - **1.** [sturdily, solidly] solide - **2.** [in degree or intensity] stark - **3.** [support] energisch; **do you feel ~ about it?** ist es Ihnen wichtig?

**strong man** *n* [in circus] starker Mann.

**strong-minded** [-'maɪndɪd] *adj* willensstark.

**strong room** *n* Tresorraum *der.*

**strong-willed** [-'wɪld] *adj* willensstark.

**stroppy** ['strɒpɪ] *(compar* **-ier;** *superl* **-iest)** *adj* Br *inf* [uncooperative] widerspenstig; **don't get ~ with me!** werd nicht pampig!

**strove** [strəuv] *pt* ⊳ **strive.**

**struck** [strʌk] *pt & pp* ⊳ **strike.**

**structural** ['strʌktʃərəl] *adj* strukturell.

**structurally** ['strʌktʃərəlɪ] *adv* strukturell.

**structure** ['strʌktʃə'] *n* - **1.** [organization, arrangement] Struktur *die* - **2.** [building, construction] Konstruktion *die* ⋄ *vt* strukturieren.

**struggle** ['strʌgl] *n* Kampf *der;* **a ~ for sthg** ein Kampf um etw; **it will be a ~ to finish on time** wir werden uns sehr anstrengen müssen, um rechtzeitig fertig zu werden ⋄ *vi* - **1.** [try hard, strive] kämpfen; **to ~ for sthg** um etw kämpfen; **she ~d to reach the switch** sie

hatte Mühe, an den Schalter zu kommen - **2.** [fight]: **to ~ (with sb)** (mit jm) kämpfen - **3.** [move with difficulty]: **he ~d up the stairs/into the lift** er kämpfte sich die Treppe hinauf/ in den Fahrstuhl.

➤ **struggle on** *vi:* **to ~ on (with sthg)** sich weiterkämpfen (durch etw).

**struggling** ['strʌglɪŋ] *adj* [business] in Schwierigkeiten; **a ~ writer** ein noch nicht anerkannter Schriftsteller.

**strum** [strʌm] *(pt & pp* **-med;** *cont* **-ming)** *vt* klimpern; [guitar] klimpern auf *(+ D)* ⋄ *vi:* **to ~ (on sthg)** (auf etw *(D))* klimpern.

**strung** [strʌŋ] *pt & pp* ⊳ **string.**

**strut** [strʌt] *(pt & pp* **-ted;** *cont* **-ting)** *n* CONSTR Strebe *die* ⋄ *vi* stolzieren.

**strychnine** ['strɪkniːn] *n* Strychnin *das.*

**stub** [stʌb] *(pt & pp* **-bed;** *cont* **-bing)** *n* - **1.** [of cigarette, pencil] Stummel *der* - **2.** [of ticket, cheque] Abschnitt *der* ⋄ *vt:* **to ~ one's toe** sich den Zeh stoßen.

➤ **stub out** *vt sep* ausldrücken.

**stubble** ['stʌbl] *n (U)* Stoppeln *pl.*

**stubborn** ['stʌbən] *adj* - **1.** [person - resolute] hartnäckig; [ - unreasonable] dickköpfig, stur - **2.** [stain] hartnäckig.

**stubbornly** ['stʌbənlɪ] *adv* [resolutely] hartnäckig; [unreasonably] störrisch, stur.

**stubby** ['stʌbɪ] *(compar* **-ier;** *superl* **-iest)** *adj* [fingers] kurz und dick.

**stucco** ['stʌkəu] *n* Stuck *der.*

**stuck** [stʌk] *pt & pp* ⊳ **stick** ⋄ *adj* - **1.** [fixed tightly, jammed - window, lid] verklemmt; [ - finger, toe, garment] eingeklemmt - **2.** [stumped]: **I'm ~** ich komme nicht weiter - **3.** [stranded]: **he got ~ in Birmingham** er saß in Birmingham fest - **4.** [in an unpleasant situation, trapped]: **to be ~** festlsitzen.

**stuck-up** *adj inf pej* hochnäsig.

**stud** [stʌd] *n* - **1.** [metal decoration] Niete *die* - **2.** [earring] Ohrstecker *der* - **3.** Br [on boot, shoe] Stollen *der* - **4.** [place for breeding horses] Gestüt *das;* **to be put out to ~** zu Zuchtzwecken verwendet werden.

**studded** ['stʌdɪd] *adj:* **~ with sthg** mit etw besetzt.

**student** ['stjuːdnt] *n* - **1.** [at college, university] Student *der,* **-in** *die* - **2.** [scholar]: **to be a ~ of history/human nature** sich für Geschichte/ die menschliche Natur interessieren ⋄ *comp* Studenten-.

**student loan** *n* Br Studentendarlehen *das.*

**students' union** *n* - **1.** [organization] Studentenvereinigung *die* - **2.** [building] *Gebäude der Studentenvereinigung, in dem sich Verwaltungsbüros, Geschäfte und Cafés befinden.*

**stud farm** *n* Gestüt *das.*

**studied** ['stʌdɪd] *adj* künstlich; [answer] einlstudiert.

**studio** ['stju:dɪəʊl] (*pl* **-s**) *n* - **1.** [artist's workroom] Atelier *das* - **2.** CINEMA, RADIO & TV Studio *das*.

**studio apartment** *n Am* = studio flat.

**studio audience** *n* Publikum *das* im Studio.

**studio flat** *Br*, **studio apartment** *Am n* Atelierwohnung *die*.

**studious** ['stju:djəs] *adj* fleißig.

**studiously** ['stju:djəslɪ] *adv* fleißig.

**study** ['stʌdɪ] (*pl* **-ies**; *pt* & *pp* **-ied**) *n* - **1.** (*U*) [learning] Studium *das* - **2.** [piece of research] Untersuchung *die* - **3.** [room] Arbeitszimmer *das* - **4.** ART & PHOT Studie *die* <> *vt* & *vi* studieren.
◆ **studies** *npl*: **how are your studies going?** [at school] wie läuft es in der Schule?; [at university] was macht das Studium?

**stuff** [stʌf] *n* (*U*) *inf* - **1.** [matter, things, substance] Zeug *das*; **to know one's ~** sich auslkennen; **and all that ~** und so weiter - **2.** [belongings] Sachen *pl* <> *vt* - **1.** [push, put] stopfen - **2.** [fill, cram]: **to ~ sthg (with sthg)** etw (mit etw) voll stopfen - **3.** [with food]: **to ~ o.s. (with sthg)** *inf* sich (mit etw) voll stopfen - **4.** CULIN füllen.

**stuffed** [stʌft] *adj* - **1.** [filled, crammed]: **~ with sthg** mit etw voll gestopft - **2.** *inf* [with food] voll - **3.** CULIN gefüllt - **4.** [animal] ausgestopft - **5.** *phr*: **get ~!** *Br vinf* du kannst mich mal!

**stuffing** ['stʌfɪŋ] *n* (*U*) - **1.** [for furniture] Polsterung *die* - **2.** [for toys & CULIN] Füllung *die*.

**stuffy** ['stʌfɪ] (*compar* **-ier**; *superl* **-iest**) *adj* - **1.** [room] stickig - **2.** [formal, old-fashioned] spießig.

**stumble** ['stʌmbl] *vi* - **1.** [trip] stolpern - **2.** [hesitate, make mistake] stocken.
◆ **stumble across, stumble on** *vt fus* stoßen auf (+ A); [person] stolpern über (+ A).

**stumbling block** ['stʌmblɪŋ-] *n* Hindernis *das*.

**stump** [stʌmp] *n* [remaining part] Stumpf *der* <> *vt* [subj: question; problem]: **to be ~ed by a problem/question** keine Lösung/Antwort wissen <> *vi* stampfen.
◆ **stumps** *npl* CRICKET Stäbe *pl*.
◆ **stump up** *vt fus inf Br* springen lassen.

**stun** [stʌn] (*pt* & *pp* **-ned**; *cont* **-ning**) *vt* - **1.** [knock unconscious] bewusstlos schlagen - **2.** [shock, surprise] verblüffen.

**stung** [stʌŋ] *pt* & *pp* ⊳ sting.

**stunk** [stʌŋk] *pt* & *pp* ⊳ stink.

**stunned** *adj* - **1.** [unconscious] bewusstlos - **2.** [shocked, surprised] verblüfft.

**stunning** ['stʌnɪŋ] *adj* - **1.** [beautiful] atemberaubend - **2.** [shocking] schrecklich; [surprising] sensationell.

**stunt** [stʌnt] *n* - **1.** [for publicity] Werbetrick *der* - **2.** CINEMA Stunt *der* <> *vt* hemmen.

**stunt man** *n* Stuntman *der*.

**stunt woman** *n* Stuntfrau *die*.

**stupefy** ['stju:pɪfaɪ] (*pt* & *pp* **-ied**) *vt* - **1.** [tire, bore] abstumpfen lassen - **2.** [surprise] verblüffen.

**stupendous** [stju:'pendəs] *adj inf* - **1.** [wonderful] toll - **2.** [very large] enorm.

**stupid** ['stju:pɪd] *adj* - **1.** [foolish] dumm - **2.** *inf* [wretched, damned] blöd.

**stupidity** [stju:'pɪdətɪ] *n* Dummheit *die*.

**stupidly** ['stju:pɪdlɪ] *adv*: **~ I had forgotten my ticket** dummerweise hatte ich mein Ticket vergessen.

**stupor** ['stju:pəʳ] *n* Betäubung *die;* **in a drunken ~** volltrunken.

**sturdy** ['stɜ:dɪ] (*compar* **-ier**; *superl* **-iest**) *adj* kräftig; [furniture, bridge] stabil.

**sturgeon** ['stɜ:dʒən] (*pl inv*) *n* Stör *der*.

**stutter** ['stʌtəʳ] *n* [speech impediment] Stottern *das* <> *vi* [in speaking] stottern.

**sty** [staɪ] (*pl* **sties**) *n* Schweinestall *der*.

**stye** [staɪ] *n* Gerstenkorn *das*.

**style** [staɪl] *n* - **1.** [gen] Stil *der;* **in ~** im großen Stil; **that's not my ~** das ist nicht meine Art - **2.** [fashion, design] Mode *die* <> *vt* [hair] stylen.

**styling mousse** ['staɪlɪŋ-] *n* (*U*) Schaumfestiger *der*.

**stylish** ['staɪlɪʃ] *adj* elegant.

**stylist** ['staɪlɪst] *n* [hairdresser] Stylist *der*, -in *die*.

**stylized, -ised** ['staɪlaɪzd] *adj* stilisiert.

**stylus** ['staɪləs] (*pl* **-es**) *n* - **1.** [on record player] Nadel *die* - **2.** COMPUT Stift *der*.

**stymie** ['staɪmɪ] *vt inf*: **to be ~d** [person] in der Klemme sitzen.

**Styrofoam**® ['staɪrəfəʊm] *n* Styropor® *das*.

**suave** [swɑ:v] *adj* gewandt; *pej* glatt.

**sub** [sʌb] *n inf* - **1.** SPORT (*abbr of* **substitute**) Ersatz *der* - **2.** *abbr of* **submarine** - **3.** *Br abbr of* **subscription** - **4.** *Am* [sandwich] belegtes Baguette.

**sub-** [sʌb] *prefix* [with nouns] Unter-, Sub-; [with adjectives] unter-, sub-.

**subcommittee** ['sʌbkə͵mɪtɪ] *n* Unterausschuss *der*.

**subconscious** [͵sʌb'kɒnʃəs] *adj* unterbewusst <> *n*: **the ~** das Unterbewusstsein.

**subconsciously** [͵sʌb'kɒnʃəslɪ] *adv* unterbewusst.

**subcontinent** [͵sʌb'kɒntɪnənt] *n* Subkontinent *der*.

**subcontract** [͵sʌbkən'trækt] *vt* an ein Subunternehmen/ Subunternehmen vergeben.

S

**subculture** ['sʌb,kʌltʃəʳ] *n* Subkultur *die*.

**subdivide** [,sʌbdɪ'vaɪd] *vt* unterteilen.

**subdue** [səb'dju:] *vt* - **1.** [enemy, rioters, crowds] unterwerfen - **2.** [feelings, passions] unterldrücken.

**subdued** [səb'dju:d] *adj* - **1.** [person] ruhig - **2.** [sound, feelings, lighting, colour] gedämpft.

**subeditor** [,sʌb'edɪtəʳ] *n* Redaktionsassistent *der*, -in *die*.

**subheading** ['sʌb,hedɪŋ] *n* Untertitel *der*.

**subhuman** [,sʌb'hju:mən] *adj pej* unmenschlich.

**subject** [*adj*, *n* & *prep* 'sʌbdʒekt, *vt* səb'dʒekt] *adj* - **1.** [subordinate]: ~ **to sthg** etw *(D)* unterworfen - **2.** [liable]: ~ **to sthg** [disease] anfällig für etw; ~ **to tax** steuerpflichtig; **prices ~ to change** COMM Preisänderungen vorbehalten; **trains are ~ to delay** es kann zu Verspätungen im Zugverkehr kommen ◇ *n* - **1.** [topic under consideration] Thema *das*; **he is the ~ of an inquiry** es wird eine Untersuchung über ihn durchgeführt - **2.** GRAMM Subjekt *das* - **3.** SCH & UNIV Fach *das* - **4.** [citizen] Staatsbürger *der*, -in *die* ◇ *vt* - **1.** [subjugate] unterwerfen - **2.** [force to experience]: **to ~ sb to sthg** [punishment, inquiry] jn einer Sache *(D)* unterziehen; **he was ~ed to harsh criticism** er war starker Kritik ausgesetzt.

➞ **subject to** *prep* [depending on] abhängig von.

**subjective** [səb'dʒektɪv] *adj* subjektiv.

**subjectively** [səb'dʒektɪvlɪ] *adv* subjektiv.

**subject matter** *n* Stoff *der*.

**sub judice** [-'dʒu:dɪsɪ] *adj* LAW: **to be ~** verhandelt werden.

**subjugate** ['sʌbdʒʊgeɪt] *vt fml* - **1.** [people, tribe, country] unterwerfen - **2.** [feelings, desires] unterldrücken.

**subjunctive** [səb'dʒʌŋktɪv] *n* GRAMM: ~ **(mood)** Konjunktiv *der*.

**sublet** [,sʌb'let] (*pt* & *pp* **sublet**; *cont* **-ting**) *vt* unterlvermieten.

**sublime** [sə'blaɪm] *adj* [wonderful] erhaben.

**sublimely** [sə'blaɪmlɪ] *adv* [completely] vollkommen.

**subliminal** [,sʌb'lɪmɪnl] *adj*: ~ **advertising** Schleichwerbung *die*.

**submachine gun** [,sʌbmə'ʃi:n-] *n* Maschinenpistole *die*.

**submarine** [,sʌbmə'ri:n] *n* U-Boot *das*.

**submerge** [səb'mɜ:dʒ] *vt* - **1.** [flood] überschwemmen - **2.** [plunge into liquid] einltauchen - **3.** *fig* [in activity]: **to ~ o.s. in sthg** sich in etw *(A)* vertiefen ◇ *vi* tauchen.

**submission** [səb'mɪʃn] *n* - **1.** [obedience, capitulation] Unterwerfung *die* - **2.** [presentation] Einreichen *das*.

**submissive** [səb'mɪsɪv] *adj* unterwürfig.

**submit** [səb'mɪt] (*pt* & *pp* **-ted**; *cont* **-ting**) *vt* [present] einlreichen ◇ *vi* [admit defeat] sich ergeben ; **to ~ to sb/sthg** sich jm/etw unterwerfen.

**subnormal** [,sʌb'nɔ:ml] *adj*: **(educationally) ~** minderbegabt.

**subordinate** [*adj* & *n* sə'bɔ:dɪnət, *vt* sə'bɔ:dɪneɪt] *adj fml* [less important]: ~ **(to sthg)** (einer Sache *(D)*) untergeordnet ◇ *n* Untergebene *der*, *die* ◇ *vt fml* unterlordnen.

**subordinate clause** [sə'bɔ:dɪnət-] *n* Nebensatz *der*.

**subordination** [sə,bɔ:dɪ'neɪʃn] *n* *(U)*: ~ **(to sthg)** Unterordnung *die* (unter etw *(A)*).

**subpoena** [sə'pi:nə] (*pt* & *pp* **-ed**) LAW *n* Vorladung *die* ◇ *vt* vorlladen.

**sub-post office** *n* Br Poststelle *die*.

**subroutine** ['sʌbru:,ti:n] *n* COMPUT Unterprogramm *das*.

**subscribe** [səb'skraɪb] *vi* - **1.** [to magazine, newspaper]: **to ~ to sthg** etw abonnieren - **2.** [to view, belief]: **to ~ to sthg** sich einer Sache *(D)* anlschließen ◇ *vt* spenden.

**subscriber** [səb'skraɪbəʳ] *n* - **1.** [to magazine, newspaper] Abonnent *der*, -in *die* - **2.** [to service] Teilnehmer *der*, -in *die* - **3.** [to charity, campaign] Spender *der*, -in *die*.

**subscription** [səb'skrɪpʃn] *n* [to newspaper, magazine] Abonnement *das*; [to club, organization] Mitgliedsbeitrag *der*.

**subsection** ['sʌb,sekʃn] *n* Unterabteilung *die*.

**subsequent** ['sʌbsɪkwənt] *adj* nachfolgend.

**subsequently** ['sʌbsɪkwəntlɪ] *adv* anschließend.

**subservient** [səb'sɜ:vjənt] *adj* - **1.** [servile]: ~ **(to sb)** (jm gegenüber) unterwürfig - **2.** [less important]: ~ **(to sthg)** (einer Sache *(D)* gegenüber) zweitrangig .

**subset** ['sʌbset] *n* MATH Teilmenge *die*.

**subside** [səb'saɪd] *vi* - **1.** [grow less intense] nachllassen - **2.** [grow quieter] leiser werden - **3.** [sink - building, ground] sich senken; [ - river] sinken.

**subsidence** [səb'saɪdns, 'sʌbsɪdns] *n* *(U)* CONSTR Bodensenkung *die*.

**subsidiarity** [səbsɪdɪ'ærɪtɪ] *n* Subsidiarität *die*.

**subsidiary** [səb'sɪdjərɪ] (*pl* **-ies**) *adj* untergeordnet ◇ *n*: ~ **(company)** Tochter(gesellschaft) *die*.

**subsidize, -ise** ['sʌbsɪdaɪz] *vt* subventionieren.

**subsidy** ['sʌbsɪdɪ] (*pl* **-ies**) *n* Subvention *die*.

**subsist** [səbˈsɪst] *vi:* to ~ (on sthg) leben (von etw).

**subsistence allowance** [səbˈsɪstəns-] *n Br* Unterhaltsbeihilfe *die.*

**subsistence farming** [səbˈsɪstəns-] *n* Subsistenzwirtschaft *die.*

**subsistence level** [səbˈsɪstəns-] *n* Existenzminimum *das.*

**substance** [ˈsʌbstəns] *n* - **1.** [material, tangibility] Substanz *die* - **2.** [essence, gist] Kern *der* - **3.** *(U)* [importance] Gewicht *das.*

**substandard** [ˌsʌbˈstændəd] *adj* minderwertig.

**substantial** [səbˈstænʃl] *adj* - **1.** [large, considerable] beträchtlich - **2.** [solid, well-built] solide.

**substantially** [səbˈstænʃəlɪ] *adv* - **1.** [quite a lot] beträchtlich - **2.** [mainly] im Wesentlichen.

**substantiate** [səbˈstænʃɪeɪt] *vt fml* untermauern.

**substantive** [sʌbˈstæntɪv] *adj fml* bedeutend.

**substitute** [ˈsʌbstɪtjuːt] *n* - **1.** [replacement]: ~ (für) Ersatz *der* (für); to be no ~ (for sthg) kein Ersatz (für etw) sein - **2.** SPORT Ersatzspieler *der,* -in *die* ◇ *vt:* to ~ sb/sthg for sb/ sthg jn/etw durch jn/etw ersetzen ◇ *vi:* to ~ for sb jn vertreten.

**substitute teacher** *n Am* Aushilfslehrer *der,* -in *die.*

**substitution** [ˌsʌbstɪˈtjuːʃn] *n* - **1.** [act of replacing] Ersetzen *das* - **2.** [replacement] Ersatz *der.*

**subterfuge** [ˈsʌbtəfjuːdʒ] *n* - **1.** *(U)* [deception] List *die* - **2.** [trick] Trick *der.*

**subterranean** [ˌsʌbtəˈreɪnjən] *adj* unterirdisch.

**subtitle** [ˈsʌbˌtaɪtl] *n* [of book] Untertitel *der.*
◆ **subtitles** *npl* CINEMA Untertitel *pl.*

**subtle** [ˈsʌtl] *adj* - **1.** [nuance, difference] fein; [colour, music] zart - **2.** [comment, method] subtil; **that wasn't very ~ of you** das war nicht sehr feinfühlig von dir.

**subtlety** [ˈsʌtltɪ] *n* - **1.** [of difference] Feinheit *die;* [of colour, music] Zartheit *die* - **2.** [of comment, method] Subtilität *die.*

**subtly** [ˈsʌtlɪ] *adv* - **1.** [different] leicht - **2.** [indirectly, cleverly] auf subtile Weise.

**subtotal** [ˈsʌbˌtəʊtl] *n* Zwischensumme *die.*

**subtract** [səbˈtrækt] *vt:* to ~ sthg (from sthg) etw (von etw) subtrahieren OR abziehen.

**subtraction** [səbˈtrækʃn] *n* Subtraktion *die.*

**subtropical** [ˌsʌbˈtrɒpɪkl] *adj* subtropisch.

**suburb** [ˈsʌbɜːb] *n* Vorort *der.*
◆ **suburbs** *npl* Vororte *pl;* **he lives in the ~s** er wohnt in einem Vorort.

**suburban** [səˈbɜːbn] *adj* - **1.** [of suburbs] Vorort- - **2.** *pej* [boring] spießig.

**suburbia** [səˈbɜːbɪə] *n (U)* die Vororte *pl.*

**subversion** [səbˈvɜːʃn] *n* Subversion *die.*

**subversive** [səbˈvɜːsɪv] *adj* subversiv ◇ *n* subversives Element.

**subvert** [səbˈvɜːt] *vt* untergraben.

**subway** [ˈsʌbweɪ] *n* - **1.** *Br* [underground walkway] Unterführung *die* - **2.** *Am* [underground railway] U-Bahn *die.*

**sub-zero** *adj* unter null.

**succeed** [səkˈsiːd] *vt* nachfolgen (+ *D*); [thing, event] folgen (+ *D*) ◇ *vi* [be successful] erfolgreich sein; **he ~ed in persuading her** es gelang ihm, sie zu überreden.

**succeeding** [səkˈsiːdɪŋ] *adj fml* nachfolgend.

**success** [səkˈses] *n* Erfolg *der.*

**successful** [səkˈsesfʊl] *adj* erfolgreich.

**successfully** [səkˈsesfʊlɪ] *adv* erfolgreich.

**succession** [səkˈseʃn] *n* - **1.** [series] Folge *die;* in (quick) ~ (rasch) hintereinander - **2.** *fml* [to high position] Nachfolge *die;* ~ (to the throne) Thronfolge *die.*

**successive** [səkˈsesɪv] *adj* aufeinander folgend.

**successor** [səkˈsesər] *n* Nachfolger *der,* -in *die.*

**success story** *n* Erfolgsstory *die.*

**succinct** [səkˈsɪŋkt] *adj* prägnant.

**succinctly** [səkˈsɪŋktlɪ] *adv* prägnant.

**succulent** [ˈsʌkjʊlənt] *adj* saftig.

**succumb** [səˈkʌm] *vi* [to a bad influence]: to ~ to sthg einer Sache *(D)* erliegen.

**such** [sʌtʃ] *adj* - **1.** [gen] solche, -r, -s; ~ **people** solche Leute; **I've never heard ~ nonsense** ich habe noch nie so einen Unsinn gehört!; **shoplifting and ~ crimes** Ladendiebstahl und derartige Delikte; **there's no ~ thing** so etwas gibt es nicht; ~ **words as "duty" and "honour"** Worte wie „Pflicht" und „Ehre"; **countries ~ as Spain and France** Länder wie Spanien und Frankreich - **2.** [whatever]: **I've spent ~ money as I had** ich habe mein bisschen Geld ausgegeben - **3.** [so great]: **there are ~ differences that ...** die Unterschiede sind so groß, dass ...; ~ **was their skill that ...** sie waren so geschickt, dass ... ◇ *adv:* ~ **big houses** so große Häuser, solche großen Häuser; ~ **a man** ein solcher Mann, so ein Mann; **it's ~ a lovely day** es ist so ein schöner Tag; ~ **a thing should never have happened** so etwas hätte nie passieren dürfen; **would you happen to have ~ a thing as a tin opener?** haben Sie zufällig einen Dosenöffner?; ~ **a lot** so viel; ~ **a long time** so lange; **in ~ a way that ...** auf solche Weise ◇ *pron:* **and ~ (like)** und dergleichen; **this is my car, ~ as it is** das ist mein Auto, wenn man es so nen-

**S**

nen will; **have some wine, ~ as there is** nimm dir Wein, was noch da ist.

➤ **as such** adv als solche, -r, -s.

➤ **such and such** adj das und das; **on ~ and ~ a day** an dem und dem Tag.

**suchlike** ['sʌtʃlaɪk] adj solche <> pron dergleichen.

**suck** [sʌk] vt **- 1.** [by mouth] saugen; [lollipop, thumb] lutschen **- 2.** [draw in] einlsaugen **- 3.** fig [involve]: **to be ~ed into sthg** in etw (A) hineingezogen werden.

➤ **suck up** vi inf: **to ~ up to sb** jm um den Bart gehen.

**sucker** ['sʌkəʳ] n **- 1.** [suction pad] Saugnapf der **- 2.** inf [gullible person] Depp der.

**suckle** ['sʌkl] vt säugen <> vi saugen.

**sucrose** ['su:krəʊz] n Saccharose die.

**suction** ['sʌkʃn] n **- 1.** [drawing in] Sogwirkung die **- 2.** [adhesion] Saugwirkung die.

**suction pump** n Saugpumpe die.

**Sudan** [su:'dɑ:n] n Sudan der; **in (the) ~** im Sudan.

**sudden** ['sʌdn] adj plötzlich; **all of a ~** plötzlich.

**sudden death** n FTBL Suddendeath der.

**suddenly** ['sʌdnlɪ] adv plötzlich.

**suddenness** ['sʌdnnɪs] n Plötzlichkeit die.

**suds** [sʌdz] npl Seifenlauge die.

**sue** [su:] vt verklagen; **to ~ sb for sthg** [libel etc] jn wegen etw verklagen; [sum of money] jn auf etw (A) verklagen.

**suede** [sweɪd] n Wildleder das <> comp Wildleder-.

**suet** ['suɪt] n Nierenfett das.

**Suez** ['suɪz] n Suez nt.

**Suez Canal** n: **the ~** der Suezkanal.

**suffer** ['sʌfəʳ] vt erleiden <> vi leiden; **to ~ from sthg** MED an etw (D) leiden.

**sufferance** ['sʌfrəns] n: **you are only here on ~** Sie werden hier nur geduldet.

**sufferer** ['sʌfrəʳ] n: **rheumatism ~** Rheumakranke der, die; **hay fever ~** an Heuschnupfen Leidende der, die.

**suffering** ['sʌfrɪŋ] n Leiden das.

**suffice** [sə'faɪs] vi fml genügen.

**sufficient** [sə'fɪʃnt] adj genügend.

**sufficiently** [sə'fɪʃntlɪ] adv genug.

**suffix** ['sʌfɪks] n Suffix das, Nachsilbe die.

**suffocate** ['sʌfəkeɪt] vt & vi ersticken.

**suffocation** [,sʌfə'keɪʃn] n Ersticken das.

**suffrage** ['sʌfrɪdʒ] n Wahlrecht das.

**suffuse** [sə'fju:z] vt: **~d with sthg** von etw durchdrungen.

**sugar** ['ʃʊgəʳ] n Zucker der <> vt zuckern.

**sugar beet** n (U) Zuckerrübe die.

**sugar bowl** n Zuckerdose die.

**sugarcane** ['ʃʊgəkeɪn] n Zuckerrohr das.

**sugar-coated** [-'kəʊtɪd] adj mit Zucker überzogen.

**sugared** ['ʃʊgəd] adj [tea, coffee] gesüßt.

**sugar lump** n Stück das Zucker.

**sugary** ['ʃʊgərɪ] adj **- 1.** [high in sugar] süß **- 2.** pej [sentimental] zuckersüß.

**suggest** [sə'dʒest] vt **- 1.** [propose] vorlschlagen **- 2.** [imply] anldeuten.

**suggestion** [sə'dʒestʃn] n **- 1.** [proposal, idea] Vorschlag der **- 2.** (U) [implication]: **there was no ~ of corruption** nichts deutete auf Korruption hin **- 3.** PSYCH Suggestion die.

**suggestive** [sə'dʒestɪv] adj **- 1.** [implying sexual connotation] anzüglich **- 2.** [implying a certain conclusion]: **to be ~ of sthg** auf etw (A) hinldeuten **- 3.** [reminiscent]: **to be ~ of sthg** an etw (A) denken lassen.

**suicidal** [sʊɪ'saɪdl] adj: **to have ~ tendencies** selbstmordgefährdet sein; **he felt ~** er war dem Selbstmord nahe; **that would be ~** das wäre reiner Selbstmord.

**suicide** ['sʊɪsaɪd] n lit & fig Selbstmord der; **to commit ~** Selbstmord begehen.

**suicide attempt** n Selbstmordversuch der.

**suit** [su:t] n **- 1.** [matching clothes] Anzug der; [for woman] Kostüm das **- 2.** [in cards] Farbe die **- 3.** LAW Prozess der **- 4.** phr: **to follow ~** fig dasselbe tun <> vt **- 1.** [look attractive on] stehen (+ D) **- 2.** [be convenient or appropriate to] passen (+ D); **~ yourself!** mach, was du willst! <> vi: **does that ~?** passt dir das?

**suitability** [,su:tə'bɪlətɪ] n [for job] Eignung die.

**suitable** ['su:təbl] adj: **~ (for)** geeignet (für).

**suitably** ['su:təblɪ] adv [dressed] passend; [impressed] gehörig.

**suitcase** ['su:tkeɪs] n Koffer der.

**suite** [swi:t] n **- 1.** [of rooms] Suite die **- 2.** [of furniture] Garnitur die.

**suited** ['su:tɪd] adj **- 1.** [suitable]: **to be ~ to/for sthg** für etw geeignet sein **- 2.** [compatible]: **to be well/ideally ~** gut/ideal zusammenlpassen.

**suitor** ['su:təʳ] n dated Verehrer der.

**sulfate** n Am = sulphate.

**sulfur** n Am = sulphur.

**sulfuric acid** n Am = sulphuric acid.

**sulk** [sʌlk] n Schmollen das <> vi schmollen.

**sulky** ['sʌlkɪ] (compar **-ier**; superl **-iest**) adj [remark] beleidigt; [child] schmollend; **to be in a ~ mood** schmollen.

**sullen** ['sʌlən] *adj* missmutig.

**sulphate** *Br,* **sulfate** *Am* ['sʌlfeɪt] *n* Sulfat *das.*

**sulphur** *Br,* **sulfur** *Am* ['sʌlfəʳ] *n* Schwefel *der.*

**sulphuric acid** *Br,* **sulfuric acid** *Am* [sʌl'fjuərɪk-] *n* Schwefelsäure *die.*

**sultan** ['sʌltən] *n* Sultan *der.*

**sultana** [səl'tɑːnə] *n Br* [dried grape] Sultanine *die.*

**sultry** ['sʌltrɪ] (*compar* -**ier**; *superl* -**iest**) *adj* - **1.** [weather, day] schwül - **2.** [woman] sinnlich.

**sum** [sʌm] (*pt* & *pp* -**med**; *cont* -**ming**) *n* Summe *die.*
➠ **sum up** *vt sep* & *vi* [summarize] zusammenfassen.

**summarily** ['sʌmərəlɪ] *adv* [dismissed] fristlos.

**summarize, -ise** ['sʌməraɪz] *vt* & *vi* zusammenfassen.

**summary** ['sʌmərɪ] (*pl* -**ies**) *adj fml* [dismissal] fristlos; [execution] standrechtlich ⬦ *n* Zusammenfassung *die.*

**summer** ['sʌməʳ] *n* Sommer *der;* **in (the) ~** im Sommer ⬦ *comp* Sommer-.

**summer camp** *n Am* Ferienlager *das.*

**summerhouse** ['sʌməhaus, *pl* -hauzɪz] *n* Gartenhaus *das.*

**summer school** *n* Ferienkurs *der.*

**summertime** ['sʌmətaɪm] *n:* **in (the) ~** im Sommer.

**Summer Time** *n Br* Sommerzeit *die.*

**summery** ['sʌmərɪ] *adj* sommerlich.

**summing-up** [ˌsʌmɪŋ-] (*pl* **summings-up**) *n* LAW Zusammenfassung *die.*

**summit** ['sʌmɪt] *n* [mountain top, meeting] Gipfel *der.*

**summon** ['sʌmən] *vt* [to sb's office] herbeizitieren; [doctor, fire brigade] rufen.
➠ **summon up** *vt sep* [courage, energy] auf lbringen.

**summons** ['sʌmənz] (*pl* **summonses**) LAW *n* Vorladung *die* ⬦ *vt* vorladen.

**sumo (wrestling)** ['suːməʊ-] *n* Sumo *das.*

**sump** [sʌmp] *n* Ölwanne *die.*

**sumptuous** ['sʌmptʃuəs] *adj* [decor, fittings] prächtig; [meal] üppig; [hotel] luxuriös.

**sum total** *n* Gesamtheit *die.*

**sun** [sʌn] (*pt* & *pp* -**ned**; *cont* -**ning**) *n* Sonne *die* ⬦ *vt:* **to ~ o.s.** sich sonnen.

**Sun.** (*abbr of* **Sunday**) So.

**sunbathe** ['sʌnbeɪð] *vi* sich sonnen.

**sunbather** ['sʌnbeɪðəʳ] *n:* **the beach was full of ~s** der Strand war voll von Leuten, die sich sonnten.

**sunbeam** ['sʌnbiːm] *n* Sonnenstrahl *der.*

**sunbed** ['sʌnbed] *n* Sonnenbank *die.*

**sunburn** ['sʌnbɜːn] *n (U)* Sonnenbrand *der.*

**sunburned** ['sʌnbɜːnd], **sunburnt** ['sʌnbɜːnt] *adj* sonnengebräunt; [excessively] sonnenverbrannt.

**sun cream** *n (U)* Sonnencreme *die.*

**sundae** ['sʌndeɪ] *n* Eisbecher *der.*

**Sunday** ['sʌndɪ] *n* Sonntag *der;* **~ lunch** Sonntagsessen *das; see also* **Saturday.**

**Sunday paper** *n Br* Sonntagszeitung *die.*

**Sunday school** *n* Sonntagsschule *die.*

**sundial** ['sʌndaɪəl] *n* Sonnenuhr *die.*

**sundown** ['sʌndaʊn] *n* Sonnenuntergang *der.*

**sun-dried** *adj* sonnengetrocknet.

**sundry** ['sʌndrɪ] *adj fml* verschiedene; **all and ~** jedermann.
➠ **sundries** *npl fml* Verschiedenes *nt.*

**sunflower** ['sʌnˌflaʊəʳ] *n* Sonnenblume *die.*

**sung** [sʌŋ] *pp* ⊳ **sing.**

**sunglasses** ['sʌnˌglɑːsɪz] *npl* Sonnenbrille *die.*

**sunhat** ['sʌnhæt] *n* Sonnenhut *der.*

**sunk** [sʌŋk] *pp* ⊳ **sink.**

**sunken** ['sʌŋkən] *adj* - **1.** [in water - treasure] versunken; [ - ship] gesunken - **2.** [low-level - garden] tiefer liegend; [ - bath] eingelassen - **3.** [cheeks] eingefallen; [eyes] tief liegend.

**sunlamp** ['sʌnlæmp] *n* Höhensonne *die.*

**sunlight** ['sʌnlaɪt] *n* Sonnenlicht *das.*

**sunlit** ['sʌnlɪt] *adj* sonnenbeschienen.

**Sunni** ['sʊnɪ] (*pl* -**s**) *adj* sunnitisch ⬦ *n* Sunnite *der,* -tin *die.*

**sunny** ['sʌnɪ] (*compar* -**ier**; *superl* -**iest**) *adj lit* & *fig* sonnig; **~ side up** *Am* [fried egg] einseitig gebraten.

**sunray lamp** ['sʌnreɪ-] *n* Höhensonne *die.*

**sunrise** ['sʌnraɪz] *n* Sonnenaufgang *der.*

**sunroof** ['sʌnruːf] *n* [of car] Schiebedach *das.*

**sunset** ['sʌnset] *n* Sonnenuntergang *der.*

**sunshade** ['sʌnʃeɪd] *n* Sonnenschirm *der.*

**sunshine** ['sʌnʃaɪn] *n* Sonnenschein *der.*

**sunspot** ['sʌnspɒt] *n* - **1.** ASTRON Sonnenfleck *der* - **2.** [holiday resort] Ferienparadies *das.*

**sunstroke** ['sʌnstrəʊk] *n* Sonnenstich *der.*

**suntan** ['sʌntæn] *n* Sonnenbräune *die* ⬦ *comp* Sonnen-.

**suntanned** ['sʌntænd] *adj* gebräunt.

**suntrap** ['sʌntræp] *n* sonnige Stelle.

**sun-up** *n Am inf* Sonnenaufgang *der.*

**super** ['suːpəʳ] *adj inf* toll.

**S**

**superabundance** [ˌsuːpərəˈbʌndəns] *n* Überfülle *die.*

**superannuation** [ˈsuːpəˌrænjuˈeɪʃn] *n (U)* [pension] Rente *die.*

**superb** [suːˈpɜːb] *adj* erstklassig.

**superbly** [suːˈpɜːblɪ] *adv* erstklassig; [built, designed] meisterhaft.

**Super Bowl** *n Am:* the ~ der Superbowl, *das jährlich zwischen den führenden US-amerikanischen Mannschaften ausgetragene Endspiel im American Football.*

**supercilious** [ˌsuːpəˈsɪlɪəs] *adj* hochnäsig.

**superficial** [ˌsuːpəˈfɪʃl] *adj* oberflächlich.

**superfluous** [suːˈpɜːfluəs] *adj* überflüssig.

**superglue** [ˈsuːpəgluː] *n* Sekundenkleber *der.*

**superhuman** [ˌsuːpəˈhjuːmən] *adj* übermenschlich.

**superimpose** [ˌsuːpərɪmˈpəuz] *vt:* to ~ sthg on sthg etw mit etw überlagern.

**superintend** [ˌsuːpərɪnˈtend] *vt* beaufsichtigen.

**superintendent** [ˌsuːpərɪnˈtendənt] *n* - **1.** *Br* [of police] Polizeikomissar *der,* -in *die* - **2.** *fml* [of department] Direktor *der,* -in *die.*

**superior** [suːˈpɪərɪəʳ] *adj* - **1.** [better] ~ **(to)** besser **(als)** - **2.** [of high quality - goods] besonders hochwertig; **a person of ~ intelligence** ein Mensch von überragender Intelligenz - **3.** [of higher rank]: ~ **(to sb)** höher **(als jd)** - **4.** *pej* [arrogant] überheblich <> *n* [senior] Vorgesetzte *der, die.*

**superiority** [suːˌpɪərɪˈɒrətɪ] *n* Überlegenheit *die; pej* [arrogance] Überheblichkeit *die.*

**superlative** [suːˈpɜːlətɪv] *adj* [of the highest quality - performance] unübertrefflich; [ - player] überragend <> *n* GRAMM Superlativ *der.*

**superman** *n:* you'd need to be a ~ to finish all that in one day! um das alles an einem Tag zu schaffen, bräuchtest du übermenschliche Kräfte!

**supermarket** [ˈsuːpəˌmɑːkɪt] *n* Supermarkt *der.*

**supernatural** [ˌsuːpəˈnætʃrəl] *adj* übernatürlich <> *n:* the ~ das Übernatürliche.

**superpower** [ˈsuːpəˌpauəʳ] *n* Supermacht *die.*

**superscript** [ˈsuːpəskrɪpt] *adj* hochgestellt.

**supersede** [ˌsuːpəˈsiːd] *vt* ablösen.

**supersonic** [ˌsuːpəˈsɒnɪk] *adj* Überschall-.

**superstar** [ˈsuːpəstɑːʳ] *n* Superstar *der.*

**superstition** [ˌsuːpəˈstɪʃn] *n* Aberglaube *der.*

**superstitious** [ˌsuːpəˈstɪʃəs] *adj* abergläubisch.

**superstore** [ˈsuːpəstɔːʳ] *n* Verbrauchermarkt *der;* DIY ~ Heimwerkermarkt *der.*

**superstructure** [ˈsuːpəˌstrʌktʃəʳ] *n lit* & *fig* Überbau *der;* [of ship] Aufbauten *pl.*

**supertanker** [ˈsuːpəˌtæŋkəʳ] *n* Riesentanker *der.*

**supertax** [ˈsuːpətæks] *n* Höchststeuer *die.*

**supervise** [ˈsuːpəvaɪz] *vt* beaufsichtigen.

**supervision** [ˌsuːpəˈvɪʒn] *n* Aufsicht *die.*

**supervisor** [ˈsuːpəvaɪzəʳ] *n* Aufsicht *die;* [of university students] Tutor *der,* -in *die.*

**supper** [ˈsʌpəʳ] *n* - **1.** [main evening meal] Abendessen *das* - **2.** [snack before bedtime] Abendbrot *das.*

**supplant** [səˈplɑːnt] *vt fml* ersetzen.

**supple** [ˈsʌpl] *adj* - **1.** [person] beweglich - **2.** [material] geschmeidig.

**supplement** [*n* ˈsʌplɪmənt, *vb* ˈsʌplɪment] *n* - **1.** [addition - to charge] Zuschlag *der;* [ - to diet] Ergänzung *die* - **2.** [of newspaper] Beilage *die;* [in book] Nachtrag *der* <> *vt* ergänzen.

**supplementary** [ˌsʌplɪˈmentərɪ] *adj* [additional] zusätzlich.

**supplier** [səˈplaɪəʳ] *n* Lieferant *der,* -in *die.*

**supply** [səˈplaɪ] (*pl* **-ies;** *pt* & *pp* **-ied**) *n* - **1.** [store, reserve] Vorrat *der;* **in short ~** knapp - **2.** [network]: **the water/electricity ~** die Wasser-/Stromversorgung - **3.** *(U)* ECON Angebot *das* <> *vt:* to ~ sthg (to sb) [deliver] etw liefern (an jn); **if you ~ the food, I'll bring the drink** wenn du dich um das Essen kümmerst, sorge ich für die Getränke; **to ~ sb (with sthg)** [deliver] jn (mit etw) beliefern; **he supplied the police with the necessary information** er lieferte der Polizei die nötigen Informationen; **to ~ sthg with sthg** etw mit etw versorgen.

◆ **supplies** *npl* Vorräte *pl;* [for office] Bürobedarf *der;* [for army] Nachschub *der.*

**supply teacher** *n Br* Aushilfslehrer *der,* -in *die.*

**support** [səˈpɔːt] *n* - **1.** [gen] Unterstützung *die* - **2.** [object, person] Stütze *die;* **he can't walk without ~** er kann nicht gehen, ohne gestützt zu werden - **3.** [of theory] Untermauerung *die* <> *vt* - **1.** [gen] unterstützen - **2.** [physically] stützen - **3.** [theory] untermauern.

**supporter** [səˈpɔːtəʳ] *n* - **1.** [of person, plan] Anhänger *der,* -in *die* - **2.** SPORT Fan *der.*

**supportive** [səˈpɔːtɪv] *adj* unterstützend; **to be ~ of** unterstützen.

**suppose** [səˈpəuz] *vt* [assume] an|nehmen; **I don't ~ you could give me a lift?** Sie könnten mich nicht vielleicht mitnehmen?; **you don't ~ she's ill?** sie wird doch wohl nicht krank sein? <> *vi* - **1.** [assume]: **I ~ (so)** das nehme ich an; **I ~ not** wahrscheinlich nicht

**- 2.** [agree]: **I ~ so** ja, gut; **I ~ not** wahrscheinlich nicht <> *conj* ▷ **supposing.**

**supposed** [sə'pəʊzd] *adj* **- 1.** [doubtful] angeblich **- 2.** [intended]: **to be ~ to do sthg** etw tun sollen **- 3.** [reputed]: **it is ~ to be good** es soll gut sein.

**supposedly** [sə'pəʊzɪdlɪ] *adv* angeblich.

**supposing** [sə'pəʊzɪŋ] *conj*: **~ you are right ...** angenommen, dass Sie Recht haben ...; **~ he came back?** wenn er nun zurückkäme?

**supposition** [sʌpə'zɪʃn] *n* Annahme *die.*

**suppository** [sə'pɒzɪtrɪ] (*pl* **-ies**) *n* Zäpfchen *das.*

**suppress** [sə'pres] *vt* unterdrücken.

**suppression** [sə'preʃn] *n* Unterdrückung *die.*

**suppressor** [sə'presə<sup>r</sup>] *n* ELEC Entstörer *der.*

**supranational** [su:prə'næʃənl] *adj* übernational.

**supremacy** [sʊ'premsɪ] *n* (U) Vormachtstellung *die.*

**supreme** [sʊ'pri:m] *adj* **- 1.** [highest in rank] Ober- **- 2.** [great] größte, -r, -s.

**Supreme Court** *n* [in US]: **the ~** der Oberste Gerichtshof.

**supremely** [sʊ'pri:mlɪ] *adv* höchst.

**supremo** [sʊ'pri:məʊ] (*pl* **-s**) *n* Br inf Oberboss *der,* -in *die.*

**Supt.** *abbr of* **superintendent.**

**surcharge** ['sɜ:tʃɑ:dʒ] *n:* **~ (on sthg)** Zuschlag *der* (auf etw (A)) <> *vt:* **to ~ sb** jn mit einem Zuschlag belegen.

**sure** [ʃʊə<sup>r</sup>] *adj* sicher; **to be ~ of sthg** sich einer Sache (G) sicher sein; **with such qualifications she can be ~ of getting a job** mit so einer Qualifikation findet sie mit Sicherheit eine Stelle; **the dollar is ~ to fall soon** der Dollar wird bestimmt bald fallen; **be ~ to lock the door** denke daran, die Tür abzuschließen; **to make ~ (that) ...** sicherstellen, dass ...; **I'm ~ (that) ...** ich bin (mir) sicher, dass ...; **to be ~ of o.s.** selbstsicher sein; [about specific matter] sich (D) seiner Sache sicher sein <> *adv* **- 1.** *esp Am inf* [yes] sicher **- 2.** *Am* [really] wirklich.

➤ **for sure** *adv:* **I don't know for ~** da bin ich nicht ganz sicher; **she'll come for ~** sie kommt bestimmt.

➤ **sure enough** *adv* tatsächlich.

**surefire** ['ʃʊəfaɪə<sup>r</sup>] *adj inf* todsicher.

**surefooted** ['ʃʊə,fʊtɪd] *adj* [steady on one's feet] sicher.

**surely** ['ʃʊəlɪ] *adv* [expressing surprise] sicherlich; **~ you can't be serious?** das ist doch nicht dein Ernst?

**sure thing** *excl Am inf* [expressing assent] klar!

**surety** ['ʃʊərətɪ] *n* [guarantee] Sicherheit *die.*

**surf** [sɜ:f] *n* Brandung *die* <> *vi* surfen <> *vt:* **to ~ the Internet** im Internet surfen.

**surface** ['sɜ:fɪs] *n lit* & *fig* Oberfläche *die;* **on the ~** [of person] äußerlich; **below** OR **beneath the ~** [of person] innerlich; **to scratch the ~ of sthg** *fig* etw oberflächlich behandeln <> *vi lit* & *fig* auf tauchen.

**surface mail** *n* Post, *die auf dem Land-/Seeweg befördert wird.*

**surface-to-air** *adj* Boden-Luft-.

**surfboard** ['sɜ:fbɔ:d] *n* Surfbrett *das.*

**surfeit** ['sɜ:fɪt] *n fml:* **~ of sthg** Übermaß *das* an etw (D).

**surfer** ['sɜ:fə<sup>r</sup>] *n* Surfer *der,* -in *die.*

**surfing** ['sɜ:fɪŋ] *n* Surfen *das.*

**surge** [sɜ:dʒ] *n* [of water] Schwall *der;* [of electricity] Stoß *der;* [of interest, support] Woge *die* <> *vi* strömen; [interest, support] an schwellen; [sales, applications] in die Höhe schießen.

**surgeon** ['sɜ:dʒən] *n* Chirurg *der,* -in *die.*

**surgery** ['sɜ:dʒərɪ] (*pl* **-ies**) *n* **- 1.** MED [performing operations] Chirurgie *die;* **to have ~** operiert werden **- 2.** *Br* MED [place] Praxis *die* **- 3.** *Br* MED & POL [consulting period] Sprechstunde *die.*

**surgical** ['sɜ:dʒɪkl] *adj* **- 1.** [connected with surgery] chirurgisch **- 2.** [worn as treatment] orthopädisch.

**surgical spirit** *n* *Br* Wunddesinfektionsmittel *das.*

**surly** ['sɜ:lɪ] (*compar* **-ier;** *superl* **-iest**) *adj* mürrisch.

**surmise** [sɜ:'maɪz] *vt fml* vermuten.

**surmount** [sɜ:'maʊnt] *vt* [overcome] überwinden.

**surname** ['sɜ:neɪm] *n* Nachname *der.*

**surpass** [sə'pɑ:s] *vt fml* [exceed] übertreffen.

**surplus** ['sɜ:pləs] *adj* überschüssig <> *n:* **~ (of sthg)** Überschuss *der* (an etw (D)).

**surprise** [sə'praɪz] *n* Überraschung *die;* **to take sb by ~** jn überraschen <> *vt* überraschen.

**surprised** [sə'praɪzd] *adj* überrascht; **I wouldn't be ~ (if ...)** es würde mich (gar) nicht überraschen(, wenn ...).

**surprising** [sə'praɪzɪŋ] *adj* überraschend.

**surprisingly** [sə'praɪzɪŋlɪ] *adv* überraschenderweise.

**surreal** [sə'rɪəl] *adj* unwirklich.

**surrealism** [sə'rɪəlɪzm] *n* Surrealismus *der.*

**surrealist** [sə'rɪəlɪst] *adj* surrealistisch <> *n* Surrealist *der,* -in *die.*

**surrender** [sə'rendə<sup>r</sup>] *n* Kapitulation *die* <> *vt* [claim, right] auf geben; [weapon, passport] abgeben ◇ *vi* - **1.** [stop fighting]: **to ~ (to sb)** sich (jm) ergeben - **2.** *fig* [give in]: **to ~ (to sthg)** (etw *(D)*) nachlgeben.

**surreptitious** [ˌsʌrəp'tɪʃəs] *adj* heimlich.

**surrogate** ['sʌrəgət] *adj* Ersatz- ◇ *n* Ersatz der.

**surrogate mother** *n* Leihmutter die.

**surround** [sə'raʊnd] *n* Umrandung die ◇ *vt* - **1.** [gen] umlgeben - **2.** [trap] umzingeln.

**surrounding** [sə'raʊndɪŋ] *adj* [area, countryside] umliegend.
 **surroundings** *npl* Umgebung die.

**surtax** ['sɜːtæks] *n (U)* Zusatzsteuer die.

**surveillance** [sɜː'veɪləns] *n (U)* Überwachung die; **to keep sb under ~** jn überwachen.

**survey** [*n* 'sɜːveɪ, *vb* sə'veɪ] *n* - **1.** [statistical investigation] Untersuchung die; [of public opinion] Umfrage die - **2.** [physical examination - of land] Vermessung die; [ - of building] Begutachtung die ◇ *vt* - **1.** [contemplate] betrachten - **2.** [investigate statistically] untersuchen - **3.** [examine, assess - land] vermessen; [ - building] begutachten.

**surveyor** [sə'veɪəʳ] *n* [of land] Landvermesser der, -in die; [of building] Baugutachter der, -in die.

**survival** [sə'vaɪvl] *n* - **1.** [continuing to live] Überleben das - **2.** [relic] Überbleibsel das.

**survive** [sə'vaɪv] *vt* überleben ◇ *vi* - **1.** [continue to exist] überleben - **2.** *inf* [cope successfully] es auslhalten.
 **survive on** *vt fus* [subsist on] leben von.

**survivor** [sə'vaɪvəʳ] *n* - **1.** [person who escapes death] Überlebende der, die - **2.** *fig* [fighter] Kämpfernatur die.

**susceptible** [sə'septəbl] *adj* - **1.** [likely to be influenced]: **~ to sthg** empfänglich für etw - **2.** MED: **~ to sthg** anfällig für etw.

**suspect** [*adj & n* 'sʌspekt, *vb* sə'spekt] *adj* verdächtig ◇ *n* Verdächtige der, die ◇ *vt* - **1.** [distrust] zweifeln an (+ *D*) - **2.** [think likely] vermuten - **3.** [consider guilty]: **to ~ sb (of sthg)** jn (einer Sache *(G)*) verdächtigen.

**suspend** [sə'spend] *vt* - **1.** [hang] auflhängen - **2.** [temporarily discontinue] zeitweilig einlstellen - **3.** [temporarily remove - from job] suspendieren; [ - from school] zeitweilig von der Schule verweisen.

**suspended sentence** [sə'spendɪd-] *n* zur Bewährung ausgesetzte Strafe.

**suspender belt** [sə'spendəʳ-] *n Br* Strumpfhaltergürtel der.

**suspenders** [sə'spendəz] *npl* - **1.** *Br* [for stockings] Strumpfhalter *pl*, Strapse *pl* - **2.** *Am* [for trousers] Hosenträger *pl*.

**suspense** [sə'spens] *n (U)* Spannung die; **to keep sb in ~** jn auf die Folter spannen.

**suspension** [sə'spenʃn] *n* - **1.** [temporary discontinuation] Einstellung die - **2.** [removal - from job] Suspendierung die; [ - from school] zeitweiliger Schulverweis - **3.** AUT Federung die.

**suspension bridge** *n* Hängebrücke die.

**suspicion** [sə'spɪʃn] *n* - **1.** *(U)* [distrust] Misstrauen das; **to be under ~** unter Verdacht stehen, verdächtigt werden - **2.** [idea, theory] Verdacht der.

**suspicious** [sə'spɪʃəs] *adj* - **1.** [having suspicions] misstrauisch - **2.** [causing suspicion] verdächtig.

**suspiciously** [sə'spɪʃəslɪ] *adv* - **1.** [showing a suspicious attitude] misstrauisch - **2.** [causing suspicion] verdächtig.

**suss** [sʌs] ◆ **suss out** *Br vt sep inf* [person] durchschauen; **to ~ out how to work sthg** rauskriegen, wie etw funktioniert.

**sustain** [sə'steɪn] *vt* - **1.** [maintain - interest, opposition, activity] aufrechtlerhalten; [ - hope] bewahren; [ - rate, speed] beilbehalten - **2.** [nourish - physically] ernähren; **he is ~ed by his faith** er wird von seinem Glauben getragen - **3.** [injury, damage] davonltragen - **4.** [withstand - weight] auslhalten.

**sustenance** ['sʌstɪnəns] *n (U) fml* Nahrung die.

**suture** ['suːtʃəʳ] *n* Naht die.

**svelte** [svelt] *adj* grazil.

**SW - 1.** (*abbr of* **short wave**) KW - **2.** (*abbr of* **southwest**) SO.

**swab** [swɒb] *n* [cotton wool] Tupfer der.

**swagger** ['swægəʳ] *n* Stolzieren das ◇ *vi* stolzieren.

**Swahili** [swɑː'hiːlɪ] *n* [language] Suaheli das.

**swallow** ['swɒləʊ] *n* - **1.** [bird] Schwalbe die - **2.** [of food, drink] Schluck der ◇ *vt* - **1.** [food, drink] schlucken - **2.** *fig* [accept] schlucken - **3.** *fig* [anger, tears] hinunterlschlucken ◇ *vi* schlucken.

**swam** [swæm] *pt* ⊳ **swim.**

**swamp** [swɒmp] *n* Sumpf der ◇ *vt* - **1.** [flood] unter Wasser setzen - **2.** [overwhelm]: **to ~ sb/sthg (with sthg)** jn/etw (mit etw) überfluten.

**swan** [swɒn] *n* [bird] Schwan der.

**swap** [swɒp] (*pt & pp* **-ped**; *cont* **-ping**) *n* [exchange] Tausch der ◇ *vt* - **1.** [exchange]: **to ~ sthg (with sb)** etw (mit jm) tauschen; **to ~ sthg (over OR round)** etw (ausl)tauschen - **2.** [replace]: **to ~ sthg for sthg** etw gegen etw einltauschen ◇ *vi* tauschen.

**swap meet** *n Am Treffen, bei dem Gebrauchtes zum Kauf angeboten oder getauscht wird.*

**swarm** [swɔːm] *n* Schwarm der ◇ *vi* schwärmen; **spectators were ~ing into the stadium** die Zuschauer strömten ins Stadion; **to be ~ing with** [place] wimmeln von.

**swarthy** ['swɔ:ðɪ] (*compar* **-ier;** *superl* **-iest**) *adj* dunkel.

**swashbuckling** ['swɒʃ͵bʌklɪŋ] *adj* verwegen.

**swastika** ['swɒstɪkə] *n* Hakenkreuz *das.*

**swat** [swɒt] (*pt &amp; pp* **-ted;** *cont* **-ting**) *vt* totlschlagen.

**swatch** [swɒtʃ] *n* Muster *das.*

**swathe** [sweɪð] *n* [large area] große Fläche.

**swathed** [sweɪðd] *adj literary* [wrapped]: ~ **in sthg** in etw *(A)* eingewickelt.

**swatter** ['swɒtəʳ] *n* Fliegenklatsche *die.*

**sway** [sweɪ] *vt* - **1.** [body, head] wiegen - **2.** [influence] beeinflussen ◇ *vi* sich wiegen; [drunk person] schwanken ◇ *n (U) fml:* **to come under the ~ of sb/sthg** unter den Einfluss von jm/ etw geraten; **to hold ~ over sb/sthg** Einfluss haben auf jn/etw.

**Swaziland** ['swɑ:zɪlænd] *n* Swasiland *nt.*

**swear** [sweəʳ] (*pt* **swore;** *pp* **sworn**) *vt* schwören; **to ~ to do sthg** schwören, etw zu tun ◇ *vi* - **1.** [state emphatically] schwören - **2.** [use swearwords] fluchen.
◆ **swear by** *vt fus inf* [have confidence in] schwören auf (+ *A).*
◆ **swear in** *vt sep* LAW vereidigen.

**swearword** ['sweəwɜːd] *n* Kraftausdruck *der.*

**sweat** [swet] *n* - **1.** [perspiration] Schweiß *der* - **2.** *inf* [hard work] Heidenarbeit *die* - **3.** *inf* [state of anxiety]: **to get into a ~ about sthg** wegen etw ins Schwitzen kommen; **he was in a cold ~** ihm brach der kalte Schweiß aus ◇ *vi lit &amp; fig* schwitzen.

**sweatband** ['swetbænd] *n* Schweißband *das.*

**sweater** ['swetəʳ] *n* Pullover *der.*

**sweatshirt** ['swetʃɜːt] *n* Sweatshirt *das.*

**sweatshop** ['swetʃɒp] *n* Ausbeuterbetrieb *der.*

**sweaty** ['swetɪ] (*compar* **-ier;** *superl* **-iest**) *adj* - **1.** [clothes] verschwitzt; [skin] schweißnass - **2.** [place, activity] schweißtreibend.

**swede** [swi:d] *n Br* Steckrübe *die.*

**Swede** [swi:d] *n* Schwede *der,* -din *die.*

**Sweden** ['swi:dn] *n* Schweden *nt.*

**Swedish** ['swi:dɪʃ] *adj* schwedisch ◇ *n* [language] Schwedisch(e) *das* ◇ *npl:* **the ~** die Schweden *pl.*

**sweep** [swi:p] (*pt &amp; pp* **swept**) *n* - **1.** [of arm, hand] Schwung *der* - **2.** [with brush]: **to give sthg a ~** etw kehren OR fegen - **3.** [chimneysweep] Schornsteinfeger *der,* -in *die* ◇ *vt* - **1.** [with brush] fegen, kehren - **2.** [scan] absuchen - **3.** [spread through] überlrollen - **4.** [subj: waves] schwemmen - **5.** [push with hand] fegen ◇ *vi* - **1.** [wind, rain] fegen - **2.** [rumour] sich ausl-

breiten; **fear swept through the crowd** die Menge wurde von Angst ergriffen - **3.** [walk quickly] rauschen.
◆ **sweep aside** *vt sep* beiseite fegen.
◆ **sweep away** *vt sep* [destroy] weglreißen.
◆ **sweep up** *vt sep &amp; vi* [with brush] zusammenl-kehren OR l-fegen.

**sweeper** ['swi:pəʳ] *n* FTBL Libero *der.*

**sweeping** ['swi:pɪŋ] *adj* - **1.** [effect, change] tief greifend - **2.** [statement] pauschal - **3.** [curve] weit ausholend.

**sweepstake** ['swi:psteɪk] *n* Sweepstake *das* OR *der.*

**sweet** [swi:t] *adj* - **1.** [gen] süß - **2.** [gentle, kind] lieb ◇ *n Br* - **1.** [candy] Bonbon *das* - **2.** [dessert] Nachtisch *der,* Dessert *das;* **what's for ~?** was gibt es als OR zum Nachtisch OR Dessert?

**sweet-and-sour** *adj* süßsauer.

**sweet corn** *n* Mais *der.*

**sweeten** ['swi:tn] *vt* [add sugar to] süßen.

**sweetener** ['swi:tnəʳ] *n* - **1.** [substance] Süßstoff *der* - **2.** *inf* [bribe] Schmiergeld *das.*

**sweetheart** ['swi:thɑːt] *n* - **1.** [term of endearment] Liebling *der* - **2.** [boyfriend or girlfriend] Freund *der,* -in *die.*

**sweetness** ['swi:tnɪs] *n* - **1.** [gen] Süße *die* - **2.** [of character, voice] Liebenswürdigkeit *die.*

**sweet pea** *n* Wicke *die.*

**sweet potato** *n* Süßkartoffel *die,* Batate *die.*

**sweet shop** *n Br* Süßwarenladen *der,* Süßwarengeschäft *das.*

**sweet-talk** *vt:* **to ~ sb (into doing sthg)** jn beschwatzen(, etw zu tun).

**sweet tooth** *n inf:* **to have a ~** gern Süßes mögen.

**swell** [swel] (*pt* **-ed;** *pp* **swollen** OR **-ed**) *vi* - **1.** [become larger]: **to ~ (up)** anlschwellen - **2.** [fill with air - lungs, balloons] sich füllen; [ - sails] sich blähen - **3.** [increase in number] anl-wachsen - **4.** [become louder] anlschwellen ◇ *vt* [increase] steigern ◇ *n* [of sea]: **there is a heavy ~ es** herrscht starker Seegang ◇ *adj Am inf* klasse, prima.

**swelling** ['swelɪŋ] *n* [on body] Schwellung *die.*

**sweltering** ['sweltərɪŋ] *adj* [heat] drückend; [weather, day] drückend heiß; **it's ~ in here** hier ist es ja wie in der Sauna.

**swept** [swept] *pt &amp; pp* ▷ **sweep.**

**swerve** [swɜːv] *vi* [vehicle, driver] ausl-schwenken.

**swift** [swɪft] *adj* - **1.** [fast] schnell - **2.** [prompt] prompt ◇ *n* [bird] Mauersegler *der.*

**swiftly** ['swɪftlɪ] *adj* - **1.** [rapidly] schnell - **2.** [promptly] prompt.

S

**swig** [swɪg] (*pt* & *pp* **-ged;** *cont* **-ging**) *inf vt* herunter|kippen ⬦ *n* Schluck *der.*

**swill** [swɪl] *n* (U) [pig food] Schweinefutter *das* ⬦ *vt Br* [wash] waschen; [glass, cup] aus|spülen; **~ (down) the floor** den Fußboden ab|schwemmen.

**swim** [swɪm] (*pt* **swam;** *pp* **swum;** *cont* **-ming**) *n:* **to have a ~** schwimmen; **to go for a ~** schwimmen gehen ⬦ *vi* **- 1.** [move through water] schwimmen **- 2.** [feel dizzy]: **my head was ~ ming** mir war ganz schwindlig.

**swimmer** [ˈswɪməʳ] *n* Schwimmer *der,* -in *die.*

**swimming** [ˈswɪmɪŋ] *n* Schwimmen *das;* **to go ~** schwimmen gehen.

**swimming baths** *npl Br* Hallenbad *das.*

**swimming cap** *n* Badekappe *die.*

**swimming costume** *n Br* Badeanzug *der.*

**swimming pool** *n* Schwimmbad *das.*

**swimming trunks** *npl* Badehose *die.*

**swimsuit** [ˈswɪmsuːt] *n* Badeanzug *der.*

**swindle** [ˈswɪndl] *n* Betrug *der* ⬦ *vt* betrügen; **to ~ sb out of sthg** jn um etw betrügen.

**swine** [swaɪn] *n inf pej* [person] Schwein *das.*

**swing** [swɪŋ] (*pt* & *pp* **swung**) *n* **- 1.** [child's toy] Schaukel *die* **- 2.** [change - in opinion, mood] Umschwung *der;* **~ to the right** POL Rechtsruck *der* **- 3.** [swaying movement] Schwingen *das* **- 4.** *inf* [blow]: **to take a ~ at sb** nach jm schlagen **- 5.** *phr:* **to be in full ~** in vollem Gange sein; **to get into the ~ of sthg** sich an etw (A) gewöhnen ⬦ *vt* **- 1.** [move back and forth] hin und her schwingen; [arms] schwingen mit; **to ~ one's legs** [dangle] seine Beine baumeln lassen **- 2.** [turn] schwenken ⬦ *vi* **- 1.** [move back and forth] hin und her schwingen; [dangle - legs] baumeln **- 2.** [turn]: **the car swung into the drive** das Auto schwenkte in die Einfahrt ein; **the door swung open** die Tür schwang auf; **he swung round** er drehte sich um **- 3.** [hit out]: **to ~ at sb** nach jm schlagen **- 4.** [change] um|schwenken; **the party has swung to the left** die Partei hat einen Linksschwenk gemacht.

**swing bridge** *n* Drehbrücke *die.*

**swing door** *n* Pendeltür *die.*

**swingeing** [ˈswɪndʒɪŋ] *adj esp Br* [cuts] drastisch; [criticism] scharf.

**swinging** [ˈswɪŋɪŋ] *adj inf* **- 1.** [lively, full of fun] schwungvoll **- 2.** [uninhibited, free] locker

**swipe** [swaɪp] *n:* **to take a ~ at sb** nach jm schlagen ⬦ *vt* **- 1.** *inf* [steal] klauen **- 2.** [plastic card] durch|ziehen ⬦ *vi:* **to ~ at sb** nach jm schlagen.

**swirl** [swɜːl] *n* Wirbel *der* ⬦ *vt* [drink] herum|schwenken ⬦ *vi* wirbeln.

**swish** [swɪʃ] *adj inf* [posh] schick ⬦ *n* [of dress]

Rascheln *das;* [of tail] Schlagen *das;* [of whip] Zischen *das* ⬦ *vt* [tail] schlagen mit ⬦ *vi* [whip] zischen; [dress] rascheln.

**Swiss** [swɪs] *adj* Schweizer, schweizerisch ⬦ *n* Schweizer *der,* -in *die* ⬦ *npl:* **the ~** die Schweizer *pl.*

**swiss roll** *n Br* Biskuitrolle *die.*

**switch** [swɪtʃ] *n* **- 1.** [control device] Schalter *der* **- 2.** [change - of policy] Änderung *die;* **the ~ to a different system** die Umstellung auf ein anderes System **- 3.** *Am* RAIL Weiche *die* ⬦ *vt* **- 1.** [transfer] wechseln; **to ~ sthg to sthg** [conversation, attention] etw auf etw (A) lenken; [allegiance] etw auf etw (A) übertragen **- 2.** [swap, exchange] vertauschen; **to ~ jobs** den Arbeitsplatz wechseln ⬦ *vi* [transfer]: **to ~ (from sthg to sthg)** (von etw auf etw (A)) (über|)wechseln; **to ~ to oil** auf Öl umstellen; **to ~ to another channel** auf einen anderen Sender umschalten.

➡ **switch off** *vt sep* [device] aus|schalten ⬦ *vi inf* [lose concentration] ab|schalten.

➡ **switch on** *vt sep* [device] an|schalten.

**switchblade** [ˈswɪtʃbleɪd] *n Am* Schnappmesser *das.*

**switchboard** [ˈswɪtʃbɔːd] *n* Zentrale *die.*

**switchboard operator** *n* Telefonist *der,* -in *die.*

**switched-on** [ˌswɪtʃt-] *adj inf* [modern]: **he's really ~** er weiß, was in ist.

**Switzerland** [ˈswɪtsələnd] *n* Schweiz *die;* **in ~** in der Schweiz.

**swivel** [ˈswɪvl] (*Br pt* & *pp* **-led;** *cont* **-ling,** *Am pt* & *pp* **-ed;** *cont* **-ing**) *vt* drehen ⬦ *vi* sich drehen.

**swivel chair** *n* Drehstuhl *der.*

**swollen** [ˈswəʊln] *pp* ➪ **swell** ⬦ *adj* [part of body] geschwollen; [river] angeschwollen; **~ with pride** stolzgeschwellt.

**swoon** [swuːn] *vi literary* OR *hum* ohnmächtig werden.

**swoop** [swuːp] *n* **- 1.** [downward flight] Sturzflug *der;* **in one fell ~** auf einen Schlag **- 2.** [raid] Razzia *die* ⬦ *vi* **- 1.** [plane] einen Sturzflug machen; [bird] herab|stoßen **- 2.** [police] eine Razzia machen; [troops] einen Überraschungsangriff machen.

**swop** [swɒp] *n, vt* & *vi* = **swap.**

**sword** [sɔːd] *n* Schwert *das;* **to cross ~s (with sb)** (mit jm) die Klingen kreuzen.

**swordfish** [ˈsɔːdfɪʃ] (*pl inv* OR **-es**) *n* Schwertfisch *der.*

**swordsman** [ˈsɔːdzmən] (*pl* **-men** [-mən]) *n* Fechter *der.*

**swore** [swɔːʳ] *pt* ➪ **swear.**

**sworn** [swɔːn] *pp* ➪ **swear** ⬦ *adj* **- 1.** [committed]: **to be ~ enemies** Todfeinde sein **- 2.** LAW: **a ~ statement** eine Aussage unter Eid.

**swot** [swɒt] (*pt & pp* **-ted;** *cont* **-ting)** *Br inf n pej* Streber *der*, -in *die* ◇ *vi:* **to ~ (for sthg)** büffeln (für etw).

◆ **swot up** *inf vt sep* büffeln ◇ *vi:* **to ~ up (on sthg)** (etw) büffeln.

**swum** [swʌm] *pp* ▷ **swim.**

**swung** [swʌŋ] *pt & pp* ▷ **swing.**

**sycamore** ['sɪkəmɔːʳ] *n* Bergahorn *der.*

**sycophant** ['sɪkəfænt] *n* Kriecher *der*, -in *die.*

**syllable** ['sɪləbl] *n* Silbe *die.*

**syllabub** ['sɪləbʌb] *n* Süßspeise aus Sahne und Wein oder Brandy.

**syllabus** ['sɪləbəs] (*pl* **-buses** OR **-bi** [-baɪ]) *n* Lehrplan *der.*

**symbol** ['sɪmbl] *n* Symbol *das.*

**symbolic** [sɪm'bɒlɪk] *adj* symbolisch; **to be ~ of sthg** etw symbolisieren.

**symbolism** ['sɪmbəlɪzm] *n* Symbolik *die.*

**symbolize, -ise** ['sɪmbəlaɪz] *vt* symbolisieren.

**symmetrical** [sɪ'metrɪkl] *adj* symmetrisch.

**symmetry** ['sɪmətrɪ] *n (U)* Symmetrie *die.*

**sympathetic** [ˌsɪmpə'θetɪk] *adj* **- 1.** [understanding] verständnisvoll **- 2.** [willing to support] wohlgesinnt; **to be ~ to sthg** einer Sache (D) wohlwollend gegenüberstehen; [new ideas] für etw zugänglich sein **- 3.** [likable] sympathisch.

**sympathize, -ise** ['sɪmpəθaɪz] *vi* **- 1.** [feel sorry] mitlfühlen, Mitleid haben; **to ~ with sb** mit jm mitlfühlen **- 2.** [understand]: **to ~ with sthg** für etw Verständnis haben **- 3.** [support]: **to ~ with sthg** mit etw sympathisieren.

**sympathizer, -iser** ['sɪmpəθaɪzəʳ] *n* [supporter] Sympathisant *der*, -in *die.*

**sympathy** ['sɪmpəθɪ] *n* **- 1.** [compassion] Mitgefühl *das*, Mitleid *das;* **to have ~ for sb** Mitleid mit jm haben; **my deepest ~** mein aufrichtiges OR herzliches Beileid **- 2.** [agreement]: **to be in ~ with sthg** mit etw sympathisieren **- 3.** [support]: **to come out** OR **strike in ~ with sb** mit jm in einen Sympathiestreik treten.

◆ **sympathies** *npl:* **my sympathies are** OR **lie with the left** ich bin auf der Seite der Linken.

**symphonic** [sɪm'fɒnɪk] *adj* sinfonisch.

**symphony** ['sɪmfənɪ] (*pl* **-ies)** *n* Sinfonie *die.*

**symphony orchestra** *n* Sinfonieorchester *das.*

**symposium** [sɪm'pəʊzjəm] (*pl* **-siums** OR **-sia** [-zjə]) *n fml* Symposium *das.*

**symptom** ['sɪmptəm] *n lit & fig* Symptom *das.*

**symptomatic** [ˌsɪmptə'mætɪk] *adj:* **~ (of sthg)** symptomatisch (für etw).

**synagogue** ['sɪnəgɒg] *n* Synagoge *die.*

**sync** [sɪŋk] *n inf:* **out of ~** nicht synchron; **in ~ synchron.**

**synchronize, -ise** ['sɪŋkrənaɪz] *vt* **- 1.** [soundtrack] synchronisieren; [movements] aufeinander ablstimmen **- 2.** [watches] gleichlstellen ◇ *vi* synchron sein.

**synchronized swimming** ['sɪŋkrənaɪzd-] *n* Synchronschwimmen *das.*

**syncopated** ['sɪŋkəpeɪtɪd] *adj* synkopiert.

**syncopation** [ˌsɪŋkə'peɪʃn] *n (U)* Synkope *die.*

**syndicate** [*n* 'sɪndɪkət, *vb* 'sɪndɪkeɪt] *n* Syndikat *das* ◇ *vt* PRESS in mehreren Zeitungen veröffentlichen.

**syndrome** ['sɪndrəʊm] *n* **- 1.** MED [set of symptoms] Syndrom *das* **- 2.** [set of characteristics] Phänomen *das.*

**synergy** ['sɪnədʒɪ] (*pl* **-ies)** *n* Synergie *die.*

**synod** ['sɪnəd] *n* Synode *die.*

**synonym** ['sɪnənɪm] *n:* **~ (for** OR **of sthg)** Synonym *das* (für OR von etw).

**synonymous** [sɪ'nɒnɪməs] *adj* **- 1.** [having the same meaning] synonym **- 2.** [associated]: **to be ~ with sthg** gleichbedeutend mit etw sein.

**synopsis** [sɪ'nɒpsɪs] (*pl* **-ses** [-siːz]) *n* Zusammenfassung *die.*

**syntax** ['sɪntæks] *n* LING Syntax *die.*

**synthesis** ['sɪnθəsɪs] (*pl* **-ses** [-siːz]) *n* Synthese *die.*

**synthesize, -ise** ['sɪnθəsaɪz] *vt* **- 1.** BIOL & CHEM synthetisieren **- 2.** [blend] eine Synthese bilden aus.

**synthesizer** ['sɪnθəsaɪzəʳ] *n* MUS Synthesizer *der.*

**synthetic** [sɪn'θetɪk] *adj* **- 1.** [man-made] synthetisch; **~ fibre** Kunstfaser *die* **- 2.** *pej* [insincere] künstlich.

**syphilis** ['sɪfɪlɪs] *n* Syphilis *die.*

**syphon** ['saɪfn] *n & vt* = **siphon.**

**Syria** ['sɪrɪə] *n* Syrien *nt.*

**Syrian** ['sɪrɪən] *adj* syrisch ◇ *n* Syrer *der*, -in *die.*

**syringe** [sɪ'rɪndʒ] (*cont* **syringeing** OR **syringing)** *n* Spritze *die* ◇ *vt* auslspülen.

**syrup** ['sɪrəp] *n (U)* **- 1.** [sugar and water] Sirup *der* **- 2.** *Br:* **(golden) ~** Sirup *der (Brotaufstrich)* **- 3.** [medicine]: **cough ~** Hustensaft *der.*

**system** ['sɪstəm] *n* System *das;* **the ~ inf** [authority] das System; **road/railway/transport ~** Straßen-/Bahn-/Transportnetz *das;* **stereo ~** Stereoanlage *die;* **to get sthg out of one's ~ inf** etw loslwerden.

**systematic** [ˌsɪstə'mætɪk] *adj* systematisch.

**systematize, -ise** ['sɪstəmətaɪz] *vt Br* systematisieren.

**system disk** *n* COMPUT Systemdiskette *die.*

**S**

**systems analyst** ['sɪstəmz-] n COMPUT System-analytiker der, -in die.

**systems engineer** ['sɪstəmz-] n COMPUT Systemtechniker der, -in die.

**system software** n COMPUT Systemsoftware die.

**t** (pl **t's** OR **ts**), **T** (pl **T's** OR **Ts**) [tiː] n t das, T das.

**ta** [tɑː] excl Br inf danke.

**TA** n abbr of **Territorial Army.**

**tab** [tæb] n - **1.** [of maker] Etikett das; [bearing owner's name] Namensschild das - **2.** [for opening can] Verschluss der - **3.** Am [bill] Rechnung die; **to pick up the ~** die Rechnung übernehmen - **4.** (abbr of **tabulator**) [on keyboard] Tab der - **5.** phr: **to keep ~s on sb** jn genau beobachten.

**Tabasco sauce**® [tə'bæskəʊ-] n Tabascosoße® die.

**tabby** ['tæbɪ] (pl **-ies**) n: **~ (cat)** getigerte Katze.

**tabernacle** ['tæbənækl] n [for Communion] Tabernakel der OR das.

**tab key** n Tabulatortaste die.

**table** ['teɪbl] n - **1.** [piece of furniture] Tisch der - **2.** [diagram] Tabelle die - **3.** phr: **to turn the ~s on sb** jm gegenüber den Spieß umldrehen <> vt - **1.** Br [propose] einlbringen - **2.** Am [postpone] auf Eis legen.

**tableau** ['tæbləʊ] (pl **-x** OR **-s** [-z]) n Tableau das.

**tablecloth** ['teɪblklɒθ] n Tischdecke die, Tischtuch das.

**table d'hôte** ['tɑːbl̩dəʊt] n: **the ~** das Tagesmenü OR Tagesgericht.

**table football** n Tischfußball der.

**table lamp** n Tischlampe die.

**table linen** n Tischwäsche pl.

**table manners** npl Tischmanieren pl.

**tablemat** ['teɪblmæt] n Set das.

**table of contents** n Inhaltsverzeichnis das.

**table salt** n Tafelsalz das.

**tablespoon** ['teɪblspuːn] n Servierlöffel der.

**tablet** ['tæblɪt] n - **1.** [pill] Tablette die - **2.** [piece of stone] Tafel die - **3.** [of soap] Stück das.

**table tennis** n Tischtennis das.

**tableware** ['teɪblweəʳ] n Tafelgeschirr das.

**table wine** n Tischwein der.

**tabloid** ['tæblɔɪd] n: **~ (newspaper)** Boulevardzeitung die; **the ~ press** die Boulevardpresse.

**taboo** [tə'buː] (pl **-s**) adj Tabu-; **to be ~** tabu sein <> n Tabu das.

**tabulate** ['tæbjʊleɪt] vt tabellarisch darlstellen.

**tachograph** ['tækəgrɑːf] n Fahrtenschreiber der.

**tachometer** [tæ'kɒmɪtəʳ] n Tachometer der OR das.

**tacit** ['tæsɪt] adj stillschweigend.

**taciturn** ['tæsɪtɜːn] adj schweigsam.

**tack** [tæk] n - **1.** [nail] kleiner Nagel - **2.** NAUT Kurs der - **3.** fig [course of action] Weg der; **to change ~** einen anderen Kurs einschlagen <> vt - **1.** [fasten with nail]: **to ~ sthg to sthg** etw an etw (A) nageln - **2.** [in sewing] heften <> vi NAUT kreuzen.

➡ **tack on** vt sep inf [add as afterthought] anlhängen.

**tackle** ['tækl] n - **1.** FTBL Tackling das - **2.** RUGBY Fassen das - **3.** [equipment, gear] Ausrüstung die - **4.** [for lifting] Flaschenzug der <> vt - **1.** [deal with] anlgehen - **2.** [attack & FTBL] anlgreifen - **3.** RUGBY fassen - **4.** [talk to]: **to ~ sb about sthg** jn auf etw (A) anlsprechen.

**tacky** ['tækɪ] (compar **-ier**; superl **-iest**) adj - **1.** inf [cheap] billig; [tasteless] geschmacklos - **2.** [sticky] klebrig.

**taco** ['tækəʊl] (pl **-s**) n Taco das.

**tact** [tækt] n Takt der; **he has no ~** er hat kein Taktgefühl.

**tactful** ['tæktfʊl] adj taktvoll.

**tactfully** ['tæktfʊlɪ] adv taktvoll.

**tactic** ['tæktɪk] n Taktik die.

➡ **tactics** n (U) MIL Taktik die.

**tactical** ['tæktɪkl] adj taktisch.

**tactical voting** n Br taktisches Wahlverhalten.

**tactile** adj: **a ~ person** eine Person, die Körperkontakt mag.

**tactless** ['tæktlɪs] adj taktlos.

**tactlessly** ['tæktlɪslɪ] adv taktlos.

**tadpole** ['tædpəʊl] n Kaulquappe die.

**taffeta** ['tæfɪtə] n Taft der.

**taffy** ['tæfɪ] (pl **-ies**) n Am Toffee das.

**tag** [tæg] (pt & pp **-ged**; cont **-ging**) n - **1.** [on clothing - of maker] Etikett *das;* [ - bearing owner's name] Namensschild *das* - **2.** [of paper] Schild *das;* **price ~** Preisschild *das;* **luggage ~** Gepäckanhänger *der* - **3.** [game] Fangen *das* - **4.** COMPUT Markierung *die* <> *vt* [label] mit einem Schild versehen; [luggage] mit Anhänger versehen.

◆ **tag along** *vi inf* mit|kommen.

**Tahiti** [tɑːˈhiːtɪ] *n* Tahiti *nt;* **in ~** auf Tahiti.

**tail** [teɪl] *n* - **1.** [of animal, bird, fish] Schwanz *der;* **with one's ~ between one's legs** [person] wie ein begossener Pudel - **2.** [of coat] Schoß *der;* [of shirt] Zipfel *der* - **3.** [of comet] Schweif *der;* [of plane] Schwanz *der* <> *vt inf* [follow - person] beschatten; [ - car] folgen (+ *D*).

◆ **tails** <> *adv* [side of coin] Zahl *die;* **heads or ~s?** Kopf oder Zahl? <> *npl* [formal dress] Frack *der.*

◆ **tail off** *vi* - **1.** [decrease in volume] leiser werden - **2.** [decrease in amount] zurück|gehen.

**tailback** [ˈteɪlbæk] *n Br* Rückstau *der.*

**tailcoat** [ˈteɪlkəʊt] *n* Frack *der.*

**tail end** *n* Ende *das.*

**tailgate** [ˈteɪlgeɪt] *n* [of hatchback car] Heckklappe *die.*

**taillight** [ˈteɪllaɪt] *n* Rücklicht *das.*

**tailor** [ˈteɪləʳ] *n* Schneider *der,* -in *die* <> *vt* [adjust]: **to ~ sthg to sthg** [plans, policy] etw auf etw *(A)* zu|schneiden; [product] etw auf etw *(A)* ab|stimmen.

**tailored** [ˈteɪləd] *adj* tailliert.

**tailor-made** *adj fig:* **to be ~ for sb** [role, job] genau auf jn zugeschnitten sein.

**tail pipe** *n Am* Auspuffrohr *das.*

**tailplane** [ˈteɪlpleɪn] *n* Höhenleitwerk *das.*

**tailwind** [ˈteɪlwɪnd] *n* Rückenwind *der.*

**taint** [teɪnt] *n* [of scandal, corruption] Makel *der* <> *vt* [reputation] beschmutzen.

**tainted** [ˈteɪntɪd] *adj* - **1.** [reputation] beschmutzt; [money] schmutzig - **2.** *Am* [food] verdorben.

**Taiwan** [ˌtaɪˈwɑːn] *n* Taiwan *nt.*

**Taiwanese** [ˌtaɪwəˈniːz] *adj* taiwanisch <> *n* Taiwaner *der,* -in *die.*

**take** [teɪk] (*pt* took, *pp* taken) *vt* - **1.** [gen] nehmen; **she took my arm** sie nahm mich beim Arm; **to ~ the train/bus** den Zug/Bus nehmen; **to ~ a bath** ein Bad nehmen; **to ~ an exam/a photo/a walk** eine Prüfung/ein Foto/einen Spaziergang machen; **to ~ risks** Risiken ein|gehen; **to ~ a decision** eine Entscheidung treffen; **to ~ an interest in sthg** sich für etw interessieren; **I ~ the view that** ... ich bin der Meinung, dass ...; **to ~ a seat** Platz nehmen; **to be ~n ill** krank werden - **2.** [bring, accompany] bringen; [take along] mit|nehmen;

**to ~ sthg to sb** jm etw bringen; **to ~ sb to the station** jn zum Bahnhof bringen; **he took her to the theatre** er ging mit ihr ins Theater; **I took it home** ich habe es mit nach Hause genommen - **3.** [remove, steal] mit|nehmen; **to ~ sthg from sb** jm etw ab|nehmen; [steal] jm etw weg|nehmen - **4.** [capture - city] ein|nehmen, erobern; [ - prisoner] machen - **5.** [control, power] übernehmen; **to ~ charge** die Leitung übernehmen - **6.** [accept] an|nehmen; [subj: machine] nehmen; [opportunity] wahr|nehmen; [responsibility] übernehmen; **do you ~ travellers' cheques?** nehmen Sie Travellerschecks?; **to ~ sb's advice** js Rat *(D)* folgen; **that's my final offer, you can ~ it or leave it** das ist mein letztes Angebot, es liegt an Ihnen - **7.** [receive - prize, praise] bekommen; **to ~ criticism** kritisiert werden - **8.** [contain] fassen; **the car can ~ six people** in dem Auto haben sechs Leute Platz - **9.** [size in clothes, shoes] haben; **what size do you ~?** welche Größe haben Sie?; **I ~ a (size) 34** ich habe Größe 34 - **10.** [bear] ertragen; **I can't ~ any more** mir reichts - **11.** [require] erfordern; **how long will it ~?** wie lange wird es dauern?, wie lange braucht es? - **12.** [react to] auf|nehmen; **to ~ sthg seriously** etw ernst nehmen; **to ~ sthg badly** etw schlecht auf|nehmen; **to ~ sthg the wrong way** etw falsch auf|fassen - **13.** [temperature, pulse] messen - **14.** [rent] mieten - **15.** [make - sum of money] ein|nehmen - **16.** GRAMM: **this verb ~s the dative** dieses Verb wird mit dem Dativ konstruiert - **17.** [assume]: **I ~ it (that)** ... ich gehe davon aus, dass ... <> *vi* [vaccination] auf|gehen; [dye] angenommen werden; [plant] Wurzel fassen; [fire] an|gehen <> *n* CINEMA Einstellung *die.*

◆ **take after** *vt fus* nach|schlagen (+ *D*); **he ~s after his mother/father** er schlägt nach seiner Mutter/seinem Vater.

◆ **take apart** *vt sep* [dismantle] auseinander|nehmen.

◆ **take away** *vt sep* - **1.** [remove]: **to ~ sthg away (from sb)** (jm) etw weg|nehmen; **is it to ~ away?** zum Mitnehmen? - **2.** [deduct] ab|ziehen.

◆ **take back** *vt sep* - **1.** [return] zurück|bringen - **2.** [faulty goods, statement] zurück|nehmen.

◆ **take down** *vt sep* - **1.** [pictures, curtains] ab|nehmen; [scaffolding, tent] ab|bauen - **2.** [from shelf] herunter|nehmen - **3.** [write down] auf|schreiben - **4.** [lower] herunter|lassen.

◆ **take in** *vt sep* - **1.** [bring inside - washing] herein|bringen - **2.** [deceive] herein|legen; **to be ~n in (by sb/sthg)** (auf jn/etw) herein|fallen - **3.** [understand] auf|nehmen - **4.** [include] ein|schließen - **5.** [provide accommodation for] auf|nehmen - **6.** [clothes] enger machen.

◆ **take off** *vt sep* - **1.** [remove] ab|nehmen; [clothing] aus|ziehen; **to ~ one's clothes off** sich aus|ziehen - **2.** [have as holiday]: **to ~ time off** sich *(D)* freilnehmen; **to ~ a week off** sich *(D)* eine Woche freilnehmen - **3.** *Br inf* [imitate] nachläffen - **4.** *inf* [go away suddenly]: **to ~ o.s. off** verschwinden <> *vi* - **1.** [plane] ablheben - **2.** [go away suddenly] verschwinden - **3.** [be successful]: **it took off when ...** der Erfolg kam, als ...

◆ **take on** *vt sep* - **1.** [job, responsibility] anlnehmen - **2.** [employ] anlstellen, einlstellen - **3.** [confront] sich anllegen mit; [competitor, sports team] anltreten gegen <> *vt fus* [colour, tone] anlnehmen; **to ~ on a new light** neue Aspekte gewinnen.

◆ **take out** *vt sep* - **1.** [remove - from container] herauslnehmen; [ - tooth] ziehen; [ - money from bank] ablheben - **2.** [library book] ausslleihen - **3.** [loan] auf lnehmen; [insurance policy] ablschließen; [patent] anlmelden - **4.** [delete] herauslnehmen - **5.** [go out with] ausslgehen mit - **6.** *phr:* **this job really ~s** OR **a lot out of you** *inf* diese Arbeit nimmt einen wirklich OR schwer mit.

◆ **take out on** *vt sep* **to ~ sthg out on sb** etw an jm ausslassen; **don't ~ it out on me!** lass deine Wut nicht an mir aus!

◆ **take over** *vt sep* [company, job] übernehmen <> *vi* - **1.** [take control] die Kontrolle übernehmen - **2.** [in job]: **to ~ over from sb** jn abllösen.

◆ **take to** *vt fus* - **1.** [come to like] mögen - **2.** [begin]: **to ~ to doing sthg** anlfangen, etw zu tun; **she's ~n to getting up earlier** sie steht nun früher auf; **to ~ to drink** zu trinken anlfangen.

◆ **take up** *vt sep* - **1.** [begin - post] anltreten; [ - job] auf lnehmen; **to ~ up the clarinet** anfangen, Klarinette zu spielen - **2.** [continue - story] fortlsetzen - **3.** [idea, question] auf lgreifen - **4.** [time, effort, space] in Anspruch nehmen - **5.** [trousers, dress] kürzen.

◆ **take up on** *vt sep* - **1.** [accept]: **to ~ sb up on an offer** js Angebot anlnehmen - **2.** [ask to explain]: **to ~ sb up on sthg** jn auf etw *(A)* hin anlsprechen.

◆ **take upon** *vt sep:* **to ~ it upon o.s. to do sthg** es auf sich *(A)* nehmen, etw zu tun.

**takeaway** *Br* ['teɪkə‚weɪ], **takeout** *Am* ['teɪkaut] *n* - **1.** [shop] *Laden, in dem warme Gerichte zum Mitnehmen angeboten werden* - **2.** [food] Essen *das* zum Mitnehmen <> *comp* [food] zum Mitnehmen.

**take-home pay** *n (U)* Nettolohn *der.*

**taken** ['teɪkn] *pp* ⊳ **take** <> *adj* [pleased]: **to be ~ with sb/sthg** von jm/etw angetan sein.

**takeoff** ['teɪkɒf] *n* [of plane] Start *der.*

**takeout** *n Am* = **takeaway.**

**takeover** ['teɪk‚əʊvəʳ] *n* Übernahme *die.*

**takeover bid** *n* Übernahmeangebot *das.*

**taker** ['teɪkəʳ] *n* [participant] Interessent *der,* -in *die.*

**takeup** ['teɪkʌp] *n:* **~ is very poor** [of offer] es gibt kaum Interessenten; **~ of housing benefit is low** Wohngeld wird nur von wenigen Leuten in Anspruch genommen.

**takings** ['teɪkɪŋz] *npl* Einnahmen *pl.*

**talc** [tælk], **talcum (powder)** ['tælkəm-] *n* Talk *der.*

**tale** [teɪl] *n* Geschichte *die.*

**talent** ['tælənt] *n* Talent *das;* **a ~ for painting/music** ein Talent zum Malen/für Musik.

**talented** ['tæləntɪd] *adj* talentiert.

**talent scout** *n* Talentsucher *der,* -in *die.*

**talisman** ['tælɪzmən] *(pl* -**s***) n* Talisman *der.*

**talk** [tɔːk] *n* - **1.** [conversation] Gespräch *das,* Unterhaltung *die;* **to have a ~** sich unterhalten; [more formal] ein Gespräch führen - **2.** [gossip] Gerede *das* - **3.** [lecture] Vortrag *der* <> *vi* - **1.** [speak] sprechen, reden; **to ~ to sb** mit jm reden OR sprechen; **to ~ to o.s.** Selbstgespräche führen; **to ~ about sb/sthg** über jn/etw sprechen OR reden; **~ing of him/that, ...** da wir gerade von ihm/davon sprechen ...; **he's ~ing of buying a car** er redet davon, dass er sich ein neues Auto kaufen will; **to ~ big** anlgeben; **look who's ~ing!, you can ~!** ausgerechnet du musst das sagen! - **2.** [gossip] klatschen - **3.** [make a speech] eine Rede halten; **to ~ on** OR **about sthg** über etw *(A)* sprechen - **4.** [betray a secret] reden <> *vt* - **1.** [politics, sport, business] reden über (+ *A)* OR von - **2.** [nonsense] reden.

◆ **talks** *npl* Gespräche *pl.*

◆ **talk down to** *vt fus* von oben herab sprechen mit.

◆ **talk into** *vt sep:* **to ~ sb into doing sthg** jn dazu überreden, etw zu tun.

◆ **talk out of** *vt sep:* **to ~ sb out of doing sthg** jm ausslreden, etw zu tun.

◆ **talk over** *vt sep* [discuss] bereden, besprechen.

**talkative** ['tɔːkətɪv] *adj* gesprächig.

**talker** ['tɔːkəʳ] *n* Redner *der,* -in *die.*

**talking point** ['tɔːkɪŋ-] *n* Gesprächsthema *das.*

**talking-to** ['tɔːkɪŋ-] *n inf* Standpauke *die;* **to give sb a (good) ~** jm eine Standpauke halten.

**talk show** *n Am* Talkshow *die.*

**tall** [tɔːl] *adj* - **1.** [person] groß; **I'm 5 feet ~** ich bin 1,50 m groß; **how ~ are you?** wie groß bist du? - **2.** [building, tree] hoch.

**tall order** *n:* **that's (a bit of) a ~** das ist ein bisschen viel verlangt.

**tall story** *n* unglaubliche Geschichte.

**tally** ['tælɪ] *(pl* -**ies;** *pt & pp* -**ied***) n* [record]: **to keep a ~ of sthg** über etw *(A)* Buch führen <> *vi* übereinlstimmen.

**talon** ['tælən] *n* Kralle *die*.

**tambourine** [ˌtæmbə'riːn] *n* Tamburin *das*.

**tame** [teɪm] *adj* - **1.** [animal, bird] zahm - **2.** *pej* [dull] lahm ◇ *vt* - **1.** [animal, bird] zähmen; [lion] bändigen - **2.** [person] bändigen.

**tamely** ['teɪmlɪ] *adv* widerstandslos.

**tamer** ['teɪməʳ] *n* Dompteur *der*, -teuse *die*.

**Tamil** ['tæmɪl] *adj* tamilisch ◇ *n* - **1.** [person] Tamile *der*, -lin *die* - **2.** [language] Tamil *das*.

**tamper** ['tæmpəʳ] ◆ **tamper with** *vt fus* sich *(D)* zu schaffen machen an *(+ D)*.

**tampon** ['tæmpɒn] *n* Tampon *der*.

**tan** [tæn] (*pt* & *pp* **-ned**; *cont* **-ning**) *adj* [light brown] hellbraun ◇ *n* [from sun] Bräune *die;* **to get a ~** braun werden ◇ *vi* braun werden.

**tandem** ['tændəm] *n* [bicycle] Tandem *das;* **in ~ (with)** zusammen (mit).

**tang** [tæŋ] *n* [taste] scharfer Geschmack; [smell] scharfer Geruch.

**tangent** ['tændʒənt] *n* GEOM Tangente *die;* **to go off at a ~** *fig* plötzlich vom Thema abschweifen.

**tangerine** [ˌtændʒə'riːn] *n* Mandarine *die*.

**tangible** ['tændʒəbl] *adj* [difference, benefit] merklich; [results] greifbar.

**tangle** ['tæŋgl] *n* - **1.** [mass] Gewirr *das;* **to get into a ~** [hair] durcheinander geraten; [string] sich verheddern - **2.** *fig* [mess] Durcheinander *das;* **to get (o.s.) into a ~** sich verstricken ◇ *vt:* **to get ~d (up)** durcheinander geraten; [wool, string] sich verheddern ◇ *vi* [hair] durcheinander geraten; [wool, string] sich verheddern.

◆ **tangle with** *vt fus inf* sich an|legen mit.

**tangled** ['tæŋgld] *adj* - **1.** [mixed together - wires] verheddert; [ - hair] durcheinander - **2.** *fig* [disordered] verworren.

**tango** ['tæŋgəʊ] (*pl* **-s**; *pt* & *pp* **-ed**; *cont* **-ing**) *n* Tango *der* ◇ *vi* Tango tanzen.

**tangy** ['tæŋɪ] (*compar* **-ier**; *superl* **-iest**) *adj* scharf; [salty] salzig.

**tank** [tæŋk] *n* - **1.** [container] Tank *der;* (fish) ~ Aquarium *das* - **2.** MIL Panzer *der*.

**tankard** ['tæŋkəd] *n* Humpen *der*.

**tanker** ['tæŋkəʳ] *n* - **1.** [ship] Tanker *der* - **2.** [truck] Tankwagen *der*.

**tanned** [tænd] *adj* [suntanned] braun (gebrannt).

**tannin** ['tænɪn] *n* Tannin *das*.

**Tannoy**® ['tænɔɪ] *n* Lautsprecheranlage *die*.

**tantalize, -ise** ['tæntəlaɪz] *vt* zappeln lassen.

**tantalizing** ['tæntəlaɪzɪŋ] *adj* verlockend.

**tantamount** ['tæntəmaʊnt] *adj:* **to be ~ to sthg** einer Sache *(D)* gleich|kommen.

**tantrum** ['tæntrəm] (*pl* **-s**) *n* Wutanfall *der*.

**Tanzania** [ˌtænzə'nɪə] *n* Tansania *nt*.

**Taoiseach** ['tiːʃək] *n* Premierminister *der*, -in *die* der Republik Irland.

**tap** [tæp] (*pt* & *pp* **-ped**; *cont* **-ping**) *n* - **1.** [device] Hahn *der;* **the hot(-water)/cold(-water)** ~ der Warmwasser-/Kaltwasserhahn - **2.** [light blow] Klaps *der;* [on door] Klopfen *das;* **she gave him a ~ on the shoulder** sie klopfte ihm auf die Schulter ◇ *vt* - **1.** [knock] klopfen - **2.** [make use of] erschließen - **3.** [listen secretly to] ab|hören ◇ *vi* [knock] klopfen.

**tap dance** *n* Stepptanz *der*.

**tap dancer** *n* Stepptänzer *der*, -in *die*.

**tape** [teɪp] *n* - **1.** [magnetic tape] Magnetband *das* - **2.** [cassette] Kassette *die* - **3.** SPORT [at finishing line] Zielband *das* - **4.** [adhesive material] Klebeband *das* ◇ *vt* - **1.** [record] auf|nehmen - **2.** [fasten with adhesive tape] (mit Klebeband) verkleben OR zu|kleben; **to ~ together** zusammen|kleben - **3.** Am [bandage] verbinden.

**tape deck** *n* Tapedeck *das*.

**tape measure** *n* Maßband *das*.

**taper** ['teɪpəʳ] *n* [candle] (dünne) Kerze ◇ *vi* [corridor] sich verengen; [trousers] nach unten enger werden; [fingers] spitz zulaufen.

◆ **taper off** *vi* langsam zurück|gehen.

**tape-record** [-rɪˌkɔːd] *vt* auf Band auf|nehmen.

**tape recorder** *n* Tonbandgerät *das;* [cassette recorder] Kassettenrekorder *der*.

**tape recording** *n* Bandaufnahme *die*.

**tapered** ['teɪpəd] *adj* [trousers] nach unten enger werdend; [fingers] spitz zulaufend.

**tapestry** ['tæpɪstrɪ] (*pl* **-ies**) *n* - **1.** [piece of work] Wandteppich *der* - **2.** (U) [craft] Tapisserie *die* - **3.** *literary:* **the rich ~ of life** die Vielfalt des Lebens.

**tapeworm** ['teɪpwɜːm] *n* Bandwurm *der*.

**tapioca** [ˌtæpɪ'əʊkə] *n* Tapioka *die*.

**tapir** ['teɪpəʳ] (*pl inv* OR **-s**) *n* Tapir *der*.

**tar** [tɑːʳ] *n* Teer *der*.

**tarantula** [tə'ræntjʊlə] *n* Tarantel *die*.

**target** ['tɑːgɪt] *n* - **1.** [of missile, bomb] Ziel *das* - **2.** [for archery, shooting] Zielscheibe *die* - **3.** *fig* [butt of criticism] Zielscheibe *die* - **4.** *fig* [goal] Ziel *das;* **we're on ~ to achieve our objective** wir sind auf dem besten Weg, unser Ziel zu erreichen ◇ *vt* - **1.** [aim weapon at] zielen auf *(+ A)* - **2.** [channel resources towards] sich *(D)* zum Ziel setzen; **to ~ the young** die Jugendlichen als Zielgruppe haben.

**tariff** ['tærɪf] *n* - **1.** [tax] Zoll *der* - **2.** Br [price list] Preisliste *die*.

**Tarmac**® ['tɑːmæk] *n* [material] Makadam *der*.
◆ **tarmac** *n* AERON: **the tarmac** die Rollbahn.

**T**

**tarnish** ['tɑːnɪʃ] vt - **1.** [make dull] stumpf werden lassen - **2.** fig [reputation] beflecken ⬦ vi [become dull] stumpf werden.

**tarnished** ['tɑːnɪʃt] adj - **1.** [dull] stumpf - **2.** fig [reputation] befleckt.

**tarot** ['tærəʊ] n: the ~ das OR der Tarock.

**tarot card** n Tarockkarte die.

**tarpaulin** [tɑːˈpɔːlɪn] n [sheet] Plane die.

**tarragon** ['tærəgən] n Estragon der.

**tart** [tɑːt] adj - **1.** [bitter-tasting] herb; [fruit] sauer - **2.** [sarcastic] scharf ⬦ n - **1.** [sweet pastry] Kuchen der; [small] Törtchen das; **fruit ~** Obstkuchen-/törtchen - **2.** Br vinf [prostitute] Nutte die.

➡ **tart up** vt sep Br inf pej [building, room] auf l-motzen; **to ~ o.s. up** sich auf ltakeln.

**tartan** ['tɑːtn] n - **1.** (U) [cloth] Schottenstoff der - **2.** [pattern] Schottenkaro das ⬦ comp im Schottenkaro.

**tartar** ['tɑːtəʳ-] n Zahnstein der.

**tartar(e) sauce** n (U) Tatarensoße die.

**task** [tɑːsk] n Aufgabe die.

**task force** n - **1.** MIL Spezialeinheit die - **2.** [group of helpers] Kommando das.

**taskmaster** ['tɑːskˌmɑːstəʳ] n: **to be a hard ~** ein strenger Vorgesetzter sein.

**Tasmania** [tæzˈmeɪnjə] n Tasmanien nt.

**tassel** ['tæsl] n Quaste die.

**taste** [teɪst] n - **1.** [sense of taste] Geschmacksinn der - **2.** [flavour] Geschmack der; **to have a funny ~** komisch schmecken - **3.** [try] Kostprobe die; **to have a ~** probieren - **4.** fig [liking, preference]: **~ (for sthg)** Vorliebe die (für etw) - **5.** fig [experience]: **his first ~ of success** sein erstes Erfolgserlebnis; **I've had a ~ of power** ich habe erfahren, wie es ist, Macht zu haben - **6.** (U) [discernment] Geschmack der; **she has (good) ~** sie hat (guten) Geschmack; **in bad ~** geschmacklos; **in good ~** geschmackvoll ⬦ vt - **1.** [food - experience flavour of] schmecken; [ - test, try] probieren, kosten - **2.** fig: **to ~ success** ein Erfolgserlebnis haben ⬦ vi schmecken; **it ~s wonderful** es schmeckt wunderbar; **to ~ of/like sthg** nach/wie etw schmecken.

**taste bud** n Geschmacksknospe die.

**tasteful** ['teɪstfʊl] adj geschmackvoll.

**tastefully** ['teɪstfʊlɪ] adv geschmackvoll.

**tasteless** ['teɪstlɪs] adj lit & fig geschmacklos.

**taster** ['teɪstəʳ] n [person] Prüfer der, -in die; **wine ~** Weinverkoster der, -in die.

**tasty** ['teɪstɪ] (compar **-ier;** superl **-iest**) adj schmackhaft; **a ~ morsel** ein Leckerbissen.

**tat** [tæt] n Br inf pej Schrott der.

**tattered** ['tætəd] adj [clothes] zerrissen; [paper] zerfleddert.

**tatters** ['tætəz] npl: **to be in ~** [clothes] in Fetzen sein; fig [confidence, reputation] sehr angeschlagen sein.

**tattle-tale** ['tætl-] n Am = telltale.

**tattoo** [təˈtuː] (pl **-s**) n - **1.** [design] Tätowierung die - **2.** [rhythmic beating] Trommeln das - **3.** Br [military display] Zapfenstreich der ⬦ vt tätowieren.

**tattooist** [təˈtuːɪst] n Tätowierer der, -in die.

**tatty** ['tætɪ] (compar **-ier;** superl **-iest**) adj Br inf pej schäbig.

**taught** [tɔːt] pt & pp ▷ **teach.**

**taunt** [tɔːnt] vt verspotten ⬦ n spöttische Bemerkung.

**Taurus** ['tɔːrəs] n Stier der; **I'm a ~** ich bin Stier.

**taut** [tɔːt] adj straff.

**tauten** ['tɔːtn] vt spannen; [muscles] anlspannen ⬦ vi sich spannen.

**tautology** [tɔːˈtɒlədʒɪl] n Tautologie die.

**tavern** ['tævn] n dated Taverne die.

**tawdry** ['tɔːdrɪ] (compar **-ier;** superl **-iest**) adj pej geschmacklos.

**tawny** ['tɔːnɪ] adj goldbraun.

**tax** [tæks] n [money paid to government] Steuer die ⬦ vt - **1.** [gen] besteuern - **2.** [patience, ingenuity] strapazieren.

**taxable** ['tæksəbl] adj steuerpflichtig.

**tax allowance** n Steuerfreibetrag der.

**taxation** [tækˈseɪʃn] n - **1.** [system] Besteuerung die - **2.** [amount] Steuer die.

**tax avoidance** [-əˈvɔɪdəns] n Steuerumgehung die.

**tax collector** n Finanzbeamte der, -tin die.

**tax cut** n Steuersenkung die.

**tax-deductible** [-dɪˈdʌktəbl] adj von der Steuer absetzbar.

**tax disc** n Br Steuermarke die.

**tax evasion** n Steuerhinterziehung die.

**tax-exempt** adj Am = tax-free.

**tax exemption** n Steuerbefreiung die.

**tax exile** n Br Steuerflüchtling der.

**tax-free** Br, **tax-exempt** Am adj steuerfrei.

**tax haven** n Steuerparadies das.

**taxi** ['tæksɪ] n Taxi das ⬦ vi [plane] rollen.

**taxicab** ['tæksɪkæb] n Taxi das.

**taxi driver** n Taxifahrer der, -in die.

**taximeter** ['tæksɪˌmiːtəʳ] n Taxameter der.

**taxing** ['tæksɪŋ] adj strapaziös.

**tax inspector** n Steuerprüfer der, -in die.

**taxi rank** Br, **taxi stand** n Taxistand der.

**taxman** ['tæksmæn] (*pl* **-men** [-men]) *n* - **1.** [tax collector] Finanzbeamter *der*, -tin *die* - **2.** *inf* [tax office]: **the ~** das Finanzamt.

**taxpayer** ['tæks‚peɪəʳ] *n* Steuerzahler *der*, -in *die*.

**tax relief** *n* Steuernachlass *der*.

**tax return** *n* Steuererklärung *die*.

**tax year** *n* Steuerjahr *das*.

**TB** (*abbr of* **tuberculosis**) *n* TB *die*.

**T-bone steak** *n* T-Bone-Steak *das*.

**tbs., tbsp.** (*abbr of* **tablespoon(ful)**) El.

**TD** *n* - **1.** (*abbr of* **Treasury Department**) *Wirtschafts- und Finanzministerium der USA* - **2.** *abbr of* **touchdown**.

**tea** [tiː] *n* - **1.** [drink] Tee *der* - **2.** *Br* [afternoon meal] Nachmittagstee *der* - **3.** *Br* [evening meal] Abendessen *das*.

> **TEA**
>
> Das britische Nationalgetränk ist nicht nur eine beliebte Erfrischung, sondern gilt auch als probates Mittel gegen Müdigkeit, Schock und alles mögliche Andere. Angestellte haben „tea breaks", Damen pflegen ihren „afternoon tea" (inklusive Sandwiches, Scones und Gebäck), und Schulkinder „have their tea" (leichte Abendmahlzeit nach der Schule). Für die Briten ist „tea" mit Essen und Behaglichkeit verbunden.

**teabag** ['tiːbæg] *n* Teebeutel *der*.

**tea ball** *n Am* Tee-Ei *das*.

**tea break** *n Br* Teepause *die*.

**tea caddy** [-‚kædɪ] *n* Teedose *die*.

**teach** [tiːtʃ] (*pt & pp* **taught**) *vt* - **1.** [gen] unterrichten; **to ~ sb sthg** jm Unterricht geben in etw (*D*), jn in etw (*D*) unterrichten; **to ~ sb to swim** jm das Schwimmen beibringen; **to ~ (sb) that** (jn) (be)lehren, dass - **2.** [advocate] lehren; **to ~ sb sthg, to ~ sthg to sb** jn etw lehren; **to ~ sb to do sthg** jn lehren, etw zu tun ◇ *vi* unterrichten.

**teacher** ['tiːtʃəʳ] *n* Lehrer *der*, -in *die*.

**teachers college** *n Am* = **teacher training college**.

**teacher's pet** *n pej* Lieblingsschüler *der*, -in *die*.

**teacher training college** *Br*, **teachers college** *Am n* ≃ pädagogische Hochschule.

**teaching** ['tiːtʃɪŋ] *n* - **1.** [profession, work] Unterrichten *das* - **2.** [thing taught] Lehre *die*.

**teaching aid** *n* Unterrichtsmittel *das*.

**teaching hospital** *n Br* Ausbildungskrankenhaus *das*.

**teaching practice** *n* (*U*) Unterrichtspraktikum *das*.

**teaching staff** *n* Lehrkörper *der*.

**tea cloth** *n* - **1.** [tablecloth] (kleine) Tischdecke *die* - **2.** [tea towel] Geschirrtuch *das*.

**tea cosy** *Br*, **tea cozy** *Am n* Teewärmer *der*.

**teacup** ['tiːkʌp] *n* Teetasse *die*.

**teak** [tiːk] *n* Teakholz *das* ◇ *comp* Teak-.

**tealeaves** ['tiːliːvz] *npl* Teeblätter *pl*.

**team** [tiːm] *n* - **1.** SPORT Team *das*, Mannschaft *die* - **2.** [group] Team *das*.
◆ **team up** *vi* sich zusammenIschließen; **to ~ up with sb** sich mit jm zusammenItun.

**team games** *n* Mannschaftsspiele *pl*.

**teammate** ['tiːmmeɪt] *n* Mannschaftsmitglied *das*.

**team spirit** *n* Teamgeist *der*.

**teamster** ['tiːmstəʳ] *n Am* Lastwagenfahrer *der*.

**teamwork** ['tiːmwɜːk] *n* (*U*) Teamarbeit *die*.

**teapot** ['tiːpɒt] *n* Teekanne *die*.

**tear**[1] [tɪəʳ] *n* [when crying] Träne *die*; **in ~s** tränenüberströmt.

**tear**[2] [teəʳ] (*pt* **tore**; *pp* **torn**) *vt* - **1.** [rip] zerreißen; **to ~ sthg open** etw aufIreißen; **to ~ sb/sthg to pieces** *fig* [criticize] jn/etw in Stücke reißen; **to be torn between** *fig* hin- und hergerissen sein zwischen (+ *D*) - **2.** [remove roughly] reißen ◇ *vi* - **1.** [rip] (zer)reißen - **2.** *inf* [move quickly] rasen; **she tore into the office** sie kam ins Büro gerast - **3.** *phr*: **to ~ loose** [get free] sich losIreißen ◇ *n* [rip] Riss *der*.
◆ **tear apart** *vt sep* - **1.** [rip up] zerreißen - **2.** [upset greatly] fertig machen.
◆ **tear at** *vt fus* zerren an (+ *D*).
◆ **tear away** *vt sep*: **to ~ o.s. away (from sthg)** sich (von etw) losIreißen.
◆ **tear down** *vt sep* [building, poster] abIreißen.
◆ **tear off** *vt sep* [clothes] herunterIreißen.
◆ **tear out** *vt sep* [coupon, page] herausIreißen.
◆ **tear up** *vt sep* zerreißen.

**tearaway** ['teərə‚weɪ] *n Br inf* Krawallmacher *der*, -in *die*.

**teardrop** ['tɪədrɒp] *n* Träne *die*.

**tearful** ['tɪəfʊl] *adj* - **1.** [person] tränenüberströmt - **2.** [event] tränenreich.

**tear gas** [tɪəʳ-] *n* Tränengas *das*.

**tearing** ['teərɪŋ] *adj inf* [pace, hurry] rasend.

**tearjerker** ['tɪə‚dʒɜːkəʳ] *n hum* Schnulze *die*.

**tearoom** ['tiːrʊm] *n* Teestube *die*.

**tease** [tiːz] *n inf* - **1.** [joker] Witzbold *der* - **2.** [sexually] Schäker *der*, -in *die* ◇ *vt*: **to ~ sb (about sthg)** jn (wegen etw) aufIziehen.

**tea service, tea set** *n* Teeservice *das*.

**tea shop** *n* Teestube *die*.

**T**

**teasing** ['ti:zɪŋ] *adj* neckend.

**Teasmade**® ['ti:zmeɪd] *n Br automatische Teemaschine.*

**teaspoon** ['ti:spu:n] *n* Teelöffel *der.*

**tea strainer** *n* Teesieb *das.*

**teat** [ti:t] *n* - **1.** [of animal] Zitze *die* - **2.** [of bottle] Sauger *der.*

**teatime** ['ti:taɪm] *n (U) Br* [in evening] Abendessenszeit *die;* [in afternoon] Teezeit *die.*

**tea towel** *n* Geschirrtuch *das.*

**technical** ['teknɪkl] *adj* [gen] technisch; ~ **term** Fachbegriff *der.*

**technical college** *n Br* ≃ Fachhochschule *die.*

**technical drawing** *n* technische Zeichnung.

**technicality** [ˌteknɪˈkælətɪ] (*pl* -ies) *n* - **1.** [intricacy] technische Einzelheit - **2.** [petty rule] Formsache *die.*

**technically** ['teknɪklɪ] *adv* - **1.** [theoretically] theoretisch - **2.** [scientifically] technisch.

**technician** [tekˈnɪʃn] *n* - **1.** [worker] Techniker *der,* -in *die* - **2.** [artist] Handwerker *der,* -in *die.*

**Technicolor**® ['teknɪˌkʌləʳ] *n* Technicolor® *das.*

**technique** [tekˈni:k] *n* Technik *die.*

**technocrat** ['teknəkræt] *n* Technokrat *der,* -in *die.*

**technological** [ˌteknəˈlɒdʒɪkl] *adj* technologisch.

**technologist** [tekˈnɒlədʒɪst] *n* Technologe *der,* -gin *die.*

**technology** [tekˈnɒlədʒɪ] (*pl* -ies) *n* Technologie *die.*

**teddy** ['tedɪ] (*pl* -ies) *n:* ~ **(bear)** Teddy(bär) *der.*

**tedious** ['ti:djəs] *adj* langweilig.

**tedium** ['ti:djəm] *n fml* Langweiligkeit *die.*

**tee** [ti:] *n GOLF* Tee *das,* Abschlag *der.*
➤ **tee off** *vi GOLF* den Ball vom Abschlag spielen.

**teem** [ti:m] *vi* - **1.** [rain] gießen - **2.** [be busy]: **to be ~ing with** wimmeln von.

**teen** [ti:n] *adj inf* Teenager-.

**teenage** ['ti:neɪdʒ] *adj* Teenager-; [children] halbwüchsig.

**teenager** ['ti:nˌeɪdʒəʳ] *n* Teenager *der.*

**teens** [ti:nz] *npl:* **to be in one's** ~ im Teenageralter sein.

**teeny (weeny)** [ˌti:nɪ('wi:nɪ)], **teensy (weensy)** [ˌti:nzɪ('wi:nzɪ)] *adj inf* klitzeklein.

**tee shirt** *n* T-Shirt *das.*

**teeter** ['ti:təʳ] *vi* - **1.** [wobble] schwanken - **2.** *fig* [be in danger]: **to be ~ing on the brink of**

disaster am Rande einer Katastrophe stehen.

**teeter-totter** *n Am* Wippe *die.*

**teeth** [ti:θ] *pl* ⊳ **tooth.**

**teethe** [ti:ð] *vi* [baby] zahnen.

**teething ring** ['ti:ðɪŋ-] *n* Beißring *der.*

**teething troubles** *npl fig* Anfangsschwierigkeiten *pl.*

**teetotal** [ti:ˈtəʊtl] *adj* abstinent.

**teetotaller** *Br,* **teetotaler** *Am* [ti:ˈtəʊtləʳ] *n* Abstinenzler *der,* -in *die.*

**TEFL** ['tefl] (*abbr of* **teaching of English as a foreign language**) *n* TEFL, *Unterrichten des Englischen als Fremdsprache.*

**Teflon**® ['teflɒn] *n* Teflon® *das* ◇ *comp* Teflon-.

**Teh(e)ran** [teəˈrɑːn] *n* Teheran *nt.*

**tel.** (*abbr of* **telephone**) Tel.

**Tel-Aviv** [ˌteləˈviːv] *n:* ~ **(-Jaffa)** Tel Aviv(-Jaffa) *nt.*

**tele-** ['telɪ] *prefix* Tele-, tele-.

**telecast** ['telɪkɑːst] *n* Fernsehsendung *die.*

**telecom** ['telɪkɒm] *n,* **telecoms** ['telɪkɒmz] *npl Br inf* Telekommunikationswesen *das.*

**telecommunications** [ˌtelɪkəˌmjuːnɪˈkeɪʃnz] *npl* Telekommunikationswesen *das.*

**telegram** ['telɪgræm] *n* Telegramm *das.*

**telegraph** ['telɪgrɑːf] *n* Telegraf *der* ◇ *vt* telegrafieren.

**telegraph pole, telegraph post** *Br n* Telegrafenmast *der.*

**telepathic** [ˌtelɪˈpæθɪk] *adj* telepathisch.

**telepathy** [tɪˈlepəθɪ] *n* Telepathie *die.*

**telephone** ['telɪfəʊn] *n* Telefon *das;* **to be on the** ~ *Br* [connected] Telefon haben; [speaking] am Telefon sein ◇ *vt* anrufen ◇ *vi* telefonieren.

**telephone book** *n* Telefonbuch *das.*

**telephone booth** *n Br* Telefonkabine *die.*

**telephone box** *n Br* Telefonzelle *die.*

**telephone call** *n* Telefonanruf *der,* Telefongespräch *das;* **to make a** ~ telefonieren.

**telephone directory** *n* Telefonbuch *das.*

**telephone exchange** *n* Fernsprechamt *das.*

**telephone kiosk** *n Br* Telefonzelle *die.*

**telephone number** *n* Telefonnummer *die.*

**telephone operator** *n* Telefonist *der,* -in *die.*

**telephone tapping** [-ˈtæpɪŋ] *n* Abhören *das* von Telefongesprächen.

**telephonist** [tɪˈlefənɪst] *n Br* Telefonist *der,* -in *die.*

**telephoto lens** [ˌtelɪˈfəʊtəʊ-] *n* Teleobjektiv *das*.

**teleprinter** [ˈtelɪˌprɪntəʳ], **teletypewriter** *Am* [ˌtelɪˈtaɪpˌraɪtəʳ] *n* Fernschreiber *der*.

**Teleprompter**® [ˈtelɪˌprɒmptəʳ] *n* Teleprompter *der*.

**telesales** [ˈtelɪseɪlz] *npl* Verkauf *der* per Telefon.

**telescope** [ˈtelɪskəʊp] *n* Teleskop *das*.

**telescopic** [ˌtelɪˈskɒpɪk] *adj* - **1.** [magnifying] teleskopisch - **2.** [contracting] ausziehbar.

**teleshopping** [ˈtelɪʃɒpɪŋ] *n* Teleshopping *das*.

**teletext** [ˈtelɪtekst] *n* Videotext *der*.

**telethon** [ˈtelɪθɒn] *n* *langes Fernsehprogramm im Zusammenhang mit einer Spendenaktion*.

**teletypewriter** *n Am* = teleprinter.

**televise** [ˈtelɪvaɪz] *vt* im Fernsehen übertragen.

**television** [ˈtelɪˌvɪʒn] *n* - **1.** [medium, industry] Fernsehen *das*; **on ~** im Fernsehen - **2.** [apparatus] Fernseher *der*.

**television licence** *n Br* [document] Fernsehgenehmigung *die*; [fee] Fernsehgebühr *die*.

**television programme** *n* Fernsehsendung *die*.

**television set** *n* Fernseher *der*.

**teleworking** [ˈtelɪˌwɜːkɪŋ] *n* Telearbeit *die*.

**telex** [ˈteleks] *n* Telex *das* ◇ *vt* (ein) Telex schicken (+ *D*); [message] telexen.

**tell** [tel] (*pt & pp* told) *vt* - **1.** [fact] sagen; [story, joke, lie] erzählen; **to ~ sb (that)** jm sagen, dass; **to ~ sb sthg, to ~ sthg to sb** jm etw erzählen; **to ~ the truth** die Wahrheit sagen; **to ~ sb the time** jm sagen, wie spät es ist; **I told you so!** das habe ich dir ja gleich gesagt! - **2.** [instruct, reveal] sagen; **to ~ sb to do sthg** jm sagen, dass er/sie etw tun soll; **to ~ sb (that)** jm sagen, dass - **3.** [judge, recognize] wissen; **to ~ the time** die Uhr lesen können; **there's no ~ing ...** man weiß nie ... ◇ *vi* - **1.** [reveal secret]: **he won't ~** er wird nichts sagen - **2.** [judge] beurteilen - **3.** [have effect] sich zeigen.

➤ **tell apart** *vt sep* unterscheiden.

➤ **tell off** *vt sep* ausschimpfen.

**teller** [ˈteləʳ] *n* - **1.** [of votes] Stimmenauszähler *der*, -in *die* - **2.** [in bank] Kassierer *der*, -in *die*.

**telling** [ˈtelɪŋ] *adj* - **1.** [effective] wirkungsvoll - **2.** [revealing] aufschlussreich.

**telling-off** (*pl* tellings-off) *n* Standpauke *die*; **to give sb a ~** jn ausschimpfen.

**telltale** [ˈtelteɪl] *adj* verräterisch ◇ *n* Petzer *der*, Petze *die*.

**telly** [ˈtelɪ] (*pl* -ies) *n Br inf* - **1.** [medium] Fernse-

hen *das*; **on ~** im Fernsehen - **2.** [apparatus] Flimmerkiste *die*.

**temerity** [tɪˈmerətɪ] *n fml* Verwegenheit *die*.

**temp** [temp] *Br inf n* (*abbr of* **temporary (employee)**) Zeitarbeitskraft *die* ◇ *vi* als Zeitarbeitskraft arbeiten.

**temp.** *abbr of* **temperature**.

**temper** [ˈtempəʳ] *n* - **1.** [state of mind, mood] Laune *die*; **to lose one's ~** die Beherrschung verlieren; **to have a short ~** leicht aufbrausend sein - **2.** [angry state]: **to be in a ~** wütend sein - **3.** [temperament] Temperament *das* ◇ *vt fml* [moderate] mäßigen.

**temperament** [ˈtemprəmənt] *n* Temperament *das*.

**temperamental** [ˌtemprəˈmentl] *adj* launenhaft.

**temperance** [ˈtemprəns] *n* - **1.** *fml* [moderation] Mäßigung *die* - **2.** [not drinking alcohol] Abstinenz *die*.

**temperate** [ˈtemprət] *adj* gemäßigt.

**temperature** [ˈtemprətʃəʳ] *n* Temperatur *die*; **to have a ~** Fieber haben; **to take sb's ~** js Temperatur messen.

**tempered** [ˈtempəd] *adj* gemäßigt.

**tempest** [ˈtempɪst] *n literary* Sturm *der*.

**tempestuous** [temˈpestjʊəs] *adj lit* & *fig* stürmisch.

**tempi** [ˈtempiː] *pl* ➩ **tempo**.

**template** [ˈtemplɪt] *n* [of shape, pattern] Schablone *die*.

**temple** [ˈtempl] *n* - **1.** RELIG Tempel *der* - **2.** ANAT Schläfe *die*.

**templet** [ˈtemplɪt] *n* = template.

**tempo** [ˈtempəʊ] (*pl* -s OR -pi [-piː]) *n* Tempo *das*.

**temporarily** [ˌtempəˈrerəlɪ] *adv* vorübergehend.

**temporary** [ˈtempərərɪ] *adj* vorübergehend; [job] befristet.

**tempt** [tempt] *vt* [entice]: **to ~ sb to do sthg** jn dazu verlocken, etw zu tun; **to be OR feel ~ed to do sthg** geneigt sein, etw zu tun.

**temptation** [tempˈteɪʃn] *n* - **1.** [state] Versuchung *die* - **2.** [tempting thing] Verlockung *die*.

**tempting** [ˈtemptɪŋ] *adj* verlockend.

**ten** [ten] *num* zehn; *see also* **six**.

**tenable** [ˈtenəbl] *adj* - **1.** [reasonable, credible] haltbar - **2.** [job, post]: **~ for** befristet auf (+ *A*).

**tenacious** [tɪˈneɪʃəs] *adj* hartnäckig.

**tenacity** [tɪˈnæsətɪ] *n* Hartnäckigkeit *die*.

**tenancy** [ˈtenənsɪ] (*pl* -ies) *n* - **1.** [period - of building] Mietdauer *die*; [ - of land] Pachtzeit *die* - **2.** [possession of building] Mieten *das*; [ - of land] Pachten *das*.

**T**

**tenant** ['tenənt] *n* Mieter *der*, -in *die*.

**Ten Commandments** *npl:* the ~ die Zehn Gebote.

**tend** [tend] *vt* - **1.** [have tendency]: to ~ to do sthg [person] dazu neigen, etw zu tun; it ~s to snow in February es schneit oft im Februar; I ~ to think (that) ... ich neige zu der Ansicht, dass ... - **2.** [look after] sich kümmern um.

**tendency** ['tendənsɪ] (*pl* -ies) *n* - **1.** [trend]: ~ towards sthg Tendenz *die* zu etw - **2.** [leaning, habit] Neigung *die;* to have the ~ to do sthg die Neigung haben, etw zu tun.

**tender** ['tendəʳ] *adj* - **1.** [caring, gentle] zärtlich - **2.** [meat] zart - **3.** [sore] empfindlich - **4.** [young, innocent]: at the ~ age of ... im zarten Alter von ... <> *n* COMM Angebot *das* <> *vt fml* [offer - money] an|bieten; [ - resignation] ein|reichen.

**tenderize, -ise** ['tendəraɪz] *vt* klopfen.

**tenderly** ['tendəlɪ] *adv* zärtlich.

**tenderness** ['tendənɪs] *n* - **1.** [care, compassion] Zärtlichkeit *die* - **2.** [soreness] Empfindlichkeit *die.*

**tendon** ['tendən] *n* Sehne *die.*

**tendril** ['tendrəl] *n* Ranke *die.*

**tenement** ['tenəmənt] *n* Mietshaus *das.*

**Tenerife** [ˌtenəˈriːf] *n* Teneriffa *nt.*

**tenet** ['tenɪt] *n fml* Grundsatz *der.*

**tenner** ['tenəʳ] *n Br inf* - **1.** [amount] zehn Pfund - **2.** [note] Zehnpfundschein *der.*

**tennis** ['tenɪs] *n* Tennis *das* <> *comp* Tennis-.

**tennis ball** *n* Tennisball *der.*

**tennis court** *n* Tennisplatz *der.*

**tennis player** *n* Tennisspieler *der*, -in *die.*

**tennis racket** *n* Tennisschläger *der.*

**tenor** ['tenəʳ] *adj* Tenor- <> *n* Tenor *der.*

**tenpin bowling** *Br* ['tenpɪn-], **tenpins** *Am* ['tenpɪnz] *n* Bowling *das.*

**tense** [tens] *adj* angespannt <> *n* GRAMM Zeit(form) *die* <> *vt* [muscles] an|spannen <> *vi* [stiffen - muscles] sich spannen; [ - person] sich verkrampfen.

**tensed up** [tenst-] *adj* angespannt.

**tension** ['tenʃn] *n (U)* - **1.** [anxiety] Anspannung *die;* [between people] Spannung *die* - **2.** TECH [tightness] Spannung *die.*
◆ **tensions** *npl* Spannungen *pl.*

**ten-spot** *n Am* Zehndollarschein *der.*

**tent** [tent] *n* Zelt *das.*

**tentacle** ['tentəkl] *n* Fangarm *der*, Tentakel *der* OR *das.*

**tentative** ['tentətɪv] *adj* - **1.** [person, step, smile] zögernd - **2.** [agreement, plan] vorläufig.

**tentatively** ['tentətɪvlɪ] *adv* - **1.** [smile, move, speak] zögernd - **2.** [agree, plan] vorläufig.

**tenterhooks** ['tentəhʊks] *npl:* to be on ~ auf glühenden Kohlen sitzen.

**tenth** [tenθ] *num* zehnte, -r, -s; *see also* sixth.

**tent peg** *n* Hering *der*, Zeltpflock *der.*

**tent pole** *n* Zeltstange *die.*

**tenuous** ['tenjʊəs] *adj* schwach.

**tenuously** ['tenjʊəslɪ] *adv* schwach.

**tenure** ['tenjəʳ] *n (U) fml* - **1.** [of property]: security of ~ Mietsicherheit *die* - **2.** [of job] Festanstellung *die.*

**tepee** ['tiːpiː] *n* Tipi *das.*

**tepid** ['tepɪd] *adj lit* & *fig* lauwarm.

**tequila** [tɪˈkiːlə] *n* Tequila *der.*

**term** [tɜːm] *n* - **1.** [word, expression] Begriff *der*, Ausdruck *der* - **2.** SCH & UNIV Trimester *das* - **3.** POL: ~ (of office) Amtszeit *die* - **4.** [period of time]: a prison ~ eine Haftstrafe; in the long/short ~ auf lange/kurze Sicht <> *vt* bezeichnen; to ~ sb/sthg sthg jn/etw als etw bezeichnen.
◆ **terms** *npl* - **1.** [of contract, agreement] Konditionen *pl* - **2.** [conditions]: in international ~s im internationalen Vergleich; in real ~s effektiv - **3.** [of relationship]: on equal OR the same ~s von Gleich zu Gleich; to be on good ~s (with sb) (mit jm) gut aus|kommen; we're no longer on speaking ~s wir reden nicht mehr miteinander - **4.** *phr:* to come to ~s with sthg sich mit etw ab|finden.
◆ **in terms of** *prep* in Bezug auf (+ A); to think in ~s of doing sthg daran denken, etw zu tun.

**terminal** ['tɜːmɪnl] *adj* MED unheilbar <> *n* - **1.** RAIL Endbahnhof *der;* AERON Terminal *der* - **2.** COMPUT Terminal *das* - **3.** ELEC Pol *der.*

**terminally** ['tɜːmɪnəlɪ] *adv* unheilbar.

**terminate** ['tɜːmɪneɪt] *vt fml* beenden; [contract] auf|lösen; [pregnancy] ab|brechen <> *vi* [bus, train] enden.

**termination** [ˌtɜːmɪˈneɪʃn] *n* - **1.** *(U) fml* [ending] Beendigung *die;* [of contract] Auflösung *die* - **2.** [abortion] Schwangerschaftsabbruch *der.*

**termini** ['tɜːmɪnaɪ] *pl* ⫸ **terminus.**

**terminology** [ˌtɜːmɪˈnɒlədʒɪ] *n* Terminologie *die.*

**terminus** ['tɜːmɪnəs] (*pl* -ni OR -nuses) *n* Endstation *die.*

**termite** ['tɜːmaɪt] *n* Termite *die.*

**Ter(r)** *abbr of* terrace.

**terrace** ['terəs] *n* - **1.** *Br* [of houses] Häuserreihe *die* - **2.** [patio] Terrasse *die.*
◆ **terraces** *npl* FTBL: the ~s die Ränge *pl.*

**terraced** ['terəst] *adj* [hillside] terrassenförmig angelegt.

**terraced house** *n Br* Reihenhaus *das.*

**terracotta** [ˌterəˈkɒtə] *n* Terrakotta *die.*

**terrain** [teˈreɪn] *n* Gelände *das*.

**terrapin** [ˈterəpɪn] *(pl inv OR* -s*)* *n* Sumpfschildkröte *die*.

**terrestrial** [təˈrestrɪəl] *adj fml* - **1.** [of the Earth] Erd-; [life, things] irdisch - **2.** [of the land] Land- - **3.** RADIO & TV terrestrisch.

**terrible** [ˈterəbl] *adj* furchtbar, schrecklich.

**terribly** [ˈterəblɪ] *adv* [extremely] furchtbar, schrecklich.

**terrier** [ˈterɪəʳ] *n* Terrier *der*.

**terrific** [təˈrɪfɪk] *adj* - **1.** [wonderful] großartig - **2.** [enormous] enorm.

**terrified** [ˈterɪfaɪd] *adj:* to be ~ (of sb/sthg) wahnsinnige Angst haben (vor jm/etw).

**terrify** [ˈterɪfaɪ] *(pt & pp* -ied*)* *vt* in Angst und Schrecken versetzen.

**terrifying** [ˈterɪfaɪɪŋ] *adj* fürchterlich.

**terrine** [teˈriːn] *n* Pastete *die*.

**territorial** [ˌterɪˈtɔːrɪəl] *adj* territorial.

**Territorial Army** *n Br:* the ~ das Territorialheer.

**territorial waters** *npl* Hoheitsgewässer *pl*.

**territory** [ˈterətrɪ] *(pl* -ies*)* *n* - **1.** [political area] Territorium *das* - **2.** [terrain] Gelände *das*.

**terror** [ˈterəʳ] *n* - **1.** [fear] panische Angst - **2.** [something feared]: the ~s of war die Schrecken des Krieges - **3.** *inf* [rascal] Teufel *der*.

**terrorism** [ˈterərɪzm] *n* Terrorismus *der*.

**terrorist** [ˈterərɪst] *n* Terrorist *der*, -in *die*.

**terrorize, -ise** [ˈterəraɪz] *vt* terrorisieren.

**terror-stricken** *adj* starr vor Schreck.

**terry(cloth)** [ˈterɪ(klɒθ)] *n* Frottee *der OR das*.

**terse** [tɜːs] *adj* - **1.** [reply, remark] knapp - **2.** [person] kurz angebunden.

**tersely** [ˈtɜːslɪ] *adv* knapp, kurz.

**tertiary** [ˈtɜːʃərɪ] *adj fml* Tertiär-, tertiär.

**tertiary education** *n* Hochschulwesen *das*.

**Terylene®** [ˈterəliːn] *n* Trevira® *das*.

**TESL** [ˈtesl] *(abbr of* teaching of English as a second language*)* *n* Unterrichten des Englischen als Zweitsprache.

**TESSA** [ˈtesə] *(abbr of* tax-exempt special savings account*)* *n* steuerbefreites Sparkonto in Großbritannien.

**test** [test] *n* - **1.** [trial] Test *der;* [of friendship, courage] Probe *die;* to put sb/sthg to the ~ jn/etw auf die Probe stellen - **2.** [examination of knowledge, skill] SCH Klassenarbeit *die;* UNIV Klausur *die;* driving ~ Fahrprüfung *die* - **3.** MED [medical check] Test *der* <> *vt* - **1.** [knowledge] testen; [friendship, courage] auf die Probe stellen; to have one's eyes ~ed seine Augen testen lassen

- **2.** [pupil] prüfen; to ~ sb on sthg jn in etw (D) prüfen.

**testament** [ˈtestəmənt] *n* - **1.** [gen] Testament *das* - **2.** [proof]: ~ to sthg Beweis *der* für etw.

**test ban** *n* Teststopp *der*.

**test card** *n Br* Testbild *das*.

**test case** *n* LAW Musterfall *der*.

**test-drive** *vt* Probe fahren.

**tester** [ˈtestəʳ] *n* - **1.** [person] Prüfer *der*, -in *die* - **2.** [sample] Muster *das*.

**test flight** *n* Testflug *der*.

**testicles** [ˈtestɪklz] *npl* Hoden *pl*.

**testify** [ˈtestɪfaɪ] *(pt & pp* -ied*)* *vt:* to ~ that bezeugen, dass <> *vi* - **1.** LAW aussagen - **2.** [be proof]: to ~ to sthg von etw zeugen.

**testimonial** [ˌtestɪˈməʊnjəl] *n* [reference] Referenz *die*.

**testimony** [*Br* ˈtestɪmənɪ, *Am* ˈtestəməʊnɪ] *n (U)* - **1.** LAW Aussage *die* - **2.** [proof, demonstration]: ~ to sthg Zeichen *das* für etw.

**testing** [ˈtestɪŋ] *adj* [difficult] schwer.

**testing ground** *n* Versuchsgelände *das*.

**test match** *n Br* internationales Cricket- oder Rugbyspiel.

**testosterone** [tesˈtɒstərəʊn] *n* Testosteron *das*.

**test paper** *n* - **1.** SCH Klassenarbeit *die* - **2.** CHEM Reagenzpapier *das*.

**test pattern** *n Am* Testbild *das*.

**test pilot** *n* Testpilot *der*, -in *die*.

**test tube** *n* Reagenzglas *das*.

**test-tube baby** *n* Retortenbaby *das*.

**testy** [ˈtestɪ] *(compar* -ier; *superl* -iest*)* *adj* gereizt.

**tetanus** [ˈtetənəs] *n* Tetanus *der*, Wundstarrkrampf *der*.

**tetchy** [ˈtetʃɪ] *(compar* -ier; *superl* -iest*)* *adj* reizbar.

**tête-à-tête** [ˌteɪtɑːˈteɪt] *n* Treffen *das* unter vier Augen.

**tether** [ˈteðəʳ] *vt* anlbinden <> *n:* to be at the end of one's ~ am Ende sein.

**Tex-Mex** [ˌteksˈmeks] *adj* Tex-Mex-.

**text** [tekst] *n* - **1.** [gen] Text *der* - **2.** [of speech, interview] Wortlaut *der*.

**textbook** [ˈtekstbʊk] *n* Lehrbuch *das*.

**textile** [ˈtekstaɪl] *n* Textilie *die;* ~s Textilien *pl* <> *comp* Textil-.

**texture** [ˈtekstʃəʳ] *n* Beschaffenheit *die*.

**TGWU** *(abbr of* Transport and General Workers' Union*)* *n* britische Gewerkschaft.

**Thai** [taɪ] *adj* thailändisch <> *n* - **1.** [person] Thailänder *der*, -in *die* - **2.** [language] Thai *das*.

**Thailand** [ˈtaɪlænd] *n* Thailand *nt*.

T

**Thames** [temz] n: the ~ die Themse.

**than** [weak form ðən, strong form ðæn] prep als; you're better ~ me du bist besser als ich; move ~ ten mehr als zehn <> conj als; I'd rather stay in ~ go out ich bleibe lieber zu Hause als auszugehen; she would do anything rather ~ let him suffer sie würde alles tun, um ihn nicht leiden zu lassen; no sooner had we arrived ~ the music began kaum waren wir angekommen, da begann die Musik zu spielen.

**thank** [θæŋk] vt: to ~ sb (for sthg) jm (für etw) danken; ~ God OR goodness OR heavens! Gott sei Dank!

&#8227; **thanks** npl Dank der <> excl danke.

&#8227; **thanks to** prep dank (+ D).

**thankful** ['θæŋkful] adj - 1. [grateful] ~ (for sthg) dankbar (für etw) - 2. [relieved] erleichtert.

**thankfully** ['θæŋkfulɪ] adv - 1. [with gratitude] dankbar - 2. [thank goodness] glücklicherweise.

**thankless** ['θæŋklɪs] adj undankbar.

**thanksgiving** ['θæŋks,gɪvɪŋ] n Danksagung die.

&#8227; **Thanksgiving (Day)** n amerikanisches Erntedankfest.

> **THANKSGIVING**
>
> In den USA ist „Thanksgiving" (Erntedankfest) ein Feiertag, der an jedem vierten Donnerstag im November zum Dank für die Ernte, aber auch für alle anderen Segnungen des vergangenen Jahres gefeiert wird. Das Fest geht auf das Jahr 1621 zurück, als die ersten Siedler aus Großbritannien, die „Pilgrims", ihre erste Ernte einbrachten. Das traditionelle Thanksgiving-Essen besteht aus Truthahnbraten und „pumpkin pie", einem Kürbisgericht.

**thank you** excl danke schön!; ~ for danke für.

&#8227; **thankyou** n Dankeschön das.

**that** [ðæt, weak form of pron senses 3–5 & conj ðət] (pl **those**) pron - 1. (demonstrative use) das, die pl; who's/what's ~? wer/was ist das?; ~'s interesting das ist interessant; is ~ Lucy? [on phone] bist du das, Lucy?; [pointing] ist das Lucy?; how much are those? wieviel kosten die (da)?; all those I saw all die, die ich sah; after ~ danach; what do you mean by ~? was willst du damit sagen? - 2. (referring to thing or person further away) jene, -r, -s, jene pl; this is new, ~ is old dies ist neu, jenes ist alt; I want those there ich möchte die da - 3. (introducing relative clause: subject) der/die/das, die pl; a shop ~ sells antiques ein Geschäft, das Antiquitäten verkauft - 4. (introducing relative clause: object) den/der/das, die pl; the film ~ I saw der Film, den ich gesehen habe; everything ~ I have done alles, was ich gemacht habe; the

best ~ he could do das Beste, was er machen konnte - 5. (introducing relative clause: after prep + D) dem/der/dem, denen pl; (introducing relative clause: after prep + A) den/die/das, die pl; the place ~ I'm looking for der Ort, nach dem ich suche; the envelope ~ I put it in der Umschlag, in den ich es steckte; the night ~ we went to the theatre der Abend, an dem wir ins Theater gingen <> adj - 1. (demonstrative use) der/die/das, die pl; ~ film was good der Film war gut; who's ~ man? wer ist der Mann?; what's ~ noise? was ist das für ein Lärm?; those chocolates are delicious die Pralinen da schmecken köstlich - 2. (referring to thing or person further away) jene, -r, -s, jene pl; I prefer ~ book ich bevorzuge das Buch da; I'll have ~ one ich nehme das da <> adv so; it wasn't ~ bad/good es war nicht so schlecht/gut <> conj dass; he recommended ~ I phone you er empfahl mir, dich anzurufen; tell him ~ I'm going to be late sag ihm, dass ich später komme.

&#8227; **at that** adv: she's a photographer, and a good one at ~ sie ist Fotografin, und dazu OR sogar eine gute.

&#8227; **that is (to say)** adv das heißt.

&#8227; **that's it** adv [that's all] das ist alles; ~'s it, I'm leaving jetzt reichts, ich gehe.

&#8227; **that's that** adv damit hat sichs.

**thatched** [θætʃt] adj: ~ roof Reetdach das.

**that's** [ðæts] = that is.

**thaw** [θɔ:] vt auftauen <> vi - 1. [ice, frozen food] tauen - 2. fig [atmosphere] sich entspannen <> n Tauwetter das.

**the** [weak form ðə, before vowel ðɪ, strong form ði:] def art - 1. [gen] der/die/das, die pl; ~ man der Mann; ~ woman die Frau; ~ book das Buch; ~ girls die Mädchen; ~ Wilsons die Wilsons; ~ highest mountain in ~ world der höchste Berg der Welt; to play ~ piano Klavier spielen; ten pence in ~ pound zehn Pence pro Pfund; you're not THE Jack Straw, are you? Sie sind nicht DER Jack Straw, oder?; it's THE place to go to in Paris da geht man in Paris hin - 2. (with an adj to form a noun): ~ British/poor die Briten/Armen; ~ impossible das Unmögliche - 3. [in dates] der; ~ twelfth (of May) der Zwölfte (Mai); ~ forties die Vierziger - 4. [in comparisons]: ~ more I see of her, ~ less I like her je mehr ich sie sehe, desto weniger mag ich sie; ~ sooner ~ better je eher, desto besser - 5. [in titles]: Elizabeth ~ Second Elisabeth die Zweite - 6. [in exclamations]: ~ impudence of it! was für eine Unverschämtheit!

**theatre** Br, **theater** Am ['θɪətə'] n - 1. [building] Theater das - 2. [art, industry]: the ~ das Theater - 3. [in hospital] Operationssaal der - 4. Am [cinema] Kino das.

**theatregoer** Br, **theatergoer** Am ['θɪətə,gəʊə'] n Theaterbesucher der, -in die.

**theatrical** [θɪˈætrɪkl] *adj* - **1.** [of the theatre] Theater- - **2.** *fig* [for effect] theatralisch.

**theft** [θeft] *n* Diebstahl *der*.

**their** [ðeəʳ] *poss adj* ihr; ~ **house** ihr Haus; ~ **children** ihre Kinder; **they brushed ~ teeth** sie putzten sich *(D)* die Zähne; **it wasn't THEIR fault** das war nicht IHRE Schuld.

**theirs** [ðeəz] *poss pron* ihre, -r, -s; **that is ~** das ist ihres; **this house is ~** dieses Haus gehört ihnen; **a friend of ~** ein Freund von ihnen; **it wasn't our fault, it was THEIRS** das war nicht unsere Schuld, es war IHRE.

**them** [*weak form* ðəm, *strong form* ðem] *pers pron pl (accusative)* sie; *(dative)* ihnen; **I know ~** ich kenne sie; **I like ~** sie gefallen mir; **it's ~** sie sind es; **send it to ~** schicke es ihnen; **tell ~** sage ihnen; **he's worse than ~** er ist schlimmer als sie; **if I were** OR **was ~** wenn ich sie wäre; **you can't expect THEM to do it** du kannst nicht erwarten, dass SIE das tun; **all of ~** sie alle; **none of ~** keiner von ihnen; **some/a few of ~** einige von ihnen; **most of ~** die meisten; **both of ~** alle beide; **there are three of ~** es gibt drei davon; [people] sie sind zu dritt; **neither of ~** keiner/keine/keines von beiden; **lay the tables and put some flowers on ~** decken Sie die Tische und stellen Sie Blumen darauf.

**thematic** [θɪˈmætɪk] *adj* thematisch.

**theme** [θiːm] *n* - **1.** [gen] Thema *das* - **2.** [theme tune - of film] Titelmelodie *die*; [ - of TV, radio programme] Erkennungsmelodie *die*.

**theme park** *n* Freizeitpark, *dessen Gestaltung einem bestimmten Thema folgt.*

**theme song** *n* [of film] Titelsong *der*; [of TV programme] Erkennungssong *der*

**theme tune** *n* [of film] Titelmelodie *die*; [of TV, radio programme] Erkennungsmelodie *die*.

**themselves** [ðemˈselvz] *pron* sich; **they washed ~** sie wuschen sich; **by ~** [alone] allein; **they did it (by) ~** sie machten es selbst; **they have the garden (all) for ~** sie haben den Garten (ganz) für sich allein.

**then** [ðen] *adv* - **1.** [not now, next, afterwards] dann; [in the past] damals; **the film starts at eight – I'll see you ~** der Film fängt um acht an – bis dann; **I had breakfast, ~ I went to work** ich frühstückte und ging dann zur Arbeit; **we were much younger ~** wir waren damals viel jünger; **before ~** vorher; **by/until ~** bis dahin; **from ~ on** von da an; **since ~** seitdem - **2.** [in that case] also; **go on, ~** also machs!; **you knew all along, ~?** du hast es also die ganze Zeit gewusst? - **3.** [therefore] also; **these, ~, were the reasons for our failure** das waren also die Gründe für unser Versagen - **4.** [with "if" clauses] dann; **if you help me now, ~ I'll help you later** wenn Sie mir jetzt helfen, dann helfe ich Ihnen später - **5.** [furthermore, also] außerdem; **... (and) ~ there are the children to consid-**

er ... und dann müssen wir an die Kinder denken ⟨⟩ *adj* damalig; **the ~ president** der damalige Präsident.

**thence** [ðens] *adv fml* & *literary* [from that place] von dort.

**theologian** [θɪəˈlɒudʒən] *n* Theologe *der*, -gin *die*.

**theology** [θɪˈɒlədʒɪ] *n* Theologie *die*.

**theorem** [ˈθɪərəm] *n* Theorem *das*.

**theoretical** [θɪəˈretɪkl] *adj* theoretisch.

**theoretically** [θɪəˈretɪklɪ] *adv* theoretisch.

**theorist** [ˈθɪərɪst] *n* Theoretiker *der*, -in *die*.

**theorize, -ise** [ˈθɪəraɪz] *vi*: **to ~ (about sthg)** theoretisieren (über etw *(A)*).

**theory** [ˈθɪərɪ] ( *pl* **-ies**) *n* Theorie *die*; **in ~** theoretisch, in der Theorie.

**therapeutic** [ˌθerəˈpjuːtɪk] *adj* therapeutisch.

**therapist** [ˈθerəpɪst] *n* Therapeut *der*, -in *die*.

**therapy** [ˈθerəpɪ] *n* Therapie *die*.

**there** [ðeəʳ] *pron* - **1.** [indicating existence]: **~ is/are** es gibt; **are ~ any left?** sind noch welche übrig?; **~ are three of us** wir sind zu dritt; **~'s a page missing** es fehlt eine Seite; **~ must be some mistake** das muss ein Irrtum sein - **2.** (with vb) *fml*: **~ comes a time when ...** es kommt eine Zeit, wo ... ⟨⟩ *adv* - **1.** [in existence, present] da; **is anyone ~?** ist da jemand?; **is John ~, please?** [on phone] ist John da? - **2.** [at/in that place] dort; [to that place] dorthin; **that man ~** der Mann dort; **I'm going ~ next week** ich gehe nächste Woche hin; **we're ~ at last!** endlich sind wir da!; **it's 6 kilometres ~ and back** es sind 6 Kilometer hin und zurück; **~ it/he is** da ist es/er; **in/over ~** da drinnen/drüben; **up ~** dort oben - **3.** [point in conversation] da; **you're wrong ~** da irrst du dich - **4.** [particular stage]: **they will take it from ~** sie werden es ab da übernehmen; **I'm nearly ~** ich bin bald soweit; **we're getting ~** wir sind fast soweit - **5.** *phr*: **he's not all ~** *inf* er hat nicht alle Tassen im Schrank ⟨⟩ *excl*: **~, I told you so!** ich habe es dir doch gleich gesagt!; **~, ~ (don't cry)** na, na (weine nicht).

➤ **there and then, then and there** *adv* auf der Stelle.

➤ **there you are** *adv* - **1.** [handing sthg to sb] bitte schön - **2.** [emphasizing that one is right]: **~ you are, what did I tell you!** ich habe es dir doch gleich gesagt! - **3.** [expressing reluctant acceptance]: **it's not ideal, but ~ you are!** es ist nicht ideal, aber was will man machen.

**thereabouts** [ðeərəˈbauts], **thereabout** *Am* [ðeərəˈbaut] *adv*: **at eight o'clock or ~** so um acht Uhr herum; **fifty or ~** so ungefähr fünfzig; **somewhere ~** da irgendwo.

**thereafter** [ˌðeərˈɑːftəʳ] *adv fml* danach.

**thereby** [ˌðeərˈbaɪ] *adv fml* damit.

**T**

**therefore** [ˈðeəfɔːʳ] *adv* deshalb, deswegen.

**therein** [ˌðeərˈɪn] *adv fml* darin.

**there's** [ðeəz] = there is.

**thereupon** [ˌðeərəˈpɒn] *adv fml* [then] daraufhin.

**thermal** [ˈθɜːml] *adj* - **1.** TECH [thermisch]: ~ insulation Wärmedämmung *die* - **2.** [clothes] Thermo-.

**thermal reactor** *n* Wärmekraftwerk *das*.

**thermal underwear** *n* Thermounterwäsche *die*.

**thermodynamics** [ˌθɜːməʊdaɪˈnæmɪks] *n (U)* Thermodynamik *die*.

**thermoelectric** [ˌθɜːməʊɪˈlektrɪk] *adj* thermoelektrisch.

**thermometer** [θəˈmɒmɪtəʳ] *n* Thermometer *das*.

**thermonuclear** [ˌθɜːməʊˈnjuːklɪəʳ] *adj* thermonuklear; ~ weapon Thermonuklearwaffe *die*.

**thermoplastic** [ˌθɜːməʊˈplæstɪk] *adj* thermoplastisch <> *n* Thermoplast *der*.

**Thermos (flask)**® [ˈθɜːməs-] *n* Thermosflasche® *die*.

**thermostat** [ˈθɜːməstæt] *n* Thermostat *der*.

**thesaurus** [θɪˈsɔːrəs] (*pl* -es) *n* Thesaurus *der*.

**these** [ðiːz] *pl* ⊳ this.

**thesis** [ˈθiːsɪs] (*pl* theses [ˈθiːsiːz]) *n* - **1.** [argument] These *die* - **2.** [doctoral dissertation] Dissertation *die*, Doktorarbeit *die*.

**they** [ðeɪ] *pers pron pl* - **1.** [gen] sie; ~'re happy sie sind glücklich; ~'re pretty earrings das sind hübsche Ohrringe; it is ~ who are responsible sie sind es, die verantwortlich sind; THEY can't do it SIE können es nicht tun - **2.** [unspecified people] man; ~ still haven't repaired the road sie haben immer noch nicht die Straße repariert; ~ say that ... man sagt, dass ...

**they'd** [ðeɪd] = they had, they would.

**they'll** [ðeɪl] = they shall, they will.

**they're** [ðeəʳ] = they are.

**they've** [ðeɪv] = they have.

**thick** [θɪk] *adj* - **1.** [gen] dick; it is one metre ~ es ist einen Meter dick; the table was ~ with dust auf dem Tisch lag eine dicke Staubschicht - **2.** [dense] dicht; ~ with smoke voller Rauch - **3.** *inf* [stupid] dumm - **4.** [accent] stark <> *n*: to be in the ~ of it mittendrin sein.
⬥ **thick and fast** *adv*: the questions came ~ and fast es kam eine Flut von Fragen.
⬥ **through thick and thin** *adv* durch dick und dünn.

**thicken** [ˈθɪkn] *vt* [soup, sauce] eindicken <> *vi* [forest, crowd, fog] dichter werden; [soup, sauce] dicker werden.

**thickener, thickening** [ˈθɪknɪŋ] *n* Bindemittel *das*.

**thicket** [ˈθɪkɪt] *n* Dickicht *das*.

**thickly** [ˈθɪklɪ] *adv* - **1.** [cut, spread] dick - **2.** [grow, populated, wooded] dicht.

**thickness** [ˈθɪknɪs] *n* - **1.** [width, depth] Dicke *die* - **2.** [density] Dichte *die* - **3.** [viscosity] Dickflüssigkeit *die*.

**thickset** [ˌθɪkˈset] *adj* gedrungen.

**thick-skinned** [-ˈskɪnd] *adj* dickfellig.

**thief** [θiːf] (*pl* thieves) *n* Dieb *der*, -in *die*.

**thieve** [θiːv] *vt* & *vi* stehlen.

**thieves** [θiːvz] *pl* ⊳ thief.

**thieving** [ˈθiːvɪŋ] *adj* diebisch; keep your ~ hands off ...! Finger weg von ...! <> *n (U)* Diebstähle *pl*.

**thigh** [θaɪ] *n* Oberschenkel *der*.

**thighbone** [ˈθaɪbəʊn] *n* Oberschenkelknochen *der*.

**thimble** [ˈθɪmbl] *n* Fingerhut *der*.

**thin** [θɪn] (*compar* -ner; *superl* -nest; *pt* & *pp* -ned; *cont* -ning) *adj* - **1.** [gen] dünn - **2.** [sparse] gering; [mist] leicht; [hair] dünn, schütter; there was a ~ crowd there es waren nur wenige Leute da; he is a bit ~ on top er hat eine leichte Glatze - **3.** [poor - excuse] fadenscheinig <> *adv*: his jokes are beginning to wear ~ seine Witze klingen reichlich abgedroschen; my patience is wearing ~ meine Geduld geht zu Ende <> *vi*: to be ~ning [hair] schütter werden.
⬥ **thin down** *vt sep* verdünnen.

**thin air** *n (U)*: to appear out of ~ aus dem Nichts auftauchen; to disappear into ~ sich in Luft auflösen.

**thing** [θɪŋ] *n* - **1.** [affair, item, subject] Sache *die*, Ding *das*; the (best) ~ to do would be ... das Beste wäre (es) ...; for one ~ erst einmal; I just couldn't get it finished, (what) with one ~ and another ich bin einfach nicht damit fertig geworden, weil so viel dazwischengekommen ist; the ~ is ... die Sache ist die, dass ...; it's just one of those ~s *inf* so was kommt schon mal vor; to have a ~ about sb/sth *inf* [like] auf jn/etw abfahren; [dislike] einen Horror vor jm/etw haben; to make a ~ (out) of sth *inf* eine große Sache aus etw machen - **2.** [anything]: not a ~ gar nichts - **3.** [object, creature] Ding *das*; the lucky ~! der/die Glückliche!; you poor ~! du Armer/Arme! - **4.** *inf* [fashion]: concern for the environment is the ~ these days Umweltschutz ist zur Zeit in; the latest ~ in sports cars das Neueste auf dem Sportwagenmarkt.
⬥ **things** *npl* - **1.** [clothes, possessions] Sachen *pl* - **2.** *inf* [life] Dinge *pl*.

**thingamabob** [ˈθɪŋəməˌbɒb], **thingummy-(jig)** *Br* [ˈθɪŋəmɪ(dʒɪɡ)], **thingie** *Br*, **thingy**

*Br* ['θɪŋɪ] ( *pl* -ies) *n* Dings(bums) *der, die, das,*
Dingsda *der, die, das.*

**think** [θɪŋk] ( *pt* & *pp* thought) *vt* - **1.** [believe]: **to**
~ (that) denken(, dass), glauben(, dass); I
~ so ich glaube schon; I don't ~ so ich glaube
nicht - **2.** [have in mind]: **to ~ (that)** denken(,
dass); **what are you ~ing?** woran denkst du?
- **3.** [imagine] sich *(D)* denken, sich *(D)* vorstellen - **4.** [remember]: **did you ~ to bring any
money?** hast du daran gedacht, etwas Geld
mitzubringen?; **try and ~ what you were
doing on that date** versuche dich zu erinnern, was du an dem Tag gemacht hast
- **5.** [in polite requests]: **do you ~ you could help
me?** könnten Sie mir vielleicht helfen?
◇ *vi* - **1.** [use mind] denken; **I thought for a long
time** ich dachte lange nach - **2.** [have stated
opinion]: **what do you ~ of** OR **about his new film?**
was hältst du von seinem neuen Film?; I
**don't ~ much of them/it** ich halte nicht viel
von ihnen/davon, **to ~ a lot of sb/sthg** viel
von jm/etw halten - **3.** *phr:* **he was going to
complain, but thought better of it** er wollte
sich beschweren, überlegte es sich dann
aber anders; **to ~ nothing of doing sthg** nichts
dabei finden, etw zu tun; **to ~ twice before
doing sthg** es sich *(D)* genau überlegen, bevor man etw tut ◇ *n inf:* **to have a ~ (about
sthg)** sich *(D)* etw überlegen; **let me have a ~**
lass mich überlegen.
➤ **think about** *vt fus* [consider] nachdenken
über *(+ A);* **to ~ about doing sthg** daran denken, etw zu tun.
➤ **think back** *vi:* **to ~ back (to sthg)** zurückdenken (an etw *(A)).*
➤ **think of** *vt fus* - **1.** [consider, remember, show consideration for] denken an *(+ A);* **to ~ of doing sthg**
daran denken, etw zu tun; I **can't ~ of her
name** ich kann mich nicht an ihren Namen
erinnern, ich komme nicht auf ihren Namen - **2.** [conceive] sich *(D)* ausdenken; **to ~ of
doing sthg** die Idee haben, etw zu tun; **we'll
~ of sthg** wir werden uns *(D)* etw einfallen
lassen.
➤ **think out, think through** *vt sep* (gründlich)
durchdenken.
➤ **think over** *vt sep* überdenken.
➤ **think up** *vt sep* sich *(D)* ausdenken.

**thinker** ['θɪŋkə^r] *n* Denker *der,* -in *die.*

**thinking** ['θɪŋkɪŋ] *adj* [person] denkend ◇ *n (U)*
- **1.** [opinion] Meinung *die;* **to my way of ~** meiner Meinung nach - **2.** [reflection]: **to do a lot of
hard ~ about sthg** gründlich über etw *(A)*
nachdenken - **3.** [theory] Überlegungen *pl.*

**think tank** *n* Expertenkommission *die.*

**thinly** ['θɪnlɪ] *adv* - **1.** [cut, spread] dünn - **2.** [forested] spärlich; [populated] dünn; [clad] leicht
- **3.** [disguised] kaum.

**thinner** ['θɪnə^r] *n (U)* Verdünner *der.*

**thinness** ['θɪnnɪs] *n* - **1.** [in width, depth] Dünne
*die* - **2.** [slim build] Magerkeit *die.*

**thin-skinned** [-'skɪnd] *adj* dünnhäutig.

**third** [θɜːd] *num* dritte, -r, -s ◇ *n* - **1.** [fraction]
Drittel *das* - **2.** *Br* UNIV Abschluss mit „befriedigend"; *see also* sixth.

**third-class** *adj Br* UNIV: ~ **degree** Abschluss mit
„Befriedigend".

**third-degree burns** *npl* Verbrennungen *pl*
dritten Grades.

**thirdly** ['θɜːdlɪ] *adv* drittens.

**third party** *n* Dritte *der, die.*

**third party insurance** *n* Haftpflichtversicherung *die.*

**third-rate** *adj pej* drittklassig.

**Third World** *n:* **the ~** die Dritte Welt.

**thirst** [θɜːst] *n* Durst *der;* **a ~ for sthg** *fig* ein
Durst nach etw; ~ **for adventure** Abenteuerlust *die.*

**thirsty** ['θɜːstɪ] ( *compar* -ier; *superl* -iest) *adj:* **to
be** OR **feel ~** Durst haben, durstig sein; **this is
~ work** diese Arbeit macht durstig.

**thirteen** [ˌθɜː'tiːn] *num* dreizehn; *see also* six.

**thirteenth** [ˌθɜː'tiːnθ] *num* dreizehnte, -r, -s;
*see also* sixth.

**thirtieth** ['θɜːtɪəθ] *num* dreißigste, -r, -s; *see
also* sixth.

**thirty** ['θɜːtɪ] ( *pl* -ies) *num* dreißig; *see also* sixty.

**thirty-something** *adj:* **to be ~** in den
Dreißigern sein.

**this** [ðɪs] ( *pl* these) *pron* - **1.** (referring to thing,
person mentioned) das; ~ **is for you** das ist für
dich; **who's/what's ~?** wer/was ist das?;
**what are these?** was ist das?; ~ **is Daphne
Logan** [introducing someone] das ist Daphne
Logan; [introducing o.s. on phone] hier ist Daphne Logan; **before ~** früher; **we talked about
~ and that** wir sprachen von diesem und jenem - **2.** (referring to thing, person nearer speaker)
diese, -r, -s, diese *pl;* **which shoes do you want,
these or those?** welche Schuhe wollen Sie,
die hier oder die da?; I **want these here** ich
möchte die hier ◇ *adj* - **1.** (referring to thing,
person) diese, -r, -s, diese *pl;* I **prefer ~ book**
ich bevorzuge dieses Buch; **these chocolates
are delicious** diese Pralinen schmecken
köstlich; **I'll have ~ one/these ones** ich nehme
dieses/diese; ~ **morning/evening** heute
Morgen/Abend; ~ **week** diese Woche;
~ **Sunday/summer** diesen Sonntag/Sommer
- **2.** *inf* [a certain]: **there was ~ man ...** da war dieser Mann ...; ~ **woman came over to my table**
diese Frau kam an meinen Tisch ◇ *adv* so;
**it was ~ big** es war so groß; ~ **far** bis hier.

**thistle** ['θɪsl] *n* Distel *die.*

**thither** ['ðɪðə^r] *adv* ▷ hither.

**tho'** [ðəʊ] conj & adv = **though.**

**thong** [θɒŋ] n - **1.** [piece of leather] Lederriemen der - **2.** Am [sandal] Sandale die.

**thorn** [θɔːn] n [prickle] Dorn der; **to be a ~ in sb's flesh** OR **side** jm ein Dorn im Auge sein.

**thorny** ['θɔːnɪ] (compar **-ier;** superl **-iest**) adj - **1.** [prickly] dornig - **2.** fig [tricky, complicated] heikel.

**thorough** ['θʌrə] adj - **1.** [exhaustive, meticulous] gründlich; [worker] sorgfältig, gewissenhaft - **2.** [complete, utter] völlig; **that's a ~ nuisance** das ist wirklich lästig.

**thoroughbred** ['θʌrəbred] n [horse] Vollblut das.

**thoroughfare** ['θʌrəfeə'] n fml Durchgangsstraße die.

**thoroughly** ['θʌrəlɪ] adv - **1.** [fully, in detail] gründlich - **2.** [completely, utterly] durch und durch.

**thoroughness** ['θʌrənɪs] n (U) Gründlichkeit die; [of worker] Sorgfältigkeit die, Gewissenhaftigkeit die.

**those** [ðəʊz] pl ⊳ **that.**

**though** [ðəʊ] conj - **1.** [in spite of the fact that] obwohl, obgleich - **2.** [even if] wenn auch ◇ adv [nevertheless] aber; **he's quite intelligent, ~** er ist aber ziemlich intelligent.

**thought** [θɔːt] pt & pp ⊳ **think** ◇ n - **1.** [notion] Gedanke der; **he hasn't a ~ in his head** er hat nichts im Kopf - **2.** (U) [act of thinking] Nachdenken das; **to give some ~ to sthg** über etw (A) nachldenken; **after much ~** nach langem Überlegen - **3.** [philosophy] Denken das - **4.** [gesture]: **it's the ~ that counts** der gute Wille zählt.

⇒ **thoughts** npl Gedanken pl; **to collect one's ~s** seine Gedanken sammeln.

**thoughtful** ['θɔːtfʊl] adj - **1.** [pensive - person, mood] nachdenklich - **2.** [considerate - person] rücksichtsvoll; [ - action, remark] wohl überlegt.

**thoughtfulness** ['θɔːtfʊlnɪs] n (U) - **1.** [pensiveness] Nachdenklichkeit die - **2.** [considerateness] Rücksichtnahme die.

**thoughtless** ['θɔːtlɪs] adj [person, behaviour] rücksichtslos; [remark] unüberlegt.

**thoughtlessness** ['θɔːtlɪsnɪs] n (U) [of person, behaviour] Rücksichtslosigkeit die; [of remark] Unüberlegtheit die.

**thousand** ['θaʊznd] num - **1.** [number] tausend; **a/one ~** (ein)tausend; **five ~ and forty-two** fünftausend(und)zweiundvierzig; **~s of** Tausende von - **2.** fig [umpteen]: **a ~** tausend; **I have a ~ things to do** ich habe tausend Dinge zu tun; see also **six.**

**thousandth** ['θaʊzntθ] num tausendste, -r, -s; see also **sixth** ◇ n [fraction] Tausendstel das.

**thrash** [θræʃ] vt - **1.** [beat, hit] prügeln - **2.** inf [trounce] fertig machen.

⇒ **thrash about, thrash around** vi sich hin und her werfen.

⇒ **thrash out** vt sep durchldiskutieren.

**thrashing** ['θræʃɪŋ] n - **1.** [beating, hitting] Prügel pl; **to give sb a ~** jm eine Tracht Prügel verpassen - **2.** inf [trouncing] Schlappe die; **to give sb a ~** jn fertig machen.

**thread** [θred] n - **1.** [of cotton, wool] Faden der - **2.** [of screw] Gewinde das - **3.** fig [theme]: **to follow the ~ of sb's argument** js Gedankengang (D) folgen; **she lost the ~ of** (of what she was saying) **sie hat den Faden verloren** ◇ vt - **1.** [needle] einlfädeln; [beads] auflziehen - **2.** [move]: **to ~ one's way through the crowd** sich durch die Menge schlängeln.

**threadbare** ['θredbeə'] adj [garment] abgetragen; [carpet] abgewetzt; [argument] fadenscheinig.

**threat** [θret] n - **1.** [warning] Drohung die - **2.** [menace]: **~ (to sb/sthg)** Bedrohung die OR Gefahr die (für jn/etw) - **3.** [risk]: **the ~ of war/inflation** die Gefahr eines Krieges/einer Inflation; **there is a ~ of storms** es kann Stürme geben.

**threaten** ['θretn] vt - **1.** [issue threat]: **to ~ sb (with sthg)** jm (mit etw) drohen; **to ~ to do sthg** drohen, etw zu tun - **2.** [be likely]: **to ~ to do sthg** drohen, etw zu tun - **3.** [endanger] bedrohen, gefährden ◇ vi drohen.

**threatening** ['θretnɪŋ] adj [person, behaviour] drohend; [situation, weather] bedrohlich; **~ letter** Drohbrief der.

**three** [θriː] num drei; see also **six.**

**three-D** adj 3-D-.

**three-dimensional** [-dɪ'menʃənl] adj dreidimensional.

**threefold** ['θriːfəʊld] adj & adv dreifach; **a ~ increase** ein Anstieg auf das Dreifache.

**three-legged race** [-'legɪd-] n Wettlauf, bei dem die beiden Läufer jeder Mannschaft an einem Bein zusammengebunden sind.

**three-piece** adj dreiteilig.

**three-ply** adj [wool] dreifädig; [wood] dreischichtig.

**three-point turn** n Br Wenden das in drei Zügen.

**three-quarters** npl drei Viertel pl; **~ of an hour** eine Dreiviertelstunde.

**threesome** ['θriːsəm] n Dreiergruppe die, Trio das.

**three-star** adj Dreisterne-.

**three-wheeler** [-'wiːlə'] n [car] dreirädriges Auto.

**thresh** [θreʃ] vt dreschen.

**threshing machine** [ˈθreʃɪŋ-] n Dreschma-
schine die.

**threshold** [ˈθreʃhəʊld] n - **1.** [doorway] Tür-
schwelle die - **2.** [level] Schwelle die - **3.** fig
[verge]: **to be on the ~ of sthg** an der Schwelle
zu etw stehen.

**threshold agreement** n Abkommen, das
bei unerwarteter Erhöhung der Inflationsrate
eine Lohnerhöhung vorsieht.

**threw** [θruː] pt ⊳ throw.

**thrift** [θrɪft] n - **1.** [prudent expenditure] Sparsamkeit die - **2.** Am = thrift institution.

**thrift institution** n Am [savings bank] Sparkasse die; [savings and loan association] Bausparkasse die.

**thrift shop** n Am Secondhandladen, dessen
Erlöse einem wohltätigen Zweck zugute kommen.

**thrifty** [ˈθrɪftɪ] (compar -ier; superl -iest) adj [per-
son] sparsam; [management] wirtschaftlich.

**thrill** [θrɪl] n - **1.** [sudden feeling] Erregung die; a
~ **of horror** ein Schauder des Entsetzens; **I
felt a ~ of joy** ich war freudig erregt - **2.** [exci-
ting experience] (aufregendes) Erlebnis <> vt
begeistern, mitlreißen <> vi: **she ~ed to the
story** sie war von der Geschichte gefesselt;
**he ~ed to the music** er wurde von der Musik
mitgerissen.

**thrilled** [θrɪld] adj: **to be ~ (with sthg)** (von etw)
begeistert sein; **I was ~ to meet her** ich fand
es sehr aufregend, sie zu treffen.

**thriller** [ˈθrɪləʳ] n Thriller der.

**thrilling** [ˈθrɪlɪŋ] adj [match, book, film] spannend; [news] umwerfend; [music] mitreißend.

**thrive** [θraɪv] (pt -d OR throve; pp -d) vi [per-
son - be successful] erfolgreich sein; [plant]
prächtig gedeihen; [business] blühen.

**thriving** [ˈθraɪvɪŋ] adj [person - successful] erfolgreich; [plant] prächtig gedeihend; [business]
blühend.

**throat** [θrəʊt] n - **1.** [inside mouth] Hals der; **to
ram** OR **force sthg down sb's ~** fig jm etw auflzwingen; **the words stuck in his ~** fig ihm blieben die Worte im Halse stecken - **2.** [front of
neck] Kehle die; **to be at each other's ~s** sich in
den Haaren liegen; **to cut sb's ~** [kill] jm die
Kehle durchlschneiden.

**throaty** [ˈθrəʊtɪ] (compar -ier; superl -iest) adj
kehlig.

**throb** [θrɒb] (pt & pp -bed; cont -bing) n [of
pulse, heart] Pochen das; [of engine, machine] Klopfen das, Hämmern das; [of music, drums] Dröhnen das <> vi - **1.** [beat - pulse, heart] pochen;
[ - blood] pulsieren; [ - engine, machine, music]
dröhnen - **2.** [be painful]: **my head is ~bing** ich
habe pochende Kopfschmerzen.

**throes** [θrəʊz] npl: **death ~** Todesqualen pl; **to
be in the ~ of sthg** mitten in etw (D) stecken.

**thrombosis** [θrɒmˈbəʊsɪs] (pl **-boses** [-ˈbəʊ-
siːz]) n Thrombose die.

**throne** [θrəʊn] n Thron der.

**throng** [θrɒŋ] n [crowd] Menschenmenge die;
**a ~ of** Scharen pl von <> vt [place] belagern;
[streets] sich drängen in (+ D) <> vi: **to ~ round
sb/sthg** sich um jn/etw drängen.

**throttle** [ˈθrɒtl] n - **1.** [valve] Drosselklappe die
- **2.** [lever] Gashebel der; [Pedal] Gaspedal das;
**at full ~** mit Vollgas <> vt [strangle] erwürgen.

**through** [θruː] adj - **1.** [finished]: **to be ~ (with
sthg)** (mit etw) fertig sein - **2.** [referring to trans-
port]: ~ **traffic** Durchgangsverkehr der; **a
~ train** ein durchgehender Zug <> adv
- **1.** [from one end to another] durch; **to let sb ~** jn
durchllassen; **wet ~** völlig durchnässt
- **2.** [until]: **I slept ~ till ten** ich schlief bis zehn
durch; **we stayed ~ till Friday** wir blieben bis
Freitag <> prep - **1.** [from one side to another]
durch; **he went ~ the park** er ging durch den
Park; **to drill ~ sthg** etw durchlbohren; **I'm
halfway ~ this book** ich habe das Buch schon
halb gelesen - **2.** [during, throughout] während
(+ G); **all ~ his life** sein ganzes Leben hindurch - **3.** [because of] wegen (+ G); **absent ~ illness** wegen Krankheit abwesend; ~ **fear** aus
Furcht; **it happened ~ no fault of his own** es
geschah ohne sein Zutun - **4.** [by means of]
durch; **I got the job ~ a friend** ich bekam die
Stelle durch einen Freund - **5.** Am [up until
and including]: **Monday ~ Thursday** Montag bis
Donnerstag.

**through and through** adv - **1.** [completely]
durch und durch - **2.** [thoroughly - know]
gründlich.

**throughout** [θruːˈaʊt] prep - **1.** [during]: ~ **the
day/morning** den ganzen Tag/Morgen
(über); ~ **the year** das ganze Jahr (hindurch); ~ **her life** ihr ganzes Leben lang
- **2.** [everywhere] überall in (+ D); ~ **the country**
im ganzen Land <> adv - **1.** [all the time] die
ganze Zeit (über) - **2.** [everywhere] überall;
[completely] ganz.

**throughput** [ˈθruːpʊt] n Br Durchsatz der.

**throve** [θrəʊv] pt ⊳ thrive.

**throw** [θrəʊ] (pt **threw**; pp **thrown**) vt - **1.** [pro-
pel, put] werfen; **to ~ one's arms around sb/sthg**
die Arme um jn/etw schlingen - **2.** [move
suddenly]: **he threw himself to the floor/onto the
bed** er warf sich auf den Boden/das Bett; **to
~ o.s. into sthg** fig sich in etw (A) stürzen
- **3.** [rider] ablwerfen - **4.** fig [force]: **to ~ sb into
confusion** jn durcheinander bringen; **he was
~n into the job at short notice** er musste die
Stelle sehr kurzfristig anltreten - **5.**: **to
~ light on sthg** etw aufklären; **to ~ doubt on
sthg** etw in Zweifel ziehen - **6.**: **to ~ a tantrum** einen Wutanfall bekommen - **7.** fig

[confuse] aus dem Konzept bringen ⬦ *n* [toss, pitch] Wurf *der.*

⬦ **throw away** *vt sep* - **1.** [discard] weglwerfen - **2.** *fig* [money, time] vergeuden; [opportunity] nicht nutzen.

⬦ **throw in** *vt sep* [include] dazulgeben.

⬦ **throw out** *vt sep* - **1.** [discard] weglwerfen - **2.** *fig* [reject] ablehnen - **3.** [force to leave] hinauslwerfen.

⬦ **throw up** *vt sep* - **1.** [ball] hochwerfen; [dust] auf lwirbeln - **2.** [problems] auf lwerfen ⬦ *vi inf* [vomit] sich übergeben.

**throwaway** ['θrəʊə,weɪ] *adj* - **1.** [product, bottle] Wegwerf- - **2.** [remark] beiläufig.

**throwback** ['θrəʊbæk] *n:* ~ **(to sthg)** Rückkehr *die* (zu etw).

**throw-in** *n Br* FTBL Einwurf *der.*

**thrown** [θrəʊn] *pp* ▷ **throw.**

**thru** [θruː] *adj, adv* & *prep Am inf* = **through.**

**thrush** [θrʌʃ] *n* - **1.** [bird] Drossel *die* - **2.** MED Soor *der.*

**thrust** [θrʌst] (*pt* & *pp* **thrust**) *n* - **1.** [forward movement - of knife, sword] Stoß *der*; [ - MIL] Vorstoß *der* - **2.** (*U*) [forward force] Schubkraft *die* - **3.** [main aspect] Tenor *der* ⬦ *vt* - **1.** [jab, shove]: **to** ~ **sthg into sthg** [knife, stick] etw in etw (*A*) stoßen; **he** ~ **the knife at me** er stieß mit dem Messer nach mir; **she** ~ **the money into her pocket** sie stopfte das Geld in ihre Tasche - **2.** [jostle]: **to** ~ **one's way through the crowd** sich (*D*) seinen Weg durch die Menge bahnen.

⬦ **thrust upon** *vt sep:* **to** ~ **sthg upon sb** jm etw auf lbürden.

**thrusting** ['θrʌstɪŋ] *adj* energisch.

**thruway** ['θruːweɪ] *n Am* Schnellstraße *die.*

**thud** [θʌd] (*pt* & *pp* **-ded**; *cont* **-ding**) *n* dumpfer Aufschlag ⬦ *vi* dumpf auf lschlagen; [feet] stampfen.

**thug** [θʌg] *n* Schläger *der.*

**thumb** [θʌm] *n* [of hand] Daumen *der*; **to twiddle one's** ~**s** Däumchen drehen ⬦ *vt inf* [hitch]: **to** ~ **a lift** per Anhalter fahren.

⬦ **thumb through** *vt fus* durchlblättern.

**thumb index** *n* Daumenregister *das.*

**thumbnail** ['θʌmneɪl] *n* Daumennagel *der.*

**thumbnail sketch** *n* [description] knappe Beschreibung.

**thumbs down** [,θʌmz-] *n:* **to get** OR **be given the** ~ abgelehnt werden.

**thumbs up** *n* [go-ahead]: **to get** OR **be given the** ~ grünes Licht bekommen.

**thumbtack** ['θʌmtæk] *n Am* Reißzwecke *die.*

**thump** [θʌmp] *n* - **1.** [blow] Schlag *der* - **2.** [thud] Bums *der* ⬦ *vt* - **1.** [punch] schlagen - **2.** [place heavily] knallen ⬦ *vi* - **1.** [move heavily] poltern - **2.** [heart] heftig pochen.

**thunder** ['θʌndəʳ] *n* (*U*) - **1.** METEOR Donner *der* - **2.** *fig* [loud sound] Donnern *das* ⬦ *vt* [say angrily] brüllen ⬦ *vi* donnern ⬦ *v impers* METEOR: **it is** ~**ing** es donnert.

**thunderbolt** ['θʌndəbəʊlt] *n* - **1.** METEOR Blitz *der* - **2.** *fig* [shock]: **the news was a** ~ die Nachricht schlug wie ein Blitz ein.

**thunderclap** ['θʌndəklæp] *n* Donnerschlag *der.*

**thundercloud** ['θʌndəklaʊd] *n* Gewitterwolke *die.*

**thundering** ['θʌndərɪŋ] *adj:* **a** ~ **success** ein Bombenerfolg.

**thunderous** ['θʌndərəs] *adj* [deafening] donnernd.

**thunderstorm** ['θʌndəstɔːm] *n* Gewitter *das.*

**thunderstruck** ['θʌndəstrʌk] *adj fig* [shocked] wie vom Donner gerührt.

**thundery** ['θʌndərɪ] *adj* gewittrig.

**Thur, Thurs** (*abbr of* **Thursday**) Do.

**Thursday** ['θɜːzdɪ] *n* Donnerstag *der; see also* **Saturday.**

**thus** [ðʌs] *adv fml* - **1.** [as a consequence] daher - **2.** [in this way] auf diese Weise - **3.** [as follows] folgendermaßen.

**thwart** [θwɔːt] *vt* vereiteln; [person] einen Strich durch die Rechnung machen (+ *D).*

**thyme** [taɪm] *n* Thymian *der.*

**thyroid** ['θaɪrɔɪd] *n:* ~ **(gland)** Schilddrüse *die.*

**tiara** [tɪˈɑːrə] *n* [piece of jewellery] Diadem *das.*

**Tibet** [tɪˈbet] *n* Tibet *nt.*

**Tibetan** [tɪˈbetn] *adj* tibetisch ⬦ *n* - **1.** [person] Tibeter *der*, -in *die* - **2.** [language] Tibetisch(e) *das.*

**tibia** ['tɪbɪə] (*pl* **-s** OR **-biae** [-bɪiː]) *n* Schienbein *das.*

**tic** [tɪk] *n* Zucken *das.*

**tick** [tɪk] *n* - **1.** [written mark] Häkchen *das* - **2.** [sound] Ticken *das* - **3.** [insect] Zecke *die* ⬦ *vt* [name] ablhaken; [answer, box on form] anlkreuzen ⬦ *vi* - **1.** [make ticking sound] ticken - **2.** *fig* [behave in a certain way]: **no one really understands what makes him** ~ keiner weiß genau, was in seinem Kopf vorgeht.

⬦ **tick away, tick by** *vi* verstreichen.

⬦ **tick off** *vt sep* - **1.** [mark off] ablhaken - **2.** [tell off] *inf:* **to** ~ **sb off (for sthg)** jn (wegen etw) rüffeln.

⬦ **tick over** *vi* - **1.** [engine] im Leerlauf sein - **2.** [business, organization] ganz gut laufen.

**ticked** [tɪkt] *adj Am inf* [annoyed] sauer.

**tickertape** ['tɪkəteɪp] *n* (*U*) Fernschreiberpapierstreifen *der.*

**ticket** ['tɪkɪt] *n* - **1.** [for match, concert] Eintrittskarte *die;* [for bus, train, tram] Fahrkarte *die,* Fahrschein *der;* [for plane] Ticket *das;* [for lottery, raffle] Los *das;* [for library] Ausweis *der;* [for car park] Parkschein *der* - **2.** [on product]: **(price)** ~ Preisschild *das* - **3.** [notice of traffic offence] Strafzettel *der* - **4.** POL: **he is running** OR **standing on a Socialist** ~ er kandidiert für die Sozialisten.

**ticket agency** *n* [for air, rail travel] Verkaufsstelle *die;* [for theatre tickets] Kartenvorverkaufsstelle *die.*

**ticket collector** *n* Br [on train] Schaffner *der,* -in *die;* [in station] Fahrkartenkontrolleur *der,* -in *die.*

**ticket holder** *n:* 'entry only for ~s' 'Eintritt nur mit Eintrittskarte'.

**ticket inspector** *n* Br [on bus, tram] Fahrkartenkontrolleur *der,* -in *die;* [on train] Schaffner *der,* -in *die.*

**ticket machine** *n* [for public transport] Fahrscheinautomat *der;* [in car park] Parkscheinautomat *der.*

**ticket office** *n* [at railway station] Fahrkartenschalter *der;* [at theatre] Theaterkasse *die.*

**ticking off** ['tɪkɪŋ-] ( *pl* **tickings off**) *n:* **to get a** ~ einen Rüffel bekommen; **to give sb a** ~ jm einen Rüffel erteilen.

**tickle** ['tɪkl] *vt* - **1.** [touch lightly] kitzeln; [subj: beard, wool] kratzen - **2.** *fig* [amuse]: **that story really ~d me!** die Geschichte war wirklich amüsant <> *vi* [foot, back] jucken; [beard, wool] kratzen.

**ticklish** ['tɪklɪʃ] *adj* - **1.** [sensitive to touch] kitzlig - **2.** *fig* [delicate] heikel.

**tick-tack-toe** *n* (U) Am [game] *Kinderspiel, bei dem Dreierreihen von Nullen und Kreuzen zu erzielen sind.*

**tidal** ['taɪdl] *adj* Gezeiten-.

**tidal wave** *n* Flutwelle *die.*

**tidbit** ['tɪdbɪt] *n* Am = **titbit.**

**tiddler** ['tɪdlər] *n* Br [fish] winziger Fisch.

**tiddly** ['tɪdlɪ] (*compar* **-ier;** *superl* **-iest**) *adj inf* - **1.** [tipsy] beschwipst - **2.** [tiny] klitzeklein.

**tiddlywinks** ['tɪdlɪwɪŋks], **tiddledywinks** Am ['tɪdldɪwɪŋks] *n* (U) [game] Flohhüpfspiel *das.*

**tide** [taɪd] *n* - **1.** [of sea] Gezeiten *pl;* **high ~** Flut *die;* **low ~** Ebbe *die;* **the ~ is in/out** es ist Flut/Ebbe - **2.** *fig* [trend]: **the ~ of (public) opinion** der Trend der öffentlichen Meinung; **to swim with/against the ~** mit dem/gegen den Strom schwimmen - **3.** *fig* [large quantity]: **a ~ of protest** eine Flut von Protesten.

➤ **tide over** *vt sep:* **to ~ sb over** jm über die Runden helfen; **I have enough to ~ me over** ich habe genug, um mich über Wasser zu halten.

**tidemark** ['taɪdmɑːk] *n* - **1.** [of sea] Flutmarke *die* - **2.** Br [round bath, neck] Schmutzrand *der.*

**tidily** ['taɪdɪlɪ] *adv* ordentlich.

**tidiness** ['taɪdɪnɪs] *n* (U) [of appearance] Gepflegtheit *die;* **the ~ of his room/desk** die Ordnung in seinem Zimmer/auf seinem Schreibtisch.

**tidings** ['taɪdɪŋz] *npl literary* Kunde *die.*

**tidy** ['taɪdɪ] (*compar* **-ier;** *superl* **-iest;** *pt* & *pp* **-ied**) *adj* - **1.** [gen] ordentlich; [appearance] gepflegt - **2.** *inf* [sizeable]: **a ~ sum** ein ganz schönes Sümmchen; **a ~ profit** ein ordentlicher Gewinn <> *vt* aufräumen.

➤ **tidy away** *vt sep* wegräumen.

➤ **tidy up** *vt sep* & *vi* aufräumen.

**tie** [taɪ] ( *pt* & *pp* **tied;** *cont* **tying**) *n* - **1.** [necktie] Krawatte *die* - **2.** [string, cord] Band *das* - **3.** [bond, link] Verbindung *die;* **family ~s** Familienbande - **4.** [in game, competition] Unentschieden *das* - **5.** Am RAIL Schwelle *die* <> *vt* - **1.** [attach]: **to ~ sthg (on)to sthg** etw an etw (A) binden; **to ~ sthg round sthg** etw um etw binden; **my hands are ~d** *fig* mir sind die Hände gebunden; **to ~ sthg with sthg** etw mit etw zusammenbinden - **2.** [do up, fasten] binden; [knot] machen - **3.** *fig* [link]: **to be ~d to sb/sthg** an jn/etw gebunden sein - **4.** *fig* [restricted]: **to be ~d to sthg** [house, office] an etw (A) gebunden sein <> *vi* [in sport] unentschieden spielen.

➤ **tie down** *vt sep fig* [restrict]: **to be ~d down by sthg** durch etw eingeschränkt sein.

➤ **tie in with** *vt fus* passen zu.

➤ **tie up** *vt sep* - **1.** [parcel, papers] verschnüren; [person] fesseln; [animal] anbinden - **2.** [shoelaces] binden - **3.** *fig* [savings] fest anlegen - **4.** *fig* [link]: **to be ~d up with sthg** mit etw zusammenhängen.

**tiebreak(er)** ['taɪbreɪk(ər)] *n* - **1.** TENNIS Tiebreak *das* - **2.** [extra question] Entscheidungsfrage *die.*

**tied** [taɪd] *adj* SPORT [drawn] unentschieden.

**tied cottage** *n* Br *vom Arbeitgeber an einen Arbeitnehmer vermietete Unterkunft.*

**tied up** *adj* [busy] beschäftigt.

**tie-dye** *vt* mittels Bindebatikverfahren färben.

**tie-in** *n* - **1.** [link]: **~ (between)** Zusammenhang *der* (zwischen (+ D)) - **2.** [promotional product]: **this book is a ~ with the TV series** dies ist das Begleitbuch zur Fernsehserie.

**tiepin** ['taɪpɪn] *n* Krawattennadel *die.*

**tier** [tɪər] *n* [of seats] Rang *der;* [of cake] Etage *die.*

**tie-up** *n* - **1.** [link]: **~ (between)** Verbindung *die* (zwischen (+ D)) - **2.** Am [interruption] Stillstand *der.*

**tiff** [tɪf] *n* Krach *der;* **to have a ~ with sb (over sthg)** mit jm (wegen etw) Krach haben.

**tiger** ['taɪgər] *n* Tiger *der.*

**tiger cub** *n* Tigerjunge *das.*

**tight** [taɪt] *adj* - **1.** [close-fitting] eng; **it was a ~ fit to get everyone into my car** wir haben uns alle in mein Auto gezwängt; **the dress was a very ~ fit** das Kleid war sehr eng - **2.** [secure - lid] fest sitzend; [ - screw] fest angezogen; [ - knot] fest - **3.** [taut] straff - **4.** [close together - bundle] fest zusammengebunden; **they stood in a ~ group** sie standen eng zusammen - **5.** [painful - chest, stomach] zusammengeschnürt - **6.** [schedule] eng; [money, match, finish] knapp - **7.** [rule, control] streng - **8.** [bend] scharf, eng - **9.** *inf* [drunk] voll - **10.** *inf* [miserly] knauserig ⟨⟩ *adv* - **1.** [firmly, securely] fest; **to hold ~** festlhalten; **to shut** OR **close sthg ~** [eyes] etw fest schließen; [lid] etw fest verschließen - **2.** [tautly] straff.

➡ **tights** *npl* Strumpfhose *die*.

**tighten** ['taɪtn] *vt* - **1.** [knot, belt, screw] anlziehen - **2.** [make tauter] straffen, spannen - **3.** [strengthen] **to ~ one's hold** OR **grip on sthg** etw fester halten; *fig* [on party, country] seine Macht in etw *(D)* auslbauen - **4.** [rule, control, security] verschärfen ⟨⟩ *vi* [grip, hold] fester werden; [rope, chain] sich spannen.

➡ **tighten up** *vt sep* - **1.** [belt, screw] anlziehen - **2.** [rule, security] verschärfen.

**tightfisted** [ˌtaɪt'fɪstɪd] *adj inf pej* knauserig.

**tightknit** [ˌtaɪt'nɪt] *adj* [closely integrated] eng.

**tight-lipped** [-'lɪpt] *adj* - **1.** [with lips pressed together] mit zusammengepressten Lippen - **2.** [silent] **to be ~ about sthg** sich zu etw nicht äußern.

**tightly** ['taɪtlɪ] *adv* - **1.** [closely] **~ packed** [train, bus] voll gestopft; [crowd] dicht gedrängt; **~ fitting** eng - **2.** [firmly, securely] fest - **3.** [tautly] straff.

**tightness** ['taɪtnɪs] *n* (U) - **1.** [of clothes, shoes] enges Anliegen - **2.** [pain - of chest, stomach] Druck *der* - **3.** [of rule, control] Strenge *die* - **4.** [of schedule] Enge *die*.

**tightrope** ['taɪtrəʊp] *n* Drahtseil *das*; **to be on** OR **walking a ~** *fig* einen Balanceakt vollführen.

**tightrope walker** *n* Seiltänzer *der*, -in *die*.

**tigress** ['taɪgrɪs] *n* Tigerin *die*.

**tilde** ['tɪldə] *n* Tilde *die*.

**tile** [taɪl] *n* - **1.** [on roof] Dachziegel *der* - **2.** [on floor, wall] Fliese *die*, Kachel *die*; **carpet ~** Teppichfliese *die*.

**tiled** [taɪld] *adj* [floor, wall, bath] gefliest; **~ roof** Ziegeldach *das*.

**tiling** ['taɪlɪŋ] *n* (U) - **1.** [act of tiling - of roof] Dachdecken *das*; [ - of floor, wall] Fliesenlegen *das* - **2.** [tiled surface - on roof] Ziegel *pl*; [ - on floor, wall] Fliesen *pl*, Kacheln *pl*

**till** [tɪl] *prep & conj* bis ⟨⟩ *n* Kasse *die*.

**tiller** ['tɪlər] *n* NAUT Pinne *die*.

**tilt** [tɪlt] *n* Neigung *die* ⟨⟩ *vt* [object, chair] kippen; [head] neigen ⟨⟩ *vi* [person, chair] kippen; [head] sich neigen.

**timber** ['tɪmbər] *n* - **1.** (U) [wood] Holz *das* - **2.** [beam] Balken *der*.

**time** [taɪm] *n* - **1.** [gen] Zeit *die*; **at that ~** zu der Zeit, damals; **now is the ~ to do it** jetzt ist der richtige Zeitpunkt OR die richtige Zeit, es zu tun; **to get the ~ to do sthg** die Zeit finden, etw zu tun; **it will take ~** es wird einige Zeit dauern; **to take ~ out to do sthg** sich *(D)* die Zeit nehmen, etw zu tun; **it's high ~ ...** es ist höchste Zeit ...; **to get paid ~ and a half** 50 % Zuschlag bezahlt bekommen; **to have no ~ for sb/sthg** keine Zeit für jn/etw haben; **to make good ~** gut OR schnell voranlkommen; **to pass the ~** sich *(D)* die Zeit vertreiben; **to play for ~** versuchen, Zeit zu gewinnen; **to take one's ~ (over sthg)** sich *(D)* (bei etw) Zeit lassen - **2.** [as measured by clock]: **what ~ is it?, what's the ~?** wie spät ist es?, wie viel Uhr ist es?; **at this ~ of the day** zu dieser Tageszeit; **in a week's/year's ~** in einer Woche/einem Jahr; **this clock keeps good ~** dies Uhr geht genau; **could you tell me the ~?** können Sie mir sagen, wie spät es ist?; **can she tell the ~?** kann sie schon die Uhr lesen? - **3.** [while, spell]: **it was a long ~ before ...** es dauerte lange, bevor ...; **in a short ~** bald; **for a ~** einige Zeit(lang) - **4.** [era] Zeit *die*; **in ancient ~s** zur Zeit der Antike; **in modern ~s** heutzutage; **to be ahead of one's ~** seiner Zeit voraus sein; **it happened before my ~** das war vor meiner Zeit; **to be behind the ~s** hinter dem Mond leben - **5.** [occasion] Mal *das*; **this ~** diesmal, dieses Mal; **(the) last ~** letztes Mal, das letzte Mal; **three ~s a week** dreimal pro OR in der Woche; **from ~ to ~** von Zeit zu Zeit; **~ after ~, ~ and again** immer wieder; **this work is exhausting even at the best of ~s** diese Arbeit ist sowieso ermüdend - **6.** [experience]: **we had a good ~** es war schön; **to have a hard ~** viel durchmachen; **to have a hard ~ doing sthg** Schwierigkeiten haben, etw zu tun - **7.** [degree of lateness]: **to be in good ~** OR **ahead of ~** früh dran sein; **on ~** pünktlich; **did you get there on ~?** warst du rechtzeitig dort? - **8.** MUS Takt *der*; **to beat ~** den Takt anlgeben; **in 4/4 ~** im Viervierteltakt ⟨⟩ *vt* - **1.** [schedule]: **the meeting was ~d to start at nine o'clock** der Beginn der Sitzung war auf neun Uhr angesetzt - **2.** [measure - race, runner] die Zeit stoppen von; **I ~d how long it took him** ich habe gestoppt, wie lange er gebraucht hat - **3.** [choose appropriate moment for] zeitlich ablstimmen.

➡ **times** *npl*: **four ~s as much/many** viermal so viel/viele; **three ~s as big** dreimal so groß ⟨⟩ *prep* MATH mal; **10 ~s 4 is 40** 10 mal 4 ist 40.

➡ **about time** *adv*: **it's about ~ (that) ...** es wird (langsam) Zeit, dass ...

➡ **at a time** *adv*: **three/four at a ~** drei/vier auf einmal; **one at a ~** eine, -r, -s nach dem anderen; **for months at a ~** monatelang.

➡ **at (any) one time** *adv* jederzeit.

➤ **at times** *adv* manchmal.

➤ **at the same time** *adv* - **1.** [simultaneously] gleichzeitig, zur gleichen Zeit - **2.** [equally] trotzdem, dennoch.

➤ **for the time being** *adv* vorläufig.

➤ **in time** *adv* - **1.** [not late] rechtzeitig; **to be in ~ for sthg** rechtzeitig für etw kommen - **2.** [eventually] schließlich; [over a long period] mit der Zeit.

**time-and-motion study** *n* Bewegungs-Zeit-Studie *die*.

**time bomb** *n lit* & *fig* Zeitbombe *die*.

**time-consuming** [-kən‚sjuːmɪŋ] *adj* zeitraubend.

**timed** [taɪmd] *adj* - **1.** [race, test] gestoppt - **2.** [opportune]: **to be well/badly ~** zum richtigen/falschen Zeitpunkt kommen.

**time difference** *n* Zeitunterschied *der*.

**time-honoured** [-‚ɒnəd] *adj* althergebracht.

**timekeeping** [ˈtaɪm‚kiːpɪŋ] *n (U)* [of employee]: **bad ~** ständiges Zuspätkommen.

**time lag** *n* Zeitabstand *der*.

**time-lapse** *adj* PHOT Zeitraffer-.

**timeless** [ˈtaɪmlɪs] *adj* zeitlos.

**time limit** *n* Frist *die*.

**timely** [ˈtaɪmlɪ] (*compar* **-ier**; *superl* **-iest**) *adj* rechtzeitig.

**time machine** *n* Zeitmaschine *die*.

**time off** *n (U)* freie Zeit; **to take ~ (from sthg)** sich *(D)* freinehmen (von etw).

**time-out** (*pl* **time-outs**) *n* SPORT Auszeit *die*.

**timepiece** [ˈtaɪmpiːs] *n dated* Uhr *die*.

**timer** [ˈtaɪmər] *n* [time switch] Schaltuhr *die*.

**timesaving** [ˈtaɪm‚seɪvɪŋ] *adj* Zeit sparend.

**time scale** *n* [for project] Zeitspanne *die*.

**time-share** *n Br* Ferienwohnung, an der man einen Besitzanteil hat.

**time sheet** *n* Stundenzettel *der*.

**time signal** *n* Zeitzeichen *das*.

**time switch** *n* Schaltuhr *die*.

**timetable** [ˈtaɪm‚teɪbl] *n* - **1.** SCH Stundenplan *der* - **2.** [of buses, trains] Fahrplan *der* - **3.** [schedule] Programm *das*.

**time zone** *n* Zeitzone *die*.

**timid** [ˈtɪmɪd] *adj* schüchtern.

**timidly** [ˈtɪmɪdlɪ] *adv* schüchtern.

**timing** [ˈtaɪmɪŋ] *n (U)* - **1.** [of actor, musician, tennis player] Timing *das* - **2.** [chosen moment]: **the ~ of the remark/election was unfortunate** der Zeitpunkt der Bemerkung/Wahlen war unglücklich gewählt - **3.** SPORT [measuring] Stoppen *das*.

**timpani** [ˈtɪmpənɪ] *npl* Kesselpauken *pl*.

**tin** [tɪn] *n* - **1.** *(U)* [metal] Blech *das* - **2.** *Br* [can] Dose *die* - **3.** [for storing] Dose *die* - **4.** [for cake] Kuchenform *die*; [for roasting] Bratform *die*.

**tin can** *n* Blechdose *die*.

**tinder** [ˈtɪndər] *n* Zunder *der*.

**tinfoil** [ˈtɪnfɔɪl] *n (U)* Alufolie *die*.

**tinge** [tɪndʒ] *n* Spur *die*.

**tinged** [tɪndʒd] *adj*: **~ with sthg** mit einer Spur von etw.

**tingle** [ˈtɪŋgl] *vi* kribbeln; **to ~ with excitement** vor Aufregung ganz kribbelig sein.

**tingling** [ˈtɪŋglɪŋ] *n* Kribbeln *das*.

**tinker** [ˈtɪŋkər] *n* Frechdachs *der* ◇ *vi*: **to ~ (with sthg)** (an etw *(D)*) herumbasteln.

**tinkle** [ˈtɪŋkl] *n* - **1.** [of bell] Klingeln *das* - **2.** *Br inf* [phone call]: **to give sb a ~** jn anklingeln ◇ *vi* [bell] klingeln.

**tin mine** *n* Zinnmine *die*.

**tinned** [tɪnd] *adj Br* Dosen-.

**tinny** [ˈtɪnɪ] (*compar* **-ier**; *superl* **-iest**) *adj* - **1.** [sound] blechern - **2.** *inf pej* [badly made] billig.

**tin opener** *n Br* Dosenöffner *der*.

**tin-pot** *adj Br pej* im Westentaschenformat.

**tinsel** [ˈtɪnsl] *n* ≃ Lametta *das*.

**tint** [tɪnt] *n* Ton *der* ◇ *vt* tönen.

**tinted** [ˈtɪntɪd] *adj* getönt.

**tiny** [ˈtaɪnɪ] (*compar* **-ier**; *superl* **-iest**) *adj* winzig.

**tip** [tɪp] (*pt* & *pp* **-ped**; *cont* **-ping**) *n* - **1.** [end] Spitze *die*; **it's on the ~ of my tongue** es liegt mir auf der Zunge - **2.** *Br* [dump] Müllkippe *die* - **3.** [gratuity] Trinkgeld *das* - **4.** [piece of advice] Tipp *der* ◇ *vt* - **1.** [tilt] kippen - **2.** [spill] schütten - **3.** [give a gratuity to] Trinkgeld geben (+ *D*) ◇ *vi* - **1.** [tilt] kippen - **2.** [spill] heraus|fallen; [liquid] sich ergießen - **3.** [give a gratuity] Trinkgeld geben.

➤ **tip off** *vt sep* [warn] einen Tipp geben (+ *D*).

➤ **tip over** *vt sep* & *vi* um|kippen.

➤ **tip up** *vi* [chair, table] kippen.

**tip-off** *n* Tipp *der*.

**tipped** [ˈtɪpt] *adj* [cigarette] mit Filter.

**Tipp-Ex**® [ˈtɪpeks] *n Br* Tipp-Ex® *das*.

➤ **tipp-ex** *vt Br* mit Tipp-Ex® korrigieren.

**tipple** [ˈtɪpl] *n inf*: **what's your ~?** was trinkst du am liebsten?

**tipsy** [ˈtɪpsɪ] (*compar* **-ier**; *superl* **-iest**) *adj inf* beschwipst.

**tiptoe** [ˈtɪptəʊ] *n*: **on ~** auf Zehenspitzen ◇ *vi* auf Zehenspitzen gehen.

**tip-top** *adj inf dated* tipptopp.

**tirade** [taɪˈreɪd] *n* Tirade *die*.

**tire** [ˈtaɪər] *n Am* = **tyre** ◇ *vt* ermüden ◇ *vi* - **1.** [get tired] müde werden - **2.** [get fed up]: **to ~ of sb/sthg** von jm/etw genug haben.

**T**

**tire out** *vt sep* erschöpfen.

**tired** ['taɪəd] *adj* - **1.** [sleepy] müde - **2.** [fed up]: **to be ~ of sthg** etw leid sein; **to be ~ of doing sthg** es leid sein, etw zu tun.

**tiredness** ['taɪədnɪs] *n* Müdigkeit *die*.

**tireless** ['taɪəlɪs] *adj* unermüdlich.

**tiresome** ['taɪəsəm] *adj* lästig.

**tiring** ['taɪərɪŋ] *adj* ermüdend.

**Tirol** *n* = Tyrol.

**tissue** ['tɪʃuː] *n* - **1.** [paper handkerchief] Tempo® *das*, Papiertaschentuch *das* - **2.** (U) BIOL Gewebe *das* - **3.** *phr:* **~ of lies** Lügengespinst *das*.

**tissue paper** *n* (U) Seidenpapier *das*.

**tit** [tɪt] *n* - **1.** [bird] Meise *die* - **2.** *vulg* [breast] Titte *die*.

**titbit** *Br* ['tɪtbɪt], **tidbit** *Am* ['tɪdbɪt] *n lit* & *fig* Leckerbissen *der*.

**tit for tat** [-'tæt] *n* wie du mir, so ich dir.

**titillate** ['tɪtɪleɪt] *vt* [person] anlregen.

**titivate** ['tɪtɪveɪt] *vt* zurechtlmachen.

**title** ['taɪtl] *n* Titel *der*.

**titled** ['taɪtld] *adj* adelig.

**title deed** *n* Eigentumsurkunde *die*.

**titleholder** ['taɪtl‚həʊldə'] *n* SPORT Titelinhaber *der*, -in *die*.

**title page** *n* Titelseite *die*.

**title role** *n* Titelrolle *die*.

**titter** ['tɪtə'] *vi* kichern.

**tittle-tattle** ['tɪtl‚tatl] *n* (U) *inf pej* Klatsch *der*.

**titular** ['tɪtjʊlə'] *adj* nominell.

**T-junction** *n* T-Kreuzung *die*.

**TM** *n abbr of* **transcendental meditation** ◇ *abbr of* **trademark**.

**TN** *abk für* Tennessee, *in Postanschrift verwendet*.

**TNT** (*abbr of* trinitrotoluene) *n* TNT *das*.

**to** [unstressed before consonant tə, unstressed before vowel tu, stressed tuː] *prep* - **1.** [indicating direction] nach; **to go ~ Liverpool/Spain** nach Liverpool/Spanien fahren; **to go ~ the USA** in die USA fahren; **to go ~ school/the cinema** in die Schule/ins Kino gehen; **to go ~ university** auf die Universität gehen; **to go ~ work/the doctor's** zur Arbeit/zum Arzt gehen; **the road ~ Bakersfield** die Straße nach Bakersfield - **2.** [indicating position]: **I nailed it ~ the wall** ich habe es an die Wand genagelt; **~ the left** links; **~ the right** rechts; **~ the east/west (of the river)** östlich/westlich (des Flusses) - **3.** (to express indirect object): **to give sthg ~ sb** jm etw geben; **to talk ~ sb** mit jm sprechen; **to listen ~ the radio** Radio hören; **to give an answer ~ a question** eine Antwort auf eine Frage geben; **we added milk ~ the mixture** wir fügten Milch zu der Mischung hinzu - **4.** [as

far as] bis; **from here ~ London** von hier bis London; **to count ~ ten** bis zehn zählen; **we work from nine ~ five** wir arbeiten von 9 bis 5; **a year ~ the day** ein Jahr auf den Tag genau - **5.** *Br* [in telling the time] vor; **it's ten ~ three** es ist zehn vor drei - **6.** [per] pro; **10 kilometres ~ the litre** 10 Kilometer pro Liter - **7.** [in ratios]: **six votes ~ four** sechs Stimmen gegen vier; **he's ten ~ one to win** es steht zehn zu eins, dass er gewinnt - **8.** [of, for]: **the key ~ the car** der Schlüssel für das Auto; **a letter ~ my daughter** ein Brief an meine Tochter - **9.** [indicating reaction, effect] zu; **~ my surprise** zu meiner Überraschung; **it would be ~ your advantage** es wäre zu Ihrem Vorteil; **what did she say ~ my suggestion?** was hat sie zu meinem Vorschlag gesagt? - **10.** [in stating opinion]: **~ me, he's lying** meiner Meinung nach lügt er; **it seemed quite unnecessary ~ me/him/etc** mir/ihm/etc erschien dies recht unnötig - **11.** [indicating process, change of state]: **to turn ~ ice** zu Eis werden; **to shoot ~ fame** plötzlich berühmt werden; **it could lead ~ trouble** das könnte Ärger geben - **12.** [accompanied by] zu; **we danced ~ the sound of guitars** wir tanzten zum Klang der Gitarren ◇ *with infinitive* - **1.** (forming simple infinitive): **~ walk** gehen; **~ laugh** lachen - **2.** (following another vb): **to begin/try ~ do sthg** anfangen/versuchen, etw zu tun; **to want ~ do sthg** etw tun wollen - **3.** (following an adj) zu; **difficult ~ do** schwer zu tun; **ready ~ go** bereit zu gehen - **4.** (indicating purpose) um zu; **we came here ~ look at the castle** wir sind hierher gekommen, um das Schloss anzuschauen - **5.** (replacing a relative clause): **he is the first ~ complain** er ist der erste, der sich beschwert; **to have a lot ~ do** viel zu tun haben; **he told me ~ leave** er sagte, ich sollte gehen - **6.** (to avoid repetition of infinitive): **I meant to call him, but I forgot ~** ich wollte ihn eigentlich anrufen, vergaß es aber; **you ought ~** du solltest es tun - **7.** [in comments]: **~ be honest ...** um ehrlich zu sein ...; **~ sum up ...** um zusammenzufassen ... ◇ *adv* [shut]: **push the door ~** drück die Tür zu.

**to and fro** *adv* hin und her; **to go ~ and fro** kommen und gehen.

**toad** [təʊd] *n* Kröte *die*.

**toadstool** ['təʊdstuːl] *n* Giftpilz *der*.

**toady** ['təʊdɪ] (*pl* -ies; *pt* & *pp* -ied) *pej n* Kriecher *der*, -in *die* ◇ *vi*: **to ~ (to sb)** (vor jm) kriechen.

**toast** [təʊst] *n* - **1.** (U) [bread, drink] Toast *der;* **to drink a ~ to sb/sthg** einen Toast auf jn/etw auslbringen - **2.** [person]: **to be the ~ of the town** der Star der Stadt sein ◇ *vt* - **1.** [bread] toasten - **2.** [person] trinken auf (+ A).

**toasted sandwich** [‚təʊstɪd-] *n* getoastetes Sandwich.

**toaster** ['təʊstə'] n Toaster der.

**toast rack** n Toastständer der.

**tobacco** [tə'bækəʊ] n Tabak der.

**tobacconist** [tə'bækənɪst] n Tabakwaren-
händler der, -in die; ~'s (shop) Tabakwaren-
handlung die.

**toboggan** [tə'bɒgən] n Schlitten der ◇ vi
Schlitten fahren.

**today** [tə'deɪ] n & adv (U) heute.

**toddle** ['tɒdl] vi - 1. [walk unsteadily] wackeln
- 2. inf [go]: to ~ off OR along loslziehen.

**toddler** ['tɒdlə'] n Kleinkind das.

**toddy** ['tɒdɪ] (pl -ies) n Toddy der, grogähnli-
ches Getränk.

**to-do** (pl -s) n inf dated Getue das.

**toe** [təʊ] n - 1. [of foot] Zeh der, Zehe die - 2. [of
sock, shoe] Spitze die ◇ vt: to ~ the line sich an
die Regeln halten; [in political party] sich an die
Parteilinie halten.

**toehold** ['təʊhəʊld] n - 1. [in rock] Halt der (für
die Zehen) - 2. fig: they've got a ~ in the market
sie sind auf diesem Markt vertreten.

**toenail** ['təʊneɪl] n Zehennagel der.

**toffee** ['tɒfɪ] n - 1. [sweet] Karamellbonbon
das - 2. [substance] Karamell das.

**toffee apple** n Br kandierter Apfel.

**tofu** ['təʊfuː] n (U) Tofu der.

**toga** ['təʊgə] n Toga die.

**together** [tə'geðə'] adv - 1. [gen] zusammen;
**to go ~** [belong together] zusammenlgehören
- 2. [at the same time] zur gleichen Zeit ◇ adj
inf: **she's very ~** sie hat den Durchblick.
➡ **together with** prep zusammen mit.

**togetherness** [tə'geðənɪs] n: feeling of ~ Zusammengehörigkeitsgefühl das.

**toggle** ['tɒgl] n [fastener] Knebelverschluss
der.

**toggle switch** n - 1. ELECTRON Kippschalter der
- 2. COMPUT Umschalttaste die.

**Togo** ['təʊgəʊ] n Togo nt.

**togs** [tɒgz] npl inf Sachen pl.

**toil** [tɔɪl] fml n Mühe die ◇ vi sich ablmühen.
➡ **toil away** vi: to ~ away (at sthg) sich (mit
etw) ablmühen.

**toilet** ['tɔɪlɪt] n Toilette die; **to go to the ~** zur
Toilette gehen.

**toilet bag** n Kulturbeutel der.

**toilet paper** n Toilettenpapier das.

**toiletries** ['tɔɪlɪtrɪz] npl Toilettenartikel pl.

**toilet roll** n Rolle die Toilettenpapier.

**toilet soap** n (U) Toilettenseife die.

**toilet tissue** n Toilettenpapier das.

**toilet-trained** [-ˌtreɪnd] adj: **to be ~** aus den
Windeln sein.

**toilet water** n (U) Eau de Toilette das.

**to-ing and fro-ing** [ˌtuːɪŋən'frəʊɪŋ] n (U) Hin
und Her das.

**token** ['təʊkn] adj symbolisch ◇ n - 1. [vou-
cher, disc] Gutschein der - 2. [symbol] Zeichen
das.
➡ **by the same token** adv ebenso.

**Tokyo** ['təʊkjəʊ] n Tokio nt.

**told** [təʊld] pt & pp ▷ tell.

**tolerable** ['tɒlərəbl] adj [reasonable] annehmbar.

**tolerably** ['tɒlərəblɪ] adv einigermaßen.

**tolerance** ['tɒlərəns] n Toleranz die.

**tolerant** ['tɒlərənt] adj - 1. [not bigoted]: ~ of sb/
sthg tolerant gegenüber jm/etw - 2. [resist-
ant]: ~ to sthg unempfindlich gegen etw.

**tolerate** ['tɒləreɪt] vt - 1. [put up with - noise, heat,
behaviour] ertragen; **I didn't like him much, but I
~d him** ich mochte ihn nicht besonders,
aber ich habe ihn so hingenommen, wie er
ist - 2. [permit] dulden, tolerieren.

**toleration** [ˌtɒlə'reɪʃn] n (U) Tolerierung die,
Duldung die.

**toll** [təʊl] n - 1. [number] Zahl die; **the death ~** die
Zahl der Toten - 2. [fee] Gebühr die - 3. phr:
**to take its ~** seinen Tribut fordern; **smoking
has taken its ~ on his health** das Rauchen ging
auf Kosten seiner Gesundheit ◇ vt & vi
[bell] läuten.

**tollbooth** ['təʊlbuːθ] n Zahlstelle die.

**toll bridge** n gebührenpflichtige Brücke.

**toll-free** Am adj & adv gebührenfrei.

**tomato** [Br tə'mɑːtəʊ, Am tə'meɪtəʊ] (pl -es) n
Tomate die.

**tomb** [tuːm] n Grab das.

**tombola** [tɒm'bəʊlə] n esp Br Tombola die.

**tomboy** ['tɒmbɔɪ] n: **she was a bit of a ~** sie war
wie ein Junge.

**tombstone** ['tuːmstəʊn] n Grabstein der.

**tomcat** ['tɒmkæt] n Kater der.

**tomfoolery** [tɒm'fuːlərɪ] n Unfug der.

**tomorrow** [tə'mɒrəʊ] n & adv [day after today]
morgen.

**ton** [tʌn] (pl inv OR -s) n - 1. Br [imperial unit of meas-
urement] ≃ Tonne die, = 1016 kg - 2. Am [unit of
measurement] ≃ Tonne die, = 907 kg - 3. [metric
unit of measurement] Tonne die, = 1000 kg - 4. phr:
**to weigh a ~** inf eine Tonne wiegen; **to come
down on sb like a ~ of bricks** jn zur Schnecke
machen.
➡ **tons** npl Br inf: **~s of** ein Haufen (+ G).

**tonal** ['təʊnl] adj klanglich.

**tone** [təʊn] n [gen] Ton der; **to lower the ~** das
Niveau senken.
➡ **tone down** vt sep mäßigen.

**tone in** *vi:* to ~ in (with sthg) (mit etw) harmonieren.

**tone up** *vt sep* in Form bringen.

**tone-deaf** *adj:* to be ~ kein musikalisches Gehör haben.

**toner** ['təʊnəʳ] *n* - **1.** [for photocopier, printer] Toner *der* - **2.** [cosmetic] Gesichtswasser *das*.

**tongs** [tɒŋz] *npl* - **1.** [for sugar] Zange *die* - **2.** [for hair] Lockenstab *der*.

**tongue** [tʌŋ] *n* - **1.** [gen] Zunge *die*; **I think he had his ~ in his cheek when he said it** *inf* ich glaube, er hat es ironisch gemeint; **to hold one's ~** *fig* den Mund halten; **to have a sharp ~** eine scharfe Zunge haben; **that set ~s wagging** das hat Gerede gegeben - **2.** *fml* [language] Sprache *die*.

**tongue-in-cheek** *adj* ironisch.

**tongue-tied** *adj:* to be ~ kein Wort herausbringen.

**tongue twister** *n* Zungenbrecher *der*.

**tonic** ['tɒnɪk] *n* - **1.** [tonic water] Tonic *das* - **2.** [medicine] Tonikum *das* - **3.** *fig* [beneficial thing] Wohltat *die*.

**tonic water** *n* Tonic *das*.

**tonight** [tə'naɪt] *n & adv* heute Abend; [during night] heute Nacht.

**tonnage** ['tʌnɪdʒ] *n (U)* NAUT Tonnage *die*.

**tonne** [tʌn] *(pl inv OR* -**s**) *n* Tonne *die*.

**tonsil** ['tɒnsɪl] *n* Mandel *die*.

**tonsil(l)itis** [ˌtɒnsɪ'laɪtɪs] *n (U)* Mandelentzündung *die*.

**too** [tuː] *adv* - **1.** [also] auch - **2.** [excessively] zu; **~ many** zu viel; **it's ~ late to go out** es ist zu spät zum Ausgehen; **I know her all** OR **only ~ well** ich kenne sie nur zu gut; **it was none ~ comfortable** es war nicht gerade bequem; **not ~ good** nicht besonders gut; **how do you feel? – not ~ bad** wie fühlst du dich? – ganz gut; **I'd be only ~ happy to help** ich würde wirklich OR nur zu gerne helfen.

**took** [tʊk] *pt* ⇨ take.

**tool** [tuːl] *n* - **1.** [implement] Werkzeug *das;* **to down ~s** *Br* die Arbeit niederlegen - **2.** *fig* [means] Hilfsmittel *das;* **words are the ~s of the writer's trade** das Handwerkzeug eines Schriftstellers sind Wörter.

**tool around** *vi Am inf* herumfahren.

**tool box** *n* Werkzeugkasten *der*.

**tool kit** *n* Werkzeugsatz *der*.

**toot** [tuːt] *n:* to give a ~ hupen ◇ *vt:* to ~ one's horn hupen ◇ *vi* hupen.

**tooth** [tuːθ] *(pl* teeth*)* *n* Zahn *der;* **to be long in the ~** *Br pej* nicht mehr der/die Jüngste sein; **to be fed up to the back teeth with sthg** *Br inf* die Nase voll von etw haben; **to grit one's teeth** die Zähne zusammenbeißen; **to have no teeth** *fig* [be powerless] keine Macht haben;

**to lie through one's teeth** das Blaue vom Himmel herunterlügen.

**toothache** ['tuːθeɪk] *n (U)* Zahnschmerzen *pl*.

**toothbrush** ['tuːθbrʌʃ] *n* Zahnbürste *die*.

**toothless** ['tuːθlɪs] *adj* zahnlos.

**toothpaste** ['tuːθpeɪst] *n* Zahnpasta *die*.

**toothpick** ['tuːθpɪk] *n* Zahnstocher *der*.

**tooth powder** *n* Zahnpulver *das*.

**tootle** ['tuːtl] *vi inf* [move unhurriedly] zotteln.

**top** [tɒp] *(pt* & *pp* -**ped**; *cont* -**ping**) *adj* - **1.** [highest] oberste, -r, -s - **2.** [most important, successful] Spitzen-; **she was ~ in the exam** sie war die Beste in der Prüfung - **3.** [maximum] Höchst- ◇ *n* - **1.** [highest point - of road] Ende *das;* [ - of stairs] oberste Stufe; [ - of hill] Gipfel *der;* [ - of tree] Krone *die;* **at the ~ of the page** oben auf der Seite; **from ~ to bottom** von oben bis unten; **on ~** oben; **over the ~** *Br* übertrieben; **at the ~ of one's voice** aus vollem Halse - **2.** [lid, cap - of bottle, jar] Deckel *der;* [ - of pen, tube] Kappe *die* - **3.** [upper side - of table] Platte *die;* [ - of box] Oberseite *die* - **4.** [clothing] Oberteil *das* - **5.** [toy] Kreisel *der* - **6.** [in organization, league, table] Spitze *die;* **to be ~ of the class** Klassenbeste, -r sein ◇ *vt* - **1.** [be first in - table, chart] anführen; [ - poll, league] an erster Stelle liegen in *(+ D)* - **2.** [better] übertreffen; [offer] überbieten - **3.** [exceed] übersteigen - **4.** [cover]: **to ~ with cream** Sahne geben auf *(+ A);* **to ~ with grated cheese** mit geriebenem Käse bestreuen; **~ped with** mit.

**on top of** *prep* - **1.** [indicating position] auf *(+ D);* [indicating direction] auf *(+ A)* - **2.** [in addition to] zusätzlich zu *(+ D)* - **3.** [in control of]: **to be on ~ of sthg** etw unter Kontrolle haben - **4.** *phr:* **to get on ~ of sb** jm über den Kopf wachsen.

**top up** *Br,* **top off** *Am vt sep* nachfüllen.

**topaz** ['təʊpæz] *n* Topas *der*.

**top brass** *n (U) inf:* the ~ die hohen Tiere *pl*.

**topcoat** ['tɒpkəʊt] *n* - **1.** [item of clothing] Mantel *der* - **2.** [paint] Deckanstrich *der*.

**top dog** *n inf* Boss *der*.

**top-flight** *adj* erstklassig; [politician, journalist] Spitzen-.

**top floor** *n* oberstes Stockwerk.

**top gear** *n* höchster Gang.

**top hat** *n* Zylinder *der*.

**top-heavy** *adj* kopflastig.

**topic** ['tɒpɪk] *n* Thema *das*.

**topical** ['tɒpɪkl] *adj* aktuell.

**topknot** ['tɒpnɒt] *n* [in hair] Haarknoten *der*.

**topless** ['tɒplɪs] *adj* [barebreasted] oben ohne.

**top-level** *adj* [meeting] Gipfel-; [talks] Spitzen-.

**topmost** ['tɒpməʊst] *adj* oberste, -r, -s.

**top-notch** *adj inf* hervorragend.

**topographer** [təˈpɒgrəfəʳ] n Vermessungs-ingenieur der, -in die.

**topography** [təˈpɒgrəfɪ] n (U) Topografie die.

**topping** [ˈtɒpɪŋ] n Garnierung die; **with a ~ of cheese/cream** mit Käse/Sahne.

**topple** [ˈtɒpl] vt [government, leader] stürzen ◇ vi fallen.
⯈ **topple over** vi umlfallen.

**top-ranking** [-ˈræŋkɪŋ] adj hochrangig.

**top-secret** adj streng geheim.

**top-security** adj [prison] Hochsicherheits-; **a ~ operation** eine Operation mit höchster Sicherheitsstufe.

**topsoil** [ˈtɒpsɔɪl] n (U) oberste Erdschicht.

**topspin** [ˈtɒpspɪn] n (U) Topspin der.

**topsy-turvy** [ˌtɒpsɪˈtɜːvɪ] adj - **1.** [messy] durcheinander - **2.** [haywire] verkehrt ◇ adv [upside down]: **to turn sthg ~** etw auf den Kopf stellen.

**tor** [tɔːʳ] n esp Br [hill] Felsenhügel der.

**torch** [tɔːtʃ] n - **1.** Br [electric] Taschenlampe die - **2.** [flaming stick] Fackel die.

**tore** [tɔːʳ] pt ▷ **tear**².

**torment** [n ˈtɔːment, vb tɔːˈment] n Qual die ◇ vt [worry, annoy] quälen.

**tormentor** [tɔːˈmentəʳ] n Peiniger der, -in die.

**torn** [tɔːn] pp ▷ **tear**².

**tornado** [tɔːˈneɪdəʊ] (pl **-es** OR **-s**) n Tornado der.

**Toronto** [təˈrɒntəʊ] n Toronto nt.

**torpedo** [tɔːˈpiːdəʊ] (pl **-es**) n Torpedo der ◇ vt torpedieren.

**torpedo boat** n Torpedoboot das.

**torpor** [ˈtɔːpəʳ] n Trägheit die.

**torque** [tɔːk] n TECH Drehmoment das.

**torrent** [ˈtɒrənt] n - **1.** [rushing water] reißender Strom - **2.** [of words] Schwall der.

**torrential** [təˈrenʃl] adj sintflutartig.

**torrid** [ˈtɒrɪd] adj lit & fig heiß.

**torso** [ˈtɔːsəʊ] (pl **-s**) n - **1.** [of person] Rumpf der; **bare ~** nackter Oberkörper - **2.** [sculpture] Torso der.

**tortoise** [ˈtɔːtəs] n Schildkröte die.

**tortoiseshell** [ˈtɔːtəʃell] adj [cat] Schildpatt- ◇ n [material] Schildpatt das ◇ comp Schildpatt-.

**tortuous** [ˈtɔːtʃʊəs] adj - **1.** [twisty] gewunden - **2.** [over-complicated] verwickelt.

**torture** [ˈtɔːtʃəʳ] n - **1.** (U) [punishment] Folter die - **2.** fig [cruel treatment] Qual die ◇ vt foltern.

**torturer** [ˈtɔːtʃərəʳ] n Folterer der, -in die.

**Tory** [ˈtɔːrɪ] (pl **-ies**) adj Tory-, konservativ ◇ n Tory der, die, Konservative der, die.

**toss** [tɒs] vt - **1.** [throw carelessly] werfen; **she ~ed back her head** sie warf ihren Kopf zurück - **2.** [food] schwenken; [salad] mischen; [pancake] wenden - **3.** [coin] werfen; **I'll ~ you for it** lass uns eine Münze werfen - **4.** [boat, passengers] hin und her werfen ◇ vi - **1.** [with coin] eine Münze werfen - **2.** [move about]: **to ~ and turn** sich hin und her werfen ◇ n - **1.** [of coin] Wurf der - **2.** [of head]: **with a ~ of his head he left the room** er warf den Kopf nach hinten und verließ den Raum.
⯈ **toss up** vi eine Münze werfen.

**toss-up** n inf: **it's a ~** es steht auf der Kippe.

**tot** [tɒt] (pt & pp **-ted**; cont **-ting**) n - **1.** inf [small child] kleines Kind - **2.** [of drink] Schluck der.
⯈ **tot up** vt sep inf zusammenlzählen.

**total** [ˈtəʊtl] (Br pt & pp **-led**; cont **-ling**, Am pt & pp **-ed**; cont **-ing**) adj - **1.** [complete - dedication, despair, darkness] völlig; [ - eclipse, failure] total; **~ fool** Volllidiot der - **2.** [amount, number] Gesamt- ◇ n Gesamtsumme die; **a ~ of 50 people** insgesamt 50 Leute; **in ~** insgesamt ◇ vt - **1.** [add up] zusammenlzählen - **2.** [amount to] sich belaufen auf (+ A) - **3.** Am inf [wreck] zu Schrott fahren.

**totalitarian** [ˌtəʊtælɪˈteərɪən] adj totalitär.

**totality** [təʊˈtælɪtɪ] n [whole] Gesamtheit die.

**totally** [ˈtəʊtəlɪ] adv völlig.

**tote bag** [təʊt-] n Am Einkaufstasche die.

**totem pole** [ˈtəʊtəm-] n Totempfahl der.

**totter** [ˈtɒtəʳ] vi - **1.** [walk unsteadily] taumeln - **2.** fig [government] schwanken.

**toucan** [ˈtuːkən] n Tukan der.

**touch** [tʌtʃ] n - **1.** (U) [act of touching] Berührung die; **to be soft to the ~** sich weich anlfühlen - **2.** [detail] Detail das; **to put the finishing ~es to sthg** einer Sache (D) den letzten Schliff geben - **3.** (U) [style] Note die - **4.** [contact]: **to get in ~ with sb** sich mit jm in Verbindung setzen; **to keep in ~ (with sb)** (mit jm) in Kontakt bleiben; **to lose ~ with sb** jn aus den Augen verlieren; **to be out of ~ with sthg** in Bezug auf etw (A) nicht auf dem Laufenden sein - **5.** [small amount]: **a ~ (of sthg)** eine Spur (von etw) - **6.** SPORT: **in ~** im Aus - **7.** phr: **it was ~ and go** es stand auf Messers Schneide; **to be a soft ~** [for money] leicht anzupumpen sein ◇ vt - **1.** [make contact with] anlfassen - **2.** [move emotionally] rühren - **3.** [eat, drink] anlrühren ◇ vi - **1.** [make contact - people, things] sich berühren; **don't ~!** nicht anfassen! - **2.** [be in contact] aneinander stoßen.
⯈ **a touch** adv: **a ~ loud/bright** eine Spur zu laut/hell.
⯈ **touch down** vi [plane] auf lsetzen.
⯈ **touch on** vt fus rühren an (+ A).
⯈ **touch up** vt sep [paintwork] auf lfrischen.

**touch-and-go** adj ungewiss.

**touchdown** [ˈtʌtʃdaʊn] n - **1.** [of plane] Aufsetzen *das* - **2.** [in American football] Touchdown *der*.

**touched** [tʌtʃt] *adj* - **1.** [moved] bewegt - **2.** *inf* [slightly mad] nicht ganz richtig im Kopf.

**touching** ['tʌtʃɪŋ] *adj* rührend.

**touch judge** *n* RUGBY Linienrichter *der*.

**touchline** ['tʌtʃlaɪn] *n* Auslinie *die*.

**touchpaper** ['tʌtʃ,peɪpəʳ] *n* Zündschnur *die (aus Papier)*.

**touch-type** *vi* blind schreiben.

**touchy** ['tʌtʃɪ] (*compar* **-ier**; *superl* **-iest**) *adj* - **1.** [person] empfindlich; **to be ~ about sthg** in Bezug auf etw (A) empfindlich sein - **2.** [subject, question] heikel.

**tough** [tʌf] *adj* - **1.** [gen] hart - **2.** [meat] zäh - **3.** [decision, life] schwer - **4.** [criminal, neighbourhood] rau - **5.** *inf* [unfortunate] hart.

**toughen** ['tʌfn] *vt* - **1.** [character] hart machen - **2.** [material] härten.

**toughened** ['tʌfnd] *adj* [glass, steel] gehärtet.

**toughness** ['tʌfnɪs] *n* (U) - **1.** [of character - strength] Stärke *die*; [ - hardness] Härte *die* - **2.** [of material] Härte *die* - **3.** [of meat] Zähigkeit *die*.

**toupee** ['tu:peɪ] *n* Toupet *das*.

**tour** [tʊəʳ] *n* - **1.** [trip] Tour *die* - **2.** [of building, town, museum] Rundgang *der* - **3.** [of pop group etc] Tournee *die*; **to be on ~** auf Tournee sein <> *vt* - **1.** [visit - city, museum] besichtigen; [ - country] reisen durch - **2.** SPORT & THEATRE eine Tournee machen durch <> *vi* [go on trip] eine Tour machen; **we ~ed round Germany** wir haben eine Deutschlandtour gemacht.

**touring** ['tʊərɪŋ] *adj*: **~ exhibition** Wanderausstellung *die*; **~ theatre group** Gastspieltruppe *die* <> *n* Herumreisen *das*; **to go ~** herumreisen.

**tourism** ['tʊərɪzm] *n* Tourismus *der*, Fremdenverkehr *der*.

**tourist** ['tʊərɪst] *n* Tourist *der*, -in *die*.

**tourist class** *n* Touristenklasse *die*.

**tourist (information) office** *n* Touristeninformation *die*, Fremdenverkehrsbüro *das*.

**touristy** ['tʊərɪstɪ] *adj pej*: **it's a very ~ pub** in der Kneipe sind nur Touristen.

**tournament** ['tɔ:nəmənt] *n* Turnier *das*.

**tourniquet** ['tʊənɪkeɪ] *n* Aderpresse *die*.

**tour operator** *n* Reiseveranstalter *der*.

**tousle** ['taʊzl] *vt* zerzausen.

**tout** [taʊt] *n* Schwarzhändler *der*, -in *die* <> *vt* [tickets, goods] an|bieten <> *vi*: **to ~ for custom** auf Kundenfang sein

**tow** [təʊ] *n*: **to give sb a ~** jn ab|schleppen; **to be on ~** *Br* abgeschleppt werden; **with sb in ~** mit jm im Schlepptau <> *vt* ab|schleppen.

**towards** *Br* [tə'wɔ:dz], **toward** *Am* [tə'wɔ:d] *prep* - **1.** [in the direction of] zu; **a move ~ self-government** eine Bewegung in Richtung Selbstregierung; **to run ~ sb** auf jn zu|laufen; **efforts ~ his release** Bemühungen um seine Freilassung - **2.** [facing] nach - **3.** [with regard to] gegenüber; **his feelings ~ me** seine Gefühle mir gegenüber OR für mich - **4.** [in time] gegen; **~ nine o'clock** gegen neun Uhr - **5.** [in space]: **to sit ~ the back/front** hinten/vorne sitzen - **6.** [as contribution] für; **he gave £20 ~ animal research** er spendete £20 für die Tierforschung; **can I pay something ~ the cost?** kann ich etwas zu den Kosten beisteuern?

**towaway zone** ['təʊəweɪ-] *n Am* absolutes Halteverbot.

**towbar** ['təʊba:] *n* Anhängerkupplung *die*.

**towel** ['taʊəl] *n* Handtuch *das*.

**towelling** *Br*, **toweling** *Am* ['taʊəlɪŋ] *n* (U) Frotteestoff *der* <> *comp* Frottee-.

**towel rail** *n* Handtuchhalter *der*.

**tower** ['taʊəʳ] *n* Turm *der*; **a ~ of strength** *Br* eine große Stütze <> *vi* hochragen; **to ~ over sb/sthg** jn/etw überragen.

**tower block** *n Br* Hochhaus *das*.

**towering** ['taʊərɪŋ] *adj* [very tall] hoch aufragend.

**town** [taʊn] *n* Stadt *die*; **to go out on the ~** einen drauf|machen; **to go to ~** *fig* [spend a lot] es sich (D) was kosten lassen; [take trouble] sich ins Zeug legen.

**town centre** *n* Stadtmitte *die*.

**town clerk** *n* Stadtdirektor *der*, -in *die*.

**town council** *n* Stadtrat *der*.

**town hall** *n* - **1.** [building] Rathaus *das* - **2.** (U) *fig* [council] Stadtrat *der*.

**town house** *n* [fashionable house] Villa *die*.

**town plan** *n* Stadtplan *der*.

**town planner** *n* Stadtplaner *der*, -in *die*.

**town planning** *n* (U) Stadtplanung *die*.

**townsfolk** ['taʊnzfəʊk], **townspeople** ['taʊnz,pi:pl] *npl*: **the ~** die Bürger *pl*.

**township** ['taʊnʃɪp] *n* - **1.** [in South Africa] Township *die* - **2.** [in US] Verwaltungsbezirk *der*.

**towpath** ['təʊpɑ:θ, *pl* -pɑ:ðz] *n* Leinpfad *der*.

**towrope** ['təʊrəʊp] *n* Abschleppseil *das*.

**tow truck** *n Am* Abschleppwagen *der*.

**toxic** ['tɒksɪk] *adj* giftig.

**toxin** ['tɒksɪn] *n* Giftstoff *der*.

**toy** [tɔɪ] *n* Spielzeug *das*.
➤ **toy with** *vt fus* spielen mit.

**toyboy** ['tɔɪbɔɪ] *n inf* junger Liebhaber *der*.

**toy shop** *n* Spielwarenladen *der*.

**trace** [treɪs] *n* Spur *die*; **to disappear without ~**

spurlos verschwinden ◇ *vt* - **1.** [find] auf lspüren - **2.** [follow progress of] verfolgen - **3.** [mark outline of] nachlzeichnen; [with tracing paper] durchlpausen.

**trace element** *n* CHEM Spurenelement *das.*

**tracer bullet** ['treɪsəʳ-] *n* Leuchtspurgeschoss *das.*

**tracing** ['treɪsɪŋ] *n* [on paper - act] Durchpausen *das;* [ - result] Pause *die.*

**tracing paper** *n (U)* Transparentpapier *das.*

**track** [træk] *n* - **1.** [path] Pfad *der;* **it's off the beaten** ~ es liegt abseits - **2.** SPORT Bahn *die* - **3.** RAIL Gleis *das* - **4.** [mark, trace] Spur *die;* **to hide** OR **cover one's ~s** seine Spuren verwischen; **to stop dead in one's ~s** wie angewurzelt stehen bleiben - **5.** [on record, tape, CD] Stück *das* - **6.** *phr:* **to keep ~ of sb/sthg** jn/etw im Auge behalten; **to lose ~ of sb/sthg** jn/etw aus den Augen verlieren; **to be on the right/wrong ~** auf der richtigen/falschen Spur sein ◇ *vt* [follow] nachlspüren (+ *D*) ◇ *vi* [camera] fahren.

◆ **track down** *vt sep* [person, animal] auf lspüren; [book, address] auf lstöbern.

**tracker dog** ['trækəʳ-] *n* Spürhund *der.*

**track event** *n* Laufwettbewerb *der.*

**tracking station** ['trækɪŋ-] *n* Bodenstation *die.*

**track record** *n:* **to have a good ~** gute Erfolge aufzuweisen haben.

**track shoes** *npl* Laufschuhe *pl.*

**tracksuit** ['træksuːt] *n* Trainingsanzug *der.*

**tract** [trækt] *n* - **1.** [pamphlet] Traktat *das* - **2.** [area]: **~ of land** Gebiet *das* - **3.** MED Trakt *der.*

**traction** ['trækʃn] *n (U)* PHYSICS Zugkraft *die;* **in ~** im Streckverband.

**traction engine** *n* Zugmaschine *die.*

**tractor** ['træktəʳ] *n* Traktor *der.*

**tractor-trailer** *n Am* Sattelschlepper *der.*

**trade** [treɪd] *n* - **1.** [commerce] Handel *der* - **2.** [job] Handwerk *das;* **by ~** von Beruf ◇ *vt* [exchange] tauschen; **to ~ sthg for sthg** etw gegen etw einltauschen ◇ *vi* - **1.** COMM [do business]: **to ~ (with sb)** (mit jm) Handel treiben - **2.** *Am* [shop]: **to ~ at** OR **with** einkaufen bei.

◆ **trade in** *vt sep* [exchange] in Zahlung geben.

**trade barrier** *n* Handelsschranke *die.*

**trade deficit** *n* Handelsdefizit *das.*

**trade discount** *n (U)* Händlerrabatt *der.*

**trade fair** *n* Messe *die.*

**trade gap** *n* Handelsdefizit *das.*

**trade-in** *n:* **they gave her a ~ on her old cooker** sie nahmen ihren alten Herd in Zahlung.

**trademark** ['treɪdmɑːk] *n* - **1.** COMM Warenzei

chen *das* - **2.** *fig* [characteristic]: **honesty is his ~** er ist für seine Ehrlichkeit bekannt.

**trade name** *n* COMM Handelsname *der.*

**trade-off** *n* Kompromiss *der.*

**trade price** *n* Großhandelspreis *der.*

**trader** ['treɪdəʳ] *n* Händler *der,* -in *die.*

**trade route** *n* Handelsweg *der.*

**trade secret** *n* Geschäftsgeheimnis *das.*

**tradesman** ['treɪdzmən] (*pl* **-men** [-mən]) *n* [shopkeeper, trader] Händler *der.*

**tradespeople** ['treɪdz,piːpl] *npl* Händler *pl.*

**trades union** *n Br* = trade union.

**Trades Union Congress** *n Br:* **the ~** der Gewerkschaftsbund.

**trades unionist** *n Br* = trade unionist.

**trade union** *n* Gewerkschaft *die.*

**trade unionist** *n* Gewerkschaftler *der,* -in *die.*

**trading** ['treɪdɪŋ] *n* Handel *der.*

**trading estate** *n Br* Industriegebiet *das.*

**tradition** [trə'dɪʃn] *n* - **1.** *(U)* [system of customs] Tradition *die* - **2.** [established practice] Brauch *der.*

**traditional** [trə'dɪʃənl] *adj* traditionell.

**traditionally** [trə'dɪʃnəlɪ] *adv* traditionsgemäß.

**traffic** ['træfɪk] (*pt & pp* **-ked;** *cont* **-king**) *n* - **1.** [vehicles] Verkehr *der* - **2.** [illegal trade] Handel *der;* **the ~ in drugs/arms** der Drogen/Waffenhandel ◇ *vi:* **to ~ in sthg** mit etw handeln.

**traffic circle** *n Am* Kreisverkehr *der.*

**traffic island** *n* Verkehrsinsel *die.*

**traffic jam** *n* Stau *der.*

**trafficker** ['træfɪkəʳ] *n* Händler *der,* -in *die.*

**traffic lights** *npl* Ampel *die.*

**traffic offence** *Br,* **traffic violation** *Am n* Verstoß *der* gegen die Straßenverkehrsordnung.

**traffic sign** *n* Verkehrsschild *das.*

**traffic violation** *n Am* = traffic offence.

**traffic warden** *n Br* Hilfspolizist *der,* Politesse *die.*

**tragedy** ['trædʒədɪ] (*pl* **-ies**) *n* Tragödie *die.*

**tragic** ['trædʒɪk] *adj* tragisch.

**tragically** ['trædʒɪklɪ] *adv* [sadly] tragischerweise; [in tragic way] auf tragische Weise.

**trail** [treɪl] *n* - **1.** [path] Weg *der;* **to blaze a ~** *fig* Pionierarbeit leisten - **2.** [traces] Spur *die;* **to be on the ~ of sb/sthg** jm/etw auf der Spur sein ◇ *vt* - **1.** [drag behind, tow] hinter sich (*D*) her schleifen - **2.** [lag behind] zurückliegen hinter (+ *D*) ◇ *vi* - **1.** [drag behind] schleifen

T

- **2.** [move slowly] trotten - **3.** SPORT [lose] zurückl-liegen.

➤ **trail away, trail off** vi: his voice ~ed away seine Stimme wurde leiser und ver-stummte schließlich.

**trailblazing** ['treɪl‚bleɪzɪŋ] adj bahnbre-chend.

**trailer** ['treɪlə'] n - **1.** [vehicle for luggage] Anhän-ger der - **2.** esp Am [for living in] Wohnwagen der - **3.** CINEMA Trailer der.

**trailer court, trailer park** n Am Platz der für Wohnwagen.

**train** [treɪn] n - **1.** RAIL Zug der; by ~ mit dem Zug - **2.** [of dress] Schleppe die - **3.** [connected se-quence]: ~ of thought Gedankengang der <> vt - **1.** [teach - animal] dressieren; to ~ sb to do sthg jm beibringen, etw zu tun - **2.** [for job] ausl-bilden; to ~ sb as sthg jn zu etw ausbilden - **3.** SPORT trainieren - **4.** [plant] über ein Spa-lier wachsen lassen - **5.** [gun, camera]: to ~ sthg on sb/sthg etw auf jn/etw richten <> vi - **1.** [for job]: to ~ (as) eine Ausbildung ma-chen (als) - **2.** SPORT: to ~ (for sthg) (für etw) trainieren.

**train driver** n Zugführer der, -in die.

**trained** [treɪnd] adj ausgebildet.

**trainee** [treɪ'niː] adj in der Ausbildung; ~ manager Trainee der; ~ nurse Kranken-pflegeschüler der, Schwesternschülerin die <> n [academic, tech-nical] Praktikant der, -in die.

**trainer** ['treɪnə'] n - **1.** [of dogs] Dresseur der, -euse die; [of horses] Trainer der, -in die - **2.** SPORT Trainer der, -in die.

➤ **trainers** npl Br [shoes] Turnschuhe pl.

**training** ['treɪnɪŋ] n - **1.** [for job] Ausbildung die - **2.** SPORT Training das.

**training college** n Br [for teachers] ≈ pädago-gische Hochschule.

**training course** n Kurs der.

**training shoes** npl Br Turnschuhe pl.

**train set** n Modelleisenbahn die.

**train spotter** [-‚spɒtə'] n Eisenbahnfan, der als Hobby Zugnummern notiert.

**train station** n Bahnhof der.

**traipse** [treɪps] vi latschen.

**trait** [treɪt] n Charakterzug der.

**traitor** ['treɪtə'] n: ~ (to sthg) Verräter der; -in die (an etw (D)).

**trajectory** [trə'dʒektərɪ] (pl -ies) n TECH Flug-bahn die.

**tram** [træm] n Br Straßenbahn die.

**tramlines** ['træmlaɪnz] npl - **1.** [for trams] Straßenbahnschienen pl - **2.** TENNIS Gasse die.

**tramp** [træmp] n - **1.** [homeless person] Land-streicher der, -in die - **2.** Am inf [loose woman]

Flittchen das <> vt trotten durch <> vi [trudge] trotten.

**trample** ['træmpl] vt niederl trampeln <> vi: to ~ on lit & fig herumltrampeln auf (+ D).

**trampoline** ['træmpəliːn] n Trampolin das.

**trance** [trɑːns] n [hypnotic state] Trance die; in a ~ in Trance.

**tranquil** ['træŋkwɪl] adj literary friedlich.

**tranquility** n Am = tranquillity.

**tranquilize** vt Am = tranquillize.

**tranquilizer** n Am = tranquillizer.

**tranquillity** Br, **tranquility** Am [træŋ-'kwɪlətɪ] n Friedlichkeit die.

**tranquillize, -ise** Br, **tranquilize** Am ['træŋkwɪlaɪz] vt beruhigen.

**tranquillizer** Br, **tranquilizer** Am ['træŋkwɪlaɪzə'] n Beruhigungsmittel das.

**transact** [træn'zækt] vt fml ablschließen.

**transaction** [træn'zækʃn] n [piece of business] Transaktion die.

**transatlantic** [‚trænzət'læntɪk] adj transat-lantisch.

**transceiver** [træn'siːvə'] n Sende-Emp-fangsgerät das.

**transcend** [træn'send] vt fml [go beyond] hi-nauslgehen über (+ A).

**transcendental meditation** [‚trænsen-'dentl-] n transzendentale Meditation.

**transcribe** [træn'skraɪb] vt - **1.** [write down - re-cording, speech] mitlschreiben; [ - manuscript] abl-schreiben - **2.** [transliterate] übertragen.

**transcript** ['trænskrɪpt] n [of speech, conversation] Mitschrift die.

**transept** ['trænsept] n Querschiff das.

**transfer** [n 'trænsfɜː', vb træns'fɜː'] (pt & pp -red; cont -ring) <> n - **1.** (U) [from one place to an-other - of money] Überweisung die; [ - of prisoner] Überführung die; [ - of patient] Verlegung die - **2.** (U) [from one person to another] Übertra-gung die - **3.** [for job] Versetzung die - **4.** SPORT Wechsel der, Transfer der - **5.** [design] Ab-ziehbild das - **6.** Am [ticket] Umsteigefahrkar-te die <> vt - **1.** (U) [from one place to another - money] überweisen; [ - prisoner] überführen; [ - patient] verlegen - **2.** [from one person to an-other]: to ~ sthg to sb jm etw übertragen - **3.** [for job] versetzen - **4.** SPORT transferieren <> vi [to different job etc & SPORT] wechseln.

**transferable** [træns'fɜːrəbl] adj übertragbar.

**transfer fee** n Br SPORT Transfersumme die.

**transfix** [træns'fɪks] vt [immobilize] erstarren lassen.

**transform** [træns'fɔːm] vt: to ~ sb/sthg (into) jn/etw verwandeln (in (+ A)).

**transformation** [‚trænsfə'meɪʃn] n Um-wandlung die.

**transformer** [træns'fɔːməʳ] *n* ELEC Transformator *der.*

**transfusion** [træns'fjuːʒn] *n* Transfusion *die.*

**transgress** [træns'gres] *fml vi* gegen die Regeln verstoßen.

**transient** ['trænzɪənt] *adj fml* [fleeting] kurzlebig ◇ *n Am* [person] Durchreisende *der, die.*

**transistor** [træn'zɪstəʳ] *n* - **1.** ELECTRON Transistor *der* - **2.** dated [portable radio] Transistorradio *das.*

**transit** ['trænsɪt] *n:* **in ~** [goods] auf dem Transport.

**transit camp** *n* Durchgangslager *das.*

**transition** [træn'zɪʃn] *n:* **~ from sthg to sthg** Übergang *der* von etw zu etw; **in ~** im Wandel.

**transitional** [træn'zɪʃənl] *adj* Übergangs-.

**transitive** ['trænzɪtɪv] *adj* GRAMM transitiv.

**transit lounge** *n* Warteraum *der.*

**transitory** ['trænzɪtrɪ] *adj* vergänglich.

**translate** [træns'leɪt] *vt* - **1.** [languages] übersetzen - **2.** fig [transform]: **to ~ a plan into action** einen Plan in die Tat umlsetzen ◇ *vi* - **1.** [words] sich übersetzen lassen - **2.** [person] übersetzen; **she ~s from English into German** sie übersetzt aus dem Englischen ins Deutsche.

**translation** [træns'leɪʃn] *n* Übersetzung *die.*

**translator** [træns'leɪtəʳ] *n* Übersetzer *der*, -in *die.*

**translucent** [trænz'luːsnt] *adj* lichtdurchlässig.

**transmission** [trænz'mɪʃn] *n* - **1.** [passing on & ELECTRON] Übertragung *die* - **2.** RADIO & TV [programme] Sendung *die.*

**transmit** [trænz'mɪt] (*pt & pp* -ted; *cont* -ting) *vt* übertragen.

**transmitter** [trænz'mɪtəʳ] *n* ELECTRON Sender *der.*

**transparency** [trans'pærənsɪ] (*pl* -ies) *n* - **1.** PHOT Dia(positiv) *das* - **2.** [for overhead projector] Folie *die* - **3.** [quality of being transparent] Durchsichtigkeit *die.*

**transparent** [træns'pærənt] *adj* - **1.** [see-through] durchsichtig - **2.** [obvious] offensichtlich.

**transpire** [træn'spaɪəʳ] *fml vt:* **it ~s that ...** es stellt sich heraus, dass ... ◇ *vi* [happen] passieren.

**transplant** [*n* 'trænsplɑːnt, *vb* træns'plɑːnt] *n* [MED - operation] Transplantation *die;* [- organ, tissue] Transplantat *das* ◇ *vt* - **1.** MED transplantieren - **2.** BOT [seedlings] umlpflanzen - **3.** [population] umlsiedeln.

**transport** [*n* 'trænspɔːt, *vb* træn'spɔːt] *n* - **1.** [system] Verkehrsmittel *pl;* **do you have your own ~?** sind Sie motorisiert? - **2.** [of goods, people] Beförderung *die,* Transport *der* ◇ *vt* [goods, people] befördern, transportieren.

**transportable** [træn'spɔːtəbl] *adj* transportierbar.

**transportation** [ˌtrænspɔː'teɪʃn] *n (U) esp Am* = transport.

**transport cafe** *n Br* Fernfahrerlokal *das.*

**transporter** [træn'spɔːtəʳ] *n* [vehicle] Autotransporter *der.*

**transpose** [træns'pəʊz] *vt* [change round] umlstellen.

**transsexual** [træns'sekʃʊəl] *n* Transsexuelle *der, die.*

**transvestite** [trænz'vestaɪt] *n* Transvestit *der.*

**trap** [træp] (*pt & pp* -ped; *cont* -ping) *n* Falle *die* ◇ *vt* - **1.** [animal, bird] fangen - **2.** fig [trick] eine Falle stellen (+ D) - **3.** [immobilize, catch]: **to be ~ped in sthg** in etw (D) festlsitzen; **to be ~ped in a relationship** in einer Beziehung gefangen sein - **4.** [energy] speichern.

**trapdoor** ['træpdɔːʳ] *n* Falltür *die.*

**trapeze** [trə'piːz] *n* Trapez *das.*

**trapper** ['træpəʳ] *n* Fallensteller *der,* -in *die.*

**trappings** ['træpɪŋz] *npl* äußere Zeichen *pl.*

**trash** [træʃ] *n* - **1.** *Am* [refuse] Abfall *der* - **2.** inf pej [sthg of poor quality] Ramsch *der;* [book, film] Schund *der* ◇ *vt Am* - **1.** [criticize] zerreißen - **2.** [damage] in ein Schlachtfeld verwandeln.

**trashcan** ['træʃkæn] *n Am* Abfalleimer *der.*

**trashy** ['træʃɪ] (*compar* -ier; *superl* -iest) *adj* inf wertlos; [film] schlecht und billig; **~ novel** Schundroman *der.*

**trauma** ['trɔːmə] *n* Trauma *das.*

**traumatic** [trɔː'mætɪk] *adj* traumatisch.

**traumatize, -ise** ['trɔːmətaɪz] *vt* [shock] traumatisieren.

**travel** ['trævl] (*Br pt & pp* -led; *cont* -ling, *Am pt & pp* -ed; *cont* -ing) *n (U)* Reisen *das* ◇ *vt* [distance] fahren; **to ~ the world/country** durch die Welt/das Land reisen ◇ *vi* - **1.** [journey] reisen - **2.** [go, move - train] fahren; [ - light] sich fortlbewegen; [ - current] fließen; [ - news] sich verbreiten.
➤ **travels** *npl* Reisen *pl.*

**travel agency** *n* Reisebüro *das.*

**travel agent** *n* Reiseveranstalter *der,* -in *die;* **~'s** Reisebüro *das.*

**travel brochure** *n* Urlaubsprospekt *der.*

**travelcard** ['trævlkɑːd] *n* Zeitkarte *die.*

**traveler** *etc n Am* = **traveller** *etc.*

**travelled** *Br,* **traveled** *Am* ['trævld] *adj* - **1.** [person]: **widely ~** weit gereist - **2.** [road, route]: **much-~** viel befahren.

**traveller** *Br*, **traveler** *Am* ['trævlə'] *n* - **1.** [person on journey] Reisende *der*, *die* - **2.** [itinerant] Herumreisende *der*, *die*.

**traveller's cheque** *n* Travellerscheck *der*.

**travelling** *Br*, **traveling** *Am* ['trævlɪŋ] *adj* - **1.** [itinerant] Wander- - **2.** [for taking on journeys, of travel] Reise-.

**travelling expenses** *npl* Reisekosten *pl*.

**travelling salesman** *n* Vertreter *der*, -in *die*.

**travelogue, travelog** *Am* ['trævəlɒg] *n* Reisebericht *der*.

**travelsick** ['trævəlsɪk] *adj* reisekrank.

**traverse** ['trævəs, ,trə'vɜ:s] *vt fml* durchqueren.

**travesty** ['trævəstɪ] (*pl* -ies) *n*: it was a ~ of justice es war eine Verhöhnung der Gerechtigkeit.

**trawl** [trɔ:l] *n* - **1.** [fishing net] Schleppnetz *das* - **2.** [search] Suche *die* ⬦ *vt* - **1.** [fish]: to ~ sthg (for sthg) in etw (*D*) mit Schleppnetzen (nach etw) fischen - **2.** [search]: to ~ sthg for sthg etw nach etw absuchen ⬦ *vi* - **1.** [fish]: to ~ for sthg nach etw fischen - **2.** [search]: to ~ for sthg nach etw suchen.

**trawler** ['trɔ:lə'] *n* Trawler *der*.

**tray** [treɪ] *n* - **1.** [for carrying] Tablett *das* - **2.** [for papers, mail] Korb *der*.

**treacherous** ['tretʃərəs] *adj* - **1.** [person, behaviour] verräterisch - **2.** [rock, tides] tückisch.

**treachery** ['tretʃərɪ] *n* Verrat *der*.

**treacle** ['tri:kl] *n Br* Sirup *der*.

**tread** [tred] (*pt* trod; *pp* trodden) *n* - **1.** [on tyre, shoe] Profil *das* - **2.** [sound or way of walking] Schritt *der*, Tritt *der* ⬦ *vt* [grapes] stampfen; to ~ sthg into sthg etw in etw (*A*) treten ⬦ *vi* - **1.** [place foot]: to ~ on sthg auf etw (*A*) treten - **2.** [walk, progress] trotten; to ~ carefully *fig* vorsichtig vorlgehen.

**treadle** ['tredl] *n* Fußhebel *der*.

**treadmill** ['tredmɪl] *n* - **1.** [wheel] Tretrad *das* - **2.** *fig* [dull routine] Tretmühle *die*.

**treason** ['tri:zn] *n* Verrat *der*.

**treasure** ['treʒə'] *n* Schatz *der* ⬦ *vt* [memory] bewahren; [object] sorgfältig auf lbewahren.

**treasure hunt** *n* Schatzsuche *die*.

**treasurer** ['treʒərə'] *n* Schatzmeister *der*, -in *die*.

**treasure trove** *n* (*U*) LAW Schatzfund *der*.

**treasury** ['treʒərɪ] (*pl* -ies) *n* [room] Schatzkammer *die*.

➤ **Treasury** *n*: the Treasury das Finanzministerium.

**treasury bill** *n* kurzfristiger Schatzwechsel.

**treat** [tri:t] *vt* - **1.** [gen] behandeln; to ~ sb as/

like sthg jn wie etw behandeln; to ~ sth as confidential etw vertraulich behandeln; to ~ sthg as a joke etw als Witz ansehen - **2.** [give sthg special]: to ~ sb (to sthg) jn (zu etw) einladen; to ~ o.s. to sthg sich (*D*) etw leisten ⬦ *n* [sthg special]: what a ~! was für ein Genuss!; to give sb a ~ jm eine Freude bereiten; this is my ~ ich lade dich ein.

**treatise** ['tri:tɪz] *n fml*: ~ (on sthg) Abhandlung *die* (über etw (*A*)).

**treatment** ['tri:tmənt] *n* [gen] Behandlung *die*; [specific method of medical care] Behandlungsmethode *die*.

**treaty** ['tri:tɪ] (*pl* -ies) *n* Vertrag *der*.

**treble** ['trebl] *adj* - **1.** MUS: ~ voice Knabensopranstimme *die* - **2.** [with numbers]: ~ 4 dreimal 4 ⬦ *n* MUS - **1.** (*U*) [musical range] Oberstimme *die* - **2.** [boy singer] Knabensopran *der* ⬦ *vt* verdreifachen ⬦ *vi* sich verdreifachen.

**treble clef** *n* Violinschlüssel *der*.

**tree** [tri:] *n* [plant & COMPUT] Baum *der*; to be barking up the wrong ~ auf dem Holzweg sein.

**tree-lined** *adj* von Bäumen gesäumt.

**treetop** ['tri:tɒp] *n* Baumkrone *die*.

**tree-trunk** *n* Baumstamm *der*.

**trek** [trek] (*pt* & *pp* -ked; *cont* -king) *n* anstrengender Marsch ⬦ *vi* - **1.** [go on long journey]: to ~ through the jungle durch den Urwald ziehen - **2.** *inf* [walk laboriously]: I had to ~ all the way home ich musste den ganzen Weg nach Hause laufen.

**trellis** ['trelɪs] *n* Spalier *das*.

**tremble** ['trembl] *vi* zittern.

**tremendous** [trɪ'mendəs] *adj* - **1.** [impressive, large] enorm - **2.** *inf* [really good] sagenhaft.

**tremendously** [trɪ'mendəslɪ] *adv* [impressively, hugely] enorm.

**tremor** ['tremə'] *n* - **1.** [of body, voice] Zittern *das* - **2.** [small earthquake] Beben *das*.

**tremulous** ['tremjʊləs] *adj literary* [voice] zitternd; [smile] zaghaft.

**trench** [trentʃ] *n* - **1.** [channel] Graben *der* - **2.** MIL Schützengraben *der*.

**trenchant** ['trentʃənt] *adj fml* scharf.

**trench coat** *n* Trenchcoat *der*.

**trench warfare** *n* (*U*) Stellungskrieg *der*.

**trend** [trend] *n* [tendency] Trend *der*, Tendenz *die*.

**trendsetter** ['trend,setə'] *n* Trendsetter *der*, -in *die*.

**trendy** [trendɪ] (*compar* -ier; *superl* -iest) *adj inf* in, angesagt.

**trepidation** [,trepɪ'deɪʃn] *n* (*U*) *fml*: in OR with ~ mit einem beklommenen Gefühl; I waited in ~ ich wartete angsterfüllt.

**trespass** ['trespəs] *vi*: to ~ (on sb's land) ein

Grundstück unbefugt betreten; 'no ~ing' 'Betreten verboten'.

**trespasser** ['trespəsə'] n Unbefugte der, die; '~s will be prosecuted' 'widerrechtliches Betreten wird strafrechtlich verfolgt'.

**trestle** ['tresl] n Bock der.

**trestle table** n Tapeziertisch der.

**trial** ['traɪəl] n - **1.** LAW Prozess der; **to be on ~ (for sthg)** (wegen etw) vor Gericht stehen - **2.** [test, experiment] Versuch der; **on ~** zur Probe; **by ~ and error** durch Ausprobieren - **3.** [unpleasant experience] Qual die; **~s and tribulations** Kummer und Sorgen.

**trial basis** n: **on a ~** versuchsweise.

**trial period** n Probezeit die.

**trial run** n [of car] Probefahrt die; [of machine] Probelauf der.

**triangle** ['traɪæŋgl] n - **1.** [shape] Dreieck das - **2.** MUS Triangel der - **3.** Am [set square] Zeichendreieck das.

**triangular** [traɪ'æŋgjʊlə'] adj [in triangle shape] dreieckig.

**triathlon** [traɪ'æθlɒn] (pl -s) n Triathlon das OR der.

**tribal** ['traɪbl] adj Stammes-.

**tribe** [traɪb] n [social group] Stamm der.

**tribulation** [ˌtrɪbjʊ'leɪʃn] n ⊳ trial.

**tribunal** [traɪ'bju:nl] n Tribunal das.

**tributary** ['trɪbjʊtrɪ] (pl -ies) n GEOGR Nebenfluss der.

**tribute** ['trɪbju:t] n - **1.** [respect] Tribut der; **to pay ~ to sb/sthg** jm/etw Tribut zollen - **2.** [evidence]: **it's a ~ to his strength of character that ...** es ist ein Beweis für seine Charakterstärke, dass ...

**trice** [traɪs] n: **in a ~** im Nu.

**triceps** ['traɪseps] (pl inv OR -cepses) n Trizeps der.

**trick** [trɪk] n - **1.** [to deceive] Streich der; **to play a ~ on sb** jm einen Streich spielen - **2.** [to entertain] Trick der - **3.** [ability, knack] Trick der; **that will do the ~** damit ist das Problem gelöst ⬦ adj [knife, moustache etc] falsch ⬦ vt austricksen; **to ~ sb into doing sthg** jn durch List dazu bringen, etw zu tun.

**trickery** ['trɪkərɪ] n Betrug der.

**trickle** ['trɪkl] n - **1.** [of liquid] Rinnsal das; [drip] Tröpfeln das - **2.**: **a ~ of people/letters** einige wenige Leute/Briefe ⬦ vi - **1.** [liquid] rinnen - **2.** [people]: **to ~ in/out** nach und nach herein-/herauskommen.

**trick or treat** n (U) Spruch, in dem verkleidete Kinder am Vorabend von Halloween bei ihrem Zug von Haus zu Haus einen Streich androhen, falls man ihnen keine Leckereien schenkt.

**trick question** n Fangfrage die.

**tricky** ['trɪkɪ] (compar -ier; superl -iest) adj [difficult] verzwickt.

**tricycle** ['traɪsɪkl] n Dreirad das.

**tried** [traɪd] pt & pp ⊳ **try** ⬦ adj: **~ and tested** erprobt, bewährt.

**trier** ['traɪə'] n: **he's a real ~** er gibt sich große Mühe.

**trifle** ['traɪfl] n - **1.** CULIN Dessert aus Biskuit, Früchten, Vanillecreme und Sahne in Schichten - **2.** [unimportant thing] Kleinigkeit die.
⬤ **a trifle** adv fml eine Spur.
⬤ **trifle with** vt fus: **he's not to be ~d with** mit ihm ist nicht zu spaßen.

**trifling** ['traɪflɪŋ] adj pej unbedeutend.

**trigger** ['trɪgə'] n [on gun] Abzug der ⬦ vt auslösen.
⬤ **trigger off** vt sep = trigger.

**trigger-happy** adj schießwütig.

**trigonometry** [ˌtrɪgə'nɒmətrɪ] n Trigonometrie die.

**trill** [trɪl] n - **1.** MUS Triller der - **2.** [of birds] Trällern das ⬦ vi [bird, woman] trällern.

**trillions** ['trɪljənz] npl inf: **~ (of)** Tausende pl (von).

**trilogy** ['trɪlədʒɪ] (pl -ies) n Trilogie die.

**trim** [trɪm] (compar -mer; superl -mest; pt & pp -med; cont -ming) adj - **1.** [neat and tidy] gepflegt - **2.** [slim] schlank ⬦ n - **1.** [cut]: **to give sb** OR **sb's hair a ~** jm die Haare nachlschneiden - **2.** [decoration] Borte die ⬦ vt - **1.** [cut - hedge] zurücklschneiden; [ - hair] nachlschneiden; [ - lawn] mähen; [ - nails] schneiden - **2.** [decorate]: **to ~ sthg (with sthg)** etw (mit etw) verzieren.
⬤ **trim away, trim off** vt sep ablschneiden.

**trimming** ['trɪmɪŋ] n [on clothing] Besatz der.
⬤ **trimmings** npl - **1.** CULIN Beilagen pl - **2.**: **a white wedding with all the ~** eine Hochzeit in Weiß mit allem, was dazugehört.

**Trinity** ['trɪnətɪ] n RELIG: **the ~** die Dreifaltigkeit.

**trinket** ['trɪŋkɪt] n Schmuckstück das.

**trio** ['tri:əʊ] (pl -s) n Trio das.

**trip** [trɪp] (pt & pp -ped; cont -ping) n - **1.** [journey] Ausflug der - **2.** drugs sl [experience] Trip der ⬦ vt [make stumble] ein Bein stellen (+ D) ⬦ vi [stumble]: **to ~ (over sthg)** (über etw (A)) stolpern.
⬤ **trip up** vt sep - **1.** [make stumble] ein Bein stellen (+ D) - **2.** [catch out] eine Falle stellen (+ D).

**tripartite** [ˌtraɪ'pɑ:taɪt] adj fml [agreement, talks] dreiseitig.

**tripe** [traɪp] n (U) - **1.** CULIN Kaldaunen pl - **2.** inf [nonsense] Quatsch der.

**triple** ['trɪpl] adj dreifach ⬦ vt verdreifachen ⬦ vi sich verdreifachen.

T

**triple jump** n: the ~ der Dreisprung.

**triplets** ['trɪplɪts] npl Drillinge pl.

**triplicate** ['trɪplɪkət] n: **in ~** in dreifacher Ausfertigung.

**tripod** ['traɪpɒd] n Stativ das.

**tripper** ['trɪpəʳ] n esp Br Ausflügler der, -in die.

**tripwire** ['trɪpwaɪəʳ] n Stolperdraht der.

**trite** [traɪt] adj pej banal.

**triumph** ['traɪəmf] n Triumph der ⬦ vi: to ~ **(over)** triumphieren (über (+ A)).

**triumphal** [traɪˈʌmfl] adj fml Triumph-.

**triumphant** [traɪˈʌmfənt] adj [exultant] triumphierend; [shout] Triumph-.

**triumphantly** [traɪˈʌmfəntlɪ] adv triumphierend.

**trivet** ['trɪvɪt] n [to protect table] Topfuntersetzer der.

**trivia** ['trɪvɪə] n (U) Belanglosigkeiten pl.

**trivial** ['trɪvɪəl] adj pej trivial.

**triviality** [ˌtrɪvɪˈælətɪ] (pl -ies) n Belanglosigkeit die.

**trivialize, -ise** ['trɪvɪəlaɪz] vt trivialisieren.

**trod** [trɒd] pt ⬦ tread.

**Trojan** ['trəʊdʒən] adj HISTORY trojanisch ⬦ n - **1.** HISTORY Trojaner der, -in die - **2.** fig [hard worker]: **to work like a ~** wie ein Pferd schuften.

**troll** [trəʊl] n Troll der.

**trolley** ['trɒlɪ] (pl trolleys) n - **1.** Br [for shopping] Einkaufswagen der; [for luggage] Gepäckwagen der - **2.** Br [for food, drinks] Servierwagen der - **3.** Am [vehicle] Straßenbahn die.

**trolleybus** ['trɒlɪbʌs] n Oberleitungsbus der.

**trombone** [trɒmˈbəʊn] n Posaune die.

**troop** [truːp] n [large group] Schar die ⬦ vi strömen.

⬤ **troops** npl MIL Truppen pl.

**trooper** ['truːpəʳ] n - **1.** MIL [in cavalry] Kavallerist der, -in die - **2.** Am [policeman] Polizist der, -in die.

**troopship** ['truːpʃɪp] n Truppentransportschiff das.

**trophy** ['trəʊfɪ] (pl -ies) n SPORT Trophäe die.

**tropical** ['trɒpɪkl] adj tropisch.

**Tropic of Cancer** ['trɒpɪk-] n: **the ~** der Wendekreis des Krebses.

**Tropic of Capricorn** n: **the ~** der Wendekreis des Steinbocks.

**tropics** ['trɒpɪks] npl: **the ~** die Tropen.

**trot** [trɒt] (pt & pp -ted; cont -ting) n Trab der ⬦ vi traben.

⬤ **on the trot** adv inf hintereinander.

⬤ **trot out** vt sep pej auf Iwarten mit

**trotter** ['trɒtəʳ] n [pig's foot] Schweinsfuß der.

**trouble** ['trʌbl] n - **1.** (U) [difficulty] Problem das; **to be in ~** [having problems] in Schwierigkeiten stecken; **to get into ~** [with sb in authority] Ärger bekommen; **to have with him/it is ...** das Problem mit ihm/damit ist ... - **2.** [bother]: **it's no ~** es macht mir keine Mühe; **to take the ~ to do sthg** sich (D) die Mühe machen, etw zu tun; **he's asking for ~** er wird dafür bezahlen müssen - **3.** (U) [pain, illness] Beschwerden pl; **to have heart/kidney ~** es mit dem Herzen/den Nieren haben - **4.** [fighting & POL] Unruhen pl ⬦ vt - **1.** [worry, upset] beunruhigen - **2.** [interrupt, disturb] stören - **3.** [cause pain to] zu schaffen machen (+ D).

⬤ **troubles** npl - **1.** [worries] Sorgen pl - **2.** POL [unrest] Unruhen pl.

**troubled** ['trʌbld] adj - **1.** [worried, upset] besorgt - **2.** [disturbed - sleep] unruhig; [ - place] von Unruhen geschüttelt; **~ times** turbulente Zeiten.

**trouble-free** adj [existence] sorgenfrei; [journey, operation] problemlos.

**troublemaker** ['trʌblˌmeɪkəʳ] n Unruhestifter der, -in die.

**troubleshooter** ['trʌblˌʃuːtəʳ] n Störungssucher der, -in die.

**troublesome** ['trʌblsəm] adj lästig.

**trouble spot** n Unruheherd der.

**trough** [trɒf] n - **1.** [for animals] Trog der - **2.** [low point] Tal das.

**trounce** [traʊns] vt inf haushoch schlagen.

**troupe** [truːp] n Truppe die.

**trouser press** ['traʊzəʳ-] n Hosenpresse die.

**trousers** ['traʊzəz] npl Hose die; **a pair of ~** eine Hose.

**trouser suit** n Br Hosenanzug der.

**trousseau** ['truːsəʊ] (pl -x OR -s [-z]) n Aussteuer die.

**trout** [traʊt] (pl inv OR -s) n Forelle die.

**trove** [trəʊv] ⬦ treasure trove.

**trowel** ['traʊəl] n - **1.** [for the garden] Pflanzkelle die - **2.** [for cement, plaster] Kelle die.

**truancy** ['truːənsɪ] n (U) unentschuldigtes Fernbleiben (von der Schule).

**truant** ['truːənt] n [child] Schwänzer der, -in die; **to play ~** (die Schule) schwänzen.

**truce** [truːs] n ~ **(between)** Waffenstillstand der (zwischen (+ D)).

**truck** [trʌk] n - **1.** esp Am [lorry] Lastwagen der - **2.** RAIL Güterwaggon der ⬦ vt Am transportieren.

**truck driver** n esp Am Lastwagenfahrer der, -in die.

**trucker** ['trʌkəʳ] n Am Lastwagenfahrer der, -in die.

**truck farm** n Am Gemüsegärtnerei die.

**trucking** ['trʌkɪŋ] *n (U)* **Am** Lastwagentransport *der.*

**truck stop** *n* **Am** Fernfahrerlokal *das.*

**truculent** ['trʌkjʊlənt] *adj* aufbrausend.

**trudge** [trʌdʒ] *n* mühsamer Marsch ⬦ *vi* sich schleppen; [through snow, mud] stapfen.

**true** ['tru:] *adj* **- 1.** [factual] wahr; **to come ~** wahr werden **- 2.** [genuine] echt, wahr **- 3.** [faithful] getreu **- 4.** [precise, exact] gerade.

**true-life** *adj* lebensecht.

**truffle** ['trʌfl] *n* Trüffel *die.*

**truism** ['tru:ɪzm] *n* Binsenweisheit *die.*

**truly** ['tru:lɪ] *adv* **- 1.** wirklich **- 2.** *phr:* **yours ~** [at end of letter] mit freundlichen Grüßen; [me] ich.

**trump** [trʌmp] *n* [card] Trumpf *der* ⬦ *vt* übertrumpfen.

**trump card** *n fig* Trumpfkarte *die.*

**trumped-up** ['trʌmpt-] *adj pej* konstruiert.

**trumpet** ['trʌmpɪt] *n* **MUS** Trompete *die* ⬦ *vi* [elephant] trompeten.

**trumpeter** ['trʌmpɪtəʳ] *n* Trompeter *der,* -in *die.*

**truncate** [trʌŋ'keɪt] *vt fml* kürzen.

**truncheon** ['trʌntʃən] *n* Knüppel *der.*

**trundle** ['trʌndl] *vt* rollen ⬦ *vi* entlanglzockeln; [downhill] hinunterlzockeln.

**trunk** [trʌŋk] *n* **- 1.** [of tree] Stamm *der* **- 2.** **ANAT** Rumpf *der* **- 3.** [of elephant] Rüssel *der* **- 4.** [luggage] Schrankkoffer *der* **- 5.** **Am** [of car] Kofferraum *der.*

➡ **trunks** *npl* [for swimming] Badehose *die.*

**trunk call** *n* **Br** Ferngespräch *das.*

**trunk road** *n* **Br** Fernstraße *die.*

**truss** [trʌs] *n* **- 1.** **MED** Bruchband *das* **- 2.** **CONSTR** Fachwerk *das.*

**trust** [trʌst] *vt* **- 1.** [have confidence in] trauen (+ D), vertrauen (+ D); **to ~ sb to do sthg** jm zutrauen, etw zu tun; **~ you!** *iron* typisch für dich! **- 2.** [entrust] **to ~ sb with sthg** jm mit etw vertrauen **- 3.** *fml* [hope] **I ~ (that)** ich hoffe (, dass) ⬦ *n* **- 1.** *(U)* [faith] Vertrauen *das;* **~ in sb/sthg** Vertrauen zu jm/etw; **to put** OR **place one's ~ in sb/sthg** Vertrauen in jn/etw setzen; **to take sthg on ~** etw (einfach) glauben **- 2.** *(U)* [responsibility] Verantwortung *die* **- 3.** **FIN** Treuhandschaft *die;* **to hold in ~** treuhänderisch verwalten **- 4.** **COMM** Trust *der.*

**trust company** *n* Treuhandgesellschaft *die.*

**trusted** ['trʌstɪd] *adj* bewährt.

**trustee** [trʌs'ti:] *n* **- 1.** **FIN** & **LAW** Treuhänder *der,* -in *die* **- 2.** [manager of institution] Verwalter *der,* -in *die.*

**trusteeship** [ˌtrʌs'ti:ʃɪp] *n (U)* Treuhandschaft *die.*

**trust fund** *n* Treuhandvermögen *das.*

**trusting** ['trʌstɪŋ] *adj* vertrauensvoll.

**trustworthy** ['trʌstˌwɜːðɪ] *adj* vertrauenswürdig.

**trusty** ['trʌstɪ] *(compar* -ier; *superl* -iest) *adj hum* treu.

**truth** [tru:θ] *n* Wahrheit *die;* **to tell the ~** die Wahrheit sagen; **to tell the ~,** ... um die Wahrheit zu sagen, ...; **in (all) ~** in aller Aufrichtigkeit.

**truth drug** *n* Wahrheitsdroge *die.*

**truthful** ['tru:θfʊl] *n* ehrlich.

**try** [traɪ] *(pt* & *pp* -ied; *pl* -ies) *vt* **- 1.** [attempt] versuchen; **to ~ to do sthg** versuchen, etw zu tun **- 2.** [sample] probieren; [test] auslprobieren **- 3.** **LAW** [case] gerichtlich verhandeln; [criminal] vor Gericht stellen **- 4.** [tax, strain] auf die Probe stellen ⬦ *vi* versuchen; **to ~ for sthg** sich um etw bemühen ⬦ *n* [attempt & **SPORT**] Versuch *der;* **to give sthg a ~** etw mal versuchen; **to have a ~ at sthg** etw mal auslprobieren.

➡ **try on** *vt sep* [clothes] anlprobieren.

➡ **try out** *vt sep* auslprobieren.

**trying** ['traɪɪŋ] *adj* schwierig.

**try-out** *n inf* Erprobung *die;* [of vehicle] Probefahrt *die.*

**tsar** [zɑːʳ] *n* Zar *der.*

**T-shirt** *n* T-Shirt *das.*

**tsp.** *(abbr of* teaspoon) Tl.

**T-square** *n* Reißschiene *die.*

**TT** *abbr of* teetotal.

**tub** [tʌb] *n* **- 1.** [of margarine, ice cream] Becher *der* **- 2.** *inf* [bath] Wanne *die.*

**tuba** ['tju:bə] *n* Tuba *die.*

**tubby** ['tʌbɪ] *(compar* -ier; *superl* -iest) *adj inf* rundlich.

**tube** [tju:b] *n* **- 1.** [hollow cylinder - inflexible] Röhrchen *das,* Rohr *das;* [ - flexible] Schlauch *der* **- 2.** **ANAT** (bronchial) **~s** Bronchien *pl* **- 3.** [of toothpaste, glue] Tube *die* **- 4.** **Br** [underground train] U-Bahn *die;* **the ~** [underground system] die U-Bahn; **by ~** mit der U-Bahn.

**tubeless** ['tju:blɪs] *adj* schlauchlos.

**tuber** ['tju:bəʳ] *n* Knolle *die.*

**tuberculosis** [tju:ˌbɜːkjʊ'ləʊsɪs] *n* Tuberkulose *die.*

**tube station** *n* **Br** U-Bahnstation *die.*

**tubing** ['tju:bɪŋ] *n (U)* [flexible] Schläuche *pl;* [inflexible] Rohre *pl.*

**tubular** ['tju:bjʊləʳ] *adj* Röhren-.

**TUC** *n abbr of* **Trades Union Congress.**

**tuck** [tʌk] *n* **SEWING** Abnäher *der* ⬦ *vt* [place neatly] stecken.

**T**

➤ **tuck away** vt sep [store] verstecken; **to be ~ed away** [hidden] abseits liegen.

➤ **tuck in** vt sep - **1.** [child, patient] zuldecken - **2.** [clothes] hineinlstecken ⬦ vi inf zullangen.

➤ **tuck up** vt sep zuldecken.

**tuck shop** n Br Schulkiosk der.

**Tudor** ['tjuːdəʳ] adj Tudor- ⬦ n: **the ~s** das Geschlecht der Tudor.

**Tue., Tues.** (abbr of Tuesday) Di.

**Tuesday** ['tjuːzdɪ] n Dienstag der; see also **Saturday**.

**tuft** [tʌft] n Büschel das.

**tug** [tʌg] (pt & pp -ged; cont -ging) n - **1.** [pull] Ruck der - **2.** [boat] Schleppkahn der ⬦ vt (ruckartig) ziehen; **she ~ged his sleeve** sie zupfte ihn am Ärmel ⬦ vi: **to ~ at sthg** (ruckartig) an etw (D) ziehen.

**tugboat** ['tʌgbəʊt] n Schleppkahn der.

**tug-of-love** n Br inf Tauziehen das um das Sorgerecht für die Kinder.

**tug-of-war** n Tauziehen das.

**tuition** [tjuːˈɪʃn] n (U) Unterricht der.

**tulip** ['tjuːlɪp] n Tulpe die.

**tulle** [tjuːl] n Tüll der.

**tumble** ['tʌmbl] vi - **1.** [person, prices] fallen - **2.** [water] stürzen ⬦ n Sturz der.

➤ **tumble down** vi [building] einlstürzen.

➤ **tumble to** vt fus Br inf kapieren.

**tumbledown** ['tʌmbldaʊn] adj baufällig.

**tumble-dry** vt im Wäschetrockner trocknen.

**tumble-dryer** [-ˌdraɪəʳ] n Wäschetrockner der.

**tumbler** ['tʌmbləʳ] n [glass - short] Whiskyglas das; [ - tall] Becherglas das.

**tummy** ['tʌmɪ] (pl -ies) n inf - **1.** [outside of stomach] Bauch der - **2.** [inside of stomach] Magen der.

**tumour** Br, **tumor** Am ['tjuːməʳ] n Tumor der.

**tumult** ['tjuːmʌlt] n fml Tumult der.

**tumultuous** ['tjuːmʌltjʊəs] adj fml stürmisch.

**tuna** [Br 'tjuːnə, Am 'tuːnə] (pl inv OR -s), **tuna fish** (pl tuna fish) n Thunfisch der.

**tundra** ['tʌndrə] n Tundra die.

**tune** [tjuːn] n [song, melody] Melodie die; **to the ~ of** fig in Höhe von; **to change one's ~** inf seine Meinung ändern ⬦ vt - **1.** MUS stimmen - **2.** [engine, RADIO & TV] einlstellen; **to ~ sthg to** sthg etw auf etw (A) einlstellen ⬦ vi RADIO & TV: **to ~ to sthg** etw einlstellen.

➤ **tune in** vi RADIO & TV einlschalten; **to ~ in to** sthg etw einlschalten.

➤ **tune up** vi MUS stimmen.

➤ **in tune** ⬦ adj MUS (richtig) gestimmt ⬦ adv - **1.** MUS richtig - **2.** [in agreement]: **to be in ~ with** sb/sthg mit jm/etw im Einklang stehen.

➤ **out of tune** ⬦ adj MUS verstimmt ⬦ adv - **1.** MUS falsch - **2.** [not in agreement]: **out of ~ with** sb/sthg mit jm/etw nicht im Einklang stehen; **the government are out of ~ with the wishes of the population** die Regierung registriert die Wünsche der Bevölkerung nicht mehr.

**tuneful** ['tjuːnfʊl] adj melodisch.

**tuneless** ['tjuːnlɪs] adj unmelodisch.

**tuner** ['tjuːnəʳ] n - **1.** RADIO & TV Tuner der - **2.** MUS Stimmer der, -in die.

**tuner amplifier** n Receiver der.

**tungsten** ['tʌŋstən] n (U) Wolfram das ⬦ comp Wolfram-.

**tunic** ['tjuːnɪk] n [clothing] Hemdbluse die; [of uniform] Uniformjacke die.

**tuning fork** ['tjuːnɪŋ-] n Stimmgabel die.

**Tunisia** [tjuːˈnɪzɪə] n Tunesien das; **in ~** in Tunesien.

**tunnel** ['tʌnl] (Br pt & pp -led; cont -ling, Am pt & pp -ed; cont -ing) n Tunnel der ⬦ vi graben; **they tunnelled through the mountain** sie trieben OR gruben einen Tunnel durch den Berg.

**tunnel vision** n (U) - **1.** MED Gesichtsfeldeinengung die - **2.** fig & pej [narrow-mindedness] Engstirnigkeit die.

**tunny** ['tʌnɪ] (pl inv OR -ies) n [fish] Thunfisch der.

**tuppence** ['tʌpəns] n Br dated zwei Pence pl.

**turban** ['tɜːbən] n [man's headdress] Turban der.

**turbid** ['tɜːbɪd] adj [mucky] trübe.

**turbine** ['tɜːbaɪn] n Turbine die.

**turbo** ['tɜːbəʊ] (pl -s) n Turbo der.

**turbocharged** ['tɜːbəʊtʃɑːdʒd] adj mit Turboaufladung.

**turbojet** [ˌtɜːbəʊˈdʒet] n - **1.** [engine] Turbinenluftstrahltriebwerk das - **2.** [plane] Düsenflugzeug das.

**turboprop** [ˌtɜːbəʊˈprɒp] n - **1.** [engine] Turbo-Prop-Triebwerk das - **2.** [plane] Turbo-Prop-Flugzeug das.

**turbot** ['tɜːbət] (pl inv OR -s) n Steinbutt der.

**turbulence** ['tɜːbjʊləns] n (U) lit & fig Turbulenz die.

**turbulent** ['tɜːbjʊlənt] adj - **1.** [period of time & PHYS] turbulent - **2.** [winds, weather] stürmisch - **3.** [crowd] ungestüm.

**tureen** [təˈriːn] n Suppenterrine die.

**turf** [tɜːf] (pl -s OR turves) n - **1.** (U) [grass surface] Rasen der - **2.** [clod] Grassode die ⬦ vt [with grass] mit Rollrasen bedecken.

➤ **turf out** vt sep Br inf [evict] rauslschmeißen.

**turf accountant** n Br fml Buchmacher der.

**turgid** ['tɜːdʒɪd] *adj fml* [style, prose] geschwollen.

**Turk** [tɜːk] *n* Türke *der*, -kin *die*.

**turkey** ['tɜːkɪ] (*pl* **turkeys**) *n* Truthahn *der*.

**Turkey** ['tɜːkɪ] *n* Türkei *die; in ~* in der Türkei.

**Turkish** ['tɜːkɪʃ] *adj* türkisch ◇ *n* [language] Türkisch(e) *das* ◇ *npl:* **the ~** die Türken *pl*.

**Turkish bath** *n* türkisches Bad.

**Turkish delight** *n* (U) türkischer Honig.

**Turkmenian** [ˌtɜːkˈmenɪən] *adj* turkmenisch.

**Turkmenistan** [ˌtɜːkmenɪˈstɑːn] *n* Turkmenistan *nt*.

**turmeric** ['tɜːmərɪk] *n* (U) [spice] Gelbwurz *die*.

**turmoil** ['tɜːmɔɪl] *n* (U) Aufruhr *der*.

**turn** [tɜːn] *n* **- 1.** [in road, river] Kurve *die* **- 2.** [of knob, key, switch] Drehung *die* **- 3.** [change] Wendung *die;* **to take a ~ for the better/worse** sich zum Guten/Schlechten wenden **- 4.** [in game, order]: **it's my ~** ich bin an der Reihe, ich bin dran; **in ~** der Reihe nach; **to take (it in) ~s to do sthg** etw abwechselnd tun **- 5.** [of year, decade] Wende *die;* **the ~ of the century** die Jahrhundertwende **- 6.** [performance] Nummer *die* **- 7.** MED Anfall *der* **- 8.** *phr:* **to do sb a good ~** jm etwas Gutes tun ◇ *vt* **- 1.** [key, head, wheel, chair] drehen **- 2.** [corner] biegen um **- 3.** [page, omelette] wenden **- 4.** [direct]: **to ~ one's attention to sb/sthg** jm/etw seine Aufmerksamkeit zuwenden **- 5.** [transform]: **to ~ sthg into sthg** etw in etw (A) verwandeln **- 6.** [make]: **to ~ sthg red** etw rot werden lassen; **to ~ sthg inside out** das Innere von etw nach außen drehen ◇ *vi* **- 1.** [change direction] wenden; **his thoughts ~ed to his family** er dachte an seine Familie **- 2.** [wheel, knob, head, person] sich drehen **- 3.** [in book]: **to ~ to sthg** etw auf|schlagen **- 4.** [for consolation, advice]: **to ~ to sb/sthg** sich an jn/etw wenden **- 5.** [become] werden; **to ~ into sthg** sich in etw (A) verwandeln.

◆ **turn against** *vt fus* sich wenden gegen.

◆ **turn around** *vt sep* & *vi* = **turn round**.

◆ **turn away** *vt sep* [refuse entry to] ab|weisen ◇ *vi* sich ab|wenden.

◆ **turn back** *vt sep* **- 1.** [force to return] zurück|schicken **- 2.** [fold back] auf|schlagen ◇ *vi* [return] um|kehren.

◆ **turn down** *vt sep* **- 1.** [reject] ab|weisen, ab|lehnen **- 2.** [heating, lighting, sound] herunter|drehen.

◆ **turn in** *vi inf* [go to bed] sich aufs Ohr legen.

◆ **turn off** *vt fus* [leave - road, path] ab|biegen von ◇ *vt sep* [switch off] ab|schalten ◇ *vi* [leave path, road] ab|biegen.

◆ **turn on** *vt sep* **- 1.** [make work] ein|schalten **- 2.** *inf* [excite sexually] an|machen ◇ *vt fus* [attack] los|gehen auf (+ A).

◆ **turn out** *vt sep* **- 1.** [switch off] aus-

schalten **- 2.** *inf* [produce] produzieren **- 3.** [eject] hinaus|werfen **- 4.** [empty] leeren ◇ *vt fus:* **to ~ out to be sthg** sich als etw erweisen; **it ~s out that ...** es stellt sich heraus, dass ... ◇ *vi* **- 1.** [end up]: **it will ~ out all right** es wird (schon) alles in Ordnung kommen **- 2.** [attend]: **to ~ out (for sthg)** (zu etw) erscheinen.

◆ **turn over** *vt sep* **- 1.** [playing card, stone, page] um|drehen **- 2.** [consider] überdenken **- 3.** [hand over]: **to ~ sb/sthg over to sb** jm jn/etw über|geben ◇ *vi* **- 1.** [roll over] sich um|drehen **- 2.** *Br* TV um|schalten.

◆ **turn round** *vt sep* **- 1.** [rotate] um|drehen **- 2.** [words, sentence] um|drehen **- 3.** [quantity of work] bearbeiten **- 4.** [company]: **the new boss managed to ~ things round** der neue Chef schaffte es, das Steuer herumzureißen ◇ *vi* [person] sich um|drehen.

◆ **turn up** *vt sep* [heat, lighting, radio, TV] auf|drehen ◇ *vi inf* **- 1.** [appear, arrive, be found] auf|tauchen **- 2.** [happen] sich ergeben.

**turnabout** ['tɜːnəbaʊt] *n* Kehrtwendung *die*.

**turnaround** *n* Am = **turnround**.

**turncoat** ['tɜːnkəʊt] *n pej* Überläufer *der*, -in *die*.

**turning** ['tɜːnɪŋ] *n* [side road] Abzweigung *die*.

**turning circle** *n* Wendekreis *der*.

**turning point** *n* Wendepunkt *der*.

**turnip** ['tɜːnɪp] *n* Rübe *die*.

**turnout** ['tɜːnaʊt] *n* [attendance] Teilnahme *die*.

**turnover** ['tɜːnˌəʊvə'] *n* (U) **- 1.** [of personnel] Fluktuation *die* **- 2.** FIN Umsatz *der*.

**turnpike** ['tɜːnpaɪk] *n* Am gebührenpflichtige Autobahn.

**turnround** *Br* ['tɜːnraʊnd], **turnaround** *Am* ['tɜːnəraʊnd] *n* **- 1.** COMM Bearbeitungszeit *die* **- 2.** [change] Umschwung *der*.

**turn signal lever** *n* Am Blinkerhebel *der*.

**turnstile** ['tɜːnstaɪl] *n* Drehkreuz *das*.

**turntable** ['tɜːnˌteɪbl] *n* [on record player] Plattenteller *der*.

**turn-up** *n* Br **- 1.** [on trousers] Aufschlag *der* **- 2.** *inf* [surprise]: **a ~ for the books** eine echte Überraschung.

**turpentine** ['tɜːpəntaɪn] *n* (U) Terpentin *das*.

**turps** [tɜːps] *n Br inf* Terpentin *das*.

**turquoise** ['tɜːkwɔɪz] *adj* türkis ◇ *n* **- 1.** [mineral, gem] Türkis *der* **- 2.** [colour] Türkis *das*.

**turret** ['tʌrɪt] *n* [on castle] Eckturm *der*.

**turtle** ['tɜːtl] (*pl inv* OR **-s**) *n* Schildkröte *die*.

**turtledove** ['tɜːtldʌv] *n* Turteltaube *die*.

**turtleneck** ['tɜːtlnek] *n* **- 1.** [garment] Rollkragenpullover *der* **- 2.** [neck] Rollkragen *der*.

**turves** [tɜːvz] *pl* ⊏▷ **turf**.

**tusk** [tʌsk] *n* Stoßzahn *der*.

**T**

**tussle** ['tʌsl] n Gerangel das <> vi: **to ~ over
sthg** lit (sich) um etw (A) raufen; fig eine Auseinandersetzung wegen etw haben.

**tut** [tʌt] excl na!

**tutor** ['tju:tə'] n - **1.** [private] Privatlehrer der,
-in die - **2.** UNIV Tutor der, -in die <> vt: **to ~ sb in
sthg** jn in etw (D) unterrichten <> vi unterrichten.

**tutorial** [tju:'tɔ:rɪəl] adj Tutoren- <> n Tuto-
rium das.

**tutu** ['tu:tu:] n Ballettröckchen das.

**tux** ['tʌks] n inf Smoking der.

**tuxedo** [tʌk'si:dəʊ] (pl -s) n Am Smoking der.

**TV** (abbr of television) n - **1.** (U) [medium, industry]
Fernsehen das; **on ~** im Fernsehen - **2.** [ap-
paratus] Fernseher der <> comp Fernseh-.

**TV dinner** n Fertiggericht das.

**twaddle** ['twɒdl] n inf pej Quatsch der.

**twang** [twæŋ] n - **1.** [of spring, guitar string] vib-
rierender Ton; [of rubber band] schnappen-
der Ton - **2.** [accent] Tonfall der <> vt zupfen
<> vi vibrieren.

**tweak** [twi:k] vt inf: **to ~ sb's ear** jn am Ohr ziehen.

**twee** [twi:] adj Br pej kitschig.

**tweed** [twi:d] Tweed der <> comp Tweed-.

**tweet** [twi:t] vi inf piepsen.

**tweezers** ['twi:zəz] npl Pinzette die.

**twelfth** [twelfθ] num zwölfte, -r, -s; see also
sixth.

**Twelfth Night** n Heiligedreikönigstag der.

**twelve** [twelv] num zwölf; see also six.

**twentieth** ['twentɪəθ] num zwanzigste, -r, -s;
see also sixth.

**twenty** ['twentɪ] (pl -ies) num zwanzig; see also
sixty.

**twenty-twenty vision** n (U) hundertpro-
zentige Sehschärfe.

**twerp** [twɜ:p] n Br inf Depp der.

**twice** [twaɪs] adv zweimal.

**twiddle** ['twɪdl] vt [knob, button] herumdrehen an (+ D) <> vi: **to ~ with sthg** an etw (D)
herumspielen.

**twig** [twɪg] n Zweig der.

**twilight** ['twaɪlaɪt] n - **1.** [in evening] Dämmerung die - **2.** fig [last stages, end] Abend der.

**twin** [twɪn] adj - **1.** [child, sibling] Zwillings-;
**~ girls** Zwillingsschwestern - **2.** [towns] Part-
ner-; [towers] Doppel-; **~ beds** zwei Einzel-
betten <> n [sibling] Zwilling der.

**twin-bedded** [-'bedɪd] adj Zweibett-.

**twin carburettor** n Doppelvergaser der.

**twine** [twaɪn] n (U) Schnur die <> vt: **to ~ sthg
round sthg** etw um etw wickeln.

**twin-engined** [-'endʒɪnd] adj zweimotorig.

**twinge** [twɪndʒ] n Stich der.

**twinkie** ['twɪŋkɪ] n Am [cake] mit Schlagsahne
gefülltes längliches Törtchen aus Biskuitteig.

**twinkle** ['twɪŋkl] n Funkeln das <> vi funkeln.

**twin room** n Zweibettzimmer das.

**twin set** n Br Twinset das.

**twin town** n Partnerstadt die.

**twin tub** n Waschmaschine die mit zwei se-
paraten Trommeln.

**twirl** [twɜ:l] vt - **1.** [spin] herumwirbeln; **he
~ed his partner** er wirbelte seine Partnerin
herum - **2.** [twist, moustache] zwirbeln <> vi
wirbeln.

**twist** [twɪst] n - **1.** [in road, staircase, river] Biegung die - **2.** [in rope]: **there's a ~ in the rope** das
Seil ist verdreht - **3.** [turn, twirl] Drehung die;
**to give sthg a ~** etw drehen - **4.** fig [in plot]
Wendung die <> vt - **1.** [gen] verdrehen
- **2.** [lid, knob, dial] drehen - **3.** MED [sprain]: **to
~ one's ankle** sich (D) den Fuß verrenken
<> vi - **1.** [road, river] sich schlängeln - **2.** [body]
sich winden; [face] sich verziehen.

**twisted** ['twɪstɪd] adj pej [person, sense of humour]
krank; [logic] verdreht.

**twister** ['twɪstə'] n Am Tornado der.

**twisty** ['twɪstɪ] (compar -ier; superl -iest) adj inf
gewunden.

**twit** [twɪt] n Br inf Trottel der.

**twitch** [twɪtʃ] n Zucken das <> vt [ears, nose] zucken mit <> vi zucken.

**twitter** ['twɪtə'] vi - **1.** [bird] zwitschern - **2.** pej
[person] schnattern.

**two** [tu:] num zwei; **in ~** in zwei Teile; see also
six.

**two-bit** adj Am pej: **a ~ gangster** ein mieser
kleiner Gangster.

**two-dimensional** [-dɪ'menʃnl] adj - **1.** [pic-
ture] zweidimensional - **2.** pej [report, descrip-
tion] oberflächlich.

**two-door** adj [car] zweitürig.

**twofaced** [ˌtu:'feɪst] adj pej falsch.

**twofold** ['tu:fəʊld] adj & adv zweifach.

**two-handed** [-'hændɪd] adj [sword, backhand]
beidhändig.

**two-piece** adj [suit, swimsuit] zweiteilig.

**two-ply** adj zweilagig.

**two-seater** n Zweisitzer der.

**twosome** ['tu:səm] n inf Paar das.

**two-stroke** adj Zweitakt- <> n Zweitakter
der.

**two-time** vt inf betrügen.

**two-tone** adj zweifarbig.

**two-way** adj - **1.** [in both directions] in beiden

Richtungen - **2.** ᴛᴇʟᴇᴄ: **~ radio** Funksprechge-
rät *das.*

**TX** *abk für Texas, in Postanschrift verwendet.*

**tycoon** [taɪˈkuːn] *n* Magnat *der.*

**Tyne and Wear** [ˌtaɪnənˈwɪəʳ] *n Gebiet um
Newcastle.*

**type** [taɪp] *n* - **1.** [sort, kind] Art *die;* **what ~ of car
are you looking for?** was für ein Auto suchen
Sie denn? - **2.** [in classification] Gruppe *die*
- **3.** [referring to person] Typ *der;* **he's/she's not my
~ inf** er/sie ist nicht mein Typ - **4.** *(U)* ᴛʏᴘᴏ
Schrift *die* <> *vt* & *vi* tippen.
➤ **type up** *vt sep* abitippen.

**typecast** [ˈtaɪpkɑːst] *(pt* & *pp* **typecast)** *vt*
festilegen (auf eine bestimmte Rolle); **to be
~ as sthg** auf etw *(A)* festgelegt werden.

**typeface** [ˈtaɪpfeɪs] *n* ᴛʏᴘᴏ Schrift *die.*

**typescript** [ˈtaɪpskrɪpt] *n* Manuskript *das.*

**typeset** [ˈtaɪpset] *(pt* & *pp* **typeset;** *cont* **-ting)**
*vt* ᴛʏᴘᴏ setzen.

**typesetter** [ˈtaɪpsetəʳ] *n* [company] Schriftset-
zer *der.*

**typesetting** [ˈtaɪpsetɪŋ] *n* Schriftsatz *der.*

**typewriter** [ˈtaɪpˌraɪtəʳ] *n* Schreibmaschine
*die.*

**typhoid (fever)** [ˈtaɪfɔɪd-] *n (U)* Typhus *der.*

**typhoon** [taɪˈfuːn] *n* Taifun *der.*

**typhus** [ˈtaɪfəs] *n (U)* Flecktyphus *der.*

**typical** [ˈtɪpɪkl] *adj* typisch; **~ of sb/sthg** typisch für jn/etw.

**typically** [ˈtɪpɪklɪ] *adv* - **1.** [usually] typischer-
weise - **2.** [characteristically]: **~ German!** typisch
Deutsch!

**typify** [ˈtɪpɪfaɪ] *(pt* & *pp* **-ied)** *vt* - **1.** [be characteristic of] bezeichnend sein für - **2.** [embody, sym-
bolize] verkörpern.

**typing** [ˈtaɪpɪŋ] *n* Tippen *das,* Maschineschreiben *das.*

**typing error** *n* Tippfehler *der.*

**typing pool** *n* Schreibzentrale *die.*

**typist** [ˈtaɪpɪst] *n* Schreibkraft *die.*

**typo** [ˈtaɪpəʊ] *n inf* Druckfehler *der.*

**typographic(al) error** [ˌtaɪpəˈgræfɪk(l)-] *n*
Druckfehler *der.*

**typography** [taɪˈpɒgrəfɪ] *n* Typografie *die.*

**tyrannical** [tɪˈrænɪkl] *adj* tyrannisch.

**tyranny** [ˈtɪrənɪ] *n (U)* [of person, government] Ty-
rannei *die.*

**tyrant** [ˈtaɪrənt] *n* Tyrann *der,* -in *die.*

**tyre** *Br,* **tire** *Am* [ˈtaɪəʳ] *n* Reifen *der.*

**tyre pressure** *n (U)* Reifendruck *der.*

**Tyrol, Tirol** [ˈtɪrɒl] *n:* **in the ~** in Tirol.

**Tyrolean** [tɪrəˈliːən], **Tyrolese** [ˌtɪrəˈliːz] *adj*
Tiroler- <> *n* Tiroler *der,* -in *die.*

**tzar** [zɑːʳ] *n* = **tsar.**

**u** *(pl* **u's** ᴏʀ **us)**, **U** *(pl* **U's** ᴏʀ **Us)** [juː] *n* [letter] u *das,*
U *das.*

**UAE** *n abbr of* **United Arab Emirates.**

**UB40** *(abbr of* **unemployment benefit form
40)** *n Arbeitslosenbescheinigung in Großbritannien.*

**U-bend** *n* U-Bogen *der.*

**ubiquitous** [juːˈbɪkwɪtəs] *adj fml* allgegenwärtig.

**UCAS** [ˈjuːkæs] *(abbr of* **Universities and Colleges Admissions Service)** *n* ≈ ZVS *die.*

**UDA** *(abbr of* **Ulster Defence Association)** *n
protestantische paramilitärische Organisation in Nordirland.*

**udder** [ˈʌdəʳ] *n* Euter *der.*

**UDI** *(abbr of* **unilateral declaration of independence)** *n* einseitige Unabhängigkeitserklärung.

**UEFA** [juːˈeɪfə] *(abbr of* **Union of European
Football Associations)** *n* UEFA *die.*

**UFO** *(abbr of* **unidentified flying object)** *n* UFO
*das.*

**Uganda** [juːˈgændə] *n* Uganda *nt.*

**Ugandan** [juːˈgændən] *adj* ugandisch <> *n*
[person] Ugander *der,* -in *die.*

**ugh** [ʌg] *excl* bah!

**ugliness** [ˈʌglɪnɪs] *n (U)* - **1.** [unattractiveness]
Hässlichkeit *die* - **2.** *fig* [unpleasantness] Uner-
freulichkeit *die.*

**ugly** [ˈʌglɪ] *(compar* **-ier;** *superl* **-iest)** *adj* - **1.** [un-
attractive] hässlich - **2.** *fig* [unpleasant] unerfreulich.

**UHF** *(abbr of* **ultra-high frequency)** *n* UHF.

**UHT** *(abbr of* **ultra-heat treated)** *adj* ultrahoch
erhitzt; **~ milk** H-Milch *die.*

**UK** *n abbr of* **United Kingdom.**

**Ukraine** [juːˈkreɪn] *n:* **the ~** die Ukraine; **in the
~** in der Ukraine.

**Ukrainian** [juːˈkreɪnjən] *adj* ukrainisch <> *n*
- **1.** [person] Ukrainer *der,* -in *die* - **2.** [language]
Ukrainisch(e) *das.*

**ukulele** [ˌjuːkəˈleɪlɪ] *n* Ukulele *die.*

**ulcer** [ˈʌlsəʳ] *n* - **1.** [in stomach] Geschwür *das*
- **2.** [in mouth, stomach] Aphthe *die.*

**U**

**ulcerated** [ˈʌlsəreɪtɪd] *adj* geschwürig.

**Ulster** [ˈʌlstəʳ] *n* Ulster *nt*.

**Ulsterman** [ˈʌlstəmən] (*pl* **-men** [-mən]) *n* Mann *der* aus Ulster.

**Ulster Unionist Party** *n* nordirische, *hauptsächlich protestantische Partei, die sich für den Verbleib von Ulster in Großbritannien einsetzt.*

**Ulsterwoman** [ˈʌlstəwumən] (*pl* **-women** [-wɪmɪn]) *n* Frau *die* aus Ulster.

**ulterior** [ʌlˈtɪərɪəʳ] *adj:* **an ~ motive** Hintergedanke *der.*

**ultimata** [ˌʌltɪˈmeɪtə] *pl* ⟶ ultimatum.

**ultimate** [ˈʌltɪmət] *adj* **- 1.** [final, long-term] letzte, -r, -s **- 2.** [most powerful] absolut ◇ *n:* **the ~ in sthg** das Höchste an etw (D).

**ultimately** [ˈʌltɪmətlɪ] *adv* [finally, in the long term] letztlich.

**ultimatum** [ˌʌltɪˈmeɪtəm] (*pl* **-tums** OR **-ta** [-tə]) *n* Ultimatum *das.*

**ultra-** [ˈʌltrə] *prefix* ultra-.

**ultramarine** [ˌʌltrəməˈriːn] *adj* Ultramarin-.

**ultrasonic** [ˌʌltrəˈsɒnɪk] *adj* Ultraschall-.

**ultrasound** [ˈʌltrəsaʊnd] *n* Ultraschall *der.*

**ultraviolet** [ˌʌltrəˈvaɪələt] *adj* ultraviolett.

**um** [ʌm] *excl* äh.

**umbilical cord** [ʌmˈbɪlɪkl-] *n* Nabelschnur *die.*

**umbrage** [ˈʌmbrɪdʒ] *n:* **to take ~ (at sthg)** (an etw (D)) Anstoß nehmen.

**umbrella** [ʌmˈbrelə] *n* **- 1.** [portable] Regenschirm *der* **- 2.** [fixed] Sonnenschirm *der* ◇ *adj* Schirm-.

**umpire** [ˈʌmpaɪəʳ] *n* Schiedsrichter *der,* -in *die* ◇ *vt* Schiedsrichter sein bei ◇ *vi* Schiedsrichter sein

**umpteen** [ˌʌmpˈtiːn] *num adj* **inf** zigmal.

**umpteenth** [ˌʌmpˈtiːnθ] *num adj* **inf: for the ~ time** zum x-ten Mal.

**UN** (*abbr of* **United Nations**) *n* UNO *die,* UN *die.*

**unabashed** [ˌʌnəˈbæʃt] *adj* unbeeindruckt.

**unabated** [ˌʌnəˈbeɪtɪd] *adj* unvermindert.

**unable** [ʌnˈeɪbl] *adj:* **to be ~ to do sthg** außer Stande sein, etw zu tun.

**unabridged** [ˌʌnəˈbrɪdʒd] *adj* ungekürzt.

**unacceptable** [ˌʌnəkˈseptəbl] *adj* unannehmbar.

**unaccompanied** [ˌʌnəˈkʌmpənɪd] *adj* [luggage] aufgegeben; [child, song] ohne Begleitung.

**unaccountable** [ˌʌnəˈkaʊntəbl] *adj* **- 1.** [inexplicable] unerklärlich **- 2.** [not responsible]: **~ for sthg** nicht verantwortlich für etw; **to be ~ to sb** sich jm gegenüber nicht verantworten müssen.

**unaccountably** [ˌʌnəˈkaʊntəblɪ] *adv* [inexplicably] unerklärlicherweise; **she felt ~ weak** sie fühlte sich unerklärlich schwach.

**unaccounted** [ˌʌnəˈkaʊntɪd] *adj:* **~ for** unauffindbar.

**unaccustomed** [ˌʌnəˈkʌstəmd] *adj* **- 1.** [unused]: **to be ~ to sthg** an etw (A) nicht gewöhnt sein; **to be ~ to doing sthg** nicht daran gewöhnt sein, etw zu tun **- 2.** **fml** [not usual] ungewohnt.

**unacquainted** [ˌʌnəˈkweɪntɪd] *adj:* **to be ~ with sb/sthg** jn/etw nicht kennen.

**unadulterated** [ˌʌnəˈdʌltəreɪtɪd] *adj* rein.

**unadventurous** [ˌʌnədˈventʃərəs] *adj* einfallslos.

**unaffected** [ˌʌnəˈfektɪd] *adj* **- 1.** [unchanged] unbeeinflusst; **~ by sthg** von etw unbeeinflusst; **the city remains ~ by the flooding** die Stadt ist von der Überschwemmung nicht betroffen; **the children were ~ by their experience of war** die Kriegserfahrung hinterließ bei den Kindern keinen seelischen Schaden **- 2.** [natural] natürlich.

**unafraid** [ˌʌnəˈfreɪd] *adj* unerschrocken.

**unaided** [ʌnˈeɪdɪd] *adj* & *adv* ohne fremde Hilfe.

**unambiguous** [ˌʌnæmˈbɪgjuəs] *adj* unzweideutig.

**un-American** [ˈʌn-] *adj* unamerikanisch.

**unanimity** [ˌjuːnəˈnɪmətɪ] *n* **fml** Einstimmigkeit *die.*

**unanimous** [juːˈnænɪməs] *adj* einstimmig.

**unanimously** [juːˈnænɪməslɪ] *adv* einstimmig.

**unannounced** [ˌʌnəˈnaʊnst] *adj* & *adv* unangemeldet.

**unanswered** [ʌnˈɑːnsəd] *adj* unbeantwortet.

**unappealing** [ˌʌnəˈpiːlɪŋ] *adj* nicht reizvoll.

**unappetizing, -ising** [ʌnˈæpɪtaɪzɪŋ] *adj* unappetitlich.

**unappreciated** [ˌʌnəˈpriːʃɪeɪtɪd] *adj* ungewürdigt.

**unappreciative** [ˌʌnəˈpriːʃɪətɪv] *adj:* **to be ~ of sthg** etw nicht zu schätzen wissen.

**unapproachable** [ˌʌnəˈprəʊtʃəbl] *adj* [person] unnahbar.

**unarmed** [ʌnˈɑːmd] *adj* unbewaffnet.

**unarmed combat** *n* (U) Nahkampf *der* ohne Waffe.

**unashamed** [ˌʌnəˈʃeɪmd] *adj* schamlos.

**unassisted** [ˌʌnəˈsɪstɪd] *adj* ohne fremde Hilfe.

**unassuming** [ˌʌnəˈsjuːmɪŋ] *adj* bescheiden.

**unattached** [ˌʌnəˈtætʃt] *adj* **- 1.** [not fastened,

linked]: ~ **to sthg** unabhängig von etw
**- 2.** [without partner] ungebunden.

**unattainable** [ˌʌnəˈteɪnəbl] *adj* unerreichbar.

**unattended** [ˌʌnəˈtendɪd] *adj* unbeaufsichtigt.

**unattractive** [ˌʌnəˈtræktɪv] *adj* unattraktiv.

**unauthorized, -ised** [ˌʌnˈɔːθəraɪzd] *adj* unrechtmäßig; [biography] nicht autorisiert.

**unavailable** [ˌʌnəˈveɪləbl] *adj* nicht verfügbar; [person] nicht zu erreichen.

**unavoidable** [ˌʌnəˈvɔɪdəbl] *adj* unvermeidlich.

**unavoidably** [ˌʌnəˈvɔɪdəblɪ] *adj:* **he was ~ de-
tained** er wurde leider aufgehalten.

**unaware** [ˌʌnəˈweəʳ] *adj:* **to be ~ of sthg** sich *(D)*
einer Sache *(G)* nicht bewusst sein; **she was
~ of my presence** sie bemerkte mich nicht.

**unawares** [ˌʌnəˈweəz] *adv:* **to catch** OR **take sb ~**
jn überraschen.

**unbalanced** [ˌʌnˈbælənst] *adj* **- 1.** [biased] unausgewogen **- 2.** [deranged] psychisch labil.

**unbearable** [ʌnˈbeərəbl] *adj* unerträglich.

**unbearably** [ʌnˈbeərəblɪ] *adv* unerträglich.

**unbeatable** [ˌʌnˈbiːtəbl] *adj* unschlagbar.

**unbecoming** [ˌʌnbɪˈkʌmɪŋ] *adj fml* [unattractive]
unvorteilhaft.

**unbeknown(st)** [ˌʌnbɪˈnəʊn(st)] *adv:* **~ to him**
ohne sein Wissen; **~ to her mother** ohne Wissen ihrer Mutter.

**unbelievable** [ˌʌnbɪˈliːvəbl] *adj* unglaublich.

**unbelievably** [ˌʌnbɪˈliːvəblɪ] *adv* [extremely] unglaublich.

**unbend** [ˌʌnˈbend] *(pt & pp* **unbent)** *vi* [relax]
sich auslstrecken.

**unbending** [ˌʌnˈbendɪŋ] *adj* [intransigent] unbeugsam.

**unbent** [ˌʌnˈbent] *pt & pp* ▷ **unbend.**

**unbia(s)sed** [ˌʌnˈbaɪəst] *adj* unvoreingenommen.

**unblemished** [ˌʌnˈblemɪʃt] *adj fig* makellos.

**unblock** [ˌʌnˈblɒk] *vt* frei machen.

**unbolt** [ˌʌnˈbəʊlt] *vt* [door] entriegeln.

**unborn** [ˌʌnˈbɔːn] *adj* [child] ungeboren.

**unbreakable** [ˌʌnˈbreɪkəbl] *adj* unzerbrechlich.

**unbridled** [ˌʌnˈbraɪdld] *adj* ungezügelt.

**unbuckle** [ˌʌnˈbʌkl] *vt* auf lschnallen.

**unbutton** [ˌʌnˈbʌtn] *vt* auf lknöpfen.

**uncalled-for** [ˌʌnˈkɔːld-] *adj* unnötig.

**uncanny** [ʌnˈkænɪ] *(compar* **-ier;** *superl* **-iest)** *adj*
unheimlich.

**uncared-for** [ˌʌnˈkeəd-] *adj* vernachlässigt.

**uncaring** [ˌʌnˈkeərɪŋ] *adj* gleichgültig; [parent]
lieblos.

**unceasing** [ˌʌnˈsiːsɪŋ] *adj fml* beständig.

**unceremonious** [ˈʌnˌserɪˈməʊnjəs] *adj* [abrupt]
brüsk.

**unceremoniously** [ˈʌnˌserɪˈməʊnjəslɪ] *adj*
[abruptly] brüsk.

**uncertain** [ʌnˈsɜːtn] *adj* **- 1.** [person, plans] unsicher; **in no ~ terms** unmissverständlich
**- 2.** [weather] unvorhersehbar; [future] ungewiss **- 3.** [cause, motive] unklar.

**unchain** [ˌʌnˈtʃeɪn] *vt* [bicycle] auf lschliessen;
[prisoner] die Ketten ablnehmen *(+ D).*

**unchallenged** [ˌʌnˈtʃælɪndʒd] *adj* [authority,
leadership, version] unangefochten.

**unchanged** [ˌʌnˈtʃeɪndʒd] *adj* unverändert.

**unchanging** [ˌʌnˈtʃeɪndʒɪŋ] *adj* unveränderlich.

**uncharacteristic** [ˈʌnˌkærəktəˈrɪstɪk] *adj* untypisch.

**uncharitable** [ˌʌnˈtʃærɪtəbl] *adj* unfreundlich.

**uncharted** [ˌʌnˈtʃɑːtɪd] *adj* **- 1.** [not recorded on
maps] nicht kartiert **- 2.** *fig* [unfamiliar] unerforscht.

**unchecked** [ˌʌnˈtʃekt] *adj & adv* [unrestrained]
uneingeschränkt.

**uncivilized, -ised** [ˌʌnˈsɪvɪlaɪzd] *adj* [barbaric]
unzivilisiert.

**unclassified** [ˌʌnˈklæsɪfaɪd] *adj* [not to be kept secret] nicht geheim.

**uncle** [ˈʌŋkl] *n* Onkel *der.*

**unclean** [ˌʌnˈkliːn] *adj* **- 1.** [dirty] schmutzig
**- 2.** RELIG unrein.

**unclear** [ˌʌnˈklɪəʳ] *adj* **- 1.** [meaning, instructions]
unklar **- 2.** [future, person] unsicher **- 3.** [motives, details] undurchsichtig.

**Uncle Sam** [-sæm] *n inf die (Regierung der)
Vereinigten Staaten, manchmal als Mann
mit weißem Bart und Zylinder dargestellt.*

**unclothed** [ˌʌnˈkləʊðd] *adj fml* unbekleidet.

**uncomfortable** [ˌʌnˈkʌmftəbl] *adj* **- 1.** [shoes,
chair, clothes] unbequem **- 2.** *fig* [fact, truth] unbequem **- 3.** [person]: **to feel ~** [in physical discomfort] sich nicht wohl fühlen; [ill at ease] sich
unbehaglich fühlen.

**uncomfortably** [ˌʌnˈkʌmftəblɪ] *adv* **- 1.** [in
physical discomfort] unbequem **- 2.** *fig* [uneasily]
verlegen **- 3.** [unpleasantly] unangenehm.

**uncommitted** [ˌʌnkəˈmɪtɪd] *adj* unbeteiligt.

**uncommon** [ʌnˈkɒmən] *adj* **- 1.** [rare] selten
**- 2.** *fml* [extreme] außergewöhnlich.

**uncommonly** [ʌnˈkɒmənlɪ] *adv fml* außergewöhnlich.

U

**uncommunicative** [ˌʌnkə'mjuːnɪkətɪv] *adj* verschlossen.

**uncomplicated** [ˌʌn'komplɪkeɪtɪd] *adj* unkompliziert.

**uncomprehending** ['ʌnˌkomprɪ'hendɪŋ] *adj* verständnislos.

**uncompromising** [ˌʌn'komprəmaɪzɪŋ] *adj* unnachgiebig.

**unconcerned** [ˌʌnkən'sɜːnd] *adj* [not anxious] unbesorgt.

**unconditional** [ˌʌnkən'dɪʃənl] *adj* bedingungslos.

**uncongenial** [ˌʌnkən'dʒiːnjəl] *adj* *fml* unangenehm.

**unconnected** [ˌʌnkə'nektɪd] *adj* ohne Zusammenhang.

**unconquered** [ˌʌn'koŋkəd] *adj* [territory] noch nie erobert; [people] unbesiegt.

**unconscious** [ʌn'konʃəs] *adj* - **1.** [having lost consciousness] bewusstlos - **2.** *fig* [unaware]: **to be ~ of** sthg sich (D) einer Sache (G) nicht bewusst sein - **3.** PSYCH unbewusst ⬦ *n* PSYCH: **the ~** das Unbewusste.

**unconsciously** [ʌn'konʃəslɪ] *adv* unbewusst.

**unconstitutional** ['ʌnˌkonstɪ'tjuːʃənl] *adj* verfassungswidrig.

**uncontested** [ˌʌnkən'testɪd] *adj* unangefochten.

**uncontrollable** [ˌʌnkən'trəʊləbl] *adj* - **1.** [irrepressible] unbezwingbar - **2.** [inflation, growth, epidemic] unkontrollierbar - **3.** [child, animal] nicht zu bändigen.

**uncontrolled** [ˌʌnkən'trəʊld] *adj* unkontrolliert.

**unconventional** [ˌʌnkən'venʃənl] *adj* unkonventionell.

**unconvinced** [ˌʌnkən'vɪnst] *adj* nicht überzeugt.

**unconvincing** [ˌʌnkən'vɪnsɪŋ] *adj* nicht überzeugend.

**uncooked** [ˌʌn'kʊkt] *adj* roh.

**uncooperative** [ˌʌnkəʊ'opərətɪv] *adj* unkooperativ.

**uncork** [ˌʌn'kɔːk] *vt* entkorken.

**uncorroborated** [ˌʌnkə'robəreɪtɪd] *adj* unbestätigt.

**uncouth** [ʌn'kuːθ] *adj* ungehobelt.

**uncover** [ʌn'kʌvər] *vt lit* & *fig* aufldecken.

**uncurl** [ˌʌn'kɜːl] *vi* - **1.** [hair, wire] sich glätten - **2.** [animal] sich strecken.

**uncut** [ˌʌn'kʌt] *adj* - **1.** [film] ungekürzt - **2.** [jewel] ungeschliffen.

**undamaged** [ˌʌn'dæmɪdʒd] *adj* unbeschädigt.

**undaunted** [ˌʌn'dɔːntɪd] *adj* unverzagt.

**undecided** [ˌʌndɪ'saɪdɪd] *adj* - **1.** [person] unentschlossen - **2.** [issue] unentschieden.

**undemanding** [ˌʌndɪ'mɑːndɪŋ] *adj* anspruchslos.

**undemonstrative** [ˌʌndɪ'monstrətɪv] *adj* zurückhaltend.

**undeniable** [ˌʌndɪ'naɪəbl] *adj* unbestreitbar.

**under** ['ʌndər] *prep* - **1.** [beneath, below] unter (+ D); (with verbs of motion) unter (+ A); **it's ~ the table** es ist unter dem Tisch; **put it ~ the table** leg es unter den Tisch - **2.** [less than] unter (+ D); **children ~ ten** Kinder unter zehn; **in ~ two hours** in weniger als zwei Stunden - **3.** [indicating conditions or circumstances]: **~ the circumstances** unter diesen Umständen; **to be ~ pressure** unter Druck sein - **4.** [undergoing]: **to be ~ review/discussion** revidiert/diskutiert werden; **~ construction** im Bau - **5.** [directed, governed by] unter (+ D); **Britain ~ Blair** Großbritannien unter Blair - **6.** [according to] nach; **~ the terms of the will** nach dem Testament - **7.** [in classification, name, title] unter (+ D) ⬦ *adv* - **1.** [beneath] unter; **how long can you stay ~?** [underwater] wie lange kannst du unter Wasser bleiben?; **she lifted the blanket and crawled ~** sie hob die Decke hoch und kroch darunter - **2.** [less]: **children of 12 and ~** Kinder bis zu 12 Jahren.

**under-** ['ʌndər] *prefix* [with nouns] Unter-; [with adjectives] unter-.

**underachiever** [ˌʌndərə'tʃiːvər] *n* Person, die trotz der vorhandenen Fähigkeiten enttäuschende Leistungen zeigt.

**underage** [ˌʌndər'eɪdʒ] *adj* minderjährig.

**underarm** ['ʌndərɑːm] *adj* - **1.** [deodorant, hair] Achsel- - **2.** SPORT [bowling] von unten ⬦ *adv* [throw, bowl] von unten.

**underbrush** ['ʌndəbrʌʃ] *n Am* Unterholz *das*.

**undercarriage** ['ʌndəˌkærɪdʒ] *n* Fahrgestell *das*.

**undercharge** [ˌʌndə'tʃɑːdʒ] *vt* zu wenig berechnen (+ D).

**underclothes** ['ʌndəkləʊðz] *npl* Unterwäsche *die*.

**undercoat** ['ʌndəkəʊt] *n* [of paint] Grundierung *die*.

**undercook** [ˌʌndə'kʊk] *vt* nicht lange genug garen.

**undercover** ['ʌndəˌkʌvər] *adj* [agent] Geheim- ⬦ *adv* verdeckt.

**undercurrent** ['ʌndəˌkʌrənt] *n fig* [tendency] Unterton *der*.

**undercut** [ˌʌndə'kʌt] (*pt* & *pp* **undercut**; *cont* **-ting**) *vt* [in price] unterbieten.

**underdeveloped** [ˌʌndədɪ'veləpt] *adj* unterentwickelt.

**underdog** [ˈʌndədɒg] n: the ~ der/die Schwächere.

**underdone** [ˌʌndəˈdʌn] adj nicht gar.

**underemployment** [ˌʌndərɪmˈplɔɪmənt] n (U) Unterbeschäftigung die.

**underestimate** [n ˌʌndərˈestɪmət, vb ˌʌndərˈestɪmeɪt] n Unterschätzung die ◇ vt - **1.** [time, money, amount] zu niedrig schätzen - **2.** [strength, abilities] unterschätzen.

**underexposed** [ˌʌndərɪkˈspəʊzd] adj PHOT unterbelichtet.

**underfinanced** [ˌʌndəˈfaɪnænst] adj unterfinanziert.

**underfoot** [ˌʌndəˈfʊt] adv unter den Füßen.

**undergo** [ˌʌndəˈgəʊ] (pt -**went**; pp -**gone** [-ˈgɒn]) vt [operation, examination] sich unterziehen (+ D); [training] teilnehmen an (+ D); [difficulties] durchlmachen; **to ~ modification** verändert werden.

**undergraduate** [ˌʌndəˈgrædjʊət] adj für Studierende ohne bereits erworbenen Hochschulabschluss ◇ n Student der, -in die.

**underground** [adj & n ˈʌndəgraʊnd, adv ˌʌndəˈgraʊnd] adj - **1.** [below ground] unterirdisch - **2.** fig [secret, illegal] Untergrund- ◇ adv: **to go/be forced ~** in den Untergrund gehen/gedrängt werden ◇ n - **1.** Br [transport system] U-Bahn die - **2.** [activist movement] Untergrund der.

**undergrowth** [ˈʌndəgrəʊθ] n (U) Unterholz das.

**underhand** [ˌʌndəˈhænd] adj hinterhältig.

**underinsured** [ˌʌndərɪnˈʃʊəd] adj unterversichert.

**underlay** [ˈʌndəleɪ] n [for carpet] Unterlage die.

**underline** [ˌʌndəˈlaɪn] vt lit & fig unterstreichen.

**underling** [ˈʌndəlɪŋ] n Untergebene der, die.

**underlying** [ˌʌndəˈlaɪŋ] adj zugrunde liegend.

**undermanned** [ˌʌndəˈmænd] adj unterbesetzt.

**undermentioned** [ˌʌndəˈmenʃnd] adj fml unten genannt.

**undermine** [ˌʌndəˈmaɪn] vt fig [weaken] untergraben.

**underneath** [ˌʌndəˈniːθ] prep [indicating location] unter (+ D); [indicating movement] unter (+ A); **from ~ sthg** unter etw (D) hervor ◇ adv darunter ◇ n [underside]: **the ~** die Unterseite.

**undernourished** [ˌʌndəˈnʌrɪʃt] adj unterernährt.

**underpaid** [pt & pp ˌʌndəˈpeɪd, adj ˈʌndəpeɪd] pt & pp ▷ **underpay** ◇ adj unterbezahlt.

**underpants** [ˈʌndəpænts] npl Unterhose die.

**underpass** [ˈʌndəpɑːs] n Unterführung die.

**underpay** [ˌʌndəˈpeɪ] (pt & pp -**paid**) vt unterbezahlen.

**underpin** [ˌʌndəˈpɪn] (pt & pp -**ned**; cont -**ning**) vt fig [back up] untermauern.

**underplay** [ˌʌndəˈpleɪ] vt [minimize the importance of] herunterlspielen.

**underprice** [ˌʌndəˈpraɪs] vt unter Preis anlbieten.

**underprivileged** [ˌʌndəˈprɪvɪlɪdʒd] adj unterprivilegiert.

**underproduction** [ˌʌndəprəˈdʌkʃn] n (U) Unterproduktion die.

**underrated** [ˌʌndəˈreɪtɪd] adj unterschätzt.

**underscore** [ˌʌndəˈskɔːr] vt lit & fig unterstreichen.

**undersea** [ˈʌndəsiː] adj Unterwasser-.

**undersell** [ˌʌndəˈsell] (pt & pp -**sold**) vt - **1.** COMM [sell at lower prices than] unterbieten - **2.** fig [underemphasize]: **to ~ o.s.** sich nicht gut genug verkaufen.

**undershirt** [ˈʌndəʃɜːt] n Am Unterhemd das.

**underside** [ˈʌndəsaɪd] n: the ~ die Unterseite.

**undersigned** [ˈʌndəsaɪnd] n fml: the ~ der/die Unterzeichnete.

**undersize(d)** [ˌʌndəˈsaɪz(d)] adj [smaller than average] unterdurchschnittlich groß; [too small] zu klein.

**underskirt** [ˈʌndəskɜːt] n Unterrock der.

**undersold** [ˌʌndəˈsəʊld] pt & pp ▷ **undersell**.

**understaffed** [ˌʌndəˈstɑːft] adj unterbesetzt.

**understand** [ˌʌndəˈstænd] (pt & pp -**stood**) vt - **1.** [gen] verstehen; **to make o.s. understood** sich verständlich machen - **2.** fml [have heard]: **to ~ that** glauben, dass; **I ~ you are looking for staff** ich habe gehört, dass Sie Mitarbeiter suchen ◇ vi verstehen.

**understandable** [ˌʌndəˈstændəbl] adj verständlich.

**understandably** [ˌʌndəˈstændəblɪ] adv verständlicherweise.

**understanding** [ˌʌndəˈstændɪŋ] n - **1.** [knowledge, insight] Kenntnis die - **2.** (U) [sympathy] Verständnis das - **3.** [interpretation, conception] Auffassung die; **it was my ~ that ...** ich dachte, dass ... - **4.** [informal agreement] Übereinkunft die; **on the ~ that ...** unter der Voraussetzung, dass ... ◇ adj [sympathetic] verständnisvoll.

**understate** [ˌʌndəˈsteɪt] vt [minimize] herunterlspielen.

**understated** [ˌʌndəˈsteɪtɪd] adj untertrieben.

**understatement** [ˌʌndəˈsteɪtmənt] n - **1.** [in-

U

adequate statement] Untertreibung *die* - **2.** *(U)* [quality of understating] Understatement *das*.

**understood** [ˌʌndə'stʊd] *pt* & *pp* ▷ **understand**.

**understudy** ['ʌndəˌstʌdɪ] *(pl* **-ies;** *pt* & *pp* **-ied)** *n* zweite Besetzung ◇ *vt* zweite Besetzung sein für.

**undertake** [ˌʌndə'teɪk] *(pt* **-took;** *pp* **-taken** [-'teɪkn]) *vt* - **1.** [take on] auf sich *(A)* nehmen - **2.** [promise]: **to ~ to do sthg** sich verpflichten, etw zu tun.

**undertaker** ['ʌndəˌteɪkər] *n* Leichenbestatter *der*, -in *die;* **~'s** [place] Bestattungsinstitut *das*.

**undertaking** [ˌʌndə'teɪkɪŋ] *n* - **1.** [task] Aufgabe *die* - **2.** [promise] Versprechen *das*.

**undertone** ['ʌndətəʊn] *n* - **1.** [quiet voice] leise Stimme - **2.** [underlying feeling] Unterton *der*.

**undertook** [ˌʌndə'tʊk] *pt* ▷ **undertake**.

**undertow** ['ʌndətəʊ] *n* Sog *der*.

**undervalue** [ˌʌndə'vælju:] *vt* unterbewerten.

**underwater** [ˌʌndə'wɔːtər] *adj* Unterwasser- ◇ *adv* unter Wasser.

**underwear** ['ʌndəweər] *n* Unterwäsche *die*.

**underweight** [ˌʌndə'weɪt] *adj* untergewichtig.

**underwent** [ˌʌndə'went] *pt* ▷ **undergo**.

**underwired** *adj* [bra] mit Drahtbügel.

**underworld** ['ʌndəˌwɜːld] *n* [criminal society]: **the ~** die Unterwelt.

**underwrite** ['ʌndəraɪt] *(pt* **-wrote;** *pp* **-written)** *vt* - **1.** *fml* [guarantee] garantieren - **2.** [in insurance business] versichern.

**underwriter** ['ʌndəˌraɪtər] *n* Versicherer *der*.

**underwritten** ['ʌndəˌrɪtn] *pp* ▷ **underwrite**.

**underwrote** ['ʌndərəʊt] *pt* ▷ **underwrite**.

**undeserved** [ˌʌndɪ'zɜːvd] *adj* unverdient.

**undesirable** [ˌʌndɪ'zaɪərəbl] *adj* unerwünscht.

**undeveloped** [ˌʌndɪ'veləpt] *adj* [land] unbebaut.

**undid** [ʌn'dɪd] *pt* ▷ **undo**.

**undies** ['ʌndɪz] *npl* *inf* Unterwäsche *die*.

**undignified** [ʌn'dɪgnɪfaɪd] *adj* würdelos.

**undiluted** [ˌʌndaɪ'lju:tɪd] *adj* - **1.** [quality, emotion] ungetrübt - **2.** [liquid] unverdünnt.

**undiplomatic** [ˌʌndɪplə'mætɪk] *adj* undiplomatisch.

**undischarged** [ˌʌndɪs'tʃɑːdʒd] *adj* - **1.** [debt] unbezahlt - **2.** [person]: **~ bankrupt** nicht entlasteter Gemeinschuldner.

**undisciplined** [ʌn'dɪsɪplɪnd] *adj* undiszipliniert.

**undiscovered** [ˌʌndɪ'skʌvəd] *adj* [unknown] unentdeckt.

**undisputed** [ˌʌndɪ'spju:tɪd] *adj* unbestritten.

**undistinguished** [ˌʌndɪ'stɪŋgwɪʃt] *adj* mittelmäßig.

**undivided** [ˌʌndɪ'vaɪdɪd] *adj* [whole] ungeteilt.

**undo** [ˌʌn'du:] *(pt* **-did;** *pp* **-done)** *vt* - **1.** [unfasten] auf lmachen - **2.** [nullify] zunichte machen.

**undoing** [ˌʌn'du:ɪŋ] *n* *(U)* *fml* Verderben *das*.

**undone** [ˌʌn'dʌn] *pp* ▷ **undo** ◇ *adj* - **1.** [unfastened] offen - **2.** *fml* [not done] ungetan.

**undoubted** [ʌn'daʊtɪd] *adj* unbestritten.

**undoubtedly** [ʌn'daʊtɪdlɪ] *adv* *fml* zweifellos.

**undreamed-of** [ʌn'dri:mdɒv], **undreamt-of** [ʌn'dremtɒv] *adj* [unimaginable] ungeahnt.

**undress** [ˌʌn'dres] *vt* auslziehen ◇ *vi* sich auslziehen.

**undressed** [ˌʌn'drest] *adj* [person] nicht angezogen; **to get ~** sich auslziehen.

**undrinkable** [ʌn'drɪŋkəbl] *adj* - **1.** [dangerous to drink] nicht trinkbar - **2.** [bad-tasting] ungenießbar.

**undue** [ʌn'dju:] *adj* *fml* unangemessen.

**undulate** ['ʌndjʊleɪt] *vi* *fml* - **1.** [in movement - snake, road] sich schlängeln - **2.** [in shape - landscape] sich wellenförmig erstrecken.

**unduly** [ʌn'dju:lɪ] *adv* *fml* unnötig.

**undying** [ʌn'daɪɪŋ] *adj* *literary* unsterblich.

**unearned income** [ʌnɜːnd-] *n* *(U)* Kapitalertrag *der*.

**unearth** [ʌn'ɜːθ] *vt* - **1.** [dig up] auslgraben - **2.** *fig* [discover] auf lstöbern.

**unearthly** [ʌn'ɜːθlɪ] *adj* - **1.** [ghostly] gespenstisch - **2.** *inf* [time of day]: **at an ~ hour** zu nächtlicher Stunde.

**unease** [ʌn'i:z] *n* *(U)* Unbehagen *das*.

**uneasy** [ʌn'i:zɪ] *(compar* **-ier;** *superl* **-iest)** *adj* - **1.** [person, feeling] unbehaglich - **2.** [silence] verlegen - **3.** [peace] unsicher.

**uneatable** [ˌʌn'i:təbl] *adj* - **1.** [dangerous to eat] nicht essbar - **2.** [bad-tasting] ungenießbar.

**uneaten** [ˌʌn'i:tn] *adj* übrig geblieben.

**uneconomic** ['ʌnˌi:kə'nɒmɪk] *adj* unökonomisch.

**uneducated** [ˌʌn'edjʊkeɪtɪd] *adj* - **1.** [person] ungebildet - **2.** [behaviour, manners, speech] unkultiviert.

**unemotional** [ˌʌnɪ'məʊʃənl] *adj* nüchtern.

**unemployable** [ˌʌnɪm'plɔɪəbl] *adj* als Arbeitskraft ungeeignet.

**unemployed** [ˌʌnɪm'plɔɪd] *adj* [out-of-work] arbeitslos ◇ *npl:* **the ~** die Arbeitslosen *pl.*

**unemployment** [ˌʌnɪm'plɔɪmənt] *n* Arbeitslosigkeit *die.*

**unemployment benefit** *Br,* **unemployment compensation** *Am n (U)* Arbeitslosenunterstützung *die.*

**unenviable** [ˌʌn'envɪəbl] *adj* nicht beneidenswert.

**unequal** [ˌʌn'iːkwəl] *adj* - **1.** [unfair] ungleich - **2.** [different] unterschiedlich.

**unequalled** *Br,* **unequaled** *Am* [ˌʌn'iːkwəld] *adj* unerreicht.

**unequivocal** [ˌʌnɪ'kwɪvəkl] *adj fml* eindeutig.

**unerring** [ˌʌn'ɜːrɪŋ] *adj* untrüglich.

**UNESCO** [juː'neskəʊ] *(abbr of* **United Nations Educational, Scientific and Cultural Organization)** *n* UNESCO *die.*

**unethical** [ʌn'eθɪkl] *adj* unmoralisch.

**uneven** [ˌʌn'iːvn] *adj* - **1.** [not flat] uneben - **2.** [inconsistent] ungleichmäßig - **3.** [unfair] ungleich.

**uneventful** [ˌʌnɪ'ventfʊl] *adj* ereignisarm.

**unexceptional** [ˌʌnɪk'sepʃənl] *adj* untadelig.

**unexpected** [ˌʌnɪk'spektɪd] *adj* unerwartet.

**unexpectedly** [ˌʌnɪk'spektɪdlɪ] *adv* unerwartet.

**unexplained** [ˌʌnɪk'spleɪnd] *adj* ungeklärt.

**unexploded** [ˌʌnɪk'spləʊdɪd] *adj* [bomb] nicht detoniert.

**unexpurgated** [ˌʌn'ekspəgeɪtɪd] *adj* ungekürzt.

**unfailing** [ʌn'feɪlɪŋ] *adj* [loyalty, support, good humour] unerschöpflich.

**unfair** [ˌʌn'feəʳ] *adj* ungerecht.

**unfair dismissal** *n (U)* ungerechtfertigte Entlassung.

**unfairly** [ˌʌn'feəlɪ] *adv* zu Unrecht.

**unfairness** [ˌʌn'feənɪs] *n* Ungerechtigkeit *die.*

**unfaithful** [ˌʌn'feɪθfʊl] *adj* [sexually] untreu.

**unfamiliar** [ˌʌnfə'mɪljəʳ] *adj* - **1.** [not well-known] unbekannt - **2.** [not acquainted]: **to be ~ with sb/ sthg** jn/etw nicht kennen.

**unfashionable** [ˌʌn'fæʃnəbl] *adj* unmodisch.

**unfasten** [ˌʌn'fɑːsn] *vt* auf|machen; [rope] auf|knoten.

**unfavourable** *Br,* **unfavorable** *Am* [ˌʌn'feɪvrəbl] *adj* - **1.** [not conducive] ungünstig - **2.** [negative] unvorteilhaft.

**unfeeling** [ʌn'fiːlɪŋ] *adj* herzlos.

**unfinished** [ˌʌn'fɪnɪʃt] *adj* unerledigt.

**unfit** [ˌʌn'fɪt] *adj* - **1.** [not in good shape] nicht fit

- **2.** [not suitable]: **~ (for sthg)** ungeeignet (für etw).

**unflagging** [ˌʌn'flægɪŋ] *adj* unermüdlich.

**unflappable** [ˌʌn'flæpəbl] *adj esp Br* nicht aus der Ruhe zu bringen.

**unflattering** [ˌʌn'flætərɪŋ] *adj* [garment] unvorteilhaft; [remark, portrait] wenig schmeichelhaft.

**unflinching** [ʌn'flɪntʃɪŋ] *adj* [courage, determination] unerschütterlich; [gaze] starr.

**unfold** [ʌn'fəʊld] *vt* - **1.** [open out] auseinander|falten - **2.** [explain] entfalten ◇ *vi* [story, truth] an den Tag kommen; **as the plot ~s** im weiteren Verlauf der Handlung.

**unforeseeable** [ˌʌnfɔː'siːəbl] *adj* unvorhersehbar.

**unforeseen** [ˌʌnfɔː'siːn] *adj* unvorhergesehen.

**unforgettable** [ˌʌnfə'getəbl] *adj* unvergesslich.

**unforgivable** [ˌʌnfə'gɪvəbl] *adj* unverzeihlich.

**unformatted** [ˌʌn'fɔːmætɪd] *adj* COMPUT nicht formatiert.

**unfortunate** [ʌn'fɔːtʃnət] *adj* - **1.** [unlucky] unglücklich - **2.** [regrettable] bedauernswert.

**unfortunately** [ʌn'fɔːtʃnətlɪ] *adv* leider.

**unfounded** [ˌʌn'faʊndɪd] *adj* unbegründet.

**unfriendly** [ˌʌn'frendlɪ] *(compar* **-ier;** *superl* **-iest)** *adj* unfreundlich.

**unfulfilled** [ˌʌnfʊl'fɪld] *adj* - **1.** [ambition, promise, prophecy] unerfüllt - **2.** [person] unausgefüllt.

**unfurl** [ˌʌn'fɜːl] *vt* entrollen; [sail] los|machen.

**unfurnished** [ˌʌn'fɜːnɪʃt] *adj* unmöbliert.

**ungainly** [ʌn'geɪnlɪ] *adj* unbeholfen.

**ungenerous** [ˌʌn'dʒenərəs] *adj* - **1.** [mean - person] kleinlich; [ - amount] bescheiden - **2.** [unkind] ungnädig.

**ungodly** [ʌn'gɒdlɪ] *adj* - **1.** [irreligious] gottlos - **2.** *inf* [unreasonable] unchristlich.

**ungrateful** [ʌn'greɪtfʊl] *adj* undankbar.

**ungratefulness** [ʌn'greɪtfʊlnɪs] *n (U)* Undankbarkeit *die.*

**unguarded** [ˌʌn'gɑːdɪd] *adj* - **1.** [not guarded] unbewacht - **2.** [careless]: **in an ~ moment** in einem unachtsamen Augenblick.

**unhappily** [ʌn'hæpɪlɪ] *adv* - **1.** [sadly] unglücklich - **2.** *fml* [unfortunately] leider.

**unhappiness** [ʌn'hæpɪnɪs] *n (U)* Traurigkeit *die.*

**unhappy** [ʌn'hæpɪ] *(compar* **-ier;** *superl* **-iest)** *adj* - **1.** [sad] unglücklich - **2.** [not pleased]: **to be ~ (about OR with sthg)** nicht glücklich (über etw (A) OR mit etw) sein - **3.** *fml* [unfortunate] unglückselig.

**unharmed** [ʌn'hɑːmd] *adj* unverletzt.

**UNHCR** (*abbr of* **United Nations High Commission for Refugees**) *n* UNHCR *die.*

**unhealthy** [ʌn'helθɪ] (*compar* **-ier;** *superl* **-iest**) *adj* ungesund.

**unheard** [ʌn'hɜːd] *adj:* **to be** OR **go ~** nicht gehört werden.

**unheard-of** [ʌn'hɜːdɒv] *adj* - **1.** [unknown] unbekannt - **2.** [unprecedented] unerhört.

**unheeded** [ʌn'hiːdɪd] *adj:* **to go ~** nicht beachtet werden.

**unhelpful** [ʌn'helpfʊl] *adj* - **1.** [unwilling to help] nicht hilfsbereit - **2.** [not useful] nicht hilfreich.

**unhindered** [ʌn'hɪndəd] *adj* unbehindert.

**unhook** [ʌn'hʊk] *vt* - **1.** [unfasten hooks of] aufIhaken - **2.** [remove from hook] abIhaken, vom Haken nehmen.

**unhurt** [ʌn'hɜːt] *adj* unverletzt.

**unhygienic** [ʌnhaɪ'dʒiːnɪk] *adj* unhygienisch.

**Uni** ['juːnɪ] *n inf* Uni *die.*

**UNICEF** ['juːnɪˌsef] (*abbr of* **United Nations International Children's Emergency Fund**) *n* UNICEF *die.*

**unicorn** ['juːnɪkɔːn] *n* Einhorn *das.*

**unicycle** ['juːnɪsaɪkl] *n* Einrad *das.*

**unidentified** [ʌnaɪ'dentɪfaɪd] *adj* nicht identifiziert.

**unidentified flying object** *n* unbekanntes Flugobjekt.

**unification** [ˌjuːnɪfɪ'keɪʃn] *n (U)* Vereinigung *die.*

**uniform** ['juːnɪfɔːm] *adj* gleichförmig ◇ *n* Uniform *die.*

**uniformity** [ˌjuːnɪ'fɔːmətɪ] *n (U)* Einheitlichkeit *die.*

**uniformly** ['juːnɪfɔːmlɪ] *adv* einheitlich.

**unify** ['juːnɪfaɪ] (*pt & pp* **-ied**) *vt* vereinen.

**unifying** ['juːnɪfaɪɪŋ] *adj* vereinigend.

**unilateral** [ˌjuːnɪ'lætərəl] *adj* einseitig.

**unimaginable** [ˌʌnɪ'mædʒɪnəbl] *adj* unvorstellbar.

**unimaginative** [ˌʌnɪ'mædʒɪnətɪv] *adj* fantasielos.

**unimpaired** [ˌʌnɪm'peəd] *adj* unbeeinträchtigt.

**unimpeded** [ˌʌnɪm'piːdɪd] *adj* ungehindert.

**unimportant** [ˌʌnɪm'pɔːtənt] *adj* unwichtig.

**unimpressed** [ˌʌnɪm'prest] *adj* unbeeindruckt.

**uninhabited** [ˌʌnɪn'hæbɪtɪd] *adj* unbewohnt.

**uninhibited** [ˌʌnɪn'hɪbɪtɪd] *adj* ungehemmt.

**uninitiated** [ˌʌnɪ'nɪʃɪeɪtɪd] *npl:* **the ~** Außenstehende *pl.*

**uninjured** [ʌn'ɪndʒəd] *adj* unverletzt.

**uninspiring** [ˌʌnɪn'spaɪrɪŋ] *adj* langweilig.

**unintelligent** [ˌʌnɪn'telɪdʒənt] *adj* nicht intelligent.

**unintentional** [ˌʌnɪn'tenʃənl] *adj* unabsichtlich.

**uninterested** [ʌn'ɪntrəstɪd] *adj* uninteressiert.

**uninterrupted** ['ʌnˌɪntə'rʌptɪd] *adj* ununterbrochen.

**uninvited** [ˌʌnɪn'vaɪtɪd] *adj* ungebeten.

**union** ['juːnjən] *n* - **1.** [trade union] Gewerkschaft *die* - **2.** [alliance] Union *die* ◇ *comp* Gewerkschafts-.

**Unionist** ['juːnjənɪst] *n* Br POL *Person, die für die Erhaltung der Union Nordirlands mit Großbritannien eintritt.*

**unionize, -ise** ['juːnjənaɪz] *vt* gewerkschaftlich organisieren.

**unionized, -ised** ['juːnjənaɪzd] *adj* gewerkschaftlich organisiert.

**Union Jack** *n:* **the ~** der Union Jack, *britische Nationalflagge.*

**union shop** *n* Am gewerkschaftspflichtiger Betrieb.

**unique** [juː'niːk] *adj* - **1.** [unparalleled] einzigartig - **2.** *fml* [peculiar, exclusive]: **this custom is ~ to our country** diesen Brauch gibt es nur in unserem Land.

**uniquely** [juː'niːklɪ] *adv* - **1.** *fml* [exclusively] ausschließlich - **2.** [exceptionally] außergewöhnlich.

**unisex** ['juːnɪseks] *adj* Unisex-, unisex.

**unison** ['juːnɪzn] *n (U)* [agreement] Einklang *der;* **in ~** [simultaneously] unisono.

**UNISON** ['juːnɪzn] *n aus kleineren britischen Gewerkschaften gebildete Großgewerkschaft des öffentlichen Dienstes.*

**unit** ['juːnɪt] *n* - **1.** [gen] Einheit *die* - **2.** [part of machine or system, piece of furniture] Element *das* - **3.** [department] Abteilung *die* - **4.** [chapter] Kapitel *das.*

**unit cost** *n* Kosten *pl* pro Einheit.

**unite** [juː'naɪt] *vt* vereinigen ◇ *vi* sich vereinigen.

**united** [juː'naɪtɪd] *adj* - **1.** [in harmony] vereint; **to be ~ in sthg** in etw (D) vereint sein - **2.** [unified] vereinigt.

**United Arab Emirates** *npl:* **the ~** die Vereinigten Arabischen Emirate *pl.*

**united front** *n:* **to present a ~** eine geschlossene Front bilden.

**United Kingdom** *n:* the ~ das Vereinigte Königreich.

**United Nations** *n:* the ~ die Vereinten Nationen *pl.*

**United States** *n:* the ~ (of America) die Vereinigten Staaten (von Amerika); in the ~ in den Vereinigten Staaten.

**unit price** *n* Preis *der* pro Einheit.

**unit trust** *n Br* Investmentfonds *der.*

**unity** ['juːnətɪ] *n* - **1.** [union] Einheit *die* - **2.** [harmony] Einigkeit *die.*

**Univ.** (*abbr of* **University**) Univ.

**universal** [ˌjuːnɪ'vɜːsl] *adj* [belief, truth] universal.

**universal joint** *n* Kardangelenk *das.*

**universe** ['juːnɪvɜːs] *n* ASTRON Universum *das.*

**university** [ˌjuːnɪ'vɜːsətɪ] (*pl* -**ies**) *n* Universität *die* <> *comp* Universitäts-; ~ **student** Student *der,* -in *die.*

**unjust** [ˌʌn'dʒʌst] *adj* ungerecht.

**unjustifiable** [ʌn'dʒʌstɪfaɪəbl] *adj* nicht zu rechtfertigen.

**unjustified** [ʌn'dʒʌstɪfaɪd] *adj* ungerechtfertigt.

**unkempt** [ˌʌn'kempt] *adj* [hair, beard, appearance] ungepflegt.

**unkind** [ʌn'kaɪnd] *adj* - **1.** [uncharitable] gemein - **2.** *fig* [climate] rau.

**unkindly** [ʌn'kaɪndlɪ] *adv* gemein; **to speak** ~ **of sb** schlecht über jn reden.

**unknown** [ˌʌn'nəʊn] *adj* unbekannt <> *n* - **1.** [unknown thing]: the ~ das Unbekannte - **2.** [unknown person] Unbekannte *der,* *die.*

**unlace** [ˌʌn'leɪs] *vt* aufschnüren.

**unladen** [ˌʌn'leɪdn] *adj* leer.

**unlawful** [ˌʌn'lɔːfʊl] *adj* ungesetzlich.

**unleaded** [ˌʌn'ledɪd] *adj* bleifrei.

**unleash** [ˌʌn'liːʃ] *vt literary* entfesseln.

**unleavened** [ˌʌn'levnd] *adj* ungesäuert.

**unless** [ən'les] *conj* es sei denn, wenn ... nicht; ~ **you know more** es sei denn, Sie wissen mehr; **you'll be late** ~ **you set off at once** wenn du dich nicht gleich auf den Weg machst, wirst du zu spät kommen; ~ **I'm mistaken** wenn ich mich nicht irre; ~ **there's a miracle** falls nicht ein Wunder geschieht; ~ **otherwise indicated** wenn nicht anders angegeben

**unlicensed, unlicenced** *Am* [ˌʌn'laɪsənst] *adj* ohne Lizenz.

**unlike** [ˌʌn'laɪk] *prep* - **1.** [different from] nicht ähnlich (+ D) - **2.** [in contrast to] im Gegensatz zu - **3.** [not typical of]: **it's very** ~ **you to complain** es sieht dir gar nicht ähnlich, dich zu beschweren.

**unlikely** [ʌn'laɪklɪ] *adj* - **1.** [not probable] unwahrscheinlich - **2.** [bizarre] merkwürdig.

**unlimited** [ʌn'lɪmɪtɪd] *adj* unbegrenzt.

**unlisted** [ʌn'lɪstɪd] *adj Am* [phone number]: **to be** ~ nicht im Telefonbuch stehen.

**unlit** [ˌʌn'lɪt] *adj* - **1.** [not burning] nicht angezündet - **2.** [dark] unbeleuchtet.

**unload** [ˌʌn'ləʊd] *vt* - **1.** [remove] ausladen - **2.** [remove load from] entladen - **3.** *fig* [unburden]: **to** ~ **one's problems on(to) sb** seine Probleme bei jm abladen.

**unlock** [ˌʌn'lɒk] *vt* aufl schließen.

**unloved** [ˌʌn'lʌvd] *adj* ungeliebt.

**unluckily** [ʌn'lʌkɪlɪ] *adv* unglücklicherweise; ~ **for us** zu unserem Pech.

**unlucky** [ʌn'lʌkɪ] (*compar* -**ier**; *superl* -**iest**) *adj* - **1.** [unfortunate] unglücklich; [person] unglücksselig - **2.** [bringing bad luck] Unglücks-.

**unmanageable** [ʌn'mænɪdʒəbl] *adj* [vehicle] schwer manövrierbar; [size] unhandlich; [situation] unkontrollierbar.

**unmanly** [ˌʌn'mænlɪ] (*compar* -**ier**; *superl* -**iest**) *adj* unmännlich.

**unmanned** [ˌʌn'mænd] *adj* unbemannt.

**unmarked** [ˌʌn'mɑːkt] *adj* - **1.** [uninjured] unverletzt - **2.** [envelope] unbeschriftet; [grave] anonym; ~ **police car** ziviles Polizeifahrzeug.

**unmarried** [ˌʌn'mærɪd] *adj* unverheiratet.

**unmask** [ˌʌn'mɑːsk] *vt* - **1.** [remove mask from] demaskieren - **2.** *fig* [expose - hypocrisy] aufl decken; [ - truth] an den Tag bringen; [ - criminal] entlarven.

**unmatched** [ˌʌn'mætʃt] *adj* [performance, intelligence] unübertroffen; [view] unvergleichlich.

**unmentionable** [ʌn'menʃnəbl] *adj* [word] unaussprechlich; **an** ~ **topic** ein Tabuthema.

**unmistakable** [ˌʌnmɪ'steɪkəbl] *adj* unverwechselbar.

**unmitigated** [ʌn'mɪtɪgeɪtɪd] *adj* vollkommen.

**unmoved** [ˌʌn'muːvd] *adj:* **to be** ~ **by sthg** von etw ungerührt sein.

**unnamed** [ˌʌn'neɪmd] *adj* [anonymous] anonym.

**unnatural** [ʌn'nætʃrəl] *adj* - **1.** [unusual, strange] unnatürlich - **2.** [affected] aufgesetzt.

**unnecessary** [ʌn'nesəsərɪ] *adj* unnötig.

**unnerving** [ˌʌn'nɜːvɪŋ] *adj* [experience] verunsichernd; [silence] beunruhigend.

**unnoticed** [ˌʌn'nəʊtɪst] *adj:* **to go** OR **pass** ~ nicht bemerkt werden.

**UNO** (*abbr of* **United Nations Organization**) *n* UNO *die.*

**unobserved** [ˌʌnəb'zɜːvd] *adj* unbeobachtet.

U

**unobtainable** [ˌʌnəb'teɪnəbl] *adj* nicht erhältlich.

**unobtrusive** [ˌʌnəb'truːsɪv] *adj* unauffällig.

**unoccupied** [ˌʌn'ɒkjʊpaɪd] *adj* - **1.** [person] unbeschäftigt - **2.** [house] unbewohnt; [seat] unbesetzt - **3.** MIL [territory, zone] nicht besetzt.

**unofficial** [ˌʌnə'fɪʃl] *adj* inoffiziell.

**unopened** [ˌʌn'əʊpənd] *adj* ungeöffnet.

**unorthodox** [ˌʌn'ɔ:θədɒks] *adj* unorthodox.

**unpack** [ˌʌn'pæk] *vt* & *vi* auslpacken.

**unpaid** [ˌʌn'peɪd] *adj* unbezahlt; ~ **volunteer** ehrenamtlicher Mitarbeiter.

**unpalatable** [ʌn'pælətəbl] *adj* - **1.** [unpleasant to taste] ungenießbar - **2.** *fig* [difficult to accept] unangenehm.

**unparalleled** [ʌn'pærəleld] *adj* einmalig.

**unpatriotic** ['ʌnˌpætrɪ'ɒtɪk] *adj* unpatriotisch.

**unpick** [ˌʌn'pɪk] *vt* auf ltrennen.

**unpin** [ˌʌn'pɪn] (*pt* & *pp* **-ned**; *cont* **-ning**) *vt* [sewing, dress] die Nadeln entfernen aus; [hair] lösen.

**unplanned** [ˌʌn'plænd] *adj* ungeplant.

**unpleasant** [ʌn'pleznt] *adj* unangenehm.

**unpleasantness** [ʌn'plezntnɪs] *n* (U) - **1.** [of person] Unfreundlichkeit *die* - **2.** [discord] Unstimmigkeit *die*.

**unplug** [ʌn'plʌg] (*pt* & *pp* **-ged**; *cont* **-ging**) *vt* ELEC: **to** ~ **sthg** den Stecker von etw herauslziehen.

**unpolished** [ˌʌn'pɒlɪʃt] *adj* - **1.** [furniture, brass, shoes] unpoliert - **2.** [person, manner] ungeschliffen.

**unpolluted** [ˌʌnpə'luːtɪd] *adj* sauber.

**unpopular** [ˌʌn'pɒpjʊləʳ] *adj* unpopulär.

**unprecedented** [ʌn'presɪdəntɪd] *adj* beispiellos.

**unpredictable** [ˌʌnprɪ'dɪktəbl] *adj* unvorhersehbar; [person] unberechenbar.

**unprejudiced** [ˌʌn'predʒʊdɪst] *adj* unvoreingenommen.

**unprepared** [ˌʌnprɪ'peəd] *adj*: **to be** ~ **(for sthg)** (auf etw (A)) nicht vorbereitet sein.

**unprepossessing** ['ʌnˌpriːpə'zesɪŋ] *adj* wenig anziehend.

**unpretentious** [ˌʌnprɪ'tenʃəs] *adj* [manner] natürlich; [meal, dress, building] einfach; [person] bescheiden.

**unprincipled** [ʌn'prɪnsəpld] *adj* skrupellos.

**unprintable** [ˌʌn'prɪntəbl] *adj* nicht druckfähig.

**unproductive** [ˌʌnprə'dʌktɪv] *adj* unproduktiv; ~ **land** unfruchtbarer Boden.

**unprofessional** [ˌʌnprə'feʃənl] *adj* unprofessionell.

**unprofitable** [ˌʌn'prɒfɪtəbl] *adj* unrentabel.

**unprompted** [ˌʌn'prɒmptɪd] *adj* unaufgefordert.

**unpronounceable** [ˌʌnprə'naʊnsəbl] *adj* unaussprechlich.

**unprotected** [ˌʌnprə'tektɪd] *adj* [person, skin, sex] ungeschützt.

**unprovoked** [ˌʌnprə'vəʊkt] *adj* grundlos.

**unpublished** [ˌʌn'pʌblɪʃt] *adj* unveröffentlicht.

**unpunished** [ˌʌn'pʌnɪʃt] *adj*: **to go** ~ [person] ungestraft davonlkommen; [crime, behaviour] ungestraft bleiben.

**unqualified** [ˌʌn'kwɒlɪfaɪd] *adj* - **1.** [not qualified] unqualifiziert; [teacher, nurse] nicht ausgebildet - **2.** [total, complete - success, support] uneingeschränkt; [ - denial] vollständig.

**unquestionable** [ʌn'kwestʃənəbl] *adj* unbestreitbar.

**unquestioning** [ʌn'kwestʃənɪŋ] *adj* bedingungslos.

**unravel** [ʌn'rævl] (*Br* *pt* & *pp* **-led**; *cont* **-ling**, *Am* *pt* & *pp* **-ed**; *cont* **-ing**) *vt* - **1.** [undo - knitting] auf ltrennen; [ - threads] entwirren - **2.** *fig* [solve] lösen <> *vi* [become undone - threads] sich lösen; [ - knitting] sich auf ltrennen.

**unreadable** [ˌʌn'riːdəbl] *adj* - **1.** [difficult, tedious to read] unlesbar - **2.** [illegible] unleserlich.

**unreal** [ˌʌn'rɪəl] *adj* [strange] unwirklich.

**unrealistic** [ˌʌnrɪə'lɪstɪk] *adj* unrealistisch.

**unreasonable** [ʌn'riːznəbl] *adj* - **1.** [person]: **he's so** ~ mit ihm kann man überhaupt nicht vernünftig reden - **2.** [demand, decision] unangemessen; **is that so** ~? ist das so viel verlangt?

**unrecognizable** [ˌʌn'rekəgnaɪzəbl] *adj*: **to be** ~ nicht wiederzuerkennen sein.

**unrecognized** [ˌʌn'rekəgnaɪzd] *adj* - **1.** [not known, noticed] unerkannt - **2.** [unacknowledged] nicht anerkannt.

**unrecorded** [ˌʌnrɪ'kɔːdɪd] *adj* - **1.** [remark, fact, event] nicht aufgezeichnet - **2.** [music, voice] nicht aufgenommen.

**unrefined** [ˌʌnrɪ'faɪnd] *adj* - **1.** [petrol, sugar] Roh-; [flour] ungebleicht - **2.** [person] unkultiviert.

**unrehearsed** [ˌʌnrɪ'hɜːst] *adj* [answer] spontan; [performance] nicht geprobt.

**unrelated** [ˌʌnrɪ'leɪtɪd] *adj*: **to be** ~ **(to sthg)** in keinem Zusammenhang (mit etw) stehen.

**unrelenting** [ˌʌnrɪ'lentɪŋ] *adj* [struggle, questions] unerbittlich; [pressure] unablässig.

**unreliable** [ˌʌnrɪ'laɪəbl] *adj* unzuverlässig.

**unrelieved** [ˌʌnrɪ'liːvd] *adj* unvermindert.

**unremarkable** [ˌʌnrɪˈmɑːkəbl] adj nicht bemerkenswert; [person] unauffällig.

**unremitting** [ˌʌnrɪˈmɪtɪŋ] adj [effort, activity] unablässig, unaufhörlich; [generosity] unvermindert.

**unrepeatable** [ˌʌnrɪˈpiːtəbl] adj - 1. [not fit to be repeated] nicht wiederholbar - 2. [exceptional] einmalig.

**unrepentant** [ˌʌnrɪˈpentənt] adj reuelos; to be ~ keine Reue zeigen.

**unrepresentative** [ˌʌnreprɪˈzentətɪv] adj: ~ (of sthg) nicht repräsentativ (für etw).

**unrequited** [ˌʌnrɪˈkwaɪtɪd] adj unerwidert.

**unreserved** [ˌʌnrɪˈzɜːvd] adj - 1. [admiration, support, approval] uneingeschränkt - 2. [seat, place] nicht reserviert.

**unresolved** [ˌʌnrɪˈzɒlvd] adj ungelöst.

**unresponsive** [ˌʌnrɪˈspɒnsɪv] adj: to be ~ to sthg [situation] gegenüber etw gleichgültig sein; [requests] unempfänglich für etw sein; [treatment] auf etw (A) nicht reagieren.

**unrest** [ʌnˈrest] n (U) Unruhen pl.

**unrestrained** [ˌʌnrɪˈstreɪnd] adj [growth] ungehemmt; [violence, joy] ungezügelt.

**unrestricted** [ˌʌnrɪˈstrɪktɪd] adj uneingeschränkt, unbeschränkt.

**unrewarding** [ˌʌnrɪˈwɔːdɪŋ] adj undankbar.

**unripe** [ʌnˈraɪp] adj unreif.

**unrivalled** Br, **unrivaled** Am [ʌnˈraɪvld] adj unübertroffen.

**unroll** [ʌnˈrəʊl] vt auf lrollen.

**unruffled** [ʌnˈrʌfld] adj [calm] gelassen.

**unruly** [ʌnˈruːlɪ] (compar -ier; superl -iest) adj - 1. [person, group] undiszipliniert; [child] unartig; [behaviour] ungezügelt - 2. [hair] widerspenstig.

**unsafe** [ʌnˈseɪf] adj - 1. [dangerous] gefährlich - 2. [in danger] nicht sicher.

**unsaid** [ʌnˈsed] adj: to leave sthg ~ etw unausgesprochen lassen.

**unsaleable, unsalable** Am [ʌnˈseɪləbl] adj unverkäuflich.

**unsatisfactory** [ˈʌnˌsætɪsˈfæktərɪ] adj unbefriedigend.

**unsavoury, unsavory** Am [ʌnˈseɪvərɪ] adj - 1. [person] zwielichtig; [appearance] abstoßend; [reputation, behaviour, area] zweifelhaft - 2. [smell] widerwärtig.

**unscathed** [ʌnˈskeɪðd] adj unversehrt.

**unscheduled** [Br ˌʌnˈʃedjuːld, Am ˌʌnˈskedʒʊld] adj außerplanmäßig.

**unscientific** [ˈʌnˌsaɪənˈtɪfɪk] adj unwissenschaftlich.

**unscrew** [ʌnˈskruː] vt - 1. [lid, bottle top] losldrehen - 2. [sign, mirror] ablschrauben.

**unscripted** [ˌʌnˈskrɪptɪd] adj [talk, speech] frei gehalten.

**unscrupulous** [ʌnˈskruːpjʊləs] adj skrupellos.

**unseat** [ʌnˈsiːt] vt - 1. [rider] ablwerfen - 2. fig [depose] ablsetzen.

**unseeded** [ʌnˈsiːdɪd] adj unplatziert.

**unseemly** [ʌnˈsiːmlɪ] (compar -ier; superl -iest) adj unpassend, unschicklich.

**unseen** [ʌnˈsiːn] adj [not observed] unbemerkt; [not visible] unsichtbar <> adv unbemerkt.

**unselfish** [ʌnˈselfɪʃ] adj selbstlos.

**unselfishly** [ʌnˈselfɪʃlɪ] adv selbstlos.

**unsettle** [ʌnˈsetl] vt beunruhigen.

**unsettled** [ʌnˈsetld] adj - 1. [disturbed - person] beunruhigt; [ - weather] unbeständig - 2. [unfinished, unresolved - argument] nicht beigelegt; [ - issue] ungeklärt - 3. [account, bill] ausstehend - 4. [area, region] unbesiedelt.

**unsettling** [ʌnˈsetlɪŋ] adj beunruhigend.

**unshak(e)able** [ʌnˈʃeɪkəbl] adj [faith, belief] unerschütterlich; [decision] unumstößlich.

**unshaven** [ʌnˈʃeɪvn] adj unrasiert.

**unsheathe** [ʌnˈʃiːð] vt ziehen, zücken.

**unsightly** [ʌnˈsaɪtlɪ] adj unansehnlich.

**unskilled** [ʌnˈskɪld] adj [worker] ungelernt; [work] einfach.

**unsociable** [ʌnˈsəʊʃəbl] adj ungesellig.

**unsocial** [ʌnˈsəʊʃl] adj: to work ~ hours früh/morgens/nachts/am Wochenende arbeiten.

**unsold** [ʌnˈsəʊld] adj unverkauft.

**unsolicited** [ˌʌnsəˈlɪsɪtɪd] adj [goods] nicht angefordert; [advice] ungebeten.

**unsolved** [ʌnˈsɒlvd] adj ungelöst.

**unsophisticated** [ˌʌnsəˈfɪstɪkeɪtɪd] adj - 1. [person] einfach; [dress, style] schlicht - 2. [device, machine, approach] simpel.

**unsound** [ʌnˈsaʊnd] adj - 1. [conclusion, theory, decision] zweifelhaft - 2. [building, structure] instabil; to be of ~ mind unzurechnungsfähig sein.

**unspeakable** [ʌnˈspiːkəbl] adj fürchterlich.

**unspeakably** [ʌnˈspiːkəblɪ] adv fürchterlich.

**unspecified** [ˌʌnˈspesɪfaɪd] adj [amount] nicht festgelegt; [reason] unbestimmt.

**unspoiled** [ʌnˈspɔɪld], **unspoilt** [ʌnˈspɔɪlt] adj - 1. [gen] unverdorben; [countryside, beach] unberührt - 2. [goods] unbeschädigt.

**unspoken** [ʌnˈspəʊkən] adj - 1. [not expressed openly] unausgesprochen - 2. [tacit] stillschweigend.

**unsporting** [ʌnˈspɔːtɪŋ] adj unsportlich, unfair.

**U**

**unstable** [ˌʌn'steɪbl] adj - **1.** [structure, government] instabil; [weather] wechselhaft - **2.** [mentally, emotionally] labil.

**unstated** [ˌʌn'steɪtɪd] adj unerwähnt.

**unsteady** [ˌʌn'stedɪ] (compar -ier; superl -iest) adj wackelig.

**unstinting** [ˌʌn'stɪntɪŋ] adj uneingeschränkt; ~ support volle Unterstützung.

**unstoppable** [ˌʌn'stɒpəbl] adj unaufhaltsam.

**unstrap** [ˌʌn'stræp] (pt & pp -ped; cont -ping) vt [bag] auf|schnallen; [baby] los|schnallen.

**unstructured** [ˌʌn'strʌktʃəd] adj unstrukturiert.

**unstuck** [ˌʌn'stʌk] adj: to come ~ [notice, stamp, label] sich ab|lösen; fig [plan, system] schief gehen; [person] auf die Nase fallen.

**unsubstantiated** [ˌʌnsəb'stænʃɪeɪtɪd] adj unbegründet.

**unsuccessful** [ˌʌnsək'sesfʊl] adj erfolglos; [attempt] vergeblich.

**unsuccessfully** [ˌʌnsək'sesfʊlɪ] adv erfolglos, vergeblich.

**unsuitable** [ˌʌn'suːtəbl] adj unpassend; to be ~ for sthg für etw ungeeignet sein.

**unsuited** [ˌʌn'suːtɪd] adj - **1.** [not appropriate]: to be ~ to OR for sthg für etw ungeeignet sein - **2.** [not compatible]: to be ~ to each other nicht zueinander passen.

**unsung** [ˌʌn'sʌŋ] adj [deed, hero] unbesungen.

**unsure** [ˌʌn'ʃɔːʳ] adj - **1.** [not confident]: to be ~ of o.s. unsicher sein - **2.** [not certain]: to be ~ (about/of sthg) sich (D) (einer Sache (G)) nicht sicher sein.

**unsurpassed** [ˌʌnsə'pɑːst] adj unübertroffen.

**unsuspecting** [ˌʌnsə'spektɪŋ] adj nichts ahnend.

**unsweetened** [ˌʌn'swiːtnd] adj ungesüßt.

**unswerving** [ʌn'swɜːvɪŋ] adj unerschütterlich.

**unsympathetic** ['ʌnˌsɪmpə'θetɪk] adj [unfeeling] nicht mitfühlend.

**untamed** [ˌʌn'teɪmd] adj - **1.** [animal] wild - **2.** [land] nicht kultiviert - **3.** [person] ungebändigt.

**untangle** [ˌʌn'tæŋgl] vt entwirren.

**untapped** [ˌʌn'tæpt] adj ungenutzt; [mineral resources] unerschlossen.

**untaxed** [ˌʌn'tækst] adj unversteuert.

**untenable** [ˌʌn'tenəbl] adj unhaltbar.

**unthinkable** [ʌn'θɪŋkəbl] adj undenkbar, unvorstellbar.

**unthinkingly** [ʌn'θɪŋkɪŋlɪ] adv bedenkenlos.

**untidy** [ʌn'taɪdɪ] (compar -ier; superl -iest) adj unordentlich.

**untie** [ˌʌn'taɪ] (cont untying) vt [string, knot, bonds] lösen; [package] auf|binden; [prisoner] los|binden.

**until** [ən'tɪl] prep bis; ~ the evening/end bis zum Abend/Ende; not ~ ... erst ...; she won't come ~ two o'clock sie kommt erst um zwei Uhr <> conj bis; wait ~ he comes warte, bis er kommt; she won't come ~ she is invited sie kommt erst, wenn sie eingeladen wird; he would not rest ~ they had all been saved er ruhte nicht eher, als bis alle gerettet waren.

**untimely** [ʌn'taɪmlɪ] adj - **1.** [premature] vorzeitig - **2.** [inopportune] ungelegen, unpassend.

**untiring** [ʌn'taɪərɪŋ] adj unermüdlich.

**untold** [ˌʌn'təʊld] adj [amount] ungezählt; [wealth] unermesslich; [suffering, joy] unsäglich.

**untouched** [ˌʌn'tʌtʃt] adj - **1.** [unchanged] unberührt, unverändert; [undamaged] unbeschädigt - **2.** [uneaten] unberührt.

**untoward** [ˌʌntə'wɔːd] adj [event] unglücklich; [behaviour] ungebührlich.

**untrained** [ˌʌn'treɪnd] adj - **1.** [person] ungelernt - **2.** [voice, mind, eye] ungeübt.

**untrammelled** Br, **untrammeled** Am [ˌʌn'træməld] adj fml uneingeschränkt.

**untranslatable** [ˌʌntræns'leɪtəbl] adj unübersetzbar.

**untreated** [ˌʌn'triːtɪd] adj unbehandelt.

**untried** [ˌʌn'traɪd] adj [method, product] ungetestet.

**untroubled** [ˌʌn'trʌbld] adj [not worried]: to be ~ by sthg etw gelassen hin|nehmen.

**untrue** [ˌʌn'truː] adj - **1.** [inaccurate] unwahr, falsch - **2.** [unfaithful, disloyal]: to be ~ to sb jm untreu sein.

**untrustworthy** [ˌʌn'trʌstˌwɜːðɪ] adj nicht vertrauenswürdig.

**untruth** [ˌʌn'truːθ] n Unwahrheit die.

**untruthful** [ˌʌn'truːθfʊl] adj unehrlich, unaufrichtig.

**unusable** [ˌʌn'juːzəbl] adj unbrauchbar.

**unused** [sense 1 ˌʌn'juːzd, sense 2 ʌn'juːst] adj - **1.** [new] unbenutzt - **2.** [unaccustomed]: to be ~ to sthg an etw (A) nicht gewöhnt sein; to be ~ to doing sthg nicht daran gewöhnt sein, etw zu tun.

**unusual** [ʌn'juːʒl] adj ungewöhnlich.

**unusually** [ʌn'juːʒəlɪ] adv außergewöhnlich.

**unvarnished** [ʌn'vɑːnɪʃt] adj fig [truth] ungeschminkt, unverhüllt; [account] ungeschönt.

**unveil** [ˌʌn'veɪl] vt lit & fig enthüllen.

**unwaged** [ˌʌn'weɪdʒd] *adj Br* ohne Einkommen.

**unwanted** [ˌʌn'wɒntɪd] *adj* [clothes, furniture] ausrangiert; [child, pregnancy] ungewollt; **to feel ~** das Gefühl haben, unerwünscht zu sein.

**unwarranted** [ʌn'wɒrəntɪd] *adj* ungerechtfertigt.

**unwavering** [ʌn'weɪvərɪŋ] *adj* unerschütterlich.

**unwelcome** [ʌn'welkəm] *adj* - **1.** [news, experience] unerfreulich - **2.** [visitor] unwillkommen.

**unwell** [ˌʌn'wel] *adj:* **to be/feel ~** sich unwohl fühlen.

**unwholesome** [ˌʌn'həʊlsəm] *adj* [food, drink] ungesund; [desire, thought] unanständig.

**unwieldy** [ʌn'wiːldɪ] (*compar* -ier; *superl* -iest) *adj* - **1.** [tool] unhandlich; [piece of furniture] sperrig - **2.** *fig* [system, method] umständlich; [organization] schwerfällig.

**unwilling** [ˌʌn'wɪlɪŋ] *adj* unwillig.

**unwind** [ˌʌn'waɪnd] (*pt* & *pp* **-wound**) *vt* ablwickeln ◇ *vi fig* [person] sich entspannen.

**unwise** [ˌʌn'waɪz] *adj* unklug.

**unwitting** [ʌn'wɪtɪŋ] *adj fml* [accomplice, victim] ahnungslos; [action] unbeabsichtigt.

**unwittingly** [ʌn'wɪtɪŋlɪ] *adv fml* unwissentlich.

**unworkable** [ˌʌn'wɜːkəbl] *adj* undurchführbar.

**unworldly** [ˌʌn'wɜːldlɪ] *adj* weltfremd.

**unworthy** [ʌn'wɜːðɪ] (*compar* -ier; *superl* -iest) *adj:* **to be ~ of sthg** einer Sache (G) unwürdig sein.

**unwound** [ʌn'waʊnd] *pt* & *pp* ▷ **unwind**.

**unwrap** [ˌʌn'ræp] (*pt* & *pp* **-ped**; *cont* **-ping**) *vt* auslpacken.

**unwritten law** [ˌʌnrɪtn-] *n* ungeschriebenes Gesetz.

**unyielding** [ʌn'jiːldɪŋ] *adj* unnachgiebig.

**unzip** [ˌʌn'zɪp] (*pt* & *pp* **-ped**; *cont* **-ping**) *vt* öffnen; **to ~ a bag** den Reißverschluss einer Tasche öffnen.

**up** [ʌp] (*pt* & *pp* **-ped**; *cont* **-ping**) *adv* - **1.** [towards higher position, level] hoch; **we walked ~ to the top** wir sind zum Gipfel gelaufen; **to pick sthg ~** etw auflheben; **to throw sthg ~** etw in die Höhe werfen; **prices are going ~** die Preise steigen; **~ and ~** immer höher - **2.** [in higher position] oben; **she's ~ in her room** sie ist oben in ihrem Zimmer; **a house ~ in the mountains** ein Haus oben in den Bergen; **~ here/there** hier/da *or* dort oben - **3.** [into an upright position]: **to stand ~** auf lstehen; **to sit ~** [from lying position] sich auf lsetzen; [sit straight] sich gerade hinlsetzen; **help me ~** hilf mir auf; **~ you get!** komm, steh auf! - **4.** [northwards]: **to live ~ north** oben im Norden wohnen; **I'm going ~ to York** ich fahre hoch nach York - **5.** [facing upwards] nach oben gerichtet; **he was lying face ~** er lag mit dem Gesicht nach oben - **6.** [along river] oben; **their house is a little further ~** ihr Haus liegt ein bisschen weiter in dieser Richtung - **7.** [close up, towards]: **to go ~ to sb** auf jn zulgehen - **8.** [ahead]: **to be two goals ~** mit zwei Toren führen ◇ *prep* - **1.** [towards higher position]: **to walk ~ a hill** einen Hügel hinauflgehen; **I went ~ the stairs** ich ging die Treppe hinauf - **2.** [in higher position]: **to be ~ a hill** oben auf einem Hügel sein - **3.** [towards far end of]: **they live ~ the road from us** sie wohnen weiter oben in unserer Straße ◇ *adj* - **1.** [out of bed] auf; **I was ~ at six today** ich war heute um sechs auf; **is she ~ yet?** ist sie schon auf?; **to be ~ all night** die ganze Nacht auflbleiben - **2.** [at an end] um, zu Ende; **time's ~** die Zeit ist um - **3.** [under repair]: **the road is ~** die Straße ist aufgerissen - **4.** *inf* [wrong]: **there's something ~** es liegt etwas in der Luft; **there's something ~ with my computer** irgendwas ist mit meinem Computer los; **what's ~ (with you)?** was ist (mit dir) los? ◇ *n:* **~s and downs** Höhen und Tiefen *pl* ◇ *vt inf* [price, cost] erhöhen; **we've ~ped our offer** wir haben unser Angebot erhöht.

➤ **up against** *prep* [confronting]: **we came ~ against a lot of opposition** wir stießen auf starken Widerstand; **she's ~ against a very strong opponent** sie hat es mit einem sehr starken Gegner zu tun; **to be ~ against it** schwer zu kämpfen haben.

➤ **up and down** *adv:* **to walk/jump ~ and down** auf und ab gehen/springen ◇ *prep* - **1.** [higher and lower]: **she's ~ and down the stairs all day** sie läuft den ganzen Tag die Treppe rauf und runter - **2.** [backwards and forwards]: **she looked ~ and down the ranks of soldiers** sie blickte die Reihen der Soldaten entlang; **we walked ~ and down the avenue** wir gingen die Allee auf und ab.

➤ **up to** *prep* - **1.** [indicating position, level] bis zu; **the water came ~ to my knees** das Wasser reichte mir bis an die Knie; **~ to this point** bis zu diesem Punkt; **~ to six weeks/ten people** bis zu sechs Wochen/zehn Personen; **it's not ~ to standard** es ist nicht gut genug - **2.** [in time] bis; **I felt fine ~ to last month** bis letzten Monat ging es mir gut - **3.** [well or able enough for]: **my French isn't ~ to much** *inf* mein Französisch ist nicht besonders gut; **to be ~ to a task** einer Aufgabe gewachsen sein; **are you ~ to travelling?** bist du reisefähig?; **I'm not ~ to going out tonight** ich schaffe es heute abend nicht auszugehen - **4.** *phr:* **what are you ~ to?** *inf* [doing] was machst du da?; [planning] was hast du vor?; **they're ~ to**

**something** sie haben etwas vor; **it's ~ to you** das liegt bei dir.

➤ **up until** *prep* bis; **~ until ten o'clock** bis um zehn Uhr.

**up-and-coming** *adj* [athlete, actor] kommend; [business] aufstrebend.

**up-and-up** *n* - **1.** *Br* [improving]: **at last his business seems to be on the ~** endlich geht es mit seiner Firma aufwärts - **2.** *Am* [honest]: **to be on the ~** vertrauenswürdig sein.

**upbeat** [ˈʌpbiːt] *adj* optimistisch.

**upbraid** [ʌpˈbreɪd] *vt fml*: **to ~ sb (for sthg)** jn (für etw) tadeln.

**upbringing** [ˈʌpˌbrɪŋɪŋ] *n* Erziehung *die*.

**update** [ˌʌpˈdeɪt] *vt* aktualisieren.

**upend** [ʌpˈend] *vt* [stand on end] hochkant stellen; [turn upside down] umdrehen.

**upfront** [ˌʌpˈfrʌnt] *adj*: **to be ~ (about sthg)** (bezüglich einer Sache *(G)*) offen sein ◇ *adv* [in advance] im Voraus.

**upgrade** [ˌʌpˈgreɪd] *vt* - **1.** [improve] verbessern; [computer system] auf|rüsten - **2.** [promote] befördern.

**upheaval** [ʌpˈhiːvl] *n* Aufruhr *der*.

**upheld** [ʌpˈheld] *pt* & *pp* ➣ **uphold**.

**uphill** [ˌʌpˈhɪl] *adj* - **1.** [rising] ansteigend - **2.** *fig* [difficult] mühsam ◇ *adv* bergauf.

**uphold** [ʌpˈhəʊld] (*pt* & *pp* -**held**) *vt* - **1.** [law] beibehalten - **2.** [decision, system] unterstützen.

**upholster** [ʌpˈhəʊlstər] *vt* polstern.

**upholstery** [ʌpˈhəʊlstərɪ] *n (U)* Polsterung *die*.

**upkeep** [ˈʌpkiːp] *n* Instandhaltung *die;* [of garden] Pflege *die*.

**upland** [ˈʌplənd] *adj* Hochland-.

➤ **uplands** *npl* Hochland *das*.

**uplift** [ʌpˈlɪft] *vt* [cheer] erfreuen.

**uplifting** [ʌpˈlɪftɪŋ] *adj* [cheering] erhebend.

**uplighter** [ˈʌplaɪtər] *n* ELEC Deckenfluter *der*.

**up-market** *adj* [hotel, restaurant, area] vornehm; [goods] edel; **we're looking for something more ~** wir suchen etwas Luxuriöseres.

**upon** [əˈpɒn] *prep fml* - **1.** [on, on top of - indicating place, position] auf (*+ D*); [ - indicating direction] auf (*+ A*); **summer/the weekend is ~ us** es ist beinahe Sommer/Wochenende - **2.** [when] als; **~ hearing the news, I rushed to the telephone** als ich die Neuigkeiten hörte, rannte ich sofort zum Telefon - **3.** [one after another]: **they asked me question ~ question** sie stellten mir eine Frage nach der anderen.

**upper** [ˈʌpər] *adj* - **1.** [physically higher & GEOGR] obere, -r, -s; **~ lip** Oberlippe *die;* **the Upper Rhine** der Oberrhein - **2.** [higher in order, rank] höher ◇ *n* [of shoe] Obermaterial *das*.

**upper class** *n:* **the ~** die Oberschicht.

➤ **upper-class** *adj* vornehm.

**upper-crust** *adj* vornehm.

**uppercut** [ˈʌpəkʌt] *n* Aufwärtshaken *der*.

**upper hand** *n:* **to have the ~** die Oberhand haben; **to gain** OR **get the ~** die Oberhand gewinnen.

**Upper House** *n* POL Oberhaus *das*.

**uppermost** [ˈʌpəməʊst] *adj* - **1.** [highest] oberste, -r, -s - **2.** [most important]: **my father's illness is ~ in my mind at the moment** die Krankheit meines Vaters beschäftigt mich momentan am meisten.

**uppity** [ˈʌpətɪ] *adj inf* hochnäsig.

**upright** [ˈʌpraɪt] *adj lit* & *fig* aufrecht ◇ *adv* aufrecht ◇ *n* [of goal] Pfosten *der;* [of bookshelf] Seitenteil *das;* [of door] Türpfosten *der*.

**upright piano** *n* Klavier *das*.

**uprising** [ˈʌpˌraɪzɪŋ] *n* Aufstand *der*.

**uproar** [ˈʌprɔːr] *n* Aufruhr *der*.

**uproarious** [ʌpˈrɔːrɪəs] *adj* [crowd] lärmend; [meeting] chaotisch; [laughter] schallend.

**uproot** [ʌpˈruːt] *vt* entwurzeln; **to ~ o.s.** seine Heimat verlassen.

**upset** [ʌpˈset] (*pt* & *pp* upset; *cont* -ting) *adj* - **1.** [distressed] aufgeregt; [shocked] bestürzt; [offended] beleidigt - **2.** MED: **to have an ~ stomach** eine Magenverstimmung haben ◇ *n* - **1.** MED: **to have a stomach ~** eine Magenverstimmung haben - **2.** [surprise result] Überraschungsergebnis *das* ◇ *vt* - **1.** [distress] auf|regen; **the news ~ him** die Nachricht bestürzte ihn - **2.** [mess up] durcheinander bringen - **3.** [overturn, knock over] um|kippen, um|stoßen; [boat] zum Kentern bringen.

**upsetting** [ʌpˈsetɪŋ] *adj* [news] bestürzend; [experience] erschütternd.

**upshot** [ˈʌpʃɒt] *n* Ergebnis *das*.

**upside down** [ˌʌpsaɪd-] *adj* [inverted] verkehrt herum ◇ *adv* verkehrt herum; **to turn sthg ~** *fig* [disorder] etw auf den Kopf stellen.

**upstage** [ˌʌpˈsteɪdʒ] *vt fig:* **to ~ sb** jm die Schau stehlen.

**upstairs** [ˌʌpˈsteəz] *adj* oben, im oberen Stockwerk ◇ *adv* - **1.** [not downstairs] oben; [with motion] nach oben - **2.** [on the floor above] oben, im oberen Stockwerk ◇ *n* oberes Stockwerk.

**upstanding** [ˌʌpˈstændɪŋ] *adj* [honest] aufrecht.

**upstart** [ˈʌpstɑːt] *n* Emporkömmling *der*.

**upstate** [ˌʌpˈsteɪt] *Am adj:* **in ~ New York** im Norden des Bundesstaates New York ◇ *adv* im Norden des Bundesstaates; [indicating direction] in den Norden des Bundesstaates.

**upstream** [ˌʌp'striːm] *adj:* ~ **(from sthg)** strom-aufwärts (von etw) <> *adv* stromaufwärts.

**upsurge** [ˈʌpsɜːdʒ] *n:* ~ **of/in sthg** Zunahme *die* an etw *(D).*

**upswing** [ˈʌpswɪŋ] *n:* ~ **(in sthg)** Aufschwung *der* (in etw *(D)).*

**uptake** [ˈʌpteɪk] *n:* **to be quick on the** ~ schnell verstehen; **to be slow on the** ~ schwer von Begriff sein.

**uptight** [ˌʌp'taɪt] *adj inf* verkrampft.

**up-to-date** *adj* - **1.** [machinery, methods] mo-dern - **2.** [news, information] neueste, -r, -s, ak-tuell; **to keep** ~ **with sthg** über etw *(A)* auf dem Laufenden bleiben.

**up-to-the-minute** *adj* allerneueste, -r, -s, aktuellste, -r, -s.

**uptown** [ˌʌp'taʊn] *Am adj:* **an** ~ **district** eine schicke Wohngegend <> *adv:* **to move** ~ **in** eine schicke Wohngegend ziehen.

**upturn** [ˈʌptɜːn] *n.* ~ **(in sthg)** Aufschwung *der* (in etw *(D)).*

**upturned** [ˌʌp'tɜːnd] *adj* - **1.** [face] nach oben gewandt; ~ **nose** Stupsnase *die* - **2.** [upside down] umgedreht.

**upward** [ˈʌpwəd] *adj* [movement, trend] Auf-wärts- <> *adv Am* = **upwards.**

**upwardly-mobile** [ˈʌpwədlɪ-] *adj* sozial aufsteigend.

**upwards** [ˈʌpwədz] *adv* - **1.** [to a higher place] nach oben - **2.** [to a higher number, degree, rate]: **to climb** OR **move** ~ anlsteigen.

➤ **upwards of** *prep* über (+ *A*), mehr als.

**upwind** [ˌʌp'wɪnd] *adj:* **he stood** ~ **from the fire to avoid the smoke** er stand so zum Feuer, dass der Wind den Rauch in die entgegen-gesetzte Richtung blies.

**Urals** [ˈjʊərəlz] *npl:* **the** ~ der Ural.

**uranium** [jʊ'reɪnjəm] *n* Uran *das.*

**Uranus** [ˈjʊərənəs] *n* [planet] Uranus *der.*

**urban** [ˈɜːbən] *adj* städtisch; ~ **development** Stadtentwicklung *die;* ~ **sprawl** Städte-wachstum *das.*

**urbane** [ɜː'beɪn] *adj* gewandt.

**urbanize, -ise** [ˈɜːbənaɪz] *vt* urbanisieren.

**urban renewal** *n* Stadterneuerung *die.*

**urchin** [ˈɜːtʃɪn] *n dated* Straßenkind *das.*

**Urdu** [ˈʊəduː] *n* Urdu *das.*

**urge** [ɜːdʒ] *n* Drang *der;* **to have an** ~ **to do sthg** den Drang verspüren, etw zu tun <> *vt* - **1.** [try to persuade]: **to** ~ **sb to do sthg** jn drän-gen, etw zu tun - **2.** [advocate] eindringlich raten zu.

**urgency** [ˈɜːdʒənsɪ] *n* Dringlichkeit *die.*

**urgent** [ˈɜːdʒənt] *adj* - **1.** [pressing] dringend - **2.** [desperate] verzweifelt.

**urgently** [ˈɜːdʒəntlɪ] *adv* dringend.

**urinal** [ˌjʊə'raɪnl] *n* [receptacle] Urinal *das;* [room] Pissoir *das.*

**urinary** [ˈjʊərɪnərɪ] *adj* Harn-.

**urinate** [ˈjʊərɪneɪt] *vi* urinieren.

**urine** [ˈjʊərɪn] *n* Urin *der.*

**urn** [ɜːn] *n* - **1.** [for ashes] Urne *die* - **2.** [for tea, cof-fee] Heißwasserbehälter *mit Zapfhahn.*

**Uruguay** [ˈjʊərəgwaɪ] *n* Uruguay *nt.*

**us** [ʌs] *pers pron* uns; **they know** ~ sie kennen uns; **they like** ~ wir gefallen ihnen; **it's** ~ wir sinds; **send it to** ~ schicke es uns; **tell** ~ sag uns; **they're worse than** ~ sie sind schlimmer als wir; **you can't expect US to do it** du kannst nicht erwarten, dass WIR das tun; **all of** ~ wir alle; **none of** ~ keiner von uns; **some/a few of** ~ einige von uns; **most of** ~ die meisten von uns; **both of** ~ wir beide; **there are three of** ~ wir sind zu dritt; **neither of** ~ keiner von uns.

**US** (*abbr of* **United States**) *n:* **the** ~ die USA *pl;* **in the** ~ in den USA.

**USA** *n* - **1.** (*abbr of* **United States of America**): **the** ~ die USA *pl;* **in the** ~ in den USA - **2.** (*abbr of* **United States Army**) Armee *der* Vereinigten Staaten.

**usable** [ˈjuːzəbl] *adj* brauchbar.

**USAF** (*abbr of* **United States Air Force**) *n* Luft-waffe *der* Vereinigten Staaten.

**usage** [ˈjuːzɪdʒ] *n* - **1.** (*U*) [use of language] Ge-brauch *der* - **2.** [meaning] Bedeutung *die* - **3.** (*U*) [treatment] Behandlung *die;* [handling] Gebrauch *der.*

**use** [*n & aux vb* juːs, *vt* juːz] *n* - **1.** [act of using] Ge-brauch *der,* Benutzung *die;* [for specific purpose] Verwendung *die;* [of method] Anwendung *die;* **to be in/out of** ~ im/außer Gebrauch sein; **to make** ~ **of sthg** von etw Gebrauch machen - **2.** [ability or right to use]: **she no longer has the** ~ **of her legs** sie kann ihre Beine nicht mehr gebrauchen - **3.** [purpose, usefulness] Nutzen *der;* **can you find a** ~ **for this?** kannst du damit etwas anfangen?; **to be of** ~ nützlich sein; **you're no** ~ **at all!** du bist zu nichts nütze!; **it's no** ~ es hat keinen Zweck!; **what's the** ~ **(of doing that)?** was hat es für einen Zweck (, das zu tun)? <> *aux vb:* **I** ~**d to go for a run every day** ich bin früher jeden Tag laufen gegangen; **he didn't** ~ **to be so fat** er war frü-her nicht so dick <> *vt* - **1.** [utilize] gebrau-chen, benutzen; [for specific purpose] verwen-den; [method] anlwenden - **2.** *pej* [exploit] benutzen.

➤ **use up** *vt sep* auflbrauchen.

**used** [*senses 1 and 2* juːzd, *sense 3* juːst] *adj* - **1.** [dirty] benutzt, schmutzig - **2.** [second-hand] gebraucht, Gebraucht- - **3.** [accustomed]: **to be** ~ **to sthg** an etw *(A)* gewöhnt sein; **to be**

**U**

~ **to doing sthg** daran gewöhnt sein OR es gewöhnt sein, etw zu tun; **to get ~ to sthg** sich an etw *(A)* gewöhnen.

**useful** ['juːsful] *adj* [handy] nützlich; **to come in ~** nützlich sein, von Nutzen sein.

**usefulness** ['juːsfulnɪs] *n* Nützlichkeit *die.*

**useless** ['juːslɪs] *adj* - **1.** [unusable] nutzlos - **2.** [pointless] zwecklos, unnütz - **3.** *inf* [hopeless]: **to be ~** zu nichts zu gebrauchen sein.

**uselessness** ['juːslɪsnɪs] *n* Nutzlosigkeit *die.*

**user** ['juːzəʳ] *n* Benutzer *der,* -in *die;* **drug ~** Drogenkonsument *der,* -in *die.*

**user-friendly** *adj* benutzerfreundlich.

**usher** ['ʌʃəʳ] *n* Platzanweiser *der,* -in *die* ◇ *vt* führen.

**usherette** [ˌʌʃə'ret] *n* Platzanweiserin *die.*

**USM** *n* - **1.** *(abbr of* **United States Mail)** *Post der Vereinigten Staaten* - **2.** *(abbr of* **United States Mint)** *Münzanstalt der Vereinigten Staaten.*

**USN** *(abbr of* **United States Navy)** *n Marine der Vereinigten Staaten.*

**USS** *(abbr of* **United States Ship)** *Kürzel vor den Namen von US-Kriegsschiffen.*

**USSR** *(abbr of* **Union of Soviet Socialist Republics)** *n* UdSSR *die.*

**usu.** *abbr of* **usually.**

**usual** ['juːʒəl] *adj* üblich; **as ~** wie üblich.

**usually** ['juːʒəlɪ] *adv* normalerweise; **more than ~ polite/careful** höflicher/vorsichtiger als sonst.

**usurp** [juː'zɜːp] *vt fml* usurpieren.

**usury** ['juːʒʊrɪ] *n (U) fml* Wucher *der.*

**UT** *abk für Utah, in Postanschrift verwendet.*

**utensil** [juː'tensɪl] *n* Utensil *das.*

**uterus** ['juːtərəs] *(pl* **-ri** [-raɪ] OR **-ruses)** *n* Uterus *der,* Gebärmutter *die*

**utilitarian** [ˌjuːtɪlɪ'teərɪən] *adj* [functional] funktionell.

**utility** [juː'tɪlətɪ] *(pl* **-ies)** *n* - **1.** [usefulness] Nützlichkeit *die* - **2.** [company]: **(public) ~** (öffentlicher) Versorgungsbetrieb - **3.** COMPUT Dienstprogramm *das.*

**utility room** *n* ≃ Waschküche *die.*

**utilize, -ise** ['juːtəlaɪz] *vt* nutzen.

**utmost** ['ʌtməust] *adj* äußerste, -r, -s ◇ *n* - **1.** [best effort]: **to do one's ~ (to achieve sthg)** sein Möglichstes tun(, um etw zu erreichen) - **2.** [maximum] Äußerste *das;* **to the ~** bis zum Äußersten.

**utopia** [juː'təupjə] *n* Utopie *die.*

**utter** ['ʌtəʳ] *adj* völlig, komplett ◇ *vt* [sound, cry] auslstoßen; [word] sagen.

**utterly** ['ʌtəlɪ] *adv* völlig.

**U-turn** *n* - **1.** [turning movement] Wende *die* - **2.** *fig* [complete change] Kehrtwendung *die.*

**UV** *(abbr of* **ultraviolet)** *adj* UV-.

**Uzbekistan** [ʊzˌbekɪ'stɑːn] *n* Usbekistan *nt.*

**v¹** *(pl* **v's** OR **vs),** **V** *(pl* **V's** OR **Vs)** [viː] *n* [letter] v *das,* V *das.*

**v²** - **1.** *abbr of* **verse** - **2.** *abbr of* **versus** - **3.** *abbr of* **volt.**

**VA** *abk für Virginia, in Postanschrift verwendet.*

**vac** [væk] *(abbr of* **vacation)** *n Br inf* Sommerferien *pl.*

**vacancy** ['veɪkənsɪ] *(pl* **-ies)** *n* - **1.** [job, position] offene Stelle, freie Position - **2.** [room available] freies Zimmer; **'vacancies'** 'frei'; **'no vacancies'** 'belegt'.

**vacant** ['veɪkənt] *adj* - **1.** [house] leer stehend; [chair] unbesetzt; [toilet] nicht besetzt; [room] frei - **2.** [post, job] offen, frei - **3.** [look] leer.

**vacant lot** *n* Baugrundstück *das.*

**vacantly** ['veɪkəntlɪ] *adv:* **to look at sb ~** jn mit leerem Blick ansehen.

**vacate** [və'keɪt] *vt* - **1.** [post, job] auflgeben - **2.** [seat] frei machen - **3.** [hotel, room] auslziehen aus.

**vacation** [və'keɪʃn] *n* - **1.** UNIV [period when closed] Ferien *pl* - **2.** *Am* [holiday] Ferien *pl,* Urlaub *der.*

**vacationer** [və'keɪʃənəʳ] *n Am* Urlauber *der,* -in *die.*

**vacation resort** *n Am* Urlaubsort *der.*

**vaccinate** ['væksɪneɪt] *vt:* **to ~ sb (against sthg)** jn (gegen etw) impfen.

**vaccination** [ˌvæksɪ'neɪʃn] *n* Impfung *die.*

**vaccine** [*Br* 'væksiːn, *Am* væk'siːn] *n* Impfstoff *der.*

**vacillate** ['væsəleɪt] *vi:* **to ~ (between)** schwanken (zwischen (+ D)).

**vacuum** ['vækjʊəm] *n* - **1.** TECH Vakuum *das* - **2.** *fig* [void] Leere *die* - **3.** [cleaning machine] Staubsauger *der;* **he gave the room a quick ~**

er saugte kurz durch das Zimmer ◇ vt & vi Staub saugen.

**vacuum cleaner** n Staubsauger der.

**vacuum-packed** adj vakuumverpackt.

**vagabond** ['vægəbɒnd] n literary Vagabund der, -in die.

**vagina** [və'dʒaɪnə] n Scheide die, Vagina die.

**vaginal** [və'dʒaɪnl] adj Scheiden-, vaginal.

**vagrant** ['veɪgrənt] n Landstreicher der, -in die.

**vague** [veɪg] adj - **1.** [imprecise, evasive] vage - **2.** [feeling] leicht - **3.** [absent-minded] zerstreut - **4.** [shape, outline] schemenhaft.

**vaguely** ['veɪglɪ] adv - **1.** [imprecisely] vage - **2.** [slightly, not very] leicht - **3.** [absent-mindedly] zerstreut - **4.** [indistinctly] undeutlich.

**vain** [veɪn] adj - **1.** pej [conceited] eitel - **2.** [attempt, hope] vergeblich.
➡ **in vain** adv vergeblich, vergebens.

**vainly** ['veɪnlɪ] adv - **1.** [in vain] vergeblich, vergebens - **2.** [conceitedly] angeberisch.

**valance** ['væləns] n - **1.** [on bed] Volant der - **2.** Am [on curtains] Blende die.

**valedictory** [,vælɪ'dɪktərɪ] adj fml Abschieds-.

**valentine card** ['væləntaɪn-] n Grußkarte die zum Valentinstag.

**Valentine's Day** ['væləntaɪnz-] n: (St) ~ Valentinstag der.

**valet** ['væleɪ, 'vælɪt] n Kammerdiener der.

**valet parking** n: '~' 'Parkservice'.

**valet service** n Reinigungsservice der.

**valiant** ['væljənt] adj kühn.

**valid** ['vælɪd] adj - **1.** [argument] stichhaltig; [explanation] einleuchtend; [decision] begründet; [claim] berechtigt - **2.** [ticket, passport, driving licence] gültig; [contract] rechtsgültig.

**validate** ['vælɪdeɪt] vt - **1.** [argument, claim] bestätigen - **2.** [document] rechtskräftig machen.

**validity** [və'lɪdətɪ] n - **1.** [of argument] Stichhaltigkeit die; [of claim] Berechtigung die - **2.** [of document] Gültigkeit die, Rechtsgültigkeit die.

**Valium®** ['vælɪəm] n Valium® das.

**valley** ['vælɪ] (pl valleys) n Tal das.

**valour** Br, **valor** Am ['vælər] n fml & literary Heldenmut der.

**valuable** ['væljuəbl] adj wertvoll.
➡ **valuables** npl Wertsachen pl.

**valuation** [,vælju'eɪʃn] n - **1.** (U) [pricing] Schätzung die - **2.** [estimated price] Schätzwert der - **3.** [opinion] Einschätzung die.

**value** ['vælju:] n Wert der; **to place a high ~ on sthg** einer Sache (D) hohen Wert beimes-

sen, auf etw (A) großen Wert legen; **to be good ~** preisgünstig sein; **to be ~ for money** ein gutes Preis-Leistungs-Verhältnis haben; **to take sthg at face ~** etw für bare Münze nehmen ◇ vt schätzen.
➡ **values** npl [morals] Werte pl, Wertvorstellungen pl.

**value-added tax** [-ædɪd-] n Mehrwertsteuer die.

**valued** ['vælju:d] adj geschätzt.

**value judg(e)ment** n Werturteil das.

**valuer** ['væljuər] n Schätzer der, -in die.

**valve** [vælv] n - **1.** [in pipe, tube] Absperrhahn der - **2.** [on tyre] Ventil das.

**vampire** ['væmpaɪər] n Vampir der.

**van** [væn] n - **1.** AUT Transporter der, Lieferwagen der - **2.** Br RAIL Wagon der, Wagen der.

**V and A** (abbr of **Victoria and Albert Museum**) n Museum für Kunsthandwerk in London.

**vandal** ['vændl] n Vandale der, -in die.

**vandalism** ['vændəlɪzml] n Vandalismus der.

**vandalize, -ise** ['vændəlaɪz] vt mutwillig beschädigen.

**vanguard** ['vænɡɑːd] n: **in the ~ of sthg** an der Spitze einer Sache (G).

**vanilla** [və'nɪlə] n Vanille die ◇ comp Vanille-.

**vanish** ['vænɪʃ] vi - **1.** [no longer be visible] verschwinden - **2.** [no longer exist - race, species] aussterben; [ - hopes, chances] schwinden.

**vanity** ['vænətɪ] n (U) pej [of person] Eitelkeit die.

**vanquish** ['væŋkwɪʃ] vt literary bezwingen.

**vantagepoint** ['vɑːntɪdʒ,pɔɪnt] n - **1.** [for view] Aussichtspunkt der - **2.** fig [advantageous position]: **from this ~** aus dieser Sicht.

**vapour** Br, **vapor** Am ['veɪpər] n (U) Dampf der.

**vapour trail** n Kondensstreifen der.

**variable** ['veərɪəbl] adj - **1.** [changeable] unbeständig - **2.** [uneven - quality] unterschiedlich; [ - performance] unbeständig ◇ n Variable die.

**variance** ['veərɪəns] n fml: **to be at ~ with sthg** mit etw nicht übereinstimmen.

**variant** ['veərɪənt] adj [alternative] andere, -r, -s; **three ~ forms** drei verschiedene Formen ◇ n [different form, spelling] Variante die.

**variation** [,veərɪ'eɪʃn] n - **1.** (U) [fact of difference] Unterschied der - **2.** [change in level or quantity] Schwankung die - **3.** [different version & MUS] Variation die; **~s on a theme** Variationen zu einem OR über ein Thema.

**varicose veins** ['værɪkəʊs-] npl Krampfadern pl.

**varied** ['veərɪd] adj [life] bewegt; [group] gemischt; [work, diet] abwechslungsreich.

**variety** [və'raɪətɪ] (pl -ies) n - **1.** (U) [difference in

**V**

type] Abwechslung *die* - **2.** [selection] Auswahl *die* - **3.** [type] Art *die*, Sorte *die* - **4.** *(U)* THEATRE Varietee *das*.

**variety show** *n* Varieteevorstellung *die;* TV Unterhaltungsshow *die*.

**various** ['veərɪəs] *adj* verschieden.

**varnish** ['vɑːnɪʃ] *n* [for wood, fingernails] Lack *der;* [for pottery] Glasur *die* <> *vt* [wood, fingernails] lackieren; [pottery] glasieren.

**vary** ['veərɪ] *(pt & pp* **-ied)** *vt* verändern, variieren <> *vi* [differ] sich unterscheiden; [fluctuate] sich ändern; [prices] schwanken; **it varies** das ist verschieden.

**varying** ['veərɪɪŋ] *adj* [different] unterschiedlich; [fluctuating] veränderlich.

**vase** [Br vɑːz, Am veɪz] *n* Vase *die*.

**vasectomy** [və'sektəmɪ] *(pl* **-ies)** *n* Vasektomie *die*.

**Vaseline®** ['væsəliːn] *n* Vaseline *die*.

**vast** [vɑːst] *adj* riesig; [expense, difference] enorm.

**vastly** ['vɑːstlɪ] *adv* [different] völlig; [popular] äußerst; [superior] weit; [improve] gewaltig.

**vastness** ['vɑːstnɪs] *n (U)* [of building] enorme Größe; [area] immense Weite.

**vat** [væt] *n* [open] Bottich *der;* [closed] Fass *das*.

**VAT** [væt, viːeɪ'tiː] *(abbr of* **value added tax)** *n* Mehrwertsteuer *die*, MwSt.

**Vatican** ['vætɪkən] *n:* **the ~** der Vatikan.

**Vatican City** *n* Vatikanstadt *die;* **in ~** in der Vatikanstadt.

**vault** [vɔːlt] *n* - **1.** [in bank] Tresorraum *der* - **2.** [under church] Gruft *die* - **3.** [roof] Gewölbe *das* - **4.** [jump] Sprung *der* <> *vt* springen über *(+ A)* <> *vi:* **to ~ over sthg** über etw *(A)* springen.

**vaulted** ['vɔːltɪd] *adj* ARCHIT gewölbt.

**vaulting horse** ['vɔːltɪŋ-] *n* SPORT Pferd *das*.

**vaunted** ['vɔːntɪd] *adj fml:* **much ~** viel gepriesen.

**VC** *n* - **1.** *abbr of* **vice-chairman** - **2.** *abbr of* **Victoria Cross**.

**VCR** *(abbr of* **video cassette recorder)** *n* Videorekorder *der*.

**VD** *n abbr of* **venereal disease**.

**VDU** *(abbr of* **visual display unit)** *n* Bildschirm *der*.

**veal** [viːl] *n* Kalbfleisch *das*.

**veer** [vɪər] *vi* - **1.** [vehicle] aus|scheren; [road] eine Kurve machen; [wind] (sich) drehen; **the car ~ed off the road** das Auto kam von der Straße ab - **2.** *fig* [conversation, mood] schwanken.

**veg** [vedʒ] *(abbr of* **vegetables)** *n inf (U)* **meat and two ~** Fleisch mit Kartoffeln und Gemüse.

**vegan** ['viːɡən] *adj* veganisch <> *n* Veganer *der,* -in *die*.

**vegetable** ['vedʒtəbl] *n* Gemüse *das* <> *adj* Gemüse-.

**vegetable garden** *n* Gemüsegarten *der*.

**vegetable knife** *n* Küchenmesser *das*.

**vegetable oil** *n* Pflanzenöl *das*.

**vegetarian** [ˌvedʒɪ'teərɪən] *adj* vegetarisch <> *n* Vegetarier *der,* -in *die*.

**vegetarianism** [ˌvedʒɪ'teərɪənɪzm] *n* Vegetarismus *der*.

**vegetate** ['vedʒɪteɪt] *vi pej* dahin|vegetieren.

**vegetation** [ˌvedʒɪ'teɪʃn] *n* Vegetation *die*.

**veggie** ['vedʒɪ] *Br inf adj* vegetarisch <> *n* Vegetarier *der,* -in *die*.

**vehement** ['viːɪmənt] *adj* heftig; [denial, protest, defence] vehement; [debate] hitzig.

**vehemently** ['viːɪməntlɪ] *adv* vehement.

**vehicle** ['viːɪkl] *n* - **1.** [for transport] Fahrzeug *das* - **2.** *fig* [medium]: **to be a ~ for sthg** ein Mittel zu etw sein.

**vehicular** [vɪ'hɪkjʊlər] *adj fml* Fahrzeug-.

**veil** [veɪl] *n* Schleier *der;* **to draw a ~ over sthg** *fig* etw verschweigen.

**veiled** [veɪld] *adj* [hidden] versteckt, verborgen.

**vein** [veɪn] *n* - **1.** [gen] Ader *die* - **2.** [mood] Stimmung *die;* [style] Art *die;* **in the same ~** in derselben Art.

**Velcro®** ['velkrəʊ] *n (U)* Klettband *das*.

**vellum** ['veləm] *n (U)* Pergament *das*.

**velocity** [vɪ'lɒsətɪ] *(pl* **-ies)** *n* PHYSICS Geschwindigkeit *die*.

**velour** [və'lʊər] *n (U)* Velours *der*.

**velvet** ['velvɪt] *n* Samt *der* <> *comp* Samt-.

**vend** [vend] *vt fml* verkaufen.

**vendetta** [ven'detə] *n* Blutrache *die;* [in the press] Hetzkampagne *die*.

**vending machine** ['vendɪŋ-] *n* Automat *der*.

**vendor** ['vendər] *n* Verkäufer *der,* -in *die;* **street ~** Straßenhändler *der,* -in *die*.

**veneer** [və'nɪər] *n* - **1.** [of wood] Furnier *das* - **2.** *fig* [appearance]: **beneath the ~ of politeness** hinter der höflichen Fassade; **to give sthg a ~ of respectability** einer Sache *(D)* einen seriösen Anstrich geben.

**venerable** ['venərəbl] *adj fml* ehrwürdig.

**venerate** ['venəreɪt] *vt fml & RELIG* verehren.

**venereal disease** [vɪ'nɪərɪəl-] *n (U)* Geschlechtskrankheit *die*.

**Venetian** [vɪ'niːʃn] *adj* venezianisch <> *n* Venezianer *der,* -in *die*.

**venetian blind** [vɪˌniːʃn-] *n* Jalousie *die*.

**Venezuela** [ˌvenɪz'weɪlə] *n* Venezuela *nt*.

**vengeance** ['vendʒəns] n (U) Vergeltung die, Rache die; **with a ~** gewaltig; **to work with a ~** hart arbeiten.

**vengeful** ['vendʒfʊl] adj literary rachsüchtig.

**Venice** ['venɪs] n Venedig nt.

**venison** ['venɪzn] n (U) Wild das (Damwild).

**venom** ['venəm] n - **1.** [poison] Gift das - **2.** fig [spite, bitterness] Gehässigkeit die.

**venomous** ['venəməs] adj - **1.** [poisonous] giftig - **2.** fig [bitter, spiteful] gehässig.

**vent** [vent] n Öffnung die; [in chimney, for ventilation] Abzug der; **to give ~ to sthg** [feelings] etw (D) freien Lauf lassen; [anger] etw (D) Luft machen ◇ vt [express - feelings] freien Lauf lassen (+ D); [ - anger] Luft machen (+ D); **to ~ one's anger on sb** seinen Ärger an jm ausllassen.

**ventilate** ['ventɪleɪt] vt (be)lüften.

**ventilation** [,ventɪ'leɪʃn] n Belüftung die.

**ventilator** ['ventɪleɪtəʳ] n - **1.** [in room, building] Ventilator der - **2.** MED Beatmungsgerät das.

**ventriloquist** [ven'trɪləkwɪst] n Bauchredner der, -in die.

**venture** ['ventʃəʳ] n Unternehmen das ◇ vt [proffer - opinion, advice] zu äußern wagen; [ - guess] wagen; [ - suggestion, remark] sich (D) erlauben; **to ~ to do sthg** sich (D) erlauben, etw zu tun ◇ vi - **1.** [go somewhere dangerous] sich wagen - **2.** [embark]: **to ~ into politics** den Schritt in die Politik wagen.

**venture capital** n (U) Risikokapital das.

**venue** ['venju:] n [for concert, conference] Veranstaltungsort der; [for match] Austragungsort der.

**Venus** ['vi:nəs] n Venus die.

**veracity** [və'ræsətɪ] n fml [of person] Aufrichtigkeit die; [of account, statement] Richtigkeit die.

**veranda (h)** [və'rændə] n Veranda die.

**verb** [vɜːb] n Verb das.

**verbal** ['vɜːbl] adj - **1.** [spoken - agreement] mündlich; [ - skills] sprachlich; **~ abuse** Beschimpfung die - **2.** GRAMM Verb-, verbal.

**verbally** ['vɜːbəlɪ] adv [communicate] mündlich; **to ~ abuse sb** jn beschimpfen.

**verbatim** [vɜː'beɪtɪm] adj & adv (wort)wörtlich.

**verbose** [vɜː'bəʊs] adj fml langatmig.

**verdict** ['vɜːdɪkt] n Urteil das; **what's your ~ on his new film?** was hältst du von seinem neuen Film?

**verge** [vɜːdʒ] n - **1.** [edge, side] Rand der; [of road] Bankett das - **2.** [brink]: **to be on the ~ of sthg** [ruin, mental breakdown] am Rand einer Sache (G) stehen; [success] kurz vor etw (D) stehen; **to be on the ~ of doing sthg** kurz davor stehen, etw zu tun.
➡ **verge (up)on** vt fus grenzen an (+ A).

**verger** ['vɜːdʒəʳ] n Küster der, -in die.

**verification** [,verɪfɪ'keɪʃn] n - **1.** (U) [check] Prüfung die, Überprüfung die - **2.** [confirmation] Bestätigung die.

**verify** ['verɪfaɪ] (pt & pp -ied) vt - **1.** [check] prüfen, überprüfen - **2.** [confirm] bestätigen.

**veritable** ['verɪtəbl] adj fml or hum wahr.

**vermilion** [və'mɪljən] adj zinnoberrot.

**vermin** ['vɜːmɪn] npl - **1.** ZOOL [insects] Ungeziefer das; [rodents] Schädlinge pl - **2.** pej [people] Abschaum der.

**vermouth** [vɜː'mu:θ] n Wermut der.

**vernacular** [və'nækjʊləʳ] adj: **~ language** [national] Landessprache die; [regional] Mundart die ◇ n: **the ~** [of country] die Landessprache; [of region] die Mundart.

**verruca** [və'ru:kə] (pl -cas OR -cae [-kaɪ]) n Warze die.

**versa** ➡ vice versa.

**versatile** ['vɜːsətaɪl] adj - **1.** [person] vielseitig - **2.** [machine, tool] vielseitig verwendbar.

**versatility** [,vɜːsə'tɪlətɪ] n - **1.** [of person] Vielseitigkeit die - **2.** [of machine, tool] vielseitige Verwendbarkeit.

**verse** [vɜːs] n - **1.** (U) [poetry] Lyrik die - **2.** [stanza] Strophe die - **3.** [in Bible] Vers der.

**versed** [vɜːst] adj: **to be well ~ in sthg** sich in etw (D) gut auslkennen.

**version** ['vɜːʃn] n - **1.** [form, account of events] Version die - **2.** [translation] Übersetzung die.

**versus** ['vɜːsəs] prep - **1.** SPORT gegen - **2.** [as opposed to] im Gegensatz zu.

**vertebra** ['vɜːtɪbrə] (pl -brae [-bri:]) n Rückenwirbel der.

**vertebrate** ['vɜːtɪbreɪt] n Wirbeltier das.

**vertical** ['vɜːtɪkl] adj senkrecht, vertikal.

**vertically** ['vɜːtɪklɪ] adv senkrecht, vertikal.

**vertigo** ['vɜːtɪgəʊ] n (U) Gleichgewichtsstörungen pl.

**verve** [vɜːv] n Schwung der.

**very** ['verɪ] adv sehr; **~ much** sehr; **not ~** nicht sehr ◇ adj genau; **the ~ opposite** genau das Gegenteil; **the ~ person I was looking for!** nach Ihnen habe ich gerade gesucht!; **that ~ afternoon** am selben Nachmittag; **the ~ next day** gleich am nächsten Tag; **my ~ own room** mein eigenes Zimmer; **the ~ best** das Allerbeste; **for the ~ first/last time** zum allerersten/allerletzten Mal; **at the ~ beginning** ganz am Anfang; **at the ~ least** you should have phoned du hättest doch zumindest anrufen können; **the ~ thought makes me shudder** mich schauderts beim bloßen Gedanken.
➡ **very well** adv - **1.** [all right] schön, also gut

**V**

**- 2.** *phr:* I/you/*etc* **can't ~ well** say no ich kann/
du kannst/*etc* wohl kaum nein sagen.

**vespers** ['vespəz] *n (U)* Vesper *die.*

**vessel** ['vesl] *n fml* **- 1.** [boat] Schiff *das* **- 2.** [container] Gefäß *das.*

**vest** [vest] *n* **- 1.** *Br* [undershirt] Unterhemd *das*
**- 2.** *Am* [waistcoat] Weste *die.*

**vested interest** ['vestɪd-] *n:* **to have a ~ in**
**sthg** [subj: individual] ein persönliches Interesse an etw *(D)* haben; [subj: party, organization] ein
ganz besonderes Interesse an etw *(D)* haben.

**vestibule** ['vestɪbjuːl] *n* **- 1.** *fml* [entrance hall]
Eingangshalle *die* **- 2.** *Am* [on train] Vorraum
*der.*

**vestige** ['vestɪdʒ] *n fml* Spur *die.*

**vestry** ['vestrɪ] *(pl* **-ies)** *n* Sakristei *die.*

**Vesuvius** [vɪ'suːvjəs] *n* der Vesuv.

**vet** [vet] *(pt & pp* **-ted;** *cont* **-ting)** *n* **- 1.** *Br abbr*
*of* **veterinary surgeon - 2.** *Am abbr of* **veteran**
◇ *vt Br* [check] überprüfen.

**veteran** ['vetrən] *adj* [experienced] mit langjähriger Erfahrung ◇ *n* Veteran *der,* -in *die.*

**veteran car** *n Br* Oldtimer *der Baujahre vor*
*1905.*

**Veterans Day** *n amerikanischer Gedenktag*
*anlässlich der Beendigung der beiden Weltkriege.*

**veterinarian** [ˌvetərɪ'neərɪən] *n Am* Tierarzt
*der,* -ärztin *die.*

**veterinary science** ['vetərɪnrɪ-] *n* Veterinärmedizin *die,* Tiermedizin *die.*

**veterinary surgeon** ['vetərɪnrɪ-] *n Br fml*
Tierarzt *der,* -ärztin *die.*

**veto** ['viːtəʊ] *(pl* **-es;** *pt & pp* **-ed;** *cont* **-ing)** *n*
Veto *das* ◇ *vt* sein Veto einllegen gegen.

**vetting** ['vetɪŋ] *n* Überprüfung *die.*

**vex** [veks] *vt fml* [annoy] (ver)ärgern.

**vexed question** [ˌvekst-] *n* viel diskutierte
Frage.

**vg** *abbr of* **very good.**

**VHF** *(abbr of* **very high frequency)** *n* UKW.

**VHS** *(abbr of* **video home system)** *n* VHS.

**VI** *abbr of* **Virgin Islands.**

**via** ['vaɪə] *prep* **- 1.** [travelling through] über *(+ A),*
via *(+ A)* **- 2.** [by means of]: **~ a friend** durch einen Freund; **~ satellite** via *OR* per Satellit.

**viability** [ˌvaɪə'bɪlətɪ] *n* **- 1.** [of plan, programme,
scheme] Durchführbarkeit *die* **- 2.** ECON Lebensfähigkeit *die.*

**viable** ['vaɪəbl] *adj* **- 1.** [plan, programme, scheme]
durchführbar **- 2.** ECON lebensfähig.

**viaduct** ['vaɪədʌkt] *n* Viadukt *der.*

**Viagra**® [vaɪ'ægrə] *n* Viagra® *das.*

**vibrant** ['vaɪbrənt] *adj* **- 1.** [colour, light] leuch-

tend **- 2.** [person] dynamisch; [city] pulsierend, voller Leben; [atmosphere] angeregt.

**vibrate** [vaɪ'breɪt] *vi* vibrieren; PHYS schwingen.

**vibration** [vaɪ'breɪʃn] *n* Vibration *die;* PHYS
Schwingung *die.*

**vicar** ['vɪkəʳ] *n* Pfarrer *der,* -in *die.*

**vicarage** ['vɪkərɪdʒ] *n* Pfarrhaus *das.*

**vicarious** [vɪ'keərɪəs] *adj* [enjoyment, pleasure] indirekt.

**vice** [vaɪs] *n* **- 1.** [immorality, fault] Laster *das*
**- 2.** [tool] Schraubstock *der.*

**vice-** [vaɪs] *prefix* Vize-.

**vice-admiral** *n* Vizeadmiral *der.*

**vice-chairman** *n* stellvertretender Vorsitzender.

**vice-chancellor** *n* UNIV *Leiter der Universitätsverwaltung und Vorsitzender des Senats.*

**vice-president** *n* Vizepräsident *der,* -in *die.*

**vice squad** *n* Sittenpolizei *die.*

**vice versa** [ˌvaɪsɪ'vɜːsə] *adv* umgekehrt.

**vicinity** [vɪ'sɪnətɪ] *n* **- 1.** [neighbourhood] Umgebung *die;* **in the ~ (of)** in der Nähe (von *OR + G)*
**- 2.** [approximate figures]: **in the ~ of £80,000 a year**
um die £80.000 pro Jahr.

**vicious** ['vɪʃəs] *adj* **- 1.** [attack, blow, killer] brutal
**- 2.** [person, gossip] boshaft, gehässig **- 3.** [dog]
bösartig.

**vicious circle** *n* Teufelskreis *der.*

**viciousness** ['vɪʃəsnɪs] *n* **- 1.** [of attack, killer]
Brutalität *die* **- 2.** [of person, gossip] Boshaftigkeit *die,* Gehässigkeit *die* **- 3.** [of dog] Bösartigkeit *die.*

**vicissitudes** [vɪ'sɪsɪtjuːdz] *npl fml* Wandel *der.*

**victim** ['vɪktɪm] *n* Opfer *das;* **to fall ~ to sb/sthg**
jm/etw zum Opfer fallen.

**victimize, -ise** ['vɪktɪmaɪz] *vt* schikanieren.

**victor** ['vɪktəʳ] *n* Sieger *der,* -in *die.*

**Victoria Cross** [vɪk'tɔːrɪə-] *n* Viktoriakreuz
*das, höchste britische Tapferkeitsauszeichnung.*

**Victoria Falls** [vɪk'tɔːrɪə-] *npl:* **the ~** die Viktoriafälle.

**Victorian** [vɪk'tɔːrɪən] *adj* **- 1.** [from Victorian era]
viktorianisch **- 2.** *usu pej* [overstrict] sittenstreng.

**victorious** [vɪk'tɔːrɪəs] *adj* [winning] siegreich.

**victory** ['vɪktərɪ] *(pl* **-ies)** *n* Sieg *der;* **to win a**
**~ over sb/sthg** jn/etw bezwingen.

**video** ['vɪdɪəʊ] *(pl* **-s;** *pt & pp* **-ed;** *cont* **-ing)** *n*
**- 1.** [gen] Video *das;* **I've got it on ~** ich habe es
auf Video **- 2.** [machine] Videorekorder *der*
◇ *comp* Video- ◇ *vt* **- 1.** [using videorecorder]
(auf Video) auf lnehmen **- 2.** [using camera] filmen.

**video camera** n Videokamera die.

**video cassette** n Videokassette die.

**videodisc** Br, **videodisk** Am ['vɪdɪəudɪsk] n Bildplatte die.

**video game** n Videospiel das.

**video machine** n Videorekorder der.

**videophone** ['vɪdɪəufəun] n Bildtelefon das.

**videorecorder** ['vɪdɪəurɪˌkɔːdəʳ] n Videorekorder der.

**video recording** n Videoaufnahme die.

**video shop** n Videothek die.

**videotape** ['vɪdɪəuteɪp] n Videoband das.

**vie** [vaɪ] (pt & pp vied; cont vying) vi: to ~ (with sb) for sthg (mit jm) um etw wetteifern; to ~ with sb to do sthg mit jm darum wetteifern, etw zu tun.

**Vienna** [vɪ'enə] n Wien nt.

**Viennese** [ˌvɪə'niːz] adj wienerisch <> n Wiener der, -in die.

**Vietnam** [Br ˌvjet'næm, Am ˌvjet'nɑːm] n Vietnam nt.

**Vietnamese** [ˌvjetnə'miːz] adj vietnamesisch <> n - **1.** [person] Vietnamese der, -sin die - **2.** [language] Vietnamesisch(e) das <> npl: the ~ die Vietnamesen.

**view** [vjuː] n - **1.** [opinion] Ansicht die, Meinung die; **what are your ~s on contraception?** wie stehen Sie zur Empfängnisverhütung?; **in my ~** meiner Ansicht OR Meinung nach; **to take the ~ that** die Ansicht vertreten, dass - **2.** [vista] Aussicht die, Blick der - **3.** [ability to see] Sicht die; **to come into ~** in Sicht kommen <> vt - **1.** [consider] sehen; **he ~ed her with suspicion** er betrachtete sie mit Argwohn - **2.** fml [house] besichtigen.

➤ **in view of** prep angesichts (+ G).

➤ **with a view to** conj: **with a ~ to doing sthg** mit der Absicht, etw zu tun.

**Viewdata**® ['vjuːdeɪtə] n Bildschirmtext der.

**viewer** ['vjuːəʳ] n - **1.** [person] Zuschauer der, -in die - **2.** [for slides] Diabetrachter der.

**viewfinder** ['vjuːˌfaɪndəʳ] n Sucher der.

**viewpoint** ['vjuːpɔɪnt] n - **1.** [opinion] Standpunkt der - **2.** [place] Aussichtspunkt der.

**vigil** ['vɪdʒɪl] n Nachtwache die.

**vigilance** ['vɪdʒɪləns] n Wachsamkeit die.

**vigilant** ['vɪdʒɪlənt] adj wachsam.

**vigilante** [ˌvɪdʒɪ'læntɪ] n (militante) Bürgerwehr.

**vigor** n Am = vigour.

**vigorous** ['vɪgərəs] adj - **1.** [walk] flott; [shake, scrub] kräftig - **2.** [protest, denial, attempt] energisch - **3.** [person, animal, plant] kräftig.

**vigour** Br, **vigor** Am ['vɪgəʳ] n (U) Kraft die, Energie die.

**Viking** ['vaɪkɪŋ] adj Wikinger- <> n Wikinger der, -in die.

**vile** [vaɪl] adj [act, person] abscheulich; [food] scheußlich.

**vilify** ['vɪlɪfaɪ] (pt & pp -ied) vt fml diffamieren.

**villa** ['vɪlə] n Villa die.

**village** ['vɪlɪdʒ] n Dorf das.

**villager** ['vɪlɪdʒəʳ] n Dorfbewohner der, -in die.

**villain** ['vɪlən] n - **1.** [of film, book, play] Bösewicht der - **2.** dated [criminal] Schurke der.

**vinaigrette** [ˌvɪnɪ'gret] n Vinaigrette die.

**vindicate** ['vɪndɪkeɪt] vt [confirm] bestätigen; [justify] rechtfertigen; **to ~ o.s.** seine Unschuld beweisen.

**vindication** [ˌvɪndɪ'keɪʃn] n [confirmation] Bestätigung die; [justification] Rechtfertigung die.

**vindictive** [vɪn'dɪktɪv] adj rachsüchtig.

**vine** [vaɪn] n [grapevine] Weinrebe die.

**vinegar** ['vɪnɪgəʳ] n Essig der.

**vine leaf** n Weinblatt das.

**vineyard** ['vɪnjəd] n Weinberg der.

**vintage** ['vɪntɪdʒ] adj - **1.** [wine] erlesen - **2.** fig [classic]: **this film is ~ Spielberg** dieser Film ist Spielberg vom Feinsten <> n [wine] Jahrgang der.

**vintage car** n Br Oldtimer der Baujahre 1919 bis 1930.

**vintner** ['vɪntnəʳ] n Weinhändler der, -in die.

**vinyl** ['vaɪnɪl] n Vinyl das <> comp Vinyl-.

**viola** [vɪ'əulə] n - **1.** MUS Bratsche die - **2.** BOT Veilchen das.

**violate** ['vaɪəleɪt] vt - **1.** [human rights, law, treaty] verstoßen gegen - **2.** [peace, privacy] stören - **3.** [grave] schänden.

**violation** [ˌvaɪə'leɪʃn] n - **1.** (U) [of human rights, law, treaty] Verstoß der gegen - **2.** [of peace, privacy] Störung die - **3.** [of grave] Schändung die.

**violence** ['vaɪələns] n (U) - **1.** [physical force] Gewalt die; [of people] Gewalttätigkeit die; [of actions] Brutalität die - **2.** [of words, reaction] Heftigkeit die.

**violent** ['vaɪələnt] adj - **1.** [person] gewalttätig; [attack] heftig; [crime] Gewalt-; [death] gewaltsam - **2.** [intense] heftig - **3.** [colour] grell.

**violently** ['vaɪələntlɪ] adv - **1.** [attack, behave] brutal; **to die ~** eines gewaltsamen Todes sterben - **2.** [react, argue, defend] heftig.

**violet** ['vaɪələt] adj violett <> n - **1.** [flower] Veilchen das - **2.** [colour] Violett das.

**violin** [ˌvaɪə'lɪn] n Violine die, Geige die.

**violinist** [ˌvaɪə'lɪnɪst] n Violinist der, -in die, Geiger der, -in die.

**V**

**VIP** (*abbr of* **very important person**) *n* Prominente *der*, *die*, VIP *der*.

**viper** ['vaɪpə'] *n* Viper *die*.

**viral** ['vaɪrəl] *adj* Virus-.

**virgin** ['vɜːdʒɪn] *adj* - **1.** [gen] jungfräulich - **2.** [forest, soil] unberührt ◇ *n* Jungfrau *die*.

**Virgin Islands** *n:* the ~ die Jungferninseln; in the ~ auf den Jungferninseln.

**virginity** [və'dʒɪnətɪ] *n* Jungfräulichkeit *die*.

**Virgo** ['vɜːgəʊ] (*pl* **-s**) *n* Jungfrau *die*.

**virile** ['vɪraɪl] *adj* männlich.

**virility** [vɪ'rɪlətɪ] *n* Männlichkeit *die*.

**virtual** ['vɜːtʃʊəl] *adj:* it is a ~ certainty das steht so gut wie fest; the traffic came to a ~ standstill der Verkehr kam praktisch zum Erliegen.

**virtually** ['vɜːtʃʊəlɪ] *adv* [almost] so gut wie, praktisch.

**virtual memory** *n* COMPUT virtueller Speicher.

**virtual reality** *n* virtuelle Realität.

**virtue** ['vɜːtjuː] *n* - **1.** [goodness] Tugendhaftigkeit *die* - **2.** [merit, quality] Tugend *die* - **3.** [benefit] Vorteil *der*.
◆ **by virtue of** *prep fml* aufgrund (+ *G*).

**virtuoso** [ˌvɜːtjʊ'əʊzəʊ] (*pl* **-sos** OR **-si** [-siː]) *n* Virtuose *der*, -sin *die*.

**virtuous** ['vɜːtʃʊəs] *adj* tugendhaft.

**virulent** ['vɪrʊlənt] *adj* - **1.** *fml* [bitter and hostile] scharf, heftig - **2.** MED [very powerful] bösartig.

**virus** ['vaɪrəs] *n* MED & COMPUT Virus *der*.

**visa** ['viːzə] *n* Visum *das*; entry/exit ~ Einreise-/Ausreisevisum *das*.

**vis-à-vis** *prep fml* [in comparison to] gegenüber (+ *D*); [regarding] bezüglich (+ *D*).

**viscose** ['vɪskəʊs] *n* Viskose *die*.

**viscosity** [vɪ'skɒsətɪ] *n* CHEM Viskosität *die*.

**viscount** ['vaɪkaʊnt] *n* Viscount *der*.

**vise** [vaɪz] *n* Am Schraubstock *der*.

**visibility** [ˌvɪzɪ'bɪlətɪ] *n* - **1.** [being visible] Sichtbarkeit *die* - **2.** [range of vision] Sichtweite *die;* good/poor ~ gute/schlechte Sicht.

**visible** ['vɪzəbl] *adj* - **1.** [which can be physically seen] sichtbar - **2.** [evident] sichtlich.

**visibly** ['vɪzəblɪ] *adv* [clearly] sichtlich.

**vision** ['vɪʒn] *n* - **1.** [ability to see] Sehvermögen *das* - **2.** *fig* [foresight] Weitblick *der;* a man of ~ ein Mann mit Weitblick - **3.** [impression, dream] Vision *die*.

**visionary** ['vɪʒənrɪ] (*pl* **-ies**) *adj* visionär ◇ *n* Visionär *der*, -in *die*.

**visit** ['vɪzɪt] *n* Besuch *der;* [stay] Aufenthalt *der;* we saw it on a ~ to the States wir haben es gesehen, als wir in Amerika waren ◇ *vt* besuchen.

◆ **visit with** *vt fus Am* - **1.** [talk with] plaudern mit - **2.** [go and see] besuchen.

**visiting card** ['vɪzɪtɪŋ-] *n* Visitenkarte *die*.

**visiting hours** ['vɪzɪtɪŋ-] *npl* Besuchszeiten *pl*.

**visitor** ['vɪzɪtə'] *n* Besucher *der*, -in *die;* she has ~s sie hat Besuch.

**visitors' book** *n* Gästebuch *das*.

**visor** ['vaɪzə'] *n* [on helmet] Visier *das*.

**vista** ['vɪstə] *n* - **1.** [view] Ausblick *der* - **2.** *fig* [perspective] Perspektive *die*.

**visual** ['vɪʒʊəl] *adj* Seh-; [joke, memory, image] visuell.

**visual aids** *npl* Anschauungsmaterial *das*.

**visual display unit** *n* Bildschirm *der*.

**visualize, -ise** ['vɪʒʊəlaɪz] *vt* sich (*D*) vorstellen.

**visually** ['vɪʒʊəlɪ] *adv:* ~ handicapped/impaired sehbehindert

**vital** ['vaɪtl] *adj* - **1.** [essential] unerlässlich, unbedingt notwendig; [essential to life] lebenswichtig; it is of ~ importance es ist von entscheidender Bedeutung - **2.** [full of life - person] vital.

**vitality** [vaɪ'tælətɪ] *n* Vitalität *die*.

**vitally** ['vaɪtəlɪ] *adv:* ~ important von entscheidender Bedeutung.

**vital statistics** *npl inf* [of woman] Maße *pl*.

**vitamin** [Br 'vɪtəmɪn, Am 'vaɪtəmɪn] *n* Vitamin *das*.

**vitreous** *adj* Glas-; ~ china Halbporzellan *das*.

**vitriolic** [ˌvɪtrɪ'ɒlɪk] *adj fml* hasserfüllt.

**viva** ['vaɪvə] *n* UNIV mündliche Prüfung.

**vivacious** [vɪ'veɪʃəs] *adj* lebhaft, lebendig.

**vivacity** [vɪ'væsətɪ] *n* Lebhaftigkeit *die*, Lebendigkeit *die*.

**vivid** ['vɪvɪd] *adj* - **1.** [colour] kräftig - **2.** [memory] lebhaft; [description] lebendig.

**vividly** ['vɪvɪdlɪ] *adv* - **1.** [painted] in kräftigen Farben - **2.** [remember] lebhaft; [describe] lebendig.

**vivisection** [ˌvɪvɪ'sekʃn] *n* Vivisektion *die*.

**vixen** ['vɪksn] *n* Füchsin *die*.

**viz** [vɪz] (*abbr of* **videlicet**) d. h.

**VLF** (*abbr of* **very low frequency**) *n* VLF, niederfrequente Radiowellen.

**V-neck** *n* - **1.** [sweater, dress] Pullover *der*/Kleid *das* mit V-Ausschnitt - **2.** [neck] V-Ausschnitt *der*.

**VOA** *n abbr of* **Voice of America**.

**vocabulary** [və'kæbjʊlərɪ] (*pl* **-ies**) *n* - **1.** [gen] Wortschatz *der*, Vokabular *das* - **2.** [list of words] Wörterverzeichnis *das*.

**vocal** [ˈvəʊkl] adj - **1.** [outspoken] lautstark
- **2.** [of the voice] stimmlich; ~ **range** Stimmumfang der.

➤ **vocals** npl: featuring Paul Jones on ~s mit
Paul Jones als Sänger.

**vocal cords** npl Stimmbänder pl.

**vocalist** [ˈvəʊkəlɪst] n Sänger der, -in die.

**vocation** [vəʊˈkeɪʃn] n [calling] Berufung die.

**vocational** [vəʊˈkeɪʃnl] adj berufsbezogen.

**vociferous** [vəˈsɪfərəs] adj fml lautstark.

**vodka** [ˈvɒdkə] n Wodka der.

**vogue** [vəʊg] adj Mode- ◇ n Mode die; **there is
a ~ for** high-heeled shoes hochnackige Schuhe sind groß in Mode; **to be in ~** in Mode
sein.

**voice** [vɔɪs] n - **1.** [gen] Stimme die; **to raise/
lower one's ~** lauter/leiser sprechen; **to
keep one's ~ down** leise OR nicht laut sprechen - **2.** [influence] Mitspracherecht das
- **3.** GRAMM Genus Verbi das; **the active/passive
voice** das Aktiv/Passiv ◇ vt [opinion, emotion]
zum Ausdruck bringen.

**voice box** n Kehlkopf der.

**Voice of America** n: **the ~** die Stimme
Amerikas.

**voice-over** n Begleitkommentar der (in
Film, Fernsehbericht).

**void** [vɔɪd] adj - **1.** [contract, result] ungültig,
nichtig ⊳ **null - 2.** fml [empty]: ~ **of interest**
ohne jegliches Interesse ◇ n - **1.** literary
[feeling of emptiness]: **the ~** left by his death die
Lücke, die sein Tod hinterlassen hat
- **2.** [chasm] Nichts das.

**voile** [vwɑːl] n Voile der.

**vol.** (abbr of **volume**) Bd.

**volatile** [Br ˈvɒlətaɪl, Am ˈvɒlətl] adj [situation]
brisant; [person] aufbrausend; [market] unbeständig.

**vol-au-vent** [ˈvɒləʊvɑ̃] n Königinpastete die.

**volcanic** [vɒlˈkænɪk] adj [eruption, landscape] Vul-
kan-; [activity, rock] vulkanisch.

**volcano** [vɒlˈkeɪnəʊ] (pl -es OR -s) n Vulkan der.

**vole** [vəʊl] n [water vole] Wühlmaus die; [common
vole] Feldmaus die.

**Volga** [ˈvɒlgə] n: **the (River) ~** die Wolga.

**volition** [vəˈlɪʃn] n fml: **of one's own ~** aus freiem Willen.

**volley** [ˈvɒlɪ] (pl **volleys**) n - **1.** [of gunfire] Salve
die - **2.** [of insults] Flut die; **a ~ of abuse** eine
Schimpfkanonade - **3.** [in tennis] Volley der;
[in football] Volleyschuss der ◇ vt [in tennis] volley spielen; [in football] volley nehmen.

**volleyball** [ˈvɒlɪbɔːl] n SPORT Volleyball der.

**volt** [vəʊlt] n Volt das.

**Volta** [ˈvɒltə] n - **1.** [river]: **the (River) ~** der Volta - **2.** [lake]: **Lake ~** der Voltasee.

**voltage** [ˈvəʊltɪdʒ] n Spannung die.

**voluble** [ˈvɒljʊbl] adj fml redselig.

**volume** [ˈvɒljuːm] n - **1.** [of sound] Lautstärke
die; **to turn the ~ up/down** lauter/leiser stellen - **2.** [of container, object] Volumen das,
Rauminhalt der - **3.** [of work] Umfang der; ~ **of
traffic** Verkehrsaufkommen das; **the ~ of letters** die Zahl der Zuschriften - **4.** [book] Band
der.

**volume control** n Lautstärkeregler der.

**voluminous** [vəˈluːmɪnəs] adj fml - **1.** [garment]
weit - **2.** [container] groß.

**voluntarily** [Br ˈvɒləntrɪlɪ, Am ˌvɒlənˈterəlɪ] adv
freiwillig; [work] ehrenamtlich.

**voluntary** [ˈvɒləntrɪ] adj - **1.** [not obligatory] freiwillig - **2.** [unpaid] ehrenamtlich.

**voluntary liquidation** n freiwillige Liquidation.

**voluntary redundancy** n Br: **to take ~** sich
abfinden lassen.

**voluntary work** n freiwillige OR ehrenamtliche Tätigkeit.

**volunteer** [ˌvɒlənˈtɪər] n - **1.** [gen & MIL] Freiwillige der, die - **2.** [unpaid worker] freiwillige
Helfer der, -in die ◇ vt - **1.** [of one's free will]: **to
~ to do sthg** sich bereit erklären, etw zu tun
- **2.** [information] geben; **to ~ advice** Ratschläge
erteilen ◇ vi sich freiwillig melden.

**voluptuous** [vəˈlʌptʃʊəs] adj [woman, mouth]
sinnlich; [body] üppig.

**vomit** [ˈvɒmɪt] n Erbrochene das ◇ vi sich
übergeben.

**voodoo** [ˈvuːduː] n Wodu der.

**voracious** [vəˈreɪʃəs] adj: **to be a ~ eater** Un-
mengen vertilgen; **to be a ~ reader** Bücher
geradezu verschlingen.

**vortex** [ˈvɔːteks] (pl **-texes** OR **-tices** [-tɪsiːz]) n
- **1.** [whirlpool, whirlwind] Wirbel der - **2.** [of events]
Strudel der.

**vote** [vəʊt] n - **1.** [individual decision] Stimme die;
**a ~ for/against sb/sthg** eine Stimme für/
gegen jn/etw - **2.** [session, ballot] Abstimmung
die; **to put sthg to the ~** über etw (A) abstimmen lassen - **3.** [result of ballot]: **the ~** das Ab-
stimmungsergebnis - **4.** [section of voters]: **the
nationalist ~ is growing** die Nationalisten gewinnen immer mehr Anhänger - **5.** [suf-
frage] Stimmrecht das ◇ vt - **1.** [gen] wählen;
**he was ~ed leader** er wurde zum Führer gewählt; **to ~ to do sthg** (per Abstimmung)
beschließen, etw zu tun - **2.** [suggest] vor-
schlagen ◇ vi wählen; **to ~ for/against sb/
sthg** für/gegen jn/etw stimmen; **to ~ on an
issue** über eine Frage abstimmen; **every responsible citizen should ~** jeder verantwor-
tungsbewusste Bürger sollte wählen gehen.

➤ **vote in** vt sep wählen.

**V**

◆ **vote out** *vt sep* ablwählen.

**vote of confidence** (*pl* **votes of confidence**) *n* Vertrauensvotum *das*; **to ask for a ~** die Vertrauensfrage stellen; **to give sb a ~** jm sein Vertrauen auslsprechen.

**vote of no confidence** (*pl* **votes of no confidence**) *n* Misstrauensvotum *das*.

**vote of thanks** (*pl* **votes of thanks**) *n:* **to propose a ~** jm seinen Dank auslsprechen.

**voter** ['vəʊtəʳ] *n* Wähler *die*, -in *die*.

**voting** ['vəʊtɪŋ] *n* Wahl *die*, Abstimmung *die*.

**vouch** [vaʊtʃ] ◆ **vouch for** *vt fus* - **1.** [person] bürgen für - **2.** [character, accuracy] sich verbürgen für.

**voucher** ['vaʊtʃəʳ] *n* Gutschein *der*.

**vow** [vaʊ] *n* Gelöbnis *das;* RELIG Gelübde *das* ◇ *vt:* **to ~ to do sthg** geloben, etw zu tun; **to ~ (that)** schwören(, dass).

**vowel** ['vaʊəl] *n* Vokal *der*.

**voyage** ['vɔɪɪdʒ] *n* Reise *die;* [by sea] Seereise *die;* [through space] Flug *der*.

**voyeur** [vwɑ:'jɜːʳ] *n* Voyeur *der*, -in *die*.

**voyeurism** [vwɑː'jɜːrɪzm] *n* Voyeurismus *der*.

**VP** *n* (*abbr of* **vice-president**) VP.

**vs** *abbr of* **versus**.

**VSO** (*abbr of* **Voluntary Service Overseas**) *n* britische Hilfsorganisation, die Freiwillige mit Berufsausbildung in Entwicklungsländern einsetzt.

**VT** *abk für* Vermont, in Postanschrift verwendet.

**VTOL** ['viːtɒl] (*abbr of* **vertical takeoff and landing**) *n* Senkrechtstart und -landung.

**vulgar** ['vʌlgəʳ] *adj* - **1.** [tasteless - décor] geschmacklos; [ - person] ordinär - **2.** [rude] vulgär.

**vulgarity** [vʌl'gærətɪ] *n* - **1.** [tastelessness - of décor, remark, joke] Geschmacklosigkeit *die;* [ - of person] Vulgarität *die* - **2.** [rudeness] Vulgarität *die*.

**vulnerability** [ˌvʌlnərə'bɪlətɪ] *n* - **1.** [to emotional harm] Verletzlichkeit *die;* [to criticism, attack] Angreifbarkeit *die* - **2.** [to influence, disease] Anfälligkeit *die;* [to bodily harm] Verwundbarkeit *die*.

**vulnerable** ['vʌlnərəbl] *adj* - **1.** [easily hurt - emotionally] verletzlich; [ - physically] verwundbar; **to be ~ to the cold** gegenüber Kälte empfindlich sein; **to be ~ to attack/criticism** leicht angreifbar sein; **the most ~ people in society** die Schwächsten in der Gesellschaft - **2.** [easily influenced]: **~ (to sthg)** anfällig (für etw).

**vulture** ['vʌltʃəʳ] *n lit* & *fig* Geier *der*.

**w** (*pl* **w's** OR **ws**), **W** (*pl* **W's** OR **Ws**) ['dʌblju:] *n* w *das*, W *das*.
◆ **W** (*abbr of* **west, watt**) W.

**WA** *abk für* Washington (State), in Postanschrift verwendet.

**wacky** ['wækɪ] (*compar* **-ier;** *superl* **-iest**) *adj inf* verrückt.

**wad** [wɒd] *n* - **1.** [of cotton wool] Bausch *der* - **2.** [of bank notes, documents] Bündel *das*.

**wadding** ['wɒdɪŋ] *n* [for packing] Material *das* zum Ausstopfen; [for clothes] Wattierung *die*.

**waddle** ['wɒdl] *vi* watscheln.

**wade** [weɪd] *vi* waten.
◆ **wade through** *vt fus fig* durchackern.

**wadge** [wɒdʒ] *n Br inf* [of food] ordentliches Stück; [of cotton wool] Bausch *der;* [of papers, banknotes] Bündel *das*.

**wading pool** ['weɪdɪŋ-] *n Am* Plantschbecken *das*.

**wafer** ['weɪfəʳ] *n* [thin biscuit] Waffel *die*.

**wafer-thin** *adj* hauchdünn.

**waffle** ['wɒfl] *n* - **1.** CULIN Waffel *die* - **2.** *Br inf* [vague talk] Geschwafel *das* ◇ *vi* schwafeln.

**waft** [wɑːft, wɒft] *vi* ziehen; [breeze] wehen.

**wag** [wæg] (*pt* & *pp* **-ged;** *cont* **-ging**) *vt* [tail] wedeln mit; **to ~ one's finger at sb** jm mit dem Finger drohen ◇ *vi* [tail] wedeln.

**wage** [weɪdʒ] *n* Lohn *der* ◇ *vt:* **to ~ war against sb/sthg** einen Kampf gegen jn/etw führen.
◆ **wages** *npl* Lohn *der*.

**wage claim** *n* Lohnforderung *die*.

**wage differential** *n* Lohnunterschied *der*.

**wage earner** [-ˌɜːnəʳ] *n* Lohnempfänger *der*, -in *die*.

**wage freeze** *n* Lohnstopp *der*.

**wage packet** *n* - **1.** [envelope] Lohntüte *die* - **2.** [pay] Lohn *der*.

**wager** ['weɪdʒəʳ] *n* Wette *die*.

**wage rise** *n Br* Lohnerhöhung *die*.

**waggish** ['wægɪʃ] *adj inf* schelmisch.

**waggle** ['wægl] *inf vt* [tail] wedeln mit; [ears] wackeln mit ◇ *vi* [tail] wedeln; [ears] wackeln.

**wagon, waggon** *Br* ['wægən] *n* - **1.** [horsedrawn vehicle] Fuhrwerk *das* - **2.** *Br* RAIL Waggon *der.*

**wagtail** *n* Bachstelze *die.*

**wail** [weɪl] *n* - **1.** [of baby] Geschrei *das;* [of mourner] Klagen *das* - **2.** [of wind, siren] Heulen *das* <> *vi* - **1.** [baby] schreien; [mourner] klagen - **2.** [wind, siren] heulen.

**wailing** ['weɪlɪŋ] *n* - **1.** [of baby] Geschrei *das;* [mourner] Klagen *das* - **2.** [of wind, siren] Heulen *das.*

**waist** [weɪst] *n* Taille *die.*

**waistband** ['weɪstbænd] *n* [of skirt] Rockbund *der;* [of trousers] Hosenbund *der.*

**waistcoat** ['weɪskəʊt] *n Br* Weste *die.*

**waistline** ['weɪstlaɪn] *n* Taille *die.*

**wait** [weɪt] *n* Wartezeit *die;* **to lie in ~ for sb** jm auflauern <> *vi* warten; **to ~ and see** abwarten(, was passiert); **~ a minute** OR **second** OR **moment** Augenblick OR Moment (mal); **(just) you ~!** warte nur!; **the washing-up can ~** der Abwasch kann warten OR hat Zeit <> *vt* - **1.** [person]: **I/he/she can't ~ to do it** ich/er/sie kann es kaum erwarten, es zu tun - **2.** *Am* [delay]: **to ~ dinner for sb** mit dem Abendessen auf jn warten - **3.**: **to ~ tables** kellnern.

◆ **wait about, wait around** *vi* warten.

◆ **wait for** *vt fus* warten auf (+ A); **to ~ for sthg to happen** darauf warten, dass etw geschieht; **to ~ for sb to do sthg** darauf warten, dass jd etw tut.

◆ **wait on** *vt fus* [serve food to] bedienen.

◆ **wait up** *vi* auf lbleiben.

**waiter** ['weɪtəʳ] *n* Kellner *der;* **waiter!** Herr Ober!

**waiting game** ['weɪtɪŋ-] *n:* **to play a ~** erst einmal abwarten, wie sich die Dinge entwickeln.

**waiting list** ['weɪtɪŋ-] *n* Warteliste *die.*

**waiting room** ['weɪtɪŋ-] *n* Warteraum *der;* [at doctor's] Wartezimmer *das;* [at railway station] Wartesaal *der.*

**waitress** ['weɪtrɪs] *n* Kellnerin *die*, Serviererin *die.*

**waive** [weɪv] *vt fml* [entrance fee] verzichten auf (+ A); [rule] nicht anwenden.

**waiver** ['weɪvəʳ] *n* Verzichtserklärung *die.*

**wake** [weɪk] (*pt* woke OR -d; *pp* woken OR -d) *n* - **1.** [of ship, boat] Kielwasser *das;* **to leave sthg in one's/its ~** etw hinterlassen; **in the ~ of** im Gefolge (+ G) - **2.** [after funeral] Totenwache *die* <> *vt* wecken <> *vi* auf lwachen.

◆ **wake up** *vt sep* auf lwecken <> *vi* - **1.** [wake] auf lwachen - **2.** [become aware]: **to ~ up to sthg** sich (D) einer Sache (G) bewusst werden.

**waken** ['weɪkən] *fml vt* wecken <> *vi* erwachen.

**waking hours** ['weɪkɪŋ-] *npl:* **to spend all one's ~ doing sthg** von früh bis spät etw tun.

**Wales** [weɪlz] *n* Wales *nt.*

**walk** [wɔːk] *n* - **1.** [stroll] Spaziergang *der;* **to go for a ~** einen Spaziergang machen; **to take the dog for a ~** mit dem Hund spazieren gehen; **it's quite a long ~ to the station** zu Fuß ist es ganz schön weit bis zum Bahnhof; **a five-mile ~** eine Wanderung von fünf Meilen - **2.** [path] Fußweg *der* - **3.** [gait] Gang *der* <> *vt* - **1.** [escort]: **I'll ~ you back to the car park** ich gehe mit dir zurück zum Parkplatz; **to ~ sb home** jn (zu Fuß) nach Hause begleiten - **2.** [dog] spazieren führen - **3.** [cover on foot] laufen, (zu Fuß) gehen; **to ~ the streets** [be homeless] obdachlos sein; [in search of sthg] durch die Straßen irren; [prostitute] auf den Strich gehen <> *vi* gehen, laufen; [hike] wandern; **he ~s to work** er geht zu Fuß zur Arbeit.

◆ **walk away with** *vt fus inf fig* [medal] mit Leichtigkeit gewinnen; [prize] kassieren, ein lsacken.

◆ **walk in on** *vt fus* [interrupt]: **to ~ in on sb/sthg** bei jm/etw hereinplatzen.

◆ **walk off** *vt sep* [headache, cramp] durch Spazierengehen vertreiben; **to ~ off a meal** einen Verdauungsspaziergang machen.

◆ **walk off with** *vt fus inf* - **1.** [steal] sich davon lmachen mit - **2.** [win easily] kassieren, ein lsacken.

◆ **walk out** *vi* - **1.** [leave suddenly] hinaus lgehen; **to ~ out of a room** einen Raum verlassen - **2.** [go on strike] in Streik treten.

◆ **walk out on** *vt fus* sitzen lassen.

**walkabout** ['wɔːkəˌbaʊt] *n Br* [by politician]: **to go on a ~** sich unters Volk mischen.

**walker** ['wɔːkəʳ] *n* [for pleasure] Spaziergänger *der*, -in *die;* [when hiking] Wanderer *der*, -derin *die;* SPORT Geher *der*, -in *die.*

**walkie-talkie** [ˌwɔːkɪˈtɔːkɪ] *n* Walkie-Talkie *das.*

**walk-in** *adj* - **1.**: **a ~ cupboard** ein begehbarer Einbauschrank OR Wandschrank - **2.** *Am* [victory] spielend.

**walking** ['wɔːkɪŋ] *n* [for pleasure] Spaziergehen *das;* [hiking] Wandern *das;* SPORT Gehen *das.*

**walking shoes** *npl* Wanderschuhe *pl.*

**walking stick** *n* Spazierstock *der.*

**Walkman**® ['wɔːkmən] *n* Walkman® *der.*

**walk of life** (*pl* walks of life) *n:* **people from all walks of life** Leute aus den verschiedensten gesellschaftlichen Gruppierungen.

**walk-on** *adj:* **~ part** Statistenrolle *die.*

**walkout** ['wɔːkaʊt] *n* [of workers] Arbeitsniederlegung *die;* [in negotiations]: **to stage a ~** demonstrativ den Verhandlungstisch verlassen.

**W**

**walkover** ['wɔːk,əʊvəʳ] n Br inf [victory] spielender Sieg.

**walkway** ['wɔːkweɪ] n Fußweg der.

**wall** [wɔːl] n - 1. [inside building, of stomach, cell] Wand die - 2. [outside] Mauer die; **to come up against a brick ~** nicht mehr weiterkommen; **to drive sb up the ~** jn auf die Palme bringen; **to go up the ~** die Wände hochgehen.

**wallaby** (pl -ies) n Wallaby das.

**wallchart** ['wɔːltʃɑːt] n Schautafel die.

**wall cupboard** n Hängeschrank der.

**walled** [wɔːld] adj von Mauern umgeben.

**wallet** ['wɒlɪt] n [for money] Brieftasche die; [for documents] Etui das.

**wallflower** ['wɔːl,flaʊəʳ] n - 1. [plant] Goldlack der - 2. inf fig [person] Mauerblümchen das.

**wallop** ['wɒləp] inf n Schlag der; **to give sthg a ~** auf etw (A) hauen ⬦ vt [person] versohlen, verdreschen; [ball] dreschen.

**wallow** ['wɒləʊ] vi - 1. [in mud] sich wälzen, sich suhlen - 2. [in emotion]: **to ~ in sthg** in etw (D) schwelgen.

**wall painting** n Wandmalerei die.

**wallpaper** ['wɔːl,peɪpəʳ] n (U) Tapete die ⬦ vt tapezieren.

**Wall Street** n Wall Street die.

**wall-to-wall** adj: **~ carpeting** Teppichboden der.

**wally** ['wɒlɪ] (pl -ies) n Br inf Dussel der.

**walnut** ['wɔːlnʌt] n - 1. [nut] Walnuss die - 2. [tree] Walnussbaum der, Nussbaum der - 3. [wood] Nussbaumholz das.

**walrus** ['wɔːlrəs] (pl inv OR -es) n Walross das.

**waltz** [wɔːls] n Walzer der ⬦ vi - 1. [dance] Walzer tanzen - 2. inf [walk confidently]: **to ~ in** (einfach) hereinlspazieren.

**wan** [wɒn] (compar -ner; superl -nest) adj [person, complexion] bleich; [smile] matt.

**wand** [wɒnd] n Zauberstab der.

**wander** ['wɒndəʳ] vi - 1. [person] herumllaufen, umherlwandern - 2. [thoughts] schweifen, wandern; **his mind ~ed during the talk** während des Vortrags schweiften seine Gedanken ab.

**wanderer** ['wɒndərəʳ] n Wandervogel der.

**wandering** ['wɒndərɪŋ] adj fahrend.

**wane** [weɪn] n: **to be on the ~** schwinden ⬦ vi - 1. [popularity, enthusiasm] schwinden - 2. [moon] abnehmen.

**wangle** ['wæŋɡl] vt inf organisieren; **to ~ sthg out of sb** jm etw aus dem Kreuz leiern.

**wanna** ['wɒnə] esp Am = want a, want to.

**wannabe** adj inf: **a ~ film-maker** ein Möchtegern-Filmemacher.

**want** [wɒnt] vt - 1. [desire] wollen; **to ~ to do sthg** etw tun wollen; **to ~ sb to do sthg** wollen, dass jd etw tut; **what do you ~ to eat?** was möchtest du (zu) essen?; **you're ~ed on the phone** Sie werden am Telefon verlangt - 2. [need] brauchen; **you ~ to be more careful** du solltest vorsichtiger sein; **the house ~s cleaning** das Haus muss gereinigt werden - 3. [seek] suchen; **he is ~ed by the police** er wird von der Polizei gesucht ⬦ n - 1. [need] Bedürfnis das - 2. [lack] Mangel der; **his ~ of understanding** seine mangelnde Einsicht; **for ~ of** aus Mangel an (+ D) - 3. [poverty] Not die; **to be in ~** Not leiden.

**want ad** n Am inf Kleinanzeige die.

**wanted** ['wɒntɪd] adj: **to be ~ (by the police)** (polizeilich) gesucht werden.

**wanting** ['wɒntɪŋ] adj fml [inadequate]: **the play is ~ in humour** dem Stück fehlt es an Humor; **to be found ~** für nicht gut genug gehalten werden.

**wanton** ['wɒntən] adj - 1. fml [destruction] mutwillig; [neglect] sträflich - 2. [immoral - behaviour, woman] schamlos.

**war** [wɔːʳ] (pt & pp -red; cont -ring) n Krieg der; **to be at ~** sich im Kriegszustand befinden; **to go to ~** [country] den Krieg erklären; **the ~ against cancer** der Kampf gegen Krebs; **you look like you've been in the ~s** Br du siehst ziemlich ramponiert aus.

**War., Warks.** abk für Warwickshire, in Postanschrift verwendet.

**warble** ['wɔːbl] vi literary [bird] trällern.

**war crime** n Kriegsverbrechen das.

**war criminal** n Kriegsverbrecher der, -in die.

**war cry** n [in battle] Kriegsruf der.

**ward** [wɔːd] n - 1. [part of hospital] Station die; [room in hospital] Krankensaal der; **maternity ~** Entbindungsstation die - 2. Br POL Wahlbezirk die - 3. LAW Mündel das.

➡ **ward off** vt fus [blow, evil spirits] ablwehren; [danger] ablwenden; [disease] schützen vor (+ D).

**war dance** n Kriegstanz der.

**warden** ['wɔːdn] n - 1. [of park] Aufseher der, -in die; [of game reserve] Wildhüter der, -in die - 2. Br [of youth hostel] Herbergsvater der, -mutter die; [of hall of residence] Heimleiter der,

-in *die* - **3.** *Am* [prison governor] Gefängnisdirektor *der,* -in *die.*

**warder** ['wɔːdəʳ] *n* [in prison] Wärter *der,* -in *die.*

**ward of court** *n* Mündel *das* unter Amtsvormundschaft.

**wardrobe** ['wɔːdrəʊb] *n* - **1.** [piece of furniture] Kleiderschrank *der,* Schrank *der* - **2.** [collection of clothes] Garderobe *die.*

**wardrobe mistress** *n Br* Gewandmeisterin *die.*

**warehouse** ['weəhaʊs, *pl* -haʊzɪz] *n* Lagerhaus *das.*

**wares** [weəz] *npl literary* Waren *pl.*

**warfare** ['wɔːfeəʳ] *n* (U) [war] Krieg *der;* [technique] Kriegsführung *die.*

**war game** *n* Kriegsspiel *das.*

**warhead** ['wɔːhed] *n* Sprengkopf *der.*

**warily** ['weərəlɪ] *adv* [carefully] vorsichtig; [suspiciously] misstrauisch.

**warlike** ['wɔːlaɪk] *adj* kriegerisch.

**warm** [wɔːm] *adj* - **1.** [gen] warm; **are you ~ enough?** ist dir warm genug? - **2.** [friendly - person, feelings, welcome] herzlich; [ - atmosphere] freundlich ⇔ *vt* [food, milk] warm machen; **to ~ one's hands** sich (D) die Hände wärmen.
- ◆ **warm over** *vt sep Am* [food, ideas] auf l-wärmen.
- ◆ **warm to** *vt fus* [idea, place] Gefallen finden an (+ D); [person]: **my heart ~ed to her** sie wurde mir sympathischer.
- ◆ **warm up** *vt sep* - **1.** [heat - food] warm machen; [ - room] heizen - **2.** [reheat] auf l wärmen ⇔ *vi* - **1.** [get warmer] wärmer werden - **2.** [machine, engine] warm laufen; [audience] in Stimmung kommen - **3.** [athlete, footballer] sich auf l wärmen; [orchestra, musician] sich ein l-spielen; [singer] sich ein l singen.

**warm-blooded** [-'blʌdɪd] *adj* warmblütig.

**war memorial** *n* Kriegerdenkmal *das.*

**warm front** *n* Warmfront *die.*

**warm-hearted** [-'hɑːtɪd] *adj* [person] warmherzig; [action, gesture] herzlich.

**warmly** ['wɔːmlɪ] *adv* - **1.** [in warm clothes]: **to dress ~** sich warm anziehen - **2.** [in a friendly way] herzlich.

**warmness** ['wɔːmnɪs] *n* Herzlichkeit *die.*

**warmonger** ['wɔːˌmʌŋgəʳ] *n* Kriegshetzer *der,* -in *die.*

**warmth** [wɔːmθ] *n* - **1.** [of temperature, clothes] Wärme *die* - **2.** [of welcome, smile, support] Herzlichkeit *die.*

**warm-up** *n* [preparation] Aufwärmen *das.*

**warn** [wɔːn] *vt* - **1.** [advise] warnen; **to ~ sb of** OR **about sthg** jn vor etw (D) warnen; **to ~ sb against doing sthg, to ~ sb not to do sthg** jn da-

vor warnen, etw zu tun - **2.** [inform] Bescheid geben (+ D); **to ~ sb that ...** jn darauf hinweisen, dass ... ⇔ *vi* [forecast]: **to ~ of sthg** vor etw (D) warnen.

**warning** ['wɔːnɪŋ] *adj* [sign, message] Warn-; [look, message] warnend ⇔ *n* - **1.** [cautionary advice] Warnung *die;* [from police, judge] Verwarnung *die* - **2.** [notice]: **to give sb ~** jm rechtzeitig Bescheid sagen; **without ~** ohne Vorwarnung.

**warning light** *n* Warnleuchte *die.*

**warning triangle** *n Br* Warndreieck *das.*

**warp** [wɔːp] *n* [of cloth] Kette *die* ⇔ *vt* - **1.** [wood]: **the sun will ~ the wood** in der Sonne wird sich das Holz verziehen - **2.** [mind] psychisch schwer schädigen ⇔ *vi* [wood] sich verziehen.

**warpath** ['wɔːpɑːθ] *n:* **to go on the ~** auf dem Kriegspfad sein.

**warped** [wɔːpt] *adj* - **1.** [wood] verzogen - **2.** [person, mind] gestört; [sense of humour] abartig.

**warrant** ['wɒrənt] *n* LAW [written order] Befehl *der;* [for arrest] Haftbefehl *der;* [for search] Durchsuchungsbefehl *der* ⇔ *vt fml* [justify] rechtfertigen.

**warrant officer** *n Dienstgrad zwischen Unteroffizier und Leutnant.*

**warranty** ['wɒrəntɪ] (*pl* -**ies**) *n* [guarantee] Garantie *die;* **it is still under ~** die Garantie ist noch nicht abgelaufen.

**warren** ['wɒrən] *n* Kaninchenbau *der.*

**warring** ['wɔːrɪŋ] *adj* [nations] Krieg führend; [factions] sich bekämpfend.

**warrior** ['wɒrɪəʳ] *n literary* Krieger *der.*

**Warsaw** ['wɔːsɔː] *n* Warschau *nt;* **the ~ Pact** der Warschauer Pakt.

**warship** ['wɔːʃɪp] *n* Kriegsschiff *das.*

**wart** [wɔːt] *n* Warze *die.*

**wartime** ['wɔːtaɪm] *adj* Kriegs- ⇔ *n* Kriegszeit *die;* **in ~** in Kriegszeiten.

**war widow** *n* Kriegerwitwe *die.*

**wary** ['weərɪ] (*compar* -**ier**; *superl* -**iest**) *adj* [careful] vorsichtig; [suspicious] misstrauisch; **to be ~ of sthg** sich vor etw (D) in Acht nehmen.

**was** [*weak form* wəz, *strong form* wɒz] *pt* ▷ **be.**

**wash** [wɒʃ] *n* - **1.** [act of washing]: **she/it needs a ~** sie/es muss gewaschen werden; **to have a ~** sich waschen; **to give sthg a ~** etw waschen - **2.** [clothes to be washed] Wäsche *die* - **3.** [from boat] Kielwasser *das* ⇔ *vt* - **1.** [clean] waschen; [dishes] spülen, abwaschen; **to ~ one's hands** sich (D) die Hände waschen - **2.** [subj: current, sea, rain] spülen; **to be ~ed ashore** an Land geschwemmt werden ⇔ *vi* [clean o.s.] sich waschen.
- ◆ **wash away** *vt sep* weglspülen.

**W**

**wash down** vt sep - **1.** [food] hinunterlspülen - **2.** [clean] (mit Wasser) ablspritzen.

**wash out** vt sep herauslwaschen; [mouth] auslspülen.

**wash up** vt sep - **1.** Br [dishes] ablwaschen, spülen - **2.** [subj: sea, river] anlschwemmen ◇ vi - **1.** Br [wash the dishes] ablwaschen, spülen - **2.** Am [wash o.s.] sich waschen.

**Wash** n: The ~ seichtes Gebiet an der englischen Ostküste.

**washable** ['wɒʃəbl] adj waschbar.

**wash-and-wear** adj bügelfrei.

**washbasin** Br ['wɒʃ,beɪsn], **washbowl** Am ['wɒʃbəʊl] n Waschbecken das.

**washcloth** ['wɒʃ,klɒθ] n Am Waschlappen der.

**washed-out** [,wɒʃt-] adj - **1.** [pale] mitgenommen - **2.** [exhausted] ausgelaugt.

**washer** ['wɒʃər] n - **1.** TECH Dichtungsring der - **2.** [washing machine] Waschmaschine die.

**washer-dryer** n Waschtrockner der.

**washing** ['wɒʃɪŋ] n - **1.** [act] Waschen das - **2.** [clothes] Wäsche die.

**washing line** n Wäscheleine die.

**washing machine** n Waschmaschine die.

**washing powder** n Br Waschpulver das.

**Washington** ['wɒʃɪŋtən] n - **1.** [state]: ~ **State** Washington nt - **2.** [city]: ~ **D.C.** Washington nt, Hauptstadt der USA.

**washing-up** n - **1.** Br [crockery, pans etc] Abwasch der - **2.** [act]: **to do the** ~ spülen, den Abwasch machen.

**washing-up liquid** n Br Spülmittel das.

**washout** ['wɒʃaʊt] n inf Reinfall der.

**washroom** ['wɒʃrʊm] n Am Toilette die.

**wasn't** [wɒznt] = was not.

**wasp** [wɒsp] n Wespe die.

**Wasp, WASP** [wɒsp] (abbr of White Anglo-Saxon Protestant) n inf weißer Angehörige des amerikanischen Bürgertums.

**waspish** ['wɒspɪʃ] adj giftig.

**wastage** ['weɪstɪdʒ] n (U) [process] Verschwendung die; [amount] Verlust der.

**waste** [weɪst] adj [fuel] ungenutzt; ~ **material** Abfallstoffe pl; ~ **water** Abwasser das ◇ n - **1.** [misuse] Verschwendung die; **to go to** ~ [talent] verkümmern; [food] verkommen; **that's a ~ of money** das ist Geldverschwendung; **a ~ of time** eine Zeitverschwendung - **2.** [refuse] Abfall der ◇ vt verschwenden; [opportunity] vertun; **such subtle distinctions are ~d on him** solch feine Anspielungen versteht er sowieso nicht; **an expensive wine would be ~d on me** mir einen teuren Wein zu servieren wäre reine Verschwendung.

**wastes** npl literary [wastelands] Wildnis die, Einöde die; **the frozen ~s of Antarctica** die Eiswüsten der Antarktis.

**waste away** vi dahinlschwinden.

**wastebasket** ['weɪst,bɑːskɪt] n Am Papierkorb der.

**wasted** ['weɪstɪd] adj [time] verschwendet; [effort] vergeblich.

**waste disposal unit** n Müllschlucker der.

**wasteful** ['weɪstfʊl] adj verschwenderisch.

**waste ground** n Ödland das.

**wasteland** ['weɪst,lænd] n lit Ödland das; fig Einöde die.

**waste paper** n Altpapier das.

**wastepaper basket, wastepaper bin** [,weɪst'peɪpə-], **wastebasket** Am ['weɪst,bɑːskɪt] n Papierkorb der.

**watch** [wɒtʃ] n - **1.** [timepiece] Uhr die, Armbanduhr die - **2.** [act of guarding]: **to keep** ~ Wache halten; **to keep (a)** ~ **on sb/sthg** auf jn/etw auflpassen - **3.** [guard - person] Wachmann der; [ - group] Wache die ◇ vt - **1.** [look at] beobachten; [game, event] zulsehen OR zulschauen bei; [film, play] sich (D) anlsehen; **to** ~ **television** fernlsehen; **to** ~ **sb playing** jm beim Spielen zulsehen OR zulschauen; ~ **this closely** sehen OR schauen Sie jetzt genau her! - **2.** [spy on] beobachten - **3.** [be careful about] auf lpassen auf (+ A); ~ **it!** inf [as threat] pass (bloß) auf! ◇ vi [observe] zulsehen, zulschauen.

**watch for** vt fus [person, thing] Ausschau halten nach; [opportunity] warten auf (+ A).

**watch out** vi - **1.** [be careful]: **to** ~ **out (for sthg)** auf lpassen (auf etw (A)), Acht geben (auf etw (A)); ~ **out!** Achtung!, Vorsicht! - **2.** [keep a lookout]: **to** ~ **out for sthg** nach etw Ausschau halten.

**watch over** vt fus [look after] wachen über (+ A).

**watchdog** ['wɒtʃdɒg] n - **1.** [dog] Wachhund der - **2.** [organization] Aufsichtsbehörde die.

**watchful** ['wɒtʃfʊl] adj [vigilant] wachsam; **to keep a** ~ **eye on sb/sthg** ein wachsames Auge auf jn/etw haben.

**watchmaker** ['wɒtʃ,meɪkər] n Uhrmacher der, -in die.

**watchman** ['wɒtʃmən] (pl -men [-mən]) n Wächter der.

**watchword** ['wɒtʃwɜːd] n Parole die.

**water** ['wɔːtər] n - **1.** [gen] Wasser das; **to pour** OR **throw cold** ~ **on sthg** fig etw mies machen; **to tread** ~ Wasser treten; **that's all** ~ **under the bridge** das ist (doch) Schnee von gestern - **2.** [urine]: **to pass** ~ Wasser lassen ◇ vt [plants] gießen; [garden, lawn] sprengen; [land, field] bewässern ◇ vi - **1.** [eyes] tränen

**- 2.** [mouth]: **my mouth was ~ing** mir lief das Wasser im Munde zusammen.

⬧ **waters** npl **- 1.** [territory at sea] Gewässer pl **- 2.** literary [of river, lake, sea] Wasser pl.

⬧ **water down** vt sep **- 1.** [drink] verdünnen **- 2.** usu pej [plan, criticism, novel] verwässern.

**water bed** n Wasserbett das.

**water bird** n Wasservogel der.

**water biscuit** n Kräcker der.

**waterborne** ['wɔːtəbɔːn] adj [disease] durch Wasser übertragen.

**water bottle** n Wasserflasche die.

**water buffalo** n Wasserbüffel der.

**water cannon** n Wasserwerfer der.

**water chestnut** n Wasserkastanie die.

**water closet** n dated Wasserklosett das.

**watercolour** ['wɔːtəˌkʌləʳ] n **- 1.** [picture] Aquarell das **- 2.** [paint] Aquarellfarbe die.

**water-cooled** [-ˌkuːld] adj wassergekühlt.

**watercourse** ['wɔːtəkɔːs] n [stream, river] Wasserlauf der; [river channel] Flussbett das; [artificial] Kanal der.

**watercress** ['wɔːtəkres] n Brunnenkresse die.

**watered-down** [ˌwɔːtəd-] adj usu pej verwässert.

**waterfall** ['wɔːtəfɔːl] n Wasserfall der.

**waterfront** ['wɔːtəfrʌnt] n Häuserzeile die am Wasser; **I live on the ~** ich wohne direkt am Wasser.

**water heater** n Heißwassergerät das, Boiler der.

**waterhole** ['wɔːtəhəʊl] n Wasserstelle die.

**watering can** ['wɔːtərɪŋ-] n Gießkanne die.

**water jump** n Wassergraben der.

**water level** n Wasserstand der.

**water lily** n Seerose die.

**waterline** ['wɔːtəlaɪn] n NAUT Wasserlinie die.

**waterlogged** ['wɔːtəlɒgd] adj **- 1.** [land, sportsfield] (völlig) aufgeweicht **- 2.** [vessel] voll Wasser.

**water main** n Hauptwasserleitung die.

**watermark** ['wɔːtəmɑːk] n **- 1.** [in paper] Wasserzeichen das **- 2.** [showing water level] Wasserstandsmarke die.

**watermelon** ['wɔːtəˌmelən] n Wassermelone die.

**water pipe** n [in building] Wasserrohr das.

**water pistol** n Wasserpistole die.

**water polo** n Wasserball der.

**waterproof** ['wɔːtəpruːf] adj [watch] wasserdicht; [anorak, shoes] wasserundurchlässig ◇ n: **~s** Regenkleidung die ◇ vt [material]

imprägnieren, wasserundurchlässig machen.

**water rates** npl Br Wassergebühren pl.

**water-resistant** adj wasserundurchlässig.

**watershed** ['wɔːtəʃed] n [turning point] Wendepunkt der.

**waterside** ['wɔːtəsaɪd] adj am Wasser ◇ n: **the ~** das Ufer.

**water skiing** n Wasserskilaufen das.

**water softener** n Wasserenthärter der.

**water-soluble** adj wasserlöslich.

**watersports** ['wɔːtəspɔːts] npl Wassersport der.

**waterspout** ['wɔːtəspaʊt] n Wasserhose die.

**water supply** n Wasserversorgung die.

**water table** n Grundwasserspiegel der.

**water tank** n Wassertank der.

**watertight** ['wɔːtətaɪt] adj **- 1.** [waterproof] wasserdicht **- 2.** [faultless] hieb- und stichfest.

**water tower** n Wasserturm der.

**waterway** ['wɔːtəweɪ] n Wasserstraße die.

**waterworks** ['wɔːtəwɜːks] (pl inv) n [building] Wasserwerk das.

**watery** ['wɔːtərɪ] adj **- 1.** [food, juice] wässrig; [coffee, tea] dünn **- 2.** [light, sun] blass.

**watt** [wɒt] n Watt das.

**wattage** ['wɒtɪdʒ] n Wattleistung die

**wave** [weɪv] n **- 1.** [gen] Welle die; **a ~ of immigrants** eine Einwanderungswelle **- 2.** [gesture]: **to give sb a ~** jm zuwinken ◇ vt **- 1.** [flag, handkerchief] schwenken; [baton] schwingen; [gun, stick] fuchteln; **to ~ one's hand at sb** jm winken **- 2.** [gesture to]: **to ~ sb on/over** jn weiterl-/herüberlwinken **- 3.** [hair] wellen ◇ vi **- 1.** [with hand] winken; **to ~ at** OR **to sb** jm zuwinken **- 2.** [flag] wehen; [branches] sich hin und her bewegen, sich wiegen.

⬧ **wave aside** vt sep [dismiss] zurücklweisen.

⬧ **wave down** vt sep anlhalten; [subj: police] herauslwinken.

**wave band** n Wellenbereich der.

**wavelength** ['weɪvleŋθ] n Wellenlänge die; **to be on the same ~ (as sb)** fig auf der gleichen Wellenlänge (wie jd) funken.

**waver** ['weɪvəʳ] vi **- 1.** [person, resolve, confidence] wanken; **she never ~ed in her determination** sie schwankte nie in ihrer Entschlossenheit **- 2.** [voice] zittern **- 3.** [flame, light] flackern.

**wavy** ['weɪvɪ] (compar **-ier**; superl **-iest**) adj **- 1.** [hair] wellig **- 2.** [line] Schlangen-.

**wax** [wæks] n **- 1.** [in candles, polish, for skis] Wachs das **- 2.** [in ears] Ohrenschmalz das ◇ vt **- 1.** [floor, table, skis] wachsen **- 2.** [legs] mit

**W**

Wachs enthaaren ◇ *vi* - **1.** *dated or hum* [become] werden; **to ~ and wane** zu-und abInehmen - **2.** [moon] zulnehmen.

**waxen** ['wæksən] *adj* [face, complexion] wächsern.

**wax paper** *n Am* Wachspapier *das.*

**waxworks** ['wækswɜːks] (*pl inv*) *n* [museum] Wachsfigurenkabinett *das.*

**way** [weɪ] *n* - **1.** [means, method] Art und Weise *die;* **this/that ~** so; **this is the best ~ to do it** man macht es am besten so; **~s and means** Mittel und Wege; **to get** *or* **have one's ~** seinen Willen durchlsetzen; **she wants to have everything her own ~** sie will in nichts nachgeben - **2.** [manner, style] Art *die;* **I feel the same ~ as you** mir geht es wie Ihnen; **she's behaving in a very odd ~** sie benimmt sich sehr seltsam; **if that's the ~ you feel ...** wenn du so denkst ...; **in the same ~** auf die gleiche Weise; **in a ~** in gewisser Hinsicht, irgendeine schon; **he's in a bad ~** es steht schlecht mit ihm; **I in no ~ wish to criticize you** ich will dich auf keinerlei Weise kritisieren - **3.** [skill]: **she has a ~ with children** sie kann gut mit Kindern umgehen; **she has a ~ with words** sie ist sehr wortgewandt; **to have a ~ of doing sthg** ein Geschick haben, etw zu tun - **4.** [thoroughfare, path] Weg *der;* **across** *or* **over the ~** gegenüber; **'give ~'** *Br* AUT 'Vorfahrt beachten' - **5.** [route] Weg *der;* **which ~ is the station?** wie kommt man zum Bahnhof ?; **what's the best ~ to the station?** wie kommt man am besten zum Bahnhof ?; **to be in the ~** im Weg sein; **to be in sb's ~** jm im Wege stehen; **their house is on the ~** ihr Haus ist auf dem Weg; **on the ~ (to the station)** auf dem Weg (zum Bahnhof); **on the ~ home/to school** auf dem Heimweg/Schulweg; **on the ~ back/there** auf dem Rückweg/Hinweg; **the town is out of our ~** die Stadt liegt nicht auf unserem Weg; **out of the ~** [place] abgelegen; **to be out of the ~** [finished] erledigt sein; [not blocking] nicht mehr im Weg sein; **get out of the** *or* **my ~!** geh mir aus dem Weg!; **to go out of one's ~ to do sthg** sich (*D*) besondere Mühe geben, etw zu tun; **to keep out of sb's ~** jm aus dem Wege gehen; **to be under ~** [ship] in Fahrt sein; [project, meeting] im Gange sein; **to get under ~** [ship] in Fahrt kommen; [project, meeting] in Gang kommen; **to lose one's ~** sich verlaufen; [in car] sich verfahren; **to make one's ~ through the crowd** sich (*D*) einen Weg durch die Menge bahnen; **make your ~ to the exit** begeben Sie sich zum Ausgang; **to make ~ for sb/sthg** jm/einer Sache Platz machen; **to stand in sb's ~** *fig* jm im Wege stehen - **6.** [direction] Richtung *die;* **which ~ are you going?** in welche Richtung gehst du?; **this/that ~** hier/dort entlang; **look this ~, please** sehen Sie bitte hierher; **~ in** Eingang *der;* **~ out** Ausgang *der* - **7.** [side]: **the right ~ round** richtig herum; **the wrong ~ round** verkehrt herum; **the right/wrong ~ up** richtig/verkehrt herum; **the other ~ round** anders herum - **8.** [distance] Weg *der;* **all the ~** den ganzen Weg; **we're with you all the ~** *fig* wir stehen voll und ganz hinter dir; **most of the ~** fast den ganzen Weg; **it's a long ~ (away) from here** es liegt weit weg *or* entfernt; **I have a long ~ to go** ich habe einen weiten Weg vor mir; **he's not as clever as her by a long ~** er ist bei weitem nicht so klug wie sie; **the takings went a long ~ towards covering expenses** die Einnahmen haben die Kosten weitgehend gedeckt - **9.** *phr:* **to give ~** [under weight, pressure] nachlgeben; **in many ~s** in vieler Hinsicht; **no ~!** auf keinen Fall! ◇ *adv inf* [far] viel; **~ ahead** weit voraus; **~ off** weit entfernt; **~ back in 1930** damals, 1930.

⬩ **ways** *npl* [customs, habits] Art *die.*
⬩ **by the way** *adv* übrigens.
⬩ **by way of** *prep* - **1.** [via] über (*+ A*) - **2.** [as a sort of] als; **by ~ of an apology** als Entschuldigung.
⬩ **in the way of** *prep* [in the form of]: **what have you got in the ~ of drinks?** was haben Sie an Getränken?

**waylay** [weɪ'leɪ] (*pt* & *pp* **-laid** [-'leɪd]) *vt* abIfangen.

**way of life** *n* [lifestyle] Lebensstil *der;* [of nation, tribe] Lebensweise *die.*

**way-out** *adj inf* verrückt.

**wayside** ['weɪsaɪd] *n:* **to fall by the ~** *fig* auf der Strecke bleiben.

**wayward** ['weɪwəd] *adj* eigenwillig.

**WC** (*abbr of* **water closet**) *n* WC *das.*

**we** [wiː] *pers pron pl* wir; **~ British** wir Briten.

**weak** [wiːk] *adj* - **1.** [gen] schwach - **2.** [lacking knowledge, skill]: **to be ~ on sthg** in etw (*D*) schwach sein.

**weaken** ['wiːkn] *vt* schwächen; [argument] entkräften ◇ *vi* - **1.** [person] schwach werden - **2.** [influence, power & FIN] schwächer werden.

**weak-kneed** [-niːd] *adj inf pej* charakterschwach.

**weakling** ['wiːklɪŋ] *n pej* Schwächling *der.*

**weakly** ['wiːklɪ] *adv* [get up, move] kraftlos; [smile] schwach.

**weak-minded** [-'maɪndɪd] *adj* [weak-willed] willensschwach.

**weakness** ['wiːknɪs] *n* - **1.** [gen] Schwäche *die;* **to have a ~ for sthg** eine Schwäche für etw haben - **2.** [in plan, argument] Schwachpunkt *der.*

**weal** [wiːl] *n* Striemen *der.*

**wealth** [welθ] *n* - **1.** (*U*) [riches] Reichtum *der* - **2.** [abundance]: **a ~ of sthg** ein Reichtum an etw (*D*).

**wealth tax** *n Br* Vermögenssteuer *die.*

**wealthy** ['welθɪ] (compar -ier; superl -iest) adj reich.

**wean** [wiːn] vt - 1. [from mother's milk] entwöhnen - 2. [from habit]: **to ~ sb from** OR **off sthg** jn von etw ablbringen.

**weapon** ['wepən] n Waffe die.

**weaponry** ['wepənrɪ] n (U) Waffen pl.

**wear** [weəʳ] (pt wore; pp worn) n - 1. [type of clothes] Kleidung die - 2. [damage]: **~ (and tear)** Abnutzung die - 3. [use]: **these shoes have had a lot of ~** diese Schuhe sind viel getragen worden; **to be the worse for ~** [tired] sehr müde sein; [drunk] betrunken sein ◇ vt - 1. [clothes, shoes, jewellery, spectacles] tragen - 2. [damage] ablnutzen ◇ vi - 1. [deteriorate] sich ablnutzen - 2. [last]: **to ~ well/badly** gut/ nicht gut halten - 3. phr: **my patience is ~ing thin** meine Geduld ist langsam erschöpft; **that excuse is starting to ~ a bit thin** diese Ausrede ist inzwischen ganz schön abgedroschen.

➤ **wear away** vt sep [steps] ausltreten; [inscription] verwittern; [grass] ablnutzen ◇ vi [steps] ausgetreten werden; [inscription] verwittern; [grass] abgenutzt werden.

➤ **wear down** vt sep - 1. [reduce size of] ablnutzen; [heel] abllaufen - 2. [weaken] auslzehren; [resistance] zermürben ◇ vi sich ablnutzen; [heel] sich abllaufen.

➤ **wear off** vi nachllassen.

➤ **wear on** vi sich hinlziehen.

➤ **wear out** vt sep - 1. [clothing, machinery] ablnutzen - 2. [person, patience, strength] erschöpfen ◇ vi [clothing, shoes] sich ablnutzen.

**wearable** ['weərəbl] adj tragbar.

**wearily** ['wɪərɪlɪ] adv müde.

**weariness** ['wɪərɪnɪs] n Müdigkeit die.

**wearing** ['weərɪŋ] adj [exhausting] anstrengend.

**weary** ['wɪərɪ] (compar -ier; superl -iest) adj - 1. [exhausted] müde - 2. [fed up]: **to be ~ of sthg** etw satt haben; **to be ~ of doing sthg** es satt haben, etw zu tun.

**weasel** ['wiːzl] n Wiesel das.

**weather** ['weðəʳ] n Wetter das; **to make heavy ~ of sthg** sich (D) etw unnötig schwer machen; **to be under the ~** nicht ganz auf der Höhe sein ◇ vt [survive] überstehen ◇ vi verwittern.

**weather-beaten** [-ˌbiːtn] adj - 1. [face, skin] wettergegerbt - 2. [stone, rocks] verwittert.

**weathercock** ['weðəkɒk] n Wetterhahn der.

**weathered** ['weðəd] adj - 1. [face] wettergegerbt - 2. [wood, building, stone] verwittert.

**weather forecast** n Wettervorhersage die.

**weatherman** ['weðəmæn] (pl -men [-men]) n Meterologe der.

**weather map** n Wetterkarte die.

**weatherproof** ['weðəpruːf] adj wetterfest.

**weather report** n Wetterbericht der.

**weather ship** n Wetterschiff das.

**weather vane** [-veɪn] n Wetterfahne die.

**weave** [wiːv] (pt wove; pp woven) n Webart die ◇ vt - 1. [using loom] weben - 2. [move along]: **to ~ one's way through the crowd/the traffic** sich durch die Menge/den Verkehr schlängeln ◇ vi [move] sich durchlschlängeln.

**weaver** ['wiːvəʳ] n Weber der, -in die.

**web** [web] n - 1. [cobweb] Spinnennetz das - 2. fig [of lies, intrigue] Netz das.

➤ **Web** n: **the Web** COMPUT das Netz, das Web.

**webbed** [webd] adj mit Schwimmhäuten.

**webbing** ['webɪŋ] n [material] Gurtband das.

**web-footed** [-ˈfʊtɪd] adj mit Schwimmfüßen.

**website** ['webˌsaɪt] n COMPUT Website die.

**wed** [wed] (pt & pp **wed** OR **-ded**) literary vt - 1. [marry] heiraten - 2. [subj: priest] trauen ◇ vi heiraten.

**we'd** [wiːd] = we had, we would.

**Wed.** (abbr of **Wednesday**) Mi.

**wedded** ['wedɪd] adj [committed]: **to be ~ to sthg** sich einer Sache (D) verschrieben haben.

**wedding** ['wedɪŋ] n Hochzeit die.

**wedding anniversary** n Hochzeitstag der.

**wedding cake** n Hochzeitskuchen der.

**wedding dress** n Hochzeitskleid das.

**wedding reception** n Hochzeitsfeier die.

**wedding ring** n Ehering der.

**wedge** [wedʒ] n - 1. [gen] Keil der; **to drive a ~ between** einen Keil treiben zwischen; **this is the thin end of the ~** das ist erst der Anfang - 2. [of cheese, cake, pie] Stück das ◇ vt - 1. [secure] festlklemmen - 2. [squeeze, push] zwängen; **she sat ~d between us** sie saß zwischen uns eingezwängt.

**wedlock** ['wedlɒk] n (U) literary Ehe die; **a child born out of ~** ein uneheliches Kind.

**Wednesday** ['wenzdɪ] n Mittwoch der; see also **Saturday.**

**wee** [wiː] adj Scot klein ◇ n inf: **to do/have a ~** Pipi machen ◇ vi inf Pipi machen.

**weed** [wiːd] n - 1. [wild plant] Unkraut das - 2. Br inf [feeble person] Schwächling der ◇ vt: **to ~ the garden** im Garten Unkraut jäten.

➤ **weed out** vt sep auslsondern.

**weeding** ['wiːdɪŋ] n: **to do the ~** Unkraut jäten.

**weedkiller** ['wiːdˌkɪləʳ] n Unkrautvertilgungsmittel das.

**W**

**weedy** ['wi:dɪ] (*compar* **-ier**; *superl* **-iest**) *adj*
- **1.** [overgrown with weeds] mit Unkraut bewachsen - **2.** *Br inf* [feeble] schwächlich.

**week** [wi:k] *n* Woche *die*; **in three ~s' time** in drei Wochen; **a ~ on Saturday, Saturday ~** Samstag in einer Woche; **a ~ last Saturday** Samstag vor einer Woche.

**weekday** ['wi:kdeɪ] *n* Wochentag *der*.

**weekend** [,wi:k'end] *n* Wochenende *das*; **at the ~** am Wochenende.

**weekend bag** *n kleine Reisetasche*.

**weekly** ['wi:klɪ] (*pl* **-ies**) *adj* wöchentlich; [newspaper] Wochen- <> *adv* wöchentlich <> *n* Wochenzeitung *die*.

**weeny** ['wi:nɪ] *adj Br inf* winzig.

**weep** [wi:p] (*pt* & *pp* **wept**) *n*: **to have a ~** weinen <> *vt* & *vi* weinen.

**weeping willow** [,wi:pɪŋ-] *n* Trauerweide *die*.

**weepy** ['wi:pɪ] (*compar* **-ier**; *superl* **-iest**) *adj* weinerlich <> *n* [sentimental film] Schmachtfetzen *der*.

**wee-wee** *n* & *vi* = **wee**.

**weft** [weft] *n* Schussfaden *der*.

**weigh** [weɪ] *vt* - **1.** [find weight of] wiegen - **2.** [consider carefully] abwägen - **3.** [raise]: **to ~ anchor** den Anker lichten <> *vi* [have specific weight] wiegen.

➤ **weigh down** *vt sep* - **1.** [physically]: **to be ~ed down with sthg** mit etw beladen sein - **2.** [mentally]: **to be ~ed down by** OR **with sthg** mit etw belastet sein.

➤ **weigh (up)on** *vt fus* lasten auf (+ D).

➤ **weigh out** *vt sep* abwiegen.

➤ **weigh up** *vt sep* [situation, pros and cons] abwägen; [person, opposition] einschätzen.

**weighbridge** ['weɪbrɪdʒ] *n Br* Brückenwaage *die*.

**weighing machine** ['weɪɪŋ-] *n* Waage *die*.

**weight** [weɪt] *n* - **1.** [of person, package, goods & SPORT] Gewicht *das*; **to put on** OR **gain ~** zunehmen; **to lose ~** abnehmen; **to take the ~ off one's feet** sich hinsetzen - **2.** *fig* [power, influence]: **the ~ of public opinion** die Übermacht der öffentlichen Meinung; **~ of evidence** Beweislast *die*; **to carry ~** von Gewicht sein; **to throw one's ~ about** sich auf-spielen - **3.** *lit* & *fig* [burden] Last *die*; **it took a ~ off my mind** damit ist mir ein Stein vom Herzen gefallen - **4.** *phr*: **to pull one's ~** seinen Beitrag leisten <> *vt*: **to ~ sthg (down)** etw beschweren.

**weighted** ['weɪtɪd] *adj*: **to be ~ in favour of/ against sb/sthg** jn/etw bevorteilen/benachteiligen.

**weighting** ['weɪtɪŋ] *n* (U) Zulage *die*.

**weightlessness** ['weɪtlɪsnɪs] *n* Schwerelosigkeit *die*.

**weight lifter** *n* Gewichtheber *der*, -in *die*.

**weight lifting** *n* Gewichtheben *das*.

**weight training** *n* Krafttraining *das*.

**weighty** ['weɪtɪ] (*compar* **-ier**; *superl* **-iest**) *adj* [serious, important] schwerwiegend.

**weir** [wɪəʳ] *n* Wehr *das*.

**weird** [wɪəd] *adj* seltsam.

**weirdo** ['wɪədəʊ] (*pl* **-s**) *n inf* seltsame Gestalt.

**welcome** ['welkəm] *adj* - **1.** [guest] willkommen; **to make sb ~** jn freundlich auf-nehmen - **2.** [free]: **to be ~ to do sthg** etw gerne tun können - **3.** [pleasant, desirable] angenehm - **4.** [in reply to thanks]: **you're ~** bitte, gern geschehen <> *n* Willkommen *das*; **to get/receive a warm ~** herzlich aufgenommen werden <> *vt* - **1.** [receive] empfangen - **2.** [approve, support] willkommen heißen <> *excl* willkommen!

**welcoming** ['welkəmɪŋ] *adj* einladend.

**weld** [weld] *n* Schweißnaht *die* <> *vt* schweißen.

**welder** [weldəʳ] *n* Schweißer *der*, -in *die*.

**welfare** ['welfeəʳ] *adj* sozial; [work, worker] Sozial- <> *n* - **1.** [state of wellbeing] Wohl *das* - **2.** *Am* [income support] Sozialhilfe *die*.

**welfare state** *n* Wohlfahrtsstaat *der*.

**well** [wel] (*compar* **better**; *superl* **best**) *adj* - **1.** [in health] gesund; **how are you?** – **(I'm) very ~, thanks** wie geht es Ihnen? – sehr gut, danke; **to feel ~** sich wohl fühlen; **to get ~** gesund werden; **get ~ soon!** gute Besserung! - **2.** [good]: **all's ~** alles ist in Ordnung; **(all) ~ and good** schön und gut; **it's just as ~ you** stayed nur gut, dass du geblieben bist <> *adv* - **1.** [gen] gut; **the patient is doing ~** der Patient macht gute Fortschritte; **to do ~ out of sthg** von etw profitieren; **you did ~ to come** immediately gut, dass du sofort gekommen bist; **~ done!** gut gemacht!; **to speak ~ of sb** jn lobend erwähnen; **~ beaten** restlos geschlagen; **'shake ~ before use'** 'vor Gebrauch gut schütteln'; **to go ~** gut gehen; **you're ~ out of it** *inf* du kannst froh sein, nichts mehr damit zu tun haben - **2.** [definitely, certainly]: **~ within one's rights** voll im Recht; **you know perfectly ~ that** ... du weißt ganz genau, dass ...; **it's ~ worth it** es lohnt sich unbedingt; **~ after six o'clock** viel später als sechs Uhr; **~ over 50** weit über 50 - **3.** [easily, possibly]: **it may ~ happen** es kann durchaus passieren; **you may ~ laugh** lachen Sie nur!; **that may ~ be true** das mag wahr sein <> *n* - **1.** [for water] Brunnen *der* - **2.** [oil well] Ölquelle *die* <> *excl* - **1.** [expressing hesitation]: **~, I don't really know** tja, das weiß ich nicht so recht

**- 2.** [expressing resignation]: **oh ~!** na ja! **- 3.** [expressing surprise]: **~, I didn't expect to see you here!** na so was, ich habe nicht erwartet, Sie hier zu sehen!; **~ I never!** na, so was! **- 4.** [after interruption]: **~, as I was saying ...** also, wie gesagt ...

➤ **as well** adv [in addition] auch; **I might as ~ go home** ich könnte genauso gut nach Hause gehen.

➤ **as well as** conj sowohl ... als auch; **children as ~ as adults** sowohl Kinder als auch Erwachsene; **she's clever as ~ as beautiful** sie ist zugleich intelligent und schön.

➤ **well up** vi hochquellen.

**we'll** [wi:l] = we shall, we will.

**well-adjusted** adj [psychologically] ausgeglichen.

**well-advised** [-əd'vaizd] adj klug; **he/you would be ~ to do sthg** er täte/du tätest gut daran, etw zu tun.

**well-appointed** [-ə'pɔintɪd] adj gut ausgestattet.

**well-balanced** adj **- 1.** [mentally] ausgeglichen **- 2.** [nutritious] ausgewogen.

**well-behaved** [-bɪ'heɪvd] adj artig.

**wellbeing** [ˌwel'biːɪŋ] n Wohl das.

**well-bred** [-'bred] adj wohlerzogen.

**well-built** adj [person] gut gebaut.

**well-chosen** adj gut gewählt.

**well-disposed** adj: **to be ~ to(wards) sb** jm wohlgesinnt sein; **to be ~ to(wards) sthg** etw befürworten.

**well-done** adj [thoroughly cooked] durchgebraten.

**well-dressed** [-'drest] adj gut gekleidet.

**well-earned** [-ɜːnd] adj wohlverdient.

**well-established** adj [company] etabliert.

**well-fed** adj wohlgenährt.

**well-groomed** [-'gruːmd] adj gepflegt.

**well-heeled** [-'hiːld] adj inf betucht.

**wellies** ['weliz] npl Br inf Gummistiefel pl.

**well-informed** adj: **to be ~ (about/on sthg)** gut informiert sein (über etw (A)).

**wellington (boot)** ['welɪŋtən-] n Gummistiefel der.

**well-intentioned** [-ɪn'tenʃnd] adj [action, suggestion] gut gemeint.

**well-kept** adj **- 1.** [garden, village] gepflegt **- 2.** [secret] wohl gehütet.

**well-known** adj bekannt.

**well-mannered** [-'mænəd] adj: **to be ~** gute Manieren haben.

**well-meaning** adj [action, suggestion] gut gemeint; **she's very ~** sie meint es gut.

**well-nigh** [-naɪ] adv nahezu.

**well-off** adj **- 1.** [financially] wohlhabend **- 2.** [in a good position]: **to be ~ for sthg** mit etw gut versorgt sein; **not to know when one is ~** inf nicht wissen, wie gut es einem geht.

**well-paid** adj gut bezahlt.

**well-preserved** adj fig [person] gut erhalten.

**well-proportioned** [-prə'pɔːʃnd] adj wohlproportioniert.

**well-read** [-'red] adj belesen.

**well-rounded** [-'raundɪd] adj [varied] vielseitig.

**well-spoken** adj: **he's very ~** er drückt sich sehr gewählt aus.

**well-thought-of** adj gut angesehen.

**well-thought-out** adj gut durchdacht.

**well-timed** [-'taɪmd] adj gut abgepasst; **his intervention was ~** er griff zur rechten Zeit ein.

**well-to-do** adj wohlhabend.

**well-wisher** [-ˌwɪʃəʳ] n Sympathisant der, -in die.

**well-woman clinic** n Br regelmäßig beim Allgemeinarzt abgehaltene Gesundheitsvorsorgesprechstunde für Frauen.

**welly** ['weli] (pl -ies) (abbr of wellington) n inf Gummistiefel der.

**Welsh** [welʃ] adj walisisch ⟨⟩ n [language] Walisisch(e) das ⟨⟩ npl: **the ~** die Waliser pl.

**Welshman** ['welʃmən] (pl -men [-mən]) n Waliser der.

**Welsh rarebit** [-'reəbɪt] n überbackenes Käsebrot.

**Welshwoman** ['welʃˌwumən] (pl -women [-ˌwɪmɪn]) n Waliserin die.

**welter** ['weltəʳ] n Flut die.

**welterweight** ['weltəweɪt] n Weltergewicht das.

**wend** [wend] vt literary: **to ~ one's way home** langsam nach Hause ziehen.

**wendy house** ['wendɪ-] n Br Spielhaus das.

**went** [went] pt ⟹ go.

**wept** [wept] pt & pp ⟹ weep.

**were** [wɜːʳ] vb ⟹ be.

**we're** [wɪəʳ] = we are.

**weren't** [wɜːnt] = were not.

**werewolf** ['wɪəwulf] (pl -wolves [-wulvz]) n Werwolf der.

**west** [west] n Westen der; **the ~** der Westen ⟨⟩ adj **- 1.** [area] West-, westlich **- 2.** [wind] West- ⟨⟩ adv nach Westen, westwärts; **~ of** westlich von.

➤ **West** n POL: **the West** der Westen.

**West Bank** n: the ~ das Westjordanland; **on the ~** im Westjordanland.

**westbound** ['westbaʊnd] adj (in) Richtung Westen.

**West Country** n: the ~ der Südwesten Englands.

**West End** n: the ~ das Westend.

**WEST END**

„West End" ist der Name des vornehmen und relativ reichen Viertels im Westen der Londoner Innenstadt mit großen Kaufhäusern, Geschäften, Theatern und Restaurants. Eine „West End Show" ist ein Theaterstück, Musical, Ballett oder Ähnliches an einem dieser Theater. Das Londoner East End gilt dagegen als die ärmere Hälfte der Innenstadt; es hat mehr Straßenmärkte und kleinere Geschäfte.

**westerly** ['westəlɪ] adj - **1.** [direction] westlich - **2.** [area] im Westen - **3.** [wind] West-.

**western** ['westən] adj - **1.** [part of country, continent] West- - **2.** POL [relating to the West] westlich <> n [film] Western der.

**Westerner** ['westənəʳ] n - **1.** POL [inhabitant of the West] Abendländer der, -in die - **2.** [inhabitant of west of country] Bewohner der, -in die des Westens.

**Western Isles** npl: the ~ die Hebriden.

**westernize, -ise** ['westənaɪz] vt verwestlichen.

**Western Seaboard** n Westküste die (der USA).

**West German** adj westdeutsch <> n [person] Westdeutsche der, die.

**West Germany** n: (former) ~ (ehemaliges) Westdeutschland nt; **in ~** in Westdeutschland.

**West Indies** [-'ɪndiːz] npl: the ~ die Westindischen Inseln; **in the ~** auf den Westindischen Inseln.

**Westminster** ['westmɪnstəʳ] n - **1.** [area] Westminster nt - **2.** fig [British parliament] britisches Parlament.

**WESTMINSTER**

Mit „Westminster" bezeichnet man das an der Themse gelegene Viertel in London in dem sich die Parlamentsgebäude („Houses of Parliament") sowie Westminster Abbey befinden. Oft wird der Ausdruck auch als Umschreibung für das britische Parlament verwendet.

**westward** ['westwəd] adj nach Westen <> adv = **westwards.**

**westwards** ['westwədz] adv nach Westen, westwärts.

**wet** [wet] (compar -**ter;** superl -**test;** pt & pp wet OR -**ted;** cont -**ting**) adj - **1.** [damp, soaked] nass - **2.** [rainy] regnerisch; [climate] feucht; **it's always ~ in Glasgow!** es regnet immer in Glasgow! - **3.** [ink, concrete] feucht; '~ **paint**' 'frisch gestrichen' - **4.** Br inf pej [weak, feeble] lasch; **he's a ~** er ist ein Weichei <> n inf Br POL Gemäßigte der, die <> vt nass machen; **to ~ the bed** ins Bett machen; **to ~ o.s.** sich in die Hosen machen.

**wet blanket** n inf pej Spielverderber der.

**wet-look** adj Glanz-.

**wetness** ['wetnɪs] n - **1.** [dampness] Nässe die - **2.** Br inf pej [feebleness] Laschheit die.

**wet nurse** n Amme die.

**wet rot** n [decay] Nassfäule die.

**wet suit** n Taucheranzug der.

**we've** [wiːv] = **we have.**

**whack** [wæk] inf n - **1.** [share] Teil der - **2.** [hit] Schlag der <> vt einen Schlag geben (+ D).

**whacked** [wækt] adj Br inf [exhausted] erschlagen.

**whacky** ['wækɪ] adj = **wacky.**

**whale** [weɪl] n [animal] Wal der; **to have a ~ of a time** inf sich mordsmäßig amüsieren.

**whaling** ['weɪlɪŋ] n (U) Walfang der.

**wham** [wæm] excl inf wumm!

**wharf** [wɔːf] (pl -**s** OR **wharves** [wɔːvz]) n Kai der.

**what** [wɒt] adj - **1.** (in questions) welche, -r, -s; **~ colour is it?** welche Farbe hat es?; **he asked me ~ colour it was** er fragte mich, welche Farbe es hatte; **~ time is it?** wie viel Uhr OR wie spät ist es?; **~ sort of (an) animal is that?** was ist das für ein Tier? - **2.** (in exclamations) was für; **~ a surprise!** was für eine Überraschung!; **~ a beautiful day!** was für ein schöner Tag! <> pron - **1.** (in questions) was; **~ is going on?** was ist los?; **~ are they doing?** was tun sie da?; **~'s your name?** wie heißt du?; **she asked me ~ happened** sie fragte mich, was passiert war; **~ is it for?** wofür ist das?; **~ are they talking about?** worüber reden sie?; **~ if it rains?** was geschieht, wenn es regnet?; **~ did you say?** wie bitte? - **2.** (introducing relative clause) was; **I didn't see ~ happened** ich habe nicht gesehen, was passiert ist; **you can't have ~ you want** du kannst nicht haben, was du willst - **3.** phr: **~ for?** wozu?; **~ about going for a meal?** wie wäre es mit Essen gehen?; **so ~?** inf na und? <> excl was!

**whatever** [wɒt'evəʳ] adj: **at ~ time you want** wann immer du willst; **they have no chance ~** sie haben überhaupt keine Chance <> pron - **1.** [no matter what]: **take ~ you want** nimm, was du willst; **~ I do, I'll lose** was ich auch tue, ich verliere; **don't let go ~ happens**

du darfst auf keinen Fall loslassen - **2.** [indicating vagueness]: **~ that may be** was auch immer das sein mag - **3.** [indicating surprise]: **~ did he say?** was hat er denn bloß gesagt? <> *excl* **Am** *inf* von mir aus!

**whatnot** ['wɒtnɒt] *n inf* [other things]: **and ~** und anderes.

**what's-his-name** *n inf* Dingsda *der, die.*

**whatsit** ['wɒtsɪt] *n inf* Dingsbums *das.*

**whatsoever** [,wɒtsəʊ'evə<sup>r</sup>] *adj*: **I had no interest ~** ich hatte keinerlei Interesse; **nothing ~** überhaupt nichts.

**wheat** [wiːt] *n* Weizen *der.*

**wheat germ** *n (U)* Weizenkeim *der.*

**wheatmeal** ['wiːtmiːl] *n* Weizenvollkornmehl *das.*

**wheedle** ['wiːdl] *vt*: **to ~ sb into doing sthg** jn dazu kriegen, etw zu tun; **to ~ sthg out of sb** jm etw ablschwatzen.

**wheel** [wiːl] *n* - **1.** [of bicycle, car, train] Rad *das* - **2.** ᴀᴜᴛ [steering wheel] Lenkrad *das* <> *vt* schieben <> *vi* - **1.** [move in circle] kreisen - **2.** [turn round]: **to ~ round** sich jäh umldrehen.

**wheelbarrow** ['wiːl,bærəʊ] *n* Schubkarre *die.*

**wheelbase** ['wiːlbeɪs] *n* Radstand *der.*

**wheelchair** ['wiːl,tʃeə<sup>r</sup>] *n* Rollstuhl *der.*

**wheel clamp** *n* Parkkralle *die.*

➡ **wheel-clamp** *vt*: **my car was ~ed** an meinem Auto war eine Parkkralle.

**wheeler-dealer** ['wiːlə<sup>r</sup>-] *n pej* Geschäftemacher *der, -in die.*

**wheelie bin** ['wiːlɪ-] *n Br* Mülltonne *die* mit Rädern.

**wheeling and dealing** ['wiːlɪŋ-] *n (U) pej* Machenschaften *pl.*

**wheeze** [wiːz] *n* [sound] pfeifender Atem <> *vi* pfeifend atmen.

**wheezy** ['wiːzɪ] (*compar* **-ier;** *superl* **-iest**) *adj* pfeifend.

**whelk** [welk] *n* Wellhornschnecke *die.*

**when** [wen] *adv* (*in questions*) wann; **~ does the plane arrive?** wann kommt das Flugzeug an?; **he asked me ~ I would be in London** er fragte mich, wann ich in London sei <> *conj* - **1.** [specifying time] wenn; [in the past] als; **on the day ~ it happened** an dem Tag, als es geschah - **2.** [although, seeing as] wo ... doch; **you said it was black ~ in fact it was white** du hast gesagt, es wäre schwarz, wo es doch weiß war.

**whenever** [wen'evə<sup>r</sup>] *conj* [every time] (immer) wenn; **~ you like** [no matter when] wann immer du willst <> *adv*: **~ did you find time to do it?** wann hast du bloß die Zeit dafür gefun-

den?; **next week or ~** nächste Woche oder wann auch immer.

**where** [weə<sup>r</sup>] *adv* (*in questions*) wo; **~ do you come from?** woher kommst du?; **~ are you going?** wohin gehst du? <> *conj* - **1.** [referring to place, situation] wo; **at the place ~ it happened** dort, wo es passiert ist; **the house ~ I was born** das Haus, in dem ich geboren wurde; **that's (just) ~ you're wrong** (genau) da irren Sie sich - **2.** [whereas] während.

**whereabouts** [adv ,weərə'baʊts, *n* 'weərəbaʊts] *adv* wo <> *npl* Aufenthaltsort *der.*

**whereas** [weər'æz] *conj* während.

**whereby** [weə'baɪ] *conj fml* wodurch.

**wheresoever** [,weəsəʊ'evə<sup>r</sup>] *conj & adv* = **wherever.**

**whereupon** [,weərə'pɒn] *conj fml* woraufhin.

**wherever** [weər'evə<sup>r</sup>] *conj* wo immer; [from any place] woher auch immer; [to any place] wohin auch immer; [everywhere] überall wo; **~ that may be** wo immer das sein mag <> *adv*: **~ did you hear that?** wo hast du das bloß gehört?

**wherewithal** ['weəwɪðɔːl] *n fml*: **to have the ~ to do sthg** das nötige Kleingeld haben, um etw zu tun.

**whet** [wet] (*pt & pp* **-ted;** *cont* **-ting**) *vt*: **to ~ sb's appetite (for doing sthg)** jn auf den Geschmack bringen(, etw zu tun).

**whether** ['weðə<sup>r</sup>] *conj* ob; **he didn't know ~ to go or not** er wusste nicht, ob er gehen sollte oder nicht; **~ I want to or not** ob ich nun will oder nicht.

**whew** [hwjuː] *excl* [when too hot] puh!; [when relieved] uff!

**whey** [weɪ] *n (U)* Molke *die.*

**which** [wɪtʃ] *adj* (*in questions*) welche, -r, -s; **~ room do you want?** welches Zimmer willst du?; **~ one?** welches?; **she asked me ~ room I wanted** sie fragte mich, welches Zimmer ich wollte <> *pron* - **1.** (*in questions – subject*) welche, -r, -s; **~ is the cheapest?** welches ist das billigste?; **he asked me ~ was the best** er fragte mich, welcher der Beste sei - **2.** (*in questions – object*) welche, -n, -s; **~ do you prefer?** welches gefällt dir besser?; **he asked me ~ I preferred** er fragte mich, welches ich bevorzugen würde - **3.** (*in questions – after prep + A*) welche, -n, -s; **~ should I put the vase on?** auf welchen soll ich die Vase stellen? - **4.** (*in questions – after prep + D*) welcher/welchem/welchem; **he asked me ~ I was talking about** er fragte mich, von welchem ich spreche - **5.** (*introducing relative clause – after subject*) der/die/das, die (*pl*); **the house ~ is on corner** das Haus, das an der Ecke steht - **6.** (*introducing relative clause – object, after prep + A*) den/die/das, die (*pl*); **the television ~ I bought** der Fernseher, den ich gekauft ha-

**W**

be; **the book through ~ he became famous** das Buch, durch das er berühmt wurde - **7.** *(introducing relative clause – object, after prep + D)* dem/der/dem, denen *(pl)*; **the settee on ~ I'm sitting** das Sofa, auf dem ich sitze; **ten apples, of ~ six are bad** zehn Äpfel, von denen *OR* wovon sechs faul sind - **8.** *(introducing relative clause – object, after prep + G)* dessen/deren/dessen, deren *(pl)* - **9.** *(referring back)* was; **he's late, ~ annoys me** er ist spät dran, was mich ärgert; **he's always late, ~ I don't like** er verspätet sich immer, was ich nicht leiden kann.

**whichever** [wɪtʃ'evə<sup>r</sup>] *adj* - **1.** [any] welche, -r, -s; **take ~ book you like** nehmen Sie, welches Buch Sie (auch immer) wollen - **2.** [no matter which] egal welche; **~ way you look** wo man auch hinsieht <> *pron* [the one which] welche, -r, -s; **take ~ you like** nimm, welches du (auch) willst.

**whiff** [wɪf] *n* - **1.** [smell] Hauch *der* - **2.** *fig* [sign] Anzeichen *das.*

**while** [waɪl] *n:* **a ~** eine Weile; **for a ~** eine Weile, eine Zeit lang; **in a ~** bald; **a short ~ ago** vor kurzem; **once in a ~** hin und wieder; **it's not worth your ~** es ist nicht der Mühe wert <> *conj* - **1.** [gen] während; **he fell asleep ~ (he was) reading** er schlief beim Lesen ein - **2.** [although] obgleich, während.
➭ **while away** *vt sep:* **to ~ away the time** sich *(D)* die Zeit vertreiben.

**whilst** [waɪlst] *conj* = **while.**

**whim** [wɪm] *n* Laune *die.*

**whimper** ['wɪmpə<sup>r</sup>] *n* [of child] Wimmern *das;* [of animal] Winseln *das* <> *vt* wimmern <> *vi* [child] wimmern; [animal] winseln.

**whimsical** ['wɪmzɪkl] *adj* wunderlich.

**whine** [waɪn] *n* Heulen *das;* [of dog] Jaulen *das* <> *vi* - **1.** [make sound] heulen; [dog] jaulen - **2.** [complain]: **to ~ (about sb/sthg)** (über jn/etw) jammern.

**whinge** [wɪndʒ] *(cont* **whingeing)** *vi Br:* **to ~ (about sb/sthg)** (über jn/etw) jammern.

**whip** [wɪp] *(pt & pp -**ped**; cont -**ping**) n* - **1.** [for hitting] Peitsche *die* - **2.** *Br Pol* Einpeitscher *der* <> *vt* - **1.** [beat with whip] auslpeitschen - **2.** *fig* [subj: rain, wind] peitschen - **3.** [take quickly]: **to ~ sthg out** etw zücken; **to ~ sthg off** etw herunterlreißen - **4.** *CULIN* [whisk] schlagen.
➭ **whip up** *vt sep* [provoke] entfachen; [hatred] schüren.

**whiplash (injury)** ['wɪplæʃ-] *n* Schleudertrauma *das.*

**whipped cream** [wɪpt-] *n* Schlagsahne *die.*

**whippet** ['wɪpɪt] *n* Whippet *der.*

**whip-round** *n Br inf:* **to have a ~** eine Sammlung machen.

**whirl** [wɜːl] *n* - **1.** [rotating movement] Wirbel *der;*

**my mind was in a complete ~** mir schwirrte der Kopf - **2.** *fig* [of activity] Trubel *der* - **3.** *phr:* **let's give it a ~** *inf* lasst es uns auslprobieren <> *vt:* **to ~ sb/sthg round** jn etw herumlwirbeln <> *vi* - **1.** [move around] wirbeln - **2.** *fig* [be confused, excited]: **his head was ~ing** ihm schwirrte der Kopf.

**whirlpool** ['wɜːlpuːl] *n* Strudel *der.*

**whirlwind** ['wɜːlwɪnd] *adj fig* [rapid] stürmisch <> *n* Wirbelsturm *der.*

**whirr** [wɜːr] *n* [of wings] Schwirren *das;* [of engine] Surren *das* <> *vi* [of wings] schwirren; [machinery, camera] surren.

**whisk** [wɪsk] *n CULIN* Schneebesen *der* <> *vt* - **1.** [put or take quickly]: **he ~ed it into his pocket** er ließ es schnell in seiner Tasche verschwinden; **she was ~ed into hospital** sie wurde schnellstens ins Krankenhaus gebracht - **2.** *CULIN* (mit dem Schneebesen) schlagen.

**whisker** ['wɪskə<sup>r</sup>] *n* [of animal] Schnurrhaar *das.*
➭ **whiskers** *npl* [of man] Backenbart *der.*

**whisky** *Br (pl* -**ies**)**, whiskey** *Am & Irish (pl* **whiskeys**) ['wɪskɪ] *n* Whisky *der.*

**whisper** ['wɪspə<sup>r</sup>] *n* Flüstern *das;* **they spoke in a ~** sie sprachen im Flüsterton <> *vt* flüstern; **to ~ sthg to sb** jm etw zulflüstern <> *vi* flüstern.

**whispering** ['wɪspərɪŋ] *n* Geflüster *das.*

**whist** [wɪst] *n* Whist *das.*

**whistle** ['wɪsl] *n* - **1.** [through lips, from whistle] Pfiff *der* - **2.** [of kettle, train] Pfeifen *das* - **3.** [object] Pfeife *die* <> *vt* pfeifen <> *vi:* **to ~ at sb** jm nachlpfeifen.

**whistle-stop tour** *n Touristenreise oder Wahlkampftour mit kurzem Stopps in vielen verschiedenen Orten.*

**whit** [wɪt] *n:* **not a ~** keine Spur.

**Whit** [wɪt] *n Br* Pfingsten *das.*

**white** [waɪt] *adj* - **1.** [gen] weiß; **to go** *OR* **turn ~** [hair] weiß werden; [face] erbleichen - **2.** [coffee, tea] mit Milch - **3.** [wine] Weiß- <> *n* - **1.** [colour] Weiß *das* - **2.** [person] Weiße *der, die* - **3.** [of egg] Eiweiß *das* - **4.** [of eye] Weiße *das.*
➭ **whites** *npl* - **1.** *SPORT* weiße Sportkleidung - **2.** [washing] weiße Wäsche.

**white blood cell** *n* weißes Blutkörperchen.

**whiteboard** ['waɪtbɔːd] *n* weiße Tafel.

**white Christmas** *n* weiße Weihnachten. ·

**white-collar** *adj:* **~ worker** Büroangestellte *der, die;* **~ job** Schreibtischarbeit *die.*

**white elephant** *n fig* Fehlinvestition *die.*

**white goods** *npl* [household machines] weiße Ware.

**white-haired** [-'heəd] adj weißhaarig.

**Whitehall** ['waɪthɔːl] n Whitehall nt.

> **WHITEHALL**
>
> Whitehall ist das Zentrum des britischen Verwaltungsapparats und Sitz zahlreicher Regierungsbüros und Behörden. Der Ausdruck bezeichnet nicht nur die Straße selber, sondern auch die britische Regierung allgemein.

**white horses** npl Br [on sea] schaumgekrönte Wellen pl.

**white-hot** adj weißglühend.

**White House** n [residence of president, US government]: **the ~** das Weiße Haus.

**white lie** n Notlüge die.

**white light** n weißes Licht.

**white magic** n weiße Magie.

**white meat** n weißes Fleisch.

**whiten** ['waɪtn] vt weiß machen; [clothes] bleichen; [walls] weißen <> vi weiß werden.

**whitener** ['waɪtnəʳ] n [for clothes] Bleichmittel das; [for shoes] Weißmacher der.

**whiteness** ['waɪtnɪs] n Weiße die.

**white noise** n weißes Rauschen.

**whiteout** ['waɪtaʊt] n Schneegestöber das.

**white paper** n POL Weißbuch das.

**white sauce** n Béchamelsoße die.

**white spirit** n (U) Br Terpentinersatz der.

**white-tie** adj mit Frackzwang.

**whitewash** ['waɪtwɒʃ] n - **1.** (U) [paint] Tünche die - **2.** pej [cover-up] Verschleierung die <> vt - **1.** [paint] tünchen - **2.** pej [cover up] verschleiern.

**whitewater rafting** ['waɪt,wɔːtəʳ-] n Whitewaterrafting das.

**white wedding** n weiße Hochzeit.

**whiting** ['waɪtɪŋ] (pl inv OR -s) n Wittling der.

**Whit Monday** n Pfingstmontag der.

**Whitsun** ['wɪtsn] n [day] Pfingstsonntag der.

**whittle** ['wɪtl] vt [reduce]: **to ~ sthg away** OR **down** etw allmählich reduzieren; **his rights have gradually been ~d away** seine Rechte sind allmählich eingeschränkt worden.

**whiz** (pt & pp -zed; cont -zing), **whizz** [wɪz] n inf: **to be a ~ at sthg** ein Genie in etw (D) sein <> vi sausen.

**whiz(z) kid** n inf Senkrechtstarter der, -in die.

**who** [huː] pron - **1.** (in questions) wer; (accusative) wen; (dative) wem; **~ are you?** wer bist du/sind Sie?; **~ does he think he is?** was bildet er sich eigentlich ein? - **2.** (in relative clauses) der/die/das, die pl; **the friend ~ came yesterday** der Freund, der gestern kam.

**WHO** (abbr of **World Health Organization**) n WHO die.

**who'd** [huːd] = who had, who would.

**whodu(n)nit** [ˌhuːˈdʌnɪt] n inf Krimi der.

**whoever** [huːˈevəʳ] pron [whichever person] wer immer; **~ it is** wer es auch ist; **~ could that be?** wer könnte das bloß sein?

**whole** [həʊl] adj - **1.** [entire, complete] ganz - **2.** esp Am [for emphasis]: **a ~ lot of questions** eine ganze Reihe von Fragen; **a ~ lot bigger** viel größer <> adv esp Am [for emphasis] völlig <> n - **1.** [all, entirety]: **the ~ of the school** die ganze Schule; **the ~ of the summer** den ganzen Sommer - **2.** [unit, complete thing] Ganze das.

➣ **as a whole** adv als Ganzes.

➣ **on the whole** adv im Großen und Ganzen.

**wholefood** ['həʊlfuːd] n Br Vollwertkost die.

**whole-hearted** [-'hɑːtɪd] adj [support, agreement] voll; **to make a ~ effort** größte Anstrengungen unternehmen.

**wholemeal** Br ['həʊlmiːl], **whole wheat** Am adj Vollkorn-.

**wholemeal bread** n Br Vollkornbrot das.

**whole note** n Am ganze Note.

**wholesale** ['həʊlseɪl] adj - **1.** [bulk] Großhandels- - **2.** pej [excessive] Massen- <> adv - **1.** [in bulk] im Großhandel - **2.** pej [excessively] massenhaft.

**wholesaler** ['həʊl,seɪləʳ] n Großhändler der, -in die.

**wholesome** ['həʊlsəm] adj gesund.

**whole wheat** adj Am = wholemeal.

**who'll** [huːl] = who will.

**wholly** ['həʊlɪ] adv völlig.

**whom** [huːm] pron fml - **1.** (in direct, indirect questions) wen; (dative) wem; **~ did you phone?** wen hast du angerufen?; **for/of/to ~?** nach/von/mit wem? - **2.** (in relative clauses) den/die/das, die (pl); (dative) dem/der/dem, denen (pl); **the girl ~ he married** das Mädchen, das er geheiratet hat; **the man of ~ you speak** der Mann, von dem du sprichst; **the man to ~ you were speaking** der Mann, mit dem du gesprochen hast; **several people came, none of ~ I knew** es kamen verschiedene Leute, von denen ich keinen kannte.

**whoop** [wuːp] n Freudenschrei der <> vi einen Freudenschrei ausstoßen.

**whoopee** [wʊˈpiː] excl juchu!, hurra!

**whooping cough** ['huːpɪŋ-] n (U) Keuchhusten der.

**whoops** [wʊps] excl huch!

**whoosh** [wʊʃ] inf n Zischen das <> vi zischen.

**whop** [wɒp] (pt & pp -ped; cont -ping) vt inf [defeat] schlagen.

**whopper** ['wɒpəʳ] n inf - **1.** [something big] Brocken der - **2.** [lie] faustdicke Lüge.

**W**

**whopping** ['wɒpɪŋ] *adj inf* Mords-; [lie] faustdick.

**whore** [hɔːʳ] *n pej* Hure *die*.

**who're** ['huːəʳ] = who are.

**whose** [huːz] *pron (in direct, indirect questions)* wessen; ~ **is this?** wem gehört das?; **tell me** ~ **this is** sag mir, wem das gehört ◇ *adj* **- 1.** *(in questions)* wessen; ~ **car is that?** wessen Auto ist das? **- 2.** *(in relative clauses)* dessen/deren/dessen, deren *(pl);* **that's the boy ~ father's an MP** das ist der Junge, dessen Vater Abgeordneter ist.

**whosoever** [ˌhuːsəʊ'evəʳ] *pron literary* wer auch immer.

**who's who** [huːz-] *n* [book] Who's who *das, Titel eines biografischen Lexikons*.

**who've** [huːv] = who have.

**why** [waɪ] *adv* warum; ~ **not?** warum nicht?; **I didn't ask** ~ ich habe nicht gefragt, weshalb ◇ *conj* warum; **there are several reasons** ~ **he left** es gibt mehrere Gründe dafür, dass er wegging ◇ *excl:* ~, **it's David!** sieh da, (da kommt) David!

➡ **why ever** *adv:* ~ **ever did you do that?** warum hast du das bloß getan?

**WI** *n abbr of* **Women's Institute** ◇ **- 1.** *abbr of* **West Indies - 2.** *abk für* Wisconsin, *in Postanschrift verwendet*.

**wick** [wɪk] *n* **- 1.** [of candle] Docht *der* **- 2.** *phr:* **to get on sb's** ~ *Br inf* jm auf die Nerven gehen.

**wicked** ['wɪkɪd] *adj* **- 1.** [evil] böse, schlecht **- 2.** [mischievous] schelmisch **- 3.** *inf* [fantastic] geil.

**wickedness** *n* [evil] Bösartigkeit *die*.

**wicker** ['wɪkəʳ] *adj:* ~ **chair** Korbstuhl *der*.

**wickerwork** ['wɪkəwɜːk] *n (U)* Korbgeflecht *das* ◇ *comp* Korb-; ~ **basket** Weidenkorb *der*.

**wicket** ['wɪkɪt] *n* CRICKET **- 1.** [stumps] Mal *das*, Wicket *das* **- 2.** [pitch] Spielbahn *die* **- 3.** [dismissal] Wicket *das;* **to take a** ~ einen Schlagmann zum Ausscheiden bringen.

**wicket keeper** *n* Torhüter *der*, -in *die*.

**wide** [waɪd] *adj* **- 1.** [broad] breit **- 2.** [variety, selection, gap, difference] groß **- 3.** [coverage, knowledge] umfassend **- 4.** [far-reaching] weit reichend **- 5.** [shot, punch, ball] weit **- 6.** [eyes] weit aufgerissen ◇ *adv* **- 1.** [as far as possible] weit **- 2.** [off-target] daneben.

**wide-angle lens** *n* PHOT Weitwinkelobjektiv *das*.

**wide-awake** *adj* hellwach.

**wide boy** *n Br inf pej* Gauner *der*.

**wide-eyed** [-'aɪd] *adj* **- 1.** [surprised, frightened] mit weit aufgerissenen Augen **- 2.** [innocent, gullible]: **the child looked at her in** ~ **innocence** das Kind sah sie mit großen unschuldigen Augen an.

**widely** ['waɪdlɪ] *adv* **- 1.** [broadly] breit **- 2.** [extensively] weit; ~ **read** belesen; **to be** ~ **experienced** viel Erfahrung haben; ~ **known** allgemein bekannt **- 3.** [considerably] beträchtlich.

**widen** ['waɪdn] *vt* **- 1.** [road, hole] verbreitern **- 2.** [search, activity, range] auslweiten; [choice] erweitern **- 3.** [gap, difference] vergrößern ◇ *vi* **- 1.** [become broader] sich verbreitern **- 2.** [search, activity, range] sich auslweiten **- 3.** [gap, difference, eyes] größer werden.

**wide open** *adj* **- 1.** [window, door] weit offen **- 2.** [eyes] weit aufgerissen **- 3.** [spaces] weit.

**wide-ranging** [-'reɪndʒɪŋ] *adj* umfassend.

**widespread** ['waɪdspred] *adj* weit verbreitet.

**widow** ['wɪdəʊ] *n* Witwe *die*.

**widowed** ['wɪdəʊd] *adj* verwitwet.

**widower** ['wɪdəʊəʳ] *n* Witwer *der*.

**width** [wɪdθ] *n* Breite *die;* **3 metres in** ~ 3 Meter breit.

**widthways** ['wɪdθweɪz] *adv* der Breite nach.

**wield** [wiːld] *vt* **- 1.** [weapon] schwingen **- 2.** [power] auslüben.

**wife** [waɪf] *(pl* wives) *n* Ehefrau *die*.

**wig** [wɪg] *n* Perücke *die*.

**wiggle** ['wɪgl] *inf n* **- 1.** [movement] Wackeln *das* **- 2.** [wavy line] Schlangenlinie *die* ◇ *vt:* **to** ~ **one's ears/toes** mit seinen Ohren/Zehen wackeln ◇ *vi* wackeln.

**wiggly** ['wɪglɪ] *(compar* -ier; *superl* -iest) *adj inf* **- 1.** [wavy] Schlangen- **- 2.** [movable] wackelig.

**wigwam** ['wɪgwæm] *n* Wigwam *der*.

**wild** [waɪld] *adj* **- 1.** [gen] wild; **to run** ~ frei herumllaufen **- 2.** [violent, dangerous] gewalttätig **- 3.** [weather, sea] stürmisch **- 4.** [hair, look] wirr **- 5.** [dream, plan] verrückt **- 6.** *inf* [very enthusiastic]: **to be** ~ **about sthg** auf etw *(A)* verrückt sein ◇ *n:* **in the** ~ in freier Wildbahn.

➡ **wilds** *npl:* **the** ~**s** die Wildnis; **he lives in the** ~**s somewhere** er wohnt irgendwo weit abgelegen.

**wild card** *n* COMPUT Platzhalter *der*, Stellvertretersymbol *das*.

**wildcat** ['waɪldkæt] *n* [animal] Wildkatze *die*.

**wildcat strike** *n* wilder Streik.

**wildebeest** ['wɪldɪbiːst] *(pl inv OR* -s) *n* Gnu *das*.

**wilderness** ['wɪldənɪs] *n* Wildnis *die;* **to be in the** ~ *fig* außerhalb des Geschehens sein.

**wildfire** ['waɪldˌfaɪəʳ] *n:* **to spread like** ~ sich wie ein Lauffeuer verbreiten.

**wild flower** *n* wilde Blume.

**wildfowl** ['waɪldfaʊl] *n* Federwild *das*.

**wild-goose chase** *n inf* hoffnungslose Suche.

**wildlife** ['waɪldlaɪf] *n* Tierwelt *die*.

**wildly** ['waɪldlɪ] adv - **1.** [gen] wild - **2.** [talk, throw] aufs Geratewohl - **3.** [very] äußerst.

**wild rice** n Wildreis der.

**wild west** n inf: the ~ der Wilde Westen.

**wiles** [waɪlz] npl List die.

**wilful** Br, **willful** Am ['wɪlfʊl] adj - **1.** [determined] stur - **2.** [deliberate] beabsichtigt.

**will¹** [wɪl] n - **1.** [gen] Wille der; against his ~ gegen seinen Willen; at ~ nach Belieben; ~ to live Lebenswille der - **2.** [document] Testament das ◇ vt: to ~ sb to do sthg (sich (D)) mit aller Kraft wünschen, dass jd etw tut; they were ~ing him to win sie wünschten seinen Sieg herbei.

**will²** [wɪl] aux vb - **1.** [expressing future tense] werden; I ~ see you next week wir sehen uns nächste Woche; ~ you be here next Friday? bist du nächsten Freitag hier?; ~ you do that for me? – no I won't/yes I ~ wirst du das für mich tun? – nein(, werde ich nicht)/ja(, werde ich); when ~ you have finished it? wann seid ihr damit fertig?; I think he WILL come ich glaube schon, dass er kommt - **2.** [expressing willingness] wollen, werden; I won't do it ich werde das nicht tun; no one ~ do it keiner wird das machen - **3.** [expressing polite question]: ~ you have some more tea? möchten Sie noch mehr Tee? - **4.** [in commands, requests]: ~ you please be quiet! sei bitte ruhig!; close that window, ~ you? mach doch das Fenster zu, bitte - **5.** [expressing possibility]: the hall ~ hold up to 1,000 people die Halle fasst bis zu 1000 Leute; pensions ~ be paid monthly Pensionen werden monatlich ausgezahlt - **6.** [expressing an assumption]: that'll be your father das wird dein Vater sein; as you ~ have gathered, ... wie Sie sich wohl gedacht haben, ... - **7.** [indicating irritation]: well, if you WILL leave your toys everywhere you la, wenn ihr auch dauernd eure Spielsachen überall herumliegen lasst; she WILL keep phoning me sie ruft mich aber auch dauernd an.

**willful** adj Am = wilful.

**willing** ['wɪlɪŋ] adj - **1.** [prepared]: to be ~ (to do sthg) bereit sein(, etw zu tun) - **2.** [eager] bereitwillig.

**willingly** ['wɪlɪŋlɪ] adv bereitwillig, gerne.

**willingness** ['wɪlɪŋnɪs] n Bereitwilligkeit die; ~ to do sthg die Bereitwilligkeit, etw zu tun.

**willow (tree)** ['wɪləʊ-] n Weide die.

**willowy** ['wɪləʊɪ] adj gertenschlank.

**willpower** ['wɪl‚paʊəʳ] n Willenskraft die.

**willy** ['wɪlɪ] (pl -ies) n Br inf Pimmel der.

**willy-nilly** [‚wɪlɪ'nɪlɪ] adv - **1.** [at random] aufs Geratewohl - **2.** [wanting or not] wohl oder übel.

**wilt** [wɪlt] vi - **1.** [plant] verwelken - **2.** fig [person] schlapp werden.

**wily** ['waɪlɪ] (compar -ier; superl -iest) adj listig.

**wimp** [wɪmp] n inf pej Waschlappen der.

**win** [wɪn] (pt & pp won; cont -ning) n Sieg der ◇ vt gewinnen ◇ vi gewinnen; [in battle] siegen; you/I/etc can't ~ da ist nichts zu machen.

⬥ **win over, win round** vt sep für sich gewinnen.

**wince** [wɪns] vi: to ~ at/with sthg bei/vor etw (D) zusammenIzucken ◇ n Zusammenzucken das.

**winch** [wɪntʃ] n Winde die ◇ vt mit einer Winde hochIziehen.

**wind¹** [wɪnd] n - **1.** METEOR Wind der - **2.** (U) [breath] Atem der - **3.** (U) [in stomach] Blähungen pl; to break ~ euphemism Winde abgehen lassen - **4.** [in orchestra]: the ~ die Bläser - **5.** phr: to get ~ of sthg inf von einer Sache Wind bekommen ◇ vt - **1.** [knock breath out of]: I was ~ed by the fall durch den Sturz blieb mir die Luft weg - **2.** Br [baby]: to ~ the baby das Baby ein Bäuerchen machen lassen.

**wind²** [waɪnd] (pt & pp wound) vt - **1.** [string, thread] wickeln - **2.** [clock] auf Iziehen - **3.** phr: to ~ one's way [river, road] sich schlängeln ◇ vi [river, road] sich schlängeln.

⬥ **wind back** vt sep [tape] zurückIspulen.

⬥ **wind down** vt sep - **1.** [car window] herunterIkurbeln - **2.** [production] allmählich einIstellen ◇ vi - **1.** [clock] abIlaufen - **2.** [relax] entspannen.

⬥ **wind forward** vt sep [tape] vorIspulen.

⬥ **wind on** vt sep weiterIspulen.

⬥ **wind up** vt sep - **1.** [finish - meeting] abIschließen; [ - business] aufIlösen - **2.** [clock] auf Iziehen - **3.** [car window] herauf Ikurbeln - **4.** Br inf [deliberately annoy] auf Iziehen ◇ vi inf [end up] enden; we wound up going to the pub schließlich gingen wir in die Kneipe.

**windbreak** ['wɪndbreɪk] n Windschutz der.

**windcheater** Br ['wɪnd‚tʃiːtəʳ], **windbreaker** Am ['wɪnd‚breɪkəʳ] n dated Windjacke die.

**windchill** ['wɪndtʃɪl] n Windauskühlung die.

**winded** ['wɪndɪd] adj außer Atem.

**windfall** ['wɪndfɔːl] n - **1.** [fruit] Fallobst das - **2.** [unexpected gift] unerhoffter Gewinn.

**winding** ['waɪndɪŋ] adj kurvenreich; [river] gewunden.

**wind instrument** [wɪnd-] n Blasinstrument das.

**windmill** ['wɪndmɪl] n Windmühle die.

**window** ['wɪndəʊ] n - **1.** [gen & COMPUT] Fenster das - **2.** [of shop] Schaufenster das - **3.** [free time] freie Zeit.

**window box** n Blumenkasten der.

**W**

**window cleaner** n Fensterputzer der, -in die.

**window display** n Schaufensterdekoration die.

**window dressing** n - **1.** [in shop] Schaufensterdekoration die - **2.** fig [non-essentials] Mache die.

**window envelope** n Fensterbriefumschlag der.

**window frame** n Fensterrahmen der.

**window ledge** n [outside] Fenstersims das; [inside] Fensterbrett das.

**windowpane** ['wɪndəʊˌpeɪn] n Fensterscheibe die.

**window shade** n Am Rollo das.

**window-shopping** n Schaufensterbummel der; **to go ~** einen Schaufensterbummel machen.

**windowsill** ['wɪndəʊsɪl] n [outside] Fenstersims der OR das; [inside] Fensterbrett das.

**windpipe** ['wɪndpaɪp] n Luftröhre die.

**windscreen** Br ['wɪndskriːn], **windshield** Am ['wɪndʃiːld] n Windschutzscheibe die.

**windscreen washer** n Scheibenwaschanlage die.

**windscreen wiper** n Scheibenwischer der.

**windshield** n Am = windscreen.

**windsock** ['wɪndsɒk] n Windsack der.

**windsurfer** ['wɪndˌsɜːfəʳ] n - **1.** [person] Windsurfer der, -in die - **2.** [board] Surfbrett das.

**windsurfing** ['wɪndˌsɜːfɪŋ] n Windsurfen das.

**windswept** ['wɪndswept] adj - **1.** [landscape] windgepeitscht - **2.** [person, hair] zerzaust.

**wind tunnel** [wɪnd-] n Windkanal der.

**windy** ['wɪndɪ] (compar -ier; superl -iest) adj windig.

**wine** [waɪn] n Wein der.

**wine bar** n Br Weinbar die.

**wine bottle** n Weinflasche die.

**wine box** n Weinkiste die.

**wine cellar** n - **1.** [stock of wine] Weinvorrat der - **2.** [place] Weinkeller der.

**wineglass** ['waɪnɡlɑːs] n Weinglas das.

**wine list** n Weinkarte die.

**wine merchant** n Br Weinhändler der.

**winepress** ['waɪnpres] n Weinpresse die.

**wine rack** n Weinregal das.

**wine tasting** [-ˌteɪstɪŋ] n - **1.** [practice] Weinverkosten n - **2.** [event] Weinprobe die.

**wine waiter** n Weinkellner der.

**wing** [wɪŋ] n - **1.** [gen] Flügel der - **2.** [of plane] Tragfläche die - **3.** [of car] Kotflügel der.

➤ **wings** npl THEATRE: **the ~s** die Kulissen.

**wing commander** n Br Oberstleutnant der der Luftwaffe.

**winger** ['wɪŋəʳ] n SPORT Außenstürmer der, -in die.

**wing nut** n Flügelmutter die.

**wingspan** ['wɪŋspæn] n Flügelspannweite die.

**wink** [wɪŋk] n [of eye] Zwinkern das; **to have forty ~s** inf ein Nickerchen machen; **not to sleep a ~, not to get a ~ of sleep** inf kein Auge zumachen ⬦ vi - **1.** [eye] zwinkern; **to ~ at sb** jm zulzwinkern - **2.** literary [lights] blinken.

**winkle** ['wɪŋkl] n Strandschnecke die.

➤ **winkle out** vt sep herauslbekommen; **to ~ sthg out of sb** fig etw aus jm herauslbekommen.

**winner** ['wɪnəʳ] n - **1.** [person] Gewinner der, -in die; [in sport] Sieger der, -in die - **2.** inf [success] Renner der; **he's onto a ~ with his new book** sein neues Buch wird garantiert ein Renner.

**winning** ['wɪnɪŋ] adj - **1.** [victorious] siegreich; [successful] erfolgreich - **2.** [pleasing] gewinnend.

➤ **winnings** npl Gewinn der.

**winning post** n Zielpfosten der.

**winsome** ['wɪnsəm] adj literary gewinnend.

**winter** ['wɪntəʳ] n Winter der; **in ~** im Winter ⬦ comp Winter-.

**winter sports** npl Wintersport der.

**wintertime** ['wɪntətaɪm] n Winterzeit die; **in ~** im Winter.

**wint(e)ry** ['wɪntrɪ] adj winterlich.

**wipe** [waɪp] n [clean]: **he gave his face/the table a ~** er wischte sein Gesicht/den Tisch ab ⬦ vt - **1.** [rub to clean - floor] wischen; [ - face, table] ablwischen - **2.** [rub to dry] abltrocknen.

➤ **wipe away** vt sep [tears] ablwischen.

➤ **wipe out** vt sep - **1.** [erase] weglwischen - **2.** [eradicate - gen] vernichten; [ - race] auslrotten.

➤ **wipe up** vt sep auf lwischen ⬦ vi [dry dishes] abltrocknen.

**wiper** ['waɪpəʳ] n [windscreen wiper] Scheibenwischer der.

**wire** ['waɪəʳ] n - **1.** [gen] Draht der; [electrical] Leitung die - **2.** esp Am [telegram] Telegramm das ⬦ comp Draht- ⬦ vt - **1.** [fasten]: **to ~ sthg to sthg** etw mit Draht an etw (D) befestigen - **2.** ELEC [plug] anlschließen; **to ~ a house** die elektrischen Leitungen in einem Haus verlegen - **3.** esp Am [send telegram to] ein Telegramm schicken.

➤ **wire up** vt sep: **to ~ up a house** die elektrischen Leitungen in einem Haus verlegen.

**wire brush** n Drahtbürste die.

**wire cutters** *npl* Drahtschere *die.*
**wireless** ['waɪəlɪs] *n dated* Radio *das.*
**wire netting** *n* Maschendraht *der.*
**wire-tapping** [-ˌtæpɪŋ] *n* Abhören *das.*
**wire wool** *n Br* Stahlwolle *die.*
**wiring** ['waɪərɪŋ] *n (U)* elektrische Leitungen *pl.*
**wiry** ['waɪərɪ] (*compar* -ier; *superl* -iest) *adj*
- **1.** [hair] borstig - **2.** [body, man] drahtig.
**wisdom** ['wɪzdəm] *n* Weisheit *die.*
**wisdom tooth** *n* Weisheitszahn *der.*
**wise** [waɪz] *adj* [prudent] weise; **to get ~ to sthg** *inf* etw spitzlbekommen; **to be no ~r** OR **none the ~r** kein bisschen schlauer sein.
➤ **wise up** *vi esp Am:* he finally ~d up to her little game er durchblickte schließlich ihr Spielchen.
**wisecrack** ['waɪzkræk] *n pej* böser Witz.
**wisely** ['waɪzlɪ] *adv* [intelligently] weise; [sensibly] klugerweise.
**wish** [wɪʃ] *n* Wunsch *der;* **~ to do sthg** der Wunsch, etw zu tun; **~ for sthg** der Wunsch nach etw *(D)* ◇ *vt* - **1.** [want]: **to ~ to do sthg** *fml* etw zu tun wünschen; **I ~ed (that) he'd come** wenn er nur käme - **2.** [desire, request by magic]: **I ~ (that) I had a million pounds** ich wünschte, ich hätte eine Million Pfund - **3.** [in greeting]: **to ~ sb sthg** jm etw wünschen ◇ *vi* [by magic]: **to ~ for sthg** sich etw herbeilwünschen.
➤ **wishes** *npl:* **best ~es** alles Gute; **(with) best ~es** [at end of letter] herzliche Grüße.
➤ **wish on** *vt sep:* **to ~ sthg on sb** jm etw wünschen.
**wishbone** ['wɪʃbəʊn] *n* Gabelbein *das.*
**wishful thinking** [ˌwɪʃfʊl-] *n* Wunschdenken *das.*
**wishy-washy** ['wɪʃɪˌwɒʃɪ] *adj inf pej* [person] kraftlos; [ideas] vage; **don't be so ~!** sage doch mal konkret, was du meinst!
**wisp** [wɪsp] *n* - **1.** [tuft] Büschel *das* - **2.** [small cloud]: **~ of smoke** Rauchfahne *die.*
**wispy** ['wɪspɪ] (*compar* -ier; *superl* -iest) *adj* [hair] dünn.
**wisteria** [wɪs'tɪərɪə] *n* Glyzinie *die.*
**wistful** ['wɪstfʊl] *adj* wehmütig.
**wit** [wɪt] *n* - **1.** [humour] Witz *der;* **a conversation full of ~** eine witzige und geistreiche Unterhaltung - **2.** [funny person]: **she's a real ~** sie ist sehr witzig - **3.** [intelligence]: **to have the ~ to do sthg** klug genug sein, etw zu tun.
➤ **wits** *npl* [intelligence, mind]: **to have** OR **keep one's ~s about one** geistesgegenwärtig sein; **to be scared out of one's ~s** *inf* sich zu Tode erschrecken; **to be at one's ~s' end** mit seinem Latein am Ende sein.
**witch** [wɪtʃ] *n* Hexe *die.*
**witchcraft** ['wɪtʃkrɑːft] *n (U)* Hexerei *die.*

**witchdoctor** ['wɪtʃˌdɒktəʳ] *n* Medizinmann *der.*
**witch-hazel** *n* - **1.** *(U)* [liquid] Hamamelisgesichtswasser *das* - **2.** [tree] Zaubernuss *die.*
**witch-hunt** *n pej* Hexenjagd *die.*
**with** [wɪð] *prep* - **1.** [gen] mit; **come ~ me** komm mit mir; **a man ~ a beard** ein Mann mit Bart; **a room ~ a bathroom** ein Zimmer mit Bad; **he hit me ~ a stick** er hat mich mit einem Stock geschlagen; **be careful ~ that!** sei vorsichtig damit!; **bring it ~ you** bringen Sie es mit; **to argue ~ sb** (sich) mit jm streiten; **the war ~ Germany** der Krieg gegen Deutschland; **I can't do it ~ you watching me** ich kann es nicht tun, wenn du mir zuschaust - **2.** [at house of, in the hands of] bei; **we stayed ~ friends** wir haben bei Freunden übernachtet; **the decision rests ~ you** die Entscheidung liegt bei dir - **3.** [indicating emotion] vor; **to tremble ~ fear** vor Angst zittern - **4.** [because of] bei; **~ the weather as it is, we decided to stay at home** angesichts des Wetters beschlossen wir zu Hause zu bleiben; **~ my luck, I'll probably lose** bei meinem Glück werde ich wahrscheinlich verlieren - **5.** *phr:* **I'll be ~ you in a moment** ich komme gleich; **I'm not quite ~ you** [I don't understand] ich komme nicht ganz mit; **I'm ~ you there** [I'm on your side] da bin ich ganz deiner Ansicht.
➤ **with it** *adj inf:* **she's very ~ it** sie weiß, was in ist.
**withdraw** [wɪð'drɔː] (*pt* -drew; *pp* -drawn) *vt*
- **1.** *fml* [remove] weglnehmen; **to ~ sthg from sthg** etw von etw weglnehmen - **2.** FIN ablheben - **3.** MIL [troops] zurücklziehen - **4.** [retract] zurücklnehmen ◇ *vi* - **1.:** **to ~ (from)** sich zurücklziehen (aus); **we withdrew to a quieter spot/a neighbouring village** wir zogen uns an einen ruhigeren Ort/in ein benachbartes Dorf zurück - **2.** [quit, give up] auflgeben; **to ~ from sthg** aus etw auslscheiden.
**withdrawal** [wɪð'drɔːl] *n* - **1.** [removal] Zurückziehen *das* - **2.** MIL Rückzug *der* - **3.** [retraction] Zurücknahme *die* - **4.** [leaving, quitting] **~ (from sthg)** Ausscheiden *das* (aus etw) - **5.** MED Entzug *der* - **6.** FIN Abheben *das.*
**withdrawal symptoms** *npl* Entzugserscheinungen *pl.*
**withdrawn** [wɪð'drɔːn] *pp* ▷ **withdraw** ◇ *adj* [shy, quiet] verschlossen.
**withdrew** [wɪð'druː] *pt* ▷ **withdraw.**
**wither** ['wɪðəʳ] *vt* verdorren lassen ◇ *vi*
- **1.** [dry up] verwelken - **2.** [become weak] schwinden.
**withered** ['wɪðəd] *adj* - **1.** [plant] verwelkt
- **2.** [skin] ausgetrocknet.
**withering** ['wɪðərɪŋ] *adj* vernichtend.

**W**

**withhold** [wɪð'həʊld] (pt & pp **-held** [-'held]) vt [information] zurücklhalten.

**within** [wɪ'ðɪn] prep innerhalb (+ G); ~ **walking distance** zu Fuß erreichbar; ~ **sight** in Sichtweite; ~ **the next week** innerhalb der nächsten Woche; ~ **10 miles** im Umkreis von 10 Meilen ◇ adv innen.

**without** [wɪð'aʊt] prep ohne; ~ **doing sthg** ohne etw zu tun; **I left** ~ **him seeing me** ich ging (weg), ohne dass er mich sah.

**withstand** [wɪð'stænd] (pt & pp **-stood** [-'stʊd]) vt standlhalten (+ D).

**witness** ['wɪtnɪs] n - **1.** [gen] Zeuge der, -gin die; **to be** ~ **to sthg** Zeuge einer Sache (G) sein - **2.** : **to bear** ~ **to sthg** [be proof of] von etw zeugen; **she bore** ~ **to the fact that** ... sie bezeugte, dass ... ◇ vt - **1.**: **to** ~ **sthg** [murder, accident] Zeuge einer Sache (G) sein; [changes] etw erleben - **2.** [countersign] als Zeuge unterschreiben.

**witness box** Br, **witness stand** Am n Zeugenstand der.

**witter** ['wɪtə'] vi Br inf pej quasseln.

**witticism** ['wɪtɪsɪzml] n geistreiche Bemerkung.

**witty** ['wɪtɪ] (compar **-ier**; superl **-iest**) adj geistreich und witzig.

**wives** [waɪvz] pl ▷ **wife**.

**wizard** ['wɪzəd] n - **1.** [man with magic powers] Zauberer der - **2.** [skilled person] Genie das.

**wizened** ['wɪznd] adj runzelig.

**wk** abbr of **week**.

**WO** n abbr of **warrant officer**.

**wobble** ['wɒbl] vi wackeln.

**wobbly** ['wɒblɪ] (compar **-ier**; superl **-iest**) adj inf wackelig.

**woe** [wəʊ] n literary Leid das.

**wok** [wɒk] n Wok der.

**woke** [wəʊk] pt ▷ **wake**.

**woken** ['wəʊkn] pp ▷ **wake**.

**wolf** [wʊlf] (pl **wolves**) n [animal] Wolf der ◇ vt inf: **to** ~ **sthg (down)** etw hinunterlschlingen.

**wolf whistle** n bewundernder Pfiff.

**wolves** ['wʊlvz] pl ▷ **wolf**

**woman** ['wʊmən] (pl **women** ['wɪmɪn]) n Frau die ◇ comp: ~ **doctor** Ärztin die; ~ **teacher** Lehrerin die.

**womanhood** ['wʊmənhʊd] n - **1.** [adult life]: **to reach** ~ zur Frau werden - **2.** [all women] Frauen pl.

**womanizer, -iser** ['wʊmənaɪzə'] n pej Frauenheld der.

**womanly** ['wʊmənlɪ] adj fraulich.

**womb** [wuːm] n Gebärmutter die.

**wombat** ['wɒmbæt] n Wombat der.

**women** ['wɪmɪn] pl ▷ **woman**.

**women's group** n Frauengruppe die.

**Women's Institute** n Br: **the** ~ britische Frauenvereinigung, in deren örtlichen Zentren sich Frauen treffen und an Kursen teilnehmen können.

**women's liberation** n - **1.** [aim] Gleichstellung die der Frau - **2.** [movement] Frauenrechtsbewegung die.

**won** [wʌn] pt & pp ▷ **win**.

**wonder** ['wʌndə'] n - **1.** [amazement] Staunen das - **2.** [cause for surprise]: **it's a** ~ **that** ... es ist ein Wunder, dass ...; **no** OR **little** OR **small** ~ kein Wunder; **no** ~ **she left!** kein Wunder, dass sie gegangen ist! - **3.** [amazing thing] Wunder das; **to work** OR **do** ~**s** Wunder wirken ◇ vt - **1.** [speculate] sich fragen; **to** ~ **if** OR **whether** sich fragen, ob - **2.** [in polite requests]: **I** ~ **whether you would mind shutting the window?** könnten sie wohl bitte das Fenster schließen? ◇ vi - **1.** [speculate] sich fragen; **to** ~ **about sthg** sich über etw (A) Fragen stellen - **2.** literary [be amazed]: **to** ~ **at sthg** sich über etw (A) wundern.

**wonderful** ['wʌndəfʊl] adj wundervoll, wunderbar.

**wonderfully** ['wʌndəfʊlɪ] adv - **1.** [very well] wunderbar - **2.** [for emphasis] sehr.

**wonderland** ['wʌndəlænd] n [fairyland] Wunderland das.

**wonky** ['wɒŋkɪ] (compar **-ier**; superl **-iest**) adj Br inf [wobbly] wackelig; [crooked] schief.

**won't** [wəʊnt] = **will not**.

**woo** [wuː] vt - **1.** literary [court - woman] den Hof machen (+ D) - **2.** fig [try to win over] umlwerben.

**wood** [wʊd] n - **1.** (U) [timber] Holz das - **2.** [group of trees] Wald der - **3.** GOLF Holzschläger der - **4.** phr: **not to see the** ~ **for the trees** Br den Wald vor lauter Bäumen nicht sehen; **touch** ~! klopf auf Holz! ◇ comp Holz-.
➡ **woods** npl [forest] Wald der.

**wooded** ['wʊdɪd] adj [forested] bewaldet.

**wooden** ['wʊdn] adj - **1.** [of wood] Holz- - **2.** pej [actor] hölzern.

**wooden spoon** n Holzlöffel der; **to win** OR **get the** ~ Br fig den Trostpreis gewinnen.

**woodland** ['wʊdlənd] n Waldland das.

**woodlouse** ['wʊdlaʊs] (pl **-lice** [laɪs]) n Kellerassel die.

**woodpecker** ['wʊd,pekə'] n Specht der.

**wood pigeon** n Ringeltaube die.

**woodshed** ['wʊdʃed] n Holzschuppen der.

**woodwind** ['wʊdwɪnd] adj Holzblas- ◇ n: **the** ~ die Holzbläser pl.

**woodwork** ['wʊdwɜːk] n - **1.** [wooden objects]

Holzarbeiten *pl;* [part of house or room] Holzteile *pl* - **2.** [craft] Tischlerei *die.*

**woodworm** ['wʊdwɜːm] *n* [beetle] Holzwurm *der;* this cupboard's got ~ in diesem Schrank ist der Holzwurm.

**woof** [wʊf] *n* [bark] Bellen *das* ⬦ *excl:* ~, ~! wau, wau!

**wool** [wʊl] *n* - **1.** [gen] Wolle *die* - **2.** *phr:* to pull the ~ over sb's eyes *inf* jn hinters Licht führen.

**woollen** *Br,* **woolen** *Am* ['wʊlən] *adj* [garment] Woll-.
⬩ **woollens** *npl* Wollwaren *pl.*

**woolly** ['wʊlɪ] (*compar* -**ier;** *superl* -**iest;** *pl* -**ies**) *adj* [woollen] Woll- ⬦ *n inf* warmer Pulli.

**woolly-headed** [-'hedɪd] *adj inf pej* verwirrt.

**woozy** ['wuːzɪ] (*compar* -**ier;** *superl* -**iest**) *adj inf* [dizzy] schwindelig.

**Worcester sauce** ['wʊstə<sup>r</sup>-] *n (U)* Worcestersoße *die.*

**word** [wɜːd] *n* - **1.** LING Wort *das;* ~ for ~ Wort für Wort; in other ~s mit anderen Worten; in your own ~s mit deinen eigenen Worten; not in so many ~s nicht direkt; in a ~ kurz gesagt; he is too stupid for ~s er ist unglaublich dumm; by ~ of mouth von Mund zu Mund; to put in a (good) ~ for sb ein gutes Wort für jn einlegen; just say the ~ du musst es nur sagen; can I have a ~ (with you)? kann ich Sie mal sprechen?; to have ~s with sb *inf* mit jm eine Auseinandersetzung haben; to have the last ~ das letzte Wort haben; she doesn't mince her ~s sie nimmt kein Blatt vor den Mund; to weigh one's ~s seine Worte sorgfältig abwägen; I/you/etc couldn't get a ~ in edgeways ich bin/du bist/etc nicht zu Wort gekommen - **2.** *(U)* [news] Nachricht *die;* have you had ~ of John recently? hast du in letzter Zeit etwas von John gehört? - **3.** [promise] Wort *das;* to give sb one's ~ jm sein Wort geben; to be as good as one's ~, to be true to one's ~ zu seinem Wort stehen ⬦ *vt* formulieren.

**word game** *n* Buchstabenspiel *das.*

**wording** ['wɜːdɪŋ] *n* Wortlaut *der.*

**word-perfect** *adj:* to be ~ at one's part seinen Rollentext perfekt beherrschen.

**wordplay** ['wɜːdpleɪ] *n (U)* Wortspiel *das.*

**word processing** *n* Textverarbeitung *die.*

**word processor** [-ˌprəʊsesə<sup>r</sup>] *n* Textverarbeitungssystem *das.*

**wordy** ['wɜːdɪ] (*compar* -**ier;** *superl* -**iest**) *adj pej* weitschweifig.

**wore** [wɔː<sup>r</sup>] *pt* ⊳ **wear.**

**work** [wɜːk] *n* - **1.** *(U)* [gen] Arbeit *die;* casual ~ Gelegenheitsarbeit *die;* temporary ~ Zeitarbeit *die;* to be in ~ Arbeit haben; to be out of ~ arbeitslos sein; at ~ [not at home] auf der Ar-

beit; [working] bei der Arbeit - **2.** ART & LITERATURE [created product] Werk *das* - **3.** *phr:* he's a nasty piece of ~ *inf* er ist ein Scheusal; you've got your ~ cut out bringing up five children es ist bestimmt schwer, fünf Kinder großzuziehen; you'll have your ~ cut out to get there on time du wirst Schwierigkeiten haben, pünktlich dort zu sein ⬦ *vt* - **1.** [person, staff]: he ~s his staff too hard er verlangt zu viel von seinen Angestellten - **2.** [machine] bedienen - **3.** [wood, clay, land] bearbeiten - **4.** [cause to become]: to ~ o.s. into sthg sich in etw *(A)* hineinsteigern - **5.** [make]: she ~ed her way through the crowd sie bahnte sich *(D)* ihren Weg durch die Menge; the painter ~ed his way along the wall der Maler arbeitete sich Schritt für Schritt an der Wand entlang; to ~ one's way to the top [in career] sich hocharbeiten ⬦ *vi* - **1.** [do a job] arbeiten - **2.** [function, be successful] funktionieren - **3.** [have effect]: to ~ against sb/sthg sich auf jn/etw negativ auswirken - **4.** [gradually become]: to ~ loose sich lockern.
⬩ **works** *n* [factory] Werk *das* ⬦ *npl* - **1.** [mechanism] Innere *das* - **2.** [digging, building] Bauarbeiten *pl* - **3.** *inf* [everything]: the ~s das ganze Drumherum.
⬩ **work at** *vt fus* [try to improve] arbeiten an (+ D).
⬩ **work off** *vt sep* [anger, frustration] loswerden.
⬩ **work on** *vt fus* - **1.** [concentrate on] arbeiten an (+ D) - **2.** [principle, assumption, belief] ausgehen von - **3.** [try to persuade] bearbeiten.
⬩ **work out** *vt sep* - **1.** [formulate] ausarbeiten - **2.** [calculate] ausrechnen ⬦ *vi* - **1.** [figure, total]: that ~s out at £10 each das macht 10 Pfund pro Person - **2.** [turn out]: to ~ out in sb's favour für jn vorteilhaft sein - **3.** [be successful] gut ausgehen - **4.** [train, exercise] trainieren.
⬩ **work up** *vt sep* - **1.** [excite]: to ~ o.s. up into sich hineinsteigern in (+ A) - **2.** [generate - enthusiasm, courage] aufbringen; [ - appetite] entwickeln.

**workable** ['wɜːkəbl] *adj* [practicable] durchführbar.

**workaday** ['wɜːkədeɪ] *adj pej* alltäglich, Alltags-.

**workaholic** [ˌwɜːkə'hɒlɪk] *n* Workaholic *der.*

**workbasket** ['wɜːkˌbɑːskɪt] *n* Nähkorb *der.*

**workbench** ['wɜːkbentʃ] *n* Werkbank *die.*

**workbook** ['wɜːkbʊk] *n* Arbeitsheft *das.*

**workday** ['wɜːkdeɪ] *n* Arbeitstag *der.*

**worked up** [ˌwɜːkt-] *adj* aufgeregt.

**worker** ['wɜːkə<sup>r</sup>] *n* [employee] Arbeiter *der,* -in *die;* a hard/fast/good ~ ein fleißiger/ schneller/guter Arbeiter.

**workforce** ['wɜːkfɔːs] *n* Belegschaft *die.*

**workhouse** ['wɜːkhaʊs] *n* - **1.** *Br* [poorhouse]

Armenhaus *das (in dem man für seine Unterbringung arbeiten musste)* - **2. Am** [prison] Arbeitshaus *das.*

**working** ['wɜːkɪŋ] *adj* - **1.** [in operation] in Betrieb; **the lift isn't ~** der Fahrstuhl ist außer Betrieb - **2.** [having employment] erwerbstätig - **3.** [relating to work] Arbeits-.
➤ **workings** *npl* - **1.** [of system, machine] Funktionsweise *die* - **2.** *fig* [of mind]: **the ~ s of his mind** seine Denkweise.

**working capital** *n* Betriebskapital *das.*

**working class** *n:* **the ~** die Arbeiterklasse.
➤ **working-class** *adj* Arbeiter-.

**working day** *n* = workday.

**working group** *n* Arbeitsgruppe *die.*

**working knowledge** *n* Grundkenntnisse *pl.*

**working man** *n* Arbeiter *der.*

**working model** *n* Versuchsmodell *das.*

**working order** *n:* **in ~** funktionstüchtig.

**working party** *n* Arbeitsgruppe *die.*

**working week** *n* Arbeitswoche *die.*

**work-in-progress** *n* laufende Arbeiten *pl.*

**workload** ['wɜːkləʊd] *n* Arbeitsvolumen *das.*

**workman** ['wɜːkmən] (*pl* **-men** [-mən]) *n* [craftsman] Handwerker *der;* [worker] Arbeiter *der.*

**workmanship** ['wɜːkmənʃɪp] *n (U)* handwerkliches Können.

**workmate** ['wɜːkmeɪt] *n* Kollege *der,* -gin *die.*

**work of art** *n lit* & *fig* Kunstwerk *das.*

**workout** ['wɜːkaʊt] *n* Training *das.*

**work permit** *n* Arbeitserlaubnis *die.*

**workplace** ['wɜːkpleɪs] *n* Arbeitsplatz *der.*

**work placement** *n* Praktikum *das.*

**workroom** ['wɜːkrʊm] *n* Arbeitszimmer *das.*

**works council** *n* Betriebsrat *der.*

**workshop** ['wɜːkʃɒp] *n* - **1.** [room, building] Werkstatt *die* - **2.** [discussion] Workshop *der.*

**workshy** ['wɜːkʃaɪ] *adj Br* arbeitsscheu.

**workstation** ['wɜːkˌsteɪʃn] *n* COMPUT Workstation *die.*

**work surface** *n* Arbeitsfläche *die.*

**worktable** ['wɜːkˌteɪbl] *n* Arbeitstisch *der.*

**worktop** ['wɜːktɒp] *n Br* Arbeitsfläche *die.*

**work-to-rule** *n Br* Dienst *der* nach Vorschrift.

**world** [wɜːld] *n* - **1.** [gen]: **the ~** die Welt; **how/ what/where/why in the ~ ...?** wie/was/wo/ warum in aller Welt ...?; **the ~ over** überall; **to be dead to the ~** schlafen wie ein Toter; **to have the best of both ~s** die Vorteile beider Seiten genießen; **the next ~** das Jenseits - **2.** [great deal]: **to think the ~ of sb** große Stücke auf jn halten; **to do sb the ~ of good** jm unwahrscheinlich gut tun; **a ~ of difference**

ein himmelweiter Unterschied ◇ *comp* Welt-.

**World Bank** *n:* **the ~** die Weltbank.

**world-class** *adj* Weltklasse-.

**World Cup** FTBL *n:* **the ~** die Weltmeisterschaft ◇ *comp* Weltmeisterschafts-.

**world-famous** *adj* weltberühmt.

**worldly** ['wɜːldlɪ] *adj* [not spiritual] weltlich; **~ goods** irdische Güter.

**world music** *n* Weltmusik *die.*

**world power** *n* Weltmacht *die.*

**World Series** *n:* **the ~** - *im amerikanischen Baseballsport die sieben Spiele umfassende Endausscheidung zwischen den Gewinnern der beiden bedeutendsten Baseballligen.*

**World Service** *n* Worldservice *der.*

**World War I** *n* Erster Weltkrieg.

**World War II** *n* Zweiter Weltkrieg.

**world-weary** *adj* daseinsmüde.

**worldwide** ['wɜːldwaɪd] *adj* & *adv* weltweit.

**World Wide Web** *n:* **the ~** COMPUT das World Wide Web.

**worm** [wɜːm] *n* [animal] Wurm *der* ◇ *vt:* **to ~ one's way** [move] sich hindurch|schlängeln; [wheedle] sich ein|schleichen.
➤ **worms** *npl* [parasites] Würmer *pl.*
➤ **worm out** *vt sep:* **to ~ sthg out of sb** jm etw aus der Nase ziehen.

**worn** [wɔːn] *pp* ▷ **wear** ◇ *adj* - **1.** [threadbare - carpet] abgenutzt; [- clothes] abgetragen; [- tyre] abgefahren - **2.** [tired] erschöpft.

**worn-out** *adj* - **1.** [old, threadbare] ganz abgenutzt; [clothes, shoes] ganz abgetragen - **2.** [tired] ausgelaugt.

**worried** ['wʌrɪd] *adj* besorgt; **I was ~ he'd be angry** ich hatte Angst, er würde böse sein; **you really had me ~** du hast mich wirklich beunruhigt; **to be ~ about sb/sthg** sich *(D)* wegen jm/etw Sorgen machen; **to be ~ sick** ganz krank sein vor Sorge.

**worrier** ['wʌrɪəʳ] *n:* **she's a terrible ~** sie macht sich immer Sorgen.

**worry** ['wʌrɪ] (*pl* **-ies;** *pt* & *pp* **-ied**) *n* Sorge *die;* **she's a real ~** sie macht uns wirklich Sorgen ◇ *vt* [cause to be troubled] Sorgen machen *(+ D)* ◇ *vi:* **to ~ about sb/sthg** sich um jn/etw sorgen OR Sorgen machen; **not to ~!** keine Sorge!

**worrying** ['wʌrɪɪŋ] *adj* beunruhigend.

**worse** [wɜːs] *adj* - **1.** [not as good] schlechter; [situation] schlimmer; **to get ~** sich verschlechtern; [situation] sich verschlimmern - **2.** [sicker]: **he's ~** es geht ihm schlechter; **she seemed to get ~** ihr Zustand schien sich zu verschlechtern ◇ *adv* [more badly] schlechter; **~ off** [having less money] schlechter dran; [in a more unpleasant situation] schlimmer dran ◇ *n*

**Schlimmeres** das; **a change for the ~** eine Verschlimmerung; [of health, weather] eine Verschlechterung.

**worsen** ['wɜːsn] vt [situation, crisis] verschlimmern ⋄ vi [situation, crisis] sich verschlimmern; [weather, work] sich verschlechtern.

**worsening** ['wɜːsnɪŋ] adj [situation, crisis] sich verschlimmernd; [weather] sich verschlechternd.

**worship** ['wɜːʃɪp] (Br pt & pp **-ped**; cont **-ping**, Am pt & pp **-ed**; cont **-ing**) vt - **1.** RELIG anlbeten - **2.** [admire, adore] vergöttern ⋄ n - **1.** (U) RELIG Verehrung die; [service] Gottesdienst der; **place of ~** Andachtstätte die; [of cult] Kultstätte die - **2.** (U) [adoration] Vergötterung die.

➤ **Worship** n: **Your Worship** Euer Ehren; **Her/ His Worship (the Mayoress/Mayor)** die sehr verehrte Frau Bürgermeister/der sehr verehrte Herr Bürgermeister.

**worshipper** Br, **worshiper** Am ['wɜːʃɪpər] n - **1.** RELIG Gläubige der, die; [of cult] Anbeter der, -in die - **2.** [admirer] Verehrer der, -in die.

**worst** [wɜːst] adj schlimmste, -r, -s, schlechteste, -r, -s ⋄ adv am schlimmsten, am schlechtesten ⋄ n: **the ~** das Schlimmste; **if the ~ comes to the ~** wenn alle Stricke reißen; **to get the ~ of it** am meisten ablbekommen.

➤ **at (the) worst** adv schlimmstenfalls.

**worsted** ['wʊstɪd] n (U) Kammgarn das.

**worth** [wɜːθ] prep: **how much is it ~?** wie viel ist das wert?; **it's ~ £50** es ist 50 Pfund wert; **it's ~ seeing** es ist sehenswert; **a book ~ reading** ein lesenswertes Buch; **it's not ~ it** es lohnt sich nicht; **he's ~ millions** er besitzt Millionen; **to run for all one is ~** fig rennen, was man nur rennen kann ⋄ n - **1.** [amount]: **£50 ~ of traveller's cheques** Reiseschecks im Wert von 50 Pfund; **a week's ~ of groceries** Lebensmittel pl für eine Woche - **2.** [value] Wert der; **he proved his ~** er hat sich bewährt.

**worthless** ['wɜːθlɪs] adj - **1.** [object] wertlos - **2.** [person] nichtsnutzig.

**worthwhile** [ˌwɜːθˈwaɪl] adj lohnend; **it was a ~ visit** der Besuch hat sich gelohnt; **to be ~** sich lohnen.

**worthy** ['wɜːðɪ] (compar **-ier**; superl **-iest**) adj - **1.** [deserving of respect] würdig; **for a ~ cause** für einen guten Zweck - **2.** [deserving]: **to be ~ of sthg** etw verdienen - **3.** pej [good but unexciting] ehrbar.

**would** [wʊd] modal vb - **1.** [in reported speech]: **she said she ~ come** sie sagte, sie würde kommen - **2.** [indicating condition]: **what ~ you do?** was würdest du tun?; **what ~ you have done?** was hättest du getan?; **I ~ be most grateful** ich wäre äußerst dankbar - **3.** [indicating willingness]: **she ~n't go** sie wollte einfach nicht gehen; **he ~ do anything for her** er würde al-

les für sie tun - **4.** [in polite questions]: **~ you like a drink?** möchtest du etwas trinken?; **~ you mind closing the window?** könntest du das Fenster zumachen? - **5.** [indicating inevitability]: **he ~ say that** er musste das sagen; **I quite forgot! – you ~!** das habe ich ganz vergessen! – das sieht dir ähnlich! - **6.** [giving advice]: **I ~ report it if I were you** an deiner Stelle würde ich es melden - **7.** [expressing opinions]: **I ~ prefer coffee** ich hätte lieber Kaffee; **I ~ prefer to go by bus** ich würde lieber mit dem Bus fahren; **I ~ have thought (that)** ... ich hätte gedacht, dass ... - **8.** [describing habitual past actions]: **she ~ often come home tired out** oft kam sie total erschöpft nach Hause.

**would-be** adj angehend.

**wouldn't** ['wʊdnt] = would not.

**would've** ['wʊdəv] = would have.

**wound**[1] [wuːnd] n Wunde die; **to lick one's ~s** seine Wunden lecken ⋄ vt - **1.** [physically] verwunden - **2.** [emotionally] verletzen.

**wound**[2] [waʊnd] pt & pp ⊳ **wind**[2].

**wounded** ['wuːndɪd] adj - **1.** [physically] verwundet - **2.** [emotionally] verletzt ⋄ npl: **the ~** die Verwundeten pl.

**wounding** ['wuːndɪŋ] adj [hurtful] verletzend.

**wove** [wəʊv] pt ⊳ **weave**.

**woven** ['wəʊvn] pp ⊳ **weave**.

**wow** [waʊ] inf n: **she's a real ~** sie ist echt toll! ⋄ vt begeistern ⋄ excl Mensch!

**WP** n - **1.** abbr of **word processing** - **2.** abbr of **word processor**.

**WPC** (abbr of **woman police constable**) n Br Polizeibeamtin die.

**wpm** (abbr of **words per minute**) WpM.

**wrangle** ['ræŋgl] n Streitigkeiten pl ⋄ vi sich streiten; **to ~ with sb (over sthg)** mit jm (über etw (A)) streiten.

**wrap** [ræp] (pt & pp **-ped**; cont **-ping**) vt - **1.** [cover in paper or cloth] einlwickeln; **to ~ sthg in sthg** etw in etw (A) einlwickeln; **to ~ sthg (a)round sthg** etw um etw wickeln - **2.** [encircle]: **to ~ sthg (a)round sthg** etw um etw legen; **to ~ one's arms round sb** seine Arme um jn schlingen ⋄ n [garment] Schultertuch das.

➤ **wrap up** vt sep - **1.** [cover in paper or cloth] einlwickeln - **2.** inf [complete] unter Dach und Fach bringen ⋄ vi [put warm clothes on]: **~ up well** OR **warmly!** zieh dich warm an!

**wrapped up** [ræpt-] adj inf [immersed]: **to be ~ in sb/sthg** nur (noch) jn/etw im Kopf haben; **she's ~ in her thoughts** sie ist in Gedanken versunken.

**wrapper** ['ræpər] n Hülle die; [of sweets] Papier das.

**wrapping** ['ræpɪŋ] n Verpackung die.

**W**

**wrapping paper** n (U) Geschenkpapier das.

**wrath** [rɒθ] n literary Zorn der.

**wreak** [ri:k] vt [destruction, havoc] anlrichten; [revenge] üben.

**wreath** [ri:θ] n [circle of flowers] Kranz der.

**wreathe** [ri:ð] vt literary hüllen.

**wreck** [rek] n Wrack das; I look a ~ ich sehe furchtbar aus; a nervous ~ ein Nervenbündel; a car ~ Am ein Autounfall ◇ vt - 1. [break, destroy] demolieren; [car] zu Schrott fahren - 2. NAUT [cause to run aground] versenken; to be ~ed [person] Schiffbruch erleiden; the ship was ~ed on the rocks das Schiff zerschellte an den Klippen - 3. [spoil, ruin] ruinieren.

**wreckage** ['rekɪdʒ] n [of plane, building] Trümmer pl; [of car] Wrack das.

**wrecker** ['rekəʳ] n Am Abschleppwagen der.

**wren** [ren] n Zaunkönig der.

**wrench** [rentʃ] n - 1. [tool] Schraubenschlüssel der - 2. [injury, twist] Verrenkung die - 3. [cause of sadness] schmerzhafter Schritt ◇ vt - 1. [pull violently] reißen - 2. [twist and injure]: to ~ one's arm/leg sich den Arm/das Bein verrenken - 3. [force away - eyes, gaze] losreißen.

**wrest** [rest] vt literary: to ~ sthg from sb jm etw entwinden.

**wrestle** ['resl] vt ringen mit; to ~ sb to the ground jn zu Boden zwingen ◇ vi - 1. [fight]: to ~ with sb mit jm ringen - 2. fig [struggle]: to ~ with sthg mit etw kämpfen.

**wrestler** ['resləʳ] n Ringer der, -in die; [as entertainer] Wrestler der, -in die.

**wrestling** ['reslɪŋ] n Ringen das; [as entertainment] Wrestling das.

**wretch** [retʃ] n [unhappy person]: poor ~! armer Tropf!

**wretched** ['retʃɪd] adj - 1. [miserable] elend; [conditions] erbärmlich - 2. inf [damned] verflixt.

**wriggle** ['rɪgl] vt [toes, shoulders] wackeln mit; to ~ one's body sich winden ◇ vi - 1. [move about - person] zappeln; [ - worm] sich winden - 2. [twist]: he ~d under the fence er wand sich unter dem Zaun hindurch; to ~ free sich loslwinden.

➤ **wriggle out of** vt fus: to ~ out of sthg sich vor etw (D) drücken; to ~ out of doing sthg sich davor drücken, etw zu tun.

**wring** [rɪŋ] (pt & pp wrung) vt - 1. [squeeze out water from] auslwringen - 2. literary: to ~ one's hands die Hände ringen - 3. [neck]: to ~ a chicken's neck einem Huhn den Hals umldrehen.

➤ **wring out** vt sep auslwringen.

**wringing** ['rɪŋɪŋ] adj: ~ (wet) tropfnass.

**wrinkle** ['rɪŋkl] n - 1. [on skin] Falte die - 2. [in cloth] Knitterfalte die ◇ vt [screw up - nose] rümpfen; [ - forehead] runzeln ◇ vi [crease] knittern.

**wrinkled** ['rɪŋkld], **wrinkly** ['rɪŋklɪ] adj - 1. [skin] faltig - 2. [cloth] zerknittert.

**wrist** [rɪst] n Handgelenk das.

**wristband** ['rɪstbænd] n [of watch] Armband das.

**wristwatch** ['rɪstwɒtʃ] n Armbanduhr die.

**writ** [rɪt] n Verfügung die.

**write** [raɪt] (pt wrote; pp written) vt - 1. [gen] schreiben; to ~ sb a letter jm einen Brief schreiben - 2. [cheque, prescription] auslstellen - 3. COMPUT speichern ◇ vi - 1. [gen] schreiben; to ~ to sb Br jm schreiben - 2. COMPUT ablspeichern.

➤ **write back** vt sep & vi zurücklschreiben.

➤ **write down** vt sep auf lschreiben.

➤ **write in** vi [to radio or TV station, shop] schreiben.

➤ **write into** vt sep: to ~ sthg into a contract etw in einen Vertrag auf lnehmen.

➤ **write off** vt sep - 1. [project] auflgeben - 2. [debt, investment, person] ablschreiben - 3. Br inf [vehicle] zu Schrott fahren ◇ vi: to ~ off to sb jn anlschreiben; to ~ off for sthg etw anlfordern.

➤ **write out** vt sep [names] auf lschreiben; [list] auf lstellen.

➤ **write up** vt sep [notes] auslarbeiten.

**write-off** n [car] Totalschaden der.

**write-protect** vt COMPUT schreibschützen.

**writer** ['raɪtəʳ] n - 1. [as profession] Schriftsteller der, -in die - 2. [of letter, article, story] Verfasser der, -in die.

**write-up** n inf Bericht der.

**writhe** [raɪð] vi sich winden; [with pain] sich krümmen.

**writing** ['raɪtɪŋ] n - 1. [gen] Schrift die; in ~ schriftlich - 2. [activity] Schreiben das.

➤ **writings** npl Werke pl; scientific ~s wissenschaftliche Schriften.

**writing case** n Br Schreibmappe die.

**writing desk** n Schreibtisch der.

**writing paper** n (U) Briefpapier das.

**written** ['rɪtn] pp ▷ write ◇ adj schriftlich.

**wrong** [rɒŋ] adj - 1. [amiss]: there's nothing ~ with me mir fehlt nichts; is something ~? stimmt etwas nicht?; what's ~? was ist los?; there's something ~ with the car mit dem Auto stimmt etwas nicht - 2. [not suitable] falsch - 3. [not correct - answer, decision, turning] falsch, verkehrt; to be ~ [person] Unrecht haben; I was ~ to ask ich hätte nicht fragen sollen - 4. [morally bad] unrecht ◇ adv [incorrectly] falsch, verkehrt; to get sth ~ sich mit etw vertun; to go ~ [make a mistake] einen Fehler machen; the printer keeps going ~ der Drucker spielt ständig verrückt; **don't get me** ~ *inf* versteh mich nicht falsch <> *n* Unrecht *das;* **to be in the** ~ Unrecht haben <> *vt literary* Unrecht tun *(+ D).*

**wrong-foot** *vt Br* - **1.** *sport* auf dem falschen Fuß erwischen - **2.** *fig* [surprise] aus dem Konzept bringen.

**wrongful** ['rɒŋfʊl] *adj* [unjust] ungerecht.

**wrongly** ['rɒŋlɪ] *adv* - **1.** [unsuitably] falsch - **2.** [mistakenly] zu Unrecht.

**wrong number** *n* falsche Nummer; **you've got the** ~ Sie haben sich verwählt.

**wrote** [rəʊt] *pt* ▷ write.

**wrought iron** [rɔːt-] *n* Schmiedeeisen *das.*

**wrung** [rʌŋ] *pt & pp* ▷ wring.

**WRVS** (*abbr of* **Women's Royal Voluntary Service**) *n* britische Hilfsorganisation für notleidende Menschen.

**wry** [raɪ] *adj* - **1.** [amused] ironisch; [humour, remark] trocken - **2.** [displeased]: **to pull a** ~ **face** das Gesicht verziehen.

**wt.** *abbr of* weight.

**WV** *abk für West Virginia, in Postanschrift verwendet.*

**WW** (*abbr of* world war) WK.

**WWW** (*abbr of* world wide web) WWW.

**WY** *abk für Wyoming, in Postanschrift verwendet.*

**WYSIWYG** ['wɪzɪwɪg] (*abbr of* what you see is what you get) *n* WYSIWYG.

**x** (*pl* **x's** *OR* **xs**), **X** (*pl* **X's** *OR* **Xs**) [eks] *n* - **1.** [letter] x *das,* X *das* - **2.** [unknown name] X - **3.** [quantity, in algebra] x - **4.** [to mark place]: **X marks the spot** ein Kreuzchen markiert die Stelle - **5.** [at end of letter] *ein Kreuzchen am Ende eines Briefes, das einen Kuss bedeutet.*

**xenophobia** [ˌzenəˈfəʊbjə] *n* Fremdenfeindlichkeit *die,* Xenophobie *die.*

**xenophobic** [ˌzenəˈfəʊbɪk] *adj* fremdenfeindlich, xenophob.

**Xerox**® ['zɪərɒks] *n* - **1.** [machine] Xerokopiergerät *das* - **2.** [copy] Xerokopie *die.*

➡ **xerox** *vt* xerokopieren.

**Xmas** ['eksməs] *n* Weihnachten *das* <> *comp* Weihnachts-.

**X-ray** *n* - **1.** [ray] Röntgenstrahl *der* - **2.** [picture] Röntgenbild *das* <> *vt* röntgen.

**xylophone** ['zaɪləfəʊn] *n* Xylofon *das.*

**y** (*pl* **y's** *OR* **ys**), **Y** (*pl* **Y's** *OR* **Ys**) [waɪ] *n* - **1.** [letter] y *das,* Y *das* - **2.** [in algebra] y.

**Y2K** (*abbr of* **year two thousand**) Jahr 2000 *das.*

**yacht** [jɒt] *n* Jacht *die.*

**yachting** ['jɒtɪŋ] *n* Segeln *das.*

**yachtsman** ['jɒtsmən] (*pl* **-men** [-mən]) *n* Segler *der.*

**yachtswoman** ['jɒtsˌwʊmən] (*pl* **-women** [-ˌwɪmɪn]) *n* Seglerin *die.*

**yahoo** [jɑːˈhuː] *n* Rüpel *der.*

**yak** [jæk] *n* [animal] Jak *der.*

**Yale lock**® [jeɪl-] *n* Sicherheitsschloss *das.*

**yam** [jæm] *n* [vegetable] Süßkartoffel *die.*

**Yangtze** ['jæntsɪ] *n:* **the** ~ **(River)** der Jangtse.

**yank** [jæŋk] *vt* ruckartig ziehen an *(+ D).*

**Yank** [jæŋk] *n Br inf pej* Ami *der.*

**Yankee** ['jæŋkɪ] *n* - **1.** *Br inf pej* [American] Ami *der* - **2.** *Am* [northerner] Nordstaatler *der.*

**yap** [jæp] (*pt & pp* **-ped;** *cont* **-ping**) *vi* - **1.** [dog] kläffen - **2.** *pej* [person] quatschen.

**yard** [jɑːd] *n* - **1.** [unit of measurement] Yard *das,* = *91,44 cm* - **2.** [enclosed area] Hof *der* - **3.** [place of work]: **ship** ~ Schiffswerft *die;* **builder's** ~ Bauhof *der* - **4.** *Am* [attached to house] Garten *der.*

**yardstick** ['jɑːdstɪk] *n* Maßstab *der.*

**yarn** [jɑːn] *n* - **1.** (*U*) [thread] Garn *das* - **2.** *inf* [story] Seemannsgarn *das;* **he can tell a good** ~ er kann gut Geschichten erzählen; **to spin sb a** ~ jm ein Märchen erzählen.

**yashmak** ['jæʃmæk] *n* Jaschmak *der.*

**yawn** [jɔːn] *n* - **1.** [when tired] Gähnen *das* - **2.** *Br inf* [boring event]: **to be a** ~ zum Gähnen sein <> *vi* gähnen.

**yd** *abbr of* **yard**.

**yeah** [jeə] *adv inf* ja.

**year** [jɪəʳ] *n* Jahr *das*; **all (the) ~ round** das ganze Jahr über; **for seven ~s** sieben Jahre (lang); **~ in ~ out** jahrein, jahraus.

**~ years** *npl* [ages] Jahre *pl*; **for ~s** jahrelang.

**yearbook** ['jɪəbʊk] *n* Jahrbuch *das*.

**yearling** ['jɪəlɪŋ] *n* Jährling *der*.

**yearly** ['jɪəlɪ] *adj* **- 1.** [event, inspection, report] jährlich **- 2.** [income, wage] Jahres- <> *adv* jährlich.

**yearn** [jɜːn] *vi:* **to ~ for sthg** sich nach etw sehnen; **to ~ to do sthg** sich danach sehnen, etw zu tun.

**yearning** ['jɜːnɪŋ] *n:* **~ (for sb/sthg)** Sehnsucht *die* (nach jm/etw); **~ for power** Machthunger *der*.

**yeast** [jiːst] *n (U)* Hefe *die*.

**yell** [jel] *n* Schrei *der* <> *vt* & *vi* schreien.

**yellow** ['jeləʊ] *adj* **- 1.** [in colour] gelb **- 2.** *inf* [cowardly] feige <> *n* Gelb *das* <> *vi* vergilben.

**yellow card** *n* FTBL gelbe Karte.

**yellow fever** *n* Gelbfieber *das*.

**yellow lines** *npl* gelbe Halteverbotslinien *pl*.

> **YELLOW LINES**
>
> In Großbritannien wird Parkverbot mit einer einfachen bzw. doppelten Linie am Straßenrand angezeigt. Eine einfache Linie bedeutet, dass zwischen 8 Uhr und 16 Uhr 30 an Werktagen Parkverbot besteht; außerhalb dieser Zeiten ist das Parken erlaubt. Eine doppelte Linie bedeutet, dass zu keiner Zeit geparkt werden darf.

**yellowness** ['jeləʊnɪs] *n (U)* gelbliche Färbung.

**Yellow Pages®** *n Br:* **the ~** die gelben Seiten *pl*.

**Yellow River** *n:* **the ~** der Gelbe Fluss.

**yelp** [jelp] *n* Aufjaulen *das*; [of person] Aufschrei *der* <> *vi* aufjaulen; [of person] aufschreien.

**Yemen** ['jemən] *n:* **(the) ~** (der) Jemen; **in (the) ~** im Jemen.

**Yemeni** ['jemənɪ] *adj* jemenitisch <> *n* Jemenit *der*, -in *die*.

**yen** [jen] *(pl sense 1 inv)* *n* **- 1.** [Japanese currency] Yen *der* **- 2.** [longing]: **to have a ~ to do sthg** den Drang verspüren, etw zu tun; **I have a sudden ~ for chocolate** ich verspüre eine plötzliche Lust auf Schokolade.

**yeoman of the guard** ['jəʊmən-] *(pl yeomen of the guard* ['jəʊmən-]) *n* königlicher Leibgardist.

**yep** [jep] *adv inf* ja.

**yes** [jes] *adv* **- 1.** [gen] ja; **~, please** ja, bitte; **to say ~ to sthg** einer Sache *(D)* zustimmen **- 2.** [to encourage further speech] so **- 3.** [expressing disagreement] doch <> *n* [vote in favour] Ja *das*.

**yes-man** *n pej* Jasager *der*.

**yesterday** ['jestədɪ] *n* Gestern *das* <> *adv* gestern.

**yet** [jet] *adv* noch; *(in questions)* schon; **have you read the book ~?** hast du das Buch schon gelesen?; **not ~** noch nicht; **aren't you ready ~?** bist du bald fertig?; **as ~** bisher, bis jetzt; **I've ~ to do it** ich muss es noch tun; **~ another delay** noch eine Verspätung; **~ again** schon wieder; **he'll win ~** er wird schon noch gewinnen <> *conj* doch; **simple ~ effective** einfach, aber wirksam; **and ~ I like him** und doch *or* dennoch mag ich ihn.

**yeti** ['jetɪ] *n* Yeti *der*.

**yew** [juː] *n* Eibe *die*.

**Y-fronts** *npl Br* Herrenunterhose *die (mit y-förmigem Saum an der Vorderseite)*.

**YHA** (*abbr of* **Youth Hostels Association**) *n* ≃ DJH *das*.

**Yiddish** ['jɪdɪʃ] *adj* jiddisch <> *n* [language] Jiddisch(e) *das*.

**yield** [jiːld] *n* Ertrag *der* <> *vt* **- 1.** [produce] hervorbringen; [fruit] tragen; [profits] abwerfen; [result, answer, clue] ergeben **- 2.** [give up] abgeben <> *vi* **- 1.** [open, give way, break] nachgeben **- 2.** *fml* [give up, surrender] sich ergeben; **to ~ to demands** Forderungen nachgeben **- 3.** *Am* AUT [give way]: '**~**' 'Vorfahrt beachten'.

**yippee** [*Br* jɪ'piː, *Am* 'jɪpɪ] *excl* hurra!, juchhu!

**YMCA** (*abbr of* **Young Men's Christian Association**) *n* CVJM *der*.

**yo** [jəʊ] *excl inf* hi!

**yob(bo)** ['jɒb(əʊ)] *n Br inf* Rowdy *der*.

**yodel** ['jəʊdl] (*Br pt* & *pp* **-led**; *cont* **-ling**, *Am pt* & *pp* **-ed**; *cont* **-ing**) *vi* jodeln.

**yoga** ['jəʊgə] *n* Yoga *der or das*.

**yoghourt, yoghurt, yogurt** [*Br* 'jɒgət, *Am* 'jəʊgərt] *n* Joghurt *der or das*.

**yoke** [jəʊk] *n* Joch *das*.

**yokel** ['jəʊkl] *n pej* Bauerntölpel *der*.

**yolk** [jəʊk] *n* Dotter *der or das*, Eigelb *das*.

**yonder** ['jɒndəʳ] *adv literary* dort drüben.

**Yorkshire pudding** ['jɔːkʃəʳ-] *n aus Pfannkuchenteig bereitete Beilage zu Rinderbraten*.

**Yorkshire terrier** *n* Yorkshire-Terrier *der*.

**you** [juː] *pers pron* **- 1.** *(subject - singular)* du; *(- plural)* ihr; *(- polite form)* Sie; **~ Germans** ihr Deutschen; **I'm shorter than ~** ich bin kleiner als du/Sie/ihr **- 2.** *(direct object, after prep + A - singular)* dich; *(- plural)* euch; *(- polite form)* Sie; **I hate ~!** ich hasse dich/Sie/euch!; **I did**

**it for** ~ ich habe es für dich/Sie/euch getan **- 3.** *(direct object, after prep + D - singular)* dir; *(- plural)* euch; *(- polite form)* Ihnen; **I told ~!** ich habe es dir/Ihnen/euch gesagt; **after ~!** nach Ihnen! **- 4.** *(indefinite use - subject)* man; *(- object)* einen; *(- indirect object)* einem; **~ never know** man kann nie wissen; **it does ~ good** es tut einem gut.

**you'd** [juːd] = **you had, you would.**

**you'll** [juːl] = **you will.**

**young** [jʌŋ] *adj* [not old] jung ⬦ *npl* **- 1.** [young people]: **the ~** die Jugend **- 2.** [baby animals] Junge *pl*.

**younger** [ˈjʌŋgəʳ] *adj* jünger.

**youngish** [ˈjʌŋɪʃ] *adj* ziemlich jung.

**young man** *n* junger Mann.

**youngster** [ˈjʌŋstəʳ] *n* **- 1.** [child] Kind *das* **- 2.** [young person] Jugendliche *der, die*.

**young woman** *n* junge Frau.

**your** [jɔːʳ] *poss adj* **- 1.** *(singular subject)* dein, -e, deine *pl; (plural subject)* euer/eure, eure *pl; (polite form)* Ihr, -e, Ihre *pl;* **~ dog** dein/euer/Ihr Hund; **~ house** dein/euer/Ihr Haus; **~ children** deine/eure/Ihre Kinder **- 2.** *(indefinite subject):* **it's good for ~ teeth** es ist gut für die Zähne; **~ average Englishman** der durchschnittliche Engländer.

**you're** [jɔːʳ] = **you are.**

**yours** [jɔːz] *poss pron (singular subject)* deiner/deine/deins, deine *pl; (plural subject)* eurer/eure/eures, eure *pl; (polite form)* Ihrer/Ihre/Ihres, Ihre *pl;* **a friend of ~** ein Freund von dir/euch/Ihnen; **that money is ~** dieses Geld gehört dir/euch/Ihnen.

➣ **Yours** *adv* [in letter - gen] Dein/Deine; [ - polite form] Ihr/Ihre; ⊏➣ **faithfully, sincerely** *etc*.

**yourself** [jɔːˈself] *(pl* **-selves** [-ˈselvz]*) pron* **- 1.** *(reflexive, after prep + A - singular)* dich; *(- plural)* euch; *(- polite form)* sich **- 2.** *(reflexive, after prep + D - singular)* dir; *(- plural)* euch; *(- polite form)* sich; **did you do it ~?** hast du/haben Sie das selbst gemacht?; **did you do it yourselves?** habt ihr/haben Sie das selbst gemacht?; **by ~/yourselves** allein.

**youth** [juːθ] *n* **- 1.** [period of life, young people] Jugend *die* **- 2.** [quality] Jugendlichkeit *die* **- 3.** [boy] Junge *der;* [young man] junger Mann.

**youth club** *n* Jugendklub *der*.

**youthful** [ˈjuːθfʊl] *adj* jugendlich.

**youthfulness** [ˈjuːθfʊlnɪs] *n* Jugendlichkeit *die*.

**youth hostel** *n* Jugendherberge *die*.

**youth hostelling** [-ˈhɒstəlɪŋ] *n Br:* **to go ~ in Scotland** eine Schottlandtour machen und in Jugendherbergen übernachten.

**you've** [juːv] = **you have.**

**yowl** [jaʊl] *n* [of dog] Jaulen *das;* [of cat] Miauen *das* ⬦ *vi* [dog] jaulen; [cat] miauen.

**yo-yo** [ˈjəʊjəʊ] *n* Jo-Jo *das*.

**yr** *abbr of* **year.**

**YT** *n abk für Yukon Territory, in Postanschrift verwendet.*

**yucca** [ˈjʌkə] *n* Yucca *die*.

**yuck** [jʌk] *excl inf* bäh!

**Yugoslav** [ˌjuːgəˈslɑːv] *adj* & *n* = **Yugoslavian.**

**Yugoslavia** [ˌjuːgəˈslɑːvɪə] *n* Jugoslawien *das;* **in ~** in Jugoslawien.

**Yugoslavian** [ˌjuːgəˈslɑːvɪən] *adj* jugoslawisch ⬦ *n* Jugoslawe *der,* -win *die*.

**yule log** [juːl-] *n* **- 1.** [piece of wood] Julscheit *der* **- 2.** [cake] *Schokoladenkuchen in Form eines Baumstammes, der zu Weihnachten serviert wird.*

**yuletide** [ˈjuːltaɪd] *n (U) literary* Weihnachtszeit *die*.

**yummy** [ˈjʌmɪ] *(compar* **-ier;** *superl* **-iest)** *adj inf* lecker.

**yuppie, yuppy** [ˈjʌpɪ] *(pl* **-ies)** *n* Yuppie *der*.

**YWCA** *(abbr of* **Young Women's Christian Association)** *n* CVJF *der*.

Z

**z** *(pl* **z's** *OR* **zs)**, **Z** *(pl* **Z's** *OR* **Zs)** [*Br* zed, *Am* ziː] *n* [letter] z *das*, Z *das*.

**Zagreb** [ˈzɑːgreb] *n* Zagreb *nt*.

**Zaïre** [zaɪˈɪəʳ] *n* Zaire *nt*.

**Zambesi, Zambezi** [zæmˈbiːzɪ] *n:* **the ~** die Sambesi.

**Zambia** [ˈzæmbɪə] *n* Sambia *nt*.

**Zambian** [ˈzæmbɪən] *adj* sambisch ⬦ *n* Sambier *der,* -in *die*.

**zany** [ˈzeɪnɪ] *(compar* **-ier;** *superl* **-iest)** *adj inf* verrückt.

**Zanzibar** [ˈzænzɪbɑːʳ] *n* Sansibar *nt*.

**zap** [zæp] *(pt* & *pp* **-ped;** *cont* **-ping)** *inf vt* abknallen ⬦ *vi* **- 1.** [rush] sausen **- 2.** tv zappen.

**zeal** [ziːl] *n fml* Eifer *der*.

**zealot** [ˈzelət] *n fml* Eiferer *der,* -in *die*.

Z

**zealous** ['zeləs] *adj fml* eifrig.

**zebra** [*Br* 'zebrə, *Am* 'zi:brə] (*pl inv* OR -s) *n* Zebra *das*.

**zebra crossing** *n Br* Zebrastreifen *der*.

**zenith** [*Br* 'zenɪθ, *Am* 'zi:nəθ] *n lit* & *fig* Zenit *der*.

**zeppelin** ['zepəlɪn] *n* Zeppelin *der*.

**zero** [*Br* 'zɪərəʊ, *Am* 'zi:rəʊ] (*pl* -s OR -es; *pt* & *pp* -ed; *cont* -ing) *adj* keinerlei; ~ **growth** Nullwachstum *das*; ~ **gravity** Schwerelosigkeit *die* ⟨⟩ *n* Null *die*.
➤ **zero in on** *vt fus* - **1.** [subj: weapon] sich ausrichten auf (+ A) - **2.** [subj: person - physically] sich stürzen auf (+ A); [ - attention] sich konzentrieren auf (+ A).

**zero-rated** [- reɪtɪd] *adj Br* nicht mehrwertsteuerpflichtig.

**zest** [zest] *n* - **1.** [excitement] Schwung *der* - **2.** (*U*) [eagerness] Begeisterung *die* - **3.** (*U*) [of orange, lemon] Schale *die*.

**zigzag** ['zɪgzæg] (*pt* & *pp* -ged; *cont* -ging) *n* Zickzack *der* ⟨⟩ *vi* [person, vehicle] im Zickzack laufen/fahren; [path] im Zickzack verlaufen.

**zilch** [zɪltʃ] *n esp Am inf* [nothing] nichts; [none] null.

**Zimbabwe** [zɪm'bɑːbwɪ] *n* Simbabwe *nt*.

**Zimbabwean** [zɪm'bɑːbwɪən] *adj* simbabwisch ⟨⟩ *n* Simbabwer *der*, -in *die*.

**Zimmer frame**® ['zɪmə*r*-] *n* Gehbock *der*.

**zinc** [zɪŋk] *n* Zink *das*.

**Zionism** ['zaɪənɪzm] *n* Zionismus *der*.

**Zionist** ['zaɪənɪst] *adj* zionistisch ⟨⟩ *n* Zionist *der*, -in *die*.

**zip** [zɪp] (*pt* & *pp* -ped; *cont* -ping) *n Br* [fastener] Reißverschluss *der*.
➤ **zip up** *vt sep* den Reißverschluss zulmachen an (+ D).

**zip code** *n Am* Postleitzahl *die*.

**zip fastener** *n Br* = zip.

**zipper** ['zɪpə*r*] *n Am* = zip.

**zippy** ['zɪpɪ] (*compar* -ier; *superl* -iest) *adj inf* [car] flott.

**zit** [zɪt] *n inf* Pickel *der*.

**zither** ['zɪðə*r*] *n* Zither *die*.

**zodiac** ['zəʊdɪæk] *n:* **the** ~ Tierkreis *der;* **sign of the** ~ Tierkreiszeichen *das*.

**zombie** ['zɒmbɪ] *n* Zombie *der*.

**zone** [zəʊn] *n* [district] Zone *die*.

**zoo** [zu:] *n* Zoo *der*.

**zoological** [ˌzəʊə'lɒdʒɪkl] *adj* zoologisch.

**zoologist** [zəʊ'ɒlədʒɪst] *n* Zoologe *der*, -gin *die*.

**zoology** [zəʊ'ɒlədʒɪ] *n* Zoologie *die*.

**zoom** [zu:m] *vi inf* - **1.** [move quickly] sausen - **2.** [rise rapidly] hochlschnellen.
➤ **zoom in** *vi* zoomen; **the camera** ~**ed in on his face** die Kamera holte sein Gesicht heran.
➤ **zoom off** *vi inf* ablrauschen.

**zoom lens** *n* Zoomobjektiv *das*.

**zucchini** [zu:'ki:nɪ] (*pl inv* OR -s) *n Am* Zucchini *die*.

**Zulu** ['zu:lu:] *adj* Zulu- ⟨⟩ *n* - **1.** [person] Zulu *der*, *die* - **2.** [language] Zulu *das*.

**Zurich** ['zjʊərɪk] *n* Zürich *nt*

# German Language and Culture
## and Culture

—

# Deutsche
# Landeskunde

Kiel

SCHLESWIG-
HOLSTEIN

MECKLEMBURG-
WEST POMERANIA

Hamburg

BREMEN    HAMBURG

Schwerin

Bremen

BRANDENBURG

LOWER SAXONY

BERLIN

Hanover

SAXONY-
ANHALT

■ Berlin

Potsdam

NORTH RHINE-
WESTPHALIA

Magdeburg

Düsseldorf

FEDERAL

SAXONY

HESSEN

Erfurt

Dresden

RHINELAND-
PALATINATE

Wiesbaden

THURINGIA

REPUBLIC OF

Mainz

SAARLAND

GERMANY

Saarbrücken

Stuttgart

BAVARIA

LOWER AUSTRIA

Linz    St Pölten    Vienna

BADEN-
WÜRTTEMBERG

Munich

UPPER AUSTRIA

VIENNA

Salzburg

Eisenstadt

Bregenz

JURA

10

3

12

2

17

1

13

Innsbruck

AUSTRIA

7    9

8

Bern

16

11

6

VORARLBERG

SALZBURG

STYRIA

BURGENLAND

Graz

VAUD

4

14

15

BERN

TYROL

TYROL

CARINTHIA

Klagenfurt

5

GRAUBÜNDEN

VALAIS

TICINO

SWITZERLAND

**Swiss Cantons**

| 1 APPENZELL | 7 LUCERNE | 13 THURGAU | ■ State capital |
| 2 AARGAU | 8 NEUCHÂTEL | 14 UNTERWALDEN | |
| 3 BASEL | 9 ST GALL | 15 URI | |
| 4 FRIBOURG | 10 SCHAFFHAUSEN | 16 ZUG | |
| 5 GENEVA | 11 SCHWYZ | 17 ZÜRICH | |
| 6 GLARUS | 12 SOLOTHURN | | |

0    100 km

## German around the world: who speaks it and where?

# German in Europe

German is spoken by more than 120 million people worldwide. Apart from being the most frequently spoken native language in Europe (with around 100 million native speakers compared to 66 million native French speakers and 64 million native English speakers), it can be found in places as diverse as Pennsylvania and Kazakhstan, Argentina and Namibia. Within Europe it is the official language of Germany, Austria and Liechtenstein, and shares official status with French and Italian in Switzerland, and with French and Luxembourgish in Luxembourg. It is also one of the three working languages of the European Union. Dialects of German are spoken in the border regions of neighboring countries including Belgium, Holland, Denmark and Italy and in the Alsace-Lorraine region of France. German-speaking communities are also to be found throughout Eastern Europe. They still survive today in Poland, the Czech Republic, Hungary, Romania, Russia and Kazakhstan but their numbers were significantly reduced by the large numbers of people relocating to Germany, Switzerland and Austria after the end of the Cold War.

# Elsewhere in the world

Further afield, German speakers are to be found in Namibia which is the former German colony of German South-West Africa, and in places to which large numbers of German speakers emigrated over the 19th and 20th centuries. Foremost among these are Brazil, Venezuela and Argentina which support large numbers of German-speaking communities. In Brazil, it is estimated that over 600,000 people speak German as a first or second language.

Of course, many immigrants of German origin made their home in the United States. The largest concentrations of German speakers can be found in Pennsylvania, Texas, Kansas, the Dakotas, Montana, Wisconsin, Ohio and Indiana, as well as in the major cities. In Pennsylvania the Amish, Hutterite and Mennonite communities speak **Pennsylvania German** which is derived from the Franconian dialect spoken in the Rhineland, and **Hutterite German** which evolved from the dialect spoken in Carinthia in Austria. Despite the slow decline of the German dialects in the US, **Pennsylvania German** is still spoken by an estimated 250,000 – 300,000 people today.

# A short history of the language and its dialects

German, English, Flemish and Dutch make up the West Germanic group of Indo-European languages and share many words and characteristics between them. A German speaker can understand a text written in Dutch or Flemish to a reasonable degree, although the understanding breaks down when these languages are spoken. The relationship between German and English is slightly more distant. The German words **Zimmer** (*room*), **Pfeife** and **Milch** have the same root as the English words *timber*, *pipe* and *milk* but demonstrate the softening of consonant sounds that took place in German after the Angles, Jutes and Saxons took their language to Britain in the mid 5th century AD.

## German dialects

The dialects from which the German spoken within the United States is derived are still alive and well within the German-speaking countries of Europe. They are so alive and well in fact that it can be very difficult for speakers of different dialects to understand one another. There are geographical reasons for this. The mountains of Austria and Switzerland, for example, used to prevent easy communication with the outside world, but there are also historical reasons. Until 1871, Germany existed as an empire of disparate city states, duchies and even kingdoms, each with their own fiercely-guarded identity. This political fragmentation influenced the language by causing the dialects to retain their individual characteristics.

## Southern dialects

German dialects fall into two general groups, those spoken in the north and in the south of the region. In the south, the dialect spoken in Bavaria and Austria is characterized by its sing-song quality, a hard rolling 'r' and the tendency to pronounce monophthongs such as 'u' as diphthongs 'u-o.' The German word **gut** (*good*) is therefore pronounced **goot** in northern Germany, but **goo-ot** in the south. The other southern dialect, Alemannic, comprises Swiss German and Swabian which is spoken in south-west Germany. Swiss German is considered to be a language in its own right, not just a dialect. Geographical isolation has led to its vowels and consonants retaining the characteristics of the language spoken in this region many hundreds of years ago. Many German speakers find Swiss German impossible to understand, not only because of its peculiarity of pronunciation but also because of the wealth of dialect words and loanwords from other languages in the Swiss Confederation. A Swiss German speaker would quite naturally thank you by saying **merci vielmals** and go for a ride on his **vélo**.

# Northern and central dialects

In the northern parts of Germany another dialect is spoken that is also regarded by some as a separate language. It is known as Low German or **Plattdeutsch** and shares an even closer similarity to English than other dialects in Germany owing to the fact that it did not undergo the same process that led to the softening of consonants. For example, the Low German word **peper** is virtually identical to *pepper* in English but has become **Pfeffer** in standard German. Similarly, the verb *to make* is **maken** in Low German as opposed to the standard German **machen**.

The central regions of Germany also have their distinct dialects including Franconian spoken around the Rhineland. Although these central regional dialects have their own flavor, they are the most accessible to all German speakers because they were the dialects closest to the Saxon chancery language on which the standard German language or **Hochdeutsch** was based. This particular written language was standardized to simplify the administration of the duchy of Saxony. The reason why it became the model for standard modern German is because it was adopted by Martin Luther in his literature and Bible translations. The advent of the printing press meant that Luther was able to reach an audience throughout the German empire and he therefore wanted to use a language which the largest number of people would understand rather than his own dialect. His influence on the age led to the language he used in his writings becoming the model for the standard language used in Germany today. This is the German which is taught as a foreign language and which is used in the media, in administration and in schools.

## Characteristics of the German language

As Mark Twain said in his famous essay *The Awful German Language* in which he describes his personal struggle to learn the language, 'it ought to be gently and reverently set aside among the dead languages, for only the dead have time to learn it.' German continues to have a reputation as a difficult language to learn. It is true that it has a relatively complex grammatical structure but this is compensated for by the fact that it is a very logical language and its spelling and pronunciation, unlike those of English, are consistent.

## Compound words

To the non-German speaker some of the most striking characteristics of German are its long words. Actually, these are compounds made up of strings of shorter words written together as one. Once broken down into their component parts they soon become less daunting. German nouns are also written with capital letters, a historical trait which continues to this day, but which, again, is consistent.

## Umlauts

The two little dots appearing above certain vowels are known as the **Umlaut** and can also look unnerving but they are simply a form of shorthand used to represent the letter **e**. They modify the vowels **a**, **o** and **u** so that they are pronounced as if combined with a following **e**. The letter **ä** corresponds to the **ai** sound in the English *air*, the letter **ö** rhymes with the **eu** sound in *chauffeur* and the letter **ü** corresponds to the vowel sound in the French word *rue*. A common vowel combination is also **äu**, which rhymes with the English *boy*, as in **Fräulein**. Another unfamiliar letter is the sharp **s** which is written **ß**. However, it is simply shorthand for double **s**, so that the word **heiß** meaning *hot* is pronounced **heiss**.

## Genders

Unlike English, German attributes different genders to its nouns. There is a choice of three, the masculine **der**, the feminine **die** and the neuter **das**. Sometimes the gender is obvious, such as in **der Mann** and **die Frau** and sometimes the ending of the noun provides a clue. Words ending in -**ung** or -**keit**, for example, are always feminine. But most of the time the student of German has no choice but to learn the gender along with the noun. It is in this area that Mark Twain perhaps had a point. However, Germans are very forgiving if a non-German native attaches the wrong gender to a noun.

# True friends and false friends

The close relationship between the English and the German languages means that there are many pairs of words that look and/or sound similar in the two languages and that do mean the same thing. These are *vrais amis* – true friends for the English native speaker who is learning German. Words such as **Haus**, **Garten**, **Schuh** or **Wein**, which mean **house, garden, shoe** and **wine,** are instantly recognizable. However, it is unwise to assume that a familiar looking word will necessarily have the same meaning in German as it has in English. Often the meaning can change over the years. **Tier**, for example, comes from the same root as the English *deer*. However, **Tier** means *animal* in German and demonstrates how the English form of the word has become very specific in meaning whereas the German has remained very general. It pays, therefore, to be wary when confronted with an apparently familiar word in German, especially since the shift in meaning of a word can be so extreme as to make it virtually unrecognizable and therefore something of a hazard.

## False friends

The close relationship between the two languages means that there are not only many helpful and familiar *vrais amis* – but also many *faux amis* or 'false friends' in German, that is, words that resemble English words but which have very different meanings. One of the more infamous ones is **Gift**, which could cause great consternation if offered to a German speaker for whom it means *poison*. Similarly, the word **Mist** on a weather report might cause alarm as it means *manure* in German. Here is a selection of other *false friends* with their real meanings:

| aktuell | *up-to-date* |
|---|---|
| bekommen | *to get* |
| eventuell | *maybe* |
| Fabrik | *factory* |
| Fantasie | *imagination* |
| Pickel | *pimple* |
| sympathisch | *nice* |

# The influence of German on the English language

As we will soon see, the influence of modern English on the German language is substantial and continues at a good pace. The same cannot be said for the influence of German on English. Only a small number of German words have been adopted into English and most of these are taken from the world of philosophy or literature, for example *weltanschauung, doppelgänger* or *leitmotiv*. Others come from the world of politics (*realpolitik*) or warfare: *flak*, for example, is an abbreviation of **Flugabwehrkanone** meaning *anti-aircraft gun*. The Second World War also gave the English language the terms *blitz* and *strafe*.

## The influence of English on the German language

English words have been entering the German language since the 18th century when British culture became highly popular in Germany. In these early years, many of the English words entering German had to do with fashion, for example **Smoking** or **Cape**, with food and drink (**Beefsteak** and **Pudding**), or with social life (**Klub** and **Gentleman**). Similar areas of influence were the field of commerce with **Scheck**, **Manager**, **Konzern**, politics with **Streik** and **Parlament**, industry (**Lokomotive**, **Tunnel**) and sports and entertainment (**Sport**, **Tennis**, **Match**). The continuing popularity of British and then, since the First World War, primarily American culture means that words from all of these areas of influence are still entering the German language today. English has come to dominate high-tech industry and is used as a *lingua franca* in commerce, banking, politics and science. As a result, words such as **Computer**, **DVD**, **Internet**, **Website**, **Global Player** and **Marketing** have been imported wholesale into German as they have into many languages around the world. However, the cultural influence still pervades, as a quick glance at the German pop charts, bestseller lists or movie charts will confirm. Pop groups from English-speaking countries continue to dominate in Germany, Austria and Switzerland and the lyrics of their songs remain untranslated.

## Loan translations

English words do not only enter the German language in an unchanged form. English words are often imported as loan translations, that is, a new German word is coined to convey the meaning of the English, usually by literally translating elements of the English word. One of the most obvious examples of this is *skyscraper*, which became **Wolkenkratzer** in German, a new coinage which literally means *cloud scraper*. Other examples include **Buchmacher** (*bookmaker*), **Anrufbeantworter** (*answering machine*) and **Bildschirmschoner** (*screen saver*). Sometimes a new word is a mixture of a loan translation and an adopted English word (admittedly with altered spelling) as in the case of **doppelklicken** or *to double-click*. Likewise, differences in grammar have led to the tendency for German inflections to be added onto English words as in the verbs **downloaden, twittern, scannen, shoppen**, **chatten** and **crashen**.

## Resistance to English

The influence of English on the German language has not been without its critics, however. In times of increased national fervor, such as during the First World War and under the Nazis, the rate of adoption of English terms slowed. In times favoring a more cosmopolitan outlook, such as during the 1920s and after the Second World War, the rate increased. Even without the influence of nationalism, attempts have been made since the 18th century to keep the German language 'pure' by discouraging the import of English words and by manufacturing loan translations in order to 'Germanify' those that did enter the language. The argument over whether something should be done to stop Anglicisms entering the German language continues. As recently as 2001 a bill was brought before the German parliament outlining measures to 'protect' the language. In 1997, the **Verein Deutsche Sprache** (*German Language Society*) was formed with the express aim of promoting German and stemming the tide of English imports into the language.

## Denglisch and Germish

Not only has the arrival of English terms into German led to loan translations being formed, it has also resulted in the creation of *Denglisch* or *Germish* words in German, i.e. words which look like English but do not actually exist in the English language. An example is **Handy** which means *cellphone* in German, or **Dressman** which means *male model*. Sometimes this process can lead to confusion for the English speaker as a rising star is referred to in German as a **Shooting Star**. Occasionally it also has rather unfortunate consequences. A **one-strap backpack** is known in German by the Denglisch term **Bodybag**.

## English as a marketing language

English has also had a profound influence on the language of marketing in Germany. In a bid to emphasize the international nature of their product or else to lend it and themselves an air of trendiness with which English is associated in German, companies often use English for product names and advertising slogans. The telecommunications giant, Deutsche Telekom, was criticized for introducing rates such as **CityCall** or **GermanCall** while the German railroad company, Deutsche Bahn, has renamed its customer service desks **ServicePoints**. Lufthansa, the leading German airline, used to advertise under the slogan *there's no better way to fly*. However, in the attempt to make their products sound sexy, advertisers have overestimated the English proficiency of the average German. In a recent poll, a target group of people aged between 14 and 59 was asked to say what they understood by Mitsubishi's slogan *Drive Alive*. Only 18% understood it as *drive in a way which makes you feel alive*. The other 82% though it meant *survive the drive in this car* – not an encouraging thought for a potential buyer. Similarly, the slogan used by the German perfume retailer, Douglas, was discovered in a survey in 2003 to be misunderstood by 92% of those surveyed. Most people thought that *come in and find out* was an invitation to go into the store and then find their way out again. In the face of the evidence that English slogans, far from being trendy and sexy, can actually lead to confusion and be detrimental to sales, the tendency among German advertisers is to now use German in their slogans and product names. Not only is there no danger of being misunderstood, the overuse of English has meant that using German in advertising is now seen as the latest cool trend.

## Youth slang

The new tendency for German to be considered hip and cool can also be seen in that most fertile area for English imports, youth slang. The familiarity of young people with new technology in particular has brought a huge influx of Anglicisms relating to the Internet, computing or mobile telephony into the language of German youth. Similarly, the influence of predominantly American youth culture on young Europeans in the form of music trends and leisure pursuits has brought even more English imports into the language. However, there are signs of a backlash against this trend with some German hip hop groups now choosing to sing in their native language, and the development of German replacements for English slang terms. This trend can be seen not so much as a rejection of English for its own sake, but as a normal reaction when new trends become mainstream and are rejected in favor of new alternatives. However, the move away from English is not yet widespread and German youth slang still abounds with English terms such as **cool** or **chillen**.

As with all youth slang, there has been a tendency in German to alter the meaning of an existing word. This corresponds to the shift in meaning of *wicked* in English. An example in German is the use of **geil** to mean *fantastic* in youth slang but in the standard language it still means *horny*. Other developments include the addition of prefixes such as **mega** or **hammer** to adjectives in order to intensify the meaning. A movie may be described as **megagut** or **hammergeil** for example.

## Kanakensprache

One other area in which youth slang has developed in Germany recently is in adopting the pidgin German known as **Kanakensprache** which is spoken by Turkish immigrant workers or immigrants from the former Yugoslavia. Although **Kanake** is a racist term for foreigners in general it has been embraced by many second and third generation immigrants. The pidgin **Kanakensprache** has become well-established throughout Germany, even generating dictionaries and comedy programs on television. Its general characteristics are simplified verb and adjectival endings and the use of the informal **du** form of address. So, for example, the perennial question posed by taxi drivers throughout Germany **wo wollen Sie hin?** (*where to?*) would be phrased in **Kanakensprache** as **wo du wolle?** There is also a tendency to use the dative form **dem** as a multipurpose definite article, for example **dem ist dem Problem** (*that's the problem*) rather than **das ist das Problem**, and to add the endings **-tu** or **-su** onto verbs to form questions, e.g. **raussu?** for **rauchst du?** (*do you smoke?*).

## German culture

Some of the more common stereotypes about German culture actually stem from Bavaria and Austria. It is only here that you will find men wearing the traditional **Lederhosen** and green hats decorated with a brush-like **Gamsbart** and the women wearing the low-cut and tightly-bodiced **Dirndl** dresses. Likewise **oompah** music is associated only with the south of Germany and Austria. This north/south divide has historical roots. It was not until the late 19th century that the different duchies, principalities and city states were formed into one German nation and the sense of regional pride remains strong today. This divide is also visible in terms of religion. Southern Germany and Austria are overwhelmingly Catholic, while the north of Germany and Switzerland are mostly Protestant.

## Food and drink

However, other German stereotypes, those of drinking beer and eating sausages, are truly national. In fact, German food and drink have become famous throughout the world. The many varieties of beer, bread and sausages created in Germany are also the result of the country's fragmented history with each area having its own specialties. Germany and Austria also have a great reputation for wines, cakes and pastries. A visit to any café in these countries will bring the visitor face to face with a mouthwatering array of cream cakes and exquisite pastries for which these countries are justly famous, and which should definitely be sampled as part of any visitor's attempts to immerse himself or herself in German culture.

## German influences on the arts and sciences

It is not only in terms of food and drink that the German-speaking countries have wielded international influence. They are also famous throughout the world for their contribution to the arts and sciences. In the field of music, there are many great German and Austrian composers and German is one of the main languages of opera and song. One need only think of such names as Bach, Mozart, Schubert, Mahler, Wagner and Beethoven, to name only the most influential. Likewise, the German-speaking countries are famous for their philosophers such as Wittgenstein, Nietzsche and Hegel. In the twentieth century the United States was able to benefit more directly from German culture in the form of German émigrés from the Nazis. In this way, American architecture, music and film-making were enriched by the talents of Mies van der Rohe, Kurt Weill and Fritz Lang. But perhaps the most famous émigré from this era was the German born physicist Albert Einstein who decided not to return to his homeland while on a speaking tour in the US in 1932.

# Christmas traditions

It is also the German-speaking countries that the US has to thank for some of its Christmas traditions. Advent calendars, for example, were first printed in Germany and the Germans were the first to decorate Christmas trees. This tradition spread from Germany to Great Britain when the German Prince Albert married Queen Victoria and introduced the custom into the British royal family. It was duly copied by their subjects and by their cousins across the pond. Some features of German Christmases may not be so familiar, however. Presents are given on Christmas Eve. Likewise, Christmas cards are not as widely sent in Germany, Switzerland and Austria as they are in the US.

## German characteristics and everyday life

The Germans, Austrians and Swiss are often seen as stereotypically humorless and serious. The humorless label is perhaps a result of the fact that the German sense of humor is very different from the American. German comedies, for example, come across to the American viewer as rather farcical and relying heavily on slapstick. In particular, there is an element of irony which is missing and this also comes across in everyday conversation. A German speaker will often take an ironic statement literally which can lead to major confusion and jokes falling rather flat. Their reputation for seriousness is well deserved but this does not necessarily mean that all German speakers are dull. It is true that in the German-speaking countries even young people love to have earnest conversations about politics or culture. It cannot be denied that they do take things seriously, but this trait also means that they tend to get things done efficiently, whether it be at work, in sports, or simply in the garden at home. They approach work and pastimes with great thoroughness, energy and dedication.

## Green thinking

This hard-working culture has led to the German-speaking countries being at the forefront of many innovations. The most obvious example of this is their dedication to environmentally-friendly living and renewable energy sources. Where other countries have been slow to take up recycling, biodegradable household products, organic farming and renewable energy, and have only come to employ them wholeheartedly when alternatives prove scarce or expensive, the Germans, Austrians and Swiss have been eager to invest in these areas right from the start, simply because it makes more sense in the long run to do so.

## Formal and informal modes of address

A further expression of this innate seriousness which might strike the foreign visitor is in the great formality with which German speakers address one another. In German, there are two options for translating the English *you*. The informal **du** is used between people who are on first-name terms, among young people and by older people when addressing children and teenagers. The formal **Sie** is used by children speaking to adults with whom they are not related and between adults who are not acquainted, who are superior in rank, or who do not share a close friendship. It would be considered very rude for a German to address an adult stranger as **du** but such slips are forgiven if made by foreigners. Although the use of the formal address is perhaps not as rigid as it used to be, it still persists among work colleagues. Whereas it is the norm for American co-workers to be on first-name terms right from the start of their acquaintance, Germans will still address a colleague they have worked alongside for decades as **Sie** and refer to him or her as **Herr X** or **Frau Y**.

## Shaking hands

This tendency toward greater formality also extends to the widespread practice of shaking hands which is normal between young or old whether they have met before or not. In a group of people it is the proper thing to go around and shake everyone's hand and introduce yourself if you are not acquainted, and it is an endearing sight to see small German children solemnly introducing themselves in this way to each member of a group. Among friends and younger people, however, it has become customary to greet each other by exchanging kisses on the cheek.

## Houses and apartments

In towns and cities in Germany, Austria and Switzerland, it is common for people to live in apartments. In the suburbs and in rural areas, however, the traditional large **Familienhaus** or *family house* is still a familiar sight. They tend to have a number of stories and the tradition is for different generations of a family to live on separate stories under the same roof. This practice is not as widespread as it used to be but is still relatively common.

## Public transportation

Even though people in German-speaking countries embrace car travel, they are also able to take advantage of the sophisticated public transportation network for getting around. The majority of towns and cities in these countries have bus and streetcar networks as well as generous cycle paths and cycling is a very popular means of transportation in urban areas. Larger towns also have suburban railways or **S-Bahn** and all the countries have large railroad networks which are internationally famous for their punctuality. Public transportation is also relatively cheap and reliable and is an excellent way for the visitor to travel around too.

## Sports and pastimes

The most popular sport in the German-speaking countries is undoubtedly soccer but other popular sports include handball, tennis and all forms of skiing. Many people also enjoy hiking and mountain climbing and take these pursuits with characteristic seriousness. A foreign visitor strolling along and admiring the view can expect to be passed by natives intent on completing their hike as quickly and efficiently as possible. Large numbers of people also keep in shape by simply taking advantage of the cycle path networks and cycling everywhere they need to go.

Handicrafts are also a popular way for people in the German-speaking countries to relax. Knitting and needlework are still extremely popular, even among the younger generations. Many children will rate **Basteln** or *crafts* as their hobby and this may include model making, painting or different dyeing techniques. Gardening is also very popular with many apartment dwellers owning a **Schrebergarten** or *allotment*. Groups of these plots sometimes cover quite large areas and each one is large enough for a vegetable patch and fruit trees and a **Gartenhaus** or small cabin. People often spend whole weekends relaxing on the *Schrebergarten* and sleeping in the cabin.

# Relaxation

Other forms of relaxation include visiting health spas or beer gardens. The latter are often found in the middle of parks or attached to a particular brewery and offer a great way to spend time outdoors, sampling the local brew. All of these relaxation pursuits will be familiar to the visitor from the US. However, there is one particular pastime which will appear unusual and about which visitors should be aware. People in the German-speaking countries tend to be very uninhibited and nudism is very common and accepted as completely normal. Often areas in parks, on the side of lakes or swimming pools or on beaches are reserved for people wanting to indulge in the **Freikörperkultur** (*free body culture*) or **FKK** for short. Often whole families go in for this pursuit and the visitor who modestly remains covered up can often feel rather outnumbered and definitely overdressed when confronted with large numbers of **FKK** enthusiasts. There is no need to feel alarmed, however. Nudism, like mountain climbing, drinking beer and shaking hands, is merely one of those national characteristics which is all part of the experience of any visit to a German-speaking country.

# DEUTSCH – ENGLISCH
# GERMAN – ENGLISH

# A

**a, A** [aː] (*pl* - *ODER* -s) *das* - **1.** [Buchstabe] a, A - **2.** MUS A - **3.** *RW:* **das ~ und O** the be-all and end-all; **von ~ bis Z** from start to finish.

➤ **A** (*pl* -) (*abk für* **Autobahn**) *die* ≃ M *Br*, ≃ I *Am* ◇ (*abk für* **Ampere**) A.

**a.** (*abk für* **am**): **Linz ~ Rhein** Linz on the Rhine.

**AA** (*abk für* **Auswärtiges Amt**) *das German Foreign Ministry*.

**Aachen** *nt* Aachen.

**Aal** (*pl* -e) *der* eel.

**aalen** ➤ **sich aalen** *ref* to bask.

**aalglatt** *adj abw* slippery.

**a.a.O.** (*abk für* **am angegebenen Ort**) loc. cit.

**Aargau** *der* Aargau.

**Aas** (*pl* -e *ODER* -Äser) *das* - **1.** (*pl* Aase) [Kadaver] carrion (*U*) - **2.** (*pl* Äser) *salopp abw* [Luder] devil; **kein ~** *salopp* not a damned single person.

**ab** *präp* (+ *D*) - **1.** [zeitlich] from; **~ 8 Uhr** from 8 o'clock; **~ 18 (Jahren)** over (the age of) 18 - **2.** [räumlich] from; **~ Werk** ex works; **9.30 ~ Köln** leaving Cologne at 9.30 - **3.** [bei einer Reihenfolge] over; **Einkünfte ~ 15.000 Euro** incomes over 15,000 euros ◇ *adv* - **1.** [räumlich] off; **weit ~ gelegen** situated a long way away - **2.** [auffordernd]: **~ ins Bett!** get to bed! - **3.** [elliptisch] off; *fig* **Hut ~!** hats off! - **4.** [im Theater] exit; **Mephisto ~** exit Mephisto; *siehe auch* **ab sein**.

➤ **ab und zu, ab und an** *adv* now and then.

**ablarbeiten** *vt* to work off.
➤ **sich abarbeiten** *ref* to work like a slave.

**Ablart** *die* variety.

**abartig** *adj* deviant.

**Abb.** (*abk für* **Abbildung**) fig.

**Abbau** *der* (*ohne pl*) - **1.** [Demontage - von Bühne,

Gerüst] taking down; [ - von Maschine] dismantling - **2.** [Reduzierung] reduction - **3.** [beim Bergbau] mining - **4.** CHEM & BIOL breaking down.

**ablbauen** *vt* - **1.** [abbrechen - Kulissen, Bühne, Zelt] to take down; [ - Maschine] to dismantle - **2.** [reduzieren] to reduce - **3.** CHEM & BIOL to break down - **4.** [beim Bergbau] to mine ◇ *vi* to go downhill.

**ablbeißen** *vt* (*unreg*) to bite off.

**ablbekommen** *vt* (*unreg*) - **1.** [Anteil, Partner, Prügel] to get; **Schaden ~** to get damaged; **hast du etwas ~?** [Verletzung] did you get hurt? - **2.** *fam* [Fleck] to get off.

**ablberufen** *vt* (*unreg*) to recall.

**ablbestellen** *vt* to cancel.

**ablbezahlen** *vt* to pay off.

**ablbiegen** (*perf* hat/ist abgebogen) (*unreg*) *vi* (*ist*) to turn off; **nach links/rechts ~** to turn left/right ◇ *vt* (*hat*) [verhindern - Vorhaben] to avert; [ - Thema] to change.

**Abbiegelspur** *die* filter lane.

**Ablbild** *das* picture.

**ablbilden** *vt* to depict.

**Ablbildung** *die* - **1.** [Bild] illustration - **2.** [Wiedergabe] depiction.

**ablbinden** *vt* (*unreg*) - **1.** [ausziehen] to undo - **2.** MED to ligature.

**ablblasen** *vt* (*unreg*) *fam* to call off.

**ablblättern** (*perf* ist abgeblättert) *vi* to flake off.

**ablbleiben** (*perf* ist abgeblieben) *vi* (*unreg*) to get to; **wo ist das Buch abgeblieben?** where has the book got to?

**ablblenden** *vt* - **1.** [Lampe] to screen - **2.** [Scheinwerfer] to dip *Br*, to dim *Am* ◇ *vi*

**- 1.** FOTO to stop down **- 2.** AUTO to dip *Br* ODER dim *Am* one's headlights.

**Abblend|licht** *das* dipped *Br* ODER dimmed *Am* headlights *(pl)*.

**ab|blitzen** *(perf* ist abgeblitzt) *vi fam:* bei jm ~ to get short shrift from sb; jn ~ lassen to send sb packing.

**ab|blocken** *vt* to block.

**ab|brechen** *(perf* hat/ist abgebrochen) *(unreg) vt (hat)* **- 1.** [Stück, Ast] to break off; [Bleistift] to break **- 2.** [Vorhaben, Beziehungen, Reise, Studium] to break off; [Streik] to call off **- 3.** EDV to abort **- 4.** RW: sich einen ~ [sich anstrengen] *salopp* to bust a gut; **brich dir mal keinen ab!** chill out! <> *vi -* **1.** *(hat)* [im Gespräch] to break off **- 2.** *(ist)* [Geräusch] to stop.

**ab|bremsen** *vi* to brake <> *vt* to slow down.

**ab|brennen** *(perf* hat/ist abgebrannt) *(unreg) vt (hat)* **- 1.** [Haus] to burn down **- 2.** [Feuerwerk] to let off <> *vi (ist)* to burn down.

**ab|bringen** *vt (unreg):* jn von seiner Meinung ~ to make sb change his/her mind; jn davon ~, aus dem Fenster zu springen to stop sb from jumping out of the window; das bringt uns vom Thema ab we're getting off the subject.

**ab|bröckeln** *(perf* ist abgebröckelt) *vi* to flake off.

**Ab|bruch** *der -* **1.** [Ende] breaking off; einer Sache *(D)* keinen ~ tun *fig* not to adversely affect sthg; das tut der Sache keinen ~ that doesn't change anything **- 2.** [Zerstörung] demolition; auf ~ at demolition value.

**abbruchreif** *adj* fit only for demolition.

**ab|buchen** *vt* WIRTSCH: ~ (von) to debit (to).

**ab|bürsten** *vt* [Mantel] to brush down; [Krümel] to brush off.

**Abc** [a(ː)beː(ː)'tseː] *das* ABC.

**ab|checken** *vt -* **1.** [Motor, Flugzeug] to check **- 2.** [auf einer Liste] to check off.

**Abc-|Schütze** *der child in first year at school.*

**ab|dampfen** *(perf* ist abgedampft) *vi fam* to hit the road.

**ab|danken** *vi* to abdicate.

**ab|decken** *vt -* **1.** [gen] to cover **- 2.** [abräumen - Tisch] to clear; [ - Dach] to take off.

**Abdeckung** *(pl -en) die -* **1.** [zum Schutz] cover **- 2.** WIRTSCH covering.

**ab|dichten** *vt* [gegen kalte Luft] to insulate; [gegen Wasser] to waterproof; [Gefäß] to make airtight; [Fenster] to draughtproof.

**Ab|dichtung** *die* [gegen kalte Luft] insulation; [gegen Wasser] waterproofing; [von Fenster] draughtproofing; [von Gefäß] making airtight.

**ab|drängen** *vt* to push aside.

**ab|drehen** *(perf* hat/ist abgedreht) *vt (hat)*

**- 1.** [Wasser, Gas] to turn off **- 2.** [Knopf, Schraube] to twist off **- 3.** [Film, Szene] to shoot <> *vi (hat, ist)* [den Kurs ändern] to turn away.

**ab|drosseln** *vt* to throttle back.

**Abdruck** *(pl -drücke) der -* **1.** [Spur] imprint; einen ~ nehmen ODER machen to take ODER make an impression **- 2.** [Druck] printing.

**ab|drucken** *vt* to print.

**ab|drücken** *vt -* **1.** [abquetschen] to constrict; jm die Luft ~ to squeeze the breath out of sb **- 2.** [umarmen] to hug <> *vi* [schießen] to pull the trigger.

➤ **sich abdrücken** *ref* to leave an impression.

**ab|ebben** *(perf* ist abgeebbt) *vi* to fade away.

**Abend** *(pl -e) der* evening; **am ~** in the evening; **gestern/heute/morgen ~** yesterday/this/tomorrow evening; **guten ~!** good evening!; **zu ~ essen** to have one's dinner ODER evening meal; **bunter ~** social evening.

**Abend|brot** *das* cold supper.

**Abend|essen** *das* dinner, evening meal.

**Abend|kasse** *die* box office *(where tickets may only be bought immediately before performance)*.

**Abend|kleid** *das* evening dress.

**Abend|kurs** *der* evening class.

**Abend|land** *das* West.

**abendlich** *adj* evening *(vor Subst).*

**Abend|mahl** *das* REL (Holy) Communion.

**Abend|programm** *das* evening programmes *(pl)* ODER viewing *(U).*

**Abend|rot** *das* sunset.

**abends** *adv* in the evening; **spät ~** late in the evening.

**Abend|schule** *die* night school.

**Abend|vorstellung** *die* evening performance.

**Abenteuer** *(pl -) das -* **1.** [Erlebnis] adventure **- 2.** [Wagnis] venture **- 3.** [Liebesverhältnis] affair.

**abenteuerlich** *adj -* **1.** [waghalsig] adventurous **- 2.** [fantastisch] fantastic.

**Abenteuerspiel|platz** *der* adventure playground.

**Abenteurer, in** *(mpl -; fpl -nen) der, die* adventurer.

**aber** *konj* but <> *adv:* **das ist ~ nett!** how nice!; **~ gerne!** of course!; **~ bitte!** go ahead!; **~ immer!** *fam* sure!; **jetzt ist ~ Schluss!** that's enough now!; **du kommst ~ spät!** you're a bit late, aren't you?

**Aber|glaube, -n** *der* superstition.

**abergläubisch** *adj* superstitious.

**aberhundert** *num* hundreds (and hundreds) of.

**ab|erkennen** *vt (unreg):* **jm etw ~** to strip sb of sthg.

**Aberkennung** *(pl -en) die* stripping.

**abermalig** *adj geh* renewed.

**abermals** *adv geh* one more time.

**ab|ernten** *vt* to harvest.

**abertausend** *num* thousands (and thousands) of.

**aberwitzig** *adj* crazy.

**ab|essen** *vt (unreg):* **etw von etw ~** to eat sthg off sthg.

**ab|fahren** *(perf* **hat/ist abgefahren)** *(unreg) vi (ist)* [losfahren] to leave; [Zug] to depart, to leave; **auf jn/etw ~** *fam fig* to be into sb/sthg ⬦ *vt (hat)* **- 1.** [Ladung] to take away **- 2.** [Strecke] to go over **- 3.** [Reifen] to wear down **- 4.** [Fahrkarte] to get full use out of **- 5.** [Gliedmaß - bei Verkehrsunfall] to sever.

**Ab|fahrt** *die* **- 1.** [Start] departure; **Vorsicht bei der ~ des Zuges!** stand clear of the doors, the train is about to depart!; **planmäßige ~** scheduled time of departure **- 2.** [Autobahnabfahrt] exit **- 3.** [Skiabfahrt] descent.

**abfahrtbereit** *adj* ready to depart.

**Abfahrts|lauf** *der* sport downhill.

**Abfahrts|zeit** *die* departure time.

**Ab|fall** *der* **- 1.** [Hausmüll] refuse; [industriell] waste **- 2.** *(ohne pl)* [Rückgang] drop, fall.

**Abfall|beseitigung** *die* waste disposal.

**ab|fallen** *(perf* **ist abgefallen)** *vi (unreg)* **- 1.** [herunterfallen] to fall off **- 2.** [übrig bleiben] to be left over; **was fällt für mich ab?** what do I get out of it? **- 3.** *geh* [sich lossagen]: **von jm/etw ~** to drift away from sb/sthg **- 4.** [schlechter sein]: **gegen jn/etw ~** to suffer by comparison with sb/sthg **- 5.** [sich neigen] to slope (down) **- 6.** [sich verringern] to drop, to fall.

**abfällig** *adj* disparaging ⬦ *adv* disparagingly.

**Abfall|produkt** *das* **- 1.** [nicht verwendbar] waste product; [verwendbar] by-product **- 2.** [aus Abfall] product made from recycled materials.

**Abfallver|wertung** *die* waste recycling.

**ab|fangen** *vt (unreg)* **- 1.** [Brief, Anruf, Transport] to intercept **- 2.** [Person] to catch **- 3.** [Schlag] to ward off **- 4.** [Flugzeug] to regain control of.

**Abfang|jäger** *der* mil interceptor.

**ab|färben** *vi* to run; **auf jn/etw ~** *fig* to rub off on sb/sthg.

**ab|fassen** *vt* to write.

**ab|federn** *vi* sport to push off ⬦ *vt* **- 1.** tech to spring **- 2.** [Schlag, Stoß] to cushion.

**ab|feiern** *vt* [Überstunden] to take time off in lieu of.

**ab|fertigen** *vt* **- 1.** [Waren] to prepare for dispatch; [Gepäck] to check in; [Schiff, Flugzeug] to prepare for departure **- 2.** [Passagier, Antragssteller] to attend to; **jn mit etw ~** to fob sb off with sthg.

**Ab|fertigung** *die* **- 1.** [von Gepäck] check-in; [von Waren] preparation for dispatch; [von Schiff, Flugzeug] preparation for departure **- 2.** [von Passagier, Antragssteller] attending to.

**ab|feuern** *vt* [Gewehr, Schuss] to fire; [Rakete] to launch.

**ab|finden** *vt (unreg)* **- 1.** [entschädigen]: **jn mit etw ~** to give sb sthg in compensation **- 2.** [zufrieden stellen]: **jn mit etw ~** to fob sth off with sthg. ⬦ **sich abfinden** *ref:* **sich mit etw ~** to come to terms with sthg.

**Abfindung** *(pl -en) die* [für einen Verlust] compensation; [für die vorzeitige Entlassung] severance pay.

**ab|flachen** *(perf* **hat/ist abgeflacht)** *vt (hat)* to flatten ⬦ *vi (ist)* to deteriorate.

**ab|flauen** *(perf* **ist abgeflaut)** *vi* **- 1.** [Interesse, Geschäfte] to fall off **- 2.** [Wind, Spannung] to die down.

**ab|fliegen** *(perf* **ist abgeflogen)** *vi (unreg)* to take off.

**ab|fließen** *(perf* **ist abgeflossen)** *vi (unreg)* [Spülwasser] to drain away; [Regenwasser] to run away.

**Ab|flug** *der* **- 1.** [von Flugzeug] take-off **- 2.** [Flughafenbereich] departures (U).

**Ab|fluss** *der* **- 1.** [Öffnung - von Waschbecken, Dusche] plughole **- 2.** [von Kapital] flight **- 3.** [von Spülwasser] draining away; [von Regenwasser] running away.

**Abfluss|rohr** *das* waste pipe.

**ab|fordern** *vt:* **jm etw ~** to demand sthg from sb.

**ab|fragen** *vt* to call up; **jn (etw) ~** to test sb (on sthg).

**ab|frottieren** *vt* to rub down.

**Abfuhr** *(pl -en) die:* **jm eine ~ erteilen** to rebuff sb; **sich (D) eine ~ holen, eine ~ einstecken** to be rebuffed.

**ab|führen** *vt* **- 1.** [festnehmen] to take away **- 2.** [vom Thema] to lead away **- 3.** [zahlen]: **etw an jn ~** to pay sthg to sb ⬦ *vi* med to act as a laxative.

**Abführ|mittel** *das* laxative.

**ab|füllen** *vt* **- 1.** [Flüssigkeit]: **Wein in Flaschen ~** to bottle wine **- 2.** [Flaschen, Säcke] to fill **- 3.** *fam* [betrunken machen]: **jn ~** to get sb plastered.

**Abgabe** *(pl -n) die* **- 1.** [Übergabe - von Gutachten] handing over; [ - von Arbeit] handing in **- 2.** [von Stimmen] casting **- 3.** [Verkauf] sale

**- 4.** [von Ball] passing **- 5.** [von Wärme, Sauerstoff] giving off.

➤ **Abgaben** pl [Steuern] taxes.

**abgabenfrei** adj exempt from tax.

**abgabenpflichtig** adj taxable.

**Abgabe|termin** der deadline.

**Ab|gang** der **- 1.** (ohne pl) [Verlassen] departure; [von der Schule] leaving; **sich einen guten ODER glänzenden ~ verschaffen** to leave on a high note **- 2.** [Personen]: **es gab fünf vorzeitige Abgänge** five people dropped out **- 3.** [Abschicken] dispatch **- 4.** MED discharge **- 5.** SPORT dismount.

**Abgangs|zeugnis** das leaving certificate.

**Abgase** pl exhaust fumes.

**Abgas|untersuchung** die emissions test.

**abgearbeitet** adj worn-out.

**ab|geben** vt (unreg) **- 1.** [abliefern - Brief, Geschenk] to hand over; [ - Arbeit] to hand in; [ - an der Garderobe] to leave **- 2.** [verkaufen] to sell **- 3.** [teilen]: **jm etw ~** to give sb sthg **- 4.** [äußern - Erklärung] to make; [ - Meinung] to give; [ - Stimme] to cast **- 5.** [abtreten] to give up **- 6.** [darstellen - Figur] to cut; **einen guten Vater ~** to make a good father **- 7.** SPORT [werfen] to pass **- 8.** [ausströmen] to give off **- 9.** [abfeuern] to fire.

➤ **sich abgeben** ref: **sich mit etw (nicht) ~** (not) to concern o.s. with sthg; **sie gibt sich mit ganz obskuren Typen ab** she mixes with some really dubious types.

**abgebrannt** adj **- 1.** [verbrannt] burnt-down **- 2.** fam [bankrott] broke.

**abgebrüht** adj fam hard-boiled, tough.

**abgedroschen** adj well-worn, hackneyed.

**abgegriffen** adj **- 1.** [Griff] worn; [Buch] well-thumbed **- 2.** [nichts sagend] well-worn, hackneyed.

**abgehackt** adj disjointed ◇ adv disjointedly.

**ab|gehen** (perf ist abgegangen) (unreg) vi **- 1.** [sich lösen] to come off **- 2.** [verlassen]: **von etw ~** to leave sthg **- 3.** [abfahren] to leave, to depart **- 4.** [abgeschickt werden] to go off **- 5.** [abgerechnet werden] to be taken off ODER deducted **- 6.** [abzweigen] to branch off **- 7.** [abweichen]: **von seiner Meinung ~** to change one's mind; **von seinen Forderungen ~** to drop one's demands **- 8.** [verlaufen] to go; **es ist gut abgegangen** it went well; **es geht ab** salopp things are really buzzing **- 9.** [fehlen]: **ihm geht jedes Feingefühl ab** he lacks any sensitivity, he has no sensitivity; **sich** (D) **nichts ~ lassen** fam not to stint on anything ◇ vt [Strecke, Straße] to walk along; [Grundstück] to walk over.

**abgekämpft** adj worn-out.

**abgekartet** adj: **ein ~es Spiel** a put-up job.

**abgeklärt** adj serene ◇ adv serenely.

**abgelegen** adj remote.

**ab|gelten** vt (unreg) to settle.

**abgemacht** adj settled; **abgemacht!** it's a deal!

**abgemagert** adj emaciated.

**abgeneigt** adj: **einer Sache** (D) **(nicht) ~ sein** (not) to be opposed to sthg.

**abgenutzt** adj [Türgriff, Fußboden] worn; [Gerät] worn-out.

**Abgeordnete** (pl **-n**) der, die [im Bundestag] member of parliament; [im Landtag] representative.

**abgeplattet** adj flattened.

**abgerissen** pp ▷ **abreißen** ◇ adj **- 1.** [heruntergekommen] ragged **- 2.** [stockend] disjointed ◇ adv **- 1.** [heruntergekommen] raggedly **- 2.** [stockend] disjointedly.

**Ab|gesandte** der, die envoy.

**abgeschieden** adj remote.

**Abgeschiedenheit** die remoteness.

**abgeschlagen** adj well-beaten.

**abgeschlossen** pp ▷ **abschließen** ◇ adj **- 1.** [vollendet] completed **- 2.** [unabhängig - Wohnung] self-contained.

**abgeschmackt** adj crude.

**abgesehen** adv: **~ von jm/etw** apart from sb/sthg.

➤ **abgesehen davon, dass ...** konj apart from the fact that ...

**abgespannt** adj exhausted.

**abgestanden** adj [Bier] flat; [Luft] stale; [Wasser] stagnant.

**abgestorben** pp ▷ **absterben** ◇ adj **- 1.** [Baum, Ast] dead **- 2.** [Fuß, Bein] numb.

**abgestumpft** adj **- 1.** [gefühllos] hardened **- 2.** [apathisch] apathetic.

**abgetragen** adj worn-out.

**abgewetzt** adj [Jacke, Stoff, Bezug] threadbare; [Leder] worn smooth.

**ab|gewinnen** vt (unreg): **jm etw ~** to win sthg from sb; **einer Sache** (D) **Geschmack ~** to acquire a taste for sthg.

**ab|gewöhnen** vt: **jm etw ~** to get sb to give sthg up; **sich** (D) **etw ~** to give sthg up.

**ab|gießen** vt (unreg) **- 1.** [Wasser] to pour away; [Kartoffeln] to drain **- 2.** [Skulptur] to cast.

**Abglanz** der pale reflection.

**ab|gleiten** (perf ist abgeglitten) vi (unreg) **- 1.** [rutschen] to slip off **- 2.** [wirkungslos bleiben]: **an jm ~** to be like water off a duck's back to sb **- 3.** [abschweifen] to stray.

**abgöttisch** adv: **jn ~ lieben/verehren** to idolize sb.

**ab|graben** vt (unreg) to dig out; **jm das Wasser ~** fig to take away sb's livelihood.

**ạb|grasen** *vt* - **1.** *fam* [absuchen, erforschen] to scour - **2.** [abweiden] to graze.

**ạb|greifen** *vt (unreg)* [Strecke] to measure off.

**ạb|grenzen** *vt* - **1.** [abtrennen - mit Zaun] to fence off; [ - mit Mauer] to wall off - **2.** [unterscheiden] to differentiate.

➤ **sich abgrenzen** *ref:* **sich von jm/etw ~** to distance o.s. from sb/sthg; **sich gegen etw ~** to isolate o.s. from sthg.

**Ạbgrenzung** *(pl -en) die* - **1.** [Grenze] boundary - **2.** [Definition] definition.

**Ạb|grund** *der* abyss; **vor dem ~ stehen** *fig* to be on the edge of the abyss.

**ạbgrundtief** *adj* profound, deep ⬦ *adv* profoundly, deeply.

**ạb|gucken** *vt fam* to copy; **etw von** *ODER* **bei jm ~** to copy sthg from sb.

**Ạb|guss** *der* cast.

**ạb|haben** *vt (unreg)* to have.

**ạb|hacken** *vt* to chop off.

**ạb|haken** *vt* to check off; **das ist längst abgehakt!** that's all ancient history *ODER* water under the bridge!

**ạb|halten** *vt (unreg)* - **1.** [veranstalten] to hold - **2.** [fern halten]: **jn von etw ~** to keep sb from sthg.

**Ạb|haltung** *die* holding.

**ạb|handeln** *vt* [behandeln] to treat.

**abhạnden** *adv:* **mir ist meine Brille ~ gekommen** my glasses have gone missing.

**Ạb|handlung** *die* treatise.

**Ạb|hang** *der* slope.

**ạb|hängen** *vt (reg)* - **1.** [Bild] to take down - **2.** [Anhänger, Wagon] to uncouple - **3.** [Konkurrenten, Verfolger] to shake off ⬦ *vi (unreg):* **von jm/etw ~** to depend on sb/sthg; **davon hängt viel ab** a lot depends on it.

**abhạngig** *adj:* **von etw ~ sein** [von Wetter, Geschmack, Zufall] to depend on sthg; [von Hilfe, Vormund] to be dependent on sthg; [von Drogen] to be addicted to sthg; **etw von etw ~ machen** to make sthg conditional on sthg.

**Ạbhängigkeit** *(pl -en) die* - **1.** [gen] dependence; **~ von etw** dependence on sthg - **2.** [von Drogen] addiction.

**ạb|härten** *vt* to toughen up ⬦ *vi:* **dieses Wetter härtet ab** this weather toughens you up.

➤ **sich abhärten** *ref* to toughen (o.s.) up.

**Ạbhärtung** *die* toughening up.

**ạb|hauen** *(perf* **ist abgehauen)** *vi fam* [verschwinden] to clear off; **hau ab!** *salopp* get lost!

**ạb|heben** *(unreg) vt* - **1.** [vom Konto] to withdraw - **2.** [am Telefon] to pick up - **3.** [beim Kartenspiel] to cut ⬦ *vi* [abfliegen] to take off.

➤ **sich abheben** *ref:* **sich von jm/etw** *ODER* **gegen jn/etw ~** to stand out against sb/sthg.

**ạb|heften** *vt* to file away.

**ạb|heilen** *(perf* **ist abgeheilt)** *vi* to heal (up).

**ạb|helfen** *vi (unreg):* **einer Sache (D) ~** to remedy sthg.

**ạb|hetzen** *vt* to drive hard.

➤ **sich abhetzen** *ref* to rush one's socks off.

**Abhilfe** *die:* **~ schaffen** to take remedial action.

**ạb|holen** *vt* [Paket, Ware] to collect; [Person] to pick up.

**ạb|holzen** *vt* [Wald, Allee] to clear; [Bäume] to cut down.

**ạb|horchen** *vt MED* to sound.

**ạb|hören** *vt* - **1.** [heimlich anhören - Gespräch] to listen in on; [ - Telefon] to tap - **2.** [abfragen] to test; **jm etw ~** to test sb on sthg - **3.** [abhorchen] to sound.

**Abhör|gerät** *das* bugging device.

**Ạbi** *(pl -s) das abk für* **Abitur.**

**Abitur** *(pl -e) das* ≃ A levels *(pl)* **Br,** ≃ SATs *(pl)* **Am,** *final examination at a German "Gymnasium", qualifying pupils for university entrance.*

**ABITUR**

The German equivalent of British A-levels, the "Abitur" is the leaving examination taken by all German pupils at the end of their school career and is a requirement if they wish to go on to university. Pupils select one main subject and a number of optional subjects. Each of the "Bundesländer" administers its own examinations.

**Abiturient, in** [abituri'ɛnt, ɪn] *(mpl -en; fpl -nen) der, die* pupil who is taking/has taken the "Abitur".

**Abitur|zeugnis** *das certificate awarded to a pupil who has passed the "Abitur".*

**ạb|jagen** *vt:* **jm etw ~** to get sthg off sb.

**ạb|kanzeln** *vt:* **jn ~** to give sb a dressing-down.

**ạb|kapseln** ➤ **sich abkapseln** *ref* to cut o.s. off.

**ạb|kaufen** *vt* - **1.** [kaufen]: **jm etw ~** to buy sthg from sb - **2.** *fam* [glauben]: **diese Geschichte kaufe ich dir nicht ab!** I'm not buying that story (of yours)!

**ạb|kehren** *vt* to sweep off.

➤ **sich abkehren** *ref geh* to turn away.

**ạb|klappern** *vt fam:* **etw (nach etw) ~** to scour sthg (for sthg).

**ạb|klären** *vt* [Missverständnis] to clear up; [Aufgabenbereiche] to clarify.

**ạb|klemmen** *vt* - **1.** [abtrennen] to cut off - **2.** [zusammenpressen] to clamp.

**ạb|klingen** *(perf* **ist abgeklungen)** *vi (unreg)* [Fieber] to die down; [Musik] to fade away.

**ab|klopfen** *vt* - **1.** [untersuchen - Vertäfelung] to tap; [ - Patienten] to sound; **etw auf etw** *(A)* **hin ~** to check sthg for sthg - **2.** [entfernen] to knock off.

**ab|knallen** *vt salopp* to blow away.

**ab|knicken** (*perf* hat/ist abgeknickt) *vt (hat)* to break, to snap ⇔ *vi (ist)* to bend sharply.

**ab|knöpfen** *vt:* **jm etw ~** to get sthg out of sb.

**ab|kochen** *vt* to sterilize *(by boiling)*.

**ab|kommandieren** *vt* MIL to send, to post.

**ab|kommen** (*perf* ist abgekommen) *vi (unreg):* **von etw ~** [Kurs, Weg] to deviate from sthg; [Thema] to get off sthg; [Gewohnheit, Vorhaben] to give sthg up, to abandon sthg.

**Abkommen** (*pl* -) *das* agreement.

**abkömmlich** *adj* available.

**ab|können** *vt (unreg) salopp:* **ich kann ihn/es nicht ab** I can't stand ODER stick *Br* him/it.

**ab|koppeln** *vt* to uncouple.

**ab|kratzen** (*perf* hat/ist abgekratzt) *vi salopp (ist)* to kick the bucket ⇔ *vt (hat)* to scrape off.

**ab|kriegen** *vt fam* - **1.** [gen] to get; **das Auto hat was abgekriegt** the car got damaged; **einen/eine ~** to get a man/woman - **2.** [Deckel, Schraube, Fleck] to get off.

**ab|kühlen** (*perf* hat/ist abgekühlt) *vi* - **1.** [Temperatur] to cool down - **2.** [Stimmung, Engagement] to cool.

➡ **sich abkühlen** *ref* [Person] to cool down ODER off; [Verhältnis] to cool; **es hat sich abgekühlt** it has got cooler.

**Abkühlung** *die* cooling.

**ab|kupfern** *vt fam* to crib.

**ab|kürzen** *vt* - **1.** [Weg]: **den Weg ~** to take a short cut - **2.** [Wort] to abbreviate - **3.** [Besuch, Reise] to cut short; [Verfahren] to shorten.

**Ab|kürzung** *die* - **1.** [von Weg] short cut - **2.** [von Wörtern] abbreviation.

**ab|laden** *vt (unreg)* - **1.** [abräumen] to unload - **2.** [erzählen]: **seinen Kummer bei jm ~** to unburden o.s. to sb.

**Ab|lage** *die* - **1.** [für Papiere, Akten] filing cabinet - **2.** [Abheften] filing.

**ab|lagern** *vt* to store ⇔ *vi* [Holz] to season; [Wein] to mature.

➡ **sich ablagern** *ref* to form a deposit.

**Ab|lagerung** *die* [Sediment] deposit.

**ab|lassen** (*unreg*) *vt* - **1.** [ausströmen lassen] to let out - **2.** *fam* [nicht aufsetzen] to leave off ⇔ *vi:* **von jm ~** [in Ruhe lassen] to leave sb alone; **von etw ~** [aufgeben] to give sthg up, to abandon sthg.

**Ab|lauf** *der* - **1.** [Verlauf] course; **um den friedlichen ~ der Veranstaltung zu gewährleisten ...** to ensure that the event passes off peace-

fully ... - **2.** [Abfluss] drain; [Rinne] outlet - **3.** [Ende] expiry.

**ab|laufen** (*perf* ist abgelaufen) *(unreg) vt* - **1.** [Strecke, Stadt] to scour - **2.** [Sohlen, Schuhe] to wear out ⇔ *vi* - **1.** [verlaufen] to go - **2.** [Frist] to expire - **3.** [Wasser] to run away - **4.** [Film, Tonband] to run; **das Tonband ~ lassen** to play the tape.

**ab|lecken** *vt* to lick.

**ab|legen** *vt* - **1.** [Mantel] to take off - **2.** [sich abgewöhnen] to get rid of - **3.** [Eid, Prüfung] to take - **4.** [Akten] to file ⇔ *vi* - **1.** [Garderobe] to take one's coat/hat/etc off - **2.** [Schiff] to cast off.

**Ableger** (*pl* -) *der* - **1.** [von Pflanzen] cutting - **2.** [Filiale] subsidiary.

**ab|lehnen** *vt* - **1.** [Angebot, Vorschlag] to reject; [Einladung] to refuse, to turn down - **2.** [Rauschgift, Schusswaffen] to disapprove of.

**Ablehnung** (*pl* -en) *die* - **1.** [von Angebot] rejection; [von Einladung] refusal; **auf ~ stoßen** to be rejected - **2.** [Missbilligung] disapproval.

**ab|leisten** *vt:* **den Wehrdienst ~** to do one's military service.

**ab|leiten** *vt* - **1.** [Rauch, Gas] to draw off - **2.** [folgern, zurückführen]: **etw von** ODER **aus etw ~** [Wort, Recht] to derive sthg from sthg - **3.** [Gleichung] to differentiate.

**Ab|leitung** *die* - **1.** [von Rauch, Gas] drawing off - **2.** [von Wort, Formel] derivation.

**ab|lenken** *vt* - **1.** [zerstreuen] to distract; **jn von der Arbeit ~** to put sb off their work - **2.** [Aufmerksamkeit, Verdacht] to divert - **3.** [weglenken - Angriff] to ward off; [ - Bewegung] to deflect.

**Ablenkung** (*pl* -en) *die* - **1.** [Zerstreuung] distraction - **2.** [Richtungsänderung] deflection.

**ab|lesen** *vt (unreg)* - **1.** [lesen] to read out - **2.** [den Stand feststellen] to read - **3.** [erraten]: **er liest ihr jeden Wunsch von den Augen ab** he can always tell what she wants from the look in her eyes.

**ab|lichten** *vt* - **1.** [fotokopieren] to photocopy - **2.** [fotografieren] to photograph.

**ab|liefern** *vt* to deliver.

**ab|lösen** *vt* - **1.** [ersetzen] to take over from - **2.** [abmachen] to take off.

➡ **sich ablösen** *ref* - **1.** [sich abwechseln] to take turns - **2.** [abgehen] to come off.

**Ablöse|summe** *die* SPORT transfer fee.

**Ablösung** *die* - **1.** [Zahlung] paying off - **2.** [Ersatzperson] relief.

**ab|luchsen** [ˈapluksn̩] *vt:* **jm etw ~** to get sthg out of sb.

**ABM** [aːbeːˈɛm] (*pl* -) (*abk für* **Arbeitsbeschaffungsmaßnahme**) *die* job creation scheme.

**ab|machen** *vt* - **1.** [entfernen] to take off - **2.** [verabreden] to agree on; **einen Termin ~** to make an appointment.

**Abmachung** (pl -en) die agreement.

**ablmagern** (perf ist abgemagert) vi to get thinner.

**Abmagerungslkur** die diet.

**ablmalen** vt to paint.

**Abmarsch** der departure.

**ablmarschieren** (perf ist abmarschiert) vi [bei Wandern] to set off; MIL to march off.

**ablmelden** vt - **1.** [Personen]: **ein Kind von der Schule ~** to give notice of a child's removal from school; **sie ist bei mir abgemeldet** fam fig I've had it ODER I'm through with her - **2.** [Gegenstände - Telefon] to have disconnected; [ - Auto] to take off the road.
➤ **sich abmelden** ref: **sich polizeilich ~** to notify the police that one is moving away; **sich bei einem Verein ~** to cancel one's membership of a club.

**Ablmeldung** die - **1.** [beim Einwohnermeldeamt] notification that one is moving away - **2.** [von der Schule] notification of a child's removal from school.

**ablmessen** vt (unreg) to measure.

**Ablmessung** die measuring.
➤ **Abmessungen** pl dimensions.

**ablmontieren** vt [Reifen, Dachgepäckträger] to take off; [Verschalung, Gerüst] to take down.

**ABM-lStelle** die job created as part of a job creation scheme.

**ablmühen** ➤ **sich abmühen** ref to struggle.

**ablmurksen** vt salopp to bump off.

**ablnabeln** vt to cut the umbilical cord of.
➤ **sich abnabeln** ref: **sich vom Elternhaus ~** to become more independent from one's parents.

**ablnagen** vt to gnaw.

**ablnähen** vt to put darts in.

**Abnahme** die - **1.** [Rückgang, Verlust] decrease - **2.** [Kauf] purchase; **~ finden** to sell - **3.** [Zulassung, Kontrolle] inspection - **4.** [Entfernen] removal.

**ablnehmen** (unreg) vt - **1.** [herunternehmen - Vorhänge, Wäsche] to take down; [ - Hut, Deckel] to take off; [ - Hörer] to pick up - **2.** [wegnehmen]: **jm etw ~** to take sthg (away) from sb - **3.** [entlasten]: **jm etw ~** to relieve sb of sthg - **4.** [kontrollieren] to inspect - **5.** [kaufen]: **jm etw ~** to buy sthg from sb - **6.** [stehlen]: **jm etw ~** to take sthg from sb - **7.** [glauben]: **das nimmt dir keiner ab!** nobody will buy that! - **8.** [entgegennehmen - Prüfung] to conduct; **jm ein Versprechen ~** to make sb give a promise - **9.** [amputieren]: **jm einen Finger ~** to take sb's finger off - **10.** [entnehmen]: **jm Blut ~** to take sb's blood - **11.** [verlieren - Gewicht] to lose ⬦ vi - **1.** [leichter werden] to lose weight - **2.** [sich verringern - Temperatur, Luftdruck, Ressourcen] to decrease; [ - Mond] to wane;

seine Interviews haben an Aggressivität abgenommen his interviews have become less aggressive.

**Abnehmer, in** (mpl -; fpl -nen) der, die buyer; **~ finden** to sell.

**Ablneigung** die aversion.

**abnorm** adj abnormal.

**ablnötigen** vt: **jm Respekt/Bewunderung ~** to win sb's respect/admiration.

**ablnutzen, ablnützen** vt to wear out.
➤ **sich abnutzen, sich abnützen** ref to wear out.

**Ablnutzung, Abnützung** die wear.

**Abo** (pl -s) das fam abk für **Abonnement**.

**Abonnement** [abɔnəˈmãː] (pl -s) das - **1.** [einer Zeitung] subscription - **2.** [im Theater] season ticket.

**abonnieren** vt to subscribe to.

**ablordnen** vt to send.

**Ablordnung** die delegation.

**ablpacken** vt to pre-pack.

**ablpassen** vt - **1.** [Person] to catch - **2.** [Moment] to wait for.

**ablperlen** (perf ist abgeperlt) vi to drip off.

**ablpflücken** vt to pick.

**ablprallen** (perf ist abgeprallt) vi - **1.** [zurückspringen - Ball] to bounce back, to rebound; [ - Kugel] to ricochet - **2.** [Vorwurf, Worte]: **an jm** ODER **von jm ~** to make no impression on sb.

**ablputzen** vt to wipe.

**ablquälen** ➤ **sich abquälen** ref - **1.** [sich plagen]: **sich mit etw ~** to struggle with sthg - **2.** [sich abzwingen]: **sich** (D) **etw ~** to force sthg out.

**ablrackern** ➤ **sich abrackern** ref fam to slave away.

**ablraten** vi (unreg): **(jm) von etw ~** to advise (sb) against sthg.

**ablräumen** vt [Geschirr] to clear away; [Tisch] to clear.

**ablreagieren** vt: **etw an jm ~** to take sthg out on sb.
➤ **sich abreagieren** ref: **sich an jm ~** to take it out on sb.

**ablrechnen** vi [Kassiererin] to cash up; **mit jm ~** [zahlen] to settle up with sb; [sich rächen] to get even with sb ⬦ vt [abziehen] to deduct.

**Ablrechnung** die - **1.** [Bilanz, Rechnung] accounts (pl) - **2.** [Rache] reckoning.

**Abrede** die (ohne pl): **etw in ~ stellen** to deny sthg.

**ablregen** ➤ **sich abregen** ref fam to calm down.

**ablreiben** vt (unreg) - **1.** [Schmutz] to rub off

**- 2.** [Hände] to wipe **- 3.** [Kind, Hund] to rub down.

**Abreibung** (pl -en) die thrashing.

**Ablreise** die departure.

**ablreisen** (perf ist abgereist) vi to depart.

**ablreißen** (perf hat/ist abgerissen) (unreg) vt (hat) **- 1.** [Papier] to tear off **- 2.** [Haus] to pull down <> vi (ist) **- 1.** [Teil, Knopf, Etikett] to come off; [Faden] to break off **- 2.** [Kontakt] to break off.

**ablrichten** vt to train.

**ablriegeln** vt **- 1.** [verschließen] to bolt **- 2.** [Gelände] to cordon off.

**ablringen** vt (unreg): jm etw ~ to force sthg out of sb; sich etw ~ to force sthg out.

**Ablriss** der **- 1.** [Zerstörung] demolition **- 2.** [Darstellung] outline.

**ablrollen** (perf hat/ist abgerollt) vt (hat) [abspulen] to unwind <> vi (ist) **- 1.** [von einer Rolle] to unwind **- 2.** [ablaufen] to go **- 3.** sport to go into a roll.

**ablrücken** (perf hat/ist abgerückt) vt (hat) to move away <> vi (ist) [wegrücken]: von jm/etw ~ [sich entfernen] to move away from sb/sthg; [sich distanzieren] to distance o.s. from sb/sthg.

**Ablruf** der EDV retrieval.
➥ **auf Abruf** adv: auf ~ bereit stehen to be standing by.

**ablrufen** vt (unreg) EDV to retrieve.

**ablrunden** vt **- 1.** [Zahl, Summe] to round down **- 2.** [Ecke, Küche, Programm] to round off.

**abrupt** adj abrupt <> adv abruptly.

**ablrüsten** vi to disarm <> vt to get rid of.

**Abrüstung** die disarmament.

**ablrutschen** (perf ist abgerutscht) vi **- 1.** [wegrutschen] to slip **- 2.** [Schüler]: er ist in Mathematik abgerutscht his marks in mathematics have gone down **- 3.** [abgleiten]: in etw (A) ~ to slide into sthg.

**Abs. - 1.** abk für **Absender - 2.** (abk für **Absatz**) para.

**ABS** [aːˈbeːˈɛs] (abk für **Antiblockiersystem**) das ABS.

**ablsacken** (perf ist abgesackt) vi **- 1.** [sinken - Flugzeug, Druck] to drop; [ - Gebäude] to subside **- 2.** [Leistung]: sie ist in Chemie abgesackt her marks in chemistry have got worse.

**Ablsage** die **- 1.** [von Termin, Veranstaltung] cancellation **- 2.** [Zurückweisung]: eine ~ an jn/etw a rejection of sb/sthg; jm/einer Sache eine ~ erteilen to reject sb/sthg.

**ablsagen** vt to cancel <> vi to cancel; jm ~ to tell sb one can't come.

**ablsägen** vt **- 1.** [sägen - Baum] to saw down; [ - Brett] to saw off **- 2.** fam [entlassen] to axe.

**ablsahnen** fam vt to cream off <> vi to make a killing.

**Ablsatz** der **- 1.** [von Schuhen] heel; auf dem ~ kehrtmachen ODER umkehren fig to turn on one's heel **- 2.** [Verkauf] sales (pl); reißenden ~ finden to sell like hot cakes **- 3.** [im Text] paragraph.

**Absatzlmarkt** der market.

**ablsaufen** (perf ist abgesoffen) vi (unreg) **- 1.** salopp [im Wasser - Schiff] to go to the bottom; [ - Person] to go to a watery grave **- 2.** fam [Motor] to flood.

**ablschaffen** vt **- 1.** [Regelung] to abolish **- 2.** [aufheben] to do away with **- 3.** [weggeben] to get rid of.

**Ablschaffung** die **- 1.** [von Regelung] abolition **- 2.** [Aufhebung] doing away with **- 3.** [Abgabe] getting rid of.

**ablschalten** vi & vt [ausschalten] to switch off.

**ablschätzen** vt **- 1.** [Menge, Zahl] to estimate **- 2.** [Menschen] to weigh up.

**abschätzig** adj disparaging <> adv disparagingly.

**Abscheu** die ODER der disgust, revulsion; vor jm/etw ~ haben ODER empfinden to find sb/sthg disgusting.

**abscheulich** adj disgusting <> adv disgustingly.

**ablschicken** vt to post Br, to mail Am.

**ablschieben** (perf hat/ist abgeschoben) (unreg) vt (hat) **- 1.** [außer Landes] to deport **- 2.** fam abw [versetzen] to shunt off <> vi (ist) salopp abw [fortgehen] to push off.

**Ablschiebung** die deportation.

**Ablschied** (pl -e) der **- 1.** [Trennung, Weggehen] parting; zum ~ hat er alle geküsst he kissed everyone goodbye; von jm/etw ~ nehmen to say goodbye to sb/sthg **- 2.** [Entlassung] resignation; seinen ~ nehmen to resign.

**ablschießen** vt (unreg) **- 1.** [Flugzeug] to shoot down **- 2.** [Kugel, Gewehr] to fire; [Pfeil] to shoot; [Rakete] to launch **- 3.** [töten] to shoot **- 4.** [Körperteil]: ihm ist ein Bein abgeschossen worden his leg has been shot off **- 5.** fam [entlassen]: jn ~ to give sb the boot, to kick sb out.

**ablschirmen** vt to shield.

**ablschlachten** vt fam to slaughter.

**Ablschlag** der **- 1.** [Preisnachlass] reduction **- 2.** [Rate]: etw auf ~ kaufen to pay for sthg by instalments **- 3.** sport [Fußball] clearance (by goalkeeper); [in Hockey] bully-off; [in Golf] tee-off.

**ablschlagen** vt (unreg) **- 1.** [verweigern]: jm etw ~ to refuse sb sthg **- 2.** [abtrennen - durch Schneiden] to chop off; [ - durch Schlagen] to knock off.

**abschlägig** adj unfavourable <> adv: etw ~ bescheiden to refuse sthg.

**Abschlagslzahlung** *die* instalment.

**ablschleifen** *vt (unreg)* - **1.** [Ecke, Unebenheit] to smooth off - **2.** [Holz] to sand (down).

➤ **sich abschleifen** *ref* - **1.** [sich abnützen] to wear away - **2.** [Benehmen] to wear off.

**Abschleppldienst** *der* (vehicle) recovery service.

**ablschleppen** *vt* - **1.** [Auto, Schiff] to tow away - **2.** *fam* [Person] to pick up.

➤ **sich abschleppen** *ref fam:* **sich mit etw ~ to** struggle along with sthg.

**Abschlepplseil** *das* towrope.

**ablschließen** *(unreg) vt* - **1.** [Tür] to lock - **2.** [Tätigkeit] to finish - **3.** [Geschäft] to conclude; [Vertrag] to sign; [Versicherung] to take out - **4.** WIRTSCH to balance <> *vi* [mit etw enden]: **mit etw ~ to** finish with sthg; **mit der Vergangenheit ~ to** draw a line under the past; **mit Verlust ~ to** show a loss; **mit einem Diplom ~ to** graduate with a diploma.

**abschließend** *adj* concluding <> *adv* in conclusion.

**Ablschluss** *der* - **1.** [Ende] end; **zum ~ der Tagung spricht Professor Schulz** Professor Schulz will bring the conference to a close; **zum ~ kommen** to draw to a close - **2.** [von Geschäft] conclusion; [von Vertrag] signing; [von Versicherung] taking out - **3.** [Abschlusszeugnis von Hochschule] degree; **die Schule ohne ~ verlassen** to leave school without any qualifications.

**Abschlusslprüfung** *die* [in Schule] *school-leaving examination;* [an Hochschule] final ODER degree examination.

**Abschlusslzeugnis** *das school-leaving certificate.*

**ablschmecken** *vt* - **1.** [würzen] to season - **2.** [kosten] to taste.

**ablschmettern** *vt* to throw out.

**ablschmieren** *vt* - **1.** [Motor] to lubricate; [Fahrradkette] to grease - **2.** *fam* [abschreiben] to crib <> *vi fam* [Flugzeug] to nosedive; [Computer, Programm] to crash.

**ablschminken** *vt:* **jn ~ to** remove sb's make-up.

➤ **sich abschminken** *ref:* **sich ~ to** remove one's make-up; **das kannst du dir ~ fam fig** you can get that out of your head.

**ablschnallen** *(perf* hat/ist abgeschnallt) *vt (hat)* to unfasten <> *vi (ist):* **da schnallst du ab salopp fig** you'll be gobsmacked.

➤ **sich abschnallen** *ref* to unfasten one's seatbelt.

**ablschneiden** *(unreg) vt* - **1.** [Stück] to cut off - **2.** [Weg]: **jm den Weg ~ to** block sb's way - **3.** [Wort]: **jm das Wort ~ to** cut sb off <> *vi:* **gut/schlecht ~ to** do well/badly.

**Ablschnitt** *der* - **1.** [im Text, von Strecke] section

- **2.** [von Formular, Karte] detachable portion; [von Scheck] counterfoil; [von Eintrittskarte] stub - **3.** [Zeitraum] period - **4.** MATH segment.

**abschnittweise** *adv* in sections.

**ablschnüren** *vt:* **jm das Blut ~ to** cut off sb's circulation; **jm die Luft ~ to** strangle sb.

**ablschöpfen** *vt* - **1.** [von einer Flüssigkeit] to skim off - **2.** [Geld] to cream off.

**ablschotten** *vt:* **jn/etw gegen jn/etw ~ to** keep sb/sthg away from sb/sthg.

**ablschrauben** *vt* to unscrew.

**ablschrecken** *vt* - **1.** [abhalten] to deter; **er ist durch nichts davon abzuschrecken** he will let nothing stop him - **2.** [mit kaltem Wasser - Eier] to put into cold water.

**abschreckend** *adj* deterrent; **eine ~e Wirkung haben** to act as a deterrent.

**Abschreckung** *(pl* -en) *die* deterrent.

**ablschreiben** *vt (unreg)* - **1.** [kopieren] to copy - **2.** WIRTSCH [aufgeben] to write off.

**Abschreibung** *(pl* -en) *die* - **1.** [von Unkosten] writing off - **2.** [von Maschine, Auto] depreciation.

**Ablschrift** *die* copy.

**ablschrubben** *vt fam* [Boden, Rücken] to scrub; [Schmutz] to scrub off.

**ablschürfen** *vt* to graze.

**Ablschuss** *der* - **1.** [von Flugzeug] shooting down - **2.** [von Gewehr] firing; [von Rakete] launching - **3.** [von Wild] shooting.

**abschüssig** *adj* sloping.

**ablschütteln** *vt eigtl* & *fig* to shake off; **sie ließ sich nicht ~ I/we/etc** couldn't shake her off.

**ablschwächen** *vt* to lessen.

➤ **sich abschwächen** *ref* to grow weaker.

**ablschwatzen** *vt:* **jm etw ~ to** talk sb into giving one sthg.

**ablschweifen** *(perf* ist abgeschweift) *vi* [Gedanken, Blick] to wander; **vom Thema ~ to** digress.

**ablschwellen** *(perf* ist abgeschwollen) *vi (unreg)* - **1.** [Schwellung] to go down - **2.** [Geräusch] to fade (away).

**ablschwirren** *(perf* ist abgeschwirrt) *vi fam* to buzz off.

**ablsegnen** *vt fam* to sanction.

**absehbar** *adj* foreseeable; **in ~er Zeit** in the foreseeable future.

**ablsehen** *(unreg) vt* - **1.** [Folgen] to foresee; **das Ergebnis ist abzusehen** it's possible to tell what the result will be; **die Konsequenzen sind gar nicht abzusehen** there's no telling what the consequences will be - **2.** [nachmachen]: **jm etw ~ to** learn sthg by watching sb <> *vi* - **1.** [verzichten]: **von etw ~ to** refrain from sth**g - 2.** [ausnehmen]: **von etw ~** to ignore sthg; **sieht man davon ab, dass er taub ist, ist er kerngesund** if you ignore the fact that he's deaf, he's perfectly healthy **- 3.** [wollen]: **es auf etw** *(A)* **abgesehen haben** to be after sthg; **es darauf abgesehen haben, alle zu verärgern** to be intent on annoying everyone **- 4.** [ärgern]: **es auf jn abgesehen haben** to have it in for sb.

**ab|seifen** *vt* [Kind] to soap down.

**ab|seilen** *vt* to lower down on a rope.
➤ **sich abseilen** *ref* **- 1.** [mit einem Seil] to abseil **- 2.** *fam* [verschwinden] to leg it.

**ab sein** *(perf* **ist ab gewesen)** *vi (unreg)* **- 1.** [entfernt]: **dieses Dorf ist weit von allem ab** this village is far away from everything **- 2.** [abgetrennt] to have come off.

**abseits** *präp:* **~ eines Ortes** ODER **von einem Ort** away from a place ◇ *adv* out of the way; **sich ~ halten** to keep oneself to oneself.

**Abseits** *das* **- 1.** SPORT offside; **im ~ stehen** to be offside **- 2.** [Isolation]: **im ~ stehen** to be out in the cold; **ins ~ geraten** to be left out in the cold.

**ab|senden** *vt* to send off.

**Ab|sender** *der* **- 1.** [Person] sender **- 2.** [Adresse] *sender's name and address.*

**Absenderin** *(pl* **-nen)** *die* sender.

**ab|senken** *vt* to lower.

**ab|servieren** ['apzɛrviːrən] *vt* **- 1.** [Tisch, Geschirr] to clear away **- 2.** *fam* [Person] to kick out.

**ab|setzen** *vt* **- 1.** [herunternehmen - Hut, Brille] to take off **- 2.** [hinstellen, hinlegen] to put down **- 3.** [aussteigen lassen] to drop off **- 4.** [Betrag]: **etw von der Steuer ~ (können)** to (be able to) deduct sthg from one's tax **- 5.** [Ware] to sell **- 6.** [entmachten - König] to depose **- 7.** [Aufführung] to drop, to take off **- 8.** [Medikament] to come off **- 9.** [Kleidung] to trim.
➤ **sich absetzen** *ref* **- 1.** [fliehen] to take off **- 2.** [sich ablagern] to be deposited **- 3.** [sich entfernen]: **sich von etw ~** to pull away from sthg **- 4.** [sich abheben]: **sich gegen etw ~** to stand out against sthg.

**ab|sichern** *vt* to make safe.
➤ **sich absichern** *ref* to cover o.s.; **sich gegen etw ~** to protect o.s. against sthg.

**Ab|sicherung** *die* making safe; [durch Versicherung] cover.

**Ab|sicht** *die* intention; **es war nicht meine ~, dir zu schaden** I didn't mean to harm you; **mit ~** intentionally; **ohne ~** unintentionally; **in bester ~** with the best of intentions.

**absichtlich** *adj* deliberate, intentional ◇ *adv* deliberately, intentionally.

**absolut** *adj* absolute ◇ *adv* absolutely; **das gefällt mir ~ nicht** I don't like that at all.

**Absolution** *(pl* **-en)** *die* absolution.

**Absolutismus** *der* absolutism.

**absolutistisch** *adj* absolutist; [Herrscher] absolute.

**Absolvent, in** [apzɔl'vɛnt, ɪn] *(mpl* **-en;** *fpl* **-nen)** *der, die geh* graduate.

**absolvieren** [apzɔl'viːrən] *vt* [Kurs] to complete; [Prüfung] to pass.

**absonderlich** *adj* strange ◇ *adv* strangely.

**ab|sondern** *vt* **- 1.** [Sekret] to secrete **- 2.** [isolieren] to isolate.
➤ **sich absondern** *ref* to isolate o.s.

**Absonderung** *(pl* **-en)** *die* **- 1.** [von Sekreten] secretion **- 2.** [Isolation] isolation.

**absorbieren** *vt eigtl* & *fig* to absorb.

**Absorption** *(pl* **-en)** *die* absorption.

**ab|spalten** *vt* CHEM to separate.
➤ **sich abspalten** *ref:* **sich (von etw) ~** to break away (from sthg).

**ab|spannen** *vt* [Pferdewagen] to unhitch; [Pferde] to unharness.

**ab|specken** *vt* **1.** *fam* [abnehmen]: **er hat drei Kilo abgespeckt** he has lost three kilos **- 2.** [reduzieren] to slim down. ◇ *vi* **1.** *fam* [abnehmen] to lose weight **- 2.** [reduzieren] to slim down.

**ab|speichern** *vt* EDV to store.

**ab|speisen** *vt:* **jn mit etw ~** to fob sb off with sthg.

**abspenstig** *adj:* **jm jn/etw ~ machen** to lure sb/sthg away from sb.

**ab|sperren** *vt* **- 1.** [abriegeln] to seal off **- 2.** [verschließen] to lock.

**Ab|sperrung** *die* **- 1.** [Schranke, Sperre] barrier **- 2.** [Absperren] sealing off.

**ab|spielen** *vt* to play.
➤ **sich abspielen** *ref* to take place.

**Ab|sprache** *die* arrangement; **nach vorheriger ~** after prior consultation.

**ab|sprechen** *vt (unreg)* **- 1.** [vereinbaren] to agree on **- 2.** [verweigern, aberkennen]: **jm etw ~** [Recht] to deny sb sthg; [Fähigkeit] to deny that sb has sthg.
➤ **sich absprechen** *ref* to come to an agreement; **wir hatten keine Zeit, uns abzusprechen** we had no time to agree on our story ODER on what to say.

**ab|springen** *(perf* **ist abgesprungen)** *vi (unreg)* **- 1.** SPORT to jump **- 2.** [sich lösen] to come off **- 3.** *fam* [zurücktreten]: **von etw ~** to back out of sthg.

**Ab|sprung** *der* **- 1.** [Sprung] jump **- 2.** [Loslösung]: **den ~ schaffen** to make the break.

**ab|spulen** *vt* to unwind.

**ab|spülen** *vt* **- 1.** [Geschirr] to wash **- 2.** [Schmutz] to wash off ◇ *vi* to wash up *Br*, to wash the dishes *Am*.

**ab|stammen** *vi:* von jm/etw ~ to be descended from sb/sthg.

**Abstammung** *die* descent.

**Ab|stand** *der* [räumlich] distance; [zeitlich] interval; **50 Meter** ~ a distance of 50 metres; **von jm/etw** ~ **halten** to keep one's distance from sb/sthg; **von etw** ~ **nehmen** to decide against sthg; **mit** ~ by far.

**ab|statten** *vt:* **jm einen Besuch** ~ to pay sb a visit; **jm Dank** ~ to express one's gratitude to sb.

**ab|stauben** *vt* - **1.** [putzen] to dust - **2.** *fam* [mitnehmen]: **etw bei jm** ~ to get sthg off sb.

**ab|stechen** *(unreg)* *vt* - **1.** [Rasen] to trim the edges of; [Torf] to cut - **2.** [töten] to slit the throat of ◇ *vi:* **von jm/etw** ~ to stand out against sb/sthg.

**Abstecher** *(pl -) der* detour.

**ab|stecken** *vt* - **1.** [markieren] to mark out - **2.** [mit Nadeln] to pin.

**ab|stehen** *(perf* hat/ist **abgestanden)** *vi (unreg):* **von etw** ~ to stick out from sthg.

**abstehend** *adj:* **er hat ~e Ohren** his ears stick out.

**Absteige** *(pl -n) die* *fam abw* cheap and shabby hotel.

**ab|steigen** *(perf* ist **abgestiegen)** *vi (unreg)* - **1.** [hinunterklettern] to get off - **2.** SPORT to be relegated - **3.** [übernachten] to stay.

**Absteiger** *(pl -) der* SPORT relegated team.

**ab|stellen** *vt* - **1.** [Gerät, Strom, Wasser] to turn off - **2.** [Last] to put down; [Möbel] to store, to put; [Auto, Fahrrad] to park - **3.** [Missstand, Problem] to put an end to - **4.** [freistellen]: **jn zu etw** ~ to assign sb to sthg - **5.** [zuschneiden]: **etw auf etw** *(A)* ~ to gear sthg towards sthg.

**Abstell|gleis** *das* siding; **jn aufs** ~ **schieben** *fig* to sideline sb.

**Abstell|raum** *der* storage room.

**ab|stempeln** *vt* - **1.** [stempeln - Dokument] to stamp; [ - Briefmarke] to postmark - **2.** *abw* [anprangern]: **jn zu** ODER **als etw** ~ to label sb sthg.

**ab|sterben** *(perf* ist **abgestorben)** *vi (unreg)* to die off.

**Abstieg** *(pl -e) der* - **1.** [vom Berg] descent - **2.** [sozial, finanziell] decline - **3.** SPORT relegation.

**ab|stimmen** *vi* [wählen] to vote; **über etw** *(A)* ~ to vote on sthg ◇ *vt* - **1.** [einstellen]: **etw auf jn/ etw** ~ to adapt sthg to sb/sthg; [Farben] to match sthg to sb/sthg - **2.** [absprechen]: **etw mit jm** ~ to agree on sthg with sb.
➤ **sich abstimmen** *ref:* **sich mit jm (über etw** *(A))* ~ to agree (on sthg) with sb.

**Ab|stimmung** *die* - **1.** [Wahl] vote - **2.** [Koordinierung] coordination - **3.** [Absprache] agreement.

**abstinent** [apsti'nɛnt] *adj* [vom Alkohol] teetotal; [von Genuss] abstinent.

**Abstinenz** [apsti'nɛnts] *die* [vom Alkohol] teetotalism, abstinence; [von Genuss] abstinence.

**ab|stoßen** *vt (unreg)* - **1.** [wegdrücken] to push off - **2.** [verkaufen] to sell off - **3.** [anekeln] to repel - **4.** [abnützen - Farbe] to knock off.
➤ **sich abstoßen** *ref* to push o.s. off.

**abstoßend** *adj* repulsive ◇ *adv* repulsively.

**ab|stottern** *vt fam* to pay for in instalments.

**abstrahieren** [apstra'hiːrən] *vt geh* to abstract.

**abstrakt** *adj* abstract ◇ *adv* in the abstract.

**Abstraktion** [apstrak'tsjoːn] *(pl -en) die* abstraction.

**ab|strampeln** ➤ **sich abstrampeln** *ref fam* to flog o.s. to death.

**ab|streichen** *vt (unreg)* - **1.** [abziehen] to knock off - **2.** [säubern] to wipe.

**ab|streifen** *vt* - **1.** [ausziehen] to take off - **2.** [ablegen] to get rid of.

**ab|streiten** *vt (unreg)* to deny.

**Ab|strich** *der* - **1.** [Einschränkungen] reservation; ~**e machen** to make concessions - **2.** MED swab; [von der Gebärmutter] smear.

**ab|stufen** *vt* - **1.** [Löhne, Preise, Farben] to grade - **2.** [Haare] to layer.

**ab|stumpfen** *(perf* hat/ist **abgestumpft)** *vt (hat)* - **1.** [Subj: Lärm, Monotonie] to dull the senses of - **2.** [Subj: Leid, Schmerz] to harden ◇ *vi (ist):* **gegen etw** ~ to become inured to sthg.

**Ab|sturz** *der* crash.

**ab|stürzen** *(perf* ist **abgestürzt)** *vi* [Flugzeug & EDV] to crash; [Bergsteiger] to fall.

**ab|stützen** *vt* to support.
➤ **sich abstützen** *ref* to support o.s.

**ab|suchen** *vt:* **etw (nach jm/etw)** ~ to search sthg (for sb/sthg).

**absurd** *adj* absurd.

**Absurdität** *(pl -en) die* absurdity.

**Abt** *(pl* Äbte) *der* abbot.

**Abt.** *(abk für* **Abteilung)** dept.

**ab|tasten** *vt* to feel.

**ab|tauen** *(perf* hat/ist **abgetaut)** *vt (hat)* to defrost ◇ *vi (ist)* [Eis] to thaw; [Kühlschrank] to defrost.

**Abtei** *(pl -en) die* abbey.

**Abteil** *das* compartment.

**ab|teilen** *vt* to divide off.

**Abteilung¹** *die* - **1.** [einer Firma, im Kaufhaus] department - **2.** MIL unit.

**Abteilung²** *die* [Trennung] dividing off.

**Abteilungs|leiter, in** *der, die* departmental manager.

**ab|tippen** *vt* to type out *ODER* up.

**Äbtissin** (*pl* -nen) *die* abbess.

**ab|törnen** *vt salopp* to turn off.

**ab|tragen** *vt (unreg)* - **1.** [Erde, Steine - Subj: Wind, Wasser] to erode; [- Subj: Person] to remove *(layer by layer)* - **2.** [Kleidung] to wear out - **3.** [Schulden] to pay off.

**abträglich** *adj geh:* jm/einer Sache ~ sein to be detrimental to sb/sthg.

**Ab|transport** *der* transportation.

**ab|transportieren** *vt* to take away.

**ab|treiben** (*perf* hat/ist abgetrieben) *(unreg) vt (hat)* - **1.** [Kind]: sie will das Kind ~ she wants to have an abortion - **2.** [Boot] to drive off course <> *vi* - **1.** *(hat)* MED [Abort vornehmen] to carry out an abortion; [Abort vornehmen lassen] to have an abortion - **2.** *(ist)* [Boot] to be driven off course.

**Abtreibung** (*pl* -en) *die* abortion.

**ab|trennen** *vt* - **1.** [abschneiden - Coupon, Blatt] to detach; [ - Ärmel, Saum] to cut off - **2.** [abteilen] to divide off.

**ab|treten** (*perf* hat/ist abgetreten) *(unreg) vt (hat)* - **1.** [Schuhe] to wear out; [Absätze] to wear down - **2.** [Rechte] to relinquish; etw an jn ~, jm etw ~ to let sb have sthg <> *vi (ist)* [fortgehen] to make one's exit.

**Abtreter** (*pl* -) *der* doormat.

**Abtretung** (*pl* -en) *die* handing over.

**ab|trocknen** *vt* to dry; sich die Hände ~ to dry one's hands.

➥ **sich abtrocknen** *ref* to dry o.s.

**ab|tropfen** (*perf* ist abgetropft) *vi* to drip; das Geschirr ~ lassen to leave the dishes to drain.

**ab|tun** *vt (unreg)* to dismiss; etw kurz ~ to brush sthg aside.

**ab|tupfen** *vt* [Blut] to dab away; [Stirn] to mop.

**ab|verlangen** *vt:* jm etw ~ to demand sthg from sb.

**ab|wägen** *vt* to weigh up; zwei Dinge gegeneinander ~ to weigh up two things against each other.

**ab|wählen** *vt* - **1.** [Politiker] to vote out (of office) - **2.** [Schulfach] to drop.

**ab|wälzen** *vt:* etw auf jn ~ to shift sthg onto sb.

**ab|wandeln** *vt* to vary.

**ab|wandern** (*perf* ist abgewandert) *vi* - **1.** [fortgehen] to migrate - **2.** [Kapital] to be removed.

**Ab|wanderung** *die* - **1.** [von Arbeitskräften] migration - **2.** [von Kapital] removal.

**Ab|wandlung** *die* adaptation.

**Abwärme** *die* waste heat.

**ab|warten** *vt* to wait for; ich kann es kaum ~, in Urlaub zu fahren I can hardly wait to go on holiday <> *vi* to wait and see.

**abwärts** *adv* downwards; alle, vom Assistenten ~ everyone from the assistant down.

**abwärts gehen** *(perf* ist abwärts gegangen) *vi (unreg)* to get worse; seit er trinkt, geht es mit ihm abwärts since he started drinking he has gone downhill.

**Abwasch** *der (ohne pl)* washing-up *Br*, dishes *Am (pl);* das ist ein ~ *fig* that will kill two birds with one stone.

**abwaschbar** *adj* washable.

**ab|waschen** *(unreg) vt* - **1.** [Geschirr] to wash - **2.** [Schmutz] to wash off <> *vi* to wash up *Br*, to wash the dishes *Am*.

**Abwaschwasser** *das* dishwater.

**Ab|wasser** *das* [von Haushalt] sewage *(U);* [von Industrie] effluent *(U)*.

**Abwasser|reinigung** *die* [von Haushalt] sewage treatment; [von Industrie] effluent treatment.

**ab|wechseln** ['apvɛksl̩n] ➥ **sich abwechseln** *ref* to alternate; sich mit jm ~ to take turns with sb.

**abwechselnd** ['apvɛksl̩nt] *adv* alternately.

**Abwechselung** ['apvɛksəluŋ], **Abwechslung** ['apvɛksluŋ] (*pl* -en) *die* change; zur ~ for a change.

**abwechslungsreich** ['apvɛksluŋsraiç] *adj* varied <> *adv:* ~ essen to eat a varied diet.

**Abwege** *pl:* auf ~ geraten to go astray.

**abwegig** *adj* bizarre.

**Abwehr** *die* - **1.** [Widerstand] resistance; auf ~ stoßen to meet with resistance - **2.** SPORT & MIL defence.

**ab|wehren** *vt* - **1.** [Schlag, Angriff] to ward off - **2.** [Störung] to deter <> *vi* to refuse.

**ab|weichen** (*perf* ist abgewichen) *vi (unreg):* von etw ~ to deviate from sthg; seine Ansichten weichen von meinen ab his opinions differ from mine.

**abweichend** *adj* different.

**Abweichung** (*pl* -en) *die* deviation.

**ab|weisen** *vt (unreg)* - **1.** [ablehnen] to reject - **2.** [Person] to turn away.

**abweisend** *adj* unfriendly <> *adv* dismissively.

**ab|wenden** *vt (unreg)* - **1.** [wegdrehen]: den Kopf ~ to turn away; den Blick ~ to look away - **2.** [Unglück] to avert.

➥ **sich abwenden** *ref* to turn away; sich von jm/etw ~ to turn one's back on sb/sthg.

**ab|werben** *vt (unreg)* to lure away.

**ab|werfen** *vt (unreg)* - **1.** [von Flugzeug] to drop - **2.** [Geld] to bring in; **Gewinn** ~ to yield a profit.

**ab|werten** *vt* to devalue.

**ab|wertend** *adj* pejorative.

**Ab|wertung** *die* - **1.** [von Geld] devaluation - **2.** [Herabsetzung] debasement.

**abwesend** *adj* - **1.** [nicht anwesend] absent - **2.** [unkonzentriert] absent, absent-minded ◇ *adv* absently.

**Abwesende** *(pl -n) der, die* absentee.

**Abwesenheit** *die* absence; **in js** ~ in sb's absence; **durch** ~ **glänzen** *iron* to be conspicuous by one's absence.

**ab|wickeln** *vt* - **1.** [Schnur] to unwind - **2.** [Geschäft] to complete - **3.** [Institution] to wind up, to close down.

**Abwicklung** *(pl -en) die* - **1.** [Abschluss] completion - **2.** [Auflösung] winding up, closing down.

**ab|wiegen** *vt (unreg)* to weigh out.

**ab|wimmeln** *vt fam* to get rid of.

**ab|winken** *vi (unreg):* **ich wollte alles erklären, aber er winkte ab** I wanted to explain everything but he waved me aside.

**ab|wirtschaften** *vi* [Staat, Firma] to go to the wall.

**ab|wischen** *vt* - **1.** [Fläche] to wipe - **2.** [Dreck] to wipe off.

**Ab|wurf** *der* - **1.** [Werfen] dropping - **2.** [in Fußball] throw-out.

**ab|würgen** *vt fam* - **1.** [Motor] to stall - **2.** [beenden, unterdrücken] to stifle.

**ab|zahlen** *vt* to pay off.

**ab|zählen** *vt* to count ◇ *vi* to use a counting-out rhyme.

**Abzähl|reim** *der* counting-out rhyme.

**Ab|zahlung** *die* repayment; [Abzahlungsrate] instalment.

**ab|zäunen** *vt* to fence off.

**Ab|zeichen** *das* badge.

**ab|zeichnen** *vt* to draw.
◆ **sich abzeichnen** *ref* - **1.** [sich ankündigen] to emerge - **2.** [sich zeigen] to stand out.

**ab|ziehen** *(perf ist/hat abgezogen) (unreg) vt (hat)* - **1.** [Schürze, Mütze] to take off; [Schlüssel] to take out - **2.** [subtrahieren - Nummer] to subtract; [ - Betrag] to deduct - **3.** [Bett] to strip - **4.** [Soldaten] to withdraw - **5.** [veranstalten]: **eine Schau** ODER **Show** ~ *salopp* to make a fuss - **6.** [Tomaten] to skin - **7.** [drucken] to print (off); [kopieren] to copy - **8.** [Haut]: **einem Kaninchen die Haut** ~ to skin a rabbit ◇ *vi (ist)* - **1.** [Gas] to clear - **2.** *fam* [Person] to clear off.

**ab|zielen** *vi:* **auf jn/etw** ~ to be aimed at sb/sthg.

**ab|zocken** *vt salopp:* **jn** ~ [ausnehmen] to fleece sb; [beim Kartenspielen] to clean sb out.

**Ab|zug** *der* - **1.** [von Kamin] flue; [Belüftung] vent - **2.** [Foto] print; [Druck] proof - **3.** [Subtraktion] deduction; **nach** ~ **der Unkosten** after costs - **4.** [Fortgehen] withdrawal; **jm freien** ~ **gewähren** to grant sb free passage - **5.** [von Wetter] moving away - **6.** [am Gewehr] trigger.

**abzüglich** *präp:* ~ **einer Sache** *(G)* less sthg.

**ab|zweigen** *(perf hat/ist abgezweigt) vi (ist)* to branch off ◇ *vt (hat)* to put aside.

**Abzweigung** *(pl -en) die* turning.

**Accessoire** [aksɛ'sŏaːʀ] *(pl -s) das* accessory.

**ach** *interj* oh!; ~ **deshalb!** oh, that's why!; ~ **ja/ nein!** oh, yes/no!; ~ **so!** (oh,) I see!

**Ach** *das:* ~ **und Weh schreien** to scream blue murder; **mit** ~ **und Krach** *fam* by the skin of one's teeth.

**Achse** ['aksə] *(pl -n) die* - **1.** [Linie & MATH] axis; **auf** ~ **sein** *fig* to be on the move - **2.** [von Auto] axle.

**Achsel** ['aksl] *(pl -n) die* shoulder; **mit den** ~**n zucken** to shrug one's shoulders.

**Achsel|höhle** *die* armpit.

**achselzuckend** ['akslˌtsʊknt] *adv* with a shrug.

**Achsen|bruch** ['aksnˌbʀʊx] *der* broken axle.

**acht** *num* eight; *siehe auch* **sechs**.

**Acht**[1] ◆ **außer Acht** *adv:* **etw außer** ~ **lassen** to disregard sthg.
◆ **in Acht** *adv:* **sich in** ~ **nehmen** to be careful; **sich vor etw** *(D)* **in** ~ **nehmen** to watch out for sthg.
◆ **Acht geben** *vi (unreg)* to take care; **auf jn/ etw** ~ **geben** to look after sb/sthg.

**Acht**[2] *(pl -en) die* eight; *siehe auch* **Sechs**.

**achtbar** *adj geh* [Leistung] worthy; [Person] respectable.

**Achte** *(pl -n) der, die, das* eighth; *siehe auch* **Sechste**.

**achte, r, s** *adj* eighth; *siehe auch* **sechste**.

**Achteck** *(pl -e) das* octagon.

**achteckig** *adj* octagonal.

**achtel** *adj (unver)* eighth; *siehe auch* **sechstel**.

**Achtel** *(pl -) das* - **1.** [der achte Teil] eighth - **2.** MUS quaver *Br,* eighth note *Am; siehe auch* **Sechstel**.

**Achtel|finale** *das* SPORT last sixteen.

**achteln** *vt* to divide into eight.

**achten** *vt* to respect ◇ *vi:* **auf etw** ~ to pay attention to sthg; **auf jn** ~ to look after sb.

**ächten** *vt* to ostracize.

**Achter** *(pl -) der* SPORT eight.

**Achter|bahn** *die* roller coaster.

**achtern** *adv* SCHIFF aft, astern.

**achtfach** *adj* eightfold ◇ *adv* eight times.

**Acht geben** *vi* ▷ **Acht**.

**achthundert** *num* eight hundred.

**achtkantig** *adv:* jn ~ hinauswerfen *fam* to throw sb out on his/her ear.

**achtlos** *adj* careless ◇ *adv* carelessly.

**achtmal** *adv* eight times.

**achtsam** *geh adj* - **1.** [aufmerksam] attentive - **2.** [vorsichtig] careful ◇ *adv* - **1.** [aufmerksam] attentively - **2.** [vorsichtig] carefully.

**Achtstunden|tag** *der* eight-hour day.

**achttausend** *num* eight thousand.

**Achtundsechziger** (*pl* -) *der person who took part in the student protests of 1968.*

**Achtung** *die* - **1.** [Respekt] respect; alle ~! well done! - **2.** [Vorsicht]: **Achtung!** look out!; [formell] attention, please!; ~, **Stufe!** mind the step!; ~, **fertig, los!** SPORT on your marks, get set, go!

**achtzehn** *num* eighteen; *siehe auch* **sechs**.

**Achtzehn** (*pl* -en) *die* eighteen; *siehe auch* **Sechs**.

**achtzig** *num* eighty; **auf ~ sein** *fam* to be livid; **jn auf ~ bringen** *fam* to make sb livid; *siehe auch* **sechs**.

**Achtzig** *die* eighty; *siehe auch* **Sechs**.

**Achtziger|jahre, achtziger Jahre** *pl:* die ~ the eighties.

**ächzen** *vi* to groan.

**Acker** (*pl* Äcker) *der* field.

**Ackerbau** *der* agriculture; ~ **treiben** to farm.

**Action** ['ɛkʃ(ə)n] *die* action.

**a. d.** (*abk für* **an der**): ~ **Donau** on the Danube.

**a. D.** (*abk für* **außer Dienst**) retd.

**A. D.** (*abk für* **Anno Domini**) A.D.

**ADAC** [a:de:'a:'tse:] (*abk für* **Allgemeiner Deutscher Automobilklub**) *der* ≈ AA *Br*, ≈ AAA *Am*.

**Adam:** **bei ~ und Eva anfangen** *fam* to begin right at the beginning.

**Adams|apfel** *der* Adam's apple.

**Adapter** (*pl* -) *der* ELEKTR adapter.

**adäquat** *adj* appropriate ◇ *adv* appropriately.

**addieren** *vt* MATH to add up.
⮑ **sich addieren** *ref:* **sich auf etw** (A) ~ to add up to sthg.

**Addition** (*pl* -en) *die* MATH addition.

**ade** *adv Süddt* cheerio.

**Adel** *der* nobility.

**adelig** = **adlig**.

**Ader** (*pl* -n) *die* vein; **eine künstlerische ~ haben** *fig* to have an artistic streak.

**Aderlass** (*pl* -lässe) *der* - **1.** [Blutentnahme] bleeding, bloodletting - **2.** *geh* [Verlust] terrible loss.

**ADFC** (*abk für* **Allgemeiner Deutscher Fahrrad-Club**) *der German cycling club.*

**Adj.** (*abk für* **Adjektiv**) adj.

**Adjektiv** (*pl* -e) *das* adjective.

**adjektivisch** ['atjɛkti:vɪʃ] GRAM *adj* adjectival ◇ *adv* adjectivally.

**Adjutant** (*pl* -en) *der* MIL adjutant.

**Adler** (*pl* -) *der* eagle.

**adlig, adelig** *adj* noble.

**Adlige** (*pl* -n) *der, die* nobleman (*f* noblewoman).

**Admiral** (*pl* -e ODER Admiräle) *der* MIL admiral.

**adoptieren** *vt* to adopt.

**Adoption** (*pl* -en) *die* adoption.

**Adoptiveltern** *pl* adoptive parents.

**Adoptiv|kind** *das* adopted child.

**Adressat** (*pl* -en) *der* addressee.

**Adress|buch** *das* - **1.** [privat] address book - **2.** [von Stadt, Gemeinde] directory.

**Adresse** (*pl* -n) *die* address; **an die falsche ~ kommen** ODER **geraten** to go to the wrong person; **sich an die richtige ~ wenden** to turn to the right person.

**adressieren** *vt* to address; **etw an jn ~** to address sthg to sb.

**adrett** *adj* smart ◇ *adv* smartly.

**Adria** *die:* **die ~** the Adriatic.

**A-Dur** *das* MUS A major.

**Adv.** (*abk für* **Adverb**) adv.

**Advent** [at'vɛnt] *der* Advent; **erster/zweiter ~** first/second Sunday in Advent.

**ADVENT**

Advent, the four weeks preceding Christmas, has a special significance in Germany and many traditions are associated with this time of year. A wreath with four candles (one of which is lit each Sunday during Advent) is hung in houses, churches and even offices and is an apt symbol of the seasonal atmosphere that prevails during this period. Advent is also however a time of intense consumerism in Germany.

**Advents|kranz** *der* Advent wreath.

**Adverb** [at'vɛrp] (*pl* -ien) *das* adverb.

**adverbial** [atvɛr'bja:l] GRAM *adj* adverbial ◇ *adv* adverbially.

**Adverbial|bestimmung** *die* GRAM adverbial qualification.

**Aerobic** [ɛ'ro:bik] *das* aerobics (*U*).

**Aerodynamik** *die* aerodynamics *(U).*

**Affäre** (*pl* -n) *die* - **1.** [Skandal, Liebschaft] affair; **sich aus der ~ ziehen** to get out of it - **2.** [Angelegenheit] matter.

**Affe** (*pl* -n) *der* - **1.** [Tier - klein] monkey; [ - groß] ape; **(ich denke,) mich laust der ~!** *fam* well, I'll be damned! - **2.** *salopp abw* [blöder Kerl] jerk, twit *Br.*

**Affekt** (*pl* -e) *der*: **im ~ handeln** *amt* to act under emotional stress.

**affektiert** *abw adj* affected ◇ *adv* affectedly.

**Affentheater** *das fam abw* to-do.

**affig** *fam abw adj* stuck-up ◇ *adv* in a stuck-up way.

**Afghane** (*pl* -n) *der* - **1.** [Person] Afghan - **2.** [Hund] Afghan hound.

**Afghanin** (*pl* -nen) *die* Afghan.

**afghanisch** *adj* Afghan.

**Afghanistan** *nt* Afghanistan.

**Afrika** *nt* Africa.

**Afrikaner, in** (*mpl* -; *fpl* -nen) *der, die* African.

**afrikanisch** *adj* African.

**After** (*pl* -) *der* anus.

**AG** [aːˈɡeː] (*pl* -s) *(abk für* **Aktiengesellschaft**) *die* ≃ plc *Br*, ≃ corp. *Am.*

**Ägäis** *die*: **die ~** the Aegean.

**Agave** [aˈɡaːvə] (*pl* -n) *die* agave.

**Agens** *das* - **1.** [Kraft] driving force - **2.** GRAM agent.

**Agent, in** (*mpl* -en; *fpl* -nen) *der, die* - **1.** [Spion] secret agent - **2.** [Vermittler] agent.

**Agentur** (*pl* -en) *die* agency.

**Aggregat** (*pl* -e) *das* unit.

**Aggregatzustand** *der* CHEM state.

**Aggression** (*pl* -en) *die* aggression.

**aggressiv** *adj* aggressive ◇ *adv* aggressively.

**agieren** *vi geh* to act.

**agil** *adj geh* [körperlich] agile; [geistig] sharp.

**Agitator** (*pl* **Agitatoren**) *der* agitator.

**agitieren** *vi*: **für/gegen jn/etw ~** to agitate for/against sb/sthg.

**Agrarpolitik** *die* agricultural policy.

**Agreement** [əˈɡriːmənt] (*pl* -s) *das* agreement.

**Ägypten** [ɛˈɡyptn̩] *nt* Egypt.

**Ägypter, in** (*mpl* -; *fpl* -nen) *der, die* Egyptian.

**ägyptisch** *adj* Egyptian.

**ah** *interj*: **ah!** [Ausdruck der Verwunderung] oh!; [Ausdruck plötzlichen Verstehens] ah!

**aha** *interj* aha!

**Aha-Erlebnis** *das* revelation.

**ahd.** (*abk für* **althochdeutsch**) OHG.

**Ahn** (*pl* -en) *der geh* forebear.

**ahnden** *vt geh* to punish.

**ähneln** *vi*: **jm/einer Sache ~** to resemble sb/sthg.

**ahnen** *vt* - **1.** [im Voraus fühlen] to have a premonition of - **2.** [vermuten] to suspect; **du ahnst es nicht!** *fam* would you believe it!

**ähnlich** *adj* similar; **jm/etw ~ sein** to be similar to ODER like sb/sthg ◇ *adv* similarly; **jm/etw ~ sehen** to look like sb/sthg; **das sieht dir/ihm ~!** that's just like you/him!

**Ähnlichkeit** (*pl* -en) *die* similarity; **mit jm/etw ~ haben** to look like sb/sthg, to be similar to sb/sthg.

**Ahnung** (*pl* -en) *die* - **1.** [Vorgefühl] premonition; **ich habe so eine ~, als ob ...** I have the feeling that ... - **2.** [Vorstellung, Vermutung] idea; **keine ~!** I've no idea!; **keine/nicht die geringste ~ haben** to have no/not the faintest idea; **hast du eine ~!** that's what you think!

**ahnungslos** *adj* unsuspecting ◇ *adv* unsuspectingly.

**Ahnungslosigkeit** *die* lack of suspicion.

**ahoi** *interj* SCHIFF ahoy!

**Ahorn** (*pl* -e) *der* maple.

**Ähre** (*pl* -n) *die* ear *(of corn).*

**ai** (*abk für* **Amnesty International**) AI.

**Aids** [ˈeidz] (*abk für* **Acquired Immune Deficiency Syndrome**) *nt* Aids.

**Aidskranke** *der, die* Aids sufferer.

**Airbag** [ˈɛːɐbɛk] (*pl* -s) *der* AUTO airbag.

**Airbus** *der* airbus.

**Akademie** (*pl* -n) *die* academy.

**Akademiker, in** (*mpl* -; *fpl* -nen) *der, die* university graduate.

**akademisch** *adj* academic.

**Akazie** (*pl* -n) *die* acacia.

**akklimatisieren** ⟿ **sich akklimatisieren** *ref geh* to acclimatize.

**Akkord** (*pl* -e) *der* chord.
⟿ **im Akkord** *adv* WIRTSCH: **im ~ arbeiten** to do piecework.

**Akkordarbeit** *die* piecework.

**Akkordeon** (*pl* -s) *das* accordion.

**Akkordlohn** *der* piece rate.

**Akku** (*pl* -s) *der* storage battery; [für Radio, Walkman] rechargeable battery.

**Akkumulator** (*pl* -en) *der* - **1.** ELEKTR storage battery - **2.** EDV accumulator.

**akkumulieren** *vt geh* to accumulate.

**akkurat** *adj* - **1.** [ordentlich] meticulous - **2.** [genau] precise <> *adv* - **1.** [ordentlich] meticulously - **2.** [genau] precisely.

**Akkusativ** (*pl -e*) *der* accusative.

**Akkusativlobjekt** *das* GRAM direct object.

**Akne** *die* acne.

**akribisch** *adj* meticulous <> *adv* meticulously.

**Akrobat, in** (*mpl -en; fpl -nen*) *der, die* acrobat.

**akrobatisch** *adj* acrobatic <> *adv* acrobatically.

**Akt** (*pl -e*) *der* - **1.** [Handlung, Aufzug] act - **2.** [Bildnis] nude - **3.** [Zeremonie] ceremony.

**Akte** (*pl -n*) *die* file; **etw zu den ~n legen** to shelve sthg.

**aktenkundig** *adj*: **ein ~er Vorgang** an occurrence which is on record.

**Aktenltasche** *die* briefcase.

**Akteur, in** [ak'tø:ɐ̯, rɪn] (*mpl -e; fpl -nen*) *der, die* player.

**Aktie** ['aktsiə] (*pl -n*) *die* share; **die ~n steigen/ fallen** share prices are rising/falling; **wie stehen die ~n?** *fam fig* how are things looking?

**Aktienlgesellschaft** *die* ≃ public limited company *Br*, ≃ corporation *Am*.

**Aktienlkurs** *der* share price.

**Aktion** (*pl -en*) *die* - **1.** [Tätigkeit] action; **in ~ sein/treten** to be in/go into action - **2.** [Verkauf] sale; [Werbung] promotion.

**Aktionär, in** [aktsio'nɛ:ɐ̯, rɪn] (*mpl -e; fpl -nen*) *der, die* shareholder.

**aktiv** *adj* active <> *adv* actively.

**Aktiv** *das* GRAM active.

**aktivieren** [akti'vi:rən] *vt* - **1.** [System, Alarm] to activate - **2.** [Person] to mobilize.

**Aktivierung** [akti'vi:rʊŋ] (*pl -en*) *die* - **1.** [von System, Alarm] activation - **2.** [von Person] mobilization.

**Aktivität** [aktivi'tɛ:t] (*pl -en*) *die* activity.

**aktualisieren** *vt* to update.

**Aktualität** *die* relevance; **an ~ gewinnen** to become topical.

**aktuell** *adj* - **1.** [Theaterstück, Buch] topical; [Thema, Problem] current - **2.** [modisch] fashionable.

**Akupressur** (*pl -en*) *die* acupressure.

**Akupunktur** (*pl -en*) *die* acupuncture.

**Akustik** (*ohne pl*) *die* - **1.** PHYS acoustics (*U*) - **2.** [Schallverhältnisse] acoustics *pl*.

**akustisch** *adj* acoustic <> *adv* acoustically.

**akut** *adj* - **1.** [vordringlich] urgent - **2.** MED acute <> *adv* - **1.** [vordringlich] urgently - **2.** MED acutely.

**AKW** [a:ka:'ve:] (*pl -s*) (*abk für* **Atomkraftwerk**) *das nuclear power station.*

**Akzent** (*pl -e*) *der* - **1.** GRAM [Betonung] stress - **2.** [Tonfall] accent - **3.** *RW:* **~e setzen** to set a new trend; **den ~ auf etw** (*A*) **legen** to lay particular stress on sthg.

**akzentfrei** *adj*: **er hat eine ~e Aussprache** he hasn't got an accent <> *adv* without an accent.

**akzeptabel** *adj* acceptable <> *adv* acceptably.

**Akzeptanz** *die* acceptance.

**akzeptieren** *vt* to accept.

**alaaf** *interj* cheer given during the Cologne carnival.

**Alabaster** *der* alabaster.

**Alarm** (*pl -e*) *der* - **1.** [Notsignal] alarm; **~ schlagen** to raise the alarm; **es war blinder ~** it was a false alarm - **2.** [Alarmzustand] state of alert.

**Alarmlanlage** *die* [von Gebäude] burglar alarm; [von Auto] car alarm.

**Alarmbereitschaft** *die*: **in ~** on standby.

**alarmieren** *vt* - **1.** [aufschrecken] to alarm - **2.** [rufen] to alert.

**Alarmzustand** *der*: **im ~** on standby.

**Alaska** *nt* Alaska.

**Albaner, in** (*mpl -; fpl -nen*) *der, die* Albanian.

**Albanien** *nt* Albania.

**albanisch** *adj* Albanian.

**Albatros** (*pl -se*) *der* albatross.

**Albdruck** *der* nightmare.

**albern** *adj* silly <> *adv* in a silly way <> *vi* to fool around.

**Albino** (*pl -s*) *der* albino.

**Albltraum** *der* nightmare.

**Album** (*pl* **Alben**) *das* album.

**Alchemie** *die* alchemy.

**Aldehyd** (*pl -e*) *der* aldehyde.

**Alemanne** (*pl -n*) *der* Alemannian.

**Alemannin** (*pl -nen*) *die* Alemannian.

**alemannisch** *adj* Alemannic.

**Alexandriner** (*pl -*) *der* alexandrine.

**Algarve**: **die ~** the Algarve.

**Alge** (*pl -n*) *die* - **1.** [Seetang] piece of seaweed; **~n** seaweed (*U*) - **2.** [Algenpest verursachend]: **~n** algae.

**Algebra** *die* algebra.

**Algerien** *nt* Algeria.

**Algerier, in** [al'ge:riɐ̯, rɪn] (*mpl -; fpl -nen*) *der, die* Algerian.

**algerisch** *adj* Algerian.

**Algier** ['alʒiːɐ̯] *nt* Algiers.

**Algorithmus** (pl -men) der algorithm.

**alias** adv alias.

**Alibi** (pl -s) das - **1.** RECHT alibi - **2.** [Ausrede] excuse.

**Alibilfunktion** die: eine ~ haben to be an excuse.

**Alimente** pl maintenance (U) Br, child support (U) Am.

**Alkali** das alkali.

**alkalisch** adj alkaline.

**Alkohol** (pl -e ODER Alkoholika) der - **1.** (pl Alkohole) CHEM alcohol - **2.** (pl Alkoholika) [Getränk] alcohol; **unter ~ stehen** amt to be under the influence (of alcohol).

**alkoholabhängig** adj: ~ **sein** to be an alcoholic.

**Alkoholeinfluss** der: **unter ~ under** the influence (of alcohol)

**alkoholfrei** adj alcohol-free.

**Alkoholgehalt** (pl -e) der alcohol content.

**Alkoholiker, in** (mpl -; fpl -nen) der, die alcoholic.

**alkoholisch** adj alcoholic <> adv alcoholically.

**Alkoholismus** der alcoholism.

**Alkohollvergiftung** die alcohol poisoning.

**all** det all (of); ~ **das Warten** all this waiting.

**All** das: **das ~** space.

**allabendlich** adj regular evening (vor Subst) <> adv every evening.

**alldem** = alledem.

**alle** (nt -s) det - **1.** [sämtliche] all; ~ **Kleider** all the clothes; ~ **beide** both (of them); ~ **fünf überlebten** all five survived; ~ **500 Angestellten** all 500 employees; **wir** ~ all of us - **2.** [verstärkend]: **in** ~**r Ruhe** in peace and quiet; **in** ~**r Öffentlichkeit** quite openly; ~ **Welt** everyone - **3.** [allerlei]: **Getränke** ~**r Art** all kinds of drinks; ~**s Mögliche** all kinds of things - **4.** [im Abstand von] every; ~ **50 Meter/zwei Wochen** every 50 metres/two weeks <> pron - **1.** [auf Personen bezogen] all, everyone; ~ **sind gekommen** everyone came, they all came; ~ **auf einmal** all at once; ~**s einsteigen!** all aboard! - **2.** [auf Sachen bezogen] all, everything; **das ist** ~**s** that's all ODER everything; **ich kann nicht** ~**s auf einmal tragen** I can't carry everything at once <> adj fam: **die Milch ist** ~ we've run out of milk.

➤ **trotz allem** adv in spite of everything.
➤ **vor allem** adv above all.

**alledem, alldem**
➤ **nach alledem** adv after all that.
➤ **trotz alledem** adv in spite of everything.
➤ **wegen alledem** adv for all those reasons.

**Allee** (pl -n) die [Straße] avenue.

**Allegorie** (pl -n) die allegory.

**allegorisch** adj allegorical <> adv allegorically.

**Allegretto** (pl -s ODER -gretti) das allegretto.

**Allegro** (pl -s) das allegro.

**allein** adj - **1.** [für sich] alone; **heute Abend war ich ~ zuhause** I was on my own at home this evening; **sie waren ~ im ganzen Kino** they were the only people in the whole cinema - **2.** [einsam] lonely <> adv - **1.** [für sich] alone - **2.** [selbstständig] on one's own, by oneself - **3.** [einsam] alone; ~ **zurückbleiben** to stay behind by oneself; ~ **herumstehen** to stand around on one's own; ~ **dastehen** to be all alone in the world - **4.** [nur] only; ~ **das Handgepäck wiegt 50 kg** the hand luggage alone weighs 50 kg; **schon ~ vom Fischgeruch wird ihm schlecht** the smell of fish alone is enough to make him ill <> konj geh however.

➤ **ganz allein** <> adj - **1.** [für sich] all alone - **2.** [einsam] all on one's own, all by oneself <> adv - **1.** [für sich, einsam] all alone - **2.** [selbstständig] all on one's own, all by oneself.
➤ **von allein** adv by oneself/itself.

**allein erziehend** adj: ~**e Mutter** single mother.

**Alleinlgang** der single-handed effort.
➤ **im Alleingang** adv single-handedly.

**Alleinlherrschaft** die autocratic rule.

**alleinig** adj sole.

**allein stehend** adj - **1.** [ledig] single - **2.** [allein wohnend]: **eine** ~**e Person** a person who lives alone.

**Alleinstehende** (pl -n) der, die - **1.** [ledig] single person - **2.** [allein wohnend] person who lives alone.

**allemal** adv fam: **dich schlage ich ~** I could beat you no sweat ▷ Mal.

**allenfalls** adv at most.

**allerbeste, r, s** adj very best.

**allerdings** adv - **1.** [als Antwort] certainly - **2.** [einschränkend] though.

**allererste, r, s** adj very first.

**Allergie** (pl -n) die allergy.

**allergisch** adj allergic; **gegen etw ~ sein** MED to be allergic to sthg; [etw nicht ausstehen können] not to be able to stand sthg <> adv - **1.** MED allergically; **auf etw ~ reagieren** to have an allergic reaction to sthg - **2.** [ablehnend]: **auf Lügen reagiere ich wirklich ~** I really can't stand people lying.

**allerhand** adj (unver) all sorts of; **das ist ja ~!** [erbost] that really is the limit!; [anerkennend] that's not bad at all! <> pron all sorts of things.

**Allerheiligen** *nt* All Saints' Day.

**allerhöchstens** ['ale'hø:kstn̩s] *adv* at the very most.

**allerlei** *det* all sorts of.

**allerletzte, r, s** *adj* - **1.** [letzte] very last - **2.** [schlecht] most awful.

**Allerletzte** *das:* **das ist ja das ~!** that's the absolute limit!

**allerliebste, r, s** *adj* - **1.** [Lieblings-] very favourite - **2.** [niedlich] delightful.

**allermeiste** *adj:* **die ~n Leute** the vast majority of the people.

**allerneuste, r, s** *adj* very latest.

**Allerseelen** *nt* (*ohne Artikel*) All Souls' Day.

**allerseits** *adv:* **guten Tag/Abend ~** good afternoon/evening everyone.

**Allerwerteste** (*pl* -n) *der hum* posterior.

**alles** ▷ **alle**.

**allesamt** *adv* all together.

**Alleslkleber** *der* all-purpose glue.

**Allgäu** *das:* **das ~** the Allgäu.

**allgemein** *adj* - **1.** [gen] general - **2.** [Interesse, Sprachgebrauch] common; [Wehrpflicht, Wahlrecht] universal ◇ *adv* generally.

➥ **im Allgemeinen** *adv* in general.

**Allgemeinbildung** *die* general education.

**allgemein gültig** *adj* universal ◇ *adv* universally.

**Allgemeinheit** (*pl* -en) *die* - **1.** [Öffentlichkeit] general public - **2.** [Undifferenziertheit] generality.

➥ **Allgemeinheiten** *pl* [Floskel] generalities.

**Allgemeinlplatz** *der* commonplace.

**allgemein verständlich** *adj* readily comprehensible ◇ *adv* in a readily comprehensible way.

**Allheillmittel** *das* cure-all, panacea.

**Allianz** (*pl* -en) *die* alliance.

**Alligator** (*pl* -gatoren) *der* alligator.

**alliiert** *adj* allied.

**Alliierte** *pl* allies; **die ~n** HIST the Allies.

**alljährlich** *adj* annual ◇ *adv* every year.

**allmächtig** *adj* almighty.

**allmählich** *adj* gradual ◇ *adv* gradually.

**allmonatlich** *adj* & *adv* monthly.

**allmorgendlich** *adj* regular morning (*vor Subst*) ◇ *adv* every morning.

**Allradlantrieb** *der* AUTO four-wheel drive.

**allseits** *adv* everywhere.

**Alltag** *der* everyday life; **der graue ~** the daily grind.

**alltäglich** *adj* - **1.** [täglich] daily - **2.** [üblich] everyday ◇ *adv* every day.

**Alltagstrott** *der* daily grind.

**allumfassend** *geh adj* comprehensive, all-embracing ◇ *adv* comprehensively.

**Allüre** (*pl* -n) *die abw:* **~n** airs and graces.

**allwissend** *adj* all-knowing, omniscient.

**allwöchentlich** *adj* weekly ◇ *adv* every week.

**allzu** *adv* far too.

➥ **allzu sehr** *adv* far too much.

➥ **allzu viel** *adv* far too much.

**Alm** (*pl* -en) *die* mountain pasture.

**Almanach** (*pl* -e) *der* almanac.

**Almosen** (*pl* -) *das* alms (*pl*).

**Aloe** ['a:loe] (*pl* -n) *die* aloe.

**Alpaka** (*pl* -s) *das* alpaca.

**Alpdruck** *der* = Albdruck.

**Alpen** *pl:* **die ~** the Alps.

**Alpenlveilchen** *das* cyclamen.

**Alpenlverein** *der organization which promotes study of the Alps and organizes mountain hikes etc.*

**Alpenlvorland** *das* (*ohne pl*) foothills (*pl*) of the Alps.

**Alpha** (*pl* -s) *das* alpha.

**Alphabet** [alfa'be:t] (*pl* -e) *das* alphabet.

**alphabetisch** *adj* alphabetical ◇ *adv* alphabetically; **~ geordnet** in alphabetical order.

**alpin** *adj* alpine.

**Alptraum** *der* = Albtraum.

**als** *konj* - **1.** [Zeitpunkt] when; **~ es dunkel wurde** when it got dark; **erst ~** only when - **2.** [Zeitspanne] as - **3.** [Vergleich]: **sie ist besser ~ ihr Bruder** she is better than her brother; **der Wein ist besser, ~ ich dachte** the wine is better than I thought it would be; **mehr ~** more than - **4.** [Vergleich vor Konjunktiv] as if, as though; **es sieht so aus, ~ würde es bald regnen** it looks like it's going to rain soon; **~ ob** as if, as though - **5.** [zur Kennzeichnung einer Eigenschaft] as; **ich verstehe es ~ Kompliment** I take it as a compliment; **~ Kind** as a child.

**also** *interj* well; **~ doch!** so I was right (after all)!; **~ gut** ODER **schön!** oh, all right then!; **na ~!** what did I tell you!, there you are!; **~ dann!** *fam* right then!; **~ bitte!** [Unmut ausdrückend] for heaven's sake!; [widerwillig nachgebend] if you must ◇ *adv* - **1.** [das heißt] that is - **2.** [demnach] so; **da lag ~ der Fehler!** so that's where the mistake was - **3.** [endlich] so; **die Sache ist ~ erledigt** so the matter is settled.

**Alsterwasser** (*pl* -wässer) *das Norddt* shandy.

**alt** (*kompar* älter; *superl* älteste) *adj* - **1.** [gen] old; **12 Jahre ~** 12 years old; **wie ~ bist du?** how old are you?; **zwei Jahre älter** two years older;

dieser ~e Schmarotzer! *abw* the old sponger! - **2.** [antik] antique - **3.** [historisch] ancient; ~e **Sprachen** classics, classical languages; das ~e **Rom** ancient Rome - **4.** *RW:* das wird nicht ~ *salopp* that won't stay here for long; ~ **aussehen** *salopp* to be up shit creek.

➤ **Alt und Jung** *pron* old and young.

**Alt** (*pl* -e *ODER* -) *der* (*pl* Alte) *MUS* alto ⟨⟩ *das* (*pl* Alt) [Bier] *type of dark German beer.*

**Altar** (*pl* Altäre) *der* altar.

**Altar|gemälde** *das* altarpiece.

**Altar|raum** *der* chancel.

**altbacken** *adj* - **1.** [alt] stale - **2.** [altmodisch] old-fashioned ⟨⟩ *adv* [altmodisch]: **sich** ~ **kleiden** to wear old-fashioned clothes.

**Altbau** (*pl* -ten) *der* old building.

**Altbau|wohnung** *die* flat *Br ODER* apartment *Am* in an old building.

**altbekannt** *adj* [Methode] well-known.

**altbewährt** *adj* proven.

**Alt|bier** *das type of dark German beer.*

**altdeutsch** *adj* [Stil] German Renaissance (*vor Subst*).

**Alte** (*pl* -n) *der, die* - **1.** [alter Mensch] old man (*f* old woman) - **2.** *salopp abw* [Elternteil, Gatte] old man (*f* old girl) - **3.** *salopp abw* [Vorgesetzter] boss, guvnor *Br* - **4.** [Gleiche]: **ganz der/die** ~ exactly the same ⟨⟩ *das* (ohne *pl*): **am** ~n **hängen** to cling to the past; ~**s und Neues** the old and the new; **alles beim** ~n **lassen** to leave everything just as it is.

**altehrwürdig** *adj* venerable.

**alteingesessen** *adj* long-established.

**Alten|heim** = Altersheim.

**Alten|hilfe** *die care for the elderly, provided by government, Church or other institutions.*

**Alten|pfleger, in** *der, die* nurse (*in old people's home*).

**Altentages|stätte** *die* old people's day centre.

**Alten|teil** *das portion of rights and property (usually farmland) retained for life by owner when handing over to his successor;* **sich aufs** ~ **zurückziehen** *fig* to retire.

**Alter** (*pl* -) *das* - **1.** [Lebensalter] age; **im** ~ **von 12 Jahren** at the age of 12; **eine Frau mittleren** ~**s** a middle-aged woman; **bis ins hohe** ~ **war er gesund** he remained healthy until a ripe old age - **2.** [Altsein] old age.

**älter** *adj* - **1.** ⊳ **alt** - **2.** [ziemlich alt] elderly.

**Ältere** (*pl* -n) *der:* **der** ~ the Elder.

**altern** (*perf* hat/ist gealtert) *vi* - **1.** [Person] to age - **2.** [Cognac, Käse] to mature.

**alternativ** *adj* alternative ⟨⟩ *adv* - **1.** [wahl-

weise] alternatively - **2.** [unkonventionell]: ~ **leben** to have an alternative lifestyle.

**Alternative** [alterna'ti:vəl] (*pl* -n) *die* alternative.

**alters** *adv:* **von** ~ **her** *geh* from time immemorial.

**Altersan|gabe** *die* age.

**altersbedingt** *adj* age-related.

**Alters|beschwerden** *pl* complaints associated with old age.

**Alters|genosse** *der* contemporary.

**Alters|genossin** *die* contemporary.

**Alters|grenze** *die* - **1.** [Höchstalter, Mindestalter] age limit - **2.** [Rentenalter] retirement age.

**Alters|gründe** *pl:* **aus** ~**n** for reasons of age.

**Alters|gruppe** *die* age group.

**Alters|heim, Altenheim** *das* old people's home.

**Alters|klasse** *die SPORT* age group.

**Alters|rente** *die* old age pension *Br,* social security *Am.*

**altersschwach** *adj* - **1.** [Person] old and infirm - **2.** [Gegenstände] decrepit.

**Alters|schwäche** *die* old age.

**Altersteil|zeit** *die optional system of reduced working hours for people over the age of 55.*

**Alters|unterschied** *der* age difference.

**Alters|versicherung** *die* old-age insurance.

**Alters|versorgung** *die* [privat] provision for one's old age; [vom Staat] provision for the elderly.

**Altertum** (*pl* -tümer) *das* [Antike] antiquity.

➤ **Altertümer** *pl* [antike Objekte] antiquities.

**altertümlich** *adj* - **1.** [antik] ancient - **2.** [altmodisch] old-fashioned ⟨⟩ *adv* in an old-fashioned way.

**Älteste** (*pl* -n) *der, die* - **1.** [ältestes Kind] eldest - **2.** [älteste Person] eldest person.

**altgedient** *adj* long-serving.

**Altglas** *das* glass for recycling.

**Altglas|container** *der* bottle bank.

**althergebracht** *adj* traditional.

**Althoch|deutsch** *das* Old High German.

**altklug** *adj* precocious ⟨⟩ *adv* precociously.

**ältlich** *adj* oldish.

**Alt|material** *das* scrap (*U*).

**Alt|metall** *das* scrap metal.

**altmodisch** *adj* old-fashioned ⟨⟩ *adv* in an old-fashioned way.

**Alt|öl** *das* oil for recycling.

**Alt|papier** *das* paper for recycling; **aus ~** made from recycled paper.

**Altpapier|container** *der* paper recycling bin.

**Altruismus** *der geh* altruism.

**altruistisch** *geh adj* altruistic ⋄ *adv* altruistically.

**altsprachlich** *adj* ⊳ **Gymnasium**.

**Alt|stadt** *die* old town.

**altvertraut** *adj* familiar.

**Altweiber|sommer** *der* Indian summer.

**Alu** *das fam* aluminium *Br*, aluminum *Am*.

**Alu|folie** *die* tinfoil *(U)*.

**Aluminium** *das* aluminium *Br*, aluminum *Am*.

**am** *präp* - **1.** *(an + dem)* at the; **~ Flughafen** at the airport; **das Schönste ~ Urlaub ist es, lange schlafen zu können** the nicest thing about holidays is being able to sleep in; **ich möchte ~ Ausflug teilnehmen** I would like to take part in the trip - **2.** *(nicht auflösbar)* [in geografischen Angaben]: **~ Meer** by the sea - **3.** *(nicht auflösbar)* [im Datum] on the; **~ Abend** in the evening; **~ Montag** on Monday; **~ 4. Oktober** on 4. October; **~ Anfang des Jahres** at the start of the year - **4.** *(nicht auflösbar)* [in Superlativen]: **~ schönsten** the most beautiful - **5.** *fam (nicht auflösbar)* [vor substantivierten Infinitiven]: **ich bin ~ Arbeiten** I am working; *siehe auch* **an**.

**Amalgam** *(pl -e) das* amalgam.

**Amateur** [ama'tø:ɐ̯] *(pl -e) der* amateur.

**amateurhaft** *abw adj* amateurish ⋄ *adv* amateurishly.

**Amateurin** [ama'tø:rɪn] *(pl -nen) die* amateur.

**Amateur|sportler** *der* amateur sportsman (*f* amateur sportswoman).

**Amazonas**: **der ~** the Amazon.

**Ambiente** [am'bi̯ɛntə] *das* ambience.

**Ambition** [ambi'tsi̯o:n] *(pl -en) die geh* ambition.

**ambitioniert** [ambitsi̯o'ni:ɐ̯t] *geh adj* ambitious ⋄ *adv* ambitiously.

**ambivalent** [ambiva'lɛnt] *adj* ambivalent ⋄ *adv* ambivalently.

**Amboss** *(pl -e) der* - **1.** [Schmiedegerät] anvil - **2.** MED incus.

**ambulant** MED *adj* outpatient ⋄ *adv* [behandeln] as an outpatient.

**Ambulanz** *(pl -en) die* MED outpatients' department.

**Ameise** *(pl -n) die* ant.

**Ameisen|haufen** *der* anthill.

**amen** *interj* amen!

**Amen** *das* [Zustimmung] blessing, approval; **es ist so sicher wie das ~ in der Kirche** you can bet your bottom dollar on it.

**Amerika** *nt* America.

**Amerikaner, in** *(mpl -; fpl -nen) der, die* American.

**amerikanisch** *adj* American.

**Amethyst** *(pl -e) der* amethyst.

**Ami** *(pl -s) der fam* Yank.

**Amino|säure** *die* amino acid.

**Ammoniak** *das* ammonia.

**Amnestie** *(pl -n) die* amnesty.

**amnestieren** *vt* to grant an amnesty to.

**Amöbe** *(pl -n) die* amoeba.

**Amok** *der:* **~ laufen** to run amok.

**a-Moll** *das* A minor.

**amoralisch** *adj* - **1.** [unmoralisch] immoral - **2.** [ohne Morale] amoral ⋄ *adv* - **1.** [unmoralisch] immorally - **2.** [ohne Morale] amorally.

**amorph** *adj* amorphous.

**amortisieren** *vt* - **1.** [Schulden, Hypothek] to pay off - **2.** [Kosten, Investitionen] to recoup.
➡ **sich amortisieren** *ref* to pay for itself.

**Ampel** *(pl -n) die* traffic lights *(pl)*; **rote ~** red light.

**Ampere** [am'pɛ:ɐ̯] *(pl -) das* amp, ampere.

**Amphibie** [am'fi:bi̯ə] *(pl -n) die* amphibian.

**amphibisch** *adj* amphibious.

**Amphi|theater** *das* amphitheatre.

**Ampulle** *(pl -n) die* ampoule.

**Amputation** *(pl -en) die* amputation.

**amputieren** *vt* to amputate; **jm das Bein ~** to amputate sb's leg.

**Amsel** *(pl -n) die* blackbird.

**Amsterdam** *nt* Amsterdam.

**Amt** *(pl Ämter) das* - **1.** [Behörde] department; [Gebäude] office; **von ~s wegen** on official orders - **2.** [Stellung] position; [wichtige politische oder kirchliche Stellung] office; **im ~ sein** to be in office; **sein ~ quittieren** to resign from one's post; **in ~ und Würden sein** *fig* to have a cushy number - **3.** [Pflicht] duty; [Aufgabe] task; **seines ~es walten** to carry out one's duties.

**amtierend** *adj:* **der damals ~e Bundeskanzler** the German chancellor in office at the time.

**amtlich** *adj* official ⋄ *adv* officially.

**Amtmann** *(pl -männer ODER -leute) der* senior civil servant.

**Amtmännin** *(pl -nen) die* senior civil servant.

**Amts|arzt, ärztin** *der, die* medical officer.

**Amts|bereich** *der* area of jurisdiction.

**Amts|deutsch** *das* (German) officialese.
**Amts|geheimnis** *das* official secret.
**Amts|gericht** *das* ≃ county court *Br*, ≃ district court *Am*.
**Amts|geschäfte** *pl* official duties.
**Amts|handlung** *die* official duty.
**Amts|schimmel** *der:* den ~ reiten to be very bureaucratic.
**Amts|sitz** *der* seat of office.
**Amts|sprache** *die* official language.
**Amts|weg** *der:* der Antrag geht den normalen ~ the application will go through the normal official channels.
**Amts|zeit** *die* term of office.
**Amulett** (*pl* -e) *das* amulet.
**amüsant** *adj* amusing ◇ *adv* amusingly.
**amüsieren** *vt* to amuse.
➡ **sich amüsieren** *ref* to have fun; **sich über jn/etw ~** [auslachen] to make fun of sb/sthg; [lustig finden] to find sb/sthg funny.

**an** *präp* - **1.** (+ D) [räumlich] at; **am Tisch sitzen** to be sitting at the table; **am See** by the lake; **~ der Wand** on the wall; **~ der Hauptstraße** on the main road; **der Ort, ~ dem wir gepicknickt haben** the place where we had a picnic; **Lehrer ~ einem Gymnasium** teacher at a grammar school - **2.** (+ A) [räumlich] to; **sich ~ den Tisch setzen** to sit down at the table; **etw ~ die Wand lehnen** to lean sthg against the wall - **3.** (+ D) [zeitlich] on; **am Freitag** on Friday; **~ diesem Tag** on that day; **~ Fulda 15.09** arriving at Fulda at 15.09 - **4.** (+ D) [stellt Bezug her]: **~ Krebs leiden** to have cancer; **~ etw zweifeln** to doubt sthg - **5.** (+ D) [aus dieser Menge]: **genug ~ Beweisen haben** to have enough proof - **6.** (+ A) [stellt Bezug her]: **~ jn denken** to think about sb; **sich ~ jn/etw erinnern** to remember sb/sthg - **7.** (+ D) [mit Hilfe von] with; **am Stock gehen** to walk with a stick; **jn ~ der Stimme erkennen** to recognize sb by their voice - **8.** (+ A) *fam* [ungefähr]: **~ die 30 Grad** about 30 degrees - **9.** *RW:* **~ und für sich** generally; **es ist ~ jm, etw zu tun** it's up to sb to do sthg; **~ sich in itself; sie hat etwas Faszinierendes ~ sich** (D) there's something fascinating about her ◇ *adv* - **1.** [elliptisch]: **Licht ~!** turn the light on!; **schnell den Schlafanzug ~!** quick, put your pyjamas on! - **2.** [zeitlich]: **von jetzt ~** from now on; **von heute ~** from today.

**Anachronismus** (*pl* -men) *der* anachronism.
**anachronistisch** *adj* anachronistic ◇ *adv* anachronistically.
**anal** *adj* anal.
**analog** *adj* - **1.** *geh* [ähnlich] analogous - **2.** EDV analogue ◇ *adv geh* analogously.
**Analogie** (*pl* -n) *die geh* analogy.

**Analphabet, in** (*mpl* -en; *fpl* -nen) *der, die* illiterate (person).
**Analyse** (*pl* -n) *die* analysis; [von Blut] test.
**analysieren** *vt* to analyse; [Blut] to test.
**Analytiker, in** (*mpl* -; *fpl* -nen) *der, die* [Psychoanalytiker] analyst.
**analytisch** *adj* analytical.
**Ananas** (*pl* - ODER -se) *die* pineapple.
**Anarchie** (*pl* -n) *die* anarchy.
**anarchisch** *adj* anarchic ◇ *adv* anarchically.
**Anarchist, in** (*mpl* -en; *fpl* -nen) *der, die* anarchist.
**anarchistisch** *adj* anarchistic ◇ *adv* anarchistically.
**Anästhesie** (*pl* -n) *die* anaesthesia.
**Anästhesist, in** (*mpl* -en; *fpl* -nen) *der, die* anaesthetist.
**Anatomie** (*pl* -n) *die* anatomy.
**anatomisch** *adj* anatomical.
**an|bahnen** *vt* [Geschäft, Treffen] to prepare; [Gespräch] to start.
➡ **sich anbahnen** *ref* to be on the way.
**Anbahnung** (*pl* -en) *die* preparation.
**an|bändeln** *vi fam:* **mit jm ~** to start going out with sb.
**An|bau** *der* - **1.** [Gebäudeteil] extension - **2.** [Bauen] building *(of extension)* - **3.** [von Pflanzen] growing.
**an|bauen** *vt* - **1.** [Gebäude] to add *(as an extension)* - **2.** [Pflanze] to grow.
**Anbau|möbel** *das* unit.
**an|behalten** *vt* (*unreg*) to keep on.
**anbei** *adv amt* enclosed.
**an|beißen** (*unreg*) *vt* to take a bite of ◇ *vi* - **1.** [Fisch] to bite - **2.** *fig* [Käufer] to take the bait.
**Anbeißen** *das:* **zum ~ sein** *fam* to look good enough to eat.
**an|bekommen** *vt* (*unreg*) - **1.** [Kleidung] to (manage to) get on - **2.** [Feuer] to (manage to) light.
**an|belangen** *vt:* **was jn/etw anbelangt** as far as sb/sthg is concerned.
**an|beraumen** *vt amt* to arrange.
**an|beten** *vt* to worship.
**Anbetracht** ➡ **in Anbetracht** *prep geh:* **in ~ einer Sache** (G) in view of sthg.
**an|betreffen** *vt* (*unreg*): **was jn/etw anbetrifft** as far as sb/sthg is concerned.
**Anbetung** (*pl* -en) *die* adoration.
**an|biedern** ➡ **sich anbiedern** *ref abw:* **sich bei jm ~** to curry favour with sb.

**an|bieten** vt (unreg) to offer.
➤ **sich anbieten** ref - **1.** [Mensch] to offer one's services; **sie bot sich an, uns die Stadt zu zeigen** she offered to show us round the city - **2.** [Sache]: **der Montag bietet sich als Termin für das Treffen an** Monday would be the best day for the meeting - **3.** [geeignet erscheinen]: **folgende Möglichkeiten bieten sich an** we have the following possibilities.

**Anbieter, in** (mpl -; fpl -nen) der, die supplier.

**an|binden** vt (unreg) to tie (up).

**An|blick** der sight.

**an|blicken** vt to look at.

**an|braten** vt (unreg) to brown.

**an|brechen** (perf hat/ist angebrochen) (unreg) vt (hat) - **1.** [Verpackung] to open - **2.** [Knochen] to crack - **3.** [Geldschein] to break into ◇ vi (ist) geh [Tag] to dawn; [Morgen] to break; [Nacht] to fall.

**an|brennen** (perf hat/ist angebrannt) (unreg) vt (hat) [mit Feuer] to set fire to ◇ vi (ist) [Essen] to burn; **nichts ~ lassen** fam fig never to let a single chance go by.

**an|bringen** vt (unreg) - **1.** [befestigen] to put up - **2.** [Kritik] to make - **3.** fam abw [mitbringen] to bring back.

**Anbruch** der [von Epoche] dawning; **bei ~ der Dunkelheit** when darkness falls/fell.

**an|brüllen** vt fam to bawl out; **gegen etw ~** to shout above sthg.

**Andacht** (pl -en) die - **1.** [Meditation] reverie; **in ~ versunken** lost in contemplation - **2.** [Gottesdienst] service.

**andächtig** adj reverent ◇ adv reverently.

**Andalusien** nt Andalusia.

**Andante** (pl -s) das mus andante.

**an|dauern** vi to continue.

**andauernd** adj continual ◇ adv continually.

**Anden** pl: **die ~** the Andes.

**Andenken** (pl -) das - **1.** [Erinnerung] memory; **zum ~ an jn/etw** in memory of sb/sthg - **2.** [Gegenstand, Souvenir] souvenir.

**andere, r, s** adj - **1.** [unterschiedlich] different; **wir sind ~r Meinung** we have a different opinion - **2.** [übrig, weitere] other ◇ pron: **der/die/das ~** the other (one); **ein ~r/eine ~** [bei Dingen] a different one; [bei Personen] someone else; **ich habe noch zwei ~** I've got two others; **unter ~m** among other things.

**andernfalls** = andernfalls.

**andererseits, andrerseits** adv on the other hand.

**andermal** ➤ **ein andermal** adv another time, some other time.

**ändern** vt to change; [Kleid] to alter; **das lässt sich nicht ~** there's nothing to be done about it; **das ändert die Sache** that changes everything.
➤ **sich ändern** ref to change.

**andernfalls, anderenfalls** adv otherwise.

**anders** adv - **1.** [andersartig, verschieden] differently; **sie sieht ganz ~ aus als ihre Schwester** she doesn't look at all like her sister; **~ ausgedrückt** put another way; **so und nicht ~!** this way only! - **2.** [sonst] else; **jemand/irgendwo ~** somebody/somewhere else; **niemand ~ als du** kann uns jetzt noch helfen only you can help us now ◇ adj different; **das muss ~ werden** this has got to change; **mir wird ganz ~** I feel weird.

**andersartig** adj different.

**Andersdenkende** (pl -n) der, die dissident.

**andersherum** adv the other way round.

**anders lautend** adj: **eine ~e Meldung** a report to the contrary.

**anderswo** adv elsewhere, somewhere else.

**anderswoher** adv from somewhere else.

**anderswohin** adv somewhere else.

**anderthalb** num one and a half.

**Änderung** (pl -en) die [gen] change; [an Kleid] alteration.

**anderweitig** adj other ◇ adv - **1.** [anderswo] elsewhere - **2.** [auf andere Weise] otherwise.

**an|deuten** vt - **1.** [ansprechen] to hint at; **~, dass ...** to hint that ... - **2.** [umreißen, skizzieren] to outline.
➤ **sich andeuten** ref to become clear.

**An|deutung** die hint; **eine ~ machen** to drop a hint.

**andeutungsweise** adv: **von etw sprechen** only to hint at sthg.

**An|drang** der crush; **es herrscht großer ~** there is a great crush.

**an|drehen** vt fam [verkaufen]: **jm etw ~** to flog sb sthg.

**andrerseits** = andererseits.

**an|drohen** vt: **jm etw ~** to threaten sb with sthg.

**An|drohung** die: **unter ~ von etw** under threat of sthg.

**an|drücken** vt to press on.

**an|lecken** (perf ist angeeckt) vi - **1.** [stoßen]: **an etw ~** to bang against sthg - **2.** [sich unbeliebt machen]: **bei jm/überall ~** to rub sb/everybody up the wrong way.

**an|eignen** vt: **sich** (D) **etw ~** [lernen] to pick sthg up; abw [nehmen] to take sthg (for o.s.).

**aneinander** adv [drücken, befestigen] together;

[reiben] against one another; [denken] about one another; **sich ~ gewöhnen** to get used to one another.

**aneinander fügen** *vt* to put together.
➤ **sich aneinander fügen** *ref* to fit together.

**aneinander geraten** (*perf* **ist aneinander geraten**) *vi* (*unreg*) to clash.

**aneinander grenzen** *vi* [Länder] to border on one another; [Gärten, Wohnungen] to be adjacent.

**aneinander hängen¹** *vi* (*unreg*) [verbunden sein] to be linked to one another <> *vt* (*reg*) [verbinden] to link together.

**aneinander hängen²** *vi* (*unreg*) [einander lieben] to be attached to one another.

**aneinander legen** *vt* to lay down next to each other.

**aneinander reihen** *vt* [Stühle, Kisten] to line up; [Worte, Sätze] to string together.
➤ **sich aneinander reihen** *ref* - **1.** [zeitlich] to follow one after the other - **2.** [räumlich] to be in a row.

**aneinander stoßen** (*perf* **hat/sind aneinander gestoßen**) (*unreg*) *vi* (*ist*) - **1.** [stoßen] to bump into each other - **2.** [grenzen] to border on each other <> *vt* (*hat*) [stoßen] to clink.

**Anekdote** (*pl* -n) *die* anecdote.

**anlekeln** *vt* to make sick.

**Anemone** (*pl* -n) *die* anemone.

**anerkannt** *adj* recognized.

**anlerkennen** *vt* (*unreg*) - **1.** [Leistung, Begabung] to acknowledge - **2.** [Meinung, Person] to accept - **3.** [Autorität, Staat, Vaterschaft] to recognize.

**Anerkennung** (*pl* -en) *die* - **1.** [von Leistung, Begabung] acknowledgement - **2.** [von Meinung, Person] acceptance - **3.** [von Autorität, Staat, Vaterschaft] recognition.

**anlfachen** *vt* to fan.

**anlfahren** (*perf* **hat/ist angefahren**) (*unreg*) *vt* (*hat*) - **1.** [bei Unfall] to run into - **2.** [Ziel] to approach - **3.** [Last] to deliver - **4.** [tadeln] to scold <> *vi* (*ist*) [losfahren] to start.

**Anlfahrt** *die* journey.

**Anfahrtslweg** *der* way (*to a place*).

**Anlfall** *der* fit; **einen ~ bekommen** ODER **kriegen** to have a fit.

**anlfallen** (*perf* **hat/ist angefallen**) (*unreg*) *vi* (*ist*) [Kosten] to be incurred <> *vt* (*hat*) [angreifen] to attack.

**anfällig** *adj*: **für etw ~ sein** to be prone ODER susceptible to sthg.

**Anlfang** *der* beginning, start; **~ April** at the beginning of April; **von ~ an** from the beginning ODER start; **den ~ machen** to begin, to start; **das ist der ~ vom Ende** this is the begin-

ning of the end; **von ~ bis Ende** from start to finish.
➤ **am Anfang** *adv* at the beginning; **am ~ des Zuges** at the front end of the train.
➤ **zu Anfang** *adv* at the beginning.

**anlfangen** (*unreg*) *vi* - **1.** [gen] to begin, to start; **mit etw ~** to start sthg, to begin sthg; **wer fängt mit dem Würfeln an?** who's going to throw first?; **das fängt ja gut an!** *iron* that's a good start!; **er fängt schon wieder an!** there he goes again! - **2.** [machen]: **er weiß nichts mit sich anzufangen** he doesn't know what to do with himself; **mit etw nichts ~ können** [verstehen] not to be able to get anywhere with sthg; [gebrauchen] not to be able to use sthg <> *vt* [beginnen] to begin, to start.

**Anfänger, in** (*mpl* -; *fpl* -nen) *der, die* beginner; **ein blutiger ~** a total beginner.

**anfänglich** *adj* initial <> *adv* initially.

**anfangs** *adv* at first.

**Anfangslbuchstabe** *der* [von Wort] first letter; [von Name] initial.

**Anfangslgehalt** *das* starting salary.

**Anfangslstadium** *das* initial stages (*pl*).

**anlfassen** *vt* - **1.** [berühren] to touch - **2.** [behandeln] to treat - **3.** [angehen] to handle <> *vi* [helfen] to lend a hand; **mit ~** to lend a hand.
➤ **sich anfassen** *ref* to feel.

**anlfechten** *vt* (*unreg*) [anzweifeln - Testament] to contest; [ - Urteil] to appeal against.

**Anfechtung** (*pl* -en) *die* [von Testament] contesting; [von Urteil] appeal.

**anlfeinden** *vt* to attack.

**Anfeindung** (*pl* -en) *die* attack.

**anlfertigen** *vt* [Anzug, Schrank] to make; [Bericht] to write; [Protokoll] to take down; **ein Porträt ~ lassen** to have a portrait done.

**Anfertigung** *die* (*ohne pl*) [von Anzug, Möbeln] making; [von Bericht] writing; [von Protokoll] taking down.

**anlfeuchten** *vt* [Lippen, Briefmarke] to moisten; [Haut] to moisturize; [Lappen] to wet.

**anlfeuern** *vt* to spur on.

**anlflehen** *vt* to beg.

**anlfliegen** (*perf* **hat/ist angeflogen**) (*unreg*) *vt* (*hat*) [Subj: Flugzeug] to approach; [Subj: Fluggesellschaft] to serve, to fly to <> *vi* (*ist*): **angeflogen kommen** to come flying up.

**Anlflug** *der* - **1.** [von Flugzeug, Hubschrauber]: **im ~ (auf etw (A)) sein** to be approaching (sthg) - **2.** [Spur] hint.

**anlfordern** *vt* to ask for; [per Post] to send off for.

**Anlforderung** *die* - **1.** [Bestellung] request - **2.** [Anspruch] demand; **~en stellen** to make demands; **einer ~ genügen** to meet a requirement; **den ~en eines Berufs gewachsen sein** to be up to the demands of a profession.

**Anlfrage** die amt enquiry.

**anlfragen** vi to enquire.

**anfreunden** ↠ sich anfreunden ref to make friends; **sich mit jm ~** to make friends with sb; **ich freunde mich langsam mit der Idee an** the idea is growing on me.

**anlfügen** vt to add.

**anlfühlen** vt to feel.
↠ **sich anfühlen** ref to feel.

**anlführen** vt - **1.** [nennen] to quote - **2.** [täuschen] to take in - **3.** [führen] to lead.

**Anlführer, in** der, die leader.

**Anlführung** die - **1.** [Zitieren] quotation - **2.** [Leitung]: **unter js ~** under sb's leadership.

**Anführungslzeichen** pl quotation marks, inverted commas.

**Anlgabe** die - **1.** [Hinweis] detail; **~n (über jn/etw) machen** to give details (about sb/sthg) - **2.** [Aufschneiderei] showing off.

**anlgeben** (unreg) vt - **1.** [nennen, zitieren - Personalien, Grund] to give; [ - Zeuge] to name - **2.** [bestimmen - Richtung, Kurs] to set - **3.** [behaupten] to claim, to allege ⬦ vi [aufschneiden] to show off; **mit etw ~** to show off about sthg.

**Angeber** (pl -) der show-off.

**Angeberei** (pl -en) die showing-off.

**Angeberin** (pl -nen) die show-off.

**angeberisch** adj [Person] boastful; [durch Gehabe, Verhalten] ostentatious ⬦ adv [mitteilen] boastfully; [sich verhalten] ostentatiously.

**angeblich** adj alleged ⬦ adv allegedly.

**angeboren** adj [Krankheit] congenital; [Talent, Abneigung] innate.

**Anlgebot** das - **1.** [Anbieten] offer; **~ und Nachfrage** supply and demand - **2.** [Sortiment] range; **etw im ~ haben** to offer sthg.

**angebracht** pp ⊳ anbringen ⬦ adj appropriate.

**angebrochen** pp ⊳ anbrechen ⬦ adj cracked.

**angebunden** pp ⊳ anbinden ⬦ adj: **kurz ~ sein** to be brusque.

**angegossen** adj: **wie ~ sitzen** fam to fit like a glove.

**angegriffen** pp ⊳ angreifen ⬦ adj [Gesundheit, Position] weakened.

**angeheiratet** adj: **eine ~e Cousine** a cousin by marriage.

**angeheitert** adj merry.

**anlgehen** (perf hat/ist angegangen) (unreg) vi (ist) - **1.** [Licht] to go on; [Feuer] to catch - **2.** [akzeptabel sein]: **es geht nicht an, etw zu tun** it's not

on to do sthg - **3.** [vorgehen]: **gegen jn/etw ~** to fight sb/sthg ⬦ vt (hat) [betreffen] to concern; **jn etwas ~** to concern sb; **das geht dich nichts an** it's none of your business.

**angehend** adj future.

**anlgehören** vi: **einer Sache (D) ~** to belong to sthg.

**Angehörige** (pl -n) der, die - **1.** [Verwandte] relative - **2.** [Mitglied] member.

**Angeklagte** (pl -n) der, die defendant.

**Angel** (pl -n) die - **1.** [zum Fischen] fishing rod - **2.** [Scharnier] hinge; **etw aus den ~n heben** fig to turn sthg upside down.

**angelaufen** pp ⊳ anlaufen ⬦ adj [Silber, Messing] tarnished; [Glas] steamed up.

**Anlgelegenheit** die matter; **kümmere dich um deine eigenen ~en!** mind your own business!

**angeln** vi - **1.** [fischen] to fish - **2.** [suchen]: **nach etw ~** [suchen] to fish around for sthg ⬦ vt - **1.** [fischen] to fish for; [fangen] to catch - **2.** [erobern]: **sich** (D) **jn ~** to land o.s. sb.

**angelsächsisch** [ˈaŋlzɛksɪʃ] adj Anglo-Saxon.

**angemessen** adj: (einer Sache (D)) **~** appropriate (to sthg) ⬦ adv appropriately.

**angenehm** adj pleasant ⬦ adv pleasantly; **(sehr) ~!** pleased to meet you!

**angenommen** pp ⊳ annehmen ⬦ adj [Kind] adopted; [Name] assumed.
↠ **angenommen, dass** adv assuming (that).

**angeregt** adj lively ⬦ adv: **sich ~ unterhalten** to have a lively conversation.

**angesagt** adj - **1.** fam [vorgesehen]: **was ist heute Abend ~?** what's the plan for this evening? - **2.** fam [notwendig]: **Vorsicht ist ~** we'd better be careful - **3.** fam [modern] in - **4.** [wichtig] important.

**angeschlagen** adj - **1.** [kaputt] chipped - **2.** [krank] groggy; **gesundheitlich ~ sein** to be in poor health.

**angesehen** pp ⊳ ansehen ⬦ adj respected.

**Angesicht** das: **im ~ einer Sache** (G) in the face of sthg; **von ~ zu ~** face to face.

**angesichts** präp: **~ einer Sache** (G) in view of sthg.

**angespannt** adj tense ⬦ adv closely.

**angestellt** adj: **~ sein** to be employed; **fest ~ sein** to have a permanent job; **bei Siemens ~ sein** to work for Siemens.

**Angestellte** (pl -n) der, die employee; [im Büro] white-collar worker.

**Angestelltenlverhältnis** das: **im ~ stehen** to be a salaried employee.

**angestrengt** adj [Miene] strained; [Versuch]

concerted ◇ *adv* [arbeiten, rudern, zuhören] hard.

**angetan** *pp* ⊳ **antun** ◇ *adj:* **von jm/etw ~ sein** to be keen on sb/sthg.

**angetrunken** *pp* ⊳ **antrinken** ◇ *adj* slightly drunk.

**angewandt** *pp* ⊳ **anwenden** ◇ *adj* applied.

**angewiesen** *pp* ⊳ **anweisen** ◇ *adj:* **auf jn/etw ~ sein** to be dependent on sb/sthg.

**an|gewöhnen** *vt:* **sich** *(D)* **~, etw zu tun** to get into the habit of doing sthg; **jm etw ~** to get sb used to sthg.

**An|gewohnheit** *die* habit.

**angewurzelt** *adv:* **wie ~ stehen bleiben** to stand rooted to the spot.

**Angina** *(pl* **Anginen)** *die* MED tonsillitis *(U);* **~ pectoris** angina.

**an|gleichen** *vt (unreg):* **etw einer Sache** *(D)* **~** to bring sthg into line with sthg.

**An|gleichung** *die* adjustment.

**Angler, in** *(mpl -; fpl -nen) der, die* angler.

**anglikanisch** *adj* Anglican ◇ *adv* [taufen] into the Anglican church.

**Anglist** *(pl -en) der* English scholar.

**Anglistik** *die (ohne pl)* English language and literature.

**Anglistin** *(pl -nen) die* English scholar.

**Angola** *nt* Angola.

**Angora|wolle** *die* angora (wool).

**angreifbar** *adj* open to attack.

**an|greifen** *(unreg) vt* **- 1.** [gen] to attack **- 2.** [Gesundheit] to affect **- 3.** [Projekt] to tackle **- 4.** [Vorrat] to draw on **- 5.** *Süddt* [anfassen] to touch ◇ *vi* to attack.

**Angreifer, in** *(mpl -; fpl -nen) der, die* attacker.

**an|grenzen** *vi:* **an etw** *(A)* **~** to border on sthg.

**An|griff** *der* attack; **etw in ~ nehmen** *fig* to set about sthg.

**Angriffs|fläche** *die:* **jm eine ~ bieten** to give sb scope for attack.

**angriffslustig** *adj* aggressive ◇ *adv* aggressively.

**angst** *adj:* **mir wird ~ und bange** I'm scared stiff.

**Angst** *(pl* **Ängste)** *die* **- 1.** [Furcht] fear; **vor jm/etw ~ haben** to be afraid of sb/sthg; **es mit der ~ zu tun bekommen** to get scared; **jm ~ machen** to frighten sb **- 2.** [Sorge]: **~ um jn/etw haben** to be anxious about sb/sthg.

**Angst|hase** *der fam abw* chicken.

**ängstigen** *vt* to frighten.

➡ **sich ängstigen** *ref:* **sich vor jm/etw ~** to be

frightened of sb/sthg; **sich um jn/etw ~** to be anxious about sb/sthg.

**ängstlich** *adj* nervous ◇ *adv* **- 1.** [furchtsam] nervously **- 2.** [genau] very carefully.

**an|gucken** *vt fam* [jn] to look at; [Fernsehsendung] to watch; **sich** *(D)* **etw ~** to look at sthg; [Fernsehsendung] to watch sthg.

**an|gurten** *vt:* **jn ~** to fasten sb's seat belt.
➡ **sich angurten** *ref* to fasten one's seat belt.

**Anh.** *abk für* **Anhang.**

**an|haben** *vt (unreg)* **- 1.** [Kleidung] to have on, to be wearing **- 2.** [Schaden]: **jm/einer Sache nichts ~ können** to be unable to harm sb/sthg.

**an|haften** *vi:* **jm/einer Sache ~** *fig* to stick to sb/sthg.

**Anhalt[1]** *der (ohne pl)* [Grund] grounds *(pl);* [Hinweis] clue.

**Anhalt[2]** *nt* Anhalt.

**an|halten** *(unreg) vi* **- 1.** [Fahrzeug] to stop **- 2.** [Zustand] to last ◇ *vt* **- 1.** [Bewegung] to stop; [Taxi] to hail; **den Atem ~** to hold one's breath **- 2.** [Person]: **jn zur Pünktlichkeit ~** to urge sb to be punctual.

**anhaltend** *adj* lasting.

**Anhalter** *(pl -) der* **- 1.** [Mitfahrer] hitchhiker; **per ~ fahren** to hitchhike **- 2.** [Einwohner von Anhalt] native/inhabitant of Anhalt ◇ *adj (unver)* of/from Anhalt.

**Anhalterin** *(pl -nen) die* **- 1.** [Mitfahrerin] hitchhiker **- 2.** [Einwohnerin von Anhalt] native/inhabitant of Anhalt.

**anhaltinisch** *adj* of/from Anhalt.

**Anhalts|punkt** *der* clue.

**anhand, an Hand** *präp:* **~ einer Sache** *(G)* with the aid of sthg.

**Anhang** *der (ohne pl)* **- 1.** [Nachwort] appendix **- 2.** *fam* [Familie] relatives *(pl);* **mit ~ auf einem Fest erscheinen** to go to a party with someone.

**an|hängen** *vt (reg)* **- 1.** [Wagen]: **etw an etw** *(A)* **~** [Waggon] to couple sthg to sthg; [Anhänger] to hitch sthg to sthg **- 2.** [Zeit]: **etw an etw** *(A)* **~** to tag sthg onto sthg **- 3.** [angebliche Schuld]: **jm etw ~** to pin sthg on sb ◇ *vi (unreg):* **einer Sache** *(D)* **~** to be an adherent of sthg.

**Anhänger** *(pl -) der* **- 1.** [von Fahrzeugen] trailer; [von Straßenbahn] carriage *(other than front carriage)* **- 2.** [Person - von Kandidat, Mannschaft] supporter; [ - von Sekte] member **- 3.** [Schmuck] pendant.

**Anhängerin** *(pl -nen) die* [von Kandidat, Mannschaft] supporter; [von Sekte] member.

**anhänglich** *adj* [Hund, Partner] devoted.

**Anhängsel** *(pl -) das* **- 1.** [Anhänger] small pendant **- 2.** *abw* [störende Person] hanger-on.

**an|hauchen** *vt* to breathe on.

**an|hauen** *vt fam* - **1.** [stoßen]: **sich den Kopf an der Schranktür ~** to bang one's head on the cupboard door - **2.** [anschnorren]: **jn um etw ~** to try to scrounge sthg off sb.

**an|häufen** *vt* to accumulate.
➡ **sich anhäufen** *ref* to pile up.

**Anhäufung** (*pl* -en) *die* accumulation.

**an|heben** *vt* (*unreg*) - **1.** [heben] to lift - **2.** [vergrößern] to raise.

**an|heften** *vt* to pin on.

**anheimelnd** *adj* homely.

**anheim stellen** *vt geh*: **jm etw ~** to leave sthg to sb's discretion.

**an|heizen** *vt* - **1.** [heizen] to light - **2.** [Stimmung, Diskussion] to liven up.

**an|herrschen** *vt* to shout at.

**an|heuern** *vt* - **1.** [Matrosen] to sign on - **2.** [Arbeitskräfte] to take on <> *vi* [auf einem Schiff] to sign on.

**Anhieb** ➡ **auf Anhieb** *adv* straight off.

**an|himmeln** *vt fam* to idolize.

**An|höhe** *die* rise.

**an|hören** *vt* - **1.** [hören]: **sich** (*D*) **etw ~** to listen to sthg; **etw mit ~** to overhear sthg; **ich kann das nicht mehr mit ~** I can't bear to listen to it any longer - **2.** [erraten]: **jm seine Freude/Wut ~** to hear the joy/anger in sb's voice - **3.** *amt* [Zeugen] to give a hearing to.
➡ **sich anhören** *ref* to sound.

**Anhörung** (*pl* -en) *die* hearing.

**Animateur, in** [anima'tøːʁ, rɪn] (*mpl* -e; *fpl* -nen) *der, die* activity organizer.

**animieren** *vt*: **jn zum Trinken ~** to persuade sb to have a drink.

**Anion** ['anjoːn] (*pl* -en) *das* PHYS anion.

**Anis** *der* aniseed.

**an|kämpfen** *vi*: **gegen jn/etw ~** to fight against sb/sthg.

**Ankara** *nt* Ankara.

**An|kauf** *der* purchase; **An- und Verkauf** buying and selling.

**an|kaufen** *vt* to buy.

**Anker** (*pl* -) *der* anchor; **vor ~ gehen/liegen** to drop/be at anchor.

**ankern** *vi* to anchor; [Anker werfen] to drop anchor; [vor Anker liegen] to be at anchor.

**an|ketten** *vt* to chain.

**An|klage** *die* - **1.** [vor Gericht] charge; **gegen jn ~ erheben** to bring a charge against sb; **unter ~ stehen** to be charged - **2.** [öffentlich] accusation - **3.** [Kläger] prosecution.

**an|klagen** *vt* - **1.** [vor Gericht] **jn (wegen etw) ~**

to charge sb (with sthg) - **2.** [öffentlich] to accuse.

**an|klammern** *vt*: **etw an etw** (*A*) **~** [mit Heftklammer] to staple sthg to sthg; [Wäsche] to hang sthg on sthg.
➡ **sich anklammern** *ref*: **sich an jn/etw ~** to cling to sb/sthg.

**An|klang** *der*: **(bei jm) ~ finden** to meet with (sb's) approval.
➡ **Anklänge** *pl*: **~ an jn/etw zeigen** to have echoes of sb/sthg.

**an|kleben** *vt* to stick.

**an|klicken** *vt* to click on.

**an|klingen** (*perf* ist angeklungen) *vi* (*unreg*) to be evident.

**an|klopfen** *vi* to knock.

**an|knüpfen** *vt* - **1.** [Seil]: **etw an etw** (*A*) **~** to tie sthg to sthg - **2.** [Gespräch] to strike up <> *vi* [Worte, Vorlesung]: **an etw** (*A*) **~** to take sthg up.

**an|kommen** (*perf* ist angekommen) *vi* (*unreg*) - **1.** [am Ziel] to arrive; **sie kommt mit dem Auto an** she's coming by car - **2.** [näher kommen] to approach - **3.** [mit Idee, Vorschlag]: **mit etw ~** to come up with sthg - **4.** [erfolgreich] to go down well; **bei jm gut/schlecht** ODER **nicht ~** to go down well/badly with sb - **5.** [sich durchsetzen]: **gegen jn/etw nicht ~** to be no match for sb/sthg - **6.** [wichtig sein]: **es kommt auf jn/etw an** it depends on sb/sthg; **es kommt darauf an** it depends; **es kommt mir vor allem auf die Qualität an** what matters to me is quality - **7.** [riskieren]: **es auf etw** (*A*) **~ lassen** to run the risk of sthg; **es darauf ~ lassen** to chance it.

**Ankömmling** (*pl* -e) *der* new arrival.

**an|können** *vi* (*unreg*) *fam*: **gegen jn/etw nicht ~** to be powerless against sb/sthg.

**an|kotzen** *vt salopp*: **jn ~** to make sb puke.

**an|kratzen** *vt* - **1.** [Oberfläche] to scratch - **2.** *fig* [Ruf] to tarnish.

**an|kreiden** *vt*: **jm etw ~** to hold sthg against sb.

**an|kreuzen** *vt* to mark with a cross.

**an|kündigen** *vt* to announce.
➡ **sich ankündigen** *ref*: **der Herbst kündigt sich an** autumn is on its way.

**An|kündigung** *die* announcement.

**An|kunft** *die* arrival; **planmäßige ~** scheduled time of arrival.

**an|kurbeln** *vt* to boost.

**Anl.** (*abk für* **Anlage**) encl.

**an|lächeln** *vt* to smile at.

**an|lachen** *vt* - **1.** [lachen] to look smilingly at - **2.** [erobern]: **sich** (*D*) **jn ~** to land o.s. sb.

**An|lage** *die* - **1.** [Park - städtisch] park; [ - von Schloss, Gebäude] grounds (*pl*) - **2.** [Gelände - militärisch] installation; [ - für Sport] facilities (*pl*)

**- 3.** [Geldanlage] investment **- 4.** [Schreiben]: **in der** ODER **als ~ amt** enclosed **- 5.** [Erbanlage]: **gute ~n zum Musiker haben** to be predisposed to become a musician **- 6.** [Bau] construction.

**Anlage|berater, in** der, die investment consultant.

**Anlass** (pl **Anlässe**) der **- 1.** [Grund] cause; **dazu gibt es keinen ~** there's no call for that; **etw zum ~ nehmen, etw zu tun** to use sthg as an opportunity to do sthg **- 2.** [Ereignis] occasion.

**an|lassen** vt (unreg) **- 1.** [eingeschaltet lassen] to leave on **- 2.** [starten] to start (up) **- 3.** [anbehalten] to keep on.

➤ **sich anlassen** ref: **sich gut/schlecht ~** to start well/badly.

**Anlasser** (pl **-**) der AUTO starter.

**anlässlich** präp: **~ einer Sache** (G) on the occasion of sthg.

**an|lasten** vt: **jm etw ~** [verantwortlich machen für] to blame sb for sthg; [Verbrechen, Charakterfehler] to accuse sb of sthg.

**An|lauf** der **- 1.** [Schwung] run-up; **~ nehmen** to take a run-up **- 2.** [Versuch] attempt.

**an|laufen** (perf **hat/ist angelaufen**) (unreg) vi (ist) **- 1.** [beginnen] to begin, to start; [Motor, Maschine] to start; [Film] to open **- 2.** [Körperteil]: **rot/blau ~** to go red/blue **- 3.** [Metall] to tarnish; [Fensterscheibe, Brille] to steam up **- 4.** [sich nähern]: **angelaufen kommen** to come running up ◇ vt (hat) [Hafen] to call at.

**Anlauf|stelle** die drop-in centre.

**Anlauf|zeit** die: **nachdem die ~ überwunden war, ...** once we were up and running, ...

**an|legen** vt **- 1.** [Garten, Park, Beet] to lay out; [Straße] to plan **- 2.** [Kartei, Sammlung] to start **- 3.** [Vorrat] to lay in **- 4.** [beabsichtigen]: **es darauf ~, etw zu tun** to be determined to do sthg **- 5.** [Geld] to invest **- 6.** [anlehnen]: **etw (an etw** (A)**) ~** to lay sthg (on sthg) **- 7.** [umbinden] to put on **- 8.** [Subj: Tier] to lay back; **die Ohren ~** to lay back its ears **- 9.** [Waffe] to raise to one's shoulder **- 10.** geh [anziehen - Geschmeide] to put on; **Trauer ~** to go into mourning ◇ vi **- 1.** [Schiff] to dock **- 2.** [mit Gewehr]: **auf jn/etw ~** to aim at sb/sthg.

➤ **sich anlegen** ref: **sich mit jm ~** to pick a fight with sb.

**Anlege|stelle** die mooring.

**an|lehnen** vt **- 1.** [Tür, Fenster] to leave ajar **- 2.** [an die Wand] to lean; **etw an etw** (A) **~** to lean sthg against sthg.

➤ **sich anlehnen** ref: **sich an etw** (A) **~** to lean against sthg; fig to draw upon sthg.

**Anlehnung** (pl **-en**) die: **der Film ist in ~ an eine Novelle entstanden** the film is based on a novel.

**an|leiern** vt fam to launch.

**Anleihe** (pl **-n**) die **- 1.** WIRTSCH loan **- 2.** [Kopie]: **bei jm/etw ~n machen** to borrow ideas from sb/sthg.

**an|leinen** vt to put on a lead.

**an|leiten** vt [Lehrling] to train; [Kind] to teach; **jn zu etw ~** to teach sb sthg.

**An|leitung** die **- 1.** [Hinweis] instruction; **unter js ~** under sb's guidance **- 2.** [Text] instructions (pl).

**an|lernen** vt to train.

**an|liefern** vt to deliver.

**an|liegen** vi (unreg) **- 1.** [sitzen]: **eng ~** to be tight **- 2.** fam [zu erledigen sein]: **was liegt heute an?** what do we have to do today?

**Anliegen** (pl **-**) das request.

**anliegend** adj **- 1.** [angrenzend] adjoining **- 2.** [sitzend]: **eng ~** tight-fitting.

**Anlieger** (pl **-**) der resident; **'~ frei**' 'residents only'.

**an|locken** vt [Kunden] to attract; [mit Köder] to lure.

**an|lügen** vt (unreg) to lie to.

**Anm.** abk für **Anmerkung**.

**an|machen** vt **- 1.** [Gerät] to turn on, to switch on **- 2.** [Salat] to dress **- 3.** salopp [ansprechen] to chat up Br, to hit on Am.

**an|malen** vt [bemalen] to paint.

➤ **sich anmalen** ref fam abw [sich schminken] to paint one's face.

**Anmarsch** der: **im ~ sein** to be on the way.

**an|maßen** vt: **sich** (D) **~, etw zu tun** to presume to do sthg.

**anmaßend** adj presumptuous.

**Anmelde|formular** das application form.

**an|melden** vt **- 1.** [beim Amt - Auto, Wohnsitz, Gewerbe] to register; [ - Fernseher] to get a licence for; [ - Patent] to apply for **- 2.** [Bedenken, Einwände] to register; [Wunsch] to make known **- 3.** [in Schule, Kurs] to enrol **- 4.** [zu Termin] to make an appointment for; **sind Sie für heute angemeldet?** do you have an appointment for today? **- 5.** [Besuch] to announce.

➤ **sich anmelden** ref **- 1.** [für Kurs] to enrol **- 2.** [zu Termin] to make an appointment.

**Anmeldung** die **- 1.** [beim Amt] registration; [eines Patents] application **- 2.** [in Schule, Kurs] enrolment **- 3.** [zu Termin] making an appointment **- 4.** [Rezeption] reception.

**an|merken** vt **- 1.** [spüren]: **jm etw ~** to notice sthg in sb; **sich** (D) **nichts ~ lassen** not to show one's feelings **- 2.** [sagen] to comment.

**Anmerkung** (pl **-en**) die **- 1.** [im Text] note **- 2.** [gesprochen] comment.

**an|mieten** vt to rent.

**anmutig** geh adj graceful ◇ adv gracefully.

**an|nageln** *vt* to nail on.

**an|nähen** *vt* to sew on.

**an|nähern** *vt* to bring closer.
➤ **sich annähern** *ref*: **sich einander ~** to approach one another.

**annähernd** *adv* nearly.

**Annäherung** (*pl* -en) *die* approach; **die ~ von Wallonien an Flandern** the rapprochement between the Walloons and the Flemish.

**Annahme** (*pl* -n) *die* - **1.** [Meinung] assumption; **in der ~, dass ...** on the assumption that ... - **2.** [von Paket, Brief] receipt; [von Geschenk] acceptance.

**annehmbar** *adj* acceptable ⬦ *adv* reasonably (well).

**an|nehmen** *vt* (*unreg*) - **1.** [empfangen, zustimmen, akzeptieren, zulassen] to accept; [Anruf] to take - **2.** [vermuten] to assume; **angenommen sie macht mit** assuming she helps - **3.** [Staatsangehörigkeit, Namen, Kind] to adopt; [Dialekt, Gewohnheit] to pick up - **4.** [Gestalt] to take on.
➤ **sich annehmen** *ref geh*: **sich js/einer Sache ~** to take care of sb/sthg.

**Annehmlichkeit** (*pl* -en) *die*: **~ en** [Vorteile] advantages; [Bequemlichkeiten] comforts.

**annektieren** *vt* to annex.

**Anno** *adv*: **~ dazumal** ODER **Tobak** the year dot; **~ Domini** Anno Domini.

**Annonce** [a'nɔ̃sə] (*pl* -n) *die* advertisement.

**annoncieren** [anɔ̃'siːrən] *vi* to place an advertisement ⬦ *vt* to advertise.

**annullieren** *vt* [Ehe] to annul; [Vertrag] to cancel.

**Anode** (*pl* -n) *die* anode.

**an|löden** *vt fam* to bore to tears.

**Anomalie** (*pl* -n) *die* anomaly.

**anonym** *adj* anonymous ⬦ *adv* anonymously.

**Anonymität** *die* (*ohne pl*) *geh* anonymity.

**Anorak** (*pl* -s) *der* anorak.

**an|ordnen** *vt* - **1.** [befehlen] to order - **2.** [Gegenstände] to arrange.

**An|ordnung** *die* - **1.** [Aufstellung] layout - **2.** [Befehl] order; **auf js ~** (A) on sb's orders; **~en treffen** to make arrangements.

**anormal** *adj* abnormal ⬦ *adv* abnormally.

**an|packen** *vt* - **1.** [mit Händen] to grab - **2.** [behandeln]: **jn hart ~** to treat sb harshly - **3.** [lösen] to tackle ⬦ *vi* [helfen]: **mit ~** to lend a hand.

**an|passen** *vt*: **etw einer Sache** (D) **~** to adapt sthg to sthg.
➤ **sich anpassen** *ref* to adapt.

**Anpassung** (*pl* -en) *die* adaptation.

**anpassungsfähig** *adj* adaptable.

**an|peilen** *vt* - **1.** SCHIFF & FLUG to take a bearing on - **2.** *fam* [anvisieren] to have one's sights on.

**an|pfeifen** *vt* (*unreg*) - **1.** SPORT: **ein Fußballspiel ~** to blow one's whistle to start a football match - **2.** *fam* [maßregeln] to have a go at.

**An|pfiff** *der* - **1.** [im Fußball] kick-off - **2.** *fam* [Tadel] ticking-off.

**an|pflanzen** *vt* to plant.

**an|pflaumen** *vt fam* to have a go at.

**an|pöbeln** *vt* to shout abuse at.

**an|prangern** *vt* to denounce.

**an|preisen** *vt* (*unreg*) [Waren] to tout.

**An|probe** *die* fitting.

**an|probieren** *vt* to try on.

**an|pumpen** *vt fam*: **jm um 100 Euro ~** to touch sb for 100 euros.

**an|quatschen** *vt fam* to chat up.

**Anrainer** (*pl* -) *der* neighbour.

**Anrainer|staat** *der*: **die ~en des Mittelmeers** the Mediterranean countries.

**an|raten** *vt* (*unreg*): **jm ~, etw zu tun** to recommend that sb do sthg.

**Anraten** *das*: **auf js ~** (A) on sb's advice.

**an|rechnen** *vt* - **1.** [einbeziehen] to take into account; **jm etw hoch ~** to think highly of sb for sthg - **2.** [berechnen] to charge for.

**An|recht** *das* - **1.** [Recht]: **ein ~ auf etw** (A) **haben** ODER **besitzen** to have the right to sthg - **2.** [Abonnement] subscription.

**An|rede** *die* form of address.

**an|reden** *vt* - **1.** [ansprechen] to speak to - **2.** [mit Titel]: **den Chef mit „Herr Professor" ~** to address the boss as "Professor"; **jn mit seinem Vornamen ~** to call sb by their first name.

**an|regen** *vt* - **1.** [beleben] to stimulate - **2.** [empfehlen] to propose - **3.** [ermutigen]: **jn ~, etw zu tun** to encourage sb to do sthg.

**anregend** *adj* stimulating ⬦ *adv* in a stimulating way.

**An|regung** *die* - **1.** [Belebung] stimulation - **2.** [Empfehlung]: **auf ~ von jm, auf js ~** (A) **(hin) at** sb's suggestion - **3.** [Anreiz] incentive.

**an|reichern** *vt* to enrich.

**Anreicherung** (*pl* -en) *die* enrichment.

**An|reise** *die* journey (there).

**an|reisen** (*perf* **ist angereist**) *vi* to travel (there).

**an|reißen** *vt* (*unreg*) - **1.** [einreißen] to tear - **2.** [erwähnen] to touch on.

**An|reiz** *der* incentive; **ein ~, etw zu tun** an incentive to do sthg.

**an|reizen** *vt* to stimulate; **jn ~, etw zu tun** to encourage sb to do sthg.

**anǀrempeln** *vt* to barge into.

**anǀrennen** *(perf* ist **angerannt)** *vi (unreg):* **gegen etw ~** [rennen] to run into sthg; **angerannt kommen** to come running up; **sich** *(D)* **das Schienbein an etw** *(D)* **~** *fam* to bang one's shin on sthg.

**anǀrichten** *vt* **- 1.** [Abendessen] to prepare **- 2.** [Schaden] to cause; **da hast du was Schönes angerichtet!** you've really gone and done it now!

**anǀrücken** *(perf* ist **angerückt)** *vi* **- 1.** [Truppen] to move in **- 2.** *fam* [auftauchen] to show up.

**Anǀruf** *der* call.

**Anrufbeantworter** *(pl* -) *der* answering machine.

**anǀrufen** *(unreg) vt* [telefonieren] to call, to phone ⬦ *vi* to call, to phone; **bei jm ~** to call *ODER* phone sb.

**anǀrühren** *vt* **- 1.** [berühren - Person, Gegenstand] to touch; [ - Thema] to touch on **- 2.** [rühren] to mix.

**ans** *präp (an* + *das):* **~ Fenster klopfen** to knock on the window; *siehe auch* **an.**

**Anǀsage** *die* announcement.

**anǀsagen** *vt* to announce; **jm/etw den Kampf ~** to declare war on sb/sthg.

⬦ **sich ansagen** *ref* to say (that) one is coming to visit.

**anǀsammeln** *vt* to collect.

⬦ **sich ansammeln** *ref* **- 1.** [anhäufen, anstauen] to pile up **- 2.** [versammeln] to gather.

**Anǀsammlung** *die* **- 1.** [Anhäufung] accumulation **- 2.** [Versammlung] gathering.

**ansässig** *adj* resident; **~ sein** to be resident.

**Anǀsatz** *der* **- 1.** [Anfang, Anzeichen] first sign; **im ~ stecken bleiben** to fall at the first hurdle; **gute Ansätze zeigen** to show promising signs; **er hat den ~ zu einem Bauch bekommen** he's started to develop a paunch; **einen ~ zu etw machen** to make a start on sthg **- 2.** [von Körperteil] base **- 3.** MATH formulation.

**anǀsaugen** *vt* to suck in.

**anǀschaffen** *vt:* **sich** *(D)* **etw ~** to get o.s. sthg ⬦ *vi fam* [Prostituierte]: **~ gehen** to be on the game.

**Anschaffung** *(pl* -en) *die* acquisition, purchase.

**Anschaffungsǀkosten** *pl* purchase cost *(U).*

**anǀschalten** *vt* to turn on.

**anǀschauen** *vt* to look at; **sich** *(D)* **etw ~** to have a look at sthg.

**anschaulich** *adj* clear ⬦ *adv* clearly.

**Anschauung** *(pl* -en) *die* **- 1.** [Meinung] opinion **- 2.** [Erfahrung]: **etw aus eigener ~ kennen** to know sthg from experience.

**AnschauungsǀmateriaI** *das* visual aids *(pl).*

**Anschein** *der* appearance; **dem** *ODER* **allem ~ nach** apparently; **es hat den ~, als ob** it looks like, it appears that; **den ~ erwecken, dass** to give the impression that.

**anscheinend** *adv* apparently.

**anǀschicken** ⬦ **sich anschicken** *ref geh:* **sich ~, etw zu tun** to get ready to do sthg.

**anǀschieben** *vt (unreg)* to push-start.

**anǀschießen** *(perf* hat/ist **angeschossen)** *(unreg) vt (hat)* **- 1.** [treffen] to shoot *(and wound)* **- 2.** *fam* [kritisieren] to have a go at ⬦ *vi (ist) fam* [sich nähern]: **angeschossen kommen** to come shooting up.

**Anschiss** *(pl* -e) *der salopp* bollocking.

**Anǀschlag** *der* **- 1.** [Attentat - auf Person] assassination attempt; [ - auf Botschaft] attack; **einen ~ auf jn verüben** to make an attempt on sb's life; **einen ~ auf etw** *(A)* **verüben** to attack sthg **- 2.** [Zettel, Plakat] notice **- 3.** [von Hahn, Knopf]: **etw bis zum ~ drehen** to turn sthg as far as it will go **- 4.** [auf der Schreibmaschine] keystroke; **50 Anschläge pro Zeile** 50 characters per line **- 5.** [am Klavier] touch.

**anǀschlagen** *(perf* hat/ist **angeschlagen)** *(unreg) vt* **- 1.** [Plakat] to put up **- 2.** [Geschirr] to chip **- 3.** [wählen] to adopt **- 4.** [Taste] to strike **- 5.** [beim Stricken] to cast on **- 6.** [verletzen]: **sich** *(D)* **den Kopf an etw** *(D)* **~** to knock one's head against sthg ⬦ *vi* **- 1.** [wirken] to work **- 2.** [bellen] to start barking.

**anǀschleichen** *(perf* hat/ist **angeschlichen)** *vi (unreg) (ist):* **angeschlichen kommen** to come with one's tail between one's legs.

⬦ **sich anschleichen** *ref* to creep up.

**anǀschleppen** *vt* **- 1.** [schleppen] to drag along **- 2.** *fam* [mitbringen] to bring along.

**anǀschließen** *vt (unreg)* **- 1.** [verbinden - Telefon, Wasserhahn] to connect; [ - Elektrogerät] to plug in **- 2.** [folgen lassen] to add **- 3.** [festschließen]: **etw an etw** *(A)* **~** to lock sthg to sthg.

⬦ **sich anschließen** *ref* **- 1.** [mitmachen]: **sich jm/einer Sache ~** to join sb/sthg; **sich einer Meinung ~** to endorse an opinion **- 2.** [folgen]: **sich an etw** *(A)* **~** to follow sthg.

**anschließend** *adv* afterwards ⬦ *adj* ensuing.

**Anǀschluss** *der* **- 1.** [an Zug, Telefon] connection; **den ~ verpassen** [Zug] to miss one's connection; **den ~ verpasst haben** *fig* to be left behind; **kein ~ unter dieser Nummer** the number you have dialled has not been recognized **- 2.** [Telefonapparat] extension **- 3.** [zu Freunden]: **~ finden** to meet people; **~ suchen zu jm** to want to meet sb **- 4.** [Folge]: **im ~ an etw** *(A)* following sthg **- 5.** POL Anschluss.

**an|schmiegen** ➡ sich anschmiegen ref: sich an jn/etw ~ to snuggle up to sb/sthg.

**an|schmieren** vt fam to fool.

**an|schnallen** vt [Skier, Rollschuhe] to put on; [Sicherheitsgurt] to fasten.
➡ **sich anschnallen** ref to fasten one's seat belt.

**an|schnauzen** vt salopp to have a go at.

**an|schneiden** vt (unreg) - **1.** [schneiden] to cut into - **2.** fig [ansprechen] to broach.

**an|schrauben** vt to screw on.

**an|schreiben** (unreg) vt - **1.** [Schulden] : sie ließ ihre Einkäufe ~ she asked to pay for her purchases later; bei jm gut/schlecht angeschrieben sein to be in sb's good/bad books - **2.** [per Brief] to write to - **3.** [aufschreiben] to write up ◇ vi: ~ lassen to pay later.

**an|schreien** vt (unreg) to shout at.

**An|schrift** die address.

**an|schuldigen** vt geh to accuse; jn wegen einer Sache (G) ~ to accuse sb of sthg.

**Anschuldigung** (pl -en) die accusation.

**an|schwellen** (perf ist angeschwollen) vi (unreg) - **1.** [Körperteil] to swell - **2.** [Gewässer] to rise - **3.** [Geräusch] to grow louder.

**an|schwemmen** vt to wash up.

**an|sehen** (unreg) vt - **1.** [anblicken] to look at; sich (D) etw ~ [zur Unterhaltung] to go and see sthg; sich (D) jn/etw ~ [zur Prüfung] to look at sb/ sthg - **2.** [erkennen] : man sieht ihm sein Alter nicht an he doesn't look his age; man sieht ihr ihre Müdigkeit nicht an her tiredness doesn't show - **3.** [erachten] : jn/etw als etw ~ to regard sb/sthg as sthg - **4.** [ertragen] : etw nicht (mit) ~ können not to be able to stand sthg ◇ vi: sieh mal an! fancy that!

**Ansehen** das - **1.** [Ruf] reputation; in hohem ~ stehen to be highly respected - **2.** [Anblick]: ich kenne ihn nur vom ~ I only know him by sight.

**ansehnlich** adj - **1.** [groß] considerable - **2.** [schön] attractive.

**an|seilen** vt to rope up.
➡ **sich anseilen** ref to rope o.s. up.

**an sein** (perf ist an gewesen) vi (unreg) to be on.

**an|setzen** vt - **1.** [in Stellung bringen - Werkzeug] to place in position; [ - Trinkgefäss, Blasinstrument] to raise to one's lips - **2.** [Termin] to arrange; [Preis] to fix - **3.** [Stück]: etw an etw (A) ~ to attach sthg to sthg - **4.** [Person]: jn auf etw (A) ~ to put sb on sthg - **5.** [zubereiten] to prepare - **6.** [anlagern]: Fett ~ to put on weight; Rost ~ to get rusty ◇ vi - **1.** [anfangen] to begin; zum Sprung ~ to get ready to jump; das Flugzeug setzte zur Landung an the plane was com-

mencing its descent - **2.** [im Kochtopf] to stick.
➡ **sich ansetzen** ref [sich ablagern - Rost, Schimmel] to form; [ - Wasserstein] to accumulate, to build up.

**Ansicht** (pl -en) die - **1.** [Meinung] opinion, view; der gleichen/anderer ~ sein to be of the same/a different opinion; meiner ~ nach in my view ODER opinion - **2.** [Betrachtung]: zur ~ [zur Probe] on trial ODER approval - **3.** [Abbildung] view.
➡ **Ansichten** pl opinions, views.

**Ansichts|karte** die postcard.

**Ansichtssache** die: das ist (reine) ~ that is (purely) a matter of opinion.

**an|siedeln** vt - **1.** [Siedler] to settle - **2.** [Industrie] to establish - **3.** [in Bereich, Epoche] to place.
➡ **sich ansiedeln** ref [Siedler] to settle; [Betrieb] to set up.

**ansonsten** adv otherwise.

**an|spannen** vt - **1.** [Muskel] to tense; [Seil] to tauten - **2.** [anstrengen] to put under strain - **3.** [Pferd] to harness.

**An|spannung** die strain; nervöse ~ nervous tension.

**an|sparen** vt to save.

**an|spielen** vi: auf jn/etw ~ to allude to sb/ sthg ◇ vt sport to play the ball to.

**Anspielung** (pl -en) die allusion.

**an|spinnen** vt (unreg) to develop.
➡ **sich anspinnen** ref: da spinnt sich was an there's sthg going on there.

**an|spitzen** vt [Bleistift] to sharpen.

**an|spornen** ['anʃpɔrnən] vt to spur on; jn zu etw ~ to spur sb on to sthg.

**Ansprache** (pl -n) die speech.

**ansprechbar** adj: nicht ~ sein [wegen Krankheit, Ohnmacht, Trunkenheit] to be in no fit state to talk to anybody; [beschäftigt sein] to be unavailable to talk to anybody.

**an|sprechen** (unreg) vt - **1.** [anreden] to speak to; jn auf etw (A) ~ to speak to sb about sthg - **2.** [erwähnen] to mention - **3.** [interessieren] to appeal to ◇ vi [reagieren] to respond; auf etw (A) ~ to respond to sthg.

**ansprechend** adj attractive ◇ adv attractively.

**an|springen** (perf hat/ist angesprungen) (unreg) vt (hat) [angreifen] to pounce on ◇ vi (ist) - **1.** [Auto, Motor] to start - **2.** fam [reagieren]: auf etw (A) ~ to jump at sthg.

**An|spruch** der - **1.** [Recht] claim; auf etw ~ haben to be entitled to sthg; auf etw ~ erheben to lay claim to sthg - **2.** [Forderung] demand; hohe Ansprüche an jn stellen to demand a lot of sb; jn/etw in ~ nehmen to make demands on sb/sthg; ich bin durch den Umzug sehr in

~ genommen I'm very busy with the move; viel Zeit in ~ nehmen to take a lot of time; ich nahm seine Hilfe gern in ~ I was happy to accept his help.

**anspruchslos** ['anʃpruxsloːs] adj - **1.** [bescheiden] unpretentious; [Leben] simple - **2.** [Publikum, Person, Lektüre] undemanding - **3.** [Pflanze] easy to look after.

**anspruchsvoll** ['anʃpruxsfɔl] adj demanding; [Zeitung] quality (vor Subst).

**an|stacheln** ['anʃtaxln] vt [Ehrgeiz] to fire; jn zu etw ~ to goad sb into sthg.

**Anstalt** (pl -en) die - **1.** [Institution] institution - **2.** [Irrenanstalt] mental hospital, institution.

➤ **Anstalten** pl arrangements; ~en/keinerlei ~en machen, etw zu tun to make/not to make a move to do sthg.

**Anstand** der [gutes Benehmen] decency.

**anständig** adj decent; eine ~e Tracht Prügel fam a real hiding ⟨⟩ adv - **1.** [ordentlich, integer] decently - **2.** fam [kräftig]: ~ bezahlen to pay well; ~ reinhauen to stuff one's face.

**anstandshalber** adv out of politeness.

**anstandslos** adv without hesitation.

**an|starren** vt to stare at.

**anstatt** präp: ~ js/einer Sache instead of sb/sthg.

➤ **anstatt dass** konj: ~ dass wir reden ... instead of talking ...

➤ **anstatt zu** konj instead of.

**an|stecken** vt - **1.** [infizieren, mitreißen] to infect; jn mit etw ~ to infect sb with sthg, to give sthg to sb; er hat uns alle mit seinem Lachen angesteckt his laughter was infectious - **2.** [Zigarette, Kerze] to light; [Haus] to set fire to - **3.** [Orden, Brosche] to pin on; [einen Ring] to put on ⟨⟩ vi to be infectious.

➤ **sich anstecken** ref: sich (bei jm) mit etw ~ to catch sthg (from sb).

**ansteckend** adj infectious.

**Ansteck|nadel** die - **1.** [Schmuckstück] pin - **2.** [Abzeichen] badge.

**Ansteckung** (pl -en) die infection.

**an|stehen** vi (unreg) - **1.** [in Schlange] to queue Br, to stand in line Am; nach etw ~ to queue for sthg Br, to stand in line for sthg Am - **2.** [Problem] to be on the agenda; [Termin] to be fixed - **3.** geh [passen]: es steht mir gut/schlecht an it befits/ill befits me.

**an|steigen** (perf ist angestiegen) vi (unreg) to rise.

**anstelle** präp: ~ js/einer Sache, ~ von jm/etw instead of sb/sthg.

**an|stellen** vt - **1.** [Gerät] to turn on - **2.** [Angestellte] to employ, to take on; in einem Großbetrieb angestellt sein to work in a big factory - **3.** [zustande bringen - Beobachtung, Vergleich] to

make; [ - Unfug] to get up to; [ - Blödsinn] to talk; sie hat alles Mögliche angestellt she tried everything; wie soll ich das ~? how am I supposed to do that?

➤ **sich anstellen** ref - **1.** [Schlange stehen] to queue Br, to stand in line Am - **2.** [sich benehmen] to act; stell dich nicht so an! don't be so stupid!; sie stellte sich sehr geschickt an she got the hang of it very quickly.

**An|stellung** die position.

**Anstich** (pl -e) der tapping.

**Anstieg** (pl -e) der - **1.** [Zunahme] rise - **2.** [Aufstieg] ascent.

**an|stiften** vt: jn zu etw ~ to incite sb to sthg.

**Anstifter** (pl -) der instigator.

**Anstiftung** (pl -en) die incitement.

**an|stimmen** vt to start; ein Geschrei ~ to start screaming.

**An|stoß** der - **1.** [Anlass] impetus (U); den ~ zu etw geben to provide the impetus for sthg - **2.** [Ärger]: (bei jm) ~ erregen to cause (sb) offence; an etw (D) ~ nehmen to take offence at sthg - **3.** [im Fußball] kick-off.

**an|stoßen** (perf hat/ist angestoßen) (unreg) vt (hat) [mit dem Fuß] to kick; [mit dem Ellenbogen - mit Gewalt] to elbow; [ - heimlich] to nudge; sich das Knie am Tisch ~ to bang one's knee on the table ⟨⟩ vi - **1.** (ist) [anecken]: mit der Schulter am Schrank ~ to bang one's shoulder on the cupboard - **2.** (hat) [angrenzen]: an etw (A) ~ to adjoin sthg - **3.** (hat) [mit Gläsern]: (mit jm) auf jn/etw ~ to drink to sb/sthg (with sb) - **4.** (hat) [im Fußball] to kick off.

**an|strahlen** vt - **1.** [beleuchten - Bauwerk] to floodlight; [ - Schauspieler] to spotlight - **2.** [anlächeln] to beam at.

**an|streben** vt geh to strive for.

**an|streichen** vt (unreg) - **1.** [streichen] to paint - **2.** [kennzeichnen] to mark.

**Anstreicher, in** (mpl -; fpl -nen) der, die painter and decorator.

**an|strengen** ['anʃtrɛŋən] vt - **1.** [ermüden] to strain - **2.** [Kräfte, Fantasie, Kopf] to use - **3.** [Prozess] to start.

➤ **sich anstrengen** ref [sich bemühen] to make an effort, to try.

**an|strengend** adj strenuous.

**Anstrengung** (pl -en) die effort; mit großer ~ with a lot of effort.

**Anstrich** der - **1.** [Farbe] coat of paint - **2.** [Schein] air; einer Sache (D) einen neuen ~ geben to breathe new life into sthg; einer Sache (D) einen seriösen ~ geben to lend authority to sthg.

**Ansturm** der - **1.** [Angriff] assault - **2.** [Andrang] rush.

**an|stürmen** (perf ist **an**gestürmt) vi: gegen etw ~ [Festung] to storm sthg.

**Antagonismus** (pl -men) der antagonism.

**an|tanzen** (perf ist **an**getanzt) vi fam to turn up; jn ~ lassen fam to call sb in.

**Antarktis** die Antarctic.

**antarktisch** adj Antarctic.

**an|tasten** vt - **1.** [Ehre] to offend; [Recht] to infringe upon - **2.** [Vermögen, Vorrat] to break into - **3.** [Essen] to touch.

**Anteil** (pl -e) der - **1.** [Teil] share - **2.** [Teilnahme]: an etw (D) ~ haben to participate in sthg; an etw (D) ~ nehmen [bemitleiden] to share in sthg; [sich beteiligen] to participate in sthg.

**Anteilnahme** die - **1.** [Mitleid] sympathy - **2.** [Interesse] interest.

**Antenne** (pl -n) die - **1.** TECH aerial - **2.** [Gefühl]: eine/keine ~ für etw haben to have a/no feel for sthg.

**Anthologie** [antolo'gi:] (pl -n) die anthology.

**Anthrax** (pl -) das anthrax.

**Anthrazit** [antra'tsi:t] der anthracite.

**Anthropologie** [antropolo'gi:] die anthropology.

**Anti|alkoholiker, in** [antialko'ho:likɐ, rɪn] (mpl -; fpl -nen) der, die teetotaller.

**antiautoritär** [antiautori'tɛːɐ] adj permissive <> adv permissively.

**Antibiotikum** [anti'bi̯o:tikum] (pl -ka) das antibiotic.

**antifaschistisch** adj antifascist.

**antik** [an'ti:k] adj - **1.** [klassisch] classical - **2.** [alt] antique.

**Antike** [an'ti:kə] die: die ~ (classical) antiquity.

**antikommunistisch** adj anticommunist.

**Anti|körper** der antibody.

**Antilope** [anti'lo:pə] (pl -n) die antelope.

**Antipathie** [antipa'ti:] (pl -n) die antipathy.

**an|tippen** vt - **1.** [Gegenstand] to tap - **2.** [Thema] to touch on.

**Antiquariat** [antikva'ri̯a:t] (pl -e) das second-hand bookshop.

**antiquarisch** adj second-hand.

**Antiquität** [antikvi'tɛ:t] (pl -en) die antique.

**Antisemit, in** [antize'mi:t, ɪn] (mpl -en; fpl -nen) der, die anti-Semite.

**antisemitisch** adj anti-Semitic.

**Antisemitismus** der anti-Semitism.

**antiseptisch** adj antiseptic.

**antistatisch** adj antistatic.

**Antithese** [anti'te:zə] die antithesis.

**antithetisch** adj antithetical.

**Antlitz** [ˈantlɪts] (pl -e) das geh countenance.

**an|törnen** vt fam to turn on.

**Antrag** [ˈantra:k] (pl Anträge) der - **1.** [Bitte] application; einen ~ auf etw (A) stellen to apply for sthg - **2.** [im Parlament] motion - **3.** [Formular] application form - **4.** [Heiratsantrag]: jm einen ~ machen to propose to sb.

**Antrags|formular** das application form.

**Antragsteller, in** (mpl -; fpl -nen) der, die amt applicant.

**an|treffen** vt (unreg) to find.

**an|treiben** vt (unreg) - **1.** [Wagen] to drive; [Motor, Gerät] to power - **2.** [Person] to urge on; jn zur Eile ~ to urge sb to hurry - **3.** [anschwemmen] to wash up.

**an|treten** (perf hat/ist **an**getreten) (unreg) vt (hat) - **1.** [beginnen] to start - **2.** [Erbschaft] to come into <> vi (ist) - **1.** [sich aufstellen] to line up - **2.** [kämpfen]: gegen jn ~ [in Fußball, Tennis] to play sb; [im Boxen] to fight sb; [in Wahl] to stand against sb.

**Antrieb** der - **1.** [Kraft] drive; ein Gerät mit elektrischem ~ an electrically-powered appliance - **2.** [Motivation] impetus; etw aus eigenem ~ tun to do sthg on one's own initiative.

**an|trinken** vt (unreg): sich (D) Mut ~ to fill o.s. with Dutch courage; sich (D) einen Schwips ~ to get tipsy.

**Antritt** der (ohne pl) - **1.** [Beginn] start - **2.** SPORT: er hat einen schnellen ~ he has a good turn of pace.

**an|trocknen** (perf ist **an**getrocknet) vi to dry.

**an|tun** vt (unreg) - **1.** [Unrecht] to do; wie konntest du mir das ~? how could you do that to me?; sich (D) etwas ~ to take one's own life - **2.** [Gutes]: jm zu viel Ehre ~ to do sb too much justice - **3.** [lieben]: das Bild hat es mir angetan I really like the picture.

**Antwort** [ˈantvɔrt] (pl -en) die - **1.** [Erwiderung] answer; [auf Brief] reply; die ~ auf etw (A) the answer to sthg; ~/keine ~ geben to reply/not to reply - **2.** [Reaktion] response; als ~ auf (+ A) in response to.

**antworten** vi - **1.** [erwidern] to answer; auf etw (A) ~ to answer sthg, to reply to sthg - **2.** [reagieren] to respond <> vt [auf Fragen] to answer, to reply.

**Antwort|schein** der reply coupon.

**an|vertrauen** vt: jm etw ~ to entrust sb with sthg.

➤ **sich anvertrauen** ref: sich jm ~ to confide in sb.

**An|verwandte** der, die geh relative.

**an|visieren** [ˈanvizi:rən] vt to set one's sights on.

**an|wachsen** [ˈanvaksn̩] (perf ist **an**gewachsen) vi (unreg) - **1.** [festwachsen] to take root - **2.** [wachsen] to increase.

**an|wählen** vt to dial.

**Anwalt** ['anvalt] (pl **Anwälte**) der - 1. [Rechtsanwalt] lawyer - 2. fig [Fürsprecher] advocate.

**Anwältin** ['anvɛltɪn] (pl **-nen**) die - 1. [Rechtsanwältin] lawyer - 2. fig [Fürsprecherin] advocate.

**Anwalts|büro** das [Firma] firm of lawyers.

**An|wandlung** die: in einer ~ von Leichtsinn/ Größenwahn in a fit of madness/ megalomania.

**an|wärmen** vt to warm.

**Anwärter, in** (mpl -; fpl -nen) der, die: ein ~ (auf etw (A)) a candidate (for sthg).

**an|weisen** vt (unreg) - 1. [zeigen] to show; jm etw ~ to show sthg to sb - 2. [beauftragen]: jn ~, etw zu tun to instruct sb to do sthg - 3. [überweisen] to transfer.

**An|weisung** die - 1. [Befehl] instruction; ~ haben, etw zu tun to have instructions to do sthg - 2. [Zahlung - per Bank] payment; [ - per Post] postal order.

**anwendbar** adj: (auf jn/etw) ~ sein to be applicable (to sb/sthg).

**an|wenden** vt - 1. [Hilfsmittel, Gewalt, List] to use - 2. [Methode, Regel]: etw auf jn/etw ~ to apply sthg to sb/sthg.

**Anwender, in** (mpl -; fpl -nen) der, die EDV user.

**An|wendung** die - 1. [Verwendung, Einsatz] use - 2. [von Methode, Regel] application; **zur ~ kommen** ODER **gelangen** amt to be applied.

**Anwendungs|programm** das EDV application.

**an|werben** vt (unreg) to recruit.

**an|werfen** vt (unreg) to start up.

**An|wesen** das estate.

**anwesend** adj present; **bei etw ~ sein** to be present at sthg.

**Anwesende** (pl -n) der, die: **die ~n** those present.

**Anwesenheit** die presence; in js ~ (D), in ~ von jm in sb's presence.

**Anwesenheits|liste** die attendance sheet.

**an|widern** ['anviːdɐn] vt to fill with repulsion.

**Anwohner, in** (mpl -; fpl -nen) der, die resident.

**Anz. - 1.** abk für **Anzahlung - 2.** abk für **Anzeige.**

**Anzahl** die number.

**an|zahlen** vt to pay a deposit on; **100 Euro ~** to pay a deposit of 100 euros.

**An|zahlung** die deposit, down payment.

**an|zapfen** vt [Fass, Leitung, Telefon] to tap.

**An|zeichen** das sign.

**Anzeige** ['antsaigə] (pl -n) die - 1. [in Zeitung] ad-

vertisement; [Brief] announcement - 2. [Instrument] display - 3. [Strafanzeige] charge; **gegen jn ~ erstatten** to bring a charge against sb.

**an|zeigen** vt - 1. [melden] to report - 2. [zeigen] to show.

**Anzeigen|blatt** das advertiser.

**Anzeigen|teil** der advertisements section.

**an|zetteln** ['antsɛtln] vt to instigate.

**an|ziehen** (unreg) vt - 1. [Kleidung] to put on; **sich (D) etw ~** to put sthg on - 2. [Person]: **jn ~** to dress sb - 3. PHYS [anlocken] to attract - 4. [Schraube, Tau] to tighten; [Bremse] to apply - 5. [Körperteil] to draw up ⬦ vi - 1. [steigen] to rise - 2. [beschleunigen] to accelerate.

➤ **sich anziehen** ref - 1. [Person] to get dressed; **sich warm ~** to dress warmly - 2. [Sachen]: **sich gegenseitig ~** to be attracted to each other.

**anziehend** adj attractive.

**Anziehungs|kraft** die - 1. PHYS (gravitational) attraction - 2. [Reiz] attractiveness, appeal.

**An|zug** der - 1. [Kleidungsstück] suit - 2. [Nähern]: **im ~ sein** to be approaching.

**anzüglich** ['antsyːklɪç] adj lewd ⬦ adv lewdly.

**an|zünden** vt [Streichholz, Kerze] to light; [Haus] to set fire to.

**an|zweifeln** vt to doubt.

**AOK** [aːʔoːˈkaː] (abk für **Allgemeine Ortskrankenkasse**) die health insurance company for German workers, students etc not covered by private insurance policies.

**Aorta** [aˈɔrta] (pl **Aorten**) die aorta.

**apart** geh adj striking ⬦ adv strikingly.

**Apartheid** [aˈpaːɐ̯thait] die apartheid.

**Apartment** = **Appartement.**

**Apathie** [apaˈtiː] (pl -n) die apathy.

**apathisch** [aˈpaːtɪʃ] adj apathetic ⬦ adv apathetically.

**Apennin** der: **der ~** the Apennines.

**Aperitif** [aperiˈtiːf] (pl -s) der aperitif.

**Apfel** ['apfl̩] (pl **Äpfel**) der apple; **in den sauren ~ beißen (müssen)** to (have to) bite the bullet.

**Apfel|baum** der apple tree.

**Apfel|kuchen** der apple cake.

**Apfel|mus** das apple sauce (usu. eaten as dessert).

**Apfel|saft** der apple juice.

**Apfelsine** [apfl̩ˈziːnə] (pl -n) die orange.

**Apfel|strudel** der apple strudel.

**Apfel|wein** der cider.

**Aphorismus** [afoˈrɪsmʊs] (pl **-men**) der aphorism.

**Apokalypse** *die* apocalypse.

**apokalyptisch** *adj* apocalyptic.

**Apostel** [a'pɔstl] (*pl* -) *der* apostle.

**Apostroph** [apo'stroːf] (*pl* -e) *der* apostrophe.

**Apotheke** [apo'teːkə] (*pl* -n) *die* pharmacy, chemist's *Br*, drugstore *Am*.

**Apotheker, in** (*mpl* -; *fpl* -nen) *der*, *die* pharmacist, chemist *Br*, druggist *Am*.

**App.** *abk für* **Appartement.**

**Apparat** [apa'raːt] (*pl* -e) *der* - **1.** [Gerät] device - **2.** [Telefon]: **am ~!** speaking! - **3.** [von Partei, Staat] apparatus - **4.** *salopp* [Riesending] whopper.

**Appartement** [apartə'mãː], **Apartment** [a'partmənt] (*pl* -s) *das* [Wohnung] flat *Br*, apartment *Am*.

**Appell** [a'pɛl] (*pl* -e) *der* - **1.** [Aufruf] appeal; einen **~ an jn richten** to make an appeal to sb - **2.** MIL roll call.

**appellieren** *vi*: **an jn/etw ~** to appeal to sb/sthg.

**Appenzell** *nt* Appenzell.

**Appenzeller** (*pl* -) *der* - **1.** [Person] native/inhabitant of Appenzell - **2.** [Käse] *type of strong Swiss cheese* <> *adj* (*unver*) of/from Appenzell.

**Appenzellerin** (*pl* -nen) *die* native/inhabitant of Appenzell.

**Appetit** [ape'tiːt] *der* appetite; **~/keinen ~ auf etw** (*A*) **haben** to feel/not to feel like sthg; **guten ~!** enjoy your meal!

**appetitanregend** *adj* appetizing.

**appetitlich** *adj* appetizing.

**Appetitlosigkeit** *die* (*ohne pl*) lack of appetite.

**Appetitzügler** (*pl* -) *der* appetite suppressant.

**applaudieren** [aplau'diːrən] *vi* to applaud; **jm ~** to applaud sb.

**Applaus** [a'plaus] *der* (*ohne pl*) applause; **jm ~ spenden** to applaud sb.

**Applikation** (*pl* -en) *die* - **1.** [Anwendung] application - **2.** [Stickerei] appliqué motif.

**Apposition** (*pl* -en) *die* GRAM apposition.

**Approbation** (*pl* -en) *die* licence to practise (*of doctor, pharmacist*).

**Après-Ski** [aprɛ'ʃiː] *das* après-ski.

**Aprikose** [apri'koːzə] (*pl* -n) *die* apricot.

**April** *der* (*ohne pl*) April; **~, ~!** April fool!; **jn in den ~ schicken** *fig* to play an April fool's trick on sb; *siehe auch* **September.**

**Aprilschauer** *der* April shower.

**Aprilscherz** *der* April fool's trick.

**Aprilwetter** *das* changeable weather.

**apropos** [apro'poː] *adv* by the way; **~ Pizza, hast du Hunger?** talking of pizza, are you hungry?

**Apsis** *die* ARCHIT apse.

**Aquaplaning** [akva'plaːnɪŋ] *das* aquaplaning.

**Aquarell** [akva'rɛl] (*pl* -e) *das* - **1.** [Bild] watercolour - **2.** [Farbe]: **in ~ malen** to paint in watercolours.

**Aquarien|fisch** *der* aquarium fish.

**Aquarium** [a'kvaːrjʊm] (*pl* **Aquarien**) *das* aquarium.

**Äquator** [ɛ'kvaːtɔr] *der* (*ohne pl*) equator.

**Aquavit** [akva'viːt] (*pl* -e) *der* aquavit.

**Äquivalent** [ɛkviva'lɛnt] (*pl* -e) *das* equivalent.

**Ar** [aːɐ] (*pl* -e ODER -) *der* ODER *das* are.

**Ära** ['ɛːra] (*pl* **Ären**) *die* era.

**Araber, in** ['arabɐ, rɪn] (*mpl* -; *fpl* -nen) *der*, *die* Arab.

**Arabien** *nt* Arabia.

**arabisch** *adj* [Kultur, Volk, Politik] Arab; [Sprache, Literatur] Arabic; [Halbinsel, Landschaft] Arabian.

**Arabisch(e)** *das* (*ohne pl*) Arabic; *siehe auch* **Englisch(e).**

**Aral|see** *der* Aral Sea, Lake Aral.

**Arbeit** ['arbaɪt] (*pl* -en) *die* - **1.** [gen] work; **die ~en am Tunnel** the work on the tunnel; **bei der ~ sein** to be working; **ihr Wagen ist in ~** your car is being worked on; **an die ~ gehen, sich an die ~ machen** to start working; **zur ~ gehen** to go to work; **ganze** ODER **gründliche ~ leisten** to do a thorough job; **nur halbe ~ machen** not to finish the job; **jm viel ~ machen** to make a lot of work for sb - **2.** [Arbeitsstelle] job; **keine ~ haben** to be out of work; **~ suchen** to be looking for work ODER a job - **3.** [Leistung, Werk] work - **4.** [Klassenarbeit] test - **5.** [wissenschaftlich] paper.

**arbeiten** *vi* - **1.** [Person] to work; **bei der Post ~** to work for the Post Office; **zu Hause ~** to work from home; **an etw** (*D*) **~** to work on sthg; **an sich** (*D*) **~** to work hard - **2.** [funktionieren - Maschine] to operate; [ - Herz] to function <> *vt* to make; **sich** (*D*) **die Finger** ODER **Hände wund ~** to work one's fingers to the bone.

➡ **sich arbeiten** *ref*: **sich müde ~** to tire o.s. out working; **sich nach oben ~** to work one's way up; **es arbeitet sich gut/schlecht mit ihm** it is/isn't easy to work with him/it.

**Arbeiter** (*pl* -) *der* worker.

**Arbeiter|bewegung** *die* labour movement.

**Arbeiterin** (*pl* -nen) *die* worker.

**Arbeiterklasse** *die* (*ohne pl*) working class ODER classes (*pl*).

**Arbeiterschaft** *die (ohne pl)* work force.

**Arbeiterwohlfahrt** *die (ohne pl)* workers' welfare organization.

**Arbeitgeber, in** (*mpl -; fpl* -nen) *der, die* employer.

**Arbeitgeberlverband** *der* employers' association.

**Arbeitnehmer, in** (*mpl -; fpl* -nen) *der, die* employee.

**Arbeitnehmerlorganisation** *die* employees' association.

**Arbeitslamt** *das* job centre *Br,* employment agency *Am.*

**Arbeitslaufwand** *der:* der ~ ist zu hoch it would take too much effort.

**Arbeitslausfall** *der* downtime.

**Arbeitslbedingungen** *pl* working conditions.

**Arbeitslbereich** *der* - **1.** [Zuständigkeitsbereich] area of work - **2.** [Arbeitsort] working area.

**Arbeitsbeschaffungslmaßnahme** *die* job creation measure.

**Arbeitsbeschaffungslprogramm** *das* job creation scheme.

**Arbeitsleifer** *der* enthusiasm for one's work.

**Arbeitslerlaubnis** *die* work permit.

**Arbeitslerleichterung** *die:* für mich war das eine große ~ that made my job a lot easier.

**Arbeitslessen** *das* [mittags] working lunch; [abends] working dinner.

**arbeitsfähig** *adj* fit for work.

**arbeitsfrei** *adj:* zwei ~e Nachmittage in der Woche two afternoons off a week.

**Arbeitslgang** *der* operation.

**Arbeitslgemeinschaft** *die* - **1.** [von Wissenschaftlern] working party; [von Schülern, Studenten] study group - **2.** [von Firmen] association.

**Arbeitslgericht** *das* industrial tribunal *Br,* labor court *Am.*

**arbeitsintensiv** *adj* labour-intensive.

**Arbeitslkampf** *der* industrial action.

**Arbeitslkleidung** *die* work clothes (*pl*).

**Arbeitslklima** *das (ohne pl)* working atmosphere.

**Arbeitslkraft** *die:* sich (*D*) seine ~ erhalten to keep o.s. fit for work.
➡ **Arbeitskräfte** *pl* workers.

**Arbeitslkreis** *der* [Lerngruppe] study group; [Ausschuss] working party.

**Arbeitslleistung** *die* [Qualität] performance; [Produktivität] productivity.

**Arbeitsllohn** *der* wages (*pl*).

**arbeitslos** *adj* unemployed.

**Arbeitslose** (*pl* -n) *der, die* unemployed person; die ~n the unemployed.

**Arbeitsloslgeld** *das (ohne pl) unemployment benefit paid for a limited period, the amount of which is based on the recipient's last wage.*

**Arbeitsloslhilfe** *die (ohne pl) lower rate of unemployment benefit paid after one's entitlement to "Arbeitslosengeld" has expired.*

**Arbeitsloslversicherung** *die* ≃ National Insurance *Br,* ≃ social insurance *Am.*

**Arbeitsloslzahl** *die* unemployment figures (*pl*); die ~ ist gestiegen unemployment has risen.

**Arbeitslosigkeit** *die (ohne pl)* unemployment.

**Arbeitslmarkt** *der* labour market.

**Arbeitslmoral** *die (ohne pl)* attitude to one's work.

**Arbeitslniederlegung** (*pl* -en) *die* walkout.

**Arbeitslort** *der* place of work.

**Arbeitslpapier** *das* [Bericht] working paper.
➡ **Arbeitspapiere** *pl* [Dokumente] cards.

**Arbeitslplan** *der* work schedule.

**Arbeitslplatz** *der* - **1.** [Stellung, Job] job - **2.** [Ort] workplace; dort am Fenster ist mein ~ I work over there by the window.

**Arbeitslrecht** *das (ohne pl)* labour law.

**arbeitsscheu** *adj* workshy.

**Arbeitslschutz** *der* health and safety.

**Arbeitslspeicher** *der* EDV RAM.

**Arbeitslstelle** *die* - **1.** [Stellung] job - **2.** [Ort, Abteilung] department.

**Arbeitslsuche** *die:* auf ~ sein to be looking for work *ODER* a job.

**Arbeitsltag** *der* working day.

**Arbeitslteilung** *die* division of labour.

**arbeitsunfähig** *adj* unfit for work.

**Arbeitslunfall** *der* industrial accident.

**Arbeitslverhältnis** *das* (employment) contract; ein neues ~ eingehen to take up new employment.

**Arbeitslvermittlung** *die* [private Agentur] employment agency.

**Arbeitslvertrag** *der* employment contract.

**Arbeitslweise** *die* [von Person] way of working; [von Maschine] mode of operation.

**Arbeitslzeit** *die* working hours (*pl*).

**Arbeitszeitlkonto** *das record of overtime worked.*

**Arbeitszeitverlkürzung** *die* reduction in working hours.

**Arbeits|zimmer** *das* study.

**archaisch** [ar'ça:ɪʃ] *adj* archaic.

**Archäologe** [arçɛo'lo:gə] (*pl* -n) *der* archaeologist.

**Archäologin** [arçɛo'lo:gɪn] (*pl* -nen) *die* archaeologist.

**archäologisch** [arçɛo'lo:gɪʃ] *adj* archaeological.

**Arche** ['arçə] (*pl* -n) *die:* **die ~ Noah** Noah's Ark.

**Arche|typ** *der* archetype.

**Archipel** [arçi'pe:l] (*pl* -e) *der* archipelago.

**Architekt, in** [arçi'tɛkt, ɪn] (*mpl* -en; *fpl* -nen) *der, die* architect.

**architektonisch** [arçitɛk'to:nɪʃ] *adj* architectural.

**Architektur** [arçitɛk'tu:ɐ̯] *die (ohne pl)* architecture.

**Archiv** [ar'çi:f] (*pl* -e) *das* archive.

**archivieren** [arçi'vi:rən] *vt* to (store in an) archive.

**ARD** [a:'ɛr'de:] (*abk für* **Arbeitsgemeinschaft der öffentlich-rechtlichen Rundfunkanstalten der Bundesrepublik Deutschland**) *die German public broadcasting network, responsible for the Erstes Programm TV channel.*

**Ardennen** *pl:* **die ~** the Ardennes.

**Areal** [are'a:l] (*pl* -e) *das* area.

**Arena** [a're:na] (*pl* **Arenen**) *die* arena.

**arg** [ark] (*kompar* **ärger;** *superl* **ärgste**) *adj* [schlimm] bad; [sehr schlimm] terrible; **js ärgster Feind** sb's arch enemy; **es liegt im Argen** it is in a terrible state ◇ *adv* [schlimm] badly; [sehr schlimm] terribly; **es zu ~ treiben** to go too far.

**Argentinien** *nt* Argentina.

**Argentinier, in** (*mpl* -; *fpl* -nen) *der, die* Argentinian.

**argentinisch** *adj* Argentinian.

**Ärger** ['ɛrgɐ] *der (ohne pl)* - **1.** [Verärgerung] annoyance; [Zorn] anger - **2.** [Problem] trouble; **mit jm/etw ~ haben** to have trouble with sb/sthg; **(jm) ~ machen** to cause (sb) trouble; **mach keinen ~!** I don't want any trouble!

**ärgerlich** *adj* - **1.** [verärgert] annoyed; [zornig] angry; **auf jn/über etw** (*A*) **~ sein** [verärgert] to be annoyed with sb/at sthg; [zornig] to be angry with sb/at sthg - **2.** [unangenehm] annoying ◇ *adv* [verärgert] angrily.

**ärgern** *vt* to annoy.
➤ **sich ärgern** *ref* to get annoyed; **sich über jn/etw ~** to get annoyed with sb/at sthg.

**Ärgernis** (*pl* -se) *das* - **1.** [Ärgerliches] nuisance - **2.** RECHT: **Erregung öffentlichen ~ses** offence against public decency.

**arglistig** *adj* malicious.

**Argument** (*pl* -e) *das* argument.

**argumentieren** *vi* to argue.

**Argwohn** *der (ohne pl)* suspicion.

**argwöhnisch** *adj* suspicious ◇ *adv* suspiciously.

**Arie** ['a:rjə] (*pl* -n) *die* aria.

**arisch** *adj* Aryan.

**Aristokrat, in** (*mpl* -en; *fpl* -nen) *der, die* aristocrat.

**aristokratisch** *adj* aristocratic.

**Arithmetik** *die (ohne pl)* arithmetic.

**arithmetisch** *adj* arithmetical.

**Arkaden** *pl* ARCHIT arcade *(sg)*.

**Arktis** *die* Arctic.

**arktisch** *adj* arctic.

**arm** (*kompar* **ärmer;** *superl* **ärmste**) *adj* poor; **~ an etw** (*D*) **sein** to lack sthg; **um etw ärmer sein** to have lost sthg; **er ist nun um 50 Mark ärmer** he's now 50 marks worse off ODER the poorer; **~ dran sein** *fam* to be in a bad way ◇ *adv* poorly; **jn ~ essen** to eat sb out of house and home.

**Arm** (*pl* -e) *der* - **1.** [gen] arm; **jn/etw im ~ halten** to hold sb/sthg in one's arms - **2.** RW: **jn auf den ~ nehmen** to pull sb's leg; **jm in den ~ fallen** to put a spoke in sb's wheel Br, to thwart sb; **jm in die ~e laufen** to walk straight into sb's arms; **jm unter die ~e greifen** to help sb out; **jn mit offenen ~en aufnehmen** to welcome sb with open arms.
➤ **Arm in Arm** *adv* arm in arm.

**Armatur** (*pl* -en) *die* [von Maschine, Auto] instrument.
➤ **Armaturen** *pl* [im Badezimmer] fittings.

**Armaturen|brett** *das* AUTO dashboard.

**Arm|band** (*pl* -bänder) *das* [Schmuck] bracelet; [von Uhr] strap.

**Armband|uhr** *die* wristwatch, watch.

**Arm|binde** *die* armband.

**Arm|brust** *die* crossbow.

**Arme** (*pl* -n) *der, die* - **1.** [Bedauernswerte] poor thing; **du ~r!** you poor thing! - **2.** [Mittellose] poor man/woman; **die ~n** the poor.

**Armee** [ar'me:] (*pl* -n) *die* army.

**Ärmel** (*pl* -) *der* sleeve; **lange/kurze ~** long/short sleeves; **die ~ hochkrempeln** *eigtl* & *fig* to roll up one's sleeves; **etw aus dem ~ schütteln** to come up with sthg just like that.

**Ärmelkanal** *der:* **der ~** the (English) Channel.

**ärmellos** *adj* sleeveless.

**Armenien** *nt* Armenia.

**Armenier, in** (*mpl* -; *fpl* -nen) *der, die* Armenian.

**armenisch** adj Armenian.

**Armllehne** die arm, armrest.

**Armlleuchter** der - **1.** [Leuchter] candelabra - **2.** fam [Idiot] cretin.

**ärmlich** adj [Wohnung, Kleidung] shabby; [Verhältnisse] miserable ◇ adv shabbily.

**armselig** adj - **1.** [ärmlich] shabby - **2.** [gering] meagre.

**Armut** die (ohne pl) poverty.

**Arnika** (pl -s) die arnica.

**Aroma** (pl -s ODER Aromen) das - **1.** [Geruch] aroma - **2.** [Würze] flavouring.

**Aromaltherapie** die aromatherapy.

**aromatisch** adj [duftend] aromatic.

**Arrak** (pl -s) der arrack.

**arrangieren** [arāŋ'ʒiːrən] vt [Treffen, Feier, Musik] to arrange.

➧ **sich arrangieren** ref: **sich mit jm ~** [sich verständigen] to come to an understanding with sb.

**Arrest** (pl -e) der detention; **jn unter ~ stellen** to put sb in detention.

**arrogant** adj arrogant ◇ adv arrogantly.

**Arroganz** die (ohne pl) arrogance.

**Arsch** (pl Ärsche) der salopp - **1.** [Gesäß] arse Br, ass Am - **2.** [Blödmann] arsehole Br, asshole Am - **3.** RW: **am ~ der Welt** in the back of beyond; **im ~ sein** vulg to be fucked; **jm in den ~ kriechen** vulg to lick sb's arse Br ODER ass Am; **leck mich am ~!** vulg fuck off!

**Arschkriecher** (pl -) der vulg arselicker Br, asslicker Am.

**Arschlloch** das vulg arsehole Br, asshole Am.

**Arsen** das (ohne pl) arsenic.

**Art** (pl -en) die - **1.** [Weise] way; **eine einfache ~, etw zuzubereiten** a simple way of preparing ODER to prepare sthg; **etw auf eine andere ~ tun** to do sthg another way; **er hat es auf seine ~ getan** he did it his way; **auf gesunde ~** healthily; **auf diese ~ wird er nie gewinnen** he'll never win like this ODER this way; **in der ~ von jm, in js ~** in the manner of sb; **in der ~ einer Sache** (G) ODER **von etw** in the manner of sthg; **die ~ und Weise(, wie)** the way (that); **Bratkartoffeln nach ~ des Hauses** the chef's special fried potatoes - **2.** (ohne pl) [Wesen] nature; [Verhalten] behaviour; **das entspricht nicht ihrer ~, sich zu beschweren** it's not like her to complain - **3.** [Sorte] sort, kind; **eine ~ Grippe** a sort ODER kind of flu; **aller** ODER **jeder ~ Pakete** all sorts ODER kinds of parcels; **in dieser ~** in this form; **das Schloss ist in seiner ~ einmalig** the castle is the only one of its kind - **4.** BIOL species; **aus der ~ schlagen** fig not to take after anyone else in the family.

**Art.** (abk für **Artikel**) art.

**Artenschutz** der (ohne pl) protection of endangered species.

**Artensterben** das (ohne pl) dying out of species.

**Arterie** (pl -n) die artery.

**arteriell** adj arterial.

**Arteriolsklerose** die arteriosclerosis (U).

**Arthritis** die arthritis.

**artig** adj good ◇ adv: **sie hat den Teller Spinat ~ aufgegessen** she ate up all her spinach like a good girl.

**Artikel** (pl -) der - **1.** [in der Zeitung, im Gesetz] article; [im Wörterbuch] entry - **2.** [Ware] item, article - **3.** GRAM: **der bestimmte/unbestimmte ~** the definite/indefinite article.

**artikulieren** vt to articulate.

➧ **sich artikulieren** ref [Person] to express o.s.; [Protest] to manifest itself.

**Artillerie** (pl -n) die MIL artillery.

**Artischocke** (pl -n) die artichoke.

**Artist, in** (mpl -en; fpl -nen) der, die [im Zirkus] (circus) performer.

**artistisch** adj acrobatic.

**Arznei** (pl -en) die medicine.

**Arzneilmittel** das medicine.

**Arzt** [aːɐ̯tst] (pl Ärzte) der doctor; **praktischer ~** general practitioner, GP.

**Ärztelhaus** das medical centre.

**Ärzteschaft** die (ohne pl) medical profession.

**Arztlhelfer, in** der, die doctor's receptionist.

**Ärztin** [ˈɛːɐ̯tstɪn] (pl -nen) die doctor.

**ärztl.** (abk für **ärztlich**) med.

**ärztlich** adj medical.

**Arztlpraxis** die doctor's practice.

**as, As** (pl as, As) das MUS A flat.

**As** (pl -se) das = **Ass.**

**Asbest** (pl -e) das asbestos.

**Asche** (pl -n) die [von Feuer] ashes (pl); [von Zigarre, Vulkan] ash.

**Aschenlbahn** die SPORT cinder track.

**Aschenlbecher** der ashtray.

**Aschenlputtel** (pl -) das Cinderella.

**Ascherlmittwoch** der Ash Wednesday.

**aschfahl** adj ashen.

**ASCII** [ˈaskiː] (abk für **American Standards Code for Information Interchange**) das EDV ASCII.

**ASCII-lTabelle** die EDV ASCII table.

**ASCII-lZeichen** das EDV ASCII character.

**Aserbaidschan** nt Azerbaijan.

**Asiat, in** (mpl -en; fpl -nen) der, die Asian.

**asiatisch** *adj* Asian.

**Asien** *nt* Asia.

**Askese** *die (ohne pl)* asceticism.

**Asket** *(pl -en) der* ascetic.

**asketisch** *adj* ascetic.

**asozial** *adj* antisocial ◇ *adv* antisocially.

**Aspekt** *(pl -e) der* aspect; **unter diesem ~** from this angle.

**Asphalt** [as'falt] *(pl -e) der* asphalt.

**asphaltieren** *vt* to asphalt.

**Aspik** *der* aspic.

**aß** *prät* ▷ essen.

**Ass** *(pl -e) das* [Spielkarte, Person] ace.

**Assel** *(pl -n) die* woodlouse.

**Assessmentcenter** *(pl -) das* assessment centre.

**Assessor** *(pl -oren) der probationer for a post in the higher civil service.*

**Assessorin** *(pl -nen) die probationer for a post in the higher civil service.*

**Assimilation** *(pl -en) die* [gen] assimilation.

**assimilieren** *vt* [gen & BIOL] to assimilate.
➤ **sich assimilieren** *ref:* **sich an etw** *(A)* **~** [sich anpassen] to adjust to sthg.

**Assistent, in** *(mpl -en; fpl -nen) der, die* assistant; **wissenschaftlicher ~** research assistant.

**Assistenzarzt, ärztin** *der, die* houseman *Br*, intern *Am*.

**assistieren** *vi* to assist; **jm bei etw ~** to assist sb with sthg.

**Assoziation** *(pl -en) die geh* [Gedankenverbindung] association.

**assoziieren** *vt geh* [Gedanken] to associate.

**Ast** *(pl Äste) der* branch; **auf dem absteigenden ~ sein** *fig* [nachlassen] to be on the way down; **den ~ absägen, auf dem man sitzt** *fig* [sich selbst schaden] to damage one's own interests; **sich** *(D)* **einen ~ lachen** *fam fig* to laugh o.s. silly.

**AStA** ['asta] *(pl ASten) (abk für Allgemeiner Studentenausschuss) der* students' union.

**Aster** *(pl -n) die* aster.

**Astgabel** *die* fork in a branch.

**Ästhetik** [ɛs'teːtɪk] *(pl -en) die* - **1.** *(ohne pl)* [das Schöne] aesthetic - **2.** [Wissenschaft] aesthetics *(U).*

**ästhetisch** *adj* aesthetic.

**Asthma** *das* asthma.

**Astloch** *das* knothole.

**astrein** *fam adj* brilliant; **nicht ganz ~** [anrüchig] a bit dodgy ◇ *adv* brilliantly.

**Astrologe** *(pl -n) der* astrologer.

**Astrologie** *die (ohne pl)* astrology.

**Astrologin** *(pl -nen) die* astrologer.

**astrologisch** *adj* astrological.

**Astronaut, in** *(mpl -en; fpl -nen) der, die* astronaut.

**Astronomie** *die (ohne pl)* astronomy.

**astronomisch** *adj eigtl* & *fig* astronomical.

**Astrophysik** *die (ohne pl)* astrophysics *(U).*

**Asyl** *(pl -e) das* - **1.** *(ohne pl)* [Zuflucht] asylum; **um ~ bitten** *ODER* **nachsuchen** to apply for asylum - **2.** [Obdachlosenasyl] hostel.

**Asylant** *(pl -en) der* asylum seeker.

**Asylantenwohnheim** *das* hostel for asylum seekers.

**Asylantin** *(pl -nen) die* asylum seeker.

**Asylbewerber, in** *der, die* asylum seeker.

**Asylrecht** *das (ohne pl)* right of asylum.

**Asymmetrie** *(pl -n) die* asymmetry.

**asymmetrisch** *adj* asymmetrical.

**Asymptote** *(pl -n) die* MATH asymptote.

**Aszendent** *(pl -en) der* ASTROL ascendant.

**AT** *(abk für Altes Testament)* OT.

**Atelier** [ate'ljeː] *(pl -s) das* - **1.** [von Künstler, Fotograf] studio - **2.** [von Schneider] workroom.

**Atelierwohnung** *die* converted loft.

**Atem** *der (ohne pl)* - **1.** [die Atmung] breathing - **2.** [die Atemluft] breath; **außer ~ sein** to be out of breath; **~ holen** [einatmen] to breathe in; [sich ausruhen] to catch one's breath - **3.** *RW:* **jn in ~ halten** [in Spannung versetzen] to keep sb on tenterhooks; **jm den ~ verschlagen** [verblüffen] to take sb's breath away.

**atemberaubend** *adj* breathtaking ◇ *adv* breathtakingly.

**Atembeschwerden** *pl* breathing problems.

**atemlos** *adj* breathless ◇ *adv* breathlessly.

**Atemnot** *die (ohne pl)* difficulty in breathing.

**Atempause** *die:* **eine ~ einlegen** *ODER* **machen** to take a breather.

**Atemzug** *der* breath; **im selben** *ODER* **in einem ~** [gleichzeitig] in the same breath.

**Atheismus** [ate'ɪsmʊs] *der (ohne pl)* atheism.

**Atheist, in** *(mpl -en; fpl -nen) der, die* atheist.

**atheistisch** *adj* atheistic.

**Athen** *nt* Athens.

**Athener** *(pl -) der* & *adj (unver)* Athenian.

**Athenerin** *(pl -nen) die* Athenian.

**Äther** *der (ohne pl)* ether.

**ätherisch** *adj* CHEM volatile.

**Äthiopien** *nt* Ethiopia.

**Äthiopier, in** *(mpl -; fpl -nen) der, die* Ethiopian.

**äthiopisch** *adj* Ethiopian.

**Athlet, in** (*mpl* -en; *fpl* -nen) *der, die* athlete.

**athletisch** *adj* athletic ⇔ *adv* athletically.

**Atlantik** *der:* der ~ the Atlantic (Ocean).

**atlantisch** *adj* Atlantic.

**Atlas** (*pl* -se oder **Atlanten**) *der* - **1.** [Buch] atlas - **2.** (*pl Atlasse*) [Satin] satin.

**atmen** *vt* & *vi* to breathe.

**Atmosphäre** (*pl* -n) *die eigtl* & *fig* atmosphere.

**Atmosphärenüberdruck** *der* (*ohne pl*) pressure above atmospheric pressure.

**atmosphärisch** *adj* atmospheric.

**Atmung** *die* (*ohne pl*) breathing.

**Ätna** *der* Mount Etna.

**Atoll** (*pl* -e) *das* atoll.

**Atom** (*pl* -e) *das* atom.

**atomar** *adj* - **1.** [von Atomen] atomic - **2.** [mit Atomkraft] nuclear.

**Atom|bombe** *die* atom ODER atomic bomb.

**Atom|energie** *die* (*ohne pl*) nuclear energy.

**Atom|gewicht** *das* atomic weight.

**Atom|kern** *der* atomic nucleus.

**Atom|kraft** *die* (*ohne pl*) nuclear power.

**Atom|kraftwerk** *das* nuclear power station.

**Atom|krieg** *der* nuclear war.

**Atom|macht** *die* nuclear power (*country*).

**Atom|meiler** *der* nuclear reactor.

**Atom|müll** *der* (*ohne pl*) nuclear waste.

**Atom|physik** *die* (*ohne pl*) nuclear physics (U).

**Atom|rakete** *die* nuclear missile.

**Atom|sprengkopf** *der* nuclear warhead.

**Atom|test** *der* nuclear test.

**Atom|waffe** *die* nuclear weapon.

**atonal** *adj* atonal.

**Atrium** (*pl* **Atrien**) *das* ARCHIT atrium.

**ätsch** *interj fam* ha-ha.

**Attaché** [ata'ʃeː] (*pl* -s) *der* attaché.

**Attacke** (*pl* -n) *die* attack.

**attackieren** *vt* [angreifen] to attack.

**Attentat** (*pl* -e) *das* [erfolglos] assassination attempt; [erfolgreich] assassination; **ein ~ auf jn verüben** [erfolglos] to make an attempt on sb's life; [erfolgreich] to assassinate sb.

**Attentäter, in** (*mpl* -; *fpl* -nen) *der, die* [erfolglos] would-be assassin; [erfolgreich] assassin.

**Attest** (*pl* -e) *das* doctor's certificate.

**attestieren** *vt:* **sie attestierten ihm das nötige Fachwissen** they certified that he had obtained the necessary specialist knowledge.

**Attraktion** (*pl* -en) *die* attraction.

**attraktiv** *adj* attractive.

**Attraktivität** [atraktivi'tɛːt] *die* (*ohne pl*) attractiveness.

**Attrappe** (*pl* -n) *die* dummy.

**Attribut** (*pl* -e) *das geh* [Merkmal & GRAM] attribute.

**attributiv** *adj* GRAM attributive.

**atü** [at'yː] (*pl* -) (*abk für* **Atmosphärenüberdruck**) *pressure above atmospheric pressure.*

**atypisch** *adj* atypical.

**ätzen** *vt* [Oberfläche] to corrode; [Wunde] to cauterize; [Bild, Initialen] to etch ⇔ *vi* [Säure, Chemikalie] to be corrosive; [Geruch] to be pungent.

**ätzend** *adj* - **1.** [Säure, Chemikalie] corrosive; [Geruch] pungent - **2.** [spöttisch] caustic - **3.** *fam* : ~ **sein** [Person] to be a pain; [Fete, Auto, Job] to be crap.

**au** *interj* - **1.** [Ausdruck von Schmerz] ouch!, ow! - **2.** [Ausdruck von Begeisterung]: ~ **ja!** oh yes!

**AU** (*pl* -s) (*abk für* **Abgasuntersuchung**) *die emissions test.*

**Aubergine** [obɛr'ʒiːnə] (*pl* -n) *die* aubergine *Br*, eggplant *Am*.

**auch** *adv* - **1.** [ebenfalls] also, too; **ich ~ me** too; **ich ~ nicht me** neither; ~ **das noch!** that's the last thing I need! - **2.** [sogar] even - **3.** [wirklich]: **das Bild schien gefälscht, und das war es ~** the picture looked like a fake and indeed it was; **sie war unkonzentriert, aber es war ja ~ schon spät** she couldn't concentrate, but it WAS late - **4.** [verstärkend]: **dass du ~ immer kleckern musst!** do you HAVE to make such a mess!; **hast du die Tür ~ wirklich zugemacht?** are you sure you closed the door? - **5.** [egal]: **wo ~ (immer)** wherever; **was ~ (immer)** whatever; **wer ~ (immer)** whoever; **wie dem ~ sei** be that as it may.

**Audienz** (*pl* -en) *die* audience.

**Audimax** (*pl* -) (*abk für* **Auditorium maximum**) *das* UNI main lecture hall.

**audiovisuell** [audiovi'zuɛl] *adj* audiovisual.

**Auditorium** (*pl* **Auditorien**) *das* - **1.** [Hörsaal] lecture hall; ~ **maximum** main lecture hall - **2.** [Publikum] audience.

**Aue** (*pl* -n) *die* water meadow.

**Auer|hahn** *der* capercaillie.

**Auer|ochse** *der* aurochs.

**auf** *präp* - **1.** (+ D, A) [räumlich] on; ~ **dem/den Tisch** on the table; ~ **dem Land** in the country; ~ **s Land** to the country; ~ **einen Berg steigen** to climb a mountain; ~ **der Post** at the post office; ~ **eine Feier gehen** to go to a party; ~ **die Uni gehen** to go to university - **2.** (+ D) [zeitlich – während]: ~ **der Reise** on the journey; ~ **der Hochzeit/Feier** at the wedding/party - **3.** (+ A) [zur Angabe der Art und Weise]: ~ **diese Art** in this way; ~ **Deutsch** in German; ~ **jeden Fall** in any case - **4.** [feste Verbindungen]: ~ **Reisen gehen** to go on a tour; ~ **js Rat hin** on sb's advice; **von heute ~ morgen** overnight; **was hat es damit ~ sich, dass ...** how come ... - **5.** (+ A) [zur Angabe eines Wunsches]: ~ **ihr Wohl!** your good health!; ~ **dass all deine Wünsche in Erfüllung gehen** may all your wishes come true - **6.** [zur Angabe eines Verhältnisses]: ~ **ein Kilo Obst kommt ein Pfund Zucker** add a pound of sugar for every kilo of fruit ⟨⟩ adv - **1.** [offen] open; **Tür ~!** open the door! - **2.** [aufgestanden] up; **ich bin seit zehn Uhr ~** I've been up since ten o'clock - **3.** [feste Verbindungen]: ~ **einmal knallte es** suddenly there was a bang; **er aß alle Süßigkeiten ~ einmal** he ate all the sweets in one go ⟨⟩ interj [los, weg]: ~ **in die Kneipe!** (let's go) to the pub!; ~ **und davon** up and away.

⇒ **auf und ab** adv - **1.** [herauf und herunter] up and down - **2.** [hin und her] back and forth.

**auflarbeiten** vt - **1.** [Korrespondenz] to finish off; [Rückstand] to clear up - **2.** [Möbel] to recondition; [Sofa] to reupholster - **3.** [Erlebnisse, Eindrücke] to work through.

**auflatmen** vi to breathe a sigh of relief; **(wieder) ~ können** to be able to breathe again.

**Aufbau** (pl -ten) der - **1.** (ohne pl) [Bauen - von Zelt, Gerüst] putting up; [ - von Ruinen] rebuilding - **2.** (ohne pl) [Gründung] building up - **3.** (ohne pl) [Struktur] structure - **4.** [Anbau] superstructure.

**auflbauen** vt - **1.** [bauen - Zelt, Gerüst] to put up; [ - Ruinen] to rebuild - **2.** [gründen, schaffen] to build up - **3.** [zusammensetzen - Kulissen, Modelleisenbahn] to build; **aus etw aufgebaut sein** to be made up ODER composed of sthg - **4.** TELEC [Verbindung] to establish - **5.** [ordnen] to structure - **6.** [fördern]: **jn zu** ODER **als etw ~** to make ODER turn sb into sthg - **7.** [trösten]: **jn ~** to give sb strength - **8.** [begründen]: **etw auf etw** (D) ~ to base sthg on sthg.

⇒ **sich aufbauen** ref - **1.** fam [sich hinstellen] to plant o.s. - **2.** [sich zusammensetzen]: **sich aus etw ~** to be made up ODER composed of sthg.

**Aufbaulgymnasium** das school taking "Realschule" leavers up to university-entrance standard in three years.

**auflbäumen** ⇒ **sich aufbäumen** ref - **1.** [Pferd] to rear (up) - **2.** [Person]: **sich gegen jn/etw ~** to rebel against sb/sthg.

**auflbauschen** vt [übertreiben] to blow up.

**auflbehalten** vt (unreg) to keep on.

**auflbekommen** vt (unreg) - **1.** [öffnen] to get open - **2.** fam [aufessen] to manage (to eat) - **3.** [Schulaufgabe] to get for homework.

**auflbereiten** vt to process; [Trinkwasser] to purify.

**Aufbereitung** (pl -en) die processing; [von Trinkwasser] purification.

**auflbessern** vt - **1.** [verbessern] to improve - **2.** [erhöhen] to increase.

**Aufbesserung** (pl -en) die - **1.** [Verbesserung] improvement - **2.** [Erhöhung] increase.

**auflbewahren** vt [in Tresor] to keep; **etw (für jn) ~** to look after sthg (for sb); **die Milch kühl ~** to store the milk in a cool place.

**Aufbewahrung** die storage.

**auflbieten** vt (unreg) - **1.** [Kraft] to summon up; [Einfluss] to use - **2.** [Polizei, Militär] to call out.

**Aufbietung** die: **unter ~ aller Kräfte** summoning up all his/her/etc strength.

**auflbinden** vt (unreg) - **1.** [lösen] to undo - **2.** [Haare] to tie up.

**auflblasen** vt (unreg) [Ballon, Luftmatratze] to blow up, to inflate; [Backen] to puff out.

**auflbleiben** (perf ist aufgeblieben) vi (unreg) - **1.** [wach bleiben] to stay up - **2.** [offen bleiben] to stay open.

**auflblenden** vt to turn on full beam Br ODER high beam Am ⟨⟩ vi to put one's headlights on full beam Br ODER high beam Am.

**auflblicken** vi - **1.** [hochsehen] to look up - **2.** [bewundern]: **zu jm ~** to look up to sb.

**auflblitzen** (perf aufgeblitzt) vi [Licht] to flash.

**auflblühen** (perf ist aufgeblüht) vi - **1.** [blühen] to blossom - **2.** [aufleben] to blossom (out) - **3.** [wachsen] to flourish.

**auflbrauchen** vt to use up.

**auflbrausen** (perf ist aufgebraust) vi - **1.** [erklingen] to break out - **2.** [hochfahren] to flare up.

**auflbrausend** adj fiery.

**auflbrechen** (perf hat/ist aufgebrochen) (unreg) vt (hat) [mit Gewalt öffnen - Tür] to force open; [ - Schloss] to force; [ - Deckel] to force off; [ - Wohnung, Auto, Tresor] to break into ⟨⟩ vi (ist) - **1.** [abreisen]: ~ **(nach)** to set off (for) - **2.** [aufreißen] to open.

**auflbringen** vt (unreg) - **1.** [beschaffen] to raise - **2.** [einsetzen] to summon up - **3.** [einführen - Gerücht] to start - **4.** [wütend machen] to make angry; **jn gegen jn/etw ~** to set sb against sb/ sthg - **5.** [öffnen können] to get open.

**Aufbruch** der (ohne pl) departure.

**auflbrühen** vt to brew.

**auflbrummen** vt fam: **jm etw ~** [Strafe] to slap sthg on sb.

**auflbürden** vt: **jm/sich etw ~** [Last, Rucksack] to load sb/o.s. down with sthg; [Verantwortung] to burden sb/o.s. with sthg.

**aufldecken** vt - **1.** [aufschlagen] to turn back - **2.** [entdecken] to uncover - **3.** [Spielkarten]: **seine**

Karten *ODER* sein Spiel ~ to show one's hand - **4.** [im Bett]: jn ~ to pull the covers off sb.

**aufdonnern** ➡ sich aufdonnern *ref fam abw* to doll o.s. up.

**aufdrängen** *vt:* jm etw ~ to force sthg onto sb.
➡ sich aufdrängen *ref* - **1.** [Person] to impose; er hat sich uns vor der Reise aufgedrängt he imposed himself on us before we set off - **2.** [Idee]: dieser Gedanke/Verdacht drängte sich mir auf I couldn't help thinking/suspecting that; diese Idee drängt sich einem ja sofort auf, wenn man seinen Bericht hört this idea comes immediately to mind on hearing his report.

**aufdrehen** *vt* - **1.** [Wasserhahn, Gas] to turn on; [Deckel] to unscrew; [Flasche, Dose] to open - **2.** *fam* [laut stellen] to turn up <> *vi fam* - **1.** [schnell fahren] to put one's foot down - **2.** [in Stimmung kommen] to get going.

**aufdringlich** *adj* [Person] pushy; [Farbe] loud; [Parfüm] overpowering <> *adv* insistently.

**aufdröseln** *vt* to undo.

**aufdrucken** *vt:* etw auf etw (A) ~ to print sthg on sthg.

**aufdrücken** *vt* - **1.** [öffnen] to push open - **2.** [anheften, anbringen]: etw auf etw (A) ~ to stamp sthg on sthg <> *vi* [drücken]: mit etw ~ to press with sthg.

**aufeinander** *adv* - **1.** [einer auf dem anderen] one on top of the other; sie liegen ~ they are lying on top of each other - **2.** [gegenseitig] one another; sie passen ~ auf they look out for each other.

**aufeinander folgen** (*perf* sind aufeinander gefolgt) *vi* to come one after the other.

**aufeinander legen** *vt* to lay one on top of the other.

**aufeinander liegen** *vi* (*unreg*) to lie on top of each other.

**aufeinander prallen** (*perf* sind aufeinander geprallt) *vi* - **1.** [zusammenstoßen] to crash into one another - **2.** [sich widersprechen] to clash.

**aufeinander stoßen** (*perf* sind aufeinander gestoßen) *vi* (*unreg*) - **1.** [Köpfe, Waggons] to bump into each other - **2.** [Meinungen] to clash.

**aufeinander treffen** (*perf* sind aufeinander getroffen) *vi* (*unreg*) to meet.

**Aufenthalt** (*pl* -e) *der* - **1.** [Anwesenheit] stay; der ~ im Bereich des Krans ist gefährlich keep well clear of the crane - **2.** [Unterbrechung] stop; in Köln haben wir über eine Stunde ~ we will have over an hour to wait in Cologne.

**Aufenthaltsgenehmigung** *die* residence permit.

**Aufenthaltsort** *der* place of residence.

**auferstehen** (*perf* ist auferstanden) *vi* (*unreg*): von den Toten ~ to rise from the dead.

**Auferstehung** *die* (*ohne pl*) resurrection.

**aufessen** *vt* (*unreg*) to eat up.

**auffädeln** *vt* to string.

**auffahren** (*perf* ist aufgefahren) (*unreg*) *vi* - **1.** [im Auto]: dicht auf den Vordermann ~ to sit right on the tail of the car in front; auf jn/etw ~ to run into sb/sthg - **2.** [erschrecken] to start; aus dem Schlaf ~ to awake with a start <> *vt* - **1.** [heranfahren] to bring up - **2.** *fam* [anbieten] to lay on - **3.** [aufschütten] to put down.

**Auffahrt** (*pl* -en) *die* - **1.** [zur Autobahn] slip road *Br*, on-ramp *Am* - **2.** [zu einem Gebäude] drive - **3.** [Aufstieg] climb - **4.** *Schweiz* [Himmelfahrt] Ascension Day.

**Auffahrunfall** *der* rear-end collision.

**auffallen** (*perf* ist aufgefallen) *vi* (*unreg*) to stand out; mir ist nichts Besonderes an ihm aufgefallen nothing in particular struck me about him; es fällt auf, dass sie sich nie grüßen it's noticeable how they never say hello; er fällt durch seine laute Stimme auf his loud voice makes him stand out; unangenehm ~ to make a bad impression.

**auffallend** *adj* striking <> *adv* strikingly.

**auffällig** *adj* [Kleidung, Auto] ostentatious; [Farbe] loud; [Verhalten] odd, unusual <> *adv* [geschminkt] ostentatiously; [häufig] surprisingly.

**auffangen** *vt* (*unreg*) - **1.** [Ball] to catch - **2.** [Worte, Spruch, Signal] to pick up - **3.** [Stoß, Schlag] to cushion; [Inflation, Preissteigerung] to offset - **4.** [sammeln] to collect.

**Auffanglager** *das* transit camp.

**auffassen** *vt* to understand; etw als etw ~ to take sthg as sthg; etw richtig ~ to understand sthg correctly; etw falsch ~ to misunderstand sthg.

**Auffassung** *die* opinion; zu der ~ kommen, dass ... to come to the conclusion that ...; nach js ~ in sb's opinion.

**Auffassungsgabe** *die* (*ohne pl*) intelligence; eine schnelle ~ haben to be quick on the uptake.

**auffinden** *vt* (*unreg*) to find, to locate.

**aufflackern** (*perf* ist aufgeflackert) *vi* [leuchten] to flicker into life.

**auffliegen** (*perf* ist aufgeflogen) *vi* (*unreg*) - **1.** [fliegen] to fly up - **2.** [sich öffnen] to fly open - **3.** *fam* [entdeckt werden - Vorhaben] to be uncovered; [- Bande] to be broken up.

**auffordern** *vt* - **1.** [bitten]: jn dazu ~, etw zu tun to ask sb to do sthg; jn zum Platznehmen ~ to ask *ODER* invite sb to be seated - **2.** [befehlen]: jn dazu ~, etw zu tun to require sb to do sthg;

jn **zur Rückkehr** ~ to require sb to return
- **3.** [zum Tanz] to ask to dance.

**Auflforderung** die - **1.** [Bitte] request, invitation - **2.** [Befehl] demand.

**auflforsten** vt to reafforest.

**auflfressen** vt (unreg) - **1.** [fressen] to devour
- **2.** fam [einnehmen]: **sie lässt sich von der Sorge
um ihren Sohn** ~ she is consumed with worry
about her son - **3.** fam [bestrafen] to eat alive.

**auflfrischen** vt - **1.** [erneuern - Bezug] to freshen up; [- Farbe] to brighten up; [- Möbel] to renovate - **2.** [erweitern - Kenntnisse] to brush up on;
[- Erinnerung] to refresh <> vi [Wind] to freshen.

**auflführen** vt - **1.** [auf der Bühne] to perform
- **2.** [nennen, auflisten] to give, to list.
➡ **sich aufführen** ref abw [sich benehmen] to behave.

**Auflführung** die [Vorstellung] performance.

**auflfüllen** vt - **1.** [nachfüllen] to top up - **2.** [füllen] to fill up - **3.** [ergänzen] to replenish.

**Auflgabe** die - **1.** [Pflicht] task; **das ist nicht meine** - that's not my responsibility; **sich** (D) **etw
zur** ~ **machen** to make sthg one's business - **2.** [Kapitulation] surrender - **3.** (ohne pl)
[von Geschäften]: **die Einzelhändler wurden zur**
~ **genötigt** the retailers were forced to give
up their businesses - **4.** [eines Pakets] posting
**Br**, mailing **Am**; [einer Anzeige] placing - **5.** [SCHU-
LE - in Prüfung] question; [- in Mathematik] problem; [- Übung] exercise; [- Schulaufgabe] homework (U).

**auflgabeln** vt fam [Buch, Frau] to pick up;
[Schnupfen] to get.

**Aufgabenlbereich** der area of responsibility.

**Aufgabenlstellung** die: **die** ~ **war unklar** it
wasn't clear what we were supposed to do.

**Aufgang** (pl **Aufgänge**) der - **1.** [Treppe] stairs
(pl) - **2.** [Leuchten] rising.

**auflgeben** (unreg) vt - **1.** [Gewohnheit, Stelle, Ge-
schäft] to give up; **das Rauchen** ~ to give up
smoking - **2.** [Person] to give up on; [Plan, Idee,
Hoffnung] to give up; [Wettkampf, Spiel] to pull
out of; **ich gebe es auf!** I give up! - **3.** [auftragen]
to set; **jm etw** ~ to set sb sthg - **4.** [Bestellung] to
place; **eine Anzeige** ~ to place an advert in
the paper - **5.** [verschicken] to send <> vi [aufhö-
ren, kapitulieren] to give up.

**aufgebläht** adj [Ballon, Verwaltungsapparat] inflated; [Bauch] swollen; [Backen] puffed-out.

**Auflgebot** das - **1.** [an Personen] contingent; [an
Maschinen, Waren] array - **2.** [für Hochzeit] banns
(pl); **das** ~ **bestellen** to publish the banns.

**aufgebracht** pp ▷ **aufbringen** <> adj [wü-
tend] angry.

**aufgedonnert** adj fam [übertrieben zurechtge-
macht] tarted up.

**aufgedreht** adj fam [aufgeregt] in high spirits.

**aufgedunsen** adj bloated.

**aufgefächert** adj fanned-out.

**auflgehen** (perf **ist aufgegangen**) vi (unreg)
- **1.** [Sonne, Mond] to rise; [Sterne] to come out
- **2.** [Knoten, Knopf] to come undone - **3.** [sich öff-
nen] to open - **4.** [Rechnung] to work out
- **5.** [verschwinden]: **in etw** (D) ~ to disappear
into sthg; **in Flammen** ~ to go up in flames
- **6.** [sich einsetzen]: **in etw** (D) ~ to be wrapped
up in sthg - **7.** [deutlich werden]: **jm** ~ to dawn
on sb - **8.** [Teig, Kuchen] to rise.

**aufgehoben** pp ▷ **aufheben** <> adj: **(bei
jm) gut/schlecht** ~ **sein** to be/not to be in good
hands (with sb).

**aufgeklärt** adj enlightened.

**aufgekratzt** adj boisterous.

**aufgelegt** adj: **gut/schlecht** ~ **sein** to be in a
good/bad mood; **zu etw** ~ **sein** to be in the
mood for sthg.

**aufgelöst** adj [fassungslos] frantic.

**aufgepasst** interj be careful!

**aufgeräumt** adj - **1.** [ordentlich] tidy - **2.** [fröh-
lich] cheerful.

**aufgeregt** adj excited <> adv excitedly.

**aufgeschlossen** pp ▷ **aufschließen** <> adj
open-minded; **etw gegenüber** ODER **für etw**
~ **sein** to be open to sthg.

**aufgeschmissen** adj fam: ~ **sein** to be stuck.

**aufgeschwemmt** adj bloated.

**aufgetakelt** adj fam [übertrieben zurechtgemacht]
tarted up.

**aufgeweckt** adj bright.

**auflgießen** vt (unreg) to make.

**auflgliedern** vt: **etw in etw** (A) ~ to split sthg
up into sthg.

**auflgreifen** vt (unreg) - **1.** [fangen] to pick up
- **2.** [übernehmen] to take up.

**aufgrund** präp: ~ **einer Sache** (G) because of
sthg; ~ **von Zeugenaussagen** on the basis of
statements made by the witnesses.

**Auflguss** der - **1.** [Tee] infusion - **2.** abw [Neufas-
sung] pale imitation.

**auflhaben** (unreg) vt - **1.** [Hausaufgaben] to have
for homework - **2.** [tragen] to have on, to be
wearing - **3.** [offen lassen - Mantel, Tür] to have
open; [- Knopf] to have undone - **4.** fam [aufge-
gessen haben] to have eaten up <> vi [geöffnet
sein] to be open.

**auflhalsen** vt fam: **jm/sich etw** ~ to lumber
sb/o.s. with sthg.

**auflhalten** vt (unreg) - **1.** [offen halten - Tür, Tasche]
to hold open; **die Hand** ~ to hold out one's
hand; **die Augen** ~ to keep one's eyes open;
**jm etw** ~ to hold sthg open for sb - **2.** [anhal-
ten - Entwicklung, Inflation] to put a check on

**- 3.** [stören] to hold up; **ich möchte Sie nicht ~** I don't want to keep you.
➤ **sich aufhalten** *ref* **- 1.** [sich befinden] to stay **- 2.** *abw* [sich aufregen]: **sich über jn/etw ~** to rant and rave about sb/sthg.

**auf|hängen** *vt* **- 1.** [hinhängen - Mantel, Plakat] to hang up; [- Bild] to hang; [- Wäsche] to hang out **- 2.** [erhängen] to hang **- 3.** [mit etw begründen]: **etw an etw** *(D)* **~** to base sthg on sthg ⬦ *vi* [am Telefon] to hang up.
➤ **sich aufhängen** *ref fam* [sich erhängen] to hang o.s.

**Aufhänger** *(pl -) der* **- 1.** [Halterung] loop **- 2.** *fig* [Grund, Anstoß] pretext.

**auf|häufen** *vt* to pile up.
➤ **sich aufhäufen** *ref* to pile up.

**auf|heben** *vt (unreg)* **- 1.** [nehmen] to pick up **- 2.** [aufbewahren] to keep; **etw gut ~** to keep sthg safe **- 3.** [Gesetz, Verordnung] to repeal; [Verbot, Embargo] to lift; [Visapflicht] to end **- 4.** [ausgleichen]: **etw/einander ~** to cancel sthg/each other out.
➤ **sich aufheben** *ref* to cancel each other out.

**Aufheben** *das:* **viel ~s von jm/etw machen** to make a great fuss about sb/sthg.

**Auf|hebung** *die* [von Gesetz, Verordnung] repeal; [von Verbot, Embargo] lifting; [von Visapflicht] ending.

**auf|heitern** *vt* [Person] to cheer up.
➤ **sich aufheitern** *ref* **- 1.** [fröhlich werden] to cheer up **- 2.** [sonnig werden] to clear up.

**auf|heizen** *vt* **- 1.** [erwärmen] to heat up **- 2.** *fig* [erregen] to whip up.
➤ **sich aufheizen** *ref* to heat up.

**auf|hellen** *vt* [heller machen] to lighten.
➤ **sich aufhellen** *ref* **- 1.** [Gesicht, Miene] to light up **- 2.** [Wetter, Himmel] to clear up.

**auf|hetzen** *vt* to stir up; **jn zu etw ~** to incite sb to sthg; **jn gegen jn/etw ~** to stir sb up against sb/sthg.

**auf|heulen** *vi* [Hund, Wolf] to howl; [Motor] to roar.

**auf|holen** *vt* [Verspätung] to make up ⬦ *vi* [Sportler, Wirtschaft] to catch up.

**auf|horchen** *vi* **- 1.** [horchen] to prick up one's ears **- 2.** [aufmerksam werden] to sit up and take notice.

**auf|hören** *vi* **- 1.** [nicht weitermachen] to stop; **~, etw zu tun** to stop doing sthg; **mit etw ~** to stop sthg; **mit dem Rauchen ~** to stop smoking **- 2.** [kündigen] to finish **- 3.** [zu Ende sein - Film, Straße, Weg] to end; [- Lärm, Regen] to stop; [- Nebel] to lift; **da hört sich doch alles auf!** *fig* that's the limit!

**auf|kaufen** *vt* to buy up.

**auf|klappen** *vt* to open.

**auf|klaren** *vi* to clear up.

**auf|klären** *vt* **- 1.** [Missverständnis] to clear up; [Mord] to solve **- 2.** [informieren]: **jn über etw** *(A)* **~** to tell sb about sthg **- 3.** [über Sexualität informieren] to explain the facts of life to.
➤ **sich aufklären** *ref* **- 1.** [sich auflösen] to be cleared up **- 2.** [sonnig werden] to clear up.

**Auf|klärung** *die* **- 1.** [von Irrtum] clearing up; [von Verbrechen] solving **- 2.** [Information] informing **- 3.** [Information über Sexualität] sex education **- 4.** HIST Enlightenment.

**auf|kleben** *vt* to stick on.

**Auf|kleber** *der* sticker.

**auf|knacken** *vt* **- 1.** [aufbrechen] to crack **- 2.** *fam* [gewaltsam aufbrechen] to break into.

**auf|knöpfen** *vt* to unbutton.

**auf|knoten** *vt* to undo.

**auf|kochen** *(perf ist aufgekocht) vi* to come to the boil; **etw ~ lassen** to bring sthg to the boil.

**auf|kommen** *(perf ist aufgekommen) vi (unreg)* **- 1.** [entstehen] to arise; [Sturm] to get up; **keine Zweifel ~ lassen** to leave no room for doubt **- 2.** [übernehmen, zahlen]: **für jn/etw ~** to pay for sb/sthg **- 3.** [aufstehen können] to get up **- 4.** [landen] to land.

**Aufkommen** *(pl -) das* **- 1.** [Anzahl] (total) number **- 2.** [Einnahme] revenue.

**auf|kratzen** *vt* [Wunde] to scratch open; [Pickel] to pick.

**auf|krempeln** *vt:* **sich** *(D)* **die Ärmel ~** to roll up one's sleeves.

**auf|kreuzen** *(perf ist aufgekreuzt) vi fam* to show up.

**auf|kriegen** *vt fam* **- 1.** [öffnen können - Tür, Paket] to get open; [- Knoten] to get undone **- 2.** [aufessen]: **etw nicht ~** not to eat sthg up.

**auf|kündigen** *vt:* **jm etw ~** [Vertrag, Freundschaft] to terminate sthg with sb.

**Aufl.** *(abk für Auflage)* ed.

**auf|lachen** *vi* to burst out laughing.

**auf|laden** *vt (unreg)* **- 1.** [Lasten]: **etw auf etw** *(A)* **~** to load sthg onto sthg **- 2.** [aufbürden]: **jm/sich etw ~** to burden sb/o.s. with sthg **- 3.** [Batterie] to charge.
➤ **sich aufladen** *ref* to charge.

**Auf|lage** *die* **- 1.** [von Büchern] edition; [von Zeitung] circulation **- 2.** [Bedingung] condition; **er hat den Betrieb gekauft mit der ~ alle Mitarbeiter zu übernehmen** he bought the company on (the) condition that all the staff remain in their jobs; **jm zur ~ machen, dass ...** to make it a condition for sb that ....

**Auflagen|höhe** *die* [von Buch] print-run; [von Zeitung] circulation.

**auf|lassen** *vt (unreg)* **- 1.** [Tür, Jacke] to leave

open; [Knopf] to leave undone - **2.** [Hut, Mütze] to keep on - **3.** [Betrieb, Anwesen] to shut down.

**auf|lauern** *vi:* jm ~ to lie in wait for sb.

**Auf|lauf** *der* - **1.** [Speise] bake - **2.** [Menschenansammlung] crowd.

**auf|laufen** (*perf* ist **aufgelaufen**) *vi (unreg)* - **1.** [sich festfahren]: **auf etw** (A) ~ to run aground on sthg - **2.** [abblocken]: **jn ~ lassen** sport to bodycheck sb - **3.** [steigen]: **auf etw** (A) ~ to mount up to sthg.

**auf|leben** (*perf* ist **aufgelebt**) *vi* - **1.** [Person] to liven up - **2.** [Gespräch, Erinnerung] to revive; **etw wieder ~ lassen** to bring sthg back to life.

**auf|legen** *vt* - **1.** [Tischtuch, Schallplatte, Schminke, Kohle] to put on; [Besteck] to put out - **2.** [Produkt, Buch] to bring out - **3.** [am Telefon] to hang up ◇ *vi* [am Telefon] to hang up.

**auf|lehnen** ➡ **sich auflehnen** *ref:* **sich gegen jn/etw ~** to rebel against sb/sthg.

**auf|lesen** *vt (unreg)* to pick up.

**auf|leuchten** (*perf* hat/ist **aufgeleuchtet**) *vi* to light up.

**auf|listen** *vt* to list.

**auf|lockern** *vt* - **1.** [Erde, Boden] to break up; [Muskeln] to loosen up - **2.** [Stimmung, Rede] to liven up.
➡ **sich auflockern** *ref* - **1.** [Sportler] to limber up - **2.** [Bewölkung] to break up; [Knoten] to loosen.

**Auflockerung** *die (ohne pl)* - **1.** [von Boden] breaking up; [von Muskeln] loosening up - **2.** [von Stimmung, Rede] livening up.

**auf|lösen** *vt* - **1.** [in Flüssigkeit, in Bestandteile] to dissolve; **etw in etw** (D) ~ to dissolve sthg in sthg - **2.** [Staatenverbund, Demonstration, Versammlung] to break up; [Vertrag] to cancel; [Verlobung] to break off; [Parlament] to dissolve - **3.** [Betrieb, Haushalt] to break up - **4.** [Missverständnis, Rätsel] to clear up.
➡ **sich auflösen** *ref* - **1.** [Tablette, Kristalle] to dissolve; [Nebel] to lift; [Bewölkung] to break up; **sich in etw** (D) ~ to dissolve in sthg; **er hat sich in Luft aufgelöst** he vanished into thin air - **2.** [Menge, Versammlung] to disperse - **3.** [Rätsel, Schwierigkeit] to be cleared up.

**Auf|lösung** *die* - **1.** [in Flüssigkeit, in Bestandteile] dissolving; **ein Bildschirm mit hoher ~** a high-resolution screen - **2.** [von Staatenverbund, Demonstration, Versammlung] breaking up; [von Vertrag] cancellation; [von Verlobung] breaking off; [von Parlament] dissolving - **3.** [von Betrieb, Haushalt] breaking up - **4.** [von Rätsel] solution.

**auf|machen** *vt* - **1.** [gen] to open; [Schnur, Knopf, Jacke] to undo - **2.** [gestalten] to make ◇ *vi* - **1.** [öffnen] to open the door; **jm ~** to let sb in - **2.** [Geschäft] to open.
➡ **sich aufmachen** *ref* [abreisen]: **sich ~ (nach)** to set off (for).

**Aufmachung** (*pl* -en) *die* - **1.** [Gestaltung] layout - **2.** [Kleidung] appearance.

**auf|malen** *vt* [zeichnen] to draw; [malen] to paint.

**Auf|marsch** *der* parade.

**auf|marschieren** (*perf* ist **aufmarschiert**) *vi* to parade.

**aufmerksam** *adj* - **1.** [konzentriert] attentive; **jn auf jn/etw ~ machen** to draw sb's attention to sb/sthg; **auf jn/etw ~ werden** to notice sb/sthg - **2.** [höflich] thoughtful ◇ *adv* attentively.

**Aufmerksamkeit** (*pl* -en) *die* - **1.** [Konzentration] attentiveness; **js ~ erregen** to draw sb's attention - **2.** [Mitbringsel] gift.

**auf|möbeln** *vt fam* - **1.** [munter machen] to cheer up - **2.** [erneuern] to do up.

**auf|muntern** *vt* [aufheitern] to cheer up; [ermutigen] to encourage.

**aufmunternd** *adj* encouraging ◇ *adv* encouragingly.

**aufmüpfig** *adj* rebellious.

**Aufnahme** (*pl* -n) *die* - **1.** [Empfang] reception; **~ in etw** (A) [Verein, Intensivstation] admission into sthg; **die Idee fand begeisterte ~** the idea was enthusiastically received; **die Kinder fanden bei Verwandten ~** the children were taken in by relatives - **2.** [Beginn - von Kontakt] establishment; [ - von Arbeit, Gespräch, Verhandlungen] start - **3.** [Aufzeichnung] recording; [von Diktat] taking down - **4.** [Fotografie] photograph.

**aufnahmefähig** *adj* receptive.

**Aufnahme|prüfung** *die* entrance examination.

**auf|nehmen** *vt (unreg)* - **1.** [aufheben, ergreifen] to pick up - **2.** [empfangen - in Klub] to admit; [ - Gast] to receive; [ - Asylant] to take in; **Namen auf einer Liste ~** to include names on a list; **ein Wort im Wörterbuch ~** to include a word in the dictionary; **jn bei sich** (D) ~ to take sb in - **3.** [essen]: **Nahrung ~** to eat - **4.** [Informationen] to take in; [Vorschlag] to take up - **5.** [reagieren auf]: **etw mit Begeisterung ~** to receive sthg enthusiastically - **6.** [beginnen - Gespräch, Arbeit, Verhandlungen] to start; [ - Thema, Tätigkeit] to take up; **mit jm Kontakt ~** to contact sb - **7.** [konkurrieren]: **es mit jm/etw ~ können** to be a match for sb/sthg - **8.** [aufschreiben] to take down - **9.** [sich leihen - Kredit, Hypothek] to get, to obtain; [ - Geld, Summe] to borrow - **10.** [Foto] to take - **11.** [auf Tonband] to record.

**auf|nötigen** *vt:* **jm etw ~** to force sthg onto sb.

**auf|opfern** ➡ **sich aufopfern** *ref:* **sich für jn/etw ~** to sacrifice o.s. for sb/sthg.

**aufopfernd** *adj* devoted ◇ *adv* devotedly.

**auf|päppeln** *vt* [nach Krankheit] to nurse back to health.

**auf|passen** *vi* to pay attention; **auf jn/etw ~** [Kind, Tasche] to keep an eye on sb/sthg; **auf Fehler ~** to watch out for mistakes; **pass auf!** [Vorsicht!] be careful!; **pass bloß auf, wenn ich dich erwische!** just you wait until I catch you!

**Aufpasser, in** (*mpl* -; *fpl* -nen) *der, die abw* [in Gefängnis] guard.

**auf|pflanzen** *vt* to plant.
➤ **sich aufpflanzen** *ref fam* to plant o.s.

**auf|platzen** (*perf* ist **aufgeplatzt**) *vi* to burst (open).

**auf|plustern** *vt* to ruffle up.
➤ **sich aufplustern** *ref* - **1.** [Vogel] to ruffle its feathers - **2.** *fam fig* [Person] to puff o.s. up.

**Aufprall** (*pl* -e) *der* impact.

**auf|prallen** (*perf* ist **aufgeprallt**) *vi*: **auf etw** (A) **~** to hit sthg.

**Aufpreis** *der* extra charge; **gegen ~** for an extra charge.

**auf|pumpen** *vt* to pump up.

**auf|putschen** *vt* to stir up.
➤ **sich aufputschen** *ref* to pep o.s. up.

**Aufputsch|mittel** *das* stimulant.

**auf|quellen** (*perf* ist **aufgequollen**) *vi* (*unreg*) to swell up.

**auf|raffen** ➤ **sich aufraffen** *ref* [sich entschließen]: **sich dazu ~, etw zu tun** to face up to doing sthg.

**auf|ragen** *vi* to rise up.

**auf|rauen** *vt* to roughen.

**auf|räumen** *vt* - **1.** [ordnen] to tidy up - **2.** [forträumen] to tidy away <> *vi* - **1.** [ordnen] to tidy up - **2.** [etw beenden]: **mit etw ~** to put an end to sthg.

**auf|rechnen** *vt*: **etw gegen etw ~** to compare sthg with sthg.

**aufrecht** *adj* - **1.** [gerade] upright - **2.** [Demokrat, Haltung] upstanding <> *adv* - **1.** [gerade] upright; **er kann sich kaum ~ halten** he can hardly stand, he's ready to drop - **2.** *fig* [bestärken]: **jn ~ halten** to sustain sb, to keep sb going.

**aufrecht|erhalten** *vt* (*unreg*) to maintain.

**Aufrecht|erhaltung** *die* maintaining.

**auf|regen** *vt* [ärgern] to annoy; [beunruhigen] to upset.
➤ **sich aufregen** *ref* to get worked up; **sich über jn/etw ~** to get worked up about sb/sthg.

**aufregend** *adj* exciting.

**Auf|regung** *die* excitement; **das schlechte Wahlergebnis versetzte die Partei in ~** the bad election result caused a great stir in the party.

**auf|reiben** *vt* (*unreg*) - **1.** [schwächen] to wear down - **2.** [vernichten] to wipe out.
➤ **sich aufreiben** *ref* [sich überanstrengen] to wear o.s. out.

**aufreibend** *adj* [anstrengend] exhausting.

**auf|reißen** (*perf* **hat/ist aufgerissen**) (*unreg*) *vt* (*hat*) - **1.** [öffnen - Brief, Verpackung] to tear open; [ - Tür, Fenster] to fling open; [ - Mund, Augen] to open wide - **2.** *salopp* [kennen lernen] to pick up <> *vi* (*ist*) [Naht] to split; [Wolkendecke] to break up.

**aufreizend** *adj* provocative <> *adv* provocatively.

**auf|richten** *vt* - **1.** [hochziehen - Kranken] to sit up; [ - Rücken] to straighten (up) - **2.** [aufstellen] to erect - **3.** [trösten] to lift.
➤ **sich aufrichten** *ref* [sich hochziehen] to sit up.

**aufrichtig** *adj* sincere <> *adv* sincerely.

**Auf|richtigkeit** *die* (*ohne pl*) sincerity.

**auf|rollen** *vt* - **1.** [zusammenrollen] to roll up - **2.** [auseinander rollen] to unroll - **3.** [besprechen, aufgreifen - Streit, Diskussion] to open up - **4.** SPORT: **das Feld von hinten ~** to move up the field.

**auf|rücken** (*perf* ist **aufgerückt**) *vi* to move up; **zum Direktor ~** to be promoted to headmaster.

**Auf|ruf** *der* appeal.

**auf|rufen** *vt* (*unreg*) - **1.** [nennen, rufen] to call - **2.** [auffordern]: **jn zu etw ~** to appeal to sb for sthg.

**Aufruhr** (*pl* -e) *der* - **1.** [Aufstand] uprising - **2.** [Unruhe] turmoil; **in ~ sein/geraten** to be in/be thrown into turmoil.

**aufrührerisch** *adj* [Versammlung] seditious; [Rede] inflammatory.

**auf|runden** *vt*: **~ (auf** (+ A)**)** to round up (to).

**auf|rüsten** *vi* to rearm; **wieder ~** to rearm.

**Auf|rüstung** *die* rearmament.

**auf|rütteln** *vt* to rouse.

**aufs** *präp* = **auf** + **das**.

**auf|sagen** *vt* [Text] to recite.

**auf|sammeln** *vt* to pick up.

**aufsässig** *adj* rebellious.

**Auf|satz** *der* - **1.** [Schularbeit] essay *Br*, paper *Am* - **2.** [Abhandlung] paper - **3.** [Aufbau] upper section.

**auf|saugen** *vt* to soak up.

**auf|schauen** *vi* - **1.** [mit Bewunderung]: **zu jm ~** to look up to sb - **2.** *Süddt* [aufblicken] to look up.

**auf|scheuchen** *vt* - **1.** [verscheuchen] to startle - **2.** *fig* [stören] to disturb.

**auf|schieben** *vt* (*unreg*) - **1.** [verschieben] to put off - **2.** [öffnen - Tür, Fenster] to slide open; [ - Riegel] to slide back.

**Auf|schlag** *der* - **1.** [Aufprall] impact - **2.** [auf den Preis] extra charge - **3**. [am Hosenbein] turn-up *Br*, cuff *Am*; [am Ärmel] cuff - **4**. sport serve; **er hat ~** it's his serve.

**auflschlagen** (*perf* hat/ist **aufgeschlagen**) (*unreg*) *vt* (*hat*) - **1**. [öffnen - Buch, Zeitung, Augen] to open - **2**. [Ei, Schale] to crack (open); [Eis] to break - **3**. [verletzen]: **sich das Knie ~** to cut one's knee - **4**. [aufbauen - Bett, Zelt] to put up; [ - Lager] to pitch - **5**. [dazurechnen]: **etw auf etw** (*A*) **~** to add sthg onto sthg <> *vi* - **1**. (*ist*) [aufprallen]: **auf etw** (*A*) **~** to hit sthg - **2**. (*hat*) sport to serve.

**auflschließen** (*unreg*) *vt* to unlock <> *vi* - **1**. [öffnen]: **jm ~** to unlock the door for sb - **2**. [nachrücken] to move up.

**auflschlitzen** *vt* [mit Messer] to slit open.

**Auflschluss** der (*ohne pl*): **über etw** (*A*) **~ geben** to provide information about sthg.

**auflschlüsseln** *vt*: **~ (nach)** to break down (into).

**aufschlussreich** *adj* informative.

**auflschnappen** *vt* fam to pick up.

**auflschneiden** (*unreg*) *vt* to cut open <> *vi* [angeben] to boast.

**Auflschnitt** der sliced cold meat and/or cheese.

**auflschnüren** *vt* to untie.

**auflschrauben** *vt* [Deckel] to unscrew; [Glas] to screw the lid off.

**auflschrecken** (*perf* hat/ist **aufgeschreckt**) *vt* (*hat*) to startle <> *vi* (*ist*) to start.

**Auflschrei** der *eigtl* & *fig* cry; **wenn die Benzinpreise erhöht werden, geht ein ~ durchs Volk** if petrol prices are put up, there will be a public outcry.

**auflschreiben** *vt* (*unreg*) - **1**. [notieren] to write down; **sich** (*D*) **etw ~** to make a note of sthg - **2**. [Strafzettel geben] to book.

**auflschreien** *vi* (*unreg*) to cry out; **vor Schmerz ~** to cry out with pain.

**Auflschrift** die inscription.

**Auflschub** der: **es duldet keinen ~** it must not be delayed; **jm ~ gewähren** to grant sb a period of grace.

**auflschütten** *vt* - **1**. [nachfüllen] to pour on - **2**. [anhäufen - Damm, Wall] to build up.

**auflschwatzen** *vt*: **jm etw ~** to talk sb into sthg.

**auflschwemmen** *vt* to make bloated.

**Auflschwung** der - **1**. [Auftrieb] upturn; **sein Optimismus gab uns ~** his optimism gave us a lift - **2**. sport swing-up.

**auflsehen** *vi* (*unreg*) [hochschauen] to look up; **zu jm ~** [bewundern] to look up to sb.

**Aufsehen** das: **~ erregen** to cause a stir; **~ erregend** sensational.

**Aufseher, in** (*mpl* -; *fpl* -nen) der, die [im Gefängnis] warder.

**auf sein** (*perf* ist **auf** gewesen) *vi* (*unreg*) fam - **1**. [offen sein] to be open - **2**. [wach sein] to be up.

**auflsetzen** *vt* - **1**. [gen] to put on - **2**. [schreiben] to draft <> *vi* [landen] to touch down.
- **sich aufsetzen** *ref* [sich aufrichten] to sit up.

**auflseufzen** *vi* to heave a sigh.

**Auflsicht** die (*ohne pl*) - **1**. [Kontrolle] supervision; **die ~ über jn/etw haben** to supervise sb/sthg; **unter js ~** (*D*) under sb's supervision - **2**. [Person] supervisor.

**Aufsichtslbehörde** die watchdog (organization).

**Aufsichtslpflicht** die [von Eltern] parental responsibility.

**Aufsichtslrat** der supervisory board, *company board comprising management and worker representatives with powers of codetermination*.

**auflsitzen** (*perf* hat/ist **aufgesessen**) *vi* (*unreg*) - **1**. (*ist*) [aufsteigen - auf Motorrad] to get on; [ - Pferd] to mount - **2**. (*ist*) [sich täuschen lassen]: **jm ~** to be taken in by sb - **3**. (*hat*) [wach bleiben] to sit up.

**auflspalten** *vt* to split.
- **sich aufspalten** *ref* to split up.

**auflspannen** *vt* to put up.

**auflsparen** *vt*: **sich** (*D*) **etw ~** to save sthg.

**auflsperren** *vt* - **1**. [aufschließen] to unlock - **2**. [offen halten] to open wide.

**auflspielen** - **sich aufspielen** *ref* [angeben] to give o.s. airs; **sich als Chef/Genie ~** to play the boss/genius.

**auflspießen** *vt* to spear.

**auflspringen** (*perf* ist **aufgesprungen**) *vi* (*unreg*) - **1**. [aufstehen]: **~ (vor** (+ *D*)**)** to jump up (with) - **2**. [sich öffnen - Blüte, Tür] to burst open; [ - Haut, Hände] to chap - **3**. [springen]: **auf etw** (*A*) **~** to jump onto sthg.

**auflspüren** *vt* to track down.

**auflstacheln** *vt*: **jn (zu etw) ~** to spur sb on (to sthg).

**auflstampfen** *vi*: **mit dem Fuß ~** to stamp one's foot.

**Auflstand** der uprising, rebellion; **wenn der Chef von der Beschwerde erfährt, macht er einen ~** fam if the boss hears of the complaint, there will be hell to pay.

**aufständisch** *adj* rebellious.

**Aufständische** (*pl* -n) der, die rebel.

**auflstapeln** *vt* to pile up.

**auflstauen** *vt* to dam.
- **sich aufstauen** *ref* [Wasser] to collect; [Gefühle, Wut] to get bottled up.

**auf|stecken** vt - **1.** [hochstecken] to pin up - **2.** fam [aufgeben, abbrechen] to give up.

**auf|stehen** (perf hat/ist aufgestanden) vi (unreg) - **1.** (ist) [sich erheben] to get up - **2.** (hat) [offen stehen] to stand open.

**auf|steigen** (perf ist aufgestiegen) vi (unreg) - **1.** [auf Motorrad, Fahrrad, Pferd] to get on; **auf etw** (A) ~ [Fahrrad, Pferd] to get on sthg - **2.** [Bergsteiger, Hubschrauber, Ballon] to climb; [Vogel] to soar; **auf einen Berg** ~ to climb a mountain - **3.** [Rauch] to rise; [Nebel] to lift - **4.** [Erfolg haben] to be promoted; **in etw** (A)/**zu etw** ~ to be promoted to sthg.

**Aufsteiger** (pl -) der - **1.** [Mannschaft] promoted team - **2.** [Person]: **sozialer** ~ social climber.

**Aufsteigerin** (pl -nen) die [Person]: **soziale** ~ social climber.

**auf|stellen** vt - **1.** [hinstellen - Schachfiguren, Kegel, Lampe] to set up; [ - Schild] to put up - **2.** [aufbauen - Gerüst, Gitter] to put up - **3.** [Liste, Plan] to draw up - **4.** [Theorie, Behauptung] to put forward - **5.** [auswählen] to select - **6.** [Ohren] to prick up; [Stacheln] to raise; [Kragen] to turn up.
➥ **sich aufstellen** ref - **1.** [sich hinstellen] to take up one's position - **2.** [sich aufrichten - Haare] to stand on end.

**Auf|stellung** die - **1.** [Hinstellen - von Schachfiguren, Kegeln, Lampe] setting up; [ - von Schild] putting up; ~ **nehmen** to take up one's position - **2.** [Aufbau - von Gerüst, Gitter] putting up - **3.** [von Liste, Plan] drawing up - **4.** [von Theorie, Behauptung] putting forward - **5.** [Wahl] selection.

**auf|stemmen** vt to prise open.

**Aufstieg** (pl -e) der - **1.** [Aufsteigen] ascent - **2.** [Erfolg] promotion.

**auf|stöbern** vt [Opfer, Sammlerstück] to track down; [Wild] to flush out.

**auf|stocken** vt - **1.** [höher bauen] to raise the height of - **2.** [vergrößern] to increase.

**auf|stoßen** (perf hat/ist aufgestoßen) (unreg) vt (hat) [öffnen] to push open <> vi - **1.** (ist) [stoßen]: **mit etw auf etw** (D) ~ to hit sthg with sthg - **2.** (hat) [rülpsen] to belch - **3.** (ist) fam [unangenehm auffallen]: **sein Verhalten ist mir sauer** ODER **übel aufgestoßen** his behaviour left a nasty taste in my mouth.

**aufstrebend** adj up-and-coming.

**auf|stützen** vt to prop up.
➥ **sich aufstützen** ref to support o.s.

**auf|suchen** vt to go to.

**Auf|takt** der - **1.** [Anfang] start - **2.** MUS upbeat.

**auf|tanken** vt [Auto] to fill up; [Flugzeug] to refuel; **Benzin** ~ to fill up with petrol Br ODER gas Am.

**auf|tauchen** (perf ist aufgetaucht) vi - **1.** [aus dem Wasser] to surface - **2.** [sichtbar werden] to appear - **3.** [aufkommen] to arise - **4.** [gefunden werden, ankommen] to turn up.

**auf|tauen** (perf hat/ist aufgetaut) vt (hat) vi (ist) [Lebensmittel] to defrost; [Boden, Eis] to thaw.

**auf|teilen** vt - **1.** [verteilen] to share out; **die Kollegen teilen die Aufgaben unter sich auf** the colleagues share out the tasks amongst themselves - **2.** [einteilen] to divide up; **jn/etw in etw** (A) ~ to divide sb/sthg up into sthg.

**Auf|teilung** die - **1.** [Verteilung]: ~ **(unter** (+D)**)** sharing out (amongst) - **2.** [Einteilung]: ~ **(in** (+A)**)** division (into).

**auf|tischen** vt - **1.** [servieren] to serve up - **2.** fam fig [erzählen] to come out with.

**Auftr.** abk für **Auftrag**.

**Auftrag** (pl **Aufträge**) der - **1.** [Befehl, Aufgabe] task; **jm einen** ~ **geben** ODER **erteilen** to give sb a task; **in js** ~ (D) **handeln** to act on sb's behalf - **2.** [Bestellung] order; **etw in** ~ **geben** [Untersuchung, Reparatur] to order sthg; [Studie, Gemälde] to commission sthg.

**auf|tragen** (unreg) vt - **1.** [aufstreichen] to apply; **etw auf etw** (A) ~ to apply sthg to sthg; **etw dick/dünn** ~ to apply sthg liberally/sparingly - **2.** [bestellen]: **jm** ~, **etw zu tun** to tell sb to do sthg; **sie hat mir Grüße an dich aufgetragen** she asked me to pass on her regards to you - **3.** [abtragen] to wear out <> vi: **dick** ~ fam [übertreiben] to go over the top.

**Auftraggeber, in** (mpl -; fpl -nen) der, die [Kunde] client; **der** ~ **einer Umfrage** the person who commissioned a survey.

**Auftrags|bestätigung** die order confirmation.

**Auftrags|lage** die order situation.

**auf|treffen** (perf ist aufgetroffen) vi (unreg) to land.

**auf|treiben** (perf hat aufgetrieben) vt (unreg) (hat) [finden] to find.

**auf|trennen** vt to unpick.

**auf|treten** (perf ist aufgetreten) vi (unreg) - **1.** [treten] to tread - **2.** [sich benehmen] to behave - **3.** [erscheinen - Person] to appear; [ - Problem, Gefahr, Frage] to arise.

**Auftreten** das - **1.** [Benehmen] behaviour - **2.** [Erscheinen] occurrence.

**Auf|trieb** der buoyancy; **jm/einer Sache** ~ **geben** fig to give sb/sthg a lift.

**auf|trumpfen** vi to show one's superiority.

**auf|tun** vt (unreg) fam [finden] to come across.
➥ **sich auftun** ref eigtl & fig to open up.

**auf|türmen** vt to pile up.
➥ **sich auftürmen** ref [Masse, Probleme] to pile up; [Berge] to tower.

**auf|wachen** (perf ist aufgewacht) vi to wake up.

**auflwachsen** [ˈaʊfvaksn̩] (*perf* ist **aufgewachsen**) *vi* (*unreg*) to grow up.

**Aufwand** *der* - **1.** [Einsatz - von Geld] expenditure; **es ist mit viel ~ verbunden** it takes a lot of time/effort/*etc* - **2.** [Luxus] extravagance; **viel** ODER **großen ~ treiben** to be very extravagant.

**aufwändig** *adj* extravagant ◇ *adv* extravagantly.

**auflwärmen** *vt* - **1.** [warm machen] to warm up - **2.** *fam fig* [wieder erwähnen] to bring up again.
➡ **sich aufwärmen** *ref* to warm o.s. up.

**auflwarten** *vi*: **mit etw ~** to offer sthg.

**aufwärts** *adv* upwards; **von 50 cm³ ~** from 50 cm³ up ODER upwards.

**aufwärts gehen** (*perf* ist **aufwärts gegangen**) *vi* (*unreg*): **mit den Verkaufszahlen geht es aufwärts** the sales figures are looking up.

**Aufwärtsltrend** *der* upward trend.

**Aufwasch** *der* (*ohne pl*) washing-up *Br*, dishes (*pl*) *Am*; **das geht in einem ~, das ist ein ~ fig** that will kill two birds with one stone.

**auflwecken** *vt* to wake up.

**auflweichen** (*perf* hat/ist **aufgeweicht**) *vt* (*hat*) - **1.** [weich machen - Boden] to make sodden; [ - Brot, Pappe] to make soggy - **2.** [Disziplin, System] to weaken; [Regeln] to water down ◇ *vi* (*ist*) [Boden] to become sodden; [Brot, Pappe] to get soggy.

**auflweisen** *vt* (*unreg*) [zeigen] to show; **der Plan weist Mängel auf** the plan contains flaws; **etwas** ODER **allerhand aufzuweisen haben** to have something to show for o.s.

**auflwenden** *vt* [Geld, Zeit] to spend; [Energie, Kraft] to use (up).

**auflwendig** *adj* & *adv* = **aufwändig**.

**Auflwendung** *die* [von Geld, Zeit] spending; [von Energie, Kraft] using (up).
➡ **Aufwendungen** *pl* [Kosten] expenditure (*U*).

**auflwerfen** *vt* (*unreg*) - **1.** [anhäufen - Erde, Kies] to pile up - **2.** [ansprechen] to raise.

**auflwerten** *vt* [Währung] to revalue; [Ansehen, Status] to enhance.

**Auflwertung** *die* [von Währung] revaluation; [von Ansehen, Status] enhancement.

**auflwickeln** *vt* to wind up.

**auflwiegeln** *vt abw* to incite; **jn gegen jn ~** to stir sb up against sb.

**Auflwind** *der* upcurrent; **~ bekommen** *fig* to get a boost; **~ haben** to be going strong.

**auflwirbeln** *vt* & *vi* to swirl up.

**auflwischen** *vt* to mop up.

**auflwühlen** *vt* - **1.** [zerwühlen] to churn up - **2.** [erregen] to stir up.

**auflzählen** *vt* to list.

**Auflzählung** *die* list.

**auflzäumen** *vt* to bridle.

**auflzehren** *vt* [verbrauchen] to exhaust.

**auflzeichnen** *vt* - **1.** [zeichnen] to draw - **2.** [aufnehmen] to record.

**Auflzeichnung** *die* [Aufnahme] recording.
➡ **Aufzeichnungen** *pl* [Notizen] notes; **sich** (*D*) **~en machen** to take notes.

**auflzeigen** *vt* [nachweisen] to show.

**auflziehen** (*perf* hat/ist **aufgezogen**) (*unreg*) *vt* (*hat*) - **1.** [Uhr, Spielzeugauto] to wind up - **2.** [erziehen - Kind] to bring up; [ - Tier] to raise - **3.** [öffnen] to open - **4.** [necken] to tease; **jn mit etw ~** to tease sb about sthg - **5.** *fam* [organisieren - Geschäft, Arbeitsgruppe] to set up; [ - Fest, Kampagne] to organize ◇ *vi* (*ist*) [Gewitter] to brew; [Wolken] to mass.

**Auflzucht** *die* rearing.

**Auflzug** *der* - **1.** [Lift] lift *Br*, elevator *Am* - **2.** *abw* [Aufmachung] get-up - **3.** [Akt] act.

**auflzwingen** *vt* (*unreg*): **jm etw ~** to force sthg onto sb.
➡ **sich aufzwingen** *ref*: **der Gedanke zwingt sich regelrecht auf** the thought is unavoidable.

**Auglapfel** *der* eyeball; **etw wie seinen ~ hüten** *fig* to be very careful with sthg.

**Auge** (*pl* -**n**) *das* - **1.** [Sehorgan] eye; **ein blaues ~** a black eye; **mit bloßem ~** with the naked eye; **etw mit eigenen ~n gesehen haben** to have seen sthg with one's own eyes; **ihm wurde schwarz vor ~** everything went black - **2.** [Würfelpunkt] dot - **3.** *RW*: (**große**) **~n machen** to stare wide-eyed; **seinen ~n nicht trauen** not to believe one's eyes; **jm aus den ~n gehen** to get out of sb's sight; **jn aus den ~n verlieren** to lose touch with sb; **die ~n offen halten** ODER **aufhalten** to keep one's eyes open; **jm die ~n öffnen** to open sb's eyes; **ein ~ auf jn/etw geworfen haben** to have an eye on sb/sthg; **ein ~ für etw haben** to have an eye for sthg; **ein ~ zudrücken** to turn a blind eye; **ihm gingen die ~n auf** his eyes were opened; **etw im ~ haben** to have one's eye on sthg; **jn/etw im ~ behalten** to keep an eye on sb/sthg; **in meinen/seinen/***etc* **~n** as I see/he sees/*etc* it; **jn/etw mit anderen** ODER **neuen ~n sehen** to see sb/sthg differently; **mit einem blauen ~ davonkommen** to get away with a bloody nose; **jn/etw nicht aus den ~n lassen** not to take one's eyes off sb/sthg; **unter vier ~n** in private; **etw vor ~n haben** to have sthg in mind.

**Augenlarzt, ärztin** *der, die* eye specialist, ophthalmologist.

**Augenlblick** *der* moment; **einen ~ bitte!** just a ODER one moment, please!; **alle ~e** all the time, constantly; **im ~** at the moment; **jeden ~** at any moment, any time.

**augenblicklich** *adj* - **1.** [sofortig] immediate

**- 2.** [jetzig] current ⬦ *adv* **- 1.** [umgehend] immediately **- 2.** [jetzig] currently.

**Augen|braue** *die* eyebrow.

**Augen|farbe** *die:* welche ~ hat sie? what colour are her eyes?

**Augen|höhe** *die:* in ~ at eye level.

**Augen|höhle** *die* eye socket.

**Augen|licht** *das (ohne pl) geh:* das ~ verlieren to lose one's eyesight.

**Augen|maß** *das* **- 1.** [visuell]: etw nach ~ schätzen to judge sthg by sight **- 2.** [Feingefühl] judgement.

**Augen|merk** *das* attention; sein ~ auf etw (A) richten to turn one's attention to sthg.

**Augen|ränder** *pl* rims of one's eyes.

**Augen|schein** *der (ohne pl) geh* appearances *(pl);* dem ersten ~ zufolge ist alles in Ordnung to judge by first appearances, everything is in order; jn/etw in ~ nehmen to have a close look at sb/sthg.

**Augen|weide** *die* feast for the eyes.

**Augen|winkel** *der:* jn/etw aus den ~n beobachten to watch sb/sthg out of the corner of one's eye.

**Augen|wischerei** *(pl -en) die:* das ist doch ~! you're kidding yourself!

**Augen|zeuge, zeugin** *der, die* eyewitness.

**augenzwinkernd** *adv* with an air of complicity.

**August** *der* August; *siehe auch* **September.**

**Auktion** [aukˈtsi̯oːn] *(pl -en) die* auction.

**Auktionator** [aukt͡si̯oˈnaːtɐ] *(pl -natoren) der* auctioneer.

**Aula** *(pl -s) die* hall.

**Aupair|mädchen, Au-pair-Mädchen** [oˈpɛːrmɛːtçən] *das* au pair.

**Aura** *die geh* aura.

**aus** *präp (+ D)* **- 1.** [heraus] out of; ~ dem Haus gehen to go out of the house, to leave the house; Rauch kam ~ dem Fenster smoke was coming out of the window **- 2.** [zur Angabe der Herkunft] from; ~ Amerika from America; ein Lied ~ den 70er Jahren a song from the seventies **- 3.** [zur Angabe des Materials]: ~ Plastik made of plastic; Möbel ~ Eschenholz ash furniture **- 4.** [zur Angabe der Zugehörigkeit]: einer ~ der Gruppe a member of the group; ein Gemälde ~ der Sammlung a picture from the collection **- 5.** [zur Angabe der Entfernung] from; ~ 50 m Entfernung from 50 m away **- 6.** [zur Angabe des Grundes]: ~ welchem Grund? for what reason?, why?; ~ Spaß for fun; ~ Habgier from greed, out of greed; ~ Wut in anger ⬦ *adv* **- 1.** [ellip-

tisch]: Licht ~! lights out! **- 2.** [zu Ende] over; ~ und vorbei all over.

**Aus** *das* end; ins ~ gehen SPORT to go out (of play).

**aus|arbeiten** *vt* [Plan, Liste, Vertrag] to draw up; [Methode, Vorschlag] to work out.

**Ausarbeitung** *(pl -en) die* [von Plan, Liste, Vertrag] drawing up; [von Methode, Vorschlag] working out.

**aus|arten** *(perf ist ausgeartet) vi* to degenerate; in *(+ A)* ODER zu etw ~ to degenerate into sthg.

**aus|atmen** *vt & vi* to breathe out.

**aus|baden** *vt:* etw ~ müssen to pay (the price) for sthg.

**aus|balancieren** *vt* to balance.

➡ **sich ausbalancieren** *ref* to balance.

**Aus|bau** *der* **- 1.** [Beseitigung] removal **- 2.** [Erweiterung - von Netz, Haus] extension; [ - von Dachboden] conversion; [ - von Kenntnissen] expansion; [ - von Kontakten] intensification, strengthening.

**aus|bauen** *vt* **- 1.** [beseitigen] to remove **- 2.** [erweitern - Netz, Haus] to extend; [ - Dachboden] to convert; [ - Kenntnisse] to expand; [ - Kontakte] to intensify, to strengthen.

**ausbaufähig** *adj* **- 1.** [Position, Beziehung] promising **- 2.** [Dachboden] convertible.

**ausbedingen** *(prät bedang aus; perf hat ausbedungen) vt:* sich *(D)* etw ~ to insist on sthg.

**aus|beißen** *vt (unreg):* sich *(D)* einen Zahn ~ to break a tooth; sich *(D)* die Zähne an etw *(D)* ~ to be getting nowhere with sthg.

**aus|bessern** *vt* [Schaden, Zaun] to repair; [Kleidungsstück] to mend.

**Ausbesserungs|arbeit** *die* repair work (U).

**aus|beulen** *vt* **- 1.** [glätten] to beat out **- 2.** [verformen] to make baggy.

➡ **sich ausbeulen** *ref* [Kleidungsstück] to go baggy.

**Aus|beute** *die* gain.

**aus|beuten** *vt* to exploit.

**Ausbeutung** *(pl -en) die* exploitation.

**aus|bezahlen** *vt* [Summe, Geld] to pay out; [Arbeiter, Erben] to pay off.

**aus|bilden** *vt* **- 1.** [schulen] to train; sich zu etw ~ lassen to train to be sthg **- 2.** [hervorbringen] to develop.

**Ausbilder, in** *(mpl -; fpl -nen) der, die* instructor (f instructress).

**Aus|bildung** *die* [beruflich, fachlich] training; [schulisch] education; in der ~ sein [beruflich, fachlich] to be a trainee; [schulisch] to be in education.

**Ausbildungs|förderung** *die financial sup-*

*port provided by Federal Government or State for students or trainees.*

**Ausbildungs|platz** *der* traineeship.

**Ausbildungs|vertrag** *der* training contract.

**Ausbildungs|zeit** *die* period of training, traineeship.

**aus|bitten** *vt (unreg):* sich *(D)* etw ~ geh to request sthg; **das möchte ich mir ausgebeten haben!** I should think so too!

**aus|blasen** *vt (unreg)* [löschen] to blow out.

**aus|bleiben** *(perf* ist ausgeblieben) *vi (unreg)* - **1.** [Besserung, Katastrophe] to fail to materialize; [Gäste, Touristen] to fail to turn up; **bei diesem Sport bleiben Verletzungen nicht aus** people are bound to get injured doing this sport - **2.** [nicht nach Hause kommen] to stay out.

**aus|blenden** *vt* TV to fade out.
➡ **sich ausblenden** *ref* TV: **wir blenden uns nun aus dieser Liveübertragung aus** we are now leaving this live broadcast.

**Aus|blick** *der* view; **ein ~ auf etw** *(A)* fig a look ahead to sthg.

**aus|bluten** *(perf* ist ausgeblutet) *vi* to bleed dry; **etw ~ lassen** to bleed sthg dry.

**ausbooten** *vt* to oust.

**aus|borgen** *vt:* jm etw ~ to lend sb sthg; **sich** *(D)* **etw (von jm) ~** to borrow sthg (from sb).

**aus|brechen** *(perf* hat/ist ausgebrochen) *(unreg) vi (ist)* - **1.** [Gefangene, Krieg, Panik, Epidemie] to break out; **aus etw ~** to break out of sthg - **2.** [verfallen]: **in Gelächter ~** to burst out laughing; **in Tränen ~** to burst into tears; **in Zorn ~** to explode with anger - **3.** [Auto] to spin out of control - **4.** [Vulkan] to erupt ◇ *vt (hat)* [herausbrechen] to break off.

**Ausbrecher, in** *(mpl* -; *fpl* -nen) *der, die* escaped prisoner.

**aus|breiten** *vt* to spread out; **etw über jm/etw ~** to spread sthg out over sb/sthg.
➡ **sich ausbreiten** *ref* - **1.** [sich verbreiten] to spread - **2.** *fam* [sich breit machen] to spread o.s. out.

**aus|brennen** *(perf* ist ausgebrannt) *vi (unreg)* - **1.** [Gebäude, Fahrzeug] to be gutted - **2.** [Person]: **ausgebrannt sein** to be burnt out.

**aus|bringen** *vt (unreg):* **einen Trinkspruch auf jn ~** to propose a toast to sb.

**Aus|bruch** *der* - **1.** [Flucht] break-out - **2.** [Beginn] outbreak; **nach einer Woche kam die Krankheit vollends zum ~** after a week the disease broke out fully - **3.** [von Vulkan] eruption - **4.** [Gefühlsäußerung] outburst.

**Ausbruchs|versuch** [ˈaʊsbrʊksfɛʀzuːx] *der* attempted break-out.

**aus|brüten** *vt eigtl &* fig to hatch.

**aus|buddeln** *vt fam* to dig up.

**aus|bügeln** *vt* - **1.** [Falte] to iron out; [Hose, Anzug] to iron - **2.** *fam* [Fehler, Mangel] to make good; [Missverständnis] to clear up, to iron out.

**Aus|bund** *der:* **ein ~ an** ODER **von etw** a model of sthg.

**aus|bürsten** *vt* [Staub, Fleck] to brush out; [Haare, Kleidungsstück] to brush.

**aus|büxen** *(perf* ist ausgebüxt) *vi fam* to scarper.

**Aus|dauer** *die* [Beharrungsvermögen] perseverance; SPORT stamina.

**ausdauernd** *adj* persevering; **ein ~er Läufer** a runner with a lot of stamina ◇ *adv* untiringly.

**ausdehnbar** *adj* expandable.

**aus|dehnen** *vt* - **1.** [Einzugsgebiet, Einfluss] to expand; [Gummiband] to extend; [Kleidungsstück] to lengthen - **2.** [zeitlich] to extend.
➡ **sich ausdehnen** *ref* - **1.** [Metall, Handel] to expand; [Feuer] to spread; [Weite] to stretch out; **sich auf etw** *(A)* **~** [Brand, Hysterie, Aktivitäten] to spread to sthg - **2.** [Besuch, Verhandlungen] to go on.

**Aus|dehnung** *die* - **1.** [von Metall, Handel] expansion; [von Feuer] spreading - **2.** [von Besuch, Verhandlungen] extension.

**aus|denken** *vt (unreg):* sich *(D)* etw ~ [Geschichte, Plan] to think sthg up; [Geschenk] to think of sthg; **da musst du dir schon etwas anderes ~!** *fam* you'll have to do better than that!; **das ist nicht auszudenken** that doesn't bear thinking about.

**aus|diskutieren** *vt* to discuss fully.

**Aus|druck** *(pl* -drücke ODER -e) *der* - **1.** *(pl* Ausdrücke) [Formulierung] expression; **das ist gar kein ~!** that isn't the word for it! - **2.** *(ohne pl)* [Zeichen] expression; **etw zum ~ bringen** to express sthg; **einer Sache** *(D)* **~ geben** ODER **verleihen** geh to express sthg - **3.** *(pl* Ausdrucke) EDV printout.

**aus|drucken** *vt* EDV to print (out).

**aus|drücken** *vt* - **1.** [Orange, Schwamm, Saft] to squeeze - **2.** [Zigarette] to stub out - **3.** [aussprechen] to express; **etw mit einfachen Worten ~** to put sthg simply - **4.** [zeigen - Gefühle, Dank] to express, to show.
➡ **sich ausdrücken** *ref* - **1.** [Person] to express o.s. - **2.** [Freude, Gier, Intoleranz] to reveal itself.

**ausdrücklich** *adj* explicit ◇ *adv* explicitly.

**ausdruckslos** *adj* expressionless ◇ *adv* expressionlessly.

**ausdrucksvoll** *adj* expressive ◇ *adv* expressively.

**Ausdrucks|weise** *die* way of expressing o.s.

**auseinander** *adv* apart; **auseinander!** break

it up!; **die Schwestern sind sechs Jahre ~** there's six years between the two sisters.

**auseinander brechen** *(perf hat/ist auseinander gebrochen) (unreg) vt (hat) vi (ist)* to break into pieces.

**auseinander bringen** *vt (unreg)* [Menschen] to drive apart.

**auseinander entwickeln** ⟿ **sich auseinander entwickeln** *ref* [Freunde] to drift apart; [Karrieren] to follow separate paths.

**auseinander fallen** *(perf ist auseinander gefallen) vi (unreg)* to fall apart.

**auseinander fliegen** *(perf ist auseinander geflogen) vi* [Vögel, Blätter] to fly in all directions; [explodieren] to be blown sky-high.

**auseinander gehen** *(perf ist auseinander gegangen) vi (unreg)* - **1.** [sich trennen - Gruppe] to break up; [ - Wege] to diverge; [ - Personen] to part - **2.** [Vorhang] to open - **3.** [Meinungen] to differ - **4.** [Ehe] to break up - **5.** *fam* [dick werden] to get fat.

**auseinander halten** *vt (unreg)* to distinguish.

**auseinander klamüsern** *vt fam* to sort out.

**auseinander laufen** *(perf ist auseinander gelaufen) vi (unreg)* - **1.** [Gruppe] to disperse - **2.** [Eis, Käse] to melt; [Farbe] to run.

**auseinander leben** ⟿ **sich auseinander leben** *ref* to drift apart.

**auseinander nehmen** *vt (unreg)* to dismantle.

**auseinander reißen** *vt (unreg)* [trennen] to tear apart.

**auseinander rücken** *(perf hat/sind auseinander gerückt) vt (hat) vi (sind)* to move apart.

**auseinander setzen** *vt:* **jm etw ~** to explain sthg to sb.
⟿ **sich auseinander setzen** *ref* - **1.** [sich beschäftigen]: **sich mit etw ~** to examine sthg - **2.** [sich streiten]: **sich mit jm ~** to argue with sb.

**Auseinandersetzung** *(pl -en) die* - **1.** [mit Thema]: **~ (mit)** examination (of) - **2.** [Streit] argument; [Debatte] debate.

**auserlesen** *adj geh* select.

**auserwählt** *adj* chosen.

**ausfahrbar** *adj* retractable.

**ausfahren** *(perf hat/ist ausgefahren) (unreg) vt (hat)* - **1.** [spazieren fahren - im Rollstuhl, Kinderwagen] to take out for a walk - **2.** [ausklappen - Antenne] to extend; [ - Fahrwerk] to lower - **3.** [liefern] to deliver - **4.** [sehr schnell fahren] to drive flat out ⟺ *vi (ist)* - **1.** [spazieren fahren - im Rollstuhl, Kinderwagen] to go for a walk - **2.** [hinausfahren - Zug] to depart.

**Ausfahrt** *die* - **1.** [Stelle] exit; '**~ freihalten!**' 'keep clear!' - **2.** [Auslaufen] departure.

**Ausfahrtsschild** *(pl -er) das* exit sign.

**Ausfahrtsstraße** *die* exit road.

**Ausfall** *der* - **1.** [von Haaren, Zähnen, Einnahmen] loss - **2.** [Nichtstattfinden] cancellation; [von Fussballspiel] postponement - **3.** [von Maschine] failure; [von Mitarbeiter] absence; [von Athlet] pulling out - **4.** [Beleidigung] attack.

**ausfallen** *(perf ist ausgefallen) vi (unreg)* - **1.** [Haare, Zahn] to fall out; **ihr sind die Haare ausgefallen** her hair has fallen out - **2.** [nicht stattfinden] to be cancelled; [Fussballspiel] to be postponed - **3.** [Verdienst, Einnahme] to be lost - **4.** [Maschine] to break down; [Bremse, Signal] to fail - **5.** [Mitarbeiter] to be absent; [Athlet] to pull out - **6.** [sich erweisen] to turn out to be; **der Sieg fiel deutlich aus** it was a clear victory; **gut/schlecht ~** to turn out well/badly.

**ausfallend** *adj* abusive; **~ werden** to become abusive.

**Ausfallserscheinung** *die* symptom *(of a medical problem)*.

**Ausfallstraße** *die* arterial road.

**ausfechten** *vt (unreg)* to fight out.

**ausfegen** *vt* to sweep out ⟺ *vi* to sweep up.

**ausfeilen** *vt* - **1.** [Rede, Aufsatz] to polish - **2.** [Gegenstand] to file.

**ausfertigen** *vt amt* [Vertrag, Testament] to draw up; [Pass, Zeugnis, Rechnung] to issue.

**Ausfertigung** *(pl -en) die amt* - **1.** [Exemplar] copy; **in doppelter ~** in duplicate - **2.** [von Vertrag, Testament] drawing up; [von Pass, Zeugnis, Rechnung] issuing.

**ausfindig** *adv:* **jn/etw ~ machen** to find sb/sthg.

**ausfliegen** *(perf hat/ist ausgeflogen) (unreg) vi (ist)* to fly away ODER off ⟺ *vt (hat)* to fly out.

**ausfließen** *(perf ist ausgeflossen) vi (unreg)* to leak.

**ausflippen** *(perf ist ausgeflippt) vi fam* to flip out.

**Ausflucht** *(pl Ausflüchte) die* excuse; **Ausflüchte machen** to make excuses.

**Ausflug** *der* trip; **einen ~ machen** ODER **unternehmen** to go on a trip.

**Ausflügler, in** *(mpl -; fpl -nen) der, die* daytripper.

**Ausflugslokal** *das* cafe or pub in the countryside to which you can drive or walk out.

**Ausflugsziel** *das* destination *(of a trip)*.

**Ausfluss** *der* - **1.** [im Waschbecken] plughole - **2.** [Ausfließen] leaking - **3.** MED discharge.

**ausformulieren** *vt* to formulate.

**ausforschen** *vt* - **1.** [Geheimnis, Versteck] to find out - **2.** [fragen]: **jn über etw ~** to pump sb for information about sthg.

**ausfragen** *vt* to interrogate.

**aus|fressen** vt (unreg): **er hat mal wieder etwas ausgefressen** fam he's been up to his tricks again.

**Ausfuhr** (pl -en) die - **1.** [Ware] export - **2.** [Tätigkeit] exporting.

**Ausfuhrbestimmungen** pl export regulations.

**aus|führen** vt - **1.** [spazieren führen - Familie, Hund] to take for a walk - **2.** [exportieren] to export - **3.** [realisieren - Reparatur, Befehl, Plan] to carry out; [ - Freistoß, Schritte] to take - **4.** [erklären] to explain.

**Ausführende** (pl -n) der, die performer.

**Ausfuhr|land** das exporter, exporting country.

**ausführlich** adj detailed ⟨⟩ adv in detail.

**Ausfuhr|sperre** die export ban.

**Aus|führung** die - **1.** [Realisierung - von Reparatur, Befehl, Plan] carrying out; [ - von Freistoß, Schritten] taking - **2.** [von Ware] design; [Modell] model - **3.** [Erklärung] explanation.

**Ausfuhr|verbot** das export ban.

**aus|füllen** vt - **1.** [Formular, Antrag] to fill in ODER out; [Kreuzworträtsel] to do; [Scheck] to make out - **2.** [füllen] to fill (up) - **3.** [verbringen]: **seine Zeit mit etw ~** to spend one's time doing sthg - **4.** [zufrieden stellen] to fulfil.

**Ausg.** (abk für **Ausgabe**) ed.

**Aus|gabe** die - **1.** [Ausgeben] distribution; [von Befehl, Banknoten] issuing; [von Essen] serving - **2.** [von Geld] expenditure; **~n** expenditure (U) - **3.** [Edition] edition.

**Aus|gang** der - **1.** [von Gebäude] exit; [von Wald] edge; [von Ort] end - **2.** (ohne pl) [Ausgeherlaubnis] time off; [von Soldaten] pass; **~ bis Mitternacht haben** to be allowed out until midnight - **3.** [Ende] outcome.

**Ausgangs|basis** die starting point, basis.

**Ausgangs|lage** die starting position.

**Ausgangs|punkt** der starting point.

**Ausgangs|sperre** die curfew.

**aus|geben** vt (unreg) - **1.** [verteilen] [Lebensmittel, Decken] to hand out; [Befehl, Banknoten] to issue; [Essen] to serve - **2.** [Geld] to spend - **3.** fam [zu Drink einladen]: **jm einen ~** fam to buy sb a drink - **4.** [bezeichnen]: **sich als jd/etw ~** to pretend to be sb/sthg; **jn/etw als** ODER **für jn/etw ~** to pass sb/sthg off as sb/sthg.

**ausgeblichen** adj faded.

**ausgebucht** adj fully booked.

**ausgebufft** adj fam slick.

**Aus|geburt** die geh & abw monstrous product; **sie ist eine ~ von Naivität** she is naive in the extreme.

**ausgedient** adj: **dieser Sessel hat nun ~** I/we/etc no longer have any use for this armchair.

**ausgedörrt** adj [Kehle, Erde] parched; [Pflanze] withered.

**ausgefallen** adj unusual ⟨⟩ adv unusually.

**ausgefeilt** adj polished.

**ausgeflippt** adj fam weird, freaky.

**ausgefranst** adj frayed.

**ausgefuchst** ['aʊsgəfʊkst] adj fam cunning.

**ausgeglichen** adj [Mensch, Persönlichkeit] balanced; [Spiel] even; [Klima] stable; [Leistung] steady.

**Ausgeglichenheit** die [von Mensch, Persönlichkeit] balanced nature; [von Spiel] evenness; [von Klima] stability, constancy; [von Leistung] steadiness.

**aus|gehen** (perf ist **ausgegangen**) vi (unreg) - **1.** [ins Kino, in die Disko] to go out - **2.** [verlöschen - Kerze, Lampe] to go out; [ - Motor] to stop; [ - Heizung, Computer] to go off - **3.** [enden] to end - **4.** [hervorgebracht werden]: **von jm ~** to come from sb - **5.** [zugrunde legen]: **von etw ~** to assume sthg; **davon ~, dass ...** to assume (that) ... - **6.** [ausfallen] to fall out - **7.** [zu Ende gehen] to run out; **mir gehen die Ideen aus** my ideas are running out ODER drying up - **8.** [abzielen]: **auf etw** (A) **~** to be looking for sthg.

**ausgehend** adj: **im ~en Zeitalter** towards the end of the age; **im ~en 20. Jahrhundert** at the end of the 20th century.

**ausgehungert** adj starved.

**ausgeklügelt** adj ingenious.

**ausgekocht** adj fam abw cunning.

**ausgelassen** adj exuberant ⟨⟩ adv exuberantly.

**Aus|gelassenheit** die exuberance.

**ausgelastet** adj [Mensch, Betrieb] at full stretch; [Maschine] at full capacity; **voll ~ sein** to have one's hands full.

**ausgelaugt** adj worn-out.

**ausgemacht** adj - **1.** [abgemacht] settled - **2.** [völlig] complete, total ⟨⟩ adv [ausgesprochen] completely, totally.

**ausgemergelt** adj [Körper, Mensch] emaciated.

**ausgenommen** konj - **1.** [es sei denn] unless - **2.** [außer] except.

**ausgepowert** ['aʊsgəpaʊɐt] adj fam whacked, bushed.

**ausgeprägt** adj pronounced ⟨⟩ adv particularly.

**ausgerechnet** adv: **~ heute** today of all days; **~ mir muss das passieren** it had to happen to me of all people.

**ausgereift** adj perfected.

**ausgeschlafen** *adj fam* [gewitzt] crafty, cunning.

**ausgeschlossen** *adj* out of the question.

**ausgespielt** *adj*: **er hat bei mir ~** I'm finished with him.

**ausgesprochen** *adj* [Ähnlichkeit, Begabung] definite; [Abneigung, Vorliebe] marked; [Glück, Zufall] real <> *adv* extremely, really.

**ausgestorben** *adj*: **wie ~** dead, deserted.

**ausgesucht** *adj* - **1.** [Wein, Zutaten] select, choice - **2.** [Höflichkeit, Hässlichkeit] extreme <> *adv* [erlesen] extremely, really.

**ausgetreten** *adj* well-worn.

**ausgewachsen** ['ausgevaksn] *adj* - **1.** [erwachsen] fully-grown - **2.** *fam* [groß] huge; **~er Blödsinn** utter nonsense.

**ausgewogen** *adj* balanced.

**Ausgewogenheit** *die* balance.

**ausgezeichnet** *adj* excellent <> *adv* excellently.

**ausgiebig** *adj* [Beratungen, Untersuchungen] extensive; [Frühstück] large; [Spaziergang] long <> *adv* extensively; **~ frühstücken** to eat a large breakfast; **sich** *(D)* **~ über etw** *(A)* **Gedanken machen** to give sthg a great deal of thought.

**aus|gießen** *vt (unreg)* to pour out.

**Ausgleich** *(pl -e) der* - **1.** [Gleichgewicht] balance; **er schafft sich einen ~ zu seiner Arbeit, indem er sich sportlich betätigt** he balances out his work by doing sport - **2.** [Wiedergutmachung] compensation; **zum** *ODER* **als ~ in return** - **3.** SPORT equalizer; [im Tennis] deuce.

**aus|gleichen** *(unreg) vt* [Unterschiede, Unregelmäßigkeiten] to even out; [Mängel, Ungerechtigkeit] to make up for; [Gegensätze] to reconcile; [Konflikt] to settle; [Konto] to balance <> *vi* SPORT to equalize.
   &#9656; **sich ausgleichen** *ref* [Unterschiede] to even out; [Konto] to balance.

**Ausgleichs|fonds** ['ausglaiçsfɔ̃:] *der* WIRTSCH equalization fund.

**Ausgleichs|sport** ['ausglaiçsfpɔrt] *der* exercise.

**aus|gleiten** *(perf ist ausgeglitten) vi (unreg) geh* - **1.** [ausrutschen] to slip - **2.** [entgleiten]: **der Teller ist ihr ausgeglitten** the plate slipped out of her hand.

**aus|gliedern** *vt* to leave out, to exclude.

**aus|graben** *vt (unreg)* to dig up.

**Aus|grabung** *die* excavation, dig.

**aus|grenzen** *vt* to exclude.

**Ausguck** *(pl -e) der* lookout (post).

**aus|gucken** *vi fam* - **1.** [Ausschau halten]: **nach jm ~** to look out for sb - **2.** [auswählen]: **sich** *(D)* **jn ~** to pick out sb.

**Aus|guss** *der* drain.

**aus|haben** *(unreg) fam vt* [ausgezogen haben] to have taken off <> *vi* [Schulschluss haben] to finish school.

**aus|haken** *vt* to unhook; **es hakt bei ihr aus** *fam fig* she goes to pieces.

**aus|halten** *(unreg) vt* - **1.** [ertragen] to stand; **den Blick von jm ~** to meet sb's gaze; **den Vergleich mit etw ~** to bear comparison with sthg; **es lässt sich ~** it's not at all bad; **mit ihr ist es nicht auszuhalten** she's unbearable - **2.** *abw* [bezahlen] to keep; **sich von jm ~ lassen** to be kept by sb <> *vi* [durchhalten] to hold out.

**aus|handeln** *vt* to negotiate.

**aus|händigen** *vt* to hand over.

**Aus|hang** *der* notice.

**aus|hängen** *vi (unreg)* [angeschlagen sein] to be up; **die Liste hängt am schwarzen Brett aus** the list is up on the noticeboard <> *vt (reg)* - **1.** [anschlagen] to put up - **2.** [ausheben] to take off its hinges.

**Aushängeschild** *(pl -er) das fig* advertisement.

**aus|harren** *vi geh* to hold out.

**aus|heben** *vt (unreg)* - **1.** [ausschaufeln] to dig out - **2.** [aushängen] to take off its hinges - **3.** [Verbrechernest] to raid.

**aus|hecken** *vt* to think up.

**aus|heilen** *(perf ist ausgeheilt) vi* [Wunde, Organ] to heal completely; [Krankheit] to be fully cured.

**aus|helfen** *vi (unreg)* to help out.

**aus|heulen** &#9656; **sich ausheulen** *ref fam*: **bei jm ~** to have a good cry on sb's shoulder.

**Aus|hilfe** *die* - **1.** [Aushelfen] assistance; **zur ~ arbeiten** to help out - **2.** [Aushilfskraft] temporary worker; [im Büro] temp.

**Aushilfs|kraft** *die* temporary worker; [im Büro] temp.

**aushilfsweise** *adv* on a temporary basis.

**aus|höhlen** *vt* [Stamm] to hollow out.

**aus|holen** *vi* - **1.** [mit dem Arm] to move one's arm back - **2.** [beim Erzählen]: **weit ~** to go back a long way.

**aus|horchen** *vt* to sound out.

**aus|hungern** *vt* to starve out.

**aus|kämmen** *vt* to comb out.

**aus|kennen** &#9656; **sich auskennen** *ref* to know one's way around; **sich in einer Stadt ~** to know one's way around a town; **sich mit Computern ~** to know a lot about computers.

**aus|kippen** *vt* to tip out.

**aus|klammern** *vt* [Thema] to leave aside.

**Aus|klang** *der* conclusion.

**ausklappbar** *adj* folding.

**aus|klappen** *vt* to open out.

**aus|kleiden** *vt* [innen ausstatten] to line.

**aus|klingen** (*perf* hat/ist ausgeklungen) *vi* (*unreg*) (hat, ist) [Musik, Tag, Fest] to come to an end.

**aus|klinken** (*perf* hat/ist ausgeklinkt) *vt* (hat) to release ⟨⟩ *vi* (ist) to come free.
➤ **sich ausklinken** *ref* to come free.

**aus|klopfen** *vt* [Teppich] to beat; [Pfeife] to knock out; [Kleidungsstück] to dust down.

**aus|klügeln** *vt* to work out.

**aus|knipsen** *vt fam* to switch off.

**aus|knobeln** *vt* - **1.** *fam* [auslosen - mit Würfeln] to throw dice to decide - **2.** [ausklügeln] to work out.

**aus|kommen** (*perf* ist ausgekommen) *vi* (*unreg*) - **1.** [genug haben] to get by, to manage; **mit etw ~** [Proviant] to make sthg last; [Gehalt] to get by on sthg; [Hilfe] to manage with sthg, to get by with sthg - **2.** [sich vertragen] to get on; **mit jm gut/schlecht ~** to get on well/badly with sb; **mit jm nicht ~** not to get on with sb.

**Auskommen** *das* (ohne *pl*) - **1.** [Lebensunterhalt]: **sein ~ haben (mit)** to get by (on) - **2.** [Zusammenleben]: **mit ihm ist kein ~** he's impossible to get on with.

**aus|kosten** *vt geh* to enjoy to the full.

**aus|kratzen** *vt* [Schüssel] to scrape out.

**aus|kugeln** *vt:* **sich** (*D*) **den rechten Arm ~** to dislocate one's right arm.

**aus|kühlen** (*perf* hat/ist ausgekühlt) *vi* (ist) [Ofen, Pudding] to cool down ODER off ⟨⟩ *vt* (hat) [Person] to chill through.

**aus|kundschaften** *vt* to spy out.

**Auskunft** (*pl* **Auskünfte**) *die* - **1.** [Information] information (*U*); **eine ~ bekommen** to get some information; **jm eine ~ geben** ODER **erteilen (über** (+ A)) to give sb some information (about) - **2.** (ohne *pl*) [Auskunftsschalter] information desk; [Fernsprechauskunft] directory enquiries.

**Auskunfts|schalter** *der* information desk.

**Auskunfts|stelle** *die* information office.

**aus|kuppeln** *vi* AUTO to disengage the clutch.

**aus|kurieren** *vt* to cure.

**aus|lachen** *vt* to laugh at.

**aus|laden** *vt* (*unreg*) - **1.** [entladen] to unload - **2.** [nach einer Einladung]: **jn ~** to tell sb not to come.

**ausladend** *adj* overhanging; [Hinterteil] protruding; [Bewegung] sweeping.

**Aus|lage** *die* display.
➤ **Auslagen** *pl* expenses.

**aus|lagern** *vt* to remove for safe storage.

**Ausland** *das* (ohne *pl*): **im ~** abroad; **ins ~** abroad.

**Ausländer** (*pl* -) *der* foreigner.

**ausländerfeindlich** *adj* xenophobic
⟨⟩ *adv:* **~ eingestellt sein** to be xenophobic.

**Ausländerfeindlichkeit** *die* (ohne *pl*) hostility to foreigners, xenophobia.

**Ausländerin** (*pl* -nen) *die* foreigner.

**ausländisch** *adj* foreign.

**Auslands|abteilung** *die* foreign operations department.

**Auslands|aufenthalt** *der* stay abroad.

**Auslandsbeziehungen** *pl* international relations; [einer Universität] foreign contacts.

**Auslands|geschäft** *das* international business.

**Auslands|gespräch** *das* international call.

**Auslands|korrespondent, in** *der, die* foreign correspondent.

**Auslands|reise** *die* trip abroad.

**Auslandsschutz|brief** *der* AUTO ≈ green card *Br, motor insurance document for travel abroad.*

**Auslands|vertretung** *die* international office.

**aus|lassen** *vt* (*unreg*) - **1.** [Absatz, Einzelheit] to leave out, to miss out; [Chance, Gelegenheit] to miss - **2.** [abreagieren]: **etw an jm ~** to take sthg out on sb.
➤ **sich auslassen** *ref fam* [sich äußern]: **er hat sich zu diesem Thema nicht näher ausgelassen** he didn't go on about the subject any more; **sich über jn/etw ~** *abw* to bitch about sb/sthg.

**aus|lasten** *vt* - **1.** [Betrieb, Maschine] to run at full capacity; **die Kapazität des Betriebs ist nicht ausgelastet** the factory isn't running at full capacity - **2.** [beanspruchen] to keep fully occupied; **mit etw ausgelastet sein** to be kept fully occupied by sthg.

**Auslauf** *der* (ohne *pl*) room (to run about).

**aus|laufen** (*perf* ist ausgelaufen) *vi* (*unreg*) - **1.** [Tank, Fass] to leak - **2.** [Flüssigkeit] to leak out - **3.** [Schiff] to set sail - **4.** [Modell, Serie] to be discontinued - **5.** [Vertrag, Amtszeit] to expire.

**Aus|läufer** *der* [eines Tiefdruckgebietes] edge; **die ~ der Alpen** the foothills of the Alps.

**aus|laugen** *vt* - **1.** [Bestandteile entziehen]: **der Boden wurde völlig ausgelaugt** the soil was completely stripped of its nutrients - **2.** [erschöpfen] to wear out.

**aus|lauten** *vi:* **auf etw** (*A*) **~** to end in sthg.

**aus|leben** *vt* [Träume, Wünsche] to live out.
➤ **sich ausleben** *ref* to enjoy life to the full.

**aus|lecken** *vt* to lick out.

**aus|leeren** *vt* to empty; [Glas, Tasse, Flasche] to drain, to empty.

**aus‖legen** vt - **1.** [Waren] to display; [Köder, Gift] to put down - **2.** [auskleiden]: **ein Zimmer mit Teppich ~** to carpet a room; **einen Schrank (mit Papier) ~** to line a cupboard (with paper) - **3.** [vorstrecken]: **jm etw ~** to lend sb sthg - **4.** [interpretieren] to interpret; **sein Zögern wurde ihm als Ängstlichkeit ausgelegt** his hesitation was interpreted as fear.

**Auslegung** (pl -en) die interpretation.

**aus‖leiern** (perf hat/ist ausgeleiert) vt (hat) vi (ist) [Kleidungsstück] to stretch.

**Ausleihe** (pl -n) die - **1.** (ohne pl) [Ausleihen] lending - **2.** [Ausleihstelle] issue desk.

**aus‖leihen** vt (unreg): **jm etw ~** to lend sb sthg; **sich** (D) **etw ~** to borrow sthg.

**aus‖lernen** vi to finish one's training.

**Auslese** die (ohne pl) - **1.** [Selektion] selection - **2.** [Wein] quality wine made from specially selected grapes.

**aus‖lesen** vt (unreg) - **1.** geh [auswählen] to select - **2.** [zu Ende lesen] to finish reading.

**aus‖liefern** vt - **1.** [Verbrecher]: **jn jm ~** to hand sb over to sb - **2.** [liefern] to deliver.

**Aus‖lieferung** die - **1.** [Übergabe] handover; [von Flüchtlingen an ihr Heimatland] extradition - **2.** [Lieferung] delivery.

**Auslieferungs‖antrag** der application for extradition.

**aus‖liegen** vi (unreg) to be on display; [Gift, Köder] to be down.

**aus‖löffeln** vt to eat up; [Suppenteller, Puddingschüssel] to empty; **nun muß er ~, was er sich eingebrockt hat** fig now he'll have to reap what he's sown.

**aus‖löschen** vt - **1.** [löschen] to extinguish, to put out - **2.** [vernichten] to erase; [Spuren] to cover; [Bevölkerung] to annihilate.

**aus‖losen** vt to draw lots for.

**aus‖lösen** vt - **1.** [Alarm, Mechanismus] to set off, to trigger - **2.** [Krieg, Panik, Freude] to cause.

**Auslöser** (pl -) der - **1.** FOTO (shutter release) button - **2.** [Ursache] trigger.

**aus‖lüften** vt to air.

**aus‖machen** vt - **1.** [Radio, Licht, Motor] to turn off; [Zigarette] to put out - **2.** [vereinbaren - Treffen] to arrange; [ - Termin] to make; **wir haben ausgemacht, nichts zu verraten** we agreed not to say anything; **ich habe mit ihr ausgemacht, dass wir ins Kino gehen** I arranged to go to the cinema with her; **ich habe einen hohen Preis mit ihm ausgemacht** I agreed on a high price with him - **3.** [stören]: **macht es Ihnen etwas aus, wenn ich rauche?** do you mind if I smoke?; **das macht ihm nichts aus** it doesn't matter to him - **4.** [betragen] to come to; **der Umweg hat eine Stunde ausgemacht** the diversion took an hour - **5.** [bedeuten]: **viel ~** to

make a big difference; **wenig ~** not to make much difference - **6.** geh [erkennen] to make out - **7.** [bilden - Reiz] to be, to constitute.

**aus‖malen** vt - **1.** [ausfüllen] to colour in - **2.** [schildern] to describe vividly - **3.** [sich vorstellen]: **sich** (D) **etw ~** to imagine sthg.

**Aus‖maß** das extent.

**aus‖merzen** vt to eradicate; [Erinnerungen] to obliterate.

**aus‖messen** vt (unreg) to measure.

**aus‖misten** vt - **1.** [reinigen] to muck out - **2.** fam [Ordnung schaffen] to clear out.

**aus‖mustern** vt - **1.** MIL: **wegen seines Herzfehlers wurde er ausgemustert** the army rejected him because of his bad heart - **2.** [aussondern] to take out of service; [abgetragene Kleidung] to sort out.

**Ausnahme** (pl -n) die exception; **mit ~ von** with the exception of; **eine ~ machen** to make an exception.

**Ausnahme‖fall** der exception, exceptional case.

**Ausnahme‖situation** die exceptional situation.

**Ausnahme‖zustand** der: **den ~ verhängen** to declare a state of emergency.

**ausnahmslos** adv without exception.

**ausnahmsweise** adv: **~ dürfen die Kinder aufbleiben** the children can stay up just this once.

**aus‖nehmen** vt (unreg) - **1.** [Tier] to gut - **2.** [ausschließen] to exclude - **3.** abw [Person] to fleece; **jn beim Kartenspiel ~** to clean sb out at cards.

**ausnehmend** adv particularly; **der Film hat mir ~ gut gefallen** I particularly liked the film.

**aus‖nüchtern** vi to sober up.

**aus‖nutzen, aus‖nützen** vt - **1.** [nutzen] to use, to make use of; [Gelegenheit, Vorteil] to use, to make the most of - **2.** [missbrauchen] to take advantage of, to exploit.

**Aus‖nutzung, Ausnützung** die - **1.** [Nutzung] use - **2.** [Missbrauch] exploitation.

**aus‖packen** vt to unpack; [Paket, Geschenk] to unwrap ⬦ vi fam to spill the beans.

**aus‖plaudern** vt to give away.

**aus‖posaunen** vt fam to tell the whole world.

**aus‖pressen** vt - **1.** [Frucht] to squeeze - **2.** [ausbeuten] to squeeze dry - **3.** [ausfragen] to press for information.

**aus‖probieren** vt to try out.

**Auspuff** (pl -e) der exhaust.

**aus|pumpen** vt to pump out; **jm den Magen ~** to pump sb's stomach out.

**aus|pusten** vt to blow out.

**aus|quartieren** vt to move out.

**aus|quetschen** vt - **1.** [auspressen] to squeeze - **2.** fam [ausfragen] to grill; **jn über etw** (A) **~** to grill sb about sthg.

**aus|radieren** vt - **1.** [durch Radieren] to rub out, to erase - **2.** fig [zerstören] to wipe out.

**aus|rangieren** vt fam [Kleidung, Möbel] to throw out; [Fahrzeug] to scrap.

**aus|rasieren** vt: **jm den Nacken ~** to shave sb's neck.

**aus|rasten** (perf ist **ausgerastet**) vi - **1.** fam [wütend werden] to go berserk - **2.** [sich lösen] to come out.

**aus|rauben** vt [Person] to rob; [Geschäft] to loot.

**aus|räumen** vt - **1.** [entfernen, leeren] to clear out - **2.** fam [ausrauben] to clean out - **3.** [Missverständnis] to clear up; [Zweifel] to dispel.

**aus|rechnen** vt to calculate, to work out; **sich** (D) **etw ~** to work sthg out for o.s.; **sie hatte sich gute Chancen ausgerechnet** she had fancied her chances.

**Aus|rede** die excuse; **faule ~** fam feeble excuse.

**aus|reden** vi to finish speaking ◇ vt: **jm etw ~** to talk sb out of sthg.

**aus|reichen** vi to be enough; **es muss bis März ~** it has to last until March.

**ausreichend** adj - **1.** [genügend] sufficient; **eine ~e Anzahl von Teilnehmern** enough participants - **2.** SCHULE mark 4 on a scale of 1 to 6, indicating a pass, but only just ◇ adv sufficiently; **wir haben ~ für die Party eingekauft** we bought enough for the party; **er hat sich ~ bemüht** he took enough trouble.

**aus|reifen** (perf ist **ausgereift**) vi - **1.** [Wein] to mature; [Obst] to ripen fully - **2.** [perfektionieren] to mature.

**Aus|reise** die: **bei der ~** on leaving the country.

**Ausreise|genehmigung** die exit visa.

**aus|reisen** (perf ist **ausgereist**) vi: **nach Deutschland ~** to leave for Germany; **aus einem Land ~** to leave a country.

**aus|reißen** (perf hat/ist **ausgerissen**) (unreg) vi (ist) fam to run away ◇ vt (hat) [Unkraut] to pull up.

**Ausreißer, in** (mpl -; fpl -nen) der, die runaway.

**aus|reiten** (perf ist **ausgeritten**) vi (unreg) to ride out, to go for a ride.

**aus|renken** vt: **jm/sich** (D) **den Arm ~** to dislocate sb's/one's arm.

**aus|richten** vt - **1.** [übermitteln]: **jm etw ~** to tell

sb sthg; **ich soll Ihnen Grüße von meiner Tante ~** my aunt sends her regards; **kann ich etwas ~?** can I take a message? - **2.** [erreichen] to achieve; **ich habe bei der Behörde nichts ~ können** I didn't get anywhere with the authorities - **3.** [Text] to align - **4.** [anpassen]: **etw auf jn/etw ~, etw nach jm/etw ~** to gear sthg towards sb/sthg; **das Angebot wurde nach der Nachfrage ausgerichtet** supply was tailored to meet demand.

**Aus|ritt** der ride; **einen ~ machen** to go for a ride.

**aus|rollen** vt to roll out.

**aus|rotten** vt [Rasse, Ungeziefer] to exterminate; [Aberglauben] to eradicate.

**aus|rücken** (perf ist **ausgerückt**) vi - **1.** MIL to move out - **2.** fam [weglaufen] to run away.

**Aus|ruf** der cry, exclamation.

**aus|rufen** vt (unreg) - **1.** [rufen] to cry, to exclaim - **2.** [öffentlich] to announce; **jn ~ lassen** to page sb - **3.** [verkünden]: **einen Streik ~** to call a strike; **jn zum König ~** to proclaim sb king.

**Ausrufe|zeichen, Ausrufungs|zeichen** das exclamation mark.

**aus|ruhen** vi to rest ◇ vt to rest; **die Beine/die Arme ~** to rest one's legs/arms.

➥ **sich ausruhen** ref to rest, to have a rest.

**aus|rupfen** vt to pull out.

**aus|rüsten** vt [Truppe] to equip; [Schiff] to fit out; **ein Auto mit einem Katalysator ~** to fit a car with a catalytic converter.

➥ **sich ausrüsten** ref to equip o.s.

**Aus|rüstung** die - **1.** [das Ausstatten - von Truppe] equipping; [ - von Schiff] fitting out - **2.** [Ausstattungsgegenstände] equipment (U).

**aus|rutschen** (perf ist **ausgerutscht**) vi to slip; **das Messer ist ihr ausgerutscht** the knife slipped out of her hand.

**Ausrutscher** (pl -) der slip.

**aus|säen** vt to sow.

**Aus|sage** die - **1.** [Äußerung - vor Gericht] statement; **nach ~ eines Fachmanns** according to an expert - **2.** [Inhalt] message.

**Aussagekraft** die expressiveness.

**aussagekräftig** adj meaningful.

**aus|sagen** vt - **1.** [ausdrücken]: **etw über jn/etw ~** to say sthg about sb/sthg, to reveal sthg about sb/sthg - **2.** [vor Gericht] to state ◇ vi to testify, to give evidence.

**aus|saugen** vt to suck out.

**aus|schaben** vt [leer machen] to scrape out.

**aus|schalten** vt - **1.** [abstellen] to switch off, to turn off - **2.** [ausschließen] to eliminate.

**Ausschank** (pl **Ausschänke**) der - **1.** (ohne pl) [Ausgabe] serving; **der ~ von Alkohol an Jugend-**

**liche ist verboten** no sale of alcohol to under-18s **- 2.** [Theke] bar.

**Ausschau** *die (ohne pl):* **nach jm/etw ~ halten** to look out for sb/sthg.

**aus|schauen** *vi* **- 1.** [ausblicken]: **nach jm/etw ~** to look out for sb/sthg, to be on the lookout for sb/sthg **- 2.** *Süddt* & *Österr* [aussehen] to look; **er schaut gut aus** he looks well; **es schaut mit jm/etw gut/schlecht aus** things are looking good/bad for sb/sthg; **wie schauts aus?** *fam* how's things?

**aus|schaufeln** *vt* to dig.

**aus|scheiden** (*perf* **hat/ist ausgeschieden**) (*unreg*) *vi (ist)* **- 1.** [aus Gruppe]: **aus etw ~** to leave sthg **- 2.** [SPORT - verlieren] to get knocked out; [ - wegen Verletzung] to pull out **- 3.** [wegfallen] to be ruled out ◇ *vt (hat)* [Giftstoff] to reject; [Eiter] to secrete.

**Aus|scheidung** *die* **- 1.** (*ohne pl*) [von Giftstoff] rejection; [von Eiter] secretion **- 2.** [Wettkampf] qualifying round; [in der Leichtathletik] heats (*pl*).

⬥ **Ausscheidungen** *pl* excretions.

**Ausscheidungs|kampf** *der* SPORT qualifying rounds (*pl*); [in der Leichtathletik] heats (*pl*).

**aus|schenken** *vt* to pour out; [in Gasthaus] to serve.

**aus|scheren** (*perf* **ist ausgeschert**) *vi* [Auto] to pull out.

**aus|schildern** *vt* to signpost.

**aus|schimpfen** *vt* to scold, to tell off.

**aus|schlachten** *vt* **- 1.** [ausbauen] to cannibalize **- 2.** *abw* [ausnutzen] to exploit.

**aus|schlafen** *vi* (*unreg*) to have a lie-in; **bist du ausgeschlafen?** do you feel fully rested?

**Aus|schlag** *der* **- 1.** [auf Haut] rash **- 2.** [das Entscheidende]: **den ~ geben** to be the decisive factor.

**aus|schlagen** (*perf* **hat/ist ausgeschlagen**) (*unreg*) *vt (hat)* **- 1.** [entfernen]: **er hat ihm einen Zahn ausgeschlagen** he knocked out one of his teeth **- 2.** [ablehnen] to turn down ◇ *vi* **- 1.** (*hat*) [treten] to kick out **- 2.** (*hat, ist*) [Zeiger, Pendel] to swing **- 3.** (*hat, ist*) [Pflanze, Baum] to produce leaves.

**ausschlaggebend** *adj* decisive.

**aus|schließen** *vt* (*unreg*) **- 1.** [Grund, Erklärung, Möglichkeit] to rule out; [Irrtum] to prevent; [Zweifel, Unsicherheit] to remove **- 2.** [ausstoßen]: **jn von etw ~** to expel sb from sthg **- 3.** [aussperren] to lock out.

⬥ **sich ausschließen** *ref* **- 1.** [sich aussperren] to lock o.s. out **- 2.** [sich fernhalten - Person] to rule o.s. out; **diese beiden Möglichkeiten schließen sich gegenseitig aus** these two possibilities rule each other out.

**ausschließlich** *adj* exclusive ◇ *adv* exclusively ◇ *präp (+ G)* excluding.

**Aus|schluss** *der* expulsion; **unter ~ der Öffentlichkeit** RECHT in camera.

**aus|schmücken** *vt* **- 1.** [Raum] to decorate **- 2.** [Geschichte] to embellish.

**aus|schneiden** *vt (unreg)* to cut out.

**Aus|schnitt** *der* **- 1.** [Zeitungsausschnitt] cutting *Br*, clipping *Am* **- 2.** [Halsausschnitt] neckline; **ein Kleid mit tiefem ~** a low-cut dress **- 3.** [Auszug] excerpt; [eines Romans] excerpt, extract; [eines Films] clip, excerpt; [eines Bilds] detail.

**aus|schöpfen** *vt* **- 1.** [Schüssel] to scoop out; [Boot] to bail out **- 2.** *fig* [ausnutzen] to exhaust.

**aus|schreiben** *vt (unreg)* **- 1.** [ganz schreiben] to write out **- 2.** [ausstellen] to make out **- 3.** [bekannt geben] to advertise.

**Aus|schreibung** *die* [von Stelle, Wettbewerb] advertisement; [von Projekt] call for tenders.

**Ausschreitungen** *pl* violent clashes.

**Aus|schuss** *der* **- 1.** [Gremium] committee **- 2.** (*ohne pl*) [Ausschussware] rejects (*pl*).

**Ausschuss|ware** *die* reject.

**aus|schütteln** *vt* to shake out.

**aus|schütten** *vt* **- 1.** [Gefäß] to empty; [Flüssigkeit] to pour out **- 2.** [auszahlen] to pay out, to distribute.

**aus|schwärmen** (*perf* **sind ausgeschwärmt**) *vi* to swarm out.

**ausschweifend** *adj* [Fantasie] wild; [Leben] debauched ◇ *adv* dissolutely; [feiern] wildly.

**aus|schweigen** (*unreg*) ⬥ **sich ausschweigen** *ref:* **sich über etw** (*A*) **~** to remain silent about sthg.

**aus|schwenken** *vt* [Glas] to swill out ◇ *vi* [sich seitwärts bewegen] to swing out.

**aus|schwitzen** *vt* [Erkältung] to sweat out.

**aus|sehen** *vi (unreg)* you look; **sie sieht gut aus** she looks good; **es sieht nach Regen aus** it looks like rain; **es sieht danach aus, als würden wir gewinnen** it looks like we will win, it looks as if we will win; **mit dem Patienten sieht es schlecht aus** things aren't looking good for the patient; **mit dem Zuschuss sieht es gut aus** things are looking good as far as the grant is concerned; **wie siehts aus?** *fam* how's things?; **sehe ich danach aus, als würde ich stehlen?** do I look as if I would steal?; **dieser Sänger sieht nach nichts aus** *fam* this singer doesn't look anything special; **so siehst du aus!** *fam* & *fig* you can think again!, nothing doing!

**Aussehen** *das (ohne pl)* appearance.

**aus sein** (*perf* **ist aus gewesen**) *vi (unreg)* **- 1.** [zu Ende sein] to be over; **mit dem Trinken ist es aus** no more drinking for me; **es ist aus mit ihm** he's had it; **es ist aus zwischen ihnen** it is over between them **- 2.** [nicht an sein] to be out **- 3.** SPORT to be out **- 4.** [erpicht sein]: **auf etw** (*A*)

**~** *fam* to be after sthg; **sie ist darauf aus, mir etw zu verkaufen** she is out to sell me sthg.

**außen** *adv* outside; **von ~** from (the) outside; **nach ~** outwards.

**✏ außen vor** *adv Norddt:* **etw ~ vor lassen** to leave sthg out.

**Außenlansicht** *die* exterior view.

**Außenlantenne** *die* outdoor aerial.

**Außenlarbeiten** *pl* work *(U)* on the exterior.

**Außenlbezirk** *der* suburb.

**Außenbordlmotor** *der* outboard motor.

**auslsenden** *vt* - **1.** [Signale] to send out - **2.** [Boten, Spion] to send.

**Außenldienst** *der:* **im ~ sein** to work in the field.

**Außenlhandel** *der (ohne pl)* foreign trade.

**Außenhandelslbilanz** *die* balance of trade.

**außenliegend** *adj* outlying.

**Außenlminister, in** *der, die* foreign minister.

**Außenlministerium** *das* foreign ministry.

**Außenlpolitik** *die (ohne pl)* foreign policy.

**außenpolitisch** *adj* foreign policy *(vor Subst);* **~e Beziehungen** foreign relations.

**Außenlseite** *die* outside.

**Außenseiter, in** *(mpl -; fpl -nen) der, die* outsider.

**Außenlspiegel** *der* wing mirror *Br,* side mirror *Am.*

**Außenstände** *pl* outstanding debts.

**Außenstehende** *(pl -n) der, die* outsider.

**Außenlstelle** *die* [von Firma] branch; [von Behörde] (local) office.

**Außenltemperatur** *die* outside temperature.

**Außenlwelt** *die (ohne pl)* outside world.

**außer** *präp (+ D)* - **1.** [außerhalb] out of; **~ Haus sein** to be away from home; **~ Atem sein** to be out of breath; **~ Betrieb** out of order; **~ sich sein (vor)** to be beside o.s. (with) - **2.** [abgesehen von] except (for), apart from; **alle ~ ihm** everyone except (for) him; **nichts ~ ...** nothing but ... - **3.** [zusätzlich] in addition to, as well as ⬦ *konj* except; **ich komme, ~ es regnet** I'll come, unless it rains.

**außerberuflich** *adj:* **sie ist vielen ~en Belastungen ausgesetzt** she's under a lot of pressure outside work.

**außerdem** *adv* also; **es ist viel zu spät, ~ regnet es** it's far too late and it's raining too.

**außerdienstlich** *adj* [Treffen] social ⬦ *adv* [sich treffen] socially.

**äußere** *adj* - **1.** [Wand, Umstände] external; [Ähnlichkeit, Schein] outward - **2.** [auswärtig] foreign.

**Äußere** *das (ohne pl)* (outward) appearance.

**außergewöhnlich** *adj* - **1.** [ungewöhnlich] unusual - **2.** [sehr gut] exceptional ⬦ *adv* exceptionally, remarkably.

**außerhalb** *präp (+ G)* outside; **~ der Stadt** outside town; **~ der Öffnungszeiten** outside opening hours ⬦ *adv* [nicht im Stadtgebiet] out of town.

**außerirdisch** *adj* extraterrestrial.

**äußerlich** *adj* - **1.** [an der Außenseite] external - **2.** [nach außen hin] outward; [oberflächlich] superficial ⬦ *adv:* **~ war sie ruhig** she was outwardly calm; **die Salbe ist ~ anzuwenden** the ointment is for external application; **~ betrachtet** on the face of it.

**Äußerlichkeiten** *pl* - **1.** [Umgangsform und Aussehen] appearances - **2.** [Unwesentliches] trivialities.

**äußern** *vt* to express.

**✏ sich äußern** *ref* - **1.** [seine Meinung sagen]: **sich über jn/etw ~** to give one's opinion on *ODER* about sb/sthg; **sich zu etw ~** to comment on sthg - **2.** [sich zeigen]: **sich in etw *(D)* ~** to reveal itself in sthg.

**außerordentlich** *adj* extraordinary ⬦ *adv* extremely, extraordinarily; **der Film hat mir ~ gut gefallen** I thought the film was extremely good.

**außerplanmäßig** *adj* [Besuch, Zwischenlandung] unscheduled; [Zug, Bus] extra, special; [Versammlung] extraordinary; [Ausgaben] additional.

**äußerst** *adv* extremely.

**außerstande, außer Stande** *adj:* **zu etw ~ sein** to be incapable of sthg; **ich sehe mich ~, diese Arbeit zu machen** I'm unable to do this job.

**äußerste** *adj* - **1.** [Ende] furthest; [Rand] outermost - **2.** [größte] extreme; **von ~r Dringlichkeit** of the utmost urgency, extremely urgent - **3.** [Termin] latest possible; [Preis, Angebot] final - **4.** [schlimmste] extreme; **falls der ~ Fall eintreten sollte** if the worst comes to the worst.

**Äußerste** *das (ohne pl):* **sein ~s geben** to give one's all; **bei etw bis zum ~n gehen** to put everything into sthg; **ich bin auf das ~ gefasst** I'm expecting the worst.

**Äußerung** *(pl -en) die* [offizielle Aussage] statement; [Bemerkung] remark.

**auslsetzen** *vt* - **1.** [verlassen] to abandon - **2.** [versprechen] to offer - **3.** [ausliefern] to expose; **wir waren auf See großer Gefahr ausgesetzt** we were exposed to great danger at sea - **4.** [beanstanden]: **dieser Kunde fand an allem etwas auszusetzen** this customer found fault with everything ⬦ *vi* [Herz] to stop; [Motor] to cut out; **sein Atem setzte kurzzeitig aus** he stopped breathing momentarily; **beim Spiel ~** to miss a go.

➤ **sich aussetzen** *ref:* **sich einer Sache** *(D)* **~** to expose o.s. to sthg.

**Aussicht** *(pl* **-en)** *die* **- 1.** [Sicht] view **- 2.** [Zukunftsperspektive] prospect; **sie hat eine Beförderung in ~** she's in line for promotion; **in ~ stehen** to be expected; **jm etw in ~ stellen** to promise sb sthg; **das sind ja schöne ~en!** *iron* what a prospect!

**aussichtslos** *adj* hopeless.

**Aussichtslosigkeit** *die (ohne pl)* hopelessness.

**aussichtsreich** *adj* [Vorhaben] promising; **ein ~er Kandidat** a candidate who stands a good chance of succeeding.

**Aussichtslturm** *der* lookout tower.

**Auslsiedler, in** *der, die* [aus Osteuropa] *person of German extraction especially from eastern Europe, who goes to live in Germany.*

**auslsöhnen** *vt* to reconcile.

➤ **sich aussöhnen** *ref:* **sich mit jm/etw ~** to become reconciled with sb/to sthg.

**Aussöhnung** *(pl* **-en)** *die* reconciliation.

**auslsondern** *vt* to pick out.

**auslsortieren** *vt* to sort out.

**auslspannen** *vt* **- 1.** [ausbreiten] to spread **- 2.** *fam* [wegnehmen]: **jm die Freundin/den Freund ~** to pinch sb's girlfriend/boyfriend ⬦ *vi* to relax.

**auslsparen** *vt* [Zimmer, Ecke] to leave empty; [Thema] to leave out.

**auslsperren** *vt* to lock out.

**Auslsperrung** *die* lockout.

**auslspielen** *vt* **- 1.** [einsetzen] to bring to bear **- 2.** [im Sport] to outplay **- 3.** [manipulieren]: **jn gegen jn ~** to play sb off against sb.

**auslspionieren** *vt* **- 1.** [Geheimnis, Versteck] to uncover **- 2.** [Person] to spy on.

**Auslsprache** *die* **- 1.** [Artikulation] pronunciation; **eine gute/schlechte ~ haben** to have a good/bad accent **- 2.** [Gespräch] discussion *(to resolve a dispute).*

**auslsprechen** *vt (unreg)* **- 1.** [artikulieren] to pronounce **- 2.** [ausdrücken] to express; [Urteil, Strafe] to deliver.

➤ **sich aussprechen** *ref* **- 1.** [sich äußern]: **sich bewundernd über jn ~** to speak admiringly of sb; **sich über etw ausführlich ~** to say what's on one's mind about sthg **- 2.** [Stellung nehmen]: **sich gegen/für jn/etw ~** to come out against/in favour of sb/sthg **- 3.** [offen sprechen]: **sich mit jm ~** to talk things through with sb.

**Auslspruch** *der* saying.

**auslspucken** *vi* to spit ⬦ *vt* **- 1.** [spucken] to

spit out **- 2.** *fam* [ausgeben, bezahlen] to cough up **- 3.** *fam* [erbrechen] to puke up.

**auslspülen** *vt* to rinse out.

**auslstaffieren** *vt* [mit Möbeln] to rig out; [mit Kleidungsstücken] to kit out.

**Auslstand** *der* **- 1.** [Streik] strike; **im ~ sein** to be on strike; **in den ~ treten** to go on strike **- 2.** [Abschied]: **seinen ~ geben** to hold a leaving party.

**auslstanzen** *vt* to punch out.

**auslstatten** *vt* [mit Geräten] to equip; [mit Lebensmitteln, Kleidung, Geld] to provide.

**Ausstattung** *(pl* **-en)** *die* **- 1.** [mit Möbeln] furnishing; [mit Geräten] equipping; [mit Lebensmitteln, Kleidung, Geld] provision **- 2.** [Ausrüstung] equipment; [von Küche, Auto] fittings *(pl)* **- 3.** [Einrichtung] furnishings *(pl).*

**auslstechen** *vt (unreg)* **- 1.** [entfernen] to dig up **- 2.** [herstellen] to cut out **- 3.** [übertreffen] to outdo.

**auslstehen** *(unreg) vt* to endure; **jn/etw nicht ~ können** *fam* not to be able to stand sb/sthg; **ausgestanden sein** to be over ⬦ *vi* [Zahlung] to be outstanding; **die Antwort steht noch aus** we're still waiting for an answer.

**auslsteigen** *(perf* **ist ausgestiegen)** *vi (unreg)* **- 1.** [heraussteigen] to get out; **aus einem Bus/Zug ~** to get off a bus/train **- 2.** *fam* [ausscheiden]: **aus einem Geschäft ~** to pull out of a deal **- 3.** [aus Gesellschaft] to drop out (from society).

**Aussteiger, in** *(mpl* **-;** *fpl* **-nen)** *der, die* dropout.

**auslstellen** *vt* **- 1.** [zeigen - Waren] to display; [ - Kunstwerke] to exhibit **- 2.** [ausfertigen - Scheck, Rezept] to make out; [ - Visum] to issue; **einen Scheck auf jn ~** to make out a cheque to sb **- 3.** [ausschalten] to turn off.

**Aussteller, in** *(mpl* **-;** *fpl* **-nen)** *der, die* [auf Messe] exhibitor.

**Auslstellung** *die* exhibition.

**Ausstellungslkatalog** *der* exhibition catalogue.

**Ausstellungslstück** *das* exhibit.

**auslsterben** *(perf* **ist ausgestorben)** *vi (unreg)* [Tierart] to become extinct; [Tradition] to die out.

**Auslsteuer** *die* dowry.

**Ausstieg** *(pl* **-e)** *der* **- 1.** [Öffnung] exit **- 2.** *(ohne pl)* [Rückzug]: **sie haben den ~ aus der Kernenergie/dem Projekt beschlossen** they have decided to abandon nuclear energy/the project.

**auslstopfen** *vt* to stuff.

**Auslstoß** *der* **- 1.** [Produktion] output **- 2.** [Emission] emission.

**auslstoßen** *vt (unreg)* **- 1.** [ausschließen] to expel

**- 2.** [hervorstoßen] [Schrei] to give; [Seufzer] to heave; [Fluch] to utter **- 3.** [produzieren] to emit.

**aus|strahlen** vt **- 1.** [verbreiten] to radiate **- 2.** [senden] to broadcast <> vi [strahlen - Licht] to shine.

**Aus|strahlung** die **- 1.** [Wirkung] charisma **- 2.** [Senden] broadcasting.

**aus|strecken** vt [Zunge] to stick out; [Fühler] to put out; **die Beine/Arme ~** to stretch one's legs/arms.

➤ **sich ausstrecken** ref to stretch out.

**aus|streichen** vt (unreg) [durchstreichen] to cross out, to delete.

**aus|strömen** (perf hat/ist ausgeströmt) vt (hat) to exude <> vi (ist) to escape.

**aus|suchen** vt to choose; **sich** (D) **etw ~** to choose sthg.

**Aus|tausch** der exchange; [von Spielern] substitution.

**austauschbar** adj interchangeable.

**aus|tauschen** vt **- 1.** [mitteilen] to exchange **- 2.** [auswechseln] to replace; **einen Spieler (gegen einen anderen) ~** to substitute a player (with another).

**aus|teilen** vt [Prospekte, Geschenke] to hand out; [Karten] to deal (out); [Essen] to dish out; [Kuchen] to share out.

**Auster** (pl -n) die oyster.

**aus|toben** vt: **seine Wut an jm ~** to vent one's fury on sb.

➤ **sich austoben** ref to let off steam.

**aus|tragen** vt (unreg) **- 1.** [Zeitung, Post] to deliver **- 2.** [ausfechten]: **einen Streit mit jm ~** to have it out with sb **- 3.** [Wettkampf] to hold **- 4.** [im Mutterleib] to carry to term.

➤ **sich austragen** ref to sign out.

**Austragung** (pl -en) die [eines Wettkampfs] holding.

**Australien** nt Australia.

**Australier, in** [aus'traːljɐ, rɪn] (mpl -; fpl -nen) der, die Australian.

**australisch** adj Australian.

**aus|treiben** vt (unreg) **- 1.** [verbannen] to exorcize **- 2.** [abgewöhnen]: **jm etw ~** to cure sb of sthg.

**aus|treten** (perf hat/ist ausgetreten) (unreg) vt (hat) **- 1.** [ersticken - Funken] to stamp out; [ - Zigarette] to tread out **- 2.** [abnutzen] to wear down **- 3.** [weiten] to break in <> vi (ist) **- 1.** [ausscheiden]: **aus etw ~** to leave sthg **- 2.** [zur Toilette gehen] to answer the call of nature.

**aus|tricksen** vt to trick.

**aus|trinken** (unreg) vt [Kaffee, Bier] to drink up, to finish; [Glas] to drain, to finish <> vi to drink up.

**Aus|tritt** der [aus Partei] resignation; **die Kirche**

hat zahlreiche **~e** zu verzeichnen a lot of people have left the Church.

**Austritts|erklärung** die [von Parteimitglied] notice of resignation.

**aus|trocknen** (perf hat/ist ausgetrocknet) vt (hat) vi (ist) [Haut, Brot, Boden] to dry out; [See] to dry up.

**aus|tüfteln** vt to work out.

**aus|üben** vt [Beruf] to practise; [Amt] to hold; [Einfluss, Druck] to exert; [Macht] to exercise, to wield; **welchen Beruf üben Sie aus?** what do you do for a living?

**Ausübung** die (ohne pl) [von Beruf] practising; [von Einfluss, Druck] exertion; [von Macht] exercising, wielding.

**aus|ufern** (perf ist ausgeufert) vi to get out of hand.

**Aus|verkauf** der sale.

**aus|verkaufen** vt to sell off.

**ausverkauft** adj sold out.

**Aus|wahl** die **- 1.** (ohne pl) [Wahl] choice; **es stehen fünf Bewerber zur ~** there are five applicants to choose from **- 2.** [Auslese] selection **- 3.** [Sortiment] range.

**aus|wählen** vt to choose, to select.

**aus|walzen** vt **- 1.** [walzen] to roll out **- 2.** abw [breittreten] to drag out.

**Aus|wanderer, Auswandrer** der emigrant.

**Aus|wanderin, Auswandrerin** die emigrant.

**aus|wandern** (perf ist ausgewandert) vi to emigrate.

**Auswanderung** die (ohne pl) emigration.

**Aus|wandrer** = Auswanderer.

**Aus|wandrerin** = Auswanderin.

**auswärtig** adj **- 1.** [extern]: **ein ~es Unternehmen** an external contractor **- 2.** [aus einem anderen Ort] from another town; [Mannschaft] away (vor Subst) **- 3.** [außenpolitisch] foreign.

**Auswärtige Amt** das foreign ministry.

**auswärts** adv [spielen, übernachten] away from home; **~ essen** to eat out.

**Auswärts|spiel** das away match.

**aus|waschen** vt (unreg) [Fleck] to wash out; [Kleidungsstück] to wash; [Pinsel] to rinse.

**aus|wechseln** ['ausvɛksln] vt [Reifen, Batterien] to replace; [Spieler] to substitute; **wie ausgewechselt sein** to be a different person.

**Aus|weg** der way out.

**ausweglos** adj hopeless.

**Ausweglosigkeit** die hopelessness.

**aus|weichen** (perf ist ausgewichen) vi (unreg) **- 1.** (+ D) [Fußgänger, Hindernis] to avoid; [Schlag] to dodge; [Auto] to get out of the way of - **2.** *(+ D)* [Frage, Entscheidung, Blick] to avoid - **3.** [zurückgreifen]: **auf etw** *(A)* **~** to switch to sthg.

**ausweichend** *adj* evasive.

**Ausweichlmanöver** *das* evasive action *(U).*

**auslweinen** ➡ **sich ausweinen** *ref:* **sich bei jm ~** to cry on sb's shoulder.

**Ausweis** *(pl* **-e)** *der* [Personalausweis] identity card; [von Mitglied] membership card; [Zugangsberechtigung] pass.

**auslweisen** *vt (unreg)* - **1.** [verbannen] to deport, to expel - **2.** [erkennen lassen]: **jn als etw ~** to identify sb as sthg.
➡ **sich ausweisen** *ref* to show one's identification.

**Ausweislkontrolle** *die* identity card check.

**Ausweispapiere** *pl* papers, identification *(U).*

**auslweiten** *vt* - **1.** [weiter machen] to stretch - **2.** [vergrößern] to expand.
➡ **sich ausweiten** *ref* - **1.** [sich weiten] to stretch - **2.** [sich vergrößern] to spread.

**Ausweitung** *(pl* **-en)** *die* - **1.** [Vergrößerung] expansion - **2.** [eines Streiks] spreading.

**auswendig** *adv* by heart; **etw ~ lernen** to learn sthg by heart; **etw ~ wissen** *ODER* **können** to know sthg by heart.

**auslwerten** *vt* to evaluate.

**Auslwertung** *die* evaluation.

**auslwiegen** *vt (unreg)* to weigh (out).

**auslwirken** ➡ **sich auswirken** *ref* to have an effect; **sich negativ ~** to have a negative effect; **sich auf jn/etw ~** to have an effect on sb/sthg.

**Auslwirkung** *die* effect, impact; **die ~ auf jn/ etw** the effect *ODER* impact on sb/sthg.

**auslwischen** *vt* to wipe; **jm eins ~** *fam fig* to get one's own back on sb.

**auslwringen** *(prät* **wrang aus;** *perf* **ausgewrungen)** *vt (unreg)* to wring out.

**Auswuchs** ['ausvu:ks] *der*
➡ **Auswüchse** *pl* excesses.

**auslwuchten** *vt* to balance.

**Auslwurf** *der* MED phlegm.

**auslzahlen** *vt* - **1.** [Gehalt, Lohn] to pay - **2.** [Teilhaber] to buy out; [Arbeiter] to pay off.
➡ **sich auszahlen** *ref* to pay off.

**auslzählen** *vt* to count up.

**Auslzahlung** *die* - **1.** [von Gehalt, Lohn] payment - **2.** [von Teilhaber] buy-out; [von Arbeiter] paying off.

**auslzeichnen** *vt* - **1.** [mit Preisschild] to price - **2.** [ehren]: **jm mit einem Preis ~** to award a prize to sb - **3.** [charakterisieren]: **große Biegsam-** keit zeichnet diesen Werkstoff aus this material is characterized by its great flexibility.
➡ **sich auszeichnen** *ref* [Person] to distinguish o.s.; [Produkt] to stand out.

**Auslzeichnung** *die* - **1.** [Ehrung] distinction; **mit ~** with distinction - **2.** [Preis] award.

**ausziehbar** *adj* [Leiter] extendable; [Tisch] pull-out.

**auslziehen** *(perf* **hat/ist ausgezogen)** *(unreg)* *vt (hat)* - **1.** [ablegen] to take off; **die Jacke ~** to take off one's jacket - **2.** [entkleiden] to undress - **3.** [vergrößern - Tisch, Antenne] to pull out - **4.** [herausziehen] to pull out <> *vi (ist)* [umziehen] to move out.
➡ **sich ausziehen** *ref* to undress; **sich die Schuhe ~** to take one's shoes off.

**Ausziehltisch** *der* pull-out table.

**Auszubildende** *(pl* **-n)** *der, die* trainee.

**Auslzug** *der* - **1.** [Ausschnitt] excerpt - **2.** [Kontoauszug] statement - **3.** [Umzug] move.

**auszugsweise** *adv:* **ein Roman ~ abdrucken** to publish a novel in instalments.

**autark** *adj* self-sufficient.

**authentisch** *adj* authentic.

**Autismus** *der (ohne pl)* MED autism.

**Auto** *(pl* **-s)** *das* car; **mit dem ~ fahren** to go by car, to drive.

**Autolatlas** *der* road atlas.

**Autolbahn** *die* motorway *Br,* freeway *Am.*

> **AUTOBAHN**
>
> At over 11,000 km, the German motorway network, construction of which began in the prewar era, is the second longest in the world after the United States. There is no speed limit on German motorways, although there is a recommended limit of 130 km/h. No toll is charged for using the motorway.

**Autobahnauflfahrt** *die* motorway access (road) *Br,* on-ramp *Am.*

**Autobahnauslfahrt** *die* motorway exit (road) *Br,* off-ramp *Am.*

**Autobahnlgebühr** *die* toll.

**Autobahnlkreuz** *das* interchange.

**Autobahnlmeisterei** *(pl* **-en)** *die* motorway *Br ODER* freeway *Am* maintenance department.

**Autobahnlpolizei** *die* motorway police *Br,* freeway police *Am.*

**Autobahnlraststätte** *die* motorway services *(pl) Br,* freeway service area *Am.*

**Autolbiografie** *die* autobiography.

**autobiografisch** *adj* autobiographical <> *adv* autobiographically.

**Auto|bombe** die car bomb.
**Auto|bus** der bus.
**Autodidakt, in** (mpl -en; fpl -nen) der, die self-taught person.
**Auto|dieb** der car thief.
**Auto|fähre** die car ferry.
**Auto|fahrer, in** der, die (car) driver.
**Auto|friedhof** der breaker's yard, scrapyard.
**autogene Training** das autogenics (U), relaxation technique based on self-hypnosis, developed by German neurologist J.H. Schultz.
**Auto|gramm** das autograph.
**Auto|industrie** die car ODER automotive industry.
**Auto|karte** die road map.
**Automat** (pl -en) der [für Getränke, Zigaretten] vending machine.
**Automatik** (pl -en) die automatic mechanism.
**Automatik|getriebe** das automatic transmission.
**automatisch** adj automatic <> adv automatically.
**automatisieren** vt to automate.
**autonom** adj - 1. [unabhängig] autonomous - 2. [anarchistisch] anarchist.
**Autonome** (pl -n) der, die anarchist.
**Autonomie** (pl -n) die autonomy.
**Auto|nummer** die (car) registration number Br, license number Am.
**Autopsie** (pl -n) die autopsy.
**Autor** (pl -toren) der author.
**Auto|radio** das car radio.
**Auto|rennen** das - 1. [Sportart] motor racing - 2. [Wettkampf] motor race.
**Autorin** (pl -nen) die author.
**autoritär** adj authoritarian.
**Autorität** (pl -en) die authority.
**Auto|schlange** die [auf Autobahn] tailback; [an Ampel, Kreuzung] queue Br ODER line Am of cars.
**Auto|telefon** das car phone.
**Auto|unfall** der car accident.
**Auto|verkehr** der car traffic.
**Auto|wrack** das wrecked car.
**avantgardistisch** [avãgar'dıstıʃ] adj avantgarde.
**Aversion** [aver'zjo:n] (pl -en) die: eine ~ gegen jn/etw haben to have an aversion to sb/sthg.
**Avocado** [avo'ka:do] (pl -s) die avocado.
**Axt** (pl Äxte) die axe; wie die ~ im Walde boorishly.

**Azalee** (pl -n) die azalea.
**Azoren** pl: die ~ the Azores.
**Azubi** (pl -s) der, die fam trainee.
**azurblau** adj azure.

# B

**b, B** [be:] (pl - ODER -s) das - 1. [Buchstabe] B, b - 2. [MUS - Note] B flat; [ - Vorzeichen] flat.
◆ B (abk für Bundesstraße) die ≈ A road Br, ≈ state highway Am.
**b.** abk für bei.
**Baby** ['be:bi] (pl -s) das baby.
**Baby|jahr** das maternity leave lasting one year for which an extra year on one's pension scheme is granted.
**Baby|nahrung** die baby food.
**Baby|sitter, in** ['be:bisitɐ, rın] (mpl -; fpl -nen) der, die babysitter.
**Bach** (pl Bäche) der stream; den ~ runtergehen fam to go down the tubes.
**Bach|stelze** ['baxʃtɛltsəl die wagtail.
**Back|blech** das baking sheet Br, cookie sheet Am.
**Backbord** das (ohne pl) SCHIFF port.
**Backe** (pl -n) die [Wange, von Po] cheek; au ~! fam oh bother!
**backen** (präs bäckt ODER backt; prät backte ODER buk; perf hat gebacken) vt - 1. [im Ofen] to bake - 2. [braten] to fry <> vi to bake.
**Backen|zahn** der molar.
**Bäcker** (pl -) der baker.
**Bäckerei** (pl -en) die bakery.
**Bäckerin** (pl -nen) die baker.
**Back|form** die baking tin.
**Background** ['bɛkgraunt] (pl -s) der background.
**Back|obst** das dried fruit.
**Back|ofen** der oven.
**Back|pflaume** die prune.
**Back|pulver** das baking powder.

**Back|stein** der brick; **ein Gebäude aus ~ a** brick building.

**bäckt** präs ▷ backen.

**Back-up, Backup** ['bɛkap] (pl -s) das EDV back-up.

**Backwaren** pl bread, cakes and pastries.

**Bad** (pl Bäder) das - **1.** [Badezimmer] bathroom - **2.** [Baden - im Meer] bathing (U); [ - in der Wanne] bath; **ein ~ im Meer** a dip in the sea; **ein ~ neh-men** to have a bath; **ein ~ in der Menge neh-men** fig to press the flesh - **3.** [Schwimmbad] (swimming) pool - **4.** [Kurort] spa town.

**Bade|anzug** der swimming costume, swim-suit.

**Bade|hose** die swimming trunks (pl).

**Bade|kappe** die swimming cap.

**Bade|mantel** der bathrobe.

**Bade|meister, in** der, die [im Schwimmbad] pool attendant; [am Strand] lifeguard.

**baden** vt [Kind] to bath Br, to bathe Am; [Wunde] to bathe ▷ vi - **1.** [in der Wanne] to have a bath - **2.** [schwimmen] to swim; **~ gehen** to go for a swim; **wenn das passiert, werde ich bei** ODER **mit meinen Plänen ~ gehen** fam if that happens, I can kiss my plans goodbye.
➤ **sich baden** ref to have a bath.

**Baden** nt Baden.

**Badener, in** (mpl -; fpl -nen) der, die native/inhabitant of Baden.

**Baden-Württemberg** nt Baden-Württem-berg.

**Baden-Württemberger, in** (mpl -; fpl -nen) der, die native/inhabitant of Baden-Württemberg.

**baden-württembergisch** adj of/from Baden-Württemberg.

**Bade|ort** der [am Meer] (seaside) resort; [Kurort] spa (town).

**Bade|sachen** pl swimming things.

**Bade|saison** die summer months during which seaside resorts are at their busiest and open-air swimming pools are open.

**Bade|tuch** das bath towel.

**Bade|wanne** die bath (tub).

**Bade|zimmer** das bathroom.

**Badminton** ['bɛtmɪntən] das badminton.

**baff** adj: (ganz) **~ sein** fam to be gobsmacked.

**Bafög** ['baːføk] (abk für **Bundesausbildungs-förderungsgesetz**) das [Stipendium] mainten-ance which is half grant and half loan awar-ded to students and trainees by the State; **~ bekommen** to get a grant.

**Bagatelle** (pl -n) die trifle.

**Bagatell|schaden** der minor damage (U).

**Bagdad** nt Baghdad.

**Bagger** (pl -) der mechanical digger.

**baggern** vt [Graben] to dig; [Fahrrinne] to dredge ▷ vi fam [Mädchen anmachen]: **er baggert schon wieder** he's on the pull again.

**Bagger|see** der artificial lake where people go to have picnics, swim etc.

**Bahamas** pl: **die ~** the Bahamas.

**Bahn** (pl -en) die - **1.** [Eisenbahn] train; **jn von der ~ abholen** to pick sb up from the (train) sta-tion; **mit der ~ fahren** to travel by train ODER rail - **2.** [Institution] railway Br, railroad Am; **die ~** [Deutsche Bahn] German rail company; **bei der ~ arbeiten** to work for the railways - **3.** [Weg] path; **wir haben freie ~** AUTO the road is clear; fig the way is clear - **4.** [von Rakete, Planet] path - **5.** SPORT [in Schwimmbad, Stadion] lane; **40 ~en schwimmen** to swim 40 lengths - **6.** [Straßen-bahn] tram Br, streetcar Am - **7.** [Streifen - von Stoff] length; [ - von Tapete] strip - **8.** RW: **auf die schiefe ~ geraten** to fall into bad ways; **jn aus der ~ werfen** to shatter sb.

**Bahn|beamte** der railway official.

**Bahn|beamtin** die railway official.

**bahnbrechend** adj pioneering.

**BahnCard®** ['baːnkaːd] (pl -s) die card offering 50% discount on German rail fares.

**Bahn|damm** der railway embankment.

**bahnen** vt: **jm/sich einen Weg ~** to clear a path for sb/o.s.

**Bahn|hof** der (railway) station; **ich verstehe nur ~** fam I haven't got a clue what you're/she's/etc on about.

**Bahnhofs|halle** die station concourse.

**Bahnhofs|mission** die room at a station where charitable organizations provide care for rail travellers.

**Bahn|polizei** die railway police Br, railroad police Am.

**Bahn|steig** (pl -e) der platform.

**Bahnsteig|kante** die platform edge.

**Bahnüber|gang** der level crossing Br, grade crossing Am; **beschrankter/unbeschrankter ~** level Br ODER grade Am crossing with/without a barrier.

**Bahn|verbindung** die (train ODER rail) con-nection.

**Bahre** (pl -n) die - **1.** [für Kranke] stretcher - **2.** [für Tote] bier.

**Baiser** [bɛ'zeː] (pl -s) das meringue.

**Bakterien** pl bacteria, germs.

**Balance** [ba'laŋsə] die balance.

**balancieren** [balaŋ'siːrən] (perf **hat/ist balan-ciert**) vt (hat) vi (ist) to balance.

**bald** adv - **1.** [in Kürze, schnell] soon - **2.** fam [fast] almost, nearly - **3.** *fam* [endlich]: **hältst du jetzt ~ den Mund?** just shut up, will you?

➡ **bis bald** *interj* see you soon *ODER* later!

**baldig** *adj* speedy; **auf ~es Wiedersehen!** hope to see you soon!

**Baldrian** (*pl* -e) *der* valerian.

**Balearen** *pl:* **die ~** the Balearic Islands, the Balearics.

**balgen** *vi* to tussle.

➡ **sich balgen** *ref:* **sich (mit jm um etw) ~** to tussle (with sb over sthg).

**Bali** *nt* Bali.

**Balkan** *der:* **der ~** the Balkans.

**Balken** (*pl* -) *der* beam.

**Balkon** [bal'kɔŋ, bal'koːn] (*pl* -s *ODER* -e) *der* balcony.

**Balkonmöbel** *pl* garden furniture (*U*) (*for patios etc*).

**Balkonltür** *die* balcony door.

**Ball** (*pl* **Bälle**) *der* ball; **am ~ bleiben** [nicht aufhören] to stick at it; [auf dem Laufenden bleiben] to keep up to date.

**Ballade** (*pl* -n) *die* ballad.

**Ballast** *der* ballast.

**Ballaststoffe** *pl* roughage (*U*).

**ballen** *vt:* **die Faust ~** to clench one's fist.

➡ **sich ballen** *ref* - **1.** [Schnee, Lehm]: **sich zu etw ~** to form into sthg - **2.** [Fehler, Schwierigkeiten] to mount, to build up.

**Ballen** (*pl* -) *der* - **1.** [Packen] bale - **2.** [von Hand] ball of the hand; [von Fuß] ball of the foot.

**ballern** *fam vi* - **1.** [schießen] to spray bullets - **2.** [schlagen]: **gegen** *ODER* **an etw** (*A*) **~** to hammer on sthg ◇ *vt* - **1.** [ohrfeigen]: **jm eine/ein paar ~** to sock sb one - **2.** [werfen]: **etw gegen etw ~** to smash sthg against sthg.

**Ballett** (*pl* -e) *das* ballet; **ins ~ gehen** to go to the ballet.

**Ballettltänzer, in** *der, die* ballet dancer (*f* ballerina).

**Ballistik** *die* ballistics (*U*).

**Ballon** [ba'lɔŋ] (*pl* -s) *der* balloon.

**Ballspiel** *das* ball game.

**Ballungslgebiet** *das,* **-raum** *der* conurbation.

**Balsam** *der eigtl* & *fig* balm.

**Balsamico-lEssig** *der* KÜCHE balsamic vinegar.

**Balte** (*pl* -n) *der* native/inhabitant of the Baltic.

**Baltikum** *das:* **das ~** the Baltic.

**Baltin** (*pl* -nen) *die* native/inhabitant of the Baltic.

**baltisch** *adj* Baltic.

**Balz** (*pl* -en) *die* courtship display (*of birds*).

**balzen** *vi* to perform a courtship display.

**Bambus** (*pl* -se) *der* bamboo.

**banal** *adj* banal ◇ *adv* banally.

**Banane** (*pl* -n) *die* banana.

**Bananenlrepublik** *die abw* banana republic.

**Banause** (*pl* -n) *der abw* philistine.

**Banausin** (*pl* -nen) *die abw* philistine.

**band** *prät* ⊏ **binden.**

**Band¹** [bɛnt] (*pl* **Bänder** *ODER* **Bände**) *das* (*pl* - *Bänder*) - **1.** [aus Stoff] band; [als Zierde] ribbon - **2.** [Tonband] tape; **etw auf ~ aufnehmen** to tape sthg - **3.** [Fließband] conveyor belt; **am laufenden ~** *fig* continuously - **4.** [aus Bindegewebe] ligament ◇ *der* (*pl Bände*) [Buch] volume; **das spricht Bände** *fig* that speaks volumes.

**Band²** [bɛnt] (*pl* -s) *die* band.

**Bandage** [ban'daːʒə] (*pl* -n) *die* [Verband] bandage; **mit harten ~n (kämpfen)** *fig* (to fight) with no holds barred.

**bandagieren** [banda'ʒiːrən] *vt* to bandage.

**Bandlbreite** *die* - **1.** ELEKTR bandwidth - **2.** *fig* [Vielzahl] range.

**Bande** (*pl* -n) *die* - **1.** [von Verbrechern, Kindern] gang - **2.** [SPORT - von Bahn, Spielfeld] barrier; [ - von Billardtisch] cushion.

**Bänderlriss** *der* torn ligament.

**Bänderlzerrung** *die* pulled ligament.

**bändigen** *vt* [Tier] to tame; [Kind] to control.

**Bandit** (*pl* -en) *der* bandit.

**Bandlmaß** *das* tape measure.

**Bandlnudeln** *pl* tagliatelle (*U*).

**Bandlsäge** *die* bandsaw.

**Bandlscheibe** *die* ANAT disc.

**Bandlwurm** *der* - **1.** [Wurm] tapeworm - **2.** *fig* [Gebilde]: **dieser Satz ist ein ~** this sentence is never-ending.

**bange** *adj* anxious; **mir ist/wird ~** I am/I'm getting worried.

**Bange** *die:* **keine ~!** don't worry!

**bangen** *vi:* **um jn/etw ~** *geh* to be worried about sb/sthg.

**Bangkok** *nt* Bangkok.

**Bangladesh** *nt* Bangladesh.

**Banjo** ['banjol] (*pl* -s) *das* banjo.

**Bank** (*pl* **Bänke** *ODER* -en) *die* - **1.** (*pl Bänke*) [in Park, Schule] bench; [in Kirche] pew; **etw auf die lange ~ schieben** *fig* to put sthg off; **durch die ~** without exception - **2.** (*pl Banken*) [Geldinstitut] bank.

**Banklangestellte** *der, die* bank employee.

**Banklanweisung** *die* banker's order.

**Banker** ['bɛŋkɐl (pl -) der ḅaɲkɪɐɪ.

**Bankett** (nl ⨾) uas banquet.

**Banklgeheimnis** das banking confidentiality.

**Banklguthaben** das bank balance.

**Bankier** [baŋ'kieː] (pl -s) der banker.

**Banklkauffrau** die bank employee who has completed a three-year training period.

**Banklkaufmann** der bank employee who has completed a three-year training period.

**Banklkonto** das bank account.

**Bankleitlzahl** die bank sort code.

**Banklnote** die banknote.

**Banklraub** der bank robbery; einen ~ verüben to rob a bank.

**Banklräuber, in** der, die bank robber.

**bankrott** adj bankrupt.

**Bankrott** (pl -e) der bankruptcy; ~ gehen to go bankrupt.

**Bankschließlfach** das safe-deposit box.

**Banklüberfall** der bank raid.

**Banklverbindung** die account details (pl).

**bannen** vt - 1. [fesseln] to hold spellbound - 2. [Gefahr] to ward off; [bösen Geist] to exorcize.

**Banner** (pl -) das banner.

**Bannlmeile** die prescribed area surrounding government buildings, within which it is forbidden to hold public demonstrations.

**Baptist, in** (mpl -en; fpl -nen) der, die Baptist.

**bar** adj - 1. [mit Bargeld] cash; ~es Geld cash - 2. [pur - Zufall] pure; [ - Unsinn] sheer ⟨⟩ adv [in Bargeld] (in) cash.
➠ **gegen bar** adv [verkaufen] for cash.
➠ **in bar** adv in cash.

**Bar** (pl -s) die - 1. [Nachtlokal] bar (often also a brothel) - 2. [Theke] bar.

**Bär** (pl -en) der bear; jm einen ~en aufbinden fig to pull sb's leg.

**Baracke** (pl -n) die hut.

**Barbar, in** (mpl -en; fpl -nen) der, die barbarian.

**barbarisch** adj barbaric ⟨⟩ adv barbarically.

**Barcelona** [bartsɛ'loːnal nt Barcelona.

**Barldame** die euph hostess (in brothel).

**Bärenlhunger** der: einen ~ haben to be ravenous.

**barfuß** adv barefoot.

**barg** prät ▷ bergen.

**Barlgeld** das cash.

**bargeldlos** adj cashless ⟨⟩ adv: ~ zahlen to use a cashless payment method.

**Barlhocker** der bar stool.

**Bariton** (pl -e) der baritone.

**Barlkauf** der cash purchase.

**Barke** (pl -n) die skiff.

**Barkeeper** ['baːɐki:pɐl (pl -) der barman.

**barmherzig** adj compassionate ⟨⟩ adv compassionately.

**Barlmixer** der barman.

**barock** adj baroque.

**Barock** der ODER das (ohne pl) baroque period.

**Barolmeter** das barometer.

**Baron** [ba'roːnl (pl -e) der baron.

**Baronesse** [baro'nɛs(ə)l (pl -n) die daughter of u baron.

**Baronin** [ba'roːnɪnl (pl -nen) die baroness.

**Barlpreis** der cash price.

**Barrel** ['bɛrəl] (pl -s ODER -) das barrel.

**Barren** (pl -) der - 1. [Block] bar - 2. [Turngerät] parallel bars (pl).

**Barriere** [ba'rieːrəl (pl -n) die barrier.

**Barrikade** (pl -n) die barricade; sie ging auf die ~n fig she was up in arms.

**barsch** (super! barsch(e)ste) adj curt ⟨⟩ adv curtly.

**Barsch** (pl -e) der [Fisch] perch.

**Barschaft** (pl -en) die cash; seine ~ belief sich auf 100 Euro he only had 100 euros (in) cash on him.

**Barlscheck** der uncrossed cheque.

**barst** prät ▷ bersten.

**Bart** (pl Bärte) der - 1. [Gesichtshaar] beard - 2. [Schlüsselbart] bit - 3. RW: jm um den ~ gehen ODER streichen to butter sb up.

**bärtig** adj bearded.

**bartlos** adj [Junge] beardless; [Mann] clean-shaven.

**Barlzahlung** die payment in cash; Verkauf nur gegen ~ cash sales only.

**Basalt** (pl -e) der basalt.

**Basar, Bazar** (pl -e) der bazaar.

**Base** (pl -n) die - 1. Süddt [Cousine] cousin - 2. Schweiz [Tante] aunt - 3. CHEM base.

**Baseball** ['beːsboːll der baseball.

**Basel** nt Basel, Basle.

**BASIC** ['beːsikl (abk für beginner's all-purpose symbolic instruction code) das EDV BASIC.

**basieren** vi: auf etw (D) ~ to be based on sthg.

**Basilika** (pl Basiliken) die basilica.

**Basilikum** das basil.

**Basis** (pl **Basen**) die - **1.** [Grundlage] basis - **2.** MIL base - **3.** POL grass roots (pl); **an der ~ arbeiten** to work at grass-roots level.

**basisch** adj CHEM basic.

**Basis|demokratie** die grass-roots democracy.

**Baske** (pl -n) der Basque.

**Baskenland** das: **das ~** the Basque Country.

**Basken|mütze** die beret.

**Basket|ball** ['ba:skətbal] der basketball.

**Baskin** (pl -nen) die Basque.

**baskisch** adj Basque.

**Baskisch(e)** das Basque; siehe auch **Englisch(e)**.

**Bass** (pl **Bässe**) der - **1.** [Stimme, Sänger] bass - **2.** [Kontrabass] double bass; [Bassgitarre] bass (guitar).

**Bassin** [ba'sɛ̃:] (pl -s) das pool.

**Bassist, in** (mpl -en; fpl -nen) der, die - **1.** [im Orchester] double bass player; [in Rockgruppe] bass player, bass guitarist - **2.** [Sänger] bass.

**Bass|schlüssel** der MUS bass clef.

**Bast** der raffia.

**basta** interj: **und damit ~!** and that's all there is to it!

**Bastelei** (pl -en) die - **1.** [Basteln] handicrafts (pl) - **2.** [Reparaturversuche]: **er hat genug von der ewigen ~** he's had enough of tinkering around all the time.

**basteln** vt to make; **Weihnachtsgeschenke ~** to make one's own Christmas presents; **ich habe es gebastelt** I made it myself ◇ vi to do handicrafts; **sie bastelt gerne** she likes making things herself; **an etw** (D) **~** to tinker with sthg.

**Bastion** (pl -en) die bastion.

**Bastler, in** (mpl -; fpl -nen) der, die handicrafts enthusiast.

**bat** prät ▷ **bitten**.

**BAT** [be':a:'te:] (abk für **Bundesangestelltentarif**) der statutory salary scale for public employees.

**Bataillon** [batal'jo:n] (pl -e) das battalion.

**Batch|betrieb** ['bɛtʃbətri:b] der EDV batch processing.

**Batch|datei** ['bɛtʃdataɪ] die EDV batch file.

**Batik** (pl -en) die batik.

**Batist** (pl -e) der cambric.

**Batterie** (pl -n) die - **1.** [Stromspeicher] battery - **2.** [große Menge] array.

**batteriebetrieben** adj battery-powered.

**Batzen** (pl -) der fam: **das hat mich einen ganz schönen ~ Geld gekostet** that cost me a packet.

**Bau** (pl -ten oder -e) der - **1.** [das Bauen] construction; **in oder im ~ sein** to be under construction - **2.** (ohne plural) [Baustelle] building site - **3.** (pl Bauten) [Gebäude] building - **4.** [Korperbau] build; **von zartem ~ sein** to be slightly built - **5.** (pl Baue) [von Kaninchen] burrow; [von Fuchs] den; [von Dachs] set.

**Bau|abschnitt** der (construction) phase.

**Bau|amt** das local planning authority.

**Bau|arbeiten** pl construction work (U).

**Bau|arbeiter, in** der, die construction worker.

**Bau|aufsicht** die [Behörde] authority responsible for the supervision of construction work.

**Bauch** (pl **Bäuche**) der stomach; **sich** (D) **den ~ voll schlagen** fam to stuff o.s. oder one's face; **mit etw auf den ~ fallen** fig to make a botch oder mess of sthg.

**Bauch|fell** das peritoneum.

**Bauch|höhle** die abdominal cavity.

**bauchig** adj bulbous.

**Bauch|landung** die [von Flugzeug] belly-landing.

**Bauch|nabel** der navel.

**Bauch|schmerzen** ['baʊxʃmɛrtsn̩] pl stomachache (U).

**Bauchspeichel|drüse** ['baʊxʃpaɪçdry:zə] die pancreas.

**Bauch|tanz** der belly dance.

**Bauch|weh** das stomachache.

**Bau|denkmal** das listed building.

**Bau|element** das component.

**bauen** vt - **1.** [anlegen, errichten] to build - **2.** [herstellen] to make; [Auto, Flugzeug] to build, to make - **3.** fam [verursachen - Unfall] to cause; **Mist ~** to mess up ◇ vi - **1.** [arbeiten, bauen lassen] to build; **an etw** (D) **~** to be building sthg - **2.** [vertrauen]: **auf jn/etw ~** to rely on sb/sthg.

**Bauer** (pl -n oder -) der (pl Bauern) - **1.** [Landwirt] farmer; HIST peasant - **2.** [Schachfigur] pawn - **3.** [Spielkarte] jack ◇ das oder der (pl Bauer) [Vogelkäfig] (bird) cage.

**Bäuerchen** (pl -) das: **ein ~ machen** [rülpsen] to burp.

**Bäuerin** (pl -nen) die [Frau des Bauern] farmer's wife; [Landwirtin] farmer.

**bäuerlich** adj rural ◇ adv: **sich ~ kleiden** to wear rustic clothes.

**Bauern|frühstück** das fried potatoes with scrambled egg and pieces of bacon.

**Bauern|haus** das farmhouse.

**Bauern|hof** der farm.

**Bauern|möbel** pl rustic furniture (U).

**baufällig** adj dilapidated.

**Bau|firma** *die* construction firm, building contractor.

**Bau|genehmigung** *die* planning permission *(U)*.

**Bau|gerüst** *das* scaffolding *(U)*.

**Bau|haus** *das* Bauhaus.

**Bau|herr, in** *der, die:* **der ~ dieses Projekts ist die Stadt** this building project is being carried out for the town council.

**Bau|jahr** *das* [von Haus] year of construction; [von Fahrzeug] year of manufacture.

**Bau|kasten** *der* construction kit; [mit Holzklötzen] box of bricks.

**Bau|klotz** *der* building brick; **Bauklötze staunen** *fam* to be gobsmacked.

**Bau|kosten** *pl* construction costs.

**Bau|land** *das (ohne pl)* development site.

**baulich** *adj* structural <> *adv* structurally.

**Baum** *(pl* **Bäume)** *der* tree; **jetzt kann ich Bäume ausreißen** *fam* I'm ready for anything now.

**Bau|material** *das* building materials *(pl)*.

**baumeln** *vi* to dangle; **die Beine ~ lassen** to dangle one's legs.

**Baum|grenze** *die* tree-line.

**Baum|kuchen** *der tall, cylindrical, hollow sponge cake with several layers, covered in chocolate.*

**Baum|schule** *die* (tree) nursery.

**Baum|stamm** *der* tree trunk.

**Baum|sterben** *das* forest dieback.

**Baum|struktur** *die* EDV tree structure.

**Baum|stumpf** *der* tree stump.

**Baum|wolle** *die* cotton.

**Bau|plan** *der* (architectural) plan.

**Bau|platz** *der* (development) site.

**Bau|polizei** *die (ohne pl)* building inspectorate.

**Bau|ruine** *die* unfinished building.

**Bau|satz** *der* kit.

**Bausch** *(pl* **-e** ODER **Bäusche)** *der* ball; **in ~ und Bogen** *fig* wholesale, completely.

**bauschen** *vt* [Kleidungsstück] to puff out; [Segel] to fill.

➤ **sich bauschen** *ref* [Vorhänge, Segel] to billow; [Ärmel] to puff out.

**bausparen** *vi* to be a member of a building society *Br* ODER savings and loan association *Am*.

**Bau|sparer, in** *der, die* member of a building society *Br* ODER savings and loan association *Am*.

**Bau|sparkasse** *die* building society *Br*, savings and loan association *Am*.

**B**

**Bau|stein** *der* - **1.** [zum Bauen] brick - **2.** [zum Spielen] building block - **3.** [Bestandteil] constituent part, component.

**Bau|stelle** *die* building site; [auf einer Straße] roadworks *(pl)*.

**Bau|stil** *der* architectural style.

**Bau|stoff** *der* building material.

**Bau|stopp** *der:* **über das Kernkraftwerk wurde ein ~ verhängt** all construction work at the nuclear power station was halted.

**Bauten** *pl* ⊳ Bau.

**Bau|träger** *der* construction firm, building contractor.

**Bau|unternehmer, in** *der, die* building contractor.

**Bau|weise** *die* construction method.

**Bau|werk** *das* building.

**Bauxit** [bau'ksi:t] *(pl* **-e)** *der* bauxite.

**Bau|zaun** *der* hoarding.

**Bayer, in** *(mpl* **-n;** *fpl* **-nen)** *der, die* Bavarian.

**bayerisch** = bayrisch.

**Bayerisch** = Bayrisch.

**Bayerische** = Bayrische.

**Bayern** *nt* Bavaria.

**Bayreuther Festspiele** *pl Wagner festival held annually in Bayreuth.*

**bayrisch, bayerisch** *adj* Bavarian <> *adv* like a Bavarian.

**Bayrisch, Bayerisch** *das* Bavarian (dialect).

**Bayrische, Bayerische** *das* Bavarian (dialect).

**Bayrischer Wald** *der* Bavarian Forest.

**Bazillus** *(pl* **-en)** *der*, **Bazille** *(pl* **-n)** *die* MED bacillus; **~n** germs.

**Bd.** *(abk für* **Band)** vol.

**BDI** [be:'de:'i:] *(abk für* **Bundesverband der Deutschen Industrie)** *der Confederation of German Industry.*

**B-Dur** *das* B flat major.

**BE** *(abk für* **Broteinheit)** bread unit.

**beabsichtigen** *vt* to intend.

**beachten** *vt* - **1.** [befolgen - Vorschriften, Verbot] to observe; [ - Ratschläge, Anweisungen] to follow - **2.** [berücksichtigen - Umstände, Gefahr] to take into consideration; **jn nicht ~** to take no notice of sb.

**beachtlich** adj [Leistung, Verbesserung, Erfolg] considerable; [Position] important ⇔ adv considerably.

**Beachtung** die - **1.** [Befolgung - von Regeln] observing - **2.** [Berücksichtigung] consideration; **unter ~ aller Umstände** taking everything into consideration; **einer Sache** (D) **~ schenken** to take sthg into consideration; **jm keine ~ schenken** to take no notice of sb; **~ finden** to be taken into consideration.

**Beamte** (pl -n) der State employee (e.g. teacher, policeman, civil servant).

**BEAMTE**

The civil service is an institution whose status is enshrined in the German constitution. Civil servants have close links with the government based on a relationship of dedication and loyalty, and they are expected to be moderate in their political views. Although they are allowed to join trade unions, they do not have the legal right to go on strike.

**Beamtenschaft** die (ohne pl) State employees (pl).

**Beamtin** (pl -nen) die State employee (e.g. teacher, policewoman, civil servant).

**beängstigend** adj frightening ⇔ adv frighteningly.

**beanspruchen** vt - **1.** [fordern] to claim - **2.** [Material, Bremsen] to wear out - **3.** [strapazieren - Geduld, Person] to tax; **wir möchten Ihre Gastfreundschaft nicht länger ~** we don't want to impose on you any longer - **4.** [Raum, Zeit, Energie] to take up.

**Beanspruchung** (pl -en) die - **1.** [von Material, Nerven] strain - **2.** [durch Beruf] demands (pl).

**beanstanden** vt to complain about.

**Beanstandung** (pl -en) die complaint.

**beantragen** vt - **1.** [verlangen] to apply for - **2.** [vorschlagen] to propose.

**beantworten** vt to answer.

**Beantwortung** (pl -en) die: **die ~ der Frage** the answer to the question.

**bearbeiten** vt - **1.** [mit Werkzeug] to work - **2.** [Text] to edit; [Musikstück] to arrange; **ein Buch für den Film ~** to adapt a book for the screen - **3.** [betreuen] to deal with - **4.** fam [misshandeln - Schlagzeug] to bang away at; **jn mit den Fäusten ~** to do sb over - **5.** fam [beeinflussen] to work on.

**Bearbeitung** (pl -en) die - **1.** [von Werkstück, Metall] working - **2.** [von Text] editing; [von Musikstück] arranging; [für Film, Fernsehen] adaptation - **3.** [von Antrag] processing.

**beatmen** vt: **jn künstlich ~** to give sb artificial respiration.

**Beatmung** (pl -en) die: **künstliche ~** artificial respiration.

**beaufsichtigen** vt to supervise.

**beauftragen** vt: **jn ~, etw zu tun** [bitten] to tell sb to do sthg; [Auftrag erteilen] to commission sb to do sthg; **beauftragt sein, etw zu tun** to be charged with doing sthg; **jn mit etw ~** to entrust sthg to sb.

**Beauftragte** (pl -n) der, die representative.

**bebauen** vt - **1.** [mit Gebäuden] to build on, to develop; **ein Gelände mit Häusern ~** to build houses on a site - **2.** [mit Pflanzen] to cultivate.

**Bebauung** (pl -en) die - **1.** [mit Gebäuden] development - **2.** [mit Pflanzung] cultivation.

**beben** vi - **1.** [durch Explosion] to shake - **2.** [Hände, Person, Lippen, Stimme] to tremble.

**Beben** (pl -) das - **1.** [von Händen, Person, Lippen, Stimme] trembling - **2.** [Erdbeben] earthquake.

**Becher** (pl -) der - **1.** [Kaffeebecher - ohne Henkel, aus Pappe, Styropor] cup; [ - ohne Henkel, aus hartem Kunststoff] beaker; [ - mit Henkel, aus Porzellan] mug - **2.** [Pokal] goblet - **3.** [für Joghurt] pot; [für Eis] tub.

**Becken** (pl -) das - **1.** [Waschbecken] basin; [Spülbecken] sink; [Schwimmbecken] pool - **2.** [Körperteil] pelvis - **3.** [Instrument] cymbal.

**Becquerel** [bɛkə'rɛl] (pl -) das becquerel.

**bedacht** pp ⊳ **bedenken** ⇔ adj - **1.** [vorsichtig] careful - **2.** [bemüht]: **auf etw** (A) **~ sein** to be concerned about sthg ⇔ adv [vorsichtig] carefully.

**Bedacht** der: **mit ~** with care; **ohne ~** without thinking.

**bedächtig** adj - **1.** [langsam] deliberate - **2.** [nachdenklich - Person, Miene] thoughtful; [ - Worte] well-considered ⇔ adv - **1.** [langsam] deliberately - **2.** [überlegt - sprechen] with well-considered words.

**bedanken ⇨ sich bedanken** ref to say thank you; **ich möchte mich herzlich ~** thank you very much; **sich bei jm für etw ~** to thank sb for sthg.

**Bedarf** der need; **ein ~ an etw** (D) a need for sthg; **~ an etw** (D) **haben** to be in need of sthg; **mein ~ ist gedeckt!** fam I've had more than enough!
**⇨ bei Bedarf** adv should the need arise.

**bedauerlich** adj regrettable.

**bedauerlicherweise** adv geh regrettably.

**bedauern** vt - **1.** [Irrtum, Unüberlegtheit] to regret - **2.** [Person] to feel sorry for; **bedaure!** I'm sorry!

**Bedauern** das - **1.** [Mitleid] sympathy - **2.** [Reue] regret; **zu meinem ~** geh to my regret.

**bedauernswert** adj - **1.** [Irrtum] regrettable - **2.** [Person] pitiable.

**bedecken** *vt* to cover.
➤ **sich bedecken** *ref* [Himmel] to cloud over.

**bedeckt** *pp* ▷ **bedecken** ◇ *adj* [Himmel] overcast; **sich ~ halten** *fig* to keep a low profile.

**bedenken** (*prät* **bedachte**; *perf* **hat bedacht**) *vt* - **1.** [überlegen] to consider - **2.** *geh* [beschenken - im Testament] to remember; **jn mit Geschenken ~** to give presents to sb; **jn mit Beifall ~** to applaud sb.

**Bedenken** (*pl* -) *das* - **1.** [Nachdenken] consideration - **2.** [Zweifel] doubt; **~ gegen etw haben** to have (one's) doubts about sthg.

**bedenkenlos** *adv* - **1.** [ohne Zweifel] unhesitatingly; **~ Geld verschleudern** to throw money away recklessly - **2.** [skrupellos] unscrupulously.

**bedenklich** *adj* - **1.** [prekär] serious - **2.** [besorgt] anxious - **3.** [fragwürdig] dubious.

**Bedenkzeit** *die:* **jm ~ geben** to give sb some time to think it over.

**bedeuten** *vt* - **1.** [gen] to mean; **viel/nichts ~** to mean a lot/nothing; **jm viel/wenig/nichts ~** to mean a lot/not to mean much/to mean nothing to sb; **das hat nichts zu ~** that doesn't matter - **2.** *geh* [zu verstehen geben]: **jm etw ~** to indicate sthg to sb.

**bedeutend** *adj* - **1.** [wichtig] important - **2.** [groß] considerable ◇ *adv* [sehr] considerably.

**bedeutsam** *adj* - **1.** [wichtig] momentous - **2.** [viel sagend] meaningful ◇ *adv* [viel sagend] meaningfully.

**Bedeutung** (*pl* -en) *die* - **1.** [Sinn] meaning - **2.** [Wichtigkeit] importance; **einer Sache** *(D)* **große/keine ~ beimessen** to attach great/no importance to sthg; **von ausschlaggebender ~ sein** to be of decisive importance.

**bedeutungslos** *adj* insignificant.

**Bedeutungs|wandel** *der* change in meaning.

**bedienen** *vt* - **1.** [Person] to serve; **mit diesem Produkt sind Sie gut bedient** this product is a good deal - **2.** [Maschine] to operate ◇ *vi* to serve.
➤ **sich bedienen** *ref* to help o.s.; **~ Sie sich!** help yourself!

**Bedienung** (*pl* -en) *die* - **1.** [Versorgung] service - **2.** [Steuerung, Anwendung] operation - **3.** [Kellner] waiter; [Kellnerin] waitress.

**Bedienungs|anleitung** *die* operating instructions *(pl)*.

**Bedienungs|fehler** *der* operating error.

**bedingen** *vt* - **1.** [verursachen] to bring about; **durch etw bedingt sein** to be caused by sthg - **2.** [verlangen] to require.

**bedingt** *adj* [Zustimmung] qualified ◇ *adv*

partly; **die Theorie ist nur ~ anwendbar** the theory is only partly applicable.

**Bedingung** (*pl* -en) *die* [Voraussetzung] condition; **eine ~ stellen** to stipulate a condition; **unter einer ~** on one condition.
➤ **Bedingungen** *pl* [Umstände] conditions.

**bedingungslos** *adj* unconditional ◇ *adv* unconditionally.

**bedrängen** *vt* [unter Druck setzen] to pressurize; [mit Truppen] to advance on; **jn mit Fragen ~** to badger sb with questions.

**Bedrängnis** (*pl* -se) *die geh:* **jn in ~ bringen** to put sb in a difficult situation.

**bedrohen** *vt* to threaten.

**bedrohlich** *adj* [Situation, Aussehen] threatening; [Nähe, Intensität] dangerous ◇ *adv* [ansehen] threateningly; [nah, schnell] dangerously.

**Bedrohung** (*pl* -en) *die* threat; **eine ~ der Freiheit** a threat to freedom.

**bedrucken** *vt* to print.

**bedrücken** *vt* to depress.

**bedrückend** *adj* [Stimmung] oppressive; [Gedanke, Neuigkeit] depressing.

**bedrückt** *adj* - **1.** [Person] depressed - **2.** [Schweigen, Stimmung] oppressive.

**bedürfen** (*präs* **bedarf**; *prät* **bedurfte**; *perf* **hat bedurft**) *vi geh:* **js/einer Sache ~** to need sb/sthg.

**Bedürfnis** (*pl* -se) *das* need.

**bedürfnislos** *adj* [Leben] simple; **~ sein** [Mensch] to have few needs.

**bedürftig** *adj* needy.

**Beef|steak** ['biːfsteːk] *das* steak.

**beehren** [bə'eːrən] *vt:* **jn mit etw ~** *geh & iron* to honour sb with sthg.

**beeiden** [bə'aɪdn̩] *vt* to give under oath.

**beeilen** [bə'aɪlən] ➤ **sich beeilen** *ref* to hurry; **beeile dich!** hurry up!

**Beeilung** [bə'aɪlʊŋ] *die:* **los** ODER **ein bisschen ~!** *fam* get a move on!

**beeindrucken** [bə'aɪndrʊkn̩] *vt* to impress ◇ *vi* to make an impression.

**beeindruckend** [bə'aɪndrʊkənt] *adj* impressive ◇ *adv* impressively.

**beeinflussbar** [bə'aɪnflʊsbaː] *adj* easily influenced.

**beeinflussen** [bə'aɪnflʊsn̩] *vt* to influence.

**beeinträchtigen** [bə'aɪntrɛçtɪɡn̩] *vt* [Bewegungsfähigkeit, Sicht] to impair; [Produktion, Stimmung] to affect adversely; [Wert, Qualität] to reduce; [Gesundheit] to damage; [Konzentration] to hamper.

**Beeinträchtigung** [bə'aɪntrɛçtɪɡʊŋ] (*pl* -en) *die* [von Bewegungsfähigkeit, Sicht] impairment; [von Produktion, Stimmung] adverse effect; [von

Wert, Qualität] reduction; [von Gesundheit] damaging; [von Konzentration] hampering.

**beenden** [bə'ɛndn̩] *vt* to end.

**beengt** [bə'ɛŋt] *adv*: ~ **wohnen** to live in cramped conditions.

**beerben** [bə'ɛrbn̩] *vt*: **jn** ~ to inherit sb's estate.

**beerdigen** [bə'e:ɐdɪgn̩] *vt* to bury.

**Beerdigung** [bə'e:ɐdigʊŋ] (*pl* **-en**) *die* funeral.

**Beerdigungslinstitut** *das* funeral directors (*pl*).

**Beere** (*pl* **-n**) *die* berry.

**Beet** (*pl* **-e**) *das* [mit Blumen] flowerbed; [mit Gemüse] vegetable patch.

**Beete** ◆ **rote Beete** beetroot.

**Befähigung** (*pl* **-en**) *die* - **1.** [Qualifikation]: **ihm fehlt die ~ zu diesem Amt** he's not qualified to do this job - **2.** [Können] ability; **die ~ für etw** ODER **zu etw** the ability for sth.

**befahl** *prät* ⊳ **befehlen**.

**befahrbar** *adj* [Straße, Weg] passable; [Fluss] navigable.

**befahren** (*präs* **befährt**; *prät* **befuhr**; *perf* **hat befahren**) *vt* to use <> *adj*: **eine stark ~e Straße** a busy street.

**Befall** *der* attack; **Schädlingsbefall** infestation.

**befallen** (*präs* **befällt**; *prät* **befiel**; *perf* **hat befallen**) *vt*: **von etw ~ sein** [Schädlingen] to be infested with sth; [Mehltau] to be struck down with sth; [Angst] to be overcome with sth.

**befangen** *adj* - **1.** [schüchtern] shy - **2.** RECHT partial - **3.** *geh* [gefangen]: **in dem Glauben ~ sein, dass ...** to labour under the misconception that ... <> *adv* shyly.

**Befangenheit** *die* - **1.** [Schüchternheit] shyness - **2.** RECHT partiality.

**befassen** (*präs* **befasst**; *prät* **befasste**; *perf* **hat befasst**) *vt*: **jn mit etw ~** *geh* to assign sth to sb.

◆ **sich befassen** *ref*: **sich mit einer Frage ~** to look into a question; **sich intensiv mit einem Thema ~** to study ODER look at a matter in great detail; **sie befasst sich viel mit diesem Thema** she deals with this subject a lot.

**Befehl** (*pl* **-e**) *der* - **1.** [Aufforderung] order - **2.** EDV command.

◆ **zu Befehl** *adv* MIL yes, sir!

**befehlen** (*präs* **befiehlt**; *prät* **befahl**; *perf* **hat befohlen**) *vt* to order; **jm** ~, **etw zu tun** to order sb to do sth; **du hast mir gar nichts zu ~** I don't take orders from you <> *vi*: **über jn/etw ~** to command sb/sth.

**Befehlslform** *die* GRAM imperative.

**Befehlslhaber** (*pl* **-**) *der* MIL commander.

**Befehlslton** *der* peremptory tone.

**Befehlslverweigerung** *die* MIL insubordination.

**befeinden** *vt geh* to be hostile towards.

◆ **sich befeinden** *ref* to be hostile towards each other.

**befestigen** *vt* - **1.** [anbringen]: **etw an etw** (D) ~ to attach sth to sth; **etw mit Schrauben an der Wand ~** to screw sth to the wall - **2.** [verstärken - Stadt, Grenze] to fortify; [ - Ufer, Damm] to reinforce; [ - Straße] to make up.

**Befestigung** (*pl* **-en**) *die* - **1.** [das Anbringen] attaching - **2.** [die Verstärkung - von Stadt] fortification; [ - von Ufer, Damm] reinforcement; [ - von Straße] making up.

**befeuchten** *vt* to moisten.

**befiehlt** *präs* ⊳ **befehlen**.

**befinden** (*prät* **befand**; *perf* **hat befunden**) *vt*: **etw für gut/richtig ~** *geh* to deem sth good/right.

◆ **sich befinden** *ref* to be; **sein Büro befindet sich im ersten Stock** his office is on the first floor.

**Befinden** *das* (state of) health; **sich nach js ~ erkundigen** to inquire after sb's health.

**befindlich** *adj geh* situated.

**befingern** *vt fam abw* to finger.

**beflecken** *vt* to stain.

**beflügeln** *vt* [Person] to inspire; [Fantasie] to fire.

**befohlen** *pp* ⊳ **befehlen**.

**befolgen** *vt* [Rat] to follow; [Befehl, Vorschrift] to obey.

**Befolgung** *die* [von Rat] following; [von Befehl, Vorschrift] obeying.

**befördern** *vt* - **1.** [transportieren] to transport - **2.** [im Beruf] to promote.

**Belförderung** *die* - **1.** [Transport] transportation - **2.** [im Beruf] promotion.

**Beförderungslmittel** *das* means of transport.

**befrachten** *vt* - **1.** [LKW, Schiff] to load (up) - **2.** [Text, Diskussion] to overburden.

**befragen** *vt* - **1.** [Person, Zeugen] to question - **2.** [Karten, Wahrsagerin] to consult.

**Befragung** (*pl* **-en**) *die* questioning.

**befreien** *vt* [Gefangenen] to free; [Land, Volk] to liberate; [Tier] to set free; **jn von etw ~** [von Diktatur, Schmerzen] to free sb from sth; [vom Unterricht] to excuse sb from sth.

**Befreiung** *die* [von Gefangenen, Tier] freeing; [von Land, Volk] liberation; [der Frau] emancipation; **eine ~ vom Unterricht kommt nicht in Frage** there's no question of you being excused from classes.

**Befreiungslbewegung** *die* liberation movement.

**Befremden** *das* dismay; **zu js ~** to sb's dismay.

**befremdend** *adj* dismaying ◇ *adv* dismayingly.

**befreunden** ➡ **sich befreunden** *ref:* **sich mit jm ~** to make friends with sb; **sich mit etw ~** to warm to sthg.

**befreundet** *adj* [Länder] friendly; **ein mit uns ~er Künstler** an artist (who is a) friend of ours; **mit jm ~ sein** to be friends with sb.

**befriedigen** *vt* to satisfy.
➡ **sich befriedigen** *ref:* **sich selbst ~** to masturbate.

**befriedigend** *adj* - **1.** [zufrieden stellend] satisfactory - **2.** SCHULE ≈ C, *mark equivalent to 3 on scale of 1 to 6* ◇ *adv* satisfactorily.

**Befriedigung** *die* - **1.** [Zufriedenheit] satisfaction - **2.** [Zufriedenstellung] satisfying.

**befristen** *vt* to put a time limit on; **ihre Tätigkeit ist auf ein Jahr befristet** her contract only runs for one year.

**befristet** *adj* [Vertrag] fixed-term, temporary.

**befruchten** *vt* to fertilize; **eine Frau künstlich ~** to inseminate a woman artificially.

**Befruchtung** *(pl -en) die* fertilization; **künstliche ~** artificial insemination.

**Befugnis** *(pl -se) die* authority *(U)*.

**befugt** *adj:* **zur Unterschrift ~ sein** to be authorized to sign.

**Belfund** *der* [ärztlich] results *(pl);* [von Fachmann] findings *(pl);* **'ohne ~ '** MED 'negative'.

**befürchten** *vt* to fear; **es ist** ODER **steht zu ~, dass ...** there is a danger that ...

**Befürchtung** *(pl -en) die* fear.

**befürworten** *vt* to support.

**Befürworter, in** *(mpl -; fpl -nen) der, die* supporter.

**begabt** *adj* talented; **für etw ~ sein** to have a talent ODER gift for sthg.

**Begabung** *(pl -en) die* talent.

**begann** *prät* ⊏⟩ **beginnen**.

**begeben** *(präs* **begibt**; *prät* **begab**; *perf* **hat begeben)** ➡ **sich begeben** *ref* - **1.** geh [gehen] to go; **sich in Gefahr ~** to put o.s. in danger - **2.** [passieren] to happen; **es begab sich aber zu der Zeit ...** REL it came to pass ...

**Begebenheit** *(pl -en) die* occurrence; **eine wahre ~** something that really happened.

**begegnen** *vi* [entgegenkommen, treffen]: **jm ~** to meet sb; **etw** *(D)* **~** [Gefahr] to face sthg; **einer Person mit Freundlichkeit ~** to treat sb in a friendly manner.
➡ **sich begegnen** *ref* [treffen] to meet.

**Begegnung** *(pl -en) die* meeting.

**begehbar** *adj* passable.

**begehen** *(prät* **beging**; *perf* **hat begangen)** *vt* - **1.** [verüben - Mord, Verbrechen] to commit; [ - Fehler] to make; **eine Dummheit ~** to do something stupid - **2.** geh [feiern] to celebrate - **3.** [benützen] to use.

**begehren** *vt* to desire; **sehr begehrt sein** to be much sought after.

**begehrenswert** *adj* desirable.

**begeistern** *vt:* **sie begeisterte das Publikum** she delighted the audience; **man kann ihn für nichts ~** you can't make him enthusiastic about anything.
➡ **sich begeistern** *ref:* **sich für etw ~** [Idee] to be enthusiastic about sthg; [Film, Hobby] really to like sthg.

**begeistert** *adj* [Reiter, Schwimmer] enthusiastic, keen; [Publikum] delighted; **von dieser Idee bin ich gar nicht ~** I'm not very enthusiastic about ODER keen on that idea; **sie war von seiner Frisur ~** she was delighted with her haircut ◇ *adv* enthusiastically.

**Begeisterung** *die* [über Idee, Beschluss, für Hobby] enthusiasm; [über Leistung] delight.

**Begierde** *(pl -n) die* desire; **~ nach jm/etw** desire for sb/sthg.

**begierig** *adj* [Blicke] longing; [Lippen, Hände] eager; **nach etw** ODER **auf etw** *(A)* **~ sein** to be eager for sthg; **darauf ~ sein, etw zu tun** to be eager to do sthg ◇ *adv* eagerly.

**begießen** *(prät* **begoss**; *perf* **hat begossen)** *vt* - **1.** [mit Wasser] to water - **2.** [feiern] to celebrate with a drink.

**Beginn** *der* beginning, start.
➡ **zu Beginn** *adv* at the beginning ODER start.

**beginnen** *(prät* **begann**; *perf* **hat begonnen)** *vt* to begin, to start ◇ *vi* to begin, to start; **mit etw ~** to begin sthg, to start sthg.

**beglaubigen** *vt* to certify.

**Beglaubigung** *(pl -en) die* - **1.** [Bescheinigung] certificate - **2.** [Handlung] certification.

**begleichen** *(prät* **beglich**; *perf* **hat beglichen)** *vt* to settle.

**begleiten** *vt* to accompany.

**Begleiter, in** *(mpl -; fpl -nen) der, die* companion; [beim Musizieren] accompanist.

**Begleitlerscheinung** *die* side effect.

**Begleitlmusik** *die* background music.

**Begleitlperson** *die* escort.

**Begleitlschreiben** *das* covering letter.

**Begleitlumstand** *der* attendant circumstance.

**Begleitung** *(pl -en) die* - **1.** [Begleiten]: **sie kam in ~** she came with someone; **in ~ einer Freundin** accompanied by a friend - **2.** MUS accompaniment - **3.** [Begleitperson] escort; [Freund] companion.

**beglücken** *vt* to make happy; **jn mit etw ~** *iron* to favour sb with sthg.

**beglückwünschen** *vt:* **jn zu etw ~** to congratulate sb on sthg.

**begnadigen** *vt* to pardon.

**Begnadigung** (*pl* -en) *die* pardon.

**begnügen** ➾ **sich begnügen** *ref:* **sich mit etw ~** to make do with sthg.

**begonnen** *pp* ▷ **beginnen.**

**begraben** (*präs* **begräbt**; *prät* **begrub**; *perf* **hat begraben**) *vt* - **1.** [beerdigen] to bury; **jn/etw unter sich** (D) **~** to bury sb/sthg - **2.** [beenden, vergessen - Streit] to bury; [ - Hoffnung, Vorhaben] to abandon.

**Begräbnis** (*pl* -se) *das* funeral.

**begradigen** *vt* to straighten.

**begreifen** (*prät* **begriff**; *perf* **hat begriffen**) *vt* & *vi* to understand.

**begreiflich** *adj* understandable; **jm etw ~ machen** to make sb understand sthg.

**begrenzen** *vt* - **1.** [Zeit, Geschwindigkeit] to limit, to restrict - **2.** [Fläche, Raum]: **der Park wird vom Fluss begrenzt** the river forms the park's boundary.

**begrenzt** *adj* limited; [Zustimmung] qualified ◇ *adv* to a limited extent.

**Begrenzung** (*pl* -en) *die* - **1.** [von Zeit, Geschwindigkeit] restriction, limit - **2.** [von Fläche, Raum] boundary.

**Be|griff** *der* - **1.** [Wort] term - **2.** [Vorstellung] idea, concept; **im ~ sein** ODER **stehen, etw zu tun** to be about to do sthg; **jm ein ~ sein** to mean something to sb; **der Name war ihr kein ~** she didn't recognize the name; **sich** (D) **einen ~ von etw machen** to get an idea of sthg; **schwer** ODER **langsam von ~ sein** *fam* to be slow on the uptake.

**begriffen** *adj:* **in etw** (D) **~ sein** to be in the process of sthg.

**begrifflich** *adj* conceptual ◇ *adv* conceptually.

**begriffsstutzig** *adj abw* slow.

**begründen** *vt* - **1.** [erklären] to justify; **sie begründete ihr Verhalten mit persönlichen Problemen** she gave personal problems as the reason for her behaviour - **2.** [gründen - Firma, Stadt, Religion] to found; [ - Theorie] to originate.

**Begründer, in** (*mpl* -; *fpl* -nen) *der, die* [von Religion, Stadt, Firma] founder; [von Theorie] originator.

**Be|gründung** *die* - **1.** [Angabe von Gründen] reason - **2.** [Gründung - von Firma, Stadt, Religion] founding; [ - von Stil] establishment.

**begrünen** *vt* to cover with greenery.

**begrüßen** *vt* - **1.** [grüßen] to greet - **2.** [gut finden] to welcome.

**begrüßenswert** *adj* welcome.

**Begrüßung** (*pl* -en) *die* greeting; [von Gästen] welcome.

**begucken** *vt fam:* **sich** (D) **jn/etw ~** to have a look at sb/sthg.
➾ **sich begucken** *ref* to look at o.s.

**begünstigen** *vt* to favour.

**begutachten** *vt* - **1.** [Subj: Fachmann] to examine and report on - **2.** [betrachten] to have a look at.

**begütert** *adj* well-to-do.

**begütigend** *adj* soothing ◇ *adv* soothingly.

**behaart** *adj* hairy.

**behäbig** *adj* [Mensch] portly; [Ausdrucksweise, Schritte] ponderous ◇ *adv* ponderously.

**behaftet** *adj:* **mit etw ~ sein** [Sache] to be marred by sthg; [Person] to be afflicted with sthg.

**behagen** *vi:* **es behagt ihr nicht** she doesn't like it.

**Behagen** *das* contentment.

**behaglich** *adj* [Sessel] comfortable; [Wärme] cosy ◇ *adv* comfortably.

**behalten** (*präs* **behält**; *prät* **behielt**; *perf* **hat behalten**) *vt* - **1.** [nicht abgeben] to keep; **etw für sich ~** [aufbewahren] to keep sthg for o.s.; [verschweigen] to keep sthg to o.s. - **2.** [sich merken] to remember.

**Behälter** (*pl* -) *der* container.

**behände** *geh adj* nimble ◇ *adv* nimbly.

**behandeln** *vt* - **1.** [gen] to treat; **jn gut/schlecht ~** to treat sb well/badly - **2.** [Problem, Thema] to deal with.

**Behändigkeit** *die geh* nimbleness.

**Be|handlung** *die* treatment; **ambulante/ stationäre ~** treatment as an out-patient/ in-patient.

**behängen** *vt* to hang.
➾ **sich behängen** *ref abw:* **sich mit etw ~** to deck o.s. out with sthg.

**beharren** *vi* to insist; **auf etw** (D) **~** to insist on sthg.

**beharrlich** *adj* persistent ◇ *adv* persistently.

**behaupten** *vt* - **1.** [versichern] to claim - **2.** [verteidigen - Vorteil, Position] to maintain.
➾ **sich behaupten** *ref* - **1.** [sich durchsetzen] to assert o.s. - **2.** [gewinnen]: **sich gegen jn ~** to overcome sb.

**Behauptung** (*pl* -en) *die* - **1.** [Aussage] claim - **2.** [Verteidigung] maintenance.

**Behausung** (*pl* -en) *die* accommodation.

**beheben** (*prät* **behob**; *perf* **hat behoben**) *vt* to rectify.

**beheimatet** *adj:* **~ in** (+ D) [Pflanze, Tierart] native to; [Person] from.

**beheizen** *vt* to heat.

**behelfen** (*präs* behilft; *prät* behalf; *perf* hat beholfen) *vi*: sich (D) mit/ohne etw ~ to make do with/without sthg.

**behelfsmäßig** *adj* [Unterkunft, Konstruktion] makeshift; [Ersatz] temporary <> *adv* temporarily.

**behelligen** *vt*: jn mit etw ~ to bother sb with sthg.

**behende** = behände.

**Behendigkeit** *die* = Behändigkeit.

**beherbergen** *vt* to put up.

**beherrschen** *vt* - **1.** [Land, Stadt] to rule - **2.** [Leidenschaft, Markt] to control - **3.** [dominieren] to dominate - **4.** [meistern - Pferd, Wagen] to have control of; [ - Arbeit, Sport, Instrument] to have mastered; [ - Sprache] to have a command of.

➡ **sich beherrschen** *ref* to control o.s.

**beherrscht** *adj* self-controlled <> *adv* with self-control.

**Beherrschung** *die* - **1.** [von Leidenschaft, Gedanken] control; **die ~ verlieren** to lose control - **2.** [von Land, Volk] rule - **3.** [von Pferd, Wagen] control; [von Instrument] mastery; [von Sprache] command.

**beherzigen** *vt* to take to heart.

**beherzt** *adj* courageous <> *adv* courageously.

**behilflich** *adj*: jm bei etw ~ sein to help sb with sthg.

**behindern** *vt* - **1.** [Verkehr, Sicht] to obstruct - **2.** [Person]: jn bei etw ~ to hinder sb in sthg.

**behindert** *adj* handicapped; **geistig/körperlich ~** mentally/physically handicapped.

**Behinderte** (*pl* -n) *der, die* handicapped person; **die ~n** the handicapped.

**behindertengerecht** *adj* suitable for disabled people; [Aufzug, Toilette] disabled (*vor Subst*) <> *adv* with the needs of the disabled in mind.

**Behinderung** (*pl* -en) *die* - **1.** [Behindern] obstruction - **2.** [Handicap] handicap.

**Behörde** (*pl* -n) *die* authority.

➡ **Behörden** *pl* authorities.

**behüten** *vt* to look after; **jn vor etw** (D) ~ to protect sb from sthg.

**behutsam** *adj* careful <> *adv* carefully.

**bei** *präp* (+ D) - **1.** [räumlich - nahe] near; [ - innen] at; **das Hotel ist gleich ~m Bahnhof** the hotel is right next to the station; **Bernau ~ Berlin** Bernau near Berlin; **~m Arzt** at the doctor's; **sie arbeitet ~ einem Verlag** she works for a publishing company; **~ meiner Tante** at my aunt's; **~ mir** at my house; **die Schuld liegt allein ~ mir** *fig* I alone am to blame; **ein Kind ~ der Hand nehmen** to take a child's hand, to take a child by the hand; **die Gelegenheit ~m Schopf packen** *fig* to seize the opportunity with both hands - **2.** [zusammen mit einer Person] with; **ich bleibe ~ dir** I'm staying with you - **3.** [zeitlich] at; **~ Beginn** at the beginning; **~ der Arbeit** at work; **~ seiner Beerdigung** at his funeral; **Vorsicht ~m Ein- und Aussteigen** be careful when getting on and off; **~m Sport brach er sich den Arm** he broke his arm (while) playing sport - **4.** [als Teil einer Menge] among; **einige dieser Stilelemente finden sich auch ~ Picasso** some of these stylistic touches are also found in Picasso's work - **5.** [zur Angabe von Umständen]: **~ Regen vorsichtig fahren** drive carefully in the rain; **~ Tag/Nacht** by day/night - **6.** [zur Angabe der Ursache]: **~ Regen fällt der Ausflug aus** if it rains the trip will be cancelled; **kannst du das Buch ~ Gelegenheit vorbeibringen?** could you bring the book round next time you get the chance?; **~ deinem Talent solltest du Maler werden** with your talent you should be an artist - **7.** [trotz] for, in spite of; **ich konnte es ~m besten Willen nicht finden** no matter how hard I tried, I couldn't find it.

➡ **bei sich** *adv*: **hast du Geld ~ dir?** have you got any money on you?; **~ sich** (D) **sein** *fig* to be (feeling) o.s.

**beibehalten** *vt* (*unreg*) [Methode] to keep to; [Gegenstände] to keep.

**Beiblatt** *das* supplementary sheet.

**beibringen** *vt* (*unreg*) - **1.** [lehren]: jm etw ~ to teach sb sthg - **2.** [mitteilen]: jm etw ~ to break sthg to sb; jm etw schonend ~ to break sthg gently to sb - **3.** [zufügen]: jm etw ~ to inflict sthg on sb - **4.** *amt* [bringen] to produce.

**Beichte** (*pl* -n) *die* confession.

**beichten** *vt* to confess; jm etw ~ to confess sthg to sb <> *vi* to confess.

**Beichtstuhl** *der* confessional.

**beide** *pron* [zwei] both; **die ~n** both of them; **diese ~n** these two; **ihr ~n** you two <> *adj* - **1.** [zwei]: **die ~n Pferde** both (of) the horses, the two horses; **diese ~n Exemplare** both (of) these copies, these two copies - **2.** [alle zwei] both.

➡ **beides** *pron* both.

**beiderlei** *det* both.

**beiderseitig** *adj* mutual.

**beiderseits** *präp* (+ G) on both sides of.

**beidhändig** *adv* with both hands.

**beidseitig** *adj* mutual <> *adv* on both sides.

**beieinander** *adv* together.

**beieinander haben** *vt* (*unreg*) to have got together; **der hat sie nicht alle beieinander** *fam abw* he's not all there.

**beieinander sein** (*perf* ist beieinander gewesen) *vi* (*unreg*) *fam:* **gut/schlecht** ~ to be in good/poor shape; **ich bin nicht ganz** ~ I'm not quite myself.

**beieinander sitzen** *vi* (*unreg*) to sit together.

**Beifahrer, in** (*mpl* -; *fpl* -nen) *der, die* front-seat passenger.

**Beifahrer|airbag** *der* AUTO passenger airbag.

**Beifahrer|sitz** *der* passenger seat.

**Beifall** *der* applause; ~ **spenden** ODER **klatschen** to applaud; **tosender** ODER **rauschender** ~ thunderous applause.

**beifällig** *adj* approving ⟨⟩ *adv* approvingly.

**Beifalls|sturm** *der* storm of applause.

**bei|fügen** *vt:* **einer Sache** (*D*) **etw** ~ to enclose sthg with sthg.

**beige** [bɛːʃ] *adj* beige.

**Beige** *das* (*ohne pl*) beige.

**bei|geben** (*unreg*) *vt* to add ⟨⟩ *vi:* **klein** ~ *fig* to back down.

**Beigeordnete** (*pl* -n) *der, die* town councillor.

**Beigeschmack** *der* - **1.** [von Esswaren] **das Bier hat einen bitteren** ~ the beer tastes slightly bitter - **2.** [von Begriff] connotation; **die ganze Affäre hatte einen bitteren** ~ the whole affair left a bitter taste in the mouth.

**Bei|hilfe** *die* - **1.** [finanziell] financial aid - **2.** [kriminell] aiding and abetting; **jm** ~ **leisten** to aid and abet sb.

**bei|kommen** (*perf* ist beigekommen) *vi* (*unreg*): **einer Sache** (*D*) ~ to overcome sthg; **ihm ist nicht beizukommen, er hat immer wieder neue Ausreden** he always has some excuse or other, you can never make him admit he's done something wrong.

**beil.** (*abk für* beiliegend) encl.

**Beil** (*pl* -e) *das* axe.

**Bei|lage** *die* - **1.** [Speise] side dish; **mit Reis als** ~ served with rice - **2.** [zu Zeitung] supplement - **3.** *amt* [Beilegen] enclosure.

**beiläufig** *adj* casual ⟨⟩ *adv* casually, in passing.

**bei|legen** *vt* - **1.** [beifügen]: **einer Sache** (*D*) **etw** ~ to enclose sthg with sthg - **2.** [schlichten] to resolve.

**Beilegung** (*pl* -en) *die* resolution.

**beileibe** *adv:* ~ **nicht!** *geh* certainly not!

**Beileid** *das* (*ohne pl*) condolences (*pl*); **herzliches** ODER **aufrichtiges** ~! my sincere condolences; **jm sein** ~ **aussprechen** to offer sb one's condolences.

**bei|liegen** *vi* (*unreg*): **etw** (*D*) ~ [einem Brief] to be enclosed with sthg; [einer Zeitung] to be inserted in sthg

**beiliegend** *adj* amt enclosed; ~ **übersenden wir Ihnen ...** please find enclosed ...

**beim** *präp* (bei + dem): **ich bin** ~ **Essen** I'm eating at the moment; ~ **letzten Test** in the last test; **sie war** ~ **Arzt** she was at the doctor's; **sie traf ihn** ~ **Einkaufen** she met him while she was shopping; ~ **Rasenmähen helfen** to help with mowing the lawn; *siehe auch* **bei.**

**bei|messen** *vt* (*unreg*): **einer Sache** (*D*) **große/keine Bedeutung** ~ to attach great/no importance to sthg.

**Bein** (*pl* -e) *das* - **1.** leg; **in die ~e gehen** [körperliche Tätigkeit] to tire one's legs out; [Musik] to get one's legs moving; **jm ein** ~ **stellen** to trip sb up - **2.** RW: **jm** ~**e machen** to make sb get a move on; **etw auf die ~e stellen** to get sthg up and running; **er kriegt im Chemieunterricht kein** ~ **auf die Erde** he just can't seem to get the hang of chemistry; **mit beiden ~en im Leben stehen** to have both feet on the ground; **sich** (*D*) **die ~e vertreten** to stretch one's legs; **sich** (*D*) **kein** ~ **ausreißen** not to overexert o.s.; **wieder auf die ~e kommen** to get back on one's feet.

**beinah, beinahe** *adv* almost, nearly.

**Bei|name** *der* epithet.

**Bein|bruch** *der* fracture of the leg; **das ist doch kein** ~! *fig* it's not the end of the world!

**beinhalten** [bə'ınhaltņ] *vt* to contain.

**Beipack|zettel** *der* instruction leaflet.

**bei|pflichten** *vi:* **jm/einer Sache** ~ to agree with sb/sthg.

**Bei|rat** *der* advisory committee.

**beirren** [bə'ırən] *vt* to disconcert; **sich durch etw nicht** ~ **lassen** not to let o.s. be put off by sthg.

**Beirut** ['baıruːt] *nt* Beirut.

**beisammen** *adv* together.

**Beisammensein** *das* get-together; **ein geselliges** ~ a social get-together.

**Beischlaf** *der* amt sexual intercourse.

**Beisein** *das:* **im** ~ **von jm, in js** ~ in the presence of sb, in sb's presence.

**beiseite** *adv* aside, to one side; ~ **lassen** to leave aside ODER to one side; ~ **legen** to put aside; ~ **schaffen** *fam* [verstecken] to stash away; ~ **treten** to move aside ODER to one side.

**bei|setzen** *vt* geh to inter.

**Beisetzung** (*pl* -en) *die* funeral.

**Beisitzer, in** (*mpl* -; *fpl* -nen) *der, die* - **1.** RECHT *judge other than the main one on a panel of judges* - **2.** [bei Prüfung] *member of an examination panel other than the chief examiner.*

**Bei|spiel** *das* example; sich *(D)* an jm ein ~ neh-
men to follow sb's example; sich *(D)* ein ~ an
etw *(D)* nehmen to take sthg as one's example; mit gutem ~ vorangehen to set a good example.
➤ **zum Beispiel** *adv* for example.

**beispielhaft** *adj* exemplary ◇ *adv* in exemplary fashion.

**beispiellos** *adj* unprecedented; [Unverschämt-
heit] unbelievable ◇ *adv* unprecedentedly.

**beispielsweise** *adv* for example.

**beißen** *(prät* biss; *perf* hat gebissen) *vt* to bite
◇ *vi* - **1.** [mit den Zähnen] to bite; in etw *(A)* ~ to
bite into sthg; nichts zu ~ haben *fig* to have
nothing to eat - **2.** [brennen] to sting; Qualm
beißt in den Augen smoke makes your eyes
sting.
➤ **sich beißen** *ref* - **1.** [mit den Zähnen] to bite
each other - **2.** [Farben] to clash.

**Bei|stand** *der* assistance.

**bei|stehen** *vi (unreg)*: jm ~ to stand by sb.

**Bei|stell|tisch** *der* occasional table.

**bei|steuern** *vt*: etw (zu etw) ~ to contribute
sthg (to sthg).

**bei|stimmen** *vi*: jm/einer Sache ~ to agree
with sb/sthg; einem Antrag ~ to approve an
application.

**Bei|trag** *(pl* **Beiträge)** *der* - **1.** [Geld, Mitarbeit]
contribution; [als Vereinsmitglied] subscription
- **2.** [Artikel] article.

**bei|tragen** *(unreg) vt* to contribute ◇ *vi*: zu
etw ~ to contribute to sthg.

**Beitrags|zahlung** *die* contribution.

**bei|treten** *(perf* ist beigetreten) *vi (unreg)*: etw
*(D)* ~ to join sthg.

**Bei|tritt** *der* [zur EU] entry; [zu Verein] joining.

**Beitritts|erklärung** *die statement accept-
ing membership terms.*

**Bei|wagen** *der* sidecar.

**Bei|werk** *das (ohne pl)* trimmings *(pl)*.

**bei|wohnen** *vi geh*: einer Sache *(D)* ~ to attend
sthg.

**Beize** *(pl* -n) *die* - **1.** [für Holz] (wood) stain - **2.** KÜ-
CHE marinade.

**beizeiten** *adv* in good time.

**beizen** *vt* [Holz] to stain.

**bejahen** *vt* [Frage] to say yes to; [Standpunkt] to
approve of.

**bejammern** *vt* to lament.

**bejubeln** *vt* to acclaim.

**bekämpfen** *vt* [Feind, Kriminalität] to fight;
[Schädlinge] to control.

**Bekämpfung** *die*: die ~ von etw the fight
against sthg; [von Schädlingen] the control of
sthg.

**bekannt** *adj* well-known; mit jm ~ sein to
know sb; etw als ~ voraussetzen to assume
sthg to be common knowledge; jm ~ vorkommen to seem familiar to sb.

**Bekannte** *(pl* -n) *der, die* acquaintance.

**Bekannten|kreis** *der* circle of acquaint-
ances.

**bekanntermaßen** *adv* as is well known.

**Bekannt|gabe** *die* announcement.

**bekannt geben** *vt (unreg)* to announce.

**Bekanntheit** *die* fame; die ~ eines Produktes
how well-known a product is.

**Bekanntheitsgrad** *der (ohne pl)*: einen hohen
~ haben to be very well-known.

**bekanntlich** *adv* as is well known.

**bekannt machen** *vt* [Beschluss, Plan] to announce; [Fremde, Gäste] to introduce; jn mit jm
~ to introduce sb to sb; jn/sich mit etw ~ to familiarize sb/o.s. with sthg.

**Bekanntmachung** *(pl* -en) *die* announcement.

**Bekanntschaft** *(pl* -en) *die* - **1.** [Kennen, Be-
kannte] acquaintance; mit etw ~ machen *iron* to
have a run-in with sthg; mit jm ~ schließen to
make sb's acquaintance - **2.** [Bekanntenkreis]
acquaintances *(pl)*.

**bekannt werden** *(perf* ist bekannt geworden) *vi (unreg)* to become known.

**bekehren** *vt* to convert.
➤ **sich bekehren** *ref*: sich (zu etw) ~ to convert
(to sthg).

**bekennen** *(prät* bekannte; *perf* hat bekannt)
*vt* [Sünde] to confess; [Fehler] to admit.
➤ **sich bekennen** *ref*: sich zu etw ~ [Glauben] to
profess sthg; [Überzeugung] to declare one's
support for sthg; [Attentat] to claim responsibility for sthg.

**Bekenner|schreiben** *das* letter claiming
responsibility.

**Bekenntnis** *(pl* -se) *das* [von Schuld] admission,
confession; ~ zu einem Glauben profession of
a faith.

**beklagen** *vt* to mourn.
➤ **sich beklagen** *ref*: sich (bei jm über jn/etw) ~
to complain (about sb/sthg to sb).

**Beklagte** *(pl* -n) *der, die* RECHT defendant.

**bekleben** *vt*: die Wand mit etw ~ to stick sthg
on the wall.

**bekleckern** *vt*: etw mit etw ~ to spill sthg on
sthg.
➤ **sich bekleckern** *ref*: sich mit etw ~ to spill
sthg on o.s.

**bekleiden** *vt geh* [Posten, Amt] to hold.

**bekleidet** *adj*: mit etw ~ sein to be wearing
sthg.

**Bekleidung** *die (ohne pl)* - **1.** [Kleidung] clothes *(pl)* - **2.** *geh* [von Posten, Amt] tenure.

**beklemmend** *adj* oppressive ⬦ *adv* oppressively.

**Beklemmung** *(pl* -en) *die* anxiety.

**beklommen** *adj* anxious ⬦ *adv* anxiously.

**beklⱷppt** *adj salopp abw* crazy.

**bekommen** *(prät* bek**a**m; *perf* hat/ist bekommen) *vt (hat)* to get; [Zug, Bus, Krankheit] to catch; **ich bekomme noch 50 Euro von dir** you owe me 50 euros; **was ~ Sie?** what would you like?; **was ~ Sie dafür?** how much is it?; **es sind keine Karten mehr zu ~** there are no more tickets available ODER to be had; **Prügel/eine Strafe bekommen~** to be beaten/punished; **sie bekommt ein Kind** she's expecting (a baby); **Besuch ~** to have visitors; **etw geschenkt/geliehen ~** to be given/lent sthg; **Angst/Hunger ~** to get frightened/hungry; **seine Stimme bekam einen zärtlichen Ton** his voice took on a gentle tone ⬦ *vi (ist):* **jm gut ~** [Essen] to agree with sb; **der Wein ist mir nicht ~** the wine disagreed with me.

**bekömmlich** *adj* digestible.

**bekräftigen** *vt* [Meinung, Kritik] to confirm, to reinforce; **jn in etw (D) ~** to confirm sb in sthg.

**bekreuzigen** ➡ **sich bekreuzigen** *ref* to cross o.s.

**bekriegen** *vt* to wage war on.
➡ **sich bekriegen** *ref* [sich bekämpfen] to be at war.

**bekritzeln** *vt* to scribble on.

**bekümmert** *adj* worried ⬦ *adv* worriedly.

**bekunden** *vt geh* to express.

**belächeln** *vt abw* to laugh at.

**beladen** *(präs* belädt; *prät* belud; *perf* hat beladen) *vt:* **etw (mit etw) ~** to load sthg (with sthg).

**Belag** *(pl* Beläge) *der* - **1.** [von Bremsen] lining; [von Straße] surface; [von Fußboden] covering - **2.** [auf Brot] topping - **3.** [auf der Zunge] fur; [auf den Zähnen] film.

**Belagerer** *(pl* -) *der* besieger.

**belagern** *vt* to besiege.

**Belagerung** *(pl* -en) *die* siege.

**Belang** *(pl* -e) *der* [Bedeutung]: **von/ohne ~ sein (für jn)** to be important/of no importance (to sb).
➡ **Belange** *pl* [Interessen] interests.

**belangen** *vt* RECHT: **jn (für etw) ~** to prosecute sb (for sthg).

**belanglos** *adj* [Gerede, Theorie] unimportant; [Summe, Menge] trifling.

**belassen** *(präs* belässt; *prät* beli**e**ß; *perf* hat belassen) *vt geh* to leave; **es dabei ~** to leave it at that.

**belastbar** *adj* - **1.** [Person] resilient - **2.** [Material] tough.

**belasten** *vt* - **1.** [mit Gewicht] to put a load on; **etw mit etw ~** to weight sthg down with sthg - **2.** [Umwelt] to pollute; [Leber] to put a strain on - **3.** [beanspruchen] to weigh heavily on; **jn mit etw ~** to burden sb with sthg - **4.** [besorgen]: **jn ~** to weigh on sb's mind - **5.** RECHT to incriminate - **6.** [finanziell - Konto] to debit; **ein Haus mit einer Hypothek ~** to mortgage a house.

**belastend** *adj* - **1.** [beanspruchend] arduous - **2.** [Besorgnis erregend] worrying - **3.** RECHT incriminating.

**belästigen** *vt* to bother; [sexuell] to harass.

**Belästigung** *(pl* -en) *die* annoyance; [sexuell] harassment.

**Belastung** *(pl* -en) *die* - **1.** [mit Gewicht] load - **2.** [Beeinträchtigung - von Umwelt] pollution - **3.** [psychisch] strain - **4.** [von Konto] debiting.

**belauern** *vt* [Person] to spy on; [Verhalten] to observe secretly.

**belaufen** *(präs* beläuft; *prät* belief; *perf* hat belaufen) ➡ **sich belaufen** *ref:* **sich auf etw (A) ~** to amount to sthg.

**belauschen** *vt* to eavesdrop on.

**beleben** *vt* - **1.** [aufleben lassen] to revive - **2.** [gestalten] to brighten up.
➡ **sich beleben** *ref* - **1.** [sich füllen] to come to life - **2.** [sich erholen, sich erhellen] to brighten up - **3.** WIRTSCH to revive.

**belebt** *adj* busy.

**Beleg** *(pl* -e) *der* - **1.** [Quittung] receipt - **2.** [Nachweis] proof.

**belegen** *vt* - **1.** [mit Belag]: **etw mit etw ~** [Brot] to top sthg with sthg; [Boden] to cover sthg with sthg - **2.** [besuchen] to enrol for - **3.** [okkupieren] to occupy - **4.** [einnehmen]: **den ersten/zweiten Platz ~** to come first/second - **5.** [versehen]: **jn/etw mit etw ~** to impose sthg on sb/sthg - **6.** [nachweisen - Zahlung] to provide proof of; [ - Behauptung, Argument] to back up; [ - Zitat] to reference.

**Belegschaft** *(pl* -en) *die* workforce.

**belegt** *adj* - **1.** [mit Aufschnitt]: **~es Brot/Brötchen** open sandwich/roll; **ein ~es Brot mit Käse** a slice of bread with cheese on it - **2.** [Zunge] furred - **3.** [besetzt - Zimmer] occupied; [ - Hotel, Kurs] full - **4.** [Stimme] hoarse.

**belehren** *vt* to instruct; **jn über etw (A) ~** to instruct sb about sthg; [Rechte] to inform sb of sthg; **jn eines Besseren/anderen ~** to teach sb better/otherwise.

**Belehrung** *(pl* -en) *die* [Belehren] instruction; [Zurechtweisung] lecture.

**beleibt** *adj* corpulent.

**beleidigen** *vt* [Person] to insult; [Empfinden] to offend.

**Beleidigung** (*pl* -en) *die* insult; ~ **des guten Geschmacks** offence against good taste.

**belesen** *adj* well-read.

**beleuchten** *vt* - **1.** [Denkmal, Brunnen] to illuminate; [Straße, Raum] to light - **2.** [Thema, Theorie] to examine.

**Beleuchtung** (*pl* -en) *die* - **1.** [mit Licht] lighting - **2.** [Lampen, Scheinwerfer] lights (*pl*) - **3.** (*ohne pl*) [von Thema, Theorie] examination.

**Belfast** *nt* Belfast.

**Belgien** *nt* Belgium.

**Belgier, in** ['bɛlgiɐ, rɪn] (*mpl* -; *fpl* -nen) *der, die* Belgian.

**belgisch** *adj* Belgian.

**Belgrad** *nt* Belgrade.

**belichten** *vt* to expose.

**Belichtung** *die* FOTO exposure.

**Belichtungsmesser** (*pl* -) *der* FOTO light meter.

**Belichtungslzeit** *die* FOTO exposure time.

**Belieben** *das*: **nach** ~ as you like; **das steht** ODER **liegt in deinem** ~ that is up to you.

**beliebig** *adj* any; **eine ~e Summe** any amount <> *adv*: ~ **viel/viele** as much/many as you like; ~ **lange** as long as you like.

**beliebt** *adj* popular; **beim jm** ~ **sein** to be popular with sb; **sich bei jm** ~ **machen** to make o.s. popular with sb.

**Beliebtheit** *die* popularity.

**beliefern** *vt*: **jn (mit etw)** ~ to supply sb (with sthg).

**Belieferung** *die* supplying.

**bellen** *vi* to bark.

**Belletristik** *die* literature.

**belletristisch** *adj*: ~**e Literatur** literature.

**belohnen** *vt* to reward.

**Belohnung** (*pl* -en) *die* - **1.** [Belohnen] rewarding - **2.** [Lohn, Entgelt] reward.

**belüften** *vt* to air.

**Belüftung** *die* ventilation.

**belügen** (*prät* belog; *perf* hat belogen) *vt* to lie to.
➤ **sich belügen** *ref*: **sich selbst** ~ to deceive o.s.

**belustigen** *vt* to amuse.

**Belustigung** *die* amusement.

**bemächtigen** ➤ **sich bemächtigen** *ref geh*: **sich einer Sache** (G) ~ to seize sthg.

**bemalen** *vt* [anmalen] to paint.
➤ **sich bemalen** *ref fam abw* to paint one's face.

**Bemalung** (*pl* -en) *die* painting.

**bemängeln** *vt* to criticize.

**bemannt** *adj* manned.

**bemerkbar** *adj* noticeable; **sich** ~ **machen** [Person] to attract attention; [Sache] to become apparent.

**bemerken** *vt* - **1.** [wahrnehmen] to notice - **2.** [sagen] to remark; **ich möchte** ~, **dass ...** I'd like to mention that ...; **nebenbei bemerkt** by the way.

**bemerkenswert** *adj* remarkable <> *adv* remarkably.

**Bemerkung** (*pl* -en) *die* remark.

**bemessen** (*präs* bemisst; *prät* bemaß; *perf* hat bemessen) *vt* to calculate; **die Zeit ist knapp** ~ time is limited.
➤ **sich bemessen** *ref*: **sich nach etw** ~ to be calculated on the basis of sthg.

**bemitleiden** *vt* to feel sorry for.

**bemitleidenswert** *adj* pitiable.

**bemühen** *vt geh* [Anwalt, Gutachter] to call on.
➤ **sich bemühen** *ref* - **1.** [sich anstrengen] to try; **sich** ~, **etw zu tun** to try to do sthg; ~ **Sie sich nicht!** don't trouble yourself! - **2.** [suchen]: **sich um jn/etw** ~ to look for sb/sthg, to try to find sb/sthg - **3.** [sich kümmern]: **sich um jn** ~ to take care of sb.

**Bemühung** (*pl* -en) *die*: ~**en** efforts.

**bemüßigt** *adv*: **sich** ~ **fühlen** ODER **sehen, etw zu tun** *geh* & *iron* to feel obliged to do sthg.

**bemuttern** *vt* to mother.

**benachbart** *adj* [Personen, Dörfer] neighbouring; [Disziplinen] related.

**benachrichtigen** *vt* to inform.

**Benachrichtigung** (*pl* -en) *die* notification.

**benachteiligen** *vt* to disadvantage; [Minderheiten] to discriminate against.

**Benachteiligung** (*pl* -en) *die* - **1.** [das Benachteiligen] disadvantaging; [von Minderheiten] discrimination - **2.** [Nachteil] disadvantage.

**Benediktiner, in** (*mpl* -; *fpl* -nen) *der, die* Benedictine.

**Benefizlkonzert** *das* charity concert.

**benehmen** (*präs* benimmt; *prät* benahm; *perf* hat benommen) ➤ **sich benehmen** *ref* to behave; **sich gut/schlecht** ~ to behave well/badly; **sich zu** ~ **wissen** to know how to behave o.s.

**Benehmen** *das* behaviour.

**beneiden** *vt*: **jn (um etw)** ~ to envy sb (sthg).

**beneidenswert** *adj* enviable <> *adv* enviably.

**Benelux-Länder** *pl* Benelux countries.

**benennen** (*prät* benannte; *perf* hat benannt) *vt* to name; RECHT to call.

**Benennung** (pl -en) die - **1.** [Benennen] naming - **2.** [Wort] name.

**Bengel** (pl -) der little rascal.

**benommen** adj groggy ◇ adv groggily.

**benoten** vt to mark.

**benötigen** vt to need.

**Benotung** (pl -en) die - **1.** [Noten geben] marking - **2.** [Note] mark.

**benutzen, benützen** vt to use.

**Benutzer, in** (mpl -; fpl -nen) der, die user.

**benutzerfreundlich** adj user-friendly.

**Benutzerlkonto** das EDV user account.

**Benutzerlname** der EDV user name.

**Benutzeroberlfläche** die EDV user interface.

**Benutzerlprogramm** das EDV user program.

**Benutzung** die use.

**Benzin** (pl -e) das petrol Br, gas Am; bleifreies/verbleites ~ unleaded/leaded petrol Br ODER gas Am; ~ tanken to fill up with petrol Br ODER gas Am.

**Benzinlkanister** der petrol can Br, gas can Am.

**Benzinlpreis** der petrol prices (pl) Br, gas prices (pl) Am.

**Benzinltank** der petrol tank Br, gas tank Am.

**Benzinlverbrauch** der fuel consumption.

**beobachten** vt - **1.** [observieren] to observe - **2.** [überwachen] to watch - **3.** [bemerken] to notice.

**Beobachter, in** (mpl -; fpl -nen) der, die observer.

**Beobachtung** (pl -en) die observation.

**Beobachtungslgabe** die powers (pl) of observation.

**bepackt** adj loaded up.

**bepflanzen** vt to plant.

**bequem** adj - **1.** [gemütlich] comfortable; es sich (D) ~ machen to make o.s. comfortable - **2.** [faul] lazy - **3.** [Lösung, Weg] easy ◇ adv - **1.** [liegen, sitzen] comfortably - **2.** [leicht] easily.

**bequemen** ⇒ **sich bequemen** ref: **sich dazu ~, etw zu tun** to deign to do sthg.

**Bequemlichkeit** (pl -en) die - **1.** [Gemütlichkeit] comfort - **2.** [Faulheit] laziness.

**beraten** (präs berät; prät beriet; perf hat beraten) vt - **1.** [Rat geben] to advise; **jn bei etw ~** to advise sb on sthg; **gut/schlecht ~ sein** to be well-advised/ill-advised - **2.** [besprechen] to discuss ◇ vi: **über etw** (A) **~** to discuss sthg. ⇒ **sich beraten** ref: **sich mit jm über etw** (A) **~** to discuss sthg with sb.

**Berater, in** (mpl -; fpl -nen) der, die adviser.

**beratschlagen** vi to discuss; **über etw** (A) **~** to discuss sthg.

**Beratung** (pl -en) die - **1.** [Ratgeben] advice - **2.** [Besprechung] discussion.

**Beratungslfirma** die consultancy.

**Beratungslstelle** die advice centre.

**berauben** vt: **jn einer Sache** (G) **~** to rob sb of sthg.

**berauschend** adj intoxicating ◇ adv: **~ wirken** to have an intoxicating effect.

**Berber** (pl -) der - **1.** [Volk] Berber - **2.** [Teppich] Berber carpet.

**Berberin** (pl -nen) die Berber.

**berechenbar** adj - **1.** [Summe, Größe] calculable - **2.** [Person, Reaktion] predictable ◇ adv predictably.

**berechnen** vt - **1.** [ausrechnen] to calculate - **2.** [anrechnen] to charge; **jm für eine Leistung 100 Euro ~** to charge sb 100 euros for a service.

**berechnend** adj calculating ◇ adv calculatingly.

**Belrechnung** die calculation; **aus ~ handeln** to act in a calculating manner.

**berechtigen** vt: **jn zu etw ~** to entitle sb to sthg.

**berechtigt** adj justified.

**berechtigterweise** adv justifiably.

**Berechtigung** (pl -en) die - **1.** [Genehmigung] right - **2.** [Korrektheit] validity, legitimacy.

**bereden** vt - **1.** [besprechen]: **etw (mit jm) ~** to discuss sthg (with sb) - **2.** fam abw [überreden]: **jn ~, etw zu tun** to talk sb into doing sthg.

**Bereich** (pl -e) der - **1.** [Gebiet] area - **2.** [Aufgabe, Thema] field - **3.** RW: **es liegt im ~ des Möglichen** it is within the bounds of possibility; **im grünen ~** normal; **im roten ~** below normal.

**bereichern** vt to enrich. ⇒ **sich bereichern** ref: **sich (an jm/etw) ~** to make money (at sb's expense/from sthg).

**Bereicherung** (pl -en) die enrichment.

**Bereifung** (pl -en) die tyres (pl).

**bereinigen** vt to settle.

**bereisen** vt to travel around.

**bereit** adj - **1.** [fertig]: **~ sein** to be ready - **2.** [gewillt]: **~ sein, etw zu tun** to be willing to do sthg; **zu allem ~ sein** to be ready to try anything; **sich ~ erklären, etw zu tun** to agree to do sthg.

**bereiten** vt - **1.** [zubereiten] to prepare - **2.** geh [machen]: **jm Sorgen/Ärger ~** to cause sb worry/trouble; **jm Freude ~** to give sb pleasure.

**bereitlhaben** vt to have ready.

**bereit|halten** *vt (unreg)* to have ready.
→ **sich bereithalten** *ref:* **sich zu** ODER **für etw** ~ to be ready for sthg.

**bereit|machen** *vt* to get ready.
→ **sich bereitmachen** *ref* to get ready.

**bereits** *adv* already; ~ **um sechs Uhr** as early as six o'clock; **wir müssen** ~ **in zwei Wochen zurück** we have to return in only two weeks' time.

**Bereitschaft** *die* - **1.** [Wille] willingness; **in** ~ **sein** to be ready - **2.** [Bereitschaftsdienst] emergency service; ~ **haben** [Polizei, Feuerwehr] to be on standby; [Arzt] to be on call.

**Bereitschafts|dienst** *der* emergency service; ~ **haben** [Polizei, Feuerwehr] to be on standby; [Arzt] to be on call.

**Bereitschafts|polizei** *die* riot police.

**Bereitschafts|zeichen** *das* EDV prompt.

**bereit|stehen** *vi (unreg)* [Fahrzeug, Koffer] to be ready; [Sanitäter, Polizei] to be on standby.

**bereit|stellen** *vt* to provide.

**Bereit|stellung** *die* provision.

**bereitwillig** *adj* willing <> *adv* willingly.

**bereuen** *vt* [Fehler, Worte, Verhalten] to regret; [Sünde] to repent of.

**Berg** *(pl* -e) *der* - **1.** [Erhöhung, große Menge] mountain; [kleiner] hill - **2.** RW: ~e **versetzen (können)** (to be able) to move mountains; **über alle** ~e **sein** to be long gone; **über den** ~ **sein** to be over the worst.
→ **Berge** *pl* mountains; **in die** ~e **fahren** to go to the mountains.

**bergab** *adv* downhill; **mit jm/etw geht es** ~ sb/ sthg is going downhill.

**bergan** = bergauf.

**Berg|arbeiter** *der* miner.

**bergauf, bergan** *adv* uphill; **mit jm/etw geht es** ~ things are looking up for sb/sthg.

**Bergbau** *der* mining.

**bergen** *(präs* **birgt**; *prät* **barg**; *perf* **hat geborgen**) *vt* - **1.** [Verunglückte] to rescue; [Leiche, Unfallwagen] to recover; [Boot] to salvage - **2.** *geh* [enthalten]: **etw in sich** *(D)* ~ to involve sthg.

**bergeweise** *adv* by the ton.

**Berg|führer, in** *der, die* mountain guide.

**Berg|hütte** *die* mountain hut.

**bergig** *adj* mountainous.

**Berg|land** *das* mountainous area.

**Berg|mann** *(pl* -leute) *der* miner.

**Berg|predigt** *die* REL Sermon on the Mount.

**Berg|schuh** *der* climbing boot.

**Berg|spitze** *die* mountain peak.

**Berg|station** *die* summit station *(of cable car)*.

**Berg|steigen** *das* (mountain) climbing.

**Berg|steiger, in** *der, die* (mountain) climber; [professionell] mountaineer.

**Berg|tour** *die* - **1.** [Wandern] mountain hike - **2.** [Klettern] mountain climb - **3.** [mit Fahrzeug] trip into the mountains.

**Bergung** *(pl* -en) *die* [von Verletzten] rescue; [von Leiche, Unfallwagen] recovery; [von Boot] salvage.

**Berg|wacht** *die (ohne pl)* mountain rescue service.

**Berg|wandern** *das* hill walking.

**Berg|werk** *das* mine.

**Bericht** *(pl* -e) *der* report; **über etw** *(A)* ~ **erstatten** to report on sthg.

**berichten** *vt* to report <> *vi* to report; **von jm/etw** ODER **über jn/etw** ~ to report on sb/ sthg.

**Berichterstatter, in** *(mpl* -; *fpl* -nen) *der, die* - **1.** [Journalist] reporter - **2.** [für Kommission] rapporteur.

**Bericht|erstattung** *die* reporting.

**berichtigen** *vt* to correct.
→ **sich berichtigen** *ref* to correct o.s.

**Berichtigung** *(pl* -en) *die* correction.

**berieseln** *vt abw* [mit Reizen]: **jn mit Musik** ~ to subject sb to a continuous stream of music.

**Berieselung** *(pl* -en) *die* - **1.** [mit Wasser] sprinkling - **2.** *abw* [mit Reizen]: **die** ~ **der Kunden mit Hintergrundmusik** subjecting customers to a continuous stream of background music.

**Beringstraße** *die* Bering Strait.

**Berlin** *nt* Berlin.

**Berliner** *(pl* -) *der* - **1.** [Person] Berliner - **2.** [Gebäck] doughnut *(filled with jam)* <> *adj (unver)* Berlin *(vor Subst);* ~ **Weiße mit Schuss** light beer with a dash of raspberry juice.

**Berlinerin** *(pl* -nen) *die* Berliner.

**berlinerisch** *adj* Berlin *(vor Subst)*.

**Berliner Mauer** *die* Berlin Wall.

**BERLINER MAUER**

> Built in 1961 to halt the exodus of citizens fleeing to the West, the Berlin Wall split the city of Berlin in two, isolating West Berlin in the middle of the GDR. A powerful symbol of the partition of Germany up until 1989, and of the predicament of the German people, it was a grim reminder of the Cold War, of state repression and of the death that lay in store for any East German who tried to escape across it.

**Berliner Philharmoniker** *pl* Berlin Philharmonic *(sg)*.

**Bern** *nt* Bern, Berne.

**Berner** *(pl -)* *der* & *adj (unver)* Bernese.

**Bernerin** *(pl -nen)* *die* Bernese.

**Berner Oberland** *das* Bernese Alps *(pl)*.

**Bernstein** *der* amber.

**bersten** *(präs* birst; *prät* barst; *perf* ist geborsten) *vi* [Schiff, Gebäude] to break up; [Glas, Eis] to shatter.

**berüchtigt** *adj* notorious; **für** ODER **wegen etw ~ sein** to be notorious for sthg.

**berücksichtigen** *vt* - **1.** [Vorschlag, Wunsch, Anliegen] to take into consideration; **wenn man berücksichtigt, dass ...** considering (that) ... - **2.** [Bewerber, Antrag] to consider.

**Berücksichtigung** *die* consideration; **unter ~ einer Sache** *(G)* taking sthg into consideration.

**Beruf** *(pl -e)* *der* profession; **was sind Sie von ~?** what do you do (for a living)?; **ich bin Mechaniker von ~** I'm a mechanic.

**berufen**[1] *adj* - **1.** [fähig] competent - **2.** [bestimmt]: **zu etw ~ sein** to have a vocation as sthg.

**berufen**[2] *(prät* berief; *perf* hat berufen) *vt* to appoint; **jn ins Ausland ~** to post sb abroad. ➤ **sich berufen** *ref:* **sich auf jn/etw ~** to quote sb/sthg as one's authority.

**beruflich** *adj* professional <> *adv* [reisen] on business.

**Berufs|anfänger, in** *der, die* person starting or looking for their first job.

**Berufs|armee** *die* professional army.

**Berufs|ausbildung** *die* vocational training.

**Berufs|berater, in** *der, die* careers adviser.

**Berufs|beratung** *die* career guidance.

**Berufs|krankheit** *die* occupational disease.

**Berufs|leben** *das* working life.

**Berufs|schule** *die* vocational school *(attended part-time by apprentices)*.

**Berufs|soldat** *der* professional soldier.

**berufstätig** *adj:* **~ sein** to have a job, to work; **sie ist nicht ~** she doesn't work.

**Berufstätige** *(pl -n)* *der, die* working person; **die ~n** the working population.

**Berufsverkehr** *der* rush-hour traffic.

**Berufung** *(pl -en)* *die* - **1.** [Ruf] appointment; [ins Ausland] posting - **2.** RECHT [Einspruch] appeal; **~ einlegen** to appeal - **3.** [Begabung] vocation - **4.** [Bezug] reference; **unter ~ auf jn/etw** with reference to sb/sthg.

**beruhen** *vi:* **auf etw** *(D)* **~** to be based on sthg; **etw auf sich** *(D)* **~ lassen** to let sthg rest.

**beruhigen** *vt* to calm (down). ➤ **sich beruhigen** *ref* [Person] to calm down; [Lage] to settle down; [Meer] to become calm.

**Beruhigung** *(pl -en)* *die* [von Person, Meer] calming; [von Lage] settling down.

**Beruhigungs|mittel** *das* sedative.

**berühmt** *adj* famous; **wegen** ODER **für etw ~ sein** to be famous for sthg.

**Berühmtheit** *(pl -en)* *die* - **1.** [Berühmtsein] fame; **~ erlangen** geh to become famous - **2.** [Person] celebrity.

**berühren** *vt* - **1.** [anfassen] to touch - **2.** [beeindrucken] to move.

**Berührung** *(pl -en)* *die* - **1.** [Anfassen] touch - **2.** [Kontakt]: **mit jm/etw in ~ kommen** to come into contact with sb/sthg.

**Berührungs|punkt** *der* point of contact.

**bes.** *(abk für* besonders*)* esp.

**besagen** *vt* to say.

**besagt** *adj* amt said.

**besaiter** *adj:* **zart ~ sein** fam abw to be very sensitive.

**besänftigen** *vt* to soothe.

**Be|satzung** *die* - **1.** [Personal] crew - **2.** MIL occupying forces *(pl)*.

**Besatzungs|macht** *die* occupying power.

**besaufen** *(präs* besäuft; *prät* besoff; *perf* hat besoffen) ➤ **sich besaufen** *ref salopp* to get plastered.

**beschädigen** *vt* to damage.

**Be|schädigung** *die* - **1.** [Beschädigen] damaging - **2.** [Schaden] damage *(U)*.

**beschaffen** *vt* to obtain; **jm etw ~** to get sb sthg; **sich** *(D)* **etw ~** to get sthg <> *adj:* **wie ist es mit seinem Sehvermögen ~?** how good is his eyesight?; **das Material ist so ~, dass es große Belastungen aushält** the nature of the material means that it can withstand heavy loads.

**Beschaffenheit** *die* - **1.** [Art] nature - **2.** [Zustand] condition.

**beschäftigen** *vt* - **1.** [anstellen] to employ; **er ist bei Siemens beschäftigt** he works for Siemens - **2.** [ablenken] to keep busy - **3.** [beanspruchen - Frage] to preoccupy; **sie ist im Moment sehr beschäftigt** she is very busy at present. ➤ **sich beschäftigen** *ref:* **sich mit jm ~** to devote one's attention to sb; **sie beschäftigt sich intensiv mit Religion** she's heavily involved in religion; **wir ~ uns gegenwärtig mit der Frage, wie ...** we are currently considering ODER looking at the issue of how to ...

**Beschäftigte** *(pl -n)* *der, die* employee.

**Beschäftigung** *(pl -en)* *die* - **1.** [Tätigkeit - Arbeit] occupation; [ - Hobby] activity - **2.** [Arbeitsstelle] job; **eine ~ suchen** to be looking for work; **ohne ~ sein** to be out of work - **3.** [Anstellen] employment - **4.** [Auseinandersetzung]: **~ mit etw** [Thema, Problem] consideration of sthg.

**Beschäftigungs|therapie** *die* occupational therapy.

**beschämen** *vt:* **jn ~** to make sb feel ashamed.

**beschämend** *adj* - **1.** [peinlich] humiliating - **2.** [schändlich] shameful <> *adv* shamefully.

**beschatten** *vt* - **1.** [überwachen] to shadow - **2.** *geh* [Schatten geben] to shade.

**beschauen** *vt* to contemplate.

**beschaulich** *adj* tranquil, peaceful <> *adv* peacefully.

**Bescheid** (*pl* -**e**) *der* [Entscheidung] decision; **den ~ vom Finanzamt erwarten** to be waiting for an answer from the tax office; **~ wissen** to know; **jm ~ sagen** *ODER* **geben** [benachrichtigen] to let sb know; *fam* [jm die Meinung sagen] to give sb a piece of one's mind.

**bescheiden¹** *adj* - **1.** [anspruchslos, einfach] modest; [Benehmen] unassuming - **2.** [Essen] frugal; [Ergebnis, Leistung] mediocre <> *adv* [sich kleiden, leben] simply.

**bescheiden²** (*prät* **beschied;** *perf* **hat beschieden**) ➡ **sich bescheiden** *ref geh* [sich begnügen]: **sich mit etw ~** to make do with sthg.

**Bescheidenheit** *die* modesty.

**bescheinigen** *vt* [mit Zeugnis] to certify; **den Empfang von etw ~** to sign for sthg; **sich etw ~ lassen** to get sthg confirmed in writing.

**Bescheinigung** (*pl* -**en**) *die* - **1.** [Bescheinigen] certification - **2.** [Schein] certificate.

**bescheißen** (*prät* **beschiss;** *perf* **hat beschissen**) *vt salopp:* **jn (um etw) ~** to con sb (out of sthg).

**beschenken** *vt:* **jn ~** to give sb gifts.

**bescheren** *vt* [schenken] to give (for Christmas).

**Bescherung** (*pl* -**en**) *die* giving of Christmas presents; **das ist ja eine schöne** *ODER* **reizende ~!** *iron* that's a nice mess!; **da haben wir die ~!** *fam iron* I told you so!

**bescheuert** *adj salopp* stupid; **du bist ja ~!** you're off your head!

**beschießen** (*prät* **beschoss;** *perf* **hat beschossen**) *vt* to fire on.

**Beschilderung** (*pl* -**en**) *die* signposting (*U*).

**beschimpfen** *vt* to insult; [mit groben Worten] to swear at; **jn als Lügner ~** to call sb a liar.

**Beschimpfung** (*pl* -**en**) *die* insult; **~en** abuse (*U*).

**Beschiss** *der vulg:* **das ist doch reiner ~!** that's a complete bloody con!

**beschissen** *vulg pp* ⊳ **bescheißen** <> *adj* shitty <> *adv* [sich benehmen] shittily; **es geht mir ~** things are going like shit for me.

**Be|schlag** *der* metal fitting; **jn/etw in ~ nehmen** *ODER* **mit ~ belegen** to monopolize sb/sthg.

**beschlagen** (*präs* **beschlägt;** *prät* **beschlug;** *perf* **hat/ist beschlagen**) *vt* (hat) [Pferd] to shoe; [Schuhsohlen] to stud <> *vi* (ist) to mist <> *adj* well-informed; **in etw** (*D*) **~ sein** to be well up on sthg.

**beschlagnahmen** *vt* to confiscate.

**beschleichen** (*prät* **beschlich;** *perf* **hat beschlichen**) *vt* - **1.** [Subj: Gefühl] to come over - **2.** [beobachten] to stalk.

**beschleunigen** *vt* [Tempo, Schritte] to quicken; [Abreise] to hasten; [Arbeitsprozess] to speed up <> *vi* to accelerate.

➡ **sich beschleunigen** *ref* to speed up.

**Beschleunigung** (*pl* -**en**) *die* [von Verfahren, Entwicklung] speeding up; [von Auto] acceleration.

**beschließen** (*prät* **beschloss;** *perf* **hat beschlossen**) *vt* - **1.** [entscheiden] to decide on; [Gesetz] to pass; [Vorhaben] to approve; **~, etw zu tun** to decide to do sthg - **2.** *geh* [beenden] to end <> *vi* [beraten]: **über etw** (*A*) **~** to decide on sthg.

**Be|schluss** *der* decision; **einen ~ fassen** to take a decision.

**beschlussfähig** *adj:* **die Versammlung ist/ist nicht ~** the meeting has/doesn't have a quorum.

**beschmieren** *vt* - **1.** [beschmutzen] to smear; **die Wände mit Graffiti ~** to daub graffiti on the walls - **2.** [bestreichen] to spread; **Brot mit Leberwurst ~** to spread pâté on bread.

➡ **sich beschmieren** *ref* to get dirty; **sich von oben bis unten mit etw ~** to get sthg all over o.s.

**beschmutzen** *vt* [Teppich, Kleidung] to soil; [Wand] to stain; **jm/sich das Kleid ~** to get sb's/one's dress dirty.

➡ **sich beschmutzen** *ref* to get dirty.

**beschneiden** (*prät* **beschnitt;** *perf* **hat beschnitten**) *vt* - **1.** [Hecke] to cut, to trim; [Baum] to prune; [Flügel] to clip - **2.** [einschränken] to curtail - **3.** MED & REL to circumcise.

**Beschneidung** (*pl* -**en**) *die* - **1.** [von Hecke] cutting, trimming; [von Baum] pruning; [von Flügel] clipping - **2.** [Einschränkung] curtailment - **3.** MED & REL circumcision.

**beschnuppern** *vt* - **1.** [beriechen] to sniff (at) - **2.** *fam* [kennen lernen] to size up.

**beschönigen** *vt* to gloss over.

**beschränken** *vt* to limit, to restrict.

**sich beschränken** *ref:* sich auf etw *(A)* ~ [Sache] to be confined to sthg; [Person] to confine o.s. to sthg; **sich in etw** *(D)* ~ [Ausgaben] to cut down on sthg.

**beschränkt** *adj* - **1.** *abw* [engstirnig] narrow-minded - **2.** [begrenzt, dürftig] limited; **in ~en Verhältnissen leben** to live in straitened circumstances - **3.** *abw* [dumm] slow, dim.

**Beschränktheit** *die* - **1.** *abw* [Engstirnigkeit] narrow-mindedness - **2.** [Begrenztheit] limited nature - **3.** *abw* [Dummheit] slowness, dimness.

**Beschränkung** *(pl* -en) *die* restriction.

**beschreiben** (*prät* beschrieb; *perf* hat beschrieben) *vt* - **1.** [darstellen, formen] to describe; [Weg] to tell - **2.** [voll schreiben] to write on.

**Beschreibung** *die* description; **aller** ODER **jeder ~ spotten** *fig* to defy description.

**beschriften** *vt* to label; [Brief] to address; [Etikett] to write on.

**Beschriftung** *(pl* -en) *die* - **1.** [Schreiben] labelling; [von Brief] addressing - **2.** [Schrift] writing.

**beschuldigen** *vt* to accuse; **jn einer Sache** *(G)* ~ to accuse sb of sthg.

**Beschuldigung** *(pl* -en) *die* accusation.

**Beschuss** *der:* **jn/etw unter ~ nehmen** to launch an attack on sb/sthg; **unter ~ geraten/stehen** to come/be under fire.

**beschützen** *vt* to protect; **jn vor etw** *(D)* ~ to protect sb from sthg.

**Beschützer, in** *(mpl* -; *fpl* -nen) *der* protector.

**Beschwerde** *(pl* -n) *die* [Klage] complaint; **~ gegen jn/etw führen** ODER **einlegen** to make ODER lodge a complaint against sb/sthg.

**Beschwerden** *pl* [Schmerzen] trouble *(U)*; **~n im Kreuz haben** to have back problems ODER trouble with one's back; **jm ~n machen** to give sb trouble.

**beschweren** *vt* [belasten] to weight down. **sich beschweren** *ref:* sich (über jn/etw) ~ to complain (about sb/sthg).

**beschwerlich** *adj* arduous.

**beschwichtigen** *vt* [Person] to placate; [Zorn] to calm.

**beschwindeln** *vt* to dupe.

**beschwingt** *adj* [Stimmung] lively; [Melodie] lilting ◇ *adv* [arbeiten] energetically; [gehen] with a spring in one's step.

**beschwipst** *adj* tipsy.

**beschwören** (*prät* beschwor; *perf* hat beschworen) *vt* - **1.** [beeiden] to swear to - **2.** [erscheinen lassen - Geister] to invoke; [ - Bilder] to conjure up; [ - Erinnerungen] to evoke - **3.** [bitten] to entreat, to implore.

**besehen** (*präs* besieht; *prät* besah; *perf* hat besehen) *vt* to look at.

**beseitigen** *vt* - **1.** [entfernen - Fleck] to remove; [ - Abfall] to get rid of, to dispose of; [ - Irrtümer, Schwierigkeiten, Missbrauch] to eliminate; [ - Schnee] to clear away - **2.** [ermorden] to eliminate.

**Beseitigung** *(pl* -en) *die* - **1.** [Entfernung - von Fleck] removal; [ - von Abfall] disposal; [ - von Irrtümer, Schwierigkeiten, Missbrauch] elimination - **2.** [Ermordung] elimination.

**Besen** *(pl* -) *der* broom; **mit eisernem ~ kehren** *fig* to make a clean sweep.

**Besen|schrank** *der* broom cupboard.

**Besen|stiel** *der* broom-handle.

**besessen** *adj* - **1.** [verrückt]: **wie ~** like someone possessed - **2.** [begeistert]: **von etw ~ sein** to be obsessed with sthg.

**besetzen** *vt* - **1.** [Stelle, Rolle] to fill - **2.** [Sitzplatz, Haus, Gebiet, Land] to occupy - **3.** [verzieren]: **etw mit etw ~** to trim sthg with sthg.

**besetzt** *adj* occupied; [Telefon] engaged; [Sitz] taken; **nicht ~** [Büro] closed.

**Besetzt|zeichen** *das* TELEKOM engaged tone.

**Besetzung** *(pl* -en) *die* - **1.** [von Posten] filling - **2.** [Team - von Schauspielern] cast; [ - von Sportlern] team - **3.** [von Land, Gebiet, Haus] occupation.

**besichtigen** *vt* [Museum] to visit; [Wohnung] to view; [Stadt] to go sightseeing in.

**Besichtigung** *(pl* -en) *die* [von Museum] visit; [von einer Wohnung] viewing; [von einer Stadt] sightseeing; [Führung] tour.

**besiedeln** *vt* - **1.** [kolonisieren] to colonize - **2.** [ansiedeln] to settle; **dicht/dünn besiedelt** densely/sparsely populated.

**besiegeln** *vt* to seal.

**besiegen** *vt* - **1.** [Feind] to defeat; [Mannschaft] to beat - **2.** [Zweifel, Neugier] to overcome.

**Besiegte** *(pl* -n) *der, die* loser.

**besinnen** (*prät* besann; *perf* hat besonnen) **sich besinnen** *ref* - **1.** [überlegen] to think, to reflect; **sich eines Besseren ~** to think better of it - **2.** [sich erinnern]: **sich auf jn/etw ~** to remember sb/sthg.

**besinnlich** *adj* [Mensch] thoughtful; [Musik] contemplative.

**Besinnung** *die:* **die ~ verlieren** to lose consciousness; **zur ~ kommen** [zu Bewusstsein] to regain consciousness; [Nachdenken] to have time for reflection.

**besinnungslos** *adj* - **1.** [bewusstlos] unconscious - **2.** [kopflos]: **~ vor Wut/Hass sein** to be beside oneself with rage/hatred.

**Besitz** *der* - **1.** [Eigentum] property - **2.** [Besitzen] possession; **etw in ~ nehmen** [Haus] to take possession of sthg; **im ~ einer Sache** *(G)* **sein** to be in possession of sthg, to possess sthg - **3.** [Landgut] estate.

**besitzen** (*prät* **besaß;** *perf* **hat besessen**) *vt* to possess, to own; [Recht, Qualität] to have.

**Besitzer, in** (*mpl* **-;** *fpl* **-nen**) *der, die* owner.

**Besitzverhältnisse** *pl* distribution (U) of wealth.

**besoffen** *pp* ⊳ **besaufen** ◇ *adj salopp* sloshed, plastered.

**besohlen** *vt* to sole.

**Besoldung** (*pl* **-en**) *die* [von Soldaten] pay; [von Beamten] salary.

**besondere, r, s** *adj* [speziell] special; [außergewöhnlich] particular; ~ **Kennzeichen** distinguishing features; **im Besonderen** (*adv*) in particular, especially.

**Besonderheit** (*pl* **-en**) *die* special feature, peculiarity.

**besonders** *adv* - **1.** [vor allem, sehr] especially, particularly - **2.** [gut]: **nicht** ~ not very well ◇ *adj*: **nicht** ~ **sein** to be not very good; **der Film ist nicht** ~ the film isn't up to much.

**besonnen** *pp* ⊳ **besinnen** ◇ *adj* prudent; [Urteil] considered ◇ *adv* prudently.

**Besonnenheit** *die* prudence.

**besorgen** *vt* - **1.** [beschaffen] to get (hold of); **jm/sich etw** ~ to get sb/o.s. sthg; **hast du etw zu** ~? do you have any shopping to do? - **2.** [sich um etw kümmern] to attend to, to see to; **es jm** ~ *salopp fig* to sort sb out.

**Besorgnis** (*pl* **-se**) *die* concern.

➡ **Besorgnis erregend** *adj* worrying.

**besorgt** *adj* worried; **um jn** ~ **sein** to be worried about sb; **rührend um jn** ~ **sein** to be concerned for sb's wellbeing ◇ *adv* anxiously; ~ **aussehen** to look worried.

**Besorgung** (*pl* **-en**) *die* - **1.** [Einkäufe] purchase; ~**en** shopping (U) - **2.** [Besorgen] obtaining.

**bespannen** *vt* [Wand] to cover; [Streichinstrument, Tennisschläger] to string.

**bespielbar** *adj* [Fußballplatz] playable.

**bespielen** *vt* to record on.

**bespitzeln** *vt* to spy on.

**besprechen** (*präs* **bespricht;** *prät* **besprach;** *perf* **hat besprochen**) *vt* - **1.** [erörtern]: **etw (mit jm)** ~ to discuss sthg (with sb) - **2.** [rezensieren] to review - **3.** [aufnehmen] to record (one's voice) on.

➡ **sich besprechen** *ref:* **sich (mit jm über etw)** ~ to confer (with sb about sthg).

**Besprechung** (*pl* **-en**) *die* - **1.** [Beratung] discussion; **in einer** ~ **sein** to be in a meeting - **2.** [Rezension] review.

**bespritzen** *vt* - **1.** [nass machen] to splash - **2.** [beschmutzen] to spatter.

**besprühen** *vt* to spray.

**besser** *adj & kompar* - **1.** [als Komparativ von gut] better; [ziemlich gut] good; **das hier ist schon ein** ~**es Gerät** this is a pretty good machine; **das Hotel ist eine** ~**e Absteige** the hotel is just a glorified dosshouse; ~ **ist** ~ better safe than sorry - **2.** [gesellschaftlich gehoben] superior ◇ *adv* better.

**Bessere** (*pl* **-n**) *der, die, das* better; ~**s zu tun haben** to have better things to do; **sich eines** ~**n besinnen** to think better of it.

**besser gehen** (*perf* **ist besser gegangen**) *vi* (*unreg*): **es geht ihr besser** she is feeling better.

**bessern** *vt* to improve; [Verbrecher] to reform.

➡ **sich bessern** *ref* [Wetter, Zustand] to improve; [Mensch] to mend one's ways.

**Besserung** *die* improvement; **auf dem Weg der** ~ on the road to recovery, on the mend.

➡ **gute Besserung** *interj* get well soon!

**Besserwisser, in** (*mpl* **-;** *fpl* **-nen**) *der, die abw* know-all, smart alec.

**Belstand** *der* - **1.** [Bestehen] survival, continued existence; **(nicht) von** ~ **sein** (not) to last; ~ **haben** to last - **2.** [Vorrat] stock.

**bestanden** *pp* ⊳ **bestehen** ◇ *adj:* **mit etw** ~ **sein** to be planted with sthg.

**beständig** *adj* - **1.** [dauernd] constant - **2.** [gleich bleibend - Wetter] settled; [ - Freund] faithful; [ - Mitarbeiter] reliable - **3.** [widerstandsfähig]: **gegen etw** ~ **sein** to be resistant to sthg ◇ *adv* - **1.** [dauernd] constantly - **2.** [zuverlässig] steadily, reliably.

**Beständigkeit** *die* - **1.** [Zuverlässigkeit] reliability - **2.** [Widerstandsfähigkeit] resistance.

**Bestandslaufnahme** *die* stocktaking; **eine** ~ **machen** to take stock.

**Bestandlteil** *der* component; **sich in seine** ~**e auflösen** to disintegrate.

**bestärken** *vt* to confirm; **jn in seinem Vorsatz** ~ to strengthen sb in his resolve; **jn in seiner Meinung** ~ to reinforce sb's opinion.

**bestätigen** *vt* to confirm; [Urteil] to uphold; **jn in einem Amt** ~ to confirm sb's appointment.

➡ **sich bestätigen** *ref* to be confirmed, to prove true.

**Bestätigung** (*pl* **-en**) *die* confirmation; [von Urteil] upholding.

**bestatten** *vt geh* to inter, to bury.

**Bestattung** (*pl* **-en**) *die geh* interment, burial.

**bestäuben** *vt* - **1.** [bestreuen] to dust, to sprinkle - **2.** BIOL to pollinate.

**bestaunen** *vt* to marvel at.

**bestbezahlt** adj highest-paid.

**beste, r, s** adj best; sich ~r Gesundheit erfreuen to enjoy the best of health ◇ adv: am ~n gehe ich jetzt I'd better go now; sie spricht am ~n Deutsch von allen she speaks the best German of everyone.

**Beste** (pl -n) der, die, das best (one); das ~ aus etw machen fig to make the best of sthg; es stent nicht zum ~n mit jm/etw things are not looking good for sb/sthg; eine Anekdote zum ~n geben to tell a story; jn zum ~n halten to pull sb's leg.

**bestechen** (präs besticht; prät bestach; perf hat bestochen) vt to bribe ◇ vi: sie besticht durch ihre Schlagfertigkeit she makes an impression with her quick-wittedness.

**bestechlich** adj open to bribery.

**Bestechung** (pl -en) die bribery.

**Besteck** (pl -e) das - 1. [Essbesteck] cutlery (U); ein ~ a place setting - 2. [von Arzt] set of surgical instruments.

**bestehen** (prät bestand; perf hat bestanden) vi - 1. [existieren] to exist; es besteht ... there is ... - 2. [sich zusammensetzen]: das Buch besteht aus zehn Kapiteln the book consists of ten chapters; der Rahmen besteht aus Kunststoff the frame is made of plastic - 3. [beinhalten]: ihre Aufgabe besteht in der Planung des Projekts her job consists of ODER involves planning the project; das Problem besteht darin, dass ... the problem is that ... - 4. [beharren]: auf etw (D) ~ to insist on sthg - 5. [standhalten]: vor jm/etw ~ to stand up to sb/sthg ◇ vt to pass.

**Bestehen** das existence; hundertjähriges ~ centenary.

**bestehen bleiben** (perf ist bestehen geblieben) vi (unreg) - 1. [übrig bleiben] to remain - 2. [Vorschrift] to be upheld.

**bestehlen** (präs bestiehlt; prät bestahl; perf hat bestohlen) vt: jn um etw ~ to steal sthg from sb.

**besteigen** (prät bestieg; perf hat bestiegen) vt - 1. [Berg] to climb; [Pferd] to mount; [Thron] to ascend - 2. [Zug, Bus, Flugzeug] to board.

**Besteigung** die [von Berg, Thron] ascent.

**bestellen** vt - 1. [anfordern] to order; sich (D) etw ~ to order sthg (for o.s.) - 2. [reservieren] to book, to reserve - 3. [kommen lassen] to summon - 4. [ausrichten]: jm Grüße ~ to give ODER send one's regards to sb; kann ich ihm etwas (von dir) ~? can I give him a message (from you)? - 5. [bearbeiten] to cultivate; es ist um jn/ etw schlecht bestellt sb/sthg is in a bad way ◇ vi to order.

**Bestellschein** der order form.

**Bestellung** (pl -en) die - 1. [Anforderung, Waren] order - 2. [Reservierung] booking, reservation - 3. [Bearbeitung] cultivation.

◆ auf Bestellung adv to order; wie auf ~ as if by command.

**Bestellzettel** der order slip.

**bestenfalls** adv at best.

**bestens** adv very well.

**besteuern** vt to tax.

**Besteuerung** die taxation.

**bestialisch** adj abw [Mord, Tat] brutal ◇ adv - 1. abw [grausam] brutally - 2. fam [unerträglich] dreadfully.

**Bestie** (pl -n) die - 1. [Raubtier] beast - 2. abw [Unmensch] brute.

**bestimmbar** adj [wissenschaftlich] classifiable.

**bestimmen** vt - 1. [Preis, Termin] to fix; jn zum Nachfolger ~ to designate sb as one's successor - 2. [vorsehen]: für jn/etw bestimmt sein to be intended for sb/sthg - 3. [ermitteln] to determine; [Pflanze] to classify; [Bedeutung] to define - 4. [Charakter] to determine; [Stadtbild, Atmosphäre] to characterize ◇ vi - 1. [entscheiden] to decide; sie bestimmt in dieser Firma she makes the decisions in this firm - 2. [verfügen]: über jn ~ to decide what sb should do; über etw (frei) ~ können to be able to do what one likes with sthg.

**bestimmend** adj decisive.

**bestimmt** adj - 1. [gewiss] certain; [genau] particular - 2. [festgelegt] fixed - 3. GRAM definite; der ~e Artikel the definite article - 4. [entscheiden] definite, firm ◇ adv - 1. [entschieden] firmly, decisively - 2. [sehr wahrscheinlich] no doubt; [sicher] certainly; das ist ~ kein Problem I'm sure that won't be a problem; etw ~ wissen to know sthg for sure ODER certain; ganz ~ definitely.

**Bestimmtheit** die firmness, decisiveness; mit ~ [entschlossen] decisively; etw mit ~ wissen to know sthg for sure ODER certain.

**Bestimmung** die - 1. (ohne pl) [von Preis, Frist] fixing - 2. [Vorschrift] regulation; eine gesetzliche ~ a legal provision - 3. [Zweck] (intended) purpose; einem Schiff seiner ~ übergeben to launch a ship - 4. [Ermitteln] determining; [von Pflanze] classification; [von Begriff, Bedeutung] definition - 5. GRAM modifier.

**Bestimmungsort** der destination.

**Bestleistung** die SPORT best performance; ihre persönliche ~ her personal best.

**Best.Nr.** (abk für Bestellnummer) order no.

**bestrafen** vt: jn (für etw) ~ to punish sb (for sthg); jn mit Gefängnis ~ to sentence sb to imprisonment.

**Bestrafung** (pl -en) die punishment; [gerichtlich] sentence.

**bestrahlen** vt - 1. MED to treat with radiotherapy - 2. [erleuchten] to illuminate, to light up.

**Bestreben** das: er hat das ~, immer behilflich zu sein he is always at pains to be helpful.

**bestrebt** adj: ~ sein, etw zu tun to be at pains to do sthg.

**Bestrebung** (pl -en) die effort.

**bestreichen** (prät **bestrich**; perf hat **bestrichen**) vt: etw mit etw ~ to spread sthg with sthg; Brot mit Butter ~ to butter bread.

**bestreiken** vt: dieser Betrieb wird seit letzter Woche bestreikt the staff of this firm have been (out) on strike since last week.

**bestreiten** (prät **bestritt**; perf hat **bestritten**) vt - **1.** [leugnen - Meinung, Aussage] to contest; [- Beschuldigung] to deny; es lässt sich nicht ~ it is indispensable - **2.** [finanzieren] to pay for - **3.** [gestalten] to carry.

**bestreuen** vt to sprinkle.

**Bestseller** ['bɛstsɛlɐ] (pl -) der best-seller.

**Bestsellerliste** die best-seller list.

**bestürmen** vt - **1.** MIL to storm - **2.** [bedrängen]: jn mit Fragen ~ to bombard sb with questions.

**bestürzt** adj: über etw (A) ~ sein to be dismayed about sthg <> adv in dismay.

**Bestürzung** die dismay.

**Bestzeit** die SPORT fastest time.

**Besuch** (pl -e) der - **1.** [Besuchen] visit; [von Schule, Kirche] attendance; jm einen ~ machen to pay sb a visit; bei jm zu ~ sein to be staying with ODER visiting sb - **2.** (ohne pl) [Gast] visitor, guest; [Gäste] visitors (pl), guests (pl); wir haben ~ we have a visitor/visitors.

**besuchen** vt to visit; [Kirche, Schule, Vorlesung] to attend.

**Besucher, in** (mpl -; fpl -nen) der, die visitor.

**Besucherzahl** die number of visitors.

**Besuchszeit** [bə'zu:xstsait] die visiting hours (pl).

**besucht** adj: gut/schlecht ~ well/poorly attended.

**betagt** adj geh elderly.

**betasten** vt [Gegenstand] to touch; [Patienten] to feel.

**betätigen** vt [Hebel] to operate; [Bremse] to apply.
➤ **sich betätigen** ref: sich politisch/sportlich ~ to engage in politics/sport; sich als etw ~ to be active as sthg.

**Betätigung** (pl -en) die - **1.** [Tätigkeit] activity - **2.** (ohne pl) [von Hebel] operation.

**betäuben** vt - **1.** MED to anaesthetize; jn örtlich ~ to give sb a local anaesthetic - **2.** [Trauer, Schmerz] to deaden, to dull.

**Betäubung** (pl -en) die - **1.** MED anaesthetization - **2.** [Benommenheit] daze.

**beteiligen** vt: jn an etw (D) ~ to give sb a share in sthg.
➤ **sich beteiligen** ref: sich an etw (D) ~ to participate in sthg; [Kosten] to contribute to sthg.

**beteiligt** adj: sie ist mit 10% ~ she has a 10% share; an etw (D) ~ sein to have a share in sthg; er war nicht daran ~ he had no part in it.

**Beteiligte** (pl -n) der, die person concerned ODER involved; [von Unternehmen] partner.

**Beteiligung** (pl -en) die - **1.** [Mitwirkung]: ~ (an etw (D)) participation (in sthg); [an Verbrechen] involvement (in sthg) - **2.** [an Gewinn] share.

**beten** vi to pray; um ODER für etw ~ to pray for sthg; für jn ~ to pray for sb <> vt to say.

**beteuern** vt to declare.

**Beteuerung** die declaration.

**Bethlehem** nt Bethlehem.

**betiteln** vt - **1.** [einen Titel geben] to entitle - **2.** fam [bezeichnen]: jn als ODER mit etw ~ to call sb sthg.

**Beton** [be'tɔŋ] (pl -s) der concrete.

**betonen** vt - **1.** [aussprechen] to stress - **2.** [hervorheben] to emphasize, to stress.

**betont** adj [Silbe] stressed; [Gleichgültigkeit, Aufmerksamkeit] studied <> adv deliberately; sich ~ lässig geben to behave with studied nonchalance.

**Betonung** (pl -en) die - **1.** [Betonen] stress - **2.** [Hervorhebung] emphasis.

**betr.** (abk für **betreffs, betreffend**) re.

**Betracht** (ohne Artikel) ➤ in Betracht adv: jn/etw in ~ ziehen [erwägen] to consider sb/sthg; [berücksichtigen] to take sb/sthg into account; (nicht) in ~ kommen (not) to be worth considering; das kommt nicht in ~ that is out of the question.
➤ **außer Betracht** adv: etw außer ~ lassen to disregard sthg.

**betrachten** vt - **1.** [ansehen] to look at; sich (D) etw (näher) ~ to have a (closer) look at sthg - **2.** [beurteilen] to regard - **3.** [überprüfen] to examine, to consider.
➤ **sich betrachten** ref to look at o.s.

**Betrachter, in** (mpl -; fpl -nen) der, die observer.

**beträchtlich** adj considerable <> adv considerably.

**Betrachtung** (pl -en) die - **1.** [Betrachten] contemplation; bei näherer ~ on closer examination - **2.** [Überlegung] reflection; über etw (A) ~en anstellen to reflect on sthg.

**Betrag** (pl Beträge) der amount (of money).

**betragen** (präs **beträgt**; prät **betrug**; perf hat **betragen**) vt [Preis, Rechnung] to amount ODER come to; die Entfernung von A zu B beträgt 10 Kilometer A is 10 kilometres away from B.
➤ **sich betragen** ref: sich gut/schlecht ~ to behave well/badly.

**Betragen** das behaviour, conduct.

**betrauen** *vt:* jn mit etw ~ to entrust sb with sthg.

**betrauern** *vt* to mourn.

**betreffen** *(präs* **betrifft;** *prät* **betraf;** *perf* **hat betroffen)** *vt* [angehen] to concern; [Auswirkungen haben auf] to affect; **was mich/diese Angelegenheit betrifft** as far as I am/this matter is concerned.

**betreffend** *adj* relevant; **der mich ~e Fall** the case concerning me.

**Betreffende** *(pl* **-n)** *der, die* person concerned.

**betreffs** *präp* *amt:* ~ **einer Sache** *(G)* concerning ODER with regard to sthg.

**betreiben** *(prät* **betrieb;** *perf* **hat betrieben)** *vt* - **1.** [vorantreiben] to pursue - **2.** [führen - Gewerbe] to carry on; [ - Laden] to run - **3.** [antreiben]: **mit etw betrieben werden** to be driven by sthg; **diese Anlage wird mit Solarenergie betrieben** this system is solar-powered.

**Betreiben** *das:* **auf js ~ (hin)** at sb's instigation.

**Betreiber, in** *(mpl* **-;** *fpl* **-nen)** *der, die* operator.

**betreten[1]** *adj* embarrassed; **über etw** *(A)* ~ **sein** to be embarrassed about sthg ◇ *adv* sheepishly.

**betreten[2]** *(präs* **betritt;** *prät* **betrat;** *perf* **hat betreten)** *vt* to enter; [Rasen] to walk on; [Bühne] to walk onto.

**Betreten** *das* entry; '~ **verboten!**' 'no entry!', 'keep out!'.

**betreuen** *vt* to look after, to take care of; [Sportler] to coach.

**Betreuer, in** *(mpl* **-;** *fpl* **-nen)** *der, die* [von Kindern] child-minder; [von Sportlern] coach; [von Touristen] guide; [von Alten] care worker.

**Betreuung** *die* care; [von Sportler] coaching.

**Betrieb** *(pl* **-e)** *der* - **1.** [Unternehmen] company, firm; [Produktionsstätte] plant; **heute ist er nicht im ~** he is not at work today - **2.** [Tätigkeit] operation - **3.** [Treiben, Verkehr]: **es ist** ODER **herrscht viel ~** it is very busy.

➤ **in Betrieb** *adv* in operation; **etw in ~ setzen** [Maschine] to start (up) sthg; [Fabrik] to commission sthg.

➤ **außer Betrieb** *adv* out of order; **etw außer ~ setzen** [Maschine] to stop sthg, to shut down sthg; [Fabrik] to decommission sthg.

**betrieblich** *adj* company-related.

**betriebsam** *adj* busy.

**Betriebsamkeit** *die* (hustle and) bustle.

**Betriebslanleitung** *die* operating instructions *(pl).*

**Betriebslausflug** *der* company ODER staff outing.

**Betriebslferien** *pl* (annual) holidays.

**Betriebslkapital** *das* working capital.

**Betriebslklima** *das* atmosphere at work.

**Betriebslkosten** *pl* operating costs.

**Betriebslleitung** *die* management.

**Betriebslrat** *der* - **1.** [Gremium] works council - **2.** [Mensch] works council member.

**betriebssicher** *adj* safe.

**Betriebslstörung** *die* breakdown.

**Betriebslsystem** *das* EDV operating system.

**Betriebslunfall** *der* accident at work, industrial accident.

**Betriebslwirt, in** *der, die* person with a business administration qualification.

**Betriebslwirtschaft** *die* business administration.

**betrinken** *(prät* **betrank;** *perf* **hat betrunken)** ➤ **sich betrinken** *ref* to get drunk.

**betroffen** *pp* ⊳ **betreffen** ◇ *adj* - **1.** [bestürzt] shaken, upset; [Schweigen] stunned; **über etw** *(A)* ~ **sein** to be upset about sthg - **2.** [nicht verschont]: **von etw ~ sein** to be affected by sthg ◇ *adv:* **jn ~ ansehen** to look at sb in consternation.

**Betroffenheit** *die* consternation.

**betrüben** *vt* to sadden.

**betrüblich** *adj* [Stimmung] gloomy; [Situation, Mitteilung] sad.

**betrübt** *adj* [Gesicht] sad; [Stimmung] gloomy; **über etw** *(A)* ~ **sein** to be sad about sthg.

**Betrug** *der* fraud; **das ist ja ~!** this is daylight robbery!

**betrügen** *(prät* **betrog;** *perf* **hat betrogen)** *vt* to cheat; [Ehepartner] to cheat on; **jn um etw ~** to cheat sb out of sthg ◇ *vi* to cheat.

**Betrüger** *(pl* **-)** *der* conman, con artist.

**Betrügerei** *(pl* **-en)** *die* swindling.

**Betrügerin** *(pl* **-nen)** *die* con artist.

**betrügerisch** *adj* [Mensch] deceitful; [Handeln] fraudulent.

**betrunken** *pp* ⊳ **betrinken** ◇ *adj* drunk.

**Bett** *(pl* **-en)** *das* - **1.** [gen] bed; **ins** ODER **zu ~ gehen** to go to bed; **das ~ machen** to make the bed; **mit jm ins ~ gehen** ODER **steigen** *fam* to go to bed with sb - **2.** [Federbett] duvet, quilt.

**Bettlbezug** *der* duvet cover.

**Bettldecke** *die* [aus Wolle] blanket; [gesteppt] quilt, duvet.

**bettelarm** *adj* desperately poor.

**betteln** *vi* to beg; **um etw ~** to beg for sthg.

**betten** *vt:* **jn auf etw** *(A)* ~ to lay sb (down) on sthg.

**Bettenwechsel** der arrival of new group of tourists at holiday resorts on Saturdays.

**bęttlägerig** adj bed-ridden.

**Bęttler, in** (mpl -; fpl -nen) der, die beggar.

**Bęttruhe** die rest.

**Bęttschwere** die: die nötige ~ haben to be ready for bed.

**Bętttuch** (pl -tücher) das sheet.

**Bęttlvorleger** (pl -) der bedside rug.

**Bęttlwäsche** die bed linen.

**Bęttlzeug** das (ohne pl) bedding, bedclothes (pl).

**betucht** adj well-to-do.

**beugen** vt - **1**. [Körper, Finger, Gesetz] to bend - **2**. [Willen] to break - **3**. [Substantiv, Adjectiv] to inflect; [Verb] to conjugate.
➤ **sich beugen** ref - **1**. [sich lehnen] to lean; **sich nach vorn** ~ to bend over - **2**. [sich unterwerfen]: **sich einer Sache** (D) ~ to submit ODER bow to sthg.

**Beule** (pl -n) die [am Kopf] lump; [am Auto] dent.

**beunruhigen** [bə'lʊnruːɪɡn̩] vt to worry; **über etw** (A) **beunruhigt sein** to be worried about sthg.
➤ **sich beunruhigen** ref to worry.

**beurlauben** [bə'luːɐlaʊbn̩] vt [suspendieren] to suspend

**beurteilen** [bə'uːɐtailn̩] vt to judge; [Größe, Qualität] to assess; **jn falsch** ~ to misjudge sb.

**Beurteilung** [bə'uːɐtailʊŋ] (pl -en) die judgement; [von Größe, Qualität] assessment.

**Beute** die - **1**. [von Einbrecher] loot - **2**. [von Raubtier] prey.

**Beutelkunst** die works of art stolen during World War II.

**Beutel** (pl -) der - **1**. [Sack] bag - **2**. BIOL pouch.

**bevölkern** vt - **1**. [bewohnen] to inhabit; **dicht bevölkert** densely populated - **2**. [füllen] to fill.
➤ **sich bevölkern** ref to fill up (with people).

**Bevölkerung** (pl -en) die population.

**Bevölkerungsldichte** die population density.

**Bevölkerungslexplosion** die population explosion.

**Bevölkerungslgruppe** die section of the population.

**bevollmächtigen** vt to authorize.

**Bevollmächtigte** (pl -n) der, die authorized representative.

**Bevollmächtigung** (pl -en) die authorization.

**bevor** konj before.

**bevormunden** vt to treat like a child.

**Bevormundung** (pl -en) die: ~ **durch jn** being treated like a child by sb.

**bevorlstehen** vi (unreg) to be imminent.

**bevorzugen** vt - **1**. [vorziehen] to prefer - **2**. [protegieren] to give preferential treatment to.

**Bevorzugung** (pl -en) die preferential treatment.

**bewachen** vt to guard.

**Bewacher, in** (mpl -; fpl -nen) der, die guard.

**bewachsen** [bə'vaksn̩] (präs **bewächst**; prät **bewuchs**; perf hat **bewachsen**) vt to cover (with plants).

**Bewachung** (pl -en) die - **1**. [Bewachen] guarding - **2**. [Wache] guard.

**bewaffnen** vt to arm.
➤ **sich bewaffnen** ref to arm o.s.

**Bewaffnung** (pl -en) die - **1**. [Ausrüstung] armament, arming - **2**. [Waffen] arms (pl).

**bewahren** vt - **1**. [Person]: **jn vor etw** (D) ~ to protect sb from sthg - **2**. [Nerven, Ruhe] to keep.

**bewähren** ➤ **sich bewähren** ref to prove one's/its worth.

**bewahrheiten** ➤ **sich bewahrheiten** ref to prove (to be) true.

**bewährt** adj [Mensch] reliable; [Methode, Mittel] proven, tried and tested.

**Bewahrung** die - **1**. [Schutz] protection - **2**. [von Ruhe] keeping.

**Bewährung** die - **1**. [Profilierung] test, trial - **2**. RECHT probation; **auf** ODER **mit** ~ on probation.

**Bewährungslhelfer** der probation officer.

**Bewährungslprobe** die (crucial) test.

**bewaldet** adj wooded.

**bewältigen** vt [Arbeit, Problem] to cope with; [js Tod, die Vergangenheit] to come to terms with; [Papierberge] to get through.

**bewandert** adj: **auf einem Gebiet/in etw** (D) ~ **sein** to be well-versed in a subject/in sthg.

**Bewandtnis** (pl -se) die geh: **damit hat es folgende** ~ ... the story behind it is (as follows) ...

**bewässern** vt to irrigate.

**Bewässerung** (pl -en) die irrigation.

**bewegen**[1] (prät **bewegte**; perf **hat bewegt**) vt (reg) - **1**. [gen] to move - **2**. [beschäftigen] to concern, to preoccupy.
➤ **sich bewegen** ref - **1**. [körperlich] to move; [im Freien] to take ODER get some exercise - **2**. [sich verhalten] to act - **3**. [in Gesellschaftsschicht]: **sich in gehobenen Kreisen** ~ to move in lofty circles.

**bewegen**² (*prät* **bewog**; *perf* **hat bewogen**) *vt* (*unreg*) **geh:** jn zu etw ~ [veranlassen] to induce sb to do sthg; [überreden] to prevail upon sb to do sthg.

**beweglich** *adj* agile; [Hebel] movable.

**bewegt** *adj* - **1.** [unruhig - Leben] eventful; [ - See, Meer] choppy - **2.** [Stimme, Worte] emotional.

**Bewegung** (*pl* -**en**) *die* - **1.** [körperlich, politisch] movement; **etw in ~ setzen** to set sthg in motion; **sich in ~ setzen** [Person] *fam* to get moving; [Zug] to start to move - **2.** [körperlich] exercise - **3.** [innerlich] emotion.

**Bewegungsfreiheit** *die* freedom of movement; [Handlungsspielraum] room for manoeuvre.

**bewegungslos** *adj* motionless ⬦ *adv:* **~ dastehen** to stand there motionless.

**beweinen** *vt* to mourn.

**Beweis** (*pl* -**e**) *der:* **ein ~** a piece of evidence; **~e** evidence, proof; **den ~ für etw erbringen** to supply *ODER* provide proof of sthg; **ein schlagender ~** convincing evidence.

**Beweislaufnahme** *die* hearing of evidence.

**beweisbar** *adj* provable.

**beweisen** (*prät* **bewies**; *perf* **hat bewiesen**) *vt* - **1.** [gen] to prove; [Unschuld] to establish - **2.** [Mut] to show.
➥ **sich beweisen** *ref* to prove o.s./itself.

**beweiskräftig** *adj:* **diese Aussage ist nicht ~** this statement does not constitute conclusive proof.

**Beweismaterial** *das* evidence.

**bewenden** (*prät* **bewandte**; *perf* **hat bewandt**) *vt:* **es dabei ~ lassen** to leave it at that.

**bewerben** (*präs* **bewirbt**; *prät* **bewarb**; *perf* **hat beworben**) ➥ **sich bewerben** *ref* to apply; **sich bei einer Firma ~** to apply for a job with a firm; **sich um etw ~** to apply for sthg.

**Bewerber, in** (*mpl* -; *fpl* -**nen**) *der, die* applicant.

**Bewerbung** *die* application.

**Bewerbungslgespräch** *das* interview (*for job, college place*).

**Bewerbungslschreiben** *das* letter of application.

**Bewerbungslunterlagen** *pl* application documents.

**bewerfen** (*präs* **bewirft**; *prät* **bewarf**; *perf* **hat beworfen**) *vt:* **jn/etw mit etw ~** to pelt sb/sthg with sthg.

**bewerkstelligen** *vt* to manage; **wie soll ich das ~?** how am I supposed to do this?

**bewerten** *vt* to assess, to evaluate; [Klassenarbeit] to mark; **etw zu hoch/niedrig ~** to overrate/underrate sthg.

**Bellwertung** *die* assessment, evaluation; [Note] mark.

**bewilligen** *vt* [Antrag] to approve; [Hilfe, Kredit] to grant.

**Bewilligung** (*pl* -**en**) *die* [von Antrag] approval; [von Hilfe, Kredit] granting.

**bewirken** *vt* to cause; **in dieser Sache kann momentan nichts bewirkt werden** nothing can be done about this matter at the moment; **es bewirkte das Gegenteil** it had the opposite effect; **wir haben bewirkt, dass jetzt Nachtbusse eingesetzt werden** we have managed to get them to lay on a night bus service.

**bewirten** *vt* to entertain; **jn mit etw ~** to give sb sthg to eat and drink.

**bewirtschaften** *vt* [Hof] to run; [Acker] to farm.

**Bewirtung** (*pl* -**en**) *die* hospitality.

**bewohnen** *vt* to inhabit.

**Bewohner, in** (*mpl* -; *fpl* -**nen**) *der, die* inhabitant.

**bewölken** ➥ **sich bewölken** *ref* to cloud over.

**bewölkt** *adj* cloudy, overcast.

**Bewölkung** *die* (*ohne pl*) - **1.** clouding over - **2.** [Wolken] clouds (*pl*).

**Bewunderer** (*pl* -) *der* admirer.

**Bewunderin** (*pl* -**nen**) *die* admirer.

**bewundern** *vt* to admire.

**bewundernswert** *adj* admirable ⬦ *adv* admirably.

**Bewunderung** *die* admiration.

**bewusst** *adj* - **1.** [absichtlich] deliberate - **2.** [bedacht] conscious; **ihre Absichten sind mir ~** I am aware of her motives; **ihre Absichten wurden mir ~** I realized what her motives were; **sich** (*D*) **einer Sache** (*G*) **~ sein** to be aware of sthg - **3.** [fraglich]: **an dem ~en Abend** on the evening in question ⬦ *adv* - **1.** [absichtlich] deliberately - **2.** [bedacht] consciously.

**bewusstlos** *adj* unconscious.

**Bewusstlosigkeit** *die* (state of) unconsciousness.

**bewusst machen** *vt:* **jm etw ~** to make sb aware of sthg; **sich** (*D*) **etw ~** to realize sthg.

**Bewusstsein** *das* - **1.** [Wissen] awareness - **2.** [geistige Klarheit] consciousness; **bei ~ sein** to be conscious; **das ~ verlieren** to lose consciousness.

**bez.** (*abk für* **bezahlt**) paid.

**Bez.** - **1.** *abk für* **Bezeichnung** - **2.** *abk für* **Bezirk.**

**bezahlen** *vt* [Ware, Leistung] to pay for; [Person, Miete, Rechnung] to pay ⬦ *vi* to pay; **wir möchten bitte ~!** may we have the bill please?

**bezahlt** *adj* paid; **die Mühe machte sich ~ the** effort paid off.

**Bezahlung** *die* - **1.** [von Ware, Rechnung] payment - **2.** [Entgelt] pay.

**bezaubern** *vt* to captivate.

**bezaubernd** *adj* captivating <> *adv* captivatingly.

**bezeichnen** *vt* - **1.** [nennen] to call; **jn/etw als etw ~** to describe sb/sthg as sthg - **2.** [markieren] to mark, to indicate.

**bezeichnend** *adj* characteristic; **~ für etw sein** to be characteristic of sthg.

**Be|zeichnung** *die* - **1.** [Benennung] name; [Beschreibung] description - **2.** [Markierung] marking.

**bezeugen** *vt* to testify to; **urkundlich bezeugt** documented.

**bezichtigen** *vt*: **jn einer Sache** *(G)* **~ geh** to accuse sb of sthg.

**beziehbar** *adj* [Haus] ready to be moved into.

**beziehen** (*prät* **bezog**; *perf* **hat bezogen**) *vt* - **1.** [Kissen, Sofa] to cover; **das Bett frisch ~ to** change the bedclothes - **2.** [Haus, Wohnung] to move into - **3.** [Ware, Zeitung, Einkünfte] to get; [Arbeitslosenhilfe] to receive - **4.** MIL [Stellung] to take up - **5.** [anwenden]: **etw auf sich** *(A)* **/jn ~** to understand sthg to refer to o.s./to sb; **eine Aussage auf sich** *(A)* **~ to take a remark personally.

➤ **sich beziehen** *ref* - **1.** [angewendet werden]: **sich auf jn/etw ~ to** refer to sb/sthg; **meine Kritik bezog sich nicht auf Sie** my criticism wasn't aimed at you - **2.** [sich berufen]: **sich auf etw** *(A)* **~ to** refer to sthg - **3.** [sich bewölken]: **der Himmel bezieht sich the** sky is clouding over.

**Be|ziehung** *die* - **1.** [Kontakt - zu Person] relationship; **~en** [politisch] relations; **gute/ schlechte ~en zu jm haben** to be on good/bad terms with sb; **er verfügt über gute ~en** he has lots of contacts - **2.** [Verhältnis] connection - **3.** [Hinsicht] respect; **in dieser/jeder ~** in this/every respect.

**beziehungsweise** *konj* - **1.** [genauer gesagt] or rather, that is - **2.** [oder] or; **die Kinder sind ins Kino, ~ ins Schwimmbad gegangen** the children have either gone to the cinema or gone swimming - **3.** [jeweils] and ... respectively; **die Uhren kosten 150 ~ 200 Euro** the watches cost 150 euros and 200 euros respectively.

**Bezirk** (*pl* -e) *der* district; [von Kirche] diocese.

**Bezug** (*pl* **Bezüge**) *der* - **1.** [Überzug] cover - **2.** [von Haus, Wohnung] entry, moving in - **3.** [Kauf] purchase; [von Tageszeitung] subscription - **4.** [Beziehung]: **auf etw** *(A)* **~ nehmen** *amt* to refer to sthg; **in ~ auf etw** *(A)* with regard to sthg.

➤ **Bezüge** *pl* income *(U)*.

**bezüglich** *präp amt*: **~ einer Sache** *(G)* concerning sthg <> *adj* [Fürwort] relative.

**Bezugs|person** *die person to whom one looks for guidance, support etc.*

**bezuschussen** *vt* to fund, to subsidize.

**bezwecken** *vt*: **etw mit etw ~ to** aim to achieve sthg by sthg.

**bezweifeln** *vt* to doubt.

**bezwingen** (*prät* **bezwang**; *perf* **hat bezwungen**) *vt* [Konkurrenz, Gegner] to defeat; [Berg] to conquer; [Wille, Gefühle] to keep under control.

**BfA** ['beːfaː] (*abk für* **Bundesversicherungsanstalt für Angestellte**) *die Federal Social Insurance Office for Salaried Employees.*

**BGB** [beːgeːˈbeː] (*abk für* **Bürgerliches Gesetzbuch**) *das German civil code.*

**BGH** [beːgeːˈhaː] (*abk für* **Bundesgerichtshof**) *der Federal Supreme Court.*

**BGS** [beːgeːˈɛs] (*abk für* **Bundesgrenzschutz**) *der Federal border guard.*

**BH** [beːˈhaː] (*pl* -**s**) (*abk für* **Büstenhalter**) *der* bra.

**Bhf.** *abk für* **Bahnhof.**

**Bibel** (*pl* -**n**) *die* bible.

**Biber** (*pl* -) *der* [Tier] beaver <> *der* ODER *das* [Stoff] flannelette.

**Bibliografie, Bibliographie** (*pl* -**n**) *die* bibliography.

**bibliografisch, bibliographisch** *adj* bibliographical.

**Bibliothek** (*pl* -**en**) *die* library.

**Bibliothekar, in** (*mpl* -**e**; *fpl* -**nen**) *der, die* librarian.

**biblisch** *adj* biblical.

**bieder** *adj* - **1.** *abw* [spießig - Person, Verhalten] bourgeois; [ - Kleidung, Einrichtung] conventional - **2.** [Person - anständig] decent, upright <> *adv abw* conventionally.

**Biedermeier** *das* Biedermeier period.

**biegen** (*prät* **bog**; *perf* **hat/ist gebogen**) *vt (hat)* to bend <> *vi (ist)* [Auto, Fahrer]: **um die Ecke ~ to** go round the corner.

➤ **sich biegen** *ref* to bend.

**biegsam** *adj* flexible, pliable.

**Biegsamkeit** *die* flexibility, pliability.

**Biegung** (*pl* -**en**) *die* bend.

**Biene** (*pl* -**n**) *die* bee.

**Bienen|honig** *der* natural honey.

**Bienen|königin** *die* queen bee.

**Bienen|stich** *der* - **1.** [Insektenstich] bee-sting - **2.** [Gebäck] *cake covered in flaked almonds and sugar, filled with cream or confectioner's custard.*

**Bienen|wachs** *das* beeswax.

**Bier** (pl -e) das beer; **ein großes/kleines ~** a half-litre/30 cl glass of beer; **~ vom Fass** draught beer; **das ist nicht dein ~!** fam fig that is none of your business!

**Bier|deckel** der beer mat.

**Bier|dose** die beer can.

**bierernst** fam adj deadly serious ◇ adv with deadly seriousness.

**Bier|flasche** die beer bottle.

**Bier|garten** der beer garden.

**Bier|glas** das beer glass.

**Bier|krug** der beer mug.

**Bier|zelt** das beer tent.

**Biest** (pl -er) das beast.

**bieten** (prät **bot**; perf **hat geboten**) vt - **1.** [anbieten] to offer; [Schutz, Chance] to provide; **zu ~ haben** to have a lot to offer; **jm etw ~** to offer sb sthg; [Gelegenheit, Schutz] to provide sb with sthg - **2.** [zeigen] to present; **einen schrecklichen Anblick ~** to look terrible - **3.** [gefallen]: **sich** (D) **etw nicht ~ lassen** not to stand for sthg.
◆ **sich bieten** ref: **es bot sich eine Gelegenheit** an opportunity came up.

**Bikini** (pl -s) der bikini.

**Bilanz** (pl -en) die - **1.** WIRTSCH balance; [schriftlich] balance sheet - **2.** [Ergebnis] outcome; **~ ziehen (aus etw)** [schlussfolgernd] to draw conclusions (about sthg); [zusammenfassend] to take stock (of sthg).

**bilateral** adv bilateral.

**Bild** (pl -er) das - **1.** [gen & TV] picture; [Gemälde] painting; [Zeichnung] drawing; [Foto] photograph - **2.** [Anblick] sight; **ein ~ für die Götter** a sight for sore eyes - **3.** [Vorstellung] idea, impression; **ein schwaches ~** fam a poor showing; **sich** (D) **ein ~ von jm/etw machen** to get an idea of sb/sthg - **4.** [Metapher] image - **5.** RW: **jn (über etw** (A)**) ins ~ setzen** to put sb in the

picture (about sthg); **(über etw** (A)**) im ~e sein** to be in the picture (about sthg).

**Bildband** (pl -bände) der coffee-table book.

**bilden** vt - **1.** [gen] to form - **2.** [Kapital] to build up - **3.** [ausbilden] to educate ◇ vi: **lesen bildet** reading improves your mind.
◆ **sich bilden** ref - **1.** [sich formen] to form - **2.** [sich informieren] to educate o.s.

**Bilder|buch** das picture book.

**Bilder|rahmen** der picture frame.

**Bild|fläche** die: **auf der ~ erscheinen** to appear on the scene; **von der ~ verschwinden** to disappear from the scene.

**Bild|hauer, in** (mpl -; fpl -nen) der, die sculptor (f sculptress).

**Bild|hauerei** (pl -en) die sculpture.

**bildhübsch** adj lovely.

**bildlich** adj - **1.** [Darstellung] pictorial - **2.** [Wendung, Ausdruck] figurative ◇ adv - **1.** [darstellen] pictorially - **2.** [gesprochen] figuratively.

**Bildnis** (pl -se) das portrait.

**Bild|schirm** der screen.

**Bildschirmschoner** (pl -) der EDV screen saver.

**Bildschirm|text** der TV German teletext system.

**bildschön** adj stunning.

**Bildung** (pl -en) die - **1.** [Ausbildung] education; **eine umfassende ~ besitzen** to be well-educated ODER cultured - **2.** [Formung] formation.

**Bildungsgrad** der level of education.

**Bildungs|politik** die education policy.

**Bildungs|urlaub** der time off for training.

**Bildungs|weg** der: **der zweite ~** second chance for people outside the education system to obtain educational qualifications.

**Bild|zeitung** die Bild.

**Billard** ['bɪljart] das billiards (U).

**billig** adj - **1.** [preiswert] cheap - **2.** abw [schlecht - Anzug, Papier, Scherz, Trick] cheap; [ - Ausrede] feeble; **ein ~er Trost** small comfort ◇ adv cheaply; **die Vase habe ich ~ gekauft** I got the vase cheap.

**Billig|angebot** das special offer.

**billigen** vt to approve.

**Billig|flug** der cheap flight.

**Billiglohn|land** das: Arbeiter aus Billiglohn-länder wie Indonesien cheap labour from countries like Indonesia.

**Billigung** (pl -en) die approval.

**Billig|ware** die cheap goods (pl).

**Billion** (pl -en) die trillion, billion Br.

**bimmeln** vi to ring.

**Bims|stein** der pumice-stone.

**bin** präs ▷ **sein.**

**Binde** (pl -n) die - **1.** [Verband] bandage - **2.** [über den Augen] blindfold; [um den Arm] armband; **den Arm in einer ~ tragen** to have one's arm in a sling; **sich** (D) **einen hinter die ~ gießen** fam to have a couple of drinks - **3.** [Damenbinde] sanitary towel.

**Binde|gewebe** das connective tissue.

**Binde|glied** das link.

**Binde|haut** die conjunctiva.

**Bindehaut|entzündung** die conjunctivitis (U).

**Binde|mittel** das binding agent.

**binden** (prät band; perf hat gebunden) vt - **1.** [zusammenbinden] to tie together - **2.** [festbinden]: **etw an etw** (A) **~** to tie sthg to sthg - **3.** [Krawatte] to knot; [Schleife, Knoten] to tie - **4.** [Soße, Buch, durch Vertrag] to bind ◇ vi to bind.

➤ **sich binden** ref [heiraten] to get married.

**bindend** adj binding ◇ adv: **~ zusagen** to commit o.s.

**Binde|strich** der hyphen.

**Bind|faden** der string; **es regnet Bindfäden** fig it's raining cats and dogs.

**Bindung** (pl -en) die - **1.** [Verbundenheit] bond; [Verpflichtung] commitment - **2.** [Skibindung] binding.

**binnen** präp (+G, +D) within.

**Binnen|hafen** der river port.

**Binnen|handel** der [eines Landes] domestic trade; [eines Staatenbundes] internal trade.

**Binnen|markt** der internal market; [von EU] single market; **der europäische ~** the European single market.

**Binse** (pl -n) die rush; **in die ~n gehen** fam [Plan] to fall through; [Geld] to go down the drain; [Fahrrad, Gerät] to pack it in.

**Binsen|weisheit** die truism.

**Biochemie** die biochemistry.

**Biolchemiker, in** der, die biochemist.

**biochemisch** adj biochemical.

**Biografie, Biographie** (pl -n) die biography.

**Biokost** die health food.

**Biolladen** der health food shop.

**Biologe** (pl -n) der biologist.

**Biologie** die biology.

**Biologin** (pl -nen) die biologist.

**biologisch** adj - **1.** [der Biologie] biological - **2.** [natürlich - Farben] natural; [ - Brot] organic.

**Biolmasse** die biomass.

**Biolphysik** die biophysics (U).

**Biolphysiker, in** der, die biophysicist.

**Biolrhythmus** der biorhythm.

**Biotop** (pl -e) der ODER das biotope.

**BIP** [beːiːˈpeː] (abk für **Bruttoinlandsprodukt**) das GDP.

**bipolar** adj bipolar.

**birgt** präs ▷ **bergen.**

**Birke** (pl -n) die birch.

**Birma** nt Burma.

**Birn|baum** der pear tree.

**Birne** (pl -n) die - **1.** [Frucht] pear - **2.** [Glühbirne] light bulb - **3.** fam [Kopf] nut.

**birst** präs ▷ **bersten.**

**bis** präp (+ A) - **1.** [zeitlich] until; **wir bleiben ~ morgen** we're staying until tomorrow; **von Montag ~ Freitag** from Monday to Friday, Monday through Friday Am; **zwei ~ drei Tage** two to three days; **~ auf weiteres** until further notice; **~ bald!** see you soon!; **~ dann!** see you then!; **~ morgen/später!** see you tomorrow/later! - **2.** [spätestens] by; **das muss ~ Mittwoch fertig sein** it must be ready by Wednesday - **3.** [räumlich] to; **es sind noch 200 km ~ Berlin** there are still 200 km to Berlin; **~ auf die Haut durchnässt** soaked to the skin ◇ konj until; **warte, ~ ich komme** wait until I'm there.

➤ **bis auf** präp (+ A) except for, apart from.

➤ **bis zu** präp up to; **~ zu 20 Personen** up to 20 people.

**Bischof** (pl Bischöfe) der bishop.

**bischöflich** adj episcopal.

**Bischofs|konferenz** die conference of bishops.

**Bischofs|sitz** der episcopal see.

**bisexuell** adj bisexual.

**Bisexuelle** (pl -n) der, die bisexual.

**bisher** adv: **~ hat sie nicht angerufen** she hasn't called so far; **wir haben das ~ immer so gemacht** until now we've always done it this way.

**bisherig** adj [ehemalig] former; **sein ~es Verhalten** his behaviour up to now.

**Biskaya** die Biscay.

**Biskuit** [bisˈkviːt] (pl -s ODER -e) der ODER das sponge.

**bislang** adv: **~ hat sie nicht angerufen** she

hasn't called so far; **wir haben das ~ immer so gemacht** until now we've always done it this way.

**Bison** (pl -s) der bison.

**biss** prät ⊏▷ **beißen.**

**Biss** (pl -e) der eigtl & fig bite.

**bisschen** adj [wenig]: **das ~ Regen macht doch nichts** that little bit of rain won't do any harm.

▸ **das bisschen** pron: **das ~ kannst du jetzt auch noch essen** you can eat that little bit up.

▸ **ein bisschen** adj [etwas] a bit of, a little; **ein ~ Kaffee** a drop of coffee ◇ adv [ein wenig] a bit; **ein ~ bleiben** to stay a while.

▸ **kein bisschen** ◇ adj: **wir haben kein ~ Brot** we have no bread at all ◇ adv [nicht] not at all.

▸ **ach du liebes bisschen** interj oh, dear!

**Bissen** (pl -) der [Stück] bite; **er rührte keinen ~ an** he didn't touch ODER eat a thing; **mir blieb der ~ im Hals(e) stecken** I nearly fell over (with surprise).

**bissig** adj eigtl & fig vicious; 'Vorsicht, ~er Hund' 'beware of the dog'.

**Bissigkeit** (pl -en) die eigtl & fig viciousness.

**bist** präs ⊏▷ **sein.**

**Bistum** (pl -tümer) das diocese.

**bisweilen** adv geh [gelegentlich, manchmal] sometimes.

**Bit** (pl -s) das EDV bit.

**bitte** adv please ◇ interj - **1.** [als Bitte, Aufforderung] please; **bedient euch, ~!** please help yourselves!; **~! Hier ist Ihr Kaffee!** here's your coffee for you; **~ sehr! Kommen Sie herein!** (do) come in!; **~ schön! was möchten Sie kaufen?** yes Sir/Madam, how can I help you? - **2.** [als Antwort]: **danke! - ~!** thanks! - don't mention it!; **Entschuldigung! - ~!** sorry! - that's all right!; **kann ich nur einen Apfel nehmen? - ~!** may I have an apple? - of course!; **~ sehr** ODER **schön!** [Antwort auf einen Dank] don't mention it!, you're welcome! - **3.** [als Nachfrage] pardon?, sorry?; **wie ~?** pardon?, sorry? - **4.** [am Telefon]: **ja ~?** hello? - **5.** [zur Selbstbestätigung]: **na ~!** there you are, you see!

**Bitte** (pl -n) die [Anliegen] request; **eine ~ an jn richten** [geh] to make a request to sb; **eine ~ um etw** a request for sthg.

**bitten** (prät bat; perf hat gebeten) vt - **1.** [höflich auffordern]: **jn ~, etw zu tun** to ask sb to do sthg; **ich bitte Sie, etwas leiser zu sein!** please be a little quieter!; **jn um etw ~** to ask sb for sthg; **ich bitte Sie um Aufmerksamkeit!** may I have your attention, please! - **2.** [einladen]: **jn zu sich ~** to ask sb to come to one; **jn zum Essen ~** geh to invite sb to dinner; **(aber) ich ~ Sie!** [drückt Unverständnis aus] come on! ◇ vi - **1.** [Bitte aussprechen]: **um etw ~** to ask for sthg; **ich bitte**

**um Ruhe!** silence, please!; **~ und betteln** to beg and plead - **2.** [einladen]: **ich bitte zu Tisch!** geh dinner is served! - **3.** RW: **da muss ich doch sehr ~!** I really must protest!; **wenn ich ~ darf!** if you don't mind!

**bitter** adj - **1.** [gen] bitter - **2.** [Ironie] biting - **3.** [Not] desperate; [Armut] abject ◇ adv - **1.** [gen] bitterly; **~ schmecken** to taste bitter - **2.** [benötigen] desperately.

**bitterböse** adj furious ◇ adv furiously.

**Bitterkeit** die eigtl & fig bitterness.

**bitterlich** adv bitterly; **~ frieren** to be bitterly cold.

**Biwak** (pl -s ODER -e) das bivouac.

**bizarr** adj bizarre.

**Bizeps** (pl -e) der biceps (sg).

**BKA** [be:ka:'a:] (abk für **Bundeskriminalamt**) das Federal Office for criminal investigation.

**Blabla** das fam abw waffle.

**Black-out, Blackout** ['blɛkaut] (pl -s) der ODER das [Gedächtnisausfall] blackout.

**blähen** vt [Segel] to fill; [Nüstern] to flare ◇ vi [Blähungen machen] to cause flatulence.

▸ **sich blähen** ref [Segel, Vorhang] to billow.

**Blähungen** pl wind (U).

**Blamage** [bla'ma:ʒə] (pl -n) die disgrace.

**blamieren** vt [kompromittieren] to disgrace.

▸ **sich blamieren** ref [sich bloßstellen] to disgrace o.s.

**blank** adj - **1.** [glänzend] shiny - **2.** [pur] sheer, pure - **3.** [unbedeckt] bare; **~ sein** fam to be broke.

**Blankoscheck** der blank cheque.

**Blase** (pl -n) die - **1.** [auf der Haut] blister; **sich** (D) **~n laufen** to get blisters on one's feet - **2.** [Luftblase] bubble - **3.** [Harnblase] bladder.

**Blasebalg** (pl -bälge) der bellows (pl).

**blasen** (präs bläst; prät blies; perf hat geblasen) vt - **1.** [gen] to blow; **jm was ~** fam to tell sb to get lost - **2.** vulg: **jm einen ~** to give sb a blow job ◇ vi - **1.** [gen] to blow; **es bläst** fam it's windy - **2.** [auf Trompete, Horn] to play.

**Bläser, in** (mpl -; fpl -nen) der, die [Musiker] wind (instrument) player; **die ~** the wind section.

**blasiert** abw adj blasé ◇ adv in a blasé manner.

**blies**

**Blas|instrument** *das* wind instrument.

**Blas|kapelle** *die* brass band.

**Blas|musik** *die* brass band music.

**blass** (*kompar* **blasser** ODER **blässer;** *superl* **blasseste** ODER **blässeste**) *adj* - **1.** [Haut] pale - **2.** [Erinnerung, Ahnung] vague; [Hoffnung] faint.

**Blässe** *die* paleness.

**bläst** *präs* ⊏▷ **blasen.**

**Blatt** (*pl* **Blätter**) *das* - **1.** [von Pflanzen] leaf - **2.** [Papier] sheet - **3.** [Seite] page - **4.** [Zeitung] paper - **5.** *RW:* **ein unbeschriebenes ~ sein** [unbekannt] to be an unknown quantity; [unerfahren] to be inexperienced; **kein ~ vor den Mund nehmen** not to mince one's words; **das ~ hat sich gewendet** the tide has turned; **das steht auf einem anderen ~** that is another matter.

**blättern** (*perf* **hat/ist geblättert**) *vi* - **1.** (*hat*) [umschlagen]: **in etw** (*D*) **~** to leaf through sthg - **2.** (*ist*) [abblättern] to flake (off) <▷ *vt* (*hat*) [Geldscheine] to count out.

**Blätter|teig** *der* puff pastry.

**Blatt|laus** *die* aphid, greenfly.

**Blatt|pflanze** *die* green plant.

**blau** (*kompar* **blauer;** *superl* **blau(e)ste**) *adj* - **1.** [Farbe] blue - **2.** [geprellt]: **ein ~es Auge** a black eye; **ein ~er Fleck** a bruise - **3.** [betrunken]: **~ sein** *fam* to be sloshed - **4.** [geschwänzt] *fam:* **einen ~en Montag machen** to skip ODER skive off *Br* work on Monday.

**Blau** *das* [Farbe] blue.

**blauäugig** *adj* - **1.** [Augen] blue-eyed - **2.** [naiv] naïve.

**Blau|beere** *die* bilberry, blueberry.

**Blaue** (*pl* -n) *das* - **1.** [Farbe] blue - **2.** [Unbekannte]: **ins ~** [fahren] with no particular place to go; [reden] aimlessly - **3.** *RW:* **das ~ vom Himmel lügen** *fam* to tell a pack of lies <▷ *der fam* [Hundertmarkschein] *a one-hundred-mark note.*

**Blau|helm** *der* blue beret.

**bläulich** *adj* bluish.

**Blau|licht** *das* [Signal] flashing blue light *(on ambulance etc.)*.

**blau|machen** *vi fam* [schwänzen] to stay away from school/work.

**Blausäure** *die* prussic acid.

**Blazer** ['bleːzɐ] (*pl* -) *der* blazer.

**Blech** (*pl* -e) *das* - **1.** [Metall] sheet metal - **2.** [Backblech] baking sheet *Br*, cookie sheet *Am* - **3.** *fam* [Unsinn] rubbish; **~ reden** to talk rubbish.

**Blech|dose** *die* tin, can.

**blechen** *fam vt* & *vi* to fork out.

**blechern** *adj* - **1.** [aus Blech] tin - **2.** [Klang] tinny.

**Blech|instrument** *das* brass instrument.

**Blech|schaden** *der* bodywork damage *(U).*

**Blei** *das* [Metall] lead.

**Bleibe** (*pl* -n) *die* place to stay.

**bleiben** (*prät* **blieb;** *perf* **ist geblieben**) *vi* - **1.** [an einem Ort] to stay; **wo bleibst du denn so lange?** [bei Eintreffen] what kept you? - **2.** [in einem Zustand] to remain; **sie ist ganz die Alte geblieben** she hasn't changed a bit; **wir ~ in Kontakt** we keep in touch; **bei etw ~** to stick to sthg; **es bleibt also dabei, morgen um zehn Uhr** ten o'clock tomorrow morning, like we said, then?; **das bleibt unter uns** it's strictly between ourselves - **3.** [als Übriges] to be left; **uns ~ nur noch wenige Tage** we only have a few days left.

**bleibend** *adj* lasting.

**bleiben lassen** *vt* (*unreg*) - **1.** [unterlassen] to leave be - **2.** [aufgeben] to give up.

**bleich** *adj* pale.

**bleichen** (*perf* **hat/ist gebleicht**) *vt* (*hat*) to bleach <▷ *vi* (*ist*) to fade.

**bleiern** *adj* - **1.** [aus Blei] lead - **2.** [schwer] leaden.

**bleifrei** *adj* unleaded.

**Bleigießen** *das New Year's Eve custom of telling fortunes from shapes produced by pouring molten lead into water.*

**Blei|stift** *der* pencil.

**Bleistiftspitzer** (*pl* -) *der* pencil sharpener.

**Blende** (*pl* -n) *die* - **1.** [vor Fenster] blind, screen; AUTO visor - **2.** [FOTO - Objektivöffnung] diaphragm; [ - Blendenzahl] aperture.

**blenden** *vt eigtl* & *fig* to dazzle <▷ *vi* [Licht] to be dazzling.

**blendend** *adj* dazzling <▷ *adv* marvellously; **du siehst ~ aus!** you look dazzling!

**Blick** (*pl* -e) *der* - **1.** [der Augen] look; [kurz] glance; **den ~ heben/senken** to raise/lower one's eyes; **einen ~ auf etw** (*A*) **werfen** to glance at sthg; **auf den ersten ~** at first sight; **einen ~ riskieren** to risk a (quick) peep; **sie würdigte mich/es keines ~es** she did not deign to look at me/it - **2.** [Ausblick] view - **3.** [Urteil] eye - **4.** *RW:* **einen ~ hinter die Kulissen werfen** to take a look behind the scenes; **keinen ~ für etw haben** not to appreciate sthg.

**blicken** *vi* to look; **sich (nicht) ~ lassen** (not) to show one's face; **das lässt tief ~** that explains a lot.

**Blick|fang** *der* eye-catcher.

**Blick|feld** *das* field of vision.

**Blick|punkt** *der:* **im ~ der Öffentlichkeit** in the public eye.

**Blick|winkel** *der* point of view.

**blieb** *prät* ⊏▷ **bleiben.**

**blies** *prät* ⊏▷ **blasen.**

**blind** *adj* - **1.** [gen] blind; ~ **für etw sein** to be blind to sthg - **2.** [Spiegel] cloudy; [Metall] tarnished - **3.** [versteckt] ⊳ **Passagier** - **4.** [falsch] ⊳ **Alarm** ⬦ *adv* blindly.

**Blind|darm** *der* appendix.

**Blinddarm|entzündung** *die* appendicitis *(U)*.

**Blinde** *(pl* **-n)** *der, die* blind man *(f* blind woman).

**Blindekuh** *die:* ~ **spielen** to play blind man's buff.

**Blinden|schrift** *die* braille

**Blind|gänger** *der* - **1.** [Geschoss] dud - **2.** [Versager] dead loss.

**Blindheit** *die eigtl* & *fig* blindness.

**blindlings** *adv* blindly.

**Blindschleiche** *(pl* **-n)** *die* slow-worm.

**blinken** *vi* - **1.** [funkeln - Metall] to gleam; [ - Sterne] to twinkle; [ - Wasser, Edelstein] to sparkle - **2.** [signalisieren - Verkehr] to indicate; [Signal geben] to signal.

**Blinker** *(pl* **-)** *der* indicator *Br*, turn signal *Am*.

**Blink|licht** *das* flashing light.

**Blink|zeichen** *das:* ~ **geben** to flash a signal.

**blinzeln** *vi* [mit einem Auge, als Zeichen] to wink; [mit beiden Augen] to blink.

**Blitz** *(pl* **-e)** *der* - **1.** [am Himmel] lightning *(U); ein* ~ **a** flash of lightning; **wie der** ~ like lightning; **wie ein** ~ **aus heiterem Himmel** like a bolt from the blue; **wie vom** ~ **getroffen** thunderstruck - **2.** [Blitzlicht] flash.

**Blitzableiter** *(pl* **-)** *der* lightning conductor.

**blitzblank** *adj* [Geschirr] sparkling clean; [Wohnung] spotless ⬦ *adv:* **die Wohnung** ~ **putzen** to clean the flat until it is spotless.

**blitzen** *vi* - **1.** [am Himmel]: **es blitzt** there is lightning - **2.** [funkeln - Schmuck, Wohnung] to sparkle; [ - Metall] to gleam - **3.** [in den Augen]: **Ärger blitzte aus ihren Augen** her eyes flashed with anger ⬦ *vt fam* [fotografieren] to take a flash photo of; **geblitzt werden** to be caught by a speed camera.

**Blitz|gerät** *das* - **1.** [zur Verkehrsüberwachung] speed camera - **2.** [von Fotoapparat] flash.

**Blitz|krieg** *der* blitzkrieg.

**Blitz|licht** *das* flash.

**Blitz|schlag** *der* flash of lightning; **vom** ~ **getroffen werden** to be struck by lightning.

**blitzschnell** *adj* lightning ⬦ *adv* like lightning.

**Block** *(pl* **Blöcke** *ODER* **-s)** *der* - **1.** *(pl* Blöcke) [Stück] block - **2.** *(pl* Blöcke) [aus Papier] pad - **3.** *(pl* Blöcke, Blocks) [Häuserblock] block - **4.** *(pl* Blocks) [Gruppe - von Staaten] bloc; [Fraktion] faction.

**Blockade** *(pl* **-n)** *die* blockade.

**Block|flöte** *die* recorder.

**Block|haus** *das* log cabin.

**blockieren** *vt* - **1.** EDV [versperren] to block - **2.** [zum Stillstand bringen] to obstruct ⬦ *vi* [Motor] to jam; [Räder] to lock.

**Block|schrift** *die* block capitals *(pl)*.

**blöd, blöde** *fam adj* stupid ⬦ *adv* stupidly.

**blödeln** *vi* to fool around.

**Blödsinn** *der fam* rubbish.

**blödsinnig** *fam adj* stupid ⬦ *adv* stupidly.

**blöken** *vi* to bleat.

**blond** *adj* blond *(f* blonde).

**blondieren** *vt* [Haare] to bleach.

**Blondine** *(pl* **-n)** *die* blonde.

**bloß** *adv* - **1.** *fam* [lediglich] only, just; **jetzt** ~ **noch etwas drehen** now just turn it some more - **2.** [zum Ausdruck von Ratlosigkeit]: **was sollen wir** ~ **machen?** what on earth shall we do? - **3.** [zum Ausdruck von Ärger]: **warum musstest du** ~ **den Schlüssel stecken lassen?** why did you have to go and leave the key in the lock?; **wenn du doch** ~ **pünktlich sein könntest!** if you could just be on time for once! - **4.** [zum Ausdruck einer Drohung]: **hau** ~ **ab!** just push off, all right?; **unterschreib das** ~ **nicht!** don't you dare sign that! - **5.** [zum Ausdruck einer Aufforderung]: ~ **keine Panik!** just don't panic! - **6.** [zum Ausdruck eines Wunsches]: **hätte ich** ~ **nichts gesagt!** if only I hadn't said anything! ⬦ *adj* - **1.** [nackt] bare; **mit** ~**en Füßen** barefoot; **mit** ~**em Auge** with the naked eye - **2.** [rein] sheer.

**Blöße** *(pl* **-n)** *die:* **jm eine** ~ **bieten** to reveal a weak spot to sb; **sich** *(D)* **eine/keine** ~ **geben** to reveal/not to reveal a weak spot.

**bloß|stellen** *vt* to show up; [Betrüger] to unmask.

**Blouson** [blu'zõ] *(pl* **-s)** *der ODER das* [Jacke] bomber jacket.

**Bluejeans** ['bluːdʒiːns] *pl* jeans.

**Blues** [bluːs] *der* - **1.** *(ohne pl)* [Musikrichtung] the blues *(pl); er spielt* ~ he plays the blues - **2.** [Musikstück] blues number.

**Bluff** [blœf] *(pl* **-s)** *der abw* bluff.

**bluffen** [blœfn] *abw vt* & *vi* to bluff.

**blühen** *vi* - **1.** [Pflanze] to bloom, to flower; [Baum] to blossom - **2.** [florieren] to flourish - **3.** *fam* [drohen]: **das kann dir auch noch** ~**!** you could still be in for it!

**blühend** *adj* - **1.** [Pflanze] blooming, flowering; [tree] blossoming - **2.** [frisch] radiant - **3.** [ausufernd]: **eine** ~**e Fantasie** a vivid imagination.

**Blume** *(pl* **-n)** *die* - **1.** [Pflanze] flower; **etw durch die** ~ **sagen** *fig* to say sthg in a roundabout way - **2.** [des Weins] bouquet - **3.** [des Bieres] head.

**Blumen|beet** das flowerbed.

**Blumen|händler, in** der, die florist.

**Blumen|kasten** der window box.

**Blumen|kohl** der cauliflower.

**Blumen|strauß** der bunch of flowers.

**Blumen|topf** der flowerpot; **damit kannst du keinen ~ gewinnen!** that won't get you anywhere!

**blumig** adj flowery.

**Bluse** (pl -n) die blouse.

**Blut** das blood; **~ spenden** to give blood; **venöses/arterielles ~** venous/arterial blood; **~ stillend** styptic; **~ (und Wasser) schwitzen** to have a nerve-racking time; **jn bis aufs ~ reizen** to push sb to the limit; **es liegt ihr im ~** it's in her blood; **ruhig ~ bewahren** to keep calm.

**Blut|abnahme** die blood test.

**blutarm** adj anaemic.

**Blut|bad** das bloodbath.

**Blut|bank** (pl -en) die blood bank.

**Blut|bild** das blood test results (pl).

**Blut|blase** die blood blister.

**Blut|druck** der blood pressure.

**blutdrucksenkend** adj antihypertensive.

**Blüte** (pl -n) die - **1.** [Pflanzenteil] flower, bloom; [von Baum] blossom - **2.** [das Blühen] flowering, blooming; [von Baum] blossoming; **in voller ~ stehen** to be in full flower; [Baum] to be in full blossom - **3.** [Aufschwung] flowering.

**Blutegel** (pl -) der leech.

**bluten** vi to bleed; **aus der Nase ~** to have a nosebleed.

**Bluter, in** (mpl -; fpl -nen) der, die haemophiliac.

**Blut|erguss** der [MED] haematoma; [blauer Fleck] bruise.

**Bluterkrankheit** die haemophilia.

**Blüte|zeit** die - **1.** [von Pflanze] flowering period - **2.** [von Kultur, Reich] heyday.

**Blut|gefäß** das blood vessel.

**Blut|gruppe** die blood group.

**Bluthochdruck** der high blood pressure.

**blutig** adj bloody <> adv - **1.** [befleckt]: **jn ~ schlagen** to beat sb to a pulp - **2.** [niederschlagen] bloodily.

**Blut|konserve** die unit of stored blood (for transfusions etc.).

**Blut|körperchen** (pl -) das corpuscle; **weiße/rote ~** white/red blood cells.

**Blut|kreislauf** der blood circulation.

**Blut|probe** die - **1.** [Untersuchung] blood test - **2.** [entnommenes Blut] blood sample.

**Blut|rache** die vendetta.

**blutrot** adj blood-red.

**Blut|spender, in** der, die blood donor.

**blutstillend** adj ⊳ Blut.

**blutsverwandt** adj related by blood.

**Blut|übertragung** die blood transfusion.

**Blutung** (pl -en) die bleeding; [MED] haemorrhage; [Monatsblutung] period.

**blutunterlaufen** adj bloodshot.

**Blut|vergiftung** die blood poisoning.

**Blut|verlust** der loss of blood.

**Blut|wurst** die black pudding Br, blood sausage Am.

**BLZ** abk für **Bankleitzahl.**

**b-Moll** das B flat minor.

**BND** [beːʔɛnˈdeː] (abk für **Bundesnachrichtendienst**) der German national intelligence agency.

**Bö** = **Böe.**

**Boa** (pl -s) die [Schlange, Schal] boa.

**Bob** (pl -s) der SPORT bobsleigh.

**Bock** (pl Böcke) der - **1.** [Kaninchen, Reh] buck; [Ziege] billy-goat; [Schaf] ram; **stur wie ein ~** as stubborn as a mule; **steif wie ein ~** as stiff as a board; **ein geiler ~** salopp a randy old goat - **2.** SPORT (vaulting) horse - **3.** [Gerüst] trestle - **4.** RW: **den ~ zum Gärtner machen** to choose the wrong person for the job; **einen ~ schießen** to slip up; **darauf hab ich keinen Bock** I can't be fagged.

**Bock|bier** das bock, strong dark beer.

**bockig** adj [störrisch] stubborn; [trotzig] contrary <> adv [störrisch] stubbornly; [trotzig] contrarily.

**Bockshorn** das: **jn ins ~ jagen** to put the wind up sb.

**Bockspringen** das - **1.** SPORT vaulting - **2.** [Spiel] leapfrog.

**Bock|wurst** die type of pork sausage, usually boiled and eaten in a bread roll with mustard.

**Boden** (pl -) der - **1.** [Grund] ground; [Erdreich] soil; **auf deutschem ~** on German soil; **er hat den ~ unter den Füßen verloren** [beim Klettern] he lost his footing; [im Leben] his world has fallen apart - **2.** [Fußboden] floor; **zu ~ gehen** [im Boxsport] to go down - **3.** [von Gefäß, Koffer, Meer] bottom - **4.** [Speicher] loft - **5.** RW: **am ~ zerstört** absolutely shattered; **an ~ gewinnen/verlieren** to gain/lose ground; **auf dem ~ der Tatsachen bleiben** to keep one's feet on the ground; **auf fruchtbaren ~ fallen** to fall on fertile ground; **den ~ für jn/etw vorbereiten** to prepare the ground for sb/sthg; **festen ~ unter den Füßen haben** to be financially secure.

**Boden|belastung** die soil pollution.

**bodenlos** *adj* - **1.** [tief] bottomless - **2.** [unglaublich] incredible.

**Bodenpersonal** *das* ground staff.

**Bodenschätze** *pl* mineral resources.

**Bodensee** *der* Lake Constance.

**bodenständig** *adj* - **1.** [einheimisch] local - **2.** [nicht experimentierfreudig] *reluctant to look beyond one's home region.*

**Bodenturnen** *das (ohne pl)* floor exercises *(pl).*

**Bodybuilding** ['bɔdibɪldɪŋ] *das* bodybuilding.

**Böe** *(pl -n)*, **Bö** *(pl -en) die* gust.

**bog** *prät* ⊳ biegen.

**Bogen** *(pl - ODER* Bögen) *der* ` - **1.** [Biegung] curve; **dort macht die Straße einen ~ nach links** the road curves to the left there; **einen ~ um jn/etw machen** to steer clear of sb/sthg; **in hohem ~** [Wasser] in a great arc; **in hohem ~ hinausgeworfen werden** *ODER* **hinausfliegen** to be thrown out on one's ear; **den ~ heraushaben** to get the hang of it - **2.** [Bauwerk] arch - **3.** [Schusswaffe & MUS] bow; **den ~ überspannen** *fig* to go too far - **4.** [Blatt] sheet.

**Bogenschießen** *das* archery.

**Bogotá** *nt* Bogota.

**Bohle** *(pl -n) die* thick plank.

**Böhmen** *nt* Bohemia.

**Böhmerwald** *der* Bohemian Forest.

**Bohne** *(pl -n) die* bean; **dicke/grüne ~n** broad/green beans; **das interessiert mich nicht die ~** *fam* I'm not in the slightest bit interested in that.

**Bohnen|stange** *die* - **1.** [für Pflanzen] cane - **2.** [Person] beanpole.

**bohnern** *vt* to polish.

**Bohner|wachs** *das* floor polish.

**bohren** *vt* - **1.** [Loch] to drill; [Brunnen, Schacht] to sink - **2.** [hineinstoßen] to stick, to thrust ◇ *vi* - **1.** [mit einem Bohrer] to drill; **nach Öl/Wasser ~** to drill for oil/water; **in** *ODER* **an einem Zahn ~** to drill a tooth; **in der Nase ~** to pick one's nose - **2.** *fam* [drängen] to keep on.
➤ **sich bohren** *ref* [eindringen]: **sich in etw (A) ~** to bore one's way into sthg.

**bohrend** *adj* [Blick] piercing; [Schmerz] gnawing; [Fragen] probing.

**Bohrer** *(pl -) der* [Gerät] drill.

**Bohr|insel** *die* oil rig.

**Bohr|maschine** *die* drill.

**Bohr|turm** *der* derrick.

**Bohrung** *(pl -en) die* drilling.

**böig** *adj* gusty.

**Boiler** [bɔylɐ] *(pl -) der* boiler.

**Boje** *(pl -n) die* buoy.

**Bolivianer, in** [boli'vjaːnɐ, rɪn] *(mpl -; fpl -nen) der, die* Bolivian.

**bolivianisch** [boli'vjaːnɪʃ] *adj* Bolivian.

**Bolivien** *nt* Bolivia.

**Boll|werk** *das* - **1.** [Festung] bulwark - **2.** *fig* [Schutzsystem] bastion.

**Bolzen** *(pl -) der* bolt.

**bombardieren** *vt* to bombard; **jn mit etw ~** *eigtl* & *fig* to bombard sb with sthg.

**bombastisch** *adj abw* [Rede] bombastic; [Aufwand] excessive; [Gebäude] grandiose.

**Bombay** ['bɔmbeː] *nt* Bombay.

**Bombe** *(pl -n) die* bomb.

**Bomben|anschlag** *der* bomb attack.

**Bomben|drohung** *die* bomb threat.

**Bomben|erfolg** *der fam* smash hit. `

**Bomben|stimmung** *die fam* wild atmosphere.

**Bon** [bɔŋ] *(pl -s) der* - **1.** [Beleg] receipt - **2.** [für Speisen und Getränke] voucher.

**Bonbon** [bɔŋ'bɔŋ] *(pl -s) der ODER das* sweet.

**Bonn** *nt* Bonn.

**Bonner** *(pl -) der* native/inhabitant of Bonn ◇ *adj (unver)* of/from Bonn.

**Bonnerin** *(pl -nen) die* native/inhabitant of Bonn.

**Bonus** *(pl -se) der* - **1.** [Extravergütung] bonus - **2.** [Rabatt] discount - **3.** [Vorteil] bonus, advantage.

**Bonze** *(pl -n) der abw* bigwig.

**Boom** [buːm] *(pl -s) der* boom.

**Boot** *(pl -e) das* boat; **mit** *ODER* **in einem ~ fahren** to go by boat; **~ fahren** to go boating; **wir sitzen alle in einem** *ODER* **im selben ~** *fig* we are all in the same boat.

**Boots|verleih** *der* boat hire.

**Bor** *das* CHEM boron.

**Bord** *(pl -e) das* [Brett] shelf ◇ *der* SCHIFF & FLUG side; **von ~ gehen** to disembark; **etw über ~ werfen** *eigtl* & *fig* to throw sthg overboard; **alle Vorsicht über ~ werfen** to throw caution to the winds.
➤ **an Bord** ◇ *adv* on board; **alle Mann an ~!** all aboard! ◇ *präp (+ G)* on board.
➤ **über Bord** *adv* overboard.

**Bordcase** ['bɔrtkeɪs] *(pl - ODER -s) der ODER das* flight bag.

**Bordell** *(pl -e) das* brothel.

**Bord|karte** *die* boarding card.

**Bord|stein** *der* kerb.

**Bordstein|kante** *die* kerb.

**borgen** *vt* - **1.** [entleihen] to borrow; **etw von**

*ODER* bei jm ~ to borrow sthg from sb; **sich** *(D)* **etw** ~ to borrow sthg - **2.** [verleihen]: **jm etw** ~ to lend sb sthg.

**Borke** *(pl -n) die* bark.

**Borneo** *nt* Borneo.

**borniert** *adj* narrow-minded.

**Börse** *(pl -n) die* - **1.** [Geldbeutel] purse - **2.** *WIRTSCH* stock market; [Gebäude] stock exchange; **das Unternehmen geht an die** ~ the company is being floated (on the stock market).

**Börsen|bericht** *der* stock market report.

**Börsen|kurs** *der* (stock) market price.

**Börsen|makler, in** *der, die* stockbroker.

**Borste** *(pl -n) die* [vom Schwein] bristle.

**borstig** *adj* - **1.** [Bart] bristly - **2.** [Wesen] surly.

**Borte** *(pl -n) die* edging.

**bösartig** *adj* - **1.** [Verhalten, Mensch, Bemerkung] malicious; [Hund] vicious - **2.** [Krankheit] malignant.

**Böschung** *(pl -en) die* bank.

**böse** *adj* - **1.** [schlecht] bad; [verwerflich] wicked, evil - **2.** [wütend]: **(über etw** *(A))* ~ **sein/werden** to be/get angry (about sthg); **auf jn** ~ **sein, jm** ~ **sein** to be angry with sb - **3.** *fam* [schlimm] bad; [Entzündung] nasty - **4.** [frech, ungezogen] naughty <> *adv* - **1.** [schlimm] badly; **sich** ~ **erkälten** to catch a nasty cold - **2.** [bösartig]: **es war nicht** ~ **gemeint** I didn't mean it nastily - **3.** [wütend] angrily.

**Böse** *(pl -n) der, die* villain <> *das:* **das ist das** ~ **an der Sache** that's the nasty thing about it; **nichts** ~**s tun/vorhaben** not to do/mean any harm; **etw** ~**s sagen** to say sthg nasty; **nichts** ~**s ahnen** to be unsuspecting.

**Bösewicht** *(pl -er ODER -e) der* - **1.** [Schuft] villain - **2.** [Schlingel] rascal.

**boshaft** *adj* - **1.** [böse] wicked, evil - **2.** [höhnisch] malicious <> *adv* [höhnisch] maliciously.

**Bosheit** *(pl -en) die* - **1.** [Gesinnung] malice - **2.** [Handlung] malicious thing.

**Bosnien-Herzegowina** *nt* Bosnia-Herzegovina.

**Bosnier, in** ['bɔsniɐ, rɪn] *(mpl -; fpl -nen) der, die* Bosnian.

**bosnisch** *adj* Bosnian.

**Bosporus** *der:* **der** ~ the Bosphorus.

**Boss** *(pl -) der* boss; [von Bande] leader.

**böswillig** *adj* malicious <> *adv* [handeln] maliciously.

**bot** *prät* ⊳ bieten.

**Botanik** *die* botany.

**botanisch** *adj* botanical ⊳ **Garten**.

**Bote** *(pl -n) der* - **1.** [gen] messenger; [von Kurierdienst] courier - **2.** [Vorbote] herald.

**Botin** *(pl -nen) die* - **1.** [gen] messenger; [von Kurierdienst] courier - **2.** [Vorbotin] herald.

**Botschaft** *(pl -en) die* - **1.** [Mitteilung] message - **2.** [diplomatische Vertretung] embassy.

**Botschafter, in** *(mpl -; fpl -nen) der, die* ambassador.

**Bottich** *(pl -e) der* tub.

**Bouillon** [bʊl'jɔŋ] *(pl -s) die* bouillon.

**Boulette** = Bulette.

**Boulevard** [bʊl(ə)'vaːɐ̯] *(pl -s) der* boulevard.

**Boulevard|blatt** *das* tabloid (newspaper), sensationalist newspaper.

**Boulevard|presse** *die* tabloid press, sensationalist press.

**Boulevard|theater** *das* light theatre.

**Boutique, Butike** [bu'tiːk] *(pl -n) die* boutique.

**Bowle** ['boːlə] *(pl -n) die* punch.

**Bowling** ['boːlɪŋ] *(pl -s) das* bowling.

**Box** *(pl -en) die* - **1.** [Lautsprecherbox] speaker - **2.** [Kasten] box - **3.** [an Rennstrecke] pit; [in Pferdestall] box; [in Garage] space.

**boxen** *vi* to box <> *vt* - **1.** *SPORT* to fight - **2.** [schlagen] to punch.
⬛ **sich boxen** *ref* [kämpfen] to fight.

**Boxen** *das* boxing.

**Boxer** *(pl -) der* [Hund & SPORT] boxer.

**Boxerin** *(pl -nen) die* SPORT boxer.

**Box|kampf** *der* boxing match.

**Boygroup** *(pl -s) die* boy band.

**Boykott** [bɔy'kɔt] *(pl -s ODER -e) der* boycott.

**boykottieren** [bɔykɔ'tiːrən] *vt* to boycott.

**Bozen** *nt* Bolzano.

**BR** [beː'ɛr] *(abk für* **Bayrischer Rundfunk**) *der* Bavarian radio and TV company.

**brach** *prät* ⊳ brechen.

**brach|liegen** *vi (unreg)* - **1.** [unbeackert] to lie fallow - **2.** [ungenützt] to remain unused.

**brachte** *prät* ⊳ bringen.

**Brackwasser** *das* brackish water.

**Brainstorming** ['breɪnstɔːmɪŋ] *das* brainstorming; **ein** ~ a brainstorming session.

**Branche** ['brãːʃə] *(pl -n) die* (branch of) industry; [Gewerbe] trade.

**Branchen|verzeichnis** *das* classified directory, ≈ Yellow Pages® *(pl).*

**Brand** *(pl Brände) der* - **1.** [Feuer] fire - **2.** [Brennen]: **vor dem** ~ **des Lagers** before the camp caught fire; **etw in** ~ **setzen** ODER **stecken** to set fire to sthg; **in** ~ **geraten** to catch fire - **3.** *fam* [Durst] raging thirst.

**Brand|anschlag** *der* arson attack.

**Brand|blase** *die* blister *(from being burned).*

**Brandenburg** *nt* Brandenburg.

**Brandenburger, in** (*mpl* -; *fpl* -nen) *der, die* Brandenburger.

**Brandenburger Tor** *das* Brandenburg Gate.

**brandenburgisch** *adj* of/from Brandenburg.

**brandmarken** *vt* [Verhältnisse] to denounce; **jn als Verräter** ~ to brand sb a traitor.

**brandneu** *adj* brand-new.

**Brandlstifter, in** *der, die* arsonist.

**Brandlstiftung** *die* arson.

**Brandlteig** *der* KÜCHE choux pastry.

**Brandung** (*pl* -en) *die* surf.

**Brandlwunde** *die* burn.

**brannte** *prät* ⊳ brennen.

**Brannt|wein** *der* spirits (*pl*); **Whisky ist ein** ~ whisky is a type of spirit.

**Brasilianer, in** (*mpl* -; *fpl* -nen) *der, die* Brazilian.

**brasilianisch** *adj* Brazilian.

**Brasilien** *nt* Brazil.

**brät** *präs* ⊳ braten.

**braten** (*präs* **brät**; *prät* **briet**; *perf* **hat gebraten**) *vt & vi* [in der Pfanne] to fry; [im Ofen mit Fett] to roast; [im Ofen ohne Fett] to bake.

**Braten** (*pl* -) *der* roast; **den** ~ **riechen** *fig* [etw Unangenehmes ahnen] to see it coming.

**Bratlhähnchen** *das* roast chicken.

**Bratlhering** *der* fried herring.

**Bratkartoffeln** *pl* fried potatoes.

**Bratlpfanne** *die* frying pan.

**Bratsche** (*pl* -n) *die* MUS viola.

**Bratlwurst** *die* (fried) sausage.

**Brauch** (*pl* **Bräuche**) *der* custom.

**brauchbar** *adj* [Vorschlag] useful; [Material, Kleidung] usable ⟨⟩ *adv* usefully; ~ **arbeiten** to do acceptable work.

**brauchen** *vt* - **1.** [benötigen] to need; **jn/etw für** ODER **zu etw** ~ to need sb/sthg for sthg - **2.** [verbrauchen] to use (up) - **3.** [verwenden]: **jn/ etw (nicht)** ~ **können** (not) to be able to use sb/sthg ⟨⟩ *aux* [müssen] to need; **ihr braucht nicht zu grinsen** there's no need for you to grin.

**Braue** (*pl* -n) *die* brow, eyebrow.

**brauen** *vt* [Bier, Tee] to brew; [Trank] to make.

**Brauerei** (*pl* -en) *die* brewery.

**braun** *adj* - **1.** [Farbe] brown; ~**e Butter** *butter melted in frying pan until brown* - **2.** [nationalsozialistisch] Nazi ⟨⟩ *adv* [farbig] brown; [braten] until brown; *siehe auch* **braun gebrannt.**

**Braun** *das* brown.

**Bräune** *die* suntan.

**bräunen** (*perf* **hat/ist gebräunt**) *vt* (hat) - **1.** [Körper, Gesicht] to tan - **2.** [Zwiebeln] to brown; [Zucker] to caramelize ⟨⟩ *vi* - **1.** (hat) [durch Sonne] to tan - **2.** (ist) [Braten] to turn brown.

⬥ **sich bräunen** *ref* [durch Sonne - Person] to get a tan; [ - Haut] to go brown; [sonnenbaden] to sunbathe.

**braun gebrannt** *adj* tanned.

**Braunkohle** *die* brown coal, lignite.

**bräunlich** *adj* brownish.

**Brause** (*pl* -n) *die* - **1.** [Getränk, Pulver] sherbet - **2.** [Dusche] shower.

**brausen** (*perf* **hat/ist gebraust**) *vi* - **1.** (hat) [Meer, Wind] to roar; [Beifall] to thunder - **2.** (ist) [sich fortbewegen] to race.

**Brauseltablette** *die* effervescent tablet.

**Braut** (*pl* **Bräute**) *die* - **1.** [am Hochzeitstag] bride - **2.** [Verlobte] fiancée - **3.** *salopp* [Mädchen] bird *Br*, chick *Am*.

**Bräutigam** (*pl* -e) *der* - **1.** [am Hochzeitstag] bridegroom - **2.** [Verlobter] fiancé.

**Brautlpaar** *das* bride and groom (*pl*).

**brav** *adj* - **1.** [artig] good - **2.** [bieder] plain ⟨⟩ *adv:* **sie hat** ~ **aufgegessen** she ate up like a good girl.

**bravo** ['braːvo] *interj* bravo!

**Bravour, Bravur** [braˈvuːɐ̯] *die:* **mit** ~ in style.

**BRD** [beːɛɐ̯ˈdeː] (*abk für* **Bundesrepublik Deutschland**) *die* FRG.

**Brechleisen** *das* crowbar.

**brechen** (*präs* **bricht**; *prät* **brach**; *perf* **hat/ist gebrochen**) *vt* - **1.** (hat) [gen] to break; [Ast] to break off; [Rose, Blume] to pluck; [Trotz, Hartnäckigkeit] to overcome; [Ehe] to break up; **jm/ sich den Arm** ~ to break sb's/one's arm - **2.** (hat) [erbrechen] to vomit (up) ⟨⟩ *vi* - **1.** (ist) [durchbrechen] to break; [Leder] to crack - **2.** (hat) [erbrechen] to vomit, to be sick - **3.** (hat) [Kontakt abbrechen]: **mit jm** ~ to break off contact with sb - **4.** (hat) [Brauch aufgeben]: **mit einer Tradition** ~ to break with a tradition - **5.** (ist) [durchkommen] to burst out.

⬥ **sich brechen** *ref* [Schall] to echo; [Licht] to be refracted; [Wellen] to break.

**brechend** *adv:* ~ **voll** full to bursting.

**Brechlmittel** *das* emetic.

**Brechlreiz** *der* nausea (*U*).

**Brechlstange** *die* crowbar.

**Brechung** (*pl* -en) *die* PHYS refraction.

**Bregenz** *nt* Bregenz.

**Brei** (*pl* -e) *der* purée; [aus Haferflocken] porridge; [aus Kartoffeln] mashed potatoes (*pl*); [aus Gries] semolina; **um den heißen** ~ **herumreden** *fig* to beat about the bush.

**breiig** [ˈbraiiç] adj mushy.

**breit** adj - **1.** [gen] wide; [Schultern, Gesicht, Hüften, Aussprache] broad; **ein ~es Lachen** a guffaw - **2.** [allgemein] general ◇ adv - **1.** [seitlich ausgedehnt]: **~ gebaut** sturdily built - **2.** [ausgedehnt - darstellen] in great detail; [ - lächeln] broadly; **~ lachen** to guffaw; siehe auch **breit gefächert**.

**breitbeinig** adv [dastehen] with one's legs apart; **~ gehen** to walk with a rolling gait.

**Breite** (pl -n) die - **1.** [Ausdehnung] width; **in die ~ gehen** fam [dicker werden] to put on weight - **2.** [geografische Lage] latitude.

**breiten** vt geh [legen]: **etw über jn/etw ~** to spread sthg over sb/sthg.
➡ **sich breiten** ref: **sich über etw (A) ~** to spread across sthg.

**Breiten|grad** der (degree of) latitude.

**breit gefächert** adj wide.

**breit machen** vt: **die Beine ~** fam to spread one's legs.
➡ **sich breit machen** ref fam - **1.** [Raum beanspruchen] to take up a lot of room - **2.** [sich einquartieren] to make o.s. at home - **3.** [sich verbreiten] to spread.

**breit|schlagen** vt (unreg) fam [überreden] to talk round; **sich zu etw ~ lassen** to let o.s. be talked into sthg.

**breitschultrig**, **breitschulterig** adj broad-shouldered.

**Breit|seite** die [von Häusern, Schiffen] side.

**breit|treten** vt (unreg) fam abw [ausgiebig erörtern] to flog to death; [weiterverbreiten] to spread.

**Breit|wand** die wide screen; **~film** film in wide screen format.

**Bremen** nt Bremen.

**Brems|belag** der brake lining.

**Bremse** (pl -n) die - **1.** [Bremsvorrichtung] brake - **2.** [Insekt] horsefly.

**bremsen** vi [halten] to brake ◇ vt - **1.** [Fahrzeug] to brake - **2.** [Entwicklung, Person] to slow down; **er ist nicht zu ~** fam there's no stopping him.
➡ **sich bremsen** ref fam: **ich kann mich ~!** no fear!

**Brems|flüssigkeit** die brake fluid.

**Brems|leuchte** die brake light.

**Brems|licht** das brake light.

**Brems|pedal** das brake pedal.

**Brems|scheibe** die brake disc.

**Brems|spur** die skid mark.

**Brems|weg** der braking distance.

**brennbar** adj flammable.

**Brenn|element** das fuel rods (pl).

**brennen** (prät brannte; perf hat gebrannt) vi

- **1.** [gen] to burn; [Haus, Wald, Gardine] to be on fire, to burn; **es brennt!** fire! - **2.** [Lampe, Birne] to be on - **3.** [Wunde, Augen] to smart; [Füße] to be sore - **4.** [erregt sein]: **vor Ungeduld ~** to be dying of impatience; **vor Ehrgeiz ~** to be burning with ambition; **auf etw (A) ~** to be dying for sthg ◇ vt - **1.** [Loch] to burn - **2.** [Ziegel, Ton] to fire; [Schnaps] to distil; [Mandeln] to roast - **3.** fam [CD-Rom] to burn.

**brennend** adj eigtl & fig burning; [Zigarette] lighted ◇ adv [sehr]: **~ eifersüchtig sein** to be burning with jealousy; **sich ~ für etw interessieren** to be extremely interested in sthg; **ich möchte es ~ gern sehen** I would absolutely love to see it.

**Brenner** der: der **~** the Brenner Pass.

**Brennerei** (pl -en) die - **1.** [Brennen] distilling - **2.** [Betrieb] distillery.

**Brennholz** das firewood.

**Brenn|nessel**, **Brenn-Nessel** die stinging nettle.

**Brenn|punkt** der - **1.** PHYS focal point - **2.** [Zentrum] focus; **im ~ des öffentlichen Interesses stehen** to be at the centre of public attention.

**Brenn|stoff** der fuel.

**Brenn|weite** die PHYS & FOTO focal length.

**brenzlig** adj - **1.** [Geschmack] burnt; **ein ~er Geruch** a smell of burning - **2.** fam [heikel] dicey.

**Bresche** (pl -n) die [Lücke] breach; **für jn in die ~ springen** [einspringen] to stand in for sb; **für jn/ etw eine ~ schlagen** to lend one's backing to sb/sthg.

**Bretagne** die Brittany.

**Brett** (pl -er) das - **1.** [aus Holz] plank; **ein ~ vor dem Kopf haben** fam fig not to be quite with it; **schwarzes ~** noticeboard - **2.** [zum Spielen] board.
➡ **Bretter** pl - **1.** [Bühne] boards - **2.** [Skier] skis

**Bretter|bude** die [gen] hut; [am Markt] stand.

**Brett|spiel** das board game.

**Brezel** (pl -n) die pretzel.

**bricht** präs ⟼ **brechen**.

**Bridge** [brɪtʃ] das bridge.

**Brief** (pl -e) der letter; **ein blauer ~** official letter giving notice of dismissal or notice that a pupil may have to repeat a year at school; **offener ~** open letter.

**Brief|bogen** der sheet of writing paper.

**Brief|bombe** die letter bomb.

**Briefdruck|sache** die letter comprising an order form, questionnaire etc, which costs less to send than an ordinary letter.

**briefen** [briːfn] (präs **brieft**; prät **briefte**; perf **hat gebrieft**) vt to brief.

**Brief|freund, in** der, die pen pal, pen friend.

**Brief|geheimnis** *das (ohne pl)* privacy of correspondence.

**Brief|karte** *die* correspondence card.

**Brief|kasten** *der* - **1.** [bei der Post] postbox *Br*, mailbox *Am* - **2.** [am Hauseingang] letterbox *Br*, mailbox *Am*.

**Briefkasten|firma** *die* fictitious company.

**Brief|kopf** *der* letterhead.

**brieflich** *adj:* **eine ~e Antwort bekommen** to receive an answer by letter <> *adv* by letter.

**Brief|marke** *die* stamp; **~n sammeln ist sein Hobby** his hobby is stamp collecting.

**Briefmarken|sammlung** *die* stamp collection.

**Brief|papier** *das* notepaper, writing paper.

**Brief|tasche** *die* wallet.

**Brief|taube** *die* carrier pigeon.

**Brief|träger, in** *der, die* postman (*f* postwoman).

**Brief|umschlag** *der* envelope.

**Brief|wahl** *die (ohne pl)* postal vote; **per ~ wählen** to use a postal vote.

**Brief|wechsel** *der* correspondence; **mit jm in ~ stehen** to correspond with sb.

**briet** *prät* [> **braten**.

**Brikett** *(pl -s) das* briquette.

**brillant** [brɪl'jant] *adj* brilliant <> *adv* brilliantly.

**Brillant** [brɪl'jant] *(pl -en) der* brilliant.

**Brille** *(pl -n) die* - **1.** [Sehhilfe, Augengläser] glasses *(pl);* **eine ~ tragen** to wear glasses; **etw durch eine rosa ~ sehen** *fig* to see sthg through rose-tinted spectacles - **2.** *fam* [Klosettbrille] toilet seat.

**Brillen|etui** *das* glasses case.

**Brillen|träger, in** *der, die* person who wears glasses.

**bringen** *(prät* **brachte;** *perf* **hat gebracht)** *vt* - **1.** [herbringen] to bring; **jm etw ~** to bring sb sthg; **er brachte mir Blumen** he brought me some flowers - **2.** [holen] to get, to fetch; **jm etw ~** to get *ODER* fetch sb sthg - **3.** [wegtragen] to take; **jm etw ~** to take sb sthg - **4.** [befördern] to take, to give a lift to; **ich bringe Sie zum Bahnhof** I'll take you *ODER* give you a lift to the station; **der Milchmann brachte die Milch** the milkman delivered the milk - **5.** [begleiten] to see; **jn zur Tür ~** to see sb to the door - **6.** *fig* [lenken]: **jn vor Gericht ~** to take sb to court; **die Rede auf etw ~** to bring the conversation round to sthg; **jn auf die Idee ~, etw zu tun** to give sb the idea of doing sthg; **jn in Gefahr ~** to put sb in danger - **7.** [Ergebnis]: **das bringt nur Ärger** that'll cause nothing but trouble; **das Projekt bringt eine Menge Arbeit mit sich** the project entails a lot of work; **jn dazu ~, dass er etw tut** to make sb do sthg, to get sb to do sthg; **jn zum Lachen ~** to make sb laugh; **jn zum Weinen/zur Verzweiflung ~** to reduce sb to tears/to despair; **Gewinn ~** to yield a profit; **das bringt nichts** *fam* that won't achieve anything - **8.** [leisten]: **es weit ~** to go far *ODER* a long way; **er brachte es bis zum Minister** he made it to minister - **9.** [veröffentlichen - in einer Zeitung] to publish; [ - im Fernsehen, Radio] to broadcast; [ - Film] to screen - **10.** *RW:* **etw hinter sich** *(A)* **~** to get sthg over and done with; **ich kann es nicht über mich ~, so etwas zu tun** I can't bring myself to do such a thing; **jn um etw ~** to do sb out of sthg; **jn um seinen guten Ruf ~** to ruin sb's reputation; **du bringst mich noch mal um den Verstand!** you're driving me mad!

**brisant** *adj* [heikel] explosive.

**Brisanz** *die* [Wichtigkeit] explosiveness.

**Brise** *(pl -n) die* breeze.

**Brite** *(pl -n) der* Briton, British person; **die ~n** the British; **ich bin ~** I'm British.

**Britin** *(pl -nen) die* Briton, British person.

**britisch** *adj* British.

**Britische Inseln** *pl* British Isles.

**Broccoli, Brokkoli** [ˈbrɔkɔli] *der* broccoli.

**bröckeln** *(perf* **hat/ist gebröckelt)** *vi* - **1.** *(hat)* [zerfallen] to crumble - **2.** *(ist)* [sich lösen]: **der Putz bröckelt von den Wänden** the plaster is flaking off the walls.

**Brocken** *(pl -) der* - **1.** [von Brot, Fleisch] bit, chunk; [von Lehm] lump - **2.** *fam* [dicker Mensch] hefty fellow - **3.** *RW:* **ein harter ~** *fam* a tough nut to crack; **ein paar ~ einer Sprache sprechen** to speak a few words of a language.

**brodeln** *vi* [Wasser, Suppe, Lava] to bubble.

**Brokat** *(pl -e) der* brocade.

**Brokkoli** = Broccoli.

**Brom** *das* bromine.

**Brom|beere** *die* blackberry.

**Bronchien** [ˈbrɔnçiən] *pl* bronchial tubes.

**Bronchitis** [brɔnˈçiːtɪs] *die* bronchitis *(U)*.

**Bronze** [ˈbrɔnsə] *die* bronze.

**Bronze|medaille** *die* bronze medal.

**Bronzezeit** *die* Bronze Age.

**Brosche** *(pl -n) die* brooch.

**Broschüre** *(pl -n) die* brochure.

**Brot** *(pl -e) das* - **1.** [als Laib] bread; **ein Laib ~** a loaf of bread - **2.** [als Scheibe] slice of bread; **ein belegtes ~** an open sandwich; **ein ~ mit Schinken** a slice of bread with ham on it - **3.** [Lebensunterhalt]: **sich sein ~ verdienen** to earn a living.

**BROT**

> Bread has an important place in the German diet. The evening meal in most German families, known as the "Abendbrot", consists of several slices of buttered bread served with cheese or cold meats. Among the 200 or so varieties of bread, the most popular - apart from the bread rolls eaten at breakfast - are brown bread, rye bread and wholemeal bread.

**Brotaufstrich** (pl -e) der spread.

**Brötchen** (pl -) das (bread) roll; **kleine ~ backen (müssen)** fam fig to (have to) rein o.s. in; **seine ~ verdienen** fam fig to earn one's pennies.

**Brot|erwerb** der livelihood.

**brotlos** adj - **1.** [arbeitslos] unemployed - **2.** [nicht einträglich]: **die Malerei ist eine ~e Kunst** there's no money in painting.

**Brot|maschine** die bread slicing machine.

**Brot|zeit** die Süddt tea break; **~ machen** to have a tea break.

**Browser** ['brauzɐ] (pl -) der EDV browser.

**Bruch** (pl Brüche) der - **1.** (ohne pl) [Brechen] breaking; [von Damm] bursting; **zu ~ gehen** [Glas] to smash, to shatter; **in die Brüche gehen** [Ehe] to break up - **2.** [von Versprechen, Wort] breaking; [von Vertrag] breach - **3.** [Trennung]: **ein ~ mit der Tradition** a break with tradition; **es kam zum ~ mit seiner Familie** he broke off contact with his family - **4.** [MED - von Knochen] fracture; [ - von Eingeweide] hernia; **sich einen ~ heben** to have ODER suffer a hernia - **5.** MATH fraction.

**Bruch|bude** die fam abw hovel.

**brüchig** adj [Material] brittle; [Teig] crumbly; [Beziehung] fragile; [Stimme] cracked.

**Bruch|landung** die crash landing.

**Bruch|rechnung** die (ohne pl) fractions (pl).

**Bruch|strich** der line (of a fraction).

**Bruch|stück** das [von Vase, Werk] fragment.

**bruchstückhaft** ['bruxʃtykhaft] adj fragmentary <> adv in fragments.

**Bruch|teil** der fraction.

**Brücke** (pl -n) die - **1.** [gen] bridge; **eine ~ schlagen** [Turnübung] to make a bridge - **2.** [Teppich] rug - **3.** RW: **alle ~n hinter sich** (D) **abbrechen** to burn one's bridges; **jm goldene ~n bauen** to make it easy for sb.

**Brücken|pfeiler** der pile (of a bridge).

**Bruder** (pl Brüder) der - **1.** [Geschwister, Mönch] brother; **wir haben die Sache unter Brüdern geregelt** we settled the matter amongst ourselves - **2.** fam [Kerl] guy.

**brüderlich** adj brotherly <> adv like brothers.

**Brüderlichkeit** die brotherliness.

**Brüderschaft** die: **mit jm ~ schließen** to agree to use the familiar "du" form with sb; **mit jm ~ trinken** to agree to use the familiar "du" form with sb and celebrate with a drink.

**Brühe** (pl -n) die - **1.** [Suppe] broth; [zum Kochen] stock - **2.** [Wasser] dirty water - **3.** fam [Schweiß]: **ihm läuft die ~ herunter** he's sweating buckets - **4.** abw [Tee, Kaffee] dishwater.

**brühwarm** adj hot off the press <> adv: **etw ~ weitererzählen** to pass sthg on straight away.

**Brüh|würfel** der stock cube.

**brüllen** vt to roar <> vi [Löwe, Person] to roar; [Stier] to bellow; [Baby, Affe] to screech; **vor Schmerz ~** to howl with pain.

**brummen** vi - **1.** [Hummel] to buzz; [Bär] to growl - **2.** [Person, Motor] to drone.

**brummig** adj [Person] grumpy; [Antwort] bad-tempered, surly <> adv grumpily.

**Brunch** [brantʃ] (pl -(e)s ODER -e) der brunch.

**brünett** adj: **eine ~e Frau** a brunette.

**Brunnen** (pl -) der - **1.** [zum Wasserholen] well - **2.** [Springbrunnen] fountain - **3.** [Wasser] mineral water.

**Brunst** (pl Brünste) die [von Reh] heat; [von Hirsch] rut; **in der ~ sein** [Reh] to be on heat; [Hirsch] to be rutting.

**brüsk** adj brusque <> adv brusquely.

**brüskieren** vt to snub.

**Brüssel** nt Brussels.

**Brüsseler, in** (mpl -; fpl -nen) der, die native/inhabitant of Brussels.

**Brust** (pl Brüste) die - **1.** (ohne pl) [Thorax] chest; **einen zur ~ nehmen** fam to have a few drinks - **2.** [Busen] breast; **jm die ~ geben** to breastfeed sb.

**Brust|beutel** der wallet (worn around the neck).

**brüsten** <> **sich brüsten** ref abw: **sich mit etw ~** to boast about sthg.

**Brust|korb** der thorax.

**Brust|schwimmen** das breaststroke.

**Brust|tasche** die breast pocket.

**Brust|ton** der: **im ~ der Überzeugung** with overriding conviction.

**Brust|umfang** der chest measurement.

**Brüstung** (pl -en) die parapet.

**Brust|warze** die nipple.

**Brut** (pl -en) die - **1.** [von Tieren] brood - **2.** [Brüten] incubation - **3.** fam abw [Pack] lot, bunch.

**brutal** adj brutal <> adv brutally.

**Brutalität** (pl -en) die brutality.

**brüten** vi - **1.** [Vögel] to brood - **2.** [nachdenken]: über etw (D) ~ to ponder sthg.

**Brüter** (pl -) der: schneller ~ fast-breeder reactor.

**Brut|kasten** der incubator.

**brutto** adv gross.

**Brutto|einkommen** das gross income.

**Brutto|gewicht** das gross weight.

**Bruttosozial|produkt** das gross national product, GNP.

**brutzeln** vi to sizzle ◇ vt fam to fry (up).

**bsd.** abk für besonders.

**BSE** (abk für Bovine Spongiforme Enzephalopathie) die BSE.

**Btx** das abk für Bildschirmtext.

**Bube** (pl -n) der - **1.** [Junge] boy - **2.** [Spielkarte] jack.

**Buch** (pl Bücher) das book; jm ein ~ mit sieben Siegeln sein to be a mystery ODER a closed book to sb; er ist ein Hochstapler wie er im ~e steht he is your typical con man; die Bücher führen to keep the books; über etw (A) ~ führen to keep a record of sthg; das neue Auto schlug mit 20000 Euro zu ~e the new car accounted for 20,000 euros.

**Buchbinder, in** (mpl -; fpl -nen) der, die book-binder.

**Buche** (pl -n) die beech.

**Buchecker** (pl -n) die beechnut.

**buchen** vt - **1.** [verbuchen] to enter - **2.** [reservieren] to book.

**Bücher|bord, -brett** das bookshelf.

**Bücherei** (pl -en) die library.

**Bücher|regal** das bookshelves (pl).

**Bücher|schrank** der bookcase.

**Bücher|stütze** die bookend.

**Buch|führung** die bookkeeping.

**Buchhalter, in** (mpl -; fpl -nen) der, die accountant, bookkeeper.

**Buch|haltung** die accountancy, bookkeeping.

**Buch|handel** der bookselling.

**Buch|händler, in** der, die bookseller.

**Buch|handlung** die, **-laden** der bookshop Br, bookstore Am.

**Buchmacher, in** (mpl -; fpl -nen) der, die bookmaker.

**Buch|markt** der book market.

**Buch|messe** die book fair.

**Buchs|baum** ['buksbaum] der box (tree).

**Buchse** ['buksə] (pl -n) die socket.

**Büchse** ['byksə] (pl -n) die - **1.** [Dose] can, tin Br - **2.** [Gewehr] shotgun.

**Büchsen|fleisch** das tinned meat Br, canned meat Am.

**Büchsen|milch** die tinned milk Br, canned milk Am.

**Büchsen|öffner** der can opener, tin opener Br.

**Buchstabe** ['buːxʃtaːbə] (pl -n) der letter; grosser ~ capital (letter); kleiner ~ lower-case letter; in fetten ~n in bold.

**buchstabieren** [buːxʃtaˈbiːrən] vt to spell.

**buchstäblich** ['buːxʃteːplɪ] adv literally.

**Bucht** (pl -en) die bay.

**Buchung** (pl -en) die - **1.** [Verbuchung] entry - **2.** [Reservierung] booking.

**Buchungs|bestätigung** die booking confirmation.

**Buchweizen** der buckwheat.

**Buckel** (pl -) der [Rücken] hump; einen ~ haben to be a hunchback; rutsch mir den ~ runter! fam abw get lost ODER stuffed!

**bücken** ➤ sich bücken ref to bend down; sich nach etw ~ to bend down to pick sthg up.

**bucklig** adj [Person] hunchbacked; [Oberfläche, Straße] bumpy.

**Bucklige** (pl -n) der, die hunchback.

**Bückling** (pl -e) der - **1.** hum [Verbeugung] bow - **2.** [Hering] smoked herring.

**Budapest** nt Budapest.

**buddeln** vt & vi to dig.

**Buddhist, in** (mpl -en; fpl -nen) der, die Buddhist.

**buddhistisch** adj Buddhist.

**Bude** (pl -n) die - **1.** [Verkaufsstand] stall - **2.** fam [kleine Wohnung, möbliertes Zimmer] pad; sturmfreie ~ haben fam to have the house to o.s.; jm auf die ~ rücken fam to pay sb an unwanted visit; die Leute rennen ihr die ~ ein fam she has people queuing on her doorstep - **3.** fam abw [Wohnung] dump.

**Budget** [byˈdʒeː] (pl -s) das budget.

**Buenos Aires** ['bueːnɔs 'airɛs] nt Buenos Aires.

**Büfett** [byˈfɛt], **buffet** [byˈfeː] (pl -s) das - **1.** [Verkaufstisch] counter - **2.** [Speisen]: kaltes ~ cold buffet - **3.** [Geschirrschrank] sideboard.

**Büffel** (pl -) der buffalo.

**büffeln** fam vi to cram, to swot Br ◇ vt: Formeln ~ to bone up on ODER swot up on Br formulas.

**Buffet** [byˈfeː] (pl -s) das Österr & Schweiz = Büfett.

**Bug** (pl -e) der [von Schiff] bow; [von Flugzeug] nose.

**BUGA** ['buːga] (pl -s) (abk für Bundesgarten-

**bauausstellung)** *die German horticultural exhibition.*

**Bügel** *(pl -) der -* **1.** [Kleiderbügel] (coat) hanger - **2.** [Griff] handle - **3.** [Steigbügel] stirrup - **4.** [Brillenbügel] side-piece.

**Bügel|brett** *das* ironing board.

**Bügel|eisen** *das* iron.

**Bügel|falte** *die* crease.

**bügelfrei** *adj* non-iron.

**bügeln** *vt & vi* to iron.

**Buggy** *(pl -s) der* buggy.

**buhen** *vi* to boo.

**Bühne** *(pl -n) die -* **1.** [Theaterraum] stage; **glatt über die ~ gehen** *fam* to go (off) smoothly - **2.** [Theater] theatre.

**Bühnen|bild** *das* set.

**Bühnenbildner, in** *(mpl -; fpl -nen) der, die* set designer.

**buk** *prät* ⊏⊐ **backen.**

**Bukarest** *nt* Bucharest.

**Bulette, Boulette** *(pl -n) die* rissole.

**Bulgare** *(pl -n) der* Bulgarian.

**Bulgarien** *nt* Bulgaria.

**Bulgarin** *(pl -nen) die* Bulgarian.

**bulgarisch** *adj* Bulgarian.

**Bulgarisch(e)** *das* Bulgarian; *siehe auch* **Englisch(e).**

**Bull|auge** *das* porthole.

**Bull|dogge** *die* bulldog.

**Bulldozer** [ˈbʊldoːzɐ] *(pl -) der* bulldozer.

**Bulle** *(pl -n) der -* **1.** [Tier] bull - **2.** *salopp abw* [Polizist] pig, cop.

**Bumerang** *(pl -s ODER -e) der* boomerang.

**Bummel** *(pl -) der* stroll; **einen ~ durch die Stadt machen** to go for a stroll round the town.

**Bummelei** *(pl -en) die abw* loafing around.

**bummeln** *(perf* hat/ist gebummelt) *vi -* **1.** *(ist)* [spazieren] to stroll - **2.** *(hat)* [langsam sein] to dawdle.

**Bummel|streik** *der* go-slow.

**Bummel|zug** *der* slow train.

**bumsen** *(perf* hat/ist gebumst) *vi -* **1.** *(hat) fam* [knallen] to bang; **es hat gebumst** [Lärm] there was a bang; [bei Unfall] there was a crash - **2.** *(ist) fam* [prallen]: **gegen** ODER **an etw** (A) **~** to bang into sthg - **3.** *(hat) fam* [koitieren] to get laid, to have it off *Br* ⟨⟩ *vt (hat) fam* to lay, to have it off with *Br.*

**Bund** *(pl* Bünde ODER -e) *der -* **1.** *(pl* Bünde) [Zusammenschluss] association; **mit jm im ~ (e) (sein)** (to be) in league with sb - **2.** [Bundesrepublik] central government - **3.** *fam* [Bundeswehr]: **der ~** the army - **4.** *(pl* Bünde) [an Kleidung] waistband ⟨⟩ *das (pl* Bunde) [von Gemüse] bunch.

**BUND** [beːʊːɛnˈdeː] *(abk für* **Bund für Umwelt und Naturschutz in Deutschland)** *der German association for the protection of the environment and the natural world.*

**Bündel** *(pl -) das -* **1.** [von Wäsche, Anträgen] bundle; [von Geldscheinen] wad; **sein ~ schnüren** ODER **packen** to pack one's bags - **2.** [aus Stroh] bale.

**bündeln** *vt -* **1.** [Heu, Stroh] to bale - **2.** [Kleidung, Papier, Banknoten] to tie into bundles - **3.** [Produkte] to combine.

**Bundes|anleihe** *die loan from German federal government.*

**Bundes|bahn** ⊏⊐ **Deutsche Bahn.**

**Bundes|bank** ⊏⊐ **Deutsche Bundesbank.**

**Bundes|bürger, in** *der, die* German citizen.

**Bundesgarten|schau** *die German horticultural exhibition.*

**Bundes|gebiet** *das* German territory.

**Bundes|genosse** *der* ally.

**Bundes|genossin** *die* ally.

**Bundesgrenz|schutz** *der (ohne pl) German border police.*

**Bundeshaupt|stadt** *die* federal capital.

**Bundes|kanzler, in** *der, die* German chancellor.

**Bundes|land** *das* federal state; **die fünf neuen Bundesländer** the five new federal states; **die alten/neuen Bundesländer** the old/new federal states.

**BUNDESLAND**

Germany is made up of 16 federal "Länder", each of which has its own constitution as well as control of various aspects of legislation. The division of responsibilities between the Federal State and each "Land" is established by law. Only certain areas (as for example foreign policy) come under the exclusive jurisdiction of the Federation. This system reflects the fundamental aim of federalism, which seeks to preserve regional diversity.

**Bundes|liga** *die German national league for football, ice hockey etc.;* **erste/zweite ~** first/second division.

**Bundes|minister, in** *der, die* federal minister; **der ~ des Inneren/der Justiz** the Federal Interior Minister/Justice Minister; **der ~ für Wirtschaft/Verkehr** the Federal Economics Minister/Transport Minister.

**Bundes|post** ⊏⊐ **Deutsche Bundespost.**

**Bundes|präsident, in** *der, die -* **1.** [in Deutschland, Österreich] president - **2.** [in der Schweiz] chair of the "Bundesrat".

**Bundes|rat** *der -* **1.** *(ohne pl)* [Parlament] Bundesrat, *upper house of German parliament, where federal states are represented* - **2.** [Parlamentarier] member of the Bundesrat.

### BUNDESRAT

> The "Bundesrat" is one of the two houses of the German parliament. It is through this chamber that the "Länder" can intervene in government. Its assent is required for more than half of all laws that are passed, to such a degree that it effectively checks the power of the government and of the Bundestag.

**Bundes|rätin** *die* member of the Bundesrat.

**Bundes|regierung** *die* German *ODER* federal government.

**Bundes|republik** *die* - **1.** [Föderation] federal republic - **2.** ⊳ **Bundesrepublik Deutschland.**

**bundesrepublikanisch** *adj:* ~e Verfassung constitution of the Federal Republic.

**Bundesrepublik Deutschland** *die* Federal Republic of Germany.

**Bundes|staat** *der* federal state.

**Bundes|straße** *die* ≈ A road *Br,* ≈ state highway *Am.*

**Bundes|tag** ⊳ Deutsche Bundestag.

**Bundesverdienst|kreuz** *das order bestowed for special services to Germany.*

**Bundesverfassungs|gericht** *das* Federal Constitutional Court.

### BUNDESVERFASSUNGSGERICHT

> The federal constitutional court which has its seat at Karlsruhe is made up of 16 judges sitting in two assemblies; they are elected for a period of twelve years, half from the Bundestag and half from the Bundesrat. Its role is to ensure that basic constitutional law is respected and it is empowered, for example, to prohibit a political party or a law which it judges to be unconstitutional.

**Bundes|wehr** *die* German army.

**bundesweit** *adj* & *adv* nationwide *(in Germany, Austria).*

**bündig** *adj* [kurz] concise ⟨⟩ *adv* [kurz] concisely.

**Bündnis** *(pl* -se) *das* alliance; mit jm ein ~ eingehen to form an alliance with sb.

**Bündnis 90/Grüne** *das German political party formed by West German environmentalists and former East German political groups.*

**Bungalow** ['bʊŋɡalo] *(pl* -s) *der* bungalow.

**Bungeejumping** ['bandʒidʒampɪŋ] *der (ohne pl)* sport bungee-jumping.

**Bunker** *(pl* -) *der* - **1.** [Schutzraum] bunker - **2.** *salopp* [Gefängnis] clink, slammer.

**bunt** *adj* - **1.** [vielfarbig] colourful - **2.** [abwechslungsreich] [Programm] varied; eine ~e Mischung a motley assortment; ein ~er Abend a social evening - **3.** [durcheinander] mixed-up; jetzt wirds mir zu ~ I've had enough ⟨⟩ *adv* - **1.** [vielfarbig] colourfully - **2.** [abwechslungsreich]: ~ gemischt assorted; es zu ~ treiben to overdo it.

**Bunt|stift** *der* coloured pencil.

**Bürde** *(pl* -n) *die* burden.

**Burg** *(pl* -en) *die* - **1.** [Gebäude] castle - **2.** [Sandburg] *circular wall of sand built on beach by holidaymakers to mark off the area where they are sitting.*

**Bürge** *(pl* -n) *der* guarantee.

**bürgen** *vi:* für jn/etw ~ *fig* to vouch for sb/sthg; für jn ~ WIRTSCH to stand surety for sb.

**Burgenland** *nt* Burgenland.

**Burgenländer, in** *(mpl* -; *fpl* -nen) *der, die* native/inhabitant of Burgenland.

**burgenländisch** *adj* of/from Burgenland.

**Bürger, in** *(mpl* -; *fpl* -nen) *der, die* - **1.** [Einwohner] citizen - **2.** [Mittelständler] middle-class person.

**Bürger|initiative** *die* [Gruppe] grass-roots pressure group.

**Bürger|krieg** *der* civil war.

**bürgerlich** *adj* - **1.** [staatlich] civil - **2.** [des Bürgertums - Partei, Familie] middle-class; [ - Küche] traditional - **3.** HIST & POL [spießig] bourgeois ⟨⟩ *adv* - **1.** [wie das Bürgertum]: Ulm ist eine ~ geprägte Stadt Ulm is a middle-class` city - **2.** *abw* [spießig]: ~ leben to have a bourgeois lifestyle.

**Bürger|meister, in** *der, die* mayor.
➤ **Regierende Bürgermeister** *der mayor and leader of local government.*

**bürgernah** *adj:* ~e Maßnahmen measures which take into account the concerns of the people.

**Bürger|recht** *das* civil rights *(pl).*

**Bürgerrechtler, in** *(mpl* -; *fpl* -nen) *der, die* civil rights activist.

**Bürgerschaft** *(pl* -en) *die* [Einwohner] citizens *(pl).*

**Bürgersteig** *(pl* -e) *der* pavement *Br,* sidewalk *Am.*

**Bürgertum** *das* bourgeoisie.

**Bürgschaft** *(pl* -en) *die* surety.

**Burgund** *nt* Burgundy.

**Burgunder** *(pl -) der -* **1.** [Person] Burgundian - **2.** [Wein] burgundy.

**Büro** [byˈroː] *(pl -s) das* office.

**Büro|angestellte** *der, die* office worker.

**Büro|arbeit** *die* office work.

**Büro|kauf|frau** *die* business administrator.

**Büro|kauf|mann** *der* business administrator.

**Büro|klammer** *die* paper clip.

**Bürokrat** *(pl -en) der* bureaucrat.

**Bürokratie** [byrokraˈtiː] *(pl -n) die* bureaucracy.

**bürokratisch** *adj* bureaucratic ⇔ *adv* bureaucratically.

**Büro|material** *das* office supplies *(pl)*.

**Bürostunden** *pl* office hours.

**Büro|zeit** *die* office hours *(pl)*.

**Bursche** *(pl -n) der -* **1.** [Junge] lad - **2.** *fam abw* [Kerl] sort, fellow - **3.** [Prachtexemplar]: **ein prächtiger ~** a magnificent specimen.

**burschikos** *adj* [Frau] mannish; [Mädchen] boyish ⇔ *adv* [Frau] mannishly; [Mädchen] boyishly.

**Bürste** *(pl -n) die* [Gerät] brush.

**bürsten** *vt* to brush; **sich** *(D)* **die Haare ~** to brush one's hair.

**Bus** *(pl -se) der -* **1.** [Omnibus] bus - **2.** [Reisebus] coach.

**Bus|bahnhof** *der* bus station.

**Busch** *(pl Büsche) der* [Strauch, Zone] bush; **bei jm auf den ~ klopfen** *fam* to sound sb out; **mit etw hinter dem ~ halten** *fam* to keep sthg under one's hat.

**Büschel** *(pl -) das* [von Gras, Haaren] tuft; [von Stroh] bundle.

**buschig** *adj* bushy.

**Busen** *(pl -) der* bosom.

**Bus|fahrer, in** *der, die -* **1.** [von Omnibus] bus driver - **2.** [von Reisebus] coach driver.

**Bushalte|stelle** *die* bus stop.

**Business Class** *die (ohne pl)* business class.

**Bussard** *(pl -e) der* buzzard.

**Buße** *(pl -n) die -* **1.** REL penance - **2.** RECHT [Geldstrafe] fine.

**büßen** *vt -* **1.** [Sünden] to atone for - **2.** [Untat] to pay for ⇔ *vi -* **1.** REL: **für etw ~** to atone for sthg - **2.** [bestraft werden]: **für etw ~** to pay for sthg.

**Buß|geld** *das* fine.

**Bußgeld|bescheid** *der* notification of a fine.

**Bus|spur** *die* bus lane.

**Buß- und Bet|tag** *der* Day of Prayer and Repentance, *German public holiday in November.*

**Büste** *(pl -n) die* bust.

**Büsten|halter** *der* bra.

**Butike** = Boutique.

**Butter** *die* butter; **alles in ~** *fam fig* everything's hunky-dory.

**Butter|brot** *das* slice of bread and butter; **du brauchst es mir nicht ständig aufs ~ zu schmieren** ODER **streichen** *fam fig* there's no need to rub it in all the time.

**Butter|dose** *die* butter dish.

**Butter|fahrt** *die* short ferry trip outside German waters to allow passengers to buy duty-free goods.

**Butter|milch** *die* buttermilk.

**BVG** [beːfauˈɡeː] *(abk für* **Bundesverfassungsgericht)** *das (ohne pl)* Federal Constitutional Court.

**b. w.** *(abk für* **bitte wenden)** PTO.

**BWL** [beːveːˈɛl] *(abk für* **Betriebswirtschaftslehre)** *die* business studies.

**Bypass** [ˈbaipas] *(pl -pässe) der* MED & TECH bypass.

**Byte** [bait] *(pl -s) das* EDV byte.

**byzantinisch** *adj* Byzantine.

**Byzanz** *nt* HIST Byzantium.

**bzg.** *(abk für* **bezüglich)** re.

**bzw.** *abk für* **beziehungsweise.**

# C

**c, C** [tseː] *(pl - ODER -s) das -* **1.** [Buchstabe] c, C - **2.** MUS C.

⬟ **C** *(abk für* **Celsius)** C.

**ca.** *(abk für* **circa)** approx.

**Cabaret** [kabaˈreː] *(pl -s) das* cabaret.

**Cabrio** [ˈkaːbrio] *(pl -s) das* = **Kabrio.**

**CAD** [tseːaːˈdeː] *(abk für* **Computer Aided Design)** *das* CAD.

**Cadmium** [ˈkatmiʊm] *das* = **Kadmium.**

**Café** [kaˈfeː] *(pl -s) das* cafe.

**Cafeteria** [kafetəˈriːal] *(pl -s) die* cafeteria.

**cal.** (abk für **Kalorie**) cal.

**Callcenter** ['kɔ:lsɛntɐ] (pl -s) das TELEKOM call centre.

**Callgirl** ['kɔ:lgø:ɐl] (pl -s) das call girl.

**Calzium** ['kaltsi̯ʊm] das = **Kalzium.**

**CAM** [tsɛ:a:'ɛm] (abk für **Computer Aided Manufacturing**) das CAM.

**Camembert** ['kaməmbe:ɐ] (pl -s) der camembert.

**campen** ['kɛmpn̩] vi to camp.

**Camper, in** ['kɛmpɐ, rɪn] (mpl -; fpl -nen) der, die camper.

**Camping** ['kɛmpɪŋ] das camping; **zum ~ fahren** to go camping.

**Camping|bus** der camper, camper van Br.

**Camping|platz** der campsite.

**canceln** ['kɛntsln̩] (präs **cancelt**; prät **cancelte**; perf **hat gecancelt**) vt to cancel.

**Cape** [ke:p] (pl -s) das cape.

**Carsharing** das car sharing.

**Carving|ski** der carving ski.

**Cäsium** ['tsɛ:zi̯ʊm] das caesium.

**catchen** ['kɛtʃn̩] vi to do all-in wrestling.

**CB-|Funker** [tsɛ:'be:fʊŋkɐ] der CB ham.

**ccm** (abk für **Kubikzentimeter**) cc.

**CD** [tsɛ:'de:] (pl -s) (abk für **Compactdisc**) die CD.

**CD-ROM** [tsɛ:de:'rɔm] (pl -) (abk für **Compact Disk read only memory**) die EDV CD-ROM.

**CD-Spieler** [tsɛ:'de:ʃpi:lɐ] (pl -) der CD player.

**CDU** [tsɛ:de:'u:] (abk für **Christlich-Demokratische Union**) die Christian Democratic Union, major German political party to the right of the political spectrum.

**C-Dur** ['tsɛ:du:ɐ] das C major.

**CeBit** ['tsɛ:bɪt] die (ohne pl) annual computing fair held in Hanover.

**Cello** ['tʃɛlo] (pl -s) das cello.

**Celsius** ['tsɛlzi̯ʊs] Celsius, centigrade; **10 Grad ~** 10 degrees Celsius ODER centigrade.

**Cembalo** ['tʃɛmbalo] (pl -s) das harpsichord.

**Cent** [(t)sɛnt] (pl -s ODER -) der cent. - **1.** [in EU] cent - **2.** (pl **cents**) [in USA] cent.

**Ceylon** nt Ceylon; **auf ~ in** Ceylon.

**Chamäleon** [ka'mɛ:leɔn] (pl -s) das chameleon.

**Champagner** [ʃam'panjɐ] (pl -) der champagne.

**Champignon** ['ʃampɪnjɔŋ] (pl -s) der mushroom.

**Champion** ['tʃɛmpi̯ən] (pl -s) der champion.

**Chance** ['ʃɑ̃:s(ə)] (pl -n) die [Möglichkeit] chance; **jm eine ~ geben** to give sb a chance; **~n (bei jm) haben** to stand a chance (with sb).

**Chancengleichheit** die (ohne pl) equal opportunities (pl).

**Chanson** [ʃɑ̃'sɔ̃] (pl -s) das satirical song.

**Chaos** ['ka:ɔs] das chaos.

**Chaot, in** [ka'o:t, ɪn] (mpl -en; fpl -nen) der, die - **1.** abw [politisch] anarchist - **2.** abw [menschlich, charakterlich] chaotic person.

**chaotisch** [ka'o:tɪʃ] adj chaotic <> adv chaotically.

**Charakter** [ka'raktɐ] (pl -tere) der character.

**Charakter|eigenschaft** die character trait.

**charakterfest** adj: **er ist ein ~er Mann** he is a strong character.

**charakterisieren** [karakteri'zi:rən] vt to characterize.

**Charakteristik** [karakte'rɪstɪk] (pl -en) die characteristic.

**charakteristisch** [karakte'rɪstɪʃ] adj characteristic; **für jn/etw ~ sein** to be characteristic of sb/sthg <> adv characteristically.

**charakterlich** [ka'raktɐlɪç] adj: **~e Schwäche** weakness of character.

**charakterlos** [ka'raktɐlo:s] adj unprincipled <> adv without principle.

**Charakter|zug** der trait.

**Charisma** ['ça:rɪsma] (pl -ismen) das charisma.

**charmant, scharmant** [ʃar'mant] adj charming <> adv charmingly.

**Charme, Scharm** [ʃarm] der charm.

**Charter|flug** ['tʃartɐflu:k] der charter flight.

**Charter|flugzeug** das charter plane.

**Charter|gesellschaft** die charter company.

**Charter|maschine** die charter plane.

**chartern** ['tʃartɐn] vt to charter.

**Chassis** [ʃa'si:] (pl -) das chassis.

**Chat** [tʃɛt] (pl -s) der EDV chat.

**Chatroom** ['tʃɛt'ru:m] (pl -s) der EDV chatroom.

**Chauffeur, in** [ʃɔ'fø:ɐ, rɪn] (mpl -e; fpl -nen) der, die chauffeur.

**chauffieren** [ʃɔ'fi:rən] vt to chauffeur.

**Chauvi** ['ʃo:vil] (pl -s) der fam abw male chauvinist pig.

**Chauvinismus** [ʃovi'nɪsmʊs] der abw chauvinism.

**Chauvinist, in** [ʃovi'nɪst] (mpl -en; fpl -nen) der, die abw chauvinist.

**chauvinistisch** [ʃovi'nɪstɪʃ] abw adj chauvinist <> adv chauvinistically.

**checken** ['tʃɛkn̩] vt - **1.** [untersuchen] to check

**- 2.** *salopp* [verstehen]: **sie checkt es einfach nicht!** she just doesn't get it!

**Check|liste** ['tʃɛklɪstə] *die* checklist.

**Cheerleaderin** [tʃɪə'liːdərɪn] (*pl* **-nen**) *die* cheerleader.

**Chef** [ʃɛf] (*pl* **-s**) *der* [von Firma, Mafiosi] boss; [von Organisation] head.

**Chef|arzt** *der* senior consultant *Br*, specialist *Am*.

**Chef|ärztin** *die* senior consultant *Br*, specialist *Am*.

**Chef|etage** *die* executive floor.

**Chefin** (*pl* **-nen**) *die* [von Firma] boss; [von Organisation] head.

**Chef|redakteur, in** *der, die* editor-in-chief.

**Chef|sekretär, in** *der, die* personal assistant (*of the boss*).

**chem.** (*abk für* **chemisch**) chem.

**Chemie** [çe'miː] *die* (*ohne pl*) **- 1.** [Wissenschaft] chemistry; **organische/anorganische ~** organic/inorganic chemistry **- 2.** *fam* [Chemikalien] chemicals (*pl*).

**Chemie|faser** *die* man-made fibre.

**Chemikalie** [çemi'kaːljə] (*pl* **-n**) *die* chemical.

**Chemiker, in** ['çeːmikɐ, rɪn] (*mpl* **-**; *fpl* **-nen**) *der, die* chemist

**chemisch** ['çeːmɪʃ] *adj* [Reaktion, Zusammensetzung] chemical; **~es Labor** chemistry lab; **~e Reinigung** dry-cleaning ⬦ *adv* chemically; **~ reinigen** to dry-clean.

**Chemo|therapie** [çemotera'piː] *die* chemotherapy.

**Chicago** *nt* Chicago.

**Chicorée, Schikoree** ['ʃikore] (*pl* **-s**) *die* ODER *der* chicory.

**Chiemsee** *der* Chiemsee.

**Chiffre** ['ʃifrə] (*pl* **-n**) *die* **- 1.** [Zeichen] (code) symbol **- 2.** [von Anzeigen] box number.

**chiffrieren** [ʃɪ'friːrən] *vt* to encode.

**Chile** ['tʃiːle] *nt* Chile.

**Chilene** ['tʃiːleːnə] (*pl* **-n**) *der* Chilean.

**Chilenin** ['tʃiːleːnɪn] (*pl* **-nen**) *die* Chilean.

**chilenisch** ['tʃiːleːnɪʃ] *adj* Chilean.

**Chili** ['tʃiːli] (*pl* **-s**) *der* **- 1.** [Schote] chilli (pepper) **- 2.** [Gewürz] chilli (powder).

**China** ['çiːna] *nt* China.

**Chinakohl** *der* (*ohne pl*) Chinese leaves (*pl*) *Br*, bok choy *Am*.

**Chinese** [çi'neːzə] (*pl* **-n**) *der* Chinese (man).

**Chinesin** [çi'neːzɪn] (*pl* **-nen**) *die* Chinese (woman).

**chinesisch** [çi'neːzɪʃ] *adj* Chinese.

**Chinesisch(e)** *das* Chinese; *siehe auch* **Englisch(e).**

**Chinin** [çi'niːn] *das* quinine.

**Chip** [tʃɪp] (*pl* **-s**) *der* [beim Spiel & ELEKTR, EDV] chip.

**Chips** [tʃɪps] *pl* crisps *Br*, chips *Am*.

**Chirurg** [çi'rʊrk] (*pl* **-en**) *der* surgeon.

**Chirurgie** [çirʊr'giː] (*pl* **-n**) *die* **- 1.** [Wissenschaft] surgery **- 2.** [Krankenhausabteilung] surgical unit; **auf der ~ liegen** to be in surgery.

**Chirurgin** [çi'rʊrgɪn] (*pl* **-nen**) *die* surgeon.

**chirurgisch** [çi'rʊrgɪʃ] *adj* surgical ⬦ *adv* surgically.

**Chlor** [kloːɐ̯] *das* chlorine.

**chlorfrei** *adj* chlorine-free ⬦ *adv* [bleichen] without using chlorine.

**Chloroform** [kloro'fɔrm] *das* chloroform.

**Chlorophyll** [kloro'fyl] *das* chlorophyll.

**Choke** [tʃoːk] (*pl* **-s**) *der* choke.

**Cholera** ['koːlera] *die* cholera.

**cholerisch** [ko'leːrɪʃ] *adj* irascible ⬦ *adv* irascibly.

**Cholesterin** [koleste'riːn] *das* cholesterol.

**Chor** [koːɐ̯] (*pl* **Chöre**) *der* MUS & ARCHIT choir; **im ~** in chorus.

**Choral** [ko'raːl] (*pl* **Choräle**) *der* [Kirchenlied] chorale; **gregorianischer ~** Gregorian chant.

**Choreograf, Choreograph** [koreo'graːf] (*pl* **-en**) *der* choreographer.

**Choreografie, Choreographie** [koreogra'fiː] (*pl* **-n**) *die* choreography.

**Choreografin** (*pl* **-nen**) *die* choreographer.

**Chor|leiter, in** *der, die* choirmaster.

**Christ** ['krɪst] (*pl* **-en**) *der* Christian.

**Christ|baum** *der* Christmas tree.

**Christ|demokrat, in** *der, die* Christian Democrat.

**Christentum** ['krɪstn̩tuːm] *das* Christianity.

**Christi Himmelfahrt** (*ohne Artikel*) [Feiertag] Ascension Day.

**Christin** ['krɪstɪn] (*pl* **-nen**) *die* Christian.

**Christkind** *das* **- 1.** [Jesuskind] baby Jesus, Christ Child **- 2.** [zu Weihnachten] ≈ Santa Claus.

**christlich** ['krɪstlɪç] *adj* Christian ⬦ *adv:* **~ handeln** to act like a Christian.

**Christmette** (*pl* **-n**) *die* [katholisch] Midnight Mass; [evangelisch] Midnight Service.

**Christ|stollen** *der* stollen, *sweet bread loaf made with dried fruit and marzipan, eaten at Christmas.*

**Christus** ['krɪstʊs] *der* Christ.

**Chrom** [kroːm] *das* [als Überzug] chrome; CHEM chromium.

**Chromosom** [kromo'zo:m] (*pl* -en) *das* chromosome.

**Chronik** ['kro:nɪk] (*pl* -en) *die* chronicle.

**chronisch** ['kro:nɪʃ] *adj* chronic.

**chronologisch** [krono'lo:gɪʃ] *adj* chronological <> *adv* chronologically.

**Chrysantheme** [kryzan'te:mə] (*pl* -n) *die* chrysanthemum.

**circa** ['tsɪrka] *adv* = zirka.

**cis, Cis** ['tsɪs] (*pl* Cis) *das* MUS C sharp.

**City** ['sɪti] (*pl* -s) *die* city centre.

**clever** ['klevɐ] *adj* clever, smart <> *adv* cleverly, smartly.

**Clinch** ['klɪntʃ] *der:* mit jm im ~ liegen to have fallen out with sb.

**Clip** ['klɪp] (*pl* -s) *der* - **1.** [Videoclip] (pop) video - **2.** [Ohrring] = Klipp.

**Clique** ['klɪkə] (*pl* -n) *die* - **1.** [Gruppe] group of friends - **2.** *abw* [Interessengemeinschaft] clique; [von Verbrechern] gang.

**Cliquenwirtschaft** *die abw:* die Regierung ist eine ~ the government just looks after its own interests.

**Clou** [klu:] (*pl* -s) *der:* der ~ an der Sache ist ... the best thing about it is ...

**Clown, in** [klaun, ɪn] (*mpl* -s; *fpl* -nen) *der, die* clown.

**Club** = Klub.

**cm** (*abk für* Zentimeter) cm.

**c-Moll** ['tse:mɔl] *das* MUS C minor.

**c/o** (*abk für* care of) c/o.

**CO₂** (*abk für* Kohlendioxid) *das* $CO_2$.

**Cockerspaniel** ['kɔkɐspa:njəl] (*pl* -s ODER -) *der* cocker spaniel.

**Cockpit** ['kɔkpɪt] (*pl* -s) *das* cockpit.

**Cocktail** ['kɔkte:l] (*pl* -s) *der* cocktail.

**Code** ['ko:t] (*pl* -s) *der* = Kode.

**codieren** [ko'di:rən] *vt* = kodieren.

**Cognac®** ['kɔnjak] (*pl* -s) *der* cognac.

**Cola** [ko:la] (*pl* -s) *die* ODER *das* Coke®.

**Collage** [kɔ'la:ʒə] (*pl* -n) *die* collage.

**Colt®** [kɔlt] (*pl* -s) *der* Colt®.

**Come-back** [kam'bɛk] (*pl* -s) *das* comeback.

**Comer See** ['ko:mɐ 'ze:] *der* Lake Como.

**Comic** ['kɔmɪk] (*pl* -s) *der* - **1.** [Geschichte] cartoon - **2.** [Heft] comic.

**Compiler** [kɔm'paɪlɐ] (*pl* -) *der* EDV compiler.

**Computer** [kɔm'pju:tɐ] (*pl* -) *der* computer.

**Computerlausdruck** *der* computer printout.

**computergesteuert** *adj* computer-controlled.

**Computerlkriminalität** *die* computer crime.

**Computerlspiel** *das* computer game.

**Computerlvirus** *der* computer virus.

**Conférencier** [kõferã'sje:] (*pl* -s) *der* MC, compere.

**Container** [kɔn'te:nɐ] (*pl* -) *der* [gen] container; [für Altglas, Papier] bank.

**Containerlschiff** *das* container ship.

**contra** ['kɔntra] *präp* = kontra.

**cool** [ku:l] *adj* & *adv salopp* cool.

**Colpilot** ['ko:pilo:t] *der* = Kopilot.

**Colpilotin** ['ko:pilo:tɪn] *die* = Kopilotin.

**Colprozessor** *der* coprocessor.

**Copyright** ['kɔpiraɪt] (*pl* -s) *das* copyright.

**Cord** [kɔrt] *der* = Kord.

**Cordlhose** ['kɔrt|ho:zə] *die* = Kordhose.

**Córdoba** ['kɔrdoba] *nt* Cordoba.

**Cornedbeef** ['kɔrnət'bi:f] *das* corned beef.

**Cornflakes** ['ko:ɐnfle:ks] *pl* cornflakes.

**Costa Rica** *nt* Costa Rica.

**Couch** [kautʃ] (*pl* -s ODER -en) *die* couch.

**Couchltisch** *der* coffee table.

**Count-down** ['kaunt'daun] (*pl* -s) *das* ODER *der* countdown.

**Countrymusic** ['kantrimju:zɪk] *die* country (and western) music.

**Coup** [ku:] (*pl* -s) *der* coup; einen (großen) ~ landen to pull off a (major) coup.

**Coupé** [ku'pe:] (*pl* -s) *das* AUTO coupé.

**Coupon** [ku'põ] (*pl* -s) *der* = Kupon.

**Cousin** [ku'zɛ̃] (*pl* -s) *der* cousin.

**Cousine, Kusine** [ku'zi:nə] (*pl* -n) *die* cousin.

**Cover** ['kavɐ] (*pl* -s ODER -) *das* - **1.** [von Schallplatten] sleeve - **2.** [von Zeitschriften] cover.

**Cowboy** ['kaubɔy] (*pl* -s) *der* cowboy.

**Creme, Krem** [kre:m, krɛ:m] (*pl* -s ODER -n) *die* - **1.** [Hautcreme] cream - **2.** [Speise] confectioner's custard.

**cremig, kremig** ['kre:mɪç] *adj* creamy <> *adv:* etw ~ schlagen to cream sthg.

**Crew** [kru:] (*pl* -s) *die* [Besatzung] crew.

**CSU** [tse:ɛs'u:] (*abk für* Christlich-Soziale Union) *die* Christian Social Union, *Bavarian political party to the right of the political spectrum, long-time alliance partners of the CDU.*

**c. t.** (*abk für* cum tempore (mit akademischem Viertel)): fängt die Vorlesung pünktlich um 14.00 an? – nein, um 14.00 c. t. does the lecture start at two o'clock on the dot? – no, it doesn't actually start until quarter past.

**Cup** [kap] (pl -s) der SPORT cup.

**Curry** ['kœri] (pl -s) das - **1.** [Gewürz] curry powder - **2.** [Gericht] curry.

**Curry|wurst** die sausage with curry sauce.

**Cursor** ['kœː(r)zɐ] (pl -s) der EDV cursor.

**CVJM** [tseːfaujɔt'ɛm] (abk für **Christlicher Verein Junger Menschen**) der [für Männer] YMCA; [für Frauen] YWCA.

**CVP** [tseːfaupeː] (abk für **Christliche Volkspartei (der Schweiz)**) die Popular Christian Democratic Party, right-wing political party in Switzerland.

**Cyberspace** ['saibɐspeis] der (ohne pl) cyberspace.

# D

**d, D** [deː] (pl - ODER -s) das - **1.** [Buchstabe] d, D - **2.** MUS D.

**da** adv - **1.** [dort] there; **guck mal ~!** look over there!; **~ kommt der Bus!** here comes the bus!; **das ~ gefällt mir am besten** I like that one best; **~ drüben** over there - **2.** fam [hier] here; **~ bin ich!** here I am!; **ist noch etwas Brot ~?** is there any bread left?; **ich bin gleich wieder ~** I'll be back in a minute - **3.** [zeitlich] then, at that time; **von ~ an** from then on - **4.** [in diesem Zusammenhang]: **~ fällt mir ein ...** I've just thought ...; **und ~ gibt es eine Geschichte dazu** and thereby hangs a tale - **5.** [in dieser Beziehung] there; **~ irren Sie sich** you're wrong there; **~ bist du selbst schuld** that's your own fault; **~ mach dir mal keine Sorgen!** don't worry about that! - **6.** [folglich] so; **der Chef war krank, ~ übernahm ich seinen Posten** the boss was ill so I went in his place - **7.** [unter dieser Bedingung] in that case; **~ gehe ich lieber gleich** in that case I'd rather go straight away <> konj - **1.** [weil] as, since; **~ ihr Vater krank war, musste sie zu Hause bleiben** as her father was ill, she had to stay at home - **2.** geh [nachdem] now (that); **jetzt, ~ Sie es erwähnen ...** now (that) you mention it ...

➡ **da und dort** adv here and there.

**d. Ä.** abk für **der Ältere**.

**DAAD** [deːaːaːˈdeː] (abk für **Deutscher Akademischer Austauschdienst**) der German Academic Exchange Service, cultural body which organizes academic exchanges for students and staff.

**da|behalten** vt (unreg) to keep (in ODER back); **jn im Betrieb ~** to keep sb on at the company.

**dabei, dabei** adv - **1.** [räumlich]: **waren Sie bei der Auktion ~?** were you at the auction?; **hast du zufällig eine Briefmarke ~?** do you happen to have a stamp on you?; **nicht ~ sein** to be missing; **ich bin ~!** fig count me in! - **2.** [zeitlich] at the same time; **sie waren gerade ~, das Haus zu verlassen** they were just leaving the house - **3.** [bei dieser Sache]: **~ kam heraus, dass ...** in the process it came out that ...; **mir ist nicht ganz wohl ~ (zumute)** I don't really feel happy about it; **und ~ bleibts!** and that's the end of it!; **es ist nichts ~** fam fig there's nothing wrong with it; **was ist schon ~!** fam fig so what! - **4.** [obwohl] although - **5.** [überdies]: **und ~ ist sie auch noch intelligent** and (what is more) she's clever too; siehe auch **dabei sein**.

**dabei|bleiben** (perf ist **dabeigeblieben**) vi (unreg) to stay on; **es bleibt dabei: wir treffen uns um fünf Uhr** let's stick to meeting at five o'clock.

**dabei|haben** vt (unreg) [Person] to have with one; [Gegenstand] to have on one; **sie wollten ihn nicht ~** they didn't want him there.

**dabei sein** (perf ist **dabei gewesen**) vi (unreg) - **1.** [anwesend sein] to be present ODER there; **ich bin dabei!** count me in! - **2.** [im Begriff sein]: **~, etw zu tun** to be just doing sthg.

**da|bleiben** (perf ist **dageblieben**) vi (unreg) to stay.

**Dach** (pl **Dächer**) das roof; **das ~ decken** to roof the house; **unterm ~ wohnen** to live in the attic; **ein ~ über dem Kopf haben** to have a roof over one's head; **unter einem ~ wohnen** ODER **leben** ODER **hausen** to live under the same roof; **jm aufs ~ steigen** fam to have a go at sb; **jm eins aufs ~ geben** fam [Ohrfeige] to clip sb round the ear; [ausschimpfen] to have a go at sb; **eins aufs ~ bekommen** ODER **kriegen** fam to get a clip round the ear.

➡ **unter Dach und Fach** adv [Vertrag] in the bag.

**Dach|boden** der attic; **auf dem ~** in the attic.

**Dach|decker** (pl -) der roofer.

**Dach|fenster** das [groß] dormer window; [Luke] skylight.

**Dach|garten** der roof garden.

**Dach|gepäckträger** der roof rack.

**Dach|geschoss** das top floor.

**Dach|kammer** die attic room.

**Dach|luke** die skylight.

**Dach|organisation** *die* umbrella organization.

**Dach|pfanne** *die* roof tile.

**Dach|rinne** *die* gutter.

**Dachs** [daks] (*pl* -e) *der* badger.

**Dach|schaden** *der* roof damage *(U)*; **einen ~ haben** *salopp fig* not to be right upstairs.

**dachte** *prät* ⊳ **denken**.

**Dach|terrasse** *die* roof terrace.

**Dach|verband** *der* umbrella organization.

**Dach|wohnung** *die* attic flat *Br* ODER apartment *Am*.

**Dach|ziegel** *der* roof tile.

**Dackel** (*pl* -) *der* dachshund.

**Dadaismus** [dada'ısmʊs] *der* Dadaism.

**Dadaist, in** [dada'ıst, ın] (*mpl* -en; *fpl* -nen) *der, die* Dadaist.

**daddeln** *vi fam:* **am Dreamcast®~** to play on one's Dreamcast®.

**dadurch, dadurch** *adv* - **1.** [auf diese Art] because of this; **~, dass** because; **~, dass wir uns viel Mühe gaben** ... because we tried very hard ...; **~ kam es, dass** ... that was why ... - **2.** [räumlich] through it.

**DAF** [daf] (*abk für* **Deutsch als Fremdsprache**) *das* German as a Foreign Language.

**dafür, dafür** *adv* - **1.** [für etwas] for it; **200 Euro ~ bezahlen** to pay 200 euros for it **er kann nichts ~** it's not his fault; **er hat kein Verständnis ~** he has no feeling for that; **er ist bekannt ~, dass er gern trinkt** he has a reputation for liking a drink [bejahend] for it, in favour of it; **~ spricht, dass** ... this is confirmed by the fact that ... - **2.** [im Ausgleich]: **er arbeitet langsam, ~ aber gründlich** he works slowly yet thoroughly - **3.** [im Tausch] in exchange; **~ mache ich für dich den Abwasch** and I'll do the washing-up for you in return - **4.** [trotzdem] nevertheless.

**Dafürhalten** *das:* **nach js ~** in sb's opinion.

**dafür|können** *vt (unreg):* **nichts ~** not to be able to help it; **ich kann doch nichts dafür, dass der Zug zu spät kommt!** it's not my fault if the train is late!; **was kann ich dafür?** it's not my fault, I can't help it.

**DAG** [deːa'geː] (*abk für* **Deutsche Angestellten-Gewerkschaft**) *die* German white-collar union.

**dagegen, dagegen** *adv* - **1.** [räumlich] against it; **das Auto fuhr ~** the car drove into it - **2.** [ablehnend] against it; **etwas ~ haben** to object; **hast du etwas ~, wenn ich rauche?** do you mind if I smoke?; **~ lässt sich nichts machen** nothing can be done about it; **es spricht nichts ~, dass wir dorthin fahren** there's no reason why we shouldn't go there - **3.** [im

Gegensatz] in comparison; **sie ist groß, er ~ ist klein** she's tall, whereas he is short; **dieser ist nichts ~!** this is nothing in comparison!

**dagegen|stellen** ⇒ **sich dagegenstellen** *ref:* **er stellt sich immer dagegen** he's never in favour of anything, he always opposes everything.

**da gewesen** *pp* ⊳ **da sein** ⇔ *adj:* **noch nie ~** unheard of.

**daheim** *adv Süddt, Österr* & *Schweiz* at home; **wann ist er mal wieder ~?** when will he be home?

**Daheim** *das Süddt, Österr* & *Schweiz* home.

**daher, daher** *adv* - **1.** [aus dieser Richtung] from there; **ach, ~ weht (also) der Wind!** *fig* so that's the way the wind is blowing! - **2.** [dadurch] that is why; **~ (auch) der Name** hence the name; **~ der ganze Ärger** that's the reason for all the hassle - **3.** [deswegen]: **~ kommt es, dass** ... that is why/how ...

**dahin, dahin** *adv* - **1.** [räumlich] there - **2.** [zeitlich]: **bis ~** until then; **bis ~ sind wir fertig** we'll be ready by then - **3.** [als Ziel]: **er antwortete ~ gehend, dass** ... he replied to the effect that ...; **seine Bemühungen gehen ~, sich selbstständig zu machen** he's trying to set up his own business ⇔ *adj fam* [kaputt, beendet, weg]: **das Kleid ist ~!** the dress has had it!; **meine Träume sind ~** my dreams have been shattered.

**dahingegen** *adv geh* on the other hand.

**dahin|gehen** (*perf* ist dahingegangen) *vi (unreg)* *geh* [verstreichen] to pass.

**dahingestellt** *pp:* **etw ~ sein lassen** to leave sthg open; **es bleibt** ODER **sei ~** it remains to be seen.

**dahinten** *adv* back there, over there.

**dahinter** *adv* behind it; **ein Haus mit einem Garten ~** a house with a garden at the back.

**dahinter kommen** (*perf* ist dahinter gekommen) *vi (unreg) fam* to find out.

**dahinter stecken** *vi* to be behind it; **es steckt nichts/nicht viel dahinter** there's nothing/nothing much behind it.

**dahinter stehen** *vi (unreg)* to be behind it.

**Dakar** *nt* Dakar.

**dalassen** *vt (unreg) fam* to leave (there).

**daliegen** *vi (unreg)* [Mensch, Gegenstand] to lie there.

**damalig** *adj* [Bedingungen, Zustände] at that time; **der ~e President** the then president.

**damals** *adv* then, in those days; **als ich ~ krank wurde** when I got ill; **seit ~** since then.

**Damaskus** *nt* Damascus.

**Damast** (*pl* -e) *der* damask.

**Dame** (*pl* -n) *die* - **1.** [Frau] lady; **der Wettbewerb der ~n** the women's competition; **meine (sehr verehrten) ~n und Herren** ladies and gentlemen - **2.** [Spielkarte] queen - **3.** [Spiel] draughts (U).

➡ **Damen** *pl* [Toilette] ladies (*sg*).

**Damen|bekleidung** *die* ladieswear.

**Damen|binde** *die* sanitary towel Br, sanitary napkin Am.

**Damen|fahrrad** *das* lady's bicycle.

**Damen|friseur** *der* ladies' hairdresser.

**damenhaft** *adj* ladylike ◇ *adv* like a lady.

**Damenmoden** *pl* ladies' fashion (U).

**Damen|toilette** *die* ladies (toilet).

**Damenwahl** *die* ladies' choice.

**damit, damit** *konj* so that ◇ *adv* - **1.** [mit dieser Sache]: **was soll ich ~?** what am I supposed to do with this?; **sie war ~ einverstanden** she agreed to it; **was meinst du ~?** what do you mean by that?; **her ~!** *fam* hand it over!; **hör auf ~!** *fam* stop it! - **2.** [zeitlich] with that; **und ~ verließ er den Raum** and with that he left the room - **3.** [somit] because of that; **und ~ war seine Unschuld bewiesen** and this proved his innocence.

**dämlich** *fam abw adj* stupid ◇ *adv* stupidly.

**Damm** (*pl* Dämme) *der* [Deich] dam; **wieder auf dem ~ sein** *fam fig* to be up and about again.

**dämmen** *vt* - **1.** [abhalten - Wasser, Fluten] to dam; [ - Ausbreitung, Seuche] to check - **2.** [Wärme] to keep in; [Schall] to absorb.

**dämmerig** = dämmrig.

**Dämmerlicht** *das* [am Abend, Morgen] twilight; [Halbdunkel] half-light.

**dämmern** *vi* - **1.** [einsetzen]: **es dämmert** [am Morgen] it's getting light, day is breaking; [am Abend] it's getting dark, night is falling - **2.** [halb schlafen]: **(vor sich hin) ~** to doze - **3.** *fam* [bewusst werden]: **eine Ahnung dämmerte ihm** a suspicion dawned on him.

**Dämmerung** (*pl* -en) *die* [am Morgen] dawn; [am Abend] dusk.

**Dämmer|zustand** *der* [schläfrig] half-sleep; [halbbewusst] semi-conscious state.

**dämmrig, dämmerig** *adj* [Licht] dim; [Tag] gloomy, dull; **es wird ~** [am Morgen] it's getting light; [am Abend] it's getting dark.

**Dämon** (*pl* Dämonen) *der* demon.

**dämonisch** *adj* demonic.

**Dampf** (*pl* Dämpfe) *der* [Dunst] steam; **giftige Dämpfe** poisonous fumes; **~ ablassen** *fam* to let off steam; **wir müssen mehr ~ dahinter machen** *fam* we need to get a move on; **jm ~ machen** *fam* to make sb get a move on.

**Dampf|bad** *das* steam bath, Turkish bath.

**Dampf|bügeleisen** *das* steam iron.

**dampfen** *vi* to steam.

**dämpfen** *vt* - **1.** [dünsten] to steam - **2.** [Geräusch, Schritte] to muffle; [Instrument, Farbton] to mute; [Licht] to dim; [Stoß] to cushion; [Stimme] to lower - **3.** [Wut, Aufregung] to calm; [Begeisterung] to dampen - **4.** [verringern] to curb.

**Dampfer** (*pl* -) *der* steamship, steamer; **du bist auf dem falschen ~!** *fam* you've got another think coming!

**Dämpfer** (*pl* -) *der*: **jm einen ~ aufsetzen** ODER **verpassen** to dampen sb's spirits.

**Dampfer|fahrt** *die* trip by steamship ODER steamer.

**Dampf|kochtopf** *der* pressure cooker.

**Dampf|lokomotive** *die* steam engine ODER locomotive.

**Dampf|maschine** *die* steam engine.

**Dampf|walze** *die* steamroller.

**danach, danach** *adv* - **1.** [zeitlich] after, afterwards; **zwei Stunden ~** two hours later; **wir können doch erst ins Theater gehen und ~ essen** why don't we go to the theatre first and eat afterwards - **2.** [nach etwas]: **~ schnappen/greifen** to snap/grab at it; **sich ~ sehnen** to long for it; **ich habe ~ gefragt** I asked about it - **3.** [entsprechend]: **es sieht ganz ~ aus** it looks like it; **mir ist jetzt nicht ~ (zumute)** I don't feel like it at the moment; **das Zimmer ist billig, es ist aber auch ~!** the room is cheap, and it looks it too!

**Däne** (*pl* -n) *der* Dane.

**daneben** *adv* - **1.** [räumlich] next to it/him/*etc*, beside it/him/*etc*; **gleich ~** right next to it; **ihr Büro ist gleich ~** her office is just next door - **2.** [vergleichend] in comparison - **3.** [außerdem] in addition (to that).

**daneben|benehmen**

➡ **sich danebenbenehmen** *ref* (*unreg*) to make an exhibition of o.s.

**daneben|gehen** (*perf* ist danebengegangen) *vi* (*unreg*) - **1.** [danebenzielen] to miss (the target) - **2.** *fam* [misslingen] to fail.

**daneben|greifen** *vi* (*unreg*) - **1.** [greifen] to miss - **2.** *fam* [sich irren] to be wide of the mark.

**daneben|hauen** *vi* - **1.** [hauen] to miss - **2.** *fam* [sich irren] to be wide of the mark.

**daneben|liegen** *vi* (*unreg*) *fam* to be wide of the mark.

**Dänemark** *nt* Denmark.

**Dänin** (*pl* -nen) *die* Dane.

**dänisch** *adj* Danish.

**Dänisch(e)** *das* Danish; *siehe auch* Englisch(e).

**dank** *präp*: **~ einer Sache** (G) thanks to sthg.

**Dank** *der* (*ohne pl*) thanks (*pl*); **zum ~ dafür** as a reward, by way of saying thank you; **vielen ~!** thank you (very much)!; **schönen** ODER **besten ~ auch!** thank you (very much)!; **jm (für etw) ~ sagen** to thank sb (for sthg),; **jm zu ~ verpflichtet sein** to owe sb a debt of gratitude.

**dankbar** adj - **1.** [voller Dank] grateful; **jm (für etw) ~ sein** to be grateful to sb (for sthg) - **2.** [lohnend] rewarding <> adv [voller Dank] gratefully.

**Dankbarkeit** die gratitude.

**danke** interj thanks!, thank you!; **~, dass du gekommen bist!** thanks ODER thank you for coming!; **noch einen Kaffee? - ~, gern/im Moment nicht** would you like another coffee? – yes, please/no thanks ODER no thank you, not just now; **~ gleichfalls!** thanks, you too!; **~ sehr** ODER **schön!** thanks (very much)!, thank you (very much)!

**danken** vi: **jm (für etw) ~** to thank sb (for sthg); **na, ich danke!** fam no thanks!, no thank you!; **nichts zu ~!** don't mention it!

**Dankeschön** das thank you.

**Dank|schreiben** das letter of thanks.

**dann** adv - **1.** [gen] then; **bis ~** see you (then) - **2.** [außerdem] then; **und ~ (noch)** ... and, on top of that ... - **3.** [konditional] in that case, then.
◆ **also dann** interj all right then.
◆ **dann und dann** adv at such and such time.
◆ **dann und wann** adv now and then.

**Danzig** nt Danzig, Gdansk.

**daran, daran** adv - **1.** [an diese Sache]: **ich denke gerade ~** I'm just thinking about it; **er arbeitete lange ~** he worked at OR on it for a long time; **es ist nichts Wahres ~** there is no truth in it; **mir liegt viel ~** it is very important to me; **er war schuld ~** it was his fault - **2.** [räumlich]: **er klebte Papier ~** he stuck paper (on)to it; **ein Tisch mit zwei Personen ~** a table with two people (sitting) at it; **wir gingen ~ vorbei** we went past it; **nahe ~** close to it - **3.** [deshalb]: **sie ist ~ gestorben** she died of it; **es liegt ~, dass ...** it is because ...

**daran|gehen** (perf ist darangegangen) vi (unreg) to get started; **~, das Essen vorzubereiten** to get started on preparing the meal.

**daran|setzen** vt [Energie, Kraft] to use; **alles ~ to** do one's utmost.

**darauf, darauf** adv - **1.** [räumlich] on it - **2.** [Richtung]: **~ zielen** to aim at it; **das deutet ~ hin, dass ...** fig this implies that ... - **3.** [zeitlich] after that; **am Tag ~** the day after, the next day; **Jahre ~** years later; **bald ~** soon after(wards) - **4.** [als Reaktion] to that; **~ steht die Todesstrafe** the penalty for that is death - **5.** [zum Ausdruck einer Intention]: **sie ist ~ aus, einen Mann zu bekommen** she's out to get a

husband; **sie wartand ~** she was most particular about it; **besonders ~ achten, dass ...** to take particular care to ...

**daraufhin** adv - **1.** [aus einem Grund] as a result - **2.** [zu einem Zweck]: **das Produkt ~ prüfen, ob es den Normen entspricht** to test the product (in order) to see if it meets the standards.

**daraus, daraus** adv - **1.** [räumlich] from it, out of it - **2.** [aus dieser Sache] from it; **~ folgt, dass ...** from this it follows that ...; **mach dir nichts ~!** don't let it bother you!; **ich mache mir nichts ~** I'm not very keen on it; **~ wird nichts!** fam nothing doing! - **3.** [aus einem Material] from it, out of it.

**dar|bieten** vt (unreg) geh to perform.
◆ **sich darbieten** ref to present itself.

**Darbietung** (pl -en) die geh [Aufführung] performance.

**darf** präs ⊳ dürfen.

**darin, darin** adv - **1.** [in etwas] in it, inside - **2.** [in diesem Sachverhalt] there; **~ hat er nicht Recht** he's wrong there ODER about that.

**dar|legen** vt to explain.

**Darlehen** (pl -) das loan; **ein ~ aufnehmen** to take out a loan.

**Darm** (pl **Därme**) der - **1.** [Organ] intestine - **2.** [Material] gut.

**Darm|flora** die intestinal flora.

**Darm|grippe** die gastric flu.

**Darm|infektion** die bowel infection.

**dar|stellen** vt - **1.** [Subj: Bild] to portray, to depict - **2.** [beschreiben] to describe - **3.** [Subj: Schauspieler] to play - **4.** [sein] to represent, to constitute; **als Wissenschaftler stellt er etwas dar** he is an impressive scientist; **die Dekoration stellt nicht viel dar** the décor is nothing special.
◆ **sich darstellen** ref - **1.** [sich erweisen] to prove to be - **2.** [sich präsentieren]: **sich als etw ~** to cultivate an image of being sthg.

**Darsteller, in** (mpl -; fpl -nen) der, die actor (f actress); **der ~ des Hamlet** the actor playing Hamlet.

**Dar|stellung** die - **1.** [als Bild] depiction, portrayal; **eine grafische ~** a graphic representation - **2.** [Bericht] account.

**darüber, darüber** adv - **1.** [räumlich - über etw] above it, over it; [ - über etw hinweg] across it, over it; **~ hinaus** fig in addition; **~ sind wir schon hinaus** we have already passed that stage - **2.** [über diese Sache] about it; **hast du ~ nachgedacht?** did you think about it?; **ich komme nicht ~ hinweg** I can't get over it; **~ hinwegsehen** to ignore it - **3.** [zeitlich] in the meantime; **sie las und vergaß ~ ganz die Nudeln** she was reading and completely forgot about the pasta - **4.** [mehr] above that, over that; **nichts geht ~!** *fig* there is nothing to beat it.

**darüber stehen** *vi (unreg)* to be above such things.

**darum, darum** *adv* - **1.** [räumlich] round it - **2.** [um diese Sache] about it; **jn ~ bitten, etw zu tun** to ask sb to do sthg; **~ geht es nicht** that's not the point; **es geht ~, dass** ... the thing is that ...; **~ wetten** to bet on it - **3.** [deswegen] that's why; **ach ~!** so that's why!, so that's the reason!; **eben ~** for that very reason; **warum? – ~!** *fam* why? – because!

**darunter, darunter** *adv* - **1.** [unter dieser Sache]: **er leidet ~** he suffers from it; **was verstehst du ~?** what do you understand by that?; **~ kann ich mir nichts vorstellen** that doesn't mean anything to me - **2.** [räumlich] under it; **sie hob das Kissen und fand ihre Kette ~** she lifted the cushion and found her necklace underneath - **3.** [weniger]: **30 Meter oder etwas ~** 30 metres or a little less; **Kinder im Alter von 5 Jahren und ~** children aged 5 and under - **4.** [in dieser Menge] among(st) them; **viele Besucher, ~ auch einige aus dem Ausland** many visitors, including some foreigners.

**darunter fallen** (*perf* ist darunter gefallen) *vi (unreg)* to be included.

**das** *det* the; **~ Rauchen** smoking <> *pron* - **1.** [Demonstrativpronomen] that; **~ da** that one there; **unser Haus? – ~ haben wir verkauft** our house? – we've sold it; **~ regnet heute wieder wie verrückt** it's raining like mad again today - **2.** [Relativpronomen - Person] who, that; [- Sache] which, that.

**da sein** (*perf* ist da gewesen) *vi (unreg)* - **1.** [vorhanden sein, anwesend sein] to be there; **es ist keine Milch mehr da** there's no more milk, there's no milk left; **ich bin gleich wieder da** I'll be back in a second - **2.** [eingetreten sein - Situation] to arise; [- Augenblick] to arrive; **er überbot alles, was bisher da gewesen war** he surpassed everything which had gone before - **3.** [leben] to live - **4.** *fam* [wach sein] to be with it; **geistig voll ~** to be all there.

**Dasein** *das* - **1.** [Leben] existence - **2.** [Anwesenheit] presence.

**Daseinsberechtigung** *die* - **1.** [Recht] right to exist - **2.** [Grund] raison d'être.

**da sitzen** *vi (unreg)* - **1.** [an einer Stelle] to sit (there) - **2.** *fam* [in einer Situation] to be left (there).

**dasjenige** *det* the; **~ Kind, das hingefallen ist** the child who fell <> *pron:* **~, was sie am liebsten tut** the thing she likes to do most; **~, das** ... the one which ...

**dass** *konj* - **1.** [im Objektsatz] that; **ich weiß, ~ du gern angelst** I know (that) you like fishing - **2.** [im Subjektsatz] the fact that; **du musst be-**

**denken, ~ er nicht mehr klein ist** you must remember (that) he's not young anymore; **~ das bloß klappt!** let it work! - **3.** [im Attributsatz] that; **unter der Bedingung, ~** ... on (the) condition that ...; **es war eine Dummheit, ~ er das gesagt hat** it was stupid of him to say that - **4.** [in festen Verbindungen]: **anstatt, ~ er selbst kam,** ... instead of coming himself, ...; **ohne ~ sie etwas gemerkt hat** without her noticing anything.

**dasselbe** *det* the same <> *pron* the same one; **genau ~ hast du gestern gesagt** you said exactly the same thing yesterday.

**da stehen** *vi (unreg)* - **1.** [an Stelle] to stand (there) - **2.** [in Situation] to find o.s.; **mit leeren Händen ~** to be left empty-handed; **gut** ODER **glänzend ~** to be in a good ODER splendid position; **wie stehe ich jetzt da?** how do you think it makes me look?

**Datei** (*pl* -en) *die* EDV file.

**Dateiname** *der* EDV filename.

**Dateiverwaltung** *die* EDV file management.

**Daten** *pl* - **1.** [Zeiten] ⊏> **Datum** - **2.** [Informationen] data; **~ verarbeitend** data-processing.

**Datenautobahn** *die* EDV information superhighway.

**Datenbank** (*pl* -en) *die* databank.

**Datenerfassung** *die* data capture.

**Datenmaterial** *das* data.

**Datennetz** *das:* **das ~** the Net; **im ~** on the Net.

**Datenschutz** *der* data protection.

**Datenschutzgesetz** *das* data protection law.

**Datentypist, in** (*mpl* -en; *fpl* -nen) *der, die* data inputter.

**datenverarbeitend** *adj* ⊏> **Daten.**

**Datenverarbeitung** *die* data processing; **elektronische ~** computing.

**datieren** *vt* to date.

**Datierung** (*pl* -en) *die* date.

**Dativ** (*pl* -e) *der* dative.

**Dativobjekt** *das* indirect object.

**dato** ⇒ **bis dato** *adv* to date.

**Datum** (*pl* Daten) *das* date; **welches ~ haben wir heute?** what's today's date?; **eine Ausgabe neueren/älteren ~s** a recent/old edition.

**Datumsangabe** *die* date.

**Datumstempel, Datumsstempel** *der* date stamp.

**Dauer** *die* length; **dieses Glück hatte keine ~** this happiness did not last; **auf (die) ~** in the long term; **seine Ehe war nicht von ~** his marriage was short-lived.

D

**Dauer|arbeitslosigkeit** *die* long-term unemployment.

**Dauer|auftrag** *der* standing order.

**Dauer|belastung** *die* constant strain.

**Dauer|beschäftigung** *die* permanent position.

**dauerhaft** *adj* [Friede, Freundschaft] lasting; [Material] durable <> *adv:* **das Problem ~ lösen** to find a lasting solution to the problem.

**Dauer|karte** *die* season ticket.

**Dauer|lauf** *der* jog.

**dauern** *vi* to last; **es dauert zu lange** it's taking too long; **eine Weile wird es schon noch ~, bis ich fertig bin** it will still be a while before I'm finished.

**dauernd** *adj* constant <> *adv* constantly.

**Dauer|regen** *der* persistent rain.

**Dauer|welle** *die* perm.

**Dauer|wurst** *die hard smoked sausage which keeps for a long time, e.g. salami.*

**Dauer|zustand** *der* permanent state.

**Däumchen** *(pl -) das:* **~ drehen** *fam* to twiddle one's thumbs.

**Daumen** *(pl -) der* thumb; **am ~ lutschen** to suck one's thumb; **jm die ~ drücken** *ODER* **halten** *fig* to keep one's fingers crossed for sb; **den ~ auf etw** *(A)* **halten** *fam* to guard sthg jealously.

**Daune** *(pl -n) die:* **~n** down *(U).*

**Daunen|decke** *die* eiderdown.

**Daunen|kissen** *das* down-filled cushion/pillow.

**davon, davon** *adv* - **1.** [räumlich] from it - **2.** [von diesem Gegenstand, aus dieser Menge] of it - **3.** [von dieser Sache] about it - **4.** [dadurch]: **er ist nicht ~ betroffen** he is not affected by it; **sie ist ~ krank geworden** it made her ill; **das kommt ~!** that's what happens!

**davon|kommen** *(perf* ist **davongekommen)** *vi (unreg)* to escape.

**davon|laufen** *(perf* ist **davongelaufen)** *vi (unreg)* to run away; **jm ~** [Ehepartner, Hausmädchen] to walk out on sb; [Verfolgter] to shake sb off.

**davon|machen** ◆ **sich davonmachen** *ref* to sneak off.

**davor, davor** *adv* - **1.** [räumlich] in front of it - **2.** [zeitlich] beforehand; **kurz ~ sein, etw zu tun** to be on the point of doing sthg - **3.** [vor dieser Sache]: **jn ~ warnen** to warn sb of it; **ich habe Angst ~** I'm scared of it.

**Davos** *nt* Davos.

**DAX** [daks] *(abk für* **Deutscher Aktienindex)** *der* DAX index, *German Share Index.*

**dazu, dazu** *adv* - **1.** [außerdem] in addition, into the bargain; **es schneit und es ist noch kalt ~**

it's snowing, and it's cold too - **2.** [zu dieser Sache]: **er hat nicht die Zeit ~** he hasn't got time for it; **ich habe keine Lust ~** I don't feel like it; **ich bin nicht ~ gekommen** I didn't get round to it.

**dazu|geben** *vt (unreg)* to add.

**dazu|gehören** *vi* - **1.** [zu etwas gehören] to belong; **gehört der Drucker dazu?** is the printer included? - **2.** [nötig sein]: **es gehört Mut dazu, das zu tun** it takes courage to do that.

**dazugehörig** *adj* belonging to it/them.

**dazu|kommen** *(perf* ist **dazugekommen)** *vi (unreg)* - **1.** [ankommen] to arrive - **2.** [hinzukommen]: **sie ist neu dazugekommen** she's a recent arrival; **kommt noch etwas dazu?** would you like anything else?

**dazu|rechnen** *vt* to add on.

**dazu|tun** *vt (unreg)* to add.

**Dazutun** *das:* **ohne js ~** without sb's help.

**dazu|zählen** *vt* to include.

**dazwischen** *adv* - **1.** [örtlich, zeitlich] in between - **2.** [dabei] among them.

**dazwischen|fahren** *(perf* ist **dazwischengefahren)** *vi (unreg)* - **1.** [bei Streit] to intervene - **2.** [ins Gespräch] to interrupt.

**dazwischen|kommen** *(perf* ist **dazwischengekommen)** *vi (unreg)* - **1.** [dazwischengeraten]: **er kam mit dem Finger dazwischen** he got his finger caught in it - **2.** [ungeplant passieren]: **mir ist etw dazwischengekommen** sthg has cropped up.

**dazwischen|rufen** *(unreg) vt:* **etw ~** to interrupt by shouting sthg <> *vi* to interrupt by shouting.

**DB** *(abk für* **Deutsche Bahn)** *German railway company.*

**DBB** [de:be:'be:] *(abk für* **Deutscher Beamtenbund)** *der German civil servants' association.*

**DCC** [de:tse:'tse:] *(abk für* **Digital Compact Cassette)** *die* DCC.

**DDR** [de:de:'er] *(abk für* **Deutsche Demokratische Republik)** *die* GDR.

**D-Dur** *das* D major.

**Deal** [di:l] *(pl -s) der* deal.

**dealen** [di:lən] *vi fam* to deal *(in drugs);* **mit etw ~** to push sthg.

**Dealer, in** ['di:lɐ, rɪn] *(mpl -; fpl -nen) der, die fam* pusher.

**Debakel** *(pl -) das* debacle.

**Debatte** *(pl -n) die* debate; **zur ~ stehen** to be on the agenda; **zur ~ stellen** to bring up for debate.

**debattieren** *vt* to debate <> *vi:* **über etw** *(A)* **~** to debate sthg.

**Debüt** [de'byː] (*pl* -s) *das* debut; **sein ~ geben** to make one's debut.

**dechiffrieren** [deʃɪ'friːrən] *vt* [Text, Geheimschrift] to decipher; [Kode] to decode.

**Deck** (*pl* -s) *das* deck; **unter ~ gehen** to go below.

➤ **an Deck** *adv* on deck.

**Deckladresse** *die* cover address.

**Decklblatt** *das* title page.

**Decke** (*pl* -n) *die* - **1.** [Tischdecke] tablecloth - **2.** [zum Zudecken - Wolldecke] blanket; [ - Steppdecke] quilt, duvet - **3.** [Zimmerdecke] ceiling - **4.** RW: **sich nach der ~ strecken (müssen)** to (have to) cut one's coat according to one's cloth; **(mit jm) unter einer ~ stecken** to be in cahoots (with sb); **mir fällt die ~ auf den Kopf** I'm sick of seeing the same four walls; **(vor Freude) an die ~ springen** to jump for joy.

**Deckel** (*pl* -) *der* - **1.** [von Gefäßen] lid - **2.** [von Büchern] cover - **3.** RW: **jm eins auf den ~ geben** *fam* to give sb a telling-off; **eins auf den ~ bekommen** ODER **kriegen** *fam* to get a telling-off.

**decken** *vt* - **1.** [bedecken - Haus] to roof; **das Dach ~** [mit Ziegeln] to tile the roof; [mit Stroh] to thatch the roof - **2.** [Tisch] to lay, to set - **3.** [legen]: **die Hand über die Augen ~** to cover one's eyes with one's hand - **4.** [schützen - Kind, Körperteil, Rückzug] to cover; [ - Komplizen] to cover up for - **5.** SPORT to mark - **6.** [Bedarf] to meet - **7.** WIRTSCH & ZOOL to cover ⬦ *vi* - **1.** [den Tisch decken] to lay ODER set the table - **2.** [Farbe] to cover.

➤ **sich decken** *ref* [Dreiecke] to be congruent; [Meinungen] to coincide; [Aussagen] to tally.

**Deckenllampe** *die* ceiling light.

**Decklfarbe** *die* thick, water-based paint.

**Decklmantel** *der*: **unter dem ~ der Wirtschaftshilfe werden Waffen geliefert** arms are being delivered under the pretext of economic aid.

**Decklname** *der* assumed name.

**Deckung** (*pl* -en) *die* - **1.** [Schutz] cover; **in ~ gehen** to take cover - **2.** SPORT [beim Boxen] guard; [Manndeckung] marking; [Verteidigung] defence - **3.** [Befriedigung - von Bedarf] covering; **zur ~ der Nachfrage** in order to meet demand - **4.** [Versicherungsschutz, von Scheck] cover - **5.** [Übereinstimmung]: **unterschiedliche Standpunkte zur ~ bringen** to bring differing points of view into line with each other - **6.** MATH congruence.

**deckungsgleich** *adj* [Dreiecke] congruent; [Ansichten, Theorien] matching.

**Decoder** [de'koːdɐ] (*pl* -) *der* ELEKTR decoder.

**decodieren** = dekodieren.

**Defätismus** *der* defeatism.

**Defätist, in** (*mpl* -en; *fpl* -nen) *der, die* defeatist.

**defätistisch** *adj* defeatist.

**defekt** *adj* faulty, defective.

**Defekt** (*pl* -e) *der* fault, defect.

**defensiv** [defen'ziːf] *adj* defensive; [Fahrweise] safe, careful ⬦ *adv* defensively; [fahren] safely, carefully.

**Defensive** [defen'ziːvə] (*pl* -n) *die* defensive; **in die ~ gedrängt** forced onto the defensive; **sich in die ~ begeben** to go onto the defensive.

**definieren** *vt* to define.

➤ **sich definieren** *ref* to be defined.

**Definition** (*pl* -en) *die* definition.

**definitiv** *adj* final ⬦ *adv*: **sich ~ entscheiden** to make a final decision; **kannst du mir ~ sagen, ob du kommst?** can you let me know for sure whether you're coming?

**Defizit** (*pl* -e) *das* - **1.** [Fehlbetrag] deficit - **2.** [Fehlen] shortage.

**Deflation** (*pl* -en) *die* WIRTSCH deflation.

**deformieren** *vt* to deform.

**deftig** *adj* - **1.** [nahrhaft] substantial, hearty - **2.** [derb] coarse.

**Degen** (*pl* -) *der* rapier.

**degenerieren** (*perf* **ist degeneriert**) *vi* to degenerate.

**degradieren** *vt* to demote; **jn/etw zu etw ~** to demote sb/sthg to sthg.

**dehnbar** *adj* [Stoff, Gummi, Begriff] elastic; [Metall] ductile.

**dehnen** *vt* - **1.** [Substanz, Glieder] to stretch - **2.** [Laut] to draw out.

➤ **sich dehnen** *ref* - **1.** [gen] to stretch - **2.** [Gespräch, Warten] to drag on.

**Dehnung** (*pl* -en) *die* stretching; [Laut] drawing out.

**Deich** (*pl* -e) *der* dyke.

**Deichsel** ['daɪksl̩] (*pl* -n) *die* shafts (*pl*).

**deichseln** ['daɪksl̩n] *vt fam* to wangle.

**dein, e** *det* your.

**deine, r, s** ODER **deins** *pron* yours.

**deiner** *pron* (Genitiv von du) of you; **ich erinnere mich ~** I remember you.

**deinerseits** *adv* - **1.** [du selbst] for your part - **2.** [von dir] on your part.

**deinesgleichen** *pron* people like you; **du und ~** you and your like.

**deinetwegen** *adv* - **1.** [dir zuliebe] for your sake - **2.** [wegen dir] because of you.

**deinetwillen** ➤ **um deinetwillen** *adv* for your sake.

**deinige** (*pl* -n) *pron* (mit Artikel) **geh: der/die/das ~** yours.

**dekadent** *adj* decadent.

**D**

**Dekadẹnz** *die* decadence.

**Dekan** (*pl* -e) *der* REL & UNI dean.

**deklamieren** *vt* & *vi* to declaim.

**deklarieren** *vt* to declare.

**Deklination** (*pl* -en) *die* declension.

**deklinieren** *vt* to decline.

**dekodieren, decodieren** [dekoˈdiːrən] *vt* to decode.

**Dekodierung** (*pl* -en) *die* decoding.

**Dekolletee, Dekolletté** [dekɔlˈteː] (*pl* -s) *das* décolleté.

**dekolletiert** *adj* with a low neckline.

**Dekor** (*pl* -s *ODER* -e) *das ODER der* [Verzierung] pattern ⬦ *das* [im Theater, Film] décor.

**Dekorateur, in** [dekoraˈtøːɐ̯, rɪn] (*mpl* -e; *fpl* -nen) *der, die* [von Innenräumen] decorator; [von Schaufenstern] window-dresser.

**Dekoration** (*pl* -en) *die* - **1.** [Ausschmückung, Auszeichnung] decoration; [von Schaufenster] window-dressing - **2.** [Kulisse] set.

**dekorativ** *adj* decorative.

**dekorieren** *vt* [schmücken, auszeichnen] to decorate; [Schaufenster] to dress.

**Dekret** (*pl* -e) *das* decree; **ein ~ erlassen** to issue a decree.

**Delegation** (*pl* -en) *die* delegation.

**delegieren** *vt* to delegate.

**Delegierte** (*pl* -n) *der, die* delegate.

**Delfin** (*pl* -e) *der* = **Delphin.**

**Delhi** [ˈdeːli] *nt* Delhi.

**delikat** *adj* - **1.** [Speise] delicious - **2.** [Person, Angelegenheit, Lage] delicate ⬦ *adv* [behutsam] delicately.

**Delikatẹsse** (*pl* -n) *die* [Leckerbissen] delicacy.

**Delikatẹssen|geschäft** *das* delicatessen.

**Delịkt** (*pl* -e) *das* offence; **ein ~ begehen** to commit an offence.

**Delinquẹnt, in** (*mpl* -en; *fpl* -nen) *der, die* offender.

**Delirium** [deˈliːrjʊm] (*pl* **Delirien**) *das* delirium; **im ~ liegen** *ODER* **sein** to be delirious.

**Dẹlle** (*pl* -n) *die* dent.

**Delphin, Delfin** (*pl* -e) *der* [Säugetier] dolphin ⬦ *das* (ohne Art) (ohne pl) [Sportart] butterfly.

**Dẹlta** (*pl* -s) *das* delta.

**dem** *det* (Dativ Singular von der, das): **mit ~ Kind** with the child ⬦ *pron* (Dativ Singular): **1.** [Demonstrativ von der, das - Person] to him; [ - Sache] to that one; **mit ~** [Person] with him; [Sache] with that one - **2.** [Relativpronomen von der, das - Person] to whom; [ - Sache] to which; **mit ~** [Person] with whom; [Sache] with which.

**Demagoge** (*pl* -n) *der abw* demagogue.

**Demagogie** *die abw* demagogy.

**Demagogin** (*pl* -nen) *die abw* demagogue.

**demagogisch** *abw adj* demagogic ⬦ *adv* demagogically.

**demaskieren** *vt* [entlarven] to unmask.
➡ **sich demaskieren** *ref* [sich entlarven] to reveal o.s.

**Demẹnti** (*pl* -s) *das* denial.

**dementieren** *vt* to deny.

**dementsprechend** *adj* appropriate ⬦ *adv* accordingly.

**demgegenüber** *adv* on the other hand.

**demgemäß** *adv* accordingly.

**demnach** *adv* so.

**demnächst** [deːmˈnɛːst] *adv* soon.

**Demografie, Demographie** (*pl* -n) *die* demography.

**demografisch** *adj* demographic.

**Demokrat** (*pl* -en) *der* democrat.

**Demokratie** (*pl* -n) *die* democracy.

**Demokratin** (*pl* -nen) *die* democrat.

**demokratisch** *adj* democratic ⬦ *adv* democratically.

**demokratisieren** *vt* to democratize.

**Demokratisierung** (*pl* -en) *die* democratization.

**demolieren** *vt* to wreck.

**Demonstrant, in** (*mpl* -en; *fpl* -nen) *der, die* demonstrator.

**Demonstration** (*pl* -en) *die* demonstration.

**Demonstrationsrecht** *das* right to demonstrate.

**demonstrativ** *adj* - **1.** [betont auffällig] pointed - **2.** [anschaulich] revealing ⬦ *adv* [betont, auffallend] pointedly.

**Demonstrativ|pronomen** *das* GRAM demonstrative pronoun.

**demonstrieren** *vi* to demonstrate; **gegen/für etw ~** to demonstrate against/in support of sthg ⬦ *vt* to demonstrate.

**Demontage** [demɔnˈtaːʒə] (*pl* -n) *die* dismantling.

**demontieren** *vt* to dismantle.

**demoralisieren** *vt* to demoralize.

**demoskopisch** *adj* opinion poll (vor Subst); **~e Untersuchung** opinion poll ⬦ *adv* through opinion polls.

**Demut** *die* - **1.** [Ergebenheit] humility - **2.** [Unterwürfigkeit] submissiveness.

**demütig** *adj* - **1.** [ergeben] humble - **2.** [unterwürfig] submissive.

**demütigen** *vt* to humiliate.

➤ **sich demütigen** *ref* to humiliate o.s.; **sich vor jm** ~ to humiliate o.s. in front of sb.

**demütigend** *adj* humiliating.

**Demütigung** (*pl* -en) *die* humiliation.

**demzufolge** *adv* consequently.

**den** *det* - **1.** *(Akkusativ Singular von der)* the - **2.** *(Dativ Plural von der, die, das)* to the; **mit ~ Kindern** with the children ◇ *pron (Akkusativ Singular)* - **1.** [Demonstrativ von der - Person] him; [ - Sache] that one - **2.** [Relativpronomen von der - Person] whom; [ - Sache] which.

**denen** *pron (Dativ Plural)* - **1.** [Demonstrativ von der, die, das] to them; **mit ~** with them - **2.** [Relativpronomen von der, die, das - Personen] to whom; [ - Sachen] to which; **mit ~** [Personen] with whom; [Sachen] with which.

**Den Haag** *nt* The Hague.

**Denkanlstoß** *der:* **jm einen ~ geben** to set sb thinking.

**Denklart** *die* way of thinking.

**denkbar** *adj* [vorstellbar] conceivable; **nicht ~ unthinkable** ◇ *adv* [äußerst] extremely; **die ~ besten/schlechtesten Bedingungen** the best/worst conditions imaginable.

**denken** (*prät* **dachte;** *perf* **hat gedacht**) *vi* - **1.** [gen] to think; **es gab mir zu ~** it made me think; **ich denke nicht** I don't think so; **denkst du, er schafft das?** do you think he'll manage?; **an jn/etw ~** to think of sb/sthg; **denk an den Kaffee!** don't forget the coffee!; **er denkt immer nur an sich** he always thinks about himself; **über jn/etw ~** to think about sb/sthg; **von jm/etw ~** to think about sb/sthg - **2.** [eingestellt sein]: **europäisch ~** to have a European outlook; **kleinlich ~** to be pettyminded - **3.** [planen]: **an etw** *(A)* ~ to think about sthg; **ich denke nicht daran, das zu tun** I have no intention of doing it ◇ *vt* - **1.** [gen] to think; **wer hätte das gedacht!** who would have thought it! - **2.** [sich vorstellen]: **sich** *(D)* **etw ~** to imagine sthg; **das hätte ich mir ~ können** I might have known; **das habe ich mir schon gedacht!** I thought as much!

**Denken** *das* - **1.** [Überlegen] thinking - **2.** [Einstellung] way of thinking.

**Denker, in** (*mpl* -; *fpl* -nen) *der, die* thinker.

**denkfaul** *adj* mentally lazy; **sei nicht so ~** use your brain.

**Denklfehler** *der* mistake in one's reasoning; **einen ~ machen** to make a mistake in one's reasoning.

**Denkmal** (*pl* -mäler *ODER* -e) *das* [Monument] monument; **jm ein ~ setzen** to commemorate sb; **sich** *(D)* **ein ~ setzen** to ensure one's place in history.

**Denkmalspflege, Denkmalpflege** *die* preservation of historical monuments.

**Denkmalsschutz, Denkmalschutz** *der* protection of historical monuments; **unter ~ stehen/stellen** to be classified/classify as a historical monument.

**Denklprozess** *der* thought process.

**denkste** *interj fam* that's what you think!

**Denkvermögen** *das* intellectual capacity.

**Denklweise** *die* way of thinking.

**denkwürdig** *adj* memorable.

**Denklzettel** *der* lesson; **jm einen ~ geben** *ODER* **verpassen** to teach sb a lesson.

**denn** *konj* - **1.** [weil] because - **2.** *geh* [als] than ◇ *adv* - **1.** [verstärkend] then; **was hast du ~?** so what's wrong?; **warum ~ nicht?** why not?; **was ist ~ eigentlich passiert?** so what ACTUALLY happened? - **2.** [dann] then.

**dennoch** *adv* nevertheless.

**Denunziant, in** (*mpl* -en; *fpl* -nen) *der, die abw* informer.

**denunzieren** *vt abw* to inform on.

**Deo** (*pl* -s) *das* deodorant.

**Deodorant** (*pl* -s *ODER* -e) *das* deodorant.

**deplatziert** *adj* out of place.

**Deponie** (*pl* -n) *die* dump.

**deponieren** *vt* to deposit.

**Deportation** (*pl* -en) *die* deportation.

**deportieren** *vt* to deport.

**Depot** [de'po:] (*pl* -s) *das* - **1.** [Aufbewahrungsort, für Verkehrsmittel] depot - **2.** [von Banken] strongroom.

**Depp** [dɛp] (*pl* -en) *der fam Österr, Schweiz & Süddt* twit.

**deppert** *adj fam* daft.

**Depression** (*pl* -en) *die* depression; **an** *ODER* **unter ~en** *(D)* **leiden** to suffer from depression.

**depressiv** *adj* - **1.** MED depressive - **2.** [Situation, Stimmung] depressing.

**deprimieren** *vt* to depress.

**deprimiert** *adj* depressed.

**der** *det* - **1.** [Nominativ] the; **~ Tod** death - **2.** [Genitiv] of the; **der Hut ~ Frau** the woman's hat; **der Duft ~ Rosen** the fragrance of the roses - **3.** [Dativ] the ◇ *pron* - **1.** [Demonstrativpronomen - Person] he; **~ war es** it was him; **~ hat es getan** he did it; **unser Sohn? - ~ geht schon längst in die Schule** our son? – he's been at school for a long time - **2.** [Demonstrativpronomen - Sache] that one; **der Wein? - ~ war fantastisch** the wine? – it was great; **~ und ~** so-and-so - **3.** [Relativpronomen - Person] who, that; [ - Sache] which, that; **die Frau, ~ ich das Buch gab** the woman I gave the book to, the woman to whom I gave the book.

**derart** *adv* so; **es hat lange nicht mehr ~ gereg-**

net it's a long time since it rained so much;
**ein ~ teures Auto kann ich mir nicht leisten** I
can't afford such an expensive car.
→ **derart ..., dass** *konj* so ... that.

**derartig** *adj* such; **eine ~e Frechheit** such (a)
cheek.

**derb** *adj* - **1.** [kräftig - Stoß, Schlag] hefty; [ - Leder]
tough - **2.** [grob] coarse, crude ⬦ *adv*
- **1.** [fest] roughly - **2.** [grob] crudely.

**deren** *det* - **1.** [Genitiv Singular von die - Person] her;
[ - Sache] its - **2.** [Genitiv Plural von der, die, das] their
- **3.** [Relativpronomen - Person] whose; [ - Sache] of
which.

**derentwegen** *adv* - **1.** [ihr zuliebe] for her
sake; [ihnen zuliebe] for their sake - **2.** [wegen
ihr] because of her; [wegen ihnen] because of
them ⬦ *rel pron* - **1.** [der, denen zuliebe - Person]
for whose sake; [ - Sache] for the sake of
which - **2.** [wegen der, denen - Person] because of
whom; [ - Sache] because of which.

**derentwillen** → **um derentwillen** *adv* for
her/their sake ⬦ *pron* for whose sake.

**dergleichen** *pron* that sort of thing.
→ **nichts dergleichen** *adv* nothing of the sort.
→ **und dergleichen mehr** *adv* and that sort of
thing, and so on.

**derjenige** *det:* **~ Mensch, der ...** the person
who ... ⬦ *pron:* **~, der das getan hat** whoever
did this; **von allen Posten erfordert ~ des Vor-**
**sitzenden besonders viel Einsatz** of all the jobs,
the chairman's is the one which requires
the most effort; **von allen Teilnehmern erhält**
**~ den Preis, der ...** the prize goes to the contestant who ....

**dermaßen** → **dermaßen ..., dass** *konj* so ...
that.

**Dermatologe** (*pl* -n) *der* dermatologist.

**Dermatologin** (*pl* -nen) *die* dermatologist.

**derselbe** *det* the same ⬦ *pron* the same
one.

**derzeit** *adv* at the moment, at present.

**derzeitig** *adj* current.

**des** *det* (Genitiv Singular von der, das) of the; **der**
**Schwanz ~ Hundes** the dog's tail.

**des, Des** (*pl* -) *das* MUS D flat.

**Desaster** (*pl* -) *das* disaster.

**desensibilisieren** *vt* MED to desensitize.

**Deserteur, in** (*mpl* -e; *fpl* -nen) *der, die*
deserter.

**desertieren** (*perf* ist desertiert) *vi* to desert;
**zum Feind ~** to go over to the enemy.

**desgleichen** *adv* likewise.

**deshalb** *adv* therefore.
→ **deshalb, weil** *konj* because.

**Design** [di'zain] (*pl* -s) *das* design.

**Designer, in** [di'zainɐ, rɪn] (*mpl* -; *fpl* -nen) *der,*
*die* designer.

**desillusionieren** *vt* to disillusion.

**Desinfektion** *die* disinfection.

**Desinfektionsmittel** *das* disinfectant.

**desinfizieren** *vt* to disinfect.

**Desinformation** *die* disinformation.

**Desinteresse** *das* lack of interest; **sein ~ an**
(+ D) ODER **für etw zeigen** to show one's lack of
interest in sthg.

**desinteressiert** *adj* uninterested; **an etw** (D)
**~ sein** to have no interest in sthg.

**deskriptiv** *adj* descriptive.

**Desktop-Publishing** ['dɛsktɔppʌbliʃɪŋ] *das*
(ohne pl) EDV desktop publishing.

**desolat** *adj* pitiful.

**desorientiert** *adj* disorientated.

**Despot, in** (*mpl* -en; *fpl* -nen) *der, die eigtl & fig*
despot.

**despotisch** *adj eigtl & fig* despotic ⬦ *adv*
*eigtl & fig* despotically.

**dessen** *det* - **1.** [Genitiv Singular von der, das - Per-
son] his; [ - Sache] its - **2.** [Relativpronomen von der,
das - Person] whose; [ - Sache] of which.

**Dessert** [dɛ'se:ɐ] (*pl* -s) *das* dessert; **zum ~** for
dessert.

**Dessous** [dɛ'su:] *pl* lingerie (U).

**destabilisieren** *vt* to destabilize.

**Destabilisierung** (*pl* -en) *die* destabiliza-
tion.

**destillieren** *vt* to distil.

**desto** *konj:* **je eher, ~ besser!** the sooner, the
better!; **je schneller du arbeitest, ~ eher bist du**
**fertig** the quicker you work, the sooner
you'll be finished.

**destruktiv** *adj* destructive ⬦ *adv* destructively.

**deswegen** *adv* therefore; **er ist krank und**
**kann ~ nicht kommen** he's ill, which is why he
can't come; **er ist gerade ~ nicht gekommen**
that's precisely the reason he didn't come;
**ach, ~!** oh, that's why! ODER the reason!; **~,**
**weil** because.

**Detail** [de'tail] (*pl* -s) *das* detail; **ins ~ gehen** to
go into detail.
→ **im Detail** *adv* [detailliert] in detail.

**Detailfrage** *die* (matter of) detail.

**detailliert** *adj* detailed ⬦ *adv* in detail.

**Detektiv, in** (*mpl* -e; *fpl* -nen) *der, die* detective.

**detektivisch** [detɛk'ti:vɪʃ] *adj* of a detective;
[Kleinarbeit] detective (vor Subst).

**determinieren** *vt* to determine.

**Detonation** (*pl* -en) *die* blast, explosion.

**detonieren** (*perf* ist detoni**e**rt) *vi* to detonate.

**Deut** ◆ keinen Deut *adv:* keinen ODER nicht einen ~ besser sein to be not a jot better.

**deuteln** *vi:* daran gibt es nichts zu ~ there is no question about it.

**deuten** *vt* [auslegen] to interpret; [Sterne] to read; **etw richtig ~** to interpret sthg correctly; **etw falsch ~** to misinterpret sthg ◇ *vi* - **1.** [zeigen]: **auf jn/etw ~** to point at sb/sthg - **2.** [schließen lassen]: **auf etw (A) ~** to point to sthg, to indicate sthg.

**deutlich** *adj* - **1.** [klar erkennbar, leicht verständlich] clear; **jm etw ~ machen** to make sthg clear to sb - **2.** [rücksichtslos offen] blunt; **~ werden** to speak one's mind ◇ *adv* - **1.** [klar, verständlich] clearly - **2.** [rücksichtslos offen] bluntly.

**Deutlichkeit** *die* - **1.** [Klarheit] clarity - **2.** [Offenheit] bluntness.
◆ **mit aller Deutlichkeit** *adv* [nachdrücklich] quite clearly.

**deutsch** *adj* German ◇ *adv* [in deutscher Sprache] in German; **mit jm ~ reden** *fam* to have a frank conversation with sb; *siehe auch* **englisch.**

**Deutsch** *das* German; **kein ~ mehr verstehen** *fam* not to understand plain English.
◆ **auf gut Deutsch** *adv fam* - **1.** [verständlich] clearly - **2.** [unverblümt] in plain English; *siehe auch* **Englisch.**

**Deutsche** (*pl* -**n**) *der, die* [Person] German; **die ~n** the Germans ◇ *das* - **1.** [deutsche Sprache] German - **2.** [deutsche Wesensart]: **das ist das typisch ~ an ihm** that is what is typically German about him; *siehe auch* **Englische.**

**Deutsche Bahn** *die (ohne pl)* German railway company.

**Deutsche Bucht** *die area of the North Sea off the German coast.*

**Deutsche Bundesbahn** *die (ohne pl)* = Deutsche Bahn.

**Deutsche Bundesbank** *die* Bundesbank.

**DEUTSCHE BUNDESBANK**

Created in 1957, the Bundesbank, the central bank of the Federal Republic of Germany, was the foundation of the German banking system. The Bundesbank enjoys a considerable degree of autonomy. Its main concern is inflation and it also issues bank notes, supplies the economy with loans and administers the country's monetary reserves. Since European monetary union, it has surrendered some of its prerogatives to the ECB (European Central Bank).

**Deutsche Bundespost** *die (ohne pl)* = Deutsche Post.

**Deutsche Bundestag** *der (ohne pl)* Bundestag, *lower house of the German Parliament.*

**DEUTSCHER BUNDESTAG**

The "Bundestag", one of the two houses of the German parliament, is the national assembly of the Federal Republic of Germany. Its members are elected by the people for a term of four years. Its main role is to pass laws, elect the Chancellor and monitor the government's activities.

**Deutsche Demokratische Republik** *die* German Democratic Republic.

**Deutsche Gewerkschaftsbund** *der* German Trade Union Federation.

**DEUTSCHER GEWERKSCHAFTSBUND**

This is the most important trade union organization in Germany. It is made up of 16 different unions, all of which belong to the industrial sector. All of these unions cater for workers and employees from the same branch of the economy, irrespective of their position in the company to which they belong. It is not bound to any political party.

**Deutsche Mark** *die (pl -)* German mark, Deutschmark.

**Deutsche Post** *die German postal service.*

**Deutsche Reich** *das* German Reich.

**deutsch-französisch** *adj* - **1.** [zwischen Deutschland und Frankreich bestehend] Franco-German - **2.** [zweisprachig] German-French.

**Deutschland** *nt* Germany.

**Deutschlandlied** *das German national anthem.*

**deutschsprachig** [ˈdɔʏtʃʃpraːxɪç] *adj* - **1.** [Bevölkerung] German-speaking - **2.** [Unterricht]: **~en Unterricht erteilen** to teach in German.

**deutschstämmig** [ˈdɔʏtʃʃtɛmɪç] *adj* of German extraction.

**Deutschunterricht** *der (ohne pl)* German lessons *(pl);* **~ geben** to teach German.

**Deutung** (*pl* -**en**) *die* interpretation; [der Sterne] reading.

**Devise** [deˈviːzə] (*pl* -**n**) *die* motto.
◆ **Devisen** *pl* foreign currency *(U).*

**Devisen|kurs** *der* exchange rate.

**Devisen|markt** *der* foreign exchange market.

**Dez.** (*abk für* **Dezember**) Dec.

**Dezember** *der* December; *siehe auch* **September.**

**dezent** *adj* - **1.** [taktvoll] discreet - **2.** [unaufdring-

lich] tasteful ◇ adv - 1. [taktvoll] discreetly
- 2. [unaufdringlich] tastefully.

**dezentral** adj decentralized ◇ adv using a
decentralized system.

**dezentralisieren** vt to decentralize

**Dezernat** (pl -e) das department.

**dezidiert** geh adj resolute ◇ adv resolutely.

**dezimal** adj decimal.

**Dezimallstelle** die decimal place.

**Dezimallsystem** das decimal system.

**Dezimallzahl** die decimal.

**Dezilmeter** das ODER der decimetre.

**dezimieren** vt to decimate.
➤ **sich dezimieren** ref to be decimated.

**DFB** [deːɛfˈbeː] (abk für **Deutscher Fußball-Bund**) der German Football Association.

**DGB** [deːgeːˈbeː] (abk für **Deutscher Gewerkschaftsbund**) der Federation of German Trade Unions.

**dgl.** abk für dergleichen.

**d. h.** (abk für **das heißt**) i.e.

**Di.** (abk für **Dienstag**) Tue., Tues.

**Dia** (pl -s) das slide.

**Diabetes** der diabetes (U).

**Diabetiker, in** (mpl -; pl -nen) der, die diabetic.

**diabolisch** geh adj diabolical ◇ adv diabolically.

**diachronisch** adj diachronic ◇ adv diachronically.

**Diagnose** (pl -n) die MED & fig diagnosis; die ~ auf etw (A) stellen to diagnose sthg; eine ~ stellen to make a diagnosis.

**diagnostizieren** vt MED & fig to diagnose.

**diagonal** adj diagonal ◇ adv: etw ~ lesen to skim-read sthg.

**Diagonale** (pl -n) die diagonal; eine ~ zeichnen to draw a diagonal line.

**Diagramm** (pl -e) das diagram.

**Diakon** (pl -e ODER -en) der - 1. [evangelisch] Church welfare worker - 2. [katholisch] deacon.

**Diakonie** die Church welfare work.

**Diakonisse** (pl -n) die - 1. [evangelisch] community nurse (working for the Church) - 2. [katholisch] deaconess.

**Dialekt** (pl -e) der dialect.

**Dialektik** die (ohne pl) dialectics (U).

**dialektisch** adj dialectical ◇ adv dialectically.

**Dialog** (pl -e) der dialogue.

**Dialyse** [diaˈlyːzə] (pl -n) die dialysis (U).

**Diamant** (pl -en) der diamond.

**diametral** adj [Punkte] diametrically opposite ◇ adv: ~ entgegengesetzt diametrically opposed.

**Dialprojektor** der slide projector.

**Diät** (pl -en) die diet; ~ halten to be on a diet; eine ~ machen to go on a diet; ~ kochen to cook dietary meals; (nach einer) ~ leben to follow a diet.

**Diätlassistent, in** der, die dietician.

**Diäten** pl [in der Politik] allowance (sg).

**Diätlkost** die (ohne pl) diet foods (pl).

**Diätlküche** die (ohne pl) [Diätkost] diet foods (pl).

**Diätlplan** der diet plan.

**dich** pron (Akkusativ von du) - 1. [Personalpronomen] you - 2. [Reflexivpronomen] yourself; hast du ~ umgezogen? have you changed?; beeil ~! hurry up!

**dicht** adj - 1. [gegen Luft] airtight; [gegen Wasser] watertight; [Schuhe, Stoff] waterproof; nicht ~ sein [Dach] to be leaking; [Schuh] to be letting water in; nicht ODER nicht mehr ganz ~ sein fam fig & abw to be funny in the head - 2. [Wald, Nebel] dense - 3. [Haar, Gefieder] thick; [Verkehr] heavy ◇ adv - 1. [undurchlässig]: ~ schließen to close tight - 2. [gedrängt] tightly; [bevölkert] densely; er ist ~ behaart he is very hairy - 3. [ganz nahe]: ~ dahinter/daneben right behind/next to it.

**Dichte** die - 1. [Undurchlässigkeit] impermeability - 2. [von Wald, Nebel] denseness - 3. [von Bevölkerung & PHYS] density; [von Verkehr] heaviness.

**dichten** vt - 1. [in Verse fassen] to write - 2. [gegen Wasser] to make watertight; [gegen Luft] to make airtight; [Fugen] to seal; [Leck] to stop ◇ vi - 1. [dicht machen] to seal - 2. [Verse schreiben] to write (poetry).

**Dichter, in** (mpl -; fpl -nen) der, die poet; [von Dramen] writer.

**dichterisch** adj poetic ◇ adv poetically.

**Dichterllesung** die poetry reading (of own works by a poet).

**dichtlhalten** vi (unreg) fam to keep one's mouth shut.

**Dichtkunst** die poetry.

**dichtlmachen** vt fam to shut, to close.

**Dichtung** (pl -en) die - 1. [Kunstwerk] poem - 2. [Literatur] literature - 3. [für Wasserhahn] washer; [im Maschinenbau] gasket.

**Dichtungsmasse** *die* sealant.

**Dichtungslring** *der* washer.

**dick** *adj* - **1.** [gen] thick; [Person, Bauch] fat - **2.** [geschwollen] swollen - **3.** *fam* [groß, bedeutend - Auto, Gehalt, Fehler] whacking great; **ein ~es Lob** a big pat on the back; **sie sind ~e Freunde** they're as thick as thieves ◇ *adv* - **1.** [stark] thickly - **2.** *fam* [sehr] really; **mit jm ~ befreundet sein** to be as thick as thieves with sb - **3.** *RW:* **es nicht so ~ haben** *fam* to be a bit short (of cash); **jn/etw ~(e) haben** *fam* to have had one's fill of sb/sthg; **mit jm durch ~ und dünn gehen** to go through thick and thin with sb.

**Dickldarm** *der* large intestine.

**Dicke** (*pl* -n) *die* [gen] thickness; [von Person, Bauch] fatness; **die Wand hat eine ~ von 20 cm** the wall is 20 cm thick ◇ *der*, *die* [Person] fatty.

**dickfellig** *adj fam* thick-skinned.

**dickflüssig** *adj* thick.

**Dickhäuter** (*pl* -) *der* pachyderm.

**Dickicht** (*pl* -e) *das* thicket.

**Dicklkopf** *der* - **1.** [Person] pig-headed person - **2.** [Haltung]: **einen ~ haben** to be pig-headed.

**dickköpfig** *adj* pig-headed.

**Dickmilch** *die* sour milk.

**dickwandig** *adj* [Behälter] with thick sides.

**Didaktik** *die* didactics (*U*).

**didaktisch** *adj* didactic; [Spielzeug] educational ◇ *adv* [lehrhaft] didactically.

**die** *det* the; **sich** (*D*) **~ Hände waschen** to wash one's hands; **~ Natur** nature ◇ *pron* - **1.** [Demonstrativpronomen - Person] she; **~ war es** it was her; **~ hat es getan** she did it; **meine Tochter? - ~ geht schon längst in die Schule** my daughter? – she's been at school for a long time - **2.** [Demonstrativpronomen - Sache] that one; **richtig, auf ~ Antwort habe ich gewartet!** that's just the answer I was waiting for!; **meine Lehre? - ~ habe ich abgebrochen** my training? – I've given it up - **3.** [Relativpronomen - Person] who, that; [ - Sache] which, that.

**Dieb** (*pl* -e) *der* thief.

**Dieblgut** *das* stolen goods (*pl*).

**Diebin** (*pl* -nen) *die* thief.

**diebisch** *adj* - **1.** [schadenfroh] gloating - **2.** [stehlend] thieving ◇ *adv:* **sich ~ freuen** to gloat.

**Diebstahl** (*pl* -stähle) *der* theft.

**diejenige** *det:* **~ Frau, die ...** the woman who ... ◇ *pron:* **~, die das gemacht hat** whoever did this; **unter allen Bewerbungen wurde ~ ausgewählt, die am originellsten war** the application that was chosen was the most original one.

**Diele** (*pl* -n) *die* - **1.** [Flur] hall - **2.** [Brett] floorboard.

**dienen** *vi* - **1.** [nützen]: **einer Sache** (*D*) **~** to help with sthg; **jm ~** to be of use to sb; **als etw ~** to serve as sthg; **der Teppich dient nur zur Zierde** the carpet is only for decoration; **das Spiel dient ihm zum Zeitvertreib** the game helps him to pass the time - **2.** [behilflich sein] to be of help; **womit kann ich ~?** can I be of help? - **3.** [für etw wirken]: **jm/einer Sache ~** to serve sb/sthg - **4.** [Subj: Butler]: **jm ~** to serve sb - **5.** [Soldat sein] to serve.

**Diener, in** (*mpl* -; *fpl* -nen) *der*, *die eigtl* & *fig* servant.

**dienlich** *adj:* **jm/einer Sache ~ sein** to be of help to sb/sthg.

**Dienst** (*pl* -e) *der* - **1.** [gen] service; **der öffentliche ~** the civil service; **jm seine ~e anbieten** to offer sb one's services; **im ~ einer Sache** (*G*) **stehen** to be in the service of sthg; **jm einen (guten) ~ erweisen** to serve sb well - **2.** [Arbeit, Pflicht] work; [von Arzt, Soldat] duty; **zum ~ gehen** to go to work; [Arzt, Soldat] to go on duty; **~ haben** to be working; [Arzt, Soldat] to be on duty; **~ habend** on duty; **~ nach Vorschrift** work-to-rule - **3.** [Arbeitsverhältnis] post; **jn in seine ~e nehmen** to engage sb.

 **außer Dienst** *adv* [Person] retired.

 **im Dienst** *adv:* **im ~ sein** to be working; [Arzt, Soldat] to be on duty.

 **vom Dienst** *adv* on duty.

**Dienstag** (*pl* -e) *der* Tuesday; *siehe auch* **Samstag.**

**dienstags** *adv* on Tuesdays; *siehe auch* **samstags.**

**Dienstlalter** *das* length of service.

**Dienstlälteste** *der*, *die* longest-serving person.

**Dienstlantritt** *der* taking up of one's post.

**dienstbereit** *adj* [geöffnet] open.

**Dienstlbote** *der* servant.

**Dienstlbotin** *die* servant.

**Dienstlgeheimnis** *das* official secret.

**Dienstlgrad** *der* rank.

**diensthabend** *adj* = Dienst habend.

**Diensthabende** (*pl* -n) *der*, *die* person on duty.

**Dienstlleistung** *die* service.

**Dienstleistungslgewerbe** *das* service industry.

**Dienstleistungslunternehmen** *das* service-sector business.

**dienstlich** *adj* - **1.** *amt* [den Dienst betreffend] business (*vor Subst*); [Befehl] official - **2.** [unpersönlich] impersonal ◇ *adv amt* [verreisen] on business.

**Dienst|reise** *die* business trip; **auf ~ sein** [geschäftlich] to be away on business; [Politiker] to be away on official business.

**Dienst|schluss** *der:* **nach ~** after work.

**Dienst|stelle** *die:* **die oberste ~** the highest authority.

**Dienst|wagen** *der* company car.

**Dienst|weg** *der:* **den ~ einhalten** to go through the proper channels.

**Dienst|wohnung** *die* company flat *Br* ODER apartment *Am.*

**Dienst|zeit** *die* **- 1.** [Dienststunden] working hours *(pl)* **- 2.** [Soldatenzeit] term of service.

**dies** *pron* this; **~ und das** ODER **jenes** *fig* this and that.

**diesbezüglich** *adj* related (to this) <> *adv* regarding this (matter).

**diese, r, s** ODER **dies** *det* this; [jene] that; **~ Tage** one of these days; **am 9. ~s Monats** on the 9th of this month <> *pron* this one; [jene] that one.

**Diesel** *(pl -)* *der* diesel.

**dieselbe** *det* the same <> *pron* the same one.

**Diesel|motor** *der* diesel engine.

**Dieselöl** *das* diesel.

**diesig** *adj* misty.

**diesjährig** *adj:* **die ~e Ernte** this year's harvest.

**diesmal** *adv* this time.

**diesseitig** *adj* **- 1.** [Ufer] on this side **- 2.** [Leben] earthly.

**diesseits** *präp* [auf dieser Seite]: **~ eines Ortes** *(G)* on this side of a place.

**Diesseits** *das:* **im ~** in this (earthly) life.

**Dietrich** *(pl -e)* *der* skeleton key.

**diffamieren** *vt* to defame.

**Diffamierung** *(pl -en)* *die* defamation; **~en** defamatory comments.

**Differential|getriebe** *das* = Differenzialgetriebe.

**Differential|rechnung** *die* = Differenzialrechnung.

**Differenz** *(pl -en)* *die* **- 1.** [gen] difference **- 2.** [Fehlbetrag] deficit.

**Differenzen** *pl* [Meinungsverschiedenheiten] differences.

**Differenzial|getriebe** *das* differential gear.

**Differenzialrechnung** *die* MATH differential calculus.

**differenzieren** *vt* to differentiate between <> *vi* to make distinctions.

**sich differenzieren** *ref* to become differentiated.

**diffus** *adj* **- 1.** [wirr] confused **- 2.** [Licht] diffuse.

**digital** *adj* digital.

**Digital|anzeige** *die* digital display.

**Digital|technik** *die* digital technology.

**Digital|uhr** *die* digital clock; [Armbanduhr] digital watch.

**DIHT** [deːiːhaːˈteː] *(abk für* **Deutscher Industrie- und Handelstag)** *der umbrella organization for German Chambers of Commerce.*

**Diktat** *(pl -e)* *das* **- 1.** [Nachschrift] dictation **- 2.** *geh* [Zwang] dictate.

**Diktator** *(pl -toren)* *der* dictator.

**Diktatorin** *(pl -nen)* *die* dictator.

**diktatorisch** *abw adj* dictatorial <> *adv* dictatorially.

**Diktatur** *(pl -en)* *die abw* dictatorship.

**diktieren** *vt* to dictate; **jm etw ~** to dictate sthg to sb.

**Diktier|gerät** *das* Dictaphone®.

**Dilemma** *(pl -s)* *das* dilemma.

**Dilettant, in** *(mpl -en; fpl -nen)* *der, die geh* dilettante.

**dilettantisch** *adj abw* amateurish.

**Dill** *der* dill.

**Dimension** *(pl -en)* *die eigtl* & *fig* dimension; **ungeahnte ~en annehmen** to take on unprecedented proportions.

**Diminutiv** *(pl -e)* *das* GRAM diminutive.

**DIN** [diːn] *(abk für* **Deutsche Industrienorm)** *die* DIN.

**Ding** *(pl -e* ODER *-er)* *das* **- 1.** *(pl Dinge)* [Gegenstand, Angelegenheit] thing; **vor allen ~en** above all; **über den ~en stehen** to be above it all; **unverrichteter ~e** without having accomplished anything; **den ~en ihren Lauf lassen** to let things take their course; **es ist nicht mit rechten ~en zugegangen** there was something odd about it; **wie die ~e liegen** as things stand; **ein ~ der Unmöglichkeit sein** to be absolutely impossible; **guter ~e sein** to be in good spirits **- 2.** *(pl Dinger)* *fam* [Sache] thing **- 3.** *(pl Dinger)* [Mädchen]: **ein junges/dummes ~** a young/stupid thing **- 4.** *(pl Dinger)* RW: **das is (ja) 'n ~!** *fam* would you believe it!, there's a thing!; **ein ~ drehen** *fam* to do a job; **krumme ~er machen** *fam* to be involved in crooked business.

**dingfest** *adj:* **jn ~ machen** to arrest sb.

**Dings** *fam der, die* [Person] thingy, thingummy <> *das* [Gegenstand, Ort] thingy, thingummy.

**Dino|saurier** *der* dinosaur.

**Dioptrie** *(pl -n)* *die* MED dioptre.

**Dioxid** *(pl -e)* *das* dioxide.

**Diözese** (pl -n) die diocese.

**Dip** (pl -s) der KÜCHE dip; **ein ~ mit Curry/Joghurt** a curry/yoghurt dip.

**Dipl.-Ing.** abk für **Diplomingenieur**.

**Dipl.-Kfm.** (abk für **Diplomkaufmann**) person with a commercial diploma.

**Diplom** (pl -e) das - **1.** [akademischer Grad] degree (in science or technology) - **2.** [Urkunde] diploma.

**Diplomlarbeit** die dissertation (submitted for a degree).

**Diplomat** (pl -en) der diplomat.

**Diplomatenlkoffer** der attaché case.

**Diplomatie** die diplomacy.

**Diplomatin** (pl -nen) die diplomat.

**diplomatisch** adj diplomatic <> adv diplomatically.

**Diplomlingenieur, in** der, die qualified engineer.

**dir** pron (Dativ von du) (to) you; **das gehört ~** it belongs to you, it's yours; **ich komme mit ~** I'm coming with you; **tun ~ die Füße weh?** do your feet hurt?

**Dir.** (abk für **Direktor**) dir.

**Directory** [daɪ'rɛktɔrɪ] (pl -s) das EDV directory.

**direkt** adj direct <> adv - **1.** [sofort] straight; TV live - **2.** [nahe] right; **~ neben** right next to - **3.** [unmittelbar]: **sie kaufen ihre Milch ~ beim Bauern** they buy their milk direct from the farmer - **4.** [unverblümt] directly.

**Direktlflug** der direct flight.

**Direktheit** die directness.

**Direktion** (pl -en) die management.

**Direktive** [dirɛk'tiːvəl] (pl -n) die geh directive.

**Direktlmandat** das POL direct mandate.

**Direktmarketing** das direct marketing.

**Direktor** (pl -toren) der [von Schule] headmaster Br, principal Am; [von Museum] director; [von Strafanstalt] governor Br, warden Am; [von Abteilung] manager.

**Direktorin** (pl -nen) die [von Schule] headmistress Br, principal Am; [von Museum] director; [von Strafanstalt] governor Br, warden Am; [von Abteilung] manager.

**Direktlübertragung** die live broadcast.

**Direktlverbindung** die - **1.** [bei der Eisenbahn, im Flugwesen] direct service; **per ~ nach München fliegen** to fly direct to Munich - **2.** TELEKOM direct line.

**Direktlverkauf** der direct selling.

**Dirigent, in** (mpl -en; fpl -nen) der, die conductor.

**dirigieren** vt - **1.** MUS to conduct - **2.** [Unterneh-

men] to manage, to run; [Verkehr] to direct <> vi to conduct.

**Dirndllkleid** das dirndl.

**Dirne** (pl -n) die prostitute.

**dis, Dis** das MUS D sharp.

**Diskette** (pl -n) die EDV (floppy) disk, .

**Diskettenlauflwerk** das EDV disk drive.

**Diskljockey** ['dɪskdʒɔkeɪ] der disc jockey.

**Disko** (pl -s) die fam disco.

**Diskontlsatz** der WIRTSCH discount rate.

**Diskothek** (pl -en) die discotheque.

**diskreditieren** vt to discredit.

**Diskrepanz** (pl -en) die discrepancy.

**diskret** adj discreet <> adv discreetly.

**Diskretion** die discretion; **in Bezug auf etw ~ wahren** to treat sthg in confidence.

**diskriminieren** vt - **1.** [benachteiligen] to discriminate against - **2.** [herabwürdigen] to disparage.

**Diskriminierung** (pl -en) die discrimination.

**Diskus** (pl -se ODER Disken) der SPORT discus.

**Diskussion** (pl -en) die discussion; **zur ~ stehen** to be under discussion; **etw zur ~ stellen** to bring sthg up for discussion.

**Diskussionslbeitrag** der contribution to the discussion.

**Diskussionslleiter, in** der, die chairperson (of a discussion).

**Diskussionslrunde** die discussion group.

**Diskuswerfen** das SPORT discus.

**diskutabel** adj worth considering.

**diskutieren** vi to discuss; **über jn/etw ~** to discuss sb/sthg <> vt to discuss.

**disponieren** vi: **in dieser Stellung muss man ~ können** in this position you have to be able to plan ahead; **über sein Geld frei ~ können** to be able to do what one wants with one's money.

**disproportional** adj badly proportioned.

**Disqualifikation** (pl -en) die disqualification.

**disqualifizieren** vt to disqualify.

**Dissens** (pl -e) der difference of opinion.

**Dissertation** (pl -en) die (doctoral) thesis.

**Dissident, in** (mpl -en; fpl -nen) der, die dissident.

**Dissonanz** (pl -en) die - **1.** MUS dissonance - **2.** [Unstimmigkeit] difference of opinion.

**Distanz** (pl -en) die - **1.** [Entfernung] distance - **2.** [persönlicher Abstand] detachment; **etw aus der ~ heraus beurteilen** to judge sthg from a distance; jm gegenüber auf ~ gehen/bleiben to distance o.s./keep one's distance from sb.

**distanzieren** → sich distanzieren *ref:* sich von jm/etw ~ to distance o.s. from sb/sthg.

**distanziert** *adj* detached ⬦ *adv:* ~ wirken to seem distant.

**Distel** (*pl* -n) *die* thistle.

**distinguiert** [dɪstɪŋ'giːɐ̯t] *adj* *geh* distinguished.

**Distrikt** (*pl* -e) *der* district.

**Disziplin** (*pl* -en) *die* discipline.

**disziplinarisch** *adj* disciplinary ⬦ *adv:* gegen jn ~ vorgehen to take disciplinary action against sb.

**Disziplinar|strafe** *die* disciplinary action (U).

**diszipliniert** *adj* disciplined ⬦ *adv* in a disciplined way.

**Diva** ['diːva] (*pl* -s *ODER* Diven) *die* [Sängerin] diva; [Filmschauspielerin] filmstar.

**Divergenz** [diver'gɛnts] (*pl* -en) *die* divergence.

**diverse** [di'vɛrzə] *adj pl* various.

**Dividende** [divi'dɛndə] (*pl* -n) *die* dividend.

**dividieren** [divi'diːrən] *vt:* etw (durch etw) ~ to divide sthg (by sthg).

**Division** [divi'zjoːn] (*pl* -en) *die* MATH & MIL division.

**Diwan** (*pl* -e) *der* divan.

**d. J.** - **1.** (*abk für* der Jüngere) the Younger - **2.** (*abk für* dieses Jahres) of this year.

**DJH** [deːjɔt'haː] (*abk für* Deutscher Jugendherbergsverband) *der* German Youth Hostel Association.

**DKP** [deːkaː'peː] (*abk für* Deutsche Kommunistische Partei) *die* German Communist Party.

**DLRG** [deːɛlɛr'geː] (*abk für* Deutsche Lebensrettungsgesellschaft) *die* German Lifesaving Association.

**d. M.** (*abk für* dieses Monats) inst.

**d-Moll** *das* D minor.

**DNA** (*abk für* desoxyribonucleic acid) *die* DNA.

**DNS** (*abk für* Desoxyribonukleinsäure) *die* = DNA.

**Do.** (*abk für* Donnerstag) Thurs.

**doch** *konj* [aber] yet, but ⬦ *adv* - **1.** [trotzdem] anyway; er wollte erst nicht, aber dann hat er es ~ gemacht at first he didn't want to, but then he did it anyway; willst du nicht? - ~ don't you want to? – yes, I do; ~ noch after all - **2.** [verstärkend]: setzen Sie sich ~! do sit down!; nicht ~, so war es nun auch nicht gemeint! okay, okay, I didn't mean it that way!; das kann ~ nicht wahr sein! but surely that can't be true!; aber das konnte ich ~ nicht wissen! but how could I have known! → nicht doch *interj* don't do that!

**Docht** (*pl* -e) *der* wick.

**Dock** (*pl* -s) *das* dock.

**Documenta** *die* international exhibition of contemporary art held every four or five years in Kassel.

**Dogge** (*pl* -n) *die* mastiff.

**Dogma** (*pl* Dogmen) *das* dogma.

**dogmatisch** *adj abw* dogmatic.

**Doktor** (*pl* -toren) *der* - **1.** [Titel] doctorate; seinen ~ machen to do one's doctorate - **2.** [Träger des Doktortitels, Arzt] doctor.

**Doktorand, in** (*mpl* -en; *fpl* -nen) *der, die* PhD student.

**Doktor|arbeit** *die* doctoral thesis.

**Doktorin** (*pl* -nen) *die* doctor.

**Doktor|titel** *der* PhD, doctorate.

**Doktor|vater** *der* supervisor.

**Doktrin** (*pl* -en) *die* doctrine.

**Dokument** (*pl* -e) *das* document.

**Dokumentar|film** *der* documentary.

**dokumentarisch** *adj* documentary ⬦ *adv* [belegen] using documentary evidence.

**Dokumentation** (*pl* -en) *die* - **1.** [Informationsmaterial] documentation (U) - **2.** [Darstellung]: eine ~ über etw (A) machen to document sthg.

**dokumentieren** *vt* - **1.** [darstellen] to document - **2.** [bekunden] to show clearly.

**Dolch** (*pl* -e) *der* dagger.

**Dolde** (*pl* -n) *die* umbel.

**Dollar** (*pl* -s *ODER* -) *der* dollar.

**dolmetschen** *vt* & *vi* to interpret.

**Dolmetscher, in** (*mpl* -; *fpl* -nen) *der, die* interpreter.

**Dolomiten** *pl* Dolomites.

**Dom** (*pl* -e) *der* cathedral.

**Domäne** (*pl* -n) *die* [Spezialgebiet] domain.

**dominant** *adj* dominant.

**Dominante** (*pl* -n) *die* MUS dominant.

**Dominanz** (*pl* -en) *die* dominance.

**dominieren** *vi* to predominate ⬦ *vt* to dominate.

**Dominikaner, in** (*mpl* -; *fpl* -nen) *der, die* GEOGR & REL Dominican.

**Dominikanische Republik** *die* Dominican Republic.

**Domino** (*pl* -s) *das* dominoes (U).

**Domizil** (*pl* -e) *das* *geh* domicile.

**Dompteur** *(pl -e) der* animal tamer.

**Dompteuse** *(pl -n) die* animal tamer.

**Donau** *die:* **die** ~ the Danube.

**Donner** *der* thunder; **wie vom ~ gerührt** thunderstruck.

**donnern** *(perf* hat/ist gedonnert) *vi* - **1.** *(hat)* [beim Gewitter]: **es donnert** it is thundering - **2.** *(ist)* [sich bewegen] to thunder - **3.** *(hat) fam* [schlagen] to hammer - **4.** *(ist) fam* [prallen]: **gegen etw ~** to slam into sthg ◇ *vt (hat) fam* to hurl.

**Donnern** *das* thunder.

**Donner|schlag** *der* thunderclap.

**Donnerstag** *(pl -e) der* Thursday; *siehe auch* **Samstag.**

**donnerstags** *adv* on Thursdays; *siehe auch* **samstags.**

**Donnerwetter** *das (ohne pl) fam* almighty row; **zum ~!** for goodness' sake!; **Donnerwetter!** my goodness!

**doof** *fam adj* stupid ◇ *adv* stupidly.

**dopen** ['doːpn̩] *vt* [Pferd] to dope.
➤ **sich dopen** *ref* [Sportler] to take drugs.

**Doping** ['doːpɪŋ] *(pl -s) das* drug-taking.

**Doping|kontrolle** *die* drugs test.

**Doppel** *(pl -) das* - **1.** [Kopie] duplicate - **2.** SPORT doubles *(U);* **im ~ spielen** to play doubles; **gemischtes ~** mixed doubles.

**Doppel|belastung** *die* double workload.

**Doppel|besteuerung** *die* double taxation.

**Doppel|bett** *das* double bed.

**Doppel|decker** *(pl -) der* - **1.** FLUG biplane - **2.** [Omnibus] double-decker (bus).

**doppeldeutig** *adj* ambiguous; **~er Witz** double entendre.

**Doppel|fenster** *das* double window.

**Doppel|gänger, in** *(mpl -; fpl -nen) der, die* double.

**Doppel|haus** *das* pair of semi-detached houses.

**Doppel|kinn** *das* double chin.

**Doppelklick** *(pl -s) der* EDV double click.

**Doppel|leben** *das* double life.

**Doppel|moral** *die (ohne pl)* double standards *(pl).*

**Doppel|name** *der* double-barrelled name.

**Doppel|punkt** *der* colon.

**doppelseitig** *adj* - **1.** [Lungenentzündung] double - **2.** [zwei Seiten umfassend] two-page.

**Doppel|stecker** *der* two-way adaptor.

**doppelt** *adj* - **1.** [zweifach] double - **2.** [gesteigert] twice as much ◇ *adv* twice; **~ so viel** twice as much; **das ist ~ gemoppelt** *fam* that is saying the same thing twice; **etw ~ und dreifach**

**prüfen** *fam* to check sthg and check it again; **~ sehen** *fam* to see double.

**Doppelte** *das:* **das** ~ twice as much.

**Doppelverdiener, in** *(mpl -; fpl -nen) der, die:* **sie sind** ~ they are both earning.

**Doppel|zimmer** *das* double room.

**Dorf** *(pl -) das* - **1.** [Ort] village; **auf dem** ~ in the country; **das olympische** ~ the Olympic Village - **2.** RW: **nie aus seinem ~ herausgekommen sein** to be parochial; **das sind für mich böhmische Dörfer** it's all Greek to me.

**Dorf|bewohner, in** *der, die* villager.

**dörflich** *adj* village *(vor Subst);* [Gegend] rural.

**Dorn** *(pl -en) der* [von Rose] thorn; [von Schnalle] prong; **jm ein ~ im Auge sein** to be a thorn in sb's side.

**dornig** *adj* thorny.

**Dornröschen** *das* Sleeping Beauty.

**Dörrobst** *das* dried fruit.

**Dorsch** *(pl -e) der* cod.

**dort** *adv* there; **~ drüben** over there; **von ~ aus** from there; **~, wo wir Fußball spielen** where we play football.

**dorther** *adv* from there.

**dorthin** *adv* there.

**dortig** *adj* local.

**Dortmund** *nt* Dortmund.

**Dose** *(pl -n) die* - **1.** [Behälter] box; [für Zucker] bowl; [für Butter] dish - **2.** [Konservendose] can, tin Br; [Bierdose] can; **Erbsen aus der** ~ tinned ODER canned peas

**dösen** *vi* to doze.

**Dosen|bier** *das* canned beer.

**Dosen|milch** *die* condensed ODER evaporated milk.

**Dosen|öffner** *der* can ODER tin Br opener.

**dosieren** *vt* to measure out.

**Dosierung** *(pl -en) die* dosage.

**Dosis** *(pl Dosen) die* dose.

**Dotter** *(pl -) das* ODER *der* yolk.

**dottergelb** *adj* deep yellow.

**Double** ['duːbl̩] *(pl -s) das* double.

**down** [daʊn] *adj fam:* **~ sein** to be down.

**down|loaden** *(präs* **loadet down;** *prät* **loadete down;** *perf* **hat downgeloadet)** *vt* EDV to download.

**Dozent, in** *(mpl -en; fpl -nen) der, die* lecturer Br, assistant professor Am.

**dpa** [deːpeːˈʔaː] *(abk für* **Deutsche Presseagentur)** *die* German Press Agency.

**Dr.** *(abk für* **Doktor)** Dr.

**Drache** *(pl -n) der* dragon.

**Drachen** (pl -) der - **1.** [Spielzeug] kite; einen ~ steigen lassen to fly a kite - **2.** abw [Frau] dragon.

**Drachenflieger, in** (mpl -; fpl -nen) der, die hang-glider.

**Draht** (pl Drähte) der - **1.** [gen] wire; ein heißer ~ a hot line - **2.** RW: auf ~ sein fam to be on the ball; jn auf ~ bringen fam to make sb pull his/her finger out; einen guten ~ zu jm haben to be well in with sb.

**drahtig** adj wiry.

**drahtlos** adj [Telefon] cordless <> adv: eine Nachricht ~ übermitteln to radio a message.

**Draht|seil** das steel cable; [im Zirkus] high wire.

**Drahtseil|bahn** die cable railway.

**Drahtzieher, in** (mpl -; fpl -nen) der, die [Hintermann] string-puller.

**drakonisch** adj draconian <> adv in a draconian manner.

**drall** adj [Mädchen] buxom; [Körperteil] well-rounded.

**Drall** (pl -e) der spin.

**Drama** (pl Dramen) das drama.

**Dramatiker, in** (mpl -z; fpl -nen) der, die playwright, dramatist.

**dramatisch** adj dramatic.

**dramatisieren** vt [hochspielen] to play up, to make a big thing of.

**Dramaturg, in** (mpl -en; fpl -nen) der, die person who selects and adapts plays for the stage.

**dramaturgisch** adj dramatic.

**dran** adv - **1.** fam = daran - **2.** [von Bedeutung]: da ist was ~! there's something in it!; da ist alles ~! it's got everything!; da ist nichts ~! there's nothing in it! - **3.** [an der Reihe]: ich bin jetzt ~ it's my turn; wer ist als Nächster ~? who's next?, whose turn is it? - **4.** RW: ~ sein to be for it; nicht wissen, wie ODER wo man ~ ist not to know where one stands; ~ glauben müssen to meet one's end.

**dran|bleiben** (perf ist drangeblieben) vi (unreg) - **1.** [am Telefon]: bleiben Sie bitte dran hold the line please - **2.** [in Rennen, Verfolgungsjagd]: an jm ~ not to let sb get away (from one) - **3.** [Entwicklung, Veränderung]: an etw (D) ~ to keep up to date with sthg.

**drang** prät ⊳ dringen.

**Drang** der urge, yearning.

**Drängelei** (pl -en) die - **1.** abw [durch Schieben] pushing (and shoving) - **2.** [durch Reden] pestering.

**drängeln** vi - **1.** [durch Schieben] to push - **2.** [durch Reden] to go on (and on) <> vt - **1.** [durch Schieben] to push - **2.** [durch Reden] to pester.

➤ **sich drängeln** ref: sich nach vorn ~ to push one's way to the front.

**drängen** vi - **1.** [schieben] to push - **2.** [nicht warten]: zum Aufbruch ~ to insist on leaving; zur Eile ~ to urge haste; auf etw (A) ~ to push ODER press for sthg <> vt - **1.** [schieben] to push - **2.** [antreiben] to urge; jn zu einem Kauf ~ to urge sb to make a purchase.

➤ **sich drängen** ref: sich nach vorn ~ to push one's way to the front.

**drangsalieren** vt abw to plague.

**dran|halten** ➤ **sich dranhalten** ref (unreg) fam to get a move on.

**dran|kommen** (perf ist drangekommen) vi (unreg) - **1.** [an die Reihe kommen] to have one's turn; ich bin als Letzter drangekommen I was last - **2.** [heranreichen] to reach.

**drastisch** adj - **1.** [einschneidend] drastic - **2.** [sehr deutlich] graphic <> adv - **1.** [stark] drastically - **2.** [sehr deutlich] graphically.

**drauf** adv fam - **1.** = darauf - **2.** RW: es kommt ~ an it depends; etw ~ haben [Fähigkeit] to be really good at sthg; er hatte hundert Sachen ~ AUTO he was doing a hundred; gut ~ sein to be in a good mood; ~ und dran sein, etw zu tun to be on the point of doing sthg.

**Draufgänger, in** (mpl -; fpl -nen) der, die daredevil.

**drauf|geben** vt (unreg) fam: jm eins ~ [schlagen] to whack sb; [zurechtweisen] to give sb what for.

**drauf|gehen** (perf ist draufgegangen) vi (unreg) fam - **1.** [umkommen] to buy it - **2.** [verbraucht werden] to be used up.

**drauf|kommen** (perf ist draufgekommen) vi (unreg) [herausfinden] to work it out; ich bin nicht gleich draufgekommen I didn't realize straight away; ich komme nicht drauf, wie sie heißt I can't think what she's called.

**drauflos|gehen** (perf ist drauflosgegangen) vi (unreg) fam to go for it.

**drauf|machen** vt fam: einen ~ to live it up.

**drauf|zahlen** vt to pay on top <> vi to lose money.

**draußen** adv outside.

➤ **nach draußen** adv outside.

➤ **von draußen** adv from outside.

**drechseln** ['drɛksln] vt to turn.

**Dreck** der fam - **1.** [Schmutz] muck, dirt; ~ machen to make a mess - **2.** RW: es interessiert mich einen ~ I don't give a damn; das geht dich einen ~ an it's none of your damn business; jn wie den letzten ~ behandeln abw to treat sb like dirt; jn/etw in den ~ ziehen to drag sb/sthg through the mud; ~ am Stecken haben to have a skeleton in the cupboard Br ODER closet Am.

**Dreck|arbeit** die fam - **1.** [schmutzige Arbeit] dirty work - **2.** [niedere Arbeit] menial jobs (pl).

**dreckig** adj - **1.** [schmutzig, unverschämt] dirty; **sich ~ machen** to get dirty - **2.** fam abw [gemein]: **du ~es Schwein!** you filthy swine! <> adv fam - **1.** abw [unverschämt] dirtily - **2.** [schlecht]: **ihr geht es ~** she is in a bad way.

**Dreck|spatz** der fam mucky pup.

**Dreh** (pl -s ODER -e) der fam: **den (richtigen) ~ heraushaben** to have got the hang of it; (so) **um den ~** round about then.

**Drehbank** (pl -bänke) die lathe.

**drehbar** adj revolving.

**Dreh|bewegung** die turn.

**Dreh|buch** das screenplay.

**Drehbuch|autor, in** der, die screenwriter.

**drehen** vt - **1.** [im Kreis bewegen] to turn - **2.** [einstellen]: **das Radio laut/leise ~** to turn the radio up/down - **3.** [formen - Seil] to twist; [- Zigarette, Pillen] to roll - **4.** TV to film, to shoot - **5.** RW: **du kannst die Sache ~ und wenden, so viel du willst, aber du wirst sie nicht ändern** whichever way you look at it, you can't change it <> vi - **1.** [wenden] to turn - **2.** [am Knopf, Schalter]: **an etw** (D) **~** to turn sthg; **am Radio ~** to turn the knob on the radio.

◆ **sich drehen** ref - **1.** [sich wenden] to turn; **mir dreht sich alles** fam my head is spinning - **2.** RW: **sich um jn/etw ~** to be about sb/sthg; **es dreht sich darum, dass ...** the thing is ...; **alles dreht sich um ihn** everything revolves around him.

**Dreh|kreuz** das turnstile.

**Dreh|orgel** die barrel organ.

**Dreh|scheibe** die [Knotenpunkt] hub.

**Dreh|stuhl** der swivel chair.

**Dreh|tür** die revolving door.

**Drehung** (pl -en) die turn.

**Dreh|wurm** der: **einen** ODER **den ~ kriegen** fam to get giddy.

**Dreh|zahl** die revs (pl).

**Drehzahlmesser** (pl -) der rev counter Br, tachometer Am.

**drei** num - **1.** [Zahl] three - **2.** RW: **für ~ essen** to eat like a horse; **nicht bis ~ zählen können** fam not to have a clue about anything; siehe auch **sechs.**

**Drei** (pl -en) die - **1.** [Zahl] three - **2.** [Schulnote] ≈ C, mark of 3 on a scale from 1 to 6; siehe auch **Sechs.**

**dreidimensional** adj three-dimensional <> adv three-dimensionally.

**Dreieck** (pl -e) das triangle.

**dreieckig** adj triangular.

**Dreier** (pl -) der - **1.** [Drei] three - **2.** [beim Lotto] three correct numbers (pl) - **3.** fam [Sprungbrett] three-metre board.

**dreierlei** adj (unver) three different; **auf ~ Weise** in three different ways.

**dreifach** adj triple; **die ~e Menge** three times as much; **in ~er Größe** three times as big; **in ~er Ausfertigung** in triplicate; **der ~e Gewinner** the three times ODER triple winner <> adv three times.

**Dreifaltigkeit** die REL Trinity.

**dreihundert** num three hundred.

**Drei|klang** der triad.

**Dreikönigs|fest** das Epiphany.

**dreimal** adv three times.

**Drei|rad** das tricycle.

**Drei|satz** der rule of three.

**Drei|sprung** der SPORT triple jump.

**dreißig** num thirty; siehe auch **sechs.**

**Dreißig** die thirty; siehe auch **Sechs.**

**Dreißigerjahre, dreißiger Jahre** pl: **die ~** the thirties.

**dreist** adj impudent <> adv impudently.

**Dreistigkeit** (pl -en) die - **1.** [Wesen, Verhalten] impudence - **2.** [Handlung]: **das ist eine ~!** what impudence!, how impudent!

**dreistöckig** adj - **1.** [Haus] three-storeyed - **2.** [Torte] three-tiered.

**dreitausend** num three thousand.

**Drei|tausender** der [Berg] peak over 3,000 metres high.

**dreiteilig** adj three-part; [Kostüm, Anzug] three-piece.

**drei viertel** num three quarters; **~ Liter** three-quarters of a litre; **~ acht** a quarter to Br ODER of Am eight.

**Dreivierteltakt** der three-four time.

**dreizehn** num thirteen; **jetzt schlägts (aber) ~!** that's the limit!; siehe auch **sechs.**

**Dreizimmer|wohnung** die three-roomed flat Br ODER apartment Am.

**Dresche** die fam: **~ kriegen** ODER **beziehen** to get a thrashing.

**dreschen** (präs drischt; prät drosch; perf hat gedroschen) vt - **1.** [Getreide] to thresh - **2.** fam [prügeln] to thrash <> vi fam [schlagen] to bang.

**Dresch|maschine** die threshing machine.

**Dresden** nt Dresden.

**Dress** (pl -e) der - **1.** SPORT kit - **2.** fam [Kleidung] outfit.

**dressieren** vt to train.

**Dressing** (pl -s) das dressing.

**Dressur** (*pl* -en) *die* - **1.** [Dressieren] training - **2.** [Pferdedressur] dressage.

**Dressurreiten** *das* dressage.

**Dr. h. c.** (*abk für* **Doktor honoris causa**) honorary doctor.

**dribbeln** (*perf* hat gedribbelt) *vi* sport to dribble.

**Drill** *der* drill.

**drillen** *vt* to drill.

**Drilling** (*pl* -e) *der* triplet.

**drin** *adv fam* - **1.** = **darin** - **2.** [möglich]: ~ **sein** to be on the cards; **bei diesem Spiel ist noch alles** ~ there is still everything to play for in this game - **3.** [gewöhnt]: ~ **sein** to have got into the swing of things.

**dringen** (*prät* **drang**; *perf* **hat/ist gedrungen**) *vi* - **1.** (*ist*) [eindringen]: **durch** oder **in etw** (*A*) ~ to penetrate sthg; **Wasser dringt durch die Decke** water is leaking through the ceiling; **Gas drang in den Raum** gas seeped into the room; **in jn** ~ to keep on at sb - **2.** (*hat*) [drängen]: **auf etw** (*A*) ~ to insist on sthg.

**dringend** *adj* urgent <> *adv* urgently.

**Dringlichkeit** *die* urgency.

**Drink** [drɪŋk] (*pl* -s) *der* drink.

**drinnen** *adv* inside; **nach** ~ **gehen** to go inside.

**drinstecken** *vi fam*: **in ihm steckt viel drin** there is a lot of potential in him.

**drischt** *präs* ⊳ **dreschen**.

**dritt** ⬤ **zu dritt** *num*: **wir sind zu** ~ there are three of us; **wir sind zu** ~ **ins Kino gegangen** three of us went to the cinema.

**dritte, r, s** *adj* third; *siehe auch* **sechste**.

**Dritte** *der, die, das* third; [außenstehende Person] third party; **der lachende** ~ **sein** to come off best *(when two others cannot agree)*; *siehe auch* **Sechste**.

**drittel** *adj (unver)* third of a; *siehe auch* **sechstel**.

**Drittel** (*pl* -) *das* third; *siehe auch* **Sechstel**.

**dritteln** *vt* to divide into three.

**drittens** *adv* thirdly.

**Dritte Reich** *das:* **das** ~ the Third Reich.

**DRK** [deːˌɛrˈkaː] (*abk für* **Deutsches Rotes Kreuz**) *das German Red Cross.*

**Dr. med.** (*abk für* **Doktor der Medizin**) MD.

**Droge** (*pl* -n) *die* drug.

**drogenabhängig** *adj:* ~ **sein** to be a drug addict.

**Drogenabhängige** (*pl* -n) *der, die* drug addict.

**Drogenberatungsstelle** *die* drug advice centre.

**Drogenhandel** *der* drug dealing.

**Drogenhändler, in** *der, die* drug dealer.

**Drogenkonsum** *der* drug taking.

**Drogenmissbrauch** *der* drug abuse.

**drogensüchtig** *adj:* ~ **sein** to be a drug addict.

**Drogenszene** *die* drug scene.

**Drogerie** (*pl* -n) *die* chemist's (shop) *(nondispensing) Br*, drugstore *Am*.

**Drohbrief** *der* threatening letter.

**drohen** *vi* to threaten; ~, **etw zu tun** to threaten to do sthg; **jm (mit etw)** ~ to threaten sb (with sthg).

**Drohne** (*pl* -n) *die* [Biene] drone.

**dröhnen** *vi* - **1.** [hallen] to boom - **2.** *salopp* [berauschen] to give you a high.

**Drohung** (*pl* -en) *die* threat.

**drollig** *adj* - **1.** [niedlich - Kind, Hund] cute; [ - Erzählung] funny, droll - **2.** [seltsam] odd <> *adv* - **1.** [niedlich] funnily - **2.** [seltsam] oddly.

**Dromedar** (*pl* -e) *das* dromedary.

**Drops** (*pl* -) *das* oder *der* fruit drop.

**drosch** *prät* ⊳ **dreschen**.

**Drossel** (*pl* -n) *die* thrush.

**drosseln** *vt* [Geschwindigkeit, Leistung] to reduce; [Heizung] to turn down.

**Drosselung** (*pl* -en) *die* [von Geschwindigkeit, Leistung] reduction.

**Dr. phil.** (*abk für* **Doktor der Philosophie**) PhD.

**drüben** *adv* [nebenan] over there.

**drüber** = **darüber**.

**Druck** (*pl* -e) *der* - **1.** [Kraft, Zwang] pressure; ~ **hinter etw** (*A*) **machen** *fam fig* to put pressure on regarding sthg; ~ **auf jn ausüben, jn unter** ~ **setzen** to put pressure on sb; ~ **machen** to put pressure on; **unter** ~ **stehen** to be under pressure - **2.** [Drucken] printing; **es ist in** oder **im** ~ it is being printed - **3.** [Gravur] print.

**Druckbuchstabe** *der* printed letter; **in** ~**n schreiben** to print.

**Drückeberger, in** (*mpl* -; *fpl* -nen) *der, die abw* shirker.

**druckempfindlich** *adj* [Körperstelle] sensitive to pressure; **Pfirsiche sind** ~ peaches bruise easily.

**drucken** *vt* to print.

**drücken** *vt* - **1.** [pressen] to press; **jn/etw an sich** (*A*) ~ to hold sb/sthg to one - **2.** *fam* [umarmen] to hug, to squeeze - **3.** [mindern] to lower <> *vi* - **1.** [pressen]: **auf etw** (*A*) ~ to press sthg; **es drückt auf die Laune** it gets you down - **2.** [Schuhe] to pinch - **3.** *salopp* [fixen] to shoot up.

⬤ **sich drücken** *ref* - **1.** [sich pressen]: **sich an etw**

*(A)* ~ to flatten o.s. against sthg - **2.** [sich entziehen]: **sich vor etw** *(D)* ~ **abw** to get out of sthg.

**drückend** *adj* - **1.** [Probleme, Sorgen] serious; [Verantwortung, Schulden] heavy; [Armut] grinding - **2.** [Hitze] oppressive.

**Drucker** *(pl -)* der printer.

**Drücker** *(pl -)* der - **1.** [Türdrücker] handle - **2.** [Hausierer] door-to-door salesman - **3.** RW: **auf den letzten** ~ **fam** at the last minute; **am** ~ **sitzen** *fam* to call the shots.

**Druckerei** *(pl -en)* die printing works, printer's.

**Druckerin** *(pl -nen)* die printer.

**Druckertreiber** *(pl -)* der EDV printer driver.

**Drucklfehler** der misprint.

**druckfertig** *adj* ready for printing.

**Drucklknopf** der press stud *Br*, snap fastener *Am*.

**Drucklluft** die compressed air.

**Drucklmittel** das means of applying pressure.

**druckreif** *adj* - **1.** [Text] ready for printing - **2.** [Ausdrucksweise] polished <> *adv* in a polished manner.

**Drucklsache** die printed matter *(U)*.

**Drucklschrift** die block capitals *(pl)*.

**drum** *fam* = darum.

**Drum** das: **das ganze** ~ **und Dran** *fam* the whole rigmarole; **mit allem** ~ **und Dran** *fam* with all the trimmings.

**drunter** *adv fam* - **1.** = darunter - **2.** RW: **alles** ODER **es geht** ~ **und drüber** everything is going haywire.

**Drüse** *(pl -n)* die gland.

**Dschungel** *(pl -)* der jungle.

**DSG** *(abk für* **Deutsche Schlafwagen- und Speisewagen-Gesellschaft)** *die company that runs sleeping and dining cars on German railways.*

**dt.** *(abk für* **deutsch)** Ger.

**DTP** *(abk für* **Desktop-Publishing)** *das (ohne pl)* EDV DTP.

**du** *pron* du; **ach,** ~ **bists!** oh, it's you!; ~ **sagen** to use the "du" form of address; **mit jm per** ~ **sein** ≈ to be on first name terms with sb.

**Duale System** *das privately run waste disposal and recycling system.*

**Dübel** *(pl -)* der Rawlplug®.

**dübeln** *vt* to fix with Rawlplugs®.

**dubios** *adj geh* dubious.

**Dublin** ['dablɪn] *nt* Dublin.

**ducken** ⟶ **sich ducken** *ref* to duck.

**dudeln** *fam abw vi* [Plattenspieler, Radio] to drone;

[auf Instrument] to tootle <> *vt* [auf Blasinstrument] to tootle on.

**Dudellsack** der bagpipes *(pl)*.

**Duell** [du'ɛl] *(pl -e)* das duel.

**duellieren** [due'liːrn̩] ⟶ **sich duellieren** *ref* to duel.

**Duett** [du'ɛt] *(pl -e)* das duet.

**Duft** *(pl Düfte)* der scent.

**duften** *vi* to smell nice; **nach etw** ~ to smell of sthg.

**duftig** *adj* dainty.

**Duftlnote** die scent.

**dulden** *vt geh* to tolerate.

**duldsam** *adj* tolerant <> *adv* tolerantly.

**Duldsamkeit** die tolerance.

**Duldung** die toleration.

**dumm** *(kompar* **dümmer;** *superl* **dümmste)** *adj* - **1.** [gen] stupid; **ich lasse mich nicht für** ~ **verkaufen fam** I won't be made a fool of; ~**es Zeug** rubbish, nonsense; **es ist** ODER **wird mir zu** ~ I've had enough of it - **2.** [unangenehm - Fehler, Zufall] annoying <> *adv* stupidly; ~ **und dämlich** *salopp fig* like crazy; **jm** ~ **kommen fam abw** to try it on with sb.

**dummdreist** *adj* impudent <> *adv* impudently.

**Dumme** *(pl -n)* der, die: **der** ~ **sein** to be the one who loses out; **einen** ~**n finden** to find some mug *Br* ODER dummy.

**dummerweise** *adv* - **1.** [ärgerlicherweise] unfortunately - **2.** [aus Dummheit] stupidly.

**Dummheit** *(pl -en)* die - **1.** [fehlende Klugheit] stupidity - **2.** [Handlung] stupid thing; **mach keine** ~**en** don't do anything stupid.

**Dummlkopf** der idiot.

**dümmlich** *adj* stupid <> *adv* stupidly.

**dumpf** *adj* - **1.** [Klang] dull, muffled - **2.** [Schmerz] dull; [Befürchtung, Verdacht] vague - **3.** [stumpfsinnig] apathetic <> *adv* - **1.** [dunkel] dully - **2.** [stumpfsinnig] apathetically.

**Dumpinglpreis** ['dampɪnpraɪs] der knockdown price.

**Düne** *(pl -n)* die dune.

**Dung** der dung.

**Düngelmittel** das fertilizer.

**düngen** *vt* to fertilize <> *vi* - **1.** [Dung] to act as a fertilizer - **2.** [Person] to fertilize one's land/garden/etc.

**Dünger** *(pl -)* der fertilizer.

**Düngung** *(pl -en)* die fertilizing.

**dunkel** *adj* - **1.** [gen] dark; **im Dunkeln tappen** *fig* to grope around in the dark - **2.** [Ton, Stimme] deep - **3.** [vage] vague; **jn über etw** *(A)* **im Dunkeln lassen** to keep sb in the dark about sthg - **4.** [dubios] shady ⬦ adv - **1.** [streichen, färben] in dark colours/a dark colour - **2.** [klingen] deep - **3.** [unklar] vaguely.

**Dünkel** der abw arrogance.

**dunkelblau** adj & adv dark blue.

**dunkelblond** adj light brown; [Person] with light brown hair ⬦ adv light brown.

**dunkelgrau** adj & adv dark grey.

**dunkelgrün** adj & adv dark green.

**dunkelhaarig** adj dark-haired.

**dunkelhäutig** adj dark-skinned.

**Dunkelheit** die darkness.

**Dunkel∣kammer** die darkroom.

**dunkelrot** adj & adv dark red.

**Dunkel∣ziffer** die number of unreported incidents.

**dünn** adj - **1.** [gen] thin; **sich ~ machen** [wenig Platz brauchen] to squeeze up - **2.** [Getränk, Stimme] weak - **3.** [Haare, Bewuchs] sparse ⬦ adv [bevölkert, bewachsen] sparsely; [auftragen] thinly.

**dünn besiedelt** adj sparsely populated.

**Dünnbrett∣bohrer** der fam abw - **1.** [fauler Mensch] lazy devil - **2.** [dummer Mensch] blockhead.

**Dünn∣darm** der small intestine.

**dünnflüssig** adj thin.

**dünnmachen** ⬥ sich dünnmachen ref fam [abhauen] to make o.s. scarce.

**Dunst** (pl **Dünste**) der - **1.** [Nebel] haze, mist - **2.** [von Zigaretten] smoke; [in der Küche] steam - **3.** RW: jm blauen ~ vormachen to pull the wool over sb's eyes; **keinen (blassen) ~ von etw haben** fam not to have the foggiest (idea) about sthg.

**dünsten** vt to steam.

**Dunst∣glocke** die cloud of smog.

**dunstig** adj [neblig] hazy, misty.

**Dunst∣kreis** der orbit.

**Dunst∣wolke** die cloud of smog.

**Duo** (pl -s) das duo.

**Duplikat** (pl -e) das duplicate.

**Dur** das major; **eine Sonate in ~** a sonata in a major key.

**durch** präp (+ A) - **1.** [räumlich, zeitlich] through; **darf ich mal bitte ~?** excuse me, please!; **~ die Schweiz reisen** to travel across Switzerland; **die ganze Nacht ~** throughout the night - **2.** [mittels] by; **~ eigene Schuld** through one's own fault; **~ Ihre Hilfe** with your help; **das Haus wurde ~ ein Erdbeben zerstört** the house was destroyed by an earthquake - **3.** MATH divided by; **sechs ~ drei** six divided by three ⬦ adv - **1.** fam [später als]: **es ist schon zwölf ~** it's gone ODER past twelve - **2.** fam [durchgebraten]

well done - **3.** fam [beendet]: **bis morgen muss ich mit dem Buch ~ sein** I have to finish the book by tomorrow - **4.** RW: **~ und ~ through and through; ~ und ~ nass** wet through; **es geht ihm ~ und ~** it went through him.

**durch∣arbeiten** vt to work through ⬦ vi to work without a break.

⬥ **sich durcharbeiten** ref: sich durch etw ~ [Menschenmenge, Text] to work one's way through sthg.

**durch∣atmen** vi to breathe deeply.

**durchaus, durchaus** adv - **1.** [gut, ohne weiteres] perfectly; **es kann ~ sein** it is perfectly possible - **2.** [unbedingt] absolutely - **3.** [absolut, überhaupt]: **~ nicht** definitely not, not at all.

**durch∣beißen** vt (unreg) to bite through.

⬥ **sich durchbeißen** ref to struggle through.

**durch∣blättern** vt to flick through.

**Durch∣blick** der fam overview; **den ~ verlieren** to lose track of things; **keinen ~ haben** fam not to have a clue.

**durch∣blicken**[1] vi - **1.** [durchsehen]: **durch etw ~** to look through sthg - **2.** fam [etw verstehen]: **da blickt doch keiner mehr durch!** it's impossible to make head or tail of it; **etw ~ lassen** fig to hint at sthg.

**durchblicken**[2] vt to see through.

**durchblutet** adj: **gut/schwach ~ sein** to have good/poor circulation.

**Durchblutung** die circulation.

**Durchblutungs∣störung** die problem with one's circulation.

**durch∣bohren**[1] vt [Brett] to drill through; [Loch] to drill ⬦ vi to drill through.

**durchbohren**[2] vt [Subj: Kugel] to go through; **jn mit Blicken ~** to fix sb with a piercing gaze.

**durch∣boxen** vt to push through.

⬥ **sich durchboxen** ref to fight one's way through.

**durch∣braten** vt (unreg) to cook well ODER through.

**durch∣brechen**[1] (perf hat/ist durchgebrochen) (unreg) vt (hat) - **1.** [zerbrechen] to break in two - **2.** [einreißen - Wand] to knock in ⬦ vi (ist) - **1.** [zerbrechen] to break in two; [Boden] to give way - **2.** [durchdringen] to break through; [Geschwür, Abszess] to perforate.

**durchbrechen**[2] (präs durchbricht; prät durchbrach; perf hat durchbrochen) vt to break through.

**durch∣brennen** (perf ist durchgebrannt) vi (unreg) - **1.** [Draht] to blow, to go - **2.** fam [weglaufen] to run away.

**durch∣bringen** vt (unreg) - **1.** [ernähren] to provide for - **2.** [Kranke] to pull through - **3.** [Geld] to get through, to blow - **4.** [Vorschlag, Gesetz] to get through.

**Durch|bruch** *der* - **1.** [Erfolg] breakthrough; jm/einer Sache zum ~ verhelfen to help sb/ sthg to make a breakthrough - **2.** [Öffnung] opening.

**durch|checken** [ˈdʊrçtʃɛkn̩] *vt* to check over.

**durchdacht** *adj* well thought out; **gut/ schlecht ~** well/badly thought out.

**durch|denken¹** *vt (unreg)* to think through.

**durchdenken²** (*prät* durchdachte; *perf* hat durchdacht) *vt* to think out.

**durch|diskutieren** *vt* to talk through.

**durch|drängen** ⇝ sich durchdrängen *ref* to push one's way through.

**durch|drehen** (*perf* hat/ist durchgedreht) *vi* - **1.** *(ist)* *fam* [verrückt werden] to crack up - **2.** *(hat)* [Räder] to spin ⟨> *vt (hat)* to mince.

**durch|dringen¹** (*perf* ist durchgedrungen) *vi (unreg)* [Geräusch, Licht, Nachricht] to get through; [Wasser] to seep through.

**durchdringen²** (*prät* durchdrang; *perf* hat durchdrungen) *vt* - **1.** [Metall, Stein, Wand] to penetrate - **2.** [Subj: Gedanke] er ist von einer Vorstellung durchdrungen one idea has completely taken hold of him.

**durch|drücken** *vt* - **1.** *fam* [durchsetzen] to push through - **2.** [Gelenk] to straighten - **3.** [passieren] to press through.

**durchdrungen** *pp* ▷ durchdringen.

**durcheinander** *adv* all over the place ⟨> *adj:* ~ sein [Zimmer, Haus] to be a mess; [Person] to be confused.

**Durcheinander** *das* [von Menschen] confusion; [von Dingen] chaos.

**durcheinander bringen** *vt (unreg)* - **1.** [Person] to confuse - **2.** [Dinge] to muddle up - **3.** [verwechseln] to mix up.

**durcheinander kommen** (*perf* ist durcheinander gekommen) *vi (unreg)* to get muddled up; mir sind die Namen durcheinander gekommen I've got the names muddled up.

**durcheinander laufen** (*perf* sind durcheinander gelaufen) *vi (unreg)* to run all over the place.

**durch|exerzieren** *vt* to go through.

**durch|fahren¹** (*perf* ist durchgefahren) *vi (unreg)* - **1.** [durchqueren] to go ODER drive through - **2.** [durchgehend fahren] to go ODER drive non-stop.

**durchfahren²** (*präs* durchfährt; *prät* durchfuhr; *perf* hat durchfahren) *vt (unreg):* ein Schreck durchfuhr ihn a wave of fear ran through him.

**Durch|fahrt** *die* - **1.** [Durchfahren]: die ~ freigeben to open the road (again); '~ verboten' 'no through road' *Br*, 'no outlet' *Am* - **2.** [Durchreise] way through; auf der ~ sein to

be travelling through - **3.** [Weg] access road.

**Durch|fahrts|straße** *die* main road *(through a place)*.

**Durch|fall** *der* - **1.** [Diarrhöe] diarrhoea - **2.** *fam* [Misserfolg] flop; [bei einer Prüfung] failure.

**durch|fallen** (*perf* ist durchgefallen) *vi (unreg)* - **1.** *fam* [versagen] to flop; [bei einer Prüfung] to fail - **2.** [durch eine Öffnung] to fall through.

**durch|feiern** *vt:* die Nacht ~ to party all night; drei Tage ~ to party for three days ⟨> *vi* to party all night.

**durch|finden** *vi (unreg)* to find one's way through.
⇝ sich durchfinden *ref* to find one's way through.

**durch|fließen** (*perf* ist durchgeflossen) *vi (unreg)* to flow through.

**durch|forschen** *vt* [Umgebung] to search; [Textmaterial] to search through.

**durch|forsten** *vt* - **1.** [durchsuchen - Gegend] to search; [ - Textmaterial] to search through - **2.** [ausdünnen - Wald] to thin out.

**durch|fragen** ⇝ sich durchfragen *ref* to ask one's way.

**durch|führbar** *adj* practicable.

**durch|führen** *vt* to carry out; [Veranstaltung] to hold ⟨> *vi* to go through.

**Durch|führung** *die* carrying out; [einer Veranstaltung] holding.

**Durch|gang** *der* - **1.** [Durchgehen]: '~ verboten' 'no right of way' - **2.** [Weg] passage - **3.** [Phase] stage; [von Wahl] round.

**durchgängig** *adj* [Auffassung] general; ein ~ Motiv in seinen Werken a motif that runs through his works ⟨> *adv* universally; ~ gute Leistungen bringen to achieve consistently good results.

**Durchgangsverkehr** *der* through traffic.

**durch|geben** *vt (unreg)* to pass on; TV & RAD to broadcast.

**durchgebraten** *pp* ▷ durchbraten ⟨> *adj:* gut ~ well done.

**durchgefroren** *adj* frozen through.

**durch|gehen** (*perf* ist durchgegangen) *(unreg)* *vi* - **1.** [gen] to go through; bitte ~! [im Bus] please move to the back of the bus! - **2.** [durchdringen] to get through - **3.** [Pferd] to bolt; mit jm ~ [Gefühle] to run away with sb - **4.** [Verkehrsmittel] to go straight through - **5.** [andauern - Sitzung, Veranstaltung] to go on non-stop - **6.** [akzeptiert werden - Fehler, Gesetzesvorlage] to get through; für vierzig Jahre ODER als Vierzigjähriger ~ to pass for forty; jm etw ~ lassen to let sb get away with sthg ⟨> *vt* to go through.

**durchgehend** adj direct; ~ geöffnet open all day.

**durch|greifen** vi (unreg) - **1.** [einschreiten] to take action - **2.** [durch eine Öffnung]: **durch etw ~** to reach through sthg.

**durch|halten** (unreg) vi to hold out <> vt [Belastung] to withstand; [Strecke, Wettkampf] to make it to the end of.

**Durchhaltevermögen** das stamina.

**durchkämmen** vt to comb.

**durch|kommen** (perf **ist durchgekommen**) vi (unreg) - **1.** [durch etw gelangen]: **durch etw ~** to get through sthg - **2.** [am Telefon, bei Prüfung] to get through - **3.** [Nachricht] to be announced - **4.** [durchfahren] to pass through - **5.** [durchdringen - Wasser, Sonne] to come through - **6.** [überleben] to pull through - **7.** [erfolgreich sein]: **mit dieser Idee wirst du beim Chef kaum ~** you won't get anywhere with the boss with that idea.

**durchkreuzen**[1] vt [zunichte machen] to thwart.

**durch|kreuzen**[2] vt [durchstreichen] to cross out.

**durch|lassen** vt (unreg) to let through.

**durchlässig** adj [Boden] porous; [Material] permeable; [Grenze] open.

**Durchlässigkeit** die [von Boden] porosity; [von Material] permeability; [von Grenze] openness.

**Durch|lauf** der sport heat.

**durch|laufen**[1] (perf **hat/ist durchgelaufen**) (unreg) vi (ist) - **1.** [durch eine Öffnung] to go through - **2.** [durchsickern] to filter through - **3.** [durchgehend laufen] to go on non-stop <> vt (hat) [kaputtlaufen] to wear through.

**durch|laufen**[2] (präs **durchläuft**; prät **durchlief**; perf **hat durchlaufen**) vt to go through.

**Durchlauferhitzer** (pl -) der instantaneous water heater.

**durchleben** vt to live through.

**durch|lesen** vt (unreg) to read through.

**durchleuchten** vt - **1.** [röntgen] to X-ray - **2.** [untersuchen] to examine, to investigate

**durchlöchern** vt to make holes in.

**durch|lüften** vt to air.

**durch|machen** vt - **1.** [Schwierigkeiten, schwere Zeiten] to go through; **sie hat viel durchgemacht** she's been through a lot - **2.** fam [feiern]: **eine Nacht ~** to party all night <> vi fam to stay up.

**Durch|messer** der diameter.

**durch|nehmen** vt (unreg) to do.

**durch|nummerieren** vt to number (consecutively).

**durchqueren** vt [Zimmer, Fluss] to cross; [Land] to go across; [Gegend] to go through.

**durch|rechnen** vt to calculate.

**durch|regnen** vi: **es regnet durch** the rain is coming through.

**Durchreiche** (pl -n) die hatch.

**Durch|reise** die: ~ **(durch)** journey through; **auf der ~** passing through.

**durch|reißen** (perf **hat/ist durchgerissen**) (unreg) vt (hat) [Papier, Stoff] to tear in two; [Faden] to break in two <> vi (ist) [Stoff] to tear in two; [Faden, Draht] to break in two.

**durch|ringen** ← **sich durchringen** ref (unreg): **sich zu etw ~** to make up one's mind finally to do sthg.

**durch|rosten** (perf **ist durchgerostet**) vi to rust through.

**Durch|sage** die announcement.

**durch|sagen** vt to announce.

**durch|schauen**[1] vt to look through.

**durchschauen**[2] vt to see through.

**durch|scheinen** vi (unreg) to shine through.

**durchscheinend** adj transparent.

**durch|schimmern** vi [Licht] to shimmer through; [Eifersucht, Misstrauen] to show through.

**durch|schlafen** (unreg) vt & vi to sleep through.

**Durch|schlag** der - **1.** [Kopie] carbon copy - **2.** [Sieb] strainer.

**durch|schlagen**[1] (perf **hat/ist durchgeschlagen**) (unreg) vt (hat) [Glas] to smash through; [Stein, Holz] to split; [Wand] to knock through; **etw durch etw ~** to knock sthg through sthg <> vi (ist) to show through. ← **sich durchschlagen** ref - **1.** [durch Gegend] to make it - **2.** [durch Zeit] to struggle through.

**durch|schlagen**[2] (präs **durchschlägt**; prät **durchschlug**; perf **hat durchschlagen**) vt to smash through.

**durch|schlagend** adj [Argumente] convincing; [Erfolg] resounding.

**Durchschlagskraft** die [von Bombe] penetrating power; [von Argument] conclusiveness.

**durch|schleusen** vt [Schiff] to take through a lock; [Person] to guide through.

**durch|schlüpfen** (perf **ist durchgeschlüpft**) vi to slip through.

**durch|schneiden** vt (unreg) [Faden, Stoff] to cut through; [Brot, Blatt Papier] to cut in half; [Kehle] to cut.

**Durch|schnitt** der average.

**durchschnittlich** adj average <> adv [im Durchschnitt] on average; abw [mittelmäßig] averagely.

**Durchschnitts|alter** das average age.

**Durchschnitts|geschwindigkeit** *die* average speed.

**Durchschnitts|mensch** *der* average person.

**Durchschnitts|wert** *der* mean value.

**Durch|schrift** *die* carbon copy.

**durch|schütteln** *vt* to shake well; **im Bus durchgeschüttelt werden** to be shaken about on the bus.

**durch|schwitzen** *vt* to soak with sweat.

**durch|sehen** *(unreg) vt* to look through ⬦ *vi:* **durch etw ~** to see through sthg.

**durch sein** *(perf* ist durch gewesen) *vi (unreg)* **fam - 1.** [Zug, Kontrolleur] to have come through; **bei jm unten ~ fig** & **abw** to be in sb's bad books - **2.** [mit Buch, Arbeit] to have finished - **3.** [Braten, Kartoffeln] to be done - **4.** [Sohle, Ärmel] to be worn out - **5.** [Gesetz] to have gone through.

**durch|setzen** *vt* [Plan, Vorhaben, Reform] to push through; [Anspruch] to assert.

➡ **sich durchsetzen** *ref* to assert o.s.; [Erfindung] to gain acceptance.

**durchsetzt** *adj:* **~ mit** interspersed with; [Partei] infiltrated by.

**Durchsetzungsvermögen** *das:* **er hat ein enormes ~** he's really able to assert himself.

**Durch|sicht** *die* inspection.

**durchsichtig** *adj* [Stoff, Folie] transparent.

**durch|sickern** *(perf* ist durchgesickert) *vi* - **1.**: **durch etw ~** [Flüssigkeit] to seep through sthg - **2.** [Gerücht] to leak out.

**durch|sprechen** *vt (unreg)* to talk over.

**durch|starten** *(perf* ist durchgestartet) *vi* to accelerate away again.

**durch|stehen** *vt (unreg)* to come through.

**durch|stellen** *vt* to put through.

**durchstöbern** *vt* to rummage through.

**durch|stoßen**[1] *vt (unreg):* **etw durch etw ~** to push sthg through sthg.

**durchstoßen**[2] *(präs* durchstößt; *prät* durchstieß; *perf* hat durchstoßen) *vt* to break through.

**durch|streichen** *vt (unreg)* to cross out.

**durch|suchen** *vt* to search.

**Durchsuchung** *(pl* -en) *die* search.

**Durchsuchungs|befehl** *der* search warrant.

**durchtrainiert** [ˈdʊrçtreːniːɐt] *adj* in peak condition.

**durch|trennen**[1] *vt* to sever.

**durchtrennen**[2] *vt* to sever.

**durchtrieben** *adj* cunning ⬦ *adv* cunningly.

**durch|wachsen**[1] [ˈdʊrçvaksn̩] *(perf* ist durchgewachsen) *vi (unreg):* **durch etw ~** to grow through sthg.

**durchwachsen**[2] *adj:* **~er Speck** streaky bacon; **~es Wetter** fair to middling weather.

**Durchwahl** *die (ohne pl)* extension.

**durch|wählen** *vi* to dial direct.

**Durchwahl|nummer** *die* extension number.

**durchweg** *adv* without exception.

**durchwühlen**[1] *vt* [Schublade] to rummage through; [Zimmer] to ransack.

**durch|wühlen**[2] *vt* [Schublade] to rummage through; [Zimmer] to ransack.

➡ **sich durchwühlen** *ref:* **sich durch etw ~** to work through sthg.

**durch|zählen** *vt* to count.

**durch|ziehen**[1] *(perf* hat/ist durchgezogen) *(unreg) vt (hat)* - **1.** [durch Öffnung] to pull through; **etw durch etw ~** to pull sthg through sthg - **2.** **fam** [Plan] to see through ⬦ *vi (ist)* - **1.** [durch Gegend] to pass through - **2.** [in Marinade - Fleisch] to marinate; [ - Gemüse] to steep.

➡ **sich durchziehen** *ref:* **sich durch etw ~** to run through sthg.

**durchziehen**[2] *vt (unreg)* to pass through.

**Durch|zug** *der* - **1.** [von Wetter] passage - **2.** *(ohne pl)* [Zugluft] draught; **auf ~ schalten fam fig** to switch off.

**dürfen** *(präs* darf; *prät* durfte; *perf* hat gedurft ODER -) *aux (perf* hat dürfen) - **1.** [als Erlaubnis]: **etw tun ~** to be allowed to do sthg; **darf ich mich setzen?** may I sit down?; **darf ich fragen ...?** may I ask ...?; **darf ich Ihnen behilflich sein?** *geh* can I be of help? - **2.** [als Überzeugung, Wunsch]: **das ~ wir nicht vergessen** we mustn't forget that; **so etwas darf einfach nicht passieren** such a thing simply should not happen; **du darfst nicht traurig sein!** don't be sad!; **das darfst du ihm nicht übel nehmen** you shouldn't hold it against him - **3.** [Veranlassung haben]: **man darf davon ausgehen, dass ...** we can assume that ... - **4.** [als Annahme]: **das dürfte genügen** that should be enough ⬦ *vi (perf* hat gedurft): **sie darf nicht ins Schwimmbad** she's not allowed to go swimming ⬦ *vt (perf* hat gedurft) **fam:** **das darf man nicht!** you're not allowed to do that!; **was darf es sein?** what can I get you?

**durfte** *prät* ⬦ dürfen.

**dürftig** *adj* - **1.** [Einkünfte, Bezahlung] meagre - **2.** **abw** [Ergebnis] poor; [Bearbeitung] sketchy; [Bewuchs] sparse ⬦ *adv* - **1.** [entlohnt] meagrely; [bekleidet] scantily - **2.** **abw** [unzureichend] poorly; [sich entschuldigen] lamely.

**Dürftigkeit** *die* [von Service] poorness; [von Einkünften] meagreness; [von Ausstattung] sparseness; [von Text] sketchiness.

**dürr** *adj* - **1.** [Person] scrawny - **2.** [Blatt] dry - **3.** [Worte] blunt.

**Dürre** (*pl* -n) *die* drought.

**Dürrelkatastrophe** *die* catastrophic drought.

**Durst** *der* - **1.** [Gefühl] thirst; ~ **haben** to be thirsty; **ich habe ~ nach einem** ODER **auf ein Glas Wein** I could just drink a glass of wine - **2.** RW: **einen über den ~ trinken** *hum* to have one too many.

**dürsten** *vi:* **nach etw ~** *geh* to thirst for sthg.

**durstig** *adj* thirsty <> *adv* thirstily.

**durstlöschend** *adj* thirst-quenching.

**Durstlstrecke** *die* lean period.

**Dusche** (*pl* -n) *die* shower; **etw ist (für jn)** ODER **wirkt (auf jn) wie eine kalte ~** sthg brings sb down to earth (with a bump).

**duschen** *vi* to have a shower <> *vt* to shower.
> **sich duschen** *ref* to have a shower.

**Duschlgel** *das* shower gel.

**Duschlraum** *der* shower room.

**Duschlvorhang** *der* shower curtain.

**Düse** (*pl* -n) *die* nozzle.

**Dusel** *der* [Glück]: ~ **haben** *fam* to be lucky.

**düsen** (*perf* **ist gedüst**) *vi fam* to rush.

**Düsenlantrieb** *der* jet propulsion.

**Düsenlflugzeug** *das* jet aircraft.

**Düsenljäger** *der* jet fighter.

**Dussel** (*pl* -) *der fam* dope.

**Düsseldorf** *nt* Düsseldorf.

**dusselig, dusslig** *fam adj* stupid <> *adv* stupidly.

**düster** *adj* gloomy <> *adv* gloomily.

**Dutyfreeshop** [ˈdjuːtiˈfriːʃɔp] (*pl* -s) *der* duty-free shop.

**Dutzend** (*pl* -) *das* [zwölf] dozen; **im ~** by the dozen.
> **Dutzende** *pl* [viele] dozens; **zu ~en** in their dozens.

**dutzendfach** *adv* dozens of times.

**dutzendmal** *adv* a dozen times.

**dutzendweise** *adv* by the dozen.

**duzen** *vt* to address someone using the familiar "du" form.
> **sich duzen** *ref* to address each other using the familiar "du" form; **sich mit jm ~** to use the "du" form with sb.

**Duzlfreund, in** *der, die* close friend.

**DVD** (*pl* -s) (*abk für* **Digital Versatile Disc**) *die* EDV DVD.

**DW** (*abk für* **Deutsche Welle**) *German public radio station.*

**Dynamik** *die (ohne pl)* - **1.** PHYS dynamics (U) - **2.** [Kraft] dynamism - **3.** MUS dynamic range.

**dynamisch** *adj* dynamic <> *adv* dynamically.

**Dynamit** *das* dynamite.

**Dynamo** (*pl* -s) *der* dynamo.

**Dynastie** (*pl* -n) *die* dynasty.

**DZ** *abk für* **Doppelzimmer.**

**D-lZug** *der* express train.

# E

**e, E** [eː] (*pl* - ODER -s) *das* - **1.** [Buchstabe] e, E - **2.** MUS E.
> **E** *der abk für* **Eilzug.**

**Ebbe** (*pl* -n) *die* tide (outgoing); **es ist ~** it is low tide; **bei Eintritt der ~** when the tide is going out; **bei uns/in unserer Kasse ist** ODER **herrscht ~** *fig* we are short of cash.

**ebd.** (*abk für* **ebenda**) ibid.

**eben** *adj* [flach - Gegend, Weg] flat; [glatt - Brett, Boden] smooth <> *adv* - **1.** just; **kannst du mal ~ vorbeikommen?** can you just come round for a minute? - **2.** [knapp]: **er hat ihn nur so ~ berührt** he just touched him; **ich mache das ~ zu Ende** I'll just finish it off - **3.** [genau]: ~ **die wollte er finden** she was the very person he wanted to find; ~ **den Anwalt meine ich** he's the very lawyer I mean; ~ **das war es, was ich sagen wollte!** that was exactly what I wanted to say! <> *interj* - **1.** [zum Ausdruck von Einverständnis] exactly - **2.** [zum Ausdruck von Widerspruch]: **aber du hast doch dein Geld!** – ~ **nicht!** but you've got your money, haven't you! – no I haven't!

**Ebenlbild** *das* image.

**ebenbürtig** *adj* equal; **jm ~ sein** to be sb's equal; **einer Sache ~ sein** to be equal to sthg.

**ebenda** *adv* [Zitat] ibidem; ~ **komme ich her** I've come from that very place.

**ebendarum** *adv* for that very reason.

**ebendeshalb** *adv* that is exactly why.

**ebendeswegen** *adv* that is exactly why.

**Ebene** (*pl* -n) *die* - **1.** [Flachland] plain - **2.** PHYS &

MATH plane - **3.** [Niveau] level; **auf gleicher** ODER **der gleichen ~** on the same level; **auf höchster ~** at the highest level.

**ebenfalls** adv as well; **danke, ~** thanks, same to you.

**Ebenholz** das ebony.

**ebenmäßig** adj well-proportioned.

**ebenso** adv just as.

**ebenso gut** adv just as well.

**Eber** (pl -) der boar.

**ebnen** vt to level; **jm den Weg ~** to smooth sb's path.

**Ebro** der: **der ~** the (River) Ebro.

**ec** abk für **Eurocheque.**

**EC** [eː'tseː] (pl -s) der abk für **Eurocity.**

**Echo** (pl -s) das echo; **ein lebhaftes** ODER **starkes ~ finden** fig to meet with a great response.

**Echse** ['ɛksəl] (pl -n) die lizard.

**echt** adj - **1.** [unverfälscht] genuine - **2.** [wahr, typisch] real - **3.** MATH proper <> adv - **1.** [rein] real; **~ italienisch essen** to eat real Italian food - **2.** fam [wirklich] really.

**Echtheit** die genuineness.

**Eck** (pl -e ODER -en) das Süddt & Österr [Ecke] corner; **über ~** diagonally.

**Eck|ball** der corner.

**Eckbank** (pl -bänke) die corner seat.

**Ecke** (pl -n) die - **1.** [gen] corner - **2.** fam [Gegend] area; **eine hübsche ~!** a pretty spot!; **das ist noch eine ganze ~!** it's still quite a way! - **3.** RW: **um die ~** fam round the corner; **jn um die ~ bringen** salopp [töten] to bump sb off, ; **es fehlt (bei uns) an allen ~n und Enden** we are short of everything; **mit jm um fünf** ODER **sechs ~n verwandt sein** fam to be distantly related to sb.

**Eck|haus** das house on a/the corner.

**eckig** adj - **1.** [Form] square - **2.** [Bewegung] awkward <> adv [ungelenk] awkwardly.

**Eck|pfeiler** der cornerstone.

**Eck|zahn** der canine tooth.

**Ecuador** nt Ecuador.

**edel** adj - **1.** geh [Person, Geste] noble - **2.** geh [Form] well-formed - **3.** [Holz, Wein] fine.

**Edel|boutique, Edelbutike** die luxury boutique.

**Edel|gas** das CHEM inert gas.

**Edel|metall** das precious metal.

**Edel|stahl** der stainless steel.

**Edel|stein** der precious stone.

**Edel|weiß** (pl -e) das edelweiss.

**Edinburgh** ['ɛdɪnburk] nt Edinburgh.

**Edition** (pl -en) die edition.

**E-Dur** das E major.

**Edutainment** [edjut'ɛɪnmənt] die edutainment.

**EDV** [eːdeː'faʊl] (abk für **elektronische Datenverarbeitung**) die data processing.

**EEG** [eːeː'geː] (pl -s) (abk für **Elektroenzephalogramm**) das EEG.

**Efeu** der (ohne pl) ivy.

**Effeff** das: **etw aus dem ~ beherrschen** fam to know sthg inside out.

**Effekt** (pl -e) der effect.

**Effekthascherei** (pl -en) die abw straining for effect (U).

**effektiv** adj effective; [Gewinn, Leistung] net <> adv effectively.

**Effektivität** [ɛfɛktivi'tɛːt] die effectiveness.

**effektvoll** adj effective <> adv effectively.

**egal** adj: **es ist mir ~** it's all the same to me; **das kann dir doch ~ sein** that's no concern of yours; **das ist ~** it doesn't matter.
➤ **egal ob** adv no matter whether.

**Egge** (pl -n) die harrow.

**Egoismus** der egoism.

**Egoist, in** (mpl -en; fpl -nen) der, die egoist.

**egoistisch** adj egoistic <> adv egoistically.

**egozentrisch** adj egocentric.

**eh** interj fam hey <> adv - **1.** [immer]: **seit ~ und je** since time immemorial; **wie ~ und je** as always - **2.** fam Süddt & Österr [sowieso] anyway.

**ehe** konj geh before; **~ es zu spät ist** before it's too late.

**Ehe** (pl -n) die marriage; **die ~ (mit jm) schließen** to get married (to sb); **in wilder ~ leben** to live in sin.

**eheähnlich** adj: **in einer ~en Gemeinschaft leben** to cohabit.

**Ehe|beratung** die marriage counselling (U).

**Ehe|bett** das double bed.

**Ehe|bruch** der adultery (U).

**Ehe|frau** die wife.

**Ehe|gatte** der geh [Ehemann] spouse, husband.
➤ **Ehegatten** pl amt [Eheleute] husband and wife.

**Ehe|gattin** die geh [Ehefrau] spouse, wife.

**Ehe|krise** die marital crisis.

**Ehe|leute** pl married couple.

**ehelich** adj marital; [Recht] conjugal.

**ehem.** abk für **ehemalig.**

**ehemalig** adj former.

**ehemals** adv formerly.

**Ehe|mann** (pl -männer) der husband.

**Ehe|paar** *das* married couple.

**Ehe|partner** *der* marriage partner.

**eher** *adv* - **1.** [vorher] earlier, sooner - **2.** [lieber] rather - **3.**: **das ist schon ~ möglich** that is more likely - **4.** [vielmehr] more.

**Ehe|ring** *der* wedding ring.

**Ehe|scheidung** *die* divorce.

**Ehe|schließung** *die* marriage ceremony.

**Ehe|vertrag** *der* marriage contract.

**ehrbar** *geh adj* respectable ◇ *adv* respectably.

**Ehre** *die* honour; **jm zu ~n** in sb's honour; **etw in ~n halten** to treasure sthg; **jm ~ machen** to do sb credit; **(wieder) zu ~n kommen** to redeem o.s.; **auf ~ und Gewissen** on one's honour; **zu viel der ~** too much honour; **keine ~ im Leib haben** not to have a shred of decency.

**ehren** *vt* [Achtung erweisen] to honour; **deine Großmut ehrt dich** your generosity does you credit; **dieses Angebot ehrt mich** I am honoured by this offer.

**ehrenamtlich** *adj* honorary ◇ *adv* in an honorary capacity.

**Ehren|bürger, in** *der, die* honorary citizen.

**Ehren|gast** *der* guest of honour.

**ehrenhaft** *adj* honourable ◇ *adv* honourably.

**ehrenhalber** *adv*: **er ist Doktor ~** he's got an honorary doctorate.

**Ehren|mann** (*pl* -männer) *der* man of honour.

**Ehren|mitglied** *das* honorary member.

**Ehren|platz** *der* place of honour.

**Ehren|runde** *die* lap of honour; **eine ~ drehen** SPORT to do a lap of honour; SCHULE to repeat a year.

**Ehren|sache** *die* point of honour; **das ist doch ~, dass ich bald wieder zurück bin** you can count on me to be back soon.

**ehrenwert** *adj geh* honourable.

**Ehrenwort** (*pl* -e) *das* word of honour; **sein ~ geben** to give one's word of honour; **(großes) ~!** *fam* I/we promise!

**ehrerbietig** [ˈeːɐ̯ɛɐ̯biːtɪç] *geh adj* respectful ◇ *adv* respectfully.

**Ehrfurcht** *die* [Verehrung] reverence; [Scheu] awe.

**ehrfürchtig** *adj* reverent ◇ *adv* reverently.

**Ehrgeiz** *der* ambition.

**ehrgeizig** *adj* ambitious ◇ *adv* ambitiously.

**ehrlich** *adj* honest; **~ währt am längsten** honesty is the best policy ◇ *adv* fairly; **~ gesagt** to be honest.

**Ehrlichkeit** *die* honesty.

**ehrlos** *adj* dishonourable ◇ *adv* dishonourably.

**Ehrung** (*pl* -en) *die* [das Ehren] honouring (*U*); [Ehre] honour.

**ehrwürdig** *adj* venerable.

**Ei** (*pl* -er) *das* - **1.** [gen] egg; **jn/etw wie ein rohes ~ behandeln** to treat sb/sthg with kid gloves; **sich** (*D*) **gleichen wie ein ~ dem anderen** to be as like as two peas in a pod; **wie aus dem ~ gepellt** ODER **geschält** well turned out - **2.** *vulg* [Hoden] ball.

**Eiche** (*pl* -n) *die* oak.

**Eichel** (*pl* -n) *die* - **1.** [Frucht] acorn - **2.** [des männlichen Gliedes] glans (penis).

**eichen** *vt* to calibrate.

**Eichhörnchen** (*pl* -) *das* squirrel.

**Eid** (*pl* -e) *der* oath; **Aussage an ~es Statt** RECHT declaration made in lieu of an oath.
⇒ **unter Eid** *adv* under oath.

**Eidechse** [ˈaɪdɛksə] (*pl* -n) *die* lizard.

**eidesstattlich** *adj* sworn ◇ *adv* solemnly.

**Eid|genosse** *der* Swiss citizen.

**Eid|genossin** *die* Swiss citizen.

**eidgenössisch** *adj* Swiss.

**Ei|dotter** *das* ODER *der* egg yolk.

**Eier|becher** *der* egg cup.

**Eier|kuchen** *der* pancake.

**Eier|likör** *der* egg flip.

**eiern** (*perf* hat/ist geeiert) *vi fam* to wobble; **er eierte auf dem alten Fahrrad um die Ecke** he came round the corner on his rickety old bike.

**Eier|schale** *die* eggshell.

**Eier|stock** *der* ovary.

**Eier|uhr** *die* egg timer.

**Eifel** *die*: **die ~** the Eifel mountains.

**Eifer** *der* eagerness; **im ~ des Gefechts** in the heat of the moment.

**Eifersucht** *die* jealousy.

**eifersüchtig** *adj* jealous; **auf jn ~ sein** to be jealous of sb ◇ *adv* jealously.

**eifrig** *adj* eager ◇ *adv* eagerly.

**Eigelb** (*pl* - ODER -e) *das* egg yolk.

**eigen** *adj* - **1.** [jm gehörend] own - **2.** [typisch] typical - **3.** [empfindlich]: **in etw** (*D*) **~ sein** to be particular about sthg.
⇒ **Eigen** *das*: **sich** (*D*) **etw zu Eigen machen** to make sthg one's own; **etw sein Eigen nennen** *geh* to call sthg one's own.
⇒ **Eigene** *der, die, das*: **etwas Eigenes haben wollen** to want to have something of one's own.

**Eigen|art** *die* characteristic.

**eigenartig** *adj* strange ⋄ *adv* strangely.

**Eigenbedarf** *der (ohne pl)* personal requirements *(pl)*; **für den ~** for one's own use.

**Eigenbrötler, in** *(mpl -; fpl -nen) der, die* recluse.

**eigenbrötlerisch** *adj* reclusive ⋄ *adv* like a recluse.

**Eigen|finanzierung** *die* WIRTSCH self-financing.

**eigenhändig** *adj* own ⋄ *adv* with one's own hands.

**Eigen|heim** *das* house of one's own.

**Eigenheit** *(pl -en) die* peculiarity.

**Eigenliebe** *die (ohne pl)* ego.

**eigenmächtig** *adj* unauthorized ⋄ *adv* on one's own authority.

**Eigen|name** *der* proper name.

**eigennützig** *adj* selfish ⋄ *adv* selfishly.

**eigens** *adv* specially.

**Eigenschaft** *(pl -en) die* characteristic; [von Auto] feature; **in seiner ~ als etw** in one's capacity as sthg.

**Eigenschaftswort** *(pl -wörter) das* adjective.

**Eigensinn** *der* stubbornness.

**eigensinnig** *adj* stubborn ⋄ *adv* stubbornly.

**eigenständig** *adj* independent ⋄ *adv* independently.

**eigentlich** *adv* - **1.** [im Grunde, wirklich] really - **2.** [übrigens] by the way; **wer ist ~ Petra?** who is Petra(, by the way)? - **3.** [zum Ausdruck von Ärger]: **was erlauben Sie sich ~?** what do you think you're doing? ⋄ *adj* [wirklich] real.

**Eigen|tor** *das* own goal.

**Eigentum** *das* - **1.** [Besitz] property - **2.** [Besitzrecht] ownership.

**Eigentümer, in** *(mpl -; fpl -nen) der, die* owner.

**eigentümlich** *adj* peculiar.

**Eigentums|wohnung** *die* owner-occupied flat *Br ODER* apartment *Am.*

**eigenverantwortlich** *adj* responsible ⋄ *adv*: **etw ~ tun** to do sthg on one's own authority.

**eigenwillig** *adj* - **1.** [eigen] original - **2.** [starrsinnig] obstinate.

**Eiger** *der*: **der ~** the Eiger.

**eignen** ◆ **sich eignen** *ref* to be suitable; **sich zu** *ODER* **für etw ~** to be suitable for sthg.

**Eignung** *die* suitability.

**Eignungs|prüfung** *die* aptitude test.

**Eignungs|test** *der* aptitude test.

**Eil|bote** *der*: **per/durch ~n zustellen** to send express.

**Eil|brief** *der* express letter.

**Eile** *die* hurry; **in ~ sein** to be in a hurry; **etw hat ~/keine ~** sthg is/is not urgent.

**eilen** *(perf* **hat/ist geeilt)** *vi* - **1.** *(ist)* [Person] to hurry - **2.** *(hat)* [Angelegenheit] to be urgent; **eilt! urgent!; mit etw eilt es/eilt es nicht** sthg is/is not urgent.

**eilig** *adj* - **1.** [Bewegung] hurried; **es ~ haben** to be in a hurry - **2.** [Angelegenheit, Brief] urgent ⋄ *adv* hurriedly.

**Eil|tempo** *das* rush; **im ~** in a rush.

**Eil|zustellung** *die* express delivery.

**Eimer** *(pl -) der* bucket; **im ~ sein** *salopp* [kaputt sein - Pläne] to be up the spout; [- Gegenstand] to be bust.

**eimerweise** *adv* by the bucketful.

**ein, e** *num* one; **~e einzelne Rose** a single rose; **~ Uhr** one o'clock; **~er Meinung sein** to have the same opinion; **~ für alle Mal** *fam fig* once and for all; **in ~em fort** *fig* non-stop; **js ~ und alles sein** *fig* to mean everything to sb ⋄ *det* **a, an** *(vor Vokal)*; **~ Hund** a dog; **~e Idee** an idea; **~ Mädchen** a girl; **~es Tages** one day; **da ist ~e Frau Schmidt am Apparat** there's a Mrs Schmidt on the phone ⋄ *pron* - **1.** [als Teil einer Menge] one; **hier ist noch ~s/~e** here's another one; **~ und dasselbe** one and the same - **2.** *fam* [jemand] someone, somebody; [man] one; **hole ~er die Polizei!** someone call the police!; **sieh mal ~er an!** well I never!; **das kann ~em schon mal passieren** these things can happen to you; **das soll nun ~er riechen!** how was I supposed to know? ⋄ *adv*: **~-aus** on-off; **~ und aus gehen** *fig* to come and go; **nicht ~ noch aus wissen** *fig* not to know whether one is coming or going.

**einander** *pron geh* each other, one another.

**ein|arbeiten** *vt* [an die Arbeit gewöhnen] to train.

◆ **sich einarbeiten** *ref* to settle in.

**Einarbeitung** *(pl -en) die* training *(U)*.

**einarmig** *adj* one-armed *(vor Subst)*; **~ sein** to have only one arm.

**ein|atmen** *vt* & *vi* to breathe in.

**einäugig** *adj* one-eyed *(vor Subst)*.

**Einbahn|straße** *die* one-way street.

**Einband** *(pl -bände) der* book cover.

**Einbau** *der* - **1.** [in Raum] fitting - **2.** [in Text] incorporation.

**ein|bauen** *vt* - **1.** [Schrank, Bad] to fit; [Motor] to install - **2.** [in Text] to incorporate.

**Einbau|küche** *die* fitted kitchen.

**Einbau|schrank** *der* [Küchenschrank] fitted cupboard; [Kleiderschrank] fitted wardrobe.

**E**

**ein\behalten** *vt (unreg)* to withhold.

**einbeinig** *adj* one-legged *(vor Subst);* ~ **sein** to have only one leg.

**ein\berufen** *vt (unreg)* **- 1.** [Sitzung] to summon **- 2.** [Wehrpflichtige] to call up *Br*, to draft *Am*.

**Ein\berufung** *die* **- 1.** [einer Sitzung] summoning *(U)* **- 2.** [von Wehrpflichtigen] call-up *Br*, draft *Am*.

**Einberufungs\befehl** *der* call-up papers *(pl) Br*, draft card *Am*.

**ein\betten** *vt* to wrap.

**ein\beziehen** *vt (unreg):* **jn/etw in etw** *(A)* ~ to include sb/sthg in sthg.

**Einbeziehung** *die* inclusion.

**ein\biegen** *(perf* hat/ist **eingebogen)** *(unreg)* *vi (ist)* [abbiegen] to turn; **nach rechts/links** ~ to turn right/left <> *vt (hat)* [verbiegen] to bend.

**ein\bilden** *vt* **- 1.** [sich einreden]: **sich** *(D)* **etw** ~ to imagine sthg; **was bildest du dir eigentlich ein, wer du bist?** who do you think you are? **- 2.** [stolz sein]: **er bildet sich ganz schön viel ein** he is really full of himself; **sich** *(D)* **viel auf etw** *(A)* ~ to be conceited about sthg; **darauf brauchst du dir nichts einzubilden** that's nothing to be proud of

**Einbildung** *(pl* **-en)** *die* **- 1.** [Fantasie] imagination **- 2.** [Hochmut] conceit.

**Einbildungskraft** *die* imagination.

**ein\binden** *vt (unreg)* **- 1.** [einschlagen] to bind **- 2.** [einbeziehen]: **jn/etw in etw** *(A)* ~ to integrate sb/sthg into sthg.

**ein\bläuen** *vt:* **jm etw** ~ to drum sthg into sb.

**ein\blenden** *vt* TV [einschalten] to insert.

➤ **sich einblenden** *ref* TV [sich einschalten] to go over; **wir blenden uns in wenigen Augenblicken in die zweite Halbzeit ein** we'll be going over to the second half in a few moments.

**einbleuen** = **einbläuen**.

**Ein\blick** *der* **- 1.** [Blick]: ~ **in die Dokumente bekommen** to get a look at the documents; ~ **in etw** *(A)* **haben** to be allowed to look at sthg; ~ **in etw** *(A)* **nehmen** to examine sthg; **jm** ~ **in etw** *(A)* **gewähren** to allow sb to examine sthg **- 2.** [Einsicht] insight.

**ein\brechen** *(perf* **hat/ist eingebrochen)** *vi (unreg)* **- 1.** *(hat)* [gewaltsam eindringen] to break in; **bei jm** ~ to burgle sb **- 2.** *(ist)* [einstürzen] to fall in **- 3.** *(ist)* [Partei, Mannschaft] to come unstuck **- 4.** *(ist)* [durchbrechen] to fall through **- 5.** *(ist)* [eindringen]: **(in ein Land)** ~ to invade a country) **- 6.** *(ist) geh* [Nacht, Dunkelheit] to fall; [Winter] to set in.

**Einbrecher, in** *(mpl* **-;** *fpl* **-nen)** *der* burglar.

**ein\bringen** *vt (unreg)* **- 1.** [Ernte] to bring in **- 2.** [Gewinn] to bring in; [Anerkennung] to bring; [Erfahrung] to give; **das bringt nichts ein** that's not worth it **- 3.** [vorlegen] to introduce **- 4.** *amt* [einsetzen - Geld, Vermögen] to invest; [ - in eine Ehe] to put in.

➤ **sich einbringen** *ref* [sich beteiligen]: **sich in etw** *(A)* ~ to make a contribution to sthg.

**ein\brocken** *vt fam:* **jm/sich etwas** ~ to land sb/o.s. in it; **dieses Problem hast du dir selbst eingebrockt!** you brought this problem on yourself!

**Ein\bruch** *der* **- 1.** [Straftat] break-in; **einen** ~ **begehen** to commit a burglary **- 2.** [Zusammenbruch] collapse **- 3.** [Eindringen] penetration **- 4.** *fam* [bei Wahl] drubbing **- 5.** [Beginn - von Winter] onset; **vor** ~ **der Nacht** before nightfall; **bei** ~ **der Dunkelheit** at nightfall.

**einbürgern** *vt* [eine Staatsangehörigkeit verleihen] to naturalize.

➤ **sich einbürgern** *ref* [üblich werden] to become established.

**Einbürgerung** *(pl* **-en)** *die* naturalization.

**Ein\buße** *die* loss.

**ein\büßen** *vt* to lose <> *vi:* **an etw** *(D)* ~ to lose sthg.

**ein\checken** ['aintʃɛkn̩] *vt* & *vi* to check in.

**ein\cremen, einkremen** *vt* to put cream on.

➤ **sich eincremen** *ref* to put cream on.

**ein\dämmen** *vt* **- 1.** [stauen] to dam **- 2.** [zurückhalten] to contain.

**ein\decken** *vt fam* [überhäufen]: **jn mit etw** ~ to swamp sb with sthg.

➤ **sich eindecken** *ref* [sich versorgen]: **sich mit etw** ~ to stock up on sthg.

**eindeutig** *adj* clear <> *adv* clearly.

**Eindeutigkeit** *die* clarity.

**ein\deutschen** *vt* to Germanize.

**eindimensional** *adj* one-dimensional.

**ein\drehen** *vt* to screw in; **sich** *(D)* **die Haare** ~ to put one's hair in curlers.

**ein\dringen** *(perf* **ist eingedrungen)** *vi (unreg)* **- 1.** [hineingelangen]: **in etw** *(A)* ~ [Wasser] to get into sthg; [Messer] to enter sthg; **in das Bewusstsein der Öffentlichkeit** ~ to enter the public consciousness **- 2.** [einbrechen]: **in etw** *(A)* ~ [Gebäude] to break into sthg; [Land] to invade sthg **- 3.** [bedrängen]: **(mit etw) auf jn** ~ [mit Waffe] to threaten sb (with sthg).

**eindringlich** *adj* insistent <> *adv* insistently.

**Eindringling** *(pl* **-e)** *der* intruder.

**Eindruck** *(pl* **-drücke)** *der* impression; ~ **auf jn machen** to make an impression on sb; **einen** ~ **von etw bekommen** ODER **erhalten** to get an impression of sthg; **einen guten/schlechten** ~ **(auf jn) machen** to make a good/bad impression (on sb); **bei jm** ~ **schinden** *fam* to impress sb.

**ein|drücken** *vt* - **1.** [beschädigen - Kotflügel, Fensterscheibe] to smash in; [ - Nase, Kissen] to flatten - **2.** [in etw hineindrücken] to press.

**eindrucksvoll** *adj* impressive <> *adv* impressively.

**ein|ebnen** *vt* to level.

**eineiig** [ˈainˌaiɪç] *adj*: **~e Zwillinge** identical twins.

**eineinhalb** *num* one and a half.

**ein|engen** *vt* - **1.** [beschränken] to constrict - **2.** [einschränken] to restrict; **jn in seiner Freiheit ~** to curb sb's freedom.

**einerlei** *adj* immaterial; **das ist mir ~** that's all the same to me.

**einerseits** *adv*: **~ ... andererseits** on the one hand ... on the other (hand).

**einfach** *adj* - **1.** [leicht, schlicht] simple - **2.** [Fahrkarte, Knoten] single <> *adv* - **1.** [leicht, schlicht] simply; **ich komme ~ mit** I'll just come with you; **es sich ~ machen** to make it easy for o.s. - **2.** [nicht mehrfach]: **etw ~ falten** to fold sthg once.

**Einfachheit** *die* simplicity; **der ~ halber** for the sake of simplicity.

**ein|fädeln** *vt* - **1.** [Faden, Nadel] to thread - **2.** [bewerkstelligen]: **sie hat die Sache schlau eingefädelt** she worked things very cleverly.
➜ **sich einfädeln** *ref* [sich einordnen] to filter in.

**ein|fahren** (*perf* **hat/ist eingefahren**) (*unreg*) *vi* (*ist*) [Zug] to arrive <> *vt* (*hat*) - **1.** [hineinschaffen - Ernte] to bring in - **2.** [beschädigen - Tor, Mauer] to knock down; [ - Kotflügel] to smash in - **3.** AUTO to run in *Br*, to break in *Am* - **4.** [einziehen - Fahrwerk] to retract.

**Ein|fahrt** *die* - **1.** [Einfahren] arrival; **der Zug hat noch keine ~** the train still hasn't arrived - **2.** [Stelle zum Hineinfahren] entrance; **'~ freihalten!'** 'keep clear'.

**Ein|fall** *der* - **1.** [Idee] idea; **ihm kam ein ~** he had an idea - **2.** [Einfallen]: **der ~ von Sonnenstrahlen** the sun's rays shining in - **3.** [Eindringen] invasion; **der ~ der Römer in Gallien** the invasion of Gaul by the Romans.

**ein|fallen** (*perf* **ist eingefallen**) *vi* (*unreg*) - **1.** [in den Sinn kommen]: **ihm fiel nichts Besseres ein** no better idea occurred to him; **ihm fällt immer eine passende Ausrede ein** he always thinks of a suitable excuse; **mir fällt nichts ein, was ich kochen könnte** I can't think of anything that I could cook; **sich** (*D*) **etwas ~ lassen** to think of something; **lass dir etwas ~, wie wir dieses Problem lösen können!** try and think of how we can solve this problem!; **was fällt dir/ Ihnen ein!** what (ever) are you thinking of! - **2.** [wieder in den Sinn kommen] to remember; **da fällt mir ein ...** that reminds me ... - **3.** [hereinkommen] to shine in - **4.** MIL: **in etw** (*A*) **~** to in-

vade sthg - **5.** [einstimmen] to join in - **6.** [einstürzen] to collapse.

**einfallslos** *adj* unimaginative <> *adv* unimaginatively.

**einfallsreich** *adj* imaginative <> *adv* imaginatively.

**Einfalt** *die* naivety.

**einfältig** *adj* - **1.** [arglos] naive; [Lächeln] innocent - **2.** [beschränkt] simple-minded.

**Einfamilien|haus** *das* house designed for one family.

**ein|fangen** *vt* (*unreg*) - **1.** [fangen und fest halten] to capture - **2.** *fam* [bekommen]: **sich** (*D*) **etw ~** to get sthg.

**einfarbig** *adj* all one colour.

**ein|fassen** *vt* - **1.** [Stoff] to edge - **2.** [mit Mauer] to enclose - **3.** [Edelstein] to set.

**Einfassung** (*pl* -en) *die* - **1.** [von Stoff] edging - **2.** [mit Mauer] enclosure - **3.** [von Edelstein] setting.

**ein|fetten** *vt* [Backform] to grease; [Schuhe, Leder] to put dubbin on.

**ein|flechten** *vt* (*unreg*) - **1.** [Band, Haare] to plait *Br*, to braid *Am* - **2.** [in Gespräch, Roman] to weave ODER slip in.

**ein|fliegen** *vt* (*unreg*) to fly in; **jn/etw ~ lassen** to fly sb/sthg in.

**ein|fließen** (*perf* **ist eingeflossen**) *vi* (*unreg*) [Wasser, Luft] to flow in; **eine Kritik ~ lassen** to slip in a criticism.

**ein|flößen** *vt* - **1.** [zu trinken geben] to help to drink - **2.** [erregen]: **jm etw ~** [Ehrfurcht, Vertrauen, Angst] to inspire sthg in sb.

**Ein|fluss** *der* influence; **unter ~ von Alkohol** under the influence of alcohol; **auf jn/etw ~ haben** [Macht] to have influence over sb/ sthg; [Effekt] to influence sb/sthg; **auf jn/etw ~ nehmen** to influence sb/sthg.

**Einfluss|bereich** *der* sphere of influence.

**einflussreich** *adj* influential.

**einförmig** *adj* monotonous <> *adv* monotonously.

**ein|frieren** (*perf* **hat/ist eingefroren**) (*unreg*) *vt* (*hat*) to freeze; [Beziehungen] to suspend <> *vi* (*ist*) [Wasserleitung] to freeze; [Teich] to freeze over.

**ein|fügen** *vt* [gen & EDV] to insert.
➜ **sich einfügen** *ref* [sich anpassen] to fit in.

**ein|fühlen** ➜ **sich einfühlen** *ref*: **er fühlte sich in ihre Lage ein** he put himself in her position.

**einfühlsam** *adj* sensitive.

**Einfühlungsvermögen** *das* empathy.

**Einfuhr** (*pl* -en) *die* - **1.** [Einführen] importation - **2.** [Ware] import.

**ein|führen** vt - **1.** [gen] to introduce; **jn in etw (A)** ~ to introduce sb to sthg; **jn bei seinen Eltern** ~ to introduce sb to one's parents; **jn in die Gesellschaft** ~ to introduce sb into society - **2.** [importieren] to import - **3.** [hineinschieben] to insert, to introduce.

◆ **sich einführen** ref [sich präsentieren] to introduce o.s.; **sich gut/schlecht** ~ to make a good/bad impression.

**Einfuhr|genehmigung** die import permit.

**Ein|führung** die introduction.

**Einfuhrzoll** (pl -zölle) der import duty.

**ein|füllen** vt to pour in; **etw in etw (A)** ~ to pour sthg into sthg.

**Ein|gabe** die - **1.** [Gesuch - an Parlament] petition; [ - an Behörden] complaint - **2.** EDV input.

**Ein|gang** der - **1.** [Eingangstür] entrance - **2.** [von Geld, Post] receipt.

**eingangs** adv at the beginning.

**Eingangs|halle** die entrance hall.

**ein|geben** vt (unreg) EDV to enter.

**eingebildet** adj - **1.** [nicht wirklich] imaginary - **2.** [hochmütig] arrogant.

**Eingeborene, Eingeborne** (pl -n) der, die native.

**Eingebung** (pl -en) die geh inspiration.

**eingefleischt** adj ▷ **Junggeselle.**

**ein|gehen** (perf ist eingegangen) (unreg) vi - **1.** [ankommen] to arrive; **bei uns ist noch keine Antwort eingegangen** we have not yet received a reply - **2.** [Tier, Pflanze] to perish - **3.** [Firma] to close down - **4.** [beachten]: **auf jn/etw** ~ to respond to sb/sthg; **auf etw (A)** ~ [Angebot, Vorschlag] to agree to sthg - **5.** [Kleidung] to shrink - **6.** geh [Einzug halten]: **in die Geschichte** ~ to go down in history ▷ vt [Bündnis, Ehe, Verpflichtung] to enter into; [Risiko] to take; [Wette] to make.

**eingehend** adj detailed ▷ adv in detail.

**ein|gemeinden** vt to incorporate.

**eingenommen** pp ▷ **einnehmen** ▷ adj: **von sich** ~ **sein** to have a high opinion of o.s.; **für/gegen etw** ~ **sein** to be taken with/biased against sthg; **von jm/etw** ~ **sein** to be taken with sb/sthg.

**eingeschlossen** pp ▷ **einschließen.**

**eingeschnappt** adj fam abw: ~ **sein** to be in a huff.

**eingespielt** adj [Team] well-practised; **aufeinander** ~ **sein** to work well together, to make a good team.

**Ein|geständnis** das confession; [von Fehler] admission.

**ein|gestehen** vt (unreg) to confess; [Fehler] to admit.

**eingetragen** pp ▷ **eintragen** ▷ adj registered ▷ **Verein;** siehe auch **Warenzeichen.**

**Eingeweide** pl entrails.

**Eingeweihte** (pl -n) der, die initiate.

**ein|gewöhnen** ◆ **sich eingewöhnen** ref to settle in.

**Eingewöhnung** die settling in.

**ein|gießen** vt (unreg) [Tasse, Glas] to pour; **jm etw** ~ to pour sb sthg.

**eingleisig** adj - **1.** [Bahnlinie] single-track - **2.** [eindimensional] simplistic ▷ adv simplistically.

**ein|gliedern** vt: **jn/etw in etw (A)** ~ to integrate sb/sthg into sthg.

◆ **sich eingliedern** ref: **sich in etw (A)** ~ to integrate into sthg.

**ein|graben** vt (unreg) - **1.** [in den Boden] to bury - **2.** [eindrücken - Spuren] to carve.

◆ **sich eingraben** ref: **sich in etw (A)** ~ [Schrift, Spuren] to be carved into sthg; [Tier] to burrow into sthg.

**ein|greifen** vi (unreg): **(in etw (A))** ~ to intervene (in sthg).

**ein|grenzen** vt - **1.** [räumlich] to enclose - **2.** [thematisch] to limit.

**Ein|griff** der - **1.** [Intervention] intervention - **2.** MED operation.

**ein|haken** vt to fasten ▷ vi to interrupt.

◆ **sich einhaken** ref: **sie hakte sich bei ihm ein** she slipped her arm through his.

**Einhalt** der geh: **jm/einer Sache** ~ **gebieten** to stop sb/sthg.

**ein|halten** (unreg) vt [befolgen, erfüllen - Termin] to keep; [ - Plan] to keep to; [ - Vorschrift] to observe ▷ vi [innehalten]: **in** ODER **mit seinem Tun** ~ to interrupt what one is doing.

**ein|handeln** vt: **Diamanten gegen Lebensmittel** ~ to trade diamonds for food; **sich (D) etw** ~ fam to let o.s. in for sthg.

**einhändig** adv one-handed.

**ein|hängen** vt - **1.** [in ein Scharnier - Tür] to hang; [ - Fenster] to put in - **2.** [auflegen - Telefonhörer] to put down ▷ vi to hang up.

◆ **sich einhängen** ref: **sich bei jm** ~ to take sb's arm.

**ein|heften** vt to file.

**einheimisch** adj local.

**Einheimische** (pl -n) der, die local.

**Einheit** (pl -en) die - **1.** [Geschlossenheit] unity - **2.** MIL [Maßeinheit] unit.

**einheitlich** adj - **1.** [geschlossen] unified - **2.** [gleich] uniform; [Standard] standardized ▷ adv uniformly; [sich kleiden] in the same way.

**Einheits|preis** der standard price.

**ein|heizen** *vt* [Wohnung] to heat; [Ofen] to light
◇ *vi:* jm ~ *fam* to give sb what for.

**einhellig** *adj* unanimous ◇ *adv* unanimously.

**ein|holen** *vt* - **1.** [Person, Wagen] to catch up with; [verlorene Zeit] to make up for - **2.** [holen] to obtain - **3.** [einziehen - Netz] to haul in; [ - Leine] to reel in - **4.** [einkaufen] to get ◇ *vi:* ~ **gehen** to go shopping.

**ein|hüllen** *vt* to wrap up.
➥ **sich einhüllen** *ref:* **sich in etw** *(A)* ~ to wrap o.s. up in sthg.

**einhundert** *num* a ODER one hundred; *siehe auch* **sechs.**

**einig** *adj* united; **(sich) über jn/etw ~ sein** to agree about sb/sthg ; **(sich) über jn/etw ~ werden** to agree on sb/sthg.

**einige** *det* - **1.** [eine gewisse Menge] a few, some; **nach ~r Zeit** after some time; ~ **Probleme** a few problems; **nur ~ waren da** there were only a few people there; ~ **wenige a few** - **2.** [beträchtlich] quite a few; **das brachte so ~ Probleme mit sich** this caused quite a lot of problems; **so ~ waren da** there were quite a lot of people there ◇ *pron* a few, some.
➥ **einiges** *pron* something; **das hat ~s für sich** there is something to be said for it; **ich könnte dir ~s erzählen** I could tell you a thing or two.

**einigen** *vt* to unite.
➥ **sich einigen** *ref:* **sich (mit jm)** ~ to reach an agreement (with sb); **sich auf etw** *(A)* ~ to agree on sthg.

**einigermaßen** *adv* fairly.

**einiges** ▷ **einige.**

**Einigkeit** *die* - **1.** [Eintracht] unity - **2.** [Übereinstimmung] agreement.

**Einigung** *(pl* -en) *die* - **1.** [Übereinkunft] agreement - **2.** [Vereinigung] unification.

**einjährig** *adj* - **1.** [Kind, Tier] one-year-old - **2.** [Vertrag, Laufzeit] one-year; [Pflanze] annual.

**ein|kalkulieren** *vt* to take into account.

**Ein|kauf** *der* - **1.** [Einkaufen] shopping - **2.** [eingekaufte Ware] purchase; **die Einkäufe aus dem Wagen holen** to get the shopping out of the car - **3.** WIRTSCH purchasing.

**ein|kaufen** *vt* to buy ◇ *vi:* ~ **gehen** to go shopping.
➥ **sich einkaufen** *ref:* **sich in ein Unternehmen** ~ to buy into ODER buy a share in a company.

**Einkaufs|bummel** *der* shopping expedition; **einen** ~ **machen** to go on a shopping expedition.

**Einkaufs|tasche** *die* shopping bag.

**Einkaufs|wagen** *der* (shopping) trolley *Br* ODER cart *Am.*

**Einkaufs|zentrum** *das* shopping centre *Br,* (shopping) mall *Am.*

**ein|kehren** *(perf* ist **eingekehrt)** *vi* to stop off.

**ein|kesseln** *vt* to surround.

**ein|klagen** *vt* [Schulden] to sue for the recovery of; [Rechte] to demand.

**ein|klammern** *vt* to put in brackets, to bracket.

**Einklang** *der* harmony.

**ein|kleben** *vt* to stick in.

**ein|kleiden** *vt* to kit out.
➥ **sich einkleiden** *ref:* **sich neu** ~ to buy o.s. a new wardrobe.

**ein|klemmen** *vt* to trap.

**ein|kochen** *(perf* hat/ist **eingekocht)** *vt (hat)* [konservieren] to preserve ◇ *vi (ist)* [eindicken] to reduce.

**Einkommen** *(pl* -) *das* income.

**Einkommens|gefälle** *das* earnings gap.

**einkommensschwach** *adj* low-income.

**Einkommens|steuer** *die* income tax.

**Einkommensteuer|erklärung** *die* (income) tax return.

**ein|kreisen** *vt* - **1.** [umzingeln] to surround - **2.** [eingrenzen] to pin down - **3.** [mit Stift] to circle.

**ein|kremen** = **eincremen.**

**ein|kriegen** ➥ **sich einkriegen** *ref:* **er kriegte sich vor Lachen nicht mehr ein** *fam* he nearly died laughing.

**Einkünfte** *pl* income *(U).*

**ein|laden** *vt (unreg)* - **1.** [Gast] to invite; **jn zu etw** ~ [Hochzeit, Party] to invite sb to sthg; **darf ich Sie zu einem Kaffee ~?** can I buy you a coffee?; **jn in ein Restaurant** ~ to take sb out for a meal - **2.** [Last] to load.

**einladend** *adj* inviting ◇ *adv* invitingly.

**Ein|ladung** *die* invitation.

**Ein|lage** *die* - **1.** [im Schuh] insole - **2.** KÜCHE *vegetables, noodles, meat etc added to a clear soup* - **3.** [im Programm] interlude - **4.** WIRTSCH [bei Bank] deposit; [bei Firma] investment.

**Einlass** *der* admission; **jm** ~ **gewähren** to admit sb.

**ein|lassen** *vt (unreg)* - **1.** [hereinlassen] to admit - **2.** [Wasser] to run; **sie ließ Wasser in die Wanne ein** she ran herself a bath - **3.** [einsetzen] to set.
➥ **sich einlassen** *ref:* **sich mit jm/auf etw** *(A)* ~ to get involved with sb/in sthg.

**Ein|lauf** *der* - **1.** SPORT placings *(pl)* - **2.** MED enema.

**ein|laufen** *(perf* hat/ist **eingelaufen)** *(unreg)* *vi (ist)* - **1.** SPORT: **ins Stadion** ~ to enter the stadium; **ins Ziel** ~ to cross the finishing line

**- 2.** [Wasser] to run in **- 3.** [einfahren] to come in **- 4.** [Stoff] to shrink ⇔ *vt (hat)* [Schuhe] to wear in.

→ **sich einlaufen** *ref* to warm up.

**ein|leben** → **sich einleben** *ref* to settle in.

**ein|legen** *vt* **- 1.** [hineintun] to put in; **den ersten Gang ~** to go into first gear **- 2.** KÜCHE to preserve; [in Essig] to pickle **- 3.** [Pause] to have, to take **- 4.** [Berufung, Bitte] to lodge; **ein gutes Wort für jn ~** to put in a good word for sb.

**Einlege|sohle** *die* insole.

**ein|leiten** *vt* **- 1.** [beginnen - Untersuchung, Verfahren] to start; [ - Schritte] to take; [ - Geburt] to induce **- 2.** [einführen] to open **- 3.** [einlassen]: **Abwässer in den Fluss ~** to let effluent into the river.

**einleitend** *adj* introductory ⇔ *adv* by way of introduction.

**Ein|leitung** *die* **- 1.** [Einführung] introduction **- 2.** [Beginn - von Untersuchung] start; [ - von Geburt] induction.

**ein|lenken** *vi* to give way.

**ein|leuchten** *vi:* **es leuchtet mir ein, dass ...** I can see that ...

**einleuchtend** *adj* convincing ⇔ *adv* convincingly.

**ein|liefern** *vt* **- 1.** [bringen - in psychiatrische Anstalt] to commit; **jn in ein Krankenhaus ~** to take sb to hospital **- 2.** [Waren] to deliver.

**Ein|lieferung** *die* **- 1.** [von Kranken] admission; [in psychiatrische Anstalt] committal **- 2.** [von Waren] delivery.

**Einlieger|wohnung** *die self-contained flat which is available for rent in a private house.*

**ein|loggen** → **sich einloggen** *ref* EDV to log on; **sich ins Internet ~** to log on to the Internet.

**ein|lösen** *vt* **- 1.** [Scheck] to cash; [Gutschein] to redeem **- 2.** [Versprechen] to keep.

**Ein|lösung** *die* [von Scheck] cashing; [von Gutschein] redemption.

**ein|machen** *vt* to preserve.

**Einmach|glas** *das* preserving jar.

**einmal** *adv* **- 1.** [ein einzelnes Mal] once; **noch ~** (once) again **- 2.** [irgendwann - zuvor] before; [ - in Zukunft] sometime; **haben wir uns nicht schon ~ gesehen?** haven't we met before?; **irgendwann ~ möchte sie nach England ziehen** she'd like to move to England someday; **es war ~ ...** once upon a time there was ... **- 3.** [mal, bitte]: **komm ~ her!** come here, will you!; **hör mir ~ gut zu!** now listen to me carefully!

→ **auf einmal** *adv* **- 1.** [plötzlich] suddenly **- 2.** [zusammen, gleichzeitig] at once.

→ **nicht einmal** *adv* not even.

**Einmaleins** *das (ohne pl)* **- 1.** [Zahlenreihe] multiplication tables *(pl)*; **das große/kleine ~** multi-

plication tables from 1 to 20/up to 10 **- 2.** [Grundwissen] ABC.

**einmalig** *adj* **- 1.** [einzeln - Zahlung] one-off **- 2.** [außergewöhnlich] unique **- 3.** [wunderbar] fantastic.

**Ein|marsch** *der* invasion.

**ein|marschieren** (*perf* **ist einmarschiert**) *vi* to invade.

**ein|massieren** *vt* to massage in.

**ein|mischen** → **sich einmischen** *ref:* **sich (in etw (A)) ~** to interfere (in sthg).

**Ein|mischung** *die* interference.

**ein|münden** (*perf* **hat/ist eingemündet**) *vi:* **in etw (A) ~** [Fluss] to flow into sthg; [Straße] to lead into sthg.

**einmütig** *adj* unanimous ⇔ *adv* unanimously.

**ein|nähen** *vt* **- 1.** [in Kleidungsstück] to sew in **- 2.** [enger nähen] to take in.

**Einnahme** (*pl* **-n**) *die* **- 1.** [Einkommen] income; [an einer Kasse] takings *(pl)*; [vom Staat] revenue; **~n und Ausgaben** income and expenditure **- 2.** [von Medikament] taking **- 3.** [Eroberung] capture.

**Einnahme|quelle** *die* source of income.

**ein|nehmen** *vt* (*unreg*) **- 1.** [Geld, Medikament, Platz] to take; **viel Raum ~** to take up a lot of room **- 2.** [erobern] to capture; **jn für sich ~** *fig* to win sb over.

**einnehmend** *adj* captivating.

**ein|nicken** (*perf* **ist eingenickt**) *vi* to nod off.

**ein|nisten** → **sich einnisten** *ref abw* [sich breit machen]: **sich bei jm ~** to park o.s. on sb.

**Ein|öde** *die* wilderness.

**ein|ordnen** *vt* to put in its place; [Akten] to file; [Dichter, Politiker] to categorize.

→ **sich einordnen** *ref* [Auto] to get into the correct lane; [Person] to fit in; **sich links ~** to get into the left-hand lane.

**ein|packen** *vt* **- 1.** [verpacken - Kleidung] to pack; [ - Geschenk] to wrap **- 2.** *fam* [anziehen] to wrap up ⇔ *vi fam:* **wenn sie den Fehler bemerkt, kannst du ~** if she notices the mistake, you've had it.

→ **sich einpacken** *ref fam* to wrap o.s. up.

**ein|parken** *vt* to park ⇔ *vi* to park; **rückwärts ~** to back in.

**ein|passen** *vt* to fit.

**ein|pendeln** → **sich einpendeln** *ref* to level off.

**ein|pflanzen** *vt* **- 1.** [pflanzen] to plant **- 2.** MED to implant.

**ein|planen** *vt* [Verlust, Verzögerung] to allow for; [Person] to count in.

**ein|prägen** *vt* **- 1.** [eingravieren] to imprint

**- 2.** [einschärfen]: **sich** (D) **etw ~** to memorize sthg; **jm etw ~** to impress sthg on sb.
 **sich einprägen** ref: **das Erlebnis hat sich mir für immer eingeprägt** the experience made an indelible impression on me.

**einprägsam** adj easily remembered; [Melodie] catchy.

**ein|quartieren** vt to put up.
 **sich einquartieren** ref to stay.

**ein|rahmen** vt to frame.

**ein|räumen** vt **- 1.** [einordnen, ordnen - Kleidung, Geschirr] to put away; **den Schrank ~** to put things away in the cupboard **- 2.** [Frist, Kredit] to grant **- 3.** [zugeben] to admit.

**ein|rechnen** vt to include.

**ein|reden** vi: **auf jn ~** to keep on at sb $\diamond$ vt: **jm etw ~** to talk sb into sthg.

**ein|reiben** vt (unreg) to rub in; **sich** (D) **die Brust mit Öl ~** to rub oil onto one's chest.

**ein|reichen** vt [Antrag] to submit; [Beschwerde] to lodge.

**ein|reihen** vt to place.
 **sich einreihen** ref: **sich in etw** (A) **~** to take one's place in ODER join sthg.

**einreihig** adj single-breasted $\diamond$ adv: **~ geknöpft** single-breasted.

**Ein|reise** die entry.

**Einreise|erlaubnis** die entry permit.

**ein|reisen** (perf **ist eingereist**) vi to enter; **nach Deutschland ~** to enter Germany.

**Einreise|visum** das entry visa.

**ein|reißen** (perf **hat/ist eingerissen**) (unreg) vt (hat) **- 1.** [Gebäude] to pull down **- 2.** [Papier, Stoff] to tear $\diamond$ vi (ist) **- 1.** [Papier, Stoff] to tear **- 2.** abw [Unsitte] to become a habit.

**ein|renken** vt **- 1.** MED to put back in its socket **- 2.** [bereinigen] to sort out.
 **sich einrenken** ref to sort itself out.

**ein|richten** vt **- 1.** [möblieren] to furnish **- 2.** [organisieren]: **etw so ~, dass ...** to organize sthg in such a way that ... **- 3.** [Stelle, Institution] to set up.
 **sich einrichten** ref **- 1.** [mit Möbeln] to furnish one's home **- 2.** [sich einstellen]: **sich auf etw** (A) **~** to prepare for sthg.

**Ein|richtung** die **- 1.** [Möbel] furnishings (pl) **- 2.** [Einrichten] furnishing **- 3.** [Schaffung] setting up **- 4.** [Institution] institution.

**ein|rollen** (perf **hat/ist eingerollt**) vt (hat) to roll up $\diamond$ vi (ist) fam to roll in.
 **sich einrollen** ref to curl up.

**ein|rosten** (perf **ist eingerostet**) vi **- 1.** [Gegenstand] to go rusty **- 2.** [Person, Gelenk] to stiffen up.

**ein|rücken** (perf **hat/ist eingerückt**) vi (ist) to enter $\diamond$ vt (hat) TYPO to indent.

**eins** num [als Zahl] one; **~ A** top-quality, A-1; **es steht ~ zu null für Dänemark** it's one-nil to Denmark; **~, zwei, drei** in no time at all $\diamond$ adj: **das ist mir ~** that's all the same to me; **mit jm ~ werden** [einig werden] to come to an agreement with sb $\diamond$ pron one; siehe auch **sechs.**

**Eins** (pl **-en**) die **- 1.** [Zahl] one **- 2.** [Schulnote] $\approx$ A, mark of 1 on a scale from 1 to 6; siehe auch **Sechs.**

**ein|sacken** vt **- 1.** [einpacken] to put into sacks **- 2.** salopp [Geld, Gewinn] to pocket.

**einsam** adj **- 1.** [Person] lonely **- 2.** [Haus, Gegend] isolated.

**Einsamkeit** die **- 1.** [von Person] loneliness **- 2.** [von Haus, Gegend] isolation.

**ein|sammeln** vt [Werkzeug, Spielzeug] to gather up; [Kinder] to pick up; [Klassenarbeiten] to collect in; [Geld] to collect.

**Ein|satz** der **- 1.** [Geld] stake **- 2.** [Einsetzen] use; **unter ~ aller Kräfte** with a huge effort; **zum ~ kommen** to be used **- 3.** [Engagement] commitment **- 4.** MIL mission; **im ~ sein** to be in action **- 5.** [Fach] compartment **- 6.** MUS entry.

**einsatzbereit** adj [Truppe] ready for action; [Maschine] ready for use.

**Einsatzbereitschaft** die **- 1.** [Engagement] commitment **- 2.**: **in ~ sein** to be on standby.

**ein|schalten** vt **- 1.** [anstellen] to switch on **- 2.** [hinzuziehen] to call in.
 **sich einschalten** ref **- 1.** [von selbst angehen] to switch on **- 2.** [eingreifen] to intervene.

**Einschalt|quote** die (programme) ratings (pl).

**ein|schärfen** vt: **jm etw ~** to impress sthg upon sb.

**ein|schätzen** vt [Gefahr, Lage] to assess; [Vermögen, Umsatz] to estimate; [Person] to judge; **jn/etw falsch ~** to misjudge sb/sthg.

**Ein|schätzung** die [von Gefahr, Lage] assessment; [von Vermögen, Umsatz] estimation; [von Person] judgement.

**ein|schenken** vt: **jm etw ~** to pour sb sthg.

**ein|schicken** vt to send in.

**ein|schieben** vt (unreg) **- 1.** [hineinschieben] to insert **- 2.** [einfügen] to fit in.

**ein|schiffen** vt [Personen] to embark; [Waren] to load.
 **sich einschiffen** ref: **sich nach Australien ~** to embark for Australia.

**einschl.** (abk für **einschließlich**) incl.

**ein|schlafen** (perf **ist eingeschlafen**) vi (unreg) **- 1.** [aus Müdigkeit] to fall asleep **- 2.** [Körperteil] to go to sleep **- 3.** [aufhören] to peter out **- 4.** [sterben] to pass away.

**ein|schläfern** vt - **1.** [töten] to put to sleep - **2.** [in Schlaf versetzen] to send to sleep.

**einschläfernd** adj soporific.

**Ein|schlag** der - **1.** [Einschuss] impact - **2.** [Qualität] element.

**ein|schlagen** (perf hat/ist eingeschlagen) (unreg) vi - **1.** (ist) [treffen] to strike - **2.** (hat) [zustimmen] to agree; [mit Händedruck] to shake on it - **3.** (hat) [lenken] to steer; **nach rechts ~** to turn right - **4.** (hat) [Furore machen - Schallplatte] to be a hit; [ - Erfindung] to be a success; [ - Enthüllungen] to cause a furore - **5.** (hat) [schlagen]: **auf jn ~** to beat sb ⇔ vt (hat) - **1.** [Nagel] to knock in - **2.** [Glas, Tür] to smash in - **3.** [Buch, Geschenk] to wrap (up) - **4.** [Weg] to take; [Richtung] to go in.

**einschlägig** adj [Literatur] relevant; [Methode] appropriate ⇔ adv: **~ vorbestraft sein** to have a previous conviction for a similar offence.

**ein|schleichen** ⇒ **sich einschleichen** ref (unreg) eigtl & fig to creep in.

**ein|schleusen** vt [Waffen] to smuggle in; [V-Leute] to infiltrate.

**ein|schließen** vt (unreg) - **1.** [einsperren] to lock up - **2.** [aufbewahren] to lock away - **3.** [umzingeln] to surround - **4.** [beinhalten] to include.

**einschließlich** präp (+ G) including; **vom 1,3 bis ~ 5,5** from 1.3 to 5.5 inclusive ⇔ adv: **bis Montag ~** up to and including Monday.

**ein|schmeicheln** ⇒ **sich einschmeicheln** ref: **sich bei jm ~** abw to curry favour with sb.

**ein|schmuggeln** vt to smuggle in.
⇒ **sich einschmuggeln** ref to smuggle o.s. in.

**ein|schnappen** (perf ist eingeschnappt) vi - **1.** [Schloss, Verschluss] to click shut - **2.** fam abw [beleidigt sein] to get in a huff.

**ein|schneiden** (unreg) vi: **das Band schneidet mir in die Haut ein** the band cuts into my skin ⇔ vt to cut.

**einschneidend** adj drastic ⇔ adv drastically.

**ein|schneien** (perf ist eingeschneit) vi to get snowed in.

**Ein|schnitt** der - **1.** [Schnitt] cut; [bei Operation] incision - **2.** [Zäsur] turning point.

**ein|schränken** vt to limit; [Rauchen, Trinken] to cut down on; [Menge, Anzahl] to reduce.
⇒ **sich einschränken** ref to economize.

**Einschränkung** (pl -en) die - **1.** [Einschränken] limitation; [von Kosten] reduction - **2.** [Vorbehalt] reservation.

**ein|schreiben** vt (unreg) - **1.** [hineinschreiben]: **eingeschrieben sein** to be registered - **2.** [Brief]: **etw ~ lassen** ODER **eingeschrieben schicken** to send sthg recorded delivery.

⇒ **sich einschreiben** ref [sich anmelden] to register.

**Ein|schreiben** das: **etw per ~ schicken** to send sthg recorded delivery.

**ein|schreiten** (perf ist eingeschritten) vi (unreg) to intervene.

**Ein|schub** der insertion.

**ein|schüchtern** vt to intimidate.

**Einschüchterung** (pl -en) die intimidation.

**ein|schulen** vt: **eingeschult werden** to start school.

**Ein|schulung** die [Tag] first day at school.

**ein|schweißen** vt - **1.** [in Folie] to shrink-wrap - **2.** [Metall] to weld in.

**ein|sehen** vt (unreg) - **1.** [Fehler, Schuld] to recognize, to admit - **2.** [Papiere] to examine.

**Einsehen** das: **ein ~ haben** [vernünftig sein] to see sense; **mit jm/etw ein/kein ~ haben** [verständnisvoll sein] to show some/no understanding towards sb/for sthg.

**ein|seifen** vt - **1.** [waschen] to soap - **2.** fam abw [überreden] to take in.

**einseitig** adj - **1.** [subjektiv] one-sided - **2.** [auf einer Seite] on one side - **3.** [Beziehung] unilateral ⇔ adv - **1.** [subjektiv] one-sidedly - **2.** [auf einer Seite] on one side - **3.** [unausgewogen]: **sich ~ ernähren** to eat an unbalanced diet.

**ein|senden** (prät sendete ein ODER sandte ein; perf hat eingesendet ODER eingesandt) vt to send in.

**Ein|sendung** die - **1.** [von Text, Ware] sending in - **2.** [bei Preisausschreiben] entry.

**ein|setzen** vt - **1.** [hineinsetzen] to put in - **2.** [gebrauchen] to use; **die Polizei/das Militär ~** to bring in the police/army - **3.** [in Amt] to appoint - **4.** [Leben] to risk; [Geld] to stake ⇔ vi to begin; [Sturm] to break.

⇒ **sich einsetzen** ref to be committed; **sich für jn ~** to stand up for sb; **sich für etw ~** to support sthg.

**Ein|setzung** die appointment.

**Ein|sicht** die - **1.** [Erkenntnis] insight; **zur ~ kommen** to see sense; **zu der ~ kommen, dass** to come to realize that - **2.** [Einblick]: **in etw** (A) **~ bekommen** to get a look at sthg.

**einsichtig** adj - **1.** [vernünftig] sensible - **2.** [verständlich] clear ⇔ adv - **1.** [vernünftig] sensibly - **2.** [verständlich] clearly.

**Ein|siedler, in** der, die hermit.

**einsilbig** adj - **1.** [Person] taciturn - **2.** [Wort, Antwort] monosyllabic ⇔ adv [antworten] in monosyllables.

**ein|sinken** (perf ist eingesunken) vi (unreg) to sink (in).

**ein|spannen** vt - **1.** [Pferd] to harness - **2.** [zur

Arbeit] to rope in - **3.** [in Schreibmaschine] to insert.

**ein|sparen** *vt* to save; [Personal] to cut back on.

**Einsparung** (*pl* -en) *die* saving; [von Personal] cutback.

**ein|sperren** *vt* to lock up.

**ein|spielen** *vt* - **1.** [Geld] to bring in; [Unkosten] to cover - **2.** [Instrument] to play in - **3.** [einfügen] to fit in.

➡ **sich einspielen** *ref* - **1.** [sich aufwärmen] to warm up - **2.** [sich abstimmen] to settle down; **die Kollegen haben sich aufeinander eingespielt** the colleagues are now working well together

**einsprachig** *adj* monolingual ◇ *adv* speaking only one language.

**ein|springen** (*perf* ist **eingesprungen**) *vi* (*unreg*): **(für jn)** ~ to stand in (for sb).

**Ein|spruch** *der* objection; ~ **(gegen etw) erheben** to object (to sthg).

**einspurig** *adj* single-lane ◇ *adv*: '**nur** ~ **befahrbar**' 'single-lane traffic only'.

**einst** *adv geh* once.

**Ein|stand** *der*: **seinen** ~ **geben** *to bring some food or drink to the office to celebrate starting one's new job.*

**ein|stecken** *vt* - **1.** [in Tasche] to put in one's pocket; **vergiss nicht, Geld einzustecken!** don't forget to take some money with you! - **2.** [Kritik, Niederlage, Verlust] to take - **3.** [Stecker] to plug in - **4.** [Brief] to post *Br*, to mail *Am* - **5.** [stehlen] to pocket.

**ein|stehen** (*perf* ist **eingestanden**) *vi* (*unreg*): **für jn/etw** ~ [sich verbürgen] to vouch for sb/sthg; [Verantwortung übernehmen] to take responsibility for sb/sthg.

**ein|steigen** (*perf* ist **eingestiegen**) *vi* (*unreg*) - **1.** [in Auto] to get in; [in Bus, Zug] to get on; **ins Auto/in den Zug** ~ to get in the car/on the train - **2.** [anfangen]: **in etw** (*A*) ~ [Beruf, Politik] to go into sthg; **er ist ins Geschäft seiner Mutter/bei Vodafone eingestiegen** he joined his mother's firm/Vodafone - **3.** [sich einkaufen]: **bei RTL/in eine Firma** ~ to buy a share in RTL/a company.

**einstellbar** *adj* adjustable.

**ein|stellen** *vt* - **1.** [Angestellte] to take on - **2.** [Gerät, Lautstärke - zum ersten Mal] to set; [ - genauer] to adjust; [Sender] to tune into - **3.** [anmachen] to switch on - **4.** [beenden] to stop.

➡ **sich einstellen** *ref* - **1.** [sich vorbereiten]: **sich auf jn/etw** ~ to prepare for sb/sthg; [sich anpassen] to get used to sb/sthg; **auf die neuen Arbeitszeiten muss ich mich noch** ~ I still have to get used to the new working hours - **2.** *geh* [anfangen] to begin.

**Ein|stellung** *die* - **1.** [von Angestellten] appoint-

ment - **2.** [von Gerät, Lautstärke - zum ersten Mal] setting; [ - genauer] adjustment; [von Sender] tuning - **3.** [Beendigung - von Verfahren, Zahlungen] termination, stopping - **4.** [Meinung, Haltung] attitude - **5.** [Szene] take.

**Einstellungs|gespräch** *das* interview.

**Einstieg** (*pl* -e) *der* - **1.** [Beginn] entry - **2.** [Einführung]: **der** ~ **in dieses Thema ist schwierig** this subject is difficult to get into - **3.** [in Bus, Zug] boarding.

**einstig** *adj geh* former.

**ein|stimmen** *vi* - **1.** [mitsingen, mitspielen]: **(in etw** (*A*)) ~ to join in (sthg) - **2.** [vorbereiten]: **jn auf etw** (*A*) ~ to get sb in the right mood for sthg.

**einstimmig** *adj* - **1.** MUS for one voice - **2.** [übereinstimmend] unanimous ◇ *adv* - **1.** MUS in unison - **2.** [übereinstimmend] unanimously.

**einstöckig** *adj* single-storey.

**ein|streichen** *vt* (*unreg*) *abw* [Geld, Gewinn] to rake in.

**ein|studieren** *vt* to rehearse.

**ein|stufen** *vt* to categorize; **jn in eine Gehaltsgruppe** ~ to put sb in an income bracket.

**einstündig** *adj* one-hour.

**Ein|sturz** *der* collapse.

**ein|stürzen** (*perf* ist **eingestürzt**) *vi* - **1.** [Haus, Mauer] to collapse - **2.** [hereinbrechen]: **neue Eindrücke stürzten auf sie ein** she was overwhelmed by new impressions.

**Einsturz|gefahr** *die*: '**Vorsicht,** ~**!**' 'danger, building unsafe!'.

**einstweilen** *adv geh* - **1.** [vorläufig] for the time being - **2.** [inzwischen] meanwhile.

**einstweilig** *amt adj* temporary ◇ *adv* temporarily.

**eintägig** *adj* one-day.

**ein|tauchen** (*perf* hat/ist **eingetaucht**) *vt* (*hat*) to dip; [völlig] to immerse; [Keks] to dunk ◇ *vi* (*ist*) to dive in.

**ein|tauschen** *vt*: **etw gegen etw** ~ to exchange sthg for sthg.

**eintausend** *num a* ODER one thousand.

**ein|teilen** *vt* - **1.** [klassifizieren] to classify - **2.** [unterteilen] to divide up - **3.** [Arbeit, Zeit] to organize - **4.** [einplanen]: **jn für** ODER **zu etw** ~ to assign sb to sthg.

**einteilig** *adj* one-piece.

**Ein|teilung** *die* - **1.** [Klassifizierung] classification - **2.** [Unterteilung] division - **3.** [von Arbeit, Zeit] organization - **4.** [Einplanung]: ~ **für** ODER **zu etw** assignment to sthg.

**eintönig** *adj* monotonous ◇ *adv* monotonously.

**Ein|topf** *der* stew.

**Eintracht** *die* harmony.

**einträchtig** *adv* harmoniously.

**Eintrag** (*pl* -träge) *der* - **1.** [Notiz] entry - **2.** [Notieren] entering.

**ein|tragen** *vt* (*unreg*) - **1.** [notieren] to write down - **2.** *amt* [registrieren] to register - **3.** [Geld] to bring in; [Ärger, Sympathie] to bring.
➤ **sich eintragen** *ref* to put one's name down.

**einträglich** *adj* lucrative.

**ein|treffen** (*perf* ist **eingetroffen**) *vi* (*unreg*) - **1.** [ankommen] to arrive - **2.** [wahr werden] to come true.

**ein|treiben** *vt* (*unreg*) to collect.

**ein|treten** (*perf* hat/ist **eingetreten**) (*unreg*) *vi* (ist) - **1.** [in Raum, Phase] to enter; **in etw** (A) ~ to enter sthg - **2.** [in Gruppe, Verein]: **in etw** (A) ~ to join sthg - **3.** [sich einsetzen]: **für jn/etw** ~ to stand up for sb/sthg - **4.** [Tod] to occur; [Fall, Umstände] to arise ◇ *vt (hat)* to kick in.

**ein|trichtern** *vt*: **jm/sich** (D) **etw** ~ to drum sthg into sb/one's head.

**Ein|tritt** *der* - **1.** [in Raum, Phase] entry; '~ frei' 'admission free'; '~ verboten' 'no entry' - **2.** [Eintrittspreis] admission; **was kostet der** ~? how much does it cost to get in? - **3.** [in Gruppe, Verein] joining - **4.** [Anfang]: **bei** ~ **der Dämmerung** at dawn.

**Eintritts|geld** *das* admission fee.

**Eintritts|karte** *die* ticket.

**ein|trocknen** (*perf* ist **eingetrocknet**) *vi* to dry up.

**ein|trüben** ➤ **sich eintrüben** *ref* to cloud over; **es trübt sich ein** it's clouding over.

**ein|trudeln** (*perf* ist **eingetrudelt**) *vi fam* to wander in.

**ein|üben** *vt* to rehearse.

**Ein|übung** *die* rehearsal.

**Einvernehmen** *das* understanding; **sich mit jm ins** ~ **setzen** *amt* to reach an understanding with sb.

**einverstanden** *adj*: **mit jm/etw** ~ **sein** to agree with sb/sthg; **sich mit etw** ~ **erklären** to agree to sthg ◇ *interj* OK!

**Ein|verständnis** *das* - **1.** [Übereinstimmung] agreement - **2.** [Billigung] consent.

**Ein|wand** *der* objection; ~ **(gegen etw) erheben** to object (to sthg).

**Ein|wanderer** *der* immigrant.

**Ein|wanderin** *die* immigrant.

**ein|wandern** (*perf* ist **eingewandert**) *vi* to immigrate.

**Ein|wanderung** *die* immigration.

**einwandfrei** *adj* perfect; [Material] flawless; [Nachweis] irrefutable ◇ *adv* perfectly.

**einwärts** *adv* inwards.

**Einweg|flasche** *die* non-returnable bottle.

**Einweg|verpackung** *die* disposable packaging.

**ein|weichen** *vt* to soak.

**ein|weihen** *vt* - **1.** [Gebäude] to open - **2.** [Wagen, Sofa] to christen, to use for the first time - **3.**: **jn in ein Geheimnis** ~ to let sb in on a secret.

**Ein|weihung** *die* [von Gebäude] opening; [von Wohnung] housewarming party.

**ein|weisen** *vt* (*unreg*) - **1.** [Patienten] to admit - **2.** [Anfänger]: **jn in etw** (A) ~ to introduce sb to sthg - **3.** [Fahrzeug] to direct.

**Ein|weisung** *die* - **1.** [von Patienten] admission - **2.** [von Anfänger] introduction - **3.** [von Fahrzeug] directing.

**ein|wenden** *vt*: ~, **dass ...** to object that...; **dagegen ist nichts einzuwenden** there's no reason why not.

**ein|werfen** *vt* (*unreg*) - **1.** [Münze] to insert; [Brief] to post *Br*, to mail *Am* - **2.** [Ball, Frage, Bemerkung] to throw in - **3.** [kaputtwerfen] to smash.

**ein|wickeln** *vt* - **1.** [einpacken] to wrap up - **2.** *fam abw* [überreden] to take in.

**ein|willigen** *vi*: **(in etw** (A)**)** ~ to agree (to sthg).

**Einwilligung** (*pl* -en) *die* consent.

**ein|wirken** *vi* - **1.** [Salbe] to take effect - **2.** [Person]: **auf jn beruhigend** ~ to have a calming influence on sb.

**Einwohner, in** (*mpl* -; *fpl* -nen) *der, die* inhabitant.

**Einwohnermelde|amt** *das local government office at which inhabitants of a town must register at the beginning and end of their residency.*

**Einwohner|zahl** *die* population, number of inhabitants.

**Ein|wurf** *der* - **1.** [Ausspruch] comment - **2.** [von Ball] throw-in - **3.** [von Münze] insertion; [von Brief] posting *Br*, mailing *Am* - **4.** [Schlitz] slot.

**Einzahl** *die* singular.

**ein|zahlen** *vt* to pay in.

**Ein|zahlung** *die* deposit.

**Einzahlungs|schein** *der* paying-in slip.

**ein|zeichnen** *vt* to mark.

**Einzel** (*pl* -) *das* singles (*pl*).

**Einzel|fall** *der* isolated case.

**Einzel|gänger, in** (*mpl* -; *fpl* -nen) *der, die* loner.

**Einzel|haft** *die* solitary confinement.

**Einzel|handel** *der* retail trade.

**Einzel|händler, in** *der, die* retailer.

**Einzelheit** *(pl -en) die* detail; **in allen ~en** down to the last detail.

**Einzel|kämpfer, in** *der, die:* **er ist ~** he fights alone.

**Einzel|kind** *das* only child.

**einzeln** *adj* - **1.** [speziell] individual - **2.** [isoliert] single; **jedes ~e Exemplar** every single copy - **3.** [Schuh, Socke] odd <> *adv* individually; [ankommen, abholen] separately; **~ stehend** solitary <> *det (nur pl)* a few.

**Einzelne** *pron sg* - **1.** [Person]: **jede/jeder ~** (each and) every one - **2.** [Sache]: **jede/jeder ~** every single one <> *pron pl* - **1.** [Personen] some (people) - **2.** [Sachen] some <> *der, die* [Mensch] individual <> *das:* **bis ins ~** down to the last detail; **ins ~ gehen** to go into detail; **im ~n** in detail.

➡ **Einzelnes** *pron* some things *(pl).*

**Einzel|person** *die* single person.

**Einzel|stück** *das* [Kunstgegenstand] piece.

**Einzel|zimmer** *das* single room.

**ein|ziehen** *(perf hat/ist eingezogen) (unreg) vt (hat)* - **1.** [Bauch, Netz] to pull in; [Krallen, Fahrgestell] to retract - **2.** [Faden, Band] to thread in - **3.** [Wand] to put in - **4.** [zur Armee] to call up - **5.** [Geld, Steuern] to collect - **6.** [beschlagnahmen] to confiscate - **7.** [Banknoten, Münzen] to withdraw (from circulation) - **8.** [einsaugen - Luft, Aroma] to breathe in - **9.** *amt* [Informationen] to gather <> *vi (ist)* - **1.** [in Wohnung] to move in - **2.** [Einzug halten] to enter; [Jahreszeit] to arrive - **3.** [Fett, Creme, Flüssigkeit] to be absorbed.

**einzig** *adj (ohne Kompar)* - **1.** [alleinig] only; **nur noch ein ~es Mal** just one more time; **ein ~er Besucher** a single visitor - **2.** *geh* [einzigartig] unique - **3.** [total] complete <> *adv* only; **~ und allein** entirely.

**einzigartig** *adj* unique <> *adv* uniquely.

**Einzige** *der, die, das:* **der/die/das ~** [Person] the only one; [Sache] the only thing; **das ~, was ...** the only thing that ...; **nur ein ~r erhob sich** only one person stood up; **sie war als ~ dafür** she was the only one in favour.

**Einzimmer|appartement** *das* one-room flat *Br* ODER apartment *Am.*

**Einzimmer|wohnung** *die* one-room flat *Br* ODER apartment *Am.*

**Ein|zug** *der* - **1.** [von Jahreszeit] arrival - **2.** [von Sportler, Sieger] entrance - **3.** MIL entry - **4.** [in Wohnung] move - **5.** [von Geld, Steuern] collection.

**Einzugs|gebiet** *das* - **1.** [von Städten] commuter belt - **2.** [von Flüssen] catchment area - **3.** [von Schulen] catchment area *Br,* school district *Am.*

**Eis** *(pl -) das* - **1.** [Gefrorenes] ice; **etw auf ~ legen**

*eigtl* & *fig* to put sthg on ice; **das ~ ist gebrochen** the ice has been broken - **2.** [Eiscreme] ice cream; **~ am Stiel** ice lolly *Br,* Popsicle® *Am.* ~

**Eis|bahn** *die* ice rink.

**Eis|bär** *der* polar bear.

**Eis|becher** *der* (ice-cream) sundae.

**Eis|bein** *das* knuckle of pork.

**Eis|berg** *der* iceberg.

**Eis|blume** *die* frost pattern.

**Eis|bombe** *die* bombe glacée.

**Eis|café** [ˈaɪskafeː] *das* ice-cream parlour.

**Eischnee** *der:* **das Eiweiß zu ~ schlagen** to beat the egg white until stiff.

**Eiscreme** [ˈaɪskreːm], **Eiskrem** *die* ice cream.

**Eis|diele** *die* ice-cream parlour.

**Eisen** *(pl -) das* - **1.** [gen] iron - **2.** *RW:* **ein heißes ~** a hot potato; **mehrere ~ im Feuer haben** *fam* to have several irons in the fire; **zum alten ~ zählen** ODER **gehören** *fam* to belong on the scrapheap.

**Eisen|bahn** *die* - **1.** [Zug] train; **mit der ~ fahren** to travel by train; **(es ist) höchste ~!** *fam fig* it's getting late! - **2.** [Institution] railway *Br,* railroad *Am* - **3.** [Modelleisenbahn] train set.

**Eisenbahn|brücke** *die* railway bridge.

**Eisenbahner, in** *(mpl -/ fpl -nen) der, die* railway worker *Br,* railroader *Am.*

**Eisenbahn|fahrplan** *der* train timetable.

**Eisenbahn|netz** *das* rail network.

**Eisen|erz** *das* iron ore.

**Eisen|gießerei** *die* iron foundry.

**eisenhaltig** *adj* [Erz] iron-bearing, ferrous; [Nahrung] containing iron.

**Eisenmangel** *der* iron deficiency.

**Eisenstadt** *nt* Eisenstadt.

**Eisen|verhüttung** *(pl -en) die* iron smelting *(U).*

**Eisenwaren|handlung** *die* hardware store.

**Eisen|zeit** *die* Iron Age.

**eisern** *adj eigtl* & *fig* iron; **~ bleiben** to remain resolute <> *adv* [unnachgiebig] resolutely.

**eisfrei** *adj* ice-free.

**eisgekühlt** *adj* chilled.

**Eisheiligen** *pl* feast days of Three Saints *(12–14 May).*

**Eis|hockey** *das* ice hockey.

**eisig** *adj* - **1.** [eiskalt] freezing - **2.** [abweisend] icy, frosty <> *adv* - **1.** [eiskalt]: **~ kalt** freezing cold - **2.** [abweisend]: **~ lächeln** to give a frosty smile.

**eiskalt** *adj* - **1.** [Körperteil, Getränk, Wind] ice-cold

**- 2.** [Mensch, Mord] cold-blooded; [Blick] frosty <> adv **- 1.** [sehr kalt] ice-cold **- 2.** [herzlos] in cold blood.

**Eiskrem** = Eiscreme.

**Eiskunstlauf** der figure skating.

**Eisschnelllauf** der speed skating.

**Eis|scholle** die ice floe.

**Eis|schrank** der fridge.

**Eis|stadion** das ice rink.

**Eisstockschießen** das sport ≈ curling.

**Eis|zapfen** der icicle.

**Eis|zeit** die Ice Age.

**eitel** adj abw vain.

**Eitelkeit** (pl -en) die abw vanity.

**Eiter** der pus.

**eitern** vi to fester.

**eitrig, eiterig** adj [Wunde] festering; [Geschwür] suppurating.

**Eiweiß** (pl -e) das **- 1.** [im Hühnerei] egg white **- 2.** BIOL & CHEM protein.

**Ei|zelle** die ovum.

**Ejakulation** (pl -en) die ejaculation.

**ejakulieren** vi to ejaculate.

**EKD** [eːˈkaːˈdeː] (abk für **Evangelische Kirche in Deutschland**) die Protestant Church in Germany.

**Ekel** (pl -) der [Abscheu] disgust; ~ **vor etw** (D) **empfinden** to find sth disgusting <> das fam abw [Person] horror.

**ekelhaft** adj **- 1.** [Ekel erregend] disgusting **- 2.** [Arbeit, Chef] nasty <> adv [Ekel erregend] disgustingly.

**ekelig** = eklig.

**ekeln** vt: **das ekelt mich** I find that disgusting; **jn aus dem Haus ~** fam to drive sb out of the house <> vi: **davor ekelt mir** I find that disgusting.

◆ **sich ekeln** ref: **sich (vor jm/etw) ~** to be disgusted (by sb/sth).

**EKG** [eːˈkaːˈgeː] (pl -s) (abk für **Elektrokardiogramm**) das ECG Br, EKG Am.

**Eklat** [eˈklaˈt] (pl -s) der [Auseinandersetzung] row; [Aufsehen] sensation; **es kam zum ~** there was a major altercation.

**eklatant** adj geh striking; [Erfolg] sensational.

**eklig, ekelig** adj **- 1.** [Ekel erregend] disgusting **- 2.** fam [gemein] nasty <> adv **- 1.** [Ekel erregend] disgustingly **- 2.** [gemein] nastily.

**Ekstase** (pl -n) die ecstasy.

**Ekzem** (pl -e) das eczema (U).

**Elan** der geh vigour.

**elastisch** adj **- 1.** [Gummi] elastic **- 2.** [Körper] supple; [Gang] springy.

**Elastizität** die **- 1.** [von Gummi] elasticity

**- 2.** [von Körper] suppleness; [von Gang] springiness.

**Elbe** die: **die ~** the (River) Elbe.

**Elch** (pl -e) der elk.

**Elefant** (pl -en) der elephant; **wie ein ~ im Porzellanladen** fam like a bull in a china shop.

**elegant** adj elegant <> adv elegantly.

**Eleganz** die elegance.

**elektrifizieren** vt to electrify.

**Elektriker, in** (mpl -; fpl -nen) der, die electrician.

**elektrisch** adj **- 1.** [elektrisch betrieben - Licht, Rasierapparat, etc] electric; **~es Gerät** electrical appliance **- 2.** [mit Elektrizität zusammenhangend - Widerstand, Ladung] electrical <> adv electrically.

**elektrisieren** vt to electrify.

**Elektrizität** die electricity.

**Elektrizitäts|werk** das power station.

**Elektrode** (pl -n) die electrode.

**Elektro|gerät** das electrical appliance.

**Elektro|geschäft** das electrical goods store.

**Elektro|herd** der electric oven.

**Elektrolyse** [elɛktroˈlyːzə] (pl -n) die electrolysis.

**Elektro|motor** der electric motor.

**Elektron** (pl -en) das electron.

**Elektronen|mikroskop** das electron microscope.

**Elektronik** die (ohne pl) **- 1.** [Wissenschaft] electronics (U) **- 2.** [Teile] electronics (pl).

**elektronisch** adj electronic <> adv electronically.

**Elektrosmog** der electromagnetic radiation, electronic smog.

**Elektrotechnik** die electrical engineering.

**Element** (pl -e) das element; **in seinem ~ sein** to be in one's element; **dunkle** ODER **zwielichtige ~e** shady characters.

**elementar** adj **- 1.** [fundamental, einfach] basic **- 2.** [Kräfte, Gefühl] elemental.

**elend** adj **- 1.** [erbärmlich] miserable **- 2.** [krank] wretched <> adv **- 1.** [erbärmlich] miserably **- 2.** [schlecht] wretchedly; **sich ~ fühlen** to feel wretched.

**Elend** das **- 1.** [Unglück] misery; **es ist ein ~ mit ihm** fam he's a hopeless case; **das heulende ~ bekommen/haben** fam to get/have the blues **- 2.** [Ärmlichkeit] poverty.

**Elends|viertel** das slum.

**elf** num eleven; siehe auch **sechs**.

**Elf** (pl -en) die [Zahl & sport] eleven <> der elf; siehe auch **Sechs**.

**Elfe** (pl -n) die elf.

**Elfenbein** das ivory.

**Elfenbeinküste** die: die ~ the Ivory Coast.

**elfhundert** num one thousand one hundred.

**elfmal** adv eleven times.

**Elflmeter** der penalty.

**elftausend** num eleven thousand.

**elfte, r, s** adj eleventh; siehe auch sechste.

**Elfte** (pl -n) der, die, das eleventh; siehe auch Sechste.

**elftel** adj (unver) eleventh; siehe auch sechstel.

**Elftel** (pl -) das eleventh; siehe auch Sechstel.

**elitär** adj elitist <> adv in an elitist way.

**Elite** (pl -n) die elite.

**Elitelschule** die prestigious school.

**Eliteluniversität** die prestigious university.

**Ellbogen, Ellenbogen** (pl -) der elbow; seine ~ gebrauchen ODER benutzen fam to be ruthless.

**Ellbogenfreiheit** die elbow-room.

**Elle** (pl -n) die - 1. [Knochen] ulna - 2. [Maßeinheit] cubit.

**Ellenbogen** = Ellbogen.

**Ellipse** (pl -n) die ellipse.

**eloquent** adj geh eloquent.

**El Salvador** nt El Salvador.

**Elsass** das Alsace.

**Elsässer** (pl -) der & adj (unver) Alsatian.

**Elsässerin** (pl -nen) die Alsatian.

**elsässisch** adj Alsatian.

**Elster** (pl -n) die magpie; diebische ~ fig thieving little so-and-so.

**elterlich** adj parental.

**Eltern** pl parents; das ist nicht von schlechten ~ fam that isn't half bad.

**Elternlabend** der SCHULE parents' evening.

**Elternlhaus** das home; aus gutem ~ kommen to come from a good family.

**elternlos** adj orphaned <> adv as an orphan.

**Elternsprechltag** der SCHULE day on which parents may meet with teachers to discuss their children's schooling.

**Elternlteil** der parent.

**EM** [ɛˈʔɛm] (pl -s) die ⊏> Europameisterschaft.

**Email** [eˈmai̯l] das enamel.

**E-Mail** [ˈiːmei̯l] (pl -s) die EDV e-mail; jm eine ~ schicken to send sb an e-mail, to e-mail sb.

**E-Mail-lAdresse** die e-mail address.

**Emaille** [eˈmaljəl] (pl -n) die enamel.

**Emanze** (pl -n) die fam abw women's libber.

**Emanzipation** (pl -en) die emancipation.

**emanzipieren** ⇒ sich emanzipieren ref to become emancipated.

**Embargo** (pl -s) das embargo.

**Emblem** [ɛmˈbleːm] (pl -e) das emblem.

**Embryo** (pl -s ODER -onen) der embryo.

**emeritieren** vt to give emeritus status to.

**Emigrant, in** (mpl -en; fpl -nen) der, die émigré.

**Emigration** (pl -en) die (voluntary) exile.

**emigrieren** (perf ist emigriert) vi to go into (voluntary) exile, to leave the country.

**Eminenz** (pl -en) die eminence; eine graue ~ an éminence grise.

**Emission** (pl -en) die emission.

**e-Moll** das E minor.

**Emotion** (pl -en) die emotion.

**emotional** adj emotional <> adv emotionally.

**empfahl** prät ⊏> empfehlen.

**empfand** prät ⊏> empfinden.

**Empfang** (pl Empfänge) der - 1. [Erhalt - von Brief, Ware] receipt; etw in ~ nehmen to receive sthg; ein Paket für die Nachbarn in ~ nehmen to take a parcel for the neighbours - 2. [Begrüßung] welcome; jn in ~ nehmen fam to welcome sb - 3. [Veranstaltung, Rezeption & TV] reception.

**empfangen** (präs empfängt; prät empfing; perf hat empfangen) vt - 1. [gen] to receive - 2. [begrüßen] to greet; Gäste ~ to receive visitors.

**Empfänger** (pl -) der - 1. [Gerät] receiver - 2. [Adressat] addressee; [von Arbeitslosengeld] recipient.

**Empfängerin** (pl -nen) die [Adressat] addressee; [von Arbeitslosengeld] recipient.

**empfänglich** adj: (für etw) ~ sein to be susceptible (to sthg).

**Empfänglichkeit** die susceptibility.

**Empfängnis** die conception.

**empfängnisverhütend** adj contraceptive.

**Empfängnisverhütung** die contraception.

**Empfangslbescheinigung** die acknowledgement of receipt.

**Empfangslchef** der receptionist.

**Empfangsldame** die receptionist.

**empfängt** präs ⊏> empfangen.

**empfehlen** (präs empfiehlt; prät empfahl;

*perf* hat empfohlen) *vt* to recommend; jm ~, etw zu tun to recommend that sb do sthg; jm etw (wärmstens ODER sehr) ~ to recommend sthg (highly) to sb.
◆ sich empfehlen *ref* - **1.** [sich anbieten] to be recommended; es empfiehlt sich, etw zu tun it is advisable to do sthg - **2.** *geh* [sich verabschieden] to take one's leave.

**empfehlenswert** *adj* - **1.** [gut] recommendable - **2.** [ratsam] advisable.

**Empfehlung** (*pl* -en) *die* - **1.** [Ratschlag] recommendation; auf js ~ hin, auf ~ von jm on sb's recommendation - **2.** [Beurteilung] reference - **3.** *geh* [Gruß] regards (*pl*).

**Empfehlungslschreiben** *das* reference.

**empfiehlt** *präs* ▷ empfehlen.

**empfinden** (*prät* empfand; *perf* hat empfunden) *vt* to feel; etw als Kränkung ~ to take offence at sthg.

**Empfinden** *das* feeling; das ~ für Gut und Böse the sense of good and evil; für ODER nach mein ~ if you ask me.

**empfindlich** *adj* - **1.** [Haut, Film, Gemüt] sensitive - **2.** [Gesundheit, Person] delicate; gegen etw ~ sein to be susceptible to sthg - **3.** [Strafe, Verlust] severe <> *adv* - **1.** [verletzlich] sensitively; ~ auf etw (A) reagieren to be touchy about sthg - **2.** [merklich] severely; jn ~ treffen to hurt sb badly - **3.** [sehr - kalt] bitterly.

**Empfindlichkeit** *die* - **1.** [von Haut, Film, Gemüt] sensitivity - **2.** [von Person] susceptibility - **3.** [von Material, Gemüt] delicacy.

**empfindsam** *adj* - **1.** [zartfühlend] sensitive - **2.** [sentimental] sentimental.

**Empfindsamkeit** *die* - **1.** [von Personen - Mitgefühl] sensitivity; [ - Sentimentalität] sentimentality - **2.** [Epoche] sentimentalism.

**Empfindung** (*pl* -en) *die* - **1.** [Wahrnehmung] sensation - **2.** [Emotion] feeling.

**empfindungslos** *adj* - **1.** [Mensch] insensitive - **2.** [Bein, Arm] numb.

**empfing** *prät* ▷ empfangen.

**empfohlen** *pp* ▷ empfehlen.

**empf. Preis** (*abk für* empfohlener Preis) MRP.

**empfunden** *pp* ▷ empfinden.

**empirisch** *adj* empirical <> *adv* empirically.

**empor** *adv geh* up.

**empören** *vt* to outrage.
◆ sich empören *ref*: sich über etw (A) ~ to be outraged by sthg.

**empörend** *adj* outrageous.

**emporlkommen** (*perf* ist emporgekommen) *vi* (unreg) *geh* - **1.** [hochkommen] to come up - **2.** [vorankommen] to get on.

**Emporkömmling** (*pl* -e) *der abw* upstart.

**emporlragen** *vi geh* to rise up.

**empört** *adj* outraged.

**Empörung** *die* outrage.

**emsig** *adj* industrious; [Biene] busy; [Treiben] bustling <> *adv* industriously.

**Enddreißiger, in** (*mpl* -; *fpl* -nen) *der, die* man in his late thirties (*f* woman in her late thirties).

**Ende** (*pl* -n) *das* - **1.** [gen] end; ~ März at the end of March; ein ~ haben to stop; zu ~ sein to be over; zu ~ gehen to come to an end; ein ~ nehmen to be over; kein ~ nehmen to go on and on; einer Sache (D) ein ~ machen ODER bereiten *geh* to put an end to sthg; ein böses ODER kein gutes ~ nehmen to come to a bad end; kein ~ finden (können) not (to be able) to stop; am ~ der Welt in the back of beyond; bis ans ~ der Welt to the ends of the earth; etw am verkehrten ~ anfassen *fig* to approach sthg the wrong way round - **2.** *fam* [Wegstrecke]: es ist noch ein ganzes ~ it's still quite a way - **3.** *RW*: am ~ sein [körperlich] to be completely exhausted; [nervlich] to be at the end of one's tether *Br* ODER rope *Am*; mit etw am ~ sein: ich bin mit meinen Kräften am ~ I'm completely exhausted; mit seiner Geduld am ~ sein to have run out of patience; mit seiner Weisheit am ~ sein to be at one's wit's end; das ~ vom Lied war ... in the end ...; das dicke ~ kommt noch *fam* the worst is yet to come.
◆ am Ende *adv* in the end.
◆ letzten Endes *adv* - **1.** [am Schluss] in the end - **2.** [im Grunde genommen] ultimately, in the final analysis.

**Endeffekt** *der*: im ~ in the end.

**enden** (*perf* hat/ist geendet) *vi* - **1.** (hat) [zu Ende gehen] to end; der Zug endet in Köln the train terminates in Cologne; gut/schlecht ~ to have a happy/an unhappy ending; nicht ~ wollend unending - **2.** (hat, ist) [sterben] to meet one's end; [schließlich landen]: im Gefängnis ~ to end up in prison.

**Endlergebnis** *das* end result.

**endgültig** *adj* final; [Antwort] definitive; [Beweis] conclusive <> *adv* finally; [erklären] definitively.

**Endivie** [ɛn'diːvjə] (*pl* -n) *die* endive.

**endlich** *adv* - **1.** [nach langem Warten] at last; wann kommst du denn ~? so when are you finally going to come? - **2.** [am Ende] finally; um neun erreichten wir ~ das Ziel we eventually got there at nine <> *adj* finite.

**Endlichkeit** *die* finite nature.

**endlos** *adj* endless <> *adv* interminably; [dauern] for ages.

**Endlprodukt** *das* final ODER end product.

**Endlrunde** *die* finals (*pl*); [bei Rennen] final lap.

**Endlsilbe** *die* final syllable.

**End|spiel** *das* final.

**End|spurt** *der* final spurt.

**End|station** *die* terminus.

**End|summe** *die* (final) total.

**Endung** (*pl* -en) *die* ending.

**End|verbraucher, in** *der, die* end user.

**Energie** (*pl* -n) *die* energy.

**Energiebedarf** *der (ohne pl)* energy requirements (*pl*).

**Energie|bündel** *das* bundle of energy.

**energiegeladen** *adj* dynamic.

**Energie|krise** *die* energy crisis.

**Energiepolitik** *die* energy policy.

**energiepolitisch** *adj* energy policy (*vor Subst*).

**Energie|quelle** *die* energy source.

**Energie|verbrauch** *der* energy consumption.

**Energie|versorgung** *die* energy supply.

**energisch** *adj* forceful <> *adv* forcefully.

**eng** *adj* - **1.** [Raum] narrow; **im Auto ist es ~** it's cramped in the car - **2.** [Kleidung] tight - **3.** [Auslegung, Interpretation] narrow; **im ~eren Sinn (des Wortes)** in the narrowest sense (of the word) - **4.** [Beziehung, Freund, Verwandte] close <> *adv* - **1.** [dicht gedrängt] close together; **~ schreiben** to have cramped handwriting - **2.** [anliegen] tightly - **3.** [auslegen, interpretieren] narrowly; **die Dinge nicht so ~ sehen** *fam fig* not to be so strict about things - **4.** [nah] close; **~ mit jm befreundet sein** to be close friends with sb.

**Engagement** [ãgaʒə'mãː] (*pl* -s) *das* - **1.** [Einsatz] commitment - **2.** [Anstellung] engagement.

**engagieren** [ãga'ʒiːrən] *vt* to engage.
&#10148; **sich engagieren** *ref:* **sie engagiert sich politisch** she's very involved in politics; **sich für jn/etw ~** to show commitment to sb/sthg.

**engagiert** [ãga'ʒiːɐt] *adj* [Mensch, Mitarbeit] committed; [Film, Roman] with a clear message <> *adv* [handeln] with commitment.

**eng anliegend** *adj* tight-fitting, close-fitting.

**eng befreundet** *adj:* **~ sein** to be close friends.

**Enge** *die* - **1.** [Schmalheit] narrowness - **2.** [Platzmangel] crampedness; **jn in die ~ treiben** *fig* to corner sb.

**Engel** (*pl* -) *der* angel.

**Engelsgeduld** *die:* **eine ~ haben** to have the patience of a saint.

**England** *nt* England.

**Engländer, in** (*mpl* -; *fpl* -nen) *der, die* Englishman (*f* Englishwoman); **die ~** the English.

**englisch** *adj* English <> *adv* [sprechen] in English.

**Englisch(e)** *das* English; **auf/in ~** in English.

**Eng|pass** *der* - **1.** [Verengung] narrow pass - **2.** [Mangel] bottleneck.

**engstirnig** *abw adj* narrow-minded <> *adv* narrow-mindedly.

**Enkel, in** (*mpl* -; *fpl* -nen) *der, die* grandson (*f* granddaughter); **unsere ~** our grandchildren.

**Enkel|kind** *das* grandchild.

**enorm** *adj* enormous, immense <> *adv* tremendously, terribly; **sich ~ anstrengen** to make a tremendous effort.

**Ensemble** [ã'sãːbl̩] (*pl* -s) *das* ensemble.

**entarten** (*perf* ist entartet) *vi* to degenerate.

**entbehren** *vt* - **1.** [verzichten auf] to do without - **2.** *geh* [vermissen] to miss <> *vi:* **einer Sache** (*G*) **~ geh** to lack sthg.

**entbehrlich** *adj* dispensable.

**Entbehrung** (*pl* -en) *die* privation.

**entbinden** (*prät* entband; *perf* hat entbunden) *vt* - **1.** [befreien] **jn von etw** ODER **einer Sache** (*G*) **~** to discharge sb from sthg - **2.** [Frau] **sie ist von einem gesunden Mädchen entbunden worden** she has given birth to a healthy girl <> *vi* [gebären] to give birth.

**Entbindung** (*pl* -en) *die* - **1.** [Befreiung] discharge - **2.** [Gebären] delivery.

**entblößen** *vt* - **1.** [Körper] to bare, to expose - **2.** [Mensch] to expose; [Gedanken, Gefühle] to reveal.
&#10148; **sich entblößen** *ref* [sich ausziehen] to undress; [Exhibitionist] to expose o.s.

**entdecken** *vt* - **1.** [gen] to discover - **2.** [Fehler] to detect; [Urheber] to identify; **kannst du ihn ~?** can you make him out?

**Entdecker, in** (*mpl* -; *fpl* -nen) *der, die* discoverer.

**Ent|deckung** *die* discovery.

**Entdeckungs|reise** *die* expedition.

**Ente** (*pl* -n) *die* - **1.** [Tier] duck; **eine lahme ~** *fam abw* & *fig* a lame duck - **2.** [Zeitungsmeldung] hoax - **3.** *fam* [Auto] Citroën 2 CV.

**entehren** *vt* to dishonour.

**enteignen** *vt* [Mensch] to dispossess; [Vermögen] to expropriate.

**Enteignung** (*pl* -en) *die* [von Mensch] dispossession; [von Vermögen] expropriation.

**enterben** *vt* to disinherit.

**entern** *vt* to board.

**Entertainer** [ˈɛntəteːnɐ] (pl -) der entertainer.

**entfachen** vt geh - **1.** [Feuer, Glut, Begeisterung] to kindle; [Brand] to start - **2.** [Krieg, Wut] to provoke.

**entfahren** (präs entfährt; prät entfuhr; perf ist entfahren) vi: ihr entfuhr ein Schrei she let out a cry.

**entfallen** (präs entfällt; prät entfiel; perf ist entfallen) vi - **1.** [vergessen]: ihr Name ist mir ~ her name has slipped my mind - **2.** [sich verteilen]: auf jn ~ to fall ODER go to sb - **3.** geh [herunterfallen]: das Messer entfiel ihr the knife slipped from her hand.

**entfalten** vt - **1.** [öffnen] to unfold - **2.** [entwickeln] to develop - **3.** [zeigen] to display, to show; [Aktivität] to launch into - **4.** [erläutern] to set out.

➤ **sich entfalten** ref - **1.** [Blüte, Fallschirm] to open; [Segel] to unfurl - **2.** [sich verwirklichen] to develop.

**Entfaltung** (pl -en) die - **1.** [von Persönlichkeit] development; [von Aktivität] launching into; etw zur ~ bringen to develop sthg to its full potential; zur ~ kommen to develop fully - **2.** [von Blüte] opening.

**entfernen** vt - **1.** [beseitigen] to remove; ein Kind von seiner Mutter ~ to take a child away from its mother - **2.** [wegführen]: jn aus seinem Amt ~ to remove sb from office - **3.** EDV to delete.

➤ **sich entfernen** ref [sich wegbegeben] to leave; sich von etw ~ [weggehen] to leave sthg; [von Pfad, Thema] to stray from sthg.

**entfernt** adj - **1.** [fort]: wenige Kilometer von hier ~ a few kilometres away ODER from here; weit ~ a long way away - **2.** [abgelegen] remote; weit davon ~ sein, etw zu tun not to have the slightest intention of doing sthg - **3.** [Verwandte] distant; [Ähnlichkeit] vague - **4.** [Ahnung] faint, vague <> adv - **1.** [weitläufig] distantly, remotely - **2.** [blass, gering] vaguely, faintly.

➤ **Entfernteste** das: nicht im Entferntesten hatte ich daran gedacht I didn't have the slightest intention of doing it.

**Entfernung** (pl -en) die - **1.** [Distanz] distance; in einer ~ von 2 km at a distance of 2 km; aus der ~ zugucken to look on from afar - **2.** [Beseitigung] removal - **3.** [Weggehen] departure.

**entfesseln** vt [Leidenschaft] to unleash; [Krieg, Diskussion] to provoke.

**entfliehen** (prät entfloh; perf ist entflohen) vi [aus Gefangenschaft] to escape; einer Sache (D) ~ [Trubel, Lärm] to flee from sthg.

**entfremden** vt - **1.** [Person] to alienate; jn jm/einer Sache ~ to alienate ODER estrange sb from sb/sthg - **2.** [zweckentfremden]: eine Flasche als Vase ~ to use a bottle as a vase.

➤ **sich entfremden** ref [Person]: sich jm/einer Sache ~ to become alienated ODER estranged from sb/sthg.

**entführen** vt [Mensch] to kidnap; [Flugzeug] to hijack.

**Entführer, in** der, die [von Menschen] kidnapper; [von Flugzeug] hijacker.

**Entführung** die [von Menschen] kidnapping; [von Flugzeug] hijacking.

**entgegen** präp (+ D) contrary to; sie kam ihm ~ she was coming towards him.

**entgegenbringen** vt (unreg): jm Verständnis/Vertrauen ~ to show ODER display understanding towards/trust in sb.

**entgegengehen** (perf ist entgegengegangen) vi (unreg): jm/einer Sache ~ to approach sb/sthg; dem Ende ~ to draw to a close.

**entgegengesetzt** adj [Richtung, Seite, Meinung] opposite; ~e Ansichten conflicting ODER opposing opinions.

**entgegenhalten** vt (unreg) - **1.** [nähern]: jm etw ~ to hold sthg out to sb - **2.** [entgegnen]: dem ist nichts entgegenzuhalten you can't argue with that; dem kann man ~, dass ... that can be countered with the argument that ...

**entgegenkommen** (perf ist entgegengekommen) vi (unreg) - **1.** [herankommen]: jm ~ to approach sb - **2.** [auf Wünsche eingehen]: mit den neuen Vorschlägen kommen wir ihnen sehr entgegen our new proposals go a long way to meeting their demands; js Wünschen/Erwartungen ~ to meet sb's wishes/expectations.

**Entgegenkommen** das goodwill; zu großem ~ bereit sein to be ready to make major concessions.

**entgegenkommend** adj [Mensch, Verhalten] accommodating, obliging <> adv accommodatingly, obligingly.

**entgegennehmen** vt (unreg) to accept.

**entgegensehen** vi (unreg): jm ~ to look in sb's direction; einer Sache (D) ~ to await sthg.

**entgegensetzen** vt: jm/etw Widerstand ~ to resist sb/sthg; einer Behauptung Beweise ~ to produce evidence that contradicts a statement; diesen Vorwürfen habe ich nichts entgegenzusetzen I have no answer to these reproaches.

**entgegenstehen** vi (unreg): einer Sache (D) ~ to stand in sthg's way; dem steht nichts entgegen there is no objection to that.

**entgegenstellen** vt to set against.

➤ **sich entgegenstellen** ref: sich jm/einer Sache ~ to resist sb/sthg.

**entgegentreten** (perf ist entgegengetreten) *vi (unreg)*: jm ~ to approach sb; einer Sache *(D)* ~ to face sthg.

**entgegnen** *vt* [antworten] to reply; [barsch] to retort.

**Entgegnung** (*pl* -en) *die* [Antwort] reply; [barsch] retort.

**entgehen** (*prät* entging; *perf* ist entgangen) *vi* - **1.** [entkommen]: einer Sache *(D)* ~ to escape sthg - **2.** [unbemerkt bleiben]: dieser Fehler ist mir entgangen this mistake escaped my notice.

**entgeistert** *adj* dumbfounded ◇ *adv* aghast.

**Entgelt** (*pl* -e) *das* payment.

**entgiften** *vt* to detoxify.

**entgleisen** (*perf* ist entgleist) *vi* - **1.** [Zug] to be derailed - **2.** [taktlos sein] to commit a faux pas.

**Entgleisung** (*pl* -en) *die* - **1.** [von Zügen] derailment - **2.** [Taktlosigkeit] faux pas.

**entgleiten** (*prät* entglitt; *perf* ist entglitten) *vi*: jm ODER js Händen ~ to slip from sb's hands.

**enthaaren** *vt* to remove the hair from; [mit Wachs] to wax.

**enthalten** (*präs* enthält; *prät* enthielt; *perf* hat enthalten) *vt* to contain.
➤ **sich enthalten** *ref* - **1.** [nicht abstimmen]: sich der Stimme ~ to abstain - **2.** *geh* [auf etw verzichten] to abstain; sich einer Sache (G) ~ to abstain from sthg; sich einer Antwort ~ to refrain from answering.

**enthaltsam** *adj* abstemious; sexuell ~ sein to abstain from sex ◇ *adv* abstemiously.

**Enthaltsamkeit** *die* abstinence.

**Ent|haltung** *die* abstention.

**entheben** (*prät* enthob; *perf* hat enthoben) *vt* *geh*: jn eines Amtes ~ to relieve sb of a post; jn einer Pflicht ~ to release sb from a duty.

**enthemmen** *vt* to disinhibit.

**enthüllen** *vt* - **1.** [Denkmal, Gemälde] to unveil - **2.** [Wahrheit, Geheimnis] to reveal.
➤ **sich enthüllen** *ref* [Wahrheit, Geheimnis] to be revealed; sich als etw ~ to reveal o.s. to be sthg.

**Enthüllung** (*pl* -en) *die* - **1.** [von Denkmal, Gemälde] unveiling - **2.** [von Wahrheit, Geheimnis] revelation.

**Enthusiasmus** *der* enthusiasm.

**enthusiastisch** *adj* enthusiastic ◇ *adv* enthusiastically.

**entjungfern** *vt* to deflower.

**entkalken** *vt* to descale.

**entkernen** *vt* [Apfel] to core; [Kirsche, Pfirsich] to stone, to pit *Am;* [Zitrusfrüchte] to remove the seeds from.

**entkleiden** *vt* to undress.

➤ **sich entkleiden** *ref* to get undressed.

**entkommen** (*präs* entkam; *perf* ist entkommen) *vi* to escape; jm ~ to elude sb.

**entkräftet** *adj* [kraftlos] exhausted.

**entkrampfen** *vt* [auflockern - Körper] to relax; [ - Atmosphäre, Situation] to ease.
➤ **sich entkrampfen** *ref* to relax.

**entladen** (*präs* entlädt; *prät* entlud; *perf* hat entladen) *vt* [Lkw, Waffe] to unload.
➤ **sich entladen** *ref* - **1.** [Gewitter] to break - **2.** [Wut, Aggressionen] to erupt - **3.** [Batterie] to discharge.

**entlang** *präp* along: die Straße ~, ~ der Straße along the road ◇ *adv:* am Fluss ~ along the river.

**entlang|fahren** (*perf* ist entlanggefahren) *vi* & *vt (unreg)* - **1.** [fahren]: etw *(A)* ODER an etw *(D)* ~ to drive along sthg - **2.** [mit Finger] to follow.

**entlang|gehen** (*perf* ist entlanggegangen) *vi* & *vt (unreg)*: etw *(A)* ODER an etw *(D)* ~ to go along sthg.

**entlang|laufen** (*perf* ist entlanggelaufen) *vi* & *vt (unreg)* - **1.** [laufen]: etw *(A)* ODER an etw *(D)* ~ to run along sthg - **2.** [Grenze]: an etw *(D)* ~ to run along sthg; der Bach läuft hier ~ the river runs along here.

**entlarven** [ɛntˈlarfn̩] *vt* to expose.

**entlassen** (*präs* entlässt; *prät* entließ; *perf* hat entlassen) *vt* - **1.** [Kranken, Soldat] to discharge; [Gefangenen] to release - **2.** [kündigen] to sack.

**Entlassung** (*pl* -en) *die* - **1.** [aus dem Krankenhaus, aus der Armee] discharge; [aus dem Gefängnis] release - **2.** [Kündigung] redundancy; [Aktion] sacking.

**Entlassungs|feier** *die* school-leaving party.

**entlasten** *vt* - **1.** [von einer Belastung befreien] to relieve the strain on; [Gewissen] to ease - **2.** RECHT to exonerate - **3.** WIRTSCH: sein Konto ~ to reduce one's overdraft.

**Entlastung** (*pl* -en) *die* - **1.** RECHT exoneration - **2.** [Mindern von Belastung] relief; [von Gewissen] easing.

**entlaufen** (*präs* entläuft; *prät* entlief; *perf* ist entlaufen) *vi* to run away, to escape; jm ~ to run away from sb.

**entledigen** ➤ **sich entledigen** *ref geh:* sich einer Sache (G) ~ [sich von etw befreien] to rid o.s. of sthg; [sich ausziehen] to remove sthg; [Aufgabe, Pflicht] to discharge sthg.

**entleeren** *vt* to empty.
➤ **sich entleeren** *ref* to empty.

**entlegen** *adj* remote.

**entleihen** (*prät* entlieh; *perf* hat entliehen) *vt* to borrow; etw von jm ~ to borrow sthg from sb.

**entlocken** *vt:* jm etw ~ to coax sthg out of sb.

**entlüften** *vt* to ventilate.

**entmachten** *vt* to remove from power.

**Entmachtung** (*pl* -en) *die* removal from power.

**entmilitarisieren** *vt* to demilitarize.

**Entmilitarisierung** (*pl* -en) *die* demilitarization.

**entmündigen** *vt:* jn ~ to declare sb unfit to manage his/her own affairs.

**Entmündigung** (*pl* -en) *die certification that a person is unfit to manage his/her own affairs.*

**entmutigen** *vt* to discourage, to dishearten.

**Entnahme** (*pl* -n) *die* removal; [von Geld, Blut] drawing.

**entnehmen** (*präs* entnimmt; *prät* entnahm; *perf* hat entnommen) *vt:* etw aus etw ~ [gen] to remove sthg from sthg; [Geld] to withdraw sthg from sthg; [schließen] to deduce sthg from sthg.

**entnervt** *adj:* ~ sein to have reached the end of one's tether *Br ODER* rope *Am.*

**entpuppen** ⇔ **sich entpuppen** *ref:* sich als etw ~ to turn out to be sthg.

**entrahmt** *adj* skimmed.

**enträtseln** *vt* [Geheimschrift] to decipher; [Geheimnis] to unravel.

**entreißen** (*prät* entriss; *perf* hat entrissen) *vt* - 1. [wegnehmen] to snatch away - 2. [retten]: jn dem Tod ~ to snatch sb from the jaws of death.

**entrichten** *vt amt* to pay.

**entrinnen** (*prät* entrann; *perf* ist entronnen) *vi geh:* jm/einer Sache ~ to escape from sb/sthg.

**entrümpeln** *vt* to clear out.

**entrüsten** *vt* to incense.
⇔ **sich entrüsten** *ref:* sich über jn/etw ~ to be incensed by sb/sthg.

**entrüstet** *adj* indignant ⇔ *adv* indignantly.

**Entrüstung** *die* indignation.

**entsagen** *vi geh:* einer Sache (D) ~ to forego sthg.

**entschädigen** *vt* to compensate; jn für etw ~ to compensate sb for sthg.

**Entlschädigung** *die* compensation.

**entschärfen** *vt* - 1. [Bombe, Debatte] to defuse - 2. [Kritik] to take the sting out of.

**entscheiden** (*prät* entschied; *perf* hat entschieden) *vi:* über etw (A) ~ to decide on sthg ⇔ *vt* [Streit] to settle; [Fußballspiel] to decide.
⇔ **sich entscheiden** *ref* - 1. [sich entschließen] to decide; sich für/gegen jn/etw ~ to decide on/

against sb/sthg; sich nicht ~ können to be unable to decide *ODER* make up one's mind - 2. [sich herausstellen]: es wird sich ~ it will be decided.

**entscheidend** *adj* [Problem, Frage] decisive; [Stimme, Tor] deciding ⇔ *adv* decisively.

**Entlscheidung** *die* decision; [von Jury] verdict; [von Gericht, Ausschuss] ruling; eine ~ treffen to make *ODER* take a decision; zu einer ~ kommen to reach a decision.

**entschieden** *pp* ▷ **entscheiden** ⇔ *adj* [Verteidiger] staunch, steadfast; [Gegner] firm, strong ⇔ *adv* firmly, emphatically; das geht ~ zu weit! that's going far too far!

**Entschiedenheit** *die* determination; mit aller ~ emphatically.

**entschlacken** *vt* to purge.

**entschlafen** (*präs* entschläft; *prät* entschlief; *perf* ist entschlafen) *vi geh* to pass away.

**entschließen** (*prät* entschloss; *perf* hat entschlossen) ⇔ **sich entschließen** *ref* to decide; sich zur Annahme des Angebots ~ to decide to accept the offer.

**entschlossen** *pp* ▷ **entschließen** ⇔ *adj* determined, resolute; (fest) ~ sein, etw zu tun to be (absolutely) determined to do sthg ⇔ *adv* without hesitation; kurz ~ without a moment's hesitation.

**Entschlossenheit** *die* determination, resolution.

**entschlüpfen** (*perf* ist entschlüpft) *vi* - 1. [weglaufen]: (jm) ~ to slip away (from sb) - 2. [entfahren]: die Bemerkung ist mir entschlüpft the remark just slipped out.

**Entlschluss** *der* decision; einen ~ fassen to make *ODER* take a decision.

**entschlüsseln** *vt* to decipher.

**entschlussfreudig** *adj* decisive ⇔ *adv* decisively.

**Entschlusskraft** *die* determination.

**entschulden** *vt* [Betrieb] to free of debt.

**entschuldigen** *vt* to excuse; entschuldige bitte! (I'm) sorry! ; ~ Sie bitte! [vor Frage, Bitte] excuse me!; [tut mir leid!] (I'm) sorry!
⇔ **sich entschuldigen** *ref* to apologize; sich für etw ~ to apologize for sthg; sich bei jm ~ to apologize to sb.

**Entschuldigung** (*pl* -en) *die* - 1. [Rechtfertigung] excuse - 2. *schule* note *(from one's parents or a doctor)* - 3. [Bitte um Verzeihung] apology - 4. [Nachsicht]: jn um ~ bitten to beg sb's pardon ⇔ *interj* [vor Frage, Bitte] excuse me!; [tut mir leid!] (I'm) sorry!

**Entschuldung** (*pl* -en) *die* [von Entwicklungsland] debt relief.

**entschwinden** (*prät* entschwand; *perf* ist entschwunden) *vi geh* to disappear.

**entsenden** (*prät* entsandte ODER entsendete; *perf* hat entsandt ODER entsendet) *vt* to send.

**entsetzen** *vt* to horrify.
➡ sich entsetzen *ref* to be horrified; sich über etw (A) ~ to be horrified at sthg.

**Entsetzen** *das* horror; zu js ~ to sb's horror.

**entsetzlich** *adj* - **1.** [schrecklich] horrible - **2.** [stark] terrible <> *adv* [sehr] terribly.

**entsetzt** *adj* horrified; über etw (A) ~ sein to be horrified at sthg <> *adv* in horror, aghast.

**entsichern** *vt* to release the safety catch of.

**entsinnen** (*prät* entsann; *perf* hat entsonnen) ➡ sich entsinnen *ref*: sich js/einer Sache ~ to remember sb/sthg.

**entsorgen** *vt* - **1.** [wegwerfen] to dispose of - **2.** [von Abfallstoffen befreien] to dispose of waste from.

**Entsorgung** (*pl* -en) *die* waste disposal.

**entspannen** *vt* to relax.
➡ sich entspannen *ref* - **1.** [Person] to relax - **2.** [Situation] to ease.

**entspannt** *adj* relaxed; [politische Lage] calm.

**Entspannung** *die* - **1.** [Erholung] relaxation - **2.** [von Situationen] reduction of tension; POL détente.

**Entspannungslpolitik** *die* policy of détente.

**Entspannungslübung** *die* relaxation exercise.

**entspinnen** (*prät* entspann; *perf* hat entsponnen) ➡ sich entspinnen *ref* to develop.

**entsprechen** (*präs* entspricht; *prät* entsprach; *perf* hat entsprochen) *vi* - **1.** [genügen]: einer Sache (D) ~ [Tatsachen] to correspond to sthg; [Erwartungen, Anforderungen] to meet sthg; 100° Celsius ~ 212° Fahrenheit 100° Celsius is equivalent to 212° Fahrenheit; einem Zweck ~ to fulfil a purpose - **2.** [nachkommen]: einer Sache (D) ~ to comply with sthg.

**entsprechend** *adj* - **1.** [angemessen, zuständig] appropriate - **2.** [dementsprechend] corresponding <> *adv* [angemessen] appropriately; [dementsprechend] correspondingly <> *präp:* einer Sache (D) ~, ~ einer Sache (D) in accordance with sthg.

**Entsprechung** (*pl* -en) *die* - **1.** [Ähnlichkeit] correspondence - **2.** [Analogie] equivalent.

**entspringen** (*prät* entsprang; *perf* ist entsprungen) *vi* - **1.** [Fluss] to rise - **2.** [entstehen aus]: einer Sache (D) ~ to arise from sthg - **3.** [entfliehen]: aus etw ~ to escape from sthg.

**entstammen** (*perf* ist entstammt) *vi:* einer Sache (D) ~ to come from sthg.

**entstehen** (*prät* entstand; *perf* ist entstanden) *vi* - **1.** [geschaffen werden] to come into being; [Gebäude] to be built; [Kunstwerk] to be created; [Beziehung] to develop; [Roman] to be written; [Streit] to arise; aus etw ODER durch etw ~ to come about as a result of sthg - **2.** [Schaden, Kosten] to be incurred.

**Entstehung** (*pl* -en) *die* - **1.** [eines Gebäudes] building; [eines Kunstwerkes] creation; [des Lebens] origins (*pl*) - **2.** [von Kosten, Schaden] incurring.

**entstellen** *vt* - **1.** [Person] to disfigure - **2.** [Sachverhalt] to distort.

**Entlstellung** *die* - **1.** [von Personen] disfigurement - **2.** [von Sachverhalten] distortion.

**entstören** *vt* to free from interference.

**enttäuschen** *vt* to disappoint; [Hoffnungen] to dash <> *vi* to be disappointing.

**enttäuscht** *adj* disappointed; [Hoffnungen] dashed; von ODER über etw (A) ~ sein to be disappointed with sthg; von jm ~ sein to be disappointed in ODER with sb <> *adv* disappointed.

**Entltäuschung** *die* disappointment.

**entwachsen** [ɛnt'vaksn̩] (*präs* entwächst; *prät* entwuchs; *perf* ist entwachsen) *vi* to outgrow.

**entwaffnen** *vt eigtl* & *fig* to disarm.

**Entlwarnung** *die* all-clear (signal).

**entwässern** *vt* to drain; MED to dehydrate.

**entweder** ➡ entweder ... oder *konj* either ... or.

**entweichen** (*prät* entwich; *perf* ist entwichen) *vi* to escape.

**entwenden** *vt geh:* jm etw ~ to steal sthg from sb.

**entwerfen** (*präs* entwirft; *prät* entwarf; *perf* hat entworfen) *vt* [Möbelstück, Kleidungsstück] to design; [Text] to draft; [Programm] to plan.

**entwerten** *vt* - **1.** [Fahrkarte] to cancel, to validate - **2.** [Geld] to devalue.

**Entwerter** (*pl* -) *der* ticket validating machine.

**entwickeln** *vt* to develop; [Gase] to produce.
➡ sich entwickeln *ref* to develop; [Gase] to be produced; sich aus etw ~ to develop out of sthg; sich zu etw ~ to develop into sthg, to become sthg.

**Entwicklung** (*pl* -en) *die* - **1.** [Entfaltung, Ausarbeitung] development; in der ~ (sein) (to be) at the development stage - **2.** FOTO developing - **3.** [von Gasen] production.

**Entwicklungsdienst** *der* ≃ Voluntary Service Overseas *Br*, ≃ Peace Corps *Am*.

**entwicklungsfähig** adj: ~ **sein** to have potential.

**Entwicklungslhelfer, in** der, die overseas aid worker.

**Entwicklungslhilfe** die development aid.

**Entwicklungslland** das developing country.

**entwirren** vt eigtl & fig to unravel.

**entwischen** (perf ist **entwischt**) vi fam to make off; **jm ~** to give sb the slip.

**entwöhnen** vt to wean.

**entwürdigend** adj degrading <> adv degradingly.

**Entlwurf** der - **1.** [Zeichnung] blueprint - **2.** [Konzept] draft.

**entwurzeln** vt eigtl & fig to uproot.

**entzerren** vt - **1.** [Signal & FOTO] to remove distortion from - **2.** [strecken] to spread, to stagger.

**entziehen** (prät **entzog**; perf hat **entzogen**) vt: **jm etw ~** to withdraw sthg from sb; **einer Sache** (D) **etw ~** to draw ODER extract sthg from sthg.
➤ **sich entziehen** ref: **sich jm/einer Sache ~** to escape sb/sthg; **sich der Verantwortung ~** to evade responsibility; **das entzieht sich meiner Kenntnis** I don't know anything about that.

**Entziehungslkur** die detox.

**entziffern** vt to decipher.

**entzücken** vt to delight; **sie war von dem Gemälde entzückt** she thought the painting was delightful.

**Entzücken** das delight.

**entzückend** adj delightful, charming.

**Entzug** der withdrawal; **im ~ sein** to be in detox.

**Entzugslerscheinung** die withdrawal symptom.

**entlzünden** vt to light.
➤ **sich entzünden** ref - **1.** [brennen] to catch fire; TECH to ignite - **2.** MED to become inflamed - **3.** [entstehen]: **sich an etw** (D) **~** to be ignited by sthg.

**Entlzündung** die inflammation.

**entzündungshemmend** adj anti-inflammatory.

**entzwei** adj: ~ **sein** to be in pieces.

**entzweilgehen** (perf ist **entzweigegangen**) vi (unreg) to break in pieces.

**Enzian** (pl -e) der - **1.** [Pflanze] gentian - **2.** [Branntwein] gentian (bitter).

**Enzyklopädie** (pl -n) die encyclopedia.

**Enzym** (pl -e) das enzyme.

**Epidemie** (pl -n) die epidemic.

**epidemisch** adj epidemic.

**Epik** die [Gattung] narrative literature.

**Epilepsie** (pl -n) die epilepsy.

**Epileptiker, in** (mpl -; fpl -nen) der, die epileptic.

**epileptisch** adj epileptic.

**episch** adj - **1.** [Werk, Gattung] narrative - **2.** [lang] epic.

**Episode** (pl -n) die episode.

**Epoche** (pl -n) die period, era.
➤ **Epoche machend** adj epoch-making.

**Epos** (pl **Epen**) das epic.

**er** pron he [bei Sachen, Tieren] it; ~ **wars!** it was him!

**erachten** vt: **jn/etw als** ODER **für etw ~** to consider sb/sthg (to be) sthg.

**Erachten** das: **meinem ~ nach, nach meinem ~, meines ~s** in my opinion.

**erahnen** vt [im Dämmerlicht] to barely make out; [Absicht] to get an inkling of.

**erarbeiten** vt - **1.** [Stellung, Wissen] to acquire (through one's own efforts) - **2.** [Bericht, Programm] to draw up; **sich** (D) **etw ~** to acquire sthg (by one's own efforts).

**Erblanlage** die hereditary disposition.

**erbarmen** ➤ **sich erbarmen** ref geh: **sich js ~** to take pity on sb.

**Erbarmen** das mercy, compassion; **mit jm/etw ~ haben** to take pity on sb/sthg; **zum ~** pitiful.

**erbärmlich** adj - **1.** [armselig, unzureichend] wretched, terrible - **2.** abw [gemein] despicable - **3.** [sehr groß] terrible <> adv [sehr] terribly.

**erbarmungslos** adj merciless <> adv mercilessly.

**erbauen** vt - **1.** [errichten] to build - **2.** geh [erheben] to uplift.
➤ **sich erbauen** ref geh: **sich an etw** (D) **~** to be uplifted by sthg.

**Erbauer, in** (mpl -; fpl -nen) der, die builder.

**erbaulich** adj [Musik, Kunst] uplifting; **nicht ~** unedifying.

**erbaut** adj: **von etw** ODER **über etw** (A) **nicht ~ sein** to be unenthusiastic about sthg.

**Erbauung** die edification.

**Erbe** (pl -n) das - **1.** [Vermögen] inheritance - **2.** [geistiges Vermächtnis] legacy <> der heir.

**erben** vt to inherit <> vi to come into an inheritance.

**erbeuten** vt to capture (as booty).

**Erblfolge** die succession.

**Erbgut** das BIOL genetic make-up.

**Erbin** (pl -nen) die heiress.

**erbittert** *adj* [Kampf] fierce; [Feind] bitter ◇ *adv* fiercely.

**Erblkrankheit** *die* hereditary disease.

**erblassen** *vi geh* to go ODER turn pale.

**erbleichen** (*perf* ist erbleicht) *vi geh* to go ODER turn pale.

**erblich** *adj* hereditary ◇ *adv*: ~ belastet sein to have a hereditary condition.

**erblicken** *vt geh* to catch sight of.

**erblinden** (*perf* ist erblindet) *vi* to go blind.

**erblühen** (*perf* ist erblüht) *vi geh* to blossom.

**Erblmasse** *die* - **1.** BIOL genetic make-up - **2.** RECHT estate.

**erbost** *adj* angry; über jn/etw ~ sein to be angry with sb/about sthg ◇ *adv* angrily.

**erbrechen** (*präs* erbricht; *prät* erbrach; *perf* hat erbrochen) *vt* to vomit (up).
➤ sich erbrechen *ref* to vomit.

**Erbrechen** *das* vomiting.

**Erbrecht** *das* RECHT right of succession.

**erbringen** (*prät* erbrachte; *perf* hat erbracht) *vt* - **1.** [ergeben] to result in; [Geldsumme] to bring in; Leistung ~ to produce; eine notwendige Leistung ~ to do some necessary work - **2.** [Nachweis] to produce.

**Erbschaft** (*pl* -en) *die* inheritance.

**Erbschaftslsteuer** *die* inheritance tax.

**Erbschleicher, in** (*mpl* -; *fpl* -nen) *der, die* legacy-hunter.

**Erbse** (*pl* -n) *die* pea.

**Erbsenlsuppe** *die* pea soup.

**Erblstück** *das* heirloom.

**Erblteil** *das* share in ODER of an inheritance.

**Erdlball** *der* globe.

**Erdlbeben** *das* earthquake.

**Erdlbeere** *die* strawberry.

**Erdlboden** *der* - **1.** [Boden] ground, earth - **2.** RW: etw dem ~ gleichmachen to raze sthg to the ground; wie vom ~ verschluckt sein to seem to have vanished from the face of the earth.

**Erde** *die* - **1.** [Erdreich] soil, earth - **2.** [fester Boden] ground; zu ebener ~ at ground level; [wohnen] on the ground floor; auf der ~ bleiben *fig* to keep one's feet on the ground; etw aus der ~ stampfen *fam* [Gebäude] to build sthg overnight; unter der ~ sein ODER liegen to be dead and buried; jn unter die ~ bringen *fam* [begraben] to bury sb; du bringst mich noch unter die ~! you'll be the death of me! - **3.** [Welt] world; auf der ganzen ~ in the whole world; auf ~n *geh* on earth - **4.** [Planet] Earth.

**erden** *vt* ELEKTR to earth.

**erdenklich** *adj* conceivable, imaginable.

➤ alles Erdenkliche *adv*: alles Erdenkliche tun to do one's utmost.

**Erdlgas** *das* natural gas.

**Erdlgeschoss** *das* ground floor *Br*, first floor *Am*.

**erdig** *adj* - **1.** [Masse] of earth - **2.** [Geruch, Geschmack] earthy - **3.** [Hände, Schuhe] covered in soil.

**Erdlkabel** *das* underground cable.

**Erdlkugel** *die* globe.

**Erdlkunde** *die* geography.

**Erdlnuss** *die* peanut.

**Erdlöl** *das* (mineral) oil.
➤ Erdöl exportierend *adj* oil-exporting.

**Erdöllproduktion** *die* oil production.

**Erdreich** *das* earth, soil.

**erdreisten** ➤ sich erdreisten *ref geh*: sich ~, etw zu tun to have the audacity to do sthg.

**erdrosseln** *vt* to strangle.

**erdrücken** *vt* - **1.** [zu Tode drücken] to crush to death - **2.** [belasten] to overwhelm.

**erdrückend** *adj* overwhelming.

**Erdlrutsch** *der* landslide.

**Erdlteil** *der* continent.

**erdulden** *vt* to endure.

**ereifern** ➤ sich ereifern *ref* to get worked up; sich über etw (A) ~ to get worked up about sthg.

**ereignen** ➤ sich ereignen *ref* to happen; [Unfall] to occur.

**Ereignis** (*pl* -se) *das* event; ein freudiges ~ a happy event.

**ereignisreich** *adj* eventful.

**Eremit, in** (*mpl* -en; *fpl* -nen) *der, die* hermit.

**erfahren** (*präs* erfährt; *prät* erfuhr; *perf* hat erfahren) *vt* - **1.** [Kenntnis erhalten von] to learn; [hören] to hear; etw von jm ~ to hear sthg from sb; etw über jn/etw ~ to find out sthg about sb/sthg; etw durch jn/etw ~ to find out about sthg from sb/sthg - **2.** *geh* [erleben - Glück, Leid] to experience; [ - Veränderung] to undergo ◇ *adj* experienced.

**Erfahrung** (*pl* -en) *die* - **1.** [Kenntnis] experience (U); ~ besitzen ODER haben to have experience - **2.** [durch Nachforschen] etw in ~ bringen to find sthg out.

**Erfahrungsausltausch** *der* exchange of experiences.

**erfahrungsgemäß** *adv* judging from experience.

**erfassen** *vt* - **1.** [Bedeutung] to grasp, to understand - **2.** [Daten, Zahlen] to record - **3.** [mitreißen - von Fahrzeug] to drag along; [ - Wasser] to sweep along - **4.** [überkommen]: **Angst erfasste sie** she was overcome with fear.

**erfinden** (*prät* **erfand**; *perf* **hat erfunden**) *vt* to invent.

**Erfinder, in** (*mpl* -; *fpl* **-nen**) *der, die* inventor.

**erfinderisch** *adj* inventive.

**Erfindung** (*pl* **-en**) *die* - **1.** [Entwicklung] invention; **eine ~ machen** to invent something - **2.** [Ausgedachtes] fabrication.

**Erfolg** (*pl* **-e**) *der* success; **~ haben** to be successful; **von ~ gekrönt werden** ODER **sein** to be crowned with success; **mit ~** successfully.
➡ **Erfolg versprechend** *adj* promising.
➡ **viel Erfolg** *interj* good luck!

**erfolgen** (*perf* **ist erfolgt**) *vi* to ensue; **auf etw (A) ~** to follow sthg; **auf das Klingeln erfolgte keine Reaktion** there was no reaction to the doorbell.

**erfolglos** *adj* unsuccessful <> *adv* unsuccessfully.

**erfolgreich** *adj* successful <> *adv* successfully.

**Erfolgslchance** *die* chance of success.

**Erfolgslerlebnis** *das* feeling of success.

**Erfolgslzwang** *der* pressure to succeed.

**erforderlich** *adj* required; **für** ODER **zu etw ~ sein** to be required for sthg.

**erfordern** *vt* to require.

**Erfordernis** (*pl* **-se**) *das* requirement.

**erforschen** *vt* [Wissensgebiet] to study; [Land, Gelände] to explore; [Möglichkeiten] to investigate.

**Erlforschung** *die* [von Wissensgebiet] study; [von Land, Gelände] exploration; [von Möglichkeiten] investigation.

**erfragen** *vt* to ask.

**erfreuen** *vt* to please.
➡ **sich erfreuen** *ref:* **sich an etw (D) ~** to take pleasure in sthg; **sich einer Sache (G) ~** to enjoy sthg.
➡ **sehr erfreut** *interj* pleased to meet you!

**erfreulich** *adj* pleasing.

**erfreulicherweise** *adv* luckily.

**erfrieren** (*prät* **erfror**; *perf* **ist erfroren**) *vi* to freeze to death; [Blüten] to be killed by frost; **sich die Hände/Füße ~** to suffer frostbite in one's hands/feet.

**erfrischen** *vt* to refresh; [geistig] to stimulate.
➡ **sich erfrischen** *ref* to refresh o.s.; [sich waschen] to freshen (o.s.) up.

**erfrischend** *adj* refreshing; [Gespräch] stimulating.

**Erfrischung** (*pl* **-en**) *die* refreshment.

**erfüllen** *vt* - **1.** [Wunsch, Vertrag, Pflicht, Bedingungen] to fulfil - **2.** [füllen, ausfüllen] to fill.

➡ **sich erfüllen** *ref* [Wunsch] to come true.

**Erfüllung** *die* fulfilment; **in ~ gehen** to come true.

**Erfurt** *nt* Erfurt.

**ergänzen** *vt* - **1.** [vervollständigen] to complete - **2.** [hinzufügen] to add.
➡ **sich ergänzen** *ref* to complement one another.

**Ergänzung** (*pl* **-en**) *die* - **1.** [Vervollständigung] completion (U) - **2.** [Zusatz] supplement; [zu Gesetz] amendment.

**ergattern** *vt fam* to manage to get hold of.

**ergeben**[1] *geh adj* devoted <> *adv* devotedly.

**ergeben**[2] (*präs* **ergibt**; *prät* **ergab**; *perf* **hat ergeben**) *vt* [Ertrag] to produce; [herausfinden] to show; **eins mal eins ergibt eins** one times one is ODER makes one; **das ergibt keinen Sinn** that doesn't make any sense.
➡ **sich ergeben** *ref* - **1.** [erfolgen] to arise; **sich aus etw ~** to result from ODER be the result of sthg; **das hat sich so ~** it just turned out like that - **2.** [sich fügen, hingeben]: **sich in etw (A) ~** to resign o.s. to sthg - **3.** [kapitulieren] to surrender.

**Ergebenheit** *die* devotion.

**Ergebnis** (*pl* **-se**) *das* result.

**ergebnislos** *adj* unsuccessful.

**ergehen** (*prät* **erging**; *perf* **hat/ist ergangen**) *vi:* **wie ist es dir ergangen?** how did you get on?; **es ist jm gut/schlecht ergangen** sb got on well/badly; **etw über sich (A) ~ lassen** [negativ] to endure sthg; [positiv] to let sthg wash over one.
➡ **sich ergehen** *ref:* **sich in etw (D) ~** to indulge in sthg.

**ergiebig** *adj* [Quelle] rich; [Thema] fertile; [Gespräch] productive.

**ergießen** (*prät* **ergoss**; *perf* **hat ergossen**) ➡ **sich ergießen** *ref* to pour.

**ergreifen** (*prät* **ergriff**; *perf* **hat ergriffen**) *vt* - **1.** [packen, Macht] to seize - **2.** [festnehmen] to capture - **3.** [Initiative, Gelegenheit] to take; [Beruf] to take up; [Maßnahmen] to adopt - **4.** [erfassen] to overcome - **5.** [bewegen] to move.

**ergreifend** *adj* moving <> *adv* movingly.

**ergriffen** *pp* ⊳ **ergreifen** <> *adj:* **~ sein** to be (deeply) moved.

**ergründen** *vt* to discover.

**erhaben** *adj* - **1.** [feierlich, großartig] magnificent - **2.** [überlegen]: **über jn/etw ~ sein** to be above sb/sthg.

**Erhalt** *der amt* receipt.

**erhalten** (*präs* **erhält**; *prät* **erhielt**; *perf* **hat erhalten**) *vt* - **1.** [bekommen] to receive, to get

**- 2.** [bewahren] to preserve; **gut ~** in good condition; **ihr Witz ist ihr ~ blieben** she kept her sense of humour.

➤ **sich erhalten** *ref* [fortdauern] to endure.

**erhältlich** *adj* available.

**Erhaltung** *die* preservation; [von Tierarten] conservation.

**erhängen** *vt* to hang.

➤ **sich erhängen** *ref* to hang o.s.

**erhärten** *vt* [Aussage, These] to support; [Verdacht] to strengthen.

➤ **sich erhärten** *ref* [Verdacht] to increase.

**erheben** *(prät* **erhob;** *perf* **hat erhoben)** *vt* **- 1.** [Arm, Stimme, Glas] to raise **- 2.** [Gebühren] to charge; [Steuern] to levy **- 3.** [Daten] to gather **- 4.** [vorbringen]: **Anklage ~** to bring charges; **auf etw** *(A)* **Anspruch ~** to make a claim for sthg; **Einspruch ~** to raise an objection; **etw zum Prinzip ~** to make sthg a principle.

➤ **sich erheben** *ref* **- 1.** [aufstehen] to rise, to get up **- 2.** [losfliegen] to rise **- 3.** [rebellieren]: **sich gegen jn/etw ~** to rise up against sb/sthg **- 4.** [überragen]: **sich über jn/etw ~** to rise above sb/sthg.

**erheblich** *adj* considerable <> *adv* considerably.

**Erl|hebung** *die* **- 1.** [Hügel] rise **- 2.** [Aufstand] uprising **- 3.** [Untersuchung] survey **- 4.** [Kassieren] levy.

**erheitern** *vt* to amuse.

➤ **sich erheitern** *ref* to brighten.

**erhellen** *vt* **- 1.** [Raum] to light up **- 2.** [Umstände] to throw light upon.

➤ **sich erhellen** *ref* [hell werden] to brighten.

**erhitzen** *vt* **- 1.** [heiß machen] to heat **- 2.** [erregen] to excite.

➤ **sich erhitzen** *ref* **- 1.** [heiß werden] to get hot **- 2.** [sich erregen] to get excited.

**erhoffen** *vt* to anticipate; **sich** *(D)* **etw von jm ~** to expect sthg from sb.

**erhöhen** *vt* **- 1.** [Preis, Einsatz, Geschwindigkeit] to increase **- 2.** [Mauer] to raise.

➤ **sich erhöhen** *ref* [steigen] to increase.

**Erhöhung** *(pl* **-en)** *die* increase.

**erholen** ➤ **sich erholen** *ref:* **sich (von etw) ~** to recover (from sthg).

**erholsam** *adj* relaxing.

**Erholung** *die* [von Krankheit] recovery; [von Anstrengung] rest.

**erholungsbedürftig** *adj* in need of a rest.

**erinnern** *vt* **- 1.** [an Aufgabe, Termin]: **jn an etw** *(A)* **~** to remind sb about *ODER* of sthg **- 2.** [an Vergangenheit]: **jn an jn/etw ~** to remind sb of sb/sthg <> *vi* **- 1.** [an Aufgabe, Termin]: **ich muss daran ~, dass ...** I must remind you that ... **- 2.** [an Vergangenes]: **an jn/etw ~** to be reminiscent of sb/sthg.

➤ **sich erinnern** *ref* to remember; **sich an jn/ etw ~** to remember sb/sthg.

**Erinnerung** *(pl* **-en)** *die* **- 1.** [Eindruck] memory; **~ an etw** *(A)* memory of sthg **- 2.** [Gedenken]: **zur ~ an jn** in memory of sb; **jn/etw in guter/ schlechter ~ behalten** to have fond/bad memories of sb/sthg **- 3.** [Gedächtnis] memory **- 4.** [Andenken] memento.

**erkälten** ➤ **sich erkälten** *ref* to catch (a) cold.

**Erkältung** *(pl* **-en)** *die* cold.

**erkämpfen** *vt* to fight for; **sich** *(D)* **etw ~** to fight for sthg.

**erkennbar** *adj* recognizable.

**erkennen** *(prät* **erkannte;** *perf* **hat erkannt)** *vt* **- 1.** [sehen können] to make out **- 2.** [Person, Fehler] to recognize; **etw zu ~ geben** to reveal sthg; **sich zu ~ geben** to reveal one's identity **- 3.** [Irrtum] to acknowledge.

**erkenntlich** *adj:* **sich ~ zeigen** to show one's gratitude.

**Erkenntnis** *(pl* **-se)** *die* **- 1.** [Entdeckung, Einsicht] realization; **wissenschaftliche ~se** scientific discoveries; **zu der ~ kommen, dass ...** to realize that ... **- 2.** [Erkennen] knowledge.

**Erker** *(pl* **-)** *der* bay window.

**erklärbar** *adj* explicable; **nicht ~** inexplicable; **leicht ~** easily explained.

**erklären** *vt* **- 1.** [erläutern] to explain; **ich kann es mir nicht ~** I can't explain it **- 2.** [bezeichnen] to declare; [Absicht] to state; [Rücktritt] to announce; **etw für ungültig ~** to declare sthg invalid; **jn für tot ~** to pronounce sb dead; **jn für vermisst ~** to declare sb missing.

➤ **sich erklären** *ref* **- 1.** [sich äußern]: **sich (mit etw) einverstanden ~** to declare that one is in agreement (with sthg); **er erklärte sich bereit, es zu tun** he said he was willing to do it **- 2.** [sich ergeben]: **etw erklärt sich aus etw** sthg is explained by sthg; **das erklärt sich von selbst** that is self-explanatory.

**erklärlich** *adj* [Verhalten, Gründe] understandable; [Phänomen] explicable.

**Erklärung** *(pl* **-en)** *die* **- 1.** [Erläuterung] explanation **- 2.** [Mitteilung] statement; **eine ~ abgeben** to make a statement.

**erklingen** *(prät* **erklang;** *perf* **ist erklungen)** *vi* [Ton, Instrument] to sound; **am Schluss erklang die Nationalhymne** at the end the national anthem was played.

**erkranken** *(perf* **ist erkrankt)** *vi* to fall ill; **an etw** *(D)* **~** to contract sthg.

**Erkrankung** *(pl* **-en)** *die* illness.

**erkunden** *vt* to explore; *MIL* to reconnoitre.

**erkundigen** ➤ **sich erkundigen** *ref* to enquire; **sich nach jm ~** to ask after sb; **sich nach etw ~** to ask about sthg.

**Erkundigung** (*pl* -en) *die* enquiry; ~en über jn/etw einziehen *ODER* einholen to make enquiries about sb/sthg.

**erlahmen** (*perf* ist erlahmt) *vi* to flag.

**erlangen** *vt* to obtain; [Kompromiss] to reach.

**Erlass** (*pl* -e *ODER* Erlässe) *der* - **1.** [von Befehl] decree - **2.** [von Schulden] remission.

**erlassen** (*präs* erlässt; *prät* erließ; *perf* hat erlassen) *vt* - **1.** [Befehl] to issue; [Gesetz] to enact - **2.** [Strafe, Schulden]: jm etw ~ to let sb off sthg.

**erlauben** *vt* to allow; jm etw ~ to allow sb sthg; sich (D) etw ~ [sich herausnehmen] to take the liberty of doing sthg; [sich gönnen] to allow o.s. sthg; was ~ Sie sich! how dare you!
➡ **erlaube mal** *interj* how dare you!

**Erlaubnis** *die* permission; jm die ~ zu etw erteilen *amt* to give sb permission to do sthg; um ~ bitten to ask (for) permission.

**erläutern** *vt* to explain.

**Erläuterung** (*pl* -en) *die* explanation.

**Erle** (*pl* -n) *die* alder.

**erleben** *vt* - **1.** [erfahren, kennen lernen] to experience; [Abenteuer] to have; du kannst was ~! *fam* you'll catch it!; hat man so was schon erlebt! *fam* did you ever hear such a thing! - **2.** [Geburtstag, Jubiläum] to live to see.

**Erlebnis** (*pl* -se) *das* experience.

**erledigen** *vt* - **1.** [Frage, Angelegenheit, Auftrag] to deal with; [Arbeit] to get through; [Einkäufe, Hausaufgaben] to do - **2.** *fam* [töten] to bump off - **3.** *fam* [besiegen] to wipe out.
➡ **sich erledigen** *ref* [sich erübrigen]: etw erledigt sich (von selbst) sthg takes care of itself.

**erledigt** *adj* - **1.** [ausgeführt, beendet - Angelegenheit] settled; [ - Auftrag] carried out; [ - Arbeit] done - **2.** *fam* [erschöpft]: ~ sein to be worn out.

**erleichtern** *vt* - **1.** [leichter machen - Arbeit, Situation] to make easier; [ - Gepäck] to make lighter; jm das Verständnis ~ to make it easier for sb to understand - **2.** [Gewissen] to ease - **3.** [bestehlen]: jn um etw ~ *hum* to relieve sb of sthg.
➡ **sich erleichtern** *ref* [sich befreien] to unburden o.s.

**erleichtert** *adj*: ~ sein to be relieved ⬦ *adv*: ~ aufatmen to breathe a sigh of relief.

**Erleichterung** (*pl* -en) *die* - **1.** [Befreiung] relief - **2.** [von Aufgabe] facilitation (U); [von Last] easing (U).

**erleiden** (*prät* erlitt; *perf* hat erlitten) *vt* to suffer.

**erlernen** *vt* to learn.

**erlesen** *adj geh* [Gemälde, Porzellan, Wein] fine; [Mahl] choice.

**erleuchten** *vt* - **1.** [erhellen] to light up - **2.** *geh* [inspirieren] to inspire.

**Erleuchtung** (*pl* -en) *die* (sudden) inspiration.

**erliegen** (*prät* erlag; *perf* ist erlegen) *vi geh*: jm/einer Sache ~ to succumb to sb/sthg.

**Erliegen** *das*: zum ~ kommen to be brought to a standstill.

**erlischt** *präs* ⬥ erlöschen.

**erlogen** *adj* made-up.

**Erlös** (*pl* -e) *der* proceeds (*pl*).

**erlöschen** (*präs* erlischt; *prät* erlosch; *perf* ist erloschen) *vi* - **1.** [Feuer, Licht] to go out; [Vulkan] to become extinct - **2.** [Gefühle] to die; [Anspruch, Mitgliedschaft] to lapse.

**erlösen** *vt* to rescue; jn von etw ~ [Leid, Schmerz] to release sb from sthg; *REL* to deliver sb from sthg.

**Erlösung** *die* [von Leiden, Schmerzen] release; [aus Zwangslage] rescue.

**Erm.** *abk für* Ermäßigung.

**ermächtigen** *vt*: jn zu etw ~ to authorize sb to do sthg.

**Ermächtigung** (*pl* -en) *die* authorization (U).

**ermahnen** *vt* to remind; jn zu mehr Vorsicht ~ to remind sb to be more careful.

**Ermahnung** *die* reminder.

**Ermangelung** ➡ in Ermangelung *präp geh*: in ~ einer Sache (G) for want *ODER* lack of sthg.

**ermäßigt** *adj* reduced.

**Ermäßigung** (*pl* -en) *die* reduction.

**ermessen** (*präs* ermisst; *prät* ermaß; *perf* hat ermessen) *vt* to assess.

**Ermessen** *das* judgement; das liegt ganz in Ihrem ~ that is entirely up to you; nach menschlichem ~ as far as it is possible to tell.

**Ermessensfrage** *die* matter of discretion.

**ermitteln** *vt* to determine; [Schuldige, Täter] to identify; [Sieger] to decide ⬦ *vi* to investigate.

**Ermittlung** (*pl* -en) *die* [Erkundigung] enquiries (*pl*); [Entdeckung] identification (U).

**ermöglichen** *vt* to make possible; jm etw ~ to make sthg possible for sb.

**ermorden** *vt* to murder.

**Ermordung** (*pl* -en) *die* murder; [von Politiker] assassination.

**ermüden** (*perf* hat/ist ermüdet) *vt* (hat) *vi* (ist) to tire.

**Ermüdung** *die* tiredness.

**ermuntern** *vt* to encourage; jn zum Studium ~ to encourage sb to study.

**ermutigen** *vt* to encourage; jn zum Studium ~ to encourage sb to study.

**ernähren** *vt* - **1.** [beköstigen] to feed - **2.** [unterhalten] to support.

➦ **sich ernähren** *ref* to eat; **sich vegetarisch ~** to eat a vegetarian diet; **sich mit** ODER **von etw ~** [Person] to live on sthg; [Tier] to feed on sthg.

**Ernährung** *die* - **1.** [Ernähren] feeding - **2.** [Mahlzeit] diet; **gesunde ~** a healthy diet.

**ernennen** (*prät* **ernannte**; *perf* **hat ernannt**) *vt* to appoint; **jn zu etw ~** to appoint sb (as) sthg.

**erneuern** [ɛɐ̯'nɔyɐn] *vt* - **1.** [ersetzen] to replace - **2.** [ausbessern - Gebäude] to renovate; [ - Gemälde] to restore; [ - kaputten Zaun] to repair - **3.** [Vertrag, Angebot] to renew.
➦ **sich erneuern** *ref* to be renewed.

**Erneuerung** [ɛɐ̯'nɔyɐrʊŋ] *die* - **1.** [Ersatz] replacement (U) - **2.** [Ausbesserung - von Gebäude] renovation (U); [ - von Gemälde] restoration (U) - **3.** [von Vertrag, Angebot] renewed.

**erneut** *adj* [Angebot, Vorschlag] new; [Kraft] renewed; [Weigerung] further ⬦ *adv* again.

**erniedrigen** *vt* to humiliate.
➦ **sich erniedrigen** *ref* [sich demütigen] to lower o.s.

**Erniedrigung** (*pl* -en) *die* humiliation (U).

**ernst** *adj* - **1.** [gen] serious; [Verhalten] solemn; **~ bleiben** to remain serious - **2.** [Absicht, Vorschlag] sincere ⬦ *adv* - **1.** [gen] seriously - **2.** [Absicht, Vorschlag] sincerely; **es mit etw ~ meinen** to be serious about sthg; **damit meine ich es ~** I really mean it; **jn/etw ~ nehmen** to take sb/sthg seriously.

**Ernst** *der* seriousness; **mit etw ~ machen** to be serious about sthg; **das ist mein voller ~** I am quite serious about it; **im ~?** really?; **der ~ der Lage** the gravity of the situation; **der ~ des Lebens beginnt** *fig* life begins in earnest.

**Ernstfall** *der* (case of) emergency.

**ernst gemeint** *adj* serious.

**ernst genommen** *adj* taken seriously.

**ernsthaft** *adj* serious; [Verhalten] solemn ⬦ *adv* - **1.** [gen] seriously - **2.** [aufrichtig] sincerely.

**Ernsthaftigkeit** *die* - **1.** [von Person] seriousness - **2.** [von Absicht] sincerity.

**ernstlich** *adv* - **1.** [gen] seriously - **2.** [beabsichtigen, bereuen] sincerely.

**Ernte** (*pl* -n) *die* harvest.

**Erntedankfest** *das* harvest festival.

**ernten** *vt* - **1.** [Früchte] to harvest; [Obst] to pick - **2.** [Beifall] to earn; [Undank] to receive.

**ernüchtern** *vt* [desillusionieren] to bring down to earth.

**Ernüchterung** (*pl* -en) *die* [Desillusion] disillusionment (U).

**Eroberer** (*pl* -) *der* conqueror.

**erobern** *vt* - **1.** [erkämpfen] to conquer - **2.** [gewinnen] to capture.

**Eroberung** (*pl* -en) *die* conquest; **eine ~ machen** *fig* to make a conquest.

**eröffnen** *vt* - **1.** [gen] to open - **2.** [bekannt geben]: **jm etw ~** to reveal sthg to sb - **3.** [Gerichtsverfahren] to institute - **4.** [Möglichkeit] to open up.
➦ **sich eröffnen** *ref*: **sich jm ~** to open up to sb.

**Eröffnung** *die* - **1.** [gen] opening (U) - **2.** [Bekanntgabe - unerwartet] revelation (U); [ - von Plan] disclosure (U) - **3.** [von Gerichtsverfahren] institution - **4.** [von Möglichkeit] opening up (U).

**erörtern** *vt* to discuss.

**Erörterung** (*pl* -en) *die* discussion.

**Erosion** (*pl* -en) *die* GEOGR erosion (U).

**Erotik** *die* eroticism.

**erotisch** *adj* erotic.

**erpicht** *adj*: **darauf ~ sein, etw zu tun** to be intent ODER set on doing sthg.

**erpressen** *vt*: **jn (mit etw) ~** to blackmail sb (with sthg); **etw von jm ~** to extort sthg from sb.

**Erpresser, in** (*mpl* -; *fpl* -nen) *der, die* blackmailer.

**Erpresserbrief** *der* blackmail letter.

**Erpressung** (*pl* -en) *die* blackmail (U).

**Erpressungsversuch** *der* attempted blackmail (U).

**erproben** *vt* [Maschine, Mittel] to test; [Ausdauer, Zuverlässigkeit] to put to the test; [Methode] to try out.

**Erprobung** (*pl* -en) *die* testing (U).

**erraten** (*präs* **errät**; *prät* **erriet**; *perf* **hat erraten**) *vt* to guess.

**errechnen** *vt* to calculate.

**erregen** *vt* - **1.** [aufregen - Person] to excite; [ - Gemüt, sexuell] to arouse - **2.** [anregen] to stimulate - **3.** [verursachen - Aufmerksamkeit, Aufsehen] to attract; [ - Widerspruch] to give rise to; [ - Mitleid, Neid] to arouse.
➦ **sich erregen** *ref* [sich aufregen] to get annoyed; **sich über etw** (A) **~** to get annoyed about sthg; **sich über jn** (A) **~** to get annoyed with sb.

**Erreger** (*pl* -) *der* [von Krankheit] cause.

**Erregung** *die* - **1.** [von Person] excitement (U); [sexuelle] arousal (U) - **2.** [von Nerven] stimulation (U) - **3.** [Verursachen - von Mitleid, Neid] arousing (U); [ - von Aufmerksamkeit] attracting (U); **die ~ öffentlichen Ärgernisses** RECHT creating a public nuisance.

**erreichbar** *adj* [Person] available; [Ort] within reach.

**erreichen** *vt* - **1.** [Ort, Person, Geschwindigkeit] to reach; [Ziel] to achieve; [Bahn] to catch - **2.** [telefonisch] to contact; **wo/wann sind Sie zu ~?** where/when can you be contacted? **- 3.** [durchsetzen] to achieve; **bei ihm kann man nichts ~** you'll not get anywhere with him.

**errichten** *vt* **- 1.** [bauen, aufbauen] to erect **- 2.** [Herrschaft] to establish.

**Errichtung** *die* **- 1.** [Bau, Aufbau] erection **- 2.** [von Herrschaft] establishment.

**erringen** (*prät* **errang**; *perf* **hat errungen**) *vt* [Sieg, Freundschaft] to win; [Vorteil, Mehrheit] to gain.

**erröten** (*perf* **ist errötet**) *vi* to blush; **vor Wut ~** to flush with anger.

**Errungenschaft** (*pl* **-en**) *die* achievement; **technische ~en** technical advances; **meine neueste ~** my latest acquisition.

**Ersatz** *der* **- 1.** [Ausgleich] substitute **- 2.** [Entschädigung] compensation.

**Ersatz|dienst** *der community work done by conscientious objectors instead of military service.*

**Ersatz|kasse** *die private health insurance scheme.*

**ersatzlos** *adv* without substitution; **~ gestrichen** abolished.

**Ersatz|mann** (*pl* **-männer** ODER **-leute**) *der* [beim Fußball] substitute; [bei der Arbeit] replacement.

**Ersatz|rad** *das* spare wheel.

**Ersatz|teil** *das* spare part.

**erschaffen** (*prät* **erschuf**; *perf* **hat erschaffen**) *vt geh* to create.

**Erschaffung** *die geh* creation.

**erscheinen** (*prät* **erschien**; *perf* **ist erschienen**) *vi* **- 1.** [kommen, sich zeigen] to appear **- 2.** [Buch, Zeitung] to come out **- 3.** [wirken] to seem.

**Erscheinung** (*pl* **-en**) *die* **- 1.** [Ereignis] phenomenon; **in ~ treten** to appear **- 2.** [Gestalt] appearance; **äußere ~** (external) appearance **- 3.** [Vision] apparition.

**erschießen** (*prät* **erschoss**; *perf* **hat erschossen**) *vt* to shoot.
➣ **sich erschießen** *ref* to shoot o.s.

**erschlaffen** (*perf* **ist erschlafft**) *vi* [Muskeln] to go limp; [Haut] to become flabby.

**erschlagen¹** *adj fig* **- 1.** [todmüde]: **~ sein** to be worn out **- 2.** [sprachlos] flabbergasted.

**erschlagen²** (*präs* **erschlägt**; *prät* **erschlug**; *perf* **hat erschlagen**) *vt* to kill; **vom Blitz ~ werden** to be struck by lightning.

**erschließen** (*prät* **erschloss**; *perf* **hat erschlossen**) *vt* [Land, Markt] to open up; [Rohstoffe, Bodenschätze] to exploit; [Bauland] to develop.
➣ **sich erschließen** *ref geh* [verständlich werden]: **sich jm ~** to become intelligible to sb.

**erschöpft** *adj* exhausted ◇ *adv* [müde] wearily.

**Erschöpfung** *die* exhaustion.

**erschrak** *prät* ▷ **erschrecken**.

**erschrecken** (*präs* **erschreckt** ODER **erschrickt**; *prät* **erschreckte** ODER **erschrak**; *perf* **hat erschreckt** ODER **ist erschrocken**) *vt (hat)* (*reg*) [überraschen] to startle; [ängstigen] to frighten ◇ *vi (ist)* (*unreg*) [überrascht sein] to be startled; [Angst haben] to be frightened; **vor jm/etw ~** to be startled by sb/sthg; **über etw** (*A*) **~** to be alarmed by sthg.
➣ **sich erschrecken** *ref* (*unreg*) to get a fright.

**erschreckend** *adj* alarming ◇ *adv* alarmingly.

**erschrickt** *präs* ▷ **erschrecken**.

**erschrocken** *pp* ▷ **erschrecken**.

**erschüttern** *vt* **- 1.** [Haus, Person] to shake; **er lässt sich durch nichts ~** he's unflappable **- 2.** [Vertrauen, Ruf] to shatter.

**erschütternd** *adj* distressing.

**Erschütterung** (*pl* **-en**) *die* **- 1.** [von Haus] shaking (*U*) **- 2.** [von Person] (state of) shock **- 3.** [von Vertrauen, Ruf] shattering.

**erschweren** *vt* to make (more) difficult.

**erschwinglich** *adj* affordable.

**ersetzbar** *adj* replaceable.

**ersetzen** *vt* **- 1.** [auswechseln, ausgleichen] to replace **- 2.** [erstatten - Auslagen] to reimburse; [ - Schaden] to make good; **jm etw ~** to compensate sb for sthg.

**ersichtlich** *adj* obvious.

**erspähen** *vt* to spot.

**ersparen** *vt* to save; **sich** (*D*) **Geld/Zeit/Mühe ~** to save o.s. money/time/trouble; **jm/sich etw Unangenehmes ~** to spare sb/o.s. sthg unpleasant.

**Ersparnis** (*pl* **-se**) *die* saving.
➣ **Ersparnisse** *pl* savings.

**erst** *adv* **- 1.** [nicht eher] not until; **er fährt ~ morgen los** he's not going until tomorrow; **~ als** only when **- 2.** [vor kurzem] (only) just; **sie war ~ gestern hier** she was here only yesterday **- 3.** [nicht später, lediglich] only; **er kommt ~ um zehn** he won't be here until ten o'clock **- 4.** [zuerst] first; [anfänglich] at first **- 5.** [emphatisierend]: **sie ist ja schon groß aber ihr Bruder ~!** she is tall but her brother is even taller; **hätte ich doch ~ alle meine Prüfungen hinter mir!** if only all my exams were finished!; **jetzt werde ich es ~ recht/nicht recht tun!** now I'm definitely going/not going to do it!
➣ **erst einmal** *adv* **- 1.** [nur einmal] only once **- 2.** [zuerst] at first.

**erstarren** (*perf* **ist erstarrt**) *vi* [vor Kälte] to go numb; [vor Schreck] to become paralysed; [Gips] to harden.

**erstatten** *vt* - **1.** [Betrag] to reimburse - **2.** [vorbringen]: **gegen jn Anzeige ~** to report sb (to the authorities); **Bericht ~** to (make a) report.

**Erstattung** *(pl -en) die* - **1.** [von Kosten] reimbursement - **2.** [von Anzeige, Bericht] making.

**Erstauflführung** *die* première.

**erstaunen** *(perf* **hat/ist erstaunt)** *vt (hat)* to astonish, to amaze <> *vi (ist):* **über etw** *(A)* **~** to be astonished ODER amazed at sthg.

**Erstaunen** *das* astonishment; **jn in ~ (ver)setzen** to astonish ODER amaze sb.

**erstaunlich** *adj* astonishing, amazing <> *adv* àstonishingly, amazingly.

**erstaunt** *adj* [Person] astonished, amazed; [Gesicht, Miene] surprised; **über etw** *(A)* **~ sein** to be astonished by sthg.

**erstbeste, r, s** *adj:* **kaufe nicht gleich den ~n Wagen!** don't simply buy the first car you look at!; **sich in das ~ Mädchen verlieben** to fall in love with the first girl that comes along.
➥ **Erstbeste** *der, die, das* first thing to come along.

**erste, r, s** *adj* - **1.** [anfänglich] first - **2.** [beste - Qualität, Wahl] top; [ - Liga, Geige] first - **3.** [Ergebnis, Erfolg] initial.

**Erste** *der, die, das* first; *siehe auch* **Sechste.**
➥ **als Erstes** *adv* first (of all).
➥ **fürs Erste** *adv* for the time being.

**erstechen** *(präs* **ersticht;** *prät* **erstach;** *perf* **hat erstochen)** *vt* to stab to death.

**erstehen** *(prät* **erstand;** *perf* **hat/ist erstanden)** *vi (ist) geh* - **1.** [Probleme, Schwierigkeiten] to arise - **2.** [auferstehen] to rise up <> *vt (hat)* to buy.

**erste Hilfe** *die* first aid; **jm ~ leisten** to give sb first aid.

**erstellen** *vt amt* - **1.** [Tabelle, Abrechnung] to draw up - **2.** [Haus] to construct.

**erstens** *adv* firstly, in the first place.

**ersticken** *(perf* **hat/ist erstickt)** *vi (ist)* to suffocate; **wir ~ zurzeit in Arbeit** we're up to our eyes in work at the moment <> *vt (hat)* [Person, Tier] to suffocate; [Feuer] to put out; **etw im Keim ~** to nip sthg in the bud.

**Erstickung** *die* suffocation.

**erstklassig** *adj* first-class <> *adv* excellently.

**Erstlkommunion** *die* REL First Communion.

**erstmalig** *adj* first <> *adv* for the first time.

**erstmals** *adv* for the first time.

**erstrangig** *adj* - **1.** [vorrangig] of prime importance - **2.** [erstklassig] first-rate <> *adv* as a matter of priority.

**erstreben** *vt* to strive for.

**erstrebenswert** *adj* worthwhile.

**erstrecken** ➥ **sich erstrecken** *ref* - **1.** [jn/etw betreffen]: **sich auf jn/etw ~** to apply to sb/sthg - **2.** [sich ausdehnen]: **sich ~ bis** [räumlich] to extend as far as; **sich über etw** *(A)* **~** [zeitlich] to last for sthg; [räumlich] to extend over sthg.

**Erstlstimme** *die* first vote.

**erstunken** *adj:* **~ und erlogen** *fam* a pack of lies.

**erstürmen** *vt* [Festung] to storm; [Gipfel] to conquer.

**ertappen** *vt* to catch; **jn bei etw ~** to catch sb doing sthg; **jn auf frischer Tat ~** to catch sb red-handed.
➥ **sich ertappen** *ref:* **sich bei etw ~** to catch o.s. doing sthg.

**erteilen** *vt:* **jm etw ~** to give sb sthg.

**ertönen** *(perf* **ist ertönt)** *vi* [Instrument] to sound; [Stimme] to ring out; [Geräusch] to be heard.

**Ertrag** *(pl -träge) der* [an Gemüse, Getreide] yield; [finanziell] profits *(pl).*

**ertragen** *(präs* **erträgt;** *prät* **ertrug;** *perf* **hat ertragen)** *vt* to bear.

**erträglich** *adj* [Zustände] tolerable; [Schmerz] bearable.

**ertragreich** *adj* [Acker] high-yielding; [Geschäft] profitable.

**Ertragsllage** *die* profit situation.

**ertränken** *vt* to drown.
➥ **sich ertränken** *ref* to drown o.s.

**erträumen** *vt:* **sich** *(D)* **etw ~** to imagine sthg.

**ertrinken** *(prät* **ertrank;** *perf* **ist ertrunken)** *vi* to drown.

**Ertüchtigung** *(pl -en) die* training *(U).*

**erübrigen** *vt* to spare.
➥ **sich erübrigen** *ref* to be unnecessary; **das erübrigt sich** there's no point.

**Erw.** *(abk für* **Erwachsene)** adult.

**erwachen** *(perf* **ist erwacht)** *vi* to awake; [Tag] to dawn.

**Erwachen** *das* awakening; **das gab ein böses ~** *fig* it was a rude awakening.

**erwachsen¹** [ɛɐˈvaksn̩] *adj* adult <> *adv* in an adult way.

**erwachsen²** *(präs* **erwächst;** *prät* **erwuchs;** *perf* **ist erwachsen)** *vi:* **aus etw ~** to arise from sthg.

**Erwachsene** [ɛɐˈvaksn̩ə] *(pl -n) der, die* adult.

**Erwachsenenbildung** *die* adult education.

**erwägen** *(prät* **erwog;** *perf* **hat erwogen)** *vt* to consider.

**Erwägung** *(pl -en) die* consideration *(U);* **etw in ~ ziehen** to consider sthg.

**erwähnen** *vt* to mention.

**erwähnenswert** *adj* worth mentioning.

**Erwähnung** (*pl* -en) *die* mention (*U*).

**erwärmen** *vt* [wärmen] to warm.

➤ **sich erwärmen** *ref* - **1.** [sich aufwärmen] to warm up - **2.** [sich begeistern]: **ich kann mich für deine Idee nicht ~** I can't generate any enthusiasm for your idea.

**Erwärmung** *die* warming.

**erwarten** *vt* - **1.** [warten auf] to wait for; **ich kann es kaum ~!** I can hardly wait! - **2.** [mit etw rechnen, erhoffen] to expect.

**Erwartung** (*pl* -en) *die* expectation.

➤ **Erwartungen** *pl* expectations; [Anforderung] requirements.

**erwartungsvoll** *adj* expectant ◇ *adv* expectantly.

**erwecken** *vt* - **1.** [Ehrgeiz, Misstrauen] to arouse; [Hoffnungen] to raise - **2.** [Tote] to awaken.

**erweichen** *vt*: **sich ~/nicht ~ lassen** *fig* to/not to yield.

**erweisen** (*prät* **erwies**; *perf* **hat erwiesen**) *vt* [Schuld] to prove; **jm einen Dienst** ODER **Gefallen ~** to do sb a favour; **es ist erwiesen, dass ...** it has been proved that ...

➤ **sich erweisen** *ref* [sich zeigen]: **sich als etw ~** to prove to be sthg.

**erweitern** *vt* [Raum, Angebot, Umfang] to extend; [Bekanntenkreis, Wissen] to expand.

➤ **sich erweitern** *ref* [Straße, Angebot] to extend; [Bekanntenkreis, Produktion] to expand; [Pupillen] to dilate.

**Erweiterung** (*pl* -en) *die* [von Raum, Angebot] extension (*U*); [von Bekanntenkreis, Wissen] expansion (*U*); [von Pupillen] dilation (*U*).

**Erwerb** *der* - **1.** [von Haus, Grundstück] purchase - **2.** [von Kenntnissen] acquisition - **3.** [aus Geschäft] earnings (*pl*).

**erwerben** (*präs* **erwirbt**; *prät* **erwarb**; *perf* **hat erworben**) *vt* - **1.** [kaufen] to purchase - **2.** [erlangen] to acquire.

**erwerbsfähig** *adj* able to work.

**erwerbslos** *adj* unemployed.

**erwerbstätig** *adj* employed; **die ~e Bevölkerung** the working population.

**erwerbsunfähig** *adj* unable to work.

**Erwerbsunfähigkeit** *die* inability to work.

**erwidern** *vt* - **1.** [antworten] to reply - **2.** [Besuch, Gruß, Gefälligkeit] to return.

**Erwiderung** (*pl* -en) *die* - **1.** [Antwort] reply - **2.** [von Besuch, Gruß, Gefälligkeit] return.

**erwiesen** *pp* ▷ **erweisen** ◇ *adj* proven.

**erwiesenermaßen** *adv* as has been proved; **~ war er der Täter** it has been proved that he was the culprit.

**erwirtschaften** *vt* to obtain by careful management.

**erwischen** *vt* - **1.** [ertappen]: **jn (bei etw) ~** to catch sb (doing sthg) - **2.** [rechtzeitig erreichen] to catch - **3.** [bekommen] to get - **4.** RW: **ihn hat es erwischt** *fam* [krank sein] he's got it; [verletzt sein] he's hurt; [verliebt sein] he's got it bad; [tot sein] he's dead.

**erwog** *prät* ▷ **erwägen**.

**erwogen** *pp* ▷ **erwägen**.

**erwünscht** *adj* [Gäste, Entwicklung] welcome; [Ergebnis] desired; **nicht ~ sein** not to be welcome.

**erwürgen** *vt* to strangle.

**Erz** (*pl* -e) *das* ore.

**erzählen** *vt* - **1.** [Geschichte, Witz] to tell; **jm von etw ~** to tell sb about sthg - **2.** RW: **du kannst mir viel ~!** *fam* pull the other one!; **dem werde ich was ~!** *fam* I'll give him a piece of my mind!

**Erzähler, in** (*mpl* -; *fpl* -nen) *der, die* - **1.** [Berichtende] narrator - **2.** [Autor] author.

**Erzählung** (*pl* -en) *die* - **1.** [Bericht] account - **2.** [Dichtung] story.

**Erzlbischof** *der* archbishop.

**Erzlbistum** *das* archbishopric.

**Erzlengel** *der* archangel.

**erzeugen** *vt* [Produkt] to produce; [Energie, Angst, Druck] to generate.

**Erzeuger** (*pl* -) *der* - **1.** [Produzent] producer - **2.** [Vater] father.

**Erzeugerin** (*pl* -nen) *die* producer.

**Erzleugnis** *das* product.

**Erzeugung** *die* [von Produkten] production; [von Energie, Druck] generation.

**Erzlfeind, in** *der, die* arch-enemy.

**Erzgebirge** *das*: **das ~** the Ore Mountains (*pl*).

**erzhaltig** *adj* containing minerals.

**erziehbar** *adj*: **ein schwer ~ es Kind** a problem child.

**erziehen** (*prät* **erzog**; *perf* **hat erzogen**) *vt* [Kinder - in der Familie] to bring up; [ - in der Schule] to educate; [Tier] to train; **jn zu jm/etw ~** to bring sb up to be sb/sthg.

**Erzieher, in** (*mpl* -; *fpl* -nen) *der, die* - **1.** [Berufsbezeichnung] teacher - **2.** [Eltern, Lehrer] educator.

**erzieherisch** *adj* educational ◇ *adv* educationally.

**Erziehung** *die* [in der Familie] upbringing; [in der Schule] education.

**Erziehungslberechtigte** *der, die* amt parent *or* guardian.

**Erziehungslgeld** *das* ≈ maternity/paternity benefit.

**Erziehungslurlaub** *der* ≈ maternity/paternity leave *(U).*

**erzielen** *vt* [Kompromiss] to reach; [Ertrag, Gewinn] to make.

**erzogen** *pp* ⊳ **erziehen** ◇ *adj:* **gut/schlecht** ~ well/badly brought up.

**erzwingen** (*prät* **erzwang**; *perf* **hat erzwungen**) *vt* to force.

**es** *pron* - **1.** [Personalpronomen im Nominativ - bei Sachen] it; [ - bei Personen] he (*f* she) - **2.** [Personalpronomen im Akkusativ - bei Sachen] it; [ - bei Personen] him (*f* her); **ich hoffe** ~ I hope so; **ich weiß** ~ I know - **3.** [unpersönliches Pronomen] it; ~ **ist drei Uhr** it's three o'clock; ~ **regnet/schneit** it's raining/snowing; ~ **freut mich, dass ...** I'm pleased that ...; **gestern gab** ~ **Nudeln** yesterday we had pasta; ~ **ist sehr interessant, sich mit Jill zu unterhalten** Jill is very interesting to talk to; ~ **wird vermutet, dass sie später kommen** they are supposed to come later; ~ **geht mir gut** I'm fine; **wer war** ~? who was it?

**Es** (*pl* -) *das* - **1.** MUS E flat - **2.** [in der Psychologie] id.

**ESA** [ˈeːza] (*abk für* **Europäische Weltraumbehörde**) *die* ESA.

**Escape** [ɛsˈkeɪp] *nt (ohne Artikel)* EDV escape.

**Esche** (*pl* -n) *die* ash.

**Esel** (*pl* -) *der* - **1.** [Tier] donkey - **2.** *fam* [Schimpfwort] ass; **ich** ~! stupid me!

**Eselin** (*pl* -nen) *die* she-ass.

**Eselslbrücke** *die* mnemonic.

**Eselslohr** *das:* **das Buch hat** ~**en** the book is dog-eared.

**ESG** [eːˈɛsˈgeː] (*pl* -s) (*abk für* **Evangelische Studentengemeinde**) *die* Protestant student society.

**Eskalation** (*pl* -en) *die* escalation.

**eskalieren** (*perf* **ist eskaliert**) *vi* to escalate.

**Eskimo** (*pl* -s) *der* Eskimo.

**Eskimolfrau** *die* Eskimo woman.

**Eskorte** (*pl* -n) *die* escort.

**Esoterik** *die* esotericism.

**Espe** (*pl* -n) *die* aspen.

**Espenllaub** *das:* **zittern wie** ~ *fig* to shake like a leaf.

**Esperanto** *das* Esperanto; *siehe auch* **Englisch(e).**

**Espresso** [ɛsˈprɛso] (*pl* - *ODER* -s) *der* espresso ◇ *das* [Lokal] coffee bar.

**Espressolmaschine** *die* espresso machine.

**Essay** [ˈɛsei] (*pl* -s) *das ODER der* essay.

**essbar** *adj* edible.

**essen** (*präs* **isst**; *prät* **aß**; *perf* **hat gegessen**) *vi* to eat; ~ **gehen** to go out for a meal; **gut** ~ to eat well; **warm/kalt** ~ to have a hot/cold meal ◇ *vt* to eat; **seinen Teller leer** ~ to eat everything on one's plate; **etw gern** ~ to like sthg.

**Essen¹** *nt* Essen.

**Essen²** (*pl* -) *das* meal; **beim** ~ **sein** to be eating; ~ **machen** *ODER* **kochen** to make *ODER* cook a meal; ~ **und Trinken** food and drink; ~ **auf Rädern** meals on wheels.

**Essenz** (*pl* -en) *die* essence.

**essenziell, essentiell** [ɛsɛnˈtsi̯ɛl] *adj geh* essential.

**Essig** (*pl* -e) *der* vinegar.

**Essigsäure** *die* acetic acid.

**Essllöffel** *der* dessertspoon.

**Essltisch** *der* dining table.

**Esslzimmer** *das* dining room.

**Este** (*pl* -n) *der* Estonian.

**Ester** (*pl* -) *der* CHEM ester.

**Estin** (*pl* -nen) *die* Estonian.

**Estland** *nt* Estonia.

**estnisch** *adj* Estonian.

**Estragon** *der* tarragon.

**etablieren** *vt* to establish.
→ **sich etablieren** *ref* - **1.** [Mode] to become established - **2.** [Firma] to set up.

**etabliert** *adj* established.

**Etage** [eˈtaːʒə] (*pl* -n) *die* floor.

**Etagenlwohnung** *die* flat *Br*, apartment *Am* (*in a block).*

**Etappe** (*pl* -n) *die* stage.

**Etat** [eˈtaː] (*pl* -s) *der* budget.

**etepetete** *adj fam:* ~ **sein** to be fussy.

**Ethik** (*pl* -en) *die* - **1.** [Lehre] ethics *(U)* - **2.** (*ohne pl*) [Moral] ethics (*pl*).

**ethisch** *adj* ethical.

**ethnisch** *adj* ethnic.

**Ethos** *das* ethos.

**Etikett** (*pl* -e(n) *ODER* -s) *das* label; **jn/etw mit einem** ~ **versehen** *fig* & *abw* to label sb/sthg.

**Etikette** *die* etiquette.

**etliche, r, s** *det* several, quite a few; ~ **Male** several times.
→ **etliches** *pron:* ~**s zahlen** to pay quite a lot; **es gibt** ~**s zu erwähnen** there are quite a few things to mention.

**Etsch** *die:* **die** ~ the (River) Adige.

**Etui** [ɛtˈviː] (*pl* -s) *das* case.

**etwa** *adv* - **1.** [zirka, ungefähr] about; **es funktioniert** ~ **so** it works roughly like this - **2.** [zum Beispiel] for example - **3.** [zum Ausdruck der Beunruhigung, eines Vorwurfs in Fragen]: **ist es** ~ **schon 24 Uhr?** don't tell me it's 12 o'clock already

**- 4.** [zur Bekräftigung]: **Edinburg ist nicht ~ groß, aber schön** Edinburgh is certainly not big but it is beautiful.
➡ **in etwa** adv roughly.

**etwaig** adj possible; **~e Fragen** any questions that arise.

**etwas** det **- 1.** [gen] something; [in Fragen] anything; **~ Anderes/Schönes** something else/nice; **möchten Sie noch ~ Anderes?** would you like anything else? **- 2.** [ein wenig] some; **möchten Sie noch ~ Kaffee?** would you like some more coffee? ⬦ pron something; [in Fragen] anything; **hast du ~ für mich?** have you got anything for me?; **das ist doch wenigstens ~!** that's something at least!; **das will ~ heißen!** that's quite something!; **so ~** such a thing ⬦ adv a little; **ihm geht es ~ besser** he is a little better; **~ spät** rather late.

**Etymologie** (pl -n) die etymology.

**etymologisch** adj etymological ⬦ adv etymologically.

**EU** (abk für **Europäische Union**) die EU.

**euch** pron (Akkusativ und Dativ von ihr) **- 1.** [Personalpronomen] you; **wir haben es ~ gesagt** we told you; **das gehört ~** this is yours, this belongs to you; **mit ~** with you **- 2.** [Reflexivpronomen] yourselves; **könnt ihr ~ das vorstellen?** can you imagine that? **- 3.** [einander] each other.

**euer, e** ODER **eure** det your; **alles Gute, Euer Thomas** yours, Thomas.

**Euphorie** die euphoria.

**euphorisch** adj euphoric ⬦ adv euphorically.

**eure, r, s** pron yours.

**eurer** pron (Genitiv von ihr) you.

**eurerseits** adv **- 1.** [ihr selbst] for your part **- 2.** [von Euch] on your part.

**euresgleichen** pron your kind.

**euretwegen** adv **- 1.** [euch zuliebe] for your sake **- 2.** [wegen euch] because of you.

**euretwillen** ➡ **um euretwillen** adv for your sake.

**eurige** (pl -n) pron (mit Artikel) geh yours.

**Euro** [ˈɔyro] (pl -) der euro.

**Eurocard®** [ˈɔyrokaːɐ̯d] (pl -s) die Eurocard®.

**Eurocent** [ˈɔyrosɛnt] der eurocent.

**Eurocheque, Euro|scheck** [ˈɔyroʃɛk] (pl -s) der Eurocheque.

**Eurocheque-|Karte, Euroscheckkarte** die Eurocheque card.

**Eurocity** [ˈɔyrosɪtɪl] (pl -s) der international train linking two or more major European cities.

**Euro|land** das Euroland.

**Europa** nt Europe.

**Europäer, in** (mpl -; fpl -nen) der, die European.

**europäisch** adj European.

**Europa|meister, in** der, die European champion.

**Europa|meisterschaft** die European championships (pl).

**Europa|parlament** das European Parliament.

**Europa|pokal** der European Cup.

**Europa|rat** der European Council.

**Euro|scheck** = Eurocheque.

**Euroscheck|karte** = Eurocheque-Karte.

**Euro|zone** die euro zone.

**Euter** (pl -) das ODER der udder.

**ev.** abk für **evangelisch**.

**e. V.** (abk für **eingetragener Verein**) registered society.

**evakuieren** [evaku'iːrən] vt to evacuate.

**Evakuierung** [evaku'iːrʊŋ] (pl -en) die evacuation.

**evangelisch** [evaŋ'geːlɪʃ] adj Protestant.

**Evangelium** [evaŋ'geːljʊm] (pl -ien) das gospel.

**eventuell** [even'tʊɛl] adj possible ⬦ adv maybe, perhaps.

**ev.-luth.** (abk für **evangelisch-lutherisch**) Lutheran.

**Evolution** [evolu'tsjoːn] (pl -en) die evolution (U).

**ev.-ref.** (abk für **evangelisch-reformiert**) Protestant Reformed.

**evtl.** abk für **eventuell**.

**EWF** [eːˈveːˈɛf] (abk für **Europäischer Währungsfonds**) der EMF.

**ewig** adj **- 1.** [nie endend] eternal **- 2.** fam abw [andauernd] constant ⬦ adv **- 1.** [endlos] eternally **- 2.** fam abw [zu lange] constantly.
➡ **auf ewig** adv [für immer] forever.

**Ewigkeit** (pl -en) die **- 1.** eternity **- 2.** RW: **bis in alle ~** fam forever and ever; **seit ~en** fam for ages; **eine halbe ~** fam an eternity.

**EWS** [eːˈveːˈɛs] (abk für **Europäisches Währungssystem**) das EMS.

**ex** adv fam: **etw (auf) ~ trinken** to drink sthg in one go; **etw ~ und hopp wegschmeißen** abw to chuck sthg away.

**exakt** adj exact; [Arbeit] precise ⬦ adv exactly; [arbeiten] with precision.

**Exaktheit** die precision.

**Examen** (pl -) das examination; **~ machen** to take one's examinations; **das ~ bestehen** to pass the examination.

**Examens|arbeit** die written work submitted as part of the "Staatsexamen".

**Examenslkandidat** *der* (examination) candidate.

**Exekution** (*pl* -en) *die* execution.

**Exekutive** [ɛksekuˈtiːvə] *die (ohne pl)* executive.

**Exempel** (*pl* -) *das* example; **ein ~ für etw** an example of sthg; **an jm ein ~ statuieren** to make an example of sb.

**Exemplar** (*pl* -e) *das* example; [von Buch] copy.

**exemplarisch** *adj* exemplary <> *adv* [vorgehen] in an exemplary fashion; [bestrafen] as an example.

**exerzieren** *vi* MIL to drill.

**Exil** (*pl* -e) *das* exile *(U)*; **ins ~ gehen** to go into exile; **im ~ leben** to live in exile.

**Exillregierung** *die* government in exile.

**existent** *adj* existing.

**Existentialismus** [ɛksɪstɛntsiaˈlɪsmʊs] *der (ohne pl)* = **Existenzialismus.**

**existentialistisch** [ɛksɪstɛntsiaˈlɪstɪʃ] = **existenzialistisch.**

**existentiell** [ɛksɪstɛnˈtsiɛll] = **existenziell.**

**Existenz** (*pl* -en) *die* - **1.** [Bestehen] existence - **2.** [Existenzgrundlage] livelihood; **eine ~ gründen** to make a life for o.s. - **3.** *abw* [Person] character; **eine verkrachte ~** *fam abw* a waster.

**Existenzlangst** *die* existential fear.

**Existenzlgrundlage** *die* basis of one's livelihood.

**Existenzialismus, Existentialismus** [ɛksɪstɛntsiaˈlɪsmʊs] *der* existentialism.

**existenzialistisch, existentialistisch** [ɛksɪstɛntsiaˈlɪstɪʃ] *adj* existentialist.

**existenziell, existentiell** [ɛksɪstɛnˈtsiɛll] *adj* existential; **eine ~ Drohung** a threat to one's life.

**Existenzlminimum** *das (ohne pl)* subsistence level.

**existieren** *vi* - **1.** [bestehen] to exist - **2.** [auskommen] to live.

**exklusiv** *adj* exclusive <> *adv* - **1.** [vornehm, abgesondert]: **~ leben** to live an exclusive lifestyle - **2.** [ausschließlich] exclusively.

**Exklusivität** [ɛkskluziviˈtɛːt] *die* - **1.** [Ausschließlichkeit] exclusivity - **2.** [Besonderheit] distinctiveness.

**Exkurs** (*pl* -e) *der* digression.

**Exkursion** (*pl* -en) *die* study trip.

**Exmatrikulation** (*pl* -en) *die* UNI *removal of someone's name from a university register.*

**exmatrikulieren** *vt* UNI *to remove someone's name from a university register.*

➤ **sich exmatrikulieren** *ref* UNI *to remove one's name from a university register.*

**Exot** (*pl* -en), **Exote** (*pl* -n) *der* [Mensch] exotic person; [Tier] exotic animal.

**Exotik** *die* exoticism.

**Exotin** (*pl* -nen) *die* exotic woman.

**exotisch** *adj* exotic <> *adv* exotically.

**expandieren** *vi* WIRTSCH to expand.

**Expansion** (*pl* -en) *die* WIRTSCH, POL expansion *(U).*

**Expedition** (*pl* -en) *die* expedition.

**Experiment** (*pl* -e) *das* - **1.** [Versuch] experiment - **2.** [Wagnis] experimentation.

**experimentell** *adj* experimental <> *adv* experimentally.

**experimentieren** *vi* to experiment; **mit etw ~** to experiment on sthg.

**Experte** (*pl* -n) *der* expert.

**Expertin** (*pl* -nen) *die* expert.

**explizit** *geh adj* explicit <> *adv* explicitly.

**explodieren** (*perf* **ist explodiert**) *vi* to explode.

**Explosion** (*pl* -en) *die* explosion.

**explosiv** *adj* explosive.

**Export** (*pl* -e) *der* export.

**Exportlartikel** *der* article for export.

**Exporteur** [ɛkspɔrˈtøːɐ̯] (*pl* -e) *der* exporter.

**exportieren** *vt* & *vi* to export.

**Express** *der (ohne pl)* *Österr* express train.

**Expressionismus** *der* expressionism.

**Expressionist, in** (*mpl* -en; *fpl* -nen) *der, die* expressionist.

**expressionistisch** *adj* expressionist.

**exquisit** *adj* exquisite <> *adv* exquisitely.

**extra** *adv* - **1.** [separat] separately - **2.** [zusätzlich] extra - **3.** [speziell] specially <> *adj (unver)* extra.

**Extra** (*pl* -s) *das* extra.

**Extralblatt** *das* special edition.

**Extrakt** (*pl* -e) *der* extract.

**extravagant** [ˈɛkstravagant] *adj* flamboyant <> *adv* flamboyantly.

**Extrawurst** *die*: **jm eine ~ braten** *fam fig* to give sb special treatment.

**extrem** *adj* extreme <> *adv* [billig, auffällig] extremely; [reagieren, denken] in an extreme way; **~ rechts stehen** to be on the extreme right.

**Extrem** (*pl* -e) *das* extreme; **von einem ~ ins anderen fallen** *fig* to go from one extreme to the other.

**Extremlfall** *der* extreme case; **im ~** in an extreme case.

**Extremist, in** (*mpl* -en; *fpl* -nen) *der, die* extremist.

**Extrem|sport** *der* extreme sports (*pl*).

**exzellent** *adj* excellent ◇ *adv* excellently.

**exzentrisch** *abw adj* eccentric ◇ *adv* eccentrically.

**Exzess** (*pl* -e) *der* excess.

**EZ** *abk für* Einzelzimmer.

**EZB** (*abk für* Europäische Zentralbank) *die* ECB.

**f, F** [ɛf] (*pl* - *ODER* -s) *das* - **1.** [Buchstabe] f, F - **2.** MUS F.

**F** (*abk für* Fahrenheit) F.

**f.** *abk für* für.

**Fa.** (*abk für* Firma) Co.

**Fabel** (*pl* -n) *die* [Erzählung] fable.

**fabelhaft** *adj* fantastic ◇ *adv* fantastically.

**Fabrik** (*pl* -en) *die* factory.

**Fabrikant, in** (*mpl* -en; *fpl* -nen) *der, die* factory owner.

**Fabrik|arbeiter, in** *der, die* factory worker.

**Fabrikat** (*pl* -e) *das* make.

**Fabrikation** (*pl* -en) *die* production (*U*).

**fabrikneu** *adj* brand new.

**fabrizieren** *vt fam abw* [machen] to throw together; **was hast du da wieder fabriziert?** what have you been up to now?

**Facette, Fassette** [fa'sɛtə] (*pl* -n) *die* facet.

**Fach** (*pl* Fächer) *das* - **1.** [in Möbel, Behälter] compartment; [für Brief, Schlüssel] pigeonhole - **2.** [in Schule, Studium] subject; **vom ~ sein** to be an expert.

**Fach|abitur** *das exam taken at the end of a secondary vocational school which enables students to enter a "Fachhochschule" but not university.*

**Fach|arbeiter, in** *der, die* skilled worker.

**Fach|arzt, ärztin** *der, die* specialist.

**fachärztlich** *adj* specialist ◇ *adv:* **~ beraten** to give specialist advice.

**Fach|ausdruck** *der* technical term.

**Fach|bereich** *der* - **1.** [Fachgebiet] field - **2.** UNI faculty.

**Fach|buch** *das* specialist book.

**Fächer** (*pl* -) *der* fan.

**Fach|frau** *die* expert.

**Fach|gebiet** *das* field.

**fachgerecht** *adj* expert ◇ *adv* expertly.

**Fach|geschäft** *das* specialist shop **Br** *ODER* store **Am.**

**Fachhoch|schule** *die college offering primarily vocational courses to the equivalent of bachelor level.*

**Fach|kenntnis** *die* specialist knowledge (*U*).

**Fach|kraft** *die* skilled worker.

**fachkundig** *adj* expert ◇ *adv* expertly.

**fachlich** *adj* [Problem] technical; [beruflich] professional ◇ *adv* technically; [beruflich] professionally; **sich ~ weiterbilden** to gain professional qualifications; **das ist ~ richtig** that's technically correct.

**Fach|literatur** *die* specialist literature.

**Fachmann** (*pl* -leute) *der* expert.

**fachmännisch** *adj* expert ◇ *adv* expertly.

**fachsimpeln** ['faxzɪmpl̩n] *vi fam* to talk shop.

**Fach|sprache** *die* specialist terminology.

**Fachwerk|haus** *das* timbered building.

**Fach|wissen** *das* specialist knowledge.

**Fackel** (*pl* -n) *die* torch.

**fackeln** *vi:* **nicht lange ~** *fam* not to think twice.

**fade** *adj abw* - **1.** [schal] bland - **2.** [stumpfsinnig] dull.

**Faden** (*pl* Fäden) *der* - **1.** [Faser] thread - **2.** MED stitch - **3.** *RW:* **an einem seidenen** *ODER* **dünnen ~ hängen** to hang by a thread; **den ~ verlieren** to lose the thread; **sich wie ein roter ~ durch etw ziehen** to run like a thread through sthg.

**fadenscheinig** *adj* - **1.** *abw* [unglaubwürdig] paltry - **2.** [abgetragen] threadbare.

**Fagott** (*pl* -e) *das* bassoon.

**fähig** *adj* capable; **zu etw ~ sein** to be capable of sthg; **zu allem ~ sein** to be capable of anything.

**Fähigkeit** (*pl* -en) *die* - **1.** [Begabung] talent - **2.** [Können] ability.

**fahnden** *vi:* **nach jm/etw ~** to search for sb/sthg.

**Fahnder, in** (mpl -; fpl -nen) der, die investigator.

**Fahndung** (pl -en) die search.

**Fahndungslliste** die wanted list.

**Fahne** (pl -n) die flag; **eine ~ haben** fam fig to smell of drink.

**Fahnenleid** der MIL oath of allegiance.

**Fahnenlflucht** die MIL desertion.

**Fahnenlmast** der flagpole.

**Fahrlausweis** der - **1.** [Fahrschein] ticket - **2.** Schweiz [Führerschein] driving licence Br, driver's license Am.

**Fahrlbahn** die road.

**Fähre** (pl -n) die ferry.

**fahren** (präs fährt; prät fuhr; perf hat/ist gefahren) vi (ist) - **1.** [Person - gen] to go; [ - mit Auto] to drive; [ - mit Fahrrad] to ride; **mit dem Zug/Bus ~** to go by train/bus; **ins Gebirge ~** to go to the mountains; **wir ~ nach England** we're going to England; **durch Wien ~** to drive through Vienna; **langsam/zu schnell ~** to drive slowly/too fast; **120 km/h ~** to drive at 120 km/h; **ein Gedanke fuhr ihm durch den Kopf** a thought flashed through his mind; **was ist denn in dich gefahren?** fig what's got into you? - **2.** [Fahrzeug] to go; [Schiff] to sail; **der Zug fährt langsam** the train is going slowly - **3.** [abfahren] to leave; **wann fährst du?** when are you leaving ODER going?; **der Bus fährt alle 30 Minuten** the bus leaves ODER runs every half hour - **4.** RW: **einen ~ lassen** fam to fart ⟨⟩ vt - **1.** (hat) [Fahrzeug] to drive; [Fahrrad] to ride - **2.** (hat) [befördern]: **ich fahre dich nach Hause** I'll drive ODER take you home - **3.** (ist) [Entfernung, Strecke] to drive; **ich fahre diese Strecke jeden Tag** I drive ODER come this way every day - **4.** (ist) SPORT: **Rollschuh ~** to rollerskate; **Ski ~** to ski; **Schlitten ~** to go sledging.

**Fahrenheit** nt Fahrenheit.

**Fahrer** (pl -) der driver.

**Fahrerlairbag** der AUTO driver's airbag.

**Fahrerflucht** die failure to stop after an accident; **~ begehen** to fail to stop after an accident.

**Fahrerin** (pl -nen) die driver.

**Fahrlerlaubnis** die amt driving licence Br, driver's license Am.

**Fahrlgast** der passenger.

**Fahrlgeld** das fare.

**Fahrlgemeinschaft** die car pool; **eine ~ zum Arbeitsplatz** a car pool for going to work.

**Fahrlgestell** das [von Auto] chassis; [von Flugzeug] undercarriage.

**fahrig** adj nervous ⟨⟩ adv nervously.

**Fahrlkarte** die ticket.

**Fahrkartenlautomat** der ticket machine.

**Fahrkartenlschalter** der ticket desk.

**fahrlässig** adj negligent; **~e Tötung** manslaughter Br, murder in the second degree Am ⟨⟩ adv negligently.

**Fahrlässigkeit** die negligence; **grobe ~** gross negligence.

**Fahrllehrer, in** der, die driving instructor.

**Fahrlplan** der timetable.

**fahrplanmäßig** adj scheduled ⟨⟩ adv on schedule.

**Fahrlpreis** der fare.

**Fahrlprüfung** die driving test.

**Fahrlrad** das bicycle; **mit dem ~ fahren** to cycle.

**Fahrradlschloss** das cycle lock.

**Fahrradlständer** der - **1.** [Dorn zum Abstellen] prop stand - **2.** [Gestell für Fahrräder] bicycle stand.

**Fahrlschein** der ticket.

**Fahrscheinlautomat** der ticket machine.

**Fahrlschule** die driving school.

**Fahrlschüler, in** der, die - **1.** [in einer Fahrschule] learner driver - **2.** [als Pendler] pupil who relies on transport to get to school.

**Fahrlstuhl** der lift Br, elevator Am.

**Fahrlstunde** die driving lesson.

**Fahrt** (pl -en) die - **1.** [gen] journey; [kurzer Ausflug] trip; **auf der ~ nach Berlin** on the way to Berlin; **freie ~ haben** to have a clear run - **2.** (ohne pl) [Geschwindigkeit] speed; **~ bekommen** to speed up - **3.** RW: **in ~ sein** [in Schwung sein] to be in the mood; fam [wütend sein] to be livid; **in ~ kommen** ODER **geraten** [in Schwung kommen] to get going; fam [wütend werden] to flare up.

⟐ **gute Fahrt** interj have a good journey!

**fährt** präs ⟐ fahren.

**Fährte** (pl -n) die trail; **auf der falschen/richtigen ~ sein** fig to be on the wrong/right track.

**Fahrtenlmesser** das sheath knife.

**Fahrtenlschreiber** der AUTO tachograph.

**Fahrtkosten, Fahrkosten** pl travelling expenses.

**Fahrtlrichtung** die [im Verkehr] direction; [im Zug] direction of travel; **die A9 in ~ Berlin/München** the northbound/southbound section of the A9; **in ~ sitzen** [im Zug] to sit facing the engine.

**fahrtüchtig** adj [Person] fit to drive; [Fahrzeug] roadworthy.

**Fahrtwind** der (ohne pl) airflow.

**Fahrlverbot** das driving ban.

**Fahrlwasser** das (ohne pl) fairway.

**Fahr|zeug** (pl -e) das vehicle.

**Fahr|zeughalter, in** (mpl -; fpl -nen) der, die registered owner.

**Fahr|zeugpapiere** pl vehicle documents.

**fair** [fɛːɐ̯] adj fair ⬦ adv fairly.

**Fairness** [ˈfɛːɐ̯nɛs] die fairness.

**Fairplay** [ˈfɛːɐ̯ˈpleː] das sport fair play.

**Fäkalien** [fɛˈkaːliən] pl faeces.

**Fakt** der: ~ ist ... the fact is ...

**faktisch** adj actual ⬦ adv actually; [praktisch] practically.

**Faktor** (pl -toren) der factor.

**Faktum** (pl -ten) das fact.

**Fakultät** (pl -en) die uni faculty.

**fakultativ** adj optional.

**Falke** (pl -n) der falcon.

**Falklandinseln** pl Falkland Islands.

**Fall** (pl Fälle) der - **1.** [gen] case; **für alle Fälle** for all eventualities; **etw ist der ~** sthg is the case; **etw von ~ zu ~ entscheiden** to decide sthg on a case-by-case basis; **klarer ~!** sure thing!; **jd/etw ist ganz sein ~** fam fig one is very keen on sb/sthg - **2.** (ohne pl) [Sturz] fall; **zu ~ kommen** to fall; **jn zu ~ bringen** fig to bring sb down; **etw zu ~ bringen** fig to thwart sthg.
➟ **auf alle Fälle** adv - **1.** [unbedingt] definitely - **2.** [vorsichtshalber] in any case.
➟ **auf jeden Fall** adv in any case.
➟ **auf keinen Fall** adv under no circumstances.
➟ **für den Fall, dass** konj in case.
➟ **gesetzt den Fall** konj supposing.
➟ **im Fall(e), dass** konj if.

**Falle** (pl -n) die - **1.** [zum Fangen] trap; **(jm) eine ~ stellen** to set a trap (for sb); **in eine ~ geraten** fig to fall into a trap - **2.** fam [Bett] bed.

**fallen** (präs fällt; prät fiel; perf ist gefallen) vi - **1.** [gen] to fall; [Preise, Niveau, Temperatur] to drop; [Haare, Stoff] to hang - **2.** [Urteil] to be passed; [Entscheidung] to be made; [Wort] to be spoken; [Schuss] to be fired; **die Würfel sind gefallen** the die is cast; **in Ungnade ~** to fall out of favour; **der Termin fällt in meinen Urlaub** the date falls during my holiday; **durch eine Prüfung ~** to fail an exam.

**fällen** vt - **1.** [Baum] to fell - **2.** [Urteil] to pass; [Entscheidung] to make.

**fallen lassen** vt (unreg) - **1.** [gen] to drop - **2.** [Bemerkung] to let drop.

**fällig** adj due.

**Fallobst** das (ohne pl) windfalls (pl).

**falls** konj if; **~ es dir nicht gefällt** in case oder if you don't like it.

**Fall|schirm** der parachute.

**Fall|schirm|jäger** der mil paratrooper.

**Fall|schirm|springer, in** der, die parachutist.

**Fall|studie** [ˈfalʃtuːdjə] die case study.

**fällt** präs ⬅ fallen.

**Fall|tür** die trapdoor.

**falsch** adj - **1.** [nicht korrekt, nicht passend] wrong - **2.** [imitiert, gefälscht, irreführend - Gebiss, Stolz, Angaben] false; [ - Pass, Geldschein] forged ⬦ adv - **1.** [nicht korrekt] wrongly; **etw ~ verstehen** to misunderstand sthg; **~ singen** to sing out of tune; **~ abbiegen** to take the wrong turning - **2.** [hinterhältig] falsely.

**Falsch|aussage** die recht false statement.

**Falsche** (pl -n) der, die, das [Person] wrong person; [Sache] wrong thing; **an den ~n** oder **die ~ geraten** fam to come to the wrong person.

**fälschen** vt to forge.

**Fälscher, in** (mpl -; fpl -nen) der, die forger.

**Falsch|fahrer, in** der, die person who drives into oncoming traffic on a motorway.

**Falschgeld** das counterfeit money.

**Falschheit** die falseness.

**fälschlich** adj false ⬦ adv falsely.

**fälschlicherweise** adv mistakenly.

**Falsch|meldung** die false report.

**Fälschung** (pl -en) die - **1.** [Fälschen] forging - **2.** [Gefälschtes] forgery.

**fälschungssicher** adj forgery-proof.

**Falt|blatt** das leaflet.

**Falte** (pl -n) die [in Stoff, Papier] fold; [in Hose, Hemd] crease; [in Haut] wrinkle; **die Stirn in ~n legen** to furrow one's brow.

**falten** vt - **1.** [Stoff, Papier, Hände] to fold - **2.** [Stirn] to furrow.

**Falten|rock** der pleated skirt.

**Falter** (pl -) der butterfly.

**faltig** adj [Haut, Hände] wrinkled; [Hemd, Tischtuch] creased.

**familiär** adj - **1.** [die Familie betreffend] family (vor Subst) ( - **2.** [zwanglos] informal ⬦ adv [zwanglos] informally.

**Familie** [faˈmiːliə] (pl -n) die family; **~ haben** to have a family.

**Familien|anschluss** der: **~ haben/suchen** to live/want to live as part of the family.

**Familien|betrieb** der family business.

**Familien|feier** die family celebration.

**Familien|kreis** der (ohne pl) family circle; **im (engsten) ~** in the presence of the immediate family.

**Familien|leben** das family life.

**Familien|mitglied** das family member.

**Familien|name** der surname.

**Familien|planung** *die* family planning.

**Familien|stand** *der* marital status.

**Fan** (*pl* -s) *der* fan.

**Fanatiker, in** (*mpl* -; *fpl* -nen) *der, die* fanatic.

**fanatisch** *adj* fanatical <> *adv* fanatically.

**Fanatismus** *der* fanaticism.

**Fanclub** *der* = Fanklub.

**fand** *prät* ⊏> finden.

**Fanfare** (*pl* -n) *die* fanfare.

**Fang** *der* - **1.** [Fangen] catching - **2.** [Beute] catch; **einen guten ~ machen** to make a good catch.

**fangen** (*präs* fängt; *prät* fing; *perf* hat gefangen) *vt* to catch.

➤ **sich fangen** *ref* - **1.** [in Falle, Netz] to get caught - **2.** [nach Schwierigkeiten] to regain one's composure.

**Fangen** *das:* **~ spielen** to play tag.

**Fang|frage** *die* trick question.

**Fango|packung** *die* fango pack.

**fängt** *präs* ⊏> fangen.

**Fan|klub, Fanclub** *der* fan club.

**Fantasie, Phantasie** [fanta'zi:] (*pl* -n) *die* - **1.** (*ohne pl*) [Vorstellungskraft] imagination - **2.** [Vorstellung] fantasy.

**fantasielos, phantasielos** *adj* unimaginative <> *adv* unimaginatively.

**fantasieren, phantasieren** *vi* - **1.** [irrereden] to be delirious - **2.** [träumen] to fantasize.

**fantasievoll, phantasievoll** *adj* imaginative <> *adv* imaginatively.

**fantastisch, phantastisch** *adj* fantastic <> *adv* fantastically.

**Farb|aufnahme** *die* colour photograph.

**Farbband** (*pl* -bänder) *das* (typewriter) ribbon.

**Farb|drucker** *der* EDV colour printer.

**Farbe** (*pl* -n) *die* - **1.** [Licht, Buntheit] colour; **~ bekommen** *fig* to get some colour - **2.** [Material] paint - **3.** [in Kartenspiel] suit; **~ bekennen** *fam fig* to put one's cards on the table.

**farbecht** *adj* colourfast.

**färben** *vt* to dye <> *vi* to run.

➤ **sich färben** *ref* to change colour; **sich rosa ~** to turn pink.

**farbenblind** *adj* colour-blind.

**farbenprächtig** *adj* gloriously colourful.

**Farb|fernsehen** *das* colour television.

**Farb|fernseher** *der* colour television.

**Farb|film** *der* colour film.

**Farb|foto** *das* colour photo.

**farbig** *adj* - **1.** [Druck, Fernsehen] colour - **2.** [bunt,

lebhaft] colourful - **3.** [Person, Papier] coloured <> *adv* colourfully.

**Farbige** (*pl* -n) *der, die* coloured person.

**farblich** *adv* as regards colour.

**farblos** *adj* colourless.

**Farb|stift** *der* coloured pencil.

**Farb|stoff** *der* colouring.

**Farb|ton** *der* shade.

**Färbung** (*pl* -en) *die* - **1.** [Farbgebung] tinge - **2.** [Tendenz] slant.

**Farce** ['fars(ə)] (*pl* -n) *die* - **1.** [Theater] farce - **2.** KÜCHE stuffing (*U*).

**Farm** (*pl* -en) *die* farm.

**Farn** (*pl* -e) *der* fern.

**Fasan** (*pl* -e ODER -en) *der* pheasant.

**Fasching** (*pl* -e ODER -s) *der* carnival before Lent.

**Faschismus** *der* fascism.

**Faschist, in** (*mpl* -en; *fpl* -nen) *der, die* fascist.

**faseln** *fam abw vi* to blather <> *vt:* **Unsinn ~** to talk rubbish.

**Faser** (*pl* -n) *die* fibre.

**faserig** *adj* [Fleisch] stringy; [Holz] coarse.

**fasern** *vi* [Holz] to splinter; [Stoff] to fray.

**Fass** (*pl* Fässer) *das* barrel; **ein ~ ohne Boden** *fig* a bottomless pit.

➤ **vom Fass** *adj* & *adv* draught.

**Fassade** (*pl* -n) *die* facade.

**fassen** (*präs* fasst; *prät* fasste; *perf* hat gefasst) *vt* - **1.** [anfassen] to take hold of; **jn/etw zu ~ bekommen** to catch hold of sb/sthg - **2.** [Dieb] to catch - **3.** [Entschluss] to make - **4.** [begreifen]: **ich kann es nicht ~** I can't take it in - **5.** [als Inhalt] to hold <> *vi:* **an etw** (*A*) **~** [kurz] to touch sthg; [lang] to feel sthg.

➤ **sich fassen** *ref* to pull o.s. together; **sich auf etw** (*A*) **gefasst machen** *fig* to prepare o.s. for sthg; **sich kurz ~** to keep it short.

**Fassette** *die* = Facette.

**Fasson** [fa'sɔŋ] (*pl* -s) *die:* **aus der ~ geraten** *fam fig* to lose one's figure; **jeder nach seiner ~** each in his/her own way.

**Fassung** (*pl* -en) *die* - **1.** [von Glühbirne] socket; [von Perle] setting - **2.** [von Text] version - **3.** [Selbstbeherrschung]: **die ~ bewahren** to maintain one's composure; **jn aus der ~ bringen** to put sb out; **etw mit ~ tragen** to bear sthg calmly.

**fassungslos** *adj* [Person] speechless; [Gesicht] astounded <> *adv* speechlessly.

**Fassungsvermögen** *das* capacity.

**fast** *adv* nearly, almost.

**fasten** *vi* to fast.

**Fasten|zeit** *die* - **1.** [Zeit religiösen Fastens] fasting period - **2.** [vor Ostern] Lent.

**Fastnacht** *die carnival before Lent.*

**Faszination** *die* fascination.

**faszinieren** *vt* to fascinate.

**fatal** *adj* - **1.** [peinlich] embarrassing - **2.** [verhängnisvoll] fatal.

**fatalistisch** *adj* fatalistic.

**fauchen** *vi* to hiss.

**faul** *adj* - **1.** [Lebensmittel, Holz] rotten - **2.** [Person] lazy - **3.** *fam* [Witz, Ausrede] dubious ⬦ *adv* [träge] lazily.

**faulen** (*perf* **hat/ist gefault**) *vi* [Holz, Fleisch] to rot; [Zahn] to decay.

**faulenzen** *vi* to laze around.

**Faulenzer, in** (*mpl* -; *fpl* -nen) *der, die* layabout.

**Faulheit** *die* laziness.

**faulig** *adj* [Obst] rotten; [Wasser] stagnant.

**Fäulnis** *die* rot; **in ~ übergehen** to begin to rot.

**Faul|pelz** *der fam* lazybones *(sg).*

**Fauna** *die* BIOL fauna.

**Faust** (*pl* **Fäuste**) *die* fist; **auf eigene ~** *fig* off one's own bat.

**Fäustchen** (*pl* -) *das:* **sich** *(D)* **(eins) ins ~ lachen** *fig* to laugh up one's sleeve.

**faustdick** *adj* [Lüge] blatant.

**Fausthand|schuh** *der* mitten.

**Fäustling** (*pl* -e) *der* mitten.

**Faust|regel** *die* rule of thumb.

**Faust|schlag** *der* punch.

**Favorit, in** (*mpl* -en; *fpl* -nen) *der, die* favourite.

**Fax** (*pl* - ODER -e) *das* fax.

**faxen** *vt* to fax.

**Faxen** *pl fam:* **~ machen** to fool around; **mach keine ~!** stop fooling around!; **die ~ dick** ODER **satt haben** to have had enough.

**FAZ** ['efa:tsɛt] (*abk für* **Frankfurter Allgemeine Zeitung**) *die German newspaper, renowned for its business and financial news.*

**Fazit** (*pl* -s ODER -e) *das* result; **das ~ (aus etw) ziehen** to sum (sthg) up.

**FC** [ɛf'tse:l] (*abk für* **Fußballclub**) *der* FC.

**FCKW** [ɛf'tse:'ka:'ve:l] (*abk für* **Fluorchlorkohlenwasserstoff**) *der (ohne pl)* CFC.

**F.D.P.** [ɛf'de:'pe:l] (*abk für* **Freie Demokratische Partei**) *die German liberal party.*

**F-Dur** *das* MUS F major.

**Februar** *der* February; *siehe auch* **September.**

**fechten** (*präs* **ficht**; *prät* **focht**; *perf* **hat gefochten**) *vi* to fence.

**Fechter, in** (*mpl* -; *fpl* -nen) *der, die* fencer.

**Feder** (*pl* -n) *die* - **1.** [von Vogel] feather; **~n lassen müssen** *fam fig* not to come out unscathed - **2.** [zum Schreiben] nib; **zur ~ greifen** to take up one's pen - **3.** [in Maschine, Matratze] spring.

➧ **Federn** *pl*: **aus den ~n** *fam* out of bed; **(noch) in den ~n liegen** *fam* to be (still) in bed.

**Feder|ball** *der* - **1.** [Spiel] badminton - **2.** [Ball] shuttlecock.

**Feder|bett** *das* quilt.

**federleicht** *adj* as light as a feather ⬦ *adv* as lightly as a feather.

**Federlesen** *das*: **ohne viel** ODER **langes ~** *fig* without further ado.

**federn** *vi* [elastisch sein] to be springy; [bei Sprung, Druck] to spring back; **in den Knien ~** to give at the knees ⬦ *vt* [Fahrzeug]: **gut gefedert sein** [Auto] to have good suspension; [Matratze] to be well sprung.

**Federung** (*pl* -en) *die* [von Wagen] suspension *(U)*; [von Bett] springs *(pl).*

**Federweiße** (*pl* -n) *der young, cloudy white wine.*

**Feder|zeichnung** *die* pen-and-ink drawing.

**Fee** (*pl* -n) *die* fairy.

**Feed-back** ['fi:dbɛk] (*pl* -s) *das* feedback *(U).*

**Feeling** ['fi:lɪŋ] (*pl* -s) *das* feeling.

**Fegefeuer** *das* purgatory.

**fegen** (*perf* **hat/ist gefegt**) *vt* (*hat*) to sweep ⬦ *vi* - **1.** (*hat*) *Norddt* [säubern] to sweep up - **2.** (*ist*) [rasen] to sweep.

**fehl** *adv*: **~ am Platz sein** to be out of place.

**Fehl|anzeige** *die fam*: **ich habe ihn zu Hause gesucht, aber da war ~** I looked for him at home but had no luck there.

**Fehl|betrag** *der* shortfall.

**Fehl|diagnose** *die* misdiagnosis.

**fehlen** *vi* - **1.** [nicht vorhanden sein] to be missing; **für ein Hobby fehlt ihr die Zeit** she doesn't have time for a hobby; **(in der Schule) ~** to miss school; **es fehlt an etw** *(D)* there is a lack of sthg; **es fehlt ihm einiges an Erfahrung** he is somewhat lacking in experience; **der/die/das fehlte gerade noch!** *fam iron* that's all I/we needed! - **2.** [vermisst werden]: **sie fehlt mir** I miss her; **die Spaziergänge am Rhein ~ mir** I miss walking along the Rhine - **3.** [irren]: **weit gefehlt!** far from it! - **4.** [erkrankt sein]: **was fehlt dir/Ihnen?** what is the matter with you?

**Fehl|entscheidung** *die* wrong decision.

**Fehler** (*pl* -) *der* - **1.** [Unrichtigkeit] mistake - **2.** [Schwäche] fault; **ist es mein ~, dass er geht?** is it my fault that he's leaving? - **3.** [Mangel] defect.

**fehlerfrei** *adj* perfect ⬦ *adv* perfectly.

**fehlerhaft** *adj* [Maschine] defective; [Aussprache] poor <> *adv* [schreiben, arbeiten] poorly; [verarbeitet] defectively.

**fehlerlos** *adj* [Aufsatz] without mistakes; [Person] perfect <> *adv* without mistakes.

**Fehler|meldung** *die* EDV error message.

**Fehler|quelle** *die* source of the fault.

**Fehl|geburt** *die* miscarriage.

**fehl|gehen** (*perf* ist fehlgegangen) *vi (unreg)* - **1.** [sich irren] to be mistaken - **2.** [Schuss] to miss.

**Fehl|griff** *der* mistake.

**Fehl|schlag** *der* failure.

**fehl|schlagen** (*perf* ist fehlgeschlagen) *vi (unreg)* to fail.

**Fehl|start** *der* - **1.** [von Sportlern] false start - **2.** [von Rakete] abortive launch.

**Fehl|urteil** *das* - **1.** [Rechtspruch - von Richter] wrong judgement; [ - von Geschworenen] wrong verdict - **2.** [Beurteilung] misjudgement.

**Fehl|verhalten** *das* inappropriate behaviour.

**Fehl|zündung** *die* misfire.

**Fehmarn** *nt* Fehmarn.

**Feier** (*pl* -n) *die* party; **zur ~ des Tages** in honour of the occasion.

**Feier|abend** *der* evening after work; **~ machen** to finish work; **nach ~** after work; **seinen ~ im Garten verbringen** to spend one's evening in the garden; **mit etw ist ~** *fam fig* it's all over with sthg.

**feierlich** *adj* - **1.** [Akt, Handlung, Stille] dignified - **2.** [Erklärung] solemn - **3.** *RW:* **das ist schon nicht mehr ~** *fam* that really is too much <> *adv* - **1.** [verabschieden, begehen] in a dignified manner - **2.** [erklären] solemnly.

**Feierlichkeit** (*pl* -en) *die* [Würde] solemnity. ➤ Feierlichkeiten *pl* celebrations.

**feiern** *vt* - **1.** [Fest, Feiertag] to celebrate - **2.** [Person] to fête <> *vi* to celebrate.

**Feier|tag** *der* holiday; **kirchlicher ~** feast day.

**feiertags** *adv* on public holidays.

**feige** *adj* cowardly.

**Feige** (*pl* -n) *die* fig.

**Feigheit** *die* cowardice.

**Feigling** (*pl* -e) *der* coward.

**Feile** (*pl* -n) *die* file.

**feilen** *vt* to file <> *vi:* **an etw** (*D*) **~** *fig* to polish sthg up.

**feilschen** *vi:* **um etw ~** to haggle over sthg.

**fein** *adj* - **1.** [Haar, Spitze, Pulver] fine; **du bist mir eine ~e Freundin!** a fine friend you are! - **2.** *fam* [erfreulich, sympathisch] great - **3.** [Gesicht] delicate - **4.** [Material, Zutat, Küche] top-quality

- **5.** [Sinne] keen - **6.** [Spott, Nuance] subtle - **7.** [Leute] refined; **sich ~ machen** to make o.s. smart <> *adv* - **1.** *fam* [lieb, brav] like a good boy/girl; **bleib ~ hier stehen!** be a good boy/girl and stay here! - **2.** [gemahlen, gezeichnet] finely - **3.** *fam* [schön, erfreulich]: **~ gemacht!** well done!; **~ heraus sein** *fig* to have done well for o.s. - **4.** [sich verhalten] nicely - **5.** [vornehm, elegant] elegantly.
➤ **vom Feinsten** *adj* top-quality.

**Fein|abstimmung** *die* fine tuning.

**Feind** (*pl* -e) *der* enemy; **sich** (*D*) **~e machen** to make enemies.

**Feindin** (*pl* -nen) *die* enemy.

**feindlich** *adj* - **1.** [Haltung, Nachbarn] hostile - **2.** [Soldaten] enemy (*vor Subst*) <> *adv* hostilely.

**Feindlichkeit** *die* [Gesinnung] hostility.

**Feindschaft** (*pl* -en) *die* enmity (*U*); **sich** (*D*) **js ~ zuziehen** to make an enemy of sb.

**feindschaftlich** *adj* hostile <> *adv* hostilely.

**feindselig** *adj* hostile <> *adv* hostilely.

**Feindseligkeit** (*pl* -en) *die* hostility. ➤ **Feindseligkeiten** *pl* hostilities.

**feinfühlig** *adj* sensitive.

**Feingefühl** *das* sensitivity.

**Feinheit** (*pl* -en) *die* - **1.** [Beschaffenheit] fineness - **2.** [Vornehmheit] refinement. ➤ **Feinheiten** *pl* subtleties.

**Feinkost|geschäft** *das* delicatessen.

**feinmaschig** *adj* fine-meshed.

**Fein|schmecker, in** (*mpl* -; *fpl* -nen) *der, die* gourmet.

**Fein|wäsche** *die (ohne pl)* delicates (*pl*).

**feixen** *vi* to smirk.

**Feld** (*pl* -er) *das* - **1.** [gen] field - **2.** [Teil - von Formular] box; [ - von Brettspiel] square - **3.** *RW:* **das ~ räumen** to bow out; **jm das ~ überlassen** to make way for sb; **etw ins ~ führen** *geh* to bring sthg forward.

**Feld|bett** *das* camp bed *Br*, cot *Am*.

**Feld|blume** *die* wild flower.

**Feld|flasche** *die* water bottle.

**Feld|jäger** *der* military policeman. ➤ **Feldjäger** *pl* military police.

**Feld|maus** *die* field mouse.

**Feld|salat** *der (ohne pl)* lamb's lettuce.

**Feld|stecher** (*pl* -) *der* binoculars (*pl*).

**Feldwebel** (*pl* -) *der* sergeant.

**Feld|weg** *der* footpath (*between fields*).

**Feld|zug** *der* campaign.

**Felge** (*pl* -n) *die* - **1.** [Teil des Rades] (wheel) rim - **2.** [Turnübung] circle.

F

**Felgen|bremse** *die* rim brake.

**Fell** (*pl* -e) *das* - **1.** [Haarkleid] fur; [von Hund, Pferd] coat; [von Schaf] fleece - **2.** *RW:* ein dickes ~ haben *fam* to be thick-skinned; jm das ~ über die Ohren ziehen *fam* to pull the wool over sb's eyes.

**Fels** (*pl* -en) *der* - **1.** (*ohne pl*) [Gestein] rock - **2.** *geh* [Felsen] cliff.

**Felsblock** (*pl* -blöcke) *der* boulder.

**Felsen** (*pl* -) *der* cliff.

**felsenfest** *adj* firm ◇ *adv* firmly; von etw ~ überzeugt sein to be firmly convinced of sthg.

**felsig** *adj* rocky.

**Fels|wand** *die* rock face.

**feminin** *adj* - **1.** [gen] feminine - **2.** *abw* [unmännlich] effeminate ◇ *adv* - **1.** [weiblich] femininely - **2.** *abw* [unmännlich] effeminately.

**Femininum** (*pl* -nina) *das* GRAM feminine noun.

**Feminismus** *der* [Frauenbewegung] feminism.

**Feminist, in** (*mpl* -en; *fpl* -nen) *der, die* feminist.

**feministisch** *adj* feminist ◇ *adv* in a feminist way.

**Fenchel** *der* fennel.

**Fenster** (*pl* -) *das* window; weg vom ~ sein *fam fig* to be out of it.

**Fenster|bank** (*pl* -bänke) *die* windowsill.

**Fenster|laden** *der* shutter.

**Fenster|platz** *der* window seat.

**Fenster|rahmen** *der* window frame.

**Fenster|scheibe** *die* window pane.

**Ferien** *pl* holiday (*sg*) *Br,* vacation (*sg*) *Am;* die großen ~ the summer holidays *Br,* the summer vacation *Am;* in die ~ fahren, ~ machen to go on holiday *Br,* to go on vacation *Am.*

**Ferien|gast** *der* holidaymaker *Br,* vacationer *Am.*

**Ferien|haus** *das* holiday home *Br,* vacation home *Am.*

**Ferien|kurs** *der* summer course.

**Ferien|lager** *das* summer camp.

**Ferien|ort** *der* resort.

**Ferien|tag** *der* day of one's holiday *Br* ODER vacation *Am.*

**Ferien|wohnung** *die* holiday flat *Br,* holiday apartment *Am.*

**Ferkel** (*pl* -) *das* - **1.** [Tier] piglet - **2.** *fam* [dreckiger Mensch] mucky pup - **3.** *fam* [unanständiger Mensch] filthy swine.

**fern** *adj* - **1.** [räumlich] far-off - **2.** [zeitlich] distant ◇ *adv* far; von ~ from a distance ◇ *präp geh:* ~ einer Sache (*D*) far from sthg.

**Fern|bedienung** *die* remote control.

**fern|bleiben** (*perf* ist ferngeblieben) *vi* (*unreg*) *geh:* einer Sache (*D*) ~ to stay away from sthg.

**Ferne** *die* (*ohne pl*) - **1.** [räumlich]: ihr Blick schweifte in die ~ she stared off into the distance; in der ~ in the distance; in die ~ ziehen *geh* to leave for far-off lands; aus der ~ [betrachten] from a distance; [Gruß] from far-off lands - **2.** [zeitlich]: in weiter ~ a long way away.

**Ferne Osten** *der* Far East.

**ferner** *konj* in addition; unter „~ liefen" rangieren to be among the also-rans ◇ *adv geh* in future ◇ *adj (Kompar)* ▷ **fern.**

**Fern|fahrer, in** *der, die* long-distance lorry driver *Br,* long-distance trucker *Am.*

**Fern|gespräch** *das* long-distance call.

**ferngesteuert** *adj* remote-controlled.

**Fern|glas** *das* binoculars (*pl*).

**fern halten** *vt* (*unreg*): jn/etw von jm/etw ~ to keep sb/sthg away from sb/sthg.

➡ **sich fern halten** *ref:* sich von jm/etw ~ to keep away from sb/sthg.

**Fern|heizung** *die* district heating.

**Fern|leihe** *die* inter-library loans system.

**Fern|licht** *das* full beam *Br,* high beam *Am.*

**fern liegen** *vi* (*unreg*): jm ~ to be far from sb's mind.

**fern liegend** *adj* distant.

**Fern|meldewesen** *das* (*ohne pl*) telecommunications (*pl*).

**Fern|rohr** *das* telescope.

**Fern|schreiben** *das* telex.

**Fern|schreiber** *der* teleprinter.

**Fernseh|ansager, in** *der, die* television announcer.

**Fernseh|apparat** *der* television set.

**fern|sehen** *vi* (*unreg*) to watch television.

**Fernsehen** *das* television; im ~ on television, on TV.

**Fernseher** (*pl* -) *der* - **1.** [Gerät] television, TV - **2.** [Fernsehzuschauer] viewer.

**Fernseh|film** *der* television ODER TV film.

**Fernseh|gerät** *das* television ODER TV set.

**Fernseh|programm** *das* - **1.** [Sendungen] television ODER TV programmes (*pl*) - **2.** [Programmheft] television ODER TV guide.

**Fernseh|übertragung** *die* television ODER TV broadcast.

**Fernseh|werbung** *die* television ODER TV commercials (*pl*).

**Fernseh|zuschauer, in** *der, die* viewer.

**Fern|sprecher** *der amt* telephone; öffentlicher ~ public telephone.

**Fern|steuerung** *die* remote control.

**Fern|straße** *die* trunk road *Br*, highway *Am*.

**Fern|studium** *das* correspondence course.

**Fern|verkehr** *der* long-distance traffic.

**Fern|wärme** *die* district heating.

**Ferse** (*pl* -n) *die* heel; jm auf den ~n sein/bleiben *fig* to be/stay on sb's heels.

**fertig** *adj* - 1. [vollendet - gen] finished; [ - Essen] ready - 2. [bereit]: ~ sein to be ready - 3. [am/zu Ende]: (mit etw) ~ sein to have finished (sthg) - 4. [müde]: ~ sein *fam* [körperlich] to be worn out; [psychisch] to be shattered; mit den Nerven ~ sein to be at the end of one's tether *Br* ODER rope *Am* - 5. RW: mit jm ~ sein *fam* to be finished ODER through with sb; mit etw ~/nicht ~ werden to cope/not cope with sthg; mit jm schon/ nicht ~ werden *fam* to cope/not cope with sb.

**fertig bringen** *vt* (*unreg*) - 1. [zustande bringen]: er hat es fertig gebracht, dass die Familien wieder miteinander reden he has managed to get the families talking to each other again - 2. [übers Herz bringen]: er bringt es nicht fertig, ihr die Wahrheit zu sagen he can't bring himself to tell her the truth - 3. [zu Ende bringen] to finish.

**Fertig|gericht** *das* ready meal.

**Fertig|haus** *das* prefabricated house.

**Fertigkeit** (*pl* -en) *die* skill.
➤ **Fertigkeiten** *pl* skills.

**fertig|machen** *vt* - 1. *fam* [zurechtweisen] to lay into - 2. *fam* [zur Verzweiflung bringen]: der macht mich fertig he does my head in - 3. *fam* [erschöpfen] to wear out.
➤ **sich fertigmachen** *ref fam* [sich überanstrengen] to do o.s. in.

**fertig machen** *vt* - 1. [abschließen] to finish - 2. [bereitmachen] to get ready - 3. *fam* [erledigen] to sort out; [zusammenschlagen] to do in.
➤ **sich fertig machen** *ref* [sich bereitmachen] to get ready.

**fertig stellen** *vt* to complete.

**fesch** *adj Österr* smart.

**Fessel** (*pl* -n) *die* - 1. [Strick, Zwang] bond - 2. [Körperteil - bei Tieren] pastern; [ - bei Menschen] ankle.

**Fessel|ballon** *der* captive balloon.

**fesseln** *vt* - 1. [anketten, binden] to tie up; jm die Hände ~ to tie sb's hands up - 2. [faszinieren] to grip.

**fesselnd** *adj* gripping ➣ *adv* grippingly.

**fest** *adj* - 1. [gut befestigt - Knoten, Verband] tight - 2. [Griff, Druck, Meinung] firm - 3. [Wohnsitz, Angestellte] permanent; [Arbeitszeiten, Gehalt, Termin] fixed - 4. [Stoff, Schuhe] strong - 5. [verbindlich - Vereinbarung, Vorgaben] binding; [ - Zusage] definite - 6. [Nahrung] solid - 7. [entschlossen - Blick, Stimme] steady ➣ *adv* - 1. [haltbar, straff] tightly - 2. [drücken, ziehen] hard - 3. [überzeugt - glauben] firmly - 4. [verbindlich - zusagen, ver-

einbaren] definitely - 5. [angestellt] permanently - 6. [schlafen] soundly - 7. *fam* [tüchtig - zugreifen] with a will.

**Fest** (*pl* -e) *das* - 1. [Veranstaltung] party - 2. [Feiertag] festival.
➤ **frohes Fest** *interj* happy Christmas!

**festangestellt** ➣ fest.

**Fest|betrag** *der* fixed amount.

**fest|binden** *vt* (*unreg*) to tie up.

**Fest|essen** *das* banquet.

**fest|halten** (*unreg*) *vt* - 1. [aufzeichnen] to record - 2. [feststellen]: wir können ~, dass ... it is clear that ... ➣ *vi*: an jm ~ to stand by sb; an etw ~ to stick to sthg.

**fest halten** (*unreg*) *vt* [halten] to hold on to.
➤ **sich fest halten** *ref*: sich an jm/etw ~ to hold on to sb/sthg.

**festigen** *vt* to strengthen.
➤ **sich festigen** *ref* to become stronger.

**Festiger** (*pl* -) *der* [Schaum] styling mousse; [Spray] hairspray.

**Festigkeit** *die* - 1. [Widerstandsfähigkeit] strength - 2. [Standhaftigkeit] steadfastness.

**Festival** ['fɛstivəl] (*pl* -s) *das* festival.

**Festland** *das* mainland.

**fest|legen** *vt* - 1. [bestimmen] to fix - 2. [verpflichten]: jn auf etw (A) ~ to pin sb down to sthg.
➤ **sich festlegen** *ref* [sich binden] to commit o.s.; sich auf etw (A) ~ to commit o.s. to sthg.

**festlich** *adj* [Essen, Veranstaltung] festive; [Kleidung] formal ➣ *adv* festively.

**Festlichkeit** (*pl* -en) *die* [Atmosphäre] festiveness.
➤ **Festlichkeiten** *pl* festivities.

**fest|liegen** *vi* (*unreg*) - 1. [nicht weiterkommen] to be held up; [Schiff] to have run aground - 2. [feststehen] to be fixed.

**fest|machen** *vt* - 1. [befestigen] to fix; [Boot] to moor - 2. [vereinbaren - Termin] to fix; [ - Geschäft] to secure.

**Fest|mahl** *das geh* banquet.

**fest|nageln** *vt* - 1. [befestigen] to nail - 2. *fam* [festlegen]: jn (auf etw (A)) ~ to pin sb down (to sthg).

**Festnahme** (*pl* -n) *die* arrest.

**fest|nehmen** *vt* (*unreg*) to arrest.

**Fest|netz** *das* TELEKOM land-line telephone network (*as opposed to mobile phones*).

**Fest|platte** *die* EDV hard disk.

**Festplattenlauf|werk** *das* EDV hard drive.

**Fest|preis** *der* fixed price.

**fest|setzen** *vt* - 1. [bestimmen] to fix - 2. [verhaften] to arrest.
➤ **sich festsetzen** *ref* [Dreck] to collect; [Erkältung, Idee] to take hold.

**F**

**fest|sitzen** *vi (unreg)* [nicht weiterkommen] to be stuck.

**fest sitzen** *vi (unreg)* **es sitzt fest** [Dübel] it won't come out; [Farbe] it won't come off.

**Festspiele** *pl* festival *(sg)*.

**fest|stehen** *vi (unreg)* - **1.** [bestimmt sein] to have been fixed - **2.** [sicher sein] to be definite.

**feststehend** *adj* [Abfolge, Tatsachen] established; [Redewendung] set.

**fest|stellen** *vt* - **1.** [in Erfahrung bringen] to find out; [diagnostizieren] to establish - **2.** [beobachten] to notice; **sie stellte fest, dass er Recht hatte** she realized that he was right - **3.** [anmerken] to state.

**Fest|stellung** *die* - **1.** [Ermittlung] establishing - **2.** [Wahrnehmung] realization; **ich machte die ~, dass ...** I realized that ... - **3.** [Erklärung] remark.

**Fest|tag** *der* [Feiertag] holiday; [Geburtstag usw.] special day.

**Festung** *(pl* -en) *die* fortress.

**festverzinslich** *adj* wirtsch fixed-interest.

**Fest|zug** *der* carnival procession.

**Fete** ['feːtə] *(pl* -n) *die fam* party.

**Fetischist, in** *(mpl* -en; *fpl* -nen) *der, die* fetishist.

**fett** *adj* - **1.** [Fleisch, Gericht] fatty - **2.** [Person, Tier, Erbe, Beute] fat <> *adv* [mit viel Fett]: **~ essen** to eat fatty food.

**Fett** *(pl* -e) *das* fat; **~ ansetzen** to get fat; **er hat sein ~ weg** *fam fig* he got what was coming to him.

**fettarm** *adj* low-fat.

**Fett|auge** *das* speck of fat.

**fetten** *vt* to grease <> *vi* to be greasy.

**Fett|fleck** *der* spot of grease.

**fett gedruckt** *adj* in bold (type).

**Fettgehalt** *der* fat content.

**fettig** *adj* greasy.

**Fettnäpfchen** *das:* **ins ~ treten** *fam* to put one's foot in it.

**fetzen** *(perf* hat/ist gefetzt) *fam vi* - **1.** *(ist)* [rennen, fahren] to tear along - **2.** *(hat)* [Begeisterung wecken] to be cool <> *vt (hat)* to tear.

**Fetzen** *(pl* -) *der* scrap; **etw in ~ zerreißen** to tear sthg to pieces; **das Kleid ist ein billiges ~!** that dress is just cheap rubbish!; **sich streiten, dass die ~ fliegen** *fam* to have an almighty row.

**fetzig** *adj fam* [toll] cool.

**feucht** *adj* [Wand, Tuch, Haar] damp; [Hände, Augen] moist; [Klima] humid <> *adv* [wischen] with a damp cloth.

**Feuchtigkeit** *die* - **1.** [leichte Nässe] moisture

- **2.** [Feuchtsein - von Wand, Tuch, Haar] dampness; [ - von Händen, Augen] moistness; [ - von Klima] humidity.

**Feuchtigkeits|creme** *die* moisturizer.

**feuchtwarm** *adj* humid.

**feudal** *adj* - **1.** [den Feudalismus betreffend] feudal - **2.** [aristokratisch] aristocratic - **3.** *fam* [vornehm] grand <> *adv fam* [vornehm] grandly.

**Feuer** *(pl* -) *das* - **1.** [gen] fire; **auf offenem ~ kochen** to cook over an open fire; **~ machen** to light a fire; **im Ofen ~ machen** to light the oven; **jn um ~ bitten** to ask sb for a light; **jm ~ geben** to give sb a light; **~ legen** to start a fire; **~ fangen** to catch fire; **das ~ einstellen/eröffnen** to cease/open fire - **2.** *(ohne pl)* [Schwung, Temperament - von Person] passion; [ - von Begeisterung, Leidenschaft] fervour - **3.** *RW:* **~ fangen** *fam* [sich verlieben] to be smitten; **mit dem ~ spielen** to play with fire; **für jn durchs ~ gehen** to walk through fire for sb; **(für jn/etw) ~ und Flamme sein** *fam* to be really keen (on sb/sthg) <> *interj* fire!

**Feueralarm** *der* fire alarm.

**Feuereifer** *der* zeal, zest.

**feuerfest** *adj* fireproof; [Backform] ovenproof.

**Feuergefahr** *die:* **es besteht ~** there is a risk of fire.

**feuergefährlich** *adj* flammable.

**Feuerland** *nt* Tierra del Fuego.

**Feuer|leiter** *die* [an Haus] fire escape; [an Löschfahrzeug] (fireman's) ladder.

**Feuer|löscher** *(pl* -) *der* fire extinguisher.

**Feuer|melder** *(pl* -) *der* fire alarm.

**feuern** *vt* - *fam* - **1.** [entlassen, heizen] to fire - **2.** [schleudern] to fling <> *vi* [schießen]: **auf jn/etw ~** to fire at sb/sthg.

**Feuer|stein** *der* flint.

**Feuer|versicherung** *die* fire insurance.

**Feuer|wehr** *(pl* -en) *die* fire brigade.

**Feuer|wehrmann** *(pl* -männer oder -leute) *der* fireman.

**Feuer|werk** *das* - **1.** [Veranstaltung] firework display - **2.** [Raketen] fireworks *(pl)*.

**Feuerwerks|körper** *der* firework.

**Feuerzangen|bowle** *die punch made of red wine, burnt rum and sugar.*

**Feuer|zeug** *das* lighter.

**Feuilleton** [fœjə'tɔ̃] *(pl* -s) *das* - **1.** [literarischer Teil einer Zeitung] arts section - **2.** [literarischer Beitrag] arts feature.

**feurig** *adj* fiery.

**ff.** *(abk für* **folgende Seiten**) ff.

**FH** [ɛf'haː] *(pl* -s) *die* ▷ **Fachhochschule.**

**Fiasko** *(pl* -s) *das* fiasco.

**Fibel** (*pl* -n) *die* - **1.** [Lesebuch] ABC-book - **2.** [Lehrbuch] handbook.

**ficht** *präs* ▷ fechten.

**Fichte** (*pl* -n) *die* spruce.

**ficken** *vt* & *vi* *vulg* to fuck.

**fidel** *adj* jolly.

**Fieber** *das* - **1.** [hohe Körpertemperatur] temperature; ~ **haben** to have a temperature; **bei jm** ~ **messen** to take sb's temperature - **2.** *geh* [Besessenheit] fever.

**fieberfrei** *adj*: **sie ist wieder** ~ her temperature is back to normal.

**fieberhaft** *adj* feverish ◇ *adv* feverishly.

**fiebern** *vi* - **1.** [Fieber haben] to have a temperature - **2.** [angespannt warten]: **vor Erregung** ~ to be in a fever of excitement; **nach etw** ~ to yearn for sthg.

**Fieberlthermometer** *das* thermometer.

**fiebrig** *adj* feverish.

**fiel** *prät* ▷ fallen.

**fies** *fam* *abw* *adj* nasty ◇ *adv* - **1.** [gemein] nastily - **2.** [ekelhaft]: ~ **schmecken** to taste horrible.

**fifty-fifty** [ˈfɪftɪˈfɪftɪ] *adv*: ~ **machen** *fam* to go fifty-fifty.

**Fig.** (*abk für* Figur) fig.

**Figur** (*pl* -en) *die* - **1.** [gen] figure; [männlich] physique - **2.** [literarische Darstellung] character - **3.** [Spielstein] piece - **4.** *RW*: **eine gute/schlechte** ~ **abgeben** *ODER* **machen** to cut a good/poor figure.

**Fiktion** (*pl* -en) *die* fiction.

**fiktiv** *adj* fictitious.

**Filet** [fiˈleː] (*pl* -s) *das* fillet.

**Filiale** (*pl* -n) *die* branch.

**Filiallleiter, in** *der, die* branch manager.

**Film** (*pl* -e) *der* film; **beim** ~ **sein** *ODER* **arbeiten** to be in the movies.

**filmen** *vt* & *vi* to film.

**Filmlkamera** *die* film camera, movie camera *Am*.

**Filmlmusik** *die* film music.

**Filmlproduzent, in** *der, die* film producer.

**Filmlriss** *der* *fam*: **ich habe einen** ~ my memory's a blank.

**Filmschaulspieler, in** *der, die* film actor (*f* film actress).

**Filmlstar** [ˈfɪlmʃtaːɐ] *der* film star, movie star.

**Filmlverleih** *der* film distributors (*pl*).

**Filter** (*pl* -) *das* *ODER* *der* filter.

**Filterkaffee** *der* filter coffee.

**filtern** *vt* to filter.

**Filterltüte** *die* filter (paper).

**Filterlzigarette** *die* filter cigarette.

**Filz** (*pl* -e) *der* - **1.** [Stoff] felt - **2.** *abw* [Vetternwirtschaft] jobs (*pl*) for the boys.

**filzen** *vt* *fam* [Person] to frisk; [Haus, Koffer] to search.

**Filzlstift** *der* felt-tip (pen).

**Fimmel** (*pl* -) *der* *fam* *abw* obsession.

**Finale** (*pl* -) *das* - **1.** [Endkampf, Endspiel] final - **2.** *MUS* finale.

**Finanzlamt** *das* tax office.

**Finanzlbeamte** *der* tax inspector.

**Finanzlbeamtin** *die* tax inspector.

**Finanzlbedarf** *der* (ohne *pl*) financial needs (*pl*).

**Finanzen** *pl* finances.

**finanziell** [finanˈtsjɛl] *adj* financial ◇ *adv* financially.

**finanzieren** *vt* to finance.

**Finanzierung** (*pl* -en) *die* financing.

**Finanzlminister, in** *der, die* finance minister, ≃ Chancellor of the Exchequer *Br*, ≃ Secretary of the Treasury *Am*.

**Finanzlministerium** *das* finance ministry, ≃ Treasury *Br*, ≃ Department of the Treasury *Am*.

**finden** (*prät* **fand**; *perf* **hat gefunden**) *vt* - **1.** [gen] to find; **wo finde ich die Post?** where is the post office?; **er fand die Kinder schlafend** he found the children sleeping; **an etw Gefallen** ~ to get *ODER* come to like sthg - **2.** [erhalten]: **Verwendung** ~ to be used; **Anerkennung** ~ to receive recognition - **3.** [beurteilen]: **ich finde sie nett** I think she's nice; **also, was du nur an ihm findest!** I don't know what you see in him!; **wie findest du ...?** what do you think of ...? ◇ *vi* - **1.** [erfolgreich suchen]: **er hat nicht zu uns gefunden** he couldn't find his way to our place - **2.** [beurteilen]: **ich finde, dass ...** I think (that) ...; **ich finde nichts dabei** I don't see anything wrong with it.

◂ **sich finden** *ref* - **1.** [wieder auftauchen]: **der Schlüssel hat sich gefunden** I/we found the key - **2.** *RW*: **das wird sich (schon) alles** ~! everything will be all right; **sie hat sich in ihr Los gefunden** she has become reconciled to her fate.

**Finder, in** (*mpl* -; *fpl* -nen) *der* finder.

**Finderllohn** *der* reward (for finding something).

**findig** *adj* resourceful.

**fing** *prät* ▷ fangen.

**Finger** (*pl* -) *der* - **1.** [Glied] finger - **2.** *RW*: **jn in die** ~ **kriegen** *ODER* **bekommen** *fam* to get one's hands on sb; **etw in die** ~ **kriegen** *ODER* **bekommen** *fam* to get hold of sthg; **jn um den (kleinen)** ~ **wickeln** to twist sb round one's little

**F**

finger; keinen ~ krumm machen *fam abw* not to lift a finger; lange ~ machen *fam abw* to be light-fingered; mit dem ~ auf jn zeigen *abw* to point one's finger at sb; sich *(D)* etw an fünf ~n abzählen können to be able to see sthg right away; sich *(D)* die ~ verbrennen *fam* to get one's fingers burnt; überall seine ~ drin ODER dazwischen haben *fam abw* to have a finger in every pie.

**Finger|abdruck** *der* fingerprint.

**fingerfertig** *adj* dexterous <> *adv* dexterously.

**Fingerhand|schuh** *der* glove.

**Finger|hut** *der* - **1.** [zum Nähen] thimble - **2.** [Blume] foxglove.

**Finger|nagel** *der* fingernail.

**Finger|spitze** *die* fingertip.

**Finger|spitzengefühl** *das* sensitivity; ~ haben ODER besitzen ODER beweisen to show sensitivity.

**Fingerzeig** *(pl -e) der:* jm einen ~ geben to give sb a tip-off.

**fingieren** *vt geh* to fake.

**Fink** *(pl -en) der* finch.

**Finne** *(pl -n) der* Finn.

**Finnin** *(pl -nen) die* Finn.

**finnisch** *adj* Finnish; *siehe auch* **englisch.**

**Finnisch(e)** *das* Finnish; *siehe auch* **Englisch(e).**

**Finnland** *nt* Finland.

**finster** *adj* - **1.** [Nacht, Straße, Zimmer, Zeiten] dark; es sieht ~ aus things are looking black - **2.** [Person, Miene] grim, sombre - **3.** [Gegend, Gestalt] sinister <> *adv* [unfreundlich] grimly.

**Finsternis** *(pl -se) die* darkness.

**Finte** *(pl -n) die* ruse.

**Firlefanz** *der (ohne pl) fam abw* - **1.** [überflüssiges Zeug] frippery - **2.** [Gehabe, Gerede] nonsense.

**firm** *adj:* in etw *(D)* ~ sein *geh* to be good at sthg.

**Firma** *(pl Firmen) die* firm, company.

**Firmen|inhaber, in** *der, die* company owner.

**Firmen|name** *der* company name.

**Firmen|wagen** *der* company car.

**Firmung** *(pl -en) die* REL confirmation.

**First Class** *die* first class.

**fis, Fis** *(pl -) das* MUS F sharp.

**Fisch** *(pl -e) der* - **1.** [Tier, Gericht] fish; stumm wie ein ~ sein [etwas verschweigen] to keep mum; [schweigsam sein] not to be very talkative; kleine ~e *fam fig* small fry - **2.** ASTROL Pisces; ~ sein to be a Pisces.

➤ **Fische** *pl* ASTROL Pisces *(U).*

**Fisch|besteck** *das* fish knives and forks *(pl).*

**Fisch|brötchen** *das* pickled herring roll.

**fischen** *vt* - **1.** [fangen] to catch - **2.** [angeln] to fish for - **3.** [holen] to fish out <> *vi* - **1.** [Fische fangen] to fish; ~ gehen to go fishing - **2.** *fam* [greifen]: nach etw ~ to fish for sthg.

**Fischer, in** *(mpl -; fpl -nen) der, die* fisherman *(f* fisherwoman).

**Fischer|boot** *das* fishing boat.

**Fischerei** *die* fishing.

**Fischerei|flotte** *die* fishing fleet.

**Fischerei|hafen** *der* fishing port.

**Fischfang** *der* fishing.

**Fisch|händler, in** *der, die* fishmonger *Br,* fish seller *Am.*

**fischig** *adj abw* fishy.

**Fisch|markt** *der* fish market.

**Fisch|stäbchen** ['fɪʃʃtɛːpçən] *das* fish finger *Br,* fish stick *Am.*

**Fiskus** *der* treasury.

**fit** *adj* [körperlich] fit; [geistig] sharp, mentally alert; ~ in Chemie sein *fam* to be good at chemistry.

**Fitness** ['fɪtnɛs] *die* [körperliche] fitness; [geistige] sharpness, mental alertness.

**Fitness|center** *das* fitness centre.

**Fittiche** *pl:* jn unter seine ~ nehmen *fam* to take sb under one's wing.

**fix** *adj* - **1.** *fam* [schnell] quick - **2.** [Kosten] fixed - **3.** [erschöpft]: ~ und fertig sein *fam* to be beat ODER knackered *Br* <> *adv fam* [schnell] quickly.

**fixen** *vt & vi fam* to shoot up.

**Fixer, in** *(mpl -; fpl -nen) der, die fam* junkie.

**fixieren** *vt* - **1.** [anstarren] to stare fixedly at - **2.** [befestigen, konservieren] to fix - **3.** *geh* [festhalten] to record.

➤ **sich fixieren** *ref:* sich auf jn/etw ~ to become fixated on sb/sthg.

**Fixierung** *(pl -en) die* - **1.** [Befestigung, Konservierung] fixing - **2.** [Festhalten] recording - **3.** [Bindung] fixation.

**Fixkosten** *pl* (fixed) overheads.

**Fjord** *(pl -e) der* fjord.

**FKK** [ɛfkaːˈkaː] *(abk für* Freikörperkultur) *das* nudism; am Strand ~ machen to sunbathe in the nude.

**flach** *adj* - **1.** [eben] flat - **2.** [niedrig, dünn - Gebäude, Absätze] low; [ - Stein, Schuhe] flat; [ - Teller] shallow - **3.** [seicht, oberflächlich] shallow <> *adv:* ~ atmen to take shallow breaths.

**Flach|dach** *das* flat roof.

**Fläche** *(pl -n) die* - **1.** [Gebiet] area - **2.** [geometrisch] plane - **3.** [Seite] surface.

**FlächenIbrand** *der* wildfire; **zum ~ werden** *fig* to spread like wildfire.

**flachIfallen** (*perf* ist flachgefallen) *vi (unreg)* *fam*: **die Party fällt flach** the party's off; **23 Stellen fallen flach** 23 people are getting the boot.

**Flachland** *das (ohne pl)* lowlands *(pl)*.

**Flachs** [flaks] *der* - **1.** [Pflanze] flax - **2.** *fam* [Unsinn] nonsense.

**flachsen** ['flaksn̩] *vi fam* to joke.

**flackern** *vi* to flicker.

**Fladen** (*pl* -) *der* - **1.** [Brotfladen] *flat, round loaf* - **2.** [Kuchen] pancake - **3.** [Kuhfladen] cowpat.

**Flagge** (*pl* -n) *die* flag.

**Flair** [flɛːɐ̯] *das ODER der* aura.

**flambieren** *vt* to flambé.

**Flame** (*pl* -n) *der* Fleming; **die ~n** the Flemish.

**Flämin** (*pl* -nen) *die* Fleming.

**Flamingo** (*pl* -s) *der* flamingo.

**flämisch** *adj* Flemish.

**Flämisch(e)** *das* Flemish; *siehe auch* **Englisch(e)**.

**Flamme** (*pl* -n) *die* - **1.** [Feuer] flame; **in ~n aufgehen/stehen** to go up/be in flames - **2.** [zum Kochen] burner; **auf kleiner/großer ~ kochen** to cook on a low/high flame.

**Flandern** *nt* Flanders *(sg)*.

**Flanell** (*pl* -e) *der* flannel.

**flanieren** (*perf* ist/hat flaniert) *vi geh* to stroll.

**Flanke** (*pl* -n) *die* flank.

**flankierend** *adj*: **~e Maßnahmen** supporting measures.

**Flasche** (*pl* -n) *die* - **1.** [Gefäß] bottle; **eine ~ Sekt** a bottle of champagne - **2.** *salopp abw* [Versager] drip.

**FlaschenIbier** *das* bottled beer.

**FlaschenIöffner** *der* bottle opener.

**FlaschenIpfand** *das* deposit *(on a bottle)*.

**FlaschenIzug** *der* block and tackle.

**flatterhaft** *adj* flighty.

**flatterig, flattrig** *adj* - **1.** [Augen, Puls] fluttering - **2.** [Person] flighty.

**flattern** (*perf* ist/hat geflattert) *vi* - **1.** [gen] to flutter - **2.** [schlagen]: **mit den Flügeln ~** to flutter its wings.

**flattrig** = flatterig.

**flau** *adj* - **1.** [übel]: **mir ist ~** I'm feeling queasy - **2.** [schlecht - Geschäft] slack <> *adv* [schlecht]: **die Geschäfte gehen** ODER **laufen ~** business is slack.

**Flaum** *der* down.

**flauschig** *adj* fleecy.

**Flausen** *pl*: **~ im Kopf haben** always to be up to some trick or other.

**Flaute** (*pl* -n) *die* - **1.** [wirtschaftlich] slack period - **2.** [Windstille] calm.

**Flechte** (*pl* -n) *die* - **1.** [Pflanze] lichen - **2.** [Hautausschlag] eczema.

**flechten** (*präs* flicht; *prät* flocht; *perf* hat geflochten) *vt* [Haare, Zopf] to plait *Br*, to braid *Am*; [Korb] to weave.

**Fleck** (*pl* -e ODER -en) *der* - **1.** [Klecks] stain - **2.** [Stelle] patch; **blauer ~** bruise - **3.** [Ort] spot.

→ **vom Fleck weg** *adv* on the spot.

**fleckenlos** *adj* spotless <> *adv* spotlessly.

**FleckIentferner** *der* stain remover.

**fleckig** *adj* - **1.** [schmutzig] stained - **2.** [gefleckt - Haut] blotchy; [ - Obst] blemished.

**FlederImaus** *die* bat.

**Flegel** (*pl* -) *der* lout.

**flegelhaft** *adj* loutish <> *adv* loutishly.

**Flegeljahre** *pl* awkward age *(sg)*.

**flehen** *vi*: **(um etw) ~** to plead (for sthg).

**Fleisch** *das* - **1.** [Nahrungsmittel] meat - **2.** [Muskelgewebe, Fruchtfleisch] flesh; **~ fressend** carnivorous - **3.** *RW*: **es ging ihr in ~ und Blut über** it became second nature to her; **sich (D) ins eigene ~ schneiden** to cut off one's nose to spite one's face.

**FleischIbrühe** *die* meat stock.

**Fleischer** (*pl* -) *der* butcher.

**Fleischerei** (*pl* -en) *die* butcher's (shop).

**Fleischerin** (*pl* -nen) *die* butcher.

**fleischfressend** = Fleisch.

**fleischig** *adj* fleshy.

**fleischlos** *adj* [vegetarisch] meat-free <> *adv*: **sich ~ ernähren** not to eat meat.

**FleischIsalat** *der* salad of strips of meat, vegetables and mayonnaise.

**FleischIvergiftung** *die* food poisoning from meat.

**FleischIwolf** *der* mincer *Br*, meat grinder *Am*.

**FleischIwurst** *die* type of cold pork sausage similar to mortadella.

**Fleiß** *der* diligence; **viel ~ auf etw (A) verwenden** to put a lot of work into sthg.

**fleißig** *adj* - **1.** [eifrig, arbeitsam] hard-working - **2.** *fam* [häufig, viel] frequent <> *adv* - **1.** [eifrig, arbeitsam] hard - **2.** *fam* [oft, viel] a lot; **~ bezahlen** to fork out money.

**flennen** *vi fam abw* to wail.

**Flensburg** *nt*: **fünf Punkte in ~ haben** to have five penalty points on one's driving licence *Br* ODER driver's license *Am*.

**fletschen** *vt:* **die Zähne** ~ to bare its teeth.

**flexibel** *adj* flexible ◇ *adv* [anpassungsfähig] flexibly.

**Flexibilität** *die* flexibility.

**flicht** *präs* ▷ **flechten.**

**flicken** *vt* to mend.

**Flicken** (*pl* -) *der* patch.

**Flickwerk** *das (ohne pl) abw* patched-up job.

**Flickzeug** *das (ohne pl)* [für Reifen] repair kit; [für Kleidung] sewing kit.

**Flieder** (*pl* -) *der* lilac.

**Fliege** (*pl* -n) *die* - **1.** [Insekt] fly - **2.** [Schleife] bow tie - **3.** *RW:* **sie kann keiner** ~ **was zuleide tun** she wouldn't hurt a fly; **zwei** ~**n mit einer Klappe schlagen** to kill two birds with one stone.

**fliegen** (*prät* **flog;** *perf* **hat/ist geflogen**) *vi (ist)* - **1.** [gen] to fly - **2.** *fam* [stürzen] to fall - **3.** *fam* [entlassen werden] to get fired, to get the sack *Br* - **4.** [attraktiv finden]: **auf jn/etw** ~ to be crazy about sb/sthg ◇ *vt (hat)* to fly.

**Fliegen|gewicht** *das* - **1.** *(ohne pl)* SPORT flyweight - **2.** *fam* [Person] little slip of a thing.

**Fliegenklatsche** (*pl* -n) *die* fly swat.

**Fliegen|pilz** *der* fly agaric.

**Flieger** (*pl* -) *der* - **1.** [Pilot] pilot - **2.** *fam* [Flugzeug] plane.

**Fliegerei** *die* flying.

**Fliegerin** (*pl* -nen) *die* pilot.

**fliehen** (*prät* **floh;** *perf* **hat/ist geflohen**) *vi (ist):* **aus dem Gefängnis** ~ to escape from jail; **sie mussten aus Deutschland** ~ they were forced to flee Germany; **vor jm/etw** ~ to flee from sb/sthg; **zu jm** ~ to flee to sb ◇ *vt (hat)* to shun.

**Fliese** (*pl* -n) *die* tile; **im Bad** ~**n legen** to tile the bathroom.

**fliesen** *vt* to tile.

**Fließband** (*pl* -bänder) *das* conveyor belt; **am** ~ **arbeiten** to be an assembly-line ODER a production-line worker.

**fließen** (*prät* **floss;** *perf* **ist geflossen**) *vi* to flow; **das Blut fließt aus der Wunde** the blood is flowing from the wound.

**fließend** *adj* - **1.** [perfekt] fluent - **2.** [ungenau, unscharf - Grenzen, Übergang] fluid - **3.** [Verkehr, Material] flowing; [Wasser] running ◇ *adv* - **1.** [sprechen] fluently - **2.** [unscharf] fluidly.

**flimmern** *vi* - **1.** [Luft, Wasser, Oberflächen] to shimmer - **2.** [Fernsehbild] to flicker.

**flink** *adj* - **1.** [geschickt] nimble - **2.** [schnell] quick ◇ *adv* - **1.** [geschickt] nimbly - **2.** [schnell] quickly.

**Flinte** (*pl* -n) *die* shotgun; **die** ~ **ins Korn werfen** *fig* to throw in the towel.

**Flipper** (*pl* -) *der* pinball machine; **(am)** ~ **spielen** to play pinball.

**flippern** *vi fam* to play pinball.

**Flirt** [flœɐt] (*pl* -s) *der* flirtation.

**flirten** ['flœɐtn̩] *vi:* **(mit jm)** ~ to flirt (with sb).

**Flittchen** (*pl* -) *das fam abw* tart.

**Flitterwochen** *pl* honeymoon *(sg);* **in die** ~ **fahren** to go on honeymoon.

**flitzen** (*perf* **ist geflitzt**) *vi fam* [Person, Wagen] to whizz.

**flocht** *prät* ▷ **flechten.**

**Flocke** (*pl* -n) *die* [von Schnee, Getreide] flake; [von Staub] ball; [von Schaum] blob.

**flockig** *adj* fluffy.

**flog** *prät* ▷ **fliegen.**

**floh** *prät* ▷ **fliehen.**

**Floh** (*pl* **Flöhe**) *der* flea; **jm einen** ~ **ins Ohr setzen** to put an idea into sb's head.

**Floh|markt** *der* flea market.

**Floppydisk** ['flɔpidɪsk] (*pl* -s) *die* EDV floppy disk.

**Flora** *die* flora.

**Florenz** *nt* Florence.

**Florett** (*pl* -e) *das* [Waffe] foil.

**Florida** *nt* Florida.

**florieren** *vi* to flourish.

**Florist, in** (*mpl* -en; *fpl* -nen) *der, die* florist.

**Floskel** (*pl* -n) *die* cliché.

**floss** *prät* ▷ **fließen.**

**Floß** (*pl* **Flöße**) *das* raft.

**Flosse** (*pl* -n) *die* - **1.** [von Fisch, Rückenflosse von Delfin] fin; [Bauchflosse von Delfin und Robbe] flipper - **2.** [Schwimmflosse] flipper - **3.** *salopp abw* [Hand] paw.

**Flöte** (*pl* -n) *die* [Querflöte] flute; [Blockflöte] recorder.

**flöten** *vi* - **1.** [Flöte spielen] to play the flute/recorder - **2.** [pfeifen - Person] to whistle - **3.** *fam abw* [einschmeichelnd sprechen] to speak in honeyed tones ◇ *vt* - **1.** [spielen] to play on the flute/recorder - **2.** [pfeifen] to whistle - **3.** *fam abw* [einschmeichelnd sagen]: **sie flötete mir Schmeicheleien ins Ohr** she murmered flattering remarks into my ear.

**flöten gehen** (*perf* **ist flöten gegangen**) *vi (unreg) fam* to get lost; [Geld] to go down the drain.

**Flötist, in** (*mpl* -en; *fpl* -nen) *der, die* flautist.

**flott** *adj* - **1.** [schick] smart, stylish - **2.** [lebhaft, schnell - Musik, Person] lively; [ - Service] speedy; [ - Auto] fast - **3.** [fahrtüchtig - Wagen] roadworthy; [ - Kahn] seaworthy ◇ *adv* - **1.** [schnell, lebhaft - arbeiten, laufen] quickly; [ - tanzen, spielen] ...1

a lively manner; **mach ~!** make it snappy!
**- 2.** [schick] smartly.

**Flotte** (pl -n) die fleet.

**Fluch** (pl Flüche) der **- 1.** [Schimpfwort] curse
**- 2.** (ohne pl) [Verwünschung] curse.

**fluchen** vi to swear; **über jn/etw ~** to swear
about sb/sthg.

**Flucht** die [aus dem Gefängnis] escape; **sie sind auf
der ~** they are fleeing; **die ~ ergreifen** to take
flight; **jn in die ~ schlagen** to put sb to flight.

**fluchtartig** adj hurried <> adv hurriedly.

**flüchten** (perf hat/ist geflüchtet) vi (ist) to
flee; **vor jm/etw ~** to flee from sb/sthg; **aus
etw ~** to escape from sthg.

➤ **sich flüchten** ref (hat): **sich in etw** (A) **~** to take
refuge in sthg.

**Fluchtlhelfer, in** der, die person who helps
escapees.

**flüchtig** adj **- 1.** [kurz] fleeting; [Gruß, Abschied]
brief **- 2.** [ungenau - Eindruck] superficial; [ - Ar-
beit] hurried **- 3.** [flüchtend - Gefangene] escaped; [ - Mörder] wanted <> adv **- 1.** [ungenau] superficially; [arbeiten] hurriedly **- 2.** [kurz]
briefly.

**Flüchtigkeitslfehler** der careless mistake.

**Flüchtling** (pl -e) der refugee.

**Flüchtlingsllager** das refugee camp.

**Fluchtlversuch** der escape attempt.

**Fluchtlweg** der escape route.

**Flug** (pl Flüge) der flight; **wie im ~(e) vergehen**
to fly by, to go by in a flash.

**Fluglbahn** die [von Rakete] trajectory.

**Fluglblatt** das leaflet.

**Flügel** (pl -) der **- 1.** [gen] wing **- 2.** [Musikinstru-
ment] grand piano **- 3.** RW: **jm ~ verleihen** to
lend sb wings.

**Flügellschraube** die wing nut.

**Fluglgast** der passenger (on plane).

**flügge** adj [Vogeljunge] fully-fledged; **~ werden**
[Kind] to be ready to leave the nest.

**Fluglgesellschaft** die airline.

**Fluglhafen** der airport.

**Flugllotse** der air traffic controller.

**Fluglplatz** der airfield.

**Fluglverkehr** der air traffic.

**Fluglzeug** das aeroplane, plane, airplane
Am; **mit dem ~ fliegen** to fly.

**Flugzeugentlführung** die hijacking.

**Flugzeuglträger** der aircraft carrier.

**Fluktuation** (pl -en) die turnover.

**Flunder** (pl -n) die flounder.

**flunkern** vi to tell stories.

**Fluor** das fluorine.

**Flur** (pl -e ODER -en) der (pl Flure) [Korridor] corridor; [am Eingang] hallway <> die (pl Fluren) [Ge-
lände] fields (pl).

**Fluss** (pl Flüsse) der **- 1.** [Wasserlauf] river
**- 2.** [Bewegung] flow.

**flussabwärts** adv downstream.

**flussaufwärts** adv upstream.

**Flusslbett** das river bed.

**flüssig** adj **- 1.** [nicht fest] liquid; [Metall] molten;
[Butter] melted **- 2.** [Stil, Verkehr] flowing; [Aus-
druck] fluent **- 3.** [zahlungsfähig, verfügbar]: **~ sein**
to be solvent; **nicht ~ sein** to be short of
money <> adv [sprechen] fluently.

**Flüssigkeit** (pl -en) die liquid.

**Flussllauf** der course (of a river).

**Flusslpferd** das hippopotamus.

**Flusslufer** das river bank.

**flüstern** vi to whisper <> vt to whisper; **jm
etw ins Ohr ~** to whisper sthg into sb's ear;
**jm was ~** fam fig to tell sb a thing or two.

**Flut** (pl -en) die **- 1.** (ohne pl) [Ansteigen des Wasser-
standes] tide (incoming); **die ~ kommt** the tide
is coming in; **bei ~** at high tide; **eine ~ von
etw** fig a flood of sthg **- 2.** geh [Wassermasse] waters (pl).

**fluten** (perf hat/ist geflutet) vt hat & vi ist geh
to flood.

**Flutlicht** das (ohne pl): **bei ~ spielen** to play
under floodlights.

**Flyer** (pl -) der flyer.

**f-Moll** das MUS F minor.

**focht** prät ⊳ fechten.

**Föderalismus** der federalism.

**föderalistisch** adj federalist.

**Föderation** (pl -en) die federation.

**föderativ** adj federal.

**Fohlen** (pl -) das foal.

**Föhn** (pl -e) der **- 1.** [Wind] hot, dry wind typical
of the Alps **- 2.** [Haartrockner] hairdryer.

**föhnen** vt: **jm/sich die Haare ~** [zum Trocknen] to
dry sb's/one's hair; **jm die Haare ~** [zum Frisie-
ren] to blow-dry sb's hair.

**Folge** (pl -n) die **- 1.** [Konsequenz] consequence;
**etw zur ~ haben** to result in sthg **- 2.** [Fortset-
zung] episode **- 3.** [Serie] succession **- 4.** amt
[Befolgung]: **jm/einem Befehl ~ leisten** to obey
sb/an order; **einer Einladung ~ leisten** to accept an invitation.

**Folgelerscheinung** die result.

**folgen** (perf ist gefolgt) vi **- 1.** [nachfolgen, verstehen, sich richten nach]: **jm/einer Sache ~** to follow
sb/sthg **- 2.** [sich anschließen]: **auf etw** (A) **~** to
follow sthg; **wie folgt** as follows **- 3.** [gehor-

chen]: **(jm/einer Sache)** ~ to obey (sb/sthg)
- **4.** [sich logisch ergeben]: **aus etw** ~ to follow
from sthg.

**folgend** adj following.
- **Folgende** das: **das Folgende** the following.
- **Folgendes** nt the following.

**folgendermaßen** adv as follows.

**folgenschwer** adj fateful.

**folgerichtig** adj logical <> adv logically.

**folgern** vt: **aus etw** ~, **dass ...** to conclude
from sthg that ...

**Folgerung** (pl -en) die conclusion.

**folglich** adv consequently.

**folgsam** adj obedient <> adv obediently.

**Folie** ['foːljə] (pl -n) die - **1.** [Verpackung - aus Plastik]
film; [ - aus Metall] foil - **2.** [für Overheadprojektor]
transparency.

**Folklore** die - **1.** [Musik] folk music - **2.** [Brauchtum] folklore.

**folkloristisch** adj folkloric; [Musik] folk.

**Folter** (pl -n) die torture; **jn auf die ~ spannen**
fig to keep sb on tenterhooks.

**foltern** vt to torture.

**Fön**® (pl -e) der = **Föhn**.

**Fonds** [fɔ̃] (pl -) der fund.

**Fondue** [fɔ̃'dyː] (pl -s) das ODER die fondue.

**fönen** = föhnen.

**Fonetik, Phonetik** die (ohne pl) phonetics.

**fonetisch, phonetisch** adj phonetic
<> adv phonetically.

**Fontäne** (pl -n) die - **1.** [von Wasser] jet
- **2.** [Springbrunnen] fountain.

**Football** ['futbɔːl] der: **(American)** ~ American
football Br, football Am.

**foppen** vt fam: **jn** ~ to pull sb's leg.

**forcieren** [fɔr'siːrən] vt [Tempo] to step up; [Entwicklung, Fortschritt] to push forward; [Angelegenheit] to force.

**forciert** [fɔr'siːɐt] adj - **1.** [verstärkt, beschleunigt]
increased - **2.** abw [gezwungen] forced.

**Förder|kreis** der patrons (pl).

**Förder|kurs** der SCHULE extra classes (pl).

**förderlich** adj geh: **jm** ~ **sein** to be beneficial
to sb; **tägliche Gymnastik ist der Gesundheit** ~
daily exercise is good for your health.

**fordern** vt - **1.** [verlangen] to demand - **2.** [beanspruchen] to make demands on; **die Aufgabe
fordert sie stark** the task really stretches
her.

**fördern** vt - **1.** [unterstützen] to support; [Handel,
Frieden] to promote; [Begabung] to foster
- **2.** [Bodenschätze] to mine.

**Forderung** (pl -en) die - **1.** [Verlangen] demand
- **2.** [finanzieller Anspruch] claim.

**Förderung** (pl -en) die - **1.** [Unterstützung] support; [von Handel, Frieden] promotion; [von Begabung] fostering - **2.** [von Bodenschätzen] mining.

**Forelle** (pl -n) die trout.

**Form** (pl -en) die - **1.** [gen] form; **in ~ einer Sache**
in the form of sthg; **in ~ sein** to be in good
form; **sich/jn in ~ bringen** to get o.s./sb into
shape; **die ~ wahren** to observe the proprieties; **in aller ~** formally - **2.** [Gestalt] shape
- **3.** [für Kuchen] baking tin.

**formal** adj formal <> adv formally.

**Formalität** (pl -en) die formality.

**Format** (pl -e) das - **1.** [Größe] size; **im ~ DIN A 3**
in A3 format - **2.** [Niveau - von Person] stature;
**die Frau hat ~** she's a woman of stature.

**formatieren** vt EDV to format.

**Formatierung** (pl -en) die EDV formatting.

**Formation** (pl -en) die - **1.** [gen] formation
- **2.** [Gruppe] group.

**formbar** adj malleable.

**formbeständig** adj: ~ **sein** to hold its
shape.

**Formel** (pl -n) die formula ; **~ 1** SPORT Formula
One.

**formell** adj formal <> adv formally.

**formen** vt - **1.** [Material] to shape - **2.** [Person] to
mould.
- **sich formen** ref [sich bilden] to take shape.

**formieren** vt to form.
- **sich formieren** ref [sich aufstellen] to get into
formation; [Organisation] to form.

**förmlich** adj formal <> adv - **1.** [gen] formally
- **2.** [regelrecht] really.

**formlos** adj - **1.** [nicht formal] informal
- **2.** [amorph] shapeless - **3.** [ungezwungen] casual <> adv - **1.** [nicht formal] informally - **2.** [ungezwungen] casually.

**Form|sache** die: **reine ~ sein** to be purely a
formality.

**Formular** (pl -e) das form.

**formulieren** vt to formulate.

**Formulierung** (pl -en) die - **1.** [Formulieren] formulation - **2.** [Textstelle] wording.

**formvollendet** adj very polite.

**forsch** adj self-confident <> adv self-confidently.

**forschen** vi - **1.** [wissenschaftlich untersuchen] to
do research - **2.** [ermitteln]: **in js Augen** ~ to
search sb's eyes; **nach jm/etw** ~ to search for
sb/sthg.

**Forscher, in** (mpl -; fpl -nen) der, die researcher.

**Forschung** (pl -en) die research; **~en** research.

**Forschungsinstitut** *das* research institute.

**Forst** (*pl* -e(n)) *der* forest.

**Forstamt** *das forestry administration office.*

**Förster, in** (*mpl* -; *fpl* -nen) *der, die* forest ranger.

**Forsthaus** *das* forest ranger's house.

**Forsythie** [fɔr'zyːtsiə] (*pl* -n) *die* forsythia.

**fort** *adv* [weg] away; ~ **sein** to be gone.
➤ **in einem fort** *adv* incessantly.
➤ **und so fort** *adv* and so forth.

**Fortbestand** *der* continued existence.

**fortbestehen** *vi (unreg)* to continue; [trotz Bedrohung] to continue to exist.

**fortbewegen** *vt* to move.
➤ **sich fortbewegen** *ref* to move.

**Fortbewegung** *die* propulsion.

**Fortbewegungsmittel** *das* means of transport.

**fortbilden** *vt* to train.
➤ **sich fortbilden** *ref* to receive training.

**Fortbildung** (*pl* -en) *die* - **1.** [Weiterbildung] training; ~ **zur Bekämpfung der Arbeitslosigkeit** lifelong learning as a means of combatting unemployment - **2.** [Kurs] training course.

**fortdauern** *vi* to continue.

**fortfahren** (*perf* **hat/ist fortgefahren**) (*unreg*) *vi* - **1.** *(ist)* [wegfahren] to leave - **2.** [nicht aufhören] to continue <> *vt (hat)* [wegfahren] to take away.

**fortfallen** (*perf* **ist fortgefallen**) *vi (unreg)* [Leistung, Zahlung] to be discontinued.

**fortführen** *vt* - **1.** [weitermachen] to carry on - **2.** [fortbringen] to take away.

**Fortführung** *die* continuation; [von Familienbetrieb] carrying on.

**Fortgang** *der (ohne pl)* - **1.** [Fortsetzung] progress - **2.** [Fortgehen] departure.

**fortgehen** (*perf* **ist fortgegangen**) *vi (unreg)* - **1.** [weggehen] to leave - **2.** [weitergehen] to continue.

**fortgeschritten** *pp* ⊳ **fortschreiten** <> *adj* advanced; **zu ~er Stunde** at a late hour.

**Fortgeschrittene** (*pl* -n) *der, die* advanced student.

**fortkommen** (*perf* **ist fortgekommen**) *vi (unreg)* - **1.** [wegkommen] to get away - **2.** [fortgebracht werden] to be taken away - **3.** [abhanden kommen] to disappear.

**fortlaufen** (*perf* **ist fortgelaufen**) *vi (unreg)* [weglaufen] to run away; **ihm ist die Frau fortgelaufen** his wife has run off and left him.

**fortlaufend** *adv* [ständig] continually; [nummerieren] consecutively.

**fortpflanzen** ➤ **sich fortpflanzen** *ref* - **1.** [sich reproduzieren] to reproduce - **2.** [sich ausbreiten] to spread.

**Fortpflanzung** *die* reproduction.

**Forts.** (*abk für* **Fortsetzung**) cont.

**fortschreiten** (*perf* **ist fortgeschritten**) *vi (unreg)* to progress; [Zeit] to move on; [Krankheit, Prozess] to advance.

**Fortschritt** *der* progress (U); ~**e** progress; ~**e machen** to make progress.

**fortschrittlich** *adj* progressive <> *adv* progressively.

**fortsetzen** *vt* to continue.

**Fortsetzung** (*pl* -en) *die* continuation; [von Film] sequel; '~ **folgt**' 'to be continued'.

**Fortsetzungsroman** *der* serialized novel.

**fortwährend** *adj* constant <> *adv* constantly.

**fortziehen** (*perf* **hat/ist fortgezogen**) (*unreg*) *vi (ist)* to move away <> *vt (hat)* to pull away.

**Fossil** (*pl* -ien) *das* fossil.

**Foto, Photo** (*pl* -s) *das* photo; **ein ~ machen** to take a photo.

**Fotoalbum** *das* photo album.

**Fotoapparat** *der* camera.

**Fotograf** (*pl* -en) *der* photographer.

**Fotografie** (*pl* -n) *die* - **1.** [Fotografieren] photography - **2.** [Foto] photograph.

**fotografieren** *vt* to photograph <> *vi* to take photographs.

**Fotografin** (*pl* -nen) *die* photographer.

**Fotokopie** *die* photocopy.

**fotokopieren** *vt* to photocopy <> *vi* to make photocopies.

**Fotokopierer** (*pl* -) *der,* **Fotokopiergerät** *das* photocopier.

**Fotomodell** *das* (photographic) model.

**Fotosynthese, Photosynthese** *die (ohne pl)* photosynthesis.

**Fotozelle, Photozelle** *die* photoelectric cell, photocell.

**Fötus** (*pl* -se *ODER* -ten) *der* foetus.

**Foul** ['faul] (*pl* -s) *das* SPORT foul.

**foulen** ['faulən] SPORT *vt* to foul <> *vi* to commit a foul.

**Foxtrott** (*pl* -e *ODER* -s) *der* foxtrot.

**FPÖ** [ɛf'peːˈøː] (*abk für* **Freiheitliche Partei Österreichs**) *die* Austrian Freedom Party.

**Fr.** - **1.** (*abk für* **Frau**) [verheiratet] Mrs; [unverheiratet] Ms, Miss - **2.** (*abk für* **Freitag**) Fri.

**Fracht** (*pl* -en) *die* freight; [mit Schiff] cargo.

F

**Frachter** (pl -) der freighter.

**Frachtlgut** das freight.

**Frack** (pl Fräcke) der tails (pl); im ~ in tails.

**Frage** (pl -n) die question; noch ~n? any more questions?; **eine rhetorische ~** a rhetorical question; **jm ~n stellen** to ask sb questions; **in diesen ~n weiß er am besten Bescheid** he knows most about these issues ODER matters; **das ist nur eine ~ des Geldes/der Zeit** it is only a question of money/time; **das kommt nicht in ~** that's out of the question; **etw in ~ stellen** [bezweifeln] to question sthg; [gefährden] to jeopardize sthg; **es steht außer ~, dass** ... there's no question that ...

➤ **ohne Frage** adv undoubtedly.

**Fragelbogen** der questionnaire.

**fragen** vt to ask; **jn um Rat ~** to ask sb for advice; **jn nach jm/etw ~** to ask sb about sb/sthg; **jn nach seinem Namen/der Uhrzeit ~** to ask sb his name/the time <> vi to ask ; **nach jm ~** [sich erkundigen] to ask about sb; [Treffen] to ask to see sb; **der Polizist fragte nach dem genauen Hergang** the policeman asked for a precise description of events ; **da fragst du noch!** you need to ASK ?

➤ **sich fragen** ref to wonder; **ich frage mich, ob** ... I wonder if ODER whether ...; **es fragt sich noch, ob** ... it is debatable whether ...

**Fragelstellung** die [Art der Frage]: **die ~ ist nicht eindeutig** the way the question is phrased isn't clear.

**Fragelstunde** die - **1.** POL: **~ im Bundestag** parliamentary question time in the "Bundestag" - **2.** [Informationsveranstaltung] consultative meeting, question and answer session.

**Fragelwort** (pl -wörter) das interrogative pronoun.

**Fragelzeichen** das question mark.

**fraglich** adj - **1.** [zweifelhaft]: **es ist ~, ob** ... it is doubtful whether ... - **2.** [in Frage kommend] in question.

**fraglos** adv undoubtedly.

**Fragment** (pl -e) das fragment.

**fragwürdig** adj dubious.

**Fraktion** [frak'tsjo:nl (pl -en) die - **1.** [im Parlament] (parliamentary) party - **2.** [innerhalb einer Partei] faction.

**Fraktionslvorsitzende** der, die leader of the (parliamentary) party.

**Franc** [frã:] (pl -s ODER -) der franc.

**frank** adv: **~ und frei** openly and honestly.

**Franke** (pl -n) der - **1.** [Einwohner von Franken] Franconian - **2.** HIST [Westgermane] Frank.

**Franken** (pl -) nt Franconia <> der Swiss franc.

**Frankenlwein** der white wine from northern Bavaria.

**Frankfurt** nt: **~ am Main/an der Oder** Frankfurt (am Main)/an der Oder.

**Frankfurter** (pl -) der Frankfurter <> adj (unver) Frankfurt (vor Subst).

**Frankfurter Buchmesse** (pl Frankfurter Buchmessen) die Frankfurt Book Fair.

**Frankfurterin** (pl -nen) die Frankfurter.

**frankieren** vt to stamp.

**Fränkin** (pl -nen) die - **1.** [Einwohnerin von Franken] Franconian - **2.** HIST [Westgermanin] Frank.

**fränkisch** adj - **1.** [aus Franken] Franconian - **2.** HIST [westgermanisch] Frankish.

**Frankreich** nt France.

**Franse** (pl -n) die strand; **ein Schal mit ~n** a scarf with a fringe.

**Franziskaner, in** (mpl -; fpl -nen) der, die Franciscan.

**Franzose** (pl -n) der Frenchman; **die ~n** the French.

**Französin** (pl -nen) die Frenchwoman.

**französisch** adj French; siehe auch **englisch**.

**Französisch(e)** das French; siehe auch **Englisch(e)**.

**frappierend** adj striking <> adv [ähnlich] strikingly.

**Fräse** (pl -n) die [für Holz] moulding machine; [für Metall] milling machine.

**fraß** prät ▷ **fressen**.

**Fraß** der - **1.** [Tiernahrung] food - **2.** abw [ungenießbares Essen] pigswill.

**Fratze** (pl -n) die [Grimasse] grotesque face; [aus Schmerz, Widerwille] grimace; **(jm) eine ~ schneiden** to pull a face at sb.

**Frau** (pl -en) die - **1.** [Erwachsene] woman - **2.** [Gattin] wife - **3.** [als Anrede - verheiratet] Mrs; [ - neutral] Ms; **~ Doktor** Doctor.

**Frauchen** (pl -) das mistress.

**Frauenlarzt, ärztin** der, die gynaecologist.

**Frauenbewegung** die women's movement.

**frauenfeindlich** adj misogynistic <> adv in a misogynistic way.

**Frauenlhaus** das women's refuge.

**Frauenlparkplatz** der parking space for women only, near exit for safety reasons.

**Fräulein** (pl -) das - **1.** [junge Frau] young lady - **2.** [als Anrede - für junge Frauen] Miss; [ - neutral] Ms; [ - für Bedienung] **~, die Rechnung bitte!** waitress, could I have the bill, please?

**fraulich** adj feminine <> adv in a feminine way.

**frdl.** ▷ **freundlich**.

**Freak** [fri:k] (pl -s) der fam freak.

**frech** adj - **1.** [gen] cheeky; [unartig] naughty; [Lüge] barefaced - **2.** [Minirock] saucy ◇ adv cheekily; [unartig] naughtily; jm ~ kommen fam to get cheeky with sb.

**Frech|dachs** ['frɛçdaks] der fam cheeky monkey.

**Frechheit** (pl -en) die - **1.** (ohne pl) [freches Verhalten] cheek - **2.** [freche Bemerkung] cheeky remark.

**Freeclimbing** ['fri:klaimbiŋ] das SPORT free climbing.

**Freelancer** (pl -) der freelancer.

**Fregatte** (pl -n) die frigate.

**frei** adj - **1.** [gen] free; ~ von etw free of sthg; ist dieser Stuhl ~? is this seat free?; das Hotel hat keine ~en Betten mehr the hotel doesn't have any more free beds; drei Wochen ~ haben to have three weeks off; jm ~e Hand lassen to give sb a free hand; bei der Reaktion wird Energie ~ energy is released during the reaction - **2.** [Mitarbeiter] freelance - **3.** [nackt] bare; machen Sie sich bitte ~ would you mind undressing? ◇ adv - **1.** [gen] freely; ~ lebende Tiere animals living in the wild; ~ sprechen to speak without notes; eine Linie ~ zeichnen to draw a line freehand - **2.** [gratis] for free; etw ~ Haus liefern to deliver sthg free.
⬥ im Freien adv in the open (air).

**Frei|bad** das open-air swimming pool.

**Freiberufler, in** (mpl -; fpl -nen) der, die - **1.** [Mitarbeiter] freelancer - **2.** [Arzt, Anwalt] doctor/lawyer in private practice.

**freiberuflich** adj [Journalist, Übersetzer, Fotograf] freelance; ~er Mitarbeiter freelancer ◇ adv: ~ tätig sein to be self-employed.

**Frei|betrag** der WIRTSCH tax allowance.

**Frei|bier** das free beer.

**Frei|brief** der excuse; er betrachtet ihre Toleranz als ~ für seine Abenteuer he thought that her tolerance gave him a licence to have affairs.

**Freiburg** nt Freiburg.
⬥ **Freiburg im Breisgau** nt Freiburg im Breisgau.

**Frei|exemplar** das free copy.

**Frei|gabe** die release; die ~ einer Brücke für den Verkehr the opening of a bridge to traffic.

**frei|geben** (unreg) vt - **1.** [gen] to release - **2.** [genehmigen - Film] to pass as fit for public viewing; [- Straße, Brücke] to open; jm einen Tag ~ to give sb a day off ◇ vi [Freizeit genehmigen]: jm ~ to give sb time off.

**freigebig** adj generous.

**frei|halten** vt (unreg) - **1.** [einladen - Person] to

treat; [- Tischrunde] to buy - **2.** [zugänglich halten] to keep clear - **3.** [reservieren] to save.

**Freihandels|zone** die free trade area.

**freihändig** adv [Fahrrad fahren] with no hands; [zeichnen] freehand.

**Freiheit** (pl -en) die - **1.** [Ungebundenheit] freedom; ein Tier in die ~ entlassen to set an animal free - **2.** [Privileg] liberty; sich (D) die ~ nehmen, etw zu tun to take the liberty of doing sthg.

**Freiheits|strafe** die prison sentence.

**freiheraus** adv freely.

**Frei|karte** die free ticket.

**Freikörperkultur** die naturism.

**frei|lassen** vt (unreg) [Gefangene] to release; [Tier] to set free.

**Freilassung** die release.

**freilich** adv - **1.** [jedoch] admittedly - **2.** Süddt [sicher] of course.

**Freilicht|bühne** die open-air theatre.

**Freilicht|museum** das open-air museum.

**frei|machen** vt - **1.** [Brief] to stamp - **2.** [ausziehen]: den Oberkörper ~ to take one's top off, to strip to the waist ◇ vi to take time off.
⬥ **sich freimachen** ref - **1.** fam [als Urlaub] to take time off; sich für den Nachmittag ~ to take the afternoon off - **2.** [sich ausziehen] to take one's clothes off.

**Frei|maurer** der freemason.

**freimütig** adj frank ◇ adv frankly.

**frei|nehmen** vt (unreg) to take off; sich (D) eine Woche ~ to take a week off.

**Frei|raum** der space (for self-fulfilment).

**freischaffend** adj freelance.

**frei|sprechen** vt (unreg) to acquit.

**Frei|spruch** der acquittal.

**frei|stehen** vi (unreg) - **1.** [Wohnung] to stand ODER be empty - **2.** [Entscheidung]: es steht ihm frei, zu gehen oder zu bleiben it's up to him whether he stays or goes.

**frei|stellen** vt - **1.** [entbinden]: jn von etw ~ to exempt sb from sthg - **2.** [überlassen]: jm etw ~ to leave sthg up to sb.

**Frei|stoß** der SPORT free kick.

**Frei|stunde** die free period.

**Freitag** (pl -e) der Friday; siehe auch **Samstag**.

**freitags** adv on Fridays; siehe auch **samstags**.

**Freiwild** das fair game.

**freiwillig** adj voluntary ◇ adv voluntarily.

**Freiwillige** (pl -n) der, die volunteer.

**Frei|zeichen** das dial tone.

**Frei|zeit** die - **1.** (ohne pl) [Mußezeit] free time - **2.** [Gruppenreise - für Kinder] holiday camp.

**Freizeit|gestaltung** *die* organizing of one's free time.

**Freizeitverhalten** *das (ohne pl)* leisure pursuits *(pl)*.

**freizügig** *adj* - **1.** [gewagt] daring - **2.** [großzügig] generous - **3.** [frei] liberal ◇ *adv* - **1.** [gewagt] daringly - **2.** [großzügig] generously - **3.** [frei] liberally.

**Freizügigkeit** *(pl -en) die* - **1.** [Großzügigkeit] generosity - **2.** [im Verhalten, Denken] permissiveness - **3.** [Ortsungebundenheit] freedom of movement.

**fremd** *adj* - **1.** [ausländisch] foreign - **2.** [nicht einem selbst gehörend]: **~e Angelegenheiten** other people's business; **in einer ~en Wohnung übernachten** to spend the night in someone else's flat - **3.** [unvertraut] strange; **er ist ~ in dieser Stadt** he is a stranger to this town.

**fremdartig** *adj* strange.

**Fremde** *(pl -n) der, die* stranger ◇ *die (ohne plural)* foreign parts *(pl)*; **in der ~** in foreign parts.

**Fremden|führer, in** *der, die* tourist guide.

**Fremden|hass** *der* xenophobia.

**Fremden|legion** *die* foreign legion.

**Fremden|verkehr** *der* tourism.

**Fremdenverkehrs|büro** *das* tourist information office.

**Fremden|zimmer** *das* (guest) room.

**fremd|gehen** *(perf* **ist fremdgegangen)** *vi (unreg):* **(mit jm) ~** to have an affair (with sb).

**Fremd|körper** *der* foreign body; **sie ist hier ein ~** she is out of place here.

**Fremd|sprache** *die* foreign language.

**Fremdsprachen|korrespondent, in** *der, die* bilingual secretary.

**fremdsprachig** *adj* in a foreign language.

**Fremdwort** *(pl -wörter) das* foreign word; **gutes Benehmen ist für ihn ein ~** he doesn't know the meaning of good behaviour.

**Fremdwörter|buch** *das* dictionary of foreign words.

**Frequenz** *(pl -en) die* - **1.** PHYS frequency - **2.** MED rate.

**Fressalien** [frɛ'sa:ljən] *pl fam* grub *(U)*.

**Fresse** *(pl -n) die vulg* - **1.** [Mund] mouth, gob *Br;* **halt die ~!** shut your trap! - **2.** [Gesicht] mug; **jm in die ~ hauen** to smack sb in the face.

**fressen** *(präs* **frisst;** *prät* **fraß;** *perf* **hat gefressen)** *vt* - **1.** [beim Tier] to eat - **2.** *fam abw* [essen] to guzzle, to scoff *Br* - **3.** *fam* [Strom, Geld] to eat up; **diese Arbeit frisst viel Zeit** this work takes up a lot of time - **4.** *RW:* **jn gefressen haben** *fam* not to be able to stand sb, to hate sb's guts ◇ *vi* - **1.** [Tier] to feed; **der Vogel frisst einem aus der Hand** the bird will eat out of your hand - **2.** *salopp abw* [Mensch] to stuff one's face - **3.** [zehren, nagen]: **an etw** *(D)* **~** to eat away at sthg.

 **sich fressen** *ref* [sich hineinfressen]: **sich in etw** *(A)* **~** to eat away at sthg.

**Fressen** *das (ohne pl)* - **1.** [Tierfutter] food - **2.** *vulg abw* [Nahrung] muck, pigswill - **3.** *RW:* **die Affäre war ein gefundenes ~ für die Presse** *fam* the affair had the press rubbing their hands with glee.

**Frettchen** *(pl -) das* ferret.

**Freude** *(pl -n) die* joy; **es ist mir eine ~ zu kommen** it would be a pleasure for me to come; **jm die ~ an etw verderben** to spoil sb's enjoyment of sthg; **an etw** *(D)* **~ haben** to take pleasure in sthg; **jm eine ~ machen** to make sb happy.

**Freuden|haus** *das* house of ill repute, brothel.

**freudestrahlend** *adj* joyous; [Gesicht] beaming ◇ *adv* joyfully.

**freudig** *adj* - **1.** [Begrüßung] joyful - **2.** [Überraschung] pleasant ◇ *adv* - **1.** [begrüßen] joyfully - **2.** [überrascht] pleasantly.

**freudlos** *adj* cheerless ◇ *adv* cheerlessly.

**freuen** *vt* to please.

 **sich freuen** *ref* to be pleased; **es freut mich, dass ...** I'm pleased that ...; **freut mich sehr!** pleased to meet you!; **sich an etw** *(D)* **~** to get a lot of pleasure from sthg; **sich über etw** *(A)* **~** to be pleased about sthg; **sich auf etw** *(A)* **~** to be looking forward to sthg.

**Freund** *(pl -e) der* - **1.** [guter Bekannter] friend; **dicke ~e sein** *fam* to be bosom pals - **2.** [Liebhaber] boyfriend - **3.** [Anhänger] lover; **ein ~ klassischer Musik** a classical music lover; **kein großer ~ von etw sein** not to be very keen on sthg.

**Freundes|kreis** *der* circle of friends.

**Freundin** *(pl -nen) die* - **1.** [gute Bekannte] friend - **2.** [Geliebte] girlfriend.

**freundlich** *adj* - **1.** [Mensch, Geste, Rat] friendly; **danke für die ~e Begrüßung** thank you for your kind welcome; **bist du so ~ und begleitest mich?** would you be so kind as to accompany me? - **2.** [Umgebung, Stimmung] nice ◇ *adv* [nett] in a friendly way; **jm ~ gesinnt sein** to be well-disposed towards sb.

**Freundlichkeit** *(pl -en) die* - **1.** *(ohne pl)* [nette Art] friendliness - **2.** [Gefälligkeit] favour; **jm ein paar ~en sagen** to say a few kind words to sb.

**Freundschaft** *(pl -en) die* friendship; **mit jm ~ schließen** to make friends with sb.

**freundschaftlich** *adj* friendly ◇ *adv* in a friendly way; **jm ~ verbunden sein** to be friends with sb.

**Freundschafts|dienst** *der* favour for a friend; **jm einen ~ erweisen** to do sb a favour.

**Freundschaftslspiel** *das* friendly (game).

**frevelhaft** *geh adj* wicked ◇ *adv* wickedly.

**Frieden, Friede** *der* peace; **dem ~ nicht recht trauen** to think things are too good to be true; **jn in ~ lassen** to leave sb in peace; **mit jm ~ schließen** to make peace with sb.

**Friedenslbewegung** *die* peace movement.

**Friedenspreis des deutschen Buchhandels** *der* annual prize awarded by German book trade to an author considered to have furthered the cause of peace.

**Friedenslvertrag** *der* peace treaty.

**friedfertig** *adj* peaceable.

**Friedllhof** *der* cemetery.

**friedlich** *adj* peaceful ◇ *adv* peacefully.

**frieren** (*prät* **fror;** *perf* **hat/ist gefroren**) *vi* **- 1.** *(hat)* [an Kälte leiden] to be cold; **es friert ihn** he is cold; **an den Füßen ~** to have cold feet; **es friert mich an den Händen** my hands are cold **- 2.** *(hat)* [sehr kalt sein]: **es friert** it is freezing **- 3.** *(ist)* [gefrieren] to freeze.

**Frikadelle** (*pl* -n) *die* rissole.

**Frikassee** [frika'seː] (*pl* -s) *das* fricassee.

**Frisbee**® [ˈfrɪsbil] (*pl* -s) *das* Frisbee®.

**frisch** *adj* **- 1.** [gen] fresh; [Verletzung] recent; [Farbe] wet; [Kraft] renewed; **diese Erinnerung ist noch ~** it's still fresh in my memory **- 2.** [sauber] clean; **sich ~ machen** to freshen up **- 3.** [kühl - unangenehm] chilly; [- angenehm] cool **- 4.** [in Form] refreshed; **~ und munter sein** to be bright and cheery ◇ *adv* [gewaschen, zubereitet] freshly; [renoviert] newly; **das Brot kommt ~ vom Bäcker** the bread is fresh from the baker's; '**~ gestrichen**' "wet paint".

**Frische** *die* **- 1.** [gen] freshness; **in alter ~** as fresh as ever **- 2.** [Kühle - unangenehm] chilliness; [- angenehm] coolness.

**Frischlkäse** *der* soft cream cheese.

**Friseur, Frisör, in** [fri'zøːɐ̯, rɪn] (*mpl* -e; *fpl* -nen) *der, die* hairdresser.

**Friseurlsalon, Frisierlsalon** *der* hairdressing salon, hairdresser's.

**Friseuse, Frisöse** [fri'zøːzə] (*pl* -n) *die* hairdresser.

**frisieren** *vt* **- 1.** [Person] **jn ~** to do sb's hair; **sie ist schick frisiert** she has a trendy hairstyle **- 2.** *fam* [Zahlen] to fiddle; **die Bilanzen ~** to cook the books **- 3.** *fam* AUTO to soup up.
  ◆ **sich frisieren** *ref* [sich kämmen] to do one's hair.

**Frisierlsalon** = Friseursalon.

**Frisör, in** = Friseur.

**Frisöse** = Friseuse.

**frisst** *präs* ▷ fressen.

**Frist** (*pl* -en) *die*: **jm eine ~ von einer Woche geben** to give sb a week; **bis zur Prüfung bleibt dir noch eine ~ von drei Tagen** you still have three days to go until the exam; **die ~ wird nicht verlängert** the deadline is not being extended; **eine ~ einhalten** to meet a deadline; **innerhalb kürzester ~** in a very short space of time.

**fristen** *vt*: **ein erbärmliches Dasein** ODER **Leben ~** to eke out a miserable existence.

**Fristenlregelung** *die* law permitting abortion to be carried out before a pregnancy has advanced beyond a certain number of weeks.

**fristgerecht** *adj* & *adv* within the specified time; **jm ~ kündigen** to give sb the correct amount of notice as specified in their contract or by law.

**fristlos** *adj* immediate ◇ *adv* without notice, with immediate effect.

**Frisur** (*pl* -en) *die* hairstyle.

**frivol** [fri'voːl] *adj* [leichtfertig] frivolous ◇ *adv* [leichtfertig] frivolously.

**Frl.** (*abk für* Fräulein) Ms.

**froh** *adj* **- 1.** [vergnügt] happy **- 2.** [erleichtert] glad; **über etw ~ sein** to be pleased ODER glad about sthg **- 3.** [Nachricht] good.

**fröhlich** *adj* **- 1.** [Mensch, Lachen] cheerful **- 2.** [Fest] jolly ◇ *adv* [vergnügt] cheerfully.

**Fröhlichkeit** *die* cheerfulness.

**fromm** (*kompar* **frommer** ODER **frömmer;** *superl* **frommste** ODER **frömmste**) *adj* **- 1.** [Mensch, Christ] devout; [Worte, Einstellung] pious **- 2.** [heuchlerisch] sanctimonious, pious ◇ *adv* **- 1.** [gläubig, gottgefällig] piously **- 2.** [heuchlerisch] sanctimoniously, piously.

**Fronleichnam** (*ohne Artikel*) Corpus Christi.

**Front** (*pl* -en) *die* front; **gegen jn/etw ~ machen** to oppose sb/sthg.

**frontal** *adj* **- 1.** [Zusammenstoß] head-on **- 2.** [Angriff, Darstellung] frontal ◇ *adv* **- 1.** [von vorn] head-on **- 2.** [angreifen] from the front.

**Frontalzusammenlstoß** *der* head-on collision.

**Frontlantrieb** *der* AUTO front-wheel drive.

**Frontlwechsel** *der* U-turn.

**fror** *prät* ▷ frieren.

**Frosch** (*pl* Frösche) *der* frog; **einen ~ im Hals haben** *fam* to have a frog in one's throat.

**Froschlmann** *der* frogman.

**Froschlschenkel** *der* frog's leg.

**Frost** (*pl* Fröste) *der* frost.

**frösteln** *vi* to shiver.

**Frostgefahr** *die* (*ohne pl*) danger of frost.

**frostig** *adj* eigtl & *fig* frosty ◇ *adv* frostily.

**Frostlschaden** *der* frost damage.

**Frottee** [frɔ'teː] (pl -s) der ODER das towelling.

**Frotteehandltuch** das terry towel.

**frottieren** vt to rub down.
→ **sich frottieren** ref to rub o.s. down.

**frotzeln** fam vt to tease <> vi: ~ (über jn/etw) to make fun (of sb/sthg).

**Frucht** (pl Früchte) die fruit; Früchte fruit (U); endlich Früchte tragen finally to bear fruit.

**fruchtbar** adj - 1. [Erde, Lebewesen] fertile - 2. [Gespräch, Idee] fruitful.

**Fruchtbarkeit** die fertility.

**Früchtchen** (pl -) das: ein schönes ODER sauberes ~ fam abw a real good-for-nothing.

**fruchten** vi to be of use; es hat nichts gefruchtet it didn't do any good.

**fruchtig** adj fruity.

**fruchtlos** adj fruitless.

**Fruchtlsaft** der fruit juice.

**früh** adj early; [Tat] premature; am ~en Morgen/Abend early in the morning/ evening <> adv early; ~ am Abend/Morgen early in the evening/morning; er ist ~ gestorben he died young; gestern/heute/morgen ~ yesterday/this/tomorrow morning; ~er oder später sooner or later; etw zu ~ verkaufen to sell sthg too soon.

**Frühaufsteher, in** (mpl -; fpl -nen) der, die early riser.

**Frühe** die
→ **in aller Frühe** adv very early in the morning.
→ **in der Frühe** adv early in the morning.

**früher** adv formerly <> adj former; in ~en Zeiten in the past.

**frühestens** adv at the earliest.

**Frühlgeburt** die - 1. [Geburt] premature birth; eine ~ haben to give birth prematurely - 2. [Baby] premature baby.

**Frühljahr** das spring; im ~ in spring.

**Frühling** (pl -e) der spring; im ~ in spring.

**Frühlingsanfang** der (ohne pl) first day of spring.

**frühlingshaft** adj spring-like.

**frühmorgens** adv early in the morning.

**frühreif** adj [Kind] precocious.

**Frühlrentner, in** der, die person who has taken early retirement.

**Frühlschoppen** der morning drink.

**Frühlsport** der early morning exercise.

**Frühlstart** der SPORT false start.

**Frühlstück** das breakfast; nach dem ~ after breakfast; zum ~ for breakfast.

**frühstücken** vi to have breakfast <> vt to have for breakfast.

**Frühstückslpause** die breakfast break taken by people who start work very early.

**frühzeitig** adj early; [Tod] premature <> adv early; [sterben] prematurely.

**Frust** der fam frustration.

**frustrieren** vt to frustrate.

**FU** [ɛf'uː] (abk für Freie Universität) die: die ~ Berlin the Berlin Free University.

**Fuchs** [fʊks] (pl Füchse) der - 1. [Tier] fox - 2. [Pelz] fox fur - 3. fam [Mensch]: ein schlauer ~ a cunning devil.

**Fuchsie** ['fʊksjə] (pl -n) die fuchsia.

**Füchsin** ['fyksɪn] (pl -nen) die vixen.

**Fuchslschwanz** der - 1. [Schwanz] fox's brush - 2. [Säge] handsaw.

**fuchsteufelswild** ['fʊkstɔyflsvɪlt] adj fam hopping mad.

**Fuchtel** die: unter js ~ stehen fam to be under sb's thumb.

**fuchteln** vi: mit etw ~ to wave sthg around.

**Fuge** (pl -n) die - 1. [Ritze] gap; aus den ~n geraten to go to pot - 2. MUS fugue.

**fügen** vt [einfügen]: etw an etw (A) ~ to join sthg to sthg; etw in etw (A) ~ to fit sthg into sthg; fest gefügt firmly established.
→ **sich fügen** ref - 1. [hineinpassen] to fit - 2. [sich unterordnen]: sich einer Sache (D) ~ to obey sthg.

**fügsam** adj obedient <> adv obediently.

**fühlbar** adj noticeable <> adv noticeably.

**fühlen** vt to feel <> vi to feel; nach etw ~ to feel for sthg.
→ **sich fühlen** ref to feel; sich krank ~ to feel ill.

**Fühler** (pl -) der feeler, antenna; seine ~ ausstrecken fig to put out feelers.

**fuhr** prät → fahren.

**Fuhre** (pl -n) die load; [von Taxi] fare.

**führen** vt - 1. [Person, Tier] to lead; jn zu einem Versteck ~ to show ODER lead sb to a hiding-place - 2. [leiten - Firma, Hotel] to run, to manage; [ - Partei] to lead; [ - Haushalt] to run; [ - Truppen] to command; [ - Krieg, Kampf] to wage; den Vorsitz ~ to be the chairperson - 3. [durchführen - Gespräch] to hold; ein Ferngespräch ~ to make a long-distance call; das Protokoll ~ to take the minutes; ein langes Gespräch geführt haben to have had a long conversation; einen Prozess gegen jn ~ to take legal action against sb - 4. [Gegenstand]: etw mit sich ODER bei sich ~ to carry sthg - 5. [Ware] to stock - 6. [Liste] to keep; sie wird als Mitglied geführt she's listed as a member - 7. [Touristen] to show around - 8. [Name, Titel] to have - 9. [bewegen] to handle <> vi - 1. SPORT to lead; knapp ~ to be just in the lead; mit 1:0 ~ to be leading 1-0, to be 1-0 up - 2. [Straße] to lead - 3. [zu einem Ergebnis]: zu etw ~ to lead to sthg; zum Er-

**folg ~** to bring success; **das führt zu nichts** that won't get us anywhere.

➤ **sich führen** *ref* to behave.

**führend** *adj* leading.

**Führer, in** (*mpl* -; *fpl* -**nen**) *der, die* - **1.** [Anführer] leader; **der ~** [Hitler] the Führer - **2.** [Fremdenführer, Buch] guide.

**Führer|schein** *der* driving licence *Br*, driver's license *Am*.

**Führung** (*pl* -**en**) *die* - **1.** [das Führen - von Firma, Hotel] running, management; [ - von Truppen] command; [ - von Partei] leadership; [ - von Haushalt] running; **unter (der) ~ von** under the direction of - **2.** [Personen - von Firma] management; [ - von Partei] leadership - **3.** [führende Stellung] lead; **in ~ liegen** to be in the lead *ODER* ahead; **in ~ gehen** to take the lead - **4.** [Besichtigung] guided tour - **5.** [Verhalten]: **wegen guter ~** on the grounds of good conduct - **6.** [Handhabung, Steuerung] operation.

**Führungsan|spruch** *der* leadership claims *(pl)*.

**Führungs|spitze** *die* [von Partei] top leadership; [von Firma] senior management.

**Führungs|zeugnis** *das*: polizeiliches ~ *police certificate stating that holder has no criminal record*.

**Fülle** *die* (*ohne pl*) [Menge, Übermaß] abundance.

**füllen** *vt* - **1.** [gen] to fill; [Geflügel, Tomate] to stuff - **2.** [hineingeben]: **etw in etw** *(A)* ~ to put sthg into sthg; **den Saft in Flaschen ~** to fill the bottles with juice.

➤ **sich füllen** *ref* [voll werden]: **sich mit etw ~** to fill up with sthg.

**Füller** (*pl* -) *der* fountain pen.

**Füllfeder|halter** *der* fountain pen.

**füllig** *adj* plump.

**Füllung** (*pl* -**en**) *die* [von Geflügel, Tomate] stuffing; [von Gebäck, in Zahn] filling.

**Fummel** (*pl* -) *der* **fam** *abw* cheap, *skimpy skirt or dress*.

**fummeln** *vi* - **1.** **fam** [tasten]: **nach etw ~** to fumble about for sthg; **an etw** *(D)* ~ to fumble around with sthg - **2.** **salopp** [sexuell berühren] to make out.

**Fund** (*pl* -**e**) *der* - **1.** [Objekt] find - **2.** [Handlung] discovery.

**Fundament** (*pl* -**e**) *das* - **1.** [Grundmauer] foundations *(pl)*; **bis auf die ~e abgerissen** to be razed to the ground - **2.** [Grundlage] basis; **etw in seinen ~en erschüttern** to strike at the very foundations of sthg.

**fundamental** *adj* fundamental ◇ *adv* fundamentally.

**Fundamentalist, in** (*mpl* -**en**; *fpl* -**nen**) *der, die* fundamentalist.

**Fund|büro** *das* lost property office *Br*, lost-and-found office *Am*.

**Fund|grube** *die* treasure trove.

**fundiert** *adj* [Wissen, Firma] sound; [Kritik, Überlegungen] well-founded; [Vortrag, Bericht] well-reasoned.

**fündig** *adj*: ~ **werden** to make a find.

**Fund|sache** *die*: ~**n** lost property *(U)*.

**fünf** *num* five; ~ **gerade sein lassen** to turn a blind eye; *siehe auch* **sechs**.

**Fünf** (*pl* -**en**) *die* - **1.** [Zahl] five - **2.** [Schulnote] ≈ E, *mark of 5 on a scale from 1 to 6*; *siehe auch* **Sechs**.

**Fünfeck** (*pl* -**e**) *das* pentagon.

**fünfeckig** *adj* pentagonal.

**Fünfeuro|schein** *der* five-euro note.

**fünffach** *adj*: **die ~e Menge** five times as much; **in ~er Größe** five times as big; **die Formulare in ~er Ausfertigung abgeben** to provide five copies of the forms; **der ~e Gewinner** the five-times winner ◇ *adv* [auffordern] five times; **~ gelagert** with five bearings.

**fünfhundert** *num* five hundred.

**Fünfjahres|plan** *der* five-year plan.

**Fünf|kampf** *der* pentathlon.

**fünfmal** *adv* five times.

**Fünfprozent|klausel** *die* five percent clause.

**FÜNFPROZENTKLAUSEL**

This clause stipulates that only parties that have managed to gain 5% of the national vote or that have a minimum of three candidates elected can be represented in the "Bundestag" (the German parliament). The purpose of this clause, enacted in the light of what happened to the parliament of the Weimar Republic, is to avoid the fragmentation of the German political system.

**fünfstellig** *adj* five-figure.

**fünfstöckig** *adj* five-storey.

**fünft** ➤ **zu fünft** *adv*: **zu ~** in a group of five; **wir waren zu ~** there were five of us.

**fünftausend** *num* five thousand.

**fünfte** *num* fifth; *siehe auch* **sechste**.

**Fünfte** (*pl* -**n**) *der, die, das* fifth; *siehe auch* **Sechste**.

**fünftel** *adj* (*unver*) fifth; *siehe auch* **sechstel**.

**Fünftel** (*pl* -) *das* fifth; *siehe auch* **Sechstel**.

**fünfzehn** *num* fifteen; *siehe auch* **sechs**.

**Fünfzehn** (*pl* -**en**) *die* fifteen; *siehe auch* **Sechs**.

**fünfzig** *num* fifty; *siehe auch* **sechs**.

**Fünfzig** *die* fifty; *siehe auch* **Sechs**.

**Fünfziger** *der* 50 euro note.

**Fünfzigerjahre, fünfziger Jahre** *pl:* die ~ the fifties.

**Fünfzigeuroschein** *der* 50 euro note.

**Funk** *der* [Übermittlung] radio.

**Funkausstellung** *die exhibition of broadcasting and communications technology.*

**Funke** (*pl* -n), **Funken** (*pl* -) *der* spark; **dass die ~n sprühen** ODER **fliegen** like crazy; **keinen ~n von etw haben** ODER **besitzen** not to have a scrap of sthg.

**funkeln** *vi* [Licht] to sparkle; [Stern] to twinkle; [Gold] to glitter.

**funkelnagelneu** *adj fam* spanking new.

**funken** *vt* to radio <> *vi:* **bei ihm hat es endlich gefunkt** *fam* [er versteht] he finally got it; **bei den beiden hat es gefunkt** *fam* [sie sind verliebt] they've fallen for each other.

**Funken** = Funke.

**Funker, in** (*mpl* -; *fpl* -nen) *der, die* radio operator.

**Funkgerät** *das* radio set; [tragbar] walkie-talkie.

**Funkhaus** *das* broadcasting centre.

**Funkloch** *das* TELEKOM *area in which mobile phone reception is not possible.*

**Funkstille** *die eigtl* & *fig* radio silence.

**Funktion** [fʊnk'tsjoːn] (*pl* -en) *die* - **1.** MATH [Aufgabe] function; [Tätigkeit] functioning; **in ~ sein/treten** to be in/come into operation - **2.** [Position] position.

**funktional** *adj* functional <> *adv* functionally.

**Funktionär, in** (*mpl* -e; *fpl* -nen) *der, die* official.

**funktionell** *adj* functional <> *adv* [funktional] functionally.

**funktionieren** *vi* to work.

**Funktionstaste** *die* EDV function key.

**funktionstüchtig** *adj* [Gerät] in good working order.

**Funkverbindung** *die* radio contact.

**Funzel** (*pl* -n) *die fam abw* dismal light.

**für** *präp* (+ A) - **1.** [gen] for; **sich ~ etw entschuldigen** to apologize for sthg; **ein Spielplatz ~ die Kinder** a playground for the children; **sich ~ Geschichte interessieren** to be interested in history; **~ jn einspringen** to stand in for sb; **jn ~ dumm halten** to think sb is stupid; **einen Mantel ~ 500 Euro kaufen** to buy a coat for 500 euros ; **~ ein halbes Jahr verreisen** to go away for half a year; **~ immer** for ever, for good; **~ sein Alter ist er noch recht munter** he's still very sprightly for his age - **2.** [zur Angabe der Unterstützung] in favour of; **~ die Abschaffung der Todesstrafe sein** to be in favour of

abolishing the death penalty; **früh aufstehen hat etwas ~ sich** getting up early has something to be said for it - **3.** [zur Angabe der Folge]: **Wort ~ Wort** word by word; **Tag ~ Tag** day after day.

**Für** *das:* **das ~ und Wider** the pros and cons.

**Furcht** *die* fear; **~ haben (vor jm/etw)** to be afraid (of sb/sthg); **aus ~ vor jm/etw** for fear of sb/sthg.

→ **Furcht erregend** *adj* frightening <> *adv* frighteningly.

**furchtbar** *adj* terrible <> *adv* [sehr] terribly; **sich ~ anstrengen** to make an enormous effort.

**fürchten** *vt* to fear; **ich fürchte, dass der Wagen kaputt ist** I'm afraid the car is out of action; **er fürchtet, zu spät zu kommen** he's afraid of arriving late <> *vi:* **um etw ~** to fear for sthg.

→ **sich fürchten** *ref:* **sich (vor jm/etw) ~** to be afraid (of sb/sthg).

**fürchterlich** *adj* terrible <> *adv* [sehr] terribly; **sich ~ anstrengen** to make an enormous effort.

**furchterregend** ⊳ Furcht.

**furchtlos** *adj* fearless <> *adv* fearlessly.

**furchtsam** *adj* [Person, Tier] easily frightened; [Blick] fearful.

**füreinander** *adv* for each other.

**Furie** ['fuːrjə] (*pl* -n) *die abw* she-devil.

**Furnier** (*pl* -e) *das* veneer.

**Furore** *die:* **~ machen** to cause a sensation.

**fürs** *präp* (für + das) ⊳ für.

**Fürsorge** *die* - **1.** [menschliche Unterstützung] care - **2.** [Sozialhilfe] social security *Br*, welfare *Am* - **3.** [Sozialamt] social services (*pl*) *Br*, welfare services (*pl*) *Am*.

**fürsorglich** *adj* attentive <> *adv* attentively.

**Fürsprache** *die* support; **bei jm ~ (für jn) einlegen** to intercede with sb (on sb's behalf).

**Fürsprecher, in** *der, die* advocate.

**Fürst** (*pl* -en) *der* prince.

**Fürstentum** (*pl* -tümer) *das* principality.

**Fürstin** (*pl* -nen) *die* princess.

**fürstlich** *adj* - **1.** [von einem Fürsten]: **der ~e Schloss** the prince's castle - **2.** [Bezahlung] handsome <> *adv* [bezahlen] handsomely; **~ leben** to live like a prince.

**Furunkel** (*pl* -) *der* ODER *das* boil.

**Furz** (*pl* Fürze) *der salopp* fart; **einen ~ lassen** to fart.

**furzen** *vi salopp* to fart.

**Fusel** *der abw* rotgut.

**Fusion** (*pl* -en) *die* - **1.** WIRTSCH merger - **2.** PHYS fusion.

**fusionieren** *vi* to merge.

**Fuß** (*pl* Füße) *der* - **1.** [Körperteil, von Berg] foot; **sich** *(D)* **die Füße vertreten** to stretch one's legs - **2.** [tragender Teil - von Lampe, Gefäß] base; [ - von Möbeln] leg - **3.** *RW:* **auf eigenen Füßen stehen** to stand on one's own two feet; **(festen) ~ fassen** to find one's feet; **jn/etw mit Füßen treten** to trample all over sb/sthg; **jm zu Füßen liegen** to adore *ODER* worship sb; **kalte Füße bekommen** *ODER* **kriegen** *fam* to get cold feet.

➡ **zu Fuß** *adv* on foot; **ich gehe oft zu ~ zur Arbeit** I often walk to work.

**Fuß|abtreter** (*pl* -) *der* doormat.

**Fuß|bad** *das* footbath.

**Fuß|ball** *der* - **1.** SPORT football *Br*, soccer *Am* - **2.** [Ball] football *Br*, soccer ball *Am*.

**Fußballer, in** (*mpl* -; *fpl* -nen) *der, die* footballer *Br*, soccer player *Am*.

**Fußball|mannschaft** *die* football team *Br*, soccer team *Am*.

**Fußball|platz** *der* football ground *Br*, soccer ground *Am*.

**Fußball|spiel** *das* football match *Br*, soccer game *Am*.

**Fußball|spieler, in** *der, die* football player *Br*, soccer player *Am*.

**Fußball|verein** *der* football club *Br*, soccer club *Am*.

**Fuß|bank** (*pl* -bänke) *die* footstool.

**Fuß|boden** *der* floor.

**Fußboden|belag** *der* floor covering.

**Fussel** (*pl* - *ODER* -n) *die ODER der* fluff (*U*); **~n** fluff.

**fusseln** *vi* to go bobbly.

**fußen** *vi:* **auf etw** *(D)* **~** to be based on sthg.

**Fuß|ende** *das* foot.

**Fußgänger** (*pl* -) *der* pedestrian.

**Fußgänger|ampel** *die* lights (*pl*) at a pedestrian crossing.

**Fußgängerin** (*pl* -nen) *die* pedestrian.

**Fußgängerüber|weg** *der* pedestrian crossing *Br*, crosswalk *Am*.

**Fußgänger|zone** *die* pedestrian precinct *Br ODER* zone *Am*.

**Fuß|gelenk** *das* ankle.

**Fuß|matte** *die* doormat.

**Fuß|note** *die* footnote.

**Fuß|pflege** *die* chiropody *Br*, podiatry *Am*; **zur ~ gehen** to go to the chiropodist's *Br ODER* podiatrist's *Am*.

**Fuß|pilz** *der* athlete's foot.

**Fuß|sohle** *die* sole (*of the foot*).

**Fuß|spur** *die* footprint.

**Fuß|stapfen** (*pl* -) *der* footprint; **in js ~ treten** *fig* to follow in sb's footsteps.

**Fuß|tritt** *der* kick.

**Fuß|weg** *der* footpath.

**futsch** *adj fam:* **~ sein** [fort] to have all gone; [kaputt] to be bust.

**Futter** (*pl* -) *das* - **1.** [für Haustiere] food; [für Vieh] feed; [Heu] fodder - **2.** [Stoff] lining.

**futtern** *fam vt* to feed ◇ *vi:* **sie kann viel ~** she can put away a lot of food.

**füttern** *vt* - **1.** [gen] to feed - **2.** [Kleidung] to line.

**Futter|napf** *der* (food) bowl.

**Futterneid** *der* jealousy.

**Fütterung** (*pl* -en) *die* - **1.** [Nähren] feeding - **2.** [von Kleidung] lining.

**Futur** (*pl* -e) *das* GRAM future (tense).

**futuristisch** *adj* futuristic ◇ *adv* in a futuristic style.

**G**

**g, G** [ge:] (*pl* - *ODER* -s) *das* - **1.** [Buchstabe] g, G - **2.** MUS G.

➡ **g** (*abk für* Gramm) g.

**gab** *prät* ⊳ geben.

**Gabe** (*pl* -n) *die* [Geschenk, Talent] gift; **eine milde ~** alms (*pl*).

**Gabel** (*pl* -n) *die* - **1.** [Besteckteil, beim Fahrrad] fork - **2.** [in der Landwirtschaft] pitchfork - **3.** [vom Telefon] cradle; **den Hörer auf die ~ legen** to hang up.

**gabeln** ➡ **sich gabeln** *ref* [sich teilen] to fork.

**Gabelung, Gablung** (*pl* -en) *die* fork.

**Gaben|tisch** *der table on which Christmas or birthday presents are placed.*

**gackern** *vi eigtl & fig* to cackle.

**gaffen** *vi fam abw* to gawp.

**Gag** [gɛ(ː)k] (*pl* -s) *der* - **1.** *fam* [Witz] gag - **2.** [Besonderheit] gimmick.

**Gage** [ˈgaːʒə] (*pl* -n) *die* fee.

**gähnen** *vi eigtl & fig* to yawn.

**Gala** (*pl* -s) *die* - **1.** [Galavorstellung] gala - **2.** [Kleidung] formal dress.

**galant** *geh adj* gallant ◇ *adv* gallantly.

**Galapagos-Inseln** *pl* Galapagos Islands.

**Galavorlstellung** *die* gala performance.

**Galaxis** (*pl* -xien) *die* - **1.** [Milchstraße]: **die ~** the Galaxy - **2.** [Sternsystem] galaxy.

**Galeere** (*pl* -n) *die* galley.

**Galerie** (*pl* -n) *die* gallery.

**Galerist, in** (*mpl* -en; *fpl* -nen) *der, die* gallery owner.

**Galgen** (*pl* -) *der* gallows (*sg*).

**Galgenfrist** *die* grace.

**Galgenhumor** *der* gallows humour.

**Galionslfigur** *die eigtl* & *fig* figurehead.

**Gälisch(e)** *das* Gaelic; *siehe auch* **Englisch(e).**

**Galizien** *nt* Galicia.

**Galle** (*pl* -n) *die* - **1.** [Organ] gall bladder - **2.** [Flüssigkeit] bile; **mir kommt die ~ hoch** *fam* it makes my blood boil.

**Gallenlstein** *der* gallstone.

**gallertartig** *adj* gelatinous.

**Gallien** [ˈgaljən] *nt* Gaul.

**Gallier, in** [ˈgaljɐ, rɪn] (*mpl* -; *fpl* -nen) *der, die* Gaul.

**Galopp** (*pl* -s *ODER* -e) *der* gallop; **im ~** [beim Pferd] at a gallop; *fam* [schnell] at top speed.

**galoppieren** (*perf* hat/ist galoppiert) *vi* to gallop.

**Galopplrennen** *das* horse race.

**Galoschen** *die fam abw* scruffy shoes.

**galt** *prät* ☞ **gelten.**

**Gamelshow** [ˈgeːmʃoː] *die* TV game show.

**gammeln** *vi fam* - **1.** *abw* [nichts tun] to loaf around - **2.** [verderben] to go off.

**Gämse** (*pl* -n) *die* chamois.

**gang** *adj:* **~ und gäbe sein** to be perfectly normal.

**Gang¹** [gɛŋ] (*pl* Gänge) *der* - **1.** [Gangart] gait; **er hat einen ~ wie John Wayne** he walks like John Wayne - **2.** [Spaziergang, Ausgang] walk; **einen ~ machen** to go for a walk - **3.** [Flur, Weg] corridor; [in Flugzeug] aisle; **unterirdischer ~** underground passage - **4.** [beim Kfz] gear; **im ersten ~** in first gear; **einen ~ zulegen** *fam* to get a move on - **5.** [Bewegung]: **etw in ~ bringen** *ODER* **setzen** [gen] to get sthg going; [Maschine] to start sthg up; **der Motor ist/kam in ~** the engine is running/started up; **die Diskussion kam erst nach einer Stunde in ~** it was an hour before the discussion got going - **6.** [Ablauf] course; **im ~e sein** to be going on - **7.** [Speisegang] course.

**Gang²** [gɛŋ] (*pl* -s) *die* gang.

**Ganglart** *die* gait.

**gangbar** *adj* [Lösung] practicable.

**gängeln** *vt abw* to treat like a child.

**Ganges** [ˈgaŋges, ˈgaŋes] *der* the (River) Ganges.

**gängig** *adj* - **1.** [üblich] common - **2.** [aktuell] current - **3.** [handelsüblich] popular.

**Ganglschaltung** *die* gears (*pl*).

**Gangster** [ˈgɛnstɐ] (*pl* -) *der* Gangster.

**Gangway** [ˈgɛŋweːl] (*pl* -s) *die* [von Schiff] gangway; [von Flugzeug] steps (*pl*).

**Ganove** [gaˈnoːvə] (*pl* -n) *der* crook.

**Gans** (*pl* Gänse) *die* goose; **dumme ~!** *fam* silly goose!

**Gänselblümchen** *das* daisy.

**Gänselbraten** *der* roast goose.

**Gänselfüßchen** *pl fam* quotation marks.

**Gänselhaut** *die* (ohne *pl*) goose-pimples (*pl*) *Br*, goosebumps *Am*.

**Gänselmarsch** *der:* **im ~** in single file.

**Gänserich** (*pl* -e) *der* gander.

**Gänseschmalz** *das* goose fat.

**ganz** *adj* - **1.** [komplett] whole, entire; **den ~en Tag** all day, the whole day; **eine ~e Zahl** a whole number; **~e Note** MUS semi-breve *Br*, whole note *Am* - **2.** [alle] all; **der ~e Kaffee** all the coffee; **~ Paris** the whole of Paris - **3.** *fam* [heil] whole, intact; **die Tasse ist noch ~** the cup is still intact *ODER* in one piece; **etw ~ machen** to repair sthg - **4.** [nur]: **wir haben ~e zehn Minuten dafür gebraucht** it took us no more than ten minutes - **5.** [verstärkend]: **eine ~e Menge** quite a lot; **was soll der ~e Quatsch!** what's all this nonsense about! ◇ *adv* - **1.** [sehr] really; **er ist ein ~ seltsamer Mensch** he's a very strange person; **~ wenig** very little - **2.** [völlig] completely; **~ bestimmt** quite certainly; **er kommt ~ bestimmt** he is sure to come; **~ und gar** completely; **~ und gar (nicht)** not at all - **3.** [einschränkend] quite; **der Film war ~ gut** the film was quite good.

**Ganze** *das* - **1.** [Einheit] whole; **eine Sache als ~s beurteilen** to judge sthg as a whole - **2.** [alles] whole thing; **das ~ war eine Farce** the whole thing was a farce; **aufs ~ gehen** to go for it; **es geht ums ~** it's all or nothing.
➡ **im Ganzen** *adv* on the whole.

**Gänze** *die:* **in seiner/ihrer ~** *geh* in its entirety; **zur ~** fully.

**ganzheitlich** *adj* - **1.** [Betrachtung] global - **2.** [Medizin] holistic ◇ *adv* globally.

**ganzjährig** *adj:* **ein ~es Angebot** an offer which is available all year round ◇ *adv* all year round.

**gänzlich** *adj* complete ◇ *adv* completely.

**ganzseitig** *adj* full-page.

**ganztägig** *adj* all-day; **ein ~er Ausflug** a day trip ◇ *adv* [geöffnet] all day; [arbeiten] full-time.

**ganztags** *adv:* **~ arbeiten** to work full-time.

**Ganztags|schule** *die* school attended in the morning and afternoon, rather than just in the morning as with most German schools.

**gar** *adv* ~ **kein** no … not … at all; **es war ~ keiner da** there was no one there at all; **auf ~ keinen Fall** under no circumstances at all; ~ **nicht** not at all; **aber du hast doch ~ nicht gefragt!** but you didn't even ask!; ~ **nichts** nothing at all; ~ **niemand** nobody at all; **sie wäre ~ zu gerne gekommen** she would have been all too happy to have come. <> *adj* [Speise] done.

**Garage** (*pl* -n) *die* garage.

**Garagen|wagen** *der* car which has always been parked in a garage rather than in the open.

**Garant** (*pl* -en) *der*: **ein ~ für etw sein** to guarantee sthg.

**Garantie** (*pl* -n) *die* guarantee; **die ~ für etw übernehmen** to guarantee sthg.
➤ **unter Garantie** *adv* under guarantee.

**garantieren** *vt* to guarantee <> *vi*: **für etw ~** to guarantee sthg.

**garantiert** *adv fam*: **er hat ~ verschlafen** I bet he's overslept; **wir werden ~ gewinnen** we're bound to win <> *adj* guaranteed.

**Garantie|schein** *der* guarantee (certificate).

**Garaus** *der*: **jm den ~ machen** *fam hum* to bump sb off; **einer Sache** (*D*) **den ~ machen** *fam hum* [Hoffnungen] to put paid to sthg.

**Gardasee** *der* Lake Garda.

**Garde** (*pl* -n) *die* [Leibgarde] guard; **noch (einer) von der alten ~ sein** *fig* to be one of the old guard.

**Garderobe** (*pl* -n) *die* - **1.** [in der Wohnung] hallstand - **2.** [in öffentlichen Räumen] cloakroom *Br*, coatroom *Am* - **3.** (*ohne pl*) [Kleidung] clothes (*pl*) (*except underwear*); **eine neue ~ kaufen** to buy a new wardrobe - **4.** [für Künstler] dressing room.

**Garderoben|frau** *die* cloakroom attendant *Br*, coatroom attendant *Am*.

**Garderoben|ständer** *der* coatstand.

**Gardine** (*pl* -n) *die* net curtain; **hinter schwedischen ~n** *fam* behind bars.

**Gardinen|stange** *die* curtain rail.

**garen** *vt* to cook.

**gären** (*prät* **gor** ODER **gärte**; *perf* **hat/ist gegoren** ODER **gegärt**) *vi* - **1.** (*ist*) (*unreg*) [in Gärung sein] to ferment - **2.** (*hat*) (*reg*) [Unzufriedenheit, Ärger]: **es gärte im Volk** the people were growing restless.

**Garn** (*pl* -e) *das* [zum Nähen] thread; [zum Weben] yarn.

**Garnele** (*pl* -n) *die* shrimp.

**garnieren** *vt* to garnish.

**Garnison** (*pl* -en) *die* garrison.

**Garnitur** (*pl* -en) *die* - **1.** [Satz] set; **eine Polstermöbel ~** a three-piece suite - **2.** [Garnierung] garnish - **3.** [Klasse, Kategorie]: **er gehört zur ersten/zweiten ~ des Vereins** *fam* he's one of the club's first-team/second-string players.

**garstig** *adj* [frech, böse] nasty <> *adv* [frech, böse] nastily.

**Garten** (*pl* **Gärten**) *der* garden; **sie hat Schallplatten quer durch den ~ gesammelt** she has a real mixture of records in her collection.
➤ **botanische Garten** *der* botanical gardens (*pl*), botanical garden.
➤ **englische Garten** *der* landscape design popular on English country estates comprising open countryside interspersed with copses.
➤ **zoologische Garten** *der* zoo.

**Garten|arbeit** *die* gardening.

**Garten|bau** *der* horticulture.

**Garten|gerät** *das* gardening tool.

**Garten|haus** *das* garden shed.

**Garten|laube** *die* summerhouse.

**Garten|schere** *die* [klein] secateurs (*pl*); [Heckenschere] shears (*pl*).

**Garten|zaun** *der* garden fence.

**Garten|zwerg** *der* garden gnome.

**Gärtner** (*pl* -) *der* gardener.

**Gärtnerei** (*pl* -en) *die* - **1.** [Betrieb] nursery - **2.** [Gartenarbeit] gardening.

**Gärtnerin** (*pl* -nen) *die* gardener.

**gärtnern** *vi* to (work in the) garden.

**Gärung** (*pl* -en) *die* fermentation.

**Gar|zeit** *die* cooking time.

**Gas** (*pl* -e) *das* - **1.** [gen] gas - **2.** [Gaspedal] accelerator *Br*, gas pedal *Am*; [Treibstoff] petrol *Br*, gas *Am*; (**das**) ~ **wegnehmen** to take one's foot off the accelerator *Br* ODER gas *Am*; ~ **geben** to accelerate.

**Gas|flasche** *die* gas cylinder.

**gasförmig** *adj* gaseous.

**Gas|hahn** *der* gas tap.

**Gas|heizung** *die* gas heating.

**Gas|herd** *der* gas cooker *Br*, gas stove *Am*.

**Gas|kocher** *der* camping stove, Primus stove®.

**Gas|leitung** *die* gas pipe.

**Gas|mann** (*pl* -männer) *der* gasman.

**Gas|maske** *die* gas mask.

**Gas|pedal** *das* accelerator *Br*, gas pedal *Am*.

**Gas|pistole** *die* pistol that fires gas cartridges.

**Gasse** (*pl* -n) *die* alley; **die Menschenmenge bil-**

G

dete eine ~ für das **Fahrzeug** the crowd parted to let the vehicle through.

**Gassi** ➠ Gassi gehen *vi (unreg) fam* to go (for) walkies.

**Gast** *(pl* Gäste) *der* - **1.** [Eingeladene] guest; **bei jm zu ~ sein** to be sb's guest; **wir sind heute Abend bei Freunden zu ~** we are visiting friends this evening; **Gäste haben** to have guests; **wir haben heute Abend Freunde zu ~** we are having some friends round *ODER* over this evening; **Sie sind mein ~, seien Sie bitte mein ~** this one's on me - **2.** [im Hotel] guest; [im Lokal] customer - **3.** [Tourist] visitor.

**Gastlarbeiter, in** *der, die* foreign worker.

**Gästelbett** *das* spare bed.

**Gästelbuch** *das* visitors' book.

**Gästelzimmer** *das* guest room.

**gastfreundlich** *adj* hospitable.

**Gastlfreundschaft** *die* hospitality.

**Gastlgeber, in** *(mpl* -; *fpl* -nen) *der, die* - **1.** [Einladende] host - **2.** [heimische Mannschaft] home team.

**Gastlhaus** *das* inn.

**Gastlhof** *der* inn.

**Gastlhörer, in** *der, die* UNI auditor *Am, person permitted to attend university lectures without being registered as a student.*

**gastieren** *vi* to give a guest performance.

**Gastlland** *das* [für Veranstaltung] host country.

**gastlich** *adj* hospitable <> *adv* hospitably.

**Gastlmannschaft** *die* away team.

**Gastronomie** *die* - **1.** [Gewerbe] catering - **2.** [Kochkunst] gastronomy.

**gastronomisch** *adj* gastronomic.

**Gastlspiel** *das* guest performance.

**Gastlstätte** *die rustic restaurant with pub attached.*

**Gastlstube** *die* dining room *(in pub).*

**Gastlwirt, in** *der, die* landlord (f landlady).

**Gastlwirtschaft** *die rustic pub where food is served.*

**Gaslvergiftung** *die* gas poisoning.

**Gaslwerk** *das* gasworks *(sg).*

**Gatte** *(pl* -n) *der* husband, spouse.

**Gatter** *(pl* -) *das* - **1.** [Tor] gate - **2.** [Zaun] fence.

**Gattin** *(pl* -nen) *die* wife, spouse.

**Gattung** *(pl* -en) *die* - **1.** BIOL genus - **2.** [Art, Untergruppe] kind, type; [von Literatur, Kunst, Musik] genre.

**GAU** [gau] *(pl* -s) *(abk für* **Größter anzunehmender Unfall)** *der* MCA, *maximum credible accident.*

**Gaudi** *die ODER das fam Süddt & Österr* fun *(U);* **eine große ~ haben** to have a real laugh.

**Gaukler, in** *(mpl* -; *fpl* -nen) *der, die* [Akrobat, Zauberkünstler] *itinerant entertainer who performs acrobatics and magic tricks.*

**Gaul** *(pl* Gäule) *der abw* nag.

**Gaumen** *(pl* -) *der* palate.

**Gauner** *(pl* -) *der* - **1.** [Betrüger] crook - **2.** *fam* [Spitzbube] cunning devil.

**Gaunerei** *(pl* -en) *die* swindle.

**Gaunerin** *(pl* -nen) *die* crook.

**Gazastreifen** *der:* der ~ the Gaza Strip.

**Gaze** [ˈgaːzə] *die* gauze.

**Gazelle** *(pl* -n) *die* gazelle.

**Gde.** *abk für* **Gemeinde.**

**G-Dur** *das* MUS G major.

**geartet** *adj:* eine wie auch immer ~e Lösung some solution or other; eine anders ~e Sprache a different kind of language.

**Geäst** *das (ohne pl)* branches *(pl).*

**geb.** - **1.** *(abk für* **geborene)** née - **2.** *(abk für* **geboren)** b.

**Gebäck** *(pl* -e) *das* pastries *(pl).*

**gebacken** *pp* ➩ **backen** <> *adj* baked; **frisch ~** freshly baked.

**Gebälk** *(pl* -e) *das* beams *(pl);* [im Dach] rafters *(pl).*

**gebar** *prät* ➩ **gebären.**

**Gebärde** *(pl* -n) *die* gesture.

**gebärden** ➠ sich gebärden *ref* to behave.

**gebären** *(präs* gebärt *ODER* gebiert; *prät* gebar; *perf* hat geboren) *vt* to give birth to.

**Gebärlmutter** *die* womb.

**Gebäude** *(pl* -) *das* - **1.** [Bauwerk] building - **2.** [gedanklich] structure; [aus Lügen] web.

**Gebäudelkomplex** *der* (building) complex.

**Gebäudelreinigung** *die* - **1.** [Reinigen] commercial cleaning - **2.** [Firma] cleaning contractors *(pl).*

**gebaut** *adj:* gut ~ sein to have a good body.

**Gebell, Gebelle** *das* barking.

**geben** *(präs* gibt; *prät* gab; *perf* hat gegeben) *vt* - **1.** [gen]: **jm etw ~** to give sb sthg, to give sthg to sb; **er gab mir 20 Euro dafür** he gave me 20 euros for it; **jm einen Kuss ~** to give sb a kiss, to kiss sb; **jm eine Spritze ~** to give sb an injection; **Unterricht ~** to teach; **eine Party ~** to have a party; **sein Einverständnis ~** to agree, to give one's consent - **2.** [platzieren]: **den Teig in die Kuchenform ~** to put the dough in the baking tin - **3.** [eine Bedeutung beimessen]: **viel/wenig auf etw (A) ~ fam** to set a lot of/little store by sthg - **4.** [telefonisch]: **~ Sie mir bitte die Personalabteilung!** could you put me through to the personnel department, please? - **5.** [kausal]: **die Kuh gibt Milch** the cow produces milk; **das gibt doch n'** etwas nothing will ever come of that; **das gibt zu denken!** it makes you think!; *fam* **das Buch gibt mir nichts** I didn't get much out of the book ◇ *v impers:* **es gibt** there is/are; **es gibt keinen Wein mehr** there is ODER there's no more wine; **hier gibt es viele Studenten** there are a lot of students here; **die schönsten Fresken gibt es in Italien** the most beautiful frescoes can be found in Italy; **was gibt es im Fernsehen?** what's on television?; **was gibt es heute zum Mittagessen?** what's for lunch today?; **was gibt es?** *fam* what's up?; **das gibt es doch nicht!** *fam fig* I don't believe it! ◇ *vi* [beim Kartenspielen] to deal; **du gibst!** it's your deal.

➤ **sich geben** *ref* - **1.** [sich verhalten] to act, to behave - **2.** [vortäuschen]: **sich als Kenner ~** to make o.s. out to be an expert - **3.** [aufhören] to sort itself out; **das gibt sich wieder** ODER **mit der Zeit** it'll sort itself out sooner or later.

**Gebet** *(pl -e) das* prayer; **ein ~ sprechen** to say a prayer; **jn ins ~ nehmen** *fam* to take sb to task.

**gebeten** *pp* ⊳ **bitten.**

**Gebiet** *(pl -e) das* - **1.** [Region, Gegend] area - **2.** [Bereich] field, area.

**gebieten** *(prät gebot; perf hat geboten) vt* - **1.** [befehlen]: **jm ~, etw zu tun** to command sb to do sthg - **2.** [verlangen] to call for; **Vorsicht ist geboten** caution is called for.

**Gebieter, in** *(mpl -; fpl -nen) der, die* master.

**gebieterisch** *adj* imperious ◇ *adv* imperiously.

**Gebietsanspruch** *der* territorial claim.

**Gebietsreform** *die* local government reorganization.

**gebietsweise** *adv* [abrechnen, gliedern] by area.

**Gebilde** *(pl -) das* structure.

**gebildet** *adj* educated ◇ *adv* eruditely.

**Gebirge** *(pl -) das* mountains *(pl);* [Bergkette] mountain range; **im ~** in the mountains.

**gebirgig** *adj* mountainous.

**Gebirgsdorf** *das* mountain village.

**Gebirgslandschaft** *die* - **1.** [Ausblick] mountain scenery *(U)* - **2.** [Gegend] mountainous region.

**Gebirgspass** *der* mountain pass.

**Gebiss** *(pl -e) das* - **1.** [Zähne] teeth *(pl)* - **2.** [Zahnersatz] dentures *(pl).*

**gebissen** *pp* ⊳ **beißen.**

**Gebläse** *(pl -) das* fan.

**geblasen** *pp* ⊳ **blasen.**

**geblieben** *pp* ⊳ **bleiben.**

**geblümt** *adj* [Kleid, Stil] flowery.

**gebogen** *pp* ⊳ **biegen** ◇ *adj* curved.

**geboren** *pp* ⊳ **gebären** ◇ *adj* born; **Frau**

**Maier, ~e Müller** Mrs. Maier, née Müller; **dazu ~ sein, etw zu tun** *fig* to be born to do sthg.

**geborgen** *pp* ⊳ **bergen** ◇ *adj* safe; **sich (bei jm) ~ fühlen** to feel secure ODER safe with sb.

**Geborgenheit** *die* security.

**geborsten** *pp* ⊳ **bersten.**

**Gebot** *(pl -e) das* - **1.** [Befehl] directive; [moralisch] precept; [göttlich] commandment - **2.** [Erfordernis] requirement; **das ~ der Stunde** the needs of the moment; **das ~ der Vernunft** the dictates of reason - **3.** [Angebot] bid.

➤ **Zehn Gebote** *pl* REL: **die Zehn ~e** the Ten Commandments.

**geboten** *pp* ⊳ **bieten** ⊳ **gebieten; etw für sein Geld ~ bekommen** to get sthg for one's money ◇ *adj* necessary, requisite.

**Gebr.** *(abk für* **Gebrüder***)* Bros.

**gebracht** *pp* ⊳ **bringen.**

**gebrannt** *pp* ⊳ **brennen** ◇ *adj* burnt; **~e Mandeln** toasted almonds.

**gebraten** *pp* ⊳ **braten** ◇ *adj* [in der Pfanne] fried; [im Backofen] roast.

**Gebräu** *(pl -e) das abw* concoction.

**Gebrauch** [gə'braux] *(pl -bräuche) der* use; **etw in ~ nehmen** to start using sthg; **von etw ~ machen** to make use of sthg.

➤ **Gebräuche** *pl* customs.

**gebrauchen** *vt* to use; **sie ist zu nichts zu ~** *fam* she is good for nothing; **ich könnte etwas zu essen ~** I could use something to eat.

**gebräuchlich** *adj* - **1.** [verbreitet] common - **2.** [üblich] usual.

**Gebrauchsanweisung** [gə'brauxsanvai-zʊŋ] *die* instructions *(pl).*

**gebrauchsfertig** [gə'brauxsfɛrtɪç] *adj* ready-to-use.

**Gebrauchsgegenstand** [gə'brauxs-ge:gnʃtant] *der* everyday object.

**gebraucht** *adj* second-hand.

**Gebrauchtwagen** *der* used ODER second-hand car.

**gebrechlich** *adj* frail.

**gebrochen** *pp* ⊳ **brechen** ◇ *adj* broken ◇ *adv* [unvollkommen]: **er spricht ~ Italienisch** he speaks broken Italian.

**Gebrüder** *pl:* **die ~ Schulze** the Schulze brothers.

**Gebrüll** *das (ohne pl)* [von Löwe, Menschenmenge] roaring; [von Stier] bellowing; [von Kind, Affe] screeching.

**Gebühr** *(pl -en) die* charge; [für Arzt, Anwalt] fee; [für Autobahn] toll; [für Post] postage.

➤ **nach Gebühr** *adv* appropriately.

➤ **über Gebühr** *adv* unduly.

**gebühren** *vi geh:* **ihm gebührt Anerkennung** he deserves recognition.

**gebührend** *adj* [Strafe, Belohnung] suitable; [Sorgfalt] due ⟷ *adv* [strafen, belohnen] suitably; **etw ~ sorgfältig machen** to do sthg with due care.

**Gebühren|einheit** *die* TELEKOM unit.

**gebührenfrei** *adj* & *adv* free of charge.

**gebührenpflichtig** *adj* subject to a charge.

**gebunden** *pp* ⟷ **binden** ⟷ *adj* - **1.** [in Beziehung]: **ich bin ~** I'm in a relationship - **2.** [vertraglich] bound - **3.** [gefesselt]: **an etw (A) ~ sein** to be tied to sthg.

**Geburt** (*pl* -en) *die* birth; **von ~ an** from birth; **von adeliger ~ sein** to be of noble birth; **er ist von ~ kein Deutscher** he is not German by birth.

**Geburten|kontrolle** *die* birth control.

**Geburten|rückgang** *der* decline in the birthrate.

**geburtenschwach** *adj* with a low birthrate.

**geburtenstark** *adj* with a high birthrate.

**gebürtig** *adj:* **sie ist ~e Bayerin, sie ist aus Bayern ~** she's Bavarian by birth.

**Geburts|anzeige** *die* birth announcement.

**Geburts|datum** *das* date of birth.

**Geburts|ort** *der* place of birth.

**Geburts|tag** *der* - **1.** [Jahrestag] birthday; **wann hast du ~?** when is your birthday?; **jm zum ~ gratulieren** to wish sb a happy birthday; **alles Gute zum ~!** happy birthday! - **2.** *amt* [Geburtsdatum] date of birth.

**Geburtstags|feier** *die* birthday party.

**Geburtstags|kind** *das* birthday boy/girl.

**Geburts|urkunde** *die* birth certificate.

**Gebüsch** (*pl* -e) *das* bushes (*pl*).

**Geck** (*pl* -en) *der abw* dandy.

**gedacht** *pp* ⟷ **denken, gedenken** ⟷ *adj:* **das Geschenk ist als Trost ~** the present is meant to be a consolation; **eigentlich war das anders ~** actually that's not what was intended; **es ist für ihn ~** it is meant for him.

**Gedächtnis** (*pl* -se) *das* memory; **kein ~ für Zahlen haben** to have no head for numbers; **etw im ~ behalten** to remember sthg; **zum ~ an jn** in memory of sb. ⟷ **aus dem Gedächtnis** *adv* from memory.

**Gedächtnis|feier** *die* commemoration.

**Gedächtnis|lücke** *die* gap in one's memory.

**Gedächtnis|schwund** *der* memory loss, amnesia; **unter ~ leiden** to suffer from memory loss ODER amnesia.

**Gedächtnis|stütze** *die* mnemonic.

**gedämpft** *adj* [Licht, Musik, Stimmung] subdued; [Geräusch, Schritte] muffled; [Farbton, Musikinstrument] muted; [Stimme] low.

**Gedanke** (*pl* -n) *der* - **1.** [Gedachte, Überlegung] thought; **sich (D) ~n über etw (A) machen** to think about sthg; **etw (ganz) in ~n tun** to do sthg (quite) without thinking; **js ~n lesen können** to be able to read sb's mind; **er hat sich entschlossen, keinen ~n daran zu verschwenden** he decided not to waste any time thinking about it; **der bloße ~, dass ...** the very idea that ... - **2.** [Vorstellung, Vorhaben] idea; **mit dem ~n spielen, etw zu tun** to toy with the idea of doing sthg - **3.** [Sorge]: **sich (D) ~n über jn/etw machen** to be worried about sb/sthg.

**Gedanken|austausch** *der* exchange of ideas.

**Gedanken|blitz** *der* brainwave.

**Gedanken|gang** *der* train of thought.

**Gedanken|gut** *das* (*ohne pl*) thought.

**gedankenlos** *adj* [ohne nachzudenken] thoughtless; [unaufmerksam] absent-minded ⟷ *adv* [ohne nachzudenken] without thinking; [unaufmerksam] absent-mindedly.

**Gedanken|strich** *der* dash.

**Gedanken|übertragung** *die* telepathy.

**gedankenverloren** *adv* lost in thought.

**gedanklich** *adj* [Problem, Zusammenhang] intellectual; [Anstrengung, Bemühung] mental ⟷ *adv* mentally.

**Gedeck** (*pl* -e) *das* - **1.** [Geschirr und Besteck] place setting - **2.** [Speisenfolge] set meal.

**Gedeih** ⟷ **auf Gedeih und Verderb** *adv* for better or for worse.

**gedeihen** (*prät* **gedieh;** *perf* **ist gediehen**) *vi* - **1.** [Mensch, Tier, Pflanze, Firma] to thrive - **2.** [Projekt, Verhandlungen] to progress.

**gedenken** (*prät* **gedachte;** *perf* **hat gedacht**) *vi geh* - **1.** [sich erinnern]: **js/einer Sache ~** to remember sb/sthg - **2.** [planen]: **etw zu tun ~** to intend to do sthg.

**Gedenken** *das* (*ohne pl*) *geh:* **zum ~ an jn/etw, jm/einer Sache zum ~** in memory of sb/sthg; **ein Feiertag zum ~ an das Kriegsende** a holiday to commemorate the end of the war.

**Gedenk|feier** *die* commemoration.

**Gedenk|minute** *die* minute's silence.

**Gedenk|stätte** *die* memorial.

**Gedenk|tafel** *die* plaque.

**Gedicht** (*pl* -e) *das* poem; **das Essen ist ein ~!** the food is just heavenly!

**gediegen** *adj* - **1.** [Gold, Silber] solid - **2.** [solide - Möbel] solid; [ - Haus] solidly-built; [ - Kleidung] well-made; [ - Kenntnisse] thorough; [ - Geschmack] discerning - **3.** [ungewöhnlich] peculiar ⟷ *adv* [solide] solidly.

**gedieh** *prät* ▷ gedeihen.

**gediehen** *pp* ▷ gedeihen.

**Gedränge** *das* crush.

**gedrängt** *adj* [Bericht, Beschreibung] succinct; [Zeitplan] busy ◇ *adv* succinctly.

**gedroschen** *pp* ▷ dreschen.

**gedrückt** *adj* depressed.

**gedrungen** *pp* ▷ dringen ◇ *adj* stocky.

**Gedudel** *das fam abw* droning.

**Geduld** *die* patience; **mit jm ~ haben** to be patient with sb; **die ~ verlieren** to lose one's patience.

**gedulden** ⇒ **sich gedulden** *ref* to be patient.

**geduldig** *adj* patient ◇ *adv* patiently.

**Geduldsfaden** *der:* **ihm reißt (gleich) der ~** he's losing his patience.

**Geduldsprobe** *die:* **es bedeutet für sie eine ~** it's trying her patience.

**gedurft** *pp* ▷ dürfen.

**geeignet** *adj* suitable; **für etw ~ sein** to be suitable for sthg; **nicht ~** unsuitable; **er ist zum Lehrer ~** he'd make a good teacher.

**Gefahr** (*pl* **-en**) *die* danger; **es besteht die ~ eines Unfalls** there's the risk of an accident; **außer ~ sein** no longer to be in danger; **~ laufen, etw zu tun** to be in danger of doing sthg. ⇒ **auf eigene Gefahr** *adv* at one's own risk.

**gefährden** *vt* [Gesundheit, Leben, Mensch] to endanger; [Unternehmen, Projekt] to jeopardize.

**Gefährdung** (*pl* **-en**) *die* [von Gesundheit, Leben, Mensch] endangering; [von Unternehmen, Projekt] jeopardizing.

**gefahren** *pp* ▷ fahren.

**Gefahren|zone** *die* danger area.

**gefährlich** *adj* dangerous ◇ *adv* dangerously.

**gefahrlos** *adj* safe ◇ *adv* safely.

**Gefährte** (*pl* **-n**) *der geh* companion.

**Gefährtin** (*pl* **-nen**) *die geh* companion.

**Gefälle** (*pl* **-**) *das* **- 1.** [von Straße, Dach] slope **- 2.** [Unterschied] difference.

**gefallen¹** (*präs* **gefällt**; *prät* **gefiel**; *perf* **hat gefallen**) *vi* **- 1.** [gut finden] **er/es gefällt mir** I like him/it **- 2.** [ertragen]: **sich** *(D)* **nichts ~ lassen** not to put up with sthg; **sich** *(D)* **nichts ~ lassen** not to put up with any nonsense; **das lasse ich mir ~!** *fam* I can handle this! ⇒ **sich gefallen** *ref:* **sie gefällt sich in der Rolle des Märtyrers** she likes to play the martyr.

**gefallen²** *pp* ▷ **fallen** ◇ *adj* [Engel, Mädchen] fallen; [Soldat] killed in action.

**Gefallen** (*pl* **-**) *der* favour; **jm einen ~ tun** to do sb a favour; **jn um einen ~ bitten** to ask sb a favour ◇ *das:* **an jm/etw ~ finden** to get ODER

come to like sb/sthg; **Ihnen zu ~** for your sake, just for you.

**gefällig** *adj* **- 1.** [entkommend] helpful; **jm ~ sein** to be of help to sb **- 2.** [angenehm] pleasant **- 3.** [genehm]: **noch ein Bier ~?** would you like another beer?

**Gefälligkeit** (*pl* **-en**) *die* [Gefallen] favour; **aus reiner ~ gebe ich dir das Geld** I'll give you the money out of the kindness of my heart.

**gefälligst** *adv* kindly.

**gefangen** *pp* ▷ **fangen** ◇ *adj:* **in etw** *(D)* **~ sein** to be a prisoner of sthg.

**Gefangene** (*pl* **-n**) *der, die* prisoner.

**gefangen halten** *vt* (*unreg*) **- 1.** [Mensch] to hold captive; [Tier] to keep in captivity **- 2.** *geh* [in Bann halten] to captivate.

**gefangen nehmen** *vt* (*unreg*) **- 1.** [festnehmen] to capture **- 2.** [in Bann ziehen] to captivate.

**Gefangenschaft** *die* captivity; **in ~ geraten** to be taken prisoner.

**Gefängnis** (*pl* **-se**) *das* **- 1.** [Haftanstalt] prison; **ins ~ kommen** to be sent to prison; **im ~ sitzen** to be in prison **- 2.** [Haftstrafe] imprisonment.

**Gefängnis|strafe** *die* prison sentence.

**Gefängnis|wärter, in** *der, die* prison guard.

**Gefängnis|zelle** *die* prison cell.

**gefärbt** *adj* dyed.

**Gefasel** *das fam abw* drivel.

**Gefäß** (*pl* **-e**) *das* **- 1.** [Behältnis] container **- 2.** [von Lebewesen] blood vessel.

**gefasst** *adj* **- 1.** [gelassen] composed **- 2.** [vorbereitet]: **auf etw** *(A)* **~ sein** to be prepared for sthg; **du kannst dich darauf ~ machen, dass ...** *fam* you'd better start getting used to the idea that ...; **sonst kannst du dich auf was ~ machen** *fam* otherwise you're in for it ◇ *adv* [gelassen] calmly.

**Gefecht** (*pl* **-e**) *das* skirmish; **jn außer ~ setzen** to put sb out of action.

**gefeit** *adj:* **(gegen etw) ~ sein** to be immune (to sthg).

**Gefieder** (*pl* **-**) *das* feathers (*pl*).

**Geflecht** (*pl* **-e**) *das:* **ein ~ aus Draht** a wire mesh; **ein Korb aus ~** a woven ODER wicker basket.

**Geflimmer** *das* flickering.

**geflissentlich** *adv* deliberately.

**geflochten** *pp* ▷ **flechten** ◇ *adj* [Band, Haar] plaited *Br*, braided *Am*; [Korb] woven, wicker.

**geflogen** *pp* ▷ fliegen.

**geflohen** *pp* ▷ fliehen.

**geflossen** *pp* ▷ fließen.

**Geflügel** *das* poultry.

**Geflügelschere** die poultry shears (pl).

**geflügelt** adj winged ⊳ **Wort**.

**Geflüster** das whispering.

**gefochten** pp ⊳ fechten.

**Gefolge** das entourage; [bei Beerdigung] cortege.

**Gefolgschaft** (pl -en) die - 1. (ohne pl) [Loyalität] allegiance; **jm die ~ verweigern** to stop supporting sb - 2. [Anhängerschaft] followers (pl).

**gefragt** adj popular; **sehr ~ sein** to be very much in demand.

**gefräßig** adj abw greedy.

**Gefreite** (pl -n) der lance corporal **Br**, private first class **Am**.

**gefressen** pp ⊳ fressen.

**gefrieren** (prät **gefror**; perf hat/ist gefroren) vi (ist) to freeze; **es hat gefroren** there has been a frost.

**Gefrier|fach** das freezer (compartment).

**Gefrier|schrank** der (upright) freezer.

**Gefrier|truhe** die (chest) freezer.

**gefroren** pp ⊳ frieren ⊳ gefrieren ⟨⟩ adj frozen.

**Gefüge** (pl -) das structure.

**gefügig** adj submissive.

**Gefühl** (pl -e) das - 1. [gen] feeling; **seine Beine sind ohne ~** he's got no feeling in his legs; **er kennt keine ~e** he doesn't have any feelings; **wenn mich mein ~ nicht trügt** if my instinct is correct; **etw im ~ haben** to know sthg instinctively - 2. [Gespür] sense; **ein ~ für etw a** sense of sthg.

**gefühllos** adj - 1. [taub] numb - 2. [herzlos] callous ⟨⟩ adv [herzlos] callously.

**gefühls|arm** adj unemotional.

**gefühlsbetont** adj emotional ⟨⟩ adv emotionally.

**Gefühlsduselei** (pl -en) die abw mawkish sentimentality.

**Gefühlsleben** das emotional life.

**gefühlsmäßig** adj emotional ⟨⟩ adv emotionally.

**gefühlvoll** adj - 1. [einfühlsam] sensitive - 2. [gefühlbetont] expressive ⟨⟩ adv - 1. [einfühlsam] sensitively - 2. [gefühlbetont] with feeling.

**gefunden** pp ⊳ finden.

**gegangen** pp ⊳ gehen.

**gegeben** pp ⊳ geben ⟨⟩ adj - 1. [vorhanden] given; **in der ~en Situation** under the circumstances; **etw als ~ annehmen** to take sthg for granted - 2. [geeignet] right; **zum ~en Zeitpunkt** in due course.

**gegebenenfalls** adv if necessary.

**Gegebenheit** (pl -en) die condition, circumstance.

**gegen** präp (+ A) - 1. [gen] against; **~ die Tür hämmern** to bang on the door; **das Schiff fährt ~ die Strömung** the ship is sailing upstream; **~ etw sein** to be opposed to ODER against sthg; **~ einen Befehl handeln** to contravene an order; **etw ~ jn haben** to have sthg against sb; **heute spielt Leipzig ~ Bremen** Leipzig are playing Bremen today; **ein Mittel ~ Grippe** a flu remedy, a medicine for flu - 2. [zeitlich]: **~ fünf Uhr** at about five o'clock; **~ Abend wurde es kühler** it cooled down towards evening - 3. [im Gegenzug] for; **~ bar** for cash - 4. [im Vergleich zu] in comparison to, compared with.

**Gegen|angriff** der counterattack.

**Gegen|antrag** der countermotion; **einen ~ stellen** to propose a countermotion.

**Gegen|argument** das counterargument.

**Gegen|beweis** der evidence (U) to the contrary.

**Gegend** (pl -en) die - 1. [Gebiet, Bereich] area; **in der ~** nearby; **in der ~ von** near; **in der Nierengegend** in the region of the kidneys; **hier in der ~** round here - 2. [Nachbarschaft] neighbourhood - 3. **RW**: **so in der ~** fam thereabouts; **die ~ unsicher machen** fam to paint the town red.

**Gegen|darstellung** die conflicting account.

**gegeneinander** adv against one another ODER each other.

**gegeneinander halten** vt (unreg) - 1. [aneinander halten] to hold side by side - 2. [vergleichen] to compare.

**gegeneinander stellen** vt - 1. [aneinander stellen] to place up against one another ODER each other - 2. [vergleichen] to compare.

**Gegenfahr|bahn** die opposite side of the road.

**Gegen|frage** die: **auf eine Frage mit einer ~ reagieren** to react to a question with another question.

**Gegen|gewicht** das counterbalance; **ein ODER das ~ zu etw bilden** to counterbalance sthg.

**Gegen|gift** das antidote.

**Gegen|kandidat, in** der, die rival candidate.

**Gegen|klage** die countercharge.

**gegenläufig** adj opposite ⟨⟩ adv in the opposite direction.

**Gegen|leistung** die: **als ~ (für etw)** in return (for sthg).

**gegen|lenken** vi to steer into a swerve.

**gegen|lesen** vt (unreg) to check.

**Gegen|liebe** *die:* er war von ihrer ~ überrascht he was surprised that she returned his affections; **auf (keine) ~ stoßen, (keine) ~ finden** to find (no) favour.

**Gegen|maßnahme** *die* countermeasure.

**Gegen|mittel** *das* antidote.

**Gegen|partei** *die* opposing side; [vor Gericht] opposing party; *sport* opposition.

**Gegen|pol** *der* - **1.** *phys* opposite pole - **2.** [Pendant] complete opposite.

**Gegen|richtung** *die* opposite direction.

**Gegen|satz** *der* contrast; **im ~ zu** in contrast to; **im ~ zu etw stehen** to contrast with sthg.

**gegensätzlich** *adj* conflicting <> *adv* completely differently.

**Gegen|schlag** *der:* **zum ~ ausholen** to strike back.

**Gegen|seite** *die* - **1.** [Gegenpartei] opposing side; [vor Gericht] opposing party; *sport* opposition - **2.** [andere Seite] other side.

**gegenseitig** *adj* mutual <> *adv* each other, one another; **sich ~ helfen** to help each other *oder* one another.

**Gegenseitigkeit** *die* reciprocity; **auf ~ beruhen** to be mutual.

**Gegen|spieler, in** *der, die* - **1.** [Gegner] opponent - **2.** [im Theater] antagonist.

**Gegensprechan|lage** *die* intercom.

**Gegen|stand** *der* - **1.** [Ding, Objekt] object - **2.** [Thema] subject.

**gegenständlich** *adj* [Kunst] representational.

**gegenstandslos** *adj* - **1.** [ungerechtfertigt] unfounded - **2.** [hinfällig] irrelevant.

**Gegen|stimme** *die* - **1.** [Stimme dagegen] vote against - **2.** [abweichende Meinung] dissenting voice.

**Gegen|stück** *das* counterpart.

**Gegen|teil** *das* opposite; **das ~ von jm/etw sein** to be the opposite of sb/sthg.

➥ **im Gegenteil** *adv* on the contrary; **ganz im ~** quite the reverse *oder* opposite.

**gegenteilig** *adj* opposite.

**gegenüber** *präp (+ D)* - **1.** [räumlich] opposite; **~ der Kirche** opposite the church; **mir ~** opposite me - **2.** [zur Angabe einer Beziehung] towards; **so kannst du dich den Schülern ~ nicht verhalten** you can't behave like that towards the pupils - **3.** [zur Angabe eines Vergleichs] compared with; **~ der alten Wohnung** compared with the old flat *Br oder* apartment *Am* <> *adv* opposite; **der Garten ~** the garden over *oder* across the road.

**Gegenüber** *das* person sitting opposite.

**gegenüber|liegen** *vi (unreg)* to be opposite; **das ~de Gebäude** the building opposite; ei-

nander ~ to face one another *oder* each other.

➥ **sich gegenüberliegen** *ref* to face one another *oder* each other.

**gegenüber|sitzen** *vi (unreg):* **jm ~** to sit opposite sb.

➥ **sich gegenübersitzen** *ref* to sit opposite one another *oder* each other.

**gegenüber|stehen** *vi (unreg)* - **1.** [zugewandt stehen]: **jm/einer Sache ~** to be facing sb/sthg - **2.** [gegenübergestellt sein]: **einer Sache (D) ~** to be faced with sthg; **jm feindlich ~** to have a hostile attitude towards sb.

➥ **sich gegenüberstehen** *ref* - **1.** [sich zugewandt stehen, gegeneinander spielen] to face one another *oder* each other - **2.** [in Konflikt stehen] to clash.

**gegenüber|stellen** *vt* - **1.** [mit jm konfrontieren]: **dem Zeugen die Verdächtigen ~** to line the suspects up in front of the witness - **2.** [nebeneinander halten]: **das Alterswerk eines Autors seinen frühen Romanen ~** to compare the late works of an author with his early novels.

**Gegenüber|stellung** *die* - **1.** [Konfrontation] confrontation - **2.** [Vergleich] comparison.

**gegenüber|treten** *(perf ist gegenübergetreten) vi (unreg):* **jm ~** to face sb.

**Gegenverkehr** *der* oncoming traffic.

**Gegen|vorschlag** *der* counterproposal.

**Gegenwart** *die* - **1.** [Zeitpunkt] present; **die Kunst der ~** contemporary art; **bis in die ~** up to the present day - **2.** [Präsenz] presence; **in js ~** in sb's presence - **3.** *gram* present (tense).

**gegenwärtig** *adj* [jetzig] current <> *adv* [jetzt] currently.

**Gegen|wehr** *die* resistance.

**Gegen|wert** *der* equivalent amount.

**Gegen|wind** *der* headwind.

**gegen|zeichnen** *vt* to countersign.

**gegessen** *pp* ⊏ essen.

**geglichen** *pp* ⊏ gleichen.

**geglitten** *pp* ⊏ gleiten.

**geglommen** *pp* ⊏ glimmen.

**Gegner, in** *(mpl -; fpl -nen) der, die* - **1.** [Widersacher, im Sport] opponent - **2.** [Feind] enemy.

**gegnerisch** *adj* opposing.

**gegolten** *pp* ⊏ gelten.

**gegoren** *pp* ⊏ gären <> *adj* fermented.

**gegossen** *pp* ⊏ gießen.

**gegr.** *(abk für gegründet)* est.

**gegraben** *pp* ⊏ graben.

**gegriffen** *pp* ⊏ greifen.

**geh.** *abk für* geheim.

**Gehabe** *das abw* affected behaviour.

G

**gehabt** *pp* ▷ haben.

**Gehackte** *das* mince *Br*, mincemeat *Am*.

**Gehalt** (*pl* **Gehälter**) *das* salary ◇ *der* - **1.** [Inhalt] content - **2.** [Anteil]: **ein geringer ~ an Gold** a low gold content.

**gehalten** *pp* ▷ halten ◇ *adj geh*: **~ sein, etw zu tun** to be obliged to do sthg.

**gehaltlos** *adj* - **1.** [Roman, Gespräch] shallow - **2.** [Lebensmittel] unnutritious; [Wein] lacking in body.

**Gehaltsabrechnung** *die* salary statement.

**Gehaltsempfänger, in** *der, die* salaried employee.

**Gehaltserhöhung** *die* salary *ODER* pay rise.

**Gehaltskürzung** *die* salary *ODER* wage cut.

**Gehaltsstufe** *die* salary bracket.

**Gehaltszahlung** *die* salary payment.

**Gehaltszulage** *die* [Erhöhung] salary *ODER* pay rise; [zusätzlich] bonus.

**gehandikapt** [gəˈhɛndikɛpt] *adj* handicapped.

**gehangen** *pp* ▷ hängen.

**gehässig** *adj* spiteful ◇ *adv* spitefully.

**Gehässigkeit** (*pl* **-en**) *die* - **1.** [Art] spitefulness - **2.** [Bemerkung] spiteful remark.

**Gehäuse** (*pl* -) *das* - **1.** [von Uhr, Fotoapparat, Radio] casing; [von Schnecke] shell - **2.** [von Apfel, Birne] core.

**gehbehindert** *adj* disabled *(used of people who have difficulty walking)*.

**Gehege** (*pl* -) *das* reserve; [im Zoo] enclosure; **jm ins ~ kommen** *fig* to encroach on sb's territory.

**geheim** *adj* - **1.** [heimlich] secret - **2.** [geheimnisvoll] mysterious ◇ *adv* [nicht offen] in secret; **~ abstimmen** to vote by secret ballot.
➠ **im Geheimen** *adv* secretly.

**Geheimagent, in** *der, die* secret agent.

**Geheimdienst** *der* secret service.

**Geheimfach** *das* hidden *ODER* secret compartment.

**geheim halten** *vt (unreg)* to keep secret.

**Geheimhaltung** *die* secrecy.

**Geheimnis** (*pl* -se) *das* - **1.** [Geheimgehaltenes] secret; **es ist ein offenes ~** it's an open secret - **2.** [Unbekanntes] mystery.

**Geheimnistuerei** *die abw* secretiveness.

**geheimnisvoll** *adj* mysterious ◇ *adv* mysteriously.

**Geheimnummer** *die* [von Telefon] ex-directory number *Br*, unlisted number *Am*; [von Scheckkarte] PIN (number); [von Tresor] combination.

**Geheimpolizei** *die* secret police.

**Geheimtipp** *der* tip (for the future).

**Geheimzahl** *die* PIN (number).

**geheißen** *pp* ▷ heißen.

**gehemmt** *adj* self-conscious ◇ *adv* self-consciously.

**gehen** (*prät* **ging**; *perf* **ist gegangen**) *vi* - **1.** [Fortbewegung] to go; **einkaufen ~** to go shopping; **wo er geht und steht hinterlässt er Unordnung** he makes a mess wherever he goes; **in die Stadt ~** to go into town; **zur Armee ~** to join the army; **in Serienproduktion ~** to go into mass production - **2.** [weggehen, abfahren] to go; **ich gehe jetzt** I'm off now; **mein Zug geht um acht Uhr** my train leaves *ODER* goes at eight o'clock - **3.** [zu Fuß gehen] to walk; **mit jm ~** *fam* [eine Beziehung haben] to go out with sb - **4.** [verkehren] to go; **der Bus geht drei Mal täglich** the bus goes *ODER* runs three times a day - **5.** [funktionieren - gen] to work; [ - Uhr, Auto] to go; **das Geschäft geht gut** business is going well - **6.** [zur Beschreibung von Vorgängen]: **wie geht das mit der Anmeldung?** how's the application going?; **das geht doch ganz einfach** it's quite simple; **es geht das Gerücht, dass ...** it is rumoured that ...; **was geht denn hier vor sich?** what's going on here, then?; **die Klingel geht!** the bell's ringing - **7.** [möglich, erlaubt sein] to be OK; **aber das geht doch nicht!** you can't do that!; **so geht das nicht, lass mich mal!** you don't do it like that, let me show you!; **ginge es vielleicht, dass wir ...?** do you think we could possibly ...? - **8.** [sich erstrecken]: **das Wasser ging ihm bis zu den Knien** the water came up to his knees; **die Straße geht bis zum Rathaus** the street goes as far as the townhall; **das Fenster geht nach Süden** the window faces *ODER* looks south; **das geht über unsere Mittel** that's beyond our means; **zu weit ~ (mit etw)** to go too far (with sthg); **es geht nichts über eine Tasse Kaffee am Morgen** there's nothing quite like a cup of coffee in the morning - **9.** [passen]: **in/durch etw ~** to go in/through sthg - **10.** [sich richten]: **es kann nicht immer nur nach dir ~** you can't always have things your own way; **wenn es nach mir ginge, ... ** if I had my way, ... - **11.** [ein Arbeitsverhältnis beenden] to leave - **12.** [Teig] to rise - **13.** [Ware] to sell ◇ *v impers* - **1.** [ergehen]: **wie geht es dir/Ihnen?** how are you?; **es geht mir gut/schlecht** I'm well/not very well; **der Firma geht es gut/schlecht** the company is doing well/badly - **2.** [sich handeln um]: **es geht um deine Mutter** it's about your mother; **worum geht es in diesem Buch?** what's this book about?; **es geht darum, alle Karten loszuwerden** the idea is to get rid of all your cards; **es geht hier nicht um Schuldzuweisungen, aber ...** we're not looking to apportion blame, but ... - **3.** [annehmbar sein]: **wie gefällt es dir? - es geht** how do you like it? - it's OK ◇ *vt* to walk.

➡ **sich gehen** *ref:* **sich ~ lassen** to let o.s. go.

**geheuer** *adj:* **das ist mir nicht (ganz) ~** [Furcht einflößend] I find that (rather) eerie; [unwohl] I'm not (too) sure about that; [verdächtig] I find that (rather) odd *ODER* suspicious.

**Geheul**, **Geheule** *das* - **1.** [Heulen] howling - **2.** *fam abw* [Heulerei] wailing.

**Gehilfe** *(pl -n) der* - **1.** [Ausgebildeter] qualified assistant *(who has successfully completed an apprenticeship)* - **2.** [Helfer] assistant.

**Gehilfin** *(pl -nen) die* - **1.** [Ausgebildete] qualified assistant *(who has successfully completed an apprenticeship)* - **2.** [Helferin] assistant.

**Gehirn** *(pl -e) das* - **1.** [Hirn] brain - **2.** *(ohne pl) fam* [Verstand] brain, brains *(pl);* **sich das ~ zermartern** to rack one's brain *ODER* brains.

**Gehirn|erschütterung** *die* concussion *(U)*.

**Gehirn|schlag** *der* stroke.

**Gehirn|wäsche** *die* brainwashing; **jm einer ~ unterziehen** to brainwash sb.

**gehoben** *pp* ➞ **heben** ⬦ *adj* - **1.** [höher - Position, Stellung] senior; [ - Einkommen, Erwartung] higher - **2.** [exklusiv] sophisticated - **3.:** **in ~er Stimmung** in high spirits.

**Gehöft** *(pl -e) das* farm(stead).

**geholfen** *pp* ➞ **helfen**.

**Gehölz** *(pl -e) das* [Wäldchen] copse.

**Gehör** *(pl -e) das* hearing; **ein schlechtes ~ haben** to be hard of hearing; **nach dem ~** by ear; **er fand bei seinem Vorgesetzten ~** his superiors listened to him; **jm/einer Sache ~/kein ~ schenken** to listen/not to listen to sb/sthg; **sich *(D)* ~ verschaffen** to make o.s. heard.

**gehorchen** *vi* to obey; **jm ~** to obey sb; **der Vernunft ~** to listen to reason.

**gehören** *vi* - **1.** [einer Person] **jm ~** to belong to sb - **2.** [an Ort] to belong; **wohin gehört das Werkzeug?** where does this tool belong? - **3.** [als Bestandteil] **zu etw ~** to be part of sthg; **sie gehört zum Krankenhauspersonal** she's a member of the hospital staff - **4.** [als Notwendigkeit] **zum Reiten gehört viel Geschick** riding requires a lot of skill; **es gehört Mut dazu, dies zu tun** it takes a lot of courage to do it - **5.** [müssen] **solche Leute ~ eingesperrt** such people ought to be locked up.

➡ **sich gehören** *ref:* **es *ODER* das gehört sich nicht** it's not the done thing.

**Gehör|gang** *der* MED auditory canal.

**gehörig** *adj* - **1.** [gebührend] proper - **2.** [beachtlich] considerable; **mit einer ~en Portion Mut** with a good deal of courage ⬦ *adv* - **1.** [gebührend] properly - **2.** [beachtlich - steigen, erhöhen] considerably; **jn ~ durchprügeln** to give sb a good thrashing.

**Gehörlose** *(pl -n) der, die* deaf person; **die ~n** the deaf.

**gehorsam** *adj* obedient.

**Gehorsam** *der* obedience; **jm den ~ verweigern** to refuse to obey sb.

**Gehorsamkeit** *die* obedience.

**Gehsteig** *(pl -e) der* pavement *Br*, sidewalk *Am*.

**Geh|weg** *der* - **1.** [Gehsteig] pavement *Br*, sidewalk *Am* - **2.** [Weg] footpath.

**Geier** *(pl -) der* vulture; **weiß der ~!** *fam* God knows!

**Geige** *(pl -n) die* [im Orchester] violin; [in Folk] fiddle; **die erste ~ spielen** *fig* to call the tune *ODER* shots; **die zweite ~ spielen** *fig* to play second fiddle.

**geigen** *vi fam* [im Orchester] to play the violin; [in Folk] to play the fiddle ⬦ *vt fam* [im Orchester] to play on the violin; [in Folk] to play on the fiddle.

**Geiger|zähler** *der* Geiger counter.

**geil** *adj* - **1.** *fam* [begierig auf Sex] horny; **er war ~ auf sie** he wanted to get into her knickers - **2.** *abw* [lüstern - Mann] lecherous; [ - Blick, Gedanke] lewd - **3.** *fam* [toll] wicked.

**Geisel** *(pl -n) die* hostage.

**Geisel|drama** *das* hostage crisis.

**Geisel|nahme** *(pl -n) die* hostage-taking.

**Geisel|nehmer, in** *(mpl -; fpl -nen) der, die* hostage-taker.

**geißeln** *vt geh* - **1.** [heftig kritisieren] to denounce - **2.** [züchtigen] to castigate.

**Geist** *(pl -e ODER -er) der* - **1.** [Verstandeskraft] mind; **den ~ aufgeben** *fam* to give up the ghost; **jm auf den ~ gehen** *fam* to get on sb's nerves - **2.** [Intellekt] intellect - **3.** [Gesinnung] spirit - **4.** *(pl Geiste)* [Spirituose] *schnapps distilled from fruit, especially berries* - **5.** *(pl Geister)* [Person, Genie] mind - **6.** *(pl Geister)* [überirdische Wesenheit]: **der Heilige ~** the Holy Ghost - **7.** *(pl Geister)* [Gespenst] ghost.

➡ **im Geist(e)** *adv* in spirit.

**Geister|bahn** *die* ghost train.

**Geister|fahrer, in** *der, die person who drives into oncoming traffic on a motorway*.

**geisterhaft** *adj* ghostly.

**Geisterhand** *die:* **wie von *ODER* durch ~** as if by magic.

**Geisterstunde** *die* witching hour.

**geistesabwesend** *adj* absent-minded ⬦ *adv* absent-mindedly.

**Geistes|blitz** *der* flash of inspiration.

**Geistesgegenwart** *die* presence of mind.

**geistesgegenwärtig** *adj* quick-witted ⬦ *adv* with great presence of mind.

**geistesgestört** adj mentally disturbed ODER unbalanced.

**Geistes|haltung** die attitude.

**geisteskrank** adj mentally ill.

**Geistes|kranke** der, die mentally ill person; [im Krankenhaus] mental patient.

**geistesverwandt** adj like-minded.

**Geistes|wissenschaft** die arts subject; die ~en the arts.

**geisteswissenschaftlich** adj arts (vor Subst).

**Geisteszustand** der mental state.

**geistig** adj - 1. [intellektuell - Mensch, Freiheit, Vermächtnis] intellectual; [ - Anstrengung, Kraft, Fähigkeit] mental - 2. [alkoholisch] alcoholic ◇ adv [intellektuell - frei, überlegen] intellectually; [ - fit, frisch, behindert] mentally; **sich ~ anstrengen** to make a mental effort.

**geistlich** adj [gen] religious; [Beistand] spiritual ◇ adv: **jm ~ beistehen** to lend sb spiritual guidance.

**Geistliche** (pl -n) der clergyman.

**geistlos** adj inane ◇ adv inanely.

**geistreich** adj intelligent ◇ adv intelligently.

**Geiz** der meanness.

**geizen** vi: **mit etw ~** [Geld] to be mean with sthg; [Lob] to be sparing with sthg.

**Geiz|hals** der fam abw skinflint.

**geizig** adj mean ◇ adv meanly.

**Geiz|kragen** der fam abw skinflint.

**Gejammer** das fam abw moaning.

**gekannt** pp ▷ kennen.

**Gekicher** das giggling.

**geklungen** pp ▷ klingen.

**gekniffen** pp ▷ kneifen.

**Geknister** das [von Papier] rustling; [von Feuer] crackling.

**gekommen** pp ▷ kommen.

**gekonnt** pp ▷ können ◇ adj masterful ◇ adv masterfully.

**Gekreisch**, **Gekreische** das [von Kindern] squealing; [von Möwen] screeching.

**Gekritzel** das abw scrawl.

**gekrochen** pp ▷ kriechen.

**gekünstelt** abw adj artificial ◇ adv artificially.

**Gel** (pl -e) das gel.

**Gelächter** (pl -) das laughter.

**gelackmeiert** adj fam conned.

**geladen** pp ▷ laden ◇ adj loaded; **~ sein** fam fig to be fuming.

**Gelage** (pl -) das banquet.

**gelähmt** adj paralysed.

**Gelähmte** (pl -n) der, die paralysed man (f woman).

**Gelände** (pl -) das - 1. [Land] country; **ein bergiges ~** mountainous terrain; **auf freiem ~** in the open country - 2. [Gebiet] area - 3. [Grundstück - zum Bau] site; [ - um Haus] grounds (pl).

**Gelände|fahrzeug** das all-terrain vehicle.

**geländegängig** adj all-terrain.

**Gelände|lauf** der - 1. SPORT cross-country (running) - 2. [Wettkampf] cross-country run.

**Geländer** (pl -) das [von Treppe] banister; [von Brücke] parapet; [von Balkon] railing.

**gelang** prät ▷ gelingen.

**gelangen** (perf ist gelangt) vi: **an etw (A) ~** to arrive at sthg; **an die Öffentlichkeit ~** to become public; **in js Besitz ~** to come into sb's possession; **zu etw ~** [Ruhm, Ansehen] to gain sthg; [Verständigung] to come to sthg; **zu Geld ~** [durch Erbe] to come into money; [durch Arbeit] to make money.

**gelassen** pp ▷ lassen ◇ adj calm ◇ adv calmly.

**Gelassenheit** die composure.

**Gelatine** die gelatine.

**gelaufen** pp ▷ laufen.

**geläufig** adj [vertraut] common; **es ist mir ~** it is familiar to me.

**gelaunt** adj: **wie ist der Chef heute ~?** what sort of mood is the boss in today?; **gut/schlecht/übel ~ sein** to be in a good/bad/terrible mood.

**gelb** adj & adv yellow.

**Gelb** das yellow.
➥ **bei Gelb** adv on amber Br, on yellow Am.

**Gelbe** das yellow; **es ist (auch nicht) das ~ vom Ei** fam it's (far from) perfect.

**Gelbe Sack** der yellow refuse bag used for recyclable packaging.

**gelblich** adj [Tapete, Papier] yellowish; [Haut] sallow.

**Gelbsucht** die jaundice.

**Geld** (pl -er) das money; **großes ~** notes (pl); **kleines ~** change, coins (pl); **ins ~ gehen** to be expensive; **etw zu ~ machen** fam [Haus, Auto] to sell sthg off; [Information, Aktien] to cash (sthg) in; **das große ~ machen** fam to make a pile; **es ist sein ~ wert** it is worth every penny; **sein ~ zum Fenster hinauswerfen** fig to throw one's money away.
➥ **Gelder** pl funds.

**Geldan|lage** die (financial) investment.

**Geld|automat** der cash machine ODER dispenser, ATM.

**Geld|beutel** der, **-börse** die [Brieftasche] wallet; [für Münzen] purse.

**Geld|buße** *die* fine.

**Geld|geber, in** *der, die* financial backer.

**geldgierig** *adj* greedy *(for money)*.

**Geld|hahn** *der:* jm den ~ abdrehen *ODER* zudrehen *fig* to cut off sb's money supply.

**Geld|karte** *die* Switch card® *Br, smart card which charges payments straight to one's bank account.*

**Geld|mittel** *pl* funds.

**Geld|quelle** *die* source of income.

**Geld|schein** *der* banknote *Br,* bill *Am.*

**Geld|schrank** *der* safe.

**Geldspiel|automat** *der* slot *ODER* fruit *Br* machine.

**Geld|strafe** *die* fine.

**Geld|stück** *das* coin.

**Geld|wert** *der* cash value.

**geleckt** *adj:* wie ~ aussehen *fam* [Person] to look one's best; [Auto] to be as shiny as a new pin.

**Gelee** [ʒɔˈleː] *(pl -s) das ODER der* jelly.

**Gelege** *(pl -) das* [von Vögeln] clutch (of eggs); [von Fröschen] spawn *(U).*

**gelegen** *pp* ⊳ liegen ⬦ *adj* - **1.** [befindlich] situated - **2.** [bedeutsam]: mir ist an deinem Besuch viel ~ *geh* your visit means a great deal to me - **3.** [passend] convenient; diese Einladung kommt mir sehr ~ this invitation comes at just the right time for me.

**Gelegenheit** *(pl -en) die* - **1.** [geeignete Möglichkeit] opportunity - **2.** [Anlass] occasion - **3.** [Angebot] bargain.
⬥ bei Gelegenheit *adv* when the opportunity arises.

**Gelegenheits|arbeit** *die* casual work *(U).*

**Gelegenheits|arbeiter, in** *der, die* casual worker.

**gelegentlich** *adj* occasional ⬦ *adv* - **1.** [manchmal] occasionally - **2.** [bei Gelegenheit] some time.

**gelehrig** *adj* quick (to learn).

**gelehrt** *adj* learned ⬦ *adv* learnedly.

**Gelehrte** *(pl -n) der, die* scholar.

**Geleit** *das geh:* freies ~ safe conduct; jm das letzte ~ geben to attend sb's funeral.

**geleiten** *vt geh* to escort.

**Geleit|schutz** *der* escort.

**Gelenk** *(pl -e) das* [beim Menschen] joint.

**Gelenk|bus** *der* articulated bus.

**gelenkig** *adj* supple ⬦ *adv* in a supple manner.

**gelernt** *adj* trained.

**gelesen** *pp* ⊳ lesen.

**Geliebte** *(pl -n) der, die* lover.

**geliefert** *adj:* ~ sein *fam* to have had it.

**geliehen** *pp* ⊳ leihen.

**gelinde** ⬥ gelinde gesagt *adv* to put it mildly.

**gelingen** *(prät* gelang*, perf* ist gelungen*) vi:* die Zeichnung ist mir gut gelungen my drawing turned out well; es gelang mir, den Brief zu schreiben I managed to write the letter; es gelang ihm, das Buch zu finden he succeeded in finding the book.

**Gelingen** *das* success.

**gelitten** *pp* ⊳ leiden.

**gellen** *vi* to ring out.

**gellend** *adj* [Geschrei] piercing; [Gelächter] shrill ⬦ *adv:* ~ schreien to give a piercing scream.

**geloben** *vt geh:* jm Treue ~ to pledge one's loyalty to sb; sie gelobte (sich), es zu tun she vowed to do it; sie haben sich Treue gelobt they have vowed to be faithful to one another.

**Gelöbnis** *(pl -se) das geh* vow.

**gelockt** *adj:* ~es Haar curly hair.

**gelogen** *pp* ⊳ lügen.

**gelöst** *adj* relaxed.

**gelten** *(präs* gilt*; prät* galt*; perf* hat gegolten*) vi* - **1.** [gültig sein] to be valid; für jn/etw ~ to apply to sb/sthg - **2.** *SPORT* to count - **3.** [anerkannt sein]: als etw ~ to be considered to be sthg - **4.** [korrekt sein]: das gilt nicht! *fam* [gen] that doesn't count!; [schummeln] that's cheating! - **5.** [akzeptieren]: etw ~ lassen to accept sthg - **6.** [wert sein] to count; Kreativität gilt hier nichts creativity counts for nothing here - **7.** [adressiert sein an]: seine Bemerkung galt nicht allein dir his remark was not only directed at you, his remark didn't only apply to you - **8.** [müssen]: in dieser Lage gilt es, einen kühlen Kopf zu bewahren in this situation you need to *ODER* it is necessary to keep a cool head.

**geltend** *adj* current; etw ~ machen [Forderung] to make sthg; [Einwand] to raise/put forward sthg.

**Geltung** *die* - **1.** [Gültigkeit] validity; dieses Gesetz hat keine ~ mehr this law is no longer valid - **2.** [Wirkung] prominence; zur ~ kommen to be shown to its best advantage; an ~ verlieren to be discredited.

**Geltungsbedürfnis** *das* need for recognition.

**gelungen** *pp* ⊳ gelingen ⬦ *adj* successful.

**gem.** *abk für* gemäß.

**gemächlich** *adj* leisurely ⬦ *adv:* ~ im Wald spazieren gehen to go for a leisurely walk in the woods.

**Gemahl, in** *(mpl -e; fpl -nen) der, die geh* husband (f wife).

G

**Gemälde** (pl -) das painting.

**Gemäldeausstellung** die exhibition (of paintings).

**Gemäldegalerie** die art ODER picture gallery.

**gemasert** adj grained.

**gemäß** präp: ~ einer Sache (D), einer Sache (D) ~ in accordance with sthg ◇ adj: jm/einer Sache ~ sein to be in keeping with sb/sthg.

**gemäßigt** adj [Politiker] moderate; [Klima] temperate.

**Gemecker, Gemeckere** das - **1.** [von Ziegen] bleating - **2.** fam abw [Nörgelei] moaning.

**gemein** adj - **1.** [niederträchtig - Person, Verhalten] mean; [- Trick, Lüge] nasty; [- Witz] dirty - **2.** fam [unfair]: **das ist ~!** that's not fair! - **3.** [gewöhnlich, allgemein] common ◇ adv - **1.** [gemeinsam]: **etw mit jm/etw ~ haben** to have sthg in common with sb/sthg - **2.** [niederträchtig] meanly - **3.** fam [sehr]: **die Verletzung hat ~ wehgetan** the injury hurt like hell; **es war ~ kalt** it was dead cold.

**Gemeinde** (pl -n) die - **1.** [Verwaltungseinheit] municipality; **sie arbeitet bei der ~** she works for the local authority - **2.** [Einwohnerschaft, Glaubensgemeinschaft] community - **3.** [Seelsorgebezirk] parish; [Gottesdienstteilnehmer] congregation.

**Gemeindeamt** das local authority.

**Gemeinderat** der local council.

**Gemeindeschwester** die district nurse.

**Gemeindewahl** die local government elections (pl).

**Gemeindezentrum** das community centre.

**gemeingefährlich** adj dangerous ◇ adv dangerously.

**Gemeingut** das geh common property.

**Gemeinheit** (pl -en) die - **1.** [verwerfliche Art] meanness - **2.** [Handlung] mean trick - **3.** fam [Ärgernis]: **so eine ~!** it's not fair!

**gemeinhin** adv generally.

**Gemeinnutz** der public good.

**gemeinnützig** adj for the benefit of the community; [Verein] charitable, non-profit-making ◇ adv for the benefit of the community.

**gemeinsam** adv - **1.** [zusammen] together; **~ verantwortlich** jointly responsible - **2.** [gleich]: **etw ~ haben** to have sthg in common ◇ adj [Weg, Interessen] common; [Verantwortung] joint; **ein ~er Urlaub/Spaziergang** a holiday/walk together.

**Gemeinsame Markt** der Common Market.

**Gemeinsamkeit** (pl -en) die - **1.** [gleiche Eigen-

schaft] common feature; **sie haben viele ~en** they have a lot in common - **2.** (ohne pl) [Zusammengehörigkeit]: **Gefühl der ~** sense of community.

**Gemeinschaft** (pl -en) die - **1.** [Gruppe] community - **2.** [Verbundenheit] company; **in unserer Klasse haben wir eine gute ~** in our class we have a good sense of community; **in ~ mit jm** together with sb; **in js ~** in sb's company.

**gemeinschaftlich** adj joint; [Interessen] common ◇ adv jointly.

**Gemeinschaftsantenne** die community aerial Br ODER antenna Am, aerial shared by all the inhabitants of a block of flats.

**Gemeinschaftsarbeit** die joint effort; **in ~** as a joint effort.

**Gemeinschaftsgeist** der team spirit.

**Gemeinschaftskunde** die (ohne pl) SCHULE social studies (pl).

**Gemeinschaftspraxis** die joint practice.

**Gemeinschaftsraum** der common room.

**gemeint** adj meant; **das war nicht so ~!** I didn't mean it like that!; **mein Rat war gut ~** my advice was well-intentioned.

**gemeinverständlich** adj generally comprehensible ◇ adv in generally comprehensible terms.

**Gemeinwohl** das common good.

**gemessen** pp ⊳ messen ◇ adj measured ◇ adv [schreiten] with a measured tread; [sprechen] in measured tones.

**Gemetzel** (pl -) das bloodbath.

**gemieden** pp ⊳ meiden.

**Gemisch** (pl -e) das mixture.

**gemischt** adj mixed.

**gemocht** pp ⊳ mögen.

**gemolken** pp ⊳ melken.

**Gemse** = Gämse.

**Gemurmel** das murmuring.

**Gemüse** (pl -) das vegetables (pl).

**Gemüseeintopf** der vegetable stew.

**Gemüsegarten** der vegetable garden.

**Gemüsehändler, in** der, die greengrocer.

**Gemüsesuppe** die vegetable soup.

**gemusst** pp ⊳ müssen.

**gemustert** adj patterned.

**Gemüt** (pl -er) das - **1.** [Wesen] disposition - **2.** (ohne pl) [Empfindungsvermögen] heart; **dieses Buch ist etwas fürs ~** this is a moving book; **der Film ist ihr aufs ~ geschlagen** the film really got her down; **sich** (D) **etw zu ~e führen** [Ratschläge] to take sthg on board; [Essen, Getränke, Roman] to indulge in sthg; [Text] to study sthg.

**Gemüter** *pl* feelings; **der Skandal hat die ~er erregt** the scandal has caused feelings to run high.

**gemütlich** *adj* - **1.** [behaglich] cosy; **es sich** *(D)* **~ machen** to make o.s. at home - **2.** [Beisammensein] informal; [Abend] pleasant; [Fahrt] leisurely - **3.** [Person] friendly ◇ *adv* - **1.** [behaglich] cosily - **2.** [zusammensitzen, sich unterhalten] pleasantly; [arbeiten] at a leisurely pace.

**Gemütlichkeit** *die* - **1.** [Behaglichkeit] cosiness - **2.** [Zwanglosigkeit, Ruhe] pleasant atmosphere; **in aller ~** at one's leisure.

**Gemüts|mensch** *der* good-natured person.

**Gemüts|ruhe** *die* composure.

**Gemützu|stand** *der* frame of mind.

**Gen** *(pl -e) das* gene.

**genannt** *pp* ▷ **nennen.**

**genau** *adj* - **1.** [exakt] exact; [Waage, Voraussage, Arbeit] accurate; **haben Sie die ~e Uhrzeit?** have you got the right time? - **2.** [gründlich] thorough; **er nimmt es mit der Pünktlichkeit nicht so ~** he doesn't take punctuality very seriously ◇ *adv* - **1.** [exakt] precisely, exactly; **genau!** precisely!, exactly!; **~ um zehn Uhr** at exactly ten o'clock; **auf die Minute/ Sekunde ~ drei Stunden** three hours to the very minute/second; **die Uhr geht ~** the clock keeps perfect time; **~ als ich hereinkam, klingelte das Telefon** the phone rang just as I came in - **2.** [zuhören, hinsehen] carefully; **ich kenne ihn ~** I know exactly what he's like.

**genau genommen** *adv* strictly speaking.

**Genauigkeit** *die* - **1.** [Exaktheit] exactness; [von Waage, Voraussage, Arbeit] accuracy - **2.** [Gründlichkeit] thoroughness.

**genauso** *adv* just as; **er sieht ~ aus** he looks just the same.

**Gen|bank** *die* gene bank.

**Gen|datei** *die* DNA database.

**genehmigen** *vt* [Antrag, Plan] to approve; [Demonstration, Aufenthalt] to authorize; **sich** *(D)* **etw ~ fam** to treat o.s. to *ODER* allow o.s. sthg; **sich** *(D)* **einen ~ fam** to have a quick one.

**Genehmigung** *(pl -en) die* - **1.** [von Antrag, Plan] approval; [von Demonstration, Aufenthalt] authorization - **2.** [Dokument] permit.

**genehmigungspflichtig** *adj* **amt** subject to official approval.

**geneigt** *adj* - **1.** [bereit]: **zu etw ~ sein** to be inclined to sthg - **2.** **geh** [freundlich gesinnt]: **jm ~ sein** to be well-disposed towards sb.

**General** *(pl -rale ODER -räle) der* general.

**General|direktor, in** *der, die* chairman (*f* chairwoman) *Br*, president *Am*.

**General|intendant, in** *der, die* artistic director.

**General|probe** *die* **eigtl** & **fig** dress rehearsal.

**General|stab** *der* general staff.

**General|streik** *der* general strike.

**generalüberholen** *vt* to give a complete overhaul.

**Generalver|sammlung** *die* annual general meeting.

**Generation** *(pl -en) die* generation.

**Generations|konflikt** *der* conflict between the generations.

**Generations|wechsel** *der:* **in dieser Partei hat ein ~ stattgefunden** a new generation has come to power in this party.

**Generator** *(pl -toren) der* generator.

**generell** *adj* general ◇ *adv* generally.

**genesen** *(prät genas; perf ist genesen) vi* **geh** to recover.

**Genesung** *die* **geh** convalescence.

**Genetik** *die* genetics *(U)*.

**genetisch** *adj* genetic ◇ *adv* genetically.

**Genf** *nt* Geneva.

**Genfer** *(pl -) der* & *adj (unver)* Genevan.

**Genferin** *(pl -nen) die* Genevan.

**Genfer See** *der* Lake Geneva.

**genial** *adj* brilliant ◇ *adv* brilliantly.

**Genick** *(pl -e) das* (back of the) neck; **sich** *(D)* **das ~ brechen** to break one's neck; **jm/einer Sache das ~ brechen fig** to ruin sb/sthg.

**Genickstarre** *die:* **~ haben** to have a stiff neck.

**Genie** [ʒeˈniː] *(pl -s) das* genius.

**genieren** [ʒeˈniːrən] *vt* to bother.
▸ **sich genieren** *ref* to be embarrassed; **sich vor jm ~** to be shy of sb, to get embarrassed in sb's presence.

**genießbar** *adj* [essbar] edible; [trinkbar] drinkable; **dieser Wein ist nicht mehr ~** this wine has gone off.

**genießen** *(prät genoss; perf hat genossen) vt* - **1.** [gen] to enjoy - **2.** [essen] to eat; [trinken] to drink.

**Genießer, in** *(mpl -; fpl -nen) der, die* pleasure lover, bon vivant; [beim Essen] gourmet.

**genießerisch** *adj* [Mensch] appreciative; [Leben] pleasurable ◇ *adv* with relish.

**Genital|bereich** *der* genital area.

**Genitalien** *pl* genitals.

**Genitiv** *(pl -e) der* **GRAM** genitive.

**genommen** *pp* ▷ **nehmen.**

**genormt** *adj* standardized.

**genoss** *prät* ▷ genießen.

**Genosse** (*pl* -n) *der* comrade.

**genossen** *pp* ▷ genießen.

**Genossenschaft** (*pl* -en) *die* cooperative.

**Genossin** (*pl* -nen) *die* comrade.

**Genre** [ˈʒãːrə] (*pl* -s) *das geh* genre.

**Gentechnik** *die* genetic engineering.

**gentechnisch** *adj:* ~e Änderungen genetic modifications ◇ *adv:* ~ veränderte Lebensmittel genetically modified foods, GM foods.

**Gentechnologie** *die* genetic engineering.

**Gentleman** [ˈdʒɛntlmɛn] (*pl* -men) *der* gentleman.

**Genua** *nt* Genoa.

**genug** *adv* enough; ~ (von etw) haben to have had enough (of sthg).

**Genüge** *die:* einer Sache (D) ~ tun *geh* to satisfy sthg; zur ~ *abw* only too well.

**genügen** *vi* - 1. [ausreichen] to be enough; ein Glas Wein genügt mir a glass of wine is enough for me; das genügt! that's enough! - 2. [entsprechen]: einer Sache (D) ~ [Anforderungen] to meet sthg; [Vorschriften] to comply with sthg.

**genügend** *adj* & *adv* enough.

**genügsam** *adj* [Mensch] modest ◇ *adv* modestly.

**Genugtuung** *die* satisfaction; ~ für etw satisfaction for sthg; mit ~ with satisfaction.

**Genus** (*pl* Genera) *das* GRAM gender.

**Genuss** (*pl* Genüsse) *der* - 1. [Konsum] consumption; in den ~ von etw kommen *fig* to receive sthg - 2. [Befriedigung] pleasure; das Konzert war ein ~ the concert was a delight.

**genüsslich** *adj* enjoyable ◇ *adv* with relish.

**Genussmittel** *das* food, drink or tobacco consumed only for pleasure or as a stimulant.

**Geograf, Geograph** (*pl* -en) *der* geographer.

**Geografie, Geographie** *die* geography.

**Geografin, Geographin** (*pl*-nen) *die* geographer.

**geografisch, geographisch** *adj* geographical ◇ *adv* geographically.

**Geologe** (*pl* -n) *der* geologist.

**Geologie** *die* geology.

**Geologin** (*pl* -nen) *die* geologist.

**geologisch** *adj* geological ◇ *adv* geologically.

**Geometrie** *die* geometry.

**geometrisch** *adj* geometric ◇ *adv* geometrically.

**Geophysik** *die* geophysics (U).

**geordnet** *adj* orderly.

**Georgien** *nt* Georgia.

**Gepäck** *das* luggage.

**Gepäckabfertigung** *die* - 1. [Handlung] luggage check-in - 2. [Schalter - am Flughafen] (baggage) check-in; [ - am Bahnhof] luggage office.

**Gepäckablage** *die* luggage rack.

**Gepäckannahme** *die* - 1. [Handlung] luggage check-in - 2. [Schalter - am Flughafen] (baggage) check-in; [ - am Bahnhof, zur Aufbewahrung] left-luggage office *Br*, baggage room *Am*; [ - am Bahnhof, zur Beförderung] luggage office.

**Gepäckaufbewahrung** *die* - 1. [Handlung] luggage storage - 2. [Schalter] left-luggage office *Br*, baggage room *Am*.

**Gepäckausgabe** *die* [am Flughafen] baggage reclaim; [am Bahnhof - zur Aufbewahrung] left-luggage office *Br*, baggage room *Am*; [ - zur Beförderung] luggage office.

**Gepäckkontrolle** *die* baggage check.

**Gepäckschalter** *der* [am Flughafen] (baggage) check-in; [am Bahnhof, zur Aufbewahrung] left-luggage office *Br*, baggage room *Am*; [am Bahnhof, zur Beförderung] luggage office.

**Gepäckschein** *der* luggage ticket.

**Gepäckstück** *das* item of luggage.

**Gepäckträger** *der* - 1. [von Fahrrad] carrier; [von Auto] luggage rack - 2. [Person] porter.

**Gepäckwagen** *der* luggage van *Br*, baggage car *Am*.

**Gepard** (*pl* -e) *der* cheetah.

**gepfeffert** *adj fam* [Preis, Rechnung] steep.

**gepfiffen** *pp* ▷ pfeifen.

**gepflegt** *adj* - 1. [Äußeres] well-groomed; [Hände] well-cared-for; [Haare, Kleidung] neat; [Garten, Haus] well-kept - 2. [von Qualität] quality (vor Subst) - 3. [Stil, Ausdruck] refined ◇ *adv* - 1. [essen] well - 2. [gewählt]: sie drückt sich sehr ~ aus she has a very refined way of speaking.

**Gepflogenheit** (*pl* -en) *die geh* habit.

**Geplauder** *das* chatting.

**Gepolter** *das* banging; mit ~ kamen sie die Straße entlang they made a din as they came down the street.

**gepr.** (*abk für geprüft*) tested.

**gepriesen** *pp* ▷ preisen.

**gepunktet** *adj* - 1. [Stoff] spotted - 2. [Linie] dotted.

**Gequassel** *das fam abw* jabbering.

**gequollen** *pp* ▷ quellen.

**gerade** *adv* - 1. [vor kurzem] just; ich bin ~ gekommen I've just arrived; ~ erst only just - 2. [jetzt] at the moment; ich bin ~ beim Saubermachen I'm just tidying up at the moment - **3.** [in jenem Moment] just; **er wollte ~ gehen** he was just about to go - **4.** [nicht schief oder gekrümmt] straight; **das Bild hängt nicht ~** the picture is not hanging straight - **5.** [besonders] exactly; **~ deshalb** precisely for that reason; **er war nicht ~ erfreut** he wasn't exactly pleased; **das war nicht ~ berauschend** it wasn't exactly exciting - **6.** [ausgerechnet]: **warum ~ ich?** why me of all people?; **dass das ~ jetzt passieren musste!** why did it have to happen now of all times? - **7.** [emphatisierend]: **das hat mir ~ noch gefehlt!** that's all I needed! - **8.** [knapp]: **~ noch** only just ⬦ adj - **1.** [nicht gekrümmt] straight - **2.** [Haltung] upright.

**Gerade** (pl -n) die - **1.** MATH straight line - **2.** SPORT straight.

**geradeaus** adv straight ahead.

**geradeǀbiegen** vt (unreg) fam [bereinigen] to straighten out.

**gerade biegen** vt (unreg) [richten] to straighten out.

**gerade halten** vt (unreg) to hold straight; **den Kopf ~** to hold one's head up.

➥ **sich gerade halten** ref to stand/sit up straight.

**geradeheraus** adj: **~ sein** to be frank ⬦ adv frankly.

**geradeǀstehen** vi (unreg) [einstehen]: **für jn/etw ~** to take responsibility for sb/sthg.

**gerade stehen** vi (unreg) [aufrecht stehen] to stand up straight.

**geradewegs** adv - **1.** [ohne Umweg] directly - **2.** [unmittelbar] immediately.

**geradezu** adv downright; **es wäre ~ ein Wunder, wenn ...** it would be downright incredible if ...

**geradlinig** adj straight ⬦ adv in a straight line.

**gerammelt** ➥ **gerammelt voll** adj: **~ voll sein** fam to be packed.

**Gerangel** das - **1.** [Rauferei] scrapping - **2.** abw [Kampf] scramble.

**Geranie** (pl -n) die geranium.

**gerannt** pp ▷ rennen.

**gerät** präs ▷ geraten.

**Gerät** (pl -e) das - **1.** [Apparat] device; [Werkzeug] tool; [in der Küche] utensil; **elektrisches ~** (electrical) appliance; **schalt das ~ ab!** switch off the set! - **2.** [Ausrüstung] equipment.

**geraten** (präs gerät; prät geriet; perf ist geraten) vi - **1.** [gelangen]: **an eine unfreundliche Verkäuferin ~** to get an unfriendly shop assistant; **in etw (A) ~** [Schwierigkeiten, Not] to get into sthg; [Verdacht] to come under sthg; [Sturm] to be caught in sthg; **in Vergessenheit ~** to be forgotten - **2.** [gelingen] to turn out; **das**

**Bild ist mir gut ~** my picture turned out well - **3.** [ähneln]: **nach jm ~** to take after sb ⬦ adj [sinnvoll] advisable ⬦ pp ▷ **raten.**

**Geräteturnen** das: **im ~** on the apparatus.

**Geratewohl** das: **sie bewarb sich aufs ~** she applied on the off-chance; **er nahm aufs ~ ein Buch aus dem Regal** he randomly selected a book from the shelf.

**geraum** adj geh: **eine ~e Weile/Zeit** a considerable while/time.

**geräumig** adj roomy.

**Geräusch** (pl -e) das noise.

**geräuschempfindlich** adj sensitive to noise.

**Geräuschǀkulisse** die background noise.

**geräuschlos** adj silent ⬦ adv silently.

**geräuschvoll** adv noisily.

**gerben** vt to tan.

**gerecht** adj fair; [Belohnung] just; **jm/einer Sache ~ werden** to do sb/sthg justice; **er konnte den Ansprüchen des Chefs nicht ~ werden** he couldn't match up to the boss's expectations ⬦ adv fairly.

**Gerechtigkeit** die justice; **ausgleichende ~** fair compensation.

**Gerede** das abw - **1.** [Geschwätz] chatter - **2.** [Klatsch]: **ins ~ kommen** to get o.s. talked about; **jn ins ~ bringen** to get sb talked about.

**geregelt** adj [Arbeit] steady; [Leben] orderly.

**gereizt** adj [Person] irritable; [Stimmung] strained ⬦ adv irritably.

**Gericht** (pl -e) das - **1.** [Speise] dish - **2.** [Institution] court; **vor ~ gehen** to go to court; **vor ~ stehen** to stand trial - **3.** [Richter]: **das ~** the bench - **4.** [Gebäude] court Br, courthouse Am - **5.** (ohne pl) [Richten] judgement; **über jn ~ halten** to sit in judgement on sb; **mit jm hart ins ~ gehen** [kritisieren] to take sb to task.

**gerichtlich** adj [Verfahren, Akte] legal; [Untersuchung] judicial ⬦ adv: **gegen jn ~ vorgehen** to start legal proceedings against sb.

**Gerichtsbeǀschluss** der (court's) verdict.

**Gerichtsǀhof** der Court of Justice.

**Gerichtsǀkosten** pl legal costs.

**Gerichtsǀmediziner, in** der, die forensic medical expert.

**Gerichtsǀsaal** der courtroom.

**Gerichtsǀurteil** das judgement (of the court).

**Gerichtsǀverfahren** das legal proceedings (pl).

**Gerichtsǀverhandlung** die hearing.

**Gerichtsvollzieher, in** (mpl -; fpl -nen) der, die bailiff.

**gerieben** pp ▷ **reiben.**

**geriet** *prät* ▷ geraten.

**gering** *adj* [Gewicht, Preis, Temperatur] low; [Menge] small; [Problem, Chance] slight; [Bedeutung, Rolle] minor; [Dauer] short.

➤ **nicht das Geringste** *adv* not at all.

➤ **nicht im Geringsten** *adv* not in the least.

**geringelt** *adj* (horizontally) striped.

**geringfügig** *adj* slight, minor ◇ *adv* slightly.

**gering schätzen** *vt* to have a low opinion of.

**geringschätzig** *adj* disdainful ◇ *adv* disdainfully.

**gerinnen** (*prät* gerann; *perf* ist geronnen) *vi* [Milch] to curdle; [Blut] to coagulate.

**Gerippe** (*pl -*) *das* skeleton.

**gerissen** *pp* ▷ reißen ◇ *adj* crafty ◇ *adv* craftily.

**geritten** *pp* ▷ reiten.

**Germane** (*pl -n*) *der* Germanic man.

**Germanin** (*pl -nen*) *die* Germanic woman.

**germanisch** *adj* Germanic.

**Germanist** (*pl -en*) *der* German scholar.

**Germanistik** *die* (*ohne pl*) German language and literature.

**Germanistin** (*pl -nen*) *die* German scholar.

**gern, gerne** (*kompar* lieber; *superl* am liebsten) *adv* - **1.** [gen] with pleasure; jn/etw ~ haben to like sb/sthg; er spielt ~ Tennis he likes to play tennis; he likes playing tennis; das kann ich ~ machen I'll gladly do it; aber ~!, ja ~! I'd love to!; ~ geschehen! don't mention it!; ich möchte ~ wissen ... I'd like to know ...; das will ich ~ glauben! I can easily believe it!; du kannst mich mal ~ haben! *salopp fig & abw* you can stuff it! - **2.** [oft]: der Computer stürzt ~ ab the computer tends to crash.

**gerochen** *pp* ▷ riechen.

**Geröll** *das* (*ohne pl*) [im Gebirge] scree; [im Bach] (loose) pebbles (*pl*).

**geronnen** *pp* ▷ rinnen.

**Gerste** *die* barley.

**Gerstenkorn** *das* - **1.** [Frucht] barleycorn - **2.** [Augenentzündung] sty.

**Gerte** (*pl -n*) *die* switch.

**Geruch** (*pl Gerüche*) *der* smell.

**geruchlos** *adj* odourless.

**Geruchssinn** [gə'ruxszɪn] *der* sense of smell.

**Gerücht** (*pl -e*) *das* rumour.

**gerufen** *pp* ▷ rufen.

**geruhen** *vi geh & iron:* ~, etw zu tun to deign to do sthg.

**geruhsam** *adj* leisurely ◇ *adv:* ~ durch den Garten gehen to go for a leisurely walk round the garden.

**Gerümpel** *das abw* junk.

**Gerundium** (*pl -dien*) *das* GRAM gerund.

**gerungen** *pp* ▷ ringen.

**Gerüst** (*pl -e*) *das* - **1.** [beim Bauen] scaffolding - **2.** [von Text] framework.

**gesalzen** *pp* ▷ salzen ◇ *adj fam* [Preis, Miete] steep; [Beschwerde] harsh.

**gesamt** *adj* whole, entire; [Einkommen, Kosten] total ◇ *adv* entirely.

**Gesamtausgabe** *die* complete edition.

**Gesamtbetrag** *der* total (amount).

**gesamtdeutsch** *adj relating to both eastern and western Germany.*

**Gesamteindruck** *der* overall impression.

**Gesamtheit** *die:* die ~ der Bevölkerung the entire population; die ~ der Probleme all the problems.

**Gesamthochschule** *die combined academic and teacher-training institution, similar to British colleges of further education, or the former "polytechnics", where the emphasis is on practical training.*

**Gesamtschule** *die* ≈ comprehensive school.

**Gesamtumsatz** *der* total turnover.

**gesandt** *pp* ▷ senden.

**Gesandte, tin** (*mpl -n; fpl -nen*) *der, die* envoy.

**Gesandtschaft** (*pl -en*) *die* legation.

**Gesang** (*pl Gesänge*) *der* - **1.** [Singen] singing - **2.** [Lied, von Vogel] song.

**Gesangbuch** *das* hymn book.

**Gesangverein** *der* choral society.

**Gesäß** (*pl -e*) *das geh* buttocks (*pl*).

**gesättigt** *adj* CHEM saturated.

**gesch.** *abk für* geschieden.

**Geschädigte** (*pl -n*) *der, die* injured party.

**geschaffen** *pp* ▷ schaffen.

**Geschäft** (*pl -e*) *das* - **1.** [Handel] business; die ~e gehen schlecht business is slack; ein ~ abschließen to close a deal; du hast damit ein gutes/schlechtes ~ gemacht that was a good/bad deal (for you); mit jm ~e machen to do business with sb - **2.** [Laden] shop, store; [Firma] business - **3.** [Gewinn] profit - **4.** [Angelegenheit] task; sich um seine ~e kümmern to go about one's business.

**geschäftig** *adj* [Treiben] bustling; [Person] busy ◇ *adv* busily.

**geschäftlich** *adj* - **1.** [beruflich] business (*vor Subst*) - **2.** [unpersönlich] businesslike ◇ *adv* - **1.** [verreisen, fliegen] on business - **2.** [unpersönlich] in a businesslike manner.

**Geschäftsauflgabe** *die:* **er wurde zur ~ ge-zwungen** he was forced to close down the business.

**Geschäftslbedingungen** *pl* terms (and conditions).

**Geschäftslbeziehungen** *pl* business contacts.

**Geschäftslbrief** *der* business letter.

**Geschäftslfrau** *die* businesswoman.

**Geschäftslfreund** *der* business associate.

**Geschäftslführer, in** *der, die* - **1.** [von Unternehmen] manager; [von GmbH] managing director - **2.** [von Organisation] secretary.

**Geschäftslführung** *die* management.

**Geschäftslinhaber, in** *der, die* proprietor.

**Geschäftsljahr** *das* financial year.

**Geschäftsllage** *die* - **1.** [wirtschaftlich] commercial situation - **2.** [örtlich] business location.

**Geschäftslleute** *pl* businessmen.

**Geschäftslmann** (*pl* -leute *ODER* -männer) *der* businessman.

**geschäftsmäßig** *adj* businesslike <> *adv* in a businesslike manner.

**Geschäftslordnung** *die* statutes (*pl*), standing orders (*pl*).

**Geschäftslpartner, in** *der, die* - **1.** [Teilhaber] business partner - **2.** [Kunde] trading partner.

**Geschäftslreise** *die* business trip.

**geschäftsschädigend** *adj* damaging to the interests of a/the company <> *adv* in a manner which is damaging to the interests of a/the company.

**Geschäftslschluss** *der* closing time.

**Geschäftslstelle** *die* office; [von Bank] branch.

**Geschäftslstraße** *die* high street *Br*, main (shopping) street *Am*.

**geschäftstüchtig** *adj* with good business acumen.

**Geschäftslverbindung** *die* business contact.

**Geschäftslzeit** *die* [von Laden] opening hours (*pl*); [von Firma] office hours (*pl*).

**Geschäftslzweig** *der* [von Unternehmen] division; [Wirtschaftssektor] branch of industry.

**geschah** *prät* ⊳ **geschehen**.

**gescheckt** *adj* [Hund, Katze, Stoff] spotted; [Pferd - braunweiß] skewbald; [ - schwarzweiß] piebald.

**geschehen** (*präs* **geschieht**; *prät* **geschah**; *perf* **ist geschehen**) *vi* - **1.** [sich ereignen] to happen - **2.** [widerfahren]: **es kann dir nichts ~** nothing can happen to you; **ihm ist ein Unrecht ~** he

has been wronged; **das geschieht dir/ihm (ganz) recht!** *abw* that serves you/him right! **- 3.** [verloren sein]: **es ist um seine Zukunft ~** he has no future; **es ist um ihn ~** he has had it; **als ich sie sah, war es um mich ~** I was lost the moment I saw her.

**Geschehen** *das* (*ohne pl*) events (*pl*).

**gescheit** *adj* - **1.** [klug] clever - **2.** [vernünftig] sensible <> *adv* - **1.** [klug] cleverly - **2.** [vernünftig] sensibly.

**Geschenk** (*pl* -e) *das* present.

**Geschenklartikel** *der* gift.

**Geschenklpackung** *die* gift box.

**Geschichte** (*pl* -n) *die* - **1.** [geschichtliche Entwicklung, Fach] history; **~ machen** to make history - **2.** [Erzählung, Bericht] story - **3.** [Begebenheit]: **es ist wieder die alte ~** it's the same old story; **mir ist heute eine seltsame ~ passiert** a strange thing happened to me today; **du machst ja ~n!** *hum* you are a one!

**geschichtlich** *adj* historical <> *adv* historically.

**Geschichtslunterricht** *der* (*ohne pl*) [Schulstunden] history lessons (*pl*).

**Geschick** (*pl* -e) *das* (*ohne pl*) [Talent, Können] skill.

◆ **Geschicke** *pl* fate (*sg*).

**Geschicklichkeit** *die* skilfulness.

**geschickt** *adj* - **1.** [fingerfertig] skilful - **2.** [raffiniert, gewandt] clever <> *adv* - **1.** [fingerfertig] skilfully - **2.** [raffiniert, gewandt] cleverly.

**geschieden** *pp* ⊳ **scheiden** <> *adj* divorced.

**geschieht** *präs* ⊳ **geschehen**.

**geschienen** *pp* ⊳ **scheinen**.

**Geschimpfe** *das* *abw* [Meckern] moaning.

**Geschirr** (*pl* -e) *das* - **1.** (*ohne pl*) [Gefäße, Service] crockery; [benutzt] dishes (*pl*); **ein ~ für sechs Personen** a dinner/tea service for six people; **~ spülen** *ODER* **abwaschen** to do the dishes, to wash up *Br* - **2.** [für Zugtiere] harness.

**Geschirrspüllmaschine** *die* dishwasher.

**Geschirrltuch** *das* tea towel *Br*, dish towel *Am*.

**geschissen** *pp* ⊳ **scheißen**.

**geschlafen** *pp* ⊳ **schlafen**.

**geschlagen** *pp* ⊳ **schlagen** <> *adj* - **1.** [ganz]: **eine ~e Stunde** a whole hour - **2.** [bestraft]: **mit jm/etw ~ sein** *fam* to be unlucky with sb/sthg.

**Geschlecht** (*pl* -er) *das* - **1.** [biologische Einteilung] sex; **das starke/schwache ~** *fam* the stronger/weaker sex - **2.** (*ohne pl*) [Geschlechtsteil] genitals (*pl*) - **3.** [Familie] lineage - **4.** [Genus] gender.

**Geschlechts|krankheit** *die* sexually transmitted disease.

**Geschlechts|merkmal** *das* sexual characteristic.

**Geschlechts|organ** *das* sexual organ.

**geschlechtsreif** *adj* sexually mature.

**Geschlechtsverkehr** *der* sexual intercourse.

**geschlichen** *pp* ▷ schleichen.

**geschliffen** *pp* ▷ schleifen ◇ *adj* polished ◇ *adv* in a polished manner.

**geschlossen** *pp* ▷ schließen ◇ *adj* - **1.** [verschlossen] closed - **2.** [Front] united - **3.** [Ortschaft] built-up; **in sich ~** [Persönlichkeit, Komposition] well-rounded ◇ *adv* [gemeinsam] unanimously.

**geschlungen** *pp* ▷ schlingen.

**Geschmack** (*pl* Geschmäcke ODER Geschmäcker) *der* - **1.** [gen] taste; **~ haben** to have taste; **guten/schlechten ~ haben** to have good/bad taste; **an etw** *(D)* **~ finden** to acquire a taste for sthg; **auf den ~ kommen** to acquire a taste for it - **2.** [Geschmackssinn] sense of taste.

**geschmacklich** *adj* as regards taste; **~e Unterschiede** differences in taste ◇ *adv* as regards taste.

**geschmacklos** *adj* tasteless ◇ *adv* tastelessly.

**Geschmacklosigkeit** (*pl* -en) *die* - **1.** [Eigenschaft] bad taste - **2.** [Handlung] tasteless behaviour *(U)*; [Äußerung] tasteless remark; **diese Geste war eine ~** this gesture was in bad taste.

**Geschmack|sache** = Geschmackssache.

**Geschmacks|richtung** *die* - **1.** [von Nahrungsmitteln] flavour - **2.** [Stilrichtung, Vorliebe] taste.

**Geschmackssache, Geschmacksache** *die*: **das ist ~** that is a matter of taste.

**Geschmackssinn** *der* sense of taste.

**Geschmacks|verirrung** *die abw*: **so eine ~!** how tasteless!

**geschmackvoll** *adj* tasteful ◇ *adv* tastefully.

**Geschmeide** (*pl* -) *das geh* jewellery.

**geschmeidig** *adj* [Material, Bewegung] supple ◇ *adv* [gewandt] supplely.

**geschmissen** *pp* ▷ schmeißen.

**geschmolzen** *pp* ▷ schmelzen.

**Geschnetzelte** *das (ohne pl)* small, thin strips of meat cooked in a sauce.

**geschnitten** *pp* ▷ schneiden ◇ *adj* - **1.** [Fleisch] sliced - **2.** [Kleid] cut; **ihr Gesicht ist hübsch ~** she has pretty features.

**geschoben** *pp* ▷ schieben.

**Geschöpf** (*pl* -e) *das* - **1.** [Lebewesen, Person] creature - **2.** [Erfindung] creation.

**geschoren** *pp* ▷ scheren.

**Geschoss** (*pl* -e) *das* - **1.** [Kugel] bullet; [Granate] shell - **2.** [Stockwerk] floor; **im dritten ~** on the third floor.

**geschossen** *pp* ▷ schießen.

**geschraubt** *abw adj* contrived ◇ *adv* in a contrived manner.

**Geschrei** *das abw* - **1.** [Schreien] shouting - **2.** [Gezeter] fuss.

**geschrieben** *pp* ▷ schreiben.

**geschrien** *pp* ▷ schreien.

**Geschütz** (*pl* -e) *das* (big) gun; **~e artillery** *(U)*; **schweres ~ auffahren** *eigtl* & *fig* to bring up the big guns.

**Geschwader** (*pl* -) *das* squadron *Br*, group *Am*.

**Geschwafel** *das fam abw* waffle.

**Geschwätz** *das abw* - **1.** [Gerede] prattle - **2.** [Tratsch] gossip.

**geschwätzig** *adj abw* prattling; [tratschend] gossipy.

**geschweige** *konj*: **~ denn** let alone.

**geschwiegen** *pp* ▷ schweigen.

**geschwind** *Süddt adj* quick ◇ *adv* quickly.

**Geschwindigkeit** (*pl* -en) *die* speed; **mit einer ~ von** at a speed of.

**Geschwindigkeits|begrenzung** *die* speed limit.

**Geschwindigkeits|überschreitung** *die* speeding.

**Geschwister** *pl* brothers and sisters.

**geschwollen** *pp* ▷ schwellen ◇ *adj* - **1.** [Finger, Gesicht] swollen - **2.** *abw* [Sätze, Ausdruck] pompous ◇ *adv abw* [pompös] pompously.

**geschwommen** *pp* ▷ schwimmen.

**geschworen** *pp* ▷ schwören.

**Geschworene** (*pl* -n) *der*, *die* juror.

**Geschwulst** (*pl* Geschwülste) *die* tumour.

**geschwunden** *pp* ▷ schwinden.

**geschwungen** *pp* ▷ schwingen ◇ *adj* curved.

**Geschwür** (*pl* -e) *das* ulcer.

**gesehen** *pp* ▷ sehen.

**Geselle** (*pl* -n) *der* - **1.** [Handwerker] qualified craftsman - **2.** [Kerl] fellow.

**gesellen** ▷ **sich gesellen** *ref*: **sich zu jm ~** to join sb; **sich zu etw ~** to be added to sthg.

**Gesellen|prüfung** *die* examination to become a qualified craftsman.

**gesellig** *adj* - **1.** [kontaktfreudig - Person] sociable;

[ - Tier] gregarious - **2.** [anregend] convivial
<> adv - **1.** [kontaktfreudig - Person] sociably;
[ - Tier] gregariously - **2.** [anregend] convivially.

**Geselligkeit** die conviviality; ~ **brauchen** to need company.

**Gesellin** (pl -nen) die qualified craftswoman.

**Gesellschaft** (pl -en) die - **1.** [Gemeinschaft] society - **2.** [Anwesenheit, Umgang] company; **jm ~ leisten** to keep sb company; **sich in guter/ schlechter ~ befinden** to be in good/bad company - **3.** [Fest] party; **geschlossene ~** private party - **4.** [Gruppe] group (of people) - **5.** [Wirtschaftsunternehmen] company.

**gesellschaftlich** adj - **1.** [Verhältnisse] social - **2.** [Ereignis] society <> adv - **1.** [sozial] socially - **2.** [in der Oberschicht] in society.

**Gesellschaftskritik** die social criticism.

**Gesellschaftsordnung** die social order.

**gesellschaftspolitisch** adj sociopolitical <> adv sociopolitically.

**Gesellschaftsspiel** das - **1.** [Brettspiel] board game - **2.** [auf Festen] party game.

**gesessen** pp ⊳ sitzen.

**Gesetz** (pl -e) das [staatliche Vorschrift, Regel] law.
⮡ **laut Gesetz** adv by law.

**Gesetzbuch** das statute book.

**Gesetzentwurf** der bill.

**Gesetzesvorlage** die bill.

**gesetzgebend** adj legislative.

**Gesetzgeber** der legislature.

**Gesetzgebung** die legislation.

**gesetzlich** adj legal; ~**er Feiertag** public holiday; **ein ~er Anspruch** a legitimate claim <> adv legally; ~ **verankert** established in law; ~ **geschützt** registered.

**gesetzlos** adj lawless <> adv lawlessly.

**gesetzmäßig** adj - **1.:** **ein ~er Prozess** a process governed by a natural law - **2.** [Macht] legal; [Inhaber] lawful.

**gesetzt** adj sedate; ~ **den Fall, dass ...** assuming that ...

**gesetzwidrig** adj illegal <> adv illegally.

**gesichert** adj secure.

**Gesicht** (pl -er ODER -e) das face; **jm etw ins ~ sagen** fig to say sthg to sb's face; **jn/etw zu ~ bekommen** fig to set eyes on sb/sthg; **sein** ODER **das ~ verlieren** fig to lose face; **sein** ODER **das ~ wahren** fig to save face.

**Gesichtsausdruck** der expression.

**Gesichtscreme** die face cream.

**Gesichtsfarbe** die (ohne pl) complexion.

**Gesichtskreis** der: **sie ist aus meinem ~ verschwunden** I have lost contact with her; **den ~ erweitern** to broaden one's horizons.

**Gesichtspunkt** der point of view.

**Gesichtswasser** (pl -wässer) das toner.

**Gesichtszüge** pl features.

**Gesindel** das abw rabble.

**gesinnt** adj: liberal ~ **sein** to be liberalminded; **jm gut/übel ~ sein** to be well/ill disposed towards sb.

**Gesinnung** (pl -en) die [Überzeugungen] convictions (pl); [Einstellung] outlook (U).

**Gesinnungsgenosse** der like-minded person.

**Gesinnungswandel** der (ohne pl) change of direction.

**gesittet** adj civilized <> adv in a civilized manner.

**Gesöff** (pl -e) das salopp abw swill.

**gesoffen** pp ⊳ saufen.

**gesogen** pp ⊳ saugen.

**gesondert** adj separate <> adv separately.

**gesonnen** pp ⊳ sinnen.

**gespannt** adj - **1.** [Stoff, Saite] taut - **2.** [Person] eager; **ich bin ~ auf seine neue Freundin** I can't wait to see his new girlfriend - **3.** [Situation] tense <> adv [erwartungsvoll, aufgeregt] eagerly.

**Gespenst** (pl -er) das ghost; [Bedrohung] spectre.

**gespenstisch** adj ghostly.

**gespien** pp ⊳ speien.

**gesponnen** pp ⊳ spinnen.

**Gespött** das mockery; **jn/sich zum ~ der Leute machen** to make sb/o.s. a laughing stock.

**Gespräch** (pl -e) das - **1.** [Konversation] conversation, talk; **etw ist im ~** fig sthg is under discussion; **mit jm im ~ bleiben** fig to keep talking with sb - **2.** [Telefonanruf] call.

**gesprächig** adj talkative.

**Gesprächseinheit** [gə'ʃprɛːçsainhait] die unit.

**Gesprächspartner, in** [gə'ʃprɛːçspartnɐ] der, die: **mein ~** the person I am/was talking to; **seine ~ bei den Verhandlungen** his partners in the negotiations.

**Gesprächsstoff** [gə'ʃprɛːçsʃtɔf] der (ohne pl) topics (pl) of conversation.

**Gesprächsthema** [gə'ʃprɛːçsteːma] das topic of conversation.

**gesprochen** pp ⊳ sprechen.

**gesprossen** pp ⊳ sprießen.

**gesprungen** pp ⊳ springen.

**Gespür** das feel; **ein/kein ~ für etw haben** to have a/no feel for sthg.

**Gestalt** (pl -en) die - **1.** [Person] figure - **2.** (ohne pl) [Körperform] build - **3.** [in Literatur] character - **4.** (ohne pl) [Form] shape; **einer Sache** (D) ~

**geben** ODER **verleihen** to give shape to sthg; **unser Plan nimmt ~ an** our plan is taking shape.
➤ **in Gestalt** *präp:* **in ~ einer Sache** *(G)* in the shape of sthg.

**gestalten** *vt* [Fest] to organize; [Schaufenster, Garten] to design.
➤ **sich gestalten** *ref* to turn out.

**gestalterisch** *adj* creative ◇ *adv* creatively.

**Gestaltung** *die* [von Fest] organizing; [von Schaufenster, Garten] designing.

**gestanden** *pp* ▷ **stehen, gestehen** ◇ *adj* experienced.

**geständig** *adj:* **~ sein** to have confessed.

**Geständnis** (*pl* **-se**) *das* confession; **ein ~ ablegen** to make a confession.

**Gestank** *der (ohne pl) abw* stench.

**gestatten** *vt:* **jm etw ~** to allow sb sthg; **sich** *(D)* **etw ~** to allow o.s. sthg.
➤ **gestatten Sie** *interj:* **~ Sie?** may I?; **~ Sie, dass ich rauche?** do you mind if I smoke?

**Geste** (*pl* **-n**) *die* gesture.

**Gesteck** (*pl* **-e**) *das* flower arrangement.

**gestehen** (*prät* **gestand;** *perf* **hat gestanden**) *vt:* **ein Verbrechen/einen Mord ~** to confess to a crime/murder; **jm die Wahrheit ~** to confess the truth to sb ◇ *vi* [aussagen] to confess.

**Gestein** (*pl* **-e**) *das* rock.

**Gestell** (*pl* **-e**) *das* stand.

**gestern** *adv* yesterday; **~ früh** first thing yesterday; **~ Morgen/Mittag/Abend** yesterday morning/lunchtime/evening; **von ~ sein** *fig* to be behind the times.

**gestiegen** *pp* ▷ **steigen.**

**Gestik** *die (ohne pl)* gestures (*pl*).

**gestikulieren** *vi* to gesticulate.

**Gestirn** (*pl* **-e**) *das* star.

**gestochen** *pp* ▷ **stechen.**

**gestohlen** *pp* ▷ **stehlen.**

**gestorben** *pp* ▷ **sterben.**

**gestoßen** *pp* ▷ **stoßen.**

**gestreift** *adj* striped.

**gestrichelt** *adj* broken.

**gestrichen** *pp* ▷ **streichen** ◇ *adj* painted; **ein ~er Teelöffel** a level teaspoon ◇ *adv:* **~ voll** full to the brim.

**gestrig** *adj* yesterday's; **am ~en Abend** yesterday evening.

**gestritten** *pp* ▷ **streiten.**

**Gestrüpp** *das* undergrowth.

**gestunken** *pp* ▷ **stinken.**

**Gestüt** (*pl* **-e**) *das* stud.

**Gesuch** (*pl* **-e**) *das* request.

**gesucht** *pp* ▷ **suchen** ◇ *adj* **- 1.** [begehrt] sought-after **- 2.** [geziert] affected ◇ *adv* [geziert] affectedly.

**gesund** (*kompar* **gesünder** ODER **gesunder;** *superl* **gesündeste** oder **gesundeste**) *adj* healthy; **~er Menschenverstand** common sense ◇ *adv* healthily; **jn ~ schreiben** to certify sb fit; **jn ~ pflegen** to nurse sb back to health.

**Gesundheit** *die* health; **auf js ~** *(A)* **trinken** ODER **anstoßen** to drink (to) sb's health ◇ *interj* bless you!

**gesundheitlich** *adj* health; **ihr ~er Zustand** the state of her health ◇ *adv* health-wise.

**Gesundheitsamt** *das* public health department.

**gesundheitsschädlich** *adj* damaging to one's health.

**Gesundheitswesen** *das* health service.

**Gesundheitszeugnis** *das* health certificate.

**Gesundheitszustand** *der* state of health.

**gesundschrumpfen** *vt* to slim down.
➤ **sich gesundschrumpfen** *ref* to slim down.

**gesungen** *pp* ▷ **singen.**

**gesunken** *pp* ▷ **sinken.**

**getan** *pp* ▷ **tun.**

**geteilt** *adj* divided; **~er Meinung sein** to have different opinions; **~ durch** divided by.

**Getöse** *das* roar.

**getragen** *pp* ▷ **tragen.**

**Getränk** (*pl* **-e**) *das* drink.

**Getränkeautomat** *der* drinks machine.

**Getreide** *das* cereals (*pl*), grain.

**Getreideanbau** *der* cereal growing.

**getrennt** *adj* separate ◇ *adv* separately; **~ zahlen** to pay separately; **(von jm) ~ leben** to be separated (from sb).

**getreten** *pp* ▷ **treten.**

**getreu** *adj* **- 1.** *geh* [Person] loyal **- 2.** [Darstellung] faithful ◇ *adv* **- 1.** *geh* [begleiten] loyally **- 2.** [darstellen] faithfully ◇ *präp:* **~ einer Sache** *(D),* **einer Sache** *(D)* **~** true to sthg.

**Getriebe** (*pl* **-**) *das* gearbox.

**getrieben** *pp* ▷ **treiben.**

**getroffen** *pp* ▷ **treffen, triefen.**

**getrogen** *pp* ▷ **trügen.**

**getrost** *adv* without any problem.

**getrunken** *pp* ▷ **trinken.**

**Getto, Ghetto** (*pl* **-s**) *das* ghetto.

**Getue** [gə'tu:ə] *das abw* fuss.

**Getümmel** *das:* **das ~ im Freibad** the hurly-burly at the swimming pool; **sich ins ~ stürzen** to throw o.s. into the fray.

**GEW** [geːeːˈveː] (*abk für* **Gewerkschaft Erziehung und Wissenschaft**) *die* German teaching union.

**Gewächs** [gəˈvɛks] (*pl* -e) *das* plant.

**gewachsen** [gəˈvaksn̩] *pp* ▷ · **wachsen** ◇ *adj:* **jm ~ sein** to be a match for sb; **etw ~ sein** to be up to sthg.

**Gewächslhaus** *das* greenhouse.

**gewagt** *adj* daring ◇ *adv* [freizügig] daringly.

**gewählt** *adj* - **1.** [durch Abstimmung bestimmt] elected - **2.** [gehoben] refined ◇ *adv* [gehoben] in a refined manner.

**Gewähr** *die* (*ohne pl*) guarantee; **~ leisten** to guarantee.

◆ **ohne Gewähr** *adv* subject to alteration.

**gewähren** *vt* to give; **jm etw ~** to grant sb sthg; **jn ~ lassen** to let sb do as he/she likes.

**gewährleisten** *vt* ▷ **Gewähr.**

**Gewahrsam** *der* - **1.** [Obhut] safekeeping; **etw in ~ nehmen** to take sthg into safekeeping - **2.** [Haft] custody.

**Gewalt** (*pl* -en) *die* - **1.** [Brutalität, Willkür] violence; **etw mit ~ öffnen** to force sthg open; **jn mit ~ zu etw zwingen** to compel sb to do sthg by (using) force; **etw mit aller ~ machen** to do sthg with all one's might; **einer Sache** (D) **~ antun** to do violence to sthg - **2.** [Macht, Beherrschung] power; **jn/sich/etw in der ~ haben** to be in control of sb/o.s./sthg - **3.** [Naturgewalt] force, power; **etw ist höhere ~** sthg is an act of God.

**Gewaltanwendung** *die* use of force.

**Gewaltenteilung** *die* separation of powers.

**Gewaltlherrschaft** *die* tyranny.

**gewaltig** *adj* [Kraft, Größe] enormous, huge; [Schönheit] tremendous ◇ *adv* enormously.

**gewaltlos** *adj* non-violent ◇ *adv* non-violently.

**gewaltsam** *adj* violent; **~e Vertreibung** forcible expulsion ◇ *adv* forcibly; [schließen] by force; **jn ~ an etw hindern** to prevent sb forcibly from doing sthg.

**Gewaltltat** *die* act of violence.

**gewalttätig** *adj* violent ◇ *adv* violently.

**Gewaltlverbrechen** *das* crime of violence.

**Gewand** (*pl* Gewänder) *das* robe.

**Gewandhauslorchester** *das* orchestra based in Leipzig.

**gewandt** *pp* ▷ **wenden** ◇ *adj* - **1.** [Ausdrucksweise, Redner] skilful - **2.** [Auftreten] confident - **3.** [Bewegung] agile ◇ *adv* - **1.** [sich ausdrücken] skilfully - **2.** [auftreten] confidently - **3.** [sich bewegen] agilely.

**Gewandtheit** *die* - **1.** [von Redner] skilfulness

- **2.** [von Umgangsformen] confidence - **3.** [von Bewegungen] agility.

**gewann** *prät* ▷ gewinnen.

**gewaschen** *pp* ▷ waschen.

**Gewässer** (*pl* -) *das* stretch of water.

◆ **Gewässer** *pl* waters.

**Gewässerlschutz** *der* prevention of water pollution.

**Gewebe** (*pl* -) *das* - **1.** [Stoff] fabric - **2.** [im Körper] tissue.

**Gewehr** (*pl* -e) *das* rifle.

**Gewehrlkolben** *der* rifle butt.

**Gewehrllauf** *der* rifle barrel.

**Geweih** (*pl* -e) *das* antlers (*pl*); [Trophäe] set of antlers.

**Gewerbe** (*pl* -) *das* - **1.** [Beruf] trade - **2.** (*ohne pl*) [Bereich] trade.

**Gewerbelfreiheit** *die* freedom of trade.

**Gewerbelgebiet** *das* business park.

**Gewerbelschein** *der* trading licence.

**Gewerbelsteuer** *die* trade tax.

**gewerblich** *adj* commercial ◇ *adv* commercially.

**gewerbsmäßig** *adj* professional ◇ *adv* professionally.

**Gewerkschaft** (*pl* -en) *die* trade union *Br*, labor union *Am*.

**Gewerkschaft(l)er, in** (*mpl* Gewerkschaft-(l)er; *fpl* -nen) *der, die* trade *Br* ODER labor *Am* unionist.

**gewerkschaftlich** *adj* trade union *Br*, labor union *Am* ◇ *adv:* **~ organisiert** unionized.

**Gewerkschaftsbund** *der* trade union federation.

**gewesen** *pp* ▷ sein.

**Gewicht** (*pl* -e) *das* weight; **etw fällt ins ~** *fig* sthg is of consequence.

**Gewichtheben** *das* weightlifting.

**Gewichtslklasse** *die* SPORT weight class.

**gewieft** *adj* smart ◇ *adv* smartly.

**gewiesen** *pp* ▷ weisen.

**gewillt** *adj:* **~/nicht ~ sein, etw zu tun** to be/not to be prepared to do sthg.

**Gewinde** (*pl* -) *das* thread.

**Gewinn** (*pl* -e) *der* - **1.** [Profit] profit; **mit ~** at a profit - **2.** (*ohne pl*) [Nutzen] benefit - **3.** [Preis] prize.

◆ **Gewinn bringend** *adj* profitable ◇ *adv* profitably.

**Gewinnlbeteiligung** *die* profit sharing.

**gewinnbringend** ▷ Gewinn.

**gewinnen** (*prät* gewann; *perf* hat gewonnen) *vi* - **1.** [siegen] to win - **2.** [wachsen]: **an etw** (D) **~** to gain in sthg - **3.** [besser werden]:

**durch etw** ~ to benefit from sthg ⬦ *vt* **- 1.** [Wettkampf, Preis] to win **- 2.** [Ansehen] to gain; **jn für etw** ~ to win sb over to sthg **- 3.** [Produkt] to produce.

**gewinnend** *adj* winning ⬦ *adv* winningly.

**Gewinner, in** (*mpl* -; *fpl* -nen) *der, die* winner.

**Gewinnlspanne** *die* profit margin.

**Gewinnung** *die* extraction.

**Gewirr, Gewirre** *das* [von Kabeln] tangle; [von Stimmen] confusion.

**gewiss** *adj* certain; **sich** (*D*) **einer Sache** (*G*) ~ **sein** to be certain of sthg; **der Sieg ist uns** ~ we are certain of victory ⬦ *adv* [sicherlich] certainly.

**Gewissen** *das* (*ohne pl*) **- 1.** [seelische Instanz] conscience; **gutes/schlechtes** ~ clear/bad conscience **- 2.** *RW:* **jn auf dem** ~ **haben** to have sb on one's conscience; **jm ins** ~ **reden** to have a serious talk with sb.

**gewissenhaft** *adj* conscientious ⬦ *adv* conscientiously.

**gewissenlos** *adj* unscrupulous ⬦ *adv* unscrupulously.

**Gewissenlosigkeit** *die* unscrupulousness.

**Gewissenslbisse** *pl* pangs of conscience.

**Gewissenslfrage** *die* (*ohne pl*) matter of conscience.

**Gewissenslgründe** *pl* conscientious reasons; **aus** ~**n** for conscientious reasons.

**Gewissenslkonflikt** *der* moral dilemma; **in einen** ~ **geraten** to be faced with a moral dilemma.

**gewissermaßen** *adv* as it were.

**Gewissheit** *die* (*ohne pl*) certainty; ~ **erlangen** to find out for certain; **etw mit** ~ **sagen/wissen** to say/know sthg for certain.

**Gewitter** (*pl* -) *das* thunderstorm.

**gewittern** *vi:* **es gewittert** it is thundering.

**gewittrig** *adj* thundery.

**gewitzt** *adj* shrewd ⬦ *adv* shrewdly.

**gewogen** *pp* ⊳ **wiegen** ⬦ *adj:* **jm/einer Sache** ~ **sein** *geh* to be well disposed towards sb/sthg.

**gewöhnen** *vt:* **jn an jn/etw** ~ to accustom sb to sb/sthg.

➥ **sich gewöhnen** *ref:* **sich an jn/etw** ~ to get used to sb/sthg; **sich daran** ~, **etw zu tun** to get used to doing sthg.

**Gewohnheit** (*pl* -en) *die* habit; **jm zur** ~ **werden** to become a habit with sb.

**Gewohnheitslrecht** *das* (*ohne pl*) customary right.

**gewöhnlich** *adj* **- 1.** [normal] normal, ordinary **- 2.** [gewohnt] usual **- 3.** *abw* [primitiv] common ⬦ *adv* **- 1.** [normalerweise] normally, usually **- 2.** *abw* [primitiv] in a common way.

➥ **wie gewöhnlich** *adv* as usual.

**gewohnt** *adj* usual; **etw** ~ **sein** to be used to sthg.

**gewöhnt** *adj:* **an etw** (*A*) ~ **sein** to be used to sthg.

**Gewöhnung** *die* (*ohne pl*): **das ist eine Frage der** ~ it's a question of getting used to it; **die** ~ **an eine neue Umgebung fällt mir schwer** I find it difficult to get used to new surroundings.

**Gewölbe** (*pl* -) *das* vault.

**gewonnen** *pp* ⊳ gewinnen.

**geworben** *pp* ⊳ werben.

**geworden** *pp* ⊳ werden.

**geworfen** *pp* ⊳ werfen.

**Gewühl** *das* **- 1.** [Menschenmenge] crush **- 2.** [Wühlen] rummaging.

**gewunden** *pp* ⊳ winden ⬦ *adj* **- 1.** [Weg] winding **- 2.** [Sätze] tortuous.

**Gewürz** (*pl* -e) *das* spice.

**Gewürzlgurke** *die* pickled gherkin.

**gewusst** *pp* ⊳ wissen.

**gez.** *abk für* gezeichnet.

**GEZ** [geːtsɛtˈtsɛt] (*abk für* Gebühreneinzugszentrale) *die* (*ohne pl*) *body which levies fees on behalf of public television and radio.*

**Gezänk, Gezanke** *das abw* quarrelling.

**gezeichnet** *pp* ⊳ zeichnen ⬦ *adj* **- 1.** [mit Stiften] hand-drawn **- 2.** [gekennzeichnet]: **von/mit etw** ~ **sein** to be marked by/with sthg.

**Gezeiten** *pl* tides.

**Gezeitenkraftlwerk** *das* tidal power station.

**Gezeter** *das abw* scolding.

**gezielt** *adj* specific; **eine** ~**e Frage/Antwort** a specific question/answer ⬦ *adv:* ~ **vorgehen** to take specific action; **jn** ~ **auf etw ansprechen** to ask sb specifically about sthg.

**geziert** *abw adj* affected ⬦ *adv* affectedly.

**gezogen** *pp* ⊳ ziehen.

**Gezwitscher** *das* twittering.

**gezwungen** *pp* ⊳ zwingen ⬦ *adj* forced ⬦ *adv* in a forced way.

**gezwungenermaßen** *adv:* **etw** ~ **machen** to be forced to do sthg.

**gg.** *abk für* gegen.

**GG** [geːˈgeː] (*abk für* Grundgesetz) *das German constitution.*

**ggf.** *abk für* gegebenenfalls.

**Ghana** *nt* Ghana.

**Ghetto** *das* = Getto.

**Gibraltar** nt Gibraltar.

**gibt** präs ▷ geben.

**Gicht** die gout.

**Giebel** (pl -) der - **1.** [auf Dach] gable - **2.** [über Tor] pediment.

**Gier** die greed; ~ nach etw craving for sthg.

**gierig** adj greedy; ~ nach ODER auf etw (A) sein to have a craving for sthg ◇ adv greedily.

**gießen** (prät goss; perf hat gegossen) vt - **1.** [schütten] to pour - **2.** [verschütten] to spill - **3.** [Blumen] to water - **4.** [Glocke, Blei] to cast; [Kerzen] to mould ◇ vi [regnen]: es gießt it's pouring.

**Gießlkanne** die watering can.

**Gift** (pl -e) das - **1.** [schädliche Substanz] poison - **2.** RW: darauf kannst du ~ nehmen! fam you can bet your life on it!

**Giftlgas** das poison gas.

**giftgrün** adj lurid green.

**giftig** adj - **1.** [Gift enthaltend, gesundheitsschädlich] poisonous - **2.** fam abw [gehässig] venomous - **3.** [grell] lurid ◇ adv fam abw [gehässig] venomously.

**Giftlmüll** der toxic waste.

**Giftlpilz** der poisonous mushroom.

**Giftlschlange** die poisonous snake.

**Giftlstoff** der poisonous substance.

**Gigant, in** (mpl -en; fpl -nen) der, die giant.

**gigantisch** adj gigantic.

**Gigolo** ['ʒiːgolol] (pl -s) der gigolo.

**gilt** präs ▷ gelten.

**Gin** [dʒɪn] der gin.

**ging** prät ▷ gehen.

**Ginster** (pl -) der broom (U); [Stechginster] gorse (U).

**Gipfel** (pl -) der - **1.** [von Bergen] summit, peak - **2.** [Höhepunkt] height; das ist (doch) der ~! that's the limit! - **3.** [Gipfeltreffen] summit.

**Gipfellkonferenz** die summit conference.

**gipfeln** vi: der Streit gipfelte in einem Schlagabtausch the argument culminated in an exchange of blows.

**Gipfelltreffen** das summit meeting.

**Gips** der - **1.** [Material] plaster - **2.** [Gipsverband] plaster cast.

**Gipslbein** das: ein ~ haben to have a leg in plaster.

**Gipslverband** der plaster cast.

**Giraffe** (pl -n) die giraffe.

**Girlande** (pl -n) die garland.

**Girlgroup** (pl -s) die girl group.

**Girolkonto** ['ʒiːrolkɔntol] das current account Br, checking account Am.

**gis, Gis** (pl Gis) das MUS G sharp.

**Gischt** der ODER die spray.

**Gitarre** (pl -n) die guitar.

**Gitarrist, in** (mpl -en; fpl -nen) der, die guitarist.

**Gitter** (pl -) das [aus Eisen] bars (pl); [gekreuzt] grille; [aus Holz] trellis; [Geländer] railings (pl).
➤ **hinter Gittern** adv fam behind bars.

**Gladiole** (pl -n) die gladiolus.

**Glanz** der - **1.** [von Stern] brightness - **2.** [von Perl] gleam - **3.** [von Augen] sparkle.

**glänzen** vi - **1.** [gen] to shine, to gleam; [Augen, Edelsteine] to sparkle; [Farbe] to be shiny - **2.** [herausragen] to shine.

**glänzend** adj - **1.** [mit Glanz] shiny; [Lack] gloss - **2.** [sehr gut] brilliant ◇ adv [sehr gut] brilliantly.

**Glanzlleistung** die brilliant achievement.

**glanzlos** adj dull.

**glanzvoll** adj [hervorragend] brilliant ◇ adv [hervorragend] brilliantly.

**Glarus** nt Glarus.

**Glas** (pl Gläser) das - **1.** [Material, Trinkglas] glass; eine Kanne aus ~ a glass pot; ein ~ Saft a glass of juice; ein ~ über den Durst trinken fig to have one too many - **2.** [für Marmelade] jar - **3.** [Brillenglas] lens.

**Glaser, in** (mpl -; fpl -nen) der, die glazier.

**Glaslfaser** die - **1.** [zur Isolierung] fibreglass - **2.** [zum Leiten von Licht] glass fibre.

**glasieren** vt - **1.** [Keramik] to glaze - **2.** [Speisen] to ice Br, to frost Am.

**glasig** adj - **1.** [Blick, Ausdruck] glazed - **2.** [beim Braten] transparent.

**glasklar** adj crystal clear ◇ adv [deutlich] in a crystal clear fashion.

**Glaslscheibe** die pane (of glass).

**Glaslscherbe** die piece of broken glass.

**Glaslsplitter** der splinter of glass.

**Glasltür** die glass door.

**Glasur** (pl -en) die - **1.** [für Keramik] glaze - **2.** [für Speisen] icing Br, frosting Am.

**glatt** adj - **1.** [Oberfläche] smooth; ~e Haare straight hair - **2.** [rutschig] slippery - **3.** [reibungslos] smooth - **4.** fam [eindeutig]: eine ~e Lüge a downright lie; eine ~e Ablehnung a flat refusal; das ist ~er Wahnsinn! that's utter madness! ◇ adv - **1.**: etw ~ streichen to smooth sthg - **2.** [verlaufen] smoothly - **3.** fam [eindeutig]: das haute ihn ~ um that completely floored him.

**Glätte** die - **1.** [Ebenheit] smoothness - **2.** [Schlüpfrigkeit] slipperiness.

**Glatteis** das (ohne pl) black ice; jn aufs ~ führen fig to catch sb out.

**glätten** *vt* [Decke] to smooth; [Falte] to smooth out.

➤ **sich glätten** *ref* [Meer] to become calm.

**glattweg** *adv* *fam* - **1.** [lügen] blatantly - **2.** [übersehen] completely - **3.** [zurückweisen] flatly.

**Glatze** (*pl* -n) *die* - **1.** [kahler Kopf] bald head; **eine ~ haben** to be bald - **2.** [kahle Stelle] bald patch; **eine ~ haben** to be going bald.

**Glaube** *der* - **1.** [Annahme] belief; **~ an etw** (A) belief in sthg; **in gutem** ODER **im guten ~n** in good faith; **jm/einer Sache ~n/keinen ~n schenken** to/not to believe sb/sthg - **2.** [Religion] faith.

**glauben** *vt* - **1.** [denken] to think - **2.** [für richtig halten] to believe; **jm ~** to believe sb; **ich glaube ihm nichts mehr** I don't believe anything he says any more; **jn etw ~ machen wollen** to try to make sb believe sthg ⬦ *vi* - **1.** [für wahr halten]: **an jn/etw ~** to believe in sb/sthg; **jm ~** to believe sb - **2.** [gläubig sein] to believe - **3.** RW: **dran ~ müssen** [umkommen] to bite the dust.

**Glaubens|bekenntnis** *das* (ohne pl) REL creed.

**Glaubens|freiheit** *die* freedom of worship.

**glaubhaft** *adj* credible ⬦ *adv* convincingly.

**gläubig** *adj* - **1.** [fromm] devout - **2.** [vertrauensselig] trusting ⬦ *adv* - **1.** [fromm] devoutly - **2.** [vertrauensselig] trustingly.

**Gläubige** (*pl* -n) *der*, *die* believer.

**Gläubiger, in** (*mpl* -; *fpl* -nen) *der*, *die* creditor.

**glaubwürdig** *adj* credible ⬦ *adv* convincingly.

**gleich** *adj* - **1.** [übereinstimmend] same; **den ~en Namen haben** to have the same name; **zwei ~e Tassen** two identical cups; **er ist immer der Gleiche geblieben** he hasn't changed a bit - **2.** [gleichwertig] equal - **3.** [egal]: **das ist mir ~** it's all the same to me; **zu ~en Teilen** in equal parts ⬦ *adv* - **1.** [ebenso] equally; **~ groß sein** to be the same size; **sie sind beide ~ alt** they're the same age - **2.** [auf gleiche Weise] the same; **die beiden Wörter werden ~ ausgesprochen** the two words are pronounced the same - **3.** [egal]: **das bleibt sich ~, ob du nun ...** it makes no difference whether you ... - **4.** [zeitlich] straight away, immediately; **ich komme ~** I'm just coming; **ich komme ~ wieder** I'll be right back; **bis ~!** see you soon! - **5.** [räumlich] right; **~ daneben** right next to it - **6.** [in Fragesätzen] again; **wie hieß er doch ~?** what's his name again? - **7.** [ebensogut] just as well; **bei dem Reparaturpreis können wir doch ~ ein neues kaufen** if it's going to cost that much to repair it, we might as well buy a new one ⬦ *präp* (+ D) *geh* like.

**gleichaltrig, gleichalterig** *adj* of the same age; **~ sein** to be the same age.

**gleichartig** *adj* of the same kind ⬦ *adv* in the same way.

**gleich bedeutend** *adj* equally important; **mit etw ~ sein** to be tantamount to sthg.

**gleichberechtigt** *adj* with equal rights; **~ sein** to have equal rights.

**Gleichberechtigung** *die* (ohne pl) equality, equal rights (pl).

**gleich bleiben** (perf **ist gleich geblieben**) *vi* (unreg) to remain the same.

**gleichen** (prät **glich**; perf **hat geglichen**) *vi*: **jm/einer Sache ~** to be like ODER resemble sb/sthg; **sich** (D) **~** to resemble each other.

**gleichermaßen** *adv* equally.

**gleichfalls** *adv* also, as well; **danke ~!** thanks, you too!

**gleichförmig** *adj* - **1.** [einheitlich] uniform - **2.** [eintönig] monotonous ⬦ *adv* - **1.** [einheitlich] uniformly - **2.** [eintönig] monotonously.

**gleich gesinnt** *adj* like-minded.

**Gleichgewicht** *das* - **1.** [Balance] balance; **im ~** balanced; **das ~ halten/verlieren** to keep/lose one's balance - **2.** [Harmonie] equilibrium; **die Veränderungen brachten sie völlig aus dem ~** the changes threw her completely off balance.

**gleichgültig** *adj* - **1.** [desinteressiert] indifferent - **2.** [einerlei - Themen] trivial; **es ist ~, ob er kommt oder nicht** it's all the same whether he comes or not; **sie ist mir ~** she means nothing to me; **Politik ist ihm völlig ~** he's completely indifferent about politics ⬦ *adv* [desinteressiert] indifferently; **~ was er macht ...** no matter what he does ...

**Gleichheit** *die* - **1.** [Übereinstimmung] similarity - **2.** [Gleichberechtigung] equality.

**Gleichheitsprinzip** *das* principle of equality.

**Gleichklang** *der* harmony.

**gleich|kommen** (perf **ist gleichgekommen**) *vi* (unreg): **einer Sache** (D) **~** to amount to sthg; **jm an etw** (D) **~** to match sb for sthg.

**gleich lautend** *adj* identical.

**gleichmäßig** *adj* - **1.** [Atmung, Schritte, Schichten] even - **2.** [Geschwindigkeit, Rhythmus] steady - **3.** [Abstände] regular ⬦ *adv* - **1.** [atmen, anordnen, verteilen] evenly - **2.** [sich vorwärts bewegen] steadily - **3.** [wiederkehrend]: **~ hohe Punktzahlen** consistently high scores.

**Gleichmäßigkeit** *die* - **1.** [von Atemzügen, Verteilung] evenness - **2.** [von Bewegung] steadiness - **3.** [von Werten] consistency.

**Gleichmut** *der* impassiveness.

**gleichmütig** *adj* impassive ⟨⟩ *adv* impassively.

**Gleichnis** (*pl* **-se**) *das* parable.

**gleichrangig** *adj* [Stellung, Mitarbeiter] of equal rank; [Problem, Arbeit, Kriterium] of equal importance ⟨⟩ *adv* equally.

**gleich|schalten** [ˈglaiçʃaltn̩] *vt abw* to bring into line.

**gleichschenklig** [ˈglaiçʃɛŋk(ə)lɪç], **gleichschenkelig** *adj* MATH: **~es Dreieck** isosceles triangle.

**Gleichschritt** *der:* **im ~** in step.

**gleichseitig** [ˈglaiçzaitɪç] *adj* equilateral; **~es Dreieck** equilateral triangle.

**gleich|setzen** [ˈglaiçzɛtsn̩] *vt* to equate.

**gleich|stellen** [ˈglaiçʃtɛlən] *vt* to treat equally; **die Arbeiter (mit) den Angestellten finanziell ~** to bring blue-collar workers' wages into line with those of white-collar workers.

**Gleichstrom** *der* direct current.

**gleich|tun** *vt (unreg):* **es jm ~** to do the same as sb.

**Gleichung** (*pl* **-en**) *die* equation.

**gleichviel** *adv* no matter.

**gleichwertig** *adj* equally good ⟨⟩ *adv* equally.

**gleichzeitig** *adj* simultaneous ⟨⟩ *adv* at the same time.

**gleich|ziehen** *vi (unreg):* **mit jm ~** to draw level with sb, to catch up with sb.

**Gleis** (*pl* **-e**) *das* **- 1.** [Schienen] track; [Bahnsteig] platform **- 2.** *RW:* **sich in ausgefahrenen ~en bewegen** to follow a well-trodden path.

**gleiten** (*prät* **glitt**, *perf* **hat/ist geglitten**) *vi* **- 1.** *(ist)* [sich bewegen] to glide; [rutschen] to slip **- 2.** *(hat)* *fam* [Arbeitnehmer] to work flexitime *Br* ODER flextime *Am.*

**Gleit|schirm** *der:* **~ fliegen** to go paragliding.

**Gleit|schirmfliegen** *das* paragliding.

**Gleit|zeit** *die* flexitime *Br,* flextime *Am.*

**Gletscher** (*pl* **-**) *der* glacier.

**glich** *prät* ⟘ **gleichen**.

**Glied** (*pl* **-er**) *das* **- 1.** [Gelenk] joint **- 2.** [Körperteil] limb; **es steckt** ODER **sitzt mir in den ~ern noch** I'm still feeling the effects of it **- 3.** [Penis] (male) member **- 4.** [Bindeglied - von Kette] link **- 5.** [Einzelteil] part; [von Satz] clause.

**gliedern** *vt* to organize, to structure.
➥ **sich gliedern** *ref:* **sich in etw** *(A)* **~** to be divided into sthg.

**Gliederung** (*pl* **-en**) *die* **- 1.** [Gliedern] organization, structuring **- 2.** [Struktur] structure.

**Gliedmaßen** *pl* limbs.

**glimmen** (*prät* **glimmte** ODER **glomm**; *perf* **hat geglimmt** ODER **geglommen**) *vi* to glow.

**glimpflich** *adj* **- 1.** [ohne Schaden]: **die Entführung nahm ein ~es Ende** the kidnapping was resolved without anyone being seriously hurt **- 2.** [nachsichtig] lenient ⟨⟩ *adv* **- 1.** [ohne Schaden] without serious consequences; **~ davonkommen** to get off lightly **- 2.** [nachsichtig] leniently.

**glitschig** *adj* slippery.

**glitt** *prät* ⟘ **gleiten**.

**glitzern** *vi* [Sterne] to twinkle; [Schmuck, Augen] to sparkle; [Schnee, Tränen] to glisten; [Silber, Gold] to glitter.

**global** *adj* **- 1.** [weltumfassend] global; [Frieden] world *(vor Subst)* **- 2.** [vielseitig, allgemein] general ⟨⟩ *adv* **- 1.** [weltumfassend] globally **- 2.** [vielseitig, allgemein] generally.

**Globalisierung** *die* globalization.

**Globus** (*pl* **-se** ODER **Globen**) *der* globe.

**Glocke** (*pl* **-n**) *die* bell; **etw an die große ~ hängen** *fam fig* to shout sthg from the rooftops.

**Glocken|blume** *die* campanula.

**Glocken|schlag** *der* chime.

**Glocken|spiel** *das* **- 1.** [von Türmen] carillon **- 2.** [Musikinstrument] glockenspiel.

**Glocken|turm** *der* belfry, bell tower.

**glomm** *prät* ⟘ **glimmen**.

**glorreich** *adj* [Sieg, Geschichte, Ergebnis] glorious; [Einfall] brilliant ⟨⟩ *adv* triumphantly.

**Glossar** (*pl* **-e**) *das* glossary.

**Glosse** (*pl* **-n**) *die* commentary.

**Glotze** *die* salopp box, telly *Br.*

**glotzen** *vi fam abw* to gawk, to gawp *Br.*

**Glück** *das* **- 1.** [Glücksfall] luck; **ein ~, dass ...** it's lucky that ...; **~ bringen** to bring luck, to be lucky; **~ haben** to be lucky; **bei jm (mit etw** *(D)***) kein ~ haben** to get no joy out of sb (with sthg); **er hat ~ mit den Frauen** he's a hit with the ladies; **er hatte mit dem Auto kein ~** he had no luck with the car; **du kannst von ~ sagen** ODER **reden** you can count yourself lucky; **sein ~ versuchen** to try one's luck **- 2.** [Fortuna] fortune; **das ~ verließ ihn** *geh* fortune ODER luck abandoned him **- 3.** [Segen] happiness; **das Kind war ihr ganzes ~** the child meant everything to her.
➥ **auf gut Glück** *adv* on the off chance.
➥ **viel Glück** *interj* good luck!
➥ **zum Glück** *adv* luckily, fortunately.

**Glucke** (*pl* **-n**) *die* mother hen.

**glücken** (*perf* **ist geglückt**) *vi* to be successful; **ihm glückt alles, was er in Angriff nimmt** he succeeds at everything he does.

**gluckern** *vi* [Wasser, Flüssigkeit] to gurgle; [Wein] to glug.

**glücklich** *adj* **- 1.** [Person, Ehe, Ende] happy **- 2.** [Zufall] happy, lucky; [Zeitpunkt, Reise] good **- 3.** [Sieger, Sieg] lucky <> *adv* **- 1.** [verheiratet, enden] happily **- 2.** [letztendlich] eventually.

**glücklicherweise** *adv* luckily, fortunately.

**Glücksbringer** (*pl* -) *der* [Sache] lucky charm; [Person] lucky mascot.

**Glücks|fall** *der* stroke of luck.

**Glücks|pilz** *der fam* lucky so-and-so.

**Glücks|sache** *die*: **es war ~** it was pure luck.

**Glücks|spiel** *das* **- 1.** [um Geld] game of chance **- 2.** [Glückssache] lottery.

**Glücks|strähne** *die* lucky streak.

**glückstrahlend** *adj* radiant, beaming (with happiness) <> *adv* radiantly.

**Glück|wunsch** *der* congratulations (*pl*); **jm seine Glückwünsche aussprechen** to congratulate sb, to offer sb one's congratulations; **herzlichen ~ zum Geburtstag!** happy birthday!; **herzliche Glückwünsche!** congratulations!

**Glückwunsch|karte** *die* greetings card.

**Glucose** = Glukose.

**Glüh|birne** *die* light bulb.

**glühen** *vi* **- 1.** [brennen] to glow **- 2.** *geh* [bewegt sein] to burn.

**glühend** *adj* **- 1.** [brennend] glowing; [Metall, Nadel] red-hot; [Hitze] scorching **- 2.** [leidenschaftlich] passionate; [Neid] deep <> *adv* [leidenschaftlich] passionately.

**Glüh|lampe** *die* light bulb.

**Glüh|wein** *der* mulled wine.

**Glukose, Glucose** *die* glucose.

**Glut** (*pl* -en) *die* **- 1.** [in Feuer] embers (*pl*) **- 2.** *geh* [Inbrunst] ardour.

**GmbH** [geːɛmbeːˈhaː] (*pl* -s) (*abk für* **Gesellschaft mit beschränkter Haftung**) *die* ≃ Ltd *Br*, ≃ Inc *Am*.

**g-Moll** *das* MUS G minor.

**Gnade** *die* **- 1.** [Gunst] favour **- 2.** [Erbarmen - menschlich] mercy; [ - göttlich] grace.

**Gnadenfrist** *die* reprieve.

**gnadenlos** *adj* merciless; [Hitze, Druck, Stress] unrelenting <> *adv* mercilessly; [heiß] mercilessly, unrelentingly.

**Gnadenstoß** *der* coup de grâce.

**gnädig** *adj* **- 1.** [wohlmeinend] kind **- 2.** [nachsichtig] lenient **- 3.** [barmherzig] merciful <> *adv* **- 1.** [wohlmeinend] kindly **- 2.** [nachsichtig] leniently.
➡ **gnädige Frau** *interj* Madam!

**Gnom** (*pl* -en) *der* gnome.

**Gockel** (*pl* -) *der* cock.

**Gold** *das* gold; **eine Uhr aus ~** a gold watch; **~ wert sein** *fig* to be invaluable.

**Gold|barren** *der* gold bar ODER ingot.

**golden** *adj* **- 1.** [aus Gold] gold **- 2.** [goldfarben] golden **- 3.** [großartig - Jahre, Zeit] golden; [ - Freiheit, Moment] glorious <> *adv* [glänzen] like gold.

**Gold|fisch** *der* goldfish.

**goldgelb** *adj* & *adv* golden yellow.

**Gold|grube** *die fam* goldmine.

**Gold|hamster** *der* golden hamster.

**goldig** *adj fam* sweet, lovely.

**Gold|medaille** *die* gold medal.

**Gold|münze** *die* gold coin.

**Gold|schmied, in** *der, die* goldsmith.

**Gold|waage** *die* gold scales (*pl*); **alles** ODER **jedes Wort auf die ~ legen** *fig* [alles wörtlich auffassen] to take everything literally; *fam* [sich bedächtig äußern] to weigh one's words carefully.

**Golf** (*pl* -e) *der* gulf <> *das* golf.

**Golf|platz** *der* golf course.

**Golf|spieler, in** *der, die* golfer.

**Golf|staaten** *pl* Gulf States.

**Golf|strom** *der* Gulf Stream.

**Gondel** (*pl* -n) *die* gondola.

**Gong** [gɔŋ] (*pl* -s) *der* gong.

**gönnen** *vt*: **jm etw ~** not to begrudge sb sthg; **sich** (D) **etw ~** to allow o.s. sthg.

**Gönner** (*pl* -) *der* patron.

**gönnerhaft** *abw adj* patronizing <> *adv* patronizingly.

**Gönnerin** (*pl* -nen) *die* patron, patroness.

**Göre** (*pl* -n) *die* **Norddt** *abw* **- 1.** [Kind] brat **- 2.** [unartiges Mädchen] little minx.

**Gorilla** (*pl* -s) *der eigtl* & *fig* gorilla.

**goss** *prät* ⊳ **gießen**.

**Gosse** (*pl* -n) *die* gutter; **in der ~ landen** ODER **enden** *abw* to end up in the gutter.

**Gote** (*pl* -n) *der* Goth.

**Gotik** *die* (*ohne pl*) [Stil] Gothic (style); [Epoche] Gothic period.

**Gotin** (*pl* -nen) *die* Goth.

**gotisch** *adj* Gothic.

**Gott** (*pl* Götter) *der* **- 1.** [christlich] God; **du lieber ~!, oh (mein) ~!** oh (my) God!; **über ~ und die Welt reden** *fam* to talk about everything under the sun; **in ~es Namen** for heaven's sake; **um ~es Willen!** [Schrecken ausdrückend] oh my God!; [flehend] for heaven's sake! **- 2.** [Gottheit] god.
➡ **Gott sei Dank** *adv* thank goodness.
➡ **grüß Gott** *interj* **Süddt, Österr** hello!
➡ **leider Gottes** *adv* unfortunately.
➡ **weiß Gott** *adv* God knows.

**Götterspeise** *die* jelly *Br*, jello *Am*.

**Gottes|dienst** *der* service; **zum ~ gehen** to go to church.

**Gotteslästerung** (*pl* -en) *die* blasphemy.

**Gottheit** (*pl* -en) *die* - **1.** [Gott, Göttin] god, deity - **2.** *geh* [Göttlichkeit] divinity.

**Göttin** (*pl* -nen) *die* goddess.

**Göttingen** *nt* Göttingen.

**göttlich** *adj eigtl* & *fig* divine <> *adv* [wunderbar] divinely.

**gottlos** *adj* - **1.** [respektlos, gottvergessen] ungodly - **2.** [ungläubig] godless <> *adv* [respektlos, gottvergessen] in an ungodly manner.

**gottverlassen** *adj* godforsaken.

**Götze** (*pl* -n) *der* idol.

**Gouverneur, in** [guvɛrˈnøːɐ̯, rɪn] (*mpl* -e; *fpl* -nen) *der, die* governor.

**GPS** [geːpeːˈʔɛs] (*abk für* **Grüne Partei der Schweiz**) *die* Swiss Green Party.

**Grab** (*pl* Gräber) *das* grave; **jn ins ~ bringen** *fig* to be the death of sb.

**graben** (*präs* gräbt; *prät* grub; *perf* hat gegraben) *vt* & *vi* to dig.
➡ **sich graben** *ref:* **sich in etw** (A) **~** [Krallen, Rad] to sink into sthg.

**Graben** (*pl* Gräben) *der* ditch; [um eine Festung] moat; [Schützengraben] trench.

**Grab|mal** (*pl* -mäler *ODER* -e) *das* tomb.

**Grab|stätte** *die* grave.

**Grab|stein** *der* gravestone, tombstone.

**gräbt** *präs* ▷ graben.

**Grabung** (*pl* -en) *die* excavation.

**Grad** (*pl* -e) *der* - **1.** [gen] degree; **es hängt in hohem ~ davon ab, ob ...** it depends to a large extent on whether ...; **die Temperatur beträgt 25 ~** the temperature is 25 degrees; **in hohem ~ verschmutzt** highly polluted - **2.** MIL rank.

**graduell** *adj* - **1.** [allmählich] gradual - **2.** [Unterschied] slight <> *adv* - **1.** [allmählich] gradually - **2.** [unterschiedlich] slightly.

**gradweise** *adv* gradually.

**Graf** (*pl* -en) *der* count.

**Graffitti** [graˈfɪti] (*pl* -s) *das* piece of graffiti; **~s** graffiti (U).

**Grafik, Graphik** (*pl* -en) *die* - **1.** [Kunst] graphic art; [Technik] graphics (U) - **2.** [Kunstwerk] graphic artwork - **3.** [Schema] diagram.

**Grafiker, Graphiker** (*pl* -) *der* graphic artist.

**Grafikerin, Graphikerin** (*pl* -nen) *die* graphic artist.

**Grafik|karte** *die* EDV graphics card.

**Grafik|programm** *das* EDV graphics program.

**Gräfin** (*pl* -nen) *die* countess.

**grafisch, graphisch** *adj* - **1.** [die Kunst betreffend] graphic - **2.** [schematisch] diagrammatic <> *adv* - **1.** [künstlerisch] graphically - **2.** [schematisch] diagrammatically.

**grafologisch, graphologisch** *adj* graphological <> *adv* graphologically.

**Grafschaft** (*pl* -en) *die* - **1.** [von Graf] count's lands (*pl*) - **2.** [Verwaltungsbezirk] county.

**Gram** *der geh* grief, sorrow.

**grämen** *vt geh* to grieve.
➡ **sich grämen** *ref geh* to be grieved.

**Gramm** (*pl* -e *ODER* -) *das* gram; **500 ~** 500 grams.

**Grammatik** (*pl* -en) *die* grammar.

**grammatikalisch, grammatisch** *adj* grammatical <> *adv* grammatically.

**Granada** *nt* Granada.

**Granat|apfel** *der* pomegranate.

**Granate** (*pl* -n) *die* shell; [Handgranate] grenade.

**grandios** *adj* superb <> *adv* superbly.

**Granit** *der* granite.

**grantig** *fam adj* grumpy <> *adv* grumpily.

**Grapefruit** [ˈɡreːpfruːt] (*pl* -s) *die* grapefruit.

**Graphik** = Grafik.

**Graphiker** = Grafiker.

**Graphikerin** = Grafikerin.

**graphisch** = grafisch.

**graphologisch** *adj* = grafologisch.

**Gras** (*pl* Gräser) *das* grass; **darüber ist ~ gewachsen** *fam* that's water under the bridge; **wir sollten warten bis ~ über die Sache gewachsen ist** we should wait until the dust has settled; **ins ~ beißen** *salopp* to bite the dust.

**grasen** *vi* to graze; **Kühe ~ lassen** to graze cattle.

**Gras|fläche** *die* area of grass.

**grasgrün** *adj* grass-green.

**Gras|halm** *der* blade of grass.

**grassieren** *vi* [Krankheit, Pest] to rage; [Mode] to be all the rage.

**grässlich** *adj* terrible <> *adv* terribly.

**Grat** (*pl* -e) *der* ridge.

**Gräte** (*pl* -n) *die* (fish) bone.

**gratis** *adj* & *adv* free (of charge).

**Gratis|probe** *die* free sample.

**Grätsche** (*pl* -n) *die:* **eine ~ über etw** (A) **machen** to hurdle sthg; **in der ~ stehen** to stand with one's legs astride.

**Gratulant, in** (*mpl* -en; *fpl* -nen) *der, die* well-wisher.

**Gratulation** (*pl* -en) *die* congratulations (*pl*).

G

**gratulieren** *vi* to offer one's congratulations; **jm (zu etw)** ~ to congratulate sb (on sthg); **jm zum Geburtstag** ~ to wish sb a happy birthday.

**grau** *adj* grey; ~ **meliert** [Haar] greying; [Wolle, Stoff] flecked with grey.

**Grau** *das* - **1.** [graue Farbe] grey - **2.** [Tristheit] greyness.

**graublau** *adj* grey-blue.

**Graulbrot** *das bread made from mixed wholemeal, rye and wheat flour.*

**Graubünden** *nt* Graubünden.

**Graubündner, in** (*mpl* -; *fpl* **-nen**) *der, die* native/inhabitant of Graubünden.

**graubündnerisch** *adj* of/from Graubünden.

**Gräuel** (*pl* -) *der* horror; **er/es ist mir ein** ~ *fig* I loathe him/it.

**Gräuelltat** *die* atrocity.

**grauen** *vi* - **1.** *geh* [dämmern]: **der Morgen** ODER **der Tag graut** day is dawning - **2.** [zum Grauen sein]: **es graut ihm vor der Prüfung** he's dreading the exam.

➡ **sich grauen** *ref* [Grauen empfinden]: **sich (vor jm/ etw)** ~ to be terrified (of sb/sthg).

**Grauen** (*pl* -) *das* - **1.** [Angst, Schrecken] dread - **2.** [Ereignis] horror.

**grauenhaft, grauenvoll** *adj* terrible ◇ *adv* terribly.

**grauhaarig** *adj* grey-haired.

**gräulich** *adj* - **1.** [grau] greyish - **2.** [entsetzlich, unerfreulich] terrible ◇ *adv* [entsetzlich, unerfreulich] terribly.

**Graupe** (*pl* -n) *die:* ~n pearl barley (*U*).

**Graupellschauer** *der* shower of fine hail.

**Graus** *der* horror.

**grausam** *adj* - **1.** [brutal] cruel - **2.** [fürchterlich, schlimm] terrible ◇ *adv* - **1.** [brutal] cruelly - **2.** [fürchterlich, äußerst] terribly.

**Grausamkeit** (*pl* -en) *die* - **1.** (*ohne pl*) [grausames Wesen] cruelty - **2.** [grausame Tat] atrocity.

**grausen** *vi*: **es grauste ihr vor ihm** she was terrified of him.

➡ **sich grausen** *ref*: **sich vor jm/etw** ~ to be terrified of sb/sthg.

**grausig** *adj* terrible ◇ *adv* terribly.

**Graulzone** *die* grey area.

**gravieren** [gra'viːrən] *vt* to engrave; **etw in etw** (*A*) ~ to engrave sthg on sthg.

**gravierend** [gra'viːrənt] *adj* [Problem, Fehler, Vorwurf] serious; [Unterschied, Änderung] significant ◇ *adv* significantly.

**Gravur** [gra'vuːɐ̯] (*pl* -en) *die* engraving.

**Graz** *nt* Graz.

**Grazie** (*pl* -n) *die* grace; **mit** ~ gracefully.

➡ **Grazien** *pl* MYTH Graces.

**graziös** *adj* graceful ◇ *adv* gracefully.

**greifbar** *adj* - **1.** [in Reichweite] to hand, handy - **2.** [parat] available - **3.** [absehbar] tangible ◇ *adv* [sehr]: ~ **nahe** within reach.

**greifen** (*prät* **griff**; *perf* **hat gegriffen**) *vt* - **1.** [fassen] to take hold of; **das liegt zum Greifen nahe** *fig* it is within grasp - **2.** [erwischen] to catch - **3.** [Akkord] to play ◇ *vi* - **1.** [fassen]: **zu etw** ~ to reach for sthg; [Maßnahmen] to resort to sthg; **zur Flasche/Zigarette** ~ *fig* to reach for the bottle/cigarettes; **nach etw** ~ to reach for sthg; [Macht] to strive for sthg - **2.** [langen] to reach; **in etw** (*A*) ~ to reach into sthg - **3.** [Halt finden] to grip; [Zahnrad] to catch - **4.** [funktionieren] to work - **5.** RW: **um sich** ~ to spread; **die Zahl ist zu hoch/niedrig gegriffen** the number is an overestimate/underestimate; **ihre Erwartungen sind zu hoch/ niedrig gegriffen** she has set her sights too high/low.

**Greiflvogel** *der* bird of prey.

**Greis, in** (*mpl* -e; *fpl* **-nen**) *der, die* old man (*f* old woman).

**grell** *adj* - **1.** [Licht, Sonne, Lampe] glaring; [Farbe, Muster] garish - **2.** [Geräusch] shrill ◇ *adv* - **1.** [scheinen, leuchten] glaringly; [bunt, gefärbt] garishly - **2.** [klingen, rufen] shrilly.

**Gremium** (*pl* **Gremien**) *das* committee.

**Grenzlbeamte** *der* customs and immigration officer.

**Grenzlbeamtin** *die* customs and immigration officer.

**Grenzlbereich** *der* - **1.** (*ohne pl*) [von Ländern] border area - **2.** [Begrenzung] limits (*pl*).

**Grenze** (*pl* -n) *die* - **1.** [Staatsgrenze] border - **2.** [Gebietsgrenze] boundary - **3.** [Trennlinie] dividing line, boundary - **4.** [Beschränkung] limit; **keine ~n kennen** to know no bounds; **ihrem Eifer sind keine ~n gesetzt** there are no limits to her enthusiasm.

➡ **grüne Grenze** *die:* **über die grüne** ~ **gehen** to cross the border at a point in the countryside where there is no border control.

**grenzen** *vi*: **an etw** (*A*) ~ [Gebiet, Land] to border sthg; [Betrug, Tollkühnheit] to border ODER verge on sthg; **aneinander** ~ to have a common border.

**grenzenlos** *adj* [Landschaft, Vertrauen, Liebe] boundless; [Verlegenheit, Sorge, Ekel] extreme ◇ *adv* [weit, lieben, begeistert] boundlessly; [verlegen, erstaunt, traurig] extremely.

**Grenzlfall** *der* borderline case.

**Grenzlkonflikt** *der* border conflict.

**Grenzlkontrolle** *die* border check.

**Grenzlposten** *der* border guard.

**Grenz|schutz** *der (ohne pl)* border police; [in Deutschland] ⊳ **Bundesgrenzschutz.**

**Grenzüber|gang** *der* - **1.** [Grenzüberschreitung]: **beim ~** while crossing the border - **2.** [Grenzkontrollstelle] border crossing.

**grenzüberschreitend** *adj* cross-border ⟨⟩ *adv* at a cross-border level.

**Grenzverkehr** *der* cross-border traffic.

**Grenz|wert** *der* limit.

**Greuel** *der* = **Gräuel.**

**Greueltat** *die* = **Gräueltat.**

**greulich** = **gräulich.**

**Grieche** (*pl* -n) *der* Greek.

**Griechenland** *nt* Greece.

**Griechin** (*pl* -nen) *die* Greek.

**griechisch** *adj* Greek.

**Griechisch(e)** *das* Greek; *siehe auch* **Englisch(e).**

**griesgrämig** *adj* grumpy ⟨⟩ *adv* grumpily.

**Grieß** *der* semolina.

**Grieß|brei** *der* semolina pudding.

**griff** *prät* ⊳ **greifen.**

**Griff** (*pl* -e) *der* - **1.** [Greifen] grip; [von Ringer] hold; **beim ~ in die Tasche** on reaching into the pocket; **der ~ nach der Flasche** reaching for the bottle; **etw mit einem ~ tun** to do sthg in next to no time; **etw im ~ haben/bekommen** *fig* to be/get on top of sthg; **jn in den ~ bekommen** *ODER* **kriegen** *fig* to gain control of sb - **2.** [Teil, Henkel] handle.

**griffbereit** *adj* & *adv* ready to hand.

**griffig** *adj* - **1.** [handlich] easy to use - **2.** [gut greifend] with a good grip.

**Grill** (*pl* -s) *der* grill.

**Grille** (*pl* -n) *die* - **1.** [Insekt] cricket - **2.** [verrückte Idee] whim.

**grillen** *vt* to grill ⟨⟩ *vi* to have a barbecue.

**Grill|fest** *das* barbecue.

**Grimasse** (*pl* -n) *die* grimace; **~n schneiden** to pull faces.

**grimmig** *adj* - **1.** [Gesicht, Ausdruck] grim; [Feind] fierce - **2.** [Kälte, Hunger] terrible ⟨⟩ *adv* [lachen] grimly.

**grinsen** *vi* to grin.

**Grinsen** *das* grin.

**Grippe** (*pl* -n) *die* flu.

**Grippeschutz|impfung** *die* flu vaccination.

**Grips** *der (ohne pl) fam* brains (*pl*); **seinen ~ anstrengen** to use one's brain.

**grob** (*kompar* **gröber;** *superl* **gröbste**) *adj* - **1.** [Sand, Salz, Züge] coarse - **2.** [Leinen, Haut, Papier, Übersicht, Skizze] rough - **3.** [unhöflich] crude - **4.** [schlimm] serious; **aus dem Gröbsten heraus**

**sein** [Kind] to be old enough to look after oneself ⟨⟩ *adv* - **1.** [mahlen, hacken] coarsely - **2.** [planen, schätzen] roughly - **3.** [schwer wiegend]: **~ fahrlässig handeln** to be grossly negligent - **4.** [unhöflich] crudely.

**Grobheit** (*pl* -en) *die* - **1.** [grobe Wesensart] crudeness - **2.** [Äußerung] crude remark.

**grobkörnig** *adj* coarse.

**grobmaschig** *adj* wide-meshed.

**Grog** (*pl* -s) *der* hot toddy.

**grölen** *abw vi* & *vt* to bawl.

**Groll** *der (ohne pl) geh* resentment; **einen ~ auf jn haben** to bear sb a grudge.

**grollen** *vi geh* - **1.** [verstimmt sein] to be sullen; **jm ~** to bear sb a grudge - **2.** [dröhnen] to rumble.

**Grönland** *nt* Greenland.

**Grönländer, in** (*mpl* -; *fpl* -nen) *der, die* Greenlander.

**grönländisch** *adj* of/from Greenland.

**Gros** [gro:] (*pl* -) *das* majority.

**Groschen** (*pl* -) *der* - **1.** [10 deutsche Pfennig] tenpfennig coin; **bei ihm ist der ~ gefallen** *fam fig* the penny dropped *Br*, he got it - **2.** [österreichische Münze] groschen.

**groß** (*kompar* **größer;** *superl* **größte**) *adj* - **1.** [räumlich] big, large; [Person] tall; **sie ist 1,80 ~** she's 1.80 m (tall) - **2.** [zahlreich]: **eine ~e Familie** a big *ODER* large family; **eine ~e Vielfalt** a wide variety - **3.** [zeitlich] big; **die ~en Ferien** the summer holidays - **4.** [intensiv] great; **eine ~e Enttäuschung** a great disappointment; **sich ~e Mühe geben** to try hard - **5.** [älter] big; **mein ~er Bruder** my big brother - **6.** [erwachsen] grown-up - **7.** [Buchstabe] capital - **8.** [bedeutend] great; **ein ~er Dichter** a great poet; **heute kommt meine ~e Stunde** it's my big moment today; **~e Fortschritte machen** to make great progress ⟨⟩ *adv* (*kompar* **größer;** *superl* **am größten**) - **1.** [räumlich]: **ein ~ angelegtes Projekt** a large-scale project - **2.** [sehr] a lot; **wir haben dann nicht mehr ~ gearbeitet** we didn't do a lot of work afterwards; **~ und breit** *fam* at great length - **3.** [im großen Stil] in style; **der Sänger ist ~ herausgekommen** the singer became a big success - **4.** [erstaunt]: **jn ~ ansehen** to stare at sb wide-eyed - **5.** [Buchstabe]: **es wird ~ geschrieben** it's written with a capital letter.

➤ **Groß und Klein** *pron*: **ein Buch für Groß und Klein** a book for young and old.

➤ **im Großen und Ganzen** *pron*: **im Großen und Ganzen** on the whole, by and large.

**großartig** *adj* - **1.** [gut] marvellous - **2.** [angeberisch] showy ⟨⟩ *adv* - **1.** [gut] marvellously - **2.** [angeberisch] showily.

**Groß|aufnahme** *die* close-up.

**Großbritannien** *nt* Great Britain.

**Groß|buchstabe** *der* capital (letter).

**Größe** (*pl* -n) *die* - **1.** [von Gegenständen, Baby, Kleidern] size - **2.** [von Personen] height - **3.** [Wichtigkeit] greatness - **4.** [Person] leading figure - **5.** MATH: eine unbekannte ~ an unknown quantity.

**großenteils** *adv* largely.

**Größen|unterschied** *der* - **1.** [von Dingen] difference in size - **2.** [von Personen] difference in height.

**Größenwahn** *der abw* megalomania.

**größenwahnsinnig** *adj* megalomaniac.

**größer** *adj* bigger, larger; eine ~e Summe quite a large sum; ohne ~e Schwierigkeiten without any great difficulty.

**Groß|familie** *die* extended family.

**Groß|format** *das* large format.

**Großglockner** *der* Grossglockner.

**Großgrund|besitzer, in** *der, die* big landowner.

**Groß|handel** *der* wholesale trade; etw im ~ beziehen to get sthg wholesale.

**Groß|händler, in** *der, die* wholesaler.

**Groß|handlung** *die* wholesale business.

**großherzig** *geh adj* magnanimous <> *adv* magnanimously.

**Groß|industrie** *die* big industry.

**Groß|macht** *die* great power.

**Groß|maul** *das fam abw* big mouth.

**großmütig** *adj* generous <> *adv* generously.

**Groß|mutter** *die* grandmother.

**Großraum|büro** *das* open-plan office.

**Großraum|wagen** *der* open carriage *Br* ODER car *Am*.

**Groß|rechner** *der* EDV mainframe.

**groß|schreiben** *vt (unreg)* [mit großem Anfangsbuchstaben] to write with a capital letter, to capitalize.

**Großschreibung** *die* capitalization.

**großspurig** *abw adj* pretentious <> *adv* pretentiously.

**Groß|stadt** *die* city (vor Subst).

**Groß|städter, in** *der, die* city-dweller.

**großstädtisch** *adj* city.

**Großteil** *der:* der ~ [Personen] the majority; [Sachen] most; ein ~ a large number/part; zum ~ for the most part.

**größtenteils** *adv* for the most part.

**größtmöglich** *adj* greatest possible.

**groß|tun** *vi (unreg) abw* to boast.
➡ sich großtun *ref:* sich mit jm/etw ~ to boast about sb/sthg.

**Groß|unternehmer, in** *der, die* big businessman (*f* big businesswoman).

**Groß|vater** *der* grandfather.

**Groß|verdiener, in** (*mpl* -; *fpl* -nen) *der, die* high earner.

**groß|ziehen** *vt (unreg)* [Kind] to bring up; [Tier] to rear.

**großzügig** *adj* - **1.** [Person, Geste] generous - **2.** [Raum] spacious <> *adv* - **1.** [freigebig, großmütig] generously - **2.** [weiträumig] spaciously.

**grotesk** *adj* grotesque.

**Grotte** (*pl* -n) *die* grotto.

**grub** *prät* ⊏➤ graben.

**Grübchen** (*pl* -) *das* dimple.

**Grube** (*pl* -n) *die* pit.

**Grübelei** (*pl* -en) *die* brooding (U).

**grübeln** *vi* to ponder.

**Grübeln** *das:* ins ~ kommen to start to ponder.

**Gruft** (*pl* Grüfte) *die* crypt.

**grün** *adj* - **1.** [farbig, unreif, ökologisch] green - **2.** RW: jn ~ und blau schlagen *fam* to beat sb black and blue <> *adv* [ökologisch]: ~ wählen to vote Green.

**Grün** (*pl* - ODER -s) *das* - **1.** green; das ist dasselbe in ~ *fig* it comes to the same thing - **2.** (ohne pl) [Pflanzen] greenery.
➡ bei Grün *adv* on green.

**Grün|anlage** *die* park.

**Grund** (*pl* Gründe) *der* - **1.** [Ursache] reason - **2.** (ohne pl) [Boden] ground; [von Meer, Bach, Glas] bottom; auf ~ laufen to run aground; ~ und Boden land - **3.** RW: einer Sache (D) auf den ~ gehen to try to get to the bottom of sthg; in ~ und Boden utterly; jn in ~ und Boden reden not to let sb get a word in edgeways.
➡ auf Grund = aufgrund.
➡ im Grunde *adv* basically.
➡ von Grund auf *adv* thoroughly.
➡ zu Grunde *adv* = zugrunde.

**Grund|ausbildung** *die* MIL basic training.

**Grund|ausstattung** *die* basic equipment.

**Grund|bedürfnis** *das* basic need.

**Grund|begriff** *der* basic principle.

**Grund|besitz** *der* land.

**Grund|buch** *das* land register.

**gründen** *vt* [Partei, Unternehmen] to found; [Familie] to start; [Stiftung] to set up <> *vi* [basieren auf]: auf etw (D) ~ to be based on sthg.
➡ sich gründen *ref:* sich auf etw (A) ~ to be based on sthg.

**Gründer, in** (*mpl* -; *fpl* -nen) *der, die* founder.

**grundfalsch** *adj* completely wrong.

**Grund|gebühr** *die* standing charge.

**Grundlgedanke** *der* basic idea.
**Grundlgesetz** *das* Basic Law.

> **GRUNDGESETZ**
>
> Originally drafted as a provisional constitution, the German constitution has proved to be a solid basis for democracy. Since it was promulgated in 1949, Germany has not undergone any serious constitutional crises. It was retained, with a few amendments, after the reunification of Germany.

**grundieren** *vt* to prime.
**Grundkenntnisse** *pl* basic knowledge *(U)*.
**Grundlkurs** *der* basic course.
**Grundllage** *die* basis.
**grundlegend** *adj* fundamental ⟨⟩ *adv* fundamentally.
**gründlich** *adj* thorough ⟨⟩ *adv* thoroughly; **sich ~ blamieren** to make a complete fool of o.s.
**Gründlichkeit** *die* thoroughness.
**Grundllohn** *der* basic wage.
**grundlos** *adj* unfounded ⟨⟩ *adv* without reason; **~ lachen** to laugh for no reason.
**Grundnahrungslmittel** *das* basic foodstuff.
**Gründonnerstag** *der* Maundy Thursday.
**Grundlrecht** *das* basic right.
**Grundlriss** *der* [von Gebäude] ground plan; [Schema] outline.
**Grundlsatz** *der* principle.
**grundsätzlich** *adj* - **1.** [wichtig] fundamental - **2.** [allgemein] basic - **3.** [bedingungslos] on principle ⟨⟩ *adv* - **1.** [allgemein] basically - **2.** [bedingungslos] on principle - **3.** [grundlegend] fundamentally; **sich ~ äußern** to state one's principles.
**Grundlschule** *die* primary school *Br*, elementary school *Am* (for pupils aged 6 to 10).
**Grundstein** *der*: **den ~ zu etw legen** to lay the foundation stone for sthg; *fig* to lay the foundations for sthg.
**Grundlsteuer** *die* real property tax.
**Grundlstück** *das* plot of land.
**Gründung** *(pl* **-en)** *die* [von Partei, Verein] foundation *(sg)*; [von Familie] starting *(U)*; [von Stiftung] setting up *(U)*.
**grundverschieden** *adj* completely different.
**Grundlwasser** *das* ground water.
**Grundwasserlspiegel** *der* water table.
**Grundlzahl** *die* MATH cardinal number.
**Grüne** *(pl* **-n)** *das* - **1.** [Farbe] green - **2.** [Natur]: **im ~n/ins ~** in/into the country ⟨⟩ *der*, *die* POL Green.

**grünen** *vi geh* to be green.
**Grünen** *pl*: **die ~** the Greens.
**Grüne Punkt** *der* (ohne pl) symbol on product packaging indicating that it is suitable for recycling.
**Grünlfläche** *die* green area.
**Grünlkohl** *der* kale.
**grünlich** *adj* greenish ⟨⟩ *adv* with a greenish colour.
**Grünlspan** *der* verdigris.
**grunzen** *vi* to grunt.
**Gruppe** *(pl* **-n)** *die* group.
**Gruppenlarbeit** *die* [im Unterricht] group work.
**Gruppenlbild** *das* group portrait.
**Gruppenldynamik** *die* (ohne pl) group dynamics *(pl)*.
**Gruppenlreise** *die* group tour.
**Gruppenlsex** *der* group sex.
**gruppenweise** *adv* in groups.
**Gruppenzwang** *der* group pressure.
**gruppieren** *vt* to arrange.
➤ **sich gruppieren** *ref* to form a group/groups.
**Gruppierung** *(pl* **-en)** *die* grouping.
**gruselig** *adj* [von Film] spine-chilling; [von Erscheinung] eerie.
**gruseln** *vt*: **es gruselt jm** ODER **jn vor jm/etw** sb/sthg makes sb's flesh creep.
➤ **sich gruseln** *ref* to be frightened; **sich vor jm/etw ~** sb/sthg makes one's flesh creep.
**Gruß** *(pl* **Grüße)** *der* greeting; **jm Grüße von jm bestellen** ODER **ausrichten** to give sb sb's regards ODER best wishes; **herzliche Grüße!** greetings!; **viele Grüße!** best wishes!; **mit freundlichen Grüßen** yours sincerely.
**grüßen** *vt* - **1.** [begrüßen] to greet - **2.** [Gruß senden]: **jn von jm ~** to give sb sb's regards ODER best wishes; **grüß deine Mutter lässt dich ~** your mother sends (you) her regards ODER best wishes ⟨⟩ *vi* [begrüßen] to say hello.
➤ **grüß dich** *interj* hello!
➤ **grüß Gott** *interj Süddt* hello!
**grußlos** *adv* without saying hello/goodbye.
**Grußwort** *(pl* **-e)** *das* welcoming address.
**Grütze** *(pl* **-n)** *die* gruel; **rote ~** jelly-like dessert made of red berries, fruit juice and sugar.
**GSG9** *(abk für* **Grenzschutzgruppe)** *die* anti-terrorist unit of the German border police.
**Guadeloupe** *nt* Guadeloupe.
**Guatemala** *nt* Guatemala.
**gucken** *fam vi* to look ⟨⟩ *vt* [Fotos, Zeitschriften] to look at; [Fernsehen] to watch.
**Guerilla** [ɡeˈrɪlja] *(pl* **-s)** *die* guerilla unit.

**Guerilla|krieg** der guerilla war.

**Guillotine** [gijo'ti:nəl (pl -n) die guillotine.

**Guinea** [gi'ne:ɐ] nt Guinea.

**Guinea-Bissau** nt Guinea-Bissau.

**Gulasch** (pl -e ODER -s) das ODER der goulash.

**Gulasch|kanone** die large tureen used to serve hot food at outdoor public events.

**Gulasch|suppe** die goulash soup.

**Gulden** (pl -) der guilder.

**Gully** (pl -s) der drain.

**gültig** adj valid; **nicht mehr ~ sein** [Kreditkarte, Reisepass] to be no longer valid.

**Gültigkeit** die validity; **seine ~ verlieren** [Kreditkarte, Reisepass] to become invalid.

**Gummi** (pl -s) das ODER der - **1.** [Material] rubber - **2.** fam [Band] rubber band <> der rubber.

**Gummi|band** (pl -bänder) das (piece of) elastic.

**Gummi|bärchen** (pl -) das small gum-like sweet in the shape of a bear.

**Gummi|baum** der rubber plant.

**Gummihand|schuh** der rubber glove.

**Gummi|knüppel** der rubber truncheon.

**Gummi|paragraf** der fam elastic clause.

**Gummi|reifen** der rubber tyre.

**Gummi|ring** der - **1.** [Band] rubber band - **2.** [Dichtung - von Wasserhahn] rubber washer; [ - zwischen Deckel und Glas] sealing ring.

**Gummi|stiefel** der rubber boot, wellington Br.

**Gunst** die favour; **die ~ der Stunde nutzen** to seize the moment; **zu js ~en** in sb's favour; siehe auch **zugunsten.**

**günstig** adj - **1.** [Gelegenheit, Umstände] favourable - **2.** [Preis] good <> adv - **1.** [beeinflussen] favourably - **2.** [kaufen] for a good price.

**Gurgel** (pl -n) die throat; **jm an die ~ springen** fam to lay into sb.

**gurgeln** vi to gurgle; [mit Mundwasser] to gargle.

**Gurke** (pl -n) die - **1.** [Salatgurke] cucumber - **2.** [Gewürzgurke] gherkin.

**gurren** vi to coo.

**Gurt** (pl -e) der - **1.** [Sicherheitsgurt] belt - **2.** [Band] strap.

**Gürtel** (pl -) der belt; **den ~ enger schnallen müssen** fig to have to tighten one's belt.

**Gürtel|linie** die: **unter der ~** [unfair] below the belt; [anzüglich] near the bone.

**Gürtel|reifen** der radial (tyre).

**Gürtel|schnalle** die (belt) buckle.

**Gurtpflicht** die obligatory use of seat belts.

**Guru** (pl -s) der guru.

**Guss** (pl Güsse) der - **1.** [Gießen] casting (U); **der Text war aus einem ~** fig the text was a unified whole - **2.** [Wasserstrahl] stream - **3.** [Regen] downpour - **4.** [Zuckerguss] icing (U) Br, frosting (U) Am.

**Gusseisen** das cast iron.

**gusseisern** adj cast-iron.

**Gusto** (pl -s) der: **nach meinem/deinem/seinem ~** to my/your/his own taste.

**gut** (kompar besser; superl beste) adj - **1.** [gen] good; **in etw ~ sein** [fähig] to be good at sthg; **für etw ~ sein** [günstig] to be good for sthg; **das Mittel ist ~ gegen Magendrücken** this medicine is good for stomach ache; **du hast es ~!** you've got it easy!; **etw ~ sein lassen** fig to leave ODER drop sthg - **2.** [mehr als] good; **das war vor einem ~en Jahr** that was a good year ago <> adv (kompar besser; superl am besten) - **1.** [gen] well; **~ kochen können** to be able to cook well, to be a good cook; **du tätest ~ daran, dich ein wenig mehr zurückhalten** you would do well to show a bit more restraint - **2.** [schön, erfreulich]: **~ schmecken/aussehen** to taste/look good; **~ gelaunt sein** to be in a good mood; **ihr ist nicht ~** she's not well - **3.** [leicht] easily; **du hast ~ reden!** it's easy for you to talk! - **4.** [freundschaftlich]: **~ befreundet sein mit jm** to be good friends with sb; **mit jm ~ auskommen** to get on well with sb - **5.** RW: **so ~ wie** as good as; **das haben wir so ~ wie geschafft** we've as good as done it.

**Gut** (pl Güter) das - **1.** [Bauernhof] estate - **2.** [Ware] goods (pl) - **3.** [Eigentum] property (U).

**Gutachten** (pl -) das report.

**Gutachter, in** (mpl -; fpl -nen) der, die expert.

**gutartig** adj - **1.** [Hund, Charakter] good-natured - **2.** [Geschwulst, Tumor] benign.

**gut aussehend** adj good-looking.

**gut bezahlt** adj well-paid.

**gutbürgerlich** adj: **~e Küche** traditional cooking.

**Gutdünken** das: **nach js ~** as sb sees fit.

**Gute** das good.
➤ **alles Gute** interj all the best!
➤ **im Guten** adv [versuchen] amicably; [sagen] nicely.

**Güte** die - **1.** [Milde] goodness; **(ach) du meine** ODER **liebe ~!** (oh) my goodness! - **2.** [Qualität] quality.

**Güte|klasse** die grade.

**Güter|bahnhof** der freight depot.

**Güter|gemeinschaft** die community of property.

**Güter|trennung** die separation of property.

**Güter|verkehr** der freight traffic.

**Güterlwagen** *der* goods wagon *Br*, freight car *Am*.

**Güterlzug** *der* freight train.

**Gütelzeichen** *das* quality mark.

**gut gehen** *(perf* ist **gut gegangen)** *vi (unreg)* - **1.** [gesundheitlich]: **es geht ihr gut** she is doing well - **2.** [glücken] to turn out well - **3.** [Geschäft] to do well - **4.** [Ware] to go well.

**gut gehend** *adj* thriving.

**gut gelaunt** *adj* cheerful.

**gut gemeint** *adj* well-meant.

**gutgläubig** *adj* trusting.

**Guthaben** *(pl -) das* (credit) balance.

**gutlheißen** *vt (unreg)* to approve of.

**gütig** *adj* kind <> *adv* kindly.

**gütlich** *adj* amicable <> *adv*: **sich ~ einigen** to come to an amicable agreement.

**gutmütig** *adj* good-natured.

**Gutmütigkeit** *die (ohne pl)* good nature; **js ~ ausnutzen** to take advantage of sb's good nature.

**Gutslbesitzer, in** *der, die* owner of an/the estate.

**Gutlschein** *der* voucher.

**gutlschreiben** *vt (unreg)*: **jm etw ~** to credit sthg to sb.

**Gutlschrift** *die* - **1.** [Handlung] crediting - **2.** [Quittung] credit slip.

**gut situiert** *adj* well-to-do.

**gut tun** *vi (unreg)*: **ein heißes Bad wird dir ~** a hot bath will do you good.

**gutwillig** *adj* willing.

**Guyana** *nt* Guyana.

**Gymnasiallehrer, in** *der, die* ≈ grammar-school teacher *Br*.

**Gymnasiast, in** *(mpl -en; fpl -nen) der, die* ≈ grammar-school pupil *Br*.

**Gymnasium** *(pl* **Gymnasien)** *das* ≈ grammar school *Br, selective secondary school attended by 10- to 19-year-olds*; **altsprachliches/neusprachliches ~** *"Gymnasium" with focus on classical/modern languages*.

**Gymnastik** *die* keep-fit.

**Gynäkologe** *(pl -n) der* gynaecologist.

**Gynäkologie** *die* gynaecology.

**Gynäkologin** *(pl -nen) die* gynaecologist.

**Gyros** *das (ohne pl)* doner kebab.

**h, H** [ha:] *(pl -* ODER **-s)** *das* - **1.** [Buchstabe] h, H - **2.** MUS B.

➠ **h** *(abk für* **Stunde, Uhr)** h, hr.

**ha¹** *(abk für* **Hektar)** ha.

**ha²** *interj* ha!

**Haager** *(pl -) der* native/inhabitant of The Hague <> *adj (unver)* of/from The Hague; **der ~ Gerichtshof** the court in The Hague.

**Haar** *(pl -e) das* - **1.** [Behaarung] hair; **graues ~** ODER **graue ~e haben** to have grey hair; **ein paar graue ~e haben** to have a few grey hairs; **sich (D) die ~e schneiden lassen** to have one's hair cut; **sich (D) die ~e raufen** to tear one's hair out - **2.** RW: **an den ~en herbeigezogen sein** to be far-fetched; **jm aufs ~ gleichen** to be the spitting image of sb; **etw aufs ~ gleichen** to be an exact copy of sthg; **der Hund hat ihm kein ~ gekrümmt** the dog didn't touch a hair on his head; **vor Angst standen ihm die ~e zu Berge** his hair stood on end with fright; **kein gutes ~ an jm/etw lassen** to pull sb/sthg to pieces; **sich in die ~e kriegen** ODER **geraten** *fam* to start squabbling; **um ein ~ hätte ich den Zug verpasst** I very nearly missed the train.

**Haarlansatz** *der* hairline.

**Haarlausfall** *der* hair loss.

**Haarlbürste** *die* hairbrush.

**haaren** *vi* to moult.

**Haaresbreite** *die*: **um ~** by a hair's breadth; **um ~ hätte es einen Unfall gegeben** there was very nearly an accident.

**Haarlfarbe** *die* hair colour.

**Haarlfestiger** *der* setting lotion.

**haargenau** *adj* exact <> *adv* exactly; **stimmt ~!** absolutely right!

**haarig** *adj* hairy.

**haarklein** *adv* in minute detail.

**Haarlnadel** *die* hairpin.

**Haarnadellkurve** *die* hairpin bend.

**haarscharf** *adj* precise; [Beobachtung] very close <> *adv* - **1.** [knapp]: **das Auto fuhr ~ an ihr vorbei** the car only just missed her - **2.** [sehr genau] precisely; [beobachten] very closely.

**Haarlschnitt** *der* haircut.

**Haar|spalterei** *die abw* hair-splitting; **das ist doch ~** that's just splitting hairs.

**Haar|spange** *die* hairclip.

**Haar|spray** *das* ODER *der* hairspray.

**haarsträubend** *adj* - **1.** [empörend] shocking - **2.** [grauenhaft] horrifying.

**Haar|teil** *das* hairpiece.

**Haarwasch|mittel** *das* shampoo.

**Haar|wasser** *das* hair lotion.

**Haar|wuchs** *der:* einen starken/spärlichen **~ haben** to have a lot of/little hair.

**Hab** ➧ **Hab und Gut** *das geh* worldly goods.

**Habe** *die (ohne pl) geh* possessions *(pl).*

**haben** *(präs* hạt; *prät* hạtte; *perf* hat gehạbt) *aux* to have; **sie hat gegessen** she has eaten ⬦ *vt* - **1.** [besitzen] to have; **ich hätte gerne ...** [im Restaurant, Geschäft] I'd like ...; **er hat zwei kleine Schwestern** he's got ODER he has two younger sisters - **2.** [zur Verfügung haben] to have; **hast du Geld dabei?** have you got any money on you?; **das Haus ist noch zu ~** the house is still available - **3.** [als Bestandteil] to have; **das Buch hat 600 Seiten** the book has (got) 600 pages - **4.** [Eigenschaft] to have; **sie hat blaue Augen** she has (got) blue eyes; **dieser Mann hat etwas Unheimliches (an sich** *(D))* there's something sinister about that man - **5.** [erleben] to have; **Angst/Durst/Hunger ~** to be afraid/thirsty/hungry; **sie hatte es schwer im Leben** she's had a hard life - **6.** [an etw leiden] to have; **das Dach hat ein Loch** there's a hole in the roof; **Kopfschmerzen ~** to have a headache; **was hast du denn?** what's wrong? - **7.** [mit Zeitangaben]: **wie spät ~ wir (es)?** *fam* what's the time?; **wir ~ (jetzt) zehn Uhr** *fam* it's ten o'clock; **wir ~ heute Dienstag** *fam* it's Tuesday today - **8.** [müssen]: **etw zu tun ~** to have to do sthg; **er hat mir gesagt, dass ich das zu tun habe** he told me I have to do it - **9.** *RW:* **... und damit hat es sich!** ... and that's that!; **was hast du davon?** what do you get out of it?; **der hat sie wohl nicht mehr alle!** *fam* he's not all there; **~ Sie etwas dagegen, wenn ...?** do ODER would you mind if ...?; **sie scheint was gegen dich zu ~** she seems to have something against you; **sie ~ hier nichts zu suchen!** they've no business here; **ich habe zu tun** I'm busy.

➧ **sich haben** *ref fam* to make a fuss.

**Haben** *das* credit.

**Habenichts** *(pl* -e) *der abw* pauper.

**Habgier** *die abw* greed.

**habgierig** *abw adj* greedy ⬦ *adv* greedily.

**Habilitation** *(pl* -en) *die university lecturer's qualification.*

**habilitieren** ➧ **sich habilitieren** *ref* to qualify as a university lecturer.

**Habseligkeiten** *pl* belongings.

**habsüchtig** *adj* greedy.

**Hack|braten** *der* meat loaf.

**Hạcke** *(pl* -n) *die* - **1.** [Ferse, Absatz] heel - **2.** [Gartengerät] hoe.

**hạcken¹** ['hɛkən] *vi* EDV to hack.

**hạcken²** ['hɛkən] *vt* - **1.** [zerkleinern] to chop - **2.** [schlagen] to hack - **3.** [bearbeiten] to hoe ⬦ *vi* [mit dem Schnabel]: **nach jm/etw ~** to peck at sb/sthg.

**Hạcker, in** ['hɛkɐ, rɪn] *(mpl* -; *fpl* -nen) *der, die* EDV hacker.

**Hackfleisch** *das* mince *Br,* mincemeat *Am.*

**Hack|ordnung** *die* pecking order.

**Hafen** *(pl* Häfen) *der* [klein] harbour; [groß] port; **in den ~ einlaufen** to come into harbour/port.

**Hafen|anlagen** *pl* docks.

**Hafen|arbeiter, in** *der, die* docker, dock worker.

**Hafen|einfahrt** *die* harbour entrance.

**Hafen|kneipe** *die* dockland pub *Br,* longshore bar *Am.*

**Hafenrund|fahrt** *die* boat trip round the harbour.

**Hafen|stadt** *die* port.

**Hafen|viertel** *das* dock area.

**Hafer** *der (ohne pl)* oats *(pl).*

**Hafer|brei** *der* porridge.

**Hafer|flocken** *pl* rolled oats.

**Hafer|schleim** *der* gruel.

**Hạft** *die* [Gewahrsam] custody; [Strafe] imprisonment; **jn in ~ nehmen** to take sb into custody; **jn aus der ~ entlassen** to release sb from custody/prison.

**Hạft|anstalt** *die* prison.

**hạftbar** *adj:* **für etw ~ sein** to be liable for sthg; **jn für etw ~ machen** to hold sb liable for sthg.

**Hạft|befehl** *der* warrant.

**Hạft|dauer** *die* term of imprisonment.

**hạften** *vi* - **1.** [kleben] to stick - **2.** [bürgen]: **für jn ~** to be responsible for sb.

**haften bleiben** *(perf* ist haften geblieben) *vi (unreg)* to stick.

**Hạft|entlassung** *die* release.

**Häftling** *(pl* -e) *der* prisoner.

**Hạftpflicht|versicherung** *die* third party insurance.

**Hạft|schale** *die* contact lens.

**Hạft|strafe** *die* prison sentence.

**Hạftung** *die* - **1.** [Verantwortung] liability; **Ge-**

**sellschaft mit beschränkter ~** limited company **- 2.** [Kontakt] adhesion.

**Hagebutte** (*pl -n*) *die* **- 1.** [Frucht] rose hip **- 2.** [Strauch] dog rose.

**Hagel** *der* hail.

**Hagel|korn** *das* hailstone.

**hageln** *vi:* **es hagelt** it is hailing ◇ *vt:* **es hagelte Beschwerden** *fig* there was a stream of complaints.

**Hagel|schauer** *der* short hailstorm.

**hager** *adj* **- 1.** [Mann, Gestalt] gaunt **- 2.** [Arme] scrawny.

**Hahn** (*pl* **Hähne**) *der* **- 1.** [Vogel] cock **- 2.** [an der Leitung] tap *Br,* faucet *Am;* **jm den ~ zudrehen** *fig* to cut off funds to sb **- 3.** *RW:* **~ im Korb sein** to be the only man there; **nach jm/etw kräht kein ~ (mehr)** nobody cares about sb/sthg (any more).

**Hähnchen** (*pl -*) *das* **- 1.** [Brathähnchen] chicken **- 2.** [kleiner Hahn] cockerel.

**Hai** (*pl -e*) *der* shark.

**Hai|fisch** *der* shark.

**Haiti** *nt* Haiti.

**Häkchen** (*pl -*) *das* **- 1.** [kleiner Haken] little hook **- 2.** [Zeichen] tick.

**häkeln** *vt & vi* to crochet.

**Häkel|nadel** *die* crochet hook.

**Haken** (*pl -*) *der* **- 1.** [Aufhänger] hook; **~ und Öse** hook and eye **- 2.** [Zeichen] tick **- 3.** [Problem] catch, snag **- 4.** SPORT hook **- 5.** *RW:* **einen ~ schlagen** to dart sideways.

**Haken|kreuz** *das* swastika.

**Haken|nase** *die* hooked nose.

**halb** *adj (ohne Kompar)* half; **ein ~er Liter** half a litre; **der ~e Tag** half the day; **~ und ~** *fam* half and half; **es ist ~ drei** it is half past two; **keine ~en Sachen machen** not to do things by halves; **~ Düsseldorf** half of Düsseldorf ◇ *adv* half; **~ lange Haare** mid-length hair.

**halbamtlich** *adj* semi-official.

**Halb|bruder** *der* half-brother.

**Halbdunkel** *das* semi-darkness.

**Halbe** (*pl -n*) *das* ODER *der* half litre; **ein ~s** [Bier] a half litre; **etw ist nichts ~s und nichts Ganzes** sthg is neither one thing nor the other.

**Halbedel|stein** *der* semi-precious stone.

**halbe-halbe** *adv* half and half, fifty-fifty; **mit jm ~ machen** to go halves with sb.

**halb fertig** *adj* half-finished.

**halbfett** *adj* **- 1.** [Lebensmittel] low-fat **- 2.** [Schrift] semibold ◇ *adv* [drucken] in semibold.

**Halb|finale** *das* semi-final.

**halbherzig** *adj* half-hearted ◇ *adv* half-heartedly.

**halbieren** *vt* **- 1.** [Kuchen, Apfel] to cut in half, to halve **- 2.** [Linie] to bisect **- 3.** [Geldsumme, Zahl] to halve. ◆ **sich halbieren** *ref* to halve.

**Halb|insel** *die* peninsula.

**Halb|jahr** *das* six months (*pl*); [Schule] ≈ term.

**halbjährig** *adj* **- 1.** [Dauer] six-month **- 2.** [Alter] six-month-old.

**halbjährlich** *adj* six-monthly, half-yearly ◇ *adv* every six months, twice a year.

**Halb|kreis** *der* semi-circle.

**Halb|kugel** *die* hemisphere.

**halblang** *adj:* **nun** ODER **jetzt mach (mal) ~!** *fig* now hang on a minute!

**halblaut** *adj* low ◇ *adv* in a low voice.

**Halb|leiter** *der* PHYS semi-conductor.

**halb links** *adv* inside left.

**halbmast** *adv:* **auf ~** at half-mast.

**Halbmond** *der* [Mondsichel] half-moon.

**halb nackt** *adj* half-naked.

**halb offen** *adj* half-open.

**Halbpension** [ˈhalppaŋzjoːn] *die* half board.

**halb rechts** *adv:* **~ spielen** to play (at) inside right.

**Halbschlaf** *der:* **im ~ sein** to be half asleep.

**Halb|schuh** *der* shoe.

**Halbschwer|gewicht** *das* SPORT light heavyweight.

**Halb|schwester** *die* half-sister.

**Halbstarke** (*pl -n*) *der, die* abw young hooligan.

**halbstündig** *adj* half-hour.

**halbstündlich** *adj* half-hourly ◇ *adv* every half hour.

**halbtags** *adv:* **~ arbeiten** to work part-time.

**Halbtags|arbeit** *die* part-time work.

**Halbtags|beschäftigung** *die* part-time work.

**Halbtags|kraft** *die* part-time employee.

**Halbton** (*pl -töne*) *der* MUS semitone.

**halb tot** *adj* half-dead.

**halbtrocken** *adj* medium-dry.

**halb voll** *adj* half-full.

**halb wach** *adj* half-asleep.

**Halb|wahrheit** *die* half-truth.

**Halb|waise** *die child with only one living parent.*

**halbwegs** *adv* reasonably, fairly.

**Halbwerts|zeit** *die* PHYS half-life.

**Halbwissen** *das abw* superficial knowledge.

**halbwüchsig** ['halpvy:ksiçl *adj* adolescent.

**Halblzeit** *die* sport - **1.** [Hälfte] half - **2.** [Pause] half-time.

**Halde** (*pl* -n) *die* - **1.** [Kohlenhalde] slag heap - **2.** [Vorrat]: **etw auf ~ haben** to have a whole pile of sthg.

**half** *prät* ⊳ **helfen.**

**Hälfte** (*pl* -n) *die* half; **die ~ der Angestellten** half (of) the employees.

➤ **zur Hälfte** *adv:* **zur ~ gefüllt** half-full; **etw zur ~ tun** to half-do sthg; **der Erlös ging zur ~ ans Rote Kreuz** half the proceeds went to the Red Cross.

**Halfter** (*pl* -) *das* ODER *der* [für Pferde] halter ⊲ *das* [für Pistole] holster.

**Halle¹** (*pl* -n) *die* [gen] hall; [von Hotel] lobby; [zum Reiten] arena; [zum Turnen] gym; [zum Tennisspielen] covered court.

**Halle²** *nt* [Stadt] Halle.

**hallen** *vi* to resound, to ring out.

**Hallenlbad** *das* indoor swimming pool.

**Hallenlhandball** *der* indoor handball.

**Hallig** (*pl* -en) *die* one of a group of small islands off the North Sea coast of Germany.

**hallo** *interj* hello.

**Hallo** (*pl* -s) *das* [Begrüßung] (noisy) welcome; [Abschied] noisy send-off ODER farewell.

**Halluzination** (*pl* -en) *die* hallucination.

**Halm** (*pl* -e) *der* [von Gras] blade; [von Getreide] stalk.

**Halma** *das* halma.

**Halogen** (*pl* -e) *das* halogen.

**Halogenllampe** *die* halogen lamp.

**Hals** (*pl* Hälse) *der* - **1.** [Körperteil - außen] neck; [ - innen] throat - **2.** [von Flasche, Instrument] neck - **3.** RW: **aus vollem ~** at the top of one's voice; **bis zum** ODER **über den ~** up to one's neck; **den ~ nicht voll kriegen können** fam to be insatiable; **es hängt mir zum ~ heraus** fam abw I'm sick of it; **etw in den falschen ~ bekommen** fam to take sthg the wrong way; **~ über Kopf** in a rush ODER hurry; **jm den ~ umdrehen** fam to wring sb's neck; **jm um den ~ fallen** to fling one's arms around sb's neck; **jn/etw am ~ haben** fam abw to be saddled with sb/sthg; **jm die Journalisten vom ~ halten** to keep the journalists off sb's back.

**Halsauslschnitt** *der* neckline.

**Halslband** (*pl* -bänder) *das* - **1.** [für Tiere] collar - **2.** [Samtband] choker.

**halsbrecherisch** *adj* [Geschwindigkeit] breakneck; [Fahrt] madcap ⊲ *adv* [fahren] at breakneck speed.

**Halslbruch** *der:* Hals- und Beinbruch! good luck!

**Halslentzündung** *die* sore throat.

**Halslkette** *die* necklace.

**Hals-Nasen-Ohren-lArzt, Ärztin** *der, die* ear, nose and throat specialist.

**Halsschlaglader** *die* carotid artery.

**Halslschmerzen** *pl* sore throat (*sg);* **~ haben** to have a sore throat.

**Halsltuch** *das* scarf.

**Halslwirbel** *der* cervical vertebra.

**halt** *interj* stop!; MIL halt!; **~ sagen** to say stop; **sag ~, wenn ich aufhören soll!** tell me when to stop ⊲ *adv* Süddt, Österr & Schweiz just, simply.

**Halt** (*pl* -e ODER -s) *der* - **1.** [Stütze] hold, grip; **die Leiter hat keinen ~** the ladder is unstable; **den ~ verlieren** to lose one's hold - **2.** [Haltestelle] stop - **3.** [Stopp]: **~ machen** to stop; **vor jm/ etw nicht ~ machen** fig to spare no one/ nothing.

**haltbar** *adj* - **1.** [konserviert]: **~ sein** to keep well; **'mindestens ~ bis ...'** 'best before ...' - **2.** [strapazierfähig] hard-wearing, durable - **3.** [glaubhaft] tenable.

**Haltbarkeit** *die* [von Lebensmitteln] life; [von Material] durability.

**Haltbarkeitsldatum** *das* 'best before' date.

**halten** (*präs* hält; *prät* hielt; *perf* hat gehalten) *vt* - **1.** [fest halten] to hold - **2.** [beibehalten] to keep; **die dicken Wände ~ die Wärme** the thick walls keep the heat in; **Kontakt ~** to keep in touch - **3.** [binden] to keep - **4.** sport to save - **5.** [behalten] to hold on to - **6.** [Rede] to make; [Vortrag, Predigt] to give; [Plädoyer] to present - **7.** [einhalten - Versprechen] to keep - **8.** [Tier] to keep - **9.** [verteidigen] to hold - **10.** [bewerten, komponieren]: **die Wohnung ist ganz in Blau gehalten** the flat is decorated entirely in blue; **das Kleid ist sehr schlicht gehalten** the dress is very simple in style - **11.** RW: **jeder, der etw auf sich hält** any self-respecting person; **jn/ etw für jn/etw ~** to take sb/sthg to be sb/ sthg; **ich habe ihn für klüger gehalten** I thought he was cleverer than that; **er war nicht zu ~** there was no holding him; **viel/wenig von jm/etw ~** to have a high/low opinion of sb/ sthg; **was hältst du von ihr?** what do you think of her? ⊲ *vi* - **1.** [anhalten, stoppen] to stop - **2.** [ganz bleiben - Gegenstand] to hold; [ - Freundschaft] to last; **zu jm ~** to stand by sb - **3.** RW: **an sich (A) ~** to control o.s.

➤ **sich halten** *ref* - **1.** [in einem Zustand - Lebensmittel] to keep; **für sein Alter hält er sich gut** he's keeping well for his age; **sich fit ~** to keep fit - **2.** [in einer Position] to stay, to remain - **3.** [an einem Ort - sich fest halten] to hold on; [ - bleiben] to

stay; **sich rechts/links ~ to** keep (to the) right/
left - **4.** [in einer Körperhaltung]: **sich gerade ~ to**
stand up straight - **5.** [bei einer Herausforderung]
to hold one's own.

**Halterung** (pl -en) die holder.

**Halte|stelle** die stop.

**Halteverbot** das [Stelle] no waiting zone,
clearway Br; **'hier herrscht ~'** 'there is no
waiting here'; **'absolutes ~'** 'no waiting'; **'ein-
geschränktes ~'** 'no parking'.

**haltlos** adj [grundlos] unfounded ⟨⟩ adv [unbe-
herrscht] uncontrollably.

**halt|machen** vi ⟶ **Halt.**

**Haltung** (pl -en) die - **1.** [Körperhaltung] posture
- **2.** [Meinung, Einstellung] attitude - **3.** [Beherr-
schung] composure; **~ bewahren/verlieren to**
keep/lose one's composure - **4.** [von Tieren]
keeping.

**Halunke** (pl -n) der - **1.** [Gauner] scoundrel
- **2.** hum [Lausejunge] young rascal.

**Hamburg** nt Hamburg.

**Hamburger** (pl -) der - **1.** [Person] native/
inhabitant of Hamburg - **2.** [Frikadelle] hamburger ⟨⟩ adj (unver) of/from Hamburg.

**Hamburgerin** (pl -nen) die native/inhab-
itant of Hamburg.

**hämisch** adj gloating; [Grinsen, Lachen] malicious ⟨⟩ adv gloatingly; [grinsen, lachen] maliciously.

**Hammel** (pl -) der - **1.** [Tier] castrated ram
- **2.** [Fleisch] mutton - **3.** fam abw [Schimpfwort]
ass, twit Br.

**Hammer** (pl Hämmer) der - **1.** [Werkzeug &
SPORT] hammer - **2.** RW fam: **das ist (ja) ein ~!**
[Frechheit] that's disgraceful!; [großartig] that's
terrific!; **einen ~ haben to** be crackers ODER
nuts; **unter den ~ kommen to** come under the
hammer.

**hämmern** vi - **1.** [mit Hammer, Faust] to hammer
- **2.** [schlagen - Herz, Puls] to pound, to throb
⟨⟩ vt - **1.** [mit Hammer] to hammer - **2.**: **auf dem
Klavier ~ to** pound away at the piano.

**Hammerwerfen** das: **das ~** the hammer.

**Hammerwerfer, in** (mpl -; fpl -nen) der, die
hammer-thrower.

**Hämorroiden** [hɛmɔroˈiːdən] pl haemorrhoids.

**Hampelmann** (pl -männer) der - **1.** [Spielzeug]
jumping jack - **2.** salopp abw [Person] spineless person.

**Hamster** (pl -) der hamster.

**Hamster|kauf** der
➡ Hamsterkäufe pl panic buying (U).

**hamstern** vt to hoard.

**Hand** (pl Hände) die - **1.** [Körperteil] hand; **per ~**
manually; **Hände hoch!** hands up!; **jn an die**
**~ nehmen to** take sb by the hand; **etw in die**
**~ nehmen** [ergreifen] to take sthg in one's
hand; [initiativ werden] to take sthg in hand
- **2.** SPORT handball - **3.** RW: **alle Hände voll zu tun**
**haben to** have one's hands full; **eine ~ voll a**
handful; **auf der ~ liegen to** be obvious; **aus**
**erster ~** second-hand (with one previous
owner); **aus zweiter ~** second-hand (with two
previous owners); **von der öffentlichen ~ bezahlt** paid for out of public funds; **etw aus der**
**~ geben to** give sthg up; **etw bei der ~ haben**
to have sthg to hand ODER handy; **etw von der**
**~ weisen to** reject sthg (out of hand); **freie**
**~ haben to** have a free hand; **für jn/etw seine**
ODER **die ~ ins Feuer legen to** vouch for sb/
sthg; **~ anlegen** [helfen] to lend a hand; **~ aufs**
**Herz!** cross my/your heart!; **~ in ~ arbeiten to**
work hand in hand; **~ und Fuß haben to** be
well thought out; **in festen Händen sein to** be
spoken for; **in js ~ sein to** be at sb's mercy; **jm**
**in die Hände fallen to** fall into sb's hands; **jm**
**zur ~ gehen to** give sb a hand; **jn an der ~ haben to** have sb on hand; **jn in der ~ haben to**
have sb at one's mercy; **er ist die rechte ~ des**
**Chefs** he's the boss's right-hand man;
**linker/rechter ~ on** the left/right, on the left-
hand/right-hand side; **mit leeren Händen**
empty-handed; **um js ~ anhalten to** ask for
sb's hand (in marriage); **unter der ~ secretly; **von der ~ in den Mund leben to** live
from hand to mouth; **zur ~ sein to** be at
hand; **zwei linke Hände haben to** be clumsy.
➡ **an Hand = anhand.**
➡ **zu Händen** (+ D) adv for the attention of.

**Hand|arbeit** die - **1.** [Herstellung]: **in ~ herge-
stellte Töpferwaren** handmade pottery
- **2.** [Artikel] handmade article - **3.** [Textilien]:
**~en needlework** (U); **eine ~ a** piece of
needlework - **4.** fam [Unterricht] needlework.

**handarbeiten** vi to do needlework.

**Hand|ball** der handball.

**Handballer, in** (mpl -; fpl -nen) der, die fam
handball player.

**Handball|spieler, in** der, die handball
player.

**Hand|betrieb** der manual operation.

**Hand|bewegung** die gesture.

**handbreit** adj about 10 cm, distance of a
hand's breadth ⟨⟩ adv: **~ offen stehen to** be
ajar.

**Hand|bremse** die handbrake Br, parking
brake Am.

**Hand|buch** das - **1.** [Lehrbuch] handbook
- **2.** [Bedienungsanleitung] manual.

**Händchen** (pl -) das: **~ halten to** hold hands;
**ein ~ für etw haben to** be a dab hand at sthg.

**Hand|creme** [ˈhantkreːm] die hand cream.

**Hände|druck** der handshake.

**Handel** *der* - **1.** [Handeln] trade; **mit jm ~ treiben** to do business with sb; **mit etw ~ treiben** to deal in sthg; **~ treibendes Volk** [Stamm, Bevölkerungsgruppe] trading nation; **einen schwungvollen ~ betreiben** to do a roaring trade - **2.** [Geschäftsleben, Laden] business; **in den ~ kommen** to come onto the market.

**handeln** *vi* - **1.** [Handel treiben]: **mit etw ~** to trade *ODER* deal in sthg; **mit jm ~** to do business with sb - **2.** [feilschen] to bargain, to haggle; **mit jm um etw ~** to bargain *ODER* haggle with sb over sthg - **3.** [agieren] to act - **4.** [behandeln]: **von etw ~** to be about sthg <> *vt* [verkaufen] to trade.

⮞ **sich handeln** *ref:* **worum handelt es sich?** what is it about?; **bei diesem Buch handelt es sich um einen Roman** this book is a novel.

**Handels|abkommen** *das* trade agreement.

**Handels|beziehungen** *pl* trade relations.

**Handels|bilanz** *die* balance of trade.

**handelseinig** *adj:* **(mit jm) ~ werden** to strike a deal (with sb).

**Handels|gericht** *das* commercial court.

**Handels|hafen** *der* trading port.

**Handels|kammer** *die* chamber of commerce.

**Handels|marine** *die* merchant navy.

**Handels|partner** *der* trading partner.

**Handels|register** *das* commercial register.

**Handels|schiff** *das* merchant ship.

**Handels|schule** *die* college attended by people who left school at 16 and wish to obtain a commercial qualification.

**handelsüblich** *adj* standard, customary.

**Handels|vertreter, in** *der, die* commercial representative, rep.

**Handels|ware** *die* commodity; **~n** merchandise (U).

**handel|treibend** *adj* ⊏⊐ Handel.

**händeringend** *adv* desperately.

**Hand|feger** *der* brush.

**handfest** *adj* - **1.** [bodenständig] sturdy - **2.** [klar, stark] solid, firm.

**Hand|fläche** *die* palm.

**Hand|gelenk** *das* wrist; **etw aus dem ~ schütteln** *fig* to do sthg effortlessly.

**Hand|gemenge** *das* scuffle.

**Hand|gepäck** *das* hand luggage.

**handgeschrieben** *adj* handwritten.

**handgestrickt** *adj* - **1.** [gestrickt] hand-knitted - **2.** *abw* [naiv] half-baked.

**Hand|granate** *die* hand grenade.

**handgreiflich** *adj:* **~ werden** to become violent.

**Handgreiflichkeit** *(pl -en) die* violence; **es kam zu ~en** they came to blows.

**Hand|griff** *der* - **1.** [Handbewegung] movement (of the hand); **mit ein paar ~en** in no time - **2.** [Haltegriff] handle.

**Hand|habe** *die:* **keine ~ gegen jn haben** RECHT to have no evidence against sb.

**handhaben** *vt* - **1.** [Werkzeug] to use; [Maschine] to operate; [Gesetze, Vorschriften] to apply - **2.** [Fall] to handle.

**Handicap, Handikap** ['hɛndikɛp] *(pl -s) das* handicap.

**Hand|koffer** *der* small suitcase.

**Hand|kuss** *der* kiss on the hand.

**Hand|langer** *(pl -) der* - **1.** [Hilfsarbeiter] labourer - **2.** *abw* [Zuarbeiter] dogsbody; [von Geheimpolizei] henchman.

**Händler, in** *(mpl -; fpl -nen) der, die* dealer.

**handlich** *adj* handy.

**Handlung** *(pl -en) die* - **1.** [Tat] act - **2.** [in Texten] plot - **3.** [Laden] shop, business.

**Handlungs|ablauf** *der* plot.

**handlungsfähig** *adj:* **~ sein** to be able to act.

**Handlungsfreiheit** *die* freedom of action.

**Handlungs|weise** *die* conduct.

**Hand-out** ['hɛndaut] *(pl -s) das* handout.

**Hand|rücken** *der* back of the hand.

**Hand|schellen** *pl* handcuffs; **jm ~ anlegen** to handcuff sb.

**Hand|schlag** *der* *(ohne pl):* **ein Geschäft durch** *ODER* **per ~ besiegeln** to shake on a deal; **er tut keinen ~** *abw* he doesn't do a stroke (of work).

**Hand|schrift** *die* - **1.** [Schrift] handwriting; **es trägt seine ~** *fig* it bears his stamp *ODER* hallmark - **2.** [Text] manuscript.

**handschriftlich** *adj* handwritten.

**Hand|schuh** *der* glove.

**Handschuh|fach** *das* glove compartment.

**Hand|stand** *der* handstand.

**Hand|tasche** *die* handbag.

**Hand|tuch** *das* towel; **das ~ werfen** *ODER* **schmeißen** *fig* to throw in the towel.

**Hand|umdrehen** *das:* **im ~** in (next to) no time.

**Handvoll** *(pl -) die* ⊏⊐ Hand.

**Hand|werk** *das* - **1.** [Beruf] trade; [künstlerisch] craft; **jm das ~ legen** to put an end to sb's misdemeanours; **sein ~ verstehen** *ODER* **kennen** to know one's job - **2.** *(ohne pl)* [Berufsstand] trade and crafts sector.

**Handlwerker, in** (*mpl* -; *fpl* -nen) *der, die* tradesman (*f* tradeswoman).

**handwerklich** *adj* [Beruf] skilled; [künstlerisch] as a craftsman/craftswoman ◇ *adv:* ~ **gut gearbeitet** well-crafted; ~ **geschickt sein** to be good with one's hands.

**Handwerkslbetrieb** *der* craft business.

**Handwerkslkammer** *die* tradesman's guild.

**Handwerkszeug** *das* (*ohne pl*) tools (*pl*) of the trade.

**Handy** ['hɛndi] (*pl* -**s**) *das* mobile (phone); **er nahm sein ~ mit** he took his mobile with him.

**Handlzeichen** *das* signal (with one's hand); **durch ~ abstimmen** to decide by a show of hands.

**Handlzettel** *der* flyer.

**Hanf** *der* hemp.

**Hang** (*pl* **Hänge**) *der* - **1.** [Abhang] slope - **2.** [Vorliebe]: **einen ~ zum Selbstmitleid haben** to be inclined to be self-pitying.

**Hängelbrücke** *die* suspension bridge.

**Hängellampe** *die* droplight.

**hangeln** (*perf* **hat/ist gehangelt**) *vi* (*ist*): **an etw** (*D*) **~** to move along sthg hand over hand.
➤ **sich hangeln** *ref* (*hat*): **sich nach unten/oben ~** to let o.s. down/pull o.s. up hand over hand.

**Hängelmatte** *die* hammock.

**hängen** (*prät* **hing** ODER **hängte**; *perf* **hat gehangen** ODER **hat gehängt**) *vt* (*reg*) - **1.** [anbringen] to hang; **etw an etw** (*A*) **~** to hang sthg on sthg; **sich einen Pullover um die Schultern ~** to drape a pullover over one's shoulders - **2.** [Körperteil] to dangle - **3.** [töten] to hang ◇ *vi* (*unreg*) - **1.** [gen] to hang - **2.** [emotional]: **an jm/etw ~** to be attached to sb/sthg - **3.** [haften] to be stuck.
➤ **sich hängen** *ref* (*reg*): **sich an etw** (*A*) **~** to hang onto sthg.

**Hängen** *das*: **mit ~ und Würgen** by the skin of one's teeth.

**hängen bleiben** (*perf* **ist hängen geblieben**) *vi* (*unreg*) - **1.** [festhängen]: **mit dem Ärmel an der Türklinke ~** to catch one's sleeve on the doorhandle - **2.** [bleiben] to stay longer than one intended - **3.** [übrig bleiben]: **von dem Gelernten blieb nichts hängen** she didn't remember any of what she'd learned; **diese Arbeit bleibt immer an mir hängen** it is always me who ends up having to do this job - **4.** *fam* [sitzen bleiben] to have to repeat the year.

**hängen lassen** *vt* (*unreg*) - **1.** [vergessen] to leave (behind) - **2.** [Person] to let down, to leave in the lurch - **3.** [Körperteil]: **die Schultern ~ lassen** to let one's shoulders droop.

➤ **sich hängen lassen** *ref* [vernachlässigen] to let o.s. go.

**Hannover** *nt* Hanover.

**Hanse** *die* Hanseatic League.

**Hanseat, in** (*mpl* -**en**; *fpl* -**nen**) *der, die* inhabitant of one of the Hanseatic towns.

**hänseln** *vt*: **jn** (**wegen etw**) **~** to tease sb (about sthg).

**Hanselstadt** *die* Hanseatic town.

**HANSESTÄDTE**

The Hanseatic League was originally a guild of merchants which grew into an association of merchant towns, formed to protect trade. It existed from the 12th to the 14th century and had a major influence on economic and cultural life. Most of the German towns that were members of the League are in the north of the country, on the North Sea and Baltic coasts. The towns that belonged to the Hanseatic League and that still exist today are Lübeck, Rostock, Wismar, Greifswald, Stralsund, Bremen and Hamburg.

**Hanswurst** *der* - **1.** [nicht ernst zu nehmender Mensch] buffoon - **2.** [Clown] clown.

**Hantel** (*pl* -**n**) *die* dumbbell.

**hapern** *vi* - **1.** [fehlen]: **es hapert an Geld** there is a shortage of money - **2.** [nicht funktionieren]: **es hapert mit etw** there are problems with sthg.

**Häppchen** (*pl* -) *das* canapé.

**happig** *fam adj* [Preis] steep ◇ *adv* greedily.

**happy** ['hɛpi] *adj fam* happy.

**Happyend** ['hɛpi'ɛnt] (*pl* -**s**) *das* happy ending.

**Hardrock** ['ha:(r)d'rɔk] *der* hard rock.

**Hardthöhe** *die Defence Ministry of the FRG*.

**Hardware** ['ha:(r)dwɛɐ] *die* EDV hardware.

**Harem** (*pl* -**s**) *der* harem.

**Harfe** (*pl* -**n**) *die* harp.

**Harke** (*pl* -**n**) *die* rake.

**harken** *vt* to rake.

**harmlos** *adj* [Tier, Person, Bemerkung] harmless; [Eingriff, Verletzung] minor; [Vergnügen] innocent ◇ *adv* [lachen, tun] innocently.

**Harmlosigkeit** (*pl* -**en**) *die* [von Tier, Person, Bemerkung] harmlessness; [von Krankheit] mildness; [von Verletzung] minor nature; [von Vergnügen] innocence.

**Harmonie** (*pl* -**n**) *die* harmony.

**harmonieren** *vi*: **miteinander ~** [Farben] to go (well) together; [Töne] to be in harmony; [Menschen] to get on (well) with one another.

**Harmonika** (*pl* -s) *die* harmonica, mouth-organ.

**harmonisch** *adj* harmonious <> *adv* - **1.** [passend] harmoniously - **2.** mus: ~ **klingen** to be harmonious.

**harmonisieren** *vt* to harmonize.

**Harn** (*pl* -e) *der* urine.

**Harnlblase** *die* bladder.

**Harpune** (*pl* -n) *die* harpoon.

**hart** (*kompar* **härter**; *superl* **härteste**) *adj* - **1.** [nicht weich - gen] hard; [ - Ei] hard-boiled; ~e **Währung** hard currency - **2.** [widerstandsfähig] tough; ~ **im Nehmen sein** to be tough - **3.** [streng - Urteil, Strafe, Winter] harsh; [ - Drogen] hard; [ - Aufprall] violent - **4.**: **es geht ~ auf ~** *fig* it's a pitched battle <> *adv (kompar* **härter**; *superl am* **härtesten**) - **1.** [nicht weich] hard; **das Ei** ~ **kochen** to hard-boil the egg - **2.** [streng - bestrafen, urteilen] harshly; [ - arbeiten, aufschlagen] hard - **3.** [räumlich]: ~ **an** (+ *D*) close to; **das war** ~ **an der Grenze des Erlaubten** *fig* it was right on the limit of what is allowed.

**Härte** (*pl* -n) *die* - **1.** [gen] hardness - **2.** [Belastung] hardship - **3.** [von Urteil, Person, Worte, Farbe, Aussprache] harshness - **4.** *fam abw* [Zumutung]: **das ist die ~!** that's a bit much!

**Härtelgrad** *der* hardness (*of water*).

**hart gekocht** *adj* hard-boiled.

**Hartgeld** *das (ohne pl)* coins (*pl*).

**hart gesotten** *adj* [Geschäftsmann, Manager] hard-headed; [Ganove, Profi] hardened.

**hartherzig** *adj* hard-hearted.

**hartnäckig** *adj* [Person] stubborn; [Verfolger, Krankheit] persistent <> *adv* [schweigen, sich weigern] stubbornly; [verfolgen, nachfragen] persistently.

**Harz** *der* resin.

**Harzer** *adj* (*unver*) of/from the Harz Mountains.

**Hasch** *das fam* hash.

**haschen** *vi* - **1.** [fangen wollen]: **nach jm/etw** ~ to snatch at sb/sthg - **2.** *fam* [Haschisch rauchen] to smoke hash.

**Haschisch** *das* ODER *der* hashish.

**Hase** (*pl* -n) *der* hare; [Kaninchen] rabbit; **(in etw)** **ein alter ~ sein** to be an old hand (at sthg); **falscher ~** KÜCHE meat loaf.

**Hasellnuss** *die* hazelnut.

**Hasenlscharte** *die* harelip.

**Hass** *der*: ~ **(auf jn/etw)** hatred (of sb/sthg).

**hassen** *vt* to hate.

**hasserfüllt** *adj* full of hatred <> *adv* with hatred.

**hässlich** *adj* - **1.** [unattraktiv] ugly - **2.** [gemein] nasty <> *adv* - **1.** [unattraktiv] tastelessly; **sich**

~ **kleiden** to wear ugly clothes - **2.** [gemein] nastily.

**Hässlichkeit** *die* [von Person, Einrichtung] ugliness.

**Hassliebe** *die* love-hate relationship.

**hast** *präs* ⊏ **haben.**

**Hast** *die* haste; **etw in ~ tun** to do sthg hastily.

**hasten** (*perf* **ist gehastet**) *vi* to hurry.

**hastig** *adv* hastily, hurriedly; ~ **laufen** to rush <> *adj* hasty.

**hat** *präs* ⊏ **haben.**

**hätscheln** *vt* to pet.

**hatschi** *interj fam* atishoo!

**hatte** *prät* ⊏ **haben.**

**Haube** (*pl* -n) *die* - **1.** [von Krankenschwester] cap; [von Nonne] veil; **unter die ~ kommen** *fig* to be married off - **2.** [Motorhaube] bonnet *Br*, hood *Am* - **3.** [Trockenhaube] hairdryer.

**Hauch** *der* - **1.** [leichter Wind] gentle breeze - **2.** [Spur]: **ein ~ von etw** a hint of sthg.

**hauchdünn** *adj* wafer-thin <> *adv* [auftragen] very sparingly; [schneiden] into very thin slices.

**hauchen** *vt* & *vi* to breathe.

**Haue** *die (ohne pl) fam* hiding; ~ **kriegen** to get a hiding.

**hauen** (*prät* **haute** ODER **hieb**; *perf* **hat gehauen**) *vt* - **1.** (*prät* **haute**) *fam* [Person] to hit - **2.** [Gegenstand]: **einen Pfahl ins Erdreich** ~ to bang a post into the ground - **3.** (*prät* **haute**) *salopp* [werfen] to chuck, to bung *Br* <> *vi fam* [auf Tisch, gegen Wand] to bang; **jm ins Gesicht** ~ to smack sb in the mouth.

➤ **sich hauen** *ref (prät* **haute**) - **1.** *fam* [sich prügeln] to scrap - **2.** *salopp* [sich hinlegen]: **sich aufs Sofa** ~ to flop down on the sofa.

**Häufchen** (*pl* -) *das* small heap; **aussehen wie ein ~ Elend** to look utterly miserable.

**Haufen** (*pl* -) *der* - **1.** [Anhäufung]: **alles auf einen** ~ **legen** to pile everything up - **2.** *fam* [Menge]: **ein ~ Freunde/Geld** loads of friends/money - **3.** RW: **einen ~ machen** *fam* [Hund] to do its business; **etw über den ~ werfen** *fam* [vereiteln] to mess up; **jn über den ~ rennen** ODER **fahren** *fam* to run ODER knock sb down.

**häufen** *vt* to pile up.

➤ **sich häufen** *ref* [Briefe, Abfälle] to pile up; [Beweise] to accumulate; [Vorfall] to be on the increase.

**haufenweise** *adv fam*: ~ **Geld verdienen** to earn heaps ODER loads of money.

**häufig** *adj* [gen] frequent; [Fehler] common <> *adv* often.

**Häufigkeit** (*pl* -en) *die* frequency.

**Häufung** (*pl* -en) *die* [von Gegenständen] accumulation; [von Vorfällen] mounting frequency.

**Haupt** (*pl* Häupter) *das geh, eigtl* & *fig* head.

**Hauptlaktionär** *der* majority shareholder.

**hauptamtlich** *adj* full-time <> *adv* full time.

**Hauptlbahnhof** *der* main station; **Leipzig ~** Leipzig central (station).

**hauptberuflich** *adj*: **~e Tätigkeit** main job <> *adv*: **~ ist er Landwirt** farming is his principal occupation.

**Hauptlbeschäftigung** *die* main occupation.

**Hauptlbestandteil** *der* main component.

**Hauptldarsteller, in** *der, die* leading man (*f* leading lady).

**Hauptleingang** *der* main entrance.

**Hauptlfach** *das* main subject; **etw im ~ studieren** to study sthg as one's main subject.

**Hauptlfigur** *die* central figure.

**Hauptlgericht** *das* main course.

**Hauptgeschäftslstelle** *die* head office.

**Hauptgeschäftslstraße** *die* main shopping street.

**Hauptgeschäftslzeit** *die* peak business hours (*pl*).

**Hauptlgewinn** *der* first prize.

**Hauptlgrund** *der* main reason.

**Häuptling** (*pl* -e) *der* chief.

**Hauptlmahlzeit** *die* main meal.

**Hauptlmann** (*pl* -leute) *der* MIL captain.

**Hauptlperson** *die* - **1.** [von Buch, Film] main character - **2.** [wichtigste Person]: **die ~ sein** to be the star of the show.

**Hauptlpost** *die* main post office.

**Hauptlquartier** *das* headquarters (*pl*).

**Hauptreiselzeit** *die* peak tourist season.

**Hauptlrolle** *die* [in Film] starring role; **Tennis spielt in ihrem Leben die ~** tennis is the most important thing in her life.

**Hauptlsache** *die* main ODER most important thing; **~, ich bestehe** the main thing is for me to pass.
➤ **in der Hauptsache** *adv* mainly, in the main.

**hauptsächlich** *adv* principally, mainly <> *adj* main, chief.

**Hauptlsaison** ['hauptzɛz] *die* high season.

**Hauptlsatz** *der* main clause.

**Hauptlschule** *die* secondary school attended by less academically gifted pupils aged between 10 and 15.

**Hauptlschüler, in** *der, die* pupil at a "Hauptschule".

**Hauptschulllehrer, in** *der, die* teacher at a "Hauptschule".

**Hauptlspeicher** *der* EDV main memory.

**Hauptlstadt** *die* capital.

**Hauptlstraße** *die* main road ODER street.

**Hauptlteil** *der* [von Text, Rede] main body; **der ~ der Fracht war beschädigt** most of the cargo was damaged.

**Hauptverkehrslstraße** *die* main thoroughfare.

**Hauptverkehrslzeit** *die* rush hour.

**Hauptlversammlung** *die* WIRTSCH (annual) general meeting, AGM.

**Hauptlwohnsitz** *der* main place of residence.

**Hauptlwort** (*pl* -wörter) *das* noun.

**Haus** (*pl* Häuser) *das* - **1.** [Wohnhaus] house - **2.** [Betrieb] firm; **er ist zurzeit nicht im ~** he is not on the premises just now; **mit den besten Empfehlungen des ~es** with the compliments of the house - **3.** [Familie] family - **4.** [Theater] auditorium; **volles ~ haben** to have a full house - **5.** RW: **altes ~ !** old thing!; **~ halten** [sparen] to budget; **mit etw ~ halten** to be careful with sthg; **mit seinen Kräften ~ halten** to conserve one's energy; **uns stehen Reformen ins ~** we are faced with reforms; **die Kinder sind von ~ aus gewöhnt mitzuhelfen** the children have been brought up to be helpful.
➤ **nach Haus(e)** *adv* home.
➤ **zu Haus(e)** *adv* at home; **zu ~e sein** [im Haus] to be at home; **in etw** (D) **zu ~e sein** [in Wissenschaftsgebiet] to be at home with sthg.

**Hauslangestellte** *der, die* domestic (servant).

**Hauslapotheke** *die* - **1.** [Medikamente] first-aid kit - **2.** [Schränkchen] medicine cabinet.

**Hauslarbeit** *die* - **1.** [im Haushalt] housework - **2.** [für die Schule, für die Universität] homework.

**Hauslarrest** *der* house arrest.

**Hauslarzt, ärztin** *der, die* family doctor.

**Hauslaufgabe** *die*: **als ~ für Morgen ...** for tomorrow's homework ...; **~n** homework (*U*).

**hausbacken** *adj* homely, plain.

**Hausbesetzer, in** (*mpl* -; *fpl* -nen) *der, die* squatter.

**Hauslbesetzung** *die* squatting.

**Hauslbesitzer, in** *der, die* home-owner; [Vermieter] landlord (*f* landlady).

**Hauslbewohner, in** *der, die* occupant.

**Häuschen** ['hɔyzçən] (*pl* -) *das* [Haus] cottage; **vor Freude ganz aus dem ~ sein** *fam* to be beside o.s. with joy.

**Hausldurchsuchung** *die* house search.

**H**

**hauseigen** *adj*: das Hotel hat einen ~en Tennisplatz the hotel has its own tennis court.

**Haus|eigentümer, in** *der, die* homeowner; [Vermieter] landlord (*f* landlady).

**hausen** *vi* - **1.** [wohnen] to live - **2.** *fam* [toben - Sturm, Krieg] to rage; [ - Eroberer, Besatzer] to rampage.

**Häuserblock** (*pl* **-blöcke**) *der* block.

**Häuser|front** *die* façade.

**Haus|flur** *der* (entrance) hall, hallway.

**Haus|frau** *die* housewife.

**Hausfriedensbruch** *der* RECHT trespass.

**Haus|gast** *der* (hotel) guest.

**hausgemacht** *adj* home-made.

**Haus|gemeinschaft** *die* all the residents of a house.

**Haushalt** (*pl* -e) *der* - **1.** [Hausarbeit] housework; im ~ helfen to help around the house - **2.** [Hausstand] estate - **3.** [Familie] household; einen ~ gründen to set up home - **4.** WIRTSCH budget.

**haus|halten** *vi (unreg)* ▷ Haus.

**Haushälter, in** (*mpl* -; *fpl* -nen) *der, die* housekeeper.

**Haushalts|artikel** *der* household article.

**Haushalts|defizit** *das* WIRTSCH budget deficit.

**Haushaltsgeld** *das* housekeeping money.

**Haushalts|jahr** *das* WIRTSCH financial year.

**Haushalts|plan** *der* WIRTSCH budget.

**Haus|herr, in** *der, die* host (*f* hostess).

**haushoch** *adj* [Flammen, Wellen] towering; [Favorit, Sieg, Überlegenheit] overwhelming ◇ *adv* [wachsen] as high as a house; [gewinnen] by a street; jm ~ überlegen sein to be head and shoulders above sb; ~ verlieren to be hammered.

**hausieren** *vi*: mit etw ~ (gehen) [verkaufen] to sell sthg from door to door; *fam* [sprechen über] to go on about sthg.

**Hausierer, in** (*mpl* -; *fpl* -nen) *der, die* door-to-door salesman (*f* -woman).

**Haus|lehrer, in** *der, die* private tutor.

**häuslich** *adj* - **1.** [im Haus - Arbeiten, Probleme, Frieden] domestic; [ - Angelegenheit] family (*vor Subst*); [ - Pflege] home (*vor Subst*) - **2.** [Person]: sie ist sehr ~ she's a real home bird ◇ *adv*: sich ~ niederlassen *fam* to make o.s. at home; sich ~ einrichten *fam* to settle in.

**Haus|mann** *der* house husband.

**Hausmannskost** *die* traditional, simple fare.

**Haus|marke** *die* - **1.** [Wein] house wine - **2.** [von Geschäft] own-brand product - **3.** [Lieblingsmarke] favourite brand.

**Haus|meister, in** *der, die* caretaker *Br*, janitor *Am*.

**Haus|mittel** *das* home remedy.

**Haus|müll** *der (ohne pl)* household waste.

**Haus|musik** *die* music played informally at home or amongst friends.

**Haus|nummer** *die* house number.

**Haus|ordnung** *die* house rules (*pl*).

**Haus|rat** *der (ohne pl)* household contents (*pl*).

**Hausrat|versicherung** *die* home and contents insurance.

**Haus|schlüssel** *der* front-door key.

**Haus|schuh** *der* slipper.

**Hausse** ['ho:s(ə)] (*pl* -n) *die* WIRTSCH boom.

**Haus|segen** *der*: bei ihm hängt der ~ schief he's having domestic trouble.

**Haus|suchung** (*pl* -en) *die* house search.

**Haus|tier** *das* pet.

**Haus|tür** *die* front door.

**Haus|verbot** *das*: meine Eltern haben meinem Freund ~ erteilt my parents have banned my friend from coming round to our house.

**Haus|verwalter, in** *der, die* property manager.

**Haus|verwaltung** *die* property managers (*pl*).

**Haus|wirt, in** *der, die* landlord (*f* -lady).

**Haus|wirtschaft** *die (ohne pl)* home economics (*U*).

**Haut** (*pl* Häute) *die* - **1.** [gen] skin; [von Tier] hide - **2.** *RW*: aus der ~ fahren to be hopping mad; es ging mir unter die ~ it got under my skin; ihm war nicht wohl in seiner ~ he felt uncomfortable; nur noch ~ und Knochen sein to be nothing but skin and bones; mit heiler ~ davonkommen to come away in one piece.

**Haut|abschürfung** (*pl* -en) *die* graze.

**Haut|arzt, ärztin** *der, die* dermatologist.

**Haut|ausschlag** *der* (skin) rash.

**Haut|creme** ['hautkre:m] *die* skin cream.

**häuten** *vt* [Früchte] to peel; [Tier] to skin.
↠ sich häuten *ref* to shed its skin.

**hauteng** *adj* skintight.

**Haut|farbe** *die* skin colour.

**Haut|krankheit** *die* skin disease.

**Haut|krebs** *der* skin cancer.

**hautnah** *adj* [Bild, Darstellung] graphic ◇ *adv* [tanzen] very closely; ~ mit etw in Kontakt kommen to come into close contact with sthg; ~ an etw (D) teilnehmen to be closely involved in sthg.

**Hautpflege** *die* skin care.

**Hawaii** *nt* Hawaii.

**Hbf.** *abk für* **Hauptbahnhof.**

**H-|Bombe** *die* H-bomb.

**H-Dur** *das* MUS B major.

**Headhunter** (*pl* -) *der* headhunter.

**Hebamme** (*pl* -n) *die* midwife.

**Hebel** (*pl* -) *der* lever; **alle ~ in Bewegung setzen** *fig* to do everything one can; **am längeren ~ sitzen** *fig* to have the whip hand.

**heben** (*prät* h**o**b; *perf* hat geh**o**ben) *vt* - **1.** [hochnehmen] to lift; [Arm, Glas] to raise; **einen ~ fam** to have a drink - **2.** [Niveau] to raise; [Umsatz, Selbstsicherheit] to boost, to improve; [Stimmung, Laune] to improve - **3.** [Wrack] to hoist, to salvage.

➥ **sich heben** *ref* - **1.** [hochgehen - Vorhang, Flugzeug, Ballon] to rise; [ - Nebel] to lift - **2.** [Niveau] to rise; [Umsatz, Laune] to improve.

**hebräisch** *adj* Hebrew.

**Hebräische, Hebräisch** *das* Hebrew; *siehe auch* **Englische.**

**Hebriden** *pl*: **die ~** the Hebrides.

**hecheln** *vi* [atmen] to pant.

**Hecht** (*pl* -e) *der* pike; **ein toller ~ sein** *fam fig* to be a great guy.

**Hecht|sprung** *der* [ins Wasser] racing dive; [über Hindernis] headlong dive.

**Heck** (*pl* -e ODER -s) *das* [von Auto, Flugzeug] rear; [von Schiff] stern.

**Hecke** (*pl* -n) *die* hedge.

**Hecken|schere** *die* hedge clippers (*pl*).

**Hecken|schütze** *der* sniper.

**Heck|klappe** *die* tailgate.

**Heckmeck** *der fam abw* fuss.

**Heck|motor** *der* rear engine.

**Heck|scheibe** *die* rear windscreen *Br* ODER windshield *Am*.

**Heckscheiben|heizung** *die* rear demister.

**Heck|scheibenwischer** *der* rear windscreen wiper *Br*, rear windshield wiper *Am*.

**Heer** (*pl* -e) *das* army.

**Hefe** (*pl* -n) *die* yeast.

**Hefe|teig** *der* leavened dough (*U*).

**Heft** (*pl* -e) *das* - **1.** [Schulheft] exercise book - **2.** [geheftetes Büchlein] booklet - **3.** [von Zeitschriften] issue.

**heften** *vt* - **1.** [befestigen]: **etw an etw** (A) **~** [gen] to attach sthg to sthg; [mit Heftmaschine] to staple sthg to sthg - **2.** [nähen] to tack - **3.** [richten]: **die Augen auf etw** (A) **~** to fix one's eyes on sthg.

➥ **sich heften** *ref* [sich richten]: **sich auf etw** (A) **~** to fix onto sthg.

**Hefter** (*pl* -) *der* folder.

**heftig** *adj* violent ◇ *adv* violently.

**Heft|klammer** *die* staple.

**Heft|pflaster** *das* (sticking) plaster *Br*, Band-Aid® *Am*.

**Heft|zwecke** (*pl* -n) *die* drawing pin *Br*, thumbtack *Am*.

**hegen** *vt* - **1.** [Verdacht, Gefühle, Hoffnung] to harbour; [Abneigung, Misstrauen, Achtung] to feel - **2.** [Wald, Wild, Garten] to tend; **jn/etw ~ und pflegen** to lavish care on sb/sthg.

**Hehl** *das* ODER *der*: **kein** ODER **keinen ~ aus etw machen** to make no secret of sthg.

**Hehler** (*pl* -) *der* receiver (of stolen goods).

**Hehlerei** (*pl* -en) *die* receiving (stolen goods).

**Hehlerin** (*pl* -nen) *die* receiver (of stolen goods).

**Heide** (*pl* -n) *die* heath ◇ *der* heathen, pagan.

**Heidekraut** *das* heather.

**Heidel|beere** *die* bilberry.

**Heiden|angst** *die fam*: **eine ~ haben** to be scared stiff.

**Heiden|geld** *das fam* fortune; **ein ~ verdienen** to earn a fortune.

**Heiden|spaß** *der fam* great fun; **einen ~ haben** to have a whale of a time.

**Heidin** (*pl* -nen) *die* heathen, pagan.

**heidnisch** *adj* heathen, pagan.

**heikel** (*kompar* h**ei**kler; *superl* h**ei**kelste) *adj* - **1.** [kompliziert] awkward, tricky - **2.** [anspruchsvoll] fussy.

**heil** *adj* - **1.** [unzerstört] intact; [Welt] perfect - **2.** [geheilt] healed.

**Heiland** *der* Saviour.

**Heil|bad** *das* - **1.** [Kurort] spa - **2.** [Baden] medicinal bath.

**heilbar** *adj* [Krankheit, Patient] curable; [Wunde] healable.

**heilen** (*perf* hat/ist geh**ei**lt) *vt* (*hat*) to cure; **jn von etw ~** [Idee] to cure sb of sthg; **jn von seinen Zweifeln ~** to allay sb's doubts ◇ *vi* (*ist*) to heal.

**heilfroh** *adj* relieved; **~ über etw** (A) **sein** to be relieved about sthg.

**heilig** *adj* - **1.** [geheiligt] holy; **der ~e Christopherus** Saint Christopher; **denen ist nichts ~** nothing is sacred to them - **2.** [Schrecken] almighty.

**Heilig|abend** *der* Christmas Eve.

**Heilige** (*pl* -n) *der, die* saint.

**Heilige Geist** *der* Holy Spirit ODER Ghost.

**Heilige Jungfrau** *die* Blessed Virgin.

**Heilige Land** *das* Holy Land.

**Heilige Nacht** die Christmas Eve.

**Heiligen|schein** der halo.

**Heilige Schrift** die Holy Scriptures (pl).

**Heiligtum** (pl -tümer) das - **1.** [Ort] shrine - **2.** [Gegenstand] relic.

**Heil|kraft** die healing power.

**Heil|kraut** das medicinal herb.

**Heilkunde** die medicine.

**heillos** adj terrible ⟨⟩ adv terribly.

**Heil|mittel** das remedy, cure.

**Heil|pflanze** die medicinal plant.

**Heil|praktiker, in** der, die alternative therapist.

**heilsam** adj salutary.

**Heilsarmee** die Salvation Army.

**Heilung** (pl -en) die [von Patient, Krankheit] curing; [von Wunde] healing.

**Heilungs|prozess** der: den ~ beschleunigen to speed up one's recovery.

**heim** adv home.

**Heim** (pl -e) das home.

**Heimarbeit** die: etw in ~ anfertigen to make sthg at home; ~ **machen** to work from home.

**Heimat** die [von Person] home, native country/region; [von Tier] original habitat.

**Heimat|anschrift** die home address.

**Heimat|film** der heimatfilm, feel-good film with a folkloric tone, mostly made in the 1950s and '60s.

**Heimat|hafen** der home port, port of registration.

**Heimat|kunde** die primary school subject covering local history, natural history and geography.

**Heimat|land** das native country.

**heimatlich** adj of/from one's native country/region; jm ein ~es Gefühl geben to remind sb of home.

**heimatlos** adj [Mensch] homeless; [Tier] stray.

**Heimat|museum** das local history museum.

**Heimat|ort** der home town.

**Heimat|vertriebene** der, die ethnic German who fled East Prussia, Silesia or Bohemia in 1945.

**Heim|computer** der home computer.

**Heim|fahrt** die journey home.

**heimisch** adj - **1.** [Bevölkerung, Industrie, Sitte] local; [Pflanze, Tier] indigenous - **2.** [zu Hause]: ~ werden to become acclimatized; sich ~ fühlen to feel at home.

**Heimkehr** die return journey.

**heim|kehren** (perf ist heimgekehrt) vi to return home.

**heim|kommen** (perf ist heimgekommen) vi (unreg) to come home.

**Heim|leiter, in** der, die warden.

**heimlich** adj secret ⟨⟩ adv secretly.

**Heimlichkeit** (pl -en) die secrecy; in aller ~ in complete secrecy.
➡ **Heimlichkeiten** pl secrets.

**Heimlichtuerei** (pl -en) die abw secretiveness.

**Heim|reise** die journey home.

**heim|reisen** (perf ist heimgereist) vi to return home.

**Heim|spiel** das home game.

**heim|suchen** vt - **1.** [Pest, Alptraum, Krankheit] to afflict; [Erdbeben] to hit - **2.** hum [belästigen] to descend on.

**Heim|trainer** [haim'trɛːnɐ] der exercise bike.

**heimtückisch** adj [Mensch, Verbrechen] malicious; [Krankheit] insidious ⟨⟩ adv maliciously.

**Heim|vorteil** der SPORT home advantage.

**heimwärts** adv homewards.

**Heim|weg** der way home.

**Heimweh** das homesickness; (nach jm/etw) ~ haben to be homesick (for sb/sthg).

**heim|zahlen** vt: jm etw ~ to pay sb back for sthg.

**Heinzel|männchen** das: das waren wohl die ~ it must have been the fairies.

**Heirat** (pl -en) die marriage.

**heiraten** vi to marry, to get married; standesamtlich ~ to get married in a registry office; kirchlich ~ to have a church wedding ⟨⟩ vt to marry.

**Heirats|annonce** die advertisement seeking a marriage partner.

**Heirats|antrag** der proposal (of marriage); jm einen ~ machen to propose to sb.

**heiratsfähig** adj marriageable.

**Heirats|schwindler** der man who pretends he is going to marry a woman in order to con her out of money etc.

**Heirats|urkunde** die marriage certificate.

**Heirats|vermittlung** die [Ort] marriage bureau.

**heiser** adj hoarse ⟨⟩ adv hoarsely; sie hat sich ~ geschrien she shouted until she was hoarse.

**Heiserkeit** (pl -en) die hoarseness.

**heiß** adj - **1.** [warm] [gen] hot; mir ist ~ I'm hot; es überläuft mich ~ und kalt I feel hot and cold all over; ~ auf jn sein fam to have the hots for sb **- 2.** [heftig - Diskussion, Auseinandersetzung] heated; [ - Liebe, Wunsch] ardent, burning **- 3.** *fam* [gut] brilliant <> *adv* **- 1.** [warm]: ~ **baden** to have a hot bath **- 2.** [heftig]: ~ **umstritten** hotly contested; jn ~ **lieben** to love sb passionately; **es ging** ~ **her** things got a bit heated.

**heißblütig** *adj* hot-blooded.

**heißen** (*prät* hieß; *perf* hat geheißen) *vi* **- 1.** [mit Namen] to be called; **er heißt Tom** he's called Tom, his name is Tom; **wie heißt du?** what's your name? **- 2.** [bedeuten] to mean; **was heißt das auf Deutsch?** how do you say that in German?; **was soll das ~!** what's the meaning of this!; **das will was ~!** that's quite something!; **das heißt** that is; **ich zeige dir das mal, das heißt, wenn du willst** I'll show you, if you want, that is; **ich komme morgen, das heißt, übermorgen** I'll be there tomorrow, or rather the day after **- 3.** [lauten] to be; **wie heißt der Titel?** what's the title?

**heiß geliebt** *adj* beloved.

**Heißhunger** *der* voracious appetite; **einen** ~ **auf etw** (A) **haben** to have a craving for sthg.

**heiß laufen** (*perf* hat/ist heiß gelaufen) *vi* (*unreg*) (*ist*) [Motor] to overheat; [Telefon] to buzz.

➤ **sich heiß laufen** *ref* [Motor] to overheat.

**Heißluft|ballon** *der* hot-air balloon.

**heiter** *adj* **- 1.** [fröhlich] cheerful **- 2.** [sonnig] fine.

**Heiterkeit** *die* **- 1.** [Fröhlichkeit] cheerfulness **- 2.** [vom Wetter] fineness.

**heizbar** *adj* heated.

**heizen** *vi* to turn on the heating; **wir** ~ **mit Gas/elektrisch** we have gas/electric heating <> *vt* to heat.

**Heizer, in** (*mpl* -; *fpl* -nen) *der, die* stoker.

**Heiz|kessel** *der* boiler.

**Heiz|kissen** *das* heated pad (*for back pain etc*).

**Heiz|körper** *der* radiator.

**Heiz|kraftwerk** *das* thermal power station.

**Heiz|lüfter** (*pl* -) *der* fan heater.

**Heiz|öl** *das* fuel oil.

**Heizung** (*pl* -en) *die* **- 1.** [System] heating **- 2.** [Heizkörper] radiator.

**Heizungs|keller** *der* boiler room.

**Hektar** (*pl* -e *oder* -) *das oder der* hectare.

**Hektik** *die* hectic pace; **bloß keine ~!** *fam* don't panic!

**hektisch** *adj* **- 1.** [Person, Bewegung] frantic; ~ **werden** to panic **- 2.** [Ort] hectic <> *adv* frantically.

**Hekto|liter** *das oder der* hectolitre.

**Held** (*pl* -en) *der* hero; **der** ~ **des Tages** *oder* **Abends sein** to be the hero of the hour.

**heldenhaft** *adj* heroic <> *adv* heroically.

**Helden|tat** *die* heroic deed.

**Heldin** (*pl* -nen) *die* heroine; **die** ~ **des Tages** *oder* **Abends sein** to be the heroine of the hour.

**helfen** (*präs* hilft; *prät* half; *perf* hat geholfen) *vi* **- 1.** [Hilfe leisten] to help; **jm (bei etw)** ~ to help sb (with sthg); **sich** (D) **zu** ~ **wissen** to know what to do **- 2.** [nützlich sein] to help; **es hilft nichts** it's no use *oder* good; **das hilft gegen Zahnschmerzen** it's good for toothache; **es hilft kein Weinen** it's no good crying.

**Helfer, in** (*mpl* -; *fpl* -nen) *der, die* helper.

**Helfers|helfer, in** *der, die abw* accomplice.

**Helgoland** *nt* Heligoland.

**Helium** *das* helium.

**hell** *adj* **- 1.** [Zimmer, Licht, Tag] bright; **es wird** ~ it's getting light **- 2.** [Farbe] light; [Haar, Haut] fair **- 3.** [Stimme] high (*esp. of child's voice*) **- 4.** [schlau] lucid **- 5.** [groß, intensiv - Freude, Begeisterung] sheer; [ - Empörung, Wahnsinn] utter <> *adv* **- 1.** [leuchtend] brightly **- 2.** [hoch]: ~ **klingen** to ring out clearly **- 3.** [sehr] totally.

**hellblau** *adj* light blue.

**hellblond** *adj* very fair.

**helle** *adj* bright.

**Heller** (*pl* -) *der*: **auf** ~ **und Pfennig** down to the last penny.

**hellgrün** *adj* light green.

**hellhörig** *adj* **- 1.** [misstrauisch]: **sie wurde** ~ her suspicions were aroused; **jn** ~ **machen** to arouse sb's suspicions **- 2.** [Raum]: **die Wohnung ist sehr** ~ you can hear everything through the walls in this flat.

**Helligkeit** (*pl* -en) *die* [von Licht] brightness.

**helllicht** *adj*: **am ~en Tage** in broad daylight.

**hellrot** *adj* light red.

**hell|sehen** *vi* (*unreg*) to see into the future.

**Hellseher, in** (*mpl* -; *fpl* -nen) *der, die* clairvoyant.

**hellwach** *adj* **- 1.** [wach] wide awake **- 2.** *fam* [rege] on the ball.

**Helm** (*pl* -e) *der* helmet.

**Helsinki** *nt* Helsinki.

**Hemd** (*pl* -en) *das* **- 1.** [Oberhemd] shirt **- 2.** [Unterhemd] vest *Br*, undershirt *Am*; **jn bis aufs** ~ **ausziehen** *fam* to have the shirt off sb's back.

**Hemd|bluse** *die* shirt (*for woman*).

**hemdsärmelig** *adj* casual.

**Hemi|sphäre** [hemi'sfɛːrə] *die* hemisphere.

**hemmen** *vt* - **1.** [bremsen - Bewegung, Geschwindigkeit] to slow down; [Fluss] to stem - **2.** [behindern] to impede, to hinder.

**Hemmlschuh** *der* brake shoe.

**Hemmlschwelle** *die* mental block.

**Hemmung** (*pl* -en) *die* [Behinderung] hindrance.
⬥ **Hemmungen** *pl* inhibitions; ~en haben to feel inhibited.

**hemmungslos** *adj* uninhibited ⬥ *adv* uninhibitedly.

**Hengst** (*pl* -e) *der* [Pferd] stallion; [Esel] jackass.

**Henkel** (*pl* -) *der* handle.

**Henker** (*pl* -) *der* [gen] executioner; [beim Erhängen] hangman.

**Henne** (*pl* -n) *die* hen.

**Hepatitis** *die* hepatitis.

**her** *adv* - **1.** [räumlich]: komm ~! come here!; ~ damit! give me that!; von Norden ~ from the north; von weit ~ from a long way away - **2.** [zeitlich]: das ist zehn Jahre ~ that was ten years ago; ich kenne sie von früher ~ I know her from before - **3.** [unter dem Aspekt]: von der Größe ~ as far as size is concerned; *siehe auch* her sein.

**herab** *adv* down; die Treppe ~ down the stairs.

**herablblicken** *vi* to look down; auf jn ~ *fig* & *geh* to look down on sb.

**herabllassen** *vt (unreg)* to lower.
⬥ **sich herablassen** *ref*: sich ~, etw zu tun to condescend to do sthg.

**herablassend** *adj* condescending, patronizing ⬥ *adv* condescendingly, patronizingly.

**herablsehen** *vi (unreg)* geh to look down; auf jn ~ *fig* to look down on sb.

**herablsetzen** *vt* - **1.** [Betrag] to reduce - **2.** [Person] to put down.

**heran, ran** *adv*: die Kiste kommt da an die Wand ~ the box goes up against the wall there; nur ~! come closer!

**heranlfahren** (*perf* hat/ist herangefahren) (*unreg*) *vi (ist)*: an etw (A) ~ to drive up to sthg ⬥ *vt (hat)*: etw an etw (A) ~ to drive sthg up to sthg.

**heranlführen** *vt*: jn an etw (A) ~ to introduce sb to sthg.

**heranlkommen** (*perf* ist herangekommen) *vi (unreg)* - **1.** [kommen] to approach; sie lässt nichts an sich (A) ~ she doesn't let anything bother her; an jn ~ [erreichen] to get hold of sb; [entsprechen] to match up to sb; an etw (A) ~ to be able to reach sthg - **2.** [bekommen]: an etw (A) ~ to get hold of sthg.

**heranllassen** *vt (unreg)*: jn an etw (A) ~ to let sb near sthg; jn nicht *ODER* niemanden *ODER* keinen an sich (A) ~ *fig* not to let anyone get close.

**heranlmachen** ⬥ sich heranmachen *ref*: sich an etw (A) ~ to get down to sthg; sich an jn ~ *fam abw* to chat sb up.

**heranlreichen** *vi*: an jn/etw ~ to match sb/sthg.

**heranlrücken** (*perf* ist/hat herangerückt) *vt (hat)* /*vi (ist)* to move closer.

**heranltasten** ⬥ sich herantasten *ref* - **1.** [sich annähern]: sich an etw (A) ~ to feel one's way towards sthg - **2.** [tasten] to feel one's way.

**heranltreten** (*perf* ist herangetreten) *vi (unreg)*: an jn ~ to approach sb.

**heranlwachsen** [hɛˈranvaksn̩] (*perf* ist herangewachsen) *vi (unreg)* to grow up.

**Heranwachsende** [hɛˈranvaksn̩də] (*pl* -n) *der, die* adolescent.

**heranlwagen** ⬥ sich heranwagen *ref*: sich an jn/etw ~ to dare to go near sb/sthg.

**heranlziehen** (*perf* hat/ist herangezogen) (*unreg*) *vt (hat)* - **1.** [ziehen]: etw an etw (A) ~ to pull sthg up to sthg - **2.** [befragen] to consult - **3.** [erziehen] to teach ⬥ *vi (ist)* [kommen] to draw near.

**herauf, rauf** *adv* up; die Treppe ~ up the stairs; vom Tal ~ up from the valley.

**herauflbeschwören** *vt (unreg)* - **1.** [verursachen] to cause - **2.** [Vergangenes] to evoke.

**herauflkommen** (*perf* ist heraufgekommen) *vi (unreg)* to come up/upstairs.

**herauflziehen** (*perf* hat/ist heraufgezogen) (*unreg*) *vi (ist)* [kommen] to approach ⬥ *vt (hat)* [ziehen] to pull up.

**heraus, raus** *adv* out; ~ aus dem Bett (get) out of bed!; ~ mit der Sprache! spit it out!, out with it!; aus dieser Überlegung ~ as a result of these reflections; es ist noch nicht ~, wer das Rennen gewonnen hat it's still unclear who won the race; *siehe auch* heraus sein.

**herauslbekommen** *vt (unreg)* - **1.** [Geheimnis] to find out; [Lösung] to work out - **2.** [entfernen] to get out - **3.** [Wechselgeld] to get back.

**herauslbilden** ⬥ sich herausbilden *ref* to develop.

**herauslbringen** *vt (unreg)* - **1.** [bringen] to bring/take out - **2.** [veröffentlichen, verkaufen] to bring out; etw (ganz) groß ~ to launch sthg amid a fanfare of publicity - **3.** *fam* [entlocken]: etw aus jm ~ to get sthg out of sb - **4.** [aussprechen, artikulieren] to utter.

**herauslfinden** (*unreg*) *vt* [entdecken] to find out ⬥ *vi* [herauskommen]: aus etw ~ to find a way out of sthg.

**herauslfliegen** (*perf* hat/ist herausgeflo-

**gen)** *(unreg)* *vt (hat)* [fliegen] to fly out <> *vi (ist)* - **1.** [fliegen - Tier, Gegenstand]: **aus etw ~** to fly out of sthg - **2.** *fam* [zur Strafe] to be thrown out - **3.** *fam* [herausfallen]: **aus etw ~** to fall out of sthg.

**herausIfließen** *(perf* ist her**aus**geflossen) *vi (unreg)* to flow out.

**Her**ausforderer *(pl -) der* challenger.

**Her**ausforderin *(pl -nen) die* challenger.

**herausIfordern** *vt* - **1.** SPORT [Feind] to challenge; **jn ~, etw zu tun** to challenge sb to do sthg - **2.** [provozieren] to provoke; **das Schicksal ~** to tempt fate.

**herausfordernd** *adj* provocative; [Frage] challenging <> *adv* provocatively.

**Her**ausIforderung *die* - **1.** SPORT [Aufgabe] challenge - **2.** [Provokation] provocation; [von Schicksal] tempting.

**Her**ausgabe *die (ohne pl)* - **1.** [Rückgabe, Freilassung] return - **2.** [von Veröffentlichung] publication.

**herausIgeben** *vt (unreg)* - **1.** [veröffentlichen] to publish - **2.** [geben]: **jm etw ~** to pass ODER hand sthg out to sb - **3.** [freilassen] to return - **4.** [Wechselgeld] to give back; **auf 50 Euro ~** to give change from 50 euros.

**Her**ausgeber, in *(mpl -; fpl -nen) der, die* - **1.** [Redakteur] editor - **2.** [Verleger] publisher.

**herausIgehen** *(perf* ist her**aus**gegangen) *vi (unreg)* - **1.** [nach draußen] to go out; **aus sich ~** *fig* to come out of one's shell - **2.** [Fleck, Schraube] to come out.

**herausIgreifen** *vt (unreg)* to pick out.

**herausIgucken** *vi fam* - **1.** [gucken] to look out - **2.** [sichtbar sein] to peep out.

**herausIhaben** *vt (unreg)* - **1.** [Lösung] to find; **~, wie ...** to find out how ... - **2.** [entfernt haben] to have got out.

**herausIhalten** *(unreg) vt* - **1.** [nach draußen] to hold out - **2.** *fam* [fern halten]: **jn aus etw ~** to keep sb out of sthg.

**~ sich heraushalten** *ref*: **sich aus etw ~** to keep out of sthg.

**herausIhängen** *vt (reg)* to hang out; **etw ~ lassen** *fam abw* to show off about sthg <> *vi (unreg)* to hang out.

**herausIholen** *vt* - **1.** [holen]: **jn/etw aus etw ~** to get sb/sthg out of sthg - **2.** [Information]: **etw aus jm ~** to get sthg out of sb - **3.** [Leistung] to get ODER squeeze out - **4.** [Geld, Gewinn] to make - **5.** SPORT to make up.

**herausIhören** *vt*: **etw aus etw ~** [erahnen] to detect sthg from sthg; [hören] to make out sthg amid sthg.

**herausIkommen** *(perf* ist her**aus**gekommen) *vi (unreg)* - **1.** [nach draußen] **(aus etw) ~** to come out (from sthg) - **2.** [Resultat]: **bei der** Rechnung kommt immer etwas anderes heraus I keep getting a different answer for the sum; **was kommt dabei heraus?** what's that going to achieve?; **das kommt auf dasselbe heraus** it amounts to the same thing, it makes no difference - **3.** [auf den Markt kommen] to come out; **(ganz) groß ~** *fig* to make a real splash - **4.** [Verbrechen] to come to light - **5.** [entkommen]: **aus etw ~** to come out ODER emerge from sthg - **6.** [deutlich werden] to stand out - **7.** [aus dem Takt kommen] to get out of time - **8.** [beim Kartenspiel] to lead - **9.** *fam* [sagen]: **mit etw ~** to come out with sthg.

**herausIkristallisieren** ~ **sich herauskristallisieren** *ref* to emerge.

**herausInehmen** *vt (unreg)* - **1.** [entfernen]: **etw (aus etw) ~** to take sthg out (of sthg) - **2.** [wagen]: **sich (D) Freiheiten ~** to take liberties.

**herausIragen** *vi* - **1.** [hervorstechen] to stand out - **2.** [herausstehen] to jut out.

**herausragend** *adj* outstanding, excellent <> *adv* outstandingly, excellently.

**herausIreden** ~ **sich herausreden** *ref*: **sich damit ~, dass ...** to make excuses for o.s. by saying that ...

**herausIreißen** *vt (unreg)* - **1.** [reißen - Blatt] to tear out; [ - Pfahl] to pull out - **2.** [entfernen] to uproot - **3.** *fam* [entlasten] to get off the hook.

**herausIrücken** *(perf* hat/ist her**aus**gerückt) *vt (hat) fam* [Geld] to cough up <> *vi (ist)* [sagen]: **mit etw ~** to come out with sthg.

**herausIschlagen** *(perf* hat/ist her**aus**geschlagen) *(unreg) vt (hat)* - **1.** [schlagen] to knock out - **2.** [Gewinn] to make <> *vi (ist)* [Feuer]: **aus etw ~** to leap out of sthg.

**heraus sein** *(perf* ist her**aus** gewesen) *vi (unreg)* - **1.** [entlassen sein]: **aus etw ~** to be out of sthg, to have left sthg - **2.** [entkommen sein]: **fein ~** to be sitting pretty - **3.** [Produkt] to be out - **4.** [herausgegangen sein]: **aus einer Phase ~** to be past a phase - **5.** [entfernt sein] to be out - **6.** [klar sein] to be known.

**herausIstellen** *vt* - **1.** [nach draußen] to put out - **2.** [hervorheben] to highlight.

**~ sich herausstellen** *ref* [klar werden] to become clear; **wer gelogen hat, wird sich noch ~** we'll soon see who has been lying; **sich als falsch/richtig ~** to turn out to be wrong/right.

**herausIstrecken** *vt* to stick out.

**herausIsuchen** *vt* to pick out; **jm etw ~** to find sthg for sb.

**herausIziehen** *vt (unreg)* to pull out.

**herb, herbe** *adj* - **1.** [Geschmack] sharp - **2.** [Enttäuschung, Erfahrung] bitter - **3.** [Kritik] harsh - **4.** [Schönheit] austere; [Gesicht, Person] dour <> *adv* - **1.** [leicht bitter]: **~ schmecken** to taste sharp - **2.** [enttäuschen] bitterly - **3.** [kritisieren] harshly.

H

**herbe** = herb.

**herbei** adv here; **alle Mann ~!** everyone come here!

**herbeilführen** vt to cause.

**herbeilschaffen** vt to get hold of.

**herlbemühen** vt geh to ask to come.
➤ **sich herbemühen** ref geh to be so good as to come.

**Herberge** (pl -n) die - **1.** [Unterkunft] lodging - **2.** [Jugendherberge] (youth) hostel.

**Herbergsleltern** pl (hostel) wardens.

**Herbergslmutter** die (hostel) warden.

**Herbergslvater** der (hostel) warden.

**herlbestellen** vt to ask to come.

**herlbitten** vt (unreg) to ask to come.

**herlbringen** vt (unreg) to bring here.

**Herbst** (pl -e) der autumn Br, fall Am; **im ~ in the autumn** Br, **in the fall** Am.

**Herbstlanfang** der beginning of autumn Br ODER fall Am.

**Herbstlferien** pl autumn holidays Br, fall vacation Am.

**herbstlich** adj autumnal.

**Herd** (pl -e) der - **1.** [Ofen] cooker - **2.** [von Revolte] seat; [von Krankheit] focus.

**Herde** (pl -n) die - **1.** [von Rindern, Elefanten] herd; [von Schafen] flock - **2.** abw [von Menschen] gang.

**Herdlplatte** die hotplate.

**herein, rein** adv in; **herein!** come in!

**hereinlbrechen** (perf ist hereingebrochen) vi (unreg) geh - **1.** [Nacht] to fall - **2.** [Unglück]: **über jn ~** to befall sb.

**hereinlfallen** (perf ist hereingefallen) vi (unreg) - **1.** [getäuscht werden] to be conned; **auf jn/etw ~** to be taken in by sb/sthg - **2.** [fallen] to fall in - **3.** [Licht] to come in, to enter.

**hereinlkommen** (perf ist hereingekommen) vi (unreg) to come in.

**hereinllassen** vt (unreg) to let in.

**hereinllegen** vt [täuschen] to take for a ride.

**hereinlspazieren** (perf ist hereinspaziert) vi fam to breeze in.
➤ **hereinspaziert** interj fam come right in!

**herlfahren** (perf hat/ist hergefahren) (unreg) vi (ist) to come here <> vt (hat) to drive here.

**Herlfahrt** die journey here.

**herlfallen** (perf ist hergefallen) vi (unreg): **über jn ~** [angreifen] to attack sb; **über etw (A) ~** [essen] to attack sthg.

**Herlgang** der: **der ~ der Tat** the course of events leading to the crime; **jm den ~ einer Sache (G) schildern** to describe to sb how sthg happened.

**herlgeben** vt (unreg) - **1.** [geben] to give; [überrei-chen] to hand over - **2.** [verschenken] to give away - **3.** [verzichten auf] to give up - **4.** [erbringen]: **der Text gibt für unser Thema nichts her** the text is of no use for our topic.
➤ **sich hergeben** ref: **sich zu etw ~** abw to allow o.s. to get involved in sthg.

**hergeholt** adj: **weit ~** far-fetched.

**hergelaufen** pp ▷ **herlaufen** <> adj abw good-for-nothing.

**herlhaben** vt (unreg) fam: **wo hast du das her?** where did you get this?

**herlhalten** (unreg) vi abw [dienen]: **als etw ~** to be used as sthg; **für jn ~** to have to take the blame for sb <> vt [halten] to hold out.

**herlholen** vt to fetch.

**herlhören** vi to listen.

**Hering** (pl -e) der - **1.** [Fisch] herring - **2.** [am Zelt] tent peg.

**Heringslsalat** der salad made from marinated herring, onion, mayonnaise and gherkins.

**herlkommen** (perf ist hergekommen) vi (unreg) - **1.** [kommen] to come here; **wo kommst du denn jetzt her?** where have you just been? - **2.** [entstehen, stammen] to come from; **wo kommen Sie her?** where do you come from?

**herkömmlich** adj conventional <> adv conventionally.

**Herkunft** die (ohne pl) [von Person] origins (pl); [von Sache] origin.

**Herkunftslland** das country of origin.

**herllaufen** (perf ist hergelaufen) vi (unreg): **neben jm/etw ~** to run alongside sb/sthg; **hinter jm/etw ~** to run after sb/sthg.

**herlmachen** vi: **viel ~** to look impressive; **wenig ~** not to look very impressive; **nichts ~** not to be up to much.
➤ **sich hermachen** ref fam: **sich über etw (A) ~** to set about sthg.

**hermetisch** adj - **1.** [Verschluss] hermetic - **2.** [Sprache, Gedicht] impenetrable <> adv [verschließen] hermetically.

**herlnehmen** vt (unreg) [nehmen, bekommen] to get.

**Heroin** das heroin.

**heroisch** adj heroic <> adv heroically.

**Herr** (pl -en) der - **1.** [Mann] gentleman; **meine ~en!** gentlemen!; '**~en**' [WC] 'gents' - **2.** [Anrede] Mr; **an ~n Müller** to Mr Müller; **~ Doktor** Doctor - **3.** [Gott] Lord - **4.** [Oberhaupt, Gebieter] lord; **der ~ des Hauses** the master of the house - **5.** RW: **aus aller ~en Länder** from every corner of the globe; **einer Sache (G) ~ werden** to get sthg under control; **~ der Lage sein** to be master of the situation; **sein eigener ~ sein** to be one's own master.

**Herrchen** (*pl* -) *das* master.

**Herren|bekleidung** *die* menswear.

**Herrenfahr|rad** *das* men's bicycle.

**Herren|friseur** *der* men's hairdresser, barber.

**herrenlos** *adj* [Tier] stray; [Koffer] abandoned.

**Herren|mode** *die* men's fashion.

**Herren|toilette** *die* men's toilet.

**Herrgott** *der*: **zum ~ beten** to pray to the Lord (God).
➤ **Herrgott noch mal** *interj* for heaven's sake!

**Herrgottsfrühe** *die*: **in aller ~** at the crack of dawn.

**her|richten** *vt* - **1.** [vorbereiten] to get ready - **2.** [reparieren] to renovate.

**Herrin** (*pl* -nen) *die* mistress.

**herrisch** *adj* [Person, Worte] overbearing; [Blick] imperious ◇ *adv* in an overbearing manner.

**herrlich** *adj* wonderful ◇ *adv* wonderfully; **~ schmecken** to taste wonderful.

**Herrlichkeit** (*pl* -en) *die* - **1.** [Qualität] glory - **2.** [herrliche Sache] wonderful thing.

**Herrschaft** (*pl* -en) *die* [über Staat, Volk] rule; **die ~ über jn/etw verlieren** to lose control of sb/sthg.
➤ **Herrschaften** *pl* people; **meine ~en!** ladies and gentlemen!

**herrschaftlich** *adj* grand ◇ *adv* grandly.

**herrschen** *vi* - **1.** [regieren]: **(über jn/etw) ~** to rule (over sb/sthg) - **2.** [bestehen] to prevail; **es herrschte allgemeine Unruhe** there was general unrest.

**Herrscher, in** (*mpl* -; *fpl* -nen) *der, die* ruler.

**herrschsüchtig** *adj* domineering.

**her|sagen** *vt* to recite.

**her|schieben** *vt (unreg)* to push here; **etw vor sich** (D) **~** [schieben] to push sthg along ahead of one; [vertagen] to put sthg off.

**her sein** (*perf* **ist her gewesen**) *vi (unreg)* - **1.** [vergangen sein]: **es ist drei Tage her, dass wir telefoniert haben** it is three days since we phoned - **2.** [herkommen]: **to come from - 3.** *RW*: **es ist nicht weit her mit jm/etw** sb/sthg is not up to much; **hinter jm/etw ~** to be after sb/sthg.

**her|stellen** *vt* - **1.** [produzieren] to produce, to make; [industriell] to manufacture - **2.** [Ruhe, Ordnung] to establish; **ihre Gesundheit ist wieder hergestellt** she has recovered, her health has been restored - **3.** [näher rücken] to put (over) here.
➤ **sich herstellen** *ref* - **1.** [Ordnung, Ruhe] to establish itself - **2.** [sich stellen]: **stell dich doch zu uns her!** come over here with us!

**Hersteller, in** (*mpl* -; *fpl* -nen) *der, die* manufacturer.

**Her|stellung** *die* - **1.** [Produktion] production; [industriell] manufacture - **2.** [von Ruhe, Ordnung] establishment.

**Hertz** (*pl* -) *das* PHYS hertz.

**herüber, rüber** *adv* over.

**herüber|kommen** (*perf* **ist herübergekommen**) *vi (unreg)* to come over.

**herüber|ziehen** (*perf* **hat/ist herübergezogen**) *(unreg) vt (hat)* [ziehen] to pull over ◇ *vi (ist)* [umziehen] to move here.

**herum** *adv* - **1.** [räumlich] round; **um etw ~** around sthg; **um den Tisch ~** around the table; **das Gerücht ist schon in der ganzen Nachbarschaft ~** the rumour has already got around the whole neighbourhood; **du trägst den Pullover verkehrt ~** your pullover is on the wrong way round; **was um sie ~ geschieht** what's going on around her - **2.** [ungefähr] around, about; **um die 50 Euro ~** around ODER about 50 euros.

**herum|ärgern** ➤ **sich herumärgern** *ref*: **sich mit jm/etw ~** to waste one's time with sb/sthg.

**herum|drehen** *vt* [Blatt, Decke] to turn over; [Schlüssel] to turn; [Pfannkuchen] to toss ◇ *vi* [drehen]: **an etw** (D) **~** to turn sthg.
➤ **sich herumdrehen** *ref* [sich umdrehen] to turn round.

**herum|fahren** (*perf* **hat/ist herumgefahren**) *(unreg) vi (ist)* - **1.** [im Kreis]: **um etw ~** to go round sthg - **2.** [umherfahren] to drive around - **3.** [sich umdrehen] to turn round - **4.** [wischen] to wipe around ◇ *vt (hat)* to drive around.

**herum|führen** *vt* - **1.** [in Stadt, Haus] to show around - **2.** [um etw herum]: **jn um etw ~** to take sb round sthg ◇ *vi* [im Kreis]: **um etw ~** to go round sthg.

**herum|geben** *vt (unreg)* to pass round.

**herum|gehen** (*perf* **ist herumgegangen**) *vi (unreg)* - **1.** [spazieren] to walk around - **2.** [zwischen Personen] to go around - **3.** [im Kreis]: **um etw ~** to go round sthg - **4.** [Gerücht] to go around - **5.** [Zeit] to pass.

**herum|hängen** *vi (unreg) fam* to hang around.

**herum|kommandieren** *vt* to order around.

**herum|kommen** (*perf* **ist herumgekommen**) *vi (unreg) fam* - **1.** [reisen] to get around - **2.** [gehen, fahren] **um etw ~** to get round sthg - **3.** [vermeiden]: **um etw ~/nicht ~** to get out of/ not to get out of sthg.

**herum|kriegen** *vt fam* - **1.** [überreden]: **sie hat mich doch noch herumgekriegt** she talked me into it in the end - **2.** [verbringen]: **die Zeit ~** to kill time - **3.** [räumlich]: **etw um etw ~** to get sthg round sthg.

**herum|laufen** (*perf* ist her**u**mgelaufen) *vi* (*unreg*) - **1.** *fam* [umhergehen] to walk around; [schneller] to run around - **2.** [im Kreis]: **um etw ~** [laufen, gehen] to go round sthg; [schneller] to run round sthg; **die Straße läuft um den Stadtkern herum** the road goes round the city centre - **3.** *fam* [gekleidet sein] to go *ODER* run around.

**herum|liegen** *vi* (*unreg*) to lie around.

**herum|lungern** (*perf* hat/ist her**u**mgelungert) *vi fam* [in der Stadt] to hang around; [auf dem Sofa] to lounge around.

**herum|posaunen** *vt fam* to broadcast.

**herum|reichen** *vt* to pass round.

**herum|reiten** (*perf* ist herumgeritten) *vi* (*unreg*): **auf etw** (D) **~** to go on about sthg.

**herum|schlagen** *vt* (*unreg*): **etw um etw ~** to wrap sthg round sthg.

➤ **sich herumschlagen** *ref*: **sich mit jm/etw ~** to battle with sb/sthg.

**herum|sitzen** *vi* (*unreg*) - **1.** [sitzen] to sit around - **2.** [im Kreis]: **um jn/etw ~** to sit round sb/sthg.

**herum|sprechen ➤ sich herumsprechen** *ref* (*unreg*) to get around.

**herum|stehen** *vi* (*unreg*) - **1.** [stehen - Person] to stand around; [ - Dinge] to sit around - **2.** [im Kreis]: **um jn/etw ~** to stand round sb/sthg.

**herum|stochern** *vi*: **in etw** (D) **~** *fam* to poke around in sthg; **im Essen ~** to pick at one's food.

**herum|treiben ➤ sich herumtreiben** *ref* (*unreg*) *fam* to hang around.

**Herumtreiber, in** (*mpl* -; *fpl* **-nen**) *der, die fam*: **er ist ein ~** he's always hanging around doing nothing.

**herum|trödeln** *vi* to dawdle around.

**herum|wickeln** *vt*: **etw um etw ~** to wrap sthg around sthg.

**herum|zeigen** *vt* to show round.

**herum|ziehen** (*perf* hat/ist herumgezogen) (*unreg*) *vi* (*ist*) - **1.** [herumfahren] to wander about; **in der Welt ~** to roam the world - **2.** [im Kreis]: **um etw ~** to go round sthg <> *vt* (*hat*): **etw um etw ~** to put sthg round sthg.

**herunter, runter** *adv* down; **~ da vom Dach!** get down from the roof!; **~ mit dir!** down you come!; [vom Stuhl] off you get!; **vom General bis ~ zum einfachen Soldaten** from the general down to the private; **auf der Fahrt von Hamburg ~** on the journey down from Hamburg.

**herunter|bekommen** *vt* (*unreg*) *fam* - **1.** [schlucken können, nach unten bekommen] to get down; **ich bekomme nichts mehr herunter** I

can't manage another thing - **2.** [entfernen können] to get off; **den Schmutz vom Teppich ~** to get the dirt out of the carpet.

**herunter|fahren** *vt* (*unreg*) - **1.** [reduzieren - Produktion] to scale down; [ - Temperatur] to reduce - **2.** EDV to shut down.

**heruntergekommen** *adj* - **1.** [Haus] dilapidated - **2.** [Person] down-at-heel.

**herunter|hauen** *vt fam*: **jm eine ~** to box sb's ears.

**herunter|holen** *vt* to bring down; **sich** (D) **einen ~** *vulg* to jerk off, to have a wank *Br*.

**herunter|laden** *vt* (*unreg*) EDV to download.

**herunter|lassen** *vt* (*unreg*) - **1.** [senken] to lower - **2.** [gehen lassen] to let down.

**herunter|laufen** (*perf* ist heruntergelaufen) *vi* (*unreg*) - **1.** [Person] to come down; [schnell] to run down - **2.** [Wasser, Tränen]: **(an etw** (D)) **~** to run down (sthg).

**herunter|machen** *vt*: **jn/etw ~** *fam* to pull sb/sthg to pieces, to knock sb/sthg.

**herunter|schlucken** *vt* to swallow.

**herunter|schrauben** *vt* - **1.** [durch Drehen] to turn down - **2.** *fig* [anpassen, Ansprüche] to lower.

**herunter|spielen** *vt* - **1.** [bagatellisieren] to play down - **2.** *abw* [Musik] to play through mechanically.

**herunter|ziehen** (*perf* hat/ist heruntergezogen) (*unreg*) *vt* (*hat*) to pull down <> *vi* (*ist*) to move down.

**hervor** *adv*: **hinter dem Sofa ~** out from behind the sofa; **~ mit euch!** out you come!

**hervor|bringen** *vt* (*unreg*) - **1.** [Ton] to utter - **2.** [entwickeln] to produce.

**hervor|gehen** (*perf* ist hervorgegangen) *vi* (*unreg*): **aus etw ~** [zu entnehmen sein] to be clear from sthg; **aus dieser Familie sind mehrere Künstler hervorgegangen** this family has produced several artists; **aus etw als Sieger ~** to emerge victorious from sthg.

**hervor|heben** *vt* (*unreg*) to emphasize; **js Leistung ~** to single out sb's performance.

**hervor|holen** *vt* to bring out.

**hervorragend** *adj* excellent <> *adv* excellently; **~ angezogen sein** to be extremely well-dressed; **~ schmecken** to taste excellent.

**hervor|rufen** *vt* (*unreg*) - **1.** [verursachen] to cause - **2.** [rufen] to call out.

**hervor|stechen** *vi* (*unreg*) to stand out.

**hervor|treten** (*perf* ist hervorgetreten) *vi* (*unreg*) - **1.** [Adern, Augen] to bulge - **2.** [nach vorne kommen] to step forward.

**hervor|tun ➤ sich hervortun** *ref* (*unreg*)

- **1.** [auffallen] to distinguish o.s. - **2.** *abw* [angeben] to show off.

**Herweg** *der* way here.

**Herz** (*pl* -en *ODER* -) *das* - **1.** [gen] heart - **2.** *(ohne Artikel)* (ohne pl) [Spielkartenfarbe] hearts (pl) - **3.** *RW:* **ein ~ für jn/etw haben** to be fond of sb/sthg; **ein ~ und eine Seele sein** to be inseparable; **es nicht übers ~ bringen, etw zu tun** not to have the heart to do sthg; **etwas auf dem ~en haben** to have sthg on one's mind; **jd/etw lässt js ~ höher schlagen** sb/sthg makes sb's heart beat faster; **jm das ~ brechen** to break sb's heart; **ich möchte dir etwas ans ~ legen** allow me to give you a piece of advice; **jm sein ~ ausschütten** to pour one's heart out to sb; **jn/etw auf ~ und Nieren prüfen** to examine sb/sthg very carefully; **sie/es liegt ihm am ~en** she/it matters to him; **jn sofort ins ~ schließen** to take to sb immediately; **sein ~ hängt an dem alten Wagen** he's very attached to the old car; **kein ~ haben** to be heartless; **leichten/schweren ~ens** with a light/heavy heart; **gib deinem ~en einen Stoß** go for it!; **seinem ~en Luft machen** to give vent to one's feelings.

◆ **von ganzem Herzen** *adv* wholeheartedly.

**Herz|anfall** *der* heart attack.

**Herzensbrecher, in** (*mpl* -; *fpl* -nen) *der, die* heartbreaker.

**herzensgut** *adj* kind-hearted.

**Herzenslust** *die:* **nach ~** to one's heart's content.

**herzerfrischend** *adj* refreshing ◇ *adv* refreshingly.

**herzergreifend** *adj* heartrending ◇ *adv* heartrendingly.

**Herz|fehler** *der* heart defect.

**herzförmig** *adj* heart-shaped.

**herzhaft** *adj* - **1.** [fest] hearty - **2.** [nahrhaft] hearty and tasty ◇ *adv* - **1.** [fest] heartily - **2.** [nahrhaft]: **~ schmecken** to be hearty and tasty.

**her|ziehen** (*perf* hat/ist hergezogen) (*unreg*) *vt* (*hat*) [heranziehen] to pull up; **jn/etw hinter sich** (*D*) **~** to drag sb/sthg along behind one ◇ *vi* - **1.** *abw* [lästern]: **über jn ~** to pull sb to pieces - **2.** (*ist*) [umziehen] to move here - **3.** (*ist*) [gehen] to walk along.

**herzig** *adj* adorable ◇ *adv* adorably.

**Herz|infarkt** *der* heart attack.

**Herz|klopfen** *das:* **ich habe ~** my heart is pounding.

**herzkrank** *adj:* **ein ~er Mensch** a person suffering from heart trouble.

**Herz|leiden** *das* heart condition.

**herzlich** *adj* - **1.** [freundlich] warm - **2.** [aufrichtig] sincere ◇ *adv* - **1.** [freundlich] warmly - **2.** [aufrichtig] sincerely - **3.** [sehr] really; **~ wenig** very little.

**herzlos** *adj* heartless ◇ *adv* heartlessly.

**Herzlosigkeit** (*pl* -en) *die* - **1.** [Eigenschaft] heartlessness - **2.** [herzlose Tat] heartless thing.

**Herz|mittel** *das* heart medication.

**Herzog, in** (*mpl* Herzöge; *fpl* -nen) *der, die* duke (*f* duchess).

**Herzogtum** (*pl* -tümer) *das* duchy.

**Herz|patient, in** *der, die* heart patient.

**Herz|schlag** *der* - **1.** [Herzrhythmus] heartbeat - **2.** [Augenblick]: **einen ~ lang** for a brief moment - **3.** [Herzstillstand] heart failure (*U*).

**Herz|schmerz** *der* chest pains (*pl*).

**Herz|schrittmacher** (*pl* -) *der* pacemaker.

**Herz|stillstand** *der* cardiac arrest.

**Herz|verpflanzung** *die* heart transplant.

**herzzerreißend** *adj* heartrending ◇ *adv* heartrendingly.

**Hesse** (*pl* -n) *der* Hessian.

**Hessen** *nt* Hesse.

**Hessin** (*pl* -nen) *die* Hessian.

**hessisch** *adj* Hessian.

**heterogen** *adj* heterogeneous ◇ *adv* heterogeneously.

**heterosexuell** [ˈheterosɛksu̯ɛl] *adj* heterosexual.

**Hetze** *die* - **1.** [Hast] (mad) rush - **2.** [Lästern] hate campaign.

**hetzen** (*perf* hat/ist gehetzt) *vi* - **1.** (*ist*) [rennen] to rush - **2.** (*hat*) [lästern]: **gegen jn ~** to stir up hatred against sb ◇ *vt* (*hat*): **jn/etw auf jn ~** to set sb/sthg on sb.

◆ **sich hetzen** *ref* [sich beeilen] to rush.

**Hetz|kampagne** *die* [durch Verleumdung] smear campaign; [Hass erregend] hate campaign.

**Heu** *das* - **1.** [getrocknetes Gras] hay - **2.** *fam* [Geld] dough, dosh *Br.*

**Heu|boden** *der* hayloft.

**Heuchelei** (*pl* -en) *die abw* - **1.** [Vortäuschen] hypocrisy - **2.** [Tat] piece of hypocrisy; [Äußerung] hypocritical remark.

**heucheln** *vt* to feign ◇ *vi* to be a hypocrite.

**Heuchler, in** (*mpl* -; *fpl* -nen) *der, die* hypocrite.

**heuchlerisch** *adj* hypocritical ◇ *adv* hypocritically.

**heuer** *adv Süddt, Österr & Schweiz* this year.

**heulen** *vi* - **1.** [Person, Tier] to howl - **2.** [Sirene] to wail.

**Heulen** *das:* **es ist zum ~** *fam* it's enough to make you weep.

**Heul|ton** der wail.

**Heuschnupfen** der hay fever.

**Heuschrecke** (pl -n) die [klein] grasshopper; [groß] locust.

**heute** adv - **1.** [als ein Tag] today; ~ früh early this morning; ~ **Morgen/Mittag/Abend** this morning/lunchtime/evening; ~ **in vierzehn Tagen/einer Woche** a fortnight/a week today; **lieber** ~ **als morgen** sooner rather than later; **von** ~ **auf morgen** from one day to the next, overnight - **2.** [gegenwärtig] nowadays.

**heutig** adj today's; **der** ~**e Tag** today; **die** ~**e Jugend** the youth of today, young people these days; **bis zum** ~**en Tag** until today.

**heutzutage** adv nowadays.

**Hexe** (pl -n) die witch.

**Hexenschuss** der: **einen** ~ **haben** to have lumbago.

**Hexerei** (pl -en) die witchcraft.

**Hibiskus** der hibiscus.

**Hieb** (pl -e) der [Schlag] blow.

➡ **Hiebe** pl fam [Prügel]: ~**e bekommen** to get a beating.

**hiebfest** adj: **hieb- und stichfest** watertight.

**hielt** prät ➾ **halten.**

**hier** adv - **1.** [räumlich] here; [in der Schule]: **hier! here!**, present!; **der/die/das** ~ this one here; **ab** ~ from here; **von** ~ **aus** from here; ~ **und da** here and there; **im Hier und Jetzt leben** to live in the here and now; „~ **spricht Stefan**" [beim Telefon] "Stefan speaking"; **ich bin nicht von** ~ I'm not from around here; ~**, nimm schon!** here, take it! - **2.** [zeitlich] now; ~ **brach sie in Tränen aus** then she broke into tears; **von** ~ **an** from now on; ~ **und da** now and then - **3.** [in dieser Sache]: ~ **täuschst du dich aber!** but that's where you're wrong.

**hieran** adv - **1.** [an dieser/diese Sache]: **ich bin** ~ **nicht interessiert** I am not interested in this; **die Erinnerung** ~ **fällt ihm schwer** he has difficulty remembering this - **2.** [an diesem/diesen Platz]: ~ **sind wir schon vorbeigekommen** we've already come past here; **das Original auf dem Kopierer** ~ **anlegen** place the original here on the photocopier.

**Hierarchie** (pl -n) die hierarchy.

**hierauf** adv - **1.** [auf dieser/diese Sache]: ~ **beharren** to insist on this; ~ **keine Antwort finden** to find no answer to this - **2.** [auf diesem/diesen Platz] on here - **3.** [daraufhin] hereupon.

**hieraufhin** adv geh hereupon.

**hieraus** adv out of this.

**hier behalten** vt (unreg) to keep here.

**hierbei** adv - **1.** [zeitlich] on this occasion - **2.** [bei dieser Sache]: ~ **ist Konzentration nötig** you need to concentrate whilst doing this.

**hier bleiben** (perf ist hier geblieben) vi (unreg) to stay here.

**hierdurch** adv - **1.** [örtlich] through here - **2.** [ursächlich] as a result of this - **3.** [hiermit] hereby.

**hierfür** adv for this.

**hierher** adv here.

**hierhin** adv here.

**hierin** adv - **1.** [örtlich] in here - **2.** [in dieser Angelegenheit] in this.

**hiermit** adv - **1.** [mit diesem Gegenstand, mit dieser Angelegenheit] with this - **2.** [mit dieser Handlung] hereby.

**hiernach** adv - **1.** [zeitlich] after this - **2.** [dieser Aussage folgend] according to this - **3.** [nach dieser Sache, Angelegenheit] for this.

**hier sein** (perf ist hier gewesen) vi (unreg) to be here.

**hierüber** adv - **1.** [räumlich] over here - **2.** [über diese Angelegenheit] about this - **3.** geh [zeitlich]: ~ **vergingen mehrere Monate** this took several months.

**hierum** adv - **1.** [örtlich] around here - **2.** [um diese Sache] about this.

**hierunter** adv - **1.** [räumlich] under here - **2.** [unter dieser Sache] by this - **3.** [bei Menge] among these.

**hiervon** adv - **1.** [von diesem Gegenstand] of this - **2.** [von dieser Angelegenheit]: ~ **hängt es ab** it depends on this; ~ **halte ich viel** I think very highly of this - **3.** [örtlich] from here - **4.** [ursächlich] from this - **5.** [von dieser Menge] of these.

**hierzu** adv - **1.** [zu dieser Angelegenheit] to this; **ich rate dir dringend** ~ I urge you to do this - **2.** [zu diesem Gegenstand] with this - **3.** [zu dieser Menge]: **stellen Sie sich bitte** ~ please stand with these people here; **legen Sie die Zeitungen bitte** ~ please add your newspapers to these.

**hierzulande** adv in this country.

**hiesig** adj local.

**hieß** prät ➾ **heißen.**

**Highsociety** ['haɪsoˈsaɪətɪ] die high society.

**Hightech** ['haɪtɛk] die [Technologie] high-tech.

**Hilfe** (pl -n) die - **1.** [Helfen] help; **mit js** ~ with sb's help; **jn/etw zu** ~ **nehmen** to use sb/sthg; **humanitäre** ~ humanitarian aid - **2.** [Geld - freiwillig] aid; [ - rechtlich garantiert] benefit - **3.** [Haushaltshilfe] cleaner ◇ interj help!

➡ **Hilfe suchend** ◇ adj [Blick] beseeching ◇ adv beseechingly.

➡ **mit Hilfe** adv = mithilfe.

**Hilfe|leistung** die aid (U); **unterlassene** ~ failing to render assistance in an emergency.

**Hilfe|ruf** der call for help.

**Hilfe|stellung** *die:* jm ~ leisten *ODER* geben *SPORT* to give sb a leg-up; *fig* to help sb out.

**hilfesuchend** ⊳ Hilfe.

**hilflos** *adj* - **1.** [hilfsbedürftig] helpless - **2.** [ratlos] clueless - **3.** [unbeholfen] awkward ⟨⟩ *adv* - **1.** [hilfsbedürftig] helplessly - **2.** [ratlos] cluelessly - **3.** [unbeholfen] awkwardly.

**hilfreich** *adj* helpful; **eine ~e Hand** a helping hand ⟨⟩ *adv:* jm ~ zur Seite stehen to be a big help to sb.

**Hilfs|aktion** *die* relief operation.

**Hilfs|arbeiter, in** *der, die* [in der Fabrik] unskilled worker; [beim Bau] labourer.

**hilfsbedürftig** *adj* in need (of help).

**hilfsbereit** *adj* helpful.

**Hilfs|kraft** *die* assistant.

**Hilfs|mittel** *das* aid.

**Hilfs|programm** *das* *EDV* utility.

**Hilfs|verb** *das* *GRAM* auxiliary verb.

**hilft** *präs* ⊳ helfen.

**Himalaya** *der:* der ~ the Himalayas.

**Him|beere** *die* raspberry.

**Himmel** (*pl* -) *der* - **1.** [Firmament] sky; **am ~** in the sky; **unter freiem ~** in the open, out of doors - **2.** [Jenseits] heaven - **3.** [Vorsehung]: **der ~ weiß, wann er endlich zurückkommt** heaven (only) knows when he will finally come back - **4.** [Baldachin] canopy - **5.** *RW:* **ach du lieber ~!** oh God!; **aus heiterem ~** out of the blue; **im siebenten ~ sein** to be in seventh heaven; **um ~s willen!** for heaven's sake!

**Himmel|bett** *das* four-poster bed.

**himmelblau** *adj* sky-blue.

**Himmel|fahrt** *die* Ascension Day.

**himmelschreiend** *adj* scandalous.

**Himmels|körper** *der* heavenly body.

**Himmels|richtung** *die* direction; **die vier ~en** the four points of the compass.

**himmelweit** *adj:* **ein ~er Unterschied** a world of difference ⟨⟩ *adv:* ~ auseinander liegen to be poles apart; **von etw ~ entfernt sein** to be nowhere near sthg.

**himmlisch** *adj* heavenly; **eine ~e Fügung** divine providence ⟨⟩ *adv* [leicht, bequem, schön] wonderfully; ~ schmecken/aussehen to taste/look divine.

**hin** *adv* - **1.** [räumlich]: **bis zum Baum ~** up to the tree; **zur Straße ~** towards the street; **zum Norden ~** (towards the) north; **wo ist er ~?** where has he gone?; ~ **und her** back and forth; **der Weg ~** the way there; **zweimal London ~ und zurück** two returns *Br ODER* round-trip tickets *Am* to London; **einmal London – nur ~, bitte!** one for London – just a single please - **2.** [zeitlich]: **zum Abend ~** towards

evening; **über viele Jahre ~** for many years; ~ **und wieder** now and then - **3.** *fig:* **er brabbelte da was vor sich ~** he was mumbling something to himself; **nach außen ~** outwardly; **auf deinen Brief ~** as soon as I got your letter; **auf deinen Rat ~** on your advice; **auf den Verdacht ~, dass ...** on the suspicion that ...; **ihr Kleid/Ruf ist ~** her dress/reputation is ruined; **er war von dem Mädchen ganz ~ (und weg)** he was completely taken with the girl.

**Hin** *das:* **das ~ und Her** the toing and froing.

**hinab** *adv* = hinunter.

**hinab|gehen** (*perf* ist hinabgegangen) (*unreg*) *vt* & *vi* geh to go down.

**hin|arbeiten** *vi:* **auf etw** (*A*) ~ to work towards sthg.

**hinauf** *adv* up; **den Berg ~** up the mountain; **von den Alpen bis an die Ostsee ~** from the Alps right up to the Baltic; **bis zum General ~** up to the general.

**hinauf|gehen** (*perf* ist hinaufgegangen) (*unreg*) *vi* to go up; **es geht hinauf** the road climbs; **mit der Miete ~** to put up *ODER* raise the rent ⟨⟩ *vt* to go up.

**hinauf|reichen** *vt* to hand up ⟨⟩ *vi* to reach; **zum Fenster ~** to reach up to the window.

**hinauf|sehen** *vi* (*unreg*): **zu jm/etw ~** to look up at sb/sthg.

**hinauf|steigen** (*perf* ist hinaufgestiegen) *vi* & *vt* (*unreg*) to climb.

**hinauf|ziehen** (*perf* hat/ist hinaufgezogen) (*unreg*) *vt* (hat) to pull up ⟨⟩ *vi* (ist) to move up.
➤ **sich hinaufziehen** *ref:* **er zieht sich an einem Seil hinauf** he pulls himself up using a rope.

**hinaus** *adv* - **1.** [räumlich] out; **das Fenster geht zur Straße ~** the window looks (out) onto the street; ~ **mit dir!** get out!; **über unsere Grenzen ~ bekannt** known beyond our borders - **2.** [zeitlich]: **über das Abendbrot ~ bleiben** to stay over dinner; **die Dame ist schon über die achtzig ~** the woman is well over eighty; **auf Monate ~** for months to come.

**hinaus|begleiten** *vt* to see out.

**hinaus|beugen** ➤ **sich hinausbeugen** *ref* to lean out.

**hinaus|gehen** (*perf* ist hinausgegangen) *vi* (*unreg*) - **1.** [nach draußen] to go out - **2.** **auf etw** (*A*) ~ [gerichtet sein - Zimmer, Fenster] to look onto sthg; [ - Tür, Gang] to lead into sthg; [ - in eine Richtung] to face sthg - **3.** [überschreiten]: **über etw** (*A*) ~ to go beyond sthg.

**hinaus|kommen** (*perf* ist hinausgekommen) *vi* (*unreg*) to come out; **über etw** (*A*) ~ to get beyond sthg.

**hinaus|laufen** (*perf* ist hinausgelaufen) *vi* (*unreg*) - **1.** [nach draußen] to run outside - **2.** [abzielen]: **auf etw** (*A*) ~ to amount to sthg; **das**

läuft auf dasselbe hinaus it amounts to the same thing.

**hinaus|lehnen** *vt* [Kopf] to stick out.
➤ **sich hinauslehnen** *ref* to lean out.

**hinaus|schicken** *vt* to send out.

**hinaus|schieben** *vt (unreg)* - **1.** [nach draußen] to push outside - **2.** [zeitlich] to put off, to postpone.
➤ **sich hinausschieben** *ref* - **1.** [örtlich] to push one's way out - **2.** [zeitlich] to be put off, to be postponed.

**hinaus|wagen** ➤ **sich hinauswagen** *ref* to venture out.

**hinaus|werfen** *vt (unreg)* to throw out.

**hinaus|wollen** *vi (unreg)* - **1.** [nach draußen] to want to go out - **2.** [auf ein Ziel]: **auf etw** *(A)* **~** to be getting at sthg; **auf eine friedliche Einigung ~** to want to achieve a peaceful agreement; **(zu) hoch ~** to aim (too) high.

**hinaus|zögern** *vt* to put off.
➤ **sich hinauszögern** *ref* to be delayed.

**hin|bekommen** *vt (unreg)*: **wie willst du denn das ~?** how do you intend to do ODER manage that?; **etw wieder ~** to mend sthg.

**hin|bestellen** *vt* to tell to come/go; **jn zu jm ~** to tell sb to come/go to sb.

**hin|biegen** *vt (unreg) fam* to sort out.

**Hinblick** *der*: **in** ODER **im ~ auf jn/etw** [in Bezug auf] with regard to sb/sthg; **in** ODER **im ~ auf etw** *(A)* [wegen] in view of sthg.

**hin|bringen** *vt (unreg)* to take (there).

**hin|denken** *vi (unreg)*: **wo denkst du (denn) hin?** what are you thinking of?

**hinderlich** *adj*: **jm/einer Sache ~ sein** to get in sb's/sthg's way.

**hindern** *vt* to prevent; **was hindert dich zu bleiben?** what is preventing you from staying?

**Hindernis** *(pl -se) das* obstacle; [in Leichtathletik] hurdle; [in Springreiten] jump.

**Hinderungs|grund** *der*: **für jn kein ~ sein** not to be an obstacle to sb.

**hin|deuten** *vi* to point; **auf jn/etw ~** [zeigen] to point at sb/sthg; [in einer Menge] to point sb/sthg out; [erkennen lassen] to point to sb/sthg.

**Hindi** *das* Hindi; *siehe auch* **Englisch(e)**.

**Hindu** *(pl -s) der* Hindu.

**hindurch** *adv* - **1.** [zeitlich]: **den ganzen Tag ~** throughout the whole day - **2.** [örtlich]: **durch den Berg ~** through the mountain.

**hinein** *adv* - **1.** [räumlich] in; **~ ins Bett!** get into bed! - **2.** [zeitlich]: **bis tief in die Nacht ~ arbeiten** to work late into the night; **in den Tag ~ leben** to live from day to day.

**hinein|bitten** *vt (unreg)* to ask in.

**hinein|denken** ➤ **sich hineindenken** *ref*

*(unreg)*: **sich in jn/etw ~** to put o.s. in sb's/sthg's position.

**hinein|fressen** *vt (unreg)*: **etw in sich** *(A)* **~** to gobble sthg up; *fam* [Sorgen] to bottle sthg up.
➤ **sich hineinfressen** *ref*: **sich in etw** *(A)* **~** to eat into sthg.

**hinein|gehen** *(perf ist hineingegangen) vi (unreg)* - **1.** [nach drinnen] to go inside - **2.** [hineinpassen]: **in diese Flasche geht nicht mehr als ein Liter hinein** this bottle won't hold more than a litre.

**hinein|geraten** *(perf ist hineingeraten) vi (unreg)*: **in etw** *(A)* **~** to get into sthg; **in einen einsamen Wald ~** to find o.s. in a lonely wood.

**hinein|reden** *vi*: **die Mutter redet ihrer Tochter in jede Entscheidung hinein** the mother interferes in all of her daughter's decisions.

**hinein|steigern** ➤ **sich hineinsteigern** *ref*: **sie hat sich in diese Sache hineingesteigert** she has become completely caught up in this affair.

**hinein|versetzen** ➤ **sich hineinversetzen** *ref*: **sich in jn** ODER **in js Lage ~** to put o.s. in sb's position.

**hinein|ziehen** *(perf hat/ist hineingezogen) (unreg) vt (hat)* - **1.** [nach drinnen] to pull in - **2.** [verwickeln]: **jn in etw** *(A)* **~** to draw sb into sthg <> *vi (ist)* - **1.** [umziehen] to move in - **2.** [gehen] to go in.

**hin|fahren** *(perf hat/ist hingefahren) (unreg) vi (ist)* to go there; [mit Auto] to drive there; **wo ist er hingefahren?** where did he go (to)? <> *vt (hat)* to take there.

**Hin|fahrt** *die* [mit dem Auto] journey there; [mit dem Zug] outward journey.

**hin|fallen** *(perf ist hingefallen) vi (unreg)* to fall (down); **sie hat die Vase ~ lassen** she dropped the vase; **wem ist der Teller hingefallen?** who dropped the plate?

**hinfällig** *adj* - **1.** [altersschwach] frail - **2.** [ungültig] invalid.

**Hin|flug** *der* outward flight.

**hin|führen** *vt* to lead there <> *vi* to lead there; **zu etw ~** to lead to sthg; **wo soll das ~?** where is it leading to?

**hing** *prät* ⊳ **hängen**.

**Hingabe** *die* devotion; **mit ~** devotedly.

**hin|geben** *vt (unreg) geh* to give up.
➤ **sich hingeben** *ref*: **sich einer Sache** *(D)* **~** to devote o.s. to sthg; **sich einer Illusion ~** to cherish an illusion; **sich jm ~** to give o.s. to sb.

**hingegen** *konj* on the other hand.

**hin|gehen** *(perf ist hingegangen) vi (unreg)* - **1.** [gehen] to go there; **zu etw ~** to go to sthg - **2.** *geh* [vergehen] to pass - **3.** [durchgehen]: **das**

mag (gerade) noch ~ that might (just) about do.

**hin|gehören** *vi* [Person, Tier] to belong; [Sache] to go, to belong.

**hin|halten** *vt (unreg)* - **1.** [reichen] to hold out - **2.** [vertrösten] to keep waiting.

**hin|hauen** *(perf* hat/ist hingehauen) *(unreg) vt (hat) fam* - **1.** [werfen] to chuck down - **2.** *abw* [flüchtig] to knock off - **3.** [erschüttern] to floor <> *vi* - **1.** *(ist) fam* [stürzen] to come a cropper - **2.** *(hat) fam* [stimmen] to work out; **das haut hin/nicht hin!** that's right/wrong!
➤ **sich hinhauen** *ref (hat) salopp* [sich hinlegen] to flop down.

**hin|hocken** ➤ **sich hinhocken** *ref* to crouch down.

**hinken** *(perf* hat/ist gehinkt) *vi* - **1.** *(hat)* [humpeln] to (have a) limp - **2.** *(ist)* [an einen Ort] to limp, to hobble.

**hin|knien** ➤ **sich hinknien** *ref* to kneel down.

**hin|kommen** *(perf* ist hingekommen) *vi (unreg)* - **1.** [ankommen] to get there; **zu etw ~** to get to sthg - **2.** [hingehören] to belong, to go - **3.** [hingeraten]: **wenn ich wüsste, wo meine Brille hingekommen ist** if I knew where my glasses had gone - **4.** [auskommen]: **mit etw ~** to manage with sthg - **5.** [zutreffen] to work out; **das kommt hin/nicht hin!** that is right/wrong!

**hin|kriegen** *vt fam* to manage; **sie hat das gut hingekriegt** she made a good job of that; **etw wieder ~** to fix sthg; **jn wieder ~** to get sb back on his/her feet.

**hinlänglich** *adj* sufficient <> *adv* sufficiently.

**hin|legen** *vt* - **1.** [Gegenstand] to put down; [Zettel] to leave - **2.** [ins Bett] to put to bed - **3.** *fam* [bezahlen] to fork out - **4.** *fam* [Darbietung] to turn in; [Prüfung] to do.
➤ **sich hinlegen** *ref* - **1.** [sich legen] to lie down - **2.** *fam* [stürzen] to come a cropper.

**hin|nehmen** *vt (unreg)* - **1.** [ertragen] to take - **2.** *fam* [mitnehmen]: **jn/etw (zu jm) mit ~** to take sb/sthg (to sb).

**hin|pflanzen** ➤ **sich hinpflanzen** *ref fam* [sich hinstellen]: **sich (vor jn) ~** to plant o.s. (in front of sb).

**hin|reichen** *vt* [zureichen]: **jm etw ~** to hand sb sthg <> *vi* - **1.** [sich erstrecken] to reach - **2.** [ausreichen] to be enough.

**Hinreise** *die* journey there.

**hin|reißen** *vt (unreg)* - **1.** [ziehen] to pull - **2.** [begeistern] to captivate - **3.** [verleiten]: **sich zu etw ~ lassen** [überzeugen] to let o.s. be carried away into doing sthg; [provozieren] to be driven to do sthg.

**hinreißend** *adj* captivating.

**hin|richten** *vt* to execute.

**Hinrichtung** *die* execution.

**hin|schauen** *vi* to look.

**hin|schicken** *vt* to send.

**hin|sehen** *vi (unreg)* to look.

**hin sein** *(perf* ist hin gewesen) *vi (unreg) fam* [kaputt] to have had it; [ruiniert] to be shattered; [vor Glück] to be overjoyed.

**hin|setzen** *vt* [Gegenstand] to put down; [Baby] to sit down.
➤ **sich hinsetzen** *ref* - **1.** [sich setzen] to sit down - **2.** *fam* [stürzen] to land on one's backside.

**Hinsicht** *die (ohne pl)*: **in dieser/jeder ~** in this/every respect; **in doppelter ~** in two respects; **in ~ auf etw** *(A)* with regard to sthg.

**hinsichtlich** *präp amt*: **~ einer Sache** *(G)* [bezüglich] with regard to sthg; [in Anbetracht] in view of sthg.

**hin|stellen** *vt* - **1.** [stellen] to put - **2.** [absetzen] to put down - **3.** [darstellen]: **jn/etw als etw ~** to describe sb/sthg as sthg.
➤ **sich hinstellen** *ref* - **1.** [sich stellen] to stand - **2.** [darstellen]: **sich als jn/etw ~** to pretend to be sb/sthg.

**hinten** *adv* - **1.** [am Ende] at the back; **da** ODER **dort ~** back there; **sie ist ~ im Garten** she's out the back (in the garden); **~ im Buch** at the back of the book; **im Auto ~ sitzen** to sit in the back of the car; **das dritte Haus von ~** the third house from the end; **das stimmt doch ~ und vorne nicht** that is totally untrue; **jn ~ und vorne bedienen** to wait on sb hand and foot - **2.** [weit entfernt]: **weit ~** a long way behind; **das liegt irgendwo ~ bei Indien** it's near India somewhere - **3.** [an der Rückseite] on the back; **~ am Radio** on the back of the radio; **das Haus hat ~ einen Balkon** the house has a balcony at the back - **4.** [als Richtungsangabe] back; **bitte nach ~ durchgehen!** please move down to the back!; **sich nach ~ lehnen** to lean back; **von ~** from behind.

**hintenherum** *adv fam* - **1.** [um etw herum] round the back - **2.** [indirekt] indirectly.

**hinter** *präp* - **1.** *(+ D, A)* [räumlich] behind; **~ dem Haus** behind the house, in back of the house Am; **~ jm herlaufen** to run after sb; **3 km ~ Köln** after Cologne; **wir stehen ~ ihnen in Produktivität zurück** we're behind them in terms of productivity - **2.** [zeitlich]: **etw ~ sich** *(A)* **bringen** to put sthg behind one; **das hätten wir endlich ~ uns!** thank God that's behind us! - **3.** *fig* behind; **~ etw kommen** to get to the bottom of sthg.

**Hinter|achse** *die* rear axle.

**Hinter|ausgang** *der* rear exit.

**Hinterbliebene** (pl -n) der, die surviving dependant.

**hintere, r, s** adj back.

**Hintere** (pl -n) der, die, das: **der/die/das ~** the one at the back.

**hintereinander** adv - **1.** [räumlich] behind each other - **2.** [zeitlich] in a row.

**Hinterleingang** der rear entrance.

**hinterfragen** vt to examine.

**Hinterlgedanke** der ulterior motive.

**hintergehen** (prät hinterging; perf hat hintergangen) vt to deceive.

**Hinterlgrund** der background; **im ~ bleiben** to remain in the background; **jn/etw in den ~ drängen** to push sb/sth into the background; **in den ~ geraten** ODER **treten** to fade into the background.

**hintergründig** adj enigmatic; [Witz] cryptic <> adv enigmatically.

**Hintergrundlinformation** die piece of background information; **~en** background information (U).

**Hinterhalt** (pl -e) der ambush; **im ~ liegen** to lie in ambush; **in einen ~ geraten** ODER **fallen** to be ambushed.

**hinterhältig** adj devious <> adv deviously.

**Hinterhand** die (ohne pl) hindquarters (pl); **(noch) etw in der ~ haben** to have sth in reserve.

**Hinterlhaus** das part of a tenement building which overlooks and is only accessible from a courtyard.

**hinterher**[1] adv [räumlich] behind; siehe auch **hinterher sein.**

**hinterher**[2] adv [zeitlich] afterwards.

**hinterherlfahren** (perf ist hinterhergefahren) vi (unreg): **jm/etw ~** to drive behind sb/sth; [verfolgen] to drive after sb/sth.

**hinterherlgehen** (perf ist hinterhergegangen) vi (unreg): **jm ~** to follow sb.

**hinterher sein** (perf ist hinterher gewesen) vi (unreg) fam: **jm/einer Sache ~** to be after sb/sth.

**Hinterlhof** der courtyard.

**Hinterlkopf** der back of the head; **etw im ~ haben/behalten** fig to have/keep sth at the back of one's mind.

**Hinterland** das hinterland.

**hinterlassen** (präs hinterlässt; prät hinterließ; perf hat hinterlassen) vt to leave; **jm etw ~** to leave sb sth.

**Hinterlassenschaft** (pl -en) die estate.

**hinterlegen** vt: **etw bei jm ~** to leave sth with sb.

**Hinterlist** die cunning.

**hinterlistig** adj cunning <> adv cunningly.

**Hintermann** (pl -männer) der - **1.** [räumlich] person behind - **2.** [in Verbrechen]: **die Hintermänner des Drogenrings** the brains behind the drugs ring.

**Hintern** (pl -) der fam backside; **jm in den ~ treten** to give sb a kick up the backside; **jm den ~ versohlen** to give sb a good hiding; **sich auf den ~ setzen** [arbeiten] to knuckle down; [hinfallen] to land on one's backside; [überrascht sein] to be flabbergasted.

**Hinterlrad** das back wheel.

**hinterrücks** adv abw from behind.

**Hinterlseite** die back.

**Hinterlteil** das fam backside.

**Hintertreffen** das (ohne pl): **ins ~ geraten** to fall behind.

**hintertreiben** (prät hintertrieb; perf hat hintertrieben) vt [Plan] to thwart; [Heirat] to prevent; [Gesetz, Reform] to block.

**Hinterltür** die back door; **durch die** ODER **eine ~** fig by the back door; **sich** (D) **eine ~ offen halten** ODER **offen lassen** fig to leave o.s. a way out.

**Hinterwäldler, in** (mpl -; fpl -nen) der, die abw yokel.

**hinterziehen** (prät hinterzog; perf hat hinterzogen) vt: **Steuern ~** to evade tax.

**hinltreten** (perf hat/ist hingetreten) vi (unreg) - **1.** (ist) [an einen Ort]: **zu jm/etw ~** to step over to sb/sth; **vor jn ~** to go up to sb - **2.** (hat) [mit Fuß] to kick.

**hinltun** vt (unreg) fam to put.

**hinüber** adv over, across; **da ~** over there; **gehen Sie links/rechts ~** go left/right; **die Reifen sind ~** fam the tyres have had it; siehe auch **hinüber sein.**

**hinüberlgehen** (perf ist hinübergegangen) vi (unreg) to go over.

**hinüberlhelfen** vi (unreg): **jm ~** to help sb over; **jm über eine schwere Zeit ~** to help sb through a difficult time.

**hinüber sein** (perf ist hinüber gewesen) vi (unreg) fam - **1.** [kaputt] to have had it; [erschöpft] to be done in; [betrunken] to be well away - **2.** [gehen] to have gone over.

**hinunter** adv down; **die Treppe ~** down the stairs; **~ nach Bayern fahren** to drive down to Bavaria; **vom General bis ~ zum einfachen Soldat** from the general down to the private.

**hinunterlblicken** vi: **in etw** (A) **~** to look down into sth; **an sich** (D) **~** to look down at o.s.; **auf jn ~** fig to look down on sb.

**hinunterlgehen** (perf ist hinuntergegangen) (unreg) vi to go down; [Flugzeug] to descend <> vt to go down.

**hinunterlreichen** *vt* to hand down ⬦ *vi* [bis zum Boden] to reach down; [Einfluss, Land] to extend down.

**hinunterlschlucken** *vt eigtl* & *fig* to swallow.

**hinunterlstürzen** (*perf* hat/ist hinuntergestürzt) *vt* - **1.** *(ist)* [hinunterfallen] to fall down - **2.** *(hat)* [werfen] to throw down - **3.** *(hat) fam* [schnell trinken] to gulp down.
➣ **sich hinunterstürzen** *ref* [sich hinunterwerfen]: **sich (von etw) ~** to throw o.s. off (sthg).

**hinweg** *adv geh* away; **über jn/etw ~** over sb/sthg; **über Jahre ~** for many years.

**Hinweg** *der* way there; **auf dem ~** on the way there.

**hinweglgehen** (*perf* ist hinweggegangen) *vi* (*unreg*): **über etw** (A) **~** to pass over sthg.

**hinweglkommen** (*perf* ist hinweggekommen) *vi* (*unreg*): **über etw** (A) **~** to get over sthg.

**hinweglsehen** *vi* (*unreg*): **über jn/etw ~** to see over sb/sthg; **über etw** (A) **~** *fig* to overlook sthg.

**hinweglsetzen** ➣ **sich hinwegsetzen** *ref*: **sich über etw** (A) **~** to disregard sthg.

**hinwegltäuschen** *vt*: **jn über etw** (A) **~** to mislead sb about sthg.

**Hinweis** (*pl* -e) *der* [Tip, Fingerzeig] tip; [Anleitung] instruction; [Indiz] sign; **jm einen ~ geben** to give sb a hint; **unter ~ auf etw** (A) with reference to sthg; **sachdienliche ~e** useful leads.

**hinlweisen** (*unreg*) *vi* - **1.** [auf etw schließen lassen]: **auf etw** (A) **~** to point to sthg - **2.** [zeigen]: **auf jn/etw ~** to point to sb/sthg ⬦ *vt*: **jn auf etw** (A) **~** to point sthg out to sb.

**Hinweisschild** (*pl* -er) *das* sign.

**Hinweisltafel** *die* sign.

**hinlwenden** *vt* to turn.
➣ **sich hinwenden** *ref* to turn.

**hinlwerfen** *vt* (*unreg*) - **1.** [werfen] to throw down - **2.** *fam* [Arbeit, Projekt] to chuck in - **3.** [Skizze] to dash off - **4.** [Bemerkung] to drop casually; [Frage] to ask casually - **5.** *fam* [fallen lassen] to drop.
➣ **sich hinwerfen** *ref* to throw o.s. down.

**Hinz** *der*: **~ und Kunz** *fam abw* every Tom, Dick and Harry.

**hinlziehen** (*perf* hat/ist hingezogen) (*unreg*) *vt* (*hat*) - **1.** [anziehen]: **jn/etw zu sich ~** to attract sb/sthg; **sich zu jm hingezogen fühlen** to feel attracted to sb/sthg - **2.** [zeitlich] to draw out ⬦ *vi* (*ist*) [umziehen] to move.
➣ **sich hinziehen** *ref* [lange dauern] to drag on.

**hinzu** *adv* in addition; **~ kommt noch ...** (and) what is more ...

**hinzulfügen** *vt* to add; **etw zu etw ~** to add sthg to sthg.

**hinzulkommen** (*perf* ist hinzugekommen) *vi* (*unreg*) - **1.** [ankommen]: **zu jm/etw ~** to join sb/sthg - **2.** [sich ergeben] to be added on; **es kommt hinzu** ODER **hinzu kommt, dass ...** moreover ...

**hinzultreten** (*perf* ist hinzugetreten) *vi* (*unreg*): **zu jm ~** to join sb.

**hinzulzählen** *vt* to add on.

**hinzulziehen** *vt* (*unreg*) to call in.

**Hiobslbotschaft** *die* bad news (U).

**Hip-hop** *der* MUS hip hop.

**Hippie** (*pl* -s) *der* hippie.

**Hirn** (*pl* -e) *das* - **1.** [Gehirn] brain - **2.** *fam* [Denkvermögen] brains (*pl*).

**Hirngespinst** (*pl* -e) *das abw* figment of one's imagination.

**Hirnhautlentzündung** *die* MED meningitis.

**hirnrissig** *fam abw adj* crazy ⬦ *adv* crazily.

**hirnverbrannt** *adj fam abw* crazy.

**Hirsch** (*pl* -e) *der* [Tier] deer; [männlich] stag; [Fleisch] venison.

**Hirschlgeweih** *das* antlers (*pl*).

**Hirschlkäfer** *der* stag beetle.

**Hirse** *die* millet.

**Hirte** (*pl* -n), **Hirt** (*pl* -en) *der* shepherd.

**Hirtin** (*pl* -nen) *die* shepherdess.

**his, His** (*pl* -) *das* MUS B sharp.

**hissen** *vt* to hoist.

**Historiker, in** (*mpl* -; *fpl* -nen) *der*, *die* historian.

**historisch** *adj* - **1.** [geschichtlich] historical - **2.** [entscheidend] historic ⬦ *adv* [geschichtlich] historically; **etw ~ betrachten** to look at sthg in historical terms.

**Hit** (*pl* -s) *der* hit.

**Hitlparade** *die* charts (*pl*).

**Hitze** *die* heat.

**hitzebeständig** *adj* heat-resistant.

**hitzefrei** *adj*: **~ haben** to have the rest of the day off school because of hot weather.

**Hitzelwelle** *die* heatwave.

**hitzig** *adj* - **1.** [Person] hot-blooded; [Temperament] fiery - **2.** [Diskussion, Streit] heated ⬦ *adv* [lebhaft] heatedly.

**hitzköpfig** *adj* [Person] hot-tempered; [Temperament] fiery.

**Hitzlschlag** *der* heat stroke.

**HIV-positiv** *adj* MED HIV-positive.

**Hiwi** (*pl* -s) *der fam* UNI undergraduate student working as an assistant to a professor.

**hl.** (*abk für* **heilig**) St.

**H-Milch** *die* long-life milk.

**h-Moll** das (ohne pl) MUS B minor.

**HNO-|Arzt, Ärztin** (abk˙ für Hals-Nasen-Ohren-Arzt) der, die ENT specialist.

**hob** prät ▷ heben.

**Hobby** ['hɔbil (pl -s) das hobby.

**Hobby|koch** der amateur cook.

**Hobby|köchin** die amateur cook.

**Hobby|raum** der hobby room.

**Hobel** (pl -) der - 1. [Werkzeug] plane - 2. [Küchengerät] slicer.

**Hobelbank** (pl -bänke) die carpenter's bench.

**hobeln** vt [Holz] to plane; [Gemüse] to slice ⟨⟩ vi to plane; **an etw** (D) ~ to plane sthg.

**hoch** (kompar höher; superl höchste) adj - 1. [räumlich] high; [Baum, Gebäude] tall; [Schnee] deep; **drei Meter** ~ three metres high/tall/deep; **im hohen Norden** in the far north - 2. [bezeichnet Ausmass - Blutdruck, Tempo, Mieten, Preis etc] high; [ - Gewicht, Strafe] heavy; [ - Anzahl, Summe] large; **in hohem Grade** to a large extent; **etw bis ins hohe Alter tun** to do sthg until one is very old; **wenn es** ~ **kommt** at the most - 3. [bezeichnet Qualität - Position, Ansprüche] high; [ - Ehre, Begabung] great; **das ist mir zu** ~ fam fig that's beyond me - 4. [gesellschaftlich gehoben]: **von hoher Geburt** of high birth; **von hohem Ansehen** highly regarded; **ein hoher Beamter** a high-ranking official - 5. [auf dem Höhepunkt]: **das hohe Mittelalter** the High Middle Ages - 6. MUS high; **jn in den höchsten Tönen loben** fig to praise sb to the skies ⟨⟩ adv (kompar höher; superl am höchsten) - 1. [räumlich]: **das Dorf ist** ~ **gelegen** the village is situated high up; **zwei Treppen** ~ two floors up; **das Flugzeug fliegt 3000 Meter** ~ the plane is flying at (a height of) 3,000 metres; **mit** ~ **erhobenem Kopf** with one's head held high; **ein** ~ **aufgeschossener Junge** a tall boy; ~ **an die Ostsee** up to the Baltic Sea - 2. [bezeichnet Ausmass, Qualität] highly; ~ **versichert sein** insured to a high value; ~ **verlieren** to lose heavily; ~ **zufrieden** very content; ~ **und heilig versprechen** to promise solemnly; ~ **lebe ...!** long live ...! - 3. [gesellschaftlich gehoben]: **sie ist eine** ~ **gestellte Persönlichkeit** she is a very important person - 4. MUS high; **du singst zu** ~! you're singing sharp! - 5. MATH: **zehn** ~ **vier** ten to the power of four.

**Hoch** (pl -s) das - 1. [Jubelruf] cheer; **jm ein dreifaches** ~ **ausbringen** to give three cheers for sb - 2. [Hochdruckgebiet] high.

**Hochachtung** die great respect; ~ **vor jm haben** to have great respect for sb.

**hochachtungsvoll** adv Yours faithfully (nach Dear Sir/Madam), Yours sincerely (nach Dear Mr/Mrs X).

**hochaktuell** adj [Thema, Buch] highly topical; [Mode] up-to-date; [Kleidungsstück] highly fashionable.

**Hoch|amt** das REL High Mass.

**hochanständig** adj [Mensch, Angebot, Benehmen] very decent ⟨⟩ adv very decently.

**hoch|arbeiten** ⟿ **sich hocharbeiten** ref to work one's way up.

**Hochbau** der building construction.

**hoch begabt** adj highly talented.

**Hochbetrieb** der: **im Büro herrscht** ~ it's very busy in the office.

**hoch bezahlt** adj highly-paid.

**Hoch|burg** die stronghold.

**hochdeutsch** adj standard German ⟨⟩ adv in standard German.

**hoch|drehen** vt - 1. [drehen] to wind up - 2. [Motor] to rev (up).

**Hochdruck** der - 1. [technisch, meteorologisch] high pressure; **unter** ~ **stehen** to be under high pressure - 2. fam fig [Hochbetrieb]: **unter** ~ **stehen** to be at full stretch.

**Hochdruck|gebiet** das high-pressure area.

**Hoch|ebene** die plateau.

**hoch empfindlich** adj highly sensitive.

**hocherfreut** adj highly delighted ⟨⟩ adv with great delight.

**hoch|fahren** (perf hat/ist hochgefahren) (unreg) vi (ist) - 1. [nach oben] to go up; [in Auto] to drive up - 2. [erschrecken] to start; **aus dem Schlaf** ~ to wake up with a start - 3. [zornig] to flare up ⟨⟩ vt (hat) fam [nach oben] to take up.

**hoch|fliegen** (perf ist hochgeflogen) vi (unreg) [Vogel, Flugzeug] to fly up; [Ballon] to go up.

**Hoch|form** die: **in** ~ **sein** to be on top form.

**Hoch|format** das vertical format.

**Hoch|frequenz** die PHYS high frequency.

**Hoch|gebirge** das high mountains (pl).

**Hoch|gefühl** das: **im** ~ **einer Sache** (G) elated by sthg.

**hoch|gehen** (perf ist hochgegangen) vi (unreg) - 1. [gehen, sich heben] to go up - 2. [Mine, Bombe] to go off; [Gebäude] to blow up; **etw** ~ **lassen** to blow sthg up - 3. fam [wütend werden] to hit the roof - 4. [aufgedeckt werden] to be uncovered; **jn** ~ **lassen** fam to squeal on sb.

**Hoch|genuss** der: **das Essen war ein echter** ~ the meal was a real treat.

**hochgeschlossen** adj [Bluse] high-necked; [Kragen] high.

**Hochgeschwindigkeits|zug** der high-speed train.

**hochgespannt** adj [Erwartungen] very high; **sie**

waren ~ auf das Ergebnis they couldn't wait for the result.

**hochgestellt** adj [Zahl] superscript.

**hoch gestellt** adj prominent.

**Hochglanz** der: ein Fotoabzug in ~ a gloss print; auf ~ poliert polished until it shines; etw auf ~ bringen fig to make sthg spick-and-span.

**hochgradig** adj extreme ◇ adv extremely.

**hoch|halten** vt (unreg) [bewahren] to uphold.

**hoch halten** vt (unreg) [nach oben] to hold up.

**Hoch|haus** das high-rise building.

**hoch|heben** vt (unreg): jn/etw ~ to lift sb/sthg (up).

**hochintelligent** adj highly intelligent.

**hochinteressant** adj very interesting.

**hoch|jubeln** vt abw to hype up.

**hochkant** adv on end; jn ~ rauswerfen fam fig to throw sb out on his/her ear.

**hoch|klappen** (perf hat/ist hochgeklappt) vt (hat) [Klapptisch] to fold up; [Verdeck, Armlehne] to fold back; [Kragen] to turn up; [Sitz] to tip up ◇ vi (ist) [Kragen, Hutkrempe] to turn up; [Sitz] to tip up.

**hoch|klettern** (perf ist hochgeklettert) vi: an etw (D) ~ to climb (up) sthg.

**hoch|kommen** (perf ist hochgekommen) vi (unreg) - 1. [nach oben] to come up - 2. [aufstehen] to get up - 3. [beruflich] to get on - 4. [erbrechen]: es kommt ihr bei dem Gedanken daran heute noch hoch the thought of it still makes her feel sick today.

**Hoch|konjunktur** die boom.

**hoch|krempeln** vt to roll up.

**Hoch|land** das uplands (pl).

**hoch|leben** vi: jn/etw ~ lassen to give three cheers for sb/sthg; er/sie/es lebe hoch! three cheers for him/her/it!

**Hochleistungssport** der top-level sport.

**hochmodisch** adj very fashionable ◇ adv very fashionably.

**Hoch|moor** das high-moor bog.

**Hochmut** der arrogance.

**hochmütig** adj arrogant ◇ adv arrogantly.

**hochnäsig** abw adj conceited ◇ adv conceitedly.

**hoch|nehmen** vt (unreg) - 1. [nehmen]: jn/etw mit ~ to take sb/sthg up - 2. fam [narren]: jn ~ to pull sb's leg - 3. [verhaften] to arrest.

**hoch nehmen** vt (unreg) [Teppich] to lift up; [Baby] to pick up.

**Hoch|ofen** der blast furnace.

**Hoch|parterre** das raised ground Br ODER first Am floor.

**hochprozentig** adj [Getränk, Spirituose] high-proof; [Lösung] highly concentrated.

**hoch qualifiziert** adj highly qualified.

**hoch|rechnen** vt to project.

**Hoch|rechnung** die projection.

**hochrot** adj bright red.

**Hoch|saison** die high season.

**hoch schätzen** ['hoːxˌʃɛtsn̩] vt geh to have a high regard for.

**hoch|schlagen** ['hoːxˌʃlaːgn̩] (perf hat/ist hochgeschlagen) (unreg) vt (hat) to turn up ◇ vi (ist) to leap up.

**hoch|schrecken** ['hoːxˌʃrɛkn̩] (prät schreckte ODER schrak hoch; perf hat/ist hochgeschreckt) vt (hat) (reg) to startle ◇ vi (ist) to start; er ist aus dem Schlaf hochgeschreckt he was startled out of sleep.

**Hochschul|abschluss** der (university) degree.

**Hoch|schule** die college; [Universität] university.

**Hochschul|lehrer, in** der, die college lecturer; [an der Universität] university lecturer.

**Hochschul|reife** die qualification required by school-leavers for university entrance.

**hochschwanger** ['hoːxˌʃvaŋɐ] adj heavily pregnant.

**Hoch|sommer** der midsummer.

**Hoch|spannung** die - 1. [Strom] high voltage - 2. [Stimmung] great tension.

**Hochspannungs|leitung** die high-tension cable.

**hoch|spielen** ['hoːxˌʃpiːlən] vt to blow up.

**hoch|springen** ['hoːxˌʃprɪŋən] (perf ist hochgesprungen) vi (unreg) to jump up.

**Hoch|springer, in** der, die SPORT high jumper.

**Hochsprung** der SPORT high jump.

**höchst** ['høːçst] adv highly.

**Höchstalter** das (ohne pl) maximum age.

**Hochstapelei** [hoːxˌʃtaːpəˈlaɪ] (pl -en) die: er ist durch ~ reich geworden he became rich through conning people.

**Hochstapler, in** ['hoːxˌʃtaːplɐ, ərɪn] (mpl -; fpl -nen) der, die con artist.

**Höchst|belastung** die extreme pressure; [eines Materials, einer Konstruktion] maximum load.

**hoch|stellen** ['hoːxˌʃtɛlən] vt - 1. [nach oben stellen] to put up; eine Zahl ~ to write a number as a superscript - 2. [Kragen] to turn up; [Sitz, Lehne] to tip up.

**höchstens** ['høːçstn̩s] adv - 1. [im äußersten Fall] at best - 2. [außer] except.

**Höchstfall** der (ohne pl): im ~ at (the) most.

**Höchstform** *die:* in ~ sein to be on top form.

**Höchst|geschwindigkeit** *die* speed limit.

**Höchst|grenze** *die* upper limit.

**Hochstimmung** *die* festive mood.

**Höchst|leistung** *die* best performance.

**Höchst|maß** *das* maximum amount.

**höchstmöglich** ['høːçstmøːklɪç] *adj* highest possible.

**Höchst|preis** *der* top price.

**Höchst|stand** *der* highest level.

**Höchst|strafe** *die* maximum penalty.

**höchstwahrscheinlich** ['høːçstvaːɐ̯ʃaɪnlɪç] *adv* most probably.

**höchstzulässig** ['høːçsttsuːlɛsɪç] *adj* maximum permissible.

**Hoch|tour** *die:* auf ~en laufen [Maschine] to run at top speed; [Vorbereitungen] to be in full swing.

**hochtrabend** *abw adj* pompous <> *adv* pompously.

**hoch treiben** *vt (unreg)* [steigern] to push up.

**Hochverrat** *der* high treason.

**Hochwasser** *das* high water; ~ haben to be in spate; *fam fig* to be at half-mast.

**hoch|werfen** *vt (unreg)* to throw up.

**hochwertig** *adj* [Produkte] high-quality; [Eiweiß] highly nutritious.

**hochwirksam** *adj* highly effective.

**Hochwürden** *(ohne Artikel) geh* [als Anrede] Father.

**Hoch|zeit** *die* wedding; silberne/goldene ~ silver/golden wedding.

**Hochzeits|geschenk** *das* wedding present.

**Hochzeits|kleid** *das* wedding dress.

**Hochzeits|nacht** *die* wedding night.

**Hochzeits|paar** *das* bride and groom.

**Hochzeits|reise** *die* honeymoon.

**Hochzeits|tag** *der* [Tag der Hochzeit] wedding day; [Jubiläum] wedding anniversary.

**hoch|ziehen** *vt (unreg)* - **1.** [Rollladen, Hose] to pull up; [Segel, Flagge] to hoist - **2.** [heben] to raise; die Nase ~ to sniff - **3.** [bauen] to put up.

➤ **sich hochziehen** *ref:* sich an etw *(D)* ~ to pull o.s. up by holding on to sthg; *fig* to take pleasure in sthg.

**Hocke** *(pl -n) die* - **1.** [Haltung]: in die ~ gehen to crouch down - **2.** [Sprung] squat vault.

**hocken** *vi* - **1.** [kauern] to crouch - **2.** *fam* [sitzen] to sit.

➤ **sich hocken** *ref* - **1.** [sich kauern] to crouch - **2.** *fam* [sich setzen] to sit o.s. down.

**Hocker** *(pl -) der* stool.

**Höcker** *(pl -) der* - **1.** [Ausbuchtung] bump - **2.** [von Kamel] hump.

**Hockey** *das* hockey.

**Hockey|spieler, in** *der, die* hockey player.

**Hoden** *(pl -) der* testicle.

**Hof** *(pl Höfe) der* - **1.** [von Häusern] courtyard - **2.** [Bauernhof] farm - **3.** [Schulhof] playground - **4.** [von Gefängnissen] yard - **5.** [von Königen] court; jm den ~ machen *fig* to court sb.

**Hofbräuhaus** *das large beer hall in Munich.*

**hoffen** *vt* to hope; ~ wir das Beste! let's hope for the best! <> *vi:* auf etw ~ to hope for sthg; auf jn ~ to pin one's hopes on sb; auf Gott ~ to trust in God.

**hoffentlich** *adv* hopefully; kommt er? – ja, ~! is he coming? – I hope so!

**Hoffnung** *(pl -en) die* hope; ohne/voller ~ sein to have given up hope/be hopeful; die ~ aufgeben/nicht aufgeben to give up/not to give up hope; seine ~en auf jn/etw setzen to pin one's hopes on sb/sthg.

**hoffnungslos** *adj* hopeless <> *adv* hopelessly.

**Hoffnungslosigkeit** *die* hopelessness.

**Hoffnungs|schimmer** *der* glimmer of hope.

**hoffnungsvoll** *adj* - **1.** [optimistisch] hopeful - **2.** [Erfolg versprechend] promising <> *adv* - **1.** [optimistisch] hopefully - **2.** [Erfolg versprechend] promisingly.

**höflich** *adj* polite <> *adv* politely.

**Höflichkeit** *(pl -en) die* - **1.** [im Auftreten] politeness - **2.** [Floskel] polite remark.

**Höflichkeits|besuch** *der* courtesy visit.

**Höhe** *(pl -n) die* - **1.** [von Schrank, Berg] height; [von Dreieck] altitude - **2.** [von Preis, Temperatur] level; ein Bußgeld in ~ von 50 Euro a fine of 50 euros - **3.** [Richtung]: in die ~ up - **4.** [Linie]: auf der ODER in ~ von etw level with sthg; auf gleicher ~ level - **5.** *RW:* auf der ~ sein [informiert sein] to be up to date; [gesund sein] to be fit; das ist die ~! *fam* that's the limit!

**Hoheit** *(pl -en) die* - **1.** [Herrschaft] sovereignty - **2.** [als Anrede] Your Highness.

**Hoheits|gebiet** *das* sovereign territory.

**Höhen|flug** *der* - **1.** [in Gedanken] flight of fancy - **2.** [mit dem Flugzeug] high-altitude flight.

**Höhen|lage** *die* altitude; in ~ at high altitude.

**Höhen|sonne** *die* sun lamp.

**Höhen|unterschied** *der* difference in altitude.

**Höhe|punkt** *der* high point.

**Hohe Tauern** *pl:* die ~ the Hohe Tauern.

**hohl** *adj* - **1.** [gen] hollow; [Augen] sunken; **in der ~en Hand** in the hollow of one's hand - **2.** *fam abw* [dumm - Phrase] empty; [ - Person] empty-headed ◇ *adv* - **1.** [dumpf] hollowly - **2.** *fam abw* [geistlos] emptily.

**Höhle** (*pl* -n) *die* - **1.** [Grotte] cave - **2.** [von Dachs] sett; [von Löwe] den; [von Fuchs] lair.

**Hohl|körper** *der* hollow body.

**Hohl|kreuz** *das (ohne pl)* hollow back.

**Hohl|maß** *das* measure of capacity.

**Hohl|raum** *der* cavity.

**Hohl|weg** *der* defile.

**Hohn** *der geh* scorn; **das ist der blanke** *ODER* **reine ~!** it is utterly ridiculous!

**höhnisch** *adj* scornful ◇ *adv* scornfully.

**Hokuspokus** *der* - **1.** [Zauberwort] hey presto - **2.** *abw* [Aufwand] fuss.

**Holding|gesellschaft** *die* holding company.

**holen** *vt* - **1.** [herbeischaffen] to fetch, to get; **sich (D) bei jm Rat ~** to ask sb for advice; **etw ~ kommen** to come for sthg; **sich (D) etw ~** [gen] to get sthg; [Krankheit] to catch sthg - **2.** [kaufen] to get - **3.** [herausnehmen]: **etw aus etw ~** to take sthg out of sthg - **4.** [Arzt, Polizei, Handwerker] to call.

**Holland** *nt* Holland.

**Holländer** (*pl* -) *der* Dutchman; **die ~** the Dutch ◇ *adj (unver)* Dutch.

**Holländerin** (*pl* -nen) *die* Dutchwoman.

**holländisch** *adj* Dutch.

**Hölle** *die* hell; **die ~ ist los!** *fam fig* all hell has broken loose!; **jm die ~ heiß machen** *fam fig* to give sb hell.

**Höllen|angst** *die fam*: **eine ~ (vor jm/etw) haben** to be scared stiff (of sb/sthg).

**Höllenlärm** *der fam* infernal din.

**höllisch** *adj* - **1.** [schrecklich] appalling - **2.** *fam* [intensiv] infernal ◇ *adv fam* [sehr] hellishly; **die Wunde tut ~ weh** the wound hurts like hell; **~ aufpassen** to be incredibly careful.

**Hollywood|schaukel** ['hɔlɪwʊdʃaʊkl̩] *die* swing hammock.

**Holm** (*pl* -e) *der sport* bar.

**Holocaust** (*pl* -s) *der* holocaust.

**Holografie, Holographie** *die* holography.

**holpern** (*perf* hat/ist geholpert) *vi* - **1.** *(ist)* [beim Fahren] to jolt - **2.** *(hat)* [beim Sprechen] to stumble.

**holprig** *adj* - **1.** [Weg] bumpy - **2.** [Fremdsprache] halting - **3.** [Stil] clumsy ◇ *adv* [sprechen, lesen] haltingly.

**Holunder** (*pl* -) *der* - **1.** [Baum] elder - **2.** [Beere] elderberry.

**Holz** (*pl* Hölzer) *das* wood; [Bauholz] timber *Br*, lumber *Am*; **aus dem gleichen** *ODER* **demselben ~ (geschnitzt) sein** *fig* to be cast from the same mould.

➤ **Holz verarbeitend** *adj* timber-processing.

**Holzblas|instrument** *das* woodwind instrument.

**Holz|boden** *der* wooden floor.

**hölzern** *adj eigtl* & *fig* wooden.

**Holzfäller, in** (*mpl* -; *fpl* -nen) *der, die* woodcutter *Br*, lumberjack *Am*.

**holzfrei** *adj* wood-free.

**Holzhammermethode** *die fam*: **jm etw mit der ~ beibringen** [Lehrstoff] to drum sthg into sb.

**Holz|haus** *das* wooden house; [Hütte im Wald] log cabin.

**holzig** *adj* woody.

**Holz|kohle** *die* charcoal.

**Holz|schnitt** *der* woodcut.

**Holz|schuh** *der* clog.

**Holz|stoß** *der* woodpile.

**holzverarbeitend** ▷ Holz.

**holzverkleidet** *adj* wood-panelled.

**Holz|weg** *der*: **auf dem ~ sein** to be barking up the wrong tree.

**Holz|wolle** *die* wood wool.

**Holz|wurm** *der* woodworm.

**Homebanking** ['hoːmbɛŋkɪŋ] *das* home banking.

**Homepage** ['hoːmpeːdʒ] (*pl* -s) *die* EDV home page.

**Homeshopping** *das (ohne pl)* home shopping.

**Hommage** [ɔ'maːʒ] (*pl* -n) *die* tribute.

**homogen** *adj* homogeneous.

**homogenisieren** *vt* to homogenize.

**Homöopath** (*pl* -en) *der* homeopathic.

**Homöopathie** *die* homeopathy.

**Homöopathin** (*pl* -nen) *die* homeopath.

**homöopathisch** *adj* homeopath.

**Homosexualität** *die* homosexuality.

**homosexuell** *adj* homosexual.

**Homosexuelle** (*pl* -n) *der, die* homosexual.

**Honduras** *nt* Honduras.

**Hongkong** *nt* Hong Kong.

**Honig** *der* honey.

**Honig|kuchen** *der* honey cake.

**honigsüß** *adj* [Lächeln] sugar-sweet; [Stimme] honeyed ◇ *adv*: **sie lächelte ~** she gave the sweetest of smiles; **~ antworten** to answer in honeyed tones.

H

**Honorar** (*pl* -e) *das* fee.

**honorieren** *vt geh* [anerkennen] to reward; [bezahlen] to remunerate.

**Hopfen** (*pl* -) *der* hops (*pl*); **bei ihm ist ~ und Malz verloren** he's a hopeless case.

**hopp** *interj* quick!; **~-~!** chop, chop!

**Hops** (*pl* -e) *der* jump.

**hopsen** (*perf* **ist gehopst**) *vi* to skip.

**hopslgehen** (*perf* **ist hopsgegangen**) *vi* (*unreg*) *salopp* - **1.** [umkommen] to buy it - **2.** [kaputtgehen]: **das Radio ist hopsgegangen** the radio's bust.

**hörbar** *adj* audible ⬦ *adv* audibly.

**hörbehindert** *adj* hard of hearing.

**Hörlbrille** *die* hearing aid glasses (*pl*).

**Hörlbuch** *das* audiobook, book on tape.

**horchen** *vi* to listen.

**Horde** (*pl* -n) *die* horde.

**hören** *vt* - **1.** [unwillkürlich] to hear; **er hat lange nichts von sich ~ lassen** we haven't heard from him for ages; **von ihm hört man nur Gutes** you only hear good things about him; **ich will nichts mehr davon ~!** that's the end of it! - **2.** [willkürlich] to listen to ⬦ *vi* - **1.** [unwillkürlich, erfahren] to hear; **schwer ~** to be hard of hearing; **Sie werden noch von mir ~!** you haven't heard the last of this! - **2.** [zuhören, gehorchen] to listen; **hör mal!** listen!; **~ auf** (+ A) to listen to; **hätte ich doch auf ihren Rat gehört!** if only I'd listened to her advice!

**Hörensagen** *das:* **etw vom ~ kennen** to know sthg from hearsay.

**hörenswert** *adj* worth listening to.

**Hörer** (*pl* -) *der* - **1.** [Zuhörer] listener - **2.** [Telefonhörer] receiver.

**Hörerin** (*pl* -nen) *die* listener.

**Hörerschaft** *die* listeners (*pl*).

**Hörlfehler** *der* hearing defect.

**Hörlfunk** *der* radio.

**Hörlgerät** *das* hearing aid.

**hörgeschädigt** *adj* hard of hearing.

**hörig** *adj:* **jm/etw ~ sein** to be in thrall to sb/sthg.

**Horizont** (*pl* -e) *der* horizon; **das geht über meinen ~** *fig* that's right over the top of my head; **seinen ~ erweitern** *fig* to broaden one's horizons.

**horizontal** *adj* horizontal ⬦ *adv* horizontally.

**Horizontale** (*pl* -n) *die* horizontal.

**Hormon** (*pl* -e) *das* hormone.

**Hörlmuschel** *die* earpiece.

**Horn** (*pl* **Hörner** ODER -e) *das* horn.

**Hornlbrille** *die* horn-rimmed glasses (*pl*).

**Hörnchen** (*pl* -) *das* - **1.** [Gebäck] croissant - **2.** [Horn] small horn.

**Hornlhaut** *die* - **1.** [Hautschicht] patch of hard skin, callus - **2.** [des Auges] cornea.

**Hornisse** (*pl* -n) *die* hornet.

**Horoskop** (*pl* -e) *das* horoscope.

**horrend** *adj* horrendous.

**Horror** *der* - **1.** [Entsetzen] horror; **einen ~ vor jm/etw haben** to be terrified of sb/sthg - **2.** *fam* [Unangenehmes]: **das war der (reine) ~** it was a (total) nightmare.

**Horrorlfilm** *der* horror film ODER movie.

**Hörlsaal** *der* lecture hall.

**Hörlspiel** *das* radio play.

**Horst** (*pl* -e) *der* eyrie.

**Hort** (*pl* -e) *der* - **1.** [Kinderhort] *day-centre where children can spend the afternoon after lessons have finished* - **2.** *geh* [Schutz] refuge.

**horten** *vt* to hoard.

**Hörweite** *die:* **in/außer ~** in/out of earshot.

**Hose** (*pl* -n) *die* trousers (*pl*) *Br*, pants (*pl*) *Am*; [Unterhose - von Männern] pants *Br*, shorts *Am*; [- von Frauen] knickers (*pl*) *Br*, panties (*pl*) *Am*; **eine neue ~ kaufen** to buy a new pair of trousers *Br* ODER pants *Am*, to buy some new trousers *Br* ODER pants *Am*; **sich** (*D*) **die ~ anziehen** to put one's trousers on; **kurze ~** shorts (*pl*); **in die ~ machen** to dirty one's pants; **die ~n anhaben** *fam fig* to wear the trousers; **die ~n voll haben** *fam fig* to be crapping o.s.; **in die ~ gehen** *fam* to be a flop; **da ist tote ~** *fam* it's totally dead there.

**Hosenlanzug** *der* trouser suit *Br*, pantsuit *Am*.

**Hosenlbein** *das* trouser leg.

**Hosenlboden** *der:* **sich auf den ~ setzen** *fam* to knuckle down.

**Hosenlbügel** *der* trouser hanger.

**Hosenlbund** *der* waistband.

**Hosenlrock** *der* culottes (*pl*).

**Hosenlschlitz** *der* fly, flies (*pl*) *Br*.

**Hosenlträger** *der* braces (*pl*) *Br*, suspenders (*pl*) *Am*.

**Hospital** (*pl* -e ODER -täler) *das* hospital.

**hospitieren** *vi* UNI to sit in (*on a class*).

**Hostess** (*pl* -en) *die* hostess.

**Hostie** (*pl* -n) *die* REL host.

**Hotdog** ['hɔt'dɔk] (*pl* -s) *das* ODER *der* hot dog.

**Hotel** (*pl* -s) *das* hotel; **~ garni** ≈ bed and breakfast.

**Hotellbett** *das* hotel bed.

**Hotellldirektor** *der* hotel manager.

**Hotellldirektorin** *die* hotel manager.

**Hotellgast** *der* hotel guest.

**Hotel|gewerbe** *das* hotel trade.
**Hotelier** [hotɛ'lje:] (*pl* -s) *der* hotelier.
**Hotel|verzeichnis** *das* hotel guide.
**Hotel|zimmer** *das* hotel room.
**Hotline** ['hotlaɪn] (*pl* -s) *die* hotline.
**HP** ▷ **Halbpension.**
**Hr.** (*abk für* **Herr**) Mr.
**HR** (*abk für* **Hessischer Rundfunk**) *der* Radio Hesse.
**hrsg.** (*abk für* **herausgegeben**) ed.
**hüben** *adv*: ~ **und drüben** on both sides (*esp. in the case of East and West Germany*).
**Hubraum** *der* cubic capacity.
**hübsch** *adj* - **1.** [Person, Anblick, Kleid, Blumen] pretty - **2.** [Idee, Umgebung] nice - **3.** *fam* [groß - Summe] tidy - **4.** *fam iron* [unangenehm]: **das ist ja eine ~e Überraschung!** what a pleasant surprise! ◇ *adv* - **1.** [schön] prettily - **2.** *fam* [sehr] jolly; **sei ~ brav!** be really good!
**Hubschrauber** (*pl* -) *der* helicopter.
**Hubschrauberlande|platz** *der* - **1.** [für Nottransporte] helicopter pad, helipad - **2.** [Flughafen] heliport.
**Hucke** (*pl* -n) *die*: **jm die ~ voll hauen** *fam* to give sb a good hiding.
**huckepack** *adv*: **jn ~ nehmen** *ODER* **tragen** *fam* to give sb a piggyback.
**Huckepackverkehr** *der* (*ohne pl*) - **1.** [für LKWs] rail trailer shipment - **2.** [für PKWs] motorail.
**Huf** (*pl* -e) *der* hoof.
**Huf|eisen** *das* horseshoe.
**Huf|schmied** *der* farrier.
**Hüfte** (*pl* -n) *die* hip.
**Hüft|gelenk** *das* hip joint.
**Huf|tier** *das* hoofed animal.
**Hüft|knochen** *der* hip bone.
**Hügel** (*pl* -) *der* - **1.** [Berg] hill - **2.** [Haufen] mound.
**hügelig** *adj* hilly.
**Huhn** (*pl* Hühner) *das* - **1.** [Vogel] chicken; **da lachen ja die Hühner!** *fam* you must be joking! - **2.** *fam* [Mädchen, Frau]: **ein dummes ~** a silly cow; **ein verrücktes ~** a queer fish.
**Hühnchen** (*pl* -) *das* chicken; **mit jm ein ~ zu rupfen haben** *fam* to have a bone to pick with sb.
**Hühner|auge** *das* corn.
**Hühner|brühe** *die* chicken broth.
**Hühner|ei** *das* hen's egg.
**Hülle** (*pl* -n) *die* cover; [Verpackung] wrapping; [von Schallplatte] sleeve; **etw in ~ und Fülle haben** to have plenty of sthg.

**hüllen** *vt*: **jn/sich/etw in etw** (A) ~ to wrap sb/o.s./sthg in sthg.
**Hülse** (*pl* -n) *die* - **1.** [Hülle] case; [von Film, Zigarre] tube - **2.** [bei Pflanzen] pod.
**Hülsen|frucht** *die* pulse.
**human** *adj* - **1.** [würdig] humane - **2.** [freundlich] lenient ◇ *adv* - **1.** [würdig] humanely - **2.** [freundlich] leniently.
**Humanismus** *der* humanism.
**Humanist, in** (*mpl* -en; *fpl* -nen) *der, die* humanist.
**humanistisch** *adj* - **1.** [altsprachlich] classical; **~es Gymnasium** secondary school providing a classical education - **2.** [philosophisch] humanistic.
**humanitär** *adj* humanitarian.
**Humanität** *die* humanity.
**Hummel** (*pl* -n) *die* bumblebee.
**Hummer** (*pl* -) *der* lobster.
**Humor** *der* humour; **viel ~ haben** to have a great sense of humour; **er hat keinen Sinn für ~** he has no sense of humour; **etw mit ~ nehmen** *ODER* **tragen** to bear sthg with good humour; **schwarzer ~** black humour.
**humoristisch** *adj* humorous ◇ *adv* humorously.
**humorlos** *adj* humourless ◇ *adv* humourlessly.
**humorvoll** *adj* humorous ◇ *adv* humorously.
**humpeln** (*perf* hat/ist gehumpelt) *vi* - **1.** (hat, ist) [hinken] to walk with *ODER* have a limp - **2.** (ist) [in eine Richtung] to limp.
**Humus** *der* humus.
**Hund** (*pl* -e) *der* - **1.** [Tier] dog; **'vorsicht, bissiger ~!'** 'beware of the dog' - **2.** *salopp* [Mann]: **er ist ein blöder ~** he's a stupid git - **3.** *RW*: **er ist bekannt wie ein bunter ~** he's a well-known face; **vor die ~e gehen** *fam* to go to the dogs; **wie ~ und Katze** like cat and dog.
**Hunde|hütte** *die* kennel.
**Hunde|leine** *die* lead *Br*, leash *Am*.
**Hunde|marke** *die* dog tag.
**hundemüde** *adj* dog-tired.
**Hunde|rasse** *die* breed (of dog).
**hundert** *num* - **1.** [Zahl] a *ODER* one hundred; **auf ~ kommen** *fam* to hit the roof - **2.** *fam* [sehr viele] hundreds of; *siehe auch* **sechs.**
**Hundert** (*pl* -e) *die* *ODER* *das* hundred.
▶ **Hunderte** *pl* [große Anzahl]: **~e von** hundreds of.
▶ **zu Hunderten** *adv*: **zu ~en kommen** to come in their hundreds; *siehe auch* **Sechs.**
**Hunderter** (*pl* -) *der* - **1.** [Geldschein] hundred euro note - **2.** [Zahl] hundred.

H

**hunderterlei** *num* - **1.** [viele verschiedene] a hundred different - **2.** [vieles] a hundred and one.

**Hunderteuro|schein** *der* hundred euro note.

**hundertfach** *adv* a hundred times.

**Hundertfache** *das (ohne pl)*: **in der Stadt muss man das ~ bezahlen** in town you have to pay a hundred times as much.

**hundertfünfzigprozentig** *adj fam* [Kommunist, Nazi] dyed-in-the-wool.

**Hundertjahr|feier** *die* centenary.

**hundertjährig** *adj* hundred-year-old.

**hundertmal** *adv* a hundred times.

**Hundertmeter|lauf** *der*: **der ~** the hundred metres.

**hundertprozentig** *adj* - **1.** [von hundert Prozent] one hundred percent - **2.** [vollkommen] complete; **er ist ein ~er Bayer** he's a Bavarian through and through ⟨⟩ *adv fam* [völlig] completely; **etw ~ wissen** to know sthg for certain.

**Hundertschaft** *(pl -en) die* group of a hundred.

**hundertste, r, s** *adj* hundredth; *siehe auch* **sechste.**

**Hundertste** *(pl -n) der, die, das* hundredth; *siehe auch* **Sechste.**

**hundertstel** *adj (unver)* hundredth; **eine ~ Sekunde** a hundredth of a second; *siehe auch* **sechstel.**

**Hundertstel** *(pl -) das* hundredth; *siehe auch* **Sechstel.**

**hunderttausend** *num* a ODER one hundred thousand.

**Hunde|salon** *der* dog parlour.

**Hunde|steuer** *die* dog licence fee.

**Hunde|zwinger** *der* dog cage.

**Hündin** *(pl -nen) die* bitch.

**Hüne** *(pl -n) der* giant.

**Hunger** *der eigtl & fig* hunger; **auf etw (A) ~ haben** to feel like eating sthg.

**Hunger|lohn** *der abw* starvation wage, pittance.

**hungern** *vi* - **1.** [nach Nahrung] to go hungry - **2.** *geh* [verlangen]: **nach etw ~** to be hungry for sthg, to crave sthg.

**Hungers|not** *die* famine.

**Hunger|streik** *der* hunger strike.

**Hunger|tuch** *das*: **am ~ nagen** to starve.

**hungrig** *adj* hungry ⟨⟩ *adv* hungrily.

**Hunsrück** *der*: **der ~** the Hunsrück mountains.

**Hupe** *(pl -n) die* horn.

**hupen** *vi* to sound one's horn.

**hüpfen** *(perf ist gehüpft) vi* to hop.

**Hürde** *(pl -n) die* hurdle; **eine ~ nehmen** *fig* to get past a hurdle.

**Hürden|lauf** *der*: **der ~** the hurdles.

**Hure** *(pl -n) die abw* whore.

**hurra** *interj* hurray!

**husch** *interj* quick!; **~, ~!** chop, chop!

**huschen** *(perf ist gehuscht) vi* to dart; [Lächeln] to flit.

**hüsteln** *vi* to give a slight cough.

**husten** *vi* to cough; **auf dieses Angebot huste ich!** *fam* you can keep your offer! ⟨⟩ *vt* [Blut, Schleim] to cough up; **jm eins** ODER **was ~** *fam* to tell sb to get lost.

**Husten** *der (ohne pl)* cough; **~ haben** to have a cough.

**Husten|anfall** *der* coughing fit.

**Husten|reiz** *der*: **~ haben** to have a tickle in one's throat.

**Husten|saft** *der* cough mixture.

**Hut** *(pl Hüte) der* - **1.** [Kleidungsstück] hat - **2.** *RW*: **das ist ein alter ~** *fam* that's old hat; **mit jm/etw nichts am ~ haben** *fam* to have no time for sb/ sthg; **seinen ~ nehmen** to pack one's bags; **dein Geld kannst du dir an den ~ stecken!** *fam* you can keep your money!; **alle unter einen ~ bringen** to get everybody to agree; **verschiedene Interessen unter einen ~ bringen** to reconcile different interests ⟨⟩ *die*: **(vor jm) auf der ~ sein** to be on one's guard (with sb); **beim Autofahren bin ich auf der ~** I'm on the alert when I'm driving.

⟹ **Hut ab** *interj*: **das hätte ich dir gar nicht zugetraut - ~ ab!** I wouldn't have thought you capable of that – hats off to you!

**hüten** *vt* [Kinder] to look after; [Geheimnis] to keep; [Tiere] to watch over.

⟹ **sich hüten** *ref*: **sich vor jm/etw ~** to be on one's guard against sb/sthg; **sich ~, etw zu tun** to take care not to do sthg.

**Hütte** *(pl -n) die* - **1.** [Haus] hut; [bewirtschaftete Berghütte] mountain lodge - **2.** [Eisenhütte] iron and steel works *(sg)*.

**Hütten|käse** *der* cottage cheese.

**Hütten|schuh** *der* slipper sock.

**Hyäne** *(pl -n) die* hyena.

**Hyazinthe** *(pl -n) die* hyacinth.

**Hydrant** *(pl -en) der* hydrant.

**Hydraulik** *die* hydraulics *(pl)*.

**hydraulisch** *adj* hydraulic ⟨⟩ *adv* hydraulically.

**Hydrokultur** *die* hydroponics *(U)*.

**Hygiene** [hy'gie:nə] *die* hygiene.

**hygienisch** [hy'giːnɪʃ] *adj* hygienic <> *adv* hygienically.

**Hymne** (*pl* -n) *die* hymn.

**Hyperbel** (*pl* -n) *die* - **1.** MATH hyperbola - **2.** [Stilfigur] hyperbole.

**Hypnose** (*pl* -n) *die* hypnosis.

**Hypnotiseur, in** [hypnoti'zøːɐ̯, rɪn] (*mpl* -e; *fpl* -nen) *der, die* hypnotist.

**hypnotisieren** *vt* to hypnotize.

**Hypochonder, in** [hypo'xɔndɐ, rɪn] (*mpl* -; *fpl* -nen) *der, die* hypochondriac.

**Hypothek** (*pl* -en) *die* mortgage; **eine ~ aufnehmen** to take out a mortgage.

**Hypo|these** *die* hypothesis.

**hypothetisch** *adj* hypothetical <> *adv* hypothetically.

**Hysterie** [hyste'riːl] (*pl* -n) *die* hysteria.

**hysterisch** *adj* hysterical; **~er Anfall** (fit of) hysterics <> *adv* hysterically.

---

**i, I** [iːl] (*pl* - ODER -s) *das* i, I.

**i.** *abk für* im.

**i.A.** (*abk für* im Auftrag) pp.

**IAA** [iːaːˈaːl] (*abk für* Internationale Automobilausstellung) *die* international motor show.

**ibd.** (*abk für* ibidem (ebenda)) ibid.

**Iberische Halbinsel** *die* Iberian peninsula.

**Ibiza** *nt* Ibiza.

**IC** [iːˈtseːl] (*pl* -s) (*abk für* Intercity) *der* intercity train.

**ICE** [iːtseːˈeːl] (*pl* -s) (*abk für* Intercity Express) *der* intercity express train.

**ich** *pron* I; **~ bins** it's me.

**Ich** *das* self; PSYCH ego.

**ichbezogen** *adj* egocentric.

**i.d.** *abk für* in der.

**ideal** *adj* ideal <> *adv* ideally.

**Ideal** (*pl* -e) *das* ideal.

**Ideal|fall** *der* ideal case; **im ~** ideally.

**idealisieren** *vt* to idealize.

**Idealismus** *der* idealism.

**Idealist, in** (*mpl* -en; *fpl* -nen) *der, die* idealist.

**idealistisch** *adj* idealistic <> *adv* idealistically.

**Idee** (*pl* -n) *die* - **1.** [gen] idea; **eine fixe ~** an obsession; **nicht die geringste** ODER **leiseste ~ von etw haben** not to have the faintest idea about sthg - **2.** [Kleinigkeit] bit; **eine ~ lauter** a bit louder.

**ideell** *adj* [Werte] spiritual <> *adv:* **jn ~ unterstützen** to give sb notional support.

**ideenreich** *adj* imaginative.

**Identifikation** (*pl* -en) *die* identification.

**identifizieren** *vt* to identify; **jn/etw mit etw ~** to identify sb/sthg with sthg.
➤ **sich identifizieren** *ref:* **sich mit jm/etw ~** to identify with sb/sthg.

**Identifizierung** (*pl* -en) *die* identification.

**identisch** *adj* identical.

**Identität** *die* identity.

**Ideologie** (*pl* -n) *die* ideology.

**ideologisch** *adj* ideological <> *adv* ideologically.

**Idiom** (*pl* -e) *das* idiom.

**idiomatisch** *adj* idiomatic.

**Idiot** (*pl* -en) *der fam abw* [Dummkopf] idiot.

**Idiotin** (*pl* -nen) *die* idiot.

**idiotisch** *fam abw adj* [dumm, unsinnig] idiotic <> *adv* [unsinnig] idiotically.

**Idol** (*pl* -e) *das* idol.

**Idylle** (*pl* -n) *die* idyll.

**idyllisch** *adj* idyllic <> *adv* idyllically.

**IFA** ['iːfal] (*abk für* Internationale Funkausstellung) *die* international radio show.

**IG** [iːˈgeːl] (*pl* -s) (*abk für* Industriegewerkschaft) *die* industry-wide union; **die ~ Metall** IG-Metall, *German metalworkers' union.*

**Igel** (*pl* -) *der* hedgehog.

**Iglu** (*pl* -s) *das* ODER *der* igloo.

**Ignorant, in** (*mpl* -en; *fpl* -nen) *der, die abw* ignoramus.

**Ignoranz** *die abw* ignorance.

**ignorieren** *vt* to ignore.

**IHK** [iːhaːˈkaːl] (*abk für* Industrie- und Handelskammer) *die* chamber of commerce and industry.

**ihm** *pron* (Dativ von er) - **1.** [Person] (to) him; **sie sagte es ~** she told him; **das gehört ~** this is his, this belongs to him; **mit ~** with him - **2.** [Sache] (to) it.

**ihn** *pron* (Akkusativ von er) - **1.** [Person] him - **2.** [Sache] it.

**ihnen** *pron* (Dativ Plural von er/sie) (to) them; **er ist**

**von ~** it's theirs, it belongs to them; **gib ~ den Schlüssel** give them the key.

**Ihnen** pron (Dativ von Sie) (to) you; **gehört das ~?** is this yours?, does this belong to you?; **wer hat es ~ gegeben?** who gave you it?, who gave it to you?; **entschuldigen Sie, meine Herren, ist der Platz neben ~ frei?** excuse me gentlemen, is the seat next to you free?

**ihr** pron - **1.** [Nominativ Plural] you - **2.** [Dativ von sie - Person] (to) her; [ - Sache] (to) it; **er sagte es ~** he told her; **das gehört ~** this is hers, this belongs to her; **mit ~** with her.

**ihr, e** det - **1.** (Singular) her - **2.** (Plural) their.

**Ihr, e** det your.

**ihre, r, s** pron - **1.** [Singular - von Person] hers; [ - von Ding] its - **2.** [Plural] theirs.

**Ihre, r, s** pron yours.

**ihrer** pron (Genitiv von sie) [Singular von Person] (of) her; [Plural] (of) them; [Singular von Ding] (of) it.

**ihrerseits** adv - **1.** [sie selbst - Singular] for her part; [ - Plural] for their part - **2.** [von ihr - Person] on her part; [ - Tier, Sache] on its part; [ - Plural] on their part.

**Ihrerseits** adv on your part.

**ihresgleichen** pron [Singular - von Person] people like her; [ - von Ding] its own kind; [Plural - von Person] people like them; [ - von Ding] their own kind.

**Ihresgleichen** pron people like you.

**ihretwegen** adv - **1.** [ihr zuliebe - von Person] for her sake; [ - von Ding] for its sake; [ihnen zuliebe] for their sake - **2.** [wegen ihr - Person] because of her; [ - Ding] because of it; [wegen ihnen] because of them.

**Ihretwegen** adv - **1.** [Ihnen zuliebe] for your sake - **2.** [wegen Ihnen] because of you.

**ihretwillen** ➡ **um ihretwillen** adv [Singular - Person] for her sake; [ - Ding] for its sake; [Plural] for their sake.

**Ihretwillen** ➡ **um Ihretwillen** adv for your sake.

**ihrige** (pl -n) pron geh: **der/die/das ~** [Singular - von Person] hers; [ - von Ding] its; [Plural] theirs.

**Ihrige** (pl -n) pron geh: **der/die/das ~** yours; **Sie sollten das ~ tun** you should do your bit ODER part.
➡ **Ihrigen** pl geh [Angehörigen]: **die ~** your people.

**Ijsselmeer** ['aisəlmeːr] das: **das ~** the Ijsselmeer.

**Ikone** (pl -n) die icon.

**illegal** adj illegal ◇ adv illegally.

**illegitim** adj [unrechtmäßig] illegitimate ◇ adv [unrechtmäßig] illegitimately.

**Illusion** (pl -en) die illusion; **mach dir keine ~en** don't kid yourself.

**illusorisch** adj illusory.

**Illustration** (pl -en) die illustration.

**illustrieren** vt to illustrate.

**Illustrierte** (pl -n) die magazine.

**Iltis** (pl -se) der polecat.

**im** präp (in + dem) ⊳ **in.**

**Image** ['ɪmɪtʃ] (pl -s) das image.

**Imagepflege** die [von Person] cultivation of one's image.

**imaginär** adj imaginary.

**Imbiss** (pl -e) der - **1.** [Mahlzeit] snack - **2.** [Imbissbude] snack bar.

**Imbiss|bude** die fam snack bar.

**Imbiss|stube** die snack bar.

**Imitation** (pl -en) die imitation.

**imitieren** vt to imitate.

**Imker, in** (mpl -; fpl -nen) der, die beekeeper.

**Immatrikulation** (pl -en) die - **1.** UNI matriculation - **2.** Schweiz [Kfz-Zulassung] registration.

**immatrikulieren** vt - **1.** UNI to enrol - **2.** Schweiz [zulassen] to register.
➡ **sich immatrikulieren** ref UNI to matriculate.

**immens** adj immense ◇ adv immensely; **~ viel** an immense amount.

**immer** adv - **1.** [zeitlich] always; **für ~** for ever, for good; **für ~ und ewig** for ever and ever; **~ wieder** again and again, time and again; **~ wenn** whenever; **~ geradeaus!** keep going straight ahead!; **~ herein!** do come in!; **~ mit der Ruhe!** take it easy!; **~ noch** still - **2.** [mit Komparativ]: **~ schwieriger** more and more difficult; **~ stärker** stronger and stronger - **3.** [egal]: **was (auch) ~** whatever; **wer (auch) ~** whoever; **wie (auch) ~** however; **wo (auch) ~** wherever.

**immerfort** adv constantly.

**immergrün** adj evergreen.

**Immer|grün** das periwinkle.

**immerhin** adv - **1.** [wenigstens] at least - **2.** [schließlich] after all - **3.** [trotzdem] nevertheless.

**immerzu** adv constantly.

**Immigrant, in** (mpl -en; fpl -nen) der, die immigrant.

**Immigration** (pl -en) die immigration.

**immigrieren** (perf ist immigriert) vi to immigrate.

**Immobilien** [ɪmo'biːljən] pl property (U).

**Immobilien|makler, in** der, die estate agent Br, realtor Am.

**immun** adj: **gegen etw ~ sein** to be immune to sthg.

**Immunität** die immunity.

**Immunschwäche** die immunodeficiency.

**Imperativ** (pl -e) der GRAM imperative.

**Imperfekt** (pl -e) das GRAM imperfect.

**Imperialismus** der imperialism.

**Imperium** (pl -perien) das empire.

**impertinent** geh adj impertinent ⬦ adv impertinently.

**impfen** vt to vaccinate; **jn gegen etw ~** to vaccinate sb against sthg.

**Impf|schein** der vaccination certificate.

**Impf|stoff** der vaccine.

**Impfung** (pl -en) die vaccination.

**implantieren** vt MED to implant.

**implizit** adj implicit ⬦ adv implicitly.

**imponieren** vi to impress; **jm (durch etw) ~** to impress sb (with sthg).

**imponierend** adj impressive ⬦ adv impressively.

**Imponiergehabe** das [Getue]: **das ist reines ~** it's pure show.

**Import** (pl -e) der - **1.** [Ware] import - **2.** [Einfuhr] importation.

**Importeur** [ɪmpɔr'tøːɐ̯] (pl -e) der importer.

**importieren** vt to import.

**imposant** adj imposing.

**impotent** adj impotent.

**Impotenz** die impotence.

**imprägnieren** vt to impregnate; [gegen Wasser] to waterproof.

**Impression** (pl -en) die impression.

**Impressionismus** der Impressionism.

**Impressionist, in** (mpl -en; fpl -nen) der, die impressionist.

**impressionistisch** adj impressionistic ⬦ adv impressionistically.

**Improvisation** [ɪmproviza'tsi̯oːn] (pl -en) die improvisation.

**improvisieren** [ɪmprovi'ziːrən] vt & vi to improvise.

**Impuls** (pl -e) der - **1.** [Anregung] stimulus; [innere Regung] impulse; **einer Sache (D) neue ~e geben** to breathe new life into sthg - **2.** [Stoß] impulse.

**impulsiv** adj impulsive ⬦ adv impulsively.

**imstande, im Stande** adj: **zu etw ~ sein** to be capable of sthg; **sie ist ~ und erzählt ihm alles** she's quite capable of telling him everything.

**in** präp - **1.** (+ D) [räumlich] in; **im Bett liegen** to be in bed; **~ der Schule** at school; **die Aufgabe hat es ~ sich** the task is a tough one - **2.** (+ A) [räumlich] into; **~ den Fluss fallen** to fall into the river; **~ die Stadt fahren** to go to ODER into town; **~ die Schule gehen** to go to school; **sich ~ jn verlieben** to fall in love with sb - **3.** (+ D) [zeitlich] in; **~ dieser Woche** this week; **im Mo-**

ment at the moment; **wir fahren ~ einer Stunde** we're going in an hour; **das schaffe ich ~ einer Stunde** I can do it in an hour - **4.** (+ A) [zeitlich] into; **wir arbeiteten bis spät ~ die Nacht** we worked late into the night - **5.** (+ D) [modal]: **~ aller Eile** hurriedly; **~ Betrieb sein** to be working; **ich habe mich ~ der Zeit geirrt** I got the time wrong - **6.** (+ A) [modal]: **etw ~ seine Einzelteile zerlegen** to take sthg to pieces - **7.** (+ D) [mit Maß- oder Mengenangaben] in; **~ Millimetern** in millimetres ⬦ adj: **~ sein** fam to be in.

**Inanspruchnahme** die (ohne pl) - **1.** amt [von Rechten, Vorteilen] utilization - **2.** [von Belegschaft] demands (pl); [von Material] use.

**Inbegriff** der embodiment, epitome.

**inbegriffen** adj: **in etw** (D) **~ sein** to be included in sthg ⬦ adv: **Steuern ~** including tax.

**Inbetriebnahme** (pl -n) die - **1.** [von Maschine, Kraftwerk] commissioning; **vor ~ des Gerätes die Gebrauchsanweisung lesen** read the instructions before switching the appliance on for the first time - **2.** [von Flughafen, Schwimmbad] opening.

**Inch** (pl -es) das ODER der inch.

**Indefinit|pronomen** das GRAM indefinite pronoun.

**indem** konj - **1.** [instrumental] by; **er vernichtete die Unterlagen, ~ er sie in den Reißwolf steckte** he destroyed the documents by putting them through the shredder - **2.** [während] while.

**Inder, in** (mpl -; fpl -nen) der, die Indian.

**indessen, indes** adv - **1.** [zeitlich] meanwhile - **2.** [gegensätzlich] however ⬦ konj geh - **1.** [zeitlich] while - **2.** [gegensätzlich] whereas.

**Index** ['ɪndɛks] (pl -e ODER Indizes) der index; **auf dem ~ stehen** to be blacklisted.

**Indianer, in** (mpl -; fpl -nen) der, die abw (Red) Indian.

**indianisch** adj Indian.

**Indien** nt India.

**Indigo** (pl -s) das ODER der indigo.

**Indikation** (pl -en) die - **1.** RECHT grounds (pl) (for abortion) - **2.** MED (recommended) treatment.

**Indikativ** (pl -e) der GRAM indicative (mood).

**Indikator** (pl -toren) der: **ein ~ (für etw)** an indicator (of sthg).

**Indio** (pl -s) der Indian.

**indirekt** adj indirect ⬦ adv indirectly.

**indisch** adj Indian.

**Indischer Ozean** der Indian Ocean.

**indiskret** adj indiscreet ⬦ adv indiscreetly.

**Indiskretion** (pl -en) die indiscretion.

**indiskutabel** adj abw out of the question.

**Individualismus** [ɪndividua'lɪsmʊs] *der* individualism.

**Individualist, in** [ɪndividua'lɪst, ɪn] *(mpl* -en; *fpl* -nen) *der, die* individualist.

**individualistisch** [ɪndividua'lɪstɪʃ] *adj* individualistic ⬦ *adv* individualistically.

**Individualität** [ɪndividuali'tɛːt] *die* individuality.

**Individualverkehr** [ɪndividu'alfɛɐ̯keːɐ̯] *der amt* private vehicle traffic.

**individuell** [ɪndividu'ɛl] *adj* individual ⬦ *adv* individually; ~ **verschieden sein** to vary from case to case.

**Individuum** [ɪndi'viːduʊm] *(pl* -viduen) *das* individual.

**Indiz** [ɪn'diːts] *(pl* -ien) *das* - **1.** RECHT piece of circumstantial evidence; ~ien circumstantial evidence - **2.** [Anzeichen] indication.

**indoeuropäisch** *adj* Indo-European.

**indogermanisch** *adj* Indo-European.

**indoktrinieren** *vt* to indoctrinate.

**Indonesien** *nt* Indonesia.

**Indonesier, in** [ɪndo'neːzi̯ɐ, rɪn] *(mpl* -; *fpl* -nen) *der, die* Indonesian.

**indonesisch** *adj* Indonesian.

**Indus** *der:* **der** ~ the (River) Indus.

**industrialisieren** *vt* to industrialize.

**Industrialisierung** *die* industrialization.

**Industrie** *(pl* -n) *die* industry.

**Industrie|betrieb** *der* factory.

**Industrie|erzeugnis** *das:* ~se manufactured goods.

**Industrie|gebiet** *das* industrial area.

**Industrie|gewerkschaft** *die* industry-wide union.

**Industriekauf|frau** *die woman with a business qualification employed on the business side of an industrial company, e.g. as an accountant.*

**Industriekauf|mann** *der man with a business qualification employed on the business side of an industrial company, e.g. as an accountant.*

**Industrie||land** *das* industrialized nation.

**industriell** *adj* industrial ⬦ *adv* industrially.

**Industrielle** *(pl* -n) *der, die* industrialist.

**Industrie- und Handels|kammer** *die* chamber of commerce and industry.

**Industrie|zweig** *der* sector, branch of industry.

**ineffektiv** *geh adj* ineffective ⬦ *adv* ineffectively.

**ineinander** *adv* in/into one another; ~ ver-

liebt sein to be in love (with one another); ~ verwickelt tangled up (in each other).

**ineinander fügen** *vt* to fit together.

➠ **sich ineinander fügen** *ref* to fit together.

**ineinander greifen** *vi (unreg)* to mesh.

**infam** *abw adj* [Lüge, Unterstellung, Verleumdung] outrageous ⬦ *adv* outrageously.

**Infanterie** ['ɪnfantəriː] *die* infantry.

**infantil** *adj* infantile ⬦ *adv abw* [kindisch] like a child.

**Infarkt** *(pl* -e) *der* heart attack.

**Infekt** *(pl* -e) *der* MED infection.

**Infektion** *(pl* -en) *die* infection.

**Infektions|krankheit** *die* infectious disease.

**Inferno** *das geh* [Ort eines entsetzlichen Geschehens] infernal scene.

**Infinitiv** *(pl* -e) *der* GRAM infinitive.

**infizieren** *vt:* jn (mit etw) ~ to infect sb (with sthg).

➠ **sich infizieren** *ref:* sich (mit etw) ~ to become infected (with sthg).

**Inflation** *(pl* -en) *die* inflation.

**inflationär** *adj* inflationary.

**Inflations|rate** *die* rate of inflation.

**inflexibel** *adj* inflexible.

**Info** *(pl* -s) *die fam* info *(U);* eine ~ some info, a piece of info.

**infolge** *präp:* ~ einer Sache *(G)* ODER von etw as a result of sthg.

**infolgedessen** *adv* consequently.

**Informatik** *die* computer science.

**Informatiker, in** *(mpl* -; *fpl* -nen) *der, die* computer scientist.

**Information** *(pl* -en) *die* - **1.** information *(U);* ~en information; eine ~ über jn/etw (a piece of) information about sb/sthg; zu js ~ for sb's information - **2.** *(ohne pl)* [in Kaufhaus, Bahnhof] information desk.

**Informations|material** *das* information.

**Informations|stand** *der* information stand.

**informativ** *adj* informative.

**informell** *adj* informal ⬦ *adv* informally.

**informieren** *vt:* jn über jn/etw ~ to inform sb about sb/sthg.

➠ **sich informieren** *ref:* sich (über jn/etw) ~ to find out (about sb/sthg).

**Infrarot** *das* infra-red.

**Infra|struktur** *die* infrastructure.

**Infusion** *(pl* -en) *die* MED infusion.

**Ing.** *(abk für* Ingenieur) eng.

**Ingenieur, in** [ɪnʒe'njøːɐ̯, rɪn] *(mpl* -e; *fpl* -nen) *der, die* engineer.

**Ingwer** *der* ginger.
**Inh.** (*abk für* Inhaber) prop.
**Inhaber, in** (*mpl* -; *fpl* -nen) *der, die* - **1.** [von Geschäft] owner - **2.** [von Amt, Titel] holder.
**inhaftieren** *vt* to take into custody.
**inhalieren** *vt* to inhale ⬦ *vi* - **1.** MED to use an inhalant - **2.** *fam* [einen Lungenzug machen] to inhale.
**Inhalt** (*pl* -e) *der* - **1.** [von Gefäß, Behälter] contents (*pl*) - **2.** [von Text, Gespräch] content; **Form und ~** form and content - **3.** [Größe - von Fläche] area; [ - von Raum] volume - **4.** [Sinn] meaning.
**inhaltlich** *adj:* **der ~e Aufbau eines Textes** the way the content of a text is structured ⬦ *adv* as far as content is concerned.
**Inhaltslangabe** *die* - **1.** [von Text] summary - **2.** [von Paket] description of contents.
**Inhaltslverzeichnis** *das* - **1.** [von Buch] table of contents; [von Paket] list of contents - **2.** EDV directory.
**inhuman** *geh adj* [unmenschlich] inhuman; [menschenunwürdig] inhumane ⬦ *adv* [unmenschlich] inhumanly; [menschenunwürdig] inhumanely.
**Inh.-Verz.** (*abk für* Inhaltsverzeichnis) cont.
**Initiale** (*pl* -n) *die* initial (letter).
**Initiative** [initsjaʹtiːvə] (*pl* -n) *die* - **1.** [gen] initiative; **die ~ ergreifen** to take the initiative; **aus eigener ~** on one's own initiative - **2.** [Gruppe] local action group.
**Initiator** (*pl* -toren) *der* initiator.
**Initiatorin** (*pl* -nen) *die* initiator.
**Injektion** (*pl* -en) *die* injection.
**Inkarnation** (*pl* -en) *die geh* embodiment.
**inkl.** (*abk für* inklusive) incl.
**inklusive** [ınkluʹziːvə] *präp:* **~ einer Sache** (G) including sthg ⬦ *adv:* **bis zum 10. August ~** until 10 August inclusive.
**inkognito** *adv* incognito.
**inkompatibel** *adj* incompatible.
**inkompetent** *adj* incompetent ⬦ *adv* incompetently.
**Inlkompetenz** *die* incompetence.
**inkonsequent** *adj* inconsistent ⬦ *adv* inconsistently.
**Inlkonsequenz** *die* inconsistency.
**Inland** *das:* **im ~** at home; **die Waren sind für das ~ bestimmt** the goods are for the domestic market; **die Reaktionen des In- und Auslandes** the reactions at home and abroad.
**inländisch** *adj* - **1.** [Waren, Produkte] domestic - **2.** [Presse] national.
**Inlandslporto** *das* inland postage rate.
**Inlandsverkehr** *der* [Handel] domestic trade.
**Inlineskates** [ʹınlainskɛits] *pl* roller-blades, inline skates; **auf/mit ~ fahren** to go roller-blading.

**inmitten** *präp:* **~ einer Sache/Gruppe** (G) in the midst of sthg/a group ⬦ *adv:* **~ von jm/etw** amidst sb/sthg.
**Inn** *der:* **der ~** the (River) Inn.
**innelhalten** *vi* (*unreg*): **in der Arbeit ~** to stop working for a moment; **er hat mitten im Singen innegehalten** he stopped ODER paused for a moment in the middle of his song.
**innen** *adv* inside; **die Schale ist ~ versilbert** the bowl is silver-plated on the inside.
➡ **nach innen** *adv* inwards.
➡ **von innen** *adv* from inside; **etw von ~ nach außen kehren** to turn sthg inside out.
**Innenanlsicht** *die* interior view.
**Innenlantenne** *die* indoor aerial Br ODER antenna Am.
**Innenlarchitekt, in** *der, die* interior designer.
**Innenlarchitektur** *die* interior design.
**Innenleinrichtung** *die* furnishings (*pl*).
**Innenlleben** *das* (*ohne pl*) - **1.** [Seele] **sein ~ vor jm ausbreiten** to tell sb one's innermost thoughts - **2.** [von Gerät] insides (*pl*).
**Innenlminister, in** *der, die* Minister of the Interior, ≃ Home Secretary *Br*, ≃ Secretary of the Interior *Am*.
**Innenlministerium** *das* Ministry of the Interior, ≃ Home Office *Br*, ≃ Department of the Interior *Am*.
**Innenlpolitik** *die* (*ohne pl*) - **1.** [Handeln] domestic policy - **2.** [Bereich der Politik] home affairs (*pl*).
**innenpolitisch** *adj* domestic policy (*vor Subst*); **~e Angelegenheiten** matters of domestic policy.
**Innenlraum** *der* interior; [Zimmer] inner room.
**Innenlseite** *die* inside.
**Innenlstadt** *die* town centre; [in Großstadt] city centre.
**innerbetrieblich** *adj* internal (*to a firm*) ⬦ *adv* internally (*to a firm*).
**innerdeutsch** *adj:* **~e Beziehungen** intra-German relations.
**innere, r, s** *adj* - **1.** [innen befindlich, persönlich] inner - **2.** [Struktur, Angelegenheit & MED] internal.
**Innere** *das* (*ohne pl*) - **1.** [Inhalt] inside - **2.** [von Raum] inside, interior; [von Land] interior; **Ministerium des ~n** Ministry of the Interior - **3.** [Geist, Seele, Basis] heart; **im tiefsten ~n** deep down (inside).
**Innereien** *pl* offal (*U*).
**innerhalb** *präp:* **~ einer Sache** (G) within sthg ⬦ *adv:* **~ von** within.
**innerlich** *adj* [Erregung] inner ⬦ *adv* inwardly.

**innerparteilich** adj internal (to the party) <> adv within the party.

**Innerste** das - **1.** [Geist, Seele] innermost being; **jm sein ~s öffnen** to bare one's soul to sb; **im ~n betroffen sein** to be cut to the quick - **2.** [Gebiet]: **bis ins ~** into the heart.

**innig** adj - **1.** [Verehrung, Wunsch, Beileid] heartfelt - **2.** [Dank] sincere - **3.** [Freundschaft] intimate <> adv [verbunden] closely.

**innovativ** [ɪnova'tiːf] adj innovative <> adv innovatively.

**Innsbruck** nt Innsbruck.

**Innung** (pl -en) die guild.

**inoffiziell** adj unofficial <> adv unofficially.

**Input** (pl -s) das ODER der EDV & WIRTSCH input.

**Inquisition** die Inquisition.

**ins** präp (in + das) [räumlich]: **~ Wohnzimmer gehen** to go into the living room; **~ Kino gehen** to go to the cinema; siehe auch **in**.

**Insasse** (pl -n) der - **1.** [im Fahrzeug] passenger - **2.** [von Gefängnis, psychiatrischer Anstalt] inmate.

**Insassin** (pl -nen) die - **1.** [im Fahrzeug] passenger - **2.** [von Gefängnis, psychiatrischer Anstalt] inmate.

**insbes.** (abk für insbesondere) esp.

**insbesondere, insbesondre** adv especially, particularly.

**Inlschrift** die inscription.

**Insekt** (pl -en) das insect.

**Insektenschutzlmittel** das insect repellent.

**Insektenlstich** der [von Wespe] insect sting; [von Mücke] insect bite.

**Insektizid** (pl -e) das insecticide.

**Insel** (pl -n) die island; **die ~ Sylt** the island of Sylt.

**Insellage** die: **die ~ Japans** Japan's island status.

**Inserat** (pl -e) das advertisement; **ein ~ aufgeben** to put an advertisement in the paper.

**Inserent, in** (mpl -en; fpl -nen) der, die advertiser.

**inserieren** vi to advertise (in a newspaper).

**insgeheim** adv secretly.

**insgesamt** adv - **1.** [in der Summe] in total - **2.** [im Großen und Ganzen] overall; **sie hat ~ einen guten Eindruck hinterlassen** she made a good overall impression.

**Insider** ['ɪnsaɪdɐ] (pl -) der insider.

**insofern**[1] adv in this respect.

**insofern**[2] konj provided that, so long as. ⟶ **insofern als** konj insofar as.

**insoweit**[1] adv in this respect.

**insoweit**[2] konj provided that, so long as. ⟶ **insoweit als** konj insofar as.

**in spe** [ɪn'speː] adj to be; **der Bürgermeister ~** the mayor-elect.

**Inspektion** (pl -en) die - **1.** [von Anlage, Schule] inspection - **2.** [von Auto] service.

**Inspektor** (pl -toren) der inspector.

**Inspektorin** (pl -nen) die inspector.

**inspirieren** vt geh to inspire; **die Gespräche haben mich zu einem Aufsatz inspiriert** the conversations have inspired me to write an essay. ⟶ **sich inspirieren** ref geh: **sich von etw ~ lassen** to get one's inspiration from sthg.

**inspizieren** vt to inspect.

**instabil** adj unstable.

**Installateur, in** [ɪnstala'tøːɐ̯, rɪn] (mpl -e; fpl -nen) der, die [Klempner] plumber; [für Strom] electrician; [für Heizung] heating engineer; [für Gas] gas-fitter.

**installieren** vt [gen & EDV] to install. ⟶ **sich installieren** ref to settle in.

**instand, in Stand** adv: **~ sein** [Maschine] to be in working order; **der Wagen ist gut ~** the car is in good repair; **etw ~ halten** [Maschine] to keep sthg in working order; [Garten] to maintain sthg; **er hält seinen Wagen schlecht ~** he doesn't look after his car very well; **etw ~ setzen** [Maschine] to overhaul sthg; [Haus] to renovate sthg.

**instandlbesetzen** vt to occupy a property illegally, especially one condemned to be demolished, in order to restore it and make it habitable.

**inständig** adv urgently <> adj urgent.

**Instantlkaffee** ['ɪnstəntkafeː] der instant coffee.

**Instantlnahrung** die instant food.

**Instantlsuppe** die instant soup.

**Instanz** (pl -en) die - **1.** [im Gerichtsverfahren] court; **in erster/zweiter ~** in the court of first instance/the appeal court - **2.** [Dienststelle] authority; **sein Antrag geht durch alle behördlichen ~en** his application is going through all the official channels.

**Instinkt** (pl -e) der instinct.

**Instinktlhandlung** die instinctive action.

**instinktiv** adj instinctive <> adv instinctively.

**Institut** (pl -e) das institute.

**Institution** (pl -en) die institution.

**Instruktion** (pl -en) die instruction.

**instruktiv** adj instructive.

**Instrument** (pl -e) das instrument.

**instrumental** MUS adj instrumental <> adv instrumentally.

**Insulaner, in** (mpl -; fpl -nen) der, die islander.

**Insulin** *das* insulin.

**inszenieren** *vt* - **1.** [Theaterstück] to direct; TV & RADIO to produce - **2.** [Skandal] to engineer; [Kampagne] to stage - **3.** *abw* [vortäuschen - Protest] to stage-manage.

**Inszenierung** (*pl* -en) *die* - **1.** [Aufführung] production - **2.** [Aufführen - von Theaterstück] direction; TV & RADIO production - **3.** [von Skandal] engineering; [von Kampagne] staging - **4.** [Vortäuschung - von Protest] *abw* stage-managing.

**intakt** *adj* [Gerät, Organ] intact; [Beziehung] healthy.

**integer** *adj:* **eine integre Person** a person of integrity ⟷ *adv* with integrity.

**Integral|helm** *der* (integral) helmet *(protecting chin as well as head).*

**Integral|rechnung** *die* integral calculus.

**Integration** (*pl* -en) *die* integration.

**integrieren** *vt* to integrate.

**Integrität** *die* integrity.

**intellektuell** [ɪntɛlɛk'tʊɛl] *adj* intellectual ⟷ *adv* intellectually.

**Intellektuelle** [ɪntɛlɛk'tʊɛlə] (*pl* -n) *der, die* intellectual.

**intelligent** *adj* intelligent ⟷ *adv* intelligently.

**Intelligenz** *die* - **1.** [Verstand, Klugheit] intelligence - **2.** [Intellektuelle] intelligentsia.

**Intelligenz|quotient** *der* IQ, intelligence quotient.

**Intendant, in** (*mpl* -en; *fpl* -nen) *der, die* - **1.** [von Theater] artistic director and theatre manager - **2.** [von Fernsehanstalt] director general.

**Intensität** (*pl* -en) *die* intensity.

**intensiv** *adj* - **1.** [Gefühl, Farbe] strong - **2.** [Licht] intense - **3.** [Arbeit] intensive ⟷ *adv* - **1.** [fühlen] strongly - **2.** [leuchten] intensely - **3.** [arbeiten] intensively.

**Intensiv|kurs** *der* crash course.

**Intensiv|station** *die* intensive care unit.

**interaktiv** *adj* EDV interactive.

**Inter|City** *der* intercity train.

**interdisziplinär** *adj* interdisciplinary.

**interessant** *adj* interesting ⟷ *adv* interestingly; **sich ~ machen** *abw* to attract attention (to o.s.).

**Interesse** (*pl* -n) *das* interest; **an jm/etw ~ haben** to be interested in sb/sthg; **~ für jn/etw zeigen** to show an interest in sb/sthg; **in js eigenem ~** in sb's own interest.
➤ **Interessen** *pl* [Neigung] interests.

**interessehalber** *adv* out of interest.

**Interessen|gemeinschaft** *die* - **1.** [von Personen] group of people with common interests - **2.** [von Firmen] syndicate.

**Interessent, in** (*mpl* -en; *fpl* -nen) *der, die* - **1.** [Interessierte] interested person - **2.** [Kunde] prospective customer.

**interessieren** *vt* to interest.
➤ **sich interessieren** *ref:* **sich für jn/etw ~** to be interested in sb/sthg.

**interessiert** *adj* interested; **an jm/etw ~ sein** to be interested in sb/sthg ⟷ *adv* with interest.

**interkulturell** *adj* cross-cultural ⟷ *adv* cross-culturally.

**Intermezzo** (*pl* -s ODER -mezzi) *das* - **1.** MUS intermezzo - **2.** [Ereignis] interlude.

**intern** *adj* internal ⟷ *adv* internally.

**Internat** (*pl* -e) *das* boarding school.

**international** *adj* international ⟷ *adv* internationally.

**Internet** ['ɪntɐ(r)nɛt] *das* Internet; **im ~** on the Internet; **im ~ surfen** to surf the Net; **etw per ~ verkaufen** to sell sthg on ODER over the Internet.

**Internet|anschluss** *der* EDV Internet connection.

**Internetbenutzer, in** (*mpl* -, *fpl* -nen) *der, die* Internet user.

**Internet|café** *das* Internet cafe, cybercafe.

**internieren** *vt* to intern.

**Interpol** *die* Interpol.

**Interpret** (*pl* -en) *der* MUS performer.

**Interpretation** (*pl* -en) *die* - **1.** [Deutung] interpretation - **2.** MUS performance.

**interpretieren** *vt* - **1.** [deuten] to interpret - **2.** MUS to perform.

**Interpretin** (*pl* -nen) *die* MUS performer.

**Interpunktion** *die* punctuation.

**InterRegio** (*pl* -s) *der* train which covers medium distances and makes frequent stops.

**Interrogativ|pronomen** *das* GRAM interrogative pronoun.

**Intervall** [ɪntɐ'val] (*pl* -e) *das* [gen & MUS] interval.

**intervenieren** [ɪntɐve'niːrən] *vi* to intervene.

**Intervention** [ɪntɐvɛn'tsi̯oːn] (*pl* -en) *die* intervention.

**Interview** [ɪntɐ'vjuː] (*pl* -s) *das* interview.

**interviewen** [ɪntɐ'vjuːən] *vt* to interview.

**intim** *adj* intimate; **mit jm ~ werden** *amt* to become intimate with sb ⟷ *adv* - **1.** [sexuell]: **mit jm ~ verkehren** to have intimate relations with sb - **2.** [nah]: **mit jm ~ befreundet sein** to be intimate friends with sb - **3.** [beleuchtet] intimately.

**Intimität** (*pl* -en) *die* intimacy.

➡ **Intimitäten** *pl* [sexuelle Handlungen] intimacy *(U)*.

**Intim|sphäre** *die* private life; **die ~ schützen** to protect one's privacy.

**intolerant** *adj* intolerant; **jm/etw gegenüber ~ sein** to be intolerant of sb/sthg.

**Intoleranz** *die* intolerance.

**intransitiv** *adj* GRAM intransitive.

**Intrige** *(pl -n) die* intrigue, plot.

**intrigieren** *vi:* **gegen jn ~** to plot against sb.

**introvertiert** [ɪntrovɛrˈtiːɐt] *adj* introverted.

**Intuition** *(pl -en) die* intuition.

**intuitiv** *adj* intuitive ⬦ *adv* intuitively.

**intus** *adj:* **einen ~ haben** *fam* to have had a few.

**Invalide** [ɪnvaˈliːdə] *(pl -n) der, die* invalid.

**Invaliden|rente** *die* disability pension.

**Invalidität** [ɪnvalidiˈtɛːt] *die* disability.

**Invasion** [ɪnvaˈzjoːn] *(pl -en) die eigtl & fig* invasion.

**Inventar** [ɪnvɛnˈtaːɐ] *(pl -e) das* - **1.** [von Geschäft] fittings *(pl)* and equipment; [von Haus] fixtures and fittings *(pl)* - **2.** [von Betrieb] machinery and equipment - **3.** [Verzeichnis] inventory.

**Inventur** [ɪnvɛnˈtuːɐ] *(pl -en) die* stocktaking; **~ machen** to stocktake.

**investieren** [ɪnvɛsˈtiːrən] *vt:* **(in etw (A)) ~** to invest (in sthg).

**Investition** [ɪnvɛstiˈtsjoːn] *(pl -en) die* investment.

**inwendig** *adj* inner; **jn/etw in- und auswendig kennen** to know sb/sthg inside out.

**inwiefern** *adv & konj* [in welcher Hinsicht] in what way; [bis zu welchem Grad] to what extent.

**inwieweit** *adv & konj* to what extent.

**Inzest** *(pl -e) der* incest.

**Inzucht** *(pl -en) die* inbreeding.

**inzwischen** *adv* - **1.** [gleichzeitig] in the meantime - **2.** [mittlerweile, jetzt] now; **~ war es Winter geworden** by now winter had arrived.

**IOK** [iːoːˈkaː] *(abk für* **Internationales Olympisches Komitee)** *das* IOC.

**Ion** [joːn] *(pl -en) das* ion.

**ionisch** [jˈoːnɪʃ] *adj* Ionic.

**IQ** [iːˈkuː, aiˈkjuː] *(pl -s) (abk für* **Intelligenzquotient)** *der* IQ.

**i.R.** *(abk für* **im Ruhestand)** retd.

**IR** *abk für* **InterRegio.**

**Irak** *der* Iraq.

**Iraker, in** *(mpl -; fpl -nen) der, die* Iraqi.

**irakisch** *adj* Iraqi.

**Iran** *der* Iran.

**Iraner, in** *(mpl -; fpl -nen) der, die* Iranian.

**iranisch** *adj* Iranian.

**irdisch** *adj* earthly, worldly.

**Ire** *(pl -n) der* Irishman.

**irgend** *adv* [irgendwie]: **wenn es ~ möglich ist** if (it's) at all possible; **wenn ich es ~ schaffe, komme ich** I'll come if I possibly can.
➡ **irgend so ein** *det fam* some.

**irgendein, e** *det* - **1.** [unbekannt] some; **das hat ~ Philosoph gesagt** some philosopher (or other) said that - **2.** [beliebig] any.

**irgendeine, -r, -s** *pron* - **1.** [Person] someone, somebody; [in Fragen] anyone; **~r von uns muss es tun** one of us has to do it - **2.** [Sache] any (one); **irgendeins von den Büchern** one or other of the books.

**irgendetwas** *pron* [unbekannte Sache] something; [beliebige Sache, in Fragen] anything.

**irgendjemand** *pron* [unbekannte Person] someone; [beliebige Person, in Fragen] anyone.

**irgendwann** *adv* [zu unbekannter Zeit] sometime; [zu beliebiger Zeit] any time.

**irgendwas** *adv* [unbekannte Sache] something; [beliebige Sache, in Fragen] anything.

**irgendwer** *pron fam* - **1.** [unbekannte Person] someone, somebody - **2.** [beliebige Person, in Fragen] anyone.

**irgendwie** *adv* [auf unbekannte Weise] somehow; [auf beliebige Weise] anyhow.

**irgendwo** *adv* [an unbekanntem Ort] somewhere; [an beliebigem Ort] anywhere.

**irgendwoher** *adv* [von unbekanntem Ort] from somewhere; [von beliebigem Ort] from anywhere.

**irgendwohin** *adv* [zu unbekanntem Ort] somewhere; [zu beliebigem Ort] anywhere.

**Irin** *(pl -nen) die* Irishwoman.

**Iris** *(pl -) die* iris.

**irisch** *adj* Irish.

**IRK** [iːɐ̯ˈkaː] *(abk für* **Internationales Rotes Kreuz)** *das* International Red Cross.

**Irland** *nt* Ireland.

**Ironie** *die* irony.

**ironisch** *adj* ironic ⬦ *adv* ironically.

**irr** = **irre.**

**irrational** *adj* irrational ⬦ *adv* irrationally.

**irre, irr** *adj* - **1.** [verrückt] crazy; **ein ~r Blick** a wild expression - **2.** *fam* [riesig] terrible - **3.** *fam* [außergewöhnlich, schön] wild ⬦ *adv* - **1.** [reden] crazily - **2.** *fam* [sehr] terribly.

**Irre** *(pl -n) der, die (pl Irren)* [Person] lunatic; **wie ein ~r** like mad ⬦ *die (ohne pl)* [Ungewissheit]: **in die ~ führen** to be misleading.

**irreal** *adj* [unwirklich] unreal.

**irre|führen** *vt* - **1.** [belügen] to mislead - **2.** [auf einem Weg] to cause to get lost.

**Irre|führung** *die* [von Meinung] deception, misleading.

**irrelevant** ['ɪrelevant] *adj* irrelevant.

**irre|machen** *vt* to disconcert, to confuse.

**irren** (*perf* hat/ist geirrt) *vi* (*ist*) to wander.
➡ **sich irren** *ref (hat)*: **sich (in jm/etw** (D)) ~ to be wrong (about sb/sthg); **wenn ich mich nicht irre** if I am not mistaken.

**Irren|anstalt** *die fam* madhouse.

**Irren|haus** *das fam abw* loony bin.

**Irr|fahrt** *die*: **eine ~ durch eine Gegend** a journey through an area where I/we/*etc* got lost.

**irrig** *adj* incorrect.

**irritieren** *vt* [stören] to annoy; **ihr Verhalten irritiert mich** I find her behaviour disconcerting *ODER* confusing.

**Irrlicht** (*pl* **-er**) *das* will-o'-the-wisp.

**Irrsinn** *der* madness.

**irrsinnig** *adj* - **1.** [verrückt] mad - **2.** *fam* [riesig] terrible <> *adv* - **1.** [verrückt] crazily - **2.** *fam* [sehr] terribly.

**Irrtum** (*pl* **-tümer**) *der* mistake; **sich im ~ befinden, im ~ sein** to be mistaken *ODER* wrong; **uns ist ein ~ unterlaufen** we have made a mistake.

**irrtümlich** *adj* mistaken <> *adv* [verwechseln, mitnehmen] by mistake.

**Irr|weg** *der*: **auf dem ~ sein** to be on the wrong track.

**Isar** *die*: **die ~** the (River) Isar.

**Ischias** *der* sciatica.

**ISDN** (*abk für* **Integrated Services Digital Network**) *das* ISDN.

**ISDN-|Anschluss** *der* TELEKOM ISDN link.

**Islam** *der* Islam.

**islamisch** *adj* Islamic.

**Island** *nt* Iceland.

**Isländer, in** (*mpl* **-**; *fpl* **-nen**) *der, die* Icelander.

**isländisch** *adj* Icelandic.

**Isländisch(e)** *das* Icelandic; *siehe auch* **Englisch(e)**.

**Isolation** (*pl* **-en**) *die* - **1.** [von Person] isolation - **2.** [Material, Abdichtung] insulation; [von Rohr, Boiler] lagging.

**Isolierband** (*pl* **-bänder**) *das* insulating tape.

**isolieren** *vt* - **1.** [Person & CHEM] to isolate - **2.** [Leitung, Wand] to insulate.

**Isolier|kanne** *die* Thermos® jug.

**Israel** *nt* Israel.

**Israeli** (*pl* **-** *ODER* **-s**) *der, die* Israeli.

**israelisch** *adj* Israeli.

**isst** *präs* ⊳ **essen**.

**ist** *präs* ⊳ **sein**.

**Istanbul** *nt* Istanbul.

**Italien** *nt* Italy.

**Italiener, in** [ita'ljeːnɐ, rɪn] (*mpl* **-**; *fpl* **-nen**) *der, die* Italian.

**italienisch** [ita'ljeːnɪʃ] *adj* Italian.

**Italienisch(e)** *das* Italian; *siehe auch* **Englisch(e)**.

**i. V.** (*abk für* **in Vertretung**) p.p.

**IWF** [iːveː'ɛf] (*abk für* **Internationaler Währungsfonds**) *der* IMF.

# J

**j, J** [jɔt] (*pl* **-** *ODER* **-s**) *das* j, J.

**ja** *interj* - **1.** [zum Ausdruck der Zustimmung] yes - **2.** [als rhetorisches Element] well; **~, wenn das so ist ...** well, if that's the case ...; **~, ich verstehe** yes, I understand - **3.** [einschränkend]: **ich würde ~ gerne, aber ...** I'd love to, but ...; **ich kann es ~ versuchen, aber ...** I can always try, but ...; **er ist ~ mein Freund** he is my friend after all - **4.** [emphatisierend]: **da bist du ~!** there you are!; **das ist ~ großartig!** that's really great!; **ich komme ~ schon!** all right, I'm coming!; **ich habe es dir ~ gesagt!** I TOLD you so!; **das ist es ~ (eben)!** that's just it!; **du kennst ihn ~!** you know what he's like - **5.** [zum Ausdruck einer Drohung]: **sag ~ nichts!** don't you dare say anything!; **dass du mir ~ pünktlich kommst!** you'd better be on time! - **6.** [zum Ausdruck einer Bitte]: **du bleibst doch, ~?** you will stay, won't you? - **7.** [drückt Überraschung aus]: **(ach) ~?** really?

**Ja** (*pl* **-s**) *das* yes.

**Jacht, Yacht** [jaxt] (*pl* **-en**) *die* yacht.

**Jacke** (*pl* **-n**) *die* - **1.** [Mantel, Jackett] jacket - **2.** [Strickjacke] cardigan.

**Jackett** [ʒa'kɛt] (*pl* **-s**) *das* jacket.

**Jade** *die* jade.

**Jagd** (*pl* **-en**) *die* - **1.** [auf Tiere] hunting; **auf die ~ gehen** to go hunting - **2.** [auf Personen, Dinge]: **~ nach jm/etw** hunt for sb/sthg; **auf jn/etw ~ machen** to hunt for sb/sthg.

**Jagd|hund** *der* hunting dog.

**Jagd|schein** *der* hunting licence.

**jagen** (*perf* hat/ist gejagt) *vt* (*hat*) to hunt; **ein Ereignis jagt das andere** one thing follows another; **der Dieb wurde aus der Stadt gejagt** the thief was driven out of town; **sich** (*D*) **eine Kugel in den Kopf ~** to shoot o.s. in the head ◇ *vi* - **1.** (*hat*) [als Sport] to hunt - **2.** (*ist*) [hetzen] to race.

**Jäger** (*pl* -) *der* - **1.** [von Tieren] hunter - **2.** [Flugzeug] fighter (plane).

**Jägerin** (*pl* -nen) *die* hunter.

**Jägerschnitzel** (*pl* -) *das escalope of pork or beef with mushroom sauce.*

**Jaguar** (*pl* -e) *der* [Tier] jaguar.

**jäh** *adj* sudden ◇ *adv* suddenly.

**Jahr** (*pl* -e) *das* year; **im ~(e)** 1992 in 1992; **die 90er ~e** the nineties; **seit ~en** for years; **(ein) gutes neues ~!** Happy New Year!; **von ~ zu ~** from year to year; **~ für ~** year after year; **in jungen ~en** at an early age.

**jahraus** *adv:* **~, jahrein** year in, year out.

**Jahr|buch** *das* yearbook.

**jahrelang** *adj:* **~e Arbeit** years of work ◇ *adv* for years.

**Jahres|abschluss** *der* end-of-year accounts (*pl*).

**Jahres|anfang** *der* beginning of the year.

**Jahres|bericht** *der* annual report.

**Jahres|einkommen** *das* annual income.

**Jahres|ende** *das* end of the year.

**Jahres|tag** *der* anniversary.

**Jahres|wagen** *der car sold at a discount to a car-factory employee which can only be resold after one year.*

**Jahres|wechsel** *der* New Year.

**Jahres|zeit** *die* season.

**Jahr|gang** *der* - **1.** [Geburtsjahr]: **der ~ 1967** the people who were born in 1967; **er ist mein ~** he was born in the same year as me - **2.** [an der Schule] year - **3.** [von Wein] vintage, year - **4.** [von Zeitschrift] year's issues (*pl*).

**Jahrgangs|stufe** *die* year (*at school*).

**Jahr|hundert** (*pl* -e) *das* century; **im 19. ~** in the 19th century.

**Jahrhundert|wende** *die* turn of the century; **um die ~** at the turn of the century.

**jährlich** *adj* annual ◇ *adv* annually; **dreimal ~** three times a year.

**Jahr|markt** *der* fair.

**Jahr|tausend** (*pl* -e) *das* millennium.

**Jahr|zehnt** (*pl* -e) *das* decade.

**Jähzorn** *der* violent temper.

**jähzornig** *adj* irascible ◇ *adv* in a violent temper.

**Jalousie** [ʒalu'ziː] (*pl* -n) *die* Venetian blind.

**Jamaika** *nt* Jamaica.

**Jammer** *der* misery; **es ist ein ~** it's a crying shame.

**jämmerlich** *adj* - **1.** [traurig] miserable - **2.** *abw* [würdelos, schlecht] pathetic ◇ *adv* - **1.** [traurig] miserably - **2.** *abw* [würdelos, schlecht] pathetically - **3.** [sehr]: **~ frieren** to be frozen stiff.

**jammern** *vi* to moan.

**jammerschade** *adj:* **~ sein** to be a crying shame.

**Januar** *der* January; *siehe auch* **September.**

**Japan** *nt* Japan.

**Japaner, in** (*mpl* -; *fpl* -nen) *der, die* Japanese.

**japanisch** *adj* Japanese.

**Japanisch(e)** *das* Japanese; *siehe auch* **Englisch(e).**

**japsen** *vi* to gasp.

**Jargon** [ʒar'gõ] (*pl* -s) *der* jargon.

**Jasmin** (*pl* -e) *der* jasmine.

**Ja|stimme** *die* vote in favour.

**jäten** *vt* [Garten] to weed; [Unkraut] to pull up.

**Jauche** (*pl* -n) *die* liquid manure.

**jauchzen** *vi* to cheer; **vor Freude ~** to shout for joy.

**jaulen** *vi* to howl.

**Java** *nt* Java.

**jawohl** *interj* certainly!

**Ja|wort** *das:* **jm sein ~ geben** to tie the knot with sb.

**Jazz** [dʒɛs] *der* jazz.

**Jazzband** ['dʒɛsbɛnt] (*pl* -s) *die* jazz band.

**je** *adv* - **1.** [jeweils] each; **drei Gruppen mit ~ fünf Personen** three groups, each of five people; **die drei Tore sind mit ~ zwei Schlössern gesichert** the three gates each have two locks - **2.** [jemals] ever; **bist du ~ mit ihm zusammengetroffen?** have you (ever) met him?; **seit eh und ~** since time immemorial; **sie ist schöner denn ~** she is more beautiful than ever ◇ *präp* [pro] per; **15 Euro ~ Stunde** 15 euros per hour; **~ nach** depending on ◇ *konj:* **~ schneller, desto besser** the quicker the better; **~ nachdem** it depends; **~ nachdem, ob ...** depending on whether ... ◇ *interj:* **oh ~!** oh no!, oh dear!

**Jeans** [dʒiːnz] (*pl* -) *die* jeans (*pl*); **eine ~** a pair of jeans.

**jede, r, s** *det* every, each; [in negativen Konstruktionen] any; **ohne ~n Zweifel** without any doubt; **~n zweiten Tag** every second day ◇ *pron* - **1.** [Person] everyone, everybody; **~ von ihnen** each of them; **da kennt ~r ~n** everybody knows everybody there; **~r Zweite** every second ODER other one; **~r kann**

**teilnehmen** anyone can take part - **2.** [Sache] each (one).

**jedenfalls** *adv* - **1.** [wenigstens] at least; **ich ~ habe keine Lust** I at any rate don't want to - **2.** [auf jeden Fall] in any case.

**jedermann** *pron* everybody, everyone.

**jederzeit** *adv* at any time.

**jedesmal** *adv* ⊳ **Mal.**

**jedoch** *adv* & *konj* however.

**Jeep**® [dʒiːp] (*pl* -**s**) *der* Jeep®.

**jegliche, r, s** *pron:* **hier kommt ~ Hilfe zu spät** all help will come too late here; **ohne ~n Sinn** without any sense; **ohne ~ s Risiko** with no risk.

**jeher** *adv:* **von ~** always.

**jemals** *adv* ever.

**jemand** *pron* someone, somebody; [in Fragen] anyone, anybody.

**Jemen** *nt* Yemen.

**jene, r, s** *geh det* that ⟷ *pron* that one.

**jenseits** *präp:* **~ einer Sache** (*G*) ODER **von etw** [räumlich] on the other side of sthg; [ideell] beyond sthg.

**Jenseits** *das:* **jn ins ~ befördern** *fam* to bump sb off.

**Jerusalem** *nt* Jerusalem.

**Jesuit** (*pl* -**en**) *der* Jesuit.

**Jet** [dʒɛt] (*pl* -**s**) *der* jet.

**Jetlag** ['dʒɛtlɛg] (*pl* -**s**) *der* jet lag.

**Jeton** [ʒa'tõ] (*pl* -**s**) *der* - **1.** [Spielmünze] chip - **2.** [Automatenmünze] token.

**jetzig** *adj* current.

**jetzt** *adv* - **1.** [momentan, mittlerweile] now; **bis ~** so far; **von ~ an** from now on; **erst ~** only just; **schon ~** already - **2.** [gegenwärtig, heute] nowadays; **das gibt es ~ nicht mehr** you don't get that any more (nowadays) - **3.** [gleich, sofort] in a moment; **~ gleich** right away; **von ~ auf gleich** on the spur of the moment - **4.** [damals] then - **5.** [zum Ausdruck des Ärgers] **das ist doch ~ kein Argument!** that's no argument!; **~ mach endlich voran!** get a move on, will you!

**jeweilig** *adj* - **1.** [zeitlich]: **nach der ~en Mode angezogen sein** to be dressed in the fashion of the day; **die Stimmung ändert sich mit der ~en Laune des Chefs** the atmosphere changes depending on what mood the boss happens to be in; **die ~e Nummer eins** the current number one - **2.** [zugehörig] respective.

**jeweils** *adv* - **1.** [jedes Mal] each time - **2.** [jeder] each; **~ drei Karten** three cards each - **3.** [momentan] at the time.

**Jg.** *abk für* **Jahrgang.**

**Jh.** (*abk für* **Jahrhundert**) C.

**JH** *abk für* **Jugendherberge.**

**Jiddisch(e)** *das* Yiddish; *siehe auch* **Englisch(e).**

**Job** [dʒɔp] (*pl* -**s**) *der* - **1.** [als Aushilfe] (temporary) job - **2.** [Arbeit] job.

**jobben** [dʒɔbn̩] *vi* to work.

**Jobsharing** ['dʒɔbˌʃɛːrɪŋ] *das* job-sharing.

**Jockey** ['dʒɔke, 'dʒɔkil] (*pl* -**s**) *der* jockey.

**Jod** *das* iodine.

**jodeln** *vi* to yodel.

**Joga, Yoga** ['joːga] = **Yoga.**

**joggen** ['dʒɔgn̩] (*perf* **hat/ist gejoggt**) *vi* to jog.

**Jogger, in** ['dʒɔgɐ, rɪn] (*mpl* -; *fpl* -**nen**) *der, die* jogger.

**Jogging** ['dʒɔgɪŋ] *das* jogging.

**Joghurt, Yoghurt, Jogurt** (*pl* - ODER -**s**) *das* ODER *der* yoghurt.

**Johannis**l**beere** *die:* **Rote ~** redcurrant; **Schwarze ~** blackcurrant.

**Johanniterunfallhilfe** *die* ≃ St John's Ambulance *Br, medical emergency service run by volunteers.*

**johlen** *vi* to howl.

**Joint** [dʒɔynt] (*pl* -**s**) *der* joint.

**Joker** ['dʒoːkɐ] (*pl* -) *der* joker.

**Jongleur, in** [ʒɔŋ'løːɐ, rɪn] (*mpl* -**e**; *fpl* -**nen**) *der, die* juggler.

**jonglieren** [ʒɔŋ'liːrən] *vi* to juggle; **mit etw ~ eigtl** & *fig* to juggle sthg ⟷ *vt* [balancieren] to juggle.

**Jordan** *der:* **der ~** the (River) Jordan; **über den ~ gehen** *fam* to kick the bucket.

**Jordanien** *nt* Jordan.

**Jordanier, in** [jɔr'daːnjɐ, rɪn] (*mpl* -; *fpl* -**nen**) *der, die* Jordanian.

**jordanisch** *adj* Jordanian.

**Joule** [dʒuːl, dʒaul] (*pl* -) *das* joule.

**Journalismus** [ʒʊrna'lɪsmʊs] *der* journalism.

**Journalist, in** [ʒʊrna'lɪst, ɪn] (*mpl* -**en**; *fpl* -**nen**) *der, die* journalist.

**journalistisch** [ʒʊrna'lɪstɪʃ] *adj* journalistic.

**jovial** [jo'vjaːl] *adj* jovial ⟷ *adv* jovially.

**Joystick** ['dʒɔystɪk] (*pl* -**s**) *der* joystick.

**jr.** (*abk für* **junior**) Jr.

**Jubel** *der* - **1.** [Freude] jubilation - **2.** [Rufen] cheering.

**jubeln** *vi* - **1.** [sich freuen] to rejoice - **2.** [rufen] to cheer.

**Jubilar, in** (*mpl* -**e**; *fpl* -**nen**) *der, die person celebrating an anniversary.*

**Jubiläum** [jubi'lɛːʊm] (*pl* **Jubiläen**) *das* anniversary; **ein ~ feiern** to celebrate an anniversary.

**juchzen** *vi* to whoop.

**jucken** *vi* - **1.** [Haut] to itch - **2.** [Material] to be itchy ⬦ *vt* - **1.** [kratzen]: **die Narbe juckt ihn** his scar is itchy - **2.** *fam* [beeinflussen]: **es juckt mich, es zu versuchen** I'm itching to try; **das juckt mich nicht** I don't care.

➤ **sich jucken** *ref* [sich kratzen] to scratch o.s.

**Juck|reiz** *der* itching; **~ verspüren** to have an itch.

**Jude** (*pl* **-n**) *der* Jew.

**Judentum** *das* Judaism.

**Jüdin** (*pl* **-nen**) *die* Jew.

**jüdisch** *adj* Jewish.

**Judo** *das* judo.

**Jugend** *die* (*ohne pl*) - **1.** [junges Alter] youth - **2.** [junge Personen] young people (*pl*); **die ~ von heute** today's youth, young people today.

**Jugend|amt** *das local authority service responsible for the welfare of young people.*

**Jugendarbeit** *die* youth work.

**jugendfrei** *adj*: 'nicht ~' 'not suitable for persons under 18'.

**Jugend|freund, in** *der, die* friend from one's youth.

**Jugend|gruppe** *die* youth group.

**Jugend|herberge** *die* youth hostel.

**jugendlich** *adj* - **1.** [jung] young - **2.** [jung wirkend] youthful ⬦ *adv*: **sich ~ geben/kleiden** to act/dress young.

**Jugendliche** (*pl* **-n**) *der, die* young person.

**Jugendschutzgesetz** *das law designed to protect young people.*

**Jugendstil** *der* art nouveau.

**Jugoslawien** *nt* Yugoslavia.

**Jukebox** ['dʒuːkbɔks] (*pl* **-es**) *die* jukebox.

**Juli** *der* July; **der 20. ~** *anniversary of failed assassination attempt on Hitler on 20 July 1944; siehe auch* **September.**

---
**20. JULI 1944**

Faced with the inevitable defeat of Germany, opponents of Hitler's regime organized a plot to assassinate Hitler before Germany was completely destroyed. One of the authors of this plot was Colonel von Stauffenberg. It was he who placed a bomb in Hitler's headquarters on the 20 July 1944. However, Hitler survived the attack with only minor injuries. The failure of this assassination attempt resulted in a large part of the German resistance movement being wiped out.

---

**Jumbojet** ['jʊmbodʒɛt], **Jumbo-Jet** (*pl* **-s**) *der* jumbo jet.

**jung** (*kompar* **jünger**; *superl* **jüngste**) *adj*

- **1.** [gen] young; [Aussehen, Stil] young, youthful; **meine jüngere Schwester** my younger sister - **2.** [nicht lange zurückliegend]: **die jüngsten Ereignisse** recent events ⬦ *adv (kompar jünger; superl am jüngsten)*: **~ sterben** to die young.

**Junge** (*pl* **-n** ODER **Jungs**) *der* (*pl* **Jungen, Jungs**) [Knabe, Mann] boy; **hallo, alter ~** hello, my old pal; **ein schwerer ~** *fam fig* a thug ⬦ *das* (*pl Jungen*) [Tier] young animal; **die ~n** the young; **~ kriegen** ODER **werfen** to give birth to young.

**Jünger, in** (*mpl* **-;** *fpl* **-nen**) *der, die* disciple.

**Jungfer** (*pl* **-n**) *die*: **alte ~** *abw* old maid.

**Jungfern|fahrt** *die* maiden voyage.

**Jung|frau** *die* - **1.** [Frau] virgin - **2.** ASTROL Virgo; **~ sein** to be a Virgo.

**jungfräulich** *adj* virginal.

**Jung|geselle** *der* bachelor; **ein eingefleischter ~** a confirmed bachelor.

**Jüngling** (*pl* **-e**) *der* - **1.** *geh* [junger Mann] youth - **2.** *abw* [unreif] spotty teenager.

**jüngst** *adv geh* recently.

**jüngste** *adj* ▷ **jung.**

**Jüngste** (*pl* **-n**) *der, die, das* youngest; **er ist nicht mehr der ~** he's not as young as he used to be.

**Jüngste Tag** *der* REL Day of Judgement.

**Jung|unternehmer, in** *der, die* young entrepreneur.

**Jungverheiratete** *der, die* newlywed man (*f* newlywed woman); **die ~n** the newlyweds.

**Juni** *der* June; **der 17. ~** *former West German holiday celebrating German unity and commemorating the uprising in the GDR on 17 June 1953; siehe auch* **September.**

**Junior** (*pl* **Junioren**) *der* - **1.** [gen] junior - **2.** [im Geschäft] junior partner.

**Juniorin** (*pl* **-nen**) *die* - **1.** [Tochter] daughter - **2.** [im Geschäft] junior partner - **3.** SPORT junior.

**Junkie** ['dʒaŋkil] (*pl* **-s**) *der fam* junkie.

**Jupiter** *der* Jupiter.

**jur.** *abk für* juristisch.

**Jura** *der* - **1.** (*ohne Artikel*) [Studienfach] law - **2.** [Gebirge]: **der ~** the Jura - **3.** [Erdzeitalter] Jurassic period.

**Jurist, in** (*mpl* **-en;** *fpl* **-nen**) *der, die* lawyer.

**juristisch** *adj* legal ⬦ *adv* legally.

**Jury** [ʒy'riː] (*pl* **-s**) *die* jury.

**Justiz** *die* - **1.** [Behörde]: **jn der deutschen ~ ausliefern** to hand sb over to the German courts; **unabhängige ~** independent judiciary - **2.** [Rechtsprechung]: **nach irischer ~** under Irish law.

**Justizlbeamte** *der* member of the judiciary.

**Justizlbeamtin** *die* member of the judiciary.

**Justizlirrtum** *der* miscarriage of justice.

**Justizlminister, in** *der, die* Minister of Justice.

**Justizlministerium** *das* Ministry of Justice.

**Justizlmord** *der* judicial murder.

**Justizvollzugslanstalt** *die amt* penal institution, penitentiary *Am*.

**Jute** *die* jute.

**Juwel** (*pl* **-en**) *das ODER der* **- 1.** (*der*) [Schmuck] piece of jewellery **- 2.** [Edelstein, Prachtstück] jewel; **sie ist ein ~** she is a gem.

**Juwelier** (*pl* **-e**) *der* jeweller.

**Juwelierlgeschäft** *das* jeweller's (shop).

**Juwelierin** (*pl* **-nen**) *die* jeweller.

**Jux** *der fam* joke; **etw aus ~ und Tollerei tun** *fam* to do sthg as a joke.

**JVA** [jɔtfau'aː] (*pl* **-s**) *die abk für* **Justizvollzugsanstalt.**

K

**k, K** [kaː] (*pl* **- ODER -s**) *das* k, K.

**Kabarett, Cabaret** [kaba'rɛt, kaba'reː] (*pl* **-s ODER -e**) *das* **- 1.** [Aufführung] satirical revue **- 2.** [Institution] *theatre where satirical revues are performed*.

**Kabarettist, in** (*mpl* **-en**; *fpl* **-nen**) *der, die* satirical revue artist.

**kabbeln** ⮞ **sich kabbeln** *ref fam*: **sich mit jm ~** to squabble with sb.

**Kabel** (*pl* **-**) *das* cable.

**Kabellanschluss** *der*: **~ haben** to have cable television.

**Kabelfernsehen** *das* cable television.

**Kabeljau** (*pl* **-s**) *der* cod.

**Kabellkanal** *der* cable TV channel.

**Kabine** (*pl* **-n**) *die* **- 1.** [von Schiff, Flugzeug] cabin **- 2.** [in Schwimmbad] cubicle; [in Kleidergeschäft] fitting room.

**Kabinett** (*pl* **-e**) *das* **- 1.** [aus Ministern] cabinet **- 2.** [Wein] *term designating a high-quality German wine*.

**Kabinettslsitzung** *die* cabinet meeting.

**Kabrio, Cabrio** (*pl* **-s**) *das* convertible.

**Kachel** (*pl* **-n**) *die* tile.

**kacheln** (*perf* **hat/ist gekachelt**) *vt* (*hat*) [auslegen] to tile ⬦ *vi* (*ist*) *fam* [rasen] to zoom along.

**Kachellofen** *der tiled stove used for heating*.

**Kacke** *die vulg* [Kot] shit; **die ~ ist am Dampfen** *vulg* the shit has hit the fan.

**kacken** *vi vulg* to shit.

**Kadaver** [ka'daːvɐ] (*pl* **-**) *der* carcass.

**Kader** (*pl* **-**) *der* **- 1.** POL cadre **- 2.** SPORT squad.

**KaDeWe**® (*abk für* **Kaufhaus des Westens**) *das large department store in Berlin*.

**Kadmium** *das* cadmium.

**Käfer** (*pl* **-**) *der* [Insekt, Auto] beetle.

**Kaff** (*pl* **-s ODER -e**) *das fam* dump.

**Kaffe, Kaffee** ['kafe, ka'feː] (*pl* **-s**) *der* **- 1.** [gen] coffee; **eine Tasse ~** a cup of coffee; **~ mit Milch** white coffee; **schwarzer ~** black coffee; **das ist kalter ~** *fam fig* that's old hat **- 2.** [Mahlzeit] afternoon coffee and cake; **~ trinken** [am Nachmittag] to have afternoon coffee; [in der Pause] to have a coffee break.

**Kaffeelbohne** *die* coffee bean.

**Kaffeelfilter** *der* filter (paper).

**Kaffeelhaus** *das* coffee house.

**Kaffeelkanne** *die* coffeepot.

**Kaffeelklatsch** (*pl* **-e**) *der*: **sich zum ~ treffen** to meet for a chat over a cup of coffee.

**Kaffeellöffel** *der* coffee spoon.

**Kaffeelmaschine** *die* coffee machine.

**Kaffeelsatz** *der* coffee grounds (*pl*).

**Kaffeeltasse** *die* coffee cup.

**Käfig** (*pl* **-e**) *der* cage.

**kahl** *adj* **- 1.** [ohne Haare] bald; **~ werden** to go bald **- 2.** [Berg, Baum] bare.

**Kahllkopf** *der* bald person.

**kahl scheren** *vt* (*unreg*) [Kopf] to shave; **jn ~** to shave sb's hair off.

**Kahllschlag** *der* **- 1.** [das Abholzen] clear felling **- 2.** [Waldfläche] clear-felled area **- 3.** [Abbau] cutbacks (*pl*).

**Kahn** (*pl* **Kähne**) *der* **- 1.** [Ruderboot] rowing boat *Br*, rowboat *Am* **- 2.** [Stechkahn] punt **- 3.** [Lastkahn] barge.

K

**Kai** (pl -s ODER -e) der quay.

**Kai|mauer** die quay wall.

**Kairo** nt Cairo.

**Kaiser** (pl -) der emperor; **wir streiten uns um des ~s Bart** this discussion is pointless.

**Kaiserin** (pl -nen) die empress.

**kaiserlich** adj imperial.

**Kaiser|reich** das empire.

**Kaiser|schmarrn** (pl -) der pancake torn into thin strips.

**Kaiser|schnitt** der MED caesarean (section).

**Kajak** (pl -s) das ODER der kayak.

**Kajüte** (pl -n) die cabin.

**Kakadu** (pl -s) der cockatoo.

**Kakao** [ka'kau] der cocoa; **jn/etw durch den ~ ziehen** fam to take the mickey out of sb/sthg.

**Kakerlake** (pl -n) die cockroach.

**Kaki** das (ohne pl) = Khaki.

**Kaktee** = Kaktus.

**Kaktus** (pl Kakteen ODER -se) der cactus.

**Kalabrien** nt Calabria.

**Kalahari** die: **die ~** the Kalahari.

**Kalauer** (pl -) der [Witz] corny joke; [Wortspiel] bad pun.

**Kalb** (pl Kälber) das **- 1.** [Tier] calf **- 2.** [Fleisch] veal.

**kalben** vi to calve.

**Kalbfleisch** das veal.

**Kaleidoskop** (pl -e) das kaleidoscope.

**Kalender** (pl -) der **- 1.** [Wandkalender] calendar **- 2.** [Taschenkalender] diary; **sich** (D) **etw im ~ rot anstreichen** fig to make sthg a red-letter day.

**Kalender|jahr** das calendar year.

**Kali** (pl -s) das potash (U).

**Kaliber** (pl -) das **- 1.** [von einem Geschütz] calibre **- 2.** [Art, Sorte] kind, ilk.

**Kalium** das potassium.

**Kalk** der (ohne pl) **- 1.** [Kalkstein] limestone **- 2.** [in Wasserkessel] lime; **ungelöschter ~** quicklime **- 3.** [zum Tünchen] whitewash.

**Kalk|stein** der limestone.

**Kalkül** (pl -e) das ODER der geh calculation.

**Kalkulation** (pl -en) die calculation.

**kalkulierbar** adj **- 1.** [Preis] calculable **- 2.** [Risiko] quantifiable.

**kalkulieren** vt [berechnen] to calculate ⟨⟩ vi to calculate; **genau/scharf ~** to make precise calculations.

**Kalorie** [kalo'ri:] (pl -n) die calorie.

**kalorienarm** [kalo'ri:ənarm] adj low-calorie ⟨⟩ adv: **~ essen** to eat low-calorie food.

**kalt** (kompar **kälter;** superl **kälteste**) adj cold; **es ist ~** it's cold; **mir ist ~** I'm cold; **~e Füße kriegen** fig to get cold feet; **das lässt mich ~** fam it leaves me cold ⟨⟩ adv (kompar **kälter;** superl am **kältesten):** **~ duschen** to have a cold shower; **das Bier ~ stellen** to chill the beer; **~ lächeln** to smile coldly.

**kaltblütig** adj cold-blooded ⟨⟩ adv in cold blood.

**Kälte** die (ohne pl) **- 1.** [gen] coldness **- 2.** [Wetter] cold; **bei ~** in cold weather; **klirrende** ODER **schneidende ~** biting cold.

**kältebeständig** adj **- 1.** [Pflanze] hardy **- 2.** [Material] frost-resistant.

**Kälte|einbruch** der cold snap.

**Kalte Krieg** der cold war.

**Kalt|front** die cold front.

**kalt lassen** vt (unreg) fam: **das lässt mich kalt** it leaves me cold.

**kalt|machen** vt fam [töten] to bump off.

**Kalt|miete** die rent not including bills.

**Kalt|schale** die KÜCHE sweet soup served cold.

**kaltschnäuzig** adj dismissive.

**kalt|stellen** vt [außer Gefecht setzen] to neutralize.

**Kalzium** das calcium.

**kam** prät ⟾ kommen.

**Kambodscha** nt Cambodia.

**Kamel** (pl -e) das **- 1.** [Tier] camel **- 2.** fig [Trottel] idiot.

**Kamelle** (pl -n) die fam: **das sind ja olle ~n** that's old hat.

**Kamera** (pl -s) die camera; **vor der ~ stehen** to appear in front of the camera.

**Kamerad, in** (mpl -en; fpl -nen) der, die friend.

**Kameradschaft** (pl -en) die friendship.

**kameradschaftlich** adj friendly ⟨⟩ adv in a friendly way.

**Kamera|frau** die camerawoman.

**Kamera|führung** die camerawork (U).

**Kamera|mann** (pl -männer) der cameraman.

**Kamerun** nt Cameroon.

**Kamille** (pl -n) die camomile.

**Kamillen|tee** der camomile tea.

**Kamin** (pl -e) der **- 1.** [Schornstein] chimney **- 2.** [Feuerstelle] fireplace; **offener ~** open fireplace.

**Kamin|feger, in** (mpl -; fpl -nen) der, die chimney sweep.

**Kamin|feuer** das open fire.

**Kamin|sims** *das ODER der* mantelpiece.

**Kamm** (*pl* Kämme) *der* - **1.** [Haarkamm, Hahnenkamm] comb; **alles über einen ~ scheren** *fig* [keinen Unterschied machen] to lump everything together - **2.** [Bergkamm] ridge.

**kämmen** *vt* to comb.

➤ **sich kämmen** *ref* to comb one's hair.

**Kammer** (*pl* -n) *die* - **1.** [kleines Zimmer] cubbyhole - **2.** POL chamber.

**Kammergericht** *das high court and court of appeal in Berlin.*

**Kammer|musik** *die* chamber music.

**Kammer|spiele** *pl* studio theatre *(sg).*

**Kammer|ton** *der* MUS concert pitch.

**Kampagne** (*pl* -n) *die* campaign; **eine ~ gegen jn/etw starten** to launch a campaign against sb/sthg.

**Kampf** (*pl* Kämpfe) *der* - **1.** [Streit] fight; [politisch, sozial] struggle, fight; [in Sport] contest; [in Krieg] battle; **~ um etw** fight for sthg; **~ gegen jn/etw** fight against sb/sthg; **jm/einer Sache den ~ ansagen** to declare war on sb/sthg - **2.** MIL fighting *(U).*

**Kampf|ansage** *die* declaration of war.

**kämpfen** *vi* to fight; **gegen jn/etw ~** to fight against sb/sthg; **für jn/etw ~** to fight for sb/sthg; **um jn/etw ~** to fight for sb/sthg; **mit etw ~** *fig* [Schlaf, Tod] to fight sthg off; [Tränen] to fight sthg back.

**Kampf|gebiet** *das* combat zone.

**Kampf|geist** *der* [kämpferische Haltung] fighting spirit.

**Kampf|hahn** *der eigtl* & *fig* fighting cock.

**Kampf|handlungen** *pl* fighting *(U).*

**Kampf|hund** *der* fighting dog.

**kampflos** *adj* MIL peaceful ◇ *adv* without a fight.

**Kampf|richter, in** *der, die* SPORT referee.

**kampfunfähig** *adj* SPORT: **jn ~ schlagen** to knock sb out of the fight.

**kampieren** *vi* - **1.** [zelten] to camp - **2.** [notdürftig] to camp down.

**Kanada** *nt* Canada.

**Kanadier** [ka'na:dɪɐ] (*pl* -) *der* - **1.** [Einwohner Kanadas] Canadian - **2.** [Sportboot] Canadian canoe.

**Kanadierin** [ka'na:dɪərɪn] (*pl* -nen) *die* Canadian.

**kanadisch** *adj* Canadian.

**Kanaille** [ka'naljə] (*pl* -n) *die abw* [Schurke] rogue.

**Kanal** (*pl* Kanäle) *der* - **1.** [Wasserweg] canal - **2.** TELEKOM channel - **3.** *RW:* **den ~ voll haben** *fam* [betrunken sein] to be plastered; *fam* [es satt haben] to be fed up to the back teeth.

**Kanal|deckel** *der* manhole cover.

**Kanalisation** (*pl* -en) *die* - **1.** [für Abwässer] sewers *(pl)* - **2.** [Ausbau eines natürlichen Wasserweges] canalization *(U).*

**kanalisieren** *vt* - **1.** [Straße, Ortsteil] to provide with a sewerage system - **2.** *fig* [Gefühle, Aggression] to channel - **3.** [Fluss] to canalize.

**Kanal|tunnel** *der* Channel Tunnel.

**Kanapee** ['kanapeː] (*pl* -s) *das* - **1.** [Sofa] sofa - **2.** KÜCHE canapé.

**Kanarien|vogel** *der* canary.

**Kanarische Inseln** *pl* Canary Islands.

**Kandidat, in** (*mpl* -en; *fpl* -nen) *der, die* candidate; **jn als ~en aufstellen** ODER **nominieren** to put sb forward as a candidate.

**Kandidatur** (*pl* -en) *die* candidacy; **seine ~ anmelden/zurückziehen** to announce/withdraw one's candidacy.

**kandidieren** *vi* to stand *Br,* to run *Am.*

**kandieren** *vt* to candy.

**Kandis|zucker** *der* sugar candy.

**Känguru** (*pl* -s) *das* kangaroo.

**Kaninchen** (*pl* -) *das* rabbit.

**Kanister** (*pl* -) *der* can.

**kann** *präs* ⊳ **können.**

**Kann|bestimmung** *die* permissive provision.

**Kännchen** (*pl* -) *das* pot.

**Kanne** (*pl* -n) *die* pot.

**Kannibale** (*pl* -n) *der* cannibal.

**Kannibalin** (*pl* -nen) *die* cannibal.

**Kannibalismus** *der* cannibalism.

**kannte** *prät* ⊳ **kennen.**

**Kanon** (*pl* -s) *der* MUS canon.

**Kanone** (*pl* -n) *die* - **1.** [Geschütz] cannon - **2.** *RW:* **unter aller ~ sein** *fam* [miserabel] to be the pits.

**Kanonen|futter** *das abw* cannon fodder.

**Kante** (*pl* -n) *die* edge; **etw auf die hohe ~ legen** *fig* to put sthg by.

**kantig** *adj* angular.

**Kantine** (*pl* -n) *die* canteen.

**Kantinen|essen** *das* canteen food.

**Kanton** (*pl* -e) *der* canton.

**kantonal** *adj* cantonal.

**Kantor** (*pl* -toren) *der* choirmaster and organist.

**Kantorin** (*pl* -nen) *die* choirmistress and organist.

**Kanu** (*pl* -s) *das* canoe.

**K**

**Kanüle** (*pl* -n) *die* [MED - Hohlnadel] hypodermic needle; [ - Röhrchen] cannula.

**Kanzel** (*pl* -n) *die* - **1.** [von Kirchen] pulpit - **2.** [von Flugzeugen] cockpit.

**Kanzlei** (*pl* -en) *die* office.

**Kanzler** (*pl* -) *der* - **1.** [Bundeskanzler] chancellor - **2.** UNI vice-chancellor *Br*, chancellor *Am*.

**KANZLER**

> The German chancellor is head of the federal government and has extensive powers. It is he who sets the agenda for government policy.

**Kanzleramt** *das* [Amtssitz des Bundeskanzlers] chancellery.

**Kanzlerin** (*pl* -nen) *die* - **1.** [Bundeskanzlerin] chancellor - **2.** UNI vice-chancellor *Br*, chancellor *Am*.

**Kap** (*pl* -s) *das* cape.

**Kap.** (*abk für* **Kapitel**) ch.

**Kapazität** (*pl* -en) *die* - **1.** [gen] capacity - **2.** [Experte] authority.

**Kap der Guten Hoffnung** *das* Cape of Good Hope.

**Kapee** *die:* schwer von ~ sein *fam* to be slow on the uptake.

**Kapelle** (*pl* -n) *die* - **1.** [kleine Kirche] chapel - **2.** MUS band.

**Kapellmeister, in** *der, die* [Leiter - einer Musikkapelle] bandmaster; [ - eines Orchesters] conductor.

**Kaper** (*pl* -n) *die* caper.

**kapern** *vt* - **1.** [erbeuten] to seize - **2.** *fam fig* [ergattern]: **sich** (*D*) **jn** ~ to hook sb.

**Kap Hoorn** *das* Cape Horn.

**kapieren** *vt fam* to get.

**kapital** [kapi'ta:l] *adj* - **1.** [Irrtum] serious - **2.** [Hirsch] magnificent.

**Kapital** (*pl* -ien ODER -e) *das* - **1.** [gen] capital - **2.** RW: aus etw ~ schlagen to make capital out of sthg; geistiges ~ intellectual assets (*pl*); totes ~ unused skills (*pl*).

**Kapitalanlage** *die* capital investment.

**Kapitalflucht** *die* flight of capital.

**Kapitalismus** *der* capitalism.

**Kapitalist, in** (*mpl* -en; *fpl* -nen) *der, die* capitalist.

**kapitalistisch** *adj* capitalist.

**kapitalkräftig** *adj* financially strong.

**Kapitalmarkt** *der* WIRTSCH capital market.

**Kapitalverbrechen** *das* RECHT serious crime.

**Kapitän** (*pl* -e) *der* captain.

**Kapitel** (*pl* -) *das* chapter; ein ~ für sich sein *fig* to be an awkward business; das ist ein anderes ~ that's another story.

**Kapitulation** (*pl* -en) *die* [Aufgabe] surrender (*U*); bedingungslose ~ unconditional surrender (*U*).

**kapitulieren** *vi* to surrender; vor jm ~ to yield to sb; vor etw (*D*) ~ to give up in the face of sthg.

**Kaplan** (*pl* Kapläne) *der* curate.

**Kappe** (*pl* -n) *die* cap; etw auf seine ~ nehmen *fam fig* to take the responsibility for sthg.

**kappen** *vt* - **1.** [beschneiden] to cut back - **2.** [durchschneiden] to cut through.

**Kapsel** (*pl* -n) *die* - **1.** [kleiner Behälter] box - **2.** [von Medikament, von Blüten] capsule.

**Kapstadt** *nt* Cape Town.

**kaputt** *adj fam* - **1.** [Vase, Gerät] broken; [Beziehung, Gesundheit] ruined - **2.** *fig* [erschöpft]: ~ sein to be done in.

**kaputtgehen** (*perf* ist kaputtgegangen) *vi* (*unreg*) *fam* - **1.** [Gerät, Gegenstand] to break; [Beziehungen, Geschäfte] to be ruined - **2.** [eingehen] to die.

**kaputtlachen** ➡ sich kaputtlachen *ref fam* to kill o.s. laughing; sich über jn/etw ~ to kill o.s. laughing at sb/sthg.

**kaputtmachen** *vt* [Gerät, Gegenstand] to break; [Beziehungen, Geschäfte] to ruin. ➡ sich kaputtmachen *ref fam* to do o.s. in.

**kaputtschlagen** *vt* (*unreg*) *fam* to smash.

**Kapuze** (*pl* -n) *die* hood.

**Kapuziner** (*pl* -) *der* - **1.** [Ordensbruder] Capuchin (friar) - **2.** *Österr* [Getränk] coffee with milk.

**Karabiner** (*pl* -) *der* carbine.

**Karabinerhaken** *der* karabiner.

**Karacho** *das fam;* mit ~ hell for leather.

**Karaffe** (*pl* -n) *die* - **1.** [mit Stöpsel] decanter - **2.** [ohne Stöpsel] carafe.

**Karambolage** [karambo'la:ʒə] (*pl* -n) *die* crash.

**Karamell** *der* caramel.

**Karamellbonbon** *das* ODER *der* toffee.

**Karat** (*pl* -e oder -) *das* - **1.** [Edelsteingewicht] carat - **2.** [Einheit]: dieser Ring hat 20 ~ this ring is 20 carats.

**Karate** *das* karate.

**Karawane** (*pl* -n) *die* caravan.

**Kardinal** (*pl* Kardinäle) *der* cardinal.

**Kardinalzahl** *die* [Grundzahl] cardinal number.

**Kardiologe** (*pl* -n) *der* MED cardiologist.

**Kardiologin** (*pl* -nen) *die* cardiologist.

**Karenz|tag** *der first day of sick leave, for which the insurer does not pay benefit.*

**Karl|freitag** *der* Good Friday.

**karg** *adj* - **1.** [Mahlzeit, Lohn] meagre - **2.** [Raum] bare - **3.** [Boden] barren.

**kärglich** *adj* meagre.

**Karibik** *die* Caribbean.

**karibisch** *adj* Caribbean.

**kariert** *adj* - **1.** [Stoff] checked - **2.** [Papier] squared ◇ *adv fam* [verwirrt]: **~ schauen** to look bewildered.

**Karies** ['kaːrjɛs] *die* MED tooth decay.

**Karikatur** (*pl* -en) *die* cartoon; [Porträt] caricature.

**Karikaturist, in** (*mpl* -en; *fpl* -nen) *der, die* cartoonist; [Porträtist] caricaturist.

**karikieren** *vt* to caricature.

**kariös** *adj* decayed.

**karitativ** *adj* charitable ◇ *adv* for charity.

**Karlsruhe** *nt* - **1.** [Stadt] Karlsruhe - **2.** [Gericht] the Federal Constitutional Court.

**Karmeliter, in** (*mpl* -; *fpl* -nen) *der, die* Carmelite.

**karminrot** *adj* carmine (red).

**Karneval** ['karnəval] (*pl* -e *ODER* -s) *der* carnival.

**KARNEVAL**

The biggest "Karneval" celebrations take place in the Rhineland (Cologne, Düsseldorf and Mainz), although the tradition is also associated with Bavaria (where it is known as "Fasching") and Swabia (where it is known as "Fasenacht" or "Fasnet"). The "Karneval" period officially begins at eleven minutes past eleven on the 11th November and ends on Ash Wednesday. On the Monday before Ash Wednesday ("Rosenmontag"), there are processions with floats carrying figures that caricature social and political life.

**Karnevalist, in** [karnəva'lıst, ın] (*mpl* -en; *fpl* -nen) *der, die* carnival participant.

**karnevalistisch** [karnəva'lıstıʃ] *adj* carnival (vor Subst).

**Karnevals|zug** *der* carnival procession.

**Karnickel** (*pl* -) *das fam* [Kaninchen] rabbit.

**Kärnten** *nt* Carinthia.

**Kärntner, in** (*mpl* -; *fpl* -nen) *der, die* Carinthian.

**kärntnerisch** *adj* Carinthian.

**Karo** (*pl* -s) *das* - **1.** [Raute] diamond - **2.** (ohne Artikel, ohne *pl*) [Spielfarbe] diamonds (*pl*) - **3.** [Spielkarte] diamond; **~bube** jack of diamonds.

**Karosserie** (*pl* -n) *die* bodywork (U).

**Karotte** (*pl* -n) *die* carrot.

**Karpaten** *pl*: **die ~** the Carpathians.

**Karpfen** (*pl* -) *der* carp.

**Karre** (*pl* -n) *die* - **1.** [Handkarre] cart - **2.** *fam* [Auto] jalopy, banger *Br*.

**karren** *vt fam* - **1.** [transportieren] to cart - **2.** [jn fahren]: **jn irgendwohin ~** to drive sb somewhere.

**Karren** (*pl* -) *der* - **1.** [kleiner Wagen] cart - **2.** *RW:* **jm den ~ aus dem Dreck ziehen** *fam* to get sb out of trouble; **jm an den ~ fahren** *fam* to take sb to task; **mir kann keiner an den ~ fahren** nobody can touch me; **ich lasse mich nicht vor deinen ~ spannen** I'm not doing your donkey work (for you).

**Karriere** [ka'rjɛːrə] (*pl* -n) *die* career; **~ machen** to make a career for o.s.

**Karriere|frau** *die* career woman.

**Karriere|typ** *der abw* careerist.

**Karl|samstag** *der* Easter Saturday.

**Karst** (*pl* -e) *der* karst.

**Kartäuser** (*pl* -) *der* Carthusian (monk).

**Karte** (*pl* -n) *die* - **1.** [Postkarte, Spielkarte] card - **2.** [Landkarte] map - **3.** *RW:* **jm die ~n legen** [wahrsagen] to tell sb's fortune from cards; **jm die gelbe/rote ~ zeigen** to show sb the yellow/ red card; **mit offenen ~n spielen** to put one's cards on the table; **alles auf eine ~ setzen** to stake everything on one chance; **schlechte ~n haben** to have been dealt a bad hand.

**Kartei** (*pl* -en) *die* card index.

**Kartei|karte** *die* index card.

**Kartei|kasten** *der* index-card box.

**Kartei|leiche** *die hum* inactive member.

**Kartell** (*pl* -e) *das* WIRTSCH cartel.

**Kartell|amt** *das* WIRTSCH ≃ Monopolies Commission *Br, government body responsible for the regulation of cartels.*

**Karten|haus** *das* house of cards; **zusammenfallen wie ein ~** *fig* to collapse like a house of cards.

**Karten|spiel** *das* - **1.** [Gesellschaftsspiel] card game - **2.** [Spielkarten] pack *Br ODER* deck *Am* of cards.

**Karten|telefon** *das* cardphone.

**Karten|vorverkauf** *der* advance booking.

**Kartoffel** (*pl* -n) *die* potato.

**Kartoffel|brei** *der* KÜCHE mashed potatoes (*pl*).

**Kartoffel|chips** *pl* crisps *Br*, chips *Am*.

**Kartoffel|puffer** *der* KÜCHE potato pancake (*made from grated potatoes*).

**Kartoffel|püree** *das* KÜCHE mashed potatoes (*pl*).

**K**

**Kartoffel|salat** *der* KÜCHE potato salad.

**Karton** (*pl* -s) *der* - **1.** [Pappe] card - **2.** [Kiste] (cardboard) box.

**Karussell** (*pl* -s) *das* merry-go-round; ~ fahren to go on the merry-go-round.

**Karlwoche** *die* Holy Week.

**Karzinom** (*pl* -e) *das* MED carcinoma.

**Kasachstan** *nt* Kazakhstan.

**Kaschemme** (*pl* -n) *die abw* sleazy bar.

**kaschieren** *vt* to conceal.

**Kaschmir** (*pl* -e) *nt* Kashmir <> *der* cashmere.

**Käse** (*pl* -) *der* cheese; **das ist ~!** *abw* & *fig* that's rubbish!

**Käse|blatt** *das fam abw* rag.

**Käse|fondue** *das* KÜCHE cheese fondue.

**Käse|gebäck** *das* KÜCHE cheese savouries (*pl*).

**Käse|glocke** *die* cheese dome.

**Käse|kuchen** *der* KÜCHE cheesecake.

**Kaserne** (*pl* -n) *die* MIL barracks (*pl*).

**kaserniert** *adj* in barracks.

**käsig** *adj* pale.

**Kasino** (*pl* -s) *das* - **1.** [Spielkasino] casino - **2.** MIL (officers') mess.

**Kasper** (*pl* -) *der* Punch.

**Kasperle|theater** *das* [Vorstellung] Punch and Judy show; [Gebäude] Punch and Judy theatre.

**Kaspische Meer** *das* Caspian Sea.

**Kasse** (*pl* -n) *die* - **1.** [Kassette] cashbox - **2.** [im Laden] till - **3.** [im Supermarkt] checkout - **4.** [im Theater, Kino] box office - **5.** *fam* [Krankenkasse] (health) insurance (*U*) - **6.** RW: ~ **machen** to cash up; **jn zur ~ bitten** to ask sb to pay up; **gemeinsame ~ machen** to share expenses; **getrennte ~ machen** to pay separately; **gut bei ~ sein** *fam* to be well-off; **knapp bei ~ sein** *fam* to be short of cash.

**Kassen|arzt, ärztin** *der, die doctor who treats patients with health insurance.*

**Kassen|bon** *der* receipt.

**Kassen|patient, in** *der, die patient with health insurance.*

**Kassen|schalter** *der* cash desk.

**Kassen|sturz** *der fam:* ~ **machen** to check one's finances.

**Kassen|zettel** *der* receipt.

**Kassette** (*pl* -n) *die* - **1.** [Musik- und Videokassette] cassette, tape; **etw auf ~ aufnehmen** to record sthg on cassette ODER tape - **2.** [für Schmuck, Schallplatten, Bücher] box.

**Kassetten|rekorder** *der* cassette recorder.

**kassieren** *vt* - **1.** [einziehen] to collect - **2.** *fam* [einnehmen] to pocket - **3.** *fam* [einheimsen - Lob, Kritik] to get; [ - Niederlage] to suffer - **4.** *fam* [Führerschein] to take away.

**Kassierer, in** (*mpl* -; *fpl* -nen) *der, die* - **1.** [von Geschäft, Bank] cashier - **2.** [von Verein] treasurer.

**Kastanie** [kas'ta:njə] (*pl* -n) *die* chestnut.

**kastanienbraun** *adj* chestnut.

**Kaste** (*pl* -n) *die* caste.

**Kasten** (*pl* Kästen) *der* - **1.** [Kiste] box - **2.** [für Flaschen] crate - **3.** [Briefkasten] postbox *Br*, mailbox *Am* - **4.** *fam* [Gebäude] great box of a building - **5.** SPORT box - **6.** *fam* [Kopf]: **etwas/viel auf dem ~ haben** [intelligent sein] to be brainy/very brainy.

**Kasten|form** *die* rectangular baking tin *Br* ODER pan *Am*.

**Kastilien** *nt* Castile.

**kastrieren** *vt* MED to castrate.

**Kasus** (*pl* -) *der* GRAM case.

**Kat** [kat] (*pl* -s) (*abk für* Katalysator) *der* AUTO cat.

**Katakombe** (*pl* -n) *die* catacomb.

**Katalanisch(e)** *das* Catalan; *siehe auch* Englisch(e).

**Katalog** (*pl* -e) *der* catalogue.

**katalogisieren** *vt* to catalogue.

**Katalonien** *nt* Catalonia.

**Katalonier, in** [kata'lo:njɐ, rɪn] (*mpl* -; *fpl* -nen) *der, die* Catalan.

**katalonisch** *adj* Catalan.

**Katalysator** (*pl* -toren) *der* [am Auto] catalytic converter; [in Chemie] catalyst.

**Katamaran** (*pl* -e) *der* catamaran.

**Katapult** (*pl* -e) *das* ODER *der* catapult.

**Katarrh, Katarr** (*pl* -e) *der* MED catarrh (*U*).

**Kataster|amt** *das* land registry.

**katastrophal** [katastro'fa:l] *adj* disastrous <> *adv* disastrously.

**Katastrophe** [katas'tro:fə] (*pl* -n) *die* disaster; **eine ~ sein** *fam* to be a disaster.

**Katastrophen|gebiet** [katas'tro:fəngəbi:t] *das* disaster area.

**Katastrophen|schutz** [katas'tro:fənʃʊts] *der* disaster relief.

**Kate** (*pl* -n) *die* cottage.

**Katechismus** (*pl* -men) *der* catechism.

**Kategorie** (*pl* -n) *die* category.

**kategorisch** *adj* categorical <> *adv* categorically.

**Kater** (*pl* -) *der* - **1.** [Tier] tomcat - **2.** *fam* [von Alkohol] hangover; **einen ~ haben** to have a hangover.

**Kater|frühstück** *das breakfast of pickled gherkins, herrings etc, intended to cure a hangover.*

**kath.** (*abk für* **katholisch**) Cath.

**Katheder** (*pl* -) *der* lectern.

**Kathedrale** (*pl* -n) *die* cathedral.

**Katheter** (*pl* -) *der* MED catheter.

**Kathode** (*pl* -n) *die* PHYS cathode.

**Katholik** (*pl* -en) *der* Catholic.

**Katholiken|tag** *der biannual congress of German Catholics.*

**Katholikin** (*pl* -nen) *die* Catholic.

**katholisch** *adj* Catholic.

**Katholizismus** *der* Catholicism.

**Kat-|Motor** *der engine of a car fitted with a catalytic converter.*

**Katz** *die:* ~ **und Maus spielen** to play cat and mouse; **für die** ~ **sein** *fam* to be a waste of time.

**Katze** (*pl* -n) *die* - 1. [Tier] cat; **die** ~ **aus dem Sack lassen** to let the cat out of the bag - 2. [weibliches Tier] she-cat.

**katzenfreundlich** *adj:* ~ **sein** to be superficially friendly.

**Katzen|sprung** *der:* **etw ist nur ein** ~ **von etw entfernt** sthg is only a stone's throw away from sthg.

**Katzen|wäsche** *die fam* catlick.

**Kauderwelsch** *das* gibberish.

**kauen** *vi* to chew; **an etw** (D) ~ [herumkauen] to chew sthg; [bewältigen] to grapple with sthg ◇ *vt* to chew.

**kauern** *vi* to crouch.
➤ **sich kauern** *ref* to crouch.

**Kauf** (*pl* Käufe) *der* purchase; **einen** ~ **abschließen** to complete a purchase; **etw in** ~ **nehmen** *fig* to accept sthg.

**kaufen** *vt* to buy; **jm/sich etw** ~ to buy sb/o.s. sthg.

**Käufer, in** (*mpl* -; *fpl* -nen) *der, die* buyer.

**Kauf|frau** *die* businesswoman.

**Kauf|haus** *das* department store.

**Kauf|kraft** *die* purchasing power.

**Kauf|leute** *pl* business people.

**käuflich** *adj* - 1. [zu erwerben]: **etw** ~ **erwerben** *amt* to purchase sthg; ~ **sein** [Ware] to be for sale; [Person] to be easily bought; **nicht** ~ **sein** [Ware] not to be for sale; [Person] not to be easily bought - 2. [prostituiert]: ~**es Mädchen** prostitute; ~**e Liebe** prostitution.

**Kaufmann** (*pl* -leute) *der* businessman.

**kaufmännisch** *adj* commercial.

**Kauf|preis** *der* purchase price.

**Kauf|rausch** *der* spending urge.

**Kauf|vertrag** *der* contract of sale.

**Kauf|zwang** *der* obligation to buy.

**Kau|gummi** *das* ODER *der* chewing gum.

**Kaukasus** *der:* **der** ~ the Caucasus.

**Kaulquappe** (*pl* -n) *die* tadpole.

**kaum** *adv* - 1. [gen] hardly; **das ist** ~ **zu glauben** that's hard to believe; ~ **dass ich angerufen hatte, standen sie schon vor der Tür** no sooner had I rung than they were at the door - 2. [höchstens] barely.

**kausal** *adj* causal ◇ *adv* causally.

**Kausal|satz** *der* GRAM causal clause.

**Kausalzusammen|hang** *der* causal connection.

**Kaution** (*pl* -en) *die* - 1. [für Wohnung] deposit - 2. [für Häftling] bail; **gegen** ~ **freikommen** to be released on bail.

**Kautschuk** *der* (India) rubber.

**Kauz** (*pl* Käuze) *der:* **ein komischer** ~ *fig* an odd bird.

**Kavalier** [kava'liɐ] (*pl* -e) *der* gentleman.

**Kavaliers|delikt** *das* trivial offence.

**Kavallerie** ['kavaləri] (*pl* -n) *die* cavalry.

**Kaviar** [ka:vjaɐ] (*pl* -e) *der* caviar.

**kcal.** (*abk für* **Kilokalorie**) kcal.

**keck** *adj* cheeky ◇ *adv* cheekily.

**Kefir** *der* (*ohne pl*) kefir, *sour-tasting drink made of fermented milk.*

**Kegel** (*pl* -) *der* - 1. MATH cone - 2. [zum Spielen] skittle.

**Kegel|bahn** *die* bowling alley.

**kegelförmig** *adj* conical.

**Kegel|klub** *der* bowling club.

**kegeln** *vi* to bowl.

**Kegel|schnitt** *der* MATH conic section.

**Kehle** (*pl* -n) *die* - 1. [gen] throat - 2. RW: **etw in die falsche** ~ **bekommen** *fam* to take sthg the wrong way; **aus voller** ~ **singen/schreien** to sing/shout at the top of one's voice.

**kehlig** *adj* throaty ◇ *adv* throatily.

**Kehl|kopf** *der* larynx.

**Kehr|besen** *der* brush.

**Kehr|blech** *das* dustpan.

**Kehre** (*pl* -n) *die* [Kurve] hairpin bend.

**kehren** *vt* - 1. [fegen] to sweep - 2. [wenden] to turn; **den starken Mann nach außen** ~ to act the tough guy; **in sich gekehrt** lost in one's own world.
➤ **sich kehren** *ref* - 1. [sich kümmern]: **sich nicht an** ODER **um etw** ~ not to care about sthg - 2. [sich richten]: **sich gegen jn** ~ to turn against sb.

**Kehr|reim** *der* refrain.

**Kehr|schaufel** *die* dustpan.

K

**Kehr|seite** *die* drawback, downside; **die ~ der Medaille** the downside.

**kehrt|machen** *vi* to turn round.

**Kehrt|wendung** *die*: **eine ~ machen** to turn round; [politisch] to do a U-turn.

**Kehr|wert** *der* MATH reciprocal.

**keifen** *vi abw* to nag.

**Keil** (*pl* -e) *der* wedge.

**Keilerei** (*pl* -en) *die fam* scrap, fight.

**Keil|riemen** *der* fan belt.

**Keim** (*pl* -e) *der* - **1.** [Pflanzentrieb] shoot; **etw im ~ ersticken** *fig* to nip sthg in the bud - **2.** [Bakterie] germ.

**keimen** *vi* [Saat] to germinate; [Kartoffeln, Zwiebeln] to sprout.

**keimfrei** *adj* [Instrumente, Milch] sterilized; [Bedingungen] sterile <> *adv* [arbeiten] in a sterile environment.

**Keimling** (*pl* -e) *der* seedling.

**keimtötend** *adj* germicidal, antiseptic.

**Keim|zelle** *die* - **1.** BIOL sex cell - **2.** [Ausgangspunkt] germ.

**kein, e** *det* no, not … any; **~ Mensch** no one; **~en einzigen Euro** not a single euro; **es gibt ~e Bananen** there are no bananas, there aren't any bananas; **ich habe ~ Geld/~e Zeit** I haven't got any money/time; **~ dummer Gedanke** not a bad idea; **das ist doch ~e Schande** it's no disgrace; **~ Wunder, dass …** it's no wonder (that) …

**keine, r, s** *pron* - **1.** [Person] no one, nobody; **~r weiß, dass …** no one *ODER* nobody knows that …; **es ist ~r da!** there's no one *ODER* nobody there!; **~r der Schüler** *ODER* **von den Schülern** none of the pupils - **2.** [Gegenstand] none; **welchen nehmen Sie? - ~n** which do you want? - neither.

**keinerlei** *adj (unver)* no … at all; **~ Bedenken haben** to have no scruples at all.

**keinesfalls** *adv* on no account; **das ist ~ schwer** that's not at all difficult.

**keineswegs** *adv* not at all; **~ besser** in no way better.

**Keks** (*pl* -e) *der* biscuit *Br*, cookie *Am*; **jm auf den ~ gehen** *fam* to get on sb's nerves.

**Kelch** (*pl* -e) *der* goblet.

**Kelle** (*pl* -n) *die* [Schöpflöffel] ladle.

**Keller** (*pl* -) *der* cellar.

**Keller|assel** *die* woodlouse.

**Keller|fenster** *das* cellar window.

**Keller|geschoss** *das* basement.

**Keller|treppe** *die* cellar stairs (*pl*).

**Keller|tür** *die* cellar door.

**Kellner, in** (*mpl* -; *fpl* -nen) *der, die* waiter (*f* waitress).

**kellnern** *vi* to wait tables.

**Kelte** (*pl* -n) *der* Celt.

**Kelter** (*pl* -n) *die* press.

**keltern** *vt* to press.

**Keltin** (*pl* -nen) *die* Celt.

**keltisch** *adj* Celtic.

**Kenia** *nt* Kenya.

**Kenianer, in** (*mpl* -; *fpl* -nen) *der, die* Kenyan.

**kenianisch** *adj* Kenyan.

**kennen** (*prät* **kannte;** *perf* **hat gekannt**) *vt* to know; **jn/etw gut ~** to know sb/sthg well; **ich kenne mich** I know what I'm like; **~ wir uns nicht?** haven't we met somewhere before?; **da kennst du ihn aber schlecht!** you don't know what he's like!

**kennen lernen** *vt* - **1.** [Person] to get to know, to meet; **freut mich, Sie kennen zu lernen!** pleased to meet you!; **du wirst mich noch ~!** *fam fig* I'll teach you! - **2.** [Sache] to get to know, to familiarize o.s. with.

➤ **sich kennen lernen** *ref* [sich begegnen] to meet.

**Kenner** (*pl* -) *der* expert; [von Wein] connoisseur.

**Kenner|blick** *der*: **mit ~** with an expert eye.

**Kennerin** (*pl* -nen) *die* expert; [von Wein] connoisseur.

**kenntlich** *adj* recognizable <> *adv*: **etw ~ machen** to mark *ODER* identify sthg.

**Kenntnis** (*pl* -nisse) *die* knowledge; **etw zur ~ nehmen** to take note of sthg, to note sthg; **jn von etw in ~ setzen** to inform sb of sthg; **dieser Vorfall entzieht sich meiner ~** *geh* I don't know anything about this incident.

➤ **Kenntnisse** *pl* knowledge (*U*).

**Kenntnisnahme** *die amt*: **zur ~** for information; **nach ~ von etw** after having seen sthg.

**Kennwort** (*pl* -wörter) *das* password.

**Kennz.** *abk für* **Kennzeichen.**

**Kenn|zahl** *die* code number.

**Kenn|zeichen** *das* - **1.** [Merkmal] symbol, sign; **besondere ~** distinguishing features - **2.** [an Kfz]: **amtliches ~** registration number *Br*, license number *Am*.

**kennzeichnen** *vt* [markieren]: **etw (mit** *ODER* **durch etw) ~** to mark sthg (with sthg); **etw als etw ~** [Produkt, Ware] to label sthg as sthg; **jn als etw ~** to describe sb as sthg.

**kennzeichnend** *adj*: **für jn/etw ~ sein** to be typical *ODER* characteristic of sb/sthg.

**Kenn|zeichnung** *die* labelling.

**Kenn|ziffer** *die* reference number.

**kentern** (*perf* **ist gekentert**) *vi* to capsize.

**Keramik** (pl -en) die - **1.** [Gefäß]: eine ~ a piece of pottery - **2.** (ohne pl) [Ton] pottery, ceramics (pl).

**Kerbe** (pl -n) die notch; **musst du denn auch noch in dieselbe ~ hauen?** fam fig do you have to go on about it too?

**Kerbel** der chervil.

**Kerbholz** das: **etwas** ODER **einiges auf dem ~ haben** fam to have blotted one's copybook.

**Kerker** (pl -) der dungeon.

**Kerl** (pl -e) der fam guy, bloke Br; **ein netter ~** a nice guy; **ein gemeiner ~** a swine.

**Kern** (pl -e) der - **1.** [von Apfel, Birne, Zitrusfrucht] pip; [von Pfirsich, Kirsche] stone, pit Am; [von Nuß] kernel - **2.** [Wichtigstes] core, crux - **3.** PHYS nucleus - **4.** [von Gruppen]: **der harte ~** the hard core.

**Kern|energie** die nuclear power.

**Kern|forschung** die nuclear research.

**Kern|fusion** die nuclear fusion.

**Kern|gehäuse** das core.

**kerngesund** adj as fit as a fiddle.

**Kern|kraft** die nuclear power.

**Kernkraft|gegner, in** der, die opponent of nuclear power.

**Kernkraft|werk** das nuclear power station.

**kernlos** adj seedless.

**Kern|physik** die nuclear physics (U).

**Kern|punkt** der [eines Vortrags] central point; [eines Problems] crux.

**Kern|reaktor** der nuclear reactor.

**Kern|seife** die household soap.

**Kern|spaltung** die nuclear fission.

**Kern|stück** das centrepiece.

**Kern|waffe** die nuclear weapon.

**Kerosin** das kerosene.

**Kerze** (pl -n) die - **1.** [zur Beleuchtung] candle - **2.** [Turnübung] shoulder stand.

**Kerzen|beleuchtung** die candlelight.

**kerzengerade** adj & adv bolt upright.

**Kerzenhalter** (pl -) der candlestick; [auf Kuchen, Weihnachtsbaum] candleholder.

**Kerzenlicht** das candlelight.

**keß** (kompar **kesser;** superl **kesseste**) adj - **1.** [Person, Verhalten] cheeky - **2.** [Kleidung] jaunty <> adv [frech] cheekily.

**Kessel** (pl -) der - **1.** [Topf] kettle; [groß] cauldron - **2.** [Tal] basin, basin-shaped valley.

**Kesseltreiben** das [Kampagne] witchhunt.

**Ketchup** ['kɛtʃap], **Ketschup** das ODER der ketchup.

**Kettcar**® (pl -s) der pedal car.

**Kette** (pl -n) die chain; [aus Perlen] string; [von Polizisten] cordon; [von Unfällen, Ereignissen] string, series; **einen Hund an die ~ legen** to put a dog on the chain.

**ketten** vt: **jn/etw an etw** (A) **~** to chain sb/sthg to sthg.

**Ketten|fahrzeug** das tracked vehicle.

**Ketten|raucher, in** der, die chain smoker.

**Ketten|reaktion** die chain reaction.

**Ketten|säge** die chain saw.

**Ketzer** (pl -) der heretic.

**Ketzerei** die heresy.

**Ketzerin** (pl -nen) die heretic.

**ketzerisch** adj heretical.

**keuchen** (perf hat/ist gekeucht) vi to pant.

**Keuchhusten** der whooping cough.

**Keule** (pl -n) die - **1.** KÜCHE leg - **2.** [Waffe & SPORT] club; **chemische ~** fig Mace®.

**keusch** adj chaste <> adv chastely.

**Keuschheit** die chastity.

**Keyboard** ['kiːbɔːd] (pl -s) das [Musikinstrument & EDV] keyboard.

**kfm.** abk für **kaufmännisch.**

**Kfz** [kaːɛfˈtsɛt] (pl -) das abk für **Kraftfahrzeug.**

**Kfz-|Steuer** die road tax.

**kg** (abk für **Kilogramm**) kg.

**KG** [kaːˈgeː] (pl -s) (abk für **Kommanditgesellschaft**) die limited partnership.

**kgl.** abk für **königlich.**

**Khaki, Kaki** das khaki.

**KHG** [kaːhaːˈgeː] (pl -s) (abk für **Katholische Hochschulgemeinde**) die ≃ CU Br, Catholic students' association.

**kHz** (abk für **Kilohertz**) kHz.

**kichern** vi to giggle.

**kicken** vi to play (football) <> vt to kick.

**Kicker, in** (mpl -s; fpl -nen) der, die footballer, football player.

**Kid** (pl -s) das fam kid.

**kidnappen** ['kɪtnɛpn̩] vt to kidnap.

**Kidnapper, in** ['kɪtnɛpɐ, rɪn] (mpl -; fpl -nen) der, die kidnapper.

**Kiefer** (pl - ODER -n) der (pl Kiefer) jaw <> die (pl Kiefern) pine.

**Kieker** der fam: **jn auf dem ~ haben** [beobachten] to have one's eye on sb; [nicht mögen] to have it in for sb.

**Kiel**[1] (pl -e) der - **1.** [von Schiff] keel - **2.** [von Federn] quill.

**Kiel**[2] nt [Stadt] Kiel.

**Kieler Woche** die annual regatta held in Kiel.

**Kieme** (*pl* -n) *die* gill.

**Kies** *der* - **1.** [auf Weg] gravel; [am Ufer] shingle - **2.** *salopp* [Geld] cash, dosh *Br.*

**Kiesel** (*pl* -) *der* pebble.

**Kiesellsäure** *die* CHEM silicic acid.

**Kiesellstein** *der* pebble.

**Kieslgrube** *die* gravel pit.

**Kieslweg** *der* gravel path.

**Kiew** ['kiːɛf] *nt* Kiev.

**Kiez** (*pl* -e) *der fam* [Stadtteil]: **der** ~ the hood.

**kiffen** *vi fam* to smoke dope.

**kikeriki** *interj* cock-a-doodle-doo!

**Kilimandscharo** *der* Kilimanjaro.

**killen** *vt salopp* to bump off.

**Killer, in** (*mpl* -; *fpl* -nen) *der, die* killer.

**Kilo** (*pl* - ODER -s) *das* kilo.

**Kilobyte** ['kiːloba̲i̲t] (*pl* -s) *das* EDV kilobyte.

**Kilolgramm** *das* kilogram.

**Kilolhertz** *das* kilohertz.

**Kilolkalorie** *die* kilocalorie.

**Kilolmeter** *der* kilometre; ~ **pro Stunde** kilometres per hour.

**Kilometergeld** *das* ≈ mileage (allowance).

**kilometerlang** *adj* ≈ miles long; **~e Strände** miles and miles of beaches.

**Kilometerlpauschale** *die* ≈ mileage allowance.

**Kilometerlstand** *der* ≈ mileage; **bei ~ 10.000** when there are 10,000 km on the clock.

**kilometerweit** *adv* [rennen] for miles; [sehen, hören] for miles (around).

**Kilometerlzähler** *der* ≈ mileometer.

**Kilolwatt** *das* kilowatt.

**Kilowattlstunde** *die* kilowatt hour.

**kiloweise** *adv* - **1.** [mehrere Kilos]: **etw ~ essen** to eat kilos of sthg - **2.** [verkaufen] by the kilo.

**Kind** (*pl* -er) *das* child; **von ~ auf** ODER **an** from childhood; **ein ~ erwarten** to be expecting (a baby); **ein ~ bekommen** ODER **kriegen** to have a baby; **das ~ beim Namen nennen** to be frank; **das ~ mit dem Bade ausschütten** to throw out the baby with the bathwater; **kein ~ von Traurigkeit sein** to enjoy life; **mit ~ und Kegel** with the whole tribe; **sich bei jm lieb ~ machen** *fam* to suck up to sb, to lick sb's boots.

**Kinderlarbeit** *die* child labour.

**Kinderlarzt, ärztin** *der, die* paediatrician.

**Kinderlbuch** *das* children's book.

**Kinderei** (*pl* -en) *die* childish behaviour (*U*).

**Kindererziehung** *die* bringing up of children.

**kinderfeindlich** *adj* [Person] unfriendly to children; [Umgebung] child-unfriendly.

**Kinderlfest** *das* children's party.

**Kinderlfrau** *die* nanny; [Tagesmutter] child minder.

**Kinderlfreibetrag** *der* child allowance.

**kinderfreundlich** *adj* [Person] fond of children; [Umgebung] child-friendly.

**Kinderlfunk** *der* children's radio.

**Kinderlgarten** *der* nursery school.

**Kinderlgärtner, in** *der, die* = **Erzieher.**

**Kinderlgeld** *das* child benefit.

**Kindergottesldienst** *der* children's service.

**Kinderlheim** *das* children's home.

**Kinderlhort** *der* *day centre where children can spend the afternoon after lessons have finished.*

**Kinderlkrankheit** *die* illness affecting children.

**Kinderlkrippe** *die* crèche.

**Kinderllähmung** *die* polio.

**kinderleicht** *adj fam* dead easy; **es war ~** it was child's play.

**kinderlieb** *adj* fond of children.

**Kinderllied** *das* nursery rhyme.

**kinderlos** *adj* childless.

**Kinderlmädchen** *das* nursemaid.

**kinderreich** *adj:* **eine ~e Familie** a large family, a family with lots of children.

**Kinderlschreck** *der* bogeyman.

**Kinderlschuh** *der* children's shoe; **noch in den ~en stecken** *fig* to be in its infancy.

**Kinderschutzlbund** *der* child protection league.

**kindersicher** *adj* childproof ◇ *adv* [aufbewahren] out of the reach of children.

**Kinderlsicherung** *die* [an Auto] childproof lock.

**Kinderlsitz** *der* child seat.

**Kinderlspiel** *das* children's game; **ein ~ sein** to be child's play; **es ist kein ~** it's not exactly child's play.

**Kinderlsprache** *die* baby talk.

**Kinderlsterblichkeit** *die* infant mortality.

**Kinderlstube** *die:* **eine gute/schlechte ~ haben** to have been well/badly brought up.

**Kinderlstunde** *die* children's hour.

**Kindertageslstätte** *die* day nursery.

**Kinderlwagen** *der* pram *Br*, baby carriage *Am.*

**Kinderlzimmer** *das* children's bedroom.

**Kindeslalter** *das* childhood; **im ~** as a child, at an early age.

**Kindeslmisshandlung** *die* child abuse.

**kindgerecht** *adj* designed for children.

**Kindheit** *die* childhood; **von ~ an** from an early age.

**kindisch** *abw adj* childish ⟨> *adv* childishly.

**kindlich** *adj* childlike ⟨> *adv* like a child.

**Kinn** (*pl* -e) *das* chin.

**Kinnlhaken** *der* hook (to the chin).

**Kinnlade** (*pl* -n) *die* (lower) jaw.

**Kino** (*pl* -s) *das* cinema, movie theater *Am;* **ins ~ gehen** to go to the movies, to go to the cinema.

**Kinolbesucher, in** *der, die* moviegoer, cinemagoer.

**Kinolprogramm** *das* movie guide, cinema guide.

**Kinshasa** *nt* Kinshasa.

**Kiosk** (*pl* -e) *der* kiosk.

**Kippe** (*pl* -n) *die* - **1.** *fam* [Zigarette] ciggy, fag *Br* - **2.** *fam* [Zigarettenstummel] cigarette butt, fag end *Br* - **3.** *RW:* **auf der ~ stehen** [zu fallen drohen] to be precariously balanced; [gefährdet oder unsicher sein] to be in the balance.

**kippelig** *adj* wobbly, unsteady.

**kippen** (*perf* **hat/ist gekippt**) *vi (ist)* to topple ⟨> *vt (hat)* - **1.** [Fenster, Möbel] to tilt - **2.** [Flüssigkeit] to tip - **3.** *fam* [Schnaps] to knock back.

**Kipplfenster** *das* tilting window.

**Kirche** (*pl* -n) *die* church; **in die ~ gehen** to go to church; **die ~ fängt um 9 Uhr an** the service starts at 9 o'clock; **lass die ~ im Dorf** *fig* don't overdo it.

**Kirchenlchor** *der* church choir.

**Kirchenlgemeinde** *die* [Bezirk] parish; [Gottesdienstteilnehmer] congregation.

**Kirchenlgeschichte** *die* church history.

**Kirchenlkonzert** *das* church concert.

**Kirchenlmaus** *die:* **arm sein wie eine ~** to be as poor as a church mouse.

**Kirchenlmusik** *die* church music.

**Kirchenlschiff** *das* ARCHIT nave.

**Kirchenlsteuer** *die* church tax.

**Kirchenltag** *der church rally.*

**KIRCHENTAG**

The Congress of German Catholics and the Congress of the German Protestant Church are huge gatherings, during which the Churches outline their respective views on various topical issues affecting aspects of social, political and religious life and give support to major charities.

**Kirchlgang** *der* churchgoing.

**Kirchgänger, in** (*mpl* -; *fpl* -nen) *der, die* churchgoer.

**kirchlich** *adj* church (*vor Subst*) ⟨> *adv:* **sich ~ trauen lassen** to have a church wedding.

**Kirchlturm** *der* [mit Spitze] steeple; [ohne Spitze] church tower.

**Kirmes** *die* fair.

**kirre** *adj fam:* **jn ~ machen** to wrap sb round one's little finger.

**Kirschlbaum** *der* cherry tree.

**Kirsche** (*pl* -n) *die* cherry; **mit ihm ist nicht gut ~n essen** he's liable to fly off the handle at any minute.

**Kirschltorte** *die:* **Schwarzwälder ~** Black Forest gâteau.

**Kirschwasser** *das* kirsch.

**Kissen** (*pl* -) *das* [auf Stuhl, Sofa] cushion; [für Bett] pillow.

**Kissenlbezug** *der* - **1.** [für Bettkissen] pillow case - **2.** [für Sofakissen] cushion cover.

**Kiste** (*pl* -n) *die* - **1.** [Behälter] crate, box; **eine ~ Wein** a case of wine - **2.** *fam* [Auto] jalopy, banger *Br.*

**kistenweise** *adv* by the crate.

**Kita** (*pl* -s) *die fam* day nursery.

**Kitsch** *der* kitsch.

**kitschig** *adj* kitschy.

**Kitt** *der* putty.

**Kittchen** (*pl* -) *das fam* nick *Br,* can *Am;* **ins ~ kommen** *fam* to get banged up; **im ~ sein** ODER **sitzen** *fam* to be in the nick *Br* ODER can *Am.*

**Kittel** (*pl* -) *der* [für Werkstatt] overalls (*pl*); [für Arzt] white coat; [für Labor] lab coat.

**Kittellschürze** (*pl* -n) *die* housecoat.

**kitten** *vt* - **1.** [kleben] to glue together - **2.** [Ehe] to patch up.

**Kitzel** (*pl* -) *der* thrill.

**kitzelig** = **kitzlig.**

**kitzeln** *vt* - **1.** [krabbeln] to tickle; **jn an den Füßen ~** to tickle sb's feet - **2.** [reizen - Ehrgeiz] *fam* to arouse.

**kịtzlig, kịtzelig** adj - **1.** [empfindlich] ticklish - **2.** [heikel] tricky.

**Kịwi** (pl -s) die kiwi fruit.

**kJ** (abk für **Kilojoule**) kJ.

**Kl.** abk für **Klasse.**

**Klạcks** (pl -e) der fam: **das ist ein ~** it's a piece of cake.

**klạffen** vi to gape.

**klạffen** vi abw to yap.

**klạffend** adj gaping.

**Klage** (pl -n) die - **1.** [Beschwerde] complaint - **2.** RECHT action, suit; **gegen jn ~ einreichen** to bring an action against sb.

**klagen** vi - **1.** [jammern] to complain; **über jn/ etw ~** to complain about sb/sthg; **über Rückenschmerzen ~** to complain of backache - **2.** [vor Gericht]: **gegen jn ~** to take legal action against sb; **auf Schadenersatz ~** to sue for damages <> vt: **jm seine Not ~** to pour out one's troubles to sb.

**Klagenfurt** nt Klagenfurt.

**Kläger, in** (mpl -; fpl -nen) der, die RECHT plaintiff.

**klaglos** adv uncomplainingly.

**Klamauk** der (ohne pl) - **1.** [Lärm] racket - **2.** [Komik] slapstick.

**klạmm** adj - **1.** [Hände] numb - **2.** [Wäsche] clammy.

**Klạmmer** (pl -n) die - **1.** [für Blätter] paper clip; [für Wäsche] (clothes) peg Br, clothespin Am; [für Wunde, von Heftmaschine] staple; [für Zähne] brace - **2.** [Symbol] bracket; **etw in ~n setzen** to bracket sthg; **in ~n stehen** to be in brackets.

**Klạmmerlaffe** der fam EDV at-sign.

**klạmmern** vt: **etw an etw** (A) **~** to attach sthg to sthg.

↪ **sich klammern** ref: **sich an jn/etw ~** eigtl & fig to cling to sb/sthg.

**klạmmheimlich** adj secret <> adv secretly.

**Klamọtten** pl fam gear (U), clothes.

**klạng** prät ▷ **klingen.**

**Klạng** (pl **Klänge**) der sound.

**klạnglich** adj tonal <> adv tonally.

**klạngvoll** adj MUS melodious.

**Klạpplbett** das folding bed.

**Klạppe** (pl -n) die - **1.** [Gegenstand] flap; [bei Blasinstrument, Motor] valve; [bei Film] clapperboard; „**~ die Fünfte**" "take five" - **2.** fam [Mund] trap; **die ~ halten** to shut one's trap; **eine große ~ haben** to have a big mouth.

**klạppen** vt: **etw nach oben/unten ~** [Sitz] to tip sthg forward/back <> vi [gelingen] to work, to come off; **hat alles geklappt?** did everything

go OK?; **es klappt (gut)** it works; **es klappt nicht** it doesn't work.

**klạpperdürr** adj fam as thin as a rake.

**klạpperig** = klapprig.

**klạppern** vi [Tür, Fensterladen] to rattle; [Kastagnette] to clack (together); **ich klappere mit den Zähnen** my teeth are chattering.

**Klạpperlstorch** der fam stork.

**Klạpplrad, Klạppfahrrad** das folding bicycle.

**klạpprig, klạpperig** adj - **1.** [Gegenstand] rickety - **2.** [Person] doddery.

**Klạpplsitz** der folding seat.

**Klạpplstuhl** der folding chair.

**Klạppltisch** der folding table.

**Klạps** (pl -e) der [leichter Schlag] pat; **einen ~ haben** fam fig to have a screw loose.

**Klạpslmühle** die fam loony bin.

**klar** adj - **1.** [gen] clear; **mir ist nicht ~, wie das funktioniert** I'm not clear how it works; **ist dir das jetzt ~?** do you understand now?; **na ~!** of course! - **2.** [bewusst]: **sich** (D) **über etw** (A) **im Klaren sein** to be aware of sthg <> adv - **1.** [deutlich] clearly - **2.** [fertig]: **~ zu etw** ready for sthg.

↪ **alles klar** interj: **alles ~?** OK?; **alles ~!** OK!

↪ **klar und deutlich** adj perfectly clear <> adv quite clearly.

**Klärlanlage** die sewage works (sg).

**Klare** (pl -n) der schnapps.

**klären** vt [Problem, Angelegenheit] to clear up.

**klarlgehen** (perf ist **klargegangen**) vi (unreg) fam to go OK.

**Klarheit** die [Gewissheit, Deutlichkeit] clarity; **über etw** (A) **~ gewinnen** ODER **bekommen** to clarify sthg; **sich** (D) **~ verschaffen** to get sthg clear.

**Klarinẹtte** (pl -n) die clarinet.

**klarlkommen** (perf ist **klargekommen**) vi (unreg): **mit jm/etw ~** to be able to cope with sb/ sthg.

**klar machen** vt: **jm etw ~** to explain sthg to sb, to make sthg clear to sb.

**klar sehen** vi (unreg) to see clearly; **in etw** (D) **~** to be able to understand sthg.

**Klarsichtlfolie** die transparent film, clingfilm Br.

**Klarsichtlhülle** die plastic cover.

**klarlstellen** vt [Problem, Frage] to clear up; **~, dass ...** to make it clear that ...

**Klartext** der: **im ~** in plain English; **~ reden** ODER **sprechen** to speak plainly.

**Klärung** (pl -en) die clearing up.

**klar werden** (perf ist **klar geworden**) vi (un-

*reg)*: **jm ~** to become clear to sb; **sich** *(D)* **über etw ~** to be able to understand sthg.

**klasse** *adj fam* great, neat *Am.*

**Klasse** *(pl -n) die* - **1.** [gen] class; **erster/zweiter ~** first/second class - **2.** [Zimmer] classroom - **3.** [Schuljahr] form *Br,* grade *Am;* **eine ~ wiederholen** to repeat a year.

**Klassenlarbeit** *die* class test.

**Klassenlfahrt** *die* class outing.

**Klassenlkamerad, in** *der, die* classmate.

**Klassenlkampf** *der* POL class war.

**Klassenllehrer, in** *der, die* class teacher.

**Klassenltreffen** *das* class reunion.

**Klassenlunterschied** *der* - **1.** POL class difference - **2.** [Leistungsvermögen] difference in class.

**Klassenlzimmer** *das* classroom.

**klassifizieren** *vt* to classify.

**Klassik** *die (ohne pl)* - **1.** [Epoche] classical period - **2.** [Antike]: **die ~** classical antiquity - **3.** [Musik] classical music - **4.** [Literatur] classical literature.

**Klassiker, in** *(mpl -; fpl -nen) der, die* - **1.** [Dichter] classical author; **die ~ lesen** to read the classics - **2.** [Referenz] classic.

**klassisch** *adj* - **1.** [Kunst, Kultur] classical - **2.** [Fehler] classic.

**Klassizismus** *der* classicism.

**Klatsch** *der fam* [Gerede] gossip.

**Klatschlbase** *die fam* gossip.

**klatschen** *(perf* **hat/ist geklatscht)** *vi* - **1.** *(hat)* [schlagen] to slap; **in die Hände ~** to clap (one's hands) - **2.** *(hat)* [Publikum] to clap - **3.** *(ist)* [Regen] to drum; [Wellen] to slap - **4.** *(hat) fam* [tratschen]: **über jn/etw ~** to gossip about sb/ sthg *vt:* **Beifall ~** to applaud; **jm eine ~** *fam* to give sb a slap.

**klatschnass** *adj fam* soaking wet.

**Klaue** *(pl -n) die* - **1.** [von Adler, Löwen] claw; [von Kühen, Schafen] hoof; **in js** ODER **jm in die ~n geraten** to fall into sb's clutches - **2.** *fam* [Schrift] scrawl.

**klauen** *fam vt* to pinch, to nick *Br;* **jm etw ~** to pinch sthg from sb, to nick sthg off sb *Br* *vi* [stehlen]: **hier wird viel geklaut** a lot of stuff gets pinched ODER nicked *Br* round here.

**Klausel** *(pl -n) die* clause.

**Klausur** *(pl -en) die* UNI exam.

**Klavier** [kla'viːɐ] *(pl -e) das* piano; **~ spielen** to play the piano.

**Klavierlkonzert** *das* - **1.** [Musikstück] piano concerto - **2.** [Konzert] piano recital.

**Klavierlstimmer, in** *(mpl -; fpl -nen) der, die* piano tuner.

**Klavierlstunde** *die* piano lesson.

**Klebeband** *(pl -bänder) das* adhesive tape.

**kleben** *vt* - **1.** [ankleben] to stick, to glue; [reparieren] to stick ODER glue together - **2.** *fam* [ohrfeigen]: **jm eine ~** to stick one on sb *vi* [halten]: **an etw** *(D)* **~ eigtl** & *fig* to stick to sthg.

**Kleber** *(pl -) der* adhesive.

**Klebelstreifen** *der* adhesive tape.

**klebrig** *adj* sticky.

**Kleblstoff** *der* adhesive, glue.

**kleckern** *vi* [verschütten] to make a mess; **du hast gekleckert** [beim Essen] you've spilt your food *vt* [verschütten] to spill.

**Klecks** *(pl -e) der* [von Farbe, Senf] blob; [von Tinte] blot.

**klecksen** *vi* to blot.

**Klee** *der* clover; **jn/etw über den grünen ~ loben** *fam* to praise sb/sthg to the skies.

**Kleelblatt** *das* clover leaf.

**Kleid** *(pl -er) das* [Frauenkleid] dress.
↞ **Kleider** *pl* [Kleidungsstücke] clothes.

**kleiden** *vt* [anziehen] to dress.
↞ **sich kleiden** *ref geh* to dress.

**Kleiderlbügel** *der* coathanger.

**Kleiderlbürste** *die* clothes brush.

**Kleiderlhaken** *der* coat hook.

**Kleiderlschrank** *der* - **1.** [Möbelstück] wardrobe, closet *Am* - **2.** *fam* [Mann] man mountain.

**Kleidung** *(pl -en) die* clothes *(pl),* clothing.

**Kleidungslstück** *das* piece of clothing, garment.

**Kleie** *(pl -n) die* bran.

**klein** *adj* - **1.** [räumlich] small, little; **mein ~er Finger** my little finger; **bis ins Kleinste** to the last detail - **2.** [temporal] short; **eine ~e Pause** a short break - **3.** [jung] little; **mein ~er Bruder** my little brother; **von ~ auf** since he/she/*etc* was little - **4.** [unerheblich] little; **meine ~ste Sorge** the least of my worries; **~e Leute** ordinary people; **ein ~er Geschäftsmann** a small businessman; **aus ~en Verhältnissen stammen** to come from a humble background; **die Herdplatte ~ stellen** to turn the hotplate down *adv:* **ein ~ wenig** a little bit; **haben Sie es nicht ~er?** *fig* don't you have anything smaller?

**Kleinlanzeige** *die* small ad *Br,* want ad *Am.*

**Kleinlasien** *das* Asia Minor.

**Kleinlbahn** *die* narrow gauge railway.

**Kleinlbürger, in** *der, die* [Spießbürger] petty bourgeois.

**kleinbürgerlich** *abw adj* petty bourgeois *adv* in a petty bourgeois way.

**K**

**Kleine** (pl -n) der, die - **1.** [Kind] little one - **2.** [als Anrede - nett] little one; [ - beleidigend] shorty ◇ das [Baby] little one.

**klein gedruckt** adj in small print.

**Kleingedruckte** das: **das ~** the small print.

**Kleingeld** das change.

**Kleinigkeit** (pl -en) die - **1.** [unwichtig] trifle; **für jn eine/keine ~ sein** to be an/no easy matter for sb - **2.** [klein, wenig]: **eine ~ mitbringen** to bring a little something; **ein paar ~en einkaufen** to buy a few little things - **3.** [zu essen] snack.

**kleinkariert** adj abw narrow-minded.

**Klein|kind** das small child.

**Kleinkram** der (ohne pl) fam - **1.** [Gegenstände] bits and pieces (pl) - **2.** [Angelegenheiten] trifling things (pl).

**klein|kriegen** vt - **1.** [Person]: **jn ~** to bring sb into line; **lass dich davon nicht ~** don't let that get you down - **2.** [Gegenstand]: **etw ist nicht kleinzukriegen** sthg will last forever - **3.** [zerkleinern - mit Messer] to chop up.

**kleinlaut** adj subdued ◇ adv in a subdued manner.

**kleinlich** adj abw petty.

**klein machen** vt - **1.** [Holz, Pappe] to chop up - **2.** [Geldschein] fam to change.
➤ **sich klein machen** ref to bend down.

**klein schneiden** vt (unreg) to chop into small pieces.

**klein|schreiben** vt (unreg) [mit kleinem Anfangsbuchstaben] to write with a small initial letter.

**Klein|schreibung** die use of small initial letters.

**Klein|staat** der small state.

**Klein|stadt** die small town.

**Kleister** (pl -) der paste.

**kleistern** vt to paste.

**Klemme** (pl -n) die - **1.** (ohne pl) fam [Bedrängnis] tight spot; **jm aus der ~ helfen** to help sb out of a tight spot; **in der ~ stecken** ODER **sitzen** ODER **sein** to be in a tight spot - **2.** ELEKTR terminal.

**klemmen** vt - **1.** [feststecken] to jam - **2.** [Finger]: **sich** (D) **etw ~** to get sthg caught ◇ vi [Tür, Schublade] to jam.
➤ **sich klemmen** ref fam: **sich dahinter ~** to get stuck in.

**Klempner, in** (mpl -; fpl -nen) der, die plumber.

**Kleptomane** (pl -n) der kleptomaniac.

**Kleptomanin** (pl -nen) die kleptomaniac.

**Klerus** der (ohne pl) clergy (pl).

**Klette** (pl -n) die - **1.** fam [Mensch] limpet; **wie ei-**
ne **~ an jm hängen** to cling to sb like a limpet - **2.** [Pflanze] burdock.

**klettern** (perf hat/ist geklettert) vi - **1.** (ist) [gen] to climb - **2.** (hat) SPORT to climb.

**Kletter|tour** die climbing expedition.

**Klett|verschluss** der Velcro® fastening.

**klicken** vi to click.

**Klient** (pl -en) der client.

**Klientel** (pl -en) die clientele.

**Klientin** (pl -nen) die client.

**Kliff** (pl -e) das cliff.

**Klima** (pl -s) das climate.

**Klima|anlage** die air conditioning (U).

**klimatisch** adj climatic.

**Klimm|zug** der pull-up.

**klimpern** vi - **1.** [spielen - auf Klavier] to tinkle away; [ - auf Gitarre] to strum - **2.** [schlagen]: **mit den Wimpern ~** to flutter one's eyelashes; **mit dem Geld ~** to jingle some coins.

**Klinge** (pl -n) die blade.

**Klingel** (pl -n) die bell.

**klingeln** vi to ring (the bell); **es hat geklingelt** [an der Tür] there's someone at the door; [in der Schule] the bell has gone; **bei jm ~** to ring sb's bell; **nach jm ~** to ring for sb.

**klingen** (prät klang; perf hat geklungen) vi - **1.** [gen] to sound - **2.** [Glocken, Gläser] to ring.

**Klinik** (pl -en) die clinic.

**klinisch** adj clinical ◇ adv clinically.

**Klinke** (pl -n) die (door) handle; **sich** (D) **die ~ in die Hand geben** fig to be constantly coming and going.

**Klinker** (pl -) der clinker.

**klipp** ➤ **klipp und klar** adv plainly.

**Klipp, Clip** (pl -s) der clip.

**Klippe** (pl -n) die rock; **alle ~n umfahren** to negotiate all obstacles.

**klirren** vi [Scheiben] to rattle; [Gläser] to clink.

**klirrend** adj: **~e Kälte** freezing cold.

**Klischee** (pl -s) das cliché.

**Klischee|vorstellung** die clichéd idea.

**Klitoris** (pl -) die clitoris.

**Klo** (pl -s) das fam loo Br, john Am; **aufs ~ gehen** to go to the loo Br ODER john Am.

**Kloake** (pl -n) die sewer.

**klobig** adj - **1.** [ungeschliffen] clumsy - **2.** [massig - Hände] massive; [ - Stuhl, Bau, Schuhe] clunky.

**Klo|brille** die fam toilet seat.

**Klo|bürste** die fam toilet brush.

**Klo|frau** die fam toilet attendant.

**Klon** (pl -s) der BIOL clone.

**klonen** vt BIOL to clone.

**Klo|papier** das fam toilet paper.

**klopfen** vi - **1.** [Person - an die Tür] to knock; [ - auf den Tisch] to rap; **es hat geklopft** there's someone at the door - **2.** [Herz] to beat <> vt [Teppich, Kissen] to beat.

**klöppeln** vt: **eine Decke ~** to make a lace tablecloth.

**Klops** (pl -e) der meatball.

**Klosett** (pl -e) das toilet.

**Kloß** (pl Klöße) der dumpling; **rohe/gekochte Klöße** dumplings made from raw/cooked potatoes; **einen ~ im Hals haben** fig to have a lump in one's throat.

**Kloster** (pl Klöster) das [für Nonnen] convent; [für Mönche] monastery.

**Kloster|kirche** die [für Nonnen] convent church; [für Mönche] monastery church.

**Klotz** (pl Klötze) der - **1.** block - **2.** [Scheit] log - **3.** abw [Gebäude] concrete block - **4.** RW: **einen ~ am Bein haben** to have a millstone round one's neck.

**klotzig** fam adj [groß] clunky <> adv: **~ verdienen** to earn a packet.

**Klub, Club** (pl -s) der club.

**Klub|mitglied** das club member.

**Klub|sessel** der club chair.

**Kluft** (pl -en ODER Klüfte) die - **1.** (pl Klüfte) [zwischen Gegensätzen] gulf - **2.** (pl Klüfte) [im Fels] cleft - **3.** (pl Kluften) [Kleidung] outfit.

**klug** (kompar klüger; superl klügste) adj - **1.** [schlau] clever - **2.** [weise] wise - **3.** RW: **jd wird aus jm/etw nicht ~** sb can't make sb/ sthg out; **der Klügere gibt nach** discretion is the better part of valour <> adv [umsichtig] wisely.

**Klugheit** (pl -en) die - **1.** [Schläue] cleverness - **2.** [Weisheit] wisdom.

➡ **Klugheiten** pl abw [Binsenweisheiten] clever remarks.

**Klumpen** (pl -) der lump.

**Klüngel** (pl -) der clique.

**klüngeln** vi to engage in cliquishness.

**Klunker** (pl -) der fam [Schmuck] rock.

**km** (abk für Kilometer) km.

**km/h** (abk für Stundenkilometer) kph.

**knabbern** vt to nibble <> vi: **an etw** (D) **~** to nibble sthg; **an etw** (D) **zu ~ haben** fam to have a hard time getting over sthg.

**Knabe** (pl -n) der - **1.** geh [Junge] boy - **2.** fam [Mann] chap.

**Knäcke|brot** das crispbread.

**knacken** vt - **1.** [Nüsse, Finger] to crack - **2.** [mit Gewalt - Schloss] to force; [ - Bank] to break into

- **3.** [Code] to crack <> vi - **1.** [Holz, Finger] to crack; [Feuer, im Radio, Telefon] to crackle - **2.** salopp [schlafen] to crash out - **3.** [an Problemen]: **an etw** (D) **zu ~ haben** fig [sich bemühen] to have one's work cut out with sthg; [die Folgen spüren] to have a hard time getting over sthg.

**knackig** adj - **1.** [Salat] crisp - **2.** salopp [Po] sexy.

**Knacks** (pl -e) der fam [psychischer Schaden]: **einen ~ haben/bekommen** to be/get screwed up.

**Knall** (pl -e) der [von Schuss, Tür] bang; [von Korken] pop; **~ auf Fall** there and then; **einen ~ haben** salopp to be crazy.

**knallen** (perf hat/ist geknallt) vi - **1.** (hat) [Schuss] to ring out; [Peitsche] to crack; [Korken] to pop - **2.** (ist) fam [aufprallen] to crash; **mit dem Kopf auf den Boden ~** to bang one's head on the floor - **3.** (hat) [Sonne] to beat down <> vt - **1.** [werfen] to fling; **die Tür ins Schloss ~** to slam the door - **2.** [ohrfeigen]: **jm eine ~** fam to clout sb.

**Knall|frosch** der jumping jack.

**knallhart** fam adj - **1.** [Geschäft, Person] tough; **sie ist ~** she's as hard as nails - **2.** [Aufschlag, Schuss] thumping <> adv brutally; **~ vorgehen** to take tough action.

**knallrot** adj bright red; **~ werden** fam to go bright red.

**knapp** adj - **1.** [Ergebnis, Rennen] close; [Vorsprung, Stimmenmehrheit] narrow - **2.** [Kleid, Schuhe] tight - **3.** [fast ganz]: **eine ~e Stunde** just under an hour; **das war ~** that was close - **4.** [wenig]: **~ bei Kasse sein** to be short of money; **~ werden** to be running short <> adv - **1.** [um weniges] narrowly - **2.** [eng] tightly; **und nicht zu ~!** fam [sehr viel] and how!

**knapp halten** vt (unreg) fam to keep short.

**knarren** vi to creak.

**Knast** (pl Knäste) der fam clink; **im ~ sein** ODER **sitzen** fam to be in the clink.

**Knatsch** der (ohne pl) fam row; **~ haben** to have trouble.

**knattern** vi [Motor] to roar; [Maschinengewehr] to rattle; [Fahne] to flap.

**Knäuel** (pl -) das ball.

**Knauf** (pl Knäufe) der knob.

**knauserig** adj stingy.

**knausern** vi: **mit etw ~** to be stingy with sthg.

**knautschen** vt & vi to crumple.

**Knautsch|zone** die AUTO crumple zone.

**Knebel** (pl -) der gag.

**knebeln** vt to gag.

**Knecht** (pl -e) der [auf Bauernhof] farmhand; [Diener] servant.

**kneifen** (prät kniff; perf hat gekniffen) vi

**- 1.** [Kleidung] to pinch **- 2.** *fam abw* [sich drücken]: **(vor etw** *(D)*) ~ to duck out (of sthg) <> *vt* to pinch.

**Kneiflzange** *die* pincers *(pl)*.

**Kneipe** *(pl -n) die fam* bar, pub *Br.*

**KNEIPE**

Unlike in British pubs, in a German "Kneipe" light meals are served not only throughout the day but also in the evening. There is usually a waiter or waitress who brings the beer to the tables, and customers pay when they are ready to leave, rather than a round at a time. A feature of many German pubs is the "Stammtisch" which is a table reserved for regular customers. In Austria, "Kneipen" are called "Beisel".

**Kneipenlbummel** *der* pub crawl *Br*, bar hop *Am.*

**Knete** *die* **- 1.** [Modelliermasse] clay **- 2.** *salopp* [Geld] dough.

**kneten** *vt* [Teig, Muskeln] to knead; [Figur] to model.

**Knick** *(pl -e ODER -s) der* **- 1.** *(pl Knicke)* [Falte] crease **- 2.** *(pl Knicke)* [in Straße] sharp bend.

**knicken** *vt* **- 1.** [falten] to fold; **'bitte nicht ~!'** 'please do not bend' **- 2.** [Äste, Blumen] to bend.

**knickrig, knickerig** *adj abw* stingy.

**Knicks** *(pl -e) der* curtsey.

**Knie** *(pl -) das* **- 1.** [Körperteil] knee; **in die ~ gehen** to bend one's knees; [nachgeben] to submit **- 2.** *RW:* **weiche ~ bekommen/haben** to go/be weak at the knees; **etw übers ~ brechen** to rush sthg.

**Knielbeuge** *(pl -n) die* knee-bend.

**Knielgelenk** *das* knee joint.

**Knielkehle** *die* hollow of the knee.

**knielang** *adj* knee-length.

**knien** *vi* to kneel.

➡ **sich knien** *ref* to kneel; **sich in etw** *(A)* **~ fig** to buckle down to sthg.

**Knielscheibe** *die* kneecap.

**Knielschützer** *(pl -) der* kneepad.

**Knielstrumpf** *der* knee-length sock.

**knietief** *adj* knee-deep.

**kniff** *prät* ⇨ **kneifen.**

**Kniff** *(pl -e) der* [Trick] trick.

**knifflig** *adj* tricky.

**knipsen** *fam vi* [fotografieren] to take snaps <> *vt* **- 1.** [Fahrkarte] to punch **- 2.** [fotografieren]: **jn/etw ~** to snap sb/sthg.

**Knirps** *(pl -e) der* [Kind] little lad.

**knirschen** *vi* **- 1.:** **mit den Zähnen ~** to grind one's teeth **- 2.** [Schnee, Sand] to crunch.

**knistern** *vi* [Feuer, brennendes Holz] to crackle; [Papier] to rustle; **mit etw ~** to rustle sthg.

**knitterfrei** *adj* crease-resistant.

**knittern** *vi* to crease.

**knobeln** *vi* **- 1.** [losen] to toss **- 2.** [spielen] to play dice **- 3.** [tüfteln]: **an etw** *(D)* **~** to puzzle over sthg.

**Knoblauch** *der* garlic.

**Knoblauchlzehe** *die* clove of garlic.

**Knöchel** *(pl -) der* ankle.

**knöchellang** *adj* ankle-length.

**Knochen** *(pl -) der* bone; **sich** *(D)* **die ~ brechen** *fam* to break one's neck; **nass bis auf die ~** *fam* soaked to the skin; **sich bis auf die ~ blamieren** *fam* to make a complete and utter fool of o.s.

**Knochenlbruch** *der* fracture.

**Knochenmark** *das* bone marrow.

**knochentrocken** *adj* **- 1.** [ausgetrocknet] bone-dry **- 2.** *fam* [langweilig] dry as dust.

**knochig** *adj* bony.

**Knock-out** [nɔk'aut] *(pl -s) der geh* knockout.

**Knödel** *(pl -) der* dumpling.

**Knolle** *(pl -n) die* BIOL tuber.

**Knopf** *(pl Knöpfe) der* button.

**Knopfdruck** *der:* **auf ~** at the push of a button.

**knöpfen** *vt* to button.

**Knopflloch** *das* buttonhole.

**Knorpel** *(pl -) der* cartilage.

**Knospe** *(pl -n) die* bud.

**knoten** *vt* to tie.

**Knoten** *(pl -) der* **- 1.** [gen] knot **- 2.** MED lump.

**Knotenlpunkt** *der* **- 1.** [von Straßen] junction **- 2.** [wichtiger Ort] centre.

**Know-how** ['nouhau] *(pl -s) das* know-how *(U)*.

**knüllen** *vt* to crumple.

**Knüller** *(pl -) der fam* sensation.

**knüpfen** *vt* to knot; [Netz] to make; **etw an etw** *(A)* **~** [mit Faden] to tie sthg to sthg; *fig* [Erwartungen, Bedingungen] to attach sthg to sthg.

**Knüppel** *(pl -) der* club; **jm einen ~ zwischen die Beine werfen** *fig* to put a spoke in sb's wheel.

**knurren** *vi* **- 1.** [Magen] to rumble **- 2.** [Hund] to growl **- 3.** [Person] to grumble.

**knusprig, knusperig** *adj* crisp <> *adv:* **~ braun** crisp and brown.

**knutschen** *fam vt* to smooch with <> *vi* to smooch.

◆ **sich knutschen** *ref* to smooch.

**Knutschlfleck** *der* lovebite.

**k. o.** [kaːˈoː] *adj:* ~ **sein** *fam* [erschöpft] to be whacked; *SPORT* to be knocked out ◇ *adv:* **jn** ~ **schlagen** to knock sb out.

**K. o.** (*pl* -) *der* knockout.

**Koala** (*pl* -s) *der* koala (bear).

**Koalition** (*pl* -en) *die* coalition.

**Kobalt** *das* *CHEM* cobalt.

**Kobold** (*pl* -e) *der* goblin.

**Koch** [kɔx] (*pl* **Köche** [ˈkœçəl] *der* cook; **viele Köche verderben den Brei** *fig* too many cooks spoil the broth.

**Kochlbuch** *das* cookbook.

**kochen** *vt* - 1. [Essen] to cook; [Kaffee] to make; **jm/sich etw** ~ to cook sb/o.s. sthg - 2. [Wäsche] to boil ◇ *vi* - 1. [Wasser, Person] to boil - 2. [Koch]: **gut/schlecht** ~ to be a good/bad cook.

**Kocher** (*pl* -) *der* stove.

**Kochlgelegenheit** *die* cooking facilities (*pl*).

**Kochlgeschirr** *das* billycan; *MIL* mess tin.

**Köchin** [kœçɪn] (*pl* -nen) *die* cook.

**Kochllöffel** *der* wooden spoon.

**Kochlrezept** *das* recipe.

**Kochlsalz** *das* cooking salt.

**Kochltopf** *der* saucepan.

**Kochlwäsche** *die* washing that needs to be boiled.

**Kode, Code** [ˈkoːt] (*pl* -s) *der* code.

**Köder** (*pl* -) *der* bait.

**ködern** *vt* to lure.

**kodieren, codieren** [koˈdiːrən] *vt* to encode.

**Koedukation** *die* *geh* coeducation.

**Koeffizient** (*pl* -en) *der* *MATH* coefficient.

**Kolexistenz** *die* *POL* coexistence.

**Koffein** *das* caffeine.

**koffeinfrei** *adj* decaffeinated.

**Koffer** (*pl* -) *der* suitcase; **die** ~ **packen** to pack one's bags; **aus dem** ~ **leben** to live out of a suitcase.

**Kofferlradio** *das* portable radio.

**Kofferlraum** *der* boot *Br*, trunk *Am*.

**Kognak** [ˈkɔnjak] (*pl* -s) *der* brandy.

**kohärent** *adj geh* coherent.

**Kohl** *der* cabbage; **das macht den** ~ **auch nicht fett** *fig* that's not much use.

**Kohldampf** *der fam:* ~ **haben** *ODER* **schieben** to be famished.

**Kohle** (*pl* -n) *die* - 1. [Brennstoff] coal *(U);* **wie auf glühenden** ~**n sitzen** *fig* to be like a cat on hot bricks - 2. *fam* [Geld] cash.

**Kohlelkraftwerk** *das* coal-fired power station.

**Kohlenldioxid** *das* carbon dioxide.

**Kohlenhydrat** (*pl* -e) *das* carbohydrate.

**Kohlenlmonoxid** *das* carbon monoxide.

**Kohlenlsäure** *die:* **Mineralwasser mit/ohne** ~ sparkling/still mineral water.

**Kohlenlstoff** *der* carbon *(U).*

**Kohlenlwasserstoff** *der* hydrocarbon.

**Kohlelpapier** *das* carbon paper.

**Kohlelstift** *der* *KUNST* stick of charcoal.

**Kohlelzeichnung** *die* *KUNST* charcoal drawing.

**Kohllkopf** *der* cabbage.

**kohlrabenschwarz** *adj* [Haare] jet-black; [Nacht] pitch-black.

**Kohlrabi** (*pl* - *ODER* -s) *der* kohlrabi.

**Kohllroulade** *die* stuffed cabbage leaves (*pl*).

**Koitus** (*pl* -) *der* *MED* coitus *(U).*

**Koje** (*pl* -n) *die* - 1. *fam* [Bett] bed - 2. [Schiffsbett] bunk.

**Kokain** *das* cocaine.

**kokett** *adj* coquettish ◇ *adv* coquettishly.

**kokettieren** *vi:* **mit jm** ~ to flirt with sb; **mit etw** ~ to make great play of sthg.

**Kokon** [koˈkõ, koˈkɔŋ] (*pl* -s) *der* cocoon.

**Kokoslnuss** *die* coconut.

**Koks** *der* coke.

**Kolben** (*pl* -) *der* - 1. *TECH* piston - 2. *CHEM* flask.

**Kolik, Kolik** (*pl* -en) *die* colic *(U).*

**Kollaps, Kollaps** (*pl* -e) *der* collapse *(sg).*

**Kollege** (*pl* -n) *der* colleague.

**kollegial** *adj* helpful.

**Kollegin** (*pl* -nen) *die* colleague.

**Kollegium** [kɔˈleːgiʊm] (*pl* -gien) *das* [in Schule] teaching staff.

**Kollekte** (*pl* -n) *die* collection.

**Kollektion** (*pl* -en) *die* collection.

**kollektiv** *adj* collective.

**Koller** *der fam:* **einen** ~ **kriegen** to fly into a rage.

**kollidieren** (*perf* ist kollidiert) *vi* - 1. [Fahrzeuge] to collide; **mit etw** ~ to collide with sthg - 2. [Interessen] to clash.

**Kollier** [kɔljeː] (*pl* -s) *das* necklace.

**Kollision** (*pl* -en) *die* collision.

**K**

**Kolloquium, Kollọquium** (pl -quien) das colloquium.

**Kọ̈ln** nt Cologne.

**Kọ̈lner** (pl -) der native/inhabitant of Cologne <> adj (unver): ~ Dom Cologne Cathedral.

**Kọ̈lnerin** (pl -nen) die native/inhabitant of Cologne.

**Kọ̈lnischwạsser**® das eau de cologne.

**Kolonialịsmus** der colonialism.

**Kolonie** [kolo'niːl] (pl -n) die colony.

**Kolọnne** (pl -n) die column; (in) ~ fahren to drive in convoy.

**Kolọss** (pl -e) der colossus.

**kolossal** adj colossal; ein ~er Irrtum a huge mistake.

**Kolumbiạner, in** (mpl -; fpl -nen) der, die Colombian.

**kolumbiạnisch** adj Colombian.

**Kolụmbien** nt Colombia.

**Kolụmne** (pl -n) die column.

**Kọma** (pl -s) das coma.

**Kombinatịon** (pl -en) die - **1.** [Zusammenfügung] combination - **2.** [Schlussfolgerung] deduction - **3.** [Arbeitsanzug] overalls (pl).

**kombinịeren** vi to reason <> vt to combine; etw mit etw ~ to combine sthg with sthg.

**Komẹt** (pl -en) der ASTRON comet.

**Komfort** [kɔm'foːɐ] der: mit allem ~ with all mod cons.

**komfortabel** adj comfortable <> adv [bequem] comfortably.

**Komik** die comic effect.

**Komiker, in** (mpl -; fpl -nen) der, die comedian.

**komisch** adj funny.

**komischerweise** adv funnily enough.

**Komitee** (pl -s) das committee.

**Kọmma** (pl -s ODER -ta) das - **1.** [Satzzeichen] comma - **2.** [mathematisches Zeichen] decimal point.

**Kommandạnt, in** (mpl -en; fpl -nen) der, die [von Festung] commandant; [von Panzer] commander.

**Kommandeur, in** [kɔman'døːɐ, rɪn] (mpl -e; fpl -nen) der, die commander.

**kommandịeren** vt [Soldaten] to command.

**Kommạndo** (pl -s) das - **1.** [gen] command; auf ~ on command; das ~ haben/übernehmen to be in/take command - **2.** [kleine Einheit] detachment.

**kọmmen** (prät kạm; perf ist gekọmmen) vi - **1.** [herkommen] to come; den Arzt ~ lassen to call the doctor - **2.** [ein Ziel erreichen] to get; wie komme ich zum Markt? how do I get to the market?; nach Hause ~ to get home; an die Macht ~ to come to power - **3.** [mit Institutionen] to go; ins/aus dem Krankenhaus ~ to go to/leave hospital; ins Gefängnis ~ to go to jail; in die Schule ~ to start school - **4.** [stammen] to come; aus Deutschland ~ to come from Germany - **5.** [folgen] to come; rechts kommt der Bahnhof the station's coming up on the right; ~ wir nun zu den Sportnachrichten now we come to the sports news; wer kommt zuerst/als Nächster? who's first/next?; von etw ~ to result from sthg; das kommt daher, dass ... it's because ...; das kommt davon! see what happens!; wie kommt es, dass ...? how is it that ...? - **6.** [passieren] to happen; das musste ja so ~! it had to happen!; überraschend ~ to come as a surprise; wie konnte es dazu ~? how could that happen?; etw ~ sehen to see sthg coming - **7.** [Programm, Film]: im Fernsehen ~ to be on (the) television; im Kino ~ to be on at the cinema Br ODER the movies Am - **8.** fam [einen Orgasmus haben] to come - **9.** [hingehören] to go, to belong; die Kisten ~ in den Keller the crates go ODER belong in the cellar - **10.** [anfangen]: ins Schleudern ~ to skid; auf etw (A) zu sprechen ~ to get around to talking about sthg; aus der Mode ~ to go out of fashion - **11.** [mit Dativ]: mir kam eine Idee an idea came to me; jm frech ~ fam to be cheeky to sb - **12.** [figurative Verwendungen mit Präposition]: sie lässt nichts auf ihn ~ she won't have a bad word said about him; auf eine Idee ~ to think of an idea; hinter etw (A) ~ to get to the bottom of sthg; um etw ~ to lose sthg; ums Leben ~ to lose one's life, to die; wieder zu Kräften ~ to regain one's strength; zu sich ~ to came round; dazu ~, etw zu tun to get round to doing sthg - **13.** RW: komm, sei nicht traurig! come on, don't be sad! <> v impers: es kam zu einem Streit there was a quarrel <> vt fam: welchen Weg bist du gekommen? which way did you come?

**Kọmmen** das: ein ~ und Gehen a coming and going; im ~ sein fig to be on the way in.

**kọmmend** adj - **1.** [Woche] coming - **2.** [Generation, Mode] future.

**Kommentar** (pl -e) der - **1.** [in Zeitung, Buch, Radio] commentary - **2.** fam [Bemerkung] comment; kein ~ no comment.

**Kommentator** (pl -toren) der commentator.

**Kommentatorin** (pl -nen) die commentator.

**kommentịeren** vt - **1.** [Ereignis] to comment on - **2.** [Text, Buch] to provide a commentary on.

**kommerziell** *adj* commercial ◇ *adv* commercially.

**Kommilitone** (*pl* -n) *der* UNI fellow student.

**Kommilitonin** (*pl* -nen) *die* UNI fellow student.

**Kommissar, in** (*mpl* -e; *fpl* -nen) *der, die* [bei der Polizei] superintendent *Br*, captain *Am*.

**Kommission** (*pl* -en) *die* commission; etw in ~ geben/nehmen to give/take sthg for sale on commission.

**Kommode** (*pl* -n) *die* chest of drawers.

**kommunal** *adj* local.

**Kommunalpolitik** *die* local politics *(U)*.

**kommunalpolitisch** *adj* of local politics.

**Kommunal|wahl** *die* local election.

**Kommune** (*pl* -n) *die* - **1.** [Gemeinde] local authority - **2.** [Wohngemeinschaft] commune.

**Kommunikation** (*pl* -en) *die* communication.

**Kommunion** (*pl* -en) *die* REL Communion *(U)*.

**Kommuniqué, Kommunikee** [kɔmyni'keː] (*pl* -s) *das* communiqué.

**Kommunismus** *der* Communism.

**Kommunist, in** (*mpl* -en; *fpl* -nen) *der, die* Communist.

**kommunistisch** *adj* Communist.

**Komödiant, in** (*mpl* -en; *fpl* -nen) *der, die* actor (*f* actress).

**Komödie** [ko'møːdjə] (*pl* -n) *die* comedy; jm eine ~ vorspielen to put on an act for sb.

**Kompagnon** ['kɔmpanjɔŋ] (*pl* -s) *der* WIRTSCH partner.

**kompakt** *adj* compact ◇ *adv* compactly.

**Kompanie** [kɔmpa'niː] (*pl* -n) *die* MIL company.

**Komparativ** (*pl* -e) *der* GRAM comparative.

**Kompass** (*pl* -e) *der* compass.

**kompatibel** *adj* EDV compatible; mit etw ~ sein to be compatible with sthg.

**Kompatibilität** *die* EDV compatibility.

**kompensieren** *vt* to compensate for.

**kompetent** *adj* competent ◇ *adv* competently.

**Kompetenz** (*pl* -en) *die* competence *(U)*.

**komplementär** *adj* complementary.

**Komplementär|farbe** *die* complementary colour.

**komplett** *adj* complete ◇ *adv* - **1.** [vollständig] fully - **2.** *fam* [völlig] completely.

**komplex** *adj* complex.

**Komplex** (*pl* -e) *der* [gen & PSYCH] complex; ~e haben to have a complex.

**Komplikation** (*pl* -en) *die* complication.

**Kompliment** (*pl* -e) *das* compliment; mein ~! my compliments!; jm ein ~ machen to pay sb a compliment.

**Komplize** (*pl* -n) *der* accomplice.

**kompliziert** *adj* complicated ◇ *adv* in a complicated way.

**Komplizin** (*pl* -nen) *die* accomplice.

**Komplott** (*pl* -e) *das* plot.

**Komponente** (*pl* -n) *die* component.

**komponieren** *vt* [zusammenstellen & MUS] to compose.

**Komponist, in** (*mpl* -en; *fpl* -nen) *der, die* composer.

**Komposition** *die* [Zusammenstellung & MUS] composition.

**Kompositum** (*pl* -ta) *das* GRAM compound.

**Kompost, Kompost** (*pl* -e) *der* compost *(U)*.

**Kompost|haufen, Komposthaufen** *der* compost heap.

**kompostieren** *vt* to compost.

**Kompott** (*pl* -e) *das* stewed fruit.

**Kompresse** (*pl* -n) *die* compress.

**Kompromiss** (*pl* -e) *der* compromise; einen ~ schließen to compromise.

**kompromissbereit** *adj* ready to compromise.

**Kompromissbereitschaft** *die* readiness to compromise.

**kompromisslos** *adj* uncompromising ◇ *adv* uncompromisingly.

**kondensieren** *vt* & *vi* to condense.

**Kondensmilch** *die* condensed milk.

**Kondenswasser** *das* condensation.

**Kondition** (*pl* -en) *die* condition.

**Konditional** (*pl* -e) *der* GRAM conditional.

**Konditions|training** *das* fitness training.

**Konditor** (*pl* -toren) *der* pastry cook.

**Konditorei** (*pl* -en) *die* cake shop.

**Konditorin** (*pl* -nen) *die* pastry cook.

**kondolieren** *vi* to express one's condolences.

**Kondom** (*pl* -e) *das* condom.

**Konfekt** (*pl* -e) *das* confectionery *(U)*.

**Konfektion** (*pl* -en) *die* - **1.** [Kleidung] ready-to-wear clothes (*pl*) - **2.** [Herstellung] manufacture of ready-to-wear clothes.

**Konferenz** (*pl* -en) *die* - **1.** [Tagung] conference - **2.** [Besprechung] meeting.

**Konferenz|schaltung** *die* TELEKOM conference system.

**Konferenz|tisch** *der* conference table.

**Konfession** (*pl* -en) *die* REL denomination.

**konfessionell** *adj* denominational ◇ *adv* denominationally.

**konfessionslos** *adj* belonging to no religious denomination.

**Konfetti** *das* confetti.

**Konfiguration** (*pl* -en) *die* EDV configuration.

**Konfirmand, in** (*mpl* -en; *fpl* -nen) *der, die* REL confirmand.

**Konfirmation** (*pl* -en) *die* REL confirmation.

**konfirmieren** *vt* REL to confirm.

**Konfitüre** (*pl* -n) *die* geh jam.

**Konflikt** (*pl* -e) *der* conflict; mit etw in ~ geraten ODER kommen to come into conflict with sthg.

**Konflikt|situation** *die* conflict situation.

**konform** *adj* concurrent; mit jm/etw ~ gehen geh to concur with sb/sthg ◇ *adv:* sich ~ verhalten to behave like everyone else.

**konformistisch** *abw adj* conformist ◇ *adv* in a conformist way.

**Konfrontation** (*pl* -en) *die* confrontation.

**konfrontieren** *vt:* jn mit jm/etw ~ to confront sb with sb/sthg.

**konfus** *adj* confused ◇ *adv* confusedly.

**Kongo** *der:* der ~ the Congo.

**Kongress** (*pl* -e) *der* - **1.** [Tagung] conference - **2.** POL Congress.

**Kongress|halle** *die* conference hall.

**König** (*pl* -e) *der* - **1.** [gen] king; die Heiligen Drei ~e the Three Wise Men - **2.** [Feiertag]: Heilige Drei ~e Epiphany.

**Königin** (*pl* -nen) *die* queen.

**königlich** *adj* - **1.** [des Monarchen] royal - **2.** [reichlich - Mahl] lavish; [ - Trinkgeld, Geschenk] handsome; [ - Vergnügen] tremendous ◇ *adv* - **1.** [riesig] tremendously - **2.** [bewirten] lavishly.

**König|reich** *das* kingdom.

**Königsberg** *nt* Königsberg.

**konisch** *adj* conical ◇ *adv* conically.

**Konjugation** (*pl* -en) *die* GRAM conjugation.

**konjugieren** *vt* GRAM to conjugate.

**Konjunktiv** (*pl* -e) *der* GRAM subjunctive.

**Konjunktur** (*pl* -en) *die* economic situation; rückläufige ~ declining economic activity; ~ haben to be in demand.

**konjunkturell** *adj* economic; [Arbeitslosigkeit] due to the economic situation ◇ *adv* economically; ~ bedingt due to the economic situation.

**konkav** *adj* concave ◇ *adv* concavely.

**konkret** *adj* concrete ◇ *adv* concretely.

**Konkurrent, in** (*mpl* -en; *fpl* -nen) *der, die* competitor.

**Konkurrenz** (*pl* -en) *die* competition; jm ~ machen to compete with sb.
➥ außer Konkurrenz *adv* as an unofficial competitor.

**konkurrenzfähig** *adj* competitive ◇ *adv* competitively.

**Konkurrenz|kampf** *der* competition.

**konkurrenzlos** *adj* unbeatable ◇ *adv* unbeatably.

**Konkurs** (*pl* -e) *der* - **1.** [Zahlungsunfähigkeit] bankruptcy; ~ anmelden to declare o.s. bankrupt - **2.** [Verfahren] bankruptcy proceedings (*pl*).

**Konkurs|verfahren** *das* bankruptcy proceedings (*pl*).

**können** (*präs* kann; *prät* konnte; *perf* hat können ODER hat gekonnt) *aux* - **1.** [vermögen, dürfen] can; etw tun ~ to be able to do sthg; ich kann Klavier spielen he can play the piano; kann ich noch ein Eis haben? can I have another ice cream?; könnte ich mal telefonieren? could I use the telephone? - **2.** [zum Ausdruck der Möglichkeit] can; es könnte verloren gegangen sein it could ODER might have got lost; etw tun ~ to be able to do sthg; sie kann nicht kommen she can't come; es kann sein, dass ich mich geirrt habe I may have been wrong; das kann schon sein that's quite possible; das kann nicht sein it can't be, it's impossible; wenn ich wollte, könnte ich ein Auto kaufen I could buy a car if I wanted to; man kann nie wissen you never know ◇ *vi:* fahren, so schnell man kann to drive as fast as you can; kann ich ins Kino? can I go to the cinema?; ich kann nicht mehr *fam* I've had it, I'm exhausted ◇ *vt (perf hat gekonnt)* - **1.** [vermögen]: kannst du Deutsch? can ODER do you speak German?; etw auswendig ~ to know sthg by heart; der kann nichts he's useless; ich kann nichts dafür I can't help it; er kann nichts dafür, dass ... it's not his fault that ... - **2.** RW: du kannst mich mal! *vulg* piss off!

**Können** *das* (*ohne pl*) ability; sein ~ unter Beweis stellen to prove one's ability.

**Könner, in** (*mpl* -; *fpl* -nen) *der, die* expert.

**könnte** *prät* ▷ können.

**Konsens** (*pl* -e) *der* geh [Übereinstimmung] consensus.

**konsequent** *adj* - **1.** [folgerichtig] consistent - **2.** [Gegner] resolute; [Nichtraucher, Christ] strict ◇ *adv* - **1.** [folgerichtig] consistently - **2.** [bekämpfen] resolutely.

**Konsequenz** (*pl* -en) *die* - **1.** [Folge] consequence; aus etw die ~en ziehen to draw the

obvious conclusion from sthg - **2.** [Unbeirr-
barkeit] resolution.

**konservativ** [kɔnzɛrva'tiːf] *adj* conservative
<> *adv* conservatively.

**Konservative** [kɔnzɛrva'tiːvə] (*pl* -n) *der, die*
Conservative.

**Konservatorium** [kɔnzɛrva'toːrjʊm] (*pl* -rien)
*das* conservatory.

**Konserve** [kɔn'zɛrvə] (*pl* -n) *die* [Dose] can, tin
*Br*; sich nur von ~n ernähren to live only on tinned *Br ODER* canned *Am* food.

**Konservenldose** *die* can, tin *Br*.

**konservieren** [kɔnzɛr'viːrən] *vt* to preserve.

**Konservierungsstoffe**        [kɔnzɛr'viːrʊŋs-
ʃtɔfəl] *pl* preservatives.

**Konsistenz** *die geh* consistency.

**Konsonant** (*pl* -en) *der* consonant.

**konspirativ** *adj* conspiratorial <> *adv* con-
spiratorially.

**konstant** *adj* constant <> *adv* constantly.

**Konstante** (*pl* -n) *die* - **1.** MATH, PHYS constant
- **2.** [konstanter Faktor] constant factor.

**Konstellation** (*pl* -en) *die* - **1.** *geh* [Lage] situation - **2.** ASTRON constellation.

**Konstitution** (*pl* -en) *die* constitution.

**konstruieren** [kɔnstru'iːrən] *vt* - **1.** [bauen] to
construct - **2.** *abw* [erfinden] to fabricate.

**Konstrukteur, in** [kɔnstrʊk'tøːʁ, rɪn] (*mpl* -e;
*fpl* -nen) *der, die* designer.

**Konstruktion** (*pl* -en) *die* construction.

**konstruktiv** *adj* - **1.** [vernünftig] constructive
- **2.** [planerisch] structural <> *adv* constructively.

**Konsul** (*pl* -n) *der* POL consul.

**Konsulat** (*pl* -e) *das* POL consulate.

**Konsulin** (*pl* -nen) *die* POL consul.

**konsultieren** *vt geh* to consult.

**Konsum** *der* [Verbrauch] consumption.

**Konsument, in** (*mpl* -en; *fpl* -nen) *der, die*
consumer.

**Konsumlgesellschaft** *die* consumer society.

**konsumieren** *vt* to consume.

**Konsumlverhalten** *das* consumer behaviour.

**Kontakt** (*pl* -e) *der* contact; mit jm ~ aufnehmen to get in touch with sb; zu *ODER* mit jm/
etw ~ haben to be in contact with sb/sthg.

**kontaktarm** *adj*: er ist ~ he finds it difficult
to make friends.

**kontaktfreudig** *adj* sociable.

**Kontaktllinse** *die* contact lens.

**kontern** *vt* & *vi* to counter.

**Kontext** (*pl* -e) *der* context.

**Kontinent, Kontinent** (*pl* -e) *der* continent.

**kontinental** *adj* continental.

**Kontingent** (*pl* -e) *das* [von Waren] quota; [von
Truppen] contingent.

**Kontinuität** [kɔntinui'tɛːt] *die* continuity.

**Konto** (*pl* Konten) *das* [Bankkonto] account; ein
~ eröffnen/auflösen to open/close an account; etw geht auf js ~ sb is to blame for
sthg.

**Kontolauszug** *der* bank statement.

**Kontolführung** *die* account management
*(U)*.

**Kontolnummer** *die* account number.

**Kontolstand** *der* bank balance.

**kontra, contra** *präp* versus <> *adv*: ~ eingestellt sein to be against.

**Kontra** (*pl* -s) *das* double; jm ~ geben *fam* to
contradict sb.

**Kontralbass** *der* double bass.

**konträr** *adj geh* contrary.

**Kontrast** (*pl* -e) *der* contrast; einen ~ zu etw
bilden to contrast with sthg.

**Kontrastlmittel** *das* contrast medium.

**Kontrolllabschnitt** *der* stub.

**Kontrolle** (*pl* -n) *die* - **1.** [Überwachung] check;
jn/etw unter ~ haben to keep a check on sb/
sthg - **2.** [Beherrschung] control; jn/etw unter
~ bekommen/haben to get/have sb/sthg
under control; die ~ über jn/etw verlieren to
lose control of sb/sthg; die ~ über sich verlieren to lose control.

**Kontrolleur, in** [kɔntrɔ'løːʁ, rɪn] (*mpl* -e; *fpl*
-nen) *der, die* inspector.

**kontrollieren** *vt* - **1.** [überprüfen] to check
- **2.** [überwachen] to keep a check on - **3.** [be-
herrschen] to control.

**Kontrolllturm** *der* FLUG control tower.

**kontrovers** [kɔntro'vɛrs] *geh adj* - **1.** [gegensätz-
lich - Standpunkt] conflicting; [ - Diskussion] adver-
sarial - **2.** [umstritten] controversial <> *adv*:
etw ~ diskutieren to discuss sthg from conflicting points of view.

**Kontroverse** [kɔntro'vɛrsə] (*pl* -n) *die geh* dispute.

**Kontur** (*pl* -en) *die* contour; [von Politiker] profile; ~ gewinnen/verlieren to take/lose
shape.

**Konvention** [kɔnvɛn'tsjoːn] (*pl* -en) *die* convention.

**konventionell** [kɔnvɛntsjo'nɛl] *adj* conventional <> *adv* conventionally.

**K**

**Konversation** [kɔnvɛrzaˈtsjoːn] (pl -en) die geh conversation; **(mit jm) ~ machen** ODER **treiben** to make conversation (with sb).

**konvertieren** [kɔnvɛrˈtiːrən] (perf **hat/ist konvertiert**) vt & vi to convert.

**konvex** [kɔnˈvɛks] adj convex <> adv convexly.

**Konvoi** [kɔnˈvɔy] (pl -s) der convoy; **im ~ fahren** to drive in convoy.

**Konzentrat** (pl -e) das concentrate.

**Konzentration** (pl -en) die concentration.

**Konzentrationsfähigkeit** die (ohne pl) powers (pl) of concentration.

**Konzentrationslager** das concentration camp.

**konzentrieren** vt - **1.** [richten]: **etw auf etw** (A) **~** to concentrate sthg on sthg - **2.** [vereinigen] to concentrate.

**~ sich konzentrieren** ref to concentrate; **sich auf etw** (A) **~** to concentrate on sthg.

**konzentriert** adj concentrated <> adv with concentration; **~ nachdenken** to concentrate.

**Konzept** (pl -e) das - **1.** [Entwurf] draft - **2.** [Plan] plan - **3.** RW: **jm nicht ins ~ passen** not to fit in with sb's plans; **jn aus dem ~ bringen** to put sb off his/her stride.

**Konzeption** (pl -en) die concept.

**Konzern** (pl -e) der group (of companies).

**Konzert** (pl -e) das [Veranstaltung] concert; [Musikstück] concerto.

**Konzertflügel** der concert grand.

**Konzertsaal** der concert hall.

**Konzession** (pl -en) die - **1.** WIRTSCH licence - **2.** [Zugeständnis] concession; **(jm/an etw** (A)) **~en machen** to make concessions (to sb/sthg).

**Koordinate** (pl -n) die coordinate.

**Koordinatensystem** das MATH coordinate system.

**koordinieren** vt to coordinate.

**Kopenhagen** nt Copenhagen.

**Kopf** (pl **Köpfe**) der - **1.** [gen] head; **mit dem** ODER **den ~ schütteln** to shake one's head; **jm etw an den ~ werfen** eigtl & fig to hurl sthg at sb - **2.** [Anführer] leader - **3.** RW: **den ~ hängen lassen** to be downhearted; **den ~ hinhalten** to take the blame; **den ~ verlieren** to lose one's head; **jm den ~ verdrehen** fam to turn sb's head; **~ und Kragen riskieren** to risk one's neck; **jm über den ~ wachsen** to overwhelm sb; **~ stehen** [vor Freude] to go wild; [durcheinander sein] to be in a jumble; **jm zu ~ steigen** to go to sb's head; **etw auf den ~ stellen** fam to turn sthg upside down; **und wenn du dich auf den ~ stellst** you're wasting your breath; **sich** (D)

**etw aus dem ~ schlagen** to get sthg out of one's head; **sich** (D) **etw durch den ~ gehen lassen** to think sthg over; **sich** (D) **etw in den ~ setzen** to get sthg into one's head; **sich** (D) **(über etw** (A)) **den ~ zerbrechen** to rack one's brains (over sthg); **über js ~** (A) **hinweg entscheiden** ODER **bestimmen** to decide over sb's head.

**~ aus dem Kopf** adv off the top of one's head.

**~ Kopf an Kopf** adv neck and neck.

**~ pro Kopf** adv per head.

**~ von Kopf bis Fuß** adv from head to toe.

**Kopfball** der header.

**Kopfbedeckung** die headgear.

**Köpfchen** (pl -) das little head; **~ haben** fam fig to have brains.

**köpfen** vt - **1.** SPORT to head - **2.** [hinrichten] to behead - **3.** fam [öffnen - Flasche] to crack open; [ - Ei] to slice the top off <> vi SPORT to head.

**Kopfende** das head.

**Kopfhaut** die scalp.

**Kopfhörer** der headphones (pl).

**Kopfkissen** das pillow.

**Kopfkissenbezug** der pillowcase.

**kopflastig** adj - **1.** [zu intellektuell] over-intellectual - **2.** [übermäßig beladen: Flugzeug] nose-heavy <> adv - **1.** [einseitig intellektuell] over-intellectually - **2.** [einseitig]: **das Flugzeug ~ beladen** to make the plane nose-heavy.

**kopflos** adj - **1.** [ohne Kopf] headless - **2.** [wirr] panicky <> adv in a state of panic.

**Kopfrechnen** das mental arithmetic.

**Kopfsalat** der lettuce.

**Kopfschmerzen** pl headache (sg); **~ haben** to have a headache.

**Kopfsprung** der dive.

**Kopfstand** der headstand.

**kopfstehen** vi (unreg) ⊳ **Kopf.**

**Kopfstütze** die headrest.

**Kopftuch** das headscarf.

**kopfüber** adv - **1.** [nach vorn] head first - **2.** [überstürzt] headlong.

**Kopfzerbrechen** das: **jm ~ machen** ODER **bereiten** to be a real headache for sb.

**Kopie** [koˈpiː] (pl -n) die copy.

**kopieren** vt to copy.

**Kopierer** (pl -) der photocopier.

**Kopiergerät** das photocopier.

**Kopilot, in, Copilot, in** [ˈkoːpiloːt, ɪn] der, die co-pilot.

**koppeln** vt - **1.** [knüpfen] to attach - **2.** [anschließen] to couple.

**Koppelung, Kopplung** (*pl* -en) *die* coupling.

**Ko|produktion** *die* coproduction.

**Koralle** (*pl* -n) *die* coral.

**Koran** (*pl* -e) *der* Koran.

**Korb** (*pl* **Körbe**) *der* - **1.** [Behälter & SPORT] basket - **2.** [Abfuhr] rebuff; **jm einen ~ geben** to turn sb down.

**Korb|stuhl** *der* wicker chair.

**Kord, Cord** [kɔrt] *der* corduroy.

**Kordel** (*pl* -n) *die* cord.

**Kord|hose, Cord|hose** ['kɔrthoːzə] *die* corduroy trousers (*pl*) Br ODER pants (*pl*) Am.

**Kordilleren** *pl:* **die ~** the Cordilleras.

**Korea** *nt* Korea.

**Koreaner, in** (*mpl* -; *fpl* -nen) *der*, *die* Korean.

**koreanisch** *adj* Korean.

**Korinthe** (*pl* -n) *die* currant.

**Kork** *der* cork.

**Korken** (*pl* -) *der* cork.

**Korkenzieher** (*pl* -) *der* corkscrew.

**Korn** (*pl* **Körner** ODER -) *das* - **1.** [Getreide] grain, corn Br - **2.** (*pl* **Körner**) [Pflanzenfrucht, kleines Partikel] grain - **3.** RW: **jn/etw aufs ~ nehmen** fam fig to hit out at sb/sthg <> *der* (*pl* **Korn**) [Schnaps] schnapps.

**Korn|blume** *die* cornflower.

**Korn|feld** *das* cornfield Br, grainfield Am.

**Körper** (*pl* -) *der* body.

**Körperbau** *der* build.

**körperbehindert** *adj* disabled.

**Körper|behinderte** *der*, *die* disabled person.

**Körper|gewicht** *das* amt weight.

**Körper|größe** *die* amt height.

**körperlich** *adj* physical <> *adv* physically.

**Körperpflege** *die* personal hygiene.

**Körperschaft** (*pl* -en) *die* RECHT corporation.

**Körper|teil** *der* part of the body.

**Körper|temperatur** *die* body temperature.

**Körper|verletzung** *die* bodily harm.

**korpulent** *adj* corpulent.

**korrekt** *adj* correct <> *adv* correctly.

**Korrektur** (*pl* -en) *die* correction; **~ lesen** to read the proofs.

**Korrekturband** (*pl* -bänder) *das* correction tape.

**Korrespondent, in** (*mpl* -en; *fpl* -nen) *der*, *die* - **1.** [Berichterstatter] correspondent - **2.** [in einer Firma] correspondence clerk.

**Korrespondenz** *die* correspondence.

**Korridor** (*pl* -e) *der* corridor.

**korrigieren** *vt* to correct.

**Korrosion** (*pl* -en) *die* corrosion (U).

**korrupt** *adj* corrupt.

**Korruption** (*pl* -en) *die* corruption (U).

**Korsett** (*pl* -s ODER -e) *das* corset.

**Korsika** *nt* Corsica.

**koscher** *adj* kosher; **nicht ganz ~** fam not quite kosher.

**Kose|name** *der* pet name.

**Kosmetik** (*pl* -ka) *die* [Pflege] beauty care.

**Kosmetika** *pl* cosmetics.

**Kosmetiker, in** (*mpl* -; *fpl* -nen) *der*, *die* beautician.

**Kosmetik|koffer** *der* vanity case.

**kosmetisch** *adj* cosmetic <> *adv* cosmetically.

**kosmisch** *adj* cosmic.

**Kosmonaut, in** (*mpl* -en; *fpl* -nen) *der*, *die* cosmonaut.

**Kosmos** *der* cosmos.

**Kost** *die* food; **leichte ~** [Nahrung] light food; **leichte/schwere ~** fig [Unterhaltung] light/heavy fare.

**kostbar** *adj* - **1.** [wertvoll, erlesen] valuable - **2.** [wichtig] precious.

**Kostbarkeit** (*pl* -en) *die* - **1.** [Wert] value - **2.** [Gegenstand] treasure.

**kosten** *vi* [probieren] to have a taste; **von der Suppe ~** to taste the soup <> *vt* - **1.** [gen] to cost; **was** ODER **wieviel kostet das?** how much is it?, how much does it cost?; **er ließ sich** (D) **die Feier etwas ~** he spent a fortune on the party; **Fragen kostet nichts** there's no harm in asking; **koste es, was es wolle** whatever the cost - **2.** [probieren] to taste, to try.

**Kosten** *pl* costs; **auf js ~** at sb's expense; **auf js ~ gehen** to be at sb's expense; **auf ~ einer Sache** (G) **gehen** to be at the expense of sthg; **auf seine ~ kommen** to get one's money's worth; [bei einer Party] to have a good time.

**Kosten|einsparung** *die* cost saving.

**Kosten|erstattung** *die* reimbursement of expenses.

**Kosten|explosion** *die* cost explosion.

**kostengünstig** *adj* economical <> *adv* economically.

**kostenlos** *adj* free <> *adv* free of charge.

**Kosten|voranschlag** *der* estimate.

**köstlich** *adj* - **1.** [im Geschmack] delicious - **2.** [amüsant] delightful <> *adv* - **1.**: **~ speisen**

K

to have a delicious meal - **2.: sich ~ amüsieren** to enjoy o.s. enormously.

**Kostlprobe** *die* [von Speise] taste; [von js Können] sample.

**kostspielig** *adj* costly.

**Kostüm** (*pl* -e) *das* - **1.** [Rock und Jacke] suit - **2.** [im Theater, zu Fasching] costume.

**Kostümlfest** *das* fancy-dress ball.

**kostümieren** ~ **sich kostümieren** *ref* to dress up *(in fancy dress)*.

**Kostverächter** (*pl* -) *der:* **kein ~ sein** [gerne essen] to like one's food; [gerne mit Frauen ausgehen] to be one for the ladies.

**Kot** *der* excrement.

**Kotelett** (*pl* -s) *das* chop, cutlet.

**Koteletten** *pl* sideboards *Br,* sideburns *Am.*

**Köter** (*pl* -) *der fam abw* mutt.

**Kotlflügel** *der* wing.

**Kotze** *die salopp* puke.

**kotzen** *vi salopp* to puke.

**Kotzen** *das salopp:* **es ist zum ~** it makes you puke; **ich finde es zum ~** it makes me puke.

**KP** [kaːˈpeː] (*pl* -s) (*abk für* **Kommunistische Partei**) *die* CP.

**Kr.** *abk für* **Kreis.**

**Krabbe** (*pl* -n) *die* [Krebs] crab; [Garnele] shrimp.

**krabbeln** (*perf* **hat/ist gekrabbelt**) *vi (ist)* to crawl <> *vt (hat) fam* [kratzen] to scratch; [kitzeln] to tickle.

**Krach** (*pl* **Kräche**) *der* - **1.** [Lärm] racket; **~ machen** to make a racket - **2.** *fam* [Ärger] row; **er hat ~ mit seiner Freundin** he's rowing with his girlfriend; **~ schlagen** to kick up a fuss - **3.** [Zusammenbruch] crash.

**krachen** (*perf* **hat/ist gekracht**) *vi* - **1.** (hat) [lärmen - Donner] to crash; [ - Schuss] to ring out; [ - Gewehr] to bang; **dann krachts!** there'll be trouble!; **an der Ecke hat es gekracht** there's been a crash on the corner - **2.** (ist) *fam* [kaputtgehen - Bett, Stuhl] to collapse; [ - Reißverschluss, Brett] to split; [ - Eis] to crack <> *vt (hat) fam* to bang.

~ **sich krachen** *ref fam* to have a row.

**krächzen** *vi* [Rabe] to caw; [Person] to croak <> *vt* to croak out.

**Kräcker** (*pl* -) *der* cracker.

**kraft** *präp amt:* **~ einer Sache** (G) by virtue of sthg.

**Kraft** (*pl* **Kräfte**) *die* - **1.** [Körperkraft] strength (U); **am Ende seiner Kräfte sein** to be completely exhausted; **~/keine ~ haben** to be strong/weak - **2.** [Fähigkeit, Wirksamkeit] power; **aus eigener ~** by oneself; **mit vereinten Kräften** by joining forces - **3.** [Hilfskraft] helper.

~ **Kräfte** *pl* [politisch] forces.

~ **außer Kraft** *adv:* **außer ~ treten/sein** to cease to be/be no longer in force.

~ **in Kraft** *adv:* **in ~ treten/setzen/sein** to come into/put into/be in force.

**Kraftlausdruck** *der* swearword.

**Kraftlfahrer, in** *der, die* driver.

**Kraftlfahrzeug** *das amt* motor vehicle.

**Kraftfahrzeuglbrief** *der amt* vehicle registration document.

**Kraftfahrzeuglschein** *der amt* vehicle registration document.

**Kraftfahrzeuglsteuer** *die amt* road tax *Br,* vehicle tax *Am.*

**kräftig** *adj* - **1.** [stark - Person] strong; [ - Schlag] powerful; [ - Körperbau, Stimme] powerful, strong - **2.** [Hunger, Farben] intense - **3.** [Mahlzeit] nourishing - **4.** [Fluch] coarse <> *adv* - **1.** [stark] hard - **2.** [fluchen] violently.

**kräftigen** *vt* to strengthen.

**kraftlos** *adj* weak <> *adv* [wanken] weakly; [herabhängen] limply.

**Kraftlprobe** *die* trial of strength.

**Kraftlstoff** *der* fuel.

**kraftvoll** *adj* powerful <> *adv* powerfully.

**Kraftlwagen** *der amt* motor car.

**Kraftlwerk** *das* power station.

**Kragen** (*pl* - *ODER* **Krägen**) *der* collar; **es geht jm an den ~ fam fig** sb is in for it; **jm an den ~ wollen fam fig** to be after sb; **ihr platzte der ~ fam fig** she blew her top.

**Krähe** (*pl* -n) *die* crow.

**krähen** *vi* to crow.

**Krakau** *nt* Cracow.

**Kralle** (*pl* -n) *die* claw.

**Kram** *der fam* - **1.** [Zeug] stuff; **jm nicht in den ~ passen fam fig** not to fit in with sb's plans - **2.** [Arbeit] business.

**kramen** *vi* to rummage about.

**Krampf** (*pl* **Krämpfe**) *der* cramp; **einen ~ bekommen/haben** to get/have cramp; **ein ~ sein fam fig** to be painful.

**Krampflader** *die* varicose vein.

**krampfen** *vt:* **die Hände/die Finger um/in etw (A) ~** to clutch sthg.

~ **sich krampfen** *ref* [Magen, Muskeln] to convulse; [Hände, Finger]: **sich um etw ~** to clutch sthg.

**krampfhaft** *adj* [Husten, Verrenkungen] convulsive; [Anstrengungen] strenuous <> *adv* [zucken] convulsively; [lächeln] in a strained way; **sich ~ bemühen** to make strenuous efforts; **~ nachdenken** to rack one's brains.

**Kran** (*pl* **Kräne**) *der* crane.

**Kranich** (*pl* -e) *der* crane.

**krank** (*kompar* **kränker;** *superl* **am kränksten**) *adj* sick, ill; **~e Menschen** sick people; **er ist ~** he is ill *ODER* sick; **~ werden** to be taken ill; **schwer ~** seriously ill; **diese ständigen Streitereien machen mich ~** these constant arguments are getting on my nerves.

**Kranke** (*pl* **-n**) *der, die* sick person; [im Krankenhaus] patient.

**kränkeln** *vi* not to be well.

**kranken** *vi:* **an etw** (*D*) **~** to suffer from sthg.

**kränken** *vt* to hurt.

**Kranken|bett** *das* sickbed.

**Kranken|geld** *das (ohne pl)* sickness benefit.

**Kranken|gymnast** (*pl* **-en**) *der* physiotherapist.

**Kranken|gymnastik** *die* physiotherapy.

**Kranken|gymnastin** (*pl* **-nen**) *die* physiotherapist.

**Kranken|haus** *das* hospital.

**Kranken|kasse** *die* health insurance association.

**KRANKENKASSE**

A "Krankenkasse" is a medical insurance organization that is responsible for national health insurance in Germany. Though there is no single state organization, there are both public and private "Krankenkassen", and all employees up to a certain income must be members of a state "Krankenkasse". The self-employed and people with incomes higher than the required limit may also take out private health insurance. Most people are covered by the "Allgemeine Ortskrankenkasse" (AOK) which operates at a regional level.

**Kranken|pflege** *die* nursing.

**Kranken|pfleger** *der* (male) nurse.

**Kranken|schein** *der* health insurance certificate.

**Kranken|schwester** *die* nurse.

**Krankenversicherten|karte** *die* health insurance card.

**Kranken|versicherung** *die* health insurance.

**Kranken|wagen** *der* ambulance.

**krank|feiern** *vi fam* to call in sick *(as an excuse to take the day off work)*.

**krankhaft** *adj* pathological <> *adv* [übertrieben] pathologically.

**Krankheit** (*pl* **-en**) *die* **- 1.** [Zustand] illness; 'wegen **~ geschlossen**' 'closed due to illness' **- 2.** [bestimmte Krankheit] disease; **eine unheilbare ~** an incurable disease.

**kränklich** *adj* sickly.

**krank|melden** ◆ **sich krankmelden** *ref* to report sick.

**krank|schreiben** *vt (unreg):* **jn ~** to give sb a medical certificate.

**Kränkung** (*pl* **-en**) *die* hurt.

**Kranz** (*pl* **Kränze**) *der* **- 1.** [Schmuck] wreath **- 2.** [Kuchen] ring.

**Krapfen** (*pl* **-**) *der* [Gebäck] doughnut.

**krass** *adj* [Gegensatz] stark; [Verstoß, Fall] blatant <> *adv* [ausdrücken] bluntly.

**Krater** (*pl* **-**) *der* crater.

**kratzen** *vi* **- 1.** [verletzen] to scratch **- 2.** [schaben] to scrape **- 3.** [jucken] to itch; **es kratzt im Hals** I've got a tickle in my throat <> *vt* **- 1.** [verletzen] to scratch **- 2.** [schaben] to scrape **- 3.** [jucken]: **jn ~** to make sb itch. ◆ **sich kratzen** *ref* to scratch o.s.

**Kratzer** (*pl* **-**) *der* scratch.

**kratzig** *adj* **- 1.** [rau] scratchy **- 2.** [heiser] rough.

**Kraul** *das* SPORT crawl.

**kraulen** (*perf* **hat/ist gekrault**) *vi (ist)* SPORT to do the crawl <> *vt (hat)* [streicheln] to tickle.

**kraus** *adj* **- 1.** [lockig] frizzy **- 2.** [gerunzelt] wrinkled **- 3.** [wirr] confused <> *adv* **- 1.** [gerunzelt]: **die Nase ~ ziehen** to wrinkle one's nose **- 2.** [wirr] confusedly.

**kräuseln** *vt* **- 1.** [in Locken] to frizz **- 2.** [in Wellen] to ripple. ◆ **sich kräuseln** *ref* [in Locken] to go frizzy.

**Kraus|kopf** *der* **- 1.** [Frisur] frizzy hair *(U)* **- 2.** [Spinner] muddlehead.

**Kraut** (*pl* **Kräuter**) *das* **- 1.** *(ohne pl)* [Kohl] cabbage **- 2.** *(ohne pl)* [Grünes] leaves *(pl)* **- 3.** *fam* [Tabak] weed **- 4.** *RW:* **dagegen ist kein ~ gewachsen** there is no cure for it; **wie ~ und Rüben** *fam* all over the place. ◆ **Kräuter** *pl* herbs.

**Kräuter|tee** *der* herbal tea.

**Krawall** (*pl* **-e**) *der* [Krach, Lärm] row; **~ machen** to make a row; **~ schlagen** *fam* to kick up a fuss. ◆ **Krawalle** *pl* [Unruhen] riots.

**Krawatte** (*pl* **-n**) *die* tie.

**kraxeln** (*perf* **ist gekraxelt**) *vi* to climb.

**kreativ** *adj* creative.

**Kreativität** [kreativi'tɛːt] *die* creativity.

**Kreatur** (*pl* **-en**) *die* creature.

**Krebs** (*pl* **-e**) *der* **- 1.** [Tier] crab **- 2.** *(ohne pl)* [Tumor] cancer; **~ haben** to have cancer **- 3.** ASTROL Cancer; **~ sein** to be a Cancer.

**Kredit** (*pl* **-e**) *der* [Darlehen] credit *(U)*; **einen**

K

~ **aufnehmen/gewähren** to take out/grant credit.

**Kreditlhai** *der abw* loan shark.

**Kreditlinstitut** *das* bank.

**Kreditlkarte** *die* credit card.

**kreditwürdig** *adj* creditworthy.

**Kreide** (*pl* -n) *die* chalk; **bei jm in der ~ stehen** *fig* to be in debt to sb.

**kreideweiß** *adj* as white as a sheet.

**kreieren** [kre'iːrən] *vt* to create.

**Kreis** (*pl* -e) *der* - **1.** [Form, Personenkreis] circle; **im ~ in a circle; im engsten ~** with close family and friends - **2.** [Verwaltungsbezirk] district - **3.** *RW*: **~e ziehen** to have repercussions; **sich im ~ drehen** to go round in circles.

**kreischen** *vi* [Person] to shriek; [Tier, Säge, Bremsen] to screech.

**Kreisel** (*pl* -) *der* top.

**kreisen** (*perf* hat/ist gekreist) *vi* - **1.** [sich drehen] to circle; **die Erde kreist um die Sonne** the earth goes round the sun - **2.** [Gedanken] : **um etw ~** to revolve around sthg.

**kreisförmig** *adj* circular <> *adv* in a circle.

**Kreisllauf** *der* - **1.** [Zyklus] cycle - **2.** [Blutkreislauf] circulation.

**Kreisllaufstörungen** *pl* circulatory trouble *(U)*.

**Kreislsäge** *die* - **1.** [Säge] circular saw - **2.** [Hut] boater.

**Kreislstadt** *die* chief town of a district.

**Kreislverkehr** *der* roundabout *Br*, traffic circle *Am*.

**Krem** (*pl* -s) *die* = Creme.

**Krematorium** [krema'toːrjʊm] (*pl* -rien) *das* crematorium.

**Kreme** (*pl* -s ODER -n) *die* = Creme.

**kremig** *adj* = cremig.

**Kreml** *der* Kremlin.

**Krempe** (*pl* -n) *die* brim.

**Krempel** *der fam* junk.

**Kreole** (*pl* -n) *der* Creole.

**Kreolin** (*pl* -nen) *die* Creole.

**kreolisch** *adj* Creole.

**krepieren** (*perf* ist krepiert) *vi* - **1.** *salopp* [sterben] to croak - **2.** [explodieren] to go off.

**Krepp** *der* crepe.

**Krepppapier** *das* crepe paper.

**Krepplsohle** *die* crepe sole.

**Kresse** (*pl* -n) *die* cress *(U)*.

**Kreta** *nt* Crete.

**kreuz** ▪ **kreuz und quer** *adv* [fahren, laufen] all over; [stellen, liegen] all over the place.

**Kreuz** (*pl* -e) *das* - **1.** [Zeichen & REL] cross; **über ~**

crosswise; **ein** ODER **das ~ schlagen** to make the sign of the cross - **2.** [Rücken] small of the back; **mir tut das ~ weh** my back aches; **jn aufs ~ legen** *fam fig* to take sb for a ride - **3.** [Autobahnkreuz] intersection - **4.** *(ohne pl)* [Qual] burden - **5.** *(ohne Artikel, ohne pl)* [Spielfarbe] clubs *(pl)* - **6.** [Spielkarte] club; **~bube** jack of clubs.

**Kreuzberg** *nt* Kreuzberg.

**Kreuz des Südens** *das* ASTRON: **das ~** the Southern Cross.

**kreuzen** (*perf* hat/ist gekreuzt) *vt* (hat) to cross <> *vi* (hat, ist) - **1.** [Boot - hin und her fahren] to cruise - **2.** [gegen den Wind segeln] to tack.
▪ **sich kreuzen** *ref* - **1.** [Weg, Brief, Linie] to cross - **2.** [Ansichten] to clash.

**Kreuzlfahrt** *die* cruise.

**Kreuzlfeuer** *das:* **im ~ stehen** to be under fire from all sides.

**Kreuzlgang** *der* cloister.

**kreuzigen** *vt* to crucify.

**Kreuzigung** (*pl* -en) *die* crucifixion.

**Kreuzlotter** *die* adder.

**Kreuzung** (*pl* -en) *die* - **1.** [Straßenkreuzung] crossroads *(sg)* - **2.** [Züchtung] cross; **eine ~ aus Pudel und Schäferhund** a cross between a poodle and an Alsatian.

**Kreuzlverhör** *das* cross-examination; **jn ins ~ nehmen** to cross-examine sb.

**Kreuzwortlrätsel** *das* crossword (puzzle).

**Kreuzlzug** *der* crusade.

**Krhs.** (*abk für* Krankenhaus) hosp.

**kribbelig** *adj* edgy.

**kribbeln** *vi* to itch; **es kribbelt mir** ODER **mich in der Nase** I've got an itchy nose.

**kriechen** (*prät* kroch; *perf* ist gekrochen) *vi* - **1.** [Wurm, Verkehr, Kind] to crawl - **2.** [Zeit] to creep by - **3.** *abw* [unterwürfig sein]: **vor jm ~** to crawl to sb.

**Kriechlspur** *die* crawler lane.

**Krieg** (*pl* -e) *der* war; **jm/einer Sache den ~ erklären** to declare war on sb/sthg.

**kriegen** *vt fam* [bekommen] to get; [Zug, Bus, Straßenbahn] to catch; **wenn wir den ~!** just wait till we get hold of him!; **Wut ~** to get angry; **es mit jm zu tun ~** to get into trouble with sb; **jn dazu ~, etw zu tun** to get sb to do sthg.

**Kriegsldienstverweigerer** (*pl* -) *der* conscientious objector.

**Kriegslerklärung** *die* declaration of war.

**Kriegslfuß** *der:* **mit jm im auf ~ stehen** to be at loggerheads with sb; **mit einer Sache auf ~ stehen** to struggle with sthg.

**Kriegslgefangene** *der, die* prisoner of war.

**Kriegs|gefangenschaft** *die* captivity *(as a prisoner of war)*; in ~ geraten to become a prisoner of war.

**Krim** *die:* die ~ the Crimea.

**Krimi** (*pl* -s) *der fam* thriller.

**Kriminal|beamte** *der* detective.

**Kriminal|beamtin** *die* detective.

**Kriminalität** *die* crime.

**Kriminalpolizei** *die* ≈ Criminal Investigation Department *Br,* ≈ Federal Bureau of Investigation *Am.*

**Kriminal|roman** *der* thriller.

**kriminell** *adj* criminal; ~ werden to turn to crime.

**Krimskrams** *der (ohne pl) fam* odds and ends (*pl*).

**Kringel** (*pl* -) *der* - 1. [Kreis] ring - 2. [Gebäck] ring-shaped biscuit.

**Kripo** (*abk für* Kriminalpolizei) *die* ≈ CID *Br,* ≈ FBI *Am.*

**Krippe** (*pl* -n) *die* - 1. [Kinderkrippe] crèche *Br,* day nursery *Am* - 2. [Futterkrippe] manger - 3. [Weihnachtskrippe] crib.

**Krise** (*pl* -n) *die* crisis; in einer ~ stecken to be in (a) crisis.

**kriseln** *vi:* es kriselt there is a crisis.

**krisenfest** *adj* crisis-proof.

**Krisen|herd** *der* trouble spot.

**Kristall** (*pl* -e) *das ODER der* crystal.

**Kriterium** (*pl* Kriterien) *das* criterion.

**Kritik** (*pl* -en) *die* - 1. [Beurteilung] criticism; an jm/etw ~ üben to criticize sb/sthg; unter aller ~ appalling - 2. [Rezension] review.

**Kritiker, in** (*mpl* -; *fpl* -nen) *der, die* critic.

**kritiklos** *adj* uncritical ⟷ *adv* uncritically.

**kritisch** *adj* critical ⟷ *adv* - 1. [prüfend, negativ] critically - 2. [gefährlich]: es steht ~ um den Kranken the patient is critical.

**kritisieren** *vt* to criticize.

**kritzeln** *vt* to scribble.

**Kroate** [kro'aːtə] (*pl* -n) *der* Croat.

**Kroatien** [kro'aːtsiən] *nt* Croatia.

**Kroatin** [kro'aːtɪn] (*pl* -nen) *die* Croat.

**kroatisch** [kro'aːtɪʃ] *adj* Croatian.

**kroch** *prät* ⟼ kriechen.

**Krokant** *der (ohne pl)* praline.

**Krokodil** (*pl* -e) *das* crocodile.

**Krokus** (*pl* -se) *der* crocus.

**Krone** (*pl* -n) *die* - 1. [gen] crown - 2. [Herrschaft] Crown - 3. [Währung - dänische] krone; [ - schwedische] krona - 4. RW: einen in der ~ haben *fam*

[betrunken sein] to have had one too many; einer Sache (*D*) die ~ aufsetzen to cap sthg.

**krönen** *vt* to crown; jn zum König ~ to crown sb king.

**Kron|leuchter** *der* chandelier.

**Krönung** (*pl* -en) *die* - 1. [das Krönen] coronation - 2. [Höhepunkt] culmination.

**Kron|zeuge** *der:* als ~ auftreten to turn Queen's/King's *Br ODER* state's *Am* evidence.

**Kron|zeugin** *die:* als ~ auftreten to turn Queen's/King's *Br ODER* state's *Am* evidence.

**Kropf** (*pl* Kröpfe) *der* goitre.

**Kröte** (*pl* -n) *die* toad.

**Krs.** *abk für* Kreis.

**Krücke** (*pl* -n) *die* - 1. [Stock] crutch - 2. *fam abw* [Person] clown.

**Krug** (*pl* Krüge) *der* [für Milch, Wein] jug; [für Bier] mug.

**Krümel** (*pl* -) *der* crumb.

**krumm** *adj* - 1. [Linie] curved; [Nagel, Rücken] bent; [Nase] hooked; [Finger, Beine] crooked - 2. *fam* [unehrlich] crooked; auf eine ~e Tour by crooked means ⟷ *adv* [gehen, stehen] with a stoop; [sitzen] bent over.

**krümmen** *vt* to bend.
⟿ **sich krümmen** *ref* to bend; [vor Schmerzen] to double up.

**krumm nehmen** *vt (unreg) fam* to take offence at; jm etw ~ to hold sthg against sb.

**Krümmung** (*pl* -en) *die* [von Horizont, Rücken] curve; [von Straße, Fluss] bend.

**Krüppel** (*pl* -) *der* cripple.

**Kruste** (*pl* -n) *die* - 1. [Rinde] crust - 2. [Schicht] scab.

**Kruzifix** (*pl* -e) *das* crucifix.

**Krypta** (*pl* Krypten) *die* crypt.

**Kt.** *abk für* Kanton.

**Kto.** (*abk für* Konto) a/c.

**Kto.-Nr.** (*abk für* Kontonummer) a/c no.

**Kuba** *nt* Cuba; auf ~ in Cuba.

**Kubaner, in** (*mpl* -; *fpl* -nen) *der, die* Cuban.

**kubanisch** *adj* Cuban.

**Kübel** (*pl* -) *der* [für Abfälle] bin; [für Pflanzen] tub.

**Kubik|meter** *der* cubic metre.

**Kubismus** *der* cubism.

**Küche** (*pl* -n) *die* - 1. [Raum] kitchen - 2. [Kochen] cooking; kalte/warme ~ cold/hot food.

**Kuchen** (*pl* -) *der* cake.

**Kuchen|blech** *das* baking sheet.

**Kuchen|form** *die* cake tin *Br ODER* pan *Am.*

**K**

**Kuchen|gabel** *die* cake fork.

**Küchen|schabe** *die* cockroach.

**Kuchen|teig** *der* cake mixture.

**Kuckuck** (*pl* -e) *der* cuckoo; **zum ~ (noch mal)!** *fam fig* for Pete's sake!

**Kufe** (*pl* -n) *die* runner.

**Kugel** (*pl* -n) *die* - **1.** [gen & sport] ball; [am Weihnachtsbaum] bauble; [beim Kugelstoßen] shot - **2.** [Form] sphere - **3.** [Geschoss] bullet - **4.** *RW:* **eine ruhige ~ schieben** *fam fig* to have it easy.

**kugelförmig** *adj* spherical.

**Kugel|gelenk** *das* ball-and-socket joint.

**Kugel|lager** *das* ball bearing.

**kugelrund** *adj* as round as a ball.

**Kugelschreiber** (*pl* -) *der* ballpoint (pen), Biro®.

**kugelsicher** *adj* bullet-proof.

**Kugelstoßen** *das* sport shot put.

**Kuh** (*pl* Kühe) *die* cow.

**Kuh|handel** *der fam* horse-trading.

**Kuhhaut** *die:* **das geht auf keine ~** *fam* it's just not on.

**kühl** *adj* cool <> *adv* coolly; **~ servieren** serve chilled; **~ und trocken lagern** keep in a cool, dry place.

**kühlen** *vt* to cool.

**Kühler** (*pl* -) *der* - **1.** auto radiator - **2.** [für Getränke] cooler.

**Kühler|haube** *die* bonnet *Br*, hood *Am*.

**Kühl|haus** *das* cold store.

**Kühl|schrank** *der* fridge.

**Kühl|tasche** *die* cool bag.

**Kühl|truhe** *die* freezer.

**Kühlung** (*pl* -en) *die* - **1.** [Erfrischung] coolness - **2.** tech cooling.

**Kühlwasser** *das* radiator water.

**kühn** *adj* bold.

**Kühnheit** *die* boldness.

**Kuh|stall** *der* cowshed.

**k. u. k.** (*abk für* kaiserlich und königlich) *Imperial and Royal.*

**Küken** (*pl* -) *das* - **1.** [Tier] chick - **2.** *fam fig* [Nesthäkchen] baby; [Mädchen] little girl.

**kulant** *adj* [Verkäufer, Geschäftspartner] obliging; [Preis] reasonable.

**Kuli** (*pl* -s) *der* - **1.** [Mensch] coolie - **2.** *fam* [Schreiber] Biro®.

**kulinarisch** *adj* culinary.

**Kulisse** (*pl* -n) *die* - **1.** [Bühnenbild] scenery (U); **hinter den ~n** *fig* behind the scenes - **2.** [Hintergrund] background.

**kullern** (*perf* ist gekullert) *vi* to roll.

**Kult** (*pl* -e) *der* cult.

**Kult|film** *der* cult film.

**kultivieren** [kulti'viːrən] *vt* to cultivate.

**kultiviert** [kulti'viːrt] *adj* refined <> *adv* in a refined manner.

**Kultur** (*pl* -en) *die* culture.

**Kultur|beutel** *der* toilet bag.

**kulturell** *adj* cultural <> *adv* culturally.

**Kultur|gut** *das* cultural assets (*pl*).

**Kultur|hoheit** *die independence of German Federal states in educational and cultural matters.*

**Kultur|kreis** *der* cultural area.

**Kultur|programm** *das* cultural programme.

**Kultus|minister, in** *der, die minister of a German Federal state responsible for education and cultural affairs.*

**Kultus|ministerium** *das ministry of education and cultural affairs within a German Federal state.*

**Kultusminister|konferenz** *die conference of the ministers of education and cultural affairs from each Federal state.*

**Kümmel** (*pl* -) *der* - **1.** (*ohne pl*) [Gewürzpflanze] caraway - **2.** [Schnaps] kümmel.

**Kümmel|brot** *das* caraway bread.

**Kummer** *der* worries (*pl*); **~ mit jm haben** to worry about sb; **jm ~ machen** to worry sb.

**kümmerlich** *adj* miserable.

**kümmern** *vt* to concern; **das kümmert sie nicht** she doesn't care about that; **was kümmert es ihn?** what is it to him?

**➥ sich kümmern** *ref:* **sich um jn ~** [helfen] to look after sb; **sich um etw ~** [organisieren, zubereiten] to see to sthg; [beachten] to worry about sthg; **kümmere dich um deine eigenen Angelegenheiten!** mind your own business!

**Kumpel** (*pl* -) *der* - **1.** [Bergarbeiter] miner - **2.** *fam* [Kamerad] pal.

**kündbar** *adj* [Stellung, Vertrag] terminable; [Mitarbeiter] dismissible.

**Kunde** (*pl* -n) *der* customer.

**Kunden|dienst** *der* - **1.** [Service] customer service - **2.** [Servicestelle] customer service department.

**Kunden|karte** *die* loyalty card.

**Kundgebung** (*pl* -en) *die* rally.

**kundig** *adj* [Person] knowledgeable; [Rat, Blick] expert.

**kündigen** *vi* [Arbeitnehmer] to hand in one's notice; [Mieter] to give notice that one is leaving; **jm ~** [Firma] to give sb his/her notice; [Vermieter] to give sb notice to quit; **jm fristlos ~** to dismiss sb without notice <> *vt* [Vertrag, Kredit] to terminate; **seine Arbeitsstelle ~** to hand in one's notice; **seine Wohnung ~** to give notice that one is leaving; **jm die Freundschaft ~** to break off one's friendship with sb.

**Kündigung** (*pl* **-en**) *die* [von Vertrag] termination; [von Arbeitsstelle] notice; [von Wohnung] notice to quit; **jm die ~ aussprechen** to give sb his/her notice.

**Kündigungslfrist** *die* period of notice.

**Kündigungsschutz** *der* [für Mieter] protection against wrongful eviction; [für Arbeitnehmer] protection against wrongful dismissal.

**Kundin** (*pl* **-nen**) *die* customer.

**Kundschaft** *die (ohne pl)* customers (*pl*).

**künftig** *adj* future <> *adv* in future.

**Kunst** (*pl* **Künste**) *die* art; **die bildende ~** fine art *(U)*; **das ist keine ~!** there is nothing to it!

**Kunstlakademie** *die* art college.

**Kunstauslstellung** *die* art exhibition.

**Kunstldünger** *der* artificial fertilizer.

**Kunstlerziehung** *die (ohne pl)* art lessons (*pl*).

**Kunstlfaser** *die* synthetic fibre.

**Kunstlfehler** *der* professional error.

**kunstfertig** *adj* skilful <> *adv* skilfully.

**Kunstgegenlstand** *der* objet d'art.

**Kunstlgeschichte** *die* history of art.

**Kunstlgewerbe** *das (ohne pl)* arts and crafts (*pl*).

**Kunstlgriff** *der* trick.

**Kunstlhändler, in** *der, die* art dealer.

**Kunsthandlwerk** *das* craft.

**Kunstlharz** *das* synthetic resin.

**Künstler, in** (*mpl* **-;** *fpl* **-nen**) *der, die* **- 1.** [Kunstschaffende] artist; **ein bildender ~** an artist (specializing in fine art) **- 2.** [Könner] master.

**künstlerisch** *adj* artistic <> *adv* artistically.

**Künstlerlname** *der* pseudonym.

**künstlich** *adj* **- 1.** [nicht natürlich] artificial **- 2.** [übertrieben] forced <> *adv* **- 1.** [nicht natürlich] artificially **- 2.** [übertrieben] in a forced way.

**Kunstlmaler, in** *der, die* painter.

**Kunstlstoff** *der* plastic.

**Kunstlstück** *das* **- 1.** [Trick] trick **- 2.** [Leistung] feat.

**Kunstlwerk** *das* work of art.

**kunterbunt** *adj* varied <> *adv* in a jumble.

**Kupfer** *das* copper.

**Kupferlstich** *der* copperplate engraving.

**Kupon, Coupon** [ku'põ] (*pl* **-s**) *der* coupon.

**Kuppe** (*pl* **-n**) *die* **- 1.** [landschaftlich] (hill)top **- 2.** [von Fingern] tip.

**Kuppel** (*pl* **-n**) *die* dome.

**Kupplung** (*pl* **-en**) *die* **- 1.** [in Auto] clutch; **die ~ kommen/schleifen lassen** to release/slip the clutch **- 2.** [für Anhänger] coupling.

**Kupplungslpedal** *das* clutch pedal.

**Kur** (*pl* **-en**) *die* health cure; **auf** ODER **zur ~ sein/gehen** to be/go on a health cure.

**Kür** (*pl* **-en**) *die* free programme.

**Kurbel** (*pl* **-n**) *die* [von Fenster, Rollo] winder; [von Drehorgel, Spieluhr] handle; [von Maschine, zum Aufziehen] crank.

**Kürbis** (*pl* **-se**) *der* pumpkin.

**Kurde** (*pl* **-n**) *der* Kurd.

**Kurdin** (*pl* **-nen**) *die* Kurd.

**kurdisch** *adj* Kurdish.

**Kurdistan** *nt* Kurdistan.

**kuren** *vi* to take a health cure.

**Kurlgast** *der visitor to a health resort.*

**Kurier** (*pl* **-e**) *der* courier.

**kurieren** *vt* to cure; **von etw kuriert sein** *fam fig* to be cured of sthg.

**kurios** *adj* curious.

**Kuriosität** (*pl* **-en**) *die* curiosity.

**Kurlkonzert** *das concert at a health resort.*

**Kurlort** *der* health resort. .

**Kurlpfuscher, in** *der, die* **abw** quack.

**Kurs** (*pl* **-e**) *der* **- 1.** [Fahrtrichtung, Lehrgang] course; **vom ~ abkommen** to go off course **- 2.** [Teilnehmer] course members (*pl*) **- 3.** [Marktpreis - von Aktien] price; [ - von Währung] exchange rate; **im ~ fallen/steigen** to fall/rise; **hoch im ~ stehen** to be very popular.

**Kurslbuch** *das* timetable.

**Kurlschatten** *der person with whom one becomes romantically involved while at a health resort.*

**kursieren** *vi* to circulate.

**kursiv** *adj* italic <> *adv* in italics.

**Kurslschwankung** *die* [von Aktien] fluctuation in price; [von Währung] fluctuation in the exchange rate.

**Kursus** (*pl* **Kurse**) *der* course.

**Kurslwechsel** *der* change of course.

**Kurltaxe** *die tax paid by visitors to health resorts.*

**Kurve** ['kʊrvə] (*pl* **-n**) *die* **- 1.** [Straßenkrümmung] bend; **die Straße macht eine ~** the road bends; **die ~ kratzen** *fam* to beat it **- 2.** [Bogenlinie] curve.

➤ **Kurven** *pl fam* [Körperform] curves.

K

**kurven** [ˈkʊrvn̩] (*perf* **ist gekurvt**) *vi* - **1.** *fam:* **durch die Stadt ~** to drive around town; **um die Ecke gekurvt kommen** to come round the corner - **2.** [Flugzeug] to circle; *fam* [umherfahren] to drive around.

**kurvenreich** *adj* [Straße] winding; [Frau] curvaceous.

**kurz** (*kompar* **kürzer;** *superl* **kürzeste**) *adj* - **1.** [räumlich] short; **was ist der kürzeste Weg zum Bahnhof?** what's the quickest way to the station? - **2.** [zeitlich] short, brief; **innerhalb ~er Zeit** within a short space of time; **vor ~em** recently; **er arbeitet erst seit ~em hier** he's only been working here for a short time *ODER* while; **über ~ oder lang** sooner or later - **3.** [gedrängt] brief; **~ und schmerzlos** *fam* short and sweet <> *adv* - **1.** [räumlich]: **~ vor/hinter** just in front of/behind; **alles ~ und klein schlagen** *fam* to smash everything to pieces; **zu ~ kommen** *fam* to get a raw deal - **2.** [zeitlich] briefly; **ich gehe mal ~ in das Geschäft dort** I'm just popping into that shop; **~ vor dem Konzert** shortly before the concert - **3.** [gedrängt]: **~ (gesagt)** in short; **sich ~ fassen** to be brief; **~ und bündig** concisely.

**Kurzarbeit** *die* short-time working.

**kurzlarbeiten** *vi* to work short time.

**Kurzlarbeiter, in** *der, die* short-time worker.

**kurzärmelig, kurzärmlig** *adj* short-sleeved <> *adv* in short sleeves.

**kurzatmig** *adj* short of breath.

**Kurze** (*pl* -n) *der* - **1.** *fam* [Kurzschluss] short - **2.** *Norddt* [Schnaps] schnapps.

**Kürze** *die* shortness.
➡ **in Kürze** *adv* shortly.

**Kürzel** (*pl* -) *das* - **1.** [Schriftzeichen] shorthand symbol - **2.** [Abkürzung] abbreviation.

**kürzen** *vt* - **1.** [Haare, Nägel, Film, Text] to cut; [Rock, Kabel] to shorten - **2.** [finanziell] to cut - **3.** MATH to cancel.

**kurzerhand** *adv* without further ado.

**kürzer treten** (*perf* **ist kürzer getreten**) *vi (unreg)* [finanziell] to cut back; [gesundheitlich] to take it easy.

**Kurzlfassung** *die* abridged version.

**Kurzlfilm** *der* short (film).

**kurzfristig** *adj* - **1.** [unangemeldet] sudden - **2.** [kurz dauernd] short-term - **3.** [rasch] quick <> *adv* - **1.** [unangemeldet] at short notice - **2.** [kurz dauernd] for a short time - **3.** [rasch] quickly.

**Kurzlgeschichte** *die* short story.

**kurzhaarig** *adj* short-haired.

**kurz halten** *vt (unreg)* *fam* to keep short.

**kurzlebig** *adj* short-lived.

**kürzlich** *adv* recently.

**Kurzlnachricht** *pl* news summary *(sg)*.

**kurzlschließen** *vt (unreg)* to short-circuit.
➡ **sich kurzschließen** *ref* to get in touch.

**Kurzlschluss** *der* - **1.** [elektrisch] short-circuit - **2.** [seelisch]: **er muss es aus einem ~ heraus getan haben** something must have snapped to make him do that.

**Kurzschlusslhandlung** *die:* **das war eine ~** something must have snapped for that to happen.

**kurzsichtig** *adj* *eigtl* & *fig* short-sighted <> *adv* short-sightedly.

**Kurzlstrecke** *die short journey on public transport, within city centre.*

**Kurzstreckenlflug** *der* short-haul flight.

**kurzum** *adv* in short.

**Kürzung** (*pl* -en) *die* cut.

**Kurzwahlltaste** *die* EDV speed-dial button.

**kurzweilig** *adj* entertaining.

**Kurzwelle** *die* short wave.

**Kurzzeitlgedächtnis** *das* short-term memory.

**kurzzeitig** *adj* brief <> *adv* briefly.

**kuschelig** *adj* cosy.

**kuscheln** *vi* to cuddle up; **mit jm ~** to cuddle sb.
➡ **sich kuscheln** *ref* to cuddle up; **sich an jn ~** to cuddle up to sb.

**Kusine** (*pl* -n) *die* cousin.

**Kuss** (*pl* **Küsse**) *der* kiss.

**kussecht** *adj* kissproof.

**küssen** *vt* & *vi* to kiss.
➡ **sich küssen** *ref* to kiss.

**Küste** (*pl* -n) *die* coast.

**Küster, in** (*mpl* -; *fpl* -nen) *der, die* verger.

**Kutsche** (*pl* -n) *die* - **1.** [Pferdewagen] coach - **2.** *fam* [Auto] jalopy, motor *Br.*

**Kutter** (*pl* -) *der* cutter.

**Kuvert** [kuˈvɛːɐ̯] (*pl* -e) *das* envelope.

**Kuwait** *nt* Kuwait.

**kW** (*abk für* **Kilowatt**) kW.

**KW** [kaːˈveː] (*abk für* **Kurzwelle**) *die* SW.

**kWh** (*abk für* **Kilowattstunde**) kWh.

**kyrillisch** *adj* Cyrillic.

**KZ** [kaːˈtsɛt] (*pl* -s) *das abk für* **Konzentrationslager.**

**L**

**l, L** [ɛl] (pl - ODER -s) das l, L.
➡ **l** (abk für **Liter**) l.

**labern** fam abw vi to prattle on ◇ vt to talk.

**labil** adj unstable; [Kreislauf] bad; [Konstitution, Gleichgewicht] delicate.

**Labor** (pl -s ODER -e) das laboratory.

**Laborant, in** (mpl -en; fpl -nen) der, die laboratory technician.

**Labyrinth** (pl -e) das maze.

**Lache¹** (pl -n) die [von Wasser] puddle; [von Blut, Öl] pool.

**Lache²** die (ohne pl) fam [Gelächter] laugh.

**lächeln** vi to smile; **über jn/etw ~** to smile about sb/at sthg.

**Lächeln** das (ohne pl) smile.

**lachen** vi to laugh; **über jn/etw ~** to laugh at sb/sthg; **bei jm/irgendwo nichts zu ~ haben** fam fig to have a hard time of it with sb/somewhere; **dass ich nicht lache!** fig don't make me laugh!; **es** ODER **das wäre doch gelacht, wenn ...** fig it would be ridiculous if ...; **du hast gut ~!** fig it's all right for you!

**Lachen** das laughter; **ein leises ~** a quiet laugh; **jn zum ~ bringen** to make sb laugh; **jm ist nicht zum ~** sb is not in a laughing mood; **etw ist zum ~** fam fig sthg is laughable; **ihm wird das ~ schon noch vergehen** he'll soon be laughing on the other side of his face.

**Lacher** (pl -) der - **1.** [Person] laugher; **die ~** the people who are/were laughing - **2.** [Lachen] laugh; **die ~ auf seiner Seite haben** fig to score points by making people laugh.

**lächerlich** adj [komisch] ridiculous; **jn/sich ~ machen** to make a fool of sb/o.s.

**Lächerliche** das: **etw ins ~ ziehen** to make a joke out of sthg.

**lachhaft** adj ludicrous.

**Lachs** [laks] (pl -e) der salmon.

**Lack** (pl -e) der [farblos] varnish; [farbig] paint; [Nagellack] varnish Br, polish Am; **der ~ ist ab** fam fig [Reiz einer Sache] the novelty has worn off; [von Person] he/she/etc has seen better days.

**lackieren** vt - **1.** [Holz] to varnish; [Auto] to spray - **2.** [mit Nagellack] to paint.

**Lackierung** (pl -en) die - **1.** [Lackieren - von Holz]

varnishing; [ - von Auto] spraying - **2.** [Lack - farblos] varnish; [ - farbig] paint.

**Lack|schaden** der damage (U) to the paintwork.

**Lack|schuh** der patent-leather shoe.

**Lade|fläche** die load area.

**laden** (präs lädt; prät lud; perf hat geladen) vt - **1.** [Fracht, Waffe & EDV] to load; **der LKW hat Kies geladen** the lorry has loaded up with gravel; **etw auf/in etw** (A) **~** to load sthg onto/into sthg - **2.** [abladen]: **etw aus/von etw ~** to unload sthg from sthg - **3.** [mit Elektrizität] to charge - **4.** geh [vorladen] to summon ◇ vi [mit einer Last] to load up; **der Laster hat schwer geladen** the truck is heavily laden.

**Laden** (pl Läden) der - **1.** [Geschäft] shop Br, store Am - **2.** [Angelegenheit] business - **3.** fam [Betrieb] outfit; **den ~ schmeißen** fam to run the show.

**Laden|dieb, in** der, die shoplifter.

**Laden|diebstahl** der shoplifting (U).

**Laden|hüter** (pl -) der non-seller.

**Laden|öffnungszeiten** pl shop Br ODER store Am opening times.

**Laden|preis** der shop Br ODER store Am price.

**Laden|schluss** der closing time.

**Ladenschluss|gesetz** das law regulating shop opening hours.

**Ladenschluss|zeiten** pl shop Br ODER store Am closing times.

**Laden|straße** die shopping street.

**Laden|tisch** der counter; **etw unter dem ~ verkaufen** fig to sell sthg under the counter.

**Lade|rampe** die loading platform.

**Lade|raum** der [von Auto] luggage space (U); [von Transporter, LKW] load space (U); [von Flugzeug, Schiff] hold.

**lädieren** vt to damage.

**lädt** präs ⊳ laden.

**Ladung** (pl -en) die - **1.** [gen] load - **2.** [zum Schießen] charge; **eine geballte ~** a load (of) - **3.** PHYS: positive/negative ~ positive/negative charge.

**Lady** ['leːdi] (pl -s) die lady.

**lag** prät ⊳ liegen.

**Lage** (pl -n) die - **1.** [Stelle, Stellung] position - **2.** [Situation] situation; **zu etw in der ~ sein** to be able to do sthg; **in der ~ sein, etw zu tun** to be able to do sthg; **nach ~ der Dinge** as things stand; **sich in js ~** (A) **versetzen** to put o.s. in sb's position - **3.** [Schicht] layer.

**Lage|bericht** der report on the situation.

**Lage|besprechung** die discussion of the situation.

**Lage|plan** *der* plan.

**Lager** (*pl* -) *das* - **1.** *eigtl* & *fig* [Feldlager, Gesinnung] camp - **2.** [für Waren] store; **etw auf ~ haben** [als Ware] to have sth in stock; [zur Unterhaltung] to be ready with sth - **3.** TECH bearing.

**Lagerbe|stand** *der* stock.

**Lager|feuer** *das* camp fire.

**Lager|halle** *die* warehouse.

**Lager|haus** *das* warehouse.

**lagern** *vt* - **1.** [aufbewahren] to store - **2.**: **einen Kranken bequem ~** to make an ill person comfortable; **den Arm hoch ~** to put one's arm in a raised position ◇ *vi* [kampieren] to camp.
➡ **sich lagern** *ref* [sich setzen] to settle (o.s.).

**Lager|platz** *der* campsite.

**Lager|raum** *der* storeroom.

**Lagerung** (*pl* -en) *die* storage (U).

**Lago Maggiore** [ˈlaːgomaˈdʒoːrə] *der* Lake Maggiore.

**Lagos** *nt* Lagos.

**Lagune** (*pl* -n) *die* lagoon.

**lahm** *adj* - **1.** [gelähmt, Ausrede] lame - **2.** [ermüdet] stiff - **3.** [matt - Mensch] dull; [ - Bewegung] sluggish ◇ *adv fam* [sich bewegen] sluggishly; [sich entschuldigen] lamely.

**lahmen** *vi* to be lame.

**lähmen** *vt eigtl* & *fig* to paralyse.

**lahm legen** *vt* to bring to a standstill.

**Lähmung** (*pl* -en) *die eigtl* & *fig* paralysis.

**Laib** (*pl* -e) *der*: **ein ~ Brot** a loaf of bread; **ein ~ Käse** a cheese.

**Laich** (*pl* -e) *der* spawn.

**Laie** [ˈlaɪə] (*pl* -n) *der* layman (*f* laywoman); **ein medizinischer ~** a layman when it comes to medicine; **blutiger ~** complete layman.

**laienhaft** [ˈlaɪənhaft] *adj* inexpert ◇ *adv* inexpertly.

**Laienspiel|gruppe** *die* amateur theatre group.

**Lake** (*pl* -n) *die* brine (U).

**Laken** (*pl* -) *das* sheet.

**lakonisch** *adj* laconic ◇ *adv* laconically.

**Lakritz** (*pl* -e) *das ODER der* liquorice.

**lallen** *vt* & *vi* to babble.

**Lama** (*pl* -s) *das* llama.

**Lambada** (*pl* -s) *der* lambada.

**Lamelle** (*pl* -n) *die* - **1.** [von Jalousie] slat - **2.** [von Heizkörper] fin - **3.** [von Pilzen] gill.

**lamentieren** *vi abw* to moan.

**Lametta** *das* angel's hair.

**Lamm** (*pl* Lämmer) *das* lamb.

**Lamm|fell** *das* lambskin.

**Lammfleisch** *das* lamb.

**lammfromm** *adj* [Person] as meek as a lamb; [Pferd, Hund] as gentle as a lamb.

**Lampe** (*pl* -n) *die* light; [Bürolampe, Stehlampe] lamp.

**Lampenfieber** *das* stage fright.

**Lampen|schirm** *der* lampshade.

**Lampion** [lamˈpjɔŋ] (*pl* -s) *der* Chinese lantern.

**lancieren** [lãˈsiːrən] *vt* - **1.** [bekannt geben] to put out - **2.** [fördern]: **jn in etw** (A) **~** to get sb into sth.

**Land** (*pl* Länder) *das* - **1.** [Staatsgebiet, ländliche Gegend] country; **jn des ~es verweisen** to deport sb; **auf dem ~** in the country - **2.** [Gelände, Festland] land; **an ~ gehen** to go ashore - **3.** [Bundesland - in Deutschland] state; [ - in Österreich] province - **4.** *RW*: **kein/wieder ~ sehen** to see no/a light at the end of the tunnel; **wieder im ~(e) sein** to be back.
➡ **hier zu Lande** *adv* = hierzulande.

**Land|arbeiter, in** *der, die* farm worker.

**Land|arzt, ärztin** *der, die* country doctor.

**landauf** *adv*: **~, landab** all over the country.

**Landbe|sitz** *der* land.

**Land|bevölkerung** *die* rural population.

**Land|brot** *das brown rye bread with a hard crust.*

**Lande|bahn** *die* runway.

**landeinwärts** *adv* inland.

**landen** (*perf* hat/ist gelandet) *vi* (*ist*) - **1.** [nach einem Flug] to land - **2.** *fam* [ankommen] to land up; **bei jm (mit etw) nicht ~ können** *fam* not to be able to get anywhere with sb (by using sth) ◇ *vt* (*hat*) *eigtl* & *fig* to land.

**Land|enge** *die* isthmus.

**Lande|platz** *der* landing strip.

**Ländereien** *pl* estates.

**Länder|spiel** *das* international match.

**Landes|ebene** *die*: **auf ~** at state level.

**Landes|farben** *pl* [von Staat] national colours; [von Bundesland] state colours.

**Landes|grenze** *die* [von Staat] national border; [von Bundesland] state boundary.

**Landeshaupt|mann** *der Österr head of a regional government in Austria.*

**Landeshaupt|stadt** *die* state capital.

**Landes|innere** *das* interior (*of the country*).

**Landes|kirche** *die Protestant Church of a German state.*

**Landes|kunde** *die study of a country and its culture.*

**landeskundlich** *adj relating to the study of a country and its culture.*

**Landes|regierung** *die* state government.

**Landes|sprache** *die* national language.

**landesüblich** *adj* national.

**Landesverrat** *der* treason.

**Landes|währung** *die* national currency.

**Land|flucht** *die* migration from the country to the town.

**Landfriedens|bruch** *der* breach of the peace.

**Land|gericht** *das* regional court.

**Land|haus** *das* country house.

**Land|karte** *die* map.

**Land|kreis** *der* district.

**landläufig** *adj* popular.

**Landleben** *das* country life.

**ländlich** *adj* rural.

**Land|luft** *die* country air.

**Land|plage** *die abw* - **1.** *eigtl* plague - **2.** *fig* menace.

**Land|regen** *der* steady rain.

**Landschaft** (*pl* -en) *die* [Gelände] countryside; [Abbildung] landscape.

**landschaftlich** *adj* [Schönheit, Besonderheit] of the countryside; [Sitte] regional <> *adv:* **der Schwarzwald ist ~ schön** the Black Forest countryside is beautiful.

**Landschul|heim** *das country retreat used by a school for short educational and recreational visits.*

**Lands|leute** *pl* compatriots.

**Lands|mann** (*pl* -leute) *der* compatriot.

**Lands|männin** (*pl* -nen) *die* compatriot.

**Land|straße** *die* country road.

**Land|streicher, in** (*mpl* -; *fpl* -nen) *der, die* tramp.

**Land|streitkräfte** *pl* land forces.

**Land|strich** *der* area.

**Land|tag** *der* - **1.** [Volksvertretung] state parliament - **2.** [Gebäude] state parliament building.

**Landtags|abgeordnete** *der, die* member of state parliament.

**Landung** (*pl* -en) *die* landing.

**Landungs|brücke** *die* landing stage.

**Land|weg** *der* overland route.

**Land|wein** *der* table wine.

**Land|wirt, in** *der, die* farmer.

**Land|wirtschaft** *die* [Agrarwesen] agriculture.

**landwirtschaftlich** *adj* agricultural <> *adv* agriculturally.

**Landwirtschafts|minister, in** *der, die* minister of agriculture.

**Land|zunge** *die* spit of land.

**lang** (*kompar* **länger;** *superl* **längste**) *adj* long; [Person] tall; **drei Meter ~** three metres long; **vor ~er Zeit** a long time ago; **vor nicht zu ~e Zeit** not (so) long ago; **drei ~e Jahre** three long years; **er arbeitet seit ~em hier** he's been working here for a long time <> *adv fam* - **1.** [entlang] along; **hier/dort ~** this/that way - **2.** [zeitlich]: **drei Jahre ~** for three years; **den ganzen Tag ~** all day; **der ~ ersehnte Tag** the long-awaited day; **~ und breit** *fam fig* & *abw* at great length.

**langärmelig, langärmlig** *adj* long-sleeved.

**langatmig** *adj* long-winded <> *adv* long-windedly.

**lange** (*kompar* **länger;** *superl* **am längsten**) *adv* [während langer Zeit] a long time; [seit langer Zeit] for a long time; **es dauert nicht mehr ~** it won't be long; **das mache ich nicht mehr länger** I won't be doing this for much longer; **das ist noch ~ nicht alles** that's not all by any means; **ich war schon ~ nicht mehr zu Hause** I haven't been home for a long time; **etw ist ~ her** sthg was a long time ago.

**Länge** (*pl* -n) *die* - **1.** [von Brett, Brief] length; **ein Stau von 5 km ~** a 5 km-long traffic jam; **der ~ nach** [teilen] lengthways; [hinstürzen] flat on one's face; **um ~n gewinnen/verlieren/voraus sein** to win/lose/be ahead by a long way - **2.** (*ohne pl*) [Körpergröße] height - **3.** GEOGR longitude - **4.** (*ohne pl*) [Dauer] length; **in die ~ ziehen** to drag out.

➤ **Längen** *pl* [von Film] tedious scenes; [von Buch] tedious passages.

**langen** *vi fam* - **1.** [ausreichen] to be enough; **mir langt es!** *fam* that's enough! - **2.** [greifen] to reach <> *vt:* **jm eine ~** *fam* to give sb a clout.

**Längen|grad** *der* degree of longitude.

**Längen|maß** *das* unit of length.

**längerfristig** *adj* longer-term <> *adv* on a longer-term basis.

**Langeweile, Langeweile** *die* boredom; **aus ~** out of boredom.

**Lang|finger** *der fam* thief; [Taschendieb] pickpocket.

**langfristig** *adj* long-term <> *adv* on a long-term basis.

**lang|gehen** (*perf* ist langgegangen) *vi* (*unreg*) to go along; **wissen, wos langgeht** *fam* to know what's what.

**lang gestreckt** *adj* long.

**langhaarig** *adj* long-haired.

**langjährig** *adj* [Beziehung] long-standing; [Erfahrung, Krankheit] long; [Kunde, Freund, Mitarbeiter] of many years' standing.

**Langlauf** *der* sport cross-country skiing.

**Langlauflski** *der* cross-country ski.

**langlebig** *adj* - **1.** [lange lebend] long-lived - **2.** [lange gebrauchsfähig] durable.

**länglich** *adj* oblong.

**längs** *präp:* ~ einer Sache *(G)* along sthg ◇ *adv* lengthways.

**Längslachse** ['lɛŋsaksəl] *die* longitudinal axis.

**langsam** *adj* - **1.** [nicht schnell] slow - **2.** [allmählich] gradual ◇ *adv* - **1.** [nicht schnell] slowly - **2.** [nach und nach] gradually; **das wird ja ~ Zeit!** it's about time!

**Langsamkeit** *die* slowness.

**Langschläfer, in** *(mpl -; fpl -nen)* *der, die* late riser.

**Langspiellplatte** *die* long-playing record.

**Längslrichtung** *die:* in ~ lengthways.

**Längslschnitt** *der* longitudinal section.

**Längslseite** *die* long side.

**Längslstreifen** *der* vertical stripe.

**längst** *adv* for a long time; **sie war ~ tot** she was long since dead, she had died a long time ago; **~ nicht** nowhere near.

**längstens** *adv fam* - **1.** [höchstens] at (the) most - **2.** [seit langem] for a long time; **es war ~ entschieden** it was long since agreed, it had been agreed a long time ago.

**Langstreckenlflug** *der* long-haul flight.

**Langstreckenllauf** *der* [Wettbewerb] long-distance race; [Sportart] long-distance running *(U)*.

**Languste** [laŋˈgustəl] *(pl -n)* *die* crayfish.

**langweilen** *vt* to bore.
◆ **sich langweilen** *ref* to be bored.

**langweilig** *adj* - **1.** [uninteressant] boring - **2.** *fam* [Zeit raubend] slow ◇ *adv* boringly.

**Langwelle** *die* long wave.

**langwierig** *adj* lengthy.

**Langzeitlarbeitslose** *der, die* long-term unemployed person.

**Langzeitlgedächtnis** *das* long-term memory.

**Langzeitlwirkung** *die* long-term effect.

**Lanze** *(pl -n)* *die* spear; **für jn/etw eine ~ brechen** *fig* to take up the fight on behalf of sb/sthg.

**Laos** *nt* Laos.

**lapidar** *adj* terse ◇ *adv* tersely.

**Lappalie** [laˈpaːljəl] *(pl -n)* *die* trifle.

**Lappe** *(pl -n)* *der* Lapp.

**Lappen** *(pl -)* *der* cloth; **etw geht jm durch die ~** *fam fig* sthg slips through sb's fingers.

**läppern** ◆ **sich läppern** *ref:* **das** *ODER* **es läppert sich** it mounts up.

**Lappin** *(pl -nen)* *die* Lapp.

**läppisch** *adj abw* - **1.** [albern] silly - **2.** [lächerlich] ridiculous.

**Lappland** *nt* Lapland.

**Laptop** [ˈlɛptɔp] *(pl -s)* *der* EDV laptop.

**Lärche** *(pl -n)* *die* larch.

**Lärm** *der* noise; **viel ~ um etw machen** *fig* to make a lot of fuss about sthg; **~ schlagen** *fam fig* to kick up a fuss.

**Lärmlbelästigung** *die* noise pollution.

**lärmempfindlich** *adj* sensitive to noise.

**lärmen** *vi* to make a noise; [Radio] to blare.

**Lärmlschutz** *der* [Schutz] protection against noise; [Vorrichtung] noise insulation *(U)*.

**Lärmschutzlwall** *der* noise barrier.

**Larve** [ˈlarfə] *(pl -n)* *die* larva.

**las** *prät* ⊳ **lesen.**

**Lasagne** [laˈzanjəl] *(pl -n)* *die* lasagne.

**lasch** *adj* - **1.** [Bewegung, Spiel] listless; [Händedruck] limp - **2.** [fade] insipid - **3.** [nachlässig] lax ◇ *adv* - **1.** [schlaff] listlessly - **2.** [fade] insipidly - **3.** [nachlässig] laxly.

**Lasche** *(pl -n)* *die* [von Umschlag] flap; [von Schuh] tongue.

**Laser** [ˈleːzɐ] *(pl -)* *der* laser.

**Laserldrucker** *der* EDV laser printer.

**Laserlstrahl** *der* laser beam.

**Laserltechnik** *die* laser technology *(U)*.

**lasieren** *vt* to varnish.

**lassen** *(präs* **lässt;** *prät* **ließ;** *perf* **hat gelassen** *ODER -) vt* - **1.** [geschehen lassen] to let; **jn nicht ins Haus ~** not to let sb in the house; **Wasser in die Badewanne ~** to run a bath; **die Luft aus den Reifen ~** to let the tyres down - **2.** [unterlassen] to stop; **das Rauchen ~** to stop smoking; **lass das!** stop it! - **3.** [überlassen] to let; **jm etw ~** to let sb have sthg; **ich lasse dir das Auto bis morgen** you can have the car until tomorrow; **eines muss man dir ja ~ ...** *fig* I'll say this much for you ... - **4.** [belassen, zurücklassen] to leave; **lass mich in Ruhe!** leave me alone!; **lass mich!** let me go!; **lass alles so, wie es ist** leave everything as it is; **das habe ich zu Hause gelassen** I left it at home ◇ *vi (perf hat gelassen)* - **1.** [belassen]: **von jm/etw ~ geh** to abandon sb/sthg - **2.** [geschehen lassen]: **lass mal, ich mach das schon!** leave it, I'll do it; **lass mal, du bist heute eingeladen** no, I'm paying today ◇ *aux* - **1.** [veranlassen]: **etw machen** *ODER* **tun ~** to have sthg done; **jn etw tun ~** to have sb do sthg; sich (D) **die Haare schneiden ~** to get ODER have one's hair cut; **sich massieren ~** to have a massage; sich (D) **einen Anzug machen ~** to have a suit made - **2.** [belassen] leave; **lass die Vase auf dem Tisch stehen** leave the vase on the table - **3.** [geschehen lassen]: **jn etw tun ~** to let sb do sthg; **ich lasse mich überraschen** I want it to be a surprise; **etw mit sich/nicht mit sich machen ~** to put up/not to put up with sthg; **ich lass mich von Ihnen nicht beleidigen!** I'm not taking any insults from you!; **lass dir das gesagt sein!** you mark my words!; **lass dich nicht stören** don't let me interrupt you; **das Licht brennen ~** to leave the light on; **die Vase fallen ~** to drop the vase; **jn warten ~** to keep sb waiting.

➤ **sich lassen** ref (perf hat lassen): **das lässt sich machen** it can be done; **es lässt sich trinken** it's drinkable; **die Fenster ~ sich nicht öffnen** the windows don't open; **hier lässt es sich aushalten** I wouldn't mind living here.

**lässig** adj casual ◇ adv - **1.** [salopp] casually - **2.** fam [leicht] easily.

**Lässigkeit** die [Lockerheit] casualness; [Leichtigkeit] ease.

**Lasso** (pl -s) das lasso.

**lässt** präs ⊳ lassen.

**Last** (pl -en) die - **1.** [Gewicht] load - **2.** geh [Bürde] burden - **3.** RW: **jm zur ~ fallen** to be a burden on sb; **jm etw zur ~ legen** to accuse sb of sthg.

➤ **Lasten** pl [Kosten] costs; **zu js ~ en** chargeable to sb.

**lasten** vi - **1.** [Gewicht]: **auf jm ~** to weigh sb down; **auf etw (D) ~** [auf Schultern] to weigh down on sthg; [auf Pfeilern] to bear down on sthg - **2.** [Verantwortung]: **auf jm ~** to weigh on sb - **3.** [finanziell]: **auf jm/etw ~** to be a burden on sb/sthg.

**Lastenaufzug** der goods lift Br ODER elevator Am.

**Laster** (pl -) das [Untugend] vice ◇ der fam [Lastwagen] truck, lorry Br.

**lasterhaft** adj depraved ◇ adv in a depraved way.

**lästern** vi: **über jn/etw ~** to make nasty remarks about sb/sthg.

**lästig** adj annoying; **jm ~ werden/sein** to become/be a nuisance to sb.

**Lastkahn** der barge.

**Lastkraftwagen** der amt heavy goods vehicle.

**Last-Minute-Angebot** [laːstˈmɪnɪt] angəboːt] das last-minute offer.

**Last-Minute-Flug** [laːstˈmɪnɪtˈfluːk] der last-minute flight.

**Lastschrift** die [Abbuchung] debit; [Mitteilung] debit advice.

**Lastwagen** der truck, lorry Br.

**Lastzug** der truck ODER lorry Br and trailer.

**Latein** das Latin; **mit seinem ~ am Ende sein** to be stuck; siehe auch **Englisch(e)**.

**Lateinamerika** nt Latin America.

**Lateinamerikaner, in** (mpl -; fpl -nen) der, die Latin American.

**lateinamerikanisch** adj Latin American.

**lateinisch** adj Latin.

**Lateinisch(e)** das Latin; siehe auch **Englisch(e)**.

**latent** adj latent ◇ adv latently.

**Laterne** (pl -n) die - **1.** [Lampion] Chinese lantern - **2.** [Straßenlaterne] streetlamp.

**Latinum** das: **großes/kleines ~** school examination in Latin taken after at least six/three years.

**latschen** (perf hat/ist gelatscht) fam vi (ist) to traipse ◇ vt (hat): **jm eine ODER ein paar ~** to give sb a clout.

**Latschen** (pl -) der fam [Schuh] worn-out shoe; [Hausschuh] worn-out slipper; **aus den ~ kippen** [ohnmächtig werden] to pass out; [sehr überrascht sein] to be flabbergasted.

**Latschenkiefer** (pl -n) die dwarf pine.

**Latte** (pl -n) die [Brett] slat; [bei Hochsprung] bar; [von Tor] crossbar; **lange ~** fam beanpole; **eine (ganze) ~** fam a (whole) string.

**Lattenrost** der slatted base.

**Latz** (pl Lätze) der bib.

**Lätzchen** (pl -) das bib.

**Latzhose** die dungarees (pl).

**lau** adj - **1.** [mäßig warm, zurückhaltend] lukewarm - **2.** [mild] mild - **3.** [mäßig] moderate ◇ adv - **1.** [zurückhaltend] lukewarmly - **2.** [mäßig] moderately well.

**Laub** das (ohne pl) leaves (pl).

**Laubbaum** der deciduous tree.

**Laubfrosch** der tree frog.

**Laubsäge** die fretsaw.

**Laubwald** der deciduous forest.

**Lauch** der leek.

**Lauer** die: **auf der ~ sitzen** ODER **liegen** fam to be on the lookout.

**lauern** vi: **auf jn/etw ~** [warten] to lie in wait for sb/sthg.

**Lauf** (pl Läufe) der - **1.** (ohne pl) [Laufen] run - **2.** [Betrieb] running - **3.** (ohne pl) [Verlauf, von Fluss] course; **im ~e des Tages** during the day; **etw nimmt seinen ~** sthg takes its course; **im ~(e) der Zeit** in the course of time; **einer Sache (D) freien** ODER **ihren ~ lassen** [Tränen, Gefühlen] to give free rein to sthg; [Angelegenheit] to let sthg take its course - **4.** [von Gewehren] barrel.

**Lauf|bahn** *die* career; **eine ~ einschlagen** to embark on a career.

**laufen** (*präs* **läuft;** *prät* **lief;** *perf* **hat/ist gelaufen**) *vi* (*ist*) - **1.** [schnell] to run - **2.** *fam* [gehen] to walk; **jn ~ lassen** to let sb go; **er läuft dauernd zum Arzt** he's always going to the doctor's - **3.** [zugange sein] to go on; **die Verhandlungen ~ noch** negotiations are still going on; **der Film läuft schon (seit) 10 Minuten** the film started ten minutes ago; **was läuft im Kino?** what's on at the cinema *Br* ODER movies? - **4.** [einen bestimmten Verlauf nehmen] to go; **es läuft gut** it's going well - **5.** [Motor, Maschine] to run, to be on; **ihr Radio läuft schon stundenlang** their radio has been on for hours; **bei ~der Maschine** when the machine is running ODER on - **6.** [funktionieren] to work - **7.** [fließen] to run; **mir läuft die Nase** my nose is running - **8.** [amtlich geführt werden]: **das Konto läuft auf ihren Namen** the account is in her name - **9.** [juristisch gültig sein] to run; **der Vertrag läuft bis zum 31.12** the contract runs ODER is valid until 31 December <> *vt* (*ist*) SPORT to run; **er ist eine neue Bestzeit gelaufen** he ran a new record; **Marathon ~** to run the marathon - **2.** (*ist*) [gehen] to walk - **3.** (*ist*) [mit Sportgerät]: **Ski ~** to ski; **Schlittschuh ~** to skate.

➠ **sich laufen** *ref:* **wie läuft es sich in den neuen Schuhen?** what are your new shoes like for walking?; **sich warm ~** to warm up.

**laufend** *adj* - **1.** [Kosten] regular; [Beschwerden, Störungen] continual - **2.** [gerade ablaufend] current - **3.** [in Betrieb] running - **4.** *RW:* **auf dem Laufenden sein/bleiben** to be/keep up-to-date; **jn auf dem Laufenden halten** to keep sb up-to-date <> *adv* [ständig] continually.

**laufen lassen** *vt* (*unreg*) to let go.

**Läufer** (*pl* -) *der* - **1.** SPORT runner - **2.** [Schachfigur] bishop.

**Läuferin** (*pl* -nen) *die* runner.

**läufig** *adj* on heat.

**Lauf|kundschaft** *die* passing trade.

**Lauf|masche** *die* ladder *Br*, run *Am*.

**Laufpass** *der:* **jm den ~ geben** to give sb his/her marching orders.

**Lauf|schritt** *der* running step; **im ~** at a run.

**Lauf|schuh** *der* [zum Spazierengehen] walking shoe; [von Sportler] running shoe.

**Lauf|steg** *der* catwalk.

**läuft** *präs* ⊏> laufen.

**Lauf|werk** *das* EDV drive.

**Lauf|zeit** *die* - **1.** [Vertragsdauer] term - **2.** [Spielzeit] running time.

**Lauge** (*pl* -n) *die* - **1.** CHEM alkaline solution - **2.** [Waschlauge] soapy water (*U*).

**Laugen|brezel** *die* pretzel.

**Laune** (*pl* -n) *die* - **1.** (*ohne pl*) [Stimmung] mood; **jn bei ~ halten** to keep sb happy; **gute/schlechte ~ haben** to be in a good/bad mood - **2.** [Einfall] whim; **etw aus einer ~ heraus tun** to do sthg on a whim.

➠ **Launen** *pl* [von Person] moods; [von Wetter] vagaries.

**launisch** *adj* moody.

**Laus** (*pl* **Läuse**) *die* louse; **was für eine ~ ist dir denn über die Leber gelaufen?** *fam fig* what's bugging you?

**Lausanne** [loˈzan] *nt* Lausanne.

**Lausbub** (*pl* -en), **Lausbube** (*pl* -n) *der* little rascal.

**lauschen** *vi* [horchen] to listen; [heimlich] to eavesdrop; **einer Sache** (*D*) **~** to listen to sthg; **auf etw** (*A*) **~** to listen to sthg.

**lausig** *fam adj* - **1.** [schlecht, Geld] lousy - **2.** [groß] terrible <> *adv* lousily; **~ kalt** *fam* freezing (cold).

**Lausitz** *die* Lusatia.

**laut** *adj* loud; [lärmend] noisy; **es wurden Zweifel ~** doubts were voiced; **~er sprechen** to speak up, to speak louder <> *adv* loudly; [lärmend] noisily <> *präp* (+ G or D) *amt* according to.

**Laut** (*pl* -e) *der* sound.

**lauten** *vi:* **die Anweisung lautet folgendermaßen ...** the instructions are as follows ...; **auf etw** (*A*) **~: die Anklage lautet auf versuchten Mord** the charge is attempted murder.

**läuten** *vi* to ring; **bei jm ~** to ring sb's bell; **es läutet** there is someone at the door; **von etw ~ hören** to hear something about sthg.

**lauter** *adv* nothing but; **vor ~ Lärm** because of all the noise.

**lauthals** *adv* at the top of one's voice.

**lautlos** *adj* silent; [Stille] complete <> *adv* silently.

**Laut|schrift** *die* phonetic alphabet.

**Laut|sprecher** *der* - **1.** [Tonverstärker] (loud)speaker - **2.** [Megafon] loudspeaker.

**lautstark** *adj* loud <> *adv* loudly.

**Laut|stärke** *die* volume.

**lauwarm** *adj* lukewarm <> *adv* [baden] in lukewarm water; **etw ~ essen/trinken** to eat/drink sthg lukewarm.

**Lava** [ˈlaːva] (*pl* **Laven**) *die* lava.

**Lavendel** [laˈvɛndl̩] *der* lavender.

**Lawine** (*pl* -n) *die* *eigtl* & *fig* avalanche.

**lax** *adj* lax <> *adv* laxly.

**Lay-out** [ˈlɛiˈaut] (*pl* -s) *das* layout.

**leasen** [li:zn̩] *vt* to lease.

**Leasing** ['li:zɪŋ] *das* leasing *(U).*

**leben** *vi* to live; **seine Mutter lebt noch** his mother is still alive; **von etw ~** to live off *ODER* on sthg; **vom Schreiben ~** to make one's living by *ODER* from writing; **es lebe der Präsident!** long live the president!; **lebe wohl!** *geh* farewell!; **damit kann ich ~** I can live with that ◇ *vt* to live; **sie lebte ein erfülltes Leben** she lived a full life.

**Leben** *(pl -) das* - **1.** [gen] life; **im täglichen ~** in everyday life; **jm das ~ schwer machen** to make life difficult for sb; **sich** *(D)* **das ~ nehmen** to take one's (own) life; **ums ~ kommen** to die - **2.** [Treiben] activity - **3.** *RW:* **etw ins ~ rufen** to bring sthg into being; **nie im ~!** not on your life!

**lebendig** *adj* - **1.** [lebend, fortwirkend] living - **2.** [lebhaft] lively ◇ *adv* [lebhaft] in a lively manner.

**Lebens|alter** *das* age.

**Lebens|art** *die* - **1.** [Umgangsformen] manners *(pl)* - **2.** [Lebensform] way of life.

**Lebens|aufgabe** *die* mission in life.

**Lebens|bedingungen** *pl* living conditions.

**Lebens|dauer** *die* - **1.** [von Lebewesen] lifespan - **2.** [von Dingen] life.

**Lebens|ende** *das:* **bis an sein ~** until the end of his life.

**Lebens|erwartung** *die* life expectancy *(U).*

**lebensfähig** *adj* capable of survival.

**Lebens|form** *die* way of life.

**Lebens|gefahr** *die* mortal danger; **außer ~ sein** to be out of danger; **Vorsicht, ~!** danger of death!

**lebensgefährlich** *adj* [Situation, Handlung] extremely dangerous; [Verletzung] critical ◇ *adv* [handeln] extremely dangerously; [sich verletzen] critically.

**Lebens|gefährte** *der* partner.

**Lebens|gefährtin** *die* partner.

**Lebens|haltungskosten** *pl* cost of living *(U).*

**Lebens|jahr** *das* year; **seit seinem zehnten ~** since he was ten.

**Lebens|künstler, in** *der, die:* **er ist ein ~** he knows how to make the best of life.

**Lebens|lage** *die* situation in life.

**lebenslänglich** *adj* & *adv* for life.

**Lebens|lauf** *der* curriculum vitae *Br*, resumé *Am.*

**lebenslustig** *adj* full of life.

**Lebens|mittel** *das* food.

**Lebensmittel|geschäft** *das* grocer's (shop).

**lebensmüde** *adj* - **1.** [den Tod herbeisehnend] tired of life - **2.** *fam* [leichtsinnig]: **du bist wohl ~** you're out of your mind.

**lebensnotwendig** *adj* essential.

**Lebens|qualität** *die (ohne pl)* quality of life.

**Lebens|retter, in** *der, die:* **er war mein ~** he saved my life.

**Lebens|standard** *der* standard of living.

**Lebens|unterhalt** *der* maintenance; **seinen ~ verdienen** to earn one's living.

**Lebens|versicherung** *die* life insurance *(U).*

**Lebens|wandel** *der (ohne pl)* lifestyle.

**Lebens|weise** *die* way of life.

**Lebens|werk** *das* life's work *(U).*

**lebenswichtig** *adj* essential.

**Lebens|zeichen** *das eigtl* & *fig* sign of life; **kein ~ von sich geben** not to show any signs of life.

**Lebens|zeit** *die* life; **auf ~** for life.

**Leber** *(pl -n) die* liver; **frei** *ODER* **frisch von der ~ weg sprechen** *ODER* **reden** *fam fig* to speak quite openly.

**Leber|fleck** *der* mole.

**Leber|käse** *der* spiced meat loaf, sliced and often fried.

**Leber|tran** *der* cod-liver oil.

**Leber|wurst** *die* liver sausage; **die beleidigte ~ spielen** *fam fig* to be in a sulk.

**Lebe|wesen** *das* living being; [tierisch, pflanzlich] living thing.

**lebhaft** *adj* - **1.** [gen] lively - **2.** [Auseinandersetzung] vigorous; [Interesse] keen; [Bedauern] deep ◇ *adv* - **1.** [angeregt] in a lively manner - **2.** [sich widersetzen] vigorously; [sich interessieren] keenly; [bedauern] deeply - **3.** [gut] well.

**Lebhaftigkeit** *die* liveliness.

**Leb|kuchen** *der* gingerbread *(U).*

**leblos** *adj* lifeless ◇ *adv* lifelessly.

**Lech** *der:* **der ~** the (River) Lech.

**lechzen** *vi geh:* **nach etw ~** to long for sthg.

**leck** *adj* leaky.

**Leck** *(pl -s) das* leak.

**lecken** *vt* to lick; **wie geleckt aussehen** *fam fig* [Wohnung] to look spick-and-span; [Person] to be all spruced up; **sich die Lippen ~** to lick one's lips; **die Katze leckte sich das Fell** the cat licked its coat ◇ *vi* - **1.** [schlecken]: **an etw** *(D)* **~** to lick sthg - **2.** [undicht sein] to leak.

➡ **sich lecken** *ref* to lick o.s.

**lecker** *adj* delicious.

**Lecker|bissen** *der* - **1.** [essbar] delicacy - **2.** [Genuss] treat.

**led.** *abk für* **ledig.**

**Leder** (*pl* -) *das* leather *(U)*; **jm ans ~ gehen/ wollen** *fam fig* to go for/want to go for sb.

**Leder|hose** *die* lederhosen *(pl)*.

**Leder|jacke** *die* leather jacket.

**Leder|waren** *pl* leather goods.

**ledig** *adj* single.

**lediglich** *adv* only.

**Lee** *das* ODER *die* lee; **nach ~** to leeward.

**leer** *adj* - **1.** [gen] empty; **~ ausgehen** to come away empty-handed - **2.** [unbeschrieben] blank.

**Leere** *die* emptiness; **sein Schlag ging ins ~** his punch missed; **ins ~ starren** to stare into space.

**leeren** *vt* to empty.
➤ **sich leeren** *ref* to empty.

**Leer|gewicht** *das* unladen weight.

**Leer|gut** *das* (ohne *pl*) empties *(pl)*.

**Leer|lauf** *der* - **1.** TECH neutral; **im ~** in neutral - **2.** [unproduktive Phase] slack period.

**leer stehend** *adj* empty.

**Leer|taste** *die* space bar.

**Leerung** (*pl* -en) *die* emptying *(U)*; [von Briefkasten] collection.

**legal** *adj* legal ⟨⟩ *adv* legally.

**legalisieren** *vt* - **1.** [legal machen] to legalize - **2.** RECHT to authenticate.

**Legalität** *die* legality.

**Legastheniker, in** (*mpl* -; *fpl* -nen) *der*, *die* dyslexic.

**legen** *vt* - **1.** [ablegen] to put; **leg den Schlüssel auf den Tisch** put the key on the table - **2.** [in horizontale Position bringen] to lay; **du musst die Flaschen ins Regal ~, nicht stellen** you should lay the bottles flat in the rack rather than upright - **3.** [Termin] to arrange; **den Urlaub auf Juli ~** to arrange one's holidays for July - **4.** [Haare] to set; **sich die Haare ~ lassen** to have one's hair set - **5.** [installieren - Rohre, Kabel] to lay; **Minen ~** to lay mines; **Feuer ~** to lay a fire - **6.** [Ei] to lay.
➤ **sich legen** *ref* - **1.** [sich hinlegen] to lie down; **sich schlafen ~** to lie down to sleep - **2.** [Staub, Nebel] to settle - **3.** [Aufregung, Sturm] to die down.

**legendär** *adj* legendary.

**Legende** (*pl* -n) *die* - **1.** [gen] legend - **2.** [Irrglaube] myth.

**leger** [leˈʒɛːɐ̯] *adj* casual ⟨⟩ *adv* casually.

**Legierung** (*pl* -en) *die* alloy.

**Legion** (*pl* -en) *die* eigtl & *fig* legion.

**Legionär, in** (*mpl* -e; *fpl* -nen) *der*, *die* legionary.

**Legislative** [leɡɪslaˈtiːvə] (*pl* -n) *die* legislature.

**Legislatur|periode** *die* parliamentary term.

**legitim** *adj* legitimate.

**Legitimation** (*pl* -en) *die* - **1.** [Befugnis] authorization *(U)* - **2.** [Daseinsberechtigung] legitimization *(U)*.

**Lehm** *der* clay.

**Lehm|boden** *der* clay soil.

**lehmig** *adj* clayey.

**Lehne** (*pl* -n) *die* [Rückenlehne] back; [Armlehne] arm.

**lehnen** *vt:* **etw gegen** ODER **an etw** *(A)* **~** to lean sthg against sthg ⟨⟩ *vi:* **an etw** *(D)* **~** to lean against sthg.
➤ **sich lehnen** *ref* - **1.** [stützen]: **sich gegen** ODER **an jn/etw ~** to lean against sb/sthg - **2.** [sich beugen] to lean.

**Lehn|stuhl** *der* armchair.

**Lehr|amt** *das* amt teaching *(U)*.

**Lehr|buch** *das* textbook.

**Lehre** (*pl* -n) *die* - **1.** [Ausbildung] apprenticeship; **in der ~ sein** to be serving one's apprenticeship - **2.** [lehrreiche Erfahrung] lesson; **aus etw eine ~ ziehen** to learn one's lesson from sthg - **3.** [Ideologie - von Propheten, Philosophen] teachings *(pl)*; [ - katholisch, marxistisch] doctrine.

**lehren** *vi* to teach ⟨⟩ *vt* to teach; **jn etw ~** to teach sb sthg.

**Lehrer, in** (*mpl* -; *fpl* -nen) *der*, *die* [in Schule] teacher; [in Sportverein] instructor.

**Lehrer|zimmer** *das* staff room.

**Lehr|gang** *der* course.

**Lehr|jahr** *das* year of one's apprenticeship.

**Lehrling** (*pl* -e) *der* apprentice.

**Lehr|methode** *die* teaching method.

**Lehr|mittel** *pl* teaching materials.

**Lehr|plan** *der* syllabus.

**lehrreich** *adj* instructive.

**Lehr|satz** *der* theorem.

**Lehr|stelle** *die* apprenticeship.

**Lehr|stuhl** *der* amt chair.

**Lehr|veranstaltung** *die* UNI class.

**Lehr|zeit** *die* apprenticeship.

**Leib** (*pl* -er) *der* - **1.** geh [Körper] body - **2.** RW: **mit ~ und Seele** body and soul; **sie ist mit ~ und Seele Krankenschwester** she is a dedicated nurse; **mit ~ und Seele dabei sein** to put one's whole heart into it; **jm jn/etw vom ~ halten** *fam* to keep sb/sthg away from sb; **sich** *(D)* **jn/ etw vom ~ halten** *fam* to keep sb/sthg at bay.

**Leibeskräfte** *pl:* **aus ~n** with all one's might.

**Leib|gericht** *das* favourite dish.

**leibhaftig** *adj* personified ◇ *adv* in person.

**leiblich** *adj* - **1.** [körperlich] physical - **2.** [blutsverwandt] natural.

**Leib|wächter, in** *der, die* bodyguard.

**Leiche** (*pl* -n) *die* corpse; **über ~n gehen** *fam fig* to stop at nothing.

**leichenblass** *adj* deathly pale.

**Leichen|halle** *die* mortuary.

**Leichnam** (*pl* -e) *der geh* body.

**leicht** *adj* - **1.** [an Gewicht] light - **2.** [geringfügig] slight; **~e Kopfschmerzen** a slight headache; **eine ~e Grippe** a mild attack of flu - **3.** [nicht schwierig] easy; **es ~ haben** to have it easy; **er hat es nicht ~** he is having a hard time - **4.** [moralisch locker] loose - **5.** [kalorienarm] diet, low-fat; [Mahlzeit] light; [Zigarette] mild ◇ *adv* - **1.** [einfach, schnell] easily; **das ist sehr ~ möglich** that's perfectly possible; **er ist ~ beleidigt** he is quick to take offence - **2.** [geringfügig] slightly; **~ nicken** to give a little nod; **es riecht ~ angebrannt** there's a slight smell of burning - **3.** [unbeschwert] lightly; **~ gebaut** lightly built; **~ bekleidet** scantily clad.

**Leicht|athlet** *der* athlete.

**Leicht|athletik** *die* athletics (*U*).

**Leicht|athletin** *die* athlete.

**leicht fallen** (*perf* ist leicht gefallen) *vi* (*unreg*): **es fällt ihm leicht/nicht leicht** it comes/doesn't come easy to him.

**leichtfertig** *abw adj* rash ◇ *adv* rashly.

**Leicht|gewicht** *das* lightweight.

**leichtgläubig** *adj* credulous.

**leichthin** *adv* casually.

**Leichtigkeit** *die* - **1.** [geringes Gewicht] lightness - **2.** [Mühelosigkeit] ease.

**leicht machen** *vt* to make easy; **jm etw ~** to make sthg easy for sb.

**Leicht|metall** *das* light metal.

**leicht nehmen** *vt* (*unreg*) not to take seriously.

**Leichtsinn** *der* recklessness.

**leichtsinnig** *adj* reckless ◇ *adv* recklessly.

**leicht verdaulich** *adj* easily digestible.

**leicht verständlich** *adj* easily understandable ◇ *adv* in an easily understandable way.

**leicht verwundet** *adj* slightly wounded.

**leid** *adj*: **jn/etw ~ sein** *ODER* **haben** to be tired of sb/sthg.

**Leid** *das* sorrow; **sie tut mir ~** I feel sorry for her; **es tut mir ~** I'm sorry; *siehe auch* **zuleide**.

**leiden** (*prät* litt; *perf* hat gelitten) *vi* to suffer; **an/unter etw** (*D*) **~** to suffer from sthg ◇ *vt*

- **1.** [erdulden] to suffer - **2.** [mögen]: **etw ~/nicht ~ können** to be able to/not to be able to stand sthg; **jn gut/nicht ~ können** to like/not to like sb.

**Leiden** (*pl* -) *das* illness.

**Leidenschaft** (*pl* -en) *die* passion.

**leidenschaftlich** *adj* passionate ◇ *adv* passionately; **~ gern tanzen** to adore dancing.

**Leidens|gefährte** *der* fellow-sufferer.

**Leidens|gefährtin** *die* fellow-sufferer.

**leider** *adv* unfortunately.

**leidig** *adj* wretched.

**leidlich** *adj* reasonable ◇ *adv* reasonably well.

**Leidtragende** (*pl* -n) *der, die*: **die Kinder sind immer die ~n** the children are always the ones to suffer.

**Leid|wesen** *das*: **zu js ~** to sb's regret.

**Leier** (*pl* -n) *die* lyre; **es ist immer die gleiche ~** *fam fig* it's always the same old story.

**Leier|kasten** *der* barrel organ.

**Leih|arbeit** *die* temporary work.

**Leih|bücherei** *die* lending library.

**leihen** (*prät* lieh; *perf* hat geliehen) *vt* - **1.** [leihweise geben]: **jm etw ~** to lend sb sthg - **2.** [ausleihen]: **sich** (*D*) **etw (von jm) ~** to borrow sthg (from sb); [mieten] to hire *Br ODER* rent *Am* sthg (from sb).

**Leih|gabe** *die* loan.

**Leih|gebühr** *die* [für Auto] hire *Br ODER* rental *Am* charge; [für Buch] lending charge.

**Leih|haus** *das* pawnshop.

**Leih|mutter** *die* surrogate mother.

**Leih|wagen** *der* hire *Br ODER* rental *Am* car.

**leihweise** *adj* & *adv* on loan.

**Leim** (*pl* -e) *der* glue; **jm auf den ~ gehen** *fam fig* to be taken in by sb; **aus dem ~ gehen** *fam* [kaputtgehen] to fall to pieces.

**leimen** *vt* - **1.** [zusammenfügen] to glue together - **2.** [ankleben] to glue.

**Leine** (*pl* -n) *die* - **1.** [Seil] cord; **~ ziehen** *salopp fig* to scram - **2.** [Wäscheleine] line - **3.** [Hundeleine] lead *Br*, leash *Am*.

**Leinen** *das* linen.

**Lein|samen** *der* linseed.

**Lein|wand** *die* [Projektionswand] screen.

**Leipzig** *nt* Leipzig.

**leise** *adj* - **1.** [nicht laut] quiet - **2.** [schwach] slight ◇ *adv* quietly.

**Leiste** (*pl* -n) *die* - **1.** [Latte] edging strip - **2.** [Körperteil] groin.

**leisten** *vt* - **1.** [vollbringen] to achieve - **2.** [machen] to do **- 3.** [Beitrag, Anzahlung] to make **- 4.** [genehmigen]: **sich** *(D)* **etw ~** [sich gönnen] to treat o.s. to sthg; [sich erlauben] to allow o.s. sthg; **sich** *(D)* **etw ~ können** [sich gönnen] to be able to afford sthg; [sich erlauben] to be able to get away with sthg.

**Leistung** *(pl -en) die* **- 1.** ᴛᴇᴄʜ [das Geleistete] performance **- 2.** [Ergebnis] achievement; **schulische ~en** school work **- 3.** [Bezahlung] payment.

➤ **Leistungen** *pl* [Zahlungen] payments.

**Leistungsdruck** *der* pressure to do well.

**leistungsfähig** *adj* **- 1.** [leistungsstark] efficient **- 2.** [zahlungsfähig] solvent; [Versicherung] with good cover.

**Leistungs|gesellschaft** *die* competitive society.

**Leistungs|kurs** *der one of two specialist subjects chosen by pupils for their "Abitur".*

**leistungsorientiert** *adj* [Gesellschaft] competitive; [Bezahlung] performance-related.

**Leistungs|prinzip** *das (ohne pl)* achievement principle.

**Leistungs|sport** *der* competitive sport.

**Leistungs|vermögen** *das* efficiency.

**Leit|artikel** *der* editorial.

**leiten** *vt* **- 1.** [anführen - Unternehmen, Projekt] to run; [ - Gruppe, Diskussion] to lead **- 2.** ᴘʜʏs to conduct **- 3.** [lenken - Bach, Verkehr] to divert; [ - Antrag] to forward; **sich von etw ~ lassen** *fig* to let o.s. be guided by sthg ⬦ *vi* to conduct.

**leitend** *adj* **- 1.** [Stellung] managerial; [Direktor] managing; [Architekt] chief; **~er Angestellter** manager **- 2.** [führend] guiding **- 3.** [weiterleitend] conductive.

**Leiter** *(pl -n* ᴏᴅᴇʀ *-) die (pl Leitern)* ladder ⬦ *der (pl Leiter)* [von Firma, Abteilung] manager; [von Gruppe, Projekt] leader.

**Leiterin** *(pl -nen) die* [von Firma, Abteilung] manager; [von Gruppe, Projekt] leader.

**Leit|faden** *der* introductory guide.

**Leit|hammel** *der* **- 1.** [von Schafherde] bellwether **- 2.** *fam fig* [Anführer] leader.

**Leit|motiv** *das* **- 1.** [Leitgedanke] guiding principle **- 2.** ᴍᴜs leitmotiv.

**Leit|planke** *die* crash barrier *Br*, guardrail *Am.*

**Leitung** *(pl -en) die* **- 1.** [Führung] running; **unter der ~ von jm** conducted by sb **- 2.** [Führungsgruppe] management *(U)* **- 3.** [Rohr] pipe **- 4.** [Draht] wire; [Kabel] cable **- 5.** [Telefonleitung] line; **eine lange ~ haben** *fam fig* to be slow on the uptake.

**Leitungs|netz** *das* **- 1.** [für Wasser, Gas] mains network **- 2.** [für Strom] electricity grid **- 3.** [für Telefon] telephone network.

**Leitungs|rohr** *das* pipe.

**Leitungs|wasser** *das* tap water.

**Leit|währung** *die* key currency.

**Leit|zins** *der* **- 1.** [Diskontsatz] discount rate **- 2.** [Eckzins] basic interest rate *(for savings at statutory notice).*

**Lektion** *(pl -en) die eigtl* & *fig* lesson; **jm eine ~ erteilen** to teach sb a lesson.

**Lektor, in** *(mpl -toren; fpl -nen) der, die* **- 1.** [bei Verlag] editor **- 2.** [an Hochschulen] language assistant.

**Lektüre** *(pl -n) die* **- 1.** [das Lesen] reading **- 2.** [Lesestoff] reading matter.

**Lende** *(pl -n) die* loin.

**lenken** *vt* **- 1.** [Fahrzeug, Gespräch] to steer **- 2.** [richten]: **die Aufmerksamkeit auf jn/etw ~** to draw attention to sb/sthg; **er lenkte den Verdacht auf sich** he attracted suspicion **- 3.** [führen] to control.

**Lenker** *(pl -) der* **- 1.** [Lenkstange] handlebars *(pl)* **- 2.** [Person] driver.

**Lenkerin** *(pl -nen) die* driver.

**Lenk|rad** *das* steering wheel.

**Lenk|stange** *die* handlebars *(pl).*

**Lenkung** *(pl -en) die* **- 1.** [Steuerung] steering *(U)* **- 2.** [Beeinflussung] control.

**Lenz** *(pl -e) der geh* [Frühling] spring; **sich** *(D)* **einen schönen** ᴏᴅᴇʀ **faulen ~ machen** *fam* to have an easy time of it.

**Leopard** *(pl -en) der* leopard.

**Lepra** *die* leprosy.

**Lerche** *(pl -n) die* lark.

**lernbehindert** *adj* with learning difficulties.

**lernen** *vt* to learn; **Klavier spielen ~** to learn to play the piano; **Bäcker ~** to train to be a baker ⬦ *vi* **- 1.** [gen] to learn; **aus der Geschichte ~** to learn from history **- 2.** [für Prüfung] to study, to revise.

**Lern|prozess** *der* learning process.

**Lern|ziel** *das* educational aim.

**lesbar** *adj* **- 1.** [Schrift] legible; **leicht/schwer ~** easy/difficult to read **- 2.** [Text, Buch] readable.

**Lesbe** *(pl -n) die* lesbian.

**Lesbierin** ['lɛsbjərɪn] *(pl -nen) die* lesbian.

**lesbisch** *adj* lesbian.

**Lese|brille** *die* reading glasses *(pl).*

**Lese|buch** *das* reader.

**Lese|lampe** *die* reading lamp.

**lesen** *(präs* **liest***; prät* **las***; perf* **hat gelesen***) vt* **- 1.** [gen] to read **- 2.** [Früchte, Trauben] to pick ⬦ *vi* **- 1.** [gen] to read; **in seiner Miene war die Verzweiflung zu ~** despair was written all over his face **- 2.** [einen Vortrag halten] to lecture.

**Leser** (*pl* -) *der* reader.

**Leseiratte** *die* bookworm.

**Leseribrief** *der* reader's letter, letter to the editor.

**Leserin** (*pl* -nen) *die* reader.

**leserlich** *adj* legible <> *adv* legibly.

**Leserschaft** (*pl* -en) *die* readership.

**Leseisaal** *der* reading room.

**Leseistoff** *der* reading material.

**Leseizeichen** *das* bookmark.

**Leseizugriff** *der* EDV read-only access.

**Lesotho** *nt* Lesotho.

**Lesung** (*pl* -en) *die* reading.

**lethargisch** *adj* lethargic <> *adv* lethargically.

**Lette** (*pl* -n) *der* Latvian.

**Lettin** (*pl* -nen) *die* Latvian.

**lettisch** *adj* Latvian.

**Lettland** *nt* Latvia.

**Letzt** ⟶ **zu guter Letzt** *adv* in the end.

**letzte, r, s** *adj* last; **das ist mein ~s Geld** that's the last of my money; **~s Jahr** last year.

**Letzte** (*pl* -n) *der, die* [Person] last; **~r werden** to come last; **sie kam als ~ an die Reihe** she had her turn last <> *der* [Tag] last day <> *das* **- 1.: er ist das ~** *fam* he's scum; **der Film ist das ~** *fam* the film is the pits **- 2.: bis ins ~** down to the last detail.

**letztemal** *adv* ⊳ Mal.

**letztendlich** *adv* **- 1.** [am Schluss] in the end **- 2.** [im Grunde genommen] ultimately, in the final analysis.

**letztenmal** *adv* ⊳ Mal.

**letztens** *adv* **- 1.** [an letzter Stelle] lastly **- 2.** [vor kurzem] recently.

**letztere, r, s** *adj* the latter; **in ~m Fall** in the latter case <> *pron* the latter.

**Letztere** *die, der, das:* **der/die/das ~** the latter.

**letztgenannte, r, s** *adj:* **die ~ Alternative** the last alternative mentioned.

**letztlich** *adv* **- 1.** [am Schluss] in the end **- 2.** [im Grunde genommen] ultimately, in the final analysis.

**Leuchte** (*pl* -n) *die:* **in der Schule war sie keine ~** *fam* she wasn't one of the brightest children at school.

**leuchten** *vi* to shine; [Feuer, Himmel] to glow.

**leuchtend** *adj* **- 1.** [Farbe] bright; **sie bekam ~e**

**Augen** her eyes lit up **- 2.** [Vorbild, Beispiel] shining <> *adv:* **~ blau/rot** bright blue/red.

**Leuchter** (*pl* -) *der* candelabrum; [für eine Kerze] candlestick.

**Leuchtifarbe** *die* luminous paint.

**Leuchtifeuer** *das* beacon; [auf Landebahn] runway light.

**Leuchtireklame** *die* neon sign.

**Leuchtistift** *der* highlighter.

**Leuchtstoffiröhre** *die* fluorescent tube.

**Leuchtiturm** *der* lighthouse.

**leugnen** *vt* to deny <> *vi* to deny everything.

**Leukämie** *die* leukaemia.

**Leukoplast**® (*pl* -e) *das* Elastoplast® Br, Band-Aid® Am.

**Leute** *pl* **- 1.** [Menschen] people; **die jungen ~** young people; **was die ~ sagen** what people say **- 2.** *RW:* **etw unter die ~ bringen** *fam* to spread sthg around; **unter (die) ~ gehen** *fam* to get out and meet people; **unter (die) ~ kommen** *fam* [bekannt werden] to get around; [ausgehen] to get out and meet people.

**Leutnant** (*pl* -s) *der* second lieutenant.

**leutselig** *adj* affable.

**Level** ['lεvḷ] (*pl* -) *der* level.

**Leviten** [le'vi:tṇ] *pl:* **jm die ~ lesen** to read sb the riot act.

**Lexikon** (*pl* -ka ODER -ken) *das* [Enzyklopädie] encyclopaedia.

**Libanese** (*pl* -n) *der* Lebanese.

**Libanesin** (*pl* -nen) *die* Lebanese.

**libanesisch** *adj* Lebanese.

**Libanon** *der:* **(der) ~** (the) Lebanon.

**Libelle** (*pl* -n) *die* [Insekt] dragonfly.

**liberal** *adj* liberal <> *adv* **- 1.** [tolerant]: **~ eingestellt sein** to be liberal-minded **- 2.** POL: **~ wählen** to vote Liberal.

**Liberale** (*pl* -n) *der, die* Liberal.

**liberalisieren** *vt* to liberalize.

**Liberalisierung** (*pl* -en) *die* liberalization.

**Liberia** *nt* Liberia.

**Libyen** *nt* Libya.

**Libyer, in** (*mpl* -; *fpl* -nen) *der, die* Libyan.

**libysch** *adj* Libyan.

**licht** *adj* **- 1.** [hell] light **- 2.** [spärlich bewachsen] sparse; [Haar] thin.

**Licht** (*pl* -er) *das* **- 1.** [Helligkeit, Lampe] light; **~ machen** to put the light on **- 2.** [Kerze] candle **- 3.** *RW:* **ans ~ kommen** to come to light; **das ~ der Welt erblicken** *geh* to come into the world; **ein günstiges/ungünstiges ~ auf jn/etw werfen** to cast sb/sthg in a favourable/an unfavourable light; **grünes ~ geben** to give the green light; **in einem guten/schlechten ~ erscheinen** to appear in a good/bad light; **jetzt geht mir ein ~ auf** now I see; **jn hinters ~ führen** to pull the wool over sb's eyes; **jn/ etw ins rechte ~ rücken** to show sb/sthg in a favourable light.

➥ **Lichter** pl lights.

**Lichtbilder|vortrag** der illustrated talk.

**Licht|blick** der bright spot.

**lichtempfindlich** adj sensitive to light; [Filmmaterial] photosensitive.

**lichten** vt to thin out.

➥ **sich lichten** ref to thin out.

**Lichter|kette** die - **1.** [als Dekoration - groß] string of light bulbs; [ - klein] fairy lights (pl) - **2.** [Demonstration] chain of demonstrators holding candles or torches.

**lichterloh** adv: **~ brennen** to blaze fiercely.

**Licht|geschwindigkeit** die speed of light.

**Licht|hupe** die AUTO: **die ~ betätigen** to flash one's headlights.

**Licht|jahr** das light year.

**Licht|maschine** die AUTO alternator.

**Licht|orgel** die disco lights (pl) (that flash in time with the music).

**Licht|quelle** die light source.

**Licht|schalter** der light switch.

**Licht|schein** der glow of light.

**lichtscheu** adj - **1.** [Tier] averse to light - **2.** [Gesindel] shady.

**Licht|schranke** die photoelectric beam.

**Lichtschutz|faktor** der (protection) factor; **~ 10** factor 10.

**Licht|strahl** der beam (of light).

**Lichtung** (pl -en) die clearing.

**Lid** (pl -er) das eyelid.

**Lid|schatten** der eye shadow.

**Lid|strich** der line drawn on eyelid with eyeliner.

**lieb** adj - **1.** [nett] kind, nice; **wie ~ von Ihnen, dass Sie daran gedacht haben!** how kind ODER nice of you to remember! - **2.** [als Anrede] dear; **Liebe Sue!** Dear Sue,; **~ Kollegen!** colleagues! - **3.** [geliebt] dear; **mein ~er Herr Freund** my dear friend; **den ~en langen Tag** all day long - **4.** [brav] good; **sei schön ~!** be a good boy/girl! <> adv nicely; siehe auch **lieb gewinnen**; siehe auch **lieb haben**.

**liebäugeln** vi: **mit etw ~** [Gegenstand, Kauf, Arbeitsstelle] to have one's eye on sthg; [Idee, Plan] to be thinking about sthg.

**Liebe** die - **1.** [gen] love; **die ~ zur Kunst** love of art; **sie war seine erste ~** she was his first love - **2.** [Sex] sex; **käufliche ~** prostitution; **~ machen** to make love - **3.** RW: **bei aller ~, aber sein**

**Benehmen ist mir zuviel** much as I love him, I've had enough of his behaviour; **~ auf den ersten Blick** love at first sight.

**Liebelei** (pl -en) die fam fling.

**lieben** vt to love.

➥ **sich lieben** ref - **1.** [lieb haben] to be in love - **2.** [sexuell] to make love.

**liebenswert** adj [Art, Geste] endearing; [Person] likable.

**liebenswürdig** adj kind.

**lieber** kompar ▷ **gern** <> adv better; **das hättest du ~ nicht sagen sollen** it would have been better if you hadn't said that; **~ nicht** maybe we shouldn't, maybe not <> adj: **das wäre mir ~** I'd prefer that.

**Liebes|brief** der love letter.

**Liebes|erklärung** die declaration of love.

**Liebes|kummer** der: **~ haben** to be lovesick.

**Liebes|paar** das lovers (pl).

**liebevoll** adj loving <> adv lovingly.

**lieb gewinnen** vt (unreg): **jn/etw ~** to grow fond of sb/sthg.

**lieb haben** vt (unreg) to love; [gern haben] to be fond of.

➥ **sich lieb haben** ref to be in love.

**Liebhaber** (pl -) der - **1.** [gen] lover - **2.** [Sammler] collector.

**Liebhaberin** (pl -nen) die - **1.** [gen] lover - **2.** [Sammler] collector.

**lieblich** adj [Wein, Kind] sweet; [Landschaft, Klang] gentle; [Anblick] charming.

**Liebling** (pl -e) der - **1.** [als Anrede, der Oma] darling - **2.** [Bevorzugte] favourite.

**Lieblings|gericht** das favourite dish.

**lieblos** adj unaffectionate <> adv - **1.** [ohne Liebe] unaffectionately - **2.** [nachlässig] **sie hat das Essen ~ zubereitet** she carelessly threw the meal together.

**Liebschaft** (pl -en) die abw casual affair.

**Liebste** (pl -n) der, die sweetheart.

**liebsten** superl ▷ **gern**.

➥ **am liebsten** adv: **am ~ würde ich jetzt nach Hause gehen** what I'd really like to do now would be to go home; **das ist mir am ~** I like it best of all.

**Liechtenstein** nt Liechtenstein.

**Lied** (pl -er) das song; REL hymn; **davon kann ich ein ~ singen** I could tell you a thing or two about that.

**Lieder|buch** das songbook.

**liederlich** adj [Person] slovenly; [Arbeit] sloppy; [Lebenswandel] dissolute.

**Liedermacher, in** (mpl -; fpl -nen) der, die singer-songwriter.

**lief** *prät* ▷ **laufen**.

**Lieferant, in** (*mpl* -en; *fpl* -nen) *der, die* supplier.

**lieferbar** *adj* available.

**liefern** *vt* - **1.** [Ware - zustellen] to deliver; [ - verkaufen] to supply; **jetzt bin ich geliefert** *fam* I've had it now - **2.** [Ernte, Eier] to produce - **3.** [Beispiel, Beweis] to provide; **sie lieferten sich ein spannendes Match** they battled out an exciting match ◇ *vi* to deliver.

**Lieferlschein** *der* delivery note.

**Lieferung** (*pl* -en) *die* [Versand] delivery; [Versorgung] supply.

**Lieferlwagen** *der* van.

**Lieferlzeit** *die* delivery time.

**Liege** (*pl* -n) *die* [für Garten] sun lounger; [zum Übernachten] camp bed *Br*, cot *Am*.

**liegen** (*prät* lag; *perf* hat gelegen) *vi* - **1.** [gen] to lie; **das Schiff liegt im Hafen** the ship is docked; **in den Bergen liegt viel Schnee** there's a lot of snow on the hills - **2.** [angelehnt sein]: **an** *ODER* **auf etw** (A) ~ to rest on sthg - **3.** [sich befinden] to be; **Dresden liegt an der Elbe** Dresden is on the Elbe; **das Haus liegt schön** the house is beautifully situated - **4.** [in Reihenfolge] to lie; **sie liegt auf dem vierten Platz** she's (lying) in fourth place; **an der Spitze** ~ to be in the lead - **5.** [mit Dativ]: **Physik liegt mir nicht** physics isn't my thing; **es liegt mir viel daran** it matters a lot to me - **6.** [mit Präpositionen]: **an mir soll es nicht** ~! don't let me stop you!; **es liegt nicht an dir** it's not your fault; **die Entscheidung liegt bei Ihnen** it's your decision; **das liegt daran, dass ...** this is because ... - **7.** [zeitlich] to be; **das liegt lange zurück** that was a long time ago.

**liegen bleiben** (*perf* ist liegen geblieben) *vi* (*unreg*) - **1.** [nicht aufstehen] to remain lying down; **(im Bett)** ~ to stay in bed - **2.** [Schnee, Laub] to lie - **3.** [vergessen werden] to be left behind - **4.** [unerledigt bleiben] to be left undone - **5.** [eine Panne haben] to break down.

**liegen lassen** (*perf* hat liegen gelassen *ODER* -) *vt* (*unreg*) to leave; **jn/etw links** ~ *fam fig* to ignore sb/sthg.

**Liegelplatz** *der* berth.

**Liegelsitz** *der* reclining seat.

**Liegelstuhl** *der* [am Strand] deckchair; [im Garten] sun lounger.

**Liegelstütz** (*pl* -e) *der* press-up.

**Liegelwagen** *der* couchette car.

**lieh** *prät* ▷ **leihen**.

**ließ** *prät* ▷ **lassen**.

**liest** *präs* ▷ **lesen**.

**Lifestyle** ['laɪfstaɪl] *der* (*ohne pl*) lifestyle.

**Lift** (*pl* -e *ODER* -s) *der* - **1.** [Aufzug] lift *Br*, elevator *Am* - **2.** (*pl* Lifte) [Skilift] ski lift.

**liften** *vt*: **sich das Gesicht** ~ **lassen** to have a face-lift.

**Liga** (*pl* Ligen) *die* league; **in der 1./2.** ~ **spielen** to be in the 1st/2nd division.

**liiert** [li'iːɐt] *adj*: **mit jm** ~ **sein** to be having an affair with sb.

**Likör** (*pl* -e) *der* liqueur.

**lila** *adj* (*unver*) lavender; [dunkler] mauve.

**Lila** *das* purple; [Zartlila] lilac; [Tieflila] mauve.

**Lilie** ['liːljə] (*pl* -n) *die* lily.

**Liliputaner, in** (*mpl* -; *fpl* -nen) *der, die* dwarf.

**Limit** (*pl* -s) *das* limit.

**Limo** (*pl* -s) *die fam* fizzy drink *Br*, soda *Am*; [mit Zitronengeschmack] lemonade; [mit Orangengeschmack] orangeade.

**Limonade** (*pl* -n) *die* fizzy drink *Br*, soda *Am*; [mit Zitronengeschmack] lemonade; [mit Orangengeschmack] orangeade.

**Linde** (*pl* -n) *die* lime tree.

**lindern** *vt* [Schmerzen] to relieve; [Not] to alleviate.

**Linderung** *die* [von Schmerzen] relief; [von Not] alleviation.

**Lineal** (*pl* -e) *das* ruler.

**linear** *adj* linear; [Tarif, Erhöhung] across-the-board ◇ *adv* [sich erhöhen] across the board.

**Linguist, in** (*mpl* -en; *fpl* -nen) *der, die* linguist.

**Linguistik** *die* linguistics (*U*).

**linguistisch** *adj* linguistic.

**Linie** ['liːnjə] (*pl* -n) *die* - **1.** [Strich, Verwandtschaftslinie] line; **sie stammt in direkter** ~ **vom Kaiser Karl ab** she is directly descended from Emperor Charles - **2.** [Denkrichtung] policy - **3.** [von Verkehrsmittel] number; **die** ~ **3** the number 3 - **4.** [Figur]: **auf die schlanke** ~ **achten** to watch one's figure - **5.** *RW*: **auf der ganzen** ~ completely; **in erster** ~ first and foremost.

**Linienlblatt** *das* ruled sheet.

**Linienlbus** *der* bus (*forming part of public transport network*).

**Linienlflug** *der* scheduled flight.

**linientreu** *adj abw* faithful to the party line.

**Linienverkehr** *der* (*ohne pl*) [Flugverkehr] scheduled flights (*pl*); [Omnibusverkehr] buses (*forming part of public transport network*).

**linieren, liniieren** *vt* to rule (lines on).

**link** *adj fam abw* shady.

**linke, r, s** *adj* - **1.** [Seitenangabe] left - **2.** [linkspolitisch] left-wing.

**Linke** (*pl* -n) *die* - **1.** [Hand] left hand; **zur** ~**n** to the left; **jm zur** ~**n** on sb's left - **2.** *POL*: **die** ~ the

Left - **3.** [Schlag] left <> *der, die* [Person] left-winger.

**linkisch** *adj* awkward, clumsy.

**links** *adv* - **1.** [Angabe der Seite] on the left; [Angabe der Richtung] left; ~ **von jm/etw** on sb's/sthg's left; **nach ~ fahren** to turn left; **von ~** from the left; **etw mit ~ machen** *fam fig* to do sthg easily - **2.** [verkehrt herum] inside out; **etw von ~ bügeln** to iron sthg on the wrong side - **3.** [linkspolitisch] left-wing; ~ **wählen** to vote for the Left <> *präp (+ G)* - **1.** [Angabe der Seite] on the left-hand side of - **2.** [politisch] to the left of.

**Links|abbieger** *der* car turning left.

**Links|außen** *(pl -)* *der* outside left.

**linksextrem** *adj* extreme left-wing; ~**e Jugendliche** young left-wing extremists; ~**e Gruppierung** extreme left-wing faction.

**Links|extremist, in** *der, die* left-wing extremist.

**linksgerichtet** *adj* left-wing.

**Linkshänder, in** *(mpl -; fpl -nen)* *der, die* left-hander.

**linkshändig** *adj* left-handed.

**linksherum** *adv* - **1.** [nach links] round to the left - **2.** [falsch herum] inside out.

**Links|kurve** *die* left-hand bend.

**linksradikal** *adj* radical left-wing.

**linksseitig** *adj & adv* on the left side.

**Linksverkehr** *der:* **in Großbritannien herrscht ~** people drive on the left in Great Britain.

**Linoleum** [li'no:leʊm] *das* linoleum.

**Linol|schnitt** *der* linocut.

**Linse** *(pl -n)* *die* - **1.** [Nahrungsmittel] lentil - **2.** [optisch] lens.

**Linz** *nt* Linz.

**Linzer** *(pl -)* *der* native/inhabitant of Linz <> *adj (unver)* of/from Linz.

**Linzerin** *(pl -nen)* *die* native/inhabitant of Linz.

**Lippe** *(pl -n)* *die* lip; **sich *(D)* die ~n lecken** to lick one's lips; **an js ~n hängen** *fig* to hang on sb's every word; **keine Klage kam über ihre ~n** she didn't utter a word of complaint.

**Lippen|bekenntnis** *das* lip-service; **ein ~ ablegen** to pay lip-service.

**Lippen|stift** *der* lipstick.

**liquidieren** *vt* - **1.** WIRTSCH [ermorden] to liquidate - **2.** [berechnen] to charge.

**lispeln** *vi* to lisp.

**Lissabon** *nt* Lisbon.

**List** *(pl -en)* *die* - **1.** [listiges Verhalten] cunning; **mit ~ und Tücke** cunningly - **2.** [listige Handlung] cunning trick.

**Liste** *(pl -n)* *die* list; **auf der schwarzen ~ stehen** to be on the blacklist.

**Listen|preis** *der* list price.

**listig** *adj* cunning <> *adv* cunningly.

**Lit.** *(abk für Literatur)* lit.

**Litanei** *(pl -en)* *die abw* [Aufzählung] litany.

**Litauen** *nt* Lithuania.

**Litauer, in** *(mpl -; fpl -nen)* *der, die* Lithuanian.

**litauisch** *adj* Lithuanian.

**Liter** *(pl -)* *der* ODER *das* litre; **ein ~ Milch** a litre of milk.

**literarisch** *adj* literary <> *adv* - **1.** [Literatur betreffend]: ~ **interessiert sein** to be interested in literature; ~ **gebildet sein** to have studied literature - **2.** [gewählt] in a literary manner.

**Literat, in** *(mpl -en; fpl -nen)* *der, die* literary figure.

**Literatur** *(pl -en)* *die* literature.

**Literatur|angabe** *die* (bibliographical) reference.

**Literatur|verzeichnis** *das* bibliography.

**Literatur|wissenschaft** *die* literary studies *(pl)*.

**Liter|flasche** *die* litre bottle.

**literweise** *adv* by the litre.

**Litfaß|säule** *die* advertising column.

**Lithografie, Lithographie** [litografi:] *(pl -n)* *die* - **1.** [Technik] lithography - **2.** [Druck] lithograph.

**litt** *prät* ⊳ leiden.

**Liturgie** *(pl -n)* *die* liturgy.

**liturgisch** *adj* liturgical.

**live** [laif] *adj (unver) adv* live.

**Lizenz** *(pl -en)* *die* licence.

**LKA** [ɛlka:'a:] *(abk für Landeskriminalamt)* *das* criminal investigation department of a federal state.

**Lkw, LKW** [ɛlka:'ve:] *(pl -s)* *(abk für Lastkraftwagen)* *der* truck, HGV *Br*, lorry *Br*.

**Lob** *das* praise; **ein hohes ~** high praise; **jm ein (großes) ~ erteilen** to praise sb (highly).

**Lobby** ['lɔbi] *(pl -s)* *die* lobby.

**loben** *vt* to praise; **das lobe ich mir!** [sehr gut] that's what I like (to see)!; **da lobe ich mir doch meine alte Schreibmaschine!** give me my old typewriter any day!

**lobenswert** *adj* commendable, praiseworthy.

**löblich** *adj* commendable, praiseworthy.

**Loch** *(pl Löcher)* *das* hole; [im Zahn] cavity; **schwarzes ~** black hole; **Löcher in die Luft gucken** *fig* to stare into space.

**lochen** *vt* to punch a hole/holes in.

**Locher** (*pl* -) *der* hole punch.

**löchern** *vt fam* to pester.

**löchrig** *adj* full of holes.

**Locke** (*pl* -n) *die* curl; ~n haben to have curly hair.

**locken** *vt* - 1. [anlocken] to entice; jn in eine Falle ~ to lure sb into a trap - 2. [wellen] to curl.

**Lockenwickler** (*pl* -) *der* curler.

**locker** *adj* - 1. [gen] loose; ein ~es Mundwerk haben to have a loose tongue - 2. [Beziehung] casual; [Haltung] laid-back ◇ *adv* - 1. [nicht fest] loosely - 2. [zwanglos] casually - 3. *fam* [mit Leichtigkeit] no sweat.

**locker|lassen** *vi (unreg)*: nicht ~ not to give up.

**lockern** *vt* - 1. [Schraube, Griff, Erde, Krawatte] to loosen; die Muskeln ~ to limber up - 2. [Gesetze, Vorschriften] to relax.

➤ **sich lockern** *ref* - 1. [Schraube, Zahn] to work itself loose - 2. [Stimmung] to become more relaxed; [Muskeln, Griff] to relax.

**Lockerungs|übung** *die* limbering-up exercise.

**lockig** *adj* [Haare] curly; [Mensch] curly-haired.

**Lock|vogel** *der* decoy.

**Loden|mantel** *der* loden coat.

**lodern** *vi* [Feuer] to blaze.

**Löffel** (*pl* -) *der* spoon.

**löffeln** *vt* to spoon.

**log** *prät* ⊳ lügen.

**Logarithmus** (*pl* -ithmen) *der* logarithm.

**Log|buch** *das* log, logbook.

**Loge** ['loːʒə] (*pl* -n) *die* - 1. [im Theater] box - 2. [von Freimaurern, Portier] lodge.

**logieren** [lo'ʒiːrən] *vi geh* to stay.

**Logik** *die* logic.

**logisch** *adj* logical ◇ *adv* logically.

**Logopäde** (*pl* -n) *der* speech therapist.

**Logopädin** (*pl* -nen) *die* speech therapist.

**Lohn** (*pl* Löhne) *der* - 1. [Bezahlung] wages (*pl*), pay - 2. [Belohnung] reward.

**Lohnabbau** *der* reduction in wages.

**lohnen** *vt* - 1. [rechtfertigen] to be worth; es lohnt eine Renovierung nicht mehr it's no longer worth repairing - 2. *geh* [vergelten]: jm etw ~ to repay sb for sthg.

➤ **sich lohnen** *ref* to be worth it; es ODER das lohnt sich (nicht) it's (not) worth it; es lohnt sich, etw zu tun it's worth doing sthg.

**lohnend** *adj* worthwhile.

**Lohn|erhöhung** *die* pay rise.

**Lohn|forderung** *die* pay claim.

**Lohn|gruppe** *die* wage bracket.

**Lohn|kürzung** *die* wage cut.

**Lohn|steuer** *die* income tax (paid by employees), ≃ PAYE *Br*.

**Lohnsteuerjahres|ausgleich** *der* annual adjustment of income tax.

**Lohnsteuer|karte** *die* form filled in by employer stating employee's annual income and tax paid.

**Lohn|tüte** *die* wage packet.

**Loire** [loaːʀ] *die*: die ~ the Loire.

**Lok** (*pl* -s) *die* (railway) engine.

**lokal** *adj* local.

**Lokal** (*pl* -e) *das* bar, pub *Br*.

**lokalisieren** *vt* - 1. [örtlich bestimmen] to locate - 2. [begrenzen] to contain.

**Lokal|nachrichten** *pl* local news (U).

**Lokal|patriotismus** *der* local pride.

**Lokal|presse** *die* local press.

**Lokal|verbot** *das*: jm ~ erteilen to bar sb.

**Lokomotive** [lokomo'tiːvə] (*pl* -n) *die* (railway) engine.

**London** *nt* London.

**Londoner, in** (*mpl* -; *fpl* -nen) *der, die* Londoner.

**Look** [luk] (*pl* -s) *der* look.

**Looping** ['luːpɪŋ] (*pl* -s) *der* loop-the-loop.

**Lorbeer** (*pl* -en) *der* [Gewürz] bay leaf.

➤ **Lorbeeren** *pl* [Ruhm]: damit kannst du ~en machen it's nothing to be proud of; sich auf seinen ~en ausruhen (können) to (be able to) rest on one's laurels.

**Lorbeer|blatt** *das* bay leaf.

**los** *adj* - 1. [lose] loose - 2. *RW*: jn/etw ~ sein *fam* to have got rid of sb/sthg; mit mir ist heute nicht viel ~ *fam abw* I'm not up to much today; es ist viel/wenig/nichts ~ *fam* there is a lot/not much/nothing going on; was ist ~? *fam* what's the matter?, what's wrong?; was ist hier ~? *fam* what's going on here? ◇ *interj* come on!

**Los** (*pl* -e) *das* - 1. [Losentscheid]: durch das ~ bestimmen to decide by drawing lots - 2. [in der Lotterie] ticket; das große ~ the jackpot; mit jm/einer Sache das große ~ ziehen *fig* to hit the jackpot with sb/sthg - 3. *geh* [Schicksal] lot.

**Los Angeles** [lɔs'endʒələs] *nt* Los Angeles.

**lösbar** *adj* solvable.

**los|binden** *vt (unreg)* to untie.

**Lösch|blatt** *das* sheet of blotting paper.

**löschen** *vt* - 1. [Kerze, Feuer] to extinguish, to put out - 2. [Konto] to close; [Schuld, Hypothek] to pay off - 3. [Tonträger] to erase - 4. [Schiff, Ladung] to unload - 5. *EDV* to delete.

**Löschen** *das* - **1.** [von Feuer] extinguishing - **2.** [von Konto] closing; [von Schuld, Hypothek] paying off - **3.** [von Tonträger] erasure - **4.** [von Schiff, Ladung] unloading - **5.** EDV deletion.

**Löschpapier** *das* blotting paper.

**lose** *adj* loose; **ein ~s Mundwerk haben** to have a loose tongue <> *adv* [locker] loosely.

**Löse|geld** *das* ransom.

**losen** *vi* [mit einem Los] to draw lots; **um etw ~** to draw lots for sthg; **darum ~, wer/wann/was ...** to draw lots to see who/when/what ...

**lösen** *vt* - **1.** [trennen - Knoten] to undo; [ - Bremse] to release; [ - Schraube] to unscrew; [ - Haare] to let down - **2.** [locker machen] to loosen - **3.** [abmachen]: **etw von etw ~** to remove sthg from sthg - **4.** [rechnen] to work out - **5.** [klären - Aufgabe, Rätsel] to solve - **6.** [Vertrag] to cancel; [Verlobung] to break off; [Ehe] to dissolve - **7.** [Fahrkarte] to buy - **8.** [auflösen] to dissolve - **9.** [Husten, Schleim] to loosen; [Krampf] to ease.
➤ **sich lösen** *ref* - **1.** [aus Versehen] to break free; [Schuss] to go off; [Lawine] to start; **sich aus etw ~** to break away from sthg - **2.** [Tapete, Briefmarke] to come off; [Knoten] to come undone; [Schraube] to work loose - **3.** [sich auflösen] to dissolve; [Schleim] to loosen - **4.** [umdenken]: **sich von etw ~** [von Vorurteilen, Vorstellung] to rid o.s. of sthg - **5.** [sich trennen]: **sich von jm ~** to break away from sb - **6.** [Muskeln] to relax; [Verkrampfung, Spannung] to ease - **7.** [Problem, Rätsel] to be solved.

**los|fahren** (*perf* ist **losgefahren**) *vi* (*unreg*) to set off.

**los|gehen** (*perf* ist **losgegangen**) *vi* (*unreg*) - **1.** [weggehen] to set off; **auf jn ~** fig to go for sb; **auf ein Ziel ~** to pursue a goal - **2.** [anfangen] to start; **gleich gehts los** it's just about to start; **jetzt geht das schon wieder los!** here we go again!; **los gehts!** off we go!

**los|kaufen** *vt* to buy the release of.

**los|kommen** (*perf* ist **losgekommen**) *vi* (*unreg*) to get away; **(nicht) von jm/etw ~** (not) to get away from sb/sthg.

**los|lassen** *vt* (*unreg*) - **1.** [Person, Gegenstand] to let go of; **lass mich los!** let go of me!, let me go! - **2.** [Tier]: **ein Hund auf jn ~** to set a dog on sb; **den Hund ~** to let the dog off the lead Br ODER leash Am - **3.** [Schrei, Fluch] to let out - **4.** [Subj: Gedanke, Problem]: **der Gedanke lässt mich nicht los** I can't get the thought out of my head.

**los|legen** *vi fam* to get started; **mit Fragen ~** to start firing questions; **na, denn leg mal los!** fire away, then!

**löslich** *adj* soluble; [Kaffeepulver, Milchpulver] instant.

**los|lösen** *vt* to remove.

➤ **sich loslösen** *ref* - **1.** [Etikett, Tapete] to come off - **2.** [Person] to break away.

**los|machen** *vt* to undo; [Hund] to let off the lead Br ODER leash Am.
➤ **sich losmachen** *ref* to free o.s.

**los|müssen** *vi* (*unreg*) *fam* to have to go.

**los|reißen** *vt* (*unreg*) to tear off.
➤ **sich losreißen** *ref* [von Kette, Griff] to break free; [von Buch, Anblick] to tear o.s. away.

**Losung** (*pl* -en) *die* - **1.** [Motto] motto; [Spruch] slogan - **2.** [Kennwort] password.

**Lösung** (*pl* -en) *die* - **1.** [gen] solution; [von Konflikt] resolution - **2.** [von Eltern, Tradition] breaking away - **3.** [von Ehe, Bündnis] breakup; [von Arbeitsverhältnis] termination.

**los|werden** (*perf* ist **losgeworden**) *vt* (*unreg*) *fam* - **1.** [gen] to get rid of; **ich werde das Gefühl nicht los, dass ...** I can't escape the feeling that ... - **2.** [Vermögen] to lose.

**Lot** (*pl* -e) *das* - **1.** [Senkblei] plumb line; **etw wieder ins ~ bringen** fig to put sthg right - **2.** SCHIFF sounding line - **3.** MATH perpendicular; **das ~ fällen** to drop a perpendicular.

**löten** *vt* to solder.

**Lothringen** *nt* Lorraine.

**Lotion** [lo'tsio:n] (*pl* -en) *die* lotion.

**Lotse** (*pl* -n) *der* - **1.** [von Schiff] pilot - **2.** [Fluglotse] air traffic controller.

**lotsen** *vt* to guide.

**Lotsin** (*pl* -nen) *die* - **1.** [von Schiff] pilot - **2.** [Fluglotsin] air traffic controller.

**Lotterie** [lɔtə'ri:] (*pl* -n) *die* lottery.

**Lotto** *das* - **1.** [Glücksspiel] (national) lottery; **im ~ gewinnen** to win the (national) lottery - **2.** [Gesellschaftsspiel] lotto.

**Lotto|gewinn** *der* (national) lottery win.

**Lotto|schein** *der* (national) lottery ticket.

**Lotus** (*pl* -) *der* lotus.

**Loveparade** ['lavpəreɪd] *die* Love Parade, *annual open-air mass rave and procession in the centre of Berlin.*

**LOVEPARADE**

The love parade has become an annual event since it first took place in Berlin in 1989. Every summer, thousands of techno fans throng through the centre of Berlin and dance through the streets to the sound of music played from carnival floats.

**Löwe** (*pl* -n) *der* - **1.** [Tier] lion - **2.** [Sternzeichen, Person] Leo; **~ sein** to be a Leo.

**Löwen|anteil** *der* lion's share.

**Löwenzahn** *der* dandelion.

**Löwin** (*pl* -nen) *die* lioness.

**loyal** [lɔa'ja:l] *adj* loyal <> *adv* loyally.

**Loyalität** [lɔajaliˈtɛːt] *die* loyalty.

**lt.** *abk für* laut.

**Lübeck** *nt* Lübeck.

**Luchs** [lʊks] (*pl* -e) *der* lynx.

**Lücke** (*pl* -n) *die* - **1.** [gen] gap; [zum Parken] space - **2.** [in Gesetz] loophole.

**Lückenbüßer, in** (*mpl* -; *fpl* -nen) *der, die abw* stopgap.

**lückenhaft** *adj* [Erinnerung, Beweisführung, Wissen] sketchy; **sein Lebenslauf ist ~** he has gaps in his CV *Br* ODER resumé *Am* ◇ *adv* [sich erinnern] sketchily.

**lückenlos** *adj* [Lebenslauf] complete; **seine Erinnerung daran ist ~** he remembers everything perfectly ◇ *adv* fully, completely.

**lud** *prät* ▷ laden.

**Luder** (*pl* -) *das fam* - **1.** *abw* [niederträchtige Frau] cow - **2.** [Person]: **armes ~** poor soul; **du kleines ~!** you little so-and-so!

**Luft** (*pl* **Lüfte**) *die* - **1.** [gen] air; **freie ~** open air; **die ~ anhalten** to hold one's breath; **~ holen** [atmen] to take a breath; [eine Pause machen] to catch one's breath; **frische ~ schöpfen** to get some fresh air; **nach ~ schnappen** to gasp - **2.** [Platz] room - **3.** RW: **aus dem Projekt ist die ~ raus** the life has gone out of the project; **nun halt mal die ~ an!** *fam* put a sock in it!; **die ~ ist rein** *fam* the coast is clear; **das ist aus der ~ gegriffen** that's pure invention; **in der ~ liegen** to be in the air; **in der ~ hängen** *fam* [Projekt, Entscheidung] to be up in the air; **jn in der ~ hängen lassen** to leave sb hanging in the air; **in die ~ gehen** *fam* to blow one's top; **mir blieb die ~ weg** *fam* I was gobsmacked; **sich** (*D*) **seinem Ärger ~ machen** to give vent to one's anger; **sich in ~ auflösen** *fam* to vanish into thin air.

**Luftangriff** *der* air raid.

**Luftaufnahme** *die* aerial photograph.

**Luftballon** *der* balloon.

**Luftblase** *die* air bubble.

**Luftbrücke** *die* airlift.

**luftdicht** *adj* airtight ◇ *adv* [verschließen] hermetically.

**Luftdruck** *der* air pressure.

**lüften** *vt* - **1.** [Zimmer, Wäsche] to air - **2.** [Geheimnis] to reveal ◇ *vi* to let some air in.

**Luftfahrt** *die* aviation.

**Luftfeuchtigkeit** *die* humidity.

**Luftgewehr** *das* air rifle.

**luftig** *adj* - **1.** [Kleidung] light - **2.** [hochgelegen]: **in ~er Höhe** high up - **3.** [Raum] airy ◇ *adv* [leicht] lightly.

**Luftkissenfahrzeug** *das* hovercraft.

**Luftkurort** *der* climatic health resort.

**luftleer** *adj*: **~er Raum** vacuum.

**Luftlinie** *die*: **600 km ~** 600 km as the crow flies.

**Luftloch** *das* - **1.** [Öffnung] air hole - **2.** [im Flug] air-pocket.

**Luftmatratze** *die* airbed.

**Luftpirat, in** *der, die* (aircraft) hijacker.

**Luftpost** *die* airmail; **mit** ODER **per ~** (by) airmail.

**Luftpumpe** *die* air pump.

**Luftraum** *der* airspace.

**Luftröhre** *die* windpipe.

**Luftschacht** *der* ventilation shaft.

**Luftschlange** *die* streamer.

**Luftschloss** *das*: **Luftschlösser bauen** to build castles in the air.

**Luftschutzraum** *der* air-raid shelter.

**Luftsprung** *der* leap; **vor Freude machte er einen ~** he leapt with joy.

**Lüftung** (*pl* -en) *die* - **1.** [Gerät] ventilation (system) - **2.** [Lüften] ventilation.

**Luftveränderung** *die* change of air.

**Luftverkehr** *der* air traffic.

**Luftverschmutzung** *die* air pollution.

**Luftwaffe** *die* airforce; HIST Luftwaffe.

**Luftweg** *der*: **auf dem ~** by air.

**Luftzug** *der* [in Gebäude] draught; [im Freien] breath of wind.

**Lug** *der geh*: **~ und Trug** lies (*pl*) and deception.

**Lüge** (*pl* -n) *die* lie.

**lügen** (*prät* **log**; *perf* **hat gelogen**) *vi* to lie; **das ist gelogen!** that's a lie!; **er lügt wie gedruckt** *fam* [Charakterzug] he's a pathological liar; [in Bezug auf etw] he's lying through his teeth.

**Lügner, in** (*mpl* -; *fpl* -nen) *der, die* liar.

**Luke** (*pl* -n) *die* [in Dach] skylight; [bei Schiff] hatch.

**lukrativ** *adj* lucrative.

**Lümmel** (*pl* -) *der fam* - **1.** [Kind] rascal - **2.** *abw* [Rüpel] lout.

**lümmeln** ⬥ **sich lümmeln** *ref fam abw* to sprawl.

**Lump** (*pl* -en) *der abw* scoundrel.

**lumpen** *vt*: **sich nicht ~ lassen** *fam* to spare no expense.

**Lumpen** (*pl* -) *der* rag.
⬥ **Lumpen** *pl abw* rags.

**lumpig** *adj* - **1.** *fam* [lausig] miserable - **2.** [gemein] mean ◇ *adv* [gemein] meanly.

**Lunchpaket** *das* packed lunch.

**Lüneburger Heide** *die* Lüneberg Heath.

**Lunge** (*pl* -n) *die* lungs (*pl*).

**➡ grüne Lunge** *die:* **die grüne ~ einer Großstadt** the lungs of a city.

**Lungenentzündung** *die* pneumonia.

**Lungenflügel** *der* lung.

**Lungenkrebs** *der* lung cancer.

**Lunte** (*pl* -n) *die* fuse; **~ riechen** *fam* [bei Gefahr] to sense danger; [Täuschung erahnen] to smell a rat.

**Lupe** (*pl* -n) *die* magnifying glass; **jn/etw unter die ~ nehmen** *fam fig* to examine sb/sthg very closely.

**lupenrein** *adj* **- 1.** [Exemplar] perfect **- 2.** [Diamant] flawless; [Alibi] watertight.

**Lurch** (*pl* -e) *der* amphibian.

**Lust** (*pl* **Lüste**) *die* **- 1.** [Bedürfnis] desire; **die ~ am Reisen ist mir vergangen** I don't feel like travelling any more; **~ bekommen/haben, etw zu tun** to feel like doing sthg; **ich habe keine ~ zum Spazierengehen** I don't feel like going for a walk; **~/keine~ auf etw** (A) **haben** to feel/ not to feel like sthg; **ich hätte jetzt ~ auf ein Eis** I fancy an ice cream; **er arbeitet ganz nach ~ und Laune** he works as and when he feels like it **- 2.** [Freude] pleasure; **die ~ an etw** (D) **verlieren** no longer to take any pleasure in sthg **- 3.** [Begierde] desires (*pl*), lust.

**lüstern** *adj* lascivious ◇ *adv:* **~ blicken** to leer.

**lustig** *adj* **- 1.** [komisch] funny; [unterhaltsam] entertaining; **sich über jn/etw ~ machen** to make fun of sb/sthg **- 2.** [fröhlich - Person, Augen] merry; [ - Abend] fun, enjoyable ◇ *adv* **- 1.** [komisch] funnily; [unterhaltsam] entertainingly **- 2.** [unbekümmert] merrily.

**lustlos** *adj* unenthusiastic ◇ *adv* unenthusiastically.

**lustvoll** *adj* pleasurable ◇ *adv* [schmatzen, spielen] with relish; [stöhnen] pleasurably.

**lutherisch** *adj* Lutheran.

**lutschen** *vt* to suck ◇ *vi:* **an etw** (D) **~** to suck sthg.

**Lutscher** (*pl* -) *der* [Süßigkeit] lollipop.

**Luv** (*ohne Artikel*) SCHIFF: **nach ~** to windward.

**Luxemburg** *nt* Luxembourg.

**Luxemburger** (*pl* -) *der* Luxemburger ◇ *adj* (*unver*) of/from Luxembourg.

**Luxemburgerin** (*pl* -nen) *die* Luxemburger.

**luxemburgisch** *adj* of/from Luxembourg.

**luxuriös** *adj* luxurious ◇ *adv* luxuriously.

**Luxus** *der* luxury.

**Luxusartikel** *der* luxury item.

**Luxushotel** *das* luxury hotel.

**Luzern** *nt* Lucerne.

**Luzerner** (*pl* -) *der* native/inhabitant of Lucerne ◇ *adj* (*unver*) of/from Lucerne.

**Luzernerin** (*pl* -nen) *die* native/inhabitant of Lucerne.

**LVA** [εl'fau'aː] (*abk für* **Landesversicherungsanstalt**) *die regional social security organization providing pensions and medical insurance for manual workers.*

**LW** [εl've:] (*abk für* **Langwelle**) *die* LW.

**Lymphdrüse** *die* lymph gland.

**Lymphknoten** *der* lymph gland.

**lynchen** *vt* **- 1.** [töten] to lynch **- 2.** *fam* [zurechtweisen] to kill.

**Lyon** [liɑ̃] *nt* Lyon.

**Lyrik** *die* lyric poetry.

**Lyriker, in** (*mpl* -; *fpl* -nen) *der, die* lyric poet.

**lyrisch** *adj* [Dichtung] lyric; [Stil] lyrical ◇ *adv* lyrically.

**m, M** [εm] (*pl* - ODER -s) *das* m, M.
**➡ m** (*abk für* **Meter**) m.

**m.** *abk für* **mit.**

**MA** *abk für* **Mittelalter.**

**M. A.** (*abk für* **Magister Artium**) M. A.

**Maas** *die:* **die ~** the (River) Maas.

**Machart** *die* [von Kleidungsstück] cut; **die ~ von etw** the way sthg has been made.

**machbar** *adj* feasible.

**machen** *vt* **- 1.** [tun] to do; **so was macht man nicht!** you can't ODER mustn't do that! **- 2.** [herstellen] to make; **ein Foto ~** to take a photo; **etw aus etw ~** to make sthg out of sthg; **sich** (D) **etw ~ lassen** to have sthg made **- 3.** [Summe, Ergebnis] to be; **zwei mal drei macht sechs** two times three is six; **das macht fünf Euro** that comes to five euros **- 4.** [mit Substantiv] **jm ein Kompliment ~** to pay sb a compliment; **mach bloß keine Dummheiten!** don't do anything silly!; **das Abendessen ~** to make dinner; **eine Prüfung ~** to take an exam; **den Doktor ~** to do a doctorate; **einen Handstand ~** to do a handstand; **die Straße macht eine Kur-**

ve there's a bend in the road; **täglich 500 Euro Umsatz ~** to turn over 500 euros a day; **einen Computerkurs ~** to do a computer course **- 5.** [erledigen] to do; **die Wäsche ~** to do the washing; **Einkäufe ~** to go shopping; **(seine) Hausaufgaben ~** to do one's homework; **sich** *(D)* **die Haare ~** to do one's hair; **da ist nichts zu ~** there's nothing we can do about it **- 6.** [durchführen]: **eine Party ~** to have a party; **eine Reise/einen Spaziergang ~** to go on a journey/for a walk; **eine Pause ~** to have a break; **einen Besuch bei jm ~** to pay sb a visit **- 7.** [verursachen]: **er machte viel Lärm um nichts** he made a lot of fuss about nothing; **Licht ~** to switch on the light; **macht nichts** never mind; **was macht das schon!** so what!; **die Hitze macht mir nichts** I don't mind the heat; **jm Angst/Freude ~** to make afraid/happy; **jm Hoffnung ~** to raise sb's hopes; **jm Mut ~** to encourage sb **- 8.** [mit Adjektiv] to make; **sich bemerkbar ~** to become noticeable; **mach die Musik leiser** turn the music down; **jn krank/glücklich ~** to make sb ill/happy; **machs gut!** take care! **- 9.** [mit Präposition]: **sie haben aus dem alten Häuschen etwas gemacht** they've really made something out of that old cottage; **sie lässt alles mit sich ~** she is very long-suffering; **etw zur Bedingung ~** to make sthg a condition <> *vi* **- 1.** [verursachen]: **macht, dass ihr bald zurück seid!** make sure you're back soon; **mach schon** ODER **doch!** **fam** get a move on! **- 2. fam** [Toilette verrichten]: **klein/groß ~** to do a number one/two; **der Hund hat vor die Haustür gemacht** the dog made a mess outside the front door; **in die Hosen ~** to wet/dirty one's pants **- 3.** [mit Adjektiv]: **Joggen macht schlank** jogging helps you lose weight; **mach schnell!** hurry up!

➤ **sich machen** *ref* **- 1. fam** [sich entwickeln] to come on; **du machst dich!** you're coming on very well **- 2.** [mit Adjektiv]: **sich beliebt/verständlich ~** to make o.s. popular/understood; **der Hut macht sich gut zu Ihrem Kleid** the hat goes well with your dress **- 3.** [mit Präposition]: **sich an die Arbeit ~** to get down to work; **sich auf den Weg ~** to set off; **sich** *(D)* **aus etw nichts ~** not to be keen on sthg; **mach dir nichts draus!** don't let it bother you!; **er machte sich zum Wortführer der Gruppe** he took on the role of the group's spokesman.

**Machenschaft** *(pl -en) die abw* intrigue.

**Macht** *(pl Mächte) die* power; **an die ~ kommen** to come to power; **an der ~ sein** to be in power; **die ~ der Gewohnheit** force of habit; **~ über jn haben** to have a hold on sb; **mit aller ~** with all one's might.

**Machtlergreifung** *die* seizure of power.

**Machthaber, in** *(mpl -/ fpl -nen) der, die:* **die ~** those in power.

**mächtig** *adj* **- 1.** [einflussreich] powerful **- 2.** [be-

herrschend]: **er ist seiner Sinne nicht mehr ~** he is no longer in full command of his senses; **sie ist des Französischen ~** she has a good command of French **- 3.** [Stimme, Hieb, Stamm] mighty; [Hunger, Angst] terrible; [Gebäude] enormous <> *adv* [enorm] terribly.

**Machtlkampf** *der* power struggle.

**machtlos** *adj* powerless; **gegen etw ~ sein** to be powerless in the face of sthg.

**Machtlprobe** *die* trial of strength.

**Machtwort** *(pl -e) das:* **ein ~ sprechen** to put one's foot down, to exercise one's authority.

**Macke** *(pl -n) die fam* **- 1.** [Tick] quirk; **eine ~ haben** *salopp* to be out of one's tiny mind **- 2.** [Fehler]: **mein Auto hat eine ~** there's something up ODER wrong with my car.

**Macker** *(pl -) der salopp* **- 1.** [Freund] man *Br,* main squeeze *Am* **- 2.** *abw* [Mann] macho jerk.

**MAD** [ɛmʔaːˈdeː] *(abk für* **Militärischer Abschirmdienst)** *der military counter-intelligence service.*

**Madagaskar** *nt* Madagascar.

**Mädchen** *(pl -) das* **- 1.** [gen] girl **- 2.** [Hausangestellte] maid; **ein ~ für alles** *fam fig* (general) dogsbody.

**mädchenhaft** *adj* girlish <> *adv* like a girl.

**Mädchenlname** *der* maiden name.

**Made** *(pl -n) die* maggot; **wie die ~ im Speck leben** to live in the lap of luxury.

**Madeira** [maˈdeːra] *nt* Madeira.

**Mädel** *(pl -* ODER **-s) das* girl.

**madig** *adj* maggoty, full of maggots; **jm etw ~ machen** *fam fig* to spoil sthg for sb.

**Madonna** *(pl Madonnen) die* **- 1.** [Muttergottes] Madonna **- 2.** [Bild, Plastik] madonna.

**Madrid** *nt* Madrid.

**Madrider** *(pl -) der* native/inhabitant of Madrid <> *adj (unver)* of/from Madrid.

**Madriderin** *(pl -nen) die* native/inhabitant of Madrid.

**mag** *präs* ⊳ **mögen.**

**Magazin** *(pl -e) das* **- 1.** [Illustrierte, Behälter für Patronen] magazine **- 2.** [Lager] storeroom **- 3.** [Fernsehsendung] magazine (programme).

**Magd** *(pl Mägde) die* **- 1.** [Dienstmagd] maid **- 2.** [Landarbeiterin] farmhand.

**Magdeburg** *nt* Magdeburg.

**Magen** *(pl Mägen* ODER **-) der** stomach; **jm auf den ~ schlagen** *fam* to upset sb; **sich** *(D)* **den ~ verderben** to get an upset stomach; **mir knurrt der ~ fam** my stomach is rumbling.

**Magenlbeschwerden** *pl* stomach trouble (U).

**Magen|geschwür** das stomach ulcer.

**Magen|schmerzen** pl stomachache (U).

**mager** adj - **1.** [Person, Tier, Gesicht] thin - **2.** [Fleisch] lean; [Quark] low-fat - **3.** [Ergebnis, Ernte] meagre <> adv [fettarm]: ~ **essen** to eat a low-fat diet.

**Magermilch** die skimmed milk.

**magersüchtig** adj anorexic.

**Maggi®** das type of brown liquid seasoning.

**Magie** [ma'giː] die magic; **schwarze** ~ black magic.

**Magier, in** ['maːgiɐ, rɪn] (mpl -; fpl -nen) der, die magician.

**magisch** adj magical; [Kräfte] magic <> adv magically.

**Magister** (pl -) der - **1.** [Person]: ~ **sein** ≃ to have a Master's degree - **2.** [Titel] ≃ Master's degree.

**Magister Artium** der ≃ Master of Arts.

**Magistrat** (pl -e) der town/city council.

**Magma** (pl Magmen) das magma.

**Magnesium** das magnesium.

**Magnet** (pl -e ODER -en) der magnet.

**Magnetband** (pl -bänder) das EDV magnetic tape.

**magnetisch** adj magnetic <> adv magnetically.

**Magnolie** [ma'gnoːljə] (pl -n) die magnolia.

**Mahagoni** das mahogany.

**Mähdrescher** (pl -) der combine harvester.

**mähen** vt [Rasen] to mow; [Getreide] to reap <> vi - **1.** [mit Mäher] to mow; [mit Sense] to reap - **2.** [blöken] to bleat.

**Mahl** (pl -e) das geh meal.

**mahlen** vt & vi to grind.

**Mahl|zeit** die meal <> interj hello! (said around lunchtime to work colleagues).

**Mahn|bescheid** der writ for payment (of a debt).

**Mähne** (pl -n) die mane.

**mahnen** vt - **1.** [ermahnen] to urge; **jn** ~, **etw zu tun** to urge sb to do sthg - **2.** [erinnern]: **jn an etw** (A) ~ to remind sb of sthg <> vi [ermahnen]: **das Ozonloch mahnt zur Vorsicht beim Sonnen** because of the hole in the ozone layer it is advisable to take care whilst sunbathing.

**Mahn|gebühr** die charge for sending out a reminder.

**Mahn|mal** das memorial.

**Mahnung** (pl -en) die - **1.** [Ermahnung] exhortation - **2.** [Schreiben] reminder.

**Mähren** nt Moravia.

**Mai** der May; **der Erste** ~ May Day; siehe auch September.

**Mai|baum** der maypole.

**Mai|glöckchen** (pl -) das lily of the valley.

**Mai|käfer** der cockchafer.

**Mailand** nt Milan.

**Mailbox** ['meilbɔks] (pl -en) die EDV mailbox.

**Main** der: **der** ~ the (River) Main.

**Mainz** nt Mainz.

**Mais** der [als Konserve] sweetcorn; [Pflanze] maize.

**Mais|kolben** der corn on the cob.

**Majestät** (pl -en) die Majesty.

**majestätisch** adj majestic <> adv majestically.

**Majonäse, Mayonnaise** [majɔ'nɛːzəl] (pl -n) die mayonnaise.

**Major** (pl -e) der major.

**Majoran** der marjoram.

**Majorin** (pl -nen) die - **1.** [Ehefrau] major's wife - **2.** [bei der Heilsarmee] major.

**makaber** adj macabre.

**Makel** (pl -) geh der - **1.** [Schandfleck] taint - **2.** [Fehler] flaw.

**makellos** adj - **1.** [tadellos] impeccable; [Figur] perfect - **2.** [fehlerlos] flawless <> adv - **1.** [tadellos] impeccably - **2.** [sauber] spotlessly.

**mäkeln** vi abw to carp; **an jm/etw** ~ to find fault with sb/sthg.

**Make-up** [meːkˈap] (pl -s) das - **1.** [Schminken] make-up - **2.** [Creme] foundation.

**Makkaroni** pl macaroni (U).

**Makler, in** (mpl -; fpl -nen) der, die [für Immobilien] estate agent Br, realtor Am; [an Börse] broker.

**Makrele** (pl -n) die mackerel.

**Makrone** (pl -n) die macaroon.

**mal** adv fam - **1.** [irgendwann - in Zukunft] sometime, someday; [ - in Vergangenheit] once; **hier stand** ~ **ein Gebäude** there was a building here once; **aus ihr wird** ~ **was werden** she'll be someone some ODER one day - **2.** [zum Ausdruck der Verbindlichkeit]: **ich komme um neun Uhr** ~ **vorbei** I'll drop by at nine o'clock; **wir müssen das am Sonntag** ~ **besprechen** we ought to discuss this on Sunday - **3.** [als Aufforderung]: **hör mir** ~ **gut zu!** now listen to me carefully!; **gib mir** ~ **bitte den Schlüssel!** would you give me the key?; **beruhige dich** ~! calm down, will you!; **sag** ~! tell me!; **hör** ~! listen! - **4.** [zur Verstärkung eines Adverbs]: **nimm schon** ~ **Platz, ich komme gleich** just take a seat, I'll be here in a minute; **vielleicht** ~ maybe; **höchstens** ~ at the very most - **5.** [einmal]: **er redet** ~ **so,** ~ **so** he says one thing one minute and another thing the next ◇ *konj* [zur Multiplikation] times.

**Mal** (*pl* -e ODER **Mäler**) *das* - **1.** (*pl Male*) [Zeitpunkt] time; **letztes/nächstes ~** last/next time; **jedes ~** every time; **ein für alle ~** *fam* once and for all; **mit einem ~(e)** all of a sudden; **von ~ zu ~** [immer mehr] more and more; [jedes Mal] every time; **beim ersten ~** the first time; **beim letzten ~** last time; **zum ersten/letzten ~** for the first/last time - **2.** (*pl Male, Mäler*) [Fleck] mark; [Muttermal] birthmark; [Pigmentmal] mole.

**Malaria** *die* malaria.

**Malaysia** [ma'laisja] *nt* Malaysia.

**Malbuch** *das* colouring book.

**Malediven** *pl:* **die ~** the Maldives.

**malen** *vt* & *vi* to paint.

**Maler** (*pl* -) *der* - **1.** [Künstler] painter, artist - **2.** [Handwerker] painter.

**Malerei** (*pl* -en) *die* painting.

**Malerin** (*pl* -nen) *die* - **1.** [Künstlerin] painter, artist - **2.** [Handwerkerin] painter.

**malerisch** *adj* [idyllisch] picturesque ◇ *adv* [schön] picturesquely.

**Mali** *nt* Mali.

**Malkasten** *der* paintbox.

**Mallorca** [ma'jɔrka] *nt* Majorca.

**malnehmen** *vt* (*unreg*): **etw mit etw ~** to multiply sthg by sthg.

**malochen** *vi salopp* to slog away.

**Malta** *nt* Malta.

**Malteser Hilfsdienst** *der* ≈ St John's Ambulance *Br*, *voluntary paramedic service*.

**Malve** ['malvə] (*pl* -n) *die* mallow.

**Malz** *das* malt.

**Malzbier** *das* malt beer.

**Malzbonbon** *der* ODER *das malted cough sweet*.

**Mama** (*pl* -s) *die fam* mummy *Br*, mommy *Am*.

**Mami** (*pl* -s) *die fam* mummy *Br*, mommy *Am*.

**Mammut** (*pl* -s ODER -e) *das* mammoth.

**mampfen** *vt* & *vi fam* to munch.

**man** *pron* - **1.** [jemand]: **~ sagte mir ...** I was told ...; **~ hat ihm eine Stelle angeboten** he was offered a job - **2.** [generalisierend] you; **wie sagt ~ das auf Deutsch?** how do you say that in German?; **das sagt ~ nicht** you don't say that; **~ sagt, dass ...** people say that ...; **~ kann deine Handschrift unmöglich lesen** your handwriting is impossible to read; **dieses Jahr trägt ~ Miniröcke** miniskirts are in this year.

**Management** ['mɛnədʒmənt] (*pl* -s) *das* management.

**managen** ['mɛnɛdʒn] *vt* - **1.** [betreuen] to man-

age; **wer managt Sie?** who is your manager? - **2.** *fam* [organisieren] to organize.

**Manager, in** ['mɛnɛdʒɐ, rɪn] (*mpl* -; *fpl* -nen) *der, die* manager.

**manche, r, s** *pron* - **1.** [bei Dingen - einige] some; [ - viele] many (things) - **2.** [bei Personen - einige] some people; [ - viele] many (people); **manch einer** many a person ◇ *det* - **1.** [einige] some - **2.** [viele] many.
➤ **so manche, r, s** *pron* & *det* quite a few.

**mancherlei** *adj* (*unver*) various ◇ *pron* various things.

**manchmal** *adv* sometimes.

**Mandant, in** (*mpl* -en; *fpl* -nen) *der, die* client (*of lawyer*).

**Mandarine** (*pl* -n) *die* mandarin.

**Mandat** (*pl* -e) *das* - **1.** [gen] mandate; [von Anwalt] brief - **2.** [POL - Amt] seat.

**Mandel** (*pl* -n) *die* almond.
➤ **Mandeln** *pl* [im Hals] tonsils.

**Mandelentzündung** *die* tonsillitis (U).

**Mandoline** (*pl* -n) *die* mandolin.

**Manege** [ma'neːʒə] (*pl* -n) *die* (circus) ring.

**Mangan** *das* CHEM manganese.

**Mangel** (*pl* **Mängel** ODER -n) *der* (*pl* Mängel) - **1.** [an Verantwortungsbewusstsein, Geistesgegenwart] lack; [an Lebensmitteln, Medikamenten] shortage; **aus ~ an etw** (*D*) for lack of sthg; **es herrscht ~ an etw** (*D*) there is a shortage of sthg - **2.** [Fehler] fault; **Mängel beheben** ODER **beseitigen** to rectify faults - **3.** [Not] hardship ◇ *die* (*pl* Mangeln) mangle.

**Mängelbericht** *der* list of defects.

**Mängelerscheinung** *die* deficiency symptom.

**mangelhaft** *adj* [unzureichend, Schulnote] poor ◇ *adv* poorly.

**mangeln** *vi:* **es mangelt jm an etw** (*D*) sb lacks sthg; **es mangelt an etw** (*D*) [nicht genug sein] there is a shortage of sthg; [fehlen] there is a lack of sthg ◇ *vt* to mangle.

**mangelnd** *adj* inadequate.

**mangels** *präp:* **~ einer Sache** (*G*) for lack of sthg.

**Mangelware** *die:* **~ sein** to be a scarce commodity; *fam fig* to be thin on the ground.

**Mango** (*pl* -s) *die* mango.

**Manie** (*pl* -n) *die* - **1.** [Tick] obsession - **2.** MED mania.

**Manier** (*pl* -en) *die* manner.
➤ **Manieren** *pl* manners.

**manierlich** *adj* correct ◇ *adv* correctly.

**Manifest** (*pl* -e) *das* manifesto.

**Maniküre** (*pl* -n) *die* - **1.** [Pflege] manicure - **2.** [Person] manicurist.

**M**

**Manila** *nt* Manila.

**Manipulation** (*pl* -en) *die* - **1.** [Verfälschung] rigging *(U)* - **2.** [Beeinflussung] manipulation *(U)* - **3.** [Vorgehen] manoeuvre.

**manipulieren** *vt* - **1.** [beeinflussen] to manipulate - **2.** [verfälschen] to rig.

**manisch** *adj* manic <> *adv* [krankhaft] manically.

**manisch-depressiv** *adj* MED manic-depressive.

**Manko** (*pl* -s) *das* - **1.** [Fehler] drawback - **2.** [Geldsumme] deficit.

**Mann** (*pl* Männer *ODER* Leute *ODER* -en) *der* - **1.** [gen] man; **von ~ zu ~** man to man - **2.** [Ehemann] husband - **3.** *RW:* **ein gemachter ~ sein** *fam* to be a made man; **etw an den ~ bringen** *fam* [durchsetzen] to push sthg; *fam* [verkaufen] to find a taker/takers for sthg; **~s genug sein** *fam* to be man enough; **seinen ~ stehen** to hold one's own <> *interj fam:* **~!, oh ~!** (my) God!; **reiß dich zusammen, ~!** pull yourself together, for God's sake.

➡ **alle Mann** *pron fam* everyone; **alle ~ an Deck!** all hands on deck!

➡ **kleine Mann** *der fam:* **der kleine ~** the ordinary man.

**Männchen** (*pl* -) *das* - **1.** [Tier] male; **~ machen** to sit up and beg - **2.** *fam* [kleiner Mann] little man.

**Mannequin** ['manəkɛ̃] (*pl* -s) *das* model.

**Männer|chor** *der* male-voice choir.

**Männersache** *die:* **das ist ~** that's a man's business.

**mannigfaltig** *adj geh* diverse.

**männlich** *adj* - **1.** [Lebewesen] male - **2.** [viril] manly - **3.** [zum Mann gehörig] man's - **4.** GRAM [Substantiv] masculine <> *adv* [viril] in a manly way.

**Männlichkeit** *die* - **1.** [Wesensart] masculinity - **2.** [Potenz] virility.

**Manns|bild** *das Süddt & Österr fam* man.

**Mannschaft** (*pl* -en) *die* - **1.** [im Sport, Team] team; **vor versammelter ~** *fam* in front of everybody - **2.** [Besatzung] crew - **3.** [Soldaten] men *(pl)*.

**Mannschafts|geist** *der* team spirit.

**Mannschafts|kapitän** *der* team captain.

**Mannschafts|sport** *der* team sport.

**mannshoch** *adj & adv* as high as a man.

**Mano|meter** *das* PHYS & TECH pressure gauge <> *interj fam* (boy) oh boy!

**Manöver** [ma'nøːvɐ] (*pl* -) *das* manoeuvre.

**Manöverkritik** *die (ohne pl) eigtl & MIL* exercise evaluation; *fig* postmortem.

**manövrieren** [manøː'vriːrən] *vt & vi eigtl & fig* to manoeuvre.

➡ **sich manövrieren** *ref* [sich bringen] to manoeuvre o.s.

**manövrierunfähig** [manøːv'riːʊnfɛːiɡ] *adj* unmanoeuvrable.

**Mansarde** (*pl* -n) *die* [Zimmer] attic room; [Wohnung] attic flat *Br ODER* apartment *Am.*

**Manschette** (*pl* -n) *die* - **1.** [von Ärmeln] cuff - **2.** [Dichtung] seal.

**Manschetten|knopf** *der* cufflink.

**Mantel** (*pl* Mäntel) *der* - **1.** [Kleidungsstück] coat - **2.** *fig* [Deckmantel] cloak - **3.** TECH casing; [von Kabel] sheath.

**Mantel|tarif** *der* framework agreement *(on working conditions).*

**manuell** *adj* manual <> *adv* manually.

**Manuskript** (*pl* -e) *das* - **1.** [Entwurf] notes *(pl)* - **2.** [Handschrift, Satzvorlage] manuscript.

**Mappe** (*pl* -n) *die* - **1.** [Hülle] folder - **2.** [Tasche] briefcase.

**Maracuja** (*pl* -s) *die* passion fruit.

**Marathon** (*pl* -s) *der ODER das* marathon.

**Marathon|läufer, in** *der, die* marathon runner.

**Märchen** (*pl* -) *das* - **1.** [Erzählung] fairy tale - **2.** [Lüge] tall story.

**Märchen|buch** *das* book of fairy tales.

**märchenhaft** *adj* - **1.** [sagenhaft] fairy-tale - **2.** [wunderschön] wonderful - **3.** [unglaublich] fantastic <> *adv* - **1.** [wunderbar] wonderfully - **2.** [unglaublich] fantastically.

**Marder** (*pl* -) *der* marten.

**Margarine** *die* margarine.

**Marge** ['marʒə] (*pl* -n) *die* WIRTSCH margin.

**Margerite** (*pl* -n) *die* daisy.

**Mariä Empfängnis** *(ohne Artikel)* Immaculate Conception.

**Mariä Himmelfahrt** *(ohne Artikel)* Assumption.

**Mariä Lichtmess** *(ohne Artikel)* Candlemas.

**Marien|käfer** *der* ladybird *Br*, ladybug *Am.*

**Marihuana** *das* marijuana.

**Marille** (*pl* -n) *die Österr* apricot.

**Marinade** (*pl* -n) *die* - **1.** [zum Einlegen] marinade - **2.** [Salatsoße] dressing - **3.** [Tunke] sauce.

**Marine** *die (ohne pl)* MIL navy.

**marineblau** *adj* navy blue.

**marinieren** *vt* to marinate.

**Marionette** (*pl* -n) *die* - **1.** [Puppe] marionette, puppet - **2.** *fig* [Person] puppet.

**Marionetten|theater** *das* puppet theatre.

**Mark**[1] (*pl* -) *die* mark; **keine müde ~** *fig* not a single penny

**Mark²** *das (ohne pl)* - **1.** [im Knochen] marrow; **es geht mir durch ~ und Bein** *fig* it goes right through me - **2.** [Konzentrat] purée.
➤ **bis ins Mark** *adv* to the core.

**markant** *adj* striking; [Kinn, Nase] prominent.

**Marke** (*pl* -n) *die* - **1.** [Lebensmittel, Verbrauchsgüter] brand; [Auto, Gebrauchsgegenstände] make - **2.** [Briefmarke] stamp - **3.** [Erkennungszeichen - von Hund] identity disc; [ - von Polizist] badge - **4.** [Wertzeichen - für Lebensmittel] coupon; [ - für Garderobe] ticket *Br*, check *Am* - **5.** *fam* [Person] character.

**Marken|artikel** *der* branded item.

**Marken|zeichen** *das* trademark.

**markerschütternd** *adj* bloodcurdling <> *adv* bloodcurdlingly.

**Marketing** *das* marketing.

**markieren** *vt* - **1.** [kennzeichnen] to mark - **2.** [hervorheben] to highlight - **3.** *fam* [vortäuschen] to play <> *vi fam* [vortäuschen] to fake.

**Markierung** (*pl* -en) *die* marking.

**markig** *adj* forceful.

**Markise** (*pl* -n) *die* awning.

**Mark|knochen** *der* marrowbone.

**Mark|stein** *der* - **1.** [Grenzstein] boundary stone - **2.** [Ereignis] milestone.

**Markt** (*pl* Märkte) *der* - **1.** [gen] market; **auf den** *ODER* **zum ~ gehen** to go to the market; **auf den ~ bringen** to put on the market - **2.** [Platz] marketplace.

**marktbeherrschend** *adj* market-dominating.

**Markt|forschung** *die* market research.

**Markt|frau** *die* market woman.

**Markt|halle** *die* covered market.

**Markt|lücke** *die* gap in the market.

**Markt|platz** *der* marketplace.

**Markt|preis** *der* market price.

**Markt|wert** *der* market value.

**Markt|wirtschaft** *die* market economy; **freie ~** free market economy; **soziale ~** social market economy.

**marktwirtschaftlich** *adj* free market <> *adv:* **~ orientiert** free market-based.

**Marmelade** (*pl* -n) *die* jam.

**Marmor** *der* marble.

**Marmor|kuchen** *der* marble cake.

**Marokkaner, in** (*mpl* -; *fpl* -nen) *der, die* Moroccan.

**marokkanisch** *adj* Moroccan.

**Marokko** *nt* Morocco.

**Marone** (*pl* -n) *die* (sweet) chestnut.

**Marotte** (*pl* -n) *die* fad.

**Mars** *der* Mars.

**marsch** *interj:* **~, an die Arbeit/ins Bett!** off to work/to bed!; **vorwärts ~!** forward march!; **~, ~!** *fam* quick march!

**Marsch** (*pl* Märsche) *der* - **1.** [Gehen] walk; **sich in ~ setzen** to set off - **2.** [beim Militär, Musikstück] march.

**Marschall** (*pl* -schälle) *der* marshal.

**marschieren** (*perf* **ist marschiert**) *vi* - **1.** [Soldaten] to march - **2.** [gehen] to walk.

**Marschmusik** *die* marching music.

**Marseille** [marˈsɛːj] *nt* Marseilles.

**Marshall-Plan** *der* Marshall Plan.

**Marter** (*pl* -n) *die* *geh* torment.

**martialisch** *geh adj* warlike <> *adv* in a warlike manner.

**Martins|tag** *der* Martinmas.

**Märtyrer, in** (*mpl* -; *fpl* -nen) *der, die* martyr.

**Marxismus** *der* Marxism.

**marxistisch** *adj* Marxist <> *adv* in a Marxist way.

**März** *der* March; *siehe auch* **September.**

**Marzipan, Marzipan** (*pl* -e) *das* marzipan *(U)*.

**Masche** (*pl* -n) *die* - **1.** [beim Stricken, Häkeln] stitch - **2.** [Art und Weise] trick; **die neueste ~ Mode** [Marotte] the latest fad; *fam* [Mode] the latest thing.

**Maschendraht** *der* wire netting.

**Maschine** (*pl* -n) *die* - **1.** [Gerät, Motorrad] machine - **2.** *fam* [Motor] engine - **3.** [Flugzeug] plane - **4.** [Schreibmaschine]: **~ schreiben** to type.

**maschinell** *adj* [Herstellung, Bearbeitung] machine (*vor Subst*); [Vorgang] mechanical <> *adv* by machine.

**Maschinenbau** *der* mechanical engineering.

**Maschinen|gewehr** *das* machine gun.

**Maschinen|pistole** *die* submachine gun.

**Maschinen|schaden** *der* engine trouble *(U)*.

**Maschinerie** (*pl* -n) *die* machinery.

**maschineschreiben, maschinenschreiben** *vi (unreg)* ⊳ **Maschine.**

**Maschinist, in** (*mpl* -en; *fpl* -nen) *der, die* machine operator.

**Masern** *pl* measles *(U)*.

**Maserung** (*pl* -en) *die* [in Holz, Leder] grain; [in Stein] vein.

**Maske** (*pl* -n) *die* - **1.** [zum Verkleiden & EDV] mask - **2.** [beim Theater] make-up.

**Masken|ball** *der* masked ball.

**M**

**Maskenbildner, in** (*mpl* -; *fpl* -nen) *der, die* make-up artist.

**maskieren** *vt eigtl* & *fig* to mask.
➡ **sich maskieren** *ref* - **1.** [sich verdecken] to disguise o.s. - **2.** [sich verkleiden] to dress up.

**Maskierung** (*pl* -en) *die* - **1.** [Verkleidung] fancy-dress costume - **2.** [Tarnung] disguise.

**Maskottchen** (*pl* -) *das* mascot.

**maskulin, maskulin** *adj* masculine.

**Maskulinum** (*pl* Maskulina) *das* GRAM masculine noun.

**Masochismus** *der* masochism.

**Masochist, in** (*mpl* -en; *fpl* -nen) *der, die* masochist.

**maß** *prät* ▷ **messen.**

**Maß** (*pl* -e ODER -) *das* (*pl* Maße) - **1.** [Maßeinheit] measure - **2.** [Messgerät] (tape) measure; **mit zweierlei ~ messen** *eigtl* to judge by different standards - **3.** [Körpermaß]: **~ nehmen** to take measurements - **4.** [Umfang, Verhältnis] degree; **in demselben/höherem ~ als** to the same/a greater degree as/than; **~ halten** to be moderate; **ein hohes ~ an etw** (*D*) a high degree of sthg ◇ *die* (*pl* Maß) *Süddt* & *Österr* [Krug] litre (of beer).
➡ **in Maßen** *adv* in moderation.
➡ **nach Maß** *adv* [Anzug] made-to-measure; [Urlaub] tailor-made.
➡ **über alle Maßen** *adv* beyond measure.
➡ **Maße** *pl* - **1.** [von Räumen] dimensions - **2.** [von Personen] measurements.

**Massage** [ma'saːʒə] (*pl* -n) *die* massage.

**Massaker** (*pl* -) *das* massacre.

**Maßangabe** *die* measurement.

**Maßarbeit** *die:* **~ sein** to be made-to-measure; **das war ~!** *fig* that was neatly done!

**Masse** (*pl* -n) *die* mass; **die breite ~** *abw* the masses (*pl*).
➡ **in Massen** *adv* [einkaufen] in bulk; **die Leute kamen in ~n** masses of people came.

**Maßeinheit** *die* unit of measurement.

**Massenabfertigung** *die* *abw* mass processing.

**Massenarbeitslosigkeit** *die* mass unemployment.

**Massengrab** *das* mass grave.

**massenhaft** *adj* in great numbers; **die ~e Hinrichtungen** the great number of executions ◇ *adv* in great numbers.

**Massenkundgebung** *die* mass rally.

**Massenmedien** *pl* mass media.

**Massenmord** *der* mass murder.

**Massenproduktion** *die* mass production.

**Massentourismus** *der* mass tourism.

**massenweise** *adv* in great numbers ◇ *adj* [Herstellung, Vernichtung] mass; [Sterben, Auftreten] in great numbers.

**Masseur, in** [ma'søːɐ, rɪn] (*mpl* -e; *fpl* -nen) *der, die* masseur (*f* masseuse).

**maßgebend, maßgeblich** *adj* [Person] influential; [Meinung] authoritative; [Urteil, Argument] decisive ◇ *adv*: **an etw** (*D*) **~ beteiligt sein** to play a decisive role in sthg.

**maßgerecht** *adj* of the right size ◇ *adv* to size.

**maßgeschneidert** *adj* made-to-measure.

**maßhalten** *vi* (*unreg*) = **Maß.**

**massieren** *vt* to massage.

**massig** *adj* massive ◇ *adv fam*: **~ zu essen** loads to eat; **~ Arbeit** loads of work.

**mäßig** *adj* - **1.** [gen] moderate - **2.** [mittelmäßig - Leistung, Wetter, Schüler] average ◇ *adv* - **1.** [maßvoll] in moderation - **2.** [wenig] moderately.

**mäßigen** *vt* [Wut] to curb; [Worte] to moderate.
➡ **sich mäßigen** *ref* [Person] to restrain o.s.; [Unwetter] to die down.

**Mäßigung** *die* restraint.

**massiv** *adj* - **1.** [Holz, Metall] solid - **2.** [wuchtig] massive - **3.** [heftig] strong ◇ *adv* - **1.** [wuchtig] massively - **2.** [heftig] strongly.

**Massiv** (*pl* -e) *das* massif.

**Maßkrug** *der Süddt* & *Österr* litre beer mug.

**maßlos** *adj* extreme ◇ *adv* extremely.

**Maßlosigkeit** *die* extremeness.

**Maßnahme** (*pl* -n) *die* measure; **~n einleiten** to introduce measures; **~n ergreifen** ODER **treffen** to take measures.

**maßregeln** *vt* to reprimand.

**Maßstab** *der* - **1.** [auf Landkarten] scale - **2.** [Richtlinie] standard.
➡ **im Maßstab** *adv*: **im ~ 1:25000** to a scale of 1:25,000.

**maßstabgetreu, maßstabsgetreu** *adj* & *adv* to scale.

**Mast** (*pl* -en ODER -e) *der* (*pl* Maste, Masten) - **1.** [auf Schiffen, für Antenne] mast - **2.** [Stange - für Fahne, Leitungen] pole; [ - für Hochspannungsleitungen] pylon ◇ *die* (*pl* Masten) [Mästen] fattening (*U*).

**mästen** *vt* to fatten.
➡ **sich mästen** *ref fam* to stuff o.s.

**masturbieren** *vi* & *vt* to masturbate.

**Masuren** *nt* Masuria.

**Match** [mɛtʃ] (*pl* -e ODER -(e)s) *das* match.

**Material** [mate'rjaːl] (*pl* -ien) *das* - **1.** [Werkstoff, Unterlagen] material - **2.** [Gerät] equipment.

**Materialfehler** *der* defect in the material.

**Materialismus** *der* materialism.

**materialistisch** *adj* materialistic <> *adv* materialistically.

**Materialkosten** *pl* cost of materials *(U)*.

**Materie** [ma'te:rjə] *(pl -n) die* - **1.** matter - **2.** *geh* [Themenbereich] subject matter.

**materiell** *adj* - **1.** [wirtschaftlich] financial - **2.** [materialistisch] materialistic - **3.** [stofflich] material <> *adv* - **1.** [materialistisch] materialistically - **2.** [wirtschaftlich] financially.

**Mathe** *die fam* maths *(U) Br*, math *(U) Am*.

**Mathematik, Mathematik** *die* mathematics *(U)*.

**Mathematiker, in** *(mpl -; fpl -nen) der, die* mathematician.

**mathematisch** *adj* mathematical <> *adv* mathematically.

**Matjes** *(pl -) der* salted herring.

**Matjeshering** *der* salted herring.

**Matratze** *(pl -n) die* mattress.

**Matriarchat** *(pl -e) das* matriarchy.

**Matrix** *(pl Matrizen) die* MATH matrix.

**Matrixdrucker** *der* EDV dot-matrix printer.

**Matrize** *(pl -n) die* stencil.

**Matrone** *(pl -n) die* matron.

**Matrose** *(pl -n) der* sailor.

**Matsch** *der* - **1.** [Schlamm] mud; [von Schnee] slush - **2.** *fam* [Brei] mush.

**matschen** *vi fam* [in Pfütze] to splash around; [in Schlamm] to squelch around; **mit etw ~** [beim Essen] to make a mush of sthg.

**matschig** *adj* - **1.** [schlammig] muddy; [Schnee] slushy - **2.** [breiig] mushy.

**matt** *adj* - **1.** [kraftlos] weak; [Händedruck, Reaktion] feeble - **2.** [nicht glänzend] matt - **3.** [trübe - Licht] dim; [ - Augen, Farbe, Glanz] dull; [ - Glühbirne] pearl; [ - Glas] frosted - **4.** [im Schach]: **~ sein** to be checkmated <> *adv* - **1.** [im Schach]: **jn ~ setzen** to checkmate sb - **2.** [trübe] dimly - **3.** [kraftlos] weakly; [reagieren] feebly.

**Matte** *(pl -n) die* mat.

**Matterhorn** *das*: **das ~** the Matterhorn.

**Mattscheibe** *die fam* [Bildschirm] telly *Br*, tube *Am*.

**Mätzchen** *pl fam* - **1.** [Unfug] nonsense *(U)* - **2.** [Trick] tricks.

**Mauer** *(pl -n) die* wall.

**Mauerblümchen** *(pl -) das* wallflower.

**mauern** *vi* - **1.** [bauen] to build - **2.** SPORT to play defensively <> *vt* [bauen] to build.

**Mauersegler** *der* swift.

**Mauerwerk** *das* masonry.

**Maul** *(pl Mäuler) das* - **1.** [bei Tieren] mouth - **2.** *salopp* [Mundwerk] trap; **halts ~!** shut your trap!; **böses ~** malicious tongue.

**maulen** *vi fam abw* to moan.

**Maulheld** *der fam abw* braggart.

**Maulkorb** *der* muzzle.

**Maultasche** *die* [Nudel] filled pasta shape served in soup.

**Maultrommel** *die* Jew's-harp.

**Maul- und Klauenseuche** *die (ohne pl)* foot-and-mouth (disease).

**Maulwurf** *der* mole.

**Maulwurfshügel** *der* molehill.

**Maurer, in** *(mpl -; fpl -nen) der, die* bricklayer.

**Maurerkelle** *die* trowel.

**Mauretanien** *nt* Mauritania.

**Mauritius** *nt* Mauritius.

**Maus** *(pl Mäuse) die* - **1.** EDV [Tier] mouse - **2.** *fam* [Mädchen] cutie - **3.** *RW*: **eine graue ~** *fam abw* a nondescript kind of woman.

**mauscheln** *vi fam* - **1.** *abw* [kungeln] to wheel and deal - **2.** [betrügen] to cheat - **3.** [nuscheln] to mumble.

**Mausefalle** *die* mousetrap.

**mausen** *vt fam* to pinch.

**Mauser** *die (ohne pl)*: **in der ~ sein** to be moulting.

**mausern ☞ sich mausern** *ref* - **1.** [Vögel] to moult - **2.** [Person] to blossom.

**mausetot** *adj fam* as dead as a doornail.

**Mausklick** *(pl -s) der* EDV mouse click; **per ~ die Adresse einfügen** to add the address by clicking the mouse.

**Mauspad** *(pl -s) das* mouse mat.

**Mautgebühr** *die Österr* toll.

**Mautstelle** *die Österr* tollgate.

**m. a. W.** *(abk für mit anderen Worten) in other words*.

**max.** *(abk für maximal)* max.

**maximal** *adj* maximum <> *adv*: **das ~ zulässige Gewicht** the maximum permitted weight; **~ 30 Personen** a maximum of 30 people.

**Maximalwert** *der* maximum value.

**maximieren** *vt* to maximize.

**Maximum** *(pl Maxima) das* maximum.

**Mayonnaise** *die* = Majonäse.

**Mazedonien** [maze'do:njən] *nt* Macedonia.

**Mäzen, in** *(mpl -e; fpl -nen) der, die* patron.

**MB** *(abk für Megabyte)* MB, Mb.

**Mbyte** ['ɛmbait] *(pl -s) (abk für Megabyte) das* EDV Mbyte.

**MdB** *(abk für Mitglied des Bundestags)* Member of the "Bundestag".

M

**MdEP** (*abk für* **Mitglied des Europäischen Parlaments**) MEP.

**MdL** (*abk für* **Mitglied des Landtags**) Member of the "Landtag".

**MDR** [ɛmˈdeːˈɛr] (*abk für* **Mitteldeutscher Rundcfunk**) *der public regional broadcasting corporation serving Saxony, Saxony-Anhalt and Thuringia.*

**m. E.** (*abk für* **meines Erachtens**) *in my opinion.*

**Mechanik** (*pl* **-en**) *die* - **1.** [Fach] mechanics (U) - **2.** [Mechanismus] mechanism.

**Mechaniker, in** (*mpl* **-**; *fpl* **-nen**) *der, die* mechanic.

**mechanisch** *adj* mechanical ⟨⟩ *adv* mechanically.

**Mechanismus** (*pl* **Mechanismen**) *der* mechanism.

**meckern** *vi* - **1.** [Ziege] to bleat - **2.** *fam* [nörgeln]: **über jn/etw ~** to moan about sb/sthg.

**Mecklenburg** *nt* Mecklenburg.

**Mecklenburger** (*pl* **-**) *der* native/inhabitant of Mecklenburg ⟨⟩ *adj* (*unver*) of/from Mecklenburg.

**Mecklenburgerin** (*pl* **-nen**) *die* native/inhabitant of Mecklenburg.

**Mecklenburger Seenplatte** *die* lake district in Mecklenburg-West Pomerania.

**mecklenburgisch** *adj* of/from Mecklenburg.

**Mecklenburg-Vorpommern** *nt* Mecklenburg-West Pomerania.

**Meckpomm** *nt fam* Mecklenburg-West Pomerania.

**Medaille** [meˈdaljə] (*pl* **-n**) *die* medal.

**Medaillenspiegel** *der* **SPORT** medals table.

**Medaillon** [medalˈjɔŋ] (*pl* **-s**) *das* - **1.** [Schmuck] locket - **2.** [Fleisch, Fisch] medallion.

**Medien** *pl* media.

**Medienverbund** *der* multimedia system.

**Medikament** (*pl* **-e**) *das* medicine; **ein ~ gegen etw** a medicine for sthg.

**Meditation** (*pl* **-en**) *die* meditation.

**meditieren** *vi* - **1.** [versunken sein] to meditate - **2.** [nachdenken]: **über etw** (A) **~** to meditate on sthg.

**Medium** [ˈmeːdjʊm] (*pl* **Medien**) *das* medium.

**Medizin** (*pl* **-en**) *die* medicine.

**Medizinball** *der* medicine ball.

**Mediziner, in** (*mpl* **-**; *fpl* **-nen**) *der, die* [Arzt] doctor; [Student] medical student.

**medizinisch** *adj* - **1.** [heilkundlich, ärztlich] medical - **2.** [heilend] medicinal ⟨⟩ *adv* medically.

**Meer** (*pl* **-e**) *das* eigtl & fig sea; **ans ~ fahren** to go to the seaside; **am ~** by the sea.

**Meerenge** *die* strait.

**Meeresfrüchte** *pl* seafood (U).

**Meeresgrund** *der* seabed; **auf dem ~** on the seabed.

**Meeresspiegel** *der* sea level; **50 Meter über/unter dem ~** 50 metres above/below sea level.

**Meerkatze** *die* guenon monkey.

**Meerrettich** *der* horseradish.

**Meerschweinchen** (*pl* **-**) *das* guinea pig.

**Meerwasser** *das* seawater.

**Meeting** [ˈmiːtɪŋ] (*pl* **-s**) *das* meeting.

**Megabyte** [ˈmegabait] (*pl* **-s**) *das* **EDV** megabyte.

**Megafon** [megaˈfoːn], **Megaphon** (*pl* **-e**) *das* megaphone.

**Megahertz** *das* megahertz.

**Mehl** *das* - **1.** [zum Backen] flour - **2.** [Pulver - von Holz] sawdust; [ - von Knochen] meal; [ - von Gestein] powder.

**mehlig** *adj* - **1.** [voller Mehl, wie Mehl] floury - **2.** [fahl] pasty.

**Mehlschwitze** (*pl* **-n**) *die* roux.

**Mehlspeise** *die* dish made from flour, eggs and milk, such as pasta, dumplings or pastries.

**mehr** *pron* [komparativ von viel] more ⟨⟩ *adv* - **1.** [komparativ von viel] more; **50 Euro, ~ nicht?** 50 euros, no more than that?; **er ist ~ Gelehrter als Künstler** he is more of a scholar than an artist - **2.** [übrig] more; **~ denn je** more than ever; **es ist keiner ~ da** there is no one left; **nichts ~** nothing more; **vom Käse ist nichts ~ da** there is nothing left of the cheese - **3.** [zeitlich]: **nicht ~** not any longer; **du bist doch kein Kind ~!** you are not a child any more; **das Konzept gibt es nicht ~** the concept doesn't exist any more - **4.** *RW*: **immer ~**, **~ und ~** more and more; **~ oder weniger** more or less.

**Mehrarbeit** *die* overtime.

**Mehraufwand** *der* extra expenditure.

**Mehrausgaben** *pl* extra expenses.

**mehrdeutig** *adj* ambiguous.

**Mehreinnahme** *die* extra income.

**mehren** *vt* to increase.
➤ **sich mehren** *ref* to increase.

**mehrere** *det* & *pron* several.
➤ **mehreres** *pron* several things.
➤ **zu mehreren** *adv*: **sie kommen ~** several (of them) are coming.

**mehrfach** *adj* multiple; [Olympiasieger] several times over; **ein Bericht in ~er Ausfertigung** several copies of a report; **in ~er Hinsicht** in more than one respect ⟨⟩ *adv* several times.

**Mehrfache** *das (ohne pl)* - **1.** MATH multiple - **2.** [an Kosten]: **ein ~s an Kosten** several times the cost.

**Mehrfamilien|haus** *das* apartment building.

**mehrfarbig** *adj* multicoloured ⬦ *adv* in many colours.

**Mehrheit** *(pl -en) die* majority; **mit großer/ knapper ~** by a large/narrow majority; **die absolute ~** an absolute majority.

**mehrheitlich** *adj* majority ⬦ *adv* by a majority.

**Mehrheits|beschluss** *der* majority decision.

**mehrheitsfähig** *adj* capable of finding majority support.

**mehrjährig** *adj* [Erfahrung] several years'; [Aufenthalt, Freundschaft] of several years; [Pflanze] perennial ⬦ *adv* perennially.

**Mehr|kampf** *der* multi-discipline event.

**Mehrkorn|brot** *das* mixed-grain bread.

**Mehr|kosten** *pl* extra costs.

**mehrmalig** *adj* repeated.

**mehrmals** *adv* several times.

**mehrsprachig** *adj* [Wörterbuch, Ausgabe, Person] multilingual; [Unterhaltung] in several languages ⬦ *adv*: **~ aufwachsen** to grow up multilingual.

**mehrstimmig** *adj* for several voices ⬦ *adv* in harmony.

**mehrtägig** *adj* [Wartezeit, Abwesenheit] of several days; [Seminar, Reise] lasting several days.

**Mehrwertsteuer** *die* VAT *Br*, sales tax *Am*.

**mehrwöchig** *adj* [Reise, Besuch, Ausbildung] lasting several weeks; [Lieferfrist, Wartezeit] of several weeks.

**Mehrzahl** *die* - **1.** [größerer Anteil] majority - **2.** [Plural] plural.

**Mehrzweck|halle** *die* multipurpose hall.

**meiden** *(prät mied; perf hat gemieden) vt geh* to avoid.
➡ **sich meiden** *ref* to avoid each other.

**Meile** *(pl -n) die* mile.

**Meilen|stein** *der geh* milestone.

**meilenweit** *adv* for miles; **~ entfernt** miles away.

**mein, e** *det* my; **~e Damen und Herren** ladies and gentlemen ⬦ *pron* mine; **sein Haus ist größer als ~s** his house is bigger than mine.

**meine, r, s** *ODER* **meins** *pron* mine.

**Mein|eid** *der* perjury (U).

**meinen** *vt* - **1.** [denken, glauben] to think; **was meinst du dazu?** what do you think?; **das will ich (aber) ~!** I should think so too! - **2.** [sagen] to say; **was meint er?** *fam* what did he say?

- **3.** [zum Ausdruck einer Intention] to mean; **etw ironisch ~** to mean sthg ironically; **wie ~ Sie das?** what do you mean by that?; **das war nicht so gemeint** it wasn't meant like that; **gut gemeint** well-intentioned; **er meint es gut mit uns** he has our interests at heart; **du warst nicht gemeint** the comment wasn't aimed at you ⬦ *vi* to think; **ich meine ja nur!** it was just a suggestion; **~ Sie?** do you think so?; **wie ~ Sie?** what did you say?; **wie Sie ~!** as you wish!

**meiner** *pron (Genitiv von ich)* of me; **er erinnert sich ~** he remembers me.

**meinerseits** *adv* - **1.** [ich selbst] for my part - **2.** [von mir] on my part.

**meinesgleichen** *pron* people like myself.

**meinetwegen** *adv* - **1.** [mir zuliebe] for my sake - **2.** [wegen mir] because of me - **3.** [von mir aus] as far as I'm concerned; **(also) ~!** if you like.

**meinetwillen** ➡ **um meinetwillen** *adv* for my sake.

**meinige** *(pl -n) pron geh*: **der/die/das ~** mine.

**Meinung** *(pl -en) die* opinion; **eine vorgefasste ~** a preconceived idea; **anderer ~ sein** to be of a different opinion; **der ~ sein, dass** to be of the opinion that; **einer** *ODER* **derselben ~ sein** to agree; **die öffentliche ~** public opinion; **jm die ~ sagen** *fam fig* to give sb a piece of one's mind; **meiner ~ nach** in my opinion.

**Meinungs|austausch** *der* exchange of views.

**Meinungs|forschung** *die* public opinion research (U).

**Meinungs|freiheit** *die* freedom of expression.

**Meinungsum|frage** *die* opinion poll.

**Meinungs|verschiedenheit** *die* difference of opinion.

**Meise** *(pl -n) die* tit; **'ne** *ODER* **eine ~ haben** *fam fig* to be bonkers.

**Meißel** *(pl -) der* chisel.

**meißeln** *vi* & *vt* to chisel.

**meist** *adv* usually, mostly.
➡ **am meisten** *adv* most; **die am ~en besuchte Ausstellung** the most visited exhibition.

**meistbietend** *adj*: **der ~e Interessent** the highest bidder ⬦ *adv* to the highest bidder.

**meiste** *adj* (the) most; **die ~n Leute** most people; **er hat das ~ Geld** he has the most money ⬦ *pron*: **das/die ~** (the) most.
➡ **die meisten** *pron* most people.

**meistens** *adv* usually, mostly.

**Meister** *(pl -) der* - **1.** [Handwerker] master craftsman; **seinen ~ machen** *fam* to get one's

**M**

master craftsman's certificate - **2.** [Experte, Künstler] master - **3.** [im Sport] champion; **(deutscher)** ~ **werden** to become (German) champion.

**meisterhaft** *adj* masterly <> *adv* brilliantly.

**Meisterin** (*pl* -nen) *die* [Handwerkerin] master craftswoman; [Expertin, Künstlerin] master; [im Sport] champion.

**meistern** *vt* - **1.** [bewältigen] to master - **2.** *geh* [zügeln] to control.

**Meisterlprüfung** *die* examination for the master craftsman's certificate.

**Meisterschaft** (*pl* -en) *die* - **1.** SPORT championship - **2.** [Können] mastery.

**Meisterlwerk** *das* masterpiece.

**meistgekauft** *adj* best-selling.

**Mekka** *nt* Mecca.

**melancholisch** [melaŋ'koːlɪʃ] *adj* melancholy <> *adv* in a melancholy way.

**Meldelfrist** *die* period of time within which somebody has to report or register something.

**melden** *vt* - **1.** [anzeigen, berichten] to report; [Geburt] to register; **(bei jm) nichts/nicht viel zu** ~ **haben** *fam* *fig* to have no/little say (with sb) - **2.** [anmelden] to announce.

➡ **sich melden** *ref* - **1.** [sich bemerkbar machen - im Unterricht] to put one's hand up; [ - Finder] to make o.s. known - **2.** [Nachricht geben]: **melde dich mal wieder!** keep in touch!; **sich bei jm** ~ [bei Freunden] to get in touch with sb; [bei Polizei] to report to sb - **3.** [am Telefon] to answer; **es meldet sich niemand** there's no answer - **4.** [sich anmelden] to register; **sich freiwillig zu etw** ~ to volunteer for sthg.

**Meldung** (*pl* -en) *die* - **1.** [Nachricht, Anzeige] report; **weitere ~en des Tages** further news (*U*) - **2.** [Mitteilung] announcement - **3.** [Anmeldung] entry.

**Melisse** (*pl* -n) *die* (lemon) balm.

**melken** (*prät* **melkte** ODER **molk**; *perf* **hat gemolken**) *vt* & *vi* to milk.

**Melodie** [melo'diː] (*pl* -n) *die* tune.

**melodisch** *adj* melodic <> *adv* melodically.

**melodramatisch** *adj* melodramatic.

**Melone** (*pl* -n) *die* - **1.** [Frucht] melon - **2.** [Hut] bowler (hat).

**Membran** (*pl* -en) *die* - **1.** TECH diaphragm - **2.** BIOL & CHEM & PHYS membrane.

**Memoiren** [me'mɔaːrən] *pl* memoirs.

**Memorandum** (*pl* -randen) *das* memorandum.

**Memory** ['mɛmɔriː] (*pl* -s) *die* EDV: **extended** ~ extended memory.

**Menge** (*pl* -n) *die* - **1.** [Anzahl] amount; **die doppelte/dreifache** ~ twice/three times the amount; **in rauen** ~**n** *fam*: **die Leute kamen in** rauen ~**n** loads of people came - **2.** [Vielzahl] a lot ODER lots; **eine** ~ **Bücher** a lot ODER lots of books - **3.** (ohne pl) [Menschenmasse] crowd - **4.** MATH set.

➡ **eine ganze Menge** *adv* quite a lot; **eine ganze** ~ **Geld** quite a lot of money.

➡ **jede Menge** *adv* *fam* loads; **jede** ~ **Arbeit** loads of work.

**Mengenanlgabe** *die* quantity.

**Mengenlehre** *die* MATH set theory.

**mengenmäßig** *adj* quantitative <> *adv* quantitatively.

**Mengenlrabatt** *der* bulk discount.

**Mengenlverhältnis** *das* relative proportions (*pl*).

**Meniskus** (*pl* -ken) *der* meniscus.

**Mensa** (*pl* **Mensen**) *die* UNI university canteen.

**Mensch** (*pl* -en) *der* - **1.** [Art, Lebewesen] human (being); **der** ~ **ist ein vernunftbegabtes Tier** man is a rational animal - **2.** [Person] person <> *interj* *fam* [wütend] for heaven's sake!; [begeistert] wow!

➡ **kein Mensch** *pron* no one.

**Menschengedenken** *das*: **seit** ~ for as long as anyone can remember.

**Menschenlhandel** *der* slave trade.

**Menschenlkenntnis** *die* knowledge of human nature.

**Menschenlleben** *das* life.

**menschenleer** *adj* deserted.

**Menschenlmenge** *die* crowd.

**Menschenrechte** *pl* human rights.

**menschenscheu** *adj* [aus Angst] shy; [aus Abneigung] unsocial.

**Menschenlseele** *die*: **keine** ~ not a soul.

**menschenunwürdig** *adj* inhumane.

**Menschenverstand** *der*: **der gesunde** ~ common sense.

**Menschenwürde** *die* human dignity.

**Menschheit** *die* humanity, mankind.

**menschlich** *adj* - **1.** [des Menschen] human - **2.** [human] humane <> *adv* [human] humanely.

**Menstruation** (*pl* -en) *die* MED menstruation.

**mental** *adj* mental <> *adv* mentally.

**Mentalität** (*pl* -en) *die* mentality.

**Menthol** *das* menthol.

**Menü** (*pl* -s) *das* - **1.** [Speisenfolge] set menu - **2.** EDV menu.

**Menuett** (*pl* -e ODER -s) *das* minuet.

**Meridian** (*pl* -e) *der* GEOGR & ASTRON meridian.

**Merk|blatt** *das* explanatory leaflet.

**merken** *vt* to notice; **sich** *(D)* **etw ~** to remember sthg; **du merkst aber auch alles!** *fam iron* how observant of you!

**merklich** *adj* noticeable <> *adv* noticeably.

**Merkmal** (*pl* -e) *das* feature.

**Merk|satz** *der* mnemonic.

**Merkur** *der* Mercury.

**merkwürdig** *adj* strange <> *adv* strangely.

**Merk|zettel** *der* note.

**messbar** *adj* measurable.

**Mess|becher** *der* measuring jug.

**Messdaten** *pl* measurements.

**Mess|diener, in** *der, die* server.

**Messe** (*pl* -n) *die* - **1.** [Gottesdienst] mass - **2.** [Ausstellung] (trade) fair.

**Messe|gelände** *das* exhibition centre.

**Messe|halle** *die* exhibition hall.

**messen** (*präs* misst; *prät* maß; *perf* hat gemessen) *vt* to measure; [Temperatur] to take <> *vi* [eine bestimmte Größe haben] to measure; **er misst 1,76 m** he is 1.76m tall.

➤ **sich messen** *ref geh* [sich vergleichen]: **sich mit jm ~** to compete with sb; **sich mit jm in etw** *(D)* **~/nicht ~ können** to be a/no match for sb in sthg.

**Messer** (*pl* -) *das* [zum Schneiden] knife; [zum Rasieren] razor; **jn ans ~ liefern** *fig* to inform on sb.

➤ **bis aufs Messer** *adv* to the bitter end.

**messerscharf** *adj* razor-sharp <> *adv* [scharfsinnig] incisively.

**Messe|stand** *der* stand at a (trade) fair.

**Messing** *das* brass.

**Messung** (*pl* -en) *die* measurement.

**Metall** (*pl* -e) *das* metal.

**Metall|arbeiter, in** *der, die* metalworker.

**Metall|industrie** *die* metalworking industry.

**metallisch** *adj* metallic <> *adv:* **~ schimmern** to have a metallic gleam.

**Metamorphose** [metamɔrˈfoːzə] (*pl* -n) *die* metamorphosis.

**Metapher** [meˈtafɐl] (*pl* -n) *die* metaphor.

**Metastase** (*pl* -n) *die* metastasis.

**Meteor** (*pl* -e) *der* meteor.

**Meteorit** (*pl* -e ODER -en) *der* meteorite.

**Meteorologe** (*pl* -n) *der* weather forecaster.

**Meteorologin** (*pl* -nen) *die* weather forecaster.

**meteorologisch** *adj* meteorological <> *adv* meteorologically.

**Meter** (*pl* -) *das* ODER *der* metre; **zwei ~ breit/** hoch/lang/tief **sein** to be two metres wide/high/long/deep.

**meterdick** *adj:* **eine ~e Schicht** a layer several metres thick <> *adv* to a thickness of several metres.

**meterhoch** *adj:* **ein ~er Zaun** a fence several metres high <> *adv* to a height of several metres; **der Schnee liegt ~** the snow is several metres deep.

**meterlang** *adj:* **ein ~es Kabel** a cable several metres long <> *adv* for several metres.

**Meter|maß** *das* tape measure.

**Methan** *das* methane.

**Methode** (*pl* -n) *die* method.

**methodisch** *adj* methodical <> *adv* methodically.

**Metronom** (*pl* -e) *das* metronome.

**Metropole** (*pl* -n) *die* **geh** metropolis.

**Mett** *das* **Norddt** raw minced **Br** ODER ground **Am** pork.

**Mett|wurst** *die* soft, smoked pork or beef sausage, usually spread on bread.

**Metzger** (*pl* -) *der* butcher.

**Metzgerei** (*pl* -en) *die* butcher's.

**Metzgerin** (*pl* -nen) *die* butcher.

**Meute** (*pl* -n) *die* - **1.** [Hunde] pack - **2.** *fam* [Menschen] mob.

**Meuterei** (*pl* -en) *die* [auf Schiff] mutiny; [in Gefängnis] revolt.

**meutern** *vi* - **1.** [sich auflehnen - Besatzung] to mutiny; [- Strafgefangene] to revolt - **2.** *fam* [sich weigern] to protest.

**Mexikaner, in** (*mpl* -; *fpl* -nen) *der, die* Mexican.

**mexikanisch** *adj* Mexican <> *adv:* **~ kochen** to cook Mexican food.

**Mexiko** *nt* Mexico.

**Mexiko-City** *nt* Mexico City.

**MEZ** [ɛmˈeːˈtsɛt] (*abk für* **mitteleuropäische Zeit**) *die* CET.

**MFG** [ɛmˈɛfˈgeː] (*pl* -s) *die* abk für **Mitfahrgelegenheit.**

**MfS** [ɛmˈɛfˈɛs] (*abk für* **Ministerium für Staatssicherheit (DDR)**) *das ministry for state security in the GDR, also called "Stasi".*

**mg** (*abk für* **Milligramm**) mg.

**MG** [ɛmˈgeː] (*pl* -s) *das* abk für **Maschinengewehr.**

**mhd.** (*abk für* **mittelhochdeutsch**) *Middle High German.*

**MHz** (*abk für* **Megahertz**) MHz.

**Mi.** (*abk für* **Mittwoch**) Wed.

**miauen** *vi* to miaow.

**mich** *pron (Akkusativ von ich)* - **1.** [Personalpronomen] me - **2.** [Reflexivpronomen] myself; **ich entschied ~ zu kündigen** I decided to hand in my notice.

**mickerig, mickrig** *adj fam abw* pathetic; [Pflanze, Tier, Person] puny; [Portion] measly.

**mickrig** = mickerig.

**mied** *prät* ⊏> **meiden.**

**Mieder** (*pl* -) *das* - **1.** [Unterwäsche] corset - **2.** [Oberteil] bodice.

**Mief** *der fam eigtl &amp; fig* stuffy atmosphere.

**Miene** (*pl* -n) *die* expression; **keine ~ verziehen** not to bat an eyelid; **gute ~ zum bösen Spiel machen** to grin and bear it.

**mies** *fam abw adj* lousy ⟨⟩ *adv:* **~ gelaunt sein** to be in a foul mood.

**Miese** *pl fam:* **in den ~n sein, ~ haben** to be in the red; **~ machen** to make a loss.

**mies machen** *vt fam abw* to run down; **jm etw ~** to spoil sthg for sb.

**Miesmuschel** *die* mussel.

**Miete** (*pl* -n) *die* [für Wohnung, Geschäftsfläche, Garage] rent; [für Fahrzeug] hire charge *Br*, rental *Am*; **zur ~ wohnen** to live in rented accommodation.

**mieten** *vt:* **(sich** (*D*)**) etw ~** [Wohnung, Geschäftsfläche, Garage] to rent; [Fahrzeug] to hire *Br*, to rent *Am*.

**Mieter, in** (*mpl* -; *fpl* -nen) *der, die* tenant.

**Mieterschutz** *der* protection of tenants' rights.

**mietfrei** *adj &amp; adv* rent-free.

**Mietpreis** *der* rent.

**Mietrecht** *das* law of landlord and tenant.

**Mietshaus** *das* block of flats *Br*, apartment building *Am*.

**Mietskaserne** *die abw* barracks.

**Mietverhältnis** *das amt* tenancy.

**Mietvertrag** *der* [für Wohnung, Geschäftsfläche] lease; [für Fahrzeug] hire *Br* ODER rental *Am* agreement.

**Mietwagen** *der* hire *Br* ODER rental *Am* car.

**Mietwohnung** *die* rented flat *Br* ODER apartment *Am*.

**Migräne** *die* migraine.

**Mikrochip** *der* microchip.

**Mikroelektronik** *die* microelectronics (*U*).

**Mikrofiche** ['mikrofi:ʃ] (*pl* -s) *das* ODER *der* microfiche.

**Mikrofilm** *der* microfilm.

**Mikrofon, Mikrophon** (*pl* -e) *das* microphone.

**Mikrokosmos** *der (ohne pl)* microcosm.

**Mikroorganismus** ['mikroɔrga'nɪsmʊs] *der* microorganism.

**Mikroprozessor** *der* EDV microprocessor.

**Mikroskop** (*pl* -e) *das* microscope.

**mikroskopisch** *adj* microscopic ⟨⟩ *adv* - **1.** [mit einem Mikroskop] under the microscope - **2.** [winzig] microscopically.

**Mikrowellenherd** *der* microwave (oven).

**Mil.** (*abk für* Militär) mil.

**Milbe** (*pl* -n) *die* mite.

**Milch** *die* milk.

**Milchflasche** *die* [für Säugling] feeding bottle; [von Molkerei] milk bottle.

**milchig** *adj* milky ⟨⟩ *adv:* **~ trüb** milky and cloudy.

**Milchkanne** *die* (milk) churn.

**Milchmädchenrechnung** *die fig* naive piece of reckoning.

**Milchprodukt** *das* dairy product.

**Milchpulver** *das* powdered milk.

**Milchreis** *der (ohne pl)* rice pudding.

**Milchshake** (*pl* -s) *der* milk shake.

**Milchstraße** *die* ASTRON Milky Way.

**Milchsuppe** *die* soup made from sweetened, thickened milk.

**Milchzahn** *der* milk tooth.

**mild, milde** *adj* - **1.** [gen] mild - **2.** [Licht, Worte, Lächeln] gentle - **3.** [Strafe, Urteil] lenient; [Herrscher] benevolent ⟨⟩ *adv* - **1.** [urteilen, strafen] leniently - **2.** [scheinen, wehen, lächeln] gently - **3.** [nicht scharf - würzen] lightly.

**Milde** *die* - **1.** [von Urteil] leniency - **2.** [von Licht] gentleness; [von Abend, Klima, Aroma] mildness.

**mildern** *vt* - **1.** [abschwächen - Wut, Worte, Urteil] to moderate; [ - Schärfe] to reduce; [ - Aufprall] to soften - **2.** [lindern] to alleviate, to relieve.

➤ **sich mildern** *ref* - **1.** [Wut, Zorn] to abate - **2.** [Klima] to become milder.

**Milderung** *die* [von Strafe] reduction; [von Wut] moderation; [von Aufprall] softening; [von Leid] alleviation, relief.

**Milieu** [mi'ljø:] (*pl* -s) *das* - **1.** [Umfeld, Umwelt] environment - **2.** [Unterwelt] world of prostitution.

**militant** *adj* militant ⟨⟩ *adv* militantly.

**Militär** (*pl* -s) *das:* **das ~** the military ⟨⟩ *der* army officer.

**Militärbündnis** *das* military alliance.

**Militärdienst** *der* military service.

**militärisch** *adj* military ⟨⟩ *adv* militarily.

**militaristisch** ⟨⟩ *adj* militaristic ⟨⟩ *adv* militaristically.

**Militärregierung** *die* military government.

**Miliz** (pl -en) die militia.

**Milliardär, in** (mpl -e; fpl -nen) der, die billionaire.

**Milliarde** (pl -n) die billion.

**Milli|gramm** das milligram.

**Milli|liter** der millilitre.

**Milli|meter** der millimetre.

**Milli|meterpapier** das graph paper.

**Million** (pl -en) die million.

**Millionär, in** (mpl -e; fpl -nen) der, die millionaire.

**Millionen|betrag** der sum running into millions.

**Millionen|stadt** die city with a population of over one million.

**Milz** (pl -en) die spleen.

**Milzbrand** der (ohne pl) anthrax.

**mimen** vt to play.

**Mimik** die (ohne pl) facial expressions and gestures.

**mimisch** adj mimic; [Darstellung] using facial expressions and gestures <> adv using facial expressions and gestures.

**Mimose** (pl -n) die **- 1.** [Pflanze] mimosa **- 2.** abw [Mensch] oversensitive person.

**min.** (abk für **Minute, minimal**) min.

**minder** adv geh less.
➝ **nicht minder** adv no less.

**minderbemittelt** adj **- 1.** fam abw [wenig intelligent] not very bright **- 2.** [arm] of limited means.

**mindere, r, s** adj [Ware, Qualität] inferior; [Bedeutung, Begabung] lesser.

**Minderheit** (pl -en) die minority; **in der ~ sein** to be in a/the minority.

**minderjährig** adj underage.

**Minderjährige** (pl -n) der, die minor.

**mindern** vt [Strafmaß, Preis, Wert] to reduce; [Ansehen] to diminish.
➝ **sich mindern** ref to decrease.

**Minderung** (pl -en) die reduction.

**minderwertig** adj inferior <> adv [herstellen] poorly.

**Minderwertigkeits|komplex** der inferiority complex.

**Minderzahl** die: **in der ~ sein** to be in a/the minority.

**Mindestalter** das minimum age.

**mindeste** adj slightest; **das ist das Mindeste, was man erwarten kann** that is the least you can expect.
➝ **nicht im Mindesten** adv not in the slightest.

**mindestens** adv at least.

**Mindest|lohn** der minimum wage.

**Mine** (pl -n) die **- 1.** [Schreibutensil - von Kugelschreiber] refill; [ - von Bleistift] lead **- 2.** [Bergwerk, Sprengsatz] mine; [Stollen] tunnel.

**Mineral** (pl -e ODER -ien) das mineral.

**mineralhaltig** adj containing minerals.

**mineralisch** adj mineral.

**Mineral|öl** das mineral oil.

**Mineralöl|steuer** die tax on oil.

**Mineral|wasser** das mineral water.

**mini** adv: **~ tragen** to wear a mini.

**Mini** (pl -s) das **- 1.** (ohne pl, ohne Artikel) [Mode] miniskirts (pl) **- 2.** fam [Kleid] mini <> der fam [Rock] mini.

**Miniatur** (pl -en) die miniature.

**Minigolf** das crazy golf.

**minimal** adj minimal <> adv minimally.

**Minimum** (pl Minima) das minimum (U).

**Minister** (pl -) der minister; **~ des Inneren/der Finanzen** interior/finance minister.

**ministeriell** adj ministerial <> adv ministerially.

**Ministerin** (pl -nen) die minister.

**Ministerium** [mɪnɪsˈteːrjʊm] (pl Ministerien) das ministry; **~ des Inneren/der Finanzen** interior/finance ministry.

**Minister|präsident, in** der, die **- 1.** [von Bundesländern] minister president, title given to leader of government in the German federal states **- 2.** [Premierminister] prime minister.

**Minister|rat** der Council of Ministers.

**Ministrant, in** (mpl -en; fpl -nen) der, die server.

**Minne|sänger** der minnesinger.

**Minsk** nt Minsk.

**minus** präp minus <> adv: **~ dreizehn Grad** minus thirteen degrees <> konj: **zehn ~ drei** ten minus three.

**Minus** das (ohne pl) **- 1.** [Fehlbetrag] deficit; **im ~ stehen** to be in the red **- 2.** [Zeichen] minus (sign).

**Minus|pol** der negative pole.

**Minus|punkt** der fig disadvantage.

**Minute** (pl -n) die minute; **auf die ~ pünktlich** on the dot; **in letzter ~** at the last minute.

**Minuten|zeiger** der minute hand.

**minutiös, minuziös** [minuˈtsjøːs] geh adj scrupulous <> adv scrupulously.

**Minze** (pl -n) die mint.

**Mio.** (abk für **Million**) m.

**mir** pron (Dativ von ich) **- 1.** (to) me; **er sagte es ~** he told me; **das gehört ~** this is mine, this belongs to me; **mit ~** with me; **ich kann ~ das**

**nicht vorstellen** I can't imagine that; **~ nichts, dir nichts** *fig* just like that - **2.** [Reflexivpronomen] myself; **ich sagte ~** I said to myself.

**Mirabelle** (*pl* -n) *die* mirabelle (plum).

**Mischlbrot** *das bread made from a mixture of rye and wheat flour.*

**mischen** *vt* [Farben, Zutaten] to mix; [Karten] to shuffle; **etw mit etw ~** to mix sthg with sthg; **etw in** ODER **unter etw** (A) **~** to mix sthg into ODER in with sthg.
➞ **sich mischen** *ref*: **sich unter etw** (A) **~** to mix with sthg; **sich in etw** (A) **~** to interfere in sthg.

**Mischling** (*pl* -e) *der* [Tier] half-breed.

**Mischmasch** (*pl* -e) *der fam* hotchpotch.

**Mischlpult** *das* mixing desk.

**Mischung** (*pl* -en) *die* mixture.

**Mischlwald** *der* mixed forest.

**miserabel** *adj* dreadful ◇ *adv* dreadfully.

**Misere** (*pl* -n) *die geh* dreadful situation.

**missachten** *vt* - **1.** [nicht befolgen] to disregard - **2.** [verachten] to despise.

**Missbehagen** *das* uneasiness; **es bereitet ihr ~** it makes her uneasy.

**missbilligen** *vt* to disapprove of.

**Misslbrauch** *der* - **1.** [sexuell, von Medikamenten, von Drogen] abuse - **2.** [schlechter Gebrauch] misuse.

**missbrauchen** *vt* - **1.** [ausnutzen - Macht, Mittel] to misuse; [ - Vertrauen] to abuse; [ - Gutmütigkeit] to take advantage of - **2.** [übermäßig nutzen, sexuell] to abuse.

**missen** *vt* to do without; **etw nicht (mehr) ~ wollen** not to want to be without sthg.

**Misslerfolg** *der* failure.

**Misslernte** *die* poor harvest.

**missfallen** (*präs* missfällt; *prät* missfiel; *perf* hat missfallen) *vi*: **es missfällt mir, wie sie ...** I dislike the way she ...; **der Plan missfiel ihm** he disliked the plan.

**Missfallen** *das* displeasure.

**missgebildet** *adj* deformed.

**Misslgeburt** *die* monster.

**Misslgeschick** *das* mishap; **jm passiert ein ~** sb has a mishap.

**missglücken** (*perf* ist missglückt) *vi* to be unsuccessful; **der Versuch ist mir missglückt** my attempt was unsuccessful.

**missgönnen** *vt*: **jm etw ~** to begrudge sb sthg.

**Misslgriff** *der* mistake.

**Missgunst** *die* resentment.

**missgünstig** *adj* resentful ◇ *adv* resentfully.

**misshandeln** *vt* to ill-treat.

**Misslhandlung** *die* ill-treatment (U).

**Mission** (*pl* -en) *die* mission; **in geheimer ~** on a secret mission.

**Mississippi** *der* [Fluss]: **der ~** the Mississippi.

**Misskredit** *der*: **jn in ~ bringen** to discredit sb; **in ~ geraten** ODER **kommen** to be discredited.

**misslang** *prät* ▷ misslingen.

**misslingen** (*prät* misslang; *perf* ist misslungen) *vi* to fail; **das Experiment ist mir misslungen** my experiment was a failure; **ein misslungener Versuch** an unsuccessful attempt.

**misslungen** *pp* ▷ misslingen.

**missmutig** *adj* [Person, Charakter] bad-tempered; [Gesicht, Laune] sullen; **~ sein** to be in a bad mood ◇ *adv* bad-temperedly; [ansehen] sullenly.

**missraten** (*präs* missrät; *prät* missriet; *perf* ist missraten) *vi*: **der Braten war ihr ~** her roast had turned out badly ◇ *adj* which/who turned out badly.

**Misslstand** *der* disgraceful state of affairs; **Missstände an den Universitäten anprangern** to make public the shortcomings of the universities.

**misst** *präs* ▷ messen.

**misstrauen** *vi*: **jm/etw ~** to mistrust sb/sthg.

**Misstrauen** *das* mistrust.

**Misstrauenslantrag** *der* motion of no confidence.

**Misstrauenslvotum** *das* vote of no confidence.

**misstrauisch** *adj* mistrustful; **jm gegenüber ~ sein** to be mistrustful of sb ◇ *adv* mistrustfully.

**Misslverhältnis** *das* discrepancy.

**missverständlich** *adj* ambiguous ◇ *adv* ambiguously.

**Missverständnis** (*pl* -nisse) *das* misunderstanding.

**missverstehen** (*prät* missverstand; *perf* hat missverstanden) *vt* to misunderstand.

**Misswirtschaft** *die* mismanagement.

**Mist** *der* - **1.** [Dung] dung; [Düngemittel] manure - **2.** *fam fig* & *abw* [Plunder, Blödsinn] rubbish; **~ machen** ODER **bauen** to make a mess of things - **3.** *fam* [als Ausruf]: **(so ein) ~!** damn it!

**Mistel** (*pl* -n) *die* mistletoe (U).

**Mistlhaufen** *der* manure heap.

**Mistlkäfer** *der* dung beetle.

**mit** *präp* (+ D) - **1.** [zusammen mit] with; **er kommt ~ seiner Frau** he's coming with his wife; **Kaffee ~ Zucker** coffee with sugar; **ein Haus ~ Gar-**

**ten** a house with a garden; **eine Scheibe Brot ~ Butter** a slice of bread and butter; **sich ~ jm unterhalten** to talk to sb **- 2.** [modal]: **~ lauter Stimme** in a loud voice; **~ Nachdruck** emphatically; **~ 100 Stundenkilometern** at 100 kilometres per hour; **~ Verspätung eintreffen** to arrive late **- 3.** [mittels] with; **~ dem Hammer** with a hammer; **~ dem Zug** by train; **~ der Post** by post; **~ Scheck bezahlen** to pay by cheque **- 4.** [stellt Bezug her]: **wie weit bist du ~ deiner Arbeit?** how far have you got with your work?; **wie wäre es ~ einer Tasse Kaffee?** how about a cup of coffee?; **die Sache ~ dem Brief** that business about the letter; **er hat es ~ dem Magen** he has stomach trouble **- 5.** [temporal] at; **~ jedem Tag** every day; **~ 16 Jahren** at (the age of) 16; **~ der Zeit** in (the course of) time <> *adv* **- 1.** [auch] too; **ich bin ~ dabei!** count me in!; **sie war nicht ~ dabei** she wasn't there; **das ist alles ~ einbegriffen** that's with everything included **- 2.** [unter anderen]: **er ist ~ der beste Schüler seiner Klasse** he is one of the best pupils in his class.

**Mitarbeit** *die* [an Projekt] collaboration; [von Schülern, Bevölkerung] participation.

**mitlarbeiten** *vi* **- 1.** [in Projekt] to collaborate; [im Haushalt] to help out; **bei/an etw** *(D)* **~** to collaborate on sthg **- 2.** [in der Schule] to participate.

**Mitlarbeiter, in** *der, die* [Betriebsangehörige] colleague, coworker *Am;* **freie ~** freelance workers.

**mitlbekommen** *vt (unreg)* **- 1.** [verstehen] to follow **- 2.** [aufschnappen]: **etw von etw ~** to hear sthg about sthg; **(von etw) nicht viel ~** not to take much (of sthg) in **- 3.** [bekommen]: **etw ~** to get sthg to take with one.

**mitlbenutzen, mitbenützen** *vt* to share.

**mitlbestimmen** *vi:* **bei etw ~** to have a say in sthg; **in einem Betrieb ~** to participate in the decision-making process in a company <> *vt:* **etw ~** to have a say in sthg.

**Mitbestimmung** *die* codetermination.

**Mitlbewohner, in** *der, die* [in Haus] other occupant; [in Wohnung] flatmate *Br,* roommate *Am.*

**mitlbringen** *vt (unreg)* **- 1.** [Geschenk, Personen] to bring (with one); [von Reise] to bring back; **jm etw ~** to bring sthg for sb **- 2.** [Fähigkeiten] to have.

**Mitbringsel** *(pl -) das fam* little present.

**Mitlbürger, in** *der, die* fellow citizen.

**mitldenken** *vi (unreg)* to think constructively.

**miteinander** *adv* [auskommen, streiten, flirten] with each other; [reden, verbinden] to each other; [gemeinsam] together.
➥ **alle miteinander** *pron* all (together).

**mitlempfinden** *vt (unreg):* **etw ~ können** to be able to share sthg.

**mitlerleben** *vt* to witness; **mit ihm habe ich schon allerhand miterlebt** he has put me through a lot.

**Mitesser** *(pl -) der* blackhead.

**mitlfahren** *(perf ist mitgefahren) vi (unreg)* to go/come along; **mit oder bei jm ~** to get a lift *Br oder* ride *Am* with sb.

**Mitfahrlgelegenheit** *die* lift *Br,* ride *Am.*

**Mitfahrlzentrale, Mitfahrerzentrale** *die agency which organizes lifts, with passengers contributing to costs.*

**mitlfühlen** *vi:* **mit jm ~** to sympathize with sb <> *vt* to share.

**mitlfühlend** *adj* sympathetic <> *adv* sympathetically.

**mitlgeben** *vt (unreg):* **jm etw ~** to give sb sthg.

**Mitgefühl** *das* sympathy.

**mitlgehen** *(perf ist mitgegangen) vi (unreg)* **- 1.** [mitkommen] to go/come along; **mit jm ~** to go/come with sb **- 2.** [teilhaben] to be carried along **- 3.** *fam* [stehlen]: **etw ~ lassen** to pinch sthg.

**mitgenommen** *pp* ⊳ **mitnehmen** <> *adj* worn out; **~ aussehen** to look worn out.

**Mitgift** *(pl -en) die* dowry.

**Mitlglied** *das* member.

**Mitgliedslbeitrag** *der* membership fee.

**Mitgliedschaft** *(pl -en) die* membership *(U).*

**mitlhalten** *vi (unreg):* **bei etw (nicht) ~ können** (not) to be able to keep up in sthg; **mit jm/ etw (nicht) ~ können** (not) to be able to keep up with sb/sthg.

**mithilfe** *adv:* **~ von etw/ jm** with the help of sthg/sb <> *präp:* **~ js/einer Sache** with the help of sb/sthg.

**Mithilfe** *die* assistance.

**mitlhören** *vi* [zufällig] to overhear; [heimlich] to listen in <> *vt* [zufällig] to overhear; [heimlich] to listen in on.

**mitlkommen** *(perf ist mitgekommen) vi (unreg)* **- 1.** [auch kommen] to come along; **kommst du mit?** are you coming? **- 2.** [folgen können] to keep up; **da komme ich nicht (mehr) mit!** *fam* it's beyond me! **- 3.** [eintreffen] to arrive.

**Mitlläufer, in** *der, die abw* hanger-on.

**Mitleid** *das* pity; **mit jm ~ haben oder empfinden** to feel pity for sb.

**Mitleidenschaft** *die:* **jn/etw in ~ ziehen** to affect sb/sthg.

**mitleidig** *adj* pitying <> *adv* pityingly.

**mitlmachen** *vt* **- 1.** [Spiel, Kurs] to take part in; [Mode] to follow; **das mache ich nicht mehr länger mit** I'm not going to put up with this any longer **- 2.** [erledigen]: **etw für jn ~** to do sthg for sb **- 3.** [aushalten] to put up with; **sie hat schon viel mitgemacht** she has been through a lot ⬦ *vi* [sich beteiligen] to take part; **bei etw (nicht) ~** (not) to take part in sthg.

**Mitmenschen** *pl* fellow human beings ODER men.

**mit|mischen** *vi fam:* **bei etw ~** [sich einmischen] to interfere in sthg; [teilnehmen] to get involved in sthg.

**mit|nehmen** *vt (unreg)* **- 1.** [mit sich nehmen] to take (with one); **ich kann dich bis zum Bahnhof ~** I can give you a lift *Br* ODER ride *Am* to the station; **sich** *(D)* **etw ~** to take sthg (with one) **- 2.** [strapazieren] to take it out of **- 3.** [kaufen] to buy **- 4.** [stehlen] to make off with **- 5.** *fam* [wahrnehmen, besuchen] to take in.

**mit|rechnen** *vi* to work it out at the same time ⬦ *vt* to include.

**mit|reden** *vi:* **~ können** to be able to join in ⬦ *vt:* **da habe ich auch noch ein Wörtchen mitzureden** I've got something to say on the subject.

**Mit|reisende** *der, die* fellow passenger.

**mit|reißen** *vt (unreg)* **- 1.** [begeistern] to carry away **- 2.** [fortreißen - bei Sturz] to pull down; [ - bei Lawine] to sweep away.

**mitsamt** *präp:* **~ einer Sache** *(D)* together with sthg.

**mit|schneiden** *vt (unreg)* to record.

**mit|schreiben** *(unreg) vt* **- 1.** [festhalten] to take down **- 2.** [Klassenarbeit, Prüfung] to do ⬦ *vi* [festhalten] to take notes.

**Mitschuld** *die* share of the blame.

**mitschuldig** *adj:* **(an etw** *(D)***) ~ sein** to be partly to blame (for sthg).

**Mit|schüler, in** *der, die* schoolmate.

**mit|sein** *(perf* **ist mitgewesen)** *vi (unreg)* to go/come along.

**mit|spielen** *vi* **- 1.** [auch spielen]: **bei/in etw** *(D)* **~** [Spiel] to join in sthg; [Mannschaft, Orchester] to play in sthg; [Theatergruppe, Film] to act in sthg **- 2.** [wichtig sein]: **bei etw ~** to play a part in sthg **- 3.** [mitmachen] to play along; **bei etw ~** to go along with sthg **- 4.** [schaden]: **jm übel ~** to give sb a hard time ⬦ *vt* [Spiel] to play.

**Mit|spieler, in** *der, die* [bei Spiel, in Mannschaft] other player.

**Mitspracherecht** *das* right to have a say; **ein/kein ~ bei etw haben** to have a/no say in sthg.

**Mittag** *(pl* **-e)** *der* midday; **am ~** at midday; **über ~** at lunchtime; **zu ~ essen** to have lunch; **gestern/heute/morgen ~** at midday yesterday/today/tomorrow.

**Mittag|essen** *das* lunch.

**mittags** *adv* at midday.

**Mittags|pause** *die* lunch break.

**Mittags|schlaf** *der (ohne pl)* afternoon nap.

**Mittags|tisch** *der* **- 1.** *geh* [Tisch]: **beim ~ sitzen** to be at the table having lunch **- 2.** [Mahlzeit] lunch.

**Mittags|zeit** *die* lunchtime.

**Mitte** *(pl* **-n)** *die* middle; **in der ~** in the middle; **jn in die ~ nehmen** to go on either side of sb; **~ vierzig** in one's mid-forties; **~ nächster Woche** in the middle of next week.

**mit|teilen** *vt:* **jm etw ~** to tell sb sthg.

➤ **sich mitteilen** *ref geh:* **sich jm ~** to confide in sb.

**Mit|teilung** *die* communication; [an Presse] statement; **jm eine ~ machen** to inform sb; **eine amtliche ~** an official announcement; **eine schriftliche ~** a written communication.

**Mittel** *(pl* **-)** *das* **- 1.** [Hilfsmittel] means *(sg)*; **mit allen ~n** by every means; **das ~ zum Zweck** the means to an end **- 2.** [Medikament] medicine; **ein ~ gegen etw** a remedy for sthg **- 3.** [zur Reinigung] cleaning agent.

➤ **Mittel** *pl* [Geldmittel] means; **öffentliche ~** public funds.

**Mittelalter** *das (ohne pl)* Middle Ages *(pl)*.

**mittelalterlich** *adj* medieval ⬦ *adv* like in medieval times.

**Mittelamerika** *nt* Central America.

**mittelbar** *adj* indirect ⬦ *adv* indirectly.

**Mittel|europa** *nt* Central Europe.

**Mittel|feld** *das* SPORT [beim Fußball] midfield; [bei Wettbewerb] pack.

**Mittel|finger** *der* middle finger.

**mittelfristig** *adj* medium-term ⬦ *adv* in the medium term.

**Mittel|gebirge** *das* low-lying mountain range.

**Mittel|gewicht** *das* [Gewichtsklasse, Sportler] middleweight.

**mittelgroß** *adj* medium-sized; [Person] of medium height.

**Mittelklasse|wagen** *der* middle-of-the-range car.

**Mittel|linie** *die* [auf Spielfeld] halfway line.

**mittellos** *adj* penniless.

**Mittel|maß** *das abw* average.

**mittelmäßig** *abw adj* average ⬦ *adv* averagely.

**Mittelmeer** *das:* **das ~** the Mediterranean (Sea).

**Mittelohr|entzündung** *die* inflammation of the middle ear.

**mittelprächtig** *adj* & *adv fam* so-so.

**Mittel|punkt** *der* centre; **im ~ stehen** to be the centre of attention.

**mittels** *präp geh:* **~ einer Sache** *(G)* by means of sthg.

**Mittel|scheitel** *der* centre parting *Br,* center part *Am.*

**Mittel|schicht** *die* middle class.

**Mittelstand** *der* middle class.

**mittelständisch** *adj* medium-sized.

**Mittel|streifen** *der* central reservation *Br,* median *Am.*

**Mittel|stürmer, in** *der, die* centre forward.

**Mittel|weg** *der* middle way; **einen ~ finden** to find a middle way; **der goldene ~** the happy medium.

**Mittel|welle** *die* medium wave.

**Mittel|wert** *der* mean.

**mitten** *adv:* **~ auf** in the middle of; **~ durch** through the middle of; **~ in etw** *(D)* in the middle of sthg; **~ in etw** *(A)* into the middle of sthg; **~ unter** among; **~ am Tag/in der Nacht** in the middle of the day/night.

**mittendrin** *adv* in the middle.

**mittendurch** *adv* through the middle.

**Mitternacht** *die* midnight.

**mitternachts** *adv* at midnight.

**mittlere, r, s** *adj* **- 1.** [zwischen den Extremen] average; **im ~n Alter** middle-aged **- 2.** [in der Mitte liegend] middle.

**Mittlere Osten** *der:* **der ~** the Middle East.

**mittlerweile** *adv* [inzwischen] in the meantime; [jetzt] now.

**Mittl|vierziger, in** *der, die* man/woman in his/her mid-forties.

**Mittwoch** *(pl -e) der* Wednesday; *siehe auch* **Samstag.**

**mittwochs** ['mɪtvɔxs] *adv* on Wednesdays; *siehe auch* **samstags.**

**mitunter** *adv* occasionally.

**mitverantwortlich** *adj* jointly responsible.

**mit|verdienen** *vi* to earn money as well.

**mit|wirken** *vi:* **(bei etw) ~** [mitarbeiten] to contribute (to sthg); [mitspielen] to take part (in sthg).

**Mitwirkende** *(pl -n) der, die* [Mitarbeiter] contributor; [Schauspieler] actor (*f* actress).

**Mitwisser, in** *(mpl -; fpl -nen) der, die* **- 1.** [bei Straftat] accessory **- 2.** [von Geheimnis]: **~ sein bei etw** to know about sthg.

**Mitwohn|zentrale** *die* agency providing shared accommodation.

**mit|zählen** *vt* & *vi* to count.

**mixen** *vt* to mix.

**Mixer** *(pl -) der* [Maschine] (food) mixer.

**Mixtur** *(pl -en) die* mixture.

**MKS** *(abk für* **Maul- und Klauenseuche**) *die (ohne pl)* foot-and-mouth (disease).

**ml** *(abk für* **Milliliter**) ml.

**mm** *(abk für* **Millimeter**) mm.

**Mo.** *(abk für* **Montag**) Mon.

**Mob** *der (ohne pl) abw* mob.

**mobben** *vt* to bully; [Kollege] to harass.

**Mobbing** *das* bullying; [von Kollege] harassment.

**Möbel** *(pl -) das* piece of furniture; **die ~** the furniture.

**Möbel|politur** *die* furniture polish.

**Möbel|stück** *das* piece of furniture.

**Möbel|wagen** *der* removal *Br* ODER moving *Am* van.

**mobil** *adj* **- 1.** [beweglich] mobile **- 2.** [munter] lively; **~ machen** MIL to mobilize; **etw ~ machen** [aufbieten] to summon up sthg; **jn ~ machen** [munter machen] to liven sb up.

**Mobile** *(pl -s) das* mobile.

**Mobil|funk** *der (ohne pl)* TELEKOM cellphone ODER mobile phone network.

**Mobiliar** *(pl -e) das* furniture and fittings *(pl).*

**mobilisieren** *vt* [gen] to mobilize; [Energie] to summon up.

**Mobilität** *die* mobility.

**Mobilmachung** *(pl -en) die* MIL mobilization.

**Mobil|telefon** *das* mobile phone.

**möblieren** *vt* to furnish.

**möbliert** *adj* furnished <> *adv:* **~ wohnen** to live in furnished accommodation.

**mochte** *prät* ⊳ **mögen.**

**Mode** *(pl -n) die* [Kleidungsstil, Zeitgeschmack] fashion; **die neueste ~** the latest fashion; **es ist jetzt groß in ~** it is very fashionable now; **mit der ~ gehen** to follow the fashion.

**Mode|haus** *das* **- 1.** [Einzelgeschäft] fashion store **- 2.** [Unternehmen] fashion house.

**Model** ['mɔdl] *(pl -s) das* model.

**Modell** *(pl -e) das* model; **~ stehen** [für Maler] to model.

**Modell|eisenbahn** *die* model railway.

**Modell|flugzeug** *das* model plane.

**modellieren** *vt* to model.

**Modem** *(pl -s) das* EDV modem.

**Moden|schau** *die* fashion show.

**Moderator** *(pl -en) der* presenter.

**Moderatorin** *(pl -nen) die* presenter.

**moderig** = **modrig.**

**modern**[1] *(perf* **hat/ist gemodert**) *vi* to moulder.

**modern**[2] *adj* modern; [modisch] fashionable

**M**

◇ adv - **1.** [zeitgemäß] in a modern way; **~ denken** to have modern ideas - **2.** [zeitgenössisch] in a modern style.

**Moderne** die (ohne pl) - **1.** HIST modern times (pl) - **2.** KUNST modern style.

**modernisieren** vt to modernize.

**Modelschmuck** der costume jewellery.

**Modelschöpfer, in** (mpl -; fpl -nen) der, die fashion designer.

**Modezeitschrift** die fashion magazine.

**modisch** adj fashionable ◇ adv fashionably.

**modrig, moderig** adj & adv musty.

**Modul** (pl -e) das EDV module.

**Modus** (pl Modi) der - **1.** geh [Verfahrensweise] method - **2.** GRAM mood.

**Mofa** (pl -s) das moped.

**mogeln** vi to cheat.

**mögen** (präs mag; prät mochte; perf hat gemocht ODER -) vt (perf hat gemocht) - **1.** [gern haben] to like; **jn/etw (nicht) ~** (not) to like sb/sthg - **2.** [wollen]: **ich möchte bitte ein Eis** I'd like an ice-cream please; **was möchten Sie?** what would you like? ◇ vi (perf hat gemocht) [wollen]: **er möchte nach Hause** he wants to go home ◇ aux (perf hat mögen): **ich möchte etwas trinken** I'd like something to drink; **möchtest du mitkommen?** would you like to come?; **mag sein** that may well be; **mag sein, dass sie noch anruft** she may still call; **das mag genügen** that should be enough.

**möglich** adj & adv possible; **so bald/schnell/früh wie ~** as soon/quickly/early as possible; **ich habe es so gut wie ~ gemacht** I did it as well as I could; **jm ist es (nicht) ~, etw zu tun** it is (not) possible for sb to do sthg; **das ist (leicht** ODER **gut) ~** that is (quite) possible.
➡ **alles Mögliche** pron absolutely everything.

**möglicherweise** adv possibly.

**Möglichkeit** (pl -en) die - **1.** [das Mögliche] possibility; **ist es denn die ~!** I don't believe it!; **es besteht die ~, dass ...** it is possible that ...; **nach ~** if possible - **2.** [Chance] opportunity.
➡ **Möglichkeiten** pl [Fähigkeiten] capabilities.

**möglichst** ['møːklɪçst] adv - **1.** [wenn möglich] if possible - **2.** [so viel wie möglich]: **~ groß/stark/viel** as big/strong/much as possible.

**Mohammedaner, in** (mpl -; fpl -nen) der, die Muslim.

**mohammedanisch** adj Muslim.

**Mohn** (pl -e) der - **1.** [Pflanze] poppy - **2.** [Samen] poppy seeds (pl).

**Mohnlblume** die poppy.

**Möhre** (pl -n) die carrot.

**Mohrenlkopf** der KÜCHE chocolate-covered marshmallow.

**Mokassin, Mokassin** (pl -s ODER -e) der moccasin.

**mokieren** ➡ **sich mokieren** ref: **sich über etw** (A) **~** to sneer at sthg.

**Mokka** (pl -s) der mocha.

**Molch** (pl -e) der newt.

**Moldau** die: **die ~** the (River) Vltava.

**Moldawien** nt Moldavia.

**Mole** (pl -n) die mole.

**Molekül** (pl -e) das molecule.

**molk** prät ➡ **melken.**

**Molke** die whey.

**Molkerei** (pl -en) die dairy.

**Moll** das minor (key).

**mollig** adj plump.

**Molotowlcocktail** ['mɔlotɔfkɔkteːl] der Molotov cocktail.

**Moment** (pl -e) der moment; **im ~** at the moment; **jeden ~** (at) any moment; **(einen) ~, bitte!** just a moment, please!; **~ mal!** fam wait a moment! ◇ das element.

**momentan** adj present ◇ adv at the moment.

**Momentlaufnahme** die snapshot.

**Monaco** nt Monaco.

**Monarch, in** (mpl -en; fpl -nen) der, die monarch.

**Monarchie** (pl -n) die monarchy.

**Monat** (pl -e) der month; **diesen/nächsten/vorigen ~** this/next/last month; **sie ist im fünften ~ (schwanger)** she is over four months pregnant.

**monatelang** adj lasting for months ◇ adv for months.

**monatlich** adj & adv monthly.

**Monatslanfang** der beginning of the month.

**Monatsleinkommen** das monthly income.

**Monatslende** das end of the month.

**Monatslgehalt** das monthly salary.

**Monatslkarte** die monthly season ticket.

**Monatslmiete** die monthly rent.

**Monatslrate** die monthly instalment.

**Mönch** (pl -e) der monk.

**Mond** (pl -e) der moon.

**mondän** adj elegant ◇ adv elegantly.

**Mondlfinsternis** die eclipse of the moon.

**Mondllandung** die moon landing.

**Mondlschein** der moonlight.

**Mond|sichel** *die* crescent moon.

**Moneten** *pl fam* dough *(U).*

**Mongole** (*pl* -n) *der* Mongolian.

**Mongolei** *die* Mongolia.

**Mongolin** (*pl* -nen) *die* Mongolian.

**mongolisch** *adj* Mongolian.

**mongoloid** *adj* MED mongoloid.

**monieren** *vt geh* to find fault with.

**Monitor** (*pl* -en ODER -e) *der* monitor.

**Mono** *das* mono.

**monogam** *adj* monogamous ◇ *adv* mono-gamously.

**Monogramm** (*pl* -e) *das* monogram.

**Monografie, Monographie** (*pl* -n) *die* monograph.

**Monokel** (*pl* -) *das* monocle.

**Monolog** (*pl* -e) *der* monologue.

**Monopol** (*pl* -e) *das* monopoly; **das ~ auf etw** *(A)* **haben** to have a monopoly on sthg.

**monoton** *adj* monotonous ◇ *adv* mono-tonously.

**Monster** (*pl* -) *das* monster.

**monströs** *adj* monstrous.

**Monstrum** (*pl* -stren) *das fam* [riesiges Teil]: **ein ~ von einem Flugzeug** a whopping great plane.

**Monsun** (*pl* -e) *der* monsoon.

**Montag** (*pl* -e) *der* Monday; **einen blauen ~ machen** to take Monday off *(unofficially);* *siehe auch* **Samstag.**

**Montage** [mɔn'taːʒə] (*pl* -n) *die* - **1.** TECH [Zusam-menbau] assembly *(U);* [Einbau] installation *(U);* **auf ~ sein** to be away on assembly/ installation work - **2.** [Schnitt] editing *(U)* - **3.** KUNST montage.

**Montageband** (*pl* -bänder) *das* assembly line.

**Montage|halle** *die* assembly shop.

**montags** *adv* on Mondays; *siehe auch* **sams-tags.**

**Montblanc** [mɔ̃'blãː] *der* Mont Blanc.

**Monteur, in** [mɔn'tøːɐ̯, rɪn] (*mpl* -e; *fpl* -nen) *der, die* fitter.

**montieren** *vt* - **1.** TECH [zusammenbauen] to as-semble; [einbauen] to install; [festmachen] to fix - **2.** [schneiden] to edit.

**Montreal** *nt* Montreal.

**Montur** (*pl* -en) *die fam* gear *(U).*

**Monument** (*pl* -e) *das* monument.

**monumental** *adj* monumental ◇ *adv* on a monumental scale.

**Moor** (*pl* -e) *das* bog.

**Moor|bad** *das* mud bath.

**Moos** (*pl* -e) *das* - **1.** [Pflanze, Pflanzengattung] moss - **2.** *fam* [Geld] dough.

**Moped** (*pl* -s) *das* moped.

**Moped|fahrer, in** *der, die* moped rider.

**Mops** (*pl* Möpse) *der* - **1.** [Hund] pug (dog) - **2.** *fam fig* [Mensch] roly-poly.

➤ **Möpse** *pl salopp* [Brüste] knockers.

**Moral** *die* - **1.** [Normen] morals *(pl)* - **2.** [Stim-mung] morale - **3.** [das Lehrreiche] moral - **4.** [Ethik] morality.

**moralisch** *adj* moral ◇ *adv* morally.

**Moral|predigt** *die abw* sermon.

**Moräne** (*pl* -n) *die* moraine.

**Morast** (*pl* -e) *der* quagmire.

**morastig** *adj* muddy.

**Morchel** (*pl* -n) *die* morel.

**Mord** (*pl* -e) *der* murder, homicide Am; [durch Attentat] assassination; **einen ~ begehen** to commit murder.

**Mord|anschlag** *der* murder attempt; [durch Attentat] assassination attempt.

**Mord|drohung** *die* death threat.

**Mörder, in** (*mpl* -; *fpl* -nen) *der, die* murderer; [durch Attentat] assassin.

**mörderisch** *adj* - **1.** [lebensgefährlich] deadly; [Tempo] breakneck - **2.** [Verbrechen, Absicht] murderous - **3.** *fam* [groß] terrible ◇ *adv* - **1.** [steil, schnell] murderously - **2.** *fam* [sehr] terribly.

**Mord|fall** *der* murder (case).

**Mord|kommission** *die* murder squad, homicide squad Am.

**Mords|kerl** *der fam:* **er ist ein ~!** he's quite a guy!

**mordsmäßig** *fam adj* [Vergnügen, Gaudi, Glück] terrific; [Krach, Geschrei, Pech] terrible ◇ *adv* terribly.

**Mord|verdacht** *der* suspicion of murder.

**Mord|versuch** *der* murder attempt.

**morgen** *adv* - **1.** [am Tag nach heute, zukünftig] to-morrow; **bis ~!** see you tomorrow!; **~ früh** tomorrow morning - **2.** [vormittag] morning.

**Morgen** (*pl* -) *der* morning; **am ~** in the morn-ing; **gestern/heute ~** yesterday/this morn-ing.

➤ **guten Morgen** *interj* good morning!

**morgendlich** *adj* morning *(vor Subst).*

**Morgen|grauen** *das* dawn.

**Morgen|gymnastik** *die* morning exerci-ses *(pl).*

**Morgen|mantel** *der* dressing gown.

**Morgen|rot** *das* red dawn sky.

**M**

**morgens** *adv* in the morning; [jeden Morgen] every morning; **von ~ bis abends** from dawn till dusk.

**morgig** *adj* [Treffen] tomorrow's; **der ~e Tag** tomorrow.

**Morphium** *das* morphine.

**morsch** *adj* rotten.

**morsen** *vt* to send in Morse (code) ◇ *vi* to use Morse (code).

**Morse|zeichen** *das* Morse signal.

**Mörtel** (*pl* -) *der* mortar.

**Mosaik** (*pl* -e *ODER* -en) *das* mosaic.

**Mosambik** *nt* Mozambique.

**Moschee** [mɔ'ʃeː] (*pl* -n) *die* mosque.

**Mosel** *die* Moselle.

**Mosel|wein** *der* Moselle (wine).

**mosern** *vi fam* to grumble.

**Moskau** *nt* Moscow.

**Moskauer** (*pl* -) *der* Muscovite ◇ *adj (unver)* of/from Moscow.

**Moskauerin** (*pl* -nen) *die* Muscovite.

**Moskito** (*pl* -s) *der* mosquito.

**Moskito|netz** *das* mosquito net.

**Moslem** (*pl* -s) *der* Muslim.

**Moslime** (*pl* -n) *die* Muslim.

**Most** (*pl* -e) *der* - **1.** [Fruchtsaft] (cloudy) fruit juice - **2.** *Süddt* [Apfelwein] cider.

**Motel, Motel** (*pl* -s) *das* motel.

**Motiv** (*pl* -e) *das* - **1.** [von Handlung] motive - **2.** [von Bild] subject - **3.** [Thema] motif.

**Motivation** [motiva'tsjoːn] (*pl* -en) *die* motivation.

**motivieren** [moti'viːrən] *vt* to motivate; **jn ~, etw zu tun** to motivate sb to do sthg.

**Motocross-|Rennen** [moto'krɔsrɛnən] *das* motocross.

**Motor, Motor** (*pl* -toren) *der* - **1.** [von Fahrzeug] engine; [von Gerät] motor - **2.** *fig* [Triebfeder] driving force.

**Motor|boot** *das* motorboat.

**Motor|haube** *die* bonnet *Br*, hood *Am*.

**motorisiert** *adj*: **~er Verkehr** motor vehicles (*pl*); **bist du ~?** *fam* have you got wheels?

**Motor|rad** *das* motorcycle, motorbike.

**Motorrad|fahrer, in** *der, die* motorcyclist.

**Motor|roller** *der* (motor) scooter.

**Motor|säge** *die* power saw.

**Motor|schaden** *der* engine trouble (*U*).

**Motor|sport** *der* motorsport.

**Motte** (*pl* -n) *die* moth.

**Motto** (*pl* -s) *das* motto; **unter dem ~ „keine**

**Steuererhöhung"** stehen to have "no tax increases" as its motto.

**motzen** *vi fam* to grumble.

**Mountainbike** ['maʊntnbaɪk] (*pl* -s) *das* mountain bike.

**Mount Everest** [maʊnt'ɛvərɛst] *der* Mount Everest.

**Mousepad** *das* = **Mauspad.**

**Möwe** (*pl* -n) *die* seagull.

**MP** [ɛm'piː] (*pl* -s) *die* abk für **Maschinenpistole.**

**Mrd.** abk für **Milliarde.**

**Ms.** (abk für **Manuskript**) ms.

**MS** (abk für **Motorschiff**) SS.

**MS-DOS** ® [ɛmɛs'dɔs] *das* EDV MS-DOS. ®

**MTA** [ɛmteː'aː] (*pl* -s) (abk für **medizinisch-technische Assistentin**) *die* medical laboratory technician.

**mtl.** abk für **monatlich.**

**Mücke** (*pl* -n) *die* [in Tropen] mosquito; [kleiner] midge, gnat.

**Mucken** *pl fam*: **(seine) ~ haben** [Auto, Maschine] to be temperamental.

**Mücken|stich** *der* mosquito bite.

**Mucks** (*pl* -e) *der*: **die Kinder haben keinen ~ gemacht** *ODER* **getan** *ODER* **von sich gegeben** the children didn't make a sound; **ich will jetzt keinen ~ mehr hören!** I don't want (to hear) another squeak out of you!

**müde** *adj* tired; **einer Sache** (*G*) **~ sein** *geh* to be tired of sthg; **nicht ~ werden, etw zu tun** never to tire of doing sthg ◇ *adv* wearily.

**Müdigkeit** *die* tiredness.

**Muff** (*pl* -e) *der* - **1.** [Handwärmer] muff - **2.** *fam* [Moder] mustiness.

**Muffel** (*pl* -) *der* sourpuss.

**muffig** *adj* - **1.** [modrig] musty - **2.** *fam* [schlecht gelaunt] grumpy ◇ *adv*: **~ riechen** to smell musty.

**Mühe** (*pl* -n) *die* effort; **es macht mir keine ~** it's no trouble (to me); **sich** (*D*) **~ machen (mit etw)** to go to trouble (over sthg); **sich** (*D*) **~ geben** to make an effort; **gib dir keine ~** don't bother; **mit Müh und Not** by the skin of one's teeth.

**mühelos** *adj* effortless ◇ *adv* effortlessly.

**muhen** *vi* to moo.

**mühevoll** *adj* laborious, painstaking ◇ *adv* laboriously, painstakingly.

**Mühle** (*pl* -n) *die* - **1.** [Mahlwerk - für Getreide] mill; [ - für Kaffee] grinder - **2.** [Gebäude] mill - **3.** [Spiel] nine men's morris - **4.** *fam* [Fahrzeug] jalopy, banger *Br*.

**mühsam** *adj* laborious ◇ *adv* laboriously.

**mühselig** *adj* [Arbeit, Tun] laborious; [Leben] arduous ◇ *adv* laboriously.

**Mulde** (*pl* -n) *die* GEOGR hollow; [Griffmulde] grip.

**Mull** (*pl* -e) *der* [Material] muslin; [für Verband] gauze.

**Müll** *der* rubbish *Br*, garbage *Am*; [radioaktiv] waste; **etw in den ~ werfen** ODER **tun** to throw sthg out ODER away.

**Müllabfuhr** *die* - **1.** [Transport] refuse *Br* ODER garbage *Am* collection - **2.** [Unternehmen] refuse *Br* ODER garbage *Am* collection service.

**Müllbinde** *die* gauze dressing.

**Mülldeponie** *die* refuse disposal site.

**Mülleimer** *der* dustbin *Br*, garbage ODER trash can *Am*.

**Müller, in** (*mpl* -; *fpl* -nen) *der*, *die* miller.

**Müller-Thurgau** (*pl* -) *der* - **1.** [wine] Müller-Thurgau wine - **2.** [Rebsorte] Müller-Thurgau grape variety.

**Müllkippe** *die* rubbish tip *Br*, garbage dump *Am*.

**Müllmann** (*pl* -männer) *der* dustman *Br*, garbage man *Am*.

**Müllschlucker** *der* rubbish *Br* ODER garbage *Am* chute.

**Mülltonne** *die* dustbin *Br*, garbage ODER trash can *Am*.

**Mülltrennung** *die* *separation of household waste for recycling purposes.*

**Müllverbrennungsanlage** *die* waste incineration plant.

**Müllwagen** *der* dustcart *Br*, garbage truck *Am*.

**mulmig** *adj* uncomfortable; **mir wird ~** [körperlich] I feel queasy.

**Multikulti** *das*: **ein Videoclip mit viel ~** *abw* a video with multicultural chic.

**multikulturell** *adj* multicultural.

**Multimillionär, in** *der*, *die* multimillionaire.

**Multiplexkino** *das* multiplex (cinema).

**Multiplikation** (*pl* -en) *die* multiplication.

**multiplizieren** *vt*: **etw mit etw ~** to multiply sthg by sthg.

**Mumie** ['muːmjə] (*pl* -n) *die* mummy.

**Mumm** *der* (ohne *pl*) *fam* guts (*pl*); **(keinen) ~ haben** to have (no) guts.

**Mumps** *der* MED mumps (*U*).

**München** *nt* Munich.

**Münchner** (*pl* -) *der* native/inhabitant of Munich ◇ *adj* (unver) of/from Munich.

**Münchnerin** (*pl* -nen) *die* native/inhabitant of Munich.

**Mund** (*pl* Münder) *der* mouth; **jm von ~ zu ~ be-**atmen to give sb mouth-to-mouth resuscitation; **den ~ (nicht) aufmachen** ODER **auftun** *fam* (not) to open one's mouth; **nimm den ~ nicht so voll!** *fam* don't be so sure of yourself!; **halt den ~!** *fam* shut up!; **in aller ~e sein** to be on everyone's lips; **jm nach dem ~ reden** *abw* to say what sb wants to hear; **nicht auf den ~ gefallen sein** *fam* to have an answer for everything.

**Mundart** *die* amt dialect.

**mundartlich** *adj* [Lied, Text] in dialect; [Vielfalt, Umgebung] dialectal.

**Munddusche** *die* water pick (for cleaning teeth).

**münden** (*perf* hat/ist gemündet) *vi* - **1.** [einmünden]: **(in etw (A)) ~** [Fluss] to flow (into sthg); [Straße] to lead (to sthg) - **2.** *geh* [enden]: **in etw (D) ~** [Vorgang] to end in sthg.

**Mundgeruch** *der* bad breath.

**Mundharmonika** *die* harmonica, mouthorgan.

**mündig** *adj* - **1.** [volljährig] of age; **~ werden** to come of age - **2.** [urteilsfähig] responsible.

**mündlich** *adj* [Vereinbarung, Versprechung] verbal; [Prüfung] oral ◇ *adv* verbally.

**mundtot** *adj*: **jn ~ machen** to silence sb.

**Mündung** (*pl* -en) *die* - **1.** [von Fluss] mouth; GEOGR estuary - **2.** [von Straße] end - **3.** [von Gewehr] muzzle.

**Mundwerk** *das* *fam*: **ein großes ~ haben** to be a bigmouth; **ein loses ~ haben** to be cheeky.

**Mundwinkel** *der* corner of one's mouth.

**Munition** (*pl* -en) *die* ammunition.

**munkeln** *vi*: **es wurde schon lange darüber gemunkelt** there had already been rumours about it for some time ◇ *vt*: **man munkelt, dass ...** it is rumoured that ...

**Münster** (*pl* -) *das* cathedral, minster.

**Münsterland** *das* Westphalian basin.

**munter** *adj* - **1.** [wach]: **~ sein** to be (wide) awake; **~ werden** to wake up; **~ machen** [Subj: Kaffee] to wake up - **2.** [lebhaft - Mensch, Tier, Spiel] lively - **3.** [fröhlich] cheerful ◇ *adv* cheerfully.

**Münzautomat** *der* slot machine.

**Münze** (*pl* -n) *die* coin; **etw für bare ~ nehmen** *fig* to take sthg at face value; **jm etw mit gleicher ~ heimzahlen** *fig* to pay sb back in his/her own coin.

**münzen** *vt* [Geld] to mint; **auf jn/etw gemünzt sein** *fig* to refer to sb/sthg.

**Münzfernsprecher** *der* amt pay phone *Br*, pay station *Am*.

**mürbe** *adj* - **1.** [Kuchen, Teig] crumbly; [Fleisch] tender; [Obst] soft - **2.** [Material] rotten, crumbling - **3.** [zermürbt]: **jn ~ machen** to wear sb down; **~ sein** to be worn down ⋄ *adv* [zart]: **Fleisch ~ klopfen** to tenderize meat.

**Mürbe|teig** *der* shortcrust pastry.

**Murmel** (*pl* **-n**) *die* marble.

**murmeln** *vt* & *vi* to murmur.

**Murmel|tier** *das* marmot; **schlafen wie ein ~** to sleep like a log.

**murren** *vi*: **(über etw** (*A*)**) ~** to grumble (about sthg); **ohne zu ~** without a word of complaint.

**mürrisch** *adj* sullen, surly ⋄ *adv* in a sullen ODER surly manner.

**Mus** (*pl* **-e**) *das* puree.

**Muschel** (*pl* **-n**) *die* **- 1.** [Tier] mussel **- 2.** [Schale] shell.

**Muse** (*pl* **-n**) *die* muse.

**Museum** [mu'zeːʊm] (*pl* **Museen**) *das* museum.

**Musical** ['mjuːzik(ə)l] (*pl* **-s**) *das* musical.

**Musik** (*pl* **-en**) *die* music; **~ machen** to make music.

**musikalisch** *adj* musical ⋄ *adv* musically.

**Musikant, in** (*mpl* **-en**; *fpl* **-nen**) *der, die* [Straßenmusikant] street musician.

**Musik|box** *die* jukebox.

**Musiker, in** (*mpl* **-**; *fpl* **-nen**) *der, die* musician.

**Musikhoch|schule** *die* music college.

**Musik|instrument** *das* musical instrument.

**Musik|kapelle** *die* band.

**Musik|lehrer, in** *der, die* music teacher.

**Musik|unterricht** *der (ohne pl)* [Schulfach] music; [Musikstunden] music lessons (*pl*).

**musisch** *adj* **- 1.** [Kunst betreffend] arts (*vor Subst*); **~e Fächer** fine arts subjects **- 2.** [künstlerisch begabt] artistic ⋄ *adv* artistically.

**musizieren** *vi* to make music.

**Muskat** *der* nutmeg.

**Muskat|nuss** *die* nutmeg.

**Muskel** (*pl* **-n**) *der* muscle.

**Muskelkater** *der*: **(einen) ~ haben** to be stiff.

**Muskulatur** (*pl* **-en**) *die* muscles (*pl*).

**muskulös** *adj* muscular.

**Müsli** (*pl* **-**) *das* muesli.

**muss** *präs* ▷ müssen.

**Muss** *das (ohne pl)* necessity, must.

**Muße** *die* leisure; **Zeit und ~ haben, etw zu tun** to have enough time to do sthg at one's leisure.

**müssen** (*präs* **muss**; *prät* **musste**; *perf* **hat gemusst** ODER **-**) *aux* (*perf* hat müssen) **- 1.** [gezwungen sein] must; **etw tun ~** to have to do sthg; **du**

**musst aufstehen** you must get up; **sie musste lachen/niesen** she had to laugh/sneeze; **du musst das Buch einfach lesen!** you simply must read this book!; **etw nicht tun ~** not to need to do sthg **- 2.** [nötig sein]: **der Brief muss noch heute weg** the letter has to go today; **das müsste geändert werden** that ought to be ODER should be changed; **muss das sein?** is that really necessary? **- 3.** [wahrscheinlich sein]: **du musst Hunger haben nach der langen Reise** you must be hungry after your long journey; **er müsste jeden Augenblick kommen** he ought to be ODER should be here any minute; **das müsste alles sein** that should be all **- 4.** [drückt Wunsch aus]: **so jung müsste man noch einmal sein!** oh, to be that young again!; **Zeit müsste man haben!** if only I had the time! ⋄ *vi* (*perf hat gemusst*) to have to; **ich muss ins Büro (gehen)** I have to go to the office; **ich muss mal** *fam* I need the toilet.

**müßig** *adj* **- 1.** [untätig] idle; **~e Stunden** leisure time **- 2.** [überflüssig] futile ⋄ *adv* [untätig] idly.

**musste** *prät* ▷ müssen.

**Muster** (*pl* **-**) *das* **- 1.** [Vorlage, Beispiel] model; **ein ~ an etw** (*D*) a model of sthg **- 2.** [Musterung] pattern **- 3.** [Warenprobe] sample.

**Musterbei|spiel** *das* perfect example.

**mustergültig** *adj* exemplary ⋄ *adv* in an exemplary fashion.

**mustern** *vt* **- 1.** [betrachten] to study, to scrutinize **- 2.** [Wehrpflichtigen] to inspect.

**Musterung** (*pl* **-en**) *die* **- 1.** [von Wehrpflichtigen] inspection **- 2.** [Betrachtung] scrutiny.

**Mut** *der* courage; **jm ~ machen** to encourage sb; **den ~ verlieren** to lose heart.

➤ **nur Mut** *interj* chin up!

➤ **zu Mute** *adv* = **zumute**.

**mutig** *adj* brave, courageous ⋄ *adv* bravely, courageously.

**mutlos** *adj* [entmutigt] despondent ⋄ *adv* [entmutigt] despondently.

**mutmaßen** *vt* to suspect.

**mutmaßlich** *adj* suspected.

**Mut|probe** *die* test of courage.

**Mutter** (*pl* **Mütter** ODER **-n**) *die* **- 1.** (*pl* Mütter) [gen] mother **- 2.** (*pl* Muttern) [von Schraube] nut.

**mütterlich** *adj* [Liebe, Frau] motherly; [Eigenschaft, Erbe] maternal ⋄ *adv* [fürsorgend] in a motherly fashion.

**mütterlicherseits** *adv* on one's mother's side.

**Mutter|liebe** *die* motherly love.

**Mutter|mal** *das* mole.

**Mutter|milch** *die* mother's milk.

**Mutterschafts|urlaub** *der* maternity leave.

**Mutter|schutz** der legal protection of pregnant women and nursing mothers against wrongful dismissal.

**mutterseelenallein** adj & adv all alone.

**Mutter|sprache** die mother tongue, native language.

**Mutter|sprachler, in** (mpl -; fpl -nen) der, die native speaker.

**Mutter|tag** der Mother's Day.

**Mutti** (pl -s) die fam mummy, mum.

**mutwillig** adj wilful ◇ adv wilfully.

**Mütze** (pl -n) die cap; [aus Wolle] hat.

**m. W.** abk für meines Wissens ▷ Wissen.

**MW** [ɛmˈveː] (abk für Mittelwelle) die MW.

**MwSt.** (abk für Mehrwertsteuer) VAT Br, sales tax Am.

**Myanmar** nt Myanmar.

**Mythologie** (pl -n) die mythology.

**Mythos** (pl Mythen) der myth; er ist schon jetzt ein ~ he is already a legend.

**n, N** [ɛn] (pl - ODER -s) das n, N.
➤ **N** (abk für Nord) N.

**na** interj well?; ~, wie gehts? so how's it going, then?; ~ los, mach schon! well go on then, do it!; ~, lass das sein! hey, leave that alone!
➤ **na also** interj there you are!
➤ **na gut** interj all right, then!
➤ **na ja** interj well!
➤ **na und** interj: na und? so (what)?

**Nabel** (pl -) der navel.

**Nabel|schnur** die umbilical cord.

**nach** präp (+ D) - 1. [zeitlich, zur Angabe einer Reihenfolge] after; ~ dem Essen after the meal; fünf (Minuten) ~ drei five (minutes) past three Br, five (minutes) after three Am; eins ~ dem anderen one after the other; ~ Ihnen! after you! - 2. [räumlich] to; ~ Frankfurt to Frankfurt; ~ Hause gehen to go home; ~ Süden south, southwards; ~ links/rechts abbiegen to turn left/right - 3. [gemäß] according to; ~ Angaben der Polizei according to the police;

~ Wunsch/Bedarf as desired/required - 4. [stellt Bezug her]: seinem Akzent ~ ist er kein Deutscher judging by his accent, he is not German; ~ französischer Art in the French style; meiner Meinung ~ in my opinion; jn nur dem Namen ~ kennen to know sb only by name.
➤ **nach und nach** adv little by little.
➤ **nach wie vor** adv as before.

**nach|ahmen** vt to imitate, to copy.

**Nachahmung** (pl -en) die imitation, copy.

**nach|arbeiten** vt - 1. [nachholen - Stunden] to make up - 2. [verbessern] to finish off.

**Nachbar, in** (mpl -n; fpl -nen) der, die neighbour.

**nachbarlich** adj - 1. [Haus, Garten] next-door - 2. [Beziehungen] neighbourly.

**Nachbar|ort** der next town/village.

**Nachbarschaft** die neighbourhood.

**nachbarschaftlich** adj neighbourly.

**nach|behandeln** vt: jn/etw ~ to give sb/sthg follow-up treatment.

**nach|bereiten** vt to revise.

**nach|bessern** vt [Vorschlag, Entwurf] to amend; [Preisangebot] to raise; sie musste ihre Arbeit ~ she had to redo the bits she had got wrong.

**nach|bestellen** vt & vi to order some more of.

**Nachbe|stellung** die repeat order.

**nach|beten** vt fam abw to parrot.

**nach|bezahlen** vt to pay later.

**Nachbildung** (pl -en) die reproduction; das ist eine billige ~ that's a cheap imitation.

**nach|blättern** vi: in etw (D) ~ to look in sthg.

**nach|blicken** vi: jm ~ to gaze after sb.

**nach|datieren** vt to backdate.

**nachdem** konj after.
➤ **je nachdem** konj depending on.

**nach|denken** vi (unreg): (über jn/etw) ~ to think (about sb/sthg).

**nachdenklich** adj thoughtful, pensive; jn ~ machen to set sb thinking ◇ adv thoughtfully, pensively.

**Nachdruck** (pl -e) der - 1. [Eindringlichkeit] emphasis; einer Sache (D) ~ verleihen to reinforce sthg; mit ~ emphatically - 2. [Nachdrucken - von Buch] reprinting; [ - von Druck] reproduction - 3. [Ausgabe] reprint.

**nach|drucken** vt to reprint.

**nachdrücklich** adj emphatic, forceful ◇ adv emphatically.

**Nachdurst** der thirst resulting from excessive consumption of alcohol.

**nach|eifern** vi: jm (in etw (D)) ~ to seek to emulate sb (in sthg).

**nacheinander** adv - **1.** [der Reihe nach] one after the other - **2.** [gegenseitig] one another.

**nach|empfinden** vt (unreg) [nachfühlen]: js Schmerz ~ to share sb's pain; **ich kann dir ~, wie du dich jetzt fühlst** I can understand how you feel.

**Nacher|zählung** die retelling (in one's own words).

**Nachfahre** (pl -n) der geh descendant.

**nach|fahren** (perf ist nachgefahren) vi (unreg): jm/einer Sache ~ to follow sb/sthg.

**nach|feiern** vt to celebrate later.

**Nachfolge** die succession.

**nach|folgen** (perf ist nachgefolgt) vi - **1.** [Nachfolge antreten]: jm (in einem Amt) ~ to succeed sb (in an office) - **2.** [nachkommen] to follow; **das ~de Fahrzeug** the vehicle behind.

**Nachfolger, in** (mpl -; fpl -nen) der, die successor.

**nach|fordern** vt [nachträglich] to make another demand for; [zusätzlich] to demand additionally.

**nach|forschen** vi to make enquiries; jm/einer Sache ~ geh to investigate sb/sthg.

**Nach|forschung** die enquiries (pl), investigations (pl); ~en (nach etw) anstellen to make enquiries (about sthg).

**Nachfrage** die - **1.** WIRTSCH demand - **2.** [Anfrage]: **wie geht es Ihnen? - danke der** ODER **für die ~** how are you? - very well, thanks.

**nach|fragen** vi - **1.** [nachhaken] to ask repeatedly - **2.** [fragen] to enquire.

**nach|fühlen** vt: js Trauer ~ to understand sb's sadness; **das kann ich ihm ~** I understand how he feels.

**nach|füllen** vt - **1.** [füllen] to refill - **2.** [nachgießen] to top up with.

**nach|geben** vi (unreg) - **1.** [bei Streit] to give in - **2.** [Brücke, Boden] to give way; [Preise, Kurse] to fall.

**Nach|gebühr** die excess postage (U).

**nach|gehen** (perf ist nachgegangen) vi (unreg) - **1.** [folgen]: jm/einer Sache ~ to follow sb/sthg - **2.** [etw prüfen]: einer Sache (D) ~ to look into sthg - **3.** [Uhr] to be slow; **meine Uhr geht zehn Minuten nach** my watch is ten minutes slow - **4.** [nachwirken]: jm ~ to stick in sb's mind - **5.** [sich widmen]: einer Sache (D) ~ to pursue sthg.

**Nachgeschmack** der aftertaste.

**nachgiebig** adj compliant; [Eltern] indulgent.

**Nachgiebigkeit** die compliance; [von Eltern] indulgence.

**nach|gießen** vt (unreg) [Öl, Kühlwasser] to top up with; **darf ich noch Kaffee ~?** would you like some more coffee?

**nach|grübeln** vi to brood.

**nach|gucken** vi fam - **1.** [nachsehen] to have a look - **2.** [hinterhersehen]: jm/einer Sache ~ to look ODER gaze after sb/sthg.

**nach|haken** vi to return to the same question.

**Nachhall** (pl -e) der echo.

**nachhaltig** adj lasting <> adv: ~ wirken to have a lasting effect.

**nach|hängen** vi (unreg) - **1.** [sich erinnern]: einer Sache (D) ~ to dwell on sthg - **2.** fam [zurückliegen]: in etw (D) ~ to lag behind in sthg.

**Nachhause|weg** der way home.

**nach|helfen** vi (unreg) - **1.** [antreiben]: bei jm ~ müssen to have to chivvy sb along - **2.** [helfen]: (jm) ~ to lend (sb) a hand.

**nachher, nachher** adv - **1.** [später] later (on) - **2.** [anschließend] afterwards.

➤ **bis nachher** interj see you later!

**Nachhilfe** die extra tuition.

**Nachhilfe|stunde** die extra lesson.

**Nachhinein** adv: im ~ with hindsight; **im ~ zeigte sich, dass er gelogen hatte** it later turned out that he had lied.

**nach|hinken** (perf ist nachgehinkt) vi: einer Sache (D) ~ to lag behind sthg; **der Zeit ~** to be behind the times.

**Nachhol|bedarf** der: ~ an etw (D) haben to have a need to catch up on sthg.

**nach|holen** vt - **1.** [nachträglich machen]: etw ~ [Versäumtes] to catch up on sthg; [Prüfung] to do sthg later - **2.** [nachziehen lassen]: **er holte seine Familie nach** his family joined him later.

**nach|jagen** (perf ist nachgejagt) vi: jm/einer Sache ~ to chase after sb/sthg.

**nach|kaufen** vt to buy more of.

**Nachkomme** (pl -n) der descendant.

**nach|kommen** (perf ist nachgekommen) vi (unreg) - **1.** [später kommen] to come (along) later - **2.** geh [entsprechen]: einer Sache (D) ~ to comply with sthg - **3.** [Schritt halten]: mit etw ~ to keep up with sthg.

**Nachkömmling** (pl -e) der late arrival (child born long after other siblings).

**Nachkriegs|zeit** die post-war period.

**Nachlass** (pl -lasse ODER -lässe) der - **1.** [Erbe] estate; literarischer ~ unpublished works (pl) - **2.** [Rabatt] discount, reduction.

**nach|lassen** (unreg) vi [Schmerz, Spannung] to ease; [Regen] to ease off; [Augen, Gehör] to fail; [Geschäft, Anstrengung] to slacken; [Qualität] to drop off ⬦ *vt* [Preis]: **jm 10% ~** to give sb a 10% discount.

**nachlässig** *adj* careless ⬦ *adv* carelessly.

**nachlaufen** *(perf ist nachgelaufen) vi (unreg):* **jm/einer Sache ~** [laufen nach] to run after sb/sthg; [folgen] to follow sb/sthg; *fam* [sich bemühen um] to pursue sb/sthg.

**Nachlese** *(pl -n) die* - **1.** [Ernte] gleanings *(pl)* - **2.** *geh* [Nachtrag, TV & RADIO] review, edited highlights *(pl)*.

**nachlesen** *vt (unreg)* to look up.

**nachliefern** *vt* to deliver later.

**nachlösen** *vt:* **eine Fahrkarte ~** to buy a ticket on the train.

**nachmachen** *vt* - **1.** [nachahmen, kopieren] to copy; [nachäffen] to mimic; [fälschen] to forge; **jm etw ~** to copy sthg off sb; **etw ~ lassen** to have sthg copied - **2.** [nachholen]: **etw** *(A)* **~** to catch up on sthg later.

**nachmessen** *vt (unreg)* to measure again.

**Nachmieter, in** *der, die* new tenant.

**Nachmittag** *der* afternoon; **am ~** in the afternoon; **gestern/heute/morgen ~** yesterday/this/tomorrow afternoon; **Dienstag ~** on Tuesday afternoon.

**nachmittags** *adv* in the afternoon.

**Nachnahme** *(pl -n) die:* **etw als ~ versenden** to send sthg cash on delivery; **per** *ODER* **gegen ~** cash on delivery.

**Nachnahmelsendung** *die* cash on delivery parcel.

**Nachname** *der* surname.

**nachplappern** *vt fam* to repeat parrot-fashion.

**Nachporto** *das* excess postage *(U)*.

**nachprüfen** *vt* - **1.** [kontrollieren] to check - **2.** [erneut prüfen] to re-examine.

**Nachprüfung** *die* - **1.** [Kontrolle] check - **2.** [zusätzliche Prüfung] re-examination.

**nachrechnen** *vt* - **1.** [nochmals rechnen] to check - **2.** [nachzählen] to work out ⬦ *vi* - **1.** [nochmals rechnen] to check - **2.** [nachzählen] to work it out.

**Nachrede** *die:* **üble ~** slander.

**Nachricht** *(pl -en) die* [Neuigkeit] piece of news; [Mitteilung] message; **eine gute ~ haben** to have (some) good news; **die ~, dass ...** the news that ...; **eine ~ von jm** [Neuigkeiten] news of sb; [Mitteilung] a message from sb; **eine ~ für jn hinterlassen** to leave a message for sb.

➡ **Nachrichten** *pl:* **die ~en** the news *(sg)*.

**Nachrichtenlagentur** *die* news agency.

**Nachrichtenldienst** *der* - **1.** [Geheimdienst] intelligence service - **2.** [Nachrichtenagentur] news agency.

**Nachrichtenlsendung** *die* news bulletin.

**Nachrichtenlsprecher, in** *der, die* newsreader.

**Nachrichtenltechnik** *die* telecommunications *(U)*.

**nachrücken** *(perf ist nachgerückt) vi* to move up.

**Nachruf** *der* obituary.

**nachrüsten** *vt* EDV to upgrade ⬦ *vi* MIL to rearm.

**Nachrüstung** *die* - **1.** [von Geräten] upgrading - **2.** [mit Waffen] rearmament.

**nachsagen** *vt* - **1.** [behaupten]: **jm etw ~** to say sthg of sb - **2.** [wiederholen] to repeat.

**Nachsaison** *die* low season.

**nachschauen** *vt* - **1.** [prüfen] to check - **2.** [nachschlagen] to look up ⬦ *vi* - **1.** [prüfen] to check - **2.** [nachblicken]: **jm/einer Sache ~** to gaze after sb/sthg.

**nachschenken** *geh vt:* **darf ich noch Kaffee ~?** would you like some more coffee? ⬦ *vi:* **darf ich ~?** can I give you a top-up?

**nachschicken** *vt* to forward.

**Nachschlag** *der* second helping.

**nachschlagen** *(perf hat/ist nachgeschlagen) (unreg) vi* - **1.** *(hat)* [nachlesen]: **in einem Wörterbuch ~** to consult a dictionary - **2.** *(ist)* [ähneln]: **jm ~** to take after sb ⬦ *vt (hat)* [nachlesen] to look up.

**Nachschlaglwerk** *das* reference work.

**Nachlschlüssel** *der* duplicate key.

**Nachschub** *der (ohne pl)* supplies *(pl)*.

**nachsehen** *(unreg) vi* - **1.** [hinterhersehen]: **jm/einer Sache ~** to gaze after sb/sthg - **2.** [suchen] to look - **3.** [prüfen] to check - **4.** [nachschlagen]: **in etw** *(D)* **~** to consult sthg ⬦ *vt* - **1.** [nachschlagen]: **etw in etw** *(D)* **~** to look sthg up in sthg - **2.** [prüfen] to check - **3.** [verzeihen]: **jm seine Fehler ~** to overlook sb's mistakes.

**Nachsehen** *das:* **das ~ haben** [unterlegen sein] to come off badly; [etw nicht bekommen] to be left empty-handed.

**nachsenden** *vt (unreg)* to forward.

**Nachsicht** *die* leniency; **mit jm ~ haben** to treat sb leniently.

**nachsichtig** *adj* lenient ⬦ *adv* leniently.

**Nachlsilbe** *die* suffix.

**nachsitzen** *vi (unreg):* **~ müssen** to get detention.

**Nachspeise** *die* dessert.

**Nachlspiel** *das* [Folgen] consequences *(pl)*; [Theaterstück] epilogue; **es wird ein ~ haben** it will have consequences.

**nachspionieren** *vi:* **jm ~** to spy on sb.

**nach|sprechen** *vt & vi (unreg)* to repeat.

**nächstbeste, r, s** *adj:* bei der ~n Gelegenheit at the first available opportunity.
➤ **Nächstbeste** *der, die, das:* der/die/das Nächstbeste *fig* the first available one.

**nächste, r, s** ['nɛːçstə, ɐ, əs] *adj* - **1.** [nah] nearest, closest - **2.** [folgend] next; **der Nächste bitte!** next, please!; **~s Mal/Jahr** next time/year; **wie heißt die ~ Haltestelle?** what's the next stop?; **die ~ Straße links** the next road on the left.

**Nächste** *(pl -n) der* - **1.** [Kunde, Patient] next; **der ~, bitte!** next, please! - **2.** REL neighbour.

**nach|stehen** *vi (unreg):* jm in nichts ~ to be (every bit) sb's equal.

**nachstehend** *adj* following ⟨⟩ *adv* below.

**nach|stellen** *vt* - **1.** [Uhr] to put back - **2.** [Satzglied] to postpone - **3.** [nachspielen] to represent - **4.** [Gerät] to adjust ⟨⟩ *vi* to hunt; jm ~ *abw* to pursue sb.

**Nächstenliebe** ['nɛːçstənliːbə] *die* charity.

**nächstens** ['nɛːçstn̩s] *adv* shortly, soon.

**nächstliegend** ['nɛːçstliːgn̩t] *adj* most obvious.

**nächstmöglich** ['nɛːçstmøːklɪç] *adj* next possible.

**Nacht** *(pl Nächte) die* night; **bei ~** at night; **in der ~** during the night; **über ~** overnight; **bei ~ und Nebel** *fig* under cover of darkness; **gestern/morgen ~** last/tomorrow night; **heute ~** tonight.
➤ **gute Nacht** *interj* good night!

**nachtblind** *adj:* ~ sein to suffer from nightblindness.

**Nacht|crème, Nachtkreme** *die* night cream.

**Nachtdienst** *der* night duty.

**Nach|teil** *der* disadvantage; **zu js ~** to sb's disadvantage.

**nachteilig** *adj* disadvantageous ⟨⟩ *adv:* etw wirkt sich für jn ~ aus sthg turns out to sb's disadvantage.

**nächtelang** *adj* lasting several nights ⟨⟩ *adv* night after night.

**Nacht|frost** *der* night frost.

**Nacht|hemd** *das* [für Frauen] nightdress; [für Männer] nightshirt.

**Nachtigall** *(pl -en) die* nightingale.

**Nachtisch** *der (ohne pl)* dessert.

**Nacht|klub** *der* nightclub.

**Nachtleben** *das* nightlife.

**nächtlich** *adj* nocturnal; [Stille] of the night.

**Nachtrag** *(pl -träge) der* [als Nachwort] postscript; [Zusatzband] supplement.

**nach|tragen** *vt (unreg)* - **1.** [übel nehmen]: jm etw ~ to hold sthg against sb - **2.** [ergänzen] to add - **3.** [hinterhertragen]: jm etw ~ to follow behind sb carrying sthg.

**nachtragend** *adj* unforgiving; **sie ist nicht ~** she doesn't bear grudges.

**nachträglich** *adj* [Glückwunsch] belated; [Beweis] subsequent ⟨⟩ *adv* [beglückwünschen] belatedly; [beweisen] subsequently.

**nach|trauern** *vi:* jm/einer Sache ~ to miss sb/sthg.

**Nachtruhe** *die* night's sleep.

**nachts** *adv* at night; **um vier Uhr ~** at four in the morning.

**Nacht|schicht** *die* night shift.

**Nacht|schwester** *die* night nurse.

**Nacht|tisch** *der* bedside table.

**Nacht|wache** *die* - **1.** [Dienst] night watch - **2.** [Person] person on night watch.

**Nacht|wächter, in** *der, die* night watchman (*f* -woman).

**Nach|untersuchung** *die* [nach Operation] post-operative checkup.

**nach|vollziehen** *vt (unreg)* to comprehend.

**nach|wachsen** ['naːxvaksn̩] *(perf ist nachgewachsen) vi (unreg)* to grow again.

**Nachweis** *(pl -e) der* proof *(U).*

**nachweisbar** *adj* [Fehler] demonstrable; [Substanz] detectable ⟨⟩ *adv:* er hat ~ gelogen it can be proved that he was lying.

**nach|weisen** *vt (unreg)* - **1.** [Fehler] to prove - **2.** [Substanz] to detect.

**nachweislich** *adv:* sie hat ~ gelogen she can be shown to have lied.

**Nach|welt** *die* posterity.

**Nach|wirkung** *die* aftereffect.

**Nach|wuchs** ['naːxvuːks] *der* - **1.** [Kind(er)] offspring - **2.** [im Beruf]: **künstlerischer/wissenschaftlicher ~** rising generation of artists/scientists; **es fehlt an ~** there is a lack of new blood.

**nach|zahlen** *vi* to pay the extra ⟨⟩ *vt:* **5 Euro ~** to pay 5 euros extra.

**nach|zählen** *vt* to check.

**Nach|zahlung** *die* back-payment *(U).*

**nach|ziehen** *(perf hat/ist nachgezogen) (unreg) vi* - **1.** *(ist)* [später umziehen] to move later - **2.** *(hat)* [nachmachen] to follow suit ⟨⟩ *vt (hat)* - **1.** [Schraube] to tighten - **2.** [Bein] to drag - **3.** [Strich] to go over; [Lippenstift] to redo.

**Nachzügler, in** *(mpl -; fpl -nen) der, die* straggler; [jüngstes Kind] youngest.

**Nạckedei** (pl -s) der fam naked child.

**Nạcken** (pl -) der back ODER nape of the neck; **jm im ~ sitzen** fig [bedrängen] to be on sb's tail; **ihm sitzt die Angst im ~** he is afraid.

**Nạcken|haar** das hair (U) on the back of the neck; [von Hund] hackles (pl); **die ~e sträubten sich** its hackles rose.

**nạckt** adj - **1.** [ohne Kleider/Fell] naked; [ Körperteil] bare - **2.** [bloß] bare; **die ~e Wahrheit** the plain truth; **~e Tatsachen** hard facts <> adv naked; **sich ~ ausziehen** to strip naked.

**Nạcktbade|strand** der nudist beach.

**Nadel** (pl -n) die [gen] needle; [Stecknadel] pin.

**Nadel|baum** der conifer.

**Nadel|drucker** der EDV dot-matrix printer.

**Nadel|öhr** das - **1.** [von Nadeln] eye - **2.** fig [enge Stelle] bottleneck.

**Nadel|wald** der coniferous forest.

**Nagel** (pl Nägel) der - **1.** nail - **2.** RW: **den ~ auf den Kopf treffen** to hit the nail on the head; **etw an den ~ hängen** to give sthg up; **dieser Brief brennt mir unter den Nägeln** fam I'm desperate to get on with this letter; **Nägel mit Köpfen machen** to do the job properly; **sich** (D) **etw unter den ~ reißen** fam abw to pinch sthg for o.s.

**Nagel|bürste** die nailbrush.

**Nagel|feile** die nail file.

**Nagel|lack** der nail varnish.

**nageln** vt to nail; [Knochen] to pin.

**nagelneu** adj brand-new.

**Nagel|schere** die nail scissors (pl).

**nagen** vi - **1.** [knabbern]: **an etw** (D) **~** to gnaw at sthg - **2.** [jn beunruhigen]: **an jm ~** [Zweifel] to prey on sb; [Hunger] to gnaw at sb <> vt to gnaw.

**Nage|tier** das rodent.

**nah, nahe** (kompar näher; superl nächste) adj near; **~ an/bei jm/etw** close to ODER near sb/sthg; **zu ~** too close; **in ~er Zukunft** in the near future; **den Tränen/dem Wahnsinn ~ sein** to be on the verge of tears/madness; **~ daran sein, etw zu tun** to be on the point ODER verge of doing sthg <> adv - **1.** [räumlich]: **eine ~e gelegene Stadt** a nearby town; **komm mir nicht zu ~e!** keep your distance!; **von ~em** from close up; **von ~ und fern** from near and far - **2.** [temporal]: **~e bevorstehen** to be imminent - **3.** [vertraut] closely; **~e verwandt** closely related; **jm zu ~ treten** fig to offend sb.

**Nah|aufnahme** die close-up.

**Nähe** die - **1.** [räumlich, zeitlich] closeness; **in meiner ~** near me; **aus der ~** from close-up; **in der ~** nearby; **in greifbarer ~** within reach

- **2.** [emotional] closeness, intimacy; **js ~ suchen** to seek sb's company.

**nahe bringen** vt (unreg) geh: **jm etw ~** to make sb appreciate sthg.

**nahe gehen** (perf ist nahe gegangen) vi (unreg): **jm ~** to affect sb deeply.

**nahe kommen** (perf ist nahe gekommen) vi (unreg): **jm ~** to get to know sb well; **einer Sache** (D) **~** to come close to sthg.

⟶ **sich nahe kommen** ref to get to know one another.

**nahe legen** vt - **1.** [Verdacht, Vermutung] to give rise to - **2.** [jn auffordern]: **jm ~, etw zu tun** to advise sb to do sthg.

**nahe liegen** vi (unreg) [Idee, Plan] to suggest itself; **der Verdacht/die Vermutung liegt nahe, dass ...** it seems reasonable to suspect/suppose that ...

**nahe liegend** adj obvious.

**nahen** (perf ist genaht) vi geh to approach.

**nähen** vt - **1.** [Kleid, Hose] to make - **2.** [Knöpfe, Flicken]: **etw an** ODER **auf etw** (A) **~** to sew sthg on ODER onto sthg - **3.** [Riss] to mend - **4.** [Wunde] vi [schneidern] to sew.

**Nahe Ọsten** der: **der ~** the Middle East.

**näher** adj - **1.** [Komparativ von nahe] closer, nearer - **2.** [Umstände, Angaben] more precise <> adv - **1.** [Komparativ von nahe] closer, nearer - **2.** [betrachten] more closely; [erklären] more precisely.

**näher bringen** vt (unreg): **jm etw ~** to make sthg more real to sb.

**Naherholungs|gebiet** das amt area close to a town, offering recreational facilities.

**näher kommen** (perf ist näher gekommen) vi (unreg) - **1.** [nahe kommen]: **jm ~** to get to know sb better - **2.** [entsprechen]: **einer Sache** (D) **~** to get closer to sthg.

⟶ **sich näher kommen** ref [sich nahe kommen] to get to know one another better.

**nähern** ⟶ **sich nähern** ref to approach.

**nahe stehen** vi (unreg): **sich/jm ~** to be close to one another/sb; **einer Idee ~** to sympathize with an idea.

**nahe stehend** adj - **1.**: **jm ~** [persönlich] close to sb; **einer Sache** (D) **~** [politisch] sympathetic to sthg - **2.** [in der Nähe] nearby.

**nahezu** adv nearly, almost.

**nahm** prät ⊳ nehmen.

**Näh|maschine** die sewing machine.

**Näh|nadel** die (sewing) needle.

**Nahọst** (ohne Artikel) the Middle East.

**Nähr|boden** der breeding ground.

**nähren** vt geh - **1.** [Vermutung, Verdacht] to nurture **- 2.** [Kinder] to feed; **sich von etw ~ geh** [essen] to live on sthg.

**nahrhaft** adj nourishing, nutritious.

**Nähr|stoff** der nutrient.

**Nahrung** die food; **feste ~** solids (pl).

**Nahrungs|mittel** das food.

**Nähr|wert** der nutritional value.

**Naht** (pl **Nähte**) die **- 1.** [an Kleidung] seam; **aus allen Nähten platzen** fig to burst at the seams **- 2.** [in der Medizin] suture **- 3.** [in der Technik] join.

**nahtlos** adj seamless; **~e Bräune** all-over tan ◇ adv [ununterbrochen] seamlessly.

**Nahverkehr** der local traffic.

**Nahverkehrs|zug** der local train.

**Nähzeug** das (ohne pl) sewing things (pl).

**Nah|ziel** das short-term aim.

**Nairobi** nt Nairobi.

**naiv** [na'iːf] adj naive ◇ adv naively.

**Naivität** [naivi'tɛːt] die naivety.

**Name** (pl **-n**) der name; **im ~n von jm** in the name of sb; **etw in js ~n tun** to do sthg on sb's behalf; **jn/etw (nur) dem ~n nach kennen** to know sb/sthg (only) by name; **sich** (D) **einen ~n machen** fig to make a name for o.s.

**Namens|tag** der name day.

**namentlich** adj & adv by name.

**namhaft** adj renowned.

**Namibia** nt Namibia.

**Namibier, in** [na'miːbiɐ, rɪn] (mpl **-**; fpl **-nen**) der, die Namibian.

**namibisch** adj Namibian.

**nämlich** adv because; **zwei von ihnen, ~ Anna und Berthold** two of them, namely Anna and Berthold; **übermorgen, ~ am Donnerstag** the day after tomorrow, that is, on Thursday; **wir treffen uns jetzt ~ am Freitag** we'll now actually be meeting on Friday.

**nannte** prät ▷ **nennen.**

**nanu** interj well (I never)!

**Napf** (pl **Näpfe**) der dish, bowl.

**Napf|kuchen** der gugelhupf (cake).

**Narbe** (pl **-n**) die scar.

**narbig** adj scarred.

**Narkose** (pl **-n**) die anaesthetic; **unter ~ stehen** to be under anaesthetic.

**Narkose|arzt, ärztin** der, die anaesthetist.

**Narr** (pl **-en**) der fool; **jn zum ~en halten** fig to make a fool of sb.

**närrisch** adj **- 1.** [verrückt] mad, crazy; **das ~e Treiben** [im Karneval] carnival festivities **- 2.** fam [unglaublich] terrific ◇ adv **- 1.** [verrückt]:

**sich ~ gebärden** to act crazy **- 2.** fam [unglaublich] terribly.

**Narzisse** (pl **-n**) die narcissus.

**nasal** adj nasal ◇ adv nasally.

**Nasal** (pl **-e**) der nasal.

**naschen** vt & vi to nibble.

**Nase** (pl **-n**) die **- 1.** nose; **sich** (D) **die ~ putzen** to blow one's nose; **jm läuft die ~** sb's nose is running; **in der ~ bohren** to pick one's nose **- 2.** RW: **über etw die ~ rümpfen** to turn one's nose up at sthg; **die ~ voll haben** fam to be fed up; **immer der ~ nach** fam just follow your nose; **jn an der ~ herumführen** to pull the wool over sb's eyes.

**Nasen|bein** das nasal bone.

**Nasen|bluten** das (ohne pl) nosebleed.

**Nasen|flügel** der side of the nose.

**Nasen|loch** das nostril.

**Nasen|spitze** die tip of the nose.

**Nashorn** (pl **-hörner**) das rhinoceros.

**nass** adj wet ◇ adv: **~ machen** to wet.

**Nässe** die wet; **vor ~ triefen** to be dripping wet; **überfrierende ~** icy patches.

**nässen** vi to weep.

**nasskalt** adj cold and damp.

**Nation** (pl **-en**) die nation.

**national** adj national ◇ adv: **~ denken** to think in national terms.

**Nationalfeier|tag** der national day.

**National|hymne** die national anthem.

**Nationalismus** der nationalism.

**nationalistisch** adj nationalistic ◇ adv: **~ orientiert** with nationalistic leanings.

**Nationalität** (pl **-en**) die nationality.

**Nationalsozialismus** der National Socialism, Nazism.

**National|sozialist, in** der, die National Socialist, Nazi.

**nationalsozialistisch** adj National Socialist, Nazi.

**NATO** ['naːtoː] (abk für **North Atlantic Treaty Organization**) die NATO.

**Natrium** das CHEM sodium.

**Natron** das CHEM soda.

**Natur** (pl **-en**) die nature; **Tiere in der freien ~** animals in the wild; **hinaus in die ~ fahren** to go out into the countryside; **es liegt in der ~ der Sache** it is in the nature of things.
➤ **von Natur aus** adv by nature.

**Naturalien** [natu'raːliən] pl: **in ~ bezahlen** to pay in kind.

**Naturalismus** der naturalism.

**naturalistisch** *adj* naturalistic ◇ *adv* naturalistically.

**naturbelassen** *adj* natural; [Obst, Gemüse] organic.

**Naturell** (*pl* -e) *das* disposition.

**Natur|ereignis** *das* natural phenomenon.

**naturgemäß** *adj* natural ◇ *adv* - **1.** [gemäß der Natur] in accordance with natural laws - **2.** [grundsätzlich] by its very nature.

**naturgetreu** *adj* [Abbildung] lifelike ◇ *adv* in a lifelike manner.

**Naturheilkunde** *die* naturopathy.

**natürlich** *adj* natural ◇ *adv* - **1.** [nicht künstlich] naturally - **2.** [selbstverständlich] of course, naturally; ~ war er wieder zu spät naturally he was too late again; ~ stimmt das, aber ... of course that's correct but ... ◇ *interj* (but) of course!

**naturrein** *adj* pure.

**Natur|schutz** *der* nature conservation; unter ~ stehen to be protected.

**Naturschutz|gebiet** *das* nature reserve.

**Natur|wissenschaft** *die* natural science.

**Natur|wissenschaftler, in** *der, die* scientist.

**Navigation** [naviga'tsjo:n] *die* navigation.

**Nazi** (*pl* -s) *der abw* Nazi.

**NB** (*abk für* nota bene) NB.

**NC** [ɛn'tse:] (*pl* -s) *der abk für* **Numerus clausus.**

**n. Chr.** (*abk für* **nach Christus**) AD.

**NDR** [ɛn'de:'ɛr] (*abk für* **Norddeutscher Rundfunk**) *der* North German Radio.

**n. E.** (*abk für* **nach Erhalt**) *on receipt.*

**Neapel** *nt* Naples.

**Nebel** (*pl* -) *der* fog; leichter ~ mist.

**Nebelhorn** (*pl* -hörner) *das* foghorn.

**nebelig** = neblig.

**Nebel|scheinwerfer** *der* fog lamp.

**Nebelschluss|leuchte** *die* rear fog lights (*pl*).

**Nebel|schwaden** *pl* swathes of mist.

**neben** *präp* - **1.** (+ D) [lokal] beside, next to - **2.** (+ D) [außer] apart from, as well as - **3.** (+ D) [verglichen mit] compared to ODER with - **4.** (+ A) beside, next to.

**nebenan** *adv* next door.

**Nebenan|schluss** *der* extension.

**Nebenaus|gang** *der* side exit.

**nebenbei** *adv* - **1.** [außerdem] in addition, as well; etw ~ erledigen to do sthg on the side - **2.** [beiläufig] in passing; ~ bemerkt by the way.

**nebenberuflich** *adj:* ~e Tätigkeit second job ◇ *adv:* ~ tätig sein to have a second job.

**Neben|beschäftigung** *die* second job.

**Nebenbuhler, in** (*mpl* -; *fpl* -nen) *der, die* rival.

**nebeneinander** *adv* - **1.** [neben jm/etw] next to each other - **2.** [gleichzeitig] simultaneously.

**Neben|fach** *das* SCHULE subsidiary subject.

**Neben|fluss** *der* tributary.

**Neben|gebäude** *das* [von Hotel] annex; [von Bauernhof] outbuilding.

**Neben|geräusch** *das* background noise.

**Neben|haus** *das* neighbouring house.

**nebenher** *adv* in addition, as well; ~ arbeiten to work on the side.

**Neben|job** *der* second job.

**Neben|kosten** *pl* - **1.** [bei Miete] additional charges - **2.** [zusätzliche Auslagen] additional costs.

**Neben|produkt** *das* by-product.

**Neben|raum** *der* next ODER adjacent room.

**Neben|rolle** *die* minor part.

**Neben|sache** *die* minor issue.

**nebensächlich** *adj* of secondary importance.

**Neben|satz** *der* GRAM subordinate clause.

**Neben|straße** *die* side street.

**Neben|strecke** *die* - **1.** [Bahnlinie] branch line - **2.** [Straße] side road.

**Neben|wirkung** *die* side effect.

**Neben|zimmer** *das* next ODER adjacent room.

**neblig, nebelig** *adj* foggy; leicht ~ misty.

**Neckar** *der:* der ~ the (River) Neckar.

**necken** *vt* to tease; jn mit jm/etw ~ to tease sb about sb/sthg.

⬧ **sich necken** *ref* to tease each other.

**neckisch** *adj* - **1.** [verschmitzt] teasing - **2.** [frech] coquettish.

**nee** *interj fam* no!

**Neffe** (*pl* -n) *der* nephew.

**neg.** (*abk für* **negativ**) neg.

**Negation** (*pl* -en) *die* - **1.** GRAM negative - **2.** *geh* [Ablehnung] negation (U).

**negativ** *adj* negative ◇ *adv* negatively; jm/etw ~ beeinflussen to have a negative influence on sb/sthg.

**Negativ** (*pl* -e) *das* negative.

**Neger, in** (*mpl* -; *fpl* -nen) *der, die abw* negro (*f* negress).

**Neger|kuss** *der* chocolate-covered marshmallow.

**N**

**nehmen** (*präs* nimmt; *prät* nahm; *perf* hat genommen) *vt* - **1.** [gen] to take; **für etw fünf Euro ~** to charge five euros for sthg; **ich nehme diese Schuhe** [kaufen] I'll take these shoes; **ich nehme ein Omelett** I'll have an omelette; **sich** (D) **etw ~** to help o.s. to sthg; **nehmt euch bitte!** please help yourselves!; **sie nimmt die Pille** she is on the pill; **jn/etw für voll ~** to take sb/sthg seriously; **es leicht/schwer nehmen** to take it lightly/hard; **wie mans nimmt** it depends (how you look at it); **jn zu sich ~** [auf Dauer] to take sb in; [vorübergehend] to have sb to stay; **etw zu sich ~** [Nahrung] to take sthg, to eat sthg; **etw an sich** (A) **~** to look after sthg; **etw auf sich** (A) **~** to take sthg on - **2.** [wegnehmen] to take away; **jm den Glauben/die Illusionen ~** to destroy sb's faith/illusions; **jm seine/ihre Freiheit ~** to deprive sb of his/her freedom; **sich etw nicht ~ lassen** *fig* to insist on doing sthg - **3.** [einstellen] to take on - **4.** [verwenden] to use; **den Zug ~** to take the train; **sich** (D) **einen Anwalt ~** to get o.s. a lawyer.

**Neid** *der* envy.

**neidisch** *adj* envious ⬦ *adv* enviously.

**neidlos** *adj* ungrudging ⬦ *adv* ungrudgingly.

**Neige** *die:* **bis zur ~** to the last drop; **zur ~ gehen** to come to an end; [Vorrat] to run out.

**neigen** *vi:* **zu etw ~** [tendieren] to have a tendency *oder* be inclined to sthg; [anfällig sein] to be prone to sthg ⬦ *vt* [beugen - Körper] to bend; [ - Kopf] to bow.

⬦ **sich neigen** *ref* [sich beugen - Gegenstand] to bend; [ - Mensch] to lean.

**Neigung** (*pl* -en) *die* - **1.** [Veranlagung] inclination; **künstlerische ~en** artistic leanings - **2.** (*ohne pl*) [Anfälligsein] susceptibility - **3.** (*ohne pl*) [Tendenz] tendency - **4.** [von Linie, Fläche] inclination.

**nein** *adv* no; **~, danke!** no thank you!; **regnet es? - ich glaube ~** is it raining? - I don't think so; **aber ~!** certainly not!; **zu etw ~ sagen** to say no to sthg; **ich glaube, ~, ich bin sogar sicher** I think so, in fact I'm sure; **~ sowas!** well I never!

**Nein** *das* no; **mit ~ antworten** to answer in the negative; **(zu etw) ~ sagen** to say no (to sthg); **nicht ~ sagen können** to be unable to say no.

**Nein|stimme** *die* no (vote).

**Nektar** (*pl* -e) *der* - **1.** [Pflanzensaft] nectar (U) - **2.** [Getränk] fruit drink.

**Nektarine** (*pl* -n) *die* nectarine.

**Nelke** (*pl* -n) *die* - **1.** [Blume] carnation - **2.** [Gewürz] clove.

**nennen** (*prät* nannte; *perf* hat genannt) *vt* - **1.** [benennen, bezeichnen] to call - **2.** [anführen] to name; [Adresse, Name] to give.

⬦ **sich nennen** *ref* - **1.** [heißen] to be called - **2.** [sich bezeichnen] to call o.s.

**nennenswert** *adj* significant ⬦ *adv* significantly.

**Nenner** (*pl* -) *der* MATH denominator; **etw auf einen (gemeinsamen) ~ bringen** *fig* to reduce sthg to a common denominator.

**Nenn|wert** *der* WIRTSCH nominal *oder* face value.

**neofaschistisch** *adj* neo-fascist.

**Neon** *das* CHEM neon.

**Neo|nazi** *der* neo-Nazi.

**Neon|farbe** *die* fluorescent colour.

**Neon|licht** (*pl* -er) *das* neon light.

**Neon|röhre** *die* neon tube.

**Nepal** *nt* Nepal.

**neppen** *vt fam abw* to rip off.

**Nerv** (*pl* -en) *der* nerve.

⬦ **Nerven** *pl* nerves; **die ~en verlieren/behalten** to lose/keep one's cool; **jm auf die ~en gehen** *oder* **fallen** to get on sb's nerves.

**nerven** *vt fam* - **1.** [Nerven kosten]: **jn ~** to get on sb's nerves - **2.** [bedrängen] to pester sb.

**Nerven|bündel** *das* bundle of nerves.

**Nerven|krieg** *der* war of nerves.

**Nerven|säge** *die fam* pain in the neck.

**Nerven|system** *das* nervous system.

**Nervenzusammen|bruch** *der* nervous breakdown.

**nervlich** *adj* nervous ⬦ *adv:* **~ völlig am Ende sein** to be a nervous wreck.

**nervös** *adj* nervous; **jn ~ machen** to make sb nervous ⬦ *adv* nervously.

**Nervosität** *die* nervousness.

**Nerz** (*pl* -e) *der* - **1.** [Pelz] mink coat - **2.** [Tier] mink.

**Nessel** (*pl* -n *oder* -) *die* (*pl Nesseln*) [Pflanze] nettle ⬦ *der* (*pl Nessel*) [Stoff] calico.

**Nest** (*pl* -er) *das* - **1.** [von Vögeln] nest - **2.** *fam abw* [Ortschaft] little place; **ein trostloses ~** a miserable hole - **3.** *fam* [Bett] bed.

**Nest|häkchen** *das* baby of the family.

**nett** *adj* nice; **wären Sie so ~ mir zu helfen?** would you mind helping me?; **eine ~e Summe** a tidy sum; **das ist ja eine ~e Bescherung!** what a nice mess! ⬦ *adv* - **1.** [ansprechend] nicely; **sich ~ unterhalten** to have a nice chat - **2.** *fam* [ziemlich]: **ganz ~ verdienen** to earn pretty well.

**netterweise** *adv* kindly.

**Nettigkeit** (*pl* -en) *die* kindness; **~en** kind words.

**netto** *adv* net.

**Netto|einkommen** *das* net income.

**Netto|gewicht** *das* net weight.

**Netz** (*pl* -e) *das* - **1.** [zum Fischen, für Haare, im Sport] net; **jm ins ~ gehen** *fig* [gefasst werden] to fall into sb's trap - **2.** [System] network; [Strom] grid; [Internet] Web; **ins ~ gehen** to go on the Web - **3.** [für Akrobaten] safety net - **4.** [von Spinnen] web - **5.** [Einkaufstasche] string bag.

**Netzan|schluss** *der* mains connection.

**Netz|haut** *die* retina.

**Netz|karte** *die* area season *ODER* rover *Br* ticket.

**Netz|teil** *das* EDV mains adaptor.

**Netz|werk** *das* EDV network.

**neu** *adj* - **1.** [gen] new; **das ist mir ~** that's news to me; **ich bin hier ~** I'm new here - **2.** [erneuert] fresh; **ein ~es Handtuch** a fresh towel; **eine ~e Flasche holen** to fetch another bottle - **3.** [aktuell]: **die ~esten Nachrichten** the latest news; **was gibts Neues?** what's new?; **seit ~estem** just lately *ODER* recently <> *adv* newly; **sie sind ~ eingezogen** they have just (recently) moved in; **~ anfangen** to start (all over) again; **etw noch mal ~ machen** to redo sthg; **~ streichen** to repaint.
➤ **aufs Neue** *adv* again.
➤ **von neuem** *adv* again.

**neuartig** *adj* new; **ein ~ Produkt** a new kind of product.

**Neubau** (*pl* -ten) *der* new building.

**Neuenburg** *nt* Neuchâtel.

**Neuenburger See** *der* Lake Neuchâtel.

**Neuengland** *nt* New England.

**neuerdings** *adv* recently, lately.

**neuerlich** *adj* further <> *adv* again.

**Neuer|öffnung** *die* reopening.

**Neu|erscheinung** *die* [von Buch] new publication; [von Platte] new release.

**Neuerung** (*pl* -en) *die* innovation; **~en einführen** to make changes.

**Neufundland** *nt* Newfoundland.

**Neufundländer** (*pl* -) *der* - **1.** [Hund] Newfoundland - **2.** [Einwohner] Newfoundlander.

**neugeboren** *adj* newborn; **sich wie ~ fühlen** to feel like a new person.

**Neugeborene** (*pl* -n) *das* newborn baby.

**Neugier, Neugierde** *die* curiosity.

**neugierig** *adj* inquisitive; **sie ist ~, ob ...** she is curious to see whether ... <> *adv* inquisitively.

**Neuguinea** *nt* New Guinea.

**Neuheit** (*pl* -en) *die* - **1.** [Produkt] innovation - **2.** [Originalität] innovativeness - **3.** [Neusein] newness.

**Neuigkeit** (*pl* -en) *die* news (U); ~ **en** news; **ich habe gute ~en** I have some good news.

**Neujahr** (*ohne Artikel*) New Year.
➤ **prost Neujahr** *interj* Happy New Year!

**Neujahrs|tag** *der* New Year's Day.

**Neukaledonien** *nt* New Caledonia.

**Neuland** *das* - **1.** [Unbekanntes] new ground - **2.** [Land] virgin land.

**neulich** *adv* recently.

**Neuling** (*pl* -e) *der* novice.

**neumodisch** *adj* *abw* newfangled.

**Neumond** *der* new moon.

**neun** *num* nine; *siehe auch* **sechs**.

**Neun** (*pl* -en) *die* nine; *siehe auch* **Sechs**.

**neunfach** *adj* ninefold <> *adv* nine times.

**neunhundert** *num* nine hundred.

**neunmal** *adv* nine times.

**neuntausend** *num* nine thousand.

**neunte, r, s** *adj* ninth; *siehe auch* **sechste**.

**Neunte** (*pl* -n) *der, die, das* ninth; *siehe auch* **Sechste**.

**neuntel** *adj* (*unver*) ninth; *siehe auch* **sechstel**.

**Neuntel** (*pl* -) *das* ninth; *siehe auch* **Sechstel**.

**neunzehn** *num* nineteen; *siehe auch* **sechs**.

**Neunzehn** (*pl* -en) *die* nineteen; *siehe auch* **Sechs**.

**neunzig** *num* ninety; *siehe auch* **sechs**.

**Neunzig** *die* ninety; *siehe auch* **Sechs**.

**Neunzigerjahre, neunziger Jahre** *pl*: **die ~** the nineties.

**Neu|ordnung** *die* reorganization.

**neureich** *adj* *abw* nouveau riche.

**Neurologe** (*pl* -n) *der* neurologist.

**Neurologin** (*pl* -nen) *die* neurologist.

**Neurose** (*pl* -n) *die* neurosis.

**Neurotiker, in** (*mpl* -; *fpl* -nen) *der, die* neurotic.

**neurotisch** *adj* neurotic <> *adv* neurotically.

**Neuschnee** *der* fresh snow.

**Neuseeland** *nt* New Zealand.

**Neuseeländer, in** (*mpl* -; *fpl* -nen) *der, die* New Zealander.

**neuseeländisch** *adj* New Zealand (*vor Subst*).

**Neusiedler See** *der* Lake Neusiedler.

**neusprachlich** *adj* ⊳ **Gymnasium**.

**neutral** *adj* neutral <> *adv* neutrally.

**neutralisieren** *vt* to neutralize.

**Neutralität** *die* neutrality.

**Neutron** (*pl* -en) *das* neutron.

**Neutrum** (*pl* **Neutra** ODER **Neutren**) *das* - **1.** GRAM neuter - **2.** *abw* [Mensch] asexual creature.

**Neu|wagen** *der* new car.

**neuwertig** *adj* nearly new.

**Neuzeit** *die* (ohne *pl*) modern times (*pl*).

**neuzeitlich** *adj* modern.

**Newsgroup** (*pl* -s) *die* EDV newsgroup.

**New York** [ˈnjuːˈjɔːk] *nt* New York.

**New Yorker** [njuːˈjɔːkɐ] (*pl* -) *der* New Yorker ◇ *adj* (*unver*) New York (*vor Subst*).

**New Yorkerin** [njuːˈjɔːkərɪn] (*pl* -nen) *die* New Yorker.

**nhd.** (*abk für* **neuhochdeutsch**) *New High German.*

**Nicaragua** *nt* Nicaragua.

**nicht** *adv* - **1.** [gen] not; **sie raucht ~** she doesn't smoke; **sie mag kein Marzipan – ich auch ~** she doesn't like marzipan – neither do I; **~ mehr und ~ weniger** neither more nor less; **warum ~?** why not? - **2.** [als Bestätigungsfrage]: **der Film war großartig, ~ wahr?** the film was great, wasn't it?; **du wusstest es schon länger, ~ (wahr)?** you've known for a while, haven't you?; **es ist wunderbar, ~ (wahr)?** it's wonderful, isn't it?; **ist das ~ schön?** isn't that nice? - **3.** [verstärkend]: **was habe ich ~ alles für dich getan!** all the things I've done for you!; **was du ~ sagst!** you don't say! ◇ *konj*: **~ dass ich ...** it's not that I ...; **~ nur ..., sondern auch ...** not only ..., but also ...

➤ **nicht einmal** *adv* not ... even; **er kann ~ einmal Englisch** he can't even speak English.

**Nichte** (*pl* -n) *die* niece.

**nichtig** *adj* - **1.** [ungültig] void - **2.** [bedeutungslos] trivial.

**Nicht|raucher** *der* - **1.** [Person] non-smoker - **2.** [Abteil] no-smoking compartment.

**Nichtraucher|abteil** *das* no-smoking compartment.

**Nicht|raucherin** *die* non-smoker.

**nicht rostend** *adj* rustproof.

**nichts** *pron* nothing; **ich weiß ~ darüber** I don't know anything about it; **für ~ und wieder ~ fam** for nothing; **das macht ~ fig** it doesn't matter; **zu danken** don't mention it; **das ist ~ für dich** it's not your kind of thing.

➤ **nichts als** *pron* nothing but.

➤ **nichts anderes** *pron* nothing else.

➤ **nichts da** *interj fam* no way!

**Nichts** *das* nothingness; **aus dem ~ auftauchen** to appear from nowhere; **vor dem ~ stehen** to have lost everything.

**nichts ahnend** *adj* unsuspecting ◇ *adv* unsuspectingly.

**Nicht|schwimmer, in** *der, die* non-swimmer.

**Nichtschwimmer|becken** *das* beginners' pool.

**nichtsdestoweniger** *adv* nevertheless.

**nichts sagend** *adj* [Worte, Geschwätz] empty.

**Nichtstun** *das* inactivity; **ich hasse dieses ~** I hate all this sitting around doing nothing.

**Nichtzutreffende** *das*: '**~s bitte streichen!**' 'delete as applicable'.

**Nickel** *das* nickel.

**Nickel|brille** *die* metal-rimmed glasses (*pl*).

**nicken** *vi* - **1.** [zustimmen] to nod; **mit dem Kopf ~** to nod (one's head) - **2.** [dösen] to doze.

**Nickerchen** (*pl* -) *das*: **ein ~ machen** to have a nap.

**nie** *adv* never; **~ im Leben!** not on your life!

➤ **nie mehr** *adv* never again.

➤ **nie und nimmer** *adv* not on your life.

**nieder** *adv*: **~ mit ...!** down with ...!

**niedere, r, s** *adj* [Einkommen, Lohn, Steuerklasse] low; [Arbeit] lowly; [Motive, Triebe] base; [Adel] lesser.

**Niedergang** *der* decline.

**niedergeschlagen** *pp* ▷ **niederschlagen** ◇ *adj* dejected ◇ *adv* dejectedly.

**Nieder|lage** *die* defeat; **jm eine ~ beibringen** ODER **zufügen** to inflict a defeat on sb.

**Niederlande** *pl*: **die ~** the Netherlands.

**Niederländer, in** (*mpl* -; *fpl* -nen) *der, die* Dutchman (*f* Dutchwoman).

**niederländisch** *adj* Dutch.

**Niederländisch(e)** *das* Dutch; *siehe auch* **Englisch(e).**

**nieder|lassen** ➤ **sich niederlassen** *ref* (*unreg*) - **1.** [sich setzen] to sit down - **2.** [beruflich]: **sich als etw ~** to set up as sthg - **3.** [sich ansiedeln] to settle.

**Niederlassung** (*pl* -en) *die* - **1.** [Unternehmen] branch - **2.** [als Arzt, Rechtsanwalt] setting up in practice.

**nieder|legen** *vt* - **1.** [Amt, Mandat] to resign from - **2.** *geh* [aufzeichnen] to put down - **3.** *geh* [hinlegen] to lay.

**nieder|machen** *vt* - **1.** [kritisieren - Person] to criticize sharply; [- Film, Buch] to slate - **2.** [ermorden] to massacre.

**Niederösterreich** *nt* Lower Austria.

**Niederösterreicher, in** (*mpl* -; *fpl* -nen) *der, die* Lower Austrian.

**niederösterreichisch** *adj* Lower Austrian.

**nieder|reißen** *vt* (*unreg*) to tear down.

**Nieder|sachse** [ˈniːdɐˈzaksə] *der* native/inhabitant of Lower Saxony.

**Niedersachsen** [ˈniːdɐzaksn̩] *nt* Lower Saxony.

**Nieder|sächsin** [ˈniːdɐˈzɛksɪn] *die* native/inhabitant of Lower Saxony.

**niedersächsisch** [ˈniːdɐˈzɛksɪʃ] *adj* of/from Lower Saxony.

**Nieder|schlag** *der* precipitation.

**nieder|schlagen** *vt (unreg)* - **1.** [zusammenschlagen] to knock down - **2.** [Blick, Augen] to lower - **3.** [Revolution] to put down.
➡ **sich niederschlagen** *ref* - **1.** [sich auswirken]: **sich in etw** *(D)* **ODER auf etw** *(A)* **~** to be reflected in sthg - **2.** [sich ablagern] to condense.

**nieder|schmettern** *vt* - **1.** [niederschlagen] to send crashing to the ground - **2.** [deprimieren] to shatter; **ein ~des Ergebnis** a shattering result.

**niederträchtig** *adj* malicious ◇ *adv* maliciously.

**Niederung** *(pl -en) die* low ground *(U)*.

**nieder|werfen** *vt (unreg)* - **1.** [niederschlagen - Person, Tier] to defeat; [ - Aufstand] to put down - **2.** *geh* [Subj: Krankheit] to lay low - **3.** *geh* [erschüttern] to shatter.
➡ **sich niederwerfen** *ref* [sich zu Boden werfen] to prostrate o.s.

**niedlich** *adj* cute ◇ *adv* cutely.

**niedrig** *adj* low; [Arbeit] lowly ◇ *adv*: **~ fliegen** to fly low; **die Preise ~ halten** to keep prices low.

**Niedrig|lohn** *der* low wages *(pl)*.

**Niedrigwasser** *(pl -) das* [von Meer] low tide; [von Fluss] low water.

**niemals** *adv* never ◇ *interj* never!

**niemand** *pron* nobody, no one; **ich habe ~en gesehen** I didn't see anybody; **~ von uns spricht Französisch** none of us speaks French; **~ anders, sonst ~** nobody else.

**Niemandsland** *das* no-man's-land.

**Niere** *(pl -n) die* kidney; **es ist mir an die ~n gegangen** *fam* it really got to me.

**Nieren|stein** *der* kidney stone.

**nieseln** *vi*: **es nieselt** it's drizzling.

**Nieselregen** *der* drizzle.

**niesen** *vi* to sneeze.

**Niete** *(pl -n) die* - **1.** [Los] losing ticket - **2.** [Bolzen, Knopf] stud - **3.** *fam* [Mensch] dead loss.

**niet- und nagelfest** *adj*: **sie haben alles, was nicht ~ war, mitgenommen** they took everything that wasn't nailed down.

**Niger** *nt* Niger.

**Nigeria** *nt* Nigeria.

**Nigerianer, in** *(mpl -; fpl -nen) der, die* Nigerian.

**nigerianisch** *adj* Nigerian.

**Nihilismus** *der* nihilism.

**nihilistisch** *geh adj* nihilistic ◇ *adv* nihilistically.

**Nikolaus** *(pl -läuse) der* - **1.** [Person]: **der ~** St Nicholas *(who brings children presents on 6 December)*, ≈ Santa Claus - **2.** [aus Schokolade] chocolate Santa Claus.

**Nikolaustag** *der* St Nicholas' Day *(6 December)*.

**Nikotin** *das* nicotine.

**Nikotingehalt** *der* nicotine content.

**Nil** *der*: **der ~** the (River) Nile.

**Nil|pferd** *das* hippopotamus.

**Nimmer|wiedersehen** ➡ **auf Nimmerwiedersehen** *adv* never to be seen again.

**nimmt** *präs* ⊃ **nehmen**.

**Nippel** *(pl -) der* nipple.

**nippen** *vi* to have a nip; **an etw** *(D)* **~** to have a sip of sthg.

**Nippes** *pl* knick-knacks.

**nirgends, nirgendwo** *adv* nowhere.

**Nische** *(pl -n) die* - **1.** [in der Wand - klein] niche; [ - groß] recess - **2.** [für Produkt, Lebewesen] niche.

**nisten** *vi* to nest.

**Nitrat** *(pl -e) das* nitrate.

**Nitroglyzerin** [niːtroˈɡlytseriːn] *das* nitroglycerine.

**Niveau** [niˈvoː] *(pl -s) das* level; **~ haben** [Person] to be cultured; **der Krimi hat ~** the detective story is quality literature.

**Nixe** *(pl -n) die* water nymph.

**Nizza** *nt* Nice.

**NN** - **1.** *(abk für* **Normalnull**) sea level - **2.** *(abk für* **nomen nescio**) name unknown.

**NO** *abk für* **Nordost**.

**nobel** *adj* - **1.** [kostspielig] luxurious - **2.** *hum* [vornehm] posh - **3.** *geh* [großzügig] noble ◇ *adv* - **1.** [kostspielig] luxuriously - **2.** *geh* [großzügig] nobly - **3.** *hum* [vornehm]: **sich ~ kleiden** to dress posh.

**Nobel|preis** *der* Nobel Prize.

**Nobel|preisträger, in** *der, die* Nobel Prize winner.

**noch** *adv* - **1.** [immer noch] still; **wir haben ~ Zeit** we still have time; **er hat ~ nichts gesagt** he still hasn't said anything; **hast du ~ Geld?** have you got any money left? - **2.** [nicht später] only; **ich habe ihn ~ letzten Monat besucht** I visited him only last month; **das muss ~ heute gemacht werden** it has to be done today; **schafft ihr das ~ bis Freitag?** do you think you'll manage it by Friday? - **3.** [zur Warnung]: **du wirst ~ an meine Worte denken!** mark my words! - **4.** [zusätzlich]: **~ eine Kaffee, bitte!** another coffee, please!; **Sie haben ~ zwei Minuten** you have two more minutes; **ich muss ~ ein paar Einkäufe machen** I have to buy a few more things; **passt das ~ in den Kofferraum?** will it fit in the boot *Br oder* trunk *Am?;* **wer ~?** who else? **- 5.** (+ *kompar*) even; **~ schneller** even quicker; **~ komplizierter** even more complicated **- 6.** [rhetorisch]: **wie war ~ sein Name?** what was his name again?; **man wird ja wohl ~ fragen dürfen** I was only asking <> *konj:* **weder ... ~ ...** neither ... nor ...

➤ **noch einmal, noch mal** *adv* again.

➤ **noch immer, immer noch** *adv* still.

➤ **noch mehr** *adv* even more.

➤ **noch nicht** *adv* not yet.

➤ **noch und noch** *adv:* **Leute ~ und ~** lots and lots of people; **es regnete ~ und ~** it rained for hours on end.

➤ **noch so** *adv:* **sei es auch ~ so klein** however small it may be; **es kann ~ so regnen** however much it rains.

**nochmals** *adv* again.

**Nomade** (*pl* -n) *der* nomad.

**Nomadin** (*pl* -nen) *die* nomad.

**Nominativ** (*pl* -e) *der* nominative.

**nominieren** *vt* to nominate.

**No-Name-|Produkt** [noːˈnɛimproːdʊkt] *das* own-label *oder* own-brand product.

**Nonne** (*pl* -n) *die* nun.

**nonstop** *adv* nonstop.

**Noppe** (*pl* -n) *die* [auf Sandale, Schläger] knobble.

**Nord** *der (ohne Artikel)* north.

**Nordamerika** *nt* North America.

**norddeutsch** *adj* Northern German.

**Norddeutschland** *nt* Northern Germany.

**norddt.** *abk für* norddeutsch.

**Norden** *der* north; **nach ~** north; **im ~** in the north.

**Nordeuropa** *nt* Northern Europe.

**Nordfriese** (*pl* -n) *der* North Frisian.

**Nordfriesin** (*pl* -nen) *die* North Frisian.

**nordfriesisch** *adj* North Frisian.

**Nordfriesische Inseln** *pl* North Frisian Islands.

**Nordfriesland** *nt* North Friesland.

**Nordirland** *nt* Northern Ireland.

**nordisch** *adj* Nordic.

**Nordkap** *das* North Cape.

**Nordkorea** *nt* North Korea.

**nördlich** *adj* northern; [Wind] northerly <> *präp:* **~ einer Sache** (G) *oder* **von etw** to the north of sthg.

**Nordost** *der (ohne Artikel)* northeast.

**Nordosten** *der* northeast.

**nordöstlich** *adj* northeastern; [Wind] north-easterly <> *präp:* **~ einer Sache** (G) *oder* **von etw** to the northeast of sthg.

**Nord-Ostsee-Kanal** *der* Kiel Canal.

**Nord|pol** *der* **- 1.** geogr North Pole **- 2.** phys north pole.

**Nordrhein-Westfalen** *nt* North Rhine-Westphalia.

**Nordsee** *die* North Sea.

**Nord|seite** *die* north side.

**nordwärts** *adv* north.

**Nordwest** *der (ohne Artikel)* northwest.

**Nordwesten** *der* northwest.

**nordwestlich** *adj* northwestern; [Wind] northwesterly <> *präp:* **~ einer Sache** (G) *oder* **von etw** to the northwest of sthg.

**Nord|wind** *der* north wind.

**nörgeln** *vi:* **(über jn/etw) ~** to moan (about sb/sthg).

**Norm** (*pl* -en) *die* **- 1.** tech [Regel] norm **- 2.** [Leistung] standard.

**normal** *adj* normal <> *adv* normally.

**Normalbenzin** *das* regular petrol *Br*, regular gas *Am*.

**normalerweise** *adv* normally, usually.

**Normal|fall** *der:* **im ~** normally, usually.

**Normalgewicht** *das* normal weight.

**normalisieren** *vt* to normalize.

➤ **sich normalisieren** *ref* to return to normal.

**Normal|zustand** *der:* **wieder im ~ sein** to be back to normal.

**Normandie** *die* Normandy.

**normen** *vt* to standardize.

**Norwegen** *nt* Norway.

**Norweger, in** (*mpl* -; *fpl* -nen) *der, die* Norwegian.

**norwegisch** *adj* Norwegian.

**Norwegisch(e)** *das* Norwegian; *siehe auch* Englisch(e).

**Nostalgie** [nɔstalˈgiːl] *die* nostalgia.

**Not** (*pl* Nöte) *die* **- 1.** [Notlage, Armut] need; **in ~ sein** to be in need; **~ leidend** needy **- 2.** [Verzweiflung] despair; **Nöte** [Sorgen] troubles **- 3.** *RW:* **mit knapper ~** by the skin of one's teeth; **wenn ~ am Mann ist** when the need arises; **~ tun** to be needed; **zur ~** *fam* if needs be.

**Notar** (*pl* -e) *der* notary.

**notariell** *adj* notarial, notary's <> *adv* by a notary.

**Notarin** (*pl* -nen) *die* notary.

**Notarzt, ärztin** *der, die* emergency doctor.

**Notausgang** *der* emergency exit.

**Not|bremse** *die* emergency brake.

**Not|dienst** *der:* ~ **haben** to be on duty.

**notdürftig** *adj* makeshift ◇ *adv* provisionally; [bekleidet] scantily.

**Note** (*pl* **-n**) *die* - **1.** [Beurteilung] mark *Br*, grade *Am* - **2.** MUS note; **nach ~n** with music ODER a score - **3.** [Eigenschaft] touch.

**Notebook** [nǝutbʊk] (*pl* **-s**) *das* EDV notebook.

**Noten|blatt** *das* sheet of music.

**Noten|schlüssel** *der* clef.

**Noten|ständer** *der* music stand.

**Not|fall** *der* emergency.

➡ **im Notfall** *adv* in an emergency.

**notfalls** *adv* if necessary.

**notgedrungen** *adv* out of necessity.

**notieren** *vt* - **1.** [aufschreiben] to note down; **sich** *(D)* **etw ~** to make a note of sthg - **2.** [Aktie] to quote ◇ *vi* WIRTSCH: **höher/niedriger ~** to rise/fall.

**nötig** *adj* necessary; **etw ~ haben** to need sthg; **du hast es gerade ~!** *iron* you can talk!; **sie hat es nicht ~ zu putzen** she doesn't have ODER need to do the cleaning ◇ *adv fam* urgently.

**Nötige** *das:* **das ~ tun** to do the necessary; **nur das Nötigste mitnehmen** only to take what is absolutely necessary.

**nötigen** *vt geh:* **jn ~, etw zu tun** [zwingen] to force sb to do sthg; [bedrängen] to press sb to do sthg.

**nötigenfalls** *adv* if necessary.

**Notiz** (*pl* **-en**) *die* note; [in der Zeitung] notice; **keine ~ von jm/etw nehmen** to take no notice of sb/sthg.

➡ **Notizen** *pl* notes.

**Notiz|block** *der* notepad.

**Notiz|buch** *das* notebook.

**Notiz|zettel** *der* note.

**Not|lage** *die* crisis.

**Not|landung** *die* emergency landing.

**notleidend** *adj* ➡ **Not.**

**Not|lösung** *die* temporary solution.

**Not|lüge** *die* white lie.

**notorisch** *adj* notorious ◇ *adv* notoriously.

**Not|ruf** *der* emergency call; [Nummer] emergency number.

**Notruf|säule** *die* emergency phone.

**Not|sitz** *der* foldaway seat.

**Not|stand** *der* - **1.** [Notlage] desperate situation - **2.** RECHT state of emergency.

**Notstands|gesetz** *das* emergency laws (*pl*).

**Notstands|gebiet** *das* disaster area.

**Notstrom|aggregat** *das* back-up electricity generator.

**Not|unterkunft** *die* emergency accommodation.

**Not|wehr** *die* self-defence.

**notwendig, notwendig** *adj* - **1.** [nötig] necessary - **2.** [logisch] inevitable ◇ *adv* necessarily.

**Notwendigkeit, Notwendigkeit** (*pl* **-en**) *die* necessity.

**Nougat** [ˈnuːgat] (*pl* **-s**) *das* ODER *der* = **Nugat.**

**Nov.** (*abk für* **November**) Nov.

**Novelle** [noˈvɛlǝ] (*pl* **-n**) *die* - **1.** [Literatur] novella - **2.** RECHT amendment.

**November** [noˈvɛmbɐ] *der* November; *siehe auch* **September.**

**NPD** [ɛnpeːˈdeː] (*abk für* **Nationaldemokratische Partei Deutschlands**) *die* German rightwing extremist party.

**Nr.** (*abk für* **Nummer**) no.

**NRW** *abk für* **Nordrhein-Westfalen.**

**NS** - **1.** (*abk für* **Nachschrift**) PS - **2.** *abk für* **Nationalsozialismus.**

**NSDAP** [ɛnɛsdeːʔaːˈpeː] (*abk für* **Nationalsozialistische Deutsche Arbeiterpartei**) *die* National Socialist German Workers' Party, *Hitler's Nazi party.*

**NS-Verbrechen** *pl* Nazi crimes.

**NT** (*abk für* **Neues Testament**) NT.

**Nu** *der:* **im ~** in an instant.

**Nuance** [ˈnyãːsǝ] (*pl* **-n**) *die* nuance; **eine ~ heller** a touch lighter.

**nüchtern** *adj* - **1.** [nicht betrunken] sober - **2.** [sachlich] matter-of-fact - **3.** [mit leerem Magen]: **~ sein** to have an empty stomach; **auf ~en Magen** on an empty stomach ◇ *adv* - **1.** [nicht betrunken] soberly - **2.** [sachlich] matter-of-factly - **3.** [mit leerem Magen] on an empty stomach.

**Nüchternheit** *die* soberness.

**Nudel** (*pl* **-n**) *die* noodle; **~n** [italienisch] pasta; [chinesisch, in Suppe] noodles.

**Nudel|holz** *das* rolling pin.

**Nudel|salat** *der* pasta salad.

**Nudel|suppe** *die* noodle soup.

**Nugat, Nougat** [ˈnuːgat] (*pl* **-s**) *der* ODER *das* nougat.

**nuklear** *adj* nuclear ◇ *adv* [aufrüsten, bewaffnen] with nuclear weapons.

**Nuklear|waffe** *die* nuclear weapon.

**null** *num* zero; **~ Komma fünf** zero ODER nought *Br* point five; **eins zu ~** one-zero, one-nil *Br*; **in ~ Komma nichts** *fam fig* in no time; **das Interesse war gleich ~** there was next to no interest; ~ **und nichtig** *fig* null and void <> *adj (unver) fam* no; *siehe auch* **sechs.**

**Null** (*pl* -en) *die* - **1.** [Zahl] zero - **2.** *fam abw* [Mensch] dead loss.

**nullachtfünfzehn** *fam abw adj (unver)* run-of-the-mill <> *adv* in a run-of-the-mill way.

**Nulllösung** (*pl* -en) *die* zero option.

**Nulllpunkt** *der* - **1.** [Tiefpunkt]: **auf den ~ sinken** to hit rock-bottom - **2.** PHYS zero.

**Nullltarif** *der*: **zum ~** free of charge.

**numerieren** = nummerieren.

**Numerus clausus** *der* UNI *limit on the number of places on certain oversubscribed university courses.*

> **NUMERUS CLAUSUS**
>
> This designates a system set up to restrict access to places on certain university courses for which there is a very high number of applicants, due to a shortage of facilities and the increase in the number of students. The average mark obtained by students at their school leaving examination is one of the selection criteria.

**Nummer** (*pl* -n) *die* - **1.** [Zahl] number; **auf ~ Sicher gehen** *fam* not to take any chances - **2.** [Größe] size - **3.** [im Zirkus] act - **4.** *fam* [Mensch] character - **5.** *salopp* [Geschlechtsakt] shag.

**nummerieren** *vt* to number.

**Nummernlkonto** *das* numbered account.

**Nummernlschild** *das* numberplate *Br*, license plate *Am*.

> **NUMMERNSCHILD**
>
> In Germany, licence plates feature two series of letters and one number: the first series of letters which consists of a maximum of three letters shows the place in which the vehicle was registered (for example: B for Berlin, M for Munich, HH for Hansestadt Hamburg) while the second series, consisting of a maximum of two letters, and the number indicate the administrative registration code of the vehicle.

**nun** *adv* - **1.** [gen] now; **von ~ an** from now on - **2.** [Ausdruck der Ungeduld]: **bist du ~ zufrieden?** are you happy now?; **was denn ~?** so what happens now? <> *interj* now; **~ denn** right ODER well then; **~ gut** oh well.

▸ **nun mal** *adv* now; **das ist ~ mal so!** that's just the way it is!

**nur** *adv* - **1.** [lediglich] only, just; **ich bin nicht krank, ~ müde** I'm not ill, just tired - **2.** [jedoch] but, yet; **sie arbeitet schnell, ~ müsste sie sorgfältiger sein** she works fast, but she should be more careful - **3.** [verstärkend]: **warum hat er**

**das ~ getan?** what made him do that?; **was meint er ~?** what does he mean?; **wenn sie ~ käme!** if only she would come!; **kommen Sie ~ herein!** do come in!; **~ keine Panik!** don't panic!; **hätte ich ~ auf dich gehört!** if only I'd listened to you!; **sie rannte, so schnell sie ~ konnte** she ran as fast as she could.

▸ **nur noch** *adv*: **ich habe ~ noch 20 Euro** I've only got 20 euros left.

▸ **nur so** *adv*: **das sagt er ~ so** *fam* he's just saying that; **der Putz bröckelt ~ so** the plaster is crumbling really badly.

▸ **nur zu** *interj* go on!

**Nürnberg** *nt* Nuremberg.

**Nürnberger** (*pl* -) *der* native/inhabitant of Nuremberg <> *adj (unver)* Nuremberg *(vor Subst)*.

**nuscheln** *vi* to mumble.

**Nuss** (*pl* Nüsse) *die* - **1.** [Frucht] nut; **eine harte ~** *fig* a tough nut to crack - **2.** *fam abw* [Mensch]: **du dumme ~!** you stupid idiot!

**Nusslbaum** *der* - **1.** [Baum] walnut tree - **2.** [Holz] walnut.

**Nussknacker** (*pl* -) *der* - **1.** [Gerät] nutcracker - **2.** [Holzfigur] *painted wooden figure of a man with a mouth that opens and closes, used as a Christmas decoration.*

**Nutte** (*pl* -n) *die salopp* - **1.** [Prostituierte] tart, hooker *Am* - **2.** *abw* [Frau] slut.

**nutzbar** *adj* usable; **(sich (D)) etw ~ machen** [Energiequelle] to harness sthg; [Boden, Land] to cultivate sthg.

**nutzbringend** *geh adj* productive <> *adv* productively.

**nütze** *adj (unver)*: **zu etwas/nichts ~ sein** to be of some/no use.

**nutzen, nützen** *vt* to use; **das nützt nichts/nicht viel** that's no/not much use <> *vi*: **jm ~** to be of use to sb.

**Nutzen** *der* benefit; **jm von ~ sein** *geh* to be of use to sb; **aus etw ~ ziehen** *geh* to exploit sthg.

**Nutzlfahrzeug** *das amt* - **1.** [Lieferwagen] commercial vehicle - **2.** [landwirtschaftlich] farm vehicle.

**Nutzlfläche** *die* [im Haus] usable floor space; **landwirtschaftliche ~** arable land.

**nützlich** *adj* useful; **sich ~ machen** to make o.s. useful.

**nutzlos** *adj* useless <> *adv* uselessly.

**Nutzung** (*pl* -en) *die* [von Bodenschätzen] exploitation; [von Energiequelle] harnessing.

**NW** (*abk für* **Nordwest**) NW.

**Nylon**® [ˈnaɪlɔn] *das* nylon.

**o, O** [o:] (pl **o** ODER **-s**) das o, O.

➡ **O** (abk für **Ost**) E.

**o. a.** (abk für **oben angegeben**) see above.

**o. Ä.** (abk für **oder Ähnliches**) and so on.

**Oase** (pl **-n**) die oasis.

**ob** konj whether; **ich weiß nicht, ~ er kommt** I don't know whether ODER if he'll come; **~ er wohl kommt?** I wonder if he'll come?; **~ ..., ~ ...** whether ... or; **und ~!** you bet!

➡ **als ob** konj as if, as though; **(so) tun als ~ ...** to pretend (that) ...; **er tat, als ~ er sie nicht gesehen hätte** he pretended not to have seen her.

**o. B.** abk für **ohne Befund** ⊳ **Befund.**

**OB** [o:'be:] (pl **-s**) der abk für **Oberbürgermeister.**

**Obb.** (abk für **Oberbayern**) Upper Bavaria.

**ÖBB** (abk für **Österreichische Bundesbahn**) Austrian Railways.

**obdachlos** adj homeless ⬦ adv: **~ werden** to become homeless.

**Obdachlose** (pl **-n**) der, die homeless person; **die ~n** the homeless.

**Obduktion** (pl **-en**) die postmortem.

**O-Beine** pl fam bow legs.

**Obelisk** (pl **-en**) der obelisk.

**oben** adv **- 1.** [räumlich] up; [obenauf] at the top; **hier/dort ~** up here/there; **ganz ~ im Schrank** right at the top of the cupboard; **ganz ~ auf dem Schrank** up on top of the cupboard; **links/rechts ~ im Bild** in the top left-hand/right-hand corner of the picture; **bis ~ hin** up to the top; **nach ~** up; [im Haus] upstairs; **mit dem Gesicht nach ~** face up; **von ~** down; **von ~ bis unten** from top to bottom; **von ~ herab** fig condescendingly; **weiter ~** further up; **~ ohne** fig topless **- 2.** [im Text] above; **siehe ~** see above; **~ erwähnt** above-mentioned **- 3.** fam [im Norden]: **da ~** up north **- 4.** fam [ranghöher]: **von ~** from above; **die da ~** the powers that be.

**obendrein** adv on top of that.

**Ober** (pl **-**) der waiter; **Herr ~!** waiter!

**Oberlarm** der upper arm.

**Oberlarzt, ärztin** der, die [Leiter einer Spezialab-

teilung] consultant; [Vertreter des Chefarztes] assistant (senior) consultant.

**Oberlbegriff** der generic term.

**Oberlbekleidung** die outer clothing.

**Oberlbürgermeister, in** der, die mayor (f mayoress) (of a large city).

**obere, r, s** adj upper.

**Oberlfläche** die **- 1.** [Außenfläche] surface **- 2.** MATH (surface) area.

**oberflächlich** adj superficial ⬦ adv superficially.

**Oberlgeschoss** das top floor; **im dritten ~** on the third Br ODER fourth Am floor.

**oberhalb** präp: **~ einer Sache** (G) above sthg ⬦ adv: **~ von jm/etw** above sb/sthg.

**Oberlhand** die: **die ~ bekommen/haben/behalten** to gain/have/keep the upper hand.

**Oberlhaupt** das head.

**Oberlhemd** das shirt.

**Oberlkiefer** der upper jaw.

**Oberlkörper** der upper body; **den ~ freimachen** to strip to the waist, to take one's top off.

**Oberlandeslgericht** das high court and court of appeal of a German federal state.

**Oberllippe** die upper lip.

**Oberlösterreich** nt Upper Austria.

**Oberlösterreicher, in** (mpl **-**; fpl **-nen**) der, die native/inhabitant of Upper Austria.

**oberösterreichisch** adj of/from Upper Austria.

**Oberlschenkel** der thigh.

**Oberlschicht** die: **die ~** the upper classes (pl).

**Oberst** (pl **-en** ODER **-e**) der colonel.

**oberste, r, s** adj top; [Gericht] supreme; **die ~ Heeresleitung** the military high command.

**Oberlstufe** die SCHULE final three years of secondary education.

**Oberlteil** das top.

**Oberlwasser** das: **~ haben** [Recht haben] to be proved right; [selbstbewusst sein] to feel confident.

**Oberlweite** die bust (measurement).

**obgleich** konj geh although.

**Obhut** die care; **er hat die Kinder meiner ~ anvertraut** he has placed the children in my care; **bei jm in guter ~ sein** to be in good hands with sb.

**obig** adj amt above (vor Subst).

**Objekt** (pl **-e**) das **- 1.** [Gegenstand, KUNST & GRAM] object **- 2.** [Immobilie] property.

**objektiv** [ɔpjɛk'tiːf] *adj* objective ⬦ *adv* objectively.

**Objektiv** (*pl* -e) *das* FOTO lens.

**Objektivität** [ɔpjɛktivi'tɛːt] *die* objectivity.

**Oblate** (*pl* -n) *die* - **1.** KÜCHE (circle of) rice paper - **2.** REL wafer.

**obliegen** (*prät* oblag; *perf* hat obgelegen) *vi geh*: jm ~ to be sb's responsibility; **es obliegt dem Käufer nachzuweisen, dass ...** it is incumbent on the purchaser to prove that ...

**obligatorisch** *adj* obligatory; [Wehrdienst, Prüfung] compulsory.

**Oboe** (*pl* -n) *die* oboe.

**obschon** *konj geh* although.

**obskur** *adj* - **1.** [geheimnisvoll] obscure - **2.** *fam* [verdächtig] dubious.

**Obst** *das* fruit.

**Obst|baum** *der* fruit tree.

**Obst|garten** *der* orchard.

**Obst|kuchen** *der* fruit flan.

**Obstler** (*pl* -) *der* fruit schnapps.

**Obst|salat** *der* fruit salad.

**obszön** *adj* obscene ⬦ *adv* obscenely.

**obwohl** *konj* although.

**Ochse** ['ɔksə] (*pl* -n) *der* [Rind] ox.

**Ochsenschwanz|suppe** *die* oxtail soup.

**Ocker** *das* ochre.

**ockergelb** *adj* yellow ochre.

**od.** *abk für* oder.

**öde** *adj* - **1.** [trostlos] desolate - **2.** *fam* [langweilig] dreary.

**oder** *konj* - **1.** [gen] or - **2.** *fam* [als Bestätigungsfrage]: **du kommst doch mit, ~?** you're going to come, aren't you?; **sie wird doch nicht zu spät kommen, ~?** she won't be late, will she?; **du hast doch kein Auto, ~?** you haven't got a car, have you?; **du hast deinen Aufsatz beendet, ~ etwa nicht?** you HAVE finished your essay, haven't you?

➤ **oder aber** *konj* or (else).

➤ **oder auch** *konj* or.

➤ **oder so** *adv* or something like that.

**Oder** *die*: **die ~** the (River) Oder.

**Oder-Neiße-Linie** *die* Oder-Neisse Line.

**Ödipus|komplex** *der* Oedipus complex.

**Odyssee** [ody'seː] (*pl* -n) *die* odyssey; **die ~** the Odyssey.

**OECD** [oːˈeːˈtseːˈdeː] (*abk für* Organization for Economic Cooperation and Development) *die* OECD.

**OEZ** (*abk für* osteuropäische Zeit) EET.

**Ofen** (*pl* **Öfen**) *der* - **1.** [Wärmespender] stove; **elektrischer ~** (electric) heater - **2.** [Backofen] oven - **3.** *fam* [Motorrad] bike.

**offen** *adj* - **1.** [gen] open; **das Geschäft hat bis 6 Uhr ~** the shop is open until 6 o'clock; **sperrangelweit ~** wide open; **mit ~en Augen** with one's eyes open; **auf ~em Meer** on the open sea; **für etw ~ sein** to have an open mind about sthg; **~ zu jm sein, jm gegenüber ~ sein** to be frank ODER open with sb; **~ und ehrlich** frank, open - **2.** [unverpackt] loose, unpacked; **~e Weine** wine by the glass/carafe - **3.** [lose] undone; **der Knopf ist ~** the button has come undone; **mit ~n Haaren** with one's hair down - **4.** [Rechnung] outstanding ⬦ *adv* openly; **etw ~ zugeben** to admit sthg openly; **~ gesagt** quite honestly; **ich habe es ihm ~ gesagt** I told him straight out.

**offenbar** *adv* obviously, clearly.

**offenbaren** *vt* to reveal.

➤ **sich offenbaren** *ref*: **sich jm ~** [Person] to confide in sb; [Lösung] to reveal itself to sb.

**Offenbarung** (*pl* -en) *die* revelation; **die ~** (the Book of) Revelations.

**Offenbarungs|eid** *der* oath of disclosure.

**offen bleiben** (*perf* ist offen geblieben) *vi (unreg)* - **1.** [Tür, Geschäft] to stay open - **2.** [Frage, Problem] to remain unresolved.

**offen halten** *vt (unreg)* [Augen] to keep open; [Tür] to hold open; **sich** (D) **eine Möglichkeit ~** to keep an option open; **sich einen Ausweg ~** to leave o.s. a way out.

➤ **sich offen halten** *ref*: **sich für etw ~** to remain open to sthg.

**Offenheit** (*pl* -en) *die* - **1.** [Ehrlichkeit] frankness; **in aller ~** in all honesty - **2.** [Aufgeschlossenheit] openness.

**offenherzig** *adj* - **1.** [Mensch] open-hearted - **2.** *fam hum* [Kleidung] revealing.

**offenkundig** *geh adj* clear ⬦ *adv* obviously, clearly.

**offen lassen** *vt (unreg) eigtl* & *fig* to leave open.

**offensichtlich** *adj* [Lüge, Betrug, Bevorzugung] blatant; [Wohlstand, Begabung] obvious; **es ist ~, dass ...** [eindeutig] it is clear that ... ⬦ *adv* obviously, clearly; [lügen] blatantly.

**offensiv** *adj* - **1.** MIL offensive - **2.** SPORT attacking ⬦ *adv* - **1.** MIL offensively - **2.** SPORT: **~ spielen** to play an attacking game.

**Offensive** [ɔfɛn'ziːvə] (pl -n) die - 1. MIL offensive - 2. SPORT attack.

**offen stehen** vi (unreg) - 1. [Tür, Fenster] to be open - 2. [zugänglich sein]: **jm ~** to be open to sb; **es steht dir offen zu fahren oder nicht** you are free to choose whether or not you go - 3. [Rechnung] to be outstanding.

**öffentlich** adj public ⬦ adv publicly; [auftreten] in public.

**Öffentlichkeit** die public; **etw an die ~ bringen** to make sthg public; **in aller ~** in front of everyone; **an die ~ dringen** to be leaked.

**Öffentlichkeitsarbeit** die (ohne pl) public relations (pl).

**öffentlich-rechtlich** adj: **~e Rundfunk- und Fernsehanstalt** ≈ public service broadcaster.

**Offerte** (pl -n) die offer.

**offiziell** adj official ⬦ adv officially.

**Offizier** (pl -e) der officer.

**offline** ['ɔflain] adv EDV offline; **~ gehen** to go offline.

**öffnen** vt - 1. [gen] to open; **mit geöffnetem Mund** with one's mouth open - 2. [lösen] to undo ⬦ vi to open; **wir ~ um neun** we open at nine; **jm ~** to open the door to sb.
➤ **sich öffnen** ref to open; [neue Märkte etc] to open up.

**Öffner** (pl -) der - 1. [für Flaschen] opener - 2. [für Türen] button used to open door in entryphone system.

**Öffnung** (pl -en) die opening; [von Körper] orifice; [von Flasche] mouth; [in Mauer] gap.

**Öffnungszeiten** pl opening hours.

**oft** (kompar **öfter**; superl **am öftesten**) adv often; **wie ~?** how often?, how many times?

**öfter, öfters** adv quite often; **warst du schon ~ hier?** have you been here often?; **~ als mir lieb ist** more often than I'd like.
➤ **des Öfteren** adv several times.

**ohne** präp (+ A) without; **ein Ehepaar ~ Kinder** a couple with no children; **das ist ~ weiteres möglich** it's perfectly possible; **~ den Fahrer waren wir sechs Personen** there were six of us, not including ODER counting the driver ⬦ konj without; **sie tat es, ~ dass er es merkte** she did it without him noticing; **sie tat es ~ zu fragen** she did it without asking.
➤ **ohne mich** interj count me out!

**ohnedies** adv geh in any case.

**ohnegleichen** adv geh unparalleled; **das war eine Dummheit ~** that was an unbelievably stupid thing to do.

**ohnehin** adv anyway.

**Ohnmacht** (pl -en) die - 1. [Bewusstlosigkeit] unconsciousness; **in ~ fallen** to faint - 2. [Machtlosigkeit] impotence.

**ohnmächtig** adj - 1. [bewusstlos] unconscious; **~ werden** to faint - 2. [machtlos] impotent ⬦ adv - 1. [bewusstlos]: **~ daliegen** to lie there unconscious - 2. [zusehen, ausgeliefert] helplessly.

**Ohr** (pl -en) das - 1. [von Person, Tier] ear - 2. RW: **ein offenes ~ für jn/etw haben** to be ready to listen to sb/sthg; **ein paar** ODER **eins** ODER **was hinter die ~en kriegen** fam to get a clip round the ear; **ganz ~ sein** to be all ears; **halt die ~en steif!** fam chin up!; **bis über beide ~en verliebt sein** to be head over heels in love; **jn übers ~ hauen** fam to take sb for a ride; **jm mit etw in den ~en liegen** to pester sb about sthg; **mit den ~en schlackern** fam to be staggered, to be gobsmacked Br; **sich aufs ~ legen** fam to have a snooze.

**Öhr** (pl -e) das eye.

**Ohr|clip** der = Ohrklipp.

**ohrenbetäubend** adj deafening ⬦ adv deafeningly.

**Ohrenschmalz** das ear wax.

**Ohr|feige** die slap (in the face); **jm eine ~ geben** to slap sb (in the face).

**ohrfeigen** vt to slap (in the face).

**Ohrklipp, Ohrclip** der clip-on earring.

**Ohr|läppchen** (pl -) das earlobe.

**Ohr|ring** der earring.

**Ohr|stecker** der (ear) stud.

**Ohr|wurm** der catchy tune; **ein ~ sein** to be catchy.

**o. J.** (abk für ohne Jahr) n.d.

**okay** [o'keː] adj & adv fam okay.

**Öko|bauer** der organic farmer.

**Öko|bäuerin** die organic farmer.

**Öko|laden** der wholefood store.

**Ökologie** [økolo'giː] die ecology.

**ökologisch** adj ecological ⬦ adv ecologically.

**Ökonomie** [økono'miː] (pl -n) die - 1. [gen] economy - 2. UNI economics (sg).

**ökonomisch** adj - 1. WIRTSCH economic - 2. [sparsam] economical ⬦ adv economically.

**Öko|steuer** die ecotax.

**Öko|system** das ecosystem.

**Okt.** (abk für Oktober) Oct.

**Oktan** (pl -e) das octane.

**Oktave** [ɔk'taːvə] (pl -n) die octave.

**Oktober** der October; **der 3. ~** German national holiday commemorating reunification on 3 October 1990; siehe auch **September**.

**O**

**Oktober|fest** *das* Munich beer festival.

**ökumenisch** REL *adj* ecumenical ◇ *adv* ecumenically.

**ö. L.** (*abk für* **östlicher Länge**): 45° ~ 45° east.

**Öl** (*pl* -e) *das* - **1.** [gen] oil - **2.** KUNST oils (*pl*).

**Oleander** (*pl* -) *der* oleander.

**ölen** *vt* to oil.

**Öl|farbe** *die* - **1.** KUNST oil paint; mit ~n malen to paint in oils - **2.** [Streichmittel] oil-based paint.

**OLG** [oːˈɛlˈgeː] *das abk für* **Oberlandesgericht**.

**Öl|gemälde** *das* oil painting.

**Öl|heizung** *die* oil-fired central heating.

**ölig** *adj* oily ◇ *adv*: ~ glänzen to have an oily sheen.

**Olive** [oˈliːvə] (*pl* -n) *die* olive.

**Oliven|öl** *das* olive oil.

**olivgrün** *adj* olive green.

**Öl|pest** *die* oil slick.

**Öl|quelle** *die* oil well.

**Öl|sardine** *die* sardine in oil.

**Öl|stand** *der* oil level; den ~ messen ODER prüfen to check the oil.

**Öl|wechsel** *der* oil change.

**Olympiade** (*pl* -n) *die* Olympic Games (*pl*), Olympics (*pl*).

**Olympia|sieger, in** *der, die* Olympic champion.

**Olympia|stadion** *das* Olympic stadium.

**olympisch** *adj* SPORT Olympic.

**Olympische Spiele** *pl* Olympic Games.

**Oma** (*pl* -s) *die* - **1.** [Großmutter] grandma, granny - **2.** *fam abw* [Frau] grandma; die ~ vor mir the old dear in front of me.

**Omelett** [ɔm(ə)ˈlɛt] (*pl* -e ODER -s) *das* omelette.

**Omni|bus** *der* [Linienbus] bus; [Reisebus] coach.

**onanieren** *vi* to masturbate.

**Onkel** (*pl* -) *der* - **1.** [Verwandter, Freund] uncle - **2.** *fam* [Mann]: gib dem ~ die Hand give the nice man your hand.

**online** [ˈɔnlain] *adj* EDV [angeschlossen] online; ~ sein to be online ◇ *adv* online.

**Online-Banking** [ˈɔnlainbɛŋkiŋ] *das* online ODER Internet banking.

**Online-|Dienst** [ˈɔnlaindiːnst] *der* EDV online service.

**o. O.** (*abk für* **ohne Ortsangabe**) n.p.

**op.** (*abk für* **opus**) op.

**OP** [oːˈpeː] (*pl* -s) (*abk für* **Operationssaal**) *der* OR *Am*, operating theatre *Br*.

**Opa** (*pl* -s) *der* - **1.** [Großvater] grandpa, grandad - **2.** *fam abw* [Mann] grandpa, grandad; der ~ vor mir the old codger in front of me.

**Opal** (*pl* -e) *der* opal.

**Open-Air-|Konzert** *das* open-air concert.

**Oper** (*pl* -n) *die* - **1.** MUS opera - **2.** [Opernhaus] opera house; in die ~ gehen to go to the opera.

**Operation** (*pl* -en) *die* operation.

**operativ** MED *adj* surgical ◇ *adv* surgically.

**Operette** (*pl* -n) *die* operetta.

**operieren** *vt* to operate on; jn am Blinddarm ~ to operate on sb's appendix; sich ~ lassen to have an operation ◇ *vi* to operate; behutsam ~ to proceed carefully.

**Opern|glas** *das* opera glasses (*pl*).

**Opern|haus** *das geh* opera house.

**Opern|sänger, in** *der, die* opera singer.

**Opfer** (*pl* -) *das* - **1.** [Mensch - von Unglück, Leidenschaften] victim - **2.** [Verzicht & REL] sacrifice - **3.** *RW*: ein ~ (für jn/etw) bringen to make a sacrifice (for sb/sthg); jm/einer Sache zum ~ fallen to fall victim to sb/sthg.

**opfern** *vt* to sacrifice; jm etw ~ to sacrifice sthg for sb; jetzt habe ich dir so viel Zeit geopfert now I've given up so much time for you; dem Orakel geopfert werden to be sacrificed to the oracle; jn/etw für etw ~ to sacrifice sb/sthg for sthg.

➤ **sich opfern** *ref* - **1.** [sich aufopfern] to sacrifice o.s. - **2.** *fam hum* [sich bereit erklären]: wer opfert sich freiwillig und geht zum Chef? who's going to volunteer to go to the boss?

**Opium** *das* opium.

**ÖPNV** [øˈpeːˈɛnˈfau] (*abk für* **öffentlicher Personennahverkehr**) *der local public transport*.

**Opportunist, in** (*mpl* -en; *fpl* -nen) *der, die* opportunist.

**opportunistisch** *adj* opportunistic ◇ *adv* opportunistically.

**Opposition** (*pl* -en) *die* opposition; in ~ zu etw stehen to be opposed to sthg.

**oppositionell** *adj* opposition (*vor Subst*); ~es Verhalten opposition.

**Optik** *die* - **1.** PHYS optics (*U*) - **2.** [Sichtweise] point of view - **3.** [Erscheinungsbild] appearance.

**Optiker, in** (*mpl* -; *fpl* -nen) *der, die* optician.

**optimal** *adj* optimal ◇ *adv* optimally.

**Optimismus** *der* optimism.

**Optimist, in** (*mpl* -en; *fpl* -nen) *der, die* optimist.

**optimistisch** *adj* optimistic ◇ *adv* optimistically.

**optisch** *adj* - **1.** PHYS optical - **2.** [visuell] visual ◇ *adv* [visuell] visually.

**Orakel** (*pl* -) *das* - **1.** [Mensch] oracle - **2.** [Weissagung] prophecy.

**oral** *adj* oral <> *adv* orally.

**orange** [oˈrãːʒ] *adj* orange.

**Orange¹** [oˈraŋːʒə, oˈrãːʒe] (*pl* -n) *die* [Frucht] orange.

**Orange²** [oˈrãːʒ] (*pl* -) *das* [Farbe] orange.

**Orangenlmarmelade** *die* (orange) marmalade.

**Orangenlsaft** *der* orange juice.

**Orang-Utan** (*pl* -s) *der* orangutang.

**Orchester** [ɔrˈkɛstɐ] (*pl* -) *das* orchestra.

**Orchidee** [ɔrçiˈdeːə] (*pl* -n) *die* orchid.

**Orden** (*pl* -) *der* - **1.** [Auszeichnung] decoration; [Medaille] medal; **jm einen ~ verleihen** to decorate sb - **2.** REL order.

**ordentlich** *adj* - **1.** [Person, Schreibtisch, Wohnung] tidy; [Schrift, Hausaufgabe] neat; [Leben] orderly - **2.** [regelgerecht - Mitglied] full; **~es Gericht** *court for civil and criminal cases* - **3.** [Note, Ergebnis] respectable - **4.** [Verdienst, Schluck] good; [Portion] good-sized; **einen ~en Schreck kriegen** to get a real fright - **5.** [anständig] proper <> *adv* - **1.** [sauber] tidily; [schreiben, gekleidet] neatly - **2.** [nach Regeln] correctly, in accordance with correct procedures - **3.** [viel] really well; **~ verdienen** to earn good money; **sie hat mit mir ~ geschimpft** she gave me a real telling-off.

**ordern** *vt* WIRTSCH to order.

**Ordinallzahl** *die* ordinal (number).

**ordinär** *adj* - **1.** *abw* [vulgär - Person, Witz] crude; [ - Benehmen, Kleidung] vulgar, common - **2.** [normal] ordinary <> *adv abw* [vulgär - lachen, fluchen] crudely; [ - sich verhalten, sich kleiden] vulgarly, commonly.

**ordnen** *vt* - **1.** [sortieren] to sort out; [Gedanken] to organize; **etw nach Datum ~** to arrange sthg according to date - **2.** [aufräumen] to tidy up - **3.** [regeln - Finanzen, Affären, Privatleben] to put in order.

➡ **sich ordnen** *ref*: **sich zu etw ~** to form sthg.

**Ordner** (*pl* -) *der* - **1.** [Hefter] file - **2.** [Person] steward.

**Ordnerin** (*pl* -nen) *die* steward.

**Ordnung** (*pl* -en) *die* - **1.** [geordneter Zustand] tidiness; **~ schaffen** to tidy up - **2.** [Disziplin, Gesetzmäßigkeit] order; **für ~ sorgen** to keep order - **3.** [Anordnung] order; **in alphabetischer ~** in alphabetical order - **4.** [Grad]: **eine Dummheit erster ~** an extremely stupid thing to do - **5.** *RW*: **das geht in ~** that's okay ODER fine; **etw in ~ bringen** [ordnen, erledigen] to sort sthg out; **in ~ sein** *fam* to be okay; **sie lässt ihre Tochter allein zu Hause? - das ist nicht in ~** she leaves her daughter alone at home? - that's not right; **der Computer ist nicht in ~**

there's something wrong with the computer; **(wieder) in ~ kommen** to sort itself out (again).

➡ **in Ordnung** *interj* okay!

**ordnungsgemäß** *adj* & *adv* in accordance with the regulations.

**Ordnungslstrafe** *die* amt fine.

**ordnungswidrig** amt *adj* [Parken] illegal; **~es Verhalten im Straßenverkehr** minor traffic offence <> *adv* [parken] illegally; **sich ~ verhalten** to contravene the regulations.

**Öre** (*pl* -) *die* ODER *das* öre.

**Oregano** *der* oregano.

**ÖRF** (*abk für* **Österreichischer Rundfunk**) *Austrian radio and television corporation.*

**Organ** (*pl* -e) *das* - **1.** [gen] organ - **2.** [Stimme] voice.

**Organisation** (*pl* -en) *die* organization.

**Organisator** (*pl* -toren) *der* organizer.

**Organisatorin** (*pl* -nen) *die* organizer.

**organisatorisch** *adj* organizational <> *adv* organizationally.

**organisch** *adj* - **1.** [eines Körperteils] physical - **2.** [natürlich & CHEM] organic <> *adv* - **1.** [physiologisch] physically - **2.** [natürlich] organically.

**organisieren** *vt* - **1.** [veranstalten, ordnen] to organize - **2.** [gründen] to form - **3.** *fam* [beschaffen] to get hold of - **4.** *fam* [stehlen] to pinch.

➡ **sich organisieren** *ref* - **1.** [sich zusammenschließen] to organize - **2.** [sich bilden] to develop.

**Organismus** (*pl* -men) *der* organism.

**Organist, in** (*mpl* -en; *fpl* -nen) *der, die* organist.

**Organizer** *der* (electronic) organizer.

**Organlspende** *die* organ donation.

**Organlspender, in** *der, die* organ donor.

**Organlverpflanzung** *die* organ transplant.

**Orgasmus** (*pl* -men) *der* orgasm.

**Orgel** (*pl* -n) *die* organ.

**Orgellkonzert** *das* organ concert.

**Orgellpfeife** *die* organ pipe; **dastehen wie die ~n** *fam* to be lined up in order of height.

**Orgie** [ˈɔrɡiə] (*pl* -n) *die* orgy.

**Orient** [ˈoːriɛnt] *der* - **1.** [der Nahe Osten] Middle East - **2.** [Asien] Orient.

**orientalisch** *adj* - **1.** [vom Nahen Osten] Middle Eastern - **2.** [vom Morgenland] oriental.

**orientieren** [oriɛnˈtiːrən] *vt* - **1.** [ausrichten]: **etw nach** ODER **an etw** (*D*) **~** to base sthg on sthg - **2.** [informieren]: **jn über etw** (*A*) **~** to inform sb about sthg.

➡ **sich orientieren** *ref* - **1.** [sich zurechtfinden] to

**O**

orientate o.s., to get one's bearings - **2.** [sich informieren]: **sich über etw** *(A)* ~ to inform o.s. about sthg - **3.** [sich ausrichten]: **sich nach** ODER **an etw** *(D)* ~ to be orientated towards sthg; **sich nach der Mutter** ~ to follow the example of one's mother.

**Orientierung** *die (ohne pl)* - **1.** [Zurechtfinden]: **die** ~ **in der Wüste ist nicht einfach** it's not easy to get one's bearings in the desert; **dieser Stadtplan ist zu Ihrer** ~ this city map is to help you find your way around; **die** ~ **verlieren** to lose one's bearings - **2.** [Information] information - **3.** [Ausrichtung]: ~ **nach** ODER **an etw** *(D)* orientation towards sthg; **vielen Jugendlichen fehlt die** ~ **an religiösen Werten** many young people have no orientation towards religious values; [nach Vorgaben, Richtlinien] conformance to sthg.

**Orientierungslsinn** *der* sense of direction.

**Orientierungslstufe** *die* SCHULE *the first two years of secondary education during which pupils at all three types of secondary school may move to a school better suited to their abilities.*

**Orientlteppich** *der* Persian rug.

**original** *adj* - **1.** [ursprünglich] original - **2.** [unverfälscht] genuine <> *adv* - **1.** [echt]: **eine** ~ **chinesische Tasse** a genuine Chinese tea cup - **2.** [direkt] live.

**Original** *(pl -e) das* - **1.** [Urform] original - **2.** [Person] character.

**Originallaufnahme** *die* [von Musik] original recording; [Foto] original print.

**originalgetreu** *adj* faithful <> *adv* faithfully.

**Originalität** *die* - **1.** [Echtheit] authenticity - **2.** [Individualität] originality.

**Originalton** *der:* **Sie hören jetzt die Rede des Präsidenten im** ~ you will now hear the original recording of the president's speech.

**Originalverlpackung** *die* original packaging.

**originell** *adj* - **1.** [ideenreich] original - **2.** *fam* [komisch] witty <> *adv* - **1.** [ideenreich] originally - **2.** *fam* [komisch] wittily.

**Orkan** *(pl -e) der* hurricane.

**Ornament** *(pl -e) das* ornament.

**Ort** *(pl -e) der* - **1.** [gen] place; [von Verbrechen] scene; **an** ~ **und Stelle** on the spot - **2.** [Ortschaft - Dorf] village; [ - Stadt] small town.
➡ **vor Ort** *adv* on the spot.

**orthodox** *adj* orthodox <> *adv* *abw* [starr] rigidly.

**Orthografie, Orthographie** [ɔrtogra'fiː] *(pl -n) die* spelling, orthography.

**Orthopäde** *(pl -n) der* orthopaedic surgeon.

**Orthopädie** *die* orthopaedics *(U)*.

**Orthopädin** *(pl -nen) die* orthopaedic surgeon.

**orthopädisch** *adj* orthopaedic <> *adv* orthopaedically.

**Örtlichkeit** *(pl -en) die* locality; **er ist mit den** ~**en bestens vertraut** he knows the area very well.
➡ **Örtlichkeiten** *pl fam* loo *(sg) Br,* john *(sg) Am.*

**Ortsanlgabe** *die:* **eine genaue** ~ **eines Unfalls machen** to give exact details of where an accident happened.

**ortsansässig** *adj* local.

**Ortschaft** *(pl -en) die* village; **geschlossene** ~ *amt* built-up area.

**ortsfremd** *adj:* **ich bin hier** ~ I'm a stranger here.

**Ortslgespräch** *das* TELEKOM local call.

**Ortslkenntnis** *die* knowledge of the area.

**ortskundig** *adj:* **ich bin hier** ~ I'm familiar with this area.

**Ortslnetz** *das* - **1.** TELEKOM local (telephone) exchange - **2.** ELEKTR local grid.

**Ortsltarif** *der* TELEKOM local rate.

**Öse** *(pl -n) die* eye; [von Schuh] eyelet.

**Oslo** *nt* Oslo.

**Ossi** *(pl -s) der fam* term used to describe citizen of the former GDR.

**Ost** *der* - **1.** [Windrichtung] east; **der Wind bläst aus** ~ the wind is blowing from the east - **2.** [Länder des Ostens, Gegend] East.

**Ostalgie** *die* nostalgia for the good things about life in the former GDR.

**Ostblock** *der* Eastern bloc.

**ostdeutsch** *adj* [Gebiet] Eastern German; POL East German.

**Ostdeutschland** *nt* [Gebiet] Eastern Germany; [DDR] East Germany.

**Osten** *der* - **1.** [Richtung] east; **nach** ~ east - **2.** [Gegend] East; **im** ~ in the East - **3.** POL: **der** ~ the East.

**Osterlei** *das* Easter egg.

**Osterlferien** *pl* Easter holidays.

**Osterlhase** *der* Easter Bunny.

**Osterlmarsch** *der* demonstration for peace held at Easter.

**Osterlmontag** *der* Easter Monday.

**Ostern** Easter; **an** ODER **zu** ~ at Easter.
➡ **frohe Ostern** *interj* Happy Easter!

**Österreich** *nt* Austria.

**Österreicher, in** *(mpl -; fpl -nen) der, die* Austrian.

**österreichisch** *adj* Austrian.

**Oster|sonntag** *der* Easter Sunday.

**Osteuropa** *nt* Eastern Europe.

**Ostfriese** (*pl* -n) *der* East Frisian.

**Ostfriesin** (*pl* -nen) *die* East Frisian.

**ostfriesisch** *adj* East Frisian.

**Ostfriesische Inseln** *pl* East Frisian Islands.

**Ostfriesland** *nt* East Frisia.

**Ost|küste** *die* east coast.

**östlich** *adj* eastern; [Wind] east ⬦ *adv:* ~ **einer Sache** (G) ODER **von etw** to the east of sthg.

**Ost|politik** *die* Ostpolitik.

**Ost|preuße** *der* East Prussian.

**Ost|preußen** *nt* East Prussia.

**Ost|preußin** *die* East Prussian.

**ostpreußisch** *adj* East Prussian.

**Östrogen** (*pl* -e) *das* oestrogen.

**Ostsee** *die:* **die** ~ the Baltic (Sea).

**Ost|seite** *die* east side.

**ostwärts** *adv* [sich bewegen] eastwards; [sich befinden] to the east.

**Ost|wind** *der* east wind.

**Ottawa** *nt* Ottawa.

**Otter** (*pl* - ODER -n) *der* (*pl* Otter) otter ⬦ *die* (*pl* Ottern) viper.

**ÖTV** [øː'teː'faʊ] (*abk für* **Gewerkschaft Öffentliche Dienste, Transport und Verkehr**) *die German public services and transport workers' union.*

**out** [aʊt] *adj* (*unver*): ~ **sein** *fam* to be out.

**Outdoor-Aktivitäten** *pl* outdoor pursuits.

**outen** *vt* to out.
➡ **sich outen** *ref* to come out.

**Outfit** ['aʊtfɪt] (*pl* -s) *das* outfit.

**Output** ['aʊtpʊt] (*pl* -s) *der* EDV output.

**Outsourcing** ['aʊtsoː(r)sɪŋ] *das* outsourcing.

**Ouvertüre** [uver'tyːrə] (*pl* -n) *die* overture.

**oval** [o'vaːl] *adj* oval ⬦ *adv* in/into an oval.

**Overall** ['oːvərɔl] (*pl* -s) *der* overalls (*pl*).

**Overhead|projektor** ['oːvɛhɛdprojɛktɔr] *der* overhead projector.

**ÖVP** [øː'faʊ'peː] (*abk für* **Österreichische Volkspartei**) *die* Austrian People's Party, *Christian Democratic political party in Austria.*

**Oxid, Oxyd** (*pl* -e) *das* oxide.

**oxidieren, oxydieren** (*perf* **hat/ist oxidiert** ODER **oxydiert**) *vt* (hat) *vi* (ist) to oxidize.

**Ozean** (*pl* -e) *der* ocean.

**Ozelot** (*pl* -e ODER -s) *der* ocelot.

**Ozon** *der* ODER *das* ozone.

**Ozonloch** *das* hole in the ozone layer.

**Ozonschicht** *die* ozone layer.

**p, P** [peː] (*pl* - ODER -s) *das* p, P.

**paar** *adj* few.
➡ **ein paar** *det* a few; **kannst du mal ein** ~ **Minuten rüberkommen?** can you come over here for a couple of minutes?

**Paar** (*pl* -e ODER -) *das* - **1.** (*pl* Paare) [zwei Personen] couple - **2.** (*pl* Paar) [zwei Dinge] pair; **ein** ~ **Strümpfe** a pair of socks.

**paaren** *vt* - **1.** [Tiere] to mate - **2.** [kombinieren] to combine.
➡ **sich paaren** *ref* [kopulieren] to mate.

**paarmal** ➡ **ein paarmal** *adv* a few times; **den Film habe ich ein** ~ **gesehen** I've seen the film a couple of times.

**Paarung** (*pl* -en) *die* - **1.** [von Tieren] mating - **2.** [von Spielern, Mannschaften] pairing.

**paarweise** *adv* in pairs.

**Pacht** (*pl* -en) *die* - **1.** [das Pachten, Vertrag] lease; **etw in** ~ **haben** to lease sthg - **2.** [Geld] rent.

**pachten** *vt* to lease; **etw (für sich) gepachtet haben** *fam fig* to have a monopoly on sthg.

**Pächter, in** (*mpl* -; *fpl* -nen) *der, die* - **1.** [von Geschäft] leaseholder - **2.** [von Grundstück] tenant.

**Pack** *das abw* rabble.

**Päckchen** (*pl* -) *das* - **1.** [Paket] small parcel - **2.** [Packung] packet.

**packen** *vt* - **1.** [voll packen] to pack; **seine Sachen** ~ to pack one's things - **2.** [legen, stellen] **etw auf/unter etw** (A) ~ to put sthg on/under sthg; **etw aus etw** ~ to take sthg out of sthg - **3.** [fassen] to seize - **4.** [übergekommen] **mich packt das Grauen** I am filled with horror - **5.** [emotional bewegen] to grip - **6.** *fam* [schaffen - Studium, Prüfung] to get through; **glaubst du, du packst es?** do you think you can manage?; **sie hat den Bus noch gepackt** she managed to catch the bus - **7.** *salopp* [begreifen] to get - **8.** RW: ~ **wirs?** *fam* [gehen wir?] shall we be off? ⬦ *vi* [vor Reisen] to pack.

➥ **sich packen** *ref fam* to clear off.

**Packen** (*pl -*) *der* pile; [zusammengeschnürt] bundle ⬦ *das* packing.

**packend** *adj* gripping ⬦ *adv* grippingly.

**Packpapier** *das* brown paper.

**Packung** (*pl -***en**) *die* - **1.** [für Waren] packet - **2.** MED compress; [aus Eis] ice pack - **3.** [Gesichtspackung] face pack - **4.** *fam* [hohe Niederlage]: **eine ~ kriegen** to get stuffed.

**Pädagoge** (*pl -***n**) *der* - **1.** [Lehrer] teacher - **2.** [Wissenschaftler] educationalist.

**Pädagogik** *die* education.

**Pädagogin** (*pl -***nen**) *die* - **1.** [Lehrerin] teacher - **2.** [Wissenschaftlerin] educationalist.

**pädagogisch** *adj* educational; **ihre ~en Fähigkeiten** her teaching ability; **meine ~e Ausbildung** my training in education ⬦ *adv* educationally.

**Pädagogische Hochschule** *die* teacher-training college.

**Paddel** (*pl -*) *das* paddle.

**Paddelboot** *das* canoe.

**paddeln** (*perf* **hat/ist gepaddelt**) *vi* - **1.** *(hat)* [rudern] to paddle - **2.** *(ist)* [Boot fahren] to canoe.

**paffen** *fam vt* [rauchen] to puff at ⬦ *vi* - **1.** *abw* [rauchen] to puff away - **2.** [nicht Lunge rauchen]: **du paffst ja nur!** you're not inhaling!

**Page** [ˈpaːʒə] (*pl -***n**) *der* [im Hotel] bellboy *Br*, bellhop *Am*.

**Pagenkopf** *der* page-boy haircut.

**Paillette** [paˈjɛtə] (*pl -***n**) *die* sequin.

**Paket** (*pl -***e**) *das* - **1.** [Postsendung] parcel - **2.** [Packung] packet - **3.** [Packen] bundle - **4.** [Zusammenstellung] package.

**Paketkarte** *die form showing sender and addressee, to be filled in when sending a parcel.*

**Paketschalter** *der* parcels counter.

**Pakistan** *nt* Pakistan.

**Pakistaner, in** (*mpl -*; *fpl -***nen**) *der, die* Pakistani.

**Pakistani** (*pl -* ODER *-***s**) *der* Pakistani.

**Pakistanin** (*pl -***nen**) *die* Pakistani.

**pakistanisch** *adj* Pakistani.

**Pakt** (*pl -***e**) *der* pact; **einen ~ schließen** to make a pact.

**paktieren** *vi abw*: **mit jm ~** to do a deal with sb.

**Palast** (*pl* **Paläste**) *der* palace.

**Palästina** *nt* Palestine.

**Palästinenser, in** (*mpl -*; *fpl -***nen**) *der, die* Palestinian.

**palästinensisch** *adj* Palestinian.

**Palette** (*pl -***n**) *die* - **1.** [für Farben] palette - **2.** [zum Transport] pallet - **3.** [Vielfalt] range.

**Palme** (*pl -***n**) *die* palm (tree); **jn auf die ~ bringen** *fam fig* to drive sb mad.

**Palmsonntag** *der* Palm Sunday.

**Pampe** *die fam* mush.

**Pampelmuse** (*pl -***n**) *die* grapefruit.

**pampig** *fam adj* - **1.** [frech] insolent - **2.** [breiig] mushy ⬦ *adv* [frech] insolently.

**Panade** (*pl -***n**) *die* breadcrumb coating.

**Panama** *nt* Panama.

**Panamakanal** *der* Panama Canal.

**Panda** (*pl -***s**) *der* panda.

**Panflöte** *die* panpipes *(pl)*.

**panieren** *vt* to coat with breadcrumbs; **paniertes Schnitzel** breaded escalope of pork.

**Paniermehl** *das (ohne pl)* breadcrumbs *(pl)*.

**Panik** *die* panic; **in ~ geraten** to panic; **(nur) keine ~!** *fam* stay cool!

**Panikmache** *die abw* scaremongering.

**panisch** *adj* [Reaktion] panic-stricken; **eine ~e Angst vor etw** *(D)* **haben** to be terrified of sthg ⬦ *adv* [reagieren] with panic; **sich ~ fürchten** to be terrified.

**Panne** (*pl -***n**) *die* - **1.** [mit Auto, Maschine] breakdown; **eine ~ haben** to break down - **2.** [Fehler] slip-up; [Versprecher] slip; **die Veranstaltung verlief ohne jede ~** the event went off without a hitch.

**Pannendienst** *der* breakdown service.

**Panorama** (*pl -***men**) *das* panorama.

**panschen** *vt* [mit Chemikalien] to adulterate; [mit Wasser] to water down ⬦ *vi* [mit Chemikalien] to adulterate the drinks; [mit Wasser] to water down the drinks.

**Panther, Panter** (*pl -*) *der* panther.

**Pantoffel** (*pl -***n**) *der* slipper; **unter dem ~ stehen** *fam* to be henpecked.

**Pantoffelheld** *der fam abw* henpecked husband.

**Pantomime** (*pl -***n**) *die* mime ⬦ *der* mime artist.

**Pantomimin** (*pl -***nen**) *die* mime artist.

**Panzer** (*pl -*) *der* - **1.** [Fahrzeug] tank - **2.** [von Insekt, Schildkröte] shell; [von Krokodil] armour - **3.** [Schutzplatte] armour plating.

**Panzerglas** *das* bulletproof glass.

**panzern** *vt* to armour-plate.
➥ **sich panzern** *ref* to shield o.s.

**Panzerschrank** *der* safe.

**Papa** (*pl -***s**) *der fam* dad, daddy.

**Papagei** (*pl -***en**) *der* parrot.

**Papi** (*pl -***s**) *der fam* dad, daddy.

**Papier** (*pl -***e**) *das* - **1.** [gen] paper; **etw zu ~ brin-**

**gen** to put sthg down on paper - **2.** [Wertpapier] security.

◆ **Papiere** *pl* [Ausweis, persönliches Dokument] documents; **Ihre ~e bitte** your papers, please; **seine ~e bekommen** ODER **kriegen** *fam fig* to get fired, to get the sack *Br*.

**Papier|geld** *das* paper money.

**Papier|korb** *der* wastepaper basket *Br*, wastebasket *Am*.

**Papier|kram** *der fam abw* paperwork.

**Papier|krieg** *der abw* tedious and long-running exchange of correspondence with an authority.

**Papier|schlange** *die* streamer.

**Papier|serviette** *die* paper napkin.

**Papiertaschen|tuch** *das* paper handkerchief.

**Papier|tüte** *die* paper bag.

**Papierwaren|geschäft** *das* stationer's.

**Papp|becher** *der* paper cup.

**Pappe** (*pl* -n) *die* cardboard; **nicht von** ODER **aus ~ sein** *fam fig* to be quite something.

**päppeln** *vt* to feed up.

**pappen** *vt:* **etw (an etw** (*A*)**) ~** to stick sthg (on sthg) <> *vi* to stick.

**Pappenstiel** *der:* **10.000 Euro sind kein ~** 10,000 euros is not to be sneezed at.

**pappig** *adj* - **1.** [haftend] sticky - **2.** [Brötchen] doughy; [Kartoffeln, Gemüse] mushy.

**Papp|karton** *der* cardboard box.

**Papp|teller** *der* paper plate.

**Paprika** (*pl* - ODER -s) *der* - **1.** [Gemüse] pepper - **2.** [Gewürz] paprika.

**Paprika|schote** *die* pepper.

**Papst** (*pl* Päpste) *der* pope.

**päpstlich** *adj* papal.

**Papyrus** *der* papyrus.

**Parabel** (*pl* -n) *die* - **1.** MATH parabola - **2.** [Gleichnis] parable.

**Parabol|antenne** *die* satellite dish.

**parabolisch** *adj* - **1.** MATH parabolic - **2.** *geh* [gleichnishaft] parable-like <> *adv* - **1.** MATH parabolically - **2.** *geh* [gleichnishaft] as a parable.

**Parade** (*pl* -n) *die* - **1.** [Aufmarsch] parade - **2.** [bei Fechten] parry; [bei Ballspiel] save; **jm in die ~ fahren** to rain on sb's parade; [ins Wort fallen] to cut sb short.

**Paradebei|spiel** *das* prime example.

**Paradies** (*pl* -e) *das* paradise.

**paradiesisch** *adj* heavenly.

**paradox** *adj* - **1.** [widersinnig] paradoxical - **2.** *fam* [unsinnig] absurd <> *adv* [widersinnig] paradoxically.

**Paraffin** (*pl* -e) *das* paraffin.

**Paragliding** ['pa:ragla̱ɪdɪŋ] *das* paragliding.

**Paragraf, Paragraph** (*pl* -en) *der* - **1.** [in Vertrag, Gesetz] section; [in Verfassung] article - **2.** [typografisches Zeichen] paragraph.

**Paragraf 218** *der article in German constitution pertaining to abortion.*

**PARAGRAF 218**

This article in the constitution is an ongoing source of controversy both in parliament and among the general public. Since 1993, it has stipulated that if an abortion is carried out during the first twelve weeks of pregnancy on medical grounds, then it is not a criminal act. It is nevertheless against the law and as such, unless an exception is made in specific cases, cannot be paid for by the country's national health service.

**Paraguay** ['paragu̱aɪ] *nt* [Staat] Paraguay <> *der* [Fluss]: **der ~** the (River) Paraguay.

**parallel** *adj* parallel <> *adv* - **1.** [gleichzeitig]: **~ zu etw** at the same time as sthg - **2.** [in gleichem Abstand]: **~ zu etw verlaufen** to run parallel to sthg.

**Parallele** (*pl* -n) *die* - **1.** MATH parallel line - **2.** [Entsprechung] parallel; **~n zu etw ziehen** to draw parallels with sthg.

**Parallel|klasse** *die* SCHULE parallel class.

**Parallelogramm** (*pl* -e) *das* parallelogram.

**Parallel|schaltung** *die* ELEKTR parallel connection.

**Parallel|schwung** *der* SPORT parallel turn.

**Parameter** (*pl* -) *der* parameter.

**paramilitärisch** *adj* paramilitary <> *adv* along paramilitary lines.

**paranoid** [parano'i:t] *adj* paranoid <> *adv:* **sich ~ verhalten** to act paranoid.

**Para|nuss** *die* brazil nut.

**Para|phrase** *die* paraphrase.

**Parapsychologie** *die* parapsychology.

**Parasit** (*pl* -en) *der eigtl & fig* parasite.

**parasitär** *adj* parasitic <> *adv* parasitically.

**parat** *adv:* **etw ~ haben/halten** to have/keep sthg ready; **auf diese Frage habe ich keine passende Antwort ~** I don't have a ready answer to this question <> *adj (unver):* **~ sein** to be ready.

**Pärchen** (*pl* -) *das* couple.

**Parfüm** (*pl* -e ODER -s) *das* perfume.

**Parfümerie** [parfymə'ri:] (*pl* -n) *die* perfumery.

**parfümieren** *vt* to perfume.

◆ **sich parfümieren** *ref:* **sich stark ~** [Frau] to wear a lot of perfume; [Mann] to wear a lot of aftershave.

**parieren** *vt* to parry ◇ *vi* to obey.

**Paris** *nt* Paris.

**Pariser** *(pl -) der* - **1.** [Einwohner] Parisian - **2.** *fam* [Kondom] rubber ◇ *adj (unver)* Parisian.

**Pariserin** *(pl -nen) die* Parisian.

**pariserisch** *adj* Parisian.

**paritätisch** *adj* [Mitbestimmung] equal; [Ausschuss] with equal representation ◇ *adv* equally.

**Park** *(pl -s) der* park.

**Parka** *(pl -s) der* parka.

**Park-and-ride-System** ['paːkɛndˈraɪtsys'-teːm] *das* park and ride system.

**Parkanlage** *die* [von Stadt] park; [von Schloss] grounds *(pl)*.

**Parkbank** *(pl -bänke) die* park bench.

**Parkbucht** *die* parking bay.

**parken** *vt* to park ◇ *vi* - **1.** [Person] to park; **falsch ~** to park illegally - **2.** [Fahrzeug]: **ein parkendes Auto** a parked car.

**Parken** *das* parking; '**~ verboten!**' 'no parking'.

**Parkett** *(pl -e ODER -s) das* - **1.** [Fußbodenbelag] parquet - **2.** [im Kino, Theater] stalls *(pl) Br*, parquet *Am*; **sich auf internationalem ~ bewegen (können)** *geh* to (be able to) move in international circles.

**Parkgebühr** *die* parking fee.

**Parkhaus** *das* multi-storey car park *Br*, parking garage *Am*.

**Parkleuchte** *die* sidelight *Br*, parking light *Am*.

**Parklicht** *das* sidelight *Br*, parking light *Am*.

**Parklücke** *die* parking space.

**Parkplatz** *der* - **1.** [Platz] car park *Br*, parking lot *Am* - **2.** [Parklücke] parking space.

**Parkscheibe** *die* parking disc.

**Parkschein** *der* (car park) ticket.

**Parksünder, in** *der, die fam* illegally parked person.

**Parkuhr** *die* parking meter.

**Parkverbot** *das:* **hier herrscht ~** there is no parking here; **im ~ stehen** to be in a no-parking zone.

**Parkwächter, in** *der, die* - **1.** [auf dem Parkplatz] car park attendant *Br*, parking lot attendant *Am* - **2.** [im Park] park attendant.

**Parlament** *(pl -e) das* parliament.

**Parlamentarier, in** [parlamɛnˈtaːrɪɐ, rɪn] *(mpl -; fpl -nen) der, die* Member of Parliament.

**parlamentarisch** *adj* parliamentary ◇ *adv* in parliament.

**Parlamentsausschuss** *der* parliamentary committee.

**Parlamentsdebatte** *die* parliamentary debate.

**Parlamentswahl** *die* parliamentary elections *(pl)*.

**Parmesan** *der* Parmesan.

**Parmesankäse** *der* Parmesan cheese.

**Parodie** [paroˈdiː] *(pl -n) die* parody; **eine ~ auf etw** a parody of sthg; **eine ~ auf jn** a take-off of sb.

**parodieren** *vt* [Roman, Film, Sprechweise] to parody; [Person] to take off.

**Parodontose** *(pl -n) die* gum disease.

**Parole** *(pl -n) die* - **1.** [Kennwort] password - **2.** [Leitspruch] slogan - **3.** *abw* [Behauptung]: **eine ausländerfeindliche ~** a racial stereotype.

**Partei** *(pl -en) die* - **1.** [gen] party; **für jn ~ ergreifen** *fig* to side with sb - **2.** [bei Streit] side.

**parteiisch** *adj* biased ◇ *adv*: **~ urteilen** to make a biased judgement.

**Parteilinie** *die* party line.

**parteilos** *adj* independent.

**Parteimitglied** *das* party member.

**Parteiprogramm** *das* party manifesto.

**Parteitag** *der* party conference *Br*, convention *Am*.

**Parteivorsitzende** *der, die* party leader.

**Parterre** [parˈtɛr] *(pl -s) das* ground floor *Br*, first floor *Am*.
➡ **im Parterre** *adv* on the ground floor *Br ODER* first floor *Am*.

**Partie** [parˈtiː] *(pl -n) die* - **1.** [Teil] part - **2.** [Spiel] game; **eine ~ Schach/Tennis spielen** to play a game of chess/tennis - **3.** *RW:* **eine gute/ schlechte ~ sein** to be/not to be a good catch; **da bin ich mit von der ~!** count me in!

**partiell** [parˈtsiɛl] *adj* partial ◇ *adv* partially.

**Partikel** *(pl -n ODER -) das (pl Partikel)* PHYS particle ◇ *die (pl Partikeln)* GRAM particle.

**Partisan, in** *(mpl -en; fpl -nen) der, die* partisan.

**Partitur** *(pl -en) die* score.

**Partizip** *(pl -ien) das* participle.
➡ **Partizip Perfekt** *das* past participle.
➡ **Partizip Präsens** *das* present participle.

**Partner, in** *(mpl -; fpl -nen) der, die* partner; [in Film] co-star.

**Partnerlook** *der* his and hers look.

**Partnerschaft** *(pl -en) die* - **1.** [zwischen Personen] partnership - **2.** [zwischen Städten] twinning.

**partnerschaftlich** *adj* [Verhältnis] based on partnership; **~e Beziehung** partnership; **~e Zusammenarbeit** cooperation ◇ *adv* - **1.** [freundschaftlich] in a spirit of partnership;

[zusammenleben] as partners - **2.** [kollegial] in partnership.

**Partner|stadt** *die* twin town.

**partout** [par'tu:] *adv fam* at all costs; **sie will ~ nicht gehorchen!** she simply refuses to obey!

**Party** ['pa:ɐ̯tiǀ (*pl* -s) *die* party.

**Pasch** (*pl* -e *ODER* **Päsche**) *der* double.

**Pascha** (*pl* -s) *der* - **1.** [Titel, Titelträger] pasha - **2.** *fam abw* [egoistischer Mann]: **den ~ spielen** to allow o.s. to be waited on hand and foot.

**Pass** (*pl* **Pässe**) *der* - **1.** [Dokument] passport - **2.** [Gebirgspass, beim Fußball] pass.

**passabel** *adj* reasonable, passable <> *adv* reasonably well, passably.

**Passage** [pa'sa:ʒə] (*pl* -n) *die* - **1.** [gen] passage - **2.** [Geschäftsstraße] arcade.

**Passagier** [pasa'ʒi:ɐ̯] (*pl* -e) *der* passenger; **blinder ~** [auf Schiff] stowaway; [im Zug] fare dodger.

**Passagier|flugzeug** *das* passenger aircraft.

**Passagierin** [pasa'ʒi:rɪn] (*pl* -nen) *die* passenger.

**Passant, in** (*mpl* -en; *fpl* -nen) *der, die* passerby.

**Pass|bild** *das* passport photo.

**passen** *vi* - **1.** [die richtige Größe haben] to fit; **die Schuhe ~ mir nicht** my shoes don't fit; **in etw** *(A)* **~ to** fit in sthg - **2.** [angenehm sein]: **passt es (dir) morgen besser?** does tomorrow suit you better?; **das passt mir nicht** that doesn't suit me; **diese ständigen Unterbrechungen ~ mir nicht** I could do without these constant interruptions; **das könnte dir so ~!** no way!; **das könnte ihm so ~!** he should be so lucky! - **3.** [zusammenpassen - Farben] to match; **zu jm ~** to suit sb; **sie passt in keinster Weise zu ihm** she isn't at all suited to him; **diese Schuhe ~ nicht zu dem Rock** these shoes don't go with the skirt - **4.** [nicht können] to pass; **da muss ich ~!** pass!

**passend** *adj* - **1.** [Gelegenheit, Methode, Kleidung] suitable; [Worte] right; **der ~e Schlüssel** the right key - **2.** [Farbe] matching <> *adv* suitably; **~ antworten** to give a fitting reply; **haben Sie es ~?** do you have the exact amount?

**Pass|foto** *das* passport photo.

**passieren** (*perf* **hat/ist passiert**) *vt (hat)* - **1.** [überschreiten, durchschreiten] to cross - **2.** [Zollkontrolle] to go through - **3.** *SPORT* to pass - **4.** *KÜCHE* to pass through a sieve <> *vi (ist)* to happen; **es ist ein Unglück passiert** there's been an accident; **mir ist etwas unglaubliches passiert** something incredible happened to me; **bei dem Unfall ist zum Glück nichts passiert**

fortunately, nobody was hurt in the accident.

**Passier|schein** *der* pass, permit.

**Passion** (*pl* -en) *die* - **1.** [gen] passion - **2.** *REL* Passion.

**passioniert** *adj* passionate.

**Passions|frucht** *die* passionfruit.

**Passionsspiele** *pl* passion plays.

**passiv, passiv** *adj* - **1.** [untätig] passive - **2.** [Mitglied] non-active <> *adv* passively.

**Passiv** ['pasiːf] (*pl* -e) *das* *GRAM* passive (voice).

**Passivität** [pasiviˈtɛːt] *die* passivity.

**Pass|kontrolle** *die* - **1.** [Kontrollieren] passport check - **2.** [Kontrollstelle] passport control.

**Pass|wort** *das* *EDV* password.

**Paste** (*pl* -n) *die* paste.

**Pastell|farbe** *die* pastel colour.

**Pastell|ton** *der* pastel shade.

**Pastete** (*pl* -n) *die* - **1.** [mit Blätterteig] vol-au-vent - **2.** [ohne Blätterteig] pâté.

**pasteurisieren** [pastøriˈziːrən] *vt* to pasteurize.

**Pastor** (*pl* -toren) *der* [katholisch] priest; [evangelisch] vicar.

**Pastorin** (*pl* -nen) *die* - **1.** [Pfarrerin] vicar - **2.** [Ehefrau des Pastors] vicar's wife.

**Pate** (*pl* -n) *der* godfather; **bei etw ~ stehen** to be the influence behind sthg.

**Paten|kind** *das* godchild.

**Paten|onkel** *der* godfather.

**Patenschaft** (*pl* -en) *die*: **die ~ für etw übernehmen** to sponsor sthg; **die ~ für jn übernehmen** to become sb's godparent.

**patent** *adj* - **1.** [lebenstüchtig] capable - **2.** [praktisch] neat - **3.** *fam* [nett] great <> *adv* [tüchtig] capably.

**Patent** (*pl* -e) *das* patent; **auf etw** *(A)* **ein ~ anmelden** to apply for a patent for sthg.

**Paten|tante** *die* godmother.

**patentieren** *vt* to patent; **sich** *(D)* **etw ~ lassen** to take out a patent on sthg.

**Pater** (*pl* -) *der* father (*priest*).

**pathetisch** *adj* melodramatic <> *adv* melodramatically.

**pathologisch** *adj* pathological <> *adv* [krankhaft] pathologically.

**Pathos** *das*: **mit ~ in der Stimme** with emotion in one's voice; **seine Rede trieft vor falschem ~** his speech is oozing with false pathos.

**Patience** [pa'sjãːs] (*pl* -n) *die* patience.

**Patient, in** (*mpl* -en; *fpl* -nen) *der, die* patient.

**Patin** (*pl* -nen) *die* godmother.

**Patina** *die* patina.

**P**

**patriarchalisch** *adj* patriarchal ◇ *adv* in a patriarchal manner.

**Patriot, in** (*mpl* -en; *fpl* -nen) *der, die* patriot.

**patriotisch** *adj* patriotic ◇ *adv* patriotically.

**Patriotismus** *der* patriotism.

**Patron, in** (*mpl* -e; *fpl* -nen) *der, die* patron saint.

**Patrone** (*pl* -n) *die* cartridge.

**patrouillieren** [patrul'(j)iːrən] (*perf* hat/ist patrouilliert) *vi* to patrol.

**Patsche** (*pl* -n) *die fam* - **1.** [Not]: in der ~ sitzen to be in a fix; jm aus der ~ helfen to help sb out of a tight spot - **2.** [Hand] paw.

**patschen** *vi fam* - **1.** [mit Händen]: jm eine ins Gesicht ~ to slap sb's face - **2.** [mit Füßen] to splash.

**patschnass** *adj fam* soaking wet.

**Patt** (*pl* -s) *das eigtl* & *fig* stalemate.

**patzen** *vi* to slip up.

**patzig** *adj* nasty ◇ *adv* nastily.

**Pauke** (*pl* -n) *die* kettledrum; auf die ~ hauen *fam fig* to paint the town red; mit ~n und Trompeten durchfallen *fig* to fail resoundingly.

**pauken** *fam vi* to swot *Br*, to grind *Am* ◇ *vt* to swot up on *Br*, to bone up on *Am*.

**Pauker, in** (*mpl* -; *fpl* -nen) *der, die fam* teacher.

**pausbäckig** *adj* chubby-cheeked.

**pauschal** *adj* - **1.** [Preis, Versicherung] all-inclusive - **2.** [Urteil] sweeping ◇ *adv* - **1.** [beurteilen] sweepingly - **2.** [abrechnen] altogether.

**Pauschale** (*pl* -n) *die* flat rate.

**Pauschallpreis** *der* all-inclusive price.

**Pauschallreise** *die* package tour.

**Pauschallurteil** *das* sweeping judgement.

**Päuschen** ['pɔysçən] (*pl* -) *das fam* breather; (ein) ~ machen to take a breather.

**Pause** (*pl* -n) *die* - **1.** [Unterbrechung] break; [im Theater, Konzert] interval - **2.** *mus* rest.

**Pausenlbrot** *das* snack (for the break).

**pausenlos** *adj* & *adv* non-stop.

**Pavian** ['paːvjaːn] (*pl* -e) *der* baboon.

**Pavillon** ['pavıljɔŋ] (*pl* -s) *der* pavilion.

**Pay-TV** ['pɛitiːviː] (*pl* -s) *das* pay TV; im ~ on pay TV.

**Pazifik** *der*: der ~ the Pacific.

**pazifisch** *adj* Pacific.

**Pazifische Ozean** *der* Pacific Ocean.

**Pazifismus** *der* pacifism.

**Pazifist, in** (*mpl* -en; *fpl* -nen) *der, die* pacifist.

**pazifistisch** *adj* pacifist ◇ *adv* in a pacifist way.

**PC** [peː'tseː] (*pl* - *ODER* -s) (*abk für* **Personal Computer**) *der* PC.

**PDS** [peːdeː'ɛs] (*abk für* **Partei des Demokratischen Sozialismus**) *die Democratic Socialist Party*.

**Pech** (*pl* -e) *das* - **1.** [Unglück] bad luck; ~ haben to be unlucky - **2.** [Erdölprodukt] pitch; zusammenhalten wie ~ und Schwefel *fig* to be as thick as thieves.

**Pechlsträhne** *die* run of bad luck.

**Pechlvogel** *der* unlucky person.

**Pedal** (*pl* -e) *das* pedal.

**Pedant, in** (*mpl* -en; *fpl* -nen) *der, die abw* pedant.

**pedantisch** *abw adj* fastidious ◇ *adv* fastidiously.

**Pegel** (*pl* -) *der* [von Fluss] water level; [von Lärm] level.

**peilen** *vt* to take a bearing on; die Lage ~ to see how the land lies ◇ *vi fam*: über den Daumen ~ to make a rough guess.

**peinigen** *vt geh* to torture.

**peinlich** *adj* - **1.** [unangenehm] embarrassing; das ist mir sehr ~ I feel very embarrassed about it - **2.** [sorgfältig] scrupulous ◇ *adv* - **1.** [unangenehm] embarrassingly - **2.** [sorgfältig] scrupulously.

**Peinlichkeit** (*pl* -en) *die* - **1.** [Zustand] awkwardness - **2.** [Handlung] embarrassment.

**Peitsche** (*pl* -n) *die* whip.

**peitschen** (*perf* hat/ist gepeitscht) *vt (hat)* to whip ◇ *vi (ist)* [Wind, Regen] to lash; [Schuss] to ring out.

**Pekinese** (*pl* -n) *der* pekinese.

**Peking** *nt* Peking.

**Pekinger** (*pl* -) *der* Pekingese ◇ *adj (unver)* Pekingese.

**Pekingerin** (*pl* -nen) *die* Pekingese.

**Pelikan** (*pl* -e) *der* pelican.

**Pelle** (*pl* -n) *die Norddt* [von Kartoffel] peel; [von Wurst] skin; jm auf die ~ rücken *fam fig* [bedrängen] to pester sb; [heranrücken] to get too close to sb.

**pellen** *vt Norddt* [Kartoffel] to peel; [Wurst] to skin.
➥ **sich pellen** *ref* to peel.

**Pelllkartoffel** *die* unpeeled boiled potato.

**Peloponnes** [pelopɔ'neːs] *der*: der ~ the Peloponnese.

**Pelz** (*pl* -e) *der* - **1.** [Fell] fur (*U*); jm auf den ~ rücken *fam fig* to pester sb - **2.** [Pelzmantel] fur (coat).

**pelzig** *adj* - **1.** [taub] numb - **2.** [pelzartig] furry.

**Pelz|mantel** *der* fur coat.

**Pendant** [pã'dã:] (*pl* -s) *das geh* counterpart.

**Pendel** (*pl* -) *das* pendulum.

**pendeln** (*perf* ist/hat gependelt) *vi* - **1.** (*ist*) [fahren] to commute - **2.** (*hat*) [schwingen - Glocken] to swing; [ - Beine] to dangle.

**Pendelverkehr** *der* [für Pendler] commuter traffic; [Hin- und Herfahren] shuttle service.

**Pendler, in** (*mpl* -; *fpl* -nen) *der, die* commuter.

**penetrant** *abw adj* [Mensch, Fragerei] obtrusive; [Geruch, Geklingel] penetrating <> *adv* [nach etw riechen] penetratingly; [auf jn einreden] obtrusively.

**peng** *interj* bang!

**penibel** *abw adj* fussy <> *adv* fussily.

**Penis** (*pl* -se) *der* penis.

**Penizillin** *das* penicillin.

**pennen** *vi fam* - **1.** [schlafen] to sleep, to kip *Br* - **2.** [nicht aufpassen] to be half-asleep - **3.** [mit jm schlafen]: mit jm ~ *salopp* to do it with sb.

**Penner, in** (*mpl* -; *fpl* -nen) *der, die fam* - **1.** [Stadtstreicher] tramp, bum *Am* - **2.** [Schlafmütze] sleepyhead.

**Pension** [paŋ'zio:n] (*pl* -en) *die* - **1.** [Hotel] guesthouse - **2.** [Ruhestand]: in ~ gehen to retire; in ~ sein to be retired - **3.** (*ohne pl*) [Bezüge] pension.

**Pensionär, in** [paŋzion'ε:ɐ̯, rın] (*mpl* -e; *fpl* -nen) *der, die* pensioner (*retired civil servant*).

**pensionieren** [paŋzio'ni:rən] *vt* to pension off.

**Pensionierung** [paŋzio'ni:roŋ] (*pl* -en) *die* retirement.

**Pensions|gast** *der* guest (*in a guesthouse*).

**Pensum** (*pl* Pensen) *das* quota.

**Pentagon** *das* pentagon.

**Penthouse** ['pɛnthaus] (*pl* -s) *das* penthouse.

**Pep** *der fam*: ~ haben to have pep.

**Peperoni** (*pl* -) *die* chilli (pepper).

**per** *präp* (+A) by.

**perfekt** *adj* - **1.** [vollkommen] perfect - **2.** [abgeschlossen]: ~ sein [Vertrag, Kauf] to be finalized; [Niederlage, Sieg] to be complete; ~ machen to finalize <> *adv* [vollkommen] perfectly.

**Perfekt** (*pl* -e) *das* GRAM perfect.

**Perfektion** *die* perfection.

**perfektionieren** *vt* to perfect.

**perforiert** *adj* perforated.

**Pergament** (*pl* -e) *das* parchment.

**Pergamentpapier** *das* greaseproof paper.

**Periode** (*pl* -n) *die* - **1.** [Epoche, Menstruation] period - **2.** MATH repetend; **1,6** ~ 1.6 recurring.

**periodisch** *adj* periodic <> *adv* periodically.

**peripher** *adj* [gen & EDV] peripheral <> *adv* - **1.** [am Rande] on the periphery - **2.** *geh* [zweitrangig] peripherally.

**Peripherie** [perife'ri:] (*pl* -n) *die* periphery; [von Stadt] outskirts (*pl*); an der ~ einer Stadt on the outskirts of a town.

**Perle** (*pl* -n) *die* - **1.** [Schmuck - aus Muschel] pearl; [ - aus Holz, Glas] bead - **2.** *geh* [Kostbarkeit] gem.

**perlen** (*perf* hat/ist geperlt) *vi* - **1.** (*hat*) [sprudeln] to bubble - **2.** (*ist*) *geh* [abperlen]: Schweiß perlt ihm auf der Stirn beads of sweat are forming on his brow.

**Perlen|kette** *die* pearl necklace.

**Perl|huhn** *das* guinea fowl.

**Perlmutt, Perlmutt** *das* mother of pearl.

**Perlon**® *das* ≈ nylon.

**permanent** *adj* permanent <> *adv* permanently.

**perplex** *adj*: (ganz) ~ sein to be stunned.

**pers.** *abk für* persönlich.

**Perser** (*pl* -) *der* - **1.** [Iraner] Persian - **2.** [Teppich] Persian carpet.

**Perserin** (*pl* -nen) *die* Persian.

**Perser|teppich** *der* Persian carpet.

**Persianer** (*pl* -) *der* Persian lamb.

**Persien** *nt* Persia.

**Persiflage** [pɛrzi'fla:ʒə] (*pl* -n) *die* satire; eine ~ auf jn/etw a satire on sb/sthg.

**persisch** *adj* Persian.

**Persischer Golf** *der*: der ~ the Persian Gulf.

**Person** (*pl* -en) *die* - **1.** [Mensch & GRAM] person; sie ist Köchin und Inhaberin in einer ~ she is chef and owner rolled into one; in (eigener) ~ in person; etw in ~ sein *fig* to be sthg personified - **2.** [Figur] character.

**Personal** *das* staff.

**Personal|abbau** *der* reduction in staff.

**Personal|abteilung** *die* personnel department.

**Personal|ausweis** *der* identity card.

**Personal|chef, in** *der, die* personnel manager.

**Personal|computer** *der* EDV personal computer.

**Personalien** [pɛrzo'na:liən] *pl* personal details.

**Personal|kosten** *pl* staff costs.

**Personal|pronomen** *das* GRAM personal pronoun.

**Personal|rat** *der* - **1.** [Gremium] staff council (*for civil servants*) - **2.** [Vertreter] staff council representative (*for civil servants*).

**Personal|rätin** *die* staff council representative *(for civil servants)*.

**personęll** *adj* staff *(vor Subst)* ◇ *adv* with regard to staff; ~ **unterbesetzt** understaffed.

**Personenkraft|wagen** *der amt* private car.

**Personen|wagen** *der* car.

**persönlich** *adj* personal; ~ **werden** to get personal ◇ *adv* personally; **etw ~ nehmen** to take sthg personally.

**Persönlichkeit** *(pl -en) die* personality.

**Perspektive** [pɛrspɛk'tiːvə] *(pl -n) die* - **1.** [Bildaufbau, Sichtweise] perspective; **aus js ~** from sb's perspective - **2.** [Aussicht] prospect.

**perspektivisch** [pɛrspɛk'tiːvɪʃ] *adj* perspective *(vor Subst)* ◇ *adv* in perspective.

**Peru** *nt* Peru.

**Peruaner, in** *(mpl -; fpl -nen) der, die* Peruvian.

**peruanisch** *adj* Peruvian.

**Perücke** *(pl -n) die* wig.

**pervęrs** [pɛr'vɛrs] *adj* perverted ◇ *adv*: ~ **veranlagt sein** to be perverted.

**Peseta, Pesete** *(pl Peseten) die* peseta.

**Pessar** *(pl -e) das* pessary.

**Pessimįsmus** *der* pessimism.

**Pessimįst, in** *(mpl -en; fpl -nen) der, die* pessimist.

**pessimįstisch** *adj* pessimistic ◇ *adv* pessimistically.

**Pęst** *die (ohne pl)* [Seuche] plague; **jn/etw hassen wie die ~** *fam fig* to absolutely hate sb/sthg; **jn/etw meiden wie die ~** *fam fig* to avoid sb/ sthg like the plague; **stinken wie die ~** *fam fig* to stink to high heaven.

**Pestizįd** *(pl -e) das* pesticide.

**Petersilie** [petɐ'ziːljə] *die* parsley.

**Petition** *(pl -en) die* petition.

**Pętrochemie** *die* petrochemistry.

**Petroleum** [pe'troːleʊm] *das* paraffin *Br,* kerosene *Am.*

**Petroleum|lampe** *die* oil lamp.

**Petunie** *(pl -n) die* petunia.

**pętzen** *vi fam* to tell tales.

**Pfad** *(pl -e) der* [gen & EDV] path.

**Pfadfinder, in** *(mpl -; fpl -nen) der, die* boy scout *(f* girl guide *Br,* girl scout *Am).*

**Pfaffe** *(pl -n) der fam abw* cleric.

**Pfahl** *(pl Pfähle) der* post.

**Pfalz** *die:* **die ~** the Palatinate.

**Pfälzer** *(pl -) der* native/inhabitant of the Palatinate ◇ *adj (unver)* of/from the Palatinate.

**Pfälzerin** *(pl -nen) die* native/inhabitant of the Palatinate.

**pfälzisch** *adj* of/from the Palatinate.

**Pfand** *(pl Pfänder) das* [von Flasche] deposit; [als Sicherheit] security; [beim Pfänderspiel] token; **etw als ~ nehmen** to take sthg as security.

**Pfand|brief** *der* mortgage bond.

**pfänden** *vt* to seize.

**Pfand|flasche** *die* returnable bottle.

**Pfand|haus** *das* pawnshop.

**Pfändung** *(pl -en) die* seizure *(U).*

**Pfanne** *(pl -n) die* (frying) pan; **jn in die ~ hauen** *fam fig* to tear sb to pieces.

**Pfann|kuchen** *der* pancake.

**Pfarrei** *(pl -en) die* parish.

**Pfarrer** *(pl -) der* [katholisch] priest; [evangelisch] minister.

**Pfarrerin** *(pl -nen) die* minister.

**Pfarr|haus** *das* [katholisch] presbytery; [evangelisch] minister's house.

**Pfau** *(pl -en) der* peacock.

**Pfd.** *(abk für Pfund)* lb.

**Pfęffer** *der* pepper.

**Pfęffer|kuchen** *der* gingerbread.

**Pfęfferminze, Pfeffermįnze** *die* peppermint.

**Pfęffer|mühle** *die* pepper mill.

**pfęffern** *vt* - **1.** [würzen] to put pepper on/in - **2.** *fam* [werfen] to chuck - **3.** *fam* [ohrfeigen]: **jm eine ~** to give sb a clout.

**Pfeife** *(pl -n) die* - **1.** [zum Rauchen, Musikinstrument] pipe; **nach js ~ tanzen** *fam fig* to dance to sb's tune; **~ rauchen** to smoke a pipe - **2.** [zum Pfeifen] whistle - **3.** *fam abw* [Mensch] dead loss.

**pfeifen** *(prät pfiff; perf hat gepfiffen) vi* to whistle; **auf jn/etw ~** *fam fig* not to give a damn about sb/sthg ◇ *vt* - **1.** [Lied] to whistle - **2.** [Spiel] to referee.

**Pfeil** *(pl -e) der* - **1.** [Waffe, Hinweiszeichen] arrow; **grüner ~** filter arrow - **2.** *fam* [Stichelei] barb.

**GRÜNER PFEIL**

The green filter arrow indicating that drivers can turn right at a crossroads when the traffic lights are red, thereby clearing traffic in the right-hand lane, is being gradually introduced in the Federal Republic, and is based on the system used in the former East Germany. It is the only East German legal measure that has been adopted by the reunited Germany.

**Pfeiler** *(pl -) der* pillar.

**Pfennig** (pl -e ODER -) der pfennig; **keinen ~ haben** fam not to have a penny.

**Pferd** (pl -e) das horse; **aufs falsche/richtige ~ setzen** to back the wrong/right horse.
➤ **zu Pferd** adv on horseback.

**Pferdeäpfel** pl horse droppings.

**Pferde|rennen** das horse race.

**Pferde|schwanz** der [Frisur] ponytail.

**Pferde|sport** der (ohne pl) equestrian sports (pl).

**Pferde|stall** der stable.

**Pferde|stärke** die horsepower (U).

**pfiff** prät ▷ pfeifen.

**Pfiff** (pl -e) der - **1.** [Ton] whistle - **2.** fig [Reiz] style; **mit ~** stylish.

**Pfifferling** (pl -e) der chanterelle; **nicht einen ODER keinen ~** fam fig not a thing.

**pfiffig** adj [Mensch, Idee] smart; [Gesicht] knowing ◇ adv cleverly.

**Pfingsten** (ohne Artikel) Whitsun.

**Pfingst|montag** der Whit Monday.

**Pfingst|rose** die peony.

**Pfingst|sonntag** der Whit Sunday.

**Pfirsich** (pl -e) der peach.

**Pflanze** (pl -n) die plant.

**pflanzen** vt to plant.

**Pflanzenschutz|mittel** das pesticide.

**pflanzlich** adj [Nährstoffe, Fasern] plant (vor Subst); [Öl] vegetable (vor Subst); **~e Ernährung** [von Person] vegetarian diet; [von Tier] herbivorous diet ◇ adv: **sich ~ ernähren** [Person] to be a vegetarian; [Tier] to be a herbivore.

**Pflaster** (pl -) das - **1.** [Verband] plaster - **2.** (ohne pl) [Straßenbelag] (road) surface; **ein teures ~ sein** fig to be an expensive place.

**pflastern** vt to pave.

**Pflaster|stein** der paving stone.

**Pflaume** (pl -n) die - **1.** [Frucht] plum - **2.** fam [Mensch] drip.

**Pflaumen|baum** der plum tree.

**Pflaumen|kuchen** der plum tart.

**Pflaumen|mus** das thick plum purée, used like jam.

**Pflege** die - **1.** [von Lebewesen] care; **bei jm in ~ sein** to be looked after by sb; **jn in ~ nehmen/haben** to look after sb; **ein Kind in ~ nehmen** to foster a child - **2.** [von Sprache, Beziehung] cultivation; [von Garten, Tradition] maintenance.

**pflegebedürftig** adj who/which needs looking after.

**Pflege|dienst** der (home) care agency, company that provides care for elderly or sick people in their own homes.

**Pflege|eltern** pl foster parents.

**Pflege|fall** der: **ein ~ sein** to be in (permanent) need of nursing care.

**Pflege|heim** das nursing home.

**Pflege|kind** das foster child.

**pflegeleicht** adj - **1.** [Material] easy-care - **2.** fam [Person] easy to deal with.

**pflegen** vt - **1.** [versorgen] to look after; **jn gesund ~** to nurse sb back to health - **2.** [schonen] to take care of - **3.** [gewohnt sein]: **etw zu tun ~** geh to be in the habit of doing sthg.

**Pflegepersonal** das nursing staff.

**Pfleger, in** (mpl -; fpl -nen) der, die nurse.

**Pflege|versicherung** die insurance covering long-term nursing costs, paid for by employer and employee.

**pfleglich** adj careful ◇ adv carefully.

**Pflicht** (pl -en) die - **1.** [Aufgabe] duty; **etw ist ~** sthg is compulsory - **2.** (ohne pl) SPORT compulsories (pl).

**pflichtbewusst** adj conscientious ◇ adv conscientiously.

**Pflicht|fach** das compulsory subject.

**Pflicht|gefühl** das sense of duty.

**Pflicht|übung** die [in Sport] compulsory exercise; fig duty.

**Pflicht|versicherung** die compulsory insurance.

**Pflock** (pl Pflöcke) der [für Tier] stake; [für Zelt] peg.

**pflücken** vt to pick.

**Pflug** (pl Pflüge) der plough.

**pflügen** vt & vi to plough.

**Pforte** (pl -n) die - **1.** [von Krankenhaus, Firma - Tor] gate; [ - Eingang] entrance - **2.** geh [kleine Tür] door.

**Pförtner, in** (mpl -; fpl -nen) der, die porter.

**Pförtner|loge** die porter's lodge.

**Pfosten** (pl -) der post.

**Pfote** (pl -n) die paw.

**Pfropf** (pl -e) der blockage; [in Ader] clot.

**Pfropfen** (pl -) der stopper.

**pfui** interj ugh!

**Pfund** (pl -e) das - **1.** [Gewicht] 500 grams, ≈ pound - **2.** [Währung] pound.

**pfundweise** adv fam by the pound.

**Pfusch** der (ohne pl) fam abw botched job; **~ machen** to make a botched job of it.

**pfuschen** vi fam abw [unsorgfältig arbeiten] to make a botched job of it; [mogeln] to cheat.

**Pfuscher, in** (mpl -; fpl -nen) der, die fam abw bungler.

**Pfütze** (pl -n) die puddle.

**PH** [peː'haː] (pl -s) die abk für **Pädagogische Hochschule.**

**Phallus** (pl Phalli) der phallus.

**Phänomen** (pl -e) das geh phenomenon.

**phänomenal** adj phenomenal <> adv phenomenally.

**Phantasie** = Fantasie.

**phantasielos** = fantasielos.

**phantasieren** = fantasieren.

**phantasievoll** = fantasievoll.

**phantastisch** = fantastisch.

**Phantom** (pl -e) das phantom.

**Phantom|bild** das Identikit® picture.

**Pharao** (pl -s ODER -aonen) der Pharaoh.

**Pharma|industrie** die pharmaceutical industry.

**Pharmazie** die pharmacy.

**Phase** (pl -n) die phase.

**Philatelie** [filate'liː] die philately.

**Philharmonie** [filharmo'niː] (pl -n) die - **1.** [Orchester] philharmonic orchestra - **2.** [Gebäude] philharmonic hall.

**Philharmoniker** pl Philharmonic (Orchestra) (sg).

**Philippinen** pl: die ~ the Philippines.

**Philologe** (pl -n) der student/teacher of language and literature.

**Philologen|verband** der association of teachers of language and literature.

**Philologie** [filolo'giː] (pl -n) die study of language and literature.

**Philologin** (pl -nen) die student/teacher of language and literature.

**philologisch** adj linguistic and literary <> adv from a linguistic and literary perspective.

**Philosoph, in** (mpl -en; fpl -nen) der, die philosopher.

**Philosophie** [filozo'fiː] (pl -n) die philosophy.

**philosophieren** vi to philosophize; über etw (A) ~ to philosophize about sthg.

**philosophisch** adj philosophical <> adv philosophically.

**phlegmatisch** adj lethargic <> adv lethargically.

**Phobie** [fo'biː] (pl -n) die MED phobia.

**Phon** (pl -s ODER -) das phon.

**Phonetik** = Fonetik.

**phonetisch** = fonetisch.

**Phosphat** (pl -e) das phosphate.

**Phosphor** der phosphorus.

**phosphoreszieren** vi to phosphoresce.

**Phosphor|säure** die phosphoric acid.

**Photosynthese** = Fotosynthese.

**Photo|zelle** = Fotozelle.

**Phrase** (pl -n) die cliché; **leere ~n** empty phrases; **~n dreschen** fam fig to spout clichés.

**pH-|Wert** [peː'haːveːɐt] der pH-value.

**Physik** die physics (U).

**physikalisch** adj - **1.** [gen] physical - **2.** [Forschung, Institut] physics (vor Subst) <> adv in terms of physics.

**Physiker, in** (mpl -; fpl -nen) der, die physicist.

**Physiologie** die physiology.

**physiologisch** adj physiological <> adv physiologically.

**physisch** adj physical <> adv physically.

**Pi** das MATH pi; **~ mal Daumen** fam fig approximately.

**Pianist, in** (mpl -en; fpl -nen) der, die pianist.

**Pickel** (pl -) der - **1.** [Entzündung] spot - **2.** [Gerät] pickaxe; [für Eis] ice-pick.

**pickelig, picklig** adj spotty.

**picken** vt & vi to peck.

**picklig** = pickelig.

**Picknick** (pl -s ODER -e) das picnic; **ein ~ machen** to have a picnic.

**pieken** vi to prick.

**piekfein** adj posh.

**Piep** der: **keinen ~ mehr sagen** fam fig [nicht reden] not to say another word; [tot sein] to have had it.

**piepegal** adj (unver): **das ist mir ~** fam I couldn't care less about that.

**piepen** vi [Vogel] to cheep; [Maus] to squeak; [Piepser] to bleep; **bei dir piepts wohl!** fam fig you're off your head!

**Piepen** das: **zum ~ sein** fam to be a scream.

**Piepser** (pl -) der TELEKOM bleeper.

**Pier** (pl -e ODER -s) der jetty.

**piercen** ⮞ sich piercen vpr: **sich die Nase ~** to have one's nose pierced.

**Piercing** ['piːrsiŋ] (pl -s) das body piercing; **ein ~ in der Zunge/Augenbraue haben** to have a pierced tongue/eyebrow.

**piesacken** vt fam to torment.

**Pietät** [pie'tɛːt] die geh reverence.

**pietätlos** geh adj irreverent <> adv irreverently.

**Pigment** (pl -e) das pigment.

**Pik** (pl -) das - **1.** (ohne Artikel, ohne pl) [Spielfarbe] spades (pl) - **2.** (pl Pik) [Spielkarte] spade; **~bube** jack of spades.

**pikant** adj spicy <> adv - **1.** [scharf]: **etw ~ würzen** to spice sthg well - **2.** [frivol] spicily.

**Pike** (*pl* -n) *die:* etw von der ~ auf lernen *fam fig* to learn sthg by working one's way up from the bottom.

**pikiert** *adj* piqued; **(über etw** (A)) ~ **sein** to be piqued (by sthg) <> *adv* [ansehen] with a piqued look; [antworten] in a piqued voice.

**Pikkolo|flöte** *die* piccolo.

**Piktogramm** (*pl* -e) *das* pictogram.

**Pilger** (*pl* -) *der* pilgrim.

**Pilger|fahrt** *die* pilgrimage.

**Pilgerin** (*pl* -nen) *die* pilgrim.

**pilgern** (*perf* ist gepilgert) *vi* - **1.** [wallfahren] to go on a pilgrimage - **2.** *fam* [laufen] to trek.

**Pille** (*pl* -n) *die* - **1.** [Verhütungsmittel]: **die** ~ the pill; **die** ~ **nehmen** to be on the pill - **2.** *fam* [Tablette] pill.

**Pilot** (*pl* -en) *der* [von Flugzeug] pilot; [von Rennwagen] driver.

**Piloten|schein** *der* pilot's licence.

**Pilotin** (*pl* -nen) *die* [von Flugzeug] pilot; [von Rennwagen] driver.

**Pilot|projekt** *das* pilot project.

**Pils** (*pl* -) *das* Pilsner.

**Pilz** (*pl* -e) *der* - **1.** [Pflanze - essbar] mushroom; [ - giftig] toadstool; **wie ~e aus dem Boden schießen** *fig* to mushroom - **2.** (ohne *pl*) [Hautpilz] fungal infection.

**Pimmel** (*pl* -) *der fam* willy *Br*, peter *Am*.

**PIN** (*pl* -s) (*abk für* **persönliche Identifikationsnummer**) *die* PIN (number).

**pingelig** *fam adj* fussy <> *adv* fussily.

**Pingpong** *das* ping-pong.

**Pinguin** ['pɪŋguiːn] (*pl* -e) *der* penguin.

**Pinie** ['piːnjə] (*pl* -n) *die* stone pine.

**pink** *adj* (unver) bright pink.

**Pink** *das* bright pink.

**pinkeln** *vi fam* to pee.

**Pinn|wand** *die* notice *Br* ODER bulletin *Am* board.

**Pinscher** (*pl* -) *der* pinscher.

**Pinsel** (*pl* -) *der* brush.

**pinseln** *vt* & *vi* to paint.

**Pinte** (*pl* -n) *die fam* bar, pub *Br*.

**Pinzette** (*pl* -n) *die* tweezers (*pl*).

**Pionier** (*pl* -e) *der* - **1.** [Vorkämpfer] pioneer - **2.** [Soldat] engineer.

**Pioniergeist** *der* pioneering spirit.

**Pionierin** (*pl* -nen) *die* pioneer.

**Pipapo** *das fam:* **mit allem** ~ with all the frills.

**Pipeline** ['paiplain] (*pl* -s) *die* pipeline.

**Pipette** (*pl* -n) *die* pipette.

**Pipi** *das fam:* ~ **machen** to do a wee-wee.

**Pirat** (*pl* -en) *der* pirate.

**Piraten|sender** *der* pirate radio station.

**Piratin** (*pl* -nen) *die* pirate.

**Pirsch** *die:* **auf die** ~ **gehen** to go stalking.

**pissen** *vi vulg* to piss.

**Pistazie** [pɪsˈtaːtsjə] (*pl* -n) *die* pistachio.

**Piste** (*pl* -n) *die* - **1.** [für Flugzeuge] runway - **2.** [Skipiste] piste - **3.** [für Fahrzeuge] track.

**Pistole** (*pl* -n) *die* pistol; **jm die** ~ **auf die Brust setzen** *fig* to hold a gun to sb's head; **wie aus der** ~ **geschossen** *fam fig* like a shot.

**pitschenass, pitschnass** *adj fam* soaking wet.

**Pizza** ['pɪtsa] (*pl* -s) *die* pizza.

**Pizzeria** [pɪtseˈriːa] (*pl* **Pizzerien** ODER -s) *die* pizzeria.

**PKK** [peːkaːˈka] (*abk für* **Kurdische Arbeiterpartei**) *die* PKK.

**Pkt.** *abk für* **Punkt.**

**Pkw** ['peːkaːveː] (*pl* -s) (*abk für* **Personenkraftwagen**) *der* car, automobile *Am*.

**plädieren** *vi* - **1.** *geh* [stimmen]: **für etw** ~ to argue for sthg - **2.** RECHT: **für** ODER **auf etw** (A) ~ to plead for sthg.

**Plädoyer** [plɛdoaˈjeː] (*pl* -s) *das* - **1.** RECHT closing argument - **2.** *geh* [Rede] plea.

**Plage** (*pl* -n) *die* nuisance.

**plagen** *vt* to torment; **von etw geplagt sein** to be tormented by sthg.

➤ **sich plagen** *ref* to slave away; **sich mit etw** ~ to slave away at sthg.

**Plagiat** (*pl* -e) *das* - **1.** [Kopieren] plagiarism (*U*) - **2.** [Produkt] imitation.

**Plakat** (*pl* -e) *das* poster.

**plakatieren** *vt* to put up posters for <> *vi* to put up posters.

**Plakette** (*pl* -n) *die* [Tafel] plaque; [Abzeichen] badge.

**Plan** (*pl* **Pläne**) *der* - **1.** [Vorgehensweise, Vorhaben] plan; **einen** ~ **aufstellen** ODER **ausarbeiten** to draw up ODER work out a plan; **Pläne schmieden** to make plans - **2.** [Karte] map - **3.** *RW:* **jn/etw auf den** ~ **rufen** to bring sb/sthg into the fray.

➤ **nach Plan** *adv* according to plan.

**Plane** (*pl* -n) *die* tarpaulin.

**planen** *vt* to plan.

**Planet** (*pl* -en) *der* planet.

**Planetarium** [planeˈtaːrjʊm] (*pl* **Planetarien**) *das* planetarium.

**planieren** *vt* to level.

**Planke** (*pl* -n) *die* plank.

**Plankton** *das* plankton.

**P**

**planlos** *adj* unsystematic ◇ *adv* unsystematically.

**planmäßig** *adj* **- 1.** [nach Plan] scheduled **- 2.** [systematisch] systematic ◇ *adv* **- 1.** [nach Plan] on time **- 2.** [systematisch] systematically.

**Planschlbecken, Plantschbecken** *das* paddling *Br* ODER wading *Am* pool.

**planschen, plantschen** *vi* to splash about.

**Plantage** [plan'ta:ʒə] (*pl* **-n**) *die* plantation.

**Planung** (*pl* **-en**) *die* **- 1.** [Vorbereitung] planning (*U*) **- 2.** [Ergebnis] plan.

**Planwirtschaft** *die* (*ohne pl*) planned economy.

**plappern** *vi* to prattle.

**plärren** *vi abw* **- 1.** [weinen] to wail **- 2.** [rufen] to yell **- 3.** [Krach machen] to blare.

**Plasma** (*pl* **Plasmen**) *das* plasma (*U*).

**Plaste** (*pl* **-n**) *die Ostdt* plastic.

**Plastik** (*pl* **-en**) *das* (*ohne pl*) plastic ◇ *die* sculpture.

**Plastikltüte** *die* plastic bag.

**plastisch** *adj* [dreidimensional] three-dimensional; **eine ~e Darstellung** a vivid description ◇ *adv* **- 1.** [dreidimensional] three-dimensionally **- 2.** [lebendig] vividly.

**Platane** (*pl* **-n**) *die* plane tree.

**Plateaulsohle** *die* platform sole; **Schuhe mit ~n** platform shoes.

**Platin** *das* platinum.

**platonisch** *adj* platonic ◇ *adv* platonically.

**plätschern** (*perf* **hat/ist geplätschert**) *vi* **- 1.** (*ist*) [fließen] to splash; [Bach] to babble **- 2.** (*hat*) [Geräusch machen] to splash.

**platt** *adj* **- 1.** [flach] flat; **einen Platten haben** *fam* to have a flat; **~ sein** *fam fig* to be flabbergasted **- 2.** [nichts sagend] trite ◇ *adv* **- 1.** [flach] flat **- 2.** [nichts sagend] tritely.

**Platt** *das* Low German, *dialect spoken in northern Germany;* **~ sprechen** to speak Low German.

**Plattdeutsch(e)** *das* Low German, *dialect spoken in northern Germany; siehe auch* **Englisch(e)**.

**Platte** (*pl* **-n**) *die* **- 1.** [Bauelement - aus Metall, Glas] sheet; [ - aus Stein, Beton] slab; [ - aus Holz] board **- 2.** [Servierplatte] plate **- 3.** [Schallplatte] record; **eine ~ auflegen** ODER **spielen** to put on ODER play a record; **die ~ kenne ich** *fam fig* I've heard it all before **- 4.** [Herdplatte] ring **- 5.** *fam* [Glatze] bald patch.

➡ **kalte Platte** *die meal of cold meats, cheese, salad etc.*

**Platten** ▷ **platt**.

**plätten** *vt Norddt* [bügeln] to iron; **geplättet sein** *fam fig* to be flabbergasted.

**Plattenlbau** *der* concrete high-rise (*made of prefabricated slabs*).

**Plattensee** *der* Lake Balaton.

**Plattenlspieler** *der* record player.

**Plattlform** *die* platform.

**Plattlfuß** *der* (*ohne pl*) *fam* flat (*tyre*).

➡ **Plattfüße** *pl:* **Plattfüße haben** to have flat feet.

**Plattheit** (*pl* **-en**) *die* **- 1.** [Flachsein] flatness **- 2.** [Banalität] triteness (*U*); [Bemerkung] platitude.

**Platz** (*pl* **Plätze**) *der* **- 1.** [Sitzplatz] seat; **~ nehmen** *geh* to take a seat **- 2.** [Freiraum] room, space; **jm/etw ~ machen** [zur Seite gehen] to make room for sb/sthg; [weichen] to make way for sb/sthg; **keinen/genug ~ haben** to have no/enough room **- 3.** [Stelle, Rang] place; **auf dem ersten/zweiten/dritten ~** in first/second/third place; **auf die Plätze, fertig, los!** on your marks, get set, go! **- 4.** [in Stadt] square **- 5.** [bei Fußball, Hockey] pitch; [bei Tennis, Volleyball] court.

➡ **fehl am Platz** *adj* out of place.

➡ **Platz sparend** *adj* space-saving ◇ *adv* in order to save space.

**Platzangst** *die* claustrophobia.

**Platzanweiser, in** (*mpl* **-**; *fpl* **-nen**) *der, die* usher (*f* usherette).

**Plätzchen** (*pl* **-**) *das* **- 1.** [Platz] spot **- 2.** [Gebäck] biscuit *Br*, cookie *Am*.

**platzen** (*perf* **ist geplatzt**) *vi* **- 1.** [bersten] to burst **- 2.** *fam* [ausfallen, scheitern - Termin, Vorstellung] to be cancelled; [ - Projekt, Vertrag] to fall through; **etw ~ lassen** to cancel sthg; **vor etw** (*D*) **~** to be seething with sthg.

**platzieren** *vt* to place.

➡ **sich platzieren** *ref* [Platz belegen] to be placed.

**Platzierung** (*pl* **-en**) *die* placing (*U*).

**Platzlkarte** *die* seat reservation.

**Platzlkonzert** *das* open-air concert.

**Platzlmangel** *der* lack of space.

**Platzlregen** *der* (*ohne pl*) cloudburst.

**platzsparend** *adj* ▷ **Platz**.

**Platzlverweis** *der* SPORT sending off.

**Platzlwunde** *die* laceration.

**plaudern** *vi* to chat.

**Plausch** *der* (*ohne pl*) chat; **mit jm einen ~ halten** to have a chat with sb.

**plausibel** *adj* plausible; **jm etw ~ machen** to make sthg clear to sb ◇ *adv* plausibly.

**Play-back** ['ple:bɛk] (*pl* **Play-backs**) *der:* **~ spielen** ODER **singen** to mime.

**Playboy** ['ple:bɔy] (*pl* **-s**) *der* playboy.

**Plazenta** (*pl* -s) *die* MED placenta.

**plazieren** *vt* = platzieren.

**Plazierung** *die* = Platzierung.

**pleite** *adj fam*: ~ **sein** to be broke.

**Pleite** (*pl* -n) *die fam* - **1.** [Ruin] bankruptcy; ~ **gehen/machen** to go bust; **vor der ~ stehen** *fam* to be faced with bankruptcy - **2.** [Reinfall] flop.

**Plenar|saal** *der* plenary chamber.

**Plenum** *das* plenary session.

**Plexiglas**® *das* ≃ Perspex®.

**Plombe** (*pl* -n) *die* - **1.** [Zahnfüllung] filling - **2.** [Siegel] lead seal.

**plombieren** *vt* - **1.** [füllen] to fill - **2.** [versiegeln] to put a lead seal on.

**plötzlich** *adj* sudden; **ganz ~** all of a sudden ⇔ *adv* suddenly; **aber ein bisschen ~!** *fam* get a move on!

**plump** *abw adj* clumsy ⇔ *adv* clumsily.

**plumpsen** (*perf* **ist geplumpst**) *vi* to crash; [ins Wasser] to splash.

**Plumps|klo** *das fam* earth closet.

**Plunder** *der fam abw* junk.

**plündern** *vt* - **1.** [ausrauben] to loot - **2.** [leeren] to raid ⇔ *vi* to loot.

**Plünderung** (*pl* -en) *die* looting *(U)*.

**Plur.** (*abk für* **Plural**) pl.

**Plural** (*pl* -e) *der* GRAM plural; **im ~** in the plural.

**pluralistisch** *adj* pluralistic ⇔ *adv* pluralistically.

**plus** *adv, präp* & *konj* plus.

**Plus** *das (ohne pl)* - **1.** [Mehrbetrag]: **(ein) ~ (von 100 Euro) machen** to make a profit (of 100 euros); **im ~ stehen** to be in credit - **2.** [Vorteil] advantage.

**Plüsch** *der* plush.

**Plüsch|tier** *das* cuddly toy.

**Plus|pol** *der* positive pole.

**Plus|punkt** *der* - **1.** [Vorteil] plus point - **2.** [Punkt] point.

**Plusquam|perfekt** *das* GRAM pluperfect.

**Plutonium** *das* CHEM plutonium.

**PLZ** *abk für* **Postleitzahl**.

**Po** (*pl* -s) *der* bottom.

**Pöbel** *der (ohne pl)* mob.

**pochen** *vi* - **1.** [klopfen] to knock; **auf etw** *(A)* ~ *fig* to insist on sthg - **2.** [pulsieren - Herz] to pound; [ - Blut] to throb.

**Pocken** *pl* MED smallpox *(U)*.

**Podest** (*pl* -e) *das* [für Redner] rostrum; [für Orchester, Chor] platform.

**Podium** ['poːdiʊm] (*pl* **Podien**) *das* podium.

**Podiums|diskussion** *die* panel discussion.

**Poesie** *die geh* poetry.

**Poesie|album** *das child's autograph book in which friends and relatives write poems and sayings.*

**Poet, in** (*mpl* -en; *fpl* -nen) *der, die* poet.

**poetisch** *adj* poetic ⇔ *adv* poetically.

**Pogrom** (*pl* -e) *der* ODER *das* pogrom.

**Pointe** ['poɛ̃ːtə] (*pl* -n) *die* punchline.

**pointiert** ['poɛ̃ˈtiːɐ̯t] *adj* trenchant ⇔ *adv* trenchantly.

**Pokal** (*pl* -e) *der* - **1.** [Trophäe] cup - **2.** [Gefäß] goblet.

**Pokal|sieger, in** *der, die* cup winner.

**Pokal|spiel** *das* cup tie.

**Poker** *der* ODER *das* poker.

**pokern** *vi* to play poker; **um etw ~** *fig* to play for high stakes to get sthg.

**Pol** (*pl* -e) *der* pole; **er ist in der Familie der ruhende ~** he is the calming influence in the family.

**polar** *adj* polar.

**Polarisierung** (*pl* -en) *die* polarization *(U)*.

**Polar|kreis** *der* polar circle.

**Polaroid|kamera**® *die* Polaroid camera®.

**Polarstern** *der* ASTRON: **der ~** the Pole Star.

**Pole** (*pl* -n) *der* Pole.

**Polemik** (*pl* -en) *die* - **1.** [Streit] polemic - **2.** [Schärfe] polemical nature.

**polemisch** *adj* polemical ⇔ *adv* polemically.

**polemisieren** *vi* to polemize.

**Polen** *nt* Poland.

**Police** [poˈliːsə] (*pl* -n) *die* policy.

**Polier** (*pl* -e) *der* foreman.

**polieren** *vt* to polish.

**Poli|klinik** *die* outpatients' clinic.

**Polin** (*pl* -nen) *die* Pole.

**Politesse** (*pl* -n) *die* traffic warden.

**Politik** *die (ohne pl)* - **1.** [des Staates] politics *(U)* - **2.** [Vorgehensweise] policy.

**Politiker, in** (*mpl* -; *fpl* -nen) *der, die* politician.

**politisch** *adj* political ⇔ *adv* politically.

**Politologie** *die* political science.

**Politur** (*pl* -en) *die* polish.

**Polizei** *die (ohne pl)* police *(pl)*.

**Polizeiauf|gebot** *das* police contingent.

**Polizei|auto** *das* police car.

**Polizei|beamte** *der* police officer.

**Polizei|beamtin** *die* police officer.

**Polizei|hund** *der* police dog.

**polizeilich** *adj* police *(vor Subst)*; **~es Kennzei**chen registration *Br ODER* license *Am* number <> *adv* by the police.

**Polizei|präsident, in** *der, die* chief constable *Br*, chief of police *Am*.

**Polizei|präsidium** *das* police headquarters *(pl)*.

**Polizei|revier** *das* - **1.** [Polizeiwache] police station - **2.** [Bereich] police district.

**Polizei|schutz** *der* police protection; **unter ~ stehen** to be under police protection.

**Polizei|streife** *die* police patrol.

**Polizei|stunde** *die (ohne pl)* closing time.

**Polizei|wache** *die* police station.

**Polizist, in** *(mpl -en; fpl -nen) der, die* policeman *(f* policewoman*)*.

**Pollen** *(pl -) der* pollen *(U)*.

**Poller** *(pl -) der* bollard.

**polnisch** *adj* Polish.

**Polnisch(e)** *das* Polish; *siehe auch* **Englisch(e)**.

**Polo** *das* polo.

**Polo|hemd** *das* polo shirt.

**Polonäse, Polonaise** [polo'nɛːzə] *(pl -n) die* polonaise.

**Polster** *(pl -) das* - **1.** [zum Sitzen, finanziell] cushion - **2.** [Schulterpolster] shoulder pad - **3.** *fam* [Fettpolster] wad of fat.

**Polstermöbel** *pl* upholstered furniture *(U)*.

**polstern** *vt* - **1.** [Möbel] to upholster - **2.** [Kleidung] to pad.

**Polsterung** *(pl -en) die* - **1.** [Polstern] upholstering - **2.** [Polster] upholstery *(U)*.

**Polter|abend** *der celebration usually held on the evening before a wedding, when crockery is broken to bring good luck.*

**poltern** *(perf* **hat/ist gepoltert***) vi* - **1.** (ist) [sich laut bewegen] to crash - **2.** (hat) [Krach machen] to make a racket; **draußen hat etwas gepoltert** there was a crash outside - **3.** (hat) [am Polterabend] *to celebrate a "Polterabend".*

**Polyester** [poli'ɛstɐ] *das* polyester.

**Polygamie** [poliga'miː] *die* polygamy.

**Polyp** [po'lyːp] *(pl -en) der* - **1.** [in der Nase] adenoid - **2.** *salopp* [Polizist] cop - **3.** [Tintenfisch] octopus.

**Pommern** *nt* Pomerania.

**Pommes** ['pɔməs] *pl fam* chips *Br*, French fries *Am*.

**Pommes frites** [pɔm'friːts] *pl* chips *Br*, French fries *Am*.

**Pomp** *der* pomp.

**pompös** *adj* lavish <> *adv* lavishly.

**Poncho** ['pɔntʃo] *(pl -s) der* poncho.

**Pony** ['pɔni] *(pl -s) das* pony <> *der* fringe *Br*, bangs *Am*.

**Pool** [puːl] *(pl -s) der* pool.

**Pop** *der* pop.

**Popcorn** *das* popcorn.

**Popel** *(pl -) der fam* [in der Nase] snot *(U)*, bogey *Br*.

**popelig, poplig** *fam abw adj* - **1.** [minderwertig] lousy - **2.** [geizig] stingy - **3.** [gewöhnlich] ordinary <> *adv* - **1.** [geizig] stingily - **2.** [billig] cheaply.

**Popelin** *der* poplin.

**popeln** *vi fam:* **in der Nase ~** to pick one's nose.

**Pop|gruppe** *die* pop group.

**Pop|konzert** *das* pop concert.

**poplig** = **popelig**.

**Popmusik** *die* pop music.

**Popo** *(pl -s) der fam* bottom.

**populär** *adj* popular <> *adv:* **~ schreiben** to write in an accessible way.

**Popularität** *die* popularity.

**populärwissenschaftlich** *adj* popular science *(vor Subst)* <> *adv* in a popular scientific way.

**Pore** *(pl -n) die* pore.

**Porno** *(pl -s) der fam* [Film] porn film; [Pornoheft] porn mag.

**Porno|film** *der* porn film.

**Pornografie, Pornographie** *die* pornography.

**pornografisch, pornographisch** *adj* pornographic <> *adv* pornographically.

**porös** *adj* porous.

**Porree** *der (ohne pl)* leek.

**Portal** *(pl -e) das* portal.

**Portier** [pɔr'tjeː] *(pl -s) der* porter.

**Portion** *(pl -en) die* - **1.** [von Essen] portion - **2.** [viel] amount.
 ➡ **halbe Portion** *die:* **eine halbe ~** *fam* a little shrimp.

**Portmonee, Portemonnaie** [pɔrtmɔ'neː] *(pl -s) das* purse.

**Porto** *(pl -s) das* postage *(U)*.

**portofrei** *adj* & *adv* post-free *Br*, postpaid *Am*.

**Porträt** [pɔr'trɛː] *(pl -s) das* portrait.

**porträtieren** *vt* to do a portrait of.

**Portugal** *nt* Portugal.

**Portugiese** *(pl -n) der* Portuguese.

**Portugiesin** *(pl -nen) die* Portuguese.

**portugiesisch** *adj* Portuguese.

**Portugiesisch(e)** *das* Portuguese; *siehe auch* Englisch(e).

**Port|wein** *der* port.

**Porzellan** (*pl* -e) *das* - **1.** [Material] porcelain - **2.** [Geschirr] china.

**pos.** (*abk für* **positiv**) pos.

**Posaune** (*pl* -n) *die* trombone.

**Pose** (*pl* -n) *die* pose.

**posieren** *vi* to pose.

**Position** (*pl* -en) *die* position.

**Positions|licht** *das* FLUG, SCHIFF navigation light.

**positiv** *adj* positive ◇ *adv* positively.

**Positur** *die*: sich in ~ setzen *ODER* stellen *fam* to strike a pose.

**Posse** (*pl* -n) *die* farce.

**Possessiv|pronomen** *das* GRAM possessive pronoun.

**possierlich** *adj* comical ◇ *adv* comically.

**Post** *die* (*ohne pl*) - **1.** [Institution, Amt] post office; etw mit der ~ schicken to send sthg by post *Br ODER* mail *Am*; auf die *ODER* zur ~ gehen to go to the post office - **2.** [Postsendung] post *Br*, mail *Am*; (und) ab (geht) die ~! *fam fig* (and) off we/you go!

**Post|amt** *das* post office.

**Post|anweisung** *die* ≈ postal order *Br*, ≈ money order *Am*.

**Post|bote** *der* postman *Br*, mailman *Am*.

**Post|botin** *die* postwoman *Br*, mailwoman *Am*.

**Posten** (*pl* -) *der* - **1.** [Ware] item - **2.** [Arbeitsstelle, Wachposten] post - **3.** *RW*: auf verlorenem ~ stehen to be fighting a losing battle; auf dem ~ sein *fam* to be fit; nicht auf dem ~ sein *fam* to be under the weather.

**Poster** (*pl* -) *der ODER das* poster.

**Postf.** *abk für* **Postfach**.

**Post|fach** *das* PO box.

**Postgiro|konto** *das* post office giro account.

**Post|karte** *die* postcard.

**postlagernd** *adj* & *adv* poste restante *Br*, general delivery *Am*.

**Postleit|zahl** *die* postcode *Br*, zip code *Am*.

**postmodern** *adj* postmodern ◇ *adv* in a postmodern manner.

**Post|scheck** *der* post office giro cheque.

**Postscheck|konto** *das* post office giro account.

**Postspar|buch** *das* post office savings book.

**Postspar|kasse** *die* post office savings bank.

**Post|stempel** *der* postmark.

**Post|weg** *der*: etw auf dem ~ schicken to send sthg by post *Br ODER* mail *Am*; auf dem ~ verloren gehen to get lost in the post *Br ODER* mail *Am*.

**postwendend** *adv* by return (of post) *Br*, by return mail *Am*.

**Postwert|zeichen** *das amt* postage stamp.

**Postwurf|sendung** *die* direct-mail item.

**potent** *adj* - **1.** [Mann] potent - **2.** *geh* [solvent] financially strong - **3.** *geh* [mächtig] powerful.

**Potenz** (*pl* -en) *die* - **1.** [sexuelle] potency - **2.** [Kraft & MATH] power; die zweite/dritte ~ von fünf the square/cube of five.

**Potenzial, Potential** [potɛn'tsiaːl] (*pl* -e) *das* potential.

**potenziell, potentiell** [potɛn'tsiɛl] *adj* potential ◇ *adv* potentially.

**Potpourri** [ˈpɔtpʊriː] (*pl* -s) *das* medley.

**Potsdam** *nt* Potsdam.

**Pott** (*pl* Pötte) *der Norddt fam* pot.

**Poularde** [puˈlardə] (*pl* -n) *die* poulard.

**Power** [ˈpaʊɐ] *die fam* oomph; ~ haben to have oomph.

**powern** [ˈpaʊɐn] *vi* to beaver away.

**pp.** (*abk für* **pergite (und so fort)**) etc.

**PR** (*abk für* **Publicrelations**) PR.

**Pracht** *die* magnificence; eine wahre ~ sein *fam* to be magnificent.

**Pracht|exemplar** *das* [Gegenstand] magnificent example; [Person] magnificent specimen.

**prächtig** *adj* - **1.** [wunderschön] magnificent - **2.** [hervorragend] marvellous ◇ *adv* - **1.** [wunderschön] magnificently - **2.** [hervorragend] marvellously.

**prachtvoll** *adj* magnificent ◇ *adv* magnificently.

**prädestinieren** *vt*: zu/für etw prädestiniert sein to be ideally suited to be sthg/for sthg.

**Prädikat** (*pl* -e) *das* - **1.** [Gütezeichen] rating - **2.** GRAM predicate.

**prädikativ** GRAM *adj* predicative ◇ *adv* predicatively.

**Präfix** (*pl* -e) *das* GRAM prefix.

**Prag** *nt* Prague.

**prägen** *vt* - **1.** [in der Entwicklung] to influence; von etw geprägt sein to be influenced by sthg - **2.** [von Anfang an] to shape - **3.** [Wort] to coin - **4.** [Münzen] to mint; [Metall, Leder] to emboss.

**Prager** (*pl* -) *der* native/inhabitant of Prague ◇ *adj (unver)* of/from Prague.

**Prager Frühling** *der* HIST: der ~ the Prague Spring.

**Pragerin** (pl -nen) die native/inhabitant of Prague.

**pragmatisch** adj pragmatic ⬦ adv pragmatically.

**prägnant** adj concise ⬦ adv concisely.

**Prägung** (pl -en) die - **1.** [Muster] impression - **2.** [in der Entwicklung] influence; **gesellschaftliche ~** social influence - **3.** [von Anfang an] shaping - **4.** [von Worten] coining (U).

**prähistorisch** adj prehistoric.

**prahlen** vi to boast; **mit etw ~** to boast about sthg.

**prakt. Arzt** (pl prakt. Ärzte) (abk für **praktischer Arzt**) der GP.

**Praktik** (pl -en) die practice.
➡ **Praktiken** pl abw practices.

**praktikabel** adj practicable ⬦ adv practicably.

**Praktikant, in** (mpl -en; fpl -nen) der, die trainee.

**Praktiker, in** (mpl -; fpl -nen) der, die practical person.

**Praktikum** (pl **Praktika**) das work placement; **ein ~ machen** ODER **absolvieren** to be on a work placement.

**praktisch** adj practical ⬦ adv - **1.** [gen] practically; **~ alles** practically everything - **2.** [nicht theoretisch] in practice.

**praktizieren** vt & vi to practise.

**Praline** (pl -n) die chocolate.

**prall** adj [Po, Busen] well-rounded; [Sack] bulging; [Tomate] firm; **in der ~en Sonne** under the blazing sun ⬦ adv: **~ gefüllt** filled to bursting.

**prallen** (perf hat/ist geprallt) vi - **1.** (ist) [stoßen]: **gegen/auf etw** (A) **~** to crash into sthg; **er ist mit dem Kopf auf den Boden geprallt** he banged his head on the floor - **2.** (hat) [Sonne] to blaze down.

**Prämie** ['prɛːmjə] (pl -n) die - **1.** [Beitrag] premium - **2.** [Belohnung] reward - **3.** [Sonderzahlung] bonus.

**Prämiensparen** das (ohne pl) premium-aided savings scheme.

**prämieren** vt to give an award to.

**Prämisse** (pl -n) die geh premise.

**prangen** vi to be prominently displayed.

**Pranger** (pl -) der: **jn/etw an den ~ stellen** fig to pillory sb/sthg.

**Pranke** (pl -n) die paw.

**Präparat** (pl -e) das geh preparation.

**Präposition** (pl -en) die GRAM preposition.

**Prärie** [prɛˈriːl] (pl -n) die prairie.

**Präsens** ['prɛːzɛns] das GRAM present (tense).

**präsent** adj geh present; **etw ~ haben** to think of sthg.

**präsentieren** vt to present.

**Präsentierteller** der: **auf dem ~ sitzen** abw & fig to be on public display.

**Präsenz** die geh presence.

**Präservativ** [prɛzɛrvaˈtiːf] (pl -e) das condom.

**Präsident, in** (mpl -en; fpl -nen) der, die president.

**Präsidentschaft** (pl -en) die presidency.

**Präsidium** [prɛˈziːdjum] (pl -dien) das - **1.** [von Verein] committee - **2.** [Polizeipräsidium] headquarters (pl).

**prasseln** (perf hat/ist geprasselt) vi - **1.** (ist) [Regen] to drum - **2.** (hat) [Feuer] to crackle.

**Prater** der (ohne pl) large park near Vienna containing permanent funfair.

**Präteritum** das GRAM preterite.

**Praxis** (pl **Praxen**) die - **1.** [Wirklichkeit] practice; **etw in die ~ umsetzen** to put sthg into practice - **2.** [Erfahrung] experience - **3.** [Räumlichkeit - von Anwalt] office; [ - von Arzt] surgery Br, office Am.
➡ **in der Praxis** adv in practice.

**praxisfern** adj impractical ⬦ adv impractically.

**praxisnah** adj practical ⬦ adv practically.

**Präzedenzlfall** der precedent.

**präzis, präzise** adj precise ⬦ adv precisely.

**präzisieren** vt geh to state more precisely.

**Präzision** die precision.

**Präzisionsarbeit** die precision work.

**predigen** vt & vi to preach.

**Prediger, in** (mpl -; fpl -nen) der, die preacher.

**Predigt** (pl -en) die sermon; **(jm) eine ~ halten** to give (sb) a sermon.

**Preis** (pl -e) der - **1.** [Geldbetrag] price - **2.** [ausgesetzte Prämie] prize - **3.** RW: **der ~ für etw** the price of sthg; **um jeden/keinen ~** at any/not at any price.
➡ **zum halben Preis** adv at half-price.

**Preisanstieg** der (ohne pl) rise in prices.

**Preislschreiben** das competition.

**preisbewusst** adj price-conscious ⬦ adv price-consciously.

**Preislbindung** die retail price maintenance.

**Preisellbeere** die cranberry.

**preisen** (prät pries; perf hat gepriesen) vt geh to praise; **sich glücklich ~** to count o.s. lucky.

**Preislerhöhung** die price increase.

**Preis|frage** *die* - **1.** [Quizfrage] prize question - **2.** [Kostenfrage] question of price.

**Preis|gabe** *die geh* [Verrat] betrayal; [Aufgabe] relinquishing.

**preis|geben** *vt (unreg) geh* - **1.** [verraten] to betray - **2.** [ausliefern] to abandon - **3.** [aufgeben] to relinquish.

**preisgekrönt** *adj* prizewinning.

**preisgünstig** *adj* cheap ◇ *adv* cheaply.

**Preis|lage** *die* price range; **in allen ~n** at all prices; **in dieser ~** in this price range.

**preislich** *adj* price *(vor Subst)* ◇ *adv* with regard to price.

**Preis|liste** *die* price list.

**Preis|nachlass** *der* price reduction.

**Preis|rätsel** *das* prize puzzle.

**Preis|richter, in** *der, die* judge.

**Preis|schild** *(pl -er) das* price tag.

**Preis|senkung** *die* price reduction.

**Preis|steigerung** *die* price increase.

**Preis|träger, in** *der, die* prizewinner.

**Preis|verleihung** *die* prize ceremony.

**preiswert** *adj* cheap ◇ *adv* cheaply.

**Prell|bock** *der* buffers *(pl).*

**prellen** *vt* - **1.** [betrügen] to cheat; **jn um etw ~** to cheat sb out of sthg - **2.** [stoßen]: **sich** *(D)* **den Schenkel/Arm ~** to bruise one's thigh/arm - **3.** [Ball] to bounce.

**Prellung** *(pl -en) die* bruise.

**Premiere** [prə'mjeːrə] *(pl -n) die* premiere.

**Premier|minister, in** [prə'mjeːminɪstɐ, rɪn] *der, die* prime minister.

**Presbyter, in** *(mpl -; fpl -nen) der, die* REL elder.

**preschen** *(perf ist gepprescht) vi* to tear.

**Presse** *(pl -n) die* press.

**Presse|agentur** *die* press agency.

**Presse|bericht** *der* press report.

**Presse|chef, in** *der, die* press officer.

**Presse|erklärung** *die* press release.

**Presse|fotograf, in** *der, die* press photographer.

**Presse|freiheit** *die* freedom of the press.

**Presse|konferenz** *die* press conference.

**Presse|meldung** *die* press report.

**pressen** *vt* to press ◇ *vi* [Schwangere] to push.

**Presse|sprecher, in** *der, die* press officer.

**Presse|stelle** *die* press office.

**Pressluft|hammer** *der* pneumatic hammer.

**Prestige** [prɛs'tiːʒə] *das* prestige.

**Preuße** *(pl -n) der* HIST Prussian.

**Preußen** *nt* HIST Prussia.

**Preußin** *(pl -nen) die* HIST Prussian.

**preußisch** *adj* HIST Prussian.

**prickeln** *vi* - **1.** [kitzeln] to tingle; **in meinen Händen prickelt es** my hands are tingling - **2.** [perlen] to sparkle.

**prickelnd** *adj* [Gefühl] thrilling; [Wein, Wasser] sparkling.

**pries** *prät* ⊳ **preisen.**

**Priester, in** *(mpl -; fpl -nen) der, die* - **1.** [katholischer] priest - **2.** [heidnischer] priest *(f* priestess).

**prima** *fam adj (unver)* fantastic ◇ *adv* fantastically.

**primär** *geh adj* primary ◇ *adv* primarily.

**Primel** *(pl -n) die* primula.

**primitiv** *adj* - **1.** [gen] primitive - **2.** [Regeln, Bedürfnisse] basic ◇ *adv* primitively.

**Prim|zahl** *die* MATH prime number.

**Prinz** *(pl -en) der* prince.

**Prinzessin** *(pl -nen) die* princess.

**Prinzip** *(pl -ien) das* principle.
➡ **aus Prinzip** *adv* on principle.
➡ **im Prinzip** *adv* in principle.

**prinzipiell** *adj* basic ◇ *adv* - **1.** [aus Prinzip] on principle; [im Prinzip] in principle - **2.** [grundsätzlich] basically.

**Priorität** *(pl -en) die* priority.
➡ **Prioritäten** *pl* priorities; **~en setzen** to prioritize.

**Prise** *(pl -n) die:* **eine ~ Salz/Pfeffer** a pinch of salt/pepper.

**Prisma** *(pl Prismen) das* prism.

**Pritsche** *(pl -n) die* plank bed.

**pritschen** *vt* SPORT to flick.

**priv.** *(abk für privat)* priv.

**privat** [pri'vaːt] *adj* private; **an ~ verkaufen** to sell privately; **von ~ kaufen** to buy privately ◇ *adv* privately.

**Privat|adresse** *die* home address.

**Privatan|gelegenheit** *die* private matter; **das ist meine ~** that is a private matter.

P

**Privatan|schrift** *die* home address.

**Privat|besitz** *der* private property.
➤ in Privatbesitz *adv* in private hands.

**Privat|detektiv, in** *der, die* private detective.

**Privat|dozent, in** *der, die* lecturer *(without a salaried position)*.

**Privat|eigentum** *das* private property.

**Privat|fernsehen** *das* commercial television.

**Privat|gespräch** *das* private conversation.

**Privat|initiative** *die* private initiative.

**privatisieren** [privati'ziːrən] *vt* to privatize.

**Privatisierung** [privati'ziːruŋ] *(pl -en) die* privatization.

**Privat|leben** *das (ohne pl)* private life.

**Privat|patient, in** *der, die* private patient.

**Privat|person** *die* private person.

**Privat|sache** *die* private matter.

**Privat|schule** *die* private school.

**Privat|sender** *der* commercial television channel.

**Privat|sphäre** *die* private life.

**Privat|unterkunft** *die* private accommodation *(U)*.

**Privat|unterricht** *der* private tuition.

**Privileg** [privi'leːk] *(pl -ien) das* privilege.

**privilegiert** [privile'giːɡt] *adj* privileged ◇ *adv:* ~ leben to have a privileged lifestyle.

**pro** *präp* per; einmal ~ Tag once a day ◇ *adv:* ~ und kontra argumentieren to argue for and against.

**Pro** *(pl -s) das:* das ~ und Kontra the pros and cons *(pl)*.

**Probe** *(pl -n) die* - 1. [Test] test; jn/etw auf die ~ stellen to put sb/sthg to the test - 2. [Stichprobe, Warenprobe] sample - 3. [Übung] rehearsal.
➤ auf Probe *adv* on a trial basis.

**Probe|alarm** *der* [für Brandfall] fire drill.

**Probe|exemplar** *das* specimen copy.

**Probe|fahrt** *die* test drive.

**Probe|lauf** *der* trial run.

**proben** *vt* & *vi* to rehearse.

**probeweise** *adv* on a trial basis.

**Probe|zeit** *die* trial period.

**probieren** *vt* to try.

**Problem** *(pl -e) das* problem; ~e mit jm/etw haben to have problems with sb/sthg; ~e wälzen to chew problems over.
➤ kein Problem *interj* no problem!

**Problematik** *die (ohne pl) geh* problems *(pl)*.

**problematisch** *adj* problematic.

**problematisieren** *vt geh* to make a problem out of.

**problemlos** *adj* problem-free ◇ *adv* without any problems.

**Produkt** *(pl -e) das* product.

**Produktion** *(pl -en) die* - 1. [Herstellung] production - 2. [Erzeugnis] product; [Film, Sendung] production.

**Produktionskosten** *pl* production costs.

**produktiv** *adj* productive ◇ *adv* productively.

**Produktivität** [produktivi'tɛːt] *die* productivity.

**Produzent, in** *(mpl -en; fpl -nen) der, die* producer.

**produzieren** *vt* - 1. [Ware, Film] to produce - 2. *fam abw* [machen] to make.
➤ sich produzieren *ref fam* to show off.

**Prof.** *(abk für Professor)* Prof.

**profan** *geh adj* mundane ◇ *adv* mundanely.

**professionell** *adj* professional ◇ *adv* professionally.

**Professor** *(pl -oren) der* professor; ordentlicher ~ (full) professor *(who holds a chair)*; außerordentlicher ~ extraordinary professor *(who does not hold a chair)*; ein zerstreuter ~ *fig* a scatterbrain.

**Professorin** *(pl -nen) die* professor.

**Professur** *(pl -en) die* professorship.

**Profi** *(pl -s) der* professional.

**Profil** *(pl -e) das* - 1. [Persönlichkeit] image - 2. [Seitenansicht] profile - 3. [von Reifen, Sohle] tread.

**profilieren** ➤ sich profilieren *ref* to make one's mark.

**profiliert** *adj* prominent.

**Profil|sohle** *die* treaded sole.

**Profit** *(pl -e) der* profit; aus etw ~ schlagen ODER ziehen *fig* to profit from sthg; *eigtl* to make a profit out of sthg; ~ machen to make a profit.

**profitieren** *vi:* von etw ~ to profit from sthg.

**pro forma** *adv* for form's sake.

**Prognose** *(pl -n) die* prognosis.

**Programm** *(pl -e) das* - 1. [Programmvorschau] listings *(pl)* - 2. [Sendungen] programmes *(pl)* - 3. [Sender] channel; das erste/zweite ~ Channel One/Two - 4. [Programmheft, Veranstaltungsablauf, Konzeption] programme; auf dem ~ stehen to be on the programme - 5. [Tagesablauf] schedule; auf dem ~ stehen to be on the agenda - 6. *EDV* program.
➤ nach Programm *adv* according to plan.

**programmgemäß** *adj* & *adv* according to plan.

**Programm|heft** *das* programme.

**Programm|hinweis** *der* programme announcement.

**programmieren** *vt* - **1.** [Computer] to program - **2.** [Videorecorder] to programme.

**Programmierer, in** (*mpl* -; *fpl* -nen) *der, die* EDV programmer.

**Programmier|sprache** *die* EDV programming language.

**Programmierung** (*pl* -en) *die* EDV programming (*U*).

**Programm|punkt** *der* item (*on programme/agenda*).

**Programmvor|schau** *die* preview.

**progressiv** *adj* progressive <> *adv* progressively.

**Projekt** (*pl* -e) *das* project.

**Projektor** (*pl* -toren) *der* projector.

**projizieren** *vt* to project.

**Prokurist, in** (*mpl* -en; *fpl* -nen) *der, die* representative of a company who holds full commercial authority.

**Prolet** (*pl* -en) *der abw* peasant.

**Proletarier, in** [proleˈtaːrjə, rɪn] (*mpl* -; *fpl* -nen) *der, die* proletarian.

**Prolog** (*pl* -e) *der* prologue.

**Promenade** (*pl* -n) *die* promenade.

**Promenaden|mischung** *die abw* mongrel.

**Promille** (*pl* -) *das* - **1.** MATH thousandth - **2.** [Alkoholgehalt] alcohol level; **er hatte 1,5 ~** he had a blood alcohol level of 1.5 parts per thousand.

**Promille|grenze** *die* legal (alcohol) limit.

**prominent** *adj* prominent.

**Prominente** (*pl* -n) *der, die* prominent figure.

**Prominenz** *die* (*ohne pl*) prominent figures (*pl*).

**Promotion¹** [proˈmoʊʃən] (*pl* -en) *die* UNI doctorate.

**Promotion²** [proˈmoʊʃən] *die* WIRTSCH promotion.

**promovieren** [promoˈviːrən] *vi* to gain a doctorate.

**promoviert** [promoˈviːɐt] *adj:* **sie ist ~e Mathematikerin** she has a doctorate in mathematics.

**prompt** *adj* prompt <> *adv* [erwartungsgemäß] of course; [sofort] promptly.

**Pronomen** (*pl* - ODER **Pronomina**) *das* GRAM pronoun.

**Propaganda** *die* - **1.** [Verbreitung] propaganda - **2.** [Werbung]: **für jn/etw ~ machen** to publicize sb/sthg.

**propagieren** *vt* to propagate.

**Propangas** *das* propane (gas).

**Propeller** (*pl* -) *der* propeller.

**proper** *fam adj* neat <> *adv* neatly.

**Prophet, in** (*mpl* -en; *fpl* -nen) *der, die* prophet (*f* prophetess).

**prophetisch** *adj* prophetic <> *adv* prophetically.

**prophezeien** *vt* to predict; [Subj: prophet] to prophesy; **jm etw ~** to predict sthg for sb.

**Proportion** (*pl* -en) *die* proportion.

**proportional** *adj* proportional <> *adv* proportionally.

**Proporz** (*pl* -e) *der* proportional representation (*U*).

**proppevoll, proppenvoll** *fam adj* chock-a-block <> *adv* to bursting point.

**Prosa** *die* prose.

**prosaisch** *geh adj* prosaic <> *adv* prosaically.

**prosit, prost** *interj* cheers!; **na denn** ODER **dann ~! fam fig** that's a fine lookout.
➔ **prost Neujahr!** *interj* Happy New Year!

**Prospekt** (*pl* -e) *der* brochure.

**Prostata** *die* prostate (gland).

**Prostituierte** (*pl* -n) *die* prostitute.

**Prostitution** *die* prostitution.

**prot.** (*abk für* **protestantisch**) Prot.

**Protagonist, in** (*mpl* -en; *fpl* -nen) *der, die* protagonist.

**Protein** (*pl* -e) *das* protein.

**Protektorat** (*pl* -e) *das* POL protectorate.

**Protest** (*pl* -e) *der* protest; **gegen etw ~ einlegen** ODER **erheben** to make a protest against sthg.

**Protestant, in** (*mpl* -en; *fpl* -nen) *der, die* Protestant.

**protestantisch** *adj* Protestant <> *adv:* **jn ~ erziehen** to bring sb up (as) a Protestant.

**protestieren** *vi* to protest; **gegen etw ~** to protest against ODER about sthg.

**Protest|kundgebung** *die* protest rally.

**Prothese** (*pl* -n) *die* [für Arm, Bein] artificial limb; [für Zähne] dentures (*pl*).

**Protokoll** (*pl* -e) *das* - **1.** [gen] record; [Aufzeichnung - wortgetreu] transcript; [ - von Sitzung] minutes (*pl*); [ - polizeilich] statement; **etw zu ~ geben** to put sthg on the record; [polizeilich] to say sthg in one's statement; **eine Aussage zu ~ nehmen** to take down a statement; **~ führen** to take the minutes; [wortgetreu] to make a transcript - **2.** [Zeremoniell] protocol.

**P**

**Protokoll|führer, in** *der, die* [von Sitzung] minute-taker; [im Gericht] clerk.

**protokollieren** *vt* to take down; [Sitzung] to minute ⬦ *vi* to keep a record; [bei Sitzung] to take the minutes.

**Proton** *(pl* -tonen) *das* PHYS proton.

**Proto|typ** *der* prototype.

**protzen** *vi abw:* mit etw ~ to show sthg off.

**protzig** *abw adj fam* showy ⬦ *adv* showily.

**prov.** *(abk für* provisorisch) temp.

**Provence** *die* Provence.

**Proviant** [pro'vi̯ant] *der (ohne pl)* provisions *(pl).*

**Provider** [pro'vaidɐ] *(pl* -) *der* EDV Internet Service Provider.

**Provinz** [pro'vɪnts] *(pl* -en) *die* - **1.** [Verwaltungs-bezirk] province - **2.** *(ohne pl) abw* [Gegend] provinces *(pl).*

**provinziell** [provɪn'tsi̯el] *abw adj* provincial ⬦ *adv* provincially.

**Provision** [provi'zi̯oːn] *(pl* -en) *die* commission.

**provisorisch** [provi'zoːrɪʃ] *adj* temporary ⬦ *adv* temporarily.

**Provokation** [provoka'tsi̯oːn] *(pl* -en) *die* provocation.

**provozieren** [provo'tsiːrən] *vt* to provoke ⬦ *vi* to be provocative.

**Prozedur** *(pl* -en) *die* procedure.

**Prozent** *(pl* - ODER -e) *das* percent; ~e bekommen to get a discount.

**Prozent|satz** *der* percentage.

**prozentual** *adj* percentage *(vor Subst)* ⬦ *adv* in percentage terms.

**Prozess** *(pl* -e) *der* - **1.** [Rechtsstreit] trial; jm den ~ machen to put sb on trial; mit jm kurzen ~ machen *fam fig* [schnell verfahren] to make short work of sb - **2.** [Vorgang] process.

**prozessieren** *vi* to go to court; gegen jn ~ to take sb to court.

**Prozession** *(pl* -en) *die* - **1.** [kirchliche] procession - **2.** *fam* [Schlange] line.

**Prozesskosten** *pl* legal costs.

**Prozessor** *(pl* -ssoren) *der* EDV processor.

**prüde** *adj* prudish ⬦ *adv* prudishly.

**prüfen** *vt* - **1.** [Gerät, Material] to test; [bei Examen] to examine; jn auf etw *(A)* ~ to examine sb on sthg; jn in etw *(D)* ~ to examine sb in sthg; etw auf etw *(A)* ~ to test sthg for sthg - **2.** [Rechnung, Aussage, Unterschrift] to check - **3.** [Angebot] to consider ⬦ *vi* [examinieren] to be an/the examiner.
➡ **sich prüfen** *ref* [sich einschätzen] to do some soul-searching.

**Prüfer, in** *(mpl* -; *fpl* -nen) *der, die* - **1.** [Lehrer] examiner - **2.** [Tester] tester.

**Prüfling** *(pl* -e) *der* candidate.

**Prüf|stand** *der* test bed.
➡ **auf dem Prüfstand** *adv* being tested.

**Prüfung** *(pl* -en) *die* - **1.** [Kontrolle] check - **2.** [Examen] exam, examination; eine ~ machen ODER haben to take an exam; eine mündliche/schriftliche ~ an oral/a written exam; eine ~ bestehen to pass an exam - **3.** *geh* [Belastung] trial - **4.** [im Sport] test.

**Prügel** *(pl* -) *der* club.
➡ **Prügel** *pl* thrashing *(U);* ~ beziehen to get a thrashing.

**Prügelei** *(pl* -en) *die* fight.

**Prügel|knabe** *der* whipping boy.

**prügeln** *vt* to beat.
➡ **sich prügeln** *ref* to fight.

**Prunk** *der abw* splendour.

**prunkvoll** *adj* magnificent ⬦ *adv* magnificently.

**prusten** *vi* to snort.

**PS** [peː'ɛs] *(pl* -) *das* - **1.** *(abk für* Pferdestärke) hp - **2.** *(abk für* Postskriptum) PS.

**Psalm** *(pl* -en) *der* psalm.

**PSch** *abk für* Postscheck.

**PSchA** *(abk für* Postscheckamt) post office account, ≈ Giro *Br.*

**Pseudonym** *(pl* -e) *das* pseudonym.

**Psyche** *(pl* -n) *die* psyche.

**Psychiater, in** *(mpl* -; *fpl* -nen) *der, die* psychiatrist.

**Psychiatrie** [psyçi̯a'triː] *(pl* -n) *die* - **1.** *(ohne pl)* [Abteilung] psychiatric department - **2.** [Wissenschaft] psychiatry.

**psychiatrisch** *adj* psychiatric ⬦ *adv:* jn ~ behandeln to give sb psychiatric treatment.

**psychisch** *adj* [Wohlbefinden, Probleme] psychological; [Krankheit] mental ⬦ *adv* mentally.

**Psychoanalyse** *die* psychoanalysis.

**Psycho|analytiker, in** *der, die* psychoanalyst.

**Psychologe** *(pl* -n) *der* psychologist.

**Psychologie** *die* psychology.

**Psychologin** *(pl* -nen) *die* psychologist.

**psychologisch** *adj* psychological ⬦ *adv* - **1.** [als Psychologe]: jn ~ begutachten to give sb a psychological examination - **2.** [mit Menschenkenntnis] psychologically.

**Psychoterror** *der* psychological terror.

**Psycho|therapeut, Psychotherapeut, in** *der, die* psychotherapist.

**Psycho|therapie** *die* psychotherapy.

**Pubertät** *die* puberty.

**Publicity** [pa'blɪsɪtɪ] *die* publicity.

**publik** *adj:* etw ~ machen to make sthg public; ~ sein/werden to be/become public.

**Publikation** [publika'tsjoːn] *(pl -en) die* publication.

**Publikum** *das (ohne pl)* - **1.** [Zuhörer, Zuschauer] audience - **2.** [Gäste] clientele - **3.** [Anhänger] public; [von Schriftsteller] readership.

**Publizist, in** *(mpl -en; fpl -nen) der, die* commentator on current affairs.

**Pudding** *(pl -e oder -s) der* blancmange.

**Pudding|pulver** *das* blancmange mix.

**Pudel** *(pl -) der* poodle; des ~s Kern the crux of the matter.

**Pudel|mütze** *die* woolly hat.

**pudelwohl** *adj fam:* sich ~ fühlen to feel on top of the world.

**Puder** *(pl -) der ODER das* powder.

**Puder|dose** *die* (powder) compact.

**pudern** *vt* to powder.
➡ **sich pudern** *ref* to powder o.s.

**Puderzucker** *der* icing sugar.

**Puff** *(pl -s) der ODER das fam* brothel.

**Puffer** *(pl -) der* - **1.** [von Bahnen] buffer - **2.** [Kartoffelpuffer] potato pancake.

**Puffer|zone** *die* buffer zone.

**Pulk** *(pl -s ODER -e) der* group; [von Läufern, Radrennfahrern] pack.

**Pulle** *(pl -n) die salopp* bottle.
➡ **volle Pulle** *adv fam* flat out.

**Pulli** *(pl -s) der fam* sweater, jumper *Br.*

**Pullover** [pʊ'loːvɐ] *(pl -) der* sweater, jumper *Br.*

**Pullunder** *(pl -) der* sleeveless sweater.

**Puls** *(pl -e) der* pulse; am ~ von etw sein to have one's finger on the pulse of sthg.

**Puls|ader** *die* artery; sich *(D)* die ~ aufschneiden to slit one's wrists.

**pulsieren** *vi* to pulsate; [Blut] to pulse.

**Puls|schlag** *der* pulse.

**Pult** *(pl -e) das* desk; [Stehpult] lectern.

**Pulver** ['pʊlfɐ, 'pʊlvɐ] *(pl -) das* - **1.** [Stoff] powder - **2.** [Schießpulver] gunpowder *(U).*

**Pulver|fass** *das* powder keg; (wie) auf einem ~ sitzen *fig* to be (like) sitting on a time bomb.

**Pulver|kaffee** *der* instant coffee.

**Pulver|schnee** *der* powder snow.

**Puma** *(pl -s) der* puma.

**pummelig** *adj* chubby.

**Pump** ➡ auf Pump *adv fam* on credit.

**Pumpe** *(pl -n) die* - **1.** [Gerät] pump - **2.** *salopp* [Herz] ticker.

**pumpen** *vt* - **1.** [saugen] to pump - **2.** *fam* [leihen]: jm etw ~ to lend sb sthg; (sich *(D)*) etw von jm ~ to borrow sthg from sb - **3.** [investieren]: Geld in etw ~ to pump money into sthg <> *vi* [saugen] to pump.

**Pumpernickel** *(pl -) der* pumpernickel, dark hard bread made from rye flour.

**Pumps** [pœmps] *(pl -) der* court shoe *Br*, pump *Am.*

**Punk** [paŋk] *(pl -s) der* punk.

**Punker, in** ['paŋkɐ, rɪn] *(mpl -; fpl -nen) der, die* punk.

**Punkt** *(pl -e) der* - **1.** [gen] point; nach ~en gewinnen/verlieren to win/lose on points - **2.** [Fleck, typografisches Zeichen] dot; [am Satzende] full stop *Br*, period *Am* - **3.** [Zeitpunkt]: ~ ein Uhr one o'clock on the dot - **4.** *RW:* der springende ~ the crux of the matter; der tote ~ the low point; an einem toten ~ angelangt [Verhandlungen] to have reached deadlock; ein wunder ODER schwacher ~ [Schwäche] a weak point; [heikles Thema] a sore point; etw auf den ~ bringen to sum sthg up; nun mach mal einen ~! *fam* all right, that's enough!

**punktgleich** *adj* level on points.

**punktieren** *vt* - **1.** MED to puncture - **2.** [tüpfeln & MUS] to dot.

**pünktlich** *adj* punctual <> *adv* punctually, on time.

**Pünktlichkeit** *die* punctuality.

**Punkt|sieg** *der* win on points.

**Punsch** *(pl -e ODER Pünsche) der* punch.

**Pupille** *(pl -n) die* pupil.

**Puppe** *(pl -n) die* - **1.** [Figur] doll; bis in die ~n *fam fig* till all hours - **2.** *salopp* [Frau, Mädchen] bird *Br*, doll *Am;* [als Anrede] baby.

**Puppen|stube** *die* doll's house.

**Puppen|theater** *das* puppet theatre.

**Puppen|wagen** *der* doll's pram *Br*, doll's baby carriage *Am.*

**pur** *adj* - **1.** [rein] pure - **2.** [Whisky] neat.

**Püree** *(pl -s) das* puree.

**Purpur** *der* crimson.

**Purzel|baum** *der:* einen ~ machen ODER schlagen to do a somersault.

**purzeln** *(perf ist gepurzelt) vi* to tumble.

**Puste** *die fam* puff; aus der ODER außer ~ sein to be out of puff; uns geht die ~ aus *fig* [Energie] we are running out of steam; [Geld] we are running out of cash.

**Pustel** *(pl -n) die* pustule; [Pickel] pimple.

**pusten** *vt & vi* to blow.

**Pute** *(pl -n) die* - **1.** [Tier] turkey (hen) - **2.** *salopp abw* [Frau] cow.

P

**Puter** (*pl* -) *der* turkey (cock).

**Puts** *pl* WIRTSCH put options.

**Putsch** (*pl* -e) *der* putsch.

**Putte** (*pl* -n) *die* cherub.

**Putz** *der* plaster; **auf den ~ hauen** *fam fig* [feiern] to party; [großtun] to boast.

**putzen** *vt* to clean; [Gemüse] to wash; **jm die Nase ~** to wipe sb's nose; **sich** (*D*) **die Zähne putzen** to clean ODER brush one's teeth; **sich** (*D*) **die Nase putzen** to blow one's nose ◇ *vi* to clean.
◆ **sich putzen** *ref* to wash o.s.; [Vogel] to preen o.s.

**Putz|frau** *die* cleaner.

**putzig** *adj fam* cute ◇ *adv* cutely.

**Putz|lappen** *der* cloth.

**Putz|mittel** *das* cleaning fluid.

**Puzzle** [ˈpazl̩] (*pl* -s) *das* jigsaw (puzzle).

**PVC** [peːfauˈtseː] (*abk für* **Polyvinylchlorid**) *das* PVC.

**Pyjama** [pyˈdʒaːma] (*pl* -s) *der* pyjamas (*pl*).

**Pyramide** (*pl* -n) *die* pyramid.

**Pyrenäen** *pl*: **die ~** the Pyrenees.

**Python** (*pl* -s) *der* python.

**q, Q** [kuː] (*pl* - ODER -s) *das* q, Q.

**q. e. d.** (*abk für* **quod erat demonstrandum**) QED.

**qm** (*abk für* **Quadratmeter**) m².

**Quacksalber, in** (*mpl* -; *fpl* -nen) *der, die abw* quack.

**Quader** (*pl* -) *der* - **1.** MATH rectangular solid - **2.** [Block] stone block.

**Quadrat** (*pl* -e) *das* square.
◆ **im Quadrat** *adv fam*: **Zufall im ~** a really lucky coincidence.

**quadratisch** *adj* square ◇ *adv* in squares.

**Quadrat|meter** *der* square metre.

**quaken** *vi* - **1.** [Frosch] to croak; [Ente] to quack - **2.** *fam abw* [reden] to squawk.

**quäken** *vi abw* to wail.

**Qual** (*pl* -en) *die* agony; [seelisch] torment; **der Zahnarztbesuch war eine einzige ~!** the visit to the dentist was agony!; **jm das Leben zur ~ machen** to make sb's life a misery; **die ~ der Wahl haben** *fig* to be spoilt for choice.
◆ **Qualen** *pl* suffering (*sg*), agony (*sg*); [seelisch] torment (*sg*); **jn von seinen/ihren ~ erlösen** to put sb out of his/her misery.

**quälen** *vt* - **1.** [gen] to torment; [foltern] to torture - **2.** *fam* [bedrängen] to pester; **jn mit etw ~** to plague sb with sthg.
◆ **sich quälen** *ref* - **1.** [leiden] to suffer - **2.** [sich abmühen] to struggle.

**Quälerei** (*pl* -en) *die* - **1.** [Peinigung] torment; [Folter] torture; [Grausamkeit] cruelty; **~ der Tiere** cruelty to animals - **2.** (*ohne pl*) [Anstrengung] struggle.

**Qualifikation** (*pl* -en) *die* - **1.** [Befähigung] ability - **2.** [Voraussetzung] qualification.

**qualifizieren** *vt* - **1.** [befähigen] to qualify - **2.** [beurteilen] to classify.
◆ **sich qualifizieren** *ref* [sich befähigen] to obtain qualifications; [für Wettbewerb] to qualify.

**Qualität** (*pl* -en) *die* quality.

**qualitativ** *adj* qualitative ◇ *adv* qualitatively.

**Qualle** (*pl* -n) *die* jellyfish.

**Qualm** *der* - **1.** [von Feuer] thick smoke - **2.** *fam abw* [von Zigaretten] fug.

**qualmen** *vi* to smoke ◇ *vt salopp* [Zigaretten] to puff away at.

**qualvoll** *adj* agonizing ◇ *adv* in agony.

**Quäntchen** *das* (*ohne pl*) little bit of; **ein ~ Glück/Wahrheit** a bit of luck/truth.

**Quantität** *die* (*ohne pl*) quantity.

**quantitativ** *adj* quantitative ◇ *adv* quantitatively.

**Quantum** (*pl* -ten) *das* quota.

**Quarantäne** [karanˈtɛːnə] (*pl* -n) *die* quarantine (*U*).

**Quark** *der* quark, *type of soft cheese*.

**Quartal** (*pl* -e) *das* quarter.

**Quartett** (*pl* -e) *das* - **1.** MUS quartet - **2.** (*ohne pl*) [Kartenspiel] *children's card game where players have to collect four of a kind*.

**Quartier** (*pl* -e) *das* accommodation (*U*).

**Quarz** (*pl* -e) *der* quartz (*U*).

**Quarz|uhr** *die* quartz watch.

**quasi** *adv* virtually.

**quasseln** *vi fam* to chatter.

**Quaste** (*pl* -n) *die* tassel.

**Quatsch** *der fam* rubbish; **~ machen** to mess about.

**quatschen** *fam vi* - **1.** [reden] to chat - **2.** *abw* [quasseln] to chatter ⬦ *vt* [reden] to talk.

**Quatsch|kopf** *der fam abw* windbag.

**Quebec** *nt* Quebec.

**Quecksilber** *das* CHEM mercury.

**Quellauf|werk** *das* EDV source drive.

**Quell|diskette** *die* EDV source disk.

**Quelle** (*pl* -n) *die* - **1.** [Wasserquelle] spring; **an der ~ sitzen** *fig* to have contacts - **2.** [Informant(en), Fundstelle] source.

**quellen** (*präs* **quillt**; *prät* **quoll**; *perf* **ist gequollen**) *vi* - **1.** [austreten - Flüssigkeit] to stream; [ - Rauch] to billow - **2.** [hervortreten] to swell; [Augen] to bulge - **3.** [Feuchtigkeit aufnehmen] to soak.

**quengeln** *vi fam* to whine.

**Quentchen** = Quäntchen.

**quer** *adv* diagonally; **~ durch etw** straight through sthg; **~ über etw** (*A*), **~ auf etw** (*D*) across sthg; **~ zu etw** at right angles to sthg; *siehe auch* **quer gestreift.**

**Quere** *die:* **jm in die ~ kommen** *fig* [behindern] to get in sb's way; [Weg abschneiden] to block sb's path; [treffen] to bump into sb.

**querfeldein** *adv* cross-country.

**Quer|flöte** *die* flute.

**Querformat** *das* landscape format.

**quer gestreift** *adj* with horizontal stripes.

**Quer|schnitt** *der* - **1.** [Auswahl, Abbildung] cross-section - **2.** [Schnitt] cut.

**querschnittsgelähmt** *adj* paraplegic.

**quer|stellen** ➠ **sich querstellen** *ref fam* to refuse.

**Quer|straße** *die:* **die nächste ~ rechts** the next turning on the right.

**Querulant, in** (*mpl* -en; *fpl* -nen) *der, die abw* moaner.

**Querver|bindung** *die* link; [Straße] connecting road.

**quetschen** *vt* - **1.** [unterbringen, drängen] to squeeze - **2.** [zerdrücken] to crush - **3.** [verletzen]: **der Baum hat mir das Bein gequetscht** the tree crushed my leg.
➠ **sich quetschen** *ref* [sich zwängen] to squeeze.

**Quetschung** (*pl* -en) *die* bruise.

**quicklebendig** *adj* very lively.

**quieken** *vi* [Ferkel] to squeal; [Maus] to squeak.

**quietschen** *vi* - **1.** [Tür, Bremse] to squeak - **2.** *fam* [juchzen] to squeal.

**quillt** *präs* ▷ quellen.

**Quint** (*pl* -en), **Quinte** (*pl* -n) *die* MUS fifth.

**Quintlessenz** *die* quintessence.

**Quintett** (*pl* -e) *das* quintet.

**Quirl** (*pl* -e) *der* whisk.

**quitt** *adj (unver):* **mit jm ~ sein** *fam* to be quits with sb.

**Quitte** (*pl* -n) *die* - **1.** [Frucht] quince - **2.** [Baum] quince tree.

**quittegelb, quittengelb** *adj* yellowish.

**quittieren** *vt* - **1.** [bestätigen] to sign for; **etw ~ lassen** to get a receipt for sthg - **2.** [erwidern] to respond to - **3.** [kündigen]: **den Dienst ~** to resign ⬦ *vi* [Empfang bestätigen] to sign.

**Quittung** (*pl* -en) *die* - **1.** [Beleg] receipt - **2.** *fig* [Konsequenz]: **da hast du die ~!** that's the price you pay!

**Quiz** [kvɪs] (*pl* -) *das* quiz.

**Quizmaster, in** [ˈkvɪsmaːstɐ, rɪn] (*mpl* -; *fpl* -nen) *der, die* quizmaster.

**quoll** *prät* ▷ quellen.

**Quote** (*pl* -n) *die* [Anteil] proportion; [festgeschriebene Zielmenge] quota; [Einschaltquote] viewing figures (*pl*).

**Quoten|regelung** *die* positive discrimination *Br*, affirmative action *Am*.

**Quotient** [kvoˈtsiɛnt] (*pl* -en) *der* quotient.

# R

**r, R** [ɛr] (*pl* - *ODER* -s) *das* r, R.

**Rabatt** (*pl* -e) *der* discount.

**Rabatte** (*pl* -n) *die* border.

**Rabatz** *der fam* racket; **~ machen** *fam* [sich beschweren] to kick up a fuss; [Krach machen] to make a racket.

**Rabbi** (*pl* -s) *der* rabbi.

**Rabe** (*pl* -n) *der* raven.

**rabenschwarz** *adj* jet-black.

**rabiat** *adj* [gewalttätig] brutal; [wütend] furious ⬦ *adv* [gewalttätig] brutally; [wütend] furiously.

**Rache** *die* revenge; **an jm ~ nehmen** to take revenge on sb.

**Rachelakt** *der* act of revenge.

**Rachen** (*pl* -) *der* throat.

**rächen** *vt* to avenge.
➠ **sich rächen** *ref* - **1.** [Rache nehmen] to get

one's revenge; **sich an jm (für** ODER **wegen etw)** ~ to take revenge on sb (for sthg) - **2.** [Konsequenzen haben]: **seine Faulheit wird sich** ~ he'll pay for his laziness.

**rackern** vi fam to slave away.

**Racket** ['rɛkət] (pl **-s)** das SPORT racquet.

**Raclette** ['raklɛt, ra'klɛt] (pl **-s)** das raclette, Swiss cheese dish.

**Rad** (pl **Räder)** das - **1.** [von Fahrzeug] wheel; **unter die Räder kommen** fam [überfahren werden] to be knocked over; fam fig [scheitern] to go to the dogs - **2.** [Fahrrad] bike; ~ **fahren** to cycle - **3.** [von Maschine] cog - **4.** [Bewegung]: **ein** ~ **schlagen** [Turnübung] to do a cartwheel; [den Schwanz fächern] to fan out its tail.

**Radar** der ODER das radar.

**Radar|kontrolle** die radar speed check.

**Radau** der racket.

**Rädchen** (pl **-)** das cog.

**radebrechen** vt: Englisch/Deutsch ~ to speak broken English/German <> vi: **er radebrechte in Englisch** he spoke broken English.

**radeln** (perf **ist geradelt)** vi to cycle.

**Rädels|führer, in** der, die ringleader.

**rad|fahren** vi (unreg) ⊳ **Rad.**

**Rad|fahrer, in** der, die cyclist.

**Radfahr|weg** der cycle track.

**Radi** (pl **-)** der Österr & Süddt fam radish.

**radieren** vt & vi - **1.** [mit Radiergummi] to erase - **2.** KUNST to etch.

**Radier|gummi** der rubber Br, eraser Am.

**Radierung** (pl **-en)** die etching.

**Radieschen** [ra'diːsçən] (pl **-)** das radish.

**radikal** adj radical <> adv radically.

**radikalisieren** vt to radicalize.

◆ **sich radikalisieren** ref to become radical.

**Radikalismus** der radicalism.

**Radikal|kur** die fam drastic measures (pl).

**Radio** (pl **-s)** das - **1.** [gen] radio; ~ **hören** to listen to the radio - **2.** (ohne pl) [Anstalt] radio station.

**radioaktiv** adj radioactive.

**Radio|aktivität** die radioactivity.

**Radio|rekorder** (pl **-)** der radio cassette recorder.

**Radio|sender** der radio station.

**Radio|sendung** die radio programme.

**Radio|wecker** der radio alarm.

**Radium** das CHEM radium.

**Radius** (pl **Radien)** der radius.

**Rad|kappe** die hubcap.

**Rad|lager** das wheel bearing.

**Radler** (pl **-)** der cyclist <> das Süddt shandy.

**Radlerin** (pl **-nen)** die cyclist.

**Radlermaß** (pl **-)** die Süddt litre of shandy.

**Radon** das CHEM radon.

**Rad|rennen** das cycle race.

**Rad|sport** der cycling.

**Rad|tour** die cycling tour.

**Rad|wechsel** der wheel change.

**Rad|weg** der cycle path.

**RAF** [ɛraː'ɛf] (abk für **Rote Armee Fraktion)** die Red Army Faction.

**raffen** vt - **1.** abw [nehmen]: **etw an sich** (A) ~ to grab sthg - **2.** [Stoff] to gather - **3.** salopp [begreifen] to get.

**raffgierig** abw adj greedy <> adv greedily.

**Raffinerie** [rafinə'riː] (pl **-n)** die refinery.

**raffiniert** adj - **1.** [Person, Plan, System] ingenious; [Geschmack, Farbe] subtle; [Kleiderschnitt] sophisticated - **2.** [gerissen] cunning <> adv - **1.** [planen, arrangieren] ingeniously; [würzen] subtly; ~ **kochen** to be a sophisticated cook - **2.** [gerissen] cunningly.

**Rafting** das SPORT whitewater rafting.

**ragen** (perf **hat/ist geragt)** vi: **aus etw** ~ to stick out of sthg; [Berg, Baum, Gebäude] to rise up out of sthg.

**Ragout** [ra'guː] (pl **-s)** das stew.

**Rahm** der cream.

**rahmen** vt to frame.

**Rahmen** (pl **-)** der - **1.** [von Bild, Fenster, Fahrrad] frame - **2.** [von Fahrzeugen] chassis - **3.** (ohne pl) [Umgebung] setting; [Kontext] context - **4.** RW: **aus dem** ~ **fallen** to be out of place; **den** ~ **einer Sache sprengen** to go beyond the scope of sthg.

◆ **im Rahmen** adv: **im** ~ **einer Sache** (G) [Zusammenhang] in the context of sthg; [Verlauf] in the course of sthg; [innerhalb der Grenzen] within the bounds of sthg; [als Teil] as part of sthg.

**Rahmen|bedingung** die general condition.

**räkeln, rekeln** ◆ **sich räkeln, sich rekeln** ref to stretch out.

**Rakete** (pl **-n)** die rocket; MIL missile.

**Rallye** ['rali, 'rɛlil] (pl **-s)** die SPORT rally.

**Rallye|fahrer, in** der, die rally driver.

**rammen** vt to ram.

**Rampe** (pl **-n)** die - **1.** [Laderampe, Auffahrt] ramp - **2.** [in Theater] apron.

**Rampenlicht** das (ohne pl) footlights (pl); **im** ~ **stehen** fig to be in the limelight.

**ramponiert** adj fam battered.

**Ramsch** der fam abw junk.

**RAM-|Speicher** ['ramʃpaiçɐ] der EDV RAM.

**ran** fam = heran.

**Rand** *(pl* **Ränder)** *der* - **1.** [von Stadt, Tisch, Teich] edge - **2.** [von Gefäßen] rim - **3.** [von Buchseite] margin - **4.** [Umrandung] edging *(U);* **(dunkle) Ränder um die Augen haben** to have dark rings around one's eyes - **5.** *RW:* **außer ~ und Band sein/geraten** *fam* to be/go completely wild; **mit jm/etw (nicht) zu ~e kommen** *fam* (not) to be able to cope with sb/sthg.

➤ **am Rande** *adv* - **1.** [nebenbei] in passing; **sich am ~e abspielen** to take place on the sidelines; **am ~e bemerkt** noticed in passing - **2.** [nahe]: **am ~e der Verzweiflung sein** to be close to despair.

**randalieren** *vi* to rampage.

**Randalierer, in** *(mpl -; fpl* **-nen)** *der, die* hooligan.

**Randlbemerkung** *die* - **1.** [schriftliche] marginal note - **2.** [mündliche] passing remark.

**Randlbezirk** *der* suburb.

**Randlerscheinung** *die* item of peripheral importance.

**Randlgruppe** *die* marginal group.

**Randlstreifen** *der* [von Autobahn] hard shoulder *Br,* shoulder *Am;* [von Straße] verge *Br,* berm *Am.*

**randvoll** *adj* full to the brim ◇ *adv* to the brim.

**rang** *prät* ⊳ **ringen.**

**Rang** *(pl* **Ränge)** *der* - **1.** [Position] rank - **2.** [Ansehen] class; **ein Wissenschaftler von ~** a renowned scientist - **3.** [in Theater, Stadion] circle; **der erste/zweite ~** [in Theater] the dress/upper circle; [im Wettbewerb] first/second place - **4.** *RW:* **alles, was ~ und Namen hat** anybody who is anybody; **jm/etw den ~ ablaufen** to overtake sb/sthg.

➤ **ersten Ranges** *adj* first-rate.

**Rangablzeichen** *das* insignia.

**Rangelei** *(pl* **-en)** *die* tussling *(U).*

**Ranglfolge** *die* order of precedence.

**rangieren** [raŋˈʒiːrən] *vt* to shunt ◇ *vi* to be ranked.

**Ranglliste** *die* (army/navy/civil service) list.

**Ranglordnung** *die* order of precedence.

**ranlhalten** ➤ **sich ranhalten** *ref (unreg) fam* to get on with it.

**rank** *adj geh:* **~ und schlank** slender.

**Ranke** *(pl* **-n)** *die* tendril.

**ranken** *(perf* **hat/ist** **gerankt)** *vi (ist)* to climb.

➤ **sich ranken** *ref* to climb; **sich um etw ~** [wachsen] to entwine itself around sthg; *fig* & *geh* [spinnen] to grow up around sthg.

**ranlassen** *vt (unreg) fam* - **1.** = **heranlassen** - **2.** [sich nähern lassen]: **jn an jn/etw ~** to let sb near sb/sthg.

**ranlmüssen** *vi (unreg) fam* [arbeiten] to have to get stuck in; [Aufgabe erledigen] to see to it.

**rann** *prät* ⊳ **rinnen.**

**rannte** *prät* ⊳ **rennen.**

**Ranzen** *(pl* **-)** *der* - **1.** [Schultasche] rucksack; [~ aus Leder] satchel - **2.** *salopp* [Bauch] belly.

**ranzig** *adj* rancid.

**Rap** [ræp] *der* MUS rap.

**rapide** *adj* rapid ◇ *adv* rapidly.

**Rappel** *der:* **einen ~ bekommen** ODER **kriegen** *fam* to go mad.

**rappeln** *vi fam* to rattle.

**Rappen** *(pl* **-)** *der* centime, *one hundredth of a Swiss franc.*

**Raps** *der* rape.

**rar** *adj* rare; **du hast dich in letzter Zeit ~ gemacht** we haven't seen much of you lately.

**Rarität** *(pl* **-en)** *die* rarity.

**rasant** *adj* - **1.** [schnell] rapid - **2.** *fam* [imponierend] stunning ◇ *adv* [schnell] rapidly.

**rasch** *adj* quick ◇ *adv* quickly.

**rascheln** *vi* to rustle.

**rasen** *(perf* **hat/ist** **gerast)** *vi* - **1.** *(ist)* [fahren] to race; **gegen etw ~** to crash into sthg - **2.** *(hat)* [toben] to rage; **das Publikum raste vor Begeisterung** the audience went wild with enthusiasm.

**Rasen** *(pl* **-)** *der* [Rasenfläche] lawn; [Gras] grass; **den ~ mähen** to mow the lawn; **den ~ sprengen** to water the grass.

**rasend** *adj* - **1.** [Entwicklung] rapid; [Geschwindigkeit] lightning *(vor Subst);* [Eile] great - **2.** [gewaltig] raging - **3.** [wütend]: **jn ~ machen** *fam* to drive sb mad ◇ *adv* - **1.**: **~ schnell** incredibly quickly - **2.** [enorm] terribly; **~ verliebt sein** to be madly in love.

**Rasenlmäher** *der* lawnmower.

**Rasensprenger** *(pl* **-)** *der* sprinkler.

**Raserei** *die (ohne pl)* - **1.** [Toben] rage; **jn zur ~ bringen** to drive sb mad - **2.** *abw* [Schnelligkeit] speeding.

**Rasierlapparat** *der* shaver.

**rasieren** *vt* to shave.

➤ **sich rasieren** *ref* to shave; **sich nass/trocken ~** to have a wet/dry shave.

**Rasierer** *(pl* **-)** *der fam* shaver.

**Rasierlklinge** *die* razor blade.

**Rasierlpinsel** *der* shaving brush.

**Rasierlschaum** *der* shaving foam.

**Rasierlwasser** *das* aftershave.

**Räson** [rɛˈzɔŋ] *die:* **jn zur ~ bringen** to make sb see reason.

**raspeln** *vt* [reiben] to grate.

**R**

**Rasse** (*pl* -n) *die* - **1.** [bei Tieren] breed - **2.** [bei Menschen] race.

**Rassel** (*pl* -n) *die* rattle.

**rasseln** (*perf* hat/ist gerasselt) *vi* - **1.** *(hat)* [Geräusch erzeugen] to rattle - **2.** *(ist) fam* [durchfallen]: **durch eine Prüfung ~** to flunk an exam.

**Rassenldiskriminierung** *die* racial discrimination *(U)*.

**Rassentrennung** *die* racial segregation.

**rassig** *adj* spirited.

**Rassismus** *der* racism.

**Rassist, in** (*mpl* -en; *fpl* -nen) *der, die* racist.

**rassistisch** *adj* racist.

**Rast** (*pl* -en) *die* rest; **~ machen** [beim Fahren] to stop for a break; [beim Gehen] to stop for a rest.

**rasten** *vi* [beim Fahren] to stop for a break; [beim Gehen] to stop for a rest.

**Raster** (*pl* -) *das* TECH screen; [System] framework.

**Rastlhaus** *das* [an Autobahnen] services *(pl)*.

**Rastlhof** *der* [an Autobahnen] services *(pl)*.

**rastlos** *adj* tireless <> *adv* tirelessly.

**Rastlplatz** *der* picnic area *(with toilet facilities)*.

**Rastlstätte** *die* [auf Autobahnen] services *(pl)*.

**Rasur** (*pl* -en) *die* shave.

**Rat** (*pl*/Räte) *der* - **1.** [Ratschlag] advice *(U)*; **jm einen ~ geben** to give sb a piece of advice; **jn/etw zu ~e ziehen** to consult sb/sthg; **jm mit ~ und Tat helfen** ODER **beistehen** ODER **zur Seite stehen** to support sb in whatever way one can; **jn um ~ fragen** ODER **bitten** to ask sb for advice; **sich** *(D)* **keinen ~ (mehr) wissen** to be at one's wits' end - **2.** [Versammlung] council - **3.** [Person] councillor.

**rät** *präs* ▷ **raten**.

**Rate** (*pl* -n) *die* - **1.** [Teilzahlung] instalment; **etw auf ~n kaufen** to buy sthg on hire purchase - **2.** [statistische] rate.

**raten** (*präs* **rät**; *prät* **riet**; *perf* hat geraten) *vt* - **1.** [erraten] to guess - **2.** [empfehlen]: **jm ~, etw zu tun** to advise sb to do sthg <> *vi* - **1.** [erraten] to guess; **dreimal darfst du ~** *fam fig* I'll give you three guesses - **2.** [Rat geben]: **jm zu etw ~** to advise sb to do sthg.

**ratenweise** *adv* in instalments.

**Ratenlzahlung** *die* payment by instalments.

**Ratelspiel** *das* guessing game.

**Ratgeber** (*pl* -) *der* - **1.** [Mensch] adviser - **2.** [Buch] guide.

**Ratgeberin** (*pl* -nen) *die* adviser.

**Ratlhaus** *das* town hall.

**ratifizieren** *vt* POL to ratify.

**Ration** (*pl* -en) *die* ration; **eiserne ~** iron rations *(pl)*.

**rational** *adj* rational <> *adv* rationally.

**rationalisieren** *vt* to rationalize.

**Rationalisierung** (*pl* -en) *die* rationalization.

**rationell** *adj* efficient <> *adv* efficiently.

**rationieren** *vt* to ration.

**rätisch** *adj* Rhaetian.

**ratlos** *adj* helpless <> *adv* helplessly.

**Rätoromanisch(e)** *das* Rhaeto-Romanic; siehe auch **Englisch(e)**.

**ratsam** *adj* advisable.

**Ratlschlag** *der* piece of advice.

**Rätsel** (*pl* -) *das* - **1.** [Aufgabe] puzzle; **jm ein ~ aufgeben** to ask sb a riddle - **2.** [Geheimnis] mystery; **etw ist jm ein ~** sthg is a mystery to sb; **vor einem ~ stehen** to be faced with a mystery.

**rätselhaft** *adj* mysterious; **es ist mir ~** it's a mystery to me.

**rätseln** *vi*: **über etw** *(A)* **~** to puzzle over sthg.

**Rätselraten** *das* guessing.

**Ratslherr** *der* councillor.

**Ratslkeller** *der* restaurant in basement of town hall.

**Ratte** (*pl* -n) *die* rat.

**rattern** (*perf* hat/ist gerattert) *vi* - **1.** *(ist)* [fahren] to clatter (along) - **2.** *(hat)* [Geräusche machen] to rattle; [Nähmaschine] to chatter.

**rau** *adj* - **1.** [Oberfläche, Person, Sitten] rough - **2.** [Klima, Leben] harsh - **3.** [angegriffen - Stimme] hoarse; [ - Hals] sore.

**Raub** *der* robbery.

**Raubbau** *der* overexploitation; **mit seiner Gesundheit ~ treiben** to ruin one's health.

**Raubdruck** (*pl* -e) *der* pirate copy.

**rauben** *vt* - **1.** [stehlen] to steal - **2.** [kosten]: **jm etw ~** to rob sb of sthg; **jm den Schlaf ~** to deprive sb of their sleep.

**Räuber, in** (*mpl* -; *fpl* -nen) *der, die* robber.

**räuberisch** *adj* predatory.

**Raublmord** *der* robbery with murder.

**Raubltier** *das* predator.

**Raubüberlfall** *der* robbery.

**Raublvogel** *der* bird of prey.

**Rauch** *der* smoke; **sich in ~ auflösen** *fig* to go up in smoke.

**rauchen** *vt* & *vi* to smoke.

**Rauchen** *das* smoking; '**~ verboten!**' 'no smoking'.

**Raucher** (*pl -*) *der* smoker.

**Raucher|abteil** *das* smoking compartment.

**Raucherin** (*pl -nen*) *die* smoker.

**räuchern** *vt* to smoke.

**Räucher|stäbchen** *das* incense sticks.

**rauchig** *adj* - **1.** [gen] smoky - **2.** [Stimme] husky.

**Rauch|verbot** *das* ban on smoking.

**Rauch|vergiftung** *die* smoke inhalation.

**Rauch|waren** *pl amt* tobacco goods.

**Rauch|wolke** *die* cloud of smoke.

**rauf** *fam* = herauf.

**Raufaser|tapete** *die* woodchip paper.

**Raufbold** (*pl -e*) *der* ruffian.

**raufen** *vi* to fight.
➡ **sich raufen** *ref* to fight.

**Rauferei** (*pl -en*) *die* fight.

**rauf|gehen** (*perf* ist r**au**fgegangen) *vt* & *vi* (*unreg*) *fam* to go up.

**rauf|kommen** (*perf* ist r**au**fgekommen) *vt* & *vi* (*unreg*) *fam* to come up.

**rauh** = rau.

**Rauhaar|dackel** *der* wire-haired dachshund.

**Rauhfaser|tapete** = Raufasertapete.

**Rauhreif** = Raureif.

**Raum** (*pl* R**äu**me) *der* - **1.** [Zimmer] room - **2.** [Platz & PHYS] space - **3.** (*ohne pl*) GEOGR area - **4.** : etw steht im ~ sthg is left in the air; etw im ~ stehen lassen to leave sthg hanging in the air.

**räumen** *vt* - **1.** [Wohnung] to vacate - **2.** [Platz, Posten] to clear.

**Raum|fähre** *die* space shuttle.

**Raum|fahrt** *die* space travel.

**Raum|forschung** *die* space research.

**Raum|inhalt** *der* volume.

**Raum|kapsel** *die* space capsule.

**räumlich** *adj* spatial <> *adv* spatially.

**Räumlichkeiten** *pl geh* premises.

**Raum|not** *die* (*ohne pl*) *geh* lack of space.

**Raum|schiff** *das* spaceship.

**Raum|station** *die* space station.

**Räumung** (*pl -en*) *die* clearing (*U*); [von Wohnung] vacation (*U*); [vor Gefahr] evacuation.

**Räumungs|arbeiten** *pl* clearance work (*sg*).

**Räumungs|klage** *die* action for eviction.

**Räumungs|verkauf** *der* clearance sale.

**Raupe** (*pl -n*) *die* - **1.** [Insekt] caterpillar - **2.** [Fahrzeug] caterpillar vehicle.

**Raupen|fahrzeug** *das* caterpillar vehicle.

**Raureif** *der* hoarfrost.

**raus** *adv fam* - **1.** = heraus - **2.** [hinaus] out; ~ hier! get out!

**Rausch** (*pl* R**äu**sche) *der* - **1.** [das Betrunkensein] intoxication; einen ~ haben to be drunk - **2.** [Ekstase] ecstasy; im ~ in ecstasy.

**rauschen** (*perf* hat/ist gerauscht) *vi* - **1.** (*hat*) [Bäume] to rustle; [Bach] to murmur; es rauscht [im Telefon] there's a crackle; [in den Ohren] there's a buzz - **2.** (*ist*) [gehen] to rush.

**rauschend** *adj*: ein ~es Fest a glittering party; ~er Beifall loud applause.

**Rausch|gift** *das* drug.

**Rauschgifthandel** *der* drug trafficking.

**rauschgiftsüchtig** *adj* addicted to drugs.

**Rauschgiftsüchtige** (*pl -n*) *der, die* drug addict.

**raus|fliegen** (*perf* ist r**au**sgeflogen) *vi* (*unreg*) *fam* [aus Schule] to be thrown out; [aus Firma] to be fired.

**raus|halten** *vt* (*unreg*) *fam* [nach draußen] to hold out.
➡ **sich raushalten** *ref fam*: sich aus etw ~ to keep out of sthg.

**raus|kriegen** *vt fam* to find out.

**räuspern** ➡ **sich räuspern** *ref* to clear one's throat.

**raus|rücken** (*perf* hat/ist r**au**sgerückt) *fam vi* (*ist*): mit etw ~ [ausdrücken] to come out with sthg; [herausgeben] to hand over sthg <> *vt* (*hat*) [herausgeben] to hand over.

**raus|schmeißen** *vt* (*unreg*) *fam* to throw out.

**Rausschmiss** (*pl -e*) *der fam* throwing out (*U*).

**Raute** (*pl -n*) *die* diamond (shape).

**rautenförmig** *adj* diamond-shaped.

**Rave** [reɪv] *der* MUS techno <> *das* ODER *der* [Veranstaltung] rave.

**Ravioli** [ra'vjoːli] *pl* ravioli (*U*).

**Razzia** (*pl* R**a**zzien) *die* (police) raid.

**RCDS** [ɛrtseːdeːˈʔɛs] (*abk für* Ring Christlich-Demokratischer Studenten) *der Christian Democrat student organization.*

**rd.** *abk für* rund.

**Reagenz|glas** *das* test tube.

**reagieren** *vi* to react; auf etw (*A*) ~ to react to sthg.

**Reaktion** (*pl -en*) *die* reaction; die ~ auf etw (*A*) the reaction to sthg.

**reaktionär** *adj abw* reactionary.

**Reaktionsvermögen** *das* (*ohne pl*) reactions (*pl*).

**Reaktor** (*pl -*t**o**ren) *der* (nuclear) reactor.

**Reaktor|fall** *der* nuclear accident.

**real** *adj* real ⬦ *adv* - **1.** [realistisch] realistically
- **2.** ᴡɪʀᴛsᴄʜ in real terms.

**Real|einkommen** *das* real income.

**realisierbar** *adj* realizable.

**realisieren** *vt geh* to realize.

**Realismus** *der* realism.

**Realist, in** (*mpl* -en; *fpl* -nen) *der, die* realist.

**realistisch** *adj* realistic ⬦ *adv* realistically.

**Realität** (*pl* -en) *die* reality.

**Real|politik** *die* realpolitik.

**Real|schule** *die secondary school for pupils up to the age of 16.*

**Real|schüler, in** *der, die* pupil at a "Real-schule".

**Rebe** (*pl* -n) *die* vine.

**Rebell** (*pl* -en) *der* rebel.

**rebellieren** *vi* to rebel; **gegen jn/etw ~** to rebel against sb/sthg.

**Rebellin** (*pl* -nen) *die* rebel.

**Rebellion** (*pl* -en) *die* rebellion.

**rebellisch** *adj* rebellious.

**Reb|huhn** *das* partridge.

**Reb|stock** *der* vine.

**Receiver** [ri'siːvɐ] (*pl* -) *der* receiver.

**Rechen** (*pl* -) *der* rake.

**Rechen|aufgabe** *die* sum.

**Rechen|fehler** *der* miscalculation.

**Rechenschaft** *die:* **von jm ~ fordern** to demand an explanation from sb; **jm (keine) ~ schuldig sein** (not) to owe sb an explanation; **jm über etw** (A) **~ ablegen** ᴏᴅᴇʀ **geben** to account to sb for sthg; **jn (für etw) zur ~ ziehen** to call sb to account (for sthg).

**Rechenschafts|bericht** *der* report.

**Rechen|zentrum** *das* computer centre.

**recherchieren** *vt* & *vi* to investigate.

**rechnen** *vi* - **1.** [berechnen] to calculate
- **2.** [schätzen] to estimate; **rund gerechnet** roughly - **3.** [erwarten]: **mit jm/etw ~** to expect sb/sthg - **4.** [sich verlassen]: **auf jn/etw ~** to count on sb/sthg; **mit jm ~** to rely on sb - **5.** [bedenken]: **mit jm/etw ~** to reckon with sb/sthg; **im Urlaub mit gutem Wetter ~** to reckon on having good weather on holiday ⬦ *vt* [berechnen] to work out.
➥ **sich rechnen** *ref* to be profitable.

**Rechner** (*pl* -) *der* ᴇᴅᴠ computer.

**rechnerisch** *adj* arithmetical ⬦ *adv* by calculation; **rein ~ gesehen lohnt sich das nicht** the figures suggest it's not worth it.

**Rechnung** (*pl* -en) *die* - **1.** ᴡɪʀᴛsᴄʜ bill; [im Restaurant] bill *Br,* check *Am;* **eine ~ begleichen** to pay a bill; **das geht auf meine ~!** this round is on me!; **jm etw in ~ stellen** to charge sb for sthg

- **2.** [Rechenaufgabe] calculation - **3.** *RW:* **auf eigene ~** on one's own account; **eine ~ begleichen** to settle a score; **einer Sache** (D) **~ tragen** *geh* to take sthg into account; **js ~ geht (nicht) auf** things (don't) work out as sb hopes.

**Rechnungs|hof** *der authority charged with auditing state institutions.*

**Rechnungs|prüfer, in** *der, die* auditor.

**Rechnungs|wesen** *das* accountancy.

**recht** *adj* - **1.** [korrekt, passend] right; **~ und billig** *fig* right and proper; **zur ~en Zeit am ~en Ort** at the right place at the right time; **ist es dir ~, wenn ich morgen vorbeikomme?** is it all right with you if I come by tomorrow?
- **2.** [besonders] particular; **es macht keinen ~en Spaß** it's not really much fun ⬦ *adv*
- **1.** [ziemlich] quite - **2.** *RW:* **man kann ihm nichts ~ machen** there's no pleasing him; **~ und schlecht** just about; **jetzt erst ~** even more.

**Recht** (*pl* -e) *das* - **1.** ʀᴇᴄʜᴛ law; **~ sprechen** to administer justice; **von ~s wegen** by law; **im ~ sein** to be in the right; **~ haben** to be right; **jm ~ geben** to admit sb is right - **2.** [Anrecht] right; **ein ~ auf etw** (A) **haben** to have a right to sthg; **das ist js gutes ~** that is sb's right.
➥ **mit** ᴏᴅᴇʀ **zu Recht** *adv* rightly.

**rechte, r, s** *adj* - **1.** [Seitenangabe] right - **2.** [rechtspolitisch] right-wing.

**Rechte** (*pl* -n) *die* - **1.** [rechte Hand] right hand; **zur ~n** on the right - **2.** ᴘᴏʟ: **die ~** the Right ⬦ *der, die* right-winger ⬦ *das:* **nach dem ~n sehen** to see to things.

**Rechteck** (*pl* -e) *das* rectangle.

**rechteckig** *adj* rectangular.

**rechtens** *adj* (*unver*): **~ sein** *fig* to be lawful.

**rechtfertigen** *vt* to justify; **etw vor jm ~** to justify sthg to sb.
➥ **sich rechtfertigen** *ref:* **sich (vor jm) ~** to justify o.s. (to sb).

**Rechtfertigung** (*pl* -en) *die* justification.

**rechthaberisch** *adj abw* opinionated; **er ist immer so ~** he always thinks he's right.

**rechtlich** *adj* legal ⬦ *adv* legally.

**rechtlos** *adj* without rights.

**rechtmäßig** *adj* lawful ⬦ *adv* lawfully.

**rechts** *adv* - **1.** [Angabe der Seite, Richtung] on the right; **~ abbiegen** turn right; **nach/von ~** to/from the right; **~ von jm** to one's right; **~ von etw** to the right of sthg - **2.** [Angabe der politischen Richtung] right wing; **~ eingestellt sein** to have right-wing leanings ⬦ *präp* (+ G) [Angabe der Seite] to the right of.

**Rechts|abbieger** (*pl* -) *der* car turning right.

**Rechtsan|spruch** *der* (legal) entitlement.

**Rechts|anwalt** *der* lawyer.

**Rechts|anwältin** *die* lawyer.

**Rechts|außen** (*pl* -) *der, die* - **1.** sport outside right - **2.** *fam* pol extreme right-winger.

**Rechts|beratung** *die* legal advice *(U).*

**Rechts|bruch** *der:* einen ~ begehen to break the law.

**rechtsbündig** *adj* right justified.

**rechtschaffen** *adj* - **1.** [Mensch, Arbeit] honest - **2.** *fam* [Hunger] real ⬦ *adv* - **1.** [leben, arbeiten] honestly - **2.** *fam* [hungrig, müde] really.

**Rechtschreib|fehler** *der* spelling mistake.

**Recht|schreibung** *die* spelling.

**Rechts|empfinden** *das* sense of right and wrong.

**rechtsextrem** *adj:* ~e Jugendliche young right-wing extremists; ~e Gruppierung extreme right-wing faction.

**Rechts|extremist, in** *der, die* abw right-wing extremist.

**Rechts|frage** *die* legal matter.

**rechtsgerichtet** *adj* right-wing.

**rechtsgültig** *adj* legally valid.

**Rechtshänder, in** (*mpl* -; *fpl* -nen) *der, die* right-hander.

**rechtshändig** *adj* right-handed.

**rechtsherum** *adv* to the right.

**rechtskräftig** *adj* final; ~ sein to be legally effective ⬦ *adv:* jn ~ verurteilen to pass a final sentence on sb.

**Rechts|kurve** *die* right-hand bend.

**Rechts|lage** *die* legal situation.

**Rechts|pfleger, in** *der, die* amt *judicial officer outside the regular judiciary who has certain judicial powers.*

**Rechtsprechung** (*pl* -en) *die* administration of justice *(U).*

**rechtsradikal** *adj* extreme right-wing.

**Rechts|radikale** *der, die* right-wing extremist.

**Rechts|schutz** *der* legal protection.

**Rechtsschutzver|sicherung** *die* legal protection insurance.

**rechtsseitig** *adj* of the right side ⬦ *adv* on the right side.

**Rechts|staat** *der* state based upon the rule of law.

**Rechts|streit** *der* amt lawsuit.

**Rechts|verkehr** *der* - **1.** [Straßenverkehr] driving on the right - **2.** recht law.

**Rechts|weg** *der* legal action; der ~ ist ausgeschlossen no legal action may be taken.

**rechtswidrig** *adj* illegal.

**rechtwinklig, rechtwinkelig** *adj* right-angled ⬦ *adv* at a right angle.

**rechtzeitig** *adj* timely ⬦ *adv* in time; ~ da sein/eintreffen to be/get there in time.

**Reck** (*pl* -e oder -s) *das* horizontal bar.

**recken** *vt* to stretch; den Hals ~ to crane one's neck.

⬧ **sich recken** *ref* to stretch (o.s.).

**Recorder** (*pl* -) *der fam* = Rekorder.

**recyclen** [riˈsaikəln] *vt* to recycle.

**Recycling** [riˈsaiklɪŋ] *das* recycling.

**Recyclingpapier** *das* recycled paper.

**Red.** - **1.** (*abk für* Redakteur) ed. - **2.** *abk für* Redaktion.

**Redakteur, in** [redakˈtøːg, rɪn] (*mpl* -e; *fpl* -nen) *der, die* editor.

**Redaktion** (*pl* -en) *die* - **1.** [Team] editorial staff - **2.** [von Texten] editing.

**Rede** (*pl* -n) *die* - **1.** [Ansprache] speech; eine ~ halten to make a speech - **2.** (*ohne pl*) [das Reden] talk; die ~ ist von jm/etw we are talking about sb/etw - **3.** gram [gebundene] verse; [ungebundene] prose; wörtliche/indirekte ~ direct/indirect speech - **4.** RW: etw ist nicht der ~ wert sthg is not worth mentioning; jm ~ und Antwort stehen to explain o.s. to sb; jn zur ~ stellen to demand an explanation from sb.

**Redefreiheit** *die* freedom of speech.

**redegewandt** *adj* eloquent.

**reden** *vi* - **1.** [gen] to talk; deutlich/langsam ~ to speak clearly/slowly; (mit jm) über jn/etw ~ to talk (to sb) about sb/sthg - **2.** [eine Rede halten] to speak - **3.** RW: darüber lässt sich ~ that may be possible; du hast gut ~ *fam* it's easy for you to talk; jn zum Reden bringen to get sb to talk; mit sich ~ lassen to be open to discussion; von sich ~ machen to cause a stir ⬦ *vt:* Unsinn ~ to talk nonsense; kein Wort ~ not to say a word.

**Redens|art** *die* saying; das ist doch nur eine ~ it's just an expression.

**Rede|wendung** *die* idiom.

**redlich** *adj* [anständig] honest ⬦ *adv:* sich ~ Mühe geben to try really hard.

**Redner, in** (*mpl* -; *fpl* -nen) *der, die* speaker.

**redselig** *adj* talkative.

**Reduktion** (*pl* -en) *die* reduction.

**reduzieren** *vt* - **1.** [verringern] to reduce - **2.** [vereinfachen]: etw auf etw (A) ~ to reduce sthg to sthg.

⬧ **sich reduzieren** *ref* to decrease.

**Reederei** (*pl* -en) *die* shipping company.

**reell** *adj* - **1.** wirtsch [Geschäft, Arbeit] honest; [Preis]

**R**

fair - **2.** [Chance] realistic - **3.** *fam* [Mahlzeit] decent.

**Reeperbahn** *die street in Hamburg famous for its bars and nightclubs.*

**Referat** (*pl* -e) *das* - **1.** [Abhandlung] paper; **ein ~ halten** to give a paper - **2.** [Abteilung] department.

**Referendar** (*pl* -e) *der person undergoing "Referendariat";* [in Schule] student teacher.

**Referendariat** (*pl* -e) *das period of practical training in teaching or legal professions, undertaken on completion of first "Staatsexamen".*

**Referendarin** (*pl* -nen) *die person undergoing "Referendariat";* [in Schule] student teacher.

**Referendum** (*pl* -den) *das* referendum.

**Referent, in** (*mpl* -en; *fpl* -nen) *der, die* - **1.** [Redner] speaker - **2.** [Beamter] adviser.

**Referenz** (*pl* -en) *die* reference.

**referieren** *vi:* **über etw** (A) **~** to give a paper on sthg.

**reflektieren** *vt* - **1.** [Licht] to reflect - **2.** *geh* [Problem] to reflect on <> *vi geh:* **über etw** (A) **~** to reflect on sthg.

**Reflektor** (*pl* -toren) *der* reflector.

**Reflex** (*pl* -e) *der* - **1.** [Reaktion] reflex - **2.** [Lichtreflex] reflection.

**Reflexion** (*pl* -en) *die* reflection.

**reflexiv** GRAM *adj* reflexive <> *adv* reflexively.

**Reflexiv|pronomen** *das* GRAM reflexive pronoun.

**Reform** (*pl* -en) *die* reform.

**Reformation** *die* REL Reformation.

**Reformations|tag** *der* REL Reformation Day, *31 October, day on which the Reformation is celebrated.*

**reformbedürftig** *adj* in need of reform.

**Reformer, in** (*mpl* -; *fpl* -nen) *der, die* reformer.

**Reform|haus** *das* health food shop.

> **REFORMHAUS**
>
> In addition to health food, these shops, which are very common in Germany, sell natural health care and beauty products. Sometimes there is also a health food café on the premises.

**reformieren** *vt* to reform.

**Reformkost** *die* health food.

**Refrain** [rə'frɛ:] (*pl* -s) *der* refrain.

**Regal** (*pl* -e) *das* shelves (*pl*).

**Regatta** (*pl* Regatten) *die* regatta.

**Reg.-Bez.** *abk für* Regierungsbezirk.

**rege** *adj* lively; [Verkehr] busy; [Handel] brisk <> *adv:* **sich ~ an etw** (D) **beteiligen** to take a lively interest in sthg.

**Regel** (*pl* -n) *die* - **1.** [Norm] rule; **in aller** ODER **der ~ as a rule; sich** (D) **etw zur ~ machen** to make sthg a rule - **2.** [Periode] period.

**Regel|blutung** *die* period.

**Regel|fall** *der* rule.

**regellos** *adj* disorderly.

**regelmäßig** *adj* regular <> *adv* regularly.

**Regelmäßigkeit** (*pl* -en) *die* regularity.

**regeln** *vt* [Temperatur, Geschwindigkeit] to regulate; [Angelegenheit] to settle; [Nachlass] to put in order; [Verkehr] to direct.
➤ **sich regeln** *ref* to sort itself out; **sich von selbst ~** to sort itself out.

**regelrecht** *adj* - **1.** *fam* [richtig] proper - **2.** [ordnungsgemäß] correct.

**Regelung** (*pl* -en) *die* regulation.

**Regel|werk** *das* system of rules.

**regelwidrig** *adj* against the rules <> *adv* [spielen] against the rules; [parken] illegally.

**regen** *vt* to move.
➤ **sich regen** *ref* to move; [Gefühl, Hoffnung] to stir.

**Regen** *der* rain; **strichweise ~** *amt* rain in places; **strömender ~** pouring rain; **saurer ~** acid rain.

**Regen|bogen** *der* rainbow.

**Regenbogenpresse** *die* (ohne *pl*) *abw* trashy magazines (*pl*).

**regenerieren** *vt geh* to regenerate.
➤ **sich regenerieren** *ref* to regenerate o.s.

**Regen|guss** *der* downpour.

**Regen|haut** *die* plastic mackintosh.

**Regen|mantel** *der* raincoat.

**Regen|rinne** *die* gutter.

**Regen|schauer** *der* shower.

**Regen|schirm** *der* umbrella.

**Regent, in** (*mpl* -en; *fpl* -nen) *der, die* sovereign.

**Regen|tonne** *die* water butt.

**Regen|tropfen** *der* raindrop.

**Regen|wald** *der* rain forest; **der tropische ~** the tropical rain forest.

**Regen|wasser** *das* rainwater.

**Regen|wetter** *das* rainy weather.

**Regen|wurm** *der* earthworm.

**Regen|zeit** *die* rainy season.

**Regie** [re'ʒi:] *die* direction; **~ führen** to direct; **etw in eigener ~ tun** ODER **durchführen** to do sthg on one's own account.

**Regie|assistent, in** *der, die* assistant director.

**regieren** *vt* to rule ⬦ *vi* to rule; **über jn/etw ~** to rule over sb/sthg.

**Regierung** (*pl* -en) *die* government.

**Regierungs|bezirk** *der administrative division of a "Land".*

**Regierungs|chef, in** *der, die* head of government.

**Regierungs|erklärung** *die* government proposals (*pl*); ≃ Queen's Speech *Br.*

**Regierungs|gebäude** *das* government building.

**Regierungs|krise** *die* governmental crisis.

**Regierungs|partei** *die* governing party.

**Regierungs|präsident, in** *der, die head of an administrative division of a "Land".*

**Regierungs|rat** *der* senior civil servant.

**Regierungs|sitz** *der* seat of government.

**Regierungs|sprecher, in** *der, die* government spokesperson.

**Regime** [re'ʒi:m] (*pl* -) *das* regime.

**Regime|kritiker, in** *der, die* dissident.

**Regiment** (*pl* -e ODER -er) *das* - **1.** (*pl Regimenter*) MIL regiment - **2.** (*pl Regimente*) [Leitung] rule; **ein strenges ~ führen** to be strict.

**Region** (*pl* -en) *die* region.

**regional** *adj* regional ⬦ *adv* regionally; **~ verschieden** different from region to region.

**Regisseur, in** [reʒɪ'søːɐ̯, rɪn] (*mpl* -e; *fpl* -nen) *der, die* director.

**Register** (*pl* -) *das* - **1.** [Verzeichnis - in Buch] index; [ - amtlich] register - **2.** [MUS - von Orgel] stop; [ - von Stimme] register; **alle ~ ziehen** *fig* to pull out all the stops.

**registrieren** *vt* - **1.** [wahrnehmen] to notice - **2.** [eintragen] to register.

**reglementieren** *vt abw* to regulate; [Person] to regiment.

**Regler** (*pl* -) *der* control.

**reglos** *adj* motionless ⬦ *adv* motionlessly.

**regnen** *vi*: **es regnet** it's raining ⬦ *vt*: **es regnet Konfetti** confetti is raining down; **es regnete Beifall** there was a storm of applause.

**regnerisch** *adj* rainy.

**regresspflichtig** *adj* liable to recourse.

**regulär** *adj* - **1.** [Preis, Arbeit] normal; [Wahl, Spiel] in accordance with the rules - **2.** MIL regular ⬦ *adv* [arbeiten] normally; [zum normalen Preis] at the normal price.

**regulieren** *vt* - **1.** [regeln - Preis, Schaden, Verkehr] to regulate - **2.** [Temperatur, Lautstärke] to adjust - **3.** [Gewässer] to straighten.

**Regulierung** (*pl* -en) *die* - **1.** [von Preis, Schaden, Verkehr] regulation - **2.** [von Temperatur, Lautstärke] adjustment - **3.** [von Gewässer] straightening.

**Regung** (*pl* -en) *die* - **1.** [Bewegung] movement - **2.** *geh* [Gefühl] stirring.

**regungslos** *adj* motionless ⬦ *adv* motionlessly.

**Reh** (*pl* -e) *das* deer.

**Reha** ['re:ha] (*abk für* **Rehabilitierung**) *die* rehab.

**rehabilitieren** *vt* to rehabilitate.
➥ **sich rehabilitieren** *ref* to redeem o.s.

**Reha-|Klinik** *die* rehab clinic.

**Reh|bock** *der* roebuck.

**Rehkitz** (*pl* -e) *das* fawn.

**Reibach** *der* (*ohne pl*) *fam* profits (*pl*); **seinen ~ machen** *fam* to make a killing.

**Reibe** (*pl* -n) *die* grater.

**Reibeisen** *das* grater.

**Reibe|kuchen** *der small pancake made from grated potatoes.*

**reiben** (*prät* **rieb**; *perf* **hat gerieben**) *vt* - **1.** [Körperteile] to rub; **sich** (D) **die Hände/die Nase/das Auge ~** to rub one's hands/nose/eye; **jm die Hände/Wangen ~** to rub sb's hands/cheeks - **2.** [Käse, Karotten] to grate ⬦ *vi* to rub.
➥ **sich reiben** *ref fam* [sich nerven]: **sich an etw** (D) **~** to come up against sthg; **sich mit jm ~** to be at loggerheads with sb.

**Reiberei** (*pl* -en) *die* friction.

**Reibung** *die* - **1.** PHYS friction - **2.** [das Reiben] rubbing.

**reibungslos** *adj* smooth ⬦ *adv* smoothly.

**reich** *adj* - **1.** [wohlhabend] rich; **~ an etw** (D) **sein** [Bodenschätzen] to be rich in sthg; [Erfahrungen] to have a wealth of sthg - **2.** [Erdölvorkommen, Ernte] rich; [Erfahrung] extensive ⬦ *adv* [geschmückt] richly.

**Reich** (*pl* -e) *das* - **1.** POL empire - **2.** [Bereich] world.

**Reiche** (*pl* -n) *der, die* rich person.

**reichen** *vi* - **1.** [Geld, Zeit] to be enough; [Vorrat] to last; **mit den Vorräten/dem Geld ~** *Norddt* to have enough supplies/money; **das reicht!** that's enough!; **mir reichts** *fam fig* I've had enough - **2.**: **(von ... bis zu ...) ~** [Grundstück, Gebiet] to extend (from ... to ...); [Kleidungsstück] to reach (from ... to ...) ⬦ *vt*: **jm etw ~** to pass sb sthg; **sich** (D) **die Hände ~** to shake hands.

**reichhaltig** *adj* rich.

**reichlich** *adj* [Essen, Zeit] ample; [Trinkgeld] generous ⬦ *adv* - **1.** [viel] amply - **2.** [ziemlich] rather.

R

**Reichs|tag** [ˈraiçstaːk] *der* [Gebäude] Reichstag.

> **REICHSTAG**
>
> The Reichstag was built between 1884 and 1894. Until 27 February 1933, when the building was burnt down, the German parliament ("deutsche Reichstag") met in session there. The fire gave the National Socialists (who had in fact orchestrated the fire) an excuse to persecute their political opponents; this marked the end of democracy in the Weimar Republic. The building was badly damaged during the Second World War and, after it was rebuilt, the Bundestag only used it for special occasions. After the reunification of Germany in 1990, the restoration of the Reichstag was completed and the building was surmounted by a glass dome. The Reichstag has been the seat of the German parliament again since 1999.

**Reichtum** (*pl* -tümer) *der* - **1.** [Vermögen] wealth - **2.** [Fülle]: **der ~ an etw** (D) the abundance of sthg.
➤ **Reichtümer** *pl* riches.

**Reich|weite** *die* - **1.** [greifbare Nähe, von Boxern] reach - **2.** TECH range.
➤ **außer Reichweite** *adv* out of reach.
➤ **in Reichweite** *adv* within reach.

**reif** *adj* - **1.** [gen] ripe; **~ für etw sein** *fam fig* to be ready for sthg; **~ fürs Irrenhaus sein** to belong in the madhouse - **2.** [erwachsen] mature; **~ für etw sein** to be old enough for sthg.

**Reif** (*pl* -e) *der* - **1.** [Schmuckstück] bracelet - **2.** [Raureif] hoarfrost.

**Reife** *die* - **1.** [von Person] maturity; **mittlere ~** SCHULE intermediate school-leaving certificate *(for those leaving at 16)* - **2.** [von Obst] ripeness.

**reifen** (*perf* hat/ist gereift) *vi* - **1.** *(ist)* [Frucht] to ripen - **2.** *(ist)* [Person, Wunsch, Entschluss] to mature - **3.** *(hat)* [Raureif geben]: **es hat gereift** there has been a frost.

**Reifen** (*pl* -) *der* - **1.** [von Fahrzeugen] tyre - **2.** [Ring] hoop.

**Reifen|druck** *der* tyre pressure.

**Reifen|panne** *die* flat tyre.

**Reifen|wechsel** *der* tyre change.

**Reife|prüfung** *die* final examination at a German "Gymnasium", required for university entrance.

**Reife|zeugnis** *das* certificate awarded to people who have passed the "Reifeprüfung".

**reiflich** *adj* very careful ⟨⟩ *adv* very carefully.

**Reih** ➤ **in Reih und Glied** in formation.

**Reihe** (*pl* -n) *die* - **1.** [Linie, Sitzreihe] row - **2.** [Menge]: **eine ~ von etw** a number of sthg - **3.** [Reihenfolge]: **du bist an der ~** it's your turn; **jn außer der ~ drannehmen** to take sb out of turn; **er kommt an die ~** it is his turn; **jetzt kommt der Garten an die ~** now it's the turn of the garden - **4.** *RW*: **aus den eigenen ~n** from one's own ranks; **aus der ~ tanzen** *fam* to be different; **etw nicht auf die ~ kriegen** *fam* not to manage sthg.
➤ **der Reihe nach** *adv* in turn.

**reihen** *vt* - **1.** [nebeneinander stellen] to line up - **2.** [auffädeln]: **etw auf etw** (A) **~** to string sthg on sthg - **3.** [nähen] to tack.
➤ **sich reihen** *ref* [sich anschließen]: **ein Misserfolg reihte sich an den anderen** failure followed failure.

**Reihen|folge** *die* order; **alphabetische ~** alphabetical order.

**Reihen|haus** *das* terraced house *Br*, row house *Am*.

**reihenweise** *adv* - **1.** [in Reihen] in rows - **2.** *fam* [in Mengen] by the score.

**Reiher** (*pl* -) *der* heron.

**reihum** *adv* round.

**Reim** (*pl* -e) *der* rhyme; **darauf kann sie sich** (D) **keinen ~ machen** *fig* she can't see any rhyme or reason in it.

**reimen** *vt* to rhyme ⟨⟩ *vi* to make up rhymes.
➤ **sich reimen** *ref* to rhyme; **'Bein' reimt sich auf 'klein'** 'Bein' rhymes with 'klein'.

**rein** *adj* - **1.** [ohne Zusätze, nicht gemischt] pure; **eine ~e Mädchenklasse** a class of just girls, an all-girl class; **eine ~e Arbeitergegend** a wholly working-class area; **~er Gewinn** net profit - **2.** [nicht als] sheer; **die ~ste Wahrheit** the absolute truth - **3.** [sauber] clean - **4.** *RW*: **etw ins Reine schreiben** to make a fair copy of sthg; **etw ins Reine bringen** to clear sthg up; **mit jm ins Reine kommen** to sort things out with sb; **mit jm im Reinen sein** to have sorted things out with sb ⟨⟩ *adv* - **1.** [ausschließlich] purely; **~ zeitlich geht es nicht** there's simply not enough time to do it - **2.** *fam* [völlig] absolutely; **~ unmöglich** utterly impossible; **er wusste auch ~ gar nichts** he didn't know anything - **3.** *fam* = **herein**.

**Rein|erlös** *der* net proceeds (*pl*).

**Rein|fall** *der fam* disaster.

**rein|fallen** (*perf* ist reingefallen) *vi* (unreg) *fam* - **1.** [hineinfallen] to fall in - **2.** [getäuscht werden] to fall for it; **auf jn/etw ~** to be taken in by sb/sthg; **mit jm/etw ~** to have nothing but trouble with sb/sthg.

**rein|gehen** (*perf* ist reingegangen) *vi* (unreg) *fam* to go in.

**Rein|gewinn** *der* net profit.

**Rein|haltung** *die:* **die ~ von etw** keeping sthg clean.

**Reinheit** *die* **- 1.** [Unverfälschtheit] purity **- 2.** [Sauberkeit] cleanness.

**reinigen** *vt* to clean; **ein Kleidungsstück chemisch ~ lassen** to have a garment drycleaned.

➡ **sich reinigen** *ref* to clean o.s.; **sich** *(D)* **die Hände ~** to clean one's hands.

**Reinigung** *(pl -en) die* **- 1.: die (chemische) ~** the (dry) cleaner's **- 2.** [Säubern] cleaning.

**Reinigungs|mittel** *das* cleaner.

**rein|kommen** *(perf* **ist reingekommen)** *vi (unreg) fam* **- 1.** [hineinkommen, hineinpassen] to get in; [hereinkommen] to come in **- 2.** [hinzukommen] to be added.

**rein|legen** *vt fam* **- 1.** [hineinlegen] to put in **- 2.** [übertölpeln] to take for a ride.

**reinlich** *adj* clean.

**reinrassig** *adj* purebred; [Pferd] thoroughbred.

**rein|reden** *vi fam* **- 1.** [ins Wort fallen] to butt in **- 2.** [sich einmischen]: **jm ~** to tread on sb's toes; **sich von niemandem ~ lassen** not to take orders from anybody.

**rein|steigern** ➡ **sich reinsteigern** *ref fam:* **sich in die Angst/Begeisterung ~** to work o.s. up into a state of fear/enthusiasm; **sich in eine Vorstellung ~** to be wrapped up in an idea.

**reinwollen** *vt fam* to want to come/go in.

**Reis** *der* rice.

**Reise** *(pl -n) die* [lang] journey; [kurz] trip; **auf ~n sein/gehen** to be/go away; **eine ~ machen** to go on a journey/trip.

➡ **gute Reise** *interj* have a good journey/trip!

**Reise|apotheke** *die* first-aid kit.

**Reise|begleiter, in** *der, die* travelling companion.

**Reise|bekanntschaft** *die acquaintance made on a journey.*

**Reise|büro** *das* travel agent's.

**Reise|bus** *der* coach.

**reisefertig** *adj & adv* ready to go.

**Reise|führer** *der* **- 1.** [Mensch] guide, courier **- 2.** [Buch] guide book.

**Reise|führerin** *die* guide, courier.

**Reise|gepäck** *das* luggage.

**Reise|gesellschaft** *die* **- 1.** [Reisegruppe] group of tourists **- 2.** [Veranstalter] tour operator.

**Reise|gruppe** *die* group of tourists.

**Reise|kosten** *pl* travelling expenses.

**Reise|land** *das* holiday destination.

**Reise|leiter, in** *der, die* guide, courier.

**reiselustig** *adj* keen on travelling.

**reisen** *(perf* **ist gereist)** *vi* to travel; **nach Athen/Schottland ~** to go to Athens/Scotland.

**Reisende** *(pl -n) der, die* [Fahrgast] passenger.

**Reise|pass** *der* passport.

**Reise|route** *die* route.

**Reise|ruf** *der emergency message for a driver, broadcast over the radio.*

**Reise|tasche** *die* travel bag.

**Reise|verkehr** *der* holiday traffic.

**Reisever|sicherung** *die* travel insurance.

**Reise|wecker** *der* travel alarm clock.

**Reisewetter|bericht** *der* holiday weather forecast.

**Reise|zeit** *die* **- 1.** [Fahrtdauer] journey time **- 2.** [Saison] holiday season.

**Reise|ziel** *das* destination.

**Reißaus** *das:* **~ nehmen** *fam* to clear off.

**Reiß|brett** *das* drawing board.

**reißen** *(prät* **riss;** *perf* **hat/ist gerissen)** *vi* **- 1.** *(ist)* [abreißen - Papier, Stoff] to tear; [ - Seil, Kette] to snap **- 2.** *(hat)* [ziehen]: **an etw** *(D)* **~** to pull at sthg ⬥ *vt (hat)* **- 1.** [zerreißen]: **etw in Stücke ~** to tear sthg into pieces **- 2.** [herunterreißen] to pull **- 3.** [herausreißen]: **sie wurde aus dem Schlaf gerissen** she was rudely awakened; **etw aus dem Zusammenhang ~** to take sthg out of context **- 4.** [wegreißen]: **jm etw aus der Hand ~** to snatch sthg from sb; **etw an sich** *(A)* **~** [Paket, Macht] to seize sthg; [Gespräch] to monopolize sthg; **hin und her gerissen sein** *fig* to be torn **- 5.** [töten] to kill.

➡ **sich reißen** *ref:* **sich um etw ~** to fight to get sthg; **sich um jn ~** to fight over sb.

**reißend** *adj* **- 1.** [Gewässer] raging **- 2.** [schnell]: **~en Absatz finden** to sell like hot cakes **- 3.** [Tier] rapacious **- 4.** [Schmerzen] searing.

**reißerisch** *abw adj* sensational ⬥ *adv* sensationally.

**reißfest** *adj* tear-resistant.

**Reißver|schluss** *der* zip *Br*, zipper *Am*.

**Reiß|wolf** *der* shredder.

**Reiß|zwecke** *die* drawing pin *Br*, thumbtack *Am*.

**reiten** *(prät* **ritt;** *perf* **hat/ist geritten)** *vi (ist)* to ride; **im Schritt/Trab/Galopp ~** to ride at a walk/trot/gallop ⬥ *vt (hat)* to ride.

**Reiter, in** *(mpl -; fpl -nen) der, die* rider.

**Reiter|hof** *der* riding stables *(pl)*.

**Reit|gerte** *die* riding crop.

**Reit|hose** *die* jodhpurs *(pl)*.

**Reit|pferd** *das* horse *(for riding)*.
**Reit|sport** *der* riding.
**Reit|stiefel** *der* riding boot.
**Reit|turnier** *das* showjumping event.
**Reit|weg** *der* bridle path.
**Reiz** *(pl* -e) *der* - **1.** [Impuls] stimulus - **2.** [Verlockung, Schönheit] appeal *(U);* **die ~e einer schönen Frau** the charms of a beautiful woman; **dem kann ich keinen ~ abgewinnen** it holds no appeal for me.
**reizbar** *adj* irritable; **sie ist leicht ~** she is very irritable.
**reizen** *vt* - **1.** [interessieren] to appeal to - **2.** [provozieren] to provoke - **3.** [Augen, Magen] to irritate - **4.** [Neugier] to arouse.
**reizend** *adj* charming <> *adv* charmingly.
**reizlos** *adj* unattractive <> *adv* unattractively.
**Reizung** *(pl* -en) *die* irritation.
**reizvoll** *adj* [verlockend] attractive; [reizend] charming <> *adv* attractively.
**Reizwäsche** *die* sexy underwear.
**rekapitulieren** *vt* to recapitulate.
**rekeln** = räkeln.
**Reklamation** *(pl* -en) *die* complaint.
**Reklame** *die* - **1.** [Werbung] advertising; **für jn/ etw ~ machen** to advertise sb/sthg; *fig* **to sing sb's/sthg's praises** - **2.** [Werbemittel] advertisement.
**reklamieren** *vt* - **1.** [beanstanden] to complain about - **2.** [einklagen] to claim <> *vi* [Einspruch erheben]: **gegen etw ~** to object to sthg.
**rekonstruieren** *vt* to reconstruct.
**Re|konstruktion** *die* reconstruction.
**Rekord** *(pl* -e) *der* [Bestleistung, Spitzenwert] record; **einen ~ aufstellen/brechen** to set/ break a record.
**Rekorder, Recorder** *(pl* -) *der* recorder.
**Rekord|zeit** *die* record time.
**Rekrut** *(pl* -en) *der* MIL recruit.
**rekrutieren** *vt* to recruit.
➡ **sich rekrutieren** *ref:* **sich aus etw ~** to be drawn from sthg.
**rektal** MED *adj* rectal <> *adv* rectally.
**Rektor** *(pl* -toren) *der* - **1.** [von Schulen] head teacher *Br*, principal *Am* - **2.** [von Hochschulen] vice-chancellor *Br*, president *Am*.
**Rektorin** *(pl* -nen) *die* - **1.** [von Schulen] head teacher *Br*, principal *Am* - **2.** [von Hochschulen] vice-chancellor *Br*, president *Am*.
**Rel.** *(abk für* **Religion**) rel.
**Relation** *(pl* -en) *die* - **1.** [Beziehung] relation; **etw steht in keiner ~ zu etw** sthg bears no relation to sthg - **2.** MATH relation.

**relativ, relativ** *adj* relative <> *adv* relatively.
**relativieren** [relat:'vi:rən] *vt* to relativize.
➡ **sich relativieren** *ref* to be relativized.
**Relativität** [relativi'tɛ:t] *die* relativity.
**Relativ|pronomen** *das* GRAM relative pronoun.
**Relativ|satz** *der* GRAM relative clause.
**relaxen** [ri'lɛksn̩] *vi fam* to take it easy.
**relevant** [rele'vant] *adj* relevant.
**Relevanz** [rele'vants] *die* relevance.
**Relief** *(pl* -s *ODER* -e) *das* relief.
**Religion** *(pl* -en) *die* - **1.** [Anschauung] religion - **2.** *(ohne pl)* [Schulfach] religious education.
**Religionsunterricht** *der* religious education.
**religiös** *adj* religious <> *adv* in a religious way; **jn ~ erziehen** to give sb a religious upbringing.
**Relikt** *(pl* -e) *das* relic.
**Reling** *(pl* -s *ODER* -e) *die* SCHIFF rail.
**Reliquie** [re'li:kvjə] *(pl* -n) *die* relic.
**remis** [rə'mi:] *adv* SPORT: **~ enden** to end in a draw.
**Remis** *(pl* -) *das* SPORT draw.
**Remoulade** *(pl* -n) *die* remoulade.
**rempeln** *vt fam* to push.
**Ren, Ren** *(pl* -s) *das* reindeer.
**Renaissance** [rənɛ'sã:s] *die* Renaissance.
**Rendezvous** [rãde'vu:] *(pl* -) *das* rendezvous.
**Rendite** *(pl* -n) *die* return, yield.
**renitent** *geh adj* refractory <> *adv* refractorily.
**Renn|bahn** *die* SPORT racetrack; [Pferdesport] racecourse.
**rennen** *(prät* **rannte**; *perf* **ist gerannt)** *vi* to run; **sie kommt immer zu mir gerannt, wenn sie etwas braucht** she's always running to me when she needs something; **gegen etw ~** to run into sthg.
**Rennen** *(pl* -) *das* - **1.** [Wettkampf] race - **2.** *RW*: **das ~ machen** to win; **ein totes ~ sein** to be a dead heat; **gut im ~ liegen** to be well placed.
**Renner** *(pl* -) *der fam* in-thing.
**Renn|fahrer, in** *der, die* racing driver.
**Renn|pferd** *das* racehorse.
**Renn|rad** *das* racing bike.
**Renn|sport** *der* racing.
**Renn|stall** *der* - **1.** [von Rennpferden] stable - **2.** [von Rennwagen] team.
**Renn|strecke** *die* racetrack.
**Renn|wagen** *der* racing car.

**renommiert** *adj* renowned.

**renovieren** [reno'viːrən] *vt* to renovate.

**Renovierung** [reno'viːruŋ] (*pl* -en) *die* renovation.

**rentabel** *adj* profitable ⋄ *adv* profitably.

**Rentabilität** *die* profitability.

**Rente** (*pl* -n) *die* pension; **auf** ODER **in ~ gehen** to retire.

**Renten|alter** *das* retirement age.

**Rentenver|sicherung** *die* pension scheme.

**Ren|tier, Rentier** *das* reindeer.

**rentieren** ⇒ **sich rentieren** *ref* [rentabel sein] to be profitable; [sich lohnen] to be worthwhile.

**Rentner, in** (*mpl* -; *fpl* -nen) *der, die* pensioner.

**Rep** [rɛp] (*pl* -s) *der abk für* **Republikaner**.

**Reparatur** (*pl* -en) *die* repair; **in ~ sein** to be being repaired.

**reparaturanfällig** *adj* liable to break down.

**reparaturbedürftig** *adj* in need of repair.

**Reparaturkosten** *pl* repair costs.

**Reparatur|werkstatt** *die* [für Autos] garage.

**reparieren** *vt* to repair.

**Repertoire** [reper'tǫaːɐ̯] (*pl* -s) *das geh* repertoire.

**Report** (*pl* -e) *der* report.

**Reportage** [repɔr'taːʒə] (*pl* -n) *die* report.

**Reporter, in** (*mpl* -; *fpl* -nen) *der, die* reporter.

**Repräsentant, in** (*mpl* -en; *fpl* -nen) *der, die* representative.

**repräsentativ** *adj* - **1.** [ausgewogen, stellvertretend] representative - **2.** [vorzeigbar] imposing ⋄ *adv* - **1.** [ausgewogen, stellvertretend] representatively - **2.** [vorzeigbar] imposingly.

**repräsentieren** *vt* to represent ⋄ *vi* [öffentlich] to perform official duties.

**Repressalie** (*pl* -n) *die* reprisal.

**repressiv** *adj* repressive ⋄ *adv* repressively.

**Re|produktion** *die* reproduction.

**reproduzieren** *vt* to reproduce. ⇒ **sich reproduzieren** *ref* to be reproduced.

**Reptil** (*pl* -ien ODER -e) *das* reptile.

**Republik** (*pl* -en) *die* republic.

**Republikaner, in** (*mpl* -; *fpl* -en) *der, die* - **1.** [Anhänger der Republik] republican - **2.** [Parteimitglied, -anhänger] *member/supporter of the German 'Republikaner'*.

**Republikaner** *pl*: **die ~** *German right-wing nationalist party.*

**republikanisch** *adj* republican ⋄ *adv:* **~ denken** to have republican views.

**Requiem** ['reːkvjɛm] (*pl* -s ODER **Requien**) *das* requiem.

**Requisit** [rekvi'ziːt] (*pl* -en) *das* prop.

**res.** (*abk für* **reserviert**) res.

**Reservat** [rezɛr'vaːt] (*pl* -e) *das* - **1.** [für Tiere, Pflanzen] reserve - **2.** [für Menschen] reservation.

**Reserve** [re'zɛrvə] (*pl* -n) *die* - **1.** [Vorrat] reserve; **jn/etw in ~ haben** ODER **halten** to have sb/sthg in reserve; **stille ~n** savings - **2.** (*ohne pl*) [Zurückhaltung] reserve; **jn aus der ~ locken** *fig* to bring sb out of his/her shell - **3.** (*ohne pl*) [beim Militär] reserves (*pl*).

**Reserve|bank** (*pl* -bänke) *die* substitutes' bench; **auf der ~ sitzen** to sit on the bench.

**Reserve|kanister** *der* spare can.

**Reserve|rad** *das* spare wheel.

**Reserve|reifen** *der* spare tyre.

**Reserve|spieler, in** *der, die* substitute.

**reservieren** [rezɛr'viːrən] *vt* to reserve.

**reserviert** [rezɛr'viːɐ̯t] *adj* reserved ⋄ *adv* in a reserved manner.

**Reservierung** [rezɛr'viːruŋ] (*pl* -en) *die* reservation.

**Reservist** [rezɛr'vɪst] (*pl* -en) *der* [von Armee] reservist.

**Reservoir** [rezɛr'vǫaːɐ̯] (*pl* -e) *das geh* reservoir.

**Reset** [ri'sɛt] (*pl* -s) *das* EDV reboot; **einen ~ machen** to reboot.

**Residenz** (*pl* -en) *die* [Wohnsitz] residence; [Stadt] royal seat.

**Resignation** (*pl* -en) *die* resignation (*U*).

**resignieren** *vi* to give up.

**resigniert** *adj* resigned ⋄ *adv* resignedly.

**resistent** *adj* resistant; **gegen etw ~ sein** to be resistant to sthg.

**resolut** *adj* resolute ⋄ *adv* resolutely.

**Resolution** (*pl* -en) *die* resolution.

**Resonanz** (*pl* -en) *die* - **1.** [Widerhall] response; **die ~ auf etw** (*A*) the response to sthg; **~/keine ~ finden** to meet with a/no response - **2.** [akustisch] resonance.

**Resozialisierung** (*pl* -en) *die* rehabilitation (*U*).

**Respekt** *der* respect; **~ vor jm haben** to have respect for sb; **Respekt!** well done!; **sich** (*D*) **~ verschaffen** to make o.s. respected.

**respektabel** *adj* respectable ⋄ *adv* [achtbar] respectably.

**respektieren** *vt* to respect.

R

**respektlos** *adj* disrespectful ◇ *adv* disrespectfully.

**Respektlosigkeit** (*pl* -en) *die* - **1.** [Wesen] disrespect - **2.** [Handlung] disrespectful act; [Bemerkung] disrespectful remark.

**Respektsperson** *die* person who commands respect.

**respektvoll** *adj* respectful ◇ *adv* respectfully.

**Ressort** [rε'soːɐ̯] (*pl* -s) *das* department; **das ist ihr ~** that's her department.

**Ressource** [rε'sʊrsə] (*pl* -n) *die* resource.

**Rest** (*pl* -e) *der* - **1.** [von Mahlzeit, Gebäude, Leichnam] remains (*pl*); [von Stoff] remnant - **2.** [von Tag, Urlaub, Erzählung] rest; **jm/etw den ~ geben** *fam fig* to finish sb/sthg off.

**Restaurant** [rεsto'rãː] (*pl* -s) *das* restaurant.

**restaurieren** *vt* to restore.

**Restaurierung** (*pl* -en) *die* restoration.

**Restbetrag** *der* balance.

**restlich** *adj* remaining.

**restlos** *adv* totally.

**restriktiv** *adj* restrictive ◇ *adv* restrictively.

**Resultat** (*pl* -e) *das* result.

**resultieren** *vi*: **aus etw/in etw** (*D*) **~** to result from/in sthg.

**Resümee** (*pl* -s) *das* summary; **das ~ ziehen** to sum up.

**Retorte** (*pl* -n) *die* CHEM retort; **aus der ~** *abw* artificial; **ein Kind aus der ~** a test-tube baby.

**Retortenbaby** *das* test-tube baby.

**Retourkutsche** [re'tuːɐ̯kʊtʃə] *die fam* retort.

**Retrospektive** [retrospεk'tiːvə] (*pl* -n) *die* - **1.** *geh* [Rückblick] retrospective view; **in der ~** in retrospect - **2.** [Ausstellung] retrospective.

**retten** *vt* to save; [aus einer Gefahr] to rescue; **jn/ etw vor jm/etw ~** to save sb/sthg from sb/ sthg; **bist du noch zu ~?** *fam fig* are you out of your mind?

➡ **sich retten** *ref* to escape; **sich vor jm/etw nicht mehr ~ können** *fam fig* to be besieged by sb/swamped with sthg.

**Retter, in** (*mpl* -; *fpl* -nen) *der, die* rescuer.

**Rettich** (*pl* -e) *der* radish (*of large red or white variety*).

**Rettung** *die* (*ohne pl*) rescue; **jd/etw ist js** (letzte) **~** *fig* sb/sthg is sb's salvation.

**Rettungsboot** *das* lifeboat.

**Rettungsdienst** *der* rescue service.

**Rettungshubschrauber** *der* rescue helicopter.

**rettungslos** *adj* [aussichtslos] hopeless ◇ *adv* - **1.** [aussichtslos] hopelessly - **2.** [total] totally.

**Rettungsring** *der* lifebelt.

**Rettungswagen** *der* ambulance.

**retuschieren** *vt* to retouch.

**Reue** *die* remorse; **die ~ über etw** (*A*) remorse for sthg.

**reuen** *vt geh*: **etw reut jn** sb deeply regrets sthg.

**reumütig** *adj* remorseful ◇ *adv* remorsefully.

**Revanche** [re'vãːʃ(ə)] (*pl* -n) *die* - **1.** [Gegenleistung]: **als ~ für etw** in return for sthg - **2.** [Vergeltung] revenge (*U*) - **3.** [beim Spiel] return game.

**revanchieren** [revã'ʃiːrən] ➡ **sich revanchieren** *ref* - **1.** [sich bedanken] to return the favour; **sich bei jm für etw ~** to repay sb for sthg - **2.** [sich rächen] to get one's revenge; **sich (bei jm) für etw ~** to get one's revenge (on sb) for sthg.

**Revers** [re'vεːɐ̯] (*pl* -) *das* lapel.

**revidieren** [revi'diːrən] *vt* - **1.** [Urteil, Ansicht] to revise - **2.** [Schriftstück] to check.

**Revier** [re'viːɐ̯] (*pl* -e) *das* - **1.** [von Tieren] territory - **2.** [Polizeirevier - Wache] (police) station; [ - Bezirk] district - **3.** [Bereich] domain - **4.** [von Jäger, Förster] area.

**Revision** [revi'zjoːn] *die* - **1.** RECHT appeal - **2.** [von Text] checking (*U*) - **3.** [von Vertrag, Richtlinien] revision.

**Revolte** [re'vɔltə] (*pl* -n) *die* revolt.

**revoltieren** [revɔl'tiːrən] *vi* to revolt; **gegen jn/etw ~** to rebel against sb/sthg.

**Revolution** [revolu'tsjoːn] (*pl* -en) *die* revolution.

**revolutionär** [revolutsjo'nεːɐ̯] *adj* revolutionary.

**Revolutionär, in** [revolutsjo'nεːrɪn] (*mpl* -e; *fpl* -nen) *der, die* revolutionary.

**revolutionieren** [revolutsjo'niːrən] *vt* to revolutionize.

**Revolver** [re'vɔlvɐ] (*pl* -) *der* revolver.

**Revue** [re'vyː] (*pl* -n) *die* - **1.** [Show] revue; **etw ~ passieren lassen** *fig* to go over sthg in one's mind - **2.** [Zeitschrift] review.

**Rezension** (*pl* -en) *die* review.

**Rezept** (*pl* -e) *das* - **1.** [ärztlich] prescription - **2.** [für Speisen] recipe.

**rezeptfrei** *adj* available without a prescription.

**Rezeption** (*pl* -en) *die* reception.

**rezeptpflichtig** *adj* available only on prescription.

**Rezession** (*pl* -en) *die* recession.

**rezitieren** *vt* to recite.

**R-lGespräch** *das* TELEKOM reverse charge *Br* ODER collect *Am* call.

**Rhabarber** *der* rhubarb.

**Rhapsodie** [rapso'di:] (*pl* -n) *die* MUS rhapsody.

**Rhein** *der:* der ~ the (River) Rhine.

**Rheingau** *der:* der ~ the Rheingau.

**Rheinhessen** *nt* Rheinhessen.

**rheinisch** *adj* Rhenish.

**Rheinland** *das:* das ~ the Rhineland.

**Rheinländer, in** (*mpl* -; *fpl* -nen) *der, die* Rhinelander.

**Rheinland-Pfalz** *nt* Rhineland-Palatinate.

**Rheinland-lPfälzer, in** *der, die* native/inhabitant of the Rhineland-Palatinate.

**Rheinlwein** *der* Rhine wine, hock *Br.*

**Rhesusfaktor** *der* MED rhesus factor.

**Rhetorik** (*pl* -en) *die* rhetoric.

**rhetorisch** *adj* rhetorical.

**Rheuma** *das* rheumatism.

**rheumatisch** *adj* rheumatic.

**Rheumatismus** (*pl* -tismen) *der* rheumatism *(U).*

**Rhododendron** (*pl* -dendren) *der* rhododendron.

**Rhodos** *nt* Rhodes.

**Rhombus** (*pl* Rhomben) *der* rhombus.

**Rhön** *die:* die ~ the Rhön Mountains.

**Rhône** *die:* die ~ the (River) Rhône.

**rhythmisch** *adj* rhythmic <> *adv* rhythmically.

**Rhythmus** (*pl* Rhythmen) *der* rhythm; aus dem ~ kommen to lose the rhythm.

**Riad** *nt* Riyadh.

**richten** *vt* - 1. [hinwenden] to point; etw auf jn/etw ~ [Waffe] to point sthg at sb/sthg; [Aufmerksamkeit] to turn sthg to sb/sthg - 2. [Brief, Appell]: etw an jn ~ to address sthg to sb - 3. [reparieren] to fix - 4. [Essen, Zimmer] to prepare <> *vi* [urteilen] to judge; über jn/etw ~ *geh* to judge sb/sthg.
  ◆ sich richten *ref* - 1. [sich einstellen auf]: sich nach jm/etw ~ to fit in with sb/sthg - 2. [abhängen von]: sich nach etw ~ to depend on sthg - 3. [sich wenden]: sich gegen jn/etw ~ to be directed at sb/sthg.

**Richter, in** (*mpl* -; *fpl* -nen) *der, die* judge.

**richterlich** *adj* judicial.

**Richter-Skala** *die* Richter scale.

**Richtlfest** *das* topping-out ceremony.

**Richtlgeschwindigkeit** *die* recommended speed limit.

**richtig** *adj* - 1. [nicht falsch, passend] right; bin ich

hier ~? am I in the right place?; er ist nicht ganz ~ im Kopf he is not quite right in the head; liege ich da ~? am I right?; sehr ~! quite right!; es für ~ halten, etw zu tun to think it right to do sthg - 2. [echt - Person] real, true; [ - Sache] real - 3. [vollwertig] proper <> *adv* - 1. [nicht falsch] correctly; meine Uhr geht ~ my watch is right ODER accurate; das hast du ~ gemacht! you were right to do it! - 2. [passend]: er kam gerade ~ he came at just the right moment - 3. *fam* [wirklich] really.

**Richtige** (*pl* -n) *das* right thing; genau das ~ just the right thing; nichts ~s nothing much <> *der, die* right person.

**richtiggehend** *adj* real <> *adv* really.

**richtig gehend** *adj* [Uhr] accurate.

**Richtigkeit** *die* correctness; mit etw hat es seine ~ sthg is in order.

**richtig liegen** *vi* (*unreg*) *fam:* mit etw ~ to be right with sthg.

**richtig stellen** *vt* to correct.

**Richtllinie** *die* guideline.

**Richtlpreis** *der* recommended price.

**Richtung** (*pl* -en) *die* - 1. [gen] direction; aus allen ~en from all directions; in eine ~ in a direction; in ~ Osten/Berlin towards the east/Berlin - 2. [Mode] trend - 3. [Geschmack] taste.

**rieb** *prät* ⊳ reiben.

**riechen** (*prät* roch; *perf* hat gerochen) *vi* to smell; jd/etw/es riecht nach etw sb/sthg/it smells of sthg; an etw (D) ~ to smell sthg <> *vt* [Duft] to smell; jn nicht ~ können *salopp fig* to hate sb's guts.

**Riecher** (*pl* -) *der:* den richtigen ODER einen ~ für etw haben *fam fig* to have a nose for sthg.

**rief** *prät* ⊳ rufen.

**Riegel** (*pl* -) *der* - 1. [von Tür] bolt; einer Sache (D) einen ~ vorschieben *fig* to put a stop to sthg - 2. [von Schokolade] bar.

**Riemen** (*pl* -) *der* - 1. [Band] strap; sich am ~ reißen *fam fig* to pull o.s. together - 2. [Ruder] oar.

**Riese** (*pl* -n) *der* giant.

**rieseln** (*perf* ist gerieselt) *vi* [Flüssigkeit] to trickle; [Schnee] to float down; [Putz, Kalk] to crumble.

**Riesenlerfolg** *der* huge success.

**Riesengebirge** *das:* das ~ the Riesengebirge.

**riesengroß** *adj* enormous.

**riesenhaft** *adj* huge.

**Riesenlrad** *das* big wheel.

**Riesenlslalom** *der* giant slalom.

**Riesenlspaß** *der* great fun *(U).*

**R**

**riesig** adj - **1.** [groß] enormous - **2.** fam [toll] fantastic ⬦ adv fam [sehr] enormously.

**Riesin** (pl -nen) die - **1.** [Frau] giant - **2.** [Sagenfigur] giantess.

**Riesling** (pl -e) der Riesling.

**riet** prät ⮕ **raten.**

**Riff** (pl -e) das reef.

**rigoros** adj rigorous ⬦ adv rigorously.

**Rille** (pl -n) die groove.

**Rind** (pl -er) das - **1.** [Tier] cow - **2.** [Fleisch] beef.

**Rinde** (pl -n) die - **1.** [von Bäumen] bark - **2.** [von Käse] rind - **3.** [von Brot] crust.

**Rinder|braten** der [roh] joint of beef; [gebraten] roast beef.

**Rinderwahnsinn, Rinderwahn** der (ohne pl) mad cow disease.

**Rindfleisch** das beef.

**Rindvieh** das (ohne pl) salopp abw ass.

**Ring** (pl -e) der - **1.** [gen] ring - **2.** [Gruppe] group - **3.** [Straße] ring road.
⮞ **Ringe** pl sport rings.

**Ring|buch** das ring binder.

**Ringel|natter** die grass snake.

**ringen** (prät rang; perf hat gerungen) vi - **1.** sport to wrestle - **2.** [sich anstrengen] to struggle; mit etw ~ geh to wrestle with sthg; mit sich ~ geh to wrestle with one's conscience; um etw ~ geh to struggle for sthg; nach Atem ODER Luft ~ to fight for breath ⬦ vt: die Hände ~ to wring one's hands.

**Ringer, in** (mpl -; fpl -nen) der, die wrestler.

**Ring|finger** der ring finger.

**ringförmig** adj ring-shaped ⬦ adv in a ring.

**Ring|kampf** der - **1.** sport wrestling match - **2.** [Rauferei] fight.

**Ring|richter, in** der, die referee.

**rings** adv: ~ um jn/etw (herum) all around sb/ sthg.

**ringsherum** adv all around.

**ringsumher** adv all around.

**Rinne** (pl -n) die - **1.** [Vertiefung] channel - **2.** [Abflussrinne] gutter.

**rinnen** (prät rann; perf ist geronnen) vi geh to flow.

**Rinnsal** (pl -e) das trickle.

**Rinn|stein** der gutter.

**Rio de Janeiro** ['ri:ode:ʒa'ne:ro] nt Rio de Janeiro.

**Rippchen** (pl -) das KÜCHE lightly smoked pork rib.

**Rippe** (pl -n) die - **1.** [Knochen] rib - **2.** [von Heizkörper] fin.

**Rippen|fell** das pleura.

**Risiko** (pl Risiken) das risk; auf eigenes ~ at one's own risk; ein ~ eingehen to take a risk.

**Risiko|gruppe** die risk group.

**riskant** adj risky ⬦ adv riskily.

**riskieren** vt to risk.

**riss** prät ⮕ **reißen.**

**Riss** (pl -e) der [in Stoff, Kleidungsstück] tear; [in Gestein, Wand] crack; [in Gesellschaft] rift.

**rissig** adj cracked.

**ritt** prät ⮕ **reiten.**

**Ritt** (pl -e) der ride.

**Ritter** (pl -) der knight.

**ritterlich** adj chivalrous ⬦ adv chivalrously.

**Ritual** (pl -e) das ritual.

**rituell** adj ritual.

**Ritus** (pl Riten) der rite.

**Ritze** (pl -n) die crack.

**ritzen** vt [gravieren] to carve.
⮞ **sich ritzen** ref [verletzen] to scratch o.s.

**Rivale** [ri'va:lə] (pl -n) der rival.

**Rivalin** [ri'va:lɪn] (pl -nen) die rival.

**rivalisieren** [rivali'si:rən] vi: (mit jm) um etw ~ to compete (with sb) for sthg.

**rivalisierend** [rivali'si:rn̩t] adj rival (vor Subst).

**Rivalität** [rivali'tɛːt] (pl -en) die rivalry.

**Riviera** (pl -ren) die: die ~ the Riviera.

**RNS** [ɛrɛn'ɛs] (abk für Ribonukleinsäure) die RNA.

**Roastbeef** ['rɔstbiːf] (pl -s) das roast beef.

**Robbe** (pl -n) die seal.

**robben** (perf ist gerobbt) vi to crawl.

**Roboter** (pl -) der robot.

**robust** adj robust.

**roch** prät ⮕ **riechen.**

**röcheln** vi to breathe with a wheezing sound; [Sterbender] to give the death rattle.

**Rochen** (pl -) der ray.

**Rock¹** (pl Röcke) der - **1.** [für Frauen] skirt - **2.** [für Männer] jacket.

**Rock²** der rock.

**rocken** vi to rock.

**Rocker, in** (mpl -; fpl -nen) der, die abw rocker.

**Rock|musik** die rock music.

**Rocky Mountains** ['rɔki'mauntɪns] pl: die ~ the Rocky Mountains.

**Rodel|bahn** die toboggan run.

**rodeln** (perf hat/ist gerodelt) vi to toboggan.

**Rodeln** das tobogganing.

**roden** vt to clear.

**Rogen** (pl -) der roe.

**Roggen** der rye.

**Roggen|brot** das rye bread (U).

**roh** adj - **1.** [ungekocht] raw - **2.** [grob, unbearbeitet] rough; ~e Gewalt brute force <> adv - **1.** [ungekocht]: etw ~ essen to eat sthg raw - **2.** [behandeln, entwerfen] roughly.

**Roh|bau** (pl -ten) der shell.

**Roh|kost** die (ohne pl) raw fruit and vegetables (pl).

**Roh|material** das raw material.

**Roh|öl** das crude oil (U).

**Rohr** (pl -e) das - **1.** [Röhre] pipe; volles ~ fam fig flat out - **2.** [Pflanze] reed.

**Rohr|bruch** der burst pipe.

**Röhrchen** (pl -) das tube; ins ~ blasen (müssen) to be breathalysed.

**Röhre** (pl -n) die - **1.** TECH pipe; in die ~ gucken ODER sehen fam fig to be left out in the cold - **2.** ELEKTR valve Br, tube Am - **3.** [Backofen] oven.

**röhren** vi [Hirsch] to bell; [Motorrad] to roar.

**Rohr|zange** die pipe wrench.

**Rohr|zucker** der cane sugar.

**Roh|seide** die raw silk (U).

**Roh|stoff** der raw material.

**Rokoko** das rococo.

**Rolladen** der = Rollladen.

**Roll|bahn** die runway.

**Rolle** (pl -n) die - **1.** [in Theater, in Gesellschaft] role - **2.** [von Garn] reel Br, spool Am - **3.** [von Möbeln] castor - **4.** SPORT roll - **5.** RW: aus der ~ fallen to forget o.s.; eine/keine ~ spielen to/not to matter.

**rollen** (perf hat/ist gerollt) vi (ist) to roll <> vt (hat) - **1.** [Zigarette] to roll; [Teig] to roll out; [Papier, Fleisch] to roll up - **2.** [fortbewegen] to roll.
➥ sich rollen ref [Papier, Foto] to curl up; [sich wälzen] to roll around.

**Rollen|spiel** das role play.

**Roller** (pl -) der scooter.

**Roller|blades**® (pl -) pl roller blades, inline skates.

**Roll|kragen** der polo neck.

**Rollladen** (pl -läden) der (rolling) shutters (pl).

**Roll|mops** der rollmop, rolled-up pickled herring.

**Rollo** (pl -s) das roller blind.

**Roll|schuh** der roller skate; ~ laufen to roller-skate.

**Roll|splitt** der (ohne pl) loose chippings (pl).

**Roll|stuhl** der wheelchair.

**Rollstuhl|fahrer, in** der, die wheelchair user.

**Roll|treppe** die escalator.

**Rom** nt Rome.

**Roma** pl Romanies.

**Roman** (pl -e) der - **1.** [Buch] novel - **2.** fam [lange Geschichte] long rigmarole.

**Romanik** die Romanesque.

**romanisch** adj - **1.** [in Bezug auf Sprache] Romance - **2.** [der Romanik] Romanesque.

**Romanistik** die Romance languages and literature.

**Romantik** die - **1.** [Gefühl] romance - **2.** [Epoche] Romantic period.

**romantisch** adj - **1.** [gefühlvoll] romantic - **2.** KUNST & MUS Romantic <> adv romantically.

**Romanze** (pl -n) die romance.

**Römer, in** (mpl -; fpl -nen) der, die Roman.

**Römer|topf** der covered clay pot for slow oven cooking.

**römisch** adj Roman.

**römisch-katholisch** adj Roman Catholic.

**röm.-kath.** (abk für römisch-katholisch) RC.

**Rommee, Rommé** (pl -s) das rummy (U).

**röntgen** vt to X-ray.

**Röntgen|aufnahme** die, **Röntgen|bild** das X-ray.

**Röntgenstrahlen** pl X-rays.

**rosa** adj (unver) pink.

**Rosa** das pink.

**rosarot** adj deep pink.

**Rose** (pl -n) die rose.

**rosé** adj (unver) pale pink.

**Rosé** (pl - ODER -s) das pale pink <> der (pl Rosés) [Wein] rosé.

**Rosen|kohl** der (ohne pl) (Brussels) sprouts (pl).

**Rosen|kranz** der rosary.

**Rosen|montag** der day before Shrove Tuesday which marks the height of the carnival season.

**Rosenmontags|zug** der carnival procession on the day before Shrove Tuesday.

**Rosette** (pl -n) die rosette.

**rosig** adj rosy.

**Rosine** (pl -n) die raisin.

**Rosmarin** der rosemary.

**Ross** (pl -e ODER Rösser) das geh steed; Süddt horse; auf dem hohen ~ sitzen fig to be on one's high horse.

**Ross|kastanie** die horse chestnut.

R

**Rost** (pl -e) der - **1.** [Eisenoxyd] rust - **2.** [Gitter - zum Braten] grill; [ - zum Abdecken] grating.

**Rostbratlwurst** die: **Nürnberger ~** Nuremberg grilled sausage.

**rostbraun** adj russet.

**rosten** (perf hat/ist gerostet) vi to rust.

**rösten** vt & vi to roast.

**rostfrei** adj [Stahl] stainless; [Messer] stainless steel; [Blech] rustproof.

**Rösti** pl Schweiz potato pancake made from grated fried potatoes.

**rostig** adj rusty.

**Rostock** nt Rostock.

**rot** (kompar **röter** ODER **roter**; superl **röteste** ODER **roteste**) adj - **1.** [Farbe] red; **~ werden** to blush - **2.** fam POL Red.

**Rot** das (ohne pl) red.
➡ **bei Rot** adv at red.

**Rotation** (pl -en) die rotation.

**rotblond** adj ginger.

**rotbraun** adj reddish brown.

**Rotlbuche** die beech.

**Röte** die redness.

**Rote Kreuz** das: das **~** the Red Cross.

**Röteln** pl MED German measles (U).

**Rote Meer** das: das **~** the Red Sea.

**röten** ➡ **sich röten** ref to turn red.

**rothaarig** adj red-haired.

**rotieren** (perf hat/ist rotiert) vi - **1.** (hat) [sich drehen, wechseln] to rotate - **2.** (hat, ist) fam [durchdrehen] to be in a flap.

**Rotlkäppchen** das Little Red Riding Hood.

**Rotlkehlchen** (pl -) das robin.

**Rotlkohl** der red cabbage.

**Rotlkraut** das Süddt red cabbage.

**rötlich** adj reddish.

**Rotlicht** das red light.

**rotlsehen** vi (unreg) to see red.

**Rotlstift** der red pen; **den ~ ansetzen** fig to make cuts.

**Rotterdam** nt Rotterdam.

**Rötung** (pl -en) die reddening.

**Rotlwein** der red wine.

**Rotwild** das red deer (pl).

**Rotz** der salopp snot.

**rotzfrech** adj fam really cheeky.

**Rouge** [ruːʒ] (pl -s) das - **1.** [Make-up] rouge - **2.** [beim Roulette] red.

**Roulade** [ru'laːdə] (pl -n) die ≈ beef olive.

**Roulette** [ru'lɛːt] (pl -s) das roulette (U).

**Route** ['ruːtə] (pl -n) die route.

**Routine** [ru'tiːnə] (pl -n) die - **1.** [Gewohnheit] routine; **zur ~ werden** to become routine - **2.** [Erfahrung]: **~ haben** to have experience.

**routinemäßig** adj routine (vor Subst) <> adv: **etw ~ erledigen** to do sthg as a matter of routine.

**Routinelluntersuchung** die routine examination.

**routiniert** [ruti'niːɐt] adj [Autofahrer, Redner] experienced; [Betrüger, Stil] skilful <> adv skilfully.

**Rowdy** ['raʊdi] (pl -s) der fam abw lout.

**Rp.** (abk für Rappen) c.

**RTL** [ɛr teːˈɛl] (abk für Radio-Télévision Luxembourg) nt RTL.

**Ruanda** nt Rwanda.

**Rubbelllos** das scratch card.

**rubbeln** vt - **1.** [abrubbeln] to rub - **2.** [Los] to scratch.

**Rübe** (pl -n) die - **1.** [Pflanze] turnip; **gelbe ~** Süddt carrot; **rote ~** beetroot - **2.** fam [Kopf] nut.

**Rubel** (pl -) der rouble; **der ~ rollt** fig the money's rolling in.

**rüber** fam - **1.** = herüber - **2.** = hinüber.

**rüberlkommen** (perf ist rübergekommen) vi (unreg) - **1.** fam [zu Besuch] to drop by - **2.** fam [über die Grenze] to come over - **3.** [mit Informationen]: **mit etw ~ salopp** to come out with sthg.

**Rubin** (pl -e) der ruby.

**Rubrik** (pl -en) die - **1.** [Kategorie] category - **2.** [von Zeitung] section; **unter der ~ XY** in the XY section.

**Ruck** (pl -e) der - **1.** [Bewegung] jerk; **sich** (D) **einen ~ geben** fam fig to make the effort - **2.** [politisch] swing.

**Rücklantwort** die reply.

**ruckartig** adj jerky <> adv jerkily.

**rückbezüglich** GRAM adj reflexive <> adv reflexively.

**Rücklblende** die flashback.

**Rücklblick** der look back; **im ~** looking back; **ein ~ auf etw** (A) a look back at sthg.

**ruckeln** (perf hat/ist geruckelt) vi - **1.** (hat) fam [zappeln] to fidget; **an etw ~** to shake sthg - **2.** (ist) [Fahrzeug] to jolt along.

**rücken** (perf hat/ist gerückt) vt (hat) vi (ist) to move.

**Rücken** (pl -) der - **1.** [gen] back; [von Buch] spine; [von Nase] bridge - **2.** SPORT [Schwimmen] backstroke - **3.** RW: **hinter js ~** behind sb's back; **jm den ~ stärken** to back sb up; **jm/einer Sache den ~ kehren** geh to turn one's back on sb/sthg; **jm in den ~ fallen** to stab sb in the back.

**Rücken|deckung** *die:* jm ~ geben to give sb one's backing.

**Rücken|lage** *die:* in ~ on one's back.

**Rücken|lehne** *die* backrest.

**Rücken|mark** *das (ohne pl)* spinal cord.

**Rücken|schmerzen** *pl* backache *(sg)*.

**Rücken|schwimmen** *das* backstroke.

**Rücken|wind** *der:* ~ haben to have a following wind.

**rück|erstatten** *vt* to reimburse; jm etw ~ to reimburse sb for sthg.

**Rückfahr|karte** *die* return (ticket) *Br*, round-trip ticket *Am*.

**Rück|fahrt** *die* return journey.

**rückfällig** *adj:* ~ werden to relapse.

**Rück|flug** *der* return flight.

**Rück|frage** *die* query.

**Rück|gabe** *die* return *(U)*.

**Rück|gang** *der* decrease.

**rückgängig** *adj* decreasing <> *adv:* etw ~ machen [Geschäft] to cancel sthg; [Entschluss] to reverse sthg.

**Rück|gewinnung** *die* recovery.

**Rück|grat** *das* spine; jm/sich das ~ brechen [verletzen] to break sb's/one's back; jm das ~ brechen *fig* [Widerstand brechen] to break sb; ~ haben *fig* to have fight in one; ~ zeigen to show fight.

**Rück|griff** *der:* ~ auf etw *(A)* [Methode] recourse to sthg; [Mode, Musik] throwback to sthg.

**Rück|halt** *der* support.

**rückhaltlos** *adj* [Vertrauen, Offenheit] complete; [Mensch] frank <> *adv* completely.

**Rückhand** *die (ohne pl)* backhand; einen Ball mit der ~ spielen to play a ball (on the) backhand.

**Rückkehr** *die* return.

**Rück|kopplung, Rückkoppelung** *die* feedback *(U)*.

**Rück|lage** *die* savings *(pl)*.

**rückläufig** *adj* declining; [Trend] downward; ~e Entwicklung decline <> *adv:* sich ~ entwickeln to decline.

**Rücklicht** *(pl -er) das* rear light.

**Rück|reise** *die* return journey.

**Rück|ruf** *der* return call.

**Rück|sack** *der* rucksack, pack; [für Reisen] backpack.

**Rück|schau** *die* look back; ~ halten *geh* to look back.

**Rück|schlag** *der* setback; einen ~ erleiden to suffer a setback.

**Rück|schluss** *der* conclusion; ein ~ auf etw *(A)* a conclusion about sthg; aus etw Rückschlüsse ziehen to draw conclusions from sthg.

**Rück|schritt** *der* backward step.

**Rück|seite** *die* back.

**Rück|sicht** *die* - **1.** [auf Person, Umstand] consideration; aus ~ auf jn/etw out of consideration for sb/sthg; auf jn/etw ~ nehmen to show consideration for sb/sthg - **2.** [nach hinten] rear view.

**Rück|sichtnahme** *die* consideration.

**rücksichtslos** *adj* [unhöflich] inconsiderate; [verantwortungslos] reckless; [erbarmungslos] ruthless <> *adv* [unhöflich] inconsiderately; [verantwortungslos] recklessly; [erbarmungslos] ruthlessly.

**Rücksichtslosigkeit** *(pl -en) die* [Unhöflichkeit] lack of consideration; [Verantwortungslosigkeit] recklessness; [Erbarmungslosigkeit] ruthlessness; so eine ~! how inconsiderate!

**rücksichtsvoll** *adj* considerate <> *adv* considerately.

**Rück|sitz** *der* back seat.

**Rück|spiegel** *der* rear-view mirror.

**Rück|spiel** *das* SPORT return game.

**Rück|sprache** *die* consultation; mit jm ~ halten ODER nehmen to consult (with) sb.

**Rück|stand** *der* - **1.** WIRTSCH arrears *(pl)*; (mit etw) im ~ sein to be in arrears (with sthg) - **2.** SPORT: in ~ geraten to fall behind; (mit etw) im ~ sein to be trailing (by sthg); den ~ aufholen to catch up - **3.** [von Gift] residue - **4.** [Abstand] gap; den ~ aufholen to close the gap.

**rückständig** *abw adj* - **1.** [Person, Politik] outdated - **2.** [Land, Technik] backward.

**Rück|stau** *der* [von Autos] tailback *Br*, backup *Am*; [von Flüssigkeiten] backing up *(U)*.

**Rück|stoß** *der* - **1.** PHYS thrust *(U)* - **2.** [von Gewehr] recoil.

**Rück|strahler** *(pl -) der* reflector.

**Rück|taste** *die* EDV backspace key.

**Rück|tritt** *der* - **1.** [aus Amt] resignation - **2.** *fam* [von Fahrrad] backpedal brake.

**Rücktritt|bremse** *die* backpedal brake.

**rückversichern** *vt* to reinsure.
➤ **sich rückversichern** *ref* to check.

**Rück|wand** *die* back.

**rückwärtig** *adj* [Teil] back; [Wohnung] at the back <> *adv* towards the back; ~ gelegen at the back.

**rückwärts** *adv* backwards; ~ einparken to reverse into a parking space; ~ orientiert backward-looking.

R

**Rückwärts|gang** *der* reverse gear; **im ~ in** reverse.

**Rück|weg** *der* way back.

**rückwirkend** *adj* [Zahlung] backdated; [Datierung, Gesetz] retrospective <> *adv:* **die Gehaltserhöhung ist ~ vom 1.1. wirksam** the salary increase is backdated to 1.1.

**Rück|zahlung** *die* repayment.

**Rück|zieher** (*pl* -) *der:* **einen ~ machen** *fam* to back out.

**Rück|zug** *der* (*ohne pl*) retreat.

**rüde** *adj* rude <> *adv* rudely.

**Rüde** (*pl* -n) *der* male.

**Rudel** (*pl* -) *das* [von Wölfen] pack; [von Hirschen] herd.

**Ruder** (*pl* -) *das* - **1.** [zum Rudern] oar - **2.** [zum Steuern] rudder - **3.** *RW:* **am ~ sein** *fam* to be at the helm; **ans ~ kommen** *fam* to take over the helm.

**Ruder|boot** *das* rowing boat *Br*, rowboat *Am*.

**Ruderer, in** (*mpl* -; *fpl* -nen) *der, die* oarsman (*f* oarswoman).

**rudern** (*perf* hat/ist gerudert) *vi* - **1.** (*hat*) SPORT to row; **mit den Armen ~** to flail one's arms - **2.** (*ist*) [in bestimmte Richtung] to row <> *vt* (*hat*) to row.

**Ruf** (*pl* -e) *der* - **1.** (*ohne pl*) [Leumund] reputation - **2.** (*ohne pl*) [Aufruf] call; **der ~ nach etw** the call for sthg - **3.** UNI offer of a chair - **4.** [von Tier] call.

**rufen** (*prät* rief; *perf* hat gerufen) *vi* to call; **nach jm/etw ~** to call for sb/sthg <> *vt* - **1.** [herbeirufen, nennen] to call; **jd/etw kommt (jm) wie gerufen** sb/sthg comes at just the right moment; **jn zu Hilfe ~** to call on sb to help - **2.** [schreien] to shout.

**Rüffel** (*pl* -) *der* telling-off.

**Ruf|name** *der* amt first name (*by which one is generally known*).

**Ruf|nummer** *die* amt telephone number.

**Rugby** ['rakbi] *das* rugby.

**Rüge** (*pl* -n) *die* reprimand.

**rügen** *vt* - **1.** [Person] to reprimand - **2.** [Mängel] to complain about.

**Rügen** *nt* Rügen.

**Ruhe** *die* - **1.** [Stille] silence; **~ bitte!** quiet please!; **~ geben to** be quiet - **2.** [Erholung] rest - **3.** [das Ungestörtsein] peace; **ich will jetzt meine ~ (haben)** I want a bit of peace and quiet; **in ~** in peace; **jn (mit etw) in ~ lassen** to stop bothering sb (with sthg); **keine ~ geben** to keep pestering - **4.** [Gelassenheit] calm; **sie ist durch nichts aus der ~ zu bringen** she won't let anything disturb her composure; **etw lässt jm keine ~** sthg gives sb no peace; **(die) be-**

wahren to keep calm - **5.** *RW:* **zur ~ kommen** to calm down; **sich zur ~ setzen** to retire.

**ruhelos** *adj* restless <> *adv* restlessly.

**ruhen** *vi* - **1.** [stillstehen - Verkehr, Arbeit, Maschinen] to be at a standstill; [ - Waffen] to be silent - **2.** *geh* [liegen] to lie; [schlafen] to sleep - **3.** [lasten, verweilen] to rest.

**Ruhe|pause** *die* break.

**Ruhe|stand** *der* retirement; **in den ~ gehen** ODER **treten** to retire; **in den ~ versetzt werden** to be retired.

**Ruhe|störung** *die:* **jn wegen ~ anzeigen** to report sb for disturbing the peace; **nächtliche ~** disturbance of the peace (*at night*).

**Ruhe|tag** *der* closing day; **'montags ~!'** 'closed on Mondays'.

**ruhig** *adj* - **1.** [still] quiet - **2.** [unbewegt] calm - **3.** [gelassen - Mensch, Stimme] calm; [ - Hand] steady; [ - Gewissen] clear - **4.** [geruhsam] peaceful <> *adv* - **1.** [still - liegen] still; [ - wohnen] in a quiet area; **sich ~ verhalten** to keep quiet - **2.** [gelassen] calmly - **3.** *fam* [gerne]: **mach ~ mit!** join in if you like!

**Ruhm** *der* fame.

**rühmen** *vt geh* to praise.

◆ **sich rühmen** *ref geh:* **sich einer Sache** (G) **~ to** pride o.s. on sthg.

**rühmlich** *adj* notable.

**Ruhr** *die* (*ohne pl*) - **1.** [Fluss]: **die ~** the (River) Ruhr - **2.** [Krankheit] dysentery.

**Rühr|ei** *das* scrambled eggs (*pl*).

**rühren** *vt* - **1.** [gen] to move; **sie war gerührt** she was moved - **2.** [umrühren] to stir <> *vi* [ansprechen]: **an etw** (*A*) **~** to touch on sthg.

◆ **sich rühren** *ref* - **1.** [sich bewegen] to move; **rührt euch!** stand at ease! - **2.** *fam* [sich melden] to be in touch.

**rührend** *adj* touching <> *adv* touchingly.

**Ruhrgebiet** *das:* **das ~** the Ruhr.

**rührselig** *adj* emotional.

**Rühr|teig** *der* cake mixture.

**Rührung** *die* emotion.

**Ruin** *der* ruin; **js ~ sein** to be the ruin of sb.

**Ruine** (*pl* -n) *die* ruin.

**ruinieren** *vt* to ruin.

◆ **sich ruinieren** *ref* to ruin o.s.

**rülpsen** *vi* to burp.

**Rülpser** (*pl* -) *der* burp.

**rum** *fam* = herum.

**Rum** (*pl* -s) *der* rum.

**Rumäne** (*pl* -n) *der* Romanian.

**Rumänien** *nt* Romania.

**Rumänin** (*pl* -nen) *die* Romanian.

**rumänisch** *adj* Romanian.

**Rumänisch(e)** *das* Romanian; *siehe auch* Englisch(e).

**rum|gammeln** *vi fam* to laze about.

**rum|hängen** *vi (unreg) fam* to hang around.

**rum|kriegen** *vt fam* - **1.** [Person] to talk round - **2.** [Zeit] to get through.

**Rummel** (*pl* -) *der* - **1.** [Jahrmarkt] fair - **2.** *fam* [Umstände]: **um jn/etw viel ~ machen** to make a big fuss about sb/sthg.

**Rummel|platz** *der* fairground.

**rumoren** *vi* - **1.** [Magen] to rumble; **bei jm rumort es im Bauch** sb's stomach is rumbling - **2.** [Person] to bang about.

**Rumpel|kammer** *die* junk room.

**rumpeln** (*perf* hat/ist gerumpelt) *vi* - **1.** *(hat)* [laut] to bang about - **2.** *(ist)* [fahren - Straßenbahn, Wagen] to rumble; [ - Fahrrad] to bump along.

**Rumpf** (*pl* Rümpfe) *der* - **1.** [Oberkörper] trunk - **2.** ⟨TECH⟩ [von Schiff] hull; [von Flugzeug] fuselage - **3.** [Rest] remnant.

**rümpfen** *vt* ⊳ Nase.

**Rump|steak** [ˈrʊmpsteːk] *das* rump steak.

**Rum|topf** *der* fruit soaked for a long time in rum.

**rum|treiben** ⟶ **sich rumtreiben** *ref* to hang around.

**rund** *adj* - **1.** [Form, Summe] round - **2.** [ungefähr]: **eine ~e Woche** a good week ⟨⟩ *adv* - **1.** [ungefähr] about; **~ gerechnet** at a rough estimate - **2.** [ohne Ecken] in a round shape; [laufen] smoothly - **3.** [um ... herum]: **~ um jn/etw** [räumlich] round sb/sthg; [thematisch] all about sb/sthg.

**Rund|bogen** *der* round arch.

**Rund|brief** *der* circular.

**Runde** (*pl* -n) *die* - **1.** [gen] round; **eine ~ drehen** to go for a walk; **eine ~ ausgeben** to buy a round - **2.** ⟨SPORT⟩ [bei Rennen] lap; [bei Boxkampf] round - **3.** [Personen] group - **4.** *RW:* **etw macht die ~** sthg is doing the rounds; **über die ~n kommen** *fam* to get by.

**runderneuert** *adj:* **~er Reifen** retreads.

**Rund|fahrt** *die* tour.

**Rund|flug** *der* sightseeing flight.

**Rund|frage** *die* survey.

**Rund|funk** *der* - **1.** [Institution] radio - **2.** [Radiosender] radio station.

**Rundfunk|anstalt** *die* amt radio station.

**Rundfunk|gebühr** *die* radio licence fee.

**Rund|gang** *der* [Spaziergang] walk; [von Wächter] round.

**rund|gehen** (*perf* ist rundgegangen) *vi (unreg):* **es geht rund** it's all go.

**rundheraus** *adv* straight out.

**rundherum** *adv* - **1.** [ganz] completely - **2.** [ringsherum] all round.

**rundlich** *adj* [Mensch] plump.

**Rund|reise** *die* tour.

**Rund|schreiben** *das* circular.

**rundum** *adv* completely.

**Rundung** (*pl* -en) *die* curve.
⟶ **Rundungen** *pl fam* [Formen] curves.

**rundweg** *adv* flatly.

**Rune** (*pl* -n) *die* rune.

**runter** *fam* = herunter, hinunter.

**runter|fallen** (*perf* ist runtergefallen) *vi (unreg) fam:* **von etw ~** to fall off sthg; **mir ist ein Glas runtergefallen** I dropped a glass.

**runter|gehen** (*perf* ist runtergegangen) *vi (unreg) fam* - **1.** [herunter] to get down - **2.** [hinunter] to go down.

**runter|hauen** *fam vt:* **jm eine ~** to slap sb.

**Runzel** (*pl* -n) *die* wrinkle.

**runzelig** = runzlig.

**runzeln** *vt* ⊳ Stirn.

**runzlig, runzelig** *adj* wrinkled.

**Rüpel** (*pl* -) *der* abw lout.

**rüpelhaft** *abw adj* loutish ⟨⟩ *adv* loutishly.

**rupfen** *vt* [Unkraut] to pull up; [Blätter] to pull off; [Huhn] to pluck.

**ruppig** *adj* [unfreundlich] gruff ⟨⟩ *adv* [unfreundlich] gruffly.

**Rüsche** (*pl* -n) *die* frill.

**Ruß** *der* soot.

**Russe** (*pl* -n) *der* Russian.

**Rüssel** (*pl* -) *der* [von Elefant] trunk; [von Schwein] snout; [von Fliege] proboscis.

**rußen** *vi* to produce soot.

**rußig** *adj* sooty.

**Russin** (*pl* -nen) *die* Russian.

**russisch** *adj* Russian.

**Russisch(e)** *das* Russian; *siehe auch* Englisch(e).

**Russland** *nt* Russia.

**rüsten** *vi* to arm.
⟶ **sich rüsten** *ref* to prepare.

**rüstig** *adj* sprightly.

**rustikal** *adj* rustic.

**Rüstung** (*pl* -en) *die* - **1.** *(ohne pl)* [von Staat] armaments *(pl)* - **2.** [von Ritter] armour.

**Rüstungs|industrie** *die* MIL armaments industry.

**R**

**Rute** (*pl* **-n**) *die* **- 1.** [Stock] switch **- 2.** [Schwanz - von Hund] tail; [ - von Fuchs] brush.

**Rutsch** (*pl* **-e**) *der:* **in einem** ODER **auf einen ~ in** one go.
➤ **guten Rutsch** *interj* Happy New Year!

**Rutsch|bahn** *die* [auf dem Spielplatz] slide; [spiral-förmig] helter-skelter; [Wasserröhre] flume.

**Rutsche** (*pl* **-n**) *die* **- 1.** [Rutschbahn] slide **- 2.** [zum Schütten] chute.

**rutschen** (*perf* **ist gerutscht**) *vi* [gleiten - ausrutschen, fallen] to slip; [ - mit dem Auto] to skid; **auf dem Stuhl hin und her ~** to shift around on one's chair; **rutsch mal ein Stück** move up a bit.

**rutschfest** *adj* non-slip.

**rutschig** *adj* slippery.

**rütteln** *vt* to shake ◇ *vi:* **an etw** (D) **~** to rattle sthg; **an etw** (D) **ist nicht zu ~** *fig* there is no changing sthg.

# S

**s, S** [ɛs] (*pl* **-**) *das* s, S.
➤ **S** (*abk für* **Süd**) S.

**s.** *abk für* **siehe.**

**S.** (*abk für* **Seite**) p.

**s. a.** (*abk für* **siehe auch**) *see also.*

**Sa.** (*abk für* **Samstag**) Sat.

**Saal** (*pl* **Säle**) *der* hall.

**Saale** *die:* **die ~** the (River) Saale.

**Saar** *die:* **die ~** the (River) Saar.

**Saarbrücken** *nt* Saarbrücken.

**Saarland** *das* Saarland.

**Saarländer** (*pl* **-**) *der* Saarlander ◇ *adj* (*unver*) Saarland (*vor Subst*).

**Saarländerin** (*pl* **-nen**) *die* Saarlander.

**saarländisch** *adj* of/from Saarland.

**Saat** (*pl* **-en**) *die* **- 1.** [das Säen] sowing **- 2.** [Körner] seed.

**Sabbat** (*pl* **-e**) *der* Sabbath.

**sabbern** *vi* [Person] to dribble; [Hund] to slober.

**Säbel** (*pl* **-**) *der* sabre.

**Sabotage** [sabo'ta:ʒə] (*pl* **-n**) *die* sabotage (*U*).

**Saboteur, in** [sabo'tø:ɐ̯, rɪn] (*mpl* **-e;** *fpl* **-nen**) *der, die* saboteur.

**sabotieren** *vt* to sabotage.

**Saccharin** [zaxa'ri:n] *das* saccharin.

**Sach|bearbeiter, in** *der, die* employee in charge of a particular matter.

**Sach|bereich** *der* area.

**Sach|beschädigung** *die* damage to property (*U*).

**sachbezogen** *adj* relevant.

**Sach|buch** *das* non-fiction book.

**sachdienlich** *adj:* **~e Hinweise** useful information.

**Sache** (*pl* **-n**) *die* **- 1.** (*ohne pl*) [Angelegenheit] matter; **das ist (nicht) deine ~** that's (none of) your business; **bei der ~ bleiben** to keep to the point; **zur ~ kommen** to get to the point; **nicht bei der ~ sein** not to be with it; **das tut nichts zur ~** *fig* that is beside the point **- 2.** (*ohne pl*) RECHT [Rechtssache] case **- 3.** RW: **das ist so eine ~** *fam* it's a bit of a problem; **hart zur ~ gehen** *fam* to really get stuck in; **mit jm gemeinsame ~ machen** *fam* to join forces with sb; **seiner ~ sicher sein** to know what one is doing.
➤ **Sachen** *pl* **- 1.** [gen] things **- 2.** *fam* [Stundenkilometer]: **100 ~n draufhaben** to be doing a hundred; **mit 180 ~n** *salopp* at 180 **- 3.** RW: **du machst vielleicht ~n!** the things you do!; **in ~n** in the matter of.

**Sach|gebiet** *das* subject area.

**sachgemäß** *adj* proper ◇ *adv* properly.

**Sach|kenntnis** *die* expertise (*U*).

**sachkundig** *adj* knowledgeable ◇ *adv* knowledgeably; **sich ~ machen** to acquaint o.s. with the matter.

**Sachlage** *die* (*ohne pl*) situation.

**sachlich** *adj* **- 1.** [Person, Diskussion] objective **- 2.** [Fehler, Unterschied] factual ◇ *adv* **- 1.** [diskutieren, bleiben] objectively **- 2.** [richtig, falsch] factually.

**sächlich** *adj* GRAM neuter.

**Sachlichkeit** *die* objectivity.

**Sach|register** *das* subject index.

**Sach|schaden** *der* material damage.

**Sachse** ['zaksə] (*pl* **-n**) *der* Saxon.

**sächseln** ['zɛksəln] *vi* *abw* to speak with a Saxon accent.

**Sachsen** ['zaksn̩] *nt* Saxony.

**Sachsen-Anhalt** [zaksn̩'anhalt] *nt* Saxony-Anhalt.

**Sächsin** ['zɛksɪn] (*pl* **-nen**) *die* Saxon.

**sächsisch** ['zɛksɪʃ] *adj* Saxon.

**sacht, sachte** *adj* - **1.** [sanft, langsam] gentle - **2.** [vorsichtig] cautious ◇ *adv* gently; **sachte!** *fam* steady on!

**Sachverhalt** (*pl* -e) *der* facts (of the matter) (*pl*).

**Sachverstand** *der* expertise.

**sachverständig** *adj* expert ◇ *adv* expertly.

**Sachlverständige** (*pl* -n) *der, die* expert.

**Sachlwert** *der* real value.

**Sachlzwang** *der* force of circumstance.

**Sack** (*pl* Säcke ODER -) *der* - **1.** (*pl* Säcke, Sack) [Behälter] sack - **2.** (*pl* Säcke) *salopp* [Mensch] bastard - **3.** (*pl* Säcke) *salopp* [Hodensack] balls (*pl*).

**Sacklgasse** *die* dead end; [in Wohngebiet] cul-de-sac; **in eine ~ geraten** [mit Fahrzeug] to go up a dead end; *fig* [in ausweglose Situation] to reach an impasse.

**Sadismus** *der* sadism.

**Sadist, in** (*mpl* -en; *fpl* -nen) *der, die* sadist.

**sadistisch** *adj* sadistic ◇ *adv* sadistically.

**säen** *vt* to sow.

**Safari** (*pl* -s) *die* safari.

**Safe** [seːf] (*pl* -s) *der* safe.

**Safran** *der* saffron.

**Saft** (*pl* Säfte) *der* - **1.** [Fruchtsaft, Strom] juice - **2.** [Pflanzensaft] sap.

**saftig** *adj* - **1.** [Obst, Fleisch] juicy - **2.** *fam* [Rechnung, Ohrfeige] hefty.

**Saftladen** *der (ohne pl) fam abw* useless outfit.

**Sage** (*pl* -n) *die* legend.

**Säge** (*pl* -n) *die* saw.

**Sägelblatt** *das* saw blade.

**Sägemehl** *das* sawdust.

**sagen** *vt* - **1.** [gen] to say; **jm etw ~** to tell sb sthg; **sich** (*D*) **etw ~** to tell o.s. sthg; **das kann je-der ~!** that's easy to say!; **ich habe es dir ja gleich gesagt** *fam* I told you!; **das hat nichts zu ~** that doesn't mean anything; **was sagst du (denn) dazu?** (so) what do you think about it? - **2.** [befehlen]: **etwas/nichts zu ~ haben** to have a/no say in things; **jm etwas/nichts zu ~ haben** to have sthg/nothing to say to sb; **er lässt sich nichts ~** you can't tell him anything; **das Sagen haben** to be in charge - **3.** *RW*: **das sage ich dir** *fam* I'm telling you; **das kann man wohl ~!** *fam* you can say that again!; **dagegen ist nichts zu ~** it's perfectly all right; **man sagt ... it is said ...; wem sagst du das!** you're telling me!; **sich** (*D*) **etw nicht zweimal ~ lassen** to jump at sthg.

➤ **sage und schreibe** *adv* believe it or not.
➤ **du sagst es** *interj* you said it!
➤ **sag bloß** *interj* you don't say.
➤ **sag mal** *interj* tell me.
➤ **wie gesagt** *interj* as I've said.

**sägen** *vt* & *vi* to saw.

**sagenhaft** *adj* fantastic ◇ *adv* fantastically.

**Sägespäne** *pl* wood shavings.

**Sägelwerk** *das* sawmill.

**Sago** *der* sago.

**sah** *prät* ⊳ sehen.

**Sahara, Sahara** *die* Sahara (Desert).

**Sahne** *die* cream.

**Sahneltorte** *die* gâteau.

**sahnig** *adj* creamy.

**Saison** [sɛˈzɔŋ] (*pl* -s) *die* season; **~ haben** to be in vogue.

**Saisonlarbeiter, in** *der, die* seasonal worker.

**saisonbedingt** *adj* seasonal.

**Saite** (*pl* -n) *die* string; **andere ~n aufziehen** *fam fig* to get tough.

**Saiteninstrument** *das* stringed instrument.

**Sakko** (*pl* -s) *der* jacket.

**sakral** *adj* sacred.

**Sakrament** (*pl* -e) *das* REL sacrament.

**Sakrileg** (*pl* -e) *das* sacrilege.

**Sakristei** (*pl* -en) *die* sacristy.

**Salamander** (*pl* -) *der* salamander.

**Salami** (*pl* -s) *die* salami.

**Salamiltaktik** *die fam* step-by-step tactics (*pl*).

**Salat** (*pl* -e) *der* - **1.** [Gericht] salad; **grüner ~** green salad - **2.** [Produkt] lettuce - **3.** *fam*: **da haben wir den ~!** *fam* I said we'd end up in this mess!

**Salatlbesteck** *das* salad servers (*pl*).

**Salatlgurke** *die* cucumber.

**Salatlschüssel** *die* salad bowl.

**Salatlsoße** *die* salad dressing.

**Salbe** (*pl* -n) *die* ointment.

**Salbei** *der* sage.

**salbungsvoll** *abw adj* unctuous.

**Saldo** (*pl* Saldi) *der* balance (*sg*).

**Salmonelle** (*pl* -n) *die* salmonella (*U*).

**Salmonellenlvergiftung** *die* salmonella poisoning.

**Salon** [saˈlɔŋ] (*pl* -s) *der* [Zimmer] drawing room.

**salonfähig** *adj* socially acceptable.

**salopp** *adj* casual; [Ausdrucksweise] slangy ◇ *adv* casually; [sich ausdrücken] slangily.

**Salpeter** *der* saltpetre.

**Salpetersäure** *die* nitric acid.

**Salto** (*pl* -s) *der* somersault.

**S**

**salutieren** *vi* MIL to salute.

**Salve** ['salvə] (*pl* -n) *die* salvo.

**Salz** (*pl* -e) *das* salt.

**salzarm** *adj* low-salt.

**Salz|bergwerk** *das* salt mine.

**Salzburg** *nt* Salzburg.

**Salzburger** (*pl* -) *der* native/inhabitant of Salzburg ◇ *adj (unver)* of/from Salzburg.

**Salzburger Festspiele** *pl annual music and theatre festival held in Salzburg.*

**Salzburgerin** (*pl* -nen) *die* native/inhabitant of Salzburg.

**salzen** (*perf* hat gesalzen) *vt* to put salt in/on.

**Salzgebäck** *das (ohne pl)* savoury snacks (*pl*).

**salzig** *adj* salty.

**Salzkartoffeln** *pl* boiled potatoes.

**salzlos** *adj* salt-free.

**Salz|säule** *die:* **zur ~ erstarren** to turn to stone.

**Salz|säure** *die* hydrochloric acid.

**Salz|stange** *die* pretzel stick.

**Salz|stock** *der* salt mine.

**Salz|streuer** (*pl* -) *der* salt cellar.

**Salz|wasser** *das* - **1.** [Meerwasser] saltwater - **2.** [Kochwasser] salted water.

**Salz|wüste** *die* salt desert.

**Samba** (*pl* -s) *die* ODER *der* samba.

**Samen** (*pl* -) *der* - **1.** [Sperma] sperm - **2.** [Pflanzensamen] seed.

**Samen|bank** (*pl* -en) *die* sperm bank.

**Samener|guss** *der* ejaculation.

**Samen|zelle** *die* sperm cell.

**sämig** *adj* thick.

**Sammel|album** *das* album.

**Sammel|band** (*pl* -bände) *der* omnibus edition.

**Sammel|becken** *das* gathering place.

**Sammelbe|griff** *der* collective term.

**Sammel|bestellung** *die* joint order.

**Sammel|büchse** *die* collecting box.

**sammeln** *vt* - **1.** [Eindrücke, Anhänger, Kräuter] to gather - **2.** [Geld, Briefmarken] to collect.
➡ **sich sammeln** *ref* - **1.** [sich konzentrieren] to collect one's thoughts - **2.** [Gruppe] to gather

**Sammel|platz** *der* assembly point.

**Sammel|stelle** *die* collection point.

**Sammelsurium** [zam|'zu:riʊm] (*pl* -surien) *das* jumble.

**Sammler, in** (*mpl* -; *fpl* -nen) *der, die* collector.

**Sammler|wert** *der* value to collectors.

**Sammlung** (*pl* -en) *die* - **1.** [gen] collection - **2.** [Ruhe] composure.

**Samstag** (*pl* -e) *der* Saturday; **am ~** on Saturday; **(am) nächsten ~ kommt sie** she's coming next Saturday; **~, den 31. Dezember** Saturday, 31 December.

**Samstag|abend** (*pl* -e) *der* Saturday evening; **~ muss ich nach Köln** I have to go to Cologne on Saturday evening.

**Samstag|morgen** (*pl* -) *der* Saturday morning; **~ muss ich nach Köln** I have to go to Cologne on Saturday morning.

**Samstag|nacht** *die* Saturday night; **~ hat es stark geregnet** it rained hard on Saturday night.

**samstags** *adv* on Saturdays; **~ morgens/abends** on Saturday mornings/evenings; **'~ geschlossen'** 'closed on Saturdays'.

**samt** *adv:* **~ und sonders** without exception ◇ *präp:* **~ jm/einer Sache** (together) with sb/sthg.

**Samt** (*pl* -e) *der* velvet.

**samtig** *adj* velvety.

**sämtlich** *adj* all; **~e Fehler verbessern** to correct all the mistakes; **er hat ~en Mut verloren** he lost all his courage; **Schillers ~e Werke** the complete works of Schiller ◇ *adv:* **sie waren ~ erschienen** they all turned up.

**Sanatorium** [zana'to:riʊm] (*pl* -torien) *das* sanatorium.

**Sand** *der* sand; **die Straßen mit ~ streuen** to grit the roads; **eine Million Euro in den ~ setzen** *fam fig* to blow a million euros; **im ~ verlaufen** *fig* to come to nothing; **~ im Getriebe** *fig* a spanner in the works.

**Sandale** (*pl* -n) *die* sandal.

**Sandbank** (*pl* -bänke) *die* sandbank.

**Sandelholz** *das* sandalwood.

**sandig** *adj* sandy.

**Sand|kasten** *der* sandpit *Br*, sandbox *Am*.

**Sandkorn** (*pl* -körner) *das* grain of sand.

**Sand|männchen** *das* sandman.

**Sand|papier** *das* sandpaper.

**Sand|stein** *der* sandstone.

**Sandstrahl|gebläse** *das* sandblaster.

**Sand|strand** *der* sandy beach.

**Sand|sturm** *der* sandstorm.

**sandte** *prät* ⊳ **senden.**

**Sand|uhr** *die* hourglass.

**Sandwich** ['sɛntvɪtʃ] (*pl* -s ODER -e) *der* ODER *das* sandwich.

**San Francisco** *nt* San Francisco.

**sanft** *adj* - **1.** [gen] gentle - **2.** [Hände, Stimme, Licht] soft - **3.** [Geburt] natural; [Energie, Tourismus] sustainable; [Tod] peaceful ◇ *adv* **- 1.** [gen] gently **- 2.** [entschlafen] peacefully.

**sanftmütig** *adj* gentle ◇ *adv* gently.

**sang** *prät* ▷ singen.

**Sang** ➡ mit **Sang und Klang** *adv*: mit ~ und **Klang durchfallen** to fail spectacularly.

**Sänger, in** (*mpl* -; *fpl* -nen) *der, die* singer.

**sanglos** *adv*: **sang- und klanglos verschwinden** to disappear unnoticed.

**Sangria** (*pl* -s) *die* sangria.

**sanieren** *vt* **- 1.** [Gebäude, Viertel] to renovate **- 2.** [Firma] to turn around **- 3.** [Finanzen] to sort out.

➡ **sich sanieren** *ref* [Person] to get o.s. out of the red.

**Sanierung** (*pl* -en) *die* **- 1.** [von Gebäude, Viertel] renovation **- 2.** [von Firma] turning round **- 3.** [von Finanzen] sorting out.

**sanierungsbedürftig** *adj* in need of renovation.

**sanitär** *adj* sanitary; ~e **Anlagen** sanitation (U).

**Sanitäter, in** (*mpl* -; *fpl* -nen) *der, die* **- 1.** MED paramedic **- 2.** MIL medical orderly.

**sank** *prät* ▷ sinken.

**Sankt Bernhard** *der*: **Großer/Kleiner ~** Great/Little St Bernard Pass.

**Sankt Gallen** *nt* St Gallen.

**Sankt Gotthard** *der* St Gotthard.

**Sanktion** (*pl* -en) *die* sanction; **~en verhängen** to impose sanctions.

**Sankt Petersburg** *nt* St Petersburg.

**San Marino** *nt* San Marino.

**sann** *prät* ▷ sinnen.

**Sansibar** *nt* Zanzibar.

**Sanskrit** *das* Sanskrit.

**Santiago** *nt*: **~ (de Chile)** Santiago; **~ de Compostela** Santiago de Compostela.

**Saphir, Saphir** (*pl* -e) *der* sapphire.

**Sardelle** (*pl* -n) *die* anchovy.

**Sardellenpaste** *die* anchovy paste.

**Sardine** (*pl* -n) *die* sardine; **wie die ~n** *fam fig* like sardines.

**Sardinenbüchse** *die* tin of sardines.

**Sardinien** [zar'di:njən] *nt* Sardinia.

**Sarg** (*pl* Särge) *der* coffin, casket *Am*.

**Sarkasmus** (*pl* -men) *der* **- 1.** [Spott] sarcasm **- 2.** [spöttische Bemerkung] sarcastic comment.

**sarkastisch** *adj* sarcastic ◇ *adv* sarcastically.

**saß** *prät* ▷ sitzen.

**SAT 1** ['zat'ains] *nt private TV channel*.

**Satan** (*pl* -e) *der* **- 1.** [Teufel] Satan **- 2.** *abw* [Mensch] fiend.

**Satellit** (*pl* -en) *der* satellite.

**Satellitenfernsehen** *das* satellite television.

**Satellitenfoto** *das* satellite picture.

**Satellitenschüssel** *die* satellite dish.

**Satellitenstadt** *die* satellite town.

**Satellitenübertragung** *die* **- 1.** [Sendemethode] satellite broadcasting **- 2.** [Sendung] satellite broadcast.

**Satin** [za'tɛ̃:, za'tɛŋ] (*pl* -s) *der* satin.

**Satire** (*pl* -n) *die* satire.

**Satiriker, in** (*mpl* -; *fpl* -nen) *der, die* satirist.

**satirisch** *adj* satirical ◇ *adv* satirically.

**satt** *adj* **- 1.** [Mensch, Tier] full; **~ sein** to be full (up); **bist du ~?** have you had enough (to eat)?; **diese Knödel machen ~** these dumplings are filling; **davon werde ich nicht ~** I won't have enough to eat with that **- 2.** [Farbe, Klang] rich ◇ *adv*: **sich ~ essen** to eat one's fill; **sich an etw ~ sehen** to gaze endlessly at sthg; **jn/etw ~ haben** *fam* to be fed up with sb/sthg.

**Sattel** (*pl* Sättel) *der* saddle.

**sattelfest** *adj*: **in etw (D) ~ sein** to have a firm grasp of sthg.

**satteln** *vt* to saddle.

**Sattelschlepper** *der* articulated lorry *Br*, semi-trailer *Am*.

**Satteltasche** *die* saddlebag; [für Fahrrad] pannier.

**Sättigung** (*pl* -en) *die* WIRTSCH & CHEM saturation.

**Saturn** *der* Saturn.

**Satz** (*pl* Sätze) *der* **- 1.** [grammatikalische Einheit] sentence; **in** *ODER* **mit einem ~** in a single *ODER* one sentence **- 2.** [Sprung] leap **- 3.** [SPORT - bei Tennis] set; [ - bei Badminton, Tischtennis] game **- 4.** [von Text - das Setzen] setting; [ - das Gesetzte] type **- 5.** MUS movement **- 6.** MATH theorem **- 7.** [von Reifen, Unterwäsche] set **- 8.** [Tarif] rate.

**Satzball** *der* [bei Tennis] set point; [bei Badminton, Tischtennis] game point.

**Satzbau** *der* syntax.

**Satzgefüge** *das* complex sentence.

**Satzglied** *das* syntagm, syntactic unit.

**Satzteil** *der* sentence part.

**Satzung** (*pl* -en) *die* statutes (*pl*).

**Satzzeichen** *das* punctuation mark.

**Satzzusammenhang** *der* context.

**Sau** (*pl* Säue *ODER* -en) *die* **- 1.** (*pl* Säue) [Schwein] sow **- 2.** (*pl* Sauen) [Wildschwein] female wild boar **- 3.** (*pl* Säue) *salopp abw* [Mensch] pig.

**sauber** *adj* **- 1.** [rein] clean **- 2.** *fam iron* [fein] fine

**S**

**- 3.** [Arbeit] neat; [Darbietung] faultless ⬦ *adv*
**- 1.** [gut] neatly **- 2.** [fehlerfrei] faultlessly.

**Sauberkeit** *die* cleanliness.

**säuberlich** *adj* neat ⬦ *adv* neatly.

**sauber machen** *vt* to clean.

**säubern** *vt* **- 1.** [reinigen] to clean **- 2.** [Institution] to purge.

**Säuberung** (*pl* -en) *die* **- 1.** [Reinigung] cleaning **- 2.** [Aussortierung] purge; **ethnische ~** ethnic cleansing.

**Sauce** ['zo:sə] (*pl* -n) *die* sauce; [Bratensoße] gravy.

**Sauciere** [zo'sjɛ:rə] (*pl* -n) *die geh* sauce boat; [für Bratensoße] gravy boat.

**Saudi** (*pl* -s) *der* Saudi.

**Saudi-Arabien** *nt* Saudi Arabia.

**saudi-arabisch** *adj* Saudi Arabian.

**sauer** *adj* **- 1.** [Essen] sour; **saure Gurken** (pickled) gherkins; **ein saurer Wein** an acidic wine **- 2.** [Stimmung] annoyed, cross; **~ auf jn sein** *fam* to be annoyed *ODER* cross with sb; **ein saures Gesicht machen** to pull a sour face **- 3.** CHEM acidic ⬦ *adv* **- 1.** [reagieren] crossly **- 2.** [nicht süß]: **~ schmecken** to taste sour **- 3.** CHEM acidically.

**Sauerampfer** *der* sorrel.

**Sauerbraten** *der* sauerbraten, *braised beef marinated in vinegar.*

**Sauerei** (*pl* -en) *die salopp* **- 1.** [Schmutz] damn mess **- 2.** [Gemeinheit] damn disgrace.

**Sauerkirsche** *die* sour cherry.

**Sauerkraut** *das* sauerkraut.

**Sauerland** *das* Sauerland.

**säuerlich** *adj* **- 1.** [Essen] slightly sour **- 2.** [Stimmung] annoyed, cross ⬦ *adv* **- 1.** [nicht süß]: **~ schmecken** to taste slightly sour **- 2.** [reagieren] crossly.

**Sauerstoff** *der* oxygen.

**Sauerstoffgerät** *das* [für Taucher] breathing apparatus *(sg).*

**Sauerteig** *der* sour dough.

**saufen** (*präs* säuft; *prät* soff; *perf* hat gesoffen) *vt* **- 1.** [Subj: Tier] to drink **- 2.** *salopp* [trinken] to knock back; **sie gehen einen ~** they're going on the booze **- 3.** *fam* [verbrauchen]: **mein Auto säuft zu viel** my car's a real gas-guzzler ⬦ *vi* **- 1.** [Tier] to drink **- 2.** *salopp* [Mensch] to booze.

**Säufer** (*pl* -) *der salopp abw* boozer.

**Sauferei** (*pl* -en) *die salopp abw* booze-up.

**Säuferin** (*pl* -nen) *die salopp abw* boozer.

**säuft** *präs* ▷ **saufen.**

**saugen** (*prät* sog *ODER* saugte; *perf* hat gesogen *ODER* gesaugt) *vt* **- 1.** [heraussaugen] to suck; **etw aus etw ~** to suck sthg out of sthg **- 2.** *(reg)* [mit Staubsauger] to vacuum ⬦ *vi*

**- 1.** [ziehen] to suck; **an etw** *(D)* **~** to suck at sthg **- 2.** *(reg)* [mit Staubsauger] to vacuum.

**säugen** *vt* to suckle.

**Säugetier** *das* mammal.

**Säugling** (*pl* -e) *der* baby.

**Säuglingsnahrung** *die* baby food.

**Säuglingspflege** *die* babycare.

**Saugnapf** *der* sucker.

**saukalt** *adj fam* damn cold.

**Säule** (*pl* -n) *die eigtl & fig* pillar.

**Saum** (*pl* Säume) *der* hem.

**saumäßig** *salopp adj* [schlecht] lousy; **~es Pech haben** to have lousy luck; **es war ein ~es Problem** it was a hell of a problem ⬦ *adv* [sehr] terribly.

**säumen** *vt* **- 1.** [Stoff] to hem **- 2.** *geh* [Weg] to line.

**saumselig** *adj geh* dilatory.

**Sauna** (*pl* -s *ODER* Saunen) *die* sauna.

**Säure** (*pl* -n) *die* **- 1.** CHEM acid **- 2.** [von Wein] acidity; [von Zitrone] sourness.

**säurefest** *adj* acid-proof.

**Saurier** ['zauriɐ] (*pl* -) *der* dinosaur.

**Saus** *der*: **in ~ und Braus leben** to live like a king.

**säuseln** *vi* [Wind] to murmur ⬦ *vt* [sprechen] to purr.

**sausen** (*perf* hat/ist gesaust) *vi* **- 1.** *(ist) fam* [schnell]: **zum Bäcker ~** to dash over to the baker's; **mit dem Fahrrad um die Ecke ~** to hurtle round the corner on one's bike **- 2.** *(hat)* [Wind] to whistle.

**Saustall** *der salopp abw* pigsty.

**Sauwetter** *das (ohne pl) fam abw* lousy weather.

**sauwohl** *adj fam* damn good; **sich ~ fühlen** to feel damn good.

**Savanne** [za'vanə] (*pl* -n) *die* savannah.

**Saxofon, Saxophon** (*pl* -e) *das* saxophone.

**SB** *abk für* **Selbstbedienung.**

**S-Bahn** *die* suburban railway.

**S-Bahnhof** *der* suburban railway station.

**S-Bahnstation** *die* suburban railway station.

**SBB** (*abk für* **Schweizerische Bundesbahn**) *Swiss federal railway company.*

**s. Br.** (*abk für* **südlicher Breite**): **60° ~** 60° S.

**SC** [ɛs'tseː] (*abk für* **Sportklub**) *der sports club.*

**Scanner** ['skɛnɐ] (*pl* -) *der* scanner.

**Schabe** (*pl* -n) *die* cockroach.

**schaben** *vt & vi* to scrape.

**Schabernack** (*pl* -e) *der* prank; **jm einen**

~ **spielen** to play a prank on sb; **mit jm ~ treiben** to play pranks on sb.

**schäbig** *abw adj* - **1.** [Kleidung, Möbel] shabby - **2.** [Bezahlung] paltry - **3.** [Person] mean ◇ *adv* - **1.** [angezogen, eingerichtet] shabbily - **2.** [ausnützen] shamelessly.

**Schablone** (*pl* -n) *die* - **1.** [zum Ausmalen] stencil; [zum Rundherummalen] template - **2.** [Schema] mould.

**Schach** (*pl* -s) *das* chess; **Schach!** check!; **jn in ~ halten** *fig* to keep sb in check.

**Schach|brett** *das* chessboard.

**Schach|figur** *die* chess piece.

**schachmatt** *adj* - **1.** [beim Spiel] checkmate - **2.** *fam* [müde] dead beat, shattered *Br.*

**Schach|spieler, in** *der, die* chess player.

**Schacht** (*pl* Schächte) *der* shaft.

**Schachtel** (*pl* -n) *die* - **1.** [Behälter] box; **eine ~ Zigaretten** a packet *Br* ODER pack *Am* of cigarettes - **2.** *salopp abw* [Frau] bag.

**Schachtel|halm** *der* horsetail.

**Schach|zug** *der eigtl* & *fig* move.

**schade** *adj:* **es ist ~ (um jn/etw)** it's a shame (about sb/sthg); **(wie) ~!** what a shame!; **zu ~ für jn/etw sein** to be too good for sb/sthg.

**Schädel** (*pl* -) *der* - **1.** [Knochen] skull - **2.** *fam* [Kopf] nut; **mir brummt der ~** *fam* my head is killing me.

**Schädel|bruch** *der* skull fracture.

**schaden** *vi* [Sache] to damage; [Person] to harm; **das schadet nichts** it won't do any harm.

**Schaden** (*pl* Schäden) *der* - **1.** [an Sachen] damage (U); **~ verursachen** to cause damage - **2.** [an Menschen] injury; **sie hat an ihrer Gesundheit ~ genommen** her health has suffered; **zu ~ kommen** to be injured; **jm (einen) ~ zufügen** to cause sb harm - **3.** [Nachteil]: **es soll dein ~ nicht sein** I'll make it worth your while.

**Schaden|ersatz** *der* compensation.

**Schadenfreiheits|rabatt** *der* no-claims bonus *Br,* safe driver discount *Am.*

**Schaden|freude** *die* malicious pleasure.

**schadenfroh** *adj* gloating; **~ sein** to gloat.

**Schadensbegrenzung** *die* damage limitation.

**Schadens|fall** *der:* **einen ~ melden** to make a claim; **im ~** in the event of damage.

**schadhaft** *adj* [mit Fabrikationsfehler] defective; [beschädigt] damaged.

**schädigen** *vt* to damage; [Person] to harm.

**schädlich** *adj* harmful; **Rauchen ist ~ für die Gesundheit** smoking damages your health.

**Schädling** (*pl* -e) *der* pest.

**Schädlingsbekämpfungs|mittel** *das* pesticide.

**schadlos** *adv:* **sich an jm/etw ~ halten** *geh* to take advantage of sb/sthg.

**Schad|stoff** *der* [im Boden, in der Luft] pollutant; [im Essen] harmful substance.

**schadstoffarm** *adj* [Motor, Maschine] low-polluting; [Essen] low in harmful substances.

**Schaf** (*pl* -e) *das* - **1.** [Tier] sheep - **2.** *fam abw* [Mensch] dope; **ein schwarzes ~** *abw* a black sheep.

**Schäfer** (*pl* -) *der* shepherd.

**Schäfer|hund** *der* [Hirtenhund] sheepdog; **Deutscher ~** German shepherd, Alsatian *Br.*

**Schäferin** (*pl* -nen) *die* shepherdess.

**schaffen**¹ *vt* - **1.** [beenden, bewältigen] to manage; **es ~, etw zu tun** to manage to do sthg; **er schafft drei Teller Spaghetti zum Abendbrot** he gets through three plates of spaghetti for his dinner; **bis wann schaffst du das?** when can you have it ready by?; **du schaffst es!** you can do it!; **er hat nicht einmal das erste Semester geschafft** he didn't even make it through the first semester; **das wäre geschafft!** that's that done! - **2.** [Prüfung] to get through - **3.** [Ärger, Unruhe] to cause - **4.** [transportieren]: **etw an einen Ort ~** to take sthg somewhere; **jn ins Bett ~** to put sb to bed; **den Verletzten vom Spielfeld ~** to carry the injured player off the pitch - **5.** [erschöpfen] to wear out; **geschafft sein** to be worn out; **du schaffst mich!** you'll be the death of me! - **6.** [erreichen] *fam:* **den Bus gerade noch ~** only just to make it in time for the bus ◇ *vi* - **1.** [tun]: **mit jm/etw nichts zu ~ haben** to have nothing to do with sb/sthg; **jm zu ~ machen** to give sb trouble; **sich an etw (D) zu ~ machen** to busy o.s. with sthg - **2.** *Süddt* [arbeiten] to work.

◆ **geschafft** *interj* [beendet] that's it!; [geglückt] done it!

**schaffen**² (*prät* schuf; *perf* hat geschaffen) *vt* to create; **Platz ~** to make room; **Ordnung ~** to restore order; **wie geschaffen für jn sein** to be made for sb.

**Schaffen** *das* (*ohne pl*) works (*pl*).

**Schaffhausen** *nt* Schaffhausen.

**Schaffner, in** (*mpl* -; *fpl* -nen) *der, die* [in Bus] conductor; [in Zug] ticket collector.

**Schaffung** *die geh* creation.

**Schafkopf** *der card game for four people where players try to get 61 points.*

**Schafs|fell** *das* - **1.** [an Tier] fleece - **2.** [Material, Teppich] sheepskin.

**Schafskäse** *der* ewe's milk cheese.

**Schaft** (*pl* Schäfte) *der* - **1.** [von Speer, Pfeil] shaft; [von Messer] handle - **2.** [von Stiefel] leg.

**Schakal** (*pl* -e) *der* jackal.

**schäkern** *vi fam* [flirten] to flirt.

**schal** *adj* [Bier] flat; [Geschmack] stale.

**Schal** (*pl* -s ODER -e) *der* scarf.

**Schälchen** (*pl* -) *das* small bowl.

**Schale** (*pl* -n) *die* - **1.** [von Zwiebel, Banane, Tomate] skin; [von Apfel, Orange, Kartoffel] peel; **Kartoffel ~n** potato peelings; **sich in ~ werfen** *fam fig* to get all dressed up - **2.** [von Krebs, Ei, Kokosnuss] shell - **3.** [Gefäß] bowl; [flach] dish.

**schälen** *vt* to peel; [Ei, Nüsse, Erbsen] to shell; **sie schälte die Erbsen aus der Hülse** she shelled the peas.
 **sich schälen** *ref* to peel.

**Schalen|sitz** *der* bucket seat.

**Schalk** (*pl* -e ODER **Schälke**) *der* rogue.

**Schall** (*pl* -e ODER **Schälle**) *der* sound.

**schalldämmend** *adj* soundproof <> *adv:* **etw ~ isolieren** to soundproof sthg.

**Schall|dämpfer** *der* - **1.** [von Auto] silencer *Br*, muffler *Am* - **2.** [von Waffe] silencer - **3.** [von Musikinstrument] mute.

**schalldicht** *adj* soundproof; **etw ~ machen** to soundproof sthg.

**schallen** (*prät* **schallte** ODER **scholl**; *perf* **hat geschallt**) *vi* to resound.

**schallend** *adj* resounding <> *adv:* **~ lachen** to roar with laughter.

**Schall|geschwindigkeit** *die* speed of sound.

**Schall|mauer** *die* sound barrier; **die ~ durchbrechen** [Flug] to break the sound barrier.

**Schall|platte** *die* record.

**Schalotte** (*pl* -n) *die* shallot.

**schalt** *prät* ⊏> **schelten.**

**schalten** *vi* - **1.** [den Gang wechseln] to change gear; **in den vierten Gang ~** to change into fourth gear - **2.** [umschalten]: **auf das zweite Programm ~** to turn to channel two; **wir ~ jetzt nach Hamburg** we're now going over to Hamburg - **3.** *fam* [reagieren] to catch on - **4.** [tun]: **~ und walten** to do as one pleases <> *vt* [anschließen] to connect; **etw parallel/in Serie** ELEKTR **~** to connect sthg in parallel/series.

**Schalter** (*pl* -) *der* - **1.** [Schaltknopf] switch - **2.** [für Auskunft, Verkauf] counter.

**Schalter|beamte** *der* counter clerk; [bei Bahn] ticket clerk.

**Schalter|beamtin** *die* counter clerk; [bei Bahn] ticket clerk.

**Schalter|halle** *die* hall; [an Bahnhof] ticket office (*at large station*).

**Schalterschluss** *der* closing time.

**Schalt|getriebe** *das* manual gearbox.

**Schalt|hebel** *der* AUTO gear lever.

**Schalt|jahr** *das* leap year.

**Schalt|plan** *der* circuit diagram.

**Schaltung** (*pl* -en) *die* - **1.** [Gangschaltung] gear change - **2.** ELEKTR circuit - **3.** TV link-up.

**Scham** *die* shame; **~ empfinden** to be ashamed.

**Scham|bein** *das* pubic bone.

**schämen** ⇒ **sich schämen** *ref* to be ashamed; **schäm dich!** shame on you!; **sich für etw ~** to be ashamed of sthg; **sich für jn ~** to be ashamed for sb; **ich schäme mich seinetwegen** I'm ashamed of him.

**Schamgefühl** *das* (sense of) modesty.

**Scham|haar** *das* pubic hair.

**schamhaft** *adj* modest <> *adv* modestly.

**schamlos** *adj* - **1.** [gen] shameless - **2.** [Lüge] barefaced <> *adv* shamelessly.

**Schande** *die* disgrace; **es ist eine ~!** it's a disgrace!; **jm/einer Sache ~ machen** to bring disgrace on sb/sthg; **zu js ~** to sb's shame; *siehe auch* **zuschanden.**

**schänden** *vt* - **1.** [Denkmal, Friedhof] to desecrate; [Leichen] to defile - **2.** [Menschen] to violate, to rape.

**Schand|fleck** *der* disgrace; **ein ~ in der Landschaft** a blot on the landscape.

**schändlich** *adj* disgraceful <> *adv* disgracefully.

**Schand|tat** *die* - **1.** [Verbrechen] heinous crime - **2.** *fam hum* [Aktion]: **zu jeder ~ bereit sein** to be game for anything.

**Schändung** (*pl* -en) *die* - **1.** [von Denkmal, Friedhof] desecration; [von Leichen] defilement - **2.** [von Menschen] violation, rape.

**Schanghai** *nt* Shanghai.

**Schanze** (*pl* -n) *die* ski jump.

**Schar** (*pl* -en) *die* [von Kindern] group; [von Vögeln] flock; **~en von ...** swarms of ...
 **in Scharen** *adv* [von Menschen] in droves; [von Tieren] in swarms.

**Scharade** (*pl* -n) *die fig* charade.

**scharen** *vt:* **jn/etw um sich ~** to gather sb/sthg around o.s.
 **sich scharen** *ref:* **sich um jn ~** to gather round sb.

**scharenweise** *adv* [von Menschen] in droves; **~ fliegen** to flock.

**scharf** (*kompar* **schärfer;** *superl* **schärfste**) *adj* - **1.** [gen] sharp - **2.** [Geschmack] hot, spicy - **3.** *fam* [toll] great; [erotisch] hot; **~ auf etw sein** to be dead keen on sthg; **~ auf jn sein** *salopp* to have the hots for sb - **4.** [Tempo] high; [Wind] biting - **5.** [Geräusch] piercing; [Geruch] pungent - **6.** [Säure] caustic - **7.** [Hund, Angriff] fierce - **8.** [Munition] live - **9.** [Prüfer] tough <> *adv* - **1.** [gen] sharply; **~ geschliffen** keenly whetted; ~ **gewürzt** hot, spicy; ~ **riechen** to be pungent; ~ **beobachten** to watch closely; ~ **nachdenken** to think hard; **jn** ~ **angreifen** to attack sb fiercely - **2.** [knapp]: **der Ball flog** ~ **an meinem Kopf vorbei** the ball flew narrowly past my head; ~ **bremsen** to brake hard, to slam on the brakes; ~ **schießen** to use live ammunition.

**Scharfblick** *der* perspicacity.

**Schärfe** (*pl* **-n**) *die* - **1.** [von Messer, Sinnen] sharpness; [von Verstand] keenness - **2.** [Bildschärfe] focus - **3.** [von Ton, Streit] severity - **4.** [von Geschmack] spiciness - **5.** [von Prüfer] toughness.

**schärfen** *vt* to sharpen.

**scharf|machen** *vt fam* [aggressiv machen] to rouse.

**scharf machen** *vt* - **1.** *fam* [sexuell erregen] to turn on - **2.** [Bombe] to prime.

**Scharf|schütze, schützin** *der, die* marksman (*f* markswoman).

**Scharfsinn** *der* astuteness.

**scharfsinnig** *adj* astute <> *adv* astutely.

**Scharlach** *der* scarlet fever.

**Scharlatan** (*pl* **-e**) *der* charlatan.

**Scharm** *der* = Charme.

**scharmant** *adj* = charmant.

**Scharmützel** (*pl* **-**) *das* skirmish.

**Scharnier** (*pl* **-e**) *das* hinge.

**Schärpe** (*pl* **-n**) *die* sash.

**scharren** *vi* to scrape; [Hund, Pferd] to paw; **mit den Füßen** ~ to shuffle one's feet.

**Scharte** (*pl* **-n**) *die* notch; **eine** ~ **auswetzen** *fig* to make amends.

**Schaschlik** (*pl* **-s**) *der ODER das* shish kebab.

**schassen** *vt fam* to chuck out.

**Schatten** (*pl* **-**) *der* - **1.** [Bereich ohne Sonne] shade; **im** ~ in the shade - **2.** [Silhouette, Fleck] shadow - **3.** *RW:* **in js** ~ **stehen** to be in sb's shadow; **jn in den** ~ **stellen** to overshadow sb; **über seinen** ~ **springen** to force o.s.

**Schatten|boxen** *das* shadow boxing.

**Schatten|dasein** *das* shadowy existence.

**Schatten|morelle** (*pl* **-n**) *die* morello cherry.

**Schatten|seite** *die* - **1.** [von Berg, Haus] dark side - **2.** [Nachteil] drawback.

**Schattierung** (*pl* **-en**) *die* - **1.** [dunkle Stelle] shading - **2.** [Farbe] shade.

**schattig** *adj* shady.

**Schatulle** (*pl* **-n**) *die* casket.

**Schatz** (*pl* **Schätze**) *der* - **1.** [Reichtum] treasure - **2.** [Liebling] darling.

**schätzen** *vt* - **1.** [Wert, Alter, Schaden] to estimate; **grob geschätzt** at a rough estimate

- **2.** [glauben, meinen] to think - **3.** [mögen]: **jn/etw** ~ to value sb/sthg; **jn/etw zu** ~ **wissen** to appreciate sb/sthg.

**schätzenswert** *adj* estimable.

**Schatz|kammer** *die* treasure chamber.

**Schatz|meister** *der* treasurer.

**Schätz|preis** *der* estimated price.

**Schatz|suche** *die* treasure hunt.

**Schätzung** (*pl* **-en**) *die* estimate; [das Schätzen] estimation; [von Gebäuden, Grundstücken] valuation.

**schätzungsweise** *adv* approximately.

**Schätz|wert** *der* estimated value.

**Schau** (*pl* **-en**) *die* show; **eine** ~ **abziehen** *fam* to put on a show; **jm die** ~ **stehlen** *fam* to steal the show from sb; **etw zur** ~ **stellen** to display sthg; **jn zur** ~ **stellen** to exhibit sb.

**Schauder** (*pl* **-**) *der* shudder; [vor Kälte] shiver.

**schauderhaft** *adj* terrible <> *adv:* ~ **aussehen** to look terrible.

**schaudern** *vt* - **1.** [vor Unbehagen] to shudder - **2.** *geh* [vor Kälte] to shiver.

**schauen** *vi* - **1.** [blicken] to look; **zu Boden** ~ to stare at the ground; **auf jn/etw** ~ to look at sb/sthg; **schau mal!** look! - **2.** [sich kümmern]: **nach jm/etw** ~ to look after sb/sthg - **3.** [kontrollieren] to check.

**Schauer** (*pl* **-**) *der* - **1.** [Regen] shower - **2.** [vor Angst] shudder; [vor Kälte] shiver.

**schauerlich** *adj* - **1.** [grausig] gruesome - **2.** *abw* [schlecht] dreadful.

**Schaufel** (*pl* **-n**) *die* shovel.

**schaufeln** *vt* - **1.** [Erde, Kies] to shovel; [Loch] to dig - **2.** *fam* [essen] to shovel down.

**Schau|fenster** *das* shop window.

**Schaufenster|bummel** *der* window-shopping trip; **einen** ~ **machen** to go window-shopping.

**Schaufenster|puppe** *die* mannequin.

**Schau|kasten** *der* display case.

**Schaukel** (*pl* **-n**) *die* swing.

**schaukeln** *vi* - **1.** [gen] to rock - **2.** [auf einer Schaukel] to swing <> *vt* - **1.** [Baby, Wiege] to rock - **2.** *fam* [erledigen]: **ich werde das schon** ~ I'll sort it out.

**Schaukel|pferd** *das* rocking horse.

**Schaukel|stuhl** *der* rocking chair.

**Schaulustige** (*pl* **-n**) *der, die* onlooker.

**Schaum** (*pl* **Schäume**) *der* foam; [von Bier] head; ~ **vor dem Mund haben** to be foaming at the mouth.

**Schaum|bad** *das* bubble bath.

**schäumen** *vi* - **1.** [Flüssigkeit] to foam; [Bier] to froth - **2.** *fam* [vor Wut] to fume.

**S**

**Schaumgummi** *der* foam rubber.

**schaumig** *adj* foamy ◇ *adv:* **etw ~ rühren** to beat sthg until light and fluffy.

**Schaum|stoff** *der* plastic foam.

**Schaum|wein** *der* sparkling wine.

**Schau|platz** *der* [von Ereignis] scene; [von Erzählung] setting.

**schaurig** *adj* - **1.** [erschreckend] gruesome - **2.** [schlecht] dreadful ◇ *adv* - **1.** [sehr] terribly - **2.** [erschreckend] gruesomely.

**Schau|spiel** *das* - **1.** [Bühnenstück] play - **2.** [Gattung] drama - **3.** *fam* [Spektakel] spectacle.

**Schau|spieler, in** *der, die* actor (*f* actress).

**schauspielern** *vi fam abw* to play-act.

**Schauspiel|haus** *das* theatre.

**Schauspiel|schule** *die* drama school.

**Schau|steller, in** (*mpl* -; *fpl* -nen) *der, die* showman (*f* showwoman).

**Schau|tafel** *die* wall chart (*often made of plastic, wood, etc*).

**Scheck** (*pl* -s) *der* cheque; **mit ~ bezahlen** to pay by cheque; **einen ~ ausstellen** to make out a cheque; **einen ~ sperren** to stop a cheque; **ungedeckter ~** bad cheque.

**Scheck|heft** *das* chequebook.

**scheckig** *adj* [Vieh] piebald ◇ *adv:* **sich ~ lachen** to laugh o.s. silly.

**Scheck|karte** *die* cheque card.

**scheel** *abw adj* [misstrauisch] sidelong ◇ *adv:* **jn ~ ansehen** [misstrauisch] to give sb a sidelong glance.

**scheffeln** *vt fam abw* [Geld] to rake in.

**scheibchenweise** *adv fam* a bit at a time.

**Scheibe** (*pl* -n) *die* - **1.** [Glas] pane (of glass); [Fensterscheibe] window pane; [von Auto] window - **2.** [von Brot, Käse, Wurst] slice; **etw in ~n schneiden** to cut sthg into slices, to slice sthg; **von ihrer Pünktlichkeit kannst du dir eine ~ abschneiden** *fam* you would do well to imitate her punctuality.

**Scheiben|bremse** *die* disc brake.

**Scheibenwaschan|lage** *die* windscreen *Br* ODER windshield *Am* washer unit.

**Scheiben|wischer** (*pl* -) *der* windscreen *Br* ODER windshield *Am* wiper.

**Scheich** (*pl* -s ODER -e) *der* sheikh.

**Scheide** (*pl* -n) *die* - **1.** [Vagina] vagina - **2.** [von Messer] sheath.

**scheiden** (*prät* schied; *perf* hat/ist geschieden) *vt* (hat) [Ehe] to dissolve; **sich ~ lassen** to get divorced ◇ *vi* (ist) *geh* - **1.** [fortgehen] to part - **2.** [entlassen werden] **aus dem Amt ~** to resign from office.

**Scheide|weg** *der:* **am ~ stehen** to be at a crossroads.

**Scheidung** (*pl* -en) *die* divorce; **die ~ einreichen** to file for divorce.

**Schein** (*pl* -e) *der* - **1.** [Lichtschein] light; **im ~ einer Taschenlampe** by torchlight - **2.** (*ohne pl*) [Anschein] appearances (*pl*); **den ~ wahren** to keep up appearances; **der ~ trügt** appearances can be deceptive - **3.** UNI ≃ credit, *certificate issued to students on successful completion of a course in a specific subject* - **4.** [Geldschein] note.

**scheinbar** *adj* apparent ◇ *adv* apparently, seemingly.

**Schein|blüte** *die* WIRTSCH bubble.

**scheinen** (*prät* schien; *perf* hat geschienen) *vi* - **1.** [leuchten] to shine - **2.** [den Eindruck erwecken] to seem, to appear; **es scheint, dass ... it** seems ODER appears that ...; **mir scheint, dass ... it** seems to me that ...; **das scheint dir nur so** it just seems that way to you.

**Schein|firma** *die* fictitious company.

**scheinheilig** *adj* [heuchlerisch] hypocritical ◇ *adv* [heuchlerisch] hypocritically.

**Schein|selbstständigkeit** *die* (*ohne pl*): **in ~ arbeiten** *to be apparently self-employed but only work for one company and pay no National Insurance contributions*.

**scheintot** *adj* MED: **~ sein** to be apparently dead.

**Scheinwerfer** (*pl* -) *der* - **1.** [am Auto] headlight - **2.** [im Theater] spotlight; [Suchscheinwerfer] searchlight.

**Scheinwerfer|licht** *das* [von Autos] headlights (*pl*); [im Theater] spotlight; **im ~** in the spotlight.

**Scheiß** *der salopp abw* shit, crap; **mach keinen ~** stop pissing around!

**Scheiß-** *präfix salopp:* **~ computer** bloody computer.

**Scheiße** *die salopp* - **1.** [gen] shit - **2.** RW: **nur ~ im Kopf haben** to be a piss-artist; **~ sein** to be shit ODER crap; **in der ~ sitzen** to be in the shit ◇ *interj salopp* shit!

**scheißegal** *adj salopp abw:* **das ist mir ~** I don't give a shit about that.

**scheißen** (*prät* schiss; *perf* hat geschissen) *vi salopp* to shit; **auf jn/etw ~** not to give a shit about sb/sthg.

**scheißfreundlich** *adj salopp* apparently very friendly.

**Scheit** (*pl* -e) *der* log.

**Scheitel** (*pl* -) *der* [Frisur] parting *Br*, part *Am*; **einen ~ ziehen** to make a parting *Br* ODER part *Am*; **vom ~ bis zur Sohle** *fig* from top to toe.

**Scheiterlhaufen** *der:* sie starben auf dem ~ they were burned at the stake.

**scheitern** (*perf* **ist gescheitert**) *vi* - **1.** [Person - gen] to fail; [ - Sport] to lose; **sie sind mit ihrem Plan am Widerstand der Bewohner gescheitert** their plan failed because of the opposition of the local population; **sie sind mit 2:0 an Italien gescheitert** they were knocked out 2–0 by Italy - **2.** [Versuch, Vorhaben] to fail; **an etw** (*D*) ~ to fail because of sthg.

**Schelle** (*pl* -**n**) *die* [an Kostüm, Zügel] bell; [an Tür] doorbell.

**schellen** *vi fam* to ring; **es schellt** the bell is ringing.

**Schelllfisch** *der* haddock.

**Schelm** (*pl* -**e**) *der* rascal.

**schelmisch** *adj* mischievous ◇ *adv* mischievously.

**schelten** (*präs* **schilt**; *prät* **schalt**; *perf* **hat gescholten**) *vt* to scold; **auf/über jn/etw** ~ to moan about sb/sthg.

**Schema** (*pl* -**s** ODER -**ta** ODER **Schemen**) *das* - **1.** [Darstellung] diagram - **2.** [Muster] routine.

**schematisch** *adj* - **1.** [grob] schematic - **2.** [routiniert] mechanical ◇ *adv* - **1.** [grob] schematically - **2.** [routiniert] mechanically.

**schematisieren** *vt* - **1.** [nach Schema erklären] to outline (using a diagram) - **2.** [vereinfachen] to oversimplify.

**Schemel** (*pl* -) *der* stool.

**schemenhaft** *adj* shadowy ◇ *adv:* **etw ~ erkennen** to make out the silhouette of sthg.

**Schenkel** (*pl* -) *der* - **1.** [Bein] thigh - **2.** MATH side.

**schenken** *vt* - **1.** [geben] to give (*as a present*); **jm etw** ~ to give sb sthg - **2.** [erlassen]: **jm etw** ~ to let sb off sthg; **sich etw** ~ to spare o.s. sthg.

**Schenkung** (*pl* -**en**) *die* gift.

**scheppern** *vi* to clatter.

**Scherbe** (*pl* -**n**) *die* piece, fragment; **die ~n zusammenkehren** to sweep up the broken pieces.

**Scherbenlhaufen** *der:* sie stand vor einem ~ her life was in ruins.

**Schere** (*pl* -**n**) *die* - **1.** [Werkzeug] pair of scissors, scissors (*pl*) - **2.** [von Krebs] pincer, claw.

**scheren** (*prät* **scherte** ODER **schor**; *perf* **hat geschert** ODER **geschoren**) *vt* (*unreg*) - **1.** [Schaf] to shear; [Hund] to clip - **2.** [Hecke] to clip; [Haare] to crop - **3.** (*reg*) [kümmern]: **das schert mich nicht** I don't care.

➤ **sich scheren** *ref* (*reg*): **sich um jn/etw** ~/**nicht** ~ to care/not to care about sb/sthg.

**Scherenlschnitt** *der* silhouette.

**Scherereien** *pl* trouble (*U*); **das gibt** ~ that will lead to trouble.

**Scherz** (*pl* -**e**) *der* joke; **etw zum** ~ **tun/sagen** to do/say sthg as a joke.

➤ **Scherz beiseite** *adv* joking apart.

**Scherzlartikel** *der* novelty (item).

**scherzen** *vi geh* to joke; **mit diesem Husten ist nicht zu** ~ this cough is no laughing matter.

**Scherzlfrage** *die* riddle.

**scherzhaft** *adv* jokingly.

**scheu** *adj* shy; **jn/etw** ~ **machen** to frighten sb/sthg ◇ *adv* shyly.

**Scheu** *die* shyness; **ohne** ~ uninhibitedly.

**scheuchen** *vt* to shoo.

**scheuen** *vt:* **keine Mühen/Kosten** ~ to spare no effort/expense ◇ *vi* [Pferd] to shy.

➤ **sich scheuen** *ref:* **sich** ~, **etw zu tun** to be afraid of doing sthg; **sich vor etw** (*D*) ~ to shy away from sthg.

**Scheuerllappen** *der* floorcloth.

**scheuern** *vt* - **1.** [putzen - Boden] to scrub; [ - Töpfe] to scour - **2.** [reiben]: **sich** (*D*) **in seinen Schuhen die Fersen wund** ~ to get sore heels because one's shoes are rubbing; **jm eine** ~ *fam fig* to slap sb in the face ◇ *vi* to rub.

**Scheuklappen** *pl* blinker.

**Scheune** (*pl* -**n**) *die* barn.

**Scheusal** (*pl* -**e**) *das fam abw* beast.

**scheußlich** *abw adj* - **1.** [Verhalten, Anblick, Wetter] terrible - **2.** [Aussehen, Geschmack] horrible ◇ *adv* - **1.** [sich verhalten, kalt] terribly - **2.** [einrichten, dekorieren] horribly.

**Schi** = Ski.

**Schicht** (*pl* -**en**) *die* - **1.** [Lage] layer - **2.** [Gesellschaftsschicht] (social) class; **alle ~en der Bevölkerung** all strata of society - **3.** [Schichtarbeit] shift; ~ **arbeiten** to work shifts.

**Schichtarbeit** *die* shift work.

**Schichtlarbeiter, in** *der, die* shift worker.

**schichten** *vt* to stack.

**Schichtlkäse** *der* low-fat "quark" with a layer of high-fat "quark"

**schichtspezifisch** *adj* appropriate to one's class.

**Schichtlwechsel** *der* change of shifts.

**schichtweise** *adv* in layers.

**schick** *adj* - **1.** [modisch] stylish - **2.** [in] trendy - **3.** [toll] great.

**Schick** *der* style; **mit** ~ stylishly.

**schicken** *vt* to send; **jm etw** ~, **etw an jn** ~ to send sb sthg, to send sthg to sb ◇ *vi:* **nach jm** ~ to send for sb.

➤ **sich schicken** *ref geh* - **1.** [sich gehören] to be proper; **es schickt sich nicht, etw zu tun** it is not

**S**

the done thing to do sthg **- 2.** [sich abfinden]: **sich in etw** (A) ~ to resign o.s. to sthg.

**Schickeria** *die fam* smart set.

**Schickimicki** (*pl* **-s**) *der abw fam* poser, trendy.

**Schicksal** (*pl* **-e**) *das* fate; **jn/etw seinem** ~ **überlassen** to leave sb/sthg to his/her/its fate; **(das ist)** ~**!** *fam fig* tough!

**Schicksalsschlag** *der* stroke of fate.

**Schiebedach** *das* sunroof.

**Schiebefenster** *das* sliding window.

**schieben** (*prät* **schob**; *perf* **hat geschoben**) *vt* **- 1.** [wegschieben] to push; **die Schuld auf einen anderen** ~ to put the blame on sb else; **ein schlechtes Ergebnis auf etw** (A) ~ to blame a poor result on sthg **- 2.** [hineinschieben] to put **- 3.** *fam* [schmuggeln] to traffic in.

➤ **sich schieben** *ref* to move; **sich durch das Gewühl** ~ to push one's way through the crowd.

**Schieber** (*pl* **-**) *der* **- 1.** [an Gerät] slider **- 2.** *fam* [Mensch] black marketeer.

**Schieberin** (*pl* **-nen**) *die fam* black marketeer.

**Schiebetür** *die* sliding door.

**Schiebung** (*pl* **-en**) *die* fixing; **das ist** ~**!** it's a fix!

**schied** *prät* ⊳ **scheiden**.

**Schiedsrichter, in** *der, die* **sport** referee; [bei Tennis] umpire.

**Schiedsstelle** *die* arbitration board.

**schief** *adj* **- 1.** [krumm] crooked; [geneigt] leaning; [Blick] wry; [Absatz] worn **- 2.** [falsch - Vergleich] false; **ein** ~**es Bild abgeben** to present a lop-sided *oder* distorted picture ⬦ *adv:* **das Sofa steht** ~ the sofa is at an angle; **das Bild hängt** ~ the picture isn't straight; **jn** ~ **ansehen** to look at sb askance.

**Schiefer** (*pl* **-**) *der* slate.

**Schiefertafel** *die* slate.

**schief gehen** (*perf* **ist schief gegangen**) *vi* (*unreg*) to go wrong; **es wird schon** ~**!** it'll be okay!

**schief gewickelt** *adj fam:* **da bist du (aber)** ~**!** you couldn't be more wrong!

**schieflachen** ➤ **sich schieflachen** *ref fam* to kill o.s. laughing.

**schief liegen** *vi* (*unreg*) *fam:* **mit einer Meinung** ~ to be out in one's opinion.

**schielen** *vi* **- 1.** [wegen Augenfehler] to squint; **sie schielt mit einem Auge** she has a squint in one eye **- 2.** *fam* [schauen] to glance; **nach jm/etw** ~ *fig* to have one's eye on sb/sthg.

**schien** *prät* ⊳ **scheinen**.

**Schienbein** *das* shin.

**Schiene** (*pl* **-n**) *die* **- 1.** [Gleis] rail **- 2.** **med** splint **- 3.** [Führungsschiene] runner.

**schienen** *vt* [Arm, Bein] to put a splint on.

**Schienenfahrzeug** *das amt:* ~**e** trains and trams.

**Schienenverkehr** *der* (*ohne pl*) trains and trams (*pl*).

**Schießbefehl** *der:* ~ **haben** to have orders to shoot.

**Schießbude** *die* shooting gallery.

**schießen** (*prät* **schoss**; *perf* **hat/ist geschossen**) *vi* **- 1.** (*hat*) [mit Gewehr] to shoot, to fire; **auf jn/etw** ~ to shoot *oder* fire at sb/sthg **- 2.** (*ist*) [wachsen] to shoot up **- 3.** (*ist*) [sich schnell bewegen] to shoot; [Flüssigkeit] to gush; **die Röte schoss ihm ins Gesicht** the colour rushed to his face **- 4.** (*hat*) **sport** to shoot ⬦ *vt* (*hat*) **- 1.** [gen] to shoot **- 2.** [Tor] to score **- 3.** [Foto] to take.

**Schießen** *das:* **das war zum** ~ *fam* it was a scream.

**Schießerei** (*pl* **-en**) *die* shoot-out.

**Schießpulver** *das* gunpowder.

**Schießscharte** *die* embrasure.

**Schießstand** *der* shooting range.

**Schiff** (*pl* **-e**) *das* **- 1.** [Wasserfahrzeug] ship; **mit dem** ~ by ship; **klar** ~ **machen** to clear the decks **- 2.** [von Kirche] nave.

**Schiffahrt** *die* = Schifffahrt.

**Schiffahrtsweg** *der* = Schifffahrtsweg.

**schiffbar** *adj* navigable.

**Schiffbruch** *der* shipwreck; ~ **erleiden** [untergehen] to be shipwrecked; **mit etw** ~ **erleiden** [scheitern] to fail in sthg.

**Schiffchen** (*pl* **-**) *das* **- 1.** [Mütze] forage cap **- 2.** [Schiff] small boat.

**Schifffahrt** *die* shipping.

**Schifffahrtsweg** *der* shipping lane.

**Schiffsjunge** *der* ship's boy.

**Schiffsreise** *die* voyage.

**Schiffsschraube** *die* ship's propeller.

**Schiffsverkehr** *der* shipping traffic.

**Schikane** (*pl* **-n**) *die* harassment; **mit allen** ~**n** *fam fig* with all the extras.

**schikanieren** *vt abw* to harass.

**Schikoree** (*pl* **-s**) *die oder* = **Chicorée**.

**Schild** (*pl* **-er** *oder* **-e**) *das* (*pl* Schilder) sign; [an Auto] numberplate *Br*, license plate *Am*; [Namensschild] nameplate ⬦ *der* (*pl Schilde*) shield; **etw im** ~ **führen** *fig* to be up to sthg.

**Schilddrüse** *die* thyroid gland.

**schildern** *vt* to describe.

**Schilderung** (*pl* **-en**) *die* description.

**Schilderwald** *der abw* maze of traffic signs.

**Schild|kröte** *die* [auf dem Land] tortoise; [im Wasser] turtle.

**Schildpatt** *das* tortoiseshell.

**Schilf** *(pl -e) das* - **1.** [Pflanze] reed - **2.** *(ohne pl)* [Gebiet] reedbed.

**schillern** *vi* to shimmer.

**Schilling** *(pl -e ODER -) der* schilling.

**Schimmel** *(pl -) der* - **1.** [Pilz] mould - **2.** [Pferd] white horse.

**schimmelig, schimmlig** *adj* mouldy.

**schimmeln** *(perf hat/ist geschimmelt) vi* to go mouldy.

**Schimmel|pilz** *der* mould.

**Schimmer** *(pl -) geh der* - **1.** [Glanz] gleam - **2.** [Spur] glimmer; **keinen (blassen) ~ von etw haben** *fam fig* not to have the faintest idea about sthg.

**schimmern** *vi* to glimmer; **durch etw ~** to show through sthg.

**schimmlig** = schimmelig.

**Schimpanse** *(pl -n) der* chimpanzee.

**Schimpf** *der:* **mit ~ und Schande** in disgrace.

**schimpfen** *vi* to grumble; **auf ODER über jn/ etw ~** to grumble about sb/sthg; **mit jm ~** to tell sb off.

**Schimpfwort** *(pl -wörter ODER -e) das* swearword.

**Schindel** *(pl -n) die* shingle.

**schinden** *(prät schund; perf hat geschunden) vt* - **1.** [quälen] to maltreat - **2.** [herausschlagen]: **Zeit ~** to play for time; **Applaus ~** to fish for applause; **Eindruck ~** to try to impress.
➥ **sich schinden** *ref* to slave away.

**Schinderei** *(pl -en) die* - **1.** [Quälerei] maltreatment - **2.** [Strapaze] struggle.

**Schindluder** *das:* **~ mit jm/etw treiben** *fam* to abuse sb/sthg.

**Schinken** *(pl -) der* - **1.** [Fleisch] ham; **roher/ gekochter/geräucherter ~** cured/cooked/ smoked ham - **2.** *fam* [Buch] enormous tome - **3.** *fam* [Film] tacky epic saga.

**Schinkenspeck** *der* bacon.

**Schippe** *(pl -n) die* shovel; **jn auf die ~ nehmen** *fam fig* to pull sb's leg.

**schippen** *vt* to shovel.

**Schirm** *(pl -e) der* - **1.** [Regenschirm] umbrella - **2.** [Sonnenschirm] sunshade; [zum Tragen] parasol; [an Mütze] visor, peak.

**Schirmherrschaft** *die* patronage.

**Schirm|mütze** *die* peaked cap.

**schiss** *prät* ▷ scheißen.

**Schiss** *der salopp:* **da hast du wohl mächtigen ~ bekommen** you got the shits big time;

**~ (vor jm/etw) haben** to be shit-scared (of sb/ sthg).

**schizophren** *adj* - **1.** MED schizophrenic - **2.** [widersprüchlich] contradictory.

**schlabberig, schlabbrig** *abw adj* - **1.** [wässrig] watery - **2.** [Pullover] baggy.

**Schlacht** *(pl -en) die* battle; **sich (D) eine ~ liefern** *fam* to do battle.

**schlachten** *vt* to slaughter.

**Schlachtenbummler, in** *(mpl -; fpl -nen) der, die* away supporter.

**Schlachter** *(pl -) der* butcher.

**Schlächter, in** *(mpl -; fpl -nen) der, die* [grausamer Mensch] butcher.

**Schlacht|feld** *das* - **1.** [Kriegsschauplatz] battlefield - **2.** *fam* [Chaos]: **ein ~ in der Küche hinterlassen** to leave the kitchen looking as if a bomb had hit it.

**Schlacht|hof** *der* slaughterhouse.

**Schlacht|plan** *der fam* battle plan.

**Schlacht|platte** *die* KÜCHE platter of various cooked meats and sausages.

**Schlacht|ruf** *der* battle cry.

**Schlacke** *(pl -n) die* clinker *(U);* [von Hochofen] slag *(U).*
➥ **Schlacken** *pl* MED waste products.

**schlackern** *vi* to shake; **mir ~ die Knie** my knees are trembling.

**Schlaf** *der* sleep; **jn um den ~ bringen** to stop sb from sleeping; **etw im ~ können** *fam fig* to be able to do sthg in one's sleep.

**Schlafan|zug** *der* pyjamas *(pl).*

**Schläfe** *(pl -n) die* temple.

**schlafen** *(präs schläft; prät schlief; perf hat geschlafen) vi* - **1.** [eingeschlafen sein] to sleep; **tief ODER fest ~** to sleep soundly; **~ gehen, sich ~ legen** to go to bed; **mit jm ~** to sleep with sb; **schlaf schön ODER gut!** sleep well! - **2.** [übernachten]: **bei jm ~** to stay the night with sb - **3.** *fam* [unaufmerksam sein] to be asleep.

**schlaff** *adj* - **1.** [nicht fest - Seil] slack; [ - Penis, Händedruck] limp; [ - Haut] loose; [ - Muskeln] flabby - **2.** [müde] listless; **Mensch, bist du ein ~er Typ!** you're such a drip! ⟨⟩ *adv* - **1.** [lose] slackly - **2.** [energielos] listlessly.

**Schlaf|gelegenheit** *die* place to sleep.

**Schlafittchen** *das fam:* **jn am ~ packen/ erwischen** to collar sb.

**Schlaf|lied** *das* lullaby.

**schlaflos** *adj* sleepless ⟨⟩ *adv* sleeplessly.

**Schlaflosigkeit** *die* insomnia.

**Schlaf|mittel** *das* sleeping pill.

**Schlaf|mütze** *die fam* - **1.** [Langschläfer] sleepyhead - **2.** [unaufmerksame Person] dopey person.

**S**

**schläfrig** *adj* sleepy ⬦ *adv* sleepily.

**Schlaf|saal** *der* dormitory.

**Schlaf|sack** *der* sleeping bag.

**Schlaf|störung** *die* insomnia *(U).*

**schläft** *präs* ⊏ **schlafen.**

**Schlaf|tablette** *die* sleeping pill.

**schlaftrunken** *adj* drowsy ⬦ *adv* drowsily.

**Schlaf|wagen** *der* sleeper.

**schlafwandeln** (*perf* hat/ist schlafgewandelt) *vi* to sleepwalk.

**Schlafwandler, in** (*mpl* -; *fpl* -nen) *der, die* sleepwalker.

**Schlaf|zimmer** *das* - **1.** [Zimmer] bedroom - **2.** [Möbel] bedroom suite.

**Schlag** (*pl* **Schläge**) *der* - **1.** [Stoß] blow; [leicht] pat; [mit der Faust] punch; [mit der Hand] slap; **ein ~ ins Gesicht** *eigtl* & *fig* a slap in the face; **jm einen ~ versetzen** [Hieb] to hit sb; [Schock] to be a blow to sb - **2.** [Geräusch - von Uhr] chime; *Süddt* [ - Knall] crash; [ - von Trommel] bang; **~ zwölf** on the stroke of twelve o'clock - **3.** *fam* [Stromstoß] (electric) shock - **4.** *RW*: **auf einen ~** in one go; **alle erschienen auf einen ~** they all turned up at once; **ein harter** ODER **schwerer ~** a heavy blow; **ein ~ ins Wasser** a washout; **mich trifft der ~** *fam* I'm flabbergasted.

➤ **Schlag auf Schlag** *adv* in quick succession; **plözlich ging es ~ auf ~** suddenly everything happened very quickly.

➤ **Schläge** *pl*: **Schläge bekommen** to get a hiding.

**Schlag|abtausch** *der* - **1.** SPORT exchange of blows - **2.** [in Diskussion] exchange.

**Schlag|ader** *die* artery.

**Schlagan|fall** *der* stroke.

**schlagartig** *adj* sudden ⬦ *adv* suddenly.

**Schlag|bohrer** *der* hammer drill.

**schlagen** (*präs* **schlägt;** *prät* **schlug;** *perf* **hat/ist geschlagen**) *vt* (*hat*) - **1.** [prügeln] to hit; [regelmäßig] to beat; [mit der Faust] to punch; [mit der Hand] to slap; [leicht] to pat; **jm etw aus der Hand ~** to knock sthg out of sb's hand - **2.** [besiegen] to beat; **jn eins zu null ~** to beat sb one-zero - **3.** [befestigen]: **jn/etw an etw** (*A*) **~** [mit Nägeln] to nail sb/sthg to sthg; **einen Nagel in die Wand ~** to bang a nail into the wall - **4.** [Ball - bei Fußball] to kick - **5.** [Eier, Sahne, Trommel] to beat - **6.** [legen]: **die Hände vor das Gesicht ~** to cover one's face with one's hands - **7.** [hinzufügen]: **etw zu etw ~** [Gebiet] to annex sthg to sthg; **etw auf etw** (*A*) **~** to add sthg to sthg ⬦ *vi* - **1.** (*ist*) [aufprallen]: **gegen etw ~** [Regen] to beat against sthg; [Wellen] to pound against sthg; **er schlug mit dem Kopf gegen die Wand** he banged his head against the wall - **2.** (*hat*) [hauen] to hit; **jm auf die Schulter ~** to slap sb on the back; **nach jm ~** to hit out at sb; **mit der Hand auf den Tisch ~** to bang one's hand on the table; **gegen etw ~** [Tür] to bang on sthg; **um sich ~** to lash out - **3.** (*ist*) [sich auswirken]: **das fette Essen schlägt mir auf den Magen** greasy food affects my stomach - **4.** (*hat*) [Uhr] to strike; [mit Glocke] to chime - **5.** (*ist*) [ähneln]: **nach jm ~** to take after sb - **6.** (*hat*) [Herz, Puls] to beat - **7.** (*hat, ist*) [einschlagen]: **in etw** (*A*) **~** to strike sthg - **8.** (*ist*) [Flammen] to leap.

➤ **sich schlagen** *ref* - **1.** [sich prügeln]: **sich (mit jm) ~** to fight (sb); **sich um etw ~** *fam* to fight for sthg; **die Gäste schlugen sich um das kalte Büfett** the guests fought over the cold buffet; **sich tapfer** ODER **wacker ~** *fig* to put up a good fight - **2.** [sich begeben]: **sich in die Büsche ~** to slip off into the bushes; **sich auf js Seite ~** to side with sb.

**schlagend** *adj* conclusive ⬦ *adv* conclusively.

**Schlager** (*pl* -) *der* [Lied] hit.

**Schläger** (*pl* -) *der* - **1.** [für Tennis, Badminton] racquet; [für Tischtennis] bat; [für Golf] club; [für Hockey] stick - **2.** *abw* [Mensch] thug.

**Schlägerei** (*pl* -en) *die* fight.

**schlagfertig** *adj* quick-witted ⬦ *adv:* **~ antworten** to give a quick-witted reply.

**Schlagfertigkeit** *die* quick-wittedness.

**schlagkräftig** *adj* - **1.** [Argument] compelling - **2.** [Truppe] powerful.

**Schlag|loch** *das* pothole.

**Schlag|sahne** *die* whipped cream.

**Schlag|seite** *die* (*ohne pl*) list; **~ bekommen** [Schiff] to start to list; **er hatte ~** *fam fig* he was swaying from side to side.

**Schlag|stock** *der* truncheon *Br*, nightstick *Am*.

**schlägt** *präs* ⊏ **schlagen.**

**Schlag|wort** (*pl* -e ODER -wörter) *das* - **1.** (*pl* Schlagworte) *abw* [Gemeinplatz] catchword - **2.** (*pl* Schlagwörter) [Stichwort] key word.

**Schlag|zeile** *die* headline; **~n machen** to make the headlines.

**Schlag|zeug** (*pl* -e) *das* [in Band] drums (*pl*); [in Orchester] percussion.

**Schlag|zeuger, in** (*mpl* -; *fpl* -nen) *der, die* [in Band] drummer; [in Orchester] percussionist.

**schlaksig** *adj* lanky ⬦ *adv* lankily.

**Schlamassel** *der fam* mess; **da haben wir den ~** we're in a real mess now!

**Schlamm** (*pl* -e ODER **Schlämme**) *der* mud; [Ablagerung] sludge.

**schlammig** *adj* muddy.

**Schlampe** (*pl* -n) *die salopp abw* slut.

**Schlamperei** (*pl* -en) *die fam* sloppiness.

**schlampig** *abw adj* - **1.** [Person] slovenly - **2.** [Arbeit] sloppy ⬦ *adv* - **1.** [sich anziehen] in a slovenly way - **2.** [arbeiten] sloppily.

**schlang** *prät* ▷ schlingen.

**Schlange** (*pl* -n) *die* - **1.** [Tier] snake - **2.** [Reihe] queue *Br*, line *Am*; ~ **stehen** to queue *Br*, to stand in line *Am*.

**schlängeln** ▶ **sich schlängeln** *ref* to wind one's/its way.

**schlank** *adj* slim; [Hals, Beine] slender ◇ *adv:* **das macht** ~ that's good for your figure.

**Schlankheitslkur** *die* diet.

**schlapp** *adj* [müde] tired out; [energielos] listless ◇ *adv* listlessly.

**Schlappe** (*pl* -n) *die fam* setback; [bei Wahl, Spiel] defeat.

**Schlapplhut** *der* slouch hat.

**schlapplmachen** *vi fam:* kurz vor dem Ziel ~ to pull out just before the finishing line.

**Schlapplschwanz** *der fam abw* drip.

**Schlaraffenland** *das* Cockaigne.

**schlau** *adj* clever; [listig] cunning; **aus jm/etw nicht ~ werden** not to be able to work sb/ sthg out ◇ *adv* cleverly; [listig] cunningly; **sich ~ machen** *fam* to put o.s. in the picture.

**Schlauch** (*pl* Schläuche) *der* hose; [in Reifen] tube.

**Schlauchlboot** *das* rubber dinghy.

**schlauchen** *vt fam* to wear out.

**Schlaufe** (*pl* -n) *die* loop.

**schlecht** *adj* - **1.** [gen] bad, poor; [Zeiten] hard; **ein ~es Gedächtnis** a bad *ODER* poor memory; **(das ist) nicht ~!** *fam* (that's) not bad!; **mehr ~ als recht** after a fashion - **2.** [gesundheitlich - Person] sick; **mir ist/wird ~** I feel sick; **~ aussehen** to look ill; **von jm ~ reden** to speak ill of sb - **3.** [Lebensmittel] off; **~ werden** to go off ◇ *adv* - **1.** [gen] badly, poorly; **die Geschäfte gehen ~** business is bad; **er sieht ~** he's got bad eyesight; **er hört ~** he's hard of hearing; **das Essen ist mir ~ bekommen** the food didn't agree with me; **es sieht ~ für jn/etw aus** it looks bad for sb/sthg; **es steht ~ um etw** [finanziell] things are looking bad for sthg; **es steht ~ um ihn** [gesundheitlich] he's not doing well - **2.** [unangenehm - schmecken, riechen] bad - **3.** [kaum] hardly; **das kann ~ sein** that's hardly possible.

**schlecht gelaunt** *adj:* ~ **sein** to be in a bad mood ◇ *adv* irritably.

**schlechthin** *adv* - **1.** [typisch]: **er ist der Gentleman ~** he is the quintessential gentleman - **2.** [absolut] simply.

**schlecht machen** *vt* to run down.

**schlecken** *vt* [lecken] to lick ◇ *vi fam* [naschen] to eat sweet things.

**schleichen** (*prät* schlich; *perf* ist geschlichen) *vi* to creep; [Auto] to crawl.

▶ **sich schleichen** *ref* to creep.

**schleichend** *adj* - **1.** [vorsichtig] creeping - **2.** [allmählich - Inflation] creeping; [ - Krankheit] insidious ◇ *adv* [langsam]: **die Autos bewegten sich ~ vorwärts** the cars crept forwards.

**Schleichlweg** *der* secret path.

**Schleichlwerbung** *die* plug.

**Schleier** (*pl* -) *der* - **1.** [Stoff] veil - **2.** [von Dunst, Nebel] haze; **auf dem Foto ist ein ~** the photo is fogged.

**schleierhaft** *adj:* **es ist mir ~, wie du das gemacht hast** it's a mystery to me how you did that.

**Schleife** (*pl* -n) *die* - **1.** [Band] bow - **2.** [Biegung] bend.

**schleifen** (*prät* schliff *ODER* schleifte; *perf* hat geschliffen *ODER* hat/ist geschleift) *vt* - **1.** (*unreg*) (hat) [abschleifen - Diamanten, Glas] to cut; [ - mit Sandpapier] to sand; [ - optische Linsen] to grind - **2.** (*unreg*) (hat) [schärfen] to sharpen, to grind - **3.** (*unreg*) (hat) [drillen] to drill hard - **4.** (*reg*) (hat) [zerren] to drag ◇ *vi* (*reg*) (hat, ist) to drag.

**Schleiflmaschine** *die* grinding machine; [für Dielenböden] sander.

**Schleim** (*pl* -e) *der* [in der Nase] mucus; [im Rachen] phlegm; [einer Schnecke] slime.

**Schleimlhaut** *die* mucous membrane.

**schleimig** *adj eigtl* & *fig* slimy ◇ *adv* slimily.

**schlemmen** *vt* to feast on ◇ *vi* to feast.

**schlendern** (*perf* ist geschlendert) *vi* to stroll.

**Schlenker** (*pl* -) *der:* **einen ~ machen** to swerve.

**schlenkern** *vi:* **mit den Armen ~** to swing one's arms.

**Schleppe** (*pl* -n) *die* train (*of dress*).

**schleppen** *vt* - **1.** [tragen] to lug; [zerren] to drag - **2.** [Fahrzeug] to tow - **3.** *fam* [mitnehmen] to drag (along) - **4.** *fam abw* [schmuggeln] to smuggle.

▶ **sich schleppen** *ref* - **1.** [gehen] to drag o.s. - **2.** [sich hinziehen] to drag on.

**schleppend** *adj* - **1.** [Schritte, Gang] dragging - **2.** [Bearbeitung, Abfertigung] slow - **3.** [Absatz] sluggish ◇ *adv* - **1.** [langsam] slowly - **2.** [mühsam]: **~ die Stufen hinaufsteigen** to drag o.s. up the steps.

**Schlepper** (*pl* -) *der* - **1.** [Schiff] tug - **2.** [Fluchthelfer] smuggler (*of refugees*) - **3.** *fam* [in Bars] tout.

**Schlepplift** *der* ski tow.

**Schleppltau** *das:* **jn ins ~ nehmen** *fam* to take sb along in tow.

**Schlesien** *nt* Silesia.

**Schlesier, in** [ˈʃleːzjɐ, rɪn] (*mpl* -; *fpl* -nen) *der, die* Silesian.

**schlesisch** *adj* Silesian.

**Schleswig-Holstein** *nt* Schleswig-Holstein.

**Schleswig-Holsteiner** (*pl* -) *der* native/inhabitant of Schleswig-Holstein ⬦ *adj* (*unver*) of/from Schleswig-Holstein.

**Schleswig-Holsteinerin** (*pl* -nen) *die* native/inhabitant of Schleswig-Holstein.

**Schleuder** (*pl* -n) *die* - **1.** [Steinschleuder] sling; [Wurfmaschine] catapult - **2.** [Wäscheschleuder] spin-dryer.

**schleudern** (*perf* hat/ist geschleudert) *vt (hat)* - **1.** *fam* [werfen] to hurl - **2.** [zentrifugieren - Wäsche] to spin; [ - Honig] to extract ⬦ *vi (ist)* to skid.

**Schleudern** *das:* ins ~ kommen *ODER* geraten [mit dem Fahrzeug] to go into a skid; *fam* [unsicher werden] to be thrown; jn ins ~ bringen *fam* to throw sb.

**Schleuder|sitz** *der* ejector seat; er sitzt auf dem ~ his future is hanging in the balance.

**schleunigst** *adv fam* - **1.** [sofort] at once - **2.** [schnell] hastily.

**Schleuse** (*pl* -n) *die* - **1.** SCHIFF lock - **2.** [Zwischenkammer] airlock.

**schleusen** *vt* [Person] to smuggle.

**Schleuser, in** (*mpl* -; *fpl* -nen) *der, die* smuggler (*of refugees*).

**schlich** *prät* ▷ schleichen.

**Schliche** *pl* tricks; jm auf *ODER* hinter die ~ kommen to get on to sb.

**schlicht** *adj* simple ⬦ *adv* simply; ~ und einfach quite simply.

**schlichten** *vt* to settle.

**schlichtweg** *adv* simply.

**Schlick** (*pl* -e) *der* silt.

**schlief** *prät* ▷ schlafen.

**schließen** (*prät* schloss; *perf* hat geschlossen) *vt* - **1.** [gen] to close; [Umschlag] to seal; [Stromkreis] to complete - **2.** [Laden, Firma] to close down - **3.** [einschließen]: jn/etw in etw (A) ~ to lock sb/sthg in sthg - **4.** [schlussfolgern] to conclude - **5.** [befestigen]: etw an etw (A) ~ to lock sthg to sthg - **6.** [umarmen]: er schloss sie in seine Arme he embraced her - **7.** [Vertrag] to conclude, to sign; [Bündnis] to form ⬦ *vi* - **1.** [zumachen] to close - **2.** [den Betrieb einstellen] to close down - **3.** [schlussfolgern] to conclude - **4.** [enden] to end.

➡ **sich schließen** *ref* - **1.** [anschließen]: sich an etw (A) ~ to follow sthg - **2.** [Wunde, Blüte, Kreis] to close.

**Schließ|fach** *das* [am Bahnhof] left-luggage *Br ODER* baggage *Am* locker; [bei der Bank] safe-deposit box.

**schließlich** *adv* - **1.** [endlich] finally; ~ und endlich *fam* finally - **2.** [nun einmal] after all.

**Schließung** (*pl* -en) *die* closure.

**schliff** *prät* ▷ schleifen.

**Schliff** (*pl* -e) *der* - **1.** [Zuschleifen - Vorgang] cutting (*U*); [ - Ergebnis] cut - **2.** [Schärfen - Vorgang] sharpening (*U*); [ - Ergebnis] edge - **3.** [Vollkommenheit]: ihm fehlt noch der ~ he lacks polish; einer Sache (*D*) den letzten ~ geben to put the finishing touches to sthg - **4.** [Benehmen] refinement.

**schlimm** *adj* - **1.** [gen] bad; [Folgen] serious; es ist ~, wie viele Leute jetzt arbeitslos werden the number of people being made redundant at the moment is terrible; halb so ~ sein to be not too bad; halb so ~! never mind! - **2.** [böse, inakzeptabel] wicked; es ist eine ~e Sache, wie er mit ihr umgeht it's terrible the way he treats her.

**Schlimmste** *das:* das ~ the worst thing; auf das ~ gefasst sein to expect the worst.

**schlimmstenfalls** *adv* at worst.

**Schlinge** (*pl* -n) *die* - **1.** [Armschlinge] sling - **2.** [in Seil] loop; [zum Aufhängen] noose - **3.** [zum Jagen] snare.

**Schlingel** (*pl* -) *der fam* rascal.

**schlingen** (*prät* schlang; *perf* hat geschlungen) *vt* - **1.** [binden] to tie; etw um/in etw (A) ~ to tie sthg round/in sthg; etw durch etw ~ to thread *ODER* pass sthg through sthg - **2.** *fam* [essen] to gobble down - **3.** [legen]: die Arme um jn/etw ~ to throw one's arms around sb/sthg ⬦ *vi fam* [essen] to gobble.

➡ **sich schlingen** *ref:* sich um etw ~ to wind o.s./itself around sthg.

**schlingern** (*perf* hat/ist geschlingert) *vi* to roll.

**Schlips** (*pl* -e) *der* tie; jm auf den ~ treten *fam fig* to tread on sb's toes.

**Schlitten** (*pl* -) *der* - **1.** [Rodelschlitten] sledge *Br,* sled *Am;* ~ fahren to go tobogganing *ODER* sledging *Br;* mit jm ~ fahren *fam* [rüde Zurechtweisen] to bawl sb out - **2.** [Pferdeschlitten] sleigh - **3.** *fam* [Auto] wheels (*pl*).

**schlittern** (*perf* ist geschlittert) *vi* - **1.** [Fahrzeug] to skid - **2.** [Mensch] to slide - **3.** [geraten]: in den Konkurs ~ to slide into bankruptcy.

**Schlitt|schuh** *der* ice skate; ~ laufen to ice-skate.

**Schlittschuh|bahn** *die* ice rink.

**Schlitz** (*pl* -e) *der* [für Geld, Briefe] slot; [Spalte] slit.

**Schlitz|auge** *das:* ~n haben to have slit eyes.

**schlitzen** *vt* to slit.

**Schlitz|ohr** *das fam* crafty devil.

**schlohweiß** *adj* snow-white.

**schloss** *prät* ▷ schließen.

**Schloss** (*pl* Schlösser) *das* - **1.** [Burg] castle; [Palast] palace - **2.** [Verschluss] lock; **hinter ~ und Riegel** *fig* behind bars.

**Schlosser, in** (*mpl* -; *fpl* -nen) *der, die* metalworker; [Autoschlosser] mechanic; [für Türschlösser] locksmith.

**Schloss|kapelle** *die* palace chapel.

**Schloss|park** *der* palace grounds (*pl*).

**Schlot** (*pl* -e) *der* chimney.

**schlottern** *vi* - **1.** [zittern] to tremble - **2.** [zu groß sein] to hang loose.

**Schlucht** (*pl* -en) *die* ravine.

**schluchzen** *vi* to sob.

**Schluck** (*pl* -e) *der* - **1.** [Menge] drop; **ein kleiner ~** a sip; **einen ~ trinken** to have a drop (to drink); **einen ~ nehmen** ODER **tun** to take a gulp - **2.** [Schlucken] gulp.

**Schluckauf** *der:* **einen ~ haben** to have hiccups.

**Schluckbeschwerden** *pl:* **haben Sie ~?** do you have difficulty swallowing?

**schlucken** *vt* - **1.** [Essen, Gefühle] to swallow - **2.** [übernehmen - Firma] to swallow up - **3.** *fam* [Alkohol, Benzin] to guzzle <> *vi* to swallow; **an etw** (*D*) **zu ~ haben** *fam fig* to find sthg hard to come to terms with.

**Schlucker** (*pl* -) *der fam:* **ein armer ~** a poor devil.

**Schluck|impfung** *die* oral vaccination.

**schluderig** = schludrig.

**schludern** *vi fam* to do sloppy work.

**schludrig, schluderig** *fam adj* sloppy <> *adv* sloppily.

**schlug** *prät* ▷ schlagen.

**schlummern** *vi geh* - **1.** [schlafen] to slumber - **2.** [vorhanden sein]: **in jm ~** to lie dormant within sb.

**Schlumpf** (*pl* Schlümpfe) *der* smurf.

**Schlund** (*pl* Schlünde) *der geh* - **1.** [Öffnung] abyss - **2.** [Rachen - von Person] back of the throat; [ - von Tier] maw.

**schlüpfen** (*perf* ist geschlüpft) *vi* - **1.** [anziehen, ausziehen]: **aus etw ~** to slip sthg off; **in etw** (*A*) **~** to slip sthg on - **2.** [sich schnell bewegen] to slip; **aus etw ~** to slip out of sthg - **3.** [Küken]: **(aus etw) ~** to hatch (out of sthg).

**Schlüpfer** (*pl* -) *der* knickers (*pl*) *Br*, panties (*pl*) *Am*.

**Schlupf|loch** *das* - **1.** [Öffnung] hole - **2.** [Versteck] hideout.

**schlüpfrig** *adj* - **1.** [anzüglich] lewd - **2.** [rutschig] slippery.

**Schlupf|winkel** *der* hideout.

**schlurfen** (*perf* ist geschlurft) *vi fam* to shuffle.

**schlürfen** *vt* & *vi* to slurp.

**Schluss** (*pl* Schlüsse) *der* - **1.** [Ende] end; **zum ~** at the end; **mit etw ~ machen** to stop sthg; **mit jm ~ machen** *fam* to break up with sb; **~ damit!** that'll do!, that's enough!; **jetzt ist aber ~ damit!** it's over now!; **~ für heute!** that'll do for today!; **damit mache ich ~ für heute** with that, I'll finish for today - **2.** [Schlussfolgerung] conclusion; **zum ~ kommen, dass ...** to reach the conclusion that ...; **Schlüsse aus etw ziehen** to draw conclusions from sthg - **3.** [Schlussstück] ending.

**Schluss|akkord** *der* [Musik] final chord; [Ausklang] finale.

**Schluss|bemerkung** *die* concluding remark.

**Schluss|bericht** *der* final report.

**Schlüssel** (*pl* -) *der* - **1.** [für Schloss, Auflösung] key; **den ~ (in der Tür) stecken lassen** to leave the key in the door; **der ~ zu etw** *fig* the key to sthg - **2.** [Schraubenschlüssel] spanner - **3.** [Code] code - **4.** [Verteilungsschlüssel] allocation base.

**Schlüssel|bein** *das* collar bone.

**Schlüssel|blume** *die* primrose.

**Schlüssel|bund** *der* bunch of keys.

**Schlüssel|dienst** *der* [für Notfälle] locksmith's; [zum Duplizieren von Schlüsseln] key-cutting service.

**Schlüssel|erlebnis** *das* crucial ODER key experience.

**schlüsselfertig** *adj:* **ein ~es Haus** a house which is ready to move into <> *adv:* **ein Haus ~ bauen** to build a house which is ready to move into.

**Schlüssel|industrie** *die* key industry.

**Schlüssel|kind** *das* latchkey child.

**Schlüssel|loch** *das* keyhole.

**Schlüssel|reiz** *der* stimulus.

**Schlüssel|ring** *der* key ring.

**Schlüssel|roman** *der* roman à clef.

**Schlüssel|stellung** *die* key position.

**Schlüssel|über|gabe** *die* handing over of the keys (*to a house*).

**schlussfolgern** *vt* to conclude; **aus etw ~** to conclude from sthg.

**Schluss|folgerung** *die* conclusion.

**schlüssig** *adj* conclusive; **sich** (*D*) **(nicht) ~ sein/werden** (not) to have made up/make up one's mind <> *adv* conclusively.

**Schluss|licht** *das* - **1.** [Letzter]: **der Verein ist das ~ in der Tabelle** the club is bottom of the table - **2.** [Rücklicht] rear light, taillight.

**Schluss|notierung** *die* closing price.

**Schluss|pfiff** *der* final whistle.

**S**

**Schluss|punkt** *der* conclusion; [von Feier] finale.

**Schluss|strich** *der:* einen ~ unter etw *(A)* ziehen to draw a line under sthg.

**Schlussver|kauf** *der* end-of-season sale.

**Schlusswort** *(pl -e) das* closing remarks *(pl)*.

**Schmach** *die geh* shame.

**schmächtig** *adj* slight ◇ *adv* [gebaut] slightly.

**Schmackes** ◆ mit Schmackes *adv fam* with gusto.

**schmackhaft** *adj* tasty ◇ *adv* [kochen] appetizingly; jm etw ~ machen to make sthg palatable to sb.

**schmal** *adj* [Straße, Treppe, Hüften] narrow; [Person] thin; [Figur] slender ◇ *adv* [geschnitten] narrowly; [gebaut] slenderly; [zusammenkneifen] tightly.

**schmälern** *vt* to diminish.

**Schmälerung** *(pl -en) die* reduction.

**Schmalfilm|kamera** *die* cine-camera *Br,* movie camera *Am.*

**Schmal|seite** *die* narrow side.

**Schmalz** *(pl -e) der* - 1. [Fett - zum Kochen] lard; [ - zum Essen] dripping - 2. *fam* [Gefühl] schmaltz.

**Schmalz|brot** *das* slice of bread and dripping.

**Schmalzgebäck** *das deep fried cakes such as doughnuts.*

**schmalzig** *adj* schmaltzy ◇ *adv* schmaltzily.

**schmarotzen** *vt abw* to scrounge ◇ *vi* - 1. *abw* [Person] to sponge; bei jm ~ to sponge off sb - 2. *BIOL* to live as a parasite.

**Schmarotzer, in** *(mpl -; fpl -nen) der, die abw* sponger.

**schmatzen** *vi* to eat noisily; mit den Lippen ~ to smack one's lips.

**schmecken** *vi* to taste; schmeckt es? does it taste good?; hat es geschmeckt? did you enjoy your meal?; es schmeckt mir I like it; nach etw ~ to taste of sthg; es schmeckt gut/schlecht it tastes good/bad; lass es dir ~! enjoy your meal! ◇ *vt* to taste.

**Schmeichelei** *(pl -en) die* flattery *(U)*.

**schmeichelhaft** *adj* flattering; das Foto ist ~ für ihn the photo flatters him ◇ *adv* flatteringly.

**schmeicheln** *vi:* jm ~ to flatter sb.

**schmeißen** *(prät* schmiss; *perf* hat geschmissen) *fam vt* - 1. [werfen] to chuck - 2. [spendieren]: eine Runde ~ to stand a round - 3. [aufgeben] to pack in - 4. [organisieren] to handle ◇ *vi:* er schmiss mit dem Ge-

schirr nach mir he chucked the crockery at me.
◆ sich schmeißen *ref:* sie schmiss sich aufs Bett she threw herself on the bed; sich in etw *(A)* ~ to get togged up in sthg.

**schmelzen** *(präs* schmilzt; *prät* schmolz; *perf* hat/ist geschmolzen) *vi (ist)* to melt ◇ *vt (hat)* to melt; [Erz] to smelt.

**schmelzend** *adj* melting.

**Schmelz|käse** *der* cheese spread.

**Schmelz|ofen** *der* smelting furnace.

**Schmelz|punkt** *der* melting point.

**Schmelz|tiegel** *der* - 1. [Behälter] crucible - 2. [Ort] melting pot.

**Schmelz|wasser** *(pl -) das* melted snow and ice.

**Schmer|bauch** *der fam abw* paunch.

**Schmerz** *(pl -en) der* - 1. *(meist pl)* [körperlich] pain; ~en lindern to relieve pain; ~en haben to be in pain - 2. [seelisch] grief.

**schmerzempfindlich** *adj* [Mensch] sensitive to pain; [Stelle] tender.

**schmerzen** *vi* & *vt* to hurt.

**Schmerzensgeld** *das* compensation.

**schmerzfrei** *adj:* der Patient ist ~ the patient is no longer feeling any pain.

**Schmerz|grenze** *die* absolute limit; mit dieser Steuererhöhung ist die ~ überschritten this is one tax increase too many.

**schmerzhaft** *adj* painful.

**schmerzlich** *adj* painful ◇ *adv* painfully.

**schmerzlindernd** *adj* pain-relieving; ~e Mittel painkillers ◇ *adv:* ~ wirken to relieve pain.

**schmerzlos** *adj* painless ◇ *adv* painlessly.

**Schmerz|mittel** *das* painkiller.

**schmerzstillend** *adj* painkilling ◇ *adv:* ~ wirken to have a painkilling effect.

**Schmerz|tablette** *die* painkiller.

**schmerzverzerrt** *adj* [Gesicht] distorted with pain.

**Schmetter|ball** *der SPORT* smash.

**Schmetterling** *(pl -e) der* [Tier & SPORT] butterfly.

**schmettern** *vt* - 1. *SPORT* to smash - 2. [werfen] to hurl - 3. [singen] to bellow out.

**Schmied** *(pl -e) der* blacksmith.

**Schmiede** *(pl -n) die* forge, smithy.

**Schmiede|eisen** *das* wrought iron.

**schmiedeeisern** *adj* wrought-iron.

**schmieden** *vt* - 1. [bearbeiten] to forge - 2. [befestigen]: jn an etw *(A)* ~ to chain sb to sthg - 3. [Pläne] to make.

**Schmiedin** (pl -nen) die blacksmith.

**schmiegen** vt to nestle.
➡ **sich schmiegen** ref: **sich an jn/etw ~** to snuggle up to sb/sthg; **sich in etw** (A) **~** to snuggle into sthg.

**schmiegsam** adj supple.

**Schmiere** (pl -n) die - 1. [Fett] grease - 2. fam [Wache]: **~ stehen** to act as a lookout.

**schmieren** vt - 1. [mit Fett] to grease; [mit Öl] to oil - 2. fam TECH to lubricate; [bestechen] to bribe - 3. [streichen] to spread; **ein Butterbrot ~** ≃ to make a sandwich - 4. RW: **jm eine ~** fam to clout sb; **wie geschmiert** fam without a hitch ◇ vi - 1. [schreiben] to scribble - 2. [klecksen] to smudge.

**Schmier|fink** der fam - 1. [Erwachsener] muckraker - 2. [Kind] mucky pup.

**Schmier|geld** das fam bribe.

**schmierig** adj - 1. [ölig] greasy - 2. abw [Witz, Anspielung] smutty - 3. abw [Typ] smarmy ◇ adv [angrinsen] smarmily; [lachen, anmachen] smuttily.

**Schmier|mittel** das lubricant.

**Schmier|papier** das fam scrap paper.

**Schmier|seife** die soft soap.

**Schmier|zettel** der fam piece of scrap paper.

**schmilzt** präs ▷ schmelzen.

**Schminke** (pl -n) die make-up.

**schminken** vt to make up.
➡ **sich schminken** ref to put on one's make-up.

**Schmink|stift** der make-up pencil.

**Schmink|tisch** der make-up table.

**schmirgeln** vt to sand.

**Schmirgel|papier** das sandpaper.

**schmiss** prät ▷ schmeißen.

**Schmiss** (pl Schmisse) der - 1. [Narbe] duelling scar - 2. fam [Pep] oomph.

**schmissig** adj spirited.

**Schmöker** (pl -) der tome (of lightweight reading).

**schmökern** vi: **in einem Buch ~** to bury o.s. in a book ◇ vt to bury o.s. in.

**schmollen** vi to sulk.

**Schmoll|mund** der pout.

**schmolz** prät ▷ schmelzen.

**schmoren** vt to braise ◇ vi - 1. [braten] to braise - 2. fam [in der Sonne] to roast - 3. fam [warten]: **jn ~ lassen** to leave sb to stew (in his/her own juice).

**Schmorfleisch** das braising steak.

**Schmu** der fam: **~ erzählen** to talk nonsense; **~ machen** to cheat.

**schmuck** adj smart ◇ adv smartly; **~ aussehen** to look smart.

**Schmuck** der - 1. [Gegenstand] jewellery - 2. [Dekoration] decoration.

**schmücken** vt to decorate.
➡ **sich schmücken** ref to adorn o.s.

**Schmuckkästchen** (pl -) das jewellery box.

**schmucklos** adj plain, unadorned ◇ adv plainly.

**Schmuck|stück** das - 1. [Schmuck] piece of jewellery - 2. [aus Sammlung, Ausstellung] jewel.

**schmuddelig** adj [schmutzig] grubby; [unordentlich] messy ◇ adv [schmutzig] in a grubby state; [unordentlich] in a mess.

**Schmuggel** der smuggling; **~ (mit etw) treiben** to smuggle (sthg).

**schmuggeln** vt & vi to smuggle.

**Schmuggler, in** (mpl -; fpl -nen) der, die smuggler.

**schmunzeln** vi: **(über etw** (A)**) ~** to smile to o.s. (at sthg).

**schmusen** vi: **(mit jm) ~** to cuddle (sb); [Liebespaar] to kiss and cuddle (with sb).

**Schmutz** der dirt; **~ abweisend** dirt-resistant; **(viel) ~ machen** to make a (terrible) mess; **jn/etw durch** ODER **in den ~ ziehen** fig to drag sb/sthg through the mud.

**schmutzen** vi to get dirty.

**Schmutz|fink** der fam - 1. [schmutziger Mensch - Erwachsener] dirty pig; [ - Kind] mucky pup - 2. [unsittlicher Mensch] creep.

**schmutzig** adj - 1. [gen] dirty; **sich ~ machen** to get dirty - 2. [Geschäftspraktiken] shady.

**Schmutzwäsche** die dirty clothes (pl).

**Schmutz|zulage** die dirty work bonus.

**Schnabel** (pl Schnäbel) der beak; **den ~ halten** fam fig to shut one's trap; **reden, wie einem der ~ gewachsen ist** fam to say exactly what one thinks.

**Schnabel|tasse** die feeding cup.

**Schnake** (pl -n) die [Weberknecht] daddy long-legs Br, crane fly Am.

**Schnalle** (pl -n) die buckle.

**schnallen** vt - 1. [festmachen] to strap; [Gürtel] to fasten, to buckle; **den Gürtel enger ~** to tighten one's belt; **etw auf etw** (A) **~** to strap sthg to sthg - 2. fam [kapieren] to get.

**schnalzen** vi: **mit der Zunge/den Fingern ~** to click one's tongue/fingers; **mit der Peitsche ~** to crack the whip.

**Schnäppchen** (pl -) das snip, bargain; **mit dem Hemd habe ich ein ~ gemacht** the shirt was a real snip ODER bargain.

**Schnäppchen|führer** der guide to warehouses selling reduced goods.

**S**

**schnappen** (*perf* hat/ist geschnappt) *vt (hat)* - **1.** *fam* [festnehmen] to catch - **2.** *fam* [nehmen]: sich (D) etw ~ to grab sthg - **3.** [packen] to grab <> *vi* - **1.** *(hat)* [beißen]: **nach jm/etw ~** to snap at sb/sthg - **2.** *(ist)* [federn] to spring up; **die Tür schnappte ins Schloss** the door clicked shut.

**Schnapplschloss** das [an Tür] spring lock; [an Tasche] clasp.

**Schnapplschuss** der snapshot.

**Schnaps** (*pl* Schnäpse) der schnapps.

**Schnapslglas** das shot glass.

**Schnapslidee** die *fam* hare-brained idea.

**Schnapslzahl** die *number in which all digits are identical, e.g. 222.*

**schnarchen** *vi* [im Schlaf] to snore.

**schnarren** *vi* [Klingel] to buzz; [Stimme] to rasp.

**schnattern** *vi* - **1.** [Gänse] to gabble; [Enten] to quack - **2.** *fam* [reden] to chatter - **3.** [zittern]: **er schnattert vor Kälte** his teeth are chattering with cold.

**schnauben** *vi eigtl & fig* to snort; **vor Wut ~** to snort with anger.

**schnaufen** *vi* to wheeze.

**Schnauzlbart** der - **1.** [Bart] moustache - **2.** *fam* [Mensch] guy with the 'tache.

**Schnauze** (*pl* -n) die - **1.** [Maul] muzzle; [von Schwein] snout - **2.** *salopp abw* [Mund] trap, gob Br; **jm eins auf die ~ hauen** to sock sb in the mouth - **3.** *RW*: **halt die ~!** *salopp* shut your trap!; **die ~ voll haben (von etw)** *salopp* to be fed up to the back teeth (with sthg); **auf die ~ fallen** *ODER* **fliegen** *salopp* [hinfallen] to fall flat on one's face; [scheitern] to come a cropper.

**schnäuzen** <> sich schnäuzen *ref*: **sich (die Nase) ~** to blow one's nose.

**Schnauzer** (*pl* -) der - **1.** [Hunderasse] Schnauzer - **2.** [Schnurrbart] large moustache.

**Schnecke** (*pl* -n) die snail; [ohne Schneckenhaus] slug; **jn zur ~ machen** *fig* to give sb a dressing-down.

**Schneckenlhaus** das snail shell.

**Schnee** der snow; **es fällt ~** snow is falling; **es liegt ~** there is snow (on the ground); **~ räumen** to clear snow; **~ von gestern sein** *fam fig* to be old hat.

**Schneelball** der snowball.

**Schneeballlschlacht** die snowball fight.

**Schneeballlsystem** das *WIRTSCH* pyramid selling.

**Schneelbesen** der whisk.

**schneeblind** *adj* snowblind.

**Schneelbrett** das frozen snow overhang.

**Schneelbrille** die snow goggles (*pl*).

**Schneeldecke** die covering of snow.

**Schneelfall** der snowfall.

**Schneelflocke** die snowflake.

**schneefrei** *adj* free of snow.

**Schneelgestöber** (*pl* -) das [leicht] snow flurry; [stärker] snowstorm.

**Schneelglätte** die packed snow (*U*).

**Schneelglöckchen** (*pl* -) das snowdrop.

**Schneelgrenze** die snow line.

**Schneelkette** die snow chain.

**Schneelmann** (*pl* -männer) der snowman.

**Schneelmatsch** der slush.

**Schneelpflug** der snowplough.

**Schneelregen** der sleet.

**Schneelschaufel** die snow shovel.

**Schneelschmelze** die thaw.

**Schneelsturm** der snowstorm.

**Schneeltreiben** das blizzard.

**Schneelverwehung** (*pl* -en), **-wehe** (*pl* -n) die snowdrift.

**schneeweiß** *adj* snow-white.

**Schneewittchen** das Snow White.

**Schneid** der (ohne pl) *fam* guts (*pl*).

**Schneidbrenner** (*pl* -) der oxyacetylene torch.

**Schneide** (*pl* -n) die [Klinge] blade; [Kante] edge.

**schneiden** (*prät* schnitt; *perf* hat geschnitten) *vt* - **1.** [gen] to cut; [Hecke] to trim; [Baum] to cut back; **sich (D) die Haare ~ lassen** to have one's hair cut - **2.** [klein schneiden - in Stücke] to chop; [ - in Scheiben] to slice; [ - Braten] to carve; **etw in Würfel ~** to cube sthg - **3.** [zurechtschneiden - Foto] to cut to size - **4.** [ausschneiden] to cut out - **5.** [beim Überholen] to cut in on; **eine Kurve ~** to cut a corner - **6.** [ignorieren]: **jn ~** to ignore sb - **7.** [überschneiden] to cut across, to cross; *MATH* to intersect - **8.** [hinzufügen]: **Schnittlauch in die Suppe ~** to chop some chives and add them to the soup - **9.** *SPORT* [Ball] to put spin on <> *vi* - **1.** [beschädigen]: **(mit etw) in etw (A) ~** to cut sthg (with sthg) - **2.** [Frisör, Messer, Schere] to cut.

<> sich schneiden *ref* - **1.** [sich verletzen] to cut o.s.; **sich in den Finger ~** to cut one's finger - **2.** [sich überschneiden] to intersect - **3.** *fam* [sich täuschen]: **wenn du das glaubst, dann hast du dich aber geschnitten!** if you think that, you've got another think *ODER* thing coming!

**schneidend** *adj* - **1.** [Wind, Kälte] biting - **2.** [Stimme] piercing <> *adv* piercingly.

**Schneider** (*pl* -) der tailor; [für Damen] dressmaker; **aus dem ~ sein** *fam fig* to be out of the woods.

**Schneiderin** (*pl* -nen) die tailor; [für Damen] dressmaker.

**schneidern** vt: (sich (D)) etw ~ to make sthg ◇ vi to make clothes.

**Schneiderlsitz** der: im ~ cross-legged.

**Schneidelzahn** der incisor.

**schneidig** adj [Bursche] dashing; [Fahrstil] daring.

**schneien** vi: es schneit it's snowing.

**Schneise** (pl -n) die firebreak.

**schnell** adj - 1. [gen] quick - 2. [Tempo] fast, quick - 3. [Person, Gefährt] fast ◇ adv - 1. [laufen] fast, quickly; nicht so ~! not so fast! - 2. [zügig] quickly; ~ machen to hurry up - 3. [bald] soon - 4. [gleich]: kannst du mal ~ vorbeikommen? could you just pop round quickly?; sag doch mal ~ just tell me again.

**Schnelle** die: auf die ~ quickly.

**schnellebig** adj = schnelllebig.

**schnellen** (perf ist geschnellt) vi to shoot; in die Höhe ~ to shoot up.

**Schnelllgericht** das ready meal.

**Schnelllhefter** der loose-leaf binder.

**Schnelligkeit** die speed.

**Schnelllimbiss** der snack bar.

**Schnellkochltopf** der pressure cooker.

**schnelllebig** adj fast-moving.

**schnellstens** adv as quickly as possible.

**Schnelllstraße** die expressway.

**Schnelllverfahren** das - 1. RECHT summary trial - 2. [Vorgang] high-speed process; im ~ fig quickly.

**Schnelllzug** der express train.

**Schnepfe** (pl -n) die - 1. [Vogel] snipe - 2. salopp abw [Frau] cow.

**schneuzen** ref = schnäuzen.

**Schnickschnack** der fam knick-knacks (pl).

**schniefen** vi to sniffle.

**Schnippchen** das: jm ein ~ schlagen fam to outsmart sb.

**schnippisch** adj pert ◇ adv pertly.

**Schnipsel** (pl -) der scrap.

**schnipsen** vt to flick ◇ vi to snap.

**schnitt** prät ▷ schneiden.

**Schnitt** (pl -e) der - 1. [Öffnung] cut; [bei Operation] incision - 2. [von Haar, Kleidung] cut; [Schnittmuster] pattern - 3. [von Film] editing (U) - 4. [Schneiden - von Baum] cutting back; [ - von Hecke] trimming - 5. fam [Durchschnitt] average; im ~ on average; einen guten ~ fahren to go at a good average speed - 6. fam [Gewinn] profit; seinen ~ machen fam to make a profit.

**Schnittlblume** die cut flower.

**Schnittchen** (pl -) das canapé.

**Schnitte** (pl -n) die - 1. [Scheibe] slice - 2. [belegtes Brot] open sandwich.

**Schnittlfläche** die - 1. [angeschnittener Teil] cut end - 2. MATH section.

**schnittig** adj sporty.

**Schnittllauch** der (ohne pl) chives (pl).

**Schnittllinie** die line of intersection.

**Schnittlmenge** die MATH intersection.

**Schnittlmuster** das pattern.

**Schnittlpunkt** der point of intersection.

**Schnittlstelle** die [gen & EDV] interface; parallele/serielle ~ parallel/serial port.

**Schnittlwunde** die cut.

**Schnitzel** (pl -) das - 1. [Fleisch] escalope - 2. [aus Papier] scrap.

**Schnitzelljagd** die paper chase.

**schnitzen** vt & vi to carve.

**Schnitzer** (pl -) der - 1. [Fehler] blunder; einen groben ~ machen to make a terrible blunder - 2. [Beruf] carver.

**Schnitzerei** (pl -en) die carving.

**Schnitzerin** (pl -nen) die carver.

**schnodderig, schnoddrig** adj brash ◇ adv brashly.

**Schnorchel** (pl -) der snorkel.

**schnorcheln** vi to snorkel.

**Schnörkel** (pl -) der curlicue; [in Schrift] flourish.

**schnorren** vt fam: etw (bei jm) ~ to scrounge sthg (off sb).

**Schnösel** (pl -) der fam abw snotty little upstart.

**schnuckelig, schnucklig** fam adj sweet ◇ adv sweetly.

**schnüffeln** vi - 1. [riechen]: an etw (D) ~ to sniff at sthg - 2. [durchsuchen] to snoop; in etw (D) ~ to snoop around in sthg ◇ vt fam [einatmen] to sniff.

**Schnuller** (pl -) der dummy Br, pacifier Am.

**Schnulze** (pl -n) die abw [Lied] slushy number.

**schnupfen** vt [Tabak] to take; [Kokain] to snort.

**Schnupfen** (pl -) der cold; einen ~ haben/bekommen to have/get a cold.

**Schnupfltabak** der snuff.

**schnuppe** adj: das ist mir ~ fam I couldn't give a damn.

**Schnupperlkurs** der taster course.

**schnuppern** vi - 1. [riechen]: (an etw (D)) ~ to sniff (at sthg) - 2. [testen]: einige Stunden ~ to try it out for a few classes ◇ vt to sniff.

**Schnur** (pl Schnüre) die string; [Zugschnur] cord; [Kabel] lead.

S

**Schnürchen** *das:* **wie am ~** *fam* without a hitch.

**schnüren** *vt* - **1.** [gen] to tie; [Mieder] to lace up - **2.** [Bündel, Paket] to tie up; **etw um etw ~** to tie sthg around sthg ⬦ *vi:* **ins Fleisch ~** to bite into one's flesh.

**schnurgerade, schnurgrade** *adj* & *adv* dead straight.

**Schnurrlbart** *der* moustache.

**schnurren** (*perf* **hat geschnurrt**) *vi eigtl* & *fig* to purr.

**Schnürlschuh** *der* lace-up (shoe).

**Schnürsenkel** (*pl* -) *der* shoelace.

**schnurstracks** *adv* straight.

**schnurz** *adj:* **das ist mir ~** *fam* I couldn't give a damn.

**Schnute** (*pl* -n) *die* mouth; **eine ~ ziehen** *fam* to pull a face.

**schob** *prät* ⬦ **schieben.**

**Schock** (*pl* -s) *der* shock; **unter ~ stehen** to be in shock; **jm einen ~ versetzen** to give a sb a shock.

**schockieren** *vt* to shock.

**schockiert** *adj* shocked; **über etw** (*A*) **~ sein** to be shocked at sthg ⬦ *adv:* **~ reagieren** to react with shock.

**schofel, schofelig** *fam abw adj* horrid ⬦ *adv* horridly.

**Schöffe** (*pl* -n) *der* lay judge, *one of two people without legal qualifications who hear cases together with a professional judge.*

**Schöffin** (*pl* -en) *die* lay judge, *one of two people without legal qualifications who hear cases together with a professional judge.*

**Schokolade** (*pl* -n) *die* - **1.** [Süßigkeit] chocolate - **2.** [Getränk - heiß] hot chocolate; [ - kalt] chocolate drink.

**Schokoladenlglasur** *die* chocolate icing *Br* ODER frosting *Am.*

**Schokoladenlpudding** *der* chocolate blancmange.

**Schokoladenlseite** *die* [vom Aussehen, Charakter] best side.

**Schokoladenltorte** *die* chocolate gâteau.

**Schokolriegel** *der* chocolate bar.

**Scholle** (*pl* -n) *die* [Fisch] plaice.

**schon** *adv* - **1.** [bereits] already; **wir essen heute ~ um elf Uhr** we're eating earlier today, at eleven o'clock; **~ damals** even then; **~ 1914** as early as 1914; **er ist ~ lange hier** he's been here for a long time; **ich bereite das ~ mal vor** I'll get that ready now; **~ jetzt** already; **~ wieder** again - **2.** [inzwischen] yet; **warst du ~ auf der Post?** have you been to the post office yet?; **warst du ~ mal in Kanada?** have you ever been to Canada?; **ich war ~ mal im Ausland** I've been abroad before; **~ längst** a long time ago; **~ oft** often - **3.** [zwar]: **es gefällt mir ~, aber ...** I DO like it, but ...; **ja ~, aber ...** yes of course, but ... - **4.** [endlich]: **komm ~!** come on!; **nun rede ~!** come on – say something! - **5.** [zur Beruhigung]: **du machst das ~** don't worry, I'm sure you'll manage it!; **es wird ~ gehen** it will work out all right; **~ gut!, ~ recht!** all right!, OK! - **6.** [wirklich] really; **das ist ~ möglich** that's quite possible; **ich glaube ~** I think so - **7.** [allein] just; **~ der Gedanke daran macht mich nervös** just thinking about it makes me nervous - **8.** [in rhetorischen Fragen]: **was nützt das ~?** what on earth is the use of that?; **was kann sie ~ wollen?** what CAN she want?

**schön** *adj* - **1.** [Frau, Kind, Sache] beautiful; [Mann] handsome - **2.** [angenehm] good; **~es Wochenende!** have a nice weekend!; **das ist ja (alles) ~ und gut, aber ...** that's all very well, but ... - **3.** [erheblich] considerable; **es ist noch ein ~es Stück** it's still quite a way - **4.** *fam iron* fine; **das kann ja ~ werden!** what a delightful prospect! - **5.** *RW:* **~en Dank!** many thanks!, thanks a lot! ⬦ *adv* - **1.** [gen] well; [gekleidet] beautifully - **2.** [verstärkend]: **~ langsam** nice and slowly; **sei ~ brav!** be a good boy/girl!

➤ **ganz schön** *adv fam* really.

➤ **na schön** *interj fam* all right!

**Schöne** (*pl* -n) *der, die, das:* **die ~** the beauty; **der ~** the handsome man; **das ~** the beautiful; **das ~ daran** the nice thing about it; **da hast du was ~s angerichtet!** *fam* you've gone and done it now!

**schonen** *vt* - **1.** [pfleglich behandeln - Kleider, Auto, Möbel] to be careful with, to treat gently - **2.** [schützen - Augen, Umwelt] to protect - **3.** [weniger verlangen von] to go easy on; **er schont den Stürmer für das nächste Spiel** he's saving ODER resting the forward for the next game - **4.** [verschonen] to ask (sb) to be spared.

➤ **sich schonen** *ref* to take it easy.

**schonend** *adj* gentle ⬦ *adv* gently; **jm etw ~ beibringen** to break sthg to sb gently; **mit jm/etw ~ umgehen** to be gentle with sb/sthg.

**schönlfärben** *vt* to paint a rosy picture of.

**Schönfärberei** *die* whitewashing.

**Schonlfrist** *die* period of grace.

**Schönheit** (*pl* -en) *die* - **1.** [gen] beauty - **2.** [Sehenswürdigkeit] attraction.

**Schönheitslfehler** *der* blemish.

**Schönheitslpflege** *die* beauty care.

**Schonkost** *die* light diet.

**schön machen** *vt* - **1.** [hübsch machen]: **etw ~** to make sthg look nice - **2.** [angenehm machen] to make agreeable; **es sich** (*D*) **~** to make things nice.

➡ **sich schön machen** *ref* to do o.s. up.

**Schön|schrift** *die*: etw in ~ schreiben to write sthg neatly.

**schön|tun** *vi (unreg) fam* to suck up.

**Schonung** (*pl* -en) *die* - **1.** [Baumschule] young plantation - **2.** [pflegliche Behandlung] careful *ODER* gentle treatment; [Schützen] protection; [verschonen] to spare; **jn um ~ bitten** [weniger verlangen von] to ask sb to go easy on one.

**schonungslos** *adj* ruthless; [Offenheit] brutal ◇ *adv* ruthlessly; [offen] brutally.

**Schönwetter|periode** *die* spell of fine weather.

**Schon|zeit** *die* close season.

**Schopf** (*pl* Schöpfe) *der* [Haar] shock of hair; **die Gelegenheit beim ~ packen** to grasp the opportunity with both hands.

**schöpfen** *vt* - **1.** [auftun] to scoop; [mit Löffel, Kelle] to ladle; **etw aus etw ~** to scoop/ladle sthg out of sthg - **2.** [Mut, Kraft, Atem] to draw; **Verdacht ~** to become suspicious; **frische Luft ~** to get a breath of fresh air.

**Schöpfer** (*pl* -) *der* - **1.** [Gott] Creator - **2.** [Gestalter] creator.

**Schöpferin** (*pl* -nen) *die* creator.

**schöpferisch** *adj* creative ◇ *adv* creatively; **~ veranlagt sein** to have creative tendencies.

**Schöpf|kelle** *die* ladle.

**Schöpf|löffel** *der* ladle.

**Schöpfung** (*pl* -en) *die* - **1.** [Welterschaffung] Creation - **2.** *geh* [Werk] creation.

**Schoppen** (*pl* -) *der* glass *(holding 1/4 or 1/2 litre of wine)*.

**schor** *prät* ⊏➢ scheren.

**Schorf** *der (ohne pl)* scab.

**Schorle** (*pl* -n) *die* [mit Wein] spritzer; [mit Apfelsaft] apple juice with mineral water.

**Schorn|stein** *der* chimney.

**Schornsteinfeger, in** (*mpl* -; *fpl* -nen) *der, die* chimney sweep.

**schoss** *prät* ⊏➢ schießen.

**Schoß** (*pl* Schöße) *der* - **1.** [Körperteil] lap; **auf js ~ sitzen** to sit on sb's lap; **das schauspielerische Können ist ihr in den ~ gefallen** acting comes easily to her; **der Erfolg ist mir nicht in den ~ gefallen** success wasn't handed to me on a plate - **2.** *geh* [Schutz] bosom - **3.** *geh* [Mutterleib] womb - **4.** [von Jacke] tail.

**Schoß|hund** *der* lapdog.

**Schote** (*pl* -n) *die* - **1.** [Frucht] pod - **2.** *fam* [erfundene Geschichte] tale.

**Schotte** (*pl* -n) *der* Scotsman, Scot.

**Schotten|rock** *der* kilt.

**Schotter** *der* gravel.

**Schotter|straße** *die* gravel road.

**Schottin** (*pl* -nen) *die* Scotswoman, Scot.

**schottisch** *adj* Scottish.

**Schottland** *nt* Scotland.

**schraffieren** *vt* to hatch.

**schräg** *adj* - **1.** [schief] sloping; [Linie] diagonal - **2.** *fam* [eigenartig] offbeat - **3.** *fam* [falsch] dodgy ◇ *adv* - **1.** [schief] at an angle; [diagonal] diagonally; **~ gegenüber** diagonally opposite; **etw ~ halten** to tilt sthg; **jn ~ ansehen** *fam* to look askance at sb - **2.** *fam* [falsch]: **das klingt ~** that sounds dodgy.

**Schräge** (*pl* -n) *die* slope; [Wand] sloping ceiling.

**Schräg|schrift** *die* TYPO italics *(pl)*.

**Schräg|strich** *der* forward slash.

**Schramme** (*pl* -n) *die* scratch.

**Schrank** (*pl* Schränke) *der* [für Geschirr, Vorräte] cupboard; [für Kleider] wardrobe *Br*, closet *Am*; [für Bücher] bookcase.

**Schranke** (*pl* -n) *die* barrier.

➡ **Schranken** *pl* [Grenzen] limits; **deiner Fantasie sind keine ~n gesetzt** your imagination has free rein; **jn in die ~n weisen** to put sb in his/her place.

**schrankenlos** *adj* [Freiheit] boundless.

**schrankfertig** *adj* washed and ironed.

**Schrank|wand** *die* wall unit.

**Schraube** (*pl* -n) *die* - **1.** [zum Befestigen] screw; [ohne Spitze] bolt; **bei ihm ist eine ~ locker** *salopp fig* he's got a screw loose - **2.** SPORT twist.

**schrauben** *vt*: **etw (auf/in etw (A)) ~** to screw sthg (onto/into sthg); **etw an etw (A) ~** to screw sthg to sthg; **etw aus** *ODER* **von etw ~** to unscrew sthg from sthg; **den Deckel von der Flasche ~** to screw the lid off the bottle; **etw nach oben/unten ~** *fig* to raise/lower sthg.

➡ **sich schrauben** *ref* [sich bewegen] to spiral.

**Schrauben|mutter** *die* nut.

**Schrauben|schlüssel** *der* spanner *Br*, wrench *Am*.

**Schrauben|zieher** (*pl* -) *der* screwdriver.

**Schraub|stock** *der* vice.

**Schraubver|schluss** *der* screw top.

**Schraub|zwinge** (*pl* -n) *die* screw clamp.

**Schreber|garten** *der* ≃ allotment.

**Schreck** *der* fright; **vor ~ in** fear *ODER* fright; **einen ~ kriegen** *fam* to get a fright; **jm einen ~ einjagen** to give sb a fright; **mit dem ~ davonkommen** to escape with no more than a fright; **ach du ~!** oh my goodness!

**Schrecken** (*pl* -) *der* terror; **die ~ des Krieges** the horrors of war; **er ist der ~ der Nachbar-**

**schaft** he's the terror of the neighbour-hood.

**Schreck|gespenst** das spectre.

**schreckhaft** adj easily scared.

**schrecklich** adj terrible ⟨> adv terribly.

**Schreckschuss|pistole** die blank gun.

**Schreck|sekunde** die moment of terror.

**Schredder, Shredder** (pl -) der shredder.

**schreddern** vt to shred.

**Schrei** (pl -e) der shout; [von Tier, Baby] cry; [aus Angst, vor Schmerz, Lust] scream; **der letzte ~** fam fig the latest thing.

**Schreib|arbeit** die clerical work (U).

**schreiben** (prät **schrieb;** perf **hat geschrieben**) vt - **1.** [gen] to write; [mit Schreibmaschine] to type - **2.** [orthografisch] to spell; **wie schreibt man das?** how do you spell that?, how's that spelt? - **3.** [Klassenarbeit, Test] to do - **4.** [Rechnung] to make out; **die Firma schreibt rote Zahlen** the company is in the red ⟨> vi - **1.** [gen] to write; **an jn ~** to write to sb; **an etw** (D) **~** to be writing sthg - **2.** [tippen] to type; siehe auch **großschreiben, kleinschreiben, krankschreiben.**
➥ **sich schreiben** ref - **1.** [korrespondieren] to correspond - **2.** [sich buchstabieren] to be spelt - **3.** [aufschreiben]: **mit diesem Kugelschreiber schreibt es sich gut** this biro writes well.

**Schreiben** (pl -) das letter.

**Schreiber, in** (mpl -; fpl -nen) der, die writer.

**schreibfaul** adj lazy about writing letters.

**Schreib|kraft** die clerical assistant; [Stenotypistin] shorthand typist.

**Schreib|maschine** die typewriter.

**Schreib|schrift** die cursive script.

**Schreib|tisch** der desk.

**Schreibtisch|lampe** die desk lamp.

**Schreibung** (pl -en) die spelling.

**Schreib|unterlage** die [auf Schreibtisch] desk pad.

**Schreib|waren** pl stationery (U).

**Schreibwaren|geschäft** das stationery shop.

**Schreib|weise** die - **1.** [Schreibung] spelling - **2.** [Ausdrucksweise] style.

**Schreib|zeug** das writing things (pl).

**schreien** (prät **schrie;** perf **hat geschrie(e)n**) vi [gen] to shout; [Tier, Baby] to cry; [aus Angst, vor Schmerz, Lust] to scream; **vor Schmerz ~** to scream with pain; **schrei nicht so!** stop shouting!; **nach etw ~** eigtl & fig to cry out for sthg.

**Schreien** das crying; [gellend] screaming; [Brüllen] shouting; **zum ~ sein** fam to be a scream.

**schreiend** adj - **1.** [Farben] garish - **2.** [Unrecht] flagrant.

**Schrei|hals** der fam bawler.

**Schreiner, in** (mpl -; fpl -nen) der, die joiner.

**schreiten** (prät **schritt;** perf **ist geschritten**) vi geh to stride; **zu etw ~** fig to get down to sthg.

**schrie** prät ▻ **schreien.**

**schrieb** prät ▻ **schreiben.**

**Schrift** (pl -en) die - **1.** [Handschrift] handwriting (U) - **2.** [das Geschriebene] writing (U) - **3.** [Alphabet] script - **4.** TYPO type.
➥ **Schriften** pl texts; [kurze Abhandlungen] papers; [Werke] works.

**schriftlich** adj written ⟨> adv in writing; **jm etw ~ geben** fam to give sb sthg in writing.

**Schrift|sprache** die written language.

**Schriftsteller, in** (mpl -; fpl -nen) der, die writer.

**schriftstellerisch** adj literary, as a writer.

**Schrift|verkehr** der correspondence.

**Schrift|zug** der - **1.** [Logo] logo - **2.** [von Unterschrift] flourish.

**schrill** adj shrill.

**schrillen** vi to shrill.

**Schrimp, Shrimp** [ʃrɪmp] (pl -s) der shrimp.

**Schritt** (pl -e) der - **1.** [gen] step; **er ist mir immer einen ~ voraus** he's always a step ahead of me; **jn am ~ erkennen** to recognize sb's step - **2.** [von Hose] crotch - **3.** [zur Angabe der Entfernung] pace; **drei ~e von mir entfernt** three paces away from me - **4.** [Gangart] walk; **im ~ reiten** to ride at a walk - **5.** RW: **~ für ~** step by step; **auf ~ und Tritt** wherever one goes; **den ersten ~ tun** to take the first step; **mit jm/etw ~ halten** to keep up with sb/sthg.

**Schrittempo** = Schritttempo.

**Schritt|macher** (pl -) der - **1.** [Vorreiter] pacesetter - **2.** [im Sport] pacemaker.

**Schritttempo** das: **(im) ~ fahren** to go dead slow.

**schrittweise** adv gradually.

**schroff** adj - **1.** [Verhalten, Antwort, Wechsel] abrupt - **2.** [Felsen, Abhang] sheer - **3.** [Gegensatz] stark ⟨> adv [abweisen, antworten] abruptly.

**schröpfen** vt fam [ausnehmen] to rip off.

**Schrot** der ODER das - **1.** [Munition] shot - **2.** [Getreide] meal; [von Weizen] wholemeal Br, wholewheat Am - **3.** RW: **er ist ein Handwerker von echtem ~ und Korn** he is a true craftsman.

**Schrott** der - **1.** [altes Metall] scrap metal; **etw zu ~ fahren** to write sthg off - **2.** fam [Plunder] junk - **3.** fam [Blödsinn] rubbish.

**Schrott|platz** der scrapyard Br, junkyard Am.

**schrottreif** *adj* fit for the scrapheap ◇ *adv:* ein Auto ~ fahren to write off a car.

**schrubben** *vt* to scrub.
➤ **sich schrubben** *ref fam* to scrub o.s.

**Schrubber** (*pl* -) *der* hard-bristled broom *(for scrubbing floors).*

**schrumpelig, schrumplig** *adj* [Haut] wrinkled; [Apfel] shrivelled.

**schrumpfen** (*perf* **ist geschrumpft**) *vi* to shrink.

**schrumplig** = schrumpelig.

**Schub** (*pl* Schübe) *der* - 1. [Kraft] thrust - 2. [Anfall] bout - 3. [Ladung, Menschengruppe] batch.

**Schublfach** *das* drawer.

**Schublkarre** *die*, **Schubkarren** *der* wheelbarrow.

**Schublkraft** *die* thrust.

**Schubllade** (*pl* -n) *die* drawer; jn in eine ~ stecken *fam fig* to pigeonhole sb.

**Schubs** (*pl* -e) *der* push; jm/etw einen ~ geben to give sb/sthg a push.

**schubsen** *vt* to push.

**schubweise** *adv* [in Gruppen] in batches; **das Fieber tritt ~ auf** the fever comes in waves.

**schüchtern** *adj* [Person, Blick] shy; [Versuch, Frage] timid ◇ *adv* [lächeln, schauen] shyly; [sich benehmen, fragen] timidly.

**Schüchternheit** *die* shyness.

**schuf** *prät* ⊳ schaffen.

**Schuft** (*pl* -e) *der abw* scoundrel.

**schuften** *vi fam* to slave away.

**Schuh** (*pl* -e) *der* shoe; **das sind zwei Paar ~e** *fam fig* those are two different things; **wissen, wo jn der ~ drückt** *fig* to know what's bothering sb; **jm etw in die ~e schieben** *fig* to pin the blame for sthg on sb.

**Schuhlbürste** *die* shoebrush.

**Schuhlcreme, Schuhkrem** *die* shoe polish.

**Schuhlgeschäft** *das* shoe shop.

**Schuhlgröße** *die* shoe size.

**Schuhlkarton** *der* shoebox.

**Schuhllöffel** *der* shoehorn.

**Schuhlmacher, in** (*mpl* -; *fpl* -nen) *der, die* cobbler, shoemaker.

**Schuhlputzer** (*pl* -) *der* - 1. [Mensch] bootblack - 2. [Gerät] shoe-cleaning machine.

**Schuhlputzerin** (*pl* -nen) *die* bootblack.

**Schuhlsohle** *die* sole.

**Schuhlspanner** *der* shoetree.

**Schuhlwerk** *das* footwear; **festes ~** stout footwear.

**Schullabgänger, in** (*mpl* -; *fpl* -nen) *der, die* school-leaver.

**Schulablschluss** *der* school-leaving qualification.

**Schullamt** *das* education authority.

**Schullanfang** *der* - 1. [Einschulung] first day of school - 2. [nach den Ferien] beginning of term.

**Schullanfänger, in** *der, die* child starting school.

**Schullaufgabe** *die* homework (U).

**Schullbank** (*pl* -bänke) *die* (school) desk; **die ~ drücken** *fam fig* to go to school.

**Schulbeilspiel** *das* classic example.

**Schullbesuch** *der* school attendance.

**Schullbildung** *die* school education, schooling.

**Schullbuch** *das* schoolbook.

**Schullbus** *der* school bus.

**schuld** *adj:* **an etw** (D) **~ sein** to be to blame for sthg; **er ist ~ daran** it's his fault.

**Schuld** (*pl* -en) *die* - 1. [Verantwortung, Ursache] blame; **es war seine ~** it was his fault; **an etw ~ haben** to be to blame for sthg; **jm (an etw** (D)**) ~ geben** to blame sb (for sthg); *siehe auch* **zuschulden** - 2. [Unrecht] guilt; **sich** (D) **keiner ~ bewusst sein** to be unaware of having done anything wrong.
➤ **Schulden** *pl* debts; **~en haben** to be in debt; **40 Milliarden Euro ~en haben** to have debts of 40 billion euros; **~en machen** to run up debts.

**Schuldbelkenntnis** *das* confession.

**schuldbewusst** *adj* guilty ◇ *adv* guiltily.

**schulden** *vt:* jm etw ~ to owe sb sthg.

**Schuldenlberg** *der* mountain of debt.

**schuldenfrei** *adj* free of debt; **unser Haus ist ~** we've paid off the mortgage on our house.

**Schuldlfrage** *die* question of guilt.

**Schuldlgefühl** *das* feeling of guilt.

**schuldig** *adj* - 1. [verantwortlich] guilty; **an etw** (D) **~ sein** to be to blame for sthg; **einer Sache** (G) **~ sein** *geh* to be guilty of sthg - 2. [nicht bezahlt] due; **jm etw ~ sein** *ODER* **bleiben** to owe sb sthg ◇ *adv:* **sich ~ bekennen** to admit one's guilt; **sich ~ machen** to be guilty; **jn ~ sprechen** to find sb guilty.

**Schuldige** (*pl* -n) *der, die* guilty party; **der ~ an dem Raub** the person responsible for the robbery.

**schuldlos** *adj* innocent ◇ *adv* innocently.

**Schuldner, in** (*mpl* -; *fpl* -nen) *der, die* debtor.

**Schuldlschein** *der* IOU.

**schuldunfähig** *adj* not responsible for one's actions.

**S**

**Schule** (pl -n) die school; in der ~ at school; zur ODER in die ~ gehen to go to school; in die ~ kommen to start school; (keine) ~ haben (not) to have to go to school; ~ machen fig to set a precedent.

**schulen** vt to train.
➡ sich schulen ref to educate o.s.; sich in etw (D) ~ to teach o.s. sthg.

**Schulenglisch** das school-level English.

**Schüler** (pl -) der pupil.

**Schüleraustausch** der (school) exchange.

**Schülerlausweis** der pupil's ID card entitling them to concessions etc.

**Schülerin** (pl -nen) die pupil.

**Schülerlkarte** die school season ticket.

**Schülerlzeitung** die school magazine.

**Schullferien** pl school holidays.

**Schullfranzösisch** das school-level French.

**schulfrei** adj: morgen ist ~ there's no school tomorrow; ~ haben to be off school.

**Schullfreund, in** der, die school friend.

**Schullheft** das exercise book.

**Schullhof** der school playground.

**schulisch** adj & adv at school.

**Schulljahr** das - 1. [Jahr] school year - 2. [Klasse] year.

**Schullkamerad, in** der, die schoolmate.

**Schullkind** das schoolchild.

**Schullklasse** die class.

**Schullleiter, in** der, die headmaster (f headmistress) Br, principal Am.

**Schullpflicht** die compulsory education; alle Kinder unter 15 Jahren unterliegen der ~ it is compulsory for all children under the age of 15 to attend school.

**schulpflichtig** adj required to attend school; im ~en Alter of school age.

**Schullrat** der schools inspector.

**Schullrätin** (pl -nen) die schools inspector.

**Schullschiff** das training ship.

**Schullschluss** der: nach ~ after school; um zwei Uhr ist ~ school finishes at two o'clock.

**Schullstunde** die period.

**Schullsystem** das school system.

**Schulltag** der school day; der erste/letzte ~ the first/last day of school.

**Schulltasche** die schoolbag.

**Schulter** (pl -n) die shoulder; jm auf die ~ klopfen to pat sb on the back; etw auf die leichte ~ nehmen to make light of sthg.

**Schulterlblatt** das shoulder blade.

**schulterfrei** adj [Abendkleid] off-the-shoul-

der; [BH] strapless ◇ adv off the shoulder.

**schultern** vt [Sack, Gepäck] to shoulder; [einen Verletzten] to put over one's shoulder.

**Schulung** (pl -en) die - 1. [gen] training - 2. [Lehrveranstaltung] training course.

**Schullweg** der way to school.

**Schullwesen** das school system.

**Schullzeit** die schooldays (pl).

**Schullzeugnis** das school report.

**schummeln** vi to cheat.

**schummerig, schummrig** adj [Licht, Beleuchtung] dim; [Ort] dimly lit.

**Schund** der abw trash.

**schunkeln** (perf hat geschunkelt) vi - 1. [sich wiegen] to link arms and sway in time to the music - 2. [Schiff] to rock.

**Schuppe** (pl -n) die - 1. [von Fischen] scale - 2. [Hautstück] flake - 3. [Kopfschuppe] dandruff (U).

**schuppen** vt to scale.
➡ sich schuppen ref to flake.

**schüren** vt - 1. [Feuer] to poke - 2. [Hass, Unzufriedenheit] to stir up.

**schürfen** vi - 1. [schleifen] to scrape - 2. [suchen]: nach Gold ~ to prospect for gold ◇ vt: sich (D) das Knie ~ to graze one's knee.

**Schürflwunde** die graze.

**Schurke** (pl -n) der abw villain.

**Schurwolle** die: reine ~ pure new wool.

**Schürze** (pl -n) die apron.

**Schuss** (pl Schüsse) der - 1. [mit Schusswaffe, beim Fußball] shot; ein ~ auf jn/etw abgeben to fire a shot at sb/sthg - 2. [ein wenig] dash; ein ~ Whisky a dash of whisky - 3. [beim Skifahren]: ~ fahren to schuss - 4. RW: weit (ab) vom ~ fam off the beaten track; gut in ~ sein fam to be in good shape.

**Schüssel** (pl -n) die bowl.

**schusselig** adj fam scatterbrained.

**Schusslinie** die: in js ~ geraten to get into sb's line of fire; fig to come under fire from sb.

**Schusslwaffe** die firearm.

**Schusslwechsel** der exchange of fire.

**Schusslwunde** die bullet wound.

**Schuster, in** (mpl -; fpl -nen) der, die shoemaker.

**Schutt** der rubble; '~ abladen verboten!' 'no dumping'; in ~ und Asche liegen to be reduced to rubble.

**Schuttabladelplatz** der rubbish Br ODER garbage Am dump.

**Schüttelfrost** der: ~ haben to be shivering.

**schütteln** *vt* to shake; **den Kopf ~** to shake one's head; 'vor Gebrauch ~' 'shake before use'; **es schüttelte ihn bei dem Gedanken** the thought made him shudder.

➤ **sich schütteln** *ref* to shake o.s.; **sich vor etw** *(D)* ~ [Lachen, Kälte] to shake with sthg; [Ekel, Entsetzen] to be filled with sthg.

**Schüttel|reim** *der rhyming couplet in which the initial consonants of the final rhyming words or syllables are exchanged for humorous effect.*

**schütten** *vt* [Flüssigkeit] to pour; [Mehl, Kartoffeln] to tip ◇ *vi:* **es schüttet** *fam* it's pouring (down).

**Schutz** *der* protection; **jn in ~ nehmen** to stand up for sb; **(vor jm/etw) ~ suchen** to take refuge (from sb/sthg).

**Schutzan|strich** *der* protective coating.

**Schutzan|zug** *der* protective clothing *(U).*

**Schutz|behauptung** *die* lie to cover o.s.

**Schutz|blech** *das* mudguard.

**Schutz|brief** *der* travel insurance certificate.

**Schutz|brille** *die* (safety) goggles *(pl).*

**Schütze** *(pl -n) der -* **1.** ASTROL Sagittarius; **~ sein** to be a Sagittarius **- 2.** [Sportschütze] marksman **- 3.** [Schützenbruder] *member of a "Schützenverein" that holds a traditional annual contest involving shooting a wooden bird off a pole* **- 4.** [bei Ballsport] scorer **- 5.** [Soldat] private.

**schützen** *vt:* **jn/etw (vor jm/etw) ~** to protect sb/sthg (from sb/sthg); **gesetzlich geschützt** registered (as a trademark).

➤ **sich schützen** *ref:* **sich gegen etw** ODER **vor etw** *(D)* **~** to protect o.s. against sthg ODER from sthg.

**Schützen|fest** *das shooting festival.*

SCHÜTZENFEST

This popular fair is still held in rural areas. The main attraction is a shooting competition organized by the local shooting club. The winner is nominated the "Schützenkönig" ("king of the marksmen").

**Schützen|graben** *der* trench.

**Schützen|hilfe** *die:* **jm ~ geben** ODER **leisten** *fam* to support sb.

**Schutz|gebiet** *das -* **1.** [Naturschutzgebiet] protected area **- 2.** [Kolonie] protectorate.

**Schutz|gebühr** *die* token fee.

**Schutz|gitter** *das* protective grille.

**Schutz|helm** *der* [für Motorradfahrer] crash helmet; [für Bauarbeiter] safety helmet.

**Schutz|hülle** *die* protective cover; [für Buch] dust jacket.

**Schutz|hütte** *die* shelter.

**Schutz|impfung** *die* vaccination.

**Schützin** *(pl -nen) die* [Sportschützin] markswoman.

**Schützling** *(pl -e) der* [Kind in Obhut] charge; [Protegé] protégé (*f* protégée).

**schutzlos** *adj* defenceless ◇ *adv:* **jm ~ ausgeliefert sein** to be completely at sb's mercy.

**Schutz|maßnahme** *die* precaution.

**Schutz|patron, in** *der, die* patron saint.

**Schutz|polizei** *die (ohne pl)* police *(pl).*

**schutzsuchend** *adj* seeking protection.

**Schutzum|schlag** *der* dust jacket.

**schwabbelig** *adj* [Körperteil] flabby; [Pudding] wobbly.

**Schwabe** *(pl -n) der* Swabian.

**Schwaben** *nt* Swabia.

**Schwäbin** *(pl -nen) die* Swabian.

**Schwabing** *nt artists' quarter in Munich.*

**schwäbisch** *adj* Swabian.

**Schwäbische Alb** *die:* **die ~** the Swabian Jura.

**schwach** *(kompar* **schwächer;** *superl* **schwächste)** *adj -* **1.** [gen] weak; **bei Kuchen werde ich immer ~** I have no willpower when it comes to cakes **- 2.** [Konstitution] delicate **- 3.** [leicht - Brise, Wärme, Ahnung, Gefühl] faint; [ - Druck] light; [ - Versuch, Entschuldigung] feeble **- 4.** [Selbstbewusstsein] low **- 5.** [Film, Leistung, Schüler] weak, poor; [Gehör, Gedächtnis] poor; **ein ~er Trost sein** to be cold comfort **- 6.** [Beteiligung] poor ◇ *adv -* **1.** [eingeschränkt, schlecht, wenig] poorly **- 2.** [leicht - wehen, strahlen, sich erinnern] faintly; [ - drücken] lightly; [ - protestieren] feebly **- 3.** GRAM: **das Verb wird ~ konjugiert** it is a weak verb.

**Schwäche** *(pl -n) die -* **1.** [gen] weakness; **eine ~ für jn/etw haben** to have a weakness for sb/sthg **- 2.** [von Geräusch] faintness **- 3.** [von Druck] lightness.

**Schwächean|fall** *der* sudden feeling of weakness.

**schwächen** *vt* to weaken.

**Schwach|kopf** *der fam abw* dummy.

**schwächlich** *adj* delicate.

**Schwächling** *(pl -e) der abw* weakling.

**Schwachsinn** *der -* **1.** *fam* [Unsinn] nonsense **- 2.** MED mental deficiency.

**schwachsinnig** *adj -* **1.** *fam* [unsinnig] stupid, ridiculous **- 2.** MED mentally deficient ◇ *adv fam* stupidly.

**Schwach|stelle** *die* weak point, weakness.

**Schwachstrom** *der* low-voltage current.

**Schwächung** *(pl -en) die* weakening.

**Schwaden** *pl* clouds.

**schwafeln** *fam abw vi* to talk drivel <> *vt* to drivel on about.

**Schwager** (*pl* Schwäger) *der* brother-in-law.

**Schwägerin** (*pl* -nen) *die* sister-in-law.

**Schwalbe** (*pl* -n) *die* swallow.

**schwamm** *prät* |> schwimmen.

**Schwamm** (*pl* Schwämme) *der* - **1.** [Tier, Haushaltsschwamm] sponge; ~ drüber! let's forget it! - **2.** [Schimmel] dry rot.

**schwammig** *adj* - **1.** [Definition, Worte] woolly; [Kontur] vague, blurred - **2.** [Gesicht] pasty - **3.** [Material] spongy <> *adv* [unklar] vaguely.

**Schwamm|tuch** *das* sponge cloth.

**Schwan** (*pl* Schwäne) *der* swan.

**schwand** *prät abk für* schwinden.

**schwanen** *vt:* ihm schwante Fürchterliches he sensed that something awful was going to happen.

**schwang** *prät* |> schwingen.

**schwanger** *adj* pregnant; ~ werden to get pregnant; im dritten Monat ~ sein to be in the third month of pregnancy.

**Schwangere** (*pl* -n) *die* pregnant woman.

**schwängern** *vt* to make pregnant; von etw geschwängert sein *geh* to be heavy with sthg.

**Schwangerschaft** (*pl* -en) *die* pregnancy.

**Schwangerschaftsab|bruch** *der* abortion, termination.

**Schwank** (*pl* Schwänke) *der* - **1.** [Anekdote] funny story - **2.** [Theaterstück] farce.

**schwanken** (*perf* hat/ist geschwankt) *vi* - **1.** (ist) [sich schwankend bewegen] to sway - **2.** (hat) [unentschlossen sein] to waver - **3.** (hat) [instabil sein] to fluctuate.

**Schwankung** (*pl* -en) *die* fluctuation.

**Schwanz** (*pl* Schwänze) *der* - **1.** [von Tieren] tail; den ~ einziehen *fam fig* to back down - **2.** *vulg* [männliches Glied] dick - **3.** *fam* [Serie] series.

**schwänzen** *vi fam* to skive *Br*, to play hookey *Am* <> *vt* [Unterricht, Stunde] to skip; die Schule ~ to skive off *Br* ODER play hookey *Am* from school.

**schwappen** (*perf* hat/ist geschwappt) *vi* - **1.** (ist) [überlaufen] to spill - **2.** (hat) [sich bewegen] to slosh <> *vt* (hat) to splash.

**Schwarm** (*pl* Schwärme) *der* - **1.** [von Kindern, Bienen] swarm; [von Fischen] shoal; [von Vögeln] flock - **2.** *fam* [Idol] heartthrob.

**schwärmen** (*perf* hat/ist geschwärmt) *vi* - **1.** (hat) [begeistert sein]: für jn/etw ~ to be mad about sb/sthg - **2.** (hat) [erzählen]: von jm/etw ~ to rave about sb/sthg - **3.** (ist) [im Schwarm fliegen] to swarm.

**Schwärmer, in** (*mpl* -; *fpl* -nen) *der, die* dreamer.

**schwärmerisch** *adj* [Blick, Stimme] rapturous; [Mensch] effusive <> *adv* [blicken, reden] rapturously.

**Schwarte** (*pl* -n) *die* - **1.** [von Speck] rind; [von Schweinebraten] crackling (U) - **2.** *fam abw* [Buch] tome.

**schwarz** (*kompar* schwärzer; *superl* schwärzeste) *adj* - **1.** [gen] black - **2.** POL pro-CDU/CSU - **3.** [Geschäfte] illicit <> *adv:* der Stift schreibt ~ the pen writes in black; ~ auf weiß *fig* in black and white; *siehe auch* schwarz sehen.

**Schwarz** *das* black.

**Schwarzafrika** *nt* Black Africa.

**Schwarzarbeit** *die* work on the black market; [als Nebentätigkeit] moonlighting.

**Schwarz|brot** *das* black bread.

**Schwarze** (*pl* -n) *der, die* black person <> *das* (ohne *pl*) black; das kleine ~ the little black number ODER dress; ins ~ treffen to hit the bull's-eye.

**Schwärze** *die* blackness.

**Schwarze Markt** *der* black market.

**Schwarze Meer** *das* Black Sea.

**schwärzen** *vt* to blacken.

**Schwarze Peter** *der* ≈ old maid; jm den Schwarzen Peter zuschieben *fig* to blame sb.

**schwarz|fahren** (*perf* ist schwarzgefahren) *vi* (unreg) to travel without a ticket.

**Schwarz|fahrer, in** *der, die* fare dodger.

**Schwarz|händler, in** *der, die* black marketeer.

**schwärzlich** *adj* blackish.

**Schwarz|markt** *der* black market.

**schwarz sehen** *vi* (unreg): (für jn/etw) ~ to be pessimistic (about sb/sthg).

**Schwarzwald** *der* Black Forest.

**Schwarzwälder Kirschtorte** *die* Black Forest gâteau.

**schwarzweiß** *adj* black and white <> *adv* in black and white.

**Schwarzweiß|film** *der* black and white film.

**Schwatz** (*pl* -e) *der fam* chat; einen ~ halten *fam* to have a chat.

**schwatzen, schwätzen** *vi* - **1.** [sich unterhalten] to chat - **2.** [in der Schule] to talk <> *vt abw:* dummes Zeug ~ to talk rubbish.

**Schwätzer, in** (*mpl* -; *fpl* -nen) *der, die abw:* ein ~ sein to talk a load of nonsense.

**schwatzhaft** *adj abw:* ein ~er Mensch a person who can't keep their mouth shut.

**Schwebe** *die:* **in der ~** in the balance.

**Schwebe|bahn** *die* overhead monorail.

**Schwebe|balken** *der* SPORT beam.

**schweben** *vi* - **1.** [fliegen, in Wasser] to float; [Vögel] to hover; [Staubteilchen] to hang - **2.** [unentschieden sein] to hover; **die Zukunft des Unternehmens schwebt noch im Ungewissen** the company's future is still in the balance - **3.** [Duft, Verdacht] to hang.

**Schweb|stoff** *der* CHEM particles *(pl)* in suspension.

**Schwede** *(pl -n) der* Swede.

**Schweden** *nt* Sweden.

**Schwedin** *(pl -nen) die* Swede.

**schwedisch** *adj* Swedish.

**Schwedisch(e)** *das* Swedish; *siehe auch* **Englisch(e)**.

**Schwefel** *der* sulphur.

**schwefeln** *vt* to sulphurize.

**Schwefel|säure** *die* sulphuric acid.

**Schwefelwasserstoff** *der* hydrogen sulphide.

**Schweif** *(pl -e) der* tail.

**schweifen** *(perf* **ist geschweift)** *vi geh* to roam.

**Schweige|minute** *die* minute's silence.

**schweigen** *(prät* **schwieg;** *perf* **hat geschwiegen)** *vi* to be silent; **wenn du ~ kannst, verrate ich dir etwas** if you can keep a secret, I'll tell you something; **über etw** *(A)* **~** to keep silent about sthg; **von jm/etw ganz zu ~** to say nothing of sb/sthg.

**Schweigen** *das* silence; **jn zum ~ bringen to** silence sb; **das ~ brechen** to break the silence; **sich in ~ hüllen** to keep silent.

**schweigend** *adj* silent ◇ *adv* silently, in silence.

**Schweigepflicht** *die* professional duty to maintain confidentiality.

**schweigsam** *adj* taciturn; **du bist heute ~** you're rather quiet today.

**Schwein** *(pl -e) das* - **1.** [Tier] pig - **2.** [Schweinefleisch] pork - **3.** *salopp abw* [Mensch] bastard - **4.** RW: **armes ~** *salopp* poor bastard; **kein ~** *salopp* not a damn soul; **~ haben** *fam* to be jammy.

**Schweine|braten** *der* roast pork.

**Schweine|fleisch** *das* pork.

**Schweine|hund** *der salopp* bastard; **den inneren ~ überwinden** *fig* to overcome one's reluctance.

**Schweinerei** *(pl -en) die fam* - **1.** [schlimme Sache] goddamn scandal; **das neue Abtreibungsgesetz ist eine ~!** the new law on abortion is bloody *Br* ODER goddamn *Am* disgraceful!

- **2.** [Schmutz] mess - **3.** [Unanständiges]: **~en** filth *(U)*.

**Schweine|stall** *der eigtl* & *fig* pigsty *Br*, pigpen *Am*.

**Schweiß** *der* sweat; **ihr brach der ~ aus** she broke out in a sweat.

**schweißen** *vt* & *vi* to weld.

**schweißgebadet** *adj* & *adv* bathed in sweat.

**schweißtreibend** *adj* - **1.** [schweißbildend] sudorific - **2.** [Arbeit] sweaty.

**Schweiß|tropfen** *der* drop of sweat.

**Schweiz** *die:* **die ~** Switzerland.

**Schweizer** *(pl -) der* & *adj (unver)* Swiss.

**Schweizerdeutsch** *das* Swiss German; *siehe auch* **Englisch(e)**.

**Schweizerin** *(pl -nen) die* Swiss.

**schweizerisch** *adj* Swiss.

**Schweizerische    Eidgenossenschaft** *die:* **die ~** the Swiss Confederation.

**Schweizer Käse** *(pl -) der* Swiss cheese.

**Schwel|brand** *der* smouldering fire.

**schwelen** *vi* - **1.** [Rauch entwickeln] to smoulder - **2.** *geh* [verborgen sein]: **in ihm schwelt die Eifersucht** he is smouldering with jealousy.

**schwelgen** *vi geh:* **in etw** *(D)* **~** to revel in sthg.

**Schwelle** *(pl -n) die* - **1.** [Türschwelle] threshold; **an der ~ einer Sache** *(D) fig* on the threshold of sthg; **an der ~ des Todes** at death's door - **2.** [der Eisenbahn] sleeper *Br*, tie *Am*.

**schwellen** *(präs* **schwillt;** *prät* **schwoll;** *perf* **ist geschwollen)** *vi* to swell.

**Schwellung** *(pl -en) die* swelling.

**schwemmen** *vt:* **die Algen wurden an Land geschwemmt** the seaweed was washed ashore.

**schwenken** *vt* - **1.** [Kran] to swing; [Kamera] to pan - **2.** [Fahne] to wave - **3.** KÜCHE to toss.

**schwer** *adj* - **1.** [Gewicht] heavy; **wie ~ bist du/ist der Koffer?** how heavy are you/is the suitcase?; **zehn Kilo ~ sein** to weigh 10 kilos - **2.** [schwierig] difficult; [beschwerlich] hard; **wir hatten einen ~en Tag** we had a hard day; **es ~ haben mit ...** to have a hard time with ... - **3.** [schlimm - Krankheit, Schaden, Unfall] serious; [ - Enttäuschung] huge, great; **es war ein ~er Schlag für ihn** it was a heavy blow for him - **4.** [stark - Geschmack, Geruch] strong; [ - Mahlzeit, Sturm] heavy ◇ *adv* - **1.** [an Gewicht] heavily - **2.** [unter Mühen]: **~ atmen** to breathe with difficulty; **~ hören** to be hard of hearing - **3.** [arbeiten] hard - **4.** [schwerlich] hardly; **das ist nur ~ möglich** it's very unlikely - **5.** [schlimm - verletzt, krank] seriously; [ - bestrafen] severely; **er**

ist ~ **gestürzt** he had a nasty fall - **6.** *fam* [sehr] really; **er ist ~ in Ordnung** he's all right.

**Schwerarbeit** *die* heavy work.

**schwerbehindert, schwer behindert** *adj* severely disabled.

**Schwer|behinderte** *der, die* severely disabled person.

**schwer beladen** *adj* heavily laden ◇ *adv:* ~ **fahren** to drive with a heavy load.

**schwerbeschädigt** *adj amt* [behindert] severely disabled.

**schwer beschädigt** *adj* [beschädigt] badly damaged ◇ *adv* in a badly damaged state.

**schwer bewaffnet** *adj* heavily armed.

**Schwere** *die* - **1.** [gen] heaviness - **2.** [von Krankheit, Schaden, Unfall] seriousness; [von Enttäuschung] enormity - **3.** [Schwierigkeitsgrad] difficulty ◇ *das:* ~**s durchmachen** to have a difficult time (of it).

**schwerelos** *adj* weightless ◇ *adv* weightlessly.

**schwer erziehbar** *adj* difficult.

**schwer fallen** (*perf* **ist schwer gefallen**) *vi* (*unreg*): **es fiel ihm schwer, Abschied zu nehmen** he found it difficult to say goodbye.

**schwerfällig** *adj* ponderous ◇ *adv* ponderously.

**Schwer|gewicht** *das* heavyweight.

**schwerhörig** *adj* hard of hearing.

**Schwerin** *nt* Schwerin.

**Schwer|industrie** *die* heavy industry.

**Schwerkraft** *die* gravity.

**schwer krank** *adj* seriously ill.

**schwerlich** *adv* hardly; **das wird dir ~ gelingen** you're never going to do that.

**schwer machen** *vt:* **jm etw ~** to make sthg difficult for sb.

**schwermütig** *adj* melancholy ◇ *adv* in a melancholy way.

**schwer nehmen** *vt* (*unreg*): **etw ~** to take sthg hard.

**Schwer|punkt** *der* - **1.** [Hauptsache] main focus; **den ~ verlagern** to shift the focus - **2.** PHYS centre of gravity.

**schwerpunktmäßig** *adj* - **1.** [Aktivität, Verlagerung] selective - **2.** [Thematik, Spezialisierung] main ◇ *adv* - **1.** [selektiv] selectively - **2.** [hauptsächlich] mainly.

**Schwert** (*pl* -**er**) *das* sword.

**schwer tun** ➥ **sich schwer tun** *ref* (*unreg*): **sich mit etw ~** to have difficulty with sthg.

**Schwer|verbrecher, in** *der, die* person who has committed a serious crime.

**schwer verdaulich** *adj eigtl* & *fig* difficult to digest.

**schwer verletzt** *adj* seriously injured.

**Schwerverletzte** *der, die:* **es gab fünf ~** five people were seriously injured.

**schwer verständlich** *adj* difficult to understand ◇ *adv* in a way that is difficult to understand.

**schwerwiegend** *adj* serious ◇ *adv* seriously.

**Schwester** (*pl* -**n**) *die* - **1.** [Verwandte] sister - **2.** [Krankenschwester] nurse - **3.** [Ordensschwester] nun, sister.

**schwesterlich** *adj* sisterly ◇ *adv* like sisters.

**schwieg** *prät* ▷ **schweigen.**

**Schwieger|eltern** *pl* parents-in-law.

**Schwieger|mutter** *die* mother-in-law.

**Schwieger|sohn** *der* son-in-law.

**Schwieger|tochter** *die* daughter-in-law.

**Schwieger|vater** *der* father-in-law.

**Schwiele** (*pl* -**n**) *die* callus.

**schwierig** *adj* difficult ◇ *adv* with difficulty.

**Schwierigkeit** (*pl* -**en**) *die* difficulty; **ohne ~en** without difficulty; **machen Sie uns keine ~en!** don't give us any trouble!; **das Atmen macht ihr ~en** she has difficulty breathing; **in ~en geraten/stecken** to get into/be in trouble.

**Schwierigkeits|grad** *der* (level of) difficulty.

**schwillt** *präs* ▷ **schwellen.**

**Schwimm|bad** *das* swimming pool.

**Schwimm|becken** *das* (swimming) pool.

**schwimmen** (*prät* **schwamm**; *perf* **hat/ist geschwommen**) *vi* - **1.** (hat, ist) [Person, Tier] to swim; **in Fett ~** *fig* to be swimming in fat; **in Geld ~** *fig* to be rolling in money - **2.** (ist) [treiben] to float ◇ *vt* to swim.

**Schwimmen** *das* swimming; **ins ~ kommen** ODER **geraten** *fig* to start to flounder.

**Schwimmer, in** (*mpl* -; *fpl* -**nen**) *der, die* swimmer.

**Schwimm|halle** *die* indoor swimming pool.

**Schwimm|sport** *der* (competitive) swimming.

**Schwimm|verein** *der* swimming club.

**Schwimm|weste** *die* life jacket *Br*, life preserver *Am*.

**Schwindel** *der* - **1.** [Gleichgewichtsstörung] dizziness; ~ **erregend** [Höhe] vertiginous; [Preis] astronomical - **2.** *abw* [Betrug] swindle; **auf einen ~ hereinfallen** to fall for a trick - **3.** *fam abw* [Lüge] lie.

**schwindelfrei** *adj:* ~ **sein** to have a head for heights.

**schwindelig, schwindlig** *adj:* mir wird (es) ~ I feel dizzy; *fig* my head is spinning.

**schwindeln** *vi* - **1.** [taumeln]: mir schwindelt I feel dizzy; mir schwindelt der Kopf *fig* my head is spinning - **2.** [lügen] to lie ⬦ *vt* [lügen]: das hat er geschwindelt! he was lying!

**schwinden** (*prät* schwand; *perf* ist geschwunden) *vi geh* - **1.** [Vorräte, Kräfte, Geld] to dwindle; [Interesse] to wane - **2.** [Erinnerung, Hoffnung] to fade.

**Schwindler, in** (*mpl* -; *fpl* -nen) *der, die* - **1.** [Betrüger] swindler - **2.** [Lügner] liar.

**schwindlig** = schwindelig.

**schwingen** (*prät* schwang; *perf* hat/ist geschwungen) *vi* - **1.** *(hat)* [vibrieren] to vibrate - **2.** [pendeln] to swing ⬦ *vt (hat)* to wave; [Axt, Schwert] to swing.

➤ **sich schwingen** *ref* - **1.** [springen]: sich auf etw (A) ~ to leap onto sthg - **2.** [überspringen]: sich über etw (A) ~ to vault over sthg - **3.** [Vogel] to soar (up).

**Schwingung** (*pl* -en) *die* - **1.** [Vibration] vibration; etw in ~ versetzen to cause sthg to vibrate - **2.** PHYS oscillation.

**Schwips** (*pl* -e) *der fam:* einen ~ haben to be tipsy.

**schwirren** (*perf* ist geschwirrt) *vi* - **1.** [Insekt] to buzz - **2.** [Geschoss] to whizz - **3.** [Gedanken]: Ideen ~ mir durch den Kopf ideas are buzzing around my head.

**schwitzen** *vi* - **1.** [Person] to sweat - **2.** [feucht werden - Fenster] to steam up; [ - Wand] to become damp.

**Schwitzkasten** *der* headlock.

**schwoll** *prät* ⬑ schwellen.

**schwor** *prät* ⬑ schwören.

**schwören** (*prät* schwor; *perf* hat geschworen) *vt* to swear; jm etw ~ to swear sthg to sb; ich schwöre dir, ich wars nicht I swear it wasn't me; ich habe mir geschworen, nie wieder zu rauchen I have sworn never to smoke again ⬦ *vi* to swear; auf jn/etw ~ to swear by sb/sthg.

**schwul** *adj fam* gay.

**schwül** *adj* - **1.** [Wetter] close, muggy - **2.** [Duft] sensuous.

**Schwule** (*pl* -n) *der fam* gay (man).

**schwülstig** *abw adj* bombastic ⬦ *adv* bombastically.

**Schwund** *der* - **1.** [von Gedächtnis, Vertrauen] decline; [von Muskeln] atrophy - **2.** WIRTSCH shrinkage.

**Schwung** (*pl* Schwünge) *der* - **1.** [Bewegung] swing; der Turner holte ~ für den Abgang the gymnast wound himself up in preparation for his dismount - **2.** [Elan] zest, verve; (viel) ~ haben to be (very) lively - **3.** [Menge] stack - **4.** *RW:* etw in ~ bringen *fam* to get sthg going; in ~ kommen *fam* [sich bewegen] to get going; [vorankommen] to get on; [Wirtschaft] to pick up; [aktiv werden] to get into one's stride.

**schwunghaft** *adj* [Handel, Geschäft] thriving; [Anstieg, Anwachsen] rapid ⬦ *adv* [ansteigen] rapidly; das Geschäft entwickelt sich ~ business is booming.

**schwungvoll** *adj* lively ⬦ *adv* in a lively fashion.

**Schwur** (*pl* Schwüre) *der* oath; einen ~ leisten to take an oath.

**Schwur|gericht** *das* court comprising two lay assessors and a professional judge, used to try serious crimes.

**Schwyz** [ˈʃviːts] *nt* Schwyz.

**Schwyzer** [ˈʃviːtsɐ] (*pl* -) *der* native/inhabitant of Schwyz ⬦ *adj (unver)* of/from Schwyz.

**Schwyzerin** [ˈʃviːtsərɪn] (*pl* -nen) *die* native/inhabitant of Schwyz.

**schwyzerisch** [ˈʃviːtsərɪʃ] *adj* of/from Schwyz.

**Sciencefiction, Science-fiction** [ˈsaiənsfɪkʃən] *die* science fiction.

**scratchen** *vi* to scratch.

**s. d.** (*abk für* siehe dies) cf.

**SDR** [ɛsdeːˈeːr] (*abk für* Süddeutscher Rundfunk) *der* South German Radio.

**sec.** (*abk für* Sekunde) sec.

**sechs** [zɛks] *num* [als Zahl, Anzahl] six; ~ Mal six times; um ~ (Uhr) at six (o'clock); fünf vor/nach ~ five to/past *Br* ODER after *Am* six; sie ist ~ she's six; mit ~ kommen die Kinder in die Schule children start school at the age of six ODER when they are six; ~ zu null six–zero ⬦ *pron* six; sie waren ~ there were six of them; ein Tisch für ~ a table for six.

**Sechs** (*pl* -en) *die* - **1.** [Zahl, Spielkarte] six - **2.** [Spieler, Bus] number six - **3.** [Schulnote] ≃ F, mark of 6 on a scale from 1 to 6.

**Sechseck** (*pl* -e) *das* hexagon.

**sechseckig** *adj* hexagonal.

**Sechserpack** (*pl* -s ODER -e) *der* pack of six; [von Bierdosen] six-pack.

**sechsfach** *adj:* die ~e Menge six times as much; in ~er Größe six times as big; die Formulare in ~er Ausfertigung abgeben to provide six copies of the forms; der ~e Gewinner the six-times winner ⬦ *adv* sixfold.

**sechshundert** *num* six hundred.

**sechsmal** *adv* six times.

**sechsstellig** *adj* six-figure.

**Sechstage|rennen** *das* six-day cycle race.

**sechstausend** *num* six thousand.

**sechste, r, s** [ˈzɛkstə, ɐ, s] *adj* sixth; **der ~ Juni** the sixth of June, June the sixth; **auf dem ~n Rang sein** to be sixth in the rankings.

**Sechste** (*pl* -n) *der, die, das* [in einer Reihenfolge] sixth; **Heinrich der ~** Henry the Sixth, Henry VI; **sie ist die ~ im Weitsprung** she is sixth in the long jump <> *der* [Angabe des Datums] sixth; **am ~n on the sixth; ich fahre Freitag, den ~n** I'm going on Friday the sixth.

**sechstel** *adj (unver)* sixth; **ein ~ Liter** a sixth of a litre.

**Sechstel** (*pl* -) *das* sixth; **etw in ~ teilen** to divide sthg in six ODER into sixths.

**sechzehn** *num* sixteen; *siehe auch* **sechs.**

**sechzehntel** *adj* sixteenth.

**Sechzehntel** (*pl* -) *das* sixteenth.

**sechzig** *num* sixty; *siehe auch* **sechs.**

**Sechzig** *die* sixty; *siehe auch* **Sechs.**

**Sechzigerjahre, sechziger Jahre** *pl:* **die ~** the sixties.

**Secondhandshop** [ˈsɛkəndˈhɛndʃɔp] (*pl* -s) *der* second-hand shop.

**SED** [ɛs eːˈdeː] (*abk für* **Sozialistische Einheitspartei Deutschlands**) *die* HIST SED, *former East German Communist Party*.

**See** (*pl* -n) *der* lake <> *die* sea; **an der ~** at the seaside; **in ~ stechen** to put to sea; **an die ~ fahren** to go to the seaside; **auf ~** at sea; **auf hoher ~** out at sea; **zur ~ fahren** to be a sailor.

**See|bad** *das* seaside resort.

**See|blick** *der* sea view; **mit ~** with a sea view.

**See|fisch** *der* saltwater fish.

**See|gang** *der:* **leichter/hoher ~** calm/rough seas (*pl*).

**See|hund** *der* - **1.** [Robbe] seal - **2.** [Fell] sealskin.

**See|igel** *der* sea urchin.

**See|karte** *die* (sea) chart.

**seekrank** *adj* seasick.

**Seele** (*pl* -n) *die* - **1.** [gen] soul; **hier lebt keine ~ mehr** there's not a soul living here any more - **2.** RW: **etw auf der ~ haben** to have sthg on one's mind; **das Problem liegt mir auf der ~** geh the problem is weighing on my mind; **er ist eine ~ von Mensch** he is an absolute dear; **du sprichst mir aus der ~** my thoughts exactly; **sich** (D) **die ~ aus dem Leib schreien** *fam* to scream one's head off; **sich** (D) **etw von der ~ reden** to get sthg off one's chest.

**Seelenruhe** *die:* **in aller ~** calmly.

**seelenruhig** *adv* calmly.

**Seeleute** *pl* <> **Seemann.**

**seelisch** *adj* psychological <> *adv* mentally; **~ bedingt sein** to have psychological causes.

**See|löwe** *der* sea lion.

**Seelsorge** *die* pastoral care.

**Seelsorger, in** (*mpl* -; *fpl* -nen) *der, die* pastor.

**See|luft** *die* sea air.

**See|mann** (*pl* -leute) *der* sailor.

**See|meile** *die* nautical mile.

**See|not** *die:* **in ~ geraten/sein** to get into/be in distress.

**See|pferdchen** (*pl* -) *das* seahorse.

**See|räuber** *der* pirate.

**See|reise** *die* voyage.

**See|rose** *die* [Pflanze] water lily.

**See|sack** *der* kitbag.

**See|schlacht** *die* sea battle.

**See|stern** *der* starfish.

**See|tang** *der* seaweed.

**seetüchtig** *adj* seaworthy.

**See|weg** *der:* **auf dem ~** by sea.

**See|zunge** *die* sole.

**Segel** (*pl* -) *das* sail.

**Segel|boot** *das* sailing boat.

**segelfliegen** *vi* to glide.

**Segel|flug** *der* - **1.** [Sport] gliding - **2.** [Flug] glider flight.

**Segel|flugzeug** *das* glider.

**segeln** (*perf* hat/ist gesegelt) *vi* to sail.

**Segel|schiff** *das* sailing ship.

**Segeltuch** (*pl* -e) *das* canvas.

**Segen** (*pl* -) *der* blessing.

**segensreich** *adj* beneficial.

**Segler** (*pl* -) *der* - **1.** [Person] yachtsman - **2.** *fam* [Segelschiff] sailing ship.

**Seglerin** (*pl* -nen) *die* yachtswoman.

**Segment** (*pl* -e) *das* segment.

**segnen** *vt* to bless; **mit etw gesegnet sein** to be blessed with sthg.

**sehbehindert** *adj* visually impaired.

**sehen** (*präs* sieht; *prät* sah; *perf* hat gesehen) *vt* - **1.** [gen] to see; [willkürlich] to watch; **etw gerne/ungerne ~** to like/dislike sthg; **sie ist stets gern gesehen** she is always welcome; **ich kann keine Kartoffeln mehr ~!** I never want to see another potato again!; **das werden wir ja gleich ~** we'll soon see; **das kann sich ~ lassen** that's remarkable; **er hat sich lange nicht ~ lassen** *fam* he hasn't shown his face for a long time - **2.** [treffen] to see, to meet <> *vi* - **1.** [gen] to see; **gut/schlecht ~** to have good/bad eyesight; **sieh mal!** look!; **lass mich mal ~**!

let me have a look!; **jm ähnlich ~** to look like sb **- 2.** [hervorstehen]: **das Wrack sieht aus dem Wasser** the wreck sticks out of the water **- 3.** [mit Präpositionen]: **auf jn/etw ~** to look at sb/sthg; **sie sieht nicht auf den Preis** she doesn't care about the price; **nach jm/etw ~** to look after sb/sthg.

➤ **sich sehen** *ref* **- 1.** [treffen] to meet **- 2.** [sich fühlen]: **sich betrogen ~** to see o.s. cheated; **sich gezwungen ~, etw zu tun** to feel obliged to do sthg.

➤ **mal sehen** *interj* we'll see!

➤ **sieh mal** *interj* look!

➤ **siehste, siehst du** *interj* there you are!

**sehenswert** *adj* worth seeing.

**Sehenswürdigkeit** (*pl* -en) *die* attraction; **~en** sights.

**Sehkraft** *die* sight.

**Sehne** (*pl* -n) *die* **- 1.** [vom Muskel] tendon **- 2.** [vom Bogen] string.

**sehnen** ➤ **sich sehnen** *ref*: **sich nach jm/etw ~** to long for sb/sthg.

**Sehnenscheidenentlzündung** *die* tendonitis (*U*).

**sehnig** *adj* **- 1.** [Fleisch] stringy **- 2.** [Körper] sinewy.

**sehnlich** *adj* [Wunsch, Verlangen] ardent ◇ *adv* longingly.

**Sehnsucht** (*pl* -süchte) *die* longing; **~ nach jm/ etw haben** to long for sb/sthg.

**sehnsüchtig** *adj* [Blick] longing ◇ *adv* longingly.

**sehr** *adv* very; [mit Verben] a lot, very much; **das gefällt mir ~** I like it a lot; **zu ~** too much; **~ viel Geld** an awful lot of money; **bitte ~!** you're welcome!; **danke ~!** thank you very much!

**Sehltest** *der* eye test.

**seicht** *adj* shallow.

**seid** *präs* ⊳ **sein**.

**Seide** (*pl* -n) *die* silk.

**seiden** *adj* **- 1.** [aus Seide] silk **- 2.** [wie Seide] silky ◇ *adv* [wie Seide] silkily.

**Seidenlmalerei** *die* silk painting.

**Seidenpapier** *das* tissue paper.

**seidig** *adj* silky.

**Seife** (*pl* -n) *die* soap.

**Seifenlblase** *die* soap bubble; **wie ~n zerplatzen** *fig* to go up in smoke.

**Seifenllauge** *die* soapsuds (*pl*).

**Seifenloper** *die* TV soap opera.

**Seifenlpulver** *das* soap powder.

**Seifenlschaum** *der* lather.

**seifig** *adj* soapy.

**Seil** (*pl* -e) *das* rope.

**Seillbahn** *die* cable railway.

**Seilschaft** (*pl* -en) *die* **- 1.** [Bergsteiger] rope **- 2.** *abw* [Clique] clique.

**Seilltänzer, in** *der, die* tightrope walker.

**sein** (*präs* **ist**; *prät* **war**; *perf* **ist gewesen**) *aux* **- 1.** [im Perfekt]: **sie ist gegangen** she has gone **- 2.** [im Konjunktiv]: **sie wäre gegangen** she would have gone ◇ *vi* **- 1.** [gen] to be; **Lehrer ~** to be a teacher; **das Hemd ist im Koffer** the shirt is in the suitcase; **das Konzert ist heute** the concert is today; **aus etw ~** to be made of sthg; **aus Indien/Zürich ~** to be from India/Zurich; **du warst es!** it was you! **- 2.** [mit Infinitiv, müssen]: **mein Befehl ist sofort auszuführen** my order is to be carried out immediately **- 3.** [mit Infinitiv, können]: **das ist nicht zu ändern** there's nothing that can be done about it; **dieses Spiel ist noch zu gewinnen** this game can still be won **- 4.** [mit Dativ]: **mir ist schlecht/kalt** I'm sick/cold; **das Buch ist mir** *fam* it's my book **- 5.** [mit unpersönlichem Pronomen] to be; **es ist zwölf Uhr** it's twelve o'clock; **es ist dunkel** it's dark; **wie wäre es mit ...?** what about ...? **- 6.** *RW*: **was ist?** what's up?; **das wärs** that's all; **etw ~ lassen** to give sthg up; **lass es gut ~!** leave it!; **ist was?** is there anything wrong?

**sein, e** *det* his.

**seine, r, s** *pron* [bei Personen] his; [bei Sachen, Tieren] its.

**Seine** [sɛːn(ə)] *die*: **die ~** the (River) Seine.

**seiner** *pron* (Genitiv von er, es): **wir gedenken ~** we remember him.

**seinerseits** *adv* **- 1.** [er selbst] for his part; [es selbst] for its part **- 2.** [von ihm - Person] on his part; [- Tier, Sache] on its part.

**seinerzeit** *adv* at that time.

**seinesgleichen** *pron abw* [Person] the likes of him; [Tier, Sache] the likes of it.

**seinetwegen** *adv* **- 1.** [ihm zuliebe - Person] for his sake; [- Tier, Sache] for its sake **- 2.** [wegen ihm - Person] because of him; [- Tier, Sache] because of it **- 3.** [von ihm aus - Person] as far as he's concerned; [- Tier] as far as it's concerned.

**seinetwillen** ➤ **um seinetwillen** *adv* [Person] for his sake; [Tier] for its sake.

**seinige** (*pl* -n) *pron* (mit Artikel) *geh*: **der/die/das ~** [Person] his; [Tier] its; **er hat das ~ getan** [Pflicht] he did her part.

**sein lassen** *vt* (*unreg*) *fam*: **lass das sein!** stop that!; **sie kann es einfach nicht ~** she just can't help herself.

**Seismograf, Seismograph** (*pl* -en) *der* seismograph.

**seit** *präp* (+ D) **- 1.** [zur Angabe des Zeitpunktes]

since; ~ **Kriegsende** since the end of the war; ~ **wann?** since when? - **2.** [zur Angabe der Dauer] for; **ich wohne hier ~ drei Jahren** I've lived here for three years; ~ **langem** for a long time ◇ *konj* since.

**seitdem** *adv* since then ◇ *konj* since.

**Seite** *(pl -n) die* - **1.** [gen] side; **etw zur ~ legen** to put sthg to one side; **zur ~ gehen** ODER **treten** to move aside; **auf der linken/rechten ~** on the left-hand/right-hand side; **er ist auf der linken ~ gelähmt** he is paralysed down the left side of his body; **auf js ~ sein** ODER **stehen** to be on sb's side - **2.** [von Buch, Heft, Zeitung] page; **auf beiden ~n** on both sides; **js schwache/starke ~** sb's weakness/strong point; **jedes Ding hat seine guten und schlechten ~n** there's a good and a bad side to everything; **sich von seiner besten ~ zeigen** to show one's best side - **3.** *RW:* **jm nicht von der ~ gehen** ODER **weichen** not to leave sb's side; **jm zur ~ stehen** to stand by sb; **jn von der ~ ansehen** to look at sb askance; **jn zur ~ nehmen** to take sb aside.

➤ **auf Seiten** *präp* (+ G) on the part of.

➤ **Seite an Seite** *adv* side by side.

➤ **von allen Seiten** *adv* from all sides.

➤ **von Seiten** *präp* (+ G) on the part of.

**Seiten|airbag** [-'ɛəbæg] *der* AUTO side airbag.

**Seitenaufprall|schutz** *der* AUTO side impact protection.

**Seitenaus|gang** *der* side exit.

**Seiten|blick** *der* sidelong glance.

**Seitenein|gang** *der* side entrance.

**Seiten|hieb** *der* sideswipe.

**seitens** *präp amt* on the part of.

**Seiten|sprung** *der* affair; **einen ~ machen** to have an affair.

**Seiten|stechen** *das* stitch; ~ **haben** to have a stitch.

**Seiten|straße** *die* side street.

**Seiten|streifen** *der* hard shoulder *Br*, shoulder *Am*.

**seitenverkehrt** *adj* mirror-image; **das Dia ist ~** the slide is the wrong way round ◇ *adv* as a mirror image.

**Seiten|wechsel** *der* SPORT change of ends.

**Seiten|zahl** *die* - **1.** [Anzahl der Seiten] number of pages - **2.** [Seitennummer] page number.

**seither** *adv* since then.

**seitlich** *adj* [Fenster, Eingang] side; [Zusammenstoß] side-on; **ein ~er Wind** a crosswind ◇ *adv:* ~ **von jm/etw** at the side of sb/sthg; **die Fahrzeuge stießen ~ zusammen** the vehicles were involved in a side-on collision ◇ *präp* ~ **einer Sache** (G) beside sthg.

**seitwärts** *adv* - **1.** [zur Seite] sideways - **2.** [auf der Seite] to one side ◇ *präp geh* [auf der Seite]: ~ **einer Sache** (G) beside sthg.

**Sek I** (*abk für* **Sekundarstufe I**) *die* ≃ junior high school *Am*, *secondary schooling from 5th to 10th schoolyear, (normally up to age 16).*

**Sek II** (*abk für* **Sekundarstufe II**) *die* ≃ sixth form *Br*, ≃ senior high school *Am*, *secondary schooling from 11th to 13th schoolyear (normally after age 16).*

**Sekret** *(pl -e) das* secretion.

**Sekretär** *(pl -e) der* - **1.** [Person] secretary - **2.** [Möbelstück] bureau.

**Sekretariat** *(pl -e) das* secretary's office.

**Sekretärin** *(pl -nen) die* secretary.

**Sekt** *(pl -e) der German sparkling wine similar to champagne.*

**Sekte** *(pl -n) die* sect.

**Sekt|glas** *das* champagne glass.

**Sektion** *(pl -en) die* [von Organisation] branch.

**Sektor** *(pl -en) der* - **1.** [gen & EDV] sector - **2.** [Fachgebiet] field.

**sekundär** *geh adj* secondary ◇ *adv* secondarily.

**Sekundar|stufe** *die* SCHULE secondary *Br* ODER high *Am* school level; ~ **I** ≃ junior high school *Am*, *secondary schooling from 5th to 10th schoolyear (normally up to age 16);* ~ **II** ≃ sixth form *Br*, ≃ senior high school *Am*, *secondary schooling from 11th to 13th schoolyear (normally after age 16).*

**Sekunde** *(pl -n) die* second.

**Sekunden|schnelle** ➤ **in Sekundenschnelle** *adv* in a matter of seconds.

**Sekunden|zeiger** *der* second hand.

**selber** *pron (unver)* = **selbst.**

**Selbermachen** *das* do-it-yourself, DIY; **Möbel zum ~** DIY furniture.

**selbst** *pron (unver):* **er ~** himself; **sie ~** herself, themselves *(pl)*; **ich ~** myself; **wir ~** ourselves; **Sie ~** yourself, yourselves *(pl)*; **ich ~ I** myself; **du bist ~ schuld** it's your own fault; **das versteht sich von ~** that goes without saying ◇ *adv* even; ~ **wenn** even if.

➤ **von selbst** *adv* - **1.** [freiwillig] of one's own accord - **2.** [automatisch] automatically, by itself; *siehe auch* **selbst gemacht.**

**Selbstachtung** *die* self-respect.

**selbständig** = **selbstständig.**

**Selbständige** = **Selbstständige.**

**Selbständigkeit** = **Selbstständigkeit.**

**Selbst|auslöser** *der* delayed-action shutter release.

**Selbst|bedienung** *die* self-service; **Restaurant mit ~** self-service restaurant.

**Selbst|befriedigung** *die* masturbation.

**Selbst|beherrschung** *die* self-control.

**Selbst|bestimmung** *die* - **1.** [von Individuen] independence - **2.** [von Völkern] self-determination.

**Selbst|beteiligung** *die* [bei Versicherungen] excess.

**Selbst|betrug** *der* self-deception.

**selbstbewusst** *adj* self-confident ◇ *adv* self-confidently.

**Selbstbewusstsein** *das* self-confidence.

**Selbst|bildnis** *das* self-portrait.

**Selbstein|schätzung** *die* self-assessment.

**Selbst|erfahrung** *die* self-discovery.

**Selbst|erkenntnis** *die* self-knowledge.

**selbst gemacht** *adj* homemade.

**selbstgerecht** *abw adj* self-righteous ◇ *adv* self-righteously.

**Selbst|gespräch** *das:* ~e führen ODER halten to talk to o.s.

**selbstherrlich** *abw adj* high-handed ◇ *adv* high-handedly.

**Selbst|hilfe** *die* self-help; **zur ~ greifen** to take matters into one's own hands.

**Selbsthilfe|gruppe** *die* self-help group.

**Selbst|justiz** *die:* ~ **üben** to take the law into one's own hands.

**selbstklebend** *adj* self-adhesive.

**Selbstkosten|preis** *der* cost price; **zum ~** at cost.

**selbstkritisch** *adj* self-critical ◇ *adv* self-critically.

**Selbst|laut** *der* vowel.

**selbstlos** *adj* unselfish, selfless ◇ *adv* unselfishly, selflessly.

**Selbst|mitleid** *das abw* self-pity.

**Selbst|mord** *der* suicide; **~ begehen** to commit suicide.

**Selbst|mörder, in** *der, die* suicide.

**selbstsicher** *adj* self-confident ◇ *adv* self-confidently.

**Selbstsicherheit** *die* self-confidence.

**selbstständig** *adj* - **1.** [unabhängig] independent - **2.** [im Beruf] self-employed; **sich ~ machen** to set up on one's own ◇ *adv* [unabhängig] independently.

**Selbstständige** (*pl* **-n**) *der, die* self-employed person.

**Selbstständigkeit** *die* independence.

**selbstsüchtig** *adj* selfish ◇ *adv* selfishly.

**selbsttätig** *adj* automatic ◇ *adv* automatically.

**Selbstüberwindung** *die:* **es kostete ihn einige ~** he had to force himself a bit.

**selbstvergessen** *adj* & *adv* geh lost in thought.

**Selbstversorger, in** (*mpl* **-;** *fpl* **-nen**) *der, die* self-reliant person.

**selbstverständlich** *adj* natural; **das ist doch ~!** that goes without saying!; **es ist für ihn ~** it is a matter of course for him ◇ *adv* naturally; **selbstverständlich!** of course!

**Selbst|verständlichkeit** (*pl* **-en**) *die* matter of course; **es ist doch eine ~, dass ich das mache** of course I'll do it; **etw mit der größter ~ tun** to do sthg as if it were the most natural thing in the world.

**Selbst|verständnis** *das* self-perception.

**Selbst|verteidigung** *die* self-defence.

**Selbst|vertrauen** *das* self-confidence.

**Selbst|verwaltung** *die* self-administration.

**Selbst|verwirklichung** *die* self-realization.

**selbstzufrieden** *abw adj* self-satisfied, smug ◇ *adv* smugly.

**Selbstzweck** *der* end in itself.

**Selektion** (*pl* **-en**) *die* selection.

**selig** *adj* - **1.** [glücklich - Person, Lächeln] blissfully happy; [ - Schlummer] blissful - **2.** [heilig gesprochen] blessed - **3.** geh [tot] late ◇ *adv* [glücklich] blissfully.

**Seligkeit** *die* bliss; **sie strahlte vor ~** she beamed blissfully.

**Sellerie** *der* celery.

**selten** *adj* rare ◇ *adv* - **1.** [kaum] rarely - **2.** [besonders] exceptionally.

**Seltenheit** (*pl* **-en**) *die* rarity; **das ist keine ~** that's not unusual.

**Selters** (*pl* **-**) *die* ODER *das* sparkling mineral water.

**Selterswasser** *das* = Selters.

**seltsam** *adj* strange ◇ *adv* strangely.

**seltsamerweise** *adv* strangely enough.

**Semantik** *die* semantics (U).

**Semester** (*pl* **-**) *das* semester; **im achten ~ sein** to be in the second half of one's fourth year.

**Semesterferien** *pl* university holidays separating semesters, lasting between one and three months.

**Semikolon** (*pl* **-s**) *das* semicolon.

**Seminar** (*pl* **-e**) *das* - **1.** [Veranstaltung] seminar - **2.** [Institut] department.

**Semmel** (*pl* **-n**) *die Österr* & *Süddt* (bread) roll; **das Buch geht weg wie warme ~n** fam the book is selling like hot cakes.

**Semmel|knödel** *der* bread dumpling.

**sen.** (*abk für* **senior**) Sen.

**Senat** (*pl* **-e**) *der* **- 1.** [gen & UNI] senate **- 2.** [von Berlin, Bremen, Hamburg] *government of one of the three German cities that have "Land" status* **- 3.** RECHT panel of judges.

**Senator** (*pl* **-en**) *der* **- 1.** [gen & UNI] senator **- 2.** [von Stadtstaat] *member of the government of one of the three German cities that have "Land" status.*

**Senatorin** (*pl* **-nen**) *die* **- 1.** [gen & UNI] senator **- 2.** [von Stadtstaat] *member of the government of one of the three German cities that have "Land" status.*

**senden** (*prät* **sendete** *ODER* **sandte**; *perf* **hat gesendet** *ODER* **gesandt**) ◇ *vt* **- 1.** (*reg*) [ausstrahlen] to broadcast **- 2.** (*reg*) [funken] to transmit, to send **- 3.** (*reg* & *unreg*) [schicken] to send; **etw an jn ~** to send sb sthg ◇ *vi (reg)* [übertragen] to broadcast.

**Sende|pause** *die* interval.

**Sender** (*pl* **-**) *der* **- 1.** [Station] station **- 2.** [Gerät] transmitter.

**Sende|reihe** *die* series.

**Sende|schluss** *der* closedown.

**Sende|zeit** *die* **- 1.** [von Sendungen] (broadcasting) time **- 2.** [von Sendern] airtime; **unsere ~ geht zu Ende** we're about to go off the air.

**Sendung** (*pl* **-en**) *die* **- 1.** [das Senden] dispatch **- 2.** [Postsendung - von Waren] consignment; [ - Brief] letter; [ - Paket] parcel **- 3.** [ausgestrahltes Programm] programme **- 4.** [Übertragung] broadcasting; **auf ~ gehen** to go on (the) air.

**Senegal** *der* Senegal.

**Senf** (*pl* **-e**) *der* mustard; **seinen ~ zu etw dazugeben** *fam abw* & *fig* to have one's say about sthg.

**Senf|gas** *das* mustard gas.

**Senf|gurke** *die* chopped gherkins pickled with mustard seeds.

**sengend** *adj* scorching.

**senil** *adj abw* senile.

**Senior** (*pl* **Senioren**) *der* **- 1.** [gen] senior **- 2.** [von Mannschaft, Gruppe] oldest member.

➤ **Senioren** *pl* **- 1.** [Alte] senior citizens **- 2.** SPORT seniors.

**Senioren|heim** *das* old people's home.

**Senioren|pass** *der* senior citizen's travel pass.

**Seniorin** (*pl* **-nen**) *die* **- 1.** [gen] senior **- 2.** [von Mannschaft, Gruppe] oldest member.

**senken** *vt* **- 1.** [gen] to lower; **beschämt senkte er den Kopf** he hung his head in shame **- 2.** [Preis, Steuern] to cut.

➤ **sich senken** *ref* **- 1.** [Wasserspiegel] to drop; [Erdreich] to subside **- 2.** [Schranken, Vorhang] to come down.

**Senk|fuß** *der* MED fallen arch.

**senkrecht** *adj* vertical ◇ *adv* vertically.

**Senk|rechte** *die* **- 1.** [Linie] vertical line **- 2.** [Lot] perpendicular.

**Senkrechtstarter, in** (*mpl* **-**; *fpl* **-nen**) *der, die* instant success.

**Senkung** (*pl* **-en**) *die* **- 1.** [Ermäßigung] reduction **- 2.** GEOL subsidence.

**Senner, in** (*mpl* **-**; *fpl* **-nen**) *der, die* **Süddt** & **Österr** *Alpine herdsman and dairyman (or -woman).*

**Sensation** (*pl* **-en**) *die* sensation.

**sensationell** *adj* sensational ◇ *adv* sensationally.

**Sense** (*pl* **-n**) *die* **- 1.** [Gerät] scythe **- 2.** *fam* [Schluss]: **nun ist ~!** that's enough!

**sensibel** *adj* sensitive ◇ *adv* sensitively.

**sensibilisieren** *vt*: **jn für etw ~** to raise sb's awareness of sthg.

**Sensibilität** *die* sensitivity.

**Sensor** (*pl* **-en**) *der* **- 1.** [Schalter] touch-sensitive button **- 2.** [Gerät] sensor.

**Sentenz** (*pl* **-en**) *die* **geh** aphorism.

**sentimental** *adj* sentimental ◇ *adv* sentimentally.

**Sentimentalität** (*pl* **-en**) *die* sentimentality.

**Seoul** [se'u:l] *nt* Seoul.

**separat** *adj* separate; [Wohnung] self-contained ◇ *adv* separately.

**Separatismus** *der* separatism.

**Sept.** (*abk für* **September**) Sept.

**September** *der* September; **der ~ war in diesem Jahr sehr schön** we had good weather this September; **am siebten ~** on the seventh of September, on September the seventh; **Sonntag, den 1. ~** Sunday, 1 September; **im ~** in September; **Anfang/Ende ~** at the beginning/end of September; **Mitte ~** in mid-September.

**Septime** (*pl* **-n**) *die* MUS seventh.

**Sequenz** (*pl* **-en**) *die* sequence.

**Serbe** (*pl* **-n**) *der* Serb.

**Serbien** *nt* Serbia.

**Serbin** (*pl* **-nen**) *die* Serb.

**serbisch** *adj* Serbian.

**Serbokroatisch(e)** *das* Serbo-Croat; *siehe auch* **Englisch(e)**.

**Serenade** (*pl* **-n**) *die* **- 1.** [Musikstück] serenade **- 2.** [Konzert] serenade concert.

**Serie** ['ze:rjə] (*pl* **-n**) *die* **- 1.** [Reihe, Sendereihe] series **- 2.** [Satz] set **- 3.** [von Produkten] line; **in ~ gehen** to go into production.

**Serienanlfertigung** *die* series production.

**serienmäßig** *adj* standard <> *adv* [konstruieren, anfertigen] on a mass scale; [mit etw ausgestattet] as standard.

**serienweise** *adv* - **1.** [in Serie] in series - **2.** [oft] by the score.

**seriös** *adj* - **1.** [vertrauenswürdig] reliable - **2.** [würdevoll, solide] respectable <> *adv* [vertrauenswürdig] reliably; [würdevoll, solide] respectably.

**Serpentine** (*pl* -n) *die* - **1.** [Straße] steeply winding road - **2.** [Kurve] hairpin bend.

**Serum** (*pl* Seren) *das* serum.

**Service**[1] ['sœːɐvɪs] (*pl* -) *das* [Ess-, Kaffeegeschirr] service.

**Service**[2] ['sœːɐvɪs] (*pl* -s) *der* service.

**servieren** [zɛrˈviːrən] *vt* [Speisen, Getränke] to serve.

**Serviererin** [sɛrˈviːrərɪn] (*pl* -nen) *die* waitress.

**Serviette** [zɛrˈvjɛtə] (*pl* -n) *die* serviette.

**Serviettenlring** *der* serviette ring.

**Servollenkung** ['zɛrvolɛŋkʊŋ] *die* power steering (U).

**Servus** ['zɛrvʊs] *interj* Süddt & Österr: Servus! [zur Begrüßung] hello!; [zur Verabschiedung] goodbye!

**Sesam** *der* sesame seeds (*pl*).

**Sessel** (*pl* -) *der* armchair.

**Sessellift** *der* chairlift.

**sesshaft** *adj* settled; ~ **werden** to settle down.

**Set** (*pl* -s) *das* ODER *der* set <> *das* (table) mat <> *der* SPORT set.

**setzen** (*perf* hat/ist gesetzt) *vt* (*hat*) - **1.** [gen] to put; **etw in jn/etw** ~ to put sthg in sb/sthg - **2.** [Denkmal, Grabmal] to put up - **3.** [Frist, Belohnung, Text] to set - **4.** [Pflanzen] to plant - **5.** [wetten]: **etw auf etw** (A) ~ to put sthg on sthg - **6.** RW: **es setzt was** *fam* there'll be trouble <> *vi* - **1.** (*hat*) [wetten] to bet; **auf jn/etw** ~ to bet on sb/sthg - **2.** (*hat, ist*) [befördern]: **über etw** (A) ~ [Fluss] to cross sthg; [Hindernis] to get over sthg.
➤ **sich setzen** *ref* - **1.** [hinsetzen] to sit down; **sich zu jm** ~ to sit with sb - **2.** [Kaffeesatz] to settle.

**Setzer, in** (*mpl* -; *fpl* -nen) *der, die* typesetter.

**Setzling** (*pl* -e) *der* seedling.

**Seuche** (*pl* -n) *die* epidemic.

**Seuchengefahr** *die* danger of an epidemic.

**seufzen** *vi* to sigh.

**Seufzer** (*pl* -) *der* sigh.

**Sevilla** [zeˈvɪlja] *nt* Seville.

**Sex** *der* sex.

**Sexlbombe** *die fam* sex bomb.

**Sexlfilm** *der* sex film.

**sexistisch** *adj* sexist <> *adv* in a sexist way.

**Sexshop** ['sɛksʃɔp] (*pl* -s) *der* sex shop.

**Sexualität** *die* sexuality.

**Sexualleben** *das* (ohne *pl*) sex life.

**Sexuallverbrechen** *das* sex crime.

**sexuell** *adj* sexual <> *adv* sexually.

**sexy** *fam adj* (*unver*) sexy <> *adv* sexily.

**Seychellen** [zeˈʃɛlən] *pl* Seychelles.

**sezieren** *vt* & *vi* to dissect.

**SFB** [ɛs ɛf ˈbeː] (*abk für* Sender Freies Berlin) *der* Radio Free Berlin.

**sfr.** (*abk für* Schweizer Franken) Swiss francs.

**Shampoo** ['ʃampu] (*pl* -s) *das* shampoo.

**Shareware** *die* EDV shareware.

**Sherry** ['ʃeri] (*pl* -s) *der* sherry.

**Shorts** ['ʃɔːɐts] *pl* shorts.

**Show** [ʃo] (*pl* -s) *die* show.

**Showgeschäft** *das* show business.

**Showmaster, in** ['ʃoːmaːstɐ, rɪn] (*mpl* -; *fpl* -nen) *der, die* compere Br, emcee Am.

**Shredder** *der* = Schredder.

**shreddern** *vt* = schreddern.

**Shrimp** *der* = Schrimp.

**Shuttle** ['ʃatl] (*pl* -s) *der* shuttle.

**Siamlkatze** *die* Siamese cat.

**Sibirien** [ziˈbiːrjən] *nt* Siberia.

**sich** *pron* - **1.** [Reflexivpronomen - unbestimmt] oneself; [ - Person] himself (f herself), themselves (*pl*); [ - Ding, Tier] itself, themselves (*pl*); [ - bei Höflichkeitsform] yourself, yourselves (*pl*); ~ (D) **etw kaufen** to buy (o.s.) sthg - **2.** [reziprokes Pronomen] each other.

**Sichel** (*pl* -n) *die* sickle.

**sicher** *adj* - **1.** [ungefährdet] safe; **in ~em Abstand** at a safe distance; **vor jm/etw** ~ **sein** to be safe from sb/sthg - **2.** [zuverlässig] reliable - **3.** [überzeugt, gewiss] sure, certain; **sich** (D) **einer Sache** (G) ~ **sein** to be sure ODER certain about sthg - **4.** [selbstbewusst] self-confident <> *adv* - **1.** [ungefährdet] safely - **2.** [zuverlässig] reliably; **etw** ~ **wissen** to know sthg for sure; **langsam aber** ~ slowly but surely - **3.** [sicherlich] certainly, definitely; **das ist** ~ **richtig, aber ...** that may be true, but ...; **Sie haben es** ~ **gemerkt** you must have noticed it - **4.** [selbstbewusst] self-confidently.
➤ **aber sicher** *interj* of course!

**sicherlgehen** (*perf* ist sichergegangen) *vi* (*unreg*) to play safe.

**S**

**Sicherheit** (*pl* -en) *die* - **1.** [Schutz - persönliche, öffentliche, im Straßenverkehr] safety; [ - soziale, wirtschaftliche, innere] security; **in ~ (vor jm/etw) sein** to be safe (from sb/sthg); **jn/etw (vor jm/etw) in ~ bringen** to rescue sb/sthg (from sb/sthg) - **2.** [Bestimmtheit] certainty; **mit ~** definitely - **3.** [Fundiertheit, Zuverlässigkeit] reliability - **4.** [Selbstbewusstsein] confidence - **5.** [Bürgschaft] surety.

**Sicherheitsab|stand** *der* safe distance.

**Sicherheits|glas** *das* safety glass.

**Sicherheits|gurt** *der* seat belt.

**sicherheitshalber** *adv* to be on the safe side.

**Sicherheits|kette** *die* safety chain.

**Sicherheits|maßnahme** *die* safety measure.

**Sicherheits|nadel** *die* safety pin.

**Sicherheits|schloss** *das* safety lock.

**sicherlich** *adv* certainly.

**sichern** *vt* to secure.
➠ **sich sichern** *ref* - **1.** [sich absichern] to secure o.s.; **sich gegen etw ~** to protect o.s. against sthg - **2.** [sich verschaffen]: **sich** (*D*) **etw ~** to secure sthg.

**sicher|stellen** *vt* - **1.** [beschlagnahmen - Geld, Fund] to seize; [ - Spuren] to secure - **2.** [gewährleisten] to safeguard.

**Sicherung** (*pl* -en) *die* - **1.** [Schutz] safeguarding - **2.** ELEKTR fuse - **3.** [Schutzmaßnahme] safeguard.

**Sicherungs|kopie** *die* EDV back-up (copy).

**Sicht** *die* - **1.** [Aussicht] visibility; **außer ~** out of sight; **die ~ auf etw** (*A*) the view of sthg; **jm die ~ versperren** to block sb's view - **2.** [Betrachtungsweise] point of view; **aus meiner ~** from my point of view.
➠ **auf lange Sicht** *adv* long-term.
➠ **in Sicht** *adv* in sight; **Land in ~!** land ahoy!

**sichtbar** *adj* - **1.** [deutlich] clear - **2.** [wahrnehmbar] visible; **es ist weithin ~** it can be seen from far away ⟨⟩ *adv* [deutlich] clearly.

**sichten** *vt* - **1.** [einsehen] to sift through - **2.** *geh* [sehen] to sight.

**sichtlich** *adj* obvious ⟨⟩ *adv* obviously.

**Sicht|weite** *die* visibility (*U*); **außer/in ~ sein** to be out of/in sight.

**sickern** (*perf* **ist gesickert**) *vi* - **1.** [fließen] to seep - **2.** [bekannt werden] to leak out.

**sie** *pron* - **1.** [Singular - Nominativ] she; [ - Akkusativ] her; **~ wars!** it was her! - **2.** [Plural - Nominativ] they; [ - Akkusativ] them - **3.** [Tier, Gegenstand] it.

**Sie** *pron* (*Singular und Plural*) you.

**Sieb** (*pl* -e) *das* [Küchensieb] sieve; [Teesieb] strainer.

**Siebdruck** (*pl* -e) *der* - **1.** [Verfahren] silk-screen printing - **2.** [Bild] silk-screen print.

**sieben**[1] *vt* - **1.** [durchsieben] to sieve - **2.** [auswählen] to weed out ⟨⟩ *vi* [auswählen] to pick and choose.

**sieben**[2] *num* seven; *siehe auch* **sechs.**

**Sieben** (*pl* - ODER -en) *die* seven; *siehe auch* **Sechs.**

**siebenarmig** *adj* seven-branched.

**Siebenbürgen** *nt* Transylvania.

**siebenfach** *adj* & *adv* sevenfold.

**siebenhundert** *num* seven hundred.

**siebenmal** *adv* seven times.

**Siebensachen** *pl fam* belongings.

**Siebenschläfer** (*pl* -) *der* - **1.** [Tier] dormouse - **2.** (*ohne Artikel, ohne pl*) [Tag] 27 June, *day whose weather is supposed to indicate the weather for the following seven weeks.*

**siebentausend** *num* seven thousand.

**siebte, siebente, r, s** *adj* seventh; *siehe auch* **sechste.**

**Siebte** (*pl* -n) *der, die, das* seventh; *siehe auch* **Sechste.**

**siebtel** *adj* (*unver*) seventh; *siehe auch* **sechstel.**

**Siebtel** (*pl* -) *das* seventh; *siehe auch* **Sechstel.**

**siebzehn** *num* seventeen; *siehe auch* **sechs.**

**Siebzehn** (*pl* -en) *die* seventeen; *siehe auch* **Sechs.**

**siebzig** *num* seventy; *siehe auch* **sechs.**

**Siebzigerjahre, siebziger Jahre** *pl:* **die ~** the seventies.

**sieden** (*prät* **siedete** ODER **sott;** *perf* **hat gesiedet** ODER **hat gesotten**) *vi* (*reg*) [Flüssigkeit] to boil ⟨⟩ *vt* to boil.

**siedend heiß** *adv:* **mir fiel ~ ein, dass ...** *fig* I remembered with horror that ...

**Siede|punkt** *der* boiling point.

**Siedler, in** (*mpl* -; *fpl* -nen) *der, die* settler.

**Siedlung** (*pl* -en) *die* - **1.** [Häusergruppe] housing estate *Br* ODER development *Am* - **2.** [Ansiedlung] settlement - **3.** [Bewohner] estate *Br*, development *Am*.

**Sieg** (*pl* -e) *der* victory; **der ~ über jn/etw** the victory over sb/sthg; **einen ~ erringen** to be victorious.

**Siegel** (*pl* -) *das* seal.

**Siegel|lack** *der* sealing wax.

**Siegel|ring** *der* signet ring.

**siegen** *vi* to win; **über jn/etw ~** to beat sb/sthg.

**Sieger** (*pl* -) *der* winner.

**Sieger|ehrung** *die* medals ceremony.

**Siegerin** (*pl* -nen) *die* winner.

**Sieger|macht** *die* victorious power.

**siegessicher** *adj* confident of victory ⬦ *adv* confidently.

**siegreich** *adj* victorious ⬦ *adv* victoriously.

**siehe** *vi* [in Text]: ~ **oben** see above; ~ **Seite 15** see page 15.

**sieht** *präs* ⟼ sehen.

**siezen** *vt* to address as "Sie".
➡ **sich siezen** *ref* to address each other as "Sie".

**Signal** (*pl* -e) *das* signal; **das ~ zu etw geben** to give the signal for sthg.

**signalisieren** *vt* to signal.

**Signalwirkung** *die:* ~ **haben** to have a knock-on effect.

**Signatur** (*pl* -en) *die* - **1.** *geh* [Unterschrift] signature - **2.** [von Büchern] shelf mark.

**signieren** *vt* to sign.

**Silbe** (*pl* -n) *die* syllable; **jn/etw mit keiner ~ erwähnen** *fig* not to say a word about sb/sthg.

**Silben|rätsel** *das* puzzle requiring the solver to put syllables together from an alphabetical list, thereby forming answers to clues.

**Silben|trennung** *die* syllabification (U).

**Silber** *das* silver.

**Silber|blick** *der* fam squint.

**silbergrau** *adj* silver-grey.

**Silberhoch|zeit** *die* silver wedding (anniversary).

**Silber|medaille** *die* silver medal.

**silbern** *adj* - **1.** [aus Silber] silver - **2.** [wie Silber] silvery ⬦ *adv* [wie Silber - glänzen] with a silvery sheen.

**Silhouette** [zi'lʊɛtə] (*pl* -n) *die* silhouette.

**Silicium, Silizium** [zi'li:tsjʊm] *das* CHEM silicon.

**Silicon, Silikon** (*pl* -e) *das* CHEM silicone (U).

**Silo** (*pl* -s) *der* ODER *das* silo.

**Silvaner** [zɪl'vaːnɐ] (*pl* -) *der* [Wein] Silvaner.

**Silvester** [zɪl'vɛstɐ] (*pl* -) *der* ODER *das* New Year's Eve; ~ **feiern** to see the New Year in.

**SILVESTER** ▓▓▓▓▓▓▓▓▓▓▓

> On New Year's Eve, Germans traditionally organize firework displays at home, in their gardens or from balconies, or in the street. They have also preserved a custom whereby the shapes obtained by melting a piece of lead and then submerging it in water are used to predict the future.

**simpel** *adj* simple ⬦ *adv* simply.

**Simplon** *der:* **der ~** the Simplon Pass.

**Sims** (*pl* -e) *das* ODER *der* ledge.

**Simulant, in** (*mpl* -en; *fpl* -nen) *der, die* abw malingerer.

**Simulation** (*pl* -en) *die* EDV simulation.

**simulieren** *vt* - **1.** [nachahmen] to simulate - **2.** abw [vortäuschen] to feign ⬦ *vi* abw [täuschen] to pretend to be ill.

**simultan** *adj* simultaneous ⬦ *adv* simultaneously.

**Simultan|dolmetscher, in** *der, die* simultaneous interpreter.

**Sinai** *der* Sinai.

**sind** *präs* ⟼ sein.

**Sinfonie** *die* = Symphonie.

**Sinfoniker, in** *der, die* = Symphoniker.

**Singapur** *nt* Singapore.

**singen** (*prät* sang; *perf* hat gesungen) *vi* - **1.** [musizieren] to sing - **2.** salopp abw [aussagen] to squeal ⬦ *vt* to sing; **jn in den Schlaf ~** to sing sb to sleep.

**Single** ['sɪŋ(g)l] (*pl* - ODER -s) *der* (*pl* Singles) single person ⬦ *die* (*pl* Single(s)) single.

**Sing|stimme** *die* singing voice.

**Singular** *der* GRAM singular; **im ~** in the singular.

**Sing|vogel** *der* songbird.

**sinken** (*prät* sank; *perf* ist gesunken) *vi* - **1.** [einsinken, versinken] to sink - **2.** [abnehmen, niedersinken] to fall.

**Sinn** (*pl* -e) *der* - **1.** [Bedeutung, Wahrnehmungsfähigkeit] sense; **im übertragenen ~** figuratively; **im weitesten ~(e)** in the broadest sense - **2.** [Gefühl]: **einen/keinen ~ für etw haben** to have a/no feeling for sthg; **er hat keinen ~ für Humor** he has no sense of humour - **3.** [Denken]: **mir steht der ~ nicht nach Urlaub** I don't feel like a holiday; **jm durch den ~ gehen** to come to sb; **jm in den ~ kommen** to enter sb's head; **jn/etw im ~ haben** to have sb/sthg in mind; **sich** (D) **etw aus dem ~ schlagen** to put sthg out of one's mind; **in js ~e handeln** to act in accordance with sb's wishes; **von ~en sein** to be out of one's mind - **4.** [Zweck]: **der ~ des Lebens** the meaning of life; **es hat keinen ~** there's no point; **ohne ~ und Verstand** without a thought for what one is doing.

**Sinn|bild** *das* symbol.

**sinnen** (*prät* sann; *perf* hat gesonnen) *vi* geh - **1.** [nachdenken] to meditate; **über etw** (A) ~ to meditate on sthg - **2.** [trachten]: **auf etw** (A) ~ to plan sthg; **gesonnen sein, etw zu tun** geh to be minded to do sthg.

**sinnentstellend** *adj* which distorts the meaning ⬦ *adv* in a way that distorts the meaning.

**Sinnes|eindruck** *der* sensory impression.

**Sinnes|organ** *das* sense organ.

**S**

**Sinnes|täuschung** *die* hallucination.

**Sinnes|wahrnehmung** *die* sensory perception.

**Sinnes|wandel** *der* change of mind.

**sinngemäß** *adj:* eine ~e Übersetzung von etw a translation which conveys the general meaning of sthg <> *adv:* etw ~ wiedergeben to give the gist of sthg.

**sinnig** *adj* clever <> *adv* cleverly.

**sinnlich** *adj* - **1.** [körperlichen Genuss betreffend] sensual - **2.** [Sinneswahrnehmung betreffend] sensory <> *adv* - **1.** [körperlichen Genuss betreffend] sensually - **2.** [Sinneswahrnehmung betreffend] through the senses.

**Sinnlichkeit** *die* sensuality.

**sinnlos** *adj* - **1.** [unsinnig] pointless - **2.** *abw* [maßlos] blind *(vor Subst)* <> *adv* - **1.** [unsinnig] pointlessly - **2.** *abw* [maßlos - zerstören] in a blind rage; sich ~ betrinken to get blind drunk.

**Sinnlosigkeit** *(pl -en) die* - **1.** [Wesen] pointlessness - **2.** [Handlung] pointless action.

**sinnverwandt** *adj* synonymous.

**sinnvoll** *adj* - **1.** [befriedigend] meaningful - **2.** [zweckmäßig] sensible <> *adv* - **1.** [befriedigend] meaningfully - **2.** [zweckmäßig] sensibly.

**Sintflut** *die* - **1.** [biblisch] Flood - **2.** [Übermaß - von Post, Anrufen] flood.

**Sinti** *pl* Sinti.

**Sinus** *(pl - ODER -se) der* MATH sine.

**Sinus|kurve** *die* MATH sine curve.

**Siphon, Sifon** [ˈziːfɔŋ] *(pl -s) der* - **1.** [Rohr] U-bend - **2.** [Flasche] siphon.

**Sippe** *(pl -n) die* clan.

**Sippschaft** *(pl -en) die fam abw* tribe.

**Sirene** *(pl -n) die* siren.

**sirren** *(perf hat/ist gesirrt) vi* - **1.** *(ist)* [fliegen] to buzz - **2.** *(hat)* [tönen] to buzz.

**Sirup** *der* - **1.** [für Saft] syrup - **2.** [aus Zucker] treacle *Br*, molasses *Am*.

**Sisal** *der* sisal.

**Sitcom** *(pl -s) die* TV sitcom.

**Sitte** *(pl -n) die* - **1.** [Gepflogenheit] custom; etw ist (bei jm) ~ sthg is the custom (with sb) - **2.** *(ohne pl) fam* [Sittenpolizei] vice squad.
➤ **Sitten** *pl* - **1.** [Benehmen] manners - **2.** [Moral] morals.

**sittenlos** *adj* immoral <> *adv* immorally.

**Sittenpolizei** *die (ohne pl)* vice squad.

**sittenstreng** *adj* morally strict <> *adv* in a morally strict way.

**Sitten|strolch** *der fam* sex fiend.

**sittenwidrig** *adj* morally offensive <> *adv* in a morally offensive way.

**Sittich** *(pl -e) der* parakeet.

**sittlich** *adj* moral <> *adv* morally.

**Sittlichkeits|verbrechen** *das* sex crime.

**sittsam** *adj* demure <> *adv* demurely.

**Situation** *(pl -en) die* situation; die ~ retten to save the situation.

**situationsbedingt** *adj* resulting from the situation <> *adv* as a result of the situation.

**Situationskomik** *die* situation comedy.

**Sitz** *(pl -e) der* - **1.** [in Parlament, Möbelstück] seat - **2.** *(ohne pl)* [von Institution, Firma] headquarters *(pl)*; [von Regierung] seat - **3.** *(ohne pl)* [von Kleidung] fit.

**Sitz|ecke** *die* corner seat.

**sitzen** *(prät saß; perf hat gesessen) vi* - **1.** [gen] to sit; bleiben Sie doch bitte ~! please don't get up!; auf etw *(D)* ~ to be sitting on sthg - **2.** [Mitglied sein]: im Vorstand ~ to sit on the board (of directors); im Parlament ~ to have a seat in parliament - **3.** [sich befinden] to be; [Firma] to be based; der Zahn sitzt locker the tooth is loose - **4.** [passen] to fit - **5.** *fam* [im Gefängnis sein] to be inside - **6.** *fam* [Gelerntes]: das Gedicht sitzt the poem has stuck; bei dem Meister sitzt jeder Handgriff the expert can do every move in his sleep - **7.** *fam* [nicht loswerden]: auf etw *(D)* ~ to be stuck with sthg - **8.** *RW:* einen ~ haben *fam* to have one too many; das hat gesessen ODER saß! *fam* that hit home!

**sitzen bleiben** *(perf ist sitzen geblieben) vi (unreg)* - **1.** [in Schule] to have to repeat a year - **2.** [auf Waren]: auf etw *(D)* ~ to be stuck with sthg.

**sitzen lassen** *vt (unreg) fam* - **1.** [Person]: jn ~ [versetzen] to stand sb up; [verlassen] to walk out on sb - **2.** [beruhen lassen]: etw (nicht) auf sich *(D)* ~ (not) to take sthg lying down.

**Sitz|fleisch** *das (ohne pl) fam* backside; ~ haben *fam hum* & *fig* [nicht gehen wollen] to be in no hurry to go; [Ausdauer haben] to have staying power; [stillsitzen können] to be able to sit still for a long time; kein ~ haben *fam hum* & *fig* [nicht stillsitzen können] to be unable to sit still for long; [keine Ausdauer haben] to lack staying power.

**Sitz|gelegenheit** *die* seat.

**Sitz|gruppe** *die* set of chairs.

**Sitz|kissen** *das* - **1.** [auf dem Boden] floor cushion - **2.** [auf einem Sitz] seat cushion.

**Sitz|ordnung** *die* seating plan.

**Sitz|platz** *der* seat.

**Sitzung** *(pl -en) die* - **1.** [Konferenz - von Vorstand, Abteilung] meeting; [ - von Bundestag] sitting - **2.** [Behandlung - beim Zahnarzt] visit; [ - beim Psychotherapeuten] session.

**Sitzungs|protokoll** *das* minutes *(pl)*.

**Sitzungs|saal** *der* conference hall.

**Sizilien** [zi'tsi:liən] *nt* Sicily.

**Skala** *(pl* **-s** ODER **-len)** *die* scale; [von Farben] range.

**Skalpell** *(pl* **-e)** *das* scalpel.

**Skandal** *(pl* **-e)** *der* scandal.

**skandalös** *adj* scandalous ⬦ *adv* scandalously.

**Skandinavien** [skandi'na:viən] *nt* Scandinavia.

**Skandinavier, in** [skandi'na:vie, rɪn] *(mpl* **-;** *fpl* **-nen)** *der, die* Scandinavian.

**skandinavisch** [skandi'na:vɪʃ] *adj* Scandinavian.

**Skat** *der* skat; **~ spielen** to play skat.

**Skateboard** ['ske:tbɔ:(r)d] *(pl* **-s)** *das* skateboard.

**Skelett** *(pl* **-e)** *das* skeleton.

**Skepsis** *die* scepticism.

**skeptisch** *adj* sceptical ⬦ *adv* sceptically.

**Sketsch, Sketch** [skɛtʃ] *(pl* **-e(s)** ODER **-s)** *der* sketch.

**Ski, Schi** [ʃi:] *(pl* **-** ODER **-er)** *der* ski; **auf ~ern** on skis; **~ fahren** ODER **laufen** to ski.

**Ski|fahren** *das* skiing.

**Ski|gebiet** *das* skiing area.

**Ski|gymnastik** *die (ohne pl)* skiing exercises *(pl)*.

**Ski|kurs** *der* skiing course.

**Ski|langlauf** *der* cross-country skiing.

**Ski|läufer, in** *der, die* skier.

**Ski|lehrer, in** *der, die* skiing instructor.

**Ski|lift** *der* ski lift.

**Skinhead** ['skɪnhɛd] *(pl* **-s)** *der* skinhead.

**Ski|piste** *die* ski run.

**Ski|springen** *das* ski jumping.

**Ski|stiefel** *der* ski boot.

**Ski|stock** *der* ski stick.

**Ski|urlaub** *der* skiing holiday *Br* ODER vacation *Am*.

**Ski|wachs** *das* ski wax *(U)*.

**Skizze** *(pl* **-n)** *die* **- 1.** [Zeichnung] sketch **- 2.** [Text] outline.

**Skizzen|block** *der* sketch pad.

**skizzieren** *vt* **- 1.** [zeichnen] to sketch **- 2.** [schreiben] to outline.

**Sklave** ['skla:və] *(pl* **-n)** *der* slave.

**Sklaverei** [sklavə'rai] *die* slavery.

**Sklavin** ['skla:vɪn] *(pl* **-nen)** *die* slave.

**Skonto** *(pl* **-s)** *der* ODER *das* discount.

**Skorbut** *der* scurvy.

**Skorpion** *(pl* **-e)** *der* **- 1.** [Tier] scorpion **- 2.** AST-ROL [Sternzeichen, Person] Scorpio; **~ sein** to be a Scorpio.

**Skript** *(pl* **-en** ODER **-s)** *das* **- 1.** UNI *printed version of a series of lectures* **- 2.** [Drehbuch] script.

**Skrupel** *(pl* **-)** *der* scruple.

**skrupellos** *adj* unscrupulous ⬦ *adv* unscrupulously.

**Skulptur** *(pl* **-en)** *die* sculpture.

**skurril** *adj* bizarre ⬦ *adv* bizarrely.

**Skyline** ['skailain] *(pl* **-s)** *die* skyline.

**Slalom** *(pl* **-s)** *der* slalom *(U)*.

**Slang** [slɛŋ] *(pl* **-s)** *der* **- 1.** *abw* [Umgangssprache] slang *(U)* **- 2.** [Fachsprache] jargon *(U)*.

**Slapstick** ['slɛpstɪk] *(pl* **-s)** *der* slapstick *(U)*.

**Slawe** *(pl* **-n)** *der* Slav.

**Slawin** *(pl* **-nen)** *die* Slav.

**slawisch** *adj* Slavonic.

**Slip** *(pl* **-s)** *der* briefs *(pl)*.

**Slipper** *(pl* **-)** *der* slip-on.

**Slogan** [slo:gn] *(pl* **-s)** *der* slogan.

**Slowakei** *die* Slovakia.

**Slowenien** *nt* Slovenia.

**Slowenisch(e)** *das* Slovene; *siehe auch* **Englisch(e)**.

**Slum** [slam] *(pl* **-s)** *der* slum.

**Smaragd** *(pl* **-e)** *der* emerald.

**smart** *adj* smart ⬦ *adv* smartly.

**Smog** [smok] *der* smog.

**Smoking** *(pl* **-s)** *der* dinner jacket *Br*, tuxedo *Am*.

**SMS** *(abk für* **Short Message System)** *die (ohne pl)* SMS.

**Snob** [snob] *(pl* **-s)** *der abw* snob.

**Snobismus** *der abw* snobbery.

**snobistisch** *abw adj* snobbish ⬦ *adv* snobbishly.

**Snowboard** *(pl* **-s)** *das* snowboard; **~ fahren** to go snowboarding.

**so** *adv* **- 1.** [auf diese Art] like this; [auf jene Art] like that; **lass es ~, wie es ist** leave it as it is; **~ ist es! fam** that's right!; **weiter ~!** keep it up!; **gut ~! fam** good; **~ was** something like that **- 2.** [mit Adjektiv, Adverb] so; **ich bin ~ froh, dass du gekommen bist** I'm so glad you came; **eine ~ schwierige Prüfung** such a difficult exam; **~ ... wie ...** as ... as ...; **sie ist ~ alt wie du** she's as old as you **- 3.** [mit Substantiv, Pronomen]: **~ einer/eine/eins** such a; **~ ein Pech!** what bad luck!; **~ ein Unsinn!** what nonsense!; **~ eine Art Jacke** a sort of jacket; **~ mancher** many (people) **- 4.** [mit Geste] this; **er war ~ groß** he was this big **- 5.** *fam* [etwa] about, around **- 6.** [bei Zitaten]: **..., ~ der Minister** ..., said the minister **- 7.** *fam* [ohne etwas] as it is; **ich trinke den Tee lieber ~** I'd rather have the tea as it is **- 8.** *fam* [kostenlos] for free; **ich bin ~ ins Kino reingekommen** I got into the cinema for free **- 9.** *fam* [im Allgemeinen]: **was hast du sonst noch ~ gemacht?** what else did you do, then?; **das sagen Sie ~** that's easy for you to say ⬦ *konj* as; **laufen, ~ schnell man kann** to run as fast as one can; **~ ..., dass** so ... that ⬦ *interj:* **~, das wars** so, that's it; **ich habe es satt! - ~?** I'm fed up with it! – are you?; **ach ~!** oh, I see!

➥ **so dass** *konj* = **sodass.**
➥ **oder so** *adv fam* or so.
➥ **so oder so** *adv* anyway.
➥ **so und so** *adv* anyway.
➥ **und so** *adv fam* and so on.

**s. o.** (*abk für* **siehe oben**) *see above.*

**So.** (*abk für* **Sonntag**) Sun.

**SO** (*abk für* **Südost**) SE.

**sobald** *konj* as soon as.

**Söckchen** (*pl* -) *das* ankle sock.

**Socke** (*pl* -n) *die* sock; **sich auf die ~n machen** *fam fig* to get moving.

**Sockel** (*pl* -) *der* [von Denkmal] plinth; [von Haus] base.

**sodass, so dass** *konj* so that.

**Sodbrennen** *das* heartburn.

**soeben** *adv* just.

**Sofa** (*pl* -s) *das* sofa.

**sofern** *konj geh* provided that.

**soff** *prät* ▷ **saufen.**

**Sofia** *nt* Sofia.

**sofort** *adv* **- 1.** [unverzüglich] immediately, straight away; **er ging ~ nach Hause** he went straight home **- 2.** *fam* [gleich] in a moment; **ich komme ~!** I'm just coming!

**Sofortbildlkamera** *die* instant camera.

**Soforthilfe** *die* emergency aid.

**sofortig** *adj* immediate.

**Sofortlmaßnahme** *die* emergency measure.

**soft** *adj fam* soft.

**Softleis** *das* soft ice cream.

**Softie** (*pl* -s) *der fam* softy.

**Software** [ˈsɔftvɛɐ] *die* EDV software.

**Softwarelfehler** *der* EDV software error.

**Softwarelpaket** *das* EDV bundled software (U), software package.

**sog** *prät* ▷ **saugen.**

**sog.** *abk für* **so genannt.**

**sogar** *adv* even.

**so genannt** *adj* so-called.

**Sohle** (*pl* -n) *die* **- 1.** [Fuß-, Schuhsohle] sole

**- 2.** [Ebene - von Tal, Stollen] floor; [ - von Fluss] bed; [ - von Bergwerk] level.

**Sohn** (*pl* **Söhne**) *der* son; **der verlorene ~** *fig* [abwesend] the prodigal son; [enttäuschend] the lost son.

**Soja** *die* soya.

**Sojalsoße** *die* soy sauce (U).

**Sojalspross** *der* beansprout.

**solang, solange** *konj* as long as.

**Solarenergie** *die* solar energy.

**Solarium** [zoˈlaːrjʊm] (*pl* -rien) *das* solarium.

**Solarlzelle** *die* solar cell.

**solch** *det* such; **~ ein/eine** such a; **~ nette Leute** such nice people; **~e wie Sie** people like you.

**solche, r, s** *det* such.

**Soldat** (*pl* -en) *der* soldier.

**Soldatenfriedlhof** *der* military cemetery.

**Soldatin** (*pl* -nen) *die* soldier.

**Söldner, in** (*mpl* -; *fpl* -nen) *der, die* mercenary.

**Sollei** *das* pickled egg.

**solid** = **solide.**

**Solidarlbeitrag** *der* contribution paid as act of solidarity between members of a particular group.

**solidarisch** *adj* [Mensch, Politik] showing solidarity; **~e Haltung zeigen** to show solidarity ⬦ *adv:* **sich ~ verhalten** to act in/show solidarity.

**solidarisieren** ➥ **sich solidarisieren** *ref:* **sich mit jm ~** to show solidarity with sb.

**Solidarität** *die* solidarity; **die ~ mit jm** solidarity with sb.

**Solidaritätslzuschlag** *der* special tax levied to help finance the reconstruction of former East Germany.

**solide, solid** *adj* **- 1.** [brav] respectable **- 2.** [stabil] solid **- 3.** [Finanzen, Wissen, Meinung] sound ⬦ *adv* **- 1.** [brav] respectably **- 2.** [stabil] solidly **- 3.** [finanzieren, ausbilden, arbeiten] soundly.

**Solidität** *die* **- 1.** [von Finanzen, Wissen] soundness **- 2.** [Stabilität] solidness **- 3.** [Bravheit] respectability.

**Solist, in** (*mpl* -en; *fpl* -nen) *der, die* soloist.

**Soll** (*pl* - ODER -s) *das* **- 1.** [Minus] debit; **~ und Haben** debit and credit **- 2.** [Sollseite] debit side **- 3.** [Leistung] target; **sein ~ erfüllen** [Pensum] to achieve one's target; [Pflicht] to fulfil one's obligations.

**sollen** (*perf* **hat gesollt** ODER -) *aux* (*perf* **hat sollen**) **- 1.** [als Aufforderung] to be supposed to; **ich soll um 10 Uhr dort sein** I'm supposed ODER meant to be there at 10; **soll ich das Fenster**

**aufmachen?** shall I open the window?; **was soll ich nur tun?** what should I do? **- 2.** [als Vermutung]: **er soll 108 Jahre alt sein** he is said to be 108 years old; **was soll das heißen?** what's that supposed to mean?; **hier soll ein Kaufhaus hinkommen** a department store is to be built here **- 3.** [konjunktivisch] should, ought to; **wir hätten nicht kommen ~** we shouldn't have come **- 4.** [als Bedingung]: **sollte sie noch kommen, sag ihr ...** if she should turn up, tell her ... ⟨⟩ *vi (perf hat gesollt):* **die Ware soll nach München** the goods are meant to go to Munich; **soll er doch!** *fam* let him!; **was soll das?** *fam* what's all this?; **was solls!** *fam* what the hell!! ⟨⟩ *vt (perf hat gesollt):* **warum soll ich das?** why should I?

**solo** *adv* **- 1.** [im Solo] solo **- 2.** *fam* [allein] on one's own ⟨⟩ *adj (unver) fam* [allein] on one's own.

**Solo** *(pl* **Soli** ODER **-s)** *das* solo.

**Solopart** *(pl* **-s** ODER **-e)** *der* solo part.

**Solothurn** *nt* Solothurn.

**solvent** [zɔl'vɛnt] *adj* solvent.

**Somalia** *nt* Somalia.

**somit[1]** *adv* so.

**somit[2]** *adv* therefore.

**Sommer** *(pl* **-)** *der* summer; **im ~** in (the) summer.

**Sommeranfang** *der* beginning of summer.

**Sommerfahrplan** *der* summer timetable.

**Sommerferien** *pl* summer holiday *Br* ODER vacation *Am*.

**Sommerfrische** *die (ohne pl)* summer holiday *Br* ODER vacation *Am*.

**Sommerkleid** *das* summer dress.

**sommerlich** *adj* summery ⟨⟩ *adv:* **~ heiß/ trocken** as hot/dry as in summer; **sich ~ kleiden** to wear summery clothes.

**Sommerpause** *die* summer break.

**Sommerreifen** *der* summer tyre.

**Sommerschlussverkauf** *der* summer sale.

**Sommersemester** *das* summer term *Br* ODER semester *Am*.

**Sommerspiele** *pl* **- 1.** [Theaterspiele] summer festival *(sg)* **- 2.** [Olympiade]: **Olympische ~** Summer Olympics.

**Sommersprosse** *die* freckle.

**Sommerzeit** *die* summertime.

**Sonate** *(pl* **-n)** *die* MUS sonata.

**Sonde** *(pl* **-n)** *die* probe.

**Sonderanfertigung** *die* special model.

**Sonderangebot** *das* special offer; **im ~** on special offer.

**Sonderausgabe** *die* special edition.

**sonderbar** *adj* strange ⟨⟩ *adv* strangely.

**Sonderbehandlung** *die* special treatment *(U)*.

**Sonderfahrt** *die amt* [Zugfahrt] special train; [Busfahrt] special bus.

**Sonderfall** *der* special case.

**Sondergenehmigung** *die* special permit.

**sondergleichen** *adj* unparalleled.

**sonderlich** *adj* **- 1.** [besondere] particular **- 2.** [sonderbar] peculiar ⟨⟩ *adv:* **nicht ~** not particularly.

**Sondermaschine** *die* special plane.

**Sondermüll** *der* hazardous waste.

**sondern** *konj* but.

**Sondernummer** *die* special issue.

**Sonderpreis** *der* **- 1.** [Sonderprämie] special prize **- 2.** [reduzierter Preis] special price.

**Sonderschule** *die* special school.

**Sonderschüler, in** *der, die* child at a special school.

**Sondersitzung** *die* [von Vorstand, Abteilung] special meeting; [von Parlament] special sitting.

**Sonderzeichen** *das* EDV special character.

**Sonderzug** *der* special train.

**sondieren** *vt geh* to sound out.

**Sonett** *(pl* **-e)** *das* sonnet.

**Song** [sɔŋ] *(pl* **-s)** *der* song.

**Sonnabend** *(pl* **-e)** *der* Saturday; *siehe auch* Samstag.

**sonnabends** *adv* on Saturdays; *siehe auch* samstags.

**Sonne** *(pl* **-n)** *die* sun; **die ~ geht auf/unter** the sun rises/sets; **die ~ scheint** the sun is shining; **in der prallen ~** in the blazing sun.

**sonnen** ⟳ **sich sonnen** *ref* **- 1.** [sich bräunen] to sun o.s. **- 2.** [in Erfolg, Ruhm]: **sich in etw** *(D)* **~** *fig* to bask in sthg.

**Sonnenaufgang** *der* sunrise.

**Sonnenbad** *das* sunbathing *(U)*; **ein ~ nehmen** to sunbathe.

**Sonnenbank** *(pl* **-bänke)** *die* sunbed.

**Sonnenblume** *die* sunflower.

**Sonnenbrand** *der* sunburn *(U)*.

**Sonnenbrille** *die* sunglasses *(pl)*.

**Sonnencreme** *die* sun cream.

**Sonnendach** *das* [von Auto] sunroof; [für Terrasse] awning.

**Sonneneinstrahlung** *die* insolation *(U)*.

**Sonnenenergie** *die* solar energy.

**Sonnen|finsternis** *die* solar eclipse.

**Sonnen|hut** *der* - **1.** [Hut] sun hat - **2.** [Pflanze] rudbeckia.

**sonnenklar** *adj fam* crystal clear.

**Sonnen|kollektor** (*pl* -ren) *der* solar collector.

**Sonnen|licht** *das* sunlight.

**Sonnen|öl** *das* suntan oil.

**Sonnen|schein** *der* sunshine.

**Sonnen|schirm** *der* sunshade.

**Sonnen|schutz** *der* protection against the sun.

**Sonnen|seite** *die* sunny side.

**Sonnen|stich** *der* sunstroke.

**Sonnen|strahl** *der* sunbeam.

**Sonnen|studio** *das* tanning studio.

**Sonnen|system** *das* solar system.

**Sonnen|uhr** *die* sundial.

**Sonnenunter|gang** *der* sunset.

**Sonnen|wende** *die* solstice.

**sonnig** *adj* sunny.

**Sonntag** (*pl* -e) *der* Sunday; *siehe auch* **Samstag.**

**sonntäglich** *adj* Sunday (*vor Subst*).

**sonntags** *adv* on Sundays; *siehe auch* **samstags.**

**Sonntags|arbeit** *die* Sunday working.

**Sonntags|fahrer, in** *der, die fam abw* Sunday driver.

**Sonntags|kind** *das* - **1.** [Glückskind] lucky person - **2.** [am Sonntag geboren] Sunday's child.

**sonor** *adj* sonorous ⟨⟩ *adv* sonorously.

**sonst** *adv* - **1.** [außerdem] else; ~ **nichts** nothing else; ~ **noch etwas/jemand?** *fam* anything/anybody else?; ~ **noch Fragen?** any more questions?; **wenn es ~ nichts ist** if that's all - **2.** [abgesehen hiervon] otherwise, apart from that; **wer/was (denn) ~?** who/what else? - **3.** [gewöhnlich] usually ⟨⟩ *konj* or (else); **jetzt beeil dich, ~ kommen wir zu spät** hurry up, or we'll be late.

**sonst.** *abk für* sonstig.

**sonstig** *adj* other.

**sonst was** *pron fam* something else; **er hätte dir ~ antun können** he could have done anything to you.

**sonst wer** *pron fam* someone else; [in Fragen] anyone else; **sie glaubt, sie ist ~** she thinks she's somebody special.

**sonst wie** *adv fam* in some other way; [in Fragen] in any other way.

**sonst wo** *adv fam* somewhere else; [in Fragen] anywhere else.

**sonst woher** *adv fam* somewhere else; [in Fragen] anywhere else; **die Leute kamen (von) ~** people came from all over; **das könnte ~ stammen** that could be from anywhere.

**sonst wohin** *adv fam* somewhere else; [in Fragen] anywhere else; **er fährt, ~ nur um seine Lieblingsband zu sehen** he travels all over just to see his favourite group.

**sooft** *konj* whenever.

**Sopran** (*pl* -e) *der* - **1.** [Stimmlage - Frau] soprano; [ - Knabe] treble - **2.** (*ohne pl*) [Stimme im Chor - Frauen] sopranos (*pl*); [ - Knaben] trebles (*pl*) - **3.** [Sängerin] soprano; [Sänger] treble.

**Sopranist, in** (*mpl* -en; *fpl* -nen) *der, die* treble (*f* soprano).

**Sorbe** (*pl* -n) *der* Sorb.

**Sorbet** [sɔr'beː] (*pl* -s) *der ODER das* sorbet.

**Sorbin** (*pl* -nen) *die* Sorb.

**sorbisch** *adj* Sorbian.

**Sorge** (*pl* -n) *die* - **1.** [Problem] worry; **sein Verhalten macht mir ~n** his behaviour worries me; **sich um jn/etw ~n machen** to worry about sb/sthg; **in ~ (um etw) sein** to be worried (about sthg) - **2.** [Pflege] care; **für jn/etw ~ tragen** *geh* to take care of sb/sthg; **~ dafür tragen, dass ...** to make sure that ...

➤ **keine Sorge** *interj* [keine Angst] don't worry!

**sorgen** *vi:* **für etw ~** to see to sthg; **für jn ~** to look after sb.

➤ **sich sorgen** *ref:* **sich um jn/etw ~** to be worried about sb/sthg.

**sorgenfrei** *adj* free from care ⟨⟩ *adv* in a carefree way.

**Sorgen|kind** *das* problem child.

**Sorgerecht** *das* custody; **das ~ für jn erhalten/haben** to get/have custody of sb.

**Sorgfalt** *die* care.

**sorgfältig** *adj* careful ⟨⟩ *adv* carefully.

**sorglos** *adj* carefree ⟨⟩ *adv* in a carefree way.

**Sorte** (*pl* -n) *die* sort, type.

➤ **Sorten** *pl* WIRTSCH foreign currency (*sg*).

**sortieren** *vt* to sort.

**sortiert** *adj:* **gut ~** well-stocked.

**Sortiment** (*pl* -e) *das* range.

**sosehr** *konj* however much.

**Soße** (*pl* -n) *die* [für Nudeln, Pudding] sauce; [für Braten] gravy; [für Salat] dressing.

**Souffleur** [su'fløːɐ] (*pl* -e) *der* prompter.

**Souffleuse** [su'fløːzə] (*pl* -n) *die* prompter.

**Soul** [soʊl] *der* soul.

**Sound** [saunt] (pl **-s**) der sound.

**Sound|karte** [] die EDV sound card.

**soundso** fam adj: **Seite ~** page such-and-such; **Frau ~** Mrs so-and-so ◇ adv [sowieso] anyway; **~ groß sein** to be of such-and-such a size; **~ viele Personen** such-and-such a number of people.

**Souterrain** [sutɛ'rɛ̃ː] (pl **-s**) der basement.

**Souvenir** [suvə'niːɐ̯] (pl **-s**) das souvenir.

**souverän** [zuvə'rɛːn] adj - **1.** POL sovereign - **2.** [überlegen] masterful ◇ adv - **1.** POL: **~ herrschen** ODER **regieren** to have sovereign power - **2.** [überlegen] masterfully.

**Souveränität** [zuvəʁɛni'tɛːt] die - **1.** POL sovereignty - **2.** [Überlegenheit] mastery.

**soviel** konj as far as; **~ ich weiß** as far as I know.

**so viel** adv so much; **~ du willst** as much as you want; **noch einmal ~** as much again; **dreimal ~** three times as much; **~ wie** as much as; **halb ~ (wie)** half as much/many (as).

**soweit** konj as far as; **~ ich weiß** as far as I know.

**so weit** adj: **~ sein** to be ready; **es ist ~** it is time ◇ adv on the whole; **~ wie möglich** as far as possible; **~ ich weiß** as far as I know.

**so wenig** adv: **~ wie möglich** as little as possible.

**sowie** konj as well as.

**sowieso** adv anyway.

**sowjetisch** adj Soviet (vor Subst).

**Sowjet|republik** die Soviet Republic.

**Sowjetunion** die: **die ehemalige ~** the former Soviet Union.

**sowohl** konj: **~ A als auch B** A as well as B, both A and B.

**Sozi** (pl **-s**) der fam Social Democrat; [Sozialist] socialist.

**sozial** adj social; [Einstellung] socially aware; **~er Beruf** caring profession ◇ adv socially; [handeln] in a socially aware manner; **~ eingestellt sein** socially aware.

**Sozial|abbau** der cuts (pl) in social services.

**Sozial|abgaben** pl social security contributions.

**Sozial|amt** das social security office.

**Sozial|arbeit** die social work.

**Sozial|arbeiter, in** der, die social worker.

**Sozial|demokrat, in** der, die Social Democrat.

**sozialdemokratisch** adj Social Democratic ◇ adv [wählen] Social Democrat; **~ eingestellt sein** to have Social Democratic views.

**Sozial|fall** der: **ein ~ sein** to be dependent on state benefit.

**Sozial|hilfe** die ≃ income support Br, ≃ welfare Am.

**Sozialisation** die socialization.

**Sozialismus** der socialism.

**Sozialist, in** (mpl **-en**; fpl **-nen**) der, die socialist.

**sozialistisch** adj socialist ◇ adv [wählen] socialist; **~ eingestellt sein** to have socialist views.

**sozialkritisch** adj socially critical ◇ adv in a socially critical way; **~ eingestellt sein** to have socially critical views.

**Sozial|kunde** die social studies (U).

**Sozial|lasten** pl social security costs.

**Sozial|leistungen** pl social security benefits.

**Sozial|minister, in** der, die social services minister.

**Sozial|pädagogik** die social education.

**Sozial|partner** der social partner.

**Sozial|plan** der scheme which seeks to alleviate the hardship resulting from mass redundancy.

**Sozial|politik** die social policy.

**Sozial|staat** der welfare state.

**Sozial|verhalten** das social behaviour.

**Sozial|ver|sicherung** die social security.

**Sozial|wohnung** die ≃ council flat Br, ≃ low-rent apartment Am.

**Soziologe** (pl **-n**) der sociologist.

**Soziologie** die sociology.

**Soziologin** (pl **-nen**) die sociologist.

**soziologisch** adj sociological ◇ adv sociologically.

**sozusagen** adv so to speak.

**Spaceshuttle** ['speːsʃat(ə)l] (pl **-s**) das space shuttle.

**Spachtel** (pl **-**) die ODER der spatula.

**Spachtel|masse** die filler.

**spachteln** vt [mit Spachtelmasse] to fill ◇ vi fam [essen] to tuck in.

**Spagat** (pl **-e**) der - **1.** SPORT: **einen ~ machen** to do the splits - **2.** fig balancing act.

**Spagetti, Spaghetti** pl spaghetti (U).

**spähen** vi - **1.** MIL to reconnoitre - **2.** geh [Ausschau halten] to peer; **nach jm/etw ~** to watch out for sb/sthg.

**Spalier** (pl **-e**) das - **1.** [von Menschen] double line; **~ stehen** to form a double line - **2.** [für Pflanzen] trellis.

**Spalt** (pl -e) der crack; **etw einen ~ weit** ODER **breit öffnen** to open sthg a crack.

**Spalte** (pl -n) die - **1.** [Öffnung] crack - **2.** TYPO column.

**spalten** vt [gen, CHEM & PHYS] to split; [Substanz, Verbindung] to break down.
➤ **sich spalten** ref - **1.** [kaputtgehen] to split - **2.** [sich aufspalten] to split up.

**Spaltung** (pl -en) die - **1.** [Teilen - von Land, Partei] splitting up (U); [Teilung - von Land, Partei] split - **2.** CHEM & PHYS splitting (U); [von Substanz] breaking down (U) - **3.** MED split.

**Span** (pl **Späne**) der shaving.

**Span|ferkel** das KÜCHE suckling pig.

**Spange** (pl -n) die - **1.** [Schmuckstück] slide Br, barrette Am - **2.** [Zahnspange] brace.

**Spanien** nt Spain.

**Spanier, in** ['ʃpaːnjɐ, rɪn] (mpl -; fpl -nen) der, die Spaniard.

**spanisch** adj Spanish ⟷ adv: **~ sprechen** to speak Spanish; **das kommt mir ~ vor** fam fig that seems weird to me.

**Spanisch(e)** das Spanish; siehe auch **Englisch(e)**.

**spann** prät ▷ **spinnen**.

**Spann** (pl -e) der instep.

**Spann|betttuch** das fitted sheet.

**Spanne** (pl -n) die period; **in der/einer ~ von ... bis** between ... and.

**spannen** vt [Bogen] to draw; [Muskeln] to tense; [Schnur] to tighten; [Netz] to stretch out ⟷ vi - **1.** fam [heimlich zusehen] to take a peep - **2.** [zu eng sein] to be too tight.
➤ **sich spannen** ref: **sich über etw** (A) **~** to span sthg.

**spannend** adj exciting ⟷ adv excitingly.

**Spanner** (pl -) der - **1.** fam abw [Mensch] peeping Tom - **2.** [Vorrichtung - für Tennisschläger] press; [ - für Hose] hanger; [ - für Schuh] tree.

**Spannerin** (pl -nen) die fam abw voyeuse.

**Spannkraft** die vigour.

**Spannung** (pl -en) die - **1.** [gen] tension; **jn/etw mit** ODER **voll ~ erwarten** to await sb/sthg eagerly - **2.** [elektrisch] voltage; **unter ~ stehen** to be live.
➤ **Spannungen** pl tension (sg).

**Spannungs|feld** das - **1.** fig [Interessensphäre] area of tension - **2.** ELEKTR electric field.

**Spannungs|gebiet** das area of tension.

**spannungsgeladen** adj tense.

**Spann|weite** die wingspan.

**Span|platte** die chipboard (U).

**Spar|buch** das savings book.

**Spar|büchse** die money box.

**Sparein|lage** die savings deposit.

**sparen** vt to save; **sich** (D) **etw ~** to save o.s. sthg; **spar dir deine dummen Bemerkungen** you can keep your silly remarks ⟷ vi to save; **an etw** (D) **~** to save on sthg; **für** ODER **auf etw** (A) **~** to save (up) for sthg; **mit etw nicht ~** geh not to stint on sthg.

**Sparer, in** (mpl -; fpl -nen) der, die saver.

**Sparflamme** die low flame; **auf ~ arbeiten** fig & hum to tick over; **auf ~ leben** fam to watch one's money.

**Spargel** (pl -) der asparagus (U).

**Spar|guthaben** das credit balance (with a savings bank).

**Spar|kasse** die savings bank.

**Spar|konto** das savings account.

**spärlich** adj [Haare] sparse; [Beifall, Maßnahmen] meagre ⟷ adv [bekleidet] scantily; [bewachsen, wachsen] sparsely; [bewaffnet] lightly.

**Spar|maßnahme** die economy measure.

**Spar|politik** die money-saving policy.

**Spar|programm** das economy drive.

**sparsam** adj economical; **mit etw ~ sein** to be economical with sthg ⟷ adv economically; **mit etw ~ umgehen** to be economical with sthg.

**Sparsamkeit** die economy.

**Spar|schwein** das piggy bank.

**spartanisch** adj - **1.** [anspruchslos] spartan - **2.** HIST Spartan ⟷ adv - **1.** [anspruchslos] spartanly - **2.** HIST in the Spartan manner.

**Sparte** (pl -n) die - **1.** WIRTSCH line of business - **2.** [in Zeitungen] section.

**Spaß** (pl **Späße**) der - **1.** [Vergnügen] fun; **zum ~** for fun; **an etw** (D) **~ haben** to enjoy sthg; **jm den ~ verderben** to spoil sb's fun; **es macht mir ~** I enjoy it; **Auto fahren macht mir keinen ~** I don't enjoy driving; **viel ~!** have fun!; **da hört der ~ auf** I draw the line at that; **mir ist der ~ vergangen** it's no fun any more - **2.** [Scherz] joke; [Streich] prank; **aus** ODER **im** ODER **zum ~** as a joke; **~ machen** [nicht ernst meinen] to be joking; **~/keinen ~ verstehen** to have a/no sense of humour.

**Spaß|bad** das swimming pool with flumes, sauna etc.

**spaßen** vi to joke; **mit jm/etw ist nicht zu ~** sb/sthg is not to be trifled with.

**spaßeshalber** adv for fun.

**spaßig** adj funny ⟷ adv in a funny way.

**Spaßmacher, in** (mpl -; fpl -nen) der, die joker.

**Spaßverderber, in** (mpl -; fpl -nen) der, die spoilsport.

**Spastiker, in** (mpl -; fpl -nen) der, die spastic.

**spastisch** *adj* spastic ◇ *adv:* ~ gelähmt sein to be a spastic.

**spät** *adj* late; **bis in die ~e Nacht** until late at night; **wie ~ ist es?** what's the time? ◇ *adv* late; **sie kam mal wieder zu ~** she was late again; **von früh bis ~** from dawn to dusk.

**spätabends** *adv* late in the evening.

**Spaten** (*pl* -) *der* spade.

**Spätentwickler, in** (*mpl* -; *fpl* -nen) *der, die* late developer.

**später** *adj & adv* later.
➡ **bis später** *interj* see you later!

**spätestens** *adv* at the latest.

**Spät|folge** *die* long-term effect.

**Spät|lese** (*pl* -n) *die* [Wein] late vintage.

**Spätnach|mittag** *der* late afternoon.

**Spät|schaden** *der* long-term damage *(U)*.

**Spät|schicht** *die* late shift.

**Spät|sommer** *der* late summer.

**Spätvor|stellung** *die* late show.

**Spatz** (*pl* -en) *der* - **1.** [Tier] sparrow - **2.** *fam* [Anrede] pet.

**Spätzle** *pl Süddt* small round noodles, similar to macaroni.

**spazieren** (*perf* ist spaziert) *vi* to stroll.

**spazieren gehen** (*perf* ist spazieren gegangen) *vi (unreg)* to go for a walk.

**Spazier|fahrt** *die* drive.

**Spazier|gang** *der* walk; **einen ~ machen** to go for a walk.

**Spazier|gänger, in** (*mpl* -; *fpl* -nen) *der, die* person going for a walk.

**Spazier|stock** *der* walking stick.

**SPD** [ɛspeː'deː] (*abk für* **Sozialdemokratische Partei Deutschlands**) *die* SPD.

**Specht** (*pl* -e) *der* woodpecker.

**Speck** *der* - **1.** [tierisch - von Schwein] pork fat; [ - geräuchert, durchwachsen] bacon; [ - von Wal, Robbe] blubber - **2.** *fam* [menschlich] flab.

**speckig** *adj* greasy.

**Speck|schwarte** *die* bacon rind *(U)*.

**Spediteur, in** [ʃpedi'tøːɐ̯, rɪn] (*mpl* -e; *fpl* -nen) *der, die* haulier; [für Umzug] furniture mover.

**Spedition** [ʃpedi'tsioːn] (*pl* -en) *die* haulage firm; [für Umzug] removal firm.

**Speer** (*pl* -e) *der* - **1.** *sport* javelin - **2.** [Waffe] spear.

**Speerwerfen** *das sport* javelin.

**Speiche** (*pl* -n) *die* spoke.

**Speichel** *der* saliva.

**Speicher** (*pl* -) *der* - **1.** [Dachboden] loft; **auf dem ~** in the loft - **2.** *EDV* memory.

**Speicher|kapazität** *die* *EDV* memory capacity.

**speichern** *vt* - **1.** [ansammeln, abspeichern] to store - **2.** *EDV* to save.

**speien** ['ʃpaiən] (*prät* spie; *perf* hat gespie(e)n) *vt* [Feuer, Lava] to spew; [Wasser] to spout ◇ *vi* to vomit.

**Speise** (*pl* -n) *die* dish; **warme ~n** hot food; **~n und Getränke** meals and drinks.

**Speise|eis** *das* ice cream.

**Speise|kammer** *die* larder.

**Speise|karte** *die* menu.

**speisen** *geh vt* - **1.** [essen] to dine on - **2.** [zu essen geben] to feed ◇ *vi* to dine.

**Speise|röhre** *die* gullet.

**Speise|saal** *der* dining room.

**Speise|salz** *das* salt *(for consumption)*.

**Speise|wagen** *der* dining car.

**Spektakel** (*pl* -) *das* [Aufführung, Ereignis] spectacle ◇ *der* racket; **~ machen** to make a racket.

**spektakulär** *adj* spectacular ◇ *adv* spectacularly.

**Spektrum** (*pl* Spektren) *das* spectrum.

**Spekulant, in** (*mpl* -en; *fpl* -nen) *der, die* speculator.

**Spekulation** (*pl* -en) *die* speculation.

**Spekulations|objekt** *das* object of speculation.

**Spekulatius** (*pl* -) *der* spiced Christmas biscuit shaped like a human or animal figure.

**spekulativ** *adj* speculative ◇ *adv* speculatively.

**spekulieren** *vi* - **1.** *fam* [hoffen]: **auf etw** (A) ~ to hope to get sthg - **2.** *wirtsch*: **(auf etw** (A)) ~ to speculate (on sthg) - **3.** [mutmaßen]: **über etw** (A) ~ to speculate about sthg.

**Spelunke** (*pl* -n) *die abw* dive.

**spendabel** *adj fam* generous.

**Spende** (*pl* -n) *die* donation; **um eine ~ bitten** to ask for donations/a donation.

**spenden** *vt* to donate; [Blut] to give ◇ *vi* to give.

**Spendenauf|ruf** *der* appeal for donations.

**Spender, in** (*mpl* -; *fpl* -nen) *der, die* donor; **wer war der edle ~?** who do I/we have to thank for this?

**spendieren** *vt:* **(jm) etw ~** to buy (sb) sthg.

**Sperling** (*pl* -e) *der* sparrow.

**Sperma** (*pl* -ta *oder* Spermen) *das* sperm.

**sperrangelweit** *adv:* **~ offen** wide open.

**Sperre** (*pl* -n) *die* - **1.** [Verbot & *sport*] ban; **eine ~ verhängen/aufheben** to impose/lift a ban

**S**

**- 2.** [Absperrung] barrier **- 3.** TECH locking device.

**sperren** vt **- 1.** [einsperren]: **jn/etw in etw** (A) **~** to shut sb/sthg in sthg **- 2.** [Konto, Kredit] to freeze; [Scheck] to stop **- 3.** [Straße] to close **- 4.** SPORT to ban.
 ➠ **sich sperren** ref: **sich (gegen etw) ~** to resist (sthg).

**Sperr|gebiet** das prohibited ODER no-go area.

**Sperrholz** das plywood.

**sperrig** adj bulky.

**Sperr|konto** das WIRTSCH blocked account.

**Sperr|müll** der bulky refuse (collected separately from normal refuse).

**Sperr|sitz** der [in Zirkus] ringside seat.

**Sperr|stunde** die closing time.

**Sperrung** (pl -en) die **- 1.** [von Straße] closing **- 2.** [von Konto, Kredit] freezing; [von Scheck] stopping.

**Spesen** pl expenses; **auf ~** on expenses.

**Spezi** (pl -s) fam der Süddt mate ⟨⟩ das cola and orangeade.

**Spezial|gebiet** das specialist field.

**spezialisieren** ➠ **sich spezialisieren** ref: **sich auf etw** (A) **~** to specialize in sthg.

**Spezialist, in** (mpl -en; fpl -nen) der, die specialist.

**Spezialität** (pl -en) die speciality Br, specialty Am.

**speziell** adj special ⟨⟩ adv specially.

**Spezies** ['∫peːtsiəs] (pl -) die species.

**spezifisch** adj specific ⟨⟩ adv specifically.

**spezifizieren** vt geh to specify.

**Sphäre** ['sfɛːrə] (pl -n) die sphere.

**Sphinx** (pl -e) die sphinx.

**spicken** vt **- 1.** KÜCHE: **etw mit etw ~** to lard sthg with sthg **- 2.** [ausstatten]: **etw mit etw ~** [Text, Rede] to pepper sthg with sthg ⟨⟩ vi to crib.

**Spick|zettel** der fam crib (sheet).

**spie** prät ⟹ speien.

**Spiegel** (pl -) der **- 1.** [Gegenstand] mirror **- 2.** [von Gewässern] surface **- 3.** MED level **- 4.** (ohne pl) [Magazin]: **der ~** German weekly news magazine.

**Spiegel|bild** das reflection.

**Spiegel|ei** das fried egg.

**spiegelglatt** adj very slippery.

**spiegeln** vi to shine.
 ➠ **sich spiegeln** ref: **sich in etw** (D) **~** to be reflected in sthg.

**Spiegelreflex|kamera** die reflex camera.

**spiegelverkehrt** adj: **eine ~e Darstellung** a mirror image ⟨⟩ adv the wrong way round.

**Spiel** (pl -e) das **- 1.** [Vergnügen, Wettkampf] game; **machen wir noch ein ~?** shall we have another game?; **das ist ein ~ mit dem Leben** you're risking your life by doing that; **ein ~ mit jm treiben** to play games with sb **- 2.** [von Musiker] playing; [von Schauspieler] acting; [von Sportler, Mannschaft] game **- 3.** TECH play **- 4.** [Glücksspiel] gambling **- 5.** RW: **auf dem ~ stehen** to be at stake; **etw aufs ~ setzen** to risk sthg; **jn/etw aus dem ~ lassen** to leave sb/sthg out of it.

**Spiel|automat** der slot machine, fruit machine Br.

**Spiel|ball** der **- 1.** [in Tennis] game point **- 2.** [Mensch] plaything.

**Spiel|bank** (pl -en) die casino.

**spielen** vi **- 1.** [gen] to play; **mit jm/etw ~** to play with sb/sthg **- 2.** [als Schauspieler] to act **- 3.** [Roman, Film] to be set **- 4.** [Glücksspiel machen] to gamble; **um etw ~** to play for sthg **- 5.** [einsetzen]: **seine Beziehungen ~ lassen** to pull strings; **seinen Charme ~ lassen** to use one's charm ⟨⟩ vt to play; **Klavier/Saxophon ~** to play the piano/saxophone; **Lotto ~** to do the lottery; **den Unschuldigen ~** to act ODER play the innocent; **den Ahnungslosen/Kranken ~** to pretend to know nothing/be ill.

**spielend** adv **- 1.** [einfach] easily **- 2.** [beim Spielen] through play.

**Spieler** (pl -) der **- 1.** [Mitspieler] player **- 2.** [Glücksspieler] gambler.

**Spielerei** (pl -en) die **- 1.** [Schnickschnack] gimmick **- 2.** abw [Herumspielen] fooling around **- 3.** fam [Leichtigkeit]: **das ist doch eine ~!** that's a piece of cake!

**Spielerin** (pl -nen) die **- 1.** [Mitspielerin] player **- 2.** [Glücksspielerin] gambler.

**spielerisch** adj **- 1.** [locker] effortless **- 2.** [Fähigkeit - in Sport, Musik] as a player; [- in Theater] as an actor ⟨⟩ adv **- 1.** [locker] effortlessly **- 2.** [in Sport]: **eine ~ enttäuschende Mannschaft** a team that gave a disappointing performance.

**Spiel|feld** das [für Fußball, Hockey] field, pitch Br; [für Tennis, Federball, Volleyball] court.

**Spiel|film** der feature film.

**Spiel|halle** die amusement arcade.

**Spiel|karte** die playing card.

**Spiel|kasino** das casino.

**Spielkonsole** (*pl* -n) *die* game ODER video console.

**Spiel|leitung** *die* [von Theaterstück, Fernsehstück] direction; **die ~ haben** [von Spielsendung] to be the quizmaster.

**Spiel|plan** *der* - **1.** [von Theatern] programme - **2.** SPORT fixture list.

**Spiel|platz** *der* playground.

**Spiel|raum** *der* leeway.

**Spiel|regel** *die* rule; **sich an die ~n halten** to stick to the rules.

**Spiel|uhr** *die* music box.

**Spiel|verderber, in** (*mpl* -; *fpl* -nen) *der, die* spoilsport.

**Spiel|waren** *pl* toys.

**Spiel|zeit** *die* - **1.** [von Theatern] season - **2.** SPORT: **die reguläre ~** normal time; [von Fußballspiel] the ninety minutes.

**Spiel|zeug** *das* - **1.** (*ohne pl*) [Spielsachen] toys (*pl*) - **2.** [einzelnes Spielgerät] toy.

**Spieß** (*pl* -e) *der* spit; **am ~** spit-roasted; **den ~ umdrehen** *fig* to turn the tables; **wie am ~ brüllen** *fig* to scream one's head off.

**Spieß|bürger, in** *der, die abw* (petit) bourgeois.

**spießen** *vt:* **etw auf etw** (*A*) **~** to skewer sthg with sthg.

**Spießer, in** (*mpl* -; *fpl* -nen) *der, die abw* (petit) bourgeois.

**spießig** *abw adj* (petit) bourgeois ⟨⟩ *adv* in a (petit) bourgeois way.

**Spieß|rute** *die:* **~n laufen** to run the gauntlet.

**Spike** [ʃpaik, spaik] (*pl* -s) *der* [von Schuh] spike; [von Reifen] stud.

➤ **Spikes** *pl* - **1.** [Schuhe] spikes - **2.** [Reifen] studded tyres.

**Spinat** (*pl* -e) *der* spinach.

**Spind** *der* locker.

**Spindel** (*pl* -n) *die* spindle.

**Spinett** (*pl* -e) *das* spinet.

**Spinne** (*pl* -n) *die* spider.

**spinnen** (*prät* **spann**; *perf* **hat gesponnen**) *vt* to spin ⟨⟩ *vi* - **1.** *fam* [verrückt sein] to be crazy; **du spinnst!, spinnst du?** are you crazy? - **2.** [arbeiten] to spin.

**Spinner** (*pl* -) *der* - **1.** *fam* [Verrückter] nutcase, nutter *Br* - **2.** [Arbeiter] spinner.

**Spinnerei** (*pl* -en) *die* - **1.** *fam* [Verrücktheit] crazy idea - **2.** [Betrieb] spinning mill.

**Spinnerin** (*pl* -nen) *die* - **1.** *fam* [Verrückte] nutcase, nutter *Br* - **2.** [Arbeiterin] spinner.

**Spinnwebe** (*pl* -n) *die* cobweb.

**Spion** (*pl* -e) *der* - **1.** [Geheimagent] spy - **2.** [Türspion] peephole.

**Spionage** [ʃpio'na:ʒə] *die* spying; **~ betreiben** to spy.

**Spionageabwehr** *die* counter-espionage.

**spionieren** *vi* - **1.** [Spionage treiben] to spy - **2.** *fam abw* [neugierig sein] to snoop.

**Spionin** (*pl* -nen) *die* spy.

**Spirale** (*pl* -n) *die* - **1.** [gewundene Linie] spiral - **2.** MED coil.

**spiritistisch** *adj* spiritualist.

**Spirituose** (*pl* -n) *die amt* spirit.

**Spiritus** (*pl* -se) *der* spirit.

**Spital** (*pl* -äler) *das Schweiz* hospital.

**spitz** *adj* - **1.** [Ende, Schuh, Bogen, Bemerkung] pointed; [Bleistift, Messer, Nadel] sharp - **2.** [Winkel] acute - **3.** *fam* [geil]: **auf jn ~ sein** to have the hots for sb; **~ darauf sein, etw zu tun** to be dying to do sthg ⟨⟩ *adv* - **1.** [zulaufen] to a point - **2.** [bemerken] pointedly.

**Spitz** (*pl* -e) *der* spitz.

**Spitz|bart** *der* goatee.

**Spitzbergen** *nt* Spitsbergen.

**Spitz|bogen** *der* pointed arch.

**Spitz|bube** *der fam* rascal.

**spitzbübisch** *adj* roguish ⟨⟩ *adv* roguishly.

**spitze** *fam adj* (unver) great ⟨⟩ *interj* great!

**Spitze** (*pl* -n) *die* - **1.** [von Messer, Bleistift] point; [von Kirchturm, Baum] top; [von Berg] peak - **2.** [Führung]: **an der ~** [in Betrieb, Partei] at the top; [in Rennen] in the lead - **3.** [Höchstwert] maximum; **etw auf die ~ treiben** *fig* to take sthg too far - **4.** *fam* [besonders gut]: **~ sein** to be great - **5.** [Bemerkung] gibe.

**Spitzel** (*pl* -) *der* informer.

**spitzen** *vt* - **1.** [spitz machen] to sharpen - **2.** [Ohren] to prick up.

**Spitzener|zeugnis** *das* top-quality product.

**Spitzen|geschwindigkeit** *die* top speed.

**Spitzen|klasse** *die* - **1.** [beste Qualität]: **~ sein** to be top-class - **2.** [die Besten] top flight.

**Spitzen|leistung** *die* top-quality performance.

**Spitzen|reiter, in** *der, die* leader.

**Spitzen|sportler, in** *der, die* top sportsman (*f* top sportswoman).

**spitzfindig** *abw adj* hairsplitting ⟨⟩ *adv:* **~ argumentieren** to split hairs.

**spitz|kriegen** *vt fam* to get wise to.

**Spitz|name** *der* nickname.

**spitzwinklig, spitzwinkelig** *adj* [Form, Dreieck] acute-angled ⟨⟩ *adv* to an acute angle.

**Spleen** [ˈʃpliːn, spliːn] (pl -s) der fam quirk.

**Splitter** (pl -) der [aus Holz, Glas] splinter; [von Bombe] fragment.

**Splitterlgruppe** die splinter group.

**splittern** (perf hat/ist gesplittert) vi to splinter.

**splitternackt** adj & adv stark naked.

**SPÖ** [ɛspeːˈøl] (abk für **Sozialdemokratische Partei Österreichs**) die Austrian Social Democratic Party.

**Spoiler** (pl -) der AUTO spoiler.

**sponsern** vt to sponsor.

**Sponsor** (pl -soren) der sponsor.

**Sponsorin** (pl -nen) die sponsor.

**spontan** adj spontaneous ⟨⟩ adv spontaneously.

**Spontaneität, Spontanität** (pl -en) die - **1.** [Eigenschaft] spontaneity - **2.** [Handlung] spontaneous act.

**sporadisch** adj sporadic ⟨⟩ adv sporadically.

**Spore** (pl -n) die spore.

**Sporn** (pl -e ODER Sporen) der - **1.** (pl Sporen) [für Pferd] spur - **2.** (pl Sporne) [Rammdorn] ram.

**Sport** der sport; ~ treiben to do sport.

**Sportlart** die sport.

**Sportlartikel** pl sports equipment (U).

**Sportlfest** das sports festival; SCHULE sports day.

**Sportfluglzeug** das light aircraft.

**Sportlgerät** das piece of sports apparatus.

**Sportlhalle** die sports hall.

**Sportlkleidung** die sportswear.

**Sportllehrer, in** der, die sports teacher.

**Sportler, in** (mpl -; fpl -nen) der, die sportsman (f sportswoman).

**sportlich** adj - **1.** [Leistung, Betätigung, Verhalten] sporting; [Person, Figur] sporty - **2.** [leger] casual ⟨⟩ adv - **1.** [den Sport betreffend]: **sich ~ betätigen** to do sport - **2.** [leger] casually - **3.** [fair] sportingly.

**Sportlmedizin** die sports medicine.

**Sportlnachrichten** pl sports news (U).

**Sportlplatz** der playing field.

**Sportlverein** der sports club.

**Sportlwagen** der - **1.** [Auto] sports car - **2.** [Kinderwagen] pushchair Br, stroller Am.

**Spot** (pl -s) der - **1.** [Werbefilm] commercial - **2.** [Scheinwerfer] spotlight.

**Spott** der mockery.

**spottbillig** adj & adv dirt-cheap.

**spotten** vi: (über jn/etw) ~ to mock (sb/sthg).

**spöttisch** adj mocking ⟨⟩ adv mockingly.

**Spottlpreis** der knockdown price.

**sprach** prät ⌐> sprechen.

**Sprache** (pl -n) die - **1.** [gen] language; **in deutscher ~** in German - **2.** RW: **jm die ~ verschlagen** to leave sb speechless; **etw zur ~ bringen** to bring sthg up; **raus mit der ~!** fam out with it!; **zur ~ kommen** to come up.

**Sprachlfehler** der speech defect.

**Sprachgelbrauch** der usage.

**Sprachlgefühl** das feeling for languages.

**Sprachlkenntnisse** pl knowledge (U) of languages.

**Sprachlkurs** der language course.

**Sprachllabor** das language laboratory.

**sprachlich** adj linguistic ⟨⟩ adv linguistically.

**sprachlos** adj [Staunen] speechless; **~ sein** to be speechless ⟨⟩ adv [dastehen] speechlessly.

**Sprachlreise** die language trip.

**Sprachlrohr** das mouthpiece.

**Sprachlwissenschaft** die linguistics (U).

**sprang** prät ⌐> springen.

**Spray** [ˈʃpreː, spreː] (pl -s) der ODER das spray.

**Sprayldose** die aerosol.

**Sprechlanlage** die intercom.

**Sprechlblase** die speech bubble.

**sprechen** (präs spricht; prät sprach; perf hat gesprochen) vi - **1.** [gen] to talk, to speak; **wer spricht da, bitte?** [am Telefon] who's speaking?; **mit jm ~** to talk to sb; **über jn/etw ~, von jm/etw ~** to talk about sb/sthg; **er sprach davon, dass ...** he mentioned that ...; **zu jm ~** to speak to sb; **auf jn/etw zu ~ kommen** to discuss sb/sthg - **2.** [als Redner auftreten] to speak; **frei ~** to speak without notes - **3.** [urteilend]: **das spricht für ihn** that's a point in his favour; **es spricht für ihn, dass ...** it's in his favour that ...; **alles spricht dafür, dass ...** there is every reason to believe that ...; **was spricht dagegen, jetzt Urlaub zu nehmen?** why shouldn't we go on holiday now? ⟨⟩ vt - **1.** [gen] to speak; **Deutsch ~** to speak German; **jn ~** to speak to sb - **2.** [Gebet] to say - **3.** [reden mit] to speak to; **er ist nicht** ODER **für niemanden zu ~ sein** he's unavailable.

**Sprecher, in** (mpl -; fpl -nen) der, die - **1.** [von Gruppe] spokesperson - **2.** [von Nachrichten] newsreader.

**Sprechlstunde** die - **1.** [beim Arzt] surgery - **2.** UNI time each week during which students can go to lecturers with individual problems.

**Sprechstundenlhilfe** die (doctor's) receptionist.

**Sprechlzimmer** das consulting room.

**spreizen** *vt* to spread.

**sprengen** *vt* - **1.** [mit Sprengstoff - Brücke, Gebäude] to blow up; [- Tür] to blow open; **etw in die Luft ~** to blow sthg up - **2.** [mit Wasser - Rasen, Garten] to water; [- Wäsche] to sprinkle with water.

**Spreng|kopf** *der* warhead.

**Spreng|kraft** *die* explosive force.

**Spreng|satz** *der* explosive charge.

**Spreng|stoff** *der* explosive.

**Spreu** *die* chaff.

**spricht** *präs* ⊳ **sprechen.**

**Sprichwort** (*pl* -wörter) *das* proverb.

**sprichwörtlich** *adj* proverbial.

**sprießen** (*prät* spross; *perf* ist gesprossen) *vi* to sprout.

**Spring|brunnen** *der* fountain.

**springen** (*prät* sprang; *perf* hat/ist gesprungen) *vi* - **1.** *(ist)* [hüpfen & SPORT] to jump; **auf etw** *(A)***/aus etw/von etw ~** to jump onto/out of/from sthg - **2.** [Ball] to bounce - **3.** *(ist)* [kaputtgehen] to crack - **4.** *RW:* **mein Vater hat 50 Euro ~ lassen** *fam* my dad gave me 50 euros ⊳ *vt (hat)* SPORT [Salto] to do.

**Springer** (*pl* -) *der* - **1.** [Sportler] jumper - **2.** [Schachfigur] knight.

**Springerin** (*pl* -nen) *die* jumper.

**Spring|form** *die* KÜCHE spring-release tin *Br*, springform pan *Am*.

**Spring|reiter, in** *der, die* show jumper.

**Sprint** (*pl* -s) *der* sprint.

**sprinten** (*perf* hat/ist gesprintet) *vi* to sprint.

**Spritze** (*pl* -n) *die* - **1.** [Injektion] injection - **2.** [Injektionsgerät, Küchengerät] syringe - **3.** [Wasserspritze] hose.

**spritzen** (*perf* hat/ist gespritzt) *vi* - **1.** *(hat)* [herumspritzen - Flüssigkeit, Person] to splash; [- Fett] to spit - **2.** *(ist)* [in bestimmte Richtung] to splash - **3.** *(hat)* [eine Spritze geben] to give an injection ⊳ *vt (hat)* - **1.** [gen] to spray; **jn nass ~** to splash sb - **2.** [Medikament, Droge] to inject; **sich/jm ein Schmerzmittel ~** to inject o.s./sb with a painkiller.

**Spritzer** (*pl* -) *der* splash; **einen ~ Würze** a dash of seasoning.

**spritzig** *adj* - **1.** [Wein] sparkling - **2.** [Auto, Läufer] lively.

**Spritz|pistole** *die* spray gun.

**Spritz|tour** *die:* **eine ~ machen** to go for a spin.

**spröde** *adj* - **1.** [trocken] dry - **2.** [brüchig] brittle - **3.** [Mensch, Art] standoffish ⊳ *adv* [unzugänglich] standoffishly.

**spross** *prät* ⊳ **sprießen.**

**Sprosse** (*pl* -n) *die* rung.

**Sprössling** (*pl* -e) *der fam hum* offspring.

**Sprotte** (*pl* -n) *die* sprat.

**Spruch** (*pl* Sprüche) *der* [Redensart] saying; **Sprüche klopfen** *fam abw* to talk big.

**Spruchband** (*pl* -bänder) *das* banner.

**spruchreif** *adj:* **die Sache ist noch nicht ~** [nicht entschieden] no decision has been taken on the matter as yet; [noch nicht offiziell] we still can't talk about the matter.

**Sprudel** (*pl* -) *der* sparkling mineral water.

**sprudeln** (*perf* hat/ist gesprudelt) *vi* - **1.** [gen] to bubble - **2.** [wenn Kohlensäure entweicht] to fizz.

**Sprüh|dose** *die* aerosol.

**sprühen** (*perf* hat/ist gesprüht) *vt (hat)* to spray ⊳ *vi* - **1.** *(ist)* [fliegen] to spray - **2.** *(hat)* [glänzen]: **vor Ideen ~** to be bubbling over with ideas; **vor Witz ~** to be sparklingly witty.

**Sprühregen** *der* drizzle.

**Sprung** (*pl* Sprünge) *der* - **1.** [Bewegung] jump - **2.** [Riss] crack; **einen ~ haben** to be cracked - **3.** *RW:* **(gerade) auf dem ~ sein** to be about to leave; **auf einen ~ vorbeikommen** *fam* to drop in for a minute; **jm auf die Sprünge helfen** to help sb out.

**Sprung|brett** *das* springboard.

**sprunghaft** *adj* - **1.** [unstet] erratic - **2.** [abrupt steigend] rapid ⊳ *adv* - **1.** [unstet] erratically - **2.** [abrupt steigend] rapidly.

**Sprung|schanze** *die* ski jump.

**SPS** [ɛs peː ɛs] (*abk für* **Sozialdemokratische Partei der Schweiz**) *die* Swiss Social Democratic Party.

**Spucke** *die* spit; **mir blieb die ~ weg** *fam* I was speechless.

**spucken** *vi* - **1.** [ausspucken] to spit; **ich spucke auf dein blödes Geld!** *salopp* I spit on your stupid money! - **2.** *fam* [sich übergeben] to puke ⊳ *vt* [Olivenstein, Blut] to spit.

**Spuk** *der* haunting; **dem ~ ein Ende machen** *fig* to return things to normal.

**spuken** *vi:* **in einem Haus ~** to haunt a house; **spukt es hier?** is this place haunted?

**Spül|becken** *das* sink.

**Spule** (*pl* -n) *die* - **1.** [Rolle] spool - **2.** ELEKTR coil.

**Spüle** (*pl* -n) *die* sink.

**spülen** *vt* - **1.** [Geschirr] to wash - **2.** [Wäsche] to rinse - **3.** [hinwegtragen]: **über Bord gespült werden** to be washed overboard ⊳ *vi* - **1.** [Geschirr reinigen] to do the dishes, to wash up *Br* - **2.** [Subj: Waschmaschine] to rinse - **3.** [hinunterspülen] to flush.

**Spül|maschine** *die* dishwasher.

**Spül|mittel** *das* washing-up liquid *Br*, dishwashing liquid *Am*.

**Spur** (*pl* -en) *die* - **1.** [Anzeichen] clue - **2.** [Abdruck] track - **3.** [Fahrstreifen] lane; **die ~ wechseln** to change lanes - **4.** [kleine Menge - von Zutat] hint; [ - von Substanz] trace - **5.** *RW:* **eine heiße ~** a strong lead; **jm/einer Sache auf der ~ sein** to be on sb's/sthg's track.

➤ **keine Spur** *interj* not at all!

**spürbar** *adj* - **1.** [fühlbar] noticeable - **2.** [deutlich] clear <> *adv* - **1.** [fühlbar] noticeably - **2.** [sichtlich] clearly.

**spuren** *vi fam* to toe the line.

**spüren** *vt* - **1.** [fühlen] to feel; **du wirst seinen Ärger zu ~ bekommen** you'll find out what it means for him to get angry; **du wirst die Konsequenzen zu ~ bekommen** you'll see what the consequences are - **2.** [ahnen] to sense.

**Spuren|element** *das* trace element.

**Spür|hund** *der* - **1.** [Hund] tracker dog - **2.** *fam* [Detektiv] sleuth.

**spurlos** *adv* - **1.** [verschwinden] without a trace - **2.** [ohne negative Auswirkungen]: **die Trennung ist nicht ~ an ihr vorübergegangen** the separation has left its mark on her.

**Spurt** (*pl* -s *ODER* -e) *der* [Endspurt] sprint for the line; [Zwischenspurt] spurt.

**spurten** (*perf* hat/ist gespurtet) *vi* - **1.** *SPORT* to put on a spurt - **2.** *fam* [schnell laufen] to sprint.

**Spur|wechsel** *der amt* change of lane.

**sputen** ➤ **sich sputen** *ref* to hurry up.

**Squash** [skvɔʃ] *das* squash.

**SR** [ɛs'ɛr] (*abk für* **Saarländischer Rundfunk**) *der Saarland regional broadcasting company.*

**SRG** [ɛsɛr'geː] (*abk für* **Schweizerische Radio- und Fernsehgesellschaft**) *die Swiss broadcasting company.*

**Sri Lanka** *nt* Sri Lanka.

**s. S.** (*abk für* **siehe Seite**) see p.

**SS** [ɛs'ɛs] *abk für* **Sommersemester** <> *die* (*abk für* **Schutzstaffel**) *MIL* SS.

**SSV** *abk für* **Sommerschlussverkauf.**

**s. t.** (*abk für* **sine tempore (ohne akademisches Viertel)**) *UNI* punctually.

**St.** - **1.** (*abk für* **Sankt**) St - **2.** *abk für* **Stück.**

**Staat** (*pl* -en) *der* state; **die ~en** *fam* the States; **mit jm/etw keinen ~ machen können** *fig* not to be able to make an impression with sb/sthg.

**Staaten|bund** *der* Confederation.

**staatenlos** *adj* stateless.

**staatl.** *abk für* **staatlich.**

**staatl. gepr.** (*abk für* **staatlich geprüft**) *government-certified.*

**staatlich** *adj* state <> *adv* by the state; **~ aner-** kannt government-approved; **~ geprüft** government-certified.

**Staats|angehörigkeit** *die* nationality; **doppelte ~** dual nationality.

**Staats|anwalt, anwältin** *der, die* public prosecutor *Br*, district attorney *Am*.

**Staats|besuch** *der* state visit.

**Staats|bürger, in** *der, die* citizen.

**Staats|dienst** *der* civil service.

**staatseigen** *adj* state-owned.

**Staats|examen** *das final exam taken by law and arts students at university.*

**Staats|feind, in** *der, die* enemy of the state.

**Staats|grenze** *die* border.

**Staats|kasse** *die* public purse.

**Staats|mann** (*pl* -männer) *der* statesman.

**Staatsober|haupt** *das* head of state.

**Staats|sekretär, in** *der, die* ≈ permanent secretary.

**Staats|sicherheitsdienst** *der security service in former GDR.*

**Staats|streich** *der* coup (d'état).

**staatstragend** *adj* pro-government.

**Staats|trauer** *die* state mourning.

**Staats|verdrossenheit** *die* political inertia.

**Staats|vertrag** *der* international treaty.

**Stab** (*pl* Stäbe) *der* rod; [von Gitter] bar; [von Dirigent] baton; *MIL* [von Pilger] staff; [zum Stabhochsprung] pole.

**Stäbchen** (*pl* -) *das* stick; [Essstäbchen] chopstick.

**Stabhoch|springer, in** *der, die SPORT* polevaulter.

**Stabhochsprung** *der SPORT* pole vault.

**stabil** *adj* - **1.** [Haus, Währung, Wetter] stable - **2.** [Person, Gesundheit] robust; [Möbel] solid.

**stabilisieren** *vt* to stabilize.

➤ **sich stabilisieren** *ref* to stabilize.

**Stabilität** *die* stability.

**Stab|reim** *der* alliteration (U).

**stach** *prät* ▷ **stechen.**

**Stachel** (pl -n) der - **1.** [von Tier] sting - **2.** [von Pflanze] thorn.

**Stachellbeere** die gooseberry.

**Stachelldraht** der barbed wire (U).

**stachelig, stachlig** adj prickly.

**Stachellschwein** das porcupine.

**stachlig** = stachelig.

**Stadion** [ˈʃtaːdjɔn] (pl **Stadien**) das stadium.

**Stadium** [ˈʃtaːdjʊm] (pl **Stadien**) das stage.

**Stadt** (pl **Städte**) die - **1.** [Ort] town; [Großstadt] city; **die ~ Köln** the city of Cologne - **2.** fam [Stadtverwaltung] town/city council.

**Stadtlauto** das city car club (run on a pay-as-you-use basis).

**stadtbekannt** adj well-known throughout the town/city.

**Stadtlbild** das [von Ort] townscape; [von Großstadt] cityscape.

**Stadtlbummel** der stroll through town.

**Städtebau** der urban development; [Planung] town planning.

**städtebaulich** adj of urban development.

**stadteinwärts** adv towards the town/city centre.

**Städter, in** (mpl -; fpl -nen) der, die town/city dweller.

**Städteltrip** der city tour.

**Stadtlflucht** die (ohne pl) town/city exodus.

**Stadtlgas** das gas (from the mains).

**Stadtlgespräch** das: **~ sein** to be the talk of the town.

**städtisch** adj - **1.** [der Stadtverwaltung] munici-pal - **2.** [der Stadt] urban.

**Stadtlkern** der town/city centre; **der histori-sche ~** the historical town/city centre.

**Stadtlmauer** die city wall.

**Stadtlmitte** die town/city centre.

**Stadtlpark** der municipal park.

**Stadtlplan** der street map.

**Stadtlrand** der outskirts (pl).

**Stadtlrat** der - **1.** [Versammlung] town/city council - **2.** [Person] town/city councillor.

**Stadtlrätin** die town/city councillor.

**Stadtrundlfahrt** die city tour.

**Stadtlstaat** der city state.

**Stadtlstreicher, in** der, die town/city tramp.

**Stadtlteil** der district.

**Stadtltor** das city gate.

**Stadtlverkehr** der town/city traffic.

**Stadtlverwaltung** die town/city council.

**Stadtlviertel** das district, quarter.

**Stadtlwerke** pl town/city services.

**Stadtlzentrum** das town/city centre, downtown area Am.

**Staffel** (pl -n) die SPORT relay race.

**Staffelei** (pl -en) die easel.

**staffeln** vt to grade.

**Stagnation** (pl -en) die stagnation (U).

**stagnieren** vi to stagnate.

**stahl** prät ▷ stehlen.

**Stahl** (pl **Stähle**) der steel (U).

**stählern** adj [aus Stahl] steel.

**Stahllindustrie** die steel industry.

**Stahllrohr** das steel pipe.

**staksen** (perf ist gestakst) vi fam to totter.

**Stalinismus** der Stalinism.

**Stall** (pl **Ställe**) der [gen] barn; [für Kühe] cow-shed; [für Pferde] stable; [für Kaninchen] hutch; [für Schweine] sty; [für Hühner] coop.

**Stamm** (pl **Stämme**) der - **1.** [von Baum] trunk - **2.** [Volk] tribe - **3.** [Wortstamm] stem.

**Stammlbaum** der family tree; [von Tier] pedi-gree.

**stammeln** vt & vi to stammer.

**stammen** vi to come; **aus etw ~** to come from sthg; **von jm ~** [herrühren] to come from sb; [gemacht sein] to be made by sb; **das Bild stammt von meiner Nachbarin** the picture was painted by my neighbour; **aus etw ~** [zeitlich] to date from sthg.

**Stammlgast** der regular.

**Stammhalter** (pl -) der fam hum son and heir.

**stämmig** adj stocky.

**Stammlkunde** der regular customer.

**Stammlkundin** die regular customer.

**Stammllokal** das local Br, favorite bar Am.

**Stammlplatz** der usual seat.

**Stammltisch** der - **1.** [Personen] group of regu-lar customers at a pub - **2.** [Treffen] meeting of regular customers at a pub - **3.** [Tisch] regulars' table at a pub.

**STAMMTISCH**

This term can refer to the table in a pub re-served for the regulars, to the group of reg-ulars who always sit there, and to their meetings. The "Stammtisch" is where the regulars play cards and talk, with politics, especially local politics, being a favourite topic for debate.

**stampfen** (perf hat/ist gestampft) vi - **1.** (hat) [auftreten] to stamp; **mit den Füßen ~** to stamp one's feet - **2.** (ist) [gehen] to stomp <> vt (hat) [Kartoffeln] to mash.

**stand** prät ▷ stehen.

**S**

**Stand** (pl **Stände**) der - **1.** [auf Messe, Markt] stand - **2.** (ohne pl) [das Stehen] standing position - **3.** (ohne pl) [Stellung - von Sonne] position; [ - von Zähler] reading; [ - von Entwicklung]: **der ~ der Dinge** the state of things; **auf dem neuesten ~ sein** to be right up-to-date - **4.** RW: **aus dem ~ heraus** just like that; **einen schweren ~ (bei jm) haben** to have a tough time (with sb); siehe auch **instand, imstande, zustande.**

**Standard** (pl **-s**) der standard.

**Standardlauflwerk** das EDV standard drive.

**Standarte** (pl **-n**) die standard.

**Standlbein** das - **1.** [Bein] supporting leg - **2.** fig & WIRTSCH mainstay (U).

**Stand-by** [stɛnt'baɪ] (pl **-s**) das [bei Elektrogeräten] standby mode; **in ~** in standby mode ⬦ der [bei Flugreisen] standby flight.

**Ständchen** (pl **-**) das serenade; **jm ein ~ bringen** to serenade sb.

**Ständer** (pl **-**) der [Gestell] stand.

**Standeslamt** das registry office.

**standesamtlich** adj registry-office ⬦ adv at the registry office.

**Standeslbeamte, beamtin** der, die registrar.

**standesgemäß** adj in keeping with one's social status ⬦ adv according to one's social status.

**Standeslunterschied** der class difference.

**standfest** adj - **1.** [Person] firm - **2.** [Möbel, Leiter] stable.

**standhaft** adj steadfast ⬦ adv: **sich ~ weigern** to refuse consistently.

**standlhalten** vi (unreg): **einer Sache** (D) **~** to withstand sthg.

**ständig** adj [Schmerzen, Belästigung] constant; [Mitglied] permanent ⬦ adv constantly.

**Standllicht** das (ohne pl) sidelights (pl).

**Standlort** der - **1.** [von Firma] location; **der ~ Deutschland** Germany as an industrial location - **2.** [von Person, Pflanze] position.

**Standlpunkt** der point of view; **auf dem ~ stehen, dass** ODER **den ~ vertreten, dass** to be of the view that.

**Standlspur** die hard shoulder Br, shoulder Am.

**Standluhr** die grandfather clock.

**Stange** (pl **-n**) die pole; [aus Metall] rod; **eine ~ Zigaretten** a carton of cigarettes; **ein Anzug von der ~** an off-the-peg suit; **bei der ~ bleiben** fam fig to stick it out; **eine ~ Geld** fam fig a fortune.

**Stängel** (pl **-**) der stalk.

**stank** prät ⬦ stinken.

**stänkern** vi fam abw to kick up a fuss.

**stanzen** vt - **1.** [Formen, Teile] to press - **2.** [Löcher] to punch.

**Stapel** (pl **-**) der - **1.** [Haufen] pile - **2.** SCHIFF: **vom ~ lassen** to launch; **vom ~ laufen** to be launched.

**Stapelllauf** der launching (of a ship).

**stapeln** vt to pile up.
⬦ **sich stapeln** ref [hingestellt werden] to be piled up; [sich türmen] to be piling up.

**stapfen** (perf **ist gestapft**) vi to tramp.

**Star** [ʃtaːɐ̯] (pl **-e** ODER **-s**) der - **1.** (pl **Stare**) [Vogel] starling - **2.** (pl **Stars**) [Person] star - **3.** (pl **Stare**) [Augenkrankheit]: **der graue ~** cataract; **der grüne ~** glaucoma (U).

**starb** prät ⬦ sterben.

**stark** (kompar **stärker**; superl **stärkste**) adj - **1.** [gen] strong - **2.** [Sturm, Schnupfen, Verkehr] heavy - **3.** fam [toll] great; **stark!** great! - **4.** [dick - Brille, Wände, Träger] thick; [ - Figur, Beine] large - **5.** [mit Maßangabe] thick - **6.** [Beteiligung] good; [Interesse] strong - **7.** GRAM: **~e Verben** strong verbs - **8.** RW: **sich für jn/etw ~ machen** to stand up for sb/sthg ⬦ adv - **1.** [intensiv - zuschlagen, schwanken, etw vermuten] strongly; [ - regnen] heavily - **2.** [viel] a lot.

**Stärke** (pl **-n**) die - **1.** [gen] strength - **2.** [von Brett, Platte, Papier] thickness - **3.** [für Wäsche] starch; [Speisestärke] cornflour Br, cornstarch Am.

**stärken** vt - **1.** [kräftigen] to strengthen - **2.** [Wäsche] to starch.
⬦ **sich stärken** ref to fortify o.s.

**Starkstrom** der (ohne pl) high-voltage current.

**Stärkung** (pl **-en**) die - **1.** [Mahlzeit] refreshment - **2.** [Aufbau] strengthening.

**starr** adj - **1.** [unbeweglich - Glieder, Material] stiff; [ - Blick] fixed; **~ vor Kälte/Schreck** stiff with cold/rigid with fear - **2.** [System, Regeln] fixed ⬦ adv [unflexibel] doggedly.

**starren** vi - **1.** [sehen] to stare; **auf jn/etw ~** to stare at sb/sthg - **2.** [emporragen]: **aus etw ~** to rise up out of sthg; **vor** ODER **von Dreck ~** to be absolutely filthy.

**starrsinnig** adj obstinate.

**Start** (pl **-s** ODER **-e**) der - **1.** [gen] start; **an den ~ gehen** to go to the starting line - **2.** [von Flugzeug] takeoff; [von Rakete] launch.

**Startlbahn** die runway.

**Startlblock** der SPORT starting block.

**starten** (perf **hat/ist gestartet**) vi (ist) - **1.** [Läufer, Pferd, Rennauto] to start - **2.** [Flugzeug] to take off - **3.** [abreisen] to set off ⬦ vt (hat) to start.

**Startlerlaubnis** die - **1.** [für Sportler] permission to participate (U) - **2.** [für Flugzeug] clearance for takeoff (U).

**Start|hilfe** *die* - **1.** [finanzielle Unterstützung] initial financial support *(U)* - **2.** [bei Panne]: **jm ~ geben** to give sb a jump-start.

**Start|kapital** *das* initial capital.

**startklar** *adj* ready to go <> *adv:* **jn/etw ~ machen** to get sb/sthg ready to go.

**Stasi** *(abk für* **Staatssicherheit)** *die* ODER *der* Stasi, *security service in former GDR.*

> **STASI**
>
> The East German secret police, an instrument of state control and repression whose methods showed no respect for human rights, was responsible for monitoring the loyalty of East German citizens towards the state and towards Communism. The Stasi kept files on all those who fell under suspicion and encouraged informers, often through blackmail and intimidation. The opening of these files has led to violent disputes throughout Germany.

**Statement** ['steːtmənt] *(pl* -**s)** *das* statement.

**Statik** *die* statics *(U).*

**Station** *(pl* -**en)** *die* - **1.** [im Krankenhaus] ward - **2.** [Haltestelle, Halt] stop; **~ machen** to stop off - **3.** [für Forschung] plant.

**stationär** *adv:* **~ behandeln** to treat as an inpatient.

**stationieren** *vt* to station.

**statisch** *adj* static.

**Statist** *(pl* -**en)** *der* extra.

**Statistik** *(pl* -**en)** *die* statistics *(pl).*

**Statistin** *(pl* -**nen)** *die* extra.

**statistisch** *adj* statistic <> *adv* statistically.

**Stativ** *(pl* -**e)** *das* tripod.

**statt** *konj* instead of; **~ früher aufzustehen, ...** instead of getting up earlier, ... <> *präp (+G)* instead of; **~ meiner** in my place, instead of me.

**stattdessen** *adv* instead.

**Stätte** *(pl* -**n)** *die* **geh** place.

**statt|finden** *vi (unreg)* to take place.

**statt|geben** *vi (unreg) amt:* **einer Sache** *(D)* **~** to approve sthg.

**stattlich** *adj* - **1.** [Erscheinung, Größe] imposing - **2.** [Summe, Anwesen] considerable <> *adv* considerably.

**Statue** ['ʃtaːtu̯ə, 'staːtu̯ə] *(pl* -**n)** *die* statue.

**Statur** *(pl* -**en)** *die* build.

**Status** *(pl* -) *der* - **1.** [Position] status - **2.** [Zustand] state.

**Status|symbol** *das* status symbol.

**Stau** *(pl* -**s** ODER -**e)** *der* - **1.** [von Autos] traffic jam; **im ~ stehen** to be stuck in a traffic jam - **2.** *(ohne pl)* [von Wasser] build-up.

**Staub** *der* dust; **~ wischen** to dust; **~ aufwirbeln** *fig* to create a stir; **sich aus dem ~ machen** *fam fig* to make one's getaway.
➤ **Staub saugen** *vi* = **staubsaugen**.

**stauben** *vi* to be dusty.

**staubig** *adj* dusty.

**staubsaugen** *vt* & *vi* to vacuum.

**Staubsauger** *(pl* -) *der* vacuum cleaner.

**Staub|tuch** *das* duster.

**Stau|damm** *der* dam.

**Staude** *(pl* -**n)** *die* perennial.

**stauen** *vt* [Wasser] to dam; [Blut] to staunch.
➤ **sich stauen** *ref* - **1.** [Autos] to form a tailback - **2.** [sich ansammeln - Wut, Hitze] to build up; [ - Luft] to accumulate.

**staunen** *vi* to be amazed; **über jn/etw ~** to be amazed at sb/sthg.

**Staunen** *das* amazement.

**Stau|see** *der* reservoir.

**Stauung** *(pl* -**en)** *die* [von Wasser] damming *(U);* [von Blut] staunching *(U);* [von Autos] build-up.

**Std.** *abk für* **Stunde.**

**Steak** [ʃteːk, steːk] *(pl* -**s)** *das* KÜCHE steak.

**stechen** *(präs* **sticht;** *prät* **stach;** *perf* **hat gestochen)** *vt* - **1.** [verletzen - mit Stachel] to sting; [ - mit Nadel] to prick; [ - mit Spritze] to stick; [ - mit Messer] to stab - **2.** [Spargel] to cut <> *vi* - **1.** [Nadel, Dorn, Stachel] to prick; **mit etw in etw** *(A)* **~** to stick sthg in sthg - **2.** [Sonne] to beat down.
➤ **sich stechen** *ref* [sich verletzen] to prick o.s.

**stechend** *adj* - **1.** [Blick] piercing - **2.** [Geruch] pungent - **3.** [Schmerz] stabbing - **4.** [Sonne] burning.

**Stech|mücke** *die* mosquito.

**Stech|uhr** *die* time clock.

**Steck|brief** *der* description *(of a criminal).*

**Steck|dose** *die* socket.

**stecken** *vt* to put; **sich** *(D)* **etw in etw** *(A)* **~** to put sthg in sthg; **etw an etw** *(A)* **~** to put sthg on sthg; **die Kinder ins Bett ~** *fam* to put the children to bed <> *vi* - **1.** [gen] to be; **wo steckst du?** where have you got to? - **2.** *RW:* **sie zeigte was in ihr steckt** she showed what she can do; **hinter etw** *(D)* **~** *fam* to be behind sthg; **voller Ideen ~** to be full of ideas.

**stecken bleiben** *(perf* **ist stecken geblieben)** *vi (unreg)* to get stuck.

**stecken lassen** *vt (unreg)* to leave; **einen Schlüssel ~** to leave the key in the lock.

**Stecken|pferd** *das* hobbyhorse.

**Stecker** *(pl* -) *der* plug.

**Steck|nadel** *die* pin.

**Steg** *(pl* -**e)** *der* - **1.** [über Bach, Fluss] footbridge - **2.** [zu Boot] jetty - **3.** [an Hosen] stirrup.

**S**

**Stegreif** *der:* aus dem ~ spielen *fig* to improvise; aus dem ~ eine Rede halten to give an impromptu speech.

**Stehauf|männchen** *das* - 1. *fam* [Mensch]: er ist ein ~ nothing gets him down - 2. [Spielzeug] tumbler.

**stehen** (*prät* stand; *perf* hat gestanden) *vi* - 1. [aufrecht stand] to stand - 2. [sich befinden] to be; die Vase steht auf dem Tisch the vase is on the table; du stehst mir im Weg you're in the way; vor Schwierigkeiten/einer Wahl ~ to be faced with difficulties/a choice; unter Alkohol ~ to be under the influence (of alcohol); es steht 15:3 the score is 15–3; wie steht es mit deiner Gesundheit? how is your health?; es steht zu hoffen, dass ... it is to be hoped that ... - 3. [geschrieben sein]: auf dem Schild steht, dass ... the notice says that ...; in der Zeitung steht, dass ... it says in the paper that ... - 4. [Uhr, Motor, Zeiger] to have stopped; der Zeiger steht auf 8 Uhr the clock says 8 o'clock - 5. [Kleid, Farbe, Frisur]: jm ~ to suit sb; jm gut/nicht ~ to suit/not to suit sb - 6. GRAMM: mit Akkusativ/Dativ ~ to take the accusative/dative; das Substantiv steht im Plural the noun is in the plural - 7. *fam* [mögen]: auf jn ~ to fancy sb; auf etw (A) ~ to be into sthg - 8. [stellvertretend]: für etw ~ to stand for sthg - 9. [verantwortlich]: zu jm/etw ~ to stand by sb/sthg; hinter jm/etw ~ to be behind sb/sthg - 10. [beurteilend]: wie stehst du dazu? what do you think about that? - 11. RW: alles ~ und liegen lassen to drop everything; wie stehts? *fam* how are things?; mit etw ~ und fallen to depend on sthg; die Arbeit steht mir bis hier *fam* I've had it up to here with this job.

◆ **sich stehen** *ref fam* - 1. [verstehen]: sich mit jm gut ~ to get on with sb; sich mit jm schlecht ~ not to get on with sb - 2. [finanziell]: sich gut/schlecht ~ to be well-/badly-off.

**Stehen** *das:* im ~ standing up.

**stehen bleiben** (*perf* ist stehen geblieben) *vi* (*unreg*) - 1. [anhalten] to stop; wo waren wir stehen geblieben? where were we?; die Zeit ist stehen geblieben time has stood still - 2. [nach Schlag, Erschütterung] to be left standing - 3. [Satz] to stay.

**stehend** *adj* - 1. [im Stand] standing - 2. [gebräuchlich] standard - 3. [unbewegt] stagnant <> *adv* [im Stand] standing.

**stehen lassen** (*perf* hat stehen lassen ODER stehen gelassen) *vt* (*unreg*) to leave; alles stehen und liegen lassen *fam fig* to drop everything.

**Steh|lampe** *die* standard lamp.

**stehlen** (*präs* stiehlt; *prät* stahl; *perf* hat gestohlen) *vt* [entwenden] to steal; sie kann mir gestohlen bleiben *fam* she can get lost; jm die Zeit ~ to waste sb's time.

◆ **sich stehlen** *ref* [sich davonmachen] to steal.

**Steh|platz** *der* standing place.

**Steh|vermögen** *das* stamina.

**Steierin** (*pl* -nen) *die* Styrian.

**Steiermark** *die* Styria.

**steif** *adj* stiff; [Sahne] thick <> *adv* stiffly; Sahne/Eiweiß ~ schlagen to beat cream until thick/egg white until stiff; ~ und fest behaupten *fig* to swear blind.

**Steig|bügel** *der* stirrup.

**Steig|eisen** *das* [beim Bergsteigen] crampon.

**steigen** (*prät* stieg; *perf* ist gestiegen) *vi* - 1. [hinaufsteigen]: auf etw (A) ~ [auf Leiter, Berg, Baum] to climb sthg; [auf Stuhl, Pferd] to climb onto sthg; [auf Fahrrad, Motorrad] to get on sthg - 2. [hineinsteigen]: in etw (A) ~ [Zug, Straßenbahn] to get on sthg; [Auto, Taxi] to get into sthg - 3. [aussteigen]: aus etw ~ [Zug, Straßenbahn] to get off sthg; [Auto, Taxi] to get out of sthg - 4. [absteigen]: von etw ~ to get off sthg - 5. [Flugzeug, Preis, Temperatur, Wasser] to rise; [Nebel] to lift; einen Drachen ~ lassen to fly a kite - 6. [Spannung, Misstrauen] to grow - 7. *fam* [Fest] to take place; ein Fest ~ lassen to have a party.

**steigend** *adj* [Zinsen, Temperatur] rising; [Tendenz, Bedarf] growing.

**steigern** *vt* - 1. [gen] to increase - 2. GRAM to compare - 3. [Leistung] to improve.

◆ **sich steigern** *ref* - 1. [sich verbessern] to improve - 2. [stärker werden] to intensify.

**Steigerung** (*pl* -en) *die* - 1. [von Preis, von Dosis] increase - 2. [von Leistung] improvement - 3. GRAM comparison.

**steil** *adj* - 1. [Wand, Berg, Weg] steep - 2. [Karriere, Aufstieg] rapid <> *adv* - 1. [senkrecht] steeply - 2. [schnell] rapidly.

**Steil|hang** *der* steep slope.

**Steil|küste** *die* cliffs (*pl*).

**Stein** (*pl* -e) *der* stone; mir fällt ein ~ vom Herzen it's a weight off my mind; bei jm einen ~ im Brett haben to be in sb's good books; jm ~e in den Weg legen to make things difficult for sb.

**Stein|bock** *der* - 1. [Tier] ibex - 2. ASTROL Capricorn; ~ sein to be a Capricorn.

**Stein|bruch** *der* quarry.

**steinern** *adj* - 1. [Treppe, Bank] stone - 2. [Miene] stony.

**Steingut** *das* earthenware.

**steinhart** *adj* rock-hard.

**steinig** *adj* stony.

**Stein|kohle** *die* coal.

**Stein|metz, in** (*mpl* -en; *fpl* -nen) *der, die* stonemason.

**Stein|pilz** *der* cep.

**steinreich** *adj* very rich.

**Stein|schlag** *der* falling rocks *(pl)*.

**Stein|zeit** *die* Stone Age.

**steinzeitlich** *adj* [der Steinzeit] Stone Age.

**Steirer** *(pl -) der* Styrian.

**steirisch** *adj* Styrian.

**Steiß** *(pl -e) der* coccyx.

**Steiß|bein** *das* coccyx.

**Stelle** *(pl -n) die* - **1.** [Platz] place; [kleine Stelle] patch; [im Text] passage; **an vierter ~** in fourth place; **- 2.** [Arbeitsplatz] job; **eine freie ~** a vacancy **- 3.** [Amt] office **- 4.** MATH figure; **eine Zahl mit vier ~n** a four-figure number; **zwei ~n nach/hinter dem Komma** two decimal places **- 5.** *RW:* **an deiner ~** if I were you; **auf der ~** immediately; **zur ~ sein** to be on the spot.

**stellen** *vt* - **1.** [hinstellen] to put - **2.** [aufrecht stellen] to place upright - **3.** [Gerät, Aufgabe] to set; **jm eine Frage ~** to ask sb a question; **der Wecker auf drei Uhr ~** to set the alarm clock for three o'clock; **das Radio lauter/leiser ~** to turn the radio up/down - **4.** [zur Verfügung stellen]: **jm etw ~** to provide sb with sthg - **5.** [Diagnose, Prognose, Bedingung] to make - **6.** [Forderung, Antrag] to submit - **7.** [Dieb, Täter] to catch - **8.** FOTO to pose - **9.** [konfrontieren mit]: **jn vor etw** *(A)* **~** to present sb with sthg - **10.** *RW:* **gut/schlecht gestellt sein** to be well/badly off; **auf sich** *(A)* **(selbst) gestellt sein** to have to fend for o.s.

➤ **sich stellen** *ref* - **1.** [sich hinstellen] to go and stand; **sich auf einen Stuhl ~** to stand on a chair - **2.** [nicht ausweichen]: **sich einer Sache** *(D)* **~** to face sthg - **3.** [Meinung äußern]: **sich kritisch zu etw ~** to take a critical view of sthg; **wie ~ Sie sich zu …?** what's your view on …? - **4.** [ablehnen]: **sich gegen jn/etw ~** to be against sb/sthg - **5.** [unterstützen]: **sich hinter jn/etw ~** to back sb/sthg - **6.** [so tun als ob]: **sich krank/schlafend ~** to pretend to be ill/asleep - **7.** [sich melden] to give o.s. up - **8.** *RW:* **sich gut mit jm ~** to get on good terms with sb.

**Stellen|angebot** *das* job offer.

**Stellen|anzeige** *die* job advertisement.

**Stellen|gesuch** *das* 'situation wanted' advertisement.

**Stellen|vermittlung** *die* employment agency.

**stellenweise** *adv* in places.

**Stellen|wert** *der* value; **die Freizeit hat einen hohen ~ in meinem Leben** leisure time occupies an important place in my life.

**Stell|platz** *der* space; [für Auto] parking space.

**Stellung** *(pl -en) die* position; **in seiner ~ als Vorsitzender** in his capacity as chairman; **meine ~ zu diesen Dingen kennst du ja bereits** you already know my position ODER where I stand on these matters; **(zu etw) ~ nehmen** to comment (on sthg); **(zu etw) ~ beziehen** to express an opinion (about sthg).

**Stellungnahme** *(pl -n) die* statement.

**stellvertretend** *adj* deputy; [vorübergehend] acting ◇ *adv* as a deputy.

**Stell|vertreter, in** *der, die* deputy.

**Stelze** *(pl -n) die* - **1.** [Krücke] stilt - **2.** [Vogel] wagtail.

**stemmen** *vt* - **1.** [drücken] to press - **2.** SPORT to lift; **ein Gewicht ~** to lift a weight above one's head; **den Körper hoch ~** to push one's body up; **die Hände in die Hüften ~** to put one's hands on one's hips.

➤ **sich stemmen** *ref* [sich drücken] to push o.s. up; **sich gegen etw ~** [sich abstemmen] to brace o.s. against sthg; **sich gegen etw ~** [sich wehren] to resist sthg.

**Stempel** *(pl -) der* [Gerät, Abdruck] stamp; [auf Briefmarke] postmark; [in Schmuckstück] hallmark; **jm/einer Sache seinen ~ aufdrücken** *fig* to leave one's mark on sb/sthg.

**Stempel|kissen** *das* inkpad.

**stempeln** *vt* [Stempel anbringen] to stamp; [Briefmarke] to cancel; [Post] to postmark; [Schmuckstück] to hallmark; **jn zu etw ~** [klassifizieren] to brand sb sthg ◇ *vi:* **~ gehen** *fam* to be on the dole *Br* ODER welfare *Am*.

**Stengel** *der* = Stängel.

**Steno** *die fam* shorthand.

**Stenografie, Stenographie** *(pl -n) die* shorthand.

**stenografieren, stenographieren** *vt* to take down in shorthand ◇ *vi* to do shorthand.

**Stenotypist, in** *(mpl -en; fpl -nen) der, die* shorthand typist.

**Stepp|decke** *die* quilt.

**Steppe** *(pl -n) die* steppe.

**steppen** *vi* [tanzen] to tap dance ◇ *vt* [nähen] to backstitch.

**Stepp|tanz** *der* tap dance.

**Sterbe|hilfe** *die* [Lebensverkürzung] euthanasia.

**sterben** *(präs* **stirbt***; prät* **starb***; perf* **ist gestorben***) vi* to die; **an etw** *(D)* **~** to die of sthg; **vor etw** *(D)* **~** *fig fam* to die of sthg; **diese Frau/ das Projekt ist für mich gestorben** *fam* as far as I'm concerned this woman/the project no longer exists.

**sterblich** *adj* mortal.

**stereo** *adj (unver)* stereo ◇ *adv* in stereo.

**Stereo** *das:* **in ~** in stereo.

**Stereoan|lage** *die* stereo (system).

**stereotyp** *adj* stereotyped ◇ *adv* in a stereotyped way.

S

**steril** adj sterile ⟷ adv - **1.** [leblos]: ~ **wirken** to be sterile - **2.** [ohne Keime]: **etw ~ machen** to sterilize sthg.

**Sterilisation** (pl -en) die sterilization.

**sterilisieren** vt to sterilize.

**Sterilität** die sterility.

**Stern** (pl -e) der star; **das steht noch in den ~en** that's impossible to say at the moment.

**Stern|bild** das constellation.

**Sternenhimmel** der (ohne pl) starry sky.

**Sternen|system** das galaxy.

**sternhagelvoll** fam adj plastered ⟷ adv drunkenly.

**Stern|schnuppe** (pl -n) die shooting star.

**Stern|stunde** die geh great moment.

**Stern|warte** (pl -n) die observatory.

**Stern|zeichen** das star sign, sign of the zodiac.

**stetig** adj steady; [Belästigungen, Wiederholung] constant ⟷ adv steadily; [wiederholen] constantly.

**stets** adv always.

**Stettin** nt Szczecin.

**Steuer** (pl -n ODER -) die - **1.** (pl -n) [Abgabe] tax; **etw von der ~ absetzen** to claim sthg against tax; **~n hinterziehen** to be guilty of tax evasion - **2.** (pl -) fam [Steuerbehörde]: **die ~** the taxman ⟷ das (pl -) [von Fahrzeug] (steering) wheel; [von Flugzeug] controls (pl); [von Schiff] helm; **am ~ sitzen** to be at the wheel.

**Steuer|berater, in** der, die tax consultant.

**Steuer|bord** das starboard.

**Steuererklärung** die tax return.

**Steuer|fahndung** die [Behörde] body responsible for carrying out investigations into cases of suspected tax evasion.

**Steuer|karte** die ≃ P60 Br, form filled in by employer stating annual income and tax paid.

**Steuer|klasse** die tax bracket (based on income, marital status and number of children).

**steuerlich** adj tax (vor Subst) ⟷ adv in terms of taxation; **~ befreien** to exempt from taxation.

**Steuer|loch** das tax shortfall.

**Steuermann** (pl -männer) der helmsman.

**steuern** vt - **1.** [lenken - Schiff, Fahrzeug] to steer; [ - Flugzeug] to fly; [ - Spielzeugauto] to control - **2.** [beeinflussen] to guide, to steer - **3.** [organisieren] to organize - **4.** [kontrollieren & TECH] to control.

**Steuer|oase** die tax haven.

**steuerpflichtig** adj [Einnahme] taxable; [Person] liable to pay tax.

**Steuer|prüfer, in** der, die tax inspector.

**Steuer|rad** das [von Auto] steering wheel; [von Flugzeug] wheel; [von Schiff] wheel, helm.

**Steuer|recht** das tax law.

**Steuer|reform** die tax reform.

**Steuer|ruder** das rudder.

**Steuerung** (pl -en) die - **1.** [Lenken - von Auto, Schiff] steering; [ - von Flugzeug] flying; [ - von Modellflugzeug] controlling - **2.** [Steuergerät] controls (pl).

**Steuer|vergünstigung** die tax break.

**Steuervoraus|zahlung** die advance payment of tax.

**Steuer|zahler, in** (mpl -; fpl -nen) der, die taxpayer.

**Steuer|zeichen** das EDV cursor.

**Steward, Stewardess** ['stjuːɐt, ʃtjuːɐt, 'stjuːɐdɛs, ʃtjuːɐdɛs] (mpl -s; fpl -en) der, die steward (f stewardess).

**StGB** [ɛsteːgeːˈbeː] (abk für **Strafgesetzbuch**) das penal code.

**stibitzen** vt fam to pinch.

**Stich** (pl -e) der - **1.** [Einstich - von Messer] stab; [ - von Biene, Wespe] sting; [ - von Mücke] bite - **2.** [Färbung] tinge - **3.** [beim Nähen & MED] stitch - **4.** [Schmerz] stabbing pain; [in der Seite] stitch - **5.** [Bemerkung] gibe; **das war ein ~ gegen dich** that was a dig at you - **6.** [beim Kartenspiel] trick - **7.** [Bild] engraving - **8.** RW: **einen ~ haben** salopp [verrückt sein] to be nuts; [ungenießbar werden] to have gone ODER be off; **jn/etw im ~ lassen** [verlassen] to leave sb/sthg; [fallen lassen] to abandon sb/sthg; **wenn mich mein Orientierungssinn nicht im ~ lässt** if my sense of direction isn't deceiving me.

**Stichelei** (pl -en) die fam abw - **1.** (ohne pl) [Handlung] gibing - **2.** [Äußerung] gibe.

**sticheln** vt to tease ⟷ vi to make snide remarks.

**Stich|flamme** die jet of flame.

**stichhaltig** adj valid; [Beweis] conclusive ⟷ adv validly; [beweisen, widerlegen] conclusively.

**Stich|probe** die - **1.** [Menge] (random) sample - **2.** [Handlung] spot check.

**sticht** präs ⊳ **stechen**.

**Stich|tag** der effective date.

**Stich|wahl** die final ballot.

**Stich|wort** (pl -e ODER -wörter) das - **1.** [Notiz] note - **2.** [Eintrag] headword - **3.** [Schlüsselwort] keyword - **4.** [im Theater] fig: **das ~ geben** to give the cue.

**sticken** vt & vi to embroider.

**Stickerei** (*pl* -en) *die* embroidery.

**stickig** *adj* stuffy.

**Stickstoff** *der* nitrogen.

**Stief|bruder** *der* stepbrother.

**Stiefel** (*pl* -) *der* boot.

**stiefeln** (*perf* ist gestiefelt) *vi fam* to stride.

**Stief|eltern** *pl* stepparents.

**Stief|geschwister** *pl* stepbrother(s) and stepsister(s).

**Stief|kind** *das* stepchild.

**Stief|mutter** *die* stepmother.

**Stief|mütterchen** (*pl* -) *das* pansy.

**Stief|schwester** *die* stepsister.

**Stief|sohn** *der* stepson.

**Stief|tochter** *die* stepdaughter.

**Stief|vater** *der* stepfather.

**stieg** *prät* ⊳ steigen.

**Stiege** (*pl* -n) *die* [aus Holz] flight of stairs; [zwischen Häusern] step (*pl*).

**Stiel** (*pl* -e) *der* - **1.** [von Blume, Frucht, Trinkglas] stem - **2.** [Griff] handle; [von Lutscher, Eis] stick.

**Stiel|auge** *das*: er machte ~n *fam fig* & *hum* his eyes nearly popped out of his head.

**Stier** (*pl* -e) *der* - **1.** [Tier] bull - **2.** [Sternzeichen, Person] Taurus; ~ sein to be a Taurus.

**stieren** *vi* to stare vacantly.

**Stier|kampf** *der* bullfight.

**stieß** *prät* ⊳ stoßen.

**Stift** (*pl* -e) *der* - **1.** [Schreibutensil] pen; [Bleistift] pencil; [Buntstift] crayon - **2.** *fam* [Lehrling] *name given to apprentices during their first year* - **3.** TECH [aus Holz] peg; [aus Metall] pin.

**stiften** *vt* - **1.** [gründen] to found - **2.** [spenden] to donate; [ausgeben] to pay for - **3.** [hervorrufen - Unruhe, Aufregung] to cause - **4.** [spendieren] to buy.

**stiften gehen** (*perf* ist stiften gegangen) *vi* (*unreg*) *fam* to hop it.

**Stifter, in** (*mpl* -; *fpl* -nen) *der*, *die* - **1.** [Gründer] founder - **2.** [Spender] donor.

**Stiftung** (*pl* -en) *die* - **1.** [Institution] foundation - **2.** [Schenkung] donation.

**Stiftung Warentest** *die* *institute which tests consumer products.*

### STIFTUNG WARENTEST

The "Stiftung Warentest" is a foundation created by the government in the context of its consumer protection policy. As it examines and analyzes consumer goods of all kinds, especially from the point of view of value for money, it is very popular with consumers.

**Stil** (*pl* -e) *der* style; in diesem ~ kann es nicht weitergehen! it can't go on like this!; im großen ~ on a grand scale; sie hat ihren Geburtstag im großen ~ gefeiert she celebrated her birthday in style.

**Stil|blüte** *die* stylistic blunder.

**stilistisch** *adj* stylistic ⬦ *adv* stylistically.

**still** *adj* - **1.** [ruhig, lautlos, stressfrei] quiet; im Stillen secretly - **2.** [bewegungslos] still - **3.** [ohne Worte - Protest, Gebet, Leiden] silent - **4.** [heimlich] secret ⬦ *adv* - **1.** [ruhig, lautlos, stressfrei] quietly - **2.** [bewegungslos] still; sie stand ~ da she was standing still - **3.** [ohne Worte - protestieren, beten, leiden] silently.

**Stille** *die* - **1.** [Ruhe] quiet - **2.** [Schweigen] silence; in aller ~ heiraten to get married in secret.

**Stillleben** *das* = Stillleben.

**stilllegen** *vt* = stilllegen.

**stillen** *vt* - **1.** [die Brust geben] to breastfeed - **2.** [Schmerz] to stop - **3.** [Hunger, Bedürfnis] to satisfy; [Durst] to quench ⬦ *vi* to breastfeed.

**Stille Ozean** *der*: der ~ the Pacific (Ocean).

**stillgestanden** *pp* ⊳ stillstehen.

**still|halten** *vi* (*unreg*) [sich nicht wehren] to offer no resistance.

**still halten** *vt* & *vi* (*unreg*) to keep still.

**stillliegen** *vi* (*unreg*) = stillliegen.

**Stillleben** (*pl* -) *das* still life.

**stilllegen** *vt* to close down.

**still|liegen** *vi* (*unreg*) to be closed down; [Produktion] to be stopped.

**stillos** *adj* lacking in style; diese Einrichtung ist ~ this décor lacks style ⬦ *adv* without any style.

**stillschweigend** *adj* tacit ⬦ *adv* tacitly.

**still|sitzen** *vi* (*unreg*) [ruhig sein] to sit still.

**still sitzen** *vi* (*unreg*) [bewegungslos] to sit still.

**Still|stand** *der* stopping; [von Maschine] stoppage; [von Verhandlung] deadlock; [von Entwicklung] halt; zum ~ kommen [Verkehr, Produktion] to come to a standstill; [Verhandlungen] to reach a deadlock; [Blutungen] to stop.

**still|stehen** *vi* (*unreg*) - **1.** [Bewegung stoppen] to stand still; stillgestanden! MIL attention! - **2.** [Telefon]: das Telefon stand keine Minute still the phone never stopped ringing - **3.** [stillliegen - Verkehr, Produktion] to be at a standstill; [ - Uhr, Maschine] to have stopped.

**Still|möbel** *das* period furniture (U).

**stilvoll** *adj* stylish ⬦ *adv* stylishly.

**Stimmband** (*pl* -bänder) *das* vocal cord.

**stimmberechtigt** *adj* entitled to vote.

**Stimm|bruch** *der*: er ist im ~ his voice is breaking.

S

**Stimme** (pl -n) die - **1.** [gen] voice - **2.** [Wähler-stimme] vote; **seine ~ abgeben** to vote; **sich der ~ enthalten** to abstain - **3.** mus part.

**stimmen** vi - **1.** [richtig sein] to be right ODER correct; [Gerücht, Aussage] to be true ODER correct; **stimmt das?** is that true?; **das stimmt nicht!** that's not true!; **stimmt!** that's true! - **2.** [wählen] **für/gegen jn/etw ~** to vote for/against sb/sthg - **3.** [übereinstimmen] to be right; **irgendetwas stimmt mit ihm nicht** he doesn't seem quite right; **da stimmt doch etwas nicht** there's something not quite right ODER fishy about that; **stimmt so!** keep the change! <> vt - **1.** mus to tune - **2.** [machen] **jn traurig/fröhlich ~** to make sb feel sad/happy.

**Stimment|haltung** die abstention.

**Stimm|gabel** die tuning fork.

**stimmhaft** adj voiced <> adv: **etw ~ aussprechen** to voice sthg.

**Stimm|lage** die voice; [beim Singen] register.

**stimmlos** adj voiceless, unvoiced <> adv: **etw ~ aussprechen** not to voice sthg.

**Stimm|recht** das right to vote.

**Stimmung** (pl -en) die - **1.** [Laune] mood; **sie trank ein Bier, um in ~ zu kommen** she drank a beer to get in the mood; **guter/schlechter ~ sein** to be in a good/bad mood - **2.** [Atmosphäre] atmosphere; **gegen jn/etw ~ machen** to stir up opinion against sb/sthg.

**stimmungsvoll** adj atmospheric <> adv atmospherically.

**Stimm|zettel** der ballot paper.

**stimulieren** vt to stimulate.

**Stink|bombe** die stink-bomb.

**stinken** (prät stank; perf hat gestunken) vi - **1.** abw [schlecht riechen]: **(nach etw) ~** to stink (of sthg) - **2.** fam [faul sein]: **dieses Geschäft stinkt** there's something fishy about this business - **3.** salopp [reichen]: **mir stinkt es** I'm fed up to the back teeth.

**stinkfaul** salopp adj bone-idle.

**Stink|tier** das skunk.

**Stipendiat, in** (mpl -en; fpl -nen) der, die [als Unterstützung] recipient of a grant; [als Auszeichnung] scholarship holder.

**Stipendium** (pl -dien) das [als Unterstützung] grant; [als Auszeichnung] scholarship.

**Stipp|visite** [ˈʃtɪpviziːtə] die flying visit.

**stirbt** präs ⊳ sterben.

**Stirn** (pl -en) die forehead; **die ~ runzeln** to frown; **jm etw an der ~ ablesen** fig to tell sthg by sb's face; **jm/einer Sache die ~ bieten** fig to stand up to sb/sthg.

**Stirnband** (pl -bänder) das headband.

**stöbern** vi to rummage (around).

**stochern** vi: **(mit etw) in etw** (A) **~** to poke at sthg (with sthg); **im Essen ~** to pick at one's food; **in den Zähnen ~** to pick one's teeth.

**Stock** (pl **Stöcke** ODER -s) der - **1.** (pl **Stöcke**) [Stab] stick; [von Dirigent] baton; **meine Oma geht am ~** my grandmother walks with a stick - **2.** (pl -s) [Stockwerk] floor, storey; **im dritten ~** on the third Br ODER fourth Am floor - **3.** (pl **Stöcke**) [Pflanze - Rosenstock] rose bush; [ - Rebstock] vine - **4.** RW: **über ~ und Stein** across country; **am ~ gehen** fam [schwach sein] to be in a bad way; fam [Geldschwierigkeiten haben] to be broke.

**stockdunkel** adj pitch-dark.

**Stöckel|schuh** der stiletto.

**stocken** vi - **1.** [zum Stillstand kommen - Verkehr] to be held up; [ - Gespräch] to falter; [ - Produktion] to be interrupted; [ - Verhandlungen] to break off - **2.** [verharren] to falter - **3.** [fest werden - Milch] to curdle; [ - Ei, Blut] to coagulate - **4.** RW: **ihr stockte der Atem** she gasped.

**stockend** adj faltering; **es herrscht ~er Verkehr** traffic is moving slowly <> adv falteringly.

**Stock|fisch** der stockfish.

**Stockholm** nt Stockholm.

**stocksteif** adj rigid <> adv rigidly.

**stocktaub** adj fam as deaf as a post.

**Stockung** (pl -en) die - **1.** [Stillstand - von Verkehr] hold-up; [ - von Verhandlungen] break; [ - von Produktion] interruption - **2.** [Festwerden - von Milch] curdling; [ - von Eigelb, Blut] coagulation.

**Stock|werk** das floor, storey.

**Stoff** (pl -e) der - **1.** [Tuch] material; **einen ~ zuschneiden** to cut out a piece of material - **2.** [Inhalt] subject matter; [zu Roman, Film] material; **~ zum Nachdenken** food for thought - **3.** [Substanz] substance.

**stofflich** adj & adv - **1.** [inhaltlich] in terms of subject matter - **2.** [einer Substanz] in terms of substance.

**Stoffwechsel** der metabolism.

**stöhnen** vi to groan; **über jn/etw ~** to moan about sb/sthg.

**Stola** (pl **Stolen**) die stole.

**Stollen** (pl -) der - **1.** [Gang] gallery, tunnel - **2.** [Gebäck] stollen, sweet bread loaf made with dried fruit and marzipan, eaten at Christmas - **3.** [unter Schuhen] stud; [unter Hufeisen] calk.

**stolpern** (perf ist gestolpert) vi to stumble; **über etw** (A) **~** to trip over sthg; **über jn ~** fig fam to bump into sb.

**stolz** adj proud; **auf jn/etw ~ sein** to be proud of sb/sthg <> adv proudly.

**Stolz** der pride; **js ganzer ~ sein** to be sb's pride and joy.

**stolzieren** (perf ist stolziert) vi to strut.

**stop** *interj* [auf Verkehrsschild] stop.

**Stop** *der* = Stopp.

**stopfen** *vt* - **1.** [ausbessern] to darn - **2.** [hineinstopfen] to stuff; **etw in etw** *(A)* ~ to stuff sthg into sthg; **sich zwei Kekse in den Mund** ~ to stuff two biscuits into one's mouth - **3.** [zustopfen] to plug - **4.** [füllen - Pfeife] to fill; [ - Geflügel] to stuff ⟨⟩ *vi* - **1.** [satt machen] to be filling - **2.** [Stuhlgang erschweren] to cause constipation.

**stopp** *interj* [halt] stop!

**Stopp** *(pl -s) der* - **1.** [Halt] stop; **ohne** ~ without stopping - **2.** [Sport] drop shot.

**Stoppel** *(pl -n) die:* ~**n** stubble *(U).*

**stoppelig, stopplig** *adj* stubbly.

**stoppen** *vt* - **1.** [anhalten] to stop - **2.** [messen - Person, Lauf] to time ⟨⟩ *vi* - **1.** [anhalten] to stop - **2.** *fam* [per Anhalter fahren] to hitchhike.

**stopplig** = stoppelig.

**Stopplschild** *das* stop sign.

**Stoppluhr** *die* stopwatch.

**Stöpsel** *(pl -) der* - **1.** [Gegenstand - von Becken] plug; [ - von Flasche] stopper - **2.** *fam hum* [Mensch] little chap.

**Stör** *(pl -e) der* sturgeon.

**störanfällig** *adj* temperamental.

**Storch** *(pl Störche) der* stork.

**stören** *vt* - **1.** [belästigen] to disturb; [unterbrechen] to interrupt; **du sollst sie nicht bei der Arbeit** ~ don't disturb *ODER* bother her while she's working - **2.** [missfallen] to bother; **das stört mich an ihm** that's one thing I don't like about him - **3.** [beeinträchtigen - Verhältnis] to spoil; [ - Radioempfang, Fernsehempfang] to interfere with ⟨⟩ *vi* - **1.** [belästigend sein]: **darf ich mal kurz** ~? may I disturb you for a moment?; **störe ich?** am I bothering you?; **'bitte nicht** ~!' 'do not disturb!' - **2.** [missfallend sein] to be annoying.

➤ **sich stören** *ref* [Anstoß nehmen]: **sich an etw** *(D)* ~ to take exception to sthg.

**Störenfried** *(pl -e) der* troublemaker.

**stornieren** *vt* to cancel.

**störrisch** *adj* stubborn ⟨⟩ *adv* stubbornly.

**Störung** *(pl -en) die* - **1.** [Belästigung] disturbance; [von Zeremonie] disruption; **bitte entschuldigen Sie die** ~! sorry to bother you! - **2.** [Funktionsstörung - von Gerät] fault; [ - von Organ] disorder - **3.** [von Signal] interference *(U).*

**Störungslstelle** *die* faults service.

**Story** ['stɔːri, 'stɔri] *(pl -s) die* story.

**Stoß** *(pl Stöße) der* - **1.** [Schlag] push, shove; [mit dem Fuß] kick; [in Auto, Schiff, Zug] jolt; **jm/einer Sache einen** ~ **versetzen** [stoßen] to give sb/sthg a push *ODER* shove; **ihre Beleidigung hat ihm einen schweren** ~ **versetzt** her insult hit him

hard; **sich** *(D)* **einen** ~ **geben** *fam fig* to make an effort - **2.** [Stapel] pile - **3.** [mit Stichwaffe] thrust; [mit Stock] poke.

**Stoßldämpfer** *der* shock absorber.

**stoßen** *(präs* **stößt;** *prät* **stieß;** *perf* **hat/ist gestoßen)** *vt (hat)* - **1.** [schubsen] to push; [mit der Faust] to punch; [mit dem Fuß] to kick - **2.** *SPORT* [Kugel] to put; [Gewichte] to press - **3.** [aufmerksam machen]: **jn auf etw** *(A)* ~ to point sthg out to sb ⟨⟩ *vi* - **1.** *(ist)* [berühren]: **an etw** *(A)* ~ to bang sthg; **er ist mit dem Kopf an den Balken gestoßen** he hit his head on the beam; **gegen etw** *(A)* ~ to bang into sthg; [Fahrzeug] to crash into sthg - **2.** *(hat)* [mit Waffe]: **nach jm** ~ to lunge at sb - **3.** *(ist)* [angrenzen]: **an etw** *(A)* ~ [Grundstück] to border on sthg; [Zimmer] to be next to sthg - **4.** *(ist)* [finden]: **auf jn/etw** ~ to come across sb/sthg; **auf Erdöl** ~ to strike oil - **5.** *(ist)* [auf Reaktion]: **auf etw** *(A)* ~ to meet with sthg - **6.** *(ist)* [sich treffen mit]: **zu jm** ~ to meet up with sb.

➤ **sich stoßen** *ref* - **1.** [sich wehtun] to bang o.s. - **2.** [nicht mögen]: **sich an etw** *(D)* ~ to take exception to sthg.

**Stoßlstange** *die* bumper *Br,* fender *Am.*

**stößt** *präs* ⟼ stoßen.

**stoßweise** *adv* - **1.** [ruckartig] in bursts - **2.** [stapelweise] in piles.

**Stoßlzahn** *der* tusk.

**Stoßlzeit** *die* - **1.** [Hauptverkehrszeit] rush hour - **2.** [in Geschäften] busy period.

**stottern** *vi* - **1.** [sprechen] to stutter, to stammer - **2.** [aussetzen] to splutter ⟨⟩ *vt* [stammeln] to stammer.

**St. Pauli** *nt* red-light district in Hamburg.

**Str.** *(abk für* **Straße)** St.

**Straflanstalt** *die amt* penal institution, penitentiary *Am.*

**Straflarbeit** *die* extra homework *(U) (as punishment).*

**Straflbank** *(pl -bänke) die SPORT* sin bin.

**strafbar** *adj* punishable; **sich** ~ **machen** *amt* to commit an offence.

**Strafe** *(pl -n) die* - **1.** [Bestrafung] punishment; **zur** ~ as a punishment; **etw unter** ~ **stellen** to make sthg a punishable offence - **2.** [Geldbuße] fine; **(50 Euro)** ~ **zahlen** to pay a (50 euros) fine - **3.** [in Gefängnis] sentence.

**strafen** *vt* to punish; **jn mit Blicken** ~ to look daggers at sb.

**straff** *adj* - **1.** [Schenkel, Brust] firm; [Haut] smooth - **2.** [Leine, Saite] taut; [Knoten] tight - **3.** [Planung, Organisation] tight ⟨⟩ *adv* - **1.** [halten, spannen] tight; **etw** ~ **ziehen** to pull sthg tight - **2.** [organisieren] tightly.

**straffällig** *adj:* ~**er Jugendlicher** young of-

**S**

fender; **~e Person** offender; **~ werden** to commit a criminal offence.

**straffen** vt **- 1.** [straff machen - Leine, Saite] to tighten; [ - Haut] to firm (up) **- 2.** [kürzen, effektiver machen] to tighten up.

**straffrei** adj: **~ bleiben** to go unpunished; **~ sein** not to carry a penalty ◇ adv: **~ davonkommen** to get off; **~ ausgehen** [Person] to go unpunished.

**Straflfreiheit** die exemption from punishment.

**sträflich** adj criminal ◇ adv criminally.

**Sträfling** (pl -e) der prisoner.

**Straflmandat** das ticket.

**Strafmaß** das sentence.

**strafmildernd** adj mitigating ◇ adv: sich **~ auswirken** to have a mitigating effect.

**Straflporto** das excess postage.

**Straflprozess** der criminal proceedings (pl).

**Straflraum** der SPORT penalty area.

**Straflrecht** das criminal law.

**Strafltat** die offence.

**Strafltäter, in** der, die criminal, offender.

**strafversetzen** vt to transfer for disciplinary reasons.

**Strafvollzug** der [Institution] penal system.

**Straflzettel** der ticket.

**Strahl** (pl -en) der **- 1.** [Wasserstrahl] jet; [dünn] trickle **- 2.** [Lichtstrahl] ray; [von Scheinwerfer, Licht, Laser] beam.
➡ **Strahlen** pl [Energiewellen] rays.

**strahlen** vi **- 1.** [lachen] to beam **- 2.** [leuchten] to shine **- 3.** [Strahlen abgeben] to radiate **- 4.** [glänzen] to sparkle.

**Strahlenlbelastung** die radioactive contamination.

**strahlend** adj **- 1.** [glücklich] beaming **- 2.** [leuchtend] radiant **- 3.** [Strahlen abgebend] radioactive **- 4.** [glänzend] sparkling; [Farbe] brilliant ◇ adv **- 1.** [glücklich] with a beaming smile **- 2.** [leuchtend] radiantly **- 3.** [glänzend] sparklingly.

**Strahlung** (pl -en) die radiation (U).

**Strähne** (pl -n) die strand.

**strähnig** adj straggly.

**stramm** adj **- 1.** [straff] tight; [Seil, Gummiband] taut **- 2.** [wohlgenährt] sturdy **- 3.** [aufrecht] upright **- 4.** fam abw [überzeugt] hardline ◇ adv **- 1.** fam [marschieren, wandern] briskly **- 2.** [straff] tightly **- 3.** [aufrecht] upright.

**strampeln** (perf hat/ist gestrampelt) vi **- 1.** (hat) [zappeln] to kick out **- 2.** (ist) fam [Fahrrad fahren] to pedal, to cycle.

**Strand** (pl Strände) der beach; **am ~** on the beach.

**Strandlbad** das bathing beach (which people pay to go to).

**stranden** (perf ist gestrandet) vi **- 1.** [festsitzen - Schiff] to run aground; [ - Wal] to become beached **- 2.** geh [scheitern] to fail.

**Strandlkorb** der wicker beach chair.

**Strandlpromenade** die promenade.

**Strang** (pl Stränge) der **- 1.** [Seil] rope **- 2.** [von Muskeln] cord; [von Nerven] bundle **- 3.** [Bündel] skein **- 4.** [Abschnitt] section **- 5.** RW: am selben **~ ziehen** to pull in the same direction; **über die Stränge schlagen** fam to kick over the traces.

**Strapaze** (pl -n) die strain; **~n auf sich** (A) nehmen to face the strain.

**strapazieren** vt **- 1.** [anstrengen] to be a strain on; [Geduld] to strain; **das Autofahren hat mich doch strapaziert!** the driving took it out of me! **- 2.** [abnutzen] to be hard on.
➡ **sich strapazieren** ref [sich anstrengen] to tax o.s.

**strapazierfähig** adj hardwearing.

**Straps** (pl -e) der suspender Br, garter Am.

**Straßburg** nt Strasbourg.

**Straße** (pl -n) die **- 1.** [in Stadt] street **- 2.** [Landstraße] road; **auf der ~ sitzen** fam [arbeitslos sein] to be out of work; [ohne Wohnung sein] to be on the streets; **auf die ~ gehen** [demonstrieren] to take to the streets; [anschaffen gehen] to walk the streets; **jn auf die ~ setzen** fam [Angestellten] to fire sb; [Mieter] to kick sb out.
➡ **auf offener Straße** adv in public.

**Straßenlarbeiten** pl roadworks.

**Straßenlbahn** die tram Br, streetcar Am.

**Straßenlbau** der roadbuilding.

**Straßenlbeleuchtung** die street lighting.

**Straßenlcafé** das street café.

**Straßenlecke** die street corner.

**Straßenfeger, in** (mpl -; fpl -nen) der, die roadsweeper.

**Straßenglätte** die (ohne pl) slippery road.

**Straßenlgraben** der ditch.

**Straßenlkarte** die road map.

**Straßenllaterne** die street light.

**Straßenlnetz** das road network.

**Straßenlschild** das road sign.

**Straßenlsperre** die roadblock.

**Straßenverhältnisse** pl road conditions.

**Straßenlverkehr** der road traffic.

**Strategie** (pl -n) die strategy.

**strategisch** adj strategic ◇ adv strategically.

**Stratosphäre** *die* stratosphere.

**sträuben** ➤ **sich sträuben** *ref* **- 1.** [Federn] to become ruffled; [Fell] to bristle; **ihr ~ sich die Haare** her hair is standing on end; **dem Hund sträubt sich das Fell** the dog's hair bristled **- 2.** [sich wehren]: **sich gegen etw ~** to resist sthg.

**Strauch** *(pl* **Sträucher)** *der* bush.

**Strauß** *(pl* **Sträuße** ODER **-e)** *der* **- 1.** *(pl Sträuße)* [Blumen] bunch of flowers **- 2.** *(pl Strauße)* [Vogel] ostrich.

**streben** *(perf* **hat/ist gestrebt)** *vi* **- 1.** *(ist)* [gehen]: **in etw** *(A)* ODER **zu etw ~** to head for sthg **- 2.** *(hat)* [trachten]: **nach etw ~** to strive for sthg **- 3.** *(hat) abw* [pauken] to swot *Br,* to grind *Am.*

**Streber, in** *(mpl* **-;** *fpl* **-nen)** *der, die abw* swot *Br,* grind *Am.*

**strebsam** *adj* [fleißig] industrious; [ehrgeizig] ambitious <> *adv* [fleißig] industriously; [ehrgeizig] ambitiously.

**Strecke** *(pl* **-n)** *die* **- 1.** [Weg] route; **diese ~ bin ich noch nie gefahren** I've never been this way before **- 2.** [Entfernung] distance **- 3.** [von Straße] stretch; **die ~ zwischen Pforzheim und Karlsruhe** the road between Pforzheim and Karlsruhe **- 4.** [von Eisenbahn] line; [von Schienen] track; **auf offener ~** between stations **- 5.** MATH (straight) line **- 6.** *RW:* **auf der ~ bleiben** *fam* [bei Wettrennen] to drop out, to pull up; [scheitern, verloren gehen] to fall by the wayside; **jn/etw zur ~ bringen** [erlegen] to kill sb/sthg; *fam* [überwältigen] to hunt sb/sthg down.

**strecken** *vt* **- 1.** [ausstrecken] to stretch **- 2.** [Hals] to crane; **den Kopf aus dem Fenster ~** to stick one's head out of the window **- 3.** [verdünnen] to thin down; [Droge] to cut.
➤ **sich strecken** *ref* **- 1.** [sich recken] to stretch **- 2.** [sich hinlegen] to stretch out.

**streckenweise** *adv* in places.

**Streetworker, in** ['striːtwœː(r)kɐ, rɪn] *(mpl* **-;** *fpl* **-nen)** *der, die* outreach worker.

**Streich** *(pl* **-e)** *der* [zum Ärgern] trick; **jm einen ~ spielen** *eigtl* & *fig* to play a trick on sb.

**streicheln** *vt* to stroke <> *vi:* **über etw** *(A)* **~** to stroke sthg.

**streichen** *(prät* **strich;** *perf* **hat/ist gestrichen)** *vt (hat)* **- 1.** [mit Farbe] to paint; 'frisch gestrichen' 'wet paint' **- 2.** [Satz, Passage] to delete; **etw von einer Liste ~** to cross sthg off a list **- 3.** [schmieren] to spread; **Brote ~** to make some sandwiches **- 4.** [Subvention, Auftrag] to cancel; **Alkohol und Zigaretten ~** to cut out alcohol and cigarettes **- 5.** [entfernen]: **sie strich sich** *(D)* **die Haare aus dem Gesicht** she pushed her hair back out of her face <> *vi* **- 1.** *(hat):* **mit der Hand über den Stoff ~** to stroke the cloth; **sich** *(D)* **über den Kopf ~** to stroke one's

head **- 2.** *(hat)* [mit Farbe] to paint **- 3.** *(ist)* [umherschleichen] to roam.

**Streicher, in** *(mpl* **-;** *fpl* **-nen)** *der, die:* **die ~** the strings.

**Streichlholz** *das* match.

**Streichlinstrument** *das* stringed instrument.

**Streichlkäse** *der* cheese spread.

**Streichlquartett** *das* string quartet.

**Streichung** *(pl* **-en)** *die* **- 1.** [von Subvention, Auftrag] cancellation; **~en** [an Etat] cuts **- 2.** [im Text] deletion.

**Streife** *(pl* **-n)** *die* patrol; **auf ~ gehen** to go on patrol.

**streifen** *(perf* **hat/ist gestreift)** *vt (hat)* **- 1.** [berühren] to brush against; **mit dem Auto die Mauer ~** to scrape against the wall with the car **- 2.** [ziehen]: **etw über etw** *(A)* **~** to pull sthg over sthg; **etw von etw ~** to pull sthg off sthg **- 3.** [Thema] to touch on **- 4.** [ansehen]: **jn/ etw mit dem Blick ~** to glance at sb/sthg <> *vi (ist)* [umherziehen]: **durch etw ~** to roam through sthg.

**Streifen** *(pl* **-)** *der* **- 1.** [Stück, Band] strip **- 2.** [Strich] stripe; [auf Fahrbahn] line.

**Streifenlwagen** *der* patrol car.

**Streik** *(pl* **-s)** *der* strike; **in (den) ~ treten** to go on strike.

**Streikbrecher, in** *(mpl* **-;** *fpl* **-nen)** *der, die* strikebreaker.

**streiken** *vi* **- 1.** [im Streik stehen] to strike **- 2.** [Motor, Maschine] to pack up.

**Streiklposten** *der* picket.

**Streit** *der* argument; **~ mit jm haben** to argue with sb.

**streiten** *(prät* **stritt;** *perf* **hat gestritten)** *vi* **- 1.** [sich auseinander setzen]: **(über etw** *(A))* **~** to argue (about sthg) **- 2.** *geh* [kämpfen]: **gegen/ für etw ~** to fight against/for sthg.
➤ **sich streiten** *ref:* **sich (mit jm/um etw) ~** to argue (with sb/about sthg).

**Streitlfrage** *die* contentious issue.

**streitig** *adv:* **jm etw ~ machen** to dispute sb's right to sthg.

**Streitigkeiten** *pl* disputes.

**Streitkräfte** *pl* armed forces.

**streitsüchtig** *adj* quarrelsome.

**streng** *adj* **- 1.** [Eltern, Kontrolle, Diät, Regel] strict; [Blick] stern; [Maßnahme] stringent **- 2.** [Geruch, Geschmack] pungent **- 3.** [Gesicht, Frisur, Winter] severe <> *adv* **- 1.** [erziehen, verbieten, einhalten] strictly; [überwachen] closely; [ansehen] sternly **- 2.** [durchdringend]: **~ riechen** to smell pungent.

**Strenge** *die* **- 1.** [von Erziehung, Kontrolle, Gesetz] strictness; [von Blick] sternness; [von Maßnahme] stringency **- 2.** [von Gesicht, Frisur, Winter] severity **- 3.** [von Geruch, Geschmack] pungency.

**streng genommen** adv strictly speaking.

**strengstens** adv strictly.

**Stress** der stress; **mach keinen ~!** fam stay cool!; **im ~ sein** to be under stress.

**stressen** (präs **stresst**; prät **stresste**; perf **hat gestresst**) vt fam to stress out.
➡ **sich stressen** ref to put o.s. under stress.

**stressig** adj fam stressful.

**Stretching** [ˈstrɛtʃɪŋ] das (ohne pl) stretch gymnastics (pl).

**Streu** die [aus Stroh] straw.

**streuen** vt [Salz, Gewürze] to sprinkle; [Dünger, Stroh, Gerüchte] to spread; [Futter, Samen] to scatter ⬦ vi [mit Sand] to grit; [mit Salz] to put down salt.

**streunen** (perf **hat/ist gestreunt**) vi **- 1.** [irgendwo] to roam around; [Hund, Katze] to stray **- 2.** (ist) [irgendwohin] to roam.

**Streusel** (pl -) der ODER das crumble topping.

**Streuselkuchen** der cake with crumble topping.

**strich** prät ⬦ streichen.

**Strich** (pl -e) der **- 1.** [Linie] line; [Gedankenstrich] dash; [von Pinsel] stroke; **einen ~ ziehen** to draw a line **- 2.** [Streichen] stroke; **Haare gegen den ~ bürsten** to brush hair the wrong way **- 3.** fam [Prostitution] prostitution; **auf dem ~ on the game**; **auf den ~ gehen** fam to walk the streets **- 4.** RW: **es geht mir gegen den ~, aber ...** fam I don't like it, but ...; **jm einen ~ durch die Rechnung machen** to wreck sb's plans; **keinen ~ tun** fam not to lift a finger; **nach ~ und Faden** fam good and proper.
➡ **unter dem Strich** adv at the end of the day.

**stricheln** vt to sketch in.

**strichweise** adj & adv in places.

**Strick** (pl -e) der rope; **jm einen ~ aus etw drehen** fig to use sthg against sb; **wenn alle ~e reißen** fig if the worst comes to the worst.

**stricken** vt & vi to knit.

**Strickjacke** die cardigan.

**Strickleiter** die rope ladder.

**Strickmuster** das knitting pattern.

**Stricknadel** die knitting needle.

**Strickzeug** das (ohne pl) [Handarbeit] knitting.

**striegeln** vt to groom.

**Striemen** (pl -) der weal.

**strikt** adj strict ⬦ adv strictly.

**Strippe** (pl -n) die fam **- 1.** [Telefon] phone; **an der ~ hängen** fam to be on the phone **- 2.** [Schnur] piece of string **- 3.** [Kabel] cable.

**Striptease** [ˈstrɪptiːs, ˈstrɪptiːs] der ODER das striptease.

**stritt** prät ⬦ streiten.

**strittig** adj contentious.

**Stroh** das straw.

**Strohblume** die everlasting flower.

**Strohdach** das thatched roof.

**Strohhalm** der straw; **sich an einen ~ klammern** fig to clutch at straws.

**Strohmann** (pl -männer) der front man.

**Strohwitwe** die hum grass widow.

**Strohwitwer** der hum grass widower.

**Strolch** (pl -e) der **- 1.** abw [Mann] ruffian **- 2.** fam hum [Schlingel] rascal.

**Strom** (pl **Ströme**) der **- 1.** [elektrisch] electricity; **unter ~ stehen** to be live **- 2.** [Fluss] river **- 3.** [Strömung] current **- 4.** [Menge] stream **- 5.** RW: **es regnet** ODER **gießt in Strömen** it's pouring down; **gegen den ~ schwimmen** to swim against the tide; **in Strömen fließen** to flow freely.

**Stromabnehmer** der [Stromkunde] electricity consumer.

**stromabwärts** adv downstream.

**stromaufwärts** adv upstream.

**Stromausfall** der power failure.

**strömen** (perf **ist geströmt**) vi to stream.

**Stromkabel** das electric cable.

**Stromkreis** der (electrical) circuit.

**stromlinienförmig** adj streamlined.

**Stromnetz** das electricity grid.

**Stromschnelle** (pl -n) die rapids (pl).

**Stromstärke** die current strength.

**Strömung** (pl -en) die **- 1.** [Strom] current **- 2.** [Bewegung] current of thought.

**Stromverbrauch** der electricity consumption.

**Stromzähler** der electricity meter.

**Strontium** [ˈstrɔntsjʊm, ˈstrɔntsjʊm] das strontium.

**Strophe** (pl -n) die verse.

**strotzen** vi: **vor Gesundheit ~** to be bursting with health; **vor Dreck ~** to be filthy.

**strubbelig, strubblig** adj tousled.

**Strudel** (pl -) der **- 1.** [Wirbel] whirlpool **- 2.** [Kuchen] strudel.

**Struktur** (pl -en) die **- 1.** [von Systemen] structure **- 2.** [von Material] texture.

**strukturell** adj structural ⬦ adv structurally.

**strukturieren** vt to structure.

**strukturschwach** adj structurally weak.

**Strukturwandel** *der* structural change.

**Strumpf** *(pl* **Strümpfe)** *der* - **1.** [beinlang] stocking - **2.** [Socke] sock.

**Strumpfhalter** *(pl* -) *der* suspender *Br*, garter *Am*.

**Strumpf|hose** *die* tights *(pl) Br*, pantyhose *(U) Am*.

**struppig** *adj* shaggy.

**Stube** *(pl* -n) *die* - **1.** *fam* [Wohnzimmer] living room - **2.** [Raum] room.

**stubenrein** *adj* house-trained.

**Stuck** *der* - **1.** [Material] stucco - **2.** [Verzierung] moulding.

**Stück** *(pl* -e) *das* - **1.** [gen] piece; [von Butter, Zucker] lump; **ein ~ vorlesen** to read a bit out; **ein ~ Papier** a piece of paper; **im** *ODER* **am ~** unsliced; **wie viele? – 10 ~, bitte** how many? – 10, please; **fünf Euro pro** *ODER* **das ~** five euros each - **2.** [Strecke]: **jn ein ~ begleiten** to accompany sb a little way; **ein ~ zur Seite rücken** to move a bit to one side - **3.** [Bühnenstück] play - **4.** *salopp abw* [Frau]: **ein dummes/freches ~** a silly/cheeky cow - **5.** *RW*: **das ist ja ein starkes ~!** *fam* that's going too far!; **große ~e auf jn halten** to think very highly of sb.

➤ **aus freien Stücken** *adv* of one's own free will.

➤ **in einem Stück** *adv* - **1.** [ganz] in one piece - **2.** *fam* [ohne Unterbrechung] non-stop.

**stückeln** *vi* to add patches.

**Stück|gut** *das* parcel *(sent by train or lorry)*.

**Stückwerk** *das (ohne pl)*: **die Reform ist/bleibt ~** the reform does not go far enough.

**Stück|zahl** *die* number of pieces.

**stud.** *abk für* Student.

**Student** *(pl* -en) *der* student.

**Studenten|verbindung** *die exclusive society for university students and alumni, with its own traditional aims and customs.*

**STUDENTENVERBINDUNG**

These student organizations no longer play as important a role as they once did in 19th century university life or, through the influence of ex-students, in politics. However, they have undergone a revival since Germany was reunited.

**Studenten|werk** *das university body responsible for running student halls, cafés, dining rooms, etc.*

**Studentenwohn|heim** *das* hall of residence.

**Studentin** *(pl* -nen) *die* student.

**studentisch** *adj* student *(vor Subst)*.

**Studie** ['ʃtuːdjə] *(pl* -n) *die* study.

**Studienab|schluss** *der* degree.

**Studien|aufenthalt** *der* study visit.

**Studien|fach** *das* subject.

**Studien|fahrt** *die* study trip.

**Studien|platz** *der* university/college place.

**Studien|rat** *der secondary school teacher*.

**Studien|rätin** *die secondary school teacher on the lowest state-employee salary scale*.

**Studien|zeit** *die* period of study.

**studieren** [ʃtuˈdiːrən] *vt* & *vi* to study.

**Studio** *(pl* -s) *das* studio.

**Studium** ['ʃtuːdjʊm] *(pl* **Studien)** *das* - **1.** [gen] study - **2.** *(ohne pl)* [Ausbildung] studies *(pl)*.

**Stufe** *(pl* -n) *die* - **1.** [von Treppen] step; '**Vorsicht ~!**' 'mind the step!' - **2.** [Stand] stage - **3.** [in einer Hierarchie] level; **sich mit jm auf die gleiche ~ stellen** [sich vergleichen] to compare o.s. with sb; [sich benehmen wie] to stoop to sb's level - **4.** [Schaltstufe] setting - **5.** [Abstufung] degree.

**Stufen|heck** *das* **ein Auto mit ~** a saloon.

**stufenweise** *adj* gradual ⬦ *adv* in stages, gradually.

**Stuhl** *(pl* **Stühle)** *der* - **1.** [Sitzmöbel] chair; **zwischen zwei Stühlen sitzen** *fig* to fall between two stools; **der elektrische ~** the electric chair - **2.** [Stuhlgang] stool.

**Stuhlgang** *der (ohne pl)* stool; **~ haben** to have a bowel movement.

**stülpen** *vt*: **etw nach außen ~** to turn sthg inside out; **etw auf/über etw *(A)* ~** to put sthg onto/over sthg.

**stumm** *adj* - **1.** [sprechunfähig] dumb - **2.** [schweigend] silent ⬦ *adv* - **1.** [sprechunfähig] dumbly - **2.** [schweigend] silently.

**Stummel** *(pl* -) *der* [von Arm, Bein, Schwanz] stump; [von Zigarette] butt; [von Kerze, Bleistift] stub.

**Stumm|film** *der* silent movie.

**Stümper** *(pl* -) *der abw* bungler.

**Stümperei** *(pl* -en) *die abw* amateur work.

**Stümperin** *(pl* -nen) *die abw* bungler.

**stumpf** *adj* - **1.** [Messer, Spitze] blunt - **2.** [Fell, Haar, Lack] dull - **3.** [Person, Ausdruck] apathetic - **4.** MATH obtuse ⬦ *adv* - **1.** [leben, blicken] apathetically - **2.** [nicht scharf, nicht spitz] bluntly - **3.** [glanzlos] dully.

**Stumpf** *(pl* **Stümpfe)** *der* stump; [von Kerze] stub.

**Stumpfsinn** *der* - **1.** [Monotonie] monotony - **2.** [geistige Abwesenheit] apathy.

**stumpfsinnig** *adj* - **1.** [monoton] monotonous - **2.** [teilnahmslos] apathetic ⬦ *adv* [teilnahmslos] apathetically.

S

**Stündchen** *(pl -) das fam:* ich habe noch ein ~ Zeit I still have an hour or so.

**Stunde** *(pl -n) die* **- 1.** [Zeiteinheit] hour; jede ~ every hour **- 2.** [Unterrichtsstunde] lesson **- 3.** *geh* [Zeit, Moment] time; **zur gewohnten ~** at the usual hour *ODER* time.

➤ **zu später Stunde** *adv geh* at a late hour.

**stunden** *vt:* jm eine Zahlung ~ to give sb longer to make a payment.

**Stunden|geschwindigkeit** *die:* eine ~ von 100 km a speed of 100 km/h.

**Stundenkilometer** *pl* kilometres per hour.

**stundenlang** *adj* lasting for hours; nach ~em Warten after waiting for hours ⬦ *adv* for hours.

**Stunden|lohn** *der* hourly rate.

**Stunden|plan** *der* timetable.

**stundenweise** *adv* [bezahlen] by the hour; ~ arbeiten to work the odd hour.

**Stunden|zeiger** *der* hour hand.

**stündlich** *adv* **- 1.** [jede Stunde] hourly, once an hour **- 2.** [jeden Augenblick] at any moment ⬦ *adj* [jede Stunde] hourly.

**Stunk** *der fam:* ~ machen to kick up a stink.

**Stuntman** ['stantmɛn] *(pl -men) der* stuntman.

**Stuntwoman** ['stantwʊmən] *(pl -women) die* stuntwoman.

**stupid, stupide** [ʃtu'piːt, ʃtu'piːdə] *adj abw* empty-headed.

**Stups** *(pl -e) der:* jm einen ~ geben to give sb a nudge.

**stupsen** *vt* to nudge.

**Stups|nase** *die* snub nose.

**stur** *abw adj* pigheaded ⬦ *adv* pigheadedly; ~ geradeaus fahren to drive straight on.

**Sturm** *(pl Stürme) der* **- 1.** [Unwetter] storm **- 2.** [von Begeisterung, Entrüstung] wave **- 3.** [Andrang, Angriff] assault; **der ~ auf die Bastille** the storming of the Bastille **- 4.** [beim Fußball] forward line **- 5.** *RW:* **gegen etw ~ laufen** to be up in arms about sthg; ~ **klingeln** to lean on the doorbell.

**stürmen** *(perf hat/ist gestürmt) vt (hat)* **- 1.** [Geschäfte, Büfett] to besiege **- 2.** [Festung, Stellung] to storm ⬦ *vi* **- 1.** *(ist)* [rennen] to rush **- 2.** *(hat)* [beim Fußball] to attack **- 3.** *(hat)* [Sturm herrschen]: **es stürmt** it's blowing a gale.

**Stürmer, in** *(mpl -; fpl -nen) der, die* forward.

**Sturm|flut** *die* storm tide.

**sturmfrei** *adj* ⊳ **Bude.**

**stürmisch** *adj* **- 1.** [windig] stormy **- 2.** [Applaus] tumultuous; [Begeisterung] wild; [Protest] vehement **- 3.** [leidenschaftlich] passionate

⬦ *adv* **- 1.** [applaudieren] tumultuously **- 2.** [leidenschaftlich] passionately **- 3.** [wehen] stormily; [regnen] violently.

**Sturm|schaden** *der* storm damage.

**Sturm|tief** *das* deep low (pressure area).

**Sturm|warnung** *die* gale warning.

**Sturz** *(pl Stürze) der* fall.

**stürzen** *(perf hat/ist gestürzt) vi (ist)* **- 1.** [fallen, zurückgehen] to fall **- 2.** [eilen] to rush ⬦ *vt (hat)* **- 1.** [Regierung, Herrscher] to bring down; [mit Gewalt] to overthrow **- 2.** [Kuchen, Pudding] to turn out **- 3.** [stoßen] to hurl.

➤ **sich stürzen** *ref* **- 1.** [springen] to jump **- 2.** [herfallen über]: **sich auf jn/etw ~** [bestürmen] to fall on sb/sthg; [angreifen] to pounce on sb/sthg **- 3.** [sich begeben]: **sich in etw (A) ~** [springen] to plunge into sthg; [sich widmen] to throw o.s. into sthg.

**Sturz|flug** *der:* **im ~** in a dive.

**Sturz|helm** *der* crash helmet.

**Stuss** *der fam abw* rubbish.

**Stute** *(pl -n) die* mare.

**Stuttgart** *nt* Stuttgart.

**Stütze** *(pl -n) die* **- 1.** [Vorrichtung] prop, support; [für Kopf, Rücken, Füße] rest; **zur ~** for support **- 2.** [Hilfe] support; [Gedächtnis] aid **- 3.** *fam* [Arbeitslosenunterstützung] dole *Br,* welfare *Am.*

**stutzen** *vt* [Bart, Haare, Hecke] to trim; [Pflanze, Baum] to cut back ⬦ *vi* [innehalten] to stop short.

**stützen** *vt* to support; **den Kopf in die Hände ~** to prop one's head on one's hands; **die Ellbogen auf den Tisch ~** to prop one's elbows on the table.

➤ **sich stützen** *ref:* **sich auf jn/etw ~** [auf Stock, Möbel] to lean on sb/sthg; [auf Vermutung, Beweis] to be based on sb/sthg.

**stutzig** *adj:* **jn ~ machen** to make sb suspicious; ~ **werden** to become suspicious.

**Stütz|punkt** *der* base.

**StVO** [ɛsteːfauˈʔoː] *(abk für* **Straßenverkehrsordnung**) *die Road Traffic Act.*

**stylen** ['staɪln] *vt* [Haare] to style.
➤ **sich stylen** *ref* to style o.s.

**Styropor**® *das* polystyrene.

**s. u.** *(abk für* **siehe unten**) see below.

**Subjekt** *(pl -e) das* **- 1.** *GRAM* subject **- 2.** *abw* [Mensch] individual, character.

**subjektiv** *adj* subjective ⬦ *adv* subjectively.

**Subjektivität** [zʊpjɛktiviˈtɛːt] *die* subjectivity.

**Sub|kultur** *die* subculture.

**Substantiv** *(pl -e) das GRAM* noun.

**Substanz** (pl -en) die substance; **das geht an die ~** it wears you down.

**subtil** geh adj subtle ◇ adv subtly.

**subtrahieren** vt & vi to subtract.

**Subtraktion** (pl -en) die subtraction.

**subtropisch** adj subtropical.

**Sublunternehmer, in** der, die subcontractor.

**Subvention** [zʊpvɛn'tsjoːn] (pl -nen) die subsidy.

**subventionieren** [zʊpvɛntsjoˈniːrən] vt to subsidize.

**subversiv** [zʊpvɛrˈziːf] adj subversive ◇ adv subversively.

**Suche** (pl -n) die search; **auf der ~ nach jm/etw sein** to be looking for sb/sthg; [angestrengt] to be searching for sb/sthg; **sich auf die ~ (nach jm/etw) machen** to start looking (for sb/sthg).

**suchen** vt - **1.** [finden wollen] to look for; [angestrengt] to search for; **er/es hat hier nichts zu ~** fam he/it has no business being here - **2.** [sich wünschen] to seek ◇ vi: **(nach jm/etw) ~** to look (for sb/sthg); [angestrengt] to search (for sb/sthg).

**Suchlmaschine** die EDV search engine.

**Sucht** (pl Süchte) die addiction; **js ~ nach etw (D)** sb's addiction to sthg.

**süchtig** adj: **(nach etw) ~ sein** to be addicted (to sthg); **~ machen** to be addictive.

**suchtkrank** adj: **~ sein** to be an addict.

**Suchltrupp** der search party.

**Sud** (pl -e) der decoction.

**Süd** (ohne Artikel) south; **aus ~en** from the south.

**Südafrika** nt South Africa.

**Südlafrikaner, in** der, die South African.

**südafrikanisch** adj South African.

**Südamerika** nt South America.

**Südlamerikaner, in** der, die South American.

**südamerikanisch** adj South American.

**Sudan** der: **der ~** (the) Sudan.

**süddeutsch** adj South German.

**Süddeutschland** nt South Germany.

**süddt.** abk für **süddeutsch.**

**Süden** der south; **nach ~** south; **im ~** in the south.

**Südeuropa** nt Southern Europe.

**Südlfrucht** die ordinary citrus fruits and certain tropical fruits, e.g. bananas.

**Südkorea** nt South Korea.

**südl.** abk für **südlich.**

**Südländer, in** (mpl -; fpl -nen) der, die: **er ist ~** he's from the Mediterranean.

**südländisch** adj Mediterranean.

**südlich** adj [Gegend] southern; [Richtung, Wind] southerly ◇ präp: **~ einer Sache** (G) ODER **von etw** (to the) south of sthg.

**Südost** (ohne Artikel) south-east.

**Südosten** der south-east.

**südöstlich** adj [Gegend] south-eastern; [Richtung, Wind] south-easterly ◇ präp: **~ einer Sache** (G) ODER **von etw** (to the) south-east of sthg.

**Südlpol** der - **1.** GEOGR South Pole - **2.** PHYS south pole.

**Südsee** die: **die ~** the South Seas (pl).

**Südlseite** die [von Haus, Garten] south side; [von Hang, Berg] south face.

**Südtirol** nt South Tyrol.

**Südltiroler, in** der, die South Tyrolean.

**südwärts** adv southwards.

**Südwest** der (ohne Artikel) south-west.

**Südwesten** der south-west.

**südwestlich** adj [Gegend] south-western; [Richtung, Wind] south-westerly ◇ präp: **~ einer Sache** (G) ODER **von etw** (to the) south-west of sthg.

**Südlwind** der south wind.

**Sueskanal** [ˈzuːɛskanaːl] der Suez Canal.

**Suff** der salopp boozing; **im ~** when one is plastered.

**süffig** adj very drinkable.

**süffisant** adj smug ◇ adv smugly.

**Suffix** (pl -e) das GRAM suffix.

**suggerieren** vt geh to suggest.

**Suggestion** (pl -en) die geh suggestion.

**suhlen** ⇒ **sich suhlen** ref eigtl & fig to wallow.

**Sühne** (pl -n) die geh atonement.

**sühnen** vt & vi geh: **etw/für etw ~** to atone for sthg.

**Suite** [ˈsviːt(ə)] (pl -n) die [im Hotel & MUS] suite.

**Sulfat** (pl -e) das CHEM sulphate.

**Sultan** (pl -e) der sultan.

**Sultanin** (pl -nen) die sultana.

**Sultanine** (pl -n) die sultana.

**Sülze** (pl -n) die brawn (U) Br, headcheese (U) Am.

**Sumatra** nt Sumatra.

**summarisch** adj summary ◇ adv summarily.

**Sümmchen** (pl -) das fam: **ein hübsches** ODER **rundes ~** a tidy sum.

**Summe** (*pl* -n) *die* sum.

**summen** (*perf* hat/ist gesummt) *vi (hat, ist)* to buzz <> *vt (hat)* to hum.

**Summer** (*pl* -) *der* buzzer.

**summieren** *vt* to add.
➡ **sich summieren** *ref* to add up.

**Sumpf** (*pl* Sümpfe) *der* [Sumpfgelände] marsh; [in Tropen] swamp.

**sumpfig** *adj* marshy.

**Sünde** (*pl* -n) *die* sin; **eine ~ begehen** to commit a sin.

**Sündenlbock** *der* scapegoat; **jn zum ~ machen** to make sb a scapegoat.

**Sünder, in** (*mpl* -; *fpl* -nen) *der, die* sinner.

**sündigen** *vi* - **1.** [religiös] to sin; **gegen etw ~** to sin against sthg - **2.** [gegen einen Vorsatz handeln] to indulge o.s.

**super** *fam adj (unver)* great <> *adv* really well <> *interj* great!

**Super** *das* four-star (petrol) *Br*, premium (gas) *Am*.

**Superlativ** (*pl* -e) *der* GRAM superlative.
➡ **Superlative** *pl* superlatives.

**Superlmacht** *die* superpower.

**Superlmarkt** *der* supermarket.

**Süppchen** (*pl* -) *das* soup.

**Suppe** (*pl* -n) *die* - **1.** [Essen] soup; **jm die ~ versalzen** *fam fig* to put a spoke in sb's wheel - **2.** *fam* [Dunst, Nebel] pea souper.

**Suppenlkelle** *die* soup ladle.

**Suppenllöffel** *der* soup spoon.

**Suppenlschüssel** *die* tureen.

**Suppenlteller** *der* soup plate.

**Suppenlwürfel** *der* stock cube.

**Surflbrett** [ˈsœːɐ̯fbʀɛt] *das* - **1.** [zum Wellensurfen] surfboard - **2.** [zum Windsurfen] sailboard.

**surfen** [ˈsœːɐ̯fn̩] (*perf* hat/ist gesurft) *vi* - **1.** [gen & EDV] to surf - **2.** [mit Segel] to windsurf.

**Surfer, in** [ˈsœːɐ̯fɐ, rɪn] (*mpl* -; *fpl* -nen) *der, die* - **1.** [gen & EDV] surfer - **2.** [Windsurfer] windsurfer.

**Surinam** *nt* Surinam.

**Surrealismus** *der* surrealism.

**surren** (*perf* hat/ist gesurrt) *vi* - **1.** *(ist)* [Pfeil] to whizz - **2.** *(hat)* [Maschine] to whirr; [Insekt] to buzz.

**suspekt** *adj* suspicious; **jm ~ sein** to make sb suspicious.

**suspendieren** *vt* to suspend; **jn von etw ~** to suspend sb from sthg.

**süß** *adj* sweet <> *adv:* **~ schmecken/aussehen** to taste/look sweet; **träume ~!** sweet dreams!

**süßen** *vt* to sweeten.

**Süßigkeiten** *pl* sweets *Br*, candy (*U*) *Am*.

**süßlich** *adj* - **1.** [süß] sweetish - **2.** [übertrieben freundlich] syrupy <> *adv* - **1.** [süß]: **~ schmecken** to have a sweetish taste - **2.** [übertrieben freundlich] in a sickly-sweet way.

**süß-sauer** *adj* sweet and sour <> *adv:* **~ schmecken** to have a sweet and sour taste.

**Süßlspeise** *die* dessert.

**Süßwasser** *das* fresh water.

**SV** [ɛsˈfaʊ] (*abk für* **Spielvereinigung**) *der (ohne pl)* sports association.

**SVP** [ɛsfaʊˈpeː] (*abk für* **Schweizer Volkspartei**) *die (ohne pl)* political party in Switzerland.

**SW** (*abk für* **Südwest**) SW.

**Sweatshirt** [ˈsvɛtʃœːɐ̯t] (*pl* -s) *das* sweatshirt.

**SWF** [ɛsveːˈɛf] (*abk für* **Südwestfunk**) *der (ohne pl)* radio station in Germany.

**Swimminglpool** [ˈsvɪmɪŋpuːl] *der* swimming pool.

**Sydney** [ˈsɪdnɪ] *nt* Sydney.

**Sylt** *nt* Sylt.

**Symbol** (*pl* -e) *das* - **1.** [Zeichen] symbol - **2.** EDV [Icon] icon.

**Symbolik** *die* symbolism.

**symbolisch** *adj* symbolic <> *adv* symbolically.

**symbolisieren** *vt* to symbolize.

**Symmetrie** (*pl* -n) *die* symmetry.

**symmetrisch** *adj* symmetrical <> *adv* symmetrically.

**Sympathie** (*pl* -n) *die* [Zuneigung] liking (*U*); **für jn/etw ~ empfinden geh** to have sympathy with sb/sthg; **sich** (*D*) **viele ~n verscherzen** to lose a lot of sympathy; **bei aller ~** *fam* with the best will in the world.

**Sympathisant, in** (*mpl* -en; *fpl* -nen) *der, die* sympathizer.

**sympathisch** *adj* nice; **sie ist mir ~** I like her <> *adv* nicely.

**sympathisieren** *vi:* **mit jm ~** to sympathize with sb.

**Symphonie** = Sinfonie.

**Symphoniker** = Sinfoniker.

**Symptom** (*pl* -e) *das* - **1.** MED symptom - **2.** [Anzeichen] sign.

**Synagoge** (*pl* -n) *die* synagogue.

**synchron** *adj* synchronous <> *adv* synchronously.

**synchronisieren** *vt* [Film, Stimme] to dub; [Bewegungen, Abläufe] to synchronize.

**Syndikat** (*pl* -e) *das* syndicate.

**Syndrom** (*pl* -e) *das* MED syndrome.

**Synode** (pl -n) die REL synod.

**Synonym** (pl -e) das synonym.

**Syntax** (pl -en) die syntax.

**Synthese** (pl -n) die: **die ~ aus etw** the synthesis of sthg.

**synthetisch** adj synthetic ◇ adv synthetically.

**Syphilis** die syphilis.

**Syrer, in** (mpl -; fpl -nen) der, die Syrian.

**Syrien** nt Syria.

**syrisch** adj Syrian.

**System** [zys'te:m] (pl -e) das system; **mit ~** systematically; **~ haben** to be systematic.

**System|absturz** der EDV system crash.

**Systematik** (pl -en) die system.

**systematisch** adj systematic ◇ adv systematically.

**System|datei** die EDV system file.

**System|diskette** die EDV system disk.

**System|software** die EDV system software.

**Szene** (pl -n) die - **1.** [im Film, Theater] scene; **sich in ~ setzen** fig to put o.s. in the limelight - **2.** [Vorfall] scene; **(jm) eine ~ machen** to make a scene (in front of sb) - **3.** [Milieu] scene.

**t, T** [te:] (pl - ODER -s) das t, T.

➡ **t** abk für **Tonne.**

**Tab.** abk für **Tabelle.**

**Tabak, Tabak** (pl -e) der tobacco (U).

**Tabak|geschäft** das tobacconist's.

**Tabak|laden** der tobacconist's.

**Tabak|steuer** die duty on tobacco.

**Tabak|waren** pl tobacco (U).

**Tabasco**® der Tabasco.®

**tabellarisch** adj tabular ◇ adv in tabular form.

**Tabelle** (pl -n) die - **1.** [Liste] table - **2.** SPORT (league) table.

**Tabellen|führer** der SPORT league leaders (pl).

**Tabellen|platz** der SPORT position in the (league) table.

**Tablett** (pl -s ODER -e) das tray.

**Tablette** (pl -n) die tablet, pill.

**tabu** adj (unver): **etw ist ~ sthg** is taboo.

**Tabu** (pl -s) das taboo.

**Tacho** (pl -s) der fam speedometer.

**Tacho|meter** der speedometer.

**Tadel** (pl -) der geh rebuke.

**tadellos** adj impeccable ◇ adv impeccably.

**tadeln** vt to rebuke.

**Tadschikistan** nt Tadzhikistan.

**Tafel** (pl -n) die - **1.** [Schreibtafel] blackboard - **2.** geh [Tisch] table - **3.** [Stück]: **eine ~ Schokolade** a bar of chocolate.

**tafelfertig** adj ready-to-eat.

**tafeln** vi geh to feast.

**täfeln** vt to panel.

**Täfelung** (pl -en) die panelling (U).

**Tafelwasser** (pl -wässer) das mineral water.

**Tafel|wein** der table wine.

**Taft** (pl -e) der taffeta.

**Tag** (pl -e) der - **1.** [24 Stunden] day; **in vierzehn ~en** in a fortnight - **2.** [in seinem Verlauf] day; **~ und Nacht geöffnet** open 24 hours - **3.** RW: **am helllichten ~** in broad daylight; **auf seine alten ~e (hin)** fam in one's old age; **bei ~(e) besehen** in the cold light of day; **dieser ~e** fam [demnächst] in the next few days; [neulich] recently; **über/unter ~(e)** above/below ground; **~ der offenen Tür** open day.

➡ **eines Tages** adv [irgendwann] one day.

➡ **guten Tag** interj hello!; [am Morgen] good morning!; [am Nachmittag] good afternoon!

➡ **Tag für Tag** adv [immer] day after day.

➡ **von Tag zu Tag** adv [immer mehr] day by day.

➡ **Tage** pl - **1.** [Zeit] days; **js ~e sind gezählt** [muss sterben/weggehen] sb's days are numbered - **2.** fam [Periode] period (sg); **sie hat/bekommt ihre ~e** fam she's got her period; siehe auch zutage.

**tagaus** adv: **~, tagein** day in, day out.

**Tag der Deutschen Einheit** der Day of German Unity.

**Tagebau** der opencast mining.

**Tage|buch** *das* diary.

**tagelang** *adj* lasting for days; **~er Regen** days of rain ⟨> *adv* for days.

**Tagelöhner, in** (*mpl* -; *fpl* -nen) *der, die* day labourer.

**tagen** *vi* - **1.** [Sitzung haben - gen] to meet; [ - Gericht] to be in session - **2.** *geh* [hell werden]: **es tagt** day is breaking.

**Tagesab|lauf** *der* day.

**Tagesan|bruch** *der* dawn.

**Tagesaus|flug** *der* day trip.

**Tagesbedarf** *der* (*ohne pl*) daily requirement.

**Tages|creme, Tages|krem** *die* day cream.

**Tages|einnahme** *die* daily takings (*pl*).

**Tages|fahrt** *die* day trip.

**Tages|gericht** *das* dish of the day.

**Tages|geschehen** *das* day's events (*pl*).

**Tages|karte** *die* day ticket.

**Tages|krem** *die* = **Tagescreme**.

**Tages|licht** *das* daylight; **etw kommt ans ~** sthg comes to light.

**Tages|mutter** *die* childminder *Br*, babysitter.

**Tages|ordnung** *die* agenda; **zur ~ übergehen** [auf einer Versammlung] to proceed with the agenda; [im täglichen Leben] to carry on as usual; **etw ist an der ~** sthg is the order of the day.

**Tagesrückfahr|karte** *die* day return (ticket) *Br*, day round-trip ticket *Am*.

**Tages|schau** *die* news.

**Tages|zeit** *die* time of day.

**Tages|zeitung** *die* daily newspaper.

**taghell** *adj* as bright as daylight.

**täglich** *adj* daily ⟨> *adv* every day; **dreimal ~** three times a day.

**tags** *adv* during the day; **~ zuvor/darauf** the day before/after.

**Tag|schicht** *die* day shift.

**tagsüber** *adv* during the day.

**tagtäglich** *adj* daily.

**Tagung** (*pl* -en) *die* conference.

**Tahiti** *nt* Tahiti.

**Taifun** (*pl* -e) *der* typhoon.

**Taille** ['taljə] (*pl* -n) *die* waist.

**tailliert** [ta'jiːɐ̯t] *adj* fitted.

**Taipeh** *nt* Taipei.

**Taiwan** *nt* Taiwan.

**Takt** (*pl* -e) *der* - **1.** [musikalische Einheit] bar - **2.** (*ohne pl*) [Feingefühl] tact - **3.** (*ohne pl*) [Rhythmus] time - **4.** *RW*: **jn aus dem ~ bringen** to put

sb off; **zu etw ein paar ~e sagen** *fam* to have a few things to say about sthg.

**Takt|frequenz** *die* EDV clock rate.

**Takt|gefühl** *das* tact.

**taktieren** *vi* to manoeuvre.

**Taktik** (*pl* -en) *die* tactics (*pl*).

**Taktiker, in** (*mpl* -; *fpl* -nen) *der, die* tactician.

**taktisch** *adj* [klug] tactical ⟨> *adv* tactically; **~ klug vorgehen** to use clever tactics.

**taktlos** *adj* tactless ⟨> *adv* tactlessly.

**Taktlosigkeit** (*pl* -en) *die* tactlessness.

**Takt|stock** *der* baton.

**taktvoll** *adj* tactful ⟨> *adv* tactfully.

**Tal** (*pl* Täler) *das* valley.

**talabwärts** *adv* down the valley.

**Talar** (*pl* -e) *der* robe.

**talaufwärts** *adv* up the valley.

**Talent** (*pl* -e) *das* talent.

**talentiert** *adj* talented ⟨> *adv* with talent.

**Taler** (*pl* -) *der* thaler.

**Tal|fahrt** *die* - **1.** [ins Tal] descent into the valley - **2.** *fig* [von Wirtschaft, Aktien] decline.

**Talg** (*pl* -e) *der* tallow; [von Menschen] sebum.

**Talisman** (*pl* -e) *der* talisman.

**Tal|kessel** *der* basin.

**Talkshow** ['tɔːkʃoː] (*pl* -s) *die* talk show.

**Tal|sohle** (*pl* -n) [von Tälern] valley floor - **2.** *fig* [von Zyklus, Entwicklung] trough.

**Tal|sperre** *die* dam.

**Tal|station** *die* valley-based terminus for ski-lift or mountain railway.

**Tamburin, Tamburin** (*pl* -e) *das* tambourine.

**Tampon** ['tampɔn, tam'poːn] (*pl* -s) *der* tampon.

**Tand** *der* (*ohne pl*) *geh* trinkets (*pl*).

**Tandem** (*pl* -s) *das* tandem.

**Tang** (*pl* -e) *der* seaweed (*U*).

**Tanga** (*pl* -s) *der* thong.

**Tangente** (*pl* -n) *die* MATH tangent.

**tangieren** *vt* - **1.** [beeinflussen] to affect; **das tangiert mich alles überhaupt nicht** I couldn't care less about all that - **2.** MATH to be tangent to.

**Tango** (*pl* -s) *der* tango.

**Tank** (*pl* -s) *der* tank.

**Tank|deckel** *der* fuel cap, petrol cap *Br*.

**tanken** *vi* to get some petrol *Br* ODER gas *Am* ⟨> *vt* - **1.** [auftanken]: **Benzin ~** to get some petrol *Br* ODER gas *Am* - **2.** [genießen] to get one's fill of.

**Tanker** (*pl* -) *der* tanker.

**Tank|schloss** *das* fuel ODER petrol *Br* cap lock.

**Tank|stelle** *die* petrol station *Br*, gas station *Am*.

**Tank|wagen** *der* tanker.

**Tankwart, in** (*mpl* -e; *fpl* -nen) *der, die* petrol *Br* ODER gas *Am* station attendant.

**Tanne** (*pl* -n) *die* - **1.** [Baum] fir tree - **2.** *(ohne pl)* [Holz] fir.

**Tannen|baum** *der* - **1.** [Tanne] fir tree - **2.** [Weihnachtsbaum] Christmas tree.

**Tannen|nadel** *die* fir needle.

**Tannen|zapfen** *der* fir cone.

**Tansania** *nt* Tanzania.

**Tantal** *das* CHEM tantalum.

**Tante** (*pl* -n) *die* - **1.** [Verwandte] aunt - **2.** *fam* [als Anrede] auntie.

**Tante-Emma-|Laden** *der* corner shop.

**Tantieme** [tã'tie:mə] (*pl* -n) *die* [für Künstler] royalty.

**Tanz** (*pl* Tänze) *der* dance.

**Tanzbein** *das (ohne pl)*: das ~ schwingen *fam hum* to hit the floor.

**tänzeln** (*perf* hat/ist getänzelt) *vi* - **1.** (ist) [geziert gehen] to skip - **2.** (hat) [sich unruhig bewegen] to prance.

**tanzen** *vt* & *vi* to dance; komm, lass uns ~ gehen let's go dancing; willst du mit mir tanzen? would you like to dance?

**Tänzer, in** (*mpl* -; *fpl* -nen) *der, die* dancer.

**Tanz|fläche** *die* dance floor.

**Tanz|kurs** *der* - **1.** [Veranstaltung] dancing lessons (*pl*) - **2.** [Teilnehmer] dancing class.

**Tanz|schule** *die* dancing school.

**Tanz|stunde** *die* - **1.** [Kurs] dancing lessons (*pl*) - **2.** [Unterrichtsstunde] dancing lesson.

**Tanz|turnier** *das* dancing competition.

**tapern** (*perf* ist getapert) *vi Norddt* to dodder.

**Tapet** *das*: etw aufs ~ bringen *fam* to bring sthg up.

**Tapete** (*pl* -n) *die* wallpaper *(U)*.

**Tapeten|wechsel** *der fig* change of scenery.

**tapezieren** *vt* & *vi* to wallpaper.

**tapfer** *adj* brave <> *adv* bravely.

**Tapferkeit** *die* bravery.

**tappen** (*perf* ist getappt) *vi*: durch das Zimmer ~ to patter through the room.

**tapsig** *adj* awkward <> *adv* awkwardly.

**Tarantel** (*pl* -n) *die* tarantula; wie von der ~ gestochen *fam fig* as if stung.

**Tarif** (*pl* -e) *der* - **1.** WIRTSCH rate - **2.** [Gebühr] charge; [Verkehrstarif] fare.

**Tarif|abschluss** *die* collective agreement.

**Tarif|autonomie** *die* right to free collective bargaining.

**Tarif|konflikt** *der* dispute over pay and conditions.

**tariflich** *adj* [Einigung, Vertrag] collective <> *adv* according to the collective agreement.

**Tarif|lohn** *der* agreed rate of pay.

**Tarif|partner** *der* social partner.

**Tarifver|handlung** *die* collective bargaining.

**Tarif|vertrag** *der* collective agreement.

**tarnen** *vt* to camouflage.
➠ **sich tarnen** *ref* to camouflage o.s.; sich als etw ~ to disguise o.s. as sthg.

**Tarnung** *die* camouflage.

**Tarock** (*pl* -s) *das* ODER *der* card game usually played with a pack of cards including 22 tarots.

**Tarot** [ta'ro:] (*pl* -s) *das* ODER *der* tarot.

**Tasche** (*pl* -n) *die* - **1.** [Tragetasche, Handtasche] bag - **2.** [Hosentasche] pocket - **3.** *RW*: etw aus eigener ~ bezahlen to pay for sthg o.s.; etw (schon) in der ~ haben *fam* to have sthg in the bag; jm auf der ~ liegen *fam* to live off sb; jn in die ~ stecken *fam* to be more than a match for sb.

**Taschen|buch** *das* paperback.

**Taschen|dieb, in** *der, die* pickpocket.

**Taschen|format** *das*: im ~ pocket-sized.

**Taschen|geld** *das* pocket money.

**Taschen|kalender** *der* pocket diary.

**Taschen|lampe** *die* torch *Br*, flashlight *Am*.

**Taschen|messer** *das* penknife, pocketknife.

**Taschen|rechner** *der* pocket calculator.

**Taschen|schirm** *der* telescopic umbrella.

**Taschentuch** (*pl* -tücher) *das* [aus Stoff] handkerchief; [aus Papier] tissue.

**Taschen|uhr** *die* pocket watch.

**Taschkent** *nt* Tashkent.

**Tasse** (*pl* -n) *die* cup; nicht alle ~n im Schrank haben *fam fig* & *abw* to have a screw loose.

**Tastatur** (*pl* -en) *die* keyboard.

**Tastaturbelegung** (*pl* -en) *die* EDV keyboard layout.

**Taste** (*pl* -n) *die* - **1.** [von Instrument, Computer] key - **2.** [von Geräten] button.

**tasten** *vi* to feel one's way; nach etw ~ to feel for sthg <> *vt* to feel.
➠ **sich tasten** *ref* to feel one's way.

**Tasten|instrument** *das* keyboard instrument.

**Tasten|telefon** *das* push-button telephone.

**Tastsinn** *der* sense of touch.

**tat** *prät* ▷ **tun.**

**Tat** (*pl* -en) *die* action; **eine verbrecherische ~** a criminal act; **eine gute ~** a good deed; **jn auf frischer ~ ertappen** *fig* to catch sb in the act; **etw in die ~ umsetzen** to put sthg into action.
↠ **in der Tat** *adv* [tatsächlich] indeed.

**Tatbe|stand** *der* - **1.** RECHT: **der ~ der Bestechung** the offence of bribery; **den ~ des Betrugs erfüllen** to constitute fraud - **2.** [Tatsache] facts (*pl*) (of the matter).

**tatenlos** *adj* idle ▷ *adv* idly; **wir mussten ~ zusehen** we could only stand and watch.

**Täter, in** (*mpl* -; *fpl* -nen) *der, die* culprit.

**Täterschaft** *die* guilt.

**Tather|gang** *der* course of events.

**tätig** *adj* - **1.** [beschäftigt]: **~ sein** to work - **2.** [aktiv] active; **wir müssen in dieser Sache ~ werden** we must take action in this matter.

**tätigen** *vt geh* [von Geschäft] to transact.

**Tätigkeit** (*pl* -en) *die* [Arbeit] job; [Aktivität] activity.

**tatkräftig** *adj* active ▷ *adv* actively.

**tätlich** *adj* physical; **~ werden** to become violent ▷ *adv* physically.

**Tätlichkeiten** *pl:* **es kam zu ~** there was violence.

**Tat|ort** *der* - **1.** [von Verbrechen] scene of the crime - **2.** [Fernsehsendung] *television detective series.*

**tätowieren** *vt* & *vi* to tattoo.

**Tätowierung** (*pl* -en) *die* - **1.** [Vorgang] tattooing (*U*) - **2.** [Ergebnis] tattoo.

**Tatra** *die* Tatra; **hohe ~** High Tatra.

**Tat|sache** *die* fact; **jn vor vollendete ~n stellen** *fig* to present sb with a fait accompli ▷ *interj* it's true!

**tatsächlich, tatsächlich** *adj* real, actual ▷ *adv* really; **du bist ja ~ pünktlich!** you're actually on time!

**tätscheln** *vt* [liebkosen] to pat.

**Tattoo** [ta'tu:] (*pl* -s) *das* = **Tätowierung.**

**Tatverdacht** *der* suspicion.

**Tatze** (*pl* -n) *die* paw.

**Tau** (*pl* -e) *der* [Niederschlag] dew ▷ *das* [Seil] rope.

**taub** *adj* - **1.** [nichts hörend] deaf; **sich ~ stellen** *fam* to turn a deaf ear - **2.** [nichts fühlend] numb.

**Taube** (*pl* -n) *der, die* [Gehörlose] deaf person ▷ *die* [Tier - gewöhnlich] pigeon; [ - weiße] dove.

**Tauben|schlag** *der* - **1.** [Unterkunft für Tauben] pigeon loft; [für Turteltauben] dovecot - **2.** [Kommen und Gehen]: **hier geht es zu wie im ~** it's like Piccadilly Circus *Br* ODER Times Square *Am* in here.

**taubstumm** *adj* deaf and dumb.

**Taubstumme** (*pl* -n) *der, die* deaf-mute.

**tauchen** (*perf* hat/ist getaucht) *vi* (hat, ist) to dive ▷ *vt* (hat) - **1.** [eintauchen] to dip - **2.** [drücken] to duck.

**Taucher, in** (*mpl* -; *fpl* -nen) *der, die* diver.

**Taucher|brille** *die* diving goggles (*pl*).

**Tauchsieder** ['tauxzi:dɐ] (*pl* -) *der* element.

**tauen** (*perf* hat/ist getaut) *vi* (hat, ist) to melt; **es taut** it's thawing ▷ *vt* (hat) to thaw.

**Tauf|becken** *das* font.

**Taufe** (*pl* -n) *die* - **1.** [Vorgang] christening - **2.** (ohne *pl*) [Sakrament] baptism; **etw aus der ~ heben** *fig* to launch sthg.

**taufen** *vt* - **1.** REL [Menschen] to baptize - **2.** [Tiere, Gegenstände] to name.

**Tauf|pate** *der* godfather.

**Tauf|patin** *die* godmother.

**taufrisch** *adj* - **1.** [Blume, Hemd] fresh - **2.** *fam* [Mensch]: **~ sein** to be as fresh as a daisy.

**Tauf|schein** *der* certificate of baptism.

**taugen** *vi:* **nichts/wenig ~** to be no/not much good; **zu** ODER **für etw ~** to be suitable for sthg.

**tauglich** *adj* - **1.** [geeignet] suitable - **2.** MIL fit (for service).

**Tauglichkeit** *die* suitability.

**Taumel** *der* (ohne *pl*) - **1.** [Rausch] frenzy; **ein ~ der Freude ergriff sie** they went into raptures - **2.** [Schwindel] (feeling of) dizziness.

**taumeln** (*perf* hat/ist getaumelt) *vi* - **1.** (ist) [schwankend gehen] to stagger - **2.** (hat) [schwanken] to reel.

**Taunus** *der:* **der ~** the Taunus.

**Tausch** (*pl* -e) *der* exchange.

**tauschen** *vt* to swap ▷ *vi:* **mit jm ~** [Arbeitszeit] to swap with sb; [an js Stelle sein, jd anderes sein] to swap places with sb.

**täuschen** *vt* to deceive; [Gegner] to trick ▷ *vi* to be deceptive.
↠ **sich täuschen** *ref* to be wrong; **sich in jm ~** to be wrong about sb.

**täuschend** *adj* deceptive ▷ *adv* deceptively.

**Tausch|handel** *der* barter.

**Tausch|objekt** *das* object for barter.

**Täuschung** (*pl* -en) *die* - **1.** [Irreführung] deception - **2.** [Verwechslung] illusion; **optische ~** optical illusion.

**Täuschungs|manöver** *das* ploy.

**tausend** *num* a ODER one thousand; *siehe auch* **sechs.**

**Tausend** (*pl* - ODER -e) *das* thousand.
↠ **Tausende** *pl* [sehr viele]: **zu ~en** by the thousand; *siehe auch* **Sechs.**

**Tausender** (pl -) der MATH thousand.

**tausenderlei** adj (unver) a thousand and one.

**tausendfach** adj thousandfold; **die ~e Menge** a thousand times the amount.

**Tausendfüßler** (pl -) der centipede.

**tausendmal** adv a thousand times.

**tausendste, r, s** adj thousandth; siehe auch sechste.

**Tausendste** (pl -n) der, die, das thousandth; siehe auch Sechste.

**tausendstel** adj (unver) thousandth; siehe auch sechstel.

**Tausendstel** (pl -) das thousandth; siehe auch Sechstel.

**Tauwetter** das thaw.

**Tauziehen** das tug-of-war.

**Taxe** (pl -n) die [Taxi] taxi.

**Taxi** (pl -s) das taxi.

**taxieren** vt - **1.** [Kunstwerk, Gebäude] to value - **2.** [Alter, Entfernung] to estimate - **3.** [Person] to size up.

**Taxifahrer, in** der, die taxi driver.

**Taxistand** der taxi rank.

**Tb** [teːˈbeː], **Tbc** [teːbeːˈtseː] die abk für **Tuberkulose**.

**Teak** [tiːk] das teak.

**Team** [tiːm] (pl -s) das team.

**Teamarbeit** die teamwork.

**Technik** (pl -en) die - **1.** (ohne pl) [Wissenschaft] technology - **2.** [Methode] technique - **3.** [Ausrüstung] equipment - **4.** (ohne pl) [Funktionsweise] workings (pl).

**Techniker, in** (mpl -; fpl -nen) der, die engineer; [im Sport, in Musik] technician.

**technisch** adj technical; [Fortschritt] technological ◇ adv technically; [fortgeschritten] technologically.

**Technische Hochschule** die technical college.

**Technische Überwachungsverein** der amt institution charged with testing roadworthiness of cars and safety of consumer goods and installations.

**Techno** der MUS techno.

**Technologie** (pl -n) die technology.

**Technologiepark** der science park.

**Technologietransfer** der transfer of technology.

**technologisch** adj technological ◇ adv technologically.

**Teddy** (pl -s), **Teddybär** (pl -en) der teddy bear.

**Tee** (pl -s) der - **1.** [gen] tea; **schwarzer ~** black tea - **2.** [Kräutertee] herbal tea.

**Teebeutel** der teabag.

**Teekanne** die teapot.

**Teekessel** der kettle.

**Teelöffel** der teaspoon.

**Teenager** (pl -) der teenager.

**Teer** der tar (U).

**teeren** vt to tar.

**Teerpappe** die roofing felt.

**Teesieb** das tea strainer.

**Teetasse** die teacup.

**Teewagen** der tea trolley.

**Teewurst** die type of soft, smoked German sausage used for spreading.

**Teflonpfanne**® die Teflon® frying pan.

**Teheran** nt Teheran.

**Teich** (pl -e) der pond.

**Teig** (pl -e) der dough (U).

**teigig** adj [Haut] pasty.

**Teigwaren** pl amt pasta (U).

**Teil** (pl -e) der [Teilmenge] part ◇ der ODER das [Anteil] share; **seinen ~ zu etw beitragen** fig to do one's share in sthg; **sich** (D) **seinen ~ denken** fig to keep one's thoughts to o.s. ◇ das [Bestandteil] part.
➡ **zum Teil** adv [teilweise] partly.

**Teilabschnitt** der section.

**Teilaspekt** der aspect.

**teilbar** adj divisible.

**Teilbereich** der branch.

**Teilchen** (pl -) das - **1.** PHYS particle - **2.** [kleines Teil] piece - **3.** Norddt [Gebäck] cake (individual).

**teilen** vt [aufteilen] to share; [zerteilen] to divide; **etw mit jm ~** to share sthg with sb; **sich** (D) **etw ~** to share sthg ◇ vi to share.
➡ **sich teilen** ref [Gruppe] to split up; [Straße] to fork; [Meinungen] to be divided.

**Teilerfolg** der partial success.

**Teilgebiet** das branch.

**teilhaben** vi (unreg): **an etw** (D) **~** to share in sthg.

**Teilhaber, in** (mpl -; fpl -nen) der, die partner.

**Teilmenge** die MATH subset.

**teilmöbliert** adj partially furnished.

**Teilnahme** (pl -n) die - **1.** [Aufmerksamkeit, Beteiligung] participation (U) - **2.** [an Kurs] attendance - **3.** [Mitgefühl] sympathy.

**Teilnahmebedingung** die conditions (pl) of entry.

**teilnahmslos** adj apathetic ◇ adv apathetically.

**T**

**teil|nehmen** *vi (unreg)* - **1.** [mitmachen]: **an etw** *(D)* ~ to take part in sthg - **2.** [mitfühlen]: **an etw** *(D)* ~ *geh* to share in sthg.

**Teilnehmer, in** *(mpl -; fpl -nen) der, die* participant.

**Teilnehmer|liste** *die* list of participants.

**teils** *adv fam* partly.
➡ **teils ..., teils ...** *adv* partly ..., partly ...

**Teil|strecke** *die* stretch.

**Teilung** *(pl -en) die* division.

**teilweise** *adv* - **1.** [zum Teil] partly - **2.** [zeitweise] sometimes ◇ *adj* partial.

**Teil|zahlung** *die* payment by instalments.

**Teilzeit|arbeit** *die* part-time work.

**Teilzeit|beschäftigte** *der, die* part-time worker.

**Teint** *(pl -s) der* - **1.** [Gesichtsfarbe] complexion - **2.** [Haut] skin.

**Tel.** *(abk für Telefon)* tel.

**Tel Aviv** [tɛla'viːf] *nt* Tel Aviv.

**Tele|arbeit** *die* teleworking.

**Telefon, Telefon** *(pl -e) das* - **1.** [Gerät] telephone; **am ~** on the telephone - **2.** *fam* [Anruf]: ~ **für dich** there's a call for you.

**Telefonan|ruf** *der* telephone call.

**Telefonan|schluss** *der* telephone line.

**Telefonat** *(pl -e) das* telephone call.

**Telefon|auskunft** *die* directory enquiries *Br*, information *Am*.

**Telefon|buch** *das* telephone book.

**Telefon|gebühr** *die* telephone charge.

**Telefon|gespräch** *das* telephone conversation.

**telefonieren** *vi* to make a telephone call; **mit jm ~** to talk to sb on the telephone.

**telefonisch** *adj* telephone *(vor Subst)* ◇ *adv* by telephone; **ich bin ~ erreichbar** you can reach me by telephone.

**Telefon|kabel** *das* telephone cable.

**Telefon|karte** *die* phonecard.

**Telefon|leitung** *die* telephone line.

**Telefon|netz** *das* telephone network.

**Telefon|nummer** *die* telephone number.

**Telefon|rechnung** *die* telephone bill.

**Telefonver|bindung** *die* telephone line.

**Telefon|zelle** *die* telephone box.

**Telefon|zentrale** *die* switchboard.

**Telegrafen|mast** *der* telegraph pole.

**telegrafieren** *vt* to telegraph.

**telegrafisch** *adj* telegraphic ◇ *adv* by telegram.

**Telegramm** *(pl -e) das* telegram.

**Telegramm|formular** *das* telegram form.

**Telegramm|stil** *der* telegraphic style.

**Tele|kolleg** *das* ≈ Open University *Br*, *course of lectures on television, forming part of a distance-learning course.*

**Telekom**® *die German telecommunications company.*

**Telekommunikation** *die (ohne pl)* telecommunications *(pl).*

**Tele|objektiv** *das* FOTO telephoto lens.

**Telepathie** *die* telepathy.

**Teleskop** *(pl -e) das* telescope.

**Telex** *(pl -e) das* telex.

**Teller** *(pl -) der* [Gefäß] plate; **seinen ~ leer essen** to finish what's on one's plate.

**Tempel** *(pl -) der* temple.

**Temperament** *(pl -e) das* - **1.** [Energie] liveliness; ~ **haben** to be lively - **2.** [Wesen] temperament.

**temperamentvoll** *adj* lively.

**Temperatur** *(pl -en) die* temperature; ~ **haben** to have a temperature.

**Temperatur|anstieg** *der* rise in temperature.

**temperaturbeständig** *adj* resistant to heat and cold.

**Temperaturrück|gang** *der* drop in temperature.

**Temperatur|schwankung** *die* temperature fluctuation.

**Tempo**[1] *(pl -s* ODER **Tempi)** *das* - **1.** *(pl Tempos)* [Geschwindigkeit] speed; **hier gilt ~ 30** there's a 30 km/h speed limit here - **2.** *(pl Tempi)* MUS tempo.

**Tempo**®[2] *(pl -s) das fam* [Papiertaschentuch] tissue.

**Tempo|limit** *das* speed limit.

**temporär** *adj geh* temporary.

**Tempo|sünder, in** *der, die person who has committed a speeding offence.*

**Tempotaschen|tuch**® *das fam* tissue.

**Tempus** *(pl Tempora) das* GRAM tense.

**Tendenz** *(pl -en) die* - **1.** [Entwicklung] trend - **2.** [Neigung] tendency.

**tendenziell** *adj* in keeping with the trend.

**tendenziös** *abw adj* biased ◇ *adv* in a biased way.

**Tendenz|wende** *die* change in a/the trend.

**tendieren** *vi* to tend; **zu etw ~** to tend towards sthg.

**Teneriffa** *nt* Tenerife.

**Tennis** *das* tennis.

**Tennis|arm** *der* tennis elbow.

**Tennis|ball** *der* tennis ball.

theatralisch

**Tennis|platz** der tennis court.

**Tennis|schläger** der tennis racquet.

**Tenor**[1] (pl Tenöre) der mus tenor.

**Tenor**[2] der (ohne pl) geh tenor.

**Tentakel** (pl -) der ODER das tentacle.

**Teppich** (pl -e) der - **1.** [Einzelstück] rug; **der rote ~** the red carpet; **etw unter den ~ kehren** fig to sweep sthg under the carpet - **2.** [Teppichboden] carpet.

**Teppich|boden** der carpet.

**Termin** (pl -e) der - **1.** [Zeitpunkt] date; [Vereinbarung] appointment; **einen ~ vereinbaren** to make an appointment - **2.** RECHT hearing.

**Terminal** ['tø:ɡminəl] (pl -s) der ODER das [Gebäude] terminal ◇ das EDV terminal.

**termingebunden** adv to a deadline.

**Termin|kalender** der diary.

**terminlich** adj scheduled; **~e Verpflichtungen** commitments; **~e Schwierigkeiten** problems regarding schedule.

**Terminologie** (pl -n) die terminology.

**Termin|plan** der schedule.

**Terminus** (pl Termini) der geh term.

**Termite** (pl -n) die termite.

**Terpentin** (pl -e) das turpentine (U).

**Terrain** [tɛ'rɛ̃:l] (pl -s) das geh terrain; **das ~ sondieren** fig to test the ground.

**Terrarium** [tɛ'ra:rjʊm] (pl Terrarien) das terrarium.

**Terrasse** (pl -n) die - **1.** [am Haus] patio - **2.** [am Berg] terrace.

**terrassenförmig** adj terraced ◇ adv in terraces.

**Terrier** ['tɛrjɐ] (pl -) der terrier.

**Terrine** (pl -n) die tureen.

**territorial** adj territorial.

**Territorium** [tɛri'to:rjʊm] (pl -torien) das territory.

**Terror** der - **1.** [Gewalt] terrorism - **2.** [Angst] terror - **3.** : **~ machen** fam to raise hell.

**Terroran|schlag** der terrorist attack.

**terrorisieren** vt to terrorize.

**Terrorismus** der terrorism.

**Terrorist, in** (mpl -en; fpl -nen) der, die terrorist.

**terroristisch** adj terrorist.

**tertiär** adj - **1.** [Erdzeitalter] Tertiary - **2.** geh [Sektor] tertiary.

**Terz** (pl -en) die mus third.

**Tesa**® der Sellotape® Br, Scotch tape® Am.

**Tesafilm**® der Sellotape® Br, Scotch tape® Am.

**Tessin** das Ticino (canton in south-east Switzerland).

**Tessiner, in** (mpl -; fpl -nen) der, die native/inhabitant of Ticino.

**Test** (pl -e ODER -s) der test.

**Testament** (pl -e) das - **1.** [letzter Wille] will; **sein ~ machen** to make one's will - **2.** REL: **das Alte/Neue ~** the Old/New Testament.

**testamentarisch** adv: **etw ~ verfügen** to put sthg in one's will.

**Test|bild** das TV test card.

**testen** vt to test.

**Test|person** die subject.

**Test|reihe** die series of tests.

**Test|strecke** die test circuit.

**Tetanus|impfung** die tetanus vaccination.

**teuer** adj - **1.** [Preis] expensive - **2.** geh [Freund] dear ◇ adv dearly; **etw kommt jm** ODER **jn ~ zu stehen** sb pays dearly for sthg.

**Teufel** (pl -) der - **1.** [gen] devil - **2.** RW: **der ~ ist los** fam all hell has broken loose; **den ~ (nicht) an die Wand malen** fam (not) to tempt fate; **in ~s Küche kommen** to be in deep water; **jn zum ~ jagen** fam to send sb packing; **scher dich** ODER geh **zum ~!** salopp go to hell!; **zum ~ mit ihr!** fam [Schluss damit] to hell with her!
➥ **auf Teufel komm raus** adv fam [unbedingt] like crazy.

**Teufels|kreis** der vicious circle.

**teuflisch** adj devilish ◇ adv devilishly.

**Texas** nt Texas.

**Text** (pl -e) der - **1.** [Geschriebenes] text; [von Lied] lyrics (pl) - **2.** [von Bild] caption.

**Text|datei** die EDV text file.

**Texter, in** (mpl -; fpl -nen) der, die copywriter.

**Textilien** pl textiles.

**Textil|industrie** die textile industry.

**Text|stelle** die passage.

**Text|verarbeitung** die EDV word processing (U).

**TH** [te:'ha:] die abk für Technische Hochschule.

**Thailand** nt Thailand.

**Thailänder, in** (mpl -; fpl -nen) der, die Thai.

**thailändisch** adj Thai.

**Theater** (pl -) das - **1.** [gen] theatre; **~ spielen** to act - **2.** fam [Ärger] fuss; **~ machen** to make a fuss; **so ein ~!** such a fuss! - **3.** fam [Vortäuschung] play-acting; **~ spielen** to put on an act.

**Theterauf|führung** die performance.

**Theater|karte** die theatre ticket.

**Theater|kasse** die theatre box office.

**Theater|stück** das play.

**Theatervor|stellung** die performance.

**theatralisch** adj dramatic.

T

**Theke** (pl -n) die - **1.** [in Kneipe] bar - **2.** [in Geschäft] counter.

**Thema** (pl **Themen**) das subject; MUS theme; **das ist doch kein ~!** fam fig that goes without saying!; **etw ist für jn kein ~** fig sthg is not important to sb; **etw ist kein ~ mehr** fig sthg is of no interest any more.

**Thematik** (pl -en) die geh theme.

**thematisch** adj thematic ◇ adv thematically.

**Themen|bereich** der field.

**Themse** die: **die ~** the (River) Thames.

**Theologe** (pl -n) der theologian.

**Theologie** (pl -n) die theology.

**Theologin** (pl -nen) die theologian.

**theor.** abk für **theoretisch**.

**Theoretiker, in** (mpl -; fpl -nen) der, die theorist.

**theoretisch** adj theoretical ◇ adv theoretically.

**theoretisieren** vi geh to theorize.

**Theorie** (pl -n) die theory.

**Therapeut, in** (mpl -en; fpl -nen) der, die therapist.

**therapeutisch** adj therapeutic ◇ adv therapeutically.

**Therapie** (pl -n) die therapy.

**Thermal|bad** das thermal bath.

**Thermo|meter** das thermometer.

**Thermos|flasche** die Thermos® (flask).

**Thermos|kanne** die Thermos® (flask).

**Thermostat** (pl -e ODER -en) der thermostat.

**These** (pl -n) die thesis.

**Thriller** (pl -) der thriller.

**Thrombose** (pl -n) die MED thrombosis.

**Thron** (pl -e) der throne.

**thronen** vi to sit imposingly.

**Thronfolger, in** (mpl -; fpl -nen) der, die heir to the throne.

**Thun|fisch, Tun|fisch** der tuna.

**Thurgau** der Thurgau.

**Thüringen** nt Thuringia.

**Thüringer** (pl -) der native/inhabitant of Thuringia ◇ adj (unver) of/from Thuringia.

**Thüringerin** (pl -nen) die native/inhabitant of Thuringia.

**Thüringer Wald** der Thuringian Forest.

**THW** [te:ha:'ve:] (abk für **Technisches Hilfswerk**) das public emergency services.

**Thymian** (pl -e) der thyme.

**Tiber** der: **der ~** the (River) Tiber.

**Tibet** nt Tibet.

**Tick** (pl -s) der quirk; [nervös] tic.

**ticken** vi to tick; **nicht ganz richtig ~** fam fig to be crazy.

**Ticket** (pl -s) das ticket.

**Tide** (pl -n) die Norddt tide.
➡ **Tiden** pl tides.

**Tiebreak** ['taibre:k] (pl -s) der SPORT tiebreak.

**tief** adj - **1.** [gen] deep; **ein ~er Fall** a long fall; **zwei Meter ~** two metres deep; **ein ~er Teller** a soup plate; **im ~sten Winter** in the depths of winter - **2.** [niedrig] low ◇ adv - **1.** [nach unten] deep - **2.** [niedrig] low; **die Sonne steht schon ~** the sun is low in the sky; **zu ~ singen** to sing flat - **3.** [zeitlich]: **bis ~ in die Nacht** far into the night - **4.** [verletzt, atmen, bewegt] deeply; **~ schlafen** to be in a deep sleep.

**Tief** (pl -s) das depression.

**Tief|bau** der underground and surface level construction.

**Tiefdruck|gebiet** das area of low pressure.

**Tiefe** (pl -n) die depth.

**Tief|ebene** die (lowland) plain.

**Tiefen|schärfe** die FOTO depth of focus.

**tiefernst** adj very serious ◇ adv very seriously.

**Tiefgang** der - **1.** [von Schiffen] draught - **2.** fam fig [von Gedanken] depth.

**Tief|garage** die underground car park Br ODER parking lot Am.

**tiefgefroren** adj frozen.

**tief gehend** adj [Wandel, Veränderung] radical; [Gespräch] profound ◇ adv radically.

**tiefgekühlt** adj frozen ◇ adv in a freezer.

**tief greifend** adj radical ◇ adv radically.

**Tiefkühl|fach** das freezer compartment.

**Tiefkühl|kost** die frozen food.

**Tiefkühl|truhe** die freezer.

**Tieflader** (pl -) der low-loader.

**tief liegend** adj [Gebiet] low-lying; [Augen] deep-set.

**Tief|punkt** der low.

**Tief|schlag** der - **1.** SPORT punch below the belt - **2.** [Schicksalsschlag] blow.

**tief schürfend** adj profound ◇ adv profoundly.

**tiefsinnig** adj profound.

**Tiefstand** der (ohne pl) low.

**Tiefst|temperatur** die minimum temperature.

**Tier** (pl -e) das animal; **ein großes** ODER **hohes ~** fam fig a big shot.

**Tier|art** die species.

**Tier|arzt, ärztin** der, die vet.

**Tier|garten** der zoo.

**Tierhalter, in** (*mpl* -; *fpl* -nen) *der, die* pet owner.

**Tier|handlung** *die* pet shop.

**Tier|heim** *das* animal home.

**tierisch** *adj* - **1.** [von Tieren] animal - **2.** *fam* [groß]: **ich habe ~e Angst** I'm really frightened <> *adv fam* really.

**Tierkreis|zeichen** *das* ASTROL star sign.

**tierlieb** *adj* animal-loving; **~ sein** to be an animal lover.

**Tier|park** *der* zoo.

**Tier|pfleger, in** *der, die* zoo-keeper.

**Tier|quälerei** *die* cruelty to animals.

**Tierschutz|verein** *der* society for the prevention of cruelty to animals.

**Tier|versuch** *der* animal experiment.

**Tiger, in** (*mpl* -; *fpl* -nen) *der, die* tiger.

**tigern** (*perf* **ist getigert**) *vi fam* to wander.

**Tigris** *der:* **der ~** the (River) Tigris.

**Tilde** (*pl* -n) *die* tilde.

**tilgen** *vt* to repay.

**Tilgung** (*pl* -en) *die* repayment.

**Tilsiter** (*pl* -) *der* [Käse] *strong cheese with small holes in it.*

**Timbre** ['tɛ̃:brə] (*pl* -s) *das* timbre.

**timen** ['taimən] *vt* to time.

**Timing** ['taimɪŋ] (*pl* -s) *das* timing (U).

**Tinktur** (*pl* -en) *die* tincture.

**Tinnef** *der fam abw* rubbish.

**Tinte** (*pl* -n) *die* ink; **in der ~ sitzen** *fam fig* to be in the soup.

**Tinten|fisch** *der* octopus; [klein] squid; [Sepia] cuttlefish.

**Tintenstrahl|drucker** *der* EDV inkjet printer.

**Tip** = Tipp.

**Tipp** (*pl* -s) *der* - **1.** [Hinweis] tip; **jm einen ~ geben** to give sb a tip - **2.** [Wette] bet.

**tippeln** (*perf* **ist getippelt**) *vi* to trot.

**tippen** *vi* - **1.** [vorhersagen, wetten] to bet; **meistens tippe ich richtig** I'm usually right; **auf etw** (A) **~** to bet on sthg; **ich tippe darauf, dass ...** I bet that ... - **2.** *fam* [Maschine schreiben] to type - **3.** [antippen] to tap; **an etw** (A) **~** to tap on sthg <> *vt* - **1.** *fam* [Schreibmaschine schreiben] to type - **2.** [antippen] to tap.

**Tipp|fehler** *der* typing mistake.

**tipptopp** *adj* (*unver*) *fam* [von Person, Garten] immaculate; [von Haus] shipshape.

**Tirol** *nt* Tyrol.

**Tiroler** (*pl* -) *der* & *adj* (*unver*) Tyrolean.

**Tirolerin** (*pl* -nen) *die* Tyrolean.

**tirolerisch** *adj* Tyrolean.

**Tisch** (*pl* -e) *der* - **1.** [Möbel] table; **den ~ decken** to set the table; **jn zu ~ bitten** ODER **rufen** *geh* to ask sb to take his/her place at the table - **2.** *RW:* **am runden ~ verhandeln** to hold round-table talks; **am grünen ~** from a purely theoretical point of view; **unter den ~ fallen** to fall by the wayside; **reinen ~ machen** [Sache bereinigen] to make a clean sweep; [alles gestehen] to make a clean breast of it; **das ist vom ~** that's been done and dusted.

**Tisch|decke** *die* tablecloth.

**tischfertig** *adj* ready to serve.

**Tischfuß|ball** *das* table football.

**Tisch|gebet** *das* grace.

**Tisch|karte** *die* place card.

**Tischler, in** (*mpl* -; *fpl* -nen) *der, die* carpenter.

**tischlern** *vt* to make.

**Tisch|nachbar, in** *der, die:* **mein ~** the person sitting next to me.

**Tisch|platte** *die* table top.

**Tisch|rede** *die* after-dinner speech.

**Tisch|tennis** *das* table tennis.

**Tischtuch** (*pl* -tücher) *das* tablecloth.

**Titan** (*pl* -en) *der* MYTH Titan <> *das* (ohne pl) CHEM titanium.

**Titel** (*pl* -) *der* title.

**Titel|bild** *das* cover picture.

**Titel|blatt** *das* title page.

**Titel|rolle** *die* title role.

**Titel|seite** *die* front page.

**Titel|verteidiger, in** *der, die* SPORT defending champion.

**Titicacasee** *der* Lake Titicaca.

**titulieren** *vt:* **jn mit** ODER **als etw ~** to call sb sthg.

**Toast** [to:st] (*pl* -e ODER -s) *der* - **1.** [Brot] toast; [Scheibe] slice of toast - **2.** [Trinkspruch] toast; **einen ~ auf jn ausbringen** *geh* to drink a toast to sb.

**Toast|brot** *das* sliced white bread (U).

**toasten** ['to:stn̩] *vt* to toast.

**Toaster** ['to:stɐ] (*pl* -) *der* toaster.

**toben** (*perf* **hat/ist getobt**) *vi* - **1.** (hat) [wild werden] to go berserk - **2.** (ist) [rennen] to charge about - **3.** (hat) [wüten] to rage.

**Tochter** (*pl* **Töchter**) *die* daughter.

**Tochter|gesellschaft** *die* subsidiary.

**Tod** (*pl* -e) *der* death; **jn zum ~(e) verurteilen** to condemn sb to death; **zu ~e kommen** to be killed; **sich** (D) **den ~ holen** *fam* to catch one's death; **zu ~e erschreckt** scared to death.

**todernst** *adj* deadly serious <> *adv* in a deadly serious way.

T

**Todes|angst** *die:* eine ~ haben/ausstehen to be scared to death.

**Todes|anzeige** *die* [in Zeitung] death notice.

**Todes|fall** *der* death.

**Todes|kampf** *der* death throes (*pl*).

**Todes|opfer** *das* casualty, fatality.

**Todes|stoß** *der:* jm/etw den ~ versetzen *eigtl* & *fig* to deliver the coup de grâce to sb/sthg.

**Todes|strafe** *die* death penalty; **auf ~ on** pain of death.

**Todes|tag** *der* anniversary of sb's death.

**Todesur|sache** *die* cause of death.

**Todesur|teil** *das* death sentence.

**Tod|feind, in** *der, die* mortal enemy.

**todkrank** *adj* terminally ill.

**tödlich** *adj* - **1.** [Krankheit, Unfall] fatal; [Gift, Biss] lethal - **2.** *fam* [Angst, Langeweile, Sicherheit] deadly; [Beleidigung] mortal <> *adv* - **1.** [verlaufen] fatally; [wirken] lethally - **2.** *fam* [langweilig] deadly; [beleidigt] mortally.

**todmüde** *adj* exhausted <> *adv* exhaustedly.

**todschick** *fam adj* dead smart <> *adv* dead smartly.

**todsicher** *fam adj* [Sache, Gewinn] sure-fire; **das ist ~** it's dead certain <> *adv* definitely.

**Tod|sünde** *die* REL mortal sin; **eine ~ sein** *fam fig* to be sacrilege.

**todunglücklich** *adj* terribly unhappy.

**Tofu** *der* tofu.

**Togo** *nt* Togo.

**Tohuwabohu** (*pl* -s) *das* chaos.

**toi, toi, toi** [ˈtɔy ˈtɔy ˈtɔy] *interj* - **1.** [unberufen] touch wood! - **2.** [viel Glück] best of luck!

**Toilette** [tɔaˈlɛtə] (*pl* -n) *die* toilet; **auf die ~ gehen** to go to the toilet.

**Toilettenpapier** *das* toilet paper.

**Tokio** *nt* Tokyo.

**tolerant** *adj* tolerant <> *adv* tolerantly.

**Toleranz** (*pl* -en) *die* tolerance.

**Toleranz|grenze** *die* limit of one's tolerance *ODER* patience.

**tolerieren** *vt* to tolerate.

**toll** *fam adj* - **1.** [schön] fantastic, brilliant - **2.** [unglaublich] far-out <> *adv* - **1.** [wunderbar] fantastically, brilliantly - **2.** [sehr] like crazy; **er hat sich ganz ~ gefreut** he was dead pleased.

**Tolle** (*pl* -n) *die* quiff.

**tollen** (*perf* **ist getollt**) *vi* to run around like crazy.

**tollkühn** *adj* reckless; **ein ~er Mensch** a daredevil <> *adv* recklessly.

**Tollpatsch** (*pl* -e) *der* clumsy devil.

**Tollwut** *die* rabies (*U*).

**Tolpatsch** = Tollpatsch.

**Tomate** (*pl* -n) *die* tomato; **die treulose ~ !** *fam hum* you unreliable old thing!

**Tomaten|mark** *das* tomato purée.

**Tombola** (*pl* -s) *die* raffle.

**Ton** (*pl* -e *ODER* **Töne**) *der* - **1.** (*pl* Tone) [Lehm] clay - **2.** (*pl* Töne) [Laut] note - **3.** (*pl* Töne) [Tonfall] tone; **hier herrscht ein rauer ~!** the atmosphere's terrible here!; **sich im ~ vergreifen** to adopt the wrong tone - **4.** (*pl* Töne) [Farbton] shade, tone - **5.** [von Platte, Film] sound - **6.** *RW:* **den ~ angeben** to be extremely influential; **zum guten ~ gehören** to be the done thing; **jn/ etw in den höchsten Tönen loben** to praise sb/ sthg to the skies; **keinen ~ sagen** *fam* to not say a word.

➡ **Ton in Ton** *adv* [farblich ähnlich] in matching shades (of the same colour).

**tonangebend** *adj* extremely influential.

**Ton|art** *die* - **1.** MUS key - **2.** [Tonfall] tone.

**Tonaus|fall** *der* TV loss of sound.

**Tonband** (*pl* -bänder) *das* - **1.** [Spule] tape - **2.** [Gerät] tape recorder.

**Tonband|gerät** *das* tape recorder.

**tönen** *vi* - **1.** [klingen] to sound - **2.** [prahlen] to boast <> *vt* [Haare] to tint.

**Ton|fall** *der* - **1.** [Tonart] tone - **2.** [Sprachmelodie] intonation.

**Ton|film** *der* sound film.

**Ton|ingenieur, in** *der, die* sound engineer.

**Ton|kopf** *der* head.

**Ton|lage** *die* pitch.

**Ton|leiter** *die* scale.

**Tonne** (*pl* -n) *die* - **1.** [Behälter] barrel - **2.** [Gewicht] tonne.

**tonnenweise** *adv* - **1.** [in Tonnen] by the tonne - **2.** [in großen Mengen] by the ton.

**Ton|störung** *die* TV sound interference.

**Ton|techniker, in** *der, die* sound technician.

**Ton|träger** *der* sound carrier.

**Tönung** (*pl* -en) *die* tint.

**top** *fam adj* (*unver*): **~ sein** to be brilliant <> *adv* brilliantly.

**Top** (*pl* -s) *das* top.

**TOP** [tɔp] (*pl* -s) (*abk für* **Tagesordnungspunkt**) *der* item on the agenda.

**Topas** (*pl* -e) *der* topaz.

**Topf** (*pl* Töpfe) *der* - **1.** [zum Kochen] pan - **2.** [für Vorräte, Blumen] pot - **3.** *fam* [Klo] loo *Br*, john *Am*.

**Töpfer** (*pl* -) *der* potter.

**Töpferei** (*pl* -en) *die* pottery.

**Töpferin** (pl -nen) die potter.

**töpfern** vt to make (pottery) ◇ vi to do pottery.

**Töpferlscheibe** die potter's wheel.

**Topfllappen** der oven cloth.

**Topflpflanze** die pot plant.

**Toplmanagement** das top management.

**topografisch, topographisch** adj topographical ◇ adv topographically.

**Topografie, Topographie** (pl -n) die topography.

**Topos** (pl **Topoi**) der recurring theme.

**Tor** (pl -e) das - 1. SPORT goal; **ein ~ schießen** to score a goal; **im ~ stehen** to be in goal - 2. [Tür] gate; [von Garage, Scheune] door.

**Toreinlfahrt** die entrance gate.

**Torf** der peat.

**Torheit** (pl -en) die **geh** - 1. [Handlung] foolish action - 2. [Dummheit] foolishness.

**Torhüter, in** (mpl -; fpl -nen) der, die goalkeeper.

**töricht** geh adj foolish ◇ adv foolishly.

**torkeln** (perf **hat/ist getorkelt**) vi to stagger.

**Torllinie** die goalline.

**Tornado** (pl -s) der tornado.

**Tornister** (pl -) der knapsack.

**Toronto** nt Toronto.

**torpedieren** vt MIL & fig to torpedo.

**Torpedo** (pl -s) das torpedo.

**Torlpfosten** der goalpost.

**Torschluss** der: **kurz vor ~** at the last minute.

**Torschlusspanik** die: **~ bekommen** to be afraid to be left on the shelf.

**Torlschütze, schützin** der, die goalscorer.

**Torso** (pl -s ODER **Torsi**) der torso.

**Torte** (pl -n) die gâteau.

**Tortenlguss** der glaze (in fruit flan), jelly.

**Tortenheber** (pl -) der cake slice.

**Tortur** (pl -en) die eigtl & fig torture.

**Torwart, in** (mpl -e; fpl -nen) der, die goalkeeper.

**tosen** (perf **hat/ist getost**) vi to roar.

**Toskana** die: **die ~** Tuscany.

**tot** adj eigtl & fig dead; **~er Winkel** blind spot; **ein ~er Punkt** a standstill; fig a deadlock; **ein ~es Gleis** a disused line ◇ adv: **~ umfallen** to drop dead; siehe auch **tot stellen.**

**total** adj total ◇ adv fam totally; **~ gut** dead good.

**Totalausverlkauf** der clearance sale.

**totalitär** adj totalitarian ◇ adv in a totalitarian way.

**Totallschaden** der write-off.

**Tote** (pl -n) der, die dead person; **es gab mehre-re ~n** several people were killed.

**Tote Meer** das: **das ~** the Dead Sea.

**töten** vt & vi to kill.
  ➡ **sich töten** ref to kill o.s.

**Totenlkopf** der - 1. [auf Arzneimittel, Piratenflagge] skull and crossbones - 2. [Schädel] skull.

**Totenlmesse** die requiem mass.

**Totenlschädel** der skull.

**Totenlschein** der death certificate.

**Totenlsonntag** der Sunday before Advent, day for commemoration of the dead in Protestant religion.

**totenstill** adj deathly silent.

**Totlgeburt** die - 1. [Projekt] non-starter - 2. [Baby] stillbirth.

**totgesagt** adj given up for dead.

**totllachen** ➡ **sich totlachen** ref fam to kill o.s. laughing.

**totllaufen** ➡ **sich totlaufen** ref (unreg) to run out of steam.

**Toto** (pl -s) das football pools (pl) Br, lottery in which participants guess the results of soccer games.

**totlschießen** vt (unreg) fam to shoot dead.

**Totschlag** der RECHT manslaughter.

**totlschlagen** vt (unreg) [töten] to beat to death.

**totlschweigen** vt (unreg) to hush up.

**tot stellen** ➡ **sich tot stellen** ref to play dead.

**Tötung** (pl -en) die killing; RECHT homicide.

**Touch** [tatʃ] (pl -s) der touch, air.

**Toulouse** [tuluz] nt Toulouse.

**Toupet** [tu'peː] (pl -s) das toupee.

**toupieren** [tu'piːrən] vt to backcomb.

**Tour** [tuːɐ] (pl -en) die - 1. [Ausflug] tour; [kürzere Fahrt] trip - 2. fam [Verhaltensweise] ploy; **etw auf die dumme/langsame ~ machen** fam to do sthg the stupid/slow way; **es auf die sanfte ~ versuchen** fam to use the gentle approach - 3. [Strecke] route - 4. TECH revolution; **auf vollen** ODER **höchsten ~en laufen** [Motor, Maschine] to run at full speed; fam [Vorbereitungen] to be in full swing - 5. RW: **auf ~en kommen** fam to get going; **in einer ~** fam [ohne Unterbrechung] without stopping; [andauernd] all the time; **krumme ~en** fam abw shady dealings.

**Tourenlski** der cross-country ski.

**Tourismus** [tu'rɪsmʊs] der tourism.

**Tourist** [tu'rɪst] (pl -en) der tourist.

**Touristenlklasse** die tourist class.

**Touristin** [tu'rɪstɪn] (pl -nen) die tourist.

**touristisch** [tu'rɪstɪʃ] adj tourist (vor Subst) ◇ adv for tourists.

**T**

**Tournee** [tʊr'neː] (pl -n) die tour; **auf ~** on tour.

**toxisch** adj toxic ⬦ adv toxically.

**Trab** der trot; **auf ~ sein** fig to be on the go; **jn auf ~ bringen** fam fig to make sb get a move on; **jn in ~ halten** fam fig to keep sb on the go; **sich in ~ setzen** fam fig to get going.

**Trabant®¹** (pl -s) der AUTO Trabant®, small car formerly manufactured in the GDR.

**Trabant²** (pl -en) der ASTRON satellite, moon.

**traben** (perf ist getrabt) vi to trot.

**Traber** (pl -) der trotter.

**Trabi** (pl -s) der fam colloquial name for a Trabant®.

**Trab|rennen** das trotting.

**Tracht** (pl -en) die - **1.** [Kleidung] traditional costume - **2.** [Schläge]: **eine ~ Prügel** fam a beating.

**trachten** vi: **nach etw ~** to strive for sthg; **jm nach dem Leben ~** to be after sb's blood.

**trächtig** adj pregnant.

**Trackball** [tr'ɛkbɔːl] (pl -s) der EDV trackball.

**Tradition** (pl -en) die tradition.

**traditionell** adj traditional ⬦ adv traditionally.

**traf** prät ⬦ **treffen**.

**tragbar** adj - **1.** [Gerät] portable - **2.** [Zustand, Verhalten] acceptable; **finanziell ~ sein** to be financially viable.

**träge** adj - **1.** [müde] lethargic - **2.** [langsam] sluggish ⬦ adv - **1.** [müde] lethargically - **2.** [langsam] sluggishly.

**tragen** (präs **trägt**; prät **trug**; perf **hat getragen**) vt - **1.** [schleppen] to carry - **2.** [am Körper haben] to wear - **3.** [bei sich haben]: **etw bei sich ~** to carry sthg (on one) - **4.** [Früchte] to produce; [Zinsen] to yield - **5.** [Kosten, Schicksal, Leid] to bear; [Anteil] to pay - **6.** [Einrichtung, Schule] to support - **7.** [Verantwortung] to take; [Folgen] to suffer - **8.** [Namen, Unterschrift] to bear ⬦ vi - **1.** [Baum] to bear fruit - **2.** [Gewicht]: **das Eis trägt noch nicht** the ice won't bear any weight yet - **3.** [Reichweite haben] to carry - **4.** [stützen] to support - **5.** RW: **an etw** (D) **schwer ~** to find sthg hard to bear.

➤ **sich tragen** ref fig - **1.** [zu tragen sein]: **dieser Stoff trägt sich sehr angenehm** this material is very pleasant to wear; **der Koffer trägt sich schlecht** the suitcase is difficult to carry - **2.** [sich selbst finanzieren] to be self-supporting - **3.** geh [planen]: **sich mit etw ~** to contemplate sthg.

➤ **Tragen** das: **zum Tragen kommen** to apply.

**tragend** adj load-bearing.

**Träger, in** (mpl -; fpl -nen) der, die - **1.** [Lastenträger] porter - **2.** [von Titel] holder - **3.** [Geldgeber]

sponsor ⬦ der - **1.** ARCHIT girder - **2.** [an Kleidung] strap.

**trägerlos** adj strapless.

**Trage|tasche** die carrier bag.

**tragfähig** adj - **1.** [Kompromiss, Politik] tenable - **2.** [Konstruktion] solid, capable of supporting a load.

**Trag|fläche** die wing.

**Trägheit** die - **1.** [Faulheit] lethargy - **2.** PHYS inertia.

**Tragik** die tragedy.

**tragikomisch** adj tragicomic.

**tragisch** adj tragic ⬦ adv tragically.

**Tragödie** [tra'gøːdjə] (pl -n) die tragedy.

**trägt** präs ⬦ **tragen**.

**Tragweite** die (ohne pl) consequences (pl); **von großer ~** of great consequence.

**Trainer, in** ['trɛːnɐ, rɪn] (mpl -; fpl -nen) der, die coach.

**trainieren** [trɛ'niːrən] vt [Verein, Sportler] to coach; [Pferd] to train; [Salto, Elfmeterschießen] to practise ⬦ vi to train.

**Training** ['trɛːnɪŋ] (pl -s) das training (U).

**Trainingsan|zug** der tracksuit.

**Trainings|lager** das training camp.

**Trakt** (pl -e) der geh wing.

**traktieren** vt to plague.

**Traktor** (pl -toren) der tractor.

**trällern** vt & vi to warble.

**Tram** (pl -s) die tram Br, streetcar Am.

**trampeln** (perf hat/ist getrampelt) vi - **1.** (ist) fam [gehen] to stamp - **2.** (hat) [stampfen]: **mit den Füßen ~** to stamp one's feet.

**Trampel|pfad** der path (trampled through undergrowth, etc).

**trampen** ['trɛmpn] (perf hat/ist getrampt) vi (hat) [an der Straße stehen] to hitchhike.

**Tramper, in** ['trɛmpɐ, rɪn] (mpl -; fpl -nen) der, die hitchhiker.

**Trampolin** (pl -e) das trampoline.

**Tran** (pl -e) der train oil; **im ~ sein** fam [unaufmerksam] to be out of it.

**Trance** ['trãːs(ə)] (pl -n) die trance; **in ~** in a trance.

**tranchieren** = transchieren.

**Träne** (pl -n) die tear; **in ~n ausbrechen** to burst into tears; **zu ~n gerührt** moved to tears; **jm/ etw keine ~ nachweinen** fam not to shed any tears for sb/sthg.

**tränen** vi to water.

**Tränen|gas** das tear gas.

**trank** prät ⬦ **trinken**.

**tränken** vt to water.

**Transaktion** (pl -en) die transaction.

**transchieren** [trãˈʃiːrən], **tranchieren** vt to carve.

**Transfer** (pl -s) der transfer.

**transferieren** vt to transfer.

**Transformator** (pl -toren) der transformer.

**Transfusion** (pl -en) die transfusion.

**Transistor** (pl -toren) der transistor.

**Transistorlradio** das transistor radio.

**Transit** (pl -e) der transit.

**transitiv** adj GRAM transitive.

**Transitverkehr** der transit traffic.

**transparent** adj transparent.

**Transparent** (pl -e) das banner.

**Transparenz** die transparency.

**Transplantation** (pl -en) die [von Organ] transplant; [von Haut] graft.

**transplantieren** vt [Organ] to transplant; [Haut] to graft.

**Transport** (pl -e) der transport.

**transportabel** adj portable.

**Transporter** (pl -) der van.

**transportfähig** adj: der Verletzte ist nicht ~ the injured man cannot be moved.

**transportieren** vt - **1.** [befördern] to transport - **2.** [Film] to wind on ⬦ vi [Kamera] to wind on; [Nähmaschine] to feed.

**Transportlmittel** das means (sg) of transport.

**transsexuell** adj transsexual.

**Transvestit** [tansvɛsˈtiːt] (pl -en) der transvestite.

**transzendental** adj transcendental.

**Transzendenz** die transcendency.

**Trapez** (pl -e) das - **1.** [im Zirkus] trapeze - **2.** MATH trapezium Br, trapezoid Am.

**trapezförmig** adj trapeziform Br, trapezoid Am.

**trappeln** (perf hat/ist getrappelt) vi - **1.** (ist) [Pferde] to clip-clop - **2.** (hat) [mit den Füßen] to patter.

**Trara** das fam: mit großem ~ with a great hullabaloo; ~ **machen** to make a fuss.

**Trasse** (pl -n) die [für Autos] route; [für Züge] line.

**trat** prät ▷ treten.

**Tratsch** der fam abw gossip.

**tratschen** vi fam abw to gossip.

**Traube** (pl -n) die - **1.** [Obst] grape - **2.** BIOL raceme - **3.** [Menge] cluster.

**Traubenlsaft** der grape juice.

**Traubenzucker** der glucose.

**trauen** vi: jm/einer Sache ~ to trust sb/sthg ⬦ vt [Brautpaar] to marry ; **sich ~ lassen** to be married; **getraut werden** to be ODER get married.

➠ **sich trauen** ref to dare.

**Trauer** die - **1.** [Schmerz] sorrow; 'in tiefer ODER stiller ~ ...' 'sadly missed by ...' - **2.** [Staatstrauer, Trauerkleidung] mourning.

**Trauerlfall** der death, bereavement.

**Trauerlfeier** die funeral service.

**Trauergottesldienst** der memorial service.

**Trauerlkloß** der fam wet blanket.

**trauern** vi: (um jn) ~ to mourn (for sb).

**Trauerlspiel** das: es ist ein ~ fam it's tragic.

**Trauerlzug** der funeral procession.

**Traufe** (pl -n) die: vom Regen in die ~ kommen to jump out of the frying pan into the fire.

**träufeln** vt: etw auf/in etw (A) ~ to trickle sthg onto/into sthg.

**Traum** (pl Träume) der dream; ein ~ von einem Haus/Mann fig a dream house/husband.

➠ **aus der Traum** interj: aus der ~ von der eigenen Wohnung we/you/etc can forget about having our/your/etc own flat.

➠ **nicht im Traum** adv fam [nie] not in my/your/etc wildest dreams.

**Trauma** (pl -ta) das trauma.

**träumen** vi - **1.** [gen] to dream; schrecklich/schön ~ to have terrible/pleasant dreams; von jm/etw ~ eigtl & fig to dream about sb/sthg - **2.** [abwesend sein] to dream, to daydream ⬦ vt to dream about; das hätte ich mir nicht ~ lassen fig I'd never have imagined it possible.

**Träumer** (pl -) der dreamer.

**Träumerei** (pl -en) die daydream.

**Träumerin** (pl -nen) die dreamer.

**träumerisch** adj [Mensch] dreamy; [Gedanken] wistful ⬦ adv dreamily.

**Traumlfrau** die fam: sie ist meine ~ she is the woman of my dreams.

**traumhaft** adj - **1.** [wunderschön] fabulous - **2.** [souverän] amazing ⬦ adv [wunderschön] fabulously.

**Traummann** (pl -männer) der fam: er ist mein ~ he is the man of my dreams.

**traurig** adj - **1.** [betrüblich] sad - **2.** [Rest, Zustand] sorry ⬦ adv sadly.

**Traurigkeit** die sadness.

**Traulring** der wedding ring.

**Traulschein** der marriage certificate.

**Trauung** (pl -en) die wedding; kirchliche/standesamtliche ~ church/civil wedding.

**Traulzeuge** der witness (at a wedding).

**Traulzeugin** die witness (at a wedding).

T

**Traveller|scheck** ['trɛvələ∫ɛk] *der* traveller's cheque.

**Treck** (*pl* -s) *der* convoy ODER column (of refugees).

**Trecker** (*pl* -) *der* tractor.

**Treff** (*pl* -s) *der* meeting place.

**treffen** (*präs* **trifft**; *prät* **traf**; *perf* **hat/ist getroffen**) *vt (hat)* - **1.** [begegnen] to meet - **2.** [Ziel] to hit; **auf dem Foto bist du gut getroffen** it's a good photo of you; **es gut/schlecht getroffen haben** *fig* to have been lucky/unlucky - **3.** [emotional verletzen] to affect - **4.** [Verabredung, Entscheidung] to make; [Maßnahmen] to take; **eine Vereinbarung ~** to come to an agreement ⬦ *vi* - **1.** *(hat)* [ins Ziel treffen] to score; **der Schuss traf nicht** the shot missed - **2.** *(ist)* [begegnen]: **auf jn/etw ~** to come across sb/sthg.
➤ **sich treffen** *ref* to meet; **sich mit jm ~** to meet sb; **es trifft sich gut/schlecht, dass ...** *fig* it's lucky/unlucky that ...; **es traf sich so, dass ...** it so happened that ...

**Treffen** (*pl* -) *das* meeting; **etw ins ~ führen** *geh* to put sthg forward.

**treffend** *adj* fitting ⬦ *adv* fittingly.

**Treffer** (*pl* -) *der* - **1.** [Tor] goal; [beim Basketball] basket - **2.** [mit Schusswaffe] hit - **3.** [Boxhieb] blow - **4.** [Losgewinn] win.

**Treff|punkt** *der* meeting place.

**treffsicher** *adj* accurate ⬦ *adv* accurately.

**treiben** (*prät* **trieb**; *perf* **hat/ist getrieben**) *vt (hat)* - **1.** [gen] to drive; **jn in etw (A) /zu etw ~** to drive sb to sthg; **du treibst mich noch in den Wahnsinn** you're driving me mad; **die Strömung trieb das Boot an den Strand** the current carried the boat ashore; **durch Windkraft getrieben** wind-powered - **2.** *fam* [anstellen] to get up to; **was treibt ihr beiden denn da wieder?** what are you two up to now? - **3.** [ansetzen] to produce - **4.** [bohren - Schacht, Tunnel] to dig - **5.** *RW:* **es zu bunt ~** *fam* to overdo it; **es mit jm ~** *salopp* to do it with sb ⬦ *vi* - **1.** *(ist)* [im Wasser] to drift; **sich ~ lassen** *fig* to drift - **2.** *(hat)* [ansetzen - Blüten] to flower; [ - Wurzeln] to root - **3.** *(hat)* [Harndrang verursachen] to be a diuretic, to have a diuretic effect.

**Treiben** *das (ohne pl)* - **1.** [Durcheinander] bustle - **2.** *abw* [Tun] activities *(pl)*.

**Treiber** (*pl* -) *der* EDV driver.

**Treib|gas** *das* propellant.

**Treib|haus** *das* greenhouse.

**Treib|hauseffekt** *der* greenhouse effect.

**Treib|holz** *das* driftwood.

**Treib|jagd** *die* shoot *(in which game is beaten)*.

**Treib|riemen** *der* drive belt.

**Treib|stoff** *der* fuel.

**Trekking, Trecking** (*pl* -s) *das* trekking.

**Trenchcoat** ['trɛnt∫koːt] (*pl* -s) *der* trench coat.

**Trend** (*pl* -s) *der* trend; **im ~ liegen** to be in vogue.

**Trendsetter** (*pl* -) *der* trendsetter.

**Trend|wende** *die* turnaround; [in der Mode, in der Industrie] trend reversal.

**trennbar** *adj* [Verb] separable; **ist das Wort „eine" ~?** can the word "eine" be hyphenated at the end of a line?

**trennen** *vt* - **1.** [gen] to separate - **2.** [unterscheiden] to distinguish.
➤ **sich trennen** *ref* - **1.** [Menschen] to separate; **sich von jm ~** to leave sb; **sich von etw ~** to part with sthg - **2.** [Wege, Leitungen *etc*] to divide.

**Trenn|linie** *die* dividing line.

**Trennung** (*pl* -en) *die* - **1.** [gen & CHEM] separation; **in ~ leben** to be separated - **2.** [Unterscheidung] distinction - **3.** GRAM end-of-line hyphenation.

**Trennungs|strich** *der* GRAM hyphen.

**Trenn|wand** *die* partition.

**treppab** *adv geh* down the stairs.

**treppauf** *adv geh* up the stairs.

**Treppe** (*pl* -n) *die* [in Gebäude] stairs *(pl)*; [im Freien] steps *(pl)*; **eine ~** [in Gebäude] a staircase; [im Freien] a flight of steps; **die ~ hinauffallen** *fam fig* to go up in the world.

**Treppenab|satz** *der* half-landing.

**Treppen|geländer** *das* banister.

**Treppen|haus** *das* stairwell.

**Treppen|stufe** *die* [in Gebäude] stair; [im Freien] step.

**Treppen|witz** *der iron:* **ein ~ der Weltgeschichte** a historical irony.

**Tresen** (*pl* -) *der* [Ausschank] bar; [Ladentisch] counter.

**Tresor** (*pl* -e) *der* safe; [Raum] strong room.

**Tret|boot** *das* pedal boat.

**treten** (*präs* **tritt**; *prät* **trat**; *perf* **hat/ist getreten**) *vt (hat)* - **1.** [mit dem Fuß] to kick; **jm auf den Fuß ~** to tread on sb's foot; **sich einen Dorn in den Fuß ~** to get a thorn in one's foot - **2.** [Kupplung, Bremse] to step on, to put one's foot down on - **3.** *fam* [antreiben]: **jn ~** to push sb ⬦ *vi* - **1.** *(hat)* [mit dem Fuß] to kick; **auf etw (A) ~** to step on sthg - **2.** *(ist)* [gehen]: **ins Zimmer ~** to enter ODER come into the room; **zu jm ~** to go up to sb; **~ Sie näher!** come closer! - **3.** [betätigen]: **auf die Bremse ~** to step on the brake, to brake - **4.** *(ist)* [hervor]: **aus etw ~** to issue from sthg - **5.** [beginnen]: **in den Staatsdienst ~** to enter government service; **in den Streik ~** to go on strike.

**treu** *adj* faithful; [Anhänger, Kunde] loyal; **einer**

**Sache** *(D)* **~ sein** to be true to sthg; **jm ~ sein** [sexuell] to be faithful to sb; **jm/einer Sache ~ bleiben** to remain faithful to sb/true to sthg ◇ *adv* [verlässlich] faithfully; [unterstützen] loyally.

**Treue** *die* **- 1.** [gen] faithfulness; [von Anhänger, Kunde] loyalty; **jm die ~ halten** to keep faith with sb **- 2.** [sexuell] fidelity.

**treuherzig** *adj* trusting ◇ *adv* trustingly.

**treulos** *adj* disloyal; [Liebhaber] unfaithful ◇ *adv* disloyally; [Liebhaber] unfaithfully.

**Triangel** *(pl -) der* MUS triangle.

**Triathlon** *(pl -s) das* triathlon.

**Tribunal** *(pl -e) das* tribunal.

**Tribüne** *(pl -n) die* **- 1.** [Sitzplätze] stand **- 2.** [Rednertribüne] rostrum.

**Tribut** *(pl -e) der* tribute; **jm/einer Sache ~ zollen** to pay tribute to sb/sthg; **einen hohen ~ fordern** to take a heavy toll.

**tributpflichtig** *adj* required to pay tribute.

**Trichine** *(pl -n) die* trichina.

**Trichter** *(pl -) der* **- 1.** [Gerät] funnel; **auf den ~ kommen** *fam fig* to catch on **- 2.** [nach Explosion] crater.

**Trick** *(pl -s) der* trick.

**Tricklfilm** *der* cartoon.

**trieb** *prät* ▷ treiben.

**Trieb** *(pl -e) der* **- 1.** [biologisch] instinct **- 2.** [psychologisch] urge **- 3.** [pflanzlich] shoot.

**Trieblfeder** *die* motive.

**triebhaft** *adj* compulsive ◇ *adv* compulsively.

**Trieblkraft** *die* driving force; [von Handeln] motive.

**Trieblwagen** *der* railcar.

**Trieblwerk** *das* FLUG engine.

**triefen** (*prät* **triefte** ODER **troff**; *perf* **hat/ist getrieft**) *vi* **- 1.** *(hat)* [nass sein]: **von** ODER **vor etw** *(D)* **~ eigtl** & *fig* to drip with sthg; **eure Kleider ~ vor Nässe** your clothes are dripping wet **- 2.** *(ist)* [fließen - in Tropfen] to drip; [ - in Rinnsalen] to run.

**triefnass** *adj* dripping wet.

**trifft** *präs* ▷ treffen.

**triftig** *adj* [Grund] good; [Argumente] valid.

**Trikot, Trikot** [tri'ko:, 'trɪkol] *(pl -s) das* [von Radrennfahrer] jersey; [von Fußballspieler] shirt; [von Tänzer] leotard.

**trillern** *vt* & *vi* to warble.

**Trillerlpfeife** *die* whistle.

**Trilogie** *(pl -n) die* trilogy.

**Trimester** *(pl -) das* [von Studienjahr] term; WIRTSCH quarter.

**trimmen** *vt* **- 1.** [fit machen]: **einen Athleten auf**

---

**Schnelligkeit ~** to do speed training with an athlete **- 2.** [zurechtmachen]: **etw auf etw** *(A)* **~** to do sthg up to look like sthg **- 3.** [schneiden] to trim.

◆ **sich trimmen** *ref* to get o.s. into shape.

**trinkbar** *adj* drinkable.

**trinken** (*prät* **trank**; *perf* **hat getrunken**) *vt* to drink; **einen ~** *fam* to have a drink; **einen ~ gehen** *fam* to go for a drink ◇ *vi* to drink; **auf jn/etw ~** to drink to sb/sthg.

**Trinker, in** (*mpl -*; *fpl* **-nen**) *der, die* alcoholic.

**trinkfest** *adj*: **er ist/ist nicht ~** he can/can't hold his drink.

**Trinklgeld** *das* tip.

**Trinklhalm** *der* (drinking) straw.

**Trinklwasser** *das* drinking water.

**Trinkwasserlversorgung** *die* drinking-water supply.

**Trio** *(pl -s) das* trio.

**Trip** *(pl -s) der fam* trip; **sie ist immer noch auf dem ökologischen ~** *fam* she's still on her ecological trip.

**trippeln** (*perf* **ist getrippelt**) *vi* to trip along.

**Tripper** *(pl -) der* gonorrhoea.

**trist** *adj* dreary.

**tritt** *präs* ▷ treten.

**Tritt** *(pl -e) der* **- 1.** [Fußtritt] kick; **jm einen ~ (in den Bauch) versetzen** to kick sb (in the stomach) **- 2.** [Schritt, Gang] step; **im ~** in step; **~ fassen** *fig* to get established.

**Trittlbrett** *das* step; [von Auto] running board.

**Trittbrettlfahrer, in** *der, die* abw parasite, free-rider *Am*.

**Trittlleiter** *die* stepladder.

**Triumph** *(pl -e) der* triumph.

**triumphal** *adj* triumphant ◇ *adv* triumphantly.

**triumphieren** *vi* **- 1.** [siegen]: **über jn/etw ~** to triumph over sb/sthg **- 2.** [frohlocken]: **innerlich ~**, to be inwardly triumphant.

**trivial** [tri'vja:l] *geh adj* **- 1.** [banal] trite **- 2.** [unbedeutend] trivial ◇ *adv* **- 1.** [banal] tritely **- 2.** [unbedeutend] trivially.

**Trivialliteratur** *die* light fiction.

**trocken** *adj* **- 1.** [gen] dry **- 2.** [ohne Beilage] plain; [Brot] dry **- 3.** *RW:* **~ sein** *fam* [keinen Alkohol mehr trinken] to be on the wagon; **auf dem Trockenen sitzen** *fam* [keinen Alkohol mehr haben] to have nothing to drink; [kein Geld haben] to be broke ◇ *adv* drily; **~ schmecken** to taste dry.

**Trockeneis** *das* dry ice.

**Trockenlhaube** *die* hair dryer *(at hairdresser's)*.

**Trockenheit** *(pl -en) die* **- 1.** [regenlose Zeit] drought **- 2.** [Zustand] dryness.

T

**trocken|legen** *vt* - **1.** [entwässern] to drain
- **2.** [Windeln wechseln] to change.

**trocknen** (*perf* hat/ist getrocknet) *vt (hat)* to
dry; **sich** *(D)* **die Tränen/Hände ~** to dry one's
tears/hands <> *vi (ist)* to dry.

**Trockner** (*pl* -) *der* dryer.

**Troddel** (*pl* -n) *die* tassel.

**Trödel** *der* junk.

**Trödel|markt** *der* flea market.

**trödeln** (*perf* hat/ist getrödelt) *vi* to dawdle.

**Trödler, in** (*mpl* -; *fpl* -nen) *der, die* junk
dealer.

**troff** *prät* [> triefen.

**trog** *prät* [> trügen.

**Trog** (*pl* Tröge) *der* trough.

**Trommel** (*pl* -n) *die* drum; [von Revolver] cylinder; [für Kabel] reel; **die ~ für jn/etw rühren** *fam*
*fig* to drum up support for sb/sthg.

**Trommel|bremse** *die* AUTO drum brake.

**Trommel|fell** *das* MED eardrum.

**trommeln** *vi* - **1.** [Musik machen, Lärm machen] to
drum; **sie trommelt sehr gut** she plays the
drums very well - **2.** [schlagen] to beat <> *vt*
- **1.** [Rhythmus] to beat out - **2.** [mit Lärm wecken]:
**jn aus dem Bett ~** to get sb up by hammering
on the door.

**Trommler, in** (*mpl* -; *fpl* -nen) *der, die* drummer.

**Trompete** (*pl* -n) *die* trumpet.

**trompeten** *vi* - **1.** [Musik machen] to play the
trumpet - **2.** [Elefant] to trumpet <> *vt:* **einen**
**Marsch ~** to play a march on the trumpet.

**Trompeter, in** (*mpl* -; *fpl* -nen) *der, die* trumpeter.

**Tropen** *pl:* **die ~** the tropics.

**Tropen|helm** *der* pith helmet.

**Tropenmedizin** *die* tropical medicine.

**tropentauglich** *adj* fit for the tropics.

**Tropf** (*pl* -e ODER Tröpfe) *der* - **1.** (*pl* Tropfe) MED
drip - **2.** (*pl* Tröpfe) [Mensch]: **armer ~!** poor
devil!

**tröpfeln** (*perf* hat/ist getröpfelt) *vi* - **1.** (ist)
[tropfen] to drip - **2.** (hat) fam [regnen]: **es tröpfelt**
it's spitting <> *vt (hat)* to drip.

**tropfen** (*perf* hat/ist getropft) *vi* to drip; **es**
**tropft** it's spitting <> *vt (hat)* to drip.

**Tropfen** (*pl* -) *der* drop; **ein edler ~** a fine wine;
**ein ~ auf den heißen Stein sein** to be a drop in
the ocean.
 **Tropfen** *pl* MED drops.

**tropfenweise** *adv* drop by drop.

**Tropfstein|höhle** *die* cave with stalactites
and/or stalagmites.

**Trophäe** (*pl* -n) *die* [Jagdtrophäe] trophy.

**tropisch** *adj* tropical <> *adv* tropically.

**Trost** *der* (ohne pl) consolation, comfort; **nicht**
**ganz bei ~ sein** *fam* to be out of one's mind.

**trösten** *vt* to console, to comfort.
 **sich trösten** *ref:* **sich (mit etw) ~** to console
o.s. (with sthg); **sie tröstete sich mit ihrem Lieb-**
**haber** she found consolation in her lover;
**tröste dich, mir geht es doch nicht besser!** if it's
any consolation, I'm not much better!

**tröstlich** *adj* comforting.

**trostlos** *adj* abw - **1.** [deprimierend] dreary
- **2.** [traurig] despairing.

**Trost|pflaster** *das* consolation.

**Trost|preis** *der* consolation prize.

**Tröstung** (*pl* -en) *die* geh comfort (U).

**Trott** (*pl* -e) *der* - **1.** [Gangart] trot - **2.** fam [Ge-
wohnheit] routine; **der alltägliche ~** the daily
grind; **in den alten ~ zurückfallen** to get back
into the old routine.

**Trottel** (*pl* -) *der* fam abw idiot.

**trotten** (*perf* ist getrottet) *vi* to trot.

**trotz** *präp* (+ G) despite, in spite of.

**trotzdem** *adv* nevertheless.

**trotzen** *vi* geh: **jm/einer Sache ~** to defy sb/
sthg; **dem Regen/der Gefahr ~** to brave the
rain/danger.

**trotzig** *adj* [Kind] difficult; [aus gutem Grund] defiant; [Gesicht, Antwort] contrary <> *adv* [aus gutem
Grund] defiantly; [uneinsichtig] contrarily.

**Trotz|kopf** *der* - **1.** [sturer Mensch] pigheaded
so-and-so - **2.** [stures Wesen] defiant streak.

**Trouble** [trabl] *der* fam trouble.

**trüb, trübe** *adj* - **1.** [Flüssigkeit] cloudy; [Augen]
dull - **2.** [Wetter, Tag, Stimmung] gloomy; **mit sei-**
**nen Berufschancen sieht ~ aus** it's looking
bleak as far as his career prospects are
concerned; **im Trüben fischen** *fam* abw to fish
in troubled waters.

**Trubel** *der* hurly-burly.

**trüben** *vt* - **1.** [verschlechtern] to mar; [gute Laune]
to dampen - **2.** [Flüssigkeit, Denken, Urteilskraft] to
cloud.
 **sich trüben** *ref* - **1.** [Wasser] to go cloudy;
[Himmel] to cloud over - **2.** [Stimmung, Laune] to
be dampened.

**Trübsal** *die* geh [Melancholie] melancholy; [Kum-
mer] grief; **~ blasen** *fig* to mope.

**trübselig** *adj* gloomy <> *adv* gloomily.

**trübsinnig** *adj* gloomy <> *adv* gloomily.

**Trübung** (*pl* -en) *die* - **1.** [von Flüssigkeit - Prozess]
clouding; [ - Resultat] cloudiness - **2.** [von Him-
mel] clouding over - **3.** [Beeinträchtigung] mar-
ring (U) - **4.** MED corneal opacity.

**trudeln** (*perf* ist getrudelt) *vi* - **1.** [fliegen] to
spin - **2.** [rollen] to roll.

**Trüffel** (*pl* -) *der* truffle.

**trug** *prät* [> tragen.

**trügen** (*prät* **trog**; *perf* **hat getrogen**) *vi* to be deceptive ⬦ *vt* to deceive.

**trügerisch** *adj* deceptive.

**Trug|schluss** *der* misconception.

**Truhe** (*pl* -n) *die* chest.

**Trumm** (*pl* -e ODER **Trümmer**) *der* ODER *das* *fam* whopper; **ihr neuer Freund ist ein ~ von einem Mann** her new boyfriend is a man mountain.

**Trümmer** *pl* [Ruinen] ruins; [Schutt] rubble *(U)*; [von Fahrzeug] wreckage *(U)*; **in ~n** *eigtl* & *fig* in ruins.

**Trümmer|haufen** *der* heap of rubble.

**Trumpf** (*pl* **Trümpfe**) *der* trump (card); **Karo ist ~!** diamonds are trumps!; **Flexibilität ist ~** flexibility is the order of the day; **einen ~ ausspielen** [im Kartenspiel] to play a trump; *fig* to play one's trump card; **seine Trümpfe aus der Hand geben** *fig* to waste one's trump card.

**Trunk** (*pl* **Trünke**) *der* *geh* drink.

**Trunkenheit** *die* *amt* inebriation; **~ am Steuer** drink-driving *Br*, drunk-driving *Am*.

**Trunksucht** *die* alcoholism.

**Trupp** (*pl* -s) *der* [von Soldaten, Polizisten] detachment, squad; [von Arbeitern] group.

**Truppe** (*pl* -n) *die* - **1.** [Einheit] unit; **nicht von der schnellen ~ sein** *fam hum* to be a slowcoach *Br* ODER slowpoke *Am* - **2.** *(ohne pl)* [Streitkräfte] forces *(pl)*; [Heer] army - **3.** [Gruppe] troupe.

➤ **Truppen** *pl* troops.

**Truppenab|zug** *der* withdrawal of troops.

**Truppenübungs|platz** *der* military training area.

**Trut|hahn** *der* turkey.

**Tschad** *der* Chad.

**Tscheche** (*pl* -n) *der* Czech.

**Tschechien** *nt* Czech Republic.

**Tschechin** (*pl* -nen) *die* Czech.

**tschechisch** *adj* Czech.

**Tschechisch(e)** *das* Czech; *siehe auch* **Englisch(e)**.

**Tschechische Republik** *die* Czech Republic.

**Tschechoslowakei** *die* Czechoslovakia.

**tschüs, tschüss** *interj* *fam* bye!

**Tsd.** *abk für* **Tausend**.

**T-Shirt** ['tiːʃœːɐ̯t] (*pl* -s) *das* T-shirt.

**TSV** [teːˈʔɛsˈfaʊ] (*abk für* **Turn- und Sportverein**) *der* *gymnastics and sports club*.

**TU** [teːˈʔuː] (*pl* -s) (*abk für* **Technische Universität**) *die* *university specializing in science and technology*.

**Tuba** (*pl* **Tuben**) *die* tuba.

**Tube** (*pl* -n) *die* tube; **auf die ~ drücken** *fam* [sich beeilen] to get a move on; [im Auto] to put one's foot down.

**Tuberkulose** (*pl* -n) *die* tuberculosis.

**Tuch** (*pl* -e ODER **Tücher**) *das* [Stoffteil, Stoff] cloth; [Halstuch] scarf; **für jn ein rotes ~ sein** *fig* to make sb see red.

**tüchtig** *adj* - **1.** [fleißig] hardworking; [fähig] competent - **2.** [groß] big; **ein ~er Schreck** a real shock ⬦ *adv* - **1.** [fleißig] hard; [fähig] competently - **2.** *fam* [viel]: **~ kalt** really cold; **jn ~ ausschimpfen** to give sb a thorough telling off.

**Tücke** (*pl* -n) *die* - **1.** [Eigenschaft] deceit - **2.** [Handlung] trick, ruse; **seine ~n haben** *fam* [Auto, Motor] to be temperamental; [Berg, Strecke] to be treacherous; **die ~ des Objekts!** *fam fig* inanimate objects can be so perverse!

**tückisch** *adj* - **1.** [hinterhältig - Person] deceitful; [ - Plan, Idee] underhand - **2.** [schwierig] devilishly difficult - **3.** [Auto, Gerät] temperamental - **4.** [gefährlich] treacherous ⬦ *adv* - **1.** [hinterhältig] deceitfully - **2.** [gefährlich] treacherously - **3.** [schwierig]: **etw ~ gestalten** to make sthg devilishly difficult.

**tüfteln** *vi*: **an etw (D) ~** to fiddle about with sthg; [geistig] to puzzle over sthg.

**Tüftler, in** (*mpl* -; *fpl* -nen) *der, die* *fam person who enjoys fiddly tasks/complex puzzles*.

**Tugend** (*pl* -en) *die* virtue.

**tugendhaft** *adj* virtuous ⬦ *adv* virtuously.

**Tulpe** (*pl* -n) *die* tulip.

**tummeln** ➤ **sich tummeln** *ref* to romp around.

**Tummel|platz** *der* - **1.** [Ort]: **dieser Markt ist ein ~ für Diebe** this marketplace is crawling with thieves - **2.** *abw* [Organisation] hotbed.

**Tumor, Tumor** (*pl* **Tumore**) *der* tumour; **ein gutartiger/bösartiger ~** a benign/malignant tumour.

**Tümpel** (*pl* -) *der* pond.

**Tumult** (*pl* -e) *der* commotion.

**tun** (*prät* **tat**; *perf* **hat getan**) *vt* - **1.** [machen] to do; **was tust du denn da?** what are you doing?; **so etwas tun man nicht** you shouldn't do that; **was kann ich für Sie ~?** what can I do for you?; **das hat damit nichts zu ~** that's got nothing to do with it - **2.** [stellen, legen] to put - **3.** [antun]: **jm/sich etwas ~** to do something to sb/o.s. - **4.** *fam* [hinreichend sein]: **ich denke, das tut es** I think that will do; **damit ist es nicht getan** that's not enough - **5.** *fam* [funktionieren]: **das Auto tut es noch/nicht mehr** the car still works/has had it ⬦ *vi* - **1.** [machen]: **zu ~ haben** to be busy; **jm gut ~** to do sb good - **2.** [vortäuschen]: **so ~, als ob** *fam* to act as if; **er tut nur so** he's only pretending - **3.** [Ausdruck einer Beziehung]: **du bekommst es mit mir zu ~, wenn ...** *fam* you'll have me to answer to if

**T**

...; **zu ~ haben mit** to be linked to; **mit jm dienstlich zu ~ haben** to know sb professionally.
➤ **sich tun** *ref:* **es tut sich etwas/nichts** something/nothing is happening.

**Tun** *das (ohne pl)* actions *(pl);* **js ~ und Treiben** sb's actions.

**tünchen** *vt* to whitewash.

**Tuner** ['tjuːnɐ] *(pl -) der* tuner.

**Tunesien** *nt* Tunisia.

**Tunesier, in** [tuˈneːziɐ, rɪn] *(mpl -; fpl -nen) der, die* Tunisian.

**tunesisch** *adj* Tunisian.

**Tun|fisch** *der* = **Thunfisch.**

**Tunis** *nt* Tunis.

**tunken** *vt* to dip; [Brot, Keks] to dunk.

**tunlichst** ['tuːnlɪçst] *adv* [unbedingt] at all costs; [möglichst] as far as possible.

**Tunnel** *(pl -) der* tunnel.

**Tunte** *(pl -n) die fam abw* pansy.

**Tüpfelchen** *(pl -) das* dot; **bis aufs I-~** *fam* to the letter; **das ~ auf dem i sein** to be the icing on the cake.

**tupfen** *vt* to dab; **etw auf etw (A) ~** to dab sthg onto sthg.

**Tupfen** *(pl -) der* spot; [kleiner] dot.

**Tupfer** *(pl -) der* - **1.** MED swab - **2.** [Fleck] dot.

**Tür** *(pl -en) die* - **1.** [gen] door; **~ an ~ wohnen** to live next door to each other; **von ~ zu ~ gehen** to go from door to door; **~ zu!** shut the door! - **2.** RW: **einer Sache (D) ~ und Tor öffnen** to open the door to sthg; **ihr stehen alle ~en offen** the world is her oyster; **jn vor die ~ setzen** *fam* [rauswerfen, entlassen] to kick sb out; **mit der ~ ins Haus fallen** to be blunt; **damit rennst du bei mir offene ~en ein** *fam* you're preaching to the converted, you don't need to convince me; **zwischen ~ und Angel** in passing.

**Tür|angel** *die* (door) hinge.

**Turban** *(pl -e) der* turban.

**Turbine** *(pl -n) die* turbine.

**Turbo** *(pl -s) der fam* turbo.

**turbulent** *adj* - **1.** [ereignisreich] eventful - **2.** [chaotisch] turbulent.

**Tür|griff** *der* doorhandle.

**Türke** *(pl -n) der* Turk.

**Türkei** *die:* **die ~** Turkey.

**Türkin** *(pl -nen) die* Turk.

**türkis** *adj* turquoise.

**Türkis** *(pl -e) der* ODER *das* turquoise.

**türkisch** *adj* Turkish.

**Türkisch(e)** *das* Turkish; *siehe auch* **Englisch(e).**

**Tür|klinke** *die* door handle.

**Turkmenistan** *nt* Turkmenistan.

**Turm** *(pl Türme) der* - **1.** [Bauwerk] tower - **2.** [Schachfigur] rook, castle.

**türmen** *(perf hat/ist getürmt) vi (ist) fam* to beat it, to do a runner *Br* <> *vt (hat)* to pile up.
➤ **sich türmen** *ref* to be piled up.

**turmhoch** *adj* [Welle] towering; [Hindernis] enormous <> *adv:* **~ aufragen** to tower up.

**Turm|spitze** *die* spire.

**Turm|uhr** *die* tower clock; [von Kirche] church clock.

**turnen** *(perf hat/ist geturnt) vt (hat)* to perform <> *vi* - **1.** *(hat)* [an einem Sportgerät] to do gymnastics; **an den Ringen/am Barren ~** to exercise on the rings/on the parallel bars - **2.** *(ist) fam* [klettern] to clamber about.

**Turnen** *das* [in der Schule] gym; [sport] gymnastics (U).

**Turner, in** *(mpl -; fpl -nen) der, die* gymnast.

**Turn|halle** *die* gymnasium.

**Turn|hose** *die* (gym) shorts *(pl).*

**Turnier** *(pl -e) das* tournament.

**Turn|schuh** *der* gym shoe *Br,* sneaker *Am.*

**Turnus** *(pl -se) der* rota; **in einem ~ von vier Jahren** every four years; **im ~** in rotation.

**turnusmäßig** *adj* regular <> *adv* regularly.

**Turn|verein** *der* sports club.

**Tür|rahmen** *der* doorframe.

**Tür|schloss** *das* lock.

**Tür|schwelle** *die* threshold.

**Tür|spalt** *der* crack (of a/the door).

**turteln** *vi fam* to bill and coo.

**Tusch** *(pl -e) der* fanfare.

**Tusche** *(pl -n) die* Indian ink.

**tuscheln** *vt & vi* to whisper.

**tuschen** *vt:* **sich die Wimpern ~** to put one's mascara on.

**Tusche|zeichnung** *die* pen-and-ink drawing.

**tut** *präs* ⊳ **tun.**

**Tütchen** *(pl -) das* sachet.

**Tüte** *(pl -n) die* bag; [mit Backpulver] packet; **das kommt nicht in die ~!** *fam fig* nothing doing!, no way!

**tuten** *vi* - **1.** [hupen] to toot; **das Schiff tutet** the ship sounds its horn - **2.** [tönen] to beep.

**Tuten** *das:* **er hat von ~ und Blasen keine Ahnung** *fam abw* he hasn't a clue.

**Tutor** *(pl -toren) der* tutor.

**Tutorin** *(pl -nen) die* tutor.

**TÜV** [tyf] [*abk für* **Technischer Überwachungsverein**] *der (ohne pl):* **ein Auto zum ~ bringen** ≈ to take a car for its MOT (test) *Br;* **das Kinder-**

**spielzeug ist vom ~ geprüft** the toy has been passed by the safety inspectorate.

**TÜV**

> Periodic testing of vehicles as well as of some machines is compulsory in Germany. It should be carried out every two years, or after three years if the vehicle is new. Anybody who fails to observe this rule is liable to be fined.

**TÜV-|Plakette** *die badge affixed to registration plates indicating that the vehicle has passed roadworthiness test.*

**TV** *(abk für* **Fernsehen***)* TV.

**Typ** *(pl* -**en***) der* - **1.** [Menschentyp, Art] type; **er ist der ~ eines Deutschen** he is a typical German; **(nicht) js ~ sein** *fam* (not) to be sb's type - **2.** *fam* [Kerl] guy, bloke *Br*.

**Typhus** *der* MED typhoid.

**typisch** *adj* typical; **etw ist ~ für jn** sthg is typical of sb ◇ *adv* typically ◇ *interj* typical!

**Typografie, Typographie** *(pl* -**n***) die* typography.

**Tyrann, in** *(mpl* -**en***; fpl* -**n***) der, die* tyrant.

**tyrannisieren** *vt abw* to tyrannize.

**Tyrrhenische Meer** *das:* **das ~** the Tyrrhenian Sea.

**u, U** [uː] *(pl* - ODER -**s***) das* u, U.

**u.** *abk für* **und**.

**u. a.** *(abk für* **unter anderem***) among other things.*

**u. Ä.** *(abk für* **und Ähnliches***) and the like.*

**u. a. m.** *(abk für* **und anderes mehr***) etc.*

**u. A. w. g.** *(abk für* **um Antwort wird gebeten***)* R.S.V.P.

**UB** [uːˈbeː] *(pl* -**s***) die abk für* **Universitätsbibliothek**.

**U-|Bahn** *die* underground *Br*, subway *Am*.

**U-Bahn|hof** *der* underground *Br* ODER subway *Am* station.

**U-Bahn-|Netz** *das* underground *Br* ODER subway *Am* system.

**übel** *(kompar* **übler***; superl* **übelste***) adj* - **1.** [Essen, Laune] bad; **nicht ~ sein** *fam* to be not bad - **2.** [moralisch] evil; **in übler Gesellschaft** in bad company - **3.** [Zustand] nasty, bad; **~ dransein** *fam* to be in a bad way - **4.** [unwohl]: **mir ist/wird ~** I feel sick ◇ *adv* - **1.** [schlimm] badly - **2.** [unwirsch]: **~ gelaunt (sein)** (to be) in a bad mood ODER temper.

**Übel** *(pl* -*) das* evil; **von ~ sein** to be an evil; **das kleinere ~** the lesser evil.

**übel nehmen** *vt (unreg):* **jm etw ~** to hold sthg against sb.

**üben** *vt* - **1.** [trainieren] to practise - **2.** *geh* [äußern]: **Nachsicht ~** to be lenient; **Kritik ~** to criticize ◇ *vi* to practise.

➤ **sich üben** *ref:* **sich in etw** *(D)* ~ *geh* [trainieren] to practise sthg; **sich in Geduld ~** [sich angewöhnen] to exercise patience.

**über** *präp* - **1.** (+ A) [eine Richtung anzeigend] over, above; [ - quer über] over; [ - bei Routen] via; **das Flugzeug flog ~ das Tal** the plane flew over the valley; **er breitete die Decke ~ das Bett** he spread the blanket over the bed; **~ die Straße gehen** to cross the road - **2.** (+ D) [eine Position anzeigend] over, above; **die Lampe hängt ~ dem Tisch** the lamp hangs above ODER over the table; **er wohnt ~ uns** he lives above us - **3.** (+ A) [zeitlich] over; **~ Wochen/Monate** for weeks/months; **~ Nacht** overnight; **~ kurz oder lang** *fig* sooner or later - **4.** (+ A) [mehr als] over; **~ eine Stunde** over an hour; **das geht ~ meinen Verstand** it's beyond me - **5.** (+ D) [mehr als] above; **~ dem Durchschnitt liegen** to be above average; **Kinder ~ zehn Jahren** children over ten (years of age); **~ Null** above zero; **seit ~ einem Jahr** for more than a year - **6.** (+ A) [mittels] through, via - **7.** (+ A) [stellt Bezug her] about; **ein Buch ~ Mozart** a book about ODER on Mozart - **8.** (+ A) [zur Angabe des Betrages] for; **eine Rechnung ~ 30 Euro** a bill for 30 euros - **9.** (+ D) [bei Rangfolge] above - **10.** (+ A) RW: **ich bringe es nicht ~ mich …** *fig* I can't bring myself to … ◇ *adv* - **1.** [mehr als] over - **2.** [zeitlich]: **den Winter ~** all winter (long); **das ganze Jahr ~** all (the) year round ◇ *adj fam* - **1.** [überdrüssig]: **etw ~ haben** to have had enough of sthg - **2.** [übrig] left (over); **ich habe noch fünf Mark ~** I still have five marks left.

➤ **über und über** *adv* all over.

**überall, überall** *adv* everywhere; **~ und nirgends (sein)** *fig* (to be) everywhere and nowhere.

**überaltert** *adj* - **1.** [Bevölkerung, Gruppe] containing a disproportionately high number of older people - **2.** [Vorstellungen, Werte] outmoded.

**Überalterung** *die (ohne pl)* disproportionate increase in the number of older people.

**Überan|gebot** *das* surplus.

**überängstlich** *adj* overanxious.

**überanstrengen** *vt* to overstrain.
➤ **sich überanstrengen** *ref* to overexert o.s.

**überantworten** *vt geh:* jn/etw jm ~ to entrust sb/sthg to sb.

**überarbeiten** *vt* to revise.
➤ **sich überarbeiten** *ref* to overwork.

**überaus, überaus** *adv geh* extremely.

**überbacken** (*präs* **überbackt** ODER **überbäckt**; *prät* **überbackte** ODER **überbuk**; *perf* **hat überbacken**) *vt* to brown; etw mit Käse ~ to bake sthg with a cheese topping.

**überbeanspruchen** *vt* [Mensch] to overtax; [Material] to overstrain.

**überbelichten** *vt* to overexpose.

**überbewerten** *vt* [Qualitäten] to overrate; [Fehler] to exaggerate.

**überbieten** (*prät* **überbot**; *perf* **hat überboten**) *vt:* einen Preis (um etw) ~ to exceed a price (by sthg); jn (um 5.000 Euro) ~ to outbid sb (by 5,000 euros); einen Rivalen ~ to outdo a rival; einen Rekord (um 10 cm) ~ to break a record (by 10 cm).
➤ **sich überbieten** *ref geh* to surpass o.s.; [Konkurrenten] to vie with each other.

**Überbleibsel** (*pl* -) *das* [Spur] remnant; [Ruinen, Scherben] remains (*pl*).

**Über|blick** *der* - **1.**: ein ~ über etw (A) [Übersicht] an overall perspective of sthg; [Zusammenfassung] a summary of sthg; den ~ verlieren to lose perspective - **2.** [Aussicht]: ein ~ über etw (A) a (panoramic) view of sthg.

**überblicken** *vt* - **1.** [einschätzen] to assess - **2.** [sehen] to overlook.

**überbringen** (*prät* **überbrachte**; *perf* **hat überbracht**) *vt:* jm etw ~ to deliver sthg to sb.

**Überbringer, in** (*mpl* -; *fpl* -nen) *der, die* bearer.

**überbrücken** *vt* [Zeit] to fill in; [Gegensätze] to reconcile.

**überdachen** *vt* to roof over.

**Überdachung** (*pl* -en) *die* - **1.** [Dach] roof - **2.** [Vorgang] construction of a/the roof.

**überdauern** *vt geh* to survive.

**überdecken** *vt* - **1.** [kaschieren] to cover up - **2.** [bedecken] to cover (over).

**überdehnen** *vt* to strain.

**überdenken** (*prät* **überdachte**; *perf* **hat überdacht**) *vt* to think over.

**überdeutlich** *adj* extremely clear ◇ *adv* extremely clearly.

**überdimensional** *adj* outsize ◇ *adv* on an outsize scale.

**Über|dosis** *die* overdose.

**überdrehen** *vt* - **1.** [zu fest anziehen - Schraube] to overtighten; [ - Uhr] to overwind - **2.** [Motor] to overrev.

**Überdruck** (*pl* -drücke) *der* excess pressure.

**Überdruss** *der* weariness; ~ an etw (D) weariness of sthg; sie haben bis zum ~ Karten gespielt *fam fig* they played cards till they got fed up with it.

**überdrüssig** *adj:* js/einer Sache ~ sein/werden *geh* to be/grow tired of sb/sthg.

**überdüngen** *vt* to overfertilize; [Zimmerpflanze] to overfeed.

**überdurchschnittlich** ['yːbɐdʊrçʃnɪtlɪç] *adj* above average ◇ *adv:* ~ schön more beautiful than average; ~ gut better than average; ~ bezahlt better paid than average.

**übereifrig** *adj* overzealous ◇ *adv* overzealously.

**übereilen** *vt* to rush; nur nichts ~ don't rush things, take your time.

**übereilt** *adj* hasty ◇ *adv* hastily.

**übereinander** *adv* - **1.** [Dinge] on top of each other - **2.** [Menschen - reden, nachdenken] about each other.

**übereinander legen** *vt* to place on top of each other; die Beine/Arme ~ to cross one's legs/fold one's arms.

**übereinander schlagen** *vt* (*unreg*): die Beine ~ to cross one's legs.

**überein|kommen** (*perf* **ist übereingekommen**) *vi* (*unreg*) *geh* to agree; mit jm ~, etw zu tun to agree with sb to do sthg.

**Übereinkunft** (*pl* -künfte) *die geh* agreement.

**überein|stimmen** *vi* - **1.** *geh* [einig sein]: mit jm (in etw (D)) ~ to agree with sb (about sthg) - **2.** [gleich sein - Zahlen, Messwerte] to tally; [ - Aussagen] to correspond.

**übereinstimmend** *adj* concurring ◇ *adv:* die Ärzte stellten ~ fest, dass der Mann schon tot war all the doctors agreed that the man was already dead.

**Überein|stimmung** *die* - **1.** [Einigung] agreement (U) - **2.** [Gleichheit] correspondence (U); etw (mit etw) in ~ bringen to bring sthg into line (with sthg).

**überempfindlich** *adj:* (gegen etw (A)) ~ sein to be oversensitive (to sthg); MED to be hypersensitive (to sthg) ◇ *adv* oversensitively; MED hypersensitively.

**überfahren**[1] (*präs* **überfährt**; *prät* **überfuhr**; *perf* **hat überfahren**) *vt* - **1.** [töten] to run over; jn ~ *fig* [überrumpeln] to catch sb unawares - **2.** [Kreuzung, Schild] to drive through.

**über|fahren**[2] (*perf* **ist übergefahren**) *vi* (*unreg*) [überqueren] to cross (over).

**Über|fahrt** *die* crossing.

**Über|fall** *der* attack; ~ auf jn/etw attack on sb/sthg; **bewaffneter** ~ armed assault.

**überfallen** (*präs* **überfällt**; *prät* **überfiel**; *perf* **hat überfallen**) *vt* - **1.** [ausrauben - gen] to attack; [ - Bank] to raid; [ - eine Frau] to assault - **2.** *fam* [überraschen] to descend on.

**überfällig** *adj* overdue.

**überfliegen** (*prät* **überflog**; *perf* **hat überflogen**) *vt* - **1.** [fliegen] to fly over - **2.** *fig* [lesen] to glance over.

**überflügeln** *vt*: jn (in etw (D)) ~ to outdo sb (in sthg).

**Überfluss** *der* [viel] abundance; [zu viel] surplus; **im** ~ **leben** to live affluently; **etw im** ~ **haben** to have sthg in abundance; **zu allem** ~ to top it all.

**überflüssig** *adj* [überzählig] superfluous; [frei] spare; [unnötig] unnecessary; **etw für** ~ **halten** to consider sthg unnecessary.

**überfluten** *vt* to flood.

**überfordern** *vt* to overtax; jn (mit etw (D)) ~ to ask too much of sb (with sthg); **die junge Mutter war überfordert** the young mother couldn't cope.

**Über|forderung** *die* overtaxing (U).

**überfragt** *adj*: da bin ich ~ I can't help you there.

**überfrierend** *adj*: ~e Nässe *amt* black ice.

**überführen** *vt* - **1.** RECHT: jn einer Sache (G) ~ to convict sb of sthg - **2.** [transportieren - gen] to transfer; [ - Tote] to transport.

**Über|führung** *die* - **1.** [Transport] transfer; [von Toten] transportation - **2.** [Brücke] bridge.

**überfüllt** *adj* overcrowded.

**überfüttern** *vt* to overfeed.

**Über|gabe** *die* - **1.** [von Gegenstand, Besitz] handing over; **die** ~ **(einer Sache** (G)**) an jn** the handing over (of sthg) to sb - **2.** MIL surrender.

**Übergang** (*pl* -gänge) *der* - **1.** (*ohne pl*) [Provisorium] temporary arrangement - **2.** [Kontrast] contrast - **3.** [Weg] crossing; [Brücke] bridge - **4.** [Phase] transition.

**Übergangs|lösung** *die* interim solution.

**Übergangs|regelung** *die* interim regulation.

**Übergangs|zeit** *die* transitional period.

**übergeben** (*präs* **übergibt**; *prät* **übergab**; *perf* **hat übergeben**) *vt* - **1.** [überreichen, weitergeben]: jm etw ~ to hand sthg over to sb; [feierlich überreichen] to present sthg to sb - **2.** [überantworten]: jm etw/jn ~ to hand sthg/sb over to sb - **3.** [freigeben] to open.

➣ **sich übergeben** *ref* to vomit.

**übergehen¹** (*prät* **überging**; *perf* **hat übergangen**) *vt* - **1.** [nicht beachten] to ignore; [überspringen] to skip - **2.** [nicht berücksichtigen]: jn bei etw ~ to pass sb over for sthg.

**über|gehen²** (*perf* **ist übergegangen**) *vi* (*unreg*) - **1.** [wechseln]: **zu etw** ~ to proceed to sthg; **dazu** ~, **etw zu tun** to proceed to do sthg - **2.** [sich verändern]: **in etw** (A) ~ to change into sthg; [Farben] to merge into sthg; **in Verwesung** ~ to decompose - **3.** [den Besitzer wechseln]: **an jn** ~ to pass to sb; **von jm an jn** ~ to pass from sb to sb.

**übergeordnet** *adj* - **1.** [wichtiger] higher; **jm/einer Sache** ~ **sein** to take precedence over sb/sthg - **2.** [allgemeiner] generic.

**Über|gewicht** *das* - **1.** [von Personen]: ~ **haben** to be overweight - **2.** [von Gegenständen] excess weight (U).

**übergießen** (*prät* **übergoß**; *perf* **hat übergossen**) *vt*: jn/etw mit etw ~ to pour sthg over sb/sthg.

**überglücklich** *adj* overjoyed.

**über|greifen** *vi* (*unreg*): **auf etw** (A) ~ to spread to sthg.

**übergreifend** *adj* comprehensive.

**Über|griff** *der* [Angriff] attack; [unrechtmäßige Handlung] encroachment.

**Über|größe** *die* outsize.

**über|haben** *vt* (*unreg*) *fam* to be sick of ODER fed up with.

**überhand nehmen** *vi* (*unreg*) to get out of hand.

**Über|hang** *der* - **1.** [Vorsprung] overhang - **2.** [Überzahl] surplus.

**überhäufen** *vt*: jn/etw mit etw ~ to inundate sb/sthg with sthg.

**überhaupt** *adv* - **1.** [verstärkend] at all; **gibt es** ~ **eine Hoffnung?** is there any hope at all?; ~ **nicht** not at all; ~ **nichts** nothing at all; **ich habe** ~ **kein Geld mehr** I've got no money left at all - **2.** [eigentlich] anyway; **wie gehts dir** ~? so, how are you, anyway? - **3.** [im Allgemeinen] on the whole ⬦ *interj* - **1.** [übrigens] by the way - **2.** [Ausdruck der Ungeduld, des Missfallens]: **und** ~ anyway.

**überheblich** *adj* arrogant ⬦ *adv* arrogantly.

**überhitzen** *vt* to overheat.

**überhöht** *adj* - **1.** [zu hoch gestiegen - Geschwindigkeit, Ansprüche] excessive; [ - Preis] exorbitant - **2.** [Gebäude] superelevated.

**überholen** *vt* - **1.** [vorbeifahren] to overtake - **2.** *fam* [übertreffen] to leave behind - **3.** [warten] to overhaul ⬦ *vi* to overtake.

**Überhol|spur** *die* overtaking lane; [auf der Autobahn] fast lane.

**überholt** *adj* outdated.

**U**

**Überhol|verbot** *das* : hier besteht ~ there is no over-taking here.

**überhören** *vt* - **1.** [nicht hören] not to hear - **2.** [ignorieren] to ignore.

**überirdisch** *adj* supernatural; [Schönheit] ethereal.

**überkandidelt** *adj fam* over-the-top.

**überkleben** *vt*: den Namensschild ~ to stick something over the nameplate.

**über|kochen** (*perf* ist **übergekocht**) *vi* - **1.** [überfließen] to boil over - **2.** *fam* [die Beherrschung verlieren] to explode.

**überkommen**[1] (*prät* **überkam**; *perf* hat **überkommen**) *vt* [Gefühl] to come over; Traurigkeit überkam sie a feeling of sadness came over her.

**überkommen**[2] *adj* traditional.

**überkreuzen** *vt* to cross; die Arme ~ to fold one's arms.

➤ sich **überkreuzen** *ref fam* to cross over one another.

**über|kriegen** *vt fam* to get sick of ODER fed up with.

**überladen**[1] (*präs* **überlädt**; *prät* **überlud**; *perf* hat **überladen**) *vt* to overload.

**überladen**[2] *adj* [bombastisch] (over)ornate.

**überlagern** *vt* [Frequenz] to mask; [Ton, Bild] to superimpose.

➤ sich **überlagern** *ref* [übereinander - Gesteinsschichten] to overlie; [ - Frequenzen] to mask each other; [ - Ereignisse] to coincide; [sich überschneiden] to overlap.

**Überland|bus** *der* coach.

**Über|länge** *die* - **1.** [zeitlich] excessive length; der Film hat ~ the film is unusually long - **2.** [von Kleidung, räumlich] extra length.

**überlappen** ➤ sich **überlappen** *ref* to overlap.

**überlassen** (*präs* **überläßt**; *prät* **überließ**; *perf* hat **überlassen**) *vt* - **1.** [leihen]: jm etw ~ to let sb have sthg - **2.** [sich nicht einmischen]: jm etw ~ to leave sthg to sb; das bleibt Ihnen ~! that is up to you! - **3.** [allein lassen]: jn seiner Verzweiflung ~ to leave sb to his/her despair; jn sich (*D*) selbst ~ to leave sb to his/her own devices.

➤ sich **überlassen** *ref*: sich einer Sache (*D*) ~ to abandon o.s. to sthg.

**überlastet** *adj* - **1.** [belastet] overloaded - **2.** [überfordert]: mit etw ~ sein to be overburdened with sthg.

**Überlastung** (*pl* **-en**) *die* [von Stromleitung] overloading (*U*); [mit Arbeit] overburdening (*U*); [von Mensch] overtaxing (*U*).

**über|laufen**[1] (*perf* ist **übergelaufen**) *vi* (*unreg*) - **1.** [überfließen] to overflow - **2.** [überwechseln] to go over to the other side; zu jm/etw ~ to go over to sb/sthg.

**überlaufen**[2] (*präs* **überläuft**; *prät* **überlief**; *perf* hat **überlaufen**) *vt* - **1.** [überkommen]: es überläuft mich shivers run down my spine - **2.** SPORT [hinter sich lassen] to outrun; [zu weit laufen] to overshoot.

**überlaufen**[3] *adj*: ~ sein to be overcrowded; [Kurs] to be oversubscribed.

**Über|läufer, in** *der, die* defector.

**überleben** *vt* - **1.** [lebend überstehen] to survive - **2.** [länger leben als]: jn ~ to outlive sb <> *vi* to survive.

➤ sich **überleben** *ref* to become outdated; sich überlebt haben to have become a thing of the past.

**Überlebende** (*pl* **-n**) *der, die* survivor.

**überlebensgroß** *adj* larger than life-size.

**überlegen**[1] *vt* to think about, to consider; sich (*D*) etw ~ [über etw nachdenken] to think sthg over; [sich etw ausdenken] to think of sthg; es sich (*D*) anders ~ to change one's mind; etw reiflich ~ to consider sthg very carefully <> *vi* to think; ohne zu ~ without thinking.

**überlegen**[2] *adj* [besser] superior; [arrogant] patronizing; jm ~ sein to be superior to sb <> *adv* [siegen] convincingly; [lächeln] patronizingly.

**Überlegenheit** *die* superiority; zahlenmäßige ~ numerical superiority.

**überlegt** *adj* deliberate <> *adv* in a considered way.

**Überlegung** (*pl* **-en**) *die* consideration (*U*); ohne ~ handeln to act without thinking; bei ODER nach reiflicher ~ after careful consideration.

**über|leiten** *vi*: zu etw ~ to lead on to sthg.

**Über|leitung** *die* link.

**überliefern** *vt* to hand down.

**Über|lieferung** *die* - **1.** [das Überliefern] handing down - **2.** [das Überlieferte] tradition.

**Übermacht** *die* superior strength; in der ~ sein to be stronger.

**übermächtig** *adj* - **1.** [emotional] overwhelming - **2.** [kräftemäßig] superior.

**übermalen** *vt* to paint over.

**Übermaß** *das* excess; ein ~ an etw (*D*) geh an excess of sthg; im ~ anwenden/genießen to use/enjoy sthg to excess.

**übermäßig** *adj* excessive <> *adv* excessively; sich ~ anstrengen to overexert o.s.; ~ ehrgeizig overambitious.

**übermitteln** *vt*: jm etw ~ to pass sthg on to sb.

**übermorgen** *adv* the day after tomorrow.

**übermüdet** *adj* overtired.

**Übermut** *der* (*ohne pl*) high spirits (*pl*).

**übermütig** *adj* highspirited; [sich überschätzend] overconfident ⬦ *adv* high-spiritedly.

**übernächste, r, s** [ˈyːbɐnɛːçstə,-,-s] *adj*: das ~ **Auto** the next car but one; ~ **Woche** the week after next.

**übernachten** *vi* to stay *ODER* spend the night; **bei jm** ~ to stay the night with sb.

**übernächtigt** *adj* bleary-eyed.

**Übernachtung** (*pl* -en) *die* overnight stay; **eine** ~ **mit Frühstück** bed and breakfast.

**Übernahme** (*pl* -n) *die* - **1.** [von Firma, Betrieb] takeover; [das Übernehmen] taking over (*U*) - **2.** [Eingliederung]: **die** ~ **in ein dauerhaftes Arbeitsverhältnis** the conversion to a permanent position - **3.** [von Kosten] meeting (*U*) - **4.** [von Wort, Brauch] adoption (*U*).

**übernatürlich** *adj* supernatural ⬦ *adv* supernaturally; ~ **klug** preternaturally clever.

**übernehmen** (*präs* übernimmt; *prät* übernahm; *perf* hat übernommen) *vt* - **1.** [Firma, Betrieb] to take over; **etw von jm** ~ to take sthg over from sb - **2.** [annehmen] to take on - **3.** [einstellen, weiterbeschäftigen] to keep on - **4.** [kopieren]: **etw von jm/etw** ~ [Verhaltensweise, Konzept] to adopt sthg from sb/sthg; [Text] to copy sthg from sb/sthg.

➡ **sich übernehmen** *ref* to overdo it; **sich mit etw** ~ [finanziell] to take on too much of sthg.

**über|ordnen** *vt* - **1.** [vorrangig behandeln]: **jm/ etw jn/etw** ~ to give sb/sthg priority over sb/sthg - **2.** [höhere Position geben]: **jm/etw jn/ etw** ~ to put sb/sthg over sb/sthg.

**überparteilich** *adj* cross-party; [Zeitung] independent ⬦ *adv* across party lines; [unabhängig] independently.

**überproportional** *adj* disproportionately large ⬦ *adv*: ~ **vertreten** overrepresented.

**überprüfen** *vt* to inspect, to check; [Verdächtigen] to screen; **jn/etw auf etw** (*A*) **(hin)** ~ to check sb/sthg for sthg.

**Über|prüfung** *die* checking (*U*); [von Verdächtigen] screening (*U*).

**überqualifiziert** *adj* overqualified.

**über|quellen** (*perf* ist übergequollen) *vi* (*unreg*): **vor etw** (*D*) ~ to overflow with sthg.

**überqueren** *vt* to cross.

**überragen** *vt* - **1.** [größer sein] to tower above - **2.** [übertreffen] to surpass; **jn/etw um etw** ~ to be taller than sb/sthg by sthg.

**überragend** *adj* outstanding ⬦ *adv* superbly.

**überraschen** *vt* to surprise; **jn mit etw** ~ to surprise sb with sthg; **jn bei etw** ~ to catch sb doing sthg; **von jm/etw überrascht werden** to be taken by surprise by sb/sthg; **vom Re-** gen überrascht werden to get caught in the rain.

**überraschend** *adj* surprising; [unerwartet] unexpected; ~ **sein** to be surprising ⬦ *adv* surprisingly; ~ **kommen** [zu Besuch] to arrive unexpectedly; [Entwicklung] to come as a surprise.

**Überraschung** (*pl* -en) *die* surprise; **eine böse** ~ **erleben** to get a nasty surprise.

**überreden** *vt* to persuade; **jn zu etw** ~ to persuade sb to do sthg; **sich zu etw** ~ **lassen** to let o.s. be talked into (doing) sthg.

**Überredung** (*pl* -en) *die* persuasion (*U*).

**überregional** *adj* [Zeitung, Sender] national; ~**e Zusammenarbeit** cooperation across regional boundaries ⬦ *adv* [im ganzen Land] at national level; [über die Region hinaus] across regional boundaries.

**überreich** *adj* abundant; [zu viel] overabundant; [Entschädigung] overgenerous ⬦ *adv*: **jn** ~ **beschenken** to lavish presents on sb.

**überreichen** *vt*: **jm etw** ~ to present sthg to sb.

**überreif** *adj* - **1.** [sehr reif] overripe - **2.** *fig* [längst fällig] (long) overdue.

**überreizt** *adj* tense; [nervös] edgy, jumpy ⬦ *adv* nervously; ~ **wirken** to seem tense.

**Über|rest** *der* remains (*pl*).

**Überroll|bügel** *der* AUTO roll-over bar.

**überrollen** *vt* - **1.** [überfahren] to run over - **2.** *fig* [überraschen] to catch unawares.

**überrumpeln** *vt*: **jn (mit etw)** ~ to take sb by surprise (with sthg).

**überrunden** *vt* - **1.** SPORT to lap - **2.** [übertreffen] to outstrip.

**übers** *präp fam* (über + das): **der Vogel fliegt** ~ **Haus** the bird is flying over the house; ~ **Jahr verteilt** spread over the year; ~ **schlechte Wetter schimpfen** to complain about the bad weather; ➪ **Ohr, Knie.**

**Übers.** *abk für* Übersetzung.

**übersät** *adj*: **mit etw** ~ **sein** to be strewn with sthg.

**übersättigt** *adj* [Zuschauer] sated; [Markt] saturated.

**Überschallgeschwindigkeit** *die* supersonic speed.

**überschatten** *vt* to overshadow.

**überschätzen** *vt* to overestimate.

➡ **sich überschätzen** *ref* to overestimate o.s.

**überschaubar** *adj* with visible limits; [Arbeit] easy to grasp; [Risiko] calculable.

**über|schäumen** (*perf* ist übergeschäumt) *vi* - **1.** [überfließen] to froth over - **2.** *fig* [emotional - vor Begeisterung, Lebenslust] to brim over; [ - vor Wut, Zorn] to boil over.

**überschlafen** (*präs* überschläft; *prät* überschlief; *perf* hat überschlafen) *vt* to sleep on.

**Überlschlag** *der* - **1.** sport somersault - **2.** [Schätzung] (rough) estimate.

**überschlagen**[1] (*präs* überschlägt; *prät* überschlug; *perf* hat überschlagen) *vt* - **1.** [rechnen] to estimate (roughly) - **2.** [überblättern] to skip.
➡ **sich überschlagen** *ref* - **1.** [Auto] to overturn; [Person] to fall head over heels - **2.** [Ereignisse] to follow one another thick and fast - **3.** [Stimme] to crack.

**überlschlagen**[2] (*perf* hat/ist übergeschlagen) (*unreg*) *vt* (*hat*) [überkreuzen]: **die Beine** ~ to cross one's legs <> *vi* (*ist*) [umschlagen]: **in etw** (*A*) ~ to turn into sthg.

**überlschnappen** (*perf* ist übergeschnappt) *vi fam* to go crazy.

**überschneiden** (*prät* überschnitt; *perf* hat überschnitten) ➡ **sich überschneiden** *ref* - **1.** [räumlich] to intersect - **2.** [zeitlich] to coincide - **3.** [inhaltlich] to overlap.

**überschreiben** (*prät* überschrieb; *perf* hat überschrieben) *vt* - **1.** [übereignen]: **jm etw** ~ to make sthg over to sb - **2.** [betiteln] to head.

**überschreiten** (*prät* überschritt; *perf* hat überschritten) *vt* - **1.** [räumlich] to cross - **2.** [inhaltlich - gen] to exceed; [ - Befugnis] to overstep - **3.** [zeitlich] to pass.

**Überlschrift** *die* heading; [in Fettdruck] headline.

**Überlschuss** *der* - **1.** [Gewinn] profit; ~ **erzielen** to make a profit - **2.** [ein Zuviel] surplus.

**überschüssig** *adj* surplus.

**überschütten** *vt*: **jn/etw mit etw** ~ to cover sb/sthg with sthg; **jn mit Lob** ~ to shower sb with praise; **jn mit Vorwürfen** ~ to heap criticism on sb.

**Überschwang** *der*: **im** ~ **der Gefühle** in a fit of exuberance.

**überschwänglich** *adj* effusive <> *adv* effusively.

**überschwemmen** *vt* - **1.** [nass machen] to flood - **2.** [überreich versehen]: **jn/etw mit etw** ~ to inundate sb/sthg with sthg.

**Überschwemmung** (*pl* -en) *die* flood.

**überschwenglich** = überschwänglich.

**Übersee** ➡ **aus Übersee** *adv* from overseas ODER abroad.
➡ **in/nach Übersee** *adv* abroad, overseas.

**überseeisch** [ˈyːbɐzeːɪʃ] *adj* overseas.

**übersehen** (*präs* übersieht; *prät* übersah; *perf* hat übersehen) *vt* - **1.** [nicht sehen, ansehen] to overlook; [absichtlich] to ignore - **2.** [einschätzen] to assess.

**übersetzen**[1] *vt* [in Sprache] to translate; **in etw** (*A*) ~ to translate into sthg; **von** ODER **aus etw** ~ to translate from sthg.

**überlsetzen**[2] (*perf* hat/ist übergesetzt) *vi* (*ist*) [überqueren] to cross <> *vt* (*hat*) [befördern] to take across.

**Überlsetzer, in** *der, die* translator.

**Übersetzung** (*pl* -en) *die* - **1.** [das Übersetzen] translation - **2.** tech gear ratio.

**Übersicht** (*pl* -en) *die* - **1.** [Fähigkeit] overview - **2.** [Darstellung]: **eine** ~ **über etw** (*A*) an outline of sthg.

**übersichtlich** *adj* - **1.** [gut strukturiert] clear - **2.** [gut zu sehen] open <> *adv* clearly.

**übersiedeln** (*perf* ist übersiedelt), **überlsiedeln** (*perf* ist übersiedelt) *vi* to move.

**übersinnlich** *adj* [Wahrnehmung] supersensory; [Kräfte] supernatural.

**überspannen** *vt* [Saite] to overtighten; [Bogen] to overdraw.

**überspannt** *adj* - **1.** [exaltiert] eccentric; [hysterisch] hysterical - **2.** [zu hoch] exaggerated <> *adv* [exaltiert] eccentrically; [hysterisch] hysterically.

**überspielen** *vt* - **1.** [verdecken] to cover up - **2.** [aufnehmen] to record

**überspitzt** *adj* exaggerated <> *adv* in an exaggerated way.

**überspringen**[1] (*prät* übersprang; *perf* hat übersprungen) *vt* - **1.** [darüber hinwegspringen] to jump - **2.** [auslassen] to skip.

**überlspringen**[2] (*perf* ist übergesprungen) *vi* (*unreg*) [Funke] to jump across.

**überlsprudeln** (*perf* ist übergesprudelt) *vi* - **1.** [Person]: **vor etw** (*D*) ~ to bubble over with sthg - **2.** [Flüssigkeit] to bubble over.

**überstehen**[1] (*prät* überstand; *perf* hat überstanden) *vt* [hinter sich bringen] to come through.

**überlstehen**[2] (*perf* hat/ist übergestanden) *vi* (*unreg*) [vorstehen] to jut out.

**übersteigen** (*prät* überstieg; *perf* hat überstiegen) *vt* - **1.** [zu viel sein] to exceed - **2.** [überklettern] to climb over.

**überstimmen** *vt* [Person] to outvote; [Antrag] to vote down.

**überlströmen** (*perf* ist übergeströmt) *vi geh* [emotional] to overflow.

**überströmt** *adj*: **sein Gesicht war von Tränen/Schweiß** ~ tears were/sweat was streaming down his face.

**Überlstunde** *die*: **eine** ~ an hour's overtime; ~**n (machen)** (to do) overtime.

**Überstundenzulschlag** *der* overtime rate.

**überstürzen** *vt* to rush into.

➤ **sich überstürzen** *ref* [Ereignisse] to follow in rapid succession.

**überstürzt** *adj* overhasty ◇ *adv* overhastily.

**überteuert** *adj* exorbitant ◇ *adv* at an exorbitant price.

**übertönen** *vt* to drown out.

**Über|topf** *der* plant-pot holder.

**Übertrag** (*pl* -träge) *der* sum carried forward.

**übertragbar** *adj* - **1.** [Fahrkarte, Recht] transferable; **nicht** ~ non-transferable - **2.** [anwendbar] applicable.

**übertragen¹** (*präs* überträgt; *prät* übertrug; *perf* hat übertragen) *vt* - **1.** [anwenden]: **etw auf jn/etw** ~ to apply sthg to sb/sthg - **2.** [senden] to broadcast - **3.** [übersetzen]: **etw in etw** (A) ~ to translate sthg into sthg - **4.** [Krankheit] to transmit - **5.** [überantworten]: **jm etw** ~ to assign sthg to sb.

➤ **sich übertragen** *ref*: **sich auf jn** ~ MED & *fig* to infect sb.

**übertragen²** *adj* [nicht wörtlich] figurative ◇ *adv* [nicht wörtlich] figuratively.

**Übertragung** (*pl* -en) *die* - **1.** [Sendung] broadcast; [das Senden] broadcasting - **2.** [von Krankheit] transmission - **3.** [Überantwortung] transfer.

**übertreffen** (*präs* übertrifft; *prät* übertraf; *perf* hat übertroffen) *vt* [Erwartungen] to surpass; [Rekord] to beat; **jn an Ausdauer/Schnelligkeit** ~ to have more stamina/be faster than sb; **sie übertrifft ihn im Tennis** she's better than him at tennis.

**übertreiben** (*prät* übertrieb; *perf* hat übertrieben) *vt* [bei Darstellung] to exaggerate; [Handlung] to overdo ◇ *vi* [bei Darstellung] to exaggerate; [bei Handlung] to overdo it.

**Übertreibung** (*pl* -en) *die* exaggeration.

**übertreten¹** (*präs* übertritt; *prät* übertrat; *perf* hat übertreten) *vt* to break.

**über|treten²** (*perf* hat/ist übergetreten) *vi* (*unreg*) - **1.** (*ist*) [beitreten]: **zu etw** (D) ~ [zu Partei] to go over to sthg; [zu Konfession] to convert to sthg - **2.** (*hat*) SPORT to overstep.

**übertrieben** *adj* [Darstellung] exaggerated; [Forderung, Ehrgeiz] excessive ◇ *adv* [darstellen] in an exaggerated manner; [ernst, höflich] excessively.

**übervoll** *adj* [Gefäß] full to overflowing; [Raum] packed, crammed full.

**übervorteilen** *vt* to cheat.

**überwachen** *vt* to keep under surveillance; [Arbeit] to oversee; **jn/etw streng** ~ to keep sb/sthg under close surveillance.

**überwältigen** *vt* - **1.** [besiegen] to overpower - **2.** [überkommen] to overwhelm.

**überwältigend** *adj* overwhelming; **nicht** ~ not exactly brilliant ◇ *adv*: ~ **aussehen** to look stunning; ~ **viele Besucher** an overwhelming number of visitors.

**über|wechseln** [ˈyːbɐvɛksl̩n] (*perf* ist übergewechselt) *vi* to switch; **ins feindliche Lager** ~ to go over to the enemy; **zu etw** ~ to switch to sthg; **zu jm** ~ [Partei, Firma] to go over to sb.

**überweisen** (*prät* überwies; *perf* hat überwiesen) *vt* - **1.** [bezahlen] to pay; **jm etw** ~, **etw an jn** ~ to pay sthg to sb; **Geld auf ein anderes Konto** ~ to transfer money to another account; **Ihr Gehalt bekommen Sie überwiesen** your salary will be paid into your account - **2.** MED: **einen Patienten ins Krankenhaus** ~ to have a patient admitted to hospital; **jn (an jn** ODER **zu jm)** ~ to refer sb (to sb).

**Über|weisung** *die* - **1.** [Zahlung] transfer; [Formular] money transfer form; **die** ~ **des Geldes dauert vier Tage** it takes four days for the money to be paid into your account - **2.** MED referral.

**Überweisungs|formular** *das* credit transfer form.

**über|werfen** *vt* (*unreg*) [anziehen]: **sich** (D) **etw** ~ to throw sthg over one's shoulders.

**überwiegen** (*prät* überwog; *perf* hat überwogen) *vi* - **1.** [Skepsis, Zweifel] to prevail - **2.** [zahlenmäßig] to predominate ◇ *vt* to outweigh.

**überwiegend, überwiegend** *adj* [Mehrheit] overwhelming; **der** ~ **Teil** the majority ◇ *adv* mainly.

**überwinden** (*prät* überwand; *perf* hat überwunden) *vt* to overcome; [Krise] to get over.

➤ **sich überwinden** *ref*: **sich zu etw** ~ to force o.s. to do sthg; **sich nicht** ~ **können, etw zu tun** not to be able to bring o.s. to do sthg.

**Überwindung** *die* - **1.** [gen] overcoming - **2.** [von Berg] conquering - **3.** [das Sichüberwinden]: **es ist für mich eine** ~ ODER **es kostet mich** ~, **es zu tun** I have to force myself to do it.

**überwintern** *vi* - **1.** [Pflanze, Vogel] to spend the winter - **2.** [Winterschlaf halten] to hibernate - **3.** *hum* [Mensch] to winter.

**überwuchern** *vt* to overgrow.

**Überzahl** *die* majority; **in der** ~ **sein** SPORT to have a numerical advantage; [mehr sein] to be in the majority.

**überzählig** *adj* spare, surplus.

**überzeugen** *vt* to convince; **jn von etw** ~ to convince sb of sthg.

➤ **sich überzeugen** *ref*: **sich (von etw)** ~ to satisfy o.s. (of sthg); ~ **Sie sich selbst!** see for yourself!

**überzeugt** *adj* convinced; **von etw** ~ **sein** to be convinced of sthg; **davon** ~ **sein, dass ...** to be convinced that ...; **sehr von sich selbst ~ sein** to be very sure of o.s.

**Über|zeugung** *die* conviction; **gegen seine ~ handeln** to go against one's convictions; **meiner ~ nach ...** it is my firm belief that ...; **zur ~ kommen** *ODER* **gelangen, dass ...** to become convinced *ODER* come to believe that ...

**überziehen¹** (*prät* **überzog;** *perf* **hat überzogen**) *vi* - **1.** [bei Bank] to go overdrawn - **2.** [zeitlich] to overrun <> *vt* - **1.** [Konto] to overdraw - **2.** [nicht pünktlich beenden] to overrun - **3.** [Sofa] to re-cover; **die Betten ~** to change the bedsheets - **4.** [übertreiben] to take too far.

**über|ziehen²** *vt* (*unreg*) [anziehen]: **sich** (D) **etw ~** to pull sthg on.

**Überziehungs|kredit** *der* overdraft facility.

**überzogen** *adj* exaggerated <> *adv:* **~ reagieren** to overreact.

**Über|zug** *der* - **1.** [Bezug] cover - **2.** [Belag] coating.

**üblich** *adj* usual; **wie ~** as usual.

**üblicherweise** *adv* usually.

**U-|Boot** *das* submarine.

**übrig** *adj* remaining; **ist noch etwas ~?** is there any left?; **die ~en Autos** the rest of the cars, the remaining cars; **die Übrigen** the rest; **ein Übriges tun** *fig* & *geh* to finish the job off <> *adv:* **für jn/etw viel/nichts ~ haben** to have a lot of/no time for sb/sthg.

➤ **im Übrigen** *adv* in addition.

**übrig bleiben** (*perf* **ist übrig geblieben**) *vi* (*unreg*) to be left over; **uns blieb nichts anderes** *ODER* **weiter übrig, als zuzustimmen** we had no alternative but to agree.

**übrigens** *adv* by the way.

**übrig lassen** *vt* (*unreg*): **jm etw ~** to leave sthg for sb.

**Übung** (*pl* **-en**) *die* - **1.** [das Üben] practice; **aus der ~ kommen/sein** to get/be out of practice - **2.** SPORT, SCHULE, MIL & MUS exercise - **3.** UNI seminar.

**u. dgl.** (*abk für* **und dergleichen**) *and the like.*

**u. d. M.** (*abk für* **unter dem Meeresspiegel**) *below sea level.*

**ü. d. M.** (*abk für* **über dem Meeresspiegel**) *above sea level.*

**UdSSR** [uːdeːɛsɛsˈɛr] (*abk für* **Union der sozialistischen Sowjetrepubliken**) *die* USSR.

**u. E.** (*abk für* **unseres Erachtens**) *in our opinion.*

**UEFA** [uˈeːfa] (*abk für* **Union der europäischen Fußballverbände**) *die* UEFA.

**UEFA-Pokal** *der* UEFA Cup.

**UFA®** [ˈuːfa] (*abk für* **Universum Film AG**) *die former Berlin-based film company.*

**Ufer** (*pl* **-**) *das* [von Fluss] bank; [von See, Meer] shore; **am ~** [von Fluss] on the bank; [von See, Meer] on the shore.

**uferlos** *adj* endless; **ins Uferlose gehen** [Kosten] to get out of hand; [Debatte] to go on and on.

**UFO, Ufo** [ˈuːfoː] (*pl* **-s**) *das* UFO.

**Uganda** *nt* Uganda.

**Ugander, in** (*mpl* **-;** *fpl* **-nen**) *der, die* Ugandan.

**ugandisch** *adj* Ugandan.

**Uhr** (*pl* **-en**) *die* - **1.** [Zeitanzeiger] clock - **2.** [Armbanduhr] watch - **3.** [Zeit]: **es ist 3 ~** it is 3 o'clock; **um 3 ~** at 3 o'clock; **um wie viel ~?** (at) what time?; **wie viel ~ ist es?** what time is it?; **rund um die ~** round the clock.

**Uhrmacher, in** (*mpl* **-;** *fpl* **-nen**) *der, die* [von Armbanduhren] watchmaker; [von größeren Uhren] clockmaker.

**Uhr|zeiger** *der* hand.

**Uhrzeiger|sinn** *der:* **im ~** clockwise; **gegen den ~** anticlockwise.

**Uhr|zeit** *die* time.

**Uhu** (*pl* **-s**) *der* eagle owl.

**Ukraine** *die* Ukraine.

**Ukrainer, in** (*mpl* **-;** *fpl* **-nen**) *der, die* Ukrainian.

**ukrainisch** *adj* Ukrainian.

**Ukrainisch(e)** *das* Ukrainian; *siehe auch* **Englisch(e).**

**UKW** [uːkaːˈveː] (*abk für* **Ultrakurzwelle**) *die* FM.

**ulkig** *adj* comical, funny <> *adv:* **~ aussehen** to look comical *ODER* funny.

**Ulme** (*pl* **-n**) *die* elm.

**ultimativ** *adj* final <> *adv:* **etw ~ fordern** to make a final demand.

**Ultimatum** (*pl* **-ten**) *das* ultimatum; **jm ein ~ stellen** to give sb an ultimatum.

**Ultrakurzwelle** *die* frequency modulation, FM.

**Ultraschall** *der* ultrasound.

**Ultraschall|untersuchung** *die* ultrasound scan.

**ultraviolett** [ˈʊltraviolɛt] *adj* ultraviolet.

**um** *präp* (+ A) - **1.** [räumlich] (a)round; **~ jn/etw herum** around sb/sthg; **gleich ~ die Ecke** just around the corner; **~ sich blicken** to look around - **2.** [zur Angabe der Uhrzeit] at; **~ drei Uhr** at three o'clock - **3.** [zur Angabe einer Differenz] by; **die Preise steigen ~ 15%** prices are rising by 15%; **~ einen Kopf größer** taller by a head - **4.** [zur Angabe von Grund]: **~ etw kämpfen** to fight for sthg; **sich ~ ein Spielzeug streiten** to quarrel over *ODER* about a toy **- 5.** [zur Angabe einer Folge] after; **Tag ~ Tag** day after day; **Schritt ~ Schritt** step by step **- 6.** [ungefähr] about, around; **es kostet ~ die 300 Euro** it costs about *ODER* around 300 euros; **so ~ Ostern herum** some time around Easter ◇ *konj:* **~ zu** (in order) to; **zu stolz, ~ nachzugeben** too proud to give in ◇ *adv* [vorüber] up; **die zehn Minuten sind ~** the ten minutes are up.

➡ **um so** *konj* = **umso**.

**um|ländern** *vt* to alter.

**umarmen** *vt* to hug.
➡ **sich umarmen** *ref* to hug.

**Umarmung** (*pl* -en) *die* hug.

**Umbau** (*pl* -e *ODER* -ten) *der* renovation.

**um|bauen¹** *vt* [verändern] to renovate; **etw zu etw ~** to convert sthg to sthg ◇ *vi* to renovate.

**umbauen²** *vt* [umgeben] to surround.

**um|benennen** *vt* (unreg) [gen & EDV] to rename; **der Karl-Marx-Platz wurde in Augustusplatz umbenannt** Karl-Marx-Platz was renamed Augustusplatz.

**um|bilden** *vt* [Regierung, Kabinett] to reshuffle.

**um|binden** *vt* (unreg): **sich** (D) **etw ~** to put sthg on.

**um|blättern** *vt* to turn over ◇ *vi* to turn over the page.

**um|bringen** *vt* (unreg) *eigtl* & *fig* to kill; **nicht umzubringen sein** *fam* *fig* to be indestructible; **diese Maloche bringt mich noch um!** this job will be the death of me!
➡ **sich umbringen** *ref* [sich töten] to kill o.s.

**Um|bruch** *der* **- 1.** [Veränderung] radical change; **sich im ~ befinden** to be undergoing an upheaval **- 2.** [von Büchern] page make-up.

**um|buchen** *vt:* **einen Flug ~** to change one's flight booking ◇ *vi* to change one's booking.

**um|denken** *vi* (unreg) to change one's way of thinking.

**um|disponieren** *vi* to make new arrangements.

**um|drehen** (*perf* hat/ist umgedreht) *vt* (hat) **- 1.** [Seite, Stein] to turn over; [Pulli] to turn round **- 2.** [Auto, Stuhl, Schlüssel] to turn ◇ *vi* (ist, hat) [umkehren] to turn back.
➡ **sich umdrehen** *ref* **- 1.** [im Stehen] to turn round; **sich nach jm/etw ~** to turn round to look at sb/sthg **- 2.** [im Liegen] to turn over.

**Um|drehung** *die* **- 1.** [um eigene Achse] turn **- 2.** TECH revolution.

**umeinander, umeinander** *adv* [sich kümmern] about each other; [wickeln] around each other.

**um|fahren¹** *vt* (unreg) [überfahren] to knock down.

**umfahren²** (*präs* umfährt; *prät* umfuhr; *perf* hat umfahren) *vt* [ausweichen] to go round; **etw weiträumig ~** to steer well clear of sthg.

**um|fallen** (*perf* ist umgefallen) *vi* (unreg) **- 1.** [umkippen] to fall over; [auf den Boden] to fall down **- 2.** [zusammenbrechen] to collapse **- 3.** *fam abw* [nachgeben] to give in.

**Umfang** (*pl* -fänge) *der* **- 1.** [Maß] circumference **- 2.** [Ausmaß - von Projekt, Untersuchung] scale; [ - von Buch, Zahlung] size; [ - von Schaden] extent; [ - von Stimme] range; **in vollem ~** fully.

**umfangreich** *adj* extensive ◇ *adv* extensively, at length.

**umfassen** (*präs* umfasst; *prät* umfasste; *perf* hat umfasst) *vt* **- 1.** [beinhalten] to cover; **das Buch umfasst 200 Seiten** the book contains 200 pages **- 2.** [umschlingen]: **jn ~** to put one's arm around sb; **etw ~** to clasp sthg.

**umfassend, umfassend** *adj* comprehensive ◇ *adv* comprehensively.

**Um|fassung** *die* **- 1.** [Umrandung] border **- 2.** [Umschlingung] hold, embrace.

**Umfeld** *das* **- 1.** [Umgebung] surroundings (*pl*) **- 2.** [Milieu] environment, milieu.

**um|formen** *vt:* **einen Satz vom Aktiv ins Passiv ~** to put a sense from the active into the passive.

**Umfrage** *die* survey.

**um|füllen** *vt:* **etw in etw** (A) **~** to pour *ODER* transfer sthg into sthg.

**um|funktionieren** *vt* to convert.

**Umgang** *der* contact; **der ~ mit Kindern/Tieren** working with children/animals; **das ist kein ~ für dich!** you shouldn't mix with people like that!; **mit jm ~ haben** *ODER* **pflegen** to associate with sb.

**umgänglich** *adj* [angenehm] friendly, affable; [gesellig] sociable.

**Umgangsformen** *pl* manners.

**Umgangssprache** *die* [informelle Sprache] colloquial speech; **in der ~** colloquially.

**umgangssprachlich** *adj* colloquial ◇ *adv* colloquially.

**umgeben** (*präs* umgibt; *prät* umgab; *perf* hat umgeben) *vt* to surround; **von jm/etw ~ sein** to be surrounded by sb/sthg.
➡ **sich umgeben** *ref:* **sich mit jm/etw ~** to surround o.s. with sb/sthg.

**Umgebung** (*pl* -en) *die* **- 1.** [Gebiet] surroundings (*pl*); **in der ~ von Heilbronn** in the vicinity of Heilbronn; **die nähere ~** the immediate vicinity **- 2.** [Umfeld] environment.

**umgehen¹** (*präs* umgeht; *prät* umging; *perf* hat umgangen) *vt* **- 1.** [Schwierigkeiten] to avoid;

**U**

[Verordnung] to get round; [Antwort] to evade - **2.** [Stau, Ortschaft] to bypass.

**um|gehen²** (*perf* **ist umgegangen**) *vi* (*unreg*) - **1.** [Grippe, Gerücht, Nachricht] to go round - **2.** [behandeln]: **mit jm/etw ~ (können)** [Maschine] to (know how to) handle sb/sthg; [Kind, Tier] to (know how to) treat sb/sthg; **kannst du mit einem Computer ~?** do you know how to use a computer? - **3.** [sich beschäftigen]: **mit dem Gedanken ~, etw zu tun** to be thinking of doing sthg.

**umgehend** *adj* immediate ◇ *adv* immediately.

**Umgehungs|straße** *die* bypass.

**umgekehrt** *adj* [Vorzeichen, Fall] opposite; [Verhältnis] inverse; [Reihenfolge] reverse; **nein, es ist gerade ~!** no, the opposite is true! ◇ *adv* the other way round; **die Sache verhält sich genau ~** the opposite is true; **... und ~** ... and vice versa.

**um|graben** *vt* (*unreg*) to dig over.

**um|gucken** ◆ **sich umgucken** *ref fam* - **1.** [zurücksehen] to look round - **2.** [sich umsehen] to have a look around; **sich nach etw ~** to look for sthg; **du wirst dich (noch) ~!** *fam* you're in for a nasty surprise!

**Um|hang** *der* cape.

**um|hängen** *vt* - **1.** [woanders hin hängen] to hang somewhere else - **2.** [umlegen]: **jm/sich etw ~** [Jacke, Decke] to put sthg round sb's/one's shoulders; [Kette] to hang sthg round sb's/one's neck.

**Umhänge|tasche** *die* shoulder bag.

**um|hauen** *vt* (*unreg*) - **1.** [fällen] to cut down - **2.** *fam* [überraschen]: **es hat mich umgehauen, als ...** I was bowled over when ... - **3.** *salopp* [Alkohol, Gestank] to knock out - **4.** *fam* [niederschlagen] to knock for six - **5.** *fam* [umwerfen] to knock over.

**umher** *adv* around.

**umher|irren** (*perf* **ist umhergeirrt**) *vi* to wander around.

**umhin|können** *vi* (*unreg*): **nicht ~, etw zu tun** to have no choice but to do sthg.

**um|hören** ◆ **sich umhören** *ref*: **sich ~** to ask around.

**U/min** (*abk für* **Umdrehungen pro Minute**) r.p.m.

**umkämpft** *adj* [Stadt, Gebiet] disputed; [Gesetz, Neuerung] controversial.

**Umkehr** *die* turning back; **jn zur ~ bewegen/ zwingen** to urge/force sb to turn back.

**um|kehren** (*perf* **hat/ist umgekehrt**) *vi* (*ist*) to turn back ◇ *vt* (*hat*) [Entwicklung, Reihenfolge, Situation] to reverse.

◆ **sich umkehren** *ref* to be reversed.

**um|kippen** (*perf* **ist umgekippt**) *vi* - **1.** [umfal-

len] to fall over; [Auto] to overturn - **2.** *fam* [bewusstlos werden] to keel over - **3.** [ökologisch] to become uninhabitable - **4.** [Stimmung] to take a turn for the worse.

**umklammern** *vt* to clasp.

**um|klappen** *vt* to fold down.

**Umkleide|kabine** *die* [in Schwimmbad] changing cubicle; [auf Sportplatz] changing room; [in Kaufhaus] fitting room.

**um|kleiden¹** ◆ **sich umkleiden** *ref geh* to change (one's clothes).

**umkleiden²** *vt* to cover.

**um|knicken** (*perf* **hat/ist umgeknickt**) *vi* (*ist*) - **1.** [verrenken]: **mit dem Fuß ~** to sprain one's ankle - **2.** [brechen] to snap in half ◇ *vt* (*hat*) [Buchseite] to crease; [Ast, Baum] to snap in half.

**um|kommen** (*perf* **ist umgekommen**) *vi* (*unreg*) to die; **vor Hunger** (*D*) **~** *fig* to be dying of hunger.

**Um|kreis** *der* - **1.** (*ohne pl*) [Umgebung] vicinity; **im ~ von 50 km** within a 50 km radius - **2.** MATH circumcircle.

**umkreisen** *vt* to circle around; [Subj: Planet, Satellit] to orbit.

**um|krempeln** *vt* - **1.** [hochkrempeln] to roll up - **2.** *fam* [verändern - Mensch] to reform; [ - Geschäft] to reorganize completely - **3.** *fam* [durchsuchen] to turn upside down.

**Umland** *das* surrounding area.

**Um|lauf** *der* [Zirkulation] circulation; **in ~ bringen** [Gerücht] to circulate; [Geld] to issue.

**Umlauf|bahn** *die* orbit.

**Um|laut** *der* umlaut.

**um|legen** *vt* - **1.** *salopp* [erschießen] to bump off - **2.** [verteilen - Kosten, Ausgaben]: **etw auf mehrere Personen ~** to share sthg between several people - **3.** [umhängen]: **sich/jm etw ~** [Jacke, Decke] to put sthg round one's/sb's shoulders; [Kette] to put sthg round one's/sb's neck - **4.** [verlegen - Patienten, Telefongespräch] to transfer; [ - Termin] to change - **5.** [umklappen] to fold down - **6.** [Kippen] to knock down; [Baum] to fell.

**um|leiten** *vt* to divert.

**Um|leitung** *die* diversion.

**umliegend** *adj* surrounding.

**Umnachtung** (*pl* **-en**) *die* (mental) derangement; **in geistiger ~** in a state of mental derangement.

**um|quartieren** *vt* to move (*to different quarters*).

**umrahmen** *vt* - **1.** [umgeben] to frame - **2.** [begleiten] to accompany.

**umranden** *vt* [Wörter, Textstellen] to circle; [Terrasse, Beet] to border.

**um|rechnen** *vt:* etw (auf/in etw *(A)*) ~ to convert sthg (into sthg).

**um|reißen¹** *vt (unreg)* [niederreißen - Baum, Mast] to tear down; [ - Person] to knock down.

**umreißen²** *(prät* umriss; *perf* hat umrissen) *vt* to outline.

**um|rennen** *vt (unreg)* to knock down.

**umringen** *vt* to surround.

**Um|riss** *der* outline; etw in groben ~en darstellen to give a rough outline of sthg.

**um|rühren** *vt* to stir.

**um|rüsten** *vt* - **1.** MIL to re-equip - **2.** [ändern] to adapt <> *vi* to re-equip.

**ums** *präp (um + das)* round the; ~ Viereck gehen to go round the block; ihm geht es dabei weniger ~ Geld, als ... for him it is not so much a question of money, as ...; du willst dich nur ~ Einkaufen drücken! you just want to get out of doing the shopping!

**um|satteln** *vi* [Arbeiter] to change jobs; [Student] to change courses; auf etw *(A)* ~ to switch to sthg.

**Um|satz** *der* turnover; wir müssen den ~ steigern we have to boost our sales ODER turnover.

**Umsatzrück|gang** *der* drop in turnover.

**Umsatz|steigerung** *die* increase in turnover.

**um|schalten** *vt* [Waschmaschine, Drucker] to switch (over) <> *vi* - **1.** [sich umstellen]: auf etw *(A)* ~ to switch (over) to sthg - **2.** TV to turn over; wir schalten um nach Hamburg we are going over to Hamburg.

**Um|schau** *die:* (nach jm/etw) ~ halten to be on the lookout (for sb/sthg).

**Um|schlag** *der* - **1.** [von Brief] envelope; [von Buch] dust jacket - **2.** [Wechsel] sudden change - **3.** MED compress - **4.** [an Ärmel] cuff; [an Hose] turn-up - **5.** [von Gütern] transfer - **6.** [Verkauf] sale.

**um|schlagen** *(perf* hat/ist umgeschlagen) *(unreg) vi (ist)* [Wetter, Stimmung] to change suddenly <> *vt (hat)* - **1.** [umlegen - Kragen] to turn down; [ - Hosenbeine] to turn up - **2.** [umblättern - Seite] to turn over - **3.** WIRTSCH to transfer - **4.** [verkaufen] to sell - **5.** [Baum] to fell.

**Umschlag|platz** *der* [im Transportwesen] transshipment centre; [von Drogen] distribution point.

**umschließen** *(prät* umschloss; *perf* hat umschlossen) *vt* - **1.** [mit Händen] to clasp; jn mit den Armen ~ to put one's arms around sb - **2.** [einbeziehen] to cover, to include - **3.** [umgeben] to surround.

**umschlingen** *(prät* umschlang; *perf* hat umschlungen) *vt* - **1.** [mit Händen] to clasp; [umar-

men] to embrace - **2.** [umwinden] to twine around.

➡ **sich umschlingen** *ref* to embrace.

**um|schmeißen** *vt (unreg) fam* - **1.** [umwerfen] to knock over - **2.** [krank machen] to knock out.

**umschreiben¹** *(prät* umschrieb; *perf* hat umschrieben) *vt* - **1.** [paraphrasieren] to paraphrase - **2.** [abgrenzen] to define - **3.** [schildern] to describe.

**um|schreiben²** *vt (unreg)* - **1.** [ändern] to rewrite - **2.** [übertragen]: etw auf jn ~ lassen to have sthg transferred to sb.

**Umschuldung** *(pl* -en) *die* debt rescheduling.

**um|schulen** *vt* - **1.** [ausbilden] to retrain - **2.** [Schule wechseln lassen] to move (to another school) <> *vi* to retrain.

**Um|schulung** *die* retraining.

**umschwärmt** *adj* - **1.** [verehrt] besieged - **2.** [umgeben] surrounded.

**Umschweife** *pl:* mach keine ~! stop beating about the bush!; etw ohne ~ sagen to say sthg straight out.

**Um|schwung** *der* sudden change.

**umsegeln** *vt* to sail round.

**um|sehen** ➡ **sich umsehen** *ref (unreg):* sich (nach jm/etw) ~ [suchen] to look around (for sb/sthg); [sich umdrehen] to look round (at sb/sthg).

**um sein** *(perf* ist um gewesen) *vi (unreg) fam* to be over.

**umseitig** *adj & adv* overleaf.

**um|setzen** *vt* - **1.** [realisieren - Plan] to implement; [ - Theorie, Idee] to put into practice; - **2.** [Umsatz machen] to turn over; wir haben Büchern im Wert von 150.000 Euro umgesetzt we have sold 150,000 euros' worth of books - **3.** [umwandeln] to convert - **4.** [umpflanzen] to transplant - **5.** [Platz verändern] to move - **6.** [ausgeben]: er setzt das ganze Geld in Drogen um he spends all his money on drugs.

➡ **sich umsetzen** *ref* - **1.** [Sitzplatz wechseln] to sit somewhere else - **2.** [sich umwandeln] to be converted.

**Umsicht** *die* prudence.

**umsichtig** *adj* prudent <> *adv* prudently.

**um|siedeln** *(perf* hat/ist umgesiedelt) *vi (ist)* to move <> *vt (hat)* to resettle.

**umso** *konj (+ kompar):* ~ schneller/mehr/wichtiger all the faster/more/more important; ~ besser! all the better!; je schneller, ~ besser the quicker the better.

**umsonst** *adj:* ~ sein [erfolglos] to be in vain; [gratis] to be free (of charge) <> *adv* - **1.** [erfolglos] in vain - **2.** [gratis] for free, for nothing; nicht ~ not without reason.

**um|springen** *(perf* ist umgesprungen) *vi (un-*

**U**

*reg)* - **1.** *abw* [umgehen]: **mit jm brutal ~** to treat sb brutally - **2.** [wechseln] to change suddenly.

**Umstand** (*pl* **-stände**) *der* - **1.** [Mühe]: **Umstände** trouble *(U);* **wenn dir das keine Umstände macht** if it's no trouble *ODER* bother; **mach dir keine Umstände** don't go to any trouble *ODER* bother; **wir wollen dir keine Umstände machen** we don't want to put you to any trouble; **nicht viele Umstände (mit jm/etw) machen** not to go to a great deal of trouble (over sb/ sthg) - **2.** [Sachlage] circumstance; **unter Umständen** in certain circumstances; **unter allen Umständen** whatever happens; **mildernde Umstände** *RECHT* mitigating circumstances; **in anderen Umständen sein** *fig* to be in the family way.

**umständehalber** *adv:* '**~ zu verkaufen**' 'genuine reason for sale'.

**umständlich** *adj* - **1.** [Methode, Arbeit] laborious - **2.** [im Denken] ponderous; [beim Sprechen] long-winded *<>* *adv* - **1.** [mühevoll] laboriously - **2.** [denken] ponderously; [sprechen] long-windedly.

**Umstands|bestimmung** *die* GRAM adverbial phrase.

**Umstands|kleid** *das* maternity dress.

**Umstandswort** (*pl* **-wörter**) *das* GRAM adverb.

**umstehend** *adj* - **1.** [umgebend] standing round about; **die Umstehenden** the bystanders - **2.** [umseitig] overleaf.

**um|steigen** (*perf* **ist umgestiegen**) *vi* (*unreg*) - **1.** [beim Reisen] to change - **2.** [wechseln]: **auf etw** *(A)* **~** to switch to sthg.

**um|stellen**[1] *vt* - **1.** [anders ausrichten - Möbel] to switch round; [ - Methode, Produktion, Weichen] to switch; [ - Kabinett] to reshuffle; **heute Nacht werden die Uhren umgestellt** the clocks go forward/back tonight; **etw auf etw** *(A)* **~** to switch sthg to sthg; **einen Betrieb auf EDV ~** to computerize a company - **2.** [Leben, Fahrplan, Mannschaft, Programm] to change.

**sich umstellen** *ref* to change; **sich in der Ernährung ~** to change one's diet; **sich auf etw** *(A)* **~** [sich anpassen] to adapt to sthg.

**umstellen**[2] *vt* [einkreisen] to surround.

**Um|stellung**[1] *die* - **1.** [von Methode, Produktion, Weichen] switch; **~ auf EDV** computerization - **2.** [Veränderung] change.

**Umstellung**[2] *die* [Einkreisung] surrounding.

**um|stimmen** *vt:* **jn ~** to make sb change his/her mind.

**um|stoßen** *vt* (*unreg*) - **1.** [Stapel, Vase, Stuhl] to knock over - **2.** [Plan, Testament, Berechnungen] to wreck.

**umstritten** *adj* controversial; **es ist ~, ob ...** it is disputed whether ...

**um|strukturieren** *vt* to restructure.

**Um|sturz** *der* coup (d'état); **der ~ der Regierung** the overthrow of the government.

**um|stürzen** (*perf* **hat/ist umgestürzt**) *vi* (*ist*) to fall over; [Auto] to overturn *<>* *vt* (*hat*) - **1.** [umwerfen] to knock over; [Auto] to overturn - **2.** [vereiteln] to upset - **3.** [ablösen] to overthrow.

**um|taufen** *vt* [anders nennen] to rename.

**Umtausch** *der* exchange; '**vom ~ ausgeschlossen**' 'no refunds or exchanges'.

**um|tauschen** *vt* - **1.** [auswechseln] to exchange; **etw gegen etw ~** to exchange sthg for sthg - **2.** [Währung tauschen] to change.

**um|tun** (*unreg*) **sich umtun** *ref fam* - **1.** [sich kümmern um]: **sich nach etw ~** to cast around for sthg - **2.** [sich kundig machen] to have a look around.

**umwälzend** *adj* [Ereignis, Veränderung] revolutionary.

**um|wandeln** *vt:* **etw in etw** *(A)/***zu etw ~** to convert sthg into sthg.

**sich umwandeln** *ref* to be converted.

**Umwandlung** (*pl* **-en**) *die* conversion.

**um|wechseln** ['ʊmvɛksln] *vt* to change; **etw in etw** *(A)* **~** to change sthg into sthg.

**Um|weg** *der* detour; **einen ~ über etw** *(A)* **machen** to make a detour via sthg; **auf ~en** *fig* in a roundabout way.

**Umwelt** *die* environment.

**umweltbedingt** *adj* caused by the environment.

**Umwelt|belastung** *die* environmental pollution *ODER* damage.

**umweltbewusst** *adj* environmentally aware *<>* *adv* in an environmentally aware way.

**Umweltbewusstsein** *das* environmental awareness.

**UMWELTBEWUSSTSEIN**

The protection of the environment is one of the chief concerns of the German people, whose vigilance and commitment in this area give added strength to the environmentalist cause.

**umweltfreundlich** *adj* environmentally friendly, eco-friendly *<>* *adv* in an environmentally friendly *ODER* eco-friendly way.

**Umwelt|minister, in** *der, die* Environment Minister.

**Umwelt|ministerium** *das* Ministry of the Environment.

**Umwelt|papier** *das* recycled paper.

**Umwelt|politik** *die* policy on the environment.

**Umwelt|schäden** *pl* ecological damage *(U)*.

**Ụmweltǀschutz** *der* environmental protection.

**Ụmweltschützer, in** (*mpl* -; *fpl* -**nen**) *der, die* environmentalist.

**Ụmweltǀsünder, in** *der, die* polluter.

**Ụmweltǀverschmutzung** *die* pollution (U).

**ụmǀwerfen** *vt* (*unreg*) - **1.** [umstürzen] to knock over - **2.** *fam:* **jn ~** [Alkohol] to knock sb out; [Nachricht] to stun sb - **3.** [umhängen]: **sich** (D) **etw ~** to put sthg round one's shoulders - **4.** [hinfällig machen] to upset.

**ụmwerfend** *fam adj* fantastic ⟨⟩ *adv:* **~ komisch** hilarious.

**umwịckeln**[1] *vt:* **etw mit etw ~** to wrap sthg round sthg.

**ụmǀwickeln**[2] *vt:* **jm/sich etw ~** to wrap sthg round sb/o.s.

**ụmǀziehen** (*perf* hat/ist ụmgezogen) (*unreg*) *vi* (*ist*) to move; **in etw** (A) **~** to move into sthg; **nach ... ~** to move to ... ⟨⟩ *vt* (*hat*) to change.
➡ **sich umziehen** *ref* to change, to get changed.

**umzịngeln** *vt* to surround.

**Ụmǀzug** *der* - **1.** [Wohnungswechsel] move - **2.** [Festzug] parade.

**UN** [uːɛn] (*abk für* **United Nations**) *die* UN.

**ụnabhängig** *adj* independent; **von jm/etw ~ sein** to be independent of sb/sthg; **~ davon, ob ...** regardless of whether ... ⟨⟩ *adv* independently.

**Ụnabhängigkeit** *die* independence.

**unabkömmlich** *adj:* **~ sein** to be tied up.

**ụnabsichtlich** *adj* unintentional ⟨⟩ *adv* unintentionally.

**ụnachtsam** *adj* - **1.** [unaufmerksam] inattentive - **2.** [nicht sorgsam] careless ⟨⟩ *adv* [nicht sorgsam] carelessly.

**Ụnachtsamkeit** (*pl* -**en**) *die* - **1.** [Unaufmerksamkeit] inattentiveness (U) - **2.** [fehlende Sorgfalt] carelessness (U).

**ụnangebracht** *adj* inappropriate.

**ụnangefochten** *adj* unchallenged ⟨⟩ *adv:* **~ führen** to be the unchallenged leader.

**ụnangemeldet** *adj & adv* - **1.** [ohne Voranmeldung - gen] unannounced; [- Patient] without an appointment - **2.** [ohne amtliche Meldung] unregistered.

**ụnangemessen** *adj* inappropriate ⟨⟩ *adv* inappropriately; **~ hoch** disproportionately high.

**ụnangenehm** *adj* unpleasant; **etw ist jm ~** sb feels embarrassed about sthg ⟨⟩ *adv:* **~ berührt** embarrassed; **~ auffallen** to make a bad impression.

**ụnangepasst** *adj* nonconformist ⟨⟩ *adv* in a nonconformist way.

**ụnangetastet** *adj:* **etw ~ lassen** [Ehre, Privileg] to leave sthg intact; [Vorräte, Ersparnisse] to leave sthg untouched.

**unangreifbar, ụnangreifbar** *adj* unassailable; [Theorie] irrefutable.

**Ụnannehmlichkeiten** *pl* trouble (U); **jm ~ bereiten** to cause sb trouble.

**ụnansehnlich** *adj* unattractive ⟨⟩ *adv* unattractively.

**ụnanständig** *adj* [obszön] indecent; [Wort, Witz] rude; **es ist ~, mit vollem Mund zu reden** it's rude to talk with your mouth full ⟨⟩ *adv* [obszön] indecently; [unhöflich] rudely.

**unantạstbar, ụnantastbar** *adj* [Rechte, Würde] inviolable.

**ụnappetitlich** *adj* [Essen] unappetizing; [Anblick, Toilette] disgusting.

**Ụnǀart** *die* bad habit.

**ụnartig** *adj* naughty ⟨⟩ *adv* naughtily.

**ụnästhetisch** *adj* unaesthetic.

**ụnauffällig** *adj* unobtrusive ⟨⟩ *adv* - **1.** [nicht auffällig] unobtrusively - **2.** [heimlich] without anyone noticing.

**unauffịndbar, ụnauffindbar** *adj:* **~ sein** to be nowhere to be found ⟨⟩ *adv:* **etw ~ verstecken** to hide sthg where it cannot be found.

**ụnaufgefordert** *adj* unasked-for ⟨⟩ *adv* without being asked.

**unaufhạltsam, ụnaufhaltsam** *adj* inexorable ⟨⟩ *adv* inexorably.

**unaufhörlich, ụnaufhörlich** *adj* constant ⟨⟩ *adv* constantly.

**ụnaufmerksam** *adj* inattentive ⟨⟩ *adv* inattentively.

**Ụnaufmerksamkeit** *die* inattentiveness.

**ụnaufrichtig** *adj* insincere; **jm gegenüber ~ sein** not to be open with sb ⟨⟩ *adv* insincerely.

**ụnausgeglichen** *adj* - **1.** [Person] unstable; [launisch] moody - **2.** [Bilanz] unsettled.

**ụnausgegoren** *adj abw* [Konzept, Plan] half-baked.

**ụnausgeschlafen** *adj & adv* half asleep.

**unaussprẹchlich, ụnaussprechlich** *adj* indescribable ⟨⟩ *adv* [glücklich, traurig] indescribably; [hassen, lieben] more than one can say.

**unausstẹhlich, ụnausstehlich** *adj* unbearable ⟨⟩ *adv* unbearably.

**unausweịchlich, ụnausweichlich** *adj* unavoidable ⟨⟩ *adv* unavoidably.

**ụnbändig** *adj* [Wut, Freude, Eifersucht] unbri-

**U**

dled; [Temperament] boisterous ◇ *adv* beyond measure.

**unbeabsichtigt** *adj* unintentional ◇ *adv* unintentionally.

**unbeachtet** *adj* unnoticed; jn/etw ~ lassen to ignore sb/sthg ◇ *adv* unnoticed.

**unbeantwortet** *adj* unanswered.

**unbedenklich** *adj* safe ◇ *adv* [Medikament einnehmen] safely; [annehmen, zustimmen] without hesitation.

**unbedeutend** *adj* - 1. [nicht bedeutend] unimportant - 2. [belanglos] slight ◇ *adv* [belanglos] slightly.

**unbedingt** *adj* absolute ◇ *adv* - 1. [auf jeden Fall] definitely; er will ~ Ski fahren he is determined to go skiing; **du** wolltest ja ~ Ski fahren it was you that wanted to go skiing; **nicht** ~ not necessarily - 2. [bedingungslos] absolutely.

**unbefahrbar, unbefahrbar** *adj* impassable.

**unbefriedigend** *adj* unsatisfactory.

**unbefristet** *adj* permanent.

**unbefugt** *adj* unauthorized ◇ *adv* without authorization.

**Unbefugte** (*pl* -n) *der, die* unauthorized person; '~n Zutritt verboten!' 'authorized personnel only'.

**unbegabt** *adj* untalented.

**unbegreiflich, unbegreiflich** *adj* incomprehensible; es ist mir ~, wie ... I can't understand how ... ◇ *adv* unbelievably.

**unbegrenzt** *adj* [Freiheit, Möglichkeiten] unlimited; [Vertrauen, Zustimmung] total ◇ *adv* [vertrauen, zustimmen] totally; [nutzen, wohnen] indefinitely.

**unbegründet** *adj* unfounded ◇ *adv* without foundation.

**unbehaglich** *adj* uncomfortable; es ist ihr ~ it makes her feel uncomfortable ◇ *adv* uncomfortably.

**unbehelligt, unbehelligt** *adj:* ~ sein ODER bleiben to be undisturbed ◇ *adv* without being stopped.

**unbeherrscht** *adj* [Wutausbruch] uncontrolled; [Bemerkung] wild; ~ sein to lack self-control ◇ *adv* without any self-control.

**unbeholfen** *adj* clumsy ◇ *adv* clumsily.

**unbeirrbar, unbeirrbar** [ʊnbə'ɪrbaːɐ̯, 'ʊnbaɪrbaːɐ̯] *adj* unwavering ◇ *adv* unwaveringly.

**unbekannt** *adj* [Künstler, Substanz, Krankheit] unknown; [Flugobjekt] unidentified; er ist mir ~ I don't know him; diese Änderung ist mir ~ I don't know about this change; Anzeige gegen ~ RECHT charge against person or per-

sons unknown ◇ *adv:* '~ verzogen' 'gone away', 'address unknown'.

**Unbekannte** *der, die* unknown person; [Fremde] stranger ◇ *die* MATH unknown.

**unbekümmert, unbekümmert** *adj* [unbeschwert] carefree; [ohne Bedenken] casual ◇ *adv* [unbeschwert] in a carefree way; [ohne Bedenken] casually.

**unbelastet** *adj* - 1. [Natur, Luft, Nahrungsmittel] unpolluted - 2. [ohne Schuld] with a clean record; [ohne Vorurteil] unprejudiced - 3.: **von Sorgen/Schulden/Verantwortung** ~ free from care/of debt/of responsibility ◇ *adv* - 1. [ohne Vorurteil] without prejudice - 2.: **von finanziellen Sorgen** ~ without any financial worries - 3. [schuldenfrei] unmortgaged.

**unbeliebt** *adj* unpopular; sich ~ machen to make o.s. unpopular.

**unbemannt** *adj* & *adv* - 1. [ohne Besatzung] unmanned - 2. *fam hum* [ohne Mann] without a man.

**unbemerkt** *adj* & *adv* unnoticed.

**unbeobachtet** *adj* unobserved; in einem ~en Moment when no one was looking ◇ *adv* unobserved.

**unbequem** *adj* - 1. [nicht bequem] uncomfortable - 2. [lästig] awkward; jm ~ sein to be a nuisance to sb ◇ *adv* [nicht bequem] uncomfortably.

**unberechenbar, unberechenbar** *adj* unpredictable ◇ *adv* unpredictably.

**unberechtigt** *adj* [Ansprüche, Vorwürfe] unjustified; [Zutritt] unauthorized ◇ *adv* [entlassen, bestrafen] without justification; [ohne Erlaubnis] without authorization.

**unberücksichtigt** *adj:* ~ bleiben ODER gelassen werden not to be taken into account.

**unberührt** *adj* - 1. [nicht berührt - Essen, Gegenstand] untouched; [ - Schnee] undisturbed; [ - Natur] unspoilt - 2. [ohne Regung] unmoved - 3. [jungfräulich]: ~ sein to be a virgin.

**unbescheiden** *adj* [Person, Gehalt] immodest; [Anspruch] presumptuous ◇ *adv* [auftreten] immodestly; [fragen] presumptuously.

**unbeschrankt** *adj* [⊏ Bahnübergang].

**unbeschränkt** *adj* [Vertrauen, Macht] absolute; [Verbrauch, Gültigkeit] unlimited ◇ *adv* [vertrauen, Macht ausüben] absolutely; [gültig, verbrauchen] without limit.

**unbeschreiblich, unbeschreiblich** *adj* indescribable ◇ *adv* indescribably; sich ~ freuen to be overjoyed.

**unbeschwert** *adj* carefree ◇ *adv* free from care.

**unbesonnen** *adj* rash ◇ *adv* rashly.

**unbeständig** *adj* changeable.

**unbestechlich, unbestechlich** *adj* [du...

Geld] incorruptible; [Kritiker] uncompromising; [Verfechter] unwavering.

**unbestimmt** *adj* [Zeitpunkt & GRAM] indefinite; [Vorstellung, Äußerung] vague <> *adv* vaguely.

**unbestritten** *adj* undisputed.

**unbeteiligt** *adj* - **1.** [nicht verwickelt] uninvolved; **an etw** (D) ~ **sein** not to be involved in sthg - **2.** [nicht interessiert] uninterested <> *adv* - **1.** [nicht verwickelt] without getting involved - **2.** [nicht interessiert] without taking an interest.

**unbewacht** *adj* [Haus, Gefangene] unguarded; [Gepäck, Parkplatz] unattended; **in einem ~en Moment** when no one was looking <> *adv* [unbeaufsichtigt] unattended; [ohne Bewachung] unguarded.

**unbewaffnet** *adj* & *adv* unarmed.

**unbewältigt** *adj* unresolved; **die Scheidung ist für sie noch ~** she hasn't come to terms with the divorce <> *adv:* **ein Problem ~ verdrängen** to suppress a problem without resolving it.

**unbeweglich** *adj* - **1.** [nicht beweglich, festgelegt] immovable - **2.** [unflexibel] inflexible - **3.** [steif] stiff - **4.** [unverändert] fixed <> *adv* - **1.** [regungslos] motionlessly - **2.** [unverändert] fixedly.

**unbewohnbar, unbewohnbar** *adj* uninhabitable.

**unbewohnt** *adj* uninhabited.

**unbewusst** *adj* unconscious <> *adv* unconsciously.

**unbezahlbar, unbezahlbar** *adj* - **1.** [nicht erschwinglich] unaffordable - **2.** [unersetzlich, unerschwinglich] priceless.

**unbrauchbar** *adj* useless.

**und** *konj* - **1.** [gen] and; ~ **wenn** even if; **eins ~ eins ist zwei** one and one is two; ~ **so weiter** and so on - **2.** [Ausdruck von Ironie] **der ~ sich entschuldigen?** him, say he's sorry?
➡ **und ob** *interj* of course!
➡ **und wie** *interj* and how!

**undankbar** *adj* - **1.** [unhöflich] ungrateful - **2.** [schwer] thankless <> *adv* ungratefully.

**undefinierbar, undefinierbar** *adj* indefinable.

**undenkbar, undenkbar** *adj* inconceivable.

**undeutlich** *adj* unclear <> *adv* unclearly.

**undicht** *adj* leaky.

**undiszipliniert** *adj* undisciplined <> *adv* in an undisciplined way.

**undurchführbar, undurchführbar** *adj* impracticable.

**undurchschaubar, undurchschaubar** *adj* unfathomable.

**undurchsichtig** *adj* - **1.** [Geschichte, Mensch] shady - **2.** [Glas, Strümpfe] opaque.

**uneben** *adj* uneven.

**unecht** *adj* - **1.** [nachgemacht - Schmuck, Leder] imitation; [ - Blumen] artificial; [ - Fingernägel] false; [ - Kunstwerk] fake - **2.** [vorgetäuscht] false - **3.** MATH improper.

**unehelich** *adj:* ~**es Kind** illegitimate child; **in einer ~en Beziehung leben** to live together <> *adv* illegitimately.

**unehrlich** *adj* dishonest <> *adv* dishonestly.

**uneigennützig** *adj* unselfish <> *adv* unselfishly.

**uneingeschränkt** *adj* [Vertrauen, Zustimmung] total; [Handlungsspielraum] unlimited; [Macht, Herrscher] absolute <> *adv* totally.

**uneinig** *adj* in disagreement; **sich** (D) **über etw** (A) ~ **sein** to disagree about sthg.

**uneins** *adj* (*unver*) *geh:* ~ **sein** to be in disagreement <> *adv* without having reached an agreement.

**unempfindlich** *adj* - **1.** [robust - Stoff, Material] hardwearing *Br*, longwearing *Am;* [ - Gerät] sturdy; [ - Pflanze] hardy - **2.** [nicht anfällig - Person] immune; [ - Haut] insensitive; **gegen etw ~ sein** [Kälte] to be insensitive to sthg; [Sticheleien, Krankheit] to be immune to sthg.

**unendlich** *adj* [Raum, Mühe & MATH] infinite; [Weite, Arbeit, Wiederholung] endless; [Geschichte] never-ending <> *adv* enormously.

**Unendlichkeit** *die* - **1.** [von Raum, Universum] infinity; [von Weite, Wüste] endlessness - **2.** *fam* [zeitlich] eternity.

**unentbehrlich, unentbehrlich** *adj* indispensable; **sich ~ machen** to make o.s. indispensable.

**unentgeltlich, unentgeltlich** *adj* free <> *adv* [benutzen] free of charge; [arbeiten, helfen] for nothing.

**unentschieden** *adj* - **1.** [nicht entschieden - Spiel] drawn; [ - Angelegenheit] undecided; **bei ~em Wahlausgang** if the election result is inconclusive - **2.** [vor Entscheidung] undecided; [nicht entschlussfreudig] indecisive <> *adv* - **1.** [nicht entschieden]: ~ **spielen** to draw; **im Spiel steht es ~** so far the game is a draw - **2.** [unentschlossen] undecidedly.

**unentschlossen** *adj* [vor Entscheidung] undecided; [nicht entschlussfreudig] indecisive <> *adv* [vor Entscheidung] undecidedly; [nicht entschlussfreudig] indecisively.

**unentschuldigt** *adj* unexcused <> *adv* without an excuse.

**unentwegt, unentwegt** *adj* constant <> *adv* constantly.

**unerbittlich, unerbittlich** *adj* - **1.** [unnachgiebig] unrelenting - **2.** [gnadenlos] relentless

◇ adv - 1. [unnachgiebig] unrelentingly; ~ bleiben to remain adamant - 2. [gnadenlos] relentlessly.

**unerfahren** adj inexperienced.

**unerfreulich** adj unpleasant.

**unerheblich** adj insignificant ◇ adv insignificantly.

**unerhört** adj - 1. [empörend] outrageous; (das ist ja) ~! that's outrageous! - 2. [Glück, Leistung] tremendous; [Preis] exorbitant ◇ adv - 1. [ungeheuer] tremendously; ~ viel a tremendous amount - 2. [empörend] outrageously.

**unerklärlich, unerklärlich** adj inexplicable; es ist mir ~ it's a mystery to me.

**unerlässlich, unerlässlich** adj essential.

**unerlaubt** adj unauthorized ◇ adv without authorization.

**unerledigt** adj [Arbeit] unfinished; [Post] unanswered ◇ adv [Post, Briefe] not dealt with.

**unermesslich, unermesslich** geh adj - 1. [unendlich] immeasurable - 2. [ungeheuer] immense ◇ adv immensely.

**unermüdlich, unermüdlich** adj tireless ◇ adv tirelessly.

**unerschöpflich, unerschöpflich** adj inexhaustible.

**unerschrocken** adj fearless ◇ adv fearlessly.

**unerschütterlich, unerschütterlich** adj [Überzeugung, Wille] unshakeable; [Person] unflinching ◇ adv unflinchingly.

**unerschwinglich, unerschwinglich** adj [Preis] prohibitive; [Luxusartikel] prohibitively expensive; für jn ~ sein to be beyond sb's means ◇ adv prohibitively.

**unersetzlich, unersetzlich** adj irreplaceable.

**unerträglich** adj unbearable ◇ adv unbearably.

**unerwähnt** adj unmentioned; ~ lassen to fail to mention; man sollte nicht ~ lassen, dass ... one should also mention that ...

**unerwartet** adj unexpected ◇ adv unexpectedly.

**unerwünscht** adj [Gast] unwelcome; [Kind] unwanted; [Benehmen] undesirable ◇ adv [kommen] although one is not welcome; [sich benehmen] undesirably.

**UNESCO** [u'nɛskɔl (abk für **United Nations Educational, Scientific and Cultural Organization**) die UNESCO.

**unfähig** adj incompetent; ~ sein, etw zu tun to be incapable of doing sthg.

**Unfähigkeit** die incompetence; die ~, etw zu tun the inability to do sthg.

**unfair** ['ʊnfɛːɐ̯] adj unfair ◇ adv unfairly.

**Unfall** der accident; tödlicher ~ fatal accident; einen ~ bauen fam to have an accident.

**Unfallflucht** die RECHT failure to stop after an accident; ~ begehen to fail to stop after an accident.

**Unfallgefahr** die risk of an accident.

**Unfallstelle** die scene of the/an accident.

**Unfallversicherung** die accident insurance.

**unfehlbar, unfehlbar** adj infallible.

**unförmig** adj shapeless; [Nase] unshapely; [Beine] huge ◇ adv: ~ angeschwollen shapeless and swollen.

**unfrei** adj - 1. [gehemmt] inhibited - 2. [abhängig]: ein ~es Volk a subject people; er war in seiner Entscheidung ~ he was not able to make a decision freely - 3. [unfrankiert] unstamped ◇ adv - 1. [gehemmt] in an inhibited manner - 2. [abhängig]: ~ entscheiden not to be able to decide freely.

**unfreiwillig** adj - 1. [nicht freiwillig] compulsory - 2. hum [unabsichtlich] unintentional ◇ adv - 1. [nicht freiwillig] without wanting to - 2. hum [unabsichtlich] unintentionally.

**unfreundlich** adj - 1. [nicht freundlich] unfriendly; zu jm ~ sein to be unfriendly to sb - 2. [unangenehm] unpleasant ◇ adv [nicht freundlich] coldly.

**unfruchtbar** adj - 1. [steril, trocken] infertile - 2. [nutzlos] fruitless.

**Unfug** der [Benehmen] mischief; [Unsinn] nonsense; grober ~ public nuisance.

**Ungar, in** (mpl -n; fpl -nen) der, die Hungarian.

**ungarisch** adj Hungarian.

**Ungarisch(e)** das Hungarian; siehe auch **Englisch(e)**.

**Ungarn** nt Hungary.

**ungeachtet** ['ungeaxtət] präp geh: ~ einer Sache (G) notwithstanding sthg.

**ungeahnt, ungeahnt** ['ungeaːnt, unge'aːnt] adj undreamt-of; [Schwierigkeiten] unsuspected.

**ungebeten** adj uninvited ◇ adv without being invited.

**ungebildet** adj uneducated.

**ungeboren** adj unborn; der Schutz ~en Lebens/~er Kinder the protection of the unborn child.

**ungebräuchlich** adj uncommon.

**ungedeckt** adj uncovered; [Tisch] laid ◇ adv without cover.

**Ungeduld** die impatience.

**ungeduldig** adj impatient ◇ adv impatiently.

**ungeeignet** *adj* unsuitable.

**ungefähr, ungefähr** *adv* about; **wann kommst du denn ~ wieder?** about when will you be back?; **die Wohnung sieht ~ so aus** the flat looks something like this; **so ~** *fam* round about; **sowas kommt nicht von ~** such a thing is no accident.

**ungefährlich** *adj* safe.

**ungehalten** *adj* indignant; **über jn/etw ~ sein** to be indignant about sb/sthg ◇ *adv* indignantly.

**ungeheizt** *adj* unheated.

**ungeheuer, ungeheuer** *adj* tremendous ◇ *adv* tremendously.

**Ungeheuer** (*pl* -) *das* monster.

**ungeheuerlich, ungeheuerlich** *adj* monstrous.

**ungehindert** *adj* unhindered ◇ *adv* without hindrance.

**ungehobelt** *adj* - **1.** *abw* [Mensch] uncouth - **2.** [Holz] unplaned ◇ *adv* *abw* [Mensch] uncouthly.

**ungehörig** *adj* [Benehmen] improper; [Antwort] impertinent ◇ *adv* [sich benehmen] improperly; [antworten] impertinently.

**ungehorsam** *adj* disobedient.

**Ungehorsam** *der* disobedience.

**ungeklärt** *adj* - **1.** [nicht entschieden - Problem, Mord] unsolved; [ - Frage] unsettled - **2.** [nicht gereinigt - Abwasser] untreated.

**ungekünstelt** *adj* unaffected ◇ *adv* unaffectedly.

**ungelegen** *adj* inconvenient; **das kommt mir ~** that's inconvenient for me.

**ungelernt** *adj* unskilled.

**ungelogen** *adv* *fam* honestly.

**ungemein, ungemein** *adj* tremendous ◇ *adv* tremendously.

**ungemütlich** *adj* - **1.** [nicht behaglich] uncomfortable; [Mensch] unfriendly - **2.** [unangenehm] unpleasant ◇ *adv* uncomfortably.

**ungenau** *adj* [Ausführungen, Erklärung] imprecise; [Übersetzung, Messung] inaccurate; [Vorstellung] vague ◇ *adv* [ausführen, erklären] imprecisely; [übersetzen, messen] inaccurately; [erkennbar] vaguely.

**Ungenauigkeit** *die* - **1.** [Ungenausein - von Formulierung] imprecision; [ - von Messung] inaccuracy - **2.** [Abweichung] inaccuracy.

**ungeniert, ungeniert** *adj* uninhibited ◇ *adv* without any inhibition; [sich äußern] openly.

**ungenießbar, ungenießbar** *adj* - **1.** [Essen] inedible; [Getränk] undrinkable - **2.** *fam* [schlecht gelaunt] unbearable.

**ungenügend** *adj* inadequate ◇ *adv* inadequately.

**ungepflegt** *adj* untidy.

**ungerade** *adj* MATH odd.

**ungerecht** *adj* unjust ◇ *adv* unjustly.

**Ungerechtigkeit** *die* injustice.

**ungereimt** *adj* - **1.** [unklar] inconsistent - **2.** [ohne Reim] unrhymed.

**ungern** *adv* reluctantly; **ich tue das nur ~** I don't like doing this.

**ungerührt** *adj* [Gesicht] impassive; [Person] unmoved ◇ *adv* impassively.

**ungeschehen** *adj:* **etw ~ machen** to undo sthg.

**Ungeschick** *das* clumsiness.

**Ungeschicklichkeit** *die* clumsiness; [Tat] piece of clumsiness.

**ungeschickt** *adj* - **1.** [nicht geschickt] clumsy; **es wäre ~, das jetzt schon zu erwähnen** it wouldn't be wise to mention that now - **2.** *fam Süddt* [ungelegen] inconvenient - **3.** *fam Süddt* [unpraktisch] impractical ◇ *adv* [nicht geschickt] clumsily.

**ungeschminkt** *adj* - **1.** [nicht geschminkt] without make-up - **2.** [unverhüllt] unvarnished ◇ *adv* - **1.** [nicht geschminkt] without make-up - **2.** [unverhüllt] openly.

**ungeschoren** *adv* *fig:* **~ davonkommen** ODER **bleiben** *fig* to get away with it; **jn ~ lassen** to be spared.

**ungeschützt** *adj* unprotected; **~ vor etw** (D) ODER **gegen etw** unprotected against sthg ◇ *adv* without protection.

**ungesetzlich** *adj* illegal ◇ *adv* illegally.

**ungespritzt** *adj* unsprayed.

**ungestört** *adj* & *adv* undisturbed.

**ungestüm** *geh* *adj* impetuous ◇ *adv* impetuously.

**ungesund** *adj* unhealthy ◇ *adv* unhealthily.

**ungeteilt** *adj* undivided.

**ungetrübt** *adj* - **1.** [Glück] perfect; [Zeit] blissful; [Zukunft] unclouded - **2.** [Glas, Wasser] clear.

**Ungetüm** (*pl* -e) *das* monster.

**ungeübt** *adj* unpractised; **in etw** (D) **~ sein** to be unpractised in sthg.

**ungewaschen** *adj* unwashed.

**ungewiss** *adj* uncertain; **sich** (D) **über etw** (A) **~ sein** to be uncertain about sthg; **jn über etw** (A) **im Ungewissen lassen** to leave sb in the dark about sthg.

**ungewöhnlich** *adj* - **1.** [unüblich] unusual - **2.** [erstaunlich] exceptional ◇ *adv* - **1.** [unüblich] unusually - **2.** [erstaunlich] exceptionally.

**ungewohnt** *adj* [fremd] unfamiliar; [Tageszeit,

Großzügigkeit] unaccustomed; **etw ist für jn ~ sb** is not used to sthg ◇ *adv* unusually.

**ungewollt** *adj* [Kind] unwanted; [Beleidigung] unintentional ◇ *adv* unintentionally.

**Ungeziefer** *das (ohne pl)* pests *(pl)*; **der Hund hat ~** the dog has fleas.

**ungezogen** *adj* naughty; [Benehmen] bad; [frech] cheeky ◇ *adv* [frech] cheekily; [sich benehmen] badly.

**ungezwungen** *adj* [Atmosphäre, Unterhaltung] informal; [Verhalten, Art] natural; [Lachen] easy ◇ *adv* [sich verhalten] naturally; [sich unterhalten] informally; [sich bewegen] easily.

**unglaubhaft** *adj* unconvincing ◇ *adv* unconvincingly.

**ungläubig** *adj* - **1.** [nicht gläubig] unbelieving - **2.** [zweifelnd] disbelieving ◇ *adv* in disbelief.

**unglaublich, unglaublich** *adj* - **1.** [nicht zu glauben] unbelievable - **2.** [ungeheuer] incredible ◇ *adv* incredibly.

**unglaubwürdig** *adj* [Mensch] untrustworthy; [Geschichte] implausible.

**ungleich** *adj* unequal; [Brüder] different ◇ *adv* - **1.** [nicht gleich] unequally; [sich verhalten] differently - **2.** [bei weitem] far.

**ungleichmäßig** *adj* - **1.** [unregelmäßig] irregular - **2.** [ungleich] unequal ◇ *adv* - **1.** [unregelmäßig] irregularly - **2.** [ungleich] unequally.

**Un|glück** *das* - **1.** [Vorfall] accident - **2.** [Pech] bad luck; **zu allem ~ brach er sich auch noch den Arm** on top of everything he broke his arm as well; **das bringt ~** that brings bad luck - **3.** *RW*: **ins/in sein ~ rennen** *fam* to rush headlong into disaster.

**unglücklich** *adj* - **1.** [nicht glücklich] unhappy - **2.** [ungünstig] unfortunate - **3.** [ungeschickt] clumsy ◇ *adv* - **1.** [nicht glücklich] unhappily - **2.** [ungeschickt] awkwardly - **3.** [ungünstig] badly.

**unglücklicherweise** *adv* unfortunately.

**Un|gnade** *die*: **bei jm in ~ fallen/sein** *fig* to fall/be out of favour with sb.

**ungültig** *adj* invalid; **etw für ~ erklären** to declare sthg null and void.

**Ungunsten** *pl*: **zu js ~** to sb's disadvantage; *siehe auch* **zuungunsten.**

**ungünstig** *adj* unfavourable; [Moment] inconvenient; [Witterung] bad ◇ *adv* unfavourably.

**ungut** *adj* bad ◇ *adv* badly; **nichts für ~!** *fig* no offence!

**unhaltbar, unhaltbar** *adj* - **1.** [Argument, Lage, These] untenable - **2.** [Schuss] unstoppable.

**unhandlich** *adj* cumbersome.

**Unheil** *das geh* disaster; **~ stiften** *geh* to cause havoc.

**unheilbar, unheilbar** *adj* incurable ◇ *adv* incurably.

**unheimlich, unheimlich** *adj* - **1.** [gruselig] eerie; **dieser Typ ist mir ~** this guy makes my flesh creep; **mir wird ~** I have an eerie feeling - **2.** *fam* [groß] terrible; [Menge] huge ◇ *adv* *fam* [ungeheuer] dead; **~ viel Geld** loads of money; **sich ~ freuen** to be dead pleased.

**unhöflich** *adj* impolite ◇ *adv* impolitely.

**unhygienisch** *adj* unhygienic ◇ *adv* unhygienically.

**Uni** *(pl -s) die fam* uni.

**UNICEF** ['u:nitsɛf] *(abk für United Nations Children's Emergency Fund) die* UNICEF.

**Uniform, Uniform** *(pl -en) die* uniform.

**uninteressant** *adj* uninteresting ◇ *adv* uninterestingly.

**Union** *(pl -en) die* union.

**Unionsparteien** *pl* "CDU" *and* "CSU".

**universal** [univɐ'za:l] *adj* universal ◇ *adv* universally.

**universell** [univɐ'zɛl] *adj* universal ◇ *adv* universally.

**Universität** [univɛrzi'tɛːt] *(pl -en) die* university.

**Universitäts|bibliothek** *die* university library.

**Universitäts|klinik** *die* university hospital.

**Universitäts|stadt** *die* university town.

**Universum** [uni'vɛrzʊm] *das* universe.

**unken** *vt* & *vi fam*: **„das geht mit Sicherheit schief", unkte sie** "it's bound to go wrong", she prophesied gloomily.

**unkenntlich** *adj* unrecognizable.

**Unkenntlichkeit** *die*: **bis zur ~** to the point of being unrecognizable.

**Unkenntnis** *die*: **in ~ einer Sache** *(G)* **sein** to be in ignorance of sthg; **etw in ~ einer Sache** *(G)* **tun** to do sthg out of ignorance of sthg.

**unklar** *adj* unclear; **jn (über etw** *(A)***) im Unklaren lassen** to leave sb in the dark (about sthg) ◇ *adv* - **1.** [unverständlich] unclearly - **2.** [vage] vaguely.

**unklug** *adj* unwise ◇ *adv* unwisely.

**unkompliziert** *adj* straightforward, uncomplicated ◇ *adv* straightforwardly.

**unkontrollierbar, unkontrollierbar** *adj* uncontrollable ◇ *adv* uncontrollably.

**unkontrolliert** *adj* uncontrolled.

**unkonventionell** ['ʊnkɔnvɛntsjɔnɛl] *adj* unconventional ◇ *adv* unconventionally.

**unkonzentriert** *adj* lacking in concentration; ~ **sein** to lack concentration ⬦ *adv* without concentrating.

**Unkosten** *pl* expenses; **allgemeine** ODER **laufende** ~ overheads *Br*, overhead *Am*; **sich in** ~ **stürzen** *fig* to go to great expense.

**Unkosten|beitrag** *der* contribution towards expenses.

**Un|kraut** *das* - **1.** *(ohne pl)* [störende Pflanzen] weeds *(pl)* - **2.** [Unkrautart] weed.

**unkritisch** *adj* uncritical ⬦ *adv* uncritically.

**unkündbar, unkündbar** *adj* [Beamte, Stelle] tenured.

**unlängst** *adv geh* recently.

**unlauter** *adj geh* dishonest; ~**er Wettbewerb** unfair competition.

**unleserlich** *adj* illegible ⬦ *adv* illegibly.

**unlogisch** *adj* illogical ⬦ *adv* illogically.

**Unlust** *die geh* [Lustlosigkeit] lack of enthusiasm; [Widerwille] reluctance.

**unlustig** *adj* [lustlos] unenthusiastic; [widerwillig] reluctant ⬦ *adv* [lustlos] unenthusiastically; [widerwillig] reluctantly.

**unmaßgeblich** *adj* of no consequence ⬦ *adv* insignificantly.

**unmäßig** *adj* - **1.** [maßlos] excessive - **2.** [ungeheuer] tremendous; ~ **viel** a tremendous amount ⬦ *adv* - **1.** [maßlos] excessively - **2.** [ungeheuer] tremendously.

**Un|menge** *die* masses *(pl)*; **eine** ~ **Arbeit** masses of work.

**Un|mensch** *der abw* monster; **ich bin kein** ~ *fam* I'm not an ogre.

**unmenschlich** *adj* - **1.** [menschenunwürdig, brutal] inhuman - **2.** *fam* [unerträglich] terrible ⬦ *adv* - **1.** [menschenunwürdig, brutal] inhumanly - **2.** *fam* [ungeheuer] terribly.

**unmerklich, unmerklich** *adj* imperceptible ⬦ *adv* imperceptibly.

**unmissverständlich** *adj* unambiguous ⬦ *adv* unambiguously.

**unmittelbar** *adj* immediate; [Verbindung] direct; **in** ~**er Nähe** in the immediate vicinity ⬦ *adv* directly; ~ **danach** immediately afterwards.

**unmöglich, unmöglich** *adj* [nicht möglich] impossible; **es ist mir** ~, **das zu tun** it is impossible for me to do that; **sich** ~ **machen** to make a fool of o.s. ⬦ *adv* - **1.** [nicht möglich, keinesfalls]: **das kann** ~ **stimmen** that can't possibly be right; **das kannst du** ~ **von ihm verlangen** you can't possibly ask that of him - **2.** *fam* [sich benehmen] impossibly.

**unmoralisch** *adj* immoral ⬦ *adv* immorally.

**unmotiviert** ['ʊnmotiviːɐ̯t] *adj* unmotivated ⬦ *adv* without motivation.

**unmündig** *adj* [Kind] underage; ~ **sein** to be under age, to be a minor; [Erwachsene] to be incapable of managing one's affairs.

**unmusikalisch** *adj* unmusical.

**Unmut** *der geh* displeasure.

**unnachgiebig** *adj* inflexible ⬦ *adv* inflexibly.

**unnachsichtig** *adj* [Behandlung, Härte] unrelenting; [Mensch] merciless ⬦ *adv* mercilessly.

**unnahbar, unnahbar** *adj* unapproachable.

**unnatürlich** *adj* unnatural ⬦ *adv* unnaturally.

**unnötig** *adj* unnecessary ⬦ *adv* unnecessarily.

**unnütz** *adj* useless ⬦ *adv* [unnötig] needlessly.

**UNO** ['uːno] *(abk für* **United Nations Organization)** *die* UN.

**unordentlich** *adj* untidy ⬦ *adv* untidily.

**Unordnung** *die* mess; **etw in** ~ **bringen** to mess sthg up; **in** ~ **geraten** to get messed up.

**unparteiisch** *adj* impartial ⬦ *adv* impartially.

**unpassend** *adj* inappropriate ⬦ *adv* inappropriately.

**unpersönlich** *adj* [gen & GRAM] impersonal ⬦ *adv* [gen & GRAM] impersonally.

**unpolitisch** *adj* unpolitical ⬦ *adv* unpolitically.

**unpopulär** *adj* unpopular.

**unpraktisch** *adj* impractical ⬦ *adv* impractically.

**unproblematisch** *adj* straightforward ⬦ *adv* straightforwardly.

**unproduktiv** *adj* unproductive ⬦ *adv* unproductively.

**unpünktlich** *adj* [Mensch] unpunctual; [Abfahrt, Zahlung] late ⬦ *adv* late.

**unqualifiziert** *adj* - **1.** [Arbeit, Arbeiter] unskilled - **2.** *abw* [dumm] idiotic ⬦ *adv abw* idiotically.

**unrasiert** *adj* & *adv* unshaven.

**unrecht** *adj* - **1.** [Zeit, Moment] inconvenient; **ist es dir** ~, **wenn ich hier warte?** would it bother you if I wait here? - **2.** *geh* [Tat, Gedanke] wicked; **es ist** ~, **so etw zu denken** it is wrong to think like that ⬦ *adv* - **1.** [ungelegen] inconveniently - **2.** *geh* [handeln, sich benehmen] wrongly; **jm** ~ **tun** to wrong sb.

**Unrecht** *das* wrong; ~ **haben, im** ~ **sein** to be wrong; **jn/sich ins** ~ **setzen** to put sb/o.s. in the wrong; **zu** ~ wrongly.

**unrechtmäßig** *adj* illegal ⟷ *adv* illegally.

**unreflektiert** *adj* unthinking ⟷ *adv* unthinkingly.

**unregelmäßig** *adj* [gen & GRAM] irregular ⟷ *adv* [gen & GRAM] irregularly.

**unreif** *adj* - **1.** [Obst] unripe - **2.** [Person] immature.

**unrein** *adj* - **1.** [Lösung, Droge] impure; [Wäsche] dirty - **2.** [Haut] blemished - **3.** REL unclean - **4.** [Text]: etw ins Unreine schreiben to write sthg out in rough.

**Unruhe** (*pl* -n) *die* (*ohne pl*) - **1.** [Treiben] commotion; er sorgt ständig für ~ he's always causing a commotion; ~ stiften to stir up trouble - **2.** [Ruhelosigkeit] unease; jn in ~ versetzen to make sb uneasy - **3.** [Aufregung] unrest, disquiet - **4.** [Bewegung]: in ~ sein to be moving restlessly.

➡ **Unruhen** *pl* [Aufruhr] riots.

**Unruhe|herd** *der* POL trouble spot.

**unruhig** *adj* - **1.** [nicht ruhig] restless - **2.** [ruhelos] uneasy; ~ werden to get anxious - **3.** [gestört - Schlaf] fitful; [ - Nacht] disturbed - **4.** [Zeit] troubled - **5.** [laut] noisy - **6.** [Muster, Bild] busy ⟷ *adv* - **1.** [nicht ruhig] restlessly - **2.** [ruhelos] uneasily - **3.** [schlafen] fitfully.

**uns** *pron* - **1.** [Personalpronomen - Akkusativ, Dativ] us; sie hat ~ gesehen she has seen us; er sagte es ~ he told us; das gehört ~ this is ours, this belongs to us; mit ~ with us; ein Freund von ~ a friend of ours - **2.** [Reflexivpronomen] ourselves; wir setzten ~ we sat down; wir konnten ~ das nicht vorstellen we couldn't imagine that - **3.** [einander] each other, one another.

**unsachgemäß** *adj* improper ⟷ *adv* improperly.

**unsachlich** *adj* subjective ⟷ *adv* subjectively.

**unsagbar, unsagbar** *adj* indescribable ⟷ *adv* indescribably.

**unsanft** *adj* rough ⟷ *adv* roughly.

**unsauber** *adj* - **1.** [Geschäft] shady - **2.** [Arbeit] sloppy, shoddy - **3.** [dreckig] dirty ⟷ *adv* - **1.** [unkorrekt] sloppily, shoddily - **2.** [dreckig]: es geht ~ zu it is dirty.

**unschädlich** *adj* harmless; jn/etw ~ machen to put sb/sthg out of action.

**unscharf** *adj* - **1.** [nicht scharf] blurred - **2.** [ungenau] vague ⟷ *adv*: ~ sehen to have blurred vision.

**unschätzbar, unschätzbar** *adj* inestimable.

**unscheinbar** *adj* inconspicuous.

**unschlagbar, unschlagbar** *adj* - **1.** [nicht zu schlagen] unbeatable - **2.** [nicht zu übertreffen] unsurpassable.

**unschlüssig** *adj* undecided; (sich (D)) über

etw (A) ~ sein to be undecided about sthg ⟷ *adv* indecisively.

**unschön** *adj* unpleasant; das war ~ von ihm that wasn't very nice of him.

**Unschuld** *die* - **1.** [gen] innocence - **2.** [Jungfräulichkeit] virginity.

**unschuldig** *adj* - **1.** [gen] innocent; an etw (D) ~ sein not to be to blame for sthg - **2.** [jungfräulich]: ein ~es Mädchen a virgin ⟷ *adv* - **1.** [gen] innocently - **2.** [verurteilen] wrongly.

**unschwer** *adv* easily.

**unselbstständig** *adj* dependent.

**unser, e** *det* our.

**unsere, r, s** ODER **unsers** *pron* ours ⟷ *det* = unser.

**unsereins** *pron* fam the likes of us.

**unsererseits, unsrerseits** *adv* - **1.** [wir selbst] for our part - **2.** [von uns] on our part.

**unseresgleichen, unsresgleichen** *pron* people like us.

**unseretwegen, unsertwegen** *adv* - **1.** [uns zuliebe] for our sake - **2.** [wegen uns] because of us - **3.** [von uns aus] as far as we are concerned.

**unseretwillen, unsertwillen** ➡ um unseretwillen *adv* for our sake.

**unseriös** *abw adj* dubious ⟷ *adv*: ~ arbeiten to be engaged in dubious work.

**unsertwegen** = unseretwegen.

**unsertwillen** = unseretwillen.

**unsicher** *adj* - **1.** [gen] uncertain - **2.** [Stimme, Hand] unsteady; ich bin mir ~, ob ... I'm uncertain whether ... - **3.** [unverlässlich] unreliable - **4.** [gefährdet] insecure - **5.** [unbeständig] unsettled - **6.** [gefährlich] unsafe; etw ~ machen fam [sich vergnügen] to hit sthg ⟷ *adv* [nicht sicher - gehen fahren] unsteadily; [ - reden, auftreten] uncertainly.

**Un|sicherheit** *die* - **1.** [Ungewissheit] uncertainty; [Eigenschaft] insecurity - **2.** [von Handlung] lapse.

**unsichtbar** *adj* invisible; sich ~ machen to make o.s. scarce ⟷ *adv* invisibly.

**Unsinn** *der* nonsense; ~ machen to fool around.

**unsinnig** *adj* - **1.** [blödsinnig] idiotic - **2.** fam [ungeheuer] tremendous ⟷ *adv* tremendously.

**Un|sitte** *die abw* bad habit.

**unsittlich** *adj* - **1.** [unmoralisch] indecent - **2.** RECHT immoral ⟷ *adv* indecently.

**unsozial** *adj* antisocial ⟷ *adv* antisocially.

**unsportlich** *adj* - **1.** [Person] unsporty - **2.** [Verhalten] unsporting.

**unsrerseits** = unsererseits.

**unsresgleichen** = unseresgleichen.

**unsrige** (pl -n) pron (mit Artikel) geh: der/die/das ~ ours.

**unsterblich, unsterblich** adj immortal; [Liebe] undying <> adv: ~ **verliebt** madly in love; **sich ~ blamieren** to make an absolute fool of o.s.

**unstillbar** adj insatiable.

**Unstimmigkeiten** pl - **1.** [Differenzen] differences of opinion - **2.** [Abweichungen] discrepancies.

**Un|summe** die huge amount of money.

**unsympathisch** adj unpleasant; **er/es ist mir ~** I don't like him/it.

**Un|tat** die evil crime.

**untätig** adj idle <> adv idly.

**untauglich** adj unsuitable; **für den Wehrdienst ~** unfit for military service.

**unteilbar, unteilbar** adj indivisible.

**unten** adv - **1.** [räumlich - im unteren Teil] at the bottom; [ - tiefer gelegen] below; [ - an der Unterseite] underneath; **~ am Tisch** at the bottom of the table; **links/rechts ~ im Bild** in the bottom left-hand/right-hand corner of the picture; **hier/dort ~** down here/there; **von ~** from below; **nach ~** down; [im Haus] downstairs; **mit dem Gesicht nach ~** face down; **weiter ~** further down - **2.** [im Text] below; **siehe ~** see below - **3.** fam [im Süden]: **~ im Süden** down south - **4.** fam [rangniedriger]: **die da ~** those at the bottom of the pile - **5.** RW: **die sind bei uns ~ durch** fam fig we're finished with them, we're through with them.

**unter** präp - **1.** (+ D) [räumlich] under; [an der Unterseite von] underneath; **~ dem Tisch liegen** to lie under the table; **~ uns wohnt Herr Braun** Mr Braun lives under ODER beneath us - **2.** (+ A) [räumlich] under; **~ den Tisch kriechen** to crawl under the table - **3.** (+ D) [weniger als] under; **Kinder ~ 12 Jahren** children under the age of 12; **~ null** below zero - **4.** (+ A) [weniger als] below - **5.** (+ D) [zur Angabe einer Teilmenge] among; **einer ~ vielen** one of many; **~ sich sein** to be in private; **~ uns (gesagt)** between you and me; **~ anderem** among other things - **6.** (+ D) [zwischen] between; **sie haben es ~ sich ausgemacht** they arranged it between themselves - **7.** (+ A) [zwischen]: **sich ~ die Menge mischen** to mingle ODER mix with the crowd - **8.** (+ D) [zur Angabe einer Hierarchie, einer Bezeichnung] under; **~ der Aufsicht/Leitung von ...** under the supervision/leadership of ...; **~ dem Namen X bekannt sein** to be known by the name of X - **9.** (+ D) [zur Angabe des Umstands] under; **~ Umständen** under ODER in certain circumstances; **~ Druck stehen** to be under pressure; **~ Berücksichtigung von** taking into consideration; **~ der Bedingung, dass ...** on the condition that ... <> adj lower; **der ~ste Knopf** the bottom button.

**Unter|arm** der forearm.

**unterbelichtet** adj - **1.** [Foto, Film] underexposed - **2.** salopp [Mensch] dim.

**unterbewerten** vt to undervalue.

**unterbewusst** adj subconscious <> adv subconsciously.

**Unterbewusstsein** das subconscious.

**unterbieten** (prät unterbot; perf hat unterboten) vt - **1.** [Preis, Angebot, Konkurrenz] to undercut - **2.** SPORT to beat.

**unterbinden** (prät unterband; perf hat unterbunden) vt to prevent.

**Unterbodenschutz** der AUTO underseal.

**unterbrechen** (präs unterbricht; prät unterbrach; perf hat unterbrochen) vt - **1.** [stören] to interrupt - **2.** [aufhören - Arbeit, Behandlung, Urlaub] to break off; **unterbrochen sein** [Telefonverbindung, Kontakt] to be cut off.

**Unterbrechung** die - **1.** [Störung] interruption - **2.** [Aufhören - von Arbeit, Behandlung, Urlaub] breaking off; **ohne ~** without a break.

**unter|bringen** vt (unreg) - **1.** [an einem Platz] to fit - **2.** [über Nacht] to put up - **3.** [bei Firma] to get a job for - **4.** [in Gedächtnis] to place.

**Unterbringung** die [Unterkunft] accommodation.

**unterderhand** adv ▷ Hand.

**unterdessen** adv meanwhile.

**unterdrücken** vt - **1.** [Volk, Minderheit] to oppress - **2.** [Gefühl, Bemerkung, Information] to suppress.

**Unterdrückung** (pl -en) die - **1.** [von Volk, Minderheiten] oppression - **2.** [von Gefühl, Bemerkung, Informationen] suppression.

**untereinander** adv - **1.** [unter sich] among ourselves/yourselves/themselves - **2.** [unter das andere] one below the other.

**unterentwickelt** adj underdeveloped.

**unterernährt** adj undernourished.

**unterfordern** vt to ask too little of.

**Unter|führung** die underpass, subway Br.

**Untergang** (pl -gänge) der - **1.** [von Volk, Kultur] decline - **2.** [von Schiff] sinking - **3.** [von Sonne, Mond] setting.

**Untergebene** (pl -n) der, die subordinate.

**unter|gehen** (perf ist untergegangen) vi (unreg) - **1.** [Sonne, Mond] to set - **2.** [Schiff, Person] to sink - **3.** [Kultur, Volk] to decline.

**untergeordnet** adj - **1.** [unterstellt & GRAM] subordinate - **2.** [Bedeutung, Rolle] secondary.

**untergliedern** vt to subdivide.

**untergraben** (präs untergräbt; prät untergrub; perf hat untergraben) vt [schaden] to undermine.

**Unter|grenze** die lower limit.

U

**Unter|grund** der - **1.** [Boden] subsoil - **2.** [Unterwelt] underground; **in den ~ gehen** to go underground - **3.** [für Farbe, Stellfläche] surface.

**Untergrund|bahn** die underground Br, subway Am.

**unter|haken** vt to link arms with.
➤ **sich unterhaken** ref: **sich (bei jm) ~** to link arms (with sb).

**unterhalb** adv: **~ von** below ⬦ präp: **~ einer Sache** (G) below sthg.

**Unterhalt** der - **1.** [Zahlung] maintenance - **2.** [von Familie, Kindern] keep - **3.** [von Gebäude, Park] upkeep.

**unterhalten¹** (präs **unterhält;** prät **unterhielt;** perf **hat unterhalten**) vt - **1.** [amüsieren] to entertain - **2.** [Kosten übernehmen für - Familie] to support; [ - Haus, Büro] to pay for the upkeep of - **3.** [Kontakte] to maintain - **4.** [betreiben] to run.
➤ **sich unterhalten** ref - **1.** [reden]: **sich (mit jm/ über etw** (A)**) ~** to talk (with sb/about sthg) - **2.** [sich amüsieren] to enjoy o.s.

**unter|halten²** vt (unreg) [darunter halten] to hold underneath.

**unterhaltsam** adj entertaining ⬦ adv entertainingly.

**Unterhaltskosten** pl [für Wagen] running costs; [für Haus] maintenance costs.

**Unter|haltung** die - **1.** [Gespräch] conversation - **2.** [Zeitvertreib] entertainment; **gute ~!** enjoy yourselves! - **3.** [von Kontakten] maintenance - **4.** [Betreibung] running.

**Unterhaltungselektronik** die electronic goods (for entertainment purposes).

**Unterhaltungsmusik** die light music.

**Unter|händler, in** der, die negotiator.

**Unter|hemd** das vest Br, undershirt Am.

**Unter|hose** die [für Herren] underpants (pl); [für Frauen] briefs (pl).

**unterirdisch** adj & adv underground.

**unter|jubeln** vt: **jm etw ~** fam to palm sthg off on sb.

**Unter|kiefer** der lower jaw.

**unter|kommen** (perf **ist untergekommen**) vi (unreg) - **1.** [über Nacht] to find accommodation - **2.** [Arbeit finden]: **bei jm ~** to get a job with sb; **so etwas ist mir noch nie untergekommen** I've never come across anything like it.

**unter|kriegen** vt fam to get down; **sich nicht ~ lassen** fam not to let things get one down.

**unterkühlt** adj - **1.** [Reaktion, Verhalten] frosty - **2.** [untertemperiert] suffering from hypothermia ⬦ adv - **1.** [reagieren, sich verhalten] frostily - **2.** [untertemperiert] suffering from hypothermia.

**Unterkunft** (pl **-künfte**) die accommodation

(U); **eine ~ suchen** to be looking for accommodation.

**Unter|lage** die [für Gymnastik] mat; [zum Schreiben] something to rest on.
➤ **Unterlagen** pl [Urkunden] documents.

**unterlassen** (präs **unterlässt;** prät **unterließ;** perf **hat unterlassen**) vt to refrain from; **es ~, etw zu tun** to refrain from doing sthg.

**unterlaufen¹** (präs **unterläuft;** prät **unterlief;** perf **ist unterlaufen**) vt [passieren]: **mir ist ein Fehler ~** I made a mistake.

**unterlaufen²** adj: **seine Augen waren mit Blut ~** his eyes were bloodshot; **blutig ~e Prellungen** severe bruising (U).

**unter|legen¹** vt [drunter legen] to put underneath.

**unterlegen²** vt - **1.** [Teppich] to underlay; [Kragen, Hosenbund] to line - **2.** [Film]: **etw mit Musik ~** to add background music to sthg.

**unterlegen³** adj inferior; **zahlenmäßig ~** outnumbered.

**Unter|leib** der abdomen.

**unterliegen** (prät **unterlag;** perf **hat/ist unterlegen**) vi - **1.** (hat) [ausgesetzt sein]: **einer Sache** (D) **~** to be subject to sthg - **2.** (ist) [verlieren] to be defeated.

**Unter|lippe** die lower lip.

**untermalen** vt: **etw mit Musik ~** to provide sthg with background music.

**untermauern** vt to underpin.

**Untermiete** die: **in** ODER **zur ~ wohnen** to be a subtenant.

**Unter|mieter, in** der, die sub-tenant.

**unternehmen** (präs **unternimmt;** prät **unternahm;** perf **hat unternommen**) vt [Versuch, Anstrengung] to make; [Reise, Ausflug] to go on; **etwas/nichts ~** to do something/nothing; **Schritte gegen jn ~** to take action against sb.

**Unternehmen** (pl -) das - **1.** [Betrieb] business, company - **2.** [Vorhaben] undertaking.

**Unternehmens|berater, in** der, die management consultant.

**Unternehmer, in** (mpl -/ fpl **-nen**) der, die entrepreneur.

**Unternehmung** (pl **-en**) die undertaking; [Ausflug] trip.

**unternehmungslustig** adj enterprising.

**Unter|offizier, in** der, die - **1.** [Mensch] non-commissioned officer - **2.** [Dienstgrad] sergeant.

**unter|ordnen** vt to subordinate; **jm/einer Sache untergeordnet sein** to be subordinate to sb/sthg.
➤ **sich unterordnen** ref: **sich (jm/einer Sache) ~** to subordinate o.s. (to sb/sthg).

**Unterprima** *(pl -men) die* SCHULE *eighth year of a "Gymnasium".*

**Unterredung** *(pl -en) die* discussion; **eine ~ mit jm haben** to have a discussion with sb.

**Unterricht** *(pl -e) der* lessons *(pl)*; **jm ~ geben** ODER **erteilen** to teach sb; **jm ~ in Englisch geben** to teach sb English; **hast du morgen ~?** do you have any classes tomorrow?; **~ in Deutsch nehmen** to have German lessons.

**unterrichten** *vt* - **1.** [Unterricht geben] to teach; **sie unterrichtet Kinder im Zeichnen** she teaches children drawing - **2.** [informieren]: **sich/jn (über etw** (A)**) ~** to inform o.s./sb (about sthg) ⬦ *vi* to teach.

**Unterrichts|fach** *das* subject.

**Unter|rock** *der* slip.

**unter|rühren** *vt* to mix in.

**untersagen** *vt* to forbid; **jm ~, etw zu tun** to forbid sb to do sthg.

**Unter|satz** *der* mat.

**unterschätzen** *vt* to underestimate.

**unterscheiden** *(prät* **unterschied**; *prät* **hat unterschieden)** *vt* - **1.** [auseinander halten, bemerken] to distinguish; **jn/etw von jm/etw ~** to tell sb/sthg from sb/sthg - **2.** [abgrenzen] to distinguish between ⬦ *vi* - **1.** [abgrenzen] to distinguish - **2.** [differenzieren] to make a distinction.

➤ **sich unterscheiden** *ref:* **sich (durch etw** ODER **in etw** (D)**) ~** to differ (in sthg).

**Unter|scheidung** *die* distinction; **eine ~ treffen** to make a distinction.

**Unter|schenkel** *der* lower leg.

**Unter|schicht** *die* lower classes *(pl)*.

**unter|schieben** *vt (unreg)* - **1.** [unterjubeln]: **jm etw ~** [Dokumente, Rauschgift] to foist sthg on sb; [Motive] to impute sthg to sb - **2.** [darunter schieben]: **(jm) etw ~** to push sthg under (sb).

**Unterschied** *(pl -e) der* - **1.** [Verschiedenheit] difference; **ein feiner/großer ~** a slight/big difference; **ein ~ wie Tag und Nacht sein** to be as different as night and day - **2.** [Unterscheidung] distinction; **im ~ zu jm/etw** unlike sb/sthg.

**unterschiedlich** *adj* different ⬦ *adv* differently; **~ groß/schnell** of varying size/speed.

**Unterschiedlichkeit** *(pl -en) die* - **1.** [Verschiedenheit] diversity - **2.** [Ungleichheit] difference.

**unterschlagen**[1] *(präs* **unterschlägt**; *prät* **unterschlug**; *perf* **hat unterschlagen)** *vt* - **1.** [sich aneignen] to misappropriate - **2.** [verschweigen] to suppress.

**unter|schlagen**[2] *vt (unreg)* [Arme] to fold; [Beine] to cross.

**Unterschlagung** *(pl -en) die* [von Geldern] misappropriation.

**Unterschlupf** *(pl -e) der* [Obdach] shelter; [Versteck] hiding place; **~ suchen/finden** [Obdach] to seek/find shelter; [Versteck] to seek/find a hiding place.

**unter|schlüpfen** *(perf* **ist untergeschlüpft)** *vi* [Obdach finden] to shelter; [sich verstecken] to hide out.

**unterschreiben** *(prät* **unterschrieb**; *perf* **hat unterschrieben)** *vt* to sign ⬦ *vi* to sign; **eigenhändig ~** to sign personally.

**unterschreiten** *(prät* **unterschritt**; *perf* **hat unterschritten)** *vt* [Maximum] to keep under; [Minimum] to fall below.

**Unter|schrift** *die* signature; **jm etw zur ~ vorlegen** to give sb sthg to be signed; **eigenhändige ~** personal signature.

**Unterschriften|sammlung** *die* petition.

**unterschwellig** *adj* subliminal ⬦ *adv* subliminally.

**Untersee|boot** *das* submarine.

**Unter|seite** *die* underside.

**Untersetzer** *(pl -) der* [für Glas] coaster; [für Topf] mat.

**untersetzt** *adj* stocky.

**Unter|stand** *der* [vor Regen, Gefahr] shelter; [für Soldaten] dugout.

**unterstehen** *(prät* **unterstand**; *perf* **hat unterstanden)** *vi* [untergeordnet sein]: **jm/einer Sache ~** to be answerable to sb/sthg.

➤ **sich unterstehen** *ref* [es wagen]: **sich ~, etw zu tun** to dare to do sthg; **untersteh dich!** don't you dare!

**unter|stellen**[1] *vt* - **1.** [zum Schutz] to store - **2.** [unter Gegenstand] to put underneath.

➤ **sich unterstellen** *ref* [zum Schutz] to shelter.

**unterstellen**[2] *vt* - **1.** [in Hierarchie]: **jm etw ~** to put sb in charge of sthg; **sie ist direkt dem Regierungspräsidenten unterstellt** she is directly answerable to the president - **2.** [Behauptung] to assume - **3.** [fälschlich]: **jm etw ~** to impute sthg to sb.

**Unter|stellung** *die* - **1.** [in Hierarchie] subordination - **2.** [fälschlich] imputation.

**unterstreichen** *(prät* **unterstrich**; *perf* **hat unterstrichen)** *vt* to underline.

**Unter|stufe** *die* SCHULE lower school.

**unterstützen** *vt* to support.

**Unterstützung** *(pl -en) die* support *(U)*; **bei jm ~ finden** to get support from sb.

**untersuchen** *vt* to examine; [polizeilich] to investigate; **etw auf etw** (A) **(hin) ~** to examine sthg for sthg; **etw näher ~** to examine sthg more closely.

**Untersuchung** *(pl -en) die* - **1.** [Untersuchen - ärztlich] examination; [ - polizeilich] investigation - **2.** [Studie] study.

**Untersuchungsaus|schuss** *der* committee of inquiry.

**Untersuchungshaft** *die* imprisonment whilst awaiting trial; **in ~ sein** ODER **sitzen** to be on remand.

**Untertan** (*pl* -en) *der* subject.

**Unter|tasse** *die* saucer; **fliegende ~** *fig* flying saucer.

**unter|tauchen** (*perf* hat/ist **untergetaucht**) *vi* (*ist*) **- 1.** [tauchen] to dive; [versinken] to sink **- 2.** *fig* [in der Menge] to disappear; [Verbrecher] to go to ground <> *vt* (*hat*) to duck.

**unterteilen** *vt* to divide up; **etw in etw** (*A*) **~** to divide sthg up into sthg.

**Unter|teilung** *die* division (*U*).

**Unter|titel** *der* subtitle; **mit ~n** with subtitles.

**Unterton** (*pl* -töne) *der* undertone.

**untertreiben** (*prät* **untertrieb**; *perf* hat untertrieben) *vi* to understate things <> *vt* to play down.

**Untertreibung** (*pl* -en) *die* understatement.

**unter|vermieten** *vt* to sublet.

**Unter|verzeichnis** *das* EDV subdirectory.

**Unterwalden** *nt* Unterwalden; **~ nid dem Wald** Nidwalden; **~ ob dem Wald** Obwalden.

**unterwandern** *vt* to infiltrate.

**Unterwäsche** *die* underwear.

**unterwegs** *adv* on the way; **~ sein** to be away.

**unterweisen** (*prät* **unterwies**; *perf* hat unterwiesen) *vt geh*: **jn in etw** (*D*) **~** to instruct sb in sthg.

**Unterwelt** *die* underworld.

**unterwerfen** (*präs* **unterwirft**; *prät* unterwarf; *perf* hat unterworfen) *vt* to subjugate.
    ➧ **sich unterwerfen** *ref* to submit.

**unterwürfig** *abw adj* servile <> *adv* servilely.

**unterzeichnen** *vt* to sign.

**unter|ziehen¹** *vt* (*unreg*) **- 1.** [darunter anziehen] to put on underneath **- 2.** KÜCHE to fold in.

**unterziehen²** (*prät* **unterzog**; *perf* hat unterzogen) *vt* [aussetzen] to subject.
    ➧ **sich unterziehen** *ref* [über sich ergehen lassen]: **sich einer Sache** (*D*) **~** to undergo sthg.

**Un|tiefe** *die* **- 1.** [seichte Stelle] shallow **- 2.** [sehr große Tiefe] depth.

**untragbar** *adj* unacceptable.

**untreu** *adj* **- 1.** [treulos] unfaithful; **jm ~ werden** to be unfaithful to sb **- 2.** *geh* [illoyal] disloyal; **er ist sich selbst ~** he is untrue to himself.

**Untreue** *die* [zu Liebhaber] infidelity; [Illoyalität] disloyalty.

**untröstlich** *adj*: **über etw** (*A*) **~ sein** to be inconsolable about sthg.

**untrüglich** *adj* unmistakable.

**unüberlegt** *adj* rash <> *adv* rashly.

**unübersehbar** *adj* [Gebiet, Weite] vast; [Schild, Hinweis, Kratzer] obvious; [Folgen] inestimable <> *adv* [groß] extremely; [aufgestellt] conspicuously.

**unübersichtlich** *adj* [Gelände] broken; [Menge] vast; [Kurve] blind; [Anordnung] confusing <> *adv* [groß] extremely; [angelegt, angeordnet] unclearly.

**unübertrefflich** *adj* unsurpassable <> *adv* brilliantly.

**unübertroffen** *adj* unsurpassed <> *adv* exceptionally.

**unumgänglich** *adj* unavoidable.

**unumwunden** *adj* frank <> *adv* frankly.

**ununterbrochen** *adj* uninterrupted <> *adv* nonstop.

**unveränderlich** *adj* unchanging.

**unverändert** *adj* unchanged.

**unverantwortlich** *adj* irresponsible <> *adv* irresponsibly.

**unverbesserlich** *adj* incorrigible.

**unverbindlich** *adj* not binding <> *adv* without obligation.

**unverblümt** *adj* blunt <> *adv* bluntly.

**unverdaulich** *adj* indigestible.

**unverdient** *adj* undeserved <> *adv* undeservedly.

**unverdorben** *adj* unspoilt.

**unverdrossen** *adj* untiring <> *adv* untiringly.

**unvereinbar** *adj* incompatible; **mit etw ~ sein** to be incompatible with sthg.

**unverfälscht** *adj* [Wein, Geschmack] unadulterated; [Brauch] genuine; [Schönheit] pure <> *adv* purely.

**unverfänglich** *adj* harmless <> *adv* harmlessly.

**unverfroren** *adj* impudent <> *adv* impudently.

**unvergesslich** *adj* unforgettable; **etw ist/ bleibt jm ~** sb will never forget sthg.

**unvergleichlich** *adj* incomparable <> *adv* incomparably.

**unverhältnismäßig** *adv* disproportionately.

**unverheiratet** *adj* unmarried.

**unverhofft** *adj* unexpected <> *adv* unexpectedly.

**unverhohlen** *adj* undisguised <> *adv* openly.

**unverkäuflich** adj not for sale; [schadhafte Ware] unsaleable.

**unverkennbar** adj unmistakable ◇ adv unmistakably.

**unvermeidlich** adj unavoidable.

**unvermindert** adj undiminished ◇ adv: ~ stark as strong as ever.

**unvermittelt** adj sudden ◇ adv suddenly.

**unvermutet** adj unexpected ◇ adv unexpectedly.

**Unvernunft** die stupidity.

**unvernünftig** adj stupid ◇ adv stupidly.

**unverrichtet** adj: ~er Dinge without having achieved anything.

**unverschämt** adj - **1.** [Mensch, Äußerung, Benehmen] impertinent; [Lüge] barefaced - **2.** [enorm - Glück] incredible; [ - Preis] outrageous ◇ adv - **1.** [taktlos] impertinently - **2.** [sehr] incredibly.

**Unverschämtheit** (pl -en) die impertinence (U); so eine ~! what a cheek!

**unverschuldet** adj & adv through no fault of one's own.

**unversehens** adv all of a sudden.

**unversehrt** adj [Person] unscathed; [Sache] intact; ~ sein/bleiben [Person] to be/remain unscathed; [Sache] to be/remain intact ◇ adv unscathed.

**unversöhnlich** adj irreconcilable ◇ adv irreconcilably.

**Unverstand** der lack of understanding.

**unverstanden** adj misunderstood.

**unverständlich** adj - **1.** [nicht deutlich] unintelligible - **2.** [unbegreiflich]: es ist mir ~, wie ... I don't understand how ...

**Unverständnis** das lack of understanding.

**unversucht** adj: nichts ~ lassen to try everything.

**unverträglich** adj - **1.** [Essen, Mahlzeit] indigestible; [Medikament] that cannot be tolerated - **2.** [unversöhnlich - Mensch, Verhalten] cantankerous; [ - Meinungen, Gegensätze] incompatible.

**unverwechselbar** [ʊnfɐˈvɛksˌbaːɐ̯] adj unmistakable.

**unverwüstlich** adj [Material] durable; [Mensch, Natur] resilient; [Gesundheit] robust; [Humor] irrepressible.

**unverzagt** adj & adv undaunted.

**unverzeihlich** adj inexcusable.

**unverzichtbar** adj essential.

**unverzüglich** adj immediate ◇ adv immediately.

**unvollendet** adj unfinished.

**unvollkommen** adj [mit Fehlern] imperfect;

[unvollständig] incomplete ◇ adv [mit Fehlern] imperfectly; [unvollständig] incompletely.

**unvollständig** adj incomplete ◇ adv incompletely.

**unvorbereitet** adj unprepared; [Rede] improvised.

**unvoreingenommen** adj impartial ◇ adv impartially.

**unvorhergesehen** adj [Ereignis, Problem] unforeseen; [Besuch] unexpected ◇ adv unexpectedly.

**unvorhersehbar** adj unforeseeable.

**unvorsichtig** adj careless ◇ adv carelessly.

**unvorstellbar** adj unimaginable ◇ adv incredibly.

**unvorteilhaft** adj unflattering.

**unwahr** adj untrue.

**Unlwahrheit** die - **1.** [Unwahrsein] untruthfulness - **2.** [Lüge] untruth.

**unwahrscheinlich** adj - **1.** [nicht wahrscheinlich] unlikely - **2.** fam [enorm] incredible ◇ adv fam [sehr] incredibly.

**unwegsam** adj impassable.

**unweigerlich** adj inevitable ◇ adv inevitably.

**unweit** präp: ~ einer Sache (G) not far from sthg ◇ adv: ~ von etw not far from sthg.

**Unwesen** das: sein ~ treiben to be up to no good.

**unwesentlich** adj insignificant ◇ adv slightly.

**Unlwetter** das storm.

**unwichtig** adj unimportant.

**unwiderruflich** adj irrevocable ◇ adv irrevocably.

**unwiderstehlich, unwiderstehlich** adj irresistible ◇ adv irresistibly.

**unwillig** adj [widerwillig] reluctant; [verärgert] angry ◇ adv [widerwillig] reluctantly; [verärgert] angrily.

**unwillkommen** adj unwelcome; jm ~ sein to be unwelcome to sb ◇ adv unwelcomely.

**unwillkürlich** adj involuntary ◇ adv involuntarily.

**unwirklich** adj unreal.

**unwirksam** adj ineffective.

**unwirsch** adj surly ◇ adv in a surly way.

**unwirtschaftlich** adj uneconomic ◇ adv uneconomically.

**Unwissenheit** die ignorance.

**unwohl** adj: jm ist ~ [krank] sb feels unwell; [unbehaglich] sb feels uneasy; sich ~ fühlen [krank] to feel unwell; [unbehaglich] to feel uneasy.

U

**Unwohlsein** *das* indisposition.

**unwürdig** *adj* undignified; **einer Sache** *(G)* ~ **sein** to be unworthy of sthg ◇ *adv* in an undignified manner.

**Unzahl** *die:* **eine** ~ **von etw** a huge quantity of sthg.

**unzählig, unzählig** *adj* innumerable ◇ *adv:* ~ **viele** a huge number (of).

**Unze** *(pl -n) die* ounce.

**Unzeit** ➤ **zur Unzeit** *adv* at the wrong moment.

**unzeitgemäß** *adj* [Kleidung, Einstellung] outmoded ◇ *adv* in an outmoded way.

**unzerbrechlich, unzerbrechlich** *adj* unbreakable.

**unzertrennlich, unzertrennlich** *adj* inseparable.

**unzüchtig** *adj* indecent ◇ *adv* indecently.

**unzufrieden** *adj* dissatisfied; **mit etw** ~ **sein** to be dissatisfied with sthg.

**Unzufriedenheit** *die* dissatisfaction.

**unzugänglich** *adj* [Person] unapproachable; [Gegend] inaccessible.

**unzulänglich** *geh adj* inadequate ◇ *adv* inadequately.

**unzulässig** *adj* inadmissible ◇ *adv* inadmissibly.

**unzumutbar** *adj* unacceptable ◇ *adv* unacceptably.

**unzurechnungsfähig** *adj* not responsible for one's actions; **jn für** ~ **erklären** to certify sb insane.

**Unzurechnungsfähigkeit** *die* unsoundness of mind.

**unzureichend** *adj* insufficient ◇ *adv* insufficiently.

**unzustellbar** *adj* undeliverable.

**unzutreffend** *adj* incorrect.

**unzuverlässig** *adj* unreliable.

**unzweideutig** *adj* unambiguous ◇ *adv* unambiguously.

**üppig** *adj* [Busen] full; [Frau] voluptuous; [Essen] lavish; [Haar] thick; [Vegetation] lush ◇ *adv* [bewachsen] thickly; [speisen, leben] lavishly; ~ **geformt** voluptuous.

**Urabstimmung** *die* strike ballot.

**Ural** *der:* **der** ~ the Urals *(pl)*.

**Uran** *das* CHEM uranium.

**Uraufführung** *die* premiere.

**urbar** *adj:* ~ **machen** [Sumpf] to reclaim; [Stück Land] to cultivate.

**Urbevölkerung** *die* original inhabitants *(pl)*.

**Urbild** *das* [Kunstwerke] original; [Inbegriffe] epitome.

**ureigen** [ˈuːɐ̯ʔaɪɡn̩] *adj* own personal.

**Ureinwohner, in** *der, die* original inhabitant.

**Urenkel, in** *der, die* great-grandson (*f* great-granddaughter).

**Urgroßeltern** *pl* great-grandparents.

**Urgroßmutter** *die* great-grandmother.

**Urgroßvater** *der* great-grandfather.

**Urheber, in** *(mpl -; fpl -nen) der, die* [von Kunstwerk] creator; [von Verbrechen] perpetrator.

**Urheberrecht** *das* copyright.

**Uri** *nt* Uri.

**Urin** *(pl -e) der* urine *(U)*.

**urinieren** *vi geh* to urinate.

**urkomisch** *adj* hilarious.

**Urkunde** *(pl -n) die* certificate.

**Urkundenfälschung** *die* forging of documents.

**Urlaub** *(pl -e) der* holiday *Br*, vacation *Am*; ~ **machen/haben** to have a holiday *Br* ODER vacation *Am*; **im** ODER **in** ~ **sein** to be on holiday *Br* ODER vacation *Am*.

**Urlauber, in** *(mpl -; fpl -nen) der, die* holidaymaker *Br*, vacationer *Am*.

**Urlaubsanschrift** *die* holiday *Br* ODER vacation *Am* address.

**Urlaubsort** *der* holiday *Br* ODER vacation *Am* resort.

**Urlaubsvertretung** *die* holiday replacement.

**Urlaubszeit** *die* holiday *Br* ODER vacation *Am* season.

**Urne** *(pl -n) die* - **1.** [Graburne] urn - **2.** [Wahlurne] ballot box.

**Urologe** *(pl -n) der* MED urologist.

**Urologin** *(pl -nen) die* MED urologist.

**urplötzlich** *adj* very sudden ◇ *adv* all of a sudden.

**Ursache** *die* cause; **die** ~ **für etw** the cause of sthg.
➤ **keine Ursache** *interj* don't mention it!

**ursächlich** *adj* causal.

**Ursprung** *der* origin.

**ursprünglich** *adj* - **1.** [anfänglich] original - **2.** [naturhaft] natural ◇ *adv* [zunächst] originally.

**Urteil** *das* - **1.** RECHT verdict; **das** ~ **lautet auf ...** RECHT the sentence is ... - **2.** [Bewertung] opinion; **sich** *(D)* **ein** ~ **bilden** to form an opinion.

**urteilen** *vi* to judge; **über jn/etw** ~ to judge sb/sthg.

**Urteilskraft** *die* judgement.
**Urteils|spruch** *der* verdict.
**Uruguay** *nt* Uruguay.
**Ur|wald** *der* primeval forest; [tropisch] jungle.
**urwüchsig** [ˈuːɐ̯vyːksɪç] *adj* [Garten, Gelände] natural; [Sprache, Humor] earthy; [Stärke] elemental.
**Urzu|stand** *der* original state.
**USA** [uːˈɛsaː] (*abk für* **United States of America**) *die* USA.
**Usbekistan** *nt* Uzbekistan.
**User** [ˈjuːzɐ] (*pl* -) *der* EDV user.
**Usus** *der:* **das ist bei jm so** ~ *fam* it's the custom with sb.
**usw.** (*abk für* **und so weiter**) etc.
**Utensilien** [utɛnˈziːliən] *pl* equipment (U).
**Uterus** *der* MED uterus.
**Utopie** [utoˈpiː] (*pl* -n) *die* utopia.
**utopisch** *adj* utopian.
**u. U.** (*abk für* **unter Umständen**) possibly.
**UV** (*abk für* **ultraviolett**) *adj* UV.
**u. v. a.** (*abk für* **und viele(s) andere**) and many others.
**u. v. a. m.** (*abk für* **und viele andere mehr**) and many others too.
**u. zw.** (*abk für* **und zwar**) to be precise.

**v, V** [faʊ] (*pl* - ODER -s) *das* v, V.
➡ **V** (*abk für* **Volt**) V.
**v.** *abk für* **von**.
**V.** (*abk für* **Vers**) v.
**v. a.** (*abk für* **vor allem**) above all.
**vage** [ˈvaːɡə], **vag** [vaːk] (*kompar* **vager**; *superl* **vagste**) *adj* vague ◇ *adv* vaguely.
**Vagina** [vaˈɡiːna] (*pl* -nen) *die* MED vagina.
**Vakuum** [ˈvaːkuʊm] (*pl* -kuen) *das* vacuum.
**vakuumverpackt** [ˈvaːkuʊmfɛɐ̯pakt] *adj* vacuum-packed.
**Vamp** [vɛmp] (*pl* -s) *der* vamp.
**Vampir** [ˈvampiːɐ̯] (*pl* -e) *der* vampire.

**Vandalismus** [vandaˈlɪsmʊs] *der* vandalism.
**Vanille** [vaˈnɪljə, vaˈnɪlə] *die* vanilla.
**Vanille|eis** *das* vanilla ice cream.
**Vanille|pudding** *der* vanilla-flavoured blancmange.
**Vanille|zucker** *der* vanilla sugar.
**variabel** [vaˈrja:bl̩] (*kompar* **variabler**; *superl* **variabelste**) *adj* variable ◇ *adv* variably.
**Variable** [vaˈrja:blə] (*pl* -n) *die* MATH & PHYS variable.
**Variante** [vaˈrjantə] (*pl* -n) *die geh* variant; **eine ~ zu etw** a variant of sthg.
**Variation** [variaˈtsjoːn] (*pl* -en) *die* variation.
**Varietee, Variété** [varjeˈteː] (*pl* -s) *das* variety show.
**variieren** [variˈiːrən] *vt* & *vi* to vary.
**Vase** [ˈvaːzə] (*pl* -n) *die* vase.
**Vaseline** [vazeˈliːnə] *die* Vaseline®.
**Vater** (*pl* **Väter**) *der* father; ~ **Staat** *hum* the State.
**Vater|land** *das* homeland.
**väterlich** *adj* - **1.** [des Vaters] paternal - **2.** [wohlwollend] fatherly ◇ *adv* [wohlwollend] in a fatherly way.
**väterlicherseits** *adv* on one's father's side; **Großeltern/Onkel/Verwandte** ~ grandparents/uncle/relations on one's father's side.
**Vater|tag** *der* Father's Day.
**Vaterunser** (*pl* -) *das* REL: **das** ~ the Lord's Prayer; **das** ~ **beten** to say the Lord's Prayer.
**Vati** (*pl* -s) *der fam* dad.
**Vatikan** [vatiˈkaːn] *der:* **der** ~ the Vatican.
**V-Aus|schnitt** *der* V-neck.
**VB** *abk für* **Verhandlungsbasis**.
**v. Chr.** (*abk für* **vor Christus**) BC.
**VDI** [faʊdeːˈiː] (*abk für* **Verband der deutschen Industrie**) *der* Association of German Industry.
**Veganer** (*pl* -) *der* vegan.
**Vegetarier, in** [vegeˈtaːrjɐ, rɪn] (*mpl* -; *fpl* -nen) *der, die* vegetarian.
**vegetarisch** [vegeˈtaːrɪʃ] *adj* vegetarian ◇ *adv:* ~ **leben/essen** to be a vegetarian.
**Vegetation** [vegetaˈtsjoːn] (*pl* -en) *die* vegetation (U).
**vegetieren** [vegeˈtiːrən] *vi abw* to live from hand to mouth.
**vehement** [veheˈmɛnt] *geh adj* vehement ◇ *adv* vehemently.
**Veilchen** [ˈfaɪlçən] (*pl* -) *das* - **1.** [Blume] violet - **2.** *fam fig* [blaues Auge] black eye.

**V**

**Velours** [vəˈluːɐ̯] (pl -) der velour.

**Vene** [ˈveːnə] (pl -n) die MED vein.

**Venedig** [veˈneːdɪç] nt Venice.

**Venezuela** nt Venezuela.

**Ventil** [vɛnˈtiːl] (pl -e) das valve.

**Ventilation** [vɛntilaˈtsi̯oːn] (pl -en) die ventilation (U).

**Ventilator** [vɛntiˈlaːtɔr] (pl -toren) der fan.

**verabreden** vt to arrange; etw mit jm ~ to arrange sthg with sb.
- sich verabreden ref to arrange to meet; sich mit jm ~ to arrange to meet sb.

**Verabredung** (pl -en) die - 1. [Treffen - geschäftlich] appointment; [ - mit Freund] date - 2. [Übereinkommen] arrangement; eine ~ treffen to come to an arrangement.

**verabreichen** vt to administer; jm etw ~ amt to administer sthg to sb.

**verabscheuen** vt to detest.

**verabschieden** vt - 1. [zum Abschied] to say goodbye to - 2. [Gesetz] to pass.
- sich verabschieden ref [Auf Wiedersehen sagen] to say goodbye; sich von jm ~ to say goodbye to sb.

**Verabschiedung** (pl -en) die - 1. [zum Abschied] farewell - 2. [von Gesetz] passing (U).

**verachten** vt to despise; das ist nicht zu ~ that's not to be sneezed at.

**verächtlich** adj - 1. [missbilligend] contemptuous - 2. [verachtenswert] despicable; jn/etw ~ machen to run sb/sthg down <> adv - 1. [missbilligend] contemptuously - 2. [verachtenswert] despicably.

**Verachtung** die contempt.

**verallgemeinern** vt & vi to generalize.

**Verallgemeinerung** (pl -en) die generalization.

**veraltet** adj obsolete.

**Veranda** [veˈranda] (pl -den) die veranda.

**veränderlich** adj [Wetter, Stimmung] changeable; [Größe] variable.

**verändern** vt to change.
- sich verändern ref - 1. [anders werden] to change - 2. [eine andere Stelle annehmen] to change one's job.

**Veränderung** die change.

**verängstigt** adj frightened.

**verankern** vt [anbringen] to fix; [Schiff] to anchor; fest verankert sein fig to be firmly established.

**Verankerung** (pl -en) die - 1. [das Anbringen] fixing (U); [Befestigung] fixture; [von Schiff] anchoring (U) - 2. [von Rechten] establishment (U).

**veranlagt** adj: melancholisch ~ sein to have a melancholic disposition; homosexuell ~ sein to have homosexual tendencies (pl).

**Veranlagung** (pl -en) die disposition; [künstlerisch] bent; homosexuelle ~ homosexual tendencies (pl).

**veranlassen** vt: jn ~, etw zu tun, jn zu etw ~ to make sb do sthg; etw ~ to arrange for sthg.

**Veranlassung** (pl -en) die - 1. [Veranlassen] instigation; auf js ~ (hin) at sb's instigation - 2. [Anlass] reason; keine ~ haben, etw zu tun to have no reason to do sthg.

**veranschaulichen** vt to illustrate.

**veranschlagen** vt to estimate; etw zu hoch/niedrig ~ to overestimate/underestimate sthg.

**veranstalten** vt - 1. [organisieren] to organize - 2. fam [machen] to make.

**Veranstalter, in** (mpl -; fpl -nen) der, die organizer.

**Veranstaltung** (pl -en) die - 1. [Ereignis] event - 2. [Organisation] organization.

**Veranstaltungskalender** der calendar of events.

**verantworten** vt to take responsibility for.
- sich verantworten ref: sich vor jm/etw ~ to answer to sb/sthg; sich für ODER wegen etw ~ to answer for sthg.

**verantwortlich** adj responsible; für jn/etw ~ sein to be responsible for sb/sthg; jn für etw ~ machen to hold sb responsible for sthg.

**Verantwortung** (pl -en) die responsibility; jn zur ~ ziehen to call sb to account; auf eigene ~ on one's own responsibility.

**verantwortungslos** adj irresponsible <> adv irresponsibly.

**verantwortungsvoll** adj responsible <> adv responsibly.

**verarbeiten** vt - 1. [Material] to process; etw zu etw ~ to make sthg into sthg - 2. [Eindruck, Erlebnis] to digest; [Misserfolg] to come to terms with.

**Verarbeitung** (pl -en) die - 1. [von Rohstoffen] processing (U) - 2. [Qualität] quality - 3. [psychisch] coming to terms with the past.

**verärgern** vt to annoy.

**Verärgerung** (pl -en) die annoyance (U).

**verarmt** adj impoverished.

**verarschen** vt salopp to take the piss out of.

**verarzten** vt to treat.

**verästelt** adj [Baum] branchy; [Fluss] with many tributaries.

**verausgaben** vt amt to spend.
- sich verausgaben ref to overexert o.s.

**veräußern** vt to dispose of.

**Verb** [vɛrp] (*pl* -en) *das* GRAM verb; **ein starkes/ schwaches ~** a strong/weak verb.

**verbal** [vɛr'baːl] *adj* verbal <> *adv* verbally.

**Verband** (*pl* -bände) *der* - **1.** [für Wunden] bandage; **einen ~ anlegen** to apply a bandage - **2.** [Organisation] association - **3.** [Gruppe] unit.

**Verband|kasten, Verbands|kasten** *der* first-aid box.

**Verbandzeug, Verbandszeug** *das* first-aid kit.

**verbannen** *vt* to exile.

**Verbannung** (*pl* -en) *die* exile (U).

**verbarrikadieren** *vt* to barricade.
➤ **sich verbarrikadieren** *ref* to barricade o.s. in.

**verbauen** *vt* - **1.** *abw* [schlecht bauen] to botch - **2.** [Aussicht] to block - **3.** *fig* [Zukunft] to spoil - **4.** [verbrauchen] to use up in building.

**verbeißen** (*prät* verbiss; *perf* hat verbissen) ➤ **sich verbeißen** *ref*: **sich in etw (A) ~** [sich festbeißen] to sink its teeth into sthg; *fig* [sich auf etw konzentrieren] to get one's teeth into sthg.

**verbergen** (*präs* verbirgt; *prät* verbarg; *perf* hat verborgen) *vt* to hide; **etw vor jm ~** to hide sthg from sb; **nichts zu ~ haben** to have nothing to hide.
➤ **sich verbergen** *ref* to hide.

**verbessern** *vt* - **1.** [Leistung] to improve - **2.** [Fehler] to correct.
➤ **sich verbessern** *ref* - **1.** [besser werden] to improve - **2.** [sich korrigieren] to correct o.s. - **3.** [sozial, finanziell] to better o.s.

**Ver|besserung** *die* - **1.** [gen] improvement - **2.** [Korrigieren, Text] correction - **3.** [Aufstieg] betterment.

**Verbesserungsvor|schlag** *der* suggestion for improvement.

**verbeugen** ➤ **sich verbeugen** *ref* to bow; **sich vor jm ~** to bow to sb.

**Verbeugung** (*pl* -en) *die* bow.

**verbiegen** (*prät* verbog; *perf* hat verbogen) *vt* to bend.
➤ **sich verbiegen** *ref* to bend.

**verbieten** (*prät* verbot; *perf* hat verboten) *vt* [Handlung] to forbid; [Partei] to ban; **jm ~, etw zu tun** to forbid sb to do sthg.
➤ **sich verbieten** *ref* to be out of the question.

**verbilligt** *adj* reduced <> *adv* at a reduced price.

**verbinden** (*prät* verband; *perf* hat verbunden) *vt* - **1.** [Wunde] to bandage - **2.** [Werkstücke, Material] to join - **3.** [Orte, Punkte] to connect - **4.** [am Telefon] to put through; **jn mit jm ~** to put sb through to sb - **5.** [zubinden]: **jm die Augen ~** to blindfold sb - **6.** [kombinieren]: **etw mit etw ~** to combine sthg with sthg

- **7.** [Freunde, Bekannte] to unite - **8.** [Gedanken] to associate <> *vi* - **1.** [am Telefon]: **ich verbinde** I'll put you through; **falsch verbunden!** wrong number! - **2.** [danken]: **jm sehr verbunden sein** *geh* to be much obliged to sb.
➤ **sich verbinden** *ref* - **1.** [Stoffe, Materialien] to combine - **2.** [zusammentreffen] to be combined - **3.** [Vorstellungen, Assoziationen]: **sich mit jm/etw ~** to be associated with sb/sthg.

**verbindlich** *adj* - **1.** [Person] friendly - **2.** [Zusage] binding; **etw ist für jn ~** sthg is binding on sb <> *adv* - **1.** [lächeln] in a friendly manner - **2.** [verpflichtend]: **er hat ~ zugesagt** he has firmly accepted.

**Ver|bindung** *die* - **1.** [Aneinanderfügen] joining (U) - **2.** [Kombination & CHEM] combination; **eine chemische ~** a chemical compound - **3.** [zwischen Orten, Punkten] link - **4.** [Zusammenhang, am Telefon, Verkehrsverbindung] connection; **keine ~ bekommen** to be unable to get through - **5.** [mit Erinnerung] association - **6.** [zu Freund, Bekannten] contact; **sich mit jm in ~ setzen** to contact sb; **in ~ bleiben** to stay in touch - **7.** [Gruppe]: **eine studentische/schlagende ~** a student/duelling fraternity.

**verbissen** *pp* ⊳ **verbeißen** <> *adj* [Kampf, Person] dogged; [Miene] grim <> *adv* [arbeiten, kämpfen] doggedly; [betrachten] grimly.

**verbitten** (*prät* verbat; *perf* hat verbeten) *vt*: **sich (D) etw ~** to refuse to put up with sthg.

**verbittert** *adj* bitter <> *adv* with bitterness.

**Verbitterung** *die* bitterness.

**verblassen** (*präs* verblasst; *prät* verblasste; *perf* ist verblasst) *vi* to fade.

**verbleiben** (*prät* verblieb; *perf* ist verblieben) *vi* - **1.** [übereinkommen]: **wie seid ihr gestern verblieben?** what did you arrange yesterday?; **wir sind damit so verblieben, dass ...** we left it that ... - **2.** [bleiben, übrig bleiben] to remain.

**verbleit** *adj*: **~es Benzin** leaded petrol; **~es Super** super leaded.

**verblendet** *adj* deluded.

**verblichen** *adj* - **1.** [blass] faded - **2.** *geh* [verstorben] departed.

**verblöden** (*perf* hat/ist verblödet) *vi (ist)* & *vt (hat)* to turn into a moron.

**verblüffen** *vt* to amaze; **verblüfft sein** to be taken aback <> *vi* to be amazing.

**verblüffend** *adj* amazing <> *adv* amazingly.

**verblüht** *adj* - **1.** [Pflanze] faded - **2.** [Person] past one's prime.

**verbluten** (*perf* ist verblutet) *vi* to bleed to death.

**verbohrt** *adj* stubborn <> *adv* stubbornly.

**verborgen** *pp* ⊳ **verbergen** <> *adj* hidden.

**V**

**Verborgene** *das (ohne pl)* ► **im Verborgenen** *adv* in obscurity.

**Verbot** *(pl -e) das* ban.

**verboten** *pp* ► **verbieten** ◇ *adj* **- 1.** [nicht erlaubt] banned; **~ sein** to be forbidden; '**streng ~!**' 'strictly prohibited!' **- 2.** *fam* [schrecklich] horrendous; **~ aussehen** *fam* to look a real sight.

**Verbotsschild** *(pl -er) das sign indicating a restriction, e.g.* "*no parking*", "*no entry*", *etc.*

**Verbrauch** *der* consumption; **der ~ von** ODER **an etw** *(D)* the consumption of sthg; **sparsam im ~** economical.

**verbrauchen** *vt* to consume.

**Verbraucher, in** *(mpl -; fpl -nen) der, die* consumer.

**Verbraucherschutz** *der* consumer protection.

**Verbrauchsgüter** [fɛɐ̯'brauxsgyːtɐ] *pl* consumer goods.

**verbrechen** *(präs* **verbricht***; prät* **verbrach***; perf* **hat verbrochen***) vt fam:* **wer hat denn das verbrochen?** who's responsible for this?; **was hat er jetzt schon wieder verbrochen?** what's he been up to now?

**Verbrechen** *(pl -) das* crime; **ein ~ begehen** to commit a crime; **ein ~ gegen etw** a crime against sthg.

**Verbrechensbekämpfung** *die* fight against crime.

**Verbrecher, in** *(mpl -; fpl -nen) der, die* criminal.

**verbrecherisch** *adj* criminal.

**verbreiten** *vt* to spread.
► **sich verbreiten** *ref* **- 1.** [sich ausbreiten] to spread; **weit verbreitet** widespread **- 2.** *abw* [sich auslassen]: **sich über etw** *(A)* **~** to hold forth about sthg.

**verbreitern** *vt* to widen.
► **sich verbreitern** *ref* to widen.

**Verbreitung** *die* spreading.

**verbrennen** *(prät* **verbrannte***; perf* **hat/ist verbrannt***) vt (hat)* **- 1.** [durch Feuer] to burn **- 2.** [Kalorien] to convert ◇ *vi (ist)* **- 1.** [durch Feuer] to burn **- 2.** [Kalorien] to be converted.
► **sich verbrennen** *ref* to burn o.s.

**Verbrennung** *(pl -en) die* **- 1.** [Verbrennen - von Holz, Kraftstoff] burning; [ - von Kohlenhydraten] conversion **- 2.** [Wunde] burn; **eine ~ ersten/zweiten/dritten Grades** a first/second/third-degree burn.

**Verbrennungslmotor** *der* internal-combustion engine.

**verbringen** *(prät* **verbrachte***; perf* **hat verbracht***) vt* **- 1.** [Zeit] to spend **- 2.** *amt* [bringen] to take.

**verbrüdern** ► **sich verbrüdern** *ref:* **sich mit jm ~** to avow eternal brotherhood with sb; [mit Feind] to fraternize with sb.

**verbrühen** *vt* to scald.
► **sich verbrühen** *ref* to scald o.s.

**verbuchen** *vt* to enter; **einen Sieg für sich ~ können** to notch up a success; **der Betrag wurde auf ihren Konto verbucht** the sum was credited to her account.

**Verbund** *(pl -e) der* WIRTSCH association.

**verbünden** ► **sich verbünden** *ref* to form an alliance; **sich mit jm ~** to form an alliance with sb.

**Verbündete** *(pl -n) der, die* ally.

**verbürgen** *vt* to guarantee.
► **sich verbürgen** *ref:* **sich für jn/etw ~** to vouch for sb/sthg.

**verbüßen** *vt* to serve.

**verchromt** *adj* chromium-plated.

**Verdacht** *(pl -e) der* suspicion; **im ~ stehen** to be under suspicion; **jn im** ODER **in ~ haben** to suspect sb; **~ schöpfen** to become suspicious.

**verdächtig** *adj* suspicious; **sich ~ machen** to arouse suspicion ◇ *adv* suspiciously.

**verdächtigen** *vt* to suspect; **jn einer Sache** *(G)* **~** to suspect sb of sthg.

**verdammt** *fam adj* & *adv* [übel] damned ◇ *interj* damn!

**verdampfen** *(perf* **ist verdampft***) vi* to vaporize.

**verdanken** *vt:* **jm etw ~** to owe sthg to sb.

**verdarb** *prät* ► **verderben**.

**verdauen** *vt* to digest.

**verdaulich** *adj:* **leicht/schwer ~** easy/hard to digest.

**Verdauung** *die* digestion.

**Verdeck** *(pl -e) das* [von Autos] hood.

**verdecken** *vt* [zudecken] to cover; [verbergen] to conceal; **jm die Sicht ~** to block sb's view.

**verdenken** *(prät* **verdachte***; perf* **hat verdacht***) vt:* **jm etw nicht ~ können** not to be able to hold sthg against sb.

**verderben** *(präs* **verdirbt***; prät* **verdarb***; perf* **hat/ist verdorben***) vi (ist)* to go off ◇ *vt (hat)* to spoil; [völlig] to ruin; **jm die Laune ~** to put sb in a bad mood; **es sich** *(D)* **mit niemandem/nicht ~ wollen** *fig* not to want to fall out with anyone.

**verderblich** *adj* perishable.

**verdeutlichen** *vt:* **jm etw ~** to explain sthg to sb.

**verdichten** ► **sich verdichten** *ref* to thicken.

**verdienen** *vt* **- 1.** [Gehalt, Gewinn] to earn

**- 2.** [Lob, Strafe] to deserve ⬦ *vi* to earn; **gut/ schlecht ~** to be well/poorly paid.

**Ver|dienst** *der* [Entgelt] earnings *(pl)* ⬦ *das* [Leistung] achievement.

**Verdienstaus|fall** *der* loss of earnings.

**verdient** *adj* outstanding; **sich um etw ~ machen** to render great service to sthg ⬦ *adv* deservedly.

**verdirbt** *präs* ▷ **verderben.**

**verdonnern** *vt:* **jn zu etw ~** *fam* to sentence sb to sthg; [zu Geldstrafe] to make sb pay sthg.

**verdoppeln** *vt* [Gewinn, Einsatz] to double; [Anstrengungen] to redouble.
◆ **sich verdoppeln** *ref* to double.

**Verdoppelung, Verdopplung** *(pl -en) die* [von Gewinn, Einsatz] doubling *(U)*; [von Anstrengungen] redoubling *(U)*.

**verdorben** *pp* ▷ **verderben.**

**verdrängen** *vt* **- 1.** [räumlich] to force out; **jn/ etw aus etw ~** to force sb/sthg out of sthg **- 2.** [psychisch] to repress.

**Verdrängung** *(pl -en) die* **- 1.** [psychisch] repression *(U)* **- 2.** [Abdrängen - von Person] ousting.

**verdreckt** *adj* filthy.

**verdrehen** *vt* to twist; **die Augen ~** to roll one's eyes.

**verdreifachen** *vt* to triple.
◆ **sich verdreifachen** *ref* to triple.

**verdrossen** *adj* sullen ⬦ *adv* sullenly.

**verdrücken** *vt fam* [essen] to put away.
◆ **sich verdrücken** *ref fam* [sich davonstehlen] to slip away.

**Verdruss** *der* annoyance.

**verduften** *(perf* ist **verduftet)** *vi fam* to make off.

**verdünnen** *vt* to dilute; [Farbe, Soße] to thin; [Kaffee, Wein] to water down.

**Verdünner** *(pl -) der* thinner.

**Verdünnung** *(pl -en) die* **- 1.** [Verdünnen - gen] dilution *(U)*; [ - von Farbe] thinning *(U)*; [ - Kaffee, Wein] watering down *(U)* **- 2.** [Substanz] thinner.

**verdunsten** *(perf* ist **verdunstet)** *vi* to evaporate.

**verdursten** *(perf* ist **verdurstet)** *vi* to die of thirst.

**verdutzt** *adj* nonplussed.

**verehren** *vt* **- 1.** [Gottheit] to worship **- 2.** *geh* [Person] to admire **- 3.** *iron* [schenken]: **jm etw ~** to present sb with sthg.

**Verehrer, in** *(mpl -; fpl -nen) der, die* admirer.

**Verehrung** *die* **- 1.** [von Gottheit] worship **- 2.** *geh* [für Person] admiration.

**vereidigen** *vt* to swear in.

**Verein** *(pl -e) der* [für Sport und Hobby] club; [gemeinnützig] society; **eingetragener ~** registered society.

**VEREIN**

A lot of people in Germany belong to associations, clubs and community groups. A club or association exists for almost every hobby. These clubs are generally purely recreational rather than political in nature.

**vereinbar** *adj* compatible; **mit etw ~ sein** to be compatible with sthg; **etw ist mit etw zeitlich ~** sthg can be fitted in with sthg.

**vereinbaren** *vt* **- 1.** [verabreden]: **etw mit jm ~** to agree sthg with sb; [Termin, Treffpunkt] to arrange sthg with sb **- 2.** [vereinen]: **etw mit etw ~** to reconcile sthg with sthg.

**Vereinbarung** *(pl -en) die* agreement; [von Termin, Treffpunkt] arrangement; **eine ~ treffen** to come to an agreement.

**vereinen** *vt* [Gruppen, Länder] to unite; [Meinungen] to reconcile; [Eigenschaften] to combine.
◆ **sich vereinen** *ref* [Gruppen, Länder] to unite; [Eigenschaften] to be combined.

**vereinfachen** *vt* to simplify.

**vereinheitlichen** *vt* to standardize.

**vereinigen** *vt* [Länder, Gebiete] to unite; [Firmen] to merge; **mehrere Titel auf sich ~** to hold several titles.
◆ **sich vereinigen** *ref* [Statten, Gruppen] to unite; [Flüsse] to join up.

**Vereinigte Arabische Emirate** *pl* United Arab Emirates.

**Vereinigte Staaten (von Amerika)** *pl* United States (of America).

**Ver|einigung** *die* **- 1.** [Vereinigen - von Staaten] uniting *(U)*; [ - von Firmen] merging *(U)* **- 2.** [Gruppe] organization.

**vereinnahmen** *vt* **- 1.** [Person] to monopolize **- 2.** [Geld] to take.

**Vereinsmit|glied** *das* [in Sportverein] club member; [gemeinnützig] member of a/the society.

**vereint** *adj* united ⬦ *adv* together.

**Vereinte Nationen** *pl* United Nations.

**vereinzelt** *adj* [Regen] occasional; [Person, Überreste] odd ⬦ *adv* occasionally.

**vereist** *adj* icy.

**vereiteln** *vt* to thwart.

**verenden** *(perf* ist **verendet)** *vi* to perish.

**vererben** *vt* **- 1.** [Güter]: **jm etw ~** to leave sthg to sb **- 2.** [Merkmal, Eigenschaft, Krankheit] to pass on; **etw auf jn ~** to pass sthg on to sb.

**Vererbung** *(pl -en) die* heredity *(U)*; **wir untersuchen die ~ von bestimmten Eigenschaften** we

**V**

are investigating the way in which certain characteristics are passed on.

**verewigen** *vt* to immortalize.
➧ **sich verewigen** *ref fam hum* to immortalize o.s.

**Verf.** *abk für* **Verfasser.**

**verfahren¹** (*präs* **verfährt;** *prät* **verfuhr;** *perf* **hat/ist verfahren**) *vi (ist)* to proceed; **mit jm/ etw ~** to deal with sb/sthg.
➧ **sich verfahren** *ref* to get lost.

**verfahren²** *adj* hopeless.

**Verfahren** (*pl* -) *das* - **1.** [Gerichtsverfahren] proceedings (*pl*) - **2.** [Methode] procedure.

**Verfall** *der* - **1.** [Niedergang - von Gebäude] decay; [ - von Person, Gesundheit] decline - **2.** [von Gutschein, Garantie] expiry.

**verfallen** (*präs* **verfällt;** *prät* **verfiel;** *perf* **ist verfallen**) *vi* - **1.** [Gebäude] to decay; [Person] to decline - **2.** [Gutschein, Garantie] to expire - **3.** [auf etw kommen]: **auf jn/etw ~** to hit on sb/ sthg - **4.** [geraten]: **in etw (A) ~** to lapse into sthg - **5.** [hörig werden]: **jm/einer Sache ~** to become a slave to sb/sthg.

**Verfalls|datum** *das* sell-by date.

**verfälschen** *vt* [Aussage, Tatsachen] to distort; [Geschmack] to adulterate.

**verfänglich** *adj* awkward.

**verfärben** *vt* to discolour.
➧ **sich verfärben** *ref* to change colour; **sich blau/schwarz ~** to turn blue/black.

**verfassen** *vt* to write.

**Verfasser, in** (*mpl* -; *fpl* -nen) *der, die* author.

**Ver|fassung** *die* - **1.** [von Staaten] constitution - **2.** [von Person] condition; **in guter/schlechter ~ sein** in good/poor shape.

**Verfassungsschutz** *der* authority responsible for protecting the German state against anti-constitutional activities.

**verfaulen** (*perf* **ist verfault**) *vi* to rot.

**verfechten** (*präs* **verficht;** *prät* **verfocht;** *perf* **hat verfochten**) *vt* to champion.

**verfehlen** *vt* to miss.

**verfehlt** *adj* misguided; **das wäre ~, ihn dafür zu bestrafen** it would be a mistake to punish him for that.

**verfeindet** *adj* [Personen] estranged; [Gruppen] enemy (*vor Subst*).

**verfeinern** *vt* to refine.

**verfeuern** *vt* - **1.** [verbrennen] to burn - **2.** [verschießen] to fire.

**verfilmen** *vt*: **einen Roman ~** to make a film of a novel.

**Verfilmung** (*pl* -en) *die* - **1.** [Verfilmen] filming (*U*) - **2.** [Film] film version.

**verfilzt** *adj* [Wolle, Pullover] felted; [Haare] matted.

**verfinstern** *vt* to darken.
➧ **sich verfinstern** *ref* to darken.

**Verflechtung** (*pl* -en) *die* interconnection.

**verfliegen** (*prät* **verflog;** *perf* **hat/ist verflogen**) *vi (ist)* - **1.** [Geruch] to disappear; [Flüssigkeit] to evaporate - **2.** [Zeit] to fly by.
➧ **sich verfliegen** *ref* to fly off course.

**verflixt** *fam adj* - **1.** [verdammt] damned - **2.** [groß] incredible <> *adv* [sehr] damned.

**verflochten** *adj*: **mit etw ~ sein** to be interconnected with sthg.

**verflossen** *adj fam* one-time.

**verfluchen** *vt* to curse.

**verflucht** *fam adj* - **1.** [verdammt] damned - **2.** [groß] incredible <> *adv* [sehr] damned.

**verflüchtigen** ➧ **sich verflüchtigen** *ref* [Geruch] to disappear; [Gas] to disperse.

**verfolgen** *vt* - **1.** [folgen, beobachten] to follow - **2.** [Verbrecher, Ziel, Plan] to pursue - **3.** [unterdrücken] to persecute - **4.** [gerichtlich nachgehen]: **etw gerichtlich ~** to prosecute sthg.

**Verfolger, in** (*mpl* -; *fpl* -nen) *der, die* pursuer.

**Verfolgte** (*pl* -n) *der, die*: **politisch ~** victim of political persecution.

**Verfolgung** (*pl* -en) *die* - **1.** [gen] pursuit (*U*) - **2.** [Unterdrückung] persecution - **3.** [gerichtliches Verfolgen]: **strafrechtliche ~** prosecution.

**Verfolgungs|jagd** *die* chase.

**Verfolgungswahn** *der* persecution mania.

**verfrachten** *vt* - **1.** [verladen] to transport - **2.** *fam hum* [transportieren] to cart off.

**Verfremdung** (*pl* -en) *die* alienation (*U*); [in Literatur, Theater] defamiliarization (*U*).

**verfressen¹** *adj salopp abw* piggish.

**verfressen²** (*präs* **verfrisst;** *prät* **verfraß;** *perf* **hat verfressen**) *vt salopp* [Geld] to blow on food.

**verfrüht** *adj* premature <> *adv* prematurely.

**verfügbar** *adj* available.

**verfügen** *vt* to order <> *vi*: **über jn/etw ~** [haben] to have sb/sthg at one's disposal; **über etw (A) ~ können** [bestimmen] to be able to do as one likes with sthg.

**Ver|fügung** *die* - **1.** [Zugriff]: **jm etw zur ~ stellen** to put sthg at sb's disposal; **jm zur ~ stehen** to be at sb's disposal - **2.** [Erlass] order; **eine einstweilige ~** a temporary injunction.

**verführen** *vt* - **1.** [verleiten]: **jn zu etw ~** to tempt sb to do sthg; **jn zum Klauen ~** to encourage sb to steal - **2.** [zum Geschlechtsverkehr] to seduce.

**verführerisch** *adj* - **1.** [anziehend] tempting - **2.** [erotisch] seductive ◇ *adv* - **1.** [anziehend] temptingly - **2.** [erotisch] seductively.

**Verführung** (*pl* -en) *die* seduction (*U*).

**Vergabe** *die* awarding.

**vergammelt** *adj fam abw* - **1.** [verdorben] spoilt - **2.** [heruntergekommen] scruffy.

**vergangen** *pp* ▷ **vergehen** ◇ *adj* [Zeiten] past; ~en Dienstag last Tuesday.

**Vergangenheit** *die* - **1.** [vergangene Zeit] past - **2.** GRAM past tense.

**Vergangenheitsbewältigung** *die* coming to terms with the past.

**vergänglich** *adj* transitory.

**vergasen** *vt* to gas.

**Vergaser** (*pl* -) *der* carburettor.

**vergaß** *prät* ▷ **vergessen**.

**vergeben** (*präs* **vergibt**; *prät* **vergab**; *perf* **hat vergeben**) *vi*: jm ~ to forgive sb ◇ *vt* - **1.** [verzeihen]: jm etw ~ to forgive sb sthg - **2.** [geben] to award - **3.** [verpassen] to miss - **4.** [schaden]: sich (*D*) etwas/nichts ~ to lose/not to lose face.

**vergebens** *adv* in vain.

**vergeblich** *adj* futile ◇ *adv* in vain.

**vergegenwärtigen** *vt*: sich (*D*) etw ~ [sich vorstellen] to imagine sthg ; [sich erinnern] to remember sthg.

**vergehen** (*prät* **verging**; *perf* **hat/ist vergangen**) *vi* (*ist*) - **1.** [Zeit] to pass - **2.** [verschwinden] to disappear; der Spaß ist mir vergangen I'm not enjoying it any more; vor etw (*D*) ~ *fig* to die of sthg. ◆ **sich vergehen** *ref* - **1.** [vergewaltigen]: sich an jm ~ to assault sb (sexually) - **2.**: sich an etw (*D*) ~ [stehlen] to misappropriate sthg.

**Vergeltung** *die* retaliation.

**vergessen** (*präs* **vergisst**; *prät* **vergaß**; *perf* **hat vergessen**) *vt* to forget; vergiss es! *fam fig* forget it! ◆ **sich vergessen** *ref* to forget o.s.

**Vergessenheit** *die*: in ~ geraten to fall into oblivion.

**vergesslich** *adj* forgetful.

**vergeuden** *vt* to waste.

**Vergeudung** (*pl* -en) *die* waste (*U*).

**vergewaltigen** *vt* [sexuell] to rape; [allgemein] to violate.

**Vergewaltigung** (*pl* -en) *die* rape.

**vergewissern** ◆ **sich vergewissern** *ref* to make sure; sich einer Sache (*G*) ~ to make sure of sthg.

**vergießen** (*prät* **vergoss**; *perf* **hat vergossen**) *vt* - **1.** [verschütten] to spill - **2.** [Blut, Tränen] to shed.

**vergiften** *vt* to poison.

◆ sich vergiften *ref* to poison o.s.

**Vergiftung** (*pl* -en) *die* poisoning (*U*).

**vergilbt** *adj* yellowing.

**Vergissmeinnicht** (*pl* -e) *das* forget-me-not.

**vergisst** *präs* ▷ **vergessen**.

**verglasen** *vt* to glaze.

**Vergleich** (*pl* -e) *der* - **1.** [Gegenüberstellung] comparison; im ~ mit ODER zu jm/etw compared to sb/sthg; einen ~ ziehen to make a comparison; der ~ hinkt *fig* that's a poor comparison - **2.** RECHT settlement - **3.** SPORT friendly.

**vergleichbar** *adj* comparable.

**vergleichen** (*prät* **verglich**; *perf* **hat verglichen**) *vt* to compare; jn/etw mit jm/etw ~ to compare sb/sthg to sb/sthg.

**Vergleichsmöglichkeit** [fɛɐ̯'glaiçsmøːklɪçkait] *die* opportunity for comparison.

**vergleichsweise** [fɛɐ̯'glaiçsvaizə] *adv* comparatively.

**vergnügen** ◆ **sich vergnügen** *ref* to enjoy o.s.

**Vergnügen** (*pl* -) *das* - **1.** [Freude] pleasure; Tanzen macht ihr großes ~ she really enjoys dancing; etw macht jm ~ sb enjoys sthg; mit ~! with pleasure! - **2.** [Unterhaltung] fun (*U*). ◆ viel Vergnügen *interj* have fun!

**vergnügt** *adj* - **1.** [Person] cheerful - **2.** [Stunden] enjoyable ◇ *adv* cheerfully.

**Vergnügungsviertel** *das* area of a town where most bars, nightclubs, cinemas, etc are situated.

**vergoldet** *adj* gold-plated.

**vergraben** (*präs* **vergräbt**; *prät* **vergrub**; *perf* **hat vergraben**) *vt* to bury. ◆ **sich vergraben** *ref* to hide o.s. away.

**vergraulen** *vt fam* to put off.

**vergreifen** (*prät* **vergriff**; *perf* **hat vergriffen**) ◆ **sich vergreifen** *ref*: sich an jm ~ [brutal werden] to assault sb; [sexuell] to assault sb (sexually); sich an etw (*D*) ~ [stehlen] to misappropriate sthg.

**vergriffen** *pp* ▷ **vergreifen** ◇ *adj* out of print.

**vergrößern** *vt* to expand; [Foto] to enlarge; [Haus] to extend; [vermehren] to increase ◇ *vi* to magnify. ◆ **sich vergrößern** *ref* - **1.** [größer werden] to expand; [zunehmen] to increase; [Tumor] to increase in size - **2.** [mehr Raum benutzen] to get more space.

**Vergrößerung** (*pl* -en) *die* - **1.** [Vergrößern] expansion (*U*); [von Haus] extension (*U*); [von Tumor] increase in size; [Vermehrung] increase - **2.** [Foto] enlargement.

**Vergrößerungsglas** *das* magnifying glass.

**Vergünstigung** (*pl* -en) *die* concession.

**vergüten** *vt:* jm etw ~ [Unkosten] to reimburse sb for sthg; [Arbeit] to remunerate sb for sthg.

**Vergütung** (*pl* -en) *die* - **1.** [von Unkosten] reimbursement - **2.** [von Arbeit] remuneration.

**verh.** (*abk für* **verheiratet**) m.

**verhaften** *vt* to arrest.

**Verlhaftung** *die* arrest.

**verhallen** (*perf* ist verhallt) *vi* to die away.

**verhalten¹** *adj* restrained ◇ *adv* in a restrained away.

**verhalten²** (*präs* verhält; *prät* verhielt; *perf* hat verhalten) ➤ sich verhalten *ref* - **1.** [sich benehmen] to behave - **2.** [sein] to be; es verhält sich so this is how matters stand; die Sache verhält sich anders this is not the case.

**Verhalten** *das* behaviour.

**Verhaltenslforschung** *die* behavioural research *(U)*.

**verhaltensgestört** *adj* with behavioural problems.

**Verhältnis** (*pl* -se) *das* - **1.** [Relation] ratio; im ~ 1 zu 2 in a ratio of 1 to 2; im ~ zum letzten Jahr compared to last year - **2.** [persönliche Beziehung] relationship; ein gutes ~ zu jm haben to have a good relationship with sb - **3.** [Liebesbeziehung] affair; ein ~ mit jm haben to have an affair with sb.
➤ **Verhältnisse** *pl* [Bedingungen] conditions; über seine ~se leben to live beyond one's means.

**verhältnismäßig** *adv* relatively.

**Verhältniswahlrecht** *das* proportional representation.

**verhandeln** *vt* - **1.** [beraten]: mit jm ~ to negotiate with sb; über etw (A) ~ to negotiate sthg - **2.** [vor Gericht] to hear a case ◇ *vt* - **1.** [aushandeln] to negotiate - **2.** [vor Gericht] to hear.

**Verlhandlung** *die* - **1.** [Beratung] negotiation - **2.** RECHT hearing.

**Verhandlungsbasis** *die* (ohne *pl*) basis for negotiation.

**verhandlungsfähig** *adj* RECHT fit to stand trial.

**verhängen** *vt* - **1.** [zuhängen] to cover - **2.** [Urteil, Verbot] to impose; etw über jn/etw ~ to impose sthg on sb/sthg.

**Verhängnis** (*pl* -se) *das:* jn zum ~ werden to be sb's downfall.

**verhängnisvoll** *adj* [Tag, Begegnung] fateful; [Fehler] disastrous ◇ *adv* disastrously.

**verharmlosen** *vt* to play down.

**verhärten** (*perf* hat/ist verhärtet) *vi* (ist) to harden ◇ *vt* (hat) to harden.

➤ sich verhärten *ref* to harden.

**verhasst** *adj* hated; diese Tricks sind mir ~ I hate these tricks.

**verhauen** *fam vt* - **1.** [schlagen] to beat up - **2.** *fig* [verderben] to mess up.
➤ sich verhauen *ref fig* [sich vertun] to mess up.

**verheddern** ➤ sich verheddern *ref* - **1.** [Fäden] to get tangled up - **2.** [Person] to get into a muddle.

**verheerend** *adj* devastating ◇ *adv* devastatingly.

**verheilen** (*perf* ist verheilt) *vi* to heal.

**verheimlichen** *vt* to keep secret; jm etw ~ to keep sthg secret from sb.

**verheiraten** *vt* to marry.
➤ sich verheiraten *ref* to get married.

**verheiratet** *adj* married; mit jm ~ sein [mit dem Ehepartner] to be married to sb; mit etw ~ sein *fam hum* [auf etw fixiert sein] to be married to sthg.

**verheißungsvoll** *adj* promising ◇ *adv* promisingly.

**verheizen** *vt* - **1.** [verbrennen] to burn - **2.** *salopp abw* [Person] to burn out.

**verhelfen** (*präs* verhilft; *prät* verhalf; *perf* hat verholfen) *vi:* jm zu etw ~ to help sb to get sthg.

**verhext** *adj:* es ist wie ~ it's a real devil.

**verhindern** *vt* to prevent.

**verhindert** *adj* - **1.** [nicht verfügbar]: ~ sein to be unable to come - **2.** [nicht professionell] would-be *(vor Subst)*.

**Verhör** (*pl* -e) *das* interrogation.

**verhören** *vt* to interrogate.
➤ sich verhören *ref* to mishear.

**verhüllen** *vt* to cover.

**verhungern** (*perf* ist verhungert) *vi* to starve to death.

**verhunzen** *vt fam abw* to mess up.

**verhüten** *vt* to prevent ◇ *vi* to take precautions.

**Verhütungslmittel** *das* contraceptive.

**verirren** ➤ sich verirren *ref* to get lost.

**verjagen** *vt* to chase away.

**verjähren** (*perf* ist verjährt) *vi* to come under the statute of limitations.

**Verjährung** (*pl* -en) *die* limitation.

**verjazzen** *vt* to jazz up.

**verjubeln** *vt fam* to blow.

**verjüngen** *vt* [Aussehen, Haut] to rejuvenate; [Belegschaft] to introduce young blood into.
➤ sich verjüngen *ref* to taper.

**verk.** - **1.** (*abk für* **verkaufen**): zu ~ for sale

**- 2.** (*abk für* **verkauft**) sold **- 3.** (*abk für* **verkürzt**) abbrev.

**verkabeln** *vt* **- 1.** [Elektrogerät] to connect up **- 2.** [an Kabelfernsehen] to connect up to cable.

**verkalkt** *adj* **- 1.** [verstopft] furred up **- 2.** *fam* [senil] senile; **~ sein** to be gaga.

**verkappt** *adj* in disguise.

**Ver|kauf** *der* **- 1.** [das Verkaufen] sale; **etw zum ~ anbieten** to offer sthg for sale; **zum ~ stehen** to be for sale **- 2.** [Abteilung] sales *(U)*.

**verkaufen** *vt* **- 1.** [Ware] to sell; **etw an jn ~** to sell sb sthg; **'zu ~!'** 'for sale' **- 2.** *fam* [darstellen]: **(jm) etw als etw ~** to sell (sb) sthg as sthg. ➡ **sich verkaufen** *ref:* **sich gut/schlecht ~** [Ware] to sell well/poorly; [sich darstellen] to sell o.s. well/poorly.

**Ver|käufer, in** *der, die* **- 1.** [beruflich] sales assistant *Br* ODER clerk *Am* **- 2.** [Verkaufende] seller.

**verkäuflich** *adj:* **~ sein** to be for sale; **schwer ~ sein** to be hard to sell.

**Verkehr** *der* **- 1.** [Straßenverkehr] traffic; **dichter ~** heavy traffic **- 2.** [Gebrauch]: **etw aus dem ~ ziehen** [Geld] to withdraw sthg from circulation; [Produkt] to withdraw sthg from sale; **jn aus dem ~ ziehen** *fam* to take sb out of circulation **- 3.** *geh* [Umgang] contact **- 4.** [Geschlechtsverkehr] intercourse.

**verkehren** (*perf* **hat/ist verkehrt**) *vi* **- 1.** (*hat*) *geh* [Person]: **mit jm ~** to associate with sb; **bei jm ~** to frequent sb's house; **in einem Lokal ~** to frequent a bar **- 2.** [Zug, Bus] to run ⬦ *vt* (*hat*): **etw ins Gegenteil ~** to reverse sthg. ➡ **sich verkehren** *ref* to turn.

**Verkehrs|ampel** *die* traffic lights *(pl)*.

**Verkehrs|aufkommen** *das:* **dichtes** ODER **hohes ~** heavy traffic.

**verkehrsberuhigt** *adj:* **~e Zone/Straße** zone/street with traffic calming.

**Verkehrsbetriebe** *pl* public transport services.

**Verkehrs|chaos** *das* chaos on the roads.

**Verkehrs|dichte** *die* volume of traffic.

**Verkehrs|funk** *der* traffic bulletin service.

**verkehrsgünstig** *adj:* **~ gelegen** conveniently situated.

**Verkehrs|kontrolle** *die* traffic check.

**Verkehrs|minister, in** *der, die* minister of transport.

**Verkehrs|ministerium** *das* ministry of transport.

**Verkehrs|mittel** *das:* **die öffentlichen ~** public transport *(U)*.

**Verkehrs|netz** *das* traffic network.

**Verkehrspolizei** *die* (*ohne pl*) traffic police *(pl)*.

**Verkehrs|polizist, in** *der, die* traffic policeman (*f* traffic policewoman).

**Verkehrs|regel** *die* traffic regulation.

**Verkehrs|teilnehmer, in** *der, die* road user.

**Verkehrs|tote** *der* person killed on the roads.

**Verkehrsun|fall** *der* road accident.

**Verkehrsver|bindung** *die* connection.

**Verkehrs|zeichen** *das* road sign.

**verkehrt** *adj* wrong ⬦ *adv* wrongly; **~ fahren** to go the wrong way. ➡ **verkehrt herum** *adv* the wrong way round.

**verkeilen** ➡ **sich verkeilen** *ref:* **sich in etw** *(A)* **~** to become wedged in sthg.

**verkennen** (*prät* **verkannte;** *perf* **hat verkannt**) *vt* [Situation] to misjudge; [Absicht] to mistake.

**Verkettung** (*pl* **-en**) *die* chain.

**verklagen** *vt* to sue.

**verklappen** *vt* to dump.

**verklausulieren** *vt* to provide with restrictive clauses.

**verkleben** (*perf* **hat/ist verklebt**) *vi* (*ist*) to become sticky ⬦ *vt* (*hat*) **- 1.** [beschmieren] to make sticky **- 2.** [Riss] to stick something over.

**verkleiden** *vt* **- 1.** [mit Kostüm] to dress up **- 2.** [Innenwand] to cover; [Gebäude] to face. ➡ **sich verkleiden** *ref* to dress up.

**Ver|kleidung** *die* **- 1.** [Kostüm] costume **- 2.** [das Verkleiden] dressing up **- 3.** [von Innenwand] covering; [von Gebäude] facing.

**verkleinern** *vt* to reduce. ➡ **sich verkleinern** *ref* to decrease.

**Verkleinerung** (*pl* **-en**) *die* reduction *(U)*.

**verklemmt** *adj* inhibited.

**verklingen** (*prät* **verklang;** *perf* **ist verklungen**) *vi* to die away.

**verknallen** ➡ **sich verknallen** *ref fam:* **sich in jn ~** to fall for sb.

**verkneifen** (*prät* **verkniff;** *perf* **hat verkniffen**) *vt:* **sich** *(D)* **etw ~** to suppress sthg.

**verkniffen** *adj* [Gesichtsausdruck] strained; [Mund] pinched.

**verknoten** *vt* to tie together. ➡ **sich verknoten** *ref* to become knotted.

**verknüpfen** *vt* **- 1.** [verknoten] to tie together **- 2.** [verbinden]: **etw mit etw ~** to connect sthg with sthg.

**verkochen** (*perf* **ist verkocht**) *vi* **- 1.** [verdampfen] to boil away **- 2.** [breiig werden] to boil to a mush.

**verkohlen** (*perf* **hat/ist verkohlt**) *vi* (*ist*) to char ⬦ *vt* (*hat*) *fam:* **jn ~** to pull sb's leg.

**V**

**verkommen**[1] (*prät* **verkam**; *perf* **ist verkommen**) *vi* - **1.** [verfallen] to become run-down - **2.** [verderben] to go bad - **3.** [verwahrlosen]: **jn ~ lassen** to let sb go to the bad.

**verkommen**[2] *adj* - **1.** [verdorben] disreputable - **2.** [verfallen] run-down.

**verkorken** *vt* to cork.

**verkorkst** *adj fam* - **1.** [unangenehm] rotten - **2.** [verdorben] upset.

**verkörpern** *vt* to embody.

**verkrachen** ➡ **sich verkrachen** *ref:* **sich mit jm ~** to have a row with sb.

**verkraften** *vt* to cope with.

**verkrampfen** ➡ **sich verkrampfen** *ref* - **1.** [Muskeln] to get cramped - **2.** [Person] to tense up.

**verkratzen** *vt* to scratch.

**verkriechen** (*prät* **verkroch**; *perf* **hat verkrochen**) ➡ **sich verkriechen** *ref* [kriechen] to crawl; [sich verstecken] to hide.

**verkrümmt** *adj* crooked.

**verkrüppelt** *adj* - **1.** [Mensch] crippled - **2.** [Baum] twisted, gnarled.

**verkrustet** *adj:* **der mit Schmutz ~e Boden** the dirt-encrusted floor.

**verkümmern** (*perf* **ist verkümmert**) *vi* to wither (away).

**verkünden** *vt* to announce; [Urteil] to pronounce; [Prophezeiung] to make; **etw lauthals ~ fam** to announce sthg at the top of one's voice.

**verkuppeln** *vt:* **jn mit jm ~** to pair sb off with sb.

**verkürzen** *vt* to shorten; [Leben, Urlaub] to cut short; [Arbeitszeit] to reduce; **die Zeit ~ to** while away the time.

**verladen** (*präs* **verlädt**; *prät* **verlud**; *perf* **hat verladen**) *vt* to load.

**Verlag** (*pl* **-e**) *der* publishing house.

**verlagern** *vt* [Gewicht, Schwerpunkt] to shift; [an einen anderen Ort] to move.
➡ **sich verlagern** *ref* to shift.

**Verllagerung** *die* shift.

**verlangen** *vt* - **1.** [fordern] to demand; [bitten] to ask for; **viel von jm ~** to ask a lot of sb; **das ist (nicht) zu viel verlangt!** that's (not) asking too much! - **2.** [erfordern] to call for - **3.** [Lohn] to ask - **4.** [Ausweis] to ask to see - **5.** [am Telefon]: **jn am Telefon ~** to ask to speak to sb on the phone; **du wirst am Telefon verlangt** there's someone on the phone for you ◇ *vi:* **nach jm/etw ~** [um etw bitten] to ask for sb/sthg; *geh* [sich sehnen] to long for sb/sthg.

**Verlangen** *das* - **1.** [Wunsch] desire - **2.** [Forderung] request.
➡ **auf Verlangen** *adv* on demand.

**verlängern** *vt* - **1.** [zeitlich, räumlich] to extend; [Ausweis] to renew - **2.** [Rock, Ärmel] to lengthen - **3.** [Soße] to thin down.
➡ **sich verlängern** *ref* - **1.** [zeitlich] to be extended - **2.** [räumlich] to grow longer.

**Verlängerung** (*pl* **-en**) *die* - **1.** [von Zeitraum, Strecke] extension - **2.** [von Rock, Ärmel] lengthening; [von Ausweis] renewal - **3.** SPORT extra time.

**Verlängerungslschnur** *die* ELEKTR extension lead *Br* ODER cord *Am*.

**verlangsamen** *vt* to slow down; **das Tempo ~** to reduce speed.
➡ **sich verlangsamen** *ref* to slow down.

**Verlass** *der:* **auf jn/etw ist ~** sb/sthg can be relied on.

**verlassen**[1] (*präs* **verlässt**; *prät* **verließ**; *perf* **hat verlassen**) *vt* to leave.
➡ **sich verlassen** *ref:* **sich auf jn/etw ~** to rely on sb/sthg.

**verlassen**[2] *adj* [menschenleer] deserted.

**verlässlich** *adj* reliable.

**Verlaub** *der geh:* **mit ~ (gesagt)** if you'll pardon me for saying so.

**Verllauf** *der* course; **im ~ von etw/einer Sache** (G) in the course of sthg.

**verlaufen** (*präs* **verläuft**; *prät* **verlief**; *perf* **hat/ist verlaufen**) *vi* (*ist*) - **1.** [Weg, Strecke, Farbe] to run - **2.** [Operation, Prüfung] to go.
➡ **sich verlaufen** *ref* - **1.** [sich verirren] to get lost - **2.** [Menge] to disperse.

**verlauten** (*perf* **ist verlautet**) *vi* to be reported; **etw (über etw) ~ lassen** to say sthg (about sthg).

**verleben** *vt* - **1.** [verbringen] to spend - **2.** [verbrauchen] to fritter away.

**verlegen**[1] *vt* - **1.** [verlieren] to mislay - **2.** [Termin] to postpone - **3.** [an anderen Ort] to move, to transfer - **4.** [Kabel, Teppichboden] to lay - **5.** [Buch] to publish.
➡ **sich verlegen** *ref:* **sich auf etw** (A) **~** to resort to sthg.

**verlegen**[2] *adj* embarrassed; **um etw nicht ~ sein** not to be short of sthg ◇ *adv* in embarrassment.

**Verlegenheit** (*pl* **-en**) *die* - **1.** [Befangenheit] embarrassment; **jn in ~ bringen** to embarrass sb; **jn in die ~ bringen, etw zu tun** to embarrass sb into doing sthg - **2.** [Notlage] difficulty; **in finanzieller ~** in financial difficulties; **jm aus der ~ helfen** to help sb out.

**Verleger, in** (*mpl* **-**; *fpl* **-nen**) *der, die* publisher.

**verleiden** *vt:* **jm etw ~** to spoil sthg for sb.

**Verleih** (*pl* **-e**) *der* - **1.** (*ohne pl*) [das Verleihen] hiring (out) - **2.** [Firma - von Videos, Fahrrädern] rental shop; [ - von Autos] car hire *Br* ODER rental *Am* company.

**verleihen** (*prät* verlieh; *perf* hat verliehen) *vt*
- **1.** [leihen] to lend; [gegen Bezahlung] to hire out
- **2.** [Orden, Titel]: jm etw ~ to award sb sthg
- **3.** [Reiz, Glanz] to give, to lend.

**verleiten** *vt*: jn dazu ~, etw zu tun to lead sb to do sthg.

**verlernen** *vt* to forget; das Klavierspielen ~ to forget how to play the piano.

**verlesen** (*präs* verliest; *prät* verlas; *perf* hat verlesen) *vt* - **1.** [vorlesen] to read out - **2.** [sortieren] to sort.
- sich verlesen *ref* to make a mistake *(when reading).*

**verletzen** *vt* - **1.** [Mensch, Körperteil] to injure; sich den Fuß ~ to injure one's foot - **2.** [Gefühle, Stolz] to hurt - **3.** [Grenze] to violate; [Abkommen] to break.
- sich verletzen *ref* to hurt o.s.; [schwer] to injure o.s.

**verletzlich** *adj* [verletzbar] vulnerable; [empfindlich] sensitive.

**verletzt** *pp* ▷ verletzen ◇ *adj*: ~ sein [eine Wunde haben] to be injured; [gekränkt sein] to be hurt; schwer ~ seriously injured; leicht ~ sein to suffer minor injuries.

**Verletzte** (*pl* -n) der, die injured person; ein Unfall mit vielen ~n an accident in which several people were injured.

**Verletzung** (*pl* -en) die - **1.** [Wunde] injury - **2.** [von Grenzraum] violation; [von Gesetz, Abkommen] infringement.

**verleugnen** *vt* to deny; [Freund] to disown.

**Verleumdung** (*pl* -en) die [mündlich] slander; [schriftlich] libel.

**verlieben** - sich verlieben *ref*: sich (in jn/ etw) ~ to fall in love (with sb/sthg).

**verliebt** *adj* [Person] in love; [Blicke] amorous; in jn ~ sein to be in love with sb ◇ *adv* amorously.

**verlieren** (*prät* verlor; *perf* hat verloren) *vt* to lose; nichts zu ~ haben to have nothing to lose; du hast hier nichts verloren *fam* you've no business here ◇ *vi* - **1.** [nicht gewinnen] to lose; gegen jn ~ to lose to sb - **2.** [einbüßen] to suffer; an etw (D) ~ [Reiz, Schönheit] to lose sthg.
- sich verlieren *ref* - **1.** [Personen] to lose one another - **2.** [Angst, Begeisterung] to evaporate.

**Verlierer, in** (*mpl* -; *fpl* -nen) der, die loser.

**verloben** - sich verloben *ref*: sich (mit jm) ~ to get engaged (to sb).

**Verlobte** (*pl* -n) der, die fiancé (*f* fiancée).

**Verlobung** (*pl* -en) die engagement.

**verlockend** *adj* tempting.

**verlogen** *adj* false.

**verlor** *prät* ▷ verlieren.

**verloren** *pp* ▷ verlieren ◇ *adj* lost.

**verloren gehen** (*perf* ist verloren gegangen) *vi* (*unreg*) to go missing, to disappear; der Geschmack geht durch das Kochen verloren it loses its taste when you boil it; an ihm ist ein Lehrer verloren gegangen he would have made a good teacher.

**verlöschen** (*präs* verlischt; *prät* verlosch ODER verlöschte; *perf* ist verloschen ODER verlöscht) *vi* to go out.

**verlosen** *vt* [kleine Preise] to raffle; [große Gewinne] to give away *(in a prize draw).*

**Verlosung** (*pl* -en) die [von kleinen Preisen] raffle; [von großen Gewinnen] prize draw.

**Verlust** (*pl* -e) der loss.

**verm.** (*abk für* vermieten): zu ~ to let.

**vermachen** *vt*: jm etw ~ to leave sthg to sb (in one's will).

**Vermächtnis** (*pl* -se) das legacy.

**vermarkten** *vt* to market.

**vermasseln** *vt fam*: jm etw ~ to ruin sthg for sb.

**vermehren** *vt* to increase.
- sich vermehren *ref* - **1.** [größer werden] to increase - **2.** [sich fortpflanzen] to reproduce.

**vermehrt** *adj* increased ◇ *adv* increasingly.

**vermeiden** (*prät* vermied; *perf* hat vermieden) *vt* to avoid; das lässt sich nicht ~ that is unavoidable.

**vermeintlich** *adj* supposed ◇ *adv* supposedly.

**vermelden** *vt* to report; es gibt nichts zu ~ there is nothing to report.

**Vermerk** (*pl* -e) der note.

**vermerken** *vt* - **1.** [notieren] to make a note of - **2.** [feststellen] to note.

**vermessen**[1] (*präs* vermisst; *prät* vermaß; *perf* hat vermessen) *vt* to measure; [Land, Wand] to survey.
- sich vermessen *ref* to get the measurements wrong.

**vermessen**[2] *adj* presumptuous.

**vermiesen** *vt fam*: jm etw ~ to spoil sthg for sb.

**vermieten** *vt*: etw (an jn) ~ to rent sthg out (to sb); 'zu ~!' 'to let'.

**Vermieter, in** der, die landlord (*f* landlady).

**Vermietung** (*pl* -en) die renting out.

**vermindern** *vt* to reduce.

**Verminderung** (*pl* -en) die reduction.

**vermischen** *vt* to mix.
- sich vermischen *ref* to mingle.

**vermissen** *vt* - **1.** [sehnsüchtig] to miss - **2.** [suchen]: **ich vermisse meinen Regenschirm** my umbrella is missing; **ich habe dich bei dem Vortrag vermisst** I didn't see you at the talk.

**vermisst** *adj* missing.

**vermitteln** *vi* to mediate ⟨⟩ *vt* - **1.** [Ehe, Kontakt] to arrange - **2.** [Job, Arbeitskraft]: **jm jn/etw ~** to find sb/sthg for sb - **3.** [Gefühl, Eindruck] to convey; [Wissen, Erfahrung] to impart, to pass on; **jm etw ~** to impart sthg to sb, to pass sthg onto sb.

**Vermittler, in** (*mpl* -; *fpl* -nen) *der, die* - **1.** [in Streitfall] mediator - **2.** [von Stellen] agent.

**Vermittlung** (*pl* -en) *die* - **1.** (*ohne pl*) [von Mitarbeitern, Jobs] finding; [von Kontakten, Ehen] arranging; **durch js ~ eine Stelle bekommen** to get a job through sb - **2.** [Firma, Büro] agency - **3.** [Telefonzentrale] exchange.

**Vermögen** (*pl* -) *das* - **1.** [Besitz] fortune; **ein ~ kosten** to cost a fortune - **2.** *geh* [Fähigkeit] ability.

**vermögend** *adj* wealthy.

**Vermögens|berater, in** *der, die* financial adviser.

**Vermögens|steuer** *die* personal wealth tax.

**vermummen** ⟶ **sich vermummen** *ref* [gegen Kälte] to wrap (o.s.) up; [zur Verkleidung] to disguise o.s.

**vermuten** *vt* - **1.** [annehmen] to assume - **2.** [für wahrscheinlich halten] to suspect.

**vermutlich** *adj* probable ⟨⟩ *adv* probably.

**Vermutung** (*pl* -en) *die* - **1.** [Annahme] supposition - **2.** [Verdacht] suspicion.

**vernachlässigen** *vt* - **1.** [gen] to neglect - **2.** [nicht beachten] to ignore.

**vernehmen** (*präs* vernimmt; *prät* vernahm; *perf* hat vernommen) *vt* - **1.** [verhören] to question; [vor Gericht] to examine - **2.** *geh* [hören] to hear.

**Vernehmung** (*pl* -en) *die* questioning; [vor Gericht] examination.

**verneinen** *vt* [Vorschlag] to reject; [Frage] to say no to.

**Verneinung** (*pl* -en) *die* - **1.** [einer Frage] negative answer; [von Vorschlag] rejection - **2.** GRAM: **die ~** the negative.

**vernetzen** *vt* - **1.** to connect, to link - **2.** EDV to network, to connect to the Internet; **vernetzt sein** to be on the Internet ODER online.

**vernichten** *vt* to destroy; [Schädlinge] to exterminate.

**vernichtend** *adj* [Kritik, Niederlage] devastating; [Blick] withering ⟨⟩ *adv* [kritisieren] devastatingly; **jn ~ ansehen** to give sb a withering look.

**Vernichtung** (*pl* -en) *die* destruction; [von Insekten] extermination.

**Vernissage** (*pl* -n) [vɛrni'saːʒ(ə)] *die private preview of a contemporary artist's work, held to open an exhibition.*

**Vernunft** *die* reason; **mit/ohne ~ handeln** to act sensibly/foolishly; **das widerspricht jeder Vernunft** that goes against all common sense; **zur ~ kommen** to come to one's senses; **jn zur ~ bringen** to bring sb to his/her senses.

**vernünftig** *adj* - **1.** [klug] sensible - **2.** [ordentlich] decent; [Preis] reasonable ⟨⟩ *adv* - **1.** [klug] sensibly - **2.** [ordentlich] decently.

**veröffentlichen** *vt* to publish.

**Veröffentlichung** (*pl* -en) *die* publication.

**verordnen** *vt*: **(jm) etw ~** to prescribe sthg (for sb).

**Verordnung** (*pl* -en) *die* - **1.** [von Medikament] prescription - **2.** [von Regel] regulation.

**verpachten** *vt* to lease.

**verpacken** *vt* [Waren] to pack; [Geschenk] to wrap (up).

**Ver|packung** *die* - **1.** [Hülle - von Ware] packaging; [ - von Geschenk] wrapping paper - **2.** [Verpacken] packing.

**verpassen** *vt* - **1.** [Bus, Gelegenheit, Film] to miss - **2.** *fam* [Schlag, Frisur] to give.

**verpatzen** *vt fam* to make a mess of.

**verpesten** *vt abw* to pollute.

**verpfänden** *vt* [Wertstück] to pawn; [Haus] to mortgage.

**verpflanzen** *vt* to transplant; [Haut] to graft.

**verpflegen** *vt* to cater for.

**Verpflegung** *die* - **1.** [das Verpflegen] catering - **2.** [Essen] food.

**verpflichten** *vt* - **1.** [auf etw festlegen] to oblige; [durch Eid] to bind; **jn zu sechs Wochen gemeinnütziger Arbeit ~** to give sb six weeks' community service - **2.** [Schauspieler] to engage; [Mannschaftssportler] to sign ⟨⟩ *vi*: **dieses Angebot verpflichtet nicht zum Kauf** no purchase necessary to take advantage of this offer.

⟶ **sich verpflichten** *ref* to commit o.s.; **sich vertraglich ~** to sign a contract.

**Verpflichtung** (*pl* -en) *die* - **1.** [Pflichten] obligation; **seine gesellschaftlichen ~en** his social commitments - **2.** [von Schauspieler] engaging; [von Mannschaftssportler] signing - **3.** [Schulden] commitment.

**verpfuschen** *vt* to make a mess of.

**verplanen** *vt* - **1.** [falsch planen] to plan badly - **2.** [festlegen - Zeit] to book up; **das Geld ist schon verplant** the money has already been earmarked for something else.

**verplempern** *vt fam* to fritter away.

**verpönt** *adj* frowned upon.

**verprellen** *vt* to drive away.

**verprügeln** vt to beat up.

**verputzen** vt - **1.** to plaster; [Außenwand] to render - **2.** fam [essen] to polish off.

**verquer** adj - **1.** [schief] crooked - **2.** [merkwürdig] weird <> adv - **1.** [schief] at an angle - **2.** [merkwürdig] weirdly.

**Verrat** der betrayal; [gegen Vaterland] treason.

**verraten** (präs **verrät;** prät **verriet;** perf hat **verraten)** vt - **1.** [Person, Gedanken] to betray; [Geheimnis, Versteck] to give away, to betray - **2.** [Gefühle] to show - **3.** [mitteilen]: **er hat mir den Preis nicht ~** he didn't tell me the price.
➡ **sich verraten** ref to give o.s. away.

**Verräter, in** (mpl -; fpl -nen) der, die traitor.

**verräterisch** adj - **1.** [zeigend] telltale - **2.** [denunzierend] treacherous.

**verrechnen** vt to include; **etw mit etw ~** to offset sthg against sthg.
➡ **sich verrechnen** ref - **1.** [falsch rechnen] to make a mistake; **sich um zwei Euro ~** to be two euros out - **2.** [sich täuschen] to miscalculate.

**Verrechnungslscheck** der crossed cheque.

**verrecken** (perf ist **verreckt)** vi fam to die a horrible death.

**verregnet** adj wet.

**verreisen** (perf ist **verreist)** vi to go away; **verreist sein** to be away.

**verreißen** (prät **verriss;** perf hat **verrissen)** vt to tear to pieces.

**verrenken** vt: **sich** (D) **den Arm ~** to dislocate one's arm.

**verrichten** vt to carry out.

**verriegeln** vt to bolt.

**verringern** vt to reduce.
➡ **sich verringern** ref to decrease.

**verrosten** (perf ist **verrostet)** vi to rust.

**verrucht** adj disreputable.

**verrücken** vt to move.

**verrückt** adj - **1.** [geistesgestört] mad; **~ spielen** [Person] to act crazy; [Computer, Auto] to play up; **nach jm/etw ~ sein** fam to be crazy about sb/sthg - **2.** [ausgefallen] crazy <> adv [ausgefallen] crazily.
➡ **wie verrückt** adv fam like mad.

**Verrückte** (pl -n) der, die lunatic.

**Verrücktwerden** das: **das ist (ja) zum ~!** fam it's enough to drive you crazy!

**Verruf** der: **in ~ bringen/kommen** to bring/fall into disrepute.

**verrufen** adj disreputable.

**verrutschen** (perf ist **verrutscht)** vi to slip.

**Vers** (pl -e) der line; **in ~en** in verse; **sich** (D) **kei-** nen **~ auf etw** (A) **machen können** fig to be unable to make sense of sthg.

**Vers.** (abk für **Versicherung)** ins.

**versacken** (perf ist **versackt)** vi - **1.** [einsinken] to sink - **2.** fam [viel trinken] to go on a bender.

**versagen** vi to fail.

**Versagen** das failure; **menschliches ~** human error.

**Versager** (pl -) der failure.

**Versagerin** (pl -nen) die failure.

**versalzen** (perf hat **versalzen)** vt - **1.** [Mahlzeit] to put too much salt in/on - **2.** [Vorhaben] to spoil.

**versammeln** vt to assemble, to gather.
➡ **sich versammeln** ref to assemble, to gather.

**Verlsammlung** die meeting; [im Freien] rally.

**Versammlungsfreiheit** die freedom of assembly.

**Versand** der - **1.** [Versenden] dispatch - **2.** [Abteilung] dispatch department.

**Versandlhaus** das mail order firm.

**Versandhauslkatalog** der mail order catalogue.

**Versandlkosten** pl delivery costs, carriage (U).

**versäumen** vt - **1.** [Zug, Termin] to miss; **du hast nichts versäumt** you didn't miss anything - **2.** [Pflicht] to neglect.

**Versäumnis** (pl -se) das omission; **durch ein ~ des Lehrers** owing to the teacher's negligence.

**versch.** (abk für **verschieden)** diff.

**verschachtelt** adj [Satz] meandering.

**verschaffen** vt: **jm etw ~** to get sb sthg; **sich** (D) **etw ~** to get (hold of) sthg; **sich** (D) **einen Vorteil ~** to gain an advantage; **sich** (D) **Respekt ~** to earn respect.

**verschämt** adj bashful <> adv bashfully.

**verschandeln** vt to ruin.

**verschärfen** vt [Kontrolle] to tighten up; [Lage, Krise] to aggravate.
➡ **sich verschärfen** ref [Gegensätze] to intensify; [Lage, Krise] to get worse.

**verschätzen** ➡ **sich verschätzen** ref to miscalculate.

**verschenken** vt - **1.** [weg geben] to give away - **2.** [als Geschenk] to give (as present) - **3.** [Punkte] to throw away; [Raum] to waste.

**verscherzen** vt: **sich** (D) **etw ~** to throw sthg away.

**verscheuchen** vt [Tier] to chase away; [Angst machen] to scare away.

**verschicken** vt to send out.

**verschieben** (prät **verschob;** perf hat **ver-**

**schoben**) vt - **1.** [Termin] to postpone - **2.** [Möbel] to move - **3.** [schmuggeln] to traffic in.
➡ **sich verschieben** ref - **1.** [Termin] to be postponed - **2.** [verrutschen] to slip.
**Verschiebung** (pl -en) die postponement.

**verschieden** adj - **1.** [unterschiedlich] different; von jm/etw ~ sein to be different from sb/sthg - **2.** [mehrere] various <> adv [unterschiedlich] differently; ~ groß sein to be different sizes; die Aufgaben waren ~ schwer the tasks were of varying degrees of difficulty.

**verschiedentlich** adv on various occasions.

**verschimmeln** (perf ist verschimmelt) vi to go mouldy.

**verschlafen¹** (präs verschläft; prät verschlief; perf hat verschlafen) vi to oversleep <> vt - **1.** [schlafend verbringen] to sleep through - **2.** fam [vergessen] to forget.
➡ **sich verschlafen** ref to oversleep.

**verschlafen²** adj sleepy.

**Verschlag** der [im Garten] shed.

**verschlagen¹** (präs verschlägt; prät verschlug; perf hat verschlagen) vt - **1.** [Appetit] to take away; jm die Sprache ~ to leave sb speechless - **2.** SPORT to mishit.

**verschlagen²** abw adj sly <> adv slyly.

**verschlechtern** vt to make worse.
➡ **sich verschlechtern** ref to get worse, to deteriorate.

**Verschlechterung** (pl -en) die deterioration.

**Verschleiß** der wear (and tear).

**verschleißen** (prät verschliss; perf hat/ist verschlissen) vi (ist) to wear out; diese Teile sind verschlissen these parts are worn out <> vt (hat) to wear out.

**verschleppen** vt - **1.** [Person] to take away (by force) - **2.** [Gegenstand] to hide - **3.** [Verhandlung] to draw out - **4.** [Krankheit] to allow to drag on.

**verschleudern** vt - **1.** [billig verkaufen] to give away - **2.** abw [verschwenden] to throw away.

**verschließen** (prät verschloss; perf hat verschlossen) vt - **1.** [Haus, Tür, Schrank] to lock - **2.** [Kunststoffbehälter] to seal; [Flasche] to stop up; die Augen vor etw (D) ~ to close one's eyes to sthg.
➡ **sich verschließen** ref to close o.s. off.

**verschlimmern** vt to make worse.
➡ **sich verschlimmern** ref to get worse.

**verschlingen** (prät verschlang; perf hat verschlungen) vt to devour; viel Geld ~ to cost a fortune.

**verschlossen** adj [Mensch] reticent; [Raum, Tür] locked; [Umschlag] sealed.

**verschlucken** vt to swallow.

➡ **sich verschlucken** ref to choke.
**Verschluss** der fastener; [von Flasche] top.
➡ **unter Verschluss** adv under lock and key.

**verschlüsseln** vt to encode.

**verschmähen** vt geh to spurn.

**verschmelzen** (präs verschmilzt; prät verschmolz; perf ist verschmolzen) vi: mit etw ~ to blend with sthg.

**verschmutzen** (perf hat/ist verschmutzt) vi (ist) [Kleidung, Wohnung] to get dirty <> vt (hat) [Kleidung, Wohnung] to get dirty; [Umwelt] to pollute.

**verschnaufen** vi to have a breather.

**verschneit** adj snow-covered.

**verschnörkelt** adj ornate.

**verschnupft** adj: ~ sein to have a cold.

**verschnüren** vt to tie up.

**verschollen** adj missing.

**verschonen** vt to spare; jn mit etw ~ to spare sb sthg.

**verschönern** vt to brighten up.

**verschossen** adj fam: in jn ~ sein to have fallen for sb.

**verschränken** vt: die Arme ~ to fold one's arms; die Beine ~ to cross one's legs.

**verschreiben** (prät verschrieb; perf hat verschrieben) vt: jm etw ~ to prescribe sb sthg.
➡ **sich verschreiben** ref: ich habe mich verschrieben I've written it down wrong.

**verschreibungspflichtig** adj available on prescription only.

**verschrieen** adj notorious.

**verschrotten** vt to scrap.

**verschrumpelt** adj shrivelled.

**verschüchtert** adj intimidated.

**verschulden** vt to be to blame for.
➡ **sich verschulden** ref to get into debt.

**Verschulden** das: ohne mein ~ through no fault of mine; durch fremdes ~ through someone else's fault.

**verschuldet** adj in debt.

**verschütten** vt - **1.** [Wasser, Getränk] to spill - **2.** [mit Erde] to bury.

**verschweigen** (prät verschwieg; perf hat verschwiegen) vt [Nachricht] to keep quiet about; [Wahrheit] to conceal; jm etw ~ to conceal sthg from sb.

**verschwenden** vt to waste.

**verschwenderisch** adj [mit Geld] extravagant; [mit Energie] wasteful <> adv [mit Geld] extravagantly; [mit Energie] wastefully.

**Verschwendung** die squandering; so eine ~! what a waste!

**verschwiegen** pp ▷ verschweigen <> adj - **1.** [Mensch] discreet - **2.** [Winkel] secluded.

**Verschwiegenheit** *die* discretion.

**verschwinden** (*prät* **verschwand**; *perf* **ist verschwunden**) *vi* to disappear; **etw ~ lassen** [wegzaubern] to make sthg disappear; *fam* [unterschlagen] to help o.s. to sthg.

**verschwommen** *adj* blurred ◇ *adv* vaguely; **ohne Brille sieht sie alles ~** without her glasses everything looks blurred to her.

**verschwören** (*prät* **verschwor**; *perf* **hat verschwören**) ➡ **sich verschwören** *ref*: **sich gegen jn ~** to conspire against sb.

**Verschwörer, in** (*mpl* -; *fpl* -**nen**) *der, die* conspirator.

**Verschwörung** (*pl* -**en**) *die* conspiracy.

**verschwunden** *pp* ▷ **verschwinden** ◇ *adj* missing.

**versehen** (*präs* **versieht**; *prät* **versah**; *perf* **hat versehen**) *vt* - **1.** [ausrüsten]: **etw mit etw ~** to equip sthg with sthg; **jm mit etw ~** to provide sb with sthg - **2.** [erledigen] to perform.

➡ **sich versehen** *ref* [sich irren] to make a mistake; **ehe man sichs versieht** before you know where you are.

**Versehen** (*pl* -) *das* accident.

➡ **aus Versehen** *adv* accidentally.

**versehentlich** *adj* accidental ◇ *adv* accidentally.

**versenden** (*prät* **versandte** ODER **versendete**; *perf* **hat versandt** ODER **versendet**) *vt* to send.

**versengen** *vt* to scorch.

**versenken** *vt* [Schiff] to sink; [Sarg] to lower.

**Versenkung** (*pl* -**en**) *die* [von Schiff] sinking; [von Sarg] lowering; **in der ~ verschwinden** *fam fig* to disappear from the scene.

**versessen** *adj*: **auf jn/etw ~ sein** to be mad about sb/sthg.

**versetzen** *vt* - **1.** [umstellen] to move; [Angestellten] to transfer, to move; [Schüler] to move up *Br*, to promote *Am* - **2.** [in einen anderen Zustand]: **sich in die Lage eines anderen ~** to put o.s. in somebody else's position; **jn in Erstaunen/Angst ~** to astonish/frighten sb; **etw in Bewegung ~** to set sthg in motion - **3.** [verpfänden] to pawn - **4.** [bei einer Verabredung]: **jn ~** to stand sb up - **5.** [austeilen]: **jm einen Stoß ~** to give sb a push; **jm einen Schlag ~** to hit sb - **6.** [antworten] to retort.

**Versetzung** (*pl* -**en**) *die* - **1.** [beruflich] transfer - **2.** SCHULE moving up *Br*, promotion *Am*.

**verseuchen** *vt* to contaminate.

**versichern** *vt* - **1.** [erklären] to affirm; **jm ~, dass ...** to assure sb that ... - **2.** [bei Versicherung] to insure.

➡ **sich versichern** *ref* - **1.** [bei Versicherung] to insure o.s. - **2.** [Gewissheit]: **sich einer Sache** (G) **~** to assure o.s. of sthg.

**Verlsicherung** *die* - **1.** [vertraglicher Schutz] insurance (U); [Vertrag] insurance policy; **eine ~ (über etw** (A)**) abschließen** to take out insurance ODER an insurance policy (for sthg) - **2.** [Firma] insurance company - **3.** [Angabe] assurance; **eidesstattliche ~** sworn statement.

**Versicherungslbeitrag** *der* insurance premium.

**Versicherungslkarte** *die* insurance card; **grüne ~** green card *Br*, *insurance card required if taking a vehicle abroad.*

**versicherungspflichtig** *adj* subject to compulsory insurance.

**Versicherungsschutz** *der* insurance cover.

**Versicherungslsumme** *die* amount insured.

**versickern** (*perf* **ist versickert**) *vi* to seep away.

**versiegeln** *vt* to seal.

**versinken** (*prät* **versank**; *perf* **ist versunken**) *vi* - **1.** [in Sumpf, Sand, Schnee]: **in etw** (A) **~** to sink into sthg - **2.** [Schiff, Sonne] to sink - **3.** [in Gedanken]: **in etw** (A) **~** to become immersed in sthg.

**Version** [vɛr'zjoːn] (*pl* -**en**) *die* version.

**versöhnen** *vt* [Feinde] to reconcile; [besänftigen] to appease; **jn mit jm ~** to reconcile sb with sb.

➡ **sich versöhnen** *ref* to become reconciled; **sich mit jm ~** to make it up with sb.

**versöhnlich** *adj* - **1.** [Antwort, Stimmung] conciliatory - **2.** [Ende, Ausgang] optimistic ◇ *adv* in a conciliatory way.

**Versöhnung** (*pl* -**en**) *die* reconciliation; [Besänftigung] appeasement.

**versorgen** *vt* - **1.** [versehen]: **jn/sich mit etw ~** to provide sb/o.s. with sthg - **2.** [beliefern - mit Strom, Wasser] to supply - **3.** [pflegen] to look after - **4.** [ernähren] to provide for.

**Versorgung** (*pl* -**en**) *die* - **1.** [mit Lebensmitteln] supply - **2.** [von Patienten] care.

**verspannt** *adj* tense.

**Verlspannung** *die* tension; **~en** tension (U).

**verspäten** ➡ **sich verspäten** *ref* to be late; **sich um eine halbe Stunde ~** to be half an hour late.

**verspätet** *adj* late; [Gratulation] belated ◇ *adv* late.

**Verspätung** (*pl* -**en**) *die* delay; **mit ~ ankommen** to arrive late; **~ haben** to be delayed; **eine Stunde ~ haben** to be an hour late.

**versperren** *vt* to block; **jm den Weg/die Sicht ~** to block sb's way/view.

**verspielen** *vt* [Geld] to gamble away; [Glück,

Chance] to throw away, to squander ⬦ *vi fam:* **er hat bei uns verspielt** he's had it as far as we're concerned.

**verspielt** *adj* [Kind] playful; [Muster] fanciful.

**versprechen** (*präs* **verspricht;** *prät* **versprach;** *perf* **hat versprochen**) *vt* - **1.** [zusagen] to promise; **jm etw ~** to promise sb sthg - **2.** [erwarten]: **sich** *(D)* **etw von jm/etw ~** to hope for sthg from sb/sthg.

➠ **sich versprechen** *ref* [etw Falsches sagen] to trip over one's words.

**Versprechen** (*pl* -) *das* promise.

**Ver|sprecher** *der* slip of the tongue.

**verspüren** *vt* to feel.

**verstaatlichen** *vt* to nationalize.

**Verstand** *der (ohne pl)* [Urteilsvermögen] reason; [Intellekt] mind; [Vernunft] sense; **den ~ verlieren** *fam fig* to go out of one's mind; **jn um den ~ bringen** *fig* to drive sb mad.

**verständig** *adj* [vernünftig] sensible ⬦ *adv* [vernünftig] sensibly.

**verständigen** *vt:* **jn (von etw** ODER **über etw** *(A))* **~** to notify sb (of sthg).

➠ **sich verständigen** *ref* - **1.** [kommunizieren] to make o.s. understood; **sich mit jm ~** to communicate with sb - **2.** [übereinkommen]: **sich über etw** *(A)* **~** to come to an agreement on sthg.

**Verständigung** (*pl* -en) *die* - **1.** [Benachrichtigung] notification - **2.** [Kommunikation] communication - **3.** [Übereinkunft] agreement.

**verständlich** *adj* - **1.** [klar - Worte, Antwort] audible - **2.** [begreiflich - Verhalten, Angst] understandable; [ - Text] comprehensible; **sich ~ machen** to make o.s. understood; **leicht/ schwer ~** easy/difficult to understand ⬦ *adv* [klar] clearly.

**Verständnis** *das* understanding; **~ für jn/ etw haben** to understand sb/sthg.

**verständnisvoll** *adj* understanding ⬦ *adv* understandingly.

**verstärken** *vt* - **1.** [stärker machen] to strengthen - **2.** [intensivieren] to increase; [Bemühungen] to intensify; [Strom] to boost; [Signal, Ton] to amplify - **3.** [Truppen, Team] to reinforce.

➠ **sich verstärken** *ref* [stärker werden] to intensify.

**Verstärker** (*pl* -) *der* amplifier.

**Verstärkung** (*pl* -en) *die* reinforcement; **~ anfordern** to call for reinforcements

**verstaubt** *adj* - **1.** [voller Staub] dusty - **2.** *abw* [veraltet] outmoded.

**verstauchen** *vt:* **sich** *(D)* **den Fuß ~** to sprain one's ankle.

**verstauen** *vt* to pack.

**Versteck** (*pl* -e) *das* hiding place; [von Verbrechern] hideout.

**verstecken** *vt* to hide.

➠ **sich verstecken** *ref:* **sich (vor jm/etw) ~** to hide (from sb/sthg).

**Verstecken** *das:* **~ spielen** to play hide-and-seek.

**versteckt** *adj* hidden; [lächeln] furtive; [Kritik, Drohung] veiled; [Eingang, Mangel] concealed ⬦ *adv* [vorbereiten] secretly; **jn ~ kritisieren** to make a veiled criticism of sb.

**verstehen** (*prät* **verstand;** *perf* **hat verstanden**) *vt* - **1.** [gen] to understand; **ich konnte kein Wort ~** I couldn't understand ODER make out a single word; **etw unter etw** *(D)* **~** to understand sthg by sthg; **versteh mich nicht falsch** don't get me wrong - **2.** [vermögen] to know; **etwas/nichts ~ von ...** to know a bit/ nothing about ...; **sie versteht es, mit Menschen umzugehen** she knows how to handle people ⬦ *vi* to understand; **jm zu ~ geben, dass ...** to give sb to understand that ...

➠ **sich verstehen** *ref* [Personen] to get on; **sich (gut) mit jm ~** to get on well with sb; **das versteht sich von selbst!** that goes without saying!

**versteifen** *vt* to stiffen.

➠ **sich versteifen** *ref* - **1.** [Glied, Gelenk] to stiffen - **2.** [sich festlegen]: **sich auf etw** *(A)* **~** to insist on sthg.

**versteigern** *vt* to auction; **etw meistbietend ~** to sell sthg to the highest bidder.

**Ver|steigerung** *die* auction.

**versteinert** *adj* - **1.** [Pflanze, Tier] fossilized; [Holz] petrified - **2.** [Miene] stony.

**Versteinerung** (*pl* -en) *die* fossil.

**verstellbar** *adj* adjustable.

**verstellen** *vt* - **1.** [verändern] to adjust - **2.** [falsch stellen] to set wrongly; [Stimme, Schrift] to disguise - **3.** [blockieren]: **jm den Weg/die Sicht ~** to block sb's path/view - **4.** [an einen falschen Ort] to put in the wrong place.

➠ **sich verstellen** *ref* - **1.** [zur Täuschung - im Wesen] to play-act - **2.** [sich anders einstellen] to be moved (out of position).

**versteuern** *vt* to pay tax on.

**verstimmt** *adj* - **1.** [Instrument] out of tune - **2.** [Person] disgruntled.

**verstockt** *abw adj* stubborn ⬦ *adv* stubbornly.

**verstohlen** *adj* furtive ⬦ *adv* furtively.

**verstopfen** (*perf* **hat/ist verstopft**) *vt* (hat) to plug (up); [Abfluss] to block ⬦ *vi* (ist) to be blocked (up).

**Verstopfung** (*pl* -en) *die* - **1.** [von Darm] constipation - **2.** [von Rohr, Straße] blockage.

**Verstorbene** (*pl* -n) *der, die geh* deceased.

**verstört** *adj* distraught.

**Ver|stoß** *der* infringement; **ein ~ gegen etw**

[gegen Gesetz] an infringement of sthg; [gegen Anstand] an offence against sthg.

**verstoßen** (*präs* **verstößt;** *prät* **verstieß;** *perf* **hat verstoßen**) *vi:* **gegen etw ~** [Regel, Gesetz] to infringe sthg; [Anstand, Geschmack] to offend against sthg <> *vt* [Kind, Ehefrau] to disown; **jn aus einer Gruppe ~** to throw sb out of a group.

**verstreichen** (*prät* **verstrich;** *perf* **hat/ist verstrichen**) *vt (hat)* [Butter] to spread; [Farbe] to apply <> *vi (ist)* [Zeit] to pass.

**verstreuen** *vt* - **1.** [verteilen] to scatter - **2.** [verschütten] to spill - **3.** [Creme] to spread.

**verstricken** *vt geh:* **jn in etw** (A) **~** to draw sb into sthg; **sich in etw** (A) **~** to get involved in sthg.

**verströmen** *vt* to exude.

**verstümmeln** *vt* to mutilate.

**verstummen** (*perf* **ist verstummt**) *vi geh* to fall silent; [Geräusch] to cease.

**Versuch** (*pl* -e) *der* - **1.** [Handlung] attempt; **einen ~ machen** ODER **unternehmen** to make an attempt - **2.** [wissenschaftlich] experiment.

**versuchen** *vt* to try; [etwas Schwieriges] to attempt; **es mit jm/etw ~** to try sb/sthg <> *vi* [kosten]: **von etw ~** to try sthg.

&#10148; **sich versuchen** *ref:* **sich an** ODER **in etw** (D) **~** to try one's hand at sthg.

**Versuchs|kaninchen** [fɛɐ̯'zuːxskaniːnçən] *das* guinea pig.

**Versuchung** (*pl* -en) *die* temptation.

**versüßen** *vt* [Leben, Befinden] to make more pleasant; [schlechte Situation] to sweeten.

**vertagen** *vt* [verschieben] to postpone; [später fortsetzen] to adjourn.

**vertauschen** *vt* - **1.** [verwechseln] to mix up - **2.** [austauschen]: **etw (gegen/mit etw) ~** to exchange sthg (for sthg).

**verteidigen** *vt* to defend.

&#10148; **sich verteidigen** *ref* to defend o.s.

**Verteidiger, in** (*mpl* -; *fpl* -nen) *der, die* RECHT counsel for the defence.

**Verteidigung** (*pl* -en) *die* defence.

**Verteidigungs|minister, in** *der, die* defence minister.

**Verteidigungs|ministerium** *das* ministry of defence *Br*, defense department *Am*.

**verteilen** *vt* - **1.** [ausgeben] to distribute; [Prospekte] to hand out - **2.** [teilen] to share out - **3.** [Creme] to spread.

&#10148; **sich verteilen** *ref* to spread out.

**Verteiler** (*pl* -) *der* TECH distributor.

**Ver|teilung** *die* distribution.

**verteuern** *vt* to make more expensive.

&#10148; **sich verteuern** *ref* to become more expensive.

**verteufeln** *vt* to condemn.

**vertiefen** *vt* to deepen.

&#10148; **sich vertiefen** *ref* - **1.** [Graben, Loch, Falten] to become deeper - **2.** [Gefühl, Freundschaft] to deepen - **3.** [sich konzentrieren]: **sich in etw** (A) **~** to become engrossed in sthg.

**vertikal** [vɛrti'kaːl] *adj* vertical <> *adv* vertically.

**vertilgen** *vt* - **1.** [aufessen] to devour - **2.** [vernichten] to exterminate.

**vertonen** *vt* [Text] to set to music.

**vertrackt** *adj* complicated <> *adv* in a complicated way.

**Vertrag** (*pl* **Verträge**) *der* contract; **jn unter ~ nehmen** to contract sb.

**vertragen** (*präs* **verträgt;** *prät* **vertrug;** *perf* **hat vertragen**) *vt* to stand, to bear; [Belastung, Kritik, Witz] to take; **sie verträgt keinen Kaffee** coffee doesn't agree with her; **sie kann viel ~ fam** she can hold her drink.

&#10148; **sich vertragen** *ref:* **sich mit jm ~** to get on with sb.

**vertraglich** *adj* contractual <> *adv* contractually.

**verträglich** *adj* [Person, Charakter] easy-going; **gut ~** [Essen] easily digestible; [Medikament] with few side-effects.

**Vertrags|bruch** *der* breach of contract.

**Vertrags|partner, in** *der, die* party to a/the contract.

**vertrauen** *vi:* **jm/einer Sache ~** to trust sb/sthg; **auf etw** (A) **~** to put one's trust in sthg; **auf sein Glück ~** to trust to luck.

**Vertrauen** *das* trust; **zu jm ~ haben** to trust sb; **jn ins ~ ziehen** to take sb into one's confidence.

&#10148; **im Vertrauen** *adv* in confidence.

&#10148; **Vertrauen erweckend** *adj:* **ein ~ erweckender Mensch** a person who inspires confidence.

**Vertrauens|basis** *die* basis of trust.

**Vertrauens|frage** *die:* **die ~ stellen** POL to ask for a vote of confidence.

**Vertrauens|sache** *die* matter of trust.

**vertrauensselig** *adj* trusting <> *adv* trustingly.

**vertrauensvoll** <> *adj* - **1.** [voller Vertrauen] trusting - **2.** [zuversichtlich] confident - **3.** [Beziehung, Zusammenarbeit] based on trust <> *adv* - **1.** [voller Vertrauen] trustingly - **2.** [zuversichtlich] confidently.

**vertrauenswürdig** *adj* trustworthy.

**vertraulich** *adj* - **1.** [geheim] confidential - **2.** [herzlich] familiar <> *adv* [geheim] confidentially.

**verträumt** *adj* dreamy <> *adv* dreamily.

**vertraut** *adj* familiar; [Freund] close; **jm ~ sein**

to be familiar to sb; **mit etw ~ sein** to be familiar with sthg; **sich mit etw ~ machen** to familiarize o.s. with sthg.

**vertreiben** (*prät* **vertrieb;** *perf* **hat vertrieben**) *vt* - **1.** [verjagen] to drive away; [aus Land] to drive out; **jn aus einem Haus ~** to turn sb out of a house - **2.** [verkaufen] to sell - **3.** [Zeit] to pass.

**Vertreibung** (*pl* -en) *die* expulsion.

**vertretbar** *adj* [Meinung] tenable; [Kosten, Risiko] justifiable.

**vertreten** (*präs* **vertritt;** *prät* **vertrat;** *perf* **hat vertreten**) *vt* - **1.** [bei Urlaub, Krankheit] to stand in for - **2.** [Interessen, Firma, Land] to represent - **3.** [Standpunkt, These, Prinzip] to support - **4.** [anwesend]: **~ sein** to be present - **5.** [verletzen]: **sich** *(D)* **den Fuß ~** to twist one's ankle.

**Vertreter, in** (*mpl* -; *fpl* -nen) *der, die* - **1.** [Stellvertreter] stand-in; [von Arzt] locum - **2.** [von Firma, Gruppe] representative - **3.** [von Meinung, Interessen] advocate.

**Vertretung** (*pl* -en) *die* - **1.** [bei Urlaub, Krankheit] replacement - **2.** [von Interessen, Firma, Land] representation - **3.** [Person] representative - **4.** [Filiale] branch; **diplomatische ~** diplomatic mission.

**Vertrieb** *der* - **1.** [Verkauf] sale - **2.** [Abteilung] sales department; **im ~ arbeiten** to work in sales.

**Vertriebene** (*pl* -n) *der, die* - **1.** [Flüchtling]: **die ~n aus dem Krisengebiet** the people driven out of the crisis region - **2.** [Heimatvertriebene] *ethnic German who fled East Prussia, Silesia or Bohemia in 1945.*

**Vertriebsab|teilung** *die* sales department.

**Vertriebskosten** *pl* sales and distribution costs.

**vertrocknen** (*perf* **ist vertrocknet**) *vi* [Boden] to dry out; [Pflanze, Gras] to wither.

**vertrödeln** *vt* to waste.

**vertrösten** *vt* to put off; **jn auf später ~** to put sb off until later.

**vertun** (*prät* **vertat;** *perf* **hat vertan**) *vt* to waste.

➤ **sich vertun** *ref* to get it wrong.

**vertuschen** *vt* [Skandal] to hush up; [Fehler, Wahrheit] to cover up.

**verübeln** *vt:* **jm etw ~** to hold sthg against sb; **ich verübele ihm seine ständige Unpünktlichkeit** I find his constant unpunctuality offensive.

**verüben** *vt* to commit.

**verulken** *vt* to make fun of.

**verunglimpfen** *vt geh* to denigrate.

**verunglücken** (*perf* **ist verunglückt**) *vi* to have an accident; **mit dem Zug ~** to be in a

train crash; **tödlich/schwer ~** to be killed/seriously injured in an accident.

**verunreinigen** *vt* to pollute.

**verunsichern** *vt* to make uneasy.

**verunstalten** *vt* to disfigure.

**veruntreuen** *vt* RECHT to embezzle.

**Veruntreuung** (*pl* -en) *die* RECHT embezzlement.

**verursachen** *vt* to cause.

**Verursacher, in** (*mpl* -; *fpl* -nen) *der, die* amt person responsible.

**Verursacherprinzip** *das principle whereby the person responsible for the damage pays for it.*

**verurteilen** *vt* - **1.** [vor Gericht]: **jn zu etw ~** to sentence sb to sthg - **2.** [kritisieren] to condemn.

**Verur|teilung** *die* - **1.** [vor Gericht] sentencing - **2.** [Missbilligung] condemnation.

**vervielfachen** *vt* to multiply.

➤ **sich vervielfachen** *ref* to multiply.

**vervielfältigen** *vt* to make copies of.

**vervollkommnen** *vt* to perfect.

➤ **sich vervollkommnen** *ref* [Person] to perfect o.s.; [Verfahren] to be perfected.

**vervollständigen** *vt* to complete.

➤ **sich vervollständigen** *ref* to be completed.

**Verw.** - **1.** (*abk für* **Verwaltung**) admin. - **2.** (*abk für* **Verweis**) ref.

**verwachsen¹** [fɛr'vaksn̩] *adj* deformed.

**verwachsen²** [fɛr'vaksn̩] (*präs* **verwächst;** *prät* **verwuchs;** *perf* **ist verwachsen**) *vi* - **1.** [heilen] to heal (up) - **2.** [verbinden]: **mit etw ~ sein** to have very close ties with sthg.

➤ **sich verwachsen** *ref fam* to correct itself with time.

**verwackelt** *adj fam* blurred.

**verwählen** ➤ **sich verwählen** *ref* to dial the wrong number.

**verwahren** *vt* to keep (safe).

➤ **sich verwahren** *ref:* **sich gegen etw ~** to protest against sthg.

**verwahrlosen** (*perf* **ist verwahrlost**) *vi* to be neglected; [Garten] to run wild.

**Verwahrung** *die* safekeeping; **etw in ~ nehmen** to take sthg into safekeeping.

**verwaist** *adj* - **1.** [Kind] orphaned - **2.** [Ort] deserted.

**verwalten** *vt* [Gebäude, Besitz] to manage; [Altenheim, Geschäft] to run; [Amt] to hold; [Geld] to administer.

**Verwalter, in** (*mpl* -; *fpl* -nen) *der, die* manager; [von Geld] administrator.

**Verwaltung** (*pl* -en) *die* administration; [von

Geschäft, Gebäude] management; **die städtische** ~ the municipal authorities.

**Verwaltungslbezirk** *der* administrative district.

**Verwaltungslgebäude** *das* administration building.

**Verwaltungslkosten** *pl* administrative costs.

**verwandeln** *vt* to transform, to change; **etw in etw** *(A)* ~ to transform *ODER* change sthg into sthg.

  &#9656; **sich verwandeln** *ref* to change.

**Verlwandlung** *die* transformation; zooL metamorphosis.

**verwandt** *pp* ▷ **verwenden** ◇ *adj* related; **mit jm ~ sein** to be related to sb; **seelisch** ~ **sein** to be kindred spirits.

**Verwandte** *(pl -n) der, die* relative.

**Verwandtschaft** *(pl -en) die* - **1.** [alle Verwandte] family - **2.** [Verwandtsein] relationship.

**verwandtschaftlich** *adj* family *(vor Subst)* ◇ *adv:* ~ **verbunden sein** to be related.

**verwarnen** *vt* to caution.

**Verlwarnung** *die* caution; **eine gebührenpflichtige** ~ a fine.

**verwaschen** *adj* faded.

**verwässern** *vt* to water down.

**verwechseln** [fɛrˈvɛksln] *vt* to mix up; **jn/etw mit jm/etw** ~ to mistake sb/sthg for sb/sthg.

**Verwechseln** *das:* **einander zum** ~ **ähnlich sehen** to be the spitting image of each other.

**Verwechslung,**     **Verwechselung** [fɛrˈvɛks(ə)lʊŋ] *(pl -en) die* mixing up; **es gab eine** ~ there was a mix-up.

**verwegen** *adj* daring ◇ *adv* daringly.

**verwehen** *vt* - **1.** [auseinanderwehen] to blow away - **2.** [zuwehen] to cover over.

**verweichlichen** *(perf hat/ist verweichlicht) vi (ist)* to grow soft.

**verweigern** *vt* to refuse; **die Annahme von etw** ~ to refuse to take sthg; **einen Befehl** ~ to refuse to obey an order; **den Kriegsdienst** ~ to be a conscientious objector; **jm etw** ~ to refuse sb sthg ◇ *vi fam* [den Wehrdienst verweigern] to be a conscientious objector.

  &#9656; **sich verweigern** *ref* to refuse; **er verweigert sich seinen Pflichten** he refuses to do his duty.

**Verlweigerung** *die* refusal; **die** ~ **eines Befehls** refusal to obey an order.

**Verweis** *(pl -e) der* - **1.** [Tadel] reprimand; **jm einen** ~ **erteilen** to reprimand sb - **2.** [in Text]: **ein** ~ **auf etw** *(A)* a reference to sthg.

**verweisen** *(prät verwies; perf hat verwiesen) vt* - **1.** [hinweisen]: **jn auf etw** *(A)* ~ to refer sb to sthg - **2.** [weiterleiten]: **jn/etw an jn/etw** ~ to refer sb/sthg to sb/sthg - **3.** [ausweisen - von Schu-

le] to expel; [ - aus Raum] to throw out - **4.** *geh* [rügen] to reprimand ◇ *vi:* **auf etw** *(A)* ~ to refer to sthg; **eine Tafel verweist auf den Eingang** a sign points to the entrance.

**verwelken** *(perf ist verwelkt) vi* to wilt.

**verwenden** *(prät verwendete ODER verwandte; perf hat verwendet ODER verwandt) vt* - **1.** [benutzen] to use - **2.** [einsetzen - Zeit, Geld] to spend; **etw für** *ODER* **zu etw** ~ to use sthg for sthg; **Kraft auf etw** *(A)* ~ to put energy into sthg; **Mühe auf etw** *(A)* ~ to take trouble over sthg.

  &#9656; **sich verwenden** *ref:* **sich für jn/etw** ~ to use one's influence to benefit sb/sthg.

**Verlwendung** *die* use; **eines Tages findet es sicher noch** ~ we're sure to find a use for it some day.

**verwerfen** *(präs verwirft; prät verwarf; perf hat verworfen) vt* to reject.

**verwerten** *vt* - **1.** [Kenntnisse] to make use of - **2.** [Abfall, Altpapier] to re-use, to recycle.

**Verlwertung** *die* - **1.** [von Kenntnissen] use - **2.** [von Abfall, Altpapier] re-use, recycling.

**verwest** *adj* decomposed.

**Verwesung** *die* decomposition.

**verwickeln** *vt:* **jn in etw** *(A)* ~ to involve sb in sthg.

  &#9656; **sich verwickeln** *ref* to get tangled up.

**verwickelt** *adj* [kompliziert] complicated.

**Verwicklung, Verwickelung** *(pl -en) die* - **1.** [Verwickeln] involvement - **2.** [Komplikation] complication.

**verwildern** *(perf ist verwildert) vi* [Garten] to become overgrown; [Tier] to become wild.

**verwinden** *(prät verwand; perf hat verwunden) vt geh* to get over; **etw nicht ~ können** not to be able to get over sthg.

**verwinkelt** *adj* [Gasse, Flur] narrow and winding; [Haus] full of nooks and crannies.

**verwirklichen** *vt* [Traum] to realize; [Plan, Ziel] to achieve; [Idee] to put into practice.

  &#9656; **sich verwirklichen** *ref* - **1.** [Hoffnung, Traum, Befürchtung] to come true - **2.** [Person]: **sich selbst** ~ to fulfil o.s.

**Verwirklichung** *(pl -en) die* [von Traum] realization; [von Plan, Ziel] achievement; [von Idee] putting into practice.

**verwirren** *vt* - **1.** [Fäden] to tangle up - **2.** [Person] to confuse.

  &#9656; **sich verwirren** *ref* - **1.** [Fäden] to become tangled up; [Haar] to get tousled - **2.** [Verstand, Sinne] to become confused.

**Verwirrung** *(pl -en) die* confusion.

**verwischen** *vt* [Spur] to cover over; [Schrift] to smudge; [Farbe] to smear; [Kontur] to blur.

  &#9656; **sich verwischen** *ref* [Grenze] to become blurred.

**V**

**verwittern** (*perf* **ist verwittert**) *vi* to weather.

**verwitwet** *adj* widowed.

**verwöhnen** *vt* to spoil.

**verwöhnt** *adj* - **1.** [Kind, Tier] spoiled - **2.** [Geschmack] discriminating.

**verworren** *adj* confused ◇ *adv* [erzählen] in a confusing manner.

**verwunden** *vt* to wound.

**verwunderlich** *adj* surprising.

**verwundern** *vt* to surprise.
➤ **sich verwundern** *ref geh* to be surprised.

**verwundert** *adj* surprised ◇ *adv* in surprise.

**Verwunderung** *die* surprise.

**Verwundete** (*pl* **-n**) *der, die* wounded person; **die ~n** the wounded.

**Verwundung** (*pl* **-en**) *die* [Wunde] wound.

**verwünschen** *vt* - **1.** [verfluchen] to curse - **2.** [verzaubern] to bewitch.

**verwüsten** *vt* to devastate.

**Verwüstung** (*pl* **-en**) *die* devastation (U).

**Verz.** *abk für* **Verzeichnis**.

**verzählen** ➤ **sich verzählen** *ref* to miscount.

**verzapfen** *vt fam abw* to come out with.

**verzaubern** *vt* to enchant; **einen Prinz in einen Frosch ~** to turn a prince into a frog.

**Verzehr** *der geh* consumption.

**verzehren** *vt geh* to consume.

**verzeichnen** *vt* to record; [Erfolg] to notch up; **ist diese Stadt auf der Landkarte verzeichnet?** is this town (marked) on the map?

**Verzeichnis** (*pl* **-se**) *das* - **1.** [Liste] list; [Katalog] catalogue; [mit Namen] index - **2.** EDV directory.

**Verzeichnis|struktur** *die* EDV directory structure.

**verzeihen** (*prät* **verzieh**; *perf* **hat verziehen**) *vt* to forgive; **jm etw ~** to forgive sb for sthg; **~ Sie bitte!** excuse me, please!; **~ Sie bitte, dass ich stören muss!** please forgive the intrusion!

**verzeihlich** *adj* forgivable.

**Verzeihung** *die* forgiveness; **jn um ~ bitten** to apologize to sb.
➤ **Verzeihung** *interj* sorry!

**verzerren** *vt* - **1.** [Gesicht] to contort - **2.** [Bild, Klang] to distort.
➤ **sich verzerren** *ref* [Gesicht] to contort.

**verzetteln** ➤ **sich verzetteln** *ref* to get bogged down.

**Verzicht** (*pl* **-e**) *der*: **der ~ auf Süßigkeiten fällt**

**ihr schwer** he finds it hard to go without sweets; **~ leisten** to do without.

**verzichten** *vi* to do without; **auf jn/etw ~** to do without sb/sthg; **wir werden zukünftig auf ihre Dienste ~** we will be dispensing with her services; **auf eine Bemerkung ~** not to make ODER to refrain from making a comment; **er verzichtete darauf, sich zu beschweren** he refrained from making a complaint; **zugunsten eines anderen auf eine Stelle ~** to let sb have a job instead of o.s.; **verzichte auf deine blöde Kommentare!** stop making your stupid comments!; **danke, ich verzichte** I'll pass (on that one), thanks.

**verzieh** *prät* ▷ **verzeihen**.

**verziehen** (*prät* **verzog**; *perf* **hat/ist verzogen**) *pp* ▷ **verzeihen** ◇ *vt (hat)* - **1.** [Miene, Mund] to screw up; **das Gesicht ~** to pull a face - **2.** [Kind] to spoil ◇ *vi (ist)* [fortziehen] to move; **unbekannt verzogen** no longer at this address.
➤ **sich verziehen** *ref* - **1.** [Gesicht, Mund] to contort - **2.** [Tür, Holz] to warp - **3.** [Nebel, Rauch] to disperse; [Unwetter] to pass - **4.** *fam* [fortgehen] to disappear; **verzieh dich** get lost!

**verzieren** *vt* to decorate.

**Verzierung** (*pl* **-en**) *die* decoration.

**verzinsen** *vt* to pay interest on.
➤ **sich verzinsen** *ref* to yield interest.

**verzögern** *vt* - **1.** [verschieben] to delay - **2.** [verlangsamen] to slow down.
➤ **sich verzögern** *ref* [sich verspäten] to be delayed.

**Verzögerung** (*pl* **-en**) *die* - **1.** [Verspätung] delay - **2.** [Verlangsamung] slowing down.

**verzollen** *vt* to declare; **haben Sie etwas zu ~?** do you have anything to declare?

**Verzug** *der* delay; **in ~ (mit etw) geraten** ODER **kommen** to fall behind (with sthg).
➤ **im Verzug** *adv*: **mit etw im ~ sein** to be behind with sthg; **Gefahr ist im ~** danger is imminent.

**verzweifeln** (*perf* **ist verzweifelt**) *vi* to despair; **an etw** (D) **/über etw** (A) **~** to despair of/at sthg.

**Verzweifeln** *das*: **es ist zum ~!** it's enough to drive you to despair!

**verzweifelt** *adj* desperate; [Blick] despairing ◇ *adv* [kämpfen, versuchen] desperately; [sagen, anblicken] despairingly.

**Verzweiflung** (*pl* **-en**) *die* despair; **vor ~** in despair; **jn zur ~ bringen** to drive sb to despair.

**verzweigt** *adj* with many branches.

**verzwickt** *adj* tricky.

**Vesuv** *der*: **der ~** Vesuvius.

**Veteran** [vete'ra:n] (*pl* **-en**) *der* veteran.

**Veto** ['veːto] (pl -s) das veto; **sein ~ gegen etw einlegen** to veto sthg.

**Vetter** (pl -n) der cousin.

**Vetternwirtschaft** die abw nepotism.

**VGA-Standard** [fauge'aːʃtandart] der EDV VGA standard.

**vgl.** (abk für **vergleiche**) cf.

**VHS** [fauhaːˈɛs] die abk für **Volkshochschule**.

**via** ['viːa] präp via.

**vibrieren** [vi'briːrən] vi to vibrate; [Stimme] to quiver.

**Video** ['viːdeo] (pl -s) das video.

**Video|clip** der video clip.

**Video|film** der video.

**Video|gerät** das video Br, VCR Am.

**Video|kamera** die video camera.

**Video|kassette** die video (tape).

**Videokonsole** (pl -n) die game console.

**Video|rekorder** der video (recorder) Br, VCR Am.

**Video|spiel** das video game.

**Video|text** der videotext.

**Videothek** [video'teːk] (pl -en) die video store.

**Vieh** das - **1.** [alle Tiere] livestock - **2.** [Rinder] cattle.

**Viehzucht** die stock breeding; [von Rindern] cattle breeding.

**viel** (kompar **mehr**; superl **meiste**), **vieles** adj: **das ~e Geld** all the money; **das Kleid mit den ~en Knöpfen** the dress with all the buttons; **~en Dank!** thank you very much! ◇ det - **1.** [Menge] much, a lot of; **zu ~** too much; **~ Tee/Zeit** a lot of tea/time - **2.** [Anzahl] many, a lot of, lots of; **zu ~** too many; **~e Bücher** a lot of books, lots of books; **~e Menschen** many ODER a lot of people ◇ adv - **1.** [intensiv, oft] a lot; **~ arbeiten** to work a lot; **sie ist ~ allein** she is alone a lot of the time - **2.** [zum Ausdruck der Verstärkung] much; **~ mehr** much more; **~ zu much too, far too; es dauert ~ zu lange** it's far too long; **nicht ~ anders** not very different ◇ pron a lot; **er sagt ~** he says a lot; **er sagt nicht ~** he doesn't say much.

◆ **nicht viel** det not much ◇ adv not much; **er schläft nicht ~** he doesn't sleep much.

◆ **nicht viele** det not many.

◆ **vieles** pron a lot of things.

◆ **viel zu viel** det & adv much too much.

◆ **viel zu viele** det far too many; siehe auch **zu viel**.

**viel beschäftigt** adj very busy.

**vielerlei** det all kinds of ◇ pron all kinds of things.

**vielfach** adj [mehrfach, wiederholt] multiple; **auf ~en Wunsch** by popular demand; **das ~e Gewicht** many times the weight ◇ adv

- **1.** [mehrfach, wiederholt] several times - **2.** [häufig] often.

**Vielfache** das [von Zahl] multiple; **um ein ~s** many times over.

**Vielfalt** die diversity, great variety.

**vielfältig** adj diverse.

**Vielflieger, in** (mpl -; fpl -nen) der frequent flier.

**vielleicht** adv - **1.** [eventuell] perhaps - **2.** fam [wirklich, außerordentlich] really; **der ist ~ gerannt!** he didn't half run! - **3.** [Ausdruck der Höflichkeit]: **wären Sie ~ so freundlich, den Termin zu bestätigen?** could you possibly confirm the date for me? - **4.** [ungefähr] about - **5.** fam [etwa]: **hast du ~ gedacht, ich würde da mitmachen?** you didn't think I would join in, did you? - **6.** fam [Ausdruck der Ungeduld]: **~ kannst du dich mal beeilen!** do you think you could possibly get a move on!

**vielmals** adv: **danke ~** thank you very much.

**vielmehr** adv geh rather.

**vielsagend** adj meaningful ◇ adv meaningfully.

**vielschichtig** adj complex ◇ adv from many different aspects.

**vielseitig** adj - **1.** [Person] versatile - **2.** [umfassend] varied ◇ adv: **~ begabt** multitalented; **~ einsetzbar** versatile.

**vielversprechend** adj promising ◇ adv promisingly.

**Vielzahl** die large number; **eine ~ von Möglichkeiten** a wealth of possibilities.

**vier** [fiːɐ̯] num four; **auf allen ~en** fam on all fours; **alle ~e von sich strecken** fam to put one's feet up; siehe auch **sechs**.

**Vier** (pl -en) die - **1.** [Zahl] four - **2.** [Schulnote] ≈ D, mark of 4 on a scale from 1 to 6; siehe auch **Sechs**.

**Vierbeiner** (pl -) der four-legged friend.

**Viereck** (pl -e) das four-sided figure; [Rechteck] rectangle; [Quadrat] square.

**viereckig** adj four-sided; [rechteckig] rectangular; [quadratisch] square.

**Vierer** (pl -) der - **1.** SPORT four - **2.** [Schulnote] ≈ D.

**vierfach** adj: **die ~e Menge** four times as much; **in ~er Größe** four times as big; **die Formulare in ~er Ausfertigung abgeben** to provide four copies of the form; **der ~e Gewinner** the four-time winner ◇ adv four times.

**vierhändig** adv as a duet ◇ adj: **ein ~es Stück** a duet.

**vierhundert** num four hundred.

**Vierhundert-Euro-Job** der low-paid job which is exempt from social security contributions.

**viermal** adv four times.

**vierspurig** adj four-lane.

**V**

**vierstellig** *adj* four-figure.

**vierstimmig** *adj* for four voices ◇ *adv* as a quartet.

**viert** ⇒ **zu viert** *adv:* wir waren zu ~ there were four of us; wir sind zu ~ ins Kino gegangen four of us went to the cinema.

**Viertaktlmotor** *der* four-stroke engine.

**viertausend** *num* four thousand.

**vierte, r, s** *adj* fourth; *siehe auch* **sechste.**

**Vierte** (*pl* **-n**) *der, die, das* fourth; *siehe auch* **Sechste.**

**viertel** *adj* (*unver*) quarter; *siehe auch* **sechstel.**

**Viertel** (*pl* **-**) *das* [Teil] quarter; ~ vor/nach drei a quarter to/past *Br* ODER after *Am* three; das akademische ~ *the quarter of an hour between the official and actual beginning of a lecture at German universities; siehe auch* **Sechstel.**

**Viertellfinale** *das* quarter-final.

**Viertelljahr** *das* quarter.

**vierteljährlich** *adj* & *adv* quarterly.

**vierteln** *vt* to divide into four.

**Viertelpfund** (*pl* **-**) *das* quarter (of a) pound.

**Viertellstunde** *die* quarter of an hour.

**viertelstündlich** *adj* & *adv* every quarter of an hour.

**viertens, viertens** *adv* fourthly.

**Vierwaldstätter See** *der* Lake Lucerne.

**vierzehn** *num* fourteen; *siehe auch* **sechs.**

**Vierzehn** (*pl* **-en**) *die* fourteen; *siehe auch* **Sechs.**

**vierzehntägig** *adv* every fortnight, fortnightly ◇ *adj* - **1.** [alle zwei Wochen] fortnightly - **2.** [zwei Wochen lang] two-week, fortnight-long.

**vierzig** *num* forty; *siehe auch* **sechs.**

**Vierzigerjahre, vierziger Jahre** *pl:* die ~ the forties.

**Vierzigstundenlwoche** *die* forty-hour week.

**Vierzimmerlwohnung** *die* four-room flat *Br* ODER apartment *Am*.

**Vierlzylinder** *der fam* four-cylinder car.

**Vietnam** [vjɛtˈnaːm] *nt* Vietnam.

**Vietnamese** [vjɛtnaˈmeːzə] (*pl* **-n**) *der* Vietnamese.

**Vietnamesin** [vjɛtnaˈmeːzɪn] (*pl* **-nen**) *die* Vietnamese.

**vietnamesisch** [vjɛtnaˈmeːzɪʃ] *adj* Vietnamese.

**Vikar, in** [viˈkaːɐ̯, rɪn] (*mpl* **-e;** *fpl* **-nen**) *der, die* [evangelisch] ≈ curate.

**Viktoriasee** *der* Lake Victoria.

**Villa** [ˈvɪla] (*pl* **Villen**) *die* villa.

**violett** [vjoˈlɛt] *adj* purple.

**Violett** *das* purple.

**Violine** [vjoˈliːnə] (*pl* **-n**) *die* violin.

**Violinlschlüssel** *der* treble clef

**Viper** [ˈviːpɐ] (*pl* **-n**) *die* viper.

**virtuell** *adj* virtual; ~e Realität virtual reality ◇ *adv* virtually.

**Virus** [ˈviːrʊs] (*pl* **Viren**) *der* ODER *das* MED & EDV virus.

**Viruslinfektion** *die* viral infection.

**Visage** [viˈzaːʒə] (*pl* **-n**) *die salopp abw* mug.

**V. i. S. d. P.** (*abk für* **Verantwortlicher im Sinne des Presserechts**) *person responsible for the contents of a publication in the eyes of German press law.*

**Visier** [viˈziːɐ̯] (*pl* **-e**) *das* - **1.** [von Helm] visor - **2.** [von Gewehr] sight; jn/etw im ~ haben [es auf jn abgesehen haben] to have it in for sb/sthg; [anpeilen] to have one's eye on sb/sthg.

**Vision** [viˈzjoːn] (*pl* **-en**) *die* vision.

**Visite** [viˈziːtə] (*pl* **-n**) *die* [privat, geschäftlich] visit; [Besuch des Arztes]: ~ machen to do one's rounds.

**Visitenlkarte** *die* visiting card.

**Viskose** [vɪsˈkoːzə] *die* viscose.

**visuell** [vizuˈɛl] *adj* visual.

**Visum** [ˈviːzʊm] (*pl* **Visa** ODER **Visen**) *das* visa.

**vital** [viˈtaːl] *adj* - **1.** [Person] full of life - **2.** [vordringlich] vital.

**Vitamin** [vitaˈmiːn] (*pl* **-e**) *das* vitamin; ~ B *fam* [Beziehungen] connections (*pl*).

**Vitaminmangel** *der* vitamin deficiency.

**Vitrine** [viˈtriːnə] (*pl* **-n**) *die* - **1.** [Schrank] display cabinet - **2.** [Ausstellungskasten] display case.

**Vizelkanzler, in** *der, die* vice-chancellor.

**Vizelpräsident, in** *der, die* vice-president.

**Vogel** (*pl* **Vögel**) *der* - **1.** [Tier] bird - **2.** *fam* [Person]: ein komischer ~ an odd customer - **3.** *RW:* den ~ abschießen *fam* to outdo everyone; einen ~ haben *salopp abw* to be off one's head; jm einen ~ zeigen *fam* to tap one's forehead at sb (*to indicate that he/she is crazy*).

**Vogelbauer** (*pl* **-**) *der* birdcage.

**Vogelfluglinie** *die ferry link between Germany and Denmark.*

**vogelfrei** *adj* outlawed; für ~ erklärt werden to be outlawed.

**Vogellfutter** *das* birdseed.

**vögeln** *vt* & *vi vulg* to screw.

**Vogelperspektive** *die:* etw aus der ~ sehen to have a bird's-eye view of sthg.

**Vogelscheuche** (*pl* **-n**) *die* scarecrow.

**Vogesen** *pl:* die ~ the Vosges.

**Vokabel** [vo'ka:bḷ] (*pl* -n) *die* word; ~n vocabulary (*U*).

**Vokabular** [vokabu'la:ɐ̯] (*pl* -e) *das* vocabulary.

**Vokal** [vo'ka:l] (*pl* -e) *der* vowel.

**Voliere** [vo'lje:r(ə)] (*pl* -n) *die* aviary.

**Volk** (*pl* Völker) *das* - **1.** [gen] people (*pl*); **das deutsche ~** the German nation *ODER* people; **sich unters ~ mischen** to mingle with the crowd - **2.** (*ohne pl*) *fam* [viele Personen] crowd; **viel ~** lots of people.

**Völker|bund** *der* HIST League of Nations.

**Völker|kunde** *die* ethnology.

**Völker|recht** *das* international law.

**völkerrechtlich** *adj* [Diskussion] of international law; [Bestimmung] under international law.

**Völker|wanderung** *die* HIST migration of the peoples, *migration of tribes such as the Huns and the Goths to the current geographical area of Germany between the 4th and 6th centuries AD.*

**Volksab|stimmung** *die* referendum.

**Volks|begehren** *das* petition for a referendum.

**Volks|entscheid** (*pl* -e) *der* referendum.

**Volks|fest** *das* festival.

**Volkshoch|schule** *die* ≈ college of adult education.

┌─────────────────────────────────┐
**VOLKSHOCHSCHULE**

Colleges of adult education in Germany offer academic as well as practical courses, usually in the form of evening classes and lectures. These courses are offered in a variety of subjects and can in some cases lead to a certificate or other recognized qualification.
└─────────────────────────────────┘

**Volks|kunst** *die* folk art.

**Volks|lied** *das* folk song.

**Volks|mund** *der* vernacular.
  ➡ **im Volksmund** *adv*: **Helmut Kohl, im ~ „Birne" genannt** Helmut Kohl, popularly known as "Birne".

**Volks|musik** *die* folk music.

**volksnah** *adj*: **ein ~er Politiker** a politician who is in touch with ordinary people.

**Volks|republik** *die* people's republic; **die ~ China** the People's Republic of China.

**Volks|tanz** *der* folk dance.

**Volkstrauer|tag** *der* ≈ Remembrance Day *Br*, ≈ Veterans' Day *Am*, *German national day of remembrance.*

**volkstümlich** *adj* - **1.** [traditionell] traditional

- **2.** [populär] popular ◇ *adv* [populär] in plain language.

**Volks|vertretung** *die* parliament.

**Volks|wirtschaft** *die* - **1.** [Wissenschaft] economics (*U*) - **2.** [Wirtschaft] economy.

**volkswirtschaftlich** *adj* economic.

**Volks|zählung** *die* census.

**voll** *adj* - **1.** [gen] full; **~ von** *ODER* **mit etw sein** to be full of sthg; **halb ~** half full; **er kann aus dem Vollen schöpfen** *fig* he has unlimited resources to draw on; **mit ~em Recht** with every justification; **in ~em Ernst** in all seriousness - **2.** *fam* [gesättigt]: **~ sein** to be full (up) - **3.** *salopp* [betrunken]: **~ sein** to be plastered - **4.** [vollwertig]: **jn nicht für ~ nehmen** *fam fig* not to take sb seriously ◇ *adv* - **1.** [völlig] totally, completely; **~ und ganz** completely - **2.** *salopp* [verstärkend] really.

**vollauf** *adv* completely.

**vollautomatisch** *adj* fully automatic ◇ *adv* fully automatically.

**Voll|bart** *der* full beard.

**Voll|blut** (*pl* -blüter) *das* thoroughbred.

**Voll|bremsung** *die*: **eine ~ machen** to slam on the brakes.

**vollbringen** (*prät* vollbrachte; *perf* hat vollbracht) *vt geh* to achieve.

**vollbusig** *adj* buxom.

**Voll|dampf** *der*: **mit ~** *fam* flat out.

**vollenden** *vt* to complete.

**vollendet** *pp* ▷ **vollenden** ◇ *adj* - **1.** [perfekt] perfect - **2.** [fertig] completed ◇ *adv* perfectly.

**vollends** *adv* completely.

**Voll|endung** *die* - **1.** [Perfektion] perfection - **2.** [Vollenden] completion; **mit** *ODER* **nach ~ des 18. Lebensjahres** on reaching the age of 18.

**voller** *adj* (*unver*) full of.

**Volley|ball** ['vɔlibal] *der* volleyball.

**vollführen** *vt* to perform.

**Voll|gas** *das*: **mit ~** at full throttle; **~ geben** to put one's foot down *Br*, to step on the gas *Am*.

**völlig** *adj* complete ◇ *adv* completely.

**volljährig** *adj*: **~ sein** to be of age.

**Vollkasko|ver|sicherung** *die* comprehensive insurance.

**vollklimatisiert** *adj* fully air-conditioned.

**vollkommen** *adj* - **1.** [perfekt] perfect - **2.** [absolut] complete ◇ *adv* - **1.** [perfekt] perfectly - **2.** [absolut] completely.

**Vollkommenheit** *die* perfection; **er bringt es im Klavierspielen zur ~** his piano playing is nothing short of perfect.

**V**

**Vollkorn|brot** *das* wholemeal *Br* ODER whole wheat *Am* bread.

**voll laufen** (*präs* **läuft voll**; *prät* **lief voll**; *perf* **ist voll gelaufen**) *vi* to fill up; **sich ~ lassen** *salopp abw* to get plastered.

**voll machen** *vt fam* - **1.** [Bett] to wet; [Windel, Hose] to dirty - **2.** [füllen] to fill - **3.** [vervollständigen] to complete.

**Voll|macht** (*pl* **-en**) *die* - **1.** (*ohne pl*) [Befugnis] authority; (*pl* **die**) RECHT power of attorney; **jm (die) ~ geben** ODER **erteilen** to authorize sb; RECHT to give sb power of attorney - **2.** [Schreiben] letter of authorization; **schriftliche ~** written authorization.

**Voll|milch** *die* full-fat milk.

**Voll|mond** *der* full moon.

**voll packen** *vt* to pack full.

**Vollpension** *die* full board.

**vollschlank** *adj:* **die ~e Dame** the woman with a fuller figure.

**vollständig** *adj* complete ◇ *adv* completely.

**Vollständigkeit** *die* completeness; **der ~ halber** for the sake of completeness.

**voll stopfen** *vt fam* to stuff full.
➤ **sich voll stopfen** *ref fam* to stuff one's face.

**vollstrecken** *vt* - **1.** RECHT [Testament] to execute; [Urteil] to carry out - **2.** SPORT to score from, to convert.

**Vollstreckung** (*pl* **-en**) *die* [von Urteil] carrying out; [von Testament] execution.

**voll tanken** *vi* to fill up; **bitte einmal ~!** fill it up, please! ◇ *vt* to fill up.

**Voll|treffer** *der* - **1.** [Schuss] direct hit - **2.** RW: **ein ~ sein** to be a hit; **einen ~ landen** *fam* to hit the bull's-eye.

**Voll|ver|sammlung** *die* general meeting.

**vollwertig** *adj* - **1.** [gleichwertig] fully-fledged - **2.** [Speisen] wholefood.

**Vollwertkost** *die* wholefood.

**vollzählig** *adj* entire ◇ *adv:* **sie sind ~ erschienen** they all turned up.

**vollziehen** (*prät* **vollzog**; *perf* **hat vollzogen**) *vt* to carry out.
➤ **sich vollziehen** *ref* to take place.

**Vollzug** *der* - **1.** [von Urteil, Beschlagnahmung] carrying out - **2.** [von Ehe] consummation - **3.** *fam* [Gefängnis] clink.

**Vollzugs|anstalt** *die* prison, penitentiary *Am*.

**Volontär** [volon'tɛːɐ̯] (*pl* **-e**) *der* trainee.

**Volontariat** [volonta'rjaːt] (*pl* **-e**) *das* - **1.** [Stelle] traineeship - **2.** [Zeit] (period of) training.

**Volontärin** [volon'tɛːrɪn] (*pl* **-nen**) *die* trainee.

**Volt** [vɔlt] (*pl* **-**) *das* volt.

**Volumen** [vo'luːmən] (*pl* **-**) *das* volume.

**vom** *präp* - **1.** (*von* + *dem*) from the; **~ Bahnhof** from the station - **2.** (*untrennbar*): **~ Fach sein** to be an expert; **müde ~ Arbeiten sein** to be tired from working.

**von** *präp* (+ *D*) - **1.** [räumlich] from; [von weg] off, from; **~ ... nach ...** from ... to ...; **~ Köln bis Paris** from Cologne to Paris; **etw vom Tisch nehmen** to take sth from ODER off the table - **2.** [zeitlich] from; **~ Montag bis Freitag** from Monday to Friday, Monday through Friday *Am*; **~ heute an** from today - **3.** [besitzanzeigend]: **ist das Buch ~ dir?** is the book yours? - **4.** [stellt Bezug her]: **die Zeitung ~ gestern** yesterday's paper; **ein Brief ~ meiner Schwester** a letter from my sister; **~ wem hast du das?** who gave it to you?; **ein Verwandter ~ mir** a relation of mine; **das war dumm/nett ~ dir** that was stupid/nice of you; **der Bürgermeister ~ Frankfurt** the mayor of Frankfurt - **5.** [in Passivsätzen] by; **~ einem Hund gebissen werden** to be bitten by a dog; **~ Hand hergestellt** made by hand - **6.** [zur Angabe der Ursache] from; **müde ~ der Reise** tired from the journey - **7.** [drückt Eigenschaften aus] of; **ein Sack ~ 25 kg** a 25 kg bag; **eine Fahrt ~ 3 Stunden** a 3-hour journey; **~ Gold** gold - **8.** [zur Angabe einer Teilmenge] of; **ein Stück ~ der Torte** a piece of the cake; **neun ~ zehn** nine out of ten - **9.** RW: **~ mir aus** *fam* I don't mind; **~ sich aus** *fam* by oneself.
➤ **von ... an** *präp* from; **~ hier an** from here; **~ jetzt an** from now on.
➤ **von ... aus** *präp* from; **~ hier aus** from here.

**voneinander** *adv* from one another; **sie sind ~ unabhängig** they are independent of one another.

**vonnöten** *adj:* **~ sein** *geh* to be necessary.

**vonstatten** *adv:* **~ gehen** *geh* to take place.

**vor** *präp* - **1.** (+ *D*) [räumlich] in front of; **~ dem Haus stehen** to stand in front of the house; **~ der Tür** at the door, in front of the door; **~ Gericht erscheinen** to appear before a court - **2.** (+ *A*) [räumlich] in front of - **3.** (+ *D*) [zur Angabe einer Reihenfolge] before, X **kommt ~** Y X comes before Y - **4.** (+ *D*) [zeitlich - zuvor] ago, **heute ~ fünf Jahren** five years ago today; **~ kurzem** recently - **5.** [zur Angabe der Uhrzeit] to *Br*, before *Am;* **fünf ~ zwölf** five to twelve *Br*, five before twelve *Am;* **fünf ~ halb neun** twenty-five past eight *Br*, twenty-five after eight *Am* - **6.** (+ *D*) [wegen] with; **~ Kälte/Angst zittern** to tremble with cold/fear; **~ Freude in die Luft springen** to jump for joy; **~ Hunger sterben** to die of hunger - **7.** [stellt Bezug her]: **Schutz ~ etw** protection from sth; **jn ~ etw warnen** to warn sb about sth - **8.** RW: **es geht etwas ~ sich** something is going on; **~ sich hin murmeln/singen** to mutter/sing to oneself ◇ *adv* forwards.
➤ **vor allem** *adv* above all.

**vorab** *adv* [im Voraus] in advance; **~ möchte ich**

**sagen, dass** ... before we start, I would like to say that ...

**Vor|abend** *der* evening before.

**Vor|abend|programm** *das* early evening schedule.

**Vor|ahnung** *die* premonition.

**voran** *adv* - **1.** [vorweg] at the front - **2.** [vorwärts] forwards.

**voran|bringen** *vt (unreg)* to make progress with.

**voran|gehen** (*perf* **ist vorangegangen**) *vi (unreg)* - **1.** [Arbeit, Projekt] to advance, to progress - **2.** [vorne gehen] to go on ahead - **3.** [vorher passieren]: **jm/etw ~** to precede sb/sthg.

**voran|kommen** (*perf* **ist vorangekommen**) *vi (unreg)* to make progress; [Arbeit, Projekt] to advance, to progress; **gut ~** to make good progress; **nicht ~** not to make any progress.

**Voran|kündigung** *die* advance notice; **ohne ~** without any advance warning.

**Voran|meldung** *die* appointment.

**vor|arbeiten** *vi:* **einen Tag ~** to work an extra day *(in order to have a day off later).*
➤ **sich vorarbeiten** *ref* to work one's way forward.

**Vor|arbeiter, in** *der, die* foreman (*f* forewoman).

**Vorarlberg** *nt* Vorarlberg.

**Vorarlberger** (*pl* -) *der* native/inhabitant of Vorarlberg ⬦ *adj (unver)* of/from Vorarlberg.

**Vorarlbergerin** (*pl* -**nen**) *die* native/ inhabitant of Vorarlberg.

**voraus** *adv* in front; **jm in etw ~ sein** *fig* to be ahead of sb in sthg; **seiner Zeit ~** ahead of one's time.

**Voraus** ➤ **im Voraus** *adv* in advance.

**voraus|berechnen** *vt* to calculate in advance.

**voraus|bezahlen** *vt* to pay for in advance.

**voraus|gehen** (*perf* **ist vorausgegangen**) *vi (unreg)* - **1.** [vorher, früher gehen] to go on ahead - **2.** [vorher passieren]: **einer Sache** *(D)* **~** to precede sthg.

**vorausgesetzt** *pp* ⊳ **voraussetzen** ⬦ *konj* provided (that).

**voraus|haben** *vt (unreg):* **jm etw ~** to have the advantage of sthg over sb.

**voraus|sagen** *vt* to predict.

**voraus|schicken** *vt* - **1.** [vorher bemerken]: **ich muss ~, dass** ... first of all, I have to say that ...; **einer Sache** *(D)* **etw ~** to begin sthg with sthg - **2.** [zuerst schicken] to send on ahead.

**voraus|sehen** *vt (unreg)* to foresee; **es war vorauszusehen, dass** ... it was to be expected that ...

**voraus|setzen** *vt* - **1.** [erfordern] to require - **2.** [für selbstverständlich halten] to take for granted; **wir müssen ~, dass** ... we must assume that ...; **etw als bekannt ~** to assume sthg is known.

**Voraussetzung** (*pl* -**en**) *die* - **1.** [Erfordernis] requirement; **ihm fehlen die nötigen ~en** he lacks the necessary qualifications; **unter der ~, dass** on condition that; **alle ~en erfüllen** to meet all the requirements - **2.** [Annahme] assumption.

**Voraussicht** *die* foresight; **aller ~ nach** in all probability.

**voraussichtlich** *adj* expected ⬦ *adv* probably.

**Voraus|wahl** *die* preliminary selection; **eine ~ treffen** to carry out a preliminary selection.

**Voraus|zahlung** *die* advance payment.

**Vorbau** (*pl* -**e**) *der* - **1.** [Bauelement] porch - **2.** *salopp abw* [Busen]: **sie hat einen ordentlichen ~** she's rather top-heavy.

**vor|bauen** *vi* to take precautions; **einer Sache** *(D)* **~** to guard against sthg.

**Vor|bedingung** *die* precondition.

**Vorbehalt** (*pl* -**e**) *der* reservation; **etw unter** *ODER* **mit ~ annehmen** to accept sthg with reservations.

**vor|behalten** *vt (unreg):* **sich etw ~** to reserve o.s. sthg; **der Swimmingpool ist den Hotelgästen ~** the swimming pool is reserved for hotel guests only.

**vorbei** *adv* - **1.** [räumlich] past, by; **an mir ~** past me - **2.** [zeitlich] over; **die Schmerzen sind ~** the pain has gone; **mit jm ist es ~** *fam* sb is finished; **mit etw ist es ~** *fam* sthg is over.

**vorbei|fahren** (*perf* **ist vorbeigefahren**) *vi (unreg)* - **1.** [vorüberfahren] to go past; [in Auto] to drive past; **an jm/etw ~** to go/drive past sb/ sthg - **2.** [aufsuchen] to drop in.

**vorbei|gehen** (*perf* **ist vorbeigegangen**) *vi (unreg)* - **1.** [entlanggehen, vergehen] to pass; **an jm/etw ~** to pass sb/sthg - **2.** [hingehen] to drop in.
➤ **im Vorbeigehen** *adv* in passing.

**vorbei|kommen** (*perf* **ist vorbeigekommen**) *vi (unreg)* - **1.** [an etw vorüber]: (**an etw** *(D)*) **~** to pass (sthg) - **2.** [besuchen]: (**bei jm**) **~** to drop in (on sb); **komm mal vorbei!** come round some time! - **3.** [vorbeikönnen] to get past.

**vorbei|lassen** *vt (unreg)* to let past.

**vorbei|reden** *vi:* **aneinander ~** to talk at cross purposes.

**vorbelastet** *adj:* **durch negative Erfahrungen ~ sein** to be biased as a result of previous bad experiences; **erblich ~ sein** to be predisposed.

**V**

**vor|bereiten** *vt* to prepare; **jn/etw auf etw**
*(A)* ~ to prepare sb/sthg for sthg.
➤ **sich vorbereiten** *ref:* **sich (auf etw** *(A)* ~ to
prepare o.s. (for sthg).

**Vor|bereitung** *die* preparation; **in** ~ **sein** to
be in preparation; ~**en für etw treffen** to
make preparations for sthg.

**vor|bestellen** *vt* to order in advance.

**vorbestraft** *adj:* ~ **sein** to have previous
convictions, to have a criminal record.

**vor|beugen** *vi:* **einer Sache** *(D)* ~ to prevent
sthg ◇ *vt* to bend forward.
➤ **sich vorbeugen** *ref* to lean forward.

**Vor|beugung** *die* prevention.

**Vor|bild** *das* model; **sich jn/etw zum** ~ **nehmen**
to model o.s. on sb/sthg.

**vorbildlich** *adj* exemplary ◇ *adv* in exemplary fashion.

**Vorbildung** *die* previous experience *(U)*.

**Vor|bote** *der* herald.

**vor|bringen** *vt (unreg)* - **1.** [Wunsch, Bedenken] to
express; [Bitte, Beschwerde] to make; **etw gegen**
**etw** ~ to raise sthg as an objection to sthg;
**etw gegen jn** ~ to say sthg against sb - **2.** [Be-
weise] to produce - **3.** [bringen] to bring.

**vor|datieren** *vt* to predate.

**Vorder|achse** *die* front axle.

**vordere, r, s** *adj* front.

**Vorder|front** *die* facade.

**Vorder|grund** *der* foreground; **etw in den**
~ **stellen** *ODER* **rücken** to place special emphasis on sthg; **im** ~ **stehen** to be to the fore.

**vordergründig** *adj* superficial ◇ *adv* superficially.

**Vorder|mann** *der:* **der Läufer überholte seinen**
~ the runner overtook the man in front of
him.

**Vorder|rad** *das* front wheel.

**Vorder|sitz** *der* front seat.

**vor|drängen** ➤ **sich vordrängen** *ref* to
push in.

**vor|dringen** *(perf* **ist vorgedrungen)** *vi (unreg)*
to advance; [in Menschenmenge] to push for-
ward; **bis zu jm** ~ to get as far as sb.

**vordringlich** *adj* priority *(vor Subst)* ◇ *adv* as
a matter of priority.

**Vor|druck** *der* form.

**voreilig** *adj* rash ◇ *adv* rashly.

**voreinander** *adv* - **1.** [in Bezug aufeinander]:
**Angst** ~ **haben** to be afraid of one another
- **2.** [räumlich] one in front of the other.

**voreingenommen** *adj* biased; **gegen jn/etw**
~ **sein** to be biased against sb/sthg ◇ *adv* in
a biased way.

**vor|enthalten** *vt (unreg):* **jm etw** ~ to with-
hold sthg from sb; [Nachricht] to keep sthg
from sb.

**Vorent|scheidung** *die* - **1.** SPORT: **der Verlust**
**des Satzes bedeutete eine** ~ the loss of the set
decided the course of the match - **2.** [vorläu-
fige Entscheidung] preliminary decision.

**vorerst** *adv* for the time being.

**Vorfahr** *(pl* -en**)**, **Vorfahre** *(pl* -n**)** *der* ancestor.

**vor|fahren** *(perf* **hat/ist vorgefahren)** *vi (ist)*
- **1.** [nach vorn fahren] to drive forward - **2.** [vo-
rausfahren] to drive on ahead - **3.** [vor Gebäude]
to drive up ◇ *vt (hat)* - **1.** [nach vorn] to drive
forward - **2.** [vor Gebäude] to drive up.

**Vorfahrt** *die* right of way; ~ **haben** to have
right of way; **jm die** ~ **nehmen** to fail to give
way to sb.

**Vorfahrts|straße** *die* major road.

**Vor|fall** *der* [Geschehnis] occurrence, incident.

**vor|fallen** *(perf* **ist vorgefallen)** *vi (unreg)* to
happen, to occur.

**Vor|feld** ➤ **im Vorfeld** *adv* in advance; **im**
~ **der Wahlen** in the run-up to the elections.

**Vor|film** *der* supporting film.

**vor|finden** *vt (unreg)* to find.

**Vor|freude** *die* anticipation.

**vor|fühlen** *vi:* **bei jm** ~ to sound sb out.

**vor|führen** *vt* - **1.** [zeigen - Film] to show;
[ - Kunststück] to perform; [ - Funktionsweise] to
demonstrate; **jm etw** ~ to show sb sthg
- **2.** *fam* [blamieren] to show up.

**Vor|führung** *die* - **1.** [im Theater, Kino, Zirkus]
performance - **2.** [von Maschine] demonstration.

**Vor|gabe** *die* - **1.** [Vorlage] guideline - **2.** [im
Sport] handicap.

**Vor|gang** *der* event, occurrence.

**Vor|gänger, in** *(mpl* -; *fpl* -nen**)** *der, die* predec-
essor.

**Vor|garten** *der* front garden.

**vorgefasst** *adj* preconceived.

**vorgefertigt** *adj* prefabricated.

**Vor|gefühl** *das* presentiment.

**vorgegeben** *adj* set in advance.

**vor|gehen** *(perf* **ist vorgegangen)** *vi (unreg)*
- **1.** [vorhergehen] to go on ahead - **2.** [passieren]
to go on; **was geht hier vor?** what's going on
here? - **3.** [handeln] to proceed; **gegen jn/etw**
~ to take action against sb/sthg - **4.** [Uhr] to
be fast - **5.** [vorne gehen] to go first.

**Vor|geschichte** *die* - **1.** [vorherige Entwicklung]
history - **2.** [Prähistorie] prehistory.

**Vorgeschmack** *der:* **ein** ~ **auf etw** *(A)* a foretaste of sthg.

**Vorgesetzte** *(pl* -n**)** *der, die* superior.

**vorgestern** *adv* [vor zwei Tagen] the day before yesterday.

➤ **von vorgestern** *adj fam abw* [uralt]: **von ~ sein** to be really old-fashioned.

**vorgestrig** *adj* - **1.** [von vor zwei Tagen] of the day before yesterday - **2.** *fam abw* [uralt] really old-fashioned.

**vor|greifen** *vi (unreg)* to get ahead of o.s.; **jm/ etw ~** to anticipate sb/sthg; **auf etw** *(A)* **~** to anticipate sthg.

**vor|haben** *vt (unreg)* to plan; **was habt ihr am Wochenende vor?** what have you got planned for the weekend?

**Vorhaben** (*pl* -) *das* plan.

**vor|halten** *(unreg) vt*: **jm etw ~** [halten] to hold sthg up to sb; [vorwerfen] to hold sthg against sb ◇ *vi* [ausreichen] to last.

**Vorhaltungen** *pl*: **jm ~ machen** to reproach sb.

**Vorhand** *die* SPORT forehand.

**vorhanden** *adj* existing; [Vorräte, Mittel] available; **~ sein** to exist; [Vorräte, Mittel] to be available; **davon ist nichts mehr ~** there's none of it left.

**Vor|hang** *der* curtain; **der eiserne ~** the Iron Curtain.

**Vorhänge|schloss** *das* padlock.

**Vorhang|stange** *die* curtain rod.

**Vor|haut** *die* foreskin.

**vorher** *adv* - **1.** [früher] before; **am Tag ~** the day before - **2.** [im Voraus] before(hand).

**vorher|bestimmen** *vt* to predetermine.

**vorherig** *adj* previous.

**Vorherrschaft** *die* supremacy.

**vor|herrschen** *vi* to prevail.

**vorherrschend** *adj* prevailing.

**Vorher|sage** *die* - **1.** [für Wetter] forecast - **2.** [des Schicksals] prediction.

**vorher|sehen** *vt (unreg)* [wahrsagen] to foresee; [voraussehen] to predict; [Wetter] to forecast.

**vorhin, vorhin** *adv* just now.

**vorig** *adj* last.

**Vor|jahr** *das* previous year.

**vorjährig** *adj*: **das ~e Treffen** the previous year's meeting.

**Vorkaufs|recht** *das* right of first refusal.

**Vorkehrungen** *pl*: **~ treffen** to take precautions.

**Vorkenntnisse** *pl* previous experience *(U)*; '**~ nicht erforderlich**' 'no experience necessary'.

**vor|knöpfen** *vt fam*: **sich** *(D)* **jn ~** [zur Kritik] to take sb to task; **sich** *(D)* **etw ~** [zur Bearbeitung] to tackle sthg.

**vor|kommen** (*perf* ist vorgekommen) *vi (unreg)* - **1.** [passieren] to happen - **2.** [auftreten] to be found, to occur - **3.** [scheinen]: **jm verdächtig ~** to seem suspicious to sb; **es kommt mir vor, als sei heute Sonntag** today feels like Sunday to me; **sich überflüssig ~** to feel unwanted - **4.** [nach vorne kommen] to come forward.

**Vorkommen** (*pl* -) *das* - **1.** [an Bodenschätzen] deposit - **2.** [Existieren] presence - **3.** [Auftreten] occurrence.

**Vorkommnis** (*pl* -se) *das* incident.

**vor|laden** *vt (unreg)* to summons.

**Vor|ladung** *die* summons *(sg)*.

**Vor|lage** *die* - **1.** [Muster] pattern - **2.** [Vorlegen] presentation - **3.** [Gesetzesvorlage] bill - **4.** SPORT [bei Fußball] assist, pass *(leading to a goal)*.

**vor|lassen** *vt (unreg)*: **jn ~** to let sb go first.

**Vor|läufer, in** *der, die* forerunner.

**vorläufig** *adj* provisional ◇ *adv* provisionally; **ich wohne ~ bei ihm** I'm staying with him for the time being; **die Polizei nahm sie ~ fest** the police held them.

**vorlaut** *adj*: **~ sein** to make comments out of turn ◇ *adv* out of turn.

**Vorleben** *das* past (life).

**vor|legen** *vt* to present; [Ausweis] to show; [Zeugnis] to submit; **jm etw ~** to present sb with sthg; **dem Professor seine Diplomarbeit ~** to hand in one's dissertation to the professor.

**vor|lesen** *vt (unreg)* to read out; **jm etw ~** to read sthg to sb.

**Vor|lesung** *die* UNI lecture.

**Vorlesungs|verzeichnis** *das* UNI lecture timetable.

**vor|letzte, r, s** *adj* penultimate, last but one.

**Vorliebe** (*pl* -n) *die* preference; **eine ~ für jn/ etw haben** to be particularly fond of sb/ sthg.

**vorlieb nehmen** *vi (unreg)*: **mit jm/etw ~** to make do with sb/sthg.

**vor|liegen** *vi (unreg)* [vorgelegt sein]: **der Antrag liegt vor** the application has been received; **die Ergebnisse liegen noch nicht vor** the results are not yet available; **gegen ihn liegt nichts vor** no charges have been brought against him.

**vor|machen** *vt* - **1.** *fam* [zeigen]: **jm etw ~** to show sb how to do sthg - **2.** [vortäuschen]: **jm etwas ~** to fool sb; **mir kannst du nichts ~** you can't fool me.

**Vormacht|stellung** *die* supremacy *(U)*.

**vormals** *adv* [früher] formerly.

**Vor|marsch** *der*: **auf dem ~ sein** *fig* to be gaining ground.

**V**

**vor|merken** _vt_ - **1.** [Termin] to make a note of - **2.** [Person]: **jn für einen Kurs ~** to put sb's name down for a course.

**Vor|mittag** _der_ morning; **gestern/heute/ morgen ~** yesterday/this/tomorrow morning.

**vormittags** _adv_ in the morning.

**Vormund** (_pl_ -e _ODER_ -münder) _der_ guardian.

**Vormundschaft** (_pl_ -en) _die_ guardianship.

**vorn, vorne** _adv_ in front, at the front; **da ~** over there; **weiter ~e** further on; **nach ~** forwards.
➤ **von vorn** _adv_ [von Anfang an] from the beginning.
➤ **von vorn bis hinten** _adv fam_ [bedienen] hand and foot; **jn von ~ bis hinten belügen** to lie through one's teeth to sb.

**Vor|name** _der_ first name.

**vorne** = vorn.

**vornehm** _adj_ - **1.** [fein - Charakter] noble; [der Oberschicht angehörend] distinguished - **2.** [elegant] upmarket ⬥ _adv_ [elegant] elegantly.

**vor|nehmen** _vt (unreg)_ - **1.** [durchführen] to carry out; [Auswahl] to make - **2.** [sich beschäftigen mit]: **sich (D) etw ~** _fam_ to tackle sthg - **3.** [sich entschließen]: **sich (D) ~, etw zu tun** to resolve to do sthg; **sich (D) etw fest vorgenommen haben** to have made up one's mind to do sthg; **sich zu viel ~** to take on too much.

**vornherein** ➤ **von vornherein** _adv_ from the start.

**vornüber** _adv_ forwards.

**Vor|ort** _der_ suburb.

**Vorort|zug** _der_ suburban train.

**Vor|platz** _der_ forecourt.

**Vor|programm** _das_ supporting programme.

**vor|programmieren** _vt_ to preprogram.

**Vorrang** _der_: **vor jm ~ haben** to take precedence over sb.

**vorrangig** _adj_ of prime importance ⬥ _adv_: **etw ~ behandeln** to treat sthg as a matter of priority.

**Vorrat** (_pl_ -räte) _der_ supply; [Reserve] store; **Vorräte** [von Geschäft] stocks; **ein ~ an etw (D)** a supply/store of sthg.
➤ **auf Vorrat** _adv_: **etw auf ~ einkaufen** to stock up on sthg.

**vorrätig** _adj_ in stock; **etw ~ haben** to have sthg in stock; **~/nicht mehr ~ sein** to be in/out of stock.

**Vor|raum** _der_ anteroom.

**Vor|recht** _das_ privilege.

**Vor|richtung** _die_ device.

**vor|rücken** (_perf_ **hat/ist vorgerückt**) _vt (hat)_ to move forward ⬥ _vi (ist)_ - **1.** [räumlich] to move forward - **2.** [in Hierarchie] to move up - **3.** [zeitlich]: **zu vorgerückter Stunde** at a late hour.

**Vorruhestand** _der_ early retirement; **in den ~ gehen** to take early retirement.

**Vor|runde** _die_ SPORT qualifying round.

**Vors.** _abk für_ Vorsitzender.

**vor|sagen** _vt_: **jm etw ~** to tell sb sthg ⬥ _vi_: **jm ~** to tell sb the answer.

**Vor|saison** _die_ low season.

**Vor|satz** _der_ resolution; **einen ~ fassen, etw zu tun** to resolve to do sthg; **gute Vorsätze** good intentions.

**vorsätzlich** _adj_ RECHT premeditated ⬥ _adv_ intentionally, on purpose.

**Vor|schau** _die_ preview.

**Vorschein** _der_: **zum ~ kommen** to turn up.

**vor|schieben** _vt (unreg)_ - **1.** [schieben] to push forward; [Riegel] to push across; **das Kinn ~** to stick one's chin out - **2.** [Vorwand] to put forward as an excuse - **3.** [Stellvertreter] to use as a front man.

**vor|schießen** _vt (unreg)_: **jm eine Summe ~** _fam_ to advance sb a sum.

**Vor|schlag** _der_ suggestion; **jm einen ~ machen** to make a suggestion to sb; **ich habe ihr den ~ gemacht, wegzufahren** I suggested to her that we should go away.

**vor|schlagen** _vt (unreg)_ to suggest; **jm etw ~** to suggest sthg to sb; **er schlug vor, ins Kino zu gehen** he suggested going to the cinema.

**vorschnell** _adj_ rash ⬥ _adv_ rashly.

**vor|schreiben** _vt (unreg)_ [Subj: Gesetz] to stipulate; **sein Vater versucht ihm alles vorzuschreiben** his father is always trying to tell him what to do; **sie lässt sich nichts ~** she won't be dictated to.

**Vor|schrift** _die_ regulation.

**Vorschub** _der_: **jm/einer Sache ~ leisten** to play into the hands of sb/sthg.

**Vorschulalter** _das_ preschool age.

**Vor|schule** _die_ nursery school.

**Vorschul|erziehung** _die_ preschool education.

**Vor|schuss** _der_ advance; **ein ~ auf etw (A)** an advance on sthg.

**vor|schützen** _vt_ to plead.

**vor|schweben** _vi_: **mir schwebt ein neues Projekt vor** I have a new project in mind.

**vor|sehen** _vt (unreg)_ - **1.** [planen] to plan; **die Feier ist für nächste Woche vorgesehen** the celebration is scheduled _ODER_ planned for next week; **es war vorgesehen, dass er mich abholt** he was supposed to pick me up; **das ist nicht vorgesehen** there are no plans for that; **jn für etw ~** to have sb in mind for sthg; **etw**

**für etw ~** to intend sthg for sthg **- 2.** [vorschreiben] to provide for.

  ➤ **sich vorsehen** *ref:* **sich vor jm/etw ~** [achtsam sein] to beware of sb/sthg.

**vor|setzen** *vt:* **jm etw ~** to serve sb sthg.

**Vorsicht** *die* care; **dieser Kollege ist mit ~ zu genießen** you should be wary of this colleague ◇ *interj* look out!; **~, Stufe!** mind the step!

**vorsichtig** *adj* careful ◇ *adv* carefully.

**vorsichtshalber** *adv* as a precaution.

**Vorsichts|maßnahme** *die* precaution; **~n treffen** to take precautions.

**Vor|silbe** *die* prefix.

**vor|singen** *(unreg) vt:* **(jm) etw ~** to sing sthg (to sb) ◇ *vi* [zur Prüfung] to do a singing test; [beim Theater] to audition.

**Vor|sitz** *der* chairmanship; **den ~ führen** ODER **haben** to be in the chair.

**Vorsitzende** *(pl -n) der, die* chairperson.

**Vorsorge** *die (ohne pl)* [gegen Krankheit, Gefahr] precautions *(pl)*; [für das Alter] provisions *(pl)*; **~ treffen** to take precautions; [für das Alter] to make provisions.

**vor|sorgen** *vi:* **für etw ~** to make provisions for sthg.

**Vorsorge|untersuchung** *die* MED precautionary examination.

**vorsorglich** *adj* precautionary ◇ *adv* as a precaution.

**Vorspann** *(pl -e) der* opening credits *(pl)*.

**Vor|speise** *die* starter.

**Vor|spiegelung** *die:* **unter ~ falscher Tatsachen** under false pretences.

**Vor|spiel** *das* **- 1.** [im Theater] prologue; [im Konzert] prelude **- 2.** [vor dem Sex] foreplay.

**vor|spielen** *vt* **- 1.** [auf einem Instrument]: **jm ein Stück ~** to play a piece for sb **- 2.** [vortäuschen] to put on an act ◇ *vi* [auf einem Instrument]: **jm ~** to play for sb.

**vor|sprechen** *(unreg) vt* **- 1.** [zum Nachsprechen]: **jm etw ~** to say sthg for sb to repeat **- 2.** [zur Prüfung] to recite ◇ *vi* **- 1.** [mit Anliegen]: **bei jm ~** to go to sb **- 2.** [im Theater] to audition.

**vor|springen** *(perf* **ist vorgesprungen)** *vi (unreg)* **- 1.** [Balkon] to jut out **- 2.** [Tiger, Kämpfer] to jump forward.

**Vor|sprung** *der* **- 1.** [von Läufer, Auto] lead **- 2.** [von Wand] ledge.

**Vor|stadt** *die* suburb.

**Vor|stand** *der* [von Firma] board of directors; [von Verein] committee; [von Partei] executive.

**Vorstandsmit|glied** *das* [von Firma] board member; [von Verein] committee member.

**Vorstands|sitzung** *die* [von Firma] board meeting; [von Verein] committee meeting.

**vor|stehen** *vi (unreg)* **- 1.** to jut out; [Backenknochen] to be prominent; [Zähne] to protrude **- 2.** [einer Gruppe, Institution]: **jm/etw ~** to be in charge of sb/sthg.

**vor|stellen** *vt* **- 1.** [bekannt machen] to introduce; **jn jm ~** to introduce sb to sb **- 2.** [sich ausdenken]: **sich** *(D)* **etw ~** to imagine sthg; **stell dir vor!** imagine! **- 3.** [Uhr] to put forward.

  ➤ **sich vorstellen** *ref* **- 1.** [bekannt machen]: **sich jm ~** to introduce o.s. to sb **- 2.** [sich bewerben]: **sich bei jm ~** to go for an interview with sb.

**Vor|stellung** *die* **- 1.** [Idee] idea; **etw entspricht (nicht) js ~en** sthg is (not) as sb imagined it; **sich keine ~ von etw machen** to have no idea about sthg **- 2.** [im Theater] performance **- 3.** [das Vorstellen] presentation.

**Vorstellungs|gespräch** *das* interview.

**Vor|stoß** *der* advance; **einen ~ bei jm machen** to approach sb.

**vor|stoßen** *(perf* **ist vorgestoßen)** *vi (unreg)* to advance.

**Vor|strafe** *die* RECHT previous conviction.

**Vorstrafen|register** *das* criminal record.

**vor|strecken** *vt* **- 1.** [Arme, Beine] to stretch out **- 2.** [Geld]: **jm etw ~** to advance sb sthg.

**Vor|stufe** *die* preliminary stage.

**Vor|tag** *der* day before.

**vor|täuschen** *vt* to feign; **jm etw ~** to pretend sthg to sb.

**Vor|teil** *der* advantage; **zu js ~** to sb's advantage; **jm gegenüber im ~ sein** to have an advantage over sb.

**vorteilhaft** *adj* [Geschäft, Lage] advantageous; [Haarschnitt] flattering.

**Vortrag** *(pl -träge) der* talk; **ein ~ über jn/etw** a talk about sb/sthg; **einen ~ halten** to give a talk.

**vor|tragen** *vt (unreg)* **- 1.** [darbieten] to perform; [Gedicht] to recite **- 2.** [aussprechen] to present; **jm eine Bitte/Beschwerde ~** to make a request/complaint to sb.

**vor|treten** *(perf* **ist vorgetreten)** *vi (unreg)* to step forward.

**Vortritt** *der:* **jm den ~ lassen** to let sb go first.

**vorüber** *adj:* **~ sein** to be over.

**vorüber|gehen** *(perf* **ist vorübergegangen)** *vi (unreg)* **- 1.** [Person] to pass by; **an jm/etw ~** to pass by sb/sthg **- 2.** [Schmerzen] to come to an end.

**vorübergehend** *adj* temporary ◇ *adv* temporarily.

**Vorur|teil** *das* prejudice; **~e gegen jn/etw haben** to be prejudiced against sb/sthg.

**Vorver|kauf** *der* advance booking; **Karten im ~ bekommen** to buy tickets in advance.

**vor|verlegen** *vt* to bring forward.

**V**

**Vor|wahl** *die* - **1.** [telefonisch] dialling code *Br*, area code *Am* - **2.** [von Wahlen] primary *Am*, *candidate selection procedure.*

**Vorwahl|nummer** *die* [telefonisch] dialling code *Br*, area code *Am*.

**Vorwand** (*pl* -wände) *der* excuse; **unter dem ~** under the pretext.

**vorwärts** *adv* forwards.

**vorwärts gehen** (*perf* **ist vorwärts gegangen**) *vi (unreg)* to progress; **mit dem Experiment geht es nicht vorwärts** the experiment isn't getting anywhere.

**vorwärts kommen** (*perf* **ist vorwärts gekommen**) *vi (unreg)* to make progress.

**Vor|wäsche** *die* pre-wash.

**vorweg** *adv* - **1.** [vorher] beforehand - **2.** [voraus] in front.

**vorweg|nehmen** *vt (unreg)* to anticipate.

**Vorweihnachtszeit** *die* pre-Christmas period.

**vor|weisen** *vt (unreg)* - **1.** [vorzeigen] to show - **2.** [bieten]: **etw ~ können** to possess sthg; **einiges vorzuweisen haben** to be very competent.

**vor|werfen** *vt (unreg)*: **jm etw ~** to accuse sb of sthg.

**vorwiegend** *adv* mainly.

**Vorwissen** *das* prior knowledge.

**vorwitzig** *adj* cheeky.

**Vor|wort** *das* preface.

**Vor|wurf** *der* accusation; **jm etw zum ~ machen** to accuse sb of sthg.

**vorwurfsvoll** *adj* reproachful <> *adv* reproachfully.

**Vor|zeichen** *das* - **1.** [Anzeichen] omen; **unter negativem ~ stehen** to be under a cloud; **unter positivem ~ stehen** to be blessed - **2.** MATH sign - **3.** MUS key signature.

**vor|zeigen** *vt*: (**jm etw**) **~** to show (sb sthg).

**vorzeitig** *adj* early; [Altern, Wehen] premature <> *adv* prematurely; **~ in Rente gehen** to take early retirement.

**vor|ziehen** *vt (unreg)* - **1.** [lieber mögen] to prefer; **jn jm ~** to prefer sb to sb; **etw einer Sache (D) ~** to prefer sthg to sthg - **2.** [Gardine] to close - **3.** [Termin] to bring forward - **4.** [nach vorn ziehen] to pull forward.

**Vor|zimmer** *das* secretary's office.

**Vor|zug** *der* - **1.** [Vorrang] advantage; **jm/etw den ~ geben** to give sb/sthg preference - **2.** [gute Eigenschaft] virtue.

**vorzüglich** *adj* excellent <> *adv* excellently.

**vorzugsweise** *adv* mainly.

**Votum** (*pl* **Voten**) *das (ohne pl)* vote.

**VP** *abk für* **Vollpension**.

**VR** (*pl* -**s**) *die abk für* **Volksrepublik**.

**vulgär** *adj* vulgar.

**Vulkan** (*pl* -**e**) *der* volcano.

**vulkanisch** *adj* volcanic.

**v. u. Z.** (*abk für* **vor unserer Zeitrechnung**) B.C.

**VWL** [faʊveːˈʔɛl] (*abk für* **Volkswirtschaftslehre**) *die* economics.

**w, W** [veː] (*pl* - *ODER* -**s**) *das* w, W.
**~ W** (*abk für* **West, Watt**) W.

**WAA** [veːaːˈʔaː] (*pl* -**s**) *die abk für* **Wiederaufbereitungsanlage**.

**Waadt** *die* Vaud.

**Waadtländer, in** (*mpl* -; *fpl* -**nen**) *der, die* native/inhabitant of Vaud.

**waadtländisch** *adj* of/from Vaud.

**Waage** (*pl* -**n**) *die* - **1.** [Gerät] scales (*pl*); **sich die ~ halten** *fig* to balance each other - **2.** ASTROL Libra; **~ sein** to be Libra.

**waagerecht, waagrecht** *adj* horizontal <> *adv* horizontally.

**Wabe** (*pl* -**n**) *die* honeycomb.

**wach** *adj* - **1.** [nicht schlafend] awake; **jn ~ machen** to wake sb; **~ halten** [Person] to keep awake; [Erinnerung] to keep alive; **~ liegen** to lie awake; **~ sein** to be awake; **~ werden** to wake up - **2.** [Geist] alert.

**Wache** (*pl* -**n**) *die* - **1.** (*ohne pl*) [Wachdienst] guard duty; **~ halten** to be on guard - **2.** [Wächter] guard - **3.** [Polizeiwache] police station.

**wachen** *vi*: (**über jn/etw**) **~** to keep watch (over sb/sthg).

**wachhabend** *adj* duty (*vor Subst*).

**Wach|hund** *der* guard dog.

**Wacholder** (*pl* -) *der* juniper.

**wach|rufen** *vt (unreg)* to awaken; **etw in jm ~** to awaken sthg in sb.

**Wachs** [vaks] (*pl* -**e**) *das* wax (*U*); **~ in js Händen sein** *fig* to be putty in sb's hands.

**wachsam** [ˈvaksaːm] *adj* vigilant.

**Wachsamkeit** [ˈvaksaːmkaɪt] *die* vigilance.

**wachsen** [vaksn̩] (*präs* **wächst** ODER **wachst**; *prät* **wuchs** ODER **wachste**; *perf* **ist gewachsen** ODER **hat gewachst**) *vi (unreg) (ist)* **- 1.** [größer werden] to grow **- 2.** [entsprechen]: **einer Sache** (D) **gewachsen sein** to be up to sthg ◇ *vt (reg) (hat)* [mit Wachs] to wax.

**wachsend** ['vaksn̩t] *adj* growing.

**Wachsfiguren|kabinett** ['vaksfigu:rn̩kabinet] *das* waxworks *(pl)*.

**Wachsmal|stift** ['vaksma:lʃtɪft] *der* wax crayon.

**wächst** [vɛkst] *präs* ▷ **wachsen**.

**Wachs|tuch** *das* oilcloth.

**Wachstum** ['vakstu:m] *das* growth.

**Wachstums|rate** *die* WIRTSCH growth rate.

**Wachtel** (*pl* -n) *die* quail.

**Wächter, in** (*mpl* -; *fpl* -nen) *der, die* guard.

**Wacht|meister, in** *der, die* constable Br, patrolman Am.

**Wacht|posten** *der* guard.

**Wacht|turm, Wachtturm** *der* watchtower.

**Wach- und Schließ|gesellschaft** *die* security firm.

**wackelig, wacklig** *adj* **- 1.** [nicht fest] wobbly **- 2.** *fam* [gefährdet] shaky; **mit seiner Versetzung steht es recht ~** his transfer is looking really uncertain.

**Wackel|kontakt** *der* ELEKTR loose contact.

**wackeln** (*perf* hat/ist gewackelt) *vi* **- 1.** *(hat)* [nicht fest sein] to be wobbly **- 2.** *(hat)* [hin und her bewegen]: **mit etw ~** to shake sthg **- 3.** *(ist)* fam [gehen] to totter **- 4.** *(hat)* fam [Posten] to be shaky.

**wacker** *adj* **- 1.** [anständig] upright **- 2.** [tüchtig] hearty ◇ *adv* valiantly.

**wacklig** = wackelig.

**Wade** (*pl* -n) *die* calf.

**Waden|bein** *das* fibula.

**Waffe** (*pl* -n) *die* weapon; **die ~n strecken** *fig* to admit defeat; **jn mit seinen eigenen ~n schlagen** *fig* to beat sb at his own game.

**Waffel** (*pl* -n) *die* waffle.

**Waffel|eisen** *das* waffle iron.

**Waffen|besitz** *der* possession of firearms.

**Waffen|gewalt** *die:* **mit ~** by force of arms.

**Waffen|handel** *der* arms trade.

**Waffen|ruhe** *die* ceasefire.

**Waffen|schein** *der* firearms licence.

**Waffenstill|stand** *der* armistice.

**wagemutig** *adj* daring.

**wagen** *vt* to risk; **einen Versuch ~** to risk an attempt; **es ~, etw zu tun** to dare to do sthg; **alles ~** to risk everything.

➤ **sich wagen** *ref* to dare; **sich nachts nicht auf die Straße ~** not to dare to go out on the street at night; **sich an etw** (A) **~** to attempt sthg.

**Wagen** (*pl* -) *der* **- 1.** [Auto] car **- 2.** [von Zug, Straßenbahn] carriage Br, car Am **- 3.** [mit Pferd] carriage.

➤ **der Große Wagen** *der* ASTRON the Plough.
➤ **der Kleine Wagen** *der* ASTRON the Little Bear.

**Wagen|heber** (*pl* -) *der* jack.

**Wagen|kolonne** *die* [Konvoi] convoy; [Autoschlange] line of traffic.

**Wagen|ladung** *die* truckload, lorryload Br.

**Wagen|park** *der* fleet of cars.

**Wagen|rad** *das* cartwheel.

**Waggon, Wagon** [va'gɔŋ] (*pl* -s) *der* carriage Br, car Am.

**waghalsig** *adj* reckless.

**Wagnis** (*pl* -se) *das* risk.

**Wagon** = Waggon.

**Wahl** (*pl* -en) *die* **- 1.** (ohne pl) [Auswahl] choice; **die ~ haben** to have the choice; **eine ~ treffen** to make a choice; **wie viel Kandidaten stehen zur ~?** how many candidates are there to choose from?; **erste/zweite ~** first/second class; **in die engere ~ kommen** to be shortlisted; **keine andere ~ haben** to have no other choice **- 2.** [Abstimmung] election; **geheime ~** secret ballot; **zur ~ gehen** to vote.

**wahlberechtigt** *adj* entitled to vote.

**Wahl|beteiligung** *die:* **hohe/niedrige ~** high/low turnout.

**Wahl|bezirk** *der* electoral district.

**wählen** *vt* **- 1.** [aussuchen] to choose **- 2.** [am Telefon] to dial **- 3.** [politisch] to elect ◇ *vi* **- 1.** [aussuchen] to choose; **zwischen etw** (D) **und etw** (D) **~** to choose between sthg and sthg **- 2.** [am Telefon] to dial **- 3.** [politisch] to vote.

**Wähler** (*pl* -) *der* voter.

**Wahl|ergebnis** *das* election result.

**Wählerin** (*pl* -nen) *die* voter.

**wählerisch** *adj* choosy.

**Wähler|stimme** *die* vote.

**Wähler|vereinigung** *die:* **eine freie ~** an independent list.

**Wahl|fach** *das* SCHULE optional subject.

**Wahl|gang** *der* ballot; **im ersten/zweiten ~** in the first/second ballot.

**Wahl|heimat** *die* adopted home.

**Wahl|helfer, in** *der, die* polling officer.

**Wahl|kabine** *die* polling booth.

**Wahl|kampf** *der* election campaign; **einen ~ führen** to conduct an election campaign.

**Wahl|kreis** *der* constituency.

**Wahl|lokal** *das* polling station.

**W**

**wahllos** *adv* at random.

**Wahlniederllage** *die* election defeat.

**Wahllprogramm** *das* election manifesto.

**Wahllrecht** *das* right to vote; **allgemeines ~** universal suffrage.

**Wahllrede** *die* election speech.

**Wähllscheibe** *die* dial.

**Wahllschein** *der* polling card.

**Wahllsieg** *der* election victory.

**Wahllspruch** *der* motto.

**Wahlverlsammlung** *die* election meeting.

**Wahllversprechen** *das* election promise.

**wahlweise** *adv*: **zum Frühstück gibt es ~ Kaffee oder Tee** for breakfast there's a choice of coffee or tea.

**Wahllzettel** *der* ballot paper.

**Wahn** *der (ohne pl)* delusion.

**Wahnsinn** *der* madness; **Wahnsinn!** amazing!; **das ist heller** ODER **reiner ~** it's utter madness.

**wahnsinnig** *adj* - **1.** [verrückt] mad; **wie ~** *fam* like mad; **das macht mich ~!** *fam* that drives me crazy! - **2.** [groß] incredible ◇ *adv fam* [sehr] incredibly.

**Wahnvorlstellung** *die* delusion.

**wahr** *adj* true; **~e Liebe/Freundschaft** true love/friendship; **das darf doch nicht ~ sein!** *fam* that can't be true!; **etw ~ machen** *fig* to carry out sthg.

➤ **nicht wahr** *interj*: **du warst doch gestern auch hier, nicht ~?** you were here yesterday too, weren't you?; **das stimmt doch, nicht ~?** that's right, isn't it?

**wahren** *vt geh* [Interessen] to protect; [Form] to preserve; **den Schein ~** to keep up appearances.

**während** *konj* [zeitlich, gegensätzlich] while ◇ *präp* during.

**währenddessen** *adv* in the meantime.

**wahrhaben** *vt*: **etw nicht ~ wollen** not to want to accept sthg.

**wahrhaftig** *adv* really.

**Wahrheit** *(pl -en) die* truth *(U)*; **es mit der ~ nicht so genau nehmen** to be economical with the truth.

➤ **in Wahrheit** *adv* in reality.

**wahrheitsgemäß** *adj* truthful ◇ *adv* truthfully.

**wahrnehmbar** *adj* perceptible.

**wahrlnehmen** *vt (unreg)* - **1.** [Veränderung, Geräusch] to notice - **2.** [Gelegenheit] to avail oneself of - **3.** [Interessen] to protect.

**Wahrnehmung** *(pl -en) die* - **1.** [Spüren] awareness *(U)* - **2.** [von Gelegenheit] seizing - **3.** [von Geschäft] representation.

**wahrlsagen** *vi* to predict the future.

**Wahrsager, in** *(mpl -; fpl -nen) der, die* fortune-teller.

**wahrscheinlich** *adj* probable ◇ *adv* probably.

**Wahrscheinlichkeit** *(pl -en) die* probability; **aller ~ nach** in all probability; **mit größter ~** most probably.

**Wahrscheinlichkeitsrechnung** *die* probability calculus.

**Wahrung** *die* protection.

**Währung** *(pl -en) die* currency; **eine harte ~** a hard currency.

**Währungsleinheit** *die* currency unit.

**Währungsrelform** *die* HIST & WIRTSCH currency reform.

**Währungslsystem** *das* monetary system.

**Wahrlzeichen** *das* symbol.

**Waise** *(pl -n) die* orphan.

**Waisenlhaus** *das* orphanage.

**Waisenlkind** *das* orphan.

**Wal** *(pl -e) der* whale.

**Wald** *(pl Wälder) der* wood; [groß] forest; **den ~ vor lauter Bäumen nicht sehen** *hum & fig* not to be able to see the wood for the trees.

**Waldlbrand** *der* forest fire.

**Wäldchen** *(pl -) das* copse.

**Waldlgebiet** *das* wooded area.

**Waldllauf** *der*: **einen ~ machen** to go for a run/jog in the woods.

**Waldmeister** *der* woodruff.

**Waldorflschule** *die* SCHULE Rudolf Steiner school.

---

**WALDORFSCHULE**

These schools were founded by the Austrian philosopher and educationalist Rudolf Steiner for the children of working-class and lower middle-class families. They give equal emphasis to pupils' scientific, artistic, manual and intellectual abilities and do not include any grading system.

---

**Waldlsterben** *das* forest dieback.

**Waldlweg** *der* forest track.

**Wales** ['weɪlz] *nt* Wales.

**Waliser, in** *(mpl -; fpl -nen) der, die* Welshman *(f Welshwoman)*.

**walisisch** *adj* Welsh.

**Walkie-Talkie** ['wɔːkɪ'tɔːkɪ] *(pl -s) das* walkie-talkie.

**Walkman**® ['wɔːkmɛn] *(pl -men) der* Walkman®.

**Wall** *(pl Wälle) der* rampart.

**Wallach** (pl -e) der gelding.

**Wall|fahrt** die pilgrimage.

**Wallfahrts|ort** der place of pilgrimage.

**Wallis** das Valais.

**Walliser** (pl -) der native/inhabitant of Valais ◇ adj (unver) of/from Valais.

**Walliserin** (pl -nen) die native/inhabitant of Valais.

**walliserisch** adj of/from Valais.

**Wallone** (pl -n) der Walloon.

**Wallonien** nt Wallonia.

**Wallonin** (pl -nen) die Walloon.

**wallonisch** adj Walloon.

**Wallung** (pl -en) die: jn in ~ versetzen [Wut] to send sb into a rage.

**Wall|nuss** die walnut.

**Wall|ross** das walrus.

**walten** vi geh to reign; etw ~ lassen to exercise sthg.

**Walze** (pl -n) die roller.

**walzen** vt to roll.

**wälzen** vt - **1.** [rollen] to roll - **2.** [Buch] to pore over.

◆ **sich wälzen** ref to roll around.

**Walzer** (pl -) der waltz; ~ tanzen to waltz.

**Wälzer** (pl -) der fam tome.

**wand** prät ⊳ winden.

**Wand** (pl Wände) die - **1.** [Mauer] wall (inside); eine tragende ~ a supporting wall - **2.** [Felswand] rock face - **3.** [von Schrank] side - **4.** RW: dass die Wände wackeln fam fit to raise the roof; die Wände haben Ohren walls have ears; in den eigenen vier Wänden in one's own home; jn an die ~ stellen fam to send sb before the firing squad.

◆ **Wand an Wand** adv next door.

**Wandel** der change; im ~ begriffen to be in a state of flux.

**wandeln** (perf hat/ist gewandelt) geh vi (ist) to stroll ◇ vt (hat) to change.

◆ **sich wandeln** ref to change; sich zu etw ~ to turn into sthg.

**Wanderer, Wandrer** (pl -) der hiker.

**Wanderin, Wandrerin** (pl -nen) die hiker.

**Wander|karte** die walking map.

**wandern** (perf ist gewandert) vi - **1.** [als Sport] to go hiking - **2.** [ziellos] to wander - **3.** fam [gebracht werden]: ins Gefängnis ~ to end up in prison.

**Wander|pokal** der challenge cup.

**Wanderschaft** (pl -en) die travels (pl).

◆ **auf Wanderschaft** adv on one's travels (pl).

**Wander|schuh** der hiking ODER walking boot.

**Wander|tag** der school outing.

**Wanderung** (pl -en) die hike; eine ~ machen to go on a hike.

**Wander|weg** der trail.

**Wand|gemälde** das fresco.

**Wand|kalender** der wall calendar.

**Wand|karte** die wall map.

**Wandlung** (pl -en) die change; eine ~ vollzieht sich a change is taking place.

**Wand|malerei** die mural.

**Wandrer** = Wanderer.

**Wandrerin** = Wanderin.

**Wand|schirm** der screen.

**Wand|schrank** der built-in cupboard Br ODER closet Am; [Kleiderschrank] built-in wardrobe Br ODER closet Am.

**Wand|tafel** die blackboard.

**wandte** prät ⊳ wenden.

**Wand|teppich** der tapestry.

**Wand|uhr** die wall clock.

**Wand|zeitung** die wall newspaper.

**Wange** (pl -n) die geh cheek.

◆ **Wange an Wange** adv cheek to cheek.

**wankelmütig** adj geh & abw irresolute.

**wanken** (perf hat/ist gewankt) vi - **1.** (ist) [Betrunkener] to stagger - **2.** (hat) [Boden, Mauer] to sway - **3.** (hat) geh [Macht] to be under threat; [Entschluss] to waver.

**Wanken** das: ins ~ kommen ODER geraten to start to waver.

**wann** adv when; bis ~? until when?, till when?; seit ~ lebst du schon hier? how long have you been living here?; von ~ bis ~? when?; ~ du willst whenever you want.

**Wanne** (pl -n) die - **1.** [Badewanne] bath; in der ~ sitzen to be in the bath - **2.** [Becken] tub.

**Wanze** (pl -n) die bug.

**Wappen** (pl -) das coat of arms.

**war** prät ⊳ sein.

**warb** prät ⊳ werben.

**Ware** (pl -n) die product; heiße ~ stolen goods.

**Waren|angebot** das range of goods.

**Waren|haus** das department store.

**Waren|lager** das warehouse.

**Waren|probe** die sample.

**Waren|sendung** die sample sent by post.

**Waren|zeichen** das: eingetragenes ~ registered trademark.

**warf** prät ⊳ werfen.

**warm** (kompar wärmer; superl wärmste) adj warm; es ist ~ it's warm; mir ist/wird ~ I'm warm/warming up; draußen ist es 30°C ~ it's

**W**

30°C outside; **mit jm ~ werden** *fam fig* to get on well with sb; **~e Miete** *rent including heating bills* ◇ *adv* warmly; **~ essen** to have a hot meal.

**Wärme** *die* warmth.

**wärmedämmend** *adj* insulating.

**wärmen** *vt* & *vi* to warm.

➤ **sich wärmen** *ref:* **sich an etw** *(D)* **~** to warm o.s.

**Wärme|pumpe** *die* TECH heat pump.

**Wärm|flasche** *die* hot-water bottle.

**warm|halten** *ref (unreg):* **sich** *(D)* **jn ~** *fig fam* to keep in with sb.

**Warmhalte|platte** *die* hotplate.

**warmherzig** *adj* warm-hearted.

**warm laufen** *(perf* **hat/ist warm gelaufen***) vi (unreg) (ist)* to warm up.

➤ **sich warm laufen** *ref* to warm up.

**Warm|miete** *die* rent including heating bills.

**wärmstens** *adv* most warmly.

**Warmwasser** *das* hot water.

**Warnblinkan|lage** *die* AUTO hazard lights *(pl).*

**Warn|dreieck** *das* AUTO warning triangle.

**warnen** *vt* to warn; **jn vor jm/etw ~** to warn sb about sb/sthg.

**Warn|schild** *(pl* **-er***) das* warning sign.

**Warn|signal** *das* warning signal.

**Warn|streik** *der* token strike.

**Warn|system** *das* warning system.

**Warnung** *(pl* **-en***) die* warning.

**Warschau** *nt* Warsaw.

**Warschauer** *(pl* **-***) der* native/inhabitant of Warsaw ◇ *adj (unver)* of/from Warsaw; **~ Pakt** HIST Warsaw Pact.

**Warschauerin** *(pl* **-nen***) die* native/inhabitant of Warsaw.

**Warte|liste** *die* waiting list; **auf der ~ stehen** to be on the waiting list; [bei Flug] to be on standby.

**warten** *vi* to wait; **auf jn/etw ~** to wait for sb/sthg; **mit etw ~** to put sthg on hold; **da kannst du lange ~** *fam* you'll have a long wait!; **na warte!** *fam* just you wait!; **nicht lange auf sich ~ lassen** not to be long in coming ◇ *vt* TECH to service.

**Wärter, in** *(mpl* **-***; fpl* **-nen***) der, die* [im Zoo, Leuchtturm] keeper; [im Gefängnis] warder.

**Warte|saal** *der* waiting room.

**Warte|zeit** *die* wait *(U).*

**Warte|zimmer** *das* waiting room.

**Wartung** *(pl* **-en***) die* servicing *(U).*

**warum** *adv* why; **~ nicht?** why not?

**Warze** *(pl* **-n***) die* wart.

**was** *pron* - **1.** [Interrogativpronomen] what; **~ ist?** what is it?; **~ ist sie (von Beruf)?** what does she do (for a living)? - **2.** [wieviel] how much, what; **~ kostet das?** how much is it? - **3.** *fam* [warum] why; **~ fragst du?** why do you ask? - **4.** *fam* [nicht wahr]: **da freust du dich, ~?** you're pleased, aren't you?; **es ist schön, ~?** it's nice, isn't it?; **gut, ~?** not bad, eh? - **5.** [Relativpronomen] which, that; **das, ~ ...** what ...; **alles, ~ ...** everything (that) ...; **das Beste, ~ ich je gehört habe** the best I've ever heard - **6.** *fam* [etwas] something - **7.** *RW:* **~ für** what sort ODER kind of; **~ sind das für Tiere?** what sort ODER kind of animals are those?; **~ für ein Lärm!** what a noise!; **~ weiß ich!** *fam* don't ask me! ◇ *interj fam* [wie bitte] what?

➤ **ach, was** *interj* no it's/*etc* not!

➤ **so was** *interj:* **na** ODER **also so ~!** really!

**Waschan|lage** *die* carwash.

**waschbar** *adj* washable.

**Wasch|bär** *der* raccoon.

**Wasch|becken** *das* washbasin.

**Wäsche** *(pl* **-n***) die* - **1.** [schmutzige Wäsche] laundry - **2.** [Unterwäsche] underwear - **3.** [Waschen] wash; **in der ~ sein** to be in the wash - **4.** *RW:* **dumm aus der ~ gucken** *fam* to look dumbfounded; **schmutzige ~ waschen** *abw* to wash one's dirty linen in public.

**waschecht** *adj* - **1.** [Stoff] colourfast - **2.** [typisch] true.

**Wäsche|klammer** *die* clothes peg *Br,* clothespin *Am.*

**Wäsche|korb** *der* laundry basket.

**Wäsche|leine** *die* washing line.

**waschen** *(präs* **wäscht***; prät* **wusch***; perf* **hat gewaschen***) vt* to wash; **sich** *(D)* **die Haare/die Hände ~** to wash one's hair/hands.

➤ **sich waschen** *ref* to have a wash; **die Fahrprüfung hatte sich gewaschen** *fam fig* the driving test was quite something; **er bekam eine Abreibung, die sich gewaschen hatte** he got one hell of a hiding.

**Wäscherei** *(pl* **-en***) die* laundrette.

**Wäsche|schleuder** *die* spin-dryer.

**Wäsche|ständer** *der* clotheshorse.

**Wäsche|trockner** *der* - **1.** [Maschine] tumbledryer - **2.** [Wäscheständer] clotheshorse.

**Wasch|gelegenheit** *die* washing facilities *(pl).*

**Wasch|lappen** *der* - **1.** [Lappen] facecloth - **2.** *fam abw* [Person] wimp.

**Wasch|maschine** *die* washing machine.

**Wasch|mittel** *das* detergent.

**Wasch|pulver** *das* washing powder.

**Wasch|raum** *der* washroom.

**Wasch|salon** *der* laundrette.

**Wasch|straße** *die* AUTO carwash.

**wäscht** *präs* ▷ waschen.

**Washington** ['wɔʃɪŋtən] *nt* Washington.

**Wasser** (*pl* - oder **Wässer**) *das* - **1.** [gen] water; ~ abstoßend water-repellent; **unter** ~ **stehen** to be under water - **2.** *(ohne pl)* [Körperflüssigkeit] fluid; **mir läuft das** ~ **im Mund zusammen** my mouth is watering; ~ **lassen** to pass water - **3.** *RW:* **ins** ~ **fallen** to fall through; **er ist mit allen** ~**n gewaschen** *fam* he wasn't born yesterday; **sich über** ~ **halten** to keep one's head above water; ~ **auf js Mühle sein** to be grist to sb's mill.

➣ **am Wasser** *adv* by the water; **nahe am** ~ **gebaut haben** *fam fig* to cry at the slightest thing.

**wasserabstoßend** ▷ Wasser.

**Wasser|bad** *das* KÜCHE bain-marie.

**Wasser|ball** *der* - **1.** [Spiel] water polo - **2.** [Ball] beach ball.

**Wasser|bett** *das* waterbed.

**Wässerchen** (*pl* -) *das:* **sie sieht aus, als ob sie kein** ~ **trüben könnte** *fig* she looks as if butter wouldn't melt in her mouth.

**Wasser|dampf** *der* steam *(U)*.

**wasserdicht** *adj* - **1.** [Bekleidung, Uhr] waterproof - **2.** *fam* [Alibi] watertight.

**Wasser|fall** *der* waterfall; **wie ein** ~ **reden** *fam fig* to talk nonstop.

**Wasser|farbe** *die* watercolours *(pl)*.

**Wasser|flugzeug** *das* seaplane.

**Wasser|glas** *das* water glass.

**Wasser|glätte** *die:* 'Vorsicht bei ~!' 'Danger! road slippery when wet'.

**Wasser|graben** *der* ditch; [Burggraben] moat.

**Wasser|hahn** *der* tap *Br*, faucet *Am*.

**Wasser|kessel** *der* kettle.

**Wasser|kopf** *der* - **1.** MED hydrocephalus *(U)* - **2.** *fig* [aufgebläht]: **der** ~ **der Verwaltung** excessive administration.

**Wasserkraft|werk** *das* hydroelectric power station.

**Wasser|lauf** *der* watercourse.

**Wasser|leitung** *die* water pipe.

**wasserlöslich** *adj* water-soluble.

**Wasser|mangel** *der* drought.

**Wasser|mann** (*pl* -**männer**) *der* ASTROL Aquarius; ~ **sein** to be an Aquarius.

**Wasser|melone** *die* watermelon.

**Wasser|mühle** *die* watermill.

**wässern** *vt* - **1.** [Pflanze, Beet] to water - **2.** KÜCHE to soak.

**Wasser|pfeife** *die* water pipe.

**Wasser|pflanze** *die* aquatic plant.

**Wasser|pistole** *die* water pistol.

**Wasser|ratte** *die* - **1.** [Tier] water rat - **2.** *fam* [Person] waterbaby.

**Wasser|rohr** *das* water pipe.

**Wasser|schaden** *der* water damage *(U)*.

**Wasser|scheide** *die* watershed.

**wasserscheu** *adj* scared of water.

**Wasser|schutzpolizei** *die* river police.

**Wasser|ski** *der* [Gerät] water ski ⟨⟩ *nt* waterskiing.

**Wasser|spiegel** *der* water level.

**Wasser|sport** *der* water sport.

**Wasser|spülung** (*pl* -**en**) *die* flush.

**Wasser|stand** *der* water level.

**Wasser|stelle** *die* watering hole.

**Wasser|stoff** *der* CHEM hydrogen.

**Wasser|straße** *die* waterway.

**Wasser|turm** *der* water tower.

**Wasser|uhr** *die* water meter.

**Wasser|verbrauch** *der* water consumption.

**Wasser|verschmutzung** *die* water pollution.

**Wasser|versorgung** *die (ohne pl)* water supply.

**Wasser|vogel** *der* waterfowl.

**Wasser|waage** *die* spirit level.

**Wasser|werfer** (*pl* -) *der* water cannon.

**Wasser|werk** *das* waterworks *(pl)*.

**Wasser|zähler** *der* water meter.

**Wasser|zeichen** *das* watermark.

**wässrig** *adj* watery.

**waten** (*perf* **ist gewatet**) *vi* to wade.

**watscheln** (*perf* **ist gewatschelt**) *vi* to waddle.

**Watt** (*pl* -**en** oder -) *das* - **1.** (*pl* **Watten**) [Küstengebiet] mudflats *(pl)* - **2.** (*pl* **Watt**) PHYS & TECH [Maßeinheit] watt.

**Watte** *die* cotton wool.

**Watte|bausch** *der* wad of cotton wool.

**Watten|meer** *das* mudflats *(pl)*.

**Watte|stäbchen** *das* cotton bud.

**wattiert** *adj* padded.

**WAZ** [vats] *(abk für* **Westdeutsche Allgemeine Zeitung***) die daily newspaper based in the west of Germany.*

**WC** [ve:'tse:] (*pl* -**s**) *(abk für* **water closet***) das* WC.

**WDR** [ve:de:'ɛr] *(abk für* **Westdeutscher Rundfunk***) der German radio station.*

**weben** (*prät* **wob**; *perf* **hat gewoben**) *vt* to weave.

➡ **sich weben** *ref geh*: **sich um jn/etw ~** to circulate about sb/sthg.

**Weber** (*pl* -) *der* weaver.

**Weberei** (*pl* -en) *die* [Unternehmen] weaving mill.

**Weberin** (*pl* -nen) *die* weaver.

**Web|kante** *die* selvage.

**Web|seite** [websaitə] *die* EDV web page, website.

**Web|stuhl** *der* loom.

**Wechsel** ['vɛksl] (*pl* -) *der* - **1.** [Tausch] change - **2.** [Zahlungsmittel] exchange.

➡ **im Wechsel** *adv* in turns.

**Wechsel|bad** *das* - **1.** [Bad] *bath in alternating hot and then cold water* - **2.** *fig* [Auf und Ab]: **~ der Gefühle** emotional rollercoaster.

**Wechsel|beziehung** *die* correlation.

**Wechsel|geld** *das* change.

**wechselhaft** ['vɛks|haft] *adj* changeable.

**Wechseljahre** *pl* menopause (*U*).

**Wechsel|kurs** *der* exchange rate.

**wechseln** ['vɛksln] (*perf* **hat/ist gewechselt**) *vt* (hat) - **1.** [Thema, Kleidung, Arbeitsplatz, Geld] to change; **etw gegen** ODER **in etw** (*A*) **~** to change sthg for sthg - **2.** [tauschen] to exchange ◇ *vi* - **1.** (hat) [sich verändern] to change - **2.** (ist) [an anderen Ort] to move.

**wechselnd** ['vɛkslnt] *adj* changing.

**Wechsel|rahmen** *der* clip frame.

**wechselseitig** *adj* mutual ◇ *adv* mutually.

**Wechsel|strom** *der* (ohne pl) ELEKTR alternating current.

**Wechsel|stube** *die* bureau de change.

**Wechsel|wähler** *der* floating voter.

**Wechsel|wirkung** *die* interaction.

**wecken** *vt* - **1.** [Person] to wake - **2.** [Neugier, Wunsch] to awaken.

**Wecker** (*pl* -) *der* alarm clock; **jm auf den ~ fallen** *fam fig* to get on sb's nerves.

**wedeln** (*perf* **hat/ist gewedelt**) *vi*: **mit etw ~** to wave sthg; **mit dem Schwanz ~** to wag its tail.

**weder** ➡ **weder … noch** *konj* neither … nor.

**weg** *adv* away; **er ist schon ~** he has already gone; **nichts wie ~ hier!** *fam* let's get out of here!; **~ damit!** *fam* take it away!; **Hände ~!** hands off!; **weit ~** far away; **über etw** (*A*) **~ sein** *fam fig* to have got over sthg.

**Weg** (*pl* -e) *der* - **1.** [Pfad] path; **am ~** by the wayside - **2.** [Strecke, Methode] way; **ein weiter ~** a long way; **jm im ~ stehen** ODER **sein** to be in sb's way; **jm über den ~ laufen** to bump into sb; **(jn) nach dem ~ fragen** to ask (sb) the way; **sich auf**

**den ~ machen** to be on one's way; **auf dem schnellsten** ODER **kürzesten ~** in the fastest possible way - **3.** [Erledigung]: **jm einen ~ abnehmen** to save sb a journey - **4.** RW: **auf dem besten ~ sein, etw zu tun** *iron* to be well on the way to doing sthg; **auf halbem ~** halfway; **etw in die ~e leiten** to set sthg in motion; **jm/etw aus dem ~ gehen** to avoid sb/sthg; **jm nicht über den ~ trauen** not to trust sb an inch.

**weg|bekommen** *vt* (unreg) *fam* [entfernen] to get rid of.

**Wegbereiter** (*pl* -) *der* pioneer.

**weg|bleiben** (*perf* **ist weggeblieben**) *vi* (unreg) - **1.** [Person] to stay away - **2.** [Abschnitt] to be left out - **3.** [Motor, Strom] to cut out; **jm bleibt die Luft weg** sb is left gasping.

**weg|bringen** *vt* (unreg) - **1.** [fortbringen] to take away - **2.** [entfernen] to get rid of.

**weg|denken** *vt* (unreg): **sich** (*D*) **etw ~** to imagine sthg as not being there; **Computer sind aus dem Arbeitsalltag nicht mehr wegzudenken** it is no longer possible to imagine daily working life without computers.

**wegen** *präp* (+ G, D) because of; **~ Umbau geschlossen** closed for refurbishment.

➡ **von wegen** *interj fam* far from it!

**weg|fahren** (*perf* **hat/ist weggefahren**) (unreg) *vi* (ist) to leave; [verreisen] to go away; **er stieg ins Auto und fuhr weg** he got in the car and drove off ◇ *vt* (hat) [transportieren] to move; [entsorgen] to take away.

**weg|fallen** (*perf* **ist weggefallen**) *vi* (unreg) to be abolished.

**Weg|gabelung** *die* fork (in the road).

**Weggang** *der* departure.

**weg|geben** *vt* (unreg) to give away.

**weg|gehen** (*perf* **ist weggegangen**) *vi* (unreg) - **1.** [fortgehen] to leave; [ausgehen] to go out; **von jm/etw ~** *fam* to leave sb/sthg; **geh weg!** go away! - **2.** [verschwinden] to go away - **3.** [Ware] to sell well.

**weggetreten** *adj*: **~ sein** *fam* [geistesabwesend] to be miles away; [benommen] to be stunned.

**weg|haben** *vt* (unreg) *fam* - **1.** [entfernen] to get rid of - **2.**: **etw ~** [verstanden haben] to get the hang of sthg; [viel wissen] to know what one is talking about.

**weg|jagen** *vt* to chase away.

**weg|kommen** (*perf* **ist weggekommen**) *vi* (unreg) - **1.** [fortgehen können] to get away; **mach, dass du wegkommst!** *fam* get out of here!; **von etw ~** to get away from sthg; [Drogen] to get off sthg - **2.** [verschwinden] to disappear - **3.** [behandelt werden]: **gut/schlecht bei etw ~** to do well/badly out of sthg.

**weg|können** *vi* (unreg) [Person] to be able to get away; [Gegenstand]: **der Sessel kann weg** the armchair can go.

**weg|lassen** *vt (unreg)* - **1.** [Person] to let go - **2.** [Abschnitt, Teil] to leave out.

**weg|laufen** (*perf* ist **weggelaufen**) *vi (unreg)* to run away; **vor** ODER **von jm/etw ~** to run away from sb/sthg; **das läuft dir nicht weg!** *fam fig* it won't run away!

**weg|legen** *vt* to put down.

**weg|machen** *vt fam* to get rid of.

**weg|müssen** *vi (unreg)* to have to go.

**weg|nehmen** *vt (unreg)* to take away; **jm etw ~** to take sthg away from sb.

**weg|räumen** *vt* to clear away.

**weg|schaffen** *vt* [sich einer Sache entledigen] to get rid of; [woandershin bringen] to move.

**weg|schicken** *vt* [Person] to send away; [Päckchen] to send.

**weg|schnappen** *vt fam:* **sie hat mir das Sonderangebot unter der Nase weggeschnappt** she snapped up the special offer from under my nose; **jm den Freund/die Freundin ~** to pinch sb's boyfriend/girlfriend.

**weg|sehen** *vi (unreg)* to look away.

**weg|stecken** *vt fam* - **1.** [Geld] to put away - **2.** [Schlag] to take.

**weg|tun** *vt (unreg)* - **1.** [weglegen] to put away - **2.** [wegwerfen] to throw away.

**Wegweiser** (*pl* -) *der* signpost.

**weg|werfen** *vt (unreg)* to throw away.

**wegwerfend** *adj* disdainful <> *adv* disdainfully.

**Wegwerf|gesellschaft** *die abw* throwaway society.

**weg|wischen** *vt* to wipe away.

**weg|wollen** *vi (unreg) fam* to want to leave.

**weg|ziehen** (*perf* **hat/ist weggezogen**) (*unreg*) *vi (ist):* **aus etw ~** [Stadt] to move away from sthg; [Wohnung, Haus] to move out of sthg <> *vt (hat)* to pull away; [Vorhang, Decke] to pull back.

**weh** *adj* painful; *siehe auch* **wehtun**.
➡ **oh weh** *interj* oh dear!; *siehe auch* **wehtun**.

**wehen** (*perf* **hat/ist geweht**) *vi* - **1.** (*hat*) [blasen] to blow; [flattern] to flutter - **2.** (*ist*) [geweht werden - Blatt, Schneeflocken] to blow about; [ - Duft, Geruch] to waft <> *vt (hat)* to blow.

**Wehen** *pl* contractions.

**wehleidig** *adj abw* self-pitying.

**wehmütig** *adj* melancholy <> *adv* melancholically.

**Wehr** (*pl* -e) *die:* **sich zur ~ setzen** to defend o.s. <> *das* (*pl* **Wehre**) weir.

**Wehr|dienst** *der* military exercise.

**Wehr|dienstverweigerer** (*pl* -) *der* conscientious objector.

**wehren** ➡ **sich wehren** *ref* to defend o.s.; **sich gegen etw ~** to defend o.s. against sthg.

**Wehrersatzdienst** *der* community service (*as alternative to military service*).

**wehrlos** *adj* defenceless <> *adv:* **jm ~ ausgeliefert sein** to be defenceless against sb.

**Wehrpflicht** *die* compulsory military service.

**wehrpflichtig** *adj* liable for military service.

**Wehrpflichtige** (*pl* -n) *der* person liable for military service.

**Wehr|übung** *die* military exercise (*for reservists*).

**weh|tun** *vi:* **jm ~** to hurt sb; **mir tun die Füße ~** my feet hurt.
➡ **sich wehtun** *ref:* to hurt o.s.

**Wehwehchen** (*pl* -) *das* little complaint.

**Weib** (*pl* -er) *das fam abw* [Frau] woman.

**Weibchen** (*pl* -) *das* female.

**weibisch** *adj abw* effeminate.

**weiblich** *adj* - **1.** [Person, Tier, Geschlecht] female - **2.** [Kleidung, Verhalten & GRAM] feminine.

**Weiblichkeit** *die* femininity.

**weich** *adj* soft; **~ werden** *fam* to soften <> *adv* [landen] softly; [bremsen] gently; [liegen] comfortably; **~ gekocht** soft-boiled; **jn ~ machen** to soften sb up.

**Weiche** (*pl* -n) *die* points (*pl*) *Br*, switch *Am;* **die ~n für etw stellen** *fig* to set the course for sthg.

**weichen** (*prät* **wich** oder **weichte;** *perf* **ist gewichen** ODER **hat geweicht**) *vi (unreg)* - **1.** [fortgehen] to move - **2.** [zurückweichen] to retreat; **vor etw** (*D*) **~** to yield to sthg <> *vt (reg)* [einweichen] to soak.

**weichgekocht** *adj* ⊳ **weich**.

**Weich|käse** *der* soft cheese.

**weichlich** *adj abw* weak.

**Weichling** (*pl* -e) *der abw* weakling.

**weichmachen** *vt* ⊳ **weich**.

**Weichsel** [ˈvaiksl̩] *die:* **die ~** the (River) Vistula.

**Weichspüler** [ˈvaiçˌʃpyːlɐ] (*pl* -) *der* fabric conditioner.

**Weichteile** *pl* privates.

**Weide** (*pl* -n) *die* - **1.** [für Vieh] meadow - **2.** [Baum] willow tree.

**Weideland** *das* pastureland.

**weiden** *vi* to graze.
➡ **sich weiden** *ref geh:* **sich an etw** (*D*) **~** to revel in sthg.

**Weidenkätzchen** (*pl* -) *das* catkin.

**weigern** ➡ **sich weigern** *ref:* **sich ~, etw zu tun** to refuse to do sthg.

**Weigerung** (*pl* -en) *die* refusal.

**W**

**weihen** vt to consecrate; **jn zu etw ~** to ordain sb as sthg.

**Weiher** (pl -) der pond.

**Weihnachten** (pl -) (ohne Artikel) Christmas; **~ feiern** to celebrate Christmas.
→ **frohe Weihnachten** interj Merry Christmas!

> ### WEIHNACHTEN
>
> German Christmas traditions differ somewhat from those in the English-speaking world. Presents are exchanged on "Heiligabend" or Christmas Eve, rather than on Christmas Day, and before going to Midnight Mass it is customary to light the candles with which the Christmas tree is decorated. The big family meal takes place at midday on Christmas Day. "Weihnachtsplätzchen" are plates of typical Christmas biscuits and cakes such as "Lebkuchen", and mulled wine is the traditional drink. In addition to Christmas Day, 26 December is also a public holiday.

**weihnachtlich** adj Christmassy ◇ adv for Christmas.

**Weihnachts|abend** der Christmas Eve.

**Weihnachts|baum** der Christmas tree.

**Weihnachts|einkäufe** pl Christmas shopping (U).

**Weihnachts|feier** die Christmas party.

**Weihnachtsfeier|tag** der: **der erste/zweite ~** Christmas/Boxing Day.

**Weihnachts|ferien** pl Christmas holidays Br ODER vacation (sg) Am.

**Weihnachts|geld** das (ohne pl) Christmas bonus.

**Weihnachts|geschenk** das Christmas present.

**Weihnachts|lied** das Christmas carol.

**Weihnachts|mann** (pl -männer) der Father Christmas.

**Weihnachts|markt** der Christmas market.

> ### WEIHNACHTSMARKT
>
> During the Christmas period, many German towns have a "Weihnachtsmarkt" or Christmas market, usually on the main square, where you can buy Christmas decorations, handmade goods, gift items, Christmas biscuits and cakes etc. There are also several stalls selling mulled wine and the local culinary specialities. The Nuremberg "Christkindlmarkt" and the Dresden Christmas market are the best known.

**Weihnachts|tag** der: **erster/zweiter ~** Christmas/Boxing Day.

**Weihnachts|zeit** die Christmas; **zur ~** at Christmas.

**Weih|rauch** der incense.

**Weih|wasser** das holy water.

**weil** konj because.

**Weilchen** → **ein Weilchen** adv a little while.

**Weile** → **eine Weile** adv a while.

**Weimar** nt Weimar.

**Weimarer Republik** die Weimar Republic.

> ### WEIMARER REPUBLIK
>
> The Weimar Republic was the first republic established in Germany after the abdication of the Emperor in November 1918. Plagued by economic difficulties and torn apart by left- and right-wing radicals hostile to democracy, it collapsed when Adolf Hitler came to power in 1933.

**Wein** (pl -e) der - **1.** [Getränk] wine; **jm reinen ~ einschenken** fig to tell sb the truth - **2.** (ohne pl) [Pflanze] vine.

**Wein|bau** der wine-growing.

**Wein|berg** der vineyard.

**Wein|brand** der brandy.

**weinen** vi to cry; **über etw** (A) **~** to cry over sthg; **um jn ~** to cry for sb; **vor etw** (D) **~** to cry with sthg; **wegen etw ~** to cry because of sthg ◇ vt to cry.

**weinerlich** adj tearful.

**Wein|essig** der wine vinegar.

**Wein|fass** das wine cask.

**Wein|flasche** die wine bottle.

**Wein|glas** das wineglass.

**Wein|karte** die wine list.

**Wein|keller** der wine cellar.

**Wein|kenner, -in** der, die wine connoisseur.

**Wein|lese** (pl -n) die grape harvest.

**Wein|probe** die wine tasting.

**weinrot** adj wine-coloured.

**Wein|stube** die wine bar.

**Wein|traube** die grape.

**weise** adj wise ◇ adv wisely.

**Weise** (pl -n) die - **1.** [Art] way - **2.** [Melodie] tune ◇ der, die wise man (f wise woman).
→ **auf diese Weise** adv in this way.
→ **auf seine Weise** adv in his own way.
→ **in gewisser Weise** adv in some respects.

**weisen** (prät **wies**; perf hat **gewiesen**) geh vt - **1.** [zeigen]: **jm etw ~** to show sb sthg - **2.** [wegschicken]: **jn aus** ODER **von etw ~** to expel sb from sthg - **3.** [abwehren]: **etw von sich ~** to reject sthg ◇ vi to point.

**Weisheit** (pl -en) die wisdom; **mit seiner ~ am**

Ende sein *fig* to be at one's wits' end; **kannst du deine ~en nicht für dich behalten?** can't you keep your pearls of wisdom to yourself?

**Weisheits|zahn** *der* wisdom tooth.

**weis|machen** *vt fam:* **jm etw ~** to make sb believe sthg; **das kannst du mir nicht ~!** you don't expect me to believe that!

**weiß** *präs* ▷ **wissen** ◇ *adj* white.

**Weiß** *das* white.

**Weiß|bier** *das Süddt* wheat beer.

**Weiß|brot** *das* white bread *(U)*.

**Weiße** *(pl -n) der, die* [Person] white person ◇ *das* [Farbe] white ◇ *die:* **Berliner ~ mit Schuss** type of wheat beer, with a shot of raspberry syrup.

**Weiße Haus** *das:* **das ~** the White House.

**weißen** *vt* to whitewash.

**Weiß|glut** *die:* **jn zur ~ bringen** *fam fig* to send sb into a rage.

**Weiß|herbst** *der* rosé (wine).

**Weiß|kohl** *der* white cabbage.

**Weißrussland** *nt* White Russia.

**Weiß|wein** *der* white wine.

**Weisung** *(pl -en) die geh* instruction; **eine ~ befolgen** to follow an instruction.

**weit** *adj* - **1.** [gen] wide; [Reise, Fahrt] long; **wie ~ ist es bis ...?** how far is it to ...?; **ist es ...?** is it far?; **es ist drei Kilometer ~ von hier** it is three kilometres away from here; **im ~esten Sinne** in the broadest sense - **2.** *RW:* **mit seinen Kenntnissen ist es nicht ~ her** he doesn't know enough; **bist du so ~?** are you ready?; **es ist so ~** the time has come ◇ *adv* - **1.** [beträchtlich] far; **~ besser** far better; **~ später** much later; **~ weg** far away; **~ bekannt** widely known; **ihre Meinungen gehen ~ auseinander** they differ widely in their opinions; **~ geöffnet** wide open; **~ verbreitet** widespread; **~ nach Mitternacht** long after midnight; **~ [gehen, fahren] a** long way; **zwei Kilometer ~ fahren** ODER **gehen** to go two kilometres - **3.** *RW:* **das geht zu ~!** that's going too far!; **so ~, so gut** so far, so good.

◆ **bei weitem** *adv* by far; **bei ~em nicht genug** not nearly enough.

◆ **von weitem** *adv* from far away.

◆ **weit und breit** *adv* far and wide.

**weitab** *adv* far away.

**weitaus** *adv* by far.

**Weitblick** *der* foresight.

**weit blickend** *adj* farsighted.

**Weite** *(pl -n) die* - **1.** *(ohne pl)* [weite Fläche] expanse; **das ~ suchen** *fig* to make o.s. scarce - **2.** SPORT distance - **3.** [von Kleidungsstücken] width.

**weiten** *vt* to widen; [Schuhe] to stretch.

◆ **sich weiten** *ref* to widen; [Schuhe] to stretch.

**weiter** *adv* further; **was geschah ~?** what happened then?; **immer ~** further and further.

◆ **nicht weiter** *adv* [nicht weiter fort] no further; [nicht mehr] no longer; **es hat mich nicht ~ interessiert** I wasn't really interested in it.

◆ **und so weiter** *adv* and so on.

◆ **weiter nichts** *adv* nothing more.

**weiter|arbeiten** *vi* to carry on working.

**Weiterbildung** *die* training; **einen Computerkurs zur ~ besuchen** to do a computer course to further one's education.

**weiter|bringen** *vt (unreg)* to move forward.

**weitere, r, s** *adj* further.

◆ **alles Weitere** *adv* all the rest.

◆ **bis auf weiteres** *adv* until further notice.

◆ **ohne weiteres** *adv* just like that.

**weiter|empfehlen** *vt (unreg)* to recommend; **jm etw ~** to recommend sthg to sb.

**weiter|entwickeln** *vt* to develop further.

◆ **sich weiterentwickeln** *ref* to develop further.

**weiter|erzählen** *vt* - **1.** [fortfahren] to continue with - **2.** [weitersagen] to pass on; **du darfst es aber nicht ~** you're not allowed to tell (anyone).

**weiter|fahren** *(perf* ist weitergefahren) *vi (unreg)* to drive on.

**weiter|führen** *vt* to continue; **das führt uns nicht weiter** this isn't getting us anywhere.

**weiter|geben** *vt (unreg)* to pass on; **etw an jn ~** to pass sthg on to sb.

**weiter|gehen** *(perf* ist weitergegangen) *vi (unreg)* - **1.** [gehen] to go on - **2.** [sich fortsetzen] to continue.

**weiter|helfen** *vi (unreg):* **jm ~** to help sb.

**weiterhin** *adv* - **1.** [immer noch] still - **2.** [künftig] in future.

**weiter|kommen** *(perf* ist weitergekommen) *vi (unreg)* - **1.** [auf Strecke, Weg] to get further - **2.** [mit Arbeit] to make progress - **3.** [im Beruf, Leben] to get ahead.

**weiter|können** *vi (unreg) fam* to be able to go on.

**weiter|laufen** *(perf* ist weitergelaufen) *vi (unreg)* - **1.** [Person] to walk/run on; [Maschine] to keep running - **2.** [Verhandlungen, Geschäfte] to continue.

**weiter|leben** *vi* to carry on living; **der Künstler lebt in seinen Werken weiter** the artist lives on in his works.

**weiter|leiten** *vt* to send on; **etw an jn ~** to pass sthg on to sb.

**weiter|machen** *vi* to carry on.

**weiter|sagen** *vt* to pass on; **jm etw ~** to tell sb sthg.

W

**weiter|sehen** *vi (unreg):* anschließend sehen wir weiter then we'll see.

**Weiterver|kauf** *der* resale.

**weiter|wissen** *vi (unreg):* nicht mehr ~ to be at one's wits' end.

**weit gehend** *adj* considerable.

**weither** *adv geh:* von ~ from far away.

**weithin** *adv* from far away.

**weitläufig** *adj* - **1.** [Haus, Grundstück] spacious - **2.** [Verwandtschaft] distant - **3.** [Schilderung] long-winded <> *adv* - **1.** [angelegt] spaciously - **2.** [verwandt] distantly - **3.** [schildern] at great length.

**weiträumig** *adj* spacious <> *adv:* etw ~ umfahren to give sthg a wide berth.

**weitsichtig** *adj* - **1.** [sehbehindert] longsighted - **2.** [umsichtig] farsighted.

**Weitsprung** *der* SPORT long jump.

**weit verbreitet** *adj* common.

**Weit|winkel** *das* FOTO wide-angle lens.

**Weitwinkel|objektiv** *das* FOTO wide-angle lens.

**Weizen** *der* wheat.

**Weizen|bier** *das* wheat beer.

**Weizen|mehl** *das* wheat flour.

**welche, r, s** *det* which <> *pron* - **1.** [Interrogativpronomen] which (one); ~r von ihnen? which (one) of them? - **2.** [Relativpronomen - Person] who, that; [ - Sache] which, that; die Bücher, ~ ich brauche the books (that) I need - **3.** [Indefinitpronomen - in Aussagesätzen] some; [ - in Frageund Konditionalsätzen] any; hast du ~? have you got any?

**welk** *adj* [Blumen] wilted; [Haut] withered.

**welken** *(perf* ist gewelkt) *vi* to wilt.

**Well|blech** *das* corrugated iron *(U).*

**Welle** *(pl -n)* die - **1.** [im Wasser] wave - **2.** [beim Rundfunk] wavelength - **3.** RW: grüne ~ phased traffic lights *(pl);* ~n schlagen to create a stir.

**wellen** ~ sich wellen *ref* [Papier] to wrinkle; [Haar] to become wavy; [Teppich] to ruck up.

**Wellen|bad** *das swimming pool with wave machine.*

**Wellenbe|reich** *der* waveband.

**Wellen|brecher** *(pl -)* der breakwater.

**Wellen|gang** *der:* hoher ~ heavy seas *(pl).*

**Wellen|länge** *die* PHYS wavelength; auf einer ~ sein *fam fig* to be on the same wavelength.

**Wellen|linie** *die* wavy line.

**Wellen|sittich** *der* budgerigar.

**wellig** *adj* [Haar] wavy; [Papier] wrinkled; [Gelände] undulating.

**Well|pappe** *die* corrugated cardboard *(U).*

**Welpe** *(pl -n)* der [von Hund] puppy; [von Fuchs, Wolf] cub.

**Welt** *(pl -en)* die world; auf der ~ in the world; in alle ~ all over the world; die Dritte ~ the Third World; alle ~ the whole world; auf die ODER zur ~ kommen to come into the world; nicht um alles in der ~ not for anything in the world; sie trennen ~en they are like chalk and cheese.

**Welt|all** *das (ohne pl)* universe.

**Welt|anschauung** *die* world view.

**Weltaus|stellung** *die* world fair.

**Welt|bank** *die* World Bank.

**weltberühmt** *adj* world-famous.

**weltfremd** *adj* unworldly.

**Welt|handel** *der* world trade.

**Welt|karte** *die* map of the world.

**Welt|krieg** *der* HIST: der Erste/Zweite ~ the First/Second World War.

**weltlich** *adj* worldly.

**Welt|literatur** *die* world literature.

**Welt|macht** *die* world power.

**Welt|markt** *der* WIRTSCH world market.

**Welt|meister, in** *der, die* world champion.

**Welt|meisterschaft** *die* world championship; [im Fußball] World Cup.

**weltoffen** *adj* open-minded.

**Welt|rang** *der:* von ~ world-class.

**Weltrang|liste** *die* SPORT world rankings *(pl).*

**Welt|raum** *der* space.

**Welt|reise** *die* round-the-world trip.

**Welt|rekord** *der* world record.

**Welt|sicherheitsrat** *der* (United Nations) Security Council.

**Welt|stadt** *die* cosmopolitan city.

**Welt|untergang** *der* end of the world.

**weltweit** *adj* worldwide.

**Welt|wirtschaft** *die* world economy.

**wem** *pron (Dativ von wer)* (to) who; ~ gehört die Tasche? whose bag is it?; mit ~ kommst du morgen? who are you coming with tomorrow?; mit ~ spreche ich? who's speaking?; von ~ hast du das? who did you get it from?

**wen** *pron (Akkusativ von wer)* who, whom; für ~ ist das? who is that for?

**Wende** *(pl -n)* die - **1.** [Veränderung] change - **2.** SPORT turn - **3.** HIST: die ~ the fall of the Berlin Wall.

**Wende|kreis** *der* - **1.** [von Auto] turning circle - **2.** GEOGR tropic.
➤ Nördliche Wendekreis *der* Tropic of Cancer.
➤ Südliche Wendekreis *der* Tropic of Capricorn.

**Wendel|treppe** *die* spiral staircase.

**wenden** (*prät* **wendete** ODER **wandte;** *perf* **hat gewendet** ODER **gewandt**) *vt (reg)* [umdrehen] to turn; [Kleidungsstück] to reverse <> *vi (reg)* to turn around; 'bitte ~' 'please turn over'.

◆ **sich wenden** *ref -* **1.** *(reg)* [sich ändern]: **sich zum Besseren/Schlechteren ~** to take a turn for the better/worse - **2.** [sich richten]: **sich an jn/etw ~** [hilfesuchend] to turn to sb/sthg; [appellierend] to address sb/sthg; **sich gegen jn/etw ~** to oppose sb/sthg.

**Wende|punkt** *der* turning point.

**wendig** *adj -* **1.** [beweglich - Auto, Boot] manoeuvrable; [- Person] agile - **2.** [geschickt] astute.

**Wendung** (*pl* **-en**) *die -* **1.** [Redewendung] idiom - **2.** [Drehung] turn - **3.** [Veränderung]: **eine ~ zum Guten/Schlechten nehmen** to take a turn for the better/worse.

**wenig** *det -* **1.** [Anzahl] a few; **mit ~en Worten** in few words - **2.** [Menge] little <> *pron -* **1.** [Anzahl] a few; **es ist nur ~en bekannt, dass ...** only a few people know that ... - **2.** [Menge] little <> *adv* a little; **~ bekannt** little known; **~ erfreulich** not very pleasant.

◆ **ein wenig** *det, pron* & *adv* a little.

◆ **nur wenig** *det -* **1.** [Anzahl] only a few - **2.** [Menge] only a little; **er hat nur ~ Zeit** he hasn't got much time <> *adv* only a little.

◆ **zu wenig** *det -* **1.** [Anzahl] too few - **2.** [Menge] too little <> *adv* & *pron* too little.

**weniger** *adv* less <> *konj:* **sieben ~ drei** seven minus three.

**wenigste** *adj* ▷ **wenig.**

◆ **am wenigsten** *adv* least.

**wenigstens** *adv* at least.

**wenn** *konj -* **1.** [zeitlich] when - **2.** [konditional] if; **~ ich das gewusst hätte** if I had known, had I known; **~ er nur käme!** if only he would come!

◆ **wenn auch** *konj* even if.

◆ **wenn bloß** *konj* if only.

**Wenn** *das:* **ohne ~ und Aber** with no ifs or buts.

**wennschon** *interj fam:* **na ~!** so what!; **~, dennschon!** no half measures!

**wer** *pron -* **1.** [Interrogativpronomen] who; **~ von euch?** which of you? - **2.** [Relativpronomen] anyone ODER anybody who; **~ mitkommen will** anyone who wants to come - **3.** *fam* [Indefinitpronomen - in Aussagesätzen] somebody, someone; [- in Frage- und Konditionalsätzen] anybody, anyone; **ist da ~?** is there anyone there?; **~ sein** *fig* to be somebody.

**Werbe|agentur** *die* advertising agency.

**Werbe|fernsehen** *das* television advertising.

**Werbe|film** *der* promotional film.

**Werbe|geschenk** *das* free gift.

**Werbe|kampagne** *die* advertising campaign.

**werben** (*präs* **wirbt;** *prät* **warb;** *perf* **hat geworben**) *vi* to advertise; **für etw ~** to advertise sthg <> *vt* to attract; **jn für etw ~** to recruit sb for sthg.

**Werbe|slogan** *der* advertising slogan.

**Werbe|spot** *der* advertisement, commercial.

**Werbe|trommel** *die:* **die ~ für etw rühren** *fig* to plug sthg.

**Werbung** (*pl* **-en**) *die* advertising; **für jn/etw ~ machen** to advertise sb/sthg.

**Werde|gang** *der* development; **der berufliche ~** professional development.

**werden** (*präs* **wird;** *prät* **wurde;** *perf* **ist geworden** ODER **worden**) *aux -* **1.** [zur Bildung des Futurs] will; **sie wird kommen** she will come, she'll come; **sie wird nicht kommen** she won't come; **es wird warm werden** it is going to be warm - **2.** [zur Bildung des Konjunktivs] would; **würdest du/würden Sie ...?** would you ...?; **ich würde gerne ...** I would like to ...; **ich würde lieber noch bleiben** I would prefer to stay a bit longer - **3.** (*Perf ist worden*) [zur Bildung des Passivs] to be; **sie wurde kritisiert** she was criticised; **nebenan wird gelacht** there's someone laughing next door <> *vi (Perf ist geworden) -* **1.** [gen] to become; **Vater ~** to become a father; **er will Lehrer ~** he wants to be a teacher; **das Kind wird groß** the child's getting bigger; **alt ~** to grow ODER get old; **rot ~** to turn ODER go red; **verrückt ~** to go mad; **krank ~** to fall ill; **schlecht ~** to go off; **ich werde morgen 25** I'll be 25 tomorrow; **es wird bald Sommer** it will soon be summer; **es wird Nacht** it's getting dark; **aus ihm wird mal ein guter Lehrer** he'll make a good teacher; **was soll aus dir ~?** what is to become of you?; **daraus wird nichts** nothing will come of it; **zu Stein ~** to turn to stone; **zum Mann ~** to become a man; **(na,) wirds bald!** *fam* get a move on! - **2.** *fam* [gelingen, sich erholen]: **sind die Fotos was geworden?** did the photos come out?; **es wird schon wieder ~** *fam* it will be all right.

**werfen** (*präs* **wirft;** *prät* **warf;** *perf* **hat geworfen**) *vt -* **1.** [Ball, Stein] to throw - **2.** [Tor, Korb] to score <> *vi* to throw; **mit etw ~** to throw sthg; **mit Geld nur so um sich ~** to throw one's money around.

◆ **sich werfen** *ref* to throw o.s.

**Werft** (*pl* **-en**) *die* shipyard.

**Werk** (*pl* **-e**) *das -* **1.** [gen] work - **2.** [Betrieb] plant.

**Werk|angehörige** = Werksangehörige.

**Werkbank** (*pl* **-bänke**) *die* workbench.

**werkeigen** = werkseigen.

**W**

**Werkslangehörige, Werkangehörige** *der, die* plant employee.

**Werkschutz** *der* plant security.

**werkseigen, werkeigen** *adj* plant-owned.

**Werklstatt** (*pl* -stätten) *die* workshop.

**Werklstoff** *der* material.

**Werklstück** *das* workpiece.

**Werkslverkauf** *der* ex-factory sale of reduced price products.

**Werkltag** *der* working day.

**werktags** *adv* on working days.

**werktätig** *adj* working.

**Werkzeug** (*pl* -e) *das* tool.

**Werkzeuglkasten** *der* tool box.

**Wermut** (*pl* -s) *der* vermouth (*U*).

**wert** *adj:* ~ sein to be worth; nichts ~ sein to be worthless; viel/tausend Euro ~ sein to be worth a lot/a thousand euros; Berlin ist eine Reise ~ Berlin is worth visiting; ~e Gäste! dear guests!

**Wert** (*pl* -e) *der* value; auf etw (*A*) ~ legen to attach importance to sthg; im ~ steigen/fallen to increase/decrease in value; das hat keinen ~! *fam* it's pointless.
➡ **Werte** *pl* values.

**Wertanlgabe** *die* registered value.

**wertbeständig** *adj* stable.

**werten** *vt* [benoten] to rate; [beurteilen] to judge; [einschätzen]: etw als Erfolg ~ to consider sthg a success.

**Wertgegenlstand** *der* valuable object.

**wertlos** *adj* worthless.

**Wertlminderung** *die* WIRTSCH depreciation (*U*).

**Wertlpapier** *das* WIRTSCH bond.

**Wertlsache** *pl* valuables.

**Wertung** (*pl* -en) *die* judgement.

**wertvoll** *adj* valuable.

**Wesen** (*pl* -) *das* - **1.** [Charakter] nature - **2.** [Mensch] being - **3.** [Lebewesen] creature.

**Wesenslart** *die* character.

**wesentlich** *adj* essential ⬦ *adv* considerably.
➡ **im Wesentlichen** *adv* essentially.

**Weser** *die:* die ~ the (River) Weser.

**weshalb** *adv* why.

**Wespe** (*pl* -n) *die* wasp.

**Wespenlnest** *das* wasp's nest; in ein ~ stechen *fig* to stir up a hornet's nest.

**wessen** *pron* (Genitiv von wer) whose.

**Wessi** (*pl* -s) *der fam* citizen of the former West Germany.

**West** (*ohne Artikel*) - **1.** [Kurs, Windrichtung] west - **2.** [Länder] West.

**westdeutsch** *adj* West German.

**Westdeutschland** *nt* western Germany; [frühere BRD] West Germany.

**Weste** (*pl* -n) *die* waistcoat *Br*, vest *Am*; eine reine ODER weiße ~ haben *fam fig* to have a clean record.

**Westen** *der* - **1.** [gen] west; aus ~ from the west; nach ~ west; im ~ in the west; der Wilde ~ the Wild West - **2.** POL West.

**Westenltasche** *die:* etw wie seine ~ kennen to know sthg like the back of one's hand.

**Western** (*pl* -) *der* western.

**Westeuropa** *nt* Western Europe.

**Westf.** *abk für* Westfalen.

**Westfale** (*pl* -n) *der* Westphalian.

**Westfalen** *nt* Westphalia.

**Westfälin** (*pl* -nen) *die* Westphalian.

**westfälisch** *adj* Westphalian.

**Westindische Inseln** *pl:* die ~ the West Indies.

**Westjordanland** *das:* das ~ the West Bank; im ~ on the West Bank.

**Westlküste** *die* West Coast.

**westl.** *abk für* westlich.

**westlich** *adj* western ⬦ *präp:* ~ einer Sache (*G*) ODER von etw (to the) west of sthg.

**Westlseite** *die* west side.

**westwärts** *adv* westwards.

**Westlwind** *der* west wind.

**weswegen** *adv* why.

**Wettbewerb** (*pl* -e) *der* competition; in ~ mit jm treten to enter into competition with sb.

**wettbewerbsfähig** *adj* competitive.

**Wettlbüro** *das* betting office.

**Wette** (*pl* -n) *die* bet.
➡ um die Wette *adv:* um die ~ laufen to have a race; um die ~ jodeln to have a yodelling competition.

**wetteifern** *vi:* mit jm um etw ~ to compete with sb for sthg.

**wetten** *vi* to bet; auf jn/etw ~ to bet on sb/sthg; mit jm ~ to bet sb; um etw ~ to bet sthg ⬦ *vt* to bet.
➡ wetten, dass? *interj* do you want to bet?

**Wetten** *das* betting.

**Wetter** (*pl* -) *das* [Klima] weather; schönes/schlechtes ~ good/bad weather.

**Wetterlamt** *das* meteorological office.

**Wetterlaussichten** *pl* weather outlook (*sg*).

**Wetterlbericht** *der* weather report.

**Wetterlfahne** *die* weather vane.

**wetterfest** *adj* weatherproof.

**wetterfühlig** *adj* sensitive to changes in the weather.

**Wetterlkarte** *die* weather map.

**Wetterllage** *die* general weather situation.

**Wetterlleuchten** *das* sheet lightning.

**wettern** *vi*: gegen jn/etw ~ to curse sb/sthg.

**Wettervorherlsage** *die* weather forecast.

**Wettlkampf** *der* contest.

**Wettllauf** *der* race.

**wettlmachen** *vt* to make up for.

**Wettlrennen** *das* race.

**Wettlrüsten** *das* arms race.

**wetzen** (*perf* hat gewetzt) *vt* to sharpen.

**WEU** (*abk für* **Westeuropäische Union**) *die* WEU.

**WEZ** (*abk für* **westeuropäische Zeit**) GMT.

**WG** [ve:'ge:] (*pl* **-s**) *die abk für* **Wohngemeinschaft**.

**Whg.** *abk für* **Wohnung**.

**Whirlpool** ['wœrlpu:l] *der* Jacuzzi®.

**Whiskey, Whisky** ['vɪskɪl] (*pl* **-s**) *der* whisky.

**WHO** [ve:ha:'o:] (*abk für* **World Health Organization**) *die* WHO.

**wich** *prät* ▷ **weichen**.

**wichtig** *adj* important; etw ~ nehmen to take sthg seriously; sich (mit etw) ~ machen *fam* to show off (about sthg).

**Wichtigkeit** *die* importance.

**Wichtigtuer** (*pl* **-**) *der fam abw* bighead.

**Wickel** (*pl* **-**) *der* compress; jn am ~ haben *fam fig* to have sb by the scruff of the neck.

**wickeln** *vt* to wind; etw um etw ~ to wrap sthg around sthg; jn/etw in etw (A) ~ to wrap sb/sthg in sthg; ein Baby ~ to change a baby's nappy *Br* ODER diaper *Am*; schief gewickelt sein *fam fig* to be very much mistaken.

**Widder** (*pl* **-**) *der* **- 1.** [Tier] ram **- 2.** ASTROL Aries; ~ sein to be an Aries.

**wider** *präp geh* against.

**Widerlhaken** *der* barb.

**widerlhallen** *vi* to echo.

**widerlegen** *vt* [Argument, Behauptung] to refute; jn ~ to prove sb wrong.

**widerlich** *adj abw* revolting.

**widerrechtlich** *adj* illegal ◇ *adv* illegally.

**Widerlrede** *die* contradiction.

▪ **keine Widerrede** *interj* don't argue!

**Widerlruf** *der* [von Aussage] retraction (*U*); [von Befehl] revocation.

▪ **bis auf Widerruf** *adv* until further notice.

**widerrufen** (*prät* widerrief; *perf* hat widerrufen) *vt* [von Aussage] to retract; [von Befehl] to revoke.

**widerlsetzen** ▪ sich widersetzen *ref*: sich einer Sache (*D*) ~ to oppose sthg; sich einem Befehl ~ to refuse to comply with an order.

**widerspenstig** *adj* unruly ◇ *adv* in an unruly manner.

**widerlspiegeln** *vt* to reflect.

▪ sich widerspiegeln *ref* to be reflected.

**widersprechen** (*präs* widerspricht; *prät* widersprach; *perf* hat widersprochen) *vi* to contradict; jm ~ to contradict sb; einer Sache/sich (*D*) ~ to contradict sthg/o.s.

**Widerlspruch** *der* **- 1.** [von Personen] protest **- 2.** [in Aussage] contradiction; in ~ zu etw stehen to contradict sthg.

**widersprüchlich** *adj* contradictory.

**widerspruchslos** ['vi:dəʃpruxslo:s] *adj* unprotesting ◇ *adv* without protest.

**Widerlstand** *der* **- 1.** [Ablehnung & ELEKTR] resistance (*U*); ~ gegen jn/etw resistance against sb/sthg; ~ leisten to put up resistance; auf ~ stoßen to meet with resistance **- 2.** [Hindernis] obstacle.

**widerstandsfähig** *adj* resilient.

**Widerstandskämpfer, in** (*mpl* **-**; *fpl* **-nen**) *der, die* resistance fighter.

**widerstandslos** *adj* & *adv* without resistance.

**widerstehen** (*prät* widerstand; *perf* hat widerstanden) *vi*: jm/einer Sache ~ to resist sb/sthg.

**widerstreben** *vi*: etw widerstrebt jm sb dislikes sthg; es widerstrebt jm, etw zu tun sb is loath to do sthg.

**widerstrebend** *adj* reluctant ◇ *adv* reluctantly.

**widerwärtig** *adj* revolting; Ratten sind mir ~ I find rats repulsive ◇ *adv*: sich ~ verhalten to behave offensively.

**Widerwille, Widerwillen** *der* reluctance; ~n gegen jn/etw empfinden to be disgusted by sb/sthg.

**widerwillig** *adj* reluctant ◇ *adv* reluctantly.

**widmen** *vt* **- 1.** [zueignen] jm etw ~ to dedicate sthg to sb **- 2.** [aufwenden] to dedicate.

▪ sich widmen *ref* [sich zuwenden]: sich jm/einer Sache ~ to devote o.s. to sb/sthg.

**Widmung** (*pl* **-en**) *die* dedication.

**wie** *adv* how; ~ heißen Sie? what's your name?; sie fragte ihn, ~ alt er sei she asked him how old he was; ~ war das Wetter? what was the weather like?; ~ gehts? how are you?; ~ spät ist es? what's the time?, what time is it?; ~ oft? how often?; ~ wäre es mit ei-

**W**

nem Gläschen? how about a drink?; **wie wäre es, wenn wir ins Schwimmbad gingen?** how about going to the (swimming) pool?; **~ bitte?** sorry?, excuse me?; **~ war das?** *fam* come again?; **~ nett von dir!** how kind of you!; **~ schade!** what a pity! <> *interj:* **er kam wohl nicht, ~?** he didn't come, did he? <> *konj* - **1.** [vergleichend - vor Substantiv] like; [ - vor Adjektiv, Verb, Partikel] as; **~ sein Vater** like his father; **so ... ~ ...** as ... as ...; **so viel, ~ du willst** as much as you want; **~ wenn** ... as if; **so groß ~ du** as big as you; **weiß ~ Schnee** as white as snow; **so schön ~ noch nie** more beautiful than ever; **~ ich schon sagte** as I said earlier; **~ gesagt** as has been said - **2.** [zum Beispiel] such as, like - **3.** [dass]: **ich hörte, ~ mein Nachbar Klavier spielte** I heard my neighbour playing the piano.

**wieder** *adv* - **1.** [gen] again; **immer ~, ~ und ~** again and again; **hin und ~** now and again; **nie ~** never again; **was hast du denn (jetzt) ~ angestellt?** what have you done this time?; **er ist ~ da** he is back; **er ging ~ ins Haus** he went back into the house - **2.** *fam* [wiederum] on the other hand.

**Wiederaufbau** *der* reconstruction.

**wiederauf|bauen** *vt* to reconstruct.

**wiederauf|bereiten** *vt* to reprocess.

**Wiederaufbereitung** (*pl* -en) *die* reprocessing *(U)*.

**Wiederaufbereitungsan|lage** *die* reprocessing plant.

**wiederauf|nehmen** *vt (unreg)* [Studium, Verhandlungen] to resume; [Thema, Vorschlag] to take up again.

**wieder|bekommen** *vt (unreg)* to get back.

**wieder|beleben** *vt* to revive.

**Wiederbelebungs|versuch** *der* attempt at resuscitation.

**wieder|bringen** *vt (unreg)* to bring back.

**wiedereinfallen** (*perf* **ist wiedereingefallen**) *vi (unreg):* **jm ~** to come back to sb.

**wiedereinführen** *vt* [Ware] to reimport.

**wieder erkennen** *vt (unreg)* to recognize.

**wieder finden** *vt (unreg)* to find again.

**Wieder|gabe** *die* [Bericht] account; [von Bild, Ton, Farben] reproduction; [von Musikstück, Gedicht] rendition.

**wieder|geben** *vt (unreg)* - **1.** [zurückgeben]: **jm etw ~** to give sthg back to sb - **2.** [mit Worten] to give an account of - **3.** [technisch] to reproduce.

**wieder gut|machen** *vt* [Schaden] to compensate for; [Fehler] to put right; [Unrecht] to repair.

**Wiedergutmachung** (*pl* -en) *die* [von Unrecht] reparation; [von Schaden] compensation *(U)*.

**wieder|haben** *vt (unreg)* to get back.

**wiederher|stellen** *vt* to restore; [Kontakt] to reestablish.

**wiederholen**[1] *vt* - **1.** [gen] to repeat - **2.** [lernen] to revise.
➤ **sich wiederholen** *ref* - **1.** [Sprecher] to repeat o.s. - **2.** [Ereignis] to recur - **3.** [Muster] to reappear.

**wieder|holen**[2] *vt* to go and fetch.

**wiederholt** *adj* repeated <> *adv* repeatedly.

**Wiederholung** (*pl* -en) *die* repetition.

**Wiederhören** ➤ **auf Wiederhören** *interj* goodbye! *(on telephone)*.

**wieder|käuen** *vt* - **1.** [kauen] to chew again - **2.** *abw* & *fig* [wiederholen] to rehash <> *vi* [Tier] to chew the cud.

**Wiederkäuer** (*pl* -) *der* ruminant.

**Wiederkehr** *die geh* - **1.** [von Person] return - **2.** [von Ereignis] recurrence.

**wieder|kommen** (*perf* **ist wiedergekommen**) *vi (unreg)* - **1.** [Person] to come back - **2.** [Ereignis] to happen again.

**Wiederschauen** ➤ **auf Wiederschauen** *interj Süddt* & *Österr* goodbye!

**wiedersehen** *vt (unreg)* to see again.

**Wiedersehen** (*pl* -) *das* reunion.
➤ **auf Wiedersehen** *interj* goodbye!

**wieder tun** *vt (unreg)* to do again.

**wiederum** *adv* - **1.** [von neuem] again - **2.** [andererseits] on the other hand.

**Wiederver|einigung** *die* HIST reunification *(U)*.

**wieder verwenden** *vt* to reuse.

**wieder verwerten** *vt* to reuse.

**Wiederver|wertung** *die* reuse *(U)*.

**Wieder|wahl** *die* reelection.

**wieder wählen** *vt* to reelect.

**Wiege** (*pl* -n) *die* cradle.

**Wiege|messer** *das* KÜCHE mezzaluna (knife).

**wiegen** (*prät* **wiegte** ODER **wog**; *perf* **hat gewiegt** ODER **gewogen**) *vt* - **1.** *(unreg)* [abwiegen] to neigh - **2.** *(reg)* [schaukeln] to rock.

**Wiegen|lied** *das* lullaby.

**wiehern** *vi* to weigh.

**Wien** *nt* Vienna.

**Wiener** (*pl* -) *der* Viennese <> *adj* (*unver*): ~ **Schnitzel** Wiener schnitzel, *escalope of veal coated with breadcrumbs;* ~ **Würstchen** Wiener, *small sausage made of beef, pork or veal.*

**Wienerin** (*pl* -nen) *die* Viennese.

**wienerisch** *adj* Viennese.

**Wienerwald** *der* (*ohne pl*) - **1.** GEOGR Vienna Woods (*pl*) - **2.** [Restaurantkette]: **Wienerwald®** *chain of restaurants serving mainly chicken dishes.*

**wies** *prät* ⊳ weisen.

**Wiesbaden** *nt* Wiesbaden.

**Wiese** (*pl* -n) *die* meadow; **auf der grünen** ~ outside town.

**Wiesel** (*pl* -) *das* weasel.

**Wiesen|blume** *die* meadow flower.

**wieso** *pron* why.

**wie viel** *pron* - **1.** [Anzahl] how many - **2.** [Menge] how much; ~ **ist zwei mal drei?** what is two times three?; ~ **Uhr ist es?** what's the time?, what time is it?; ~ **älter/schneller?** how much older/faster?; ~ **Geld das kostet!** what a lot of money it costs!

**wievielmal** *pron* how many times.

**wievielt** *adj* which.
➡ **zu wievielt** *adv:* **zu** ~ **seid ihr in Urlaub gefahren?** how many of you went on holiday?

**Wievielte** *der, die, das:* **der** ~ **ist heute?** what's today's date?

**wieweit** *konj* how far.

**wild** *adj* - **1.** [gen] wild; ~ **auf etw** (A) **sein** *fam* to be crazy about sthg; **wie** ~ *fam* like crazy; ~ **werden** to go crazy; **halb so** ~ **sein** *fam fig* not to be so bad - **2.** [unzivilisiert] savage - **3.** [illegal] illegal <> *adv* - **1.** [gen] wildly - **2.** [illegal] illegally.

**Wild** *das* game.

**Wilde** (*pl* -n) *der, die* savage; **wie ein** ~**r** *fam* like a madman.

**wildern** *vi* [jagen - Mensch] to poach; [ - Tier] to hunt <> *vt* to poach.

**wildfremd** *adj* completely strange; **ein** ~**er Mensch** a complete stranger.

**wild lebend** *adj* wild.

**Wild|leder** *das* suede (*U*).

**Wildnis** (*pl* -se) *die* wilderness.

**Wild|schwein** *das* wild boar.

**wild wachsend** [ˈvɪltvaksn̩t] *adj* wild.

**Wildwasser** (*pl* -) *das* white water (*U*).

**Wild|wechsel** *der* [Pfad] game path.

**will** *präs* ⊳ wollen.

**Wille** (*pl* -n), **Willen** *der* will; **aus freiem** ~**n** of one's own free will; **beim besten** ~**n** with the best will in the world; **sie musste wider** ~ **n lachen** she couldn't help laughing.

**willen** *präp:* **um js/einer Sache** ~ for the sake of sb/sthg.

**willenlos** *adj* & *adv* with a total lack of will.

**willens** *adj:* ~ **sein, etw zu tun** *geh* to be willing to do sthg.

**Willenskraft** *die* willpower.

**willensschwach** *adj* weak-willed.

**willensstark** *adj* strong-willed.

**willig** *adj* willing <> *adv* willingly.

**willkommen** *adj* welcome; **sein Besuch ist uns** ~ we welcome his visit; **ihr seid uns jederzeit** ~ you are always welcome.
➡ **herzlich willkommen** *interj* welcome!

**Willkommen** (*pl* -) *das* welcome.

**Willkür** *die* arbitrariness.

**willkürlich** *adj* arbitrary <> *adv* arbitrarily.

**wimmeln** *vi:* **es wimmelt von** ... it's crawling with ...

**wimmern** *vi* to whimper.

**Wimpel** (*pl* -) *der* pennant.

**Wimper** (*pl* -n) *die* eyelash; **ohne mit der** ~ **zu zucken** *fig* without batting an eyelid.

**Wimpern|tusche** *die* mascara (*U*).

**Wind** (*pl* -e) *der* wind; **bei** ~ **und Wetter** in all weathers; **etw in den** ~ **schlagen** *fig* to ignore sthg; **in alle** ~**e verstreut** *fig* scattered to the four winds; **jm den** ~ **aus den Segeln nehmen** *fig* to take the wind out of sb's sails; ~ **von etw bekommen** *fam fig* to get wind of sthg.

**Wind|beutel** *der* KÜCHE ≈ profiterole.

**Winde** (*pl* -n) *die* - **1.** [Hebevorrichtung] winch - **2.** [Pflanze] bindweed (*U*).

**Windel** (*pl* -n) *die* nappy *Br*, diaper *Am*.

**windelweich** *adv fam:* **jn** ~ **schlagen** to beat sb to a pulp.

**winden** (*prät* wand; *perf* hat gewunden) *vt geh* [flechten] to wind; [Kranz] to make; **etw um etw** ~ to wind sthg around sthg.
➡ **sich winden** *ref* - **1.** [sich schlängeln - Schlange, Aal] to slither; [ - vor Schmerz] to writhe - **2.** *geh* [Pflanze] to wind o.s. - **3.** [Weg] to wind - **4.** [vor Verlegenheit] to squirm.

**Windenergie** *die* wind energy.

**Windeseile** *die:* **in** ~ in a flash.

**Wind|fang** *der* porch.

**windgeschützt** *adj* sheltered.

**Wind|hose** *die* whirlwind.

**Wind|hund** *der* - **1.** [Tier] greyhound - **2.** *fam abw* [Mensch] dodgy character.

**W**

**windig** adj - 1. [Wetter] windy - 2. fam abw [Person, Ausrede] dodgy.

**Wind|jacke** die windcheater Br, windbreaker Am.

**Wind|jammer** (pl -) der SCHIFF windjammer.

**Wind|kanal** der wind tunnel.

**Windkraft|anlage** die wind turbine.

**Wind|mühle** die windmill.

**Wind|pocken** pl chickenpox (U).

**Wind|richtung** die wind direction.

**Wind|rose** die compass card.

**Wind|schatten** der lee.

**windschief** adj lop-sided.

**Windschutz|scheibe** die windscreen Br, windshield Am.

**Wind|stärke** die wind force.

**windstill** adj [Tag] still; [Ecke] sheltered.

**Wind|stoß** der gust of wind.

**Windsurfing** [ˈvɪntˌsœrfɪŋ] das windsurfing.

**Windung** (pl -en) die winding.

**Wink** (pl -e) der - 1. [Geste] sign - 2. [Bemerkung] hint; **jm einen ~ geben** to give sb a tip; **ein ~ mit dem Zaunpfahl** fig a clear hint.

**Winkel** (pl -) der - 1. MATH angle; **ein stumpfer/spitzer/rechter ~** an obtuse/an acute/a right angle; **toter ~** fig blind spot - 2. [Ecke] corner - 3. [Platz] spot.

**winken** (perf hat gewinkt ODER gewunken) vi - 1. [zur Begrüßung, zum Abschied] to wave; **jm ~** to wave to sb - 2. [als Aufforderung]: **einem Taxi ~** to hail a taxi; **dem Kellner ~** to call the waiter - 3. [Belohnung] to get <> vt: **jn zu sich (hin) ~** to beckon sb over; **jn an einen Ort ~** to direct sb to a place.

**winseln** vi - 1. [Tier] to whine - 2. abw [Person] to whimper.

**Winter** (pl -) der winter; **den ~ über** for the winter; **im ~** in winter.

**Winter|anfang** der beginning of winter.

**Winterfahr|plan** der winter timetable.

**Winter|ferien** pl winter holidays Br ODER vacation (sg) Am.

**Winter|garten** der conservatory.

**winterlich** adj wintery; [Kleidung, Landschaft] winter <> adv: **~ kalt** cold and wintery.

**Winter|mantel** der winter coat.

**Winter|pause** die winter break.

**Winter|reifen** der winter tyre.

**Winter|schlaf** der hibernation.

**Winterschlussver|kauf** der January sale.

**Winter|semester** das UNI winter semester.

**Winter|spiele** pl: **Olympische ~** Winter Olympics.

**Winter|sport** der winter sport.

**Winter|zeit** die wintertime.

**Winzer, in** (mpl -; fpl -nen) der, die wine grower.

**winzig** adj tiny.

**Wippe** (pl -n) die seesaw Br, teeter-totter Am.

**wippen** vi to rock.

**wir** pron we; **~ beide** both of us; **~ waren es** it was us.

**Wirbel** (pl -) der - 1. [von Wasser] whirlpool; [von Wind] whirlwind - 2. [Aufregung] stir; **viel ~ um etw machen** to make a big fuss about sthg - 3. [im Haar] cowlick - 4. [im Rücken] vertebra.

**wirbeln** (perf hat/ist gewirbelt) vi (ist) to whirl; [Schneeflocken, Blätter] to swirl <> vt (hat) to whirl; [Schneeflocken, Blätter] to swirl.

**Wirbel|säule** die spine.

**Wirbel|sturm** der tornado.

**Wirbel|tier** das BIOL vertebrate.

**wirbt** präs ⊳ werben.

**wird** präs ⊳ werden.

**wirft** präs ⊳ werfen.

**wirken** vi - 1. [erscheinen] to seem; **sie wirkt auf jeden sympathisch** everybody finds her nice - 2. [wirksam sein] to have an effect; **beruhigend ~** to have a calming effect; **gegen etw ~** to be effective against sthg - 3. [beruflich, Bild, Muster] to work.

**wirklich** adj real <> adv really.

**Wirklichkeit** (pl -en) die reality. **➥ in Wirklichkeit** adv in reality.

**wirksam** adj effective <> adv effectively.

**Wirk|stoff** der active substance.

**Wirkung** (pl -en) die effect; **eine ~ auf jn/etw haben** to have an effect on sb/sthg; **ohne ~ bleiben** to have no effect.

**wirkungslos** adj ineffective.

**wirkungsvoll** adj effective.

**wirr** adj - 1. [unordentlich] tangled - 2. [konfus] confused <> adv - 1. [unordentlich] in a tangle - 2. [konfus] in a confused way.

**Wirren** pl chaos (U).

**Wirrwarr** der ODER das confusion.

**Wirsing, Wirsingkohl** der savoy cabbage.

**Wirt, in** (mpl -e; fpl -nen) der, die landlord (f landlady).

**Wirtschaft** (pl -en) die - 1. [Ökonomie] economy; **die freie ~** the private sector - 2. [Gaststätte] pub Br, bar Am.

**wirtschaften** vi - 1. [leiten]: **Gewinn bringend ~** to run things at a profit; **wer wirtschaftet auf diesem Gut?** who runs this estate?; **mit Geld ~** to manage finances - 2. [tätig sein] to be busy

◇ *vt* [leiten]: **eine Firma in den Ruin ~** to ruin a company.

**wirtschaftlich** *adj* - **1.** [materiell] economic - **2.** [sparsam] economical ◇ *adv* economically.

**Wirtschaftslabkommen** *das* economic agreement.

**Wirtschaftslbeziehungen** *pl* economic relations.

**Wirtschaftslgeld** *das* housekeeping money.

**Wirtschaftslgipfel** *der* economic summit.

**Wirtschaftslhilfe** *die* economic aid *(U)*.

**Wirtschaftsljahr** *das* financial year.

**Wirtschaftslkriminalität** *die* economic crime.

**Wirtschaftslkrise** *die* economic crisis.

**Wirtschaftsllage** *die* economic situation.

**Wirtschaftslmacht** *die* economic power.

**Wirtschaftslminister, in** *der, die* Minister of Economic Affairs.

**Wirtschaftslministerium** *das* Ministry of the Economy.

**Wirtschaftslpolitik** *die* (ohne pl) economic policy.

**Wirtschaftslprüfer, in** *der, die* auditor.

**Wirtschaftslsystem** *das* economic system.

**Wirtschaftslteil** *der* business section.

**Wirtschaftslwachstum** *das* economic growth.

**Wirtschaftslwissenschaft** *die* economics *(U)*.

**Wirtschaftslwunder** *das* HIST (post-war) economic miracle.

**WIRTSCHAFTSWUNDER**

This is the name given to the rebuilding of the German economy that began in 1948, following monetary reform and financial assistance from America. Ludwig Erhard, the minister for economic affairs at the time, embodied the "economic miracle", which reached its height in the sixties when Germany became the leading European economic power.

**Wirtschaftslzweig** *der* economic sector.

**Wirtslhaus** *das* pub, often with accommodation.

**Wirtslleute** *pl* landlord and landlady.

**Wirtslstube** *die* bar.

**wischen** *vt* [Boden, Mund] to wipe; [Dreck] to wipe away; [putzen] to clean ◇ *vi*: **mit der Hand über die Stirn ~** to wipe one's hand across one's brow.

**Wischer** (pl -) *der* wiper.

**Wischerlblatt** *das* AUTO wiper blade.

**wischfest** *adj* washable.

**wispern** *vt* & *vi* to whisper.

**wiss.** *abk für* **wissenschaftlich.**

**wissbegierig** *adj* thirsty for knowledge.

**wissen** (präs **weiß**; prät **wusste**; perf **hat gewusst**) *vt* to know; **etw über jn/etw ~** to know sthg about sb/sthg; **jn etw ~ lassen** to let sb know sthg; **immer alles besser ~** to always know better; **weißt du was?** *fam* you know what?; **ich will nichts von ihm/davon ~** I don't want to have anything to do with him/it; **das musst du ~** that's up to you; **was weiß ich!** *fam* don't ask me! ◇ *vi* to know; **ich weiß!** I know!; **soviel** ODER **soweit ich weiß, ...** as far as I know ...; **nicht, dass ich wüsste** *fam* not as far as I know; **weißt du noch?** do you remember?; **von/um etw ~** to know about sthg; **man kann nie ~** you never know.

**Wissen** *das* knowledge; **wider besseres ~** against my/your/etc better judgement; **nach bestem ~ und Gewissen** to the best of one's knowledge and ability; **meines ~s** to my knowledge.

**Wissenschaft** (pl -en) *die* science.

**Wissenschaftler, in** (mpl -; fpl -nen) *der, die* scientist; [in Geisteswissenschaften] academic.

**wissenschaftlich** *adj* academic; [naturwissenschaftlich] scientific ◇ *adv* academically; [naturwissenschaftlich] scientifically.

**Wissensllücke** *die* gap in one's knowledge.

**wissenswert** *adj* worth knowing; [Fakten] valuable.

**Wissenswerte** *das* useful knowledge.

**wissentlich** *adj* deliberate ◇ *adv* deliberately.

**wittern** *vt* - **1.** [riechen] to scent - **2.** [vermuten] to sense.

**Witterung** (pl -en) *die* - **1.** [Wetter] weather - **2.** [Geruch] scent.

**Witwe** (pl -n) *die* widow.

**Witwenlrente** *die* widow's pension.

**Witwer** (pl -) *der* widower.

**Witz** (pl -e) *der* - **1.** [Scherz] joke; **der ~ an der Sache war ...** *fam* the funny thing was ...; **ein fauler ~** fam a bad joke; **~e machen** ODER **reißen** fam to crack jokes; **du machst wohl ~e!** you can't be serious! - **2.** [Humor] wit.

**Witzbold** (pl -e) *der fam* joker.

**witzeln** *vi*: **über jn/etw ~** to make fun of sb/sthg.

**Witzlfigur** *die fam abw* figure of fun.

**witzig** *adj* funny; [Idee] original ◇ *adv* [lustig] funnily.

**W**

**witzlos** *adj* - **1.** [langweilig] dull - **2.** *fam* [überflüssig] pointless.

**w. L.** (*abk für* **westlicher Länge**): 50° ~ 50° W.

**WM** [veːˈɛm] (*pl* **-s**) *die abk für* **Weltmeisterschaft**.

**wo** *adv* where; **von ~ kam das Geräusch?** where did that noise come from? ◇ *pron* where ◇ *konj fam* - **1.** [obwohl] when - **2.** [da] since; **jetzt, ~ alles vorbei ist** now that it's all over.

**w. o.** (*abk für* **wie oben**) *see above*.

**woanders** *adv* somewhere else.

**wob** *prät* ▷ **weben**.

**wobei** *pron* - **1.** [als Frage]: **~ ist es passiert?** how did it happen?; **~ hast du ihn gestört?** what was he doing when you disturbed him? - **2.** [zeitlich]: **sie stürzte von der Leiter, ~ sie sich ein Arm brach** she fell off the ladder and broke her arm - **3.** [allerdings] although.

**Woche** (*pl* **-n**) *die* week; **vorige** ODER **letzte ~** last week; **diese/nächste ~** this/next week.

**Wochenarbeitslzeit** *die* working week.

**Wochenlblatt** *das* weekly (newspaper).

**Wochenlende** *das* weekend; **am ~** at the weekend.

▶ **schönes Wochenende** *interj* have a nice weekend!

**Wochenendlhaus** *das* weekend house.

**Wochenlkarte** *die* weekly ticket.

**wochenlang** *adj* lasting for weeks; **nach ~em Warten** after waiting for weeks ◇ *adv* for weeks.

**Wochenllohn** *der* weekly wages (*pl*).

**Wochenlmarkt** *der* weekly market.

**Wochenltag** *der* weekday.

**wochentags** *adv* on weekdays.

**wöchentlich** *adj* & *adv* weekly.

**Wodka** (*pl* **-s**) *der* vodka.

**wodurch, wodurch** *pron* - **1.** [als Frage] how - **2.** [Relativpronomen] as a result of which.

**wofür, wofür** *pron* - **1.** [als Frage] what ... for? - **2.** [Relativpronomen] for which.

**wog** *prät* ▷ **wiegen**.

**Woge** (*pl* **-n**) *die geh* wave.

**wogegen, wogegen** *pron* - **1.** [als Frage] against what - **2.** [Relativpronomen] against which ◇ *konj* [wohingegen] whereas.

**wogen** *vi geh* [Meer] to swell; [Kornfeld] to wave.

**woher, woher** *pron* - **1.** [als Frage] where ... from; **~ kommen Sie?** where do you come from?; **~ weißt du das?** how do you know that? - **2.** [Relativpronomen] from where.

**wohin, wohin** *pron* - **1.** [als Frage] where; **~ damit?** *fam* where shall I put it? - **2.** [Relativpronomen] where.

**wohl** (*kompar* **wohler** ODER **besser;** *superl* **am wohlsten** ODER **besten**) *adv* - **1.** (*kompar wohler, superl am wohlsten*) [zufrieden] well; **sich ~ fühlen** [gesundheitlich] to feel well; [angenehm] to feel at home; **~ oder übel** *fig* like it or not - **2.** [wahrscheinlich] probably; **das ist ~ möglich** quite possibly; **du bist ~ wahnsinnig!** you must be crazy! - **3.** [zum Ausdruck der Unbeantwortbarkeit]: **ob sie ~ gut angekommen sind?** I wonder if they have arrived safely - **4.** (*kompar besser, superl am besten*) *geh* [gut] well; **er weiß sehr ~, dass ...** he knows perfectly well that ...

▶ **wohl aber** *konj* but.

**Wohl** *das* well-being; **zum ~e der Allgemeinheit** for the common good; **zum ~!** cheers!

**wohlauf** *adj geh*: **~ sein** to be in good health.

**wohlbehalten** *adv* safe and sound.

**wohlerzogen** *adj geh* well brought up.

**Wohlfahrt** *die* welfare.

**Wohlfahrtslstaat** *der* welfare state.

**wohlgemerkt** *adv* mind you.

**wohlhabend** *adj* well-to-do.

**wohlig** *adj* [Wärme, Gefühl] pleasant; [Seufzer] contented ◇ *adv* contentedly.

**wohlmeinend** *adj* well-meaning.

**Wohllstand** *der* affluence.

**Wohlstandslgesellschaft** *die abw* affluent society.

**Wohlltat** *die* - **1.** [Hilfe] charitable deed - **2.** [Genuss]: **eine ~ sein** to be very welcome.

**wohltätig** *adj* charitable.

**wohl tuend** *adj* pleasant ◇ *adv* pleasantly.

**wohl tun** *vi* (*unreg*) *geh* to do good.

**wohlverdient** *adj* well-earned.

**wohlweislich** *adv* very wisely.

**wohlwollend** *adj* benevolent ◇ *adv* benevolently.

**Wohnanllage** *die* (housing) development.

**Wohnlblock** *der* block of flats *Br*, apartment house *Am*.

**wohnen** *vi* to live; **wir ~ vorübergehend bei Freunden** we're staying with friends at the moment; **zur Miete ~** to rent, to live in rented accommodation.

**Wohnlgebiet** *das* residential area.

**Wohnlgegend** *die*: **eine gute/schlechte ~** a good/bad area (to live).

**Wohnlgeld** *das amt* rent rebate.

**Wohnlgemeinschaft** *die* shared flat/house; **in einer ~ wohnen** to share a flat/house.

**wohnhaft** *adj amt* resident.

**Wohnlhaus** *das* house.

**Wohn|heim** *das* [für Studenten] hall of residence; [für Obdachlose] hostel.

**Wohn|lage** *die:* **eine gute/schlechte ~** a good/bad place to live.

**wohnlich** *adj* homely ◇ *adv* in a homely way.

**Wohn|mobil** (*pl* **-e**) *das* camper *Br,* RV *Am.*

**Wohn|ort** *der* place of residence.

**Wohn|raum** *der* **- 1.** [Wohngebiet] living space **- 2.** [Zimmer] room.

**Wohn|sitz** *der* place of residence; **ohne festen ~** of no fixed abode.

**Wohnung** (*pl* **-en**) *die* flat *Br,* apartment *Am.*

**Wohnungs|amt** *das* housing office.

**Wohnungs|bau** *der* housebuilding; **der soziale ~** *amt* social housing.

**Wohnungs|eigentümer, in** *der, die* flat owner *Br,* apartment owner *Am.*

**Wohnungs|inhaber, in** *der, die* occupant.

**Wohnungs|not** *die* housing shortage.

**Wohnungs|suche** *die* flat-hunting; **auf ~ sein** to be flat-hunting.

**Wohnungs|tür** *die* front door.

**Wohn|viertel** *das* residential area.

**Wohn|wagen** *der* caravan *Br,* trailer *Am.*

**Wohn|zimmer** *das* living room.

**Wok** (*pl* **-s**) *der* wok.

**wölben** ◆ **sich wölben** *ref* [Oberfläche] to curve; [Segel, Material] to bulge; **sich über etw** (*A*) **~** to arch over sthg.

**Wölbung** (*pl* **-en**) *die* [von Himmel] dome; [von Oberfläche] curvature.

**Wolf** (*pl* **Wölfe**) *der* **- 1.** [Tier] wolf; **mit den Wölfen heulen** *fam fig* to follow the herd **- 2.** *fam* [Fleischwolf] mincer; **jn durch den ~ drehen** *fig* to give sb a hard time.

**Wolga** *die:* **die ~** the (River) Volga.

**Wolke** (*pl* **-n**) *die* cloud; **aus allen ~n fallen** *fig* to be astounded.

**Wolken|bruch** *der* cloudburst.

**Wolken|kratzer** *der* skyscraper.

**wolkenlos** *adj* cloudless.

**wolkig** *adj* cloudy.

**Woll|decke** *die* blanket.

**Wolle** *die* wool; **aus ~ woollen; sich in die ~ kriegen** *fam fig* to start arguing.

**wollen** (*präs* **will;** *prät* **wollte;** *perf* **hat gewollt** ODER **-**) *aux* (*perf* hat wollen): **er will anrufen** he wants to make a call; **~ wir aufstehen?** shall we get up?; **ich wollte gerade gehen, da ...** I was just about to go when ...; **was willst du damit sagen?** what do you mean by that?; **diese Entscheidung will überlegt sein** this decision needs to be thought through ◇ *vi (perf*

*hat gewollt):* **das Kind will nicht** the child doesn't want to; **sie will nach Hause** she wants to go home; **ich wollte, es wäre nur schon vorbei** I wish it were over; **dann ~ wir mal!** *fam* let's do it!; **ganz wie du willst** *fam* it's up to you! ◇ *vt (perf hat gewollt)* **- 1.** [gen] to want; **ich will ein Eis** I want an ice-cream; **mach, was du willst** do as you like; **~, dass jd etw tut** to want sb to do sthg; **willst du, dass ich dir helfe?** do you want me to help you?; **was willst du mit dem Messer?** what do you want a knife for?; **von jm etwas ~** *fam* to fancy sb **- 2.** *fam* [brauchen] to need **- 3.** *RW:* **da ist nichts (mehr) zu ~** *fam* there's nothing that we/*etc* can do about it.

**Woll|knäuel** *das* ball of wool.

**Woll|pullover** *der* woollen jumper *Br* ODER sweater *Am.*

**Woll|socke** *die* woollen sock.

**womit¹** *pron* [Interrogativpronomen] what ... with; **~ habe ich das verdient?** what did I do to deserve that?

**womit²** *pron* [Relativpronomen] with which; ..., **~ ich sagen will ... ...,** by which I mean ...

**womöglich** *adv* possibly.

**wonach¹** *pron* [als Frage] for what; **~ suchst du?** what are you looking for?; **~ schmeckt es?** what does it taste of?

**wonach²** *pron* [nach was] for which; **das Kleid, ~ ich solange gesucht habe** the dress I have been looking for for so long.

**Wonne** (*pl* **-n**) *die geh* joy.

**woran¹** *pron* [Interrogativpronomen] what ... on; **~ denkst du?** what are you thinking about?

**woran²** *pron* [Relativpronomen] on which; **alles, ~ du dich noch erinnern kannst** everything you can remember; **ich möchte wissen, ~ ich bei ihm bin** I'd like to know where I stand with him.

**worauf¹** *pron* [Interrogativpronomen] what ... on; **~ wartest du?** what are you waiting for?

**worauf²** *pron* **- 1.** [räumlich] on which **- 2.** [woraufhin] whereupon.

**woraus¹** *pron* [Interrogativpronomen] what ... from; **~ ist die Tasche?** what is the bag made of?

**woraus²** *pron* [Relativpronomen] from which.

**worin¹** *pron* [Interrogativpronomen] what ... in; **~ besteht der Unterschied?** what's the difference?

**worin²** *pron* [Relativpronomen] in which.

**Workaholic** [wɔ:(r)kə'hɔlik] (*pl* **-s**) *der* workaholic.

**Workshop** ['wœ:(r)kʃɔp] (*pl* **-s**) *der* workshop.

**World Wide Web** [wɜ:ld waid web] *das* EDV World Wide Web; **im ~** on the (World Wide) Web.

**W**

**Wort** (pl -e ODER **Wörter**) das - **1.** (pl Wörter) [sprachliche Einheit] word; ~ **für** ~ word for word - **2.** (pl Worte) [Äußerung] word; **etw aufs** ~ **glauben** to believe every word of sthg; **sein Hund gehorcht ihm aufs** ~ his dog obeys his every word; **kein** ~ **sagen/glauben** not to say/ believe a word; **mir fehlen die** ~**e!** I'm speechless!; **mit anderen** ~**en** in other words; **sie ließ mich nicht zu** ~ **kommen** she wouldn't let me speak ODER have my say - **3.** (pl Worte) [Zitat] quotation - **4.** (pl Worte) geh [Text] words (pl) - **5.** (ohne pl) [Zusage] word; **jm sein** ~ **geben** to give sb one's word - **6.** RW: **das letzte** ~ **haben** to have the last word; **das** ~ **haben/erteilen/ergreifen** to have/give/take the floor; **ein geflügeltes** ~ a well-known quotation; **für jn ein gutes** ~ **einlegen** to put in a good word for sb; **jm ins** ~ **fallen** to interrupt sb; **über etw** (A) **kein** ~ **verlieren** not to breathe a word about sthg.

**Wort|art** die GRAM part of speech.

**wortbrüchig** adj: ~ **werden** to break one's word.

**Wörtchen** (pl -) das little word; **ein (ernstes)** ~ **mit jm reden** to have words with sb; **ein** ~ **mitzureden haben** fam fig to have a say.

**Wörter|buch** das dictionary.

**Wort|führer, in** der, die spokesman (f spokeswoman).

**wortgetreu** adj word-for-word ◇ adv word for word.

**wortgewandt** adj eloquent ◇ adv eloquently.

**wortkarg** adj laconic ◇ adv laconically.

**Wortklauberei** (pl -en) die abw quibbling.

**Wortlaut** der wording; **im vollen** ~ verbatim.

**wörtlich** adj word-for-word ◇ adv [übersetzen] word for word; **etw** ~ **nehmen** to take sthg literally.

**wortlos** adj silent ◇ adv without a word.

**Wort|meldung** die request for the floor; **eine** ~ **liegt vor** someone would like the floor.

**wortreich** adj wordy ◇ adv at length; **sich** ~ **entschuldigen** to apologize profusely.

**Wort|spiel** das pun.

**Wort|wahl** die choice of words.

**Wort|wechsel** der heated exchange (of words).

**wortwörtlich** adj word-for-word ◇ adv word for word.

**worüber¹** pron [Interrogativpronomen] what ... about; ~ **lachst du?** what are you laughing about?

**worüber²** pron [Relativpronomen] about which.

**worum¹** pron [Interrogativpronomen] what ... about; ~ **geht es?** what's it about?

**worum²** pron [Relativpronomen] about which.

**worunter¹** pron [Interrogativpronomen] under what; ~ **hat er gelitten?** what did he suffer from?

**worunter²** pron [unter was] under which.

**wovon¹** pron [Interrogativpronomen] what ... from; ~ **hast du geträumt?** what did you dream about?

**wovon²** pron [Relativpronomen] from which.

**wovor¹** pron [Interrogativpronomen] what ... of; ~ **hast du Angst?** what are you frightened of?

**wovor²** pron - **1.** [räumlich] in front of which - **2.** [stellt Bezug her]: ~ **ich mich am meisten fürchte** ... what I'm most frightened of ...

**wozu¹** pron [Interrogativpronomen] why; ~ **dient dieser Schalter?** what's this switch for?

**wozu²** pron [Relativpronomen] for which.

**Wrack** (pl -s ODER -e) das wreck.

**WS** abk für **Wintersemester.**

**WSV** abk für **Winterschlussverkauf.**

**WTO** [veːteːoː] (abk für **World Trade Organization**) die WTO.

**Wttbg.** abk für **Württemberg.**

**Wucher** der abw extortion; **5 Euro für ein Sandwich? das ist** ~**!** 5 euros for a sandwich? that's daylight robbery!

**wuchern** (perf hat/ist gewuchert) vi - **1.** (ist) [wild wachsen] to grow uncontrollably - **2.** (hat) [Wucher treiben] to profiteer.

**Wucher|preis** der abw extortionate price.

**Wucherung** (pl -en) die MED growth.

**Wucherzinsen** pl abw extortionate interest (sg).

**wuchs** [vuːks] prät ⊳ **wachsen.**

**Wuchs** [vuːks] der - **1.** [Wachstum] growth - **2.** [Gestalt] stature.

**Wucht** die force; **mit voller** ~ **gegen einen Baum fahren** to smash into a tree.

**wuchtig** adj - **1.** [plump] massive - **2.** [Schlag, Stoß] violent.

**wühlen** vi - **1.** [graben] to dig - **2.** [stöbern] to rummage; **in etw** (D) ~ fam to rummage through sthg.

➤ **sich wühlen** ref [sich graben] to burrow; **sich in etw** (A) ~ to dig into sthg.

**Wühl|tisch** der bargain counter.

**Wulst** (pl **Wülste**) der roll.

**wulstig** adj thick.

**wund** adj sore ◇ adv: **sich die Füße** ~ **laufen** to walk until one's feet are sore.

**Wunde** (pl -n) die wound.

**Wunder** (pl -) das miracle; ~ **wirken** to work wonders; **kein** ~**!** no wonder!; **er glaubt, er**

sei ~ was für ein toller **Kerl** *fam* he thinks he's God's gift; **sein** *ODER* **ein blaues ~ erleben** *fam fig* to get a nasty surprise.

**wunderbar** *adj* **- 1.** [großartig] wonderful **- 2.** [übernatürlich] miraculous ◇ *adv* [großartig] wonderfully.

**wunderhübsch** *adj* quite beautiful ◇ *adv* quite beautifully.

**Wunderlkerze** *die* sparkler.

**Wunderlkind** *das* child prodigy.

**wunderlich** *adj* strange ◇ *adv* strangely.

**wundern** *vt* to surprise.
➨ **sich wundern** *ref:* **sich (über jn/etw) ~** to be surprised (at sb/sthg); **du wirst dich noch ~** you're in for a nasty surprise.

**wunderschön** *adj* beautiful ◇ *adv* beautifully.

**wundervoll** *adj* wonderful ◇ *adv* wonderfully.

**Wunderlwerk** *das* marvel.

**Wundstarrkrampf** *der* MED tetanus.

**Wunsch** (*pl* Wünsche) *der* wish; **ein ~ nach etw** a wish for sthg; **auf js ~** at sb's request; **nach ~ verlaufen** to go as planned; **die besten Wünsche für etw** best wishes for sthg.

**Wunschdenken** *das* wishful thinking.

**Wünschellrute** *die* divining rod.

**wünschen** *vt* **- 1.** [haben wollen]: **sich** (*D*) **etw ~** to want sthg; **was wünschst du dir zum Geburtstag?** what would you like for your birthday?; **wünsch dir etwas** make a wish; **dich würde ich mir als Tante ~** I wish you were my aunt; **(sich** (*D*) **) ~, dass** to hope that; **ich wünschte, das wäre schon zu Ende** I wish it was already over **- 2.** [erhoffen]: **jm etw ~** to wish sb sthg **- 3.** [verlangen] to want; **ich wünsche eine Auskunft** I would like some information; **wie viel Kilo ~ Sie?** how many kilos would you like?; **ich wünsche das nicht, dass du so spät heimkommst** I don't want you coming home so late; **was ~ Sie?** can I help you?; **~, dass jd etw macht** to want sb to do sthg **- 4.** [zu erhoffen]: **es ist zu ~, dass** it is to be hoped that **- 5.** [an einen Ort]: **jn weit weg ~** to wish sb far away **- 6.** *RW:* **zu ~ übrig lassen** to leave a lot to be desired; **ganz wie Sie ~!** certainly!

**wünschenswert** *adj* desirable.

**wunschgemäß** *adv* as requested.

**Wunschlkind** *das* wanted child.

**wunschlos** *adv:* **~ glücklich sein** *hum* to be perfectly happy with what one has.

**Wunschltraum** *der* dream.

**Wunschvorlstellung** *die* dream.

**Wunschlzettel** *der* ≈ letter to Santa Claus (*asking for presents*).

**wurde** *prät* ⊏> werden.

**Würde** (*pl* -n) *die* **- 1.** [Selbstachtung] dignity; **unter js ~ sein** to be beneath sb **- 2.** [Stellung] rank.

**Würdenträger** (*pl* -) *der* dignitary.

**würdevoll** *adj* dignified ◇ *adv* with dignity.

**würdig** *adj* **- 1.** [würdevoll] dignified **- 2.** [entsprechend] worthy; **einer Sache** (*G*) **~ sein** to be worthy of sthg ◇ *adv* **- 1.** [würdevoll] with dignity **- 2.** [entsprechend] appropriately.

**würdigen** *vt* **- 1.** [mit Auszeichnung] to honour; [in Ansprache] to pay tribute to **- 2.** [schätzen] to appreciate.

**Würdigung** (*pl* -en) *die* appreciation.

**Wurf** (*pl* Würfe) *der* **- 1.** [Werfen] throw; **ein großer ~** *fig* a resounding success **- 2.** [bei Säugetieren] litter.

**Würfel** (*pl* -) *der* **- 1.** [Kubus] cube **- 2.** [Spielwürfel] dice.

**würfeln** *vi* [Würfel werfen] to throw the dice; **um etw ~** to throw for sthg ◇ *vt* **- 1.** [mit dem Würfel] to throw **- 2.** [in Würfel schneiden] to dice.

**Würfelzucker** *der* (*ohne pl*) sugar cubes (*pl*).

**Wurflgeschoss** *das* projectile (*thrown, not fired*).

**Wurflsendung** *die* mailshot.

**würgen** *vt* [Subj: Person] to strangle; [Subj: Krawatte] to choke ◇ *vi* **- 1.** [schlucken]: **an etw** (*D*) **~** to choke on sthg **- 2.** [Brechreiz haben] to retch.

**Wurm** (*pl* Würmer) *der* worm; **da ist** *ODER* **sitzt der ~ drin** *fam fig* there's something wrong there.

**wurmen** *vt* to rankle with.

**wurmstichig** *adj* worm-ridden.

**Wurst** (*pl* Würste) *die* **- 1.** [gen] sausage **- 2.** [Aufschnitt] cold meats (*pl*) **- 3.** *RW:* **es geht um die ~** *fam* it's the moment of truth; **es ist mir ~** *fam* I couldn't care less.

---

**WURST**

Sausages are extremely popular in Germany and there is a wide variety, with every region having its own speciality. Some sausages are always eaten hot - they may be fried, grilled or boiled. These include "Bratwurst", "Bockwurst", "Wiener" and "Frankfurter". Others, such as "Leberwurst" (liver sausage) and "Blutwurst" (black pudding), can be served hot or cold. Cold meats such as salami are also popular and are eaten with bread for supper or even for breakfast.

---

**Wurstlbrot** *das* slice of bread topped with salami etc.

**Würstchen** (*pl* -) *das* **- 1.** [kleine Wurst] frankfurter-style sausage **- 2.** *fam* [unwichtige Person] nobody; **ein armes ~** a poor thing.

**Württemberg** *nt* Württemberg.

**W**

**Württemberger** (*pl -*) *der* native/inhabitant of Württemberg <> *adj (unver)* of/from Württemberg.

**Württembergerin** (*pl -nen*) *die* native/inhabitant of Württemberg.

**württembergisch** *adj* of/from Württemberg.

**Würze** (*pl -n*) *die* seasoning; *fig* spice.

**Wurzel** (*pl -n*) *die* [gen & MATH] root; ~n schlagen *lit* & *fig* to put down roots.

**Wurzel|bürste** *die* scrubbing brush.

**würzen** *vt* - **1.** [Speise] to season - **2.** [Bericht] to spice up.

**würzig** *adj* [gut gewürzt] well-seasoned; [Bier] rich; [stark duftend] aromatic.

**wusch** *prät* ▷ waschen.

**wusste** *prät* ▷ wissen.

**Wust** *der abw* jumble.

**wüst** *adj* - **1.** [vereinsamt - Gegend] desolate - **2.** [wirr - Haare] wild; [ - Durcheinander] chaotic - **3.** *abw* [Schlägerei, Beschimpfung] savage <> *adv* - **1.** [wirr] chaotically - **2.** *abw* [fluchen, schimpfen] savagely.

**Wüste** (*pl -n*) *die* desert; jn in die ~ schicken *fam fig* to fire sb.

**Wut** *die* rage; eine ~ auf jn haben to be furious with sb; seine ~ an jm/etw auslassen to vent one's anger on sb/sthg.

**Wutan|fall** *der* fit of rage.

**wüten** *vi* to rage.

**wütend** *adj* furious; auf ODER über jn ~ sein to be furious with sb <> *adv* furiously.

**wutentbrannt** *adv* in a rage.

**Wwe.** *abk für* Witwe.

**WWF** [veɪveːef] (*abk für* World Wide Fund for Nature) *der* WWF.

**WWW** *abk für* World Wide Web.

**x, X** [ɪks] (*pl -*) *das* x, X; jm ein X für ein U vormachen *fig* to fool sb.

**X-Beine** *pl* knock-knees.

**x-beinig, X-beinig** *adj* knock-kneed.

**x-beliebig** *adj fam* any old.

**x-mal** *adv fam* countless times.

**XXL-|Größe** *die* XXL, extra large.

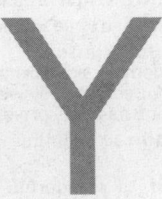

**y, Y** [ˈypsilɔn] (*pl - ODER -s*) *das* y, Y.

**Yacht** [jaxt] (*pl -en*) *die* = Jacht.

**Yen** [jɛn] (*pl - ODER -s*) *der* yen.

**Yoga, Joga** [ˈjoːga] *der* ODER *das* yoga.

**Yuppie** [ˈjupi] (*pl -s*) *der* yuppie.

**z, Z** [tsɛt] (*pl - ODER -s*) *das* z, Z.

**z.** *abk für* zur.

**Z.** *abk für* Zeile.

**zack** *interj fam* pow!; ~, ~ ! chop, chop!

**Zack** *der:* auf ~ sein *fam* to be on one's toes.

**Zacke** (*pl -n*) *die* [von Gabel, Harke] prong; [von Stern] point.

**Zacken** (*pl -*) *der* [von Krone] point; [von Gabel, Harke] prong; du brichst dir keinen ~ aus der Krone *fam fig* it won't hurt you.

**zackig** *adj* - **1.** [gezackt - Felsen, Kante, Blatt] jagged; [ - Stern] pointed - **2.** *fam* [forsch] brisk <> *adv* - **1.** [gezackt] jaggedly - **2.** *fam* [forsch] briskly.

**zaghaft** *adj* hesitant <> *adv* hesitantly.

**Zagreb** *nt* Zagreb.

**zäh** *adj* - **1.** [widerstandsfähig] tough - **2.** [zähflüssig] thick - **3.** [hartnäckig] tenacious ◇ *adv* - **1.** [langsam] slowly - **2.** [hartnäckig] firmly.

**zähflüssig** *adj* thick; [Verkehr] slow-moving.

**Zähigkeit** *die* - **1.** [von Material] toughness - **2.** [von Mensch] tenacity.

**Zahl** (*pl* -en) *die* number; römische ~en Roman numerals; **wir haben keine genauen ~en** we don't have exact figures; **eine gerade/ungerade** ~ an even/odd number; **in den roten/schwarzen ~en sein** *fig* to be in the red/black.

**zahlbar** *adj* payable; ~ **an/in** payable to/in.

**zählbar** *adj* countable.

**zahlen** *vt* - **1.** [gen] to pay; **jm etw** ~ to pay sb sthg, to pay sthg to sb - **2.** [Taxi, Hotelzimmer, Reparatur] to pay for ◇ *vi* to pay; **bitte** ~! the bill, please! *Br*, the check, please! *Am*; **im Voraus** ~ to pay in advance.

**zählen** *vt* - **1.** [die Anzahl ermitteln] to count - **2.** [rechnen]: **ich zähle ihn zu den bedeutendsten Malern dieses Jahrhunderts** I would count him as one of the greatest painters of the century; **etw zu etw** ~ to count sthg as sthg - **3.** [wert sein] to be worth ◇ *vi* - **1.** [gen] to count - **2.** [gehören]: **Monet zählt zu meinen Lieblingsmalern** Monet is one of my favourite painters - **3.** [vertrauen]: **auf jn/etw** ~ to count on sb/sthg.

**Zahlen|kombination** *die* combination.

**zahlenmäßig** *adj* numerical ◇ *adv*: ~ **überlegen sein** to have a numerical advantage.

**Zahlen|material** *das* (*ohne pl*) figures (*pl*).

**Zahlen|schloss** *das* combination lock.

**Zähler** (*pl* -) *der* - **1.** [Gerät] meter - **2.** MATH numerator.

**Zahl|grenze** *die* fare stage.

**zahllos** *adj* innumerable.

**zahlreich** *adj* numerous ◇ *adv* in great numbers.

**Zahlung** (*pl* -en) *die* payment; **etw in** ~ **geben** to trade sthg in; **etw in** ~ **nehmen** to take sthg in part exchange.

**Zählung** (*pl* -en) *die* count; [der Bevölkerung] census.

**Zahlungsan|weisung** *die* money transfer order.

**Zahlungsauf|forderung** *die* request for payment.

**Zahlungs|bedingungen** *pl* terms of payment.

**Zahlungs|bilanz** *die* balance of payments.

**zahlungsfähig** *adj* solvent.

**Zahlungs|frist** *die* payment deadline.

**Zahlungs|mittel** *das* method of payment.

**Zahlungs|schwierigkeiten** *pl*: ~ **stecken** to be having difficulty paying one's debts.

**Zahlungs|termin** *der* due date.

**zahlungsunfähig** *adj* insolvent.

**Zahlwort** (*pl* -wörter) *das* GRAM numeral.

**zahm** *adj* tame ◇ *adv* tamely.

**zähmen** *vt* - **1.** [Tier, Natur] to tame - **2.** *geh* [Neugier, Ungeduld] to curb; [Kinder] to control.

**Zähmung** (*pl* -en) *die* - **1.** [von Tier] taming - **2.** [von Neugier, Ungeduld] curbing.

**Zahn** (*pl* Zähne) *der* - **1.** [im Mund] tooth; **einen** ~ **ziehen** to extract a tooth; **sich einen** ~ **ziehen lassen** to have a tooth out; **sie klapperte mit den Zähnen** her teeth were chattering; **sich** (*D*) **die Zähne putzen** to clean ODER brush one's teeth; **die dritten Zähne** [Gebiss] false teeth - **2.** *RW*: **die Zähne zusammenbeißen** *fam* to grit one's teeth; **einen ganz schönen** ~ **draufhaben** *fam* to drive at breakneck speed; **jm auf den** ~ **fühlen** to grill sb; **jm die Zähne zeigen** *fam* to show sb one's teeth; **jm einen** ~ **ziehen** to pour cold water on sb's idea; **daran habe ich mir die Zähne ausgebissen** *fam* I didn't get anywhere with it.

**Zahn|arzt** *der* dentist.

**Zahnarzt|helfer, in** *der, die* dental nurse.

**Zahn|ärztin** *die* dentist.

**zahnärztlich** *adj* dental.

**Zahnarzt|praxis** *die* dental practice.

**Zahnbe|handlung** *die* dental treatment.

**Zahn|bürste** *die* toothbrush.

**zähneklappernd** *adv* with chattering teeth.

**zähneknirschend** *adv* with bad grace.

**zahnen** *vi* to teethe.

**Zahn|ersatz** *der* (*ohne pl*) false teeth (*pl*).

**Zahn|fleisch** *das* (*ohne pl*) gums (*pl*); **auf dem** ~ **kriechen** *fam fig* to be on one's last legs.

**Zahn|klammer** *die* brace.

**Zahn|krone** *die* crown.

**zahnlos** *adj* toothless.

**Zahn|lücke** *die* gap in one's teeth.

**Zahn|medizin** *die* dentistry.

**Zahn|pasta** (*pl* -ten), **Zahnpaste** (*pl* -n) *die* toothpaste.

**Zahnputz|becher** *der* tooth mug.

**Zahn|rad** *das* cog.

**Zahnrad|bahn** *die* cog railway.

**Zahn|schmelz** *der* (tooth) enamel.

**Zahn|schmerzen** *pl* toothache (*U*); ~ **haben** to have toothache.

**Z**

**Zahn|seide** *die* dental floss.

**Zahn|spange** *die* brace.

**Zahn|stein** *der* tartar.

**Zahn|stocher** (*pl* -) *der* toothpick.

**Zahn|wurzel** *die* root (*of a tooth*).

**Zaire** [za'iːr(ə)] *nt* Zaire.

**Zange** (*pl* -n) *die* pliers (*pl*); [Beißzange, von Insekt] pincers (*pl*); [für Kohlen, Zucker] tongs (*pl*); MED forceps (*pl*); **jn in die ~ nehmen** *fam fig* to put the screws on sb.

**Zank** *der* quarrelling.

**zanken** ➡ **sich zanken** *ref:* **sich (mit jm um etw) ~** to quarrel (with sb about sthg).

**zänkisch** *adj* quarrelsome.

**Zäpfchen** (*pl* -) *das* [Medikament] suppository.

**zapfen** *vt:* **ein großes Bier ~** ≈ to pull a pint.

**Zapfen** (*pl* -) *der* - **1.** [aus Holz] tenon - **2.** [von Bäumen] cone - **3.** [aus Eis] icicle.

**Zapfenstreich** *der:* **um 23 Uhr ist ~** lights out is at eleven o'clock.

**Zapf|hahn** *der* tap.

**Zapf|pistole** *die* petrol pump nozzle.

**Zapf|säule** *die* petrol *Br* ODER gas *Am* pump.

**zappelig, zapplig** *adj* [Kind] fidgety.

**zappeln** *vi* to wriggle; **auf seinem Stuhl ~** to fidget in one's chair; **jn ~ lassen** *fam fig* to let sb sweat.

**Zappelphilipp** ['tsap(ə)lfilɪp] (*pl* -e ODER -s) *der fam abw* fidget.

**zappen** *vi* to channel-hop.

**zappenduster** *adj fam* pitch-black.

**zapplig** = zappelig.

**zart** *adj* - **1.** [gen] delicate - **2.** [weich - Haut] soft; [- Fleisch, Gemüse, Pflänzchen] tender - **3.** [Gebäck] fine - **4.** [Berührung, Kuss] gentle; [Farbton] soft ⟶ *adv* [berühren, küssen, lächeln] gently.

**zart besaitet** *adj* very sensitive.

**zartbitter** *adj* [Schokolade] dark.

**zart fühlend** *adj* sensitive ⟶ *adv* sensitively.

**zärtlich** *adj* tender, affectionate; [Fürsorge] loving; **zu jm ~ sein** to be tender ODER affectionate towards sb ⟶ *adv* tenderly, affectionately.

**Zärtlichkeit** (*pl* -en) *die* [Gefühl] tenderness. ➡ **Zärtlichkeiten** *pl* [Liebkosungen] caresses.

**Zauber** (*pl* -) *der* magic; **das ist doch fauler ~!** *fam abw* that's a con!

**Zauberei** (*pl* -en) *die* magic.

**Zauberer** (*pl* -) *der* magician.

**Zauber|formel** *die* - **1.** [Zauberspruch] (magic) spell - **2.** [Patentlösung] magic formula.

**zauberhaft** *adj* enchanting ⟶ *adv* enchantingly.

**Zauberin** (*pl* -nen) *die* magician.

**Zauber|kraft** *die* magic power.

**Zauber|künstler, in** *der, die* magician.

**Zauberkunst|stück** *das* magic trick.

**zaubern** *vi* to do magic ⟶ *vt:* **etw aus etw ~** *fig* to conjure sthg from sthg.

**Zauber|spruch** *der* (magic) spell.

**Zauber|stab** *der* magic wand.

**Zauber|trick** *der* magic trick.

**Zaum** (*pl* Zäume) *der* bridle; **sich/etw im ~ halten** *fig* to keep o.s./sthg in check.

**zäumen** *vt* to bridle.

**Zaumzeug** (*pl* -e) *das* bridle.

**Zaun** (*pl* Zäune) *der* fence.

**Zaun|gast** *der* person who watches an event, e.g. a football match, from a distance to avoid paying.

**Zaun|pfahl** *der* fencepost.

**z. B.** (*abk für* zum Beispiel) e.g.

**ZDF** [tsɛtdeː'ʔɛf] (*abk für* Zweites Deutsches Fernsehen) *das* second German public television channel.

**Zebra** (*pl* -s) *das* zebra.

**Zebra|streifen** *der* zebra crossing *Br*, crosswalk *Am*.

**Zeche** (*pl* -n) *die* - **1.** [Rechnung] bill *Br*, check *Am*; **die ~ prellen** *fam* to leave without paying - **2.** [Mine] pit.

**zechen** *vi hum* to booze.

**Zechpreller, in** (*mpl* -; *fpl* -nen) *der, die* person who leaves without paying.

**Zech|tour** *die* pub crawl.

**Zeder** (*pl* -n) *die* cedar.

**Zeh** (*pl* -en) *der* toe; **großer/kleiner ~** big/little toe.

**Zehe** (*pl* -n) *die* - **1.** [Fußglied] toe; **jm auf die ~n treten** *fam fig* to tread on sb's toes - **2.** [Knoblauchzehe] clove.

**Zehen|nagel** *der* toenail.

**Zehen|spitze** *die* tip of one's toes; **auf ~n** on tiptoe.

**zehn** *num* ten; *siehe auch* **sechs**.

**Zehn** (*pl* -en) *die* ten; *siehe auch* **Sechs**.

**Zehner** (*pl* -) *der* - **1.** MATH [Zahl] ten - **2.** *fam* [Zehnmeterbrett] ten-metre board.

**Zehner|karte** *die* book of ten tickets.

**Zehneuro|schein** *der* ten-euro note.

**zehnfach** *adj* tenfold ⟶ *adv* ten times.

**Zehn|kampf** *der* SPORT decathlon.

**Zehn|kämpfer** *der* SPORT decathlete.

**zehnmal** *adv* ten times.

**zehntausend** *num* ten thousand; **die oberen Zehntausend** *fig* the upper crust; *siehe auch* **sechs**.

**zehnte, r, s** *adj* tenth; *siehe auch* **sechste**.

**Zehnte** (*pl* -n) *der, die, das* tenth; *siehe auch* **Sechste**.

**zehntel** *adj (unver)* tenth; *siehe auch* **sechstel**.

**Zehntel** (*pl* -) *das* tenth; *siehe auch* **Sechstel**.

**Zehntel|sekunde** *die* tenth of a second.

**zehren** *vi*: **von etw ~** to live on sthg; **an jm/etw ~** to wear sb/sthg down.

**Zeichen** (*pl* -) *das* - **1.** [gen] sign; **jm ein ~ geben** to give sb a signal ODER sign; **zum ~ seiner Dankbarkeit** as a token of his appreciation; **zum ~, dass sie ihm folgen solle** to let her know that she should follow him; **er hat die ~ der Zeit erkannt, und ist ausgewandert** he saw which way things were going and left the country - **2.** [Symbol] symbol - **3.** [Tierkreiszeichen] (star) sign - **4.** EDV character.

**Zeichen|block** (*pl* -blöcke ODER -s) *der* drawing pad.

**Zeichener|klärung** *die* key.

**Zeichen|kohle** *die* charcoal.

**Zeichen|papier** *das* drawing paper.

**Zeichen|setzung** *die* punctuation.

**Zeichen|sprache** *die* sign language.

**Zeichen|stift** *der* drawing pencil.

**Zeichen|tabelle** *die* EDV character set.

**Zeichentrick|film** *der* cartoon.

**zeichnen** *vt* - **1.** [darstellen] to draw - **2.** [kennzeichnen] to mark; **das Fell ist interessant gezeichnet** its coat has interesting markings - **3.** [unterzeichnen - Scheck] to sign; [ - Aktien, Anleihe] to subscribe <> *vi* to draw.

**Zeichner, in** (*mpl* -; *fpl* -nen) *der, die* draughtsman (*f* draughtswoman); **technischer ~** technical draughtsman (*f* technical draughtswoman).

**Zeichnung** (*pl* -en) *die* - **1.** [Bild] drawing - **2.** [von Fell, Tier, Blüte] markings (*pl*).

**Zeige|finger** *der* index finger; **mit erhobenem ~** *fig* in a moralizing tone.

**zeigen** *vt* - **1.** [gen] to show; **jm etw ~** to show sb sthg; **den Gästen die neue Wohnung ~** to show the guests round the new flat; **der habe ich es gezeigt!** *fam* I showed her! - **2.** [Uhr] to say; [Waage] to read <> *vi* to point; **nach Südost ~** to point south-east; **auf jn/etw ~** to point at sb/sthg; **zeig mal!** *fam* let's/let me see!

➤ **sich zeigen** *ref* - **1.** [sich verhalten] to show o.s.; **sich nachsichtig ~** to show lenience, to show o.s. to be lenient - **2.** [sich präsentieren]: **sich in**

**der Öffentlichkeit ~** to appear in public - **3.** [erkennbar werden]: **schon ~ sich die ersten Fehler** the first mistakes are already starting to appear; **es hat sich gezeigt, dass ...** it has been shown ODER demonstrated that ...; **es wird sich ~, ob ...** time will tell whether ...

**Zeiger** (*pl* -) *der* hand; **der große/kleine ~** the big/little hand.

**Zeile** (*pl* -n) *die* - **1.** [von Texten] line; **zwischen den ~n** between the lines - **2.** [Nachricht]: **jm ein paar ~n schreiben** to drop sb a line.

**Zeilenab|stand** *der* (line) spacing.

**Zeit** (*pl* -en) *die* - **1.** [gen] time; **in letzter ~** lately; **im Laufe der ~** in the course of time; **von ~ zu ~** from time to time; **die ~ stoppen** to stop the clock; **~ raubend** time-consuming; **~ sparend** time-saving; **sich** *(D)* **für jn/etw ~ nehmen** to spend time on sb/sthg; **die ~ drängt** *fig* time is short; **wir dürfen keine ~ verlieren** we have no time to lose; **sich** *(D)* **die ~ (mit Kartenspielen) vertreiben** to pass the time (playing cards); **sich** *(D)* **~ lassen** to take one's time - **2.** GRAM tense - **3.** [Zeitung]: **Die ~** *weekly German newspaper*.

➤ **auf Zeit** *adv* temporarily.

➤ **eine Zeit lang** *adv* for a while.

➤ **mit der Zeit** *adv* - **1.** in time - **2.** = zurzeit.

**DIE ZEIT**

> Die Zeit is a weekly newspaper that is published at national level. Its feature articles, analyses and reports have established its reputation as a serious newspaper, especially in terms of its coverage of political, economic and cultural affairs.

**Zeit|alter** *das* age.

**Zeitan|sage** *die* speaking clock.

**Zeit|arbeit** *die* temporary work.

**Zeit|bombe** *die eigtl* & *fig* time bomb.

**Zeit|dokument** *das* document of contemporary events.

**Zeit|druck** *der*: **in ~ sein, unter ~ stehen** to be under time pressure.

**Zeitein|teilung** *die*: **freie ~** freedom to manage one's own time.

**Zeit|ersparnis** *die* time saving.

**Zeit|gefühl** *das* sense of time.

**Zeit|geist** *der* spirit of the times, zeitgeist.

**zeitgemäß** *adj* contemporary, modern.

**Zeit|genosse** *der* contemporary.

**Zeit|genossin** *die* contemporary.

**zeitgenössisch** *adj* contemporary.

**Zeit|geschehen** *das (ohne pl)* current affairs (*pl*).

Z

**Zeit|geschichte** *die* contemporary history.

**Zeit|gewinn** *der* time saving.

**zeitgleich** *adj* simultaneous ⟷ *adv* simultaneously, at the same time.

**zeitig** *adj* & *adv* early.

**Zeit|karte** *die* travel pass.

**Zeitlang** *die* ⊏▷ **Zeit.**

**zeitlebens** *adv* all my/his/her/*etc* life.

**zeitlich** *adj* chronological ⟷ *adv*: **~ begrenzt sein** to be of limited duration.

**Zeitliche** *das*: **das ~ segnen** to give up the ghost.

**zeitlos** *adj* timeless.

**Zeitlupe** ◆ **in Zeitlupe** *adv* TV in slow motion.

**Zeitmangel** *der* lack of time.

**Zeit|not** *die* lack of time; **in ~ sein** to be short of time.

**Zeit|plan** *der* timetable.

**Zeit|punkt** *der* time; **etw zum richtigen ~ tun** to do sthg at the right moment ODER time; **zu diesem ~** at this point in time.

**Zeit|raffer** *der* time-lapse photography.

**zeitraubend** *adj* = **Zeit.**

**Zeit|raum** *der* period.

**Zeit|rechnung** *die*: **vor unserer ~** Before Christ; **nach unserer ~** Anno Domini.

**Zeit|schrift** *die* [Illustrierte] magazine; [wissenschaftlich] journal.

**Zeit|soldat** *der soldier who enlists for a fixed period of time.*

**Zeit|spanne** *die* timespan.

**zeitsparend** *adj* = **Zeit.**

**Zeitung** (*pl* -en) *die* newspaper.

**Zeitungs|abonnement** *das* newspaper subscription.

**Zeitungs|annonce** *die* newspaper advertisement.

**Zeitungs|anzeige** *die* newspaper advertisement.

**Zeitungs|artikel** *der* newspaper article.

**Zeitungsaus|schnitt** *der* newspaper cutting.

**Zeitungs|bericht** *der* newspaper report.

**Zeitungs|kiosk** *der* newspaper kiosk.

**Zeitungs|leser, in** *der*, *die* newspaper reader.

**Zeitungs|notiz** *die* newspaper item.

**Zeitungs|papier** *das* newspaper.

**Zeit|unterschied** *der* time difference.

**Zeit|verlust** *der* lost time.

**Zeit|verschiebung** *die* time difference.

**Zeit|verschwendung** *die* waste of time.

**Zeit|vertrag** *der* fixed-term ODER temporary contract.

**Zeit|vertreib** (*pl* -e) *der* pastime; **zum ~** to pass the time.

**zeitweilig** *adj* temporary ⟷ *adv* from time to time, on and off.

**zeitweise** *adv* - **1.** [gelegentlich] occasionally - **2.** [vorübergehend] temporarily.

**Zeit|wert** *der* current value.

**Zeit|zeichen** *das* time signal.

**Zeit|zünder** *der* time fuse.

**Zelle** (*pl* -n) *die* cell.

**Zell|kern** *der* BIOL nucleus.

**Zell|stoff** *der* cellulose.

**Zell|teilung** *die* BIOL cell division.

**Zellulitis** *die* cellulite.

**Zelluloid** [tsɛluˈlɔyt] *das* celluloid.

**Zellulose** (*pl* -n) *die* cellulose.

**Zelt** (*pl* -e) *das* tent; **die ~e abbrechen** *fig* to up sticks; **die ~e aufschlagen** *fig* to settle.

**zelten** *vi* to camp.

**Zelt|lager** *das* camp.

**Zelt|plane** *die* tarpaulin.

**Zelt|platz** *der* campsite.

**Zelt|stange** *die* tent pole.

**Zement** *der* cement.

**zementieren** *vt* to cement.

**zensieren** *vt* - **1.** [benoten] to mark - **2.** [kontrollieren] to censor ⟷ *vi* to mark.

**Zensur** (*pl* -en) *die* - **1.** [Benotung] mark - **2.** [Kontrolle] censorship - **3.** [Behörde] censorship board, censors (*pl*).

**Zenti|gramm** *das* centigram.

**Zenti|liter** *der* centilitre.

**Zenti|meter** *der* centimetre.

**Zentimeter|maß** *das* tape measure.

**Zentner** (*pl* -) *der unit of measurement equivalent to 50 kg in Germany and 100 kg in Austria and Switzerland.*

**Zentner|last** *die* heavy load.

**zentral** *adj* central ⟷ *adv* [wohnen, gelegen] centrally.

**Zentralafrika** *nt* Central Africa.

**Zentralafrikanische Republik** *die* Central African Republic.

**Zentralbank** (*pl* -en) *die* central bank.

**Zentrale** (*pl* -n) *die* - **1.** [zentrale Stelle] headquarters (*pl*) - **2.** [Telefonzentrale] switchboard.

**Zentral|heizung** *die* central heating.

**zentralisieren** *vt* to centralize.

**Zentralismus** *der* centralism.

**zentrieren** *vt* to centre.

**Zentrifuge** (*pl* -n) *die* centrifuge.

**Zentrum** (*pl* Zentren) *das* centre.

**Zeppelin** (*pl* -e) *der* zeppelin.

**Zepter** (*pl* -) *der ODER das* sceptre; **das ~ führen** *ODER* **schwingen** *fam* to rule the roost.

**zerbeißen** (*prät* zerbiss; *perf* hat zerbissen) *vt* [mit den Zähnen] to crunch; **von Flöhen zerbissen werden** to get bitten all over by fleas.

**zerbomben** *vt* to flatten (with bombs).

**zerbrechen** (*präs* zerbricht; *prät* zerbrach; *perf* hat/ist zerbrochen) *vi (ist)* [Glas, Vase] to break into pieces, to smash; [Freundschaft, Ehe] to break up; **an etw** (*D*) **~** *fig* to be broken by sthg <> *vt (hat)* to smash.

**zerbrechlich** *adj* fragile.

**zerbröckeln** (*perf* hat/ist zerbröckelt) *vt (hat)* & *vi (ist)* to crumble.

**zerdrücken** *vt* [Kartoffeln, Bananen] to mash; [Knoblauch, Insekt] to crush.

**Zeremonie** (*pl* -n) *die* ceremony.

**Zerfall** *der* [von Gebäude, Denkmal] decay; [von Moral, Diktatur] decline.

**zerfallen** (*präs* zerfällt; *prät* zerfiel; *perf* ist zerfallen) *vi* to disintegrate; [Mauer, Kuchen, Reich] to crumble; [Molekül] to decay; **in etw** (*A*) **~** [Molekül] to decay into sthg; [Mauer, Kuchen] to crumble into sthg.

**zerfetzen** *vt* to tear to pieces; [Brief] to tear up.

**zerfleddern** *vt* to make tatty.

**zerfleischen** *vt* to tear apart.

**zerfließen** (*prät* zerfloss; *perf* ist zerflossen) *vi* - **1.** [schmelzen] to melt - **2.** [auseinander fließen] to run.

**zerfressen** (*präs* zerfrisst; *prät* zerfraß; *perf* hat zerfressen) *vt* - **1.** [durch Insekten]: **ein von Motten ~er Mantel** a moth-eaten coat - **2.** [durch Rost, Säure] to corrode.

**zergehen** (*prät* zerging; *perf* ist zergangen) *vi* to melt; **etw im Mund ~ lassen** to allow sthg to dissolve in one's mouth.

**zerhacken** *vt* to chop up.

**zerkauen** *vt* to chew thoroughly.

**zerkleinern** *vt* to cut up; [mit Gabel] to mash.

**zerklüftet** *adj* [Landschaft, Tal] rugged; [Felsen] jagged.

**zerknirscht** *adj* remorseful; **über etw** (*A*) **~ sein** to be full of remorse for sthg.

**zerknittern** *vt* to crumple.

**zerknüllen** *vt* to screw up (into a ball).

**zerkratzen** *vt* to scratch.

**zerkrümeln** (*perf* hat/ist zerkrümelt) *vt (hat)* & *vi (ist)* to crumble.

**zerlassen** (*präs* zerlässt; *prät* zerließ; *perf* hat zerlassen) *vt* to melt.

**zerlegen** *vt* - **1.** [auseinander nehmen] to take apart; **etw in (seine) Einzelteile ~** to dismantle sthg into its constituent parts - **2.** [Geflügel, Wild] to carve up.

**zerlumpt** *adj* ragged.

**zermalmen** *vt* to crush.

**Zermatt** *nt* Zermatt.

**zermürben** *vt* to wear down.

**zerpflücken** *vt* - **1.** [Kopfsalat] to pull the leaves off; [Blume] to pull the petals off - **2.** [kritisieren] to pull to pieces.

**zerplatzen** (*perf* ist zerplatzt) *vi* [Ballon, Reifen] to burst; [Kessel] to explode.

**zerquetschen** *vt* to crush; [Kartoffeln] to mash.

**Zerrbild** *das* distorted picture.

**zerreden** *vt* to discuss at great length.

**zerreiben** (*prät* zerrieb; *perf* hat zerrieben) *vt* [Kräuter] to rub between one's fingers; [Farben, Feind] to pulverize.

**zerreißen** (*prät* zerriss; *perf* hat/ist zerrissen) *vt (hat)* - **1.** [in Stücke] to tear to pieces; [Brief] to tear up - **2.** [Strümpfe, Hose] to tear <> *vi (ist)* to tear.

**Zerreißprobe** *die*: **eine ~ für die Koalition** a serious test of the strength of the coalition.

**zerren** *vt* to drag; **sich** (*D*) **einen Muskel ~** to pull a muscle <> *vi*: **an etw** (*D*) **~** to pull on sthg.

**zerrinnen** (*prät* zerronn; *perf* ist zerronnen) *vi* - **1.** [Butter] to melt - **2.** [Träume] to fade away - **3.** [Zeit] to slip by.

**zerrissen** *adj* torn.

**Zerrung** (*pl* -en) *die* pulled muscle *ODER* ligament.

**zerrüttet** *adj* [Gesundheit] ruined; [Ehe] broken; **aus ~en Verhältnissen** from a broken home.

**zersägen** *vt* to saw up.

**zerschellen** (*perf* ist zerschellt) *vi* to be dashed to pieces.

**zerschlagen**[1] (*präs* zerschlägt; *prät* zerschlug; *perf* hat zerschlagen) *vt* to smash.
➥ **sich zerschlagen** *ref* [Pläne] to fall through.

**zerschlagen**[2] *adj* shattered.

**zerschmettern** *vt* to shatter.

**zerschneiden** (*prät* zerschnitt; *perf* hat zerschnitten) *vt* - **1.** [in Stücke] to cut up - **2.** [verletzen] to cut.

Z

**zersetzen** *vt* - **1.** [Subj: Säure, Rost] to corrode; [Subj: Fäulnis] to decompose - **2.** [untergraben] to undermine.

◆ **sich zersetzen** *ref* [durch Säure, Rost] to corrode; [durch Fäulnis] to decompose.

**Zersetzung** *die* [durch Säure, Rost] corrosion; [durch Fäulnis] decomposition.

**zersiedelt** *adj* overdeveloped.

**zerspalten** (*perf* **hat zerspalten** ODER **zerspaltet**) *vt* to split.

**zersplittern** (*perf* **ist zersplittert**) *vi* [Holz, Knochen] to splinter; [Glas, Fenster] to shatter.

**zerspringen** (*prät* **zersprang**; *perf* **ist zersprungen**) *vi* to shatter.

**zerstampfen** *vt* - **1.** [Kartoffeln] to mash; [Gewürze] to grind - **2.** [zerstören] to trample.

**zerstäuben** *vt* to spray.

**Zerstäuber** (*pl* -) *der* atomizer.

**zerstechen** (*präs* **zersticht**; *prät* **zerstach**; *perf* **hat zerstochen**) *vt* - **1.** [beschädigen] to puncture - **2.** [Subj: Insekten] to bite all over.

**zerstören** *vt* to destroy.

**Zerstörer** (*pl* -) *der* SCHIFF destroyer.

**zerstörerisch** *adj* destructive.

**Zerstörung** *die* destruction.

**zerstreuen** *vt* - **1.** [Blätter] to scatter - **2.** [Demonstranten] to disperse - **3.** [vom Alltag ablenken] to distract - **4.** [Zweifel] to dispel.

◆ **sich zerstreuen** *ref* - **1.** [Menschenmenge] to disperse - **2.** [sich vom Alltag ablenken] to distract o.s.

**zerstreut** *adj* absent-minded ◇ *adv* absent-mindedly.

**Zerstreutheit** *die* absent-mindedness.

**Zerstreuung** (*pl* -en) *die* distraction.

**zerstückeln** *vt* [Land] to divide up; [Leiche] to dismember; [Stoff] to cut up.

**zerteilen** *vt* [Wild, Geflügel] to carve up; [Stoff] to cut up; **den Kuchen in kleine Stücke ~** to divide the cake into small pieces.

◆ **sich zerteilen** *ref* [Wolken] to part.

**Zertifikat** (*pl* -e) *das* certificate.

**zertrampeln** *vt* to trample (on).

**zertreten** (*präs* **zertritt**; *prät* **zertrat**; *perf* **hat zertreten**) *vt* [Insekt] to stamp on; [Zigarettenkippe] to stub out with one's foot.

**zertrümmern** *vt* [Schrank, Felsbrocken] to smash up; [Spiegel] to smash.

**zerzaust** *adj* [Haare] dishevelled.

**zetern** *vi abw* to moan.

**Zettel** (*pl* -) *der* piece of paper; [Nachricht] note; [Einkaufszettel] (shopping) list.

**Zettel|kasten** *der* file-card box.

**Zettelwirtschaft** *die abw:* **bei so einer ~ findet man nichts wieder** you'll never find anything with notes strewn everywhere like that.

**Zeug** *das fam* [Sachen] stuff; [Kleidung] gear; **das ~ zu etw haben** *fam fig* to have the makings of sthg; **jm am ~ flicken** *fam fig* to put sb down; **wir müssen uns ins ~ legen** we're going to have to put our backs into it; **arbeiten, was das ~ hält** *fam fig* to work flat out.

◆ **dummes Zeug** *interj fam* rubbish!

**Zeuge** (*pl* -n) *der* witness; **die ~n Jehovas** the Jehovah's Witnesses.

**zeugen** *vi:* **von etw ~ geh** to show sthg ◇ *vt* to father.

**Zeugenaus|sage** *die* statement.

**Zeugin** (*pl* -nen) *die* witness.

**Zeugnis** (*pl* -se) *das* - **1.** [von Arbeitgeber] reference - **2.** [von Prüfung] certificate - **3.** SCHULE report.

**Zeugung** (*pl* -en) *die* fathering (U).

**z. H.** (*abk für* **zu Händen**) attn.

**Zi.** *abk für* **Zimmer**.

**Zicke** (*pl* -n) *die* nanny goat.

◆ **Zicken** *pl fam:* **~n machen** to cause trouble.

**Zickzack** (*pl* -e) *der* zigzag.

◆ **im Zickzack** *adv:* **im ~ laufen/fahren** to zigzag.

**Ziege** (*pl* -n) *die* - **1.** [Tier] goat - **2.** *fam* [als Schimpfwort] cow.

**Ziegel** (*pl* -) *der* - **1.** [Stein] brick - **2.** [Dachziegel] tile.

**Ziegel|dach** *das* tiled roof.

**Ziegel|stein** *der* brick.

**Ziegen|bock** *der* billy goat.

**Ziegen|käse** *der* goat's cheese.

**ziehen** (*prät* **zog**; *perf* **hat/ist gezogen**) *vt* (*hat*) - **1.** [gen] to pull; [Subj: Tier - Karren] to draw; **etw durch etw ~** to pull sthg through sthg; **etw von etw ~** to pull sthg off sthg; **jn am Ärmel ~** to tug sb's sleeve; **jn an den Haaren ~** to pull sb's hair - **2.** [herausziehen - Zahn, Korken] to pull out; [ - Rüben, Unkraut] to pull up - **3.** MED [Fäden] to take out - **4.** [Brieftasche, Waffe] to take out; [Hut] to doff; **etw aus etw ~** to take sthg out of sthg - **5.** [zeichnen] to draw - **6.** [züchten - Pflanzen] to grow; [ - Tiere] to breed - **7.** [anziehen]: **Aufmerksamkeit auf sich** (A) **~** to draw attention to o.s.; **du hast ihren Hass auf dich gezogen** you've incurred her hatred - **8.** [zur Folge haben]: **etw nach sich ~** to lead to sthg; **Probleme nach sich ~** to cause problems - **9.** [aus dem Automaten] to get (*from a vending machine*) - **10.** [anlegen - Mauer, Zaun] to put up; [ - Graben] to dig; [ - Grenze] to draw ◇ *vi* - **1.** (*hat*) [zerren] to pull; **an etw** (D) **~** to pull sthg; **der Hund zog**

an der Leine the dog was pulling on the lead *Br* ODER leash *Am* - **2.** *(ist)* [umziehen, sich bewegen] to move; **durch die Straßen ~** to wander through the streets; **eine Blaskapelle zog durchs Dorf** a brass band trooped through the village; **die Vögel ~ nach Süden** the birds are going ODER flying south - **3.** *(hat)* [saugen]: **an etw** *(D)* **~** [Pfeife, Zigarette] to take a puff on sthg - **4.** *(hat)* [Auto, Motor] to run - **5.** *(ist)* [dringen]: **der Duft zog durchs ganze Haus** the scent floated throughout the house; **in etw** *(A)* **~** [Flüssigkeit] to soak into sthg - **6.** *(hat)* [Kaffee, Tee] to brew - **7.** *(hat)* [bei Brettspiel] to move; **du musst ~!** it's your move! - **8.** *(hat) fam* [Eindruck machen] to go down well; **das zieht bei mir nicht!** that doesn't wash with me! - **9.** *(hat)* [Luftzug haben]: **es zieht** there's a draught; **in eurer Wohnung zieht es ja furchtbar** it's terribly draughty in your flat.

➤ **sich ziehen** *ref* - **1.** [nicht enden wollen] to drag on - **2.** [sich erstrecken] to stretch - **3.** [sich hochziehen] to pull o.s. up.

**Ziehlharmonika** *die* concertina.

**Ziehung** *(pl* -en) *die:* **die ~ der Lottozahlen** the lottery draw; **die ~ der Lose** the drawing of lots.

**Ziel** *(pl* -e) *das* - **1.** [Zielort] destination; **am ~ sein** to have reached one's destination - **2.** SPORT finish - **3.** [Zweck] goal; **sich** *(D)* **ein ~ setzen** to set o.s. a goal ODER target; **etw zum ~ haben** to have sthg as a goal.

**zielbewusst** *adj* purposeful <> *adv* purposefully.

**zielen** *vi* to aim; **auf jn/etw ~** to aim at sb/sthg.

**Zielfernrohr** *das* telescopic sight.

**Zielgerade** *die* SPORT finishing straight.

**Zielgruppe** *die* target group.

**Ziellaufwerk** *das* EDV destination drive.

**Ziellinie** *die* SPORT finishing line.

**ziellos** *adj* aimless <> *adv* aimlessly.

**Zielscheibe** *die* - **1.** [beim Schießen] target - **2.** [Opfer] butt.

**Zielsetzung** *(pl* -en) *die* objective.

**zielsicher** *adj* purposeful <> *adv* purposefully.

**zielstrebig** *adj* single-minded <> *adv* single-mindedly.

**ziemlich** *adj fam:* **mit ~er Genugtuung/Sicherheit** with some satisfaction/certainty; **das war eine ~e Gemeinheit** that was a rather mean thing to do <> *adv* - **1.** [sehr] quite; **~ viel** quite a lot - **2.** *fam* [fast] almost.

**Zierde** *(pl* -n) *die* decoration.

**zieren** ➤ **sich zieren** *ref* to be coy.

**Zierlfisch** *der* ornamental fish.

**zierlich** *adj* [Person] petite; [Hände] dainty; [Porzellanfigur] delicate <> *adv* daintily.

**Zierlpflanze** *die* ornamental plant.

**Ziffer** *(pl* -n) *die* figure.

** Zifferlblatt** *das* face.

**zig** *adj fam* umpteen.

**Zigarette** *(pl* -n) *die* cigarette.

**Zigarettenlautomat** *der* cigarette machine.

**Zigarettenlpause** *die* cigarette break.

**Zigarettenlschachtel** *die* cigarette packet.

**Zigarettenlstummel** *der* cigarette stub.

**Zigarillo** *(pl* -s) *der* ODER *das* cigarillo.

**Zigarre** *(pl* -n) *die* cigar.

**Zigeuner, in** *(mpl* -; *fpl* -nen) *der, die* gypsy.

**zigmal** *adv fam* umpteen times.

**Zimbabwe** [zɪmˈbabvə] *nt* Zimbabwe.

**Zimmer** *(pl* -) *das* room; **'~ frei!** 'vacancies'.

**Zimmerllautstärke** *die:* **in ~** at low volume.

**Zimmerlmädchen** *das* chambermaid.

**Zimmerlmann** *(pl* -leute) *der* carpenter.

**zimmern** *vt* to make *(from wood)* <> *vi* to do carpentry.

**Zimmerlnachweis** *der* accommodation service.

**Zimmerlnummer** *die* room number.

**Zimmerlpflanze** *die* house plant.

**Zimmerlservice** *der* room service.

**Zimmerlsuche** *die:* **auf ~ sein** to be looking for a room.

**Zimmerlvermittlung** *die* accommodation service.

**zimperlich** *abw adj:* **sei nicht so ~!** don't be such a wimp!; **sie ist nicht gerade ~** she doesn't exactly hold back <> *adv:* **nicht ~ mit jm umgehen** not to treat sb with kid gloves.

**Zimt** *der* cinnamon.

**Zimtlstange** *die* cinnamon stick.

**Zink** *das* zinc.

**Zinke** *(pl* -n) *die* [von Gabel] prong; [von Kamm] tooth.

**Zinn** *das* - **1.** [Metall] tin - **2.** [Gegenstände] pewter.

**Zins** *(pl* -en) *der:* **~en** interest *(U);* **~en bringen** to earn interest.

**Zinseslzins** *der* compound interest.

**Zinslfuß** *der* interest rate.

**zinsgünstig** *adj* WIRTSCH with a favourable interest rate.

**zinslos** *adj* interest-free.

Z

**Zins|satz** *der* interest rate.

**Zipfel** (*pl* -) *der* corner.

**Zipfel|mütze** *die* pointed hat.

**zirka, circa** ['tsɪrka] *adv* about, approximately; ~ **1900** circa 1900.

**Zirkel** (*pl* -) *der* - **1.** [Gerät] compasses (*pl*) - **2.** [Gruppe] circle.

**zirkulieren** (*perf* hat/ist zirkuliert) *vi* to circulate.

**Zirkus** (*pl* -se) *der* circus.

**Zirkus|zelt** *das* big top.

**zirpen** *vi* to chirp.

**zischen** (*perf* hat/ist gezischt) *vi* - **1.** *(hat)* [Geräusch] to hiss - **2.** *(ist)* [Fahrzeug] to whizz <> *vt (hat)* - **1.** [sagen] to hiss - **2.** *salopp* [trinken] to knock back.

**Zisterne** (*pl* -n) *die* well.

**Zisterzienser, in** (*mpl* -; *fpl* -nen) *der, die* Cistercian.

**Zitadelle** (*pl* -n) *die* citadel.

**Zitat** (*pl* -e) *das* quotation, quote.

**Zither** (*pl* -n) *die* zither.

**zitieren** *vt* - **1.** [wiedergeben] to quote - **2.** [rufen]: jn zu jm/vor etw (*A*) ~ to summon sb to sb/ before sthg <> *vi:* aus etw ~ to quote from sthg; **ich zitiere** and I quote.

**Zitronat** *das* küche candied lemon peel.

**Zitrone** (*pl* -n) *die* lemon.

**Zitronen|presse** *die* lemon squeezer.

**Zitronen|saft** *der* lemon juice.

**Zitronen|schale** *die* lemon zest.

**Zitrus|frucht** *die* citrus fruit.

**zitterig, zittrig** *adj* shaky.

**zittern** *vi* - **1.** [vibrieren - Hände, Körper] to tremble; [ - Stimme] to shake; **vor Kälte** ~ to shiver with cold - **2.** [Angst haben]: **vor jm/etw** ~ to be terrified of sb/sthg - **3.** [sich sorgen]: **um** ODER **für jn/etw** ~ to be very worried about sb/ sthg.

**zittrig** = zitterig.

**Zivi** ['tsiːvi] (*pl* -s) *der* fam man doing his "Zivildienst".

**zivil** [tsi'viːl] *adj* - **1.** [Bevölkerung, Leben] civilian - **2.** [Preise] *fam* reasonable <> *adv fam* [anständig] reasonably.

**Zivil** [tsi'viːl] ➔ **in Zivil** *adv* [Soldat] in civilian clothes; [Polizist] in plain clothes.

**Zivil|bevölkerung** *die* civilian population.

**Zivil|courage** *die* courage of one's convictions.

**Zivil|dienst** *der community service done by conscientious objectors instead of military service.*

**Zivil|dienstleistende** (*pl* -n) *der man doing his "Zivildienst".*

**Zivilisation** [tsiviliza'tsioːn] (*pl* -en) *die* civilization.

**Zivilisations|krankheit** *die* disease of modern society.

**zivilisiert** [tsivili'ziːɐt] *adj* civilized.

**Zivilist, in** [tsivi'lɪst, ɪn] (*mpl* -en; *fpl* -nen) *der, die* civilian.

**Zivil|recht** *das* recht civil law.

**ZKB** (*abk für* **Zimmer, Küche, Bad**) room(s), kitchen, bathroom.

**ZOB** (*abk für* **Zentraler Omnibusbahnhof**) central bus station.

**Zoff** *der salopp:* ~ **machen** to cause a lot of hassle; **es gibt** ~ there is trouble.

**zog** *prät* ⊳ ziehen.

**zögern** *vi* to hesitate; **mit etw** ~ to delay sthg; **ohne zu** ~ without hesitation.

**Zögern** *das* hesitation.

**Zölibat** *das* ODER *der* rel celibacy.

**Zoll** (*pl* Zölle ODER -) *der* - **1.** (*pl* Zölle) [Abgabe] duty - **2.** (*ohne pl*) [Behörde] customs (*pl*) - **3.** (*pl* Zoll) [Maßeinheit] inch.

**Zoll|abfertigung** *die* customs clearance.

**Zoll|amt** *das* customs office.

**Zoll|beamte** *der* customs officer.

**Zoll|beamtin** *die* customs officer.

**zollen** *vt geh:* **jm Beifall** ~ to applaud sb.

**Zoller|klärung** *die* customs declaration.

**Zoll|fahndung** *die* customs investigation.

**zollfrei** *adj* duty-free.

**Zoll|kontrolle** *die* customs check.

**Zöllner** (*pl* -) *der* customs officer.

**zollpflichtig** *adj* liable for duty.

**Zoll|schranke** *die* customs barrier.

**Zoll|stock** *der* folding rule.

**Zombie** (*pl* -s) *der* zombie.

**Zone** (*pl* -n) *die* zone.

**Zonen|grenze** *die* border between the former East and West Germany.

**Zoo** [tsoː] (*pl* -s) *der* zoo.

**Zoo|handlung** *die* pet shop.

**Zoologie** [tsoolo'giː] *die* zoology.

**zoologisch** [tsoo'loːgɪʃ] *adj* zoological; ▷ Garten.

**Zoom** [zuːm] (*pl* **-s**) *das* FOTO zoom.

**Zopf** (*pl* **Zöpfe**) *der* plait *Br*, braid *Am*; **Zöpfe flechten** to plait *Br* ODER braid *Am* one's hair.

**Zopf|muster** *das* cable pattern.

**Zorn** *der* anger; **der ~ auf jn/etw** anger at sb/sthg.
➤ **im Zorn** *adv* in anger.

**zornig** *adj* angry; **auf jn/über etw** *(A)* **~ sein** to be angry with sb/about sthg ⬦ *adv* angrily.

**Zote** (*pl* **-n**) *die abw* smutty joke.

**zottig** *adj* shaggy.

**z. T.** (*abk für* **zum Teil**) partly.

**Ztr.** *abk für* **Zentner**.

**zu** *präp (+ D)* **- 1.** [räumlich - Richtung] to; [ - Position] at; **~ jm/etw hin** towards sb/sthg; **~ Hause** (at) home; **~ beiden Seiten** on both sides **- 2.** [zeitlich] at; **~ Beginn** at the beginning; **~ Ostern/ Weihnachten** at Easter/Christmas **- 3.** [modal]: **~ Pferd** by horse; **~ Fuß** on foot; **~ Fuß gehen** to walk; **~ meiner großen Enttäuschung** to my great disappointment **- 4.** [stellt Bezug her] about **- 5.** [in Kombination mit] with; **stell das Glas ~ den anderen** put that glass with the others **- 6.** [für einen bestimmten Zweck] for **- 7.** [mit Nennung eines Endzustandes] into; **~ Eis werden** to turn into ice **- 8.** [aus einem bestimmten Anlass] on **- 9.** [in Mengenangaben]: **~ viert** in fours; **wir sind ~ viert** there are four of us; **~ Tausenden** in thousands; **Säcke ~ 50 kg** 50 kg bags; **Orangen ~ 50 Cent das Stück** oranges at 50 cents each **- 10.** SPORT: **3 ~ 2** 3–2 ⬦ *adv* **- 1.** [übermäßig] too; **~ alt** too old; **~ sehr** too much **- 2.** *fam* [zumachen]: **Tür ~!** shut the door! **- 3.** [zur Angabe der Richtung] towards ⬦ *konj* **- 1.** (+ *Infinitiv*) to; **etwas ~ essen** something to eat; **es fängt an ~ schneien** it's starting to snow; **~ verkaufen** for sale; **ohne ~ fragen** without asking **- 2.** (+ *pp*) to; **die ~ erledigende Sache** the matter to be dealt with.
➤ **nur zu** *interj* go ahead!; *siehe auch* **zu sein**.

**zuallererst, zuallererst** *adv* first of all.

**zuallerletzt, zuallerletzt** *adv* last of all.

**Zubehör** (*pl* **-e**) *das* accessories *(pl)*.

**zu|beißen** *vi (unreg)* to bite.

**zu|bekommen** *vt (unreg)* [Tür, Koffer] to get shut.

**zu|bereiten** *vt* to prepare.

**Zubereitung** (*pl* **-en**) *die* preparation.

**zu|betonieren** *vt* to concrete over.

**zu|bewegen** *vt*: **etw auf jn/etw ~** to move sthg towards sb/sthg.
➤ **sich zubewegen** *ref*: **sich auf jn/etw ~** to make one's way towards sb/sthg.

**zu|billigen** *vt*: **jm etw ~** to allow sb sthg.

**zu|binden** *vt (unreg)* to tie up.

**zu|bleiben** (*perf* **ist zugeblieben**) *vi (unreg) fam* to stay shut.

**zu|blinzeln** *vi*: **jm ~** to wink at sb.

**zu|bringen** *vt (unreg)* **- 1.** [Zeit] to spend **- 2.** [Tür, Koffer] to get shut.

**Zubringer** (*pl* **-**) *der* feeder road.

**zu|buttern** *vt fam* to chip in.

**Zucchini** [tsʊ'kiːni] (*pl* **-s**) *die* courgette *Br*, zucchini *Am*.

**Zucht** (*pl* **-en**) *die* **- 1.** [Züchten - von Tieren] breeding; [ - von Pflanzen] growing; [ - von Perlen] cultivation **- 2.** *geh* [Disziplin] discipline; **~ und Ordnung** order and discipline.

**züchten** *vt* [Tiere] to breed; [Pflanzen] to grow; [Bakterien, Perlen] to cultivate.

**Züchter, in** (*mpl* **-**; *fpl* **-nen**) *der, die* [von Tieren] breeder; [von Pflanzen] grower; [von Austern] cultivator.

**Zucht|perle** *die* cultured pearl.

**Züchtung** (*pl* **-en**) *die* [Züchten - von Tieren] breeding; [ - von Pflanzen] growing; [ - von Bakterien, Perlen] cultivation; [Zuchtergebnis - Tiere] breed; [ - Pflanzen] variety.

**zucken** (*perf* **hat/ist gezuckt**) *vi* **- 1.** (*hat*) [unwillkürlich] to twitch; **mit den Schultern ~** to shrug (one's shoulders) **- 2.** (*ist*) [in eine Richtung - Flamme] to leap up; [ - Blitz] to flash.

**zücken** *vt* **- 1.** *geh* [Waffe] to draw **- 2.** *hum* [Portmonee, Notizbuch] to whip out.

**Zucker** *der* **- 1.** [Nahrungsmittel] sugar *(U)* **- 2.** *fam* [Krankheit] diabetes; **~ haben** to be diabetic.

**Zucker|dose** *die* sugar bowl.

**Zucker|guss** *der* icing.

**Zucker|hut** *der* sugar loaf.

**zuckerkrank** *adj* diabetic.

**zuckern** *vt* [Nachspeise, Kuchen] to put sugar in/on; [Kaffee] to sugar.

**Zucker|rohr** *das* sugarcane.

**Zucker|rübe** *die* sugar beet.

**zuckersüß** *adj* **- 1.** [sehr süß] as sweet as sugar **- 2.** *abw* [übertrieben freundlich] sickly sweet.

**Zuckerwatte** *die* candyfloss *Br*, cotton candy *Am*.

**Zuckung** (*pl* **-en**) *die* twitch.

**zu|decken** *vt* to cover; **sich/jn/etw mit etw ~** to cover o.s./sb/sthg with sthg.

**zudem** *adv geh* moreover.

**z**

**zu|drehen** vt - **1.** [schließen] to turn off - **2.** [zuwenden]: **jm den Rücken ~** to turn one's back on sb.

➤ **sich zudrehen** ref [sich zuwenden]: **sich jm ~** to turn to sb.

**zu|dringlich** adj pushy.

**Zudringlichkeit** (pl **-en**) die [zudringliche Art] pushiness; **~en** (pl) pushy behaviour (U).

**zu|drücken** vt [Auge, Koffer] to close; [Tür] to push shut.

**zueinander** adv to each other; **~ passen** to go together.

**zueinander halten** vi (unreg) to stick together.

**zu|erkennen** vt (unreg): **jm etw ~** to award sthg to sb.

**zuerst** adv - **1.** [als Erstes] first - **2.** [am Anfang] at first - **3.** [zum ersten Mal] for the first time.

**zu|fahren** (perf **ist zugefahren**) vi (unreg) - **1.** [sich zubewegen]: **auf jn/etw ~** to drive towards sb/sthg - **2.** fam: **fahr zu!** get a move on!

**Zu|fahrt** die - **1.** [Zufahrtsweg] access road; [zu einem Haus] drive; **die ~ sperren** to block access - **2.** [Zufahren] access.

**Zufahrts|straße** die access road.

**Zu|fall** der coincidence; **so ein ~!** what a coincidence!; **etw dem ~ überlassen** to leave sthg to chance.

➤ **durch Zufall** adv by chance.

**zu|fallen** (perf **ist zugefallen**) vi (unreg) - **1.** [Tür, Deckel] to slam shut; [Augen] to close - **2.**: **jm ~** [Preis] to go to sb; [Aufgabe] to fall to sb; **sie ist ein Glückspilz, alles fällt ihr zu** she's very lucky, everything falls into her lap.

**zufällig** adj chance (vor Subst) ◇ adv by chance.

**zufälligerweise** adv by chance.

**Zufalls|bekanntschaft** die chance acquaintance.

**zu|fassen** vi: **schnell ~, ehe die Vase umkippt** to make a grab for the vase before it falls over; **fest ~** to grip tightly.

**zu|fliegen** (perf **ist zugeflogen**) vi (unreg): **jm ~** [Vogel] to fly into sb's house; [Ideen] to come easily to sb; **auf jn/etw ~** to fly towards sb/sthg.

**Zu|flucht** die refuge; **~ suchen** to seek refuge; **zu etw ~ nehmen** fig to resort to sthg.

**zu|flüstern** vt: **jm etw ~** to whisper sthg to sb.

**zufolge** präp: **jm/einer Sache ~** according to sb/sthg.

**zufrieden** adj contented; [mit Befriedigung] satisfied; **mit jm/etw ~ sein** to be satisfied with sb/sthg ◇ adv contentedly.

**zufrieden geben** ➤ **sich zufrieden geben** ref (unreg): **sich mit etw ~** to be satisfied with sthg.

**Zufriedenheit** die contentment; [Befriedigung] satisfaction; **zu js vollster ~** to sb's complete satisfaction.

**zufrieden lassen** vt (unreg) to leave in peace; **jn mit etw ~** to stop going on at sb about sthg.

**zufrieden stellen** vt to satisfy.

**zufrieden stellend** adj satisfactory.

**zu|frieren** (perf **ist zugefroren**) vi (unreg) to freeze over.

**zu|fügen** vt: **jm Schaden/Unrecht ~** to do sb harm/an injustice.

**Zufuhr** die [von Energie] supply; [von Luft] influx.

**zu|führen** vt amt: **jn seiner Strafe ~** to punish sb; **dem Geschäft neue Kunden ~** to bring the company in new customers ◇ vi: **auf etw** (A) **~** to lead to sthg.

**Zug¹** (pl **Züge**) der - **1.** [Bahn] train; **mit dem ~ fahren** to go by train - **2.** [Schar] procession - **3.** [Bewegung - von Vögeln] migration; [- von Wolken] drifting; **im ~e einer Sache** (G) amt in the course of sthg - **4.** [mit Spielfigur] move; **er ist am ~** eigtl & fig it is his move - **5.** [Schluck] gulp; **in einem ~** in one go - **6.** [beim Rauchen] puff - **7.** [Atemzug] breath; **in vollen Zügen** in deep breaths; fig to the full - **8.** (ohne pl) [Durchzug] draught - **9.** [Gesichtszug]: **Züge** features - **10.** [Charakterzug] characteristic - **11.** [beim Schwimmen] stroke - **12.** RW: **in groben Zügen** in broad outline; **zum ~(e) kommen** to get a chance.

**Zug²** nt Zug.

**Zu|gabe** die - **1.** [Zugeben] addition - **2.** [Zugegebenes] free gift ◇ interj encore!

**Zugab|teil** das compartment.

**Zu|gang** der - **1.** [gen & EDV] access; '**~ verboten!**' 'no entry!'; **~ zu etw haben** to have access to sthg - **2.** [Zugangsweg] entrance.

**zugange** adj: **mit etw ~ sein** fam to be busy with sthg.

**zugänglich** adj - **1.** [Raum, Ort] accessible; **schwer ~** difficult to get to - **2.** [Information] available; **jm etw ~ machen** to make sthg available to sb - **3.** [Person] approachable; **für etw ~ sein** to be receptive to sthg.

**Zug|begleiter, in** der, die [Person] guard Br, conductor Am ◇ der [Faltblatt] train information leaflet.

**Zug|brücke** die drawbridge.

**zu|geben** vt (unreg) - **1.** [hinzugeben] to add

**- 2.** [gestehen] to admit; **zugegeben, ...** admittedly ...

**zugegebenermaßen** *adv* admittedly.

**zugegen** *adj:* **bei etw ~ sein** *geh* to be present at sthg.

**zulgehen** (*perf* **ist zugegangen**) *vi* (*unreg*)
**- 1.** [sich zubewegen]: **auf jn/etw ~** to approach sb/sthg **- 2.** [verlaufen]: **auf der Party gehts lustig zu** the party is going with a swing **- 3.** *fam* [schneller gehen]: **geh zu!** get a move on! **- 4.** [sich schließen - Tür, Koffer] to close; [ - Knopf, Reißverschluss] to do up.

**zugehörig** *adj* that belongs with it/them; **sich jm/einer Sache ~ fühlen** to feel a part of sb/sthg.

**Zugehörigkeit** *die* [zu Verein, Familie] membership.

**zugeknöpft** *adj* buttoned up.

**Zügel** (*pl* -) *der* reins (*pl*); **die ~ in der Hand haben** *fig* to have things under control; **die ~ schleifen lassen** *fig* to slacken the reins.

**zügellos** *adj* unrestrained ◇ *adv* in an unrestrained manner.

**zügeln** *vt* **- 1.** [Pferd] to rein in **- 2.** [Gefühl] to restrain.

➡ **sich zügeln** *ref* [sich zurückhalten] to restrain o.s.

**Zulgeständnis** *das* concession; **~se an jn/etw machen** to make concessions to sb/sthg.

**zulgestehen** *vt* (*unreg*): **jm etw ~** [gestatten] to grant sb sthg; [zugeben] to admit sthg to sb.

**zugetan** *adj:* **jm/etw ~ sein** *geh* to be fond of sb/sthg.

**Zulgewinn** *der* gain.

**Zugewinnlgemeinschaft** *die* RECHT *agreement whereby only those possessions acquired jointly since marriage are divided up equally on divorce.*

**Zuglführer, in** *der, die* senior guard *Br* ODER conductor *Am.*

**zugig** *adj* draughty.

**zügig** *adj* rapid ◇ *adv* rapidly.

**Zuglkraft** *die* PHYS traction (*U*).

**zugkräftig** *adj* with popular appeal; [Name] influential; [Werbung, Titel] catchy.

**zugleich** *adv* at the same time.

**Zuglluft** *die* (*ohne pl*) draught.

**Zuglmaschine** *die* tractor.

**Zuglpersonal** *das* (*ohne pl*) train crew.

**zulgreifen** *vi* (*unreg*) **- 1.** [zufassen] to grab it/them; **sie greift schnell zu und hält die Leiter fest** she grabs the ladder and holds it firmly **- 2.** [sich bedienen] to help o.s.; **greifen Sie zu!**

help yourself! **- 3.** [mithelfen] to do one's bit; **kräftig ~** to really get stuck in.

**Zulgriff** *der* **- 1.** [Zugang]: **~ auf etw** (*A*) **haben** to have access to sthg; **sich js ~ entziehen** to escape sb's clutches **- 2.** EDV access (*U*).

**Zugriffslzeit** *die* EDV access time.

**zugrunde, zu Grunde** *adv:* **an etw** (*D*) **~ gehen** [sterben] to perish from sthg; [ruiniert werden] to be wrecked by sthg; **einer Sache** (*D*) **~ liegen** to form the basis of sthg; **jn ~ richten** to ruin sb.

**Zuglschaffner, in** *der, die* ticket inspector.

**Zugspitze** *die:* **die ~** the Zugspitze.

**Zugltelefon** *das* train telephone.

**Zuglunglück** *das* train accident.

**zugunsten, zu Gunsten** *präp:* **~ js/einer Sache** in favour of sb/sthg ◇ *adv:* **~ von jm/etw** in favour of sb/sthg.

**zugute** *adv:* **jm/etw ~ kommen** to prove beneficial to sb/sthg; **jm etw ~ halten** *geh* to make sb due allowance for sthg.

**Zugverlbindung** *die* train connection.

**Zuglverkehr** *der* (*ohne pl*) train services (*pl*).

**Zuglvogel** *der* migratory bird.

**Zuglzwang** *der:* **unter ~ stehen** to be forced to act; **in ~ geraten** to find o.s. forced to act.

**zulhaben** *vi* (*unreg*) *fam* to be shut.

**zulhalten** *vt* (*unreg*) [Tür, Mund, Augen] to keep closed; [Nase] to hold; [Ohren] to cover ◇ *vi:* **auf jn/etw ~** to head for sb/sthg.

**Zuhälter** (*pl* -) *der* pimp.

**zuhause** *adv Schweiz* & *Österr* at home; *siehe auch* **Haus.**

**Zuhause** *das* home.

**zulheilen** (*perf* **ist zugeheilt**) *vi* to heal up.

**zulhören** *vi* to listen; **jm/einer Sache ~** to listen to sb/sthg.

**Zulhörer, in** *der, die* listener.

**zulkehren** *vt:* **jm den Rücken ~** to turn one's back on sb.

**zulklappen** (*perf* **hat/ist zugeklappt**) *vt* (*hat*) [Fenster, Deckel] to slam shut; [Taschenmesser] to snap shut ◇ *vi* (*ist*) [Fenster, Deckel] to slam shut.

**zulkleben** *vt* **- 1.** [schließen] to seal **- 2.** [bekleben]: **etw mit etw ~** to stick sthg all over sthg.

**zulknallen** (*perf* **hat/ist zugeknallt**) *vt* (*hat*) & *vi* (*ist*) *fam* to slam.

**zulkneifen** *vt* (*unreg*) to shut tightly.

**zulknöpfen** *vt* to button up.

**zulkommen** (*perf* **ist zugekommen**) *vi* (*unreg*)
**- 1.** [sich bewegen]: **auf jn/etw ~** to approach sb/sthg; **etw auf sich** (*A*) **~ lassen** *fig* to take

sthg as it comes - **2.** [zustehen]: **jm ~** to befit sb
- **3.** *geh* [zuteil werden]: **etw kommt jm zu** sb re-
ceives sthg; **jm etw ~ lassen** to send sb sthg.

**Zukunft** *die* [künftige Zeit & GRAM] future; **etw hat
~/keine ~** *fig* to have a/no future.
> **in Zukunft** *adv* in future.

**zukünftig** *adj* future ◇ *adv* in future.

**Zukunfts|musik** *die* pie in the sky.

**Zukunfts|perspektive** *die* future pros-
pects *(pl)*.

**Zukunfts|pläne** *pl* plans for the future.

**zul.** *abk für* **zulässig.**

**zu|lächeln** *vi:* **jm ~** to smile at sb.

**Zu|lage** *die* bonus.

**zu|lassen** *vt (unreg)* - **1.** [erlauben] to allow
- **2.** [amtlich - Medikament] to license; [ - Auto] to
register; **jn zu einer Prüfung ~** to permit sb to
take an examination - **3.** [nicht öffnen] to
leave closed.

**zulässig** *adj* permissible.

**Zulassung** *(pl* -en*) die* - **1.** [Zulassen - von Medika-
ment] licensing; [ - von Arzt, Auto] registration;
**die ~ zum Studium** acceptance to study at
university; **die ~ zur Prüfung** permission to
take an examination - **2.** AUTO [Schein] vehicle
registration document.

**Zulassungs|stelle** *die* vehicle registration
office.

**Zulauf** *der:* **regen** ODER **großen ~ haben** to be
very popular.

**zu|laufen** *(perf* ist zugelaufen*) vi (unreg)*
- **1.** [sich bewegen]: **auf jn/etw ~** to run towards
sb/sthg - **2.** [Tier]: **jm ~** to adopt sb - **3.** [auslau-
fen] to taper; **spitz ~** to end in a point.

**zu|legen** *vt* - **1.** [anschaffen]: **sich** *(D)* **etw ~** to get
o.s. sthg - **2.** [dazutun - Geld] to put in; [ - Tempo]
to put on ◇ *vi* [schneller werden] to get moving.

**zuleide, zu Leide** *adv:* **jm etwas ~ tun** to
harm sb.

**zuletzt** *adv* - **1.** [gen] last; **nicht ~** not least
- **2.** [am Ende] in the end; **bis ~** to the very end.

**zuliebe** *präp:* **jm ~** for sb's sake; **einer Sache** *(D)*
**~** for the sake of sthg.

**Zulieferbe|trieb** *der* supplier.

**Zulieferer** *(pl* -*) der* supplier.

**Zu|lieferung** *die* supply.

**zum** *präp* - **1.** *(zu + dem)* to the; **~ Friseur gehen** -
to go to the hairdresser's - **2.** *(untrennbar):*
**~ Tanzen gehen** to go dancing; **~ Teil** partly;
**~ Beispiel** for example; **~ Thema ...** on the
subject of ...; **Fenster ~ Garten** window over-
looking the garden; *siehe auch* **zu.**

**zu|machen** *vt* & *vi* to close; [Mantel] to do up.

**zumal** *adv* especially ◇ *konj* especially as.

**zu|mauern** *vt* to brick up.

**zumindest** *adv* at least.

**zumutbar** *adj* reasonable.

**zumute, zu Mute** *adj:* **jm ist/wird ... ~** sb
feels ...; **ihm ist nicht zum Lachen ~** he doesn't
feel like laughing.

**zu|muten** *vt:* **jm etw ~** to expect sthg of sb;
**das kannst du ihr nicht ~** you can't ask her to
do that.

**Zumutung** *(pl* -en*) die:* **etw als ~ empfinden** to
feel that sthg is unreasonable; **eine ~ sein** to
be unreasonable.

**zunächst** [tsu'nɛːçst] *adv* - **1.** [zuerst] first
- **2.** [einstweilen] for the moment.

**zu|nageln** *vt* [Kiste] to nail up; [Fenster] to board
up.

**zu|nähen** *vt* to sew up.

**Zunahme** *(pl* -n*) die* increase.

**Zu|name** *der* surname.

**zünden** *vt* [Bombe, Sprengladung] to detonate;
[Triebwerk] to fire ◇ *vi* [Triebwerk] to fire; [Treib-
stoff] to ignite.

**zündend** *adj fig* [Aussprache] rousing; [Idee] exciting.

**Zünder** *(pl* -*) der* detonator.

**Zünd|holz** *das Süddt* & *Österr* match.

**Zünd|kerze** *die* AUTO spark plug.

**Zünd|schloss** *das* AUTO ignition.

**Zünd|schlüssel** *der* AUTO ignition key.

**Zünd|schnur** *die* fuse.

**Zünd|stoff** *der fig* dynamite *(U).*

**Zündung** *(pl* -en*) die* - **1.** [Zünden] detonation
- **2.** AUTO ignition.

**zu|nehmen** *(unreg) vi* - **1.** [gewinnen]: **an etw** *(D)*
**~** to gain in sthg - **2.** [dicker werden] to put on
weight ◇ *vt:* **5 Kilo ~** to put on 5 kilos.

**zunehmend** *adj* [Alter, Einfluss] increasing;
[Mond] waxing; **in ~em Maße** increasingly
◇ *adv* increasingly.

**zu|neigen** *vi* [zu etw tendieren]: **jm/einer Sache ~**
to lean towards sb/sthg ◇ *vt geh* [zuwenden]:
**jm etw ~** to lean sthg towards sb.
> **sich zuneigen** *ref geh* [sich hinneigen]: **sich jm ~**
to lean towards sb.

**Zuneigung** *die* affection; **~ zu jm/etw** affection for sb/sthg.

**Zunft** *(pl* Zünfte*) die* HIST guild.

**zünftig** *adj* proper ◇ *adv* properly.

**Zunge** *(pl* -n*) die* tongue; **auf der ~ zergehen** to
melt in the mouth; **die ~ herausstrecken** to
stick one's tongue out; **es liegt mir auf der
~** *fig* it's on the tip of my tongue; **seine ~ im
Zaum halten** *fig* to watch one's tongue.

**Zungenbrecher** (*pl -*) *der* tongue twister.

**Zungen|spitze** *die* tip of the tongue.

**Zünglein** (*pl -*) *das:* **das ~ an der Waage sein** *fig* to tip the scales.

**zunichte** *adj:* **etw ~ machen** to ruin sthg.

**zu|nicken** *vi:* **jm ~** to nod to sb.

**zunutze, zu Nutze** *adj:* **sich** (*D*) **etw ~ machen** to take advantage of sthg.

**zuoberst** *adv* on top.

**zu|ordnen** *vt:* **jn/etw jm/einer Sache ~** to assign sb/sthg to sb/sthg; **Katzen werden den Raubtieren zugeordnet** cats are classified as carnivores.

**zu|packen** *vi* **- 1.** [greifen] to grab it/them **- 2.** [mitarbeiten] to knuckle down to it.

**zu|parken** *vt* to block with one's vehicle.

**zupass** *adv:* **jm ~ kommen** *geh* to come at the right moment for sb.

**zupfen** *vi:* **an etw** (*D*) **~** to tug at sthg <> *vt* **- 1.** [Unkraut] to pull up **- 2.** [Instrument, Augenbrauen, Haar] to pluck.

**Zupf|instrument** *das* plucked instrument.

**zu|prosten** *vi:* **jm ~** to raise one's glass to sb.

**zur** *präp* **- 1.** (*zu + der*) to the; **~ Post gehen** to go to the post office **- 2.** (*untrennbar*): **~ Zeit** at the moment; **~ Straße liegen** to face the street; **~ allgemeinen Verwunderung** to everyone's amazement; *siehe auch* **zu.**

**zu|raten** *vi* (*unreg*): **jm ~** to advise sb.

**Zürcher, Züricher** (*pl -*) *der* native/inhabitant of Zurich <> *adj* (*unver*) of/from Zurich.

**Zürcherin, Züricherin** (*pl -nen*) *die* native/inhabitant of Zurich.

**zu|rechnen** *vt:* **jn/etw jm/einer Sache ~** to class sb/sthg as sb/sthg.

**zurechnungsfähig** *adj* of sound mind.

**Zurechnungsfähigkeit** *die* soundness of mind.

**zurecht|finden** ⬥ **sich zurechtfinden** *ref* (*unreg*) to find one's way around.

**zurecht|kommen** (*perf* **ist zurechtgekommen**) *vi* (*unreg*) to get on; **mit jm ~** to get on with sb; **mit etw ~** to cope with sthg.

**zurecht|legen** *vt* **- 1.** [Kleidung, Werkzeug] to lay out ready **- 2.** [Ausrede] to get ready.

**zurecht|machen** *vt* [herrichten] to get ready. ⬥ **sich zurechtmachen** *ref* [schminken] to put one's make-up on.

**zurecht|rücken** *vt* to straighten.

**zurecht|weisen** *vt* (*unreg*) to reprimand.

**Zurecht|weisung** *die* reprimand.

**zu|reden** *vi:* **jm ~** to persuade sb; **jm gut ~** to talk nicely to sb.

**zu|reichen** *vt:* **jm etw ~** to pass sb sthg.

**Zürich** *nt* Zurich.

**Züricher** = Zürcher.

**Züricherin** = Zürcherin.

**Zürichsee** ['tsy:rıçze:] *der* Lake Zurich.

**zu|richten** *vt* to mess up; **jn übel ~** to beat sb up.

**zurück** *adv* **- 1.** [gen] back; **ich bin um 5 Uhr ~** I'll be back at 5 o'clock; **einmal Berlin und ~** a return to Berlin *Br*, a round-trip ticket to Berlin *Am* **- 2.** [im Rückstand] behind.

**Zurück** *das:* **es gibt kein ~ mehr** there's no going back.

**zurück|behalten** *vt* (*unreg*) **- 1.** [als Pfand] to keep back **- 2.** [als Erinnerung] to be left with.

**zurück|bekommen** *vt* (*unreg*) to get back.

**zurück|bilden** ⬥ **sich zurückbilden** *ref* to go down.

**zurück|bleiben** (*perf* **ist zurückgeblieben**) *vi* (*unreg*) **- 1.** [nicht folgen] to stay behind; **hinter jm/etw ~** to fall behind sb/sthg **- 2.** [sich nicht nähern] to keep back **- 3.** [mit Leistung, Ergebnis] to fall behind **- 4.** [Erinnerung, Schaden] to be left.

**zurück|blicken** *vi* to look back; **auf etw** (*A*) **~** to look back at sthg; *fig* to look back on sthg.

**zurück|bringen** *vt* (*unreg*) to bring/take back; **jm etw ~** to bring sthg back.

**zurück|datieren** *vt* to backdate.

**zurück|erhalten** *vt* (*unreg*) to get back.

**zurück|erobern** *vt* to recapture.

**zurück|erstatten** *vt:* **jm etw ~** to refund sb sthg.

**zurück|erwarten** *vt* to expect back.

**zurück|fahren** (*perf* **hat/ist zurückgefahren**) (*unreg*) *vi* (*ist*) **- 1.** [zurückkehren] to go back **- 2.** [rückwärts fahren] to drive back <> *vt* (*hat*) to drive back.

**zurück|fallen** (*perf* **ist zurückgefallen**) *vi* (*unreg*) **- 1.** [gen] to fall back **- 2.** [in Rückstand geraten] to fall behind **- 3.** [zurückgegeben werden]: **an jn ~** to revert to sb **- 4.** [zurückgeführt werden]: **auf jn ~** to reflect on sb.

**zurück|finden** *vi* (*unreg*) to find one's way back.

**zurück|fliegen** (*perf* **hat/ist zurückgeflogen**) *vi* (*ist*) (*unreg*) to fly back.

**zurück|fordern** *vt:* **etw ~** to ask for sthg back.

**zurück|führen** *vt* **- 1.** [von etwas herleiten]: **etw auf etw** (*A*) **~** to put sthg down to sthg

**z**

**- 2.** [Person, Sache] to take back ◇ *vi* [Weg] to lead back.

**zurück|geben** *vt (unreg)* **- 1.** [wiedergeben - Geliehenes, Führerschein] to give back; [ - Ware] to return; [ - Mandat] to give up; **jm etw ~** to give sb sthg back **- 2.** [antworten] to answer **- 3.** [zurückspielen] to return.

**zurückgeblieben** *adj* retarded.

**zurück|gehen** *(perf* ist zurückgegangen*) vi (unreg)* **- 1.** [gen] to go back **- 2.** [weniger werden] to go down **- 3.** [zurückzuführen sein]: **auf jn/etw ~** to go back to sb/sthg **- 4.** [zurückgesandt werden]: **etw ~ lassen** to send sthg back.

**zurückgezogen** *adj* [Mensch] retiring; [Leben] secluded ◇ *adv* in seclusion.

**zurück|greifen** *vi (unreg):* **auf jn/etw ~** to fall back on sb/sthg.

**zurück|halten** *vt (unreg)* **- 1.** [Person, Meinung, Gefühl] to hold back **- 2.** [Nachricht, Sendung] to withhold **- 3.** [an etw hindern]: **jn von etw ~** to stop sb from doing sthg.
  ➤ **sich zurückhalten** *ref* [sich bremsen] to restrain o.s.; **sich mit Kritik ~** to stop being critical; **sich mit dem Trinken ~** to watch what one drinks.

**zurückhaltend** *adj* [Mensch] reserved; [Beifall, Äußerung] restrained ◇ *adv* with restraint.

**Zurückhaltung** *die* restraint.

**zurück|holen** *vt* to fetch back.

**zurück|kämmen** *vt* to comb back.

**zurück|kehren** *(perf* ist zurückgekehrt*) vi geh* to return; **zu jm/etw ~** to return to sb/sthg.

**zurück|kommen** *(perf* ist zurückgekommen*) vi (unreg)* **- 1.** [zurückkehren] to come back **- 2.** [zurückgreifen]: **auf jn/etw ~** to come back to sb/sthg.

**zurück|können** *vi (unreg)* to be able to get back.

**zurück|lassen** *vt (unreg)* **- 1.** [hinterlassen] to leave behind **- 2.** [zurückgehen lassen] to let go back.

**zurück|legen** *vt* **- 1.** [wieder hinlegen] to put back **- 2.** [Kopf] to lean back **- 3.** [Geld, Ware] to put aside **- 4.** [Strecke] to cover.
  ➤ **sich zurücklegen** *ref* [sich zurücklehnen] to lie back.

**zurück|liegen** *vi (unreg)* **- 1.** [vergangen sein]: **es liegt zwei Jahre zurück** it was two years ago **- 2.** [im Rückstand sein] to be behind.

**zurück|müssen** *vi (unreg)* to have to go back.

**zurück|nehmen** *vt (unreg)* **- 1.** [Ware] to take back **- 2.** [widerrufen - Äußerung, Vorwurf] to take back; [ - Antrag] to withdraw; [ - Entscheidung, Befehl] to rescind.

**zurück|rufen** *(unreg) vt* to call back; **sich etw**

**in Bewusstsein ~** to recall sthg ◇ *vi* [am Telefon] to call back.

**zurück|schicken** *vt* to send back.

**zurück|schlagen** *(perf* hat/ist zurückgeschlagen*) (unreg) vi* **- 1.** *(hat)* [schlagen] to hit back **- 2.** *(ist)* [sich zurückbewegen - Pendel] to swing back; [ - Wellen] to fall back **- 3.** *(hat)* [sich auswirken]: **auf etw** *(A)* **~** to have a detrimental effect on sthg ◇ *vt (hat)* **- 1.** [Kragen, Decke, Verdeck] to turn back **- 2.** [Ball] to hit back; [mit Fuß] to kick back **- 3.** [Gegner, Angriff] to repulse.

**zurück|schrecken** *(perf* ist zurückgeschreckt*) vi* **- 1.** [vor Schreck] to start back in fright **- 2.** [sich scheuen]: **vor etw** *(D)* **~** to shy away from sthg; **vor nichts ~** to stop at nothing.

**zurück|setzen** *vt* **- 1.** [wieder zurück] to put back **- 2.** [nach hinten] to move back **- 3.** [Auto] to reverse **- 4.** [benachteiligen] to neglect; **sich zurückgesetzt fühlen** to feel neglected ◇ *vi* [mit Auto] to reverse.
  ➤ **sich zurücksetzen** *ref* **- 1.** [wieder zurück] to sit down again **- 2.** [nach hinten] to move back.

**zurück|stecken** *vt* **- 1.** [wieder zurück] to put back **- 2.** [nach hinten] to move back ◇ *vi* [mit weniger zufrieden sein] to lower one's sights; **hinter jm nicht ~** to lag behind sb.

**zurück|stellen** *vt* **- 1.** [wieder zurück] to put back **- 2.** [nach hinten] to move back **- 3.** [Heizung, Lautstärke] to turn down **- 4.** [verschieben - Plan, Projekt] to put off; [ - Wünsche, Zweifel] to set aside.

**zurück|stoßen** *vt (unreg)* **- 1.** [wieder zurück] to push back **- 2.** [wegstoßen] to push away.

**zurück|strahlen** *vt* to reflect ◇ *vi* to be reflected.

**zurück|treten** *(perf* ist zurückgetreten*) vi (unreg)* **- 1.** [nach hinten] to step back **- 2.** [von Kauf, Zusage]: **von etw ~** to withdraw from sthg **- 3.** [von Amt] to resign; **von etw ~** to resign from sthg.

**zurück|verfolgen** *vt* to trace back.

**zurück|versetzen** *vt* **- 1.** [an Ausgangspunkt] to move back **- 2.** [in frühere Zeit] to take back.
  ➤ **sich zurückversetzen** *ref* [in frühere Zeit] to imagine o.s. back.

**zurück|weichen** *(perf* ist zurückgewichen*) vi (unreg)* to shrink back; **vor jm/etw ~** to shrink away from sb; **vor etw ~** to shrink from sthg.

**zurück|weisen** *vt (unreg)* **- 1.** [abweisen] to reject **- 2.** [Vorwurf] to repudiate.

**Zurück|weisung** *die* rejection.

**zurück|werfen** *vt (unreg)* **- 1.** [an Ausgangspunkt] to throw back **- 2.** [Licht, Schall] to reflect **- 3.** [in Rückstand bringen] to set back.

**zurück|zahlen** *vt* to pay back; **jm etw ~** [Schulden] to pay sb back sthg; *fam* [aus Rache] to pay sb back for sthg.

**zurück|ziehen** (*perf* hat/ist zurückgezogen) (*unreg*) *vt (hat)* - **1.** [gen] to withdraw - **2.** [nach hinten] to pull back ⟷ *vi (ist)* [umziehen] to move back.

➡ **sich zurückziehen** *ref* [sich isolieren] to withdraw; **sich aus etw ~** to retire from sthg.

**Zu|ruf** *der* shout.

**zu|rufen** *vt (unreg)* to shout; **jm etw ~** to shout sthg to sb.

**zurzeit** *adv* at present.

**zus.** *abk für* zusammen.

**Zu|sage** *die* - **1.** [zu Einladung] acceptance *(U)* - **2.** [Versprechen] promise.

**zu|sagen** *vt* [versprechen] to promise; **jm etw ~** to promise sb sthg ⟷ *vi* - **1.** [bei Einladung] to accept - **2.** [gefallen]: **jm ~** to appeal to sb.

**zusammen** *adv* - **1.** [gen] together - **2.** [insgesamt] altogether; **das macht ~ 10 Euro** that's 10 euros altogether; *siehe auch* **zusammen sein.**

**Zusammenarbeit** *die* collaboration; **in ~ mit jm/etw** in collaboration with sb/sthg.

**zusammen|arbeiten** *vi* to work together; **mit jm ~** to work with sb.

**zusammen|beißen** *vt (unreg)* ⊳ **Zahn.**

**zusammen|bekommen** *vt (unreg)* - **1.** [Geldsumme] to get together - **2.** [zusammensetzen können] to be able to put together.

**zusammen|binden** *vt (unreg)* [Blumen, Fäden] to tie together; [Haare] to tie up.

**zusammen|bleiben** (*perf* ist zusammengeblieben) *vi (unreg)* to stay together.

**zusammen|brauen** *vt fam* to concoct.

➡ **sich zusammenbrauen** *ref* to be brewing.

**zusammen|brechen** (*perf* ist zusammengebrochen) *vi (unreg)* - **1.** [gen] to collapse - **2.** [Verkehr] to come to a standstill.

**zusammen|bringen** *vt (unreg)* - **1.** [beschaffen] to get together - **2.** [Personen] to bring together - **3.** [Gelerntes] to manage.

**Zusammen|bruch** *der* collapse.

**zusammen|drängen** *vt* [Menge] to herd together; [Termine] to pack together.

➡ **sich zusammendrängen** *ref* [Menschen] to crowd together; [Termine] to be packed together.

**zusammen|fahren** (*perf* ist zusammengefahren) *vi (unreg)* - **1.** [erschrecken] to start - **2.** [zusammenstoßen] to collide ⟷ *vt fam* [kaputtfahren - Auto] to smash up; [ - Person, Tier] to knock down.

**zusammen|fallen** (*perf* ist zusammengefallen) *vi (unreg)* - **1.** [einsinken]: **(in sich) ~** to col-

lapse - **2.** [abmagern] to become emaciated - **3.** [Termine, Flächen] to coincide.

**zusammen|falten** *vt* to fold up.

**zusammen|fassen** *vt* to summarize.

**Zusammen|fassung** *die* summary.

**zusammen|flicken** *vt fam* to patch up.

**zusammen|fügen** *vt geh* to fit together.

➡ **sich zusammenfügen** *ref geh* to fit together.

**zusammen|führen** *vt* to bring together.

**zusammen|gehören** *vi* to belong together.

**zusammengehörig** *adj* [Teile] that belongs together; [Fragen, Aspekte] related.

**Zusammengehörigkeitsgefühl** *das (ohne pl)* feeling of belonging together.

**zusammengewürfelt** *adj* [Gruppe] motley; [Mobiliar, Kleidungsstücke] assorted.

**Zusammenhalt** *der* solidarity.

**zusammen|halten** (*unreg*) *vi* - **1.** [Personen] to stick together - **2.** [Teile] to hold together ⟷ *vt* - **1.** [verbunden halten] to hold together - **2.** [beisammenhalten - Herde, Gruppe] to keep together; [ - Geld] to hang on to.

**Zusammen|hang** *der* connection; **etw in ~ mit etw bringen** to make a connection between sthg and sthg; **etw aus dem ~ reißen** to take sthg out of context; **im ~ mit etw stehen** to be connected with sthg.

**zusammen|hängen** *vi (unreg)* - **1.** [befestigt sein] to be joined (together) - **2.** [ursächlich]: **mit etw ~** to be connected with sthg.

**zusammenhängend** *adj* coherent.

**zusammenhanglos,            zusammenhangslos** *adj* incoherent ⟷ *adv* incoherently.

**zusammen|klappen** (*perf* hat/ist zusammengeklappt) *vt (hat)* to fold up ⟷ *vi (ist) fam* to collapse.

**zusammen|kommen** (*perf* ist zusammengekommen) *vi (unreg)* - **1.** [Personen] to meet; **mit jm ~** to meet sb - **2.** [Ereignisse, Unglück] to happen together; **heute kam wirklich alles zusammen** everything that could go wrong today, did go wrong - **3.** [sich sammeln - Spenden] to be collected; [ - Unkosten, Verluste] to mount up.

**Zusammenkunft** (*pl* -künfte) *die* meeting.

**zusammen|laufen** (*perf* ist zusammengelaufen) *vi (unreg)* - **1.** [Personen, Tiere] to gather - **2.** [Linien, Flüsse] to meet - **3.** *fam* [Flüssigkeit] to run together.

**zusammen|leben** *vi* to live together; **mit jm ~** to live together with sb.

**zusammen|legen** *vt* - **1.** [sammeln, zusammen

**z**

unterbringen] to put together **- 2.** [falten] to fold up **- 3.** [Termine, Gruppen] to combine ◇ *vi* [gemeinsam bezahlen] to club together.

**zusammen|nehmen** *vt (unreg)* to summon up.

➤ **sich zusammennehmen** *ref* to pull o.s. together.

**zusammen|packen** *vt* & *vi* to pack up.

**zusammen|passen** *vi* [Farben, Kleidungsstücke] to go together; [Menschen] to suit each other.

**zusammen|prallen** *(perf* ist zusammengeprallt) *vi* to collide; **mit jm/etw ~** to collide with sb/sthg.

**zusammen|pressen** *vt* [Mund, Hände] to press together; [Schwamm] to squeeze.

**zusammen|rechnen** *vt* to add up.

**zusammen|reimen** *vt:* sich *(D)* etw ~ to figure sthg out.

**zusammen|reißen** ➤ sich zusammenreißen *ref (unreg) fam* to pull o.s. together.

**zusammen|rotten** ➤ sich zusammenrotten *ref abw* to band together.

**zusammenrücken** *(perf* hat/ist zusammengerückt) *vi (ist)* to move closer together ◇ *vt (hat)* to move together.

**zusammen|schlagen** *(perf* hat/ist zusammengeschlagen) *(unreg) vt (hat)* **- 1.** [gegeneinanderschlagen - Hände] to clap; [ - Absätze] to click **- 2.** *fam* [niederschlagen] to beat up ◇ *vi (ist):* **über jm/etw ~** to engulf sb/sthg.

**zusammen|schließen** *vt (unreg)* to lock together.

➤ **sich zusammenschließen** *ref* to join forces.

**Zusammen|schluss** *der* joining together *(U).*

**zusammen sein** *(perf* sind zusammen gewesen) *vi (unreg)* to be together.

**Zusammensein** *das* being together.

**zusammen|setzen** *vt* to put together.

➤ **sich zusammensetzen** *ref* **- 1.** [bestehen]: **sich aus etw ~** to be composed of sthg **- 2.** [zusammentreffen] to get together; **sich mit jm ~** to get together with sb.

**Zusammensetzung** *(pl* -en) *die* composition.

**Zusammen|spiel** *das* [von Team] teamwork; [von Kräften] interaction.

**zusammen|stellen** *vt* to put together.

**Zusammen|stellung** *die:* **die ~ von etw** putting sthg together.

**Zusammen|stoß** *der* [von Fahrzeugen] crash; *fig* [von Menschen] clash.

**zusammen|stoßen** *(perf* ist zusammengestoßen) *vi (unreg)* to crash; **mit jm/etw ~** [als Un-

fall] to crash into sb/sthg; *fig* [als Streit] to clash with sb/sthg.

**zusammen|suchen** *vt* to collect together.

**zusammen|tragen** *vt (unreg)* to collect.

**zusammen|treffen** *(perf* ist zusammengetroffen) *vi (unreg)* **- 1.** [Personen] to meet; **mit jm ~** to meet sb **- 2.** [Ereignisse] to coincide.

**Zusammen|treffen** *das* [mit Freunden] meeting; [von Ereignissen] coincidence.

**zusammen|treten** *(perf* hat/ist zusammengetreten) *(unreg) vi (ist)* to assemble ◇ *vt (hat)* fam: **jn ~** to kick sb's head in.

**zusammen|tun** *vt (unreg) fam* to put together.

➤ **sich zusammentun** *ref* to get together; **sich mit jm ~** to get together with sb.

**zusammen|wachsen** [tsu'zamənvaksn̩] *(perf* ist zusammengewachsen) *vi (unreg)* to grow together; [Städte] to merge; [Knochen] to knit.

**zusammen|zählen** *vt* to count up.

**zusammen|ziehen** *(perf* hat/ist zusammengezogen) *(unreg) vt (hat)* **- 1.** [enger machen - Schlinge, Netz] to pull tight; [ - Augenbrauen] to knit **- 2.** [sammeln] to mass ◇ *vi (ist)* [in eine Wohnung] to move in together; **mit jm ~** to move in with sb.

➤ **sich zusammenziehen** *ref* [enger, kleiner werden] to contract.

**zusammen|zucken** *(perf* ist zusammengezuckt) *vi* to give a start.

**Zu|satz** *der* addition; [in Nahrungsmittel] additive; [in Vertrag] rider.

**Zusatz|gerät** *das* attachment.

**zusätzlich** *adj* additional ◇ *adv* in addition.

**zuschanden, zu Schanden** *adv:* **etw ~ machen** to ruin sthg.

**zu|schauen** *vi Süddt, Österr &* **Schweiz** to watch; **~, dass ...** to make sure that ...; **jm bei etw ~** to watch sb doing sthg.

**Zuschauer, in** *(mpl* -; *fpl* -nen) *der, die* [im Theater, Kino] member of the audience; [im Stadion] spectator; [bei Unfall, Prügelei] onlooker.

➤ **Zuschauer** *pl* [im Theater, Kino] audience *(sg).*

**Zuschauer|raum** *der* auditorium.

**zu|schicken** *vt:* **jm etw ~** to send sthg to sb.

**zu|schieben** *vt (unreg)* **- 1.** [schließen] to push shut **- 2.** [hinschieben]: **jm etw ~** to push sthg over to sb **- 3.** [Schuld]: **jm etw ~** to push sthg onto sb.

**zu|schießen** *(perf* hat/ist zugeschossen) *(unreg) vt (hat)* **- 1.** [Ball] to pass **- 2.** [Geld]: **jm etw ~** to give sb sthg as a contribution ◇ *vi (ist)* [sich schnell zubewegen]: **auf jn ~** to rush towards sb.

**Zu|schlag** *der* **- 1.** [zusätzlicher Betrag - auf Lohn] additional pay *(U);* [ - auf Ware] surcharge

**- 2.** [zur Fahrkarte] supplement **- 3.** [Zusage]: **den ~ erhalten** [Firma] to be awarded the contract; [Gebot] to be successful.

**zu|schlagen** *(perf hat/ist zugeschlagen) (un- reg) vi* **- 1.** *(ist)* [Tür, Deckel] to slam shut **- 2.** *(hat)* [Person] to hit out **- 3.** *(hat)* [Einsatztruppe, Terrorist] to strike **- 4.** *(hat) fam* [kaufen] to go for it ◇ *vt (hat)* **- 1.** [Tür, Deckel] to slam shut **- 2.** [zusprechen]: **jm etw ~** [einem Bieter] to knock sthg down to sb; [einer Firma] to award sthg to sb.

**zuschlagpflichtig** *adj* subject to a supplement.

**zu|schließen** *(unreg) vt* to lock ◇ *vi* to lock up.

**zu|schnappen** *(perf hat/ist zugeschnappt) vi* **- 1.** *(hat)* [Hund] to snap **- 2.** *(ist)* [Falle, Tür] to click shut.

**zu|schneiden** *vt (unreg)* [Stoff, Kleidungsstück] to cut out; [Brett] to cut to size; **auf jn/etw zugeschnitten sein** *fig* to be tailor-made for sb/ sthg.

**Zu|schnitt** *der* **- 1.** [Zuschneiden] cutting out **- 2.** [Schnitt] cut.

**zu|schnüren** *vt* to tie up.

**zu|schrauben** *vt* [Flasche, Glas] to screw the top on; [Deckel] to screw on.

**zu|schreiben** *vt (unreg):* **jm etw ~** to attribute sthg to sb; **sich** *(D)* **etw selbst zuzuschreiben haben** to have o.s. to blame for sthg.

**Zu|schrift** *die* reply.

**zuschulden, zu Schulden** *adv:* **sich** *(D)* **etwas ~ kommen lassen** to do wrong; **sich** *(D)* **nichts ~ kommen lassen** to do no wrong.

**Zu|schuss** *der* [öffentlich] grant; [privat] contribution.

**zu|sehen** *vi (unreg)* **- 1.** [zuschauen] to watch; **jm bei etw ~** to watch sb doing sthg; **bei etw ~** to watch sthg **- 2.** [veranlassen]: **~, dass ...** to make sure that ...; **sieh zu, dass du wegkommst!** *fam* go away!

**zusehends** *adv* visibly.

**zu sein** *(perf ist zu gewesen) vi (unreg)* to be closed.

**zu|setzen** *vt* **- 1.** [Zutat] to add **- 2.** [Geld] to pay out ◇ *vi* [schaden]: **jm ~** to take it out of sb.

**zu|sichern** *vt:* **jm etw ~** to assure sb of sthg.

**zu|spielen** *vt:* **jm etw ~** [Ball] to pass sthg to sb; [Nachricht] to pass sthg on to sb.

**zu|spitzen** ⬤ **sich zuspitzen** *ref* to intensify.

**Zu|spruch** *der (ohne pl) geh* **- 1.** [Trost] words *(pl)* of comfort; [Aufmunterung] words *(pl)* of encouragement **- 2.** [Zulauf]: **großen ~ finden** to be very popular.

**Zu|stand** *der* state; [Gesundheitszustand] condition; **in gutem/schlechtem ~** in good/bad condition.

⬤ **Zustände** *pl* situation; **Zustände bekommen** ODER **kriegen** *fam fig* to have a fit.

**zustande, zu Stande** *adv:* **etw ~ bringen** to bring sthg about; **~ kommen** to come about.

**zuständig** *adj* [verantwortlich] responsible; [Amtssprache] relevant.

**zustatten** *adv:* **jm/etw ~ kommen** to come in useful for sb/sthg.

**zu|stecken** *vt:* **jm etw ~** to slip sb sthg.

**zu|stehen** *vi (unreg):* **etw steht jm zu** sb is entitled to sthg; **das/es steht mir nicht zu** that's/ it's not up to me.

**zu|steigen** *(perf ist zugestiegen) vi (unreg)* to get on; **noch jemand zugestiegen?** any more tickets?

**zu|stellen** *vt* **- 1.** [Weg] to block **- 2.** *amt* [Brief]: **jm etw ~** [bringen] to deliver sthg to sb; [schicken] to send sb sthg.

**Zu|stellung** *die amt* delivery.

**zu|steuern** *(perf hat/ist zugesteuert) vi (ist):* **auf jn/etw ~** to head for sb/sthg ◇ *vt (hat):* **etw auf jn/etw ~** to steer sthg towards sb/ sthg.

**zu|stimmen** *vi* to agree; **jm ~** to agree with sb.

**Zu|stimmung** *die* agreement; **zu etw seine ~ geben** to give one's consent to sthg; **~ finden** to meet with approval.

**zu|stoßen** *(perf hat/ist zugestoßen) (unreg) vt (hat)* [schließen] to push shut ◇ *vi* **- 1.** *(hat)* [mit Waffe] to make a stab **- 2.** *(ist)* [geschehen]: **jm ~** to happen to sb.

**Zustrom** *der (ohne pl)* stream.

**zutage, zu Tage** *adv:* **etw ~ fördern** to bring sthg to light; **klar** ODER **offen ~ liegen** to be as clear as day; **~ treten** ODER **kommen** to come to the surface; *fig* to come to light.

**Zutaten** *pl* ingredients.

**zu|teilen** *vt:* **jm etw ~** to allocate sthg to sb.

**Zu|teilung** *die* allocation.

**zutiefst** *adv* deeply.

**zu|tragen** *vt (unreg):* **jm etw ~** to take sb sthg. ⬤ **sich zutragen** *ref geh* to come to pass.

**zu|trauen** *vt:* **jm/sich etw ~** to think sb/one is capable of sthg; **ich hätte ihm mehr Geschick zugetraut** I would have expected him to show more skill.

**Zutrauen** *das* confidence; **~ zu jm haben** to have confidence in sb.

**zutraulich** *adj* trusting ◇ *adv* trustingly.

**zu|treffen** *vi (unreg)* to be correct; **auf jn/etw ~** to apply to sb/sthg.

**Zutreffendes** *(ohne Artikel) amt:* '**~ bitte ankreuzen**' 'tick as applicable'.

**Z**

**zu|trinken** *vi (unreg):* **jm ~** to drink to sb.

**Zutritt** *der* entry; **~ haben** to have access; **'~ verboten!'** 'no entry'.

**Zutun** *das: ohne js* **~** without sb's involvement.

**zuungunsten, zu Ungunsten** *präp:* **~ js/ einer Sache** against sb/sthg ⬦ *adv:* **~ von jm** against sb.

**zuverlässig** *adj* reliable ⬦ *adv* reliably.

**Zuverlässigkeit** *die* reliability.

**Zuversicht** *die* confidence.

**zuversichtlich** *adj* confident ⬦ *adv* confidently.

**zu viel** *pron* too much; **~ kriegen** *fam* [sich aufregen] to blow one's top; [nicht aushalten] not to be able to stand it.

**zuvor** *adv* before.

**zuvor|kommen** (*perf* **ist zuvorgekommen**) *vi (unreg):* **jm ~** to beat sb to it.

**zuvorkommend** *adj* obliging.

**Zuwachs** ['tsu:vaks] *der* growth; **etw auf ~ kaufen** to buy sthg big enough to allow room for growth.

**zu|wachsen** ['tsu:vaksn̩] (*perf* **ist zugewachsen**) *vi (unreg)* to become overgrown.

**Zu|wanderung** *die* immigration (*U*).

**zuwege, zu Wege** *adv:* **etw ~ bringen** to bring sthg about.

**zuweilen** *adv* *geh* now and again.

**zu|weisen** *vt (unreg):* **jm etw ~** to allocate sthg to sb.

**zu|wenden** *vt:* **jm den Rücken ~** to turn one's back on sb; **sein Interesse der Zeitung ~** to turn one's attention to the newspaper.

➧ **sich zuwenden** *ref:* **sich jm/etw ~** to turn to sb/sthg.

**Zu|wendung** *die* - **1.** [Aufmerksamkeit] attention - **2.** [Geld] contribution.

**zu wenig** *pron* not enough.

**zu|werfen** *vt (unreg):* **jm etw ~** to throw sthg to sb.

**zuwider** *adv:* **Würmer sind mir ~** I find worms revolting.

**zuwider|handeln** *vi:* **einer Sache** (*D*) **~** to contravene sthg.

**zu|winken** *vi:* **jm ~** to wave to sb.

**zu|zahlen** *vt* to pay extra.

**zu|ziehen** (*perf* **hat/ist zugezogen**) (*unreg*) *vt* (*hat*) - **1.** [schließen - Tür, Fenster] to pull shut; [ - Vorhang, Reißverschluss] to close; [ - Schlinge, Knoten] to pull tight - **2.** [Spezialist] to bring in - **3.** [verschaffen]: **sich** (*D*) **etw ~** [Erkältung] to catch sthg; [Zorn, Neid] to incur sthg ⬦ *vi (ist)* [an einen Ort ziehen] to move into the area/town/*etc*.

**zuzüglich** *präp* (+G, D) plus.

**ZVS** [tsɛtfau'ɛs] (*abk für* **Zentralstelle für die Vergabe von Studienplätzen**) *die* ≃ UCAS *Br*, *German organization responsible for the allocation of student places.*

**zw.** (*abk für* **zwischen**) bet.

**zwang** *prät* ⊏⊐ **zwingen**.

**Zwang** (*pl* **Zwänge**) *der* [körperlich] force; [Druck] pressure; [gesellschaftlich] constraint; [innerer] compulsion; **sich keinen ~ antun** to feel free.

**zwängen** *vt* to force; **sich/etw in etw** (*A*) **~** to force o.s./sthg into sthg.

**zwanglos** *adj* informal ⬦ *adv* informally.

**Zwangs|arbeit** *die* forced labour.

**Zwangs|jacke** *die* straitjacket.

**Zwangs|lage** *die* predicament.

**zwangsläufig** *adj* inevitable ⬦ *adv* inevitably; **etw ~ tun müssen** to be bound to do sthg.

**Zwangs|maßnahme** *die* coercive measure.

**Zwangsver|steigerung** *die* forced sale (*by auction*).

**zwanzig** *num* twenty; *siehe auch* **sechs**.

**Zwanzig** *die (ohne pl)* twenty; *siehe auch* **Sechs**.

**Zwanziger** (*pl* **-**) *der* [Banknote] twenty euro note.

**Zwanzigerjahre, zwanziger Jahre** *pl* twenties; **die ~** the twenties.

**Zwanzigeuro|schein** *der* twenty-euro note *Br* ODER bill *Am*.

**zwanzigste, r, s** *adj* twentieth; *siehe auch* **sechste**.

**Zwanzigste** (*pl* **-n**) *der, die, das* twentieth; *siehe auch* **Sechste**.

**zwar** *adv:* **das ist ~ schön, aber viel zu teuer** it's nice but far too expensive; **dieses Hotel ist ~ teuer, aber nicht sehr komfortabel** while this hotel is expensive, it's not very comfortable; **und ~** to be exact; **ihr geht jetzt ins Bett, und ~ sofort!** go to bed right now, and I mean right now!

**Zweck** (*pl* **-e**) *der* - **1.** [Ziel] purpose; **für einen guten ~** for a good cause; **seinen ~ erfüllen** to serve its purpose; **zu diesem ~** for this purpose - **2.** [Sinn] point; **keinen ~ haben** to be pointless.

**zweckdienlich** *adj* appropriate.

**zweckentfremden** *vt:* **etw als etw ~** to use sthg as sthg.

**zweckentsprechend** *adj* appropriate.

**zwecklos** *adj* pointless.

**zweckmäßig** *adj* appropriate ⬦ *adv* appropriately.

**zwecks** *präp amt:* ~ **einer Sache** *(G)* for the purpose of sthg.

**zwei** *num* two; **für** ~ **essen** *fig* to eat enough for two; *siehe auch* **sechs.**

**Zwei** *(pl* **-en)** *die* **- 1.** [Zahl] two **- 2.** [Schulnote] ≃ B, *mark of 2 on a scale from 1 to 6; siehe auch* **Sechs.**

**Zweibett|zimmer** *das* twin room.

**Zweicent|stück** *das* two-cent piece.

**zweideutig** *adj* **- 1.** [mehrdeutig] ambiguous **- 2.** [frivol] suggestive ⇔ *adv* **- 1.** [mehrdeutig] ambiguously **- 2.** [frivol] suggestively.

**zweidimensional** *adj* two-dimensional.

**Zweidrittel|mehrheit** *die* two-thirds majority.

**Zweier** *(pl* **-)** *der* **- 1.** [Schulnote] ≃ B **- 2.** [Ruderboot] double scull.

**zweierlei** *num* **- 1.** [zwei verschiedene] odd **- 2.** [etwas anderes]: **es ist ~** it is two different things.

**zweifach** *adj* double; **die ~e Menge** twice as much; **in ~er Ausfertigung** in duplicate; **der ~e Gewinner** the two-times winner ⇔ *adv* twice.

**Zweifamilien|haus** *das* two-family house.

**Zweifel** *(pl* **-)** *der* doubt; ~ **an etw** *(D)* doubts *(pl)* about sthg; **außer ~ stehen** to be beyond doubt; **ohne ~** without doubt.

**zweifelhaft** *adj* **- 1.** [unsicher] doubtful **- 2.** [anrüchig] dubious.

**zweifellos** *adv* undoubtedly.

**zweifeln** *vi* to doubt; **an etw** *(D)* ~ to doubt sthg.

**Zweifels|fall** *der:* **im** ~ in case of doubt.

**zweifelsfrei** *adj* definite ⇔ *adv* beyond doubt.

**Zweig** *(pl* **-e)** *der* branch; **auf keinen grünen ~ kommen** *fig* not to get anywhere.

**zweigleisig** *adj* **- 1.** [mit zwei Gleisen] double-track *(vor Subst)* **- 2.** [doppelt] twin-track *(vor Subst)* ⇔ *adv* [mit zwei Gleisen] on two tracks.

**Zweig|stelle** *die* branch.

**zweihundert** *num* two hundred.

**Zweihunderteuro|schein** *der* two-hundred-euro note *Br* ODER bill *Am.*

**Zweikanalton** *der* TV feature utilizing stereo TV channels for simultaneous transmission of film dialogue in the original and a foreign language.

**zweimal** *adv* twice.

**Zwei|rad** *das* two-wheeler.

**zweireihig** *adj* double-breasted.

**zweischneidig** *adj* double-edged.

**zweiseitig** *adj* **- 1.** [zwei Seiten umfassend] two-page *(vor Subst)* **- 2.** [gegenseitig] bilateral.

**Zweisitzer** *(pl* **-)** *der* AUTO two-seater.

**zweisprachig** *adj* bilingual ⇔ *adv* [aufwachsen] bilingually; [geschrieben] in two languages.

**zweistellig** *adj* two-figure *(vor Subst).*

**zweistimmig** *adj* two-part *(vor Subst)* ⇔ *adv* in two parts.

**zweistöckig** *adj* two-storey *(vor Subst).*

**zweit** ⇒ **zu zweit** *adv:* **sie waren zu** ~ there were two of them; **wir sind zu** ~ **ins Kino gegangen** two of us went to the cinema.

**Zweitakt|motor** *der* AUTO two-stroke engine.

**zweitausend** *num* two thousand.

**zweitbeste, r, s** *adj* second best.

**zweite, r, s** *adj* second; *siehe auch* **sechste.**

**Zweite** *(pl* **-n)** *der, die, das* second; **wie kein ~r** like nobody else; *siehe auch* **Sechste.**

**zweiteilig** *adj* [Kleid, Badeanzug] two-piece *(vor Subst);* [Film] two-part *(vor Subst);* [Ausgabe] two-volume *(vor Subst).*

**zweitens** *adv* secondly.

**zweitrangig** *adj* [Frage, Aufgabe] of secondary importance; [Bedeutung] secondary.

**Zweit|stimme** *die* POL second vote.

**zweitürig** *adj* two-door *(vor Subst).*

**Zweit|wagen** *der* second car.

**Zweizimmer|wohnung** *die* two-room flat *Br* ODER apartment *Am.*

**Zwerch|fell** *das* diaphragm.

**Zwerg** *(pl* **-e)** *der* dwarf.

**Zwetsche, Zwetschge** *(pl* **-n)** *die* plum.

**zwicken** *vt* & *vi* to pinch.

**Zwick|mühle** *die* **- 1.** [schwierige Situation] dilemma **- 2.** [beim Mühlespiel] *winning position in "Nine Men's Morris".*

**Zwieback** *(pl* **Zwiebäcke** ODER **-e)** *der* rusk.

**Zwiebel** *(pl* **-n)** *die* onion.

**Zwiebel|kuchen** *der pizza-like dish consisting of dough base with topping of onion, ham and sour cream.*

**Zwielicht** *das* twilight; **ins** ~ **geraten** *fig* to fall under suspicion.

**zwielichtig** *adj* shady.

**Zwiespalt** *(pl* **-e** ODER **-spälte)** *der* conflict.

**zwiespältig** *adj* [Gefühle] conflicting; [Charakter] contradictory.

**Zwilling** *(pl* **-e)** *der* **- 1.** [Person] twin; **eineiige/**

zweieiige ~e identical/non-identical twins
- **2.** ASTROL Gemini; ~ **sein** to be a Gemini.
➤ **Zwillinge** *pl* ASTROL Gemini *(sg)*.

**Zwillings|bruder** *der* twin brother.

**Zwillings|schwester** *die* twin sister.

**zwingen** *(prät* **zwang**; *perf* **hat gezwungen)** *vt*
to force; **jn zu etw ~** to force sb to do sthg.
➤ **sich zwingen** *ref* to force o.s.; **sich zu etw ~**
to force o.s. to do sthg.

**zwinkern** *vi* [als Reflex] to blink; [als Zeichen] to
wink.

**Zwirn** *(pl* -**e)** *der* thread.

**zwischen** *präp (+D, A)* - **1.** [gen] between
- **2.** [inmitten] amongst.

**Zwischen|aufenthalt** *der* stopover.

**Zwischen|bemerkung** *die* interjection.

**Zwischen|ding** *das fam* cross.

**zwischendurch** *adv* - **1.** [zeitlich] in the
meantime - **2.** [räumlich] here and there.

**Zwischen|ergebnis** *das* provisional re-
sult.

**Zwischen|fall** *der* incident.
➤ **Zwischenfälle** *pl* clashes.

**Zwischen|händler, in** *der, die* middleman.

**Zwischen|landung** *die* stopover.

**zwischenmenschlich** *adj* interpersonal.

**Zwischen|prüfung** *die* UNI intermediate
examination.

**Zwischen|raum** *der* gap.

**Zwischen|ruf** *der* interjection.

**Zwischen|speicher** *der* EDV cache.

**Zwischen|wand** *die* partition.

**Zwischen|zeit** *die* time in between; **in der ~**
in the meantime.

**zwischenzeitlich** *amt adj* during the interim period ◇ *adv* in the meantime.

**Zwist** *(pl* -**e)** *der geh* strife *(U)*.

**Zwistigkeiten** *pl geh* disputes.

**zwitschern** *vi* to twitter.

**Zwitter** *(pl* -**)** *der* hermaphrodite.

**zwölf** *num* twelve; **es ist fünf vor ~** *fig* time has
almost run out; *siehe auch* **sechs.**

**Zwölf** *(pl* -**en)** *die* twelve; *siehe auch* **Sechs.**

**zwölfhundert** *num* twelve hundred.

**zwölfte, r, s** *adj* twelfth; *siehe auch* **sechste.**

**Zwölfte** *(pl* -**n)** *der, die, das* twelfth; *siehe auch*
**Sechste.**

**zwölftel** *adj (unver)* twelfth; *siehe auch* **sechstel.**

**Zwölftel** *(pl* -**)** *das* twelfth; *siehe auch* **Sechstel.**

**Zyankali** [tsÿan'ka:li] *das* potassium cyanide.

**zyklisch** [tsy:klɪʃ] *adj* cyclical ◇ *adv* cyclical-
ly.

**Zyklus** ['tsy:klʊs] *(pl* **Zyklen)** *der* cycle.

**Zylinder** [tsi'lɪndɐ] *(pl* -**)** *der* - **1.** [Hut] top hat
- **2.** MATH & TECH cylinder.

**zynisch** ['tsy:nɪʃ] *adj* cynical.

**Zynismus** [tsy'nɪsmʊs] *der* cynicism.

**Zypern** *nt* Cyprus.

**Zypresse** [tsy'prɛsə] *(pl* -**n)** *die* cypress.

**Zyste** ['tsystə] *(pl* -**n)** *die* MED cyst.

**z. Z.** = zurzeit.

**zzgl.** *abk für* **zuzüglich.**

# unregelmäßige englische Verben

| Infinitive _Infinitiv_ | Past Tense _Präteritum_ | Past Participle _Perfekt_ |
|---|---|---|
| arise | arose | arisen |
| awake | awoke | awoken |
| be | was, were | been |
| bear | bore | born(e) |
| beat | beat | beaten |
| become | became | become |
| begin | began | begun |
| bend | bent | bent |
| beseech | besought | besought |
| bet | bet (_also_ betted) | bet (_also_ betted) |
| bid | bid (_also_ bade) | bid (_also_ bidden) |
| bind | bound | bound |
| bite | bit | bitten |
| bleed | bled | bled |
| blow | blew | blown |
| break | broke | broken |
| breed | bred | bred |
| bring | brought | brought |
| build | built | built |
| burn | burnt (_also_ burned) | burnt (_also_ burned) |
| burst | burst | burst |
| buy | bought | bought |
| can | could | - |
| cast | cast | cast |
| catch | caught | caught |
| choose | chose | chosen |
| cling | clung | clung |
| come | came | come |
| cost | cost | cost |
| creep | crept | crept |
| cut | cut | cut |
| deal | dealt | dealt |
| dig | dug | dug |
| do | did | done |
| draw | drew | drawn |
| dream | dreamed (_also_ dreamt) | dreamed (_also_ dreamt) |
| drink | drank | drunk |
| drive | drove | driven |
| dwell | dwelt | dwelt |
| eat | ate | eaten |
| fall | fell | fallen |
| feed | fed | fed |
| feel | felt | felt |
| fight | fought | fought |
| find | found | found |
| flee | fled | fled |
| fling | flung | flung |
| fly | flew | flown |
| forbid | forbade | forbidden |
| forget | forgot | forgotten |
| forsake | forsook | forsaken |
| freeze | froze | frozen |
| get | got | got (_Am_ gotten) |
| give | gave | given |

| Infinitive<br>*Infinitiv* | Past Tense<br>*Präteritum* | Past Participle<br>*Perfekt* |
|---|---|---|
| go | went | gone |
| grind | ground | ground |
| grow | grew | grown |
| hang | hung (*also* hanged) | hung (*also* hanged) |
| have | had | had |
| hear | heard | heard |
| hide | hid | hidden |
| hit | hit | hit |
| hold | held | held |
| hurt | hurt | hurt |
| keep | kept | kept |
| kneel | knelt (*also* kneeled) | knelt (*also* kneeled) |
| know | knew | known |
| lay | laid | laid |
| lead | led | led |
| lean | leant (*also* leaned) | leant (*also* leaned) |
| leap | leapt (*also* leaped) | leapt (*also* leaped) |
| learn | learnt (*also* learned) | learnt (*also* learned) |
| leave | left | left |
| lend | lent | lent |
| let | let | let |
| lie | lay | lain |
| light | lit (*also* lighted) | lit (*also* lighted) |
| lose | lost | lost |
| make | made | made |
| may | might | - |
| mean | meant | meant |
| meet | met | met |
| mistake | mistook | mistaken |
| mow | mowed | mown (*also* mowed) |
| pay | paid | paid |
| put | put | put |
| quit | quit (*also* quitted) | quit (*also* quitted) |
| read | read | read |
| rend | rent | rent |
| rid | rid | rid |
| ride | rode | ridden |
| ring | rang | rung |
| rise | rose | risen |
| run | ran | run |
| saw | sawed | sawn |
| say | said | said |
| see | saw | seen |
| seek | sought | sought |
| sell | sold | sold |
| send | sent | sent |
| set | set | set |
| shake | shook | shaken |
| shall | should | - |
| shear | sheared | shorn (*also* sheared) |
| shed | shed | shed |
| shine | shone | shone |
| shoot | shot | shot |

| Infinitive<br>*Infinitiv* | Past Tense<br>*Präteritum* | Past Participle<br>*Perfekt* |
|---|---|---|
| show | showed | shown |
| shrink | shrank | shrunk |
| shut | shut | shut |
| sing | sang | sung |
| sink | sank | sunk |
| sit | sat | sat |
| slay | slew | slain |
| sleep | slept | slept |
| slide | slid | slid |
| sling | slung | slung |
| slit | slit | slit |
| smell | smelt (*also* smelled) | smelt (*also* smelled) |
| sow | sowed | sown (*also* sowed) |
| speak | spoke | spoken |
| speed | sped (*also* speeded) | sped (*also* speeded) |
| spell | spelt (*also* spelled) | spelt (*also* spelled) |
| spend | spent | spent |
| spill | spilt (*also* spilled) | spilt (*also* spilled) |
| spin | spun | spun |
| spit | spat | spat |
| split | split | split |
| spoil | spoiled (*also* spoilt) | spoiled (*also* spoilt) |
| spread | spread | spread |
| spring | sprang | sprung |
| stand | stood | stood |
| steal | stole | stolen |
| stick | stuck | stuck |
| sting | stung | stung |
| stink | stank | stunk |
| stride | strode | stridden |
| strike | struck | struck (*also* stricken) |
| strive | strove | striven |
| swear | swore | sworn |
| sweep | swept | swept |
| swell | swelled | swollen (*also* swelled) |
| swim | swam | swum |
| swing | swung | swung |
| take | took | taken |
| teach | taught | taught |
| tear | tore | torn |
| tell | told | told |
| think | thought | thought |
| throw | threw | thrown |
| thrust | thrust | thrust |
| tread | trod | trodden |
| wake | woke (*also* waked) | woken (*also* waked) |
| wear | wore | worn |
| weave | wove (*also* weaved) | woven (*also* weaved) |
| wed | wedded | wedded |
| weep | wept | wept |
| win | won | won |
| wind | wound | wound |
| wring | wrung | wrung |
| write | wrote | written |

# German
# Irregular
# Verbs

| Infinitiv *Infinitive* | Präsens *Present* | Präteritum *Preterite* | Perfekt *Past Participle* |
|---|---|---|---|
| beginnen | beginnt | begann | hat begonnen |
| beißen | beißt | biss | hat gebissen |
| bergen | birgt | barg | hat geborgen |
| bersten | birst | barst | ist geborsten |
| bewegen | bewegt | bewegte | hat bewegt |
| biegen | biegt | bog | hat gebogen |
| bieten | bietet | bot | hat geboten |
| binden | bindet | band | hat gebunden |
| bitten | bittet | bat | hat gebeten |
| blasen | bläst | blies | hat geblasen |
| bleiben | bleibt | blieb | ist geblieben |
| bleichen | bleicht | blich | hat geblichen |
| braten | brät | briet | hat gebraten |
| brechen | bricht | brach | hat/ist gebrochen |
| bringen | bringt | brachte | hat gebracht |
| denken | denkt | dachte | hat gedacht |
| dürfen | darf | durfte | hat gedurft/dürfen |
| empfehlen | empfiehlt | empfahl | hat empfohlen |
| essen | isst | aß | hat gegessen |
| fahren | fährt | fuhr | hat/ist gefahren |
| fallen | fällt | fiel | ist gefallen |
| fangen | fängt | fing | hat gefangen |
| fechten | ficht | focht | hat gefochten |
| finden | findet | fand | hat gefunden |
| flechten | flicht | flocht | hat geflochten |
| fliegen | fliegt | flog | hat/ist geflogen |
| fliehen | flieht | floh | ist geflohen |
| fließen | fließt | floss | ist geflossen |
| fragen | fragt | fragte | hat gefragt |
| fressen | frisst | fraß | hat gefressen |
| frieren | friert | fror | hat gefroren |
| gären | gärt | gor | hat/ist gegoren |
| geben | gibt | gab | hat gegeben |
| gedeihen | gedeiht | gedieh | ist gediehen |
| gehen | geht | ging | ist gegangen |
| gelten | gilt | galt | hat gegolten |
| genießen | genießt | genoss | hat genossen |
| gelingen | gelingt | gelang | ist gelungen |
| geschehen | geschieht | geschah | ist geschehen |
| gewinnen | gewinnt | gewann | hat gewonnen |
| gießen | gießt | goss | hat gegossen |
| gleichen | gleicht | glich | hat geglichen |
| gleiten | gleitet | glitt | ist geglitten |
| graben | gräbt | grub | hat gegraben |
| greifen | greift | griff | hat gegriffen |
| haben | hat | hatte | hat gehabt |
| halten | hält | hielt | hat gehalten |
| hängen | hängt | hing/hängte | hat gehangen/gehängt |
| hauen | haut | haute | hat gehauen |
| heben | hebt | hob | hat gehoben |
| heißen | heißt | hieß | hat geheißen |
| helfen | hilft | half | hat geholfen |
| kennen | kennt | kannte | hat gekannt |
| klingen | klingt | klang | hat geklungen |

| Infinitiv *Infinitive* | Präsens *Present* | Präteritum *Preterite* | Perfekt *Past Participle* |
|---|---|---|---|
| kneifen | kneift | kniff | hat gekniffen |
| kommen | kommt | kam | ist gekommen |
| können | kann | konnte | hat können/gekonnt |
| kriechen | kriecht | kroch | ist gekrochen |
| lassen | lässt | ließ | hat gelassen/lassen |
| laufen | läuft | lief | hat/ist gelaufen |
| leiden | leidet | litt | hat gelitten |
| leihen | leiht | lieh | hat geliehen |
| lesen | liest | las | hat gelesen |
| liegen | liegt | lag | hat gelegen |
| lügen | lügt | log | hat gelogen |
| mahlen | mahlt | mahlte | hat gemahlen |
| meiden | meidet | mied | hat gemieden |
| messen | misst | maß | hat gemessen |
| mögen | mag | mochte | hat gemocht/mögen |
| müssen | muss | musste | hat gemusst/müssen |
| nehmen | nimmt | nahm | hat genommen |
| nennen | nennt | nannte | hat genannt |
| pfeifen | pfeift | pfiff | hat gepfiffen |
| pflegen | pflegt | pflegte | hat gepflegt |
| quellen | quillt | quoll | ist gequollen |
| raten | rät | riet | hat geraten |
| reiben | reibt | rieb | hat gerieben |
| reißen | reißt | riss | hat/ist gerissen |
| reiten | reitet | ritt | hat/ist geritten |
| rennen | rennt | rannte | ist gerannt |
| riechen | riecht | roch | hat gerochen |
| ringen | ringt | rang | hat gerungen |
| rinnen | rinnt | rann | ist geronnen |
| rufen | ruft | rief | hat gerufen |
| salzen | salzt | salzte | hat gesalzen |
| saufen | säuft | soff | hat gesoffen |
| schaffen | schafft | schuf | hat geschaffen |
| schallen | schallt | schallte | hat geschallt |
| scheinen | scheint | schien | hat geschienen |
| schieben | schiebt | schob | hat geschoben |
| schießen | schießt | schoss | hat/ist geschossen |
| schlafen | schläft | schlief | hat geschlafen |
| schlagen | schlägt | schlug | hat/ist geschlagen |
| schleichen | schleicht | schlich | ist geschlichen |
| schließen | schließt | schloss | hat geschlossen |
| schlingen | schlingt | schlang | hat geschlungen |
| schmeißen | schmeißt | schmiss | hat geschmissen |
| schmelzen | schmilzt | schmolz | ist geschmolzen |
| schneiden | schneidet | schnitt | hat geschnitten |
| schreiben | schreibt | schrieb | hat geschrieben |
| schreien | schreit | schrie | hat geschrie(e)n |
| schreiten | schreitet | schritt | ist geschritten |
| schweigen | schweigt | schwieg | hat geschwiegen |
| schwellen | schwillt | schwoll | ist geschwollen |
| schwimmen | schwimmt | schwamm | hat/ist geschwommen |
| schwinden | schwindet | schwand | ist geschwunden |
| schwingen | schwingt | schwang | hat geschwungen |
| schwören | schwört | schwor | hat geschworen |

| Infinitiv<br>*Infinitive* | Präsens<br>*Present* | Präteritum<br>*Preterite* | Perfekt<br>*Past Participle* |
|---|---|---|---|
| sehen | sieht | sah | hat gesehen |
| sein | ist | war | ist gewesen |
| senden | sendet | sandte | hat gesendet/gesandt |
| sieden | siedet | sott | hat gesotten |
| singen | singt | sang | hat gesungen |
| sinnen | sinnt | sann | hat gesonnen |
| sitzen | sitzt | saß | hat gesessen |
| sollen | soll | sollte | hat gesollt |
| spalten | spaltet | spaltete | hat gespalten |
| sprechen | spricht | sprach | hat gesprochen |
| springen | springt | sprang | hat/ist gesprungen |
| stehen | steht | stand | hat gestanden |
| stehlen | stiehlt | stahl | hat gestohlen |
| steigen | steigt | stieg | ist gestiegen |
| sterben | stirbt | starb | ist gestorben |
| stoßen | stößt | stieß | hat/ist gestoßen |
| streichen | streicht | strich | hat gestrichen |
| streiten | streitet | stritt | hat gestritten |
| tragen | trägt | trug | hat getragen |
| treffen | trifft | traf | hat getroffen |
| treiben | treibt | trieb | hat/ist getrieben |
| treten | tritt | trat | hat/ist getreten |
| trinken | trinkt | trank | hat getrunken |
| tun | tut | tat | hat getan |
| verderben | verdirbt | verdarb | hat verdorben |
| vergessen | vergisst | vergaß | hat vergessen |
| verlieren | verliert | verlor | hat verloren |
| wachsen | wächst | wuchs | ist gewachsen |
| waschen | wäscht | wusch | hat gewaschen |
| wenden | wendet | wendete/<br>wandte | hat gewendet/<br>gewandt |
| werden | wird | wurde | ist geworden/worden |
| werfen | wirft | warf | hat geworfen |
| winken | winkt | winkte | hat gewunken |
| wissen | weiß | wusste | hat gewusst |
| wollen | will | wollte | hat gewollt/wollen |
| ziehen | zieht | zog | hat/ist gezogen |
| zwingen | zwingt | zwang | hat gezwungen |

Achevé d'imprimer en Italie chez Rotolito Lombarda.
Dépôt légal : juin 2010. 304106.
N° de projet : 11014306. Juin 2011